THE NEW OXFORD ANNOTATED BIBLE

New Revised
Standard Version

Fully Revised Fourth Edition

THE NEW OXFORD ANNOTATED BIBLE

New Revised
Standard Version
With The Apocrypha

An Ecumenical Study Bible

Michael D. Coogan, *Editor*

Marc Z. Brettler, Carol A. Newsom,
and Pheme Perkins, *Associate Editors*

OXFORD
UNIVERSITY PRESS

OXFORD
UNIVERSITY PRESS

Oxford New York
Auckland Cape Town Dar es Salaam Hong Kong Karachi Kuala Lumpur
Madrid Melbourne Mexico City Nairobi New Delhi Shanghai Taipei Toronto

With offices in
Argentina Austria Brazil Chile Czech Republic France Greece Guatemala
Hungary Italy Japan Poland Portugal Singapore South Korea Switzerland
Thailand Turkey Ukraine Vietnam

Published by Oxford University Press, Inc.
198 Madison Avenue, New York, New York 10016

http://www.oup.com/us

Oxford is a registered trademark of Oxford University Press, Inc.

Design and typesetting by 2Krogh AS, Denmark.

10   9   8   7   6   5   4   3   2
Printed in the Netherlands

CONTRIBUTORS

Contributor	Book(s)	Contributor	Book(s)
Yairah Amit	Judges	Bernard M. Levinson	Deuteronomy
John R. Bartlett	1 Maccabees	Christopher R. Matthews	Acts
Jennifer K. Berenson	Ephesians, Colossians	Steven L. McKenzie	1, 2 Samuel
Theodore A. Bergren	2 Esdras	Carol Meyers	Exodus
Adele Berlin	Lamentations	Margaret M. Mitchell	1, 2 Timothy, Titus,
M. Eugene Boring	1 Peter		Philemon
Sheila Briggs	Galatians	Gregory Mobley	Hosea, Amos, Micah
Timothy B. Cargal	James	Judith H. Newman	Psalm 151
David M. Carr	Genesis	Jerome H. Neyrey, S.J.	John
Richard J. Clifford	Psalms	Julia M. O'Brien	Obadiah, Nahum, Habakkuk,
David J. A. Clines	Job		Zephaniah
John J. Collins	3 Maccabees	Carolyn Osiek	Philippians
Stephen L. Cook	Ezekiel	Pheme Perkins	1, 2, 3 John
J. R. C. Cousland	Matthew	David L. Petersen	Joel, Haggai, Zechariah,
Katharine Dell	Proverbs		Malachi
Neil Elliott	Romans	Thomas Römer	1, 2 Kings
Tamara Cohn Eskenazi	Ezra, Nehemiah, 1 Esdras	Jean-Pierre Ruiz	Revelation
J. Cheryl Exum	Song of Solomon	Daniel R. Schwartz	2 Maccabees
Terence E. Fretheim	Numbers	Choon-Leong Seow	Ecclesiastes
Matthew Goff	Baruch, Letter of Jeremiah	David A. de Silva	4 Maccabees
Lester Grabbe	Wisdom of Solomon	Marion L. Soards	Luke
Daniel J. Harrington	Sirach	Jeffrey Stackert	Leviticus
David G. Horrell	1, 2 Thessalonians	Marvin A. Sweeney	Isaiah
Richard A. Horsley	Mark	Patrick A. Tiller	2 Peter, Jude
Rodney R. Hutton	Jeremiah	Sze-kar Wan	2 Corinthians
Cynthia Briggs Kittredge	Hebrews	Laurence L. Welborn	1 Corinthians
Gary N. Knoppers	1, 2 Chronicles	Lawrence M. Wills	Judith
David Lambert	Prayer of Manasseh	K. Lawson Younger, Jr.	Joshua
Mary Joan Winn Leith	Esther, Greek Esther	Yair Zakovitch	Ruth, Jonah
Amy-Jill Levine	Daniel, Additions to Daniel,		
	Tobit		

Marc Z. Brettler: *The Pentateuch; The Historical Books; The Poetical and Wisdom Books, The Canons of the Bible* [with Pheme Perkins]; *The Hebrew Bible's Interpretation of Itself; Jewish Interpretation in the Premodern Era*

Michael D. Coogan: *Textual Criticism* [with Pheme Perkins]; *The Interpretation of the Bible: From the Nineteenth to the Mid-twentieth Centuries; The Geography of the Bible; The Ancient Near East*

Carol A. Newsom: *The Prophetic Books; Introduction to the Apocryphal/Deuterocanonical Books; Christian Interpretation in the Premodern Era; Contemporary Methods in Biblical Study; The Persian and Hellenistic Periods*

Pheme Perkins: *The Gospels; Letters/Epistles in the New Testament; The Canons of the Bible* [with Marc Z. Brettler]; *Textual Criticism* [with Michael D. Coogan]; *Translation of the Bible into English; The New Testament Interprets the Jewish Scriptures; The Roman Period*

CONTENTS

The Apocryphal/Deuterocanonical Books

The Apocryphal/Deuterocanonical Books are listed here in four groupings, as follows:

The New Testament

THE GOSPELS

General Essays, Tables

MAPS, CHARTS, AND DIAGRAMS

THE EDITORS' PREFACE

For nearly five decades *The Oxford Annotated Bible* and its successor *The New Oxford Annotated Bible* have served generations of readers and students as a study Bible. That extraordinary longevity alone is eloquent testimony to its success. This new edition retains the format and features that have proven so attractive. At the same time, the field of biblical studies has not been static, and this edition is a thoroughgoing revision of the previous ones. In particular, the editors have recruited contributors from a wide diversity of backgrounds and of scholarly approaches to the biblical traditions. In order to present this diversity more fully, the introductions to the biblical books, the maps and charts, the annotations, and the study materials at the end of the book have been significantly enhanced and lengthened since the third edition.

We recognize that no single interpretation or approach is sufficient for informed reading of these ancient texts, and have aimed at inclusivity of interpretive strategies. On a great number of issues there is a consensus among scholars, and the contributors have been encouraged to present such consensus when it exists. Where it has broken down, and has not yet re-formed, alternatives are mentioned. Moreover, in order to respect the canonical status of various parts of the Bible for different communities, and to avoid privileging any book or part of the Bible, we have kept both introductions and annotations roughly proportionate to the length of the books, while recognizing that some parts require more elaboration than others.

The editorial process was collaborative. Each contribution was read in its entirety by at least three of the editors, and revised with a view toward consistency of tone, coherence of approach, and completeness of coverage. We have also wanted to allow the contributors' own voices to be heard, and we have avoided imposing a superficial uniformity of style and approach. Throughout, we have kept the needs of the general audience firmly in mind during the editorial stages, and our aim has been a congruity of experience as a reader turns from book to book and from section to section of the finished volume.

CONTENTS OF THE ANNOTATED BIBLE

The biblical text stands apart from any editorial contributions, in both placement and format. This will enable anyone who wishes to do so to read the text unprejudiced by editorial judgments.

The footnotes that are part of the New Revised Standard Version (indicated by an italic superscript letter after the word or phrase in question) are printed at the bottom of the right-hand column of the biblical text on each page where they occur. In these notes, divergent textual readings and alternate translations are printed in italics. The phrase "Other ancient authorities read" means that the reading (i.e., the wording) of the passage is different in various manuscripts and early versions, and the word "Or" signifies that the Hebrew, Aramaic, Greek, or Latin text permits an alternate rendering besides the one given in the text. (See "Textual Criticism," p. 2192.)

Discussion of larger units in the Bible is provided by essays introducing each of them: "The Pentateuch," "The Historical Books," "The Poetical and Wisdom Books," "The Prophetic Books," "The Apocryphal/Deuterocanonical Books," "The Gospels," and "Letters/Epistles in the New Testament."

Each book is preceded by its own introduction, which sketches the book's structure, main themes, literary history, and historical context, as well as broad lines of interpretation; they therefore present a clear overview and guide to reading. For this edition we have not only made the introductions longer than in previous editions but have also organized them so that they cover the same topics in the same order.

At the bottom of each page of the biblical text, in a different font from it and in a single column, are the annotations. The annotations are just that, notes rather than paraphrase or commentary, although these genres admittedly overlap. They are intended to enhance the reader's understanding of the text, providing essential information, background, and interpretation, rather than only summarizing what it says. The boldface headings delineate the larger units of the book and provide a detailed consecutive outline of its contents. The word or phrase being glossed is given in italics. Quotation marks are used for words quoted from elsewhere in the Bible as well as for transliterations of ancient languages. Since we desire each book to stand on its own, as much as possible the annotations are self-contained. We have thus tried to avoid both cross-references to fuller discussions elsewhere, and the misconception that a book or larger part of the Bible is merely a perfunctory reworking of other material, or that a particular passage can only be understood fully in the light of later biblical traditions. At the same time, we recognize that the Bible is often a progressive text, and that later parts of the Bible often contain the oldest interpretations of earlier traditions. The best starting point for interpreting a particular passage is often another passage, and we have encouraged contributors to point out interconnections in the biblical material by means of cross-references. (The cross-references that end with "n." refer to the annotation as well as to the biblical text.)

A listing of abbreviations for the books of the Bible used in this edition is found on p. xxi. The chapter and verse divisions in a reference are separated by a period; thus, Gen 3.8 refers to the book of Genesis, chapter 3, verse 8. Inclusive references are used for both chapters and verses; thus, Ex 1–15 refers to the first fifteen chapters of the book of Exodus; Rom 11.33–36 to verses 33 through 36 of chapter 11 of the letter to the Romans; and so forth. When a book of the Bible is referred to within an annotation on that book, the name of the book is not repeated unless there is ambiguity.

In keeping with our general desire to take account of the diversity of the users of this study Bible, we have adopted two widely accepted conventions: We have referred to the first portion of the text as "the Hebrew Bible," since it is a collection preserved by the Jewish community and that is how Jews regard it; and we have cited all dates in the notes as BCE or CE ("Before the Common Era" and "Common Era") instead of BC or AD ("Before Christ" and "Anno Domini" ["in the year of the Lord"]), which imply a Christian view of the status of Jesus of Nazareth. Use of the title "Old Testament" for those books here designated as "the Hebrew Bible" is confined to instances expressing the historical view of various Christian interpreters. These conventions are followed in the study materials that we have produced; the translation has its own conventions, which we are not at liberty to alter.

Several dozen maps and plans are interspersed in the biblical text. These will assist readers to locate important places mentioned in the text or to clarify the prose descriptions of such structures as the Tabernacle and the Temple.

The study materials at the end of the volume are a series of interconnected essays that provide background information for understanding the Bible, the processes by which it was formed, the contexts in which it was produced, and the ways in which it has been interpreted through the ages. These essays are followed by tables of rulers, of weights and measures, of the calendar, and of parallel passages in the biblical traditions. There is also a brief bibliography to English translations of ancient writings that are referred to in the notes. A select chronology provides a quick reference for major events, rulers, and other persons contemporaneous with the biblical accounts. The study materials also include a glossary of important terms and concepts.

At the end of the book is a comprehensive subject index to all of the study materials, including the annotations. Finally, there is a separate set of fourteen color maps, with a separate index to them, that constitute a brief historical atlas to the Bible.

ACKNOWLEDGMENTS

It remains to express our gratitude, first and above all to the contributors, whose learning has made this a work of which we are immensely proud, and whose uncommon patience with the editorial process made our task light. Donald Kraus, Executive Editor in the Bible department at Oxford University Press, U.S.A., has guided this edition from its inception with wisdom and tact. Elisabeth Nelson carried out with efficiency and accuracy a wide variety of editorial tasks that are needed in a project of this complexity. Mary Sutherland prepared the text for composition, and 2Krogh AS, Denmark, designed and typeset the entire text. We thank them all.

MICHAEL D. COOGAN, MARC Z. BRETTLER,
CAROL A. NEWSOM, PHEME PERKINS
August, 2009

TO THE READER

[The following prefatory essay, "To the Reader," is part of the New Revised Standard Version Bible translation (NRSV), and is reprinted here in accordance with the requirements of the National Council of the Churches of Christ in the U.S.A., which holds copyright to the NRSV.]

This preface is addressed to you by the Committee of translators, who wish to explain, as briefly as possible, the origin and character of our work. The publication of our revision is yet another step in the long, continual process of making the Bible available in the form of the English language that is most widely current in our day. To summarize in a single sentence: the New Revised Standard Version of the Bible is an authorized revision of the Revised Standard Version, published in 1952, which was a revision of the American Standard Version, published in 1901, which, in turn, embodied earlier revisions of the King James Version, published in 1611.

In the course of time, the King James Version came to be regarded as "the Authorized Version." With good reason it has been termed "the noblest monument of English prose," and it has entered, as no other book has, into the making of the personal character and the public institutions of the English-speaking peoples. We owe to it an incalculable debt.

Yet the King James Version has serious defects. By the middle of the nineteenth century, the development of biblical studies and the discovery of many biblical manuscripts more ancient than those on which the King James Version was based made it apparent that these defects were so many as to call for revision. The task was begun, by authority of the Church of England, in 1870. The (British) Revised Version of the Bible was published in 1881–1885; and the American Standard Version, its variant embodying the preferences of the American scholars associated with the work, was published, as was mentioned above, in 1901. In 1928 the copyright of the latter was acquired by the International Council of Religious Education and thus passed into the ownership of the Churches of the United States and Canada that were associated in this Council through their boards of education and publication.

The Council appointed a committee of scholars to have charge of the text of the American Standard Version and to undertake inquiry concerning the need for further revision. After studying the questions whether or not revision should be undertaken, and if so, what its nature and extent should be, in 1937 the Council authorized a revision. The scholars who served as members of the Committee worked in two sections, one dealing with the Old Testament and one with the New Testament. In 1946 the Revised Standard Version of the New Testament was published. The publication of the Revised Standard Version of the Bible, containing the Old and New Testaments, took place on September 30, 1952. A translation of the Apocryphal/Deuterocanonical Books of the Old Testament followed in 1957. In 1977 this collection was issued in an expanded edition, containing three additional texts received by Eastern Orthodox communions (3 and 4 Maccabees and Psalm 151). Thereafter the Revised Standard Version gained the distinction of being officially authorized for use by all major Christian churches: Protestant, Anglican, Roman Catholic, and Eastern Orthodox.

The Revised Standard Version Bible Committee is a continuing body, comprising about thirty members, both men and women. Ecumenical in representation, it includes scholars affiliated with various Protestant denominations, as well as several Roman Catholic members, an Eastern Orthodox member, and a Jewish member who serves in the Old Testament section. For a period of time the Committee included several members from Canada and from England.

Because no translation of the Bible is perfect or is acceptable to all groups of readers, and because discoveries of older manuscripts and further investigation of linguistic features of the text continue to become available, renderings of the Bible have proliferated. During the years following the publication of the Revised Standard Version, twenty-six other English translations and revisions of the Bible were produced by committees and by individual scholars—not to mention twenty-five other translations and revisions of the New Testament alone. One of the latter was the second edition of the RSV New Testament, issued in 1971, twenty-five years after its initial publication.

Following the publication of the RSV Old Testament in 1952, significant advances were made in the discovery and interpretation of documents in Semitic languages related to Hebrew. In addition to the information that had become available in the late 1940s from the Dead Sea texts of Isaiah and Habakkuk, subsequent acquisitions from the same area brought to light many other early copies of all the books of the Hebrew Scriptures (except Esther), though most of these copies are fragmentary. During the same period early Greek manuscript copies of books of the New Testament also became available.

In order to take these discoveries into account, along with recent studies of documents in Semitic languages related to Hebrew, in 1974 the Policies Committee of the Revised Standard Version, which is a standing committee of the National Council of the Churches of Christ in the U.S.A., authorized the preparation of a revision of the entire RSV Bible.

For the Old Testament the Committee has made use of the *Biblia Hebraica Stuttgartensia* (1977; ed. sec. emendata, 1983). This is an edition of the Hebrew and Aramaic text as current early in the Christian era and fixed by Jewish scholars (the "Masoretes") of the sixth to the ninth centuries. The vowel signs, which were added by the Masoretes, are accepted in the main, but where a more probable and convincing reading can be obtained by assuming different vowels, this has been done. No notes are given in such cases, because the vowel points are less ancient and reliable than the consonants. When an alternative reading given by the Masoretes is translated in a footnote, this is identified by the words "Another reading is."

Departures from the consonantal text of the best manuscripts have been made only where it seems clear that errors in copying had been made before the text was standardized. Most of the corrections adopted are based on the ancient versions (translations into Greek, Aramaic, Syriac, and Latin), which were made prior to the time of the work of the Masoretes and which therefore may reflect earlier forms of the Hebrew text. In such instances a footnote specifies the version or versions from which the correction has been derived and also gives a translation of the Masoretic Text. Where it was deemed appropriate to do so, information is supplied in footnotes from subsidiary Jewish traditions concerning other textual readings (the *Tiqqune Sopherim*, "emendations of the scribes"). These are identified in the footnotes as "Ancient Heb tradition."

Occasionally it is evident that the text has suffered in transmission and that none of the versions provides a satisfactory restoration. Here we can only follow the best judgment of competent scholars as to the most probable reconstruction of the original text. Such reconstructions are indicated in footnotes by the abbreviation Cn ("Correction"), and a translation of the Masoretic Text is added.

For the Apocryphal/Deuterocanonical Books of the Old Testament the Committee has made use of a number of texts. For most of these books the basic Greek text from which the present translation was made is the edition of the Septuagint prepared by Alfred Rahlfs and published by the Württemberg Bible Society (Stuttgart, 1935). For several of the books the more recently published individual volumes of the Göttingen Septuagint project were utilized. For the book of Tobit it was decided to follow the form of the Greek text found in codex Sinaiticus (supported as it is by evidence from Qumran); where this text is defective, it was supplemented and corrected by other Greek manuscripts. For the three Additions to Daniel (namely, Susanna, the Prayer of Azariah and the Song of the Three Jews, and Bel and the Dragon) the Committee continued to use the Greek version attributed to Theodotion (the so-called "Theodotion-Daniel"). In translating Ecclesiasticus (Sirach), while constant reference was made to the Hebrew fragments of a large portion of this book (those discovered at Qumran and Masada as well as those recovered from the Cairo Geniza), the Committee generally followed the Greek text (including verse numbers) published by Joseph Ziegler in the Göttingen Septuagint (1965). But in many places the Committee has translated the Hebrew text when this provides a reading that is clearly superior to the Greek; the Syriac and Latin versions were also consulted throughout and occasionally adopted. The basic text adopted in rendering 2 Esdras is the Latin version given in *Biblia Sacra*, edited by Robert Weber (Stuttgart, 1971). This was supplemented by consulting the Latin text as edited by R. L. Bensly (1895) and by Bruno Violet (1910), as well as by taking into account the several Oriental versions of 2 Esdras, namely, the Syriac, Ethiopic, Arabic (two forms, referred to as Arabic 1 and Arabic 2), Armenian, and Georgian versions. Finally, since the Additions to the Book of Esther are disjointed and quite unintelligible as they stand in most editions of the Apocrypha, we have provided them with their original context by translating the whole of the Greek version of Esther from Robert Hanhart's Göttingen edition (1983).

For the New Testament the Committee has based its work on the most recent edition of *The Greek New Testament*, prepared by an interconfessional and international committee and published by the United Bible Societies (1966; 3rd ed. corrected, 1983; information concerning changes to be introduced into the critical apparatus of the forthcoming 4th edition was available to the Committee). As in that edition, double brackets are used to enclose a few passages that are generally regarded to be later additions to the text, but which we have retained because of their evident antiquity and their importance in the textual tradition. Only in very rare instances have we replaced the text or the punctuation of the Bible Societies' edition by an alternative that seemed to us to be superior. Here and there in the footnotes the phrase, "Other ancient authorities read," identifies alternative readings preserved by Greek manuscripts and early versions. In both Testaments, alternative renderings of the text are indicated by the word "Or."

As for the style of English adopted for the present revision, among the mandates given to the Committee in 1980 by the Division of Education and Ministry of the National Council of Churches of Christ (which now holds the copyright of the RSV Bible) was the directive to continue in the tradition of the King James Bible, but to introduce such changes as are warranted on the basis of accuracy, clarity, euphony, and current English usage. Within the constraints set by the original texts and by the mandates of the Division, the Committee has followed the maxim, "As literal as possible, as free as necessary." As a consequence, the New Revised Standard Version (NRSV) remains essentially a literal translation. Paraphrastic renderings have been adopted only sparingly, and then chiefly to compensate for a deficiency in the English language—the lack of a common gender third person singular pronoun.

During the almost half a century since the publication of the RSV, many in the churches have become sensitive to the danger of linguistic sexism arising from the inherent bias of the English language towards the masculine gender, a bias that in the case of the Bible has often restricted or obscured the meaning of the original text. The mandates from the Division specified that, in references to men and women, masculine-oriented language should be eliminated as far as this can be done without altering passages that reflect the historical situation of ancient patriarchal culture. As can be appreciated, more than once the Committee found that the several mandates stood in tension and even in conflict. The various concerns had to be balanced case by case in order to provide a faithful and acceptable rendering without using contrived English. Only very occasionally has the pronoun "he" or "him" been retained in passages where the reference may have been to a woman as well as to a man; for example, in several legal texts in Leviticus and Deuteronomy. In such instances of formal, legal language, the options of either putting the passage in the plural or of introducing additional nouns to avoid masculine pronouns in English seemed to the Committee to obscure the historic structure and literary character of the original. In the vast majority of cases, however, inclusiveness has been attained by simple rephrasing or by introducing plural forms when this does not distort the meaning of the passage. Of course, in narrative and in parable no attempt was made to generalize the sex of individual persons.

Another aspect of style will be detected by readers who compare the more stately English rendering of the Old Testament with the less formal rendering adopted for the New Testament. For example, the traditional distinction between *shall* and *will* in English has been retained in the Old Testament as appropriate in rendering a document that embodies what may be termed the classic form of Hebrew, while in the New Testament the abandonment of such distinctions in the usage of the future tense in English reflects the more colloquial nature of the koine Greek used by most New Testament authors except when they are quoting the Old Testament.

Careful readers will notice that here and there in the Old Testament the word LORD (or in certain cases GOD) is printed in capital letters. This represents the traditional manner in English versions of rendering the Divine Name, the "Tetragrammaton" (see the notes on Exodus 3.14, 15), following the precedent of the ancient Greek and Latin translators and the long established practice in the reading of the Hebrew Scriptures in the synagogue. While it is almost if not quite certain that the Name was originally pronounced "Yahweh," this pronunciation was not indicated when the Masoretes added vowel sounds to the consonantal Hebrew text. To the four consonants YHWH of the Name, which had come to be regarded as too sacred to be pronounced, they attached vowel signs indicating that in its place should be read the Hebrew word *Adonai* meaning "Lord" (or *Elohim* meaning "God"). Ancient Greek translators employed the word *Kyrios* ("Lord") for the Name. The Vulgate likewise used the Latin word *Dominus* ("Lord"). The form "Jehovah" is of late medieval origin; it is a combination of the consonants of the Divine Name and the vowels attached to it by the Masoretes but belonging to an entirely different word. Although the American Standard Version (1901) had used "Jehovah" to render the Tetragrammaton (the sound of Y being represented by J and the sound of W by V, as in Latin), for two reasons the Committees that produced the RSV and the NRSV returned to the more familiar usage of the King James Version. (1) The word "Jehovah" does not accurately represent any form of the Name ever used in Hebrew. (2) The use of any proper name for the one and only God, as though there were other gods from whom the true

God had to be distinguished, began to be discontinued in Judaism before the Christian era and is inappropriate for the universal faith of the Christian Church.

It will be seen that in the Psalms and in other prayers addressed to God the archaic second person singular pronouns *thee, thou, thine*) and verb forms (*art, hast, hadst*) are no longer used. Although some readers may regret this change, it should be pointed out that in the original languages neither the Old Testament nor the New makes any linguistic distinction between addressing a human being and addressing the Deity. Furthermore, in the tradition of the King James Version one will not expect to find the use of capital letters for pronouns that refer to the Deity—such capitalization is an unnecessary innovation that has only recently been introduced into a few English translations of the Bible. Finally, we have left to the discretion of the licensed publishers such matters as section headings, cross-references, and clues to the pronunciation of proper names.

This new version seeks to preserve all that is best in the English Bible as it has been known and used through the years. It is intended for use in public reading and congregational worship, as well as in private study, instruction, and meditation. We have resisted the temptation to introduce terms and phrases that merely reflect current moods, and have tried to put the message of the Scriptures in simple, enduring words and expressions that are worthy to stand in the great tradition of the King James Bible and its predecessors.

In traditional Judaism and Christianity, the Bible has been more than a historical document to be preserved or a classic of literature to be cherished and admired; it is recognized as the unique record of God's dealings with people over the ages. The Old Testament sets forth the call of a special people to enter into covenant relation with the God of justice and steadfast love and to bring God's law to the nations. The New Testament records the life and work of Jesus Christ, the one in whom "the Word became flesh," as well as describes the rise and spread of the early Christian Church. The Bible carries its full message, not to those who regard it simply as a noble literary heritage of the past or who wish to use it to enhance political purposes and advance otherwise desirable goals, but to all persons and communities who read it so that they may discern and understand what God is saying to them. That message must not be disguised in phrases that are no longer clear, or hidden under words that have changed or lost their meaning; it must be presented in language that is direct and plain and meaningful to people today. It is the hope and prayer of the translators that this version of the Bible may continue to hold a large place in congregational life and to speak to all readers, young and old alike, helping them to understand and believe and respond to its message.

For the Committee,
BRUCE M. METZGER

ALPHABETICAL LISTING OF THE BOOKS OF THE BIBLE

Including the Apocryphal/Deuterocanonical Books

LIST OF ABBREVIATIONS

Books of the Bible: Abbreviation First

HEBREW BIBLE

Gen	Genesis	2 Chr	2 Chronicles	Dan	Daniel
Ex	Exodus	Ezra	Ezra	Hos	Hosea
Lev	Leviticus	Neh	Nehemiah	Joel	Joel
Num	Numbers	Esth	Esther	Am	Amos
Deut	Deuteronomy	Job	Job	Ob	Obadiah
Josh	Joshua	Ps	Psalms	Jon	Jonah
Judg	Judges	Prov	Proverbs	Mic	Micah
Ruth	Ruth	Eccl	Ecclesiastes	Nah	Nahum
1 Sam	1 Samuel	Song	Song of Solomon	Hah	Habakkuk
2 Sam	2 Samuel	Isa	Isaiah	Zeph	Zephaniah
1 Kings	1 Kings	Jer	Jeremiah	Hag	Haggai
2 Kings	2 Kings	Lam	Lamentations	Zech	Zechariah
1 Chr	1 Chronicles	Ezek	Ezekiel	Mal	Malachi

THE APOCRYPHAL/DEUTEROCANONICAL BOOKS

Tob	Tobit	Song of Thr	Azariah and the Three Jews	Pr Man	The Prayer of Manasseh
Jdt	Judith			Ps 151	Psalm 151
Add Esth	Esther (Greek)	Sus	Susanna	3 Macc	3 Maccabees
Wis	The Wisdom of Solomon	Bel	Bel and the Dragon	2 Esd	2 Esdras
Sir	Sirach	1 Macc	1 Maccabees	4 Macc	4 Maccabees
Bar	Baruch	2 Macc	2 Maccabees		
Let Jer	The Letter of Jeremiah	1 Esd	1 Esdras		

NEW TESTAMENT

Mt	Matthew	Eph	Ephesians	Heb	Hebrews
Mk	Mark	Phil	Philippians	Jas	James
Lk	Luke	Col	Colossians	1 Pet	1 Peter
Jn	John	1 Thess	1 Thessalonians	2 Pet	2 Peter
Acts	Acts of the Apostles	2 Thess	2 Thessalonians	1 Jn	1 John
Rom	Romans	1 Tim	1 Timothy	2 Jn	2 John
1 Cor	1 Corinthians	2 Tim	2 Timothy	3 Jn	3 John
2 Cor	2 Corinthians	Titus	Titus	Jude	Jude
Gal	Galatians	Philem	Philemon	Rev	Revelation

In the textual notes to the books of the Bible, the following abbreviations are used:

Ant.	Josephus, *Antiquities of the Jews*
Aram	Aramaic
Ch, chs	Chapter, chapters
Cn	Correction; made where the text has suffered in transmission and the versions provide no satisfactory restoration but where the Standard Bible Committee agrees with the judgment of competent scholars as to the most probable reconstruction of the original text.
Gk	Septuagint, Greek version of the Old Testament [also used in the NT, where it means simply Greek]
Heb	Hebrew of the consonantal Masoretic Text of the Old Testament
Josephus	Flavius Josephus (Jewish historian, about A.D. 37 to about 95)
Macc.	The book(s) of the Maccabees
Ms(s)	Manuscript(s)
MT	The Hebrew of the pointed Masoretic Text of the Old Testament
OL	Old Latin
Q Ms(s)	Manuscript(s) found at Qumran by the Dead Sea
Sam	Samaritan Hebrew text of the Old Testament
Syr	Syriac Version of the Old Testament
Syr H	Syriac Version of Origen's Hexapla
Tg	Targum
Vg	Vulgate, Latin Version of the Old Testament

For a detailed discussion of these terms, see "Textual Criticism," p. 2192.

The following abbreviations of additional ancient works are used in the introductions and annotations to the biblical books, and in the General Essays at the end of the volume:

Ag. Ap.	Josephus, *Against Apion*	*b. Yoma*	Babylonian Talmud, Tractate *Yoma*
Apoc. Bar.	*Apocalypse of Baruch*	CD	Cairo Genizah, Damascus Document
Apoc. Zeph.	*Apocalypse of Zephaniah*		
Aristophanes, *Ran.*	Aristophanes, *Ranae* (*Frogs*)	Cicero, *Fin.*	Cicero, *De finibus*
Aristotle, *Pol.*	Aristotle, *Politics*	*1 Clem*	*1 Clement* (First Epistle of Clement)
Aristotle, *Rh.*	Aristotle, *Rhetoric*	CoS	*The Context of Scripture: Canonical Compositions, Monumental Inscriptions, and Archival Documents from the Ancient World*, 3 vols. (ed. W.W. Hallo; Leiden: Brill, 1997-2002)
Aristotle, *Virt.*	Aristotle, *Virtues and Vices*		
2 Bar.	*2 Baruch* (another name for the Apocalypse of Baruch)		
b. B. Bat.	Babylonian Talmud, Tractate *Baba Bathra*		
b. Ber.	Babylonian Talmud, Tractate *Berakot*	*Did.*	*Didache*
		Dio Chrys., *Or.*	Dio Chrysostom, *Orationes*
b. Eruv.	Babylonian Talmud, Tractate *Eruvim*	Diod. Sic.	Diodorus of Sicily (*Library of History*)
b. Git.	Babylonian Talmud, Tractate *Gittin*		
b. Meg.	Babylonian Talmud, Tractate *Megillah*	*1 En.*	*1 Enoch*
		Ep. Arist.	*Letter of Aristeas*
b. Ned.	Babylonian Talmud, Tractate *Nedarim*	Euripides, *Tro.*	Euripides, *Trojan Women*
		Eusebius, *Hist. eccl.*	Eusebius, *Historia ecclesiastica*
b. San.	Babylonian Talmud, Tractate *Sanhedrin*	Eusebius, *Praep. Ev.*	Eusebius, *Praeparatio Evangelica*
		Gen. Rab.	*Genesis Rabbah*
b. Shabb.	Babylonian Talmud, Tractate *Shabbat*	Gk	Greek
		Hermas, *Mand.*	*Shepherd of Hermas, Mandate*

Hermas, *Sim.*	Shepherd of Hermas, *Similitude*	Plato, *Phaedr.*	Plato, *Phaedrus*
Hist.	Herodotus, *Histories*	Plato, *Symp.*	Plato, *Symposium*
Homer, *Od.*	Homer, *Odyssey*	Pliny, *Nat. Hist.*	Pliny, *Naturalis Historia*
HS	Holiness School	Plutarch, *Mor.*	Plutarch, *Moralia*
Ignatius, *Philad.*	Ignatius, *Epistle to the Philadelphians*	*Pro Rabirio*	Cicero, *Pro Rabirio Postuma*
		Pss. Sol.	*Psalms of Solomon*
Irenaeus, *Adv. Haer.*	Irenaeus, *Adversus omnes Haereses*	11QTemple	The Temple Scroll from Qumran Cave 11 (11Q19)
JB	Jerusalem Bible		
Jer. Sot.	Jerusalem Talmud, *Sotah* (see *y. Sot.*)	1QH	Hodayot (Thanksgiving Hymns) from Qumran Cave 1
Josephus, *Ant.*	Josephus, *Jewish Antiquities*	1QM	Milhamah (War Scroll) from Qumran Cave 1
Josephus, *Ap.*	Josephus, *Against Apion*		
Josephus, *J.W.*	Josephus, *Jewish War*	11QMelch	Melchizedek Scroll from Qumran Cave 11 (11Q13)
Jub.	*Jubilees*		
Juvenal, *Sat.*	Juvenal, *Satires*	1QpHab	Pesher to Habakkuk from Qumran Cave 1
KJV	King James Version (1611)		
l	liter	11QPs^a	The Psalms^a Scroll from Qumran Cave 11 (11Q5)
Lam. Rab.	*Lamentations Rabbah*		
lit.	literally	1QS	Rule of the Community (Serek Hayahad) from Qumran Cave 1
LXX	the Septuagint		
m. Abot	*Mishnah Abot*	Quintilian, *Inst.*	*Institutio Oratoria*
m. Avoda Zara	*Mishnah Avoda Zara*	REB	REVISED ENGLISH BIBLE
m. Ber.	*Mishnah Berakot*	RSV	REVISED STANDARD VERSION
m. Ketub.	*Mishnah Ketubim*	Seder Olam R.	*Seder Olam Rabbah*
m. Ned.	*Mishnah Nedarim*	Shab.	*Shabbat*
m. Ohalot	*Mishnah Ohalot*	Sifre Num.	*Sifre Numbers*
Midr.	Midrash	Sib. Or.	*Sibylline Oracles*
Midr. Pss.	Midrash Psalms	Sophocles, *Ant.*	Sophocles, *Antigone*
Midr. Rab.	Midrash Rabbah	Strom.	Clement of Alexandria, *Stromateis*
m. Shabb.	*Mishnah Shabbat*	Tacitus, *Hist.*	Tacitus, *Historiae*
m. Sot.	*Mishnah Sotah*	T. Abr.	*Testament of Abraham*
NIV	New International Version	T. Jos.	*Testament of Joseph*
NT	New Testament	T. Jud. (Test. Jud.)	*Testament of Judah*
P. Oxy.	Oxyrhynchus Papyri	T. Levi	*Testament of Levi*
Philo, *De Conf.Ling.*	Philo, *De Confusione Linguarum*	T. Moses	*Testament of Moses*
Philo, *De spec. leg.*	Philo, *De specialibus Legibus*	T. Naph.	*Testament of Naphtali*
Philo, *Flaccus*	Philo, *Against Flaccus*	T. Reuben	*Testament of Reuben*
Philo, *Her.*	Philo, *Quis rerum divinarum heres sit*	T. Sol.	*Testament of Solomon*
Philo, *Leg. all.*	Philo, *Legum allegoriae*	Tg. Ps-.J.	*Targum Pseudo-Jonathan*
Philo, *Leg. Gai.*	Philo, *Legatio ad Gaium*	Tr. Eruv.	Babylonian Talmud, *Tractate Eruvim* (see *b. Eruv.*)
Philo, *Migr.*	Philo, *De migratione Abrahami*		
Philo, *Opif.*	Philo, *De opificio mundi*	*y.*	Jerusalem Talmud
Philo, *Quest. in Gen.*	Philo, *Quaestiones in Genesis*	*y. Sot.*	Jerusalem Talmud, *Sotah*
Plato, *Cri.*	Plato, *Crito*	v., vv.	verse, verses
Plato, *Gorg.*	Plato, *Gorgias*		

Note: The abbreviation "Q," unless specified as "Quelle" ("Source") for the posited New Testament document of non-Markan common material in Matthew and Luke, refers to Qumran, and manuscripts from Qumran are identified by the cave number, which precedes the Q, and the official manuscript number, which follows it; thus, 1Q34 = Manuscript 34 from Cave 1 at Qumran; 4Q174 = Manuscript 174 from Cave 4; etc.

THE NEW OXFORD ANNOTATED BIBLE

Fully Revised
Fourth Edition

New Revised Standard Version

THE HEBREW BIBLE

The Hebrew Scriptures
commonly called
The Old Testament

New Revised Standard Version

INTRODUCTION TO THE PENTATEUCH

TERMINOLOGY, CONTENTS, AND TRADITIONAL VIEWS OF AUTHORSHIP

The word "Pentateuch," from the Greek for "five (*penta*) books (*teuchos*)," has entered English by way of Latin as the designation for the first group of books in the Bible, comprising Genesis, Exodus, Leviticus, Numbers, and Deuteronomy. Unlike other canonical divisions, where there is significant debate within and between different religious traditions, both Jewish and Christian traditions view these five books in this order as a single unit, introducing the Bible. The unanimity of tradition and the initial placement of these five books reflect their significance within both Judaism and Christianity.

Despite this unanimity of tradition, it is not so obvious how these five books cohere. They certainly do not form a single book in the modern sense, with a single author; modern scholarship has persuasively argued that each of these books is composite, consisting of several sources from different periods in Israel's history (see below). Nor is there complete coherence of plot among them. Moses is the central human character of much of the Pentateuch, but he is only introduced in ch 2 of Exodus, the second book. Nor is the early development of Israel as a people the Pentateuch's unifying theme, as may be seen from the first eleven chapters of the Bible, which are concerned with the world from creation to the birth of Abraham (Gen 11.27). Other suggested unifying themes for the Pentateuch, such as covenant, are also inadequate, since they do not explicitly appear at the beginning of the Pentateuch and continue well beyond it. The suggestion that the promise of the land unifies the Pentateuch is especially problematic, since this theme, though introduced in Gen 12, is only fulfilled with the conquest of the land in the book of Joshua, in which case the Hexateuch ("six books": the Pentateuch plus Joshua) rather than the Pentateuch should be seen as the decisive unit.

The Hebrew terms *torah*, *torat moshe* ("the Torah of Moses"), *torat YHWH* ("the Torah of the Lord"), and *torat ha'elohim* ("the Torah of God"), already in use in late biblical literature to describe what is later called the Pentateuch (e.g., 2 Chr 23.18; Ezra 7.6,10; Neh 8.1,18; Dan 9.11), offer a better clue to the nature and unity of these books. *Torah* is often understood as "law," and indeed this is one of its frequent meanings in the Bible, as in Ex 12.49; "There shall be one law [Heb *torah*] for the native and for the alien who resides among you." Law is a predominant genre of the Pentateuch, which contains extensive legal collections in Ex 21–23, Lev 17–26, and Deut 12–26, as well as selected laws within various narratives, such as the law of circumcision in the narrative about Abraham in Gen 17 and the law concerning inheritance of the land by women in Num 36, embedded within a section about the possession of the land. Many narrative sections also contain material that is of legal significance. For example, the first creation account in Genesis culminates with the "creation" of the sabbath (Gen 2.2–3), though this would only be legislated in Exodus, first in ch 16, and then as part of the Decalogue, in Ex 20.8–11. Similarly, the account of the construction of the tabernacle (Ex 25–40), a temporary temple for God in the wilderness, is not narrated for its own sake, but as an introduction to the various laws of sacrifice, narrated at the beginning of Leviticus, the book that immediately follows these chapters.

Yet "law" is not the only possible translation of *torah*, and the Pentateuch should not be described as a book of law. The Hebrew term *torah* also means "instruction" or "teaching," as in Prov 1.8, "Hear, my child, your father's instruction, and do not reject your mother's teaching [Heb *torah*]." Teaching is not confined to law; indeed narratives or stories are as effective a medium of instruction. Thus, given the predominance of narrative in significant portions of the Pentateuch, especially in Genesis, the beginning of Exodus, and Numbers, it is best to understand the biblical term *torat moshe* as "the instruction of Moses." This instruction was realized through narratives and laws, which together elucidate the proper norms of living and the relationship between God and the world.

The term *torat moshe*, in various late biblical books such as Ezra, Nehemiah, and Chronicles, refers to the Pentateuch more or less as it now exists, but it is not found in the Pentateuch. In fact, the Torah does not explicitly suggest that it was compiled by Moses himself. (The phrase "the Torah" in passages such as Deut 4.44, "This is the law [Heb *torah*] that Moses set before the Israelites," never refers to the complete Pentateuch.) It is easy to see how the tradition ascribing these five books as a whole to Moses developed. In several places, the Bible suggests that Moses stayed on Mount Sinai for forty days and forty nights (Ex 24.18; 34.28; Deut 9.9; 10.10). Clearly, this was too long a time for short legal collections such as Ex 21–23 to have been conveyed to him, and thus traditions developed that Moses received the entire written Torah from God at that point. According to the classical rabbis, Moses simultaneously received the oral law, which served as the authoritative interpretation of the written law. The written Torah would include, according to all rabbinic sources (which are followed by the early church), even the book of Genesis, which represents God's narration to Moses of the early history of the world and of Abraham and his family. Some rabbinic sources even suggest that the final chapter of the Torah, Deut 34, which narrates the death of Moses, was dictated by God to Moses, who wrote it with his tears. The view that the Torah should be understood as the divine word mediated by Moses was the standard view of synagogue and church through the Renaissance.

This view is explicitly contradicted by the Torah's narrative, as was sometimes (though rarely) recognized in the Middle Ages. Thus, Abraham ibn Ezra, a scholar active in the twelfth century CE, noted that Gen 12.6 states in reference to Abraham that "at that time the Canaanites were in the land." The words "at that time" suggest that for the author, the Canaanites were no longer in the land; in other words, it appears that the text was written after the time of Moses, because during his time the Canaanites were still in the land. A small number of other places that indicate authorship later than Moses were pointed out by a few medieval scholars, but these were not systematized into a thesis that could challenge the dominant view concerning Moses' authorship of the Torah.

MODERN SOURCE THEORIES

Slowly, with the rise of rationalism, particularly as associated with figures such as Thomas Hobbes (1588–1679) and Benedict (Baruch) Spinoza (1632–1677), the view that the Torah was a unified whole, written by Moses, began to be questioned. (For additional information on this development, see the essays on "The Interpretation of the Bible.") This culminated in the development of the Documentary Hypothesis in the nineteenth century, according to which the Pentateuch (or Hexateuch) is composed of four main sources or documents that were edited or redacted together: J, E, P, and D. Each of these sources or documents is embedded in a (relatively) complete form in the current Pentateuch, and each has a distinct vocabulary and theological perspective.

J and E are so called after the names for God that each of them uses in Genesis: J uses the name "Yahweh" (German "Jahwe," hence "J"), translated in the NRSV as "Lord," though it is really a personal name, whose exact meaning is unknown, from the root "to be"; E prefers to call the deity "Elohim" (translated "God"), an epithet that also serves as the generic term for God or gods in the Bible. P, which also uses "Elohim," is an abbreviation for the Priestly material, and D refers to Deuteronomy.

The difference in divine names, however, is not the main criterion used by scholars for suggesting that the Torah is not a unified composition. Much more significant are doublets and contradictions, in both narrative and legal material. For example, it has long been noted that chs 1–3 of Genesis twice narrate the creation of the world. People are created first in 1.27—"So God created humankind in his image, in the image of God he created them; male and female he created them"—and then again in 2.7—"Then the Lord God formed man from the dust of the ground, and breathed into his nostrils the breath of life; and the man became a living being." Furthermore, the second creation account does not simply mirror or repeat the first, but differs from the first both in outline and in detail. Gen 1.1–2.3, the first account, narrates the creation of a highly symmetrical world by a very powerful deity who creates through the word. In this account, for example, man and woman are created together (1.27) after the creation of the land animals (1.25). In contrast, the second account, in Gen 2.4–3.24, suggests that man was created (2.7), then the animals (2.19), and then woman (2.21–22). Its focus is on the creation of humanity, not of the entire physical world, and God experiments and anthropomorphically "forms" various beings, rather than creating them with the word. Thus, these are two distinct accounts, written by two authors, representing different worldviews about the nature of creation, humanity, and God.

The two creation accounts appear as two totally separate blocks of material in Gen 1.1–2.3 and 2.4–3.24. In several cases, however, such a clear-cut division of sources is impossible. For example, the flood story culminates in a tradition that God will never again bring a flood on the land (Gen 9.11); for this reason, the J and P flood narratives cannot appear as separate and complete narratives, so they are intertwined. Similarly, the story of the plague of blood (Ex 7.14–24) contains two intertwined accounts; in one (J), Moses is the protagonist, and the blood affects only the Nile, and the main plague is death of fish (e.g., vv. 17–18), while in the other (P), Aaron appears as well, and blood affects all Egyptian water sources (e.g., vv. 19, 24). In such cases, the narratives are combined with skill, though careful attention to plot and vocabulary help to discern the original building blocks or sources of the story.

In addition to narrative, the legal material in the Torah is also the product of several sources. For example, slave laws concerning Hebrew or Israelite slaves are found in the Torah in Ex 21.1–6, Lev 25.39–46, and Deut 15.12–18. These laws cannot be reconciled in a straightforward fashion since three different notions of slavery underlie them. Most significant is the way in which Exodus differentiates between the treatment of male and female slaves, whereas Deuteronomy claims that they should both be treated similarly. While Exodus and Deuteronomy agree that a slave who loves his master may opt to remain a slave "for life" (Ex 21.6) or "forever" (Deut 15.17), Lev 25 insists that slavery does not really exist, since slaves must be treated "as hired or bound laborers," and they may only serve "until the year of the jubilee" (v. 40). Such legal differences are not surprising given that the Bible is composite, and that the different legal collections reflect norms or ideals of different groups living in different times.

In fact, it is possible to trace distinctive styles and theological notions that typify individual Pentateuchal sources. For example, the J source is well known for its highly anthropomorphic God, who has a close relationship with humans, as seen in Gen 2.4–3.24, which includes, for example, a description of the Lord God "walking in the garden" (3.8) and says that the Lord God "made garments of skins for the man and for his wife, and clothed them" (3.21). On the other hand, in E, the Elohist source, God is more distant from people, typically communicating with them by dreams or through intermediaries, such as heavenly messengers (NRSV "angels") and prophets. The P or Priestly source is characterized by a strong interest in order and boundaries (see Gen 1), as well as an overriding concern with the priestly family of Aaron and the Temple-based religious system, which is prefigured by worship at the tabernacle in the wilderness. D, or Deuteronomy, is characterized by a unique hortatory or preaching style and insists strongly that God cannot be seen, as in this source's description of revelation: "Then the Lord spoke to you out of the fire. You heard the sound of words but saw no form; there was only a voice" (Deut 4.12). This explains why this source, uniquely, insists that God does not physically dwell in the Temple or tabernacle; rather, the Temple is "the place that the Lord your God will choose as a dwelling for his name" (Deut 12.11). D further emphasizes that this one God must be worshiped in one place only (see especially Deut 12); this place is later understood to be Jerusalem. Deuteronomy also shows exceptional concern for the underclasses, such as the widow and orphan, and it focuses on Moses.

The narrative sources J, E, P, and D also have legal collections associated with them. The Covenant Collection or Covenant Code (see Ex 24.7) in Ex 20.22–23.33 is associated with J or E. The Holiness Collection or Holiness Code of Lev 17–26 is so named because of its central injunction, "You shall be holy, for I the Lord your God am holy" (Lev 19.2). Though not composed by the Priestly author (P), it represents Priestly theology. The Deuteronomic law collection appears in Deut 12–26. These blocks of material were called "codes" by earlier scholars; but since the blocks are neither complete nor organized for the law court, as a "code" might be, the term "collection" is more suitable.

Critical biblical scholarship, through the latter part of the twentieth century, was quite confident in dating each of these Pentateuchal sources along with the legal collections they incorporated. Thus, J was seen as the earliest collection, often dated to the period of David and Solomon in the tenth century BCE, followed by E, which was often associated with the Northern Kingdom of Israel, established after the death of Solomon. D was connected to the reform of King Josiah of Judah in the late seventh century, and P was seen as deriving from the Babylonian exile in the sixth century. Scholars now agree that the reasons usually given for assigning these dates are problematic, and a lively debate has developed concerning such fundamental issues as the relative order of these sources and the extent to which any of them are as early as previous scholars had suggested. The existence of E as a complete source has been questioned as well, especially since E first appears well after the beginning of the Torah and is very difficult to disentangle from J after the beginning of Exodus. Thus, many scholars now talk of JE together as an early narrative source, incorporating diverse traditions. Additionally, most scholars no longer see each source as the work of a single author writing at one particular time but recognize that each is the product of a single group or "school" over a long time. Thus, it is best to speak of streams or strands of tradition and to contrast their basic underpinnings, rather than to speak of a source coming from a single author, period, and locale. Some scholars are also exploring the possibility that Genesis–2 Kings, rather than Genesis–Deuteronomy, should be considered a book. Yet, despite the unraveling of a consensus on the exact date and nature of the sources, it is still valid to contrast the ideologies and worldviews of the sources, contrasting, for example, the Deuteronomic view of Israel's fundamental, intrinsic holiness—as seen, in Deut 7.6, "For you are a people holy to the LORD your God"—with the Priestly view, articulated most clearly in the Holiness Collection, which suggests that Israel must aspire to holiness—as in Lev 19.2, "You shall be holy."

COMPILATION AND REDACTION OF THE PENTATEUCH

It is unclear how these various sources and legal collections, which now comprise the Torah, came together to form a single book. A number of scholars have recently posited that the Torah was compiled by Ezra on the basis of a request by the Persian authorities, but this goes beyond the evidence available. Most scholars posit an editor or series of editors or redactors, conventionally called R, who combined the various sources, perhaps in several stages, over a long time. Not all ancient Israelite legal and narrative traditions were collected and redacted as part of the Torah, as the Torah itself occasionally indicates when it refers to other sources (see Num 21.14,27). Much was certainly lost. Without access to this lost material, it is impossible to suggest in detail how and why the redactor(s), R, functioned in a particular way. It is sufficient to notice that in contrast to modern editing, which is fundamentally interested in developing a single viewpoint, the redaction of the Torah, like the editing of other ancient works, was not interested in creating a purely consistent, singular perspective but incorporated a variety of voices and perspectives and wished to preserve them despite their repetitions and contradictions. This is part of the process of the formation of authoritative scripture.

The ultimate result of this redaction, which most likely took place during the Babylonian exile (586–538 BCE) or soon thereafter in the early Persian period, was the creation of a very long book, narrating what must have been thought to be the formative period of Israel, from the period of the creation of the world through the death of Moses. Perhaps the events narrated in Gen 1–11 were included as a type of introduction to the choosing of Abraham, describing in detail the failures of humanity, as seen especially in the flood narrative (Gen 6–9) and the Tower of Babel episode (Gen 11.1–9), which necessitated the choosing of a particular nation by God.

No other work of comparable length or inclusiveness, in terms of the time covered and the sources systematically incorporated, was produced in the ancient Near East. This extensive, inclusive nature of the Torah has created a fundamental and interesting problem with which all serious biblical interpreters have either consciously or subconsciously grappled: Do we concentrate on interpreting the individual sources, on hearing the voices of the constituent parts of the text before redaction took place? Or do we focus on the final product, an approach that has been called holistic reading? The annotations of the following books will draw attention to this issue, showing how meaning may be uncovered by looking both at the early building blocks of the text, and at the text in its final, redacted form.

Marc Z. Brettler

GENESIS

NAME

Jewish tradition calls the first book of the Bible after its first significant word, *Bereshit*, which can be translated as "in the beginning" or "when first." It was common in the ancient world to name a book after its first word(s); for example, the great Mesopotamian epic of creation, *Enuma Elish*, gets its name from its first words, which mean "When on high." *Bereshit* also highlights the character of the book as the beginning of the Bible.

Christian tradition takes its name for the first book of the Bible, "Genesis," from the old Greek translation of the Torah, the Septuagint. *Genesis* in Greek means "origin" or "birth," and it appears in labels throughout the Greek translation of book, starting with two labels that refer to a "book of origins/births" (2.4 and 5.1 in the Septuagint). This name highlights an important dimension of the book of Genesis: its focus on genealogical origins. Though Genesis contains some of the most powerful narratives in the Bible, these stories occur within a genealogical structure, starting with 2.4 and ending with 37.2. Within this framework, the book may be understood as an expanded genealogy of the "children of Israel" who will be the focus of attention in the book of Exodus and subsequent books.

CANONICAL STATUS AND LOCATION

The book of Genesis, along with the rest of the Pentateuch/Torah, is one of the most central parts of both the Jewish Tanakh and the Christian Old Testament. Every ordering of the Bible places it first, and as such it sets the stage for what follows. Jews have long revered Genesis as the first book in the Torah, the most authoritative part of the Hebrew Bible. Christians have paid particular attention to Genesis because of its focus on God's work with humanity prior to the giving of the law. When Islam arose, it too featured a prominent focus on traditions from Genesis, such as the stories of Adam and Eve, Abraham and Ishmael, and Joseph. As a result, three major religious traditions—Judaism, Christianity, and Islam—all lay claim to the characters and stories of Genesis, each with their distinct understanding of the meaning of this important book of beginnings.

AUTHORSHIP

Ancient manuscripts of Genesis lack any claim of authorship. In the ancient Near East, most literary compositions were anonymous. Only during the Greco-Roman period do we start to see statements in early Jewish texts that Moses wrote Genesis and the rest of the Pentateuch. By this time Judaism had been influenced by Greek culture, where authorship was important and the writings of Homer enjoyed the highest prestige. In response, the Jewish authors of texts such as Jubilees (second century BCE) claimed that their Pentateuch had an ancient author as well—Moses. This identification of authorship made some sense since the four books of the Pentateuch that follow Genesis all are set during the lifetime of Moses, and Moses is by far the most prominent human character in the Pentateuch. In addition, verses such as Deut 4.44, "This is the law [Heb *torah*] that Moses set before the Israelites," were understood by later tradition as attributing the authorship of the entire Pentateuch to Moses.

Nevertheless, careful readers of the Bible realized in subsequent centuries that there were problems with this claim of authorship by Moses. Some verses in Genesis refer to events after the time of Moses, such as when the Canaanites were no longer in the land (12.6). In addition, a few rabbis wondered how Moses would have written a narrative about his own death and burial (Deut 34). To be sure, interpreters who have made it an article of faith to affirm Moses' authorship of the Pentateuch have found ways to explain these and other problems. These discussions, however, highlight ways that Genesis and other books of the Pentateuch do not seem to have been written originally in the voice of Moses. Like other ancient texts, it was originally anonymous, and only attributed to Moses in the context of later, author-oriented cultures.

DATES OF COMPOSITION, HISTORICAL CONTEXTS, AND LITERARY HISTORY

Two hundred and fifty years of historical scholarship on Genesis have established that Genesis was written over many centuries, using oral and written traditions. "In the beginning," so to speak, were oral traditions, since

Genesis was composed in a largely oral culture. We can see marks of that oral culture in the way similar stories about wife endangerment, wells, and oaths were attached to different patriarchs; compare, for example, stories about Abraham in Philistia in 20.1–18; 21.22–34 with stories about Isaac in the same location in 26.6–33. Indeed, these sorts of oral traditions about beginnings were important at every stage in the composition of Genesis.

Most scholars agree that the texts now found in Genesis began to be written down sometime after the establishment of the monarchy in Israel in the tenth century BCE. Building on German scholarship from the nineteenth century, many scholars think they can find (fragments of) two early sources in Genesis, a tenth-century BCE Yahwistic source ("J" for German "Jahwist") written in Judah during the reign of David or Solomon, and an Elohistic source ("E") written in the Northern Kingdom of Israel sometime during the eighth century BCE. Much recent scholarship, however, has doubted the existence of such sources and preferred to see the earliest written origins of Genesis in separate compositions, such as a Yahwistic primeval history covering the creation and flood, an originally Northern Israelite narrative about Jacob and Joseph, and a separate Moses story. In either case, the earliest works now embedded in Genesis were products of scribes working in the context of the monarchies of early Judah and Israel.

Many important parts of Genesis, however, were not written until after the monarchy had fallen in 586 BCE and Judean leaders were living in exile in Babylon. According to many scholars, this is the time when the Abraham narrative was written, and the theme of the promise of the land and much progeny was added to earlier stories about Jacob and Joseph. Through such new compositions and additions, former royal scribes adapted earlier writings about creation and ancestors to reassure the exiles of God's intent to bless them as God once blessed their ancestors. Moreover, they used this theme of promise to link earlier separate stories to each other and to the Moses story that followed. Alongside these scribal adaptations, a priestly group of authors wrote a parallel version of many stories in Genesis, starting with the seven-day creation account in 1.1–2.3 and the genealogy in ch 5, continuing with a priestly version of the flood story, and moving on from God's covenant of circumcision with Abraham (ch 17) to short stories about the inheritance of this covenant promise by his descendants. This layer of texts in Genesis, parallel to the non-Priestly texts, is called "P" for "Priestly source," because of its strong links to other Pentateuchal texts in Exodus–Numbers that focus on the priesthood of Aaron and sacrificial worship. For example, in structure and vocabulary, the seven-day creation account in 1.1–2.3 anticipates the story of the creation of the Priestly tabernacle at the end of the book of Exodus (Ex 35–40).

The last major stage in the composition of Genesis was the combination of the older non-Priestly writings about creation–flood and ancestors with their priestly counterparts. This probably happened during the postexilic period, when exiles such as Nehemiah and Ezra had returned and were rebuilding Jerusalem and its Temple. The consolidation of parallel traditions now in Genesis (and the rest of the Pentateuch) resulted in a common Torah around which the community could unite. This consolidation, however, also produced powerful contrasts in Genesis that can be seen by the attentive reader, such as between the seven-day creation in 1.1–2.3 (P) and the earlier non-Priestly story of creation and aftermath in 2.4–3.24, or between a version of the flood culminating in Noah's sacrifice (e.g., 7.1–5 and 8.20–22) and a Priestly version of the flood that lacks such a sacrifice and does not describe the provision of extra animals for it (e.g., 6.11–22 and 9.1–17). The contrasts are so clear that historical scholars already started to distinguish between the Priestly layer and the other parts of Genesis almost three hundred years ago, and the specifics of this distinction of P and non-P throughout the Pentateuch has remained an assured result of historical scholarship.

In sum, we do not know many of the details of the earliest composition of Genesis, and the oral stories that stand behind the book are lost. Nevertheless, we do know that the book was written over centuries by multiple authors, and we have a more specific and assured picture of the final stages of its composition. This picture highlights the way Genesis is not limited to just one situation or set of perspectives. Instead, it is a chorus of different voices, a distillate of ancient Israel's experiences with God over the centuries, written in the form of continually adapted stories about beginnings.

STRUCTURE AND CONTENTS

There are two main sections in Genesis, the primeval history in chs 1–11 and the ancestral history in chs 12–50. The latter section is often divided into the story of Abraham and Sarah (chs 12–25), the story of Jacob and Esau (chs 26–36), and the story of Joseph and his brothers (chs 37–50). Notably, despite the male focus of headings like this and in the book itself, it is matriarchs of ancient Israel, Sarah, Rebekah, Rachel, and Leah, who often play a determinative role in the Genesis narratives of birth and the fulfillment of God's promise.

The primeval history has two major sections that parallel each other: (1) the creation of the cosmos and stories of the first humans (1.1–6.4); and (2) the flood and dispersal of post-flood humanity (6.5–11.9). It features universal traditions similar to myths in other cultures, particularly in the ancient Near East and Greece. For example, the Mesopotamian Atrahasis epic was written hundreds of years before chs 1–11, yet it parallels numerous particulars of the biblical narrative as it describes the creation of the world, a flood, and the vow of the gods (here plural) not to destroy life with a flood again.

The ancestral history picks up where the primeval history left off and tells the story of God's choice of Abraham and the transmission of the promise (12.1–3) through Isaac and Jacob (whose name is changed to Israel in 32.28; 35.10), down to Jacob's twelve sons, the progenitors of the twelve tribes of Israel. These stories are closest to oral folklore, so it is often difficult to find ancient written parallels to chs 12–50. Nevertheless, recent scholarship has found similarities between Israelite tales about the matriarchs and patriarchs and modern legends told in oral cultures. For example, there are some striking parallels between the depiction of the clever deceptions of Jacob and others (e.g., 25.27–34; 27.1–45) and the celebration of wily "tricksters" in Native American and other traditions.

These different parts of Genesis are brought together through the framework of *toledot* ("generations" or "descendants") headings (originally from the Priestly source), each of which guides the reader to the major focus of the section that follows it (2.4; 5.1; 6.9; 10.1; 11.10; 11.27; 25.12; 25.19; 36.1,9; 37.2). After an initial focus on all the peoples of the world descending from Adam (5.1) and Noah (6.9; 10.1), they highlight a narrowing focus in Genesis on those who receive the divine promise. The headings first lead us to Abraham, the first to receive God's promise (11.10,27). Then they distinguish between descendants of Abraham who receive the promise (Isaac and Jacob/Israel) and those who do not (Ishmael and Esau).

Using these kinds of guides, we can outline Genesis as follows:

I. The primeval history   1.1–11.26
   A. Creation and violence before the flood   1.1–6.4
   B. Re-creation through flood and multiplication of humanity   6.5–11.26
II. The ancestral history   11.27–50.26
   A. Gift of the divine promise to Abraham and his descendants   11.27–25.11
   B. The divergent destinies of the descendants of Ishmael and Isaac (Jacob/Esau)   25.12–35.29
   C. The divergent destinies of the descendants of Esau and Jacob/Israel   36.1–50.26

By the end of the book, the lens of the narrative camera has moved from a wide-angle overview of all the peoples of the world to a narrow focus on one small group, the sons of Jacob (also named "Israel"). As the book concludes, this family is stuck together in Egypt because of famine in their homeland, but they all are heirs of the promise of their fathers, Abraham, Isaac, and Jacob. This family of promise will become the people of promise featured at the outset of the book of Exodus.

INTERPRETATION

The history of interpretation of Genesis begins with its gradual composition over centuries. Early monarchic scribes reinterpreted oral traditions in writing the first preexilic compositions behind Genesis. Later exilic scribes expanded and joined earlier compositions in the process of addressing an audience of Judeans exiled in Babylon. Priests (exilic or postexilic) wrote their own versions of the beginnings of Israel, "P." Later postexilic writers consolidated the non-Priestly and Priestly writings into a common Torah that was the foundation for later Judaism. Each of these stages involved interpretation of how earlier writings pertained to the present. Genesis as we have it now is a crystallization of these multiple interpretations.

As discussed, the book has continued to be centrally important to Jews, Christians, and Muslims. It was a major focus of early Jewish writings from the fifth century BCE to the first century CE. Later Jewish rabbinic scholars built on these traditions, writing midrashic interpretations of Genesis and expansive Aramaic translations of the book. Some of these Jewish traditions adapted the stories of Genesis so that they linked better with Torah law. For example, already in the book of Jubilees (written in the second century BCE), Abraham was portrayed as the first monotheist, destroying his father's idols before departing for the promised land. Moreover, the story of Abraham's virtual sacrifice of Isaac (22.1–19), termed the "Akedah" (the "binding") in Jewish tradition, was adapted by some readers into an account of how Isaac actually was sacrificed by Abraham and resurrected by God—anticipating later Jewish suffering and hopes for redemption.

Christian communities likewise focused on the stories of Genesis. For example, Paul, the central figure behind the outreach of Christians to Gentiles, argued that Abraham was an important example of how grace, through faith, came before the giving of the law. In his letter to the Romans (4.1–15) he notes that Abraham had his faith "reckoned to him as righteousness" (Gen 15.6) before he had undergone circumcision (Gen 17). Based on this and other arguments, Paul argued that Gentiles did not have to fulfill Torah requirements such as circumcision in order to partake of God's promise, as long as they joined themselves to Jesus Christ, whom Paul affirmed as the true spiritual offspring and heir of Abraham. Thus, whereas earlier and later Jewish interpreters tended to stress Abraham's and other patriarchs' Torah obedience, Paul, himself also a Jew, reinterpreted Abraham apart from Torah obedience in order to create a place for non-Jews to have a full relationship with the God of Israel.

Stories originating from Genesis also play a prominent role in Islam. Building on older Jewish traditions about Abraham destroying his father's idols, the Koran and other Muslim traditions revere Abraham as one of the first monotheists. Yet within Islam, Ishmael and not Isaac is the most important of his sons. It is Ishmael and not Isaac whom Abraham almost sacrifices (cf. Gen 22) according to Islamic tradition. Moreover, after that, Islamic tradition holds that Abraham and Ishmael went on to find and rebuild the Kaaba shrine at Mecca, Islam's most holy site. In this way, stories from Genesis are linked to two of the five central pillars of Islam: monotheism and pilgrimage.

In the modern era, Genesis has been an important battleground as communities have worked to live out ancient faiths in a modern world. For example, much discussion of Genesis, at least among Christians in the West, has focused on whether the stories of Genesis are historically true. Astronomers, biologists, and other scientists have offered accounts of the origins of the cosmos and humanity different from those in Gen 1–2. Some believers, however, insist on the importance of affirming the historical accuracy of every part of Genesis, and have come to see such belief as a defining characteristic of what it means to be truly faithful. This definition is relatively new: the historicity of Genesis was not a significant concern prior to the rise of modern science and the historical method; in fact, in premodern times, the stories of Genesis were often read metaphorically or allegorically. Moreover, many would argue that an ancient document such as Genesis is not ideally treated as scientific treatise or a modern-style historical source. Instead, its rich store of narratives offer nonscientific, narrative, and poetic perspectives on values and the meaning of the cosmos that pertain to other dimensions of human life.

Finally, recent years have seen a proliferation of other approaches to Genesis, particularly literary studies of Genesis in its final form and feminist rereadings of many narratives in Genesis. For example, some feminist scholars have questioned whether the typical reading of the garden of Eden story, which is highly critical of women, is correct. Others have highlighted the crucial role of the matriarchs as actors in the Genesis drama, especially as determiners of which son of a given patriarch will inherit the promise (e.g., Sarah and Rebekah) or as influencers of the levels of privilege among brothers (e.g., Rachel). Reading from another perspective, African American interpreters have traced the misuse of the story of Ham to reinforce racism and slavery, and a wide variety of interpreters have called into question the traditional interpretation of the story of Sodom and Gomorrah as a judgment on homosexuality. In these ways and many others, an ever more diverse range of interpreters of the Bible have offered new perspectives on a text centrally important to readers for many centuries.

GUIDE TO READING

Many who have resolved to read the whole Bible actually have made it through Genesis, but what they find often surprises them. Those who know the stories of Genesis through the lens of later interpretation often assume that the characters in the book are saints. A closer reading reveals otherwise. The supposedly "faithful" Abraham often seems doubtful of God's intent to protect and provide for him, and Jacob and his family are distinguished by their ability to survive in the world through bargaining and trickery. Such stories pose a challenge to those who would use the Bible as a source of role models for ethical behavior. Standing at the Bible's outset, they challenge readers to develop other models for understanding and appreciating this ancient text.

Genesis has been a major focus for literary approaches to the Bible. These approaches adopt techniques from study of contemporary literature to illuminate the artistry and poetics of the Bible. The story of Joseph and his brothers is a particularly constructive place to explore this kind of approach. Note how the narrator subtly leads the reader through an arc extending from Joseph's initial dreams of rule of his brothers in ch 37 to their submission to him and his provision of food for them in chs 42–50. Along the way, the speeches of Joseph and his brothers often do not correspond precisely to the reality described by the narrator, and the divergences reveal much about their characters. For example, Joseph's brothers trick their father about Joseph being killed (37.31–35), but their failure to report that their money was back in their sacks (42.25–34) is found out by Jacob, who guesses that they were planning to take Benjamin from him (42.35–38) as they actually took Joseph. Later, Joseph puts his brothers in a position where they can save themselves from slavery by betraying Benjamin, Joseph's full brother, as they once betrayed Joseph himself (44.1–17). Only when Judah, who formerly initiated the sale of Joseph into slavery (37.26–28), offers himself in place of Benjamin (44.18–34) does Joseph break down and reveal his true identity to his brothers (45.1–15). In this way the Joseph story artfully describes the first movement in Genesis from the urge toward fratricide (cf. 4.1–16; 27.41–45; see 33.12–17n.) to full reunion. Reading the Joseph story for such turns and characterizations can be an excellent introduction to the elegance of biblical narrative more generally.

Finally, one strategy in reading Genesis is to observe the differences between some of the writings embedded in it. The reader can compare parallel stories in Genesis, such as the different stories of creation in 1.1–2.3 and 2.4–3.24 or the parallel and yet different accounts about Hagar (chs 16 and 21), the covenant with Abraham (chs 15 and 17), or Abraham and Sarah (12.10–20 and 20.1–18), or Abraham, Abimelech, and Isaac (20.1–18; 21.22–34 and 26.6–33). Comparing these different accounts helps uncover the distinct perspectives of each and their contribution to the book of Genesis as a whole.

David M. Carr

1 In the beginning when God created[a] the heavens and the earth, [2] the earth was a formless void and darkness covered the face of the deep, while a wind from God[b] swept over the face of the waters. [3] Then God said, "Let there be light"; and there was light. [4] And God saw that the light was good; and God separated the light from the darkness. [5] God called the light Day, and the darkness he called Night. And there was

[a] Or *when God began to create* or *In the beginning God created*

[b] Or *while the spirit of God* or *while a mighty wind*

1.1–11.26: The primeval history: from creation to the birth of Abraham. This unit is composed of two principal layers, a Priestly source that also provides an editorial framework (1.1–2.3; 5.1–28,30–32; 6.9–22; 7.6,11,13–16a,18–21,24; 8.1–2a,3–5,14–19; 9.1–17; 10.10–27), and an earlier non-Priestly primeval history that uses the divine name Yahweh (represented as Lᴏʀᴅ in the translation) found in the rest of 2.4–11.9. As seen in the chart on correspondences spanning the primeval history (see p. 13), the present combined text is an intricate narrative, with echoes of creation and un-creation, struggles surrounding human god-likeness, and other themes.

1.1–2.3: Creation culminating in sabbath. This Priestly account of creation presents God as a king, creating the universe by decree in six days and resting on the seventh. **1.1:** Scholars differ on whether this verse is to be translated as an independent sentence summarizing what follows (e.g., "In the beginning God created") or as a temporal phrase describing what things were like when God started (e.g., "When God began to create . . . the earth was a formless void"; cf. 2.4–6). In either case, the text does not describe creation out of nothing (contrast 2 Macc 7.28). Instead, the story emphasizes how God creates order from a watery chaos. **2:** As elsewhere in the Bible, *the deep* (Heb "tehom") has no definite article attached to it in Hebrew. Some scholars understand "tehom" to be related to the Babylonian goddess Tiamat, a deity representing primeval oceanic chaos, whom the head god, Marduk, defeated in *Enuma Elish*, a major Babylonian myth that includes an account of creation. Christian interpreters have often seen the "Spirit" of the Trinity later in this verse. *Wind* fits the ancient context better (see 8.1). **3:** The first of eight acts of creation through decree. Like a divine king God pronounces his will and it is accomplished. **4–5:** These verses introduce two other themes crucial to this account: the goodness of creation and the idea that creation is accomplished through God's separating, ordering, and naming elements of the universe. The seven-day scheme of 1.1–2.3 requires the creation of light, day, and night at the outset.

evening and there was morning, the first day.

⁶ And God said, "Let there be a dome in the midst of the waters, and let it separate the waters from the waters." ⁷ So God made the dome and separated the waters that were under the dome from the waters that were above the dome. And it was so. ⁸ God called the dome Sky. And there was evening and there was morning, the second day.

⁹ And God said, "Let the waters under the sky be gathered together into one place, and let the dry land appear." And it was so. ¹⁰ God called the dry land Earth, and the waters that were gathered together he called Seas. And God saw that it was good. ¹¹ Then God said, "Let the earth put forth vegetation: plants yielding seed, and fruit trees of every kind on earth that bear fruit with the seed in it." And it was so. ¹² The earth brought forth vegetation: plants yielding seed of every kind, and trees of every kind bearing fruit with the seed in it. And God saw that it was good. ¹³ And there was evening and there was morning, the third day.

¹⁴ And God said, "Let there be lights in the dome of the sky to separate the day from the night; and let them be for signs and for seasons and for days and years, ¹⁵ and let them be lights in the dome of the sky to give light upon the earth." And it was so. ¹⁶ God made the two great lights—the greater light to rule the day

and the lesser light to rule the night—and the stars. ¹⁷ God set them in the dome of the sky to give light upon the earth, ¹⁸ to rule over the day and over the night, and to separate the light from the darkness. And God saw that it was good. ¹⁹ And there was evening and there was morning, the fourth day.

²⁰ And God said, "Let the waters bring forth swarms of living creatures, and let birds fly above the earth across the dome of the sky." ²¹ So God created the great sea monsters and every living creature that moves, of every kind, with which the waters swarm, and every winged bird of every kind. And God saw that it was good. ²² God blessed them, saying, "Be fruitful and multiply and fill the waters in the seas, and let birds multiply on the earth." ²³ And there was evening and there was morning, the fifth day.

²⁴ And God said, "Let the earth bring forth living creatures of every kind: cattle and creeping things and wild animals of the earth of every kind." And it was so. ²⁵ God made the wild animals of the earth of every kind, and the cattle of every kind, and everything that creeps upon the ground of every kind. And God saw that it was good.

²⁶ Then God said, "Let us make humankind[a] in our image, according to our likeness;

___

[a] Heb *adam*

___

6–8: The *dome/Sky* made on the second day separates an upper ocean (Ps 148.4; see Gen 7.11) from a lower one. This creates a space in which subsequent creation can take place. **9–13:** Two creative acts: creation of dry land and command that the land bring forth vegetation. *Earth* is a feminine noun in Heb. The text thus echoes other ancient mythologies and the life cycle in having a feminine earth bring forth the first life in the universe (cf. Job 1.21). God is involved only indirectly here, commanding the earth to *put forth*. **14–19:** There is a correspondence between days one to three and days four to six (1 || 4, 2 || 5, 3 || 6), which heightens the symmetry and order of God's creation. Here, God's creation of heavenly *lights* on the fourth day corresponds to creation of light, day, and night on the first. In a critical response to non-Israelite cultures who worshiped these heavenly bodies, the bodies are not named and are identified as mere timekeepers. **20–23:** See vv. 14–19n. The second day featured the dome separating upper and lower oceans; the corresponding fifth day features the creation of birds to fly *across the dome* and ocean creatures, including sea monsters (Ps 104.25–26)—this is probably a polemic against other ancient Israelite traditions, which suggested that the sea monsters rebelled against God (e.g., Isa 51.9). God's blessing of the swarming creatures (1.22) anticipates a similar blessing that God will give humanity (1.28). **24–30:** The third day described creation of land and plants in turn, the corresponding sixth day involves the creation of two types of plant-eating land-dwellers: animals and then humans. **24–25:** Again, earth is involved in bringing forth life (see 1.9–13n.). **26:** The plural *us, our* (3.22; 11.7) probably refers to the divine beings who compose God's heavenly court (1 Kings 22.19; Job 1.6). *Image, likeness* is often interpreted to be a spiritual likeness between God and humanity. Another view is that this text builds on ancient concepts of the king physically resembling the god and thus bearing a bodily stamp of his authority to rule. Here this idea is democratized, as all of humanity appears godlike. This appearance equips humans for godlike rule over the fish, birds,

and let them have dominion over the fish of the sea, and over the birds of the air, and over the cattle, and over all the wild animals of the earth,[a] and over every creeping thing that creeps upon the earth."

27 So God created humankind[b] in his image,

in the image of God he created them;[c]

male and female he created them.

28 God blessed them, and God said to them, "Be fruitful and multiply, and fill the earth and subdue it; and have dominion over the fish of the sea and over the birds of the air and over every living thing that moves upon the earth." 29 God said, "See, I have given you every plant yielding seed that is upon the face of all the earth, and every tree with seed in its fruit; you shall have them for food. 30 And to every beast of the earth, and to every bird of the air, and to everything that creeps on the earth, everything that has the breath of life, I have given every green plant for food." And it was so. 31 God saw everything that he had made, and indeed, it was very good. And there was evening and there was morning, the sixth day.

2 Thus the heavens and the earth were finished, and all their multitude. 2 And on the seventh day God finished the work that he had done, and he rested on the seventh day from all the work that he had done. 3 So God blessed the seventh day and hallowed it, because on it God rested from all the work that he had done in creation.

4 These are the generations of the heavens and the earth when they were created.

In the day that the LORD[d] God made the earth and the heavens, 5 when no plant of the field was yet in the earth and no herb of the field had yet sprung up—for the LORD God had not caused it to rain upon the earth, and there was no one to till the ground; 6 but a stream would rise from the earth, and water the whole face of the ground— 7 then the LORD God formed man from the dust of the

a Syr: Heb *and over all the earth*
b Heb *adam*
c Heb *him*
d Heb YHWH, as in other places where "LORD" is spelled with capital letters (see also Exod 3.14-15 with notes).

and animals. **27–28:** The text stresses the creation of humanity as simultaneously male and female. This leads to the emphasis in the blessing of v. 28 and the book of Genesis as a whole on the multiplication of humanity in general (6.1; 9.1–7) and Israel in particular (17.2–6; 47.27). **29 30:** The text envisions an ancient mythological time before violence disturbs God's perfect order (cf. 6.11). **31:** Where individual elements of creation were "good" (vv. 4,10, etc.), the whole is *very good,* perfectly corresponding to God's intention. **2.1–3:** This day is the climax to which the whole seven-day scheme has led. God does not command the sabbath, but does rest (Heb "shabat") on the seventh day and bless it, weaving the seven-day rhythm into creation. The establishment of institutions is found in other ancient creation stories as well.

2.4a: Although many scholars view this as the conclusion to the Priestly creation account, it is probably a separate introduction to the following material, as elsewhere in Genesis (e.g., 5.1; 6.9; 10.1).

CORRESPONDENCES SPANNING THE PRIMEVAL HISTORY

Creation (1.1–2.3)	
Crime and punishment with <u>eating of fruit</u> (2.4–3.24)	Crime and punishment with *brother conflict* (4.1–16)
Prevention of godlike immortality (3.23–24)	Origins of cultures (4.17–24 origins of peoples, ch 10)
Flood: un-creation and re-creation (6.5–9.17)	
Spreading of **peoples** (10.1–11.9) as part of divine prevention of people gaining godlike power (11.1–9)	*Brother separation*: subjugation of a **people** (9.20–27) as a result of the <u>first drinking of wine</u>

2.4b–25: Creation in a garden. This non-Priestly Yahwistic tradition is different from 1.1–2.3, as evidenced by the different style and order of events. Though distinct from the Priestly account of 1.1–2.3, it nevertheless reflects ancient temple imagery. **4b–6:** A description of how things were prior to creation (cf. 1.1–2) is common in ancient Near Eastern creation stories. **7:** The wordplay on Heb "'adam" (human being; here translated "man" [cf. 1.26]) and "'adamah" (arable land; here *ground*) introduces a motif characteristic of this tradition: the relation of humankind to the soil from which it was *formed.* Human nature is not a duality of body and soul; rather

ground,[a] and breathed into his nostrils the breath of life; and the man became a living being. [8] And the LORD God planted a garden in Eden, in the east; and there he put the man whom he had formed. [9] Out of the ground the LORD God made to grow every tree that is pleasant to the sight and good for food, the tree of life also in the midst of the garden, and the tree of the knowledge of good and evil.

[10] A river flows out of Eden to water the garden, and from there it divides and becomes four branches. [11] The name of the first is Pishon; it is the one that flows around the whole land of Havilah, where there is gold; [12] and the gold of that land is good; bdellium and onyx stone are there. [13] The name of the second river is Gihon; it is the one that flows around the whole land of Cush. [14] The name of the third river is Tigris, which flows east of Assyria. And the fourth river is the Euphrates.

[15] The LORD God took the man and put him in the garden of Eden to till it and keep it. [16] And the LORD God commanded the man, "You may freely eat of every tree of the garden; [17] but of the tree of the knowledge of good and evil you shall not eat, for in the day that you eat of it you shall die."

[18] Then the LORD God said, "It is not good that the man should be alone; I will make him a helper as his partner." [19] So out of the ground the LORD God formed every animal of the field and every bird of the air, and brought them to the man to see what he would call them; and whatever the man called every living creature, that was its name. [20] The man gave names to all cattle, and to the birds of the air, and to every animal of the field; but for the man[b] there was not found a helper as his partner. [21] So the LORD God caused a deep sleep to fall upon the man, and he slept; then he took one of his ribs and closed up its place with flesh. [22] And the rib that the LORD God had taken from the man he made into a woman and brought her to the man. [23] Then the man said,

"This at last is bone of my bones
    and flesh of my flesh;
this one shall be called Woman,[c]
    for out of Man[d] this one was taken."

[24] Therefore a man leaves his father and his mother and clings to his wife, and they be-

a Or *formed a man* (Heb *adam*) *of dust from the ground* (Heb *adamah*)

b Or *for Adam*

c Heb *ishshah*

d Heb *ish*

God's *breath* animates the *dust* and it becomes a single *living being* (Ps 104.29; Job 34.14–15). **8–9:** *Eden* means "delight." This divine garden recalls the "garden of God/the LORD" mentioned elsewhere in the Bible (13.10; Ezek 28.13–16; 31.8–9; Isa 51.3; Joel 2.3); such sacred gardens are known in other ancient Near Eastern temple traditions. In addition, ancient Near Eastern art and texts feature a prominent focus on trees, often associated with feminine powers of fertility. Usually such trees symbolize life, as in the *tree of life* here (3.22; see Prov 3.18; Rev 22.2,14,19). But this story focuses more on the *tree of the knowledge of good and evil,* symbolizing wisdom (2 Sam 14.17; 1 Kings 3.9). See further 12.6–8n. **10–14:** This section, along with the preceding one describing the "stream" rising up to water the ground (2.6), may draw on the ancient tradition that a temple is built on a primal mountain of creation from which the waters of the earth flow. The rivers mentioned here combine world rivers like the *Tigris* and *Euphrates* (both in Mesopotamia) with the local *Gihon* that flowed from Mount Zion in Jerusalem (Ps 46.4; Isa 7.6; Zech 14.8), although *Cush* is generally either Ethiopia or in Arabia. *Pishon* is unknown; *Havilah* is probably in Arabia. **16–17:** The speech concludes with a legal prohibition using technical Priestly death-penalty language (e.g., Lev 20.9,11,12). **18–20:** Animals are created after the first human rather than before (cf. 1.24–25). The human's naming of the animals implies a dominion over them analogous to that seen in 1.26–28. Yet the LORD God here contrasts with the all-powerful deity depicted in ch 1. The LORD God creates the animals in a comical, failed attempt to make a *helper* for the human that "corresponds to him" (NRSV: *as his partner*). **21–23:** Just as the connection of humanity to the ground is affirmed in the making of the first human (Heb *'adam*") from earthy "humus" ("*'adamah*") (2.7), so also the connection of men and women is affirmed here through the crowning event of creation: the making of the woman from a part of the man (2.21–22). The man affirms this connection in a jubilant poem (2.23) featuring a wordplay on "man" (Heb *'ish*") and "woman" ("*'ishshah*"). This concluding song of praise of the woman corresponds to God's concluding affirmation of all of creation as "very good" in 1.31. **24–25:** Sex between a *man* and *his wife* is regarded here as reflecting the essence

come one flesh. [25] And the man and his wife were both naked, and were not ashamed.

3 Now the serpent was more crafty than any other wild animal that the LORD God had made. He said to the woman, "Did God say, 'You shall not eat from any tree in the garden'?" [2] The woman said to the serpent, "We may eat of the fruit of the trees in the garden; [3] but God said, 'You shall not eat of the fruit of the tree that is in the middle of the garden, nor shall you touch it, or you shall die.'" [4] But the serpent said to the woman, "You will not die; [5] for God knows that when you eat of it your eyes will be opened, and you will be like God,[a] knowing good and evil." [6] So when the woman saw that the tree was good for food, and that it was a delight to the eyes, and that the tree was to be desired to make one wise, she took of its fruit and ate; and she also gave some to her husband, who was with her, and he ate. [7] Then the eyes of both were opened, and they knew that they were naked; and they sewed fig leaves together and made loincloths for themselves.

[8] They heard the sound of the LORD God walking in the garden at the time of the evening breeze, and the man and his wife hid themselves from the presence of the LORD God among the trees of the garden. [9] But the LORD God called to the man, and said to him, "Where are you?" [10] He said, "I heard the sound of you in the garden, and I was afraid, because I was naked; and I hid myself." [11] He said, "Who told you that you were naked? Have you eaten from the tree of which I commanded you not to eat?" [12] The man said, "The woman whom you gave to be with me, she gave me fruit from the tree, and I ate." [13] Then the LORD God said to the woman, "What is this that you have done?" The woman said, "The serpent tricked me, and I ate." [14] The LORD God said to the serpent,

"Because you have done this,
cursed are you among all animals
and among all wild creatures;
upon your belly you shall go,
and dust you shall eat
all the days of your life.
[15] I will put enmity between you and the woman,
and between your offspring and hers;
he will strike your head,
and you will strike his heel."

[16] To the woman he said,

"I will greatly increase your pangs in childbearing;

a   Or *gods*

of the connection God created between men and women. The unashamed nakedness of the man and woman indicates their still uncivilized and innocent status.

3.1–24: Garden disobedience and punishment. Though this story is often taken by Christians as an account of "original sin," the word "sin" never occurs in it. Instead, it describes how the maturing of humans into civilized life involved damage of connections established in 2.4–25 between the LORD God, man, woman, and earth. **1:** This characterization of the snake emphasizes his wise craftiness (Heb "'arum"), a characteristic that contrasts with the innocent nakedness ("'arum") of the man and woman. Snakes were a symbol in the ancient world of wisdom, fertility, and immortality. Only later was the snake in this story seen by interpreters as the devil (see Wis 2.24). **4–5:** The snake introduces doubt by rightly predicting the consequences of eating the fruit—the humans will not be put to death as implied in the language of 2.17 and their eyes will be *opened* (see v. 7) so they gain wisdom, *knowing good and evil.* **6–7:** The woman sees that the pleasant fruit of the tree is desirable *to make one wise;* she eats it and shares it with her husband. The result is enlightenment: *the eyes of both were opened.* Such wisdom takes them from the earlier unashamed nakedness (2.25) to clothing, a mark of civilization. **8–13:** Legal forms recur as the LORD God interrogates first the man and then the woman (see 2.16–17n.). The disintegration of earlier connectedness is shown by the hiding of the humans from the LORD God and the tendency of the man to blame the woman (and implicitly the LORD God) for his action. Later interpreters of the story have shown a similar tendency to blame the woman (e.g., Sir 25.24; 1 Tim 2.14). **14–19:** A proclamation of sentence or penalty follows the interrogation, starting with the snake and concluding with the man. **14–15:** Here the crawl of the snake is linked to the LORD God's punishing curse. As a result, later audiences can look to the crawling snake as a reminder of the story and testimony to its truth. **16–19:** Though this is often understood as a curse of the woman to pain in childbirth, the word "curse" is not used in these verses. Another interpretation is that the woman is sentenced to endless "toil" (not *pain*) of reproduction, much as the man is condemned in vv. 17–19 to endless toil in food production. The man's *rule* over the woman here is a tragic reflection of the disintegration of

The descendants of Adam
according to the Yahwistic source (Gen 4)

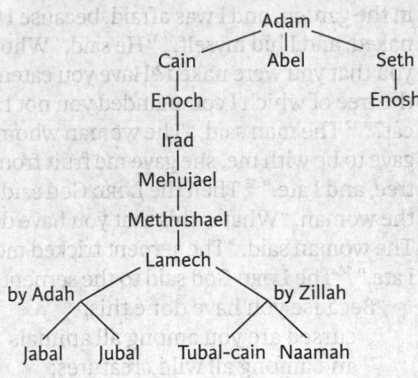

The descendants of Adam
according to the Priestly source (Gen 5)

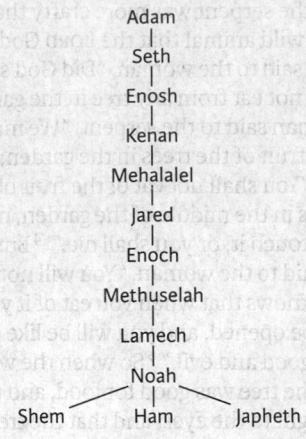

in pain you shall bring forth children,
yet your desire shall be for your husband,
and he shall rule over you."
[17] And to the man[a] he said,
"Because you have listened to the voice of
your wife,
and have eaten of the tree
about which I commanded you,
'You shall not eat of it,'
cursed is the ground because of you;
in toil you shall eat of it all the days of
your life;
[18] thorns and thistles it shall bring forth
for you;
and you shall eat the plants of the
field.
[19] By the sweat of your face
you shall eat bread
until you return to the ground,
for out of it you were taken;
you are dust,
and to dust you shall return."

[20] The man named his wife Eve,[b] because
she was the mother of all living. [21] And the
LORD God made garments of skins for the
man[c] and for his wife, and clothed them.
[22] Then the LORD God said, "See, the man
has become like one of us, knowing good and
evil; and now, he might reach out his hand and
take also from the tree of life, and eat, and live
forever"— [23] therefore the LORD God sent him
forth from the garden of Eden, to till the ground
from which he was taken. [24] He drove out the
man; and at the east of the garden of Eden he
placed the cherubim, and a sword flaming and
turning to guard the way to the tree of life.

4 Now the man knew his wife Eve, and
she conceived and bore Cain, saying, "I
have produced[d] a man with the help of the

a   Or to Adam
b   In Heb Eve resembles the word for living
c   Or for Adam
d   The verb in Heb resembles the word for Cain

original connectedness between them. 21: The LORD God's clothing of the humans here reflects care for them in
the process of becoming civilized, even though that process involved disobedience. 22: As elsewhere in the ancient Near East, humans here are depicted as having a brief opportunity for immortality. The LORD God's fear of
humans becoming godlike (cf. 1.26–27) recalls the snake's assertions in 3.4–5. The term "us" probably refers to
the heavenly court (see 1.26n.). 24: Cf. Ezek 28.13–16. The last echoes of temple imagery (see 2.8–9n.; 2.20–11n.)
occur here. The cherubim are composite, winged creatures like the Sphinx of Egypt, half human and half lion.
Representations of them guarded sanctuaries like the one in Jerusalem (1 Kings 6.23–28,32,35). The gate to the
garden of Eden is in the east, like the processional gate to the Temple (Ezek 10.19).

4.1–16: Cain and Abel. While 2.4–3.24 featured relations between men and women, 4.1–16 turns to relations
between brothers, paralleling 3.1–24 in many respects. 1: This first verse emphasizes the wonder of creative

LORD." [2] Next she bore his brother Abel. Now Abel was a keeper of sheep, and Cain a tiller of the ground. [3] In the course of time Cain brought to the LORD an offering of the fruit of the ground, [4] and Abel for his part brought of the firstlings of his flock, their fat portions. And the LORD had regard for Abel and his offering, [5] but for Cain and his offering he had no regard. So Cain was very angry, and his countenance fell. [6] The LORD said to Cain, "Why are you angry, and why has your countenance fallen? [7] If you do well, will you not be accepted? And if you do not do well, sin is lurking at the door; its desire is for you, but you must master it."

[8] Cain said to his brother Abel, "Let us go out to the field."[a] And when they were in the field, Cain rose up against his brother Abel, and killed him. [9] Then the LORD said to Cain, "Where is your brother Abel?" He said, "I do not know; am I my brother's keeper?" [10] And the LORD said, "What have you done? Listen; your brother's blood is crying out to me from the ground! [11] And now you are cursed from the ground, which has opened its mouth to receive your brother's blood from your hand. [12] When you till the ground, it will no longer yield to you its strength; you will be a fugitive and a wanderer on the earth." [13] Cain said to the LORD, "My punishment is greater than I can bear! [14] Today you have driven me away from the soil, and I shall be hidden from your face; I shall be a fugitive and a wanderer on the earth, and anyone who meets me may kill me." [15] Then the LORD said to him, "Not so![b] Whoever kills Cain will suffer a sevenfold vengeance." And the LORD put a mark on Cain, so that no one who came upon him would kill him. [16] Then Cain went away from the presence of the LORD, and settled in the land of Nod,[c] east of Eden.

[17] Cain knew his wife, and she conceived and bore Enoch; and he built a city, and named it Enoch after his son Enoch. [18] To Enoch was born Irad; and Irad was the father of Mehujael, and Mehujael the father of Methushael, and Methushael the father of Lamech. [19] Lamech took two wives; the name of the one was Adah, and the name of the other Zillah. [20] Adah bore Jabal; he was the ancestor of those who live in tents and have livestock. [21] His brother's name was Jubal; he was the ancestor of all those who play the lyre and pipe. [22] Zillah bore Tubal-cain, who made all kinds of bronze and iron tools. The sister of Tubal-cain was Naamah.

[23] Lamech said to his wives:

"Adah and Zillah, hear my voice;
    you wives of Lamech, listen to what I say:
I have killed a man for wounding me,
    a young man for striking me.

a   Sam Gk Syr Compare Vg: MT lacks *Let us go out to the field*
b   Gk Syr Vg: Heb *Therefore*
c   That is *Wandering*

power in the first birth of a child. The child's name, "Cain," derives from a Hebrew word for create, "qanah." Ancient Israelites may have associated this Cain with the Kenite tribe (Num 24.21–22). 2: The name "Abel" is the same word translated as "vanity" (or "emptiness") in the book of Ecclesiastes. His name anticipates his destiny. The distinction between Cain and Abel's occupations implies a further step toward culture. 3–5: The story does not explain why the LORD *had regard for Abel and his offering* but not *for Cain and his offering*. Instead, it focuses on Cain's reaction to this unexplained divine preference for the sacrifice of his younger brother. 6–7: This is the first mention of *sin* in the Bible. It is depicted as a predatory animal, *lurking at the door*. 10–11: Blood is sacred, for it is the seat of life (9.4; Deut 12.23), and blood of unpunished murders pollutes the ground (Num 35.30–34). 13–14: The importance of arable ground in these chapters can be seen in Cain's conclusion that expulsion from the *soil* means being *hidden* from the LORD's *face*. 16: See 11.1–9n.

4.17–26: First overview of generations from creation to flood. Though the order of the names is different, most of them are variants of those in 5.1–32. 17: Cain's marriage, along with his fear of others (4.14), presumes the presence of a broader population, indicating that the narratives about him were not originally connected with creation. 19–22: The emphasis on civilization seen in 3.1–24 emerges again here in the depiction of the occupations of Lamech's sons. This tradition does not anticipate a flood narrative. 23–24: The first half of this song may once have been used to brag about the ability of Lamech and his family to avenge their honor. Placed where it is and including v. 24, it now functions to demonstrate a major consequence of the expansion of civilization: an expansion of the violence with which the family tree began (see 4.1–16). 25: A parallel to 4.1,

²⁴ If Cain is avenged sevenfold,
 truly Lamech seventy-sevenfold."
²⁵ Adam knew his wife again, and she bore a son and named him Seth, for she said, "God has appointed[a] for me another child instead of Abel, because Cain killed him." ²⁶ To Seth also a son was born, and he named him Enosh. At that time people began to invoke the name of the LORD.

5 This is the list of the descendants of Adam. When God created humankind,[b] he made them[c] in the likeness of God. ² Male and female he created them, and he blessed them and named them "Humankind"[b] when they were created.
³ When Adam had lived one hundred thirty years, he became the father of a son in his likeness, according to his image, and named him Seth. ⁴ The days of Adam after he became the father of Seth were eight hundred years; and he had other sons and daughters. ⁵ Thus all the days that Adam lived were nine hundred thirty years; and he died.
⁶ When Seth had lived one hundred five years, he became the father of Enosh. ⁷ Seth lived after the birth of Enosh eight hundred seven years, and had other sons and daughters. ⁸ Thus all the days of Seth were nine hundred twelve years; and he died.
⁹ When Enosh had lived ninety years, he became the father of Kenan. ¹⁰ Enosh lived after the birth of Kenan eight hundred fifteen years, and had other sons and daughters. ¹¹ Thus all the days of Enosh were nine hundred five years; and he died.
¹² When Kenan had lived seventy years, he became the father of Mahalalel. ¹³ Kenan lived after the birth of Mahalalel eight hundred and forty years, and had other sons and daughters. ¹⁴ Thus all the days of Kenan were nine hundred and ten years; and he died.
¹⁵ When Mahalalel had lived sixty-five years, he became the father of Jared. ¹⁶ Mahalalel lived after the birth of Jared eight hundred thirty years, and had other sons and daughters. ¹⁷ Thus all the days of Mahalalel were eight hundred ninety-five years; and he died.
¹⁸ When Jared had lived one hundred sixty-two years he became the father of Enoch. ¹⁹ Jared lived after the birth of Enoch eight hundred years, and had other sons and daughters. ²⁰ Thus all the days of Jared were nine hundred sixty-two years; and he died.
²¹ When Enoch had lived sixty-five years, he became the father of Methuselah. ²² Enoch walked with God after the birth of Methuselah three hundred years, and had other sons and daughters. ²³ Thus all the days of Enoch were three hundred sixty-five years. ²⁴ Enoch walked with God; then he was no more, because God took him.
²⁵ When Methuselah had lived one hundred eighty-seven years, he became the father of Lamech. ²⁶ Methuselah lived after the birth of Lamech seven hundred eighty-two years, and had other sons and daughters. ²⁷ Thus all the days of Methuselah were nine hundred sixty-nine years; and he died.

a The verb in Heb resembles the word for *Seth*
b Heb *adam*
c Heb *him*

5.1–32: Second overview of generations from creation to flood. This Priestly genealogy parallels 4.1–26, building from the P creation story (1.1–2.3) to the Priestly strand of the flood narrative. 1a: *The list of the descendants of Adam* was evidently a separate source which the Priestly writer drew upon for this chapter and used as a model for later notices (6.9; 10.1; etc.). 1b–2: The Priestly writer uses this reprise of 1.26–28 to bind his genealogical source (where "'adam" designates a particular person) to 1.1–2.3 (where "'adam" designates humanity as a whole). 3: The divine *likeness* (v. 1; see 1.26n.) was continued in Adam's son Seth and thus transmitted to succeeding generations (9.6). 4–32: Ancient Babylonian lists similarly survey a series of heroes before the flood, each of whom lived fantastically long times. Like those lists, the list in 5.4–32 gives extraordinary ages for pre-flood figures, with ages declining over time to the 100–200 years of Israel's ancestors. The names in this list resemble those of 4.17–26 (see 4.17–26n.). 24: Babylonian traditions also report that some individuals—e.g., Emmeduranki (a pre-flood figure), Etana, and Adapa—were taken up into heaven by God. Later Jewish tradition

²⁸ When Lamech had lived one hundred eighty-two years, he became the father of a son; ²⁹ he named him Noah, saying, "Out of the ground that the LORD has cursed this one shall bring us relief from our work and from the toil of our hands." ³⁰ Lamech lived after the birth of Noah five hundred ninety-five years, and had other sons and daughters. ³¹ Thus all the days of Lamech were seven hundred seventy-seven years; and he died.

³² After Noah was five hundred years old, Noah became the father of Shem, Ham, and Japheth.

6 When people began to multiply on the face of the ground, and daughters were born to them, ² the sons of God saw that they were fair; and they took wives for themselves of all that they chose. ³ Then the LORD said, "My spirit shall not abide^a in mortals forever, for they are flesh; their days shall be one hundred twenty years." ⁴ The Nephilim were on the earth in those days—and also afterward—when the sons of God went in to the daughters of humans, who bore children to them. These were the heroes that were of old, warriors of renown.

⁵ The LORD saw that the wickedness of humankind was great in the earth, and that every inclination of the thoughts of their hearts was only evil continually. ⁶ And the LORD was sorry that he had made humankind on the earth, and it grieved him to his heart. ⁷ So the LORD said, "I will blot out from the earth the human beings I have created— people together with animals and creeping things and birds of the air, for I am sorry that I have made them." ⁸ But Noah found favor in the sight of the LORD.

⁹ These are the descendants of Noah. Noah was a righteous man, blameless in his generation; Noah walked with God. ¹⁰ And Noah had three sons, Shem, Ham, and Japheth.

¹¹ Now the earth was corrupt in God's sight, and the earth was filled with violence. ¹² And God saw that the earth was corrupt; for all flesh had corrupted its ways upon the earth. ¹³ And God said to Noah, "I have determined to make an end of all flesh, for the earth is filled with violence because of them; now I am going to destroy them along with the earth. ¹⁴ Make yourself an ark of cypress^a wood; make rooms in the ark, and cover it inside and out with pitch. ¹⁵ This is how you are to make it: the length of the ark three hundred cubits, its width fifty cubits, and its

^a Meaning of Heb uncertain

speculated at length on Enoch's travels. **29:** This (non-Priestly) verse links the curse of the ground in 3.17–19 and viticulture, which was inaugurated by Noah (9.20).

6.1–4: Divine-human reproduction illustrates the breaching of the divine-human boundary that the LORD God feared in 3.22. There the LORD God drove humans away from the tree of life. Here, in an abbreviated narrative often attributed to the Yahwistic primeval history, the LORD God limits their life span to *one hundred twenty* years, the life span of Moses (Deut 31.2); another interpretation is that the *one hundred twenty* years refer to a reprieve from punishment for several generations. Nothing appears to happen to the *sons of God* (see the "heavenly court" in 1.26n.) who instigated it all. **4:** The products of divine-human intercourse are legendary *warriors of renown*. They are distinguished here from the *Nephilim*, a race of giants said to exist both prior to and after those times (cf. Num 13.33; Deut 2.10–11).

6.5–8.19: The great flood. This story describes God's un-creation and re-creation of the world. The version preserved here is an interweaving of parallel accounts, one of which links with the Priestly traditions of 1.1–2.3; 5.1–32 and the other of which links with the Yahwistic primeval history in 2.4b–4.26. This type of intertwining of traditions is less usual but is necessary here to avoid describing two consecutive floods. **6.5–8:** This introduction links with the non-Priestly material, particularly 2.7 (compare 6.7). **5:** Though the biblical account is quite close in many respects to Mesopotamian flood stories, one significant difference is that this text attributes the flood to God's judgment on *the wickedness of humankind* rather than divine frustration with human overpopulation and noise. **9–22:** This section begins the Priestly account of the flood. **11–13:** Here the Priestly writers attribute the flood to corruption of the earth and *violence* filling it (see 4.8,10,23–24). **14–16:** In the Babylonian epic of Gilgamesh, the hero, named Utnapishtim, is told to build a similar houseboat, sealing it with pitch. The description of a three-leveled ark may be based on an ancient idea that the ark reflects the

height thirty cubits. ¹⁶ Make a roof² for the ark, and finish it to a cubit above; and put the door of the ark in its side; make it with lower, second, and third decks. ¹⁷ For my part, I am going to bring a flood of waters on the earth, to destroy from under heaven all flesh in which is the breath of life; everything that is on the earth shall die. ¹⁸ But I will establish my covenant with you; and you shall come into the ark, you, your sons, your wife, and your sons' wives with you. ¹⁹ And of every living thing, of all flesh, you shall bring two of every kind into the ark, to keep them alive with you; they shall be male and female. ²⁰ Of the birds according to their kinds, and of the animals according to their kinds, of every creeping thing of the ground according to its kind, two of every kind shall come in to you, to keep them alive. ²¹ Also take with you every kind of food that is eaten, and store it up; and it shall serve as food for you and for them." ²² Noah did this; he did all that God commanded him.

7 Then the LORD said to Noah, "Go into the ark, you and all your household, for I have seen that you alone are righteous before me in this generation. ² Take with you seven pairs of all clean animals, the male and its mate; and a pair of the animals that are not clean, the male and its mate; ³ and seven pairs of the birds of the air also, male and female, to keep their kind alive on the face of all the earth. ⁴ For in seven days I will send rain on the earth for forty days and forty nights; and every living thing that I have made I will blot out from the face of the ground." ⁵ And Noah did all that the LORD had commanded him.

⁶ Noah was six hundred years old when the flood of waters came on the earth. ⁷ And Noah with his sons and his wife and his sons' wives went into the ark to escape the waters of the flood. ⁸ Of clean animals, and of animals that are not clean, and of birds, and of everything that creeps on the ground, ⁹ two and two, male and female, went into the ark with Noah, as God had commanded Noah. ¹⁰ And after seven days the waters of the flood came on the earth.

¹¹ In the six hundredth year of Noah's life, in the second month, on the seventeenth day of the month, on that day all the fountains of the great deep burst forth, and the windows of the heavens were opened. ¹² The rain fell on the earth forty days and forty nights. ¹³ On the very same day Noah with his sons, Shem and Ham and Japheth, and Noah's wife and the three wives of his sons entered the ark, ¹⁴ they and every wild animal of every kind, and all domestic animals of every kind, and every creeping thing that creeps on the earth, and every bird of every kind—every bird, every winged creature. ¹⁵ They went into the ark with Noah, two and two of all flesh in which there was the breath of life. ¹⁶ And those that entered, male and female of all flesh, went in as God had commanded him; and the LORD shut him in.

¹⁷ The flood continued forty days on the earth; and the waters increased, and bore up the ark, and it rose high above the earth. ¹⁸ The waters swelled and increased greatly on the earth; and the ark floated on the face of the waters. ¹⁹ The waters swelled so mightily on the earth that all the high mountains under the whole heaven were covered; ²⁰ the

ª Or *window*

three-part structure of both universe and temple. It is about 437 x 73 x 44 ft (133 x 22 x 13 m). **18:** *Covenant,* see 9.8–17n. **19–20:** See 7.2–3n. **7.1–5:** This non-Priestly text parallels P in 6.11–22 and continues the tradition seen in 6.5–8. **2–3:** The provision of extra *clean* animals allows for the sacrifice that will occur in 8.20. If only one pair of each animal were taken, every sacrifice would eliminate a species. In contrast, the Priestly tradition presumes that both sacrifice and the distinction between clean and unclean animals (see Lev 11) were not introduced until Sinai. Therefore only one pair of each species is taken in that tradition (6.19–20; 7.14–15; cf. 7.9), and there is no concluding sacrifice (9.1–17). **6–16:** Noah, his family, and the animals enter the ark twice (7.7–9 || 7.13–16), reflecting the interweaving of the two flood accounts discussed earlier. Whereas the non-Priestly account has the flood caused by forty days of rain (7.4,12), the Priestly account attributes the flood to God's opening of the protective dome created on the second day (1.6–8), thus allowing the upper and lower oceans to meet (7.11). **17–24:** The P and non-P strands are thoroughly interwoven in this description of the flood itself, including multiple descriptions of the extinction of life outside the ark (7.21–23). Such flood imagery seems to have been a powerful image of worldwide chaos. Though many world traditions speak of floods, there is no geological

waters swelled above the mountains, covering them fifteen cubits deep. ²¹ And all flesh died that moved on the earth, birds, domestic animals, wild animals, all swarming creatures that swarm on the earth, and all human beings; ²² everything on dry land in whose nostrils was the breath of life died. ²³ He blotted out every living thing that was on the face of the ground, human beings and animals and creeping things and birds of the air; they were blotted out from the earth. Only Noah was left, and those that were with him in the ark. ²⁴ And the waters swelled on the earth for one hundred fifty days.

8 But God remembered Noah and all the wild animals and all the domestic animals that were with him in the ark. And God made a wind blow over the earth, and the waters subsided; ² the fountains of the deep and the windows of the heavens were closed, the rain from the heavens was restrained, ³ and the waters gradually receded from the earth. At the end of one hundred fifty days the waters had abated; ⁴ and in the seventh month, on the seventeenth day of the month, the ark came to rest on the mountains of Ararat. ⁵ The waters continued to abate until the tenth month; in the tenth month, on the first day of the month, the tops of the mountains appeared.

⁶ At the end of forty days Noah opened the window of the ark that he had made ⁷ and sent out the raven; and it went to and fro until the waters were dried up from the earth. ⁸ Then he sent out the dove from him, to see if the waters had subsided from the face of the ground; ⁹ but the dove found no place to set its foot, and it returned to him to the ark, for the waters were still on the face of the whole earth. So he put out his hand and took it and brought it into the ark with him. ¹⁰ He waited another seven days, and again he sent out the dove from the ark; ¹¹ and the dove came back to him in the evening, and there in its beak was a freshly plucked olive leaf; so Noah knew that the waters had subsided from the earth. ¹² Then he waited another seven days, and sent out the dove; and it did not return to him any more.

¹³ In the six hundred first year, in the first month, on the first day of the month, the waters were dried up from the earth; and Noah removed the covering of the ark, and looked, and saw that the face of the ground was drying. ¹⁴ In the second month, on the twenty-seventh day of the month, the earth was dry. ¹⁵ Then God said to Noah, ¹⁶ "Go out of the ark, you and your wife, and your sons and your sons' wives with you. ¹⁷ Bring out with you every living thing that is with you of all flesh—birds and animals and every creeping thing that creeps on the earth—so that they may abound on the earth, and be fruitful and multiply on the earth." ¹⁸ So Noah went out with his sons and his wife and his sons' wives. ¹⁹ And every animal, every creeping thing, and every bird, everything that moves on the earth, went out of the ark by families.

²⁰ Then Noah built an altar to the LORD, and took of every clean animal and of every

evidence of a global flood of the sort described here. **8.1–5:** With the exception of 8.2b–3a, this unit comes from the Priestly writer. **1–2a:** God's wind echoes the first creation (1.2) in the process of starting the re-creation process. The closing of the *fountains of the deep and the windows of the heavens* reestablishes the space for life that was first created on the second day (1.6–8). **4:** In the Gilgamesh epic the boat also rested on a mountain. *Ararat,* a region in Armenia. **6–12:** Part of the non-Priestly account. In the Gilgamesh epic the hero sent out two birds, a dove and a swallow, each of which came back; the third, a raven, did not return. **13–19:** The Priestly account resumes here with a description of the exit from the ark of Noah, his family, and the animals.

8.20–9.17: Divine commitments after the flood. This section features two accounts of God's commitments after the flood (8.20–22 [non-P]; 9.1–17 [P]), both of which include God's promise not to destroy life through such a flood ever again. **8.20–22:** The non-Priestly tradition describes Noah's *burnt offerings* of clean animals (see 7.2–3n.). In the Gilgamesh epic (see 6.14–16n.; 8.4n.; 8.6–12n.) the hero offered sacrifices and "the gods smelled the pleasant fragrance" and repented of their decision to destroy humanity. Here the LORD smells the *pleasing odor* of Noah's offering and resolves never again to curse the ground or destroy all creatures (v. 21). The LORD does this despite full recognition that the human heart has not changed (cf. 6.5–7). The final result of Noah's sacrifice is the LORD's promise to preserve the cycle of agricultural seasons (v. 22). A central aim of temple sacrifice in Israel and elsewhere was to preserve that cycle. The echo of that idea here is yet another way in which the "non-Priestly" primeval history reflects temple concerns (see also the focus on responses to

clean bird, and offered burnt offerings on the altar. [21] And when the LORD smelled the pleasing odor, the LORD said in his heart, "I will never again curse the ground because of humankind, for the inclination of the human heart is evil from youth; nor will I ever again destroy every living creature as I have done.
[22] As long as the earth endures,
  seedtime and harvest, cold and heat,
  summer and winter, day and night,
    shall not cease."

9 God blessed Noah and his sons, and said to them, "Be fruitful and multiply, and fill the earth. [2] The fear and dread of you shall rest on every animal of the earth, and on every bird of the air, on everything that creeps on the ground, and on all the fish of the sea; into your hand they are delivered. [3] Every moving thing that lives shall be food for you; and just as I gave you the green plants, I give you everything. [4] Only, you shall not eat flesh with its life, that is, its blood. [5] For your own lifeblood I will surely require a reckoning: from every animal I will require it and from human beings, each one for the blood of another, I will require a reckoning for human life.
[6] Whoever sheds the blood of a human,
  by a human shall that person's blood be shed;
  for in his own image
    God made humankind.
[7] And you, be fruitful and multiply, abound on the earth and multiply in it."

[8] Then God said to Noah and to his sons with him, [9] "As for me, I am establishing my covenant with you and your descendants after you, [10] and with every living creature that is with you, the birds, the domestic animals, and every animal of the earth with you, as many as came out of the ark.[a] [11] I establish my covenant with you, that never again shall all flesh be cut off by the waters of a flood, and never again shall there be a flood to destroy the earth." [12] God said, "This is the sign of the covenant that I make between me and you and every living creature that is with you, for all future generations: [13] I have set my bow in the clouds, and it shall be a sign of the covenant between me and the earth. [14] When I bring clouds over the earth and the bow is seen in the clouds, [15] I will remember my covenant that is between me and you and every living creature of all flesh; and the waters shall never again become a flood to destroy all flesh. [16] When the bow is in the clouds, I will see it and remember the everlasting covenant between God and every living creature of all flesh that is on the earth." [17] God said to Noah, "This is the sign of the covenant that I have established between me and all flesh that is on the earth."

[18] The sons of Noah who went out of the ark were Shem, Ham, and Japheth. Ham was the father of Canaan. [19] These three were the

[a] Gk: Heb adds *every animal of the earth*

sacrifice in 4.1–8 and notes on 2.8–9,10–14; 3.24). **9.1–17:** The Priestly tradition lacks an account of sacrifice (see 7.2–3n.). Instead it focuses on affirmations of some aspects of the creation in 1.1–31 and revisions of others. **1–7:** This section begins and ends with a reaffirmation of the fertility blessing (vv. 1,7; cf. 1.28). **2–6:** Here God revises the earlier command of vegetarianism (1.29–30). This is a partial concession to the "violence" observed prior to the flood (6.11,13) and an extension of the human dominion over creation described in 1.26–28. At the same time, God regulates this violence through stipulating that humans may not eat the blood in which life resides (see 4.10–11n.) and that humans as bearers of God's image (1.26–27) may not be killed. Since these laws are given to Noah and his sons, the ancestors of all post-flood humanity, they were used in later Jewish tradition as the basis for a set of seven Noachide laws that were seen as binding upon Gentiles as well as Jews (see Acts 15.20; 21.25; *b. San.* 58b). **8–17:** This is the first covenant explicitly described as such in the Bible, and it encompasses all of humanity, as well as the animal world (vv. 10,12,15) and even the earth (v. 13). A "covenant" is a formal agreement, often between a superior and inferior party, the former "making" or "establishing" (vv. 9,11) the bond with the latter, and the superior protecting the weaker party. This agreement is often sealed through ceremonies. In this case, God sets his weapon, the bow (Ps 7.12–13; Hab 3.9–11), in the sky facing away from humanity as a sign of God's commitment not to flood the earth again.
    9.18–29: Noah and his sons. Aside from P in vv. 18–19 and 28–29, this text is part of the Yahwistic primeval history. It repeats major themes from the pre-flood period: farming (see 3.17; 5.29), nakedness, alienation in

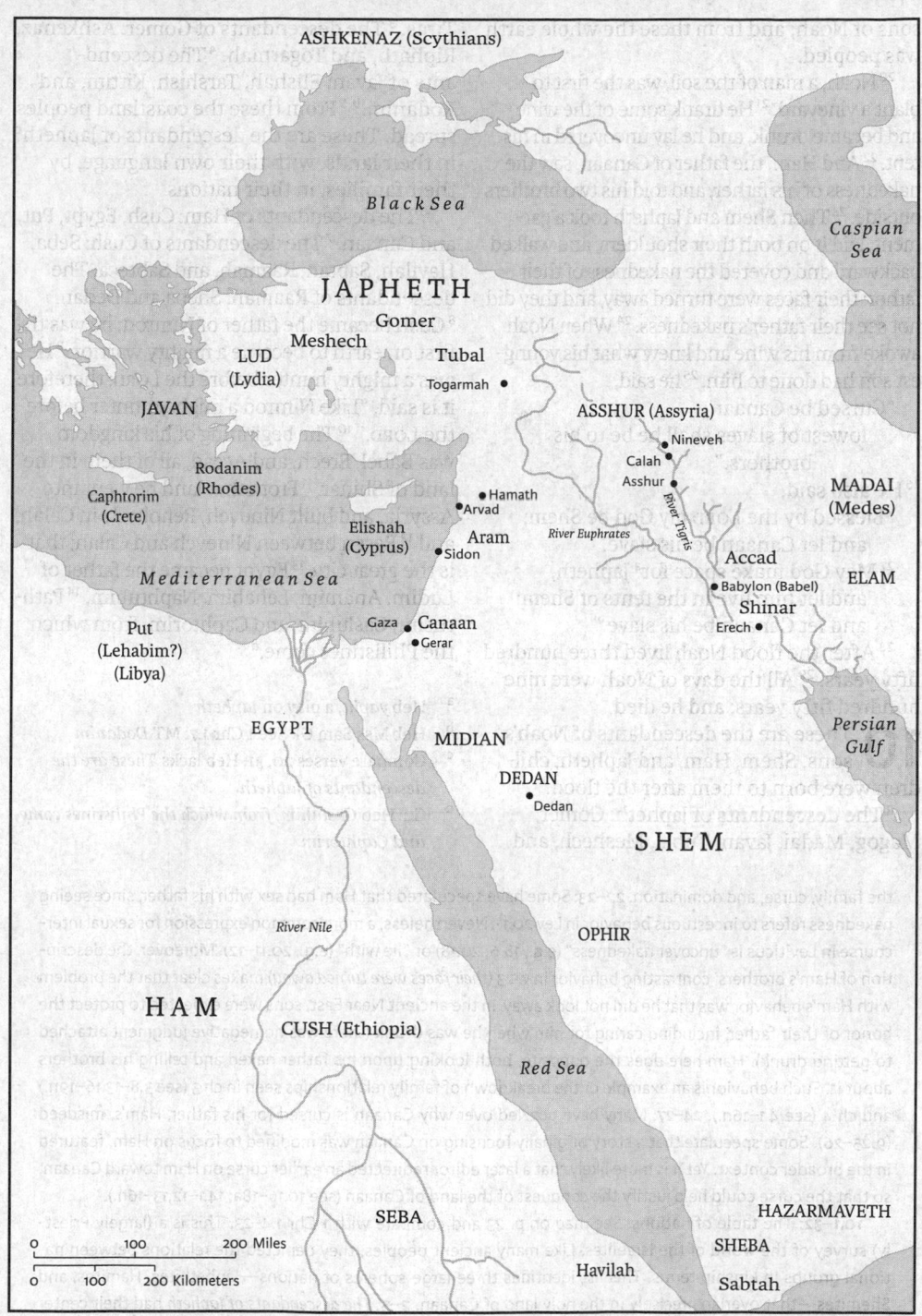

ASHKENAZ (Scythians)

Black Sea

Caspian Sea

JAPHETH

Gomer

Meshech

LUD
(Lydia)

Tubal

Togarmah

ASSHUR (Assyria)

JAVAN

Nineveh

Calah

Asshur

MADAI
(Medes)

Rodanim
(Rhodes)

Hamath

Arvad

Caphtorim
(Crete)

Elishah
(Cyprus)

Aram

Sidon

River Euphrates

River Tigris

Accad

ELAM

Babylon (Babel)

Mediterranean Sea

Shinar

Erech

Put
(Lehabim?)
(Libya)

Gaza

Gerar

Canaan

Persian Gulf

EGYPT

MIDIAN

DEDAN

Dedan

SHEM

River Nile

OPHIR

HAM

CUSH (Ethiopia)

Red Sea

HAZARMAVETH

SEBA

SHEBA

Havilah

Sabtah

0   100   200 Miles

0   100   200 Kilometers

Ch 10: The table of nations. Only places that can be identified with probability are shown.

sons of Noah; and from these the whole earth was peopled.

[20] Noah, a man of the soil, was the first to plant a vineyard. [21] He drank some of the wine and became drunk, and he lay uncovered in his tent. [22] And Ham, the father of Canaan, saw the nakedness of his father, and told his two brothers outside. [23] Then Shem and Japheth took a garment, laid it on both their shoulders, and walked backward and covered the nakedness of their father; their faces were turned away, and they did not see their father's nakedness. [24] When Noah awoke from his wine and knew what his youngest son had done to him, [25] he said,

"Cursed be Canaan;
lowest of slaves shall he be to his
brothers."

[26] He also said,

"Blessed by the LORD my God be Shem;
and let Canaan be his slave.
[27] May God make space for[a] Japheth,
and let him live in the tents of Shem;
and let Canaan be his slave."

[28] After the flood Noah lived three hundred fifty years. [29] All the days of Noah were nine hundred fifty years; and he died.

10 These are the descendants of Noah's sons, Shem, Ham, and Japheth; children were born to them after the flood.

[2] The descendants of Japheth: Gomer, Magog, Madai, Javan, Tubal, Meshech, and Tiras. [3] The descendants of Gomer: Ashkenaz, Riphath, and Togarmah. [4] The descendants of Javan: Elishah, Tarshish, Kittim, and Rodanim.[b] [5] From these the coastland peoples spread. These are the descendants of Japheth[c] in their lands, with their own language, by their families, in their nations.

[6] The descendants of Ham: Cush, Egypt, Put, and Canaan. [7] The descendants of Cush: Seba, Havilah, Sabtah, Raamah, and Sabteca. The descendants of Raamah: Sheba and Dedan. [8] Cush became the father of Nimrod; he was the first on earth to become a mighty warrior. [9] He was a mighty hunter before the LORD; therefore it is said, "Like Nimrod a mighty hunter before the LORD." [10] The beginning of his kingdom was Babel, Erech, and Accad, all of them in the land of Shinar. [11] From that land he went into Assyria, and built Nineveh, Rehoboth-ir, Calah, and [12] Resen between Nineveh and Calah; that is the great city. [13] Egypt became the father of Ludim, Anamim, Lehabim, Naphtuhim, [14] Pathrusim, Casluhim, and Caphtorim, from which the Philistines come.[d]

---

a   Heb *yapht*, a play on *Japheth*
b   Heb Mss Sam Gk See 1 Chr 1.7: MT *Dodanim*
c   Compare verses 20, 31. Heb lacks *These are the descendants of Japheth*
d   Cn: Heb *Casluhim, from which the Philistines come, and Caphtorim*

---

the family, curse, and domination. **22–23:** Some have speculated that Ham had sex with his father, since seeing nakedness refers to incestuous behavior in Lev 20.17. Nevertheless, a more common expression for sexual intercourse in Leviticus is "uncover nakedness" (e.g., 18.6; 20.18) or "lie with" (e.g., 20.11–12). Moreover, the description of Ham's brothers' contrasting behavior in v. 23 (*their faces were turned away*) makes clear that the problem with Ham's behavior was that he did not look away. In the ancient Near East, sons were expected to protect the honor of their father, including caring for him when he was drunk (there was no negative judgment attached to getting drunk). Ham here does the opposite, both looking upon his father naked and telling his brothers about it. Such behavior is an example of the breakdown of family relationships seen in ch 3 (see 3.8–13,16–19n.) and ch 4 (see 4.1–16n.). **24–27:** Many have puzzled over why Canaan is cursed for his father, Ham's, misdeed (9.25–26). Some speculate that a story originally focusing on Canaan was modified to focus on Ham, featured in the broader context. Yet it is more likely that a later editor redirected an earlier curse on Ham toward Canaan, so that the curse could help justify the conquest of the land of Canaan (see 10.16–18a; 14.1–12,13–16n.).

10.1–32: The table of nations. See map on p. 23 and compare with 1 Chr 1.4–23. This is a (largely Priestly) survey of the world of the Israelites. Like many ancient peoples, they depicted the relations between national groups in kinship terms. This list identifies three large spheres of nations—Japhethites, Hamites, and Shemites—that overlap precisely in the holy land of Canaan. **2–5:** *The descendants of Japheth* had their center in Asia Minor (present-day Turkey). **6–20:** *The descendants of Ham* lived in the Egyptian orbit. **8–15:** A fragment of the non-Priestly primeval history. It features a legend regarding Nimrod's building a kingdom in *Shinar* (southern Mesopotamia) and Assyria (vv. 8–12). Canaan is the father of two sons, *Heth* (representing the Hittites originally of Asia Minor) and *Sidon* (who represents the Phoenician coastal cities). **14:** See Jer 47.4; Am

¹⁵ Canaan became the father of Sidon his firstborn, and Heth, ¹⁶ and the Jebusites, the Amorites, the Girgashites, ¹⁷ the Hivites, the Arkites, the Sinites, ¹⁸ the Arvadites, the Zemarites, and the Hamathites. Afterward the families of the Canaanites spread abroad. ¹⁹ And the territory of the Canaanites extended from Sidon, in the direction of Gerar, as far as Gaza, and in the direction of Sodom, Gomorrah, Admah, and Zeboiim, as far as Lasha. ²⁰ These are the descendants of Ham, by their families, their languages, their lands, and their nations.

²¹ To Shem also, the father of all the children of Eber, the elder brother of Japheth, children were born. ²² The descendants of Shem: Elam, Asshur, Arpachshad, Lud, and Aram. ²³ The descendants of Aram: Uz, Hul, Gether, and Mash. ²⁴ Arpachshad became the father of Shelah; and Shelah became the father of Eber. ²⁵ To Eber were born two sons: the name of the one was Peleg,ᵃ for in his days the earth was divided, and his brother's name was Joktan. ²⁶ Joktan became the father of Almodad, Sheleph, Hazarmaveth, Jerah, ²⁷ Hadoram, Uzal, Diklah, ²⁸ Obal, Abimael, Sheba, ²⁹ Ophir, Havilah, and Jobab; all these were the descendants of Joktan. ³⁰ The territory in which they lived extended from Mesha in the direction of Sephar, the hill country of the east. ³¹ These are the descendants of Shem, by their families, their languages, their lands, and their nations.

³² These are the families of Noah's sons, according to their genealogies, in their nations; and from these the nations spread abroad on the earth after the flood.

11 Now the whole earth had one language and the same words. ² And as they migrated from the east,ᵇ they came upon a plain in the land of Shinar and settled there. ³ And they said to one another, "Come, let us make bricks, and burn them thoroughly." And they had brick for stone, and bitumen for mortar. ⁴ Then they said, "Come, let us build ourselves a city, and a tower with its top in the heavens, and let us make a name for ourselves; otherwise we shall be scattered abroad upon the face of the whole earth." ⁵ The LORD came down to see the city and the tower, which mortals had built. ⁶ And the LORD said, "Look, they are one people, and they have all one language; and this is only the beginning of what they will do; nothing that they propose to do will now be impossible for them. ⁷ Come, let us go down, and confuse their language there, so that they will not understand one another's speech." ⁸ So the LORD scattered

ᵃ That is *Division*
ᵇ Or *migrated eastward*

9.7. 16–18a: This survey of Canaanite peoples lists ethnic groups rather than ancestors, including the *Jebusites* (centered in Jerusalem), *Amorites* (natives of the hill country), and the *Hivites* (a group in central Palestine). The list resembles later lists of peoples displaced by Israel (e.g., 15.19–21; Deut 7.1) and may be an addition from the same hand that directed Noah's curse toward Canaan (see 9.18–27n.). 21–31: *Shem* is the father of the Semitic peoples, including Israel. Another pair of fragments of the non-Priestly primeval history (vv. 21,24–30) focuses on the *children of Eber*. The name *Eber* may be related to "Hebrew." If so, then this text postulates a wider group of *children of Eber* of which the Israelites are a part.

11.1–9: The tower of Babel. This narrative (from the non-Priestly Yahwistic primeval history) revisits the theme of preservation of the divine-human boundary. The threat to that boundary, self-reflective speech by the LORD, and act of divine prevention all parallel 3.22–24 and 6.1–4. With 11.2 the human family completes the eastward movement begun in 3.22–24 (cf. 4.16). Yet this story will focus on a scattering of the human family into different ethnic, linguistic, and territorial groups. As such, it now gives background for the table of nations in ch 10, although it was not originally written with that in view. 2: *Shinar*, see 10.8–15n. 4: The humans are depicted as fearful of being scattered and thus aiming to make a name for themselves through a *tower* reaching into heaven. The humans' intention here to stay together contradicts the divine imperative to "fill the earth" now found in Priestly traditions (1.28; 9.1,7). 6: The LORD is described here as fearing the human power that might result from ethnic and linguistic unity (see 3.22). 7: *Let us*, see 1.26n. 8–9: The LORD's scattering of humanity and confusing of language is the final step in creation of civilized humanity, with its multiple territorial and linguistic groups. The movement toward cultural maturity begun in ch 3 is complete. Each step toward this end has been fraught with conflict and loss. The name "Babel," interpreted here as "confusion" but originally meaning "gate of god" (cf. 28.15n.) serves as a final testimony to the ambiguous results of this process.

them abroad from there over the face of all the earth, and they left off building the city. [9] Therefore it was called Babel, because there the LORD confused[a] the language of all the earth; and from there the LORD scattered them abroad over the face of all the earth.

[10] These are the descendants of Shem. When Shem was one hundred years old, he became the father of Arpachshad two years after the flood; [11] and Shem lived after the birth of Arpachshad five hundred years, and had other sons and daughters.

[12] When Arpachshad had lived thirty-five years, he became the father of Shelah; [13] and Arpachshad lived after the birth of Shelah four hundred three years, and had other sons and daughters.

[14] When Shelah had lived thirty years, he became the father of Eber; [15] and Shelah lived after the birth of Eber four hundred three years, and had other sons and daughters.

[16] When Eber had lived thirty-four years, he became the father of Peleg; [17] and Eber lived after the birth of Peleg four hundred thirty years, and had other sons and daughters.

[18] When Peleg had lived thirty years, he became the father of Reu; [19] and Peleg lived

after the birth of Reu two hundred nine years, and had other sons and daughters.

[20] When Reu had lived thirty-two years, he became the father of Serug; [21] and Reu lived after the birth of Serug two hundred seven years, and had other sons and daughters.

[22] When Serug had lived thirty years, he became the father of Nahor; [23] and Serug lived after the birth of Nahor two hundred years, and had other sons and daughters.

[24] When Nahor had lived twenty-nine years, he became the father of Terah; [25] and Nahor lived after the birth of Terah one hundred nineteen years, and had other sons and daughters.

[26] When Terah had lived seventy years, he became the father of Abram, Nahor, and Haran.

[27] Now these are the descendants of Terah. Terah was the father of Abram, Nahor, and Haran; and Haran was the father of Lot. [28] Haran died before his father Terah in the land of his birth, in Ur of the Chaldeans. [29] Abram and Nahor took wives; the name of Abram's wife was Sarai, and the name of Nahor's wife was Milcah. She was the daughter of Haran

[a] Heb *balal*, meaning *to confuse*

11.20–26: The descendants of Shem. This genealogy from the Priestly tradition closely parallels 5.1–32 (though it lacks death notices). It builds a genealogical bridge from Shem to Terah, the father of Abraham. Parts of the genealogy of Shem (10.21–31) are repeated, but now the text focuses exclusively on those descendants who will lead to Abraham. The text implies that all these descendants are firstborn sons, thus setting up Abraham as the firstborn heir of Shem, the eldest of Noah's sons.

11.27–25.11: The story of Abraham and his family. The bulk of this section is a non-Priestly narrative about Abraham. It builds on a blend of oral traditions about him, such as the stories standing behind the present narratives about his descent into Egypt (12.10–20), the Abraham and Lot cycle (13.2–13; 18.1–16; 19.1–28,30–37), a pair of Hagar and Ishmael narratives (16.1–14 and 21.8–20), and the tradition about Abraham's stay in Philistine Gerar (20.1–18; 21.22–34; cf. 26.6–33). Some scholars think that these once were part of two separate written J and E sources, with remnants of J (the Yahwistic source) found primarily in chs 12–19 (along with ch 24) and E (Elohistic source) fragments in chs 20–22. Others see indicators that these chapters, though building on a range of separate traditions, were composed as a single whole (see the Introduction and 20.1–18n.). Scholars generally agree, however, that other parts of the Abraham story were added later, such as the story of conquest and covenant in 14.1–15.21 and Priestly materials found in 17.1–27 and elsewhere (see 11.27–32n.; 12.4b–5n; 16.3n; 17.1–27n; 21.3–5n; 25.7–11n). For patterns uniting this complex whole, see "Chiasm in the Abraham Story" on p. 38.

11.27–32: Introduction to the Abraham story. The genealogical heading (v. 27) and the concluding notices regarding Terah's travels and death (vv. 31–32) are Priestly, but most scholars consider vv. 28–30 to be earlier, non-Priestly material. **27:** *Abram*, see 17.5n. The designation "Abraham" is used here in the annotations as the better-known name of Abra(ha)m. Aside from his birth, nothing is told about the early life of Abraham; this lack is filled in by later postbiblical tradition. **29–30:** *Sarai*, see 17.15n. This is the first appearance of the theme of barrenness of the three most central matriarchs: Sarai/Sarah, Rebekah (25.21), and Rachel (29.31). Their initial

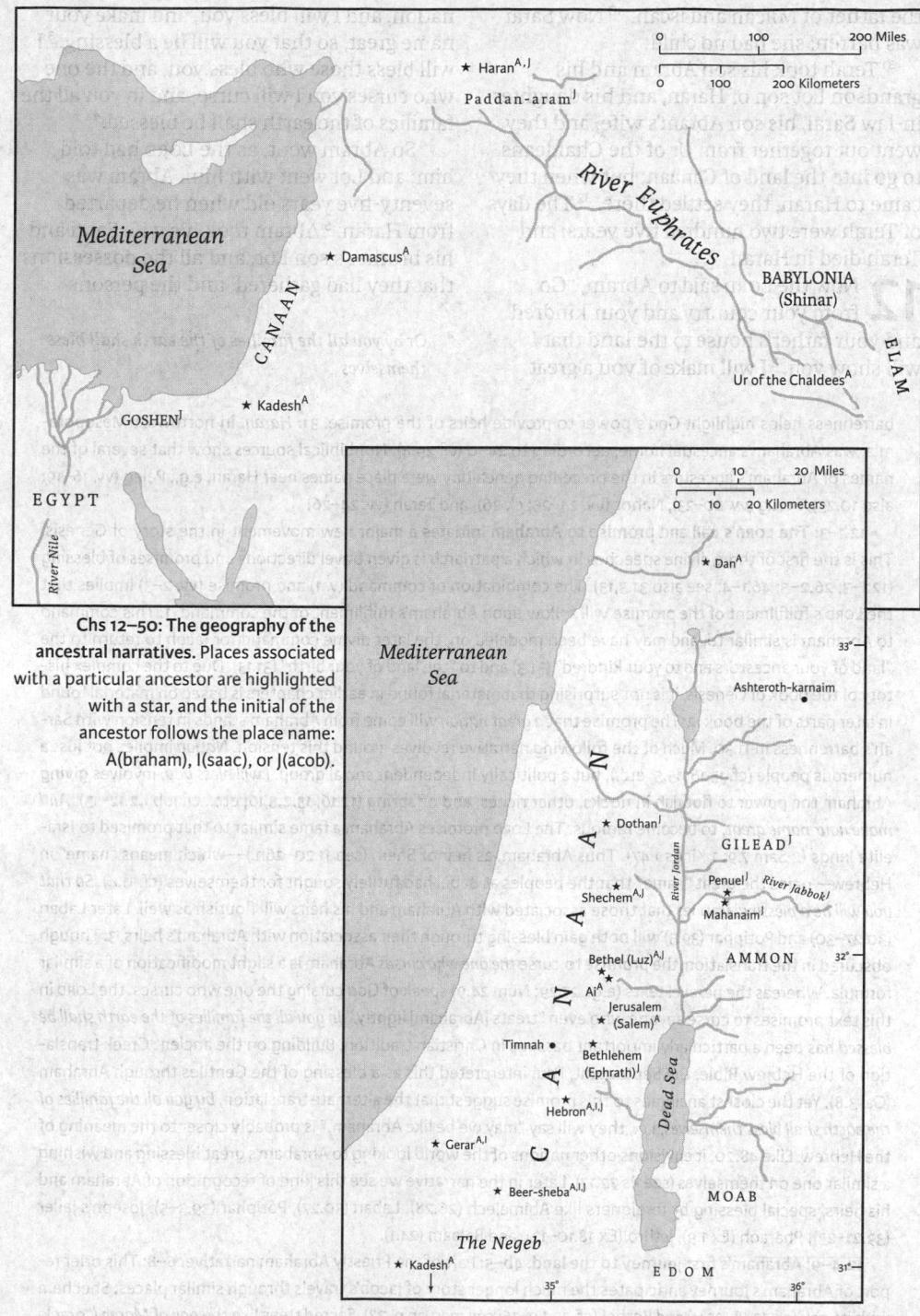

Chs 12–50: The geography of the ancestral narratives. Places associated with a particular ancestor are highlighted with a star, and the initial of the ancestor follows the place name: A(braham), I(saac), or J(acob).

Map labels:

0   100   200 Miles
0   100   200 Kilometers

Haran[A, J]
Paddan-aram[J]
River Euphrates
BABYLONIA (Shinar)
Mediterranean Sea
CANAAN
Damascus[A]
ELAM
Kadesh[A]
GOSHEN[J]
Ur of the Chaldees[A]
EGYPT
River Nile
Dan[A]

0   10   20 Miles
0   10   20 Kilometers

Mediterranean Sea
C A N A A N
Dothan[J]
GILEAD[J]
Ashteroth-karnaim
Shechem[A, J]
River Jordan
Penuel[J]   River Jabbok[J]
Mahanaim[J]
Bethel (Luz)[A, J]
Ai[A]
AMMON
Jerusalem (Salem)[A]
Timnah
Bethlehem (Ephrath)[J]
Dead Sea
Hebron[A, I, J]
Gerar[A, I]
Beer-sheba[A, I, J]
MOAB
The Negeb
Kadesh[A]
E D O M

33°
32°
31°
35°   36°

the father of Milcah and Iscah. [30] Now Sarai was barren; she had no child.

[31] Terah took his son Abram and his grandson Lot son of Haran, and his daughter-in-law Sarai, his son Abram's wife, and they went out together from Ur of the Chaldeans to go into the land of Canaan; but when they came to Haran, they settled there. [32] The days of Terah were two hundred five years; and Terah died in Haran.

12 Now the LORD said to Abram, "Go from your country and your kindred and your father's house to the land that I will show you. [2] I will make of you a great nation, and I will bless you, and make your name great, so that you will be a blessing. [3] I will bless those who bless you, and the one who curses you I will curse; and in you all the families of the earth shall be blessed."[a]

[4] So Abram went, as the LORD had told him; and Lot went with him. Abram was seventy-five years old when he departed from Haran. [5] Abram took his wife Sarai and his brother's son Lot, and all the possessions that they had gathered, and the persons

[a] Or *by you all the families of the earth shall bless themselves*

barrenness helps highlight God's power to provide heirs of the promise. **31:** *Haran,* in northwest Mesopotamia, was Abraham's ancestral home, according to 24.10 (cf. 29.4). Nonbiblical sources show that several of the names of Abraham's ancestors in the preceding genealogy were place names near Haran; e.g., Peleg (vv. 16–19; also 10.25), Serug (vv. 20–23), Nahor (vv. 24–25; cf. 26), and Terah (vv. 24–26).

12.1–3: The LORD's call and promise to Abraham initiates a major new movement in the story of Genesis. This is the first of three divine speeches in which a patriarch is given travel directions and promises of blessing (12.1–3; 26.2–5; 46.1–4; see also 31.3,13). The combination of command (v. 1) and promise (vv. 2–3) implies that the LORD's fulfillment of the promise will follow upon Abraham's fulfillment of the command. **1:** This command to Abraham is similar to, and may have been modeled on, the later divine command for Jacob to return to the "land of your ancestors and to your kindred" (31.3) and to "the land of your birth" (31.13). Due to the complex history of the book of Genesis, it is not surprising that material found in earlier chapters is based on material found in later parts of the book. **2:** The promise that *a great nation* will come from Abraham stands in tension with Sarah's barrenness in 11.30. Much of the following narrative revolves around this tension. *Nation* implies not just a numerous people (cf. 13.16; 15.5; etc.), but a politically independent social group. *I will bless you,* involves giving Abraham the power to flourish in flocks, other riches, and offspring (12.16; 13.2,5,16; etc.; cf. Job 42.12–13). *And make your name great,* to become famous. The LORD promises Abraham a fame similar to that promised to Israelite kings (2 Sam 7.9; 1 Kings 1.47). Thus Abraham, as heir of Shem (see 11.20–26n.)—which means "name" in Hebrew—gains the great "name" that the peoples at Babel had futilely sought for themselves (cf. 11.4). *So that you will be a blessing,* implies that those associated with Abraham and his heirs will flourish as well. Later Laban (30.27–30) and Potiphar (39.5) will both gain blessing through their association with Abraham's heirs. **3:** Though obscured in the translation, the promise to curse *the one who curses* Abraham is a slight modification of a similar formula. Whereas the parallel texts (e.g., 27.29; Num 24.9) speak of God cursing the one who curses, the LORD in this text promises to curse anyone who even "treats [Abraham] lightly." *In you all the families of the earth shall be blessed* has been a particularly important passage in Christian tradition. Building on the ancient Greek translation of the Hebrew Bible, the Septuagint, Paul interpreted this as a blessing of the Gentiles through Abraham (Gal 3.8). Yet the closest analogies to this promise suggest that the alternate translation, *by you all the families of the earth shall bless themselves,* i.e., they will say "may we be like Abraham," is probably closer to the meaning of the Hebrew. Like 48.20, it envisions other nations of the world looking to Abraham's great blessing and wishing a similar one on themselves (see Ps 72.17). Later in the narrative we see this kind of recognition of Abraham and his heirs' special blessing by foreigners like Abimelech (26.28), Laban (30.27), Potiphar (39.3–5), Joseph's jailer (39.21–23), Pharaoh (Ex 1.9), Jethro (Ex 18.10–12), and Balaam (24.1).

12.4–9: Abraham's first journey to the land. 4b–5: Part of the Priestly Abraham narrative. **6–8:** This brief report of Abraham's journey anticipates the much longer story of Jacob's travels through similar places: Shechem with its oak (cf. 33.18–35.4) and Bethel (cf. 35.1,9–16; see map on p. 27). Sacred trees like the *oak of Moreh* ("oracle giver"; cf. 13.18; 18.1; 35.4; Deut 11.30; Josh 24.26; Judg 9.37) occur elsewhere in Genesis (e.g., 21.33; 35.8) and seem to have played an important role in the religion of the ancient Israelites and surrounding peoples (see 2.8–9n.).

whom they had acquired in Haran; and they set forth to go to the land of Canaan. When they had come to the land of Canaan, [6] Abram passed through the land to the place at Shechem, to the oak[a] of Moreh. At that time the Canaanites were in the land. [7] Then the LORD appeared to Abram, and said, "To your offspring[b] I will give this land." So he built there an altar to the LORD, who had appeared to him. [8] From there he moved on to the hill country on the east of Bethel, and pitched his tent, with Bethel on the west and Ai on the east; and there he built an altar to the LORD and invoked the name of the LORD. [9] And Abram journeyed on by stages toward the Negeb.

[10] Now there was a famine in the land. So Abram went down to Egypt to reside there as an alien, for the famine was severe in the land. [11] When he was about to enter Egypt, he said to his wife Sarai, "I know well that you are a woman beautiful in appearance; [12] and when the Egyptians see you, they will say, 'This is his wife'; then they will kill me, but they will let you live. [13] Say you are my sister, so that it may go well with me because of you, and that my life may be spared on your account." [14] When Abram entered Egypt the Egyptians saw that the woman was very beautiful. [15] When the officials of Pharaoh saw her, they praised her to Pharaoh. And the woman was taken into Pharaoh's house. [16] And for her sake he dealt well with Abram; and he had sheep, oxen, male donkeys, male and female slaves, female donkeys, and camels.

[17] But the LORD afflicted Pharaoh and his house with great plagues because of Sarai, Abram's wife. [18] So Pharaoh called Abram, and said, "What is this you have done to me? Why did you not tell me that she was your wife? [19] Why did you say, 'She is my sister,' so that I took her for my wife? Now then, here is your wife, take her, and be gone." [20] And Pharaoh gave his men orders concerning him; and they set him on the way, with his wife and all that he had.

13 So Abram went up from Egypt, he and his wife, and all that he had, and Lot with him, into the Negeb.

[2] Now Abram was very rich in livestock, in silver, and in gold. [3] He journeyed on by stages from the Negeb as far as Bethel, to the place where his tent had been at the beginning, between Bethel and Ai, [4] to the place where he had made an altar at the first; and there Abram called on the name of the LORD. [5] Now Lot, who went with Abram, also had flocks and herds and tents, [6] so that the land could not support both of them living together; for their possessions were so great that they could not live together, [7] and there was strife between the herders of Abram's livestock and the herders of Lot's livestock. At that time the Canaanites and the Perizzites lived in the land.

[8] Then Abram said to Lot, "Let there be no strife between you and me, and between your herders and my herders; for we are kindred. [9] Is not the whole land before you? Separate yourself from me. If you take the left hand, then I will go to the right; or if you take the right hand, then I will go to the left." [10] Lot looked about him, and saw that the plain of the Jordan was well watered everywhere like the garden of the LORD, like the land of Egypt, in the direction of Zoar; this was before the LORD had destroyed Sodom and Gomorrah. [11] So Lot chose for himself all the plain of the Jordan, and Lot journeyed eastward; thus they separated from each other. [12] Abram settled in the land of Canaan, while Lot settled among the cities of the Plain and moved his

a   Or terebinth
b   Heb seed

12.10–13.1: First story of endangerment of the matriarch (cf. ch 20; 26.6–11). Putting Sarah in jeopardy to protect himself, Abraham appears not to trust the promise of protection just offered him. On Abraham's later claim to be Sarah's half-brother, see 20.12n. Overall, this story of descent into Egypt because of famine and rescue through plagues anticipates many aspects of the later narrative about Israel's descent into Egypt and Exodus from it (Gen 45–Ex 14).

13.2–18: Split of Abraham and Lot. 2–7: This narrative describing huge flocks and riches in Abraham's household testifies to the preliminary fulfillment of the promises of blessing in 12.2–3. Lot, see 11.27,31. 8–13: The narrative anticipates the Sodom and Gomorrah narrative (ch 19) through mention of those cities, the wickedness of their inhabitants (13.13), and references to Zoar (19.19–23). It also notes that Lot, the heir apparent, does

tent as far as Sodom. [13] Now the people of Sodom were wicked, great sinners against the LORD.

[14] The LORD said to Abram, after Lot had separated from him, "Raise your eyes now, and look from the place where you are, northward and southward and eastward and westward; [15] for all the land that you see I will give to you and to your offspring[a] forever. [16] I will make your offspring like the dust of the earth; so that if one can count the dust of the earth, your offspring also can be counted. [17] Rise up, walk through the length and the breadth of the land, for I will give it to you." [18] So Abram moved his tent, and came and settled by the oaks[b] of Mamre, which are at Hebron; and there he built an altar to the LORD.

14 In the days of King Amraphel of Shinar, King Arioch of Ellasar, King Chedorlaomer of Elam, and King Tidal of Goiim, [2] these kings made war with King Bera of Sodom, King Birsha of Gomorrah, King Shinab of Admah, King Shemeber of Zeboiim, and the king of Bela (that is, Zoar). [3] All these joined forces in the Valley of Siddim (that is, the Dead Sea).[c] [4] Twelve years they had served Chedorlaomer, but in the thirteenth year they rebelled. [5] In the fourteenth year Chedorlaomer and the kings who were with him came and subdued the Rephaim in Ashteroth-karnaim, the Zuzim in Ham, the Emim in Shaveh-kiriathaim, [6] and the Horites in the hill country of Seir as far as El-paran on the edge of the wilderness; [7] then they turned back and came to

En-mishpat (that is, Kadesh), and subdued all the country of the Amalekites, and also the Amorites who lived in Hazazon-tamar. [8] Then the king of Sodom, the king of Gomorrah, the king of Admah, the king of Zeboiim, and the king of Bela (that is, Zoar) went out, and they joined battle in the Valley of Siddim [9] with King Chedorlaomer of Elam, King Tidal of Goiim, King Amraphel of Shinar, and King Arioch of Ellasar, four kings against five. [10] Now the Valley of Siddim was full of bitumen pits; and as the kings of Sodom and Gomorrah fled, some fell into them, and the rest fled to the hill country. [11] So the enemy took all the goods of Sodom and Gomorrah, and all their provisions, and went their way; [12] they also took Lot, the son of Abram's brother, who lived in Sodom, and his goods, and departed.

[13] Then one who had escaped came and told Abram the Hebrew, who was living by the oaks[b] of Mamre the Amorite, brother of Eshcol and of Aner; these were allies of Abram. [14] When Abram heard that his nephew had been taken captive, he led forth his trained men, born in his house, three hundred eighteen of them, and went in pursuit as far as Dan. [15] He divided his forces against them by night, he and his servants, and routed them and pursued them to Hobah, north of Damascus. [16] Then he brought back all the goods, and also brought

a Heb *seed*
b Or *terebinths*
c Heb *Salt Sea*

not choose to stay in the land of Canaan (vv. 10–12). **14–17:** Only after Abraham has split from Lot and settled in *Canaan* does God show him the land (cf. 12.7). This certifies that Abraham has fulfilled God's command to go to the land that God "will show" him (12.1). Similarly, Jacob is promised the land after he has split from Esau (28.13–14). **18:** *Mamre* was an ancient southern sacred place, slightly north of Hebron, with which Abraham was associated (see ch 23).

14.1–24: Abraham's rescue of Lot from the eastern kings. This and ch 15 are closely related (see 15.1n., 15.12–16n.) and link in multiple ways with late layers of the primeval history (see 9.18–27n.; 10.16–18a n.). **1–12:** Here an alliance of four eastern kings conquers five Canaanite kings associated with the Dead Sea region where Lot is said to have settled. In a fulfillment of the curse of Noah predicting the enslavement of Canaan by Shem (9.25–26), these Canaanite kings had been subject for twelve years to an eastern alliance of kings headed by the Shemite king, *Chedorlaomer* (cf. 10.22). When the Canaanite kings rebel, the eastern kings crush the revolt and seize Lot and his household and take them back toward their home. Neither the battle nor any of the kings can be identified in nonbiblical sources. **13–16:** Abraham's ability to pursue and overcome the Shemite conquerors testifies to his status as heir of Shem and recipient of Shem's blessing (9.25–27). Moreover, this demonstrates the fulfillment of the divine promise to protect Abraham and his household (12.3). **13:** *Hebrew,* probably meaning

back his nephew Lot with his goods, and the women and the people.

¹⁷ After his return from the defeat of Chedorlaomer and the kings who were with him, the king of Sodom went out to meet him at the Valley of Shaveh (that is, the King's Valley). ¹⁸ And King Melchizedek of Salem brought out bread and wine; he was priest of God Most High.[a] ¹⁹ He blessed him and said,

"Blessed be Abram by God
    Most High,[a]
  maker of heaven and earth;
²⁰ and blessed be God Most High,[a]
  who has delivered your enemies into
    your hand!"

And Abram gave him one-tenth of everything. ²¹ Then the king of Sodom said to Abram, "Give me the persons, but take the goods for yourself." ²² But Abram said to the king of Sodom, "I have sworn to the LORD, God Most High,[a] maker of heaven and earth, ²³ that I would not take a thread or a sandal-thong or anything that is yours, so that you might not say, 'I have made Abram rich.' ²⁴ I will take nothing but what the young men have eaten, and the share of the men who went with me—Aner, Eshcol, and Mamre. Let them take their share."

15 After these things the word of the LORD came to Abram in a vision, "Do not be afraid, Abram, I am your shield; your reward shall be very great." ² But Abram said, "O Lord GOD, what will you give me, for I continue childless, and the heir of my house is Eliezer of Damascus?"[b] ³ And Abram said, "You have given me no offspring, and so a slave born in my house is to be my heir." ⁴ But the word of the LORD came to him, "This man shall not be your heir; no one but your very own issue shall be your heir." ⁵ He brought him outside and said, "Look toward heaven and count the stars, if you are able to count them." Then he said to him, "So shall your descendants be." ⁶ And he believed the LORD; and the LORD[c] reckoned it to him as righteousness.

⁷ Then he said to him, "I am the LORD who brought you from Ur of the Chaldeans, to give you this land to possess." ⁸ But he said, "O Lord GOD, how am I to know that I shall possess it?" ⁹ He said to him, "Bring me a heifer three years old, a female goat three years old, a ram three years old, a turtledove,

a   Heb *El Elyon*
b   Meaning of Heb uncertain
c   Heb *he*

an outsider, as often in the Bible (see 39.14; Ex 1.15; 1 Sam 29.3; Jon 1.9). **17–20:** This is the only section of Genesis associating a patriarch with Jerusalem; indeed, it is the only place in the entire Torah where Jerusalem is referred to by name. As heir of Shem, Abraham now receives the blessing of the priest in what will become Israel's royal and religious center. *Salem* is a name for Jerusalem (Ps 76.2), where the ancient high god of the Canaanite pantheon, El Elyon (*God Most High*), was worshiped in pre- and early Israelite times. The *King's Valley* is near Jerusalem (2 Sam 18.18), and the priest *Melchizedek* appears as the founder of a royal priesthood in an ancient Jerusalemite psalm (110.4). This mysterious Melchizedek was later interpreted eschatologically at Qumran and typologically by early Christians (Heb 7.1–17). **20:** *One-tenth,* i.e., a tithe; cf. 28.22; Num 18.21–28.

15.1–21: The first covenant with Abraham. The LORD promises Abraham protection, reward, and an heir in the wake of his recent military encounter with the eastern kings. **1:** The promise to be a *shield* (Heb "magen") for Abraham echoes Melchizedek's praise of the god who "delivered" ("miggen") Abraham (14.20), and the *reward* replaces the goods he had refused from the king of Sodom (14.21–24). **2–5:** The parallel objections from Abraham (vv. 2 and 3) and parallel divine responses (vv. 4 and 5) may be indicators of growth in this text, whether parallel sources (J and E; see the Introduction) or the supplementation of an earlier story by later material. **6:** This verse indicates that Abraham considered his objections answered. Though later tradition has generally understood God to be the one who reckoned righteousness to Abraham (e.g., Rom 4.9; Gal 3.6), the subject and object are not specified in Hebrew. *Righteousness* is being true to one's social obligations and commitments. It is possible that it is Abraham here who reckons righteousness to the LORD, certifying that he now believes that the LORD will be true to his commitments in 15.1 (cf. 15.2–3). **7–21:** This section parallels the promise-objection-reassurance pattern of 15.1–6, but with the added component of a covenant ceremony sealing God's promise to give Abraham the land. **9–17:** The ceremony (9–11,17) reflects an ancient practice in which the participants in a covenant oath passed through the dismembered parts of an animal and proclaimed a similar fate on themselves if they

and a young pigeon." [10] He brought him all these and cut them in two, laying each half over against the other; but he did not cut the birds in two. [11] And when birds of prey came down on the carcasses, Abram drove them away.

[12] As the sun was going down, a deep sleep fell upon Abram, and a deep and terrifying darkness descended upon him. [13] Then the LORD[a] said to Abram, "Know this for certain, that your offspring shall be aliens in a land that is not theirs, and shall be slaves there, and they shall be oppressed for four hundred years; [14] but I will bring judgment on the nation that they serve, and afterward they shall come out with great possessions. [15] As for yourself, you shall go to your ancestors in peace; you shall be buried in a good old age. [16] And they shall

come back here in the fourth generation; for the iniquity of the Amorites is not yet complete."

[17] When the sun had gone down and it was dark, a smoking fire pot and a flaming torch passed between these pieces. [18] On that day the LORD made a covenant with Abram, saying, "To your descendants I give this land, from the river of Egypt to the great river, the river Euphrates, [19] the land of the Kenites, the Kenizzites, the Kadmonites, [20] the Hittites, the Perizzites, the Rephaim, [21] the Amorites, the Canaanites, the Girgashites, and the Jebusites."

16

Now Sarai, Abram's wife, bore him no children. She had an Egyptian slave-girl whose name was Hagar, [2] and Sarai

---

a   Heb *he*

---

disobeyed the terms of the agreement (see Jer 34.18). Likely because of this, the Hebrew word for "making" a covenant is literally to "cut" a covenant (found in 15.18). In this case, God passes between the pieces in the form of fire (see Ex 3.2; 13.21). **12–16:** A speech has been inserted into this ceremony that echoes Abraham's earlier triumph over the eastern kings at "Dan" and return from there with "goods" (Heb "rekush"; 14.14–16). Here in v. 14 God promises a future *judgment* (Heb "dan") on Egypt and escape of Abraham's descendants from there with yet more goods (again "rekush" in 15.14; see Ex 3.21–22; 12.33–36). Though this is promised in four generations at the end of the speech (15.16), a Priestly editor may have modified this in v. 13 to four hundred years in order to better match Priestly material in Exodus (Ex 12.40). **16:** *The iniquity of the Amorites,* see Lev 20.23; Deut 9.4. **18–21:** The ceremony is concluded with God's promise to give the land of the Canaanite peoples (cf. 10.16–18) to Abraham. **18:** The boundaries given here are the broadest definition of the promised land in the Bible. They correspond to similarly broad, ideal descriptions of the land in the Deuteronomistic History (e.g., 2 Sam 8.3; 1 Kings 4.21; cf. Deut 1.7; 11.24; Josh 1.4). The phrase *river of Egypt* occurs only here, and may refer to the Nile. But elsewhere in the Bible (e.g., Num 34.5; 2 Kings 24.7; Isa 27.12) and in other sources, the "Wadi of Egypt" is apparently either the Wadi Besor or the Wadi el-Arish, both south of Gaza. **19–21:** The form of this list of ten nations to be displaced resembles the list of Canaanite groups in Gen 10.16–18, but its contents more resemble lists of Canaanite peoples in the Tetrateuch (e.g., Ex 3.8,17; 13.5) and Deuteronomistic History (e.g., Deut 7.1; 20.17; Josh 3.10). This list, however, is longer than others. Though it is missing the "Hivites" (see 10.16–18a n.), who occur on most other lists, this list is unique in including the *Kenites, Kenizzites, Kadmonites,* and *Rephaim.*

16.1–16: Hagar's encounter with God and the birth of Ishmael stand at the heart of the Abraham story (see "Chiasm in the Abraham Story" on p. 38), enveloped by parallel traditions dealing with covenant (chs 15 and 17), Lot and Abraham (chs 13–14 and 18–19), the endangerment of Sarah (12.10–20 and ch 20), and the promise (12.1–6 and 22.1–19). This story echoes the story of Abraham's endangerment of Sarah in 12.10–20 in describing the complications resulting from human attempts to fulfill the promise, in this case the promise of offspring. In addition, like that story, this one links with the Exodus, though offering a quite different picture. In the book of Exodus Israelites are "oppressed" (Heb "'anah") by the Egyptians (Ex 1.12), flee east toward Israel through the wilderness, and meet God there (Ex 19.24.1–2,10–11). In this chapter, however, it is an *Egyptian,* Hagar, who is "oppressed" (Heb "'anah"; "dealt harshly with" in the NRSV of v. 6) by the Israelite matriarch Sarah; Hagar flees west from Israel toward Egypt and meets God in the wilderness. Later, in Gen 21.8–21, we will see a doublet of this story, where Hagar again must leave Abraham's clan, go into the desert, and hear an oracle that will revolve around an interpretation of the name of Hagar's son, Ishmael (Heb for "God hears"). Both stories have their origins in ancient traditions surrounding the origins of the Ishmaelites, seen in Genesis as ancestors of the Arab peoples (see Gen 25.12–18), but the version here in Gen 16 is distinguished by its echoes of the Exodus story

said to Abram, "You see that the LORD has prevented me from bearing children; go in to my slave-girl; it may be that I shall obtain children by her." And Abram listened to the voice of Sarai. [3] So, after Abram had lived ten years in the land of Canaan, Sarai, Abram's wife, took Hagar the Egyptian, her slave-girl, and gave her to her husband Abram as a wife. [4] He went in to Hagar, and she conceived; and when she saw that she had conceived, she looked with contempt on her mistress. [5] Then Sarai said to Abram, "May the wrong done to me be on you! I gave my slave-girl to your embrace, and when she saw that she had conceived, she looked on me with contempt. May the LORD judge between you and me!" [6] But Abram said to Sarai, "Your slave-girl is in your power; do to her as you please." Then Sarai dealt harshly with her, and she ran away from her.

[7] The angel of the LORD found her by a spring of water in the wilderness, the spring on the way to Shur. [8] And he said, "Hagar, slave-girl of Sarai, where have you come from and where are you going?" She said, "I am running away from my mistress Sarai." [9] The angel of the LORD said to her, "Return to your mistress, and submit to her." [10] The angel of the LORD also said to her, "I will so greatly multiply your offspring that they cannot be counted for multitude." [11] And the angel of the LORD said to her,

"Now you have conceived and shall bear
  a son;

you shall call him Ishmael,[a]
  for the LORD has given heed to your
    affliction.
[12] He shall be a wild ass of a man,
  with his hand against everyone,
    and everyone's hand against him;
  and he shall live at odds with all his kin."

[13] So she named the LORD who spoke to her, "You are El-roi";[b] for she said, "Have I really seen God and remained alive after seeing him?"[c] [14] Therefore the well was called Beer-lahai-roi;[d] it lies between Kadesh and Bered.

[15] Hagar bore Abram a son; and Abram named his son, whom Hagar bore, Ishmael. [16] Abram was eighty-six years old when Hagar bore him[e] Ishmael.

17 When Abram was ninety-nine years old, the LORD appeared to Abram, and said to him, "I am God Almighty;[f] walk before me, and be blameless. [2] And I will make my covenant between me and you, and will make you exceedingly numerous." [3] Then Abram fell on his face; and God said to him, [4] "As for me, this is my covenant with you: You shall be the ancestor of a multitude of nations. [5] No longer shall your name be Abram,[g] but your

a That is *God hears*
b Perhaps *God of seeing* or *God who sees*
c Meaning of Heb uncertain
d That is *the Well of the Living One who sees me*
e Heb *Abram*
f Traditional rendering of Heb *El Shaddai*
g That is *exalted ancestor*

and ultimately sympathetic focus on Hagar. **2:** According to ancient surrogate motherhood customs, a wife could give her maid to her husband and claim the child as her own (30.3,9). **3:** This duplicate notice of Sarah's transfer of Hagar to Abraham as a surrogate mother probably comes from the Priestly source. **4–5:** The translation *looked with contempt* implies that Hagar disdained her mistress, whereas the Hebrew verb ("qll," "to treat lightly") only implies that Hagar did not look up to her mistress the way she once did. Having had a child, Hagar is now derisively seen by her mistress as a slave who is not sufficiently submissive. **7:** Here *the angel of the LORD* is not a heavenly being subordinate to God but the LORD (Yahweh) in earthly manifestation, as is clear from v. 13 (cf. 21.17,19; Ex 14.19). **11:** *The LORD has given heed,* lit., "The LORD has heard," an explanation of the name Ishmael (see note *a* and 21.17n.). **13:** *God of seeing* (see note *b*) was the name of the deity at the Beer-lahai-roi well, now identified with Israel's God. On Hagar's question, cf. 32.30; Ex 33.20; Judg 6.22–23; 13.22. **15–16:** Priestly material focusing more on Ishmael than on Hagar.

17.1–27: The everlasting covenant and sign of circumcision. This account from the Priestly tradition is parallel to that in 15.1–21 and links to the Priestly covenant with Noah in 9.8–17; see further 9.8–17n. **1:** The phrase translated as *God Almighty* (Heb "El Shadday") is variously understood as "God [or "El"], the one of the mountains," "God of the Shadday [deities]," or even "fertile God" (literally, "God with breasts," see 49.25). Whatever its original meaning, the Priestly tradition understands this epithet to be what the early ancestors of Israel called God before they learned the name Yahweh (Ex 6.2–8). **2–6:** In a parallel to 15.1–6 this text includes the

name shall be Abraham;[a] for I have made you the ancestor of a multitude of nations. [6] I will make you exceedingly fruitful; and I will make nations of you, and kings shall come from you. [7] I will establish my covenant between me and you, and your offspring after you throughout their generations, for an everlasting covenant, to be God to you and to your offspring[b] after you. [8] And I will give to you, and to your offspring after you, the land where you are now an alien, all the land of Canaan, for a perpetual holding; and I will be their God."

[9] God said to Abraham, "As for you, you shall keep my covenant, you and your offspring after you throughout their generations. [10] This is my covenant, which you shall keep, between me and you and your offspring after you: Every male among you shall be circumcised. [11] You shall circumcise the flesh of your foreskins, and it shall be a sign of the covenant between me and you. [12] Throughout your generations every male among you shall be circumcised when he is eight days old, including the slave born in your house and the one bought with your money from any foreigner who is not of your offspring. [13] Both the slave born in your house and the one bought with your money must be circumcised. So shall my covenant be in your flesh an everlasting covenant. [14] Any uncircumcised male who is not circumcised in the flesh of his foreskin shall be cut off from his people; he has broken my covenant."

[15] God said to Abraham, "As for Sarai your wife, you shall not call her Sarai, but Sarah shall be her name. [16] I will bless her, and moreover I will give you a son by her. I will bless her, and she shall give rise to nations; kings of peoples shall come from her." [17] Then Abraham fell on his face and laughed, and said to himself, "Can a child be born to a man who is a hundred years old? Can Sarah, who is ninety years old, bear a child?" [18] And Abraham said to God, "O that Ishmael might live in your sight!" [19] God said, "No, but your wife Sarah shall bear you a son, and you shall name him Isaac.[c] I will establish my covenant with him as an everlasting covenant for his offspring after him. [20] As for Ishmael, I have heard you; I will bless him and make him fruitful and exceedingly numerous; he shall be the father of twelve princes, and I will make him a great nation. [21] But my covenant I will establish with Isaac, whom Sarah shall bear to you at this season next year." [22] And when he had finished talking with him, God went up from Abraham.

[23] Then Abraham took his son Ishmael and all the slaves born in his house or bought with his money, every male among the men of Abraham's house, and he circumcised the flesh of their foreskins that very day, as God had said to him. [24] Abraham was ninety-nine years old when he was circumcised in the

---

a   Here taken to mean *ancestor of a multitude*
b   Heb *seed*
c   That is *he laughs*

promise of offspring in the covenant. **5:** A new name signifies a new relationship or status (see 32.28). *Abraham,* a dialectal variant of *Abram,* means "the [divine] ancestor is exalted." Here the name is explained by its similarity to the Hebrew for *ancestor of a multitude,* referring to nations whose ancestry was traced to Abraham (v. 16; 28.3; 35.11; 48.4), such as Edomites and Ishmaelites. The promise to make Abraham "exceedingly numerous" (v. 2) and *exceedingly fruitful* (v. 6) echoes the broader fertility blessing given animals (1.22; 8.17) and humanity (1.28; 9.1,7) in the primeval history. **7:** Within the Priestly tradition, the promise to be God to Abraham and his offspring leads to the divine provision of religious laws and a tabernacle sanctuary into which God comes to dwell in Israel's midst (Ex 25–31; 35–40). Like the covenant with Noah (9.8–17), this covenant to be bound to Israel is *an everlasting covenant* (vv. 13,19) because it is grounded in the will of God, not human behavior. It is a covenant of grant, rather than a conditional covenant. **9–14:** Circumcision was an ancient rite practiced among some Semitic groups, perhaps originally connected to marriage (see 34.14–17), probably having to do with warding off demons (see Ex 4.24–26). Here, however, it is moved to early childhood and reinterpreted as a sign of God's everlasting covenant with Israel, a mark of membership in the covenant community. Unlike the covenant with Noah (9.1–17), this one pertains only to the household and heirs of Abraham. **15:** *Sarah,* meaning "princess," is a variant of *Sarai;* see v. 5n. **17:** Abraham's laughter here in the Priestly tradition anticipates Sarah's laughter in the non-Priestly account (18.9–15n.).

flesh of his foreskin. ²⁵ And his son Ishmael was thirteen years old when he was circumcised in the flesh of his foreskin. ²⁶ That very day Abraham and his son Ishmael were circumcised; ²⁷ and all the men of his house, slaves born in the house and those bought with money from a foreigner, were circumcised with him.

18 The LORD appeared to Abraham[a] by the oaks[b] of Mamre, as he sat at the entrance of his tent in the heat of the day. ² He looked up and saw three men standing near him. When he saw them, he ran from the tent entrance to meet them, and bowed down to the ground. ³ He said, "My lord, if I find favor with you, do not pass by your servant. ⁴ Let a little water be brought, and wash your feet, and rest yourselves under the tree. ⁵ Let me bring a little bread, that you may refresh yourselves, and after that you may pass on—since you have come to your servant." So they said, "Do as you have said." ⁶ And Abraham hastened into the tent to Sarah, and said, "Make ready quickly three measures[c] of choice flour, knead it, and make cakes." ⁷ Abraham ran to the herd, and took a calf, tender and good, and gave it to the servant, who hastened to prepare it. ⁸ Then he took curds and milk and the calf that he had prepared, and set it before them; and he stood by them under the tree while they ate.

⁹ They said to him, "Where is your wife Sarah?" And he said, "There, in the tent." ¹⁰ Then one said, "I will surely return to you in due season, and your wife Sarah shall have a son." And Sarah was listening at the tent entrance behind him. ¹¹ Now Abraham and Sarah were old, advanced in age; it had ceased to be with Sarah after the manner of women. ¹² So Sarah laughed to herself, saying, "After I have grown old, and my husband is old, shall I have pleasure?" ¹³ The LORD said to Abraham, "Why did Sarah laugh, and say, 'Shall I indeed bear a child, now that I am old?' ¹⁴ Is anything too wonderful for the LORD? At the set time I will return to you, in due season, and Sarah shall have a son." ¹⁵ But Sarah denied, saying, "I did not laugh"; for she was afraid. He said, "Oh yes, you did laugh."

¹⁶ Then the men set out from there, and they looked toward Sodom; and Abraham went with them to set them on their way. ¹⁷ The LORD said, "Shall I hide from Abraham what I am about to do, ¹⁸ seeing that Abraham shall become a great and mighty nation, and all the nations of the earth shall be blessed in him?[d] ¹⁹ No, for I have chosen[e] him, that he may charge his children and his household after him to keep the way of the LORD by doing righteousness and justice; so that the LORD may bring about for Abraham what he has promised him." ²⁰ Then the LORD said, "How great is the outcry against Sodom and Gomorrah and how very grave their sin! ²¹ I must go down and see whether they have done altogether according to the outcry that has come to me; and if not, I will know."

a Heb *him*
b Or *terebinths*
c Heb *seahs*
d Or *and all the nations of the earth shall bless themselves by him*
e Heb *known*

18.1–15: The LORD's visit to Abraham and Sarah. 1: The *oaks of Mamre*, see 12.6–8n.; 13.18n. **2–8:** A description of ideal hospitality of Abraham parallel to that of Lot in 19.1–11. This motif of secretly divine visitors is widespread in folklore. The relation between the three visitors and the LORD (v. 1) is unclear. The narrative fluidly shifts from speaking of them as a group (e.g., v. 9) to having "the LORD" speak alone (e.g., v. 13; cf. v. 10). Later materials in v. 22 and 19.1 conceive of "the LORD" as one of the three angels (see 16.7n.), though this is not specified in the preceding narrative ("one" in the NRSV of v. 10 is a translator's addition). **9–15:** The narrator uses the theme of Sarah's laughter (cf. 17.17) to stress the incredibility of God's promise of a son (eventually Isaac, 21.1–3). **11:** *Ceased . . . after the manner of women*, a circumlocution for menopause. **12:** Isaac's name means "he [God] laughs," and other traditions develop the link with laughter as well (17.17–19; 21.6,8; 26.8).

18.16–33: Abraham's intercession for Sodom and Gomorrah. 17–19: This first speech by the LORD stresses that he speaks to Abraham because he chose him to teach his household the ways of righteousness. In vv. 22–32 the LORD will model such righteousness in his responsiveness to Abraham. **18:** See 12.3n. **20–21:** This second speech by the LORD echoes his decision at Babel to *go down* and *see* what was going on there (11.5; cf. divine self-reflection in 3.22; 6.3,5–7; 11.6–7). Unlike vv. 17–19, this speech suggests that the LORD has not yet

²² So the men turned from there, and went toward Sodom, while Abraham remained standing before the LORD.ᵃ ²³ Then Abraham came near and said, "Will you indeed sweep away the righteous with the wicked? ²⁴ Suppose there are fifty righteous within the city; will you then sweep away the place and not forgive it for the fifty righteous who are in it? ²⁵ Far be it from you to do such a thing, to slay the righteous with the wicked, so that the righteous fare as the wicked! Far be that from you! Shall not the Judge of all the earth do what is just?" ²⁶ And the LORD said, "If I find at Sodom fifty righteous in the city, I will forgive the whole place for their sake." ²⁷ Abraham answered, "Let me take it upon myself to speak to the Lord, I who am but dust and ashes. ²⁸ Suppose five of the fifty righteous are lacking? Will you destroy the whole city for lack of five?" And he said, "I will not destroy it if I find forty-five there." ²⁹ Again he spoke to him, "Suppose forty are found there." He answered, "For the sake of forty I will not do it." ³⁰ Then he said, "Oh do not let the Lord be angry if I speak. Suppose thirty are found there." He answered, "I will not do it, if I find thirty there." ³¹ He said, "Let me take it upon myself to speak to the Lord. Suppose twenty are found there." He answered, "For the sake of twenty I will not destroy it." ³² Then he said, "Oh do not let the Lord be angry if I speak just once more. Suppose ten are found there." He answered, "For the sake of ten I will not destroy it." ³³ And the LORD went his way, when he had finished speaking to Abraham; and Abraham returned to his place.

19 The two angels came to Sodom in the evening, and Lot was sitting in the gateway of Sodom. When Lot saw them, he rose to meet them, and bowed down with his face to the ground. ² He said, "Please, my lords, turn aside to your servant's house and spend the night, and wash your feet; then you can rise early and go on your way." They said, "No; we will spend the night in the square." ³ But he urged them strongly; so they turned aside to him and entered his house; and he made them a feast, and baked unleavened bread, and they ate. ⁴ But before they lay down, the men of the city, the men of Sodom, both young and old, all the people to the last man, surrounded the house; ⁵ and they called to Lot, "Where are the men who came to you tonight? Bring them out to us, so that we may know them." ⁶ Lot went out of the door to the men, shut the door after him, ⁷ and said, "I beg you, my brothers, do not act so wickedly. ⁸ Look, I have two daughters who have not known a man; let me bring them out to you, and do to them as you please; only do nothing to these men, for they have come under the shelter of my roof." ⁹ But they replied, "Stand back!" And they said, "This fellow came here as an alien, and he would play the judge! Now we will deal worse with you than with them." Then they pressed hard against the man Lot, and came near the door to break it down. ¹⁰ But the men inside reached out their hands and brought Lot into the house with them, and shut the door. ¹¹ And they

ᵃ Another ancient tradition reads *while the LORD remained standing before Abraham*

decided what to do. **22–33:** Like Moses (e.g., Ex 32.9–14), Abraham negotiates with an angry God, appealing to God's righteousness. In this case, however, the terms he ends up winning—aversion of disaster if ten righteous people can be found—do not avert destruction. Thus, this text appears to be a theoretical reflection on God's righteousness and how many righteous people are required to save a broader group; cf. Ezek 14.12–23.

19.1–38: The rescue of Lot and his family from the destruction of Sodom and Gomorrah. The destruction of Sodom and Gomorrah was a prominent example in Israelite tradition of God's total judgment (Deut 29.23; Isa 1.9; Jer 49.18; Am 4.11). **1:** *Two angels,* see 18.2–8n. **1–11:** As in the case of 18.1–8, the main issue here is hospitality to secretly divine visitors. Here, however, the sanctity of hospitality is threatened by *the men of the city* who wish to rape (*know*) the guests (cf. Judg 19.22–30). The primary point of this text is how this threat by the townspeople violates the value of hospitality (contrast 18.1–16). Hospitality is valued so strongly in this context that Lot offers his virgin daughters in place of his guests (vv. 7–8). Nevertheless, this foolish and cruel act has the opposite of its intended effect, leading the townspeople to threaten worse things to Lot than the rape they were going to inflict on his guests (v. 9), and requiring the guests to protect their host (vv. 10–11). Where Abraham was the model of hospitality (Gen 18.1–16), Lot's actions show him to be a bungling, almost heartless

struck with blindness the men who were at the door of the house, both small and great, so that they were unable to find the door.

¹² Then the men said to Lot, "Have you anyone else here? Sons-in-law, sons, daughters, or anyone you have in the city—bring them out of the place. ¹³ For we are about to destroy this place, because the outcry against its people has become great before the LORD, and the LORD has sent us to destroy it." ¹⁴ So Lot went out and said to his sons-in-law, who were to marry his daughters, "Up, get out of this place; for the LORD is about to destroy the city." But he seemed to his sons-in-law to be jesting.

¹⁵ When morning dawned, the angels urged Lot, saying, "Get up, take your wife and your two daughters who are here, or else you will be consumed in the punishment of the city." ¹⁶ But he lingered; so the men seized him and his wife and his two daughters by the hand, the LORD being merciful to him, and they brought him out and left him outside the city. ¹⁷ When they had brought them outside, theyª said, "Flee for your life; do not look back or stop anywhere in the Plain; flee to the hills, or else you will be consumed." ¹⁸ And Lot said to them, "Oh, no, my lords; ¹⁹ your servant has found favor with you, and you have shown me great kindness in saving my life; but I cannot flee to the hills, for fear the disaster will overtake me and I die. ²⁰ Look, that city is near enough to flee to, and it is a little one. Let me escape there—is it not a little one?—and my life will be saved!" ²¹ He said to him, "Very well, I grant you this favor too, and will not overthrow the city of which you have spoken. ²² Hurry, escape there, for I can do nothing until you arrive there." Therefore the city was called Zoar.ᵇ ²³ The sun had risen on the earth when Lot came to Zoar.

²⁴ Then the LORD rained on Sodom and Gomorrah sulfur and fire from the LORD out of heaven; ²⁵ and he overthrew those cities, and all the Plain, and all the inhabitants of the cities, and what grew on the ground. ²⁶ But Lot's wife, behind him, looked back, and she became a pillar of salt.

²⁷ Abraham went early in the morning to the place where he had stood before the LORD; ²⁸ and he looked down toward Sodom and Gomorrah and toward all the land of the Plain and saw the smoke of the land going up like the smoke of a furnace.

²⁹ So it was that, when God destroyed the cities of the Plain, God remembered Abraham, and sent Lot out of the midst of the overthrow, when he overthrew the cities in which Lot had settled.

³⁰ Now Lot went up out of Zoar and settled in the hills with his two daughters, for he was afraid to stay in Zoar; so he lived in a cave with his two daughters. ³¹ And the firstborn said to the younger, "Our father is old, and there is not a man on earth to come in to us after the manner of all the world. ³² Come, let us make our father drink wine, and we will lie with him, so that we may preserve offspring through our father." ³³ So they made their father drink wine that night; and the firstborn went in, and lay with her father; he did not know when she lay down or when she rose. ³⁴ On the next day, the firstborn said to the younger, "Look, I lay last night with my father; let us make him drink wine tonight also; then you go in and lie with him, so that we may preserve

ª Gk Syr Vg: Heb *he*
ᵇ That is *Little*

imitator who does not deserve to be the heir of the promise to Abraham. **12–14:** In place of Sarah's laughter (Heb "tsḥq") in the preceding hospitality scene (18.11–14), we have here the Sodomite *sons-in-law* assuming that Lot is *jesting* (Heb "tsḥq"). **15–23:** Once again, Lot is unfavorably contrasted with Abraham. Where Abraham hurried to serve his angelic guests (18.2,6,7), Lot hesitates at their urging to leave Sodom, requiring them to take him away by force (vv. 15–16). Then, doubting their rescue plan, he asks them to let him stop in a nearby city (Zoar, which means "little"; see note *b* and v. 20) lest he be caught up in the coming destruction (vv. 17–22). In the end, though Lot claims that he has found a Noah-like favor with his angelic rescuers (19.19; cf. Gen 6.8), this is not affirmed by the angels or the narrator. **24–25:** The *rain* of destruction continues the echoes of the Noah story. **26:** This text turns salt formations in the Dead Sea area into a testimony to the truth of the story, asserting that one of those formations was Lot's wife, who disobediently looked back at the cities God was destroying. **29:** This is a Priestly summary of the story, echoing 8.1 and attributing Lot's rescue to his relation with Abraham.

offspring through our father." [35] So they made their father drink wine that night also; and the younger rose, and lay with him; and he did not know when she lay down or when she rose. [36] Thus both the daughters of Lot became pregnant by their father. [37] The firstborn bore a son, and named him Moab; he is the ancestor of the Moabites to this day. [38] The younger also bore a son and named him Ben-ammi; he is the ancestor of the Ammonites to this day.

20 From there Abraham journeyed toward the region of the Negeb, and settled between Kadesh and Shur. While residing in Gerar as an alien, [2] Abraham said of his wife Sarah, "She is my sister." And King Abimelech of Gerar sent and took Sarah. [3] But God came to Abimelech in a dream by night, and said to him, "You are about to die because of the woman whom you have taken; for she is a married woman." [4] Now Abimelech had not approached her; so he said, "Lord, will you destroy an innocent people? [5] Did he not himself say to me, 'She is my sister'? And she herself said, 'He is my brother.' I did this in the integrity of my heart and the innocence of my hands." [6] Then God said to him in the dream, "Yes, I know that you did this in the integrity of your heart; fur-

37–38: This story suggests that two of Israel's closest neighbors, the Moabites and Ammonites in Transjordan, originated in incest. Mistakenly assuming that the destruction of Sodom and Gomorrah was so total that there is no one else on earth by whom to have children (19.31), Lot's daughters get their father drunk so that he will conceive with them. The themes of drunkenness and (implicit) nakedness are reminiscent of the story of Noah and his sons (9.20–27).

20.1–18: The second story of endangerment of the matriarch (cf. 12.10–20; 26.6–11). Many scholars have argued that chs 20–22 contain the first major block of an Elohistic (E) source parallel to the Yahwistic (J) source found in chs 12–19 and extending through the rest of the Pentateuch (see further 15.2–5n. and the Introduction). Note parallels between stories of endangerment of Sarah in 20.1–18 (E) and 12.10–20 (J); the Hagar stories 21.8–19 (E) and 16.1–14 (J), and even stories about Abimelech in 21.22–34 (E) and 26.17–33 (J). These similarities indicate that the author of the non-Priestly Abraham narrative probably drew upon cycles of Yahwistic and Elohistic traditions that were parallel at some points. Nevertheless, there are some important indicators that the Elohistic traditions seen in Gen 20–22 were written down as part of a larger whole that included the preceding narratives in Gen 12–19 and thus do not reflect (in their present form) a separate written source. Not only are the Elohistic accounts organized as part of a broader chiasm that includes the narratives of Genesis 12–19, but details of Genesis 20–22 are understandable only when these chapters are read following Genesis 12–19.

CHIASM IN THE ABRAHAM STORY

There are a series of correspondences between different parts of the Abraham story, where themes introduced at the outset of a narrative are resumed in reverse order in its second half. This chiastic pattern binds many parts of the Abraham story together and puts a heightened emphasis on the sections that occur at the center (in **boldface**).

    A. Prologue (11.28–30)
        B. First challenge: call for Abraham to leave family of origin (12:1–3)
            C. Wife-sister story 12:10–13:1
                D. Separation from Lot (13:2–18)
                    E. Covenant of pieces with Abraham (14–15)
                        F. Hagar-Ishmael story (Gen 16:1–14)
                    E.' Covenant of circumcision with Abraham (17)
                D.' Hospitality/progeny episodes; Abraham contrasted with Lot (18–19)
            C.' Wife-sister story (20)
        B.' Final challenge: calls for Abraham to let go of family of future (21.8–21 and 22.1–19)
    A.' Epilogue 22.20–24

For example, Abraham's brief claim in 20.2 that Sarah is his sister would not make sense without the explanation of his request to her to make the same claim in 12.11–13. **3–7:** The depiction of Abimelech is far more detailed and sympathetic than that of the foreign king in either of the parallel accounts (cf. 12.15–19; 26.9–10).

thermore it was I who kept you from sinning against me. Therefore I did not let you touch her. [7] Now then, return the man's wife; for he is a prophet, and he will pray for you and you shall live. But if you do not restore her, know that you shall surely die, you and all that are yours."

[8] So Abimelech rose early in the morning, and called all his servants and told them all these things; and the men were very much afraid. [9] Then Abimelech called Abraham, and said to him, "What have you done to us? How have I sinned against you, that you have brought such great guilt on me and my kingdom? You have done things to me that ought not to be done." [10] And Abimelech said to Abraham, "What were you thinking of, that you did this thing?" [11] Abraham said, "I did it because I thought, There is no fear of God at all in this place, and they will kill me because of my wife. [12] Besides, she is indeed my sister, the daughter of my father but not the daughter of my mother; and she became my wife. [13] And when God caused me to wander from my father's house, I said to her, 'This is the kindness you must do me: at every place to which we come, say of me, He is my brother.'" [14] Then Abimelech took sheep and oxen, and male and female slaves, and gave them to Abraham, and restored his wife Sarah to him. [15] Abimelech said, "My land is before you; settle where it pleases you." [16] To Sarah he said, "Look, I have given your brother a thousand pieces of silver; it is your exoneration before all who are with you; you are completely vindicated." [17] Then Abraham prayed to God; and God healed Abimelech, and also healed his wife and female slaves so that they bore children. [18] For the LORD had closed fast all the wombs of the house of Abimelech because of Sarah, Abraham's wife.

21 The LORD dealt with Sarah as he had said, and the LORD did for Sarah as he had promised. [2] Sarah conceived and bore Abraham a son in his old age, at the time of which God had spoken to him. [3] Abraham gave the name Isaac to his son whom Sarah bore him. [4] And Abraham circumcised his son Isaac when he was eight days old, as God had commanded him. [5] Abraham was a hundred years old when his son Isaac was born to him. [6] Now Sarah said, "God has brought laughter for me; everyone who hears will laugh with me." [7] And she said, "Who would ever have said to Abraham that Sarah would nurse children? Yet I have borne him a son in his old age."

[8] The child grew, and was weaned; and Abraham made a great feast on the day that Isaac was weaned. [9] But Sarah saw the son of Hagar the Egyptian, whom she had borne to Abraham, playing with her son Isaac.[a] [10] So she said to Abraham, "Cast out this slave woman with her son; for the son of this slave woman shall not inherit along with my son Isaac." [11] The matter was very distress-

a   Gk Vg: Heb lacks *with her son Isaac*

7: To Abraham is attributed the intercessory role of *prophet;* this is the Bible's first use of the term, and the only designation of Abraham as a prophet in the Torah (but see Ps 105.15). 12: The narrator never asserts that Sarah is Terah's daughter (cf. 11.27–30). Nevertheless, faced with Abimelech's passionate questioning, Abraham claims to be her half-brother by way of his father. Though many have taken his assertion at face value, it may be an attempt to provide as many excuses for his behavior as possible (cf. 20.11).

21.1–21: Isaac and Ishmael. 3–5: A notice of Isaac's birth and circumcision taken from the Priestly source (see 17.1–24). On *the name Isaac,* see 18.12n. 6: See 18.9–15n. 8–21: This story of endangerment of Ishmael parallels the following one of endangerment of Isaac. After God gives Abraham the command to let his child go (v. 12; 22.2), he rises *early in the morning* to fulfill it (v. 14 || 22.3), the child is delivered when an *angel of God/the LORD* cries out from heaven (v. 17; 22.11–12), and Hagar and Abraham both see a way to save the child (v. 19 || 22.13). These features distinguish this story of Hagar and Ishmael from its parallel in ch. 16, where Hagar likewise left Abraham's clan, went into the desert, and heard a message from an angel of God (there an "angel of the LORD") about her child's destiny. Though the divinity is referred to in ch. 16 as "the LORD" and here in ch. 21 as "God," the angel in both cases promises that Hagar's offspring will be numerous (16.10; 21.18) and assures her that God has "heard" hers (ch. 16.11) or her child's (ch. 21.17) suffering, wordplays on Ishmael's name, which means "God hears" (see also 17.20, part of the Priestly tradition). These are probably oral variants of a story about the origin of the Ishmaelites (see 25.12–18). 9: *Playing with,* literally "making [him] laugh," another reference to Isaac's

ing to Abraham on account of his son. [12] But God said to Abraham, "Do not be distressed because of the boy and because of your slave woman; whatever Sarah says to you, do as she tells you, for it is through Isaac that offspring shall be named for you. [13] As for the son of the slave woman, I will make a nation of him also, because he is your offspring." [14] So Abraham rose early in the morning, and took bread and a skin of water, and gave it to Hagar, putting it on her shoulder, along with the child, and sent her away. And she departed, and wandered about in the wilderness of Beer-sheba.

[15] When the water in the skin was gone, she cast the child under one of the bushes. [16] Then she went and sat down opposite him a good way off, about the distance of a bowshot; for she said, "Do not let me look on the death of the child." And as she sat opposite him, she lifted up her voice and wept. [17] And God heard the voice of the boy; and the angel of God called to Hagar from heaven, and said to her, "What troubles you, Hagar? Do not be afraid; for God has heard the voice of the boy where he is. [18] Come, lift up the boy and hold him fast with your hand, for I will make a great nation of him." [19] Then God opened her eyes and she saw a well of water. She went, and filled the skin with water, and gave the boy a drink.

[20] God was with the boy, and he grew up; he lived in the wilderness, and became an expert with the bow. [21] He lived in the wilderness of Paran; and his mother got a wife for him from the land of Egypt.

[22] At that time Abimelech, with Phicol the commander of his army, said to Abraham,

"God is with you in all that you do; [23] now therefore swear to me here by God that you will not deal falsely with me or with my offspring or with my posterity, but as I have dealt loyally with you, you will deal with me and with the land where you have resided as an alien." [24] And Abraham said, "I swear it."

[25] When Abraham complained to Abimelech about a well of water that Abimelech's servants had seized, [26] Abimelech said, "I do not know who has done this; you did not tell me, and I have not heard of it until today." [27] So Abraham took sheep and oxen and gave them to Abimelech, and the two men made a covenant. [28] Abraham set apart seven ewe lambs of the flock. [29] And Abimelech said to Abraham, "What is the meaning of these seven ewe lambs that you have set apart?" [30] He said, "These seven ewe lambs you shall accept from my hand, in order that you may be a witness for me that I dug this well." [31] Therefore that place was called Beer-sheba;[a] because there both of them swore an oath. [32] When they had made a covenant at Beer-sheba, Abimelech, with Phicol the commander of his army, left and returned to the land of the Philistines. [33] Abraham[b] planted a tamarisk tree in Beer-sheba, and called there on the name of the LORD, the Everlasting God.[c] [34] And Abraham resided as an alien many days in the land of the Philistines.

22

After these things God tested Abraham. He said to him, "Abraham!" And he said, "Here I am." [2] He said, "Take your

---

[a] That is *Well of seven* or *Well of the oath*
[b] Heb *He*
[c] Or *the* LORD, *El Olam*

---

name; see 18.12n. **14–17:** In these verses Ishmael is a little boy, a stark contrast to the presentation of him as a teenager in the preceding Priestly traditions (16.16; 17.25; 21.5). This is just one sign that stories like this one about Hagar and Ishmael were not originally written with the Priestly tradition in view. **17:** See 16.7n.

21.22–34: Abraham's dispute with Abimelech. This text continues the story about Abraham and Abimelech that was begun in ch 20. Together, the narratives of Abraham's sojourn in Gerar in ch 20 and 21.22–34 resemble that of Isaac's sojourn in Gerar in 26.6–33, and they may have a common oral background. This story combines a tradition that explains the name *Beer-sheba* as meaning "well of seven" (see 22.28–30) with an explanation (parallel to 26.31–33) that it means "well of oath." **33:** On the tamarisk tree, see 12.6–8n. *Everlasting God* ("El Olam") may be an ancient divine name once associated with the sanctuary at Beer-sheba.

22.1–19: The testing of Abraham. Although in later tradition this is one of the most significant chapters in the ancestral narratives, nothing in the text marks it as such. **1a:** The narrative begins by informing the reader of something that Abraham does not know, that *God tested Abraham.* Abraham's "fear" of God is not proven (v. 12) until he has reached out his hand to slaughter his son (v. 10). **1b–2:** After giving up Ishmael earlier (see

son, your only son Isaac, whom you love, and go to the land of Moriah, and offer him there as a burnt offering on one of the mountains that I shall show you." ³ So Abraham rose early in the morning, saddled his donkey, and took two of his young men with him, and his son Isaac; he cut the wood for the burnt offering, and set out and went to the place in the distance that God had shown him. ⁴ On the third day Abraham looked up and saw the place far away. ⁵ Then Abraham said to his young men, "Stay here with the donkey; the boy and I will go over there; we will worship, and then we will come back to you." ⁶ Abraham took the wood of the burnt offering and laid it on his son Isaac, and he himself carried the fire and the knife. So the two of them walked on together. ⁷ Isaac said to his father Abraham, "Father!" And he said, "Here I am, my son." He said, "The fire and the wood are here, but where is the lamb for a burnt offering?" ⁸ Abraham said, "God himself will provide the lamb for a burnt offering, my son." So the two of them walked on together.

⁹ When they came to the place that God had shown him, Abraham built an altar there and laid the wood in order. He bound his son Isaac, and laid him on the altar, on top of the wood. ¹⁰ Then Abraham reached out his hand and took the knife to kill[a] his son. ¹¹ But the angel of the LORD called to him from heaven, and said, "Abraham, Abraham!" And he said, "Here I am." ¹² He said, "Do not lay your hand on the boy or do anything to him; for now I know that you fear God, since you have not withheld your son, your only son, from me." ¹³ And Abraham looked up and saw a ram, caught in a thicket by its horns. Abraham went and took the ram and offered it up as a burnt offering instead of his son. ¹⁴ So Abraham called that place "The LORD will provide";[b] as it is said to this day, "On the mount of the LORD it shall be provided."[c]

¹⁵ The angel of the LORD called to Abraham a second time from heaven, ¹⁶ and said, "By myself I have sworn, says the LORD: Because you have done this, and have not withheld your son, your only son, ¹⁷ I will indeed bless you, and I will make your offspring as numerous as the stars of heaven and as the sand that is on the seashore. And your offspring shall possess the gate of their enemies, ¹⁸ and by your offspring shall all the nations of the earth gain blessing for themselves, because you have obeyed my voice." ¹⁹ So Abraham returned to his young men, and they arose and went together to Beer-sheba; and Abraham lived at Beer-sheba.

²⁰ Now after these things it was told Abraham, "Milcah also has borne children, to your brother Nahor: ²¹ Uz the firstborn, Buz his brother, Kemuel the father of Aram, ²² Che-

a   Or to slaughter
b   Or will see; Heb traditionally transliterated Jehovah Jireh
c   Or he shall be seen

21.8–21n.), Abraham must prepare to give up Isaac, his promised heir, as well. The story echoes the opening of the Abraham story. Just as he was once asked to go (Heb "lek leka") from his family of origin and travel to a land God would show him (12.1), so now he must go ("lek leka") and sacrifice his future family on a mountain that God will show him (v. 2). The way the command is stated (your only son . . . whom you love), which parallels the syntax of 12.1, presupposes that what is being asked of Abraham is extraordinary and extremely difficult. The narrative is not a polemic against child sacrifice: while it does not presuppose a general practice of sacrifice of the firstborn, it does suggest that such a practice could be performed under extraordinary circumstances (see 2 Kings 3.27). 3: As in 12.4–6 Abraham obeys the command immediately. 5: Abraham's promise that he and Isaac will return may suggest a faith that God will work out an alternative sacrifice (see v. 8). 9–13: The narration slows down here, showing how close Abraham came to fulfilling the command. Some later Jewish traditions understood Abraham to have actually sacrificed (an obedient) Isaac, making both men models for later generations of Jewish martyrs. A similar image stands behind the Christian understanding of Isaac as a prefiguration of Jesus. 12: See 22.1a n. 14: Like other characters in Genesis (e.g., Jacob in 28.19 and 32.2,30), Abraham names the place in response to his encounter with God (see 22.8; cf. 28.19; 32.30). The name The LORD will provide is not attested elsewhere as a place name. The mention of Moriah in v. 2 and of the mount of the LORD in v. 14 may be allusions to Jerusalem (see 1 Chr 3.1). 15–18: This second divine call stands out as an additional divine response to his obedience (cf. vv. 11–12), this time providing a reward for Abraham's passing of the "test." 18: See 12.3n.

22.20–24: The descendants of Abraham's brother Nahor. See 11.27–29; 24.15.

sed, Hazo, Pildash, Jidlaph, and Bethuel." [23] Bethuel became the father of Rebekah. These eight Milcah bore to Nahor, Abraham's brother. [24] Moreover, his concubine, whose name was Reumah, bore Tebah, Gaham, Tahash, and Maacah.

23 Sarah lived one hundred twenty-seven years; this was the length of Sarah's life. [2] And Sarah died at Kiriath-arba (that is, Hebron) in the land of Canaan; and Abraham went in to mourn for Sarah and to weep for her. [3] Abraham rose up from beside his dead, and said to the Hittites, [4] "I am a stranger and an alien residing among you; give me property among you for a burying place, so that I may bury my dead out of my sight." [5] The Hittites answered Abraham, [6] "Hear us, my lord; you are a mighty prince among us. Bury your dead in the choicest of our burial places; none of us will withhold from you any burial ground for burying your dead." [7] Abraham rose and bowed to the Hittites, the people of the land. [8] He said to them, "If you are willing that I should bury my dead out of my sight, hear me, and entreat for me Ephron son of Zohar, [9] so that he may give me the cave of Machpelah, which he owns; it is at the end of his field. For the full price let him give it to me in your presence as a possession for a burying place." [10] Now Ephron was sitting among the Hittites; and Ephron the Hittite answered Abraham in the hearing of the Hittites, of all who went in at the gate of his city, [11] "No, my lord, hear me; I give you the field, and I give you the cave that is in it; in the presence of my people I give it to you; bury your dead." [12] Then Abraham bowed down before the people of the land. [13] He said to Ephron in the hearing of the people of the land, "If you only will listen to me! I will give the price of the field; accept it from me, so that I may bury my dead there." [14] Ephron answered Abraham, [15] "My lord, listen to me; a piece of land worth four hundred shekels of silver—what is that between you and me? Bury your dead." [16] Abraham agreed with Ephron; and Abraham weighed out for Ephron the silver that he had named in the hearing of the Hittites, four hundred shekels of silver, according to the weights current among the merchants.

[17] So the field of Ephron in Machpelah, which was to the east of Mamre, the field with the cave that was in it and all the trees that were in the field, throughout its whole area, passed [18] to Abraham as a possession in the presence of the Hittites, in the presence of all who went in at the gate of his city. [19] After this, Abraham buried Sarah his wife in the cave of the field of Machpelah facing Mamre (that is, Hebron) in the land of Canaan. [20] The field and the cave that is in it passed from the Hittites into Abraham's possession as a burying place.

24 Now Abraham was old, well advanced in years; and the LORD had blessed Abraham in all things. [2] Abraham said to his servant, the oldest of his house, who had charge of all that he had, "Put your hand under my thigh [3] and I will make you swear by the LORD, the God of heaven and earth, that you will not get a wife for my son from the daughters of the Canaanites, among whom I live, [4] but will go to my country and to my kindred and get a wife for my son Isaac." [5] The servant said to him, "Perhaps the woman may not be willing to follow me to this land; must I then take your son back to the land from which you came?" [6] Abraham

23.1–20: **Abraham's purchase of a family burial place.** A late Priestly tradition. 2: *Kiriath-arba,* the older name of Hebron (Josh 14.15; 15.13; Judg 1.10). 3: The *Hittites* are considered at this point to be among the Canaanite peoples (see v. 7 and 10.15; 15.9). 4–16: The narrative stresses the legitimacy of the Israelites' claim to this burial plot. 10: Legal transactions often took place at the city gate; see 34.20; Deut 20.19; 25.7; Ruth 4.1–11; 2 Sam 15.2). 15: *Four hundred shekels,* about 10 lb (4.5 kg). 17–20: As in many ancient cultures, the Israelites believed that burial of ancestors in a plot of land gave their heirs a sacred claim to it. The Priestly notices of the Genesis story indicate that descendants of Abraham who did not inherit the promise ended up outside Canaan (e.g., Ishmael in 25.12–18 and Esau in 36.1–43; cf. 25.1–6), while Israel's early patriarchs and matriarchs were buried in the land (25.9–10; 35.27–29; 49.29–32; 50.12–13; etc.; cf. non-Priestly traditions in 35.19–20; 50.5,25).

24.1–67: **Finding a wife for Isaac** among kinfolk in Haran. 2: Putting the hand under the thigh, an old form of oath taking (47.29), reflected the view that reproductive organs were sacred. 3: The text describes a concern by Abraham about intermarriage with Canaanites that is otherwise seen primarily in late materials from Deuter-

said to him, "See to it that you do not take my son back there. [7] The LORD, the God of heaven, who took me from my father's house and from the land of my birth, and who spoke to me and swore to me, 'To your offspring I will give this land,' he will send his angel before you, and you shall take a wife for my son from there. [8] But if the woman is not willing to follow you, then you will be free from this oath of mine; only you must not take my son back there." [9] So the servant put his hand under the thigh of Abraham his master and swore to him concerning this matter.

[10] Then the servant took ten of his master's camels and departed, taking all kinds of choice gifts from his master; and he set out and went to Aram-naharaim, to the city of Nahor. [11] He made the camels kneel down outside the city by the well of water; it was toward evening, the time when women go out to draw water. [12] And he said, "O LORD, God of my master Abraham, please grant me success today and show steadfast love to my master Abraham. [13] I am standing here by the spring of water, and the daughters of the townspeople are coming out to draw water. [14] Let the girl to whom I shall say, 'Please offer your jar that I may drink,' and who shall say, 'Drink, and I will water your camels'—let her be the one whom you have appointed for your servant Isaac. By this I shall know that you have shown steadfast love to my master."

[15] Before he had finished speaking, there was Rebekah, who was born to Bethuel son of Milcah, the wife of Nahor, Abraham's brother, coming out with her water jar on her shoulder. [16] The girl was very fair to look upon, a virgin, whom no man had known. She went down to the spring, filled her jar, and came up. [17] Then the servant ran to meet her and said, "Please let me sip a little water from your jar." [18] "Drink, my lord," she said, and quickly lowered her jar upon her hand and gave him a drink. [19] When she had finished giving him a drink, she said, "I will draw for your camels also, until they have finished drinking." [20] So she quickly emptied her jar

into the trough and ran again to the well to draw, and she drew for all his camels. [21] The man gazed at her in silence to learn whether or not the LORD had made his journey successful.

[22] When the camels had finished drinking, the man took a gold nose-ring weighing a half shekel, and two bracelets for her arms weighing ten gold shekels, [23] and said, "Tell me whose daughter you are. Is there room in your father's house for us to spend the night?" [24] She said to him, "I am the daughter of Bethuel son of Milcah, whom she bore to Nahor." [25] She added, "We have plenty of straw and fodder and a place to spend the night." [26] The man bowed his head and worshiped the LORD [27] and said, "Blessed be the LORD, the God of my master Abraham, who has not forsaken his steadfast love and his faithfulness toward my master. As for me, the LORD has led me on the way to the house of my master's kin."

[28] Then the girl ran and told her mother's household about these things. [29] Rebekah had a brother whose name was Laban; and Laban ran out to the man, to the spring. [30] As soon as he had seen the nose-ring, and the bracelets on his sister's arms, and when he heard the words of his sister Rebekah, "Thus the man spoke to me," he went to the man; and there he was, standing by the camels at the spring. [31] He said, "Come in, O blessed of the LORD. Why do you stand outside when I have prepared the house and a place for the camels?" [32] So the man came into the house; and Laban unloaded the camels, and gave him straw and fodder for the camels, and water to wash his feet and the feet of the men who were with him. [33] Then food was set before him to eat; but he said, "I will not eat until I have told my errand." He said, "Speak on."

[34] So he said, "I am Abraham's servant. [35] The LORD has greatly blessed my master, and he has become wealthy; he has given him flocks and herds, silver and gold, male and female slaves, camels and donkeys. [36] And Sarah my master's wife bore a son to my

onomy (e.g., Deut 7.3–4) and texts influenced by Deuteronomy. **10:** *Aram-naharaim*, the upper Euphrates region of northern Syria, in which Haran, Abraham's original home, was located (see 12.4). **12:** *Steadfast love*, NRSV's translation of Heb "ḥesed" that signifies the loyalty arising from a relationship (e.g., friendship; see 1 Sam 20.8). Applied to God, it means benevolent action, loyalty manifest in deeds. **15:** See 22.20–23. **22:** A *shekel* weighed

master when she was old; and he has given him all that he has. ³⁷ My master made me swear, saying, 'You shall not take a wife for my son from the daughters of the Canaanites, in whose land I live; ³⁸ but you shall go to my father's house, to my kindred, and get a wife for my son.' ³⁹ I said to my master, 'Perhaps the woman will not follow me.' ⁴⁰ But he said to me, 'The LORD, before whom I walk, will send his angel with you and make your way successful. You shall get a wife for my son from my kindred, from my father's house. ⁴¹ Then you will be free from my oath, when you come to my kindred; even if they will not give her to you, you will be free from my oath.'

⁴² "I came today to the spring, and said, 'O LORD, the God of my master Abraham, if now you will only make successful the way I am going! ⁴³ I am standing here by the spring of water; let the young woman who comes out to draw, to whom I shall say, "Please give me a little water from your jar to drink," ⁴⁴ and who will say to me, "Drink, and I will draw for your camels also"—let her be the woman whom the LORD has appointed for my master's son.'

⁴⁵ "Before I had finished speaking in my heart, there was Rebekah coming out with her water jar on her shoulder; and she went down to the spring, and drew. I said to her, 'Please let me drink.' ⁴⁶ She quickly let down her jar from her shoulder, and said, 'Drink, and I will also water your camels.' So I drank, and she also watered the camels. ⁴⁷ Then I asked her, 'Whose daughter are you?' She said, 'The daughter of Bethuel, Nahor's son, whom Milcah bore to him.' So I put the ring on her nose, and the bracelets on her arms. ⁴⁸ Then I bowed my head and worshiped the LORD, and blessed the LORD, the God of my master Abraham, who had led me by the right way to obtain the daughter of my master's kinsman for his son. ⁴⁹ Now then, if you will deal loyally and truly with my master, tell me; and if not, tell me, so that I may turn either to the right hand or to the left."

⁵⁰ Then Laban and Bethuel answered, "The thing comes from the LORD; we cannot speak to you anything bad or good. ⁵¹ Look, Rebekah is before you, take her and go, and let her be the wife of your master's son, as the LORD has spoken."

⁵² When Abraham's servant heard their words, he bowed himself to the ground before the LORD. ⁵³ And the servant brought out jewelry of silver and of gold, and garments, and gave them to Rebekah; he also gave to her brother and to her mother costly ornaments. ⁵⁴ Then he and the men who were with him ate and drank, and they spent the night there. When they rose in the morning, he said, "Send me back to my master." ⁵⁵ Her brother and her mother said, "Let the girl remain with us a while, at least ten days; after that she may go." ⁵⁶ But he said to them, "Do not delay me, since the LORD has made my journey successful; let me go that I may go to my master." ⁵⁷ They said, "We will call the girl, and ask her." ⁵⁸ And they called Rebekah, and said to her, "Will you go with this man?" She said, "I will." ⁵⁹ So they sent away their sister Rebekah and her nurse along with Abraham's servant and his men. ⁶⁰ And they blessed Rebekah and said to her,

"May you, our sister, become
    thousands of myriads;
may your offspring gain possession
    of the gates of their foes."

⁶¹ Then Rebekah and her maids rose up, mounted the camels, and followed the man; thus the servant took Rebekah, and went his way.

⁶² Now Isaac had come from[a] Beer-lahai-roi, and was settled in the Negeb. ⁶³ Isaac went out in the evening to walk[b] in the field; and looking up, he saw camels coming. ⁶⁴ And Rebekah looked up, and when she saw Isaac, she slipped quickly from the camel, ⁶⁵ and said to the servant, "Who is the man over there, walking in the field to meet us?" The servant said, "It is my master." So she took her veil and covered herself. ⁶⁶ And the servant told Isaac all the things that he had done. ⁶⁷ Then Isaac brought her into his mother Sarah's tent. He took Rebekah, and she became his wife; and he loved her. So Isaac was comforted after his mother's death.

25 Abraham took another wife, whose name was Keturah. ² She bore him Zimran, Jokshan, Medan, Midian, Ishbak, and

---

a Syr Tg: Heb *from coming to*
b Meaning of Heb word is uncertain

Shuah. [3] Jokshan was the father of Sheba and Dedan. The sons of Dedan were Asshurim, Letushim, and Leummim. [4] The sons of Midian were Ephah, Epher, Hanoch, Abida, and Eldaah. All these were the children of Keturah. [5] Abraham gave all he had to Isaac. [6] But to the sons of his concubines Abraham gave gifts, while he was still living, and he sent them away from his son Isaac, eastward to the east country.

[7] This is the length of Abraham's life, one hundred seventy-five years. [8] Abraham breathed his last and died in a good old age, an old man and full of years, and was gathered to his people. [9] His sons Isaac and Ishmael buried him in the cave of Machpelah, in the field of Ephron son of Zohar the Hittite, east of Mamre, [10] the field that Abraham purchased from the Hittites.

There Abraham was buried, with his wife Sarah. [11] After the death of Abraham God blessed his son Isaac. And Isaac settled at Beer-lahai-roi.

[12] These are the descendants of Ishmael, Abraham's son, whom Hagar the Egyptian, Sarah's slave-girl, bore to Abraham. [13] These are the names of the sons of Ishmael, named in the order of their birth: Nebaioth, the firstborn of Ishmael; and Kedar, Adbeel, Mibsam, [14] Mishma, Dumah, Massa, [15] Hadad, Tema, Jetur, Naphish, and Kedemah. [16] These are the sons of Ishmael and these are their names, by their villages and by their encampments, twelve princes according to their tribes. [17] (This is the length of the life of Ishmael, one hundred thirty-seven years; he breathed his last and died, and was gathered to his people.) [18] They settled from Havilah to

about .4 oz (11.5 gr). **62**: *Beer-lahai-roi*, see 16.14; 25.11.

25.1–11: The death of Abraham. 1–6: The ancestry of Arabian tribes, including Midian (Ex 2.15b–22; 18.1–27), is traced to Abraham through another wife, Keturah. **7–11**: A conclusion to the Abraham story taken from the Priestly source. On the cave of Machpelah, see ch 23. **11**: *Beer-lahai-roi*, see 16.14; 24.62.

25.12–18: Overview of the descendants of Ishmael (cf. 36.1–43). Before the narrative discusses the descendants of Isaac (25.19–35.29), it gives an overview of the descendants of Ishmael, the firstborn son of Abraham. For the genealogy of Abraham, see chart on p. 52. **16**: Like Israel, the Ishmaelites are said to have twelve tribes. **18**: The Ishmaelites are placed in the desert on either side of the Red Sea. See map on p. 23.

25.19–35.29: The story of Jacob and his family. The bulk of this section of Genesis goes back to early traditions about Jacob/Israel, the father of the Israelite tribes. Though many originated as ancient Israelite oral traditions, this written version of the Jacob story shows multiple connections to places that were important in the Northern Kingdom of Israel (see 28.10–11n., 20–22n., 31.13n., 32.1–2n., 32.30–31n., and 33.18n.), and it thus likely originated there. This story has been enriched through additions that balance the early northern focus on Jacob with an emphasis on Judah, King David's ancestor (see 30.21n.; 34.1–31n. and 49.1–28n.). Later, still other texts were added, such as the interlude about Jacob's father, Isaac (26.1–33), the gift of the Abrahamic promise to Jacob at Bethel (28.13-16), and fragments of Priestly material (25.19–20; 26.34–35; 27.46–28.9; 31.17–18; 35.9–15,22b–29).

CHIASM IN THE JACOB STORY

As in the Abraham story [see p. 38], there may be a chiastic pattern in the Jacob story, where themes introduced in its first half are resumed in reverse order in the second. This kind of pattern places emphasis on its center (in **boldface**), in this case the fertility of Jacob himself and of his flocks:

  A. Encounter between Jacob/Esau (25.21–34; 27)

      B. Encounter with God and departure from home (28)

         C. Acquisition of wives, Leah and Rachel (29.1–30)

            D. Fertility: the birth of Jacob's children (29.31–30.24)

            D.' Fertility: the growth of Jacob's flocks (30.25–43)

         C.' Jacob's removal of his wives from their father's household (31.1–32.1)

      B.' Encounter with God on return home (32.22–32)

  A.' Reunion encounter between Jacob and Esau (33.1–33.17)

Shur, which is opposite Egypt in the direction of Assyria; he settled down[a] alongside of[b] all his people.

[19] These are the descendants of Isaac, Abraham's son: Abraham was the father of Isaac, [20] and Isaac was forty years old when he married Rebekah, daughter of Bethuel the Aramean of Paddan-aram, sister of Laban the Aramean. [21] Isaac prayed to the LORD for his wife, because she was barren; and the LORD granted his prayer, and his wife Rebekah conceived. [22] The children struggled together within her; and she said, "If it is to be this way, why do I live?"[c] So she went to inquire of the LORD. [23] And the LORD said to her,

"Two nations are in your womb,
    and two peoples born of you shall be
        divided;
the one shall be stronger than the other,
    the elder shall serve the younger."

[24] When her time to give birth was at hand, there were twins in her womb. [25] The first came out red, all his body like a hairy mantle; so they named him Esau. [26] Afterward his brother came out, with his hand gripping Esau's heel; so he was named Jacob.[d] Isaac was sixty years old when she bore them.

[27] When the boys grew up, Esau was a skillful hunter, a man of the field, while Jacob was a quiet man, living in tents. [28] Isaac loved Esau, because he was fond of game; but Rebekah loved Jacob.

[29] Once when Jacob was cooking a stew, Esau came in from the field, and he was famished. [30] Esau said to Jacob, "Let me eat some of that red stuff, for I am famished!" (Therefore he was called Edom.[e]) [31] Jacob said, "First sell me your birthright." [32] Esau said, "I am about to die; of what use is a birthright to me?" [33] Jacob said, "Swear to me first."[f] So he swore to him, and sold his birthright to Jacob. [34] Then Jacob gave Esau bread and lentil stew, and he ate and drank, and rose and went his way. Thus Esau despised his birthright.

26 Now there was a famine in the land, besides the former famine that had occurred in the days of Abraham. And Isaac went to Gerar, to King Abimelech of the Philistines. [2] The LORD appeared to Isaac[g] and said, "Do not go down to Egypt; settle in the land that I shall show you. [3] Reside in this land as an alien, and I will be with you, and will bless you; for to you and to your descendants I will give all these lands, and I will fulfill the oath that I swore to your father Abraham. [4] I will make your offspring as numerous as the

a   Heb *he fell*
b   Or *down in opposition to*
c   Syr: Meaning of Heb uncertain
d   That is *He takes by the heel* or *He supplants*
e   That is *Red*
f   Heb *today*
g   Heb *him*

25.19–28: Introduction of the descendants of Isaac. 19–20: Introductory Priestly material. For the genealogy of Isaac, see chart on p. 52. **22–23:** The narrative presupposes an ancient practice of seeking a divine oracle at a local sanctuary. **25:** The Hebrew word for *red* ("'admoni") is a play on the word "Edom" ("'edom"; v. 30); *hairy* ("se'ar") is a play on Seir, the region of the Edomites (32.3). **26:** *Jacob,* which probably means "may (God) protect," is interpreted here by a play on the Hebrew word for "heel," i.e., "he takes by the heel" or "he supplants"; see Hos 12.3. **27–28:** As in the Cain and Abel story, this narrative plays on the tension between the hunter and the shepherd (4.2), as well as between the older and the younger brother.

25.29–34: Jacob buys Esau's birthright. 30: See 25.25n. **31–34:** The *birthright* refers to the extra rights that normally go to the eldest son: leadership of the family and a double share of the inheritance (Deut 21.15–17). This caricature of Esau as a dull person, outwitted on an empty stomach, is intended to explain Israel's domination of Edom (2 Sam 8.9–14; 1 Kings 11.14–22; 1 Kings 3.9–12; 8.20–22).

26.1–33: Interlude on Isaac. Whereas the surrounding sections focus primarily on Isaac's descendants, this chapter focuses on Isaac apart from his children. Although relatively little is told about Isaac, it is significant that each element makes him parallel to his father Abraham: the initial note linking his trip to Gerar with Abraham's initial journey to Egypt (v. 1; cf. 12.10), the travel command and promise (vv. 2–5; see 12.1–3n.; 22.18n.), the story of endangerment of the matriarch (vv. 6–11; cf. 12.10–13.1 and 20.1–18), the manifestation of blessing on Isaac (vv. 12–14; cf. 12.16; 20.14), the recognition of that blessing by Abimelech (v. 28; cf. 21.22), and the well stories (vv. 17–33; see 21.22–34n.). The narratives of Abraham and Isaac have clearly influenced one another. By the end of the chapter it is clear that Isaac has successfully inherited Abraham's blessing and is thus prepared

stars of heaven, and will give to your offspring all these lands; and all the nations of the earth shall gain blessing for themselves through your offspring, [5] because Abraham obeyed my voice and kept my charge, my commandments, my statutes, and my laws."

[6] So Isaac settled in Gerar. [7] When the men of the place asked him about his wife, he said, "She is my sister"; for he was afraid to say, "My wife," thinking, "or else the men of the place might kill me for the sake of Rebekah, because she is attractive in appearance." [8] When Isaac had been there a long time, King Abimelech of the Philistines looked out of a window and saw him fondling his wife Rebekah. [9] So Abimelech called for Isaac, and said, "So she is your wife! Why then did you say, 'She is my sister'?" Isaac said to him, "Because I thought I might die because of her." [10] Abimelech said, "What is this you have done to us? One of the people might easily have lain with your wife, and you would have brought guilt upon us." [11] So Abimelech warned all the people, saying, "Whoever touches this man or his wife shall be put to death."

[12] Isaac sowed seed in that land, and in the same year reaped a hundredfold. The LORD blessed him, [13] and the man became rich; he prospered more and more until he became very wealthy. [14] He had possessions of flocks and herds, and a great household, so that the Philistines envied him. [15] (Now the Philistines had stopped up and filled with earth all the wells that his father's servants had dug in the days of his father Abraham.) [16] And Abimelech said to Isaac, "Go away from us; you have become too powerful for us."

[17] So Isaac departed from there and camped in the valley of Gerar and settled there. [18] Isaac dug again the wells of water that had been dug in the days of his father Abraham; for the Philistines had stopped them up after the death of Abraham; and he gave them the names that his father had given them. [19] But when Isaac's servants dug in the valley and found there a well of spring water, [20] the herders of Gerar quarreled with Isaac's herders, saying, "The water is ours." So he called the well Esek,[a] because they contended with him. [21] Then they dug another well, and they quarreled over that one also; so he called it Sitnah.[b] [22] He moved from there and dug another well, and they did not quarrel over it; so he called it Rehoboth,[c] saying, "Now the LORD has made room for us, and we shall be fruitful in the land."

[23] From there he went up to Beer-sheba. [24] And that very night the LORD appeared to him and said, "I am the God of your father Abraham; do not be afraid, for I am with you and will bless you and make your offspring numerous for my servant Abraham's sake." [25] So he built an altar there, called on the name of the LORD, and pitched his tent there. And there Isaac's servants dug a well.

[26] Then Abimelech went to him from Gerar, with Ahuzzath his adviser and Phicol the commander of his army. [27] Isaac said to them, "Why have you come to me, seeing that you hate me and have sent me away from you?" [28] They said, "We see plainly that the LORD has been with you; so we say, let there be an oath between you and us, and let us make a covenant with you [29] so that you will do us no harm, just as we have not touched you and have done to you nothing but good and have sent you away in peace. You are now the blessed of the LORD." [30] So he made them a feast, and they ate and drank. [31] In the morning they rose early and exchanged oaths; and Isaac set them on their way, and they departed from him in peace. [32] That same day Isaac's servants came and told him about the well that they had dug, and said to him, "We have found water!" [33] He called it Shibah;[d] therefore the name of the city is Beer-sheba[e] to this day.

[34] When Esau was forty years old, he married Judith daughter of Beeri the Hittite, and

---

[a] That is Contention

[b] That is Enmity

[c] That is Broad places or Room

[d] A word resembling the word for oath

[e] That is Well of the oath or Well of seven

---

to pass it on to one of his sons (see ch 27). **8:** *Fondling*, Heb "metsaḥeq," another reference to Isaac's name; see 18.12n. **33:** Another explanation of the name "Beer-sheba"; see 21.22–34n.

26.34–28.4: The transfer of blessing to Jacob and not Esau. 26.34–35 (cf. 28.8–9 and 36.2–3): This Priestly

Basemath daughter of Elon the Hittite; [35] and they made life bitter for Isaac and Rebekah.

27 When Isaac was old and his eyes were dim so that he could not see, he called his elder son Esau and said to him, "My son"; and he answered, "Here I am." [2] He said, "See, I am old; I do not know the day of my death. [3] Now then, take your weapons, your quiver and your bow, and go out to the field, and hunt game for me. [4] Then prepare for me savory food, such as I like, and bring it to me to eat, so that I may bless you before I die."

[5] Now Rebekah was listening when Isaac spoke to his son Esau. So when Esau went to the field to hunt for game and bring it, [6] Rebekah said to her son Jacob, "I heard your father say to your brother Esau, [7] 'Bring me game, and prepare for me savory food to eat, that I may bless you before the LORD before I die.' [8] Now therefore, my son, obey my word as I command you. [9] Go to the flock, and get me two choice kids, so that I may prepare from them savory food for your father, such as he likes; [10] and you shall take it to your father to eat, so that he may bless you before he dies." [11] But Jacob said to his mother Rebekah, "Look, my brother Esau is a hairy man, and I am a man of smooth skin. [12] Perhaps my father will feel me, and I shall seem to be mocking him, and bring a curse on myself and not a blessing." [13] His mother said to him, "Let your curse be on me, my son; only obey my word, and go, get them for me." [14] So he went and got them and brought them to his mother; and his mother prepared savory food, such as his father loved. [15] Then Rebekah took the best garments of her elder son Esau, which were with her in the house, and put them on her younger son Jacob; [16] and she put the skins of the kids on his hands and on the smooth part of his neck. [17] Then she handed the savory food, and the bread that she had prepared, to her son Jacob.

[18] So he went in to his father, and said, "My father"; and he said, "Here I am; who are you, my son?" [19] Jacob said to his father, "I am Esau your firstborn. I have done as you told me; now sit up and eat of my game, so that you may bless me." [20] But Isaac said to his son, "How is it that you have found it so quickly, my son?" He answered, "Because the LORD your God granted me success." [21] Then Isaac said to Jacob, "Come near, that I may feel you, my son, to know whether you are really my son Esau or not." [22] So Jacob went up to his father Isaac, who felt him and said, "The voice is Jacob's voice, but the hands are the hands of Esau." [23] He did not recognize him, because his hands were hairy like his brother Esau's hands; so he blessed him. [24] He said, "Are you really my son Esau?" He answered, "I am." [25] Then he said, "Bring it to me, that I may eat of my son's game and bless you." So he brought it to him, and he ate; and he brought him wine, and he drank. [26] Then his father Isaac said to him, "Come near and kiss me, my son." [27] So he came near and kissed him; and he smelled the smell of his garments, and blessed him, and said,

"Ah, the smell of my son
  is like the smell of a field that the LORD
    has blessed.
[28] May God give you of the dew of heaven,
  and of the fatness of the earth,
  and plenty of grain and wine.
[29] Let peoples serve you,
  and nations bow down to you.
Be lord over your brothers,
  and may your mother's sons bow down
    to you.
Cursed be everyone who curses you,
  and blessed be everyone who blesses
    you!"

[30] As soon as Isaac had finished blessing Jacob, when Jacob had scarcely gone out from the presence of his father Isaac, his brother

note on Esau's difficult marriages was originally connected with 27.46–28.9 (P). Now, however, it helps legitimate the following story about how he was tricked out of his father's blessing. **27.1–45:** This non-Priestly story of Rebekah and Jacob's cunning resembles "trickster" traditions in other cultures, where a culture hero flourishes through underhanded tactics (cf. 29.23–25; 31.19–35; 34.1–31; 38.1–30). Women had little power and often had to use unconventional means to accomplish their goals. **4:** Deathbed blessings (and curses) were important in the life and literature of ancient peoples (e.g., 48.8–20; 49.1–28). It was believed that such blessings irrevocably released a tangible power that determined the character and destiny of the recipient. Ch 27 itself focuses exclusively on Isaac's blessing, but the preceding chapter (ch 26) makes clear that this is Isaac's transfer of

Esau came in from his hunting. [31] He also prepared savory food, and brought it to his father. And he said to his father, "Let my father sit up and eat of his son's game, so that you may bless me." [32] His father Isaac said to him, "Who are you?" He answered, "I am your firstborn son, Esau." [33] Then Isaac trembled violently, and said, "Who was it then that hunted game and brought it to me, and I ate it all[a] before you came, and I have blessed him?—yes, and blessed he shall be!" [34] When Esau heard his father's words, he cried out with an exceedingly great and bitter cry, and said to his father, "Bless me, me also, father!" [35] But he said, "Your brother came deceitfully, and he has taken away your blessing." [36] Esau said, "Is he not rightly named Jacob?[b] For he has supplanted me these two times. He took away my birthright; and look, now he has taken away my blessing." Then he said, "Have you not reserved a blessing for me?" [37] Isaac answered Esau, "I have already made him your lord, and I have given him all his brothers as servants, and with grain and wine I have sustained him. What then can I do for you, my son?" [38] Esau said to his father, "Have you only one blessing, father? Bless me, me also, father!" And Esau lifted up his voice and wept.

[39] Then his father Isaac answered him:
"See, away from[c] the fatness of the earth
  shall your home be,
  and away from[d] the dew of heaven on
    high.
[40] By your sword you shall live,
  and you shall serve your brother;
but when you break loose,[e]
  you shall break his yoke from your
    neck."
[41] Now Esau hated Jacob because of the blessing with which his father had blessed him, and Esau said to himself, "The days of mourning for my father are approaching; then I will kill my brother Jacob." [42] But the words of her elder son Esau were told to Rebekah; so she sent and called her younger son Jacob and said to him, "Your brother Esau is consoling himself by planning to kill you. [43] Now therefore, my son, obey my voice; flee at once to my brother Laban in Haran, [44] and stay with him a while, until your brother's fury turns away— [45] until your brother's anger against you turns away, and he forgets what you have done to him; then I will send, and bring you back from there. Why should I lose both of you in one day?"

[46] Then Rebekah said to Isaac, "I am weary of my life because of the Hittite women. If Jacob marries one of the Hittite women such as these, one of the women of the land, what good will my life be to me?"

28 Then Isaac called Jacob and blessed him, and charged him, "You shall not marry one of the Canaanite women. [2] Go at once to Paddan-aram to the house of Bethuel, your mother's father; and take as wife from there one of the daughters of Laban, your mother's brother. [3] May God Almighty[f] bless you and make you fruitful and numerous, that you may become a company of peoples. [4] May he give to you the blessing of Abraham, to you and to your offspring with you, so that you may take possession of the land where you now live as an alien—land that God gave to Abraham." [5] Thus Isaac sent Jacob away;

---

a   Cn: Heb *of all*
b   That is *He supplants* or *He takes by the heel*
c   Or *See, of*
d   Or *and of*
e   Meaning of Heb uncertain
f   Traditional rendering of Heb *El Shaddai*

---

a divine blessing first given to Abraham (12.1–3; etc.). **11:** See 25.25n. **34–35:** The blessing was believed to release a power that could not be retracted (see v. 4n.). **36:** See 25.26n.; 29.29–34. There is a wordplay in the Heb words for *my birthright* ("bekorati") and *my blessing* ("birkati"). **39:** An inversion of the same words in v. 28. **40:** See 25.31–34n. Edom repeatedly revolted from subjection by Judah (1 Kings 11.14–22; 2 Kings 8.20–22). **43:** See 24.4,29. *Haran* was the home of Abraham's brother Nahor, whose son was Laban. Like Isaac, Jacob will marry within the extended family; see 24.4,10n.,29; 29. **46:** See 26.34–35n. **27.46–28.2:** On intermarriage, see 24.3n. **28.1–4:** A Priestly parallel to the preceding story (27.27–29) where Isaac was not tricked into blessing Jacob, but intended from the outset to bless him in the process of sending him away to find a proper wife (see 26.34–35n.). Compare with P in 17.1–8; 35.11–12; 48.3–4. **3:** *God Almighty*, see 17.1n.

28.5–22: The split between Jacob and Esau occurs twice here, the Priestly version in 28.5–9 and the non-

and he went to Paddan-aram, to Laban son of Bethuel the Aramean, the brother of Rebekah, Jacob's and Esau's mother.

⁶ Now Esau saw that Isaac had blessed Jacob and sent him away to Paddan-aram to take a wife from there, and that as he blessed him he charged him, "You shall not marry one of the Canaanite women," ⁷ and that Jacob had obeyed his father and his mother and gone to Paddan-aram. ⁸ So when Esau saw that the Canaanite women did not please his father Isaac, ⁹ Esau went to Ishmael and took Mahalath daughter of Abraham's son Ishmael, and sister of Nebaioth, to be his wife in addition to the wives he had.

¹⁰ Jacob left Beer-sheba and went toward Haran. ¹¹ He came to a certain place and stayed there for the night, because the sun had set. Taking one of the stones of the place, he put it under his head and lay down in that place. ¹² And he dreamed that there was a ladder[a] set up on the earth, the top of it reaching to heaven; and the angels of God were ascending and descending on it. ¹³ And the LORD stood beside him[b] and said, "I am the LORD, the God of Abraham your father and the God of Isaac; the land on which you lie I will give to you and to your offspring; ¹⁴ and your offspring shall be like the dust of the earth, and you shall spread abroad to the west and to the east and to the north and to the south; and

all the families of the earth shall be blessed[c] in you and in your offspring. ¹⁵ Know that I am with you and will keep you wherever you go, and will bring you back to this land; for I will not leave you until I have done what I have promised you." ¹⁶ Then Jacob woke from his sleep and said, "Surely the LORD is in this place—and I did not know it!" ¹⁷ And he was afraid, and said, "How awesome is this place! This is none other than the house of God, and this is the gate of heaven."

¹⁸ So Jacob rose early in the morning, and he took the stone that he had put under his head and set it up for a pillar and poured oil on the top of it. ¹⁹ He called that place Bethel;[d] but the name of the city was Luz at the first. ²⁰ Then Jacob made a vow, saying, "If God will be with me, and will keep me in this way that I go, and will give me bread to eat and clothing to wear, ²¹ so that I come again to my father's house in peace, then the LORD shall be my God, ²² and this stone, which I have set up for a pillar, shall be God's house; and of all that you give me I will surely give one-tenth to you."

29

Then Jacob went on his journey, and came to the land of the people of the east. ² As he looked, he saw a well in the field

ᵃ Or *stairway* or *ramp*

ᵇ Or *stood above it*

ᶜ Or *shall bless themselves*

ᵈ That is *House of God*

Priestly account in 28.10–22. **8–9:** See 26.34–35 and compare 36.2–3. **10–11:** Bethel (see 12.6–8n.; map on p. 27) was one of the two major royal sanctuaries of the Northern Kingdom (1 Kings 12.26–13.10; Am 7.10–13). Here it is depicted as an unsettled place. **12:** The earliest version of this oracle described divine messengers (NRSV *angels*) ascending and descending a stairway (a better translation than NRSV's *ladder*) to heaven. This is reflected in v. 17. **13–15:** God's appearance here is awkwardly linked to the preceding stairway vision. Therefore, many scholars see another authorial hand here, adding the Abrahamic promise to an early Bethel narrative that lacked it. **13–14:** The promise to Jacob here after his split from Esau is similar to the promise to Abraham in 13.14–17 just after his split from Lot. On the formulation of these promises, see 12.1–3n. **15:** This portion of the divine promise relates specifically to Jacob's journey and anticipates both his vow (vv. 20–22) and later references to this event (35.3; cf. 31.13). It may be the earliest layer of the promise speech. **16–17:** Some scholars have seen a doubled response here by Jacob, a response to God's appearance and speech in v. 16 and a (possibly earlier) response to the vision of the stairway in v. 17 (see v. 12n.). Verse 17 explains the name "Bethel" ("house of El") as *house of God. Gate of heaven* suggests the ancient view that a sanctuary was a place where the god came to earth, like "Babel" ("gate of god," 11.1–9). **18:** Ancient Israelite local sanctuaries featured sacred pillars, perhaps signifying male powers of fertility (see v. 22; 31.13,45–54; 35.14,20). For feminine tree imagery, see 2.8–9n. **19:** *Bethel,* see vv. 16–17n. **20–22:** This text looks toward both Jacob's immediate trip to Haran and the longer range future of the sanctuary at Bethel (see 28.10–11n.). **22:** *One-tenth,* see 14.20n.

29.1–30: Jacob's marriages to Laban's daughters. **2–12:** Wells often serve as meeting places for men and women in the cultures of the Near East. The Bible describes several such well scenes (e.g., 24.10–27; Ex 2.15–22).

and three flocks of sheep lying there beside it; for out of that well the flocks were watered. The stone on the well's mouth was large, ³ and when all the flocks were gathered there, the shepherds would roll the stone from the mouth of the well, and water the sheep, and put the stone back in its place on the mouth of the well.

⁴ Jacob said to them, "My brothers, where do you come from?" They said, "We are from Haran." ⁵ He said to them, "Do you know Laban son of Nahor?" They said, "We do." ⁶ He said to them, "Is it well with him?" "Yes," they replied, "and here is his daughter Rachel, coming with the sheep." ⁷ He said, "Look, it is still broad daylight; it is not time for the animals to be gathered together. Water the sheep, and go, pasture them." ⁸ But they said, "We cannot until all the flocks are gathered together, and the stone is rolled from the mouth of the well; then we water the sheep."

⁹ While he was still speaking with them, Rachel came with her father's sheep; for she kept them. ¹⁰ Now when Jacob saw Rachel, the daughter of his mother's brother Laban, and the sheep of his mother's brother Laban, Jacob went up and rolled the stone from the well's mouth, and watered the flock of his mother's brother Laban. ¹¹ Then Jacob kissed Rachel, and wept aloud. ¹² And Jacob told Rachel that he was her father's kinsman, and that he was Rebekah's son; and she ran and told her father.

¹³ When Laban heard the news about his sister's son Jacob, he ran to meet him; he embraced him and kissed him, and brought him to his house. Jacobᵃ told Laban all these things, ¹⁴ and Laban said to him, "Surely you are my bone and my flesh!" And he stayed with him a month.

¹⁵ Then Laban said to Jacob, "Because you are my kinsman, should you therefore serve me for nothing? Tell me, what shall your wages be?" ¹⁶ Now Laban had two daughters;

the name of the elder was Leah, and the name of the younger was Rachel. ¹⁷ Leah's eyes were lovely,ᵇ and Rachel was graceful and beautiful. ¹⁸ Jacob loved Rachel; so he said, "I will serve you seven years for your younger daughter Rachel." ¹⁹ Laban said, "It is better that I give her to you than that I should give her to any other man; stay with me." ²⁰ So Jacob served seven years for Rachel, and they seemed to him but a few days because of the love he had for her.

²¹ Then Jacob said to Laban, "Give me my wife that I may go in to her, for my time is completed." ²² So Laban gathered together all the people of the place, and made a feast. ²³ But in the evening he took his daughter Leah and brought her to Jacob; and he went in to her. ²⁴ (Laban gave his maid Zilpah to his daughter Leah to be her maid.) ²⁵ When morning came, it was Leah! And Jacob said to Laban, "What is this you have done to me? Did I not serve with you for Rachel? Why then have you deceived me?" ²⁶ Laban said, "This is not done in our country—giving the younger before the firstborn. ²⁷ Complete the week of this one, and we will give you the other also in return for serving me another seven years." ²⁸ Jacob did so, and completed her week; then Laban gave him his daughter Rachel as a wife. ²⁹ (Laban gave his maid Bilhah to his daughter Rachel to be her maid.) ³⁰ So Jacob went in to Rachel also, and he loved Rachel more than Leah. He served Labanᶜ for another seven years.

³¹ When the LORD saw that Leah was unloved, he opened her womb; but Rachel was barren. ³² Leah conceived and bore a son, and she named him Reuben;ᵈ for she said, "Because the LORD has looked on my affliction; surely

ᵃ Heb *He*
ᵇ Meaning of Heb uncertain
ᶜ Heb *him*
ᵈ That is *See, a son*

4-5: See 24.10n.; 26.43. 10: Jacob, the folk hero, has superhuman strength (see v. 3). 18: Jacob asks for Rachel as a reward for service (cf. Josh 15.16–17; 1 Sam 17.25; 18.17) instead of paying the usual marriage price (34.12; Ex 22.16–17; Deut 22.29). 23–25: Here Jacob the trickster (see 27.1–45n.) is tricked; this motif will continue throughout the Jacob story. The exchange could be made because the bride was brought veiled to the bridegroom (24.65). 27: *The week* refers to the week of marriage festivity (Judg 14.12).

29.31–30.24: The birth of eleven of Jacob's sons and Dinah (for Benjamin's birth, see 35.16–18). This birth of children and the later birth of flocks (30.25–43) stand at the heart of the Jacob story. The pathos of the conflict

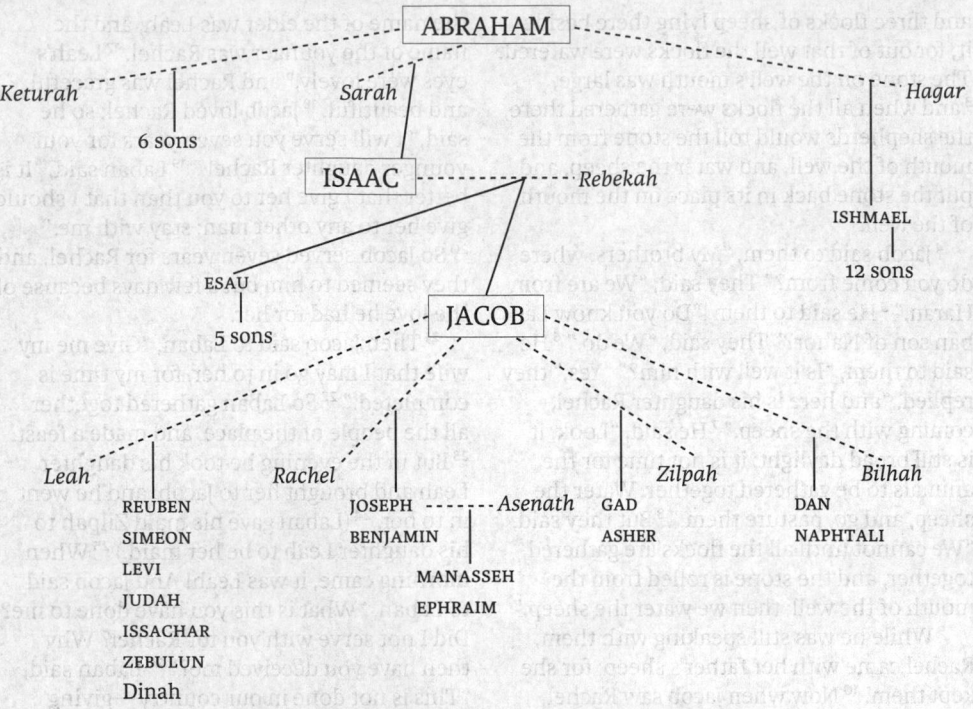

Chs 12–50: The genealogy of Abraham, Isaac, and Jacob. Dashed lines show wives or concubines; solid lines show descendants.

now my husband will love me." [33] She conceived again and bore a son, and said, "Because the LORD has heard[a] that I am hated, he has given me this son also"; and she named him Simeon. [34] Again she conceived and bore a son, and said, "Now this time my husband will be joined[b] to me, because I have borne him three sons"; therefore he was named Levi. [35] She conceived again and bore a son, and said, "This time I will praise[c] the LORD"; therefore she named him Judah; then she ceased bearing.

30 When Rachel saw that she bore Jacob no children, she envied her sister; and she said to Jacob, "Give me children, or I shall die!" [2] Jacob became very angry with Rachel and said, "Am I in the place of God, who has withheld from you the fruit of the womb?" [3] Then she said, "Here is my maid Bilhah; go in to her, that she may bear upon my knees and that I too may have children through her." [4] So she gave him her maid Bilhah as a wife; and

Jacob went in to her. [5] And Bilhah conceived and bore Jacob a son. [6] Then Rachel said, "God has judged me, and has also heard my voice and given me a son"; therefore she named him Dan.[d] [7] Rachel's maid Bilhah conceived again and bore Jacob a second son. [8] Then Rachel said, "With mighty wrestlings I have wrestled[e] with my sister, and have prevailed"; so she named him Naphtali.

[9] When Leah saw that she had ceased bearing children, she took her maid Zilpah and gave her to Jacob as a wife. [10] Then Leah's maid Zilpah bore Jacob a son. [11] And Leah said, "Good fortune!" so she named him Gad.[f]

a Heb *shama*
b Heb *lawah*
c Heb *hodah*
d That is *He judged*
e Heb *niphtal*
f That is *Fortune*

between women is expressed through folk-explanations of the names (see NRSV text notes). 30.3,9: Like Sarah, Rachel and Leah give their servants to Jacob as surrogate wives; see 16.2n. 14: *Mandrakes*, roots of a potato-like

[12] Leah's maid Zilpah bore Jacob a second son. [13] And Leah said, "Happy am I! For the women will call me happy"; so she named him Asher.[a]

[14] In the days of wheat harvest Reuben went and found mandrakes in the field, and brought them to his mother Leah. Then Rachel said to Leah, "Please give me some of your son's mandrakes." [15] But she said to her, "Is it a small matter that you have taken away my husband? Would you take away my son's mandrakes also?" Rachel said, "Then he may lie with you tonight for your son's mandrakes." [16] When Jacob came from the field in the evening, Leah went out to meet him, and said, "You must come in to me; for I have hired you with my son's mandrakes." So he lay with her that night. [17] And God heeded Leah, and she conceived and bore Jacob a fifth son. [18] Leah said, "God has given me my hire[b] because I gave my maid to my husband"; so she named him Issachar. [19] And Leah conceived again, and she bore Jacob a sixth son. [20] Then Leah said, "God has endowed me with a good dowry; now my husband will honor[c] me, because I have borne him six sons"; so she named him Zebulun. [21] Afterwards she bore a daughter, and named her Dinah.

[22] Then God remembered Rachel, and God heeded her and opened her womb. [23] She conceived and bore a son, and said, "God has taken away my reproach"; [24] and she named him Joseph,[d] saying, "May the LORD add to me another son!"

[25] When Rachel had borne Joseph, Jacob said to Laban, "Send me away, that I may go to my own home and country. [26] Give me my wives and my children for whom I have served you, and let me go; for you know very well the service I have given you." [27] But Laban said to him, "If you will allow me to say so, I have learned by divination that the LORD has blessed me because of you; [28] name your wages, and I will give it." [29] Jacob said to him, "You yourself know how I have served

you, and how your cattle have fared with me. [30] For you had little before I came, and it has increased abundantly; and the LORD has blessed you wherever I turned. But now when shall I provide for my own household also?" [31] He said, "What shall I give you?" Jacob said, "You shall not give me anything; if you will do this for me, I will again feed your flock and keep it: [32] let me pass through all your flock today, removing from it every speckled and spotted sheep and every black lamb, and the spotted and speckled among the goats; and such shall be my wages. [33] So my honesty will answer for me later, when you come to look into my wages with you. Every one that is not speckled and spotted among the goats and black among the lambs, if found with me, shall be counted stolen." [34] Laban said, "Good! Let it be as you have said." [35] But that day Laban removed the male goats that were striped and spotted, and all the female goats that were speckled and spotted, every one that had white on it, and every lamb that was black, and put them in charge of his sons; [36] and he set a distance of three days' journey between himself and Jacob, while Jacob was pasturing the rest of Laban's flock.

[37] Then Jacob took fresh rods of poplar and almond and plane, and peeled white streaks in them, exposing the white of the rods. [38] He set the rods that he had peeled in front of the flocks in the troughs, that is, the watering places, where the flocks came to drink. And since they bred when they came to drink, [39] the flocks bred in front of the rods, and so the flocks produced young that were striped, speckled, and spotted. [40] Jacob separated the lambs, and set the faces of the flocks toward the striped and the completely black animals in the flock of Laban; and he put his

---

a That is *Happy*
b Heb *sakar*
c Heb *zabal*
d That is *He adds*

---

plant, were thought to have aphrodisiac properties. **21:** The note about the birth of Dinah is inserted (without a story or explanation of the name) to anticipate the story about her in ch 34.

30.25–43: The birth of Jacob's flocks. Since striped or speckled coloration was unusual, Laban seemingly had nothing to lose. **37–40:** Ancient breeders believed that the female, at the time of conception, was influenced by visual impressions that affect the color of the offspring. Jacob produced striped animals by putting striped sticks before the females' eyes while they were breeding.

own droves apart, and did not put them with Laban's flock. [41] Whenever the stronger of the flock were breeding, Jacob laid the rods in the troughs before the eyes of the flock, that they might breed among the rods, [42] but for the feebler of the flock he did not lay them there; so the feebler were Laban's, and the stronger Jacob's. [43] Thus the man grew exceedingly rich, and had large flocks, and male and female slaves, and camels and donkeys.

31

Now Jacob heard that the sons of Laban were saying, "Jacob has taken all that was our father's; he has gained all this wealth from what belonged to our father." [2] And Jacob saw that Laban did not regard him as favorably as he did before. [3] Then the LORD said to Jacob, "Return to the land of your ancestors and to your kindred, and I will be with you." [4] So Jacob sent and called Rachel and Leah into the field where his flock was, [5] and said to them, "I see that your father does not regard me as favorably as he did before. But the God of my father has been with me. [6] You know that I have served your father with all my strength; [7] yet your father has cheated me and changed my wages ten times, but God did not permit him to harm me. [8] If he said, 'The speckled shall be your wages,' then all the flock bore speckled; and if he said, 'The striped shall be your wages,' then all the flock bore striped. [9] Thus God has taken away the livestock of your father, and given them to me.

[10] "During the mating of the flock I once had a dream in which I looked up and saw that the male goats that leaped upon the flock were striped, speckled, and mottled. [11] Then the angel of God said to me in the dream, 'Jacob,' and I said, 'Here I am!' [12] And he said, 'Look up and see that all the goats that leap on the flock are striped, speckled, and mottled; for I have seen all that Laban is doing to you. [13] I am the God of Bethel,[a] where

you anointed a pillar and made a vow to me. Now leave this land at once and return to the land of your birth.'" [14] Then Rachel and Leah answered him, "Is there any portion or inheritance left to us in our father's house? [15] Are we not regarded by him as foreigners? For he has sold us, and he has been using up the money given for us. [16] All the property that God has taken away from our father belongs to us and to our children; now then, do whatever God has said to you."

[17] So Jacob arose, and set his children and his wives on camels; [18] and he drove away all his livestock, all the property that he had gained, the livestock in his possession that he had acquired in Paddan-aram, to go to his father Isaac in the land of Canaan.

[19] Now Laban had gone to shear his sheep, and Rachel stole her father's household gods. [20] And Jacob deceived Laban the Aramean, in that he did not tell him that he intended to flee. [21] So he fled with all that he had; starting out he crossed the Euphrates,[b] and set his face toward the hill country of Gilead.

[22] On the third day Laban was told that Jacob had fled. [23] So he took his kinsfolk with him and pursued him for seven days until he caught up with him in the hill country of Gilead. [24] But God came to Laban the Aramean in a dream by night, and said to him, "Take heed that you say not a word to Jacob, either good or bad."

[25] Laban overtook Jacob. Now Jacob had pitched his tent in the hill country, and Laban with his kinsfolk camped in the hill country of Gilead. [26] Laban said to Jacob, "What have you done? You have deceived me, and carried away my daughters like captives of the sword. [27] Why did you flee secretly and deceive me and not tell me? I would have sent you away

a   Cn: Meaning of Heb uncertain
b   Heb *the river*

31.1–55: Jacob's departure from Laban's family. 4–16: This speech by Jacob and reply by his wives is often assigned by scholars to a different author than the surrounding verses, generally identified as J. In it Jacob presents to his wives a particular perspective on the previously narrated events (cf. 30.25–43). 13: Where Jerusalem Zion traditions claimed that the LORD dwells in Zion (Ps's 9.12; 135.21), God claims in this text to be "the god of Bethel" (see 28.10–11n.). This probably reflects the particular perspective of this originally northern Jacob story in comparison with Jerusalem-oriented traditions that predominate in the Bible. 19–35: The *household gods* (see 1 Sam 19.13–17) may have been figures representing ancestral deities. Possession of them ensured leadership of the family and legitimated property claims. Here Jacob's favored wife, Rachel, is the trickster (see

with mirth and songs, with tambourine and lyre. [28] And why did you not permit me to kiss my sons and my daughters farewell? What you have done is foolish. [29] It is in my power to do you harm; but the God of your father spoke to me last night, saying, 'Take heed that you speak to Jacob neither good nor bad.' [30] Even though you had to go because you longed greatly for your father's house, why did you steal my gods?" [31] Jacob answered Laban, "Because I was afraid, for I thought that you would take your daughters from me by force. [32] But anyone with whom you find your gods shall not live. In the presence of our kinsfolk, point out what I have that is yours, and take it." Now Jacob did not know that Rachel had stolen the gods.[a]

[33] So Laban went into Jacob's tent, and into Leah's tent, and into the tent of the two maids, but he did not find them. And he went out of Leah's tent, and entered Rachel's. [34] Now Rachel had taken the household gods and put them in the camel's saddle, and sat on them. Laban felt all about in the tent, but did not find them. [35] And she said to her father, "Let not my lord be angry that I cannot rise before you, for the way of women is upon me." So he searched, but did not find the household gods.

[36] Then Jacob became angry, and upbraided Laban. Jacob said to Laban, "What is my offense? What is my sin, that you have hotly pursued me? [37] Although you have felt about through all my goods, what have you found of all your household goods? Set it here before my kinsfolk and your kinsfolk, so that they may decide between us two. [38] These twenty years I have been with you; your ewes and your female goats have not miscarried, and I have not eaten the rams of your flocks. [39] That which was torn by wild beasts I did not bring to you; I bore the loss of it myself; of my hand you required it, whether stolen by day or stolen by night. [40] It was like this

with me: by day the heat consumed me, and the cold by night, and my sleep fled from my eyes. [41] These twenty years I have been in your house; I served you fourteen years for your two daughters, and six years for your flock, and you have changed my wages ten times. [42] If the God of my father, the God of Abraham and the Fear[b] of Isaac, had not been on my side, surely now you would have sent me away empty-handed. God saw my affliction and the labor of my hands, and rebuked you last night."

[43] Then Laban answered and said to Jacob, "The daughters are my daughters, the children are my children, the flocks are my flocks, and all that you see is mine. But what can I do today about these daughters of mine, or about their children whom they have borne? [44] Come now, let us make a covenant, you and I; and let it be a witness between you and me." [45] So Jacob took a stone, and set it up as a pillar. [46] And Jacob said to his kinsfolk, "Gather stones," and they took stones, and made a heap; and they ate there by the heap. [47] Laban called it Jegar-sahadutha:[c] but Jacob called it Galeed.[d] [48] Laban said, "This heap is a witness between you and me today." Therefore he called it Galeed, [49] and the pillar[e] Mizpah,[f] for he said, "The LORD watch between you and me, when we are absent one from the other. [50] If you ill-treat my daughters, or if you take wives in addition to my daughters, though no one else is with us, remember that God is witness between you and me."

[51] Then Laban said to Jacob, "See this heap and see the pillar, which I have set between

a Heb them
b Meaning of Heb uncertain
c In Aramaic The heap of witness
d In Hebrew The heap of witness
e Compare Sam: MT lacks the pillar
f That is Watchpost

27.1–45n.). 35: The way of women, menstruation. 42: The Hebrew word rendered as Fear in Fear of Isaac, is different from the Hebrew word usually used for "fear" of the LORD. The same word clearly means "terror" or "dread" elsewhere, as in the "terror of the LORD" refrain in Isa 2.10,19,21. Some scholars, however, have proposed alternative understandings of the word in this context, such as "refuge" of Isaac. 43–54: The story is built around an older tradition regarding a boundary covenant between Arameans and Israelites (vv. 44,52), both of whom laid claim to the region of Gilead in northern Transjordan (see map on p. 252). On the pillar, see 28.18n. 47: The stone heap is given two names (see notes c and d), one in Laban's language (Aramaic) and one in Jacob's (Hebrew).

you and me. [52] This heap is a witness, and the pillar is a witness, that I will not pass beyond this heap to you, and you will not pass beyond this heap and this pillar to me, for harm. [53] May the God of Abraham and the God of Nahor"—the God of their father—"judge between us." So Jacob swore by the Fear[a] of his father Isaac, [54] and Jacob offered a sacrifice on the height and called his kinsfolk to eat bread; and they ate bread and tarried all night in the hill country.

[55] [b]Early in the morning Laban rose up, and kissed his grandchildren and his daughters and blessed them; then he departed and returned home.

32 Jacob went on his way and the angels of God met him; [2] and when Jacob saw them he said, "This is God's camp!" So he called that place Mahanaim.[c]

[3] Jacob sent messengers before him to his brother Esau in the land of Seir, the country of Edom, [4] instructing them, "Thus you shall say to my lord Esau: Thus says your servant Jacob, 'I have lived with Laban as an alien, and stayed until now; [5] and I have oxen, donkeys, flocks, male and female slaves; and I have sent to tell my lord, in order that I may find favor in your sight.'"

[6] The messengers returned to Jacob, saying, "We came to your brother Esau, and he is coming to meet you, and four hundred men are with him." [7] Then Jacob was greatly afraid and distressed; and he divided the people that were with him, and the flocks and herds and camels, into two companies, [8] thinking, "If Esau comes to the one company and destroys it, then the company that is left will escape."

[9] And Jacob said, "O God of my father Abraham and God of my father Isaac, O LORD who said to me, 'Return to your country and to your kindred, and I will do you good,' [10] I am not worthy of the least of all the steadfast love and all the faithfulness that you have

shown to your servant, for with only my staff I crossed this Jordan; and now I have become two companies. [11] Deliver me, please, from the hand of my brother, from the hand of Esau, for I am afraid of him; he may come and kill us all, the mothers with the children. [12] Yet you have said, 'I will surely do you good, and make your offspring as the sand of the sea, which cannot be counted because of their number.'"

[13] So he spent that night there, and from what he had with him he took a present for his brother Esau, [14] two hundred female goats and twenty male goats, two hundred ewes and twenty rams, [15] thirty milch camels and their colts, forty cows and ten bulls, twenty female donkeys and ten male donkeys. [16] These he delivered into the hand of his servants, every drove by itself, and said to his servants, "Pass on ahead of me, and put a space between drove and drove." [17] He instructed the foremost, "When Esau my brother meets you, and asks you, 'To whom do you belong? Where are you going? And whose are these ahead of you?' [18] then you shall say, 'They belong to your servant Jacob; they are a present sent to my lord Esau; and moreover he is behind us.'" [19] He likewise instructed the second and the third and all who followed the droves, "You shall say the same thing to Esau when you meet him, [20] and you shall say, 'Moreover your servant Jacob is behind us.'" For he thought, "I may appease him with the present that goes ahead of me, and afterwards I shall see his face; perhaps he will accept me." [21] So the present passed on ahead of him; and he himself spent that night in the camp.

[22] The same night he got up and took his two wives, his two maids, and his eleven chil-

---

a Meaning of Heb uncertain

b Ch 32.1 in Heb

c Here taken to mean *Two camps*

53: *Nahor,* Laban's father, and *Abraham,* Jacob's father, were brothers (11.27).

32.1–32: **Journey toward Esau. 1–2:** The Transjordanian town of Mahanaim (see map on p. 252) may have been a capital of the Northern Kingdom during the brief reign of Ishbaal, Saul's heir (2 Sam 2.8–9); was a site to which David fled during Absalom's rebellion (17.24–29) and was an administrative center in the time of Solomon (1 Kings 4.14). *Angels,* see 28.12n. **3–21:** The ever-clever Jacob develops multiple strategies to appease his brother: dividing his camp (vv. 6–8), praying for divine help (vv. 9–12), and then sending several waves of livestock as a gift to Esau (vv. 13–21). **22–32:** Abraham unknowingly hosted divine visitors (18.1–15); now Jacob unknowingly

dren, and crossed the ford of the Jabbok. [23] He took them and sent them across the stream, and likewise everything that he had. [24] Jacob was left alone; and a man wrestled with him until daybreak. [25] When the man saw that he did not prevail against Jacob, he struck him on the hip socket; and Jacob's hip was put out of joint as he wrestled with him. [26] Then he said, "Let me go, for the day is breaking." But Jacob said, "I will not let you go, unless you bless me." [27] So he said to him, "What is your name?" And he said, "Jacob." [28] Then the man[a] said, "You shall no longer be called Jacob, but Israel,[b] for you have striven with God and with humans,[c] and have prevailed." [29] Then Jacob asked him, "Please tell me your name." But he said, "Why is it that you ask my name?" And there he blessed him. [30] So Jacob called the place Peniel,[d] saying, "For I have seen God face to face, and yet my life is preserved." [31] The sun rose upon him as he passed Penuel, limping because of his hip. [32] Therefore to this day the Israelites do not eat the thigh muscle that is on the hip socket, because he struck Jacob on the hip socket at the thigh muscle.

33 Now Jacob looked up and saw Esau coming, and four hundred men with him. So he divided the children among Leah and Rachel and the two maids. [2] He put the maids with their children in front, then Leah with her children, and Rachel and Joseph last of all. [3] He himself went on ahead of them, bowing himself to the ground seven times, until he came near his brother.

[4] But Esau ran to meet him, and embraced him, and fell on his neck and kissed him, and they wept. [5] When Esau looked up and saw the women and children, he said, "Who are these with you?" Jacob said, "The children whom God has graciously given your servant." [6] Then the maids drew near, they and their children, and bowed down; [7] Leah likewise and her children drew near and bowed down; and finally Joseph and Rachel drew near, and they bowed down. [8] Esau said, "What do you mean by all this company that I met?" Jacob answered, "To find favor with my lord." [9] But Esau said, "I have enough, my brother; keep what you have for yourself." [10] Jacob said, "No, please; if I find favor with you, then accept my present from my hand; for truly to see your face is like seeing the face of God—since you have received me with such favor. [11] Please accept my gift that is brought to you, because God has dealt graciously with me, and because I have everything I want." So he urged him, and he took it.

[12] Then Esau said, "Let us journey on our way, and I will go alongside you." [13] But Jacob said to him, "My lord knows that the children are frail and that the flocks and herds, which are nursing, are a care to me; and if they are overdriven for one day, all the flocks will die. [14] Let my lord pass on ahead of his servant,

a   Heb *he*
b   That is *The one who strives with God* or *God strives*
c   Or *with divine and human beings*
d   That is *The face of God*

fights with God (cf. Ex 4.24–26). The narrative includes a complicated wordplay on the names of Jacob (Heb "ya'aqob"), the river Jabbok ("yabboq"; modern Nahr ez-Zerqa), and *wrestled* ("wayye'abeq"; v. 24). **25**: Jacob is so strong (29.10) that he is winning the contest until his divine opponent pulls Jacob's hip out of joint. **26**: The divine being had to vanish before sunrise—a mark of the antiquity of the tradition on which this story is based. **28**: Jacob's new name reflects a new self: no longer was he the "supplanter" (25.26; 27.36), but *Israel* (35.10), which probably originally meant "El rules" (the god El was the head of the Northwest Semitic pantheon). Here, however, it is interpreted to mean "the one who strives with God" (cf. Hos 12.3–4). *And with humans* refers to Jacob's strife with Esau and Laban. In this way, the community of Israel, as descendants of this god-wrestler, is depicted as a group that successfully strives with God and humans. **29**: The divine being refuses lest Jacob, by possessing the name, gain power over him. **30**: Jacob had feared to see Esau's face (v. 20), but instead saw God *face to face* and lived (see 16.13n.). **30–31**: The story is located at Penuel/Peniel ("face of El"), one of the first capitals of the Northern Kingdom (1 Kings 12.25). **32**: An Israelite prohibition against eating the thigh muscle of an animal is cited as testimony to the truth of the story. This prohibition is not mentioned elsewhere in the Bible.

33.1–17: Partial reunion with Esau. 10: *Like seeing the face of God,* who at Penuel (or Peniel) also proved to be gracious (32.30–31). **12–17**: Esau proposes to stay with Jacob, but Jacob sends him ahead, promising to join with him (v. 14). Jacob does not join him, however (v. 17), perhaps noting that Esau had always planned to wait

and I will lead on slowly, according to the pace of the cattle that are before me and according to the pace of the children, until I come to my lord in Seir."

[15] So Esau said, "Let me leave with you some of the people who are with me." But he said, "Why should my lord be so kind to me?" [16] So Esau returned that day on his way to Seir. [17] But Jacob journeyed to Succoth,[a] and built himself a house, and made booths for his cattle; therefore the place is called Succoth.

[18] Jacob came safely to the city of Shechem, which is in the land of Canaan, on his way from Paddan-aram; and he camped before the city. [19] And from the sons of Hamor, Shechem's father, he bought for one hundred pieces of money[b] the plot of land on which he had pitched his tent. [20] There he erected an altar and called it El-Elohe-Israel.[c]

34 Now Dinah the daughter of Leah, whom she had borne to Jacob, went out to visit the women of the region. [2] When Shechem son of Hamor the Hivite, prince of the region, saw her, he seized her and lay with her by force. [3] And his soul was drawn to Dinah daughter of Jacob; he loved the girl, and spoke tenderly to her. [4] So Shechem spoke to his father Hamor, saying, "Get me this girl to be my wife."

[5] Now Jacob heard that Shechem[d] had defiled his daughter Dinah; but his sons were with his cattle in the field, so Jacob held his peace until they came. [6] And Hamor the father of Shechem went out to Jacob to speak with him, [7] just as the sons of Jacob came in from the field. When they heard of it, the men were indignant and very angry, because

he had committed an outrage in Israel by lying with Jacob's daughter, for such a thing ought not to be done.

[8] But Hamor spoke with them, saying, "The heart of my son Shechem longs for your daughter; please give her to him in marriage. [9] Make marriages with us; give your daughters to us, and take our daughters for yourselves. [10] You shall live with us; and the land shall be open to you; live and trade in it, and get property in it." [11] Shechem also said to her father and to her brothers, "Let me find favor with you, and whatever you say to me I will give. [12] Put the marriage present and gift as high as you like, and I will give whatever you ask me; only give me the girl to be my wife."

[13] The sons of Jacob answered Shechem and his father Hamor deceitfully, because he had defiled their sister Dinah. [14] They said to them, "We cannot do this thing, to give our sister to one who is uncircumcised, for that would be a disgrace to us. [15] Only on this condition will we consent to you: that you will become as we are and every male among you be circumcised. [16] Then we will give our daughters to you, and we will take your daughters for ourselves, and we will live among you and become one people. [17] But if you will not listen to us and be circumcised, then we will take our daughter and be gone."

[18] Their words pleased Hamor and Hamor's son Shechem. [19] And the young man did not delay to do the thing, because he was

a   That is *Booths*
b   Heb *one hundred qesitah*
c   That is *God, the God of Israel*
d   Heb *he*

to kill him until their father died (27.41; cf. 35.29). **17:** *Succoth* means "booths." Its precise location is uncertain.
33.18–35.5: The stay in Shechem and the rape of Dinah. 33.18: *Shechem,* see 12.6–8n., was an important town in early Israel and one of the first capitals of the Northern Kingdom (1 Kings 12.25). **19:** Here and in ch 34 *Shechem* is a personal name. As elsewhere in Genesis, the story portrays, in the guise of individuals, relations between Israel and non-Israelite groups. **20:** The name of the altar ("El is the God of Israel") may be another reflection of the worship of El in early Israel (see 28.16–17n.; 32.28,31–32n.). **34.1–31:** In its broader context, this story explains why Simeon and Levi, two of Jacob's elder sons, did not receive his highest blessing; see 49.1–28n. **2:** See 33.19n. *Lay with her by force,* raped her, though some scholars interpret the Hebrew verbs as suggesting illicit sexual intercourse rather than rape. **7:** *Committed an outrage in Israel* is an old expression for ultimate offenses, such as violations of the sexual honor of the tribal group (here), the ban on booty in holy war (Josh 7.15), and the sanctity of hospitality (Judg 19.23–24; 20.6,10). **8–12:** Israelite law stipulates that a man who has sex with an unbetrothed woman must retroactively marry her by paying her father a high marriage price (Ex 22.16–17; Deut 22.28–29). This narrative either does not recognize this law, or assumes that it does not apply outside the

delighted with Jacob's daughter. Now he was the most honored of all his family. [20] So Hamor and his son Shechem came to the gate of their city and spoke to the men of their city, saying, [21] "These people are friendly with us; let them live in the land and trade in it, for the land is large enough for them; let us take their daughters in marriage, and let us give them our daughters. [22] Only on this condition will they agree to live among us, to become one people: that every male among us be circumcised as they are circumcised. [23] Will not their livestock, their property, and all their animals be ours? Only let us agree with them, and they will live among us." [24] And all who went out of the city gate heeded Hamor and his son Shechem; and every male was circumcised, all who went out of the gate of his city.

[25] On the third day, when they were still in pain, two of the sons of Jacob, Simeon and Levi, Dinah's brothers, took their swords and came against the city unawares, and killed all the males. [26] They killed Hamor and his son Shechem with the sword, and took Dinah out of Shechem's house, and went away. [27] And the other sons of Jacob came upon the slain, and plundered the city, because their sister had been defiled. [28] They took their flocks and their herds, their donkeys, and whatever was in the city and in the field. [29] All their wealth, all their little ones and their wives, all that was in the houses, they captured and made their prey. [30] Then Jacob said to Simeon and Levi, "You have brought trouble on me by making me odious to the inhabitants of the land, the Canaanites and the Perizzites; my numbers are few, and if they gather themselves against me and attack me, I shall be destroyed, both I and my household." [31] But they said, "Should our sister be treated like a whore?"

35 God said to Jacob, "Arise, go up to Bethel, and settle there. Make an altar there to the God who appeared to you when you fled from your brother Esau." [2] So Jacob said to his household and to all who were with him, "Put away the foreign gods that are among you, and purify yourselves, and change your clothes; [3] then come, let us go up to Bethel, that I may make an altar there to the God who answered me in the day of my distress and has been with me wherever I have gone." [4] So they gave to Jacob all the foreign gods that they had, and the rings that were in their ears; and Jacob hid them under the oak that was near Shechem.

[5] As they journeyed, a terror from God fell upon the cities all around them, so that no one pursued them. [6] Jacob came to Luz (that is, Bethel), which is in the land of Canaan, he and all the people who were with him, [7] and there he built an altar and called the place El-bethel,[a] because it was there that God had revealed himself to him when he fled from his brother. [8] And Deborah, Rebekah's nurse, died, and she was buried under an oak below Bethel. So it was called Allon-bacuth.[b]

---

[a] That is *God of Bethel*

[b] That is *Oak of weeping*

---

people of Israel. **13–17**: Jacob's sons now are the tricksters (see 27.1–45n.). On circumcision see 17.9–14n. **21–23**: In contrast to Hamor's proposal to the Israelites of intermarriage and acquisition of land (vv. 8–10), his speech to his countrymen here betrays an interest in impoverishing the Israelites through assimilating them. On concern about intermarriage, see 24.3n. **25–26**: Simeon and Levi lead the killing and recapture of Dinah because, as older full brothers of Dinah (29.33–34; 30.21), they were responsible for avenging the violation of the family's honor through her. **27–29**: In a reversal of what the Shechemites had planned for them (vv. 21–23), the Israelites take all the Shechemites' possessions. **30–31**: Jacob is depicted here as less concerned about family honor than about good relations with the Canaanites (see 35.5). His sons' question is left unanswered at the end of the story (cf. Jon 4.11), but is ultimately addressed in 49.5–7. **35.1–4**: The present narrative reflects a later judgment on non-Yahwistic ritual objects. Like its parallels (Josh 24.23; Judg 10.16; 1 Sam 7.3), it may presuppose, however, a more ancient practice of burial of divine images in sacred places, i.e., by a sacred tree (see 12.6–8n.). **5**: Jacob's fears (see 34.30) prove to be unfounded.

35.6–15: Jacob's return to Bethel (cf. 28.10–22). **6–7**: In the ancient world deities had local manifestations (e.g., on two ancient inscriptions we find "Yahweh of Samaria"). Jacob honors the local manifestation of El at Bethel by calling the sanctuary there "El of Bethel." **8**: Once again a tree is associated with a revered sanctuary

⁹ God appeared to Jacob again when he came from Paddan-aram, and he blessed him. ¹⁰ God said to him, "Your name is Jacob; no longer shall you be called Jacob, but Israel shall be your name." So he was called Israel. ¹¹ God said to him, "I am God Almighty:ᵃ be fruitful and multiply; a nation and a company of nations shall come from you, and kings shall spring from you. ¹² The land that I gave to Abraham and Isaac I will give to you, and I will give the land to your offspring after you." ¹³ Then God went up from him at the place where he had spoken with him. ¹⁴ Jacob set up a pillar in the place where he had spoken with him, a pillar of stone; and he poured out a drink offering on it, and poured oil on it. ¹⁵ So Jacob called the place where God had spoken with him Bethel.

¹⁶ Then they journeyed from Bethel; and when they were still some distance from Ephrath, Rachel was in childbirth, and she had hard labor. ¹⁷ When she was in her hard labor, the midwife said to her, "Do not be afraid; for now you will have another son." ¹⁸ As her soul was departing (for she died), she named him Ben-oni;ᵇ but his father called him Benjamin.ᶜ ¹⁹ So Rachel died, and she was buried on the way to Ephrath (that is, Bethlehem), ²⁰ and Jacob set up a pillar at her grave; it is the pillar of Rachel's tomb, which is there

to this day. ²¹ Israel journeyed on, and pitched his tent beyond the tower of Eder.

²² While Israel lived in that land, Reuben went and lay with Bilhah his father's concubine; and Israel heard of it.

Now the sons of Jacob were twelve. ²³ The sons of Leah: Reuben (Jacob's firstborn), Simeon, Levi, Judah, Issachar, and Zebulun. ²⁴ The sons of Rachel: Joseph and Benjamin. ²⁵ The sons of Bilhah, Rachel's maid: Dan and Naphtali. ²⁶ The sons of Zilpah, Leah's maid: Gad and Asher. These were the sons of Jacob who were born to him in Paddan-aram.

²⁷ Jacob came to his father Isaac at Mamre, or Kiriath-arba (that is, Hebron), where Abraham and Isaac had resided as aliens. ²⁸ Now the days of Isaac were one hundred eighty years. ²⁹ And Isaac breathed his last; he died and was gathered to his people, old and full of days; and his sons Esau and Jacob buried him.

36 These are the descendants of Esau (that is, Edom). ² Esau took his wives from the Canaanites: Adah daughter of Elon the Hittite, Oholibamah daughter of Anah sonᵈ of Zibeon the Hivite, ³ and

ᵃ Traditional rendering of Heb *El Shaddai*
ᵇ That is *Son of my sorrow*
ᶜ That is *Son of the right hand* or *Son of the South*
ᵈ Sam Gk Syr: Heb *daughter*

(see 12.6–8n.). **9–15:** A Priestly parallel to the non-Priestly renaming tradition in 32.28 and the Bethel tradition in 28.10–22. **10:** Cf. 32.28. **11–12:** Cf. non-P, 28.13–15. The divine fulfillment of Isaac's wish (28.3–4) that God bestow Abraham's blessing (17.1–8) on Jacob. **11:** *God Almighty,* see 17.1n. **13:** P stresses that God is not bound to Bethel in the way asserted in the non-Priestly Bethel narratives (28.10–22; 36.6–7). God merely spoke there and left. **14:** In a P doublet of 28.18–19, Jacob sets up a pillar at Bethel (see 28.18n.) and (re)names the place.

35.16–21: The birth of Benjamin and death of Rachel. 18: Dying in childbirth, Rachel gives an ominous name ("son of my sorrow") to the baby. In this instance (cf. 29.31–30.24) the father overrules his wife's naming and gives him a more propitious one. *Benjamin* (see note c) refers either to the right hand as a symbol of power or to the tribe's position south ("right") of Ephraim. **19:** Here and in 48.7 the tomb of Rachel is located near Bethlehem (south of Jerusalem). Compare 1 Sam 10.2 and Jer 31.15. **20:** On pillars, see 28.18n. **21:** From this point on the name *Israel* is often used to refer to Jacob (32.28).

35.22–29: Concluding materials on Jacob's sons and Isaac's death and burial. 22a: This aside describes how Reuben violated his father's honor by sleeping with Jacob's concubine, the servant of recently deceased Rachel, Bilhah (29.29; 30.3–8). Later he will be cursed for this act (see 49.3–4n.). This is a part of a series of texts added to the early Jacob and Joseph narratives that explain Jacob's preference for Judah (see 49.1–28n.), and thus Judean kingship under David and his successors. **22b–29:** A Priestly listing of Jacob's sons and the death and burial notice of Isaac.

36.1–43: Overview of the descendants of Esau and prior inhabitants of Edom/Seir. Cf. 25.12–18. Before the narrative goes into detail on the descendants of Jacob (37.2–50.26), it gives an overview (largely Priestly) of the descendants of Esau, the firstborn son of Isaac. **2–3:** Though this note agrees with other Priestly material in stressing his intermarriage with foreigners, the names or parentage of Esau's wives are different here (cf.

Basemath, Ishmael's daughter, sister of Nebaioth. [4] Adah bore Eliphaz to Esau; Basemath bore Reuel; [5] and Oholibamah bore Jeush, Jalam, and Korah. These are the sons of Esau who were born to him in the land of Canaan.

[6] Then Esau took his wives, his sons, his daughters, and all the members of his household, his cattle, all his livestock, and all the property he had acquired in the land of Canaan; and he moved to a land some distance from his brother Jacob. [7] For their possessions were too great for them to live together; the land where they were staying could not support them because of their livestock. [8] So Esau settled in the hill country of Seir; Esau is Edom.

[9] These are the descendants of Esau, ancestor of the Edomites, in the hill country of Seir. [10] These are the names of Esau's sons: Eliphaz son of Adah the wife of Esau; Reuel, the son of Esau's wife Basemath. [11] The sons of Eliphaz were Teman, Omar, Zepho, Gatam, and Kenaz. [12] (Timna was a concubine of Eliphaz, Esau's son; she bore Amalek to Eliphaz.) These were the sons of Adah, Esau's wife. [13] These were the sons of Reuel: Nahath, Zerah, Shammah, and Mizzah. These were the sons of Esau's wife, Basemath. [14] These were the sons of Esau's wife Oholibamah, daughter of Anah son[a] of Zibeon: she bore to Esau Jeush, Jalam, and Korah.

[15] These are the clans[b] of the sons of Esau. The sons of Eliphaz the firstborn of Esau: the clans[b] Teman, Omar, Zepho, Kenaz, [16] Korah, Gatam, and Amalek; these are the clans[b] of Eliphaz in the land of Edom; they are the sons of Adah. [17] These are the sons of Esau's son Reuel: the clans[b] Nahath, Zerah, Shammah, and Mizzah; these are the clans[b] of Reuel in the land of Edom; they are the sons of Esau's wife Basemath. [18] These are the sons of Esau's wife Oholibamah: the clans[b] Jeush, Jalam, and Korah; these are

the clans[b] born of Esau's wife Oholibamah, the daughter of Anah. [19] These are the sons of Esau (that is, Edom), and these are their clans.[b]

[20] These are the sons of Seir the Horite, the inhabitants of the land: Lotan, Shobal, Zibeon, Anah, [21] Dishon, Ezer, and Dishan; these are the clans[b] of the Horites, the sons of Seir in the land of Edom. [22] The sons of Lotan were Hori and Heman; and Lotan's sister was Timna. [23] These are the sons of Shobal: Alvan, Manahath, Ebal, Shepho, and Onam. [24] These are the sons of Zibeon: Aiah and Anah; he is the Anah who found the springs[c] in the wilderness, as he pastured the donkeys of his father Zibeon. [25] These are the children of Anah: Dishon and Oholibamah daughter of Anah. [26] These are the sons of Dishon: Hemdan, Eshban, Ithran, and Cheran. [27] These are the sons of Ezer: Bilhan, Zaavan, and Akan. [28] These are the sons of Dishan: Uz and Aran. [29] These are the clans[b] of the Horites: the clans[b] Lotan, Shobal, Zibeon, Anah, [30] Dishon, Ezer, and Dishan; these are the clans[b] of the Horites, clan by clan[d] in the land of Seir.

[31] These are the kings who reigned in the land of Edom, before any king reigned over the Israelites. [32] Bela son of Beor reigned in Edom, the name of his city being Dinhabah. [33] Bela died, and Jobab son of Zerah of Bozrah succeeded him as king. [34] Jobab died, and Husham of the land of the Temanites succeeded him as king. [35] Husham died, and Hadad son of Bedad, who defeated Midian in the country of Moab, succeeded him as king, the name of his city being Avith.

a   Gk Syr: Heb daughter
b   Or chiefs
c   Meaning of Heb uncertain
d   Or chief by chief

26.34–35; 28.8–9). 6–8: Echoes the (non-Priestly) story of Abraham's split from Lot (13.2–13). 9–14: A list of Esau's descendants organized by the mother (cf. 35.23–26). 9: The repeated introduction (cf. 36.1) may indicate that an earlier Priestly overview of Esau's descendants began here. 15–19: A list of clans of the sons of Esau that diverges slightly from vv. 9–14 in its list of offspring of Eliphaz (cf. 36.11 and 15–16). 20–30: A list of clans of Horite inhabitants of Seir (see 14.6), which may have been originally understood as a region in Transjordan different from Edom. In Deut 2.12,22 Esau (Edom) is described as having expelled the Horites from Seir. 31–39: A

³⁶ Hadad died, and Samlah of Masrekah succeeded him as king. ³⁷ Samlah died, and Shaul of Rehoboth on the Euphrates succeeded him as king. ³⁸ Shaul died, and Baal-hanan son of Achbor succeeded him as king. ³⁹ Baal-hanan son of Achbor died, and Hadar succeeded him as king, the name of his city being Pau; his wife's name was Mehetabel, the daughter of Matred, daughter of Me-zahab.

⁴⁰ These are the names of the clansᵃ of Esau, according to their families and their localities by their names: the clansᵃ Timna, Alvah, Jetheth, ⁴¹ Oholibamah, Elah, Pinon, ⁴² Kenaz, Teman, Mibzar, ⁴³ Magdiel, and Iram; these are the clansᵃ of Edom (that is, Esau, the father of Edom), according to their settlements in the land that they held.

37 Jacob settled in the land where his father had lived as an alien, the land of Canaan. ² This is the story of the family of Jacob.

Joseph, being seventeen years old, was shepherding the flock with his brothers; he was a helper to the sons of Bilhah and Zilpah, his father's wives; and Joseph brought a bad report of them to their father. ³ Now Israel loved Joseph more than any other of his children, because he was the son of his old age; and he had made him a long robe with sleeves.ᵇ ⁴ But when his brothers saw that their father loved him more than all his brothers, they hated him, and could not speak peaceably to him.

⁵ Once Joseph had a dream, and when he told it to his brothers, they hated him even more. ⁶ He said to them, "Listen to this dream that I dreamed. ⁷ There we were, binding sheaves in the field. Suddenly my sheaf rose and stood upright; then your sheaves

ᵃ Or *chiefs*
ᵇ Traditional rendering (compare Gk): *a coat of many colors*; meaning of Heb uncertain

list of early kings of Edom (see Num 20.14). **40–43:** A list of a slightly different kind of clan group (Heb "'alup") in Edom that partially overlaps with names occurring in 36.9–19.

37.1–50.26: The story of Joseph and his family. As indicated in the Introduction, this portion of Genesis features an intricate depiction of Joseph's relations with his brothers and father. Starting with a pair of dreams (37.5–11), the narrative follows a trajectory from his brothers' murderous hatred of Joseph to Joseph's eventual testing of and reunion with them (chs 42–45; 50). Like the Jacob story, this narrative has Northern connections, especially with the addition of the story in 48.8–14 of Joseph's special blessing on his son, Ephraim. The first king of the Northern Kingdom, Jeroboam, was a member of the tribe of Ephraim (1 Kings 11.26), and stories like these about early Israelite ancestors would have reinforced his claim to rule. Yet over time the story evolved in significance, through additions assuming *Judah's* destiny to rule (see 49.1–28n.), inserted echoes of the promise theme first introduced in the Abraham story (such as 46.1–4; 48.15–16 and 12.1–3n.), connections leading to the book of Joshua (50.24–25), and a few fragments that may come from the Priestly source (e.g. 37.1–2; 46.8–27; 47.27–28; 48.3–6; 49.29–33).

37.1–11: Joseph's dreams of power. These narratives open the remarkably cohesive story of Joseph and his brothers in chs 37–50. Source critics have attempted to trace strands of the hypothesized Yahwistic and Elohistic source documents (see Introduction) through the Joseph story; thus sections focusing on Reuben and Midianites (e.g., 37.22–24,28–36) were assigned to E, while sections focusing on Judah and the Ishmaelites (e.g., 37.25–28) were assigned to J. Others suggested that an early Joseph story focused on Reuben was revised by an author who focused on Judah and referred to Jacob as "Israel." Despite the presence of some additions and modifications (e.g., 37.2a; 41.46), however, the essential unity of the Joseph story is clear. **2a:** *This is the story,* despite the different translation here in the NRSV, this heading is identical with those in 5.1; 6.9; 10.1; 11.27; 25.12,18; 36.1,9 that refer to the "descendants" of a given figure. Here it identifies what follows as concerning the "descendants of Jacob," that is Joseph and his brothers. **2b–4:** According to the Priestly narrative (vv. 1–2), Joseph tattled on his brothers. The non-Priestly narrative (vv. 3–4) explains his brothers' antagonism toward him as resulting from jealousy about Jacob's love. Joseph is favored as the eldest of the children of Jacob by his favorite wife, Rachel (30.22–24). The *long robe with sleeves* (v. 3; see note *b*) is a royal garment (2 Sam 13.18–19) anticipating Joseph's future status. At this point in the story neither the reader nor the brothers know how this will come about. **5–8:** This first dream report predicts Joseph's domination of his brothers (43.26; 50.18; cf. 42.6). The story may intend to predict the future rule of Jeroboam, a member of the

gathered around it, and bowed down to my sheaf." [8] His brothers said to him, "Are you indeed to reign over us? Are you indeed to have dominion over us?" So they hated him even more because of his dreams and his words.

[9] He had another dream, and told it to his brothers, saying, "Look, I have had another dream: the sun, the moon, and eleven stars were bowing down to me." [10] But when he told it to his father and to his brothers, his father rebuked him, and said to him, "What kind of dream is this that you have had? Shall we indeed come, I and your mother and your brothers, and bow to the ground before you?" [11] So his brothers were jealous of him, but his father kept the matter in mind.

[12] Now his brothers went to pasture their father's flock near Shechem. [13] And Israel said to Joseph, "Are not your brothers pasturing the flock at Shechem? Come, I will send you to them." He answered, "Here I am." [14] So he said to him, "Go now, see if it is well with your brothers and with the flock; and bring word back to me." So he sent him from the valley of Hebron.

He came to Shechem, [15] and a man found him wandering in the fields; the man asked him, "What are you seeking?" [16] "I am seeking my brothers," he said; "tell me, please, where they are pasturing the flock." [17] The man said, "They have gone away, for I heard them say, 'Let us go to Dothan.'" So Joseph went after his brothers, and found them at Dothan. [18] They saw him from a distance, and before he came near to them, they conspired to kill him. [19] They said to one another, "Here comes this dreamer. [20] Come now, let us kill him and throw him into one of the pits; then we shall say that a wild animal has devoured him, and we shall see what will become of his dreams." [21] But when Reuben heard it, he delivered him out of their hands, saying, "Let us not take his life." [22] Reuben said to them, "Shed no blood; throw him into this pit here in the wilderness, but lay no hand on him"— that he might rescue him out of their hand and restore him to his father. [23] So when Joseph came to his brothers, they stripped him of his robe, the long robe with sleeves[a] that he wore; [24] and they took him and threw him into a pit. The pit was empty; there was no water in it.

[25] Then they sat down to eat; and looking up they saw a caravan of Ishmaelites coming from Gilead, with their camels carrying gum, balm, and resin, on their way to carry it down to Egypt. [26] Then Judah said to his brothers, "What profit is it if we kill our brother and conceal his blood? [27] Come, let us sell him to the Ishmaelites, and not lay our hands on him, for he is our brother, our own flesh." And his brothers agreed. [28] When some Midianite traders passed by, they drew Joseph up, lifting him out of the pit, and sold him to the Ishmaelites for twenty pieces of silver. And they took Joseph to Egypt.

[29] When Reuben returned to the pit and saw that Joseph was not in the pit, he tore his clothes. [30] He returned to his brothers, and said, "The boy is gone; and I, where can I turn?" [31] Then they took Joseph's robe,

[a] See note on 37.3

Joseph tribe of Ephraim, over the other tribes of northern Israel (1 Kings 11.26; 12.1–14.20). 9–11: Jacob sees this dream as predicting that he and Joseph's mother, Rachel, will join the brothers in submitting to Joseph. This episode was probably part of an independent Joseph story that originally did not follow an account of Rachel's death (see 35.16–20).

37.12–36: Joseph is sold into slavery. 17: Dothan is about 15 mi (24 km) north of Shechem and lay along a trade route from Syria to Egypt. 20: *The pits* were cisterns for storing rain water and sometimes used to imprison people (Jer 38.6). 22–27: The advice of Reuben and Judah reflects the ancient idea that blood cannot be "concealed" (v. 26), but cries out for requital (see 4.10–11n.). 25–36: Most scholars agree that some combination or modification of traditions has occurred here. Though the brothers decide here to sell Joseph (v. 27) and Joseph later says that they did so (45.4–5), this narrative describes the *Midianites* as drawing him out and selling him to the *Ishmaelites* (v. 28). Later, both the *Midianites* (37.36) and the *Ishmaelites* (39.1; cf. 37.25) are identified as the ones who sold Joseph to Potiphar. 25: *Gilead*, in northern Transjordan, was famous for its *balm*, an aromatic resin used in healing (see Jer 8.22). 26–27: On the role of Judah, see 44.18–34n. 31–34: Now Jacob is tricked by an

slaughtered a goat, and dipped the robe in the blood. [32] They had the long robe with sleeves[a] taken to their father, and they said, "This we have found; see now whether it is your son's robe or not." [33] He recognized it, and said, "It is my son's robe! A wild animal has devoured him; Joseph is without doubt torn to pieces." [34] Then Jacob tore his garments, and put sackcloth on his loins, and mourned for his son many days. [35] All his sons and all his daughters sought to comfort him; but he refused to be comforted, and said, "No, I shall go down to Sheol to my son, mourning." Thus his father bewailed him. [36] Meanwhile the Midianites had sold him in Egypt to Potiphar, one of Pharaoh's officials, the captain of the guard.

38

It happened at that time that Judah went down from his brothers and settled near a certain Adullamite whose name was Hirah. [2] There Judah saw the daughter of a certain Canaanite whose name was Shua; he married her and went in to her. [3] She conceived and bore a son; and he named him Er. [4] Again she conceived and bore a son whom she named Onan. [5] Yet again she bore a son, and she named him Shelah. She[b] was in Chezib when she bore him. [6] Judah took a wife for Er his firstborn; her name was Tamar. [7] But Er, Judah's firstborn, was wicked in the sight of the LORD, and the LORD put him to death. [8] Then Judah said to Onan, "Go in to

your brother's wife and perform the duty of a brother-in-law to her; raise up offspring for your brother." [9] But since Onan knew that the offspring would not be his, he spilled his semen on the ground whenever he went in to his brother's wife, so that he would not give offspring to his brother. [10] What he did was displeasing in the sight of the LORD, and he put him to death also. [11] Then Judah said to his daughter-in-law Tamar, "Remain a widow in your father's house until my son Shelah grows up"—for he feared that he too would die, like his brothers. So Tamar went to live in her father's house.

[12] In course of time the wife of Judah, Shua's daughter, died; when Judah's time of mourning was over,[c] he went up to Timnah to his sheepshearers, he and his friend Hirah the Adullamite. [13] When Tamar was told, "Your father-in-law is going up to Timnah to shear his sheep," [14] she put off her widow's garments, put on a veil, wrapped herself up, and sat down at the entrance to Enaim, which is on the road to Timnah. She saw that Shelah was grown up, yet she had not been given to him in marriage. [15] When Judah saw her, he thought her to be a prostitute, for she had covered her face. [16] He went over to her at

a See note on 37.3
b Gk: Heb *He*
c Heb *when Judah was comforted*

article of clothing (contrast 27.15; see 29.23–25n.). **35:** *Sheol,* the underworld to which a person went at death—the Hebrew Bible does not recognize a differentiated heaven and hell. Since this afterlife was at best a shadowy existence (see Ps 6.5; Eccl 9.10), Jacob's going to his son there was not a comforting expectation. **36:** Multiple traditions testify to some kind of connection between Joseph and an Egyptian *Potiphar/*" Potiphera." *Potiphar* is a form of "Potiphera," the name of the Egyptian priest who is Joseph's father-in-law in 41.45 and 46.20.

38.1–30: Judah and Tamar. Though an apparent interlude in the Joseph story, this chapter echoes elements of ch 37 and anticipates themes from the upcoming Joseph story. Yet this story contrasts with most of this part of Genesis in its focus on Judah, not Joseph. Moreover, it has striking parallels with later narratives about David (see 38.1–2n., 6n.). Both elements—the focus on Judah and anticipation of David—link 38.1–30 with a sequence of episodes, starting in 30.21; 34.1–31; 35.22, that prepare for Jacob's blessing of Judah and prediction of the Davidic dynasty in 49.8–12. See 49.1–28n. and 8–12n. **1–2:** *Adullam,* a town where David later built up his mercenary army (1 Sam 22.1; 2 Sam 23.13). The locales in this narrative are appropriately in the territory of the tribe of Judah. Judah's wife, the daughter of Shua (Heb "Bat Shu'a," v. 12), anticipates the later "Bathsheba" of the David and Solomon narratives (2 Sam 11; cf. 1 Chr 3.5). **6:** Links to the David and Solomon story continue with mention of "Tamar" (see 2 Sam 13). **8–10:** According to the ancient custom of levirate marriage (Deut 25.5–10), *the duty of a brother-in-law* was to father a male descendant for his deceased brother and thus perpetuate his name and inheritance. Onan's death is attributed to his refusal to perform this duty (thus endangering Judah's line), probably by coitus interruptus (rather than "onanism," masturbation). **11:** Judah apparently fears that the death of his sons resulted from Tamar's sinister power. **12–19:** Tamar tricks Judah into playing the role of the brother-

the roadside, and said, "Come, let me come in to you," for he did not know that she was his daughter-in-law. She said, "What will you give me, that you may come in to me?" ¹⁷ He answered, "I will send you a kid from the flock." And she said, "Only if you give me a pledge, until you send it." ¹⁸ He said, "What pledge shall I give you?" She replied, "Your signet and your cord, and the staff that is in your hand." So he gave them to her, and went in to her, and she conceived by him. ¹⁹ Then she got up and went away, and taking off her veil she put on the garments of her widowhood.

²⁰ When Judah sent the kid by his friend the Adullamite, to recover the pledge from the woman, he could not find her. ²¹ He asked the townspeople, "Where is the temple prostitute who was at Enaim by the wayside?" But they said, "No prostitute has been here." ²² So he returned to Judah, and said, "I have not found her; moreover the townspeople said, 'No prostitute has been here.'" ²³ Judah replied, "Let her keep the things as her own, otherwise we will be laughed at; you see, I sent this kid, and you could not find her."

²⁴ About three months later Judah was told, "Your daughter-in-law Tamar has played the whore; moreover she is pregnant as a result of whoredom." And Judah said, "Bring her out, and let her be burned." ²⁵ As she was being brought out, she sent word to her father-in-law, "It was the owner of these who made me pregnant." And she said, "Take note, please, whose these are, the signet and the cord and the staff." ²⁶ Then Judah acknowledged them and said, "She is more in the right than I, since I did not give her to my son Shelah." And he did not lie with her again.

²⁷ When the time of her delivery came, there were twins in her womb. ²⁸ While she was in labor, one put out a hand; and the midwife took and bound on his hand a crimson thread, saying, "This one came out first." ²⁹ But just then he drew back his hand, and out came his brother; and she said, "What a breach you have made for yourself!" Therefore he was named Perez.^a ³⁰ Afterward his brother came out with the crimson thread on his hand; and he was named Zerah.^b

39 Now Joseph was taken down to Egypt, and Potiphar, an officer of Pharaoh, the captain of the guard, an Egyptian, bought him from the Ishmaelites who had brought him down there. ² The LORD was with Joseph, and he became a successful man; he was in the house of his Egyptian master. ³ His master saw that the LORD was with him, and that the LORD caused all that he did to prosper in his hands. ⁴ So Joseph found favor in his sight and attended him; he made him overseer of his house and put him in charge of all that he had. ⁵ From the time that he made him overseer in his house and over all that he had, the LORD blessed the Egyptian's house for Joseph's sake; the blessing of the LORD was on all that he had, in house and field. ⁶ So he left all that he had in Joseph's charge; and, with him there, he had no concern for anything but the food that he ate.

Now Joseph was handsome and good-looking. ⁷ And after a time his master's wife

^a That is *A breach*
^b That is *Brightness*; perhaps alluding to the crimson thread

in-law by dressing as a prostitute and allowing him to hire her to have sex (see 27.1–45n.). **18:** The *signet* was a seal, often suspended from the neck with a *cord,* used to "sign" documents. **20–22:** Though some interpret the Hebrew here for "holy woman" ("qedeshah") as referring to a *temple prostitute* (so NRSV), it is unlikely that there was an institution of sacred prostitution in ancient Israel. Some commentators propose that Judah's Adullamite friend is just delicately referring to the missing "prostitute" as a similarly unattached "holy woman." **24:** Stoning was the usual punishment for adultery (Deut 22.23–24; cf. Jn 8.5), although burning was prescribed for exceptional cases (Lev 21.9). **25–26:** The presentation of evidence to Judah here echoes the presentation of the bloody robe to Jacob in 37.32–33. **27–30:** The birth of Judah's twins is depicted in terms similar to that of Jacob and Esau (25.24–26). The final link of this chapter to the David narrative (see 38.1–2,6n.) occurs with Perez, the firstborn and ancestor of David (Ruth 4.18–22; see 49.1–28 and 8–12n.).

39.1–23: Joseph's success, temptation, and imprisonment. 1–6: Joseph's enjoyment of blessing and Potiphar's recognition of it are an outgrowth of the promise to Abraham in 12.1–3 (see 12.2n.). **7–20:** A parallel Egyptian "Tale of Two Brothers" also tells a tale of how a man rejected the advances of another's wife, who then

cast her eyes on Joseph and said, "Lie with me." [8] But he refused and said to his master's wife, "Look, with me here, my master has no concern about anything in the house, and he has put everything that he has in my hand. [9] He is not greater in this house than I am, nor has he kept back anything from me except yourself, because you are his wife. How then could I do this great wickedness, and sin against God?" [10] And although she spoke to Joseph day after day, he would not consent to lie beside her or to be with her. [11] One day, however, when he went into the house to do his work, and while no one else was in the house, [12] she caught hold of his garment, saying, "Lie with me!" But he left his garment in her hand, and fled and ran outside. [13] When she saw that he had left his garment in her hand and had fled outside, [14] she called out to the members of her household and said to them, "See, my husband[a] has brought among us a Hebrew to insult us! He came in to me to lie with me, and I cried out with a loud voice; [15] and when he heard me raise my voice and cry out, he left his garment beside me, and fled outside." [16] Then she kept his garment by her until his master came home, [17] and she told him the same story, saying, "The Hebrew servant, whom you have brought among us, came in to me to insult me; [18] but as soon as I raised my voice and cried out, he left his garment beside me, and fled outside."

[19] When his master heard the words that his wife spoke to him, saying, "This is the way your servant treated me," he became enraged. [20] And Joseph's master took him and put him into the prison, the place where the king's prisoners were confined; he remained there in prison. [21] But the LORD was with Joseph and showed him steadfast love; he gave him favor in the sight of the chief jailer. [22] The chief jailer committed to Joseph's care all the prisoners who were in the prison, and whatever was done there, he was the one who did it. [23] The chief jailer paid no heed to anything that was in Joseph's care, because the LORD was with him; and whatever he did, the LORD made it prosper.

40 Some time after this, the cupbearer of the king of Egypt and his baker offended their lord the king of Egypt. [2] Pharaoh was angry with his two officers, the chief cupbearer and the chief baker, [3] and he put them in custody in the house of the captain of the guard, in the prison where Joseph was confined. [4] The captain of the guard charged Joseph with them, and he waited on them; and they continued for some time in custody. [5] One night they both dreamed—the cupbearer and the baker of the king of Egypt, who were confined in the prison—each his own dream, and each dream with its own meaning. [6] When Joseph came to them in the morning, he saw that they were troubled. [7] So he asked Pharaoh's officers, who were with him in custody in his master's house, "Why are your faces downcast today?" [8] They said to him, "We have had dreams, and there is no one to interpret them." And Joseph said to them, "Do not interpretations belong to God? Please tell them to me."

[9] So the chief cupbearer told his dream to Joseph, and said to him, "In my dream there was a vine before me, [10] and on the vine there were three branches. As soon as it budded, its blossoms came out and the clusters ripened into grapes. [11] Pharaoh's cup was in my hand; and I took the grapes and pressed them into Pharaoh's cup, and placed the cup in Pharaoh's hand." [12] Then Joseph said to him, "This is its interpretation: the three branches are three days; [13] within three days Pharaoh will lift up your head and restore you to your office; and you shall place Pharaoh's cup in his hand, just as you used to do when you were his cupbearer. [14] But remember me when it is well with you; please do me the kindness to make mention of me to Pharaoh, and so get me out of this place. [15] For in fact I was stolen out of the land of the Hebrews; and here also

---

a Heb *he*

laid false accusations against him and almost brought about his death. **12–15:** Again (see 37.31–33), Joseph's *garment* is used as misleading evidence. **14:** *Hebrew*, see 14.13n. **21–23:** Abraham's blessing is again evident here.

40.1–23: Joseph establishes his expertise as dream interpreter. Doubled dreams are a recurring motif in the Joseph narrative (see 37.5–10; 41.1–7,32; 42.9). **13:** *Lift up your head*, i.e., graciously free you from prison (2 Kings 25.27). The same expression is applied ironically to the baker's fate in v. 19. **15:** *Stolen*, 37.28.

I have done nothing that they should have put me into the dungeon." [16] When the chief baker saw that the interpretation was favorable, he said to Joseph, "I also had a dream: there were three cake baskets on my head, [17] and in the uppermost basket there were all sorts of baked food for Pharaoh, but the birds were eating it out of the basket on my head." [18] And Joseph answered, "This is its interpretation: the three baskets are three days; [19] within three days Pharaoh will lift up your head—from you!—and hang you on a pole; and the birds will eat the flesh from you."

[20] On the third day, which was Pharaoh's birthday, he made a feast for all his servants, and lifted up the head of the chief cupbearer and the head of the chief baker among his servants. [21] He restored the chief cupbearer to his cupbearing, and he placed the cup in Pharaoh's hand; [22] but the chief baker he hanged, just as Joseph had interpreted to them. [23] Yet the chief cupbearer did not remember Joseph, but forgot him.

41 After two whole years, Pharaoh dreamed that he was standing by the Nile, [2] and there came up out of the Nile seven sleek and fat cows, and they grazed in the reed grass. [3] Then seven other cows, ugly and thin, came up out of the Nile after them, and stood by the other cows on the bank of the Nile. [4] The ugly and thin cows ate up the seven sleek and fat cows. And Pharaoh awoke. [5] Then he fell asleep and dreamed a second time; seven ears of grain, plump and good, were growing on one stalk. [6] Then seven ears, thin and blighted by the east wind, sprouted after them. [7] The thin ears swallowed up the seven plump and full ears. Pharaoh awoke, and it was a dream. [8] In the morning his spirit was troubled; so he sent and called for all the magicians of Egypt and all its wise men. Pharaoh told them his dreams, but there was no one who could interpret them to Pharaoh.

[9] Then the chief cupbearer said to Pharaoh, "I remember my faults today. [10] Once Pharaoh was angry with his servants, and put me and the chief baker in custody in the house of the captain of the guard. [11] We dreamed on the same night, he and I, each having a dream with its own meaning. [12] A young Hebrew was there with us, a servant of the captain of the guard. When we told him, he interpreted our dreams to us, giving an interpretation to each according to his dream. [13] As he interpreted to us, so it turned out; I was restored to my office, and the baker was hanged."

[14] Then Pharaoh sent for Joseph, and he was hurriedly brought out of the dungeon. When he had shaved himself and changed his clothes, he came in before Pharaoh. [15] And Pharaoh said to Joseph, "I have had a dream, and there is no one who can interpret it. I have heard it said of you that when you hear a dream you can interpret it." [16] Joseph answered Pharaoh, "It is not I; God will give Pharaoh a favorable answer." [17] Then Pharaoh said to Joseph, "In my dream I was standing on the banks of the Nile; [18] and seven cows, fat and sleek, came up out of the Nile and fed in the reed grass. [19] Then seven other cows came up after them, poor, very ugly, and thin. Never had I seen such ugly ones in all the land of Egypt. [20] The thin and ugly cows ate up the first seven fat cows, [21] but when they had eaten them no one would have known that they had done so, for they were still as ugly as before. Then I awoke. [22] I fell asleep a second time[a] and I saw in my dream seven ears of grain, full and good, growing on one stalk, [23] and seven ears, withered, thin, and blighted by the east wind, sprouting after them; [24] and the thin ears swallowed up the seven good ears. But when I told it to the magicians, there was no one who could explain it to me."

[25] Then Joseph said to Pharaoh, "Pharaoh's dreams are one and the same; God has revealed to Pharaoh what he is about to do. [26] The seven good cows are seven years, and the seven good ears are seven years; the dreams are one. [27] The seven lean and ugly cows that came up after them are seven years, as are the seven empty ears blighted by the east wind. They are seven years of

---

[a] Gk Syr Vg: Heb lacks *I fell asleep a second time*

41.1–57: Joseph's elevation as the result of successful dream interpretation. **8:** The narrator intends to demonstrate the superiority of Israel's God over Egyptian magic and wisdom (cf. Ex 8.18–19; 9.11; Dan 2.2–19; 5.8,15–

famine. [28] It is as I told Pharaoh; God has shown to Pharaoh what he is about to do. [29] There will come seven years of great plenty throughout all the land of Egypt. [30] After them there will arise seven years of famine, and all the plenty will be forgotten in the land of Egypt; the famine will consume the land. [31] The plenty will no longer be known in the land because of the famine that will follow, for it will be very grievous. [32] And the doubling of Pharaoh's dream means that the thing is fixed by God, and God will shortly bring it about. [33] Now therefore let Pharaoh select a man who is discerning and wise, and set him over the land of Egypt. [34] Let Pharaoh proceed to appoint overseers over the land, and take one-fifth of the produce of the land of Egypt during the seven plenteous years. [35] Let them gather all the food of these good years that are coming, and lay up grain under the authority of Pharaoh for food in the cities, and let them keep it. [36] That food shall be a reserve for the land against the seven years of famine that are to befall the land of Egypt, so that the land may not perish through the famine."

[37] The proposal pleased Pharaoh and all his servants. [38] Pharaoh said to his servants, "Can we find anyone else like this—one in whom is the spirit of God?" [39] So Pharaoh said to Joseph, "Since God has shown you all this, there is no one so discerning and wise as you. [40] You shall be over my house, and all my people shall order themselves as you command; only with regard to the throne will I be greater than you." [41] And Pharaoh said to Joseph, "See, I have set you over all the land of Egypt." [42] Removing his signet ring from his hand, Pharaoh put it on Joseph's hand; he arrayed him in garments of fine linen, and put a gold chain around his neck. [43] He had him ride in the chariot of his second-in-command; and they cried out in front of him, "Bow the knee!"[a] Thus he set him over all the land of Egypt. [44] Moreover Pharaoh said

to Joseph, "I am Pharaoh, and without your consent no one shall lift up hand or foot in all the land of Egypt." [45] Pharaoh gave Joseph the name Zaphenath-paneah; and he gave him Asenath daughter of Potiphera, priest of On, as his wife. Thus Joseph gained authority over the land of Egypt.

[46] Joseph was thirty years old when he entered the service of Pharaoh king of Egypt. And Joseph went out from the presence of Pharaoh, and went through all the land of Egypt. [47] During the seven plenteous years the earth produced abundantly. [48] He gathered up all the food of the seven years when there was plenty[b] in the land of Egypt, and stored up food in the cities; he stored up in every city the food from the fields around it. [49] So Joseph stored up grain in such abundance— like the sand of the sea—that he stopped measuring it; it was beyond measure.

[50] Before the years of famine came, Joseph had two sons, whom Asenath daughter of Potiphera, priest of On, bore to him. [51] Joseph named the firstborn Manasseh,[c] "For," he said, "God has made me forget all my hardship and all my father's house." [52] The second he named Ephraim,[d] "For God has made me fruitful in the land of my misfortunes."

[53] The seven years of plenty that prevailed in the land of Egypt came to an end; [54] and the seven years of famine began to come, just as Joseph had said. There was famine in every country, but throughout the land of Egypt there was bread. [55] When all the land of Egypt was famished, the people cried to Pharaoh for bread. Pharaoh said to all the Egyptians, "Go to Joseph; what he says to you, do." [56] And since the famine had spread over all the land,

---

a   *Abrek*, apparently an Egyptian word similar in sound to the Hebrew word meaning *to kneel*

b   Sam Gk: MT *the seven years that were*

c   That is *Making to forget*

d   From a Hebrew word meaning *to be fruitful*

---

28). **16:** Joseph denies having any occult art and ascribes his skill solely to God. **42:** *His signet ring* (see 38.18n.) empowered Joseph to act as Pharaoh's representative. **45:** The installation rites culminate in the bestowal of an Egyptian name on Joseph. Joseph's adoption into the Egyptian court is further indicated by his marriage into the priesthood of *On* or Heliopolis. No judgment is attached to this intermarriage with an Egyptian foreigner (see Deut 23.8–9). *Potiphera*, see 37.36n. **46:** This is the first Priestly notice since the outset of the Joseph story (37.2). **50–52:** The birth of Joseph's two sons; see 46.20; ch 48.

Joseph opened all the storehouses,[a] and sold to the Egyptians, for the famine was severe in the land of Egypt. [57] Moreover, all the world came to Joseph in Egypt to buy grain, because the famine became severe throughout the world.

42 When Jacob learned that there was grain in Egypt, he said to his sons, "Why do you keep looking at one another? [2] I have heard," he said, "that there is grain in Egypt; go down and buy grain for us there, that we may live and not die." [3] So ten of Joseph's brothers went down to buy grain in Egypt. [4] But Jacob did not send Joseph's brother Benjamin with his brothers, for he feared that harm might come to him. [5] Thus the sons of Israel were among the other people who came to buy grain, for the famine had reached the land of Canaan.

[6] Now Joseph was governor over the land; it was he who sold to all the people of the land. And Joseph's brothers came and bowed themselves before him with their faces to the ground. [7] When Joseph saw his brothers, he recognized them, but he treated them like strangers and spoke harshly to them. "Where do you come from?" he said. They said, "From the land of Canaan, to buy food." [8] Although Joseph had recognized his brothers, they did not recognize him. [9] Joseph also remembered the dreams that he had dreamed about them. He said to them, "You are spies; you have come to see the nakedness of the land!" [10] They said to him, "No, my lord; your servants have come to buy food. [11] We are all sons of one man; we are honest men; your servants have never been spies." [12] But he said to them, "No, you have come to see the nakedness of the land!" [13] They said, "We, your servants, are twelve brothers, the sons of a certain man in the land of Canaan; the youngest, however, is now with our father, and one is no more.". [14] But Joseph said to them, "It is just as I have

said to you; you are spies! [15] Here is how you shall be tested: as Pharaoh lives, you shall not leave this place unless your youngest brother comes here! [16] Let one of you go and bring your brother, while the rest of you remain in prison, in order that your words may be tested, whether there is truth in you; or else, as Pharaoh lives, surely you are spies." [17] And he put them all together in prison for three days.

[18] On the third day Joseph said to them, "Do this and you will live, for I fear God: [19] if you are honest men, let one of your brothers stay here where you are imprisoned. The rest of you shall go and carry grain for the famine of your households, [20] and bring your youngest brother to me. Thus your words will be verified, and you shall not die." And they agreed to do so. [21] They said to one another, "Alas, we are paying the penalty for what we did to our brother; we saw his anguish when he pleaded with us, but we would not listen. That is why this anguish has come upon us." [22] Then Reuben answered them, "Did I not tell you not to wrong the boy? But you would not listen. So now there comes a reckoning for his blood." [23] They did not know that Joseph understood them, since he spoke with them through an interpreter. [24] He turned away from them and wept; then he returned and spoke to them. And he picked out Simeon and had him bound before their eyes. [25] Joseph then gave orders to fill their bags with grain, to return every man's money to his sack, and to give them provisions for their journey. This was done for them.

[26] They loaded their donkeys with their grain, and departed. [27] When one of them opened his sack to give his donkey fodder at the lodging place, he saw his money at the top of the sack. [28] He said to his brothers, "My money has been put back; here it is in

---

[a] Gk Vg Compare Syr: Heb *opened all that was in* (or, *among*) *them*

42.1–38: Joseph's brothers' first journey to Egypt. **5:** See 12.10; 26.1. **6:** *Bowed themselves before him,* since all but Benjamin are present, Joseph's first dream (37.5–8) is almost fulfilled (cf. 43.26). **9–14:** The charge of spying is natural, since Egypt's frontier, facing Canaan, was vulnerable to attack (Ex 1.10). Nevertheless, the narrator (v. 9) explains Joseph's accusation as related to his memory of his dreams (37.5–11). **15–17:** Though Joseph claims to be "testing" whether his brothers are spies, he actually seems to be "testing" whether they will betray his full brother and father's favorite (v. 4), Benjamin, the way they once betrayed him (see chs 43–44). The reader, however, does not yet know this and is left to wonder about Joseph's motives for putting his brothers through the following ordeal. **21–23:** The brothers' expression of guilt at their earlier betrayal of Joseph hints at the change

my sack!" At this they lost heart and turned trembling to one another, saying, "What is this that God has done to us?"

²⁹ When they came to their father Jacob in the land of Canaan, they told him all that had happened to them, saying, ³⁰ "The man, the lord of the land, spoke harshly to us, and charged us with spying on the land. ³¹ But we said to him, 'We are honest men, we are not spies. ³² We are twelve brothers, sons of our father; one is no more, and the youngest is now with our father in the land of Canaan.' ³³ Then the man, the lord of the land, said to us, 'By this I shall know that you are honest men: leave one of your brothers with me, take grain for the famine of your households, and go your way. ³⁴ Bring your youngest brother to me, and I shall know that you are not spies but honest men. Then I will release your brother to you, and you may trade in the land.'"

³⁵ As they were emptying their sacks, there in each one's sack was his bag of money. When they and their father saw their bundles of money, they were dismayed. ³⁶ And their father Jacob said to them, "I am the one you have bereaved of children: Joseph is no more, and Simeon is no more, and now you would take Benjamin. All this has happened to me!" ³⁷ Then Reuben said to his father, "You may kill my two sons if I do not bring him back to you. Put him in my hands, and I will bring him back to you." ³⁸ But he said, "My son shall not go down with you, for his brother is dead, and he alone is left. If harm should come to him on the journey that you are to make, you would bring down my gray hairs with sorrow to Sheol."

43 Now the famine was severe in the land. ² And when they had eaten up the grain that they had brought from Egypt, their father said to them, "Go again, buy us a little more food." ³ But Judah said to him, "The man solemnly warned us, saying, 'You shall not see my face unless your brother is with you.' ⁴ If you will send our brother with us, we will go down and buy you food; ⁵ but if you will not send him, we will not go down, for the man said to us, 'You shall not see my

face, unless your brother is with you.'" ⁶ Israel said, "Why did you treat me so badly as to tell the man that you had another brother?" ⁷ They replied, "The man questioned us carefully about ourselves and our kindred, saying, 'Is your father still alive? Have you another brother?' What we told him was in answer to these questions. Could we in any way know that he would say, 'Bring your brother down'?" ⁸ Then Judah said to his father Israel, "Send the boy with me, and let us be on our way, so that we may live and not die—you and we and also our little ones. ⁹ I myself will be surety for him; you can hold me accountable for him. If I do not bring him back to you and set him before you, then let me bear the blame forever. ¹⁰ If we had not delayed, we would now have returned twice."

¹¹ Then their father Israel said to them, "If it must be so, then do this: take some of the choice fruits of the land in your bags, and carry them down as a present to the man— a little balm and a little honey, gum, resin, pistachio nuts, and almonds. ¹² Take double the money with you. Carry back with you the money that was returned in the top of your sacks; perhaps it was an oversight. ¹³ Take your brother also, and be on your way again to the man; ¹⁴ may God Almighty[a] grant you mercy before the man, so that he may send back your other brother and Benjamin. As for me, if I am bereaved of my children, I am bereaved." ¹⁵ So the men took the present, and they took double the money with them, as well as Benjamin. Then they went on their way down to Egypt, and stood before Joseph.

¹⁶ When Joseph saw Benjamin with them, he said to the steward of his house, "Bring the men into the house, and slaughter an animal and make ready, for the men are to dine with me at noon." ¹⁷ The man did as Joseph said, and brought the men to Joseph's house. ¹⁸ Now the men were afraid because they were brought to Joseph's house, and they said, "It is because of the money, replaced in

a   Traditional rendering of Heb *El Shaddai*

---

of heart for which Joseph is looking. **25:** *Money,* lit., "silver." **38:** *Sheol,* see 37.35n.

43.1–34: Joseph's brothers' second journey to Egypt. **1–2:** Simeon, left as a hostage in Egypt (vv. 14,23), is apparently forgotten, for the brothers return only when more grain is needed. **3–7:** Cf. 42.29–34. **8–10:** Again (see 37.26–27) *Judah* is depicted as the hero; see 44.18–34n. **11:** *Balm . . . gum,* and *resin,* echoing 37.25. **14:** *God*

our sacks the first time, that we have been brought in, so that he may have an opportunity to fall upon us, to make slaves of us and take our donkeys." ¹⁹ So they went up to the steward of Joseph's house and spoke with him at the entrance to the house. ²⁰ They said, "Oh, my lord, we came down the first time to buy food; ²¹ and when we came to the lodging place we opened our sacks, and there was each one's money in the top of his sack, our money in full weight. So we have brought it back with us. ²² Moreover we have brought down with us additional money to buy food. We do not know who put our money in our sacks." ²³ He replied, "Rest assured, do not be afraid; your God and the God of your father must have put treasure in your sacks for you; I received your money." Then he brought Simeon out to them. ²⁴ When the steward[a] had brought the men into Joseph's house, and given them water, and they had washed their feet, and when he had given their donkeys fodder, ²⁵ they made the present ready for Joseph's coming at noon, for they had heard that they would dine there.

²⁶ When Joseph came home, they brought him the present that they had carried into the house, and bowed to the ground before him. ²⁷ He inquired about their welfare, and said, "Is your father well, the old man of whom you spoke? Is he still alive?" ²⁸ They said, "Your servant our father is well; he is still alive." And they bowed their heads and did obeisance. ²⁹ Then he looked up and saw his brother Benjamin, his mother's son, and said, "Is this your youngest brother, of whom you spoke to me? God be gracious to you, my son!" ³⁰ With that, Joseph hurried out, because he was overcome with affection for his brother, and he was about to weep. So he went into a private

room and wept there. ³¹ Then he washed his face and came out; and controlling himself he said, "Serve the meal." ³² They served him by himself, and them by themselves, and the Egyptians who ate with him by themselves, because the Egyptians could not eat with the Hebrews, for that is an abomination to the Egyptians. ³³ When they were seated before him, the firstborn according to his birthright and the youngest according to his youth, the men looked at one another in amazement. ³⁴ Portions were taken to them from Joseph's table, but Benjamin's portion was five times as much as any of theirs. So they drank and were merry with him.

44 Then he commanded the steward of his house, "Fill the men's sacks with food, as much as they can carry, and put each man's money in the top of his sack. ² Put my cup, the silver cup, in the top of the sack of the youngest, with his money for the grain." And he did as Joseph told him. ³ As soon as the morning was light, the men were sent away with their donkeys. ⁴ When they had gone only a short distance from the city, Joseph said to his steward, "Go, follow after the men; and when you overtake them, say to them, 'Why have you returned evil for good? Why have you stolen my silver cup?[b] ⁵ Is it not from this that my lord drinks? Does he not indeed use it for divination? You have done wrong in doing this.'"

⁶ When he overtook them, he repeated these words to them. ⁷ They said to him, "Why does my lord speak such words as these? Far be it from your servants that they should

---

a Heb *the man*
b Gk Compare Vg: Heb lacks *Why have you stolen my silver cup?*

Almighty, see 17.1n. **23:** The Egyptian steward anticipates the emphasis of the story on divine providence (44.16; 45.5–8; 50.20). **26:** With all eleven brothers now bowing down (cf. v. 15), they unknowingly fulfill the first dream in 37.5–8 (see 50.18n.). **29–30:** Joseph *was overcome with affection* for Benjamin, his only full brother (through Rachel). **34:** Just as Benjamin (42.4,38; 43.6–14) and before him Joseph (37.3–4) was favored by Jacob, so here—through Joseph's actions—the brothers watch a son of Rachel enjoy special privilege in the Egyptian court. The stage is set for a reprise of their murderous envy once shown toward Joseph in Gen 37 and now potentially directed at Benjamin.

44.1–34: Joseph's final test of his brothers. 1–5: Here the focus is on Joseph's cup, a sacred vessel for divination, prediction of the future (cf. 42.25–28). The brothers' (unknowing) taking of the cup and pronouncement of a death penalty on the thief (v. 9) echo the earlier story of Rachel's stealing of Laban's household gods (31.19) and Jacob's pronouncement of the death penalty on the thief (31.32). In a narrative that parallels those stories,

do such a thing! [8] Look, the money that we found at the top of our sacks, we brought back to you from the land of Canaan; why then would we steal silver or gold from your lord's house? [9] Should it be found with any one of your servants, let him die; moreover the rest of us will become my lord's slaves." [10] He said, "Even so; in accordance with your words, let it be: he with whom it is found shall become my slave, but the rest of you shall go free." [11] Then each one quickly lowered his sack to the ground, and each opened his sack. [12] He searched, beginning with the eldest and ending with the youngest; and the cup was found in Benjamin's sack. [13] At this they tore their clothes. Then each one loaded his donkey, and they returned to the city.

[14] Judah and his brothers came to Joseph's house while he was still there; and they fell to the ground before him. [15] Joseph said to them, "What deed is this that you have done? Do you not know that one such as I can practice divination?" [16] And Judah said, "What can we say to my lord? What can we speak? How can we clear ourselves? God has found out the guilt of your servants; here we are then, my lord's slaves, both we and also the one in whose possession the cup has been found." [17] But he said, "Far be it from me that I should do so! Only the one in whose possession the cup was found shall be my slave; but as for you, go up in peace to your father."

[18] Then Judah stepped up to him and said, "O my lord, let your servant please speak a word in my lord's ears, and do not be angry with your servant; for you are like Pharaoh himself. [19] My lord asked his servants, saying, 'Have you a father or a brother?' [20] And we said to my lord, 'We have a father, an old man, and a young brother, the child of his old age. His brother is dead; he alone is left of his mother's children, and his father loves him.' [21] Then you said to your servants, 'Bring him down to me, so that I may set my eyes on him.' [22] We said to my lord, 'The boy cannot leave his father, for if he should leave his father, his father would die.' [23] Then you said to your servants, 'Unless your youngest brother comes down with you, you shall see my face no more.' [24] When we went back to your servant my father we told him the words of my lord. [25] And when our father said, 'Go again, buy us a little food,' [26] we said, 'We cannot go down. Only if our youngest brother goes with us, will we go down; for we cannot see the man's face unless our youngest brother is with us.' [27] Then your servant my father said to us, 'You know that my wife bore me two sons; [28] one left me, and I said, Surely he has been torn to pieces; and I have never seen him since. [29] If you take this one also from me, and harm comes to him, you will bring down my gray hairs in sorrow to Sheol.' [30] Now therefore, when I come to your servant my father and the boy is not with us, then, as his life is bound up in the boy's life, [31] when he sees that the boy is not with us, he will die; and your servants will bring down the gray hairs of your servant our father with sorrow to Sheol. [32] For your servant became surety for the boy to my father, saying, 'If I do not bring him back to you, then I will bear the blame in the sight of my father all my life.' [33] Now therefore, please let your servant remain as a slave to my lord in place of the boy; and let the boy go back with his brothers. [34] For how can I go back to my father if the boy is not with me? I fear to see the suffering that would come upon my father."

45 Then Joseph could no longer control himself before all those who stood by him, and he cried out, "Send everyone away

Joseph lays a trap for his brothers. **17**: Joseph tests his brothers (see 42.15–17) to see whether they will let Benjamin go into slavery as they once did with him (37.25–35). In this case, the stakes are higher, since the brothers now think that they themselves will go into slavery if they do not betray Benjamin. **18–34**: Judah had secured Jacob's release of Benjamin through offering himself as collateral (43.8–10; see v. 32). Now he steps forth to express a respect for their father's bond to Rachel's son(s) that had not been evident among the brothers before (cf. 37.19–35). This is a prime example of a passage in the Joseph narrative where Judah, rather than the elder Reuben, plays the role of the most powerful and prominent son (see also 37.26–27; ch 38; 43.3–5,8–10; 46.28). Such texts have typically been assigned to a Judah-Israel (or J) layer of the story (see Introduction and 37.1–11n.), but may rather reflect an attempt in the Joseph story as a whole (perhaps an early Northern text) to show even Judah, King David's ancestor, eventually recognizing Joseph's right to rule over his brothers.

from me." So no one stayed with him when Joseph made himself known to his brothers. ² And he wept so loudly that the Egyptians heard it, and the household of Pharaoh heard it. ³ Joseph said to his brothers, "I am Joseph. Is my father still alive?" But his brothers could not answer him, so dismayed were they at his presence.

⁴ Then Joseph said to his brothers, "Come closer to me." And they came closer. He said, "I am your brother, Joseph, whom you sold into Egypt. ⁵ And now do not be distressed, or angry with yourselves, because you sold me here; for God sent me before you to preserve life. ⁶ For the famine has been in the land these two years; and there are five more years in which there will be neither plowing nor harvest. ⁷ God sent me before you to preserve for you a remnant on earth, and to keep alive for you many survivors. ⁸ So it was not you who sent me here, but God; he has made me a father to Pharaoh, and lord of all his house and ruler over all the land of Egypt. ⁹ Hurry and go up to my father and say to him, 'Thus says your son Joseph, God has made me lord of all Egypt; come down to me, do not delay. ¹⁰ You shall settle in the land of Goshen, and you shall be near me, you and your children and your children's children, as well as your flocks, your herds, and all that you have. ¹¹ I will provide for you there—since there are five more years of famine to come—so that you and your household, and all that you have, will not come to poverty.' ¹² And now your eyes and the eyes of my brother Benjamin see that it is my own mouth that speaks to you. ¹³ You must tell my father how greatly I am honored in Egypt, and all that you have seen. Hurry and bring my father down here." ¹⁴ Then he fell upon his brother Benjamin's neck and wept, while Benjamin wept upon his neck. ¹⁵ And he kissed all his brothers and wept upon them; and after that his brothers talked with him.

¹⁶ When the report was heard in Pharaoh's house, "Joseph's brothers have come," Pharaoh and his servants were pleased. ¹⁷ Pharaoh said to Joseph, "Say to your brothers, 'Do this: load your animals and go back to the land of Canaan. ¹⁸ Take your father and your households and come to me, so that I may give you the best of the land of Egypt, and you may enjoy the fat of the land.' ¹⁹ You are further charged to say, 'Do this: take wagons from the land of Egypt for your little ones and for your wives, and bring your father, and come. ²⁰ Give no thought to your possessions, for the best of all the land of Egypt is yours.'"

²¹ The sons of Israel did so. Joseph gave them wagons according to the instruction of Pharaoh, and he gave them provisions for the journey. ²² To each one of them he gave a set of garments; but to Benjamin he gave three hundred pieces of silver and five sets of garments. ²³ To his father he sent the following: ten donkeys loaded with the good things of Egypt, and ten female donkeys loaded with grain, bread, and provision for his father on the journey. ²⁴ Then he sent his brothers on their way, and as they were leaving he said to them, "Do not quarrel[a] along the way."

²⁵ So they went up out of Egypt and came to their father Jacob in the land of Canaan. ²⁶ And they told him, "Joseph is still alive! He is even ruler over all the land of Egypt." He was stunned; he could not believe them. ²⁷ But when they told him all the words of Joseph that he had said to them, and when he saw the wagons that Joseph had sent to carry him, the spirit of their father Jacob revived. ²⁸ Israel said, "Enough! My son Joseph is still alive. I must go and see him before I die."

46 When Israel set out on his journey with all that he had and came to Beersheba, he offered sacrifices to the God of his father Isaac. ² God spoke to Israel in visions

---

a   Or *be agitated*

45.1–28: Joseph makes himself known to his brothers and father. 1–3: The brothers initially react with shock to the knowledge that they face the brother whom they sold into slavery. 4–13: Joseph reassures his brothers by telling them that God—not they—sent him into slavery. God sent him there so that he might feed his family in the famine. 10: *The land of Goshen,* probably located in the eastern Nile Delta. 16–20: Asiatics are frequently attested as living in Egypt, though no Egyptian records refer specifically to the Israelites living there.

46.1–27: Jacob's migration to Egypt. 1–4: Jacob's first stop on the way out of the land is *Beer-sheba,* where the same God who told Isaac to stay in the land and not to go to Egypt (26.2–3) now tells his son, Jacob, to leave

of the night, and said, "Jacob, Jacob." And he said, "Here I am." [3] Then he said, "I am God,[a] the God of your father; do not be afraid to go down to Egypt, for I will make of you a great nation there. [4] I myself will go down with you to Egypt, and I will also bring you up again; and Joseph's own hand shall close your eyes."

[5] Then Jacob set out from Beer-sheba; and the sons of Israel carried their father Jacob, their little ones, and their wives, in the wagons that Pharaoh had sent to carry him. [6] They also took their livestock and the goods that they had acquired in the land of Canaan, and they came into Egypt, Jacob and all his offspring with him, [7] his sons, and his sons' sons with him, his daughters, and his sons' daughters; all his offspring he brought with him into Egypt.

[8] Now these are the names of the Israelites, Jacob and his offspring, who came to Egypt. Reuben, Jacob's firstborn, [9] and the children of Reuben: Hanoch, Pallu, Hezron, and Carmi. [10] The children of Simeon: Jemuel, Jamin, Ohad, Jachin, Zohar, and Shaul,[b] the son of a Canaanite woman. [11] The children of Levi: Gershon, Kohath, and Merari. [12] The children of Judah: Er, Onan, Shelah, Perez, and Zerah (but Er and Onan died in the land of Canaan); and the children of Perez were Hezron and Hamul. [13] The children of Issachar: Tola, Puvah, Jashub,[c] and Shimron. [14] The children of Zebulun: Sered, Elon, and Jahleel [15] (these are the sons of Leah, whom she bore to Jacob in Paddan-aram, together with his daughter Dinah; in all his sons and his daughters numbered thirty-three). [16] The children of Gad: Ziphion, Haggi, Shuni, Ezbon, Eri, Arodi, and Areli. [17] The children of Asher: Imnah, Ishvah, Ishvi, Beriah, and their sister Serah. The children of Beriah: Heber and Malchiel [18] (these are the children of Zilpah, whom Laban gave to his daughter Leah; and these she bore to Jacob—sixteen persons). [19] The children of Jacob's wife Rachel: Joseph and Benjamin. [20] To Joseph in the land of Egypt were born Manasseh and Ephraim, whom Asenath daughter

of Potiphera, priest of On, bore to him. [21] The children of Benjamin: Bela, Becher, Ashbel, Gera, Naaman, Ehi, Rosh, Muppim, Huppim, and Ard [22] (these are the children of Rachel, who were born to Jacob—fourteen persons in all). [23] The children of Dan: Hashum.[d] [24] The children of Naphtali: Jahzeel, Guni, Jezer, and Shillem [25] (these are the children of Bilhah, whom Laban gave to his daughter Rachel, and these she bore to Jacob—seven persons in all). [26] All the persons belonging to Jacob who came into Egypt, who were his own offspring, not including the wives of his sons, were sixty-six persons in all. [27] The children of Joseph, who were born to him in Egypt, were two; all the persons of the house of Jacob who came into Egypt were seventy.

[28] Israel[e] sent Judah ahead to Joseph to lead the way before him into Goshen. When they came to the land of Goshen, [29] Joseph made ready his chariot and went up to meet his father Israel in Goshen. He presented himself to him, fell on his neck, and wept on his neck a good while. [30] Israel said to Joseph, "I can die now, having seen for myself that you are still alive." [31] Joseph said to his brothers and to his father's household, "I will go up and tell Pharaoh, and will say to him, 'My brothers and my father's household, who were in the land of Canaan, have come to me. [32] The men are shepherds, for they have been keepers of livestock; and they have brought their flocks, and their herds, and all that they have.' [33] When Pharaoh calls you, and says, 'What is your occupation?' [34] you shall say, 'Your servants have been keepers of livestock from our youth even until now, both we and our ancestors'—in order that you may settle in the land of Goshen, because all shepherds are abhorrent to the Egyptians."

a Heb *the God*
b Or *Saul*
c Compare Sam Gk Num 26.24; 1 Chr 7.1: MT *Iob*
d Gk: Heb *Hushim*
e Heb *He*

the land for Egypt (see 12.1–3n.; 28.13–15n.). God also expands the earlier promise that Abraham would be a *great nation* (see 12.2n.) by saying that God will make Jacob a great nation in *Egypt* (v. 3; see 47.27; Ex 1.7,9). **8–27:** A Priestly section listing Jacob's descendants by their mothers, using the traditional number seventy (v. 27; Ex 1.5; Deut 10.22). Most names of the clan leaders are in the Priestly list in Num 26. **12:** See ch 38.

46.28–47.28: Jacob's family settles in Egypt. **46.34:** *All shepherds are abhorrent,* there is no nonbiblical evi-

47 So Joseph went and told Pharaoh, "My father and my brothers, with their flocks and herds and all that they possess, have come from the land of Canaan; they are now in the land of Goshen." [2] From among his brothers he took five men and presented them to Pharaoh. [3] Pharaoh said to his brothers, "What is your occupation?" And they said to Pharaoh, "Your servants are shepherds, as our ancestors were." [4] They said to Pharaoh, "We have come to reside as aliens in the land; for there is no pasture for your servants' flocks because the famine is severe in the land of Canaan. Now, we ask you, let your servants settle in the land of Goshen." [5] Then Pharaoh said to Joseph, "Your father and your brothers have come to you. [6] The land of Egypt is before you; settle your father and your brothers in the best part of the land; let them live in the land of Goshen; and if you know that there are capable men among them, put them in charge of my livestock."

[7] Then Joseph brought in his father Jacob, and presented him before Pharaoh, and Jacob blessed Pharaoh. [8] Pharaoh said to Jacob, "How many are the years of your life?" [9] Jacob said to Pharaoh, "The years of my earthly sojourn are one hundred thirty; few and hard have been the years of my life. They do not compare with the years of the life of my ancestors during their long sojourn." [10] Then Jacob blessed Pharaoh, and went out from the presence of Pharaoh. [11] Joseph settled his father and his brothers, and granted them a holding in the land of Egypt, in the best part of the land, in the land of Rameses, as Pharaoh had instructed. [12] And Joseph provided his father, his brothers, and all his father's household with food, according to the number of their dependents.

[13] Now there was no food in all the land, for the famine was very severe. The land of Egypt and the land of Canaan languished because of the famine. [14] Joseph collected all the money to be found in the land of Egypt and in the land of Canaan, in exchange for the grain that they bought; and Joseph brought the money into Pharaoh's house. [15] When the money from the land of Egypt and from the land of Canaan was spent, all the Egyptians came to Joseph, and said, "Give us food! Why should we die before your eyes? For our money is gone." [16] And Joseph answered, "Give me your livestock, and I will give you food in exchange for your livestock, if your money is gone." [17] So they brought their livestock to Joseph; and Joseph gave them food in exchange for the horses, the flocks, the herds, and the donkeys. That year he supplied them with food in exchange for all their livestock. [18] When that year was ended, they came to him the following year, and said to him, "We can not hide from my lord that our money is all spent; and the herds of cattle are my lord's. There is nothing left in the sight of my lord but our bodies and our lands. [19] Shall we die before your eyes, both we and our land? Buy us and our land in exchange for food. We with our land will become slaves to Pharaoh; just give us seed, so that we may live and not die, and that the land may not become desolate."

[20] So Joseph bought all the land of Egypt for Pharaoh. All the Egyptians sold their fields, because the famine was severe upon them; and the land became Pharaoh's. [21] As for the people, he made slaves of them[a] from one end of Egypt to the other. [22] Only the land of the priests he did not buy; for the priests had a fixed allowance from Pharaoh, and lived on the allowance that Pharaoh gave them; therefore they did not sell their land. [23] Then Joseph said to the people, "Now that I have this day bought you and your land for Pharaoh, here is seed for you; sow the land. [24] And at the harvests you shall give one-fifth to Pharaoh, and four-fifths shall be your own, as seed for the field and as food for yourselves and your households, and as food for your little ones." [25] They said, "You have saved our lives; may it please my lord, we will be slaves to Pharaoh." [26] So Joseph made it a statute concerning the land of Egypt, and it stands to this day, that Pharaoh should have

[a] Sam Gk Compare Vg: MT *He removed them to the cities*

dence for this assertion. **47.7,12:** According to this Priestly tradition, *Jacob blessed Pharaoh.* **11:** A Priestly notice. *The land of Rameses* cannot be identified with certainty. The first Egyptian pharaoh with that name ruled at the beginning of the thirteenth century BCE. **13–26:** Joseph's clever impoverishment of the Egyptians here contrasts

the fifth. The land of the priests alone did not become Pharaoh's.

27 Thus Israel settled in the land of Egypt, in the region of Goshen; and they gained possessions in it, and were fruitful and multiplied exceedingly. 28 Jacob lived in the land of Egypt seventeen years; so the days of Jacob, the years of his life, were one hundred forty-seven years.

29 When the time of Israel's death drew near, he called his son Joseph and said to him, "If I have found favor with you, put your hand under my thigh and promise to deal loyally and truly with me. Do not bury me in Egypt. 30 When I lie down with my ancestors, carry me out of Egypt and bury me in their burial place." He answered, "I will do as you have said." 31 And he said, "Swear to me"; and he swore to him. Then Israel bowed himself on the head of his bed.

48 After this Joseph was told, "Your father is ill." So he took with him his two sons, Manasseh and Ephraim. 2 When Jacob was told, "Your son Joseph has come to you," he[a] summoned his strength and sat up in bed. 3 And Jacob said to Joseph, "God Almighty[b] appeared to me at Luz in the land of Canaan, and he blessed me, 4 and said to me, 'I am going to make you fruitful and increase your numbers; I will make of you a company of peoples, and will give this land to your offspring after you for a perpetual holding.' 5 Therefore your two sons, who were born to you in the land of Egypt before I came to you in Egypt, are now mine; Ephraim and Manasseh shall be mine, just as Reuben and Simeon are. 6 As

for the offspring born to you after them, they shall be yours. They shall be recorded under the names of their brothers with regard to their inheritance. 7 For when I came from Paddan, Rachel, alas, died in the land of Canaan on the way, while there was still some distance to go to Ephrath; and I buried her there on the way to Ephrath" (that is, Bethlehem).

8 When Israel saw Joseph's sons, he said, "Who are these?" 9 Joseph said to his father, "They are my sons, whom God has given me here." And he said, "Bring them to me, please, that I may bless them." 10 Now the eyes of Israel were dim with age, and he could not see well. So Joseph brought them near him; and he kissed them and embraced them. 11 Israel said to Joseph, "I did not expect to see your face; and here God has let me see your children also." 12 Then Joseph removed them from his father's knees,[c] and he bowed himself with his face to the earth. 13 Joseph took them both, Ephraim in his right hand toward Israel's left, and Manasseh in his left hand toward Israel's right, and brought them near him. 14 But Israel stretched out his right hand and laid it on the head of Ephraim, who was the younger, and his left hand on the head of Manasseh, crossing his hands, for Manasseh was the firstborn. 15 He blessed Joseph, and said,

"The God before whom my ancestors
    Abraham and Isaac walked,

a Heb *Israel*
b Traditional rendering of Heb *El Shaddai*
c Heb *from his knees*

with his beneficent provision for his own family (see 45.5–11; 50.20–21). **27–28:** Another fragment from P. Here the Priestly fertility promise to Abraham (17.2,6; cf. 1.28; 9.1,7) is fulfilled in Egypt. **27:** *Goshen,* see 45.10n.

47.29–49.33: Jacob's preparations for death, including the adoption and blessing of Ephraim and Manasseh. This section is viewed by many scholars as a series of later insertions into the Joseph story, linking it back to the Jacob story and forward to the story of the Israelites. **47.29:** *Put your hand under my thigh,* see 24.2n. **30–31:** Joseph binds himself by oath to bury Jacob in an ancestral burial place, perhaps in Transjordan (see 50.10n.). This non-Priestly notice parallels the Priestly notice where Jacob orders his sons to bury him in the cave at Machpelah (49.29–33; see ch 23). **48.3–6:** This Priestly narrative refers to the Priestly Bethel (Luz) account (35.9–13) in describing Jacob's adoption of his two grandsons by Joseph. The narrative accounts for the division of the "house of Joseph" (Josh 17.17; 18.5; Judg 1.23,35) into two tribes, Manasseh and Ephraim. **7:** 35.16–20. **8–14:** In having Jacob favor the younger son, Ephraim, over the older, Manasseh, this non-Priestly narrative echoes the previous accounts of Jacob's achievement of ascendancy over Esau (25.22–34; 27.1–45). Like the older Joseph story into which this scene is inserted (see 47.28–49.33n.), this section may intend to predict the Ephraimite Jeroboam's ascendancy over the Northern Kingdom (1 Kings 11.26; 12.1–14.20; see 37.5–8n.). **10:** Cf. 27.1. **15–16:** Jacob passes

the God who has been my shepherd all my
life to this day,
[16] the angel who has redeemed me from all
harm, bless the boys;
and in them let my name be perpetuated,
and the name of my ancestors
Abraham and Isaac;
and let them grow into a multitude on the
earth."
[17] When Joseph saw that his father laid his
right hand on the head of Ephraim, it displeased him; so he took his father's hand, to
remove it from Ephraim's head to Manasseh's
head. [18] Joseph said to his father, "Not so, my
father! Since this one is the firstborn, put
your right hand on his head." [19] But his father
refused, and said, "I know, my son, I know; he
also shall become a people, and he also shall
be great. Nevertheless his younger brother
shall be greater than he, and his offspring
shall become a multitude of nations." [20] So he
blessed them that day, saying,

"By you[a] Israel will invoke blessings,
saying,
'God make you[a] like Ephraim and like
Manasseh.'"
So he put Ephraim ahead of Manasseh.
[21] Then Israel said to Joseph, "I am about to
die, but God will be with you and will bring
you again to the land of your ancestors. [22] I
now give to you one portion[b] more than to
your brothers, the portion[b] that I took from
the hand of the Amorites with my sword and
with my bow."

49

Then Jacob called his sons, and said:
"Gather around, that I may tell you
what will happen to you in days to come.
[2] Assemble and hear, O sons of Jacob;
listen to Israel your father.

[3] Reuben, you are my firstborn,
my might and the first fruits of my
vigor,
excelling in rank and excelling in
power.
[4] Unstable as water, you shall no longer
excel
because you went up onto your father's
bed;
then you defiled it—you[c] went up onto
my couch!

[5] Simeon and Levi are brothers;
weapons of violence are their
swords.
[6] May I never come into their council;
may I not be joined to their
company—
for in their anger they killed men,
and at their whim they hamstrung
oxen.
[7] Cursed be their anger, for it is fierce,
and their wrath, for it is cruel!

[a] *you* here is singular in Heb
[b] Or *mountain slope* (Heb *shekem*, a play on the
name of the town and district of Shechem)
[c] Gk Syr Tg: Heb *he*

onto the Joseph tribes the special blessing of Abraham and Isaac (12.1–3; 26.2–5; etc.). **17–19:** See 8–14n. **20:** This
older version of the blessing on Ephraim and Manasseh (cf. vv. 15–16) is an example of people "blessing themselves by" another (see 12.3n.). **22:** In Hebrew *one portion* (or "shoulder," Heb "shekem") is a play on the name
"Shechem" (see 12.6n.). *With my sword and with my bow,* cf. 33.19–34.31. *Amorites,* see 10.16–18a n.
49.1–28: Jacob's blessing on his twelve sons. Though the poem is depicted as a deathbed *blessing* by the
text following it (49.28; cf. 27.4 and n.), this poem seems to have been originally designed as a prediction of
the destinies, good and bad, of the tribes of Israel. Many scholars have argued that the poem is ancient on the
basis of its language and resemblance to tribal poems in Deut 33 and Judg 5. Nevertheless, the present form
of the poem appears to have been modified to fit the narrative context in which it has been put. Its first part
follows the birth order of 29.31–35 and legitimates rule for Judah and—by extension—the Davidic dynasty. The
author of these changes may be responsible for inserting the whole poem into its present context, as well as
for the addition to the Jacob-Joseph story of the narratives referred to in 49.3–7 (30.21; 34.1–31; 35.21–22a; cf.
37.36–38.30). **3–4:** This section justifies Reuben's ejection from favor as firstborn by recalling the story of his
sleeping with his father's concubine (see 35.22n.). **5–7:** Judah's older brothers, Simeon and Levi, fail to take Reuben's place because of their role in the despoiling of Shechem (34.25–31). **8–12:** With his three older brothers
out of favor (vv. 3–7), Judah receives the greatest part of his father's blessing. The narrative of the succession
to David features a similar displacement of older sons: Amnon (2 Sam 13), Absalom (2 Sam 15–18), and Adonijah

I will divide them in Jacob,
    and scatter them in Israel.

[8] Judah, your brothers shall praise you;
    your hand shall be on the neck of your
        enemies;
    your father's sons shall bow down
        before you.
[9] Judah is a lion's whelp;
    from the prey, my son, you have gone
        up.
He crouches down, he stretches out like a
        lion,
    like a lioness—who dares rouse him
        up?
[10] The scepter shall not depart from Judah,
    nor the ruler's staff from between his
        feet,
until tribute comes to him;[a]
    and the obedience of the peoples is his.
[11] Binding his foal to the vine
    and his donkey's colt to the choice vine,
he washes his garments in wine
    and his robe in the blood of grapes;
[12] his eyes are darker than wine,
    and his teeth whiter than milk.

[13] Zebulun shall settle at the shore of the sea;
    he shall be a haven for ships,
    and his border shall be at Sidon.

[14] Issachar is a strong donkey,
    lying down between the sheepfolds;
[15] he saw that a resting place was good,
    and that the land was pleasant;
so he bowed his shoulder to the burden,
    and became a slave at forced labor.

[16] Dan shall judge his people
    as one of the tribes of Israel.
[17] Dan shall be a snake by the roadside,
    a viper along the path,

that bites the horse's heels
    so that its rider falls backward.

[18] I wait for your salvation, O LORD.

[19] Gad shall be raided by raiders,
    but he shall raid at their heels.

[20] Asher's[b] food shall be rich,
    and he shall provide royal
        delicacies.

[21] Naphtali is a doe let loose
    that bears lovely fawns.[c]

[22] Joseph is a fruitful bough,
    a fruitful bough by a spring;
    his branches run over the wall.[d]
[23] The archers fiercely attacked him;
    they shot at him and pressed him
        hard.
[24] Yet his bow remained taut,
    and his arms[e] were made agile
by the hands of the Mighty One
        of Jacob,
    by the name of the Shepherd, the Rock
        of Israel,
[25] by the God of your father, who will help
        you,
    by the Almighty[f] who will bless you
with blessings of heaven above,
blessings of the deep that lies beneath,
    blessings of the breasts and of the
        womb.

---

[a] Or until *Shiloh* comes or until he comes to *Shiloh* or
     (with Syr) *until he comes to whom it belongs*
[b] Gk Vg Syr: Heb *From Asher*
[c] Or *that gives beautiful words*
[d] Meaning of Heb uncertain
[e] Heb *the arms of his hands*
[f] Traditional rendering of Heb *Shaddai*

(1 Kings 1–2). See 38.27–30n. **10:** The *scepter* and *staff* are symbols of sovereignty. The latter part of the verse, however, is obscure (see note *a*). It appears to predict rule for Judean royalty until Judah's Davidic descendants achieve universal dominion (Num 24.17; Pss 2, 110) and is therefore preexilic. **13–27:** This latter part of the blessing (vv. 13–27) diverges from the birth order of 30.1–24. This section appears to predate placement into its present context in the story of Jacob and Joseph. **16:** The tribal name *Dan* is derived from the Hebrew verb for "judge" ("dan"). **18:** Probably a late scribal addition; cf. Ps 119.166. **22–26:** The lengthy blessing on Joseph and its triumphant conclusion (v. 26) suggest that he may have been the original focus of the early blessing (see 49.1–28n.). **25:** *The Almighty,* see 17.1n. *Blessings of heaven,* i.e., rain, dew, sun. *The deep that lies beneath,* an allusion to the subterranean ocean (see 1.6; 2.6). Compare Deut 33.13.

26 The blessings of your father
are stronger than the blessings of the
eternal mountains,
the bounties[a] of the everlasting hills;
may they be on the head of Joseph,
on the brow of him who was set apart
from his brothers.

27 Benjamin is a ravenous wolf,
in the morning devouring the prey,
and at evening dividing the spoil."

28 All these are the twelve tribes of Israel, and this is what their father said to them when he blessed them, blessing each one of them with a suitable blessing. 29 Then he charged them, saying to them, "I am about to be gathered to my people. Bury me with my ancestors—in the cave in the field of Ephron the Hittite, 30 in the cave in the field at Machpelah, near Mamre, in the land of Canaan, in the field that Abraham bought from Ephron the Hittite as a burial site. 31 There Abraham and his wife Sarah were buried; there Isaac and his wife Rebekah were buried; and there I buried Leah— 32 the field and the cave that is in it were purchased from the Hittites." 33 When Jacob ended his charge to his sons, he drew up his feet into the bed, breathed his last, and was gathered to his people.

50 Then Joseph threw himself on his father's face and wept over him and kissed him. 2 Joseph commanded the physicians in his service to embalm his father. So the physicians embalmed Israel; 3 they spent forty days in doing this, for that is the time required for embalming. And the Egyptians wept for him seventy days.

4 When the days of weeping for him were past, Joseph addressed the household of Pharaoh, "If now I have found favor with you, please speak to Pharaoh as follows: 5 My father made me swear an oath; he said, 'I am about to die. In the tomb that I hewed out for myself in the land of Canaan, there you shall bury me.' Now therefore let me go up, so that I may bury my father; then I will return." 6 Pharaoh answered, "Go up, and bury your father, as he made you swear to do."

7 So Joseph went up to bury his father. With him went up all the servants of Pharaoh, the elders of his household, and all the elders of the land of Egypt, 8 as well as all the household of Joseph, his brothers, and his father's household. Only their children, their flocks, and their herds were left in the land of Goshen. 9 Both chariots and charioteers went up with him. It was a very great company. 10 When they came to the threshing floor of Atad, which is beyond the Jordan, they held there a very great and sorrowful lamentation; and he observed a time of mourning for his father seven days. 11 When the Canaanite inhabitants of the land saw the mourning on the threshing floor of Atad, they said, "This is a grievous mourning on the part of the Egyptians." Therefore the place was named Abel-mizraim;[b] it is beyond the Jordan. 12 Thus his sons did for him as he had instructed them. 13 They carried him to the land of Canaan and buried him in the cave of the field at Machpelah, the field near Mamre, which Abraham bought as a burial site from Ephron the Hittite. 14 After he had buried his father, Joseph returned to Egypt with his brothers and all who had gone up with him to bury his father.

15 Realizing that their father was dead, Joseph's brothers said, "What if Joseph still bears a grudge against us and pays us back in full for all the wrong that we did to him?"

a   Cn Compare Gk: Heb *of my progenitors to the boundaries*
b   That is *mourning* (or *meadow*) *of Egypt*

49.29–33: This Priestly section includes an order to bury Jacob at Machpelah (see ch 23) that parallels the earlier non-Priestly burial order (47.29–31).

50.1–26: Burial of Jacob and final days of Joseph. 1–11: This non-Priestly narrative seems to presuppose that the burial and mourning occurred in Transjordan, not at the cave at Machpelah (23.1,19). **2–3:** Jacob is provided with Egyptian honors: embalming and lengthy mourning. **5:** This speech by Joseph links to the non-Priestly order to bury him at an ancestral burial place, here a tomb that Jacob had hewn out for himself (see 47.30–31n.). **10:** Hebron/Mamre (see v. 13) is much closer to Egypt than this unidentified location in Transjordan. **12–13:** The Priestly narrative. **15–16:** In fear now that their father is dead (cf. 27.41 and 33.12–17n.), Joseph's brothers attempt

[16] So they approached[a] Joseph, saying, "Your father gave this instruction before he died, [17] 'Say to Joseph: I beg you, forgive the crime of your brothers and the wrong they did in harming you.' Now therefore please forgive the crime of the servants of the God of your father." Joseph wept when they spoke to him. [18] Then his brothers also wept,[b] fell down before him, and said, "We are here as your slaves." [19] But Joseph said to them, "Do not be afraid! Am I in the place of God? [20] Even though you intended to do harm to me, God intended it for good, in order to preserve a numerous people, as he is doing today. [21] So have no fear; I myself will provide for you and your little ones." In this way he reassured them, speaking kindly to them.

[22] So Joseph remained in Egypt, he and his father's household; and Joseph lived one hundred ten years. [23] Joseph saw Ephraim's children of the third generation; the children of Machir son of Manasseh were also born on Joseph's knees.

[24] Then Joseph said to his brothers, "I am about to die; but God will surely come to you, and bring you up out of this land to the land that he swore to Abraham, to Isaac, and to Jacob." [25] So Joseph made the Israelites swear, saying, "When God comes to you, you shall carry up my bones from here." [26] And Joseph died, being one hundred ten years old; he was embalmed and placed in a coffin in Egypt.

a   Gk Syr: Heb *they commanded*
b   Cn: Heb *also came*

to protect themselves through reporting that Jacob had ordered Joseph to forgive them (vv. 16–17). **18–21:** For the first time, the brothers knowingly subject themselves to Joseph (cf. 43.26), fulfilling Joseph's first dream (37.5–7) and thus refuting their challenge of his destiny to rule them (37.8). Since they had just spoken of themselves as God's slaves (v. 17; translated in the NRSV as *servants*), their description of themselves here as Joseph's slaves implicitly equates him with God. Echoing his father's words to Rachel (30.2), Joseph rejects this equation, attributing his dominion over his brothers as resulting from God's plan. Later readers could have taken this as an implicit endorsement of the divine destiny of Joseph's descendants—such as the Ephraimite king Jeroboam (1 Kings 11.26)—to rule over the other tribes. **23:** *Machir* was an early tribal group (Judg 5.14), later viewed as a clan within Manasseh that laid claim to Gilead (Num 32.39–40; Deut 3.15). *Born on Joseph's knees,* see 30.3. **24:** A reference to God's covenant oath to give the land to Abraham (15.9–17n.; 22.15–18). It closely resembles similar texts in Deut 1.8; 6.10 and related materials. **25:** This request will be fulfilled in Ex 13.19; Josh 24.2, one of the links between Genesis and the narrative extending to the end of Joshua.

EXODUS

NAME

The English name "Exodus" derives from a Latinized abbreviation of the Greek title *exodos aigyptou* ("exit from Egypt"); this title highlights the storyline of the first third of the book. In keeping with the ancient practice of naming books after their opening words, the Hebrew title is *Shemot* ("names"), taken from the beginning ("These are the names").

CANONICAL STATUS AND LOCATION

The second book of the Bible in all canonical traditions, Exodus is not an independent work but rather is an integral part of the Torah, or Pentateuch. Its opening verses connect it to Gen 46.8–27; and it closes with the completion of the tabernacle, the wilderness shrine that prefigures the Temple and its endowment with the divine presence. Details of worship at that shrine dominate the next book, Leviticus; and Numbers and Deuteronomy continue the journey narrative.

AUTHORSHIP

Traditional authorship is ascribed to Moses in part based on passages such as 24.4 and 34.27. Modern biblical scholarship, however, has noted many problems with the view that Moses wrote the entire Torah, including Exodus. Like the rest of the Pentateuch, Exodus contains contradictions and redundancies. For example, Moses' father-in-law is sometimes called Reuel and sometimes Jethro; and the mountain of revelation is Sinai in some passages and Horeb in others. The narratives of Moses on the mountain in chs 19 and 24 have many overlapping and conflicting details, as does the account of the nine marvels in 7.8–10.29. Differences in vocabulary, style, and ideas are also discernible. Thus Exodus is best understood as a composite of traditions shaped over many centuries by an unknown number of anonymous storytellers and writers. Those traditions eventually comprised four major sources (known as J, E, D, and P) that were skillfully combined into the present canonical book by one or more redactors or editors who felt that all the sources were valid. The redactor(s) or editor(s) can be credited with the overall interweaving of disparate materials—narratives, legal texts, priestly records, lists, and one long poem. Redaction also introduced patterns, such as the repetition of a thematic word or phrase a symbolic number of times (usually seven or ten) in a literary unit (see, e.g., 4.21n.; 5.1n.; 18.26n.; 40.16n.), and also the triadic arrangement of the account of the nine marvels (see 7.8–10.29n.).

HISTORICAL CONTEXT

The diverse materials in Exodus are situated within a storyline describing the departure of a group of oppressed people from Egypt to a sacred mountain in Sinai where they enter into a covenant with the God they believed rescued them; at God's direction, they construct a portable shrine for their deity before continuing their journey. The historicity of that story has been questioned, partly because the sources comprising Exodus date from many centuries after the events they purport to describe. The events themselves, which involve the escape of a component of the Pharaoh's workforce, the disruption of Egyptian agriculture, and the loss of many Egyptian lives, are not mentioned in Egyptian sources (although the Egyptians would not necessarily record such events). Similarly, the larger-than-life leader Moses is not mentioned in contemporaneous nonbiblical sources; and no trace of a large group of people moving across the Sinai Peninsula has been found by archaeological surveys or excavations. Moreover, virtually none of the places mentioned in Exodus, including the holy mountain, can be identified with sites discovered in Sinai or with names known from other sources (see 12.37n.; 19.1n.). In addition, features of the story, such as the signs and wonders performed in Egypt and the exceedingly large number of people said to have left Egypt (see 12.37n.), defy credibility. Finally, the Exodus story culminates in Joshua, with the conquest of the land of Israel; and here too the archaeological record does not corroborate the main biblical narrative.

Despite these problems, the basic storyline is supported by evidence from Egyptian and other sources. Foreigners from western Asia, called "Asiatics" in Egyptian documents, periodically did migrate to Egypt, especially during times of famine (see Gen 12.10; 41.57; 43.1–2); others were taken to Egypt as military captives or were forcibly sent there as human tribute by Canaanite rulers. Moreover, many of these groups, including those who had voluntarily entered Egypt, were vulnerable to conscription for state projects. This pattern was especially strong toward the end of the Late Bronze Age (ca. 1400–1200 BCE). And, although virtually all of the foreigners in Egypt were assimilated into local culture, there is at least one documented instance of several workers escaping into the Sinai wilderness. Thus the overall pattern of descent into Egypt followed by servitude and escape is based on information in ancient documents. In addition, the end of the Late Bronze Age, by which time the Israelites would have left Egypt, coincides with the date of inscriptional evidence—a stele erected by the pharaoh Merneptah in ca. 1209 BCE, which contains the first mention of Israel outside the Bible—for a people called "Israel" in the land of Canaan.

A plausible reconstruction is that a relatively small group of people, descendants of western Asiatics who had entered Egypt generations before, managed to escape from servitude. So improbable was such an event that the people, or their leader, attributed it to miraculous divine intervention. This experience bonded them in their loyalty to that deity and gave them a collective identity. This story was originally oral and developed like other oral tales. Upon entering Canaan, they told their story and spread word about their unusual saving God, Yahweh, a name perhaps learned from Midianites with whom they interacted (see 3.15n.). Their stories about securing freedom are collective memories meant to re-create for others the intense emotional experience of liberation rather than to record accurate details of their flight. As time passed, major features of Israelite culture—such as the main agricultural festivals (especially passover), the custom of redeeming firstborn males, the idea of a people in a covenant relationship with God, prophets as the transmitters of God's word, the sabbath, the construction of a central shrine as God's earthly abode, a sacrificial system administered by priests—were assimilated into the core Exodus story, which gives them their emotional power and authority (see 11.1–13.16n.). This commemoration of the past makes the experience of a few the collective story, the very identity, of the community taking shape and expanding in the highlands of Canaan and later struggling to survive the traumas of division and exile.

LITERARY HISTORY

The components of the book of Exodus have been so skillfully woven together that it is no longer possible to reconstruct the process by which they emerged and were ultimately combined. The overall story comprises elements of both the J source (which may have its origin when the monarchy was established in the tenth century BCE and then circulated in the Southern Kingdom of Judah) and the E source (formed and circulated in the Northern Kingdom of Israel by the eighth century BCE). Deuteronomic elements (D, usually linked to seventh-century developments) can also be identified; it is even possible that all three—J, E, and D—drew from a common commemorative tradition but developed it in their own particular ways. A strong P (Priestly) component is present not only in the passages dealing with the sanctuary, priests, and rituals, but also in several points of the story line, notably in the accounts of the marvels in Egypt and the deliverance at the sea. The final redaction reflects priestly emphases of the sixth century BCE or later but also preserves ritual and ceremonial practices many centuries older.

STRUCTURE

The book can be subdivided into thematic and literary units in various ways; this one positions the revelation at Sinai and the covenant in the center:

Part I: Israel in and out of Egypt (1.1–15.21): God sees Israelite suffering in Egypt (chs 1–2), Moses becomes God's spokesperson (3.1–7.7), and a series of marvels (7.7–10.29) and a plague (11.1–13.16) culminate in the escape of the people (13.17–15.21).

Part II: Sinai and Covenant (15.22–24.18): After traveling through the wilderness (15.22–18.27), the Israelites arrive at Sinai, where they experience a theophany, a divine appearance (ch 19), and receive the covenant (chs 20–24).

Part III: Sanctuary and New Covenant. An episode of apostasy followed by covenant renewal (chs 32–34) separates instructions for building the sanctuary (chs 25–31) from the account of its construction (chs 35–40).

INTERPRETATION

Exodus is arguably the most important book in the Hebrew Bible. It presents an explanation of God's name YHWH and central biblical ideas about God, especially that God responds to and saves people who are suffering or oppressed. Major institutions of ancient Israel—such as prophecy, covenant, community regulations, a central shrine, festivals, sacrifice, and the sabbath—are grounded in the narrative of liberation. Exodus likely struck a resonant cord for Judeans experiencing defeat and exile in the sixth century BCE and later; for them, maintaining or restoring the institutions set forth in Exodus contributed to their emerging identity and to their very survival as a dispersed people. A similar dynamic can be posited for subsequent Jewish history. Although the institutions of Exodus played a lesser role in Christian tradition, the concept of divine self-revelation as manifest in Jesus Christ is rooted in the prominence of God's self-revelation in Exodus; and the story of suffering leading to redemption shapes key Christian beliefs. For both Jews and Christians, identification with the suffering in Egypt contributes to the moral imperative to alleviate the suffering of others. As a story of liberation, Exodus has infused hope into many peoples. Despite its many positive features, however, some aspects of Exodus—such as the loss of innocent Egyptian lives and the investment of community resources in an elaborate shrine—continue to trouble readers.

GUIDE TO READING

An awareness of literary patterns and the repetition of words and phrases, as pointed out in the notes, can contribute to the reader's awareness of the power of the unfolding drama of the story and an understanding of important themes.

Carol Meyers

1 These are the names of the sons of Israel who came to Egypt with Jacob, each with his household: ² Reuben, Simeon, Levi, and Judah, ³ Issachar, Zebulun, and Benjamin, ⁴ Dan and Naphtali, Gad and Asher. ⁵ The total number of people born to Jacob was seventy. Joseph was already in Egypt. ⁶ Then Joseph died, and all his brothers, and that whole generation. ⁷ But the Israelites were fruitful and prolific; they multiplied and grew exceedingly strong, so that the land was filled with them.

⁸ Now a new king arose over Egypt, who did not know Joseph. ⁹ He said to his people, "Look, the Israelite people are more numerous and more powerful than we. ¹⁰ Come, let us deal shrewdly with them, or they will increase and, in the event of war, join our enemies and fight against us and escape from the land." ¹¹ Therefore they set taskmasters

1.1–15.21: Israel in and out of Egypt. The Israelites are oppressed in Egypt; but they escape from Pharaoh's control through the intervention of their God, whose identity is revealed to their heroic leader Moses, who then carries out God's directives to secure their release.

1.1–22: The oppression of the Israelites. The introductory chapter connects Exodus with Genesis and serves as a prologue to the story of deliverance by describing how the Israelites became oppressed (in fulfillment of Gen 15.13). 1–7: A brief retelling of the account in Gen 46.8–27 of Jacob's family relocating in Egypt. 1: *Israel* here refers to the patriarch Jacob. 2–4: The sons of Jacob, the ancestors of the twelve tribes of Israel, are listed by groups according to their mothers (see Gen 29.31–30.24; 35.16–20,23–26): the six sons of Leah; Rachel's second son; two each of the handmaids Bilhah and Zilpah; and Rachel's firstborn *Joseph*, the one with a position of power in the Egyptian court (Gen 41.37–45). 5: Because the number seven and its multiples symbolize totality, the notion of *seventy* descendants of Jacob signifies that all Israel is present in Egypt (cf. Gen 46.27; Deut 10.22). 7: The language of Israelite increase echoes God's commands at creation (Gen 1.28) and after the flood (Gen 9.1,7) and also God's promises to the ancestors (Gen 12.2; 15.5; 17.2; 18.18; 22.17; 26.4; 28.14; 46.3; 48.4), suggesting that the divine promise is now fulfilled through Israel. 8–14: The Egyptian ruler considers the increased Israelite population a threat and attempts to restrict their growth, first by subjecting them to *forced labor*. 8: The *new king* is often identified by modern scholars as Rameses II (1279–1213 BCE), but he is not named here (or anywhere in the Bible). This anonymity perhaps demeans him and gives the narrative an ahistorical character. 10: The possibility of *escape* is mentioned, foreshadowing what will eventually happen. 11: *Forced labor* probably does not designate chattel slavery but rather corvée or compulsory unpaid labor, a typical way to mobilize labor for state projects in the ancient Near East (e.g., 1 Kings 5.13). *Supply cities* in border areas served military

over them to oppress them with forced labor. They built supply cities, Pithom and Rameses, for Pharaoh. [12] But the more they were oppressed, the more they multiplied and spread, so that the Egyptians came to dread the Israelites. [13] The Egyptians became ruthless in imposing tasks on the Israelites, [14] and made their lives bitter with hard service in mortar and brick and in every kind of field labor. They were ruthless in all the tasks that they imposed on them.

[15] The king of Egypt said to the Hebrew midwives, one of whom was named Shiphrah and the other Puah, [16] "When you act as midwives to the Hebrew women, and see them on the birthstool, if it is a boy, kill him; but if it is a girl, she shall live." [17] But the midwives feared God; they did not do as the king of Egypt commanded them, but they let the boys live. [18] So the king of Egypt summoned the midwives and said to them, "Why have you done this, and allowed the boys to live?" [19] The midwives said to Pharaoh, "Because the Hebrew women are not like the Egyptian women; for they are vigorous and give birth before the midwife comes to them." [20] So God dealt well with the midwives;

and the people multiplied and became very strong. [21] And because the midwives feared God, he gave them families. [22] Then Pharaoh commanded all his people, "Every boy that is born to the Hebrews[a] you shall throw into the Nile, but you shall let every girl live."

2 Now a man from the house of Levi went and married a Levite woman. [2] The woman conceived and bore a son; and when she saw that he was a fine baby, she hid him three months. [3] When she could hide him no longer she got a papyrus basket for him, and plastered it with bitumen and pitch; she put the child in it and placed it among the reeds on the bank of the river. [4] His sister stood at a distance, to see what would happen to him.

[5] The daughter of Pharaoh came down to bathe at the river, while her attendants walked beside the river. She saw the basket among the reeds and sent her maid to bring it. [6] When she opened it, she saw the child. He was crying, and she took pity on him. "This must be one of the Hebrews' children," she said. [7] Then his sister said to Pharaoh's

---

[a] Sam Gk Tg: Heb lacks *to the Hebrews*

---

purposes. *Pithom* and *Rameses* were probably located in the eastern Nile Delta, protecting the northeastern frontier of Egypt; attempts to identify them with sites dating to the reign of Rameses II are inconclusive. **13–14:** Words using the root "to serve" appear five times in these two verses (translated *imposing tasks*, *service*, *labor*, *tasks*, and *imposed*), emphasizing the difficult lives of the Israelites; they are forced to work in state agriculture as well as construction. **15–22:** Forced labor apparently has failed to deplete the Israelite population, so another strategy, selective infanticide, is implemented. **15:** The term *Hebrew* seems to denote the Israelites as a people rather than a social class, usually when contrasting them with non-Israelites, as in Gen 14.13; Ex 21.2; 1 Sam 29.3. *Shiphrah* and *Puah* are the first two of a series of twelve women featured in the life of Moses, the deliverer of the twelve tribes. Although some interpreters and ancient traditions consider them Egyptians who are "midwives *to the Hebrews*" rather than *Hebrew midwives*, their Semitic names make it more likely that they are Hebrew professionals. **16:** *Birthstool*, the two bricks or stones on which a woman in labor was positioned. The instruction to *kill* infant boys, and not girls, in order to limit population growth suggests the king's ineptitude and introduces the violence that will recur as the story of oppression and liberation continues. **22:** *Every boy . . . you shall throw into the Nile*, the final strategy for depleting the Israelite population anticipates the appearance of the baby Moses.

2.1–25: The emergence of Moses. 1–10: As in the birth legends of other heroic figures in ancient Near Eastern literature, the miraculous rescue of the doomed infant Moses signifies that he is destined for greatness. **1:** Moses' parents, both from the priestly tribe of *Levi*, are named in 6.20. *Woman*, Moses' mother, the third in a series of twelve women featured in chs 1–2; see 1.15n. **2:** *Saw that he was a fine baby*, lit., "saw that he was good," echoes the language of creation in Gen 1. **3:** The Hebrew word for *basket* appears elsewhere in the Bible only as a designation for Noah's ark (Gen 6.14) as the instrument for saving God's creation. Here it is the means for rescuing the person who will save the Israelites. *Reeds*, see 13.18n. **4:** Moses' *sister*, elsewhere called Miriam—the fourth woman of the story (see 1.15n.)—is not named until 15.20. She appears in four additional books of the Hebrew Bible (Numbers, Deuteronomy, 1 Chronicles, and Micah), more than any other woman. **5:** The royal *daughter* is the fifth woman of chs 1–2; see 1.15n. **6:** *Hebrew*, see 1.15n. **7:** Hiring a wet *nurse* was usually a practice

daughter, "Shall I go and get you a nurse from the Hebrew women to nurse the child for you?" [8] Pharaoh's daughter said to her, "Yes." So the girl went and called the child's mother. [9] Pharaoh's daughter said to her, "Take this child and nurse it for me, and I will give you your wages." So the woman took the child and nursed it. [10] When the child grew up, she brought him to Pharaoh's daughter, and she took him as her son. She named him Moses,[a] "because," she said, "I drew him out[b] of the water."

[11] One day, after Moses had grown up, he went out to his people and saw their forced labor. He saw an Egyptian beating a Hebrew, one of his kinsfolk. [12] He looked this way and that, and seeing no one he killed the Egyptian and hid him in the sand. [13] When he went out the next day, he saw two Hebrews fighting; and he said to the one who was in the wrong, "Why do you strike your fellow Hebrew?" [14] He answered, "Who made you a ruler and judge over us? Do you mean to kill me as you killed the Egyptian?" Then Moses was afraid and thought, "Surely the thing is known." [15] When Pharaoh heard of it, he sought to kill Moses.

But Moses fled from Pharaoh. He settled in the land of Midian, and sat down by a well.

[16] The priest of Midian had seven daughters. They came to draw water, and filled the troughs to water their father's flock. [17] But some shepherds came and drove them away. Moses got up and came to their defense and watered their flock. [18] When they returned to their father Reuel, he said, "How is it that you have come back so soon today?" [19] They said, "An Egyptian helped us against the shepherds; he even drew water for us and watered the flock." [20] He said to his daughters, "Where is he? Why did you leave the man? Invite him to break bread." [21] Moses agreed to stay with the man, and he gave Moses his daughter Zipporah in marriage. [22] She bore a son, and he named him Gershom; for he said, "I have been an alien[c] residing in a foreign land."

[23] After a long time the king of Egypt died. The Israelites groaned under their slavery, and cried out. Out of the slavery their cry for help rose up to God. [24] God heard their groaning, and God remembered his covenant with Abraham, Isaac, and Jacob. [25] God looked upon the Israelites, and God took notice of them.

a Heb *Mosheh*
b Heb *mashah*
c Heb *ger*

of elites in the ancient Near East. **10:** *Moses*, an Egyptian name meaning "give birth" and often part of Egyptian names joined with the name of a god (e.g., Thutmoses, Ahmoses, Rameses), is given a Hebrew etymology ("he who draws out") in anticipation of Moses' role in drawing his people through the sea (14.21–29). Such folk etymologies are common in the Torah. **11–15:** In the first two episodes of his adult life, Moses saves one Hebrew and tries to adjudicate between two others; both roles will recur but will involve all his people. **11:** *His kinsfolk*, he identifies with his people even though he was raised in the royal court. **14–15a:** Moses is rejected by his own people, and the pharaoh seeks his life. **14:** *Ruler*, Heb "sar;" cf. 18.21,25. *Judge*, one of Moses' roles as a ruler or administrator; see 18.13–27n. **15b–22:** Moses flees to Midian and marries. **15b:** *Midian*, probably in northwest Arabia. The Midianites, said to be descendants of Abraham and Keturah (Gen 25.2), were caravaneers whose routes stretched across Sinai to southern Palestine. Moses meets his future wife at a *well*, a pattern appearing in the stories of Rebekah (Gen 24) and Rachel (Gen 29). **16:** Moses' future father-in-law is a *priest*, an important role in ch 18. **16:** *Seven daughters*, making a total of twelve female figures (see 1.15n.). **17:** Saved by the daughter of a king, Moses now saves the daughters of a priest, one of whom will save him (4.24–26); the motif of saving recurs, anticipating the ultimate deliverance at the sea (13.17–15.21). **18:** *Reuel*, elsewhere called Jethro (as 3.1) or Hobab (Judg 4.11); these may reflect different ancient sources. **19:** Probably because of his manner of dress, Moses is mistaken for an *Egyptian*. **21:** *Gave . . . in marriage*, lit., "gave . . . as a wife," the usual idiom for marriage in biblical Hebrew. **23–25:** A postscript to the marriage episode provides a transition to the account of Moses becoming deliverer of his people in response to God's call. *God* is mentioned in the midwives episode but only now is said to be aware of the Israelites' plight. **23:** They *cried*, the Egyptians eventually will cry louder (11.6), and the Israelites will cry again at the sea (14.10). *Their slavery*, that is, "their work." **24:** Referring to the ancestral *covenant* (Heb "berit," as in 6.4–5; cf. 25.16n.) links the book of Exodus with Genesis and anticipates the Sinai covenant (Ex 19–24).

3 Moses was keeping the flock of his father-in-law Jethro, the priest of Midian; he led his flock beyond the wilderness, and came to Horeb, the mountain of God. [2] There the angel of the LORD appeared to him in a flame of fire out of a bush; he looked, and the bush was blazing, yet it was not consumed. [3] Then Moses said, "I must turn aside and look at this great sight, and see why the bush is not burned up." [4] When the LORD saw that he had turned aside to see, God called to him out of the bush, "Moses, Moses!" And he said, "Here I am." [5] Then he said, "Come no closer! Remove the sandals from your feet, for the place on which you are standing is holy ground." [6] He said further, "I am the God of your father, the God of Abraham, the God of Isaac, and the God of Jacob." And Moses hid his face, for he was afraid to look at God.

[7] Then the LORD said, "I have observed the misery of my people who are in Egypt; I have heard their cry on account of their taskmasters. Indeed, I know their sufferings, [8] and I have come down to deliver them from the Egyptians, and to bring them up out of that land to a good and broad land, a land flowing with milk and honey, to the country of the Canaanites, the Hittites, the Amorites, the Perizzites, the Hivites, and the Jebusites. [9] The cry of the Israelites has now come to me; I have also seen how the Egyptians oppress them. [10] So come, I will send you to Pharaoh to bring my people, the Israelites, out of Egypt." [11] But Moses said to God, "Who am I that I should go to Pharaoh, and bring the Israelites out of Egypt?" [12] He said, "I will be with you; and this shall be the sign for you that it is I who sent you: when you have brought the people out of Egypt, you shall worship God on this mountain."

[13] But Moses said to God, "If I come to the Israelites and say to them, 'The God of your ancestors has sent me to you,' and they ask me, 'What is his name?' what shall I say to them?" [14] God said to Moses, "I AM WHO I AM."[a] He said further, "Thus you shall say to the Israelites, 'I AM has sent me to you.'" [15] God also said to Moses, "Thus you shall say

---

[a] Or *I AM WHAT I AM* or *I WILL BE WHAT I WILL BE*

3.1–4.17: Moses' call and mission. The god of the ancestors appears to Moses in Midian, reveals the divine name, and commissions him to deliver his people. The term "prophet" is not used for Moses in Exodus, but this call narrative presents him as one. **3.1–10:** Theophany: divine revelation at the bush. **1:** *Keeping the flock*, the role of the shepherd signifies both human (e.g., 1 Sam 17.15; 2 Sam 5.2; 7.8) and divine (e.g., Pss 23.1; 80.1; 100.3) kingship. *Horeb* (or Sinai; see 19.1n.) is called *mountain of God*, perhaps indicating its sanctity for Midianites. **2:** An *angel* (lit., "messenger") is a manifestation of God who sometimes takes human form. God's presence also appears in clouds and especially *fire* (e.g., Gen 15.17; Ex 19.9; 24.15–18; 33.9; 40.34–38), which are sometimes depicted as pillars (Ex 13.21; 14.19,24). *Bush*, (Heb "seneh") is an unidentifiable but specific type of bush, perhaps alluding to Sinai (as also Deut 33.16), another place of divine presence and revelation. God's appearance in a bush may also reflect the role of plants or trees as symbols of fertility and divine presence (see 25.31–40n.). **5:** *Place* (Heb "maqom") often signifies holy space (Gen 28.11; Josh 5.15), as does *holy ground*; both indicate a site of theophany. **6:** Divine presence represents such intense, mysterious, and powerful holiness that it was considered dangerous to humans, hence Moses' reluctance to *look* at God's manifestation (see 19.10–15n.; cf. 24.10; 33.20,23; 34.29–35; contrast 33.11). **8:** *Come down* implies that God resides in a heavenly abode (see 25.9n.). *Flowing with milk and honey* (and 33.3), a recurrent vision of a fertile land, is a reality only when people obey God (Deut 28). The *honey* is probably not bees' honey but rather syrup made from cooking dates or grapes. *Canaanites . . . Jebusites* is one of several lists in the Torah (Pentateuch) of the indigenous inhabitants of the land; the longest appears in Gen 15.19–21; cf. 23.23,28; 33.2; 34.11. **10:** Prophets are called and then *sent* to deliver God's message (Isa 6.8; Jer 1.7). **3.11–4.17:** Moses is in dialogue with God about four issues. **3.11–12:** Moses' first problem is a sense of unworthiness for the mission; and the *sign* of divine help will be *worship* at the *mountain*, although it is not clear if present or future worship is implied. **13–15:** The next problem is not knowing God's name, for deities are identified by their proper names (not by generic "God") in the polytheistic world of the Israelites. Moses needs to know which deity is calling him. **14:** *I am who I am* renders the first name (Heb "'ehyeh 'asher 'ehyeh") that God provides; a shortened form, *I am* ("'ehyeh") renders the second. Because the Hebrew is grammatically problematic, these translations are uncertain. **15:** The third name is LORD. In Hebrew the name has four letters, "yhwh" (perhaps pronounced Yahweh), and is thus known as the Tetragrammaton. Like the first two

to the Israelites, 'The LORD,[a] the God of your ancestors, the God of Abraham, the God of Isaac, and the God of Jacob, has sent me to you':

This is my name forever,
and this my title for all generations.
[16] Go and assemble the elders of Israel, and say to them, 'The LORD, the God of your ancestors, the God of Abraham, of Isaac, and of Jacob, has appeared to me, saying: I have given heed to you and to what has been done to you in Egypt. [17] I declare that I will bring you up out of the misery of Egypt, to the land of the Canaanites, the Hittites, the Amorites, the Perizzites, the Hivites, and the Jebusites, a land flowing with milk and honey.' [18] They will listen to your voice; and you and the elders of Israel shall go to the king of Egypt and say to him, 'The LORD, the God of the Hebrews, has met with us; let us now go a three days' journey into the wilderness, so that we may sacrifice to the LORD our God.' [19] I know, however, that the king of Egypt will not let you go unless compelled by a mighty hand.[b] [20] So I will stretch out my hand and strike Egypt with all my wonders that I will perform in it; after that he will let you go. [21] I will bring this people into such favor with the Egyptians that, when you go, you will not go empty-handed; [22] each woman shall ask her neighbor and any woman living in the neighbor's house for jewelry of silver and of gold, and clothing, and you shall put them on your sons and on your daughters; and so you shall plunder the Egyptians."

4 Then Moses answered, "But suppose they do not believe me or listen to me, but say, 'The LORD did not appear to you.'" [2] The LORD said to him, "What is that in your hand?" He said, "A staff." [3] And he said, "Throw it on the ground." So he threw the staff on the ground, and it became a snake; and Moses drew back from it. [4] Then the LORD said to Moses, "Reach out your hand, and seize it by the tail"—so he reached out his hand and grasped it, and it became a staff in his hand— [5] "so that they may believe that the LORD, the God of their ancestors, the God of Abraham, the God of Isaac, and the God of Jacob, has appeared to you."

[6] Again, the LORD said to him, "Put your hand inside your cloak." He put his hand into his cloak; and when he took it out, his hand was leprous,[c] as white as snow. [7] Then God said, "Put your hand back into your cloak"—so he put his hand back into his cloak, and when he took it out, it was restored like the rest of his body— [8] "If they will not believe you or heed the first sign, they may believe the second sign. [9] If they will not believe even these two signs or heed you, you shall take some water from the Nile and pour it on the dry ground; and the water that you shall take from the Nile will become blood on the dry ground."

a The word "LORD" when spelled with capital letters stands for the divine name, YHWH, which is here connected with the verb hayah, "to be"
b Gk Vg: Heb no, not by a mighty hand
c A term for several skin diseases; precise meaning uncertain

versions of God's name, it is from a root meaning "to be." God's name thus has a verbal rather than a noun form, but its specific meaning is uncertain. Because of the great sanctity of the divine name, early Jewish tradition avoided pronouncing it and used the Heb word "'adonay" ("my lord") as a substitute. Most translations respect that tradition and use LORD for the deity's proper name. According to Gen 4.26 (see also Gen 13.4) people knew God's name early in human history; but this passage along with 6.3 suggests a different tradition, that Moses is the first to hear it. In contemporaneous nonbiblical sources this divine name is known only from a Late Bronze Age inscription that mentions the "Shasu of ya-h-wa [or yhw]"; the Shasu were desert-dwellers, and probably included Midianites. **16–22:** A directive to Moses about speaking to his people and Pharaoh comes before the other two problems. **18:** *God of the Hebrews*, which relates the LORD to a specific people, is used when Moses is addressing non-Israelites (5.3; 7.16; 9.1; 9.13; 10.3); see 1.15n. Egyptians did allow their state workers time off, so the request to make a *three days' journey* is reasonable. **19:** *Mighty hand* is an image of divine power in the ancient Near East (13.9; 15.6). **22:** That an Israelite woman can request jewelry (see also 11.2–3; 12.35–36; 32.2–3) and clothing from her Egyptian *neighbor* suggests that they live peacefully together in workers' villages; yet this transfer of goods is called *plunder*, perhaps in reference to Gen 15.14. **4.1–9:** God responds to Moses' third problem, that the people will not heed him, by providing three supernatural signs: changing a *staff* (see 4.20n.) to a *snake* (4.2–5), making Moses' *hand* diseased and then restoring it (4.6–8), and turning *water* bloody (4.9).

[10] But Moses said to the LORD, "O my Lord, I have never been eloquent, neither in the past nor even now that you have spoken to your servant; but I am slow of speech and slow of tongue." [11] Then the LORD said to him, "Who gives speech to mortals? Who makes them mute or deaf, seeing or blind? Is it not I, the LORD? [12] Now go, and I will be with your mouth and teach you what you are to speak." [13] But he said, "O my Lord, please send someone else." [14] Then the anger of the LORD was kindled against Moses and he said, "What of your brother Aaron the Levite? I know that he can speak fluently; even now he is coming out to meet you, and when he sees you his heart will be glad. [15] You shall speak to him and put the words in his mouth; and I will be with your mouth and with his mouth, and will teach you what you shall do. [16] He indeed shall speak for you to the people; he shall serve as a mouth for you, and you shall serve as God for him. [17] Take in your hand this staff, with which you shall perform the signs."

[18] Moses went back to his father-in-law Jethro and said to him, "Please let me go back to my kindred in Egypt and see whether they are still living." And Jethro said to Moses, "Go in peace." [19] The LORD said to Moses in Mid-ian, "Go back to Egypt; for all those who were seeking your life are dead." [20] So Moses took his wife and his sons, put them on a donkey, and went back to the land of Egypt; and Moses carried the staff of God in his hand.

[21] And the LORD said to Moses, "When you go back to Egypt, see that you perform before Pharaoh all the wonders that I have put in your power; but I will harden his heart, so that he will not let the people go. [22] Then you shall say to Pharaoh, 'Thus says the LORD: Israel is my firstborn son. [23] I said to you, "Let my son go that he may worship me." But you refused to let him go; now I will kill your firstborn son.'"

[24] On the way, at a place where they spent the night, the LORD met him and tried to kill him. [25] But Zipporah took a flint and cut off her son's foreskin, and touched Moses'[a] feet with it, and said, "Truly you are a bridegroom of blood to me!" [26] So he let him alone. It was then she said, "A bridegroom of blood by circumcision."

[27] The LORD said to Aaron, "Go into the wilderness to meet Moses." So he went; and he met him at the mountain of God and kissed him. [28] Moses told Aaron all the words of the

a Heb *his*

The last sign anticipates the first of the marvels (7.14–25). **10-17:** God answers Moses' fourth problem – that he cannot speak – by assuring him of divine help and then assigning his brother to speak for him. **10:** *Slow of speech* may indicate a speech impediment (cf. 6.12,30) or perhaps a prophet's reluctance to accept a commission from God (cf. Jer 1.6–7). **14:** The first mention of *Aaron*. **15–16:** As Moses' spokesperson, Aaron will be to Moses as Moses is to God. **17:** *Staff,* see 4.20n.

4.18–31: Moses returns to Egypt. 20: Two *sons,* as in 18.3, although only one is mentioned in 2.22 and 4.25. **20:** Moses' staff, which he used as a shepherd (see 3.1; 4.2), has now become *the staff of God,* the instrument through which he and Aaron exert divine power; see further 17.9n. **21:** The motif of the Pharaoh's hardened *heart* (stubbornness) appears frequently in the narrative of Moses' negotiations with the Egyptian ruler, serving to increase dramatic tension. The number ten plays a role: ten times the Pharaoh hardens his own heart (e.g., 8.15), although even then it is part of God's plan (7.3; 11.9); and ten times God hardens it directly (e.g., 9.12). **22:** Based on the formulaic words of heralds bearing messages in the ancient Near East, the biblical expression *thus says the LORD* introduces words conveyed by a prophetic messenger of God. The prominent *firstborn son* motif, here used for Israel as the child of God (who will live), in v. 23 and in chs 11 and 12 designates the Egyptians' offspring (who will die). Firstborn of animals as well as humans have special status—they open their mothers' wombs and represent all future progeny (cf. 34.19–20). **24–26:** In this enigmatic episode, God attacks Moses for reasons that are unclear. **24:** Moses again is saved by a woman, his wife Zipporah; see 2.17n. In performing her son's circumcision, she may be carrying out a female role in Midianite and Israelite culture (1 Macc 1.60; 2 Macc 6.10; 4 Macc 4.25; cf. Gen 17.23–27 and Josh 5.2–7, where men are the circumcisers). **25:** *Feet,* a euphemism for genitals (see Isa 7.20). *Bridegroom of blood* may connote an ancient apotropaic function of circumcision as a rite of passage, for the Heb word for bridegroom ("ḥatan") in other Semitic languages can mean "protect" as well as "circumcise." Marriage and circumcision are also associated in Gen 34.14–24. **27–31:** Aaron joins Moses and convinces the people with words and signs that God sees their plight. **27:** *The mountain of God,* 3.1.

LORD with which he had sent him, and all the signs with which he had charged him. ²⁹ Then Moses and Aaron went and assembled all the elders of the Israelites. ³⁰ Aaron spoke all the words that the LORD had spoken to Moses, and performed the signs in the sight of the people. ³¹ The people believed; and when they heard that the LORD had given heed to the Israelites and that he had seen their misery, they bowed down and worshiped.

5 Afterward Moses and Aaron went to Pharaoh and said, "Thus says the LORD, the God of Israel, 'Let my people go, so that they may celebrate a festival to me in the wilderness.'" ² But Pharaoh said, "Who is the LORD, that I should heed him and let Israel go? I do not know the LORD, and I will not let Israel go." ³ Then they said, "The God of the Hebrews has revealed himself to us; let us go a three days' journey into the wilderness to sacrifice to the LORD our God, or he will fall upon us with pestilence or sword." ⁴ But the king of Egypt said to them, "Moses and Aaron, why are you taking the people away from their work? Get to your labors!" ⁵ Pharaoh continued, "Now they are more numerous than the people of the land[a] and yet you want them to stop working!" ⁶ That same day Pharaoh commanded the taskmasters of the people, as well as their supervisors, ⁷ "You shall no longer give the people straw to make bricks, as before; let them go and gather straw for themselves. ⁸ But you shall require of them the same quantity of bricks as they have made previously; do not diminish it, for they are lazy; that is why they cry, 'Let us go and offer sacrifice to our God.' ⁹ Let heavier work be laid on them; then they will labor at it and pay no attention to deceptive words."

¹⁰ So the taskmasters and the supervisors of the people went out and said to the people, "Thus says Pharaoh, 'I will not give you straw. ¹¹ Go and get straw yourselves, wherever you can find it; but your work will not be lessened in the least.'" ¹² So the people scattered throughout the land of Egypt, to gather stubble for straw. ¹³ The taskmasters were urgent, saying, "Complete your work, the same daily assignment as when you were given straw." ¹⁴ And the supervisors of the Israelites, whom Pharaoh's taskmasters had set over them, were beaten, and were asked, "Why did you not finish the required quantity of bricks yesterday and today, as you did before?"

¹⁵ Then the Israelite supervisors came to Pharaoh and cried, "Why do you treat your servants like this? ¹⁶ No straw is given to your servants, yet they say to us, 'Make bricks!' Look how your servants are beaten! You are unjust to your own people."[b] ¹⁷ He said, "You are lazy, lazy; that is why you say, 'Let us go and sacrifice to the LORD.' ¹⁸ Go now, and work; for no straw shall be given you, but you shall still deliver the same number of bricks." ¹⁹ The Israelite supervisors saw that they were in trouble when they were told, "You shall not lessen your daily number of bricks." ²⁰ As they left Pharaoh, they came upon Moses and Aaron who were waiting to meet them. ²¹ They said to them, "The LORD look upon

a Sam: Heb *The people of the land are now many*
b Gk Compare Syr Vg: Heb *beaten, and the sin of your people*

5.1–6.1: Moses and Aaron have their first encounter with Pharaoh. **5.1–3:** They request only a three-day leave, not permanent freedom; but Pharaoh refuses as anticipated in 3.19. **1:** *God of Israel*, rather than the usual "God of the Hebrews" (see 3.18n.), is used uniquely here to identify the LORD to the Egyptians. The imperative *Let my people go* appears for the first time and anticipates its sevenfold use in the account of nine divine marvels; see 7.16n. **2:** *Know the LORD*, which entails acknowledging the LORD's authority, is a recurrent theme in Exodus; God's mighty deeds finally convince the Egyptians of God's reality and power (14.4,18) and cause the Israelites to affirm their belief (16.12; 29.46). Knowing God means experiencing God's powerful deeds (1 Kings 20.13). **3:** *God of the Hebrews*, see 3.18n. *Fall . . . sword* indicates that failure to carry out religious obligations would cause more Israelite suffering (and Pharaoh would lose his laborers). **4–19:** Pharaoh again employs strategies, now also punitive, to deal with the burgeoning Israelite population. **7:** *Straw*, an essential component in brick-making, binds the particles of Nile mud. **9:** *Deceptive words* probably refers to Moses' promise of liberation. **10:** Introducing Pharaoh's words with *Thus says Pharaoh* sets him in opposition to the LORD, whose words are similarly announced (see 4.22n). **5.20–6.1:** The Israelites are disheartened, and Moses turns to God who promises to take action.

you and judge! You have brought us into bad odor with Pharaoh and his officials, and have put a sword in their hand to kill us."

[22] Then Moses turned again to the LORD and said, "O LORD, why have you mistreated this people? Why did you ever send me? [23] Since I first came to Pharaoh to speak in your name, he has mistreated this people, and you have done nothing at all to deliver your people."

6 Then the LORD said to Moses, "Now you shall see what I will do to Pharaoh: Indeed, by a mighty hand he will let them go; by a mighty hand he will drive them out of his land."

[2] God also spoke to Moses and said to him: "I am the LORD. [3] I appeared to Abraham, Isaac, and Jacob as God Almighty,[a] but by my name 'The LORD'[b] I did not make myself known to them. [4] I also established my covenant with them, to give them the land of Canaan, the land in which they resided as aliens. [5] I have also heard the groaning of the Israelites whom the Egyptians are holding as slaves, and I have remembered my covenant. [6] Say therefore to the Israelites, 'I am the LORD, and I will free you from the burdens of the Egyptians and deliver you from slavery to them. I will redeem you with an outstretched arm and with mighty acts of judgment. [7] I will take you as my people, and I will be your God. You shall know that I am the LORD your God, who has freed you from the burdens of the Egyptians. [8] I will bring you into the land that I swore to give to Abraham, Isaac, and Jacob; I will give it to you for a possession. I am the LORD.'" [9] Moses told this to the Israelites; but

they would not listen to Moses, because of their broken spirit and their cruel slavery.

[10] Then the LORD spoke to Moses, [11] "Go and tell Pharaoh king of Egypt to let the Israelites go out of his land." [12] But Moses spoke to the LORD, "The Israelites have not listened to me; how then shall Pharaoh listen to me, poor speaker that I am?"[c] [13] Thus the LORD spoke to Moses and Aaron, and gave them orders regarding the Israelites and Pharaoh king of Egypt, charging them to free the Israelites from the land of Egypt.

[14] The following are the heads of their ancestral houses: the sons of Reuben, the firstborn of Israel: Hanoch, Pallu, Hezron, and Carmi; these are the families of Reuben. [15] The sons of Simeon: Jemuel, Jamin, Ohad, Jachin, Zohar, and Shaul,[d] the son of a Canaanite woman; these are the families of Simeon. [16] The following are the names of the sons of Levi according to their genealogies: Gershon,[e] Kohath, and Merari, and the length of Levi's life was one hundred thirty-seven years. [17] The sons of Gershon:[e] Libni and Shimei, by their families. [18] The sons of Kohath: Amram, Izhar, Hebron, and Uzziel, and the length of Kohath's life was one hundred thirty-three years. [19] The sons of Merari: Mahli and Mushi. These are the families of the Levites according to their genealogies. [20] Amram married Jochebed his father's sister

[a] Traditional rendering of Heb *El Shaddai*

[b] Heb *YHWH*; see note at 3.15

[c] Heb *me? I am uncircumcised of lips*

[d] Or *Saul*

[e] Also spelled *Gershom*; see 2.22

6.2–7.7: **God reaffirms the mission of Moses and Aaron** in the light of the worsened circumstances of the people. This section from the Priestly source parallels 3.1–4.17. 6.2: God's self-identification (also vv. 5 and 6) emphasizes the connection of God's identity to the promise. 3: *Almighty* (Heb "shadday"), an epithet of God (Gen 17.1n.; 35.11), probably meaning "the one of the mountains." 4: The ancestral *covenant* promised the land (Gen 15.7–21; 17.1–8; see 2.24n.). 5: Similar to 2.23–25. 6-8: Seven dynamic verbs (*will free, deliver, redeem, take, will be, will bring, will give*), with God as the first-person subject, connote the totality of God's commitment. Two other verbs in dependent clauses (*swore, freed*) bring the total up to nine divine actions, anticipating the nine signs and wonders of the next section. 7: *I will take you as my people, and I will be your God* is formulaic language emphasizing the two partners of a covenant (Jer 31.33). *Know*, see 5.2n. 9: *Cruel slavery*, or "hard work," referring to their predicament rather than their status. 12: *Poor speaker* (also v. 30) is another expression of a prophet's reluctance; see 4.10n. 14-25: A genealogy, similar to other genealogies in the Pentateuch (Gen 46.8–27; Num 3.1–37; 26), gives authority to Moses, Aaron, and Aaron's sons and grandsons by tracing their lineage in the priestly tribe of Levi. 20: Moses' mother *Jochebed*, whose name probably means "Yah [Yahweh] is glory," is the first person in the Bible to have a name formed with the name of Israel's God. *Aaron and Moses* but not Miriam;

and she bore him Aaron and Moses, and the length of Amram's life was one hundred thirty-seven years. [21] The sons of Izhar: Korah, Nepheg, and Zichri. [22] The sons of Uzziel: Mishael, Elzaphan, and Sithri. [23] Aaron married Elisheba, daughter of Amminadab and sister of Nahshon, and she bore him Nadab, Abihu, Eleazar, and Ithamar. [24] The sons of Korah: Assir, Elkanah, and Abiasaph; these are the families of the Korahites. [25] Aaron's son Eleazar married one of the daughters of Putiel, and she bore him Phinehas. These are the heads of the ancestral houses of the Levites by their families.

[26] It was this same Aaron and Moses to whom the LORD said, "Bring the Israelites out of the land of Egypt, company by company." [27] It was they who spoke to Pharaoh king of Egypt to bring the Israelites out of Egypt, the same Moses and Aaron.

[28] On the day when the LORD spoke to Moses in the land of Egypt, [29] he said to him, "I am the LORD; tell Pharaoh king of Egypt all that I am speaking to you." [30] But Moses said in the LORD's presence, "Since I am a poor speaker,[a] why would Pharaoh listen to me?"

7 The LORD said to Moses, "See, I have made you like God to Pharaoh, and your brother Aaron shall be your prophet. [2] You shall speak all that I command you, and your brother Aaron shall tell Pharaoh to let the Israelites go out of his land. [3] But I will harden Pharaoh's heart, and I will multiply my signs and wonders in the land of Egypt. [4] When Pharaoh does not listen to you, I will lay my hand upon Egypt and bring my people the Israelites, company by company, out of the land of Egypt by great acts of judgment. [5] The Egyptians shall know that I am the LORD, when I stretch out my hand against Egypt and bring the Israelites out from among them." [6] Moses and Aaron did so; they did just as the LORD commanded them. [7] Moses was eighty years old and Aaron eighty-three when they spoke to Pharaoh.

[8] The LORD said to Moses and Aaron, [9] "When Pharaoh says to you, 'Perform a wonder,' then you shall say to Aaron, 'Take your staff and throw it down before Pharaoh, and it will become a snake.'" [10] So Moses and Aaron went to Pharaoh and did as the LORD had commanded; Aaron threw

a   Heb *am uncircumcised of lips*; see 6.12

---

several women appear in this lineage but only as wives and mothers (vv. 15,23,25). **23:** *Nadab* and *Abihu*, priestly leaders with Aaron in the Sinai narrative (24.1). **25:** *Eleazar . . . Phinehas*, the successors of Aaron (not Moses) conclude the genealogy, revealing its priestly interest; see 28.1. **26–30:** The narrative resumes with a brief recapitulation of 6.2–12. **26:** *Company by company*, military language depicts the fleeing Israelites (also 12.17; 12.37n.; 13.18). **7.1–7:** Another account of the affirmation of Moses' mission. **1:** See 4.15–16n. **3:** *Harden*, see 4.21n. *Signs and wonders* anticipates the nine marvels of the next section; these acts of God, together with the plague (slaying of Egyptian firstborn), are the source of knowing God. **5:** *Know*, see 5.2n.

7.8–10.29: The nine marvels. The designation "ten plagues" is not used in the Bible. Fewer than ten catastrophes appear in the two psalms that mention them, Pss 78.44–51 and 105.28–36. The narrative in the book of Exodus likely draws from several sources to form a three-triad pattern, totaling nine marvels: Pharaoh receives a warning, in the morning, for the first, fourth, and seventh marvels; Pharaoh receives a warning, time unspecified, for the second, fifth, and eighth ones; the third, sixth, and ninth happen unannounced. Each triad has the same sequence, an arrangement suggesting that nine is the appropriate number, with the slaying of the firstborn coming as a separate, tenth, climactic event. The noun "plague" appears only for the tenth calamity, the death of firstborn (11.1), except for once at 9.14 (see n.). "Signs and wonders" (or, marvels) appears to be the Bible's designation (as in 7.3; cf. 10.1–2; 11.9–10; Pss 78.43; 105.27) for the first nine, which do not fit the meaning of "plague" as an epidemic of deadly disease understood to be a punitive measure (cf. 32.35; Num 25). The marvels unfold in a dramatic series of encounters between God's emissaries, Moses and Aaron, and the deified Pharaoh and his officials and magicians; and they result in the Pharaoh's acknowledging ("knowing") God. Although each of the first nine alone might reflect a natural occurrence, the intensity and rapid-fire timing are not natural; grouped together, they are a vivid expression of God's extraordinary power, as is the wholly supernatural tenth event, the slaying of the firstborn.

7.8–13: Preface to the marvels. The introduction to the marvels, like 4.1–5, features a staff turning into a snake in a competition with Egyptian magicians. **9:** *Aaron*, not Moses, has the leading role in this episode and in

down his staff before Pharaoh and his officials, and it became a snake. [11] Then Pharaoh summoned the wise men and the sorcerers; and they also, the magicians of Egypt, did the same by their secret arts. [12] Each one threw down his staff, and they became snakes; but Aaron's staff swallowed up theirs. [13] Still Pharaoh's heart was hardened, and he would not listen to them, as the LORD had said.

[14] Then the LORD said to Moses, "Pharaoh's heart is hardened; he refuses to let the people go. [15] Go to Pharaoh in the morning, as he is going out to the water; stand by at the river bank to meet him, and take in your hand the staff that was turned into a snake. [16] Say to him, 'The LORD, the God of the Hebrews, sent me to you to say, "Let my people go, so that they may worship me in the wilderness." But until now you have not listened. [17] Thus says the LORD, "By this you shall know that I am the LORD." See, with the staff that is in my hand I will strike the water that is in the Nile, and it shall be turned to blood. [18] The fish in the river shall die, the river itself shall stink, and the Egyptians shall be unable to drink water from the Nile.'" [19] The LORD said to Moses, "Say to Aaron, 'Take your staff and stretch out your hand over the waters of Egypt—over its rivers, its canals, and its ponds, and all its pools of water—so that they may become blood; and there shall be blood throughout the whole land of Egypt, even in vessels of wood and in vessels of stone.'"

[20] Moses and Aaron did just as the LORD commanded. In the sight of Pharaoh and of his officials he lifted up the staff and struck the water in the river, and all the water in the river was turned into blood, [21] and the fish in the river died. The river stank so that the Egyptians could not drink its water, and there was blood throughout the whole land of Egypt. [22] But the magicians of Egypt did the same by their secret arts; so Pharaoh's heart remained hardened, and he would not listen to them, as the LORD had said. [23] Pharaoh turned and went into his house, and he did not take even this to heart. [24] And all the Egyptians had to dig along the Nile for water to drink, for they could not drink the water of the river.

[25] Seven days passed after the LORD had struck the Nile.

8 [a] Then the LORD said to Moses, "Go to Pharaoh and say to him, 'Thus says the LORD: Let my people go, so that they may worship me. [2] If you refuse to let them go, I will plague your whole country with frogs. [3] The river shall swarm with frogs; they shall come up into your palace, into your bedchamber and your bed, and into the houses

[a] Ch 7.26 in Heb

the first three marvels. **11:** *Magicians* appear for the first time; the Hebrew term is derived from an Egyptian word denoting a priestly official. **11:** *Secret arts* refers to spells or incantations that the Egyptians use, whereas Aaron simply casts his staff down. **13:** *Hardened*, appearing in the preface, anticipates Pharaoh's response to every marvel and to the climactic plague; see 4.21n. *As . . . said*, noting the veracity of God's predictions, similarly anticipates what will be said for most of the marvels.

7.14–8.19: First three marvels. Aaron's staff is the instrument of divine power. **7.14–25: First marvel, bloody waters.** This marvel, like some others, combines two traditions: in one, Moses' action pollutes the Nile only, while in the other, Aaron turns all Egyptian water into blood. **15:** *Water* and *river bank* evoke the image of the infant Moses in the river (2.3) and anticipate the role of water in the final water event, when the Red (Reed) Sea splits and the Egyptian troops drown (14.21–29). **16–17:** The Israelites have heard what God will do (6.6–8), as has Moses (7.1–5); now the Pharaoh is told. **16:** *God of the Hebrews*, see 3.18n. *Let my people go* appears six more times in the marvels sequence (8.20,21; 9.1,13; 10.3,4; cf. 5.1); this sevenfold usage emphases the theme of securing freedom for the Israelites. **17:** The entire *Nile* turns bloody, making this far more extensive than the bloody-water sign to the Israelites (4.9). **18:** The *Egyptians* (but apparently not the Israelites) will be affected (as in vv. 21,24, and in the next marvel, 8:3–4,9–11). **19:** The abundance of water terms, *rivers . . . water*, stresses the role of water; see 7.15n. **22:** The magicians can duplicate this calamity, but again (as in 7.11) they must use spells. The text here and elsewhere reflects humor—the Egyptian magicians make the calamity even worse! **22:** *Hardened*, see 4.21n. **8.1–15: Second marvel, frogs. 3:** The Pharaoh, his *officials*, and the *people*, that is, all Egyptians, are affected. These three elements of Egypt's hierarchical society are mentioned nine times in the account of

of your officials and of your people,[a] and into your ovens and your kneading bowls. [4] The frogs shall come up on you and on your people and on all your officials.'" [5][b] And the LORD said to Moses, "Say to Aaron, 'Stretch out your hand with your staff over the rivers, the canals, and the pools, and make frogs come up on the land of Egypt.'" [6] So Aaron stretched out his hand over the waters of Egypt; and the frogs came up and covered the land of Egypt. [7] But the magicians did the same by their secret arts, and brought frogs up on the land of Egypt.

[8] Then Pharaoh called Moses and Aaron, and said, "Pray to the LORD to take away the frogs from me and my people, and I will let the people go to sacrifice to the LORD." [9] Moses said to Pharaoh, "Kindly tell me when I am to pray for you and for your officials and for your people, that the frogs may be removed from you and your houses and be left only in the Nile." [10] And he said, "Tomorrow." Moses said, "As you say! So that you may know that there is no one like the LORD our God, [11] the frogs shall leave you and your houses and your officials and your people; they shall be left only in the Nile." [12] Then Moses and Aaron went out from Pharaoh; and Moses cried out to the LORD concerning the frogs that he had brought upon Pharaoh.[c] [13] And the LORD did as Moses requested: the frogs died in the houses, the courtyards, and the fields. [14] And they gathered them together in heaps, and the land stank. [15] But when Pharaoh saw that there was a respite, he hardened his heart, and would not listen to them, just as the LORD had said.

[16] Then the LORD said to Moses, "Say to Aaron, 'Stretch out your staff and strike the dust of the earth, so that it may become gnats throughout the whole land of Egypt.'" [17] And they did so; Aaron stretched out his hand with his staff and struck the dust of the earth, and gnats came on humans and animals alike; all the dust of the earth turned into gnats throughout the whole land of Egypt. [18] The magicians tried to produce gnats by their secret arts, but they could not. There were gnats on both humans and animals. [19] And the magicians said to Pharaoh, "This is the finger of God!" But Pharaoh's heart was hardened, and he would not listen to them, just as the LORD had said.

[20] Then the LORD said to Moses, "Rise early in the morning and present yourself before Pharaoh, as he goes out to the water, and say to him, 'Thus says the LORD: Let my people go, so that they may worship me. [21] For if you will not let my people go, I will send swarms of flies on you, your officials, and your people, and into your houses; and the houses of the Egyptians shall be filled with swarms of flies; so also the land where they live. [22] But on that day I will set apart the land of Goshen, where my people live, so that no swarms of flies shall be there, that you may know that I the LORD am in this land. [23] Thus I will make a distinction[d] between my people and your people. This sign shall appear tomorrow.'" [24] The LORD did so, and great swarms of flies came into the house of Pharaoh

a   Gk: Heb *upon your people*
b   Ch 8.1 in Heb
c   Or *frogs, as he had agreed with Pharaoh*
d   Gk Vg: Heb *will set redemption*

the nine marvels and once more in the account of the slaying of the firstborn (12.30). **8:** Despite the magicians' replication of this event (v. 7), the Pharaoh momentarily relents and seems to recognize Israel's god by asking Moses and Aaron to *pray* (lit., "plead") on behalf of the Egyptians (cf. 8.28–30; 9.28; 10.17–18). **10:** *Tomorrow,* a one-day delay; see 8.23n. Here too Pharaoh is depicted as a buffoon, as he does not opt to cease the plague immediately. **15:** *Hardened,* see 4.21n. **8. 16–19: Third marvel, gnats. 16:** *Dust* represents what is countless (Gen 13.16). **18–19:** Failing this time to replicate the calamity, the magicians—but not Pharaoh—recognize the infestation as an act of Israel's god. **19:** *Hardened,* see 4.21n.

8.20–9.12: Second group of three marvels. Instrumentality shifts: God is the direct agent (8.24; 9.6), and then Moses and Aaron are agents together (9.8). **8.20–32: Fourth marvel, flies.** The meaning of the Hebrew term for this marvel is uncertain; some scholars understand it as a plague of mixed animals. **20:** Although Aaron is sometimes mentioned, *Moses* dominates the accounts of the remaining six marvels. **22:** *Goshen,* unknown in Egyptian sources, appears here and in 9.26 as the location of the Israelite work camps, probably in the eastern Nile Delta; see 1.11n. and Gen 45.10. **23:** *Distinction,* now God explicitly excludes the Israelites from the calamities; see 7.18n. *Tomorrow* introduces a time element; a delay in the onset of the marvel (as also in 9.5,18; 10.4) is

and into his officials' houses; in all of Egypt the land was ruined because of the flies.

[25] Then Pharaoh summoned Moses and Aaron, and said, "Go, sacrifice to your God within the land." [26] But Moses said, "It would not be right to do so; for the sacrifices that we offer to the LORD our God are offensive to the Egyptians. If we offer in the sight of the Egyptians sacrifices that are offensive to them, will they not stone us? [27] We must go a three days' journey into the wilderness and sacrifice to the LORD our God as he commands us." [28] So Pharaoh said, "I will let you go to sacrifice to the LORD your God in the wilderness, provided you do not go very far away. Pray for me." [29] Then Moses said, "As soon as I leave you, I will pray to the LORD that the swarms of flies may depart tomorrow from Pharaoh, from his officials, and from his people; only do not let Pharaoh again deal falsely by not letting the people go to sacrifice to the LORD."

[30] So Moses went out from Pharaoh and prayed to the LORD. [31] And the LORD did as Moses asked: he removed the swarms of flies from Pharaoh, from his officials, and from his people; not one remained. [32] But Pharaoh hardened his heart this time also, and would not let the people go.

9 Then the LORD said to Moses, "Go to Pharaoh, and say to him, 'Thus says the LORD, the God of the Hebrews: Let my people go, so that they may worship me. [2] For if you refuse to let them go and still hold them, [3] the hand of the LORD will strike with a deadly pestilence your livestock in the field: the horses, the donkeys, the camels, the herds, and the flocks. [4] But the LORD will make a distinction between the livestock of Israel and the livestock of Egypt, so that nothing shall die of all that belongs to the Israelites.'" [5] The LORD set a time, saying, "Tomorrow the

LORD will do this thing in the land." [6] And on the next day the LORD did so; all the livestock of the Egyptians died, but of the livestock of the Israelites not one died. [7] Pharaoh inquired and found that not one of the livestock of the Israelites was dead. But the heart of Pharaoh was hardened, and he would not let the people go.

[8] Then the LORD said to Moses and Aaron, "Take handfuls of soot from the kiln, and let Moses throw it in the air in the sight of Pharaoh. [9] It shall become fine dust all over the land of Egypt, and shall cause festering boils on humans and animals throughout the whole land of Egypt." [10] So they took soot from the kiln, and stood before Pharaoh, and Moses threw it in the air, and it caused festering boils on humans and animals. [11] The magicians could not stand before Moses because of the boils, for the boils afflicted the magicians as well as all the Egyptians. [12] But the LORD hardened the heart of Pharaoh, and he would not listen to them, just as the LORD had spoken to Moses.

[13] Then the LORD said to Moses, "Rise up early in the morning and present yourself before Pharaoh, and say to him, 'Thus says the LORD, the God of the Hebrews: Let my people go, so that they may worship me. [14] For this time I will send all my plagues upon you yourself, and upon your officials, and upon your people, so that you may know that there is no one like me in all the earth. [15] For by now I could have stretched out my hand and struck you and your people with pestilence, and you would have been cut off from the earth. [16] But this is why I have let you live: to show you my power, and to make my name resound through all the earth. [17] You are still exalting yourself against my people, and will not let them go. [18] Tomorrow at this time I will

a twist on the delay of Moses' wonder-ending prayer (8.10n.). **25:** As in 8.8, Pharaoh seems to relent; but in v. 32 he reneges. **26:** *Offensive*, practices of one people are odious to another. **28–29:** *Pray*, as in 8.9. **32:** *Hardened*, see 4.21n. **9.1–7: Fifth marvel, pestilence. 1:** *God of the Hebrews*, see 3.18n. **3:** *Hand*, see 3.19n. *Pestilence* in Deuteronomic and prophetic texts kills humans as well as animals but here only animals. **4:** *Distinction*, see 8.23n. **5:** *Tomorrow*, see 8.23n. **7:** *Hardened*, see 4.21n. **9.8–12: Sixth marvel, boils. 11:** *Magicians* cannot compete and are themselves afflicted (cf. 7.11,22; 8.7,18–19). **12:** Now Pharaoh's heart is *hardened* by God; see 4.21n.

9.13–10.29: Third group of three marvels. Moses' outstretched hand is now the instrument, and the severity of the calamities escalates. **9.13–35: Seventh marvel, hail. 13:** *God of the Hebrews*, see 3.18n. **14:** Only here is *plagues* used for one of the first nine calamities, perhaps because, as for the climactic slaying of the firstborn, there is extensive loss of human as well as animal life; see 7.8–10.29n. and 11.1n. **18:** *Tomorrow*, see 8.23n. So

cause the heaviest hail to fall that has ever fallen in Egypt from the day it was founded until now. [19] Send, therefore, and have your livestock and everything that you have in the open field brought to a secure place; every human or animal that is in the open field and is not brought under shelter will die when the hail comes down upon them.'" [20] Those officials of Pharaoh who feared the word of the LORD hurried their slaves and livestock off to a secure place. [21] Those who did not regard the word of the LORD left their slaves and livestock in the open field.

[22] The LORD said to Moses, "Stretch out your hand toward heaven so that hail may fall on the whole land of Egypt, on humans and animals and all the plants of the field in the land of Egypt." [23] Then Moses stretched out his staff toward heaven, and the LORD sent thunder and hail, and fire came down on the earth. And the LORD rained hail on the land of Egypt; [24] there was hail with fire flashing continually in the midst of it, such heavy hail as had never fallen in all the land of Egypt since it became a nation. [25] The hail struck down everything that was in the open field throughout all the land of Egypt, both human and animal; the hail also struck down all the plants of the field, and shattered every tree in the field. [26] Only in the land of Goshen, where the Israelites were, there was no hail.

[27] Then Pharaoh summoned Moses and Aaron, and said to them, "This time I have sinned; the LORD is in the right, and I and my people are in the wrong. [28] Pray to the LORD! Enough of God's thunder and hail! I will let you go; you need stay no longer." [29] Moses said to him, "As soon as I have gone out of the city, I will stretch out my hands to the LORD; the thunder will cease, and there will be no more hail, so that you may know that the earth is the LORD's. [30] But as for you and your officials, I know that you do not yet fear the LORD God." [31] (Now the flax and the barley were ruined, for the barley was in the ear and the flax was in bud. [32] But the wheat and the spelt were not ruined, for they are late in coming up.) [33] So Moses left Pharaoh, went out of the city, and stretched out his hands to the LORD; then the thunder and the hail ceased, and the rain no longer poured down on the earth. [34] But when Pharaoh saw that the rain and the hail and the thunder had ceased, he sinned once more and hardened his heart, he and his officials. [35] So the heart of Pharaoh was hardened, and he would not let the Israelites go, just as the LORD had spoken through Moses.

10 Then the LORD said to Moses, "Go to Pharaoh; for I have hardened his heart and the heart of his officials, in order that I may show these signs of mine among them, [2] and that you may tell your children and grandchildren how I have made fools of the Egyptians and what signs I have done among them—so that you may know that I am the LORD."

[3] So Moses and Aaron went to Pharaoh, and said to him, "Thus says the LORD, the God of the Hebrews, 'How long will you refuse to humble yourself before me? Let my people go, so that they may worship me. [4] For if you refuse to let my people go, tomorrow I will bring locusts into your country. [5] They shall cover the surface of the land, so that no one will be able to see the land. They shall devour the last remnant left you after the hail, and they shall devour every tree of yours that grows in the field. [6] They shall fill your houses, and the houses of all your officials and of all the Egyptians—something that neither your parents nor your grandparents have seen, from the day they came on earth to this day.'" Then he turned and went out from Pharaoh.

[7] Pharaoh's officials said to him, "How long shall this fellow be a snare to us? Let

severe is the *hail* that it figures in the next calamity (10.5,15). **19:** The severity prompts God, uniquely, to suggest a protective measure. **24:** *Fire flashing*, probably lightning, along with thunder accompanies the hail (vv. 23–24) to deadly effect, in contrast to the thunder and lightning in the theophany at Sinai (19.16,19). **26:** See 8.22n. and 8.23n. **27:** *Sinned*, an apparently unqualified admission; but Pharaoh continues to sin by reneging again (v. 34; 8.15,32). **28:** *Pray*, see 8.8n. **35:** *Hardened*, apparently by God; see 4.21n. **10.1–20: Eighth marvel, locusts. 1:** God *hardened* the hearts of both the Pharaoh and his officers; see 4.21n. **2:** *Tell . . . grandchildren* heralds the importance of remembering; see 11.1–13.16n. **3:** *God of the Hebrews*, see 3.18n. **4:** *Tomorrow*, see 8.23n. *Locusts* are extremely damaging; they reflect disaster (Joel 1.2–2.27) and divine judgment (as Amos 4.9). **5:** *No one . . . see*,

the people go, so that they may worship the LORD their God; do you not yet understand that Egypt is ruined?" [8] So Moses and Aaron were brought back to Pharaoh, and he said to them, "Go, worship the LORD your God! But which ones are to go?" [9] Moses said, "We will go with our young and our old; we will go with our sons and daughters and with our flocks and herds, because we have the LORD's festival to celebrate." [10] He said to them, "The LORD indeed will be with you, if ever I let your little ones go with you! Plainly, you have some evil purpose in mind. [11] No, never! Your men may go and worship the LORD, for that is what you are asking." And they were driven out from Pharaoh's presence.

[12] Then the LORD said to Moses, "Stretch out your hand over the land of Egypt, so that the locusts may come upon it and eat every plant in the land, all that the hail has left." [13] So Moses stretched out his staff over the land of Egypt, and the LORD brought an east wind upon the land all that day and all that night; when morning came, the east wind had brought the locusts. [14] The locusts came upon all the land of Egypt and settled on the whole country of Egypt, such a dense swarm of locusts as had never been before, nor ever shall be again. [15] They covered the surface of the whole land, so that the land was black; and they ate all the plants in the land and all the fruit of the trees that the hail had left; nothing green was left, no tree, no plant in the field, in all the land of Egypt. [16] Pharaoh hurriedly summoned Moses and Aaron and said, "I have sinned against the LORD your God, and against you. [17] Do forgive my sin just this once, and pray to the LORD your God that at the least he remove this deadly thing from me." [18] So he went out from Pharaoh

and prayed to the LORD. [19] The LORD changed the wind into a very strong west wind, which lifted the locusts and drove them into the Red Sea;[a] not a single locust was left in all the country of Egypt. [20] But the LORD hardened Pharaoh's heart, and he would not let the Israelites go.

[21] Then the LORD said to Moses, "Stretch out your hand toward heaven so that there may be darkness over the land of Egypt, a darkness that can be felt." [22] So Moses stretched out his hand toward heaven, and there was dense darkness in all the land of Egypt for three days. [23] People could not see one another, and for three days they could not move from where they were; but all the Israelites had light where they lived. [24] Then Pharaoh summoned Moses, and said, "Go, worship the LORD. Only your flocks and your herds shall remain behind. Even your children may go with you." [25] But Moses said, "You must also let us have sacrifices and burnt offerings to sacrifice to the LORD our God. [26] Our livestock also must go with us; not a hoof shall be left behind, for we must choose some of them for the worship of the LORD our God, and we will not know what to use to worship the LORD until we arrive there." [27] But the LORD hardened Pharaoh's heart, and he was unwilling to let them go. [28] Then Pharaoh said to him, "Get away from me! Take care that you do not see my face again, for on the day you see my face you shall die." [29] Moses said, "Just as you say! I will never see your face again."

11 The LORD said to Moses, "I will bring one more plague upon Pharaoh and upon Egypt; afterwards he will let you go from here; indeed, when he lets you go, he

---

[a]   Or *Sea of Reeds*

a result replicated by the ninth wonder (10.23). **13:** An *east wind*, which will also part the Red (Reed) Sea (14.21), brings the locusts; and a "west wind" will remove them by casting them into that sea, v. 19. **16:** *Sinned*, see 9.27n. **17–18:** *Pray*, see 8.8n. **19:** *Red Sea*, see 13.18n. **20:** *Hardened* by God; see 4.21n. **10:21–29: Ninth marvel, darkness.** **21:** *Darkness . . . felt*, perhaps reflecting the thick air of Near Eastern sandstorms. Darkness anticipates the midnight setting of the climactic death of the firstborn (12.29) and the nighttime sea crossing (14.20). **22:** *Three days* mirrors the requested three-day journey for sacrifice (3.18; 5.3; 8.27) and anticipates the three-day duration of the first post-Sinai journey (15.22). **27:** *Hardened* by God; see 4.21n. **28–29:** Rejecting further direct encounters with Pharaoh, who has divine pretensions, Moses will uniquely meet the LORD directly (33.11; but cf. 33.20–23).

   11.1–13.16: Plague, commemorative rituals, and departure. After the firstborn plague is announced, detailed commands for commemorative rituals appear interspersed with accounts of the Egyptian deaths and the Is-

will drive you away. [2] Tell the people that every man is to ask his neighbor and every woman is to ask her neighbor for objects of silver and gold." [3] The LORD gave the people favor in the sight of the Egyptians. Moreover, Moses himself was a man of great importance in the land of Egypt, in the sight of Pharaoh's officials and in the sight of the people.

[4] Moses said, "Thus says the LORD: About midnight I will go out through Egypt. [5] Every firstborn in the land of Egypt shall die, from the firstborn of Pharaoh who sits on his throne to the firstborn of the female slave who is behind the handmill, and all the firstborn of the livestock. [6] Then there will be a loud cry throughout the whole land of Egypt, such as has never been or will ever be again. [7] But not a dog shall growl at any of the Israelites—not at people, not at animals—so that you may know that the LORD makes a distinction between Egypt and Israel. [8] Then all these officials of yours shall come down to me, and bow low to me, saying, 'Leave us, you and all the people who follow you.' After

that I will leave." And in hot anger he left Pharaoh.

[9] The LORD said to Moses, "Pharaoh will not listen to you, in order that my wonders may be multiplied in the land of Egypt." [10] Moses and Aaron performed all these wonders before Pharaoh; but the LORD hardened Pharaoh's heart, and he did not let the people of Israel go out of his land.

12 The LORD said to Moses and Aaron in the land of Egypt: [2] This month shall mark for you the beginning of months; it shall be the first month of the year for you. [3] Tell the whole congregation of Israel that on the tenth of this month they are to take a lamb for each family, a lamb for each household. [4] If a household is too small for a whole lamb, it shall join its closest neighbor in obtaining one; the lamb shall be divided in proportion to the number of people who eat of it. [5] Your lamb shall be without blemish, a year-old male; you may take it from the sheep or from the goats. [6] You shall keep it until the fourteenth day of this month; then the whole assembled con-

raelite Exodus. Although addressed to the Israelites as they leave Egypt, the directives for various rituals also mandate future behaviors that will commemorate the radical change from servitude to freedom through God's intervention. The miraculous departure from Egypt becomes part of the collective memory of future generations, kept alive through religious practices that enable later generations to recall and relive the experiences of the Exodus generation. The rituals will contribute to Israelite communal identity and help maintain community values. Present and future merge in this composite and somewhat redundant account drawing on Priestly and other sources.

11.1–10: Announcement of the plague. 1: *Plague* is now the appropriate term for the horrific loss of life that ensues; see 7.8–10.29n. and 9.14n. *Drive* echoes the prediction of 6.1. **2:** That Israelite women would acquire Egyptian goods is announced in 3.22 (also 12.35–36; cf. 35.22,29). Here men too will obtain jewelry; but the clothing of 3.22 is omitted, as is the involvement of children. **5:** *Firstborn,* see 4.22n. *Pharaoh . . . female slave,* opposite ends of the socioeconomic spectrum form a merism indicating that all Egyptians will be affected. **6:** The Egyptians' unique *loud cry* surpasses the Israelites' cry (see 2.2n.). Uniqueness also features in the seventh marvel, which similarly involves human and animal death (see 9.18,25 and 9.14n.), and the eighth (10.14). **7:** *Distinction between Egypt and Israel,* again indicating the selective nature of what will happen (see 8.23n. and 9.4). **10:** *Hardened* by God, see 4.21n.

12.1–28: Preparations for departure: passover and unleavened bread festivals. Here, in vv. 43–49, and in 13.3–10, God ordains what will become a major Israelite festival (Deut 16.1–8; Num 9.1–14; 2 Kings 23.21–23; Ezek 45.21–24). Agricultural and pastoral components of the Canaanite ritual calendar—springtime birth of lambs, growth of green herbs, and ripening of grains—are given antecedents in Israel's story. Linked to the Exodus, the heightened emotions of such celebrations help re-create for later generations the exultant experience of liberation. This historicization of festivals contributes to their enduring nature (see 11.1–13.16n.). **1–13: Passover. 2:** *This month* (March-April), called Aviv in 13.4 and 23.15, is later called Nisan (Neh 2.1; Esth 3.7). This spring New Year (*the first month of the year*) probably reflects a priestly reckoning (Lev 23.5; Num 9.1–5) in contrast to an older tradition of an autumn New Year (23.16; 34.22). **3:** *Whole congregation of Israel,* repeated in v. 47, denotes gender and probably age inclusiveness (throughout time; vv. 14,17). **4:** *Household* likely indicates an extended (not a nuclear) family—enough people to consume a lamb in one sitting. **5:** *Without blemish* introduces the

gregation of Israel shall slaughter it at twilight. [7] They shall take some of the blood and put it on the two doorposts and the lintel of the houses in which they eat it. [8] They shall eat the lamb that same night; they shall eat it roasted over the fire with unleavened bread and bitter herbs. [9] Do not eat any of it raw or boiled in water, but roasted over the fire, with its head, legs, and inner organs. [10] You shall let none of it remain until the morning; anything that remains until the morning you shall burn. [11] This is how you shall eat it: your loins girded, your sandals on your feet, and your staff in your hand; and you shall eat it hurriedly. It is the passover of the LORD. [12] For I will pass through the land of Egypt that night, and I will strike down every firstborn in the land of Egypt, both human beings and animals; on all the gods of Egypt I will execute judgments: I am the LORD. [13] The blood shall be a sign for you on the houses where you live: when I see the blood, I will pass over you, and no plague shall destroy you when I strike the land of Egypt.

[14] This day shall be a day of remembrance for you. You shall celebrate it as a festival to the LORD; throughout your generations you shall observe it as a perpetual ordinance. [15] Seven days you shall eat unleavened bread; on the first day you shall remove leaven from your houses, for whoever eats leavened bread from the first day until the seventh day shall be cut off from Israel. [16] On the first day you shall hold a solemn assembly, and on the seventh day a solemn assembly; no work shall be done on those days; only what everyone must eat, that alone may be prepared by you. [17] You shall observe the festival of unleavened bread, for on this very day I brought your companies out of the land of Egypt: you shall observe this day throughout your generations as a perpetual ordinance. [18] In the first month, from the evening of the fourteenth day until the evening of the twenty-first day, you shall eat unleavened bread. [19] For seven days no leaven shall be found in your houses; for whoever eats what is leavened shall be cut off from the congregation of Israel, whether an alien or a native of the land. [20] You shall eat nothing leavened; in all your settlements you shall eat unleavened bread.

[21] Then Moses called all the elders of Israel and said to them, "Go, select lambs for your families, and slaughter the passover lamb. [22] Take a bunch of hyssop, dip it in the blood that is in the basin, and touch the lintel and the two doorposts with the blood in the basin. None of you shall go outside the door of your house until morning. [23] For the LORD will

language of sacrifice, for offerings to God are to be perfect (Lev 22.19–25; Deut 15.21; 17.1). **7:** *Blood* can have an apotropaic (evil-averting) quality; see 4.25n. and 12.11n. **8:** Unlike other sacrifices, this one is *roasted. Unleavened bread* appears here without comment, as if it were already known and incorporated into the passover festival; see 12.15n. *Bitter herbs*, probably a green plant serving as a condiment. **11:** The people must be ready to travel while they consume the lamb. *Passover* ("pesaḥ"), is often understood as "passing over," but is more likely from a word meaning "protect" ("spare," Isa 31.5), which is in accord with the apotropaic role of the blood smeared on doorways (12.5n.). Here (and in vv. 27,43) "passover" refers to the lamb sacrifice; eventually, it designates a longer commemorative festival (Deut 16.1–8; Ezek 45.21) that includes the seven-day festival of unleavened bread with which it is associated (12.14–20; 13.2–10). **12:** *I will strike* has God slaying the firstborn, but see 12.23n. **13:** *Pass over*, see 12.11n. **14–20: Unleavened bread. 14:** *This day* is the fifteenth day, after the passover of the fourteenth of Nisan; see 12.2n. and 12.6. Thus, the nighttime passover is followed by a seven-day festival of unleavened bread (see Lev 23.5–8). *Remembrance* proclaims the commemorative aspect of the festival, and *throughout . . . perpetual* applies it to all future Israelites (see 10.2n. and 11.1–13.16n.). **15:** *Unleavened bread* (Heb "matsah," spelled "matzah" or "matzo" in English), which originated in an ancient spring harvest festival, is given an explanation (vv. 34,39; 23.15; 34.18) connecting it to the hasty departure from Egypt; cf. the similar "historicization" of the lamb festival with which it is ultimately combined (see 12.11n. and 11.1–13.16n.). *Cut off*, the penalty for many serious violations of priestly law (e.g., 30.33,38; 31.14), probably does not mean excommunication but rather signifies dying without heirs, that is, having one's lineage ended; it would thus be implemented by God, not humans. **16:** *No work* signifies a holy day, as on the sabbath (20.8–11). **17:** *Companies*, a military term; see 6.26n. **19:** Although not obliged to celebrate the passover (v. 48), an *alien* (non-Israelite) must refrain from eating leavened bread. **21–28: Passover again. 22:** *Hyssop*, an aromatic plant used in rituals, including for sprinkling a liquid (Num 19.18). **23:** *Pass over*, that is "protect;" see 12.11n. Representing a variant tradition, a divine agent,

pass through to strike down the Egyptians; when he sees the blood on the lintel and on the two doorposts, the LORD will pass over that door and will not allow the destroyer to enter your houses to strike you down. ²⁴ You shall observe this rite as a perpetual ordinance for you and your children. ²⁵ When you come to the land that the LORD will give you, as he has promised, you shall keep this observance. ²⁶ And when your children ask you, 'What do you mean by this observance?' ²⁷ you shall say, 'It is the passover sacrifice to the LORD, for he passed over the houses of the Israelites in Egypt, when he struck down the Egyptians but spared our houses.'" And the people bowed down and worshiped. ²⁸ The Israelites went and did just as the LORD had commanded Moses and Aaron.

²⁹ At midnight the LORD struck down all the firstborn in the land of Egypt, from the firstborn of Pharaoh who sat on his throne to the firstborn of the prisoner who was in the dungeon, and all the firstborn of the livestock. ³⁰ Pharaoh arose in the night, he and all his officials and all the Egyptians; and there was a loud cry in Egypt, for there was not a house without someone dead. ³¹ Then he summoned Moses and Aaron in the night, and said, "Rise up, go away from my people, both you and the Israelites! Go, worship the LORD, as you said. ³² Take your flocks and your herds, as you said, and be gone. And bring a blessing on me too!"

³³ The Egyptians urged the people to hasten their departure from the land, for they said, "We shall all be dead." ³⁴ So the people took their dough before it was leavened, with their kneading bowls wrapped up in their cloaks on their shoulders. ³⁵ The Israelites had done as Moses told them; they had asked the Egyptians for jewelry of silver and gold, and for clothing, ³⁶ and the LORD had given the people favor in the sight of the Egyptians, so that they let them have what they asked. And so they plundered the Egyptians.

³⁷ The Israelites journeyed from Rameses to Succoth, about six hundred thousand men on foot, besides children. ³⁸ A mixed crowd also went up with them, and livestock in great numbers, both flocks and herds. ³⁹ They baked unleavened cakes of the dough that they had brought out of Egypt; it was not leavened, because they were driven out of Egypt and could not wait, nor had they prepared any provisions for themselves.

⁴⁰ The time that the Israelites had lived in Egypt was four hundred thirty years. ⁴¹ At the end of four hundred thirty years, on that very day, all the companies of the LORD went out from the land of Egypt. ⁴² That was for the LORD a night of vigil, to bring them out of the land of Egypt. That same night is a vigil to be kept for the LORD by all the Israelites throughout their generations.

the destroyer, rather than God, carries out the mission. **24–27:** Commands for future observance emphasize the educational function of the passover (also 10.2; 13.8–9,14–16; cf. Deut 6.6–7); see 11.1–13.16n.

12.29–52: Plague, departure, and passover. As soon as the firstborn of the Egyptians die, the Israelites leave Egypt and are reminded to celebrate the passover. **29–36: Plague.** What God announced in 11.1–8 is carried out. **29:** *Firstborn*, see 4.22n. *Pharaoh . . . prisoner* represent the two ends of the Egyptian social continuum; see 11.5n. **30:** *Cry*, see 11.6n. **32:** Cf. 10.24. A master who releases servants receives a *blessing* (Deut 15.18). **33:** *Urge*, perhaps fulfilling the notion of driving out the Israelites (6.1; 11.1). **35:** *Jewelry . . . clothing*, rather than "plunder" (in v. 36; see 3.22n.), may represent the goods given to released servants (Deut 15.13–15). **12.37–42: Exodus**, departing Egypt and beginning the wilderness journey (which continues in Numbers). **37:** Each stage of the journey is marked by formulaic language: traveling from Place A to Place B. Both *Rameses* (see 1.11n.) and *Succoth* are probably in the eastern Nile Delta; like virtually all the stops on the journey, however, they cannot be clearly identified and may not reflect accurate or actual memories. *Six hundred thousand* (as Num 11.21; cf. 38.26) is likely hyperbole meant to reflect the proliferation of Israelites (1.7–9,20; 5.5) and the concept of all Israel experiencing the Exodus; cf. 14.7n. *Men on foot*, or infantry, continues the military imagery; see 6.26n. *Children* are mentioned, but not the elderly or women; the latter may be subsumed into the "men" who are their husbands (see 20.8–11n). **38:** *Mixed crowd* suggests that non-Israelites were among those escaping. **39:** See 12.15n. **40–41:** *Four hundred and thirty years* is close to the period of "four hundred years" foreordained in Gen 15.13 (but cf. Gen 15.16); suggested reasons for the additional thirty years are speculative. **41:** *Companies*, see 12.17n. **42:** *Vigil*, from a root meaning "to guard" and also "to observe, perform (an obligation)" appears twice, forming a wordplay

⁴³ The Lᴏʀᴅ said to Moses and Aaron: This is the ordinance for the passover: no foreigner shall eat of it, ⁴⁴ but any slave who has been purchased may eat of it after he has been circumcised; ⁴⁵ no bound or hired servant may eat of it. ⁴⁶ It shall be eaten in one house; you shall not take any of the animal outside the house, and you shall not break any of its bones. ⁴⁷ The whole congregation of Israel shall celebrate it. ⁴⁸ If an alien who resides with you wants to celebrate the passover to the Lᴏʀᴅ, all his males shall be circumcised; then he may draw near to celebrate it; he shall be regarded as a native of the land. But no uncircumcised person shall eat of it; ⁴⁹ there shall be one law for the native and for the alien who resides among you.

⁵⁰ All the Israelites did just as the Lᴏʀᴅ had commanded Moses and Aaron. ⁵¹ That very day the Lᴏʀᴅ brought the Israelites out of the land of Egypt, company by company.

13 The Lᴏʀᴅ said to Moses: ² Consecrate to me all the firstborn; whatever is the first to open the womb among the Israelites, of human beings and animals, is mine.

³ Moses said to the people, "Remember this day on which you came out of Egypt, out of the house of slavery, because the Lᴏʀᴅ brought you out from there by strength of hand; no leavened bread shall be eaten. ⁴ Today, in the month of Abib, you are going out. ⁵ When the Lᴏʀᴅ brings you into the land of the Canaanites, the Hittites, the Amorites, the Hivites, and the Jebusites, which he swore to your ancestors to give you, a land flowing with milk and honey, you shall keep this observance in this month. ⁶ Seven days you shall eat unleavened bread, and on the seventh day there shall be a festival to the Lᴏʀᴅ. ⁷ Unleavened bread shall be eaten for seven days; no leavened bread shall be seen in your possession, and no leaven shall be seen among you in all your territory. ⁸ You shall tell your child on that day, 'It is because of what the Lᴏʀᴅ did for me when I came out of Egypt.' ⁹ It shall serve for you as a sign on your hand and as a reminder on your forehead, so that the teaching of the Lᴏʀᴅ may be on your lips; for with a strong hand the Lᴏʀᴅ brought you out of Egypt. ¹⁰ You shall keep this ordinance at its proper time from year to year.

¹¹ "When the Lᴏʀᴅ has brought you into the land of the Canaanites, as he swore to you and your ancestors, and has given it to you, ¹² you shall set apart to the Lᴏʀᴅ all that first opens the womb. All the firstborn of your livestock that are males shall be the Lᴏʀᴅ's. ¹³ But every firstborn donkey you shall

connoting present divine protection and future Israelite commemoration. **43–51: Further passover instructions,** explicitly for future observances. **43:** *Ordinance for the passover* (also cited in Num 9.12 and probably in Ex 13.10) is likely the title of a priestly document containing rules for passover observance. *Foreigner*, non-Israelite living temporarily in the land. **44:** A *slave* who is *purchased* is *circumcised* and considered part of the household (Gen 17.12–13). **45:** *Bound or hired servant* denotes a temporary member of a household. **46:** *In one house*, see 12.4n. **47:** *Whole congregation*, see 12.3n. **48:** Unlike the "foreigner" of v. 43, an *alien* is usually a permanent, non-Israelite resident and must be *circumcised* in order to celebrate the passover. Circumcision in this instance is not a conversion rite. **49:** *Law* (Heb "torah") is better translated "instruction" or "teaching" (as 13.9; 18.20) because the regulations for Israelite communal life are considered divinely revealed instruction. *Native*, or citizen, that is Israelite. **50–51:** These verses resume the narrative of vv. 37–41. **51:** *Company*, see 12.17n.

13.1–16: More commemorative rituals: consecration of the firstborn and unleavened bread festival. 2: The *consecration* of the *firstborn*, which reflects the special status of the first offspring of a woman or animal (see 4.22n.; 13.12n; 22.29–30; 34.19–20; Num 8.16–18), will receive its commemorative connection in vv. 11–16. **3:** The charge to *remember* prescribes commemoration; see 10.2n. and 11.1–13.16n. *House of slavery*, parallel to *Egypt* (also 13.14; 20.2), suggests that the entire country is the site of forced labor. **4:** *Abib*, meaning "new grain," is an older name for this springtime month; see 12.2n. **5:** See 3.8n. **8:** See 11.1–13.16n. and 12.24–27n. **9:** *Sign . . . forehead* (also v. 16; Deut 6.6–8) probably denotes metaphoric modes of commemoration (as Prov 6.20–21; 7.1–3) but is interpreted literally in postexilic times, giving rise to the Jewish custom of phylacteries. The phrase *teaching* (Heb "torah") *of the Lᴏʀᴅ* appears for the first time in the Bible; see 12.49n. *Hand*, see 3.19n. **11:** Instructions for the consecration of the firstborn resume. **12:** *Set apart to the Lᴏʀᴅ*, for the firstborn belong to God; see 4.22n. *Males*, specifying for the first time the gender of the firstborn to be consecrated. **13:** Because the *donkey* is an impure animal (according to the categories in Lev 11; Deut 14.3–21), it is redeemed by a pure one, a

redeem with a sheep; if you do not redeem it, you must break its neck. Every firstborn male among your children you shall redeem. [14] When in the future your child asks you, 'What does this mean?' you shall answer, 'By strength of hand the LORD brought us out of Egypt, from the house of slavery. [15] When Pharaoh stubbornly refused to let us go, the LORD killed all the firstborn in the land of Egypt, from human firstborn to the firstborn of animals. Therefore I sacrifice to the LORD every male that first opens the womb, but every firstborn of my sons I redeem.' [16] It shall serve as a sign on your hand and as an emblem[a] on your forehead that by strength of hand the LORD brought us out of Egypt."

[17] When Pharaoh let the people go, God did not lead them by way of the land of the Philistines, although that was nearer; for God thought, "If the people face war, they may change their minds and return to Egypt." [18] So God led the people by the roundabout way of the wilderness toward the Red Sea.[b] The Israelites went up out of the land of Egypt prepared for battle. [19] And Moses took with him the bones of Joseph who had required a solemn oath of the Israelites, saying, "God will surely take notice of you, and then you must carry my bones with you from here." [20] They set out from Succoth, and camped at Etham, on the edge of the wilderness. [21] The LORD went in front of them in a pillar of cloud by day, to lead them along the way, and in a pillar of fire by night, to give them light, so that they might travel by day and by night. [22] Neither the pillar of cloud by day nor the pillar of fire by night left its place in front of the people.

14 Then the LORD said to Moses: [2] Tell the Israelites to turn back and camp in front of Pi-hahiroth, between Migdol and the sea, in front of Baal-zephon; you shall camp opposite it, by the sea. [3] Pharaoh will say of the Israelites, "They are wandering aimlessly in the land; the wilderness has closed in on them." [4] I will harden Pharaoh's heart, and he will pursue them, so that I will gain glory for myself over Pharaoh and all his army; and the Egyptians shall know that I am the LORD. And they did so.

[5] When the king of Egypt was told that the people had fled, the minds of Pharaoh and his officials were changed toward the people, and they said, "What have we done, letting Israel leave our service?" [6] So he had his chariot made ready, and took his army with him; [7] he took six hundred picked chariots and all the other chariots of Egypt with officers over all of them. [8] The LORD hardened the heart of Pharaoh king of Egypt and he pursued Israelites, who were going out boldly. [9] The Egyptians pursued them, all Pharaoh's horses and chariots, his chariot drivers and his

---

a   Or *as a frontlet*; meaning of Heb uncertain
b   Or *Sea of Reeds*

---

sheep; see also 34.20. The procedure for redeeming the human *firstborn male* is not specified. **14–15:** Linking the consecration of the firstborn to the firstborn slain in the plague gives the custom a pedagogical function; see 10.2n. and 11.1–13.16n. **16:** See 13.9n.

   13.17–15.21: Journey to and through the sea, described in prose and poetry.

   13.17–14.31: The narrative account, somewhat repetitive and inconsistent, is probably composite. **13.17:** *Way of the land of the Philistines*, the shortest land route from Egypt to Canaan, runs parallel to the Mediterranean coast toward southwest Canaan where the Philistines, a people from the Aegean, settled in the late thirteenth and early twelfth centuries BCE. **18:** *Roundabout way of the wilderness*, that is, not a specific route. This vague description fits the ahistorical character of the places along the way; see 12.37n. *Red Sea* (Heb "yam sup"), properly Reed Sea, probably designates the reedy marshes of northeastern Egypt; but the miraculous sea-splitting account (14.21–29) does not fit the marshland referent and may reflect a different, perhaps imaginary or mythological, sea tradition. *Battle*, in keeping with the military language for the journeying Israelites; see 6.26n. **19:** Gen 50.24–26. **20:** Next stage of the journey; see 12.37n. **21:** *Pillar of cloud* and *pillar of fire*, probably one column manifesting the divine presence as a shielding cloud by day and a guiding light by night; see 3.2n. **14.1:** *Moses* acts alone, without Aaron, in the sea-crossing episode. **2:** Next stage of the journey; see 12.37n. *Sea*, see 13.18n. **4:** *Harden*, by God; see 4.21n. *Glory*, or more likely "power" and thus "authority" (also v. 17). *Know*, see 5.2n. **7:** *Six hundred*, perhaps a stock military unit (cf. Judg 18.11), provides a 1:1000 ratio with the Israelite infantry (12.37n.). **8:** *Hardened* by God; see 4.21n. **9:** *Pursued . . . overtook* is formulaic language (15.9; Deut 19.6; etc.). **10:** *Cried*, see

army; they overtook them camped by the sea, by Pi-hahiroth, in front of Baal-zephon.

[10] As Pharaoh drew near, the Israelites looked back, and there were the Egyptians advancing on them. In great fear the Israelites cried out to the LORD. [11] They said to Moses, "Was it because there were no graves in Egypt that you have taken us away to die in the wilderness? What have you done to us, bringing us out of Egypt? [12] Is this not the very thing we told you in Egypt, 'Let us alone and let us serve the Egyptians'? For it would have been better for us to serve the Egyptians than to die in the wilderness." [13] But Moses said to the people, "Do not be afraid, stand firm, and see the deliverance that the LORD will accomplish for you today; for the Egyptians whom you see today you shall never see again. [14] The LORD will fight for you, and you have only to keep still."

[15] Then the LORD said to Moses, "Why do you cry out to me? Tell the Israelites to go forward. [16] But you lift up your staff, and stretch out your hand over the sea and divide it, that the Israelites may go into the sea on dry ground. [17] Then I will harden the hearts of the Egyptians so that they will go in after them; and so I will gain glory for myself over Pharaoh and all his army, his chariots, and his chariot drivers. [18] And the Egyptians shall know that I am the LORD, when I have gained glory for myself over Pharaoh, his chariots, and his chariot drivers."

[19] The angel of God who was going before the Israelite army moved and went behind them; and the pillar of cloud moved from in front of them and took its place behind them. [20] It came between the army of Egypt and the army of Israel. And so the cloud was there with the darkness, and it lit up the night; one did not come near the other all night.

[21] Then Moses stretched out his hand over the sea. The LORD drove the sea back by a strong east wind all night, and turned the sea into dry land; and the waters were divided. [22] The Israelites went into the sea on dry ground, the waters forming a wall for them on their right and on their left. [23] The Egyptians pursued, and went into the sea after them, all of Pharaoh's horses, chariots, and chariot drivers. [24] At the morning watch the LORD in the pillar of fire and cloud looked down upon the Egyptian army, and threw the Egyptian army into panic. [25] He clogged[a] their chariot wheels so that they turned with difficulty. The Egyptians said, "Let us flee from the Israelites, for the LORD is fighting for them against Egypt."

[26] Then the LORD said to Moses, "Stretch out your hand over the sea, so that the water may come back upon the Egyptians, upon their chariots and chariot drivers." [27] So Moses stretched out his hand over the sea, and at dawn the sea returned to its normal depth. As the Egyptians fled before it, the LORD tossed the Egyptians into the sea. [28] The waters returned and covered the chariots and the chariot drivers, the entire army of Pharaoh that had followed them into the sea; not one of them remained. [29] But the Israelites walked on dry ground through the sea, the waters forming a wall for them on their right and on their left.

[30] Thus the LORD saved Israel that day from the Egyptians; and Israel saw the Egyptians dead on the seashore. [31] Israel saw the great work that the LORD did against the Egyptians. So the people feared the LORD and believed in the LORD and in his servant Moses.

15 Then Moses and the Israelites sang this song to the LORD:

"I will sing to the LORD, for he has
    triumphed gloriously;

---

[a] Sam Gk Syr: MT *removed*

2.23n. **11–12:** For the first but not the last time the Israelites complain in a crisis situation, challenging Moses' authority (15.24; 16.2–3; 17.3; and frequently in Numbers). **14:** *The LORD will fight* introduces the concept of the Divine Warrior, based on the Canaanite deity Baal who battles watery chaos often depicted as a sea monster. The image is used metaphorically in the Bible to represent divine might wielded to save Israel (v. 25; 15.3; Deut 20.4; 1 Sam 17.47; Zech 9.13–14.) **15:** *Cry,* see 2.23n. **16:** Moses' *staff* (see 4.17n.) is not mentioned in vv. 21,26,27. **17:** *Harden* appears for the last time; see 4.21n. *Glory,* see 14.4n. **18:** *Know,* see 5.2n. **19–20:** *Angel* and *pillar,* both manifestations of God's presence (see 3.2n. and 13.21n.), are used sequentially, perhaps indicating a composite. **21:** *Wind, dry land,* and *divided waters,* which evoke creation (Gen 1.2,6,9; cf. Gen 8.2), are from a Priestly hand. **24:** *Pillar,* see 3.2n. **31:** The Hebrew for *believed* means to "trust" in God rather than to affirm God's existence.

  15.1–21: The Song of the Sea is a lyric victory hymn generally considered one of the oldest literary units

horse and rider he has thrown into the
sea.
2 The Lᴏʀᴅ is my strength and my
might,[a]
and he has become my salvation;
this is my God, and I will praise him,
my father's God, and I will exalt him.
3 The Lᴏʀᴅ is a warrior;
the Lᴏʀᴅ is his name.

4 "Pharaoh's chariots and his army he cast
into the sea;
his picked officers were sunk in the Red
Sea.[b]
5 The floods covered them;
they went down into the depths like a
stone.
6 Your right hand, O Lᴏʀᴅ, glorious in
power—
your right hand, O Lᴏʀᴅ, shattered the
enemy.
7 In the greatness of your majesty you
overthrew your adversaries;
you sent out your fury, it consumed
them like stubble.
8 At the blast of your nostrils the waters
piled up,
the floods stood up in a heap;
the deeps congealed in the heart of the
sea.

9 The enemy said, 'I will pursue, I will
overtake,
I will divide the spoil, my desire shall
have its fill of them.
I will draw my sword, my hand shall
destroy them.'
10 You blew with your wind, the sea
covered them;
they sank like lead in the mighty
waters.

11 "Who is like you, O Lᴏʀᴅ, among the
gods?
Who is like you, majestic in
holiness,
awesome in splendor,
doing wonders?
12 You stretched out your right hand,
the earth swallowed them.

13 "In your steadfast love you led the people
whom you redeemed;
you guided them by your strength to
your holy abode.
14 The peoples heard, they trembled;
pangs seized the inhabitants of
Philistia.

a Or song
b Or Sea of Reeds

in the Bible, perhaps from the twelfth century BCE; it probably was an independent composition, not part of one of the other sources of Exodus. Influenced by mythic accounts of the Divine Warrior's battle with watery chaos (see 14.14n.), it is rich in metaphors and terms that preclude single explanations and at times even defy comprehension; its general meaning would be less clear without the prose version, although in some details it diverges from that version. **1:** Although attributed to *Moses*, female authorship cannot be ruled out (see 15.21n.); note that *I* need not be Moses. **2:** *The Lᴏʀᴅ . . . salvation*, a hymnic bicolon appearing (perhaps as a quotation) in Isa 12.2 and Ps 118.14. *My father's God*, Israel's ancestral deity (3.6,13,15; 4.5; 6.2–4). **3:** *Warrior*, see 14.14n. *Name*, see 3.13–15n. **4:** *Red Sea*, see 14.18n. **5:** Hebrew for *floods* is the same term used for the watery chaos in Genesis 1 ("deep," Gen 1.2) **6:** The *right hand* of God (also v. 12), not Moses' hand (as 14.16,21,26), directly vanquishes the enemy; see 3.19n. **7:** *Consumed . . . stubble* evokes imagery of fire, which can be paired with water as elements of devastation (Isa 43.2,16–17). **8:** *Blast of your nostrils*, poetic language for a strong wind (v. 10), usually destructive (see Job 4.9). **9:** *Pursue . . . overtake*, see 14.9n. **11:** *Among the gods* may be language of Israelite monolatry in which the existence of other (inferior) gods is not denied (18.11; 20.3; 23.32–33) until universal monotheism emerges in the seventh or sixth century BCE. Another possibility is that *gods* denotes the lesser divine manifestations or angels in God's heavenly court (Pss 82.1; 89.5–8). Either way, the incomparability of Israel's god is forcefully proclaimed by the rhetorical questions of this verse. **12:** *Right hand*, see 15.6n. *Earth*, seemingly incompatible with the water imagery, refers to the underworld (Sheol or death), which swallows the living (Num 16.32; Isa 29.4; Prov 1.12). **13:** The Hebrew for *love* ("ḥesed") also connotes "kindness" and especially "faithfulness." *Holy abode* most likely refers to God's heavenly dwelling (as do the terms of v. 17b) or mythical home in the north (Ps 48.1–2); but it perhaps also alludes to the Promised Land as God's mountainous possession (v. 17a; Ps 78.54–55) and to the Israelites as God's sanctuary (Ps 114.1–2). If this is not a premonarchic poem, it may also refer to the

¹⁵ Then the chiefs of Edom were
  dismayed;
    trembling seized the leaders of Moab;
    all the inhabitants of Canaan melted
      away.
¹⁶ Terror and dread fell upon them;
    by the might of your arm, they became
      still as a stone
until your people, O LORD, passed by,
    until the people whom you acquired
      passed by.
¹⁷ You brought them in and planted them
    on the mountain of your own
      possession,
    the place, O LORD, that you made your
      abode,
    the sanctuary, O LORD, that your hands
      have established.
¹⁸ The LORD will reign forever and ever."
¹⁹ When the horses of Pharaoh with his
chariots and his chariot drivers went into
the sea, the LORD brought back the waters of
the sea upon them; but the Israelites walked
through the sea on dry ground.

²⁰ Then the prophet Miriam, Aaron's sister,
took a tambourine in her hand; and all the
women went out after her with tambourines
and with dancing. ²¹ And Miriam sang to
them:
  "Sing to the LORD, for he has triumphed
    gloriously;
    horse and rider he has thrown into the sea."
²² Then Moses ordered Israel to set out
from the Red Sea,ᵃ and they went into the
wilderness of Shur. They went three days in
the wilderness and found no water. ²³ When
they came to Marah, they could not drink the
water of Marah because it was bitter. That is
why it was called Marah.ᵇ ²⁴ And the people
complained against Moses, saying, "What
shall we drink?" ²⁵ He cried out to the LORD;
and the LORD showed him a piece of wood;ᶜ
he threw it into the water, and the water
became sweet.

ᵃ Or *Sea of Reeds*
ᵇ That is *Bitterness*
ᶜ Or *a tree*

Jerusalem Temple (v. 17b). **14:** *Philistia*, see 13.17n. **15:** The Transjordanian kingdoms of *Edom* and *Moab*, as well as many inhabitants of *Canaan*, figure among the early enemies of the Israelites. **16:** *Arm*, instead of "hand" (see 15.6n.), as in 6.6. **17:** This verse contains overlapping and multileveled imagery similar to that of ancient Canaanite poetry (see 15.13n.). *Mountain of your possession* can refer to Israel's homeland in Canaan, conceptualized as God's inheritance (see v. 13n.; 34.9); other biblical references to God's mountain as the Temple mount (e.g., Isa 2.3) may derive from this verse. The Hebrew for *abode*, not the same as for "abode" in v. 13, designates God's heavenly throne. *Sanctuary*, "holy place" in Hebrew, is never used in 1 Kings for the Jerusalem Temple; and elsewhere it designates places or objects possessing sanctity, including celestial dwellings of deities (see 25.9n.). *Your hands have established*, indicates that God made the sanctuary, implying that it is the heavenly one, not the copy constructed in Jerusalem by humans; or, it could give God credit for building the earthly shrine (cf. Ps 78.69). Either way, the verb also connotes God's creative activity (Ps 8.3). **18:** *Reign* introduces the prominent biblical metaphor of God as king. **19–21:** A brief narrative with a final poetic section. **19:** A summary of 14.23–29. **20:** The title *prophet* is used for Miriam (whose name appears here for the first time) but not Moses in Exodus. *Tambourine* is an anachronistic translation of Hebrew "top," a small handheld frame drum (without jingles) played mainly by women in the ancient Near East. *All the women . . . dancing* indicate a woman's performance genre—usually involving drums, dance, and song—for victory celebrations (1 Sam 18.6–7; Jer 31.4,13). **21:** This poem, similar to 15.1, may be an abbreviation or title of 15.1–18, in which case Miriam would be the composer of the song attributed to Moses (see 15.1n.), a possibility also suggested by the association of women with the victory song genre (15.20n.).

15.22–24.18. Sinai and Covenant. Facing recurrent difficulties, the Israelites cross the wilderness to Sinai (15.22–18.27) where they experience a theophany (ch 19) and receive the covenant (chs 20–24).

15.22–18.27: Crises and reorganization in the wilderness. The journey resumes; four crises foreshadowing the difficulties of life in Canaan—two water shortages, lack of food, and a military threat—and a meeting with Jethro prepare Moses for the Sinai experience.

15.22–27: First crisis, lack of water. 22–23: Next stage of the journey; see 12.37n. **22:** *Red Sea*, see 13.18n. **24:** *Complained*, see 14.11–12n. **25b:** *Statute . . . ordinance*, necessary because a community cannot exist without regulations; see 21.1–22.17n. The wilderness crises constitute a *test* of the Israelites (also 16.4) and of God (17.2,7);

There the Lord[a] made for them a statute and an ordinance and there he put them to the test. [26] He said, "If you will listen carefully to the voice of the Lord your God, and do what is right in his sight, and give heed to his commandments and keep all his statutes, I will not bring upon you any of the diseases that I brought upon the Egyptians; for I am the Lord who heals you."

[27] Then they came to Elim, where there were twelve springs of water and seventy palm trees; and they camped there by the water.

16 The whole congregation of the Israelites set out from Elim; and Israel came to the wilderness of Sin, which is between Elim and Sinai, on the fifteenth day of the second month after they had departed from the land of Egypt. [2] The whole congregation of the Israelites complained against Moses and Aaron in the wilderness. [3] The Israelites said to them, "If only we had died by the hand of the Lord in the land of Egypt, when we sat by the fleshpots and ate our fill of bread; for you have brought us out into this wilderness to kill this whole assembly with hunger."

[4] Then the Lord said to Moses, "I am going to rain bread from heaven for you, and each day the people shall go out and gather enough for that day. In that way I will test them, whether they will follow my instruction or not. [5] On the sixth day, when they prepare what they bring in, it will be twice as much as they gather on other days." [6] So Moses and Aaron said to all the Israelites, "In the evening you shall know that it was the Lord who brought you out of the land of Egypt, [7] and in the morning you shall see the glory of the Lord, because he has heard your complaining against the Lord. For what are we, that you complain against us?" [8] And Moses said, "When the Lord gives you meat to eat in the evening and your fill of bread in the morning, because the Lord has heard the complaining that you utter against him— what are we? Your complaining is not against us but against the Lord."

[9] Then Moses said to Aaron, "Say to the whole congregation of the Israelites, 'Draw near to the Lord, for he has heard your complaining.'" [10] And as Aaron spoke to the whole congregation of the Israelites, they looked toward the wilderness, and the glory of the Lord appeared in the cloud. [11] The Lord spoke to Moses and said, [12] "I have heard the complaining of the Israelites; say to them, 'At twilight you shall eat meat, and in the morning you shall have your fill of bread; then you shall know that I am the Lord your God.'"

[13] In the evening quails came up and covered the camp; and in the morning there was a layer of dew around the camp. [14] When the layer of dew lifted, there on the surface of the wilderness was a fine flaky substance, as fine as frost on the ground. [15] When the Israelites saw it, they said to one another, "What is it?"[b] For they did not know what it was. Moses said to them, "It is the bread that the Lord has given you to eat. [16] This is what the Lord has commanded: 'Gather as much of it as each of you needs, an omer to a person according to the number of persons, all providing for those in their own tents.'" [17] The Israelites did so, some gathering more, some less. [18] But when they measured it with an omer, those who gathered much had noth-

---

[a] Heb *he*

[b] Or *"It is manna"* (Heb *man hu*, see verse 31)

---

see Deut 8.1–3,16. **26**: The term *diseases*, although not used in the marvels episodes (7.8–10.29), may allude to them or to general Egyptian maladies or to both. **27**: Next stage of the journey; see 12.37n.

16.1–36: Second crisis, lack of food (cf. Num 11). **1**: Next stage of the journey, see 12.37n. *Fifteenth day . . . second month* is a month after departing Egypt (12.17–18). The name *Sinai* appears for the first time (see 19.1n.); cf. Horeb in 3.1. **2**: *Complained*, see 14.11–12n. **3**: *Hand of the Lord*, see 9.3n. *Fleshpots* (referring to meat) and *bread*, their food in Egypt, will be matched by quails (v. 13) and bread (v. 4; or manna, vv. 15,31) in the wilderness. **4**: This *test* (see 15.25n.) may be about obeying God's instructions (Heb "torah"; see 12.49n.) as well as about believing God will provide for them. **6**: To *know* God here (and v. 12) is to recognize that God can miraculously provide sustenance; cf. 5.2n. **7**: The phrase *glory of the Lord*, signifying (the cloud of) divine presence, appears for the first time in the Bible (also v. 10; 24.16,17; 40.34,35); see 3.2n. **9**: *Aaron* again speaks for Moses; see 4.15–16n. **12**: *Know*, see 16.6n. **13**: *Dew*, like rain, signifies divine favor (e.g., Gen 27.28)—both were essential for agriculture in an-

ing over, and those who gathered little had no shortage; they gathered as much as each of them needed. [19] And Moses said to them, "Let no one leave any of it over until morning." [20] But they did not listen to Moses; some left part of it until morning, and it bred worms and became foul. And Moses was angry with them. [21] Morning by morning they gathered it, as much as each needed; but when the sun grew hot, it melted.

[22] On the sixth day they gathered twice as much food, two omers apiece. When all the leaders of the congregation came and told Moses, [23] he said to them, "This is what the LORD has commanded: 'Tomorrow is a day of solemn rest, a holy sabbath to the LORD; bake what you want to bake and boil what you want to boil, and all that is left over put aside to be kept until morning.'" [24] So they put it aside until morning, as Moses commanded them; and it did not become foul, and there were no worms in it. [25] Moses said, "Eat it today, for today is a sabbath to the LORD; today you will not find it in the field. [26] Six days you shall gather it; but on the seventh day, which is a sabbath, there will be none."

[27] On the seventh day some of the people went out to gather, and they found none. [28] The LORD said to Moses, "How long will you refuse to keep my commandments and instructions? [29] See! The LORD has given you the sabbath, therefore on the sixth day he gives you food for two days; each of you stay where you are; do not leave your place on the seventh day." [30] So the people rested on the seventh day.

[31] The house of Israel called it manna; it was like coriander seed, white, and the taste of it was like wafers made with honey. [32] Moses said, "This is what the LORD has commanded: 'Let an omer of it be kept throughout your generations, in order that they may see the food with which I fed you in the wilderness, when I brought you out of the land of Egypt.'" [33] And Moses said to Aaron, "Take a jar, and put an omer of manna in it, and place it before the LORD, to be kept throughout your generations." [34] As the LORD commanded Moses, so Aaron placed it before the covenant,[a] for safekeeping. [35] The Israelites ate manna forty years, until they came to a habitable land; they ate manna, until they came to the border of the land of Canaan. [36] An omer is a tenth of an ephah.

17 From the wilderness of Sin the whole congregation of the Israelites journeyed by stages, as the LORD commanded. They camped at Rephidim, but there was no water for the people to drink. [2] The people quarreled with Moses, and said, "Give us water to drink." Moses said to them, "Why do you quarrel with me? Why do you test the LORD?" [3] But the people thirsted there for water; and the people complained against Moses and said, "Why did you bring us out of Egypt, to kill us and our children and livestock with thirst?" [4] So Moses cried out to the LORD, "What shall I do with this people? They are almost ready to stone me." [5] The LORD said to Moses, "Go on ahead of the people, and take some of the elders of Israel with you; take in your hand the staff with which you struck the Nile, and go. [6] I will be standing there in front of you on the rock at Horeb. Strike the

---

a   Or *treaty* or *testimony*; Heb *eduth*

cient Israel. **16:** *Omer*, see 16.36n. **19:** This will indicate trust in God. **23–30:** Instructions for the *sabbath* as a *day of rest* on the *seventh day* (cf. Gen 2.2–3) are presented as preceding the Decalogue's sabbath commandment (see 20.8–11n.); observing the sabbath is part of Israel's learning to obey God (see 16.4n.); see also 20.8–11; 23.12; 31.12–17; 34.21; 35.1–3. **31:** *House of Israel*, see 40.34n. Verse 15 provides an etymology for *manna*, which cannot be identified and may be a mythic substance (cf. Num 11.7–9). **32:** *Kept throughout your generations* alludes to an otherwise unknown commemorative ritual; see 11.1–13.16n. **34:** *Covenant*, elliptical for the not-yet-announced "ark of the covenant" (25.10–22), is parallel to LORD (v. 33), indicating that the ark signifies God's presence (see 25.17–22n.). **35:** *Forty years*, the first mention of the length of the wilderness sojourn. **36:** *Ephah* (ca. 21 qts [23 liters]) and *omer* (2 qts [2.3 liters]) are dry measures, usually for grain.

17.1–7: Third crisis, lack of water (cf. Num 20.2–13). **1:** Further stages of the journey; see 12.27n. **2–3:** The people *complain* again (see 14.11–12n.), with the synonym *quarrel* (Heb "rib") providing an etymology for Meribah (v. 7). Similarly, *test* (Heb "nissah") provides an etymology for Massah (v. 7). **6:** *Water* coming from a *rock* at the mountain *Horeb* (see 3.1n.) invokes mythic imagery of the cosmic mountain, source of all water and the

rock, and water will come out of it, so that the people may drink." Moses did so, in the sight of the elders of Israel. ⁷ He called the place Massahᵃ and Meribah,ᵇ because the Israelites quarreled and tested the Lord, saying, "Is the Lord among us or not?"

⁸ Then Amalek came and fought with Israel at Rephidim. ⁹ Moses said to Joshua, "Choose some men for us and go out, fight with Amalek. Tomorrow I will stand on the top of the hill with the staff of God in my hand." ¹⁰ So Joshua did as Moses told him, and fought with Amalek, while Moses, Aaron, and Hur went up to the top of the hill. ¹¹ Whenever Moses held up his hand, Israel prevailed; and whenever he lowered his hand, Amalek prevailed. ¹² But Moses' hands grew weary; so they took a stone and put it under him, and he sat on it. Aaron and Hur held up his hands, one on one side, and the other on the other side; so his hands were steady until the sun set. ¹³ And Joshua defeated Amalek and his people with the sword.

¹⁴ Then the Lord said to Moses, "Write this as a reminder in a book and recite it in the hearing of Joshua: I will utterly blot out the remembrance of Amalek from under heaven." ¹⁵ And Moses built an altar and called it, The Lord is my banner. ¹⁶ He said, "A hand upon the banner of the Lord!ᶜ The Lord will have war with Amalek from generation to generation."

18 Jethro, the priest of Midian, Moses' father-in-law, heard of all that God had done for Moses and for his people Israel,

how the Lord had brought Israel out of Egypt. ² After Moses had sent away his wife Zipporah, his father-in-law Jethro took her back, ³ along with her two sons. The name of the one was Gershom (for he said, "I have been an alienᵈ in a foreign land"), ⁴ and the name of the other, Eliezerᵉ (for he said, "The God of my father was my help, and delivered me from the sword of Pharaoh"). ⁵ Jethro, Moses' father-in-law, came into the wilderness where Moses was encamped at the mountain of God, bringing Moses' sons and wife to him. ⁶ He sent word to Moses, "I, your father-in-law Jethro, am coming to you, with your wife and her two sons." ⁷ Moses went out to meet his father-in-law; he bowed down and kissed him; each asked after the other's welfare, and they went into the tent. ⁸ Then Moses told his father-in-law all that the Lord had done to Pharaoh and to the Egyptians for Israel's sake, all the hardship that had beset them on the way, and how the Lord had delivered them. ⁹ Jethro rejoiced for all the good that the Lord had done to Israel, in delivering them from the Egyptians.

¹⁰ Jethro said, "Blessed be the Lord, who has delivered you from the Egyptians and

ᵃ That is *Test*
ᵇ That is *Quarrel*
ᶜ Cn: Meaning of Heb uncertain
ᵈ Heb *ger*
ᵉ Heb *Eli*, my God; *ezer*, help

---

divine home. **7:** *Among us*, or "with you/us," an expression denoting God's potent presence, which provides food or water for Israelites and protects them (Judg 8.12–13).

17.8–16. Fourth crisis, military threat. 8: *Amalek* refers to a seminomadic group and habitual enemy of Israel (v. 16; Deut 25.17–19; Judg 6.1–3; etc.). It is not attested in nonbiblical records. **9:** Moses' successor *Joshua*, whose name appears seven times in Exodus, is first mentioned here. Moses' *staff* (presumably held in his hand, vv. 11–12) can secure military victory (as also in the sea crossing, 14.16) and produce water (17.5–6) or make it undrinkable (7.15–19); see 4.2on. **10:** *Hur*, with an Egyptian name and as an associate of Moses and Aaron (also 24.14), is likely a Levite; but he is a Judahite in 31.2. **14:** The instruction to *write* is the first biblical mention of Israelite literacy. *Reminder*, another indication of the commemorative aspects of the Exodus narrative; cf. 11.1–13.16n. *Book*, or "document." *Recite* implies oral as well as written recollection. **15–16:** The construction of an *altar* may be a third commemorative act.

18.1–27: Meeting with Jethro, who solves an organizational crisis. **1:** *Jethro*, see 2.18n. Because the Hebrew for *father-in-law* ("ḥoten") connotes the concept of marriage as a bond between two families, not just between the conjugal pair, its frequent and redundant use in ch 18 emphasizes Moses' connection with the Midianites. **2:** *Sent away* may be a mistranslation of "dowry" (1 Kings 9.16), meaning that Zipporah (2.21–22; 4.20) had been Moses' *wife* since receiving it. **3–4:** *Gershom*'s symbolic name appears in 2.22 but *Eliezer*'s only here. **5:** *Mountain of God*, i.e., Sinai/Horeb (see 3.1n.); compare 19.2, a tradition implying that the Israelites reach the mountain

from Pharaoh. [11] Now I know that the LORD is greater than all gods, because he delivered the people from the Egyptians,[a] when they dealt arrogantly with them." [12] And Jethro, Moses' father-in-law, brought a burnt offering and sacrifices to God; and Aaron came with all the elders of Israel to eat bread with Moses' father-in-law in the presence of God.

[13] The next day Moses sat as judge for the people, while the people stood around him from morning until evening. [14] When Moses' father-in-law saw all that he was doing for the people, he said, "What is this that you are doing for the people? Why do you sit alone, while all the people stand around you from morning until evening?" [15] Moses said to his father-in-law, "Because the people come to me to inquire of God. [16] When they have a dispute, they come to me and I decide between one person and another, and I make known to them the statutes and instructions of God." [17] Moses' father-in-law said to him, "What you are doing is not good. [18] You will surely wear yourself out, both you and these people with you. For the task is too heavy for you; you cannot do it alone. [19] Now listen to me. I will give you counsel, and God be with you! You should represent the people before God, and you should bring their cases before God; [20] teach them the statutes and instructions and make known to them the way they are to go and the things they are to do. [21] You should also look for able men among all the people, men who fear God, are trustworthy, and hate dishonest gain; set such men over

them as officers over thousands, hundreds, fifties, and tens. [22] Let them sit as judges for the people at all times; let them bring every important case to you, but decide every minor case themselves. So it will be easier for you, and they will bear the burden with you. [23] If you do this, and God so commands you, then you will be able to endure, and all these people will go to their home in peace."

[24] So Moses listened to his father-in-law and did all that he had said. [25] Moses chose able men from all Israel and appointed them as heads over the people, as officers over thousands, hundreds, fifties, and tens. [26] And they judged the people at all times; hard cases they brought to Moses, but any minor case they decided themselves. [27] Then Moses let his father-in-law depart, and he went off to his own country.

19 On the third new moon after the Israelites had gone out of the land of Egypt, on that very day, they came into the wilderness of Sinai. [2] They had journeyed from Rephidim, entered the wilderness of Sinai, and camped in the wilderness; Israel camped there in front of the mountain. [3] Then Moses went up to God; the LORD called to him from the mountain, saying, "Thus you shall say to the house of Jacob, and tell the Israelites: [4] You have seen what I did to the Egyptians, and how I bore you on eagles' wings and brought you to myself. [5] Now therefore, if you obey my

[a] The clause *because ... Egyptians* has been transposed from verse 10

after the Jethro episode. **10–12:** As a priest (v. 1, see 2.16n.) who blesses the LORD, acknowledges the LORD (see 5.2n.) as greater than other deities (see 15.11n.), and sacrifices to the LORD, Jethro may reflect Midianite familiarity with this deity; see 3.15n. **12:** *Eat bread* denotes a communal sacrificial meal binding the Israelites, Jethro, and God (see 24.5n.). **13–27** (cf. Deut 1.9–18): Rendering justice will be the responsibility of a hierarchy of administrative officials (vv. 13,22; NRSV "judges"). **20:** *Statutes*, see 15.25b n. *Instructions* (Heb "torot," pl. of "torah"), see 12.49n. **26:** *Case* (also, "thing, word, matter") translates a Hebrew root ("dbr") appearing ten times in ch 18, anticipating the ten "words" of the Decalogue; see 20.1–17n. **27:** *Depart*, cf. Deut 10.29–32.

19.1–25: Revelation at the mountain, God's second appearance at Sinai/Horeb (cf. ch 3) is a composite of traditions, at times contradictory or redundant; but at the same time conveying the mystery of this momentous theophany. Sinai/Horeb is depicted as an earthly manifestation of the cosmic mountain (see 17.6n.), the axis of the mythic connection between the divine and the human realms. **1:** The precise location of *Sinai* (or Horeb; see 3.1n.) is uncertain. Some passages locate it in southern Jordan (Deut 33.2; Judg 5.4; Hab 3.3,7); the traditional site in the southern Sinai Peninsula is unlikely. **3:** *House of Jacob* is parallel with "sons of Israel" (Israelites), the two names of the ancestor of the twelve tribes (Gen 32.28). **4:** The reminder of God's past actions for the Israelites, as preface to the covenant, is typical of Near Eastern treaties in which an overlord states past benefactions; also 20.2. *Eagle's wings*, an image of parental protection and nurturance (Deut 32.11–13). **5:** *Obey*

voice and keep my covenant, you shall be my treasured possession out of all the peoples. Indeed, the whole earth is mine, ⁶ but you shall be for me a priestly kingdom and a holy nation. These are the words that you shall speak to the Israelites."

⁷ So Moses came, summoned the elders of the people, and set before them all these words that the LORD had commanded him. ⁸ The people all answered as one: "Everything that the LORD has spoken we will do." Moses reported the words of the people to the LORD. ⁹ Then the LORD said to Moses, "I am going to come to you in a dense cloud, in order that the people may hear when I speak with you and so trust you ever after."

When Moses had told the words of the people to the LORD, ¹⁰ the LORD said to Moses: "Go to the people and consecrate them today and tomorrow. Have them wash their clothes ¹¹ and prepare for the third day, because on the third day the LORD will come down upon Mount Sinai in the sight of all the people. ¹² You shall set limits for the people all around, saying, 'Be careful not to go up the mountain or to touch the edge of it. Any who touch the mountain shall be put to death. ¹³ No hand shall touch them, but they shall be stoned or shot with arrows;ᵃ whether animal or human being, they shall not live.' When the trumpet sounds a long blast, they may go up on the mountain." ¹⁴ So Moses went down from the mountain to the people. He consecrated the people, and they washed their clothes. ¹⁵ And he said to the people, "Prepare for the third day; do not go near a woman."

¹⁶ On the morning of the third day there was thunder and lightning, as well as a thick cloud on the mountain, and a blast of a trumpet so loud that all the people who were in the camp trembled. ¹⁷ Moses brought the people out of the camp to meet God. They took their stand at the foot of the mountain. ¹⁸ Now Mount Sinai was wrapped in smoke, because the LORD had descended upon it in fire; the smoke went up like the smoke of a kiln, while the whole mountain shook violently. ¹⁹ As the blast of the trumpet grew louder and louder, Moses would speak and God would answer him in thunder. ²⁰ When the LORD descended upon Mount Sinai, to the top of the mountain, the LORD summoned Moses to the top of the mountain, and Moses went up. ²¹ Then the LORD said

ᵃ Heb lacks *with arrows*

. . . *keep* signifies the people's responsibilities to the god who saved them, thus anticipating the Sinai *covenant*, first mentioned here (cf. 2.24; 6.4–5). The concept of a pact between God and Israel is a theologized form of Near Eastern treaty agreements in which a ruler is the patron of a vassal, who has obligations in return. Unlike most vassals, Israel will have special status as the *treasured possession* of its overlord (Deut 7.6; 14.2; 26.18). **6:** *Priestly kingdom . . . holy nation* poetically expresses the idea that all Israelites are priestly; that is, they will have privileges of intimacy with God and responsibilities of physical and moral purity—both associated with priests in the ancient world. **8:** This unanimous agreement is reaffirmed after the covenant is presented (24.7). **9:** *Cloud*, see 3.2n. *Hear*, denoting an auditory theophany; v. 11 implies a visual one. **10–15:** God's presence will render the mountain intensely holy and too dangerous for people and for priests (v. 22; cf. 24.11) to approach (see 3.6n.); even being at a slight remove requires purification. **10:** *People*, perhaps only men; see v. 15n. *Consecrate*, that is, make ritually fit to approach divine sanctity (Josh 3.5). *Wash* as an antidote to ritual impurity (see 29.4). **12:** *Limits* (and v. 23), the border around dangerous sanctity. *Death*, because the intense holiness of God's presence has a dangerous quality (also v. 21; 20.19); see 24.9–11n. and Num 4.15. **13:** *Go up on the mountain*, after the theophany when the mountain is no longer holy, or reflecting a different tradition in which the people do ascend the mountain. **14:** *Consecrated . . . washed*, see v. 10n. **15:** *Go near a woman*, that is, have sex, which causes ritual impurity (Lev 15.18). Addressed to men, this seems to exclude women from experiencing the theophany; but see 20.1–17n. **16–19:** Intense natural phenomena of a thunderstorm and a volcano (*thunder, lightning,* a thick *cloud,* dense *smoke, violent* shaking) in combination connote the extraordinary phenomenon of revelation (Judg 5.4–5; Pss 18.7–15; 68.7–8; Hab 3.3–6; cf. 1 Kings 19.11–13). A blaring *trumpet,* otherwise used to herald sovereigns (as 1 Kings 1.34) or signal momentous (as 1 Sam 13.3; Isa 18.3) and sacred events (as Lev 25.9), augments the sensory images. **20–25:** Three zones of sanctity are established—holiest at the top for God and Moses (vv. 20,24); a middle stage for Aaron (v. 24) and perhaps leaders (v. 22; 24.1–2,9–11); least holy at the bottom for the people (vv. 12,17,21,23). These zones correspond to the tabernacle's three levels of holiness (see 25.1–31.17n.).

to Moses, "Go down and warn the people not to break through to the LORD to look; otherwise many of them will perish. ²² Even the priests who approach the LORD must consecrate themselves or the LORD will break out against them." ²³ Moses said to the LORD, "The people are not permitted to come up to Mount Sinai; for you yourself warned us, saying, 'Set limits around the mountain and keep it holy.'" ²⁴ The LORD said to him, "Go down, and come up bringing Aaron with you; but do not let either the priests or the people break through to come up to the LORD; otherwise he will break out against them." ²⁵ So Moses went down to the people and told them.

20 Then God spoke all these words: ² I am the LORD your God, who brought you out of the land of Egypt, out of the house of slavery; ³ you shall have no other gods before[a] me.

⁴ You shall not make for yourself an idol, whether in the form of anything that is in heaven above, or that is on the earth beneath, or that is in the water under the earth. ⁵ You shall not bow down to them or worship them; for I the LORD your God am a jealous God, punishing children for the iniquity of parents, to the third and the fourth generation of those who reject me, ⁶ but showing steadfast

a Or *besides*

20.1–24.18: Covenant. The stipulations of the covenant—Decalogue (20.1–17) and Covenant Rules (20.22–23.19)—are interspersed with additional Sinai narratives (20.18–21; 23.20–24.18). 20.1–17: Decalogue (also Deut 5.6–21). These ten precepts (see 18.26n.; also called the "Ten Commandments") are not titled here but are called "ten words" or "ten sayings" in 34.28; Deut 4.13; 10.4. Set forth in apodictic (absolute) form, they constitute unconditional community policy rather than law. Not numbered in the Bible, they are counted in diverse ways.

NUMBERING OF THE TEN COMMANDMENTS IN EXODUS 20.1–17			
	MOST JEWISH TRADITION	EASTERN ORTHODOX, ANGLICAN, MOST PROTESTANT CHURCHES	ROMAN CATHOLIC AND LUTHERAN CHURCHES
Ex 20.2	1	1	1
20.3	2	1	1
20.4–6	2	2	1
20.7	3	3	2
20.8–11	4	4	3
20.12	5	5	4
20.13	6	6	5
20.14	7	7	6
20.15	8	8	7
20.16	9	9	8
20.17a	10	10	9
20.17b	10	10	10

The first several deal with human obligations to God and are accompanied by explanations (called motive clauses); the others concern social issues and usually do not mention God. Because its pronouns are all second-person masculine singular, the Decalogue seems to address the adult men responsible for Israelite households (as v. 17), with its stipulations otherwise applying to all people as appropriate. However, the masculine singular sometimes represents both members of the conjugal pair (as v. 10; see Gen 2.24). 1: *God spoke* these words to the people directly, not through Moses. 2: Divine self-identification and recapitulation of past benefaction (see 19.4n.). 3: Worship of the LORD alone, without denying other deities; see 15.11n. 4–6: Imageless worship of God distinguished Israelite religion from those of their neighbors. 5: *To the . . . generation*, transgenerational

love to the thousandth generation[a] of those who love me and keep my commandments.

[7] You shall not make wrongful use of the name of the LORD your God, for the LORD will not acquit anyone who misuses his name.

[8] Remember the sabbath day, and keep it holy. [9] Six days you shall labor and do all your work. [10] But the seventh day is a sabbath to the LORD your God; you shall not do any work—you, your son or your daughter, your male or female slave, your livestock, or the alien resident in your towns. [11] For in six days the LORD made heaven and earth, the sea, and all that is in them, but rested the seventh day; therefore the LORD blessed the sabbath day and consecrated it.

[12] Honor your father and your mother, so that your days may be long in the land that the LORD your God is giving you.

[13] You shall not murder.[b]

[14] You shall not commit adultery.

[15] You shall not steal.

[16] You shall not bear false witness against your neighbor.

[17] You shall not covet your neighbor's house; you shall not covet your neighbor's wife, or male or female slave, or ox, or donkey, or anything that belongs to your neighbor.

[18] When all the people witnessed the thunder and lightning, the sound of the trumpet, and the mountain smoking, they were afraid[c] and trembled and stood at a distance, [19] and said to Moses, "You speak to us, and we will listen; but do not let God speak to us, or we will die." [20] Moses said to the people, "Do not be afraid; for God has come only to test you and to put the fear of him upon you so that you do not sin." [21] Then the people stood at a distance, while Moses drew near to the thick darkness where God was.

[22] The LORD said to Moses: Thus you shall say to the Israelites: "You have seen for yourselves that I spoke with you from heaven. [23] You shall not make gods of silver alongside me, nor shall you make for yourselves gods of gold. [24] You need make for me only an altar of earth and sacrifice on it your burnt offerings

a   Or to thousands
b   Or kill
c   Sam Gk Syr Vg: MT they saw

guilt (see 34.7; cf. Gen 15.16) is sometimes rejected (Jer 31.29–30; Ezek 18). 7: As a metaphor for divine presence (20.24; Deut 12.5; etc.), God's *name* is potent and cannot be misused (as in false oaths, Jer 7.9). 8–11: The *sabbath* is to be *holy* (v. 8; the same Heb word is translated "consecrated" in v. 11), that is, distinct from other days (see 16.23–30n.), and is directed to God as creator (v. 11, as in the Priestly creation story [Gen 1.1–2.3; contrast Deut 5.15]). "Wife" is omitted from the otherwise inclusive list because she is included in *you*; see 20.1–17n. 12: Parental authority, akin to that of God, likewise deserves *honor* (see 14.4n., where "glory" is from the same root as *honor*, and 21.15,17n). 13: *Murder* is forbidden, but not killing in war or in capital punishment. 14: *Adultery*, sexual intercourse between a man and a married or betrothed woman, is a grave offense (Lev 20.10; Deut 22.22) because lineages could be compromised by this infidelity. 15: Theft of both persons and property is prohibited; the Hebrew word for "kidnap" (21.16) is the same as for *steal*. 16: Forbidding *false witness* is indicative of strong concerns for justice (23.1–3). 17: Considered two separate "words" in some traditions, this prohibition addresses the male head of household; see 20.1–17n.

20.18–21: The Sinai account resumes, with the people insisting that Moses transmit God's word. In the re-telling of this in Deut 18.15–22, he becomes the prototype of a true prophet. 18: *Thunder . . . lightning . . . trumpet . . . smoking*, see 19.16–19n. 19: *Die*, see 19.13n.

20.22–23.33: Community regulations. This collection of legal materials, sometimes called the Book of the Covenant (24.7) or Covenant Code or Covenant Collection (cf. Josh 24.26, "book of the law [Heb 'torah']"), is diverse in content and form. Introductory instructions (20.22–26) and a concluding narrative (23.20–33) frame a two-part enumeration of community rulings (ordinances) and rules (statutes). The first part (21.1–22.17) con-sists mainly of casuistic materials—case laws with attached punishments. The second part (22.18–23.19) com-prises ethical or religious norms and exhortations typically expressed in apodictic or absolute form. These two parts may reflect the merging of ancient customary regulations with covenant-oriented materials.

20.22–26: Introductory instructions are given in the second-person plural. The forbidden statues (see 20.4–5) made of costly *silver* and *gold* are contrasted with the simple, low altars of *earth* or unhewn *stone* for sacrificing to God, which (unlike the single "place" in Deuteronomic tradition; see Deut 12.5–14; etc.) can take

and your offerings of well-being, your sheep and your oxen; in every place where I cause my name to be remembered I will come to you and bless you. [25] But if you make for me an altar of stone, do not build it of hewn stones; for if you use a chisel upon it you profane it. [26] You shall not go up by steps to my altar, so that your nakedness may not be exposed on it."

21
These are the ordinances that you shall set before them:

[2] When you buy a male Hebrew slave, he shall serve six years, but in the seventh he shall go out a free person, without debt. [3] If he comes in single, he shall go out single; if he comes in married, then his wife shall go out with him. [4] If his master gives him a wife and she bears him sons or daughters, the wife and her children shall be her master's and he shall go out alone. [5] But if the slave declares, "I love my master, my wife, and my children; I will not go out a free person," [6] then his master shall bring him before God.[a] He shall be brought to the door or the doorpost; and his master shall pierce his ear with an awl; and he shall serve him for life.

[7] When a man sells his daughter as a slave, she shall not go out as the male slaves do. [8] If she does not please her master, who designated her for himself, then he shall let her be redeemed; he shall have no right to sell her to a foreign people, since he has dealt unfairly with her. [9] If he designates her for his son, he shall deal with her as with a daughter. [10] If he

takes another wife to himself, he shall not diminish the food, clothing, or marital rights of the first wife.[b] [11] And if he does not do these three things for her, she shall go out without debt, without payment of money.

[12] Whoever strikes a person mortally shall be put to death. [13] If it was not premeditated, but came about by an act of God, then I will appoint for you a place to which the killer may flee. [14] But if someone willfully attacks and kills another by treachery, you shall take the killer from my altar for execution.

[15] Whoever strikes father or mother shall be put to death.

[16] Whoever kidnaps a person, whether that person has been sold or is still held in possession, shall be put to death.

[17] Whoever curses father or mother shall be put to death.

[18] When individuals quarrel and one strikes the other with a stone or fist so that the injured party, though not dead, is confined to bed, [19] but recovers and walks around outside with the help of a staff, then the assailant shall be free of liability, except to pay for the loss of time, and to arrange for full recovery.

[20] When a slaveowner strikes a male or female slave with a rod and the slave dies immediately, the owner shall be punished. [21] But if the slave survives a day or two, there

[a] Or *to the judges*
[b] Heb *of her*

place wherever people invoke God's *name* (presence); cf. 27.1–8. **26:** *Nakedness may not be exposed*, probably because undergarments were not normally worn; contrast 28.42.

21.1–22.20: Ordinances (rulings) and statutes (rules). In form and content, this section resembles other ancient Near Eastern legal collections. It comprises four sections: two groups of rulings (*ordinances*, v. 1), beginning with *when* or *if*, on specific cases (21.1–11; 21.18–22.17), and stringent rules (statutes) beginning with *whoever* or *you* (21.12–17; 22.18–20).

21.2–11: Manumission regulations (cf. Deut 15.12–18; Lev 25.39–55) for indentured Israelite (*Hebrew*, v. 2; see 1.15n.) servants, which provide procedures rather than penalties. **2:** *Buy*, better "acquire." *Slave*, better "servant" (and v. 7). *Six years* limits the duration of service. **5–6:** The servant can irrevocably forego independence; a physical mark involving little trauma signifies that status (v. 6). **6:** *Before God*, probably either by swearing an oath in God's name or by holding this ceremony at a local sanctuary. **7–11:** The rights of an indentured female who becomes a wife in the household where she serves are established.

21.12–32: Violence regulations include absolute rules for capital offenses (vv. 12–17) and case rulings concerning assault on people by humans (18–27) and animals (28–32). **12–14:** Distinction between deliberate and accidental homicide. **13:** *Place to . . . flee* because the victim's kin would seek revenge (cf. Num 35.12; Deut 4.41–43; 19.1–13; Josh 20). **15,17:** Two rules supporting parental authority, probably over adult children in an extended family (also Lev 20.9). **16:** *Kidnap*, lit., "steal"; see 20.15n. **17:** *Curses* had potency and were as serious as physi-

is no punishment; for the slave is the owner's property.

[22] When people who are fighting injure a pregnant woman so that there is a miscarriage, and yet no further harm follows, the one responsible shall be fined what the woman's husband demands, paying as much as the judges determine. [23] If any harm follows, then you shall give life for life, [24] eye for eye, tooth for tooth, hand for hand, foot for foot, [25] burn for burn, wound for wound, stripe for stripe.

[26] When a slaveowner strikes the eye of a male or female slave, destroying it, the owner shall let the slave go, a free person, to compensate for the eye. [27] If the owner knocks out a tooth of a male or female slave, the slave shall be let go, a free person, to compensate for the tooth.

[28] When an ox gores a man or a woman to death, the ox shall be stoned, and its flesh shall not be eaten; but the owner of the ox shall not be liable. [29] If the ox has been accustomed to gore in the past, and its owner has been warned but has not restrained it, and it kills a man or a woman, the ox shall be stoned, and its owner also shall be put to death. [30] If a ransom is imposed on the owner, then the owner shall pay whatever is imposed for the redemption of the victim's life. [31] If it gores a boy or a girl, the owner shall be dealt with according to this same rule. [32] If the ox gores a male or female slave, the owner shall pay to the slaveowner thirty shekels of silver, and the ox shall be stoned.

[33] If someone leaves a pit open, or digs a pit and does not cover it, and an ox or a donkey falls into it, [34] the owner of the pit shall make restitution, giving money to its owner, but keeping the dead animal.

[35] If someone's ox hurts the ox of another, so that it dies, then they shall sell the live ox and divide the price of it; and the dead animal they shall also divide. [36] But if it was known that the ox was accustomed to gore in the past, and its owner has not restrained it, the owner shall restore ox for ox, but keep the dead animal.

22 [a] When someone steals an ox or a sheep, and slaughters it or sells it, the thief shall pay five oxen for an ox, and four sheep for a sheep.[b] The thief shall make restitution, but if unable to do so, shall be sold for the theft. [4] When the animal, whether ox or donkey or sheep, is found alive in the thief's possession, the thief shall pay double.

[2][c] If a thief is found breaking in, and is beaten to death, no bloodguilt is incurred; [3] but if it happens after sunrise, bloodguilt is incurred.

[5] When someone causes a field or vineyard to be grazed over, or lets livestock loose to graze in someone else's field, restitution shall be made from the best in the owner's field or vineyard.

[6] When fire breaks out and catches in thorns so that the stacked grain or the standing grain or the field is consumed, the one who started the fire shall make full restitution.

[7] When someone delivers to a neighbor money or goods for safekeeping, and they are stolen from the neighbor's house, then the thief, if caught, shall pay double. [8] If the thief is not caught, the owner of the house shall be brought before God,[d] to determine whether or not the owner had laid hands on the neighbor's goods.

[9] In any case of disputed ownership involving ox, donkey, sheep, clothing, or any other

---

a   Ch 21.37 in Heb
b   Verses 2, 3, and 4 rearranged thus: 3b, 4, 2, 3a
c   Ch 22.1 in Heb
d   Or *before the judges*

---

cal assault. **20:** *Slave*, probably a non-Israelite (cf. vv. 21,32). **22–27:** Measure-for-measure punishment, or "lex talionis" (Lev 24.19–20; Deut 19.21) is a principle of fair treatment of assailants rather than a literal prescription for retaliatory treatment in all cases; note that indemnity and compensation are sometimes acceptable (vv. 22,26,27). **28–32:** Goring ox cases mandate liability for accidental or negligent homicide. **32:** A chattel *slave* (as in v. 21) rather than an indentured servant (as in vv. 2–11), because monetary value is assigned. A *shekel* weighed about .4 oz (11.4 gm).

21.33–22.15: Property and restitution, more case rulings. **21.33–36:** Compensation for death or injury to animals because of negligence. **22.1–4:** Theft of property (cf. 22.16n.). **1:** *Sold*, to secure funds for the fine. **2–3:** Nighttime theft is more serious, presumably because the intruder's intent is less clear. **5–6:** Restitution for agri-

loss, of which one party says, "This is mine," the case of both parties shall come before God;[a] the one whom God condemns[b] shall pay double to the other.

[10] When someone delivers to another a donkey, ox, sheep, or any other animal for safekeeping, and it dies or is injured or is carried off, without anyone seeing it, [11] an oath before the LORD shall decide between the two of them that the one has not laid hands on the property of the other; the owner shall accept the oath, and no restitution shall be made. [12] But if it was stolen, restitution shall be made to its owner. [13] If it was mangled by beasts, let it be brought as evidence; restitution shall not be made for the mangled remains.

[14] When someone borrows an animal from another and it is injured or dies, the owner not being present, full restitution shall be made. [15] If the owner was present, there shall be no restitution; if it was hired, only the hiring fee is due.

[16] When a man seduces a virgin who is not engaged to be married, and lies with her, he shall give the bride-price for her and make her his wife. [17] But if her father refuses to give her to him, he shall pay an amount equal to the bride-price for virgins.

[18] You shall not permit a female sorcerer to live.

[19] Whoever lies with an animal shall be put to death.

[20] Whoever sacrifices to any god, other than the LORD alone, shall be devoted to destruction.

[21] You shall not wrong or oppress a resident alien, for you were aliens in the land of Egypt. [22] You shall not abuse any widow or orphan. [23] If you do abuse them, when they cry out to me, I will surely heed their cry; [24] my wrath will burn, and I will kill you with the sword, and your wives shall become widows and your children orphans.

[25] If you lend money to my people, to the poor among you, you shall not deal with them as a creditor; you shall not exact interest from them. [26] If you take your neighbor's cloak in pawn, you shall restore it before the sun goes down; [27] for it may be your neighbor's only clothing to use as cover; in what else shall that person sleep? And if your neighbor cries out to me, I will listen, for I am compassionate.

[28] You shall not revile God, or curse a leader of your people.

[29] You shall not delay to make offerings from the fullness of your harvest and from the outflow of your presses.[c]

The firstborn of your sons you shall give to me. [30] You shall do the same with your oxen and with your sheep: seven days it shall remain with its mother; on the eighth day you shall give it to me.

[31] You shall be people consecrated to me; therefore you shall not eat any meat that is mangled by beasts in the field; you shall throw it to the dogs.

a Or *before the judges*
b Or *the judges condemn*
c Meaning of Heb uncertain

cultural damages caused by negligence. **7–15:** Restitution for loss of property in another's care. **9–11:** Two cases of judicial impasse. Disputes lacking evidence or witnesses are decided using unspecified priestly mechanisms; cf. Num 5.11–31.

22.16–20: Social and religious stipulations, including one case ruling (22.16–17) and three rules (22.18–20). **16–17:** Consensual premarital sex obligates the man to marry the woman or compensate her father for the decrease, because of her lost virginity, in the *bride-price* (better "marital gift") a future husband might pay. **16:** *Seduces*, not coerces, implying her consent. **18–20:** Like 21.12–17, this second group of absolute rules—prohibiting sorcery (cf. Deut 18.10–11), bestiality (cf. Lev 18.23; 20.15–16; Deut 27.21), and apostasy—are unequivocal and involve capital punishment. **20:** *Devoted to destruction* (execution) may also entail eradicating the offender's family and confiscating their property (Lev 27.28–29).

22.21–23.19. Ethical and religious exhortations and norms. The stipulations of the second part of the community regulations (see 20.22–23.33n.) are mostly unconditional. Some concern social relationships and justice (22.21–27; 23.1–12) and the others present obligations to God (22.28–31; 23.13–19), thus linking humanitarian and religious matters. **22.21–27:** Concern for the disadvantaged appears repeatedly in the Pentateuch (e.g., 23.6,9–12; Lev 19.33–34; 23.22; Deut 1.16; 10.18–19; 24.17–22). **28–31:** Several religious matters: prohibitions (vv. 28,31) and prescriptions (vv. 29–30). **28:** Cf. Lev 24.15–16; 1 Kings 21.10,13. **29–30:** See 13.2.n.; 34.19–20; Num

23

You shall not spread a false report. You shall not join hands with the wicked to act as a malicious witness. ² You shall not follow a majority in wrongdoing; when you bear witness in a lawsuit, you shall not side with the majority so as to pervert justice; ³ nor shall you be partial to the poor in a lawsuit.

⁴ When you come upon your enemy's ox or donkey going astray, you shall bring it back.

⁵ When you see the donkey of one who hates you lying under its burden and you would hold back from setting it free, you must help to set it free.ᵃ

⁶ You shall not pervert the justice due to your poor in their lawsuits. ⁷ Keep far from a false charge, and do not kill the innocent and those in the right, for I will not acquit the guilty. ⁸ You shall take no bribe, for a bribe blinds the officials, and subverts the cause of those who are in the right.

⁹ You shall not oppress a resident alien; you know the heart of an alien, for you were aliens in the land of Egypt.

¹⁰ For six years you shall sow your land and gather in its yield; ¹¹ but the seventh year you shall let it rest and lie fallow, so that the poor of your people may eat; and what they leave the wild animals may eat. You shall do the same with your vineyard, and with your olive orchard.

¹² Six days you shall do your work, but on the seventh day you shall rest, so that your ox and your donkey may have relief, and your homeborn slave and the resident alien may be refreshed. ¹³ Be attentive to all that I have said to you. Do not invoke the names of other gods; do not let them be heard on your lips.

¹⁴ Three times in the year you shall hold a festival for me. ¹⁵ You shall observe the festival of unleavened bread; as I commanded you, you shall eat unleavened bread for seven days at the appointed time in the month of Abib, for in it you came out of Egypt.

No one shall appear before me empty-handed.

¹⁶ You shall observe the festival of harvest, of the first fruits of your labor, of what you sow in the field. You shall observe the festival of ingathering at the end of the year, when you gather in from the field the fruit of your labor. ¹⁷ Three times in the year all your males shall appear before the Lord GOD.

¹⁸ You shall not offer the blood of my sacrifice with anything leavened, or let the fat of my festival remain until the morning.

¹⁹ The choicest of the first fruits of your ground you shall bring into the house of the LORD your God.

You shall not boil a kid in its mother's milk.

²⁰ I am going to send an angel in front of you, to guard you on the way and to bring you to the place that I have prepared. ²¹ Be attentive to him and listen to his voice; do not rebel against him, for he will not pardon your transgression; for my name is in him.

²² But if you listen attentively to his voice and do all that I say, then I will be an enemy to your enemies and a foe to your foes.

ᵃ Meaning of Heb uncertain

18.27. 31: *Consecrated* (lit., "holy"), see 19.6n. Elsewhere, to be edible animals must be drained of their blood (Lev 7.24; 17.13–15). 23.1–12: Judicial integrity (vv. 1–3,6–8) and the protection of animals and marginal groups (vv. 4–5,6,9–12). 1–3: 20.16; Lev 19.12,15; Deut 19.15–19. 4–5: Cf. Deut 22.1–4. 6–9: See 22.21–27n. 10–12: A seventh-year agricultural hiatus favors the poor; and the seventh-day rest (see 16.23–30n.) benefits animals, servants, and foreigners. 13–19: Obligations to God. 13: See 15.11n; 20.3. 14–19a: The three major agricultural festivals (cf. 34.22–23)—*unleavened bread* (linked to passover and the Exodus; see 12.15n.); *harvest*, or *first fruits*, also called Shavuot or Festival of Weeks (34.22,26; Lev 23.15–21; Deut 16.9–12); *ingathering*, also called Sukkot or Festival of Booths (Lev 23.33–43; Deut 16.13–15). 17: *All your males*; cf. Deut 31.11–12. *Before the Lord GOD*, presumably wherever there is an altar (20.22–26n.); cf. Deut 16.2,6,7,11,15,16, which stipulates pilgrimage to one place, presumably Jerusalem. 18: The blood prohibition probably applies to all sacrifices, not just festival ones. *Until the morning*, cf. 12.8. 19a: *House*, a general designation for a shrine (Gen 28.22). 19b: *Milk*, perhaps "fat," prohibiting the slaughter of the kid's mother to protect its breeding potential (also 34.26; Deut 14.21).

23.20–33: The Sinai narrative resumes with further divine promises and admonitions. 20–23: The *angel* (lit., "messenger") represents God's presence (see 3.2n.) as does God's *name*. 22: *Enemy . . . foes* employs Near East-

²³ When my angel goes in front of you, and brings you to the Amorites, the Hittites, the Perizzites, the Canaanites, the Hivites, and the Jebusites, and I blot them out, ²⁴ you shall not bow down to their gods, or worship them, or follow their practices, but you shall utterly demolish them and break their pillars in pieces. ²⁵ You shall worship the LORD your God, and I[a] will bless your bread and your water; and I will take sickness away from among you. ²⁶ No one shall miscarry or be barren in your land; I will fulfill the number of your days. ²⁷ I will send my terror in front of you, and will throw into confusion all the people against whom you shall come, and I will make all your enemies turn their backs to you. ²⁸ And I will send the pestilence[b] in front of you, which shall drive out the Hivites, the Canaanites, and the Hittites from before you. ²⁹ I will not drive them out from before you in one year, or the land would become desolate and the wild animals would multiply against you. ³⁰ Little by little I will drive them out from before you, until you have increased and possess the land. ³¹ I will set your borders from the Red Sea[c] to the sea of the Philistines, and from the wilderness to the Euphrates; for I will hand over to you the inhabitants of the land, and you shall drive them out before you. ³² You shall make no covenant with them and their gods. ³³ They shall not live in your land, or they will make you sin against me; for if you worship their gods, it will surely be a snare to you.

24 Then he said to Moses, "Come up to the LORD, you and Aaron, Nadab, and Abihu, and seventy of the elders of Israel, and worship at a distance. ² Moses alone shall come near the LORD; but the others shall not come near, and the people shall not come up with him."

³ Moses came and told the people all the words of the LORD and all the ordinances; and all the people answered with one voice, and said, "All the words that the LORD has spoken we will do." ⁴ And Moses wrote down all the words of the LORD. He rose early in the morning, and built an altar at the foot of the mountain, and set up twelve pillars, corresponding to the twelve tribes of Israel. ⁵ He sent young men of the people of Israel, who offered burnt offerings and sacrificed oxen as offerings of well-being to the LORD. ⁶ Moses took half of the blood and put it in basins, and half of the blood he dashed against the altar. ⁷ Then he took the book of the covenant, and read it in the hearing of the people; and they said, "All that the LORD has spoken we will do, and we will be obedient." ⁸ Moses took the blood and dashed it on the people, and said, "See the blood of the covenant that the LORD has made with you in accordance with all these words."

a Gk Vg: Heb *he*
b Or *hornets*: Meaning of Heb uncertain
c Or *Sea of Reeds*

ern treaty language. **23–33:** Cf. 34.11–17. **23,28:** See 3.8n. **24:** Cf. 20.3; 23.13. *Pillars,* upright stones sometimes acceptable, when signifying social or political groups (24.4) or embodying God's presence (Gen 28.16–22), but otherwise considered idolatrous (34.13; Lev 26.1; Deut 12.3, etc.). **25–26:** Sustenance and progeny are the blessings produced by covenant fealty (Lev 26.3–10; Deut 28.1–6). **27–30:** The indigenous inhabitants of the land are driven away; using "holy war" language; other passages say they are to be exterminated (e.g., Deut 7.2; Josh 10–11). **31:** This territorial delineation is one of several traditions about the extent of the land (e.g., Gen 15.18; Num 34.1–12). *The sea of the Philistines,* the Mediterranean. **32–33:** *Their gods,* see 15.11n.

24.1–18: Theophanies and covenant ceremonies. Repetitive or conflicting details again (see 19.1–25n.) indicate a composite narrative about God's appearance—to Moses and the leaders (vv. 1–2,9–11), and to Moses alone (vv. 12–18). Covenant ratification rituals are known from ancient Near Eastern documents. **1–2:** Several zones of sanctity are implied; see 19.20–25n. **1:** *Nadab* and *Abihu,* 6.23. **3–8:** Covenant ceremony. **3:** *Words* and *ordinances,* referring to the Decalogue (see 20.1–17n.) and community rulings (see 20.22–23.33n.); cf. Josh 24.25. *One voice,* unanimous agreement, as in 19.8. **4:** *Moses wrote,* see 24.12n. *Pillars,* see 23.24n. **5:** *Burnt offerings . . . offerings of well-being* (cf. 18.12), the former burned entirely with the rising smoke constituting God's portion (Lev 1) and the latter providing food for the participants (Deut 27.6–7); a ceremonial feast is implied (cf. v. 11). Celebratory repasts are vehicles for creating relationships between the parties (here, God and the people) sharing the meal; see also 18.12n. **6–8:** Another ratification ritual draws on the life-death quality of blood (see 22.31n.); throwing half on the people and half on the altar (for God, as 20.24) serves to bind the two parties. **7:**

⁹ Then Moses and Aaron, Nadab, and Abihu, and seventy of the elders of Israel went up, ¹⁰ and they saw the God of Israel. Under his feet there was something like a pavement of sapphire stone, like the very heaven for clearness. ¹¹ God[a] did not lay his hand on the chief men of the people of Israel; also they beheld God, and they ate and drank.

¹² The LORD said to Moses, "Come up to me on the mountain, and wait there; and I will give you the tablets of stone, with the law and the commandment, which I have written for their instruction." ¹³ So Moses set out with his assistant Joshua, and Moses went up into the mountain of God. ¹⁴ To the elders he had said, "Wait here for us, until we come to you again; for Aaron and Hur are with you; whoever has a dispute may go to them."

¹⁵ Then Moses went up on the mountain, and the cloud covered the mountain. ¹⁶ The glory of the LORD settled on Mount Sinai, and the cloud covered it for six days; on the seventh day he called to Moses out of the cloud. ¹⁷ Now the appearance of the glory of the LORD was like a devouring fire on the top of the mountain in the sight of the people of Israel. ¹⁸ Moses entered the cloud, and went up on the mountain. Moses was on the mountain for forty days and forty nights.

25 The LORD said to Moses: ² Tell the Israelites to take for me an offering; from all whose hearts prompt them to give you shall receive the offering for me. ³ This is the offering that you shall receive from them: gold, silver, and bronze, ⁴ blue, purple, and crimson yarns and fine linen, goats' hair, ⁵ tanned rams' skins, fine leather,[b]

---

[a] Heb *He*

[b] Meaning of Heb uncertain

Book of the covenant, see 19.8n. **8:** *On the people,* perhaps on the pillars (v. 4) representing them. **9–11:** Partway up the mountain (continuing from vv. 1–2), the leaders too partake of a ceremonial meal and, despite the danger (see 3.6n.), have a visual experience of God. **10:** *Sapphire,* cf. Ezek 1.26. **12–18:** The theophany to Moses alone in the holiest zone will resume in the golden calf episode of 31.18–34.35. **12:** *Tablets,* probably two (31.18; 32.15); important documents were thus recorded. *I have written* (also 31.18; 32.16; 34.1; Deut 9.10) has God writing the document; contrast 24.4; 34.27–28. **13–14:** *Joshua* and *Hur* each appear for the second time (17.9–10). **15–17:** *Cloud* and *fire,* see 3.2n. and 19.16–19n. *Glory of the LORD,* see 16.7n. **15:** *Covered,* see 40.34n. **16:** *Settled,* better "dwelled," uses the same Heb root as the noun for God's wilderness dwelling, the tabernacle; see 25.9n.

Chs 25–40: Building the tabernacle and receiving a new covenant. The remaining chapters of Exodus have as their main focus the construction of the tabernacle as an earthly home for God. Directions for building the portable wilderness shrine (25.1–27.21; 30.1–31.18) and for clothing and inaugurating the priests who would be custodians of the shrine and its rituals (28.1–29.46) are followed by an account of how the directions are carried out so that the divine presence can enter (35.1–40.38). Much of the information in the second section is exactly the same as in the first, although the internal order differs. Between the two sections comes the golden calf episode (chs 32–34), which results in a restored covenant.

25.1–31.18: Instructions for building the tabernacle and inaugurating the priesthood. Unlike religious edifices today, which are places for people to enter and worship, temples and shrines in the ancient world were considered earthly residences for deities (see 25.8) and were off-limits for most humans. They were costly, well-furnished structures, befitting their divine occupants. Although a modest tent shrine, perhaps reflected in the designation "tent of meeting" (see 27.21n.), would have been possible, the elaborate and costly structure of Exodus likely draws in part from knowledge of the Jerusalem Temple. Like Mount Sinai (and the Jerusalem Temple), the portable wilderness shrine of the Israelites would have three zones of sanctity; see 19.20–25n. Following an introduction (25.1–9) and instructions for making its sacred furnishings (25.10–40), come directions for making the structure itself (ch 26) and then its courtyard and altar (27.1–19); an addendum prescribes lamp oil (27.20–21). A concluding section (28.1–31.18) gives instructions for the priestly vestments (ch 28) and for consecrating the priests (ch 29), and ends with God's announcing the two chief artisans and calling for sabbath observance (ch 31).

25.1–9: Introduction: the materials (also 35.4–29). Seven kinds of substances (metals, yarn, skins, wood, oil, spices, and gemstones) signify the totality of supplies. **2:** *Offering . . . hearts,* indicating that materials for the shrine will come from donations, not taxes. **3:** Three precious metals for components will be used according to the three zones of sanctity (see 19.20–25n.), with *gold* for those most holy or

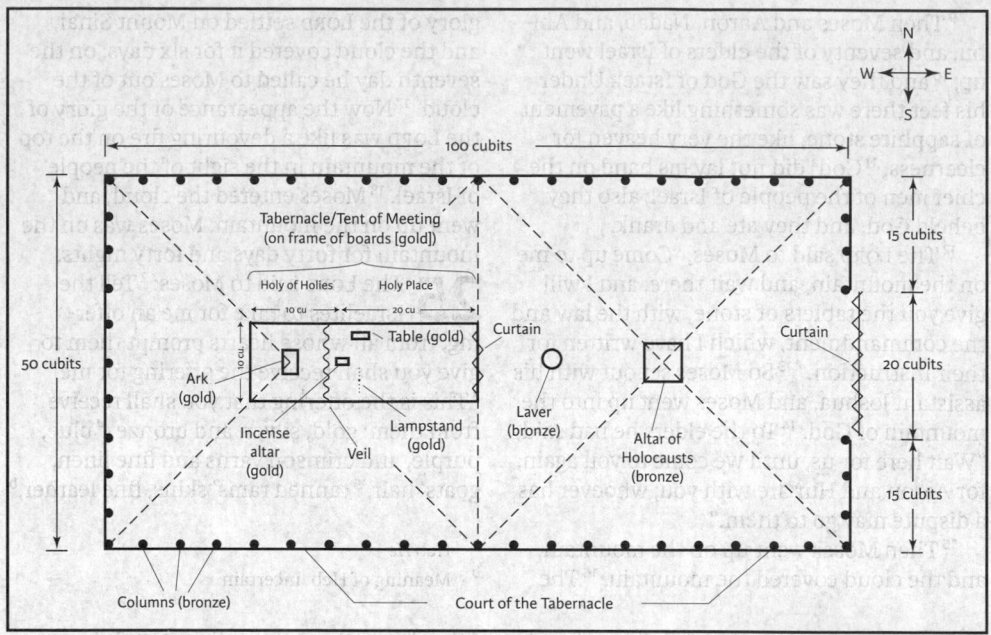

Chs 25–31; 36–39: The structure of the Tabernacle as described in the book of Exodus.

acacia wood, ⁶ oil for the lamps, spices for the anointing oil and for the fragrant incense, ⁷ onyx stones and gems to be set in the ephod and for the breastpiece. ⁸ And have them make me a sanctuary, so that I may dwell among them. ⁹ In accordance with all that I show you concerning the pattern of the tabernacle and of all its furniture, so you shall make it.

¹⁰ They shall make an ark of acacia wood; it shall be two and a half cubits long, a cubit and a half wide, and a cubit and a half high. ¹¹ You shall overlay it with pure gold, inside and outside you shall overlay it, and you shall make a molding of gold upon it all around. ¹² You shall cast four rings of gold for it and put them on its four feet, two rings on the one side of it, and two rings on the other side. ¹³ You shall make poles of acacia wood, and overlay them with gold. ¹⁴ And you shall put the poles into the rings on the sides of the ark, by which to carry the ark. ¹⁵ The

closest to the most holy and bronze for the least holy. **8:** *Sanctuary*, see 15.17n. *Dwell among them*, indicating that the shrine will be God's earthly residence (see 25.1–31.17n.). The Hebrew term for *dwell* denotes a portable presence rather than one tied to a fixed location. **9:** *Pattern* likely designates the heavenly abode after which the earthly one is to be modeled (see 3.8n.). *Tabernacle* is a noun formed from the Hebrew verb "to dwell" (see 25.8n.) and suggests God's indwelling presence. Used fifty-eight times in the book of Exodus, here it refers to the entire sacred complex; in other passages (e.g., 26.1) it denotes just the tent structure.

25.10–40: Interior furnishings. The most holy item, the gold-covered ark (vv. 10–22), will be situated in the inner sanctum. Three more gold items—table (vv. 23–30), lampstand (vv. 31–40), and incense altar (which is not prescribed in this section; see 30.1–10)—will be near the ark, in the main room of the shrine.

25.10–22: The ark and its cover (also 37.1–9). A gilded chest that will contain the sacred covenant document, the ark has a lid surmounted by winged creatures over which God's invisible presence rests. In ancient Israel's aniconic tradition, the ark comes closest to a physical symbol of God (see 1 Sam 4.4; 2 Sam 6.2). **10:** Its size (ca. 114 × 69 × 69 cm = 45 × 27 × 27 in) is similar to that of chests known from ancient Egypt for keeping valuables. **12–15:** *Rings* and *poles* for transport are also known from ancient Egypt. **16:** The Hebrew word for *covenant* here ("ʿedut"; see 2.24n.) is favored by the Priestly writer; perhaps referring to the tablets of 24.12,

poles shall remain in the rings of the ark; they shall not be taken from it. ¹⁶ You shall put into the ark the covenantᵃ that I shall give you.

¹⁷ Then you shall make a mercy seatᵇ of pure gold; two cubits and a half shall be its length, and a cubit and a half its width. ¹⁸ You shall make two cherubim of gold; you shall make them of hammered work, at the two ends of the mercy seat.ᶜ ¹⁹ Make one cherub at the one end, and one cherub at the other; of one piece with the mercy seatᶜ you shall make the cherubim at its two ends. ²⁰ The cherubim shall spread out their wings above, overshadowing the mercy seatᶜ with their wings. They shall face one to another; the faces of the cherubim shall be turned toward the mercy seat.ᶜ ²¹ You shall put the mercy seatᶜ on the top of the ark; and in the ark you shall put the covenantᵃ that I shall give you. ²² There I will meet with you, and from above the mercy seat,ᶜ from between the two cherubim that are on the ark of the covenant,ᵃ I will deliver to you all my commands for the Israelites.

²³ You shall make a table of acacia wood, two cubits long, one cubit wide, and a cubit and a half high. ²⁴ You shall overlay it with pure gold, and make a molding of gold around it. ²⁵ You shall make around it a rim a handbreadth wide, and a molding of gold around the rim. ²⁶ You shall make for it four rings of gold, and fasten the rings to the four corners at its four legs. ²⁷ The rings that hold the poles used for carrying the table shall be close to the rim. ²⁸ You shall make the poles of acacia wood, and overlay them with gold, and the table shall be carried with these. ²⁹ You shall make its plates and dishes for incense, and its flagons and bowls with which to pour drink offerings; you shall make them of pure gold. ³⁰ And you shall set the bread of the Presence on the table before me always.

³¹ You shall make a lampstand of pure gold. The base and the shaft of the lampstand shall be made of hammered work; its cups, its calyxes, and its petals shall be of one piece with it; ³² and there shall be six branches going out of its sides, three branches of the lampstand out of one side of it and three branches of the lampstand out of the other side of it; ³³ three cups shaped like almond blossoms, each with calyx and petals, on one branch, and three cups shaped like almond blossoms, each with calyx and petals, on the other branch—so for the six branches going out of the lampstand. ³⁴ On the lampstand itself

ᵃ Or *treaty*, or *testimony*; Heb *eduth*
ᵇ Or *a cover*
ᶜ Or *the cover*

it is similar to the word for "meet," thus signifying the role of the ark as a place for oracular revelations (v. 22; 29.42–43; 33.7–10) and alluding to another name for the tabernacle, "tent of meeting" (see 27.21n.). **17–22:** The ark's cover (*mercy seat*) features imaginary composite beings (*cherubim*) whose wings form the throne, with the ark as its footstool, on which God's invisible presence rests (1 Sam 4.4; 1 Chr 28.2; Pss 99.1,5; 132.7); see 16.34n. Such composite figures as components of thrones are known from ancient Near Eastern art. **22:** *Meet*, see v. 16n.

25.23–30: The table (also 37.10–16; cf. 1 Kings 7.48) is the repository for sacred vessels and for the bread offering. A dwelling place for a deity, as for humans, needs a table for food. Bread and libations (and animals) are among the comestibles brought to God, though elsewhere the Torah makes it clear that the priests, not God consume the bread (Lev 24.5–9). **23:** Its dimensions (1 × .5 m = 36 × 18 in; height: .75 m = 27 in) are similar to those of offering tables depicted in ancient Near Eastern art. **27–28:** Its *rings* and *poles* provide portability. **29:** *Incense*, see 30.34–38. **30:** *Bread of the Presence*, or "bread [set] before [God]," refers to loaves offered to God on the sabbath.

25.31–40: The lampstand (Heb "menorah"; also 37.17–24) will hold oil lamps for illuminating God's dwelling (cf. the ten lampstands of the Jerusalem Temple, 1 Kings 7.49). No dimensions are provided. The wealth of botanical terms (branches, calyxes, almond blossoms, petals) suggests that in shape and decoration, it represented a sacred tree and perhaps even God as source of fertility (see 3.2n.). **31:** *Base and shaft* together denote a cylindrical stand flared at the bottom. **37:** *Seven lamps*, perhaps one on each branch; otherwise, a

there shall be four cups shaped like almond blossoms, each with its calyxes and petals. [35] There shall be a calyx of one piece with it under the first pair of branches, a calyx of one piece with it under the next pair of branches, and a calyx of one piece with it under the last pair of branches—so for the six branches that go out of the lampstand. [36] Their calyxes and their branches shall be of one piece with it, the whole of it one hammered piece of pure gold. [37] You shall make the seven lamps for it; and the lamps shall be set up so as to give light on the space in front of it. [38] Its snuffers and trays shall be of pure gold. [39] It, and all these utensils, shall be made from a talent of pure gold. [40] And see that you make them according to the pattern for them, which is being shown you on the mountain.

26 Moreover you shall make the tabernacle with ten curtains of fine twisted linen, and blue, purple, and crimson yarns; you shall make them with cherubim skillfully worked into them. [2] The length of each curtain shall be twenty-eight cubits, and the width of each curtain four cubits; all the curtains shall be of the same size. [3] Five curtains shall be joined to one another; and the other five curtains shall be joined to one another. [4] You shall make loops of blue on the edge of the outermost curtain in the first set; and likewise you shall make loops on the edge of the outermost curtain in the second set. [5] You shall make fifty loops on the one curtain, and you shall make fifty loops on the edge of the curtain that is in the second set; the loops shall be opposite one another. [6] You shall make fifty clasps of gold, and join the curtains to one another with the clasps, so that the tabernacle may be one whole.

[7] You shall also make curtains of goats' hair for a tent over the tabernacle; you shall make eleven curtains. [8] The length of each curtain shall be thirty cubits, and the width of each curtain four cubits; the eleven curtains shall be of the same size. [9] You shall join five curtains by themselves, and six curtains by themselves, and the sixth curtain you shall double over at the front of the tent. [10] You shall make fifty loops on the edge of the curtain that is outermost in one set, and fifty loops on the edge of the curtain that is outermost in the second set.

[11] You shall make fifty clasps of bronze, and put the clasps into the loops, and join the tent together, so that it may be one whole. [12] The part that remains of the curtains of the tent, the half curtain that remains, shall hang over the back of the tabernacle. [13] The cubit on the one side, and the cubit on the other side, of what remains in the length of the curtains of the tent, shall hang over the sides of the tabernacle, on this side and that side, to cover it. [14] You shall make for the tent a covering of tanned rams' skins and an outer covering of fine leather.[a]

[15] You shall make upright frames of acacia wood for the tabernacle. [16] Ten cubits shall be the length of a frame, and a cubit and a half the width of each frame. [17] There shall be two pegs in each frame to fit the frames together; you shall make these for all the frames of the tabernacle. [18] You shall make the frames for the tabernacle: twenty frames for the south side; [19] and you shall make forty bases of silver under the twenty frames, two bases under the first frame for its two pegs, and two bases under the next frame for its two pegs; [20] and for the second side of the tabernacle,

---

a   Meaning of Heb uncertain

single lamp in the middle (see 27.20n.; Lev 24.2). **39:** A *talent*, or 3,000 shekels, is about 34 kg = 75.5 lb. **40:** *Pattern*, see 25.9n.

26.1–37: The tabernacle structure (also 36.8–38). The tent itself consists of coverings (vv. 1–14), frames (vv. 15–30), and textile partitions (31–37) that form two interior spaces: the most holy place for the ark, and the holy place where the furnishings will be placed. **1–14: Coverings.** The tentlike structure will be formed with two fabric layers—panels of linen and tricolored wools decorated with *cherubim* (see 25.17–22n.), and unadorned goat hair panels—covered with two layers of animal skins (v. 14). **1:** *Tabernacle*, referring to the tent itself; see 25.9n. *Linen* renders an Egyptian term for a luxury fabric. *Blue, purple, and crimson* were the most costly and highly prized dyes. **15–30: Frames.** A complex system of wooden boards and bars, with metal fastenings and bases, will form frames for the hangings. The information is incomplete, with the exact size and manner of assembly

on the north side twenty frames, [21] and their forty bases of silver, two bases under the first frame, and two bases under the next frame; [22] and for the rear of the tabernacle westward you shall make six frames. [23] You shall make two frames for corners of the tabernacle in the rear; [24] they shall be separate beneath, but joined at the top, at the first ring; it shall be the same with both of them; they shall form the two corners. [25] And so there shall be eight frames, with their bases of silver, sixteen bases; two bases under the first frame, and two bases under the next frame.

[26] You shall make bars of acacia wood, five for the frames of the one side of the tabernacle, [27] and five bars for the frames of the other side of the tabernacle, and five bars for the frames of the side of the tabernacle at the rear westward. [28] The middle bar, halfway up the frames, shall pass through from end to end. [29] You shall overlay the frames with gold, and shall make their rings of gold to hold the bars; and you shall overlay the bars with gold. [30] Then you shall erect the tabernacle according to the plan for it that you were shown on the mountain.

[31] You shall make a curtain of blue, purple, and crimson yarns, and of fine twisted linen; it shall be made with cherubim skillfully worked into it. [32] You shall hang it on four pillars of acacia overlaid with gold, which have hooks of gold and rest on four bases of silver. [33] You shall hang the curtain under the clasps, and bring the ark of the covenant[a] in there, within the curtain; and the curtain shall separate for you the holy place from the most holy. [34] You shall put the mercy seat[b] on the ark of the covenant[a] in the most holy place.

[35] You shall set the table outside the curtain, and the lampstand on the south side of the tabernacle opposite the table; and you shall put the table on the north side.

[36] You shall make a screen for the entrance of the tent, of blue, purple, and crimson yarns, and of fine twisted linen, embroidered with needlework. [37] You shall make for the screen five pillars of acacia, and overlay them with gold; their hooks shall be of gold, and you shall cast five bases of bronze for them.

27 You shall make the altar of acacia wood, five cubits long and five cubits wide; the altar shall be square, and it shall be three cubits high. [2] You shall make horns for it on its four corners; its horns shall be of one piece with it, and you shall overlay it with bronze. [3] You shall make pots for it to receive its ashes, and shovels and basins and forks and firepans; you shall make all its utensils of bronze. [4] You shall also make for it a grating, a network of bronze; and on the net you shall make four bronze rings at its four corners. [5] You shall set it under the ledge of the altar so that the net shall extend halfway down the altar. [6] You shall make poles for the altar, poles of acacia wood, and overlay them with bronze; [7] the poles shall be put through the rings, so that the poles shall be on the two sides of the altar when it is carried. [8] You shall make it hollow, with boards. They shall be made just as you were shown on the mountain.

[9] You shall make the court of the tabernacle. On the south side the court shall have

---

a Or *treaty*, or *testimony*; Heb *eduth*
b Or *the cover*

---

remaining conjectural. But the tent is clearly rectangular and measures ca. 13.8 × 4.6 m = 45 × 15 ft. **31–37: Partitions.** A textile curtain with *cherubim* decorations (see 25.17–22n.) will subdivide the interior space into two zones of holiness (v. 33), and a textile panel will form the entrance; both will be made of linen and tricolored wool (see 26.1–14n.). **33:** *Most holy [place]*, or inner sanctuary (1 Kings 6.16).

27.1–19: The courtyard and its altar (also 38.1–20). Directions for making the courtyard altar (27.1–8) precede instructions for making the enclosure wall, ca. 2.3 m. = 7.5 ft high, forming a courtyard (27.9–19) measuring ca. 45.7 × 22.9 m = 150 × 75 ft. **1–8: Altar.** The sole courtyard appurtenance in this passage (see 30.17–21 for the courtyard basin) is the large and elaborate altar (ca. 7.5 × 7.5 × 4.5 ft = 2.3 × 2.3 × 1.4 m); contrast the earthen altar of 20.24–26. **2:** *Horns*, quarter-round pieces, on the corners (as for the incense altar, 30.2), are attested in many excavated examples; they are used in the ritual of 29.12. **9–19: Enclosure.** As the least sacred zone, the courtyard will have unadorned textiles and metal fittings and utensils mainly of bronze; the linen panel for the entrance, however, will be decorated with tricolored wool (see 26.1n.). The location of the tent within the court is unspecified.

hangings of fine twisted linen one hundred cubits long for that side; [10] its twenty pillars and their twenty bases shall be of bronze, but the hooks of the pillars and their bands shall be of silver. [11] Likewise for its length on the north side there shall be hangings one hundred cubits long, their pillars twenty and their bases twenty, of bronze, but the hooks of the pillars and their bands shall be of silver. [12] For the width of the court on the west side there shall be fifty cubits of hangings, with ten pillars and ten bases. [13] The width of the court on the front to the east shall be fifty cubits. [14] There shall be fifteen cubits of hangings on the one side, with three pillars and three bases. [15] There shall be fifteen cubits of hangings on the other side, with three pillars and three bases. [16] For the gate of the court there shall be a screen twenty cubits long, of blue, purple, and crimson yarns, and of fine twisted linen, embroidered with needlework; it shall have four pillars and with them four bases. [17] All the pillars around the court shall be banded with silver; their hooks shall be of silver, and their bases of bronze. [18] The length of the court shall be one hundred cubits, the width fifty, and the height five cubits, with hangings of fine twisted linen and bases of bronze. [19] All the utensils of the tabernacle for every use, and all its pegs and all the pegs of the court, shall be of bronze.

[20] You shall further command the Israelites to bring you pure oil of beaten olives for the light, so that a lamp may be set up to burn regularly. [21] In the tent of meeting, outside the curtain that is before the covenant,[a] Aaron and his sons shall tend it from evening to morning before the LORD. It shall be a perpetual ordinance to be observed throughout their generations by the Israelites.

28

Then bring near to you your brother Aaron, and his sons with him, from among the Israelites, to serve me as priests— Aaron and Aaron's sons, Nadab and Abihu, Eleazar and Ithamar. [2] You shall make sacred vestments for the glorious adornment of your brother Aaron. [3] And you shall speak to all who have ability, whom I have endowed with skill, that they make Aaron's vestments to consecrate him for my priesthood. [4] These are the vestments that they shall make: a breastpiece, an ephod, a robe, a checkered tunic, a turban, and a sash. When they make these sacred vestments for your brother Aaron and his sons to serve me as priests, [5] they shall use gold, blue, purple, and crimson yarns, and fine linen.

[6] They shall make the ephod of gold, of blue, purple, and crimson yarns, and of fine

---

a   Or *treaty*, or *testimony*; Heb *eduth*

27.20–21: Lamp oil (also 35.8,28). 20: A single *lamp* may belong to the tradition that uses "tent of meeting" for the wilderness shrine; see v. 21n. (cf. 25.37n.). *Regularly* probably means perpetually; light symbolizing divine presence will always be there. 21: *Tent of meeting*, designating the place where the Israelites or their representatives meet God, is used thirty-four times in the book of Exodus to refer to the tent-shrine (see 25.16n.); it may reflect a tradition that is separate from and older than that of texts using "tabernacle" (see 25.9n). *Covenant*, perhaps elliptical for "ark [or tablets] of the covenant." *Aaron* appears for the first time in the tabernacle texts.

28.1–43: Vestments for the priests (also 39.1–31). After an introduction (vv. 1–5), the focus is on Aaron's apparel (vv. 6–39) with less attention to the garb of his sons, who were second-tier priests (vv. 40–43). No title is given for Aaron in the Pentateuch; the titles "high priest" (as Hag 1.12; Zech 3.1) or "chief priest" (2 Kings 25.18) are in non-Torah texts only. 1–5: Introduction. The priestly lineage is announced, followed by a summary of the six prescribed vestments for which fabric of linen and tricolored wool is to be used. 1: See the genealogy of 6.16–25, especially v. 23. *Aaron* has appeared frequently, but the term *priest* is first used here. 2: *Sacred*, better "holy," because they are worn in and correspond to the holy space of the shrine. 3: *All . . . ability*, including women; see 35.4–29n. 5: Sumptuous fabrics, like those of the holy space of the shrine; see 26.1n. 6–39: Aaron's garments. The first two—ephod (vv. 6–14) and breastpiece (vv. 15–30)—and possibly the fourth (turban) have ritual functions; the others—robe (vv. 31–35), turban (vv. 36–38), tunic (v. 39), and sash (v. 39)—are opulent garments like those clothing royalty and statues of the gods in Near Eastern shrines. 6–14: The somewhat enigmatic *ephod* (contrast other biblical uses, e.g., Judg 8.27; 1 Sam 2.18; 14.3) is a ceremonial garment like a bib or apron, adorned with engraved stones (vv. 9–12) representing the Israelite tribes. Oracles from God to the

twisted linen, skillfully worked. [7] It shall have two shoulder-pieces attached to its two edges, so that it may be joined together. [8] The decorated band on it shall be of the same workmanship and materials, of gold, of blue, purple, and crimson yarns, and of fine twisted linen. [9] You shall take two onyx stones, and engrave on them the names of the sons of Israel, [10] six of their names on the one stone, and the names of the remaining six on the other stone, in the order of their birth. [11] As a gem-cutter engraves signets, so you shall engrave the two stones with the names of the sons of Israel; you shall mount them in settings of gold filigree. [12] You shall set the two stones on the shoulder-pieces of the ephod, as stones of remembrance for the sons of Israel; and Aaron shall bear their names before the LORD on his two shoulders for remembrance. [13] You shall make settings of gold filigree, [14] and two chains of pure gold, twisted like cords; and you shall attach the corded chains to the settings.

[15] You shall make a breastpiece of judgment, in skilled work; you shall make it in the style of the ephod; of gold, of blue and purple and crimson yarns, and of fine twisted linen you shall make it. [16] It shall be square and doubled, a span in length and a span in width. [17] You shall set in it four rows of stones. A row of carnelian,[a] chrysolite, and emerald shall be the first row; [18] and the second row a turquoise, a sapphire,[b] and a moonstone; [19] and the third row a jacinth, an agate, and an amethyst; [20] and the fourth row a beryl, an onyx, and a jasper; they shall be set in gold filigree. [21] There shall be twelve stones with names corresponding to the names of the sons of Israel; they shall be like signets, each engraved with its name, for the twelve tribes. [22] You shall make for the breastpiece chains of pure gold, twisted like cords; [23] and you

shall make for the breastpiece two rings of gold, and put the two rings on the two edges of the breastpiece. [24] You shall put the two cords of gold in the two rings at the edges of the breastpiece; [25] the two ends of the two cords you shall attach to the two settings, and so attach it in front to the shoulder-pieces of the ephod. [26] You shall make two rings of gold, and put them at the two ends of the breastpiece, on its inside edge next to the ephod. [27] You shall make two rings of gold, and attach them in front to the lower part of the two shoulder-pieces of the ephod, at its joining above the decorated band of the ephod. [28] The breastpiece shall be bound by its rings to the rings of the ephod with a blue cord, so that it may lie on the decorated band of the ephod, and so that the breastpiece shall not come loose from the ephod. [29] So Aaron shall bear the names of the sons of Israel in the breastpiece of judgment on his heart when he goes into the holy place, for a continual remembrance before the LORD. [30] In the breastpiece of judgment you shall put the Urim and the Thummim, and they shall be on Aaron's heart when he goes in before the LORD; thus Aaron shall bear the judgment of the Israelites on his heart before the LORD continually.

[31] You shall make the robe of the ephod all of blue. [32] It shall have an opening for the head in the middle of it, with a woven binding around the opening, like the opening in a coat of mail,[c] so that it may not be torn. [33] On its lower hem you shall make pomegranates of blue, purple, and crimson yarns, all around the lower hem, with bells of gold between them all around— [34] a golden bell and a

---

a   The identity of several of these stones is uncertain
b   Or *lapis lazuli*
c   Meaning of Heb uncertain

---

priest (v. 30) would thus be given to all Israelites. **15–30:** Just as enigmatic in design, despite or because of its detailed presentation, is the *breastpiece of judgment*. Like the *ephod* to which it is attached, it has gemstones (twelve of them) representing the Israelite tribes (vv. 17–21). Also, it has a pouch for the *Urim* and *Thummim* (v. 30), whose exact meaning and mode of functioning are uncertain. They are specially marked pebbles or rocks cast or thrown to secure divine decisions, a form of divination. Set close to its wearer's *heart*, the site of intellect and wisdom, the breastpiece was to be used in seeking divine *judgment* on matters brought to God by the chief priestly official. **31–35:** The *robe* is adorned at its hem with tricolor woolen *pomegranates*, like the tassels appearing in iconographic representations of the clothing of deities and royalty in the ancient Near East. The golden *bells* at the hem bring the auditory sense into the shrine; the jingling was perhaps apotropaic as the

pomegranate alternating all around the lower hem of the robe. [35] Aaron shall wear it when he ministers, and its sound shall be heard when he goes into the holy place before the LORD, and when he comes out, so that he may not die.

[36] You shall make a rosette of pure gold, and engrave on it, like the engraving of a signet, "Holy to the LORD." [37] You shall fasten it on the turban with a blue cord; it shall be on the front of the turban. [38] It shall be on Aaron's forehead, and Aaron shall take on himself any guilt incurred in the holy offering that the Israelites consecrate as their sacred donations; it shall always be on his forehead, in order that they may find favor before the LORD.

[39] You shall make the checkered tunic of fine linen, and you shall make a turban of fine linen, and you shall make a sash embroidered with needlework.

[40] For Aaron's sons you shall make tunics and sashes and headdresses; you shall make them for their glorious adornment. [41] You shall put them on your brother Aaron, and on his sons with him, and shall anoint them and ordain them and consecrate them, so that they may serve me as priests. [42] You shall make for them linen undergarments to cover their naked flesh; they shall reach from the hips to the thighs; [43] Aaron and his sons shall wear them when they go into the tent of meeting, or when they come near the altar to minister in the holy place; or they will bring guilt on themselves and die. This shall be a perpetual ordinance for him and for his descendants after him.

29 Now this is what you shall do to them to consecrate them, so that they may serve me as priests. Take one young bull and two rams without blemish, [2] and unleavened bread, unleavened cakes mixed with oil, and unleavened wafers spread with oil. You shall make them of choice wheat flour. [3] You shall put them in one basket and bring them in the basket, and bring the bull and the two rams. [4] You shall bring Aaron and his sons to the entrance of the tent of meeting, and wash them with water. [5] Then you shall take the vestments, and put on Aaron the tunic and the robe of the ephod, and the ephod, and the breastpiece, and gird him with the decorated band of the ephod; [6] and you shall set the turban on his head, and put the holy diadem on the turban. [7] You shall take the anointing oil, and pour it on his head and anoint him. [8] Then you shall bring his sons, and put tunics on them, [9] and you shall gird them with sashes[a] and tie headdresses on them; and the priesthood shall be theirs by a perpetual ordinance. You shall then ordain Aaron and his sons.

[10] You shall bring the bull in front of the tent of meeting. Aaron and his sons shall lay

---

a   Gk: Heb *sashes, Aaron and his sons*

---

priest approached the dangerous, most holy zone (v. 35; see 3.6n.; 19.13n.; 30.7n.). **36–38:** The headpiece was to be a *turban* (also v. 39) notable for its golden *rosette* (and also a crown; see *diadem*, 29.6). The rosette's engraved words were perhaps part of a ritual purifying the priest and thus protecting him as he approached the perfect (and dangerous) purity of God's presence; see preceding note. **39:** An embroidered *sash* and a *checkered* (more likely, "fringed") *tunic* complete the vestments for Aaron. **40–43: Vestments for other priests,** less elaborate and costly than those for Aaron. **42:** *Undergarments,* see 20.26n. **43:** *Perpetual . . . descendants,* that is, the hereditary priestly lineage.

29.1–46: Consecration of the priests. The authority of priests derives from the installation rites they undergo as well as from the symbolic garments they wear. The rites are set forth (vv. 1–37), followed by instructions for a regular sacrifice (vv. 38–43) and then a final summation (vv. 44–46). **1–37: Installation procedures** (also Lev 8), which will last seven days and are performed by Moses acting as priest, comprise three rites and the sacrifice of three animals for expiatory and purificatory purposes. **1–9: Three rites**—washing, dressing, anointing. **1:** *Consecrate* (to make holy) appears seven times in this chapter. **4:** *Wash,* see 19.10n. **7:** *Anointing* Aaron (but not his sons; contrast 28.41; 30.30) is a symbolic procedure marking transition to a new status (as for royalty, 1 Sam 24.6); here it gives priests the requisite holiness for entering the tabernacle's holy space. **5:** *Vestments,* see notes to ch 28. **9:** *Ordain,* lit., "fill the hand," is an idiom alluding to the scepter or staff often held by an officer; it thus indicates taking on the rights and duties of a position. **10–37: Animal sacrifices.** The first two—bull of purification (vv. 10–14; see Lev 4.1–12) and ram for burnt offering (vv. 15–18; see Lev 1)—prepare the priests;

their hands on the head of the bull, [11] and you shall slaughter the bull before the LORD, at the entrance of the tent of meeting, [12] and shall take some of the blood of the bull and put it on the horns of the altar with your finger, and all the rest of the blood you shall pour out at the base of the altar. [13] You shall take all the fat that covers the entrails, and the appendage of the liver, and the two kidneys with the fat that is on them, and turn them into smoke on the altar. [14] But the flesh of the bull, and its skin, and its dung, you shall burn with fire outside the camp; it is a sin offering.

[15] Then you shall take one of the rams, and Aaron and his sons shall lay their hands on the head of the ram, [16] and you shall slaughter the ram, and shall take its blood and dash it against all sides of the altar. [17] Then you shall cut the ram into its parts, and wash its entrails and its legs, and put them with its parts and its head, [18] and turn the whole ram into smoke on the altar; it is a burnt offering to the LORD; it is a pleasing odor, an offering by fire to the LORD.

[19] You shall take the other ram; and Aaron and his sons shall lay their hands on the head of the ram, [20] and you shall slaughter the ram, and take some of its blood and put it on the lobe of Aaron's right ear and on the lobes of the right ears of his sons, and on the thumbs of their right hands, and on the big toes of their right feet, and dash the rest of the blood against all sides of the altar. [21] Then you shall take some of the blood that is on the altar, and some of the anointing oil, and sprinkle it on Aaron and his vestments and on his sons and his sons' vestments with him; then he and his vestments shall be holy, as well as his sons and his sons' vestments.

[22] You shall also take the fat of the ram, the fat tail, the fat that covers the entrails, the appendage of the liver, the two kidneys with the fat that is on them, and the right thigh (for it is a ram of ordination), [23] and one loaf of bread, one cake of bread made with oil, and one wafer, out of the basket of unleavened bread that is before the LORD; [24] and you shall place all these on the palms of Aaron and on the palms of his sons, and raise them as an elevation offering before the LORD. [25] Then you shall take them from their hands, and turn them into smoke on the altar on top of the burnt offering of pleasing odor before the LORD; it is an offering by fire to the LORD.

[26] You shall take the breast of the ram of Aaron's ordination and raise it as an elevation offering before the LORD; and it shall be your portion. [27] You shall consecrate the breast that was raised as an elevation offering and the thigh that was raised as an elevation offering from the ram of ordination, from that which belonged to Aaron and his sons. [28] These things shall be a perpetual ordinance for Aaron and his sons from the Israelites, for this is an offering; and it shall be an offering by the Israelites from their sacrifice of offerings of well-being, their offering to the LORD.

[29] The sacred vestments of Aaron shall be passed on to his sons after him; they shall be anointed in them and ordained in them. [30] The son who is priest in his place shall wear them seven days, when he comes into the tent of meeting to minister in the holy place.

[31] You shall take the ram of ordination, and boil its flesh in a holy place; [32] and Aaron and his sons shall eat the flesh of the ram and the bread that is in the basket, at the entrance of the tent of meeting. [33] They themselves shall eat the food by which atonement is made, to ordain and consecrate them, but no one else shall eat of them, because they are holy. [34] If any of the flesh for the ordination, or of the bread, remains until the morning, then you shall burn the remainder with fire; it shall not be eaten, because it is holy.

the third and most elaborate is the ram for ordination (vv. 19–34; see the well-being offering, Lev 3). **12:** *Horns*, see 27.2n. The altar itself must be purified. **14:** The *sin offering* brings about the moral purification necessary for approaching God's total purity. Some scholars understand this as an offering that cleanses sections of the tabernacle from ritual impurity. **18:** *Burnt offering*, see 24.5n. *Pleasing odor*, see Gen 8.21. **20:** Sprinkling the ram's blood on the priests' extremities (*lobes . . . thumbs . . . toes*), which represent their entire bodies, substitutes animal blood and death for that of the priests; their symbolic death means they belong to God. **22:** *Ordination*, see v. 9n. **24:** *Elevation offering*, lifted to God. **26–34:** Without lands or agricultural holdings, priests depended on a *portion* of the sacrifice for their maintenance (Lev 7.31–36; 22.1–16); the meat and accompanying bread are

³⁵ Thus you shall do to Aaron and to his sons, just as I have commanded you; through seven days you shall ordain them. ³⁶ Also every day you shall offer a bull as a sin offering for atonement. Also you shall offer a sin offering for the altar, when you make atonement for it, and shall anoint it, to consecrate it. ³⁷ Seven days you shall make atonement for the altar, and consecrate it, and the altar shall be most holy; whatever touches the altar shall become holy.

³⁸ Now this is what you shall offer on the altar: two lambs a year old regularly each day. ³⁹ One lamb you shall offer in the morning, and the other lamb you shall offer in the evening; ⁴⁰ and with the first lamb one-tenth of a measure of choice flour mixed with one-fourth of a hin of beaten oil, and one-fourth of a hin of wine for a drink offering. ⁴¹ And the other lamb you shall offer in the evening, and shall offer with it a grain offering and its drink offering, as in the morning, for a pleasing odor, an offering by fire to the Lord. ⁴² It shall be a regular burnt offering throughout your generations at the entrance of the tent of meeting before the Lord, where I will meet with you, to speak to you there. ⁴³ I will meet with the Israelites there, and it shall be sanctified by my glory; ⁴⁴ I will consecrate the tent of meeting and the altar; Aaron also and his sons I will consecrate, to serve me as priests. ⁴⁵ I will dwell among the Israelites, and I will be their God. ⁴⁶ And they shall know that I am the Lord their God, who brought them out of the land of Egypt that I might dwell among them; I am the Lord their God.

30 You shall make an altar on which to offer incense; you shall make it of acacia wood. ² It shall be one cubit long, and one cubit wide; it shall be square, and shall be two cubits high; its horns shall be of one piece with it. ³ You shall overlay it with pure gold, its top, and its sides all around and its horns; and you shall make for it a molding of gold all around. ⁴ And you shall make two golden rings for it; under its molding on two opposite sides of it you shall make them, and they shall hold the poles with which to carry it. ⁵ You shall make the poles of acacia wood, and overlay them with gold. ⁶ You shall place it in front of the curtain that is above the ark of the covenant,ᵃ in front of the mercy seatᵇ that is over the covenant,ᵃ where I will meet with you. ⁷ Aaron shall offer fragrant incense on it; every morning when he dresses the lamps he shall offer it, ⁸ and when Aaron sets up the lamps in the evening, he shall offer it, a regular incense offering before the Lord throughout your generations. ⁹ You shall not offer unholy incense on it, or a burnt offering, or a grain offering; and you shall not pour a drink offering on it. ¹⁰ Once a year Aaron shall perform the rite of atonement on its horns. Throughout your generations he shall perform the atonement for it once a year with the blood of the atoning sin offering. It is most holy to the Lord.

¹¹ The Lord spoke to Moses: ¹² When you take a census of the Israelites to register them, at registration all of them shall give a ransom for their lives to the Lord, so that no plague may come upon them for being registered. ¹³ This is what each one who is

ᵃ Or *treaty*, or *testimony*; Heb *eduth*
ᵇ Or *the cover*

eaten in sacred space, affirming their special relationship with God (see 24.5n.). **35–37:** During the seven-day installation ceremonies, the altar too must be purified and sanctified (also v. 12). **38–42: Regular sacrifices.** A daily *burnt offering* (see 24.5n.) of animals with grain, oil, and wine is prescribed. **40:** *Hin*, a liquid measure (3.8 liters = 4 qts). **42–43:** *Meet*, see 25.16n. **44–46: Summation,** using covenant language (see 6.7n.; 19.4n.; 20.2n.). **45–46:** *Dwell*, see 25.8n.

30.1–31.18. Additional instructions. The divine instructions conclude with information about four more components of the shrine (incense altar, laver, oil, and incense) and about a census, the artisans, and the sabbath. **30.1–10: Incense altar** (also 37.25–28). Smaller (ca. .5 × .5 × 1.0 m = 18 × 18 × 36 in) than the horned courtyard altar (see 27.2n.), it is the third golden object to be placed in front of the inner sanctum (see 25.10–40n.). **7:** *Fragrant incense* (vv. 34–38) involves the olfactory senses; and its smoke would be apotropaic, shielding the priest from the potent divine presence (Lev 16.13); see 28.31–35n. **9:** Food is not offered on this altar. **10:** See Lev 16.29–34; cf. Num 16.46. *Sin offering,* see 29.14n. **11–16: Census.** People are counted for taxes or for conscription (Num 1); but ancient peoples believed that counting people could bring disaster (as 2 Sam 24), and the

registered shall give: half a shekel according to the shekel of the sanctuary (the shekel is twenty gerahs), half a shekel as an offering to the Lord. [14] Each one who is registered, from twenty years old and upward, shall give the Lord's offering. [15] The rich shall not give more, and the poor shall not give less, than the half shekel, when you bring this offering to the Lord to make atonement for your lives. [16] You shall take the atonement money from the Israelites and shall designate it for the service of the tent of meeting; before the Lord it will be a reminder to the Israelites of the ransom given for your lives.

[17] The Lord spoke to Moses: [18] You shall make a bronze basin with a bronze stand for washing. You shall put it between the tent of meeting and the altar, and you shall put water in it; [19] with the water[a] Aaron and his sons shall wash their hands and their feet. [20] When they go into the tent of meeting, or when they come near the altar to minister, to make an offering by fire to the Lord, they shall wash with water, so that they may not die. [21] They shall wash their hands and their feet, so that they may not die: it shall be a perpetual ordinance for them, for him and for his descendants throughout their generations.

[22] The Lord spoke to Moses: [23] Take the finest spices: of liquid myrrh five hundred shekels, and of sweet-smelling cinnamon half as much, that is, two hundred fifty, and two hundred fifty of aromatic cane, [24] and five hundred of cassia—measured by the sanctuary shekel—and a hin of olive oil; [25] and you shall make of these a sacred anointing oil blended as by the perfumer; it shall be a holy anointing oil. [26] With it you shall anoint the tent of meeting and the ark of the covenant,[b] [27] and the table and all its uten-

sils, and the lampstand and its utensils, and the altar of incense, [28] and the altar of burnt offering with all its utensils, and the basin with its stand; [29] you shall consecrate them, so that they may be most holy; whatever touches them will become holy. [30] You shall anoint Aaron and his sons, and consecrate them, in order that they may serve me as priests. [31] You shall say to the Israelites, "This shall be my holy anointing oil throughout your generations. [32] It shall not be used in any ordinary anointing of the body, and you shall make no other like it in composition; it is holy, and it shall be holy to you. [33] Whoever compounds any like it or whoever puts any of it on an unqualified person shall be cut off from the people."

[34] The Lord said to Moses: Take sweet spices, stacte, and onycha, and galbanum, sweet spices with pure frankincense (an equal part of each), [35] and make an incense blended as by the perfumer, seasoned with salt, pure and holy; [36] and you shall beat some of it into powder, and put part of it before the covenant[b] in the tent of meeting where I shall meet with you; it shall be for you most holy. [37] When you make incense according to this composition, you shall not make it for yourselves; it shall be regarded by you as holy to the Lord. [38] Whoever makes any like it to use as perfume shall be cut off from the people.

31 The Lord spoke to Moses: [2] See, I have called by name Bezalel son of Uri son of Hur, of the tribe of Judah: [3] and I have filled him with divine spirit,[c] with ability, intelligence, and knowledge in every

a Heb *it*
b Or *treaty*, or *testimony*; Heb *eduth*
c Or *with the spirit of God*

payment here is to forestall misfortune. **13:** *Shekel*, a weight (ca. .4 oz = 11.4 gm), not a coin. The half-shekel (Heb "beka") of the census is mentioned in the metal inventory (38.26). *Shekel of the sanctuary* may allude to a priestly role in maintaining standard weights. **17–21: Laver** (also 38.8; 40.7,30). Made of bronze, the least holy metal, the washstand will be in the courtyard, the least sacred zone. Washing is part of the process of purification before approaching the perfect purity of God's presence (see 19.10n.). **22–38: Oil and incense** (also 37.29) are to be made of costly aromatic substances. For the oil (vv. 22–25), these include myrrh, a resin, and cassia, a variety of cinnamon; for the incense, stacte, galbanum, and frankincense, different varies of resin, and onycha, a perfume from a mollusk found in the Red Sea. Anointing will change the status of the shrine, its furnishings, and its personnel from profane to holy; see 29.7n. **23–24:** *Shekels*, see 30.13n. *Hin*, see 29.40n. **36:** *Tent of meeting . . . meet*, see 27.21n. **31.1–11: Artisans** (also 35.30–36.7). Two chief artisans are designated, one from the southernmost tribe (Judah) and one from the northernmost (Dan). **2:** *Bezalel*, see 1 Chr 2.18–20. *Hur*, see 17.10n. **3:** *Divine spirit*, see v. 11n. *Ability* (or, "wisdom, skill"), *intelligence, and knowledge* constitute artistic genius (cf.

kind of craft, [4] to devise artistic designs, to work in gold, silver, and bronze, [5] in cutting stones for setting, and in carving wood, in every kind of craft. [6] Moreover, I have appointed with him Oholiab son of Ahisamach, of the tribe of Dan; and I have given skill to all the skillful, so that they may make all that I have commanded you: [7] the tent of meeting, and the ark of the covenant,[a] and the mercy seat[b] that is on it, and all the furnishings of the tent, [8] the table and its utensils, and the pure lampstand with all its utensils, and the altar of incense, [9] and the altar of burnt offering with all its utensils, and the basin with its stand, [10] and the finely worked vestments, the holy vestments for the priest Aaron and the vestments of his sons, for their service as priests, [11] and the anointing oil and the fragrant incense for the holy place. They shall do just as I have commanded you.

[12] The LORD said to Moses: [13] You yourself are to speak to the Israelites: "You shall keep my sabbaths, for this is a sign between me and you throughout your generations, given in order that you may know that I, the LORD, sanctify you. [14] You shall keep the sabbath, because it is holy for you; everyone who profanes it shall be put to death; whoever does any work on it shall be cut off from among the people. [15] Six days shall work be done, but the seventh day is a sabbath of solemn rest, holy to the LORD; whoever does any work on the sabbath day shall be put to death. [16] Therefore the Israelites shall keep the sabbath, observing the sabbath throughout their generations, as a perpetual covenant. [17] It is a sign forever between me and the people of Israel that in six days the LORD made heaven and earth, and on the seventh day he rested, and was refreshed."

[18] When God[c] finished speaking with Moses on Mount Sinai, he gave him the two tablets of the covenant,[a] tablets of stone, written with the finger of God.

32 When the people saw that Moses delayed to come down from the mountain, the people gathered around Aaron, and said to him, "Come, make gods for us, who shall go before us; as for this Moses, the man who brought us up out of the land of Egypt, we do not know what has become of him." [2] Aaron said to them, "Take off the gold rings that are on the ears of your wives, your sons, and your daughters, and bring them to me." [3] So all the people took off the gold rings from their ears, and brought them to Aaron. [4] He took the gold from them, formed it in a mold,[d] and cast an image of

[a] Or *treaty*, or *testimony*; Heb *eduth*

[b] Or *the cover*

[c] Heb *he*

[d] Or *fashioned it with a graving tool*; Meaning of Heb uncertain

1 Kings 7.14). **6:** *Oholiab* is otherwise unknown. **11:** *Do . . . commanded* implies that human creativity is subordinated to divine inspiration. **12–17: Sabbath** (also 35.1–3), see 16.23–30n. Its mention here combines sacred time with sacred space, and serves as an introduction to the episode of the golden calf, which separates the divine instructions from the account of their being carried out. **12:** The command for the seventh-day observance is fittingly introduced by a phrase (*The LORD said/spoke to Moses*) used here for the seventh time in this section (25.1; 30.11,17,22,34; 31.1,12). This directive for *holy* time (vv. 14,15) is the climax of the directives for holy space. **17:** As circumcision is the sign of the covenant with Abraham in Priestly tradition (Gen 17), so the sabbath is the *sign* of the covenant with Israel. **18:** This verse concludes the divine instructions and resumes the narrative of the Sinai theophany (24.18). *Two tablets . . . written*, see 24.12n.

32.1–34.35: Covenant violation and restoration. The golden-calf apostasy interrupts the tabernacle sequence. The people arouse divine wrath by their sins; Moses too is angry but intercedes several times (ch 32). After Moses seeks God's presence and pleads once more for his people (ch 33), God reestablishes the covenant (ch 34).

32.1–35: Sin, divine anger, and several intercessions by Moses. 1: *Delayed*, for forty days and nights (24.18). *Make gods*, that is, provide visible evidence of divine presence. **2–3:** *Gold rings* (earrings); cf. 3.22; Gen 35.4; Judg 8.24. **4:** A *calf* (better "young bull"), like cherubim, could form the pedestal or throne of the invisible deity (see 25.17–22n.); or it may itself have been the object of worship, representing bovine strength and fertility associated with the LORD. *Gods*, a plural form (also vv. 1,8), is probably influenced by 1 Kings 12.25–30; contrast Neh

a calf; and they said, "These are your gods, O Israel, who brought you up out of the land of Egypt!" [5] When Aaron saw this, he built an altar before it; and Aaron made proclamation and said, "Tomorrow shall be a festival to the LORD." [6] They rose early the next day, and offered burnt offerings and brought sacrifices of well-being; and the people sat down to eat and drink, and rose up to revel.

[7] The LORD said to Moses, "Go down at once! Your people, whom you brought up out of the land of Egypt, have acted perversely; [8] they have been quick to turn aside from the way that I commanded them; they have cast for themselves an image of a calf, and have worshiped it and sacrificed to it, and said, 'These are your gods, O Israel, who brought you up out of the land of Egypt!'" [9] The LORD said to Moses, "I have seen this people, how stiff-necked they are. [10] Now let me alone, so that my wrath may burn hot against them and I may consume them; and of you I will make a great nation."

[11] But Moses implored the LORD his God, and said, "O LORD, why does your wrath burn hot against your people, whom you brought out of the land of Egypt with great power and with a mighty hand? [12] Why should the Egyptians say, 'It was with evil intent that he brought them out to kill them in the mountains, and to consume them from the face of the earth'? Turn from your fierce wrath; change your mind and do not bring disaster on your people. [13] Remember Abraham, Isaac, and Israel, your servants, how you swore to them by your own self, saying to them, 'I will multiply your descendants like the stars of heaven, and all this land that I have promised I will give to your descendants, and they shall inherit it forever.'" [14] And the LORD changed his mind

about the disaster that he planned to bring on his people.

[15] Then Moses turned and went down from the mountain, carrying the two tablets of the covenant[a] in his hands, tablets that were written on both sides, written on the front and on the back. [16] The tablets were the work of God, and the writing was the writing of God, engraved upon the tablets. [17] When Joshua heard the noise of the people as they shouted, he said to Moses, "There is a noise of war in the camp." [18] But he said,

"It is not the sound made by victors,
    or the sound made by losers;
it is the sound of revelers that I hear."

[19] As soon as he came near the camp and saw the calf and the dancing, Moses' anger burned hot, and he threw the tablets from his hands and broke them at the foot of the mountain. [20] He took the calf that they had made, burned it with fire, ground it to powder, scattered it on the water, and made the Israelites drink it.

[21] Moses said to Aaron, "What did this people do to you that you have brought so great a sin upon them?" [22] And Aaron said, "Do not let the anger of my lord burn hot; you know the people, that they are bent on evil. [23] They said to me, 'Make us gods, who shall go before us; as for this Moses, the man who brought us up out of the land of Egypt, we do not know what has become of him.' [24] So I said to them, 'Whoever has gold, take it off'; so they gave it to me, and I threw it into the fire, and out came this calf!"

[25] When Moses saw that the people were running wild (for Aaron had let them run wild, to the derision of their enemies), [26] then

---

[a] Or treaty, or testimony; Heb eduth

9.18; Ps 106.19–20. **5–6:** The festival is for the LORD, indicating that the calf is not the image of another deity. **6:** Burnt offerings . . . well-being, see 24.5n. **7:** Your people, not "my people" (3.7; 5.1; etc). You, that is, Moses (also 33.1; cf. 20.2; 32.11–12, where God secures Israel's freedom). **10–12:** Wrath . . . hot . . . consume, language associated with punitive plagues (Num 11.33; 16.35,46; 25.4,8–9,11). **11:** Mighty hand, see 3.19n. **13:** Moses reminds God that the ancestral covenant (see 2.24n.) is unconditional and irrevocable (Gen 13.15–16; etc.). **15–16:** Tablets . . . written, see 24.12n. **17:** Joshua is partway up the mountain (24.9–14). **19:** The Heb term for dancing denotes circle dancing, usually done by women (as 15.20). **20:** Burned . . . ground is idiomatic language for complete demolition (cf. 2 Kings 23.15). Moses subjects the people to a trial by ordeal (cf. Num 5.16–28). Those who suffer ill effects from drinking the water and pulverized metal are considered guilty and die in a plague (v. 35). **21–24:** Aaron, however, remains unpunished (cf. Num 12). **26–29:** The shocking violence of the Levites, perhaps reflecting

Moses stood in the gate of the camp, and said, "Who is on the LORD's side? Come to me!" And all the sons of Levi gathered around him. [27] He said to them, "Thus says the LORD, the God of Israel, 'Put your sword on your side, each of you! Go back and forth from gate to gate throughout the camp, and each of you kill your brother, your friend, and your neighbor.'" [28] The sons of Levi did as Moses commanded, and about three thousand of the people fell on that day. [29] Moses said, "Today you have ordained yourselves[a] for the service of the LORD, each one at the cost of a son or a brother, and so have brought a blessing on yourselves this day."

[30] On the next day Moses said to the people, "You have sinned a great sin. But now I will go up to the LORD; perhaps I can make atonement for your sin." [31] So Moses returned to the LORD and said, "Alas, this people has sinned a great sin; they have made for themselves gods of gold. [32] But now, if you will only forgive their sin—but if not, blot me out of the book that you have written." [33] But the LORD said to Moses, "Whoever has sinned against me I will blot out of my book. [34] But now go, lead the people to the place about which I have spoken to you; see, my angel shall go in front of you. Nevertheless, when the day comes for punishment, I will punish them for their sin."

[35] Then the LORD sent a plague on the people, because they made the calf—the one that Aaron made.

33

The LORD said to Moses, "Go, leave this place, you and the people whom you have brought up out of the land of Egypt, and go to the land of which I swore to Abraham, Isaac, and Jacob, saying, 'To your descendants I will give it.' [2] I will send an angel before you, and I will drive out the Canaanites, the Amorites, the Hittites, the Perizzites, the Hivites, and the Jebusites. [3] Go up to a land flowing with milk and honey; but I will not go up among you, or I would consume you on the way, for you are a stiff-necked people."

[4] When the people heard these harsh words, they mourned, and no one put on ornaments. [5] For the LORD had said to Moses, "Say to the Israelites, 'You are a stiff-necked people; if for a single moment I should go up among you, I would consume you. So now take off your ornaments, and I will decide what to do to you.'" [6] Therefore the Israelites stripped themselves of their ornaments, from Mount Horeb onward.

[7] Now Moses used to take the tent and pitch it outside the camp, far off from the camp; he called it the tent of meeting. And everyone who sought the LORD would go out to the tent of meeting, which was outside the camp. [8] Whenever Moses went out to the tent, all the people would rise and stand, each of them, at the entrance of their tents and watch Moses until he had gone into the tent. [9] When Moses entered the tent, the pillar of cloud would descend and stand at the entrance of the tent, and the LORD would speak with Moses. [10] When all the people saw the pillar of cloud standing at the entrance of the tent, all the people would rise and bow down, all of them, at the entrance of their tent. [11] Thus the LORD used to speak to Moses face to face, as one speaks to a friend. Then he would return to the camp; but his young assistant, Joshua son of Nun, would not leave the tent.

[12] Moses said to the LORD, "See, you have said to me, 'Bring up this people'; but you have not let me know whom you will send with me. Yet you have said, 'I know you by name, and you have also found favor in my sight.' [13] Now if I have found favor in your

---

a   Gk Vg Compare Tg: Heb *Today ordain yourselves*

an ancient power struggle, earns them eternal priesthood. **33:** *My book*, cf. Ps 69.28; Dan 12.1; Mal 3.16. **34:** *The people*, not "my people"; see v. 7n. *Angel*, see 3.2n.; 23.23. **35:** The *plague* is punitive (see 7.8–10.29n.; 32.10–12n.).

33.1–23. The divine presence is secured through further intercession by Moses. 1: *You*, see 32.7n. *The people*, see 32.34n. **2:** *Angel*, see 3.2n. *Canaanites . . . Hivites*, see 3.8n. **3:** *Flowing . . . honey*, see 3.8n. *Among*, see 17.6n.; the divine presence can be punitive as well as beneficial. *Consume*, see 32.10–12n. **7:** *Tent of meeting*, see 25.16n.; 27.21n. *Sought the LORD*, elliptical for seeking an oracular pronouncement from God, here procured by Moses, not priests; see 28.6–14n., 15–30n. **9–10:** *Pillar of cloud*, divine presence; see 3.2n. **11:** *Face to face*, intimacy available only to Moses (see Num 12.7–8; Deut 34.10–12); but cf. 3.6n. **13:** *Your people* is covenant terminology (see

sight, show me your ways, so that I may know you and find favor in your sight. Consider too that this nation is your people." ¹⁴ He said, "My presence will go with you, and I will give you rest." ¹⁵ And he said to him, "If your presence will not go, do not carry us up from here. ¹⁶ For how shall it be known that I have found favor in your sight, I and your people, unless you go with us? In this way, we shall be distinct, I and your people, from every people on the face of the earth."

¹⁷ The LORD said to Moses, "I will do the very thing that you have asked; for you have found favor in my sight, and I know you by name." ¹⁸ Moses said, "Show me your glory, I pray." ¹⁹ And he said, "I will make all my goodness pass before you, and will proclaim before you the name, 'The LORD';ᵃ and I will be gracious to whom I will be gracious, and will show mercy on whom I will show mercy. ²⁰ But," he said, "you cannot see my face; for no one shall see me and live." ²¹ And the LORD continued, "See, there is a place by me where you shall stand on the rock; ²² and while my glory passes by I will put you in a cleft of the rock, and I will cover you with my hand until I have passed by; ²³ then I will take away my hand, and you shall see my back; but my face shall not be seen."

34 The LORD said to Moses, "Cut two tablets of stone like the former ones, and I will write on the tablets the words that were on the former tablets, which you broke. ² Be ready in the morning, and come up in the morning to Mount Sinai and present yourself there to me, on the top of the mountain. ³ No one shall come up with you, and do not let anyone be seen throughout all the mountain; and do not let flocks or herds graze in front of that mountain." ⁴ So Moses cut two tablets of stone like the former ones; and he rose early in the morning and went up on Mount Sinai, as the LORD had commanded him, and took in his hand the two tablets of stone. ⁵ The LORD descended in the cloud and stood with him there, and proclaimed the name, "The LORD."ᵃ ⁶ The LORD passed before him, and proclaimed,

"The LORD, the LORD,
a God merciful and gracious,
slow to anger,
and abounding in steadfast love and
    faithfulness,
⁷ keeping steadfast love for the thousandth
    generation,ᵇ
forgiving iniquity and transgression and
    sin,
yet by no means clearing the guilty,
but visiting the iniquity of the parents
upon the children
and the children's children,
to the third and the fourth generation."

⁸ And Moses quickly bowed his head toward the earth, and worshiped. ⁹ He said, "If now I have found favor in your sight, O Lord, I pray, let the Lord go with us. Although this is a stiff-necked people, pardon our iniquity and our sin, and take us for your inheritance."

¹⁰ He said: I hereby make a covenant. Before all your people I will perform marvels, such as have not been performed in all the earth or in any nation; and all the people among whom you live shall see the work of the LORD; for it is an awesome thing that I will do with you.

ᵃ Heb YHWH; see note at 3.15
ᵇ Or for thousands

6.7n.); Moses reminds God of this relationship (contrast 32.7; 33.1). **14:** *My presence will go*, better, "I personally will go." **18:** *Glory*, see 16.7n. **19:** Just as God knows Moses' name (v. 17), Moses will know God's (see 3.15n), an expression of reciprocal intimacy. *I will be gracious . . . mercy*, see 34.6. **20,23:** *Face*, see 3.6n.; cf. 33.11n. **23:** *Back* (like arm, hand, and face) refers to God in anthropomorphic, metaphorical terms.

34.1–35: Covenant restoration and Moses' fourth plea to God. 1: Moses is to *cut* the tablets; contrast 32.16, where God makes them. *Tablets . . . write*, see 24.12n. *Words*, referring to the ten *words* (sayings) of the covenant (the Decalogue), v. 28; see 20.17n. **3:** As a holy zone, access to the mountain is restricted; cf. 19.13n., 20–25n. **5:** *Cloud*, see 3.2n. **5:** *Name*, see 33.19n. **6–7:** This catalogue of divine qualities, known in Jewish tradition as the Thirteen Attributes of God, appears fully or in part frequently in the Bible, at times omitting transgenerational punishment (20.5–6; Num 14.18–19; Deut 7.9–10; etc.). *Generation*, see 20.5n. **9:** *Inheritance*, or "possession," that is, the promised land; see 15.17n. **11–26:** These stipulations concerning religious obligations and festivals

¹¹ Observe what I command you today. See, I will drive out before you the Amorites, the Canaanites, the Hittites, the Perizzites, the Hivites, and the Jebusites. ¹² Take care not to make a covenant with the inhabitants of the land to which you are going, or it will become a snare among you. ¹³ You shall tear down their altars, break their pillars, and cut down their sacred poles[a] ¹⁴ (for you shall worship no other god, because the LORD, whose name is Jealous, is a jealous God). ¹⁵ You shall not make a covenant with the inhabitants of the land, for when they prostitute themselves to their gods and sacrifice to their gods, someone among them will invite you, and you will eat of the sacrifice. ¹⁶ And you will take wives from among their daughters for your sons, and their daughters who prostitute themselves to their gods will make your sons also prostitute themselves to their gods.

¹⁷ You shall not make cast idols.

¹⁸ You shall keep the festival of unleavened bread. Seven days you shall eat unleavened bread, as I commanded you, at the time appointed in the month of Abib; for in the month of Abib you came out from Egypt.

¹⁹ All that first opens the womb is mine, all your male[b] livestock, the firstborn of cow and sheep. ²⁰ The firstborn of a donkey you shall redeem with a lamb, or if you will not redeem it you shall break its neck. All the firstborn of your sons you shall redeem.

No one shall appear before me empty-handed.

²¹ Six days you shall work, but on the seventh day you shall rest; even in plowing time and in harvest time you shall rest. ²² You shall observe the festival of weeks, the first fruits of wheat harvest, and the festival of ingather-ing at the turn of the year. ²³ Three times in the year all your males shall appear before the LORD God, the God of Israel. ²⁴ For I will cast out nations before you, and enlarge your borders; no one shall covet your land when you go up to appear before the LORD your God three times in the year.

²⁵ You shall not offer the blood of my sacrifice with leaven, and the sacrifice of the festival of the passover shall not be left until the morning.

²⁶ The best of the first fruits of your ground you shall bring to the house of the LORD your God.

You shall not boil a kid in its mother's milk.

²⁷ The LORD said to Moses: Write these words; in accordance with these words I have made a covenant with you and with Israel. ²⁸ He was there with the LORD forty days and forty nights; he neither ate bread nor drank water. And he wrote on the tablets the words of the covenant, the ten commandments.[c]

²⁹ Moses came down from Mount Sinai. As he came down from the mountain with the two tablets of the covenant[d] in his hand, Moses did not know that the skin of his face shone because he had been talking with God. ³⁰ When Aaron and all the Israelites saw Moses, the skin of his face was shining, and they were afraid to come near him. ³¹ But Moses called to them; and Aaron and all the leaders of the congregation returned to him,

a Heb *Asherim*
b Gk Theodotion Vg Tg: Meaning of Heb uncertain
c Heb *words*
d Or *treaty*, or *testimony*; Heb *eduth*

include features of the Decalogue (especially 20.3,4,8–11) and of the community regulations (especially 23.14–19); because its primary focus is on worship, it is often called the Ritual Decalogue. **11:** *Drive*, see 23.27–30n. *Amorites . . . Jebusites*, see 3.8n. **13:** *Altars* and *pillars* (see 23.24n.) dedicated to the gods of other peoples are forbidden. *Sacred poles* probably were symbols of Asherah, a Canaanite goddess associated with the LORD in several ancient inscriptions. See also Deut 7.5; 12.3. **14:** See 20.3n. **15–16:** *Prostitute*, sexual metaphors are used in the Bible to characterize human-deity relationships, both positively and negatively (e.g., Isa 62.4–5; Jer 2.2; Ezek 16; 23; Hos 1–3). **16:** Intermarriage with local peoples—but not with all other peoples—is prohibited only for men (Gen 24.3; Ezra 9.2; etc.; but cf. Deut 7.3; Josh 23.12–13; etc.). **18–26:** For the three festivals, see 23.14–19a n.; for the sabbath (v. 21), see 16.23–30n.; for the kid-cooking regulation, see 23.19bn.; for the firstborn redemption, see 13.2n.,13n. **27–28:** Moses is to *write*; see 24.12n. *Words*, see 34.1n. **28:** *Forty . . . nights*, like the first time, 24.18. **29–35:** Moses' special status, as mediator between the people and God, is manifest in his radiating countenance, akin to divine luminosity (Ps 104.2; Ezek 1.27–28; Hab 3.4) and thus too intense to be routinely visible. **29,35:** *Shone* and *shining*, better "radiant," for the Hebrew word may denote emanating rays.

and Moses spoke with them. ³² Afterward all the Israelites came near, and he gave them in commandment all that the Lord had spoken with him on Mount Sinai. ³³ When Moses had finished speaking with them, he put a veil on his face; ³⁴ but whenever Moses went in before the Lord to speak with him, he would take the veil off, until he came out; and when he came out, and told the Israelites what he had been commanded, ³⁵ the Israelites would see the face of Moses, that the skin of his face was shining; and Moses would put the veil on his face again, until he went in to speak with him.

35 Moses assembled all the congregation of the Israelites and said to them: These are the things that the Lord has commanded you to do:

² Six days shall work be done, but on the seventh day you shall have a holy sabbath of solemn rest to the Lord; whoever does any work on it shall be put to death. ³ You shall kindle no fire in all your dwellings on the sabbath day.

⁴ Moses said to all the congregation of the Israelites: This is the thing that the Lord has commanded: ⁵ Take from among you an offering to the Lord; let whoever is of a generous heart bring the Lord's offering: gold, silver, and bronze; ⁶ blue, purple, and crimson yarns, and fine linen; goats' hair, ⁷ tanned rams' skins, and fine leather;ᵃ acacia wood, ⁸ oil for the light, spices for the anointing oil and for the fragrant incense, ⁹ and onyx stones and gems to be set in the ephod and the breastpiece.

¹⁰ All who are skillful among you shall come and make all that the Lord has commanded: the tabernacle, ¹¹ its tent and its covering, its clasps and its frames, its bars, its pillars, and its bases; ¹² the ark with its poles, the mercy seat,ᵇ and the curtain for the screen; ¹³ the table with its poles and all its utensils, and the bread of the Presence; ¹⁴ the lampstand also for the light, with its utensils and its lamps, and the oil for the light; ¹⁵ and the altar of incense, with its poles, and the anointing oil and the fragrant incense, and the screen for the entrance, the entrance of the tabernacle; ¹⁶ the altar of burnt offering, with its grating of bronze, its poles, and all its utensils, the basin with its stand; ¹⁷ the hangings of the court, its pillars and its bases, and the screen for the gate of the court; ¹⁸ the pegs of the tabernacle and the pegs of the court, and their cords; ¹⁹ the finely worked vestments for ministering in the holy place, the holy vestments for the priest Aaron, and the vestments of his sons, for their service as priests.

²⁰ Then all the congregation of the Israelites withdrew from the presence of Moses. ²¹ And they came, everyone whose heart was stirred, and everyone whose spirit was willing, and brought the Lord's offering to be used for the tent of meeting, and for all its service, and for the sacred vestments. ²² So they came, both men and women; all who were of a willing heart brought brooches and earrings and signet rings and pendants, all sorts of gold objects, everyone bringing an offering of gold to the Lord. ²³ And everyone who possessed blue or purple or crimson yarn or fine linen or goats' hair or tanned rams' skins or fine leather,ᵃ brought them. ²⁴ Everyone who could make an offering of silver or bronze brought it as the Lord's offering; and everyone who possessed acacia wood of any use in the work, brought it. ²⁵ All the skillful women spun with their hands, and brought what they had spun in blue and

ᵃ Meaning of Heb uncertain
ᵇ Or *the cover*

Chs 35–40: The tabernacle is constructed and God's presence enters it. The tabernacle narrative (which began with the divine instructions of chs 25–31) resumes: carrying out preliminary procedures (35.2–36.7); making the tabernacle components (36.8–39.43); erecting the tabernacle and God's presence filling it (40.1–38). These chapters contain nearly verbatim repetitions of many passages of chs 25–31, except that they describe action taken (rather than commanded) and are arranged according to pragmatic construction concerns rather than according to degree of sanctity.

35.1–36.7: Preliminary procedures. 35.1–3: Sabbath instructions concluded the prescriptive texts (31.12–17; see 16.23–30n.) and begin the descriptive ones. 1: *Things*, or "words"; see 18.26n. 4–29: Materials (25.1–9), provided by both women and men (vv. 22,29; see 11.2n.) and including fabrics made by female craftspersons (vv.

purple and crimson yarns and fine linen; [26] all the women whose hearts moved them to use their skill spun the goats' hair. [27] And the leaders brought onyx stones and gems to be set in the ephod and the breastpiece, [28] and spices and oil for the light, and for the anointing oil, and for the fragrant incense. [29] All the Israelite men and women whose hearts made them willing to bring anything for the work that the LORD had commanded by Moses to be done, brought it as a freewill offering to the LORD.

[30] Then Moses said to the Israelites: See, the LORD has called by name Bezalel son of Uri son of Hur, of the tribe of Judah; [31] he has filled him with divine spirit,[a] with skill, intelligence, and knowledge in every kind of craft, [32] to devise artistic designs, to work in gold, silver, and bronze, [33] in cutting stones for setting, and in carving wood, in every kind of craft. [34] And he has inspired him to teach, both him and Oholiab son of Ahisamach, of the tribe of Dan. [35] He has filled them with skill to do every kind of work done by an artisan or by a designer or by an embroiderer in blue, purple, and crimson yarns, and in fine linen, or by a weaver—by any sort of artisan or skilled designer.

36 Bezalel and Oholiab and every skillful one to whom the LORD has given skill and understanding to know how to do any work in the construction of the sanctuary shall work in accordance with all that the LORD has commanded.

[2] Moses then called Bezalel and Oholiab and every skillful one to whom the LORD had given skill, everyone whose heart was stirred to come to do the work; [3] and they received from Moses all the freewill offerings that the Israelites had brought for doing the work on the sanctuary. They still kept bringing him freewill offerings every morning, [4] so that all the artisans who were doing every sort of task on the sanctuary came,

each from the task being performed, [5] and said to Moses, "The people are bringing much more than enough for doing the work that the LORD has commanded us to do." [6] So Moses gave command, and word was proclaimed throughout the camp: "No man or woman is to make anything else as an offering for the sanctuary." So the people were restrained from bringing; [7] for what they had already brought was more than enough to do all the work.

[8] All those with skill among the workers made the tabernacle with ten curtains; they were made of fine twisted linen, and blue, purple, and crimson yarns, with cherubim skillfully worked into them. [9] The length of each curtain was twenty-eight cubits, and the width of each curtain four cubits; all the curtains were of the same size. [10] He joined five curtains to one another, and the other five curtains he joined to one another. [11] He made loops of blue on the edge of the outermost curtain of the first set; likewise he made them on the edge of the outermost curtain of the second set; [12] he made fifty loops on the one curtain, and he made fifty loops on the edge of the curtain that was in the second set; the loops were opposite one another. [13] And he made fifty clasps of gold, and joined the curtains one to the other with clasps; so the tabernacle was one whole.

[14] He also made curtains of goats' hair for a tent over the tabernacle; he made eleven curtains. [15] The length of each curtain was thirty cubits, and the width of each curtain four cubits; the eleven curtains were of the same size. [16] He joined five curtains by themselves, and six curtains by themselves. [17] He made fifty loops on the edge of the outermost curtain of the one set, and fifty loops on the edge of the other connecting

[a] Or *the spirit of God*

25–26; cf. 2 Kings 23.7), are donated. **35.30–36.7: Artisans** (31.1–11), who have the added role of teachers (v. 34), receive the materials.

36.8–39.42: The tabernacle components are made: structure (36.8–38), interior furnishings (37.1–29), courtyard and its furnishings (38.1–20), inserted inventory (38.21–31), vestments (39.1–31). Then the work is completed (39.32–42).

36.8–38: Structure (26.1–37), consisting of fabrics (vv. 8–19) over frames (vv. 20–34) followed by the internal fabric divider and entry screen (vv. 35–38).

curtain. [18] He made fifty clasps of bronze to join the tent together so that it might be one whole. [19] And he made for the tent a covering of tanned rams' skins and an outer covering of fine leather.[a]

[20] Then he made the upright frames for the tabernacle of acacia wood. [21] Ten cubits was the length of a frame, and a cubit and a half the width of each frame. [22] Each frame had two pegs for fitting together; he did this for all the frames of the tabernacle. [23] The frames for the tabernacle he made in this way: twenty frames for the south side; [24] and he made forty bases of silver under the twenty frames, two bases under the first frame for its two pegs, and two bases under the next frame for its two pegs. [25] For the second side of the tabernacle, on the north side, he made twenty frames [26] and their forty bases of silver, two bases under the first frame and two bases under the next frame. [27] For the rear of the tabernacle westward he made six frames. [28] He made two frames for corners of the tabernacle in the rear. [29] They were separate beneath, but joined at the top, at the first ring; he made two of them in this way, for the two corners. [30] There were eight frames with their bases of silver: sixteen bases, under every frame two bases.

[31] He made bars of acacia wood, five for the frames of the one side of the tabernacle, [32] and five bars for the frames of the other side of the tabernacle, and five bars for the frames of the tabernacle at the rear westward. [33] He made the middle bar to pass through from end to end halfway up the frames. [34] And he overlaid the frames with gold, and made rings of gold for them to hold the bars, and overlaid the bars with gold.

[35] He made the curtain of blue, purple, and crimson yarns, and fine twisted linen, with cherubim skillfully worked into it. [36] For it he made four pillars of acacia, and overlaid them with gold; their hooks were of gold, and he cast for them four bases of silver.

[37] He also made a screen for the entrance to the tent, of blue, purple, and crimson yarns, and fine twisted linen, embroidered with needlework; [38] and its five pillars with their hooks. He overlaid their capitals and their bases with gold, but their five bases were of bronze.

37

Bezalel made the ark of acacia wood; it was two and a half cubits long, a cubit and a half wide, and a cubit and a half high. [2] He overlaid it with pure gold inside and outside, and made a molding of gold around it. [3] He cast for it four rings of gold for its four feet, two rings on its one side and two rings on its other side. [4] He made poles of acacia wood, and overlaid them with gold, [5] and put the poles into the rings on the sides of the ark, to carry the ark. [6] He made a mercy seat[b] of pure gold; two cubits and a half was its length, and a cubit and a half its width. [7] He made two cherubim of hammered gold; at the two ends of the mercy seat[c] he made them, [8] one cherub at the one end, and one cherub at the other end; of one piece with the mercy seat[c] he made the cherubim at its two ends. [9] The cherubim spread out their wings above, overshadowing the mercy seat[c] with their wings. They faced one another; the faces of the cherubim were turned toward the mercy seat.[c]

[10] He also made the table of acacia wood, two cubits long, one cubit wide, and a cubit and a half high. [11] He overlaid it with pure gold, and made a molding of gold around it. [12] He made around it a rim a handbreadth wide, and made a molding of gold around the rim. [13] He cast for it four rings of gold, and fastened the rings to the four corners at its four legs. [14] The rings that held the poles used for carrying the table were close to the rim. [15] He made the poles of acacia wood to carry the table, and overlaid them with gold.

a   Meaning of Heb uncertain
b   Or *a cover*
c   Or *the cover*

37.1–29: Interior furnishings (25.10–40; 30.1–10) and anointing oil and incense (30.22–28). The ark for the holiest space is again first (vv. 1–9), followed by all three objects for the holy space: lampstand (vv. 17–24), table, and incense altar (vv. 25–28); the incense altar does not come immediately after the table and the lampstand in the earlier instructions. This section ends with an account of making the anointing oil and incense (v. 29), much shorter than in the instructions.

[16] And he made the vessels of pure gold that were to be on the table, its plates and dishes for incense, and its bowls and flagons with which to pour drink offerings.

[17] He also made the lampstand of pure gold. The base and the shaft of the lampstand were made of hammered work; its cups, its calyxes, and its petals were of one piece with it. [18] There were six branches going out of its sides, three branches of the lampstand out of one side of it and three branches of the lampstand out of the other side of it; [19] three cups shaped like almond blossoms, each with calyx and petals, on one branch, and three cups shaped like almond blossoms, each with calyx and petals, on the other branch—so for the six branches going out of the lampstand. [20] On the lampstand itself there were four cups shaped like almond blossoms, each with its calyxes and petals. [21] There was a calyx of one piece with it under the first pair of branches, a calyx of one piece with it under the next pair of branches, and a calyx of one piece with it under the last pair of branches. [22] Their calyxes and their branches were of one piece with it, the whole of it one hammered piece of pure gold. [23] He made its seven lamps and its snuffers and its trays of pure gold. [24] He made it and all its utensils of a talent of pure gold.

[25] He made the altar of incense of acacia wood, one cubit long, and one cubit wide; it was square, and was two cubits high; its horns were of one piece with it. [26] He overlaid it with pure gold, its top, and its sides all around, and its horns; and he made for it a molding of gold all around, [27] and made two golden rings for it under its molding, on two opposite sides of it, to hold the poles with which to carry it. [28] And he made the poles of acacia wood, and overlaid them with gold.

[29] He made the holy anointing oil also, and the pure fragrant incense, blended as by the perfumer.

38 He made the altar of burnt offering also of acacia wood; it was five cubits long, and five cubits wide; it was square, and three cubits high. [2] He made horns for it on its four corners; its horns were of one piece with it, and he overlaid it with bronze. [3] He made all the utensils of the altar, the pots, the shovels, the basins, the forks, and the firepans: all its utensils he made of bronze. [4] He made for the altar a grating, a network of bronze, under its ledge, extending halfway down. [5] He cast four rings on the four corners of the bronze grating to hold the poles; [6] he made the poles of acacia wood, and overlaid them with bronze. [7] And he put the poles through the rings on the sides of the altar, to carry it with them; he made it hollow, with boards.

[8] He made the basin of bronze with its stand of bronze, from the mirrors of the women who served at the entrance to the tent of meeting.

[9] He made the court; for the south side the hangings of the court were of fine twisted linen, one hundred cubits long; [10] its twenty pillars and their twenty bases were of bronze, but the hooks of the pillars and their bands were of silver. [11] For the north side there were hangings one hundred cubits long; its twenty pillars and their twenty bases were of bronze, but the hooks of the pillars and their bands were of silver. [12] For the west side there were hangings fifty cubits long, with ten pillars and ten bases; the hooks of the pillars and their bands were of silver. [13] And for the front to the east, fifty cubits. [14] The hangings for one side of the gate were fifteen cubits, with three pillars and three bases. [15] And so for the other side; on each side of the gate of the court were hangings of fifteen cubits, with three pillars and three bases. [16] All the hangings around the court were of fine twisted linen. [17] The bases for the pillars were of bronze, but the hooks of the pillars and their bands were of silver; the overlaying

38.1–20: Altar (27.1–8), **laver** (30.17–21), **and courtyard** (27.9–19). Unlike in the earlier instructions, the two ritual items—altar (vv. 1–7) and laver (v. 8)—appear sequentially, the latter without the functional details given earlier but with the added information that its *bronze* comes from the *mirrors* of women (also mentioned in 1 Sam 2.22), who were probably low-rank temple servitors. **8:** The *entrance to the tent of meeting*, a highly significant location as the site of Moses' oracular interactions with God (33.9–10), was not off-limits to women (see Num 27.1–2).

of their capitals was also of silver, and all the pillars of the court were banded with silver. [18] The screen for the entrance to the court was embroidered with needlework in blue, purple, and crimson yarns and fine twisted linen. It was twenty cubits long and, along the width of it, five cubits high, corresponding to the hangings of the court. [19] There were four pillars; their four bases were of bronze, their hooks of silver, and the overlaying of their capitals and their bands of silver. [20] All the pegs for the tabernacle and for the court all around were of bronze.

[21] These are the records of the tabernacle, the tabernacle of the covenant,[a] which were drawn up at the commandment of Moses, the work of the Levites being under the direction of Ithamar son of the priest Aaron. [22] Bezalel son of Uri son of Hur, of the tribe of Judah, made all that the LORD commanded Moses; [23] and with him was Oholiab son of Ahisamach, of the tribe of Dan, engraver, designer, and embroiderer in blue, purple, and crimson yarns, and in fine linen.

[24] All the gold that was used for the work, in all the construction of the sanctuary, the gold from the offering, was twenty-nine talents and seven hundred thirty shekels, measured by the sanctuary shekel. [25] The silver from those of the congregation who were counted was one hundred talents and one thousand seven hundred seventy-five shekels, measured by the sanctuary shekel; [26] a beka a head (that is, half a shekel, measured by the sanctuary shekel), for everyone who was counted in the census, from twenty years old and upward, for six hundred three thousand, five hundred fifty men. [27] The hundred talents of silver were for casting the bases of the sanctuary, and the bases of the curtain; one hundred bases for the hundred talents, a talent for a base. [28] Of the thousand seven hundred seventy-five shekels he made hooks for the pillars, and overlaid their capitals and made bands for them. [29] The bronze that was contributed was seventy talents, and two thousand four hundred shekels; [30] with it he made the bases for the entrance of the tent of meeting, the bronze altar and the bronze grating for it and all the utensils of the altar, [31] the bases all around the court, and the bases of the gate of the court, all the pegs of the tabernacle, and all the pegs around the court.

39 Of the blue, purple, and crimson yarns they made finely worked vestments, for ministering in the holy place; they made the sacred vestments for Aaron; as the LORD had commanded Moses.

[2] He made the ephod of gold, of blue, purple, and crimson yarns, and of fine twisted linen. [3] Gold leaf was hammered out and cut

a   Or *treaty,* or *testimony;* Heb *eduth*

38.21–31: The **inventory of work and metal materials**, beginning with the most valuable (gold), has no parallel in the instructions except for the reference in v. 26 to the silver acquired at the census assessment (30.11–16), where it was earmarked for operating, not construction, expenses. **21:** *Records,* tallies of resources about to be enumerated rather than accounts of work done. *Tabernacle of the covenant,* meaning that the tabernacle houses a receptacle (ark) for the covenant document (tablets). The *work of the Levites* is collecting and accounting; later it will include maintaining and moving the shrine (Num 4; 7.1–8). *Ithamar,* Aaron's youngest son (6.23; 28.1), has a major administrative role. **22–23:** *Bezalel . . . Oholiab,* see 31.1–11n. **24:** *Talent,* see 25.39n. The amount of gold is slightly less than Hezekiah's tribute to Sennacherib (2 Kings 18.14). *Sanctuary shekel,* see 30.13n. **25–26:** For the collected silver, see 30.11–16. The number of men is slightly more than the earlier enumeration; see 12.37n. **27–28:** Information about the uses of the census (but not the donated) silver is provided; such information is absent for the gold. **30–31:** The uses of the bronze (as of the silver but not the gold) are specified; but the lavers made of women's mirrors (38.8) are omitted.

39.1–31: **Vestments** (28.1–43). This section includes some technical details, such as how the ephod's golden threads were made (v. 3), absent in the earlier commands. It also omits some aspects of function: the breastpiece is called "breastpiece of judgment" three times in ch 28 (vv. 15,29,30; see 28.15–30n.) in reference to its oracular function but not once here; and the Urim and Thummim, used for divination (28.30), are not mentioned. **1:** *Aaron* is named only here and in v. 27, at the beginning and end of this section, whereas he appears throughout (sixteen times) the earlier instructions on vestments. The name *Moses* appears seven times here as part of a formula punctuating the narrative (*as the LORD had commanded Moses;* vv. 1,5,7,21,26,29,31; cf. 40.16n.).

into threads to work into the blue, purple, and crimson yarns and into the fine twisted linen, in skilled design. [4] They made for the ephod shoulder-pieces, joined to it at its two edges. [5] The decorated band on it was of the same materials and workmanship, of gold, of blue, purple, and crimson yarns, and of fine twisted linen; as the LORD had commanded Moses.

[6] The onyx stones were prepared, enclosed in settings of gold filigree and engraved like the engravings of a signet, according to the names of the sons of Israel. [7] He set them on the shoulder-pieces of the ephod, to be stones of remembrance for the sons of Israel; as the LORD had commanded Moses.

[8] He made the breastpiece, in skilled work, like the work of the ephod, of gold, of blue, purple, and crimson yarns, and of fine twisted linen. [9] It was square; the breastpiece was made double, a span in length and a span in width when doubled. [10] They set in it four rows of stones. A row of carnelian,[a] chrysolite, and emerald was the first row; [11] and the second row, a turquoise, a sapphire,[b] and a moonstone; [12] and the third row, a jacinth, an agate, and an amethyst; [13] and the fourth row, a beryl, an onyx, and a jasper; they were enclosed in settings of gold filigree. [14] There were twelve stones with names corresponding to the names of the sons of Israel; they were like signets, each engraved with its name, for the twelve tribes. [15] They made on the breastpiece chains of pure gold, twisted like cords; [16] and they made two settings of gold filigree and two gold rings, and put the two rings on the two edges of the breastpiece; [17] and they put the two cords of gold in the two rings at the edges of the breastpiece. [18] Two ends of the two cords they had attached to the two settings of filigree; in this way they attached it in front to the shoulder-pieces of the ephod. [19] Then they made two rings of gold, and put them at the two ends of the breastpiece, on its inside edge next to the ephod. [20] They made two rings of gold,

and attached them in front to the lower part of the two shoulder-pieces of the ephod, at its joining above the decorated band of the ephod. [21] They bound the breastpiece by its rings to the rings of the ephod with a blue cord, so that it should lie on the decorated band of the ephod, and that the breastpiece should not come loose from the ephod; as the LORD had commanded Moses.

[22] He also made the robe of the ephod woven all of blue yarn; [23] and the opening of the robe in the middle of it was like the opening in a coat of mail,[c] with a binding around the opening, so that it might not be torn. [24] On the lower hem of the robe they made pomegranates of blue, purple, and crimson yarns, and of fine twisted linen. [25] They also made bells of pure gold, and put the bells between the pomegranates on the lower hem of the robe all around, between the pomegranates; [26] a bell and a pomegranate, a bell and a pomegranate all around on the lower hem of the robe for ministering; as the LORD had commanded Moses.

[27] They also made the tunics, woven of fine linen, for Aaron and his sons, [28] and the turban of fine linen, and the headdresses of fine linen, and the linen undergarments of fine twisted linen, [29] and the sash of fine twisted linen, and of blue, purple, and crimson yarns, embroidered with needlework; as the LORD had commanded Moses.

[30] They made the rosette of the holy diadem of pure gold, and wrote on it an inscription, like the engraving of a signet, "Holy to the LORD." [31] They tied to it a blue cord, to fasten it on the turban above; as the LORD had commanded Moses.

[32] In this way all the work of the tabernacle of the tent of meeting was finished; the Israelites had done everything just as the LORD had commanded Moses. [33] Then

[a] The identification of several of these stones is uncertain
[b] Or *lapis lazuli*
[c] Meaning of Heb uncertain

39.32–43: Completing and inspecting the work, listing the components of the tabernacle in the same order as in chs 35–39 (rather than the order of chs 25–31). **32:** *Work . . . finished* echoes the Priestly language of Gen 2.2, as does 40.33; thus the construction of the tabernacle, a microcosm of the cosmos, echoes its creation. *Tabernacle of the tent of meeting*, used only here and in 40.2,6,29, combines the two designations of the wilderness shrine and thus its two functions: a place for God's earthly presence, and a locale for oracular interactions; see

they brought the tabernacle to Moses, the tent and all its utensils, its hooks, its frames, its bars, its pillars, and its bases; [34] the covering of tanned rams' skins and the covering of fine leather,[a] and the curtain for the screen; [35] the ark of the covenant[b] with its poles and the mercy seat;[c] [36] the table with all its utensils, and the bread of the Presence; [37] the pure lampstand with its lamps set on it and all its utensils, and the oil for the light; [38] the golden altar, the anointing oil and the fragrant incense, and the screen for the entrance of the tent; [39] the bronze altar, and its grating of bronze, its poles, and all its utensils; the basin with its stand; [40] the hangings of the court, its pillars, and its bases, and the screen for the gate of the court, its cords, and its pegs; and all the utensils for the service of the tabernacle, for the tent of meeting; [41] the finely worked vestments for ministering in the holy place, the sacred vestments for the priest Aaron, and the vestments of his sons to serve as priests. [42] The Israelites had done all of the work just as the LORD had commanded Moses. [43] When Moses saw that they had done all the work just as the LORD had commanded, he blessed them.

40 The LORD spoke to Moses: [2] On the first day of the first month you shall set up the tabernacle of the tent of meeting. [3] You shall put in it the ark of the covenant,[b] and you shall screen the ark with the curtain. [4] You shall bring in the table, and arrange its setting; and you shall bring in the lampstand, and set up its lamps. [5] You shall put the golden altar for incense before the ark of the covenant,[b] and set up the screen for the entrance of the tabernacle. [6] You shall set the altar of burnt offering before the entrance of the tabernacle of the tent of meeting, [7] and place the basin between the tent of meeting and the altar, and put water in it. [8] You shall set up the court all around, and hang up the screen for the gate of the court. [9] Then you shall take the anointing oil, and anoint the tabernacle and all that is in it, and consecrate it and all its furniture, so that it shall become holy. [10] You shall also anoint the altar of burnt offering and all its utensils, and consecrate the altar, so that the altar shall be most holy. [11] You shall also anoint the basin with its stand, and consecrate it. [12] Then you shall bring Aaron and his sons to the entrance of the tent of meeting, and shall wash them with water, [13] and put on Aaron the sacred vestments, and you shall anoint him and consecrate him, so that he may serve me as priest. [14] You shall bring his sons also and put tunics on them, [15] and anoint them, as you anointed their father, that they may serve me as priests: and their anointing shall admit them to a perpetual priesthood throughout all generations to come.

[16] Moses did everything just as the LORD had commanded him. [17] In the first month in the second year, on the first day of the month, the tabernacle was set up. [18] Moses set up the tabernacle; he laid its bases, and set up its frames, and put in its poles, and raised up its pillars; [19] and he spread the tent over the tabernacle, and put the covering of the tent over it; as the LORD had commanded Moses. [20] He took the covenant[b] and put it into the ark, and put the poles on the ark, and set the mercy seat[c] above the ark; [21] and he brought the ark into the tabernacle, and set up the curtain for screening, and

---

a   Meaning of Heb uncertain
b   Or *treaty*, or *testimony*; Heb *eduth*
c   Or *the cover*

25.9,16n.; 27.21n. **43:** *Saw*, reminiscent of God seeing the completion of creation (Gen 1.31). *Blessed*, just as God offers blessings in the creation account (Gen 1.22,28; 2.3).

   40.1–38: Erection of the tabernacle and God's presence filling it. After the final instructions for assembling and anointing God's earthly abode (vv. 1–15; cf. 29.4–9; 30.26–30; Lev 8.10–13) are carried out (vv. 16–33), God's presence enters it (vv. 34–38). Moses alone assembles and sanctifies the tabernacle's components and consecrates the priests and their vestments. **2:** Setting up the tabernacle on the *first day of the first month* (of the second year after the Exodus; v. 17), that is, New Year's Day, keys it to the beginning of creation, to the new creation after the flood (Gen 8.13), and to the beginning of freedom (see 12.2n.). **16:** *As the LORD had commanded him* appears in this introductory command and then seven more times, following seven units of assembly

screened the ark of the covenant;[a] as the Lord had commanded Moses. [22] He put the table in the tent of meeting, on the north side of the tabernacle, outside the curtain, [23] and set the bread in order on it before the Lord; as the Lord had commanded Moses. [24] He put the lampstand in the tent of meeting, opposite the table on the south side of the tabernacle, [25] and set up the lamps before the Lord; as the Lord had commanded Moses. [26] He put the golden altar in the tent of meeting before the curtain, [27] and offered fragrant incense on it; as the Lord had commanded Moses. [28] He also put in place the screen for the entrance of the tabernacle. [29] He set the altar of burnt offering at the entrance of the tabernacle of the tent of meeting, and offered on it the burnt offering and the grain offering as the Lord had commanded Moses. [30] He set the basin between the tent of meeting and the altar, and put water in it for washing, [31] with which Moses and Aaron and his sons washed their hands and their feet. [32] When they went into the tent of meeting, and when they approached the altar, they washed; as the Lord had commanded Moses. [33] He set up the court around the tabernacle and the altar, and put up the screen at the gate of the court. So Moses finished the work.

[34] Then the cloud covered the tent of meeting, and the glory of the Lord filled the tabernacle. [35] Moses was not able to enter the tent of meeting because the cloud settled upon it, and the glory of the Lord filled the tabernacle. [36] Whenever the cloud was taken up from the tabernacle, the Israelites would set out on each stage of their journey; [37] but if the cloud was not taken up, then they did not set out until the day that it was taken up. [38] For the cloud of the Lord was on the tabernacle by day, and fire was in the cloud[b] by night, before the eyes of all the house of Israel at each stage of their journey.

a Or *treaty*, or *testimony*; Heb *eduth*
b Heb *it*

(vv. 19,21,23,25,27,29,32), perhaps replicating the seven days of creation (see 39.2n.). **33:** *Finished the work*, see 39.32n. **34–38:** *Cloud*, see 3.2n.; 13.21n. *Glory of the Lord*, see 16.7n. **34:** The cloud *covered* the shrine, just as it covered the mountain of revelation (24.15). Here the cloud indicates divine satisfaction with the construction of the tabernacle as a residence for the divine. **38:** *House of Israel*, which designates the Israelites only here and 16.31 in the book of Exodus, may be a wordplay: the Israelites are a house and the Lord now has an earthly house (cf. 2 Sam 7.11,13,16). The cloud and fire of divine presence will guide the people on the remaining *stages* of their journey (see 12.37n.; 13.21n.; Num 9.15–23; 10.11–28).

LEVITICUS

NAME AND LOCATION IN CANON

Leviticus is situated at the center of the Torah, the Pentateuch. It derives its English name from the ancient Greek translation of the Hebrew Bible, the Septuagint, where the book is titled "Leviticus" because its main concern is worship practices officiated by the high priest Aaron and his descendants, who belong to the tribe of Levi. Because Levites not belonging to Aaron's line are mentioned only briefly in Leviticus (25.32–33), the early rabbinic title, "The Priests' Instruction" (*torat kohanim*), is perhaps more fitting. The book's Hebrew name, *wayyiqra'* ("And he [the LORD] summoned"), follows the custom of titling ancient literary works according to their opening word(s).

AUTHORSHIP AND DATE

Though traditionally attributed to Moses, the book of Leviticus is part of the larger Priestly source in the Pentateuch, which appears primarily in Genesis–Numbers and is so named because its content, theological ideas, and literary style reflect priestly perspectives. This Priestly source was penned by several different anonymous authors or groups of authors. The two main compositional strata in Leviticus are known as P ("Priestly"), which comprises most of chs 1–16; and H ("Holiness"), which includes the "Holiness Collection" (chs 17–26; so named because of its repeated exhortation to the Israelites to be holy), the addendum on vows, dedications, and tithes in ch 27, and brief interpolations in chs 1–16. These two strata are distinguishable on the basis of ideological and stylistic differences.

Recent scholarship has demonstrated that H was composed to revise, supplement, and complete the earlier P strata of the Priestly source, even as it agrees with P's basic historical myth and religious ideology. Many of H's innovations over against P are mediating positions between P and non-Priestly Pentateuchal legislation. For example, in P the only Israelites who are holy are priests. In Deuteronomy, all of Israel is holy. H mediates between these positions by providing a means for lay Israelites to attain holiness by obeying the divine commandments. H also introduces ethical commandments that parallel non-Priestly Pentateuchal laws but fall outside the scope of P's ritual concerns.

Scholars have proposed various methods for dating Leviticus. One of the most promising exploits correspondences between its H portions and laws in the book of Deuteronomy. Strong evidence suggests that at least the core of Deuteronomy originated in the late seventh century BCE. Because H seems to revise this Deuteronomic core, it must postdate Deuteronomy. The P portions of Leviticus, which predate H, exhibit little or no correspondence with Deuteronomy and thus may be contemporary with or older than Deuteronomy; at the very least, they did not know Deuteronomy. Thus, Leviticus, like other books of the Torah, was composed over a long period: it preserves some preexilic traditions, but its literary form likely originated in the exilic period. Correlations between Leviticus and the exilic book of Ezekiel also support this view.

CONTENTS AND STRUCTURE

Though its content is primarily religious ritual and law, Leviticus is part of the larger Priestly story in the Pentateuch. It recounts the delivery of its divine instructions to Moses at the tent of meeting (1.1; 7.38). The book also includes two sections of narratives not dominated by divine instruction (8.1–10.20; 24.10–23); yet even these narrative sections serve as historical context and rationale for the laws embedded within them. Situated in Leviticus, however, the priestly legislation receives powerful validation through its narrative setting. The larger Priestly narrative secures the proper pedigree for these laws: they are divine revelation mediated by Moses in the wilderness.

Set at Mount Sinai, Leviticus begins exactly one year after the Israelites' departure from Egypt, immediately following Moses's construction of the tent of meeting and its indwelling by the deity at the end of the book of Exodus (Ex 40.17–35). The Priestly source's plot continues in the book of Numbers from the exact moment that Leviticus ends. The date in Num 1.1 ("the first day of the second month, in the second year") confirms that the series of divine speeches delivered in Leviticus and the other events recorded in the book ostensibly occurred over a period of one month.

Leviticus can be divided into five major sections:

1. Sacrifice (chs 1–7). In the Priestly source, the Israelites present no sacrificial offerings prior to receiving these laws. The sacrificial laws must precede the consecration of the priests and dedication of the

tabernacle in chs 8–9 because Moses and the priests must know how to perform the sacrifices at these events. This section is subdivided into two parts: (a) basic prescriptions for presenting sacrificial offerings (1.1–6.7); and (b) elaborations on the preceding instructions (6.8–7.38), with particular emphasis on priestly concerns.

2. The dedication of the tabernacle and priests and the transgression of Aaron's sons (chs 8–10). This unit is subdivided into two sections: (a) the seven-day consecration of the priests by Moses, including the dedication of the tabernacle (ch 8); and (b) the inaugural service of the priests on the eighth day, culminating in the revelation of the divine glory, and the subsequent transgression of Aaron's sons Nadab and Abihu (9.1–10.20).

3. Ritual purity (chs 11–16). This section is subdivided into two parts: (a) the impurity laws (chs 11–15); and (b) the Day of Atonement (ch 16). The impurity laws are enumerated prior to the description of the Day of Atonement in order to clarify the impurities cleansed in the annual ritual.

4 The Holiness Collection (chs 17–26). This unit (also called the Holiness Code; see 17.1–26.46n.) has six subdivisions: (a) laws governing sacrifice and meat consumption (ch 17); (b) miscellaneous ethical laws (chs 18–20); (c) priestly and sacrificial rules (chs 21–22); (d) laws governing calendrical observances (23.1–24.9; 25.1–26.2); (e) the account of the blasphemer, with related measure-for-measure laws, which interrupt the calendrical observance laws (24.10–23); and (f) inducements for Israel's obedience, with summary postscript (26.3–46).

5. An addendum concerning vows, dedications, and tithes (ch 27).

INTERPRETATION

Leviticus is difficult to understand and appreciate because it is highly technical and regularly assumes knowledge of its ritual system. Its sparse narrative structure is also easily obscured due to the large blocks of laws that dominate the book. In addition, its authors' approaches to the issues they treat and their assumptions about them are often far removed from modern Western views.

One attempt by the translators of the NRSV to bridge the gap between the ancient text of Leviticus and its modern readers is their substitution of gender-neutral language for many of the masculine pronouns and verbal forms in the book. While the intent motivating this effort is laudable, elimination of male-centered language has resulted in sometimes confusing alterations to the original Hebrew text. For example, laws expressed with third-person masculine forms ("If *his* offering is from the herd, *he* shall make it an unblemished male") are regularly left untranslated or rendered into English with (nongendered) second-person forms ("If *the* offering is from the herd, *you* shall offer a male without blemish"). Likewise, singular verbs ("When any of you *brings* an offering") are translated as plurals ("When any of you *bring* an offering") or converted from active ("*he shall slaughter* the bull") to passive voice ("the bull *shall be slaughtered*"). The foregoing examples, drawn from Lev 1.2–5, are representative of similar changes elsewhere in the book and are problematic for two reasons. First, such changes prevent the reader from understanding both individual verses and the larger religious program of the Priestly authors. Second, these alterations obscure the formal characteristics of biblical legislation and distinguishing features of both smaller, preexisting units assembled by P and, at times, even differences between P and H.

In their ancient context, the primary concern of the laws in Leviticus is to establish the requisite circumstances for the deity's habitation among the Israelites. The Priestly authors claim that following the commandments in Leviticus will ensure the tangible benefits and protection of the divine presence in the Israelites' midst. Failure to adhere to these laws will result in the deity's departure from the tabernacle and the loss of divine benefaction.

With the later emergence of Judaism, the laws of Leviticus became a major source for rabbinic Jewish *halakhah* (law) and remain the basis for many modern Jewish religious practices, such as dietary rules, purity rules, and holidays. The laws of Leviticus also inform many New Testament texts.

GUIDE TO READING

Because the focus of Leviticus's narrative is the law in its divine speeches, the book is most profitably read first according to legal topic rather than from beginning to end. An initial reading might begin with a sampling of Leviticus's purity and ethical laws in chs 11–12 and 19 and rules for removal of impurity and sin, as found in chs 4 and 16. The reader could then turn to other exemplary chapters: chs 8 and 21 on the priesthood, ch 17 on slaughter and meat consumption, ch 23 on festivals, ch 25 on the sabbatical and jubilee years, and ch 26 on divine inducements for obedience. Further study may focus on a particular chapter or group of thematically related chapters, as outlined earlier. The distinctiveness of the laws in Leviticus and the theological perspectives they express can also be appreciated through comparison with topically related laws in Exodus, Numbers, Deuteronomy, and Ezekiel 40–48. The authors of the book of Leviticus created a remarkably coherent system of ritual and theology, and the different parts of the book should be read with an eye toward this larger internal logic.

Jeffrey Stackert

1 The LORD summoned Moses and spoke to him from the tent of meeting, saying: ² Speak to the people of Israel and say to them: When any of you bring an offering of livestock to the LORD, you shall bring your offering from the herd or from the flock.

³ If the offering is a burnt offering from the herd, you shall offer a male without blemish; you shall bring it to the entrance of the tent of meeting, for acceptance in your behalf before the LORD. ⁴ You shall lay your hand on the head of the burnt offering, and it shall be

1.1–7.38: Sacrificial prescriptions. This section comprises two parts: 1.1–6.7 and 6.8–7.38. In Priestly thought, sacrifice, a ritualized meal for the deity at times shared with its offerers, is the basic mode of interaction with God. To be accepted, sacrifices must be performed according to the divine instructions. **1.1–6.7: Basic sacrificial instructions.** These laws address basic procedures for presenting food gift offerings (1.1–3.17) and purification and atonement offerings (4.1–6.7). These sacrifices can also be categorized according to the quality of each offering's sanctity. The grain, purification, and reparation offerings are each "most holy," a designation that reserves their edible portions for the priests (cf. 6.17; Num 18.8–10). Well-being offerings, portions of which are consumed by lay Israelites, are less holy sacrifices. Because burnt offerings are not eaten by humans, their holiness status is undesignated. All offerings in Leviticus share the underlying rationale for sacrifice in Israel and the ancient Near East: sacrifice is an enticement to the deity to engender good will or to mitigate potential threats. **1.1–3.17: Instructions for gift offerings of food.** The burnt offering, grain offering, and well-being offerings (thanksgiving, votive, or freewill; cf. 7.11–18) presented by Israelite laypersons are impromptu sacrifices. Each is described as "an offering by fire" (e.g., 1.9; 2.2; 3.3), better translated "a gift offering (of food)" (cf. 3.11,17). Presentation of gift offerings provides laypersons a specific means of expressing devotion to the deity and of favorably disposing God toward the offerer. As gifts, sacrifices become personal possessions of the deity. Further, God is understood to consume the sacrificial portions burned on the altar (cf. 21.6,8), though this view is partially sublimated in Priestly theology. **1.1–17: The burnt offering.** The burnt offering is completely consumed in fire on the altar. Its name literally means "that which goes up" (in smoke from the altar; cf. 1.9). Three different types of animals for burnt offerings are listed (in descending order of value): a bull (vv. 3–9), a male sheep or goat (vv. 10–13), and turtledoves or pigeons (vv. 14–17). **1:** *Tent of meeting,* see Ex 26; 29.42–46; 40.34–38. The tent of meeting is situated in the middle of the Israelite wilderness camp (Num 2.2) and is the dwelling place of the LORD. **2:** This is a general introduction to the burnt offering here and the well-being offering in ch 3. It clarifies that all animal food gift offerings must be from domesticated animals (cf. 17.1–16n.). Omission of birds here suggests that vv. 14–17 are a secondary addition. *You shall bring your offering,* lit. "he shall bring his offering." Throughout this chapter, the offerer is described in the grammatical third-person masculine singular. **3:** *Without blemish,* cf. Mal 1.6–14. Burnt offerings are impromptu sacrifices of religious devotion (cf. 22.18–20). They are also regularly included in statutory religious observances (Ex 29.38–42; Num 28–29). Because of the prominence of burnt offerings in sacrificial worship, the main altar in the tabernacle courtyard is called the "altar of burnt offering" (Ex 38.1; 40.6). *The entrance of the tent of meeting* is the courtyard area between the altar of burnt offering and the tent (Ex 29.4; 30.17–21). **4:** *Lay your hand,* one hand only, to designate ownership of the animal prior to sacrifice. *And it shall be acceptable,* better, "and it will be accepted" (cf. 19.5–8). The language of acceptance in vv. 3–4 underscores the sacrifice as a gift eliciting divine favor (cf. Mal 1.6–14). *As atonement for you,* better, "as a ransom for him"; see

acceptable in your behalf as atonement for you. [5] The bull shall be slaughtered before the LORD; and Aaron's sons the priests shall offer the blood, dashing the blood against all sides of the altar that is at the entrance of the tent of meeting. [6] The burnt offering shall be flayed and cut up into its parts. [7] The sons of the priest Aaron shall put fire on the altar and arrange wood on the fire. [8] Aaron's sons the priests shall arrange the parts, with the head and the suet, on the wood that is on the fire on the altar; [9] but its entrails and its legs shall be washed with water. Then the priest shall turn the whole into smoke on the altar as a burnt offering, an offering by fire of pleasing odor to the LORD.

[10] If your gift for a burnt offering is from the flock, from the sheep or goats, your offering shall be a male without blemish. [11] It shall be slaughtered on the north side of the altar before the LORD, and Aaron's sons the priests shall dash its blood against all sides of the altar. [12] It shall be cut up into its parts, with its head and its suet, and the priest shall arrange them on the wood that is on the fire on the altar; [13] but the entrails and the legs shall be washed with water. Then the priest shall offer the whole and turn it into smoke on the altar;

it is a burnt offering, an offering by fire of pleasing odor to the LORD.

[14] If your offering to the LORD is a burnt offering of birds, you shall choose your offering from turtledoves or pigeons. [15] The priest shall bring it to the altar and wring off its head, and turn it into smoke on the altar; and its blood shall be drained out against the side of the altar. [16] He shall remove its crop with its contents[a] and throw it at the east side of the altar, in the place for ashes. [17] He shall tear it open by its wings without severing it. Then the priest shall turn it into smoke on the altar, on the wood that is on the fire; it is a burnt offering, an offering by fire of pleasing odor to the LORD.

2 When anyone presents a grain offering to the LORD, the offering shall be of choice flour; the worshiper shall pour oil on it, and put frankincense on it, [2] and bring it to Aaron's sons the priests. After taking from it a handful of the choice flour and oil, with all its frankincense, the priest shall turn this token portion into smoke on the altar, an offering by fire of pleasing odor to the LORD. [3] And what is left of the grain offering shall

[a] Meaning of Heb uncertain

17.11n. **5:** *The bull shall be slaughtered*, lit. "he [the offerer] shall slaughter the bull" (contrast Ezek 44.11). Dashing blood on the altar ransoms the life of the offerer who kills the animal (cf. 17.4,11); it is also found in the cases of the well-being offering (3.2,8,13), the reparation offering (7.2), and the offering of firstborn animals (Num 18.17); cf. Ex 24.6. **7:** *The sons of the priest Aaron*, though referring immediately to the male children of Aaron, these include all subsequent priests from Aaron's clan (cf. v. 8). **9:** *Turn the whole into smoke*, emphasizing that God enjoys the entire sacrifice and concretizing the image of the sacrifice's *pleasing odor* (cf. Gen 8.21). Though the Priestly authors view the earthly tabernacle as God's dwelling place, the imagery of smoke rising from the altar suggests that the deity is in the heavens. Burning sacrificial portions is a ritualized manner of effecting divine consumption.

2.1–16: The grain offering. Instructions for the grain offering, whose name literally means "gift, tribute (eliciting favor)," interrupt the animal food gift offerings in chs 1 and 3 (cf. 1.2). Like the passage on the birds in 1.14–17, these instructions are inserted into an earlier unit and were likely added in order to provide a still more affordable alternative for the burnt offering (cf. 1.1–17n.; 5.1–13). The second-person address of vv. 4–16, which accurately reflects the underlying Hebrew text, further sets these verses apart from vv. 1–3 and chs 1 and 3, all of which employ third-person language to describe the offerer (see Introduction). The grain offering is also a regular accompaniment to the burnt offering presented in statutory religious observances and on other occasions (cf. Ex 29.38–42; 40.29; Lev 9.17; Num 15.1–12; 28.4–6). Two main types of grain offerings are described: raw (vv. 1–3) and cooked (vv. 4–10). The cooked type is further subdivided according to method of preparation. While the raw variety is accompanied by oil and frankincense, only oil accompanies the cooked varieties, perhaps to make them more affordable for the poor. The required preparation may compensate for the lack of frankincense. **1:** *Frankincense*, an aromatic resin from shrubs found in Arabia and East Africa. **2–3:** *Token portion*, unlike the burnt offering, only a portion of the grain offering is burned. The remainder is designated as compensation for the priests (cf. Num 18.8–10). *Offering by fire*, see 1.1–3.17n. *Pleasing odor*, see 1.9n. While the

be for Aaron and his sons, a most holy part of the offerings by fire to the LORD.

⁴ When you present a grain offering baked in the oven, it shall be of choice flour: unleavened cakes mixed with oil, or unleavened wafers spread with oil. ⁵ If your offering is grain prepared on a griddle, it shall be of choice flour mixed with oil, unleavened; ⁶ break it in pieces, and pour oil on it; it is a grain offering. ⁷ If your offering is grain prepared in a pan, it shall be made of choice flour in oil. ⁸ You shall bring to the LORD the grain offering that is prepared in any of these ways; and when it is presented to the priest, he shall take it to the altar. ⁹ The priest shall remove from the grain offering its token portion and turn this into smoke on the altar, an offering by fire of pleasing odor to the LORD. ¹⁰ And what is left of the grain offering shall be for Aaron and his sons; it is a most holy part of the offerings by fire to the LORD.

¹¹ No grain offering that you bring to the LORD shall be made with leaven, for you must not turn any leaven or honey into smoke as an offering by fire to the LORD. ¹² You may bring them to the LORD as an offering of choice products, but they shall not be offered on the altar for a pleasing odor. ¹³ You shall not omit from your grain offerings the salt of the covenant with your God; with all your offerings you shall offer salt.

¹⁴ If you bring a grain offering of first fruits to the LORD, you shall bring as the grain offering of your first fruits coarse new grain from fresh ears, parched with fire. ¹⁵ You shall add oil to it and lay frankincense on it; it is a grain offering. ¹⁶ And the priest shall turn a token portion of it into smoke—some of the coarse grain and oil with all its frankincense; it is an offering by fire to the LORD.

3 If the offering is a sacrifice of well-being, if you offer an animal of the herd, whether male or female, you shall offer one without blemish before the LORD. ² You shall lay your hand on the head of the offering and slaughter it at the entrance of the tent of meeting; and Aaron's sons the priests shall dash the blood against all sides of the altar. ³ You shall offer from the sacrifice of well-being, as an offering by fire to the LORD, the fat that covers the entrails and all the fat that is around the entrails; ⁴ the two kidneys with the fat that is on them at the loins, and the appendage of the liver, which he shall remove

frankincense is aromatic, the pleasing smell to God is not from incense, for the grain offering without frankincense produces the same effect (cf. v. 9). *Most holy part*, see 1.1–6.7n. **11:** *Honey*, fruit syrup made from dates or grapes, not bees' honey (cf. 2 Chr 31.5). Leavening agents (including honey, which supports fermentation) are prohibited from grain offerings, perhaps to expedite their preparation (cf. Ex 12.39; Deut 16.3). **12:** *Choice products*, first-processed products, such as oil, wine, grain, and dough (cf. Num 15.20–21; 18.12–13). Contrast the first-harvested grain offering of vv. 14–16. **13:** NRSV omits the beginning of this verse: "You shall season each of your grain offerings with salt." *Salt* inhibits fermentation and thus may be a corollary to the prohibitions against leaven and honey. It is more likely, however, that salt functions as a flavor enhancer for the deity's food, as it does in Mesopotamian food offerings (cf. 1.1–3.17n.; 1.9n.; Job 6:6). *Salt of the covenant*, the term *covenant* (Heb, "berit") here refers to a statutory requirement (cf. Ex 31:16; contrast Lev 24.8–9, Num 18.19, and Num 25.13, where *covenant* refers to a due or allotment). The text is better translated, "You shall not omit from your grain offering the salt required by your God." **14–16:** The first ripe offering may be a form of the offering in 23.10–11.

3.1–17: The well-being offering. There are three subtypes of well-being offerings: thanksgiving, votive, and freewill (7.11–18; 22.21). The meaning of the Hebrew name of the offering, "shelamim," is uncertain. Proposals include "gift," "payment," "communion," "covenant," "peace," "whole," and "salvific," among others. "Well-being" is preferable because the offering is motivated by the positive circumstance of its offerer. It is the only sacrifice whose meat may be consumed by laypersons (rather than priests). As such, it is a less holy offering (cf. 1.1–6.7n.; 7.19–21). According to the Priestly authors, all sacrificeable animals must be presented as offerings at the tabernacle if their meat is to be eaten (cf. 17.3–7)—they serve as a communal feast between the Israelites and God. Both male and female herd (vv. 1–5) and flock animals (vv. 6–16) are eligible as well-being sacrifices, for their primary purpose is to provide meat for lay consumption. Portions of the sacrifice are burned on the altar (3.9–10,14–15), and portions are designated for the priests (7.28–36), but the main share is retained by the offerer (7.15–21; 19.6–8). **1:** *Without blemish*, see 22.21–30. **2:** *Lay your hand*, see 1.4n. *Dash the blood*, see 1.5n. **3–5:** The visceral fat and the organs are considered the most desirable portions and are thus reserved for God

with the kidneys. [5] Then Aaron's sons shall turn these into smoke on the altar, with the burnt offering that is on the wood on the fire, as an offering by fire of pleasing odor to the LORD.

[6] If your offering for a sacrifice of well-being to the LORD is from the flock, male or female, you shall offer one without blemish. [7] If you present a sheep as your offering, you shall bring it before the LORD [8] and lay your hand on the head of the offering. It shall be slaughtered before the tent of meeting, and Aaron's sons shall dash its blood against all sides of the altar. [9] You shall present its fat from the sacrifice of well-being, as an offering by fire to the LORD: the whole broad tail, which shall be removed close to the backbone, the fat that covers the entrails, and all the fat that is around the entrails; [10] the two kidneys with the fat that is on them at the loins, and the appendage of the liver, which you shall remove with the kidneys. [11] Then the priest shall turn these into smoke on the altar as a food offering by fire to the LORD.

[12] If your offering is a goat, you shall bring it before the LORD [13] and lay your hand on its head; it shall be slaughtered before the tent of meeting; and the sons of Aaron shall dash its blood against all sides of the altar. [14] You

shall present as your offering from it, as an offering by fire to the LORD, the fat that covers the entrails, and all the fat that is around the entrails; [15] the two kidneys with the fat that is on them at the loins, and the appendage of the liver, which you shall remove with the kidneys. [16] Then the priest shall turn these into smoke on the altar as a food offering by fire for a pleasing odor.

All fat is the LORD's. [17] It shall be a perpetual statute throughout your generations, in all your settlements: you must not eat any fat or any blood.

4 The LORD spoke to Moses, saying, [2] Speak to the people of Israel, saying: When anyone sins unintentionally in any of the LORD's commandments about things not to be done, and does any one of them:

[3] If it is the anointed priest who sins, thus bringing guilt on the people, he shall offer for the sin that he has committed a bull of the herd without blemish as a sin offering to the LORD. [4] He shall bring the bull to the entrance of the tent of meeting before the LORD and lay his hand on the head of the bull; the bull shall be slaughtered before the LORD. [5] The anointed priest shall take some of the blood of the bull and bring it into the tent of meeting. [6] The priest shall dip his finger

alone (cf. vv. 16–17). In Hebrew, *fat* often connotes "best." **5:** *With the burnt offering*, referring to the statutory daily morning offering (Ex 29.38–42); *pleasing odor*, see 1.9n. **9:** *Broad tail*, the predominant species of sheep in the Levant has a fatty area surrounding the tail that can weight up to 33 lb (15 kg). **16b–17:** See 17.10–14n.; Gen 9.4; Ezek 44.7. These verses are an H addition to P.

4.1–6.7: Instructions for atonement offerings. Unlike gift offerings, which are spontaneous acts of worship, atonement offerings are required to purge the sanctuary of ritual contamination caused by various sins and impurities. Left unpurged, the accumulation of sin and impurity in the tabernacle threatens the abiding presence of the deity. If God departs, Israel loses all divine protection and benefaction (cf. Ezek 8–11).

4.1–35: The purification offering. Traditionally translated "sin offering," this sacrifice actually purifies the sanctuary from defilement, not the individual from sin; it is thus better translated "purification offering." The purification offering's blood acts as a ritual detergent, cleansing the tabernacle complex from inadvertent transgressions of divine prohibitions. Numbers 15.22–31 expands the application of the purification offering to inadvertent transgression of all divine prescriptions, including explicit commandments. Ch 4 considers inadvertent sins of four different parties: the high priest (vv. 3–12), the entire Israelite congregation (vv. 13–21), a chieftain (vv. 22–26), and an ordinary Israelite (vv. 27–35). The severity of the resulting sanctuary pollution relates to the status of the sinner and is reflected by the animal required for the offering and the locations where its blood is applied. Sins of the high priest and entire community penetrate into the outer room of the tabernacle (vv. 5–7,16–18), while sins of a chieftain or ordinary layperson are less potent, accumulating only on the outer sacrificial altar (vv. 25,30,34). Ch 16 adds a third tier to this gradation: deliberate sins penetrate into and pollute the holy of holies, the inner sanctum of the deity (16.11–17). **2:** *Unintentionally*, lit. "in error," referring to actions done in negligence or ignorance (cf. vv. 13–14). **3–12:** Offering of the high priest. **4:** *Entrance of the tent of meeting*, see 1.3n. *Lay his hand*, see 1.4n. **6:** *Curtain*, Ex 26.31–33. Sprinkling blood purges the outer room of the

in the blood and sprinkle some of the blood seven times before the LORD in front of the curtain of the sanctuary. ⁷ The priest shall put some of the blood on the horns of the altar of fragrant incense that is in the tent of meeting before the LORD; and the rest of the blood of the bull he shall pour out at the base of the altar of burnt offering, which is at the entrance of the tent of meeting. ⁸ He shall remove all the fat from the bull of sin offering: the fat that covers the entrails and all the fat that is around the entrails; ⁹ the two kidneys with the fat that is on them at the loins; and the appendage of the liver, which he shall remove with the kidneys, ¹⁰ just as these are removed from the ox of the sacrifice of well-being. The priest shall turn them into smoke upon the altar of burnt offering. ¹¹ But the skin of the bull and all its flesh, as well as its head, its legs, its entrails, and its dung— ¹² all the rest of the bull—he shall carry out to a clean place outside the camp, to the ash heap, and shall burn it on a wood fire; at the ash heap it shall be burned.

¹³ If the whole congregation of Israel errs unintentionally and the matter escapes the notice of the assembly, and they do any one of the things that by the LORD's command- ments ought not to be done and incur guilt; ¹⁴ when the sin that they have committed becomes known, the assembly shall offer a bull of the herd for a sin offering and bring it before the tent of meeting. ¹⁵ The elders of the congregation shall lay their hands on the head of the bull before the LORD, and the bull shall be slaughtered before the LORD. ¹⁶ The anointed priest shall bring some of the blood of the bull into the tent of meet- ing, ¹⁷ and the priest shall dip his finger in the blood and sprinkle it seven times before the LORD, in front of the curtain. ¹⁸ He shall put some of the blood on the horns of the altar

that is before the LORD in the tent of meeting; and the rest of the blood he shall pour out at the base of the altar of burnt offering that is at the entrance of the tent of meeting. ¹⁹ He shall remove all its fat and turn it into smoke on the altar. ²⁰ He shall do with the bull just as is done with the bull of sin offering; he shall do the same with this. The priest shall make atonement for them, and they shall be forgiven. ²¹ He shall carry the bull outside the camp, and burn it as he burned the first bull; it is the sin offering for the assembly.

²² When a ruler sins, doing unintentionally any one of all the things that by command- ments of the LORD his God ought not to be done and incurs guilt, ²³ once the sin that he has committed is made known to him, he shall bring as his offering a male goat without blemish. ²⁴ He shall lay his hand on the head of the goat; it shall be slaughtered at the spot where the burnt offering is slaughtered be- fore the LORD; it is a sin offering. ²⁵ The priest shall take some of the blood of the sin offer- ing with his finger and put it on the horns of the altar of burnt offering, and pour out the rest of its blood at the base of the altar of burnt offering. ²⁶ All its fat he shall turn into smoke on the altar, like the fat of the sacrifice of well-being. Thus the priest shall make atonement on his behalf for his sin, and he shall be forgiven.

²⁷ If anyone of the ordinary people among you sins unintentionally in doing any one of the things that by the LORD's commandments ought not to be done and incurs guilt, ²⁸ when the sin that you have committed is made known to you, you shall bring a female goat without blemish as your offering, for the sin that you have committed. ²⁹ You shall lay your hand on the head of the sin offering; and the sin offering shall be slaughtered at the place of the burnt offering. ³⁰ The priest shall take

tent. **7:** *Horns*, see Ex 27.2; 30.2–3. *The altar of fragrant incense* is in the outer room of the tabernacle (Ex 30.1–10); see plan on p. 118. Daubing blood on the altar's horns purges it from sin and pollution. The remainder of the blood is poured on the ground for disposal (cf. 17.13; Deut 12.16,27). **8–10:** see 3.3–5. **11–12:** Unlike purification offerings from the flock (cf. 6.24–29), no meat from the bull purification offering may be eaten (cf. 6.30), for the priest may not benefit from his own transgression. **13–21:** Offering for the entire congregation. **20:** *For them*, meaning "on their behalf," i.e., in response to their sin. *And they shall be forgiven*, forgiveness is assured once the required ritual procedure is accomplished. Though this concluding formula is omitted from the high priest's offering, it should be assumed there as well (cf. vv. 26,31,35). **22–26:** Offering for a chieftain. **22:** *Ruler* probably means "chieftain" or "clan leader" (see Num 1.16). **27–35:** Offering for an ordinary Israelite.

some of its blood with his finger and put it on the horns of the altar of burnt offering, and he shall pour out the rest of its blood at the base of the altar. [31] He shall remove all its fat, as the fat is removed from the offering of well-being, and the priest shall turn it into smoke on the altar for a pleasing odor to the Lord. Thus the priest shall make atonement on your behalf, and you shall be forgiven.

[32] If the offering you bring as a sin offering is a sheep, you shall bring a female without blemish. [33] You shall lay your hand on the head of the sin offering; and it shall be slaughtered as a sin offering at the spot where the burnt offering is slaughtered. [34] The priest shall take some of the blood of the sin offering with his finger and put it on the horns of the altar of burnt offering, and pour out the rest of its blood at the base of the altar. [35] You shall remove all its fat, as the fat of the sheep is removed from the sacrifice of well-being, and the priest shall turn it into smoke on the altar, with the offerings by fire to the Lord. Thus the priest shall make atonement on your behalf for the sin that you have committed, and you shall be forgiven.

5 When any of you sin in that you have heard a public adjuration to testify and— though able to testify as one who has seen or learned of the matter—do not speak up, you are subject to punishment. [2] Or when any of you touch any unclean thing—whether the carcass of an unclean beast or the carcass of unclean livestock or the carcass of an unclean swarming thing—and are unaware of it, you have become unclean, and are guilty. [3] Or when you touch human uncleanness— any uncleanness by which one can become unclean—and are unaware of it, when you come to know it, you shall be guilty. [4] Or when any of you utter aloud a rash oath for a bad or a good purpose, whatever people utter in an oath, and are unaware of it, when you come to know it, you shall in any of these be guilty. [5] When you realize your guilt in any of these, you shall confess the sin that you have committed. [6] And you shall bring to the Lord, as your penalty for the sin that you have committed, a female from the flock, a sheep or a goat, as a sin offering; and the priest shall make atonement on your behalf for your sin.

[7] But if you cannot afford a sheep, you shall bring to the Lord, as your penalty for the sin that you have committed, two turtledoves or two pigeons, one for a sin offering and the other for a burnt offering. [8] You shall bring them to the priest, who shall offer first the one for the sin offering, wringing its head at the nape without severing it. [9] He shall sprinkle some of the blood of the sin offering on the side of the altar, while the rest of the blood shall be drained out at the base of the

5.1–13: Purification offerings for specific offenses. This passage extends the scope of ch 4, detailing four specific sins that require purification offerings. In each case (v. 1, withholding testimony; v. 2, contracting impurity from an animal; v. 3, contracting impurity from a person; v. 4, failure to fulfill an oath due to negligence), the sin or pollution has persisted over a prolonged period (vv. 4–5). This lapse of time, which in no case diminishes the gravity of sin or pollution but instead exacerbates it, unites the case of withholding testimony, which is premeditated, with the final three cases, which involve inadvertent actions. Verses 1–4 each present the circumstance of a person's actions and state of mind but do not render a verdict or outline a required response, which comes only in v. 5ff. **1:** *You are subject to punishment,* lit. "and he bears his sin" (cf. 1.2n.). P portrays sin both as a weight of guilt shouldered by the offender until it is borne away through forgiveness and as a defiling object attracted to the sanctuary like certain metals to a magnet. Left unremedied, such sins will accumulate in the sanctuary and drive the deity from it (cf. 16.1–34n.). **2–3:** *You have become unclean, and are guilty,* emendation yields, "but he has realized it and now feels guilt." For impurity contracted by touching animal carcasses, see 11.8,24–40. *When you come to know it, you shall be guilty,* lit. "but he has realized it and now feels guilt." For impurity contracted by touching a human, see 15.4–10,19–24,26–27; Num 19.11–13,16. In each of these cases, had the person who contracted pollution immediately purified him- or herself, no purification offering would have been required. **4:** *When you come to know it . . . be guilty,* lit. "but he has realized it and now feels guilt." *In any of these* was inadvertently inserted here from v. 5 because the scribe's eye skipped. **5–6:** The ritual procedure for sanctuary purification in these four cases requires confession as well as a purification offering, unlike the unintentional sins in ch 4. **7–13:** Less costly alternatives for the purification offering. It is not clear whether these substitutions may be made only in cases of the four sins in vv. 1–4 or for any purification offering. **7:** Two

altar; it is a sin offering. ¹⁰ And the second he shall offer for a burnt offering according to the regulation. Thus the priest shall make atonement on your behalf for the sin that you have committed, and you shall be forgiven.

¹¹ But if you cannot afford two turtledoves or two pigeons, you shall bring as your offering for the sin that you have committed one-tenth of an ephah of choice flour for a sin offering; you shall not put oil on it or lay frankincense on it, for it is a sin offering. ¹² You shall bring it to the priest, and the priest shall scoop up a handful of it as its memorial portion, and turn this into smoke on the altar, with the offerings by fire to the LORD; it is a sin offering. ¹³ Thus the priest shall make atonement on your behalf for whichever of these sins you have committed, and you shall be forgiven. Like the grain offering, the rest shall be for the priest.

¹⁴ The LORD spoke to Moses, saying: ¹⁵ When any of you commit a trespass and sin unintentionally in any of the holy things of the LORD, you shall bring, as your guilt offering to the LORD, a ram without blemish from the flock, convertible into silver by the sanctuary shekel; it is a guilt offering. ¹⁶ And you shall make restitution for the holy thing in which you were remiss, and shall add one-fifth to it and give it to the priest. The priest shall make atonement on your behalf with the ram of the guilt offering, and you shall be forgiven.

¹⁷ If any of you sin without knowing it, doing any of the things that by the LORD's com-

mandments ought not to be done, you have incurred guilt, and are subject to punishment. ¹⁸ You shall bring to the priest a ram without blemish from the flock, or the equivalent, as a guilt offering; and the priest shall make atonement on your behalf for the error that you committed unintentionally, and you shall be forgiven. ¹⁹ It is a guilt offering; you have incurred guilt before the LORD.

6 ᵃ The LORD spoke to Moses, saying: ² When any of you sin and commit a trespass against the LORD by deceiving a neighbor in a matter of a deposit or a pledge, or by robbery, or if you have defrauded a neighbor, ³ or have found something lost and lied about it—if you swear falsely regarding any of the various things that one may do and sin thereby— ⁴ when you have sinned and realize your guilt, and would restore what you took by robbery or by fraud or the deposit that was committed to you, or the lost thing that you found, ⁵ or anything else about which you have sworn falsely, you shall repay the principal amount and shall add one-fifth to it. You shall pay it to its owner when you realize your guilt. ⁶ And you shall bring to the priest, as your guilt offering to the LORD, a ram without blemish from the flock, or its equivalent, for a guilt offering. ⁷ The priest shall make atonement on your behalf before the LORD, and you shall be forgiven for any of the things that one may do and incur guilt thereby.

ᵃ Ch 5.20 in Heb

birds are necessary, one for the purifying blood, and the other for the fat pieces to be burned on the altar. **10:** *According to the regulation,* see 1.14–17. **11–13:** The substitution of a grain offering is a noteworthy accommodation because it includes no blood, the essential component of the purification offering. Because this grain offering is presented in response to wrongdoing, frankincense and oil, symbols of joy, are excluded from it. **11:** *Ephah,* about 21 qts (23 l).

5.14–6.7: The reparation offering. Traditionally translated "guilt offering," this sacrifice actually serves as compensation for sacrilege against the sacred items (vv. 14–16), an unknown sin (vv. 17–19; the "unknown sin" is a common motif in Near Eastern texts), or fraud arising from a false oath (presumably spoken in the name of the LORD and thus sacrilege; 6.1–7). The cases of sacrilege require the offering and restitution plus damages (cf. 22.14). This sacrifice is thus better understood as a "reparation offering." The ritual procedure for this "most holy" sacrifice is found in 7.1–6. **14–16:** Inadvertent trespass against sacred items. **15:** *Holy things,* the most holy sacrificial portions, the altar, and the tabernacle and its furnishings belong to and exist in close proximity to the deity. They are thus sacred. **5.15,18; 6.6:** *Convertible into silver,* a person may bring the *equivalent* value of the offering in silver. **5.16,18; 6.7:** *Make atonement,* appease the deity on behalf of the sinner (cf. 7.1–6n.). **17–19:** Unknown sin. Though ambiguous, this case may differ from those addressed by the purification offering because here the person senses that he or she sinned, but the act itself is unknown. **6.1–7:** See Num 5.5–10 and contrast damages in Ex 22.7–15.

8 [a]The LORD spoke to Moses, saying: [9] Command Aaron and his sons, saying: This is the ritual of the burnt offering. The burnt offering itself shall remain on the hearth upon the altar all night until the morning, while the fire on the altar shall be kept burning. [10] The priest shall put on his linen vestments after putting on his linen undergarments next to his body; and he shall take up the ashes to which the fire has reduced the burnt offering on the altar, and place them beside the altar. [11] Then he shall take off his vestments and put on other garments, and carry the ashes out to a clean place outside the camp. [12] The fire on the altar shall be kept burning; it shall not go out. Every morning the priest shall add wood to it, lay out the burnt offering on it, and turn into smoke the fat pieces of the offerings of well-being. [13] A perpetual fire shall be kept burning on the altar; it shall not go out.

[14] This is the ritual of the grain offering: The sons of Aaron shall offer it before the LORD, in front of the altar. [15] They shall take from it a handful of the choice flour and oil of the grain offering, with all the frankincense that is on the offering, and they shall turn its memorial portion into smoke on the altar as a pleasing odor to the LORD. [16] Aaron

and his sons shall eat what is left of it; it shall be eaten as unleavened cakes in a holy place; in the court of the tent of meeting they shall eat it. [17] It shall not be baked with leaven. I have given it as their portion of my offerings by fire; it is most holy, like the sin offering and the guilt offering. [18] Every male among the descendants of Aaron shall eat of it, as their perpetual due throughout your generations, from the LORD's offerings by fire; anything that touches them shall become holy.

[19] The LORD spoke to Moses, saying: [20] This is the offering that Aaron and his sons shall offer to the LORD on the day when he is anointed: one-tenth of an ephah of choice flour as a regular offering, half of it in the morning and half in the evening. [21] It shall be made with oil on a griddle; you shall bring it well soaked, as a grain offering of baked[b] pieces, and you shall present it as a pleasing odor to the LORD. [22] And so the priest, anointed from among Aaron's descendants as a successor, shall prepare it; it is the LORD's— a perpetual due—to be turned entirely into

[a] Ch 6.1 in Heb
[b] Meaning of Heb uncertain

6.8–7.38: Elaborations on the sacrificial instructions. This section, which contains five divine speeches, offers further instructions for each of the offerings detailed in 1.1–6.7 and focuses especially upon ritual performance, distribution of sacrificial pieces, and disposal procedures. The first three are ostensibly directed to the priests alone (6.9–7.21), although the instructions in 7.11–21 are pertinent to both priests and laypersons. The final two speeches are directed to all of the Israelites (7.22–36), and 7.37–38 serves as a subscript to this section. 6.8–13: The burnt offering. Cf. 1.3–13. Alternatively, this may refer to the statutory daily burnt offerings (cf. Ex 29.38–42; Num 28.3–8). 10–11: The priestly garb is described in Ex 28.39–43. The linen garments must be worn in approaching the sacred altar, while nonsacral garb is worn for ash disposal outside the camp. 12: This verse may be punctuated differently: lay out the burnt offering on it may actually be a new sentence, viz., "He shall arrange the burnt offering upon it and turn into smoke the fat pieces of the well-being offering." If so, this burnt offering is likely not the daily statutory offering (cf. 3.5). 12–13: The perpetual fire maintains a direct link to the divine fire that ignites the altar in 9.24. It is God who consumes all sacrificial pieces burned on the altar. 6.14–23: The grain offerings. 14–18: These verses provide instructions for the grain offering described in 2.1–13. 15: Frankincense, see 2.1n. Pleasing odor, see 1.9n. 16: Holy place, the priests' portions of most holy offerings must be consumed within the sanctuary complex in order to ensure their sanctity and to avoid communicating holiness (cf. v. 18). Court, see Ex 27.9–19. 17: Offerings by fire, see 1.1–3.17n. 18: Shall eat, better, "may eat." All males of Aaron's line are priests and thus may share in most holy sacrificial portions (cf. 21.22). Women belonging to priestly families may partake of lesser holy sacrificial portions assigned to the priests (22.10–13). Become holy, holiness is conceptualized as an invisible divine essence that is communicable through physical contact (cf. v. 27; Ex 29.37; 30.29; Ezek 44.19). 19–23: These verses provide instructions for the statutory grain offerings that the high priest must present daily. 20: On the day when he is anointed, better, "once he has been anointed." Aaron, the first high priest, is not anointed until ch 8. This statute is also applicable to all future high priests (cf. v. 22).

smoke. [23] Every grain offering of a priest shall be wholly burned; it shall not be eaten.

[24] The LORD spoke to Moses, saying: [25] Speak to Aaron and his sons, saying: This is the ritual of the sin offering. The sin offering shall be slaughtered before the LORD at the spot where the burnt offering is slaughtered; it is most holy. [26] The priest who offers it as a sin offering shall eat of it; it shall be eaten in a holy place, in the court of the tent of meeting. [27] Whatever touches its flesh shall become holy; and when any of its blood is spattered on a garment, you shall wash the bespattered part in a holy place. [28] An earthen vessel in which it was boiled shall be broken; but if it is boiled in a bronze vessel, that shall be scoured and rinsed in water. [29] Every male among the priests shall eat of it; it is most holy. [30] But no sin offering shall be eaten from which any blood is brought into the tent of meeting for atonement in the holy place; it shall be burned with fire.

7 This is the ritual of the guilt offering. It is most holy; [2] at the spot where the burnt offering is slaughtered, they shall slaughter the guilt offering, and its blood shall be dashed against all sides of the altar. [3] All its fat shall be offered: the broad tail, the fat that covers the entrails, [4] the two kidneys with the fat that is on them at the loins, and the appendage of the liver, which shall be removed with the kidneys. [5] The priest shall turn them into smoke on the altar as an offering by fire to the LORD; it is a guilt offering. [6] Every male among the priests shall eat of it; it shall be eaten in a holy place; it is most holy.

[7] The guilt offering is like the sin offering, there is the same ritual for them; the priest who makes atonement with it shall have it. [8] So, too, the priest who offers anyone's burnt offering shall keep the skin of the burnt offering that he has offered. [9] And every grain offering baked in the oven, and all that is prepared in a pan or on a griddle, shall belong to the priest who offers it. [10] But every other grain offering, mixed with oil or dry, shall belong to all the sons of Aaron equally.

[11] This is the ritual of the sacrifice of the offering of well-being that one may offer to the LORD. [12] If you offer it for thanksgiving, you shall offer with the thank offering unleavened cakes mixed with oil, unleavened wafers spread with oil, and cakes of choice flour well soaked in oil. [13] With your thanksgiving sacrifice of well-being you shall bring your offering with cakes of leavened bread. [14] From this you shall offer one cake from each offering, as a gift to the LORD; it shall belong to the priest who dashes the blood of the offering of well-being. [15] And the flesh of your thanksgiving sacrifice of well-being shall be eaten on the day it is offered; you shall not leave any of it until morning. [16] But if the sacrifice you offer is a votive offering or a freewill offering, it shall be eaten on the day that you offer your sacrifice, and what is left of it shall be eaten the next day; [17] but what is left of the flesh of the sacrifice shall be burned up on the third day. [18] If any of the flesh of your sacrifice of well-being is eaten on the third

---

6.24–30: The purification offering. 24–29: These verses provide instructions for purification offerings whose blood is applied to the outer altar (cf. 4.22–35). Portions of these most holy offerings may be eaten by the priests (see 1.1–6.7n.). 25: *Sin offering*, see 4.1–35n. 26: *Holy place*, see 6.16n. *Court*, see Ex 27.9–19. 27–28: *Become holy*, see 6.18n. The blood of the offering seems to decontaminate by absorbing impurities, which explains how it contaminates garments and vessels. 29: *Shall eat*, better, "may eat" (cf. 6.18n.). 30: This verse refers to the purification offering for more virulent contamination and any purification offering of a priest (cf. Ex 29.14; Lev 4.1–21; 6.23; 8.17; 9.11; 16.27).

7.1–10: The reparation offering. Cf. 5.14–6.7. 1: *Guilt offering*, see 5.14–6.7n. 2: *Its blood shall be dashed*, see 1.5n. 6: *Shall eat*, better, "may eat" (cf. 6.18n.). 7: *Ritual*, better, "instruction." 7–10: These verses summarize some of the compensation given to the priests for their ritual activities (cf. Num 18.8–20).

7.11–38: The well-being offerings. Cf. 3.1–17; 22.21–23. This unit provides instructions for three different types of well-being offerings: thanksgiving, votive, and freewill. The thanksgiving offering is more complex than the votive and freewill offerings, requiring accompanying grain offerings (cf. 2.4–10) and leavened bread (contrast 2.11–12). In addition, the thanksgiving offering may be eaten only on the day it is presented, while other well-being sacrifices may be consumed for two days. 13: Lit. "The foregoing he shall offer with loaves of leavened bread, together with his well-being offering of thanksgiving." 18: *Acceptable*, lit. "accepted" (cf. 1.4n.;

day, it shall not be acceptable, nor shall it be credited to the one who offers it; it shall be an abomination, and the one who eats of it shall incur guilt.

[19] Flesh that touches any unclean thing shall not be eaten; it shall be burned up. As for other flesh, all who are clean may eat such flesh. [20] But those who eat flesh from the Lord's sacrifice of well-being while in a state of uncleanness shall be cut off from their kin. [21] When any one of you touches any unclean thing—human uncleanness or an unclean animal or any unclean creature—and then eats flesh from the Lord's sacrifice of well-being, you shall be cut off from your kin.

[22] The Lord spoke to Moses, saying: [23] Speak to the people of Israel, saying: You shall eat no fat of ox or sheep or goat. [24] The fat of an animal that died or was torn by wild animals may be put to any other use, but you must not eat it. [25] If any one of you eats the fat from an animal of which an offering by fire may be made to the Lord, you who eat it shall be cut off from your kin. [26] You must not eat any blood whatever, either of bird or of animal, in any of your settlements. [27] Any one of you who eats any blood shall be cut off from your kin.

[28] The Lord spoke to Moses, saying: [29] Speak to the people of Israel, saying: Any one of you who would offer to the Lord your sacrifice of well-being must yourself bring to the Lord your offering from your sacrifice of well-being. [30] Your own hands shall bring the Lord's offering by fire; you shall bring the fat with the breast, so that the breast may be raised as an elevation offering before the Lord. [31] The priest shall turn the fat into smoke on the altar, but the breast shall belong to Aaron and his sons. [32] And the right thigh from your sacrifices of well-being you shall give to the priest as an offering; [33] the one among the sons of Aaron who offers the blood and fat of the offering of well-being shall have the right thigh for a portion. [34] For I have taken the breast of the elevation offering, and the thigh that is offered, from the people of Israel, from their sacrifices of well-being, and have given them to Aaron the priest and to his sons, as a perpetual due from the people of Israel. [35] This is the portion allotted to Aaron and to his sons from the offerings made by fire to the Lord, once they have been brought forward to serve the Lord as priests; [36] these the Lord commanded to be given them, when he anointed them, as a perpetual due from the people of Israel throughout their generations.

[37] This is the ritual of the burnt offering, the grain offering, the sin offering, the guilt offering, the offering of ordination, and the sacrifice of well-being, [38] which the Lord commanded Moses on Mount Sinai, when he commanded the people of Israel to bring their offerings to the Lord, in the wilderness of Sinai.

8 The Lord spoke to Moses, saying: [2] Take Aaron and his sons with him, the vestments, the anointing oil, the bull of sin offering, the two rams, and the basket of unleavened bread; [3] and assemble the whole congregation at the entrance of the tent

19.5–8; 22.17–30). *Incur guilt*, cf. 5.1n. **19–21**: Sacrificial portions are to be kept from impurity because, as holy food, they belong to God, whose presence is threatened by impurity (cf. 4.1–35n.; 11.1–16.34n.; 19.8). *Cut off*, this penalty is applied by the Priestly authors to several offenses against God and likely refers to the complete destruction of the offender's lineage. **22–27**: These commands develop further the prohibition against fat and blood in 3.17. **23**: *Ox or sheep or goat*, i.e., sacrificeable animals. **25,27**: *Cut off*, see 7.19–21n. **28–36**: The priests' portion of the well-being offering. **30**: *Elevation*, a ritual act dedicating the offering to the deity. **31–33**: The breast belongs to all of the priests, while the thigh is designated for the priest who officiates over the sacrifice. **37–38**: A summarizing postscript to 6.8–7.36. The inclusion of the ordination offering here may be due to its similarity to the well-being offering (cf. 8.22–32n.). **38**: *On Mount Sinai*, better, "at Mount Sinai," namely at the tabernacle erected at the foot of the mountain after Moses's descent (Ex 34.29).

8.1–10.20: The dedication of the tabernacle and priests and the transgression of Aaron's sons. Chs 8–10 narrate the consecration of the tabernacle complex, the seven-day ordination of the priests, the inaugural priestly service on the eighth day that culminates in the revelation of the divine presence through fire, and the subsequent illicit ritual of Aaron's sons, Nadab and Abihu.

8.1–36: The dedication of the tabernacle and priests. A fulfillment of the consecration rituals as instructed

of meeting. ⁴ And Moses did as the LORD commanded him. When the congregation was assembled at the entrance of the tent of meeting, ⁵ Moses said to the congregation, "This is what the LORD has commanded to be done."

⁶ Then Moses brought Aaron and his sons forward, and washed them with water. ⁷ He put the tunic on him, fastened the sash around him, clothed him with the robe, and put the ephod on him. He then put the decorated band of the ephod around him, tying the ephod to him with it. ⁸ He placed the breastpiece on him, and in the breastpiece he put the Urim and the Thummim. ⁹ And he set the turban on his head, and on the turban, in front, he set the golden ornament, the holy crown, as the LORD commanded Moses.

¹⁰ Then Moses took the anointing oil and anointed the tabernacle and all that was in it, and consecrated them. ¹¹ He sprinkled some of it on the altar seven times, and anointed the altar and all its utensils, and the basin and its base, to consecrate them. ¹² He poured some of the anointing oil on Aaron's head and anointed him, to consecrate him. ¹³ And Moses brought forward Aaron's sons, and clothed them with tunics, and fastened sashes around them, and tied headdresses on them, as the LORD commanded Moses.

¹⁴ He led forward the bull of sin offering; and Aaron and his sons laid their hands upon the head of the bull of sin offering, ¹⁵ and it was slaughtered. Moses took the blood and with his finger put some on each of the horns of the altar, purifying the altar; then he poured out the blood at the base of the altar. Thus he consecrated it, to make atonement for it. ¹⁶ Moses took all the fat that was around the entrails, and the appendage of the liver, and the two kidneys with their fat, and turned them into smoke on the altar. ¹⁷ But the bull itself, its skin and flesh and its dung, he burned with fire outside the camp, as the LORD commanded Moses.

¹⁸ Then he brought forward the ram of burnt offering. Aaron and his sons laid their hands on the head of the ram, ¹⁹ and it was slaughtered. Moses dashed the blood against all sides of the altar. ²⁰ The ram was cut into its parts, and Moses turned into smoke the head and the parts and the suet. ²¹ And after the entrails and the legs were washed with water, Moses turned into smoke the whole ram on the altar; it was a burnt offering for a pleasing odor, an offering by fire to the LORD, as the LORD commanded Moses.

²² Then he brought forward the second ram, the ram of ordination. Aaron and his sons laid their hands on the head of the ram, ²³ and it was slaughtered. Moses took some of its blood and put it on the lobe of Aaron's right ear and on the thumb of his right hand and on the big toe of his right foot. ²⁴ After Aaron's sons were brought forward, Moses put some of the blood on the lobes of their right ears and on the thumbs of their right hands and on the big toes of their right feet; and Moses dashed the rest of the blood against all sides of the altar. ²⁵ He took the fat—the broad tail, all the fat that was around the entrails, the appendage of the liver, and the two kidneys with their fat—and the right thigh. ²⁶ From the basket of unleavened bread that was before the LORD, he took one cake of unleavened bread, one cake of bread with oil, and one wafer, and placed them on the fat and on the right thigh. ²⁷ He placed all these

by God (cf. vv. 5,9,13,17,21,29,31,34) to Moses in Ex 28–29; 30.26–30; 40.9–15. **2**: *Anointing oil*, Ex 30.22–33; 37.29. *Bull of sin offering*, see Lev 4.3. For the offerings listed here, see Ex 29.1–3. **5**: *What the LORD has commanded*, i.e., Ex 29. **7–9,13**: For descriptions of the priestly vestments, see Ex 28.1–43; 39.1–31. The high priest's clothing is intended for his "honor and beauty" (Ex 28.2) and distinguishes him from the other priests, whose ritual attire is simpler. **10–12,30**: Anointing infuses the tabernacle, its furnishings, and the priests with ritual holiness, setting them apart as the personal possessions of the deity and his ceremonial servants. Anointing with oil was a common transition rite for persons and objects in the ancient Near East (cf. 14.15–18,26–29), and was therefore also used in Israel to change the status of a commoner to king (e.g., 1 Sam 10.1; 16.13). **14–17**: 4.1–12. **18–21**: 1.10–13. **22–32**: *Ram of ordination*, cf. Ex 29.22–28,31–34. The ordination offering is similar (but not identical) to the well-being offering. It inaugurates the system for priestly compensation, as indicated by its name: *ordination*, literally, "filling (the hand)," refers to the assignment of part of the offerings to the priests. **23–24**: *Ear . . . thumb . . . big toe*, treating the bodily extremities symbolizes application

on the palms of Aaron and on the palms of his sons, and raised them as an elevation offering before the LORD. [28] Then Moses took them from their hands and turned them into smoke on the altar with the burnt offering. This was an ordination offering for a pleasing odor, an offering by fire to the LORD. [29] Moses took the breast and raised it as an elevation offering before the LORD; it was Moses' portion of the ram of ordination, as the LORD commanded Moses.

[30] Then Moses took some of the anointing oil and some of the blood that was on the altar and sprinkled them on Aaron and his vestments, and also on his sons and their vestments. Thus he consecrated Aaron and his vestments, and also his sons and their vestments.

[31] And Moses said to Aaron and his sons, "Boil the flesh at the entrance of the tent of meeting, and eat it there with the bread that is in the basket of ordination offerings, as I was commanded, 'Aaron and his sons shall eat it'; [32] and what remains of the flesh and the bread you shall burn with fire. [33] You shall not go outside the entrance of the tent of meeting for seven days, until the day when your period of ordination is completed. For it will take seven days to ordain you; [34] as has been done today, the LORD has commanded to be done to make atonement for you. [35] You shall remain at the entrance of the tent of meeting day and night for seven days, keeping the LORD's charge so that you do not die; for so I am commanded." [36] Aaron and his

sons did all the things that the LORD commanded through Moses.

9 On the eighth day Moses summoned Aaron and his sons and the elders of Israel. [2] He said to Aaron, "Take a bull calf for a sin offering and a ram for a burnt offering, without blemish, and offer them before the LORD. [3] And say to the people of Israel, 'Take a male goat for a sin offering; a calf and a lamb, yearlings without blemish, for a burnt offering; [4] and an ox and a ram for an offering of well-being to sacrifice before the LORD; and a grain offering mixed with oil. For today the LORD will appear to you.'" [5] They brought what Moses commanded to the front of the tent of meeting; and the whole congregation drew near and stood before the LORD. [6] And Moses said, "This is the thing that the LORD commanded you to do, so that the glory of the LORD may appear to you." [7] Then Moses said to Aaron, "Draw near to the altar and sacrifice your sin offering and your burnt offering, and make atonement for yourself and for the people; and sacrifice the offering of the people, and make atonement for them; as the LORD has commanded."

[8] Aaron drew near to the altar, and slaughtered the calf of the sin offering, which was for himself. [9] The sons of Aaron presented the blood to him, and he dipped his finger in the blood and put it on the horns of the altar; and the rest of the blood he poured out at the base of the altar. [10] But the fat, the kidneys, and the appendage of the liver from the sin offering he turned into smoke on the altar, as

to the entire person. **31:** Once the ordination process has begun, the priests may partake of the sacred offering portions. **33:** *It will take seven days to ordain you,* better, "He (i.e., God) will fill your hand for seven days." Sacrifices are the possession of the deity, who shares a portion with the priests. **33–35:** The purification and ordination ritual is to be repeated for seven days (cf. Ex 29.35–37), during which the priests must remain in the sanctuary complex to preserve their purity. **36:** This verse covers the time period of the six remaining days of the priestly ordination. Priestly literature often describes the fulfillment of complex instructions through short report statements (cf. 16.34b).

9.1–10.20: The inauguration of priestly service and the transgression of Nadab and Abihu. Chs 9–10 narrate the events of the eighth day, i.e., the day after the consecration of the priests is completed. The priests perform their first sacrifices, and the glory of the LORD appears to the people with fire, confirming the deity's presence and approval of the priests' ritual activities. Immediately following this joyous occasion, however, Aaron's sons, Nadab and Abihu, commit sacrilege by making an unauthorized incense offering, which prompts the divine fire to emerge once more to consume them. The deaths of Nadab and Abihu occasion further instructions for the priests.

9.1–24: The inauguration of priestly service. 4,6: The deity's appearance is the fire that emerges from the tabernacle (vv. 23–24; cf. Ex 40.38). **6–21:** While Moses performed the sacrificial ritual in lieu of the priests in

the LORD commanded Moses; [11] and the flesh and the skin he burned with fire outside the camp.

[12] Then he slaughtered the burnt offering. Aaron's sons brought him the blood, and he dashed it against all sides of the altar. [13] And they brought him the burnt offering piece by piece, and the head, which he turned into smoke on the altar. [14] He washed the entrails and the legs and, with the burnt offering, turned them into smoke on the altar.

[15] Next he presented the people's offering. He took the goat of the sin offering that was for the people, and slaughtered it, and presented it as a sin offering like the first one. [16] He presented the burnt offering, and sacrificed it according to regulation. [17] He presented the grain offering, and, taking a handful of it, he turned it into smoke on the altar, in addition to the burnt offering of the morning.

[18] He slaughtered the ox and the ram as a sacrifice of well-being for the people. Aaron's sons brought him the blood, which he dashed against all sides of the altar, [19] and the fat of the ox and of the ram—the broad tail, the fat that covers the entrails, the two kidneys and the fat on them,[a] and the appendage of the liver. [20] They first laid the fat on the breasts, and the fat was turned into smoke on the altar; [21] and the breasts and the right thigh Aaron raised as an elevation offering before the LORD, as Moses had commanded.

[22] Aaron lifted his hands toward the people and blessed them; and he came down after sacrificing the sin offering, the burnt offering, and the offering of well-being. [23] Moses and Aaron entered the tent of meeting, and then came out and blessed the people; and the glory of the LORD appeared to all the people. [24] Fire came out from the LORD and consumed the burnt offering and the fat on the altar; and when all the people saw it, they shouted and fell on their faces.

10 Now Aaron's sons, Nadab and Abihu, each took his censer, put fire in it, and laid incense on it; and they offered unholy fire before the LORD, such as he had not commanded them. [2] And fire came out from the presence of the LORD and consumed them, and they died before the LORD. [3] Then Moses said to Aaron, "This is what the LORD meant when he said,

'Through those who are near me
    I will show myself holy,
and before all the people
    I will be glorified.'"

And Aaron was silent.

[4] Moses summoned Mishael and Elzaphan, sons of Uzziel the uncle of Aaron, and said to them, "Come forward, and carry your kinsmen away from the front of the sanctuary to a place outside the camp." [5] They came forward and carried them by their tunics out of the camp, as Moses had ordered. [6] And Moses said to Aaron and to his sons Eleazar and Ithamar, "Do not dishevel your hair, and do not tear your vestments, or you will die and wrath will strike all the congregation; but your kindred, the whole house of Israel, may mourn the burning that the LORD has sent. [7] You shall not go outside the entrance

---

a   Gk: Heb the broad tail, and that which covers, and the kidneys

---

ch 8, here the priests, having been fully ordained, perform the sacrifices as described in chs 1–5. **22–23:** *Lifted his hands*, a ritual action accompanying the blessing. The people receive two blessings—one from Aaron and one from Moses and Aaron together. For a priestly blessing, see Num 6.22–27. **22:** *Came down*, an anachronistic reference to the altar of burnt offering in the Temple, which was elevated (cf. 2 Kings 16.10–13; Ezek 43.13–17). The tabernacle's altar was portable and had no steps (Ex 27.1). **23–24:** God's fiery *glory* is also manifested in the cloud and fire pillar that led the Israelites out of Egypt and through the wilderness, and that rested over the tent of meeting (Ex 13.21; 40.38; Num 9.15–23); see also Ex 24.17; Ezek 1.27–28. **24:** *They shouted*, for joy, not out of fear. Prostration is a ritual act of submission.

10.1–20: The transgression of Nadab and Abihu. 1: *Unholy fire*, lit. "strange fire," referring to the unauthorized incense offering. **2:** *Fire*, because God had not instructed the priests to present incense offerings, the fire that would consume the offerings instead consumed Nadab and Abihu. The Korah rebellion ends similarly with divine fire consuming the offerers of illicit incense (Num 16.35). For God viewed as a consuming fire in P, see Ex 24.17. **3:** *When he said*, perhaps referring to Ex 29.43–44, but more likely referencing a text that is now lost. **4–7:** Because of their ritual holiness, the priests are not allowed to contact a corpse or to mourn for the dead

of the tent of meeting, or you will die; for the anointing oil of the LORD is on you." And they did as Moses had ordered.

[8] And the LORD spoke to Aaron: [9] Drink no wine or strong drink, neither you nor your sons, when you enter the tent of meeting, that you may not die; it is a statute forever throughout your generations. [10] You are to distinguish between the holy and the common, and between the unclean and the clean; [11] and you are to teach the people of Israel all the statutes that the LORD has spoken to them through Moses.

[12] Moses spoke to Aaron and to his remaining sons, Eleazar and Ithamar: Take the grain offering that is left from the LORD's offerings by fire, and eat it unleavened beside the altar, for it is most holy; [13] you shall eat it in a holy place, because it is your due and your sons' due, from the offerings by fire to the LORD; for so I am commanded. [14] But the breast that is elevated and the thigh that is raised, you and your sons and daughters as well may eat in any clean place; for they have been assigned to you and your children from the sacrifices of the offerings of well-being of the people of Israel. [15] The thigh that is raised and the breast that is elevated they shall bring, together with the offerings by fire of the fat, to raise for an elevation offering before the

LORD; they are to be your due and that of your children forever, as the LORD has commanded.

[16] Then Moses made inquiry about the goat of the sin offering, and—it had already been burned! He was angry with Eleazar and Ithamar, Aaron's remaining sons, and said, [17] "Why did you not eat the sin offering in the sacred area? For it is most holy, and God[a] has given it to you that you may remove the guilt of the congregation, to make atonement on their behalf before the LORD. [18] Its blood was not brought into the inner part of the sanctuary. You should certainly have eaten it in the sanctuary, as I commanded." [19] And Aaron spoke to Moses, "See, today they offered their sin offering and their burnt offering before the LORD; and yet such things as these have befallen me! If I had eaten the sin offering today, would it have been agreeable to the LORD?" [20] And when Moses heard that, he agreed.

11 The LORD spoke to Moses and Aaron, saying to them: [2] Speak to the people of Israel, saying:

From among all the land animals, these are the creatures that you may eat. [3] Any animal that has divided hoofs and is cleft-

---

[a] Heb *he*

(cf. 21.1–6,10–12). **8–11:** These verses, the only instance in Leviticus of God speaking to Aaron alone, are likely an H insertion into P. The stated mourning restrictions motivate the introduction of further priestly responsibilities. **10:** *The holy and the common . . . the unclean and the clean*, the two fundamental binary distinctions in Priestly literature. All persons, objects, and places are characterized by one quality of each pair: holy and clean (e.g., the properly functioning sanctuary, including its priests); common and clean (the default status of lay Israelites not suffering from impurities such as found in chs 11–15 and Num 19); common and impure (e.g., lay Israelites suffering from impurity); and, less frequently, holy and impure (such as holy ritual items that become impure during the course of purification rituals, e.g., purification offering carcasses, cf. 6.27–28; 16.26–28). **11:** *To teach . . . all the statutes*, better, "to give rulings regarding all the statutes." The priests do not actively instruct the people in the law (cf. Hag 2.11–13). **12–15:** Cf. 7.11–14,28–36. Aaron and his remaining sons must complete the rituals as prescribed, even after the deaths of Nadab and Abihu. **16–20:** A somewhat enigmatic section, in which Moses is upset that the priests did not consume the people's purification offering, although he never explicitly commanded them to do so in ch 9. Verse 17 suggests that the priestly consumption of the offering itself is expiatory (cf. 6.24–30, although these verses imply that eating the purification offering is a privilege, not a requirement). Aaron's response is unclear, yet Moses accepts it, perhaps because of the unique circumstance of the eighth day.

11.1–16.34: Ritual impurity and purification. Chs 11–16 narrate divine instructions concerning impurity and various processes for purification. In Priestly literature, impurity is a real, though invisible, film that adheres to persons and objects and is attracted to the tabernacle as some metals are attracted to a magnet. However, impurity is fundamentally different from sin: impurity is contracted in the course of normal, daily activities and carries no moral stigma (see further 10.10n.). Yet because impurity is contagious and threatens the continued

footed and chews the cud—such you may eat. [4] But among those that chew the cud or have divided hoofs, you shall not eat the following: the camel, for even though it chews the cud, it does not have divided hoofs; it is unclean for you. [5] The rock badger, for even though it chews the cud, it does not have divided hoofs; it is unclean for you. [6] The hare, for even though it chews the cud, it does not have divided hoofs; it is unclean for you. [7] The pig, for even though it has divided hoofs and is cleft-footed, it does not chew the cud; it is unclean for you. [8] Of their flesh you shall not eat, and their carcasses you shall not touch; they are unclean for you.

[9] These you may eat, of all that are in the waters. Everything in the waters that has fins and scales, whether in the seas or in the streams—such you may eat. [10] But anything in the seas or the streams that does not have fins and scales, of the swarming creatures in the waters and among all the other living creatures that are in the waters—they are detestable to you [11] and detestable they shall remain. Of their flesh you shall not eat, and their carcasses you shall regard as detestable.

[12] Everything in the waters that does not have fins and scales is detestable to you.

[13] These you shall regard as detestable among the birds. They shall not be eaten; they are an abomination: the eagle, the vulture, the osprey, [14] the buzzard, the kite of any kind; [15] every raven of any kind; [16] the ostrich, the nighthawk, the sea gull, the hawk of any kind; [17] the little owl, the cormorant, the great owl, [18] the water hen, the desert owl,[a] the carrion vulture, [19] the stork, the heron of any kind, the hoopoe, and the bat.[b]

[20] All winged insects that walk upon all fours are detestable to you. [21] But among the winged insects that walk on all fours you may eat those that have jointed legs above their feet, with which to leap on the ground. [22] Of them you may eat: the locust according to its kind, the bald locust according to its kind, the cricket according to its kind, and the grasshopper according to its kind. [23] But all other winged insects that have four feet are detestable to you.

a   Or *pelican*
b   Identification of several of the birds in verses 13-19 is uncertain

presence of the deity in the sanctuary, its disposal must be accomplished fastidiously. Failure to purify is sinful and carries dire consequences (cf. 15.31). The sources of impurity are human and animal corpses (ch 11; Num 19), normal and abnormal genital discharges (chs 12; 15), and a disease, "surface affliction," often mistranslated as "leprosy" (chs 13–14). The common denominator among these sources of impurity is their association with death or at least a loss of life force. In cases of minor impurity, purification is accomplished through some combination of bathing, laundering, and the passage of time. In addition to these rites, major impurities also require presentation of a purification offering to cleanse the altar, for major impurities penetrate into the tabernacle complex. Because of their regular contact with the sanctuary and the threat of its contamination, priests are required to avoid virtually all impurity (cf. 21.1–15).

11.1–47: Dietary laws. The dietary laws provide a bridge between the sacrificial instructions that precede them and the following purity rules. In their concern for meat consumption, the instructions in ch 11 correlate strongly with the sacrificial laws, which themselves outline the foods that the deity eats and restrict meat consumption according to its sanctity. A comparison of the sacrificial and dietary laws reveals that the Israelite God has the most restrictive diet, followed by the priests, the Israelite laypersons, and finally non-Israelites. By following the dietary rules, the Israelites observe the order of creation and are separated from the other nations. Such separateness is a fundamental component of holiness (vv. 44–45). Ch 11 also looks forward to the issues of impurity and its disposal in chs 12–16, for animals deemed unsuitable for consumption are termed impure, and contact with their corpses explicitly defiles. **2b–23:** Cf. Deut 14.3–21. **2b–8:** Permitted large land animals must have split hooves and chew their cud. The examples of prohibited animals suggests that undomesticated animals are the special focus of this chapter (see 1.2n.; 17.1–16n.). **9–12:** Permitted sea creatures must have fins and scales. **13–19:** Rather than providing dual characteristics, as with large land animals and sea creatures, a list of prohibited birds is provided. **20–23:** Winged insects are generally forbidden. The only exceptions are those with jumping legs, which are specifically enumerated. **24–40:** Laws concerning impurity contracted through contact with animal corpses. Generally speaking, more intense contact (e.g., carrying or eating vs. touching) requires

24 By these you shall become unclean; whoever touches the carcass of any of them shall be unclean until the evening, 25 and whoever carries any part of the carcass of any of them shall wash his clothes and be unclean until the evening. 26 Every animal that has divided hoofs but is not cleft-footed or does not chew the cud is unclean for you; everyone who touches one of them shall be unclean. 27 All that walk on their paws, among the animals that walk on all fours, are unclean for you; whoever touches the carcass of any of them shall be unclean until the evening, 28 and the one who carries the carcass shall wash his clothes and be unclean until the evening; they are unclean for you. 29 These are unclean for you among the creatures that swarm upon the earth: the weasel, the mouse, the great lizard according to its kind, 30 the gecko, the land crocodile, the lizard, the sand lizard, and the chameleon. 31 These are unclean for you among all that swarm; whoever touches one of them when they are dead shall be unclean until the evening. 32 And anything upon which any of them falls when they are dead shall be unclean, whether an article of wood or cloth or skin or sacking, any article that is used for any purpose; it shall be dipped into water, and it shall be unclean until the evening, and then it shall be clean. 33 And if any of them falls into any earthen vessel, all that is in it shall be unclean, and you shall break the vessel. 34 Any food that could be eaten shall be unclean if water from any such vessel comes upon it; and any liquid that could be drunk shall be unclean if it was in any such vessel. 35 Everything on which any part of the carcass falls shall be unclean; whether an oven or stove, it shall be broken in pieces; they are unclean, and shall remain unclean for you.

36 But a spring or a cistern holding water shall be clean, while whatever touches the carcass in it shall be unclean. 37 If any part of their carcass falls upon any seed set aside for sowing, it is clean; 38 but if water is put on the seed and any part of their carcass falls on it, it is unclean for you.

39 If an animal of which you may eat dies, anyone who touches its carcass shall be unclean until the evening. 40 Those who eat of its carcass shall wash their clothes and be unclean until the evening; and those who carry the carcass shall wash their clothes and be unclean until the evening.

41 All creatures that swarm upon the earth are detestable; they shall not be eaten. 42 Whatever moves on its belly, and whatever moves on all fours, or whatever has many feet, all the creatures that swarm upon the earth, you shall not eat; for they are detestable. 43 You shall not make yourselves detestable with any creature that swarms; you shall not defile yourselves with them, and so become unclean. 44 For I am the LORD your God; sanctify yourselves therefore, and be holy, for I am holy. You shall not defile yourselves with any swarming creature that moves on the earth. 45 For I am the LORD who brought you up from the land of Egypt, to be your God; you shall be holy, for I am holy.

46 This is the law pertaining to land animal and bird and every living creature that moves through the waters and every creature that swarms upon the earth, 47 to make a distinction between the unclean and the clean, and between the living creature that may be eaten and the living creature that may not be eaten.

12 The LORD spoke to Moses, saying: 2 Speak to the people of Israel, saying: If a woman conceives and bears a male child, she shall be ceremonially unclean

---

more complex purification rites. **41–45**: Small land animals are forbidden. *Be holy, for I am holy*, see 11.1–47n., 19.2n. **43,44**: *Defile yourselves*, see 18.20n. **46–47**: A typical Priestly summary postscript.

12.1–8: Childbirth. Childbirth produces impurity because of the mother's postpartum flow of blood, which is viewed as analogous to menstruation (cf. vv. 2,5). The period of impurity differs according to the sex of the child and is divided into a shorter, major phase (seven or fourteen days) and a longer, minor phase (thirty-three or sixty-six days). In each case, the entire period of impurity is a multiple of forty, a common biblical number representing completion. **2–5**: *As at the time of her menstruation*, see 15.19–24. Because this reference anticipates ch 15, it is possible that the purity laws were once ordered differently, with ch 12 following ch 15. During the initial, major phase, the parturient can contaminate the sanctuary as well as common objects and persons through physical contact. During the subsequent, minor phase, her impurity only threatens the sanctuary. **3**:

seven days; as at the time of her menstruation, she shall be unclean. [3] On the eighth day the flesh of his foreskin shall be circumcised. [4] Her time of blood purification shall be thirty-three days; she shall not touch any holy thing, or come into the sanctuary, until the days of her purification are completed. [5] If she bears a female child, she shall be unclean two weeks, as in her menstruation; her time of blood purification shall be sixty-six days.

[6] When the days of her purification are completed, whether for a son or for a daughter, she shall bring to the priest at the entrance of the tent of meeting a lamb in its first year for a burnt offering, and a pigeon or a turtledove for a sin offering. [7] He shall offer it before the LORD, and make atonement on her behalf; then she shall be clean from her flow of blood. This is the law for her who bears a child, male or female. [8] If she cannot afford a sheep, she shall take two turtledoves or two pigeons, one for a burnt offering and the other for a sin offering; and the priest shall make atonement on her behalf, and she shall be clean.

13 The LORD spoke to Moses and Aaron, saying:

[2] When a person has on the skin of his body a swelling or an eruption or a spot, and it turns into a leprous[a] disease on the skin of his body, he shall be brought to Aaron the priest or to one of his sons the priests. [3] The priest shall examine the disease on the skin of his body, and if the hair in the diseased area has turned white and the disease appears to be deeper than the skin of his body, it is a leprous[a] disease; after the priest has examined him he shall pronounce him ceremonially unclean. [4] But if the spot is white in the skin of his body, and appears no deeper than the skin, and the hair in it has not turned white, the priest shall confine the diseased person for seven days. [5] The priest shall examine him on the seventh day, and if he sees that the disease is checked and the disease has not spread in the skin, then the priest shall confine him seven days more. [6] The priest shall examine him again on the seventh day, and if the disease has abated and the disease has not spread in the skin, the priest shall pronounce him clean; it is only an eruption; and he shall wash his clothes, and be clean. [7] But if the eruption spreads in the skin after he has shown himself to the priest for his cleansing, he shall appear again before the priest. [8] The priest shall make an examination, and if the eruption has spread in the skin, the priest shall pronounce him unclean; it is a leprous[a] disease.

[9] When a person contracts a leprous[a] disease, he shall be brought to the priest. [10] The priest shall make an examination, and

[a] A term for several skin diseases; precise meaning uncertain

Circumcision is unrelated to impurity or purification. It is mentioned here because it is performed on the eighth day after birth and thus immediately follows the initial seven-day period of impurity. 6–8: *Sin offering*, lit. "purification offering." The new mother has committed no sin. She must present a purification offering because her impurity polluted the altar (see 4.1–35n.). Verse 8 is an addendum that follows the original ending of the law in v. 7b, providing a more affordable sacrificial option for a poor mother.

13.1–14.57: **Surface afflictions.** Though consolidated under a single term (Heb "tsara'at") traditionally translated "leprosy," the surface afflictions described in these chapters are not modern leprosy (Hansen's disease), which was unknown in the ancient Near East when these texts were written. The inclusion of conditions affecting fabrics and houses alongside human disease also rules out modern leprosy, as do the symptoms of the human diseases described. The Priestly authors do not view disease in general as causing impurity; surface affliction causes impurity because it is associated with death (cf. Num 12.12).

13.1–46: **Surface affliction on humans.** Various symptoms are enumerated for determining whether a condition is surface affliction. In each case, the priest must give a ruling regarding the skin disease, differentiating between clean and unclean (cf. 10.10). The skin conditions most consistent with the various symptoms described include eczema, psoriasis, and vitiligo. 2: *He shall be brought*, or perhaps, "It shall be reported." In either case, others in the community have an interest in diagnosing surface affliction not because the disease is contagious but because the impurity it produces threatens the sanctuary. 3: *Examine*, without touching the affected skin, for the impurity of surface affliction is communicable. *His body*, or her body: the law applies to both men and women (cf. vv. 2,29). 4: *The priest shall confine*, in order to determine whether the skin disease produces

if there is a white swelling in the skin that has turned the hair white, and there is quick raw flesh in the swelling, [11] it is a chronic leprous[a] disease in the skin of his body. The priest shall pronounce him unclean; he shall not confine him, for he is unclean. [12] But if the disease breaks out in the skin, so that it covers all the skin of the diseased person from head to foot, so far as the priest can see, [13] then the priest shall make an examination, and if the disease has covered all his body, he shall pronounce him clean of the disease; since it has all turned white, he is clean. [14] But if raw flesh ever appears on him, he shall be unclean; [15] the priest shall examine the raw flesh and pronounce him unclean. Raw flesh is unclean, for it is a leprous[a] disease. [16] But if the raw flesh again turns white, he shall come to the priest; [17] the priest shall examine him, and if the disease has turned white, the priest shall pronounce the diseased person clean. He is clean.

[18] When there is on the skin of one's body a boil that has healed, [19] and in the place of the boil there appears a white swelling or a reddish-white spot, it shall be shown to the priest. [20] The priest shall make an examination, and if it appears deeper than the skin and its hair has turned white, the priest shall pronounce him unclean; this is a leprous[a] disease, broken out in the boil. [21] But if the priest examines it and the hair on it is not white, nor is it deeper than the skin but has abated, the priest shall confine him seven days. [22] If it spreads in the skin, the priest shall pronounce him unclean; it is diseased. [23] But if the spot remains in one place and does not spread, it is the scar of the boil; the priest shall pronounce him clean.

[24] Or, when the body has a burn on the skin and the raw flesh of the burn becomes a spot, reddish-white or white, [25] the priest shall examine it. If the hair in the spot has turned white and it appears deeper than the skin, it is a leprous[a] disease; it has broken out in the burn, and the priest shall pronounce him unclean. This is a leprous[a] disease. [26] But if the priest examines it and the hair in the spot is not white, and it is no deeper than the skin but has abated, the priest shall confine him seven days. [27] The

priest shall examine him the seventh day; if it is spreading in the skin, the priest shall pronounce him unclean. This is a leprous[a] disease. [28] But if the spot remains in one place and does not spread in the skin but has abated, it is a swelling from the burn, and the priest shall pronounce him clean; for it is the scar of the burn.

[29] When a man or woman has a disease on the head or in the beard, [30] the priest shall examine the disease. If it appears deeper than the skin and the hair in it is yellow and thin, the priest shall pronounce him unclean; it is an itch, a leprous[a] disease of the head or the beard. [31] If the priest examines the itching disease, and it appears no deeper than the skin and there is no black hair in it, the priest shall confine the person with the itching disease for seven days. [32] On the seventh day the priest shall examine the itch; if the itch has not spread, and there is no yellow hair in it, and the itch appears to be no deeper than the skin, [33] he shall shave, but the itch he shall not shave. The priest shall confine the person with the itch for seven days more. [34] On the seventh day the priest shall examine the itch; if the itch has not spread in the skin and it appears to be no deeper than the skin, the priest shall pronounce him clean. He shall wash his clothes and be clean. [35] But if the itch spreads in the skin after he was pronounced clean, [36] the priest shall examine him. If the itch has spread in the skin, the priest need not seek for the yellow hair; he is unclean. [37] But if in his eyes the itch is checked, and black hair has grown in it, the itch is healed, he is clean; and the priest shall pronounce him clean.

[38] When a man or a woman has spots on the skin of the body, white spots, [39] the priest shall make an examination, and if the spots on the skin of the body are of a dull white, it is a rash that has broken out on the skin; he is clean.

[40] If anyone loses the hair from his head, he is bald but he is clean. [41] If he loses the hair from his forehead and temples, he has baldness of the forehead but he is clean.

[a] A term for several skin diseases; precise meaning uncertain

⁴² But if there is on the bald head or the bald forehead a reddish-white diseased spot, it is a leprousᵃ disease breaking out on his bald head or his bald forehead. ⁴³ The priest shall examine him; if the diseased swelling is reddish-white on his bald head or on his bald forehead, which resembles a leprousᵃ disease in the skin of the body, ⁴⁴ he is leprous,ᵃ he is unclean. The priest shall pronounce him unclean; the disease is on his head.

⁴⁵ The person who has the leprousᵃ disease shall wear torn clothes and let the hair of his head be disheveled; and he shall cover his upper lip and cry out, "Unclean, unclean." ⁴⁶ He shall remain unclean as long as he has the disease; he is unclean. He shall live alone; his dwelling shall be outside the camp.

⁴⁷ Concerning clothing: when a leprousᵃ disease appears in it, in woolen or linen cloth, ⁴⁸ in warp or woof of linen or wool, or in a skin or in anything made of skin, ⁴⁹ if the disease shows greenish or reddish in the garment, whether in warp or woof or in skin or in anything made of skin, it is a leprousᵃ disease and shall be shown to the priest. ⁵⁰ The priest shall examine the disease, and put the diseased article aside for seven days. ⁵¹ He shall examine the disease on the seventh day. If the disease has spread in the cloth, in warp or woof, or in the skin, whatever be the use of the skin, this is a spreading leprousᵃ disease; it is unclean. ⁵² He shall burn the clothing, whether diseased in warp or woof, woolen or linen, or anything of skin, for it is a spreading leprousᵃ disease; it shall be burned in fire.

⁵³ If the priest makes an examination, and the disease has not spread in the clothing, in warp or woof or in anything of skin, ⁵⁴ the priest shall command them to wash the article in which the disease appears, and he shall put it aside seven days more. ⁵⁵ The priest shall examine the diseased article after it has been washed. If the diseased spot has not changed color, though the disease has not spread, it is unclean; you shall burn it in fire, whether the leprousᵃ spot is on the inside or on the outside.

⁵⁶ If the priest makes an examination, and the disease has abated after it is washed, he shall tear the spot out of the cloth, in warp or woof, or out of skin. ⁵⁷ If it appears again in the garment, in warp or woof, or in anything of skin, it is spreading; you shall burn with fire that in which the disease appears. ⁵⁸ But the cloth, warp or woof, or anything of skin from which the disease disappears when you have washed it, shall then be washed a second time, and it shall be clean.

⁵⁹ This is the ritual for a leprousᵃ disease in a cloth of wool or linen, either in warp or woof, or in anything of skin, to decide whether it is clean or unclean.

14 The LORD spoke to Moses, saying: ² This shall be the ritual for the leprousᵃ person at the time of his cleansing:

He shall be brought to the priest; ³ the priest shall go out of the camp, and the priest shall make an examination. If the disease is healed in the leprousᵃ person, ⁴ the priest shall command that two living clean birds and cedarwood and crimson yarn and hyssop be brought for the one

ᵃ A term for several skin diseases; precise meaning uncertain

impurity and to limit exposure to impurity in the event that it is surface affliction. **38–44:** These verses consider difficult cases and supplement vv. 2–37 by focusing upon skin conditions that do not cause impurity. **45–46:** The afflicted person dresses as a mourner (cf. 10.6; Ezek 24.17,22) because of the association between surface affliction and death. *He shall live alone . . . outside the camp*, cf. 2 Kings 7.3–8; 15.5; 2 Chr 26.21; Lk 17.12. Separation from the camp limits the spread of impurity, but impurity still contaminates the sanctuary (cf. 14.1–32).

13.47–59: Surface affliction on cloth. Illustrating the systematization of Priestly thought, the instructions for fabrics are similar in structure and detail to the preceding instructions for skin diseases. The surface affliction includes various forms of mold, fungus, and mildew. **51:** *Spreading*, meaning uncertain. Unlike a person with surface affliction, an afflicted fabric, like the twice-afflicted house (14.45), cannot be cleansed. **59:** Summary postscript for vv. 47–59, which interrupts 13.1–46 and 14.1–32.

14.1–32: Purification after surface affliction. The ritual here does not heal surface affliction; it only purifies

who is to be cleansed. [5] The priest shall command that one of the birds be slaughtered over fresh water in an earthen vessel. [6] He shall take the living bird with the cedarwood and the crimson yarn and the hyssop, and dip them and the living bird in the blood of the bird that was slaughtered over the fresh water. [7] He shall sprinkle it seven times upon the one who is to be cleansed of the leprous[a] disease; then he shall pronounce him clean, and he shall let the living bird go into the open field. [8] The one who is to be cleansed shall wash his clothes, and shave off all his hair, and bathe himself in water, and he shall be clean. After that he shall come into the camp, but shall live outside his tent seven days. [9] On the seventh day he shall shave all his hair: of head, beard, eyebrows; he shall shave all his hair. Then he shall wash his clothes, and bathe his body in water, and he shall be clean.

[10] On the eighth day he shall take two male lambs without blemish, and one ewe lamb in its first year without blemish, and a grain offering of three-tenths of an ephah of choice flour mixed with oil, and one log[b] of oil. [11] The priest who cleanses shall set the person to be cleansed, along with these things, before the LORD, at the entrance of the tent of meeting. [12] The priest shall take one of the lambs, and offer it as a guilt offering, along with the log[b] of oil, and raise them as an elevation offering before the LORD. [13] He shall slaughter the lamb in the place where the sin offering and the burnt offering are slaughtered in the holy place; for the guilt offering, like the sin offering, belongs to the priest: it is most holy. [14] The priest shall take some of the blood of the guilt offering and put it on the lobe of the right ear of the one to be cleansed, and on the thumb of the right hand, and on the big toe of the right foot. [15] The priest shall take some of the log[b] of oil and pour it into the palm of his own left hand, [16] and dip his right finger in the oil that is in his left hand and sprinkle some oil with his finger seven times before the LORD. [17] Some of the oil that remains in his hand the priest shall put on the lobe of the right ear of the one to be cleansed, and on the thumb of the right hand, and on the big toe of the right foot, on top of the blood of the guilt offering. [18] The rest of the oil that is in the priest's hand he shall put on the head of the one to be cleansed. Then the priest shall make atonement on his behalf before the LORD: [19] the priest shall offer the sin offering, to make atonement for the one to be cleansed from his uncleanness. Afterward he shall slaughter the burnt offering; [20] and the priest shall offer the burnt offering and the grain offering on the altar. Thus the priest shall make atonement on his behalf and he shall be clean.

[21] But if he is poor and cannot afford so much, he shall take one male lamb for a guilt offering to be elevated, to make atonement on his behalf, and one-tenth of an ephah of choice flour mixed with oil for a grain offer-

---

a   A term for several skin diseases; precise meaning uncertain

b   A liquid measure

---

a person. Note that the priest only performs the rites after confirming the person's recovery (v. 3). **2:** *He shall be brought*, better, "It shall be reported," cf. v. 3. **4–7:** The same rite is found in vv. 49–53 for purifying houses. **4:** Many of the materials in this verse probably have symbolic significance and are well attested in biblical and other ancient Near Eastern rituals (cf. Ex 12.22; Num 19.6; Job 9.19; Ps 51.7). **6–7:** The person's impurity is purged by the sprinkling of blood and transferred to the living bird, which carries it away (cf. the goat in 16.21–22). **8–9:** The staged transition constitutes a rite of passage from impure to pure and underscores the severity of impurity caused by surface affliction. **10–20:** The eighth-day sacrifices purge the tabernacle of impurity (cf. 4.1–6.7). **10:** *Ephah*, about 21 qts (23 liters). *Log*, about 11 oz (.32 l). **12:** *Guilt offering*, better, "reparation offering"; see 5.14–6.7n. *Elevation offering*, see 7.30n. **14,17,25,28:** For smearing of blood and oil and the significance of the ear, thumb, and toe, see 8.10–12,30n.; 8.23–24n. **20:** *And he shall be clean*, a summary statement for the foregoing purification rituals. The sacrifices purify the tabernacle, not the person. **21–32:** More affordable provisions for purification (cf. 2.1–16n.; 5.7–13n.; 12.6–8n.).

ing and a log[a] of oil; [22] also two turtledoves or two pigeons, such as he can afford, one for a sin offering and the other for a burnt offering. [23] On the eighth day he shall bring them for his cleansing to the priest, to the entrance of the tent of meeting, before the LORD; [24] and the priest shall take the lamb of the guilt offering and the log[a] of oil, and the priest shall raise them as an elevation offering before the LORD. [25] The priest shall slaughter the lamb of the guilt offering and shall take some of the blood of the guilt offering, and put it on the lobe of the right ear of the one to be cleansed, and on the thumb of the right hand, and on the big toe of the right foot. [26] The priest shall pour some of the oil into the palm of his own left hand, [27] and shall sprinkle with his right finger some of the oil that is in his left hand seven times before the LORD. [28] The priest shall put some of the oil that is in his hand on the lobe of the right ear of the one to be cleansed, and on the thumb of the right hand, and the big toe of the right foot, where the blood of the guilt offering was placed. [29] The rest of the oil that is in the priest's hand he shall put on the head of the one to be cleansed, to make atonement on his behalf before the LORD. [30] And he shall offer, of the turtledoves or pigeons such as he can afford, [31] one[b] for a sin offering and the other for a burnt offering, along with a grain offering; and the priest shall make atonement before the LORD on behalf of the one being cleansed. [32] This is the ritual for the one who has a leprous[c] disease, who cannot afford the offerings for his cleansing.

[33] The LORD spoke to Moses and Aaron, saying:

[34] When you come into the land of Canaan, which I give you for a possession, and I put a leprous[c] disease in a house in the land of your possession, [35] the owner of the house shall come and tell the priest, saying, "There seems to me to be some sort of disease in my house." [36] The priest shall command that they empty the house before the priest goes to examine the disease, or all that is in the house will become unclean; and afterward the priest shall go in to inspect the house. [37] He shall examine the disease; if the disease is in the walls of the house with greenish or reddish spots, and if it appears to be deeper than the surface, [38] the priest shall go outside to the door of the house and shut up the house seven days. [39] The priest shall come again on the seventh day and make an inspection; if the disease has spread in the walls of the house, [40] the priest shall command that the stones in which the disease appears be taken out and thrown into an unclean place outside the city. [41] He shall have the inside of the house scraped thoroughly, and the plaster that is scraped off shall be dumped in an unclean place outside the city. [42] They shall take other stones and put them in the place of those stones, and take other plaster and plaster the house.

[43] If the disease breaks out again in the house, after he has taken out the stones and scraped the house and plastered it, [44] the priest shall go and make inspection; if the disease has spread in the house, it is a spreading leprous[c] disease in the house; it is unclean. [45] He shall have the house torn down, its stones and timber and all the plaster of the house, and taken outside the city to an unclean place. [46] All who

---

[a] A liquid measure

[b] Gk Syr: Heb *afford*, [31]*such as he can afford, one*

[c] A term for several skin diseases; precise meaning uncertain

---

14.33–53: Surface affliction in houses. 34: *When you come into the land*, in the narrative, the Israelites are living in the wilderness camp; they therefore do not currently live in houses. *I put*, surface affliction is viewed as divine punishment (Num 12.10; Deut 28.27,35; 2 Sam 3.29; 2 Kings 5.26–27; 2 Chr 26.16–21). **35:** *The owner*, though it is potentially inconvenient and even a potentially significant financial loss (cf. vv. 43–45), the homeowner is expected to report possible surface affliction because of the threat of contamination and its effect on the entire community. **36:** The impurity caused by surface affliction will contaminate other objects and persons in the house (cf. vv. 46–47), but an allowance is made for removing objects before the priest officially diagnoses surface affliction. **40–41,45:** Disposal outside the city parallels the exclusion of surface-afflicted persons out-

enter the house while it is shut up shall be unclean until the evening; [47] and all who sleep in the house shall wash their clothes; and all who eat in the house shall wash their clothes.

[48] If the priest comes and makes an inspection, and the disease has not spread in the house after the house was plastered, the priest shall pronounce the house clean; the disease is healed. [49] For the cleansing of the house he shall take two birds, with cedarwood and crimson yarn and hyssop, [50] and shall slaughter one of the birds over fresh water in an earthen vessel, [51] and shall take the cedarwood and the hyssop and the crimson yarn, along with the living bird, and dip them in the blood of the slaughtered bird and the fresh water, and sprinkle the house seven times. [52] Thus he shall cleanse the house with the blood of the bird, and with the fresh water, and with the living bird, and with the cedarwood and hyssop and crimson yarn; [53] and he shall let the living bird go out of the city into the open field; so he shall make atonement for the house, and it shall be clean.

[54] This is the ritual for any leprous[a] disease: for an itch, [55] for leprous[a] diseases in clothing and houses, [56] and for a swelling or an eruption or a spot, [57] to determine when it is unclean and when it is clean. This is the ritual for leprous[a] diseases.

15

The LORD spoke to Moses and Aaron, saying: [2] Speak to the people of Israel and say to them:

When any man has a discharge from his member,[b] his discharge makes him ceremonially unclean. [3] The uncleanness of his discharge is this: whether his member[b] flows with his discharge, or his member[b] is stopped from discharging, it is uncleanness for him. [4] Every bed on which the one with the discharge lies shall be unclean; and everything on which he sits shall be unclean. [5] Anyone who touches his bed shall wash his clothes, and bathe in water, and be unclean until the evening. [6] All who sit on anything on which the one with the discharge has sat shall wash their clothes, and bathe in water, and be unclean until the evening. [7] All who touch the body of the one with the discharge shall wash their clothes, and bathe in water, and be unclean until the evening. [8] If the one with the discharge spits on persons who are clean, then they shall wash their clothes, and bathe in water, and be unclean until the evening. [9] Any saddle on which the one with the discharge rides shall be unclean. [10] All who touch anything that was under him shall be unclean until the evening, and all who carry such a thing shall wash their clothes, and bathe in water, and be unclean until the evening. [11] All those whom the one with the discharge touches without his having rinsed his hands in water shall wash their clothes, and bathe in water, and be unclean until the evening. [12] Any earthen vessel that the one with the discharge touches shall be broken; and every vessel of wood shall be rinsed in water.

---

[a] A term for several skin diseases; precise meaning uncertain
[b] Heb *flesh*

---

side the camp (13.46). **46–47:** See 11.24–40n. **54–57:** A typical Priestly conclusion formula for chs 13–14, though the items in the summary are ordered differently in the chapters.

15.1–33: Sexual discharges. This chapter outlines impurities caused by regular and irregular discharges from the genitals. As with other causes of contamination, sexual flows generate impurity because of the perceived loss of life that accompanies them. The chapter exhibits a chiastic structure of impurity sources: A: Abnormal male discharge (vv. 2–15); B: Normal male discharge (seminal emission; vv. 16–17); C: Seminal discharge during sexual intercourse, affecting both men and women (v. 18); B': Normal female discharge (menstruation; vv. 19–24); A': Abnormal female discharge (vv. 25–30). None of these sexual discharges is considered sinful; rather, the contamination caused by them threatens the presence of the deity and thus requires careful measures for containment and purification (cf. 11.1–16.34n.). **3:** *Flows . . . stopped*, likely due to one of several infections of the urethra, including gonorrhea. **4–12:** Impurity is contagious through physical contact with the impure person or objects contaminated by him. **13–15:** See 14.8–9n.; 14.10–20n. *Sin offering*, lit. "purification offering." **18:** Normal

¹³ When the one with a discharge is cleansed of his discharge, he shall count seven days for his cleansing; he shall wash his clothes and bathe his body in fresh water, and he shall be clean. ¹⁴ On the eighth day he shall take two turtledoves or two pigeons and come before the Lord to the entrance of the tent of meeting and give them to the priest. ¹⁵ The priest shall offer them, one for a sin offering and the other for a burnt offering; and the priest shall make atonement on his behalf before the Lord for his discharge.

¹⁶ If a man has an emission of semen, he shall bathe his whole body in water, and be unclean until the evening. ¹⁷ Everything made of cloth or of skin on which the semen falls shall be washed with water, and be unclean until the evening. ¹⁸ If a man lies with a woman and has an emission of semen, both of them shall bathe in water, and be unclean until the evening.

¹⁹ When a woman has a discharge of blood that is her regular discharge from her body, she shall be in her impurity for seven days, and whoever touches her shall be unclean until the evening. ²⁰ Everything upon which she lies during her impurity shall be unclean; everything also upon which she sits shall be unclean. ²¹ Whoever touches her bed shall wash his clothes, and bathe in water, and be unclean until the evening. ²² Whoever touches anything upon which she sits shall wash his clothes, and bathe in water, and be unclean until the evening; ²³ whether it is the bed or anything upon which she sits, when he touches it he shall be unclean until the evening. ²⁴ If any man lies with her, and her impurity falls on him, he shall be unclean seven days; and every bed on which he lies shall be unclean.

²⁵ If a woman has a discharge of blood for many days, not at the time of her impurity, or if she has a discharge beyond the time of her impurity, all the days of the discharge she shall continue in uncleanness; as in the days of her impurity, she shall be unclean. ²⁶ Every bed on which she lies during all the days of her discharge shall be treated as the bed of her impurity; and everything on which she sits shall be unclean, as in the uncleanness of her impurity. ²⁷ Whoever touches these things shall be unclean, and shall wash his clothes, and bathe in water, and be unclean until the evening. ²⁸ If she is cleansed of her discharge, she shall count seven days, and after that she shall be clean. ²⁹ On the eighth day she shall take two turtledoves or two pigeons and bring them to the priest at the entrance of the tent of meeting. ³⁰ The priest shall offer one for a sin offering and the other for a burnt offering; and the priest shall make atonement on her behalf before the Lord for her unclean discharge.

³¹ Thus you shall keep the people of Israel separate from their uncleanness, so that they do not die in their uncleanness by defiling my tabernacle that is in their midst.

³² This is the ritual for those who have a discharge: for him who has an emission of semen, becoming unclean thereby, ³³ for her who is in the infirmity of her period, for anyone, male or female, who has a discharge, and for the man who lies with a woman who is unclean.

sexual relations cause impurity, yet according to the Priestly authors, God commands humans to "be fruitful and multiply" (e.g., Gen 1.28; 9.1,7). It is thus clear that sources of impurity are generally unrelated to sin. **19–24:** Menstrual impurity persists for seven days, presumably approximating the longest duration of regular menstruation. The strength of the impurity communicated by the menstruant is related to the intensity of contact with her (cf. 11.24–40n.). No rules for purification are given; presumably the woman bathes and launders on the seventh day, and waits until evening (2 Sam 11.2,4; cf. Num 19.19). **24:** *If any man lies with her, and her impurity falls on him*, lit., "If any man lies with her, with the result that her impurity falls on him." Although it communicates impurity, intercourse with a menstruant is permitted by P (contrast 18.19 and 20.18, which are H). **25–30:** Irregular female blood flow, like irregular male discharge, produces impurity until the flow stops and requires a seven-day waiting period and sacrificial blood for sanctuary purification (cf. vv. 13–15). **31:** The rationale for proper disposal of impurity: impurity is attracted to the sanctuary, where it will accumulate and threaten the divine presence (cf. 4.1–6.7n.; 11.1–16.34n.). **32–33:** A typical Priestly summary postscript (cf. 7.37–38; 11.46–47; 13.59; 14.54–57).

16

The LORD spoke to Moses after the death of the two sons of Aaron, when they drew near before the LORD and died. [2] The LORD said to Moses:

Tell your brother Aaron not to come just at any time into the sanctuary inside the curtain before the mercy seat[a] that is upon the ark, or he will die; for I appear in the cloud upon the mercy seat.[a] [3] Thus shall Aaron come into the holy place: with a young bull for a sin offering and a ram for a burnt offering. [4] He shall put on the holy linen tunic, and shall have the linen undergarments next to his body, fasten the linen sash, and wear the linen turban; these are the holy vestments. He shall bathe his body in water, and then put them on. [5] He shall take from the congregation of the people of Israel two male goats for a sin offering, and one ram for a burnt offering.

[6] Aaron shall offer the bull as a sin offering for himself, and shall make atonement for himself and for his house. [7] He shall take the two goats and set them before the LORD at the entrance of the tent of meeting; [8] and Aaron shall cast lots on the two goats, one lot for the LORD and the other lot for Azazel.[b] [9] Aaron shall present the goat on which the lot fell for the LORD, and offer it as a sin offering; [10] but the goat on which the lot fell for Azazel[b] shall be presented alive before the LORD to make atonement over it, that it may be sent away into the wilderness to Azazel.[b]

[11] Aaron shall present the bull as a sin offering for himself, and shall make atonement for himself and for his house; he shall slaughter the bull as a sin offering for himself. [12] He shall take a censer full of coals of fire from the altar before the LORD, and two handfuls of crushed sweet incense, and he shall bring it inside the curtain [13] and put the incense on the fire before the LORD, that the cloud of the incense may cover the mercy seat[a] that is upon the covenant,[c] or he will die. [14] He shall take some of the blood of the bull, and sprinkle it with his finger on the front of the mercy seat,[a] and before the mercy seat[a] he shall sprinkle the blood with his finger seven times.

[15] He shall slaughter the goat of the sin offering that is for the people and bring its blood inside the curtain, and do with its blood as he did with the blood of the bull,

---

a   Or *the cover*
b   Traditionally rendered *a scapegoat*
c   Or *treaty*, or *testament*; Heb *eduth*

16.1–34: The Day of Atonement. This chapter describes the annual purification of the entire tabernacle complex, including the purgation (Heb "kippur") of the inner sanctum of the deity, the holy of holies. According to v. 29, "yom hakkippurim" ("the day of purifications," cf. 23.26–32; 25.9)—in later Judaism, Yom Kippur (often mistranslated as the Day of Atonement)—is the tenth day of the seventh month. Though the sanctuary complex is regularly purged by the blood of purification offerings, further purification ensures thorough cleansing. Moreover, routine purification does not purge the contamination of intentional sins, which penetrates all the way into the holy of holies and is therefore especially threatening to the deity (cf. 4.1–35n.). This system creates the remarkable circumstance that the holy of holies, purged only once each year, could become the most polluted area in the tabernacle complex. This potential flaw in the Priestly system of purification reveals the fundamental optimism of its authors: in their view, once Israel knows the commandments of God, they will carefully obey them. Intentional sin is expected to be a rare occurrence; unintentional sin and impurities, by contrast, are unavoidable and thus greater concerns. 1: *After the death of the two sons of Aaron*, some interpreters have argued that ch 16 originally followed ch 10 and that its purification ritual was intended to purge the tabernacle of corpse contamination after the deaths of Nadab and Abihu, and after other emergencies, rather than once a year on Yom Kippur. Alternatively, this reference simply situates ch 16 in the chronology of the overall narrative, perhaps indicating that chs 11–15 were not actually narrated immediately after the events of ch 10 (cf. 16.34b n.). 2: *Mercy seat*, the cover of the ark upon which the cherubim are set (cf. Ex 25.17–22). 3: See 4.3. *Sin offering*, lit. "purification offering" (cf. 4.1–35n.) 4: See 8.6–9. 6–22: Aaron applies the sacrificial blood to the sanctuary and its furnishings, effecting their purification. In later Judaism, after the Temple is destroyed, the focus of the Day of Atonement shifts to the repentance and forgiveness of individuals. 7: *Tent of meeting*, see 1.1n. 8: *Azazel*, probably, "angry" or "fierce god," a demonic figure (cf. 17.7), in contrast to the Israelite deity. Rabbinic interpreters understood *Azazel* as "the goat that goes away," i.e., the "scapegoat." 13: When he enters

sprinkling it upon the mercy seat[a] and before the mercy seat.[a] [16] Thus he shall make atonement for the sanctuary, because of the uncleannesses of the people of Israel, and because of their transgressions, all their sins; and so he shall do for the tent of meeting, which remains with them in the midst of their uncleannesses. [17] No one shall be in the tent of meeting from the time he enters to make atonement in the sanctuary until he comes out and has made atonement for himself and for his house and for all the assembly of Israel. [18] Then he shall go out to the altar that is before the LORD and make atonement on its behalf, and shall take some of the blood of the bull and of the blood of the goat, and put it on each of the horns of the altar. [19] He shall sprinkle some of the blood on it with his finger seven times, and cleanse it and hallow it from the uncleannesses of the people of Israel.

[20] When he has finished atoning for the holy place and the tent of meeting and the altar, he shall present the live goat. [21] Then Aaron shall lay both his hands on the head of the live goat, and confess over it all the iniquities of the people of Israel, and all their transgressions, all their sins, putting them on the head of the goat, and sending it away into the wilderness by means of someone designated for the task.[b] [22] The goat shall bear on itself all their iniquities to a barren region; and the goat shall be set free in the wilderness.

[23] Then Aaron shall enter the tent of meeting, and shall take off the linen vestments that he put on when he went into the holy place, and shall leave them there. [24] He shall bathe his body in water in a holy place, and put on his vestments; then he shall come out and offer his burnt offering and the burnt offering of the people, making atonement for himself and for the people. [25] The fat of the sin offering he shall turn into smoke on the altar. [26] The one who sets the goat free for Azazel[c] shall wash his clothes and bathe his body in water, and afterward may come into the camp. [27] The bull of the sin offering and the goat of the sin offering, whose blood was brought in to make atonement in the holy place, shall be taken outside the camp; their skin and their flesh and their dung shall be consumed in fire. [28] The one who burns them shall wash his clothes and bathe his body in water, and afterward may come into the camp.

[29] This shall be a statute to you forever: In the seventh month, on the tenth day of the month, you shall deny yourselves,[d] and shall do no work, neither the citizen nor the alien who resides among you. [30] For on this day atonement shall be made for you, to cleanse you; from all your sins you shall be clean before the LORD. [31] It is a sabbath of complete rest to you, and you shall deny yourselves;[d] it is a statute forever. [32] The priest who is anointed and consecrated as priest in his

a   Or the cover
b   Meaning of Heb uncertain
c   Traditionally rendered a scapegoat
d   Or shall fast

the holy of holies, Aaron must burn incense to conceal the deity from his sight (cf. v. 2). **16:** The beginning of the verse is better translated, "He shall purify the sanctuary from the Israelites' impurities and, of all their sins, from their rebellious acts." Impurity and intentional sins are hereby both purged from the inner sanctum. *And so he shall do for the tent of meeting*, referring to the cleansing of the outer room of the tabernacle (cf. 4.5–7,16–18; Ex 30.10). *Remains*, better, "dwells." **18–19:** Working out from the inner and outer rooms of the tabernacle, Aaron is to purify the altar of burnt offerings in the courtyard. **21–22:** Aaron slaughtered one of the people's goats as a purification offering (v. 15). The other carries away their sins, which Aaron loads onto it by reciting them while placing *both his hands* on its head (contrast 1.4). *Wilderness*, a region viewed in the ancient Near East as the domain of demons. **29–34a:** An H addition to vv. 1–28+34b, which are P. H expands the ritual to include fasting and work cessation and thereby provides the laity a role in the Day of Atonement. **31:** *Sabbath of complete rest*, lit. "sabbath of sabbaths," emphasizing the requirement for a complete cessation of work. This term is also applied to the sabbath day (Ex 31.15; 35.2; Lev 23.3,32) and to the sabbath year (Lev 25.4). **34b:** Moses delivers the divine commands to Aaron, but Aaron does not perform them immediately because the Day of Atonement is six months away (see Introduction).

father's place shall make atonement, wearing the linen vestments, the holy vestments. [33] He shall make atonement for the sanctuary, and he shall make atonement for the tent of meeting and for the altar, and he shall make atonement for the priests and for all the people of the assembly. [34] This shall be an everlasting statute for you, to make atonement for the people of Israel once in the year for all their sins. And Moses did as the LORD had commanded him.

17 The LORD spoke to Moses: [2] Speak to Aaron and his sons and to all the people of Israel and say to them: This is what the LORD has commanded. [3] If anyone of the house of Israel slaughters an ox or a lamb or a goat in the camp, or slaughters it outside the camp, [4] and does not bring it to the entrance of the tent of meeting, to present it as an offering to the LORD before the tabernacle of the LORD, he shall be held guilty of bloodshed; he has shed blood, and he shall be cut off from the people. [5] This is in order that the people of Israel may bring their

sacrifices that they offer in the open field, that they may bring them to the LORD, to the priest at the entrance of the tent of meeting, and offer them as sacrifices of well-being to the LORD. [6] The priest shall dash the blood against the altar of the LORD at the entrance of the tent of meeting, and turn the fat into smoke as a pleasing odor to the LORD, [7] so that they may no longer offer their sacrifices for goat-demons, to whom they prostitute themselves. This shall be a statute forever to them throughout their generations.

[8] And say to them further: Anyone of the house of Israel or of the aliens who reside among them who offers a burnt offering or sacrifice, [9] and does not bring it to the entrance of the tent of meeting, to sacrifice it to the LORD, shall be cut off from the people.

[10] If anyone of the house of Israel or of the aliens who reside among them eats any blood, I will set my face against that person who eats blood, and will cut that person off from the people. [11] For the life of the flesh is in the blood; and I have given it to you for mak-

17.1–26.46: The Holiness Collection. Most scholars agree that chs 17–26 (H) comprise a compositional stratum in the book of Leviticus separate from chs 1–16 (P). Chs 17–26 are especially concerned with holiness and extend the potential for holiness to the Israelite laity. For this reason, chs 17–26 are titled the Holiness Collection (see Introduction). Many scholars call this the Holiness Code, but like other ancient Near Eastern law collections, it is not a code: it has redundancies and contradictions, is not organized for use by judges, and is not complete. Though initially believed to be older than chs 1–16, recent scholarship has demonstrated that chs 17–26, as well as ch 27, are later additions to the preceding chapters meant to revise and supplement them. It is likely that H supplements P in part by borrowing and revising non-Priestly laws from the books of Exodus and Deuteronomy.

17.1–16: Slaughter. In light of the sacrificial laws in chs 1–7, H here provides a new set of regulations concerning eating meat. Most notably, H requires that the Israelites present as offerings at the sanctuary all sacrificeable animals that are slaughtered (vv. 3–7). This command supplements the P rules in Gen 9.3–4, which permit nonsacrificial slaughter of animals for meat, provided that no blood is consumed. Having received the sacrificial laws, Israel is obligated to treat every slaughter of a domesticated animal as a sacrifice. The Priestly source thus divides culinary history into three epochs: (1) Creation to Flood (vegetarianism, Gen 1.29–31); (2) Post-Flood to Sinai (nonsacrificial slaughter, Gen 9.3–4); (3) After Sinai (sacrificial slaughter of all domesticated animals, Lev 1–7; 17.3–7). Lev 17 contrasts markedly with Deut 12.15–27, which expressly permit profane slaughter of sacrificeable animals. 3–4: All slaughtered sacrificeable animals must be presented as offerings. Such sacrifices, intended to provide meat for eating, are undoubtedly well-being offerings (cf. 3.1–17; 7.11–34). Within its wilderness setting, H envisions a single sanctuary, making adherence to this command possible. 4: Nonsacrificial slaughter is tantamount to murder (cf. 1.4; 17.11), a view that enforces sanctuary slaughter. 5,7: With the introduction of sacrifice, what was once nonsacrificial slaughter is perceived as sacrificial. Any slaughter of sacrificeable animals outside of the sanctuary is viewed as sacrifice to other deities or to demons. Prostitution is a frequent metaphor for worshiping other gods. Goat demons, cf. 16.8n.; 2 Chr 11.15; Isa 13.21; 34.14. 8–9: Foreigners residing among the Israelites presumably may slaughter domesticated animals nonsacrificially, but neither Israelites nor foreigners may offer sacrifices to any deity but the LORD. 10–14: Consumption of blood from both wild and domesticated animals is prohibited (cf. Gen 9.4; Lev 3.17; Deut 12.23–25). Once the blood

ing atonement for your lives on the altar; for, as life, it is the blood that makes atonement. [12] Therefore I have said to the people of Israel: No person among you shall eat blood, nor shall any alien who resides among you eat blood. [13] And anyone of the people of Israel, or of the aliens who reside among them, who hunts down an animal or bird that may be eaten shall pour out its blood and cover it with earth.

[14] For the life of every creature—its blood is its life; therefore I have said to the people of Israel: You shall not eat the blood of any creature, for the life of every creature is its blood; whoever eats it shall be cut off. [15] All persons, citizens or aliens, who eat what dies of itself or what has been torn by wild animals, shall wash their clothes, and bathe themselves in water, and be unclean until the evening; then they shall be clean. [16] But if they do not wash themselves or bathe their body, they shall bear their guilt.

18 The LORD spoke to Moses, saying: [2] Speak to the people of Israel and say to them: I am the LORD your God. [3] You shall not do as they do in the land of Egypt, where you lived, and you shall not do as they do in the land of Canaan, to which I am bringing you. You shall not follow their statutes. [4] My ordinances you shall observe and my statutes you shall keep, following them: I am the LORD your God. [5] You shall keep my statutes and my ordinances; by doing so one shall live: I am the LORD.

[6] None of you shall approach anyone near of kin to uncover nakedness: I am the LORD. [7] You shall not uncover the nakedness of your father, which is the nakedness of your mother; she is your mother, you shall not uncover her nakedness. [8] You shall not uncover the nakedness of your father's wife; it is the nakedness of your father. [9] You shall not uncover the nakedness of your sister, your father's daughter or your mother's daughter, whether born at home or born abroad. [10] You shall not uncover the nakedness of your son's daughter or of your daughter's daughter, for their nakedness is your own nakedness. [11] You shall not uncover the nakedness of your father's wife's daughter, begotten by your father, since she is your sister. [12] You shall not uncover the nakedness of your father's sister; she is your father's flesh. [13] You shall not uncover the nakedness of your mother's sister, for she is your mother's flesh. [14] You shall not uncover the nakedness of your father's brother, that is, you shall not approach his wife; she is your aunt. [15] You shall not uncover the nakedness of your daughter-in-law: she is your son's wife; you shall not uncover her nakedness. [16] You shall not uncover the nakedness of your brother's wife; it is your brother's nakedness. [17] You shall not uncover the nakedness of a woman and her daughter, and you shall not take[a] her son's daughter or her daughter's daughter to uncover her nakedness; they are your[b] flesh; it is depravity. [18] And you shall not take[a] a woman as a

a Or *marry*
b Gk: Heb lacks *your*

is drained, the meat may be eaten. **11:** *For making atonement for your lives*, better, "as a ransom for your lives." According to H, sacrificial blood on the altar not only purifies but also ransoms (Heb "kipper") the offerer from shedding the animal's blood (cf. 1.4; 17.4). Compare the payment of a ransom in Ex 30.11–16 and Num 31.48–50 to appease divine wrath. **15–16:** Laypersons (but not priests; cf. 22.8) may eat an animal that died naturally or was killed by other animals, but they must purify afterwards (cf. 11.40; contrast Ex 22.30; Deut 14.21). Later Judaism prohibits such eating, following Deut 14.21.

18.1–30: Foreign abominations. The prohibitions in this chapter are primarily sexual in nature, though child sacrifice to Molech is also included. These sins are associated with foreigners and especially the Canaanites, whom God will remove from their land so that Israel may dwell in it. There is no evidence that the Canaanites actually engaged in these practices. **1–5:** A general prohibition against following the statutes of the Egyptians and Canaanites, and adjuration instead to obey the LORD's commands, which follow in vv. 6–23. **2,4:** *I am the LORD your God*, a characteristic H expression, underscoring that because the Israelites belong to the LORD, they must be distinct from other nations and follow the rules of their god alone. **6–20,22–23:** Sexual prohibitions, with special focus on various forms of incest. 20.10–21 enumerates punishments for sexual sins; cf. Deut 27.20–23. **6:** *Uncover nakedness*, nakedness is a euphemism for the genitals, and the entire phrase refers to intercourse.

rival to her sister, uncovering her nakedness while her sister is still alive. ¹⁹ You shall not approach a woman to uncover her nakedness while she is in her menstrual uncleanness. ²⁰ You shall not have sexual relations with your kinsman's wife, and defile yourself with her. ²¹ You shall not give any of your offspring to sacrifice themᵃ to Molech, and so profane the name of your God: I am the LORD. ²² You shall not lie with a male as with a woman; it is an abomination. ²³ You shall not have sexual relations with any animal and defile yourself with it, nor shall any woman give herself to an animal to have sexual relations with it: it is perversion.

²⁴ Do not defile yourselves in any of these ways, for by all these practices the nations I am casting out before you have defiled themselves. ²⁵ Thus the land became defiled; and I punished it for its iniquity, and the land vomited out its inhabitants. ²⁶ But you shall keep my statutes and my ordinances and commit none of these abominations, either the citizen or the alien who resides among you ²⁷ (for the inhabitants of the land, who were before you, committed all of these abominations, and the land became defiled); ²⁸ otherwise the land will vomit you out for defiling it, as it vomited out the nation that was before you. ²⁹ For whoever commits any of these abominations shall be cut off from

their people. ³⁰ So keep my charge not to commit any of these abominations that were done before you, and not to defile yourselves by them: I am the LORD your God.

19 The LORD spoke to Moses, saying: ² Speak to all the congregation of the people of Israel and say to them: You shall be holy, for I the LORD your God am holy. ³ You shall each revere your mother and father, and you shall keep my sabbaths: I am the LORD your God. ⁴ Do not turn to idols or make cast images for yourselves: I am the LORD your God.

⁵ When you offer a sacrifice of well-being to the LORD, offer it in such a way that it is acceptable in your behalf. ⁶ It shall be eaten on the same day you offer it, or on the next day; and anything left over until the third day shall be consumed in fire. ⁷ If it is eaten at all on the third day, it is an abomination; it will not be acceptable. ⁸ All who eat it shall be subject to punishment, because they have profaned what is holy to the LORD; and any such person shall be cut off from the people.

⁹ When you reap the harvest of your land, you shall not reap to the very edges of your field, or gather the gleanings of your harvest. ¹⁰ You shall not strip your vineyard bare, or gather the fallen grapes of your vineyard; you

ᵃ Heb *to pass them over*

17: *Depravity*, a term of opprobrium employed by H for sexual sins. 19: Contrast 15.24, which allows intercourse with a menstruant. 20: *Defile yourself*, referring to moral impurity, which is prohibited by H. Ritual impurity, by contrast, is permitted (cf. 15.18n.). 21: *Molech*, a Canaanite deity associated with child sacrifice; see 20.2–5. *Profane the name*, to deny the Israelite God the honor and fame due him or to dishonor him directly. It also seems to connote diminishing the deity's holiness. 24–30: God avenged the land for the defilement caused by its inhabitants, whom the land in turn expelled. Such will be the fate of the Israelites if they too commit the sins prohibited in vv. 6–23. Punishment for prohibited moral impurity is often exile or other destruction (Isa 64.4–11; Ezek 20.38; 22.2–16; 39.23–24; cf. Lev 26.33–39). 25: For crimes and sins polluting the land, see Num 35.33–34; Isa 24.5–7; Ezek 22.24; Ezra 9.11. 29: *Cut off*, see 7.19–21n.

19.1–37: Holiness of Israelite laypersons. This chapter is a miscellany of ethical and ritual laws introduced by the command for all Israelites to be holy (v. 2), an imperative fulfilled through careful observance of all the statutes presented by the Priestly authors. 2: Lay holiness expresses the separateness of Israel from the other peoples (cf. vv. 36–37; 25.38,55): Israelites worship the LORD and express their fidelity through obedience to the LORD's commands (cf. 11.44–45; 20.7–8,24–26; Num 15.40–41). Cf. Ex 19.6; Deut 14.2,21; 26.19; 28.6. 3–4,11–13: These verses have close correspondence with the Decalogue (cf. Ex 20.2–17; Deut 5.6–21). 5–8: Cf. 7.15–18. The grammatical formulation here differs in part from 7.15–18 (here, genuine second-person plural construction; in ch 7, third-person singular). Note too that 7.15–18 is addressed to the priests alone (6.24) while this chapter is addressed to the Israelite laity (v. 2). Verse 8 also clarifies the nature of the penalty for one who eats the well-being offering on the third day: as in the case of consuming the sacrifice in an impure state, eating on the third day leads to complete destruction of the offender's lineage (cf. 7.19–21). 9–10: Cf. Ex 23.10–11; Lev 23.22;

shall leave them for the poor and the alien: I am the Lord your God.

¹¹ You shall not steal; you shall not deal falsely; and you shall not lie to one another. ¹² And you shall not swear falsely by my name, profaning the name of your God: I am the Lord.

¹³ You shall not defraud your neighbor; you shall not steal; and you shall not keep for yourself the wages of a laborer until morning. ¹⁴ You shall not revile the deaf or put a stumbling block before the blind; you shall fear your God: I am the Lord.

¹⁵ You shall not render an unjust judgment; you shall not be partial to the poor or defer to the great: with justice you shall judge your neighbor. ¹⁶ You shall not go around as a slanderer[a] among your people, and you shall not profit by the blood[b] of your neighbor: I am the Lord.

¹⁷ You shall not hate in your heart anyone of your kin; you shall reprove your neighbor, or you will incur guilt yourself. ¹⁸ You shall not take vengeance or bear a grudge against any of your people, but you shall love your neighbor as yourself: I am the Lord.

¹⁹ You shall keep my statutes. You shall not let your animals breed with a different kind; you shall not sow your field with two kinds of seed; nor shall you put on a garment made of two different materials.

²⁰ If a man has sexual relations with a woman who is a slave, designated for another man but not ransomed or given her freedom, an inquiry shall be held. They shall not be put to death, since she has not been freed; ²¹ but he shall bring a guilt offering for himself to the Lord, at the entrance of the tent of meeting, a ram as guilt offering. ²² And the priest shall make atonement for him with the ram of guilt offering before the Lord for his sin that he committed; and the sin he committed shall be forgiven him.

²³ When you come into the land and plant all kinds of trees for food, then you shall regard their fruit as forbidden;[c] three years it shall be forbidden[d] to you, it must not be eaten. ²⁴ In the fourth year all their fruit shall be set apart for rejoicing in the Lord. ²⁵ But in the fifth year you may eat of their fruit, that their yield may be increased for you: I am the Lord your God.

²⁶ You shall not eat anything with its blood. You shall not practice augury or witchcraft. ²⁷ You shall not round off the hair on your temples or mar the edges of your beard. ²⁸ You shall not make any gashes in your flesh for the dead or tattoo any marks upon you: I am the Lord.

²⁹ Do not profane your daughter by making her a prostitute, that the land not become prostituted and full of depravity. ³⁰ You shall keep my sabbaths and reverence my sanctuary: I am the Lord.

³¹ Do not turn to mediums or wizards; do not seek them out, to be defiled by them: I am the Lord your God.

³² You shall rise before the aged, and defer to the old; and you shall fear your God: I am the Lord.

³³ When an alien resides with you in your land, you shall not oppress the alien. ³⁴ The alien who resides with you shall be to you as the citizen among you; you shall love the alien as yourself, for you were aliens in the land of Egypt: I am the Lord your God.

³⁵ You shall not cheat in measuring length, weight, or quantity. ³⁶ You shall have honest balances, honest weights, an honest ephah,

a Meaning of Heb uncertain
b Heb *stand against the blood*
c Heb *as their uncircumcision*
d Heb *uncircumcision*

25.2–7; Deut 24.19–22; Ruth 2.1–10. **15:** Cf. Ex 22.2–3; Deut 1.17; 16.18–20. **17–18:** For attitudes and actions toward foreigners, see 17.8–9; 19.33–34; 25.39–46. **18b:** This verse, along with Deut 6.5, is quoted in Mt 22.37–40 (cf. Mk 12.28–33; Lk 10.27; Rom 13.9; Gal 5.14). The neighbor here is a fellow Israelite (cf. vv. 17,34). **19:** One reason mixtures are prohibited is to remind the people to keep themselves distinct, i.e., holy (cf. Deut 22.9–11). The mixture of wool and linen is reserved for the priestly vestments (Ex 28.6; 39.29) and fringes to be worn (Num 15.37–41). **20–22:** Contrast the case of the free, betrothed woman in 20.10; cf. Ex 22.16–17; Deut 22.23–27. **26:** *Blood*, cf. 3.17n.; 17.10–14n. For prohibitions against various forms of divination, see also v. 31; Ex 22.18; Deut 18.9–14. **27–28:** Cf. 21.5n. **35–36:** Cf. Deut 25.13–16; Am 8.5; Mic 6.11. An *ephah* was a dry measure equivalent to ca. 21 qts (23 liters); a *hin* was a liquid measure equivalent to ca. 1 gal (3.8 liters).

and an honest hin: I am the LORD your God, who brought you out of the land of Egypt. [37] You shall keep all my statutes and all my ordinances, and observe them: I am the LORD.

20 The LORD spoke to Moses, saying: [2] Say further to the people of Israel:

Any of the people of Israel, or of the aliens who reside in Israel, who give any of their offspring to Molech shall be put to death; the people of the land shall stone them to death. [3] I myself will set my face against them, and will cut them off from the people, because they have given of their offspring to Molech, defiling my sanctuary and profaning my holy name. [4] And if the people of the land should ever close their eyes to them, when they give of their offspring to Molech, and do not put them to death, [5] I myself will set my face against them and against their family, and will cut them off from among their people, them and all who follow them in prostituting themselves to Molech.

[6] If any turn to mediums and wizards, prostituting themselves to them, I will set my face against them, and will cut them off from the people. [7] Consecrate yourselves therefore, and be holy; for I am the LORD your God. [8] Keep my statutes, and observe them; I am the LORD; I sanctify you. [9] All who curse father or mother shall be put to death; having cursed father or mother, their blood is upon them.

[10] If a man commits adultery with the wife of[a] his neighbor, both the adulterer and the adulteress shall be put to death. [11] The man who lies with his father's wife has uncovered his father's nakedness; both of them shall be put to death; their blood is upon them. [12] If a man lies with his daughter-in-law, both of them shall be put to death; they have committed perversion, their blood is upon them. [13] If a man lies with a male as with a woman, both of them have committed an abomination; they shall be put to death; their blood

is upon them. [14] If a man takes a wife and her mother also, it is depravity; they shall be burned to death, both he and they, that there may be no depravity among you. [15] If a man has sexual relations with an animal, he shall be put to death; and you shall kill the animal. [16] If a woman approaches any animal and has sexual relations with it, you shall kill the woman and the animal; they shall be put to death, their blood is upon them.

[17] If a man takes his sister, a daughter of his father or a daughter of his mother, and sees her nakedness, and she sees his nakedness, it is a disgrace, and they shall be cut off in the sight of their people; he has uncovered his sister's nakedness, he shall be subject to punishment. [18] If a man lies with a woman having her sickness and uncovers her nakedness, he has laid bare her flow and she has laid bare her flow of blood; both of them shall be cut off from their people. [19] You shall not uncover the nakedness of your mother's sister or of your father's sister, for that is to lay bare one's own flesh; they shall be subject to punishment. [20] If a man lies with his uncle's wife, he has uncovered his uncle's nakedness; they shall be subject to punishment; they shall die childless. [21] If a man takes his brother's wife, it is impurity; he has uncovered his brother's nakedness; they shall be childless.

[22] You shall keep all my statutes and all my ordinances, and observe them, so that the land to which I bring you to settle in may not vomit you out. [23] You shall not follow the practices of the nation that I am driving out before you. Because they did all these things, I abhorred them. [24] But I have said to you: You shall inherit their land, and I will give it to you to possess, a land flowing with milk and honey. I am the LORD your God; I have

---

a   Heb repeats *if a man commits adultery with the wife of*

20.1–27: Various prohibitions. Some of the laws in chs 18–19 are repeated here, although many are in a different legal form (some of the absolute prohibitions [apodictic laws] of ch 18 are here formulated as legal cases [casuistic laws] with stated penalties). Other laws are also added. The significant overlap between the two chapters suggests that they are independent reflections of a common tradition subsequently compiled by H. **2:** *Molech*, see 18.21n. **5:** *Cut them off*, see 7.19–21n. **5–6:** *Prostituting*, cf. 17.5,7n. **7–8:** *Consecrate yourselves*, i.e., separate from foreign worship practices by following the LORD's commands (cf. vv. 24–26). **9:** Cf. Ex 21.17. **10–21:** Cf. 18.6–20,22–23. **18:** *Sickness*, i.e., her menstrual period (cf. 15.33). Contrast 15.24. **20–21:** *Die childless*, perhaps a variant of the "cut off" formula (cf. 7.19–21n.). **22–26:** A concluding exhortation similar to 18.24–30;

separated you from the peoples. [25] You shall therefore make a distinction between the clean animal and the unclean, and between the unclean bird and the clean; you shall not bring abomination on yourselves by animal or by bird or by anything with which the ground teems, which I have set apart for you to hold unclean. [26] You shall be holy to me; for I the LORD am holy, and I have separated you from the other peoples to be mine.

[27] A man or a woman who is a medium or a wizard shall be put to death; they shall be stoned to death, their blood is upon them.

21

The LORD said to Moses: Speak to the priests, the sons of Aaron, and say to them:

No one shall defile himself for a dead person among his relatives, [2] except for his nearest kin: his mother, his father, his son, his daughter, his brother; [3] likewise, for a virgin sister, close to him because she has had no husband, he may defile himself for her. [4] But he shall not defile himself as a husband among his people and so profane himself. [5] They shall not make bald spots upon their heads, or shave off the edges of their beards, or make any gashes in their flesh. [6] They shall be holy to their God, and not profane the name of their God; for they offer the LORD's offerings by fire, the food of their God; therefore they shall be holy. [7] They shall not marry a prostitute or a woman who has been defiled; neither shall they marry a woman divorced from her husband. For they are holy to their God, [8] and you shall treat them as holy, since they offer the food of your God; they shall be holy to you, for I the LORD, I who sanctify you, am holy. [9] When the daughter

of a priest profanes herself through prostitution, she profanes her father; she shall be burned to death.

[10] The priest who is exalted above his fellows, on whose head the anointing oil has been poured and who has been consecrated to wear the vestments, shall not dishevel his hair, nor tear his vestments. [11] He shall not go where there is a dead body; he shall not defile himself even for his father or mother. [12] He shall not go outside the sanctuary and thus profane the sanctuary of his God; for the consecration of the anointing oil of his God is upon him: I am the LORD. [13] He shall marry only a woman who is a virgin. [14] A widow, or a divorced woman, or a woman who has been defiled, a prostitute, these he shall not marry. He shall marry a virgin of his own kin, [15] that he may not profane his offspring among his kin; for I am the LORD; I sanctify him.

[16] The LORD spoke to Moses, saying: [17] Speak to Aaron and say: No one of your offspring throughout their generations who has a blemish may approach to offer the food of his God. [18] For no one who has a blemish shall draw near, one who is blind or lame, or one who has a mutilated face or a limb too long, [19] or one who has a broken foot or a broken hand, [20] or a hunchback, or a dwarf, or a man with a blemish in his eyes or an itching disease or scabs or crushed testicles. [21] No descendant of Aaron the priest who has a blemish shall come near to offer the LORD's offerings by fire; since he has a blemish, he shall not come near to offer the food of his God. [22] He may eat the food of his God, of the most holy as well as of the holy. [23] But he shall not come near the curtain or approach

---

cf. 20.7–8n. **24:** *Milk and honey,* a typical biblical description of the land of Canaan (e.g., Ex 3.8; Deut 6.3). **27:** Because it follows the concluding paragraph, this verse is likely a later insertion; cf. v. 6; 19.31.

21.1–22.33: Priestly restrictions and sacrificial rules. These chapters are directed primarily to the priests (21.1,17; 22.2; cf. 21.24; 22.18) and are especially concerned with maintaining their ritual holiness, which was granted to them through ordination (ch 8), as well as the holiness of the sacrifices.

21.1–15: Because of their regular contact with the sanctuary, priests must avoid impurities otherwise tolerated for lay Israelites. The high priest must observe greater restrictions (vv. 10–15) because of his closer contact with the sacred. **1:** *Defile himself,* through corpse contamination (cf. 10.4–7n.; Num 19). **5:** Apparently mourning rituals, also prohibited to nonpriests (19.27–28); cf. Deut 14.1–2; Isa 22.12; Jer 16.6. **6:** *Profane the name,* cf. 18.21n. *Offerings by fire,* see 1.1–3.17n. *Food of their God,* cf. 1.1–3.17n.; 1.9n. **8:** Though vv. 1b–15 are ostensibly directed to the priests and not the Israelite laity, this verse addresses all Israelites. **10–15:** Stricter regulations for the high priest. **10:** See 8.10–12,30n. **16–23:** Bodily defects disqualify priests from altar service, for they undermine the wholeness of the priest (cf. 22.17–25). However, such defects do not render them impure. Such priests may still

the altar, because he has a blemish, that he may not profane my sanctuaries; for I am the LORD; I sanctify them. [24] Thus Moses spoke to Aaron and to his sons and to all the people of Israel.

22 The LORD spoke to Moses, saying: [2] Direct Aaron and his sons to deal carefully with the sacred donations of the people of Israel, which they dedicate to me, so that they may not profane my holy name; I am the LORD. [3] Say to them: If anyone among all your offspring throughout your generations comes near the sacred donations, which the people of Israel dedicate to the LORD, while he is in a state of uncleanness, that person shall be cut off from my presence: I am the LORD. [4] No one of Aaron's offspring who has a leprous[a] disease or suffers a discharge may eat of the sacred donations until he is clean. Whoever touches anything made unclean by a corpse or a man who has had an emission of semen, [5] and whoever touches any swarming thing by which he may be made unclean or any human being by whom he may be made unclean—whatever his uncleanness may be— [6] the person who touches any such shall be unclean until evening and shall not eat of the sacred donations unless he has washed his body in water. [7] When the sun sets he shall be clean; and afterward he may eat of the sacred donations, for they are his food. [8] That which died or was torn by wild animals he shall not eat, becoming unclean by it: I am the LORD. [9] They shall keep my charge, so that they may not incur guilt and die in the sanctuary[b] for having profaned it: I am the LORD; I sanctify them.

[10] No lay person shall eat of the sacred donations. No bound or hired servant of the priest shall eat of the sacred donations; [11] but if a priest acquires anyone by purchase, the person may eat of them; and those that are born in his house may eat of his food. [12] If a priest's daughter marries a layman, she shall not eat of the offering of the sacred donations; [13] but if a priest's daughter is widowed or divorced, without offspring, and returns to her father's house, as in her youth, she may eat of her father's food. No lay person shall eat of it. [14] If a man eats of the sacred donation unintentionally, he shall add one-fifth of its value to it, and give the sacred donation to the priest. [15] No one shall profane the sacred donations of the people of Israel, which they offer to the LORD, [16] causing them to bear guilt requiring a guilt offering, by eating their sacred donations: for I am the LORD; I sanctify them.

[17] The LORD spoke to Moses, saying: [18] Speak to Aaron and his sons and all the people of Israel and say to them: When anyone of the house of Israel or of the aliens residing in Israel presents an offering, whether in payment of a vow or as a freewill offering that is offered to the LORD as a burnt offering, [19] to be acceptable in your behalf it shall be a male without blemish, of the cattle or the sheep or the goats. [20] You shall not offer anything that has a blemish, for it will not be acceptable in your behalf.

[21] When anyone offers a sacrifice of well-being to the LORD, in fulfillment of a vow or as a freewill offering, from the herd or from the flock, to be acceptable it must be perfect; there shall be no blemish in it. [22] Anything blind, or injured, or maimed, or having a discharge or an itch or scabs—these you shall not offer to the LORD or put any of them on the altar as offerings by fire to the LORD. [23] An ox or a lamb that has a limb too long or too short you may present for a freewill

---

a   A term for several skin diseases; precise meaning uncertain

b   Vg: Heb *incur guilt for it and die in it*

---

eat of the offering portions designated for the priests (cf. Num 18.8–10). **22.1–16:** Rules for avoiding defilement of offerings. Verses 1–9 focus on priests and their impurity (cf. 11.1–16.34n.), while vv. 10–16 focus on laypersons. **2:** *Direct Aaron . . . sacred donations,* better, "Speak to Aaron and his sons so that they will keep themselves from the sacred donations," referring to times when priests who have contracted impurity are therefore barred from eating holy offering portions (cf. 7.20–21). **7:** *For they are his food,* offering portions are the priests' primary remuneration (Num 18.8–10). **8:** Unlike laypersons (cf. 11.39–40; 17.15–16), priests are prohibited from eating such animals. **9:** Death is the assumed penalty for trespass upon the sacred (cf. 10.2; 16.2). **14–16:** Cf. 5.14–16. **17–30:** Animals not accepted as well-being offerings. **17–25:** The topic of physical defect or impurity-causing disease connects these verses to 21.16–22.9. Anything or anyone contacting the altar must be without defect; cf. Mal

offering; but it will not be accepted for a vow. ²⁴ Any animal that has its testicles bruised or crushed or torn or cut, you shall not offer to the LORD; such you shall not do within your land, ²⁵ nor shall you accept any such animals from a foreigner to offer as food to your God; since they are mutilated, with a blemish in them, they shall not be accepted in your behalf.

²⁶ The LORD spoke to Moses, saying: ²⁷ When an ox or a sheep or a goat is born, it shall remain seven days with its mother, and from the eighth day on it shall be acceptable as the LORD's offering by fire. ²⁸ But you shall not slaughter, from the herd or the flock, an animal with its young on the same day. ²⁹ When you sacrifice a thanksgiving offering to the LORD, you shall sacrifice it so that it may be acceptable in your behalf. ³⁰ It shall be eaten on the same day; you shall not leave any of it until morning: I am the LORD.

³¹ Thus you shall keep my commandments and observe them: I am the LORD. ³² You shall not profane my holy name, that I may be sanctified among the people of Israel: I am the LORD; I sanctify you, ³³ I who brought you out of the land of Egypt to be your God: I am the LORD.

23 The LORD spoke to Moses, saying: ² Speak to the people of Israel and say to them: These are the appointed festivals of the LORD that you shall proclaim as holy convocations, my appointed festivals.

³ Six days shall work be done; but the seventh day is a sabbath of complete rest, a holy convocation; you shall do no work: it is a sabbath to the LORD throughout your settlements.

⁴ These are the appointed festivals of the LORD, the holy convocations, which you shall celebrate at the time appointed for them. ⁵ In the first month, on the fourteenth day of the month, at twilight,ᵃ there shall be a passover offering to the LORD, ⁶ and on the fifteenth day of the same month is the festival of unleavened bread to the LORD; seven days you shall eat unleavened bread. ⁷ On the first day you shall have a holy convocation; you shall not work at your occupations. ⁸ For seven days you shall present the LORD's offerings by fire; on the seventh day there shall be a holy convocation: you shall not work at your occupations.

⁹ The LORD spoke to Moses: ¹⁰ Speak to the people of Israel and say to them: When you enter the land that I am giving you and you reap its harvest, you shall bring the sheaf of the first fruits of your harvest to the priest. ¹¹ He shall raise the sheaf before the LORD, that you may find acceptance; on the day after the sabbath the priest shall raise it. ¹² On the day when you raise the sheaf, you shall offer a lamb a year old, without blemish, as a burnt offering to the LORD. ¹³ And the grain offering with it shall be two-tenths of an ephah of choice flour mixed with oil,

ᵃ Heb *between the two evenings*

1.6–14. **19–21:** *Acceptable*, lit. "accepted." See 1.4n.; cf. 22.25. **23:** This verse asserts differentiation and hierarchical valuation among freewill offerings (cf. 7.15–16). **30:** Cf. 7.15–18; 19.5–8. **31–33:** The Israelites' adherence to the commandments brings honor to the deity and assures his presence among the people. Failure to follow the commandments profanes that aspect of the holy God that is directly accessible to the people, his "name," i.e., his reputation (cf. 19.2,37; 20.7–8,24–26).

23.1–44: **Calendar of sacred occasions.** Alongside Num 28–29, which focus on the offerings required for each sacred occasion, this chapter outlines the Priestly calendar of religious holidays. For non-Priestly calendars, see Ex 23.10–17; 34.18–24; Deut 16. **2:** *Convocations*, better, "occasions." **2b–3:** An interpolation that elevates the sabbath to the level of the other sacred festivals. Note the nearly identical formulation of v. 2b and v. 4, which originally followed v. 2a. The equation of sabbath and sacred festivals may have led to the prohibition of work on the festivals, which is not attested in the non-Priestly calendars. *Sabbath of complete rest*, referring to the prohibition of all work (cf. v. 28; Num 29.7; Lev 16.31n.). On other holy occasions, regular occupational work is prohibited but not light work such as food preparation (23.7–8,21,25,35–36; Num 28.18,25–26; 29.1,12,35). **5–8:** The combined observance of Passover and the immediately following pilgrimage festival of unleavened bread is the first sacred occasion of the year. It coincides with the barley harvest. For further Priestly prescriptions concerning Passover and the festival of unleavened bread, see Ex 12.1–20,43–49; Num 9.1–14; 28.16–25. **5:** *First month*, March–April. **9–14:** The first-fruits offering from the barley harvest; cf. 19.23–25. **13:** *Ephah . . . hin*, see

an offering by fire of pleasing odor to the Lord; and the drink offering with it shall be of wine, one-fourth of a hin. [14] You shall eat no bread or parched grain or fresh ears until that very day, until you have brought the offering of your God: it is a statute forever throughout your generations in all your settlements.

[15] And from the day after the sabbath, from the day on which you bring the sheaf of the elevation offering, you shall count off seven weeks; they shall be complete. [16] You shall count until the day after the seventh sabbath, fifty days; then you shall present an offering of new grain to the Lord. [17] You shall bring from your settlements two loaves of bread as an elevation offering, each made of two-tenths of an ephah; they shall be of choice flour, baked with leaven, as first fruits to the Lord. [18] You shall present with the bread seven lambs a year old without blemish, one young bull, and two rams; they shall be a burnt offering to the Lord, along with their grain offering and their drink offerings, an offering by fire of pleasing odor to the Lord. [19] You shall also offer one male goat for a sin offering, and two male lambs a year old as a sacrifice of well-being. [20] The priest shall raise them with the bread of the first fruits as an elevation offering before the Lord, together with the two lambs; they shall be holy to the Lord for the priest. [21] On that same day you shall make proclamation; you shall hold a holy convocation; you shall not work at your occupations. This is a statute forever in all your settlements throughout your generations.

[22] When you reap the harvest of your land, you shall not reap to the very edges of your field, or gather the gleanings of your harvest; you shall leave them for the poor and for the alien: I am the Lord your God.

[23] The Lord spoke to Moses, saying: [24] Speak to the people of Israel, saying: In the seventh month, on the first day of the month, you shall observe a day of complete rest, a holy convocation commemorated with trumpet blasts. [25] You shall not work at your occupations; and you shall present the Lord's offering by fire.

[26] The Lord spoke to Moses, saying: [27] Now, the tenth day of this seventh month is the day of atonement; it shall be a holy convocation for you: you shall deny yourselves[a] and present the Lord's offering by fire; [28] and you shall do no work during that entire day; for it is a day of atonement, to make atonement on your behalf before the Lord your God. [29] For anyone who does not practice self-denial[b] during that entire day shall be cut off from the people. [30] And anyone who does any work during that entire day, such a one I will destroy from the midst of the people. [31] You shall do no work: it is a statute forever throughout your generations in all your settlements. [32] It shall be to you a sabbath of complete rest, and you shall deny yourselves;[a] on the ninth day of the month at evening, from evening to evening you shall keep your sabbath.

[33] The Lord spoke to Moses, saying: [34] Speak to the people of Israel, saying: On the fifteenth day of this seventh month, and lasting seven days, there shall be the festival of booths[c] to the Lord. [35] The first day shall be a holy convocation; you shall not work at your occupations. [36] Seven days you shall present the Lord's offerings by fire; on the eighth day you shall observe a holy convocation and present the Lord's offerings by fire; it is a solemn assembly; you shall not work at your occupations.

[37] These are the appointed festivals of the Lord, which you shall celebrate as times of

a Or *shall fast*
b Or *does not fast*
c Or *tabernacles*: Heb *succoth*

19.35–36n. **14:** *Statute forever . . . all your settlements,* hallmark H language (cf. vv. 21,31,41). **15–21:** Though this observance coincides with the "pilgrimage festival of weeks" elsewhere (Ex 34.22; Deut 16.10,16; cf. Ex 23.16), H leaves it unnamed and does not require any pilgrimage for it, perhaps because the community was occupied with the wheat harvest. **22:** See 19.9–10n. **23–25:** The beginning of the agricultural calendar. In later Jewish tradition, this calendar became preeminent, and thus the first day of the seventh month became the new year. **24:** The *trumpet blasts* (or, alternatively, "shouts") are intended to remind God of his people (cf. Num 10.10). **26–32:** Cf. ch 16. These verses correspond especially with 16.29–34a (H). **33–36:** The *festival of booths,* celebrating the

holy convocation, for presenting to the LORD offerings by fire—burnt offerings and grain offerings, sacrifices and drink offerings, each on its proper day— **38** apart from the sabbaths of the LORD, and apart from your gifts, and apart from all your votive offerings, and apart from all your freewill offerings, which you give to the LORD.

39 Now, the fifteenth day of the seventh month, when you have gathered in the produce of the land, you shall keep the festival of the LORD, lasting seven days; a complete rest on the first day, and a complete rest on the eighth day. **40** On the first day you shall take the fruit of majestic[a] trees, branches of palm trees, boughs of leafy trees, and willows of the brook; and you shall rejoice before the LORD your God for seven days. **41** You shall keep it as a festival to the LORD seven days in the year; you shall keep it in the seventh month as a statute forever throughout your generations. **42** You shall live in booths for seven days; all that are citizens in Israel shall live in booths, **43** so that your generations may know that I made the people of Israel live in booths when I brought them out of the land of Egypt: I am the LORD your God.

44 Thus Moses declared to the people of Israel the appointed festivals of the LORD.

24 The LORD spoke to Moses, saying: **2** Command the people of Israel to bring you pure oil of beaten olives for

the lamp, that a light may be kept burning regularly. **3** Aaron shall set it up in the tent of meeting, outside the curtain of the covenant,[b] to burn from evening to morning before the LORD regularly; it shall be a statute forever throughout your generations. **4** He shall set up the lamps on the lampstand of pure gold[c] before the LORD regularly.

5 You shall take choice flour, and bake twelve loaves of it; two-tenths of an ephah shall be in each loaf. **6** You shall place them in two rows, six in a row, on the table of pure gold.[d] **7** You shall put pure frankincense with each row, to be a token offering for the bread, as an offering by fire to the LORD. **8** Every sabbath day Aaron shall set them in order before the LORD regularly as a commitment of the people of Israel, as a covenant forever. **9** They shall be for Aaron and his descendants, who shall eat them in a holy place, for they are most holy portions for him from the offerings by fire to the LORD, a perpetual due.

10 A man whose mother was an Israelite and whose father was an Egyptian came out among the people of Israel; and the Israelite woman's son and a certain Israelite began fighting in the camp. **11** The Israelite woman's

a Meaning of Heb uncertain
b Or *treaty*, or *testament*; Heb *eduth*
c Heb *pure lampstand*
d Heb *pure table*

fruit harvest (cf. Ex 23.16; 34.22; Deut 16.13; 1 Kings 8.65). **37–38:** An earlier conclusion to the chapter. **39–42:** Further instructions for the festival of booths. **40:** In Neh 8.14–17, these branches are used to construct booths. **43:** Only here is the festival of booths historicized. There is no mention of the Israelites living in booths in the stories of the Exodus and wilderness period. This claim may originate by analogy to the deity's wilderness tent sanctuary.

24.1–9: Ritual lamps and bread. These two regular rites (lighting lamps and displaying bread) performed by the high priest effect the perpetual worship of God in his sanctuary. As such, they are an appropriate sequel to the ritual calendar in ch 23. **1–4:** The lampstand and its maintenance; cf. Ex 27.20–21. **2:** *Lamp,* cf. Ex 25.31–40; 26.35; 27.20–21; 30.7–8; 37.17–24; 40.24–25; Num 8.1–4. **5–9:** On this bread and its table, see Ex 25.23–30; 26.35; 37.10–16; 40.22–23. **8:** This verse is better translated, "Every sabbath day in perpetuity he shall arrange it before the LORD; it is required from the Israelites until the end of time." Cf. 2.13n. **9:** The bread is not eaten by the deity, but is given to the priests as remuneration for their ritual service. It must be eaten in the sanctuary complex because of its absorption of holiness by close and prolonged proximity to the deity.

24.10–23: The case of the blasphemer and laws arising from it. The incident of the blasphemer unexpectedly interrupts the divine revelation of law, as in the case of Nadab and Abihu (cf. 9.1–10.20n.). Because no law had yet been given to address such a case of blasphemy (v. 12), God intervenes to resolve the issue and gives further legislation prompted by this case (cf. Num 9.6–14; 15.32–36; 27.1–11). **10:** The incident involves a "half-Israelite" of matrilineal descent, which prompts the question of his culpability. Verse 16 clarifies this issue. **11:** *Blasphemed,* likely referring to uttering a curse against the LORD (cf. v. 15), not simply pronouncing

son blasphemed the Name in a curse. And they brought him to Moses—now his mother's name was Shelomith, daughter of Dibri, of the tribe of Dan— ¹²and they put him in custody, until the decision of the LORD should be made clear to them.

¹³The LORD said to Moses, saying: ¹⁴Take the blasphemer outside the camp; and let all who were within hearing lay their hands on his head, and let the whole congregation stone him. ¹⁵And speak to the people of Israel, saying: Anyone who curses God shall bear the sin. ¹⁶One who blasphemes the name of the LORD shall be put to death; the whole congregation shall stone the blasphemer. Aliens as well as citizens, when they blaspheme the Name, shall be put to death. ¹⁷Anyone who kills a human being shall be put to death. ¹⁸Anyone who kills an animal shall make restitution for it, life for life. ¹⁹Anyone who maims another shall suffer the same injury in return: ²⁰fracture for fracture, eye for eye, tooth for tooth; the injury inflicted is the injury to be suffered. ²¹One who kills an animal shall make restitution for it; but one who kills a human being shall be put to death. ²²You shall have one law for the alien and for the citizen: for I am the LORD your God. ²³Moses spoke thus to the people of Israel; and they took the blasphemer outside the camp, and stoned him to death. The people of Israel did as the LORD had commanded Moses.

25

The LORD spoke to Moses on Mount Sinai, saying: ²Speak to the people of Israel and say to them: When you enter the land that I am giving you, the land shall observe a sabbath for the LORD. ³Six years you shall sow your field, and six years you shall prune your vineyard, and gather in their yield; ⁴but in the seventh year there shall be a sabbath of complete rest for the land, a sabbath for the LORD: you shall not sow your field or prune your vineyard. ⁵You shall not reap the aftergrowth of your harvest or gather the grapes of your unpruned vine: it shall be a year of complete rest for the land. ⁶You may eat what the land yields during its sabbath—you, your male and female slaves, your hired and your bound laborers who live with you; ⁷for your livestock also, and for the wild animals in your land all its yield shall be for food.

⁸You shall count off seven weeks[a] of years, seven times seven years, so that the period of seven weeks of years gives forty-nine years. ⁹Then you shall have the trumpet sounded loud; on the tenth day of the seventh month—on the day of atonement—you shall have the trumpet sounded throughout all your land. ¹⁰And you shall hallow the fiftieth year and you shall proclaim liberty throughout the land to all its inhabitants. It shall be a jubilee for you: you shall return, every one of you, to your property and every one of you to your family. ¹¹That fiftieth year shall be a jubilee for you: you shall not sow, or reap the

---

ᵃ Or *sabbaths*

his *Name* (a circumlocution for the divine proper name, Yahweh). The name is holy—belonging to God—but is accessible to all and thus particularly vulnerable to trespass. **14:** *Lay their hands*, ritually placing guilt upon the blasphemer (cf. 1.4n.; 16.21–22n.). **17–22:** Further laws arising from the blasphemer's case, each of which exhibits the measure-for-measure (talion) principle (cf. Ex 21.23–35; Deut 19.21). **23b:** The enactment of the divine command in v. 14.

25.1–26.2: The sabbatical and jubilee years. This unit institutes a fixed seventh-year and fiftieth-year rest for the land that is likely based on the seventh-year laws in Ex 23.10–11 and Deut 15.1–18. It also ties manumission of Hebrew slaves (called "hired servants") to the fiftieth year, termed the "jubilee." The sabbatical and jubilee years are coordinated numerically, and each is part of the larger system of social welfare legislated here. These laws are motivated by the conviction that the land and the Israelites each belong to God (vv. 23,42,55). **2–7:** In every seventh year all agricultural work must cease so that the land may observe a *sabbath of complete rest* (see 16.31n.); cf. Ex 23.10–12. **5–6:** The *aftergrowth* of the seventh year may be eaten, but it must not be harvested for use as in the preceding six years. **8–17:** The jubilee (from Heb "yobel," meaning "ram's horn," blown to signal the holy day) is to begin on the Day of Atonement in the fiftieth year, counted according to the sabbatical years. All agricultural work must cease, debts and indentured servants are released, and ancestral property that was sold reverts to its original owners. Contrast Ex 21.2–6; Deut 15.1–3,12–18; Jer 34.8–22, where the seventh year serves some of these purposes. There is no evidence for the practice of the jubilee in the bibli-

aftergrowth, or harvest the unpruned vines. [12] For it is a jubilee; it shall be holy to you: you shall eat only what the field itself produces.

[13] In this year of jubilee you shall return, every one of you, to your property. [14] When you make a sale to your neighbor or buy from your neighbor, you shall not cheat one another. [15] When you buy from your neighbor, you shall pay only for the number of years since the jubilee; the seller shall charge you only for the remaining crop years. [16] If the years are more, you shall increase the price, and if the years are fewer, you shall diminish the price; for it is a certain number of harvests that are being sold to you. [17] You shall not cheat one another, but you shall fear your God; for I am the LORD your God.

[18] You shall observe my statutes and faithfully keep my ordinances, so that you may live on the land securely. [19] The land will yield its fruit, and you will eat your fill and live on it securely. [20] Should you ask, "What shall we eat in the seventh year, if we may not sow or gather in our crop?" [21] I will order my blessing for you in the sixth year, so that it will yield a crop for three years. [22] When you sow in the eighth year, you will be eating from the old crop; until the ninth year, when its produce comes in, you shall eat the old. [23] The land shall not be sold in perpetuity, for the land is mine; with me you are but aliens and tenants. [24] Throughout the land that you hold, you shall provide for the redemption of the land.

[25] If anyone of your kin falls into difficulty and sells a piece of property, then the next of kin shall come and redeem what the relative has sold. [26] If the person has no one to redeem it, but then prospers and finds sufficient means to do so, [27] the years since its sale shall be computed and the difference shall be refunded to the person to whom it was sold, and the property shall be returned. [28] But if there are not sufficient means to

recover it, what was sold shall remain with the purchaser until the year of jubilee; in the jubilee it shall be released, and the property shall be returned.

[29] If anyone sells a dwelling house in a walled city, it may be redeemed until a year has elapsed since its sale; the right of redemption shall be one year. [30] If it is not redeemed before a full year has elapsed, a house that is in a walled city shall pass in perpetuity to the purchaser, throughout the generations; it shall not be released in the jubilee. [31] But houses in villages that have no walls around them shall be classed as open country; they may be redeemed, and they shall be released in the jubilee. [32] As for the cities of the Levites, the Levites shall forever have the right of redemption of the houses in the cities belonging to them. [33] Such property as may be redeemed from the Levites—houses sold in a city belonging to them—shall be released in the jubilee; because the houses in the cities of the Levites are their possession among the people of Israel. [34] But the open land around their cities may not be sold; for that is their possession for all time.

[35] If any of your kin fall into difficulty and become dependent on you,[a] you shall support them; they shall live with you as though resident aliens. [36] Do not take interest in advance or otherwise make a profit from them, but fear your God; let them live with you. [37] You shall not lend them your money at interest taken in advance, or provide them food at a profit. [38] I am the LORD your God, who brought you out of the land of Egypt, to give you the land of Canaan, to be your God.

[39] If any who are dependent on you become so impoverished that they sell themselves to you, you shall not make them serve as slaves. [40] They shall remain with you as

[a] Meaning of Heb uncertain

cal period. **13–17:** Because nonancestral property cannot be held in perpetuity, land "sales" are leases calculated according to the jubilee calendar. **18–22:** God will provide a miraculous bumper crop in the sixth year so that no one will suffer by observing the sabbatical or jubilee years. The sabbatical year thus should not be viewed as land fallowing, which would presume the least agricultural fertility in the sixth year. **23–55:** Successively greater levels of poverty are considered: property sale and redemption (vv. 25–34); dependence upon fellow Israelites' support (loans) (vv. 35–38); "hired service" (enslavement) to a fellow Israelite (vv. 39–43; vv. 44–46 address permanent enslavement of foreigners); "hired service" (enslavement) to a resident alien (vv. 47–55). **32:** *Cities of the Levites,* see Num 35.1–8; Josh 21.1–42. This is the only mention of Levites in the book. **36–37:** Cf. Ex 22.24;

hired or bound laborers. They shall serve with you until the year of the jubilee. ⁴¹ Then they and their children with them shall be free from your authority; they shall go back to their own family and return to their ancestral property. ⁴² For they are my servants, whom I brought out of the land of Egypt; they shall not be sold as slaves are sold. ⁴³ You shall not rule over them with harshness, but shall fear your God. ⁴⁴ As for the male and female slaves whom you may have, it is from the nations around you that you may acquire male and female slaves. ⁴⁵ You may also acquire them from among the aliens residing with you, and from their families that are with you, who have been born in your land; and they may be your property. ⁴⁶ You may keep them as a possession for your children after you, for them to inherit as property. These you may treat as slaves, but as for your fellow Israelites, no one shall rule over the other with harshness.

⁴⁷ If resident aliens among you prosper, and if any of your kin fall into difficulty with one of them and sell themselves to an alien, or to a branch of the alien's family, ⁴⁸ after they have sold themselves they shall have the right of redemption; one of their brothers may redeem them, ⁴⁹ or their uncle or their uncle's son may redeem them, or anyone of their family who is of their own flesh may redeem them; or if they prosper they may redeem themselves. ⁵⁰ They shall compute with the purchaser the total from the year when they sold themselves to the alien until the jubilee year; the price of the sale shall be applied to the number of years: the time they were with the owner shall be rated as the time of a hired laborer. ⁵¹ If many years

remain, they shall pay for their redemption in proportion to the purchase price; ⁵² and if few years remain until the jubilee year, they shall compute thus: according to the years involved they shall make payment for their redemption. ⁵³ As a laborer hired by the year they shall be under the alien's authority, who shall not, however, rule with harshness over them in your sight. ⁵⁴ And if they have not been redeemed in any of these ways, they and their children with them shall go free in the jubilee year. ⁵⁵ For to me the people of Israel are servants; they are my servants whom I brought out from the land of Egypt: I am the LORD your God.

26 You shall make for yourselves no idols and erect no carved images or pillars, and you shall not place figured stones in your land, to worship at them; for I am the LORD your God. ² You shall keep my sabbaths and reverence my sanctuary: I am the LORD.

³ If you follow my statutes and keep my commandments and observe them faithfully, ⁴ I will give you your rains in their season, and the land shall yield its produce, and the trees of the field shall yield their fruit. ⁵ Your threshing shall overtake the vintage, and the vintage shall overtake the sowing; you shall eat your bread to the full, and live securely in your land. ⁶ And I will grant peace in the land, and you shall lie down, and no one shall make you afraid; I will remove dangerous animals from the land, and no sword shall go through your land. ⁷ You shall give chase to your enemies, and they shall fall before you by the sword. ⁸ Five of you shall give chase to a hundred, and a hundred of you shall give chase to ten thousand; your enemies shall fall before you by the sword. ⁹ I will look with

Deut 23.21. **42,55:** Israelites may not be enslaved because they are already enslaved to God (cf. 26.13). Contrast Ex 21.2–11; Deut 15.12–18. **26.1–2:** These verses conclude the H legislation and thus belong with the preceding (cf. ch 19), not with the rest of ch 26, which moves from legislation to inducements for obeying God's laws.

26.3–46: Inducements for obedience. This unit is the conclusion to chs 17–26, the Holiness Collection (ch 27 is a later addition). Although similar in structure and content to the blessings and curses in Deut 28 and in ancient Near Eastern political treaties, these verses never use that terminology. Moreover, unlike the curse sections of Deut 28 and Near Eastern treaties, the threatened punishments in vv. 14–39 proceed incrementally and are explicitly aimed at compelling obedience (cf. vv. 18,21,23–24,27–28). For H, Israel's disobedience does not abrogate God's commitment (covenant) to his people. Because he owns them as slaves (cf. 25.42,55), God will punish his people, but in so doing he never gives up ownership of them. The prominent use of covenant language and strong ties to Deut 28 suggest that H here may have borrowed from and revised D. **3–13:** Rewards for obedience. **9:** *Covenant,* for P and H, this is the divine promise of land and progeny (Gen 17.1–8; 28.3–4;

favor upon you and make you fruitful and multiply you; and I will maintain my covenant with you. [10] You shall eat old grain long stored, and you shall have to clear out the old to make way for the new. [11] I will place my dwelling in your midst, and I shall not abhor you. [12] And I will walk among you, and will be your God, and you shall be my people. [13] I am the LORD your God who brought you out of the land of Egypt, to be their slaves no more; I have broken the bars of your yoke and made you walk erect.

[14] But if you will not obey me, and do not observe all these commandments, [15] if you spurn my statutes, and abhor my ordinances, so that you will not observe all my commandments, and you break my covenant, [16] I in turn will do this to you: I will bring terror on you; consumption and fever that waste the eyes and cause life to pine away. You shall sow your seed in vain, for your enemies shall eat it. [17] I will set my face against you, and you shall be struck down by your enemies; your foes shall rule over you, and you shall flee though no one pursues you. [18] And if in spite of this you will not obey me, I will continue to punish you sevenfold for your sins. [19] I will break your proud glory, and I will make your sky like iron and your earth like copper. [20] Your strength shall be spent to no purpose: your land shall not yield its produce, and the trees of the land shall not yield their fruit.

[21] If you continue hostile to me, and will not obey me, I will continue to plague you sevenfold for your sins. [22] I will let loose wild animals against you, and they shall bereave you of your children and destroy your livestock; they shall make you few in number, and your roads shall be deserted.

[23] If in spite of these punishments you have not turned back to me, but continue hostile to me, [24] then I too will continue hostile to you: I myself will strike you sevenfold for your sins. [25] I will bring the sword against you, executing vengeance for the covenant; and if you withdraw within your cities, I will send pestilence among you, and you shall be delivered into enemy hands. [26] When I break your staff of bread, ten women shall bake your bread in a single oven, and they shall dole out your bread by weight; and though you eat, you shall not be satisfied.

[27] But if, despite this, you disobey me, and continue hostile to me, [28] I will continue hostile to you in fury; I in turn will punish you myself sevenfold for your sins. [29] You shall eat the flesh of your sons, and you shall eat the flesh of your daughters. [30] I will destroy your high places and cut down your incense altars; I will heap your carcasses on the carcasses of your idols. I will abhor you. [31] I will lay your cities waste, will make your sanctuaries desolate, and I will not smell your pleasing odors. [32] I will devastate the land, so that your enemies who come to settle in it shall be appalled at it. [33] And you I will scatter among the nations, and I will unsheathe the sword against you; your land shall be a desolation, and your cities a waste.

[34] Then the land shall enjoy[a] its sabbath years as long as it lies desolate, while you are in the land of your enemies; then the land shall rest, and enjoy[a] its sabbath years. [35] As long as it lies desolate, it shall have the rest it did not have on your sabbaths when you were living on it. [36] And as for those of you who survive, I will send faintness into their hearts in the lands of their enemies; the sound of a driven leaf shall put them to flight, and they shall flee as one flees from the sword, and they shall fall though no one pursues. [37] They shall stumble over one another, as if to escape a sword, though no one pursues; and you shall have no power to stand against your enemies. [38] You shall perish among the nations, and the land of your enemies shall devour you. [39] And those of you who survive

[a] Or *make up for*

35.11–12; Ex 6.2–8). **11:** The ultimate reward for obedience is the divine presence in Israel; cf. Ex 6.7; Jer 7.23; 30.22. **14–39:** Threats of successive punishments intended to ensure Israel's compliance. The punishments address the reverse topics mentioned in the rewards section. As in Deut 28 and Near Eastern treaties, rhetorical impact is heightened by focusing more on punishments than rewards. **31:** *Sanctuaries*, multiple sanctuaries are not endorsed but presented as evidence of disobedience (cf. v. 30; 17.3–4n.). **33–45:** These verses address exile, indicating that this chapter may have been written or edited after Babylonian conquest of Judah in 586 BCE. **34:**

shall languish in the land of your enemies because of their iniquities; also they shall languish because of the iniquities of their ancestors.

[40] But if they confess their iniquity and the iniquity of their ancestors, in that they committed treachery against me and, moreover, that they continued hostile to me— [41] so that I, in turn, continued hostile to them and brought them into the land of their enemies; if then their uncircumcised heart is humbled and they make amends for their iniquity, [42] then will I remember my covenant with Jacob; I will remember also my covenant with Isaac and also my covenant with Abraham, and I will remember the land. [43] For the land shall be deserted by them, and enjoy[a] its sabbath years by lying desolate without them, while they shall make amends for their iniquity, because they dared to spurn my ordinances, and they abhorred my statutes. [44] Yet for all that, when they are in the land of their enemies, I will not spurn them, or abhor them so as to destroy them utterly and break my covenant with them; for I am the LORD their God; [45] but I will remember in their favor the covenant with their ancestors whom I brought out of the land of Egypt in the sight of the nations, to be their God: I am the LORD.

[46] These are the statutes and ordinances and laws that the LORD established between himself and the people of Israel on Mount Sinai through Moses.

27

The LORD spoke to Moses, saying: [2] Speak to the people of Israel and say to them: When a person makes an explicit vow to the LORD concerning the equivalent for a human being, [3] the equivalent for a male shall be: from twenty to sixty years of age the equivalent shall be fifty shekels of

silver by the sanctuary shekel. [4] If the person is a female, the equivalent is thirty shekels. [5] If the age is from five to twenty years of age, the equivalent is twenty shekels for a male and ten shekels for a female. [6] If the age is from one month to five years, the equivalent for a male is five shekels of silver, and for a female the equivalent is three shekels of silver. [7] And if the person is sixty years old or over, then the equivalent for a male is fifteen shekels, and for a female ten shekels. [8] If any cannot afford the equivalent, they shall be brought before the priest and the priest shall assess them; the priest shall assess them according to what each one making a vow can afford.

[9] If it concerns an animal that may be brought as an offering to the LORD, any such that may be given to the LORD shall be holy. [10] Another shall not be exchanged or substituted for it, either good for bad or bad for good; and if one animal is substituted for another, both that one and its substitute shall be holy. [11] If it concerns any unclean animal that may not be brought as an offering to the LORD, the animal shall be presented before the priest. [12] The priest shall assess it: whether good or bad, according to the assessment of the priest, so it shall be. [13] But if it is to be redeemed, one-fifth must be added to the assessment.

[14] If a person consecrates a house to the LORD, the priest shall assess it: whether good or bad, as the priest assesses it, so it shall stand. [15] And if the one who consecrates the house wishes to redeem it, one-fifth shall be added to its assessed value, and it shall revert to the original owner.

a   Or make up for

Sabbath years, cf. 25.2–7; 2 Chr 36.21. 40–45: Those who remain and repent will be restored, for God's commitment to Israel is unmoved. This was likely a particularly meaningful promise to the exiles. 46: Concluding summary to chs 1–26 (cf. 27.34). On Mount Sinai, better, "at Mount Sinai" (see 7.38n.).

27.1–34: Vows, dedications, and tithes. This chapter is a later addition to Leviticus, inserted as an appendix. Its author(s) attempted to integrate it into the book by repeating the concluding summary from 26.46 in 27.34. 2–13: Procedures for vows of persons and animals; cf. Num 30.1–16. Vows are promised gifts to God in exchange for divine favor. In the case of vows of humans (oneself or another), an equivalent monetary gift is presented in lieu of human sacrifice. Calculations are made according to the vowed person's socioeconomic worth. 3: A shekel weighed about .4 oz (11.4 gr). 9–10: Sacrificeable animals offered as vows are viewed as the deity's food and are thus holy. 11–12: Nonsacrificeable animals vowed to God are intended to be sold by the sanctuary according to their valuation. 13: One-fifth, cf. 5.16; 6.5. 14–24: Dedications of houses, ancestral land, and non-

[16] If a person consecrates to the LORD any inherited landholding, its assessment shall be in accordance with its seed requirements: fifty shekels of silver to a homer of barley seed. [17] If the person consecrates the field as of the year of jubilee, that assessment shall stand; [18] but if the field is consecrated after the jubilee, the priest shall compute the price for it according to the years that remain until the year of jubilee, and the assessment shall be reduced. [19] And if the one who consecrates the field wishes to redeem it, then one-fifth shall be added to its assessed value, and it shall revert to the original owner; [20] but if the field is not redeemed, or if it has been sold to someone else, it shall no longer be redeemable. [21] But when the field is released in the jubilee, it shall be holy to the LORD as a devoted field; it becomes the priest's holding. [22] If someone consecrates to the LORD a field that has been purchased, which is not a part of the inherited landholding, [23] the priest shall compute for it the proportionate assessment up to the year of jubilee, and the assessment shall be paid as of that day, a sacred donation to the LORD. [24] In the year of jubilee the field shall return to the one from whom it was bought, whose holding the land is. [25] All assessments shall be by the sanctuary shekel: twenty gerahs shall make a shekel.

[26] A firstling of animals, however, which as a firstling belongs to the LORD, cannot be consecrated by anyone; whether ox or sheep, it is the LORD's. [27] If it is an unclean animal, it shall be ransomed at its assessment, with one-fifth added; if it is not redeemed, it shall be sold at its assessment.

[28] Nothing that a person owns that has been devoted to destruction for the LORD, be it human or animal, or inherited landholding, may be sold or redeemed; every devoted thing is most holy to the LORD. [29] No human beings who have been devoted to destruction can be ransomed; they shall be put to death.

[30] All tithes from the land, whether the seed from the ground or the fruit from the tree, are the LORD's; they are holy to the LORD. [31] If persons wish to redeem any of their tithes, they must add one-fifth to them. [32] All tithes of herd and flock, every tenth one that passes under the shepherd's staff, shall be holy to the LORD. [33] Let no one inquire whether it is good or bad, or make substitution for it; if one makes substitution for it, then both it and the substitute shall be holy and cannot be redeemed.

[34] These are the commandments that the LORD gave to Moses for the people of Israel on Mount Sinai.

---

ancestral land. Valuations of land are accounted according to the jubilee calendar (cf. 25.13–17n.). **16:** A *homer* was about 6.5 bushels (230 l). **26–27:** Firstborn animals already belong to God (Ex 13.1–2,12; 22.29–30; 34.19; Num 3.40–51; 18.17; Deut 15.19–20) and therefore cannot be dedicated or vowed. *It shall be ransomed*, better, "It may be ransomed"; cf. Num 18.15. **28:** *Devoted to destruction*, a type of dedication found mostly in biblical war texts (e.g., Num 21.2; Deut 2.34; 3.6; 7.2; Josh 6.17–21; 8.26; 10.1,28; 1 Sam 15) and in the Moabite Mesha Inscription. Here, such dedication (Heb "ḥerem") is applied to one's own property. **30–33:** Tithes (cf. Num 18.20–32; Deut 14.22–29; 26.12). This is the only occurrence of an animal tithe in Pentateuchal law, but see Gen 14.20; 28.22; 1 Sam 8.15–17; 2 Chr 31.5–6. **34:** A variation on the conclusion in 26.46.

NUMBERS

NAME AND LOCATION IN CANON

Numbers is the fourth of the five books of the Pentateuch. Its narrative tells the story of Israel's journey from the final stages of the stay at Mount Sinai through the wilderness to the eastern border of the promised land of Canaan. The English title, "Numbers," derived from the Greek (*Arithmoi*) and Latin (*Numeri*) translations, is based on its census lists (chs 1; 26). In early Jewish tradition, it is called "The Fifth of the Census," based on its opening theme; later, it was known by its first significant Hebrew word, *bemidbar*, "In the wilderness (of)."

AUTHORSHIP, DATES OF COMPOSITION, AND LITERARY HISTORY

The issue of authorship is part of the larger question pertaining to the Pentateuch (see pp. 3–6). Moses was traditionally considered its author. Biblical scholars have now come to view the Pentateuch as a work of many authors and editors from various periods of Israel's history.

The origin of Numbers is disputed and difficult to discern. The book itself speaks of sources: the "Book of the Wars of the LORD" (21.14) and popular songs (21.17–18,27–30). The tradition most identifiable is the Priestly (P) writing, with its interest in matters of worship and the priesthood of Aaron and his descendants; it is most attested in chs 1–10; 26–36. Other sources, such as J and E (esp. in chs 11–25), are more difficult to discern; scholars often speak simply of combined JE or a non-Priestly stratum. Earlier scholars called this an "epic tradition," even though it is not certain that it originally had the form of a poetic epic. The association of texts with three primary locales (Sinai: 1.1–10.10; Kadesh: chs 13–20; Moab: chs 22–36) could reflect a way in which traditions were gathered over time. Editorial activity, combining these disparate materials, is unusually frequent.

Scholars have also studied individual traditions and their development, such as the Balaam cycle, the murmuring stories, the censuses, the wilderness encampment, the Transjordan conquest, the cities of refuge, land apportionment, and the priesthood. This research shows that various Israelite interests from different settings underlie the present text. These traditions have been brought together, most likely during and after the exile to Babylon in the early sixth century BCE, to form a single composition.

STRUCTURE AND CONTENTS

The complex character of Numbers is evident in the genres it includes: lists, itineraries, statutes, ritual and priestly prescriptions, poetic oracles, songs, wilderness stories, and even a well-known benediction (6.22–27). The interweaving of law and narrative characteristic of the books of Exodus through Deuteronomy is most evident in Numbers; statutes regularly emerge from specific situations, revealing a dynamic relationship of law and life.

Moreover, several texts border on the bizarre, with talking donkeys, curses from a non-Israelite diviner turned into blessings with messianic implications, the earth swallowing up people, copper snakes with healing powers, an almond-producing rod, an execution for picking up sticks on the sabbath, Miriam turning leprous, and anomalous procedures for discerning a wife's faithlessness. Might these unusual goings-on have been constructed to match the incredible character of Israel's response to God? Moreover, God is often depicted in ways that challenge traditional understandings.

The structure of Numbers is best seen from two angles:

1. *The census lists*. The book's overarching structure is laid out in terms of two census lists (chs 1; 26). The first registers the generation of the Exodus and Sinai prepared to move toward the promised land. When faced with dangers, however, they do not trust the promise; they experience God's judgment (14.32–33) and finally, in the wake of apostasy, die off in a plague (25.9). Even Moses and Aaron mistrust God and are prohibited from entering the land (20.12); only the faithful scouts, Caleb and Joshua, and the young (14.29) are allowed to do so. The oracles of Balaam (chs 22–24) provide a positive sign, as God blesses the insiders through this outsider.

   The second census (ch 26) lists the members of the new generation. They signal God's continuing faithfulness to ancestral promises and to those who will enter the land. The following texts (chs 27–36) deal with issues regarding that future. No deaths, murmurings, or rebellions against the leadership are narrated, while hopeful signs are presented.

2. *The geography of a journey toward the promised land*, with all the problems encountered along the way in spite of careful preparations. The itinerary of 33.2–49, toward the book's conclusion, offers a detailed itinerary of that journey.

A. Numbers begins with the people preparing to leave Sinai (1.1–10.10). That includes the camp's organization and various statutes, especially regarding the sanctuary and its leadership. An idealized picture emerges: a community ordered in all ways appropriate to God's dwelling in the center of the camp and the precise obedience to every divine command (e.g., 1.17–19,54). The reader may wonder how anything could go wrong.

B. In episodic fashion, Israel moves through the wilderness from Sinai to Transjordan (10.11–25.18). The disjunction of the opening and closing chapters of this section is remarkable: obedience turns to rebellion; trust becomes mistrust; the holy is profaned; order becomes disorder; the future of God's people is threatened. Continuities with the wilderness stories in Ex 15.22–19.1 are seen in the gifts of quail and manna, the ongoing complaints, and military victory; but discontinuities are also sharp, evident especially in sin and judgment. Integrated with the journey reports are various statutes (15; 18; 19), focused on purification and leadership support, the need for which grows out of these experiences.

C. The journey concludes in the plains of Moab (26.1–36.13), an entirely positive stage. Conflicts are resolved through negotiation and compromise and land begins to be settled. Various statutes anticipate a future in the land; the community is to order its life so that this dwelling place of both God and people is not ritually polluted.

These three stages may also be characterized in terms of Israel's changing relationship with God, moving from fidelity to unfaithfulness and back. Through all these developments, God remains faithful to the unconditional ancestral promises. Though Israel's journey involves judgment, that judgment finally serves God's objectives of blessing.

INTERPRETATION

Such portrayals of a journey mirror the situation of the implied readers, especially if this book was compiled in the Babylonian exile. Israel's apostasy and experience of judgment lie in their recent past; signs of a hopeful future are articulated in both law and promise. The paradigm of old generation and new generation would be pertinent both for the years of exile as well as for the uncertainties of the postexilic period. Certain themes provide compass points for navigating the journey through Numbers:

1. *A wilderness book*. The entire book is set in the wilderness. This setting presents problems and possibilities for shaping a community identity for the newly redeemed people of God. As a long-oppressed community, Israel has a deeply ingrained identity as "slaves." It does not have the resources to move quickly to a "slaves no more" (Lev 26.13) mentality; God must be at work to enable them to "walk erect" once again. For the purpose of forming such a new identity, the period of wandering is a necessary buffer between liberation from Egypt and residence in the new land. Such a process does not unfold easily for Israel or for God; even the most meticulous preparations do not make things go right.

Israel's time in the wilderness is shaped by God's extraordinary patience and mercy, and the divine will to stay with Israel in this time of adolescence. If God wants a mature child, defiance must be risked. It soon becomes clear that the maturation process will take longer than a single generation.

2. *Ancestral promises*. God is committed to the ancestral promise of the gift of the land. As Israel moves out from Sinai, the goal is the land God is "giving" (10.29, and often). Conditions regarding the promise of the land are expressed (14.8), but they affect the future of individuals—even an entire generation—not Israel as such. Beyond that, Balaam's oracles ironically gather the clearest references to promises in Numbers; no Israelite, including Moses, has standing enough left to bring them to expression.

The middle section (chs 11–25) reveals the complexities and the problems in the movement toward fulfillment; the wilderness is a time of endangered promises. Again and again the people trust the deceptive securities of the past more than God's promised future (11.5; 21.5). Hence, they experience disasters of various kinds that threaten progress toward the goal, including plagues (11.33; 16.49), abortive conquest (chs 13–14), and snake infestation (21.6).

The final section (chs 26–36), with the new generation in place, expresses confidence in the promise with the apportionment of lands and the specification of boundaries. Initial settlements in Transjordan initiate the fulfillment of the promise. Moreover, various laws dealing with emerging issues constitute a hopeful sign in the midst of much failure and grief: a community will exist to obey them.

3. *Divine presence and guidance*. God, not Moses, has birthed this people (11.12) and chosen to stay with them and to dwell in the heart of their camp (5.3). From this womblike center blessings flow out into the encircled community. This intense kind of presence is promised for Israel's future in the land as well (35.34), as even Balaam testifies (23.21–22).

Because of the presence of God in Israel's midst in the tabernacle, it was to be protected from casual contact. The tribe of Levi was consecrated for tabernacle service and made responsible for guarding this holy place (1.50–53). Sharp warnings about intrusion are issued (1.51–53; 3.10,38), even for Levites (4.17–20). Strikingly, encroachment is not a serious problem in the subsequent narratives (see ch 16). The more problematic issue is mistrust and rebellion with respect to God and God's chosen leaders. These forms of sinfulness pervade chs 11–25, deeply affecting the character of the journey and the shape of Israel's future.

Israel's God not only dwells in the midst of Israel, but also goes before them. The accompanying presence of God is marked by the pillar of cloud and fire (9.15–23). This symbol is linked to the ark of the covenant, representing God's presence (10.35–36). God's ongoing presence is the decisive factor in Israel's journey, but various texts witness also to the import of human leaders (e.g., 10.29–32). God works in and through what is available, even characters like Balaam.

4. *Divine revelation and human leadership*. Revelation is not confined to Sinai; it occurs throughout Israel's journey. Statutes and other divine words newly enjoin Israel all along the way. God's word is a dynamic reality, intersecting with life and all of its contingencies. This is demonstrated in the very form of this material, interweaving law and narrative. God's word is usually mediated through Moses, but not uniquely so. This becomes an issue during the journey. Challenges to Moses' (and Aaron's) leadership that began before Sinai are intensified and other leaders take up the argument.

This issue is voiced most sharply by Miriam and Aaron: Has God spoken only through Moses? (12.2). The response is negative. God's spirit even rests upon the outsider Balaam who mediates remarkably clear words of God (24.2–4,15–16). Yet Moses does have a special relationship with God and challenges to his role are not countenanced.

God often communicates to and through Moses; indeed, 7.89 speaks of Moses' contact with God as routine. In 12.8 Moses actually "beholds the form of the LORD" and lives to report it. One facet of this relationship is especially remarkable: the genuine give-and-take between them as they engage issues confronting the wandering community. This interaction says something about both Moses and God. Moses' leadership credentials are considerable, including a capacity to tolerate threats to his authority (11.29) and to persevere with God (chs 11; 14; 16), calling forth the strong statement regarding his unique devotion (12.3). God also is remarkably open to such discourse and honors Moses' insights. Indeed, God may shape a different future in view of the encounter (14.13–20; 16.20–22). But such divine openness to change will always be in the service of God's unchanging goals for Israel and the creation (Balaam's point in 23.19).

Some disputes are focused on Aaron (and his sons) and their priestly leadership (chs 16; 17). Actual tests are carried out, which substantiate their unique role with respect to the sanctuary. Members of this family also assume an intercessory function; they "stand between the dead and the living" and a plague is averted (16.47–50; see 25.7–13). This correlates with their mediating role in various rituals (chs 5; 15). Interest in the proper succession of leaders (Eleazar: 20.22–29; Joshua: 27.12–23) demonstrates their importance for the stability of the community. Rebellion against God-chosen leaders is subversive of God's intentions for the community and risks death. But the leaders themselves are not exempt from strict standards (20.10–12).

5. *Holy people and holy priests*. The call in Leviticus for the people to be holy is continued here (15.40). What constitutes a holy life, or is inimical to it, is central. Various uncleannesses—whether moral or ritual—are incompatible with holiness (chs 5; 6).

A case for more democratic forms of priestly leadership is pursued by Korah on the basis of the holiness of all (16.3). Moses' reply assumes gradations of holiness; even if all are holy, God chooses certain persons to exercise priestly leadership, and this status constitutes a holiness that sets them apart from other holy ones. The disaster experienced by Korah and his company (16.23–35) demonstrates the special status of Aaron's family (16.40), as does the test with staffs (ch 17).

Gradations of holiness are also evident within the members of the tribe of Levi. The Levites are set aside to care for the tabernacle, symbolized by their encampment between tabernacle and people. Among the Levites the family of Aaron is set aside for priestly duties (16.40; 17; 18.7–11,19). Indeed, a "covenant of perpetual priesthood" is made with this family because of the mediating actions of Phinehas (25.10–13). Specific groups of Aaron's descendants are differentiated based on their roles of caring for the tabernacle; for example, the family of Kohath alone is responsible for the "the most holy things" (4.1–20).

GUIDE TO READING

When first reading the book, one might begin with the main narrative (chs 1; 10–14; 16–17; 20–27; 31–33). The legal sections may best be read according to different topics: the Levites (chs 3–4; 7–8; 18; 35); priestly and levitical duties (chs 3–4; 16–17; 18; 35); the arrangement of the camp (chs 2–3; 10); laws pertaining to women (ch 5; 27.1–11; 30; 36); holy days (9.1–14; 15.32–36; 28–29); impurity and holiness (5.1–4; 6; 16–17; 19; 35); sacrifices and offerings (chs 7; 15; 28–29); and distribution of the land (27.1–11; 32; 34–36). Numbers also contains poetic passages (6.24–26; 10.35–36; 20.14–15,17–18, 27–30; 23.7–10,18–24; 24.3–9,15–24), which might be studied together and in connection with the style of the Psalms.

Terence E. Fretheim

1 The LORD spoke to Moses in the wilderness of Sinai, in the tent of meeting, on the first day of the second month, in the second year after they had come out of the land of Egypt, saying: ² Take a census of the whole congregation of Israelites, in their clans, by ancestral houses, according to the number of names, every male individually; ³ from twenty years old and upward, everyone in Israel able to go to war. You and Aaron shall enroll them, company by company. ⁴ A man from each tribe shall be with you, each man the head of his ancestral house. ⁵ These are the names of the men who shall assist you:

From Reuben, Elizur son of Shedeur.

⁶ From Simeon, Shelumiel son of Zurishaddai.
⁷ From Judah, Nahshon son of Amminadab.
⁸ From Issachar, Nethanel son of Zuar.
⁹ From Zebulun, Eliab son of Helon.
¹⁰ From the sons of Joseph:
from Ephraim, Elishama son of Ammihud;
from Manasseh, Gamaliel son of Pedahzur.
¹¹ From Benjamin, Abidan son of Gideoni.
¹² From Dan, Ahiezer son of Ammishaddai.
¹³ From Asher, Pagiel son of Ochran.
¹⁴ From Gad, Eliasaph son of Deuel.
¹⁵ From Naphtali, Ahira son of Enan.
¹⁶ These were the ones chosen from the congregation, the leaders of their ancestral tribes, the heads of the divisions of Israel.

1.1–10.10: Israel prepares to leave Sinai for the promised land. This task includes the organization of the camp and various statutes, especially regarding the sanctuary and its leadership.

1.1–54: The first census of the tribes. Moses is commanded to conduct a census of each tribe. **1:** The census (see Ex 38.26) occurs one month after the completion of the tabernacle, here called *the tent of meeting* (Ex 40.17; compare Ex 33.7–11), shortly before the departure from Sinai (10.11), where Israel had been for almost a year (Ex 19.1). **2–3:** The *census* is of males twenty years and older; and seeks to determine those *able to go to war*. Each tribe was divided into *clans*, which included several *ancestral houses* (family groups). **4–16:** God names *a man from each tribe, . . . head of his ancestral house*, to assist Moses. Most of the individuals named do not occur elsewhere in the Bible outside of the book of Numbers (see also chs 2; 7; 10). The tribe of Levi is omitted, and the tribe of Joseph is subdivided into Ephraim and Manasseh (see Gen 48), thus keeping the number of the tribes at

¹⁷ Moses and Aaron took these men who had been designated by name, ¹⁸ and on the first day of the second month they assembled the whole congregation together. They registered themselves in their clans, by their ancestral houses, according to the number of names from twenty years old and upward, individually, ¹⁹ as the LORD commanded Moses. So he enrolled them in the wilderness of Sinai.

²⁰ The descendants of Reuben, Israel's firstborn, their lineage, in their clans, by their ancestral houses, according to the number of names, individually, every male from twenty years old and upward, everyone able to go to war: ²¹ those enrolled of the tribe of Reuben were forty-six thousand five hundred.

²² The descendants of Simeon, their lineage, in their clans, by their ancestral houses, those of them that were numbered, according to the number of names, individually, every male from twenty years old and upward, everyone able to go to war: ²³ those enrolled of the tribe of Simeon were fifty-nine thousand three hundred.

²⁴ The descendants of Gad, their lineage, in their clans, by their ancestral houses, according to the number of the names, from twenty years old and upward, everyone able to go to war: ²⁵ those enrolled of the tribe of Gad were forty-five thousand six hundred fifty.

²⁶ The descendants of Judah, their lineage, in their clans, by their ancestral houses, according to the number of names, from twenty years old and upward, everyone able to go to war: ²⁷ those enrolled of the tribe of Judah were seventy-four thousand six hundred.

²⁸ The descendants of Issachar, their lineage, in their clans, by their ancestral houses, according to the number of names, from twenty years old and upward, everyone able to go to war: ²⁹ those enrolled of the tribe of Issachar were fifty-four thousand four hundred.

³⁰ The descendants of Zebulun, their lineage, in their clans, by their ancestral houses, according to the number of names, from twenty years old and upward, everyone able to go to war: ³¹ those enrolled of the tribe

of Zebulun were fifty-seven thousand four hundred.

³² The descendants of Joseph, namely, the descendants of Ephraim, their lineage, in their clans, by their ancestral houses, according to the number of names, from twenty years old and upward, everyone able to go to war: ³³ those enrolled of the tribe of Ephraim were forty thousand five hundred.

³⁴ The descendants of Manasseh, their lineage, in their clans, by their ancestral houses, according to the number of names, from twenty years old and upward, everyone able to go to war: ³⁵ those enrolled of the tribe of Manasseh were thirty-two thousand two hundred.

³⁶ The descendants of Benjamin, their lineage, in their clans, by their ancestral houses, according to the number of names, from twenty years old and upward, everyone able to go to war: ³⁷ those enrolled of the tribe of Benjamin were thirty-five thousand four hundred.

³⁸ The descendants of Dan, their lineage, in their clans, by their ancestral houses, according to the number of names, from twenty years old and upward, everyone able to go to war: ³⁹ those enrolled of the tribe of Dan were sixty-two thousand seven hundred.

⁴⁰ The descendants of Asher, their lineage, in their clans, by their ancestral houses, according to the number of names, from twenty years old and upward, everyone able to go to war: ⁴¹ those enrolled of the tribe of Asher were forty-one thousand five hundred.

⁴² The descendants of Naphtali, their lineage, in their clans, by their ancestral houses, according to the number of names, from twenty years old and upward, everyone able to go to war: ⁴³ those enrolled of the tribe of Naphtali were fifty-three thousand four hundred.

⁴⁴ These are those who were enrolled, whom Moses and Aaron enrolled with the help of the leaders of Israel, twelve men, each representing his ancestral house. ⁴⁵ So the whole number of the Israelites, by their ancestral houses, from twenty years old and upward, everyone able to go to war in Israel— ⁴⁶ their whole number was six hun-

twelve. Having a name on this list assured each tribal group of their present identity. 17–46: The census. 27: The largest tribe is Judah, probably because of its importance to the author. 46: The results of the census: 603,550

dred three thousand five hundred fifty. [47] The Levites, however, were not numbered by their ancestral tribe along with them.

[48] The LORD had said to Moses: [49] Only the tribe of Levi you shall not enroll, and you shall not take a census of them with the other Israelites. [50] Rather you shall appoint the Levites over the tabernacle of the covenant,[a] and over all its equipment, and over all that belongs to it; they are to carry the tabernacle and all its equipment, and they shall tend it, and shall camp around the tabernacle. [51] When the tabernacle is to set out, the Levites shall take it down; and when the tabernacle is to be pitched, the Levites shall set it up. And any outsider who comes near shall be put to death. [52] The other Israelites shall camp in their respective regimental camps, by companies; [53] but the Levites shall camp around the tabernacle of the covenant,[a] that there may be no wrath on the congregation of the Israelites; and the Levites shall perform the guard duty of the tabernacle of the covenant.[a] [54] The Israelites did so; they did just as the LORD commanded Moses.

2 The LORD spoke to Moses and Aaron, saying: [2] The Israelites shall camp each in their respective regiments, under ensigns by their ancestral houses; they shall camp facing the tent of meeting on every side. [3] Those

to camp on the east side toward the sunrise shall be of the regimental encampment of Judah by companies. The leader of the people of Judah shall be Nahshon son of Amminadab, [4] with a company as enrolled of seventy-four thousand six hundred. [5] Those to camp next to him shall be the tribe of Issachar. The leader of the Issacharites shall be Nethanel son of Zuar, [6] with a company as enrolled of fifty-four thousand four hundred. [7] Then the tribe of Zebulun: The leader of the Zebulunites shall be Eliab son of Helon, [8] with a company as enrolled of fifty-seven thousand four hundred. [9] The total enrollment of the camp of Judah, by companies, is one hundred eighty-six thousand four hundred. They shall set out first on the march.

[10] On the south side shall be the regimental encampment of Reuben by companies. The leader of the Reubenites shall be Elizur son of Shedeur, [11] with a company as enrolled of forty-six thousand five hundred. [12] And those to camp next to him shall be the tribe of Simeon. The leader of the Simeonites shall be Shelumiel son of Zurishaddai, [13] with a company as enrolled of fifty-nine thousand three hundred. [14] Then the tribe of Gad: The leader of the Gadites shall be Eliasaph son of Reuel, [15] with a company as enrolled of forty-five

---

a   Or *treaty*, or *testimony*; Heb *eduth*

males (see 11.21; Ex 12.37); the second census yields 601,730 (26.51). When women, children, and Levites are added, the total is well over two million. This impossibly high number testifies to God's blessing this people, keeping promises. At the same time, this generation will prove unfaithful and will die off in the wilderness (see 14.22–30; 26.65). **47–54:** The Levites, who do not bear arms and are not registered here, are given duties regarding the tabernacle (chs 3–4). They are charged to encamp around it, protect it from casual contact, maintain it, carry it during the journey, and pitch it at each stop. The rare phrase, *tabernacle of the covenant* (vv. 50,53; 10.11; Ex 38.21), extends the designation for its major sacred object, the ark of the covenant. **51:** The *outsider* refers to non-Levites, Israelite or alien (see 16.40). The sense of *comes near* is encroach; the encroacher is executed on the spot by levitical guards (see 18.7). **53:** This action is in the interests of the community, so that it not experience the *wrath* of God, which may cause death, often through a plague (16.46–50; 31.16). These strict measures are instituted to preserve a proper relationship between God and the people. **54:** Throughout chs 1–9, the Israelites are reported to have done exactly as God commanded. Later failures cannot be blamed on faulty preparations.

2.1–34: The tribal arrangement around the tabernacle. With the *tent of meeting* (the tabernacle) centered in the camp, and the *Levites* camped immediately around it (2.17; see ch 3), God commands that the tribes be precisely ordered around the perimeter. They are to be ordered as *companies* (or *regiments*, 2.17,34), specifying military readiness. Three tribes are to be positioned at each side of the tent, under their distinctive banners; each triad named for the dominant tribe of the three from the perspective of Israel's later history, which is flanked by the other two tribes in each case—*the regimental encampment of Judah* (v. 3; the most dominant; see 1.27n.) to the east; Reuben to the south; Ephraim to the west; Dan to the north. This order of the tribes is

thousand six hundred fifty. ¹⁶ The total enrollment of the camp of Reuben, by companies, is one hundred fifty-one thousand four hundred fifty. They shall set out second.

¹⁷ The tent of meeting, with the camp of the Levites, shall set out in the center of the camps; they shall set out just as they camp, each in position, by their regiments.

¹⁸ On the west side shall be the regimental encampment of Ephraim by companies. The leader of the people of Ephraim shall be Elishama son of Ammihud, ¹⁹ with a company as enrolled of forty thousand five hundred. ²⁰ Next to him shall be the tribe of Manasseh. The leader of the people of Manasseh shall be Gamaliel son of Pedahzur, ²¹ with a company as enrolled of thirty-two thousand two hundred. ²² Then the tribe of Benjamin: The leader of the Benjaminites shall be Abidan son of Gideoni, ²³ with a company as enrolled of thirty-five thousand four hundred. ²⁴ The total enrollment of the camp of Ephraim, by companies, is one hundred eight thousand one hundred. They shall set out third on the march.

²⁵ On the north side shall be the regimental encampment of Dan by companies. The leader of the Danites shall be Ahiezer son of Ammishaddai, ²⁶ with a company as enrolled of sixty-two thousand seven hundred. ²⁷ Those to camp next to him shall be the tribe of Asher. The leader of the Asherites shall be Pagiel son of Ochran, ²⁸ with a company as enrolled of forty-one thousand five hundred. ²⁹ Then the tribe of Naphtali: The leader of the Naphtalites shall be Ahira son of Enan, ³⁰ with a company as enrolled of fifty-three thousand four hundred. ³¹ The total enrollment of the camp of Dan is one hundred fifty-seven thousand six hundred. They shall set out last, by companies.ᵃ

³² This was the enrollment of the Israelites by their ancestral houses; the total enrollment in the camps by their companies was six hundred three thousand five hundred fifty. ³³ Just as the LORD had commanded Moses, the Levites were not enrolled among the other Israelites.

³⁴ The Israelites did just as the LORD had commanded Moses: They camped by regiments, and they set out the same way, everyone by clans, according to ancestral houses.

3 This is the lineage of Aaron and Moses at the time when the LORD spoke with Moses on Mount Sinai. ² These are the names of the sons of Aaron: Nadab the firstborn, and Abihu, Eleazar, and Ithamar; ³ these are the names of the sons of Aaron, the anointed priests, whom he ordained to minister as priests. ⁴ Nadab and Abihu died before the LORD when they offered unholy fire before the LORD in the wilderness of Sinai, and they had no children. Eleazar and Ithamar served as priests in the lifetime of their father Aaron.

⁵ Then the LORD spoke to Moses, saying: ⁶ Bring the tribe of Levi near, and set them before Aaron the priest, so that they may assist him. ⁷ They shall perform duties for him and for the whole congregation in front of the tent of meeting, doing service at the tabernacle; ⁸ they shall be in charge of all the furnishings of the tent of meeting, and attend to the duties for the Israelites as they do service at the tabernacle. ⁹ You shall give the Levites to Aaron and his descendants; they are unreservedly given to him from among the Israelites. ¹⁰ But you shall make a register of Aaron and his descendants; it is they who shall attend to the priesthood, and any outsider who comes near shall be put to death.

¹¹ Then the LORD spoke to Moses, saying: ¹² I hereby accept the Levites from among the Israelites as substitutes for all the firstborn that open the womb among the Israelites.

ᵃ Compare verses 9, 16, 24: Heb *by their regiments*

the order for the march, beginning with Judah (see 10.14–28). **17:** The tent, transported by Levites, is to move between the camps of Reuben and Ephraim. **34:** God's commands are again followed.

3.1–4.49: The Levites are set apart; organization and responsibilities. 3.1: The formula links Moses and Aaron with the genealogies in Genesis (the last is Gen 37.2; see Ex 6.23–25). **3–4:** Moses (*he*) ordains the two remaining sons of Aaron, *Eleazar and Ithamar* (Lev 8.30). On Nadab and Abihu, see Lev 10.1–20. **5–10:** A distinction is made within the tribe of Levi between descendants of Aaron, who attend to priestly duties, and other Levites, who assist the priests, with responsibilities for *service at the tabernacle* (see 1.50–53). **11–13:** Restated in 8.16–18, recalls the sparing of Israel's firstborn (Ex 13.1–2,11–15), in remembrance of which God had consecrated them;

The Levites shall be mine, [13] for all the first-born are mine; when I killed all the firstborn in the land of Egypt, I consecrated for my own all the firstborn in Israel, both human and animal; they shall be mine. I am the LORD.

[14] Then the LORD spoke to Moses in the wilderness of Sinai, saying: [15] Enroll the Levites by ancestral houses and by clans. You shall enroll every male from a month old and upward. [16] So Moses enrolled them according to the word of the LORD, as he was command-ed. [17] The following were the sons of Levi, by their names: Gershon, Kohath, and Merari. [18] These are the names of the sons of Ger-shon by their clans: Libni and Shimei. [19] The sons of Kohath by their clans: Amram, Izhar, Hebron, and Uzziel. [20] The sons of Merari by their clans: Mahli and Mushi. These are the clans of the Levites, by their ancestral houses.

[21] To Gershon belonged the clan of the Libnites and the clan of the Shimeites; these were the clans of the Gershonites. [22] Their enrollment, counting all the males from a month old and upward, was seven thousand five hundred. [23] The clans of the Gershonites were to camp behind the tabernacle on the west, [24] with Eliasaph son of Lael as head of the ancestral house of the Gershonites. [25] The responsibility of the sons of Gershon in the tent of meeting was to be the tabernacle, the tent with its covering, the screen for the entrance of the tent of meeting, [26] the hang-ings of the court, the screen for the entrance of the court that is around the tabernacle and the altar, and its cords—all the service pertaining to these.

[27] To Kohath belonged the clan of the Am-ramites, the clan of the Izharites, the clan of the Hebronites, and the clan of the Uzzielites; these are the clans of the Kohathites. [28] Counting all the males, from a month old and upward, there were eight thousand six hundred, attending to the duties of the sanctuary. [29] The clans of the Kohathites were to camp on the south side of the tabernacle, [30] with Elizaphan son of Uzziel as head of the ancestral house of the clans of the Kohathites. [31] Their responsibility was to be the ark, the table, the lampstand, the altars, the vessels of the sanctuary with which the priests minister, and the screen—all the service pertaining to these. [32] Eleazar son of Aaron the priest was to be chief over the leaders of the Levites, and to have oversight of those who had charge of the sanctuary.

[33] To Merari belonged the clan of the Mahlites and the clan of the Mushites: these are the clans of Merari. [34] Their enrollment, counting all the males from a month old and upward, was six thousand two hundred. [35] The head of the ancestral house of the clans of Merari was Zuriel son of Abihail; they were to camp on the north side of the tabernacle. [36] The responsibility assigned to the sons of Merari was to be the frames of the tabernacle, the bars, the pillars, the bases, and all their accessories—all the service pertaining to these; [37] also the pillars of the court all around, with their bases and pegs and cords.

[38] Those who were to camp in front of the tabernacle on the east—in front of the tent of meeting toward the east—were Moses and Aaron and Aaron's sons, having charge of the rites within the sanctuary, whatever had to be done for the Israelites; and any outsider who came near was to be put to death. [39] The total enrollment of the Levites whom Moses and Aaron enrolled at the commandment of the LORD, by their clans, all the males from a month old and upward, was twenty-two thousand.

[40] Then the LORD said to Moses: Enroll all the firstborn males of the Israelites, from

the Levites serve in their stead as representatives of all Israel. **14–39:** Continues the narrative from 2.34, describ-ing a census of the non-Aaronide *Levites* (actual total: 22,300; see 3.39), their encampment positions, and their nonmilitary responsibilities (see 1.47–49). Their camp is ordered in terms of Levi's sons; their clans encamp on three sides of the tabernacle and have varying duties with respect to its transit. **25–37:** The Kohathites (Moses and Aaron are descendants of Kohath; Ex 6.18–20) are responsible for the most sacred objects, the Gershonites for the fabrics, and the Merarites for the supporting structures (detailed in 4.1–33; for the objects, see Ex 25–30). **38:** Aaron and his sons are preeminent, encamping on the entrance (eastern) side of the tabernacle. Aaron's son, Eleazar, is in charge of the leaders of the three clans (3.32) and has general oversight of the tabernacle

a month old and upward, and count their names. [41] But you shall accept the Levites for me—I am the LORD—as substitutes for all the firstborn among the Israelites, and the livestock of the Levites as substitutes for all the firstborn among the livestock of the Israelites. [42] So Moses enrolled all the firstborn among the Israelites, as the LORD commanded him. [43] The total enrollment, all the firstborn males from a month old and upward, counting the number of names, was twenty-two thousand two hundred seventy-three.

[44] Then the LORD spoke to Moses, saying: [45] Accept the Levites as substitutes for all the firstborn among the Israelites, and the livestock of the Levites as substitutes for their livestock; and the Levites shall be mine. I am the LORD. [46] As the price of redemption of the two hundred seventy-three of the firstborn of the Israelites, over and above the number of the Levites, [47] you shall accept five shekels apiece, reckoning by the shekel of the sanctuary, a shekel of twenty gerahs. [48] Give to Aaron and his sons the money by which the excess number of them is redeemed. [49] So Moses took the redemption money from those who were over and above those redeemed by the Levites; [50] from the firstborn of the Israelites he took the money, one thousand three hundred sixty-five shekels, reckoned by the shekel of the sanctuary; [51] and Moses gave the redemption money to Aaron and his sons, according to the word of the LORD, as the LORD had commanded Moses.

4 The LORD spoke to Moses and Aaron, saying: [2] Take a census of the Kohathites separate from the other Levites, by their clans and their ancestral houses, [3] from thirty years old up to fifty years old, all who qualify to do work relating to the tent of meeting. [4] The service of the Kohathites relating to the tent of meeting concerns the most holy things.

[5] When the camp is to set out, Aaron and his sons shall go in and take down the screening curtain, and cover the ark of the covenant[a] with it; [6] then they shall put on it a covering of fine leather,[b] and spread over that a cloth all of blue, and shall put its poles in place. [7] Over the table of the bread of the Presence they shall spread a blue cloth, and put on it the plates, the dishes for incense, the bowls, and the flagons for the drink offering; the regular bread also shall be on it; [8] then they shall spread over them a crimson cloth, and cover it with a covering of fine leather,[b] and shall put its poles in place. [9] They shall take a blue cloth, and cover the lampstand for the light, with its lamps, its snuffers, its trays, and all the vessels for oil with which it is supplied; [10] and they shall put it with all its utensils in a covering of fine leather,[b] and put it on the carrying frame. [11] Over the golden altar they shall spread a blue cloth, and cover it with a covering of fine leather,[b] and shall put its poles in place; [12] and they shall take all the utensils of the service that are used in the sanctuary, and put them in a blue cloth, and cover them with a covering of fine leather,[b] and put them on the carrying frame. [13] They shall take away the ashes from the altar, and spread a purple cloth over it; [14] and they shall

---

a Or *treaty*, or *testimony*; Heb *eduth*
b Meaning of Heb uncertain

(4.16), his brother Ithamar over the work of the Gershonites and Merarites (4.28,33). **40–51:** The *firstborn males* of Israel are numbered; see 3.11–13. **43–48:** The total of 22,273 seems much too low in view of the census (1.32); no satisfactory explanation is available. Given the one-to-one ransom of Levites for firstborn males, the 273 persons over 22,000 are redeemed by five shekels apiece (cf. Lev 27.6). *I am the LORD*, see Lev 19. **49–51:** The ransom, reckoned by *the shekel of the sanctuary* (Ex 30.13), is paid by the firstborn to Moses and given to the priests; a shekel weighed about .4 oz (11.4 gr). **4.1–49:** The second levitical census (compare 3.15), taken to determine those Levites (ages thirty to fifty) who are to perform the duties detailed in 4.4–33; the differing ages in 8.24–26 (compare Ezra 3.8) may reflect expanding community needs. The responsibilities for certain sanctuary items are commanded in detail, so that each item is accounted for. **2–20:** The Kohathites are distinguished by their responsibility for *the most holy things*, with different colors of cloth marking gradations of holiness. **5–15:** Aaron and his sons are responsible for packing and unpacking the most holy things; only they are allowed to see and

put on it all the utensils of the altar, which are used for the service there, the firepans, the forks, the shovels, and the basins, all the utensils of the altar; and they shall spread on it a covering of fine leather,[a] and shall put its poles in place. [15] When Aaron and his sons have finished covering the sanctuary and all the furnishings of the sanctuary, as the camp sets out, after that the Kohathites shall come to carry these, but they must not touch the holy things, or they will die. These are the things of the tent of meeting that the Kohathites are to carry.

[16] Eleazar son of Aaron the priest shall have charge of the oil for the light, the fragrant incense, the regular grain offering, and the anointing oil, the oversight of all the tabernacle and all that is in it, in the sanctuary and in its utensils.

[17] Then the LORD spoke to Moses and Aaron, saying: [18] You must not let the tribe of the clans of the Kohathites be destroyed from among the Levites. [19] This is how you must deal with them in order that they may live and not die when they come near to the most holy things: Aaron and his sons shall go in and assign each to a particular task or burden. [20] But the Kohathites[b] must not go in to look on the holy things even for a moment; otherwise they will die.

[21] Then the LORD spoke to Moses, saying: [22] Take a census of the Gershonites also, by their ancestral houses and by their clans; [23] from thirty years old up to fifty years old you shall enroll them, all who qualify to do work in the tent of meeting. [24] This is the service of the clans of the Gershonites, in serving and bearing burdens: [25] They shall carry the curtains of the tabernacle, and the tent of meeting with its covering, and the outer covering of fine leather[a] that is on top of it, and the screen for the entrance of the tent of meeting, [26] and the hangings of the court, and the screen for the entrance of the gate of the court that is around the tabernacle and the altar, and their cords, and all the equipment for their service; and they shall

do all that needs to be done with regard to them. [27] All the service of the Gershonites shall be at the command of Aaron and his sons, in all that they are to carry, and in all that they have to do; and you shall assign to their charge all that they are to carry. [28] This is the service of the clans of the Gershonites relating to the tent of meeting, and their responsibilities are to be under the oversight of Ithamar son of Aaron the priest.

[29] As for the Merarites, you shall enroll them by their clans and their ancestral houses; [30] from thirty years old up to fifty years old you shall enroll them, everyone who qualifies to do the work of the tent of meeting. [31] This is what they are charged to carry, as the whole of their service in the tent of meeting: the frames of the tabernacle, with its bars, pillars, and bases, [32] and the pillars of the court all around with their bases, pegs, and cords, with all their equipment and all their related service; and you shall assign by name the objects that they are required to carry. [33] This is the service of the clans of the Merarites, the whole of their service relating to the tent of meeting, under the hand of Ithamar son of Aaron the priest.

[34] So Moses and Aaron and the leaders of the congregation enrolled the Kohathites, by their clans and their ancestral houses, [35] from thirty years old up to fifty years old, everyone who qualified for work relating to the tent of meeting; [36] and their enrollment by clans was two thousand seven hundred fifty. [37] This was the enrollment of the clans of the Kohathites, all who served at the tent of meeting, whom Moses and Aaron enrolled according to the commandment of the LORD by Moses.

[38] The enrollment of the Gershonites, by their clans and their ancestral houses, [39] from thirty years old up to fifty years old, everyone who qualified for work relating to the tent of meeting— [40] their enrollment by their clans

a Meaning of Heb uncertain
b Heb *they*

touch them. **15–16:** The (other) Kohathites carry the items prepared by Aaron and his sons; they are supervised by Eleazar. *Oil for the light,* Ex 27.20; *incense,* Ex 30.7; *grain offering,* Lev 6.14–18; *anointing oil,* Ex 30.22–34. **17–20:** God takes the greater risk of the Kohathites into account and specifies precautionary procedures. **21–28:** The service of the Gershonites; see 3.25–26. **29–33:** The service of the Merarites; see 3.36–37. **34–45:** The implemen-

and their ancestral houses was two thousand six hundred thirty. [41] This was the enrollment of the clans of the Gershonites, all who served at the tent of meeting, whom Moses and Aaron enrolled according to the commandment of the LORD.

[42] The enrollment of the clans of the Merarites, by their clans and their ancestral houses, [43] from thirty years old up to fifty years old, everyone who qualified for work relating to the tent of meeting— [44] their enrollment by their clans was three thousand two hundred. [45] This is the enrollment of the clans of the Merarites, whom Moses and Aaron enrolled according to the commandment of the LORD by Moses.

[46] All those who were enrolled of the Levites, whom Moses and Aaron and the leaders of Israel enrolled, by their clans and their ancestral houses, [47] from thirty years old up to fifty years old, everyone who qualified to do the work of service and the work of bearing burdens relating to the tent of meeting, [48] their enrollment was eight thousand five hundred eighty. [49] According to the commandment of the LORD through Moses they were appointed to their several tasks of serving or carrying; thus they were enrolled by him, as the LORD commanded Moses.

5 The LORD spoke to Moses, saying. [2] Command the Israelites to put out of the camp everyone who is leprous,[a] or has a discharge, and everyone who is unclean through contact with a corpse; [3] you shall put out both male and female, putting them outside the camp; they must not defile their camp, where I dwell among them. [4] The Israelites did so, putting them outside the camp; as the LORD had spoken to Moses, so the Israelites did.

[5] The LORD spoke to Moses, saying: [6] Speak to the Israelites: When a man or a woman wrongs another, breaking faith with the LORD, that person incurs guilt [7] and shall confess the sin that has been committed. The person shall make full restitution for the wrong, adding one-fifth to it, and giving it to the one who was wronged. [8] If the injured party has no next of kin to whom restitution may be made for the wrong, the restitution for wrong shall go to the LORD for the priest, in addition to the ram of atonement with which atonement is made for the guilty party. [9] Among all the sacred donations of the Israelites, every gift that they bring to the priest shall be his. [10] The sacred donations of all are their own; whatever anyone gives to the priest shall be his.

[11] The LORD spoke to Moses, saying: [12] Speak to the Israelites and say to them: If any man's wife goes astray and is unfaithful to him, [13] if a man has had intercourse with her but it is hidden from her husband, so that she is undetected though she has defiled herself, and there is no witness against her since she was not caught in the act; [14] if a spirit of jealousy comes on him, and he is jealous of his wife who has defiled herself; or if a spirit of jealousy comes on him, and he is jealous of his wife, though she has not defiled herself; [15] then the man shall bring his wife

---

[a] A term for several skin diseases; precise meaning uncertain

---

tation of the divine commands. **46–49:** Summary. The reason for the difference in the number of Levites from 3.39 is not clear. The encampment is now fully prepared for the journey.

5.1–6.21: Purification of the camp. Matters needing attention for the journey to come.

5.1–4: Persons who are ritually and communicably impure for various reasons are to be put outside the camp, so as not to contaminate the community or defile the tabernacle (see Lev 13.45–46; 15.31–33; 21.1–3,11). **5–10:** This case law extends Lev 6.1–7: when the wronged party dies without next of kin, priests receive the appropriate restitution. The public confession of this deliberate sin (see Lev 5.5) is also new. **11–31:** This case law regarding a woman suspected of adultery has many difficulties. Though often called a trial by ordeal, the coalescence of verdict and sanction, effected by God not the community, suggests a dramatized oath. **12–14:** The focus is a wife, possibly pregnant, whose husband suspects (*a spirit of jealousy*) her of adultery but has no evidence, whether she has actually done so (5.12–14a) or is only suspected (5.14b). In the former case, this text softens the penalty prescribed for an adulteress in Lev 20.10, probably because there was no evidence. In the latter case, a woman unjustly accused could be vindicated; the jealous husband (or the community) could not arbitrarily decide her fate. **15:** In either case, the man brings his wife (who is *under [his] authority*, vv.19,20,29) to the priest with a simple grain offering, without the usual oil and frankincense (Lev 2.1–10; 5.11). *One-tenth of an*

to the priest. And he shall bring the offering required for her, one-tenth of an ephah of barley flour. He shall pour no oil on it and put no frankincense on it, for it is a grain offering of jealousy, a grain offering of remembrance, bringing iniquity to remembrance.

[16] Then the priest shall bring her near, and set her before the LORD; [17] the priest shall take holy water in an earthen vessel, and take some of the dust that is on the floor of the tabernacle and put it into the water. [18] The priest shall set the woman before the LORD, dishevel the woman's hair, and place in her hands the grain offering of remembrance, which is the grain offering of jealousy. In his own hand the priest shall have the water of bitterness that brings the curse. [19] Then the priest shall make her take an oath, saying, "If no man has lain with you, if you have not turned aside to uncleanness while under your husband's authority, be immune to this water of bitterness that brings the curse. [20] But if you have gone astray while under your husband's authority, if you have defiled yourself and some man other than your husband has had intercourse with you," [21]—let the priest make the woman take the oath of the curse and say to the woman—"the LORD make you an execration and an oath among your people, when the LORD makes your uterus drop, your womb discharge; [22] now may this water that brings the curse enter your bowels and make your womb discharge, your uterus drop!" And the woman shall say, "Amen. Amen."

[23] Then the priest shall put these curses in writing, and wash them off into the water of bitterness. [24] He shall make the woman drink the water of bitterness that brings the curse, and the water that brings the curse shall enter her and cause bitter pain. [25] The priest shall take the grain offering of jealousy out of the woman's hand, and shall elevate the grain offering before the LORD and bring it to the altar; [26] and the priest shall take a handful of the grain offering, as its memorial portion, and turn it into smoke on the altar, and afterward shall make the woman drink the water. [27] When he has made her drink the water, then, if she has defiled herself and has been unfaithful to her husband, the water that brings the curse shall enter into her and cause bitter pain, and her womb shall discharge, her uterus drop, and the woman shall become an execration among her people. [28] But if the woman has not defiled herself and is clean, then she shall be immune and be able to conceive children.

[29] This is the law in cases of jealousy, when a wife, while under her husband's authority,

ephah, ca. 2 qts (2.3 liters). *Frankincense* is an aromatic resin from shrubs in Arabia and East Africa. Such offerings *bring the* (potential) *iniquity to remembrance* before God. **16–28:** The procedure: the priest prepares a mixture of holy water (see Ex 30.17–21) and tabernacle floor dust, potent because of its contact with holy things, in an earthen vessel (which could be broken after use; see Lev 11.33). The priest then brings the woman *before the* LORD (the altar), loosens her hair (a sign of humiliation or [potential] uncleanness; Lev 13.45), and puts the grain offering in her hands. **19–22:** She takes an oath regarding the suspicions registered: if she has been faithful, she will be immune from the water; if unfaithful, the water will cause her sexual organs to be affected adversely in some way (correlated with the crime) and she will be ostracized among the people and precluded from having children. If the woman is pregnant, the effect may have been a miscarriage. The effect of the water upon the woman is considered a sign as to whether the woman has told the truth. **22:***"Amen. Amen"* expresses willingness to accept either result (see Deut 27.15–26). Unlike her husband, she is given no other voice in the ritual. **23–28:** 5.24 anticipates 5.26b, as 5.16a does 5.18a. The priest writes the curses on a surface from which the ink could be washed off into the water the woman is to drink; the imbibed water is thought to contain the curses' power (Ex 32.20,35). The priest takes the offering from her and burns a portion on the altar, after which she drinks the water. If the woman has been unfaithful, she will experience distress (no time frame is specified), hence the phrase *water of bitterness.* The potion has no bitter taste nor brings pain, but this would be the effect if God adjudged the woman guilty (5.21; see Zech 5.1–4; Jer 8.14; 9.15). **26:** *Memorial portion,* see Lev 2.2–3. **28:** The effect for the guiltless woman is that she will *conceive children.* **29–31:** A summary of the two cases for which this ordeal would be applied. The man is freed from responsibility for a false accusation. If the woman is guilty, she bears the consequences by divine agency. The ritual could not certainly verify suspicions; but, as with sacrifices, God is believed to effect the proper result. In this polygynous society, where men could have many sexual partners,

goes astray and defiles herself, [30] or when a spirit of jealousy comes on a man and he is jealous of his wife; then he shall set the woman before the Lord, and the priest shall apply this entire law to her. [31] The man shall be free from iniquity, but the woman shall bear her iniquity.

6 The Lord spoke to Moses, saying: [2] Speak to the Israelites and say to them: When either men or women make a special vow, the vow of a nazirite,[a] to separate themselves to the Lord, [3] they shall separate themselves from wine and strong drink; they shall drink no wine vinegar or other vinegar, and shall not drink any grape juice or eat grapes, fresh or dried. [4] All their days as nazirites[b] they shall eat nothing that is produced by the grapevine, not even the seeds or the skins.

[5] All the days of their nazirite vow no razor shall come upon the head; until the time is completed for which they separate themselves to the Lord, they shall be holy; they shall let the locks of the head grow long.

[6] All the days that they separate themselves to the Lord they shall not go near a corpse. [7] Even if their father or mother, brother or sister, should die, they may not defile themselves; because their consecration to God is upon the head. [8] All their days as nazirites[b] they are holy to the Lord.

[9] If someone dies very suddenly nearby, defiling the consecrated head, then they shall shave the head on the day of their cleansing; on the seventh day they shall shave it. [10] On the eighth day they shall bring two turtledoves or two young pigeons to the priest at the entrance of the tent of meeting, [11] and the priest shall offer one as a sin offering and the other as a burnt offering, and make atonement for them, because they incurred guilt by reason of the corpse. They shall sanctify the head that same day, [12] and separate themselves to the Lord for their days as nazirites,[b] and bring a male lamb a year old as a guilt offering. The former time shall be void, because the consecrated head was defiled.

[13] This is the law for the nazirites[b] when the time of their consecration has been completed: they shall be brought to the entrance of the tent of meeting, [14] and they shall offer their gift to the Lord, one male lamb a year old without blemish as a burnt offering, one ewe lamb a year old without blemish as a sin offering, one ram without blemish as an offering of well-being, [15] and a basket of unleavened bread, cakes of choice flour mixed with oil and unleavened wafers spread with oil, with their grain offering and their drink offerings. [16] The priest shall present them before the Lord and offer their sin offering and burnt offering, [17] and shall offer the ram as a sacrifice of well-being to the Lord, with the basket of unleavened bread; the priest also shall make the accompanying grain offering and drink offering. [18] Then the nazirites[b] shall shave the consecrated head at the entrance of the tent of meeting, and shall take the hair from the consecrated head and put it on the fire under the sacrifice of well-being. [19] The priest shall take the shoulder of the ram, when it is boiled, and one unleavened cake out of the basket, and one unleavened wafer, and shall put them in the palms of the

---

a   That is *one separated* or *one consecrated*
b   That is *those separated* or *those consecrated*

but women could have only one, women lived under the threat of this ritual.

6.1–21: A temporary, voluntary nazirite vow. 2: Nazirites were male or female individuals who took a vow of consecration for a special vocation *to separate themselves to the Lord*. The precise purpose for becoming a nazirite remains elusive; they function as temporary priests in some fashion. Other texts describe both lifetime and temporary nazirites (Judg 13.5; 1 Sam 1.11; Am 2.11–12). **3–5:** The nazirite vow entailed separation from products of the vineyard (and other intoxicants), haircuts, and corpses; their return to secular life was signified by cutting the hair. Highly visible members of the community, they were public signs of total dedication to God, similar to the Rechabites (2 Kings 10.15; Jer 35). **6–12:** Nazirites were not to come into contact with (or even within sight of) a corpse; accidental contact defiled *the consecrated head* (long hair) and required rites of purification (19.1–22; Lev 21.1–12). Upon being purified, they were to *sanctify the head*, i.e., be reconsecrated. **13–20:** The law for terminating the vow. For the range of offerings see Lev 1–7. The ritual includes the shaving of the

nazirites,[a] after they have shaved the conse-crated head. [20] Then the priest shall elevate them as an elevation offering before the LORD; they are a holy portion for the priest, together with the breast that is elevated and the thigh that is offered. After that the nazi-rites[a] may drink wine.

[21] This is the law for the nazirites[a] who take a vow. Their offering to the LORD must be in accordance with the nazirite[b] vow, apart from what else they can afford. In accordance with whatever vow they take, so they shall do, fol-lowing the law for their consecration.

[22] The LORD spoke to Moses, saying: [23] Speak to Aaron and his sons, saying, Thus you shall bless the Israelites: You shall say to them,

[24] The LORD bless you and keep you;
[25] the LORD make his face to shine upon you, and be gracious to you;
[26] the LORD lift up his countenance upon you, and give you peace.
[27] So they shall put my name on the Israel-ites, and I will bless them.

7 On the day when Moses had finished set-ting up the tabernacle, and had anointed and consecrated it with all its furnishings, and had anointed and consecrated the altar with all its utensils, [2] the leaders of Israel, heads of their ancestral houses, the leaders of the tribes, who were over those who were enrolled, made offerings. [3] They brought their offerings before the LORD, six covered wagons and twelve oxen, a wagon for every two of the leaders, and for each one an ox; they presented them before the tabernacle. [4] Then the LORD said to Moses: [5] Accept these from them, that they may be used in doing the service of the tent of meeting, and give them to the Levites, to each according to his service. [6] So Moses took the wagons and the oxen, and gave them to the Levites. [7] Two wagons and four oxen he gave to the Gershonites, according to their service; [8] and four wagons and eight oxen he gave to the Merarites, according to their service, under the direction of Ithamar son of Aaron the priest. [9] But to the Kohathites he gave none, because they were charged with the care of the holy things that had to be carried on the shoulders.

[10] The leaders also presented offerings for the dedication of the altar at the time when it was anointed; the leaders presented their offering before the altar. [11] The LORD said to Moses: They shall present their offerings, one leader each day, for the dedication of the altar.

[12] The one who presented his offering the first day was Nahshon son of Amminadab,

---

[a] That is *those separated* or *those consecrated*
[b] That is *one separated* or *one consecrated*

---

head and the burning of the hair (because it was holy). **20**: *Elevation offering*, see Lev 7.27–36. **21**: A summary.

6.22–27: The priestly blessing. Almost identical forms of this blessing were found on two small silver plaques in a tomb near Jerusalem, dating to the late seventh or early sixth century BCE. **24–26**: Each line, with God as subject, is progressively longer (three, five, seven Hebrew words). Perhaps the second verb in each case defines the first more specifically; together the six verbs cover God's benevolent activity from various angles and state God's gracious will for Israel. To *bless* signifies any divine gift that serves the life and well-being of individuals and communities. To *keep* is a specific blessing to those with safety concerns, focusing on God's protection from all forms of evil (cf. Ps 121.7–8). The shining *face* of God (contrast the hiding face) signifies God's benevolent disposition (cf. Ps 67.1). *Lift up his countenance* signifies a favorable movement toward the other in granting *peace*, that is, wholeness and fullness of life. **27**: To *put my name on the Israelites* emphasizes that the priests are representatives—only God can bless.

7.1–8.26: Final preparations for tabernacle worship. 7.1–88: The consecration of the tabernacle with offer-ings made by the tribal leaders. **1**: A flashback occurs (through 10.10), one month earlier than 1.1, coinciding with the day Moses set up the tabernacle (Ex 40); it returns the reader to God's descent to dwell among the people and their response. **2–9**: One offering: six wagons and twelve oxen to carry the tabernacle and its furnishings. The Merarites receive two-thirds of the wagons and oxen because they carry the supporting structure; the Kohathites carry the *holy things* by hand, reflecting the importance of these items (4.1–15). **10**: Refers to the *offerings* presented in both 7.1–9 and 7.12–88. **11–83**: Another offering: necessities for the public altar sacri-fices and the priesthood, to be offered at the altar whenever needed. The tribal leaders (see 2.3–31) each give the same offerings on twelve successive days of the celebration; the names are the same as in 1.5–15, but the

of the tribe of Judah; [13] his offering was one silver plate weighing one hundred thirty shekels, one silver basin weighing seventy shekels, according to the shekel of the sanctuary, both of them full of choice flour mixed with oil for a grain offering; [14] one golden dish weighing ten shekels, full of incense; [15] one young bull, one ram, one male lamb a year old, for a burnt offering; [16] one male goat for a sin offering; [17] and for the sacrifice of well-being, two oxen, five rams, five male goats, and five male lambs a year old. This was the offering of Nahshon son of Amminadab.

[18] On the second day Nethanel son of Zuar, the leader of Issachar, presented an offering; [19] he presented for his offering one silver plate weighing one hundred thirty shekels, one silver basin weighing seventy shekels, according to the shekel of the sanctuary, both of them full of choice flour mixed with oil for a grain offering; [20] one golden dish weighing ten shekels, full of incense; [21] one young bull, one ram, one male lamb a year old, as a burnt offering; [22] one male goat as a sin offering; [23] and for the sacrifice of well-being, two oxen, five rams, five male goats, and five male lambs a year old. This was the offering of Nethanel son of Zuar.

[24] On the third day Eliab son of Helon, the leader of the Zebulunites: [25] his offering was one silver plate weighing one hundred thirty shekels, one silver basin weighing seventy shekels, according to the shekel of the sanctuary, both of them full of choice flour mixed with oil for a grain offering; [26] one golden dish weighing ten shekels, full of incense; [27] one young bull, one ram, one male lamb a year old, for a burnt offering; [28] one male goat for a sin offering; [29] and for the sacrifice of well-being, two oxen, five rams, five male goats, and five male lambs a year old. This was the offering of Eliab son of Helon.

[30] On the fourth day Elizur son of Shedeur, the leader of the Reubenites: [31] his offering was one silver plate weighing one hundred thirty shekels, one silver basin weighing seventy shekels, according to the shekel of the sanctuary, both of them full of choice flour mixed with oil for a grain offering; [32] one golden dish weighing ten shekels, full of incense; [33] one young bull, one ram, one male lamb a year old, for a burnt offering;

[34] one male goat for a sin offering; [35] and for the sacrifice of well-being, two oxen, five rams, five male goats, and five male lambs a year old. This was the offering of Elizur son of Shedeur.

[36] On the fifth day Shelumiel son of Zurishaddai, the leader of the Simeonites: [37] his offering was one silver plate weighing one hundred thirty shekels, one silver basin weighing seventy shekels, according to the shekel of the sanctuary, both of them full of choice flour mixed with oil for a grain offering; [38] one golden dish weighing ten shekels, full of incense; [39] one young bull, one ram, one male lamb a year old, for a burnt offering; [40] one male goat for a sin offering; [41] and for the sacrifice of well-being, two oxen, five rams, five male goats, and five male lambs a year old. This was the offering of Shelumiel son of Zurishaddai.

[42] On the sixth day Eliasaph son of Deuel, the leader of the Gadites: [43] his offering was one silver plate weighing one hundred thirty shekels, one silver basin weighing seventy shekels, according to the shekel of the sanctuary, both of them full of choice flour mixed with oil for a grain offering; [44] one golden dish weighing ten shekels, full of incense; [45] one young bull, one ram, one male lamb a year old, for a burnt offering; [46] one male goat for a sin offering; [47] and for the sacrifice of well-being, two oxen, five rams, five male goats, and five male lambs a year old. This was the offering of Eliasaph son of Deuel.

[48] On the seventh day Elishama son of Ammihud, the leader of the Ephraimites: [49] his offering was one silver plate weighing one hundred thirty shekels, one silver basin weighing seventy shekels, according to the shekel of the sanctuary, both of them full of choice flour mixed with oil for a grain offering; [50] one golden dish weighing ten shekels, full of incense; [51] one young bull, one ram, one male lamb a year old, for a burnt offering; [52] one male goat for a sin offering; [53] and for the sacrifice of well-being, two oxen, five rams, five male goats, and five male lambs a year old. This was the offering of Elishama son of Ammihud.

[54] On the eighth day Gamaliel son of Pedahzur, the leader of the Manassites:

[55] his offering was one silver plate weighing one hundred thirty shekels, one silver basin weighing seventy shekels, according to the shekel of the sanctuary, both of them full of choice flour mixed with oil for a grain offering; [56] one golden dish weighing ten shekels, full of incense; [57] one young bull, one ram, one male lamb a year old, for a burnt offering; [58] one male goat for a sin offering; [59] and for the sacrifice of well-being, two oxen, five rams, five male goats, and five male lambs a year old. This was the offering of Gamaliel son of Pedahzur.

[60] On the ninth day Abidan son of Gideoni, the leader of the Benjaminites: [61] his offering was one silver plate weighing one hundred thirty shekels, one silver basin weighing seventy shekels, according to the shekel of the sanctuary, both of them full of choice flour mixed with oil for a grain offering; [62] one golden dish weighing ten shekels, full of incense; [63] one young bull, one ram, one male lamb a year old, for a burnt offering; [64] one male goat for a sin offering; [65] and for the sacrifice of well-being, two oxen, five rams, five male goats, and five male lambs a year old. This was the offering of Abidan son of Gideoni.

[66] On the tenth day Ahiezer son of Ammishaddai, the leader of the Danites: [67] his offering was one silver plate weighing one hundred thirty shekels, one silver basin weighing seventy shekels, according to the shekel of the sanctuary, both of them full of choice flour mixed with oil for a grain offering; [68] one golden dish weighing ten shekels, full of incense; [69] one young bull, one ram, one male lamb a year old, for a burnt offering; [70] one male goat for a sin offering; [71] and for the sacrifice of well-being, two oxen, five rams, five male goats, and five male lambs a year old. This was the offering of Ahiezer son of Ammishaddai.

[72] On the eleventh day Pagiel son of Ochran, the leader of the Asherites: [73] his offering was one silver plate weighing one hundred thirty shekels, one silver basin weighing seventy shekels, according to the shekel of the sanctuary, both of them full of choice flour mixed with oil for a grain offering; [74] one golden dish weighing ten shekels, full of incense; [75] one young bull, one ram, one male lamb a year old, for a burnt offering; [76] one male goat for a sin offering; [77] and for the sacrifice of well-being, two oxen, five rams, five male goats, and five male lambs a year old. This was the offering of Pagiel son of Ochran.

[78] On the twelfth day Ahira son of Enan, the leader of the Naphtalites: [79] his offering was one silver plate weighing one hundred thirty shekels, one silver basin weighing seventy shekels, according to the shekel of the sanctuary, both of them full of choice flour mixed with oil for a grain offering; [80] one golden dish weighing ten shekels, full of incense; [81] one young bull, one ram, one male lamb a year old, for a burnt offering; [82] one male goat for a sin offering; [83] and for the sacrifice of well-being, two oxen, five rams, five male goats, and five male lambs a year old. This was the offering of Ahira son of Enan.

[84] This was the dedication offering for the altar, at the time when it was anointed, from the leaders of Israel: twelve silver plates, twelve silver basins, twelve golden dishes, [85] each silver plate weighing one hundred thirty shekels and each basin seventy, all the silver of the vessels two thousand four hundred shekels according to the shekel of the sanctuary, [86] the twelve golden dishes, full of incense, weighing ten shekels apiece according to the shekel of the sanctuary, all the gold of the dishes being one hundred twenty shekels; [87] all the livestock for the burnt offering twelve bulls, twelve rams, twelve male lambs a year old, with their grain offering; and twelve male goats for a sin offering; [88] and all the livestock for the sacrifice of well-being twenty-four bulls, the rams sixty, the male goats sixty, the male lambs a year old sixty. This was the dedication offering for the altar, after it was anointed.

[89] When Moses went into the tent of meeting to speak with the Lord,[a] he would

---

[a] Heb *him*

---

order of tribes is different, with Judah first. **13:** *Shekel,* see 3.49–51n. **84–88:** Summary and total. The repetition underlines the unity and equality of the tribal groups and their support for the tabernacle. **89:** God's ongoing commitment to Israel (to dwell among them; to speak to Moses) matches the people's obedient response. The

hear the voice speaking to him from above the mercy seat[a] that was on the ark of the covenant[b] from between the two cherubim; thus it spoke to him.

8 The LORD spoke to Moses, saying: [2] Speak to Aaron and say to him: When you set up the lamps, the seven lamps shall give light in front of the lampstand. [3] Aaron did so; he set up its lamps to give light in front of the lampstand, as the LORD had commanded Moses. [4] Now this was how the lampstand was made, out of hammered work of gold. From its base to its flowers, it was hammered work; according to the pattern that the LORD had shown Moses, so he made the lampstand.

[5] The LORD spoke to Moses, saying: [6] Take the Levites from among the Israelites and cleanse them. [7] Thus you shall do to them, to cleanse them: sprinkle the water of purification on them, have them shave their whole body with a razor and wash their clothes, and so cleanse themselves. [8] Then let them take a young bull and its grain offering of choice flour mixed with oil, and you shall take another young bull for a sin offering. [9] You shall bring the Levites before the tent of meeting, and assemble the whole congregation of the Israelites. [10] When you bring the Levites before the LORD, the Israelites shall lay their hands on the Levites, [11] and Aaron shall present the Levites before the LORD as an elevation offering from the Israelites, that they may do the service of the LORD. [12] The Levites shall lay their hands on the heads of the bulls,

and he shall offer the one for a sin offering and the other for a burnt offering to the LORD, to make atonement for the Levites. [13] Then you shall have the Levites stand before Aaron and his sons, and you shall present them as an elevation offering to the LORD.

[14] Thus you shall separate the Levites from among the other Israelites, and the Levites shall be mine. [15] Thereafter the Levites may go in to do service at the tent of meeting, once you have cleansed them and presented them as an elevation offering. [16] For they are unreservedly given to me from among the Israelites; I have taken them for myself, in place of all that open the womb, the firstborn of all the Israelites. [17] For all the firstborn among the Israelites are mine, both human and animal. On the day that I struck down all the firstborn in the land of Egypt I consecrated them for myself, [18] but I have taken the Levites in place of all the firstborn among the Israelites. [19] Moreover, I have given the Levites as a gift to Aaron and his sons from among the Israelites, to do the service for the Israelites at the tent of meeting, and to make atonement for the Israelites, in order that there may be no plague among the Israelites for coming too close to the sanctuary.

[20] Moses and Aaron and the whole congregation of the Israelites did with the Levites accordingly; the Israelites did with

a   Or *the cover*
b   Or *treaty*, or *testimony*; Heb *eduth*

---

mercy seat is the cover of *the ark of the covenant*, upon which were fixed two *cherubim*, sphinxlike creatures, shaped to form a throne for the invisible God (1 Sam 4.4; 2 Sam 6.2); the ark functioned as God's footstool (1 Chr 28.2; Ex 25.17–21), where God speaks to Moses when he enters the tabernacle, fulfilling God's promise in Ex 25.22 (see Num 11.16–30). **8.1–26:** Consecration of the Levites. **1–4:** Lighting directions for the tabernacle lamps (Ex 25.37), with a reminder of the *pattern* of their construction (Ex 25.9). The seven branches and flowery design may have symbolized the tree of life (see 1 Kings 7.49; Zech 4.1–14); the branched lampstand (Heb "menorah") remains an important symbol of light. **5–26:** The Levites are consecrated *to do service at the tent of meeting* (v. 15; see Lev 8; the priests are sanctified; the Levites are purified). **5–8:** This entails participation in a purification rite (see Lev 14.8–9) so they can perform this service without endangering themselves or the community. **9–18:** The Levites are presented *before the tent of meeting* and before *Aaron and his sons*. The people *lay their hands* on them, symbolizing the Levites as a living sacrifice dedicated to the service of God instead of their firstborn (vv. 16–17; see 3.11–13,40–51). The Levites in turn *lay their hands* on the bulls—sacrificed *to make atonement* for sins committed (v. 12b; see Lev 1; 4). God claims that the Levites are *mine . . . unreservedly given to me from among the Israelites* (vv.14–16; 3.9); God in turn gives them to the Aaronides for service at the tabernacle. **19:** This action is *to make atonement* for Israelites to prevent any plague resulting from too close contact with the holy things. **20–26:** The divine commands are obeyed: a summary of the cleansing, age requirements (see 4.47), and a clarification that they *assist* the Aaronides.

the Levites just as the LORD had commanded Moses concerning them. [21] The Levites purified themselves from sin and washed their clothes; then Aaron presented them as an elevation offering before the LORD, and Aaron made atonement for them to cleanse them. [22] Thereafter the Levites went in to do their service in the tent of meeting in attendance on Aaron and his sons. As the LORD had commanded Moses concerning the Levites, so they did with them.

[23] The LORD spoke to Moses, saying: [24] This applies to the Levites: from twenty-five years old and upward they shall begin to do duty in the service of the tent of meeting; [25] and from the age of fifty years they shall retire from the duty of the service and serve no more. [26] They may assist their brothers in the tent of meeting in carrying out their duties, but they shall perform no service. Thus you shall do with the Levites in assigning their duties.

9 The LORD spoke to Moses in the wilderness of Sinai, in the first month of the second year after they had come out of the land of Egypt, saying: [2] Let the Israelites keep the passover at its appointed time. [3] On the fourteenth day of this month, at twilight,[a] you shall keep it at its appointed time; according to all its statutes and all its regulations you shall keep it. [4] So Moses told the Israelites that they should keep the passover. [5] They kept the passover in the first month, on the fourteenth day of the month, at twilight,[a] in the wilderness of Sinai. Just as the LORD had commanded Moses, so the Israelites did. [6] Now there were certain people who were unclean through touching a corpse, so that they could not keep the passover on that day. They came before Moses and Aaron on that day, [7] and said to him, "Although we are unclean through touching a corpse, why must we be kept from presenting the LORD's offering at its appointed time among the Israelites?" [8] Moses spoke to them, "Wait, so that I may hear what the LORD will command concerning you."

[9] The LORD spoke to Moses, saying: [10] Speak to the Israelites, saying: Anyone of you or your descendants who is unclean through touching a corpse, or is away on a journey, shall still keep the passover to the LORD. [11] In the second month on the fourteenth day, at twilight,[a] they shall keep it; they shall eat it with unleavened bread and bitter herbs. [12] They shall leave none of it until morning, nor break a bone of it; according to all the statute for the passover they shall keep it. [13] But anyone who is clean and is not on a journey, and yet refrains from keeping the passover, shall be cut off from the people for not presenting the LORD's offering at its appointed time; such a one shall bear the consequences for the sin. [14] Any alien residing among you who wishes to keep the passover to the LORD shall do so according to the statute of the passover and according to its regulation; you shall have one statute for both the resident alien and the native.

[15] On the day the tabernacle was set up, the cloud covered the tabernacle, the tent of the

---

a   Heb between the two evenings

9.1–14: The passover at Sinai. The flashback begun at 7.1 continues. 1–5: A second celebration of passover (see Ex 12.24). 6–14: A question to Moses regarding passover celebration upon touching a corpse (5.1–4; 19.11–20) results in new legislation from the LORD: such persons shall keep the same regulations one month later (see Ex 12). The case of persons *away on a journey* is another adjustment. 12: Not *break a bone* of the passover lamb: see Ex 12.46; Jn 19.36. 13: Those *not on a journey* that refrain from passover shall be *cut off from the people*, that is, *bear the consequences for the sin*, most likely extermination of the family line. 14: A permissive rubric for the *resident alien*, a non-Israelite residing permanently in the land.

9.15–23: Divine guidance in the wilderness. A supplement to Ex 40.34–38, anticipating 10.11–13. The (single) pillar of cloud and fire (Ex 13.21–22; 14.24; 40.38) in which God was present was an ongoing feature of the wilderness journey. Linked to the tabernacle (and the ark, 10.33–36), the pillar's lifting and resting scheduled the stages of Israel's journey. The cloud would rest on the tabernacle and, while the tabernacle remained in the middle of the marching people, the cloud would proceed to the front of the procession (9.17; 14.14). Israel's obedience to these signs is stressed.

covenant;[a] and from evening until morning it was over the tabernacle, having the appearance of fire. [16] It was always so: the cloud covered it by day[b] and the appearance of fire by night. [17] Whenever the cloud lifted from over the tent, then the Israelites would set out; and in the place where the cloud settled down, there the Israelites would camp. [18] At the command of the LORD the Israelites would set out, and at the command of the LORD they would camp. As long as the cloud rested over the tabernacle, they would remain in camp. [19] Even when the cloud continued over the tabernacle many days, the Israelites would keep the charge of the LORD, and would not set out. [20] Sometimes the cloud would remain a few days over the tabernacle, and according to the command of the LORD they would remain in camp; then according to the command of the LORD they would set out. [21] Sometimes the cloud would remain from evening until morning; and when the cloud lifted in the morning, they would set out, or if it continued for a day and a night, when the cloud lifted they would set out. [22] Whether it was two days, or a month, or a longer time, that the cloud continued over the tabernacle, resting upon it, the Israelites would remain in camp and would not set out; but when it lifted they would set out. [23] At the command of the LORD they would camp, and at the command of the LORD they would set out. They kept the charge of the LORD, at the command of the LORD by Moses.

10 The LORD spoke to Moses, saying: [2] Make two silver trumpets; you shall make them of hammered work; and you shall use them for summoning the congregation, and for breaking camp. [3] When both are blown, the whole congregation shall assemble before you at the entrance of the tent of meeting. [4] But if only one is blown, then the leaders, the heads of the tribes of Israel, shall assemble before you. [5] When you blow an alarm, the camps on the east side shall set out; [6] when you blow a second alarm, the camps on the south side shall set out. An alarm is to be blown whenever they are to set out. [7] But when the assembly is to be gathered, you shall blow, but you shall not sound an alarm. [8] The sons of Aaron, the priests, shall blow the trumpets; this shall be a perpetual institution for you throughout your generations. [9] When you go to war in your land against the adversary who oppresses you, you shall sound an alarm with the trumpets, so that you may be remembered before the LORD your God and be saved from your enemies. [10] Also on your days of rejoicing, at your appointed festivals, and at the beginnings of your months, you shall blow the trumpets over your burnt offerings and over your sacrifices of well-being; they shall serve as a reminder on your behalf before the LORD your God: I am the LORD your God.

[11] In the second year, in the second month, on the twentieth day of the month, the cloud lifted from over the tabernacle of the covenant.[a] [12] Then the Israelites set out by stages from the wilderness of Sinai, and the cloud settled down in the wilderness of Paran. [13] They set out for the first time at the command of the LORD by Moses. [14] The

---

a Or *treaty*, or *testimony*; Heb *eduth*
b Gk Syr Vg: Heb lacks *by day*

10.1–10: Two silver trumpets. God commands Moses to make two trumpets of hammered silver to be blown by priests on various occasions. **7:** *Blow*, one long blast; *alarm*, a series of short blasts. **9–10:** The rationale: to bring Israel's situation before God, who is called to act on their behalf, either in battle (salvation from enemies) or in and through the offerings (forgiveness and well-being).

10.11–25.18: The wilderness journey, from Sinai to the plains of Moab, east of the Jordan River, the border of the promised land. Israel's obedience to this point stands in sharp contrast to what follows. Warnings of divine judgment go unheeded, with disastrous results (1.53; 8.19). Many of these narratives mirror Ex 15.22–18.27: manna, rocks producing water, battles with desert tribes, and nonstop complaints, and may be from different sources than the accounts of these events in the book of Exodus. But Numbers is different: the people are sharply identified as rebellious, against both God and Moses and Aaron.

10.11–28: Departure from Sinai. 11: Nineteen days after the census (1.1) and eleven months after arrival at Sinai (Ex 19.1). The time of departure is set by divine command, signaled by the cloud (9.15–23). **12:** *By stages*, see ch 33. The end of the first stage is signaled by the cloud settling in *the wilderness of Paran*, the arid region

standard of the camp of Judah set out first, company by company, and over the whole company was Nahshon son of Amminadab. [15] Over the company of the tribe of Issachar was Nethanel son of Zuar; [16] and over the company of the tribe of Zebulun was Eliab son of Helon.

[17] Then the tabernacle was taken down, and the Gershonites and the Merarites, who carried the tabernacle, set out. [18] Next the standard of the camp of Reuben set out, company by company; and over the whole company was Elizur son of Shedeur. [19] Over the company of the tribe of Simeon was Shelumiel son of Zurishaddai, [20] and over the company of the tribe of Gad was Eliasaph son of Deuel.

[21] Then the Kohathites, who carried the holy things, set out; and the tabernacle was set up before their arrival. [22] Next the standard of the Ephraimite camp set out, company by company, and over the whole company was Elishama son of Ammihud. [23] Over the company of the tribe of Manasseh was Gamaliel son of Pedahzur, [24] and over the company of the tribe of Benjamin was Abidan son of Gideoni.

[25] Then the standard of the camp of Dan, acting as the rear guard of all the camps, set out, company by company, and over the whole company was Ahiezer son of Ammishaddai. [26] Over the company of the tribe of Asher was Pagiel son of Ochran, [27] and over the company of the tribe of Naphtali was Ahira son of Enan. [28] This was the order of march of the Israelites, company by company, when they set out.

[29] Moses said to Hobab son of Reuel the Midianite, Moses' father-in-law, "We are setting out for the place of which the LORD said, 'I will give it to you'; come with us, and we will treat you well; for the LORD has promised good to Israel." [30] But he said to him, "I will not go, but I will go back to my own land and to my kindred." [31] He said, "Do not leave us, for you know where we should camp in the wilderness, and you will serve as eyes for us. [32] Moreover, if you go with us, whatever good the LORD does for us, the same we will do for you."

[33] So they set out from the mount of the LORD three days' journey with the ark of the covenant of the LORD going before them three days' journey, to seek out a resting place for them, [34] the cloud of the LORD being over them by day when they set out from the camp.

[35] Whenever the ark set out, Moses would say,
"Arise, O LORD, let your enemies be scattered,
and your foes flee before you."
[36] And whenever it came to rest, he would say,
"Return, O LORD of the ten thousand thousands of Israel."[a]

11 Now when the people complained in the hearing of the LORD about their misfortunes, the LORD heard it and his

---

[a] Meaning of Heb uncertain

south of Canaan. **14–28:** The marching order and levitical responsibilities follow the arrangement in chs 2–3.

10.29–36: Human and divine guidance. 29: The name of Moses' father-in-law varies: *Hobab* (here and Judg 4.11); *Jethro* (Ex 3.1; 18.1); *Reuel* (here and Ex 2.18). Hobab was leader of the Kenites (Judg 1.16), a desert tribe; they would know the wilderness. Moses' invitation shows that the cloud's guidance is not deemed sufficient: both divine and human activities are necessary for the people to find their way. **33–36:** The ark with the cloud precedes the community. **33:** The second *three days' journey* is probably an erroneous scribal repetition. **35–36:** Moses' directives to the LORD, at the departure and arrival of the ark, are old poetic pieces, portraying the march as a liturgical procession. God was intensely present with the ark (7.89; see Ps 68.1; 132.7–8). God, the "LORD of Hosts" (*the ten thousand thousands of Israel*), leads Israel in battle against its enemies (1 Sam 4.1–7.2). That Moses invites God to become active on Israel's behalf again demonstrates the integration of human activity and divine.

11.1–3: A paradigm of rebellion. Provides a pattern in both form and content for several episodes that follow: murmuring; judgment; cry (of repentance); intercession; deliverance.

The people's complaints of unidentified misfortunes are not specifically directed to God, but God hears them. The divine anger is provoked by the people's *complaining*; *the fire of the LORD*, perhaps lightning (see Ex 9.23–24), consumes outlying areas of the camp. Moses intercedes and the storm stops.

anger was kindled. Then the fire of the LORD burned against them, and consumed some outlying parts of the camp. [2] But the people cried out to Moses; and Moses prayed to the LORD, and the fire abated. [3] So that place was called Taberah,[a] because the fire of the LORD burned against them.

[4] The rabble among them had a strong craving; and the Israelites also wept again, and said, "If only we had meat to eat! [5] We remember the fish we used to eat in Egypt for nothing, the cucumbers, the melons, the leeks, the onions, and the garlic; [6] but now our strength is dried up, and there is nothing at all but this manna to look at."

[7] Now the manna was like coriander seed, and its color was like the color of gum resin. [8] The people went around and gathered it, ground it in mills or beat it in mortars, then boiled it in pots and made cakes of it; and the taste of it was like the taste of cakes baked with oil. [9] When the dew fell on the camp in the night, the manna would fall with it.

[10] Moses heard the people weeping throughout their families, all at the entrances of their tents. Then the LORD became very angry, and Moses was displeased. [11] So Moses said to the LORD, "Why have you treated your servant so badly? Why have I not found favor in your sight, that you lay the burden of all this people on me? [12] Did I conceive all this people? Did I give birth to them, that you should say to me, 'Carry them in your bosom, as a nurse carries a sucking child, to the land that you promised on oath to their ancestors'? [13] Where am I to get meat to give to all this people? For they come weeping to me and say, 'Give us

meat to eat!' [14] I am not able to carry all this people alone, for they are too heavy for me. [15] If this is the way you are going to treat me, put me to death at once—if I have found favor in your sight—and do not let me see my misery."

[16] So the LORD said to Moses, "Gather for me seventy of the elders of Israel, whom you know to be the elders of the people and officers over them; bring them to the tent of meeting, and have them take their place there with you. [17] I will come down and talk with you there; and I will take some of the spirit that is on you and put it on them; and they shall bear the burden of the people along with you so that you will not bear it all by yourself. [18] And say to the people: Consecrate yourselves for tomorrow, and you shall eat meat; for you have wailed in the hearing of the LORD, saying, 'If only we had meat to eat! Surely it was better for us in Egypt.' Therefore the LORD will give you meat, and you shall eat. [19] You shall eat not only one day, or two days, or five days, or ten days, or twenty days, [20] but for a whole month—until it comes out of your nostrils and becomes loathsome to you—because you have rejected the LORD who is among you, and have wailed before him, saying, 'Why did we ever leave Egypt?'" [21] But Moses said, "The people I am with number six hundred thousand on foot; and you say, 'I will give them meat, that they may eat for a whole month'! [22] Are there enough flocks and herds to slaughter for them? Are there enough fish in the sea to catch for them?" [23] The LORD said to Moses, "Is the LORD's

a   That is Burning

11.4–35: Rebellion and leadership. The coherence is difficult and likely reflects different interwoven traditions about food and Moses' leadership. On the provision of food, see 20.1–13. 4–15: The *rabble* (non-Israelites, Ex 12.38), along with the Israelites, despise God's gifts of food (and deliverance, v. 20). Nostalgic for Egyptian food, they consider the *manna* (see Ex 16.14–21) insufficient. In response to God's anger, Moses complains that given what the people have become, God has mistreated him, placing too heavy a leadership burden on him (see Ex 18.18) and not providing sufficient resources. Moses uses maternal imagery for God: God has conceived and birthed this people (Deut 32.18) and should assume the responsibilities of a wet nurse. Moses should not have to carry this burden *alone*, implying that God is negligent. Feeling caught in the middle, Moses asks for either relief or death. 16–20: God's reply: God will share the spirit given to Moses with others, who will share the burden (vv. 24–30), and God will provide the asked-for meat (vv. 31–35). Repeating the complaints, God declares that they are to prepare for an encounter with God; they will indeed get meat, but too much! 21–22: Moses wonders about the numbers to feed. 23: God's response: God's hand is not *too short* (see textual note

power limited?[a] Now you shall see whether my word will come true for you or not."

[24] So Moses went out and told the people the words of the Lord; and he gathered seventy elders of the people, and placed them all around the tent. [25] Then the Lord came down in the cloud and spoke to him, and took some of the spirit that was on him and put it on the seventy elders; and when the spirit rested upon them, they prophesied. But they did not do so again.

[26] Two men remained in the camp, one named Eldad, and the other named Medad, and the spirit rested on them; they were among those registered, but they had not gone out to the tent, and so they prophesied in the camp. [27] And a young man ran and told Moses, "Eldad and Medad are prophesying in the camp." [28] And Joshua son of Nun, the assistant of Moses, one of his chosen men,[b] said, "My lord Moses, stop them!" [29] But Moses said to him, "Are you jealous for my sake? Would that all the Lord's people were prophets, and that the Lord would put his spirit on them!" [30] And Moses and the elders of Israel returned to the camp.

[31] Then a wind went out from the Lord, and it brought quails from the sea and let them fall beside the camp, about a day's journey on this side and a day's journey on the other side, all around the camp, about two cubits deep on the ground. [32] So the people worked all that day and night and all the next day, gathering the quails; the least anyone gathered was ten homers; and they spread them out for themselves all around the camp. [33] But while the meat was still between their teeth, before it was consumed, the anger of the Lord was kindled against the people, and the Lord struck the people with a very great plague. [34] So that place was called Kibroth-hattaavah,[c] because there they buried the people who had the craving. [35] From Kibroth-hattaavah the people journeyed to Hazeroth.

12 While they were at Hazeroth, Miriam and Aaron spoke against Moses because of the Cushite woman whom he had married (for he had indeed married a Cushite woman); [2] and they said, "Has the Lord spoken only through Moses? Has he not spoken through us also?" And the Lord heard it. [3] Now the man Moses was very humble,[d] more so than anyone else on the face of the earth. [4] Suddenly the Lord said to Moses, Aaron, and Miriam, "Come out, you three, to the tent of meeting." So the three of them came out. [5] Then the Lord came down in a pillar of cloud, and stood at the entrance of the tent, and called Aaron and Miriam; and

a   Heb Lord's hand too short?
b   Or of Moses from his youth
c   That is Graves of craving
d   Or devout

a) to provide this food. God will show that his word is effective. **24–30:** As for burden-sharing, Moses gathers seventy elders; God shares Moses' spirit with them, and *they prophesied*. Such a charisma was given to various leaders (24.2; 27.18; 1 Sam 10.5–10) and was transferable (2 Kings 2.9). Unlike Moses, they prophesy only once. Even two elders who remained in the camp (Eldad and Medad) receive a share of God's spirit. Despite efforts by Joshua, Moses refuses restriction of God's word to himself only; indeed, he wishes that *all the Lord's people* could receive this charisma. **31–35:** Food provision (see vv.18–23) comes in the form of *quails* (see Ex 16.13; Ps 78.26–31), carried into the camp on a wind from *the sea*, the Gulf of Aqaba/Eilat. They cover the ground for miles to a depth of *two cubits* (ca. 3 ft [.9 m]); the least gathered was *ten homers* (65 bu [230 liters])! Before they had finished eating, God's anger was provoked and a plague swept the camp.

12.1–16: Familial challenge to Moses' leadership. 1–2: Moses' status as a unique spokesperson for God is challenged by Miriam (see Ex 15.19–21) and Aaron. Although some sources identify Miriam as Moses' sister (see Num 26.59), in Ex 15.20 she is called "the sister of Aaron," and underlying the challenge may be rivalry between two families. The stated basis for the challenge is that Moses had married a *Cushite woman*. Cush may refer to Ethiopia or to an area in Midian (see Hab 3.7) and hence the woman may be Zipporah (10.29; Ex 2.15–22), in which case Aaron and Miriam may be complaining of Zipporah's leadership role or influence with Moses (see Ex 4.24–26; 18.2). **3–8:** Challenges to Moses' unique relationship with God are not countenanced, stated generally (v. 3) and by God to Aaron and Miriam in Moses' presence. God customarily speaks to prophets in visions and dreams, but Moses is different for two reasons: he is uniquely entrusted with the house of Israel (Ex 40.38); God speaks to him directly (Ex 33.11; Deut 34.10) and he sees *the form of the Lord*, a human form that God assumes (see 14.14; Ex 24.9–11). The issue pertains both to what is heard (clarity) and what is seen (God). God assumes

Lebo-hamath •

Great Sea
(Mediterranean Sea)

Damascus •

Sea of
Gennesaret

C A N A A N

Hill Country

River Jordan

Jerusalem •

Hebron •

Dead Sea

Negeb

Wilderness
of Zin

• Kadesh

- - - - *Spies' route*

| 0 | 10 | 20 Miles |
| 0 | 10 | 20 Kilometers |

The route of the spies in chapter 13.

they both came forward. [6] And he said, "Hear my words:

> When there are prophets among you,
> I the LORD make myself known to them
> in visions;
> I speak to them in dreams.
> [7] Not so with my servant Moses;
> he is entrusted with all my house.
> [8] With him I speak face to face— clearly,
> not in riddles;
> and he beholds the form of the LORD.

Why then were you not afraid to speak against my servant Moses?" [9] And the anger of the LORD was kindled against them, and he departed.

[10] When the cloud went away from over the tent, Miriam had become leprous,[a] as white as snow. And Aaron turned towards Miriam and saw that she was leprous. [11] Then Aaron said to Moses, "Oh, my lord, do not punish us[b] for a sin that we have so foolishly committed. [12] Do not let her be like one stillborn, whose flesh is half consumed when it comes out of its mother's womb." [13] And Moses cried to the LORD, "O God, please heal her." [14] But the LORD said to Moses, "If her father had but spit in her face, would she not bear her shame for seven days? Let her be shut out of the camp for seven days, and after that she may be brought in again." [15] So Miriam was shut out of the camp for seven days; and the people did not set out on the march until Miriam had been brought in again. [16] After that the people set out from Hazeroth, and camped in the wilderness of Paran.

13 The LORD said to Moses, [2] "Send men to spy out the land of Canaan, which I am giving to the Israelites; from each of their ancestral tribes you shall send a man, every one a leader among them." [3] So Moses sent them from the wilderness of Paran, according to the command of the LORD, all of them leading men among the Israelites. [4] These were their names: From the tribe of Reuben, Shammua son of Zaccur; [5] from the tribe of Simeon, Shaphat son of Hori; [6] from the tribe of Judah, Caleb son of Jephunneh; [7] from the tribe of Issachar, Igal son of Joseph; [8] from the tribe of Ephraim, Hoshea son of Nun; [9] from the tribe of Benjamin, Palti son of Raphu; [10] from the tribe of Zebulun, Gaddiel son of Sodi; [11] from the tribe of Joseph (that is, from the tribe of Manasseh), Gaddi son of Susi; [12] from the tribe of Dan, Ammiel son of Gemalli; [13] from the tribe of Asher, Sethur son of Michael; [14] from the tribe of Naphtali, Nahbi son of Vophsi; [15] from the tribe of Gad, Geuel son of Machi. [16] These were the names of the men whom Moses sent to spy out the land. And Moses changed the name of Hoshea son of Nun to Joshua.

[17] Moses sent them to spy out the land of Canaan, and said to them, "Go up there into the Negeb, and go up into the hill country, [18] and see what the land is like, and whether the people who live in it are strong or weak, whether they are few or many, [19] and whether the land they live in is good or bad, and whether the towns that they live in are unwalled or fortified, [20] and whether the land is rich or poor, and whether there are trees in it or not. Be bold, and bring some of the fruit of

---

a   A term for several skin diseases; precise meaning uncertain

b   Heb *do not lay sin upon us*

---

that Miriam and Aaron were aware of this and is angry (11.33). **10–16**: Miriam becomes *leprous* (an unidentified skin disease); Aaron interprets it as a consequence of their foolish sin and pleads ironically that *"my lord"* Moses spare them. **11–12**: *Do not lay sin upon us* (see textual note b) is preferable; the effect is intrinsic to the deed. The whiteness of Miriam's skin occasions the stillborn analogy. Why Aaron does not suffer the same effects is unknown; cf. Ex 32.21–24n. **13–15**: Moses prays on Miriam's behalf; God responds with banishment from the camp *for seven days*, either an external sign of shame, or the period required for purification after skin disease (see Lev 13.4; 14.8). The people honor her by delaying the march until she returns, apparently healed.

13.1–14.45: *The spy mission and decision to attack.* The setting for chs 13–20 is *Kadesh*(-barnea), 13.26, about 50 mi (80 km) south of Beersheba in the wilderness of Paran (or Zin, 20.1). This rebellion is decisive for Israel's future. Two sources are combined here: in one, only Caleb is righteous, while in the other, both Joshua and Caleb are righteous. **13.1–33**: Twelve scouts, one from each tribe, are chosen to spy on Canaan at God's command (see 32.6–13; Deut 1.22–45); most of those named do not occur elsewhere. **17–20**: Moses gives instructions regarding destination and observations to be made. **17**: *The Negeb* is the semidesert region in southern

the land." Now it was the season of the first ripe grapes.

²¹ So they went up and spied out the land from the wilderness of Zin to Rehob, near Lebo-hamath. ²² They went up into the Negeb, and came to Hebron; and Ahiman, Sheshai, and Talmai, the Anakites, were there. (Hebron was built seven years before Zoan in Egypt.) ²³ And they came to the Wadi Eshcol, and cut down from there a branch with a single cluster of grapes, and they carried it on a pole between two of them. They also brought some pomegranates and figs. ²⁴ That place was called the Wadi Eshcol,ᵃ because of the cluster that the Israelites cut down from there.

²⁵ At the end of forty days they returned from spying out the land. ²⁶ And they came to Moses and Aaron and to all the congregation of the Israelites in the wilderness of Paran, at Kadesh; they brought back word to them and to all the congregation, and showed them the fruit of the land. ²⁷ And they told him, "We came to the land to which you sent us; it flows with milk and honey, and this is its fruit. ²⁸ Yet the people who live in the land are strong, and the towns are fortified and very large; and besides, we saw the descendants of Anak there. ²⁹ The Amalekites live in the land of the Negeb; the Hittites, the Jebusites, and the Amorites live in the hill country; and the Canaanites live by the sea, and along the Jordan."

³⁰ But Caleb quieted the people before Moses, and said, "Let us go up at once and occupy it, for we are well able to overcome it." ³¹ Then the men who had gone up with him said, "We are not able to go up against this people, for they are stronger than we." ³² So

they brought to the Israelites an unfavorable report of the land that they had spied out, saying, "The land that we have gone through as spies is a land that devours its inhabitants; and all the people that we saw in it are of great size. ³³ There we saw the Nephilim (the Anakites come from the Nephilim); and to ourselves we seemed like grasshoppers, and so we seemed to them."

14 Then all the congregation raised a loud cry, and the people wept that night. ² And all the Israelites complained against Moses and Aaron; the whole congregation said to them, "Would that we had died in the land of Egypt! Or would that we had died in this wilderness! ³ Why is the LORD bringing us into this land to fall by the sword? Our wives and our little ones will become booty; would it not be better for us to go back to Egypt?" ⁴ So they said to one another, "Let us choose a captain, and go back to Egypt."

⁵ Then Moses and Aaron fell on their faces before all the assembly of the congregation of the Israelites. ⁶ And Joshua son of Nun and Caleb son of Jephunneh, who were among those who had spied out the land, tore their clothes ⁷ and said to all the congregation of the Israelites, "The land that we went through as spies is an exceedingly good land. ⁸ If the LORD is pleased with us, he will bring us into this land and give it to us, a land that flows with milk and honey. ⁹ Only, do not rebel against the LORD; and do not fear the people of the land, for they are no more than bread for us; their protection is removed from

---

ᵃ That is *Cluster*

Israel. **20:** *Season of the first ripe grapes,* late summer. **21–24:** They scout the length of the country, to *Rehob, near Lebo-hamath* in the far north (see 34.7–9n.), though vv. 22–24 report only on the Negeb and Judah, from which they bring back fruit; especially noted is a cluster of grapes (hence the name Eshcol, near Hebron; see translators' note *a*). **22:** *The Anakites,* see v. 33n. **25–33:** After forty days the scouts bring back a mixed report. The initial report is realistic (vv. 28–29); the land is bountiful but filled with strong people and fortified cities. The identity and placement of indigenous peoples is not always clear (compare 13.29 with 14.25,45; Gen 15.19–21), reflecting different traditions. **28:** *Anak,* see v. 33n. **29:** The *Amalekites,* a perennial enemy of Israel (Ex 17.8–16). **30–33:** A division occurs among the scouts; Caleb expresses confidence, while others give *an unfavorable report,* voicing alarm at the size of its inhabitants. This report is exaggerated for effect; it succeeds. **33:** *The Anakites* (vv. 22,28,33), a people giant in stature and associated with the *Nephilim* (see Gen 6.4; Josh 15.14). **14.1–45:** Seduced by the negative report, the people despise God's promise of land and complain against Moses and Aaron for fear of their lives and the fate of their dependents (see 31.13–18). **4:** They plot to choose a new leader and reverse the Exodus. **5–10a:** They persist in spite of the leaders' urgent pleas (*fell on their faces*; 16.4,22), expressions of

them, and the LORD is with us; do not fear them." [10] But the whole congregation threatened to stone them.

Then the glory of the LORD appeared at the tent of meeting to all the Israelites. [11] And the LORD said to Moses, "How long will this people despise me? And how long will they refuse to believe in me, in spite of all the signs that I have done among them? [12] I will strike them with pestilence and disinherit them, and I will make of you a nation greater and mightier than they."

[13] But Moses said to the LORD, "Then the Egyptians will hear of it, for in your might you brought up this people from among them, [14] and they will tell the inhabitants of this land. They have heard that you, O LORD, are in the midst of this people; for you, O LORD, are seen face to face, and your cloud stands over them and you go in front of them, in a pillar of cloud by day and in a pillar of fire by night. [15] Now if you kill this people all at one time, then the nations who have heard about you will say, [16] 'It is because the LORD was not able to bring this people into the land he swore to give them that he has slaughtered them in the wilderness.' [17] And now, therefore, let the power of the LORD be great in the way that you promised when you spoke, saying,

[18] 'The LORD is slow to anger,
and abounding in steadfast love,
forgiving iniquity and transgression,
but by no means clearing the guilty,
visiting the iniquity of the parents

upon the children
to the third and the fourth generation.'
[19] Forgive the iniquity of this people according to the greatness of your steadfast love, just as you have pardoned this people, from Egypt even until now."

[20] Then the LORD said, "I do forgive, just as you have asked; [21] nevertheless—as I live, and as all the earth shall be filled with the glory of the LORD— [22] none of the people who have seen my glory and the signs that I did in Egypt and in the wilderness, and yet have tested me these ten times and have not obeyed my voice, [23] shall see the land that I swore to give to their ancestors; none of those who despised me shall see it. [24] But my servant Caleb, because he has a different spirit and has followed me wholeheartedly, I will bring into the land into which he went, and his descendants shall possess it. [25] Now, since the Amalekites and the Canaanites live in the valleys, turn tomorrow and set out for the wilderness by the way to the Red Sea."[a]

[26] And the LORD spoke to Moses and to Aaron, saying: [27] How long shall this wicked congregation complain against me? I have heard the complaints of the Israelites, which they complain against me. [28] Say to them, "As I live," says the LORD, "I will do to you the very things I heard you say: [29] your dead bodies shall fall in this very wilderness; and of all your number, included in the census, from twenty years old and upward, who have

[a] Or *Sea of Reeds*

distress (*tore their clothes*; Gen 37.34), and assurances that the indigenous peoples are but *bread* to eat (compare 13.32; Ps 14.4) and their gods will provide no *protection*, . . . *the LORD is with us*. Rather than rejoice in the report of *an exceedingly good land* and trust that God will see to the promise, the people *rebel against the LORD* and threaten the leaders with death. **10b–38:** To these developments God responds (*glory* is the divine manifestation in a fiery cloud; see 9.15–23n.). This response has several dimensions. **11–12:** God voices a lament (repeated in v. 26), echoing those of the people and Moses (11.11–14). God announces a disastrous judgment (cf. Ex 9.15); God will disown Israel and start over with Moses (cf. Ex 32.9–10). This announcement is preliminary, a point for debate with Moses (see 16.20–21). **13–38:** God engages Moses in conversation. Moses argues (compare Ex 32.11–14) that God's reputation among the nations is at stake; they will conclude that God failed them. Their opinion should count with God. Moses also appeals to God's promise (see Ex 34.6–7), pleading for God to act according to his *steadfast love*: *forgiving* the people as God had done *ten times* (v. 22; cf. Gen 31.7). God forgives Israel (v. 20), but forgiveness does not cut off all consequences; the old generation will die in the wilderness and their children suffer for the adults' infidelity (vv. 27–35; 26.64–65; 32.10–12). *I will do to you the very things I heard you say* (v. 28). In effect: your will, not mine, is granted. Judgment is intrinsic to the deed (*you shall bear your iniquity*, v. 34; 32.23). Yet, the consequences are softened: the children and the clans of Caleb and Joshua (vv. 24,30,38; see Josh 14.6–14) will enter the land. But the rest of the people must continue their wandering for

complained against me, ³⁰ not one of you shall come into the land in which I swore to settle you, except Caleb son of Jephunneh and Joshua son of Nun. ³¹ But your little ones, who you said would become booty, I will bring in, and they shall know the land that you have despised. ³² But as for you, your dead bodies shall fall in this wilderness. ³³ And your children shall be shepherds in the wilderness for forty years, and shall suffer for your faithlessness, until the last of your dead bodies lies in the wilderness. ³⁴ According to the number of the days in which you spied out the land, forty days, for every day a year, you shall bear your iniquity, forty years, and you shall know my displeasure." ³⁵ I the LORD have spoken; surely I will do thus to all this wicked congregation gathered together against me: in this wilderness they shall come to a full end, and there they shall die.

³⁶ And the men whom Moses sent to spy out the land, who returned and made all the congregation complain against him by bringing a bad report about the land— ³⁷ the men who brought an unfavorable report about the land died by a plague before the LORD. ³⁸ But Joshua son of Nun and Caleb son of Jephunneh alone remained alive, of those men who went to spy out the land.

³⁹ When Moses told these words to all the Israelites, the people mourned greatly. ⁴⁰ They rose early in the morning and went up to the heights of the hill country, saying, "Here we are. We will go up to the place that the LORD has promised, for we have sinned." ⁴¹ But Moses said, "Why do you continue to transgress the command of the LORD? That will not succeed. ⁴² Do not go up, for the LORD is not with you; do not let yourselves be struck down before your enemies. ⁴³ For the Amalekites and the Canaanites will confront you there, and you shall fall by the sword; because you have turned back from following the LORD, the LORD will not be with you." ⁴⁴ But they presumed to go up to the heights of the hill country, even though the ark of the covenant of the LORD, and Moses, had not left the camp. ⁴⁵ Then the Amalekites and the Canaanites who lived in that hill country came down and defeated them, pursuing them as far as Hormah.

15 The LORD spoke to Moses, saying: ² Speak to the Israelites and say to them: When you come into the land you are to inhabit, which I am giving you, ³ and you make an offering by fire to the LORD from the herd or from the flock—whether a burnt offering or a sacrifice, to fulfill a vow or as a freewill offering or at your appointed festivals—to make a pleasing odor for the LORD, ⁴ then whoever presents such an offering to the LORD shall present also a grain offering, one-tenth of an ephah of choice flour, mixed with one-fourth of a hin of oil. ⁵ Moreover, you shall offer one-fourth of a hin of wine as a drink offering with the burnt offering or the sacrifice, for each lamb. ⁶ For a ram, you shall offer a grain offering, two-tenths of an ephah of choice flour mixed with one-third of a hin of oil; ⁷ and as a drink offering you shall offer one-third of a hin of wine, a pleasing odor to the LORD. ⁸ When you offer a bull as a burnt offering or a sacrifice, to fulfill a vow or as an offering of well-being to the LORD, ⁹ then you shall present with the bull a grain offering, three-tenths of an ephah of choice flour, mixed with half a hin of oil, ¹⁰ and you shall present as a drink offering half a hin of wine, as an offering by fire, a pleasing odor to the LORD.

¹¹ Thus it shall be done for each ox or ram, or for each of the male lambs or the kids. ¹² According to the number that you offer, so you shall do with each and every one. ¹³ Every native Israelite shall do these things in this way, in presenting an offering by fire,

a generation until they die. **39–45:** The people mourn over the loss, confess their sin, and seek to make things right by taking the land on their own; but they are defeated, for neither God (in the ark) nor Moses goes with them. **45:** *Hormah*, a city near Beersheba (see 21.2–3).

15.1–41: Statutes for life in the land. The narrative is interrupted by a series of statutes for *when you come into the land* (15.2,18); God still intends a future for them. The statutes also apply to outsiders, who have equal status before God concerning many issues relating to the land: *you and the alien shall be alike before the LORD* (v. 15). **1–16:** A grain offering (flour mixed with oil) and a drink offering (wine)—agricultural products—shall accompany each *offering by fire* listed in 15.3, rather than selective instances (see Lev 1–7). **3:** *Pleasing odor,* see Gen

a pleasing odor to the LORD. [14] An alien who lives with you, or who takes up permanent residence among you, and wishes to offer an offering by fire, a pleasing odor to the LORD, shall do as you do. [15] As for the assembly, there shall be for both you and the resident alien a single statute, a perpetual statute throughout your generations; you and the alien shall be alike before the LORD. [16] You and the alien who resides with you shall have the same law and the same ordinance.

[17] The LORD spoke to Moses, saying: [18] Speak to the Israelites and say to them: After you come into the land to which I am bringing you, [19] whenever you eat of the bread of the land, you shall present a donation to the LORD. [20] From your first batch of dough you shall present a loaf as a donation; you shall present it just as you present a donation from the threshing floor. [21] Throughout your generations you shall give to the LORD a donation from the first of your batch of dough.

[22] But if you unintentionally fail to observe all these commandments that the LORD has spoken to Moses— [23] everything that the LORD has commanded you by Moses, from the day the LORD gave commandment and thereafter, throughout your generations— [24] then if it was done unintentionally without the knowledge of the congregation, the whole congregation shall offer one young bull for a burnt offering, a pleasing odor to the LORD, together with its grain offering and its drink offering, according to the ordinance, and one male goat for a sin offering. [25] The priest shall make atonement for all the congregation of the Israelites, and they shall be forgiven; it was unintentional, and they have brought their offering, an offering by fire to the LORD, and their sin offering before the LORD, for their error. [26] All the congregation of the Israelites shall be forgiven, as well as the aliens residing among them, because the whole people was involved in the error.

[27] An individual who sins unintentionally shall present a female goat a year old for a sin offering. [28] And the priest shall make atonement before the LORD for the one who commits an error, when it is unintentional, to make atonement for the person, who then shall be forgiven. [29] For both the native among the Israelites and the alien residing among them—you shall have the same law for anyone who acts in error. [30] But whoever acts high-handedly, whether a native or an alien, affronts the LORD, and shall be cut off from among the people. [31] Because of having despised the word of the LORD and broken his commandment, such a person shall be utterly cut off and bear the guilt.

[32] When the Israelites were in the wilderness, they found a man gathering sticks on the sabbath day. [33] Those who found him gathering sticks brought him to Moses, Aaron, and to the whole congregation. [34] They put him in custody, because it was not clear what should be done to him. [35] Then the LORD said to Moses, "The man shall be put to death; all the congregation shall stone him outside the camp." [36] The whole congregation brought him outside the camp and stoned him to death, just as the LORD had commanded Moses.

[37] The LORD said to Moses: [38] Speak to the Israelites, and tell them to make fringes on

8.21; Ex 29.18; Lev 1.9; etc. 4: *One-tenth of an ephah,* ca. 2 qts (2.3 liters). *Hin,* ca. 1 gal (3.8 liters). 17–21: Prescribes a *donation* of one loaf from the first batch of dough to acknowledge that all such gifts come from God. Broadens earlier statutes regarding first fruits to include that produced by humans (see Lev 23.9–14; Num 18.13–18). 22–36: Sacrifices for atonement for unintentional sins (Lev 4.13–21), for the *whole people* (vv. 22–26) and for the *individual* (vv. 27–29), and penalties for individuals who *act high-handedly,* i.e., who are unrepentant (vv. 30–31). In 5.5–8 (Lev 6.7) intentional sins can be atoned for, apparently because the persons are repentant. Sacrifices are a God-given means through which to obtain forgiveness. 30–31: *Cut off,* see 9.13n. 32–36: Intentional sabbath-breaking illustrates such defiance. The man's labor carried the death penalty (Ex 31.14–15; 35.2–3); yet it was not clear how to proceed—perhaps some thought that this was too minor a violation, or it was unclear if the penalty should be enforced by the community or by God. Lev 24.10–23 and Num 9.6–14 narrate other cases requiring a divine oracle to clarify a law's applicability. 37–41: Pertains to clothing (see Deut 22.12). Tassels, worn in the ancient Near East by royalty, are to be attached to each corner of everyone's garments, with a blue(-purple) cord on each, a public sign of Israel's status as a holy people and a reminder of what that entailed.

the corners of their garments throughout their generations and to put a blue cord on the fringe at each corner. ³⁹ You have the fringe so that, when you see it, you will remember all the commandments of the LORD and do them, and not follow the lust of your own heart and your own eyes. ⁴⁰ So you shall remember and do all my commandments, and you shall be holy to your God. ⁴¹ I am the LORD your God, who brought you out of the land of Egypt, to be your God: I am the LORD your God.

16 Now Korah son of Izhar son of Kohath son of Levi, along with Dathan and Abiram sons of Eliab, and On son of Peleth— descendants of Reuben—took ² two hundred fifty Israelite men, leaders of the congregation, chosen from the assembly, well-known men,ᵃ and they confronted Moses. ³ They assembled against Moses and against Aaron, and said to them, "You have gone too far! All the congregation are holy, every one of them, and the LORD is among them. So why then do you exalt yourselves above the assembly of the LORD?" ⁴ When Moses heard it, he fell on his face. ⁵ Then he said to Korah and all his company, "In the morning the LORD will make known who is his, and who is holy, and who will be allowed to approach him; the one whom he will choose he will allow to approach him. ⁶ Do this: take censers, Korah and all yourᵇ company, ⁷ and tomorrow put fire in them, and lay

incense on them before the LORD; and the man whom the LORD chooses shall be the holy one. You Levites have gone too far!" ⁸ Then Moses said to Korah, "Hear now, you Levites! ⁹ Is it too little for you that the God of Israel has separated you from the congregation of Israel, to allow you to approach him in order to perform the duties of the LORD's tabernacle, and to stand before the congregation and serve them? ¹⁰ He has allowed you to approach him, and all your brother Levites with you; yet you seek the priesthood as well! ¹¹ Therefore you and all your company have gathered together against the LORD. What is Aaron that you rail against him?"

¹² Moses sent for Dathan and Abiram sons of Eliab; but they said, "We will not come! ¹³ Is it too little that you have brought us up out of a land flowing with milk and honey to kill us in the wilderness, that you must also lord it over us? ¹⁴ It is clear you have not brought us into a land flowing with milk and honey, or given us an inheritance of fields and vineyards. Would you put out the eyes of these men? We will not come!"

¹⁵ Moses was very angry and said to the LORD, "Pay no attention to their offering. I

ᵃ Cn: Heb *and they confronted Moses, and two hundred fifty men… well-known men*
ᵇ Heb *his*

The call to be holy (v. 40; Lev 19.2) is a call to be true to the relationship in which they already stand.
16.1–50: The rebellions of Korah and others. Numbers 16–18 focus on issues relating to legitimacy of leadership, especially service in the tabernacle. Two rebellions are reported, one by Korah and others (vv. 1–40); a second by the whole congregation in response to their deaths (vv. 41–50). Conflict between Levites and Aaronides may reflect later controversies among rival priestly groups (see 12.1–16; 17.1–13). The first rebellion is composite, combining separate rebellions by Korah and his band, and of Dathan and Abiram and their followers. **1–21:** Korah belonged to the Levite clan responsible for the tabernacle's most holy things (4.4). **2–3:** He is joined by other Levites, the Reubenites Dathan, Abiram, and On, along with two hundred fifty other leaders; they challenge Moses and Aaron: *You have gone too far . . . you exalt yourselves* (see v. 13). Their claim that *every one* is holy is correct (15.40; Deut 7.6); the problem is the implication that Aaron and Moses are not more holy than they. The issue is not simply priestly status for all Levites (so Moses, v. 10), though this is primary. The presence of the group from Reuben reveals another interest: extending secular leadership prerogatives to representatives from all twelve tribes. **4–21:** After he *fell on his face* (14.5), Moses proposes a test. The antagonists are to bring *censers* (metal trays on which incense is burned, Lev 10.1–2) to the tabernacle and prepare them for offering incense. If God accepts their offerings, priestly status would be recognized. **5–7:** *And who is holy* assumes gradations of holiness. God will decide the identity of *the holy one* who is to *approach him* (i.e., the altar); this entails a holiness that sets him apart from other holy ones. **8–11:** The Levites' challenge to Aaron's leadership is a move *against the LORD*, elevating privilege above service. **12–14:** Speaking to challenges to his own leadership, Moses sends for Dathan and Abiram. They twice refuse, and ironically even call Egypt a land of milk and honey. **15–21:** Reverting to the Korah story of vv. 8–11, Moses tells God to ignore their offerings and repeats his instructions

have not taken one donkey from them, and I have not harmed any one of them." [16] And Moses said to Korah, "As for you and all your company, be present tomorrow before the LORD, you and they and Aaron; [17] and let each one of you take his censer, and put incense on it, and each one of you present his censer before the LORD, two hundred fifty censers; you also, and Aaron, each his censer." [18] So each man took his censer, and they put fire in the censers and laid incense on them, and they stood at the entrance of the tent of meeting with Moses and Aaron. [19] Then Korah assembled the whole congregation against them at the entrance of the tent of meeting. And the glory of the LORD appeared to the whole congregation.

[20] Then the LORD spoke to Moses and to Aaron, saying: [21] Separate yourselves from this congregation, so that I may consume them in a moment. [22] They fell on their faces, and said, "O God, the God of the spirits of all flesh, shall one person sin and you become angry with the whole congregation?"

[23] And the LORD spoke to Moses, saying: [24] Say to the congregation: Get away from the dwellings of Korah, Dathan, and Abiram. [25] So Moses got up and went to Dathan and Abiram; the elders of Israel followed him. [26] He said to the congregation, "Turn away from the tents of these wicked men, and touch nothing of theirs, or you will be swept away for all their sins." [27] So they got away from the dwellings of Korah, Dathan, and Abiram; and Dathan and Abiram came out and stood at the entrance of their tents, together with their wives, their children, and their little ones. [28] And Moses said, "This is how you shall know that the LORD has sent me to do all these works; it has not been of my own

accord: [29] If these people die a natural death, or if a natural fate comes on them, then the LORD has not sent me. [30] But if the LORD creates something new, and the ground opens its mouth and swallows them up, with all that belongs to them, and they go down alive into Sheol, then you shall know that these men have despised the LORD."

[31] As soon as he finished speaking all these words, the ground under them was split apart. [32] The earth opened its mouth and swallowed them up, along with their households—everyone who belonged to Korah and all their goods. [33] So they with all that belonged to them went down alive into Sheol; the earth closed over them, and they perished from the midst of the assembly. [34] All Israel around them fled at their outcry, for they said, "The earth will swallow us too!" [35] And fire came out from the LORD and consumed the two hundred fifty men offering the incense.

[36] [a] Then the LORD spoke to Moses, saying: [37] Tell Eleazar son of Aaron the priest to take the censers out of the blaze; then scatter the fire far and wide. [38] For the censers of these sinners have become holy at the cost of their lives. Make them into hammered plates as a covering for the altar, for they presented them before the LORD and they became holy. Thus they shall be a sign to the Israelites. [39] So Eleazar the priest took the bronze censers that had been presented by those who were burned; and they were hammered out as a covering for the altar— [40] a reminder to the Israelites that no outsider, who is not of the descendants of Aaron, shall approach to offer incense before the LORD, so as not to become

[a]   Ch 17.1 in Heb

to Korah, adding that Aaron is also to appear. Each man stands before the LORD at the tent with their censers prepared. Korah assembles the entire congregation, apparently sympathetic. The glory of the LORD appears (cf. 9.15–16); God determines to destroy the congregation. 22–34: Moses and Aaron intercede; not all should bear the consequences for *one person*. The phrase *the God of the spirits of all flesh* (see 27.16) appeals to God as creator, who gives breath to all. God responds positively, separating the congregation from the rebels and their families. Moses sets up a test to demonstrate that this is God's decision. 29–30: If these people die a natural death, then he is wrong; if God *creates something new* (a creation for this moment) and the ground opens up and swallows them, and they descend alive to *Sheol* (the abode of the dead), then they have *despised the LORD*. 32–34: The latter happens immediately to *everyone who belonged to Korah* (see 26.9–10; Deut 11.6; Ps 106.17). 35–40: Upon the killing of the two hundred fifty men, attention is given to their censers, which became holy because of the use to which they were put. Gathered from the fire by Eleazar, Aaron's son (see Lev 21.11), they are hammered into

like Korah and his company—just as the LORD had said to him through Moses.

⁴¹ On the next day, however, the whole congregation of the Israelites rebelled against Moses and against Aaron, saying, "You have killed the people of the LORD." ⁴² And when the congregation had assembled against them, Moses and Aaron turned toward the tent of meeting; the cloud had covered it and the glory of the LORD appeared. ⁴³ Then Moses and Aaron came to the front of the tent of meeting, ⁴⁴ and the LORD spoke to Moses, saying, ⁴⁵ "Get away from this congregation, so that I may consume them in a moment." And they fell on their faces. ⁴⁶ Moses said to Aaron, "Take your censer, put fire on it from the altar and lay incense on it, and carry it quickly to the congregation and make atonement for them. For wrath has gone out from the LORD; the plague has begun." ⁴⁷ So Aaron took it as Moses had ordered, and ran into the middle of the assembly, where the plague had already begun among the people. He put on the incense, and made atonement for the people. ⁴⁸ He stood between the dead and the living; and the plague was stopped. ⁴⁹ Those who died by the plague were fourteen thousand seven hundred, besides those who died in the affair of Korah. ⁵⁰ When the plague was stopped, Aaron returned to Moses at the entrance of the tent of meeting.

17
ᵃThe LORD spoke to Moses, saying: ² Speak to the Israelites, and get twelve staffs from them, one for each ancestral house, from all the leaders of their ancestral houses. Write each man's name on his staff, ³ and write Aaron's name on the staff of Levi. For there shall be one staff for the head of each ancestral house. ⁴ Place them in the tent of meeting before the covenant,ᵇ where I meet with you. ⁵ And the staff of the man whom I choose shall sprout; thus I will put a stop to the complaints of the Israelites that they continually make against you. ⁶ Moses spoke to the Israelites; and all their leaders gave him staffs, one for each leader, according to their ancestral houses, twelve staffs; and the staff of Aaron was among theirs. ⁷ So Moses placed the staffs before the LORD in the tent of the covenant.ᵇ

⁸ When Moses went into the tent of the covenantᵇ on the next day, the staff of Aaron for the house of Levi had sprouted. It put forth buds, produced blossoms, and bore ripe almonds. ⁹ Then Moses brought out all the staffs from before the LORD to all the Israelites; and they looked, and each man took his staff. ¹⁰ And the LORD said to Moses, "Put back the staff of Aaron before the covenant,ᵇ to be kept as a warning to rebels, so that you may make an end of their complaints against me, or else they will die." ¹¹ Moses did so; just as the LORD commanded him, so he did.

¹² The Israelites said to Moses, "We are perishing; we are lost, all of us are lost! ¹³ Everyone who approaches the tabernacle of the LORD will die. Are we all to perish?"

ᵃ Ch 17.16 in Heb
ᵇ Or treaty, or testimony; Heb eduth

---

an altar covering, to serve as a reminder that only Aaronides can approach the LORD. 41–50: The congregation blames Moses and Aaron, threatening them. The glory of the LORD appears and God threatens to annihilate them (see 16.19–22). Moses and Aaron intercede and act to atone for the intentional sins of the people. 48: They *stood between the dead and the living*, because a plague had already broken out. The action stops the plague, but not before 14,700 died.

17.1–13: Aaron's blossoming staff. God again demonstrates the priestly status of Aaron. Like the bronze covering for the altar (16.38), Aaron's staff serves as an ongoing visual sign of God's choice of Aaron. This story is best designated a legend, with parallels in many cultures. God's effort on Aaron's behalf is settled by another ordeal. 4–7: Moses places twelve staffs, each inscribed with a leader's name, *before the covenant*, i.e., the ark (10.33–36; Ex 16.33–34; 25.16,21). Aaron's staff, (of the house of Levi) the powers of which have been demonstrated (Ex 7.8–12,19; 8.16–17), was added to them. God set the terms: the staff that sprouts indicates the leader God had chosen for priestly prerogatives. 8–13: The following morning only Aaron's staff had flowered and it bore ripe almonds (symbolic of life-enhancing capacities of priests). Showing the evidence to the people, Moses puts the staff before the ark, to be kept as a *warning* (sign) to the rebels. God had performed such a sign to *put a stop to the complaints . . . against you* (pl.; v. 5) and *me* (v. 10). For prophetic usage of this image, see Isa 11.1–2.

18

The LORD said to Aaron: You and your sons and your ancestral house with you shall bear responsibility for offenses connected with the sanctuary, while you and your sons alone shall bear responsibility for offenses connected with the priesthood. [2] So bring with you also your brothers of the tribe of Levi, your ancestral tribe, in order that they may be joined to you, and serve you while you and your sons with you are in front of the tent of the covenant.[a] [3] They shall perform duties for you and for the whole tent. But they must not approach either the utensils of the sanctuary or the altar, otherwise both they and you will die. [4] They are attached to you in order to perform the duties of the tent of meeting, for all the service of the tent; no outsider shall approach you. [5] You yourselves shall perform the duties of the sanctuary and the duties of the altar, so that wrath may never again come upon the Israelites. [6] It is I who now take your brother Levites from among the Israelites; they are now yours as a gift, dedicated to the LORD, to perform the service of the tent of meeting. [7] But you and your sons with you shall diligently perform your priestly duties in all that concerns the altar and the area behind the curtain. I give your priesthood as a gift;[b] any outsider who approaches shall be put to death.

[8] The LORD spoke to Aaron: I have given you charge of the offerings made to me, all the holy gifts of the Israelites; I have given them to you and your sons as a priestly portion due you in perpetuity. [9] This shall be yours from the most holy things, reserved from the fire: every offering of theirs that they render to me as a most holy thing, whether grain offering, sin offering, or guilt offering, shall belong to you and your sons. [10] As a most holy thing you shall eat it; every male may eat it; it shall be holy to you. [11] This also is yours: I have given to you, together with your sons and daughters, as a perpetual due, whatever is set aside from the gifts of all the elevation offerings of the Israelites; everyone who is clean in your house may eat them. [12] All the best of the oil and all the best of the wine and of the grain, the choice produce that they give to the LORD, I have given to you. [13] The first fruits of all that is in their land, which they bring to the LORD, shall be yours; everyone who is clean in your house may eat of it. [14] Every devoted thing in Israel shall be yours. [15] The first issue of the womb of all creatures, human and animal, which is offered to the LORD, shall be yours; but the firstborn of human beings you shall redeem, and the firstborn of unclean animals you shall redeem. [16] Their redemption price, reckoned from one month of age, you shall fix at five shekels of silver, according to the shekel of the sanctuary (that is, twenty gerahs). [17] But the firstborn of a cow, or the firstborn of a sheep, or the firstborn of a goat, you shall not redeem; they are holy. You shall dash their blood on the altar, and shall turn their fat into smoke as an offering by fire for a pleasing odor to the LORD; [18] but their flesh shall be yours, just as the breast that is elevated and as the right thigh are yours. [19] All the holy offerings that the Israelites present to the LORD I have given to you, together with your sons and daughters, as a perpetual due;

---

a Or *treaty*, or *testimony*; Heb *eduth*
b Heb *as a service of gift*

18.1–32: Rights and responsibilities of priests and Levites. In response to the people's lament of 17.13, ch 18 is a recapitulation and redefinition of the responsibilities of priests and Levites along with their means of support. 1–7: Gathers previous material (see 1.50–53; 3.5–10,14–39; 4.1–33; 8.14–19) and delineates the relationship among the various groups regarding their duties at the tent of meeting. The protection of the community (i.e., outsiders, including Levites; vv. 4,7) from wrath (v. 5; see 1.53) is a prime concern (18.1,4–5,7,22). Priesthood is a gift from God as is the sanctuary service of their brother Levites (vv. 2, 6; see 8.19). 8–32: A review (from Lev 6–7; 27) of the God-commanded portion due the Aaronides from the people (vv. 8–20), and from the Levites (vv. 25–32, a new provision), and that due to the Levites (18.21–24), in *perpetuity* (vv. 8,11,19,23). 8–20: The *portion* due to the Aaronides consists of those *holy gifts* the people give to God, who in turn gives it to the priests and Levites for their support and for the sanctuary. 9–10: *The most holy things* are offerings for the priests (parts *reserved from the fire*, not burned). 11–19: Specifies the *holy offerings*; they are *a covenant of salt forever before the LORD* (v. 19). Salt, a preservative presented with all offerings, becomes a symbol for an everlasting covenant

it is a covenant of salt forever before the LORD for you and your descendants as well. [20] Then the LORD said to Aaron: You shall have no allotment in their land, nor shall you have any share among them; I am your share and your possession among the Israelites.

[21] To the Levites I have given every tithe in Israel for a possession in return for the service that they perform, the service in the tent of meeting. [22] From now on the Israelites shall no longer approach the tent of meeting, or else they will incur guilt and die. [23] But the Levites shall perform the service of the tent of meeting, and they shall bear responsibility for their own offenses; it shall be a perpetual statute throughout your generations. But among the Israelites they shall have no allotment, [24] because I have given to the Levites as their portion the tithe of the Israelites, which they set apart as an offering to the LORD. Therefore I have said of them that they shall have no allotment among the Israelites.

[25] Then the LORD spoke to Moses, saying: [26] You shall speak to the Levites, saying: When you receive from the Israelites the tithe that I have given you from them for your portion, you shall set apart an offering from it to the LORD, a tithe of the tithe. [27] It shall be reckoned to you as your gift, the same as the grain of the threshing floor and the fullness of the wine press. [28] Thus you also shall set apart an offering to the LORD from all the tithes that you receive from the Israelites; and from them you shall give the LORD's offering to the priest Aaron. [29] Out of all the gifts to you, you shall set apart every offering due to the LORD; the best of all of them is the part to be consecrated. [30] Say also to them: When you have set apart the best of it, then the rest shall be reckoned to the Levites as produce of the threshing floor, and as produce of the wine press. [31] You may eat it in any place, you and your households; for it is your payment for your service in the tent of meeting. [32] You shall incur no guilt by reason of it, when you have offered the best of it. But you shall not profane the holy gifts of the Israelites, on pain of death.

19 The LORD spoke to Moses and Aaron, saying: [2] This is a statute of the law that the LORD has commanded: Tell the Israelites to bring you a red heifer without defect, in which there is no blemish and on which no yoke has been laid. [3] You shall give it to the priest Eleazar, and it shall be taken outside the camp and slaughtered in his presence. [4] The priest Eleazar shall take some of its blood with his finger and sprinkle it seven times towards the front of the tent of meeting. [5] Then the heifer shall be burned in his sight; its skin, its flesh, and its blood, with its dung, shall be burned. [6] The priest shall take cedarwood, hyssop, and crimson material, and throw them into the fire in which the heifer is burning. [7] Then the priest shall wash his clothes and bathe his body in water, and afterwards he may come into the camp; but the priest shall remain unclean until evening.

(Lev 2.13; 2 Chr 13.5). *Firstborn*, see Ex 13.11–13. **20:** God's commitment to the Aaronides in perpetuity, for they have no *allotment*, that is, property. *I am your share*; they are dependent for life and health upon the gifts of God, mediated through human beings. **21–24:** The Levites' portion is the Israelites' tithe of agricultural produce. The tithe (one-tenth) belongs to God (v. 24) but is given to the Levites. They also have no tribal territory, but are given forty-eight cities with pasture land (see 35.1–8). **25–32:** The Levites are to give *a tithe of the tithe* they have received (*the best of it*) to the Aaronides, reflecting the highest status of that group. The other nine-tenths is no longer holy and becomes their own—*as your payment for your service*. But, if they do not give their tithe, that will *profane* the holy gifts, and they shall die.

19.1–22: Ritual of the red heifer. Provisions for rituals of purification upon contact with a corpse (expanding 5.1–4). **1–10:** Specifies the procedure by which a cleansing agent was prepared under the supervision of the priest. Eleazar is charged with this duty (Aaron dies at 20.28); he and his assistants must be ritually clean, but they become unclean upon contact with the holy and short-term decontamination rituals are prescribed for each. The unblemished (brown-) red heifer (more precisely, cow) perhaps symbolized blood/life. The burning of the animal (including its blood/life, v. 5, uniquely here) may have concentrated life in the ashes, which, when mixed with water and applied to the unclean person or thing, would counteract the contagious impurity of death. The placement of *cedarwood, hyssop,* and *crimson* yarn (probably symbolizing blood), during the burning

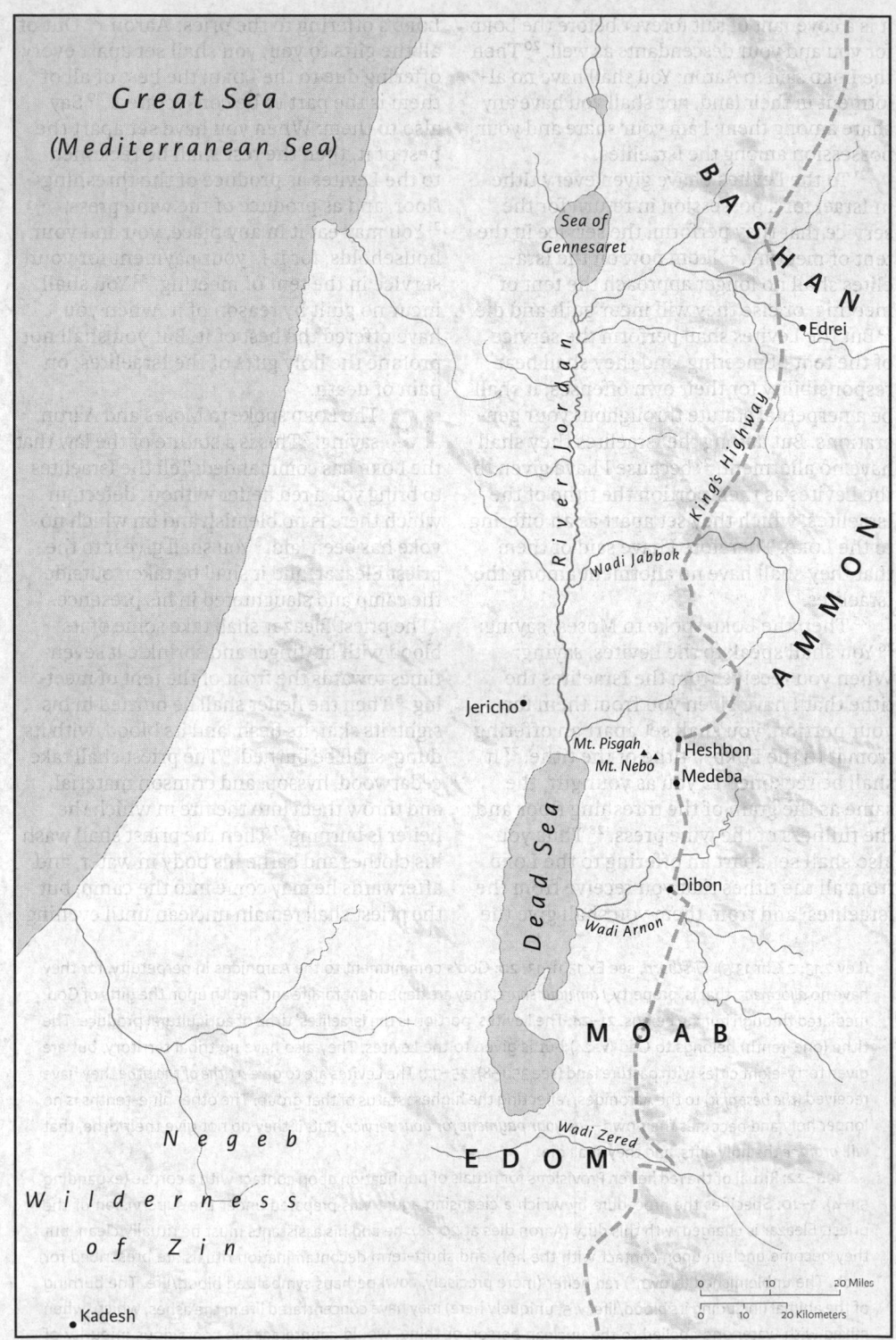

Conflicts in the Negreb and Transjordan.

[8] The one who burns the heifer[a] shall wash his clothes in water and bathe his body in water; he shall remain unclean until evening. [9] Then someone who is clean shall gather up the ashes of the heifer, and deposit them outside the camp in a clean place; and they shall be kept for the congregation of the Israelites for the water for cleansing. It is a purification offering. [10] The one who gathers the ashes of the heifer shall wash his clothes and be unclean until evening.

This shall be a perpetual statute for the Israelites and for the alien residing among them. [11] Those who touch the dead body of any human being shall be unclean seven days. [12] They shall purify themselves with the water on the third day and on the seventh day, and so be clean; but if they do not purify themselves on the third day and on the seventh day, they will not become clean. [13] All who touch a corpse, the body of a human being who has died, and do not purify themselves, defile the tabernacle of the LORD; such persons shall be cut off from Israel. Since water for cleansing was not dashed on them, they remain unclean; their uncleanness is still on them.

[14] This is the law when someone dies in a tent: everyone who comes into the tent, and everyone who is in the tent, shall be unclean seven days. [15] And every open vessel with no cover fastened on it is unclean. [16] Whoever in the open field touches one who has been killed by a sword, or who has died naturally,[b] or a human bone, or a grave, shall be unclean seven days. [17] For the unclean they shall take some ashes of the burnt purification offering, and running water shall be added in a vessel; [18] then a clean person shall take hyssop, dip it in the water, and sprinkle it on the tent, on all the furnishings, on the persons who were there, and on whoever touched the bone, the slain, the corpse, or the grave. [19] The clean person shall sprinkle the unclean ones on the third day and on the seventh day, thus purifying them on the seventh day. Then they shall wash their clothes and bathe themselves in water, and at evening they shall be clean. [20] Any who are unclean but do not purify themselves, those persons shall be cut off from the assembly, for they have defiled the sanctuary of the LORD. Since the water for cleansing has not been dashed on them, they are unclean.

[21] It shall be a perpetual statute for them. The one who sprinkles the water for cleansing shall wash his clothes, and whoever touches the water for cleansing shall be unclean until evening. [22] Whatever the unclean person touches shall be unclean, and anyone who touches it shall be unclean until evening.

20 The Israelites, the whole congregation, came into the wilderness of Zin in the first month, and the people stayed in Kadesh. Miriam died there, and was buried there.

[2] Now there was no water for the congregation; so they gathered together against Moses and against Aaron. [3] The people quarreled with Moses and said, "Would that we had died when our kindred died before the LORD! [4] Why have you brought the assembly of the LORD into this wilderness for us and our livestock to die here? [5] Why have you brought us up out of Egypt, to bring us to this wretched place? It is no place for grain, or figs, or vines, or pomegranates; and there is no water to

---

a Heb *it*
b Heb lacks *naturally*

---

intensified the ashes' purifying quality. **11–22:** Verses 11–13, detailed in vv. 14–22, specify the use to which the ashes and *running water* are put for persons and things that have had contact with death. As in other cases (see Lev 12.2) they are unclean for seven days; to become clean, they must twice be sprinkled with this mixture by a clean person (vv. 17–19; 19.9; 5.3–4). Otherwise, they *defile the tabernacle* where God dwells (5.3) and shall be *cut off from Israel* (vv. 13,20; see 9.13) for the sake of the community's wholeness.

20.1–29: The disobedience of Moses and Aaron. Explains why Israel's key leaders did not enter Canaan, marked especially by the *rebellion* of Moses and Aaron (compare Ex 17.1–7, also at Meribah, "quarrel"). **1:** *Kadesh*, see 13.26. God's command to journey back toward Egypt (14.25) was carried out and so they arrive again in Kadesh (setting out again in 20.22). **2–13:** The people again complain about wilderness conditions, this time that *there was no water* (vv. 2,5; compare 14.2–4). Moses and Aaron fall on their faces and turn toward God (14.5; 16.4); again the glory of the LORD appears (9.15–16). The reader expects judgment, but God recognizes that the

drink." ⁶ Then Moses and Aaron went away from the assembly to the entrance of the tent of meeting; they fell on their faces, and the glory of the LORD appeared to them. ⁷ The LORD spoke to Moses, saying: ⁸ Take the staff, and assemble the congregation, you and your brother Aaron, and command the rock before their eyes to yield its water. Thus you shall bring water out of the rock for them; thus you shall provide drink for the congregation and their livestock.

⁹ So Moses took the staff from before the LORD, as he had commanded him. ¹⁰ Moses and Aaron gathered the assembly together before the rock, and he said to them, "Listen, you rebels, shall we bring water for you out of this rock?" ¹¹ Then Moses lifted up his hand and struck the rock twice with his staff; water came out abundantly, and the congregation and their livestock drank. ¹² But the LORD said to Moses and Aaron, "Because you did not trust in me, to show my holiness before the eyes of the Israelites, therefore you shall not bring this assembly into the land that I have given them." ¹³ These are the waters of Meribah,ᵃ where the people of Israel quarreled with the LORD, and by which he showed his holiness.

¹⁴ Moses sent messengers from Kadesh to the king of Edom, "Thus says your brother Israel: You know all the adversity that has befallen us: ¹⁵ how our ancestors went down to Egypt, and we lived in Egypt a long time; and the Egyptians oppressed us and our ancestors; ¹⁶ and when we cried to the LORD,

he heard our voice, and sent an angel and brought us out of Egypt; and here we are in Kadesh, a town on the edge of your territory. ¹⁷ Now let us pass through your land. We will not pass through field or vineyard, or drink water from any well; we will go along the King's Highway, not turning aside to the right hand or to the left until we have passed through your territory."

¹⁸ But Edom said to him, "You shall not pass through, or we will come out with the sword against you." ¹⁹ The Israelites said to him, "We will stay on the highway; and if we drink of your water, we and our livestock, then we will pay for it. It is only a small matter; just let us pass through on foot." ²⁰ But he said, "You shall not pass through." And Edom came out against them with a large force, heavily armed. ²¹ Thus Edom refused to give Israel passage through their territory; so Israel turned away from them.

²² They set out from Kadesh, and the Israelites, the whole congregation, came to Mount Hor. ²³ Then the LORD said to Moses and Aaron at Mount Hor, on the border of the land of Edom, ²⁴ "Let Aaron be gathered to his people. For he shall not enter the land that I have given to the Israelites, because you rebelled against my command at the waters of Meribah. ²⁵ Take Aaron and his son Eleazar, and bring them up Mount Hor; ²⁶ strip Aaron of his vestments, and put them on his son Eleazar. But Aaron shall be

ᵃ That is *Quarrel*

need for water is real. **8–9:** God commands Moses to take *the staff . . . from before the* LORD (in the tent, 17.10–11) and *command* [i.e., speak to] *the rock before their eyes to yield its water.* **10–13:** Moses asks the people: *Shall we bring water for you out of the rock?* With this self-reference rather than God, he strikes (rather than commands) *the rock twice with his staff,* and water flows. God's response is negative: Moses and Aaron did not *trust in* God (Deut 32.51, "broke faith") to *show my holiness* before the people (but see v. 13) and hence they will not lead the people into the land. They *rebelled against my command* or *word* (20.24; 27.14); Deut 1.37; 3.26; 4.21; Ps 106.32–33 qualify Moses' fault. The text is unclear about the precise offense, and the judgment seems not to match the action, but the point seems to be that they compromised God's holiness *before the eyes of the Israelites.* The end result (here, water to drink) is not the only thing that counts as a witness to God, but also the means by which it is achieved. Water does not materialize out of thin air but courses through rock formations. God works in and through the natural to provide (see ch 11). **14–21:** Request to pass through Edom, to enter Canaan from the east (compare 14.39–45). **14:** *King of Edom,* Gen 36.31–39. *Your brother,* Gen 25.24–26. Edom refuses. **16:** *Angel,* Ex 14.19; 23.20–23; 33.2. **17:** *The King's Highway* is the major north-south route through Transjordan. A show of military force convinces Israel to go around Edom (see Judg 11.17–18; Deut 2.4–8). **22–29:** Death of Aaron and installation of Eleazar (see v. 12). **22:** *Mount Hor*'s location is unknown. **26–28:** Aaron's *vestments* (Ex 28) are transferred to Eleazar before *the whole congregation,* signifying continuity (Deut 32.50). Aaron dies (*gathered [to*

gathered to his people,[a] and shall die there." [27] Moses did as the LORD had commanded; they went up Mount Hor in the sight of the whole congregation. [28] Moses stripped Aaron of his vestments, and put them on his son Eleazar; and Aaron died there on the top of the mountain. Moses and Eleazar came down from the mountain. [29] When all the congregation saw that Aaron had died, all the house of Israel mourned for Aaron thirty days.

21 When the Canaanite, the king of Arad, who lived in the Negeb, heard that Israel was coming by the way of Atharim, he fought against Israel and took some of them captive. [2] Then Israel made a vow to the LORD and said, "If you will indeed give this people into our hands, then we will utterly destroy their towns." [3] The LORD listened to the voice of Israel, and handed over the Canaanites; and they utterly destroyed them and their towns; so the place was called Hormah.[b]

[4] From Mount Hor they set out by the way to the Red Sea,[c] to go around the land of Edom; but the people became impatient on the way. [5] The people spoke against God and against Moses, "Why have you brought us up out of Egypt to die in the wilderness? For there is no food and no water, and we detest this miserable food." [6] Then the LORD sent poisonous[d] serpents among the people, and they bit the people, so that many Israelites died. [7] The people came to Moses and said, "We have sinned by speaking against the LORD and against you; pray to the LORD to take away the serpents from us." So Moses

prayed for the people. [8] And the LORD said to Moses, "Make a poisonous[e] serpent, and set it on a pole; and everyone who is bitten shall look at it and live." [9] So Moses made a serpent of bronze, and put it upon a pole; and whenever a serpent bit someone, that person would look at the serpent of bronze and live.

[10] The Israelites set out, and camped in Oboth. [11] They set out from Oboth, and camped at Iye-abarim, in the wilderness bordering Moab toward the sunrise. [12] From there they set out, and camped in the Wadi Zered. [13] From there they set out, and camped on the other side of the Arnon, in[f] the wilderness that extends from the boundary of the Amorites; for the Arnon is the boundary of Moab, between Moab and the Amorites. [14] Wherefore it is said in the Book of the Wars of the LORD,

"Waheb in Suphah and the wadis.
The Arnon [15] and the slopes of the wadis
     that extend to the seat of Ar,
and lie along the border of Moab."[g]

[16] From there they continued to Beer;[h] that is the well of which the LORD said to Moses, "Gather the people together, and I will give them water." [17] Then Israel sang this song:

a Heb lacks *to his people*
b Heb *Destruction*
c Or *Sea of Reeds*
d Or *fiery*; Heb *seraphim*
e Or *fiery*; Heb *seraph*
f Gk: Heb *which is in*
g Meaning of Heb uncertain
h That is *Well*

---

his people], see Gen 25.8) and is mourned for thirty days (see Deut 34.8) rather than the usual seven.

21.1–35: Victory, complaint, and healing. Positive signs become more frequent. **1–3:** This text functions paradigmatically for other texts concerning the conquest, called holy war texts (compare 11.1–3). Israel makes a vow to wage war against *Hormah* (see 14.45), if God would give victory. Israel's victory at *Arad* (east of Beer-sheba) reverses the failure at Hormah earlier. *Atharim*, unknown. Israel fulfills the vow, destroying people and towns. Such problematic texts (compare ch 31) in which the Canaanite population is killed and dedicated to God are grounded in a concern about danger to Israel's future (Deut 20.16–18). **4–9:** This final complaint is directed for the first time against both God and Moses (see 14.2–3; Ex 16.3); the people confess their sin, and the segment ends on a healing note. **6:** The judgment for the complaining is an infestation of *poisonous serpents* (or *fiery*, because of the burning) resulting in many deaths. **7:** Though the people repent (and are presumably forgiven), the snakes are not removed. The effects of sin may continue beyond forgiveness. **8–9:** God responds to those effects by commanding a means of healing (*serpent of bronze*, a homeopathic Egyptian technique to heal snakebite); those who look to the bronze serpent are healed. According to 2 Kings 18.4, the serpent, placed in the Temple in Jerusalem, was destroyed by the reforming king Hezekiah. **10–20:** Travel in Transjordan, around Edom and Moab (see map on p. 218); several sites are unidentified (see 33.41–49). **13:** *Amorites*, see 13.29. **14–18:** Water is provided at God's initiative and the people sing songs of appreciation (see vv. 27–30). The *Book of the*

"Spring up, O well!—Sing to it!—
[18] the well that the leaders sank,
that the nobles of the people dug,
with the scepter, with the staff."
From the wilderness to Mattanah, [19] from
Mattanah to Nahaliel, from Nahaliel to
Bamoth, [20] and from Bamoth to the valley lying in the region of Moab by the top of Pisgah
that overlooks the wasteland.[a]

[21] Then Israel sent messengers to King
Sihon of the Amorites, saying, [22] "Let me pass
through your land; we will not turn aside
into field or vineyard; we will not drink the
water of any well; we will go by the King's
Highway until we have passed through your
territory." [23] But Sihon would not allow Israel
to pass through his territory. Sihon gathered
all his people together, and went out against
Israel to the wilderness; he came to Jahaz, and
fought against Israel. [24] Israel put him to the
sword, and took possession of his land from
the Arnon to the Jabbok, as far as to the Ammonites; for the boundary of the Ammonites
was strong. [25] Israel took all these towns, and
Israel settled in all the towns of the Amorites,
in Heshbon, and in all its villages. [26] For Heshbon was the city of King Sihon of the Amorites, who had fought against the former king
of Moab and captured all his land as far as the
Arnon. [27] Therefore the ballad singers say,

"Come to Heshbon, let it be built;
    let the city of Sihon be established.
[28] For fire came out from Heshbon,
    flame from the city of Sihon.
It devoured Ar of Moab,

and swallowed up[b] the heights of the
    Arnon.
[29] Woe to you, O Moab!
You are undone, O people of Chemosh!
He has made his sons fugitives,
    and his daughters captives,
    to an Amorite king, Sihon.
[30] So their posterity perished
    from Heshbon[c] to Dibon,
    and we laid waste until fire spread to
        Medeba."[d]

[31] Thus Israel settled in the land of the
Amorites. [32] Moses sent to spy out Jazer; and
they captured its villages, and dispossessed
the Amorites who were there.

[33] Then they turned and went up the road
to Bashan; and King Og of Bashan came out
against them, he and all his people, to battle
at Edrei. [34] But the LORD said to Moses, "Do
not be afraid of him; for I have given him into
your hand, with all his people, and all his
land. You shall do to him as you did to King
Sihon of the Amorites, who ruled in Heshbon." [35] So they killed him, his sons, and all
his people, until there was no survivor left;
and they took possession of his land.

22 The Israelites set out, and camped in
the plains of Moab across the Jordan
from Jericho. [2] Now Balak son of Zippor saw

a   Or *Jeshimon*
b   Gk: Heb *and the lords of*
c   Gk: Heb *we have shot at them; Heshbon has
    perished*
d   Compare Sam Gk: Meaning of MT uncertain

Wars of the LORD was apparently an early collection of poems about Israel's conquests (Josh 10.13). **20:** *Pisgah*, a ridge across the Jordan from Jericho (22.1; Deut 34.1). **21–35:** Victories over the Amorites, north of Moab (com- pare Deut 2.24–3.7). The location of several sites is uncertain. **21–26:** A request of King Sihon for safe passage is denied; Sihon pursues Israel, but Israel defeats him and possesses his lands. **22:** *King's Highway,* see 20.17n. **25:** *Heshbon,* probably Tel Hisban, ca. 20 km (12 mi) south of Amman. **27–30:** These include former Moabite lands, and the taunt song praises the victory of the Amorites over the Moabites and their god Chemosh and the cap- ture of their lands (see ch. 32). **30:** *Dibon,* modern Dhiban, ca. 34 mi (55 km) south of Amman. *Medeba,* between Heshbon (v. 25) and Dibon. **33–35:** The victory over Og's lands (north of Sihon's land and across from Galilee) secures the Transjordan for tribal settlement (32.33); it mirrors 21.1–3 with its stress upon total destruction. **33:** *Edrei,* modern Der'a, ca. 65 mi (105 km) south of Damascus.

22.1–24.25: The story of Balaam. Balaam is a traveling professional seer whom God uses to bring blessing to Is- rael (some traditions assess him negatively; see 31.18; Josh 13.22; Rev 2.14). This material also functions ironically; a non-Israelite with less than sterling credentials voices God's promises clearly. Coherence issues, the various divine names, and the admixture of prose and poetry may reflect a long history of transmission. An Aramaic inscription from the eighth century BCE, found at Tell Deir 'Alla in Jordan, ascribes its contents to a "seer of the gods" named "Balaam, son of Beor." This text and chs 22–24 probably have common roots in Transjordanian traditions.

all that Israel had done to the Amorites. ³ Moab was in great dread of the people, because they were so numerous; Moab was overcome with fear of the people of Israel. ⁴ And Moab said to the elders of Midian, "This horde will now lick up all that is around us, as an ox licks up the grass of the field." Now Balak son of Zippor was king of Moab at that time. ⁵ He sent messengers to Balaam son of Beor at Pethor, which is on the Euphrates, in the land of Amaw,ᵃ to summon him, saying, "A people has come out of Egypt; they have spread over the face of the earth, and they have settled next to me. ⁶ Come now, curse this people for me, since they are stronger than I; perhaps I shall be able to defeat them and drive them from the land; for I know that whomever you bless is blessed, and whomever you curse is cursed."

⁷ So the elders of Moab and the elders of Midian departed with the fees for divination in their hand; and they came to Balaam, and gave him Balak's message. ⁸ He said to them, "Stay here tonight, and I will bring back word to you, just as the Lord speaks to me"; so the officials of Moab stayed with Balaam. ⁹ God came to Balaam and said, "Who are these men with you?" ¹⁰ Balaam said to God, "King Balak son of Zippor of Moab, has sent me this message: ¹¹ 'A people has come out of Egypt and has spread over the face of the earth; now come, curse them for me; perhaps I shall be able to fight against them

and drive them out.'" ¹² God said to Balaam, "You shall not go with them; you shall not curse the people, for they are blessed." ¹³ So Balaam rose in the morning, and said to the officials of Balak, "Go to your own land, for the Lord has refused to let me go with you." ¹⁴ So the officials of Moab rose and went to Balak, and said, "Balaam refuses to come with us."

¹⁵ Once again Balak sent officials, more numerous and more distinguished than these. ¹⁶ They came to Balaam and said to him, "Thus says Balak son of Zippor: 'Do not let anything hinder you from coming to me; ¹⁷ for I will surely do you great honor, and whatever you say to me I will do; come, curse this people for me.'" ¹⁸ But Balaam replied to the servants of Balak, "Although Balak were to give me his house full of silver and gold, I could not go beyond the command of the Lord my God, to do less or more. ¹⁹ You remain here, as the others did, so that I may learn what more the Lord may say to me." ²⁰ That night God came to Balaam and said to him, "If the men have come to summon you, get up and go with them; but do only what I tell you to do." ²¹ So Balaam got up in the morning, saddled his donkey, and went with the officials of Moab.

²² God's anger was kindled because he was going, and the angel of the Lord took his

ᵃ Or *land of his kinsfolk*

22.1–40: Balaam's three encounters with God. 1–6: *Balak,* king of Moab, fearful of Israel, hires Balaam, a famous mercenary diviner from Syria (*Pethor,* uncertain location; cf. "Aram," 23.7), to *curse this people* to insure their defeat. **7–21:** *Divination* (see 23.23; Deut 18.9–14) was a widely practiced art in that world. Asking for a delay to consult with the Lord, Balaam has his first encounter with God. That Balaam refers to *the Lord* (YHWH), that he calls the Lord *my God,* and that the Lord converses with Balaam, is remarkable. God prohibits Balaam from cursing Israel, for they are blessed. **13–17:** Balaam recounts the divine refusal to officials who report back to Balak. Balak makes a more attractive offer—a *great honor.* **18–21:** Balaam again consults with *the Lord my God* and tells officials he is subject exactly (not *less or more*) to the divine command. In view of Balaam's faithfulness, God changes the strategy and commands him to go and *do only what I tell you to do.* Balaam goes. **22–35:** What follows contains disjunctions with what has preceded, and may be from another tradition. The reader (but not Balaam) is told of *God's anger* because he departed; indeed, God has become Balaam's *adversary.* The narrator delays the rationale until v. 32. God's command to Balaam in v. 35 remains essentially as it was in v. 20. To get to that repeated command, the narrator uses fable motifs regarding a talking donkey (see Judg 9.7–15), which God uses in what amounts to a test of Balaam. The *angel* (lit., "messenger") *of the Lord* (see 9.15–23), with *drawn sword* (cf. Josh 5.13; 1 Chr 21.16), confronts Balaam and his donkey three times in increasingly restrictive circumstances. The donkey alone sees the angel and seeks to avoid him; Balaam strikes the animal repeatedly, which signals his *perverse* ways (v. 32; contrast v. 20). With God's aid, the donkey questions Balaam, who thinks he has been *made a fool* and threatens the donkey (vv.

stand in the road as his adversary. Now he was riding on the donkey, and his two servants were with him. [23] The donkey saw the angel of the LORD standing in the road, with a drawn sword in his hand; so the donkey turned off the road, and went into the field; and Balaam struck the donkey, to turn it back onto the road. [24] Then the angel of the LORD stood in a narrow path between the vineyards, with a wall on either side. [25] When the donkey saw the angel of the LORD, it scraped against the wall, and scraped Balaam's foot against the wall; so he struck it again. [26] Then the angel of the LORD went ahead, and stood in a narrow place, where there was no way to turn either to the right or to the left. [27] When the donkey saw the angel of the LORD, it lay down under Balaam; and Balaam's anger was kindled, and he struck the donkey with his staff. [28] Then the LORD opened the mouth of the donkey, and it said to Balaam, "What have I done to you, that you have struck me these three times?" [29] Balaam said to the donkey, "Because you have made a fool of me! I wish I had a sword in my hand! I would kill you right now!" [30] But the donkey said to Balaam, "Am I not your donkey, which you have ridden all your life to this day? Have I been in the habit of treating you this way?" And he said, "No."

[31] Then the LORD opened the eyes of Balaam, and he saw the angel of the LORD standing in the road, with his drawn sword in his hand; and he bowed down, falling on his face.

[32] The angel of the LORD said to him, "Why have you struck your donkey these three times? I have come out as an adversary, because your way is perverse[a] before me. [33] The donkey saw me, and turned away from me these three times. If it had not turned away from me, surely just now I would have killed you and let it live." [34] Then Balaam said to the angel of the LORD, "I have sinned, for I did not know that you were standing in the road to oppose me. Now therefore, if it is displeasing to you, I will return home." [35] The angel of the LORD said to Balaam, "Go with the men; but speak only what I tell you to speak." So Balaam went on with the officials of Balak.

[36] When Balak heard that Balaam had come, he went out to meet him at Ir-moab, on the boundary formed by the Arnon, at the farthest point of the boundary. [37] Balak said to Balaam, "Did I not send to summon you? Why did you not come to me? Am I not able to honor you?" [38] Balaam said to Balak, "I have come to you now, but do I have power to say just anything? The word God puts in my mouth, that is what I must say." [39] Then Balaam went with Balak, and they came to Kiriath-huzoth. [40] Balak sacrificed oxen and sheep, and sent them to Balaam and to the officials who were with him.

[41] On the next day Balak took Balaam and brought him up to Bamoth-baal; and from there he could see part of the people of

---

a   Meaning of Heb uncertain

28–29). The donkey's appeal to their long history together stops the threat. God opens Balaam's eyes to see as the donkey sees. Balaam responds that, though he did not know of God's opposition, he has sinned. God renews the commission and Balaam proceeds. Through the use of irony and humor, God uses the donkey as Balaam's teacher. **36–40**: Having arrived at the boundary of Moab, Balaam is greeted by a chiding Balak. Balaam responds: what God *puts in my mouth*, as with the prophets (Jer 1.9; Ezek 2.8–3.3; 1 Kings 22.14), *is what I must say* (compare Jer 20.7–9).

22.41–24.13: Balaam's first three oracles. These mirror the three episodes of Balaam with his donkey. The first two oracles follow a pattern (22.41–23.11; 23.13–25), while the third breaks the pattern in some ways (23.27–24.13): (a) Balak brings Balaam to a high point overlooking Israel's camp; (b) Balak builds seven altars and offers bulls and rams. Sacrifices were typical in the diviner's art, perhaps to *look for omens* in the entrails; (c) Balaam twice turns to consult with the LORD; the third time he does not *as at other times . . . look for omens* (24.1), so consulting with the LORD is diviner's language. *Divination* is seen to be a bankrupt means of revelation (23.23);. (d) God twice puts a word in Balaam's mouth and commands him to speak that word. In the third case (24.2), *the spirit of God* comes upon him (see 11.17,25–26); (e) Balaam speaks God's blessings on Israel rather than curses (23.7–10; 23.18–24; 24.3–9); (f) Balak's reactions are increasingly negative, issuing finally in dismissal (24.10–11); (g) Balaam's response to Balak is testimony to God's word. That he *must take care to say* (23.12) what God puts in his mouth indicates that he has other options. That Balaam *falls down, but with eyes uncovered* (is alert; 24.4,16) may refer to a qualified ecstatic reception of God's word. Balaam "sees" Israel's history, moving from past to

23 Israel.[a] [1] Then Balaam said to Balak, "Build me seven altars here, and prepare seven bulls and seven rams for me." [2] Balak did as Balaam had said; and Balak and Balaam offered a bull and a ram on each altar. [3] Then Balaam said to Balak, "Stay here beside your burnt offerings while I go aside. Perhaps the Lord will come to meet me. Whatever he shows me I will tell you." And he went to a bare height.

[4] Then God met Balaam; and Balaam said to him, "I have arranged the seven altars, and have offered a bull and a ram on each altar." [5] The Lord put a word in Balaam's mouth, and said, "Return to Balak, and this is what you must say." [6] So he returned to Balak,[b] who was standing beside his burnt offerings with all the officials of Moab. [7] Then Balaam[c] uttered his oracle, saying:

"Balak has brought me from Aram,
    the king of Moab from the eastern
        mountains:
'Come, curse Jacob for me;
    Come, denounce Israel!'
[8] How can I curse whom God has not
        cursed?
    How can I denounce those whom the
        Lord has not denounced?
[9] For from the top of the crags I see him,
    from the hills I behold him.
Here is a people living alone,
    and not reckoning itself among the
        nations!
[10] Who can count the dust of Jacob,
    or number the dust-cloud[d] of
        Israel?
Let me die the death of the upright,
    and let my end be like his!"

[11] Then Balak said to Balaam, "What have you done to me? I brought you to curse my enemies, but now you have done nothing but bless them." [12] He answered, "Must I not take care to say what the Lord puts into my mouth?"

[13] So Balak said to him, "Come with me to another place from which you may see them; you shall see only part of them, and shall not see them all; then curse them for me from there." [14] So he took him to the field of Zophim, to the top of Pisgah. He built seven altars, and offered a bull and a ram on each altar. [15] Balaam said to Balak, "Stand here beside your burnt offerings, while I meet the Lord over there." [16] The Lord met Balaam, put a word into his mouth, and said, "Return to Balak, and this is what you shall say." [17] When he came to him, he was standing beside his burnt offerings with the officials of Moab. Balak said to him, "What has the Lord said?" [18] Then Balaam uttered his oracle, saying:

"Rise, Balak, and hear;
    listen to me, O son of Zippor:
[19] God is not a human being, that he should
        lie,
    or a mortal, that he should change his
        mind.
Has he promised, and will he not do it?
    Has he spoken, and will he not fulfill it?
[20] See, I received a command to bless;
    he has blessed, and I cannot revoke it.
[21] He has not beheld misfortune in Jacob;
    nor has he seen trouble in Israel.
The Lord their God is with them,
    acclaimed as a king among them.
[22] God, who brings them out of Egypt,
    is like the horns of a wild ox for them.
[23] Surely there is no enchantment against
        Jacob,

a Heb lacks of Israel
b Heb him
c Heb he
d Or fourth part

present to a more and more specific future: election *among the nations* (23.9); promise (and fulfillment) of many descendants, like a *dust-cloud* (23.10; see Gen 13.16); blessing (24.9; see Gen 12.3); Exodus (23.22; 24.8); God's presence and care in the wilderness (23.21; see 24.5–6). He anticipates a successful conquest (23.24; 24.6–9) and the rise of the monarchy (24.7,17–19). The overall scene for Balaam is a blessed people, confident and flourishing. In Balaam's words (23.10): *let my end be like his!* The oracles are highly poetic and often obscure in their current form. **23.14:** *Pisgah*, see 21.20n. **19–22:** Balaam also sees some of Israel's basic convictions about God. God is not a human being, not deceptive, blesses Israel, reveals his word, and makes and keeps promises. That God will not *change his mind* refers to promises and is not a generalization about divine immutability (see Ex 32.14) or prophecy (see Jer 18.7–10). God chooses to dwell among them, is *acclaimed as a king*, and is a deliverer,

no divination against Israel;
now it shall be said of Jacob and Israel,
  'See what God has done!'
[24] Look, a people rising up like a lioness,
  and rousing itself like a lion!
It does not lie down until it has eaten the
  prey
  and drunk the blood of the slain.''

[25] Then Balak said to Balaam, "Do not curse them at all, and do not bless them at all." [26] But Balaam answered Balak, "Did I not tell you, 'Whatever the LORD says, that is what I must do'?"

[27] So Balak said to Balaam, "Come now, I will take you to another place; perhaps it will please God that you may curse them for me from there." [28] So Balak took Balaam to the top of Peor, which overlooks the wasteland.[a] [29] Balaam said to Balak, "Build me seven altars here, and prepare seven bulls and seven rams for me." [30] So Balak did as Balaam had said, and offered a bull and a ram on each altar.

24 Now Balaam saw that it pleased the LORD to bless Israel, so he did not go, as at other times, to look for omens, but set his face toward the wilderness. [2] Balaam looked up and saw Israel camping tribe by tribe. Then the spirit of God came upon him, [3] and he uttered his oracle, saying:
  "The oracle of Balaam son of Beor,
    the oracle of the man whose eye is
      clear,[b]
[4] the oracle of one who hears the words of
    God,
  who sees the vision of the Almighty,[c]
  who falls down, but with eyes
      uncovered:
[5] how fair are your tents, O Jacob,
  your encampments, O Israel!
[6] Like palm groves that stretch
    far away,
  like gardens beside a river,

like aloes that the LORD has planted,
  like cedar trees beside the waters.
[7] Water shall flow from his buckets,
  and his seed shall have abundant
    water,
his king shall be higher than Agag,
  and his kingdom shall be exalted.
[8] God who brings him out of Egypt,
  is like the horns of a wild ox for him;
he shall devour the nations that are his
    foes
  and break their bones.
  He shall strike with his arrows.[d]
[9] He crouched, he lay down like a lion,
  and like a lioness; who will rouse him
    up?
Blessed is everyone who blesses you,
  and cursed is everyone who curses
    you."

[10] Then Balak's anger was kindled against Balaam, and he struck his hands together. Balak said to Balaam, "I summoned you to curse my enemies, but instead you have blessed them these three times. [11] Now be off with you! Go home! I said, 'I will reward you richly,' but the LORD has denied you any reward." [12] And Balaam said to Balak, "Did I not tell your messengers whom you sent to me, [13] 'If Balak should give me his house full of silver and gold, I would not be able to go beyond the word of the LORD, to do either good or bad of my own will; what the LORD says, that is what I will say'? [14] So now, I am going to my people; let me advise you what this people will do to your people in days to come."

[15] So he uttered his oracle, saying:
  "The oracle of Balaam son of Beor,

---

a Or *overlooks Jeshimon*
b Or *closed* or *open*
c Traditional rendering of Heb *Shaddai*
d Meaning of Heb uncertain

---

depicted as strong animals that will defeat Israel's enemies (23.22; 24.8–9; see Gen 49.9). **28:** *Peor,* cf. Baal-peor, 25.3; 31.16.

24.14–25: Balaam's fourth oracle. 7: *Agag,* the name of a king of Amalek (see 24.20; 13.29) in 1 Sam 15.8. **15–19:** His *eye is clear,* he himself has *the knowledge of the Most High* and can see the future (*see him, but not now . . . not near*). Israel will bring Moab, Edom, and other peoples in the region under their aegis and its God will be exalted among the nations. How this will occur is stated in 24.17 (see 24.7); God will raise up a star and scepter (24.17a; royal images, Gen 49.10) from the tribe of Judah (lion imagery is used in 23.24; 24.9; see Gen 49.9) and Israel will be established among the nations (24.17–24). These images are usually associated with the

the oracle of the man whose eye is
clear,[a]
[16] the oracle of one who hears the words
of God,
and knows the knowledge of the Most
High,[b]
who sees the vision of the Almighty,[c]
who falls down, but with his eyes
uncovered:
[17] I see him, but not now;
I behold him, but not near—
a star shall come out of Jacob,
and a scepter shall rise out of Israel;
it shall crush the borderlands[d] of Moab,
and the territory[e] of all the
Shethites.
[18] Edom will become a possession,
Seir a possession of its enemies,[f]
while Israel does valiantly.
[19] One out of Jacob shall rule,
and destroy the survivors of Ir."
[20] Then he looked on Amalek, and uttered
his oracle, saying:
"First among the nations was Amalek,
but its end is to perish forever."
[21] Then he looked on the Kenite, and uttered his oracle, saying:
"Enduring is your dwelling place,
and your nest is set in the rock;
[22] yet Kain is destined for burning.
How long shall Asshur take you away
captive?"
[23] Again he uttered his oracle, saying:

"Alas, who shall live when God does this?
[24] But ships shall come from Kittim
and shall afflict Asshur and Eber;
and he also shall perish forever."
[25] Then Balaam got up and went back to
his place, and Balak also went his way.

25 While Israel was staying at Shittim,
the people began to have sexual
relations with the women of Moab. [2] These
invited the people to the sacrifices of their
gods, and the people ate and bowed down
to their gods. [3] Thus Israel yoked itself to the
Baal of Peor, and the LORD's anger was kindled against Israel. [4] The LORD said to Moses,
"Take all the chiefs of the people, and impale
them in the sun before the LORD, in order that
the fierce anger of the LORD may turn away
from Israel." [5] And Moses said to the judges
of Israel, "Each of you shall kill any of your
people who have yoked themselves to the
Baal of Peor."

[6] Just then one of the Israelites came and
brought a Midianite woman into his family,
in the sight of Moses and in the sight of the
whole congregation of the Israelites, while
they were weeping at the entrance of the tent

a   Or *closed* or *open*
b   Or *of Elyon*
c   Traditional rendering of Heb *Shaddai*
d   Or *forehead*
e   Some Mss read *skull*
f   Heb *Seir, its enemies, a possession*

Davidic dynasty and its victories over Moab and Edom (Seir) (2 Sam 8.2,12–14) and have been messianically
interpreted. *Shethites*; uncertain; *Ir* is Moab (22.36). **20–25**: Obscure brief oracles against the nations, with God
acting (24.23): *Amalek*, see v. 7n.; *Kain*, the Kenites, a subgroup of the Midianites (see 22.4); *Asshur* (Assyria, or
an obscure tribal group, Gen 25.3); *Eber* (perhaps Mesopotamia, see Gen 10.25); and the Philistines or other sea
people (*Kittim*; see Gen 10.4).

25.1–18: The final rebellion. Two stories about Israelite men and foreign women (vv. 1–5; 6–16) have been
interwoven, with the second now providing an illustration of the first (the conclusion assumes both, vv. 16–18;
see Ps 106.28–31). The focus is idolatry (vv. 2–3). The old generation will finally die off. **1–5**: *Shittim* (see Josh 2.1;
3.1). The first story (see Deut 4.3–4) involves Moabite women who, through illicit sexual activity, invite Israelite
males into idolatrous practices associated with Baal, the Canaanite god of Peor (see 31.16). God tells Moses to
impale the chiefs of Israel to turn *the fierce anger of the LORD* away (see 1.53). Moses issues another command:
kill any idolaters. Because the wrath of God is not turned away by following God's command to execute a few, a
plague follows (see 25.8–9; compare 25.18; 31.8–16). **6–15**: Describes a relationship between a Midianite woman
and a *Simeonite* (vv.14–15 specify their status and may link the man with v. 4). *Into his family* (v. 6) better reads
"to his brothers"; the tabernacle setting suggests something more sinister as does *trickery* in v.18. He did this
in the sight of Moses and all Israelites as *they were weeping* (probably over the plague). The wrong committed is
unclear: marriage to a non-Israelite was not permitted, and according to some scholars the parading before the
people near the tabernacle may imply ritual prostitution. Because Moses had married a Midianite (Ex 2.15–22)

of meeting. [7] When Phinehas son of Eleazar, son of Aaron the priest, saw it, he got up and left the congregation. Taking a spear in his hand, [8] he went after the Israelite man into the tent, and pierced the two of them, the Israelite and the woman, through the belly. So the plague was stopped among the people of Israel. [9] Nevertheless those that died by the plague were twenty-four thousand.

[10] The LORD spoke to Moses, saying: [11] "Phinehas son of Eleazar, son of Aaron the priest, has turned back my wrath from the Israelites by manifesting such zeal among them on my behalf that in my jealousy I did not consume the Israelites. [12] Therefore say, 'I hereby grant him my covenant of peace. [13] It shall be for him and for his descendants after him a covenant of perpetual priesthood, because he was zealous for his God, and made atonement for the Israelites.'"

[14] The name of the slain Israelite man, who was killed with the Midianite woman, was Zimri son of Salu, head of an ancestral house belonging to the Simeonites. [15] The name of the Midianite woman who was killed was Cozbi daughter of Zur, who was the head of a clan, an ancestral house in Midian.

[16] The LORD said to Moses, [17] "Harass the Midianites, and defeat them; [18] for they have harassed you by the trickery with which they deceived you in the affair of Peor, and in the affair of Cozbi, the daughter of a leader of Midian, their sister; she was killed on the day of the plague that resulted from Peor."

26

After the plague the LORD said to Moses and to Eleazar son of Aaron the priest, [2] "Take a census of the whole congregation of the Israelites, from twenty years old and upward, by their ancestral houses, everyone in Israel able to go to war." [3] Moses and Eleazar the priest spoke with them in the plains of Moab by the Jordan opposite Jericho, saying, [4] "Take a census of the people,[a] from twenty years old and upward," as the LORD commanded Moses.

The Israelites, who came out of the land of Egypt, were:

[5] Reuben, the firstborn of Israel. The descendants of Reuben: of Hanoch, the clan of the Hanochites; of Pallu, the clan of the Palluites; [6] of Hezron, the clan of the Hezronites; of Carmi, the clan of the Carmites. [7] These are the clans of the Reubenites; the number of those enrolled was forty-three thousand seven hundred thirty. [8] And the descendants of Pallu: Eliab. [9] The descendants of Eliab:

---

a   Heb lacks *take a census of the people*: Compare verse 2

---

perhaps he had difficulty responding, but the deed called for decisive action. **7–13:** *Phinehas*, grandson of Aaron, does not hesitate. He enters *the tent* (a rare word, occurring only here in the Bible, perhaps implying some ritual function) and pierces them through, apparently in a single thrust, suggesting that they were engaged in sexual intercourse. The effect of his action, called for by God in v. 4, is that he *made atonement for the Israelites* (cf. 16.46–48). God interprets this act as *zeal* exercised on behalf of the divine *jealousy* (the related words show that God's zeal became Phinehas's; see Ex 34.14–16; Hos 9.10). Phinehas's action is the basis for God's establishing with the Aaronides a *covenant of peace* (see Isa 54.10; Ezek 34.25), interpreted to mean a covenant of perpetual priesthood (see Jer 33.17–22; Mal 2.4–8). However, Aaron had already received this commitment (Ex 29.9; 40.15), so this may reflect a different tradition, or formalization of the prior commitment. **16–18:** God's command to *harass* (be an enemy to) *the Midianites* corresponds to *they have harassed you*. The consequence grows out of the sin (see ch 31 for fulfillment). This text may reflect priestly rivalries. Phinehas is elevated over Moses and Aaron's other son Ithamar (see 1 Kings 2.26–27) and God's commitment to Phinehas (see 1 Chr 6.4–10; Ezek 44.15), is eternal.

26.1–36.13: The new generation on the plains of Moab. The balance of Numbers contains little narrative, though enough to provide a framework for the legal material. Various statutes and lists are presented that prepare Israel for life in the land. Balaam's oracles have made clear that God keeps promises and the assumptions of land ownership and allocation in chs 27–36 have a promissory force. Yet, this does not lessen the call to be faithful, and chs 27–36 assist Israel in its faithfulness by new orderings of its life. New experience is drawn into the orbit of the law in the service of the life of the flourishing of community.

26.1–65: Census of the new generation. It begins with military service in mind, Eleazar replacing his father Aaron, and land allotment issues paramount (compare 1.2–3). The twelve-tribe structure remains intact. The

Nemuel, Dathan, and Abiram. These are the same Dathan and Abiram, chosen from the congregation, who rebelled against Moses and Aaron in the company of Korah, when they rebelled against the LORD, [10] and the earth opened its mouth and swallowed them up along with Korah, when that company died, when the fire devoured two hundred fifty men; and they became a warning. [11] Notwithstanding, the sons of Korah did not die.

[12] The descendants of Simeon by their clans: of Nemuel, the clan of the Nemuelites; of Jamin, the clan of the Jaminites; of Jachin, the clan of the Jachinites; [13] of Zerah, the clan of the Zerahites; of Shaul, the clan of the Shaulites.[a] [14] These are the clans of the Simeonites, twenty-two thousand two hundred.

[15] The children of Gad by their clans: of Zephon, the clan of the Zephonites; of Haggi, the clan of the Haggites; of Shuni, the clan of the Shunites; [16] of Ozni, the clan of the Oznites; of Eri, the clan of the Erites; [17] of Arod, the clan of the Arodites; of Areli, the clan of the Arelites. [18] These are the clans of the Gadites: the number of those enrolled was forty thousand five hundred.

[19] The sons of Judah: Er and Onan; Er and Onan died in the land of Canaan. [20] The descendants of Judah by their clans were: of Shelah, the clan of the Shelanites; of Perez, the clan of the Perezites; of Zerah, the clan of the Zerahites. [21] The descendants of Perez were: of Hezron, the clan of the Hezronites; of Hamul, the clan of the Hamulites. [22] These are the clans of Judah: the number of those enrolled was seventy-six thousand five hundred.

[23] The descendants of Issachar by their clans: of Tola, the clan of the Tolaites; of Puvah, the clan of the Punites; [24] of Jashub, the clan of the Jashubites; of Shimron, the clan of the Shimronites. [25] These are the clans of Issachar: sixty-four thousand three hundred enrolled.

[26] The descendants of Zebulun by their clans: of Sered, the clan of the Seredites; of Elon, the clan of the Elonites; of Jahleel, the clan of the Jahleelites. [27] These are the clans

of the Zebulunites; the number of those enrolled was sixty thousand five hundred.

[28] The sons of Joseph by their clans: Manasseh and Ephraim. [29] The descendants of Manasseh: of Machir, the clan of the Machirites; and Machir was the father of Gilead; of Gilead, the clan of the Gileadites. [30] These are the descendants of Gilead: of Iezer, the clan of the Iezerites; of Helek, the clan of the Helekites; [31] and of Asriel, the clan of the Asrielites; and of Shechem, the clan of the Shechemites; [32] and of Shemida, the clan of the Shemidaites; and of Hepher, the clan of the Hepherites. [33] Now Zelophehad son of Hepher had no sons, but daughters: and the names of the daughters of Zelophehad were Mahlah, Noah, Hoglah, Milcah, and Tirzah. [34] These are the clans of Manasseh; the number of those enrolled was fifty-two thousand seven hundred.

[35] These are the descendants of Ephraim according to their clans: of Shuthelah, the clan of the Shuthelahites; of Becher, the clan of the Becherites; of Tahan, the clan of the Tahanites. [36] And these are the descendants of Shuthelah: of Eran, the clan of the Eranites. [37] These are the clans of the Ephraimites: the number of those enrolled was thirty-two thousand five hundred. These are the descendants of Joseph by their clans.

[38] The descendants of Benjamin by their clans: of Bela, the clan of the Belaites; of Ashbel, the clan of the Ashbelites; of Ahiram, the clan of the Ahiramites; [39] of Shephupham, the clan of the Shuphamites; of Hupham, the clan of the Huphamites. [40] And the sons of Bela were Ard and Naaman: of Ard, the clan of the Ardites; of Naaman, the clan of the Naamites. [41] These are the descendants of Benjamin by their clans; the number of those enrolled was forty-five thousand six hundred.

[42] These are the descendants of Dan by their clans: of Shuham, the clan of the Shuhamites. These are the clans of Dan by their clans. [43] All the clans of the Shuhamites: sixty-four thousand four hundred enrolled.

[44] The descendants of Asher by their families: of Imnah, the clan of the Imnites; of

---

[a] Or *Saul ... Saulites*

listing focuses on clans rather than individuals (for land allotment); the totals are given for each tribe. **9:** *Dathan and Abiram ... Korah,* see ch 16. **19:** *Er and Onan,* see Gen 38.1–10. **33:** On *the daughters of Zelophehad,* see 27.1–11;

Ishvi, the clan of the Ishvites; of Beriah, the clan of the Beriites. [45] Of the descendants of Beriah: of Heber, the clan of the Heberites; of Malchiel, the clan of the Malchielites. [46] And the name of the daughter of Asher was Serah. [47] These are the clans of the Asherites: the number of those enrolled was fifty-three thousand four hundred.

[48] The descendants of Naphtali by their clans: of Jahzeel, the clan of the Jahzeelites; of Guni, the clan of the Gunites; [49] of Jezer, the clan of the Jezerites; of Shillem, the clan of the Shillemites. [50] These are the Naphtalites[a] by their clans: the number of those enrolled was forty-five thousand four hundred.

[51] This was the number of the Israelites enrolled: six hundred and one thousand seven hundred thirty.

[52] The LORD spoke to Moses, saying: [53] To these the land shall be apportioned for inheritance according to the number of names. [54] To a large tribe you shall give a large inheritance, and to a small tribe you shall give a small inheritance; every tribe shall be given its inheritance according to its enrollment. [55] But the land shall be apportioned by lot; according to the names of their ancestral tribes they shall inherit. [56] Their inheritance shall be apportioned according to lot between the larger and the smaller.

[57] This is the enrollment of the Levites by their clans: of Gershon, the clan of the Gershonites; of Kohath, the clan of the Kohathites; of Merari, the clan of the Merarites. [58] These are the clans of Levi: the clan of the Libnites, the clan of the Hebronites, the clan of the Mahlites, the clan of the Mushites, the clan of the Korahites. Now Kohath was the father of Amram. [59] The name of Amram's wife was Jochebed daughter of Levi, who was born to Levi in Egypt; and she bore to Amram:

Aaron, Moses, and their sister Miriam. [60] To Aaron were born Nadab, Abihu, Eleazar, and Ithamar. [61] But Nadab and Abihu died when they offered unholy fire before the LORD. [62] The number of those enrolled was twenty-three thousand, every male one month old and upward; for they were not enrolled among the Israelites because there was no allotment given to them among the Israelites.

[63] These were those enrolled by Moses and Eleazar the priest, who enrolled the Israelites in the plains of Moab by the Jordan opposite Jericho. [64] Among these there was not one of those enrolled by Moses and Aaron the priest, who had enrolled the Israelites in the wilderness of Sinai. [65] For the LORD had said of them, "They shall die in the wilderness." Not one of them was left, except Caleb son of Jephunneh and Joshua son of Nun.

27 Then the daughters of Zelophehad came forward. Zelophehad was son of Hepher son of Gilead son of Machir son of Manasseh son of Joseph, a member of the Manassite clans. The names of his daughters were: Mahlah, Noah, Hoglah, Milcah, and Tirzah. [2] They stood before Moses, Eleazar the priest, the leaders, and all the congregation, at the entrance of the tent of meeting, and they said, [3] "Our father died in the wilderness; he was not among the company of those who gathered themselves together against the LORD in the company of Korah, but died for his own sin; and he had no sons. [4] Why should the name of our father be taken away from his clan because he had no son? Give to us a possession among our father's brothers."

[5] Moses brought their case before the LORD. [6] And the LORD spoke to Moses, saying:

---

a   Heb *clans of Naphtali*

36.1–12. 51: The grand total is 601,730 compared to 603,550 in 1.46. 52–56: A new reason for the census is given in 26.52–56: land apportionment is to be based on tribal size after the conquest is complete; the location of land will be determined *by lot*, a means of eliminating human bias. 57–62: The Levites are newly and separately enrolled (see 3.14–39, an increase of 1,000), with no tribal allotment (18.23–24). 65: See 14.20–35.

27.1–11: **The daughters of Zelophehad**. Because ancestral lands are to be kept within the tribe (see Lev 25.25–34; 1 Kings 21.1–4), a way to pass on the inheritance must be found if a man has no sons. In such cases daughters may inherit, here given Moses' blessing (see Josh 17.3–6). A restriction is added in 36.1–2, providing an inclusio for chs 27–36. 3–4: The daughters take the initiative with Moses in pursuing inheritance rights inasmuch as their father had no sons (26.33). The allusion to their father not *in the company of Korah* likely refers to the two hundred fifty leaders of 16.2; *his own sin* may reference the old generation (26.64–65). Their father's

⁷ The daughters of Zelophehad are right in what they are saying; you shall indeed let them possess an inheritance among their father's brothers and pass the inheritance of their father on to them. ⁸ You shall also say to the Israelites, "If a man dies, and has no son, then you shall pass his inheritance on to his daughter. ⁹ If he has no daughter, then you shall give his inheritance to his brothers. ¹⁰ If he has no brothers, then you shall give his inheritance to his father's brothers. ¹¹ And if his father has no brothers, then you shall give his inheritance to the nearest kinsman of his clan, and he shall possess it. It shall be for the Israelites a statute and ordinance, as the LORD commanded Moses."

¹² The LORD said to Moses, "Go up this mountain of the Abarim range, and see the land that I have given to the Israelites. ¹³ When you have seen it, you also shall be gathered to your people, as your brother Aaron was, ¹⁴ because you rebelled against my word in the wilderness of Zin when the congregation quarreled with me.ᵃ You did not show my holiness before their eyes at the waters." (These are the waters of Meribath-kadesh in the wilderness of Zin.) ¹⁵ Moses spoke to the LORD, saying, ¹⁶ "Let the LORD, the God of the spirits of all flesh,

appoint someone over the congregation ¹⁷ who shall go out before them and come in before them, who shall lead them out and bring them in, so that the congregation of the LORD may not be like sheep without a shepherd." ¹⁸ So the LORD said to Moses, "Take Joshua son of Nun, a man in whom is the spirit, and lay your hand upon him; ¹⁹ have him stand before Eleazar the priest and all the congregation, and commission him in their sight. ²⁰ You shall give him some of your authority, so that all the congregation of the Israelites may obey. ²¹ But he shall stand before Eleazar the priest, who shall inquire for him by the decision of the Urim before the LORD; at his word they shall go out, and at his word they shall come in, both he and all the Israelites with him, the whole congregation." ²² So Moses did as the LORD commanded him. He took Joshua and had him stand before Eleazar the priest and the whole congregation; ²³ he laid his hands on him and commissioned him—as the LORD had directed through Moses.

28

The LORD spoke to Moses, saying: ² Command the Israelites, and say to them: My offering, the food for my offerings

ᵃ Heb lacks with me

---

name would still be associated with this land, for their sons would pass on the name (Ezra 2.61). 6–11: God agrees with the daughters and decrees other ways in which the inheritance can be transmitted in the absence of sons, with preference given to direct lineage both to ensure the endurance of the family name and to safeguard a just distribution of land among the tribes.

27.12–23: From Moses to Joshua. Authority is transferred to Joshua, one of the good spies in chs 13–14, from Moses, whose earlier rebellion is recalled (see 20.12). Moses is given a glimpse of the promised land from *the Abarim range* (Mount Nebo, Deut 32.49). 16–17: Moses initiates the issue of succession, appealing to God as Creator, *the God of the spirits of all flesh* (see 16.22; Gen 2.7). This God, who gives breath to all, has given Joshua *the spirit*, a specific charisma for leadership and prophecy (v.18; see 11.17,26; Deut 34.9). Joshua has been Moses' assistant since the Exodus (11.28; Ex 24.13; 33.11). Here his responsibilities are especially associated with military leadership (see Ex 17.8–14), the basic sense of *go out before them and come in before them* (27.17,21; Josh 14.11). Yet, the image of *sheep without a shepherd* suggests a more comprehensive, almost royal leadership role, as Moses had (see 2 Sam 5.2). 18–21: God commands Moses to *commission* Joshua by laying his *hand upon him*, a symbolic act signifying the transfer of *authority* (cf. 8.10–11). The investiture is public, before *all the congregation*, so it is clear that the people are to *obey* this one. The act is also to take place before *Eleazar the priest* (see 20.22–29), to whom Joshua is responsible with respect to the discernment of the will of God (especially regarding battle) through the use of *Urim* (and Thummim; see Ex 28.29–30; Lev 8.8). The latter responsibility explains why only *some of his authority* was given to Joshua (see Moses' role in 12.6–8; Deut 34.10; Josh 1.7–8).

28.1–29.40: Offerings for life in the land, for various occasions. Building upon other Pentateuchal texts regarding these matters (see Lev 23; Deut 16.1–17), these texts focus on sacrificial offerings through which Israel places itself in tune with God's temporal order in creation. In and through these offerings God acted for the sake of the life and well-being of the community. The totals: thirty days of the year, besides the daily and

by fire, my pleasing odor, you shall take care to offer to me at its appointed time. [3] And you shall say to them, This is the offering by fire that you shall offer to the LORD: two male lambs a year old without blemish, daily, as a regular offering. [4] One lamb you shall offer in the morning, and the other lamb you shall offer at twilight;[a] [5] also one-tenth of an ephah of choice flour for a grain offering, mixed with one-fourth of a hin of beaten oil. [6] It is a regular burnt offering, ordained at Mount Sinai for a pleasing odor, an offering by fire to the LORD. [7] Its drink offering shall be one-fourth of a hin for each lamb; in the sanctuary you shall pour out a drink offering of strong drink to the LORD. [8] The other lamb you shall offer at twilight[a] with a grain offering and a drink offering like the one in the morning; you shall offer it as an offering by fire, a pleasing odor to the LORD.

[9] On the sabbath day: two male lambs a year old without blemish, and two-tenths of an ephah of choice flour for a grain offering, mixed with oil, and its drink offering— [10] this is the burnt offering for every sabbath, in addition to the regular burnt offering and its drink offering.

[11] At the beginnings of your months you shall offer a burnt offering to the LORD: two young bulls, one ram, seven male lambs a year old without blemish; [12] also three-tenths of an ephah of choice flour for a grain offering, mixed with oil, for each bull; and two-tenths of choice flour for a grain offering, mixed with oil, for the one ram; [13] and one-tenth of choice flour mixed with oil as a grain offering for every lamb—a burnt offering of pleasing odor, an offering by fire to the LORD. [14] Their drink offerings shall be half a hin of wine for a bull, one-third of a hin for a ram, and one-fourth of a hin for a lamb.

This is the burnt offering of every month throughout the months of the year. [15] And there shall be one male goat for a sin offering to the LORD; it shall be offered in addition to the regular burnt offering and its drink offering.

[16] On the fourteenth day of the first month there shall be a passover offering to the LORD. [17] And on the fifteenth day of this month is a festival; seven days shall unleavened bread be eaten. [18] On the first day there shall be a holy convocation. You shall not work at your occupations. [19] You shall offer an offering by fire, a burnt offering to the LORD: two young bulls, one ram, and seven male lambs a year old; see that they are without blemish. [20] Their grain offering shall be of choice flour mixed with oil: three-tenths of an ephah shall you offer for a bull, and two-tenths for a ram; [21] one-tenth shall you offer for each of the seven lambs; [22] also one male goat for a sin offering, to make atonement for you. [23] You shall offer these in addition to the burnt offering of the morning, which belongs to the regular burnt offering. [24] In the same way you shall offer daily, for seven days, the food of an offering by fire, a pleasing odor to the LORD; it shall be offered in addition to the regular burnt offering and its drink offering. [25] And on the seventh day you shall have a holy convocation; you shall not work at your occupations.

[26] On the day of the first fruits, when you offer a grain offering of new grain to the LORD at your festival of weeks, you shall have a holy convocation; you shall not work at your occupations. [27] You shall offer a burnt offering, a pleasing odor to the LORD: two young bulls, one ram, seven male lambs a year old.

a   Heb *between the two evenings*

sabbath offerings. The first three offerings mark the basic temporal frame of days, weeks, and months. The others mark out the festival year: the first month (March-April; Passover and Unleavened Bread), fifty days later (Weeks) , and the seventh month (Rosh Hashanah, Day of Atonement, and Booths). These festivals are timed to Israel's harvests; later they are associated with key events of Israel's history (Exodus; giving of the law; wilderness wanderings). **28.2:** Introduces the offerings (brought by the people) that belong wholly to God (whole burnt offerings; purification or sin offerings; each with meal and drink offerings, see 15.2–16) for the various times. *Pleasing odor,* see 15.3. **3–8:** Daily burnt offering, offered at dawn and dusk (see Ex 29.38–42; Lev 6.9–13). **9–10:** Sabbath offerings relate to the hallowed seventh day of creation. **11–15:** Monthly (new moon) offerings (see 1 Sam 20.5; Isa 1.13; Am 8.5). **16–25:** Passover and, on the seven days following, Unleavened Bread (see 9.1–14; Lev 23.2–8; Ex 12.1–27; 13.3–10; Deut 16.1–8). **26–31:** Festival of First Fruits (Weeks; Harvest; Pentecost;

[28] Their grain offering shall be of choice flour mixed with oil, three-tenths of an ephah for each bull, two-tenths for one ram, [29] one-tenth for each of the seven lambs; [30] with one male goat, to make atonement for you. [31] In addition to the regular burnt offering with its grain offering, you shall offer them and their drink offering. They shall be without blemish.

29

On the first day of the seventh month you shall have a holy convocation; you shall not work at your occupations. It is a day for you to blow the trumpets, [2] and you shall offer a burnt offering, a pleasing odor to the LORD: one young bull, one ram, seven male lambs a year old without blemish. [3] Their grain offering shall be of choice flour mixed with oil, three-tenths of one ephah for the bull, two-tenths for the ram, [4] and one-tenth for each of the seven lambs; [5] with one male goat for a sin offering, to make atonement for you. [6] These are in addition to the burnt offering of the new moon and its grain offering, and the regular burnt offering and its grain offering, and their drink offerings, according to the ordinance for them, a pleasing odor, an offering by fire to the LORD.

[7] On the tenth day of this seventh month you shall have a holy convocation, and deny yourselves;[a] you shall do no work. [8] You shall offer a burnt offering to the LORD, a pleasing odor: one young bull, one ram, seven male lambs a year old. They shall be without blemish. [9] Their grain offering shall be of choice flour mixed with oil, three-tenths of an ephah for the bull, two-tenths for the one ram, [10] one-tenth for each of the seven lambs; [11] with one male goat for a sin offering, in addition to the sin offering of atonement, and the regular burnt offering and its grain offering, and their drink offerings.

[12] On the fifteenth day of the seventh month you shall have a holy convocation; you shall not work at your occupations. You shall celebrate a festival to the LORD seven days. [13] You shall offer a burnt offering, an offering by fire, a pleasing odor to the LORD: thirteen young bulls, two rams, fourteen male lambs a year old. They shall be without blemish. [14] Their grain offering shall be of choice flour mixed with oil, three-tenths of an ephah for each of the thirteen bulls, two-tenths for each of the two rams, [15] and one-tenth for each of the fourteen lambs; [16] also one male goat for a sin offering, in addition to the regular burnt offering, its grain offering and its drink offering.

[17] On the second day: twelve young bulls, two rams, fourteen male lambs a year old without blemish, [18] with the grain offering and the drink offerings for the bulls, for the rams, and for the lambs, as prescribed in accordance with their number; [19] also one male goat for a sin offering, in addition to the regular burnt offering and its grain offering, and their drink offerings.

[20] On the third day: eleven bulls, two rams, fourteen male lambs a year old without blemish, [21] with the grain offering and the drink offerings for the bulls, for the rams, and for the lambs, as prescribed in accordance with their number; [22] also one male goat for a sin offering, in addition to the regular burnt offering and its grain offering and its drink offering.

[23] On the fourth day: ten bulls, two rams, fourteen male lambs a year old without blemish, [24] with the grain offering and the drink offerings for the bulls, for the rams, and for the lambs, as prescribed in accordance with their number; [25] also one male goat for a sin offering, in addition to the regular burnt offering, its grain offering and its drink offering.

[26] On the fifth day: nine bulls, two rams, fourteen male lambs a year old without blemish, [27] with the grain offering and the drink offerings for the bulls, for the rams, and for the lambs, as prescribed in accordance with their number; [28] also one male goat for a sin offering, in addition to the regular burnt offering and its grain offering and its drink offering.

[a] Or and fast

see Lev 23.15–21; Deut 16.9–12). **29.1–6:** *The first day of the seventh month* (see Lev 23.23–25), later called Rosh Hashanah (New Year's Day). **7–11:** Day of Atonement (Yom Kippur), tenth day of the seventh month (Lev 16.1–34; 23.26–32). **12–38:** Tabernacles (Booths, Sukkot, Ingathering), the autumn harvest festival, from the fifteenth day of the month for seven or eight days (Lev 23.33–36,39–43; Deut 16.13–15). The extensive list of produce and animals anticipates abundance in the promised land.

²⁹ On the sixth day: eight bulls, two rams, fourteen male lambs a year old without blemish, ³⁰ with the grain offering and the drink offerings for the bulls, for the rams, and for the lambs, as prescribed in accordance with their number; ³¹ also one male goat for a sin offering, in addition to the regular burnt offering, its grain offering, and its drink offerings.

³² On the seventh day: seven bulls, two rams, fourteen male lambs a year old without blemish, ³³ with the grain offering and the drink offerings for the bulls, for the rams, and for the lambs, as prescribed in accordance with their number; ³⁴ also one male goat for a sin offering, besides the regular burnt offering, its grain offering, and its drink offering.

³⁵ On the eighth day you shall have a solemn assembly; you shall not work at your occupations. ³⁶ You shall offer a burnt offering, an offering by fire, a pleasing odor to the LORD: one bull, one ram, seven male lambs a year old without blemish, ³⁷ and the grain offering and the drink offerings for the bull, for the ram, and for the lambs, as prescribed in accordance with their number; ³⁸ also one male goat for a sin offering, in addition to the regular burnt offering and its grain offering and its drink offering.

³⁹ These you shall offer to the LORD at your appointed festivals, in addition to your votive offerings and your freewill offerings, as your burnt offerings, your grain offerings, your drink offerings, and your offerings of well-being.

⁴⁰ ªSo Moses told the Israelites everything just as the LORD had commanded Moses.

30 Then Moses said to the heads of the tribes of the Israelites: This is what the LORD has commanded. ² When a man makes a vow to the LORD, or swears an oath to bind himself by a pledge, he shall not break his word; he shall do according to all that proceeds out of his mouth.

³ When a woman makes a vow to the LORD, or binds herself by a pledge, while within her father's house, in her youth, ⁴ and her father hears of her vow or her pledge by which she has bound herself, and says nothing to her; then all her vows shall stand, and any pledge by which she has bound herself shall stand. ⁵ But if her father expresses disapproval to her at the time that he hears of it, no vow of hers, and no pledge by which she has bound herself, shall stand; and the LORD will forgive her, because her father had expressed to her his disapproval.

⁶ If she marries, while obligated by her vows or any thoughtless utterance of her lips by which she has bound herself, ⁷ and her husband hears of it and says nothing to her at the time that he hears, then her vows shall stand, and her pledges by which she has bound herself shall stand. ⁸ But if, at the time that her husband hears of it, he expresses disapproval to her, then he shall nullify the vow by which she was obligated, or the thoughtless utterance of her lips, by which she bound herself; and the LORD will forgive her. ⁹ (But every vow of a widow or of a divorced woman, by which she has bound herself, shall be binding upon her.) ¹⁰ And if she made a vow in her husband's house, or bound herself by a pledge with an oath, ¹¹ and her husband heard

ª Ch 30.1 in Heb

30.1–16: Vows and their limits. These statutes concern vows or pledges made by men (30.2) and by women (30.3–15) and the lines of responsibility. Vows are (sworn) promises *to the LORD*, related to service (Nazirite, 6.2) or the (potential) fulfillment of a request, often in crisis (see 21.2–3). The basic concern is to bind persons to their word, though women are bound within limits placed by the actions of father or husband (except widows and divorcees, who are independent, v. 9). Failed promises adversely affect the relationship to God and disrupt the stability of a community. A single case concerning men is followed by three cases concerning women: those still in their father's house and under his authority (vv. 3–5); those under vows at the time they are married (vv. 6–8); those who are married and under their husband's authority (vv. 10–15). Essentially the same patriarchal principles are operative. If the father or husband disapproves, the vow is annulled; *the LORD will forgive her* (vv. 5,8,12) and she is to suffer no consequences. If a father or husband disapproves, he must speak up at the time he hears (of) the vow or the vow stands; then if it is broken, he (not she) will be guilty (3.14–15). These statutes protect both men (from responsibility to fulfill a woman's vow) and, to a lesser extent, women (whose vows remain intact unless there is immediate male response).

it and said nothing to her, and did not express disapproval to her, then all her vows shall stand, and any pledge by which she bound herself shall stand. [12] But if her husband nullifies them at the time that he hears them, then whatever proceeds out of her lips concerning her vows, or concerning her pledge of herself, shall not stand. Her husband has nullified them, and the LORD will forgive her. [13] Any vow or any binding oath to deny herself,[a] her husband may allow to stand, or her husband may nullify. [14] But if her husband says nothing to her from day to day,[b] then he validates all her vows, or all her pledges, by which she is obligated; he has validated them, because he said nothing to her at the time that he heard of them. [15] But if he nullifies them some time after he has heard of them, then he shall bear her guilt.

[16] These are the statutes that the LORD commanded Moses concerning a husband and his wife, and a father and his daughter while she is still young and in her father's house.

31 The LORD spoke to Moses, saying, [2] "Avenge the Israelites on the Midianites; afterward you shall be gathered to your people." [3] So Moses said to the people, "Arm some of your number for the war, so that they may go against Midian, to execute the LORD's vengeance on Midian. [4] You shall send a thousand from each of the tribes of Israel to the war." [5] So out of the thousands of Israel, a thousand from each tribe were conscripted,

twelve thousand armed for battle. [6] Moses sent them to the war, a thousand from each tribe, along with Phinehas son of Eleazar the priest,[c] with the vessels of the sanctuary and the trumpets for sounding the alarm in his hand. [7] They did battle against Midian, as the LORD had commanded Moses, and killed every male. [8] They killed the kings of Midian: Evi, Rekem, Zur, Hur, and Reba, the five kings of Midian, in addition to others who were slain by them; and they also killed Balaam son of Beor with the sword. [9] The Israelites took the women of Midian and their little ones captive; and they took all their cattle, their flocks, and all their goods as booty. [10] All their towns where they had settled, and all their encampments, they burned, [11] but they took all the spoil and all the booty, both people and animals. [12] Then they brought the captives and the booty and the spoil to Moses, to Eleazar the priest, and to the congregation of the Israelites, at the camp on the plains of Moab by the Jordan at Jericho.

[13] Moses, Eleazar the priest, and all the leaders of the congregation went to meet them outside the camp. [14] Moses became angry with the officers of the army, the commanders of thousands and the commanders of hundreds, who had come from service in the war. [15] Moses said to them, "Have

---

a Or *to fast*
b Or *from that day to the next*
c Gk: Heb adds *to the war*

31.1–54: War against the Midianites. This narrative (with ch 32) focuses on traditions associated with Israel's conquests and settlement in Transjordan. The story is idealized (no Israelite is lost in battle, v. 49), enhancing the portrayal of the new generation. 1–2: Continuing from 25.17–18, God commands Israel to attack the Midianites in response to their attacks on Israel; v. 16 interprets this in terms of women seducing Israelites into idolatry, urged on by Balaam. 3–11: Israel's military response to God's command is interpreted as *executing the LORD's vengeance*; but the sense of "vindication" (of the honor of God and Israel) is preferable. This battle has the earmarks of a holy war (see 21.1–3,21–35), with the presence of the priest (see Deut 20.2–4; Phinehas rather than Eleazar, see 27.21; Lev 21.11–12) and the sanctuary *vessels* (probably including the ark; see 10.35–36), and the *sounding of alarm* (10.1–10). Only a thousand men from each tribe are engaged, a small percentage of those available (26.51; see Judg 7.2–8). Every male (including Balaam) is killed and their towns destroyed (see Josh 13.21–22). 12–18: In contrast to ch 21, the women and children (and animals) are not killed but taken captive and (with other booty) brought before Moses, Eleazar, and the congregation. This may reflect the practice of holy war outlined in Deut 20.13–18, where a distinction is made between Canaanites and others more distant (e.g., Midianites). Moses is angry that captives have been taken, or at least that *all the women* have. He isolates *these women here* (perhaps because they are assumed to be involved in the Peor apostasy in ch 25, or may lead the men astray) and commands that *every woman who has known a man* and all male children be killed. But all female virgins can be preserved alive *for yourselves*, as wives or slaves. The text informs the reader only indirectly

you allowed all the women to live? [16] These women here, on Balaam's advice, made the Israelites act treacherously against the LORD in the affair of Peor, so that the plague came among the congregation of the LORD. [17] Now therefore, kill every male among the little ones, and kill every woman who has known a man by sleeping with him. [18] But all the young girls who have not known a man by sleeping with him, keep alive for yourselves. [19] Camp outside the camp seven days; whoever of you has killed any person or touched a corpse, purify yourselves and your captives on the third and on the seventh day. [20] You shall purify every garment, every article of skin, everything made of goats' hair, and every article of wood."

[21] Eleazar the priest said to the troops who had gone to battle: "This is the statute of the law that the LORD has commanded Moses: [22] gold, silver, bronze, iron, tin, and lead— [23] everything that can withstand fire, shall be passed through fire, and it shall be clean. Nevertheless it shall also be purified with the water for purification; and whatever cannot withstand fire, shall be passed through the water. [24] You must wash your clothes on the seventh day, and you shall be clean; afterward you may come into the camp."

[25] The LORD spoke to Moses, saying, [26] "You and Eleazar the priest and the heads of the ancestral houses of the congregation make an inventory of the booty captured, both human and animal. [27] Divide the booty into two parts, between the warriors who went out to battle and all the congregation. [28] From the share of the warriors who went out to battle, set aside as tribute for the LORD, one item out of every five hundred, whether persons, oxen, donkeys, sheep, or goats. [29] Take it from their half and give it to Eleazar the priest as an offering to the LORD. [30] But from the Israelites' half you shall take one out of every fifty, whether persons, oxen, donkeys, sheep, or goats—all the animals—and give them to

the Levites who have charge of the tabernacle of the LORD."

[31] Then Moses and Eleazar the priest did as the LORD had commanded Moses:

[32] The booty remaining from the spoil that the troops had taken totaled six hundred seventy-five thousand sheep, [33] seventy-two thousand oxen, [34] sixty-one thousand donkeys, [35] and thirty-two thousand persons in all, women who had not known a man by sleeping with him.

[36] The half-share, the portion of those who had gone out to war, was in number three hundred thirty-seven thousand five hundred sheep and goats, [37] and the LORD's tribute of sheep and goats was six hundred seventy-five. [38] The oxen were thirty-six thousand, of which the LORD's tribute was seventy-two. [39] The donkeys were thirty thousand five hundred, of which the LORD's tribute was sixty-one. [40] The persons were sixteen thousand, of which the LORD's tribute was thirty-two persons. [41] Moses gave the tribute, the offering for the LORD, to Eleazar the priest, as the LORD had commanded Moses.

[42] As for the Israelites' half, which Moses separated from that of the troops, [43] the congregation's half was three hundred thirty-seven thousand five hundred sheep and goats, [44] thirty-six thousand oxen, [45] thirty thousand five hundred donkeys, [46] and sixteen thousand persons. [47] From the Israelites' half Moses took one of every fifty, both of persons and of animals, and gave them to the Levites who had charge of the tabernacle of the LORD; as the LORD had commanded Moses.

[48] Then the officers who were over the thousands of the army, the commanders of thousands and the commanders of hundreds, approached Moses, [49] and said to Moses, "Your servants have counted the warriors who are under our command, and not one of us is missing. [50] And we have brought the LORD's offering, what each of us found, articles of gold, armlets and bracelets, signet

that these commands of Moses were carried out (31.35). **19–24:** See 19.1–22, with new distinctions between flammable and nonflammable (metal) items. **25–47:** God issues commands regarding the disposition of captives and booty. They are to be divided evenly between the warriors and the rest of the congregation (see 1 Sam 30.24). One in five hundred of the warriors' items is to be given to the priests as *tribute for the LORD*; one in fifty of the congregation's items to the Levites (see 18.8–32). This command is carried out (v. 31) and details follow regarding disposition and quantity of the spoil; the total—just of the officers—is immense and surely exagger-

rings, earrings, and pendants, to make atonement for ourselves before the LORD." [51] Moses and Eleazar the priest received the gold from them, all in the form of crafted articles. [52] And all the gold of the offering that they offered to the LORD, from the commanders of thousands and the commanders of hundreds, was sixteen thousand seven hundred fifty shekels. [53] (The troops had all taken plunder for themselves.) [54] So Moses and Eleazar the priest received the gold from the commanders of thousands and of hundreds, and brought it into the tent of meeting as a memorial for the Israelites before the LORD.

32 Now the Reubenites and the Gadites owned a very great number of cattle. When they saw that the land of Jazer and the land of Gilead was a good place for cattle, [2] the Gadites and the Reubenites came and spoke to Moses, to Eleazar the priest, and to the leaders of the congregation, saying, [3] "Ataroth, Dibon, Jazer, Nimrah, Heshbon, Elealeh, Sebam, Nebo, and Beon— [4] the land that the LORD subdued before the congregation of Israel—is a land for cattle; and your servants have cattle." [5] They continued, "If we have found favor in your sight, let this land be given to your servants for a possession; do not make us cross the Jordan."

[6] But Moses said to the Gadites and to the Reubenites, "Shall your brothers go to war while you sit here? [7] Why will you discourage the hearts of the Israelites from going over into the land that the LORD has given them? [8] Your fathers did this, when I sent them from Kadesh-barnea to see the land. [9] When they went up to the Wadi Eshcol and

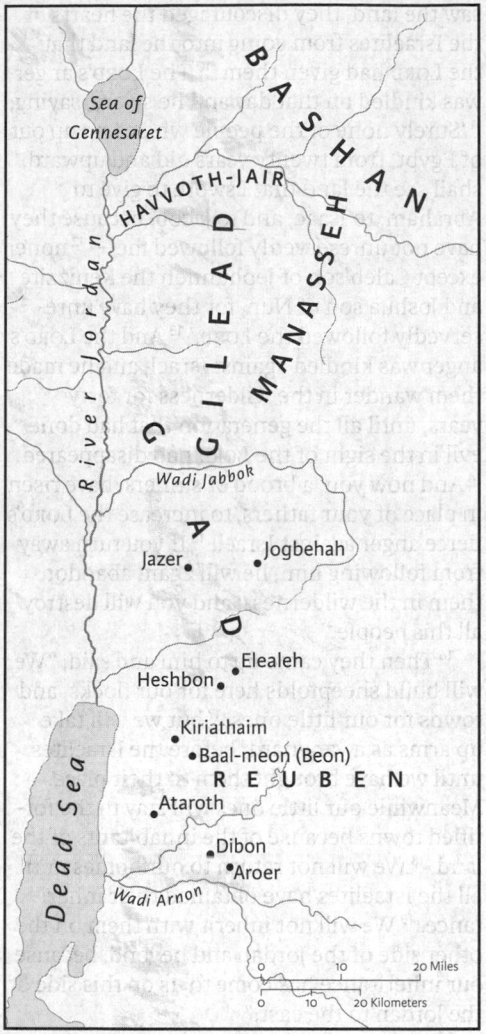

The territory of the Transjordan tribes.

ated: 808,000 animals, 32,000 young women, and 16,750 shekels of gold (v. 52). **52:** A shekel, about .5 oz (11.4 gr). **48–54:** Nonliving booty. The officers approach Moses with their gift to God of the precious metals each soldier had taken. These valuables are brought to *make atonement* for themselves (perhaps because of the taking of human life) and as *a memorial . . . before the LORD*—through tabernacle furnishings made from the metals.

32.1–42: Early land settlement issues. The focus is on tribes who settled east of the Jordan—Reuben, Gad, and the half-tribe of Manasseh (see Gen 15.18; Deut 1.7–8; 3.12–20; Josh 13.8–32; 22.1–34). A crisis arises among these members of the new generation, and its resolution by means of compromise stands in sharp contrast to earlier experiences. **3–5:** The cities listed are east of the Jordan, between the Arnon and Jabbok rivers (see vv. 33–38). *The land that the LORD subdued*, see 21.21–35. These areas with their pasture lands were now available and attracted the attention of the cattle-rich tribes of Reuben and Gad (later joined by the half-tribe of Manasseh, vv. 33–42). **6–15:** But their words, "Do not make us cross the Jordan," trigger Moses' memories of past disasters associated with reluctance to enter the *land* (Canaan; see chs 13–14). Moses questions their motives; indeed, he considers them *a brood of sinners* who repeat the unfaithfulness of the old generation, the effects of which he rehearses. This could trigger *the LORD's fierce anger* (see 1.53) with even more disastrous conse-

saw the land, they discouraged the hearts of the Israelites from going into the land that the LORD had given them. [10] The LORD's anger was kindled on that day and he swore, saying, [11] 'Surely none of the people who came up out of Egypt, from twenty years old and upward, shall see the land that I swore to give to Abraham, to Isaac, and to Jacob, because they have not unreservedly followed me— [12] none except Caleb son of Jephunneh the Kenizzite and Joshua son of Nun, for they have unreservedly followed the LORD.' [13] And the LORD's anger was kindled against Israel, and he made them wander in the wilderness for forty years, until all the generation that had done evil in the sight of the LORD had disappeared. [14] And now you, a brood of sinners, have risen in place of your fathers, to increase the LORD's fierce anger against Israel! [15] If you turn away from following him, he will again abandon them in the wilderness; and you will destroy all this people."

[16] Then they came up to him and said, "We will build sheepfolds here for our flocks, and towns for our little ones, [17] but we will take up arms as a vanguard[a] before the Israelites, until we have brought them to their place. Meanwhile our little ones will stay in the fortified towns because of the inhabitants of the land. [18] We will not return to our homes until all the Israelites have obtained their inheritance. [19] We will not inherit with them on the other side of the Jordan and beyond, because our inheritance has come to us on this side of the Jordan to the east."

[20] So Moses said to them, "If you do this— if you take up arms to go before the LORD for the war, [21] and all those of you who bear arms cross the Jordan before the LORD, until he has driven out his enemies from before him [22] and the land is subdued before the LORD—

then after that you may return and be free of obligation to the LORD and to Israel, and this land shall be your possession before the LORD. [23] But if you do not do this, you have sinned against the LORD; and be sure your sin will find you out. [24] Build towns for your little ones, and folds for your flocks; but do what you have promised."

[25] Then the Gadites and the Reubenites said to Moses, "Your servants will do as my lord commands. [26] Our little ones, our wives, our flocks, and all our livestock shall remain there in the towns of Gilead; [27] but your servants will cross over, everyone armed for war, to do battle for the LORD, just as my lord orders."

[28] So Moses gave command concerning them to Eleazar the priest, to Joshua son of Nun, and to the heads of the ancestral houses of the Israelite tribes. [29] And Moses said to them, "If the Gadites and the Reubenites, everyone armed for battle before the LORD, will cross over the Jordan with you and the land shall be subdued before you, then you shall give them the land of Gilead for a possession; [30] but if they will not cross over with you armed, they shall have possessions among you in the land of Canaan." [31] The Gadites and the Reubenites answered, "As the LORD has spoken to your servants, so we will do. [32] We will cross over armed before the LORD into the land of Canaan, but the possession of our inheritance shall remain with us on this side of[b] the Jordan."

[33] Moses gave to them—to the Gadites and to the Reubenites and to the half-tribe of Manasseh son of Joseph—the kingdom of King Sihon of the Amorites and the kingdom

---

a   Cn: Heb *hurrying*

b   Heb *beyond*

---

quences. **16–19:** These tribes propose a compromise: they will settle in the Transjordan, leave their families and animals behind, and proceed to fight *as a vanguard before the Israelites*, in the front line of the assault against Canaan (compare 34.10–12). They will not return to their homes until *all the Israelites* are secure and they will not inherit those lands. **20–24:** Moses responds positively, if cautiously; references to God are especially prominent. They are to go *before the LORD*, that is, before the ark (see Josh 4.12–13; 6.7–8). If they follow through, they are *free of obligation to the LORD*, that is, regarding this matter (see Josh 22.9). If they do not, *your sin will find you out*: the effects of sin have an intrinsic relationship to the deed. **25–32:** Gad and Reuben deferentially (*your servants . . . my lord*) agree with those terms. Eleazar, Joshua, and tribal heads publicly agree to witness this agreement. If these tribes fail, they must move to lands west of the Jordan. They agree, *as the LORD has spoken*: Moses' word seems to be as good as God's. **33–38:** Moses gives the lands to these tribes, who rebuild Amorite cities and rename some

of King Og of Bashan, the land and its towns, with the territories of the surrounding towns. [34] And the Gadites rebuilt Dibon, Ataroth, Aroer, [35] Atroth-shophan, Jazer, Jogbehah, [36] Beth-nimrah, and Beth-haran, fortified cities, and folds for sheep. [37] And the Reubenites rebuilt Heshbon, Elealeh, Kiriathaim, [38] Nebo, and Baal-meon (some names being changed), and Sibmah; and they gave names to the towns that they rebuilt. [39] The descendants of Machir son of Manasseh went to Gilead, captured it, and dispossessed the Amorites who were there; [40] so Moses gave Gilead to Machir son of Manasseh, and he settled there. [41] Jair son of Manasseh went and captured their villages, and renamed them Havvoth-jair.[a]

[42] And Nobah went and captured Kenath and its villages, and renamed it Nobah after himself.

33 These are the stages by which the Israelites went out of the land of Egypt in military formation under the leadership of Moses and Aaron. [2] Moses wrote down their starting points, stage by stage, by command of the Lord; and these are their stages according to their starting places. [3] They set out from Rameses in the first month, on the fifteenth day of the first month; on the day after the passover the Israelites went out boldly in the sight of all the Egyptians, [4] while the Egyptians were burying all their firstborn, whom the Lord had struck down among them. The Lord executed judgments even against their gods.

[5] So the Israelites set out from Rameses, and camped at Succoth. [6] They set out from Succoth, and camped at Etham, which is on the edge of the wilderness. [7] They set out from Etham, and turned back to Pi-hahiroth, which faces Baal-zephon; and they camped before Migdol. [8] They set out from Pi-hahiroth, passed through the sea into the wilderness, went a three days' journey in the wilderness of Etham, and camped at Marah. [9] They set out from Marah and came to Elim; at Elim there were twelve springs of water and seventy palm trees, and they camped there. [10] They set out from Elim and camped by the Red Sea.[b] [11] They set out from the Red Sea[b] and camped in the wilderness of Sin. [12] They set out from the wilderness of Sin and camped at Dophkah. [13] They set out from Dophkah and camped at Alush. [14] They set out from Alush and camped at Rephidim, where there was no water for the people to drink. [15] They set out from Rephidim and camped in the wilderness of Sinai. [16] They set out from the wilderness of Sinai and camped at Kibroth-hattaavah. [17] They set out from Kibroth-hattaavah and camped at Hazeroth. [18] They set out from Hazeroth and camped at Rithmah. [19] They set out from Rithmah and camped at Rimmon-perez. [20] They set out from Rimmon-perez and camped at Libnah. [21] They set out from Libnah and camped at Rissah. [22] They set out from Rissah and camped at Kehelathah. [23] They set out from Kehelathah and camped at Mount Shepher. [24] They set out from

[a] That is *the villages of Jair*
[b] Or *Sea of Reeds*

(see Josh 13.8–32 for land allotments; for *Sihon* and *Og*, see ch 21). **39–42:** The integration of the half-tribe of Manasseh; their land holdings, on both sides of the Jordan, lie north of Gad's. They oust more Amorites for their lands. The land for two and one-half tribes is thus already in place before the Jordan is crossed.

33.1–49: The wilderness journey remembered. A recollection of the forty-two stages of Israel's journey through the wilderness, from Egypt to their present situation across the Jordan. Its placement recognizes the transition from wilderness journey to land settlement. Represented as Moses' writing at God's command (v. 2), its origin may lie in one or more ancient itineraries circulating in Israel (for another summary, Deut 1.1–3.28). Many sites are not mentioned elsewhere (33.13,18–29); most are not geographically identifiable. The itinerary is surprisingly secular; God's activity is mentioned only at v. 4 and at Aaron's death (v. 38), accentuating the importance of human activity. The reader can recognize two uneven segments, up to and following the death of Aaron (vv. 38–39; see 20.23–29), perhaps betraying priestly interests. Only v. 8 speaks of the travel time. The bare bones character of the description highlights the journey in and of itself. **3–37:** The first segment. **3–4:** Passover is considered a battle among the gods (see v. 52; Ex 12.12; 15.11), while Sinai and the sea crossing are mentioned only in passing. *Rameses*, see Ex 12.37. **5–6:** See Ex 13.20. **7:** See Ex 14.2. **8:** See Ex 15.22–23. **9:** See Ex 15.27. **10:** See Ex 15.22. **11:** See Ex 16.1. **14:** See Ex 17.1. **15:** See Ex 19.1–2. **16–17:** See 11.34–35. **30–34:** Cf. Deut 10.6–7.

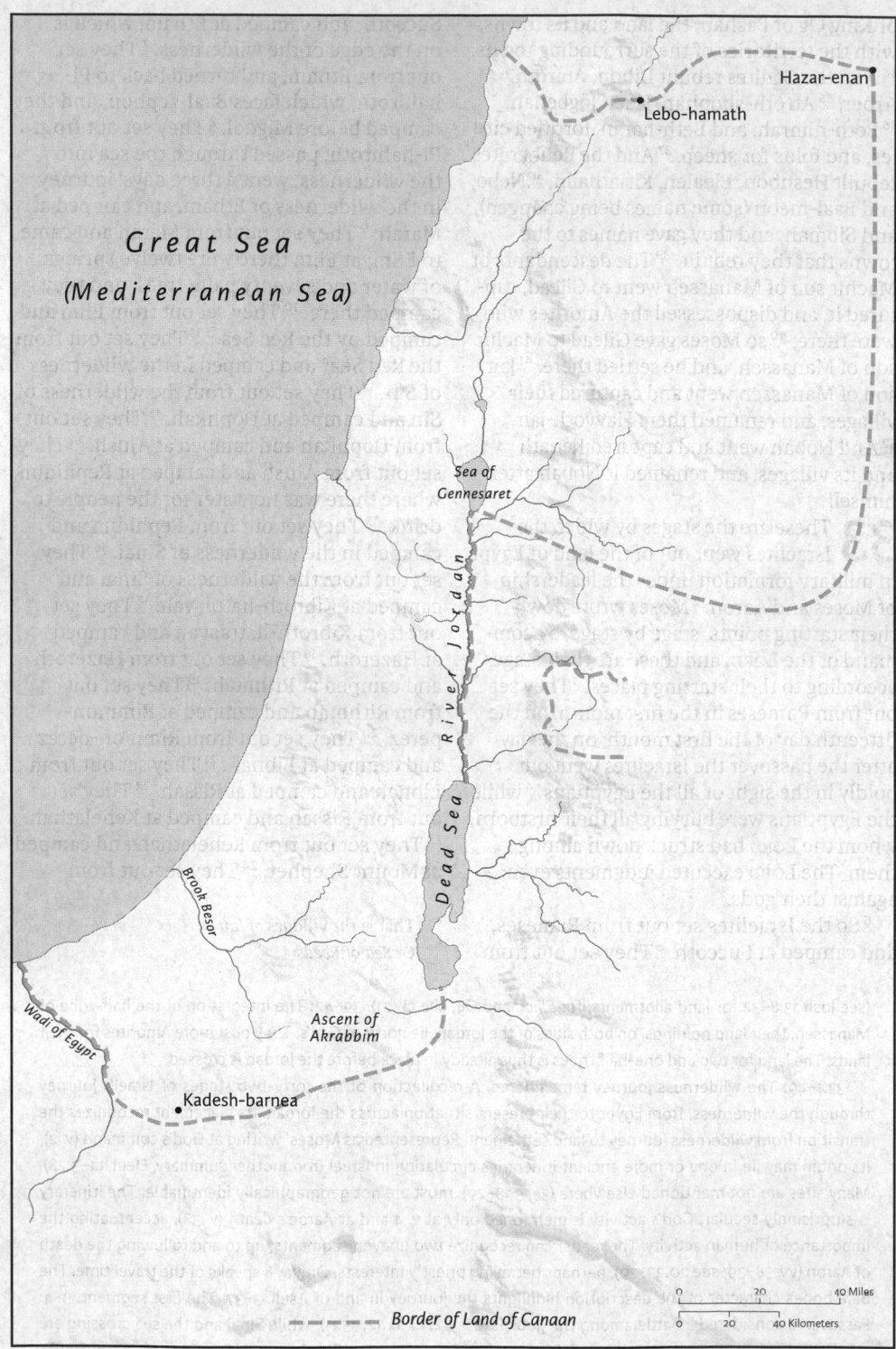

Great Sea
(Mediterranean Sea)

Hazar-enan

Lebo-hamath

Sea of
Gennesaret

River Jordan

Brook Besor

Dead Sea

Wadi of Egypt

Ascent of
Akrabbim

Kadesh-barnea

0   20   40 Miles

0   20   40 Kilometers

- - - - Border of Land of Canaan

The boundaries of the promised land.

Mount Shepher and camped at Haradah. ²⁵ They set out from Haradah and camped at Makheloth. ²⁶ They set out from Makheloth and camped at Tahath. ²⁷ They set out from Tahath and camped at Terah. ²⁸ They set out from Terah and camped at Mithkah. ²⁹ They set out from Mithkah and camped at Hashmonah. ³⁰ They set out from Hashmonah and camped at Moseroth. ³¹ They set out from Moseroth and camped at Bene-jaakan. ³² They set out from Bene-jaakan and camped at Hor-haggidgad. ³³ They set out from Hor-haggidgad and camped at Jotbathah. ³⁴ They set out from Jotbathah and camped at Abronah. ³⁵ They set out from Abronah and camped at Ezion-geber. ³⁶ They set out from Ezion-geber and camped in the wilderness of Zin (that is, Kadesh). ³⁷ They set out from Kadesh and camped at Mount Hor, on the edge of the land of Edom.

³⁸ Aaron the priest went up Mount Hor at the command of the LORD and died there in the fortieth year after the Israelites had come out of the land of Egypt, on the first day of the fifth month. ³⁹ Aaron was one hundred twenty-three years old when he died on Mount Hor.

⁴⁰ The Canaanite, the king of Arad, who lived in the Negeb in the land of Canaan, heard of the coming of the Israelites.

⁴¹ They set out from Mount Hor and camped at Zalmonah. ⁴² They set out from Zalmonah and camped at Punon. ⁴³ They set out from Punon and camped at Oboth. ⁴⁴ They set out from Oboth and camped at Iye-abarim, in the territory of Moab. ⁴⁵ They set out from Iyim and camped at Dibon-gad. ⁴⁶ They set out from Dibon-gad and camped at Almon-diblathaim. ⁴⁷ They set out from Almon-diblathaim and camped in the mountains of Abarim, before Nebo. ⁴⁸ They set out from the mountains of Abarim and camped in the plains of Moab by the Jordan at Jericho; ⁴⁹ they camped by the Jordan from Beth-jeshimoth as far as Abel-shittim in the plains of Moab.

⁵⁰ In the plains of Moab by the Jordan at Jericho, the LORD spoke to Moses, saying: ⁵¹ Speak to the Israelites, and say to them: When you cross over the Jordan into the land of Canaan, ⁵² you shall drive out all the inhabitants of the land from before you, destroy all their figured stones, destroy all their cast images, and demolish all their high places. ⁵³ You shall take possession of the land and settle in it, for I have given you the land to possess. ⁵⁴ You shall apportion the land by lot according to your clans; to a large one you shall give a large inheritance, and to a small one you shall give a small inheritance; the inheritance shall belong to the person on whom the lot falls; according to your ancestral tribes you shall inherit. ⁵⁵ But if you do not drive out the inhabitants of the land from before you, then those whom you let remain shall be as barbs in your eyes and thorns in your sides; they shall trouble you in the land where you are settling. ⁵⁶ And I will do to you as I thought to do to them.

34 The LORD spoke to Moses, saying: ² Command the Israelites, and say to them: When you enter the land of Canaan

36: Cf. 13.26; 20.1. 37: *Mount Hor, see* 20.22; *Edom, see* 20.14–21. 38–39: See 20.23–29. 40: See 20.1–3. 41–49: The second segment (compare 21.1–22.1) moves quickly to the present situation (a passing reference to Mount Nebo, the site of Moses' death and burial). 43: 21.10–11. 45: *Dibon-gad,* cf. 32.34; 21.30n. 48: See 22.1. 49: Cf. 25.1.

33.50–56: **Directions for conquest of Canaan.** These hortatory instructions from God to Moses specify the nature of the possession of the land and its allotment. Israel is to *drive out* (not exterminate; contrast Ex 23.23; Deut 7.1–6) the present inhabitants, destroy their images and sanctuaries (*high places* are open-air sanctuaries; see Lev 26.30), and apportion the land by lot according to the size of the clans (see 26.54–55). If they do not drive out the inhabitants (which actually happens; see Judg 1.1–2.5; 1 Kings 9.21), those left *shall be as barbs in your eyes and thorns in your sides*, which is what they prove to be over the years (Josh 23.13; see Ex 23.23–33; 34.11–16; Deut 7.16; 12.2–4; Judg 2.11–3.6).

34.1–29: **The apportionment of the land. 1–15:** The boundaries of the promised land are idealized; they do not correspond to the boundaries known from other biblical sources (such as Josh 13–19; Ezek 47.13–20), yet the boundaries correspond well to Canaan as described in Egyptian sources prior to the Israelite settlement and a few other texts (see Josh 13–19; Ezek 47.13–20). Many sites are unknown and so the boundaries cannot be determined with precision. **2–6:** The southern border moves from the southern end of the Dead Sea south and

(this is the land that shall fall to you for an inheritance, the land of Canaan, defined by its boundaries), [3] your south sector shall extend from the wilderness of Zin along the side of Edom. Your southern boundary shall begin from the end of the Dead Sea[a] on the east; [4] your boundary shall turn south of the ascent of Akrabbim, and cross to Zin, and its outer limit shall be south of Kadesh-barnea; then it shall go on to Hazar-addar, and cross to Azmon; [5] the boundary shall turn from Azmon to the Wadi of Egypt, and its termination shall be at the Sea.

[6] For the western boundary, you shall have the Great Sea and its[b] coast; this shall be your western boundary.

[7] This shall be your northern boundary: from the Great Sea you shall mark out your line to Mount Hor; [8] from Mount Hor you shall mark it out to Lebo-hamath, and the outer limit of the boundary shall be at Zedad; [9] then the boundary shall extend to Ziphron, and its end shall be at Hazar-enan; this shall be your northern boundary.

[10] You shall mark out your eastern boundary from Hazar-enan to Shepham; [11] and the boundary shall continue down from Shepham to Riblah on the east side of Ain; and the boundary shall go down, and reach the eastern slope of the sea of Chinnereth; [12] and the boundary shall go down to the Jordan, and its end shall be at the Dead Sea.[a] This shall be your land with its boundaries all around.

[13] Moses commanded the Israelites, saying: This is the land that you shall inherit by lot, which the LORD has commanded to give to the nine tribes and to the half-tribe; [14] for

the tribe of the Reubenites by their ancestral houses and the tribe of the Gadites by their ancestral houses have taken their inheritance, and also the half-tribe of Manasseh; [15] the two tribes and the half-tribe have taken their inheritance beyond the Jordan at Jericho eastward, toward the sunrise.

[16] The LORD spoke to Moses, saying: [17] These are the names of the men who shall apportion the land to you for inheritance: the priest Eleazar and Joshua son of Nun. [18] You shall take one leader of every tribe to apportion the land for inheritance. [19] These are the names of the men: Of the tribe of Judah, Caleb son of Jephunneh. [20] Of the tribe of the Simeonites, Shemuel son of Ammihud. [21] Of the tribe of Benjamin, Elidad son of Chislon. [22] Of the tribe of the Danites a leader, Bukki son of Jogli. [23] Of the Josephites: of the tribe of the Manassites a leader, Hanniel son of Ephod, [24] and of the tribe of the Ephraimites a leader, Kemuel son of Shiphtan. [25] Of the tribe of the Zebulunites a leader, Eli-zaphan son of Parnach. [26] Of the tribe of the Issacharites a leader, Paltiel son of Azzan. [27] And of the tribe of the Asherites a leader, Ahihud son of Shelomi. [28] Of the tribe of the Naphtalites a leader, Pedahel son of Ammihud. [29] These were the ones whom the LORD commanded to apportion the inheritance for the Israelites in the land of Canaan.

35

In the plains of Moab by the Jordan at Jericho, the LORD spoke to Moses, saying: [2] Command the Israelites to give, from

[a] Heb Salt Sea
[b] Syr: Heb lacks its

west across the wilderness of Zin to south of Kadesh to the Wadi of Egypt to the Mediterranean (*Great Sea*), the western boundary. 7–9: The northern border is less clear, extending from the Mediterranean to Mount Hor (not the southern mountain of 20.22) into southern Syria (Lebo-hamath). 10–12: The eastern boundary moves from a line north of the eastern slope of the sea of *Chinnereth* (Galilee) down the Jordan to the Dead Sea. 14–15: See ch 32. 16–29: Ten tribal leaders (not Reuben and Gad) are appointed to apportion the land, generally listed from south to north; they are the new generation, different from those listed in 13.2–15 (except for Caleb). Eleazar and Joshua are chosen to supervise the work.

35.1–34: **Special cities and refinements in the law**. These stipulations are given by God to Moses for the enhancement of life for various persons in the new land. The taking of human life puts the land in special danger. 1–8: Cities for the Levites (see Lev 25.32–34; for lists, see Josh 21.1–42; 1 Chr 6.54–81). Stipulations for land distribution are continued, with provision for the Levites, who have no territorial rights (see 18.21–24; 26.62). Inasmuch as they will be active throughout the land (unspecified functions beyond care for the tabernacle), they are to be allotted forty-eight cities (six of which are cities of refuge, vv. 9–15). These cities provide for their housing and for grazing lands for their livestock, though not as permanent possessions (and others would

the inheritance that they possess, towns for the Levites to live in; you shall also give to the Levites pasture lands surrounding the towns. ³ The towns shall be theirs to live in, and their pasture lands shall be for their cattle, for their livestock, and for all their animals. ⁴ The pasture lands of the towns, which you shall give to the Levites, shall reach from the wall of the town outward a thousand cubits all around. ⁵ You shall measure, outside the town, for the east side two thousand cubits, for the south side two thousand cubits, for the west side two thousand cubits, and for the north side two thousand cubits, with the town in the middle; this shall belong to them as pasture land for their towns.

⁶ The towns that you give to the Levites shall include the six cities of refuge, where you shall permit a slayer to flee, and in addition to them you shall give forty-two towns. ⁷ The towns that you give to the Levites shall total forty-eight, with their pasture lands. ⁸ And as for the towns that you shall give from the possession of the Israelites, from the larger tribes you shall take many, and from the smaller tribes you shall take few; each, in proportion to the inheritance that it obtains, shall give of its towns to the Levites.

⁹ The LORD spoke to Moses, saying: ¹⁰ Speak to the Israelites, and say to them: When you cross the Jordan into the land of Canaan, ¹¹ then you shall select cities to be cities of refuge for you, so that a slayer who kills a person without intent may flee there. ¹² The cit-

ies shall be for you a refuge from the avenger, so that the slayer may not die until there is a trial before the congregation.

¹³ The cities that you designate shall be six cities of refuge for you: ¹⁴ you shall designate three cities beyond the Jordan, and three cities in the land of Canaan, to be cities of refuge. ¹⁵ These six cities shall serve as refuge for the Israelites, for the resident or transient alien among them, so that anyone who kills a person without intent may flee there.

¹⁶ But anyone who strikes another with an iron object, and death ensues, is a murderer; the murderer shall be put to death. ¹⁷ Or anyone who strikes another with a stone in hand that could cause death, and death ensues, is a murderer; the murderer shall be put to death. ¹⁸ Or anyone who strikes another with a weapon of wood in hand that could cause death, and death ensues, is a murderer; the murderer shall be put to death. ¹⁹ The avenger of blood is the one who shall put the murderer to death; when they meet, the avenger of blood shall execute the sentence. ²⁰ Likewise, if someone pushes another from hatred, or hurls something at another, lying in wait, and death ensues, ²¹ or in enmity strikes another with the hand, and death ensues, then the one who struck the blow shall be put to death; that person is a murderer; the avenger of blood shall put the murderer to death, when they meet.

²² But if someone pushes another suddenly without enmity, or hurls any object without

live there). **4–5:** *A thousand cubits* (ca. 433 m [1,457 ft]). The various tribes will contribute cities according to their size. **9–15:** *Cities of refuge* (cf. Deut 4.41–43; 19.1–13; for a list, see Josh 20.1–9). Six well-distributed cities of refuge were set aside as places of asylum for persons (Israelite or alien) who killed someone *without intent* until their case could be properly tried. Their purpose was to prevent blood feuds. **12:** As long as such persons remained within one of these cities they were secure from the *avenger* (or redeemer; see Lev 25.25,47–49), the relative of the deceased charged to ensure proper retribution for the sake of the land (see v. 33). **16–34:** Distinctions in the homicide laws, between murder and unpremeditated killing (on intentional/unintentional distinction, see 15.22–31; Ex 21.13–14). The burden of proof is on the slayer. **16–21:** Those who murder another with intent, regardless of means or motivation (six examples are given), are to be put to death by the *avenger*, after a trial (see supplement, vv. 30–32). The avenger's action is necessary for the sake of the future of the land. **22–29:** In the case of killing without intent and hostility, a trial is to be held, outside the city of refuge, with national judges representing the congregation to decide whether the killing was truly unintentional (see Josh 20.6). If so decided, the slayer was returned to the city where he originally took refuge, where he remained until the death of the high priest. The cities of refuge were a kind of exile. Because they only masked the polluting effects of the murder, expiation was still necessary. This was accomplished through the (natural) death of the high priest, which had expiatory significance, issuing in a kind of general amnesty. Only then was release possible. If the slayer left the city before this occurred, he was not protected from the avenger, whose actions would not incur

lying in wait, [23] or, while handling any stone that could cause death, unintentionally[a] drops it on another and death ensues, though they were not enemies, and no harm was intended, [24] then the congregation shall judge between the slayer and the avenger of blood, in accordance with these ordinances; [25] and the congregation shall rescue the slayer from the avenger of blood. Then the congregation shall send the slayer back to the original city of refuge. The slayer shall live in it until the death of the high priest who was anointed with the holy oil. [26] But if the slayer shall at any time go outside the bounds of the original city of refuge, [27] and is found by the avenger of blood outside the bounds of the city of refuge, and is killed by the avenger, no bloodguilt shall be incurred. [28] For the slayer must remain in the city of refuge until the death of the high priest; but after the death of the high priest the slayer may return home.

[29] These things shall be a statute and ordinance for you throughout your generations wherever you live.

[30] If anyone kills another, the murderer shall be put to death on the evidence of witnesses; but no one shall be put to death on the testimony of a single witness. [31] Moreover you shall accept no ransom for the life of a murderer who is subject to the death penalty; a murderer must be put to death. [32] Nor shall you accept ransom for one who has fled to a city of refuge, enabling the fugitive to return to live in the land before the death of the high priest. [33] You shall not pollute the land in which you live; for blood pollutes the land, and no expiation can be made for the land,

for the blood that is shed in it, except by the blood of the one who shed it. [34] You shall not defile the land in which you live, in which I also dwell; for I the LORD dwell among the Israelites.

36

The heads of the ancestral houses of the clans of the descendants of Gilead son of Machir son of Manasseh, of the Josephite clans, came forward and spoke in the presence of Moses and the leaders, the heads of the ancestral houses of the Israelites; [2] they said, "The LORD commanded my lord to give the land for inheritance by lot to the Israelites; and my lord was commanded by the LORD to give the inheritance of our brother Zelophehad to his daughters. [3] But if they are married into another Israelite tribe, then their inheritance will be taken from the inheritance of our ancestors and added to the inheritance of the tribe into which they marry; so it will be taken away from the allotted portion of our inheritance. [4] And when the jubilee of the Israelites comes, then their inheritance will be added to the inheritance of the tribe into which they have married; and their inheritance will be taken from the inheritance of our ancestral tribe."

[5] Then Moses commanded the Israelites according to the word of the LORD, saying, "The descendants of the tribe of Joseph are right in what they are saying. [6] This is what the LORD commands concerning the daughters of Zelophehad, 'Let them marry whom they think best; only it must be into a clan of their father's tribe that they are married,

[a] Heb *without seeing*

guilt. 30–32: A supplement stating that evidence of more than one witness is needed (see Deut 19.15–21) and no monetary ransom is possible. 33–34: Murder is not simply a matter between two families—it pollutes the land and its wholeness, threatening the divine presence among Israel; only the blood of the killer can make *expiation* for the land (remove the impurity the murder has let loose; compare Deut 21.1–9).

36.1–13: Once again: the daughters of Zelophehad. Issues raised concerning the effects of the decision earlier rendered to the daughters of Zelophehad (27.1–11). They based their case on the continuance of their father's name and his property in their clan (27.4). 1–4: Members of their tribe Manasseh come to Moses and ask for an interpretation in view of the fact that upon marriage any property held by the wife became that of her husband. Hence, if a daughter were to marry outside of her tribe, the property would transfer to that tribe and Manasseh (in this case) would lose its full original allotment. Even the property transfer in the *jubilee* year (every fiftieth year) would not return it to the family, because only sold, not inherited, property is so returned (see Lev 25.13–34; 27.16–25). 5–9: Moses agrees and apparently receives a *word of the LORD* on the matter (it may be his interpretation more generally; see Ex 18.23). The daughters may marry within their own tribe (as was common in patrilineal systems) so that the original tribal allotment remains intact. 10–12: The five daughters of

⁷ so that no inheritance of the Israelites shall be transferred from one tribe to another; for all Israelites shall retain the inheritance of their ancestral tribes. ⁸ Every daughter who possesses an inheritance in any tribe of the Israelites shall marry one from the clan of her father's tribe, so that all Israelites may continue to possess their ancestral inheritance. ⁹ No inheritance shall be transferred from one tribe to another; for each of the tribes of the Israelites shall retain its own inheritance.'"

¹⁰ The daughters of Zelophehad did as the Lord had commanded Moses. ¹¹ Mahlah, Tirzah, Hoglah, Milcah, and Noah, the daughters of Zelophehad, married sons of their father's brothers. ¹² They were married into the clans of the descendants of Manasseh son of Joseph, and their inheritance remained in the tribe of their father's clan.

¹³ These are the commandments and the ordinances that the Lord commanded through Moses to the Israelites in the plains of Moab by the Jordan at Jericho.

Zelophehad actually do marry first cousins within their clan. 13: The final verse speaks of God's commandments given through Moses since 22.1, when Israel arrived by the Jordan. These commandments have been essentially forward-looking, anticipating Israel's future life in the land.

DEUTERONOMY

NAME

The English name of the book comes from the ancient Greek translation, the Septuagint, and means "second law" (see 17.18n.). That title reflects the early Jewish perspective that Deuteronomy is Moses' rehearsal of the earlier legal sections of the Torah. The Hebrew name of the book is *Debarim* ("words"), and comes from the book's opening: "These are the words" (1.1).

AUTHORSHIP, DATE, AND HISTORICAL CONTEXT

Deuteronomy directly addresses the problem of the historical distance between past and present, between tradition and the needs of the contemporary generation, between revelation and interpretation. In that way, it is a remarkably modern text that instructs its audience how to become more thoughtful readers of scripture. In narrative terms, Deuteronomy comes just as the Israelites, encamped on the plains of Moab, finally stand poised to enter the promised land. This entry into Canaan would provide the long-awaited climax of the story that had begun with the promises to the ancestors in Genesis, and whose fulfillment had been delayed by the enslavement in Egypt and the wandering in the wilderness. Now, on the eve both of his death and of the nation's entry into the land without him, Moses, as Deuteronomy's speaker, arrests the narrative action in order to deliver a series of three speeches, grouped together as a long farewell address. He reviews the nation's history, expounds upon their laws, and instructs them about the importance of loyalty to God. He also requires that the nation swear upon oath to uphold this combination of law and theological instruction as a covenant upon the plains of Moab, one that supplements the prior covenant of Horeb (Deuteronomy's name for Sinai; 28.69). Only after the conclusion of these discourses and a following appendix (chs 31–34) does the overall narrative line resume with the account of the nation's entry into Canaan in the books of Joshua and Judges.

Despite this perspective and the text's own self-presentation, however, Deuteronomy is likely not from Moses himself but originates in the seventh century BCE. It has long been recognized that there are striking similarities between the distinctive religious and legal requirements of Deuteronomy and the account of the major religious reform carried out by Josiah, the king of Judah, in 622 BCE (2 Kings 22–23). That reform had been inspired by the discovery in the Temple of a "scroll of the Torah" (2 Kings 22.8; NRSV "book of the law"). Josiah's reform restricted all sacrificial worship of God to Jerusalem and removed foreign elements from the system of worship; it culminated in the celebration of the first nationally centralized Passover at the Temple in Jerusalem (2 Kings 23.21–23). So strongly do these royal initiatives correspond to the distinctive requirements of Deuteronomy that scholars, both traditional and critical, have long identified the "scroll of the Torah" discovered in Josiah's Temple as Deuteronomy.

Josiah's reform, with Deuteronomy as its catalyst, was much more a revolution than a simple return to older forms of worship. Previously, it was entirely legitimate to sacrifice to God throughout the land, as did Abraham at Shechem and near Bethel (Gen 12.7–8); Jacob at Bethel (Gen 35.1–7); Samuel at Mizpah, Ramah, Gilgal, and Bethlehem (1 Sam 7.9,17; 9.11–14; 10.8; 16.1–5); and Elijah upon Mount Carmel (1 Kings 18.20–46). Indeed, earlier biblical law stipulated that God would grant blessing "in every place where I cause my name to be remembered" (Ex 20.24). Deuteronomy challenged that older norm, prohibiting sacrifice "at any place" (lit. "in every place") and restricting it to a single site, implicitly Jerusalem (Deut 12.13–14). In this way, Deuteronomy's self-presentation as a rehearsal or explication of prior law (1.1–5) or as a simple supplement to the prior covenant (29.1) obscures the extent to which Deuteronomy actually challenges and revises earlier law in support of its new religious vision.

A century of Assyrian imperial domination serves as the historical background of Josiah's reforms. The Northern Kingdom of Israel had fallen to the Assyrians in 722 BCE (2 Kings 17). Continuing Assyrian incursions down the southeastern coast of the Mediterranean had all but reduced Judah to a rump-state (2 Kings 18.13). In a desperate bid to preserve the nation's autonomy, King Hezekiah of Judah made a pact with Assyria (2 Kings 18.13–18), as had his predecessor Ahaz (2 Kings 16.7–8). The resulting military allegiances led to religious syncretism, as foreign forms of worship were introduced into the Temple (2 Kings 16.10–20; 21.1–6).

By the last quarter of the seventh century BCE, however, Assyria's might was in decline. In this context, Josiah's religious reforms represented an important bid for Judean cultural, political, and religious autonomy. The monarch extended his reforms into the area of the former Northern Kingdom of Israel (2 Kings 23.15–20), territory formerly under Assyrian control. Deuteronomy, apparently written sometime during this historical crisis, likewise reflects the desire to preserve Judean cultural and religious integrity. Its authors were convinced that older conventions of worship and social organization were no longer viable. If the religion of the LORD was to survive the crisis, renewal and adaptation were necessary. The collection of laws that form the core of Deuteronomy (chs 12–26) provides a remarkably comprehensive program for cultural renewal. The laws deal with worship; the festival calendar; the major institutions of public life (justice, kingship, priesthood, prophecy); criminal, family, and civil law; and ethics. These laws are presented as the requirements of a covenant between God and the nation, which the people take an oath to uphold, upon penalty of sanctions, while maintaining unconditional loyalty to their God. That covenant structure closely corresponds to Neo-Assyrian state treaties that have been recovered from this period, the most famous of which is the *Vassal Treaty of Esarhaddon* (672 BCE). At a number of points, the authors of Deuteronomy seem consciously to have patterned their covenant after such treaties, treaties that had been repeatedly imposed upon Judah in the late eighth and seventh centuries BCE. From this perspective, Deuteronomy is a countertreaty: Its authors turned the weapon of imperialism into a bid for freedom, shifting its oath of loyalty from the Assyrian overlord to their divine sovereign.

The authors of Deuteronomy were thus tutored in international treaty conventions, and elsewhere reveal their knowledge of the literary traditions of ancient Near Eastern law (see 15.1–18n.; 17.8–13n.,14–20n.; 22.13–30n.) and wisdom literature (1.13n.; 4.2n.). The authors of Deuteronomy made use of another common ancient Near Eastern convention as well. They did not directly attach their names to their compositions or write in their own voices; instead, they attributed their composition to a prestigious figure from the past. By employing Moses as their spokesperson, they established a link with tradition at precisely the time when tradition, for the sake of survival, had to be transformed. This convention of ascribing a text to an ancient personage, technically called "pseudepigraphy," is particularly well known in the later literature of the Second Temple period; examples include *Jubilees*, *4 Ezra*, the *Testament of Abraham*, and (among the Dead Sea Scrolls) the *Temple Scroll*.

LITERARY HISTORY

It is important to note that Deuteronomy has its own internal literary history as well, preserving several layers of tradition within itself—the structure of three different speeches given by Moses, with an appendix, already suggests a process of literary growth. That growth is closely connected to the gradual formation of the Hebrew Bible. To appreciate what is involved, it helps imaginatively to turn the clock back to the time before the Bible achieved its present form.

When Deuteronomy was first promulgated, it would not have been part of any larger whole. Instead, it would have been complete by itself as a "scroll of the Torah" ("book of the law"). It would have consisted of most of the laws of chs 12–26, framed by a relatively simple introduction and conclusion. This form of Deuteronomy presented itself as a treaty concluded between the nation and its God in a formal ceremony whereby each citizen took an oath of under penalty of strict sanctions (28.1–46). This was very likely the preexilic form of Deuteronomy.

At a later stage, presumably sometime during the exile in the mid-sixth century BCE, Deuteronomy would have been incorporated into the Deuteronomistic History (the books of Joshua, Judges, Samuel, and Kings) to serve as its introduction. At this point, the Deuteronomistic editors would have given the book its literary frame (1.1–4.40; chs 31–34), while also adding to the collection of laws, selectively tying its promises or expectations to the later historical material. Expansions in Deuteronomy that reflect the Babylonian exile may derive from this stage (see 4.25–31; 28.47–56; 30.1–10).

At a still later point, in the exilic or postexilic period, Priestly editors appended Deuteronomy to the newly formed Pentateuch, to serve as its conclusion. Ironically, the decision to conclude the Pentateuch with Deuteronomy separated the overall narrative plan of Genesis through Numbers from its logical fulfillment in an account of the conquest of the land. This narrative climax was delayed to the books of Joshua and Judges.

In the final chapters of Deuteronomy, these three viewpoints operate simultaneously, creating a complex interplay of perspectives. The legal section is brought to its conclusion with a formal ratification ceremony involving the swearing of an oath to assume the penalties for transgressing the covenant (chs 29–31). At the same time, other editors worked to embed Deuteronomy in the Deuteronomistic History. Still other editors tied the book to Genesis-Numbers and thus make the creation of Torah—no longer the occupation of the land—the climax of the newly created Pentateuch. The three perspectives operate concurrently, spinning like Ezekiel's vision of "a wheel within a wheel" (Ezek 1.16).

STRUCTURE AND CONTENTS

GUIDE TO READING

Part of the continuing relevance of Deuteronomy is that it does not permit itself to be read literally or passively. It challenges its readers actively to confront the problem of the relation between revelation and interpretation, and breaks down conventional boundaries between scripture and tradition. It makes paradox central to its structure: The book distinctively narrates the process of its own formation (31.1–12) while also anticipating its existence and completion (17.18; 28.58; 30.10). Interpretation is directly and indirectly a theme of Deuteronomy (see 1.5). At many points, the authors of Deuteronomy reinterpret earlier narratives (see 6.1n.) and laws (particularly from the Covenant Collection or Covenant Code in Ex 20–23). Moreover, the process of the book's editing intentionally preserves conflicting perspectives on a full range of issues central to Israelite religion: on whether the revelation of the Decalogue at Mount Horeb (Deuteronomy's name for Mount Sinai) was direct or required the mediation of Moses (5.5n.); on the stature of Moses relative to other prophets (34.10n.); on the nature of divine punishment for sin (5.9–10n.; 7.10n.); on whether God rules as head of a pantheon or is the only God who exists (4.7–8n., 15–31n., 35n.; 32.8n.); and even on Deuteronomy's own setting in time and place (1.1n.; 2.12n.; 3.11n.). These mutually exclusive positions preserve an ongoing ancient debate about fundamental religious assumptions. The editors of Deuteronomy opted against closure: They preserved these different schools of thought in their full integrity. Accordingly, there is in Deuteronomy no access to God in the covenant without entering into this debate. The modern reader of Deuteronomy must become, like the authors of Deuteronomy, an interpreter.

Bernard M. Levinson

1 These are the words that Moses spoke to all Israel beyond the Jordan—in the wilderness, on the plain opposite Suph, between Paran and Tophel, Laban, Hazeroth, and Di-zahab. ² (By the way of Mount Seir it takes eleven days to reach Kadesh-barnea from Horeb.) ³ In the fortieth year, on the first day of the eleventh month, Moses spoke to the Israelites just as the LORD had commanded him to speak to them. ⁴ This was after he had defeated King Sihon of the Amorites, who reigned in Heshbon, and King Og of Bashan, who reigned in Ashtaroth andª in Edrei. ⁵ Beyond the Jordan in the land of Moab, Moses undertook to expound this law as follows:

⁶ The LORD our God spoke to us at Horeb, saying, "You have stayed long enough at this mountain. ⁷ Resume your journey, and go into the hill country of the Amorites as well as into the neighboring regions—the Arabah, the hill country, the Shephelah, the Negeb, and the seacoast—the land of the Canaanites and the Lebanon, as far as the great river, the river Euphrates. ⁸ See, I have set the land before you; go in and take possession of the land that Iᵇ swore to your ancestors, to Abraham, to Isaac, and to Jacob, to give to them and to their descendants after them."

⁹ At that time I said to you, "I am unable by myself to bear you. ¹⁰ The LORD your God has multiplied you, so that today you are as numerous as the stars of heaven. ¹¹ May the LORD, the God of your ancestors, increase you

---

ª Gk Syr Vg Compare Josh 12.4: Heb lacks *and*
ᵇ Sam Gk: MT *the LORD*

1.1–4.43: The first discourse of Moses has two subsections: a historical retrospective (1.6–3.29) and a sermon on the importance of obeying the teaching of Moses (4.1–40). An editorial heading (1.1–5) and an appendix (4.41–43) frame the discourse. **1.1–5: Editorial heading. 1:** *Beyond the Jordan,* the land east of the Jordan river (Transjordan), "the land of Moab" (v. 5), where the Israelites have stopped, awaiting entry into the land. The reference places the editor west of the Jordan, in Canaan. According to the narrative line, however, the Israelites have not yet reached the promised land, and Moses never does. From this and similar anachronisms, medieval Jewish commentators already recognized that not all of the Pentateuch could be attributed to Moses (see also 2.12; 3.11n.; 20.15; 34.5; Gen 12.6). *The plain* (lit. "the Arabah"), the Rift Valley that includes the Jordan River and stretches south from the Dead Sea through Eilat and the Red Sea into Africa. The places mentioned cannot be identified with certainty. **2:** *Eleven days* implies a scathing indictment of the nation. As a result of their rebellion in the desert (Num 13–14), it actually took them thirty-eight years, eight months, and twenty days to reach this point after they first broke camp (Num 10.11). *Kadesh-barnea,* see Num 13.26n. *Horeb* (Ex 3.1; 17.6; 33.6) is Deuteronomy's term for the mount of revelation. "(Mount) Sinai," in contrast, is the more standard term used by the Yahwistic and Priestly writers (see Ex 19.11; 34.29); it occurs in Deuteronomy only at 33.1, where it refers more generally to a mountainous region in the south. **4:** Num 21.21–35. **5:** *Expound* seems intentionally ambiguous about whether Moses here proclaims new religious teachings or simply explicates material already proclaimed. *This law,* better, "this teaching" (Heb "torah," 4.8,44; 27.3,8,26; 28.58,61; 29.20,28; 30.10; 31.9,11–12; 32.46). The word designates not only the combination of ritual, civil, family, and ethical law found in chs 12–26, but also the religious instruction of chs 5–11. For later editors, as here, the same word seems to refer to the entire book of Deuteronomy.

1.6–3.29: Historical review. Moses rehearses the Exodus, the revelation at Horeb/Sinai, and the rebellion in the desert for the generation who arose after these events, so that they may understand what brought them to the present moment. At a number of points, this narrative diverges from that of Exodus-Numbers. **1.6:** The original of the divine command quoted has not been preserved (cf. Num 10). **7:** *Amorites,* as at Gen 15.16, seems to be used generically for the family of nations who are the original inhabitants of Canaan, rather than technically to designate one of those nations (contrast Gen 15.19–21; Ex 3.8,17). *The Shephelah* is the region of foothills between the hill country on the east and the *seacoast* on the west. *The Negeb* is the semi-arid region south of the hill country. *Great river,* the ideal borders of the Israelite empire extended to the Euphrates (Gen 15.18), the northern limit of David's conquests (2 Sam 8.3). **8:** *See . . . set the land before you,* God symbolically displays the land and transfers its legal title to Israel (similarly, Gen 13.14–15). **9–18:** This account combines and reinterprets two previous accounts of the creation of a military-judicial system to share the burden of leadership (compare vv. 9–12 with Num 11.14–17 and vv. 13–17 with Ex 18.13–27), placing the institutionalization of leadership after the departure from Sinai rather than before it and omitting the advisory role of Jethro, the non-Israelite (con-

a thousand times more and bless you, as he has promised you! [12] But how can I bear the heavy burden of your disputes all by myself? [13] Choose for each of your tribes individuals who are wise, discerning, and reputable to be your leaders." [14] You answered me, "The plan you have proposed is a good one." [15] So I took the leaders of your tribes, wise and reputable individuals, and installed them as leaders over you, commanders of thousands, commanders of hundreds, commanders of fifties, commanders of tens, and officials, throughout your tribes. [16] I charged your judges at that time: "Give the members of your community a fair hearing, and judge rightly between one person and another, whether citizen or resident alien. [17] You must not be partial in judging: hear out the small and the great alike; you shall not be intimidated by anyone, for the judgment is God's. Any case that is too hard for you, bring to me, and I will hear it." [18] So I charged you at that time with all the things that you should do.

[19] Then, just as the LORD our God had ordered us, we set out from Horeb and went through all that great and terrible wilderness that you saw, on the way to the hill country of the Amorites, until we reached Kadesh-barnea. [20] I said to you, "You have reached the hill country of the Amorites, which the LORD our God is giving us. [21] See, the LORD your God has given the land to you; go up, take possession, as the LORD, the God of your ancestors, has promised you; do not fear or be dismayed."

[22] All of you came to me and said, "Let us send men ahead of us to explore the land for us and bring back a report to us regarding the route by which we should go up and the cities we will come to." [23] The plan seemed good to me, and I selected twelve of you, one from each tribe. [24] They set out and went up into the hill country, and when they reached the Valley of Eshcol they spied it out [25] and gathered some of the land's produce, which they brought down to us. They brought back a report to us, and said, "It is a good land that the LORD our God is giving us."

[26] But you were unwilling to go up. You rebelled against the command of the LORD your God; [27] you grumbled in your tents and said, "It is because the LORD hates us that he has brought us out of the land of Egypt, to hand us over to the Amorites to destroy us. [28] Where are we headed? Our kindred have made our hearts melt by reporting, 'The people are stronger and taller than we; the cities are large and fortified up to heaven! We actually saw there the offspring of the Anakim!'" [29] I said to you, "Have no dread or fear of them. [30] The LORD your God, who goes before you, is the one who will fight for you, just as he did for you in Egypt before your very eyes, [31] and in the wilderness, where you saw how the LORD your God carried you, just as one carries a child, all the way that you traveled until you reached this place. [32] But in spite of this, you have no trust in the LORD your God, [33] who goes before you on the way to seek out a place for you to camp, in fire by night, and in the cloud by day, to show you the route you should take."

[34] When the LORD heard your words, he was wrathful and swore: [35] "Not one of these—not one of this evil generation—shall see the good land that I swore to give to your ancestors, [36] except Caleb son of Jephunneh. He shall see it, and to him and to his descen-

trast Ex 18). **10**: *Stars of heaven,* fulfilling the promises made to the ancestors (Gen 15.5; 22.17; 26.4; Ex 32.13). **11**: *God of your ancestors,* Deuteronomy's normal phrase is "the LORD your/our God" (i.e., vv. 6,10). This departure from that formula ties this new generation to its past by recalling God's earlier promises (Gen 26.24; 32.9; Ex 3.6). **13**: *Wise* (contrast Ex 18.21), an attribute regularly stressed by Deuteronomy (4.6; 16.19; 32.29), suggesting the influence of wisdom literature upon its authors. *Reputable* (lit. "knowing"), continuing the emphasis upon wisdom as a criterion for leadership. **16**: *Resident alien,* the non-Israelite who lives in the community without title to land and who is therefore economically vulnerable; Deuteronomy insists upon a single law that applies to Israelite and non-Israelite alike (5.14; 10.18–19; 14.29; 16.11; 24.14,17,19–21). **17**: Similarly, 16.18–20.

1.19–46: From Horeb to Kadesh. A retelling, with significant variations, of the spies' reconnaissance of the land (Num 13), the people's complaining of God's inability to fulfill the promises made to Israel's ancestors (Num 14.1–38), and the abortive attempt to penetrate Canaan from the south despite the divine command not to do so (Num 14.39–45; cf. 21.1–3). **28**: *Anakim,* see Num 13.22,33n. **30**: Ex 14.14. **33**: *Fire . . . cloud,* see Ex 13.21–22n.

The circuit via Transjordan.

dants I will give the land on which he set foot, because of his complete fidelity to the LORD." [37] Even with me the LORD was angry on your account, saying, "You also shall not enter there. [38] Joshua son of Nun, your assistant, shall enter there; encourage him, for he is the one who will secure Israel's possession of it. [39] And as for your little ones, who you thought would become booty, your children, who today do not yet know right from wrong, they shall enter there; to them I will give it, and they shall take possession of it. [40] But as for you, journey back into the wilderness, in the direction of the Red Sea."[a]

[41] You answered me, "We have sinned against the LORD! We are ready to go up and fight, just as the LORD our God commanded us." So all of you strapped on your battle gear, and thought it easy to go up into the hill country. [42] The LORD said to me, "Say to them, 'Do not go up and do not fight, for I am not in the midst of you; otherwise you will be defeated by your enemies.'" [43] Although I told you, you would not listen. You rebelled against the command of the LORD and presumptuously went up into the hill country. [44] The Amorites who lived in that hill country then came out against you and chased you as bees do. They beat you down in Seir as far as Hormah. [45] When you returned and wept before the LORD, the LORD would neither heed your voice nor pay you any attention.

[46] After you had stayed at Kadesh as many days as you did,

2 [1] we journeyed back into the wilderness, in the direction of the Red Sea,[a] as the LORD had told me and skirted Mount Seir for many days. [2] Then the LORD said to me: [3] "You have been skirting this hill country long enough. Head north,

[4] and charge the people as follows: You are about to pass through the territory of your kindred, the descendants of Esau, who live in Seir. They will be afraid of you, so, be very careful [5] not to engage in battle with them, for I will not give you even so much as a foot's length of their land, since I have given Mount Seir to Esau as a possession. [6] You shall purchase food from them for money, so that you may eat; and you shall also buy water from them for money, so that you may drink. [7] Surely the LORD your God has blessed you in all your undertakings; he knows your going through this great wilderness. These forty years the LORD your God has been with you; you have lacked nothing." [8] So we passed by our kin, the descendants of Esau who live in Seir, leaving behind the route of the Arabah, and leaving behind Elath and Ezion-geber.

When we had headed out along the route of the wilderness of Moab, [9] the LORD said to me: "Do not harass Moab or engage them in battle, for I will not give you any of its land as a possession, since I have given Ar as a possession to the descendants of Lot." [10] (The Emim—a large and numerous people, as tall as the Anakim—had formerly inhabited it. [11] Like the Anakim, they are usually reckoned as Rephaim, though the Moabites call them Emim. [12] Moreover, the Horim had formerly inhabited Seir, but the descendants of Esau dispossessed them, destroying them and settling in their place, as Israel has done in the land that the LORD gave them as a possession.) [13] "Now then, proceed to cross over the Wadi Zered."

[a] Or *Sea of Reeds*

34–38: See Num 14.28–30. 37: Here Moses is not punished for his own sin (contrast 32.51; Num 20.10–13; 27.12–23). Instead, the narrator presents Moses as innocent and as vicariously bearing the punishment due Israel for its sin (see 3.24–28; 4.21).

2.1–3.29: The circuit via Transjordan. 1–8a: Num 20.14–21. From Kadesh, Israel turned south through the Arabah to the Gulf of Aqaba in order to go around *Seir* (Edom; Num 21.4; cf. 33.47–49). 4: *Descendants of Esau*, see Gen 36.1. 6: *Money*, silver or gold that was weighed out. 8a: *Elath*, see 1 Kings 9.26. *Ezion-geber*, see Num 33.35. 8b–25: Num 21.4–20, significantly revised. Turning along the brook Zered (modern Wadi el-Hasa), which formed Edom's southern boundary, Israel detoured through the wilderness of Moab toward the Amorite kingdom of Sihon. 9: Moab and Ammon (v. 19) were traditionally related through Lot (Gen 19.36–38). 10–12: NRSV attempts to mitigate the anachronistic post-conquest perspective by confining it to parentheses (see v. 12n.). 10–11: *Emim . . . Rephaim* (cf. v. 20; 3.11–13), names reflecting the legendary view that the aboriginal inhabitants of the land were fearsome giants. 12: *Horim*, see Gen 36.20–30n. *As Israel has done . . . possession*, the conquest is

So we crossed over the Wadi Zered. [14] And the length of time we had traveled from Kadesh-barnea until we crossed the Wadi Zered was thirty-eight years, until the entire generation of warriors had perished from the camp, as the LORD had sworn concerning them. [15] Indeed, the LORD's own hand was against them, to root them out from the camp, until all had perished.

[16] Just as soon as all the warriors had died off from among the people, [17] the LORD spoke to me, saying, [18] "Today you are going to cross the boundary of Moab at Ar. [19] When you approach the frontier of the Ammonites, do not harass them or engage them in battle, for I will not give the land of the Ammonites to you as a possession, because I have given it to the descendants of Lot." [20] (It also is usually reckoned as a land of Rephaim. Rephaim formerly inhabited it, though the Ammonites call them Zamzummim, [21] a strong and numerous people, as tall as the Anakim. But the LORD destroyed them from before the Ammonites so that they could dispossess them and settle in their place. [22] He did the same for the descendants of Esau, who live in Seir, by destroying the Horim before them so that they could dispossess them and settle in their place even to this day. [23] As for the Avvim, who had lived in settlements in the vicinity of Gaza, the Caphtorim, who came from Caphtor, destroyed them and settled in their place.) [24] "Proceed on your journey and cross the Wadi Arnon. See, I have handed over to you King Sihon the Amorite of Heshbon, and his land. Begin to take possession by engaging him in battle. [25] This day I will begin to put the dread and fear of you upon the peoples everywhere under heaven; when they hear report of you, they will tremble and be in anguish because of you."

[26] So I sent messengers from the wilderness of Kedemoth to King Sihon of Heshbon with the following terms of peace: [27] "If you let me pass through your land, I will travel only along the road; I will turn aside neither to the right nor to the left. [28] You shall sell me food for money, so that I may eat, and supply me water for money, so that I may drink. Only allow me to pass through on foot— [29] just as the descendants of Esau who live in Seir have done for me and likewise the Moabites who live in Ar—until I cross the Jordan into the land that the LORD our God is giving us." [30] But King Sihon of Heshbon was not willing to let us pass through, for the LORD your God had hardened his spirit and made his heart defiant in order to hand him over to you, as he has now done.

[31] The LORD said to me, "See, I have begun to give Sihon and his land over to you. Begin now to take possession of his land." [32] So when Sihon came out against us, he and all his people for battle at Jahaz, [33] the LORD our God gave him over to us; and we struck him down, along with his offspring and all his people. [34] At that time we captured all his towns, and in each town we utterly destroyed men, women, and children. We left not a single survivor. [35] Only the livestock we kept as spoil for ourselves, as well as the plunder of the towns that we had captured. [36] From Aroer on the edge of the Wadi Arnon (including the town that is in the wadi itself) as far as Gilead, there was no citadel too high for us. The LORD our God gave everything to us. [37] You did not encroach, however, on the land of the Ammonites, avoiding the whole upper region of the Wadi Jabbok as well as the towns of the hill country, just as[a] the LORD our God had charged.

3 When we headed up the road to Bashan, King Og of Bashan came out against us, he and all his people, for battle at Edrei.

[a] Gk Tg: Heb *and all*

---

represented anachronistically as already having been completed (see 1.1n.; 3.11n.). **13:** *Wadi,* a seasonal stream. **14:** Fulfilling God's angry oath (1.34–35; Num 14.28–30). Without the death of the generation of the Exodus, here marked as accomplished, there can be no entry into the promised land. **15:** *LORD's own hand,* they did not die of natural causes. The imagery reverses the standard idea of holy war: God had turned against Israel rather than fighting on its behalf (see 3.22; 7.1–5; 12.29–31; 20.1–20). **20:** Cf. vv. 10–12n.; Gen 14.5. **23:** *Caphtor,* Crete, referring to the conquest of the coastal plain by "Sea Peoples" such as Philistines shortly after 1200 BCE (see Gen 10.2–5,14; Am 9.7). **24:** *Arnon,* see Num 21.12–13. **26–37:** The victory over Sihon, whose capital was at Heshbon. The earlier source in Num 21.21–32 is here supplemented and revised. **30:** See Ex 4.21n. **34:** *Utterly destroyed,* see

² The LORD said to me, "Do not fear him, for I have handed him over to you, along with his people and his land. Do to him as you did to King Sihon of the Amorites, who reigned in Heshbon." ³ So the LORD our God also handed over to us King Og of Bashan and all his people. We struck him down until not a single survivor was left. ⁴ At that time we captured all his towns; there was no citadel that we did not take from them—sixty towns, the whole region of Argob, the kingdom of Og in Bashan. ⁵ All these were fortress towns with high walls, double gates, and bars, besides a great many villages. ⁶ And we utterly destroyed them, as we had done to King Sihon of Heshbon, in each city utterly destroying men, women, and children. ⁷ But all the livestock and the plunder of the towns we kept as spoil for ourselves.

⁸ So at that time we took from the two kings of the Amorites the land beyond the Jordan, from the Wadi Arnon to Mount Hermon ⁹ (the Sidonians call Hermon Sirion, while the Amorites call it Senir), ¹⁰ all the towns of the tableland, the whole of Gilead, and all of Bashan, as far as Salecah and Edrei, towns of Og's kingdom in Bashan. ¹¹ (Now only King Og of Bashan was left of the remnant of the Rephaim. In fact his bed, an iron bed, can still be seen in Rabbah of the Ammonites. By the common cubit it is nine cubits long and four cubits wide.) ¹² As for the land that we took possession of at that time, I gave to the Reubenites and Gadites the territory north of Aroer,ᵃ that is on the edge of the Wadi Arnon, as well as half the hill country of Gilead with its towns, ¹³ and I gave to the half-tribe of Manasseh the rest of Gilead and all of Bashan, Og's kingdom. (The whole region of Argob: all that portion of Bashan used to be called a land of Rephaim; ¹⁴ Jair

the Manassite acquired the whole region of Argob as far as the border of the Geshurites and the Maacathites, and he named them—that is, Bashan—after himself, Havvoth-jair,ᵇ as it is to this day.) ¹⁵ To Machir I gave Gilead. ¹⁶ And to the Reubenites and the Gadites I gave the territory from Gilead as far as the Wadi Arnon, with the middle of the wadi as a boundary, and up to the Jabbok, the wadi being boundary of the Ammonites; ¹⁷ the Arabah also, with the Jordan and its banks, from Chinnereth down to the sea of the Arabah, the Dead Sea,ᶜ with the lower slopes of Pisgah on the east.

¹⁸ At that time, I charged you as follows: "Although the LORD your God has given you this land to occupy, all your troops shall cross over armed as the vanguard of your Israelite kin. ¹⁹ Only your wives, your children, and your livestock—I know that you have much livestock—shall stay behind in the towns that I have given to you. ²⁰ When the LORD gives rest to your kindred, as to you, and they too have occupied the land that the LORD your God is giving them beyond the Jordan, then each of you may return to the property that I have given to you." ²¹ And I charged Joshua as well at that time, saying: "Your own eyes have seen everything that the LORD your God has done to these two kings; so the LORD will do to all the kingdoms into which you are about to cross. ²² Do not fear them, for it is the LORD your God who fights for you."

²³ At that time, too, I entreated the LORD, saying: ²⁴ "O Lord GOD, you have only begun to show your servant your greatness and your

ᵃ Heb territory from Aroer
ᵇ That is Settlement of Jair
ᶜ Heb Salt Sea

7.2n. 37: The river Jabbok makes a wide bend south and thus forms the western border of Ammon (3.16). 3.1–11: The victory over Bashan (Num 21.33–35). 1: Edrei, on the extreme south border of Bashan; see Num 21.33–35n. 11: The oversized bed of Og, one of the legendary Rephaim (2.10–11), was a "museum piece" in Rabbah, a city on the Ammonite border. The emphasis that this bed can still be seen there places the historical perspective of the narrator, and thus of Deuteronomy's composition, long after the events here recounted (1.1n.; 2.12n.). A cubit was about 44 cm (17.5 in). 12–22: The allotment of tribal territories in Transjordan (Num 32; Josh 13). 14: Num 32.41. 17: The territory included the eastern part of the Jordan Valley or Arabah. 22: The whole story of the Exodus, wilderness journey, and invasion of Canaan is governed by the convictions of holy war, whereby God is a divine warrior who engages in battle on behalf of Israel. 23–29: Num 27.12–23. 24: What god . . . can perform, the assertion of God's superior power, relative to other gods in heaven, assumes the existence of other gods

might; what god in heaven or on earth can perform deeds and mighty acts like yours! [25] Let me cross over to see the good land beyond the Jordan, that good hill country and the Lebanon." [26] But the LORD was angry with me on your account and would not heed me. The LORD said to me, "Enough from you! Never speak to me of this matter again! [27] Go up to the top of Pisgah and look around you to the west, to the north, to the south, and to the east. Look well, for you shall not cross over this Jordan. [28] But charge Joshua, and encourage and strengthen him, because it is he who shall cross over at the head of this people and who shall secure their possession of the land that you will see." [29] So we remained in the valley opposite Beth-peor.

4 So now, Israel, give heed to the statutes and ordinances that I am teaching you to observe, so that you may live to enter and occupy the land that the LORD, the God of your ancestors, is giving you. [2] You must neither add anything to what I command you nor take away anything from it, but keep the commandments of the LORD your God with which I am charging you. [3] You have seen for yourselves what the LORD did with regard to the Baal of Peor—how the LORD your God destroyed from among you everyone who followed the Baal of Peor, [4] while those of you who held fast to the LORD your God are all alive today.

[5] See, just as the LORD my God has charged me, I now teach you statutes and ordinances for you to observe in the land that you are about to enter and occupy. [6] You must observe them diligently, for this will show your wisdom and discernment to the peoples, who, when they hear all these statutes, will say, "Surely this great nation is a wise and discerning people!" [7] For what other great nation has a god so near to it as the LORD our God is whenever we call to him? [8] And what other great nation has statutes and ordinances as just as this entire law that I am setting before you today?

[9] But take care and watch yourselves closely, so as neither to forget the things that your eyes

(5.7n.; 6.4n.; 32.8n.; Ex 15.11; Ps 89.5–8). For the later perspective of monotheism, see 4.35n. **26:** See 1.37n. **27:** Mount *Pisgah*, see 34.1n.

4.1–40: Exhortation to obey the teachings of Moses. While preceding the Decalogue (5.6–21), this unit provides a later theological reflection upon it, focusing on the second commandment and broadening its significance. Admonitions to obedience (vv. 1,40) frame the unit, which systematically contrasts obedience (vv. 5–24)/disobedience (vv. 25–31); remembering/forgetting (vv. 9,23); the LORD/other gods (vv. 7,34); Israel's revealed Torah/the laws of other nations (vv. 8,28); and God/idols (vv. 12–20). The correct worship of God is aniconic: Images (whether of God or of natural phenomena) should play no role in Israelite religion. This becomes so strong a theme that idolatry by itself is asserted to be the cause of the nation's exile from its land (vv. 25–31). The explicit reference to exile suggests that the unit is a late theological explanation for the Babylonian exile in the early sixth century BCE. The focus on idolatry as the basis for the divine punishment diverges significantly from the perspective elsewhere that views failure to heed "all his [God's] commandments and decrees" as the cause of exile (28.15; cf. 28.1,45,58–59). **1–4:** The incident at Peor (Num 25.1–9) is recalled to emphasize the importance of fidelity to God and the dire consequences of worshiping other gods. **2:** This admonition not to alter the teaching of Moses, whether by addition or subtraction (cf. 12.32), parallels similar admonitions in wisdom literature (Prov 30.6; Eccl 3.14; 12.12–13; Sir 42.21; cf. Rev 22.18–19) and in ancient Near Eastern legal traditions. **5–8:** The author here challenges the prevailing Near Eastern idea that wisdom was a royal prerogative. Whereas, for example, the ancient Babylonian *Laws of Hammurabi* (ca. 1755 BCE) praised the "just decisions" of its "wise" king (cols 47.1; 4.7), here it is the nation Israel who will be internationally renowned as "wise" for its "just" laws (vv. 6,8). See also 29.29n.; 30.11–14n. **7–8:** Israel is distinguished both by its God and by its law: The two ideas are interlocked. God is *near*, both in having entered history on behalf of Israel and in revealing his will as Torah (30.14). The laws are *just* (better, "righteous"), not only in their morality but also as embodying the will of God. **9–14:** The revelation at Sinai/Horeb (Ex 19–20; Deut 5) is recalled in order to instruct this generation, who did not experience it. **9:** The paired injunctions not to *forget* the powerful experience of God's actions and to educate *your children*, so that the past becomes "present" also to them, represent a prominent aim of Deuteronomy: to overcome the distance of the past and maintain it as a source of identity (vv. 23,25; 6.2,7,20–25; 8.11; 9.7; 31.13; 32.18). *Your eyes have seen*, as well as the following "how you once stood" (v. 10), are highly paradoxical assertions. Nei-

have seen nor to let them slip from your mind all the days of your life; make them known to your children and your children's children— [10] how you once stood before the LORD your God at Horeb, when the LORD said to me, "Assemble the people for me, and I will let them hear my words, so that they may learn to fear me as long as they live on the earth, and may teach their children so"; [11] you approached and stood at the foot of the mountain while the mountain was blazing up to the very heavens, shrouded in dark clouds. [12] Then the LORD spoke to you out of the fire. You heard the sound of words but saw no form; there was only a voice. [13] He declared to you his covenant, which he charged you to observe, that is, the ten commandments;[a] and he wrote them on two stone tablets. [14] And the LORD charged me at that time to teach you statutes and ordinances for you to observe in the land that you are about to cross into and occupy.

[15] Since you saw no form when the LORD spoke to you at Horeb out of the fire, take care and watch yourselves closely, [16] so that you do not act corruptly by making an idol for yourselves, in the form of any figure—the likeness of male or female, [17] the likeness of any animal that is on the earth, the likeness of any winged bird that flies in the air, [18] the likeness of anything that creeps on the ground, the likeness of any fish that is in the water under the earth. [19] And when you look up to the heavens and see the sun, the moon, and the stars, all the host of heaven, do not be led astray and bow down to them and serve them, things that the LORD your God has allotted to all the peoples everywhere under heaven. [20] But the LORD has taken you and brought you out of the iron-smelter, out of Egypt, to become a people of his very own possession, as you are now.

[21] The LORD was angry with me because of you, and he vowed that I should not cross the Jordan and that I should not enter the good

a   Heb *the ten words*

ther is literally true: The actual generation of the Exodus had died off (2.14–15n.). This paradoxical structure of thought, whereby Moses addresses those who had not witnessed the events as if they had, while insisting that they inculcate the events to posterity, is central to Deuteronomy's theology of history (5.3–4,23; 11.7; 29.14–15). 10: *My words*, the Decalogue ("ten commandments"; v. 13; 5.22; 9.10; 10.2,4). Elsewhere, however, the phrase refers comprehensively to the legal corpus of chs 12–26 (12.28). *Fear*, respectful reverence, not intimidation (see Job 28.28; Prov 1.7). 11: The manifestation of a god ("theophany") was often associated with disturbances of nature in Ugaritic (Canaanite) literature. This motif was taken over by Israelite writers and applied to God (Ex 19.16–19; 20.21; Ps 18.7–15; 29.3–9). 12: *Form* (also vv. 15–16,23,25), directly alluding to the second commandment of the Decalogue (5.8 = Ex 20.4). 13: A subtle reinterpretation of Sinai: The specification of that event as one where God proclaimed *ten commandments* occurs only here, at 10.4, and at Ex 34.28. There is no special number of or name for the commandments (lit. "words") in Ex 19–20 or Deut 5. The rationale for *two stone tablets* (as at 5.22) derives from ancient Near Eastern treaties, whereby both sovereign and vassal would retain a separate complete copy of the treaty. 15–31: Reinterpretation of the second commandment. The Decalogue concedes the existence of other gods, while prohibiting Israel from worshiping them (5.7; cf. 32.8; Ex 15.11; Ps 82.1). It then separately prohibits the making of images (5.8). The distinction between those two commandments is dissolved here. The existence of other gods is no longer conceivable; the sole focus is the prohibition against idols. Here and elsewhere (see v. 19n.) key ideas in Deuteronomy are reinterpreted from a later theological perspective; such passages therefore represent a later textual layer that dates to the exilic period. 16b–19a: This catalogue follows the order of creation in Gen 1 in reverse order, consistent with ancient scribal practice when quoting an earlier text. 18: *Water under the earth*, seas, rivers, and lakes. Ancient cosmology conceived the earth to be a disk floating on such waters (cf. Gen 1.9). 19: *Sun . . . host of heaven* may reflect images derived from the Neo-Assyrian pantheon brought into the Jerusalem Temple by Manasseh but removed by Josiah (2 Kings 21.5; 23.4–5; Jer 8.2). The idea of idols or of celestial phenomena literally being worshiped sharply distorts ancient Near Eastern religion, which regarded such phenomena as visible manifestations or emblems of a deity, not as themselves divine. This polemic, with the idea that God *allotted* the celestial phenomena to other nations while reserving Israel as "his very own possession" (v. 20; cf. 7.6n.; 32.8–9), reinterprets the earlier idea that God, as head of the pantheon, assigned other nations to the supervision of lesser gods but retained Israel as "his allotted share" (lit. "his very own possession"; 32.8–9). The author deanimates those gods, reducing

land that the LORD your God is giving for your possession. [22] For I am going to die in this land without crossing over the Jordan, but you are going to cross over to take possession of that good land. [23] So be careful not to forget the covenant that the LORD your God made with you, and not to make for yourselves an idol in the form of anything that the LORD your God has forbidden you. [24] For the LORD your God is a devouring fire, a jealous God.

[25] When you have had children and children's children, and become complacent in the land, if you act corruptly by making an idol in the form of anything, thus doing what is evil in the sight of the LORD your God, and provoking him to anger, [26] I call heaven and earth to witness against you today that you will soon utterly perish from the land that you are crossing the Jordan to occupy; you will not live long on it, but will be utterly destroyed. [27] The LORD will scatter you among the peoples; only a few of you will be left among the nations where the LORD will lead you. [28] There you will serve other gods made by human hands, objects of wood and stone that neither see, nor hear, nor eat, nor smell. [29] From there you will seek the LORD your God, and you will find him if you search after him with all your heart and soul. [30] In your distress, when all these things have happened to you in time to come, you will return to the LORD your God and heed him. [31] Because the LORD your God is a merciful God, he will neither abandon you nor destroy you; he will not forget the covenant with your ancestors that he swore to them.

[32] For ask now about former ages, long before your own, ever since the day that God created human beings on the earth; ask from one end of heaven to the other: has anything so great as this ever happened or has its like ever been heard of? [33] Has any people ever heard the voice of a god speaking out of a fire, as you have heard, and lived? [34] Or has any god ever attempted to go and take a nation for himself from the midst of another nation, by trials, by signs and wonders, by war, by a mighty hand and an outstretched arm, and by terrifying displays of power, as the LORD your God did for you in Egypt before your very eyes? [35] To you it was shown so that you would acknowledge that the LORD is God; there is no other besides him. [36] From heaven he made you hear his voice to discipline you. On earth he showed you his great fire, while you heard his words coming out of the fire. [37] And because he loved your ancestors, he chose their descendants after them. He brought you out of Egypt with his own presence, by his great power, [38] driving out before you nations greater and mightier than yourselves, to bring you in, giving you their land for a possession, as it is still today. [39] So acknowledge today and take to heart that the LORD is God in heaven above and on the earth beneath; there is no other. [40] Keep his statutes and his commandments, which I am commanding you today for your own well-being and that of your descendants after you, so that you may long remain in the land that the LORD your God is giving you for all time.

[41] Then Moses set apart on the east side of the Jordan three cities [42] to which a homicide could flee, someone who unintentionally kills another person, the two not having been

them to lifeless celestial objects. **21:** See 1.37n. **26:** *Heaven . . . witness,* similarly, 30.19; 31.28; 32.1; Isa 1.2; 44.23; Ps 69.34; 96.11. **27–28:** These verses allude to the exile of conquered populations, a policy used effectively by the Assyrians and the Babylonians. **32–40:** Continuation of the double focus on the uniqueness of God's revelation to Israel and of the covenant he made with the nation. Several passages fit best in the historical context of the Babylonian exile (see v. 35n.). **33:** Alludes to the normal expectation that no human can look directly upon God and survive (Gen 16.13; 32.30; Ex 3.6; 19.21; 33.20). **34:** *Attempted,* better, "ventured" (as at 28.56). *Trials . . . wonders* refers to the signs performed by Moses and Aaron in Egypt, including the plagues, to persuade Pharaoh to release Israel (Ex 7.3; 8.23; 10.1–2; 11.9–10). **35:** *There is no other,* this affirmation of full monotheism (contrast v. 7; 5.7) corresponds to the thought of the exilic Second Isaiah (Isa 43.10–13; 44.6–8; 45.6–7,22).

4.41–43: An appendix. The cities of refuge to be established in Transjordan. Since the law concerned with these cities (ch 19) does not refer to this passage, these verses are most likely an editorial appendix composed after the completion of ch 19 (cf. Num 35.9–15; Josh 20.8). Similar disconnected appendixes often appear in the Bible at the conclusion of longer literary units (e.g., Lev 27).

at enmity before; the homicide could flee to one of these cities and live: [43] Bezer in the wilderness on the tableland belonging to the Reubenites, Ramoth in Gilead belonging to the Gadites, and Golan in Bashan belonging to the Manassites.

[44] This is the law that Moses set before the Israelites. [45] These are the decrees and the statutes and ordinances that Moses spoke to the Israelites when they had come out of Egypt, [46] beyond the Jordan in the valley opposite Beth-peor, in the land of King Sihon of the Amorites, who reigned at Heshbon, whom Moses and the Israelites defeated when they came out of Egypt. [47] They occupied his land and the land of King Og of Bashan, the two kings of the Amorites on the eastern side of the Jordan: [48] from Aroer, which is on the edge of the Wadi Arnon, as far as Mount Sirion[a] (that is, Hermon), [49] together with all the Arabah on the east side of the Jordan as far as the Sea of the Arabah, under the slopes of Pisgah.

5 Moses convened all Israel, and said to them: Hear, O Israel, the statutes and ordinances that I am addressing to you today; you shall learn them and observe them diligently. [2] The LORD our God made a covenant with us at Horeb. [3] Not with our ancestors did the LORD make this covenant, but with us, who are all of us here alive today. [4] The LORD spoke with you face to face at the mountain, out of the fire. [5] (At that time I was standing between the LORD and you to declare to you the words[b] of the LORD; for you were afraid because of the fire and did not go up the mountain.) And he said:

[6] I am the LORD your God, who brought you out of the land of Egypt, out of the house of slavery; [7] you shall have no other gods before[c] me.

[8] You shall not make for yourself an idol, whether in the form of anything that

a Syr: Heb *Sion*
b Q Mss Sam Gk Syr Vg Tg: MT *word*
c Or *besides*

4.44–28.68: The second discourse of Moses.

4.44–49: Introduction. Cf. 1.1–5. 49: *Sea of the Arabah,* the Dead Sea.

5.1–33: The revelation at Sinai/Horeb. Ostensibly a retelling of Ex 19–20, this version introduces significant changes in both detail and theology. The central idea is that God publicly reveals the law to the entire nation across boundaries of gender, race, and class, including non-Israelites (Ex 12.38). Near Eastern legal collections, in contrast, were attributed to a human monarch and were concerned to preserve class distinctions. Moreover, a deity disclosing himself to an entire nation was unprecedented. The Decalogue has God address each Israelite individually as a grammatically masculine singular "you," rather than the expected plural. In contrast to Near Eastern law, the prohibitions are universal and absolute: The aim of the law is to transform society by creating a moral community in which murder, theft, etc. will no longer exist. Obedience to God's will (vv. 6–16) demands active respect for the integrity of the neighbor (vv. 17–21). The editing drives home the point that there is no access to God or revelation without mediation and interpretation (vv. 5,28–32), preserving two mutually independent viewpoints about whether God spoke directly to the people (v. 4) or only through the mediation of Moses (v. 5n.). Similarly, the editing retains a debate about the terror involved in hearing directly the divine voice (vv. 24–25).

5.1–5: Making the past present. 3: *Not with our ancestors . . . but with us,* inconsistent with the earlier emphasis that the generation who experienced these events has now died off (2.14–15). The aim is to overcome the limits of historical time and place through participation in the covenant, which makes revelation "present" (see 4.9n.; 11.2; 29.14–15n.). *Our ancestors* may refer either to the Exodus generation (2.14–15n.) or to the patriarchs Abraham, Isaac, and Jacob (1.11n.). 5: NRSV suggests that the first sentence intends merely to clarify v. 4. More likely, it presents an independent view that challenges the assumption of v. 4. *I was standing between . . . you,* contrast "face to face" (v. 4). *You . . . did not go up the mountain,* contradicting v. 4, "with you . . . at the mountain" (Heb). *And he said,* in Hebrew, the original transition from the end of v. 4 directly to the Decalogue.

5.6–21: The Decalogue. This version differs at several points from that in Ex 20.2–17. 7–10: See 4.15–31n. 9: Punishment for sins against God extends across three generations. This principle of vicarious punishment contrasts sharply with the Israelite norm for civil and criminal law, which restricts punishment to the agent alone (24.16). Later layers of tradition challenged this theological principle of divine justice (see 7.10n.; Jer 31.29–30;

The Numbering of the Ten Commandments in Deuteronomy 5.6-18

Command	Jewish Tradition	Eastern Orthodox, Anglican and Most Protestant Churches	Roman Catholic and Lutheran Churches
1	Self-identification of God as separate command (v. 6)	Other Gods (vv. 6-7)	Other Gods & Idols (vv. 6-10)
2	Other Gods & Idols (vv. 7-10)	Idols (vv. 8-10)	False Oath (v. 11)
3	False Oath (v. 11)	False Oath (v. 11)	Sabbath (vv. 12-15)
4	Sabbath (vv. 12-15)	Sabbath (vv. 12-15)	Parents (v. 16)
5	Parents (v. 16)	Parents (v. 16)	Murder (v. 17)
6	Murder (v. 17)	Murder (v. 17)	Adultery (v. 17)
7	Adultery (v. 17)	Adultery (v. 17)	Theft (v. 17)
8	Theft (v. 17)	Theft (v. 17)	False Witness (v. 17)
9	False Witness (v. 17)	False Witness (v. 17)	Coveting Wife (v. 18)
10	Coveting (v. 18)	Coveting (v. 18)	Coveting Property (v. 18)

is in heaven above, or that is on the earth beneath, or that is in the water under the earth. ⁹ You shall not bow down to them or worship them; for I the LORD your God am a jealous God, punishing children for the iniquity of parents, to the third and fourth generation of those who reject me, ¹⁰ but showing steadfast love to the thousandth generationᵃ of those who love me and keep my commandments.

¹¹ You shall not make wrongful use of the name of the LORD your God, for the LORD will not acquit anyone who misuses his name. ¹² Observe the sabbath day and keep it holy, as the LORD your God commanded you. ¹³ Six days you shall labor and do all your work. ¹⁴ But the seventh day is a sabbath to the LORD your God; you shall not do any work—you, or your son or your daughter, or your male or female slave, or your ox or your donkey, or any of your livestock, or the resident alien in your towns, so that your male and female slave may rest as well as you. ¹⁵ Remember that you were a slave in the land of Egypt, and the LORD your God brought you out from there with a mighty hand and an outstretched arm; therefore the LORD your God commanded you to keep the sabbath day.

¹⁶ Honor your father and your mother, as the LORD your God commanded you, so that your days may be long and that it may go well with you in the land that the LORD your God is giving you.

¹⁷ You shall not murder.ᵇ

¹⁸ Neither shall you commit adultery.

¹⁹ Neither shall you steal.

a   Or to thousands
b   Or kill

Ezek 18). 10: *Steadfast love* or "grace," loyalty of action as an expectation of the covenant (2 Sam 7.15; Hos 6.6). *Who love me,* technical language of Near Eastern treaties, whereby "love" refers to the loyalty of action that the vassal owes the sovereign. 11: The intent is to prohibit careless use of the divine name in the context of swearing an oath ("May God do X to me unless I do Y"); such oaths were viewed as legally binding (see Judg 11.29–40). 12: *Observe,* contrast Ex 20.8. 14: The law equally benefits slaves and non-Israelites (1.16n.; 15.15; 16.11; 24.17). 15: Contrast the rationale provided for the sabbath at Ex 20.11. Deuteronomy here, as elsewhere, emphasizes the Exodus as a central motivation for religious and social practices. 16: *As . . . commanded you,* the ostensible precise repetition of the Decalogue here diverges from the original (Ex 20.12) by shifting to the perspective of Moses as speaker, whose annotation is now included in the revelation. 17: *Murder* is correct; text note *b* is an inaccurate translation ("kill," as a global prohibition). 18: The absolute prohibition of adultery transforms it from the breach of the contractual rights of the woman's husband into an offense against both God and the larger community. Near Eastern law normally granted the husband the sole right of deciding whether to execute or otherwise punish the wife for adultery (see *Laws of Hammurabi* § 129). Biblical law here removes the wife from

20 Neither shall you bear false witness against your neighbor.

21 Neither shall you covet your neighbor's wife.

Neither shall you desire your neighbor's house, or field, or male or female slave, or ox, or donkey, or anything that belongs to your neighbor.

22 These words the LORD spoke with a loud voice to your whole assembly at the mountain, out of the fire, the cloud, and the thick darkness, and he added no more. He wrote them on two stone tablets, and gave them to me. 23 When you heard the voice out of the darkness, while the mountain was burning with fire, you approached me, all the heads of your tribes and your elders; 24 and you said, "Look, the LORD our God has shown us his glory and greatness, and we have heard his voice out of the fire. Today we have seen that God may speak to someone and the person may still live. 25 So now why should we die? For this great fire will consume us; if we hear the voice of the LORD our God any longer, we shall die. 26 For who is there of all flesh that has heard the voice of the living God speaking out of fire, as we have, and remained alive? 27 Go near, you yourself, and hear all that the LORD our God will say. Then tell us everything that the LORD our God tells you, and we will listen and do it."

28 The LORD heard your words when you spoke to me, and the LORD said to me: "I have heard the words of this people, which they have spoken to you; they are right in all that they have spoken. 29 If only they had such a mind as this, to fear me and to keep all my commandments always, so that it might go well with them and with their children forever! 30 Go say to them, 'Return to your tents.' 31 But you, stand here by me, and I will tell you all the commandments, the statutes and the ordinances, that you shall teach them, so that they may do them in the land that I am giving them to possess." 32 You must therefore be careful to do as the LORD your God has commanded you; you shall not turn to the right or to the left. 33 You must follow exactly the path that the LORD your God has commanded you, so that you may live, and that it may go well with you, and that you may live long in the land that you are to possess.

6 Now this is the commandment—the statutes and the ordinances—that the LORD your God charged me to teach you to observe in the land that you are about to cross into and occupy, 2 so that you and your children and your children's children may fear the LORD your God all the days of your life, and keep all his decrees and his commandments that I am commanding you, so that your days may be long. 3 Hear therefore, O Israel, and observe them diligently, so that it may go well with you, and so that you may multiply greatly in a land flowing with milk and honey, as the LORD, the God of your ancestors, has promised you.

the disposal of the husband and grants her the status of legal person (see 22.22n.). **21:** *Wife . . . house,* contrast the sequence of Ex 20.17. **22:** *Two . . . tablets,* see 4.12n.

5.22–33: Moses as mediator. While the Decalogue was given directly to the people (v. 4; 4.10–13), the rest of the laws were mediated to the people by Moses, at their plea (v. 27; 4.14). **23–27:** 4.33; cf. Ex 20.18–21. **24–25:** An awkward juxtaposition; v. 24 may be an insertion reflecting 4.33. The anxiety explains the request that Moses serve as mediator. **28–31:** The idea that Moses mediates between God and the people will be used in two ways: to justify the laws that Moses subsequently propounds as revelation (chs 12–26), and to justify the institution of prophecy (18.15–22).

6.1–11.32: The requirement of loyalty to God. A sermonic preamble to the laws of chs 12–26. **6.1–3:** Introduction, stressing the rewards of obedience to the covenant. **1:** *The commandment . . . occupy,* the Hebrew is nearly identical to 5.31. The precise repetition of terminology legitimates the entire second discourse—both *the commandment* (chs 6–11) and *the statutes and the ordinances* (the legal corpus of chs 12–26; see 12.1)—as originating in direct divine revelation from God on Horeb (5.31). The Book of the Covenant Collection (Ex 21–23), with its "ordinances" (Ex 21.1), and the "statutes and the ordinances" of Deuteronomic law (6.1; 12.1), now in implicit tension, are independently presented as God's words to Moses on the mountain immediately following the Decalogue (Ex 20.21; 24.3,12). **2:** *Fear,* better, "revere" (see 4.10n.). **4–25:** A sermon on the first commandment of the Decalogue, incorporating direct allusions to it: vv. 4 and 14 refer to 5.7; vv. 12,21,23 refer to 5.6; v. 15 ("jealous God")

⁴ Hear, O Israel: The LORD is our God, the LORD alone.ᵃ ⁵ You shall love the LORD your God with all your heart, and with all your soul, and with all your might. ⁶ Keep these words that I am commanding you today in your heart. ⁷ Recite them to your children and talk about them when you are at home and when you are away, when you lie down and when you rise. ⁸ Bind them as a sign on your hand, fix them as an emblemᵇ on your forehead, ⁹ and write them on the doorposts of your house and on your gates.

¹⁰ When the LORD your God has brought you into the land that he swore to your ancestors, to Abraham, to Isaac, and to Jacob, to give you—a land with fine, large cities that you did not build, ¹¹ houses filled with all sorts of goods that you did not fill, hewn cisterns that you did not hew, vineyards and olive groves that you did not plant—and when you have eaten your fill, ¹² take care that you do not forget the LORD, who brought you out of the land of Egypt, out of the house of slavery. ¹³ The LORD your God you shall fear; him you shall serve, and by his name alone you shall swear. ¹⁴ Do not follow other gods, any of the gods of the peoples who are all around you, ¹⁵ because the LORD your God, who is present with you, is a jealous God. The anger of the LORD your God would be kindled against you and he would destroy you from the face of the earth.

¹⁶ Do not put the LORD your God to the test, as you tested him at Massah. ¹⁷ You must diligently keep the commandments of the LORD your God, and his decrees, and his statutes that he has commanded you. ¹⁸ Do what is right and good in the sight of the LORD, so that it may go well with you, and so that you may go in and occupy the good land that the LORD swore to your ancestors to give you, ¹⁹ thrusting out all your enemies from before you, as the LORD has promised.

²⁰ When your children ask you in time to come, "What is the meaning of the decrees and the statutes and the ordinances that the LORD our God has commanded you?" ²¹ then you shall say to your children, "We were Pharaoh's slaves in Egypt, but the LORD brought us out of Egypt with a mighty hand. ²² The LORD displayed before our eyes great and awesome signs and wonders against Egypt, against Pharaoh and all his household. ²³ He brought us out from there in order to bring us in, to

ᵃ Or *The LORD our God is one LORD*, or *The LORD our God, the LORD is one*, or *The LORD is our God, the LORD is one*

ᵇ Or *as a frontlet*

refers to 5.9; vv. 5,17 refer to 5.10. **4–9:** In Jewish tradition these verses begin the important prayer known as the Shema ("Hear!"). **4–5:** This "first" commandment (Mk 12.29–30) restates the first Decalogue commandment in positive form. *Hear, O Israel* (5.1; 9.1; 20.3; 27.9), an imperative modeled on a wisdom teacher's call for attention (Prov 1.8; 4.1,10; 5.7; 7.24; 23.19). *The LORD . . . alone*, as text note *a* indicates, the Hebrew is difficult; the translation selected makes most sense historically. The focus is not on God's nature in the abstract but on the quality of Israel's relationship to God. The proclamation, like 5.7, does not deny the existence of other gods but is concerned with the exclusivity of Israel's loyalty to God (as in ch 13). This vision is universalized in later prophecy (Zech 14.9). **5:** *Love*, see 5.10n. The paradox of commanding a feeling (as in Lev 19.17–18) is resolved with the recognition that covenantal "love" is not private emotion but loyalty of action toward both deity and neighbor (see 5.1–33n.). **7:** *At home . . . away*, using paired opposites as a merism (28.3–6n.) to indicate totality: One should always *talk about* the commandments. **8:** *Bind them*, based on the wisdom teacher's symbolically urging his students to focus on the lesson (Prov 3.3; 6.21; 7.3). This law, literally interpreted, provides the basis for the Jewish convention of binding phylacteries, containing selected texts from the Torah, upon the arm and forehead. **9:** *Doorposts*, important transitional spaces in which religious-legal ceremonies were performed and where divine images might be stored (see Ex 12.7,21–23; 21.6; Isa 57.8). Perhaps partially reacting against a formerly magical background, this law devotes that space to the teaching of Moses. The law provides the basis for the Jewish convention of placing a small box containing this and related texts upon the upper portion of the right doorpost (Heb "mezuzah"). **10–11:** The list, *land . . . houses . . . cisterns . . . olive groves* (cf. Josh 24.13; Neh 9.24–25), defines the elements of an established civilization, which Israel is about to both inherit and become. **12:** The threat of forgetting and the risk of apostasy are repeatedly stressed (4.9–14n.; 8.11–20; 32.18; cf. 5.29; Hos 2.5–13). **16:** *Test . . . Massah,* for the incident and the Hebrew pun, see Ex 17.2–7; see also Mt 4.7. **20:** The Jewish Passover text ("Haggadah") includes this and similar didactic questions (Ex 12.21–27; 13.1–10,11–16). **22:** See 4.34n.

give us the land that he promised on oath to our ancestors. ²⁴ Then the Lᴏʀᴅ commanded us to observe all these statutes, to fear the Lᴏʀᴅ our God, for our lasting good, so as to keep us alive, as is now the case. ²⁵ If we diligently observe this entire commandment before the Lᴏʀᴅ our God, as he has commanded us, we will be in the right."

7 When the Lᴏʀᴅ your God brings you into the land that you are about to enter and occupy, and he clears away many nations before you—the Hittites, the Girgashites, the Amorites, the Canaanites, the Perizzites, the Hivites, and the Jebusites, seven nations mightier and more numerous than you— ² and when the Lᴏʀᴅ your God gives them over to you and you defeat them, then you

must utterly destroy them. Make no covenant with them and show them no mercy. ³ Do not intermarry with them, giving your daughters to their sons or taking their daughters for your sons, ⁴ for that would turn away your children from following me, to serve other gods. Then the anger of the Lᴏʀᴅ would be kindled against you, and he would destroy you quickly. ⁵ But this is how you must deal with them: break down their altars, smash their pillars, hew down their sacred poles,ᵃ and burn their idols with fire. ⁶ For you are a people holy to the Lᴏʀᴅ your God; the Lᴏʀᴅ your God has chosen you out of all the peoples on earth to be his people, his treasured possession.

ᵃ Heb *Asherim*

7.1–10.11: Risks to covenantal faith upon entry to the land. The first issue is that Israel enters an already inhabited land, whose greater population and worship apparatus it must confront (ch 7). Thereafter, successful habitation carries its own risks: complacency and loss of historical memory (ch 8).

7.1–26: The war of conquest. Two topics are treated: the command to destroy the original occupants of Canaan (vv. 1–3,6,17–24); and the command not to worship their gods (vv. 4–5,7–15,25–26). The editors join the two themes at v. 16. **1:** An after-the-fact literary compilation more than a historical portrayal: The peoples included in the "table of nations" vary considerably (Gen 15.19–21; Ex 3.8,17; 13.5; 23.23; 33.2; 34.11; Deut 20.17; Josh 3.10; 9.1; 11.3; 12.8; 24.11; Judg 3.5; 1 Kings 9.20; Ezra 9.1; Neh 9.8; 2 Chr 8.7). *Hittites* (Gen 23.10; 25.9; 49.29–30; 50.13; Num 13.29, etc.), the Hittite Empire (ca. 1700–1200 BCE) in fact flourished not in Canaan but in Anatolia, in central Turkey. The *Jebusites*, the pre-Israelite inhabitants of Jerusalem, retained control of the city until conquered by David several centuries after the conquest (2 Sam 5.6–7). The latter narrative implies the nonimplementation of this law. The ideal number *seven*, which signifies completion or totality (28.7; Gen 1; the plague list of Ps 78.44–51 and 105.28–36 in contrast to Ex 7–12), suggests that the enumeration may be artificial. **2:** This requirement for destruction is anomalous: Earlier sources contemplate only expulsion (Ex 23.23–33; cf. 34.11). The definition and requirements of the "ban" vary considerably throughout the Bible: total destruction of people and property (here; 13.15–17; 20.16–17; 1 Sam 15.3); sparing of property (2.34–35; 3.6–7); sparing of women, children, and property (20.10–14). Finally, other narratives more realistically speak of the failure of conquest except in limited areas and the use of conquered populations for labor (Josh 15–17; Judg 1; 3.1–6). These factors suggest that the law of the ban is an anachronistic literary formulation. It first arose centuries after the settlement; it was never implemented because there was no population extant against whom it could be implemented. Its polemic is directed at internal issues of religious purity in postexilic Judah. Often the authors of Deuteronomy stigmatize as "Canaanite" older forms of Israelite religion that they no longer accept (see v. 5n.; 16.22n.; 18.9–14n.). *Utterly destroy*, or "place under the ban," or "devote." That which is "devoted" is set aside for divine use and denied to humans. The war of conquest, as a holy war, should not be one where the individual profits through plunder (see 12.29–31n.; 13.15n.; 20.1–20n.; Josh 7). The law addresses apostasy as opposed to ethnicity; it is directed against apostate Israelites in 8.20; 13.15–17. **3:** This prohibition against intermarriage does not fit easily after v. 2, suggesting several layers of editing. It is also inconsistent with 21.10–14, which seems more likely to reflect the original policy. **5:** See Ex 34.13. *Pillars*, stone monuments that marked places where God appeared and were thus originally legitimate in worship (Gen 35.14; Ex 24.4; Hos 3.4). Only subsequently were they prohibited as alien (Ex 23.24; 34.13; Lev 26.1; Deut 12.3; 16.22; 2 Kings 18.4). *Sacred poles*, or, with text note *a, Asherim*. The singular, "Asherah," preserves the name of an important Canaanite goddess (1 Kings 18.19) known from Ugarit; here the word designates merely the wooden pole, tree, or image that represented her (16.21; Judg 6.25–26,28). **6–16:** The meaning of Israel's covenantal relationship to God. **6:** *For* suggests that the verse (also 14.2) originally continued v. 3, since it provides the rationale for total separation from

⁷ It was not because you were more numerous than any other people that the LORD set his heart on you and chose you—for you were the fewest of all peoples. ⁸ It was because the LORD loved you and kept the oath that he swore to your ancestors, that the LORD has brought you out with a mighty hand, and redeemed you from the house of slavery, from the hand of Pharaoh king of Egypt. ⁹ Know therefore that the LORD your God is God, the faithful God who maintains covenant loyalty with those who love him and keep his commandments, to a thousand generations, ¹⁰ and who repays in their own person those who reject him. He does not delay but repays in their own person those who reject him. ¹¹ Therefore, observe diligently the commandment—the statutes and the ordinances—that I am commanding you today.

¹² If you heed these ordinances, by diligently observing them, the LORD your God will maintain with you the covenant loyalty that he swore to your ancestors; ¹³ he will love you, bless you, and multiply you; he will bless the fruit of your womb and the fruit of your ground, your grain and your wine and your oil, the increase of your cattle and the issue of your flock, in the land that he swore to your ancestors to give you. ¹⁴ You shall be the most blessed of peoples, with neither sterility nor barrenness among you or your livestock. ¹⁵ The LORD will turn away from you every illness; all the dread diseases of Egypt that you experienced, he will not inflict on you, but he will lay them on all who hate you. ¹⁶ You shall devour all the peoples that the LORD your God is giving over to you, showing them no pity; you shall not serve their gods, for that would be a snare to you.

¹⁷ If you say to yourself, "These nations are more numerous than I; how can I dispossess them?" ¹⁸ do not be afraid of them. Just remember what the LORD your God did to Pharaoh and to all Egypt, ¹⁹ the great trials that your eyes saw, the signs and wonders, the mighty hand and the outstretched arm by which the LORD your God brought you out. The LORD your God will do the same to all the peoples of whom you are afraid. ²⁰ Moreover, the LORD your God will send the pestilence[a] against them, until even the survivors and the fugitives are destroyed. ²¹ Have no dread of them, for the LORD your God, who is present with you, is a great and awesome God. ²² The LORD your God will clear away these nations before you little by little; you will not be able to make a quick end of them, otherwise the wild animals would become too numerous for you. ²³ But the LORD your God will give them over to you, and throw them into great panic, until they are destroyed. ²⁴ He will hand their kings over to you and you shall blot out their name from under heaven; no one will be able to stand against you, until you have destroyed them. ²⁵ The images of their gods you shall burn with fire. Do not covet the silver or the gold that is on them and take it for yourself, because you could be ensnared by it; for it is abhorrent to the LORD your God. ²⁶ Do not bring an abhorrent thing into your house, or you will be set apart for destruction like it.

---

[a] Or *hornets*: Meaning of Heb uncertain

the Canaanites, not for the destruction of their cult sites. This verse summarizes Deuteronomy's view of Israel's relation to God. *Holy*, lit. "set aside as separate," as is clear here. *Chosen*, the precondition of Israel's elected status. *His treasured possession* (14.2; 26.18; Ex 19.5; Ps 135.4; Mal 3.17), designating Israel as the exclusive property of God; cf. 4.20n., where a different Heb word is used. Just as the monarch is entitled to private "treasure" not in the public domain (1 Chr 29.3), so does God single Israel out for a special relationship. **9–11**: A discourse on the second commandment that radically revises its meaning. The reuse of key phrases and inversion of the order of punishment and blessing in 5.9–10 mark the citation. **9**: *Covenant loyalty*, NRSV translates the same word as "steadfast love" at 5.10 (see note). **10**: *In their own person*, individually or personally. The repetition of the phrase, bracketing the key idea that God *does not delay*, highlights the rejection of vicarious punishment (5.9n.; Ex 34.7). Instead, the sermon argues for individual retribution, as in criminal law (24.16), while deleting any reference to the transmission of punishment across generations. **12–14**: Natural fertility is here made contingent upon obedience to the covenant. **17–26**: Israel need not fear nations more powerful than it since, according to the idea of the holy war, God "is present with you" in battle (v. 21; 6.15; cf. 20.1–4). These verses echo ideas found in Ex 23.20–33. **20**: *Pestilence*, see Ex 23.27–28n.; Josh 24.12. **22**: Abbreviating Ex 23.29–30; contrast 9.3.

You must utterly detest and abhor it, for it is set apart for destruction.

8 This entire commandment that I command you today you must diligently observe, so that you may live and increase, and go in and occupy the land that the LORD promised on oath to your ancestors. ² Remember the long way that the LORD your God has led you these forty years in the wilderness, in order to humble you, testing you to know what was in your heart, whether or not you would keep his commandments. ³ He humbled you by letting you hunger, then by feeding you with manna, with which neither you nor your ancestors were acquainted, in order to make you understand that one does not live by bread alone, but by every word that comes from the mouth of the LORD.ᵃ ⁴ The clothes on your back did not wear out and your feet did not swell these forty years. ⁵ Know then in your heart that as a parent disciplines a child so the LORD your God disciplines you. ⁶ Therefore keep the commandments of the LORD your God, by walking in his ways and by fearing him. ⁷ For the LORD your God is bringing you into a good land, a land with flowing streams, with springs and underground waters welling up in valleys and hills, ⁸ a land of wheat and barley, of vines and fig trees and pomegranates, a land of olive trees and honey, ⁹ a land where you may eat bread without scarcity, where you will lack nothing, a land whose stones are iron and from whose hills you may mine copper. ¹⁰ You shall eat your fill and bless the LORD your God for the good land that he has given you.

¹¹ Take care that you do not forget the LORD your God, by failing to keep his commandments, his ordinances, and his statutes, which I am commanding you today. ¹² When you have eaten your fill and have built fine houses and live in them, ¹³ and when your herds and flocks have multiplied, and your silver and gold is multiplied, and all that you have is multiplied, ¹⁴ then do not exalt yourself, forgetting the LORD your God, who brought you out of the land of Egypt, out of the house of slavery, ¹⁵ who led you through the great and terrible wilderness, an arid wasteland with poisonousᵇ snakes and scorpions. He made water flow for you from flint rock, ¹⁶ and fed you in the wilderness with manna that your ancestors did not know, to humble you and to test you, and in the end to do you good. ¹⁷ Do not say to yourself, "My power and the might of my own hand have gotten me this wealth." ¹⁸ But remember the LORD your God, for it is he who gives you power to get wealth, so that he may confirm his covenant that he swore to your ancestors, as he is doing today. ¹⁹ If you do forget the LORD your God and follow other gods to serve and worship them, I solemnly warn you today that you shall surely perish. ²⁰ Like the nations that the LORD is destroying before you, so shall you perish, because you would not obey the voice of the LORD your God.

ᵃ Or *by anything that the LORD decrees*
ᵇ Or *fiery*; Heb *seraph*

8.1–20: The temptation to pride and self-sufficiency in the land. Moses warns the people that success in Canaan will tempt them to forget the wilderness lesson of complete dependence upon God. 1–10: An appeal to Israel's memory: In the wilderness God sustained the people daily (Ex 12.37–17.16; Num 11–14). 3: *Manna*, see Ex 16; Num 11.7–8. 5: Suffering is here interpreted as discipline, as in a parent's correction of a child (Hos 11); this metaphor reflects the influence of wisdom literature (see Prov 3.11–12; cf. 1.13n.; 4.2n.; 4.5–8n.; 4.10n.; 6.4n.; 11.2).

8.11–20: The peril of prosperity. 11: A bold equation between *the LORD* and the legal corpus (*his commandments . . . ordinances . . . statutes . . . today*). Disobedience of Deuteronomy's laws becomes tantamount to forgetting God and transgressing the first commandment (see v. 19n.). 15: *Poisonous snakes,* Num 21.6–9. *Water . . . from flint rock,* Ex 17.1–7; Num 20.2–13; Ps 114.8. 16: *Manna,* see v. 3n. 19: *Other gods . . . serve . . . worship,* citing the first and second commandments (5.7,9). *Worship,* translated "bow down to" at 5.9. 20: *Like the nations,* here Israel is itself placed under the ban if it commits apostasy (see 7.1–26n.). *Destroying . . . perish,* in Hebrew, the same word is used to underscore the precise "measure for measure" nature of the punishment. Israel's election (7.6n.) grants no exemption from upholding the law. Rightful habitation in the promised land, like its fertility (7.12–14n.), depends upon covenantal obedience, not ethnic identity (7.2n.).

9 Hear, O Israel! You are about to cross the Jordan today, to go in and dispossess nations larger and mightier than you, great cities, fortified to the heavens, ² a strong and tall people, the offspring of the Anakim, whom you know. You have heard it said of them, "Who can stand up to the Anakim?" ³ Know then today that the LORD your God is the one who crosses over before you as a devouring fire; he will defeat them and subdue them before you, so that you may dispossess and destroy them quickly, as the LORD has promised you.

⁴ When the LORD your God thrusts them out before you, do not say to yourself, "It is because of my righteousness that the LORD has brought me in to occupy this land"; it is rather because of the wickedness of these nations that the LORD is dispossessing them before you. ⁵ It is not because of your righteousness or the uprightness of your heart that you are going in to occupy their land; but because of the wickedness of these nations the LORD your God is dispossessing them before you, in order to fulfill the promise that the LORD made on oath to your ancestors, to Abraham, to Isaac, and to Jacob.

⁶ Know, then, that the LORD your God is not giving you this good land to occupy because of your righteousness; for you are a stubborn people. ⁷ Remember and do not forget how you provoked the LORD your God to wrath in the wilderness; you have been rebellious against the LORD from the day you came out of the land of Egypt until you came to this place.

⁸ Even at Horeb you provoked the LORD to wrath, and the LORD was so angry with you that he was ready to destroy you. ⁹ When I went up the mountain to receive the stone tablets, the tablets of the covenant that the LORD made with you, I remained on the mountain forty days and forty nights; I neither ate bread nor drank water. ¹⁰ And the LORD gave me the two stone tablets written with the finger of God; on them were all the words that the LORD had spoken to you at the mountain out of the fire on the day of the assembly. ¹¹ At the end of forty days and forty nights the LORD gave me the two stone tablets, the tablets of the covenant. ¹² Then the LORD said to me, "Get up, go down quickly from here, for your people whom you have brought from Egypt have acted corruptly. They have been quick to turn from the way that I commanded them; they have cast an image for themselves." ¹³ Furthermore the LORD said to me, "I have seen that this people is indeed a stubborn people. ¹⁴ Let me alone that I may destroy them and blot out their name from under heaven; and I will make of you a nation mightier and more numerous than they."

¹⁵ So I turned and went down from the mountain, while the mountain was ablaze; the two tablets of the covenant were in my two hands. ¹⁶ Then I saw that you had indeed sinned against the LORD your God, by casting for yourselves an image of a calf; you had been quick to turn from the way that the LORD had commanded you. ¹⁷ So I took hold of the two tablets and flung them from my two hands, smashing them before your eyes. ¹⁸ Then I lay prostrate before the LORD as before, forty days and forty nights; I neither ate bread nor drank water, because of all the sin you had committed, provoking the LORD by doing what was evil in his sight. ¹⁹ For I was afraid that the anger that the LORD bore against you was so fierce that he would destroy you. But the LORD listened to me that time also. ²⁰ The LORD was so angry with Aaron that he was ready to destroy him, but I interceded also on behalf of Aaron at that same time. ²¹ Then I took the sinful thing you had made, the calf, and burned it with fire and crushed it, grinding it thoroughly, until it was reduced to dust; and I threw the dust of it into the stream that runs down the mountain.

²² At Taberah also, and at Massah, and at Kibroth-hattaavah, you provoked the LORD to wrath. ²³ And when the LORD sent you from

---

9.1–10.11: The already broken and renewed covenant. God does not give the land to the people as a reward for righteousness, for in the wilderness they acted rebelliously. **9.2:** See 1.28n.; 2.10. **4–5:** Victory will be given in the holy war because (negatively) Canaan has been irrevocably corrupted by the actions of its present occupants and because (positively) of God's enduring commitment to the promises made to Israel's ancestors. **6–24:** The historical record shows that Israel has been rebellious since the Exodus (Ezek 20.5–8; contrast Hos 2.14–20; Jer 2.2–3). **8–10:** Ex 24.12–18; 31.18. **11–21:** Ex 32, revised. **17:** *Smashing them,* not in simple anger but reflecting

Kadesh-barnea, saying, "Go up and occupy the land that I have given you," you rebelled against the command of the LORD your God, neither trusting him nor obeying him. [24] You have been rebellious against the LORD as long as he has[a] known you.

[25] Throughout the forty days and forty nights that I lay prostrate before the LORD when the LORD intended to destroy you, [26] I prayed to the LORD and said, "Lord GOD, do not destroy the people who are your very own possession, whom you redeemed in your greatness, whom you brought out of Egypt with a mighty hand. [27] Remember your servants, Abraham, Isaac, and Jacob; pay no attention to the stubbornness of this people, their wickedness and their sin, [28] otherwise the land from which you have brought us might say, 'Because the LORD was not able to bring them into the land that he promised them, and because he hated them, he has brought them out to let them die in the wilderness.' [29] For they are the people of your very own possession, whom you brought out by your great power and by your outstretched arm."

10 At that time the LORD said to me, "Carve out two tablets of stone like the former ones, and come up to me on the mountain, and make an ark of wood. [2] I will write on the tablets the words that were on the former tablets, which you smashed, and you shall put them in the ark." [3] So I made an ark of acacia wood, cut two tablets of stone like the former ones, and went up the mountain with the two tablets in my hand. [4] Then

he wrote on the tablets the same words as before, the ten commandments[b] that the LORD had spoken to you on the mountain out of the fire on the day of the assembly; and the LORD gave them to me. [5] So I turned and came down from the mountain, and put the tablets in the ark that I had made; and there they are, as the LORD commanded me.

[6] (The Israelites journeyed from Beeroth-bene-jaakan[c] to Moserah. There Aaron died, and there he was buried; his son Eleazar succeeded him as priest. [7] From there they journeyed to Gudgodah, and from Gudgodah to Jotbathah, a land with flowing streams. [8] At that time the LORD set apart the tribe of Levi to carry the ark of the covenant of the LORD, to stand before the LORD to minister to him, and to bless in his name, to this day. [9] Therefore Levi has no allotment or inheritance with his kindred; the LORD is his inheritance, as the LORD your God promised him.)

[10] I stayed on the mountain forty days and forty nights, as I had done the first time. And once again the LORD listened to me. The LORD was unwilling to destroy you. [11] The LORD said to me, "Get up, go on your journey at the head of the people, that they may go in and occupy the land that I swore to their ancestors to give them."

[12] So now, O Israel, what does the LORD your God require of you? Only to fear the LORD your God, to walk in all his ways, to love

a   Sam Gk: MT *I have*
b   Heb *the ten words*
c   Or *the wells of the Bene-jaakan*

a legal ceremony to confirm breach of treaty. **22:** Num 11.1–3; Ex 17.1–7; Num 11.31–34. **23:** Num 13–14. **25–29:** A paraphrase of Ex 32.11–14. Deuteronomy portrays Moses as the ideal prophet (34.10–12); he intercedes for the people and vicariously suffers for them (1.37n.; cf. Isa 53).

   10.1–11: The second ascent of the mountain (cf. Ex 34.1–4,27–28). **1–3:** These verses reflect a tradition that Moses made the ark and put the stone tablets in it (1 Kings 8.9). **6–9:** An editorial insertion; vv. 6–7 seem to quote a wilderness itinerary from the Priestly literature (cf. Num 33.30–38). **6:** Num 20.22–29. **8:** Ex 32.25–29. The Levites' role is to bear the ark (Num 4.4–15), to *minister,* i.e., conduct the sacrificial services (Num 18), and to *bless* the people (Num 6.22–27). **9:** See 12.12n.; 18.2n.

   10.12–11.32: Obedience as the condition for prosperity in the land. This section provides the climax and conclusion of the historical review found in 8.1–10.11. **10.12–13:** A striking transformation of the Decalogue. Earlier, breach of the first and second commandments, with their focus specifically on God, had been redefined and equated with "failing to keep his commandments . . . ordinances . . . and . . . statutes" (8.11n.). Now obedience to God is similarly redefined as compliance with the fixed *commandments . . . and . . . decrees* (v. 13) of Deuteronomy, i.e., the laws of chs 12–26 (see 28.15,45). For a similar catechism that does not extend the traditional focus upon God to law, see Mic 6.8. *And to keep* (lit. "by keeping") the precise antithesis of 8.11. The

him, to serve the LORD your God with all your heart and with all your soul, [13] and to keep the commandments of the LORD your God[a] and his decrees that I am commanding you today, for your own well-being. [14] Although heaven and the heaven of heavens belong to the LORD your God, the earth with all that is in it, [15] yet the LORD set his heart in love on your ancestors alone and chose you, their descendants after them, out of all the peoples, as it is today. [16] Circumcise, then, the foreskin of your heart, and do not be stubborn any longer. [17] For the LORD your God is God of gods and Lord of lords, the great God, mighty and awesome, who is not partial and takes no bribe, [18] who executes justice for the orphan and the widow, and who loves the strangers, providing them food and clothing. [19] You shall also love the stranger, for you were strangers in the land of Egypt. [20] You shall fear the LORD your God; him alone you shall worship; to him you shall hold fast, and by his name you shall swear. [21] He is your praise; he is your God, who has done for you these great and awesome things that your own eyes have seen. [22] Your ancestors went down to Egypt seventy persons; and now the LORD your God has made you as numerous as the stars in heaven.

11 You shall love the LORD your God, therefore, and keep his charge, his decrees, his ordinances, and his command-

ments always. [2] Remember today that it was not your children (who have not known or seen the discipline of the LORD your God), but it is you who must acknowledge his greatness, his mighty hand and his outstretched arm, [3] his signs and his deeds that he did in Egypt to Pharaoh, the king of Egypt, and to all his land; [4] what he did to the Egyptian army, to their horses and chariots, how he made the water of the Red Sea[b] flow over them as they pursued you, so that the LORD has destroyed them to this day; [5] what he did to you in the wilderness, until you came to this place; [6] and what he did to Dathan and Abiram, sons of Eliab son of Reuben, how in the midst of all Israel the earth opened its mouth and swallowed them up, along with their households, their tents, and every living being in their company; [7] for it is your own eyes that have seen every great deed that the LORD did.

[8] Keep, then, this entire commandment that I am commanding you today, so that you may have strength to go in and occupy the land that you are crossing over to occupy, [9] and so that you may live long in the land that the LORD swore to your ancestors to give them and to their descendants, a land flowing with milk and honey. [10] For the land

a   Q Ms Gk Syr: MT lacks *your God*
b   Or *Sea of Reeds*

sequence *love . . . keep . . . commandments* cites 5.10. **16:** *Circumcise . . . the . . . heart* means to open oneself to God (Lev 26.41); no distinction is intended between mind, will, and emotion. The metaphorical formulation, which challenges any attempt to reduce Deuteronomy to narrow "legalism," corresponds to prophetic ideals (cf. Jer 4.4; 31.33). **17–18:** Integrity in the administration of court justice (v. 17; cf. 1.17; 16.19) and protection of the marginalized (v. 18) are given a theological foundation, making the remarkable argument that human social ethics amounts to "imitatio dei." Responsibility for ensuring justice in court and for defending the marginalized were conventional royal prerogatives (*Laws of Hammurabi* prologue; Ps 72.4). Deuteronomy contemplates no such role for the monarch (17.14–20n.). Instead, here it is God who protects the rights of the marginalized, entering history to do so (cf. Ex 3.7–10; Phil 2.6–7). Love of neighbor thus originates in divine action. **18–19:** *Strangers . . . stranger,* better, the legal term "resident alien" in both cases. Just as justice must be rendered to Israelite and alien alike (see 1.16n.), so must "love" reach across national or ethnic lines (cf. Lev 19.33–34). **18:** *Loves . . . providing,* note love's concrete expression in action and service (see 5.10n.; 6.5n.). **19:** *For you were,* see Ex 22.21; 23.9. **22:** *Seventy persons* (Gen 46.27; Ex 1.5) comes first in the Hebrew, emphasizing Israel's miraculous transformation into a nation. *Stars in heaven,* see 1.10n.

11.1–32: Loyalty to the covenant provides the condition for life in Canaan. The punishments and rewards noted in this section are predominantly addressed to a plural "you," stressing communal rather than individual responsibility. **2:** The frequent word *today* in Deuteronomy emphasizes the contemporaneity of the covenant (see 5.3n.). *Discipline,* see 8.5n. **4:** See Ex 14. **6:** The address is based upon the early tradition of the revolt of Dathan and Abiram (Num 16). There is no mention of Korah's rebellion (Num 16.3–11), which was very likely

that you are about to enter to occupy is not like the land of Egypt, from which you have come, where you sow your seed and irrigate by foot like a vegetable garden. [11] But the land that you are crossing over to occupy is a land of hills and valleys, watered by rain from the sky, [12] a land that the LORD your God looks after. The eyes of the LORD your God are always on it, from the beginning of the year to the end of the year.

[13] If you will only heed his every commandment[a] that I am commanding you today—loving the LORD your God, and serving him with all your heart and with all your soul— [14] then he[b] will give the rain for your land in its season, the early rain and the later rain, and you will gather in your grain, your wine, and your oil; [15] and he[b] will give grass in your fields for your livestock, and you will eat your fill. [16] Take care, or you will be seduced into turning away, serving other gods and worshiping them, [17] for then the anger of the LORD will be kindled against you and he will shut up the heavens, so that there will be no rain and the land will yield no fruit; then you will perish quickly off the good land that the LORD is giving you.

[18] You shall put these words of mine in your heart and soul, and you shall bind them as a sign on your hand, and fix them as an emblem[c] on your forehead. [19] Teach them to your children, talking about them when you are at home and when you are away, when you lie down and when you rise. [20] Write them on the doorposts of your house and on your gates, [21] so that your days and the days of your children may be multiplied in the land that the LORD swore to your ancestors to give them, as long as the heavens are above the earth.

[22] If you will diligently observe this entire commandment that I am commanding you, loving the LORD your God, walking in all his ways, and holding fast to him, [23] then the LORD will drive out all these nations before you, and you will dispossess nations larger and mightier than yourselves. [24] Every place on which you set foot shall be yours; your territory shall extend from the wilderness to the Lebanon and from the River, the river Euphrates, to the Western Sea. [25] No one will be able to stand against you; the LORD your God will put the fear and dread of you on all the land on which you set foot, as he promised you.

[26] See, I am setting before you today a blessing and a curse: [27] the blessing, if you obey the commandments of the LORD your God that I am commanding you today; [28] and the curse, if you do not obey the commandments of the LORD your God, but turn from the way that I am commanding you today, to follow other gods that you have not known.

[29] When the LORD your God has brought you into the land that you are entering to occupy, you shall set the blessing on Mount Gerizim and the curse on Mount Ebal. [30] As you know, they are beyond the Jordan, some distance to the west, in the land of the

a Compare Gk: Heb *my commandments*
b Sam Gk Vg: MT *I*
c Or *as a frontlet*

added by the Priestly school after this abstract was made. **10–12:** The Nile valley must be irrigated through human effort; Canaan depends upon seasonal rainfall. The difference is mentioned to stress Israel's dependence upon God, who gives and withholds rain (Am 4.7–8), as well as the fundamental sanctity of the land of Israel. **14:** The *early rain* comes at the end of the summer drought (October-November); the *later rain* comes in the spring (March-April). **16–17:** See 7.12–14n. **18–21:** See 6.6–9. **24:** *Every place . . . yours,* a legal ritual that effected transfer of title by pacing out the perimeter of the territory (see 25.9n.; Gen 13.17). The territory is described in terms of the ideal limits of David's empire (see 1.7n.). *The Western Sea,* the Mediterranean. **26–32:** The two ways (see ch 28; 30.15–20). **26:** *Curse,* the sanctions for violating a treaty, which a vassal assumes in a sworn oath (see 28.15–68). **29–30:** These verses represent an editorial intrusion. Previously, *blessing . . . and the curse* identify the benefits of covenantal obedience and the sanctions for breach of covenant (vv. 26–28; 28.2,15). That theme is the expected climax of this chapter. Here they are restricted to a series of positive and negative sayings shouted from mounts *Gerizim and . . . Ebal,* in anticipation of ch 27. *Gerizim,* on the south, and *Ebal,* on the north, flank the pass guarded by the city of Shechem in the central hill country. This geographic restriction fits poorly in a chapter otherwise directed to the entire land (vv. 22–25,31–32). **30:** *The oak of Moreh,* at Shechem (see Gen 12.6).

Canaanites who live in the Arabah, opposite Gilgal, beside the oak[a] of Moreh. [31] When you cross the Jordan to go in to occupy the land that the LORD your God is giving you, and when you occupy it and live in it, [32] you must diligently observe all the statutes and ordinances that I am setting before you today.

12 These are the statutes and ordinances that you must diligently observe in the land that the LORD, the God of your ancestors, has given you to occupy all the days that you live on the earth.

[2] You must demolish completely all the places where the nations whom you are about to dispossess served their gods, on the mountain heights, on the hills, and under every leafy tree. [3] Break down their altars, smash their pillars, burn their sacred poles[b] with fire, and hew down the idols of their gods, and thus blot out their name from their places. [4] You shall not worship the LORD your God in such ways. [5] But you shall seek the place that the LORD your God will choose out of all your tribes as his habitation to put his name there. You shall go there, [6] bringing there your burnt offerings and your sacrifices, your tithes and your donations, your votive gifts, your freewill offerings, and the firstlings of your herds and flocks. [7] And you shall eat there in the presence of the LORD your God, you and your households together, rejoicing in all the undertakings in which the LORD your God has blessed you.

[8] You shall not act as we are acting here today, all of us according to our own desires, [9] for you have not yet come into the rest and the possession that the LORD your God is giving you. [10] When you cross over the Jordan and live in the land that the LORD your God is allotting to you, and when he gives you rest from your enemies all around so that you live in safety, [11] then you shall bring everything that I command you to the place that the LORD your God will choose as a dwelling for his name: your burnt offerings and your sacrifices, your tithes and your donations, and all your choice votive gifts that you vow to the LORD. [12] And you shall rejoice before the LORD your God, you together with your sons and your daughters, your male and female slaves, and the Levites who reside in your towns (since they have no allotment or inheritance with you).

[13] Take care that you do not offer your burnt offerings at any place you happen to

---

[a] Gk Syr: Compare Gen 12.6; Heb *oaks* or *terebinths*
[b] Heb *Asherim*

31–32: Transition to the legal corpus. **32:** *Diligently observe . . . statutes and ordinances*, cited in reverse order at 12.1 to effect the transition from the literary frame of Deuteronomy (chs 1–11) into the laws (chs 12–26). **12.1–26.15: The legal corpus: Deuteronomy's transformation of Israelite religion. 12.1–32: Centralization of worship.** Centralization and purification of worship, restriction to a single sanctuary, and removal of foreign influence distinguish Deuteronomy. Four paragraphs (vv. 2–7,8–12,13–19,20–28) command centralization; a fifth (vv. 29–31) warns against alien worship. **1:** An editorial superscription. *Earth*, more accurately, "land (of Israel)." **2–7:** Israel must reject the Canaanite precedent of multiple sanctuaries. **2:** *You*, The chapter alternates between plural (vv. 1–12) and singular (vv. 13–31), which, combined with six repetitions of the centralization command (vv. 5,11,14,18,21,26), suggests a long compositional history. *Demolish*, see Ex 23.23–24; 34.11–14; Deut 7.5. *Heights . . . leafy tree*, Canaanite sanctuaries, "high places" (1 Kings 3.2; 2 Kings 16.4), but used to worship God as well (1 Kings 3.4). **3:** See 7.5n. **5:** *The place that the LORD . . . will choose*, Jerusalem played no role in Israel's history until the period of David. Consequently the city cannot be named explicitly without undermining the literary form of Deuteronomy as an address by Moses. *As his habitation*, better, "to establish it" (the divine name), indicating possession and special relationship. *Put his name there*, Deuteronomy rejects the idea that a nation's God would inhabit the Temple (contrast 1 Kings 8.12–13). **6:** *Burnt offerings*, in which all of the flesh was burnt on the altar (v. 27; Lev 1.3–17). *Sacrifices*, other offerings where portions of the animal were assigned to the priests or shared by worshipers (v. 27; 18.1–3; Lev 3; 7.29–36). **8–12:** That worship at multiple sanctuaries was to have limited temporal validity differs from Ex 20.24. **8:** *Our own desires*, a negative judgment, as in Judg 17.6; 21.25. **9–10:** *Rest and . . . possession*, territorial security (Josh 21.44) would allow centralization. This was fulfilled with David's conquest of Jerusalem, which allowed the construction of the Temple (2 Sam 7.1,11; 1 Kings 8.56). **12:** Since *the Levites* were not assigned land (see Josh 13.14; cf. Ezek 44.28), they had to depend upon voluntary offerings (see 10.9; 18.1–2). **13–19:** The earliest of the chapter's five paragraphs is

see. [14] But only at the place that the LORD will choose in one of your tribes—there you shall offer your burnt offerings and there you shall do everything I command you.

[15] Yet whenever you desire you may slaughter and eat meat within any of your towns, according to the blessing that the LORD your God has given you; the unclean and the clean may eat of it, as they would of gazelle or deer. [16] The blood, however, you must not eat; you shall pour it out on the ground like water. [17] Nor may you eat within your towns the tithe of your grain, your wine, and your oil, the firstlings of your herds and your flocks, any of your votive gifts that you vow, your freewill offerings, or your donations; [18] these you shall eat in the presence of the LORD your God at the place that the LORD your God will choose, you together with your son and your daughter, your male and female slaves, and the Levites resident in your towns, rejoicing in the presence of the LORD your God in all your undertakings. [19] Take care that you do not neglect the Levite as long as you live in your land.

[20] When the LORD your God enlarges your territory, as he has promised you, and you say, "I am going to eat some meat," because you wish to eat meat, you may eat meat whenever you have the desire. [21] If the place where the LORD your God will choose to put his name is too far from you, and you slaughter as I have commanded you any of your herd or flock that the LORD has given you,

then you may eat within your towns whenever you desire. [22] Indeed, just as gazelle or deer is eaten, so you may eat it; the unclean and the clean alike may eat it. [23] Only be sure that you do not eat the blood; for the blood is the life, and you shall not eat the life with the meat. [24] Do not eat it; you shall pour it out on the ground like water. [25] Do not eat it, so that all may go well with you and your children after you, because you do what is right in the sight of the LORD. [26] But the sacred donations that are due from you, and your votive gifts, you shall bring to the place that the LORD will choose. [27] You shall present your burnt offerings, both the meat and the blood, on the altar of the LORD your God; the blood of your other sacrifices shall be poured out beside[a] the altar of the LORD your God, but the meat you may eat.

[28] Be careful to obey all these words that I command you today,[b] so that it may go well with you and with your children after you forever, because you will be doing what is good and right in the sight of the LORD your God.

[29] When the LORD your God has cut off before you the nations whom you are about to enter to dispossess them, when you have dispossessed them and live in their land, [30] take care that you are not snared into imi-

[a] Or on
[b] Gk Sam Syr: MT lacks today

concentrically arranged in a chiasm to structure diverse material in an ABC:C´B´A´ pattern.

   A *Take care that* (13)
      B *but only* (Heb "ki 'im") + centralization (14)
         C *yet* ("raq") + secular slaughter (15)
         C´ *but* ("raq") + secular slaughter (16)
      B´ *rather* ("ki 'im" [untranslated in NRSV]) + centralization (18)
   A´ *Take care that* (19)

13–16: Two important, revolutionary distinctions: First, between sacrificial worship at random sites, *any place*, rejected as illegitimate, and legitimate sacrifice performed at a single sanctuary, *the place that the LORD will choose*. This contrasts with previous norms, when altars were common throughout the land (Gen 12.7; 35.1–7; 1 Sam 3.1; 7.17; 1 Kings 18.20–46). Second, between ritual sacrifice and secular slaughter of domestic animals for food. Prior to Deuteronomy, all slaughter, even for food, was sacrificial and took place at an altar. With altars throughout the land, that rule imposed no burden upon Israelites. The prohibition of all local altars, however, created a real difficulty for those without easy access to the central sanctuary. The permission granted here for local, secular slaughter answers that need. By analogy to the rules for hunting wild game (*gazelle or deer*), domestic animals may be slaughtered throughout the land, on condition that their blood is poured out *on the ground like water* (cf. Lev 17.13). Blood symbolizes "life" (v. 23; 15.23; Gen 9.4–5; Lev 17.14; 19.26). **17:** *Tithe,* see 14.22–29n. **20–28:** Permission

tating them, after they have been destroyed before you: do not inquire concerning their gods, saying, "How did these nations worship their gods? I also want to do the same." [31] You must not do the same for the Lord your God, because every abhorrent thing that the Lord hates they have done for their gods. They would even burn their sons and their daughters in the fire to their gods. [32] [a] You must diligently observe everything that I command you; do not add to it or take anything from it.

13 [b] If prophets or those who divine by dreams appear among you and promise you omens or portents, [2] and the omens or the portents declared by them take place, and they say, "Let us follow other gods" (whom you have not known) "and let us serve them," [3] you must not heed the words of those prophets or those who divine by dreams; for the Lord your God is testing you, to know whether you indeed love the Lord your God with all your heart and soul. [4] The Lord your God you shall follow, him alone you shall fear, his commandments you shall keep, his voice you shall obey, him you shall serve, and to him you shall hold fast. [5] But those prophets or those who divine by dreams shall be put to death for having spoken treason against the Lord your God—who brought you out of the land of Egypt and redeemed you from the house of slavery—to turn you from the way in which the Lord your God commanded you to walk. So you shall purge the evil from your midst.

[6] If anyone secretly entices you—even if it is your brother, your father's son or[c] your mother's son, or your own son or daughter, or the wife you embrace, or your most intimate friend—saying, "Let us go worship other gods," whom neither you nor your ancestors have known, [7] any of the gods of the peoples that are around you, whether near you or far away from you, from one end of the earth to the other, [8] you must not yield to or heed any such persons. Show them no pity or compassion and do not shield them. [9] But you shall surely kill them; your own hand shall be first against them to execute them, and afterwards

a   Ch 13.1 in Heb
b   Ch 13.2 in Heb
c   Sam Gk Compare Tg: MT lacks *your father's son or*

for secular slaughter is now justified by the expansion of Israel's boundaries. **30:** Elsewhere, the corruption of Israelite religion is presented as resulting from the attractions of marital contract (7.1–5,25) or political treaty (Ex 23.33; 34.12). **31:** *Burn their sons and their daughters,* the Canaanites are accused of child sacrifice (see 2 Kings 3.27; 23.10; Jer 19.5–6; ch 31), elsewhere associated with the deity Molech (Lev 18.21; 20.2–5). **32:** An exhortation to preserve the law unchanged. *Diligently observe,* the same idiom found at 12.1 (also 11.32) frames the unit with an inclusio. *Do not add to it or take anything from it,* an ancient Near Eastern scribal formula often included in the epilogues of treaties, inscriptions, and law collections to protect them from being defaced, altered, or written over (see 4.2n.).

13.1–18: Unconditional loyalty to God. Various hypothetical situations involving conflict of covenant loyalty to God, treated analogously to ancient Near Eastern suzerainty treaties, which stipulated absolute loyalty. **1–5:** A prophet or diviner invites listeners to commit idolatry. While Deuteronomy presents Moses as the founder of Israelite prophecy, establishing both its standard (18.15–22) and its pinnacle (34.10–12), Deuteronomy nonetheless regulates prophecy, requiring the execution of the prophet who contravenes Deuteronomy's teaching (vv. 1–5; 18.19–22) and subordinating prophecy to covenantal law. No longer is the power to perform signs the test of a prophet's legitimacy (contrast v. 2 with 34.11–12; Ex 4.1–9,21; 1 Kings 18.20–40). **1:** The religious stature of prophets makes it difficult to resist their incitement to commit apostasy. *Dreams,* the two sources of religious authority correspond to the nearly contemporary Neo-Assyrian *Vassal Treaty of Esarhaddon* (672 BCE), which requires loyalty even in the face of conspiracy from "your brothers, your sons, your daughters, or from the mouth of a prophet, an ecstatic, or an inquirer of oracles" (§ 10). *Omens or portents* were used by legitimate prophets to authenticate their proclamations (34.11; Ex 4.1–9,21; 7.9; Judg 6.17). **5:** *Treason,* as betrayal of the divine suzerain. *Purge the evil from your midst,* a formula emphasizing the obligation to eliminate particularly offensive religious transgressions (17.7,12; 19.19; 21.21; etc.). **6–11:** Conflict between family love, marriage, or friendship and covenantal fidelity (cf. Lk 14.26). **6:** *Secretly,* i.e., there are no witnesses. *Father's son,* this addition of the half-brother (see text note c) provides a poor reading. The Heb deliberately selects the most intimate of human relations in this verse; thus the full brother (*mother's son*). **9:** *But you shall surely kill them,* i.e., summary execution. The absence of witnesses and a trial conflicts with Deuteronomy's own requirements elsewhere (17.4,6; 19.15), but

the hand of all the people. [10] Stone them to death for trying to turn you away from the LORD your God, who brought you out of the land of Egypt, out of the house of slavery. [11] Then all Israel shall hear and be afraid, and never again do any such wickedness.

[12] If you hear it said about one of the towns that the LORD your God is giving you to live in, [13] that scoundrels from among you have gone out and led the inhabitants of the town astray, saying, "Let us go and worship other gods," whom you have not known, [14] then you shall inquire and make a thorough investigation. If the charge is established that such an abhorrent thing has been done among you, [15] you shall put the inhabitants of that town to the sword, utterly destroying it and everything in it—even putting its livestock to the sword. [16] All of its spoil you shall gather into its public square; then burn the town and all its spoil with fire, as a whole burnt offering to the LORD your God. It shall remain a perpetual ruin, never to be rebuilt. [17] Do not let anything devoted to destruction stick to your hand, so that the LORD may turn from his fierce anger and show you compassion, and in his compassion multiply you, as he swore to your ancestors, [18] if you obey the voice of the LORD your God by keeping all his commandments that I am commanding you today, doing what is right in the sight of the LORD your God.

14 You are children of the LORD your God. You must not lacerate yourselves or shave your forelocks for the dead. [2] For you are a people holy to the LORD your God; it is you the LORD has chosen out of all the peoples on earth to be his people, his treasured possession.

[3] You shall not eat any abhorrent thing. [4] These are the animals you may eat: the ox, the sheep, the goat, [5] the deer, the gazelle, the roebuck, the wild goat, the ibex, the antelope, and the mountain-sheep. [6] Any animal that divides the hoof and has the hoof cleft in two, and chews the cud, among the animals, you may eat. [7] Yet of those that chew the cud or have the hoof cleft you shall not eat these: the camel, the hare, and the rock badger, because they chew the cud but do not divide the hoof; they are unclean for you. [8] And the pig, because it divides the hoof but does not chew the cud, is unclean for you. You shall not eat their meat, and you shall not touch their carcasses.

[9] Of all that live in water you may eat these: whatever has fins and scales you may eat. [10] And whatever does not have fins and scales you shall not eat; it is unclean for you.

[11] You may eat any clean birds. [12] But these are the ones that you shall not eat: the eagle, the vulture, the osprey, [13] the buzzard, the kite of any kind; [14] every raven of any kind;

arises from the grave threat to the covenant (Ex 32.25–27; Num 25.6–9). **10**: *Stone,* the penalty carried out by the community for violations of its fundamental values or sources of authority: apostasy or treason (see 17.2–7; Lev 20.2; Josh 7.10–26; 1 Kings 21.8–14), blasphemy (Lev 24.13–23), defying parental authority (21.18–21; 22.20–21), and betraying marriage (22.23–24). Each is prohibited by the Decalogue (5.6,11,16,18). **13**: *Scoundrels,* lit. "sons of worthlessness," or "children of Belial" (KJV). **15–17**: The infidelity of the Israelite town requires that its entire population be placed under the same ban as that used for the Canaanites (7.1–6,25–26; 12.29–30; 20.16–18). **16**: Normally new occupants would rebuild cities after destruction right on top of the *ruin* (Heb "tel").

14.1–29: The obligations of holiness. 1–22: Special status entails special obligations, one of which is dietary. The affirmation of holiness (vv. 2,21) therefore frames the list of permitted and prohibited foods. **1**: *Children of the LORD,* the first of three metaphors to emphasize the special relation between God and Israel. The divine parent has special custody for the child (Ex 4.22–23; Hos 1.10) but, equally, special indignation at wrongdoing (32.5–6,19–20; Isa 1.2). *Lacerate . . . shave . . . dead,* laceration and head shaving, common mourning rituals, were associated with Canaanite customs and perhaps with ancestor worship (Lev 19.27–28; 1 Kings 18.28; Jer 16.6–7; 41.4–5; 47.5; Am 8.10). **2**: *Holy,* Israel must distinguish itself from other nations by observing special requirements. *Treasured possession,* see 7.6n. **3–21**: Deuteronomy's dietary restrictions differ from the more detailed list of permitted and prohibited foods provided by the Priestly source (Lev 11.2–23). A binary classification system, permitted vs. forbidden, is systematically applied to each of the three basic divisions of species within creation (Gen 1.20–25; 9.2–3), which are grouped according to their habitat as creatures of the land (vv. 1–8), water (vv. 9–10), or air (vv. 11–20). Animals that do not satisfy the defining characteristics for their group are not to be eaten: the pig (v. 8) and shellfish (v. 10). The terms *unclean* (v. 8) and *clean* (v. 11) do not refer to hygiene. Ritu-

¹⁵ the ostrich, the nighthawk, the sea gull, the hawk of any kind; ¹⁶ the little owl and the great owl, the water hen ¹⁷ and the desert owl,ᵃ the carrion vulture and the cormorant, ¹⁸ the stork, the heron of any kind; the hoopoe and the bat.ᵇ ¹⁹ And all winged insects are unclean for you; they shall not be eaten. ²⁰ You may eat any clean winged creature.

²¹ You shall not eat anything that dies of itself; you may give it to aliens residing in your towns for them to eat, or you may sell it to a foreigner. For you are a people holy to the LORD your God.

You shall not boil a kid in its mother's milk.

²² Set apart a tithe of all the yield of your seed that is brought in yearly from the field. ²³ In the presence of the LORD your God, in the place that he will choose as a dwelling for his name, you shall eat the tithe of your grain, your wine, and your oil, as well as the firstlings of your herd and flock, so that you may learn to fear the LORD your God always. ²⁴ But if, when the LORD your God has blessed you, the distance is so great that you are unable to transport it, because the place where the LORD your God will choose to set his name is too far away from you, ²⁵ then you may turn it

into money. With the money secure in hand, go to the place that the LORD your God will choose; ²⁶ spend the money for whatever you wish—oxen, sheep, wine, strong drink, or whatever you desire. And you shall eat there in the presence of the LORD your God, you and your household rejoicing together. ²⁷ As for the Levites resident in your towns, do not neglect them, because they have no allotment or inheritance with you.

²⁸ Every third year you shall bring out the full tithe of your produce for that year, and store it within your towns; ²⁹ the Levites, because they have no allotment or inheritance with you, as well as the resident aliens, the orphans, and the widows in your towns, may come and eat their fill so that the LORD your God may bless you in all the work that you undertake.

15 Every seventh year you shall grant a remission of debts. ² And this is the manner of the remission: every creditor shall remit the claim that is held against a neighbor, not exacting it of a neighbor who

ᵃ Or *pelican*
ᵇ Identification of several of the birds in verses 12–18 is uncertain

ally "impure" and "pure" convey the idea more clearly. Not all of the species mentioned can be identified. **21:** *Anything that dies of itself,* carrion (Ex 22.31) or any animal not slaughtered so that the blood can be drained (12.16,23–25). *Boil a kid,* Deuteronomy extends an older law specifically connected to the pilgrimage festival offerings (Ex 23.19; 34.26) into a general dietary rule. Some view it as directed against Canaanite religious rituals; others view it as concerned to prevent the abuse of animals. **22–29:** An annual *tithe* of ten percent of crops and livestock was a common tax or honorarium paid to a monarch (Gen 14.20; 28.22; 1 Sam 8.15,17). Here the rule signifies that Israel is God's steward, working but not owning the land; see Lev 25.23. **23:** The standard rules of the tithe (Lev 27.30–33; Num 18.21–32; cf. Ex 22.30) are revised to direct offerings to the single sanctuary (12.17). *You shall eat,* whereas Deuteronomy assigns the tithe to the landholder, Lev 27.30 assigns it to the sanctuary and Num 18.21 to the Levites. **24–25:** In light of centralization, the sanctified crops (designated for the sanctuary) may be converted *into money* (see 2.6n.), to facilitate the journey. That "firstlings" (v. 23) may also be sold for cash is at variance with Lev 27.32. *Too far,* as in 12.21. **27:** *Levites,* see 12.12n. **28–29:** One out of every three years the tithe law is shifted away from the central sanctuary to focus on the needs of the disadvantaged and the marginalized in the local community, to ensure they too may *eat their fill.*

15.1–18: Remission of debts (vv. 1–11) **and manumission of slaves** (vv. 12–18). On accession to the throne, ancient Near Eastern rulers would sometimes grant one-time cancellation of debts, return land confiscated by the crown, and free indentured slaves. That custom, Akkadian "duraru," is reflected in the Heb "deror," "jubilee" or "release," of Lev 25.10; Isa 61.1; Jer 34.15,17. Deuteronomy's conception of the covenant between Israel and God entails a similar fresh start as a covenantal obligation that recurs every seven years, adjusting earlier laws In the Covenant Collection (Ex 21–23) to the innovation of centralization of worship. The sequence reflects increasingly severe stages of financial distress: from debt to indentured servitude, an ancient form of bankruptcy (see Lev 25.13–55 for a similar sequence).

15.1–6: Cancellation of debts. 1: *Seventh year,* this law presupposes Ex 23.10–11, which stipulates that ag-

is a member of the community, because the LORD's remission has been proclaimed. ³ Of a foreigner you may exact it, but you must remit your claim on whatever any member of your community owes you. ⁴ There will, however, be no one in need among you, because the LORD is sure to bless you in the land that the LORD your God is giving you as a possession to occupy, ⁵ if only you will obey the LORD your God by diligently observing this entire commandment that I command you today. ⁶ When the LORD your God has blessed you, as he promised you, you will lend to many nations, but you will not borrow; you will rule over many nations, but they will not rule over you.

⁷ If there is among you anyone in need, a member of your community in any of your towns within the land that the LORD your God is giving you, do not be hard-hearted or tight-fisted toward your needy neighbor. ⁸ You should rather open your hand, willingly lending enough to meet the need, whatever it may be. ⁹ Be careful that you do not entertain a mean thought, thinking, "The seventh year, the year of remission, is near," and therefore view your needy neighbor with hostility and give nothing; your neighbor might cry to the LORD against you, and you would incur guilt. ¹⁰ Give liberally and be ungrudging when you do so, for on this account the LORD your God will bless you in all your work and in all that

you undertake. ¹¹ Since there will never cease to be some in need on the earth, I therefore command you, "Open your hand to the poor and needy neighbor in your land."

¹² If a member of your community, whether a Hebrew man or a Hebrew woman, is soldᵃ to you and works for you six years, in the seventh year you shall set that person free. ¹³ And when you send a male slaveᵇ out from you a free person, you shall not send him out empty-handed. ¹⁴ Provide liberally out of your flock, your threshing floor, and your wine press, thus giving to him some of the bounty with which the LORD your God has blessed you. ¹⁵ Remember that you were a slave in the land of Egypt, and the LORD your God redeemed you; for this reason I lay this command upon you today. ¹⁶ But if he says to you, "I will not go out from you," because he loves you and your household, since he is well off with you, ¹⁷ then you shall take an awl and thrust it through his earlobe into the door, and he shall be your slaveᶜ forever.

You shall do the same with regard to your female slave.ᵈ

¹⁸ Do not consider it a hardship when you send them out from you free persons,

a   Or *sells himself or herself*
b   Heb *him*
c   Or *bondman*
d   Or *bondwoman*

ricultural land should be permitted to lie fallow each "seventh year." **2**: *Remission*, the same verb in Ex 23.11, "lie fallow," now means cancellation of debts. **3**: In not canceling debts of foreigners, the legislator makes a concession to the pragmatic concerns of the creditor. **4**: *There will . . . be no one in need*, or, "no poor." Contrast the pragmatism of v. 7.

15.7–11: An appeal to conscience, anticipating the problem of implementing and enforcing such a law. **9**: *Cry . . . guilt*, the law has no judicial penalty or sanction (similarly 24.15; Ex 22.23–24).

15.12–18: Manumission. This adjusts the older laws regulating male (Ex 21.2–6) and female (Ex 21.7–11) slaves in four ways: (1) A single law applies to both genders, abrogating the older law (contrast v. 17b with Ex 21.7b); (2) the ceremony where the slave relinquishes freedom is secularized (vv. 16–17), so that it now takes place at the house rather than at a local sanctuary (Ex 21.6); (3) the master must now grant the slave a gift (vv. 13–14; contrast Ex 21.2); (4) by conjoining the Covenant Collection's manumission (Ex 21.2–6) and land sabbatical (Ex 23.10–11) laws, Deuteronomy creates a single year of release and transforms manumission, formerly based in the individual household, into a year of universal liberty. The delay of manumission to the fiftieth year by the Holiness Collection may reflect the difficulty of implementing this idealistic law (Lev 25.39–44). **12**: *Hebrew*, see Ex 21.2n. *Is sold* or "sells himself" (see text note *a*); a court might require a thief, unable to repay a theft, to indenture his labor as compensation (Ex 22.1–4); or, overcome by debt, a serf might assign his labor to repay a loan (Lev 25.39–44). **14–15**: The gift provided the manumitted slave recalls and reenacts the nation's own manumission by God from slavery in Egypt. **18**: As in vv. 8–10, an appeal to conscience that anticipates the difficulty of enforcing a law that lacks judicial sanction.

because for six years they have given you services worth the wages of hired laborers; and the LORD your God will bless you in all that you do.

¹⁹ Every firstling male born of your herd and flock you shall consecrate to the LORD your God; you shall not do work with your firstling ox nor shear the firstling of your flock. ²⁰ You shall eat it, you together with your household, in the presence of the LORD your God year by year at the place that the LORD will choose. ²¹ But if it has any defect—any serious defect, such as lameness or blindness—you shall not sacrifice it to the LORD your God; ²² within your towns you may eat it, the unclean and the clean alike, as you would a gazelle or deer. ²³ Its blood, however, you must not eat; you shall pour it out on the ground like water.

16 Observe the month[a] of Abib by keeping the passover to the LORD your God, for in the month of Abib the LORD your God brought you out of Egypt by night. ² You shall offer the passover sacrifice to the LORD your God, from the flock and the herd,

at the place that the LORD will choose as a dwelling for his name. ³ You must not eat with it anything leavened. For seven days you shall eat unleavened bread with it—the bread of affliction—because you came out of the land of Egypt in great haste, so that all the days of your life you may remember the day of your departure from the land of Egypt. ⁴ No leaven shall be seen with you in all your territory for seven days; and none of the meat of what you slaughter on the evening of the first day shall remain until morning. ⁵ You are not permitted to offer the passover sacrifice within any of your towns that the LORD your God is giving you. ⁶ But at the place that the LORD your God will choose as a dwelling for his name, only there shall you offer the passover sacrifice, in the evening at sunset, the time of day when you departed from Egypt. ⁷ You shall cook it and eat it at the place that the LORD your God will choose; the next morning you may go back to your tents. ⁸ For six days you

a   Or *new moon*

15.19–23: **Sacrifice:** Older convention required that each firstborn male domestic animal be offered as a sacrifice to God at one of the local sanctuaries (Ex 13.1–2,11–16; 22.29–30; 34.19–20). The author now adjusts that law to the new one stipulating a single sanctuary. **19:** *Not do work,* thereby reserving the animal for God. **20:** *In the presence of the LORD,* at the central sanctuary in Jerusalem. **21–23:** Blemished firstborn livestock need not be taken to the central sanctuary. They may be slaughtered locally, following the requirements for secular slaughter (12.15–16,21–25).

16.1–17: **The festival calendar.** Previously, each male Israelite was commanded to undertake three pilgrimages to "appear before the LORD": to make an offering at one of the multiple local sanctuaries (v. 16; Ex 23.14–18). These occasions, which Deuteronomy redirects to the central sanctuary, were called "pilgrimage festivals" (v. 16; Ex 23.14). The three festivals were unleavened bread (Heb "mazzot"), harvest, and ingathering (Ex 23.14–17; 34.18,23). Deuteronomy renames the latter two "weeks" (Heb "shavuot," v. 10) and "booths" (Heb "sukkoth," v. 13), their current names. **1–8:** Passover was originally a separate, family observance (Ex 12.1–13,21–23), involving a nighttime slaughter of a sheep or goat in the doorway of the house, where the blood was smeared to mark the house as Israelite. Deuteronomy's centralization of worship necessitated the redirection of the paschal slaughter to the central sanctuary (vv. 2,6–7). The older blood ritual then merges with the festival of unleavened bread, also celebrated in early spring. In contrast to Deuteronomy, the festivals of passover and unleavened bread remain distinct in Lev 23.5–6; Num 28.16,17–25. **1:** *Abib* (lit. "new ear" of grain), in early spring, when ears of barley, the first crop, began to ripen (Ex 13.4; 23.15; 34.18). Originally the first month of the Hebrew calendar (Ex 12.2), later called "Nisan." **2:** *From the flock and the herd,* earlier the offering was restricted to the flock only (Ex 12.4–5,21). **3:** *For seven days,* combining the seven-day observance of the festival of unleavened bread (Ex 12.14–20; 23.15) and the one-day observance of passover (vv. 1–3a,4b–7). **7:** *Cook,* more accurately, "boil," like other standard sacrifices (Ex 29.1; Lev 6.28; 8.31; Num 6.19; Zech 14.21). This provision conflicts with the stipulation that the paschal offering be "roasted over the fire," not "boiled in water" (Ex 12.8–9). The two inconsistent requirements for preparing the Passover are harmonized at 2 Chr 35.13. **8:** The Heb reads simply, "For six days you shall eat unleavened bread." The NRSV's addition, *continue,* results in an eight-day total for the festivals of passover and unleavened bread, modeled after the Priestly version of the calendar: 1 day (Passover) + 6 days

shall continue to eat unleavened bread, and on the seventh day there shall be a solemn assembly for the LORD your God, when you shall do no work.

⁹ You shall count seven weeks; begin to count the seven weeks from the time the sickle is first put to the standing grain. ¹⁰ Then you shall keep the festival of weeks to the LORD your God, contributing a freewill offering in proportion to the blessing that you have received from the LORD your God. ¹¹ Rejoice before the LORD your God—you and your sons and your daughters, your male and female slaves, the Levites resident in your towns, as well as the strangers, the orphans, and the widows who are among you—at the place that the LORD your God will choose as a dwelling for his name. ¹² Remember that you were a slave in Egypt, and diligently observe these statutes.

¹³ You shall keep the festival of booths[a] for seven days, when you have gathered in the produce from your threshing floor and your wine press. ¹⁴ Rejoice during your festival, you and your sons and your daughters, your male and female slaves, as well as the Levites, the strangers, the orphans, and the widows resident in your towns. ¹⁵ Seven days you shall keep the festival to the LORD your God at the place that the LORD will choose; for the LORD your God will bless you in all your produce and in all your undertakings, and you shall surely celebrate.

¹⁶ Three times a year all your males shall appear before the LORD your God at the place that he will choose: at the festival of unleavened bread, at the festival of weeks, and at the festival of booths.[a] They shall not appear before the LORD empty-handed; ¹⁷ all shall give as they are able, according to the blessing of the LORD your God that he has given you.

¹⁸ You shall appoint judges and officials throughout your tribes, in all your towns that the LORD your God is giving you, and they shall render just decisions for the people.

a Or *tabernacles*; Heb *succoth*

(unleavened bread) + 1 day (the solemn assembly); see Lev 23.3–8. In contrast, Deuteronomy intended to fuse the two holidays into a single seven-day observance. **9–12:** The festival of weeks (Ex 34.22; Lev 23.15–16; Num 28.26), originally a "festival of harvest" (Ex 23.16) celebrated in June. In postbiblical Judaism, the festival came to be associated with the revelation at Mount Sinai (Ex 19–20); in the New Testament it is called Pentecost because it begins on the fiftieth day after Passover (Acts 2.1; 20.16; 1 Cor 16.8). **9:** *Begin to count . . . from the time the sickle is first put to the standing grain,* the seven weeks begin when the grain is ripe, delaying the celebration until the conclusion of the harvest. The Holiness Collection offers a slightly different date for this festival (Lev 23.15). **11:** *You and your sons and your daughters,* the command to rejoice specifies the inclusion of women (as v. 14; 12.12,18). *Slaves . . . widows,* the marginalized and the disadvantaged are also included. *Strangers,* better, "resident aliens"; see 1.16n. **13–15:** *The festival of booths,* originally the fall harvest festival, called "ingathering" (Ex 23.16; 34.22; cf. Lev 23.33–43). **16–17:** The formulaic summary ("colophon") reuses the conclusion of the older festival calendar in the Covenant Collection (Ex 23.17). Two elements, however, reflect older assumptions inconsistent with the rest of this chapter: Passover (vv. 1–8) is not mentioned, and the pilgrimage requirement is directed to *all your males* (as Ex 23.17).

16.18–18.22: Laws of public officials. The proposed government has judicial, executive, and religious branches: local and central courts (16.18–17.13), kingship (17.14–20), levitical priesthood (18.1–8), and prophecy (18.9–22). Each relates to the others and is subordinated to the authority of the word of God, the teaching of Deuteronomy. Even institutions that might claim absolute authority, such as king or prophet, are integrated into a comprehensive vision. The continual concern with centralization of worship connects this section with the preceding legislation on the sacrificial system. The ritual laws (16.21–17.1) seem to intrude between two paragraphs each concerned with justice (16.18–20; 17.2–7), but the repetition provides a transition into the new section, while establishing the underlying unity of both areas of community life: (A) worship (12.1–16.17); (B) justice (16.18–20); (A′) worship (16.21–17.1); (B′) justice (17.2–7,8–13).

16.18–17.13: The organization of justice. 16.18–20: Deuteronomy here establishes a professionalized local judiciary. **18:** *Towns* (lit. "gates"), the local sphere (12.15,17,21; 16.5), as distinguished from the central sanctuary; also the traditional place where the village elders dispensed justice (Job 29.7; Ruth 4.1,11; Lam 5.14). By leaving the elders unmentioned, Deuteronomy contracts or eliminates their authority, though they are mentioned

¹⁹ You must not distort justice; you must not show partiality; and you must not accept bribes, for a bribe blinds the eyes of the wise and subverts the cause of those who are in the right. ²⁰ Justice, and only justice, you shall pursue, so that you may live and occupy the land that the LORD your God is giving you.

²¹ You shall not plant any tree as a sacred pole[a] beside the altar that you make for the LORD your God; ²² nor shall you set up a stone pillar—things that the LORD your God hates.

17 You must not sacrifice to the LORD your God an ox or a sheep that has a defect, anything seriously wrong; for that is abhorrent to the LORD your God.

² If there is found among you, in one of your towns that the LORD your God is giving you, a man or woman who does what is evil in the sight of the LORD your God, and transgresses his covenant ³ by going to serve other gods and worshiping them—whether the sun or the moon or any of the host of heaven, which I have forbidden— ⁴ and if it is reported to you or you hear of it, and you make a thorough inquiry, and the charge is proved true that such an abhorrent thing has occurred in Israel, ⁵ then you shall bring out to your gates that man or that woman who has committed this crime and you shall stone the man or woman to death. ⁶ On the evidence of two or three witnesses the death sentence shall be executed; a person must not be put to death on the evidence of only one witness. ⁷ The hands of the witnesses shall be the first raised against the person to execute the death penalty, and afterward the hands of all the people. So you shall purge the evil from your midst.

⁸ If a judicial decision is too difficult for you to make between one kind of bloodshed and another, one kind of legal right and another, or one kind of assault and another— any such matters of dispute in your towns— then you shall immediately go up to the place that the LORD your God will choose, ⁹ where you shall consult with the levitical priests and the judge who is in office in those days; they shall announce to you the decision in the case. ¹⁰ Carry out exactly the decision that they announce to you from the place that the LORD will choose, diligently observing everything they instruct you. ¹¹ You must carry out

a   Heb *Asherah*

elsewhere in older sections of Deuteronomy (e.g., 19.12; 21.2; 22.15). **19:** *You must not distort justice,* an admonition, quoting Ex 23.6a (where the same verb is translated "pervert"). *For a bribe blinds the eyes of the wise,* the older law in Ex 23.8, whose reference to "those with sight" (NRSV's "officials" is not correct) is revised in light of Deuteronomy's stress upon wisdom (see notes on 1.13; 34.9).

16.21–17.1: Prohibitions against Canaanite cultic objects (7.5; 12.3; Ex 34.13). **16.21:** *Sacred pole,* see 7.5n. **22:** *Stone pillar,* see 7.5n. **17.1:** See 15.21, here broadened into a general law of sacrifice.

17.2–7: Local justice. This law overlaps with 13.6–11, but is placed here because it deals with the procedures and jurisdiction of the local courts. The law grants the local courts maximum autonomy (see 16.8), provided that a trial is conducted according to rational standards that assure empirical proof. **2:** *A man or woman,* the law views the woman as a legally responsible individual. The viewpoint in marriage and family law differs, however (see 22.13–29). **3:** Contravening the Decalogue (5.8–9). **6:** *Two or three witnesses,* the condition for establishing proof. The prohibition against execution on the basis of testimony by *one witness* is also found at 19.15–16; Num 35.30.

17.8–13: Justice at the central sanctuary. In the pre-Deuteronomic period, legal cases in which there was an absence of physical evidence or of witnesses were remanded to the local sanctuary, where the parties to the dispute would swear a judicial oath at the altar (19.17; Ex 22.7–11; 1 Kings 8.31–32; note also Ex 21.6). These two laws (17.2–7,8–13) thus fill the judicial void created by Deuteronomy's prohibition of the local sanctuaries (ch 12). Now, any case that requires recourse to the altar is remanded to the central sanctuary; all other cases, even capital ones, may be tried locally (vv. 2–7). **8:** These cases must be referred to the central sanctuary because, in the absence of witnesses or evidence, local officials cannot make a ruling. *Between one kind of bloodshed and another,* the legal distinction between murder and manslaughter (Ex 21.12–14; Num 35.16–23). In each pair, the distinction is between premeditated or unintentional offenses. **9:** The tribunal at the sanctuary includes both priestly and lay members. The account of Jehoshaphat's setting up tribunals throughout Judah composed of lay and clerical judges reflects this law (2 Chr 19.5–11).

fully the law that they interpret for you or the ruling that they announce to you; do not turn aside from the decision that they announce to you, either to the right or to the left. ¹² As for anyone who presumes to disobey the priest appointed to minister there to the LORD your God, or the judge, that person shall die. So you shall purge the evil from Israel. ¹³ All the people will hear and be afraid, and will not act presumptuously again.

¹⁴ When you have come into the land that the LORD your God is giving you, and have taken possession of it and settled in it, and you say, "I will set a king over me, like all the nations that are around me," ¹⁵ you may indeed set over you a king whom the LORD your God will choose. One of your own community you may set as king over you; you are not permitted to put a foreigner over you, who is not of your own community. ¹⁶ Even so, he must not acquire many horses for himself, or return the people to Egypt in order to acquire more horses, since the LORD has said to you, "You must never return that way again." ¹⁷ And he must not acquire many wives for himself, or else his heart will turn away; also silver and gold he must not acquire in great quantity for himself. ¹⁸ When he has taken the throne of his kingdom, he shall have a copy of this law written for him in the presence of the levitical priests. ¹⁹ It shall remain

with him and he shall read in it all the days of his life, so that he may learn to fear the LORD his God, diligently observing all the words of this law and these statutes, ²⁰ neither exalting himself above other members of the community nor turning aside from the commandment, either to the right or to the left, so that he and his descendants may reign long over his kingdom in Israel.

18 The levitical priests, the whole tribe of Levi, shall have no allotment or inheritance within Israel. They may eat the sacrifices that are the LORD's portionᵃ ² but they shall have no inheritance among the other members of the community; the LORD is their inheritance, as he promised them.

³ This shall be the priests' due from the people, from those offering a sacrifice, whether an ox or a sheep: they shall give to the priest the shoulder, the two jowls, and the stomach. ⁴ The first fruits of your grain, your wine, and your oil, as well as the first of the fleece of your sheep, you shall give him. ⁵ For the LORD your God has chosen Leviᵇ out of all your tribes, to stand and minister in the name of the LORD, him and his sons for all time.

⁶ If a Levite leaves any of your towns, from wherever he has been residing in Israel, and

ᵃ Meaning of Heb uncertain
ᵇ Heb *him*

17.14–20: The law of the king. Deuteronomy greatly restricts royal authority. Generally Near Eastern monarchs promulgated law; here the monarch is subject to the law and required to read it daily (v. 19). Deuteronomy even denies the king his typical judicial role as court of last appeal (cf. Ps 72.1–4; 2 Sam 12.1–14; 14.1–24; 1 Kings 3.16–28). This law far more emphasizes what the king cannot do than what he may do. 14: *Like all the nations,* see 1 Sam 8.10–18. 16–18: The offenses parallel warnings against royal autocracy outlined at the very founding of the monarchy (1 Sam 8.10–18). They likely presuppose Solomon's trade in horses (1 Kings 10.26–29) and his wealth (1 Kings 10.14–22). The Deuteronomistic Historian believed those marriages led to idolatry (1 Kings 11.9–13). *A copy of this law,* the Septuagint reads "this repetition of the law" (Gk "to deuteronomion touto"), the source of the book's name. Like later traditional views, it sees Deuteronomy as a reprise of Exodus, Leviticus, and Numbers, ignoring the extent to which it revises and challenges earlier law.

18.1–8: The levitical priesthood. Centralization also affected the Israelite priesthood. A "job description" (vv. 1–5) precedes discussion of this impact (vv. 6–8). 1: *Levitical priests,* the Deuteronomic conception differs from that of Priestly literature, which speaks of two distinct groups, "the priests" and "the Levites." The Priestly source sees a hierarchy within the tribe of Levi between direct descendants of Aaron and the rest. Only the Aaronide priests officiate at the altar (Num 18.5,7) and receive the priestly share of the offerings (Num 18.8–20). The Levites serve the priests, and are prohibited from officiating (Num 18.3–4,6); they receive tithes and in turn tithe to the priests (Num 18.21–31). Here, in Deuteronomy, all within the tribe are levitical priests and both serve at the altar and receive sacrifices. 2: *No inheritance,* see 12.12n. *The LORD is their inheritance,* God grants them a share of the sacrificial offerings, making them dependent upon other Israelites for support. In contrast, the priest-prophet Ezekiel allocates land to the priests and the Levites in his vision of the future restoration

comes to the place that the LORD will choose (and he may come whenever he wishes), [7] then he may minister in the name of the LORD his God, like all his fellow-Levites who stand to minister there before the LORD. [8] They shall have equal portions to eat, even though they have income from the sale of family possessions.[a]

[9] When you come into the land that the LORD your God is giving you, you must not learn to imitate the abhorrent practices of those nations. [10] No one shall be found among you who makes a son or daughter pass through fire, or who practices divination, or is a soothsayer, or an augur, or a sorcerer, [11] or one who casts spells, or who consults ghosts or spirits, or who seeks oracles from the dead. [12] For whoever does these things is abhorrent to the LORD; it is because of such abhorrent practices that the LORD your God is driving them out before you. [13] You must remain completely loyal to the LORD your God. [14] Although these nations that you are about to dispossess do give heed to soothsayers and diviners, as for you, the LORD your God does not permit you to do so.

[15] The LORD your God will raise up for you a prophet[b] like me from among your own people; you shall heed such a prophet.[c] [16] This is what you requested of the LORD your God at Horeb on the day of the assembly when you said: "If I hear the voice of the LORD my God any more, or ever again see this great fire, I will die." [17] Then the LORD replied to me: "They are right in what they have said. [18] I will raise up for them a prophet[b] like you from among their own people; I will put my words in the mouth of the prophet,[d] who shall speak to them everything that I command. [19] Anyone who does not heed the words that the prophet[e] shall speak in my name, I myself will hold accountable. [20] But any prophet who speaks in the name of other gods, or who pre-

a   Meaning of Heb uncertain
b   Or *prophets*
c   Or *such prophets*
d   Or *mouths of the prophets*
e   Heb *he*

of Judah (Ezek 48.10–14). **5:** *Stand and minister,* officiate at the altar. **6–8:** When the local altars throughout the land are outlawed (12.8–12,13–15), the Levites serving there would be unemployed and, owning no land, would become destitute. Accordingly a Levite who *leaves any of your towns . . . and comes* to the central sanctuary in Jerusalem must be provided for (contrast 2 Kings 23.9). This emphasis underscores that the countryside altars were not entirely Canaanite sanctuaries (as 12.2–4 asserts). **8:** *Equal portions,* the choice meats, grains, and oil assigned the tribe in vv. 3–4.

18.9–22: A prophet like Moses. **9–14:** Just as the legal corpus prohibits sacrificial worship it condemns as Canaanite (12.1–4,29–31; also 7.1–6,25–26; Ex 23.24; 34.11–16), it prohibits forms of divination it brands as foreign and abhorrent. In each case it requires its own alternative: here, prophecy rather than divination. However, divination is not elsewhere typified as foreign (1 Sam 28.3–25; Isa 8.19–22; 28.4). Thus, describing the practice as foreign may actually cloak a condemnation of Israelite popular religion. **10:** *Pass through fire,* child sacrifice (see 12.31n.), joined with divination for condemnation because each is "abhorrent" (v. 9). *Practices divination, or is a soothsayer,* the most comprehensive compilation of such activities in the Bible (Ex 22.18; Lev 19.30–31; 20.6,27; Isa 8.19; Ezek 21.21). **11:** *Who consults ghosts or spirits . . . dead,* necromancy or conjuring the dead (1 Sam 28.7–15; Isa 8.19–20; 29.4). Popular religion in antiquity devoted extensive attention to communicating with the dead, especially with ancestors. **12:** *Abhorrent,* more commonly "abomination," as at Lev 26.26–27,29. There is no claim that divination is ineffective; it is, however, illegitimate (see 1 Sam 28.7–25). **15–22:** Deuteronomy transforms prophecy, viewing the prophet as the spokesperson of Torah (see 13.1–5n.) and defining Moses as the paradigmatic prophet. **15:** *The LORD . . . will raise up,* prophecy by divine election. That God alone appoints the prophet makes the prophet independent of all institutions and able to challenge them. More than one prophet is clearly intended. *Like me,* at Horeb (5.23–33), Moses established the model of prophecy as mediating God's word to the people. Thus the prophet, like the king (17.15), should be *from among your own people.* **16–17:** See 5.23–31; Ex 20.18–21. **18:** Cf. Jer 1.9; the prophet's oracles do not originate from other deities, from dead spirits, from skilled manipulation of objects, or from the prophet's own reflections. **20–23:** Having established an Israelite model of prophecy, the law provides two criteria to distinguish true from false prophecy. The first is that the prophet should speak exclusively on behalf of God, and report only God's words. The second makes

sumes to speak in my name a word that I have not commanded the prophet to speak—that prophet shall die." [21] You may say to yourself, "How can we recognize a word that the LORD has not spoken?" [22] If a prophet speaks in the name of the LORD but the thing does not take place or prove true, it is a word that the LORD has not spoken. The prophet has spoken it presumptuously; do not be frightened by it.

19 When the LORD your God has cut off the nations whose land the LORD your God is giving you, and you have dispossessed them and settled in their towns and in their houses, [2] you shall set apart three cities in the land that the LORD your God is giving you to possess. [3] You shall calculate the distances[a] and divide into three regions the land that the LORD your God gives you as a possession, so that any homicide can flee to one of them.

[4] Now this is the case of a homicide who might flee there and live, that is, someone who has killed another person unintentionally when the two had not been at enmity before: [5] Suppose someone goes into the forest with another to cut wood, and when one of them swings the ax to cut down a tree, the head slips from the handle and strikes the other person who then dies; the killer may flee to one of these cities and live. [6] But if the distance is too great, the avenger of blood in hot anger might pursue and overtake and put the killer to death, although a death

sentence was not deserved, since the two had not been at enmity before. [7] Therefore I command you: You shall set apart three cities.

[8] If the LORD your God enlarges your territory, as he swore to your ancestors—and he will give you all the land that he promised your ancestors to give you, [9] provided you diligently observe this entire commandment that I command you today, by loving the LORD your God and walking always in his ways— then you shall add three more cities to these three, [10] so that the blood of an innocent person may not be shed in the land that the LORD your God is giving you as an inheritance, thereby bringing bloodguilt upon you.

[11] But if someone at enmity with another lies in wait and attacks and takes the life of that person, and flees into one of these cities, [12] then the elders of the killer's city shall send to have the culprit taken from there and handed over to the avenger of blood to be put to death. [13] Show no pity; you shall purge the guilt of innocent blood from Israel, so that it may go well with you.

[14] You must not move your neighbor's boundary marker, set up by former generations, on the property that will be allotted to you in the land that the LORD your God is giving you to possess.

a   Or *prepare roads to them*

the fulfillment of a prophet's oracle the measure of its truth (Jer 28.9). That approach attempts to solve a critical problem: If two prophets each claim to speak on behalf of God yet make mutually exclusive claims (1 Kings 22.6 versus v. 17; Jer 27.8 versus 28.2), how may one decide which speaks the truth? The solution offered is not free of difficulty. If a false prophet is distinguished by the failure of his oracle to come true, then making a decision in the present about which prophet to obey becomes impossible. Nor can this criterion easily be reconciled with 13.2, which concedes that the oracles of false prophets might come true.

19.1–13: Cities of refuge (see 4.41–43n.). Sanctuary for those who killed unintentionally shielded them from revenge killing by the kin of the dead person (vv. 6,12). In light of centralization, Deuteronomy proscribes the previous site of refuge, the local altar (Ex 21.13), and instead designates three "neutral" cities. **1:** For the formulaic introduction, see 12.29. **4:** *Who might flee there,* more literally, "where he might flee (there)," an exact citation of Ex 21.13b, the older law that requires revision. **5:** *May flee to one of these cities,* explicitly amended to include the city reference. **6:** *But if the distance is too great,* Deuteronomy's updating of older law; see 14.24. *In hot anger,* if the kinsman kills the slayer in hot pursuit, the law is powerless. **8:** *Enlarges your territory,* a means for updating older law to address present realities by casting the provision for change as intended from the beginning (see 12.20; Ex 34.20). **10:** *The blood of an innocent person,* killing someone who has unintentionally committed homicide would constitute murder. *Bloodguilt,* the spilling of innocent blood, which defiles the land (see 21.1–9n.). **12:** Revising Ex 21.14. *Handed over to the avenger,* the law regulates but does not replace the clan-based system of justice. **14:** A transitional verse. The sacrosanct status of a *boundary marker* was a legal tradition in the ancient Near East (see 27.17; Isa 5.8; Hos 5.10; Job 24.2; Prov 22.28).

¹⁵ A single witness shall not suffice to convict a person of any crime or wrongdoing in connection with any offense that may be committed. Only on the evidence of two or three witnesses shall a charge be sustained. ¹⁶ If a malicious witness comes forward to accuse someone of wrongdoing, ¹⁷ then both parties to the dispute shall appear before the LORD, before the priests and the judges who are in office in those days, ¹⁸ and the judges shall make a thorough inquiry. If the witness is a false witness, having testified falsely against another, ¹⁹ then you shall do to the false witness just as the false witness had meant to do to the other. So you shall purge the evil from your midst. ²⁰ The rest shall hear and be afraid, and a crime such as this shall never again be committed among you. ²¹ Show no pity: life for life, eye for eye, tooth for tooth, hand for hand, foot for foot.

20 When you go out to war against your enemies, and see horses and chariots, an army larger than your own, you shall not be afraid of them; for the LORD your God is with you, who brought you up from the land of Egypt. ² Before you engage in battle, the priest shall come forward and speak to the troops, ³ and shall say to them: "Hear, O Israel! Today you are drawing near to do battle against your enemies. Do not lose heart, or be afraid, or panic, or be in dread of them; ⁴ for it is the LORD your God who goes with you, to fight for you against your enemies, to give you victory." ⁵ Then the officials shall address the troops, saying, "Has anyone built a new house but not dedicated it? He should go back to his house, or he might die in the battle and another dedicate it. ⁶ Has anyone planted a vineyard but not yet enjoyed its fruit? He should go back to his house, or he might die in the battle and another be first to enjoy its fruit. ⁷ Has anyone become engaged to a woman but not yet married her? He should go back to his house, or he might die in the battle and another marry her." ⁸ The

19.15–21: The integrity of the judicial system. A law that requires probity on the part of the newly established judges (16.18) and a law that demands corresponding integrity from witnesses (19.21) form an inclusio around this large unit by emphasizing the honesty required of all participants in the judicial system. **15:** *A single witness,* the same Heb phrase as "only one witness" at 17.6. *On the evidence of two or three witnesses shall a charge be sustained,* broadening the focus of 17.6 on capital crimes and prohibiting hearsay or spurious accusation (one person's word against another's). **17:** *Both parties,* the accuser and the accused. *Before the LORD,* testimony before the altar at the central sanctuary (12.7; 14.23; 17.8–13). **19:** *Do to the false witness . . . meant to do to the other,* reciprocal justice, called "talion," the technical term for "an eye for an eye," elsewhere employed for bodily injury or homicide (Ex 21.23–25; Lev 24.17–21). It distinguishes crimes against the person (requiring talion) from property crimes (where alone financial compensation is permitted). By applying it to crimes against the judicial system, the legislators here seek to ensure the integrity of the law by using the highest sanction available to them.

20.1–20: Rules for waging holy war. In contrast to other legal collections, which include only brief sections concerning military engagement (Ex 23.23–33; 34.11–16; Num 35.50–56), Deuteronomy, reflecting a literary setting of Israel about to enter the land, concerns itself extensively with the laws of holy war. God as divine warrior directly confronts the adversary on behalf of the nation, and God's presence in the camp imposes additional purity requirements on the people (23.10–14). The holy war is fought to extirpate iniquity and to create a covenantal community organized by divine law (Lev 18.24–29; 20.22–24). Accordingly, seizing the spoils of war, including human prisoners, is prohibited; all had to be devoted exclusively to God, like the "whole burnt offering" (13.16). Contemporary inscriptions like the Moabite Stone (ca. 850 BCE) establish that similar theologies of holy war were shared by a number of nations. In Deuteronomy, the conception of the conquest as a holy war represents a highly schematized idealization, formulated half a millennium after the settlement, at a time when ethnic Canaanites would already long have assimilated into the Israelite population. **1:** *Horses and chariots,* the adversary is superior both in numbers and in military equipment (see Ex 14.9; 15.4; Josh 11.4). *Army,* lit. "people." **3–4:** See 9.1–3; 31.3–6; cf. Ex 14.14,25; 15.1–4. **5–9:** A reverse muster, designed to thin the ranks by removing conscripts who have competing priorities because they are in a transitional state. **5:** *Dedicated* (or "inaugurated"), although Solomon's dedication of the Temple is narrated (1 Kings 8), there are no specific rituals of home dedication recorded in the Bible. The parallel curse employs "live" (28.30). **6:** *Enjoyed its fruit,* priestly law required that newly planted fruit trees could only be harvested in the fifth year (Lev 19.23–25). **7:** *Engaged . . . married,* see

officials shall continue to address the troops, saying, "Is anyone afraid or disheartened? He should go back to his house, or he might cause the heart of his comrades to melt like his own." ⁹ When the officials have finished addressing the troops, then the commanders shall take charge of them.

¹⁰ When you draw near to a town to fight against it, offer it terms of peace. ¹¹ If it accepts your terms of peace and surrenders to you, then all the people in it shall serve you at forced labor. ¹² If it does not submit to you peacefully, but makes war against you, then you shall besiege it; ¹³ and when the LORD your God gives it into your hand, you shall put all its males to the sword. ¹⁴ You may, however, take as your booty the women, the children, livestock, and everything else in the town, all its spoil. You may enjoy the spoil of your enemies, which the LORD your God has given you. ¹⁵ Thus you shall treat all the towns that are very far from you, which are not towns of the nations here. ¹⁶ But as for the towns of these peoples that the LORD your God is giving you as an inheritance, you must not let anything that breathes remain alive. ¹⁷ You shall annihilate them—the Hittites and the Amorites, the Canaanites and the Per-

izzites, the Hivites and the Jebusites—just as the LORD your God has commanded, ¹⁸ so that they may not teach you to do all the abhorrent things that they do for their gods, and you thus sin against the LORD your God.

¹⁹ If you besiege a town for a long time, making war against it in order to take it, you must not destroy its trees by wielding an ax against them. Although you may take food from them, you must not cut them down. Are trees in the field human beings that they should come under siege from you? ²⁰ You may destroy only the trees that you know do not produce food; you may cut them down for use in building siegeworks against the town that makes war with you, until it falls.

21 If, in the land that the LORD your God is giving you to possess, a body is found lying in open country, and it is not known who struck the person down, ² then your elders and your judges shall come out to measure the distances to the towns that are near the body. ³ The elders of the town nearest the body shall take a heifer that has never been worked, one that has not pulled in the yoke; ⁴ the elders of that town shall bring the heifer down to a wadi with running water, which is neither plowed nor sown,

22.13–30n. 8: *Comrades*, lit. "brothers," to which Deuteronomy frequently, and distinctively, gives the meaning, "fellow citizens" (cf. 24.7); NRSV also translates the same word as "neighbor" (15.7,9,11; 22.1–4; 24.13; 25.3) and "Israelite" (23.19–20; 24.14). **11:** The use of a defeated people for *forced labor* was widespread. Israelites so used the indigenous population of Canaan (Judg 1.27–36). David's cabinet included an official responsible for "forced labor" (2 Sam 20.24). **15–18:** *Thus you shall treat all the towns that are very far from you,* a secondary addition retroactively restricts the preceding rules of engagement (vv. 10–14), which tolerate the taking of captives as "forced labor," so that they apply only to foreign wars. The stipulation that the indigenous population of Canaan should uniformly be exterminated is a literary fiction (see v. 11n.; 7.2n.). **15:** *The nations,* the Canaanites. *Here,* on the anachronism, see 1.1n.; 2.12n. **16:** *But as for the towns of these peoples that the LORD . . . is giving you* refers to the inhabitants of the land (v. 17). **17:** *You shall annihilate them,* the Heb phrase is elsewhere translated as "utterly destroy" (7.2; 13.15); it refers to killing and sanctifying the dead to a deity. **19–20:** Wars often involved the kind of "scorched earth policy" prohibited here (2 Kings 3.19,25). **20:** *Siegeworks* were regularly built against walled cities (1 Sam 20.15; 2 Kings 25.1).

21.1–9: Atonement for an unsolved murder. Since a murder victim's blood tainted the land (Gen 4.10; Num 35.33–34), it was imperative to "purge the guilt of innocent blood from Israel" (19.13). This law, which has gone through several stages of reworking, addresses how to do so when the perpetrator cannot be identified. There are similar ancient Near Eastern laws for corpses discovered outside cities; these emphasize financial liability rather than atoning for the spilled blood (*Laws of Hammurabi* §§ 23–24; *Hittite Laws* § 6). The original significance of the law's rituals is difficult to recover. **1:** *Open country,* beyond the legal jurisdiction of any particular town (see 22.23,25), and where witnesses are unlikely. **2:** *Elders . . . judges,* see 16.18n. *Measure the distances* to establish legal jurisdiction, as in the similar *Hittite Laws* § 6. **3:** *Never been worked . . . not pulled in the yoke,* symbolizing the human victim's innocence (similarly, Num 19.2). **4:** *Wadi with running water* (Am 5.24), lit. "with reliable water," in contrast to unreliable seasonal streams (Jer 15.18). *Break the heifer's neck,* nonsacrificial killing;

and shall break the heifer's neck there in the wadi. [5] Then the priests, the sons of Levi, shall come forward, for the LORD your God has chosen them to minister to him and to pronounce blessings in the name of the LORD, and by their decision all cases of dispute and assault shall be settled. [6] All the elders of that town nearest the body shall wash their hands over the heifer whose neck was broken in the wadi, [7] and they shall declare: "Our hands did not shed this blood, nor were we witnesses to it. [8] Absolve, O LORD, your people Israel, whom you redeemed; do not let the guilt of innocent blood remain in the midst of your people Israel." Then they will be absolved of bloodguilt. [9] So you shall purge the guilt of innocent blood from your midst, because you must do what is right in the sight of the LORD.

[10] When you go out to war against your enemies, and the LORD your God hands them over to you and you take them captive, [11] suppose you see among the captives a beautiful woman whom you desire and want to marry, [12] and so you bring her home to your house: she shall shave her head, pare her nails, [13] discard her captive's garb, and shall remain in your house a full month, mourning for her father and mother; after that you may go in to her and be her husband, and she shall be your wife. [14] But if you are not satisfied with her, you shall let her go free and not sell her for money. You must not treat her as a slave, since you have dishonored her.

[15] If a man has two wives, one of them loved and the other disliked, and if both the loved and the disliked have borne him sons, the firstborn being the son of the one who is disliked, [16] then on the day when he wills his possessions to his sons, he is not permitted to treat the son of the loved as the firstborn in preference to the son of the disliked, who is the firstborn. [17] He must acknowledge as firstborn the son of the one who is disliked, giving him a double portion[a] of all that he has; since he is the first issue of his virility, the right of the firstborn is his.

[18] If someone has a stubborn and rebellious son who will not obey his father and

a Heb *two-thirds*

sacrifice requires slitting the throat (see Ex 13.13; 34.20). **5**: *Priests,* not mentioned in v. 2, and likely a later addition. *All cases* contrasts with 17.9, where the levitical priests at the central sanctuary adjudicated only cases that could not be resolved locally. **6**: *Wash their hands over the heifer,* with no laying on of hands, and thus without symbolic transfer of culpability to the animal (contrast Lev 16.21–22). **7**: *Our hands . . . witnesses,* stronger in Heb: "As for our hands, they did not shed this blood nor did our eyes see," covering both direct action and failure to avert or report a crime (cf. Lev 5.1). **8**: *Absolve, O LORD,* the ritual of vv. 3–6 has no intrinsic efficacy; prayer is the means of absolution. *They will be absolved,* better, "that they may be absolved," since absolution ultimately depends upon divine action, not human ritual.

21.10–25.19: Miscellaneous civil and family laws. The following laws are concerned with family, civil, and ethical issues. Laws to extend legal protection to women when they would otherwise be disenfranchised concern female captives (21.10–14), property rights of the less-favored wife (21.15–17), and false charges of infidelity (22.13–19).

21.10–14: Legal obligations toward female captives. This procedure most likely originally applied to the Canaanite population (20.15–18n.). Female war captives routinely became concubines. This law accords such women dignity and protection against enslavement. **12–13**: The rituals provide both captive and captor means to effect a transition from one status to another. **13**: *Full month,* full period of mourning, as for Aaron and Moses (Num 20.29; Deut 34.8). *Mourning,* it is unclear whether the parents actually died in the war or are lost to her because of her captivity. The time to grieve implies legal respect for the female captive as a person. *Go in to her,* approach her sexually; consummation provides the legal means to become *husband, and . . . wife.* **14**: Cf. Ex 21.7–8. *Money,* see 2.6n. *Dishonored,* "violated" sexually (22.24,29; Gen 34.2; Judg 19.24; 2 Sam 13.12).

21.15–17: Legal protection of the less-favored wife. The law uses the norm of primogeniture (Gen 25.29–34; *Laws of Hammurabi* §§ 165–70) to protect the son of the less-favored wife from disinheritance. **17**: *Double portion,* as text note *a* indicates, two-thirds (see Zech 13.8), leaving one-third for the other son. *Right of the firstborn,* ironically, the foundation narratives concerning Isaac, Jacob, and Joseph subvert the legal norm here affirmed (Gen 17.15–22; 21.8–14; 27.1–40; 48.8–22).

21.18–21: The rebellious son. The Decalogue requirement to honor the parents (5.16; Ex 20.12) carries no ex-

mother, who does not heed them when they discipline him, [19] then his father and his mother shall take hold of him and bring him out to the elders of his town at the gate of that place. [20] They shall say to the elders of his town, "This son of ours is stubborn and rebellious. He will not obey us. He is a glutton and a drunkard." [21] Then all the men of the town shall stone him to death. So you shall purge the evil from your midst; and all Israel will hear, and be afraid.

[22] When someone is convicted of a crime punishable by death and is executed, and you hang him on a tree, [23] his corpse must not remain all night upon the tree; you shall bury him that same day, for anyone hung on a tree is under God's curse. You must not defile the land that the LORD your God is giving you for possession.

22 You shall not watch your neighbor's ox or sheep straying away and ignore them; you shall take them back to their owner. [2] If the owner does not reside near you or you do not know who the owner is, you shall bring it to your own house, and it shall remain with you until the owner claims it; then you shall return it. [3] You shall do the same with a neighbor's donkey; you shall do the same with a neighbor's garment; and you shall do the same with anything else that your neighbor loses and you find. You may not withhold your help.

[4] You shall not see your neighbor's donkey or ox fallen on the road and ignore it; you shall help to lift it up.

[5] A woman shall not wear a man's apparel, nor shall a man put on a woman's garment; for whoever does such things is abhorrent to the LORD your God.

[6] If you come on a bird's nest, in any tree or on the ground, with fledglings or eggs, with the mother sitting on the fledglings or on the eggs, you shall not take the mother with the young. [7] Let the mother go, taking only the young for yourself, in order that it may go well with you and you may live long.

[8] When you build a new house, you shall make a parapet for your roof; otherwise you might have bloodguilt on your house, if anyone should fall from it.

[9] You shall not sow your vineyard with a second kind of seed, or the whole yield will have to be forfeited, both the crop that you have sown and the yield of the vineyard itself.

[10] You shall not plow with an ox and a donkey yoked together.

plicit sanction; here flagrant and sustained disobedience is a capital offense. **19:** *Elders* were judges of family law and held court at the city *gate,* a public forum (22.15; 25.7; Job 29.7; Ruth 4.1–2,11; Lam 5.14). The professionalized judiciary established at the same site (16.18) may have had jurisdiction specifically over religious and criminal law (17.2–7). **21:** Here, mere parental testimony suffices (contrast 13.14; 17.4). *Stone him,* see 13.10n.

21.22–23: Treatment of the executed. Public exposure of the corpse of an executed criminal, which was not the norm, was a form of reproach directed against enemies of the state (Josh 8.29; 10.26; 1 Sam 31.10; Esth 9.6–14). Out of respect for the body, to prevent it from serving as carrion (2 Sam 21.10), this law sets stringent limits to that procedure. **22:** *Hang . . . on a tree,* the Heb word for "tree" is broader; the law could also refer to suspension from "gallows" (Esth 9.13) or a "pole" (Gen 40.19), or possibly, based upon Neo-Assyrian precedent, impalement upon a stake.

22.1–12: Various moral and religious responsibilities of citizenship. The rationale for the sequence and selection of these laws is often unclear.

22.1–4: Moral duties toward the neighbor. Two laws (vv. 1–3,4) that develop two corresponding laws from the earlier Covenant Collection. **1–3:** The earlier law governing the return of wandering animals (Ex 21.1–3) is here revised and extended. **1:** *Your neighbor's ox,* in contrast to "your enemy's ox" (Ex 23.4). *Neighbor,* lit. "brother"; see 20.8n. **3:** *Anything else,* the earlier law is universalized to apply to any lost property. **4:** Reworking Ex 23.5 to emphasize the neighbor, as in v. 1.

22.5–12: Miscellaneous laws. 5: The prohibition against cross-dressing seeks to maintain gender boundaries; a similar concern for boundaries is evident in vv. 9–11. **6–7:** Avoiding simultaneous consumption of two generations of the same creature is also evident in other laws (14.21; Ex 23.19; 34.26; Lev 22.28). **8:** The *roof* was used as living space (Josh 2.6; Judg 3.20–25; 2 Sam 11.2). *Bloodguilt,* criminal negligence; a capital offense (see 19.10n.). **9–10:** Corresponding to Lev 19.19, these laws attempt to maintain specific boundaries between cat-

[11] You shall not wear clothes made of wool and linen woven together.

[12] You shall make tassels on the four corners of the cloak with which you cover yourself.

[13] Suppose a man marries a woman, but after going in to her, he dislikes her [14] and makes up charges against her, slandering her by saying, "I married this woman; but when I lay with her, I did not find evidence of her virginity." [15] The father of the young woman and her mother shall then submit the evidence of the young woman's virginity to the elders of the city at the gate. [16] The father of the young woman shall say to the elders: "I gave my daughter in marriage to this man but he dislikes her; [17] now he has made up charges against her, saying, 'I did not find evidence of your daughter's virginity.' But here is the evidence of my daughter's virginity." Then they shall spread out the cloth before the elders of the town. [18] The elders of that town shall take the man and punish him; [19] they shall fine him one hundred shekels of silver (which they shall give to the young woman's father) because he has slandered a virgin of Israel. She shall remain his wife; he shall not be permitted to divorce her as long as he lives.

[20] If, however, this charge is true, that evidence of the young woman's virginity was not found, [21] then they shall bring the young woman out to the entrance of her father's house and the men of her town shall stone her to death, because she committed a disgraceful act in Israel by prostituting herself in her father's house. So you shall purge the evil from your midst.

[22] If a man is caught lying with the wife of another man, both of them shall die, the man who lay with the woman as well as the woman. So you shall purge the evil from Israel.

[23] If there is a young woman, a virgin already engaged to be married, and a man meets her in the town and lies with her, [24] you shall bring both of them to the gate of that town and stone them to death, the young woman because she did not cry for help in the town and the man because he violated his neighbor's wife. So you shall purge the evil from your midst.

[25] But if the man meets the engaged woman in the open country, and the man

egories seen as incompatible (as in v. 5; 14.3–20). **9:** *Forfeited,* not permitted for human consumption. **12:** *Tassels,* this may reflect an application of royal garb, seen, for example, in Neo-Assyrian palace reliefs, to the nation as a whole. Num 15.37–40 gives a theological rationale.

22.13–30: Violations of marriage law. In the ancient Near East, marriage was a contractual relationship. The woman could not act independently: She remained in her father's household until a suitor paid a bride-price (vv. 28–29; Ex 22.16–17) to compensate for the reduction of the household. At that point she became formally "engaged," although still residing with her father (v. 21). Later, at the marriage feast, the union was consummated (Gen 29.22–25) and the woman took up residence in her husband's house.

22.13–21: False accusation of breach of marital contract. 14: *Makes up charges against her,* possibly for mercenary reasons, since nonfulfillment of the marital contract would entail refund of the bride-price and possibly a payment of a penalty for breach of contract. The *evidence,* the bloodstained cloth of v. 17. **15:** *Elders,* see 16.18n.; 21.19n. **17:** *The cloth* upon which husband and wife slept upon consummation of the relationship. It was understood that the cloth should have been bloodstained from the couple's first intercourse; there is scant medical support for this widespread assumption. **19:** *They shall fine him,* the penalty for his slanderous accusation is financial, although the penalty for her infidelity, if proven true, is capital (vv. 20–21); contrast 19.19. *One hundred shekels,* about 1.1 kg (2.5 lb), twice the fine for rape (v. 29). **21:** *Entrance of her father's house,* at the very site of the offense. *Stone her to death,* see 13.10n. *Disgraceful act in Israel,* a violation of basic community sexual and religious norms (Gen 34.7; Josh 7.15; Judg 19.23–34; 20.6,10). *Purge the evil,* see 13.5n.

22.22–30: Adultery and rape. 22: Adultery is a violation of the seventh commandment (5.18) and a capital offense (Lev 18.20; 20.10). *Both of them shall die,* a contrast with ancient Near Eastern norms, which required the male's death but left the wife's fate to her husband. The law removes the wife from her husband's authority and defines her as a legal person accountable for her actions. **23–27:** Two laws to determine culpability (vv. 23–24) or nonculpability (vv. 25–27) in cases of rape. Both laws show detailed points of contact with *Middle Assyrian Laws* (*M.A.L.;* ca. 1076 BCE). **23:** *Engaged to be married,* this legal status permits the transition from adultery to rape: Although the woman still resides with her father, she is contractually bound to her future husband.

seizes her and lies with her, then only the man who lay with her shall die. [26] You shall do nothing to the young woman; the young woman has not committed an offense punishable by death, because this case is like that of someone who attacks and murders a neighbor. [27] Since he found her in the open country, the engaged woman may have cried for help, but there was no one to rescue her.

[28] If a man meets a virgin who is not engaged, and seizes her and lies with her, and they are caught in the act, [29] the man who lay with her shall give fifty shekels of silver to the young woman's father, and she shall become his wife. Because he violated her he shall not be permitted to divorce her as long as he lives.

[30] [a]A man shall not marry his father's wife, thereby violating his father's rights.[b]

23 No one whose testicles are crushed or whose penis is cut off shall be admitted to the assembly of the LORD.

[2] Those born of an illicit union shall not be admitted to the assembly of the LORD. Even to the tenth generation, none of their descen-

dants shall be admitted to the assembly of the LORD.

[3] No Ammonite or Moabite shall be admitted to the assembly of the LORD. Even to the tenth generation, none of their descendants shall be admitted to the assembly of the LORD, [4] because they did not meet you with food and water on your journey out of Egypt, and because they hired against you Balaam son of Beor, from Pethor of Mesopotamia, to curse you. [5] (Yet the LORD your God refused to heed Balaam; the LORD your God turned the curse into a blessing for you, because the LORD your God loved you.) [6] You shall never promote their welfare or their prosperity as long as you live.

[7] You shall not abhor any of the Edomites, for they are your kin. You shall not abhor any of the Egyptians, because you were an alien residing in their land. [8] The children of the third generation that are born to them may be admitted to the assembly of the LORD.

---

[a] Ch 23.1 in Heb

[b] Heb *uncovering his father's skirt*

In the town, where there are potential witnesses (*M.A.L.* § A 12). **25:** The assault in *open country,* where there are no likely witnesses, suggests planned malice. **26:** *Like . . . someone who attacks and murders a neighbor,* i.e., premeditated (19.11–13). Rape is a criminal assault rather than a sex crime. **28–29.** These conditions correspond to *M.A.L.* § A 55, which implies forced rape. In contrast, Ex 22.16–17 specifies intercourse with, but not forced rape of, a "virgin who is not engaged." The conflation of these two models in this law leaves it unclear whether or not it refers to consensual intercourse. **28:** *And lies with her,* as in Ex 22.16, placing the woman in a legally ambiguous position, unavailable to others (v. 14). **29:** *Fifty shekels,* presumably the bride-price. In contrast to Ex 22.17, the father's consent is not sought. Postbiblical Jewish law granted both father and daughter the right to refuse. **30:** A transition to the next section. *Father's wife,* i.e., a widowed stepmother (see Lev 18.7–8). *Violating his father's rights,* lit. "uncovering his father's skirt" (text note *b*); i.e., even indirect sexual contact with him must be avoided (Gen 9.23–24; 49.4; Lev 18.8; 20.11).

23.1–8: Restrictions on access to Israel's assembly. *The assembly of the LORD* (v. 1), the national governing body, or popular legislature, was charged with a broad range of judicial, political, and policy matters (Judg 20.2). **1:** *Testicles . . . penis,* the same physiological qualification that the Holiness Collection requires of the priesthood (Lev 21.17–23), now extended to all Israel (see 14.2n.). **2:** *Illicit union,* incestuous marriages (v. 3; 22.30; Lev 18.6–18). *Tenth generation,* see v. 3n. **3–8:** The restrictions do not entail denial of residence rights, and those named would retain the protection afforded by the legal status of "resident alien" (see 1.16; 5.14; Lev 19.10,33–34; 23.22). **3–6:** These laws were reused in the postexilic context to prohibit intermarriage (Ezra 9–10; Neh 13.1–3). **3:** *Ammonite or Moabite,* perhaps introduced after v. 2 because of an older tradition concerning their incestuous origins (Gen 19.30–38). *Tenth generation,* "forever," as explicitly stated in the Hebrew. **4:** The rationale varies from the earlier report that Israel detoured around Ammon without requesting assistance and received food and water from Moab (2.19,29,37). *Balaam,* see Num 22–24. **7:** *Not abhor . . . Edomites,* an extraordinary inclusion, since the Edomites participated in the destruction of Jerusalem (Ps 137.7; Obadiah). *Kin,* through Esau (Gen 25.24–26; 36.1). *Egyptians,* this injunction remarkably overlooks the enslavement (26.6; 28.60,68; Ex 1–15), going back to the provision of sanctuary (Gen 12; 37–50).

⁹ When you are encamped against your enemies you shall guard against any impropriety.

¹⁰ If one of you becomes unclean because of a nocturnal emission, then he shall go outside the camp; he must not come within the camp. ¹¹ When evening comes, he shall wash himself with water, and when the sun has set, he may come back into the camp.

¹² You shall have a designated area outside the camp to which you shall go. ¹³ With your utensils you shall have a trowel; when you relieve yourself outside, you shall dig a hole with it and then cover up your excrement. ¹⁴ Because the LORD your God travels along with your camp, to save you and to hand over your enemies to you, therefore your camp must be holy, so that he may not see anything indecent among you and turn away from you.

¹⁵ Slaves who have escaped to you from their owners shall not be given back to them. ¹⁶ They shall reside with you, in your midst, in any place they choose in any one of your towns, wherever they please; you shall not oppress them.

¹⁷ None of the daughters of Israel shall be a temple prostitute; none of the sons of Israel shall be a temple prostitute. ¹⁸ You shall not bring the fee of a prostitute or the wages of a male prostitute[a] into the house of the LORD your God in payment for any vow, for both of these are abhorrent to the LORD your God.

¹⁹ You shall not charge interest on loans to another Israelite, interest on money, interest on provisions, interest on anything that is lent. ²⁰ On loans to a foreigner you may charge interest, but on loans to another Israelite you may not charge interest, so that the LORD your God may bless you in all your undertakings in the land that you are about to enter and possess.

²¹ If you make a vow to the LORD your God, do not postpone fulfilling it; for the LORD your God will surely require it of you, and you would incur guilt. ²² But if you refrain from vowing, you will not incur guilt. ²³ Whatever your lips utter you must diligently perform, just as you have freely vowed to the LORD your God with your own mouth.

²⁴ If you go into your neighbor's vineyard, you may eat your fill of grapes, as many as you wish, but you shall not put any in a container.

a   Heb *a dog*

23.9–14: **Special rules for the military camp.** The theology of holy war assumes God's direct participation in the campaign (7.17–24; 20.4), creating a demand for heightened purity, like that required of the entire people at Sinai (Ex 19.10,14). Sexual abstinence seems also to have been required (1 Sam 21.4–5; 2 Sam 11.8–11; cf. Ex 19.15). 10–11: Cf. Lev 15.16–18. 12: *Designated area*, a latrine. 14: *Travels along*, see 20.4; 31.6. *Anything indecent*, as in 24.1.

23.15–25.19: **The heightened moral responsibilities of the covenant community.**

23.15–16: **Prohibition of the return of escaped slaves.** The law rejects the almost universal stipulation within ancient Near Eastern law that escaped slaves must be returned (*Laws of Hammurabi* §§ 16–20; *Hittite Laws* §§ 22–24). 16: The extraordinary repetition emphasizes that the entire community must be open to them.

23.17–18: **Restrictions on prostitution.** These verses presuppose the inevitability of prostitution, while proscribing it for Israelites and regulating it in such a way as to preserve the Temple's sanctity. 17: *Temple prostitute* (Heb "qedesha"), the translation reflects belief in the existence of sacred prostitution in Israel and the ancient Near East, for which there is scant evidence; more likely "qedesha" is a standard euphemism for the coarser term for prostitute (v. 18). The same alternation between the two terms appears in Gen 38.15,21. The word might better be translated as "one set aside." 18: *Prostitute*, Heb "zonah," closer to "whore" (Hos 1.2). *Male prostitute* (lit. "dog"), in context, the male counterpart to a common female prostitute. To maintain holiness, the law forbids donating income gained from prostitution to the Temple (cf. Hos 4.14; Mic 1.7).

23.19–25: **Financial ethics, vows, gathering by the needy.** 19–20: This law builds on Ex 22.25, which clarifies that lending served primarily as a means of social support for "the poor among you" (similarly Lev 25.36–37). Charging interest would amount to profiteering from the misfortunes of others. *Money*, see 2.6n. 20: *A foreigner*, as distinct from the "resident alien," who fully participated in Israel's social welfare system (see 1.16n.); for similar distinctions, see 15.3; Lev 25.44–45. 21–23: A *vow* (v. 21) promises payment of something to God (usually a sacrifice at a temple) in exchange for receiving something (see 1 Sam 1.11). This cautious reserve about vows, understandable in light of Judg 11.29–40, closely corresponds to wisdom teachings (Eccl 5.4–6). For a more positive view, see Ps 50.14. 24–25: These rules prohibit exploitation of Deuteronomy's extensive support system for

²⁵ If you go into your neighbor's standing grain, you may pluck the ears with your hand, but you shall not put a sickle to your neighbor's standing grain.

24 Suppose a man enters into marriage with a woman, but she does not please him because he finds something objectionable about her, and so he writes her a certificate of divorce, puts it in her hand, and sends her out of his house; she then leaves his house ² and goes off to become another man's wife. ³ Then suppose the second man dislikes her, writes her a bill of divorce, puts it in her hand, and sends her out of his house (or the second man who married her dies); ⁴ her first husband, who sent her away, is not permitted to take her again to be his wife after she has been defiled; for that would be abhorrent to the LORD, and you shall not bring guilt on the land that the LORD your God is giving you as a possession.

⁵ When a man is newly married, he shall not go out with the army or be charged with any related duty. He shall be free at home one year, to be happy with the wife whom he has married.

⁶ No one shall take a mill or an upper millstone in pledge, for that would be taking a life in pledge.

⁷ If someone is caught kidnaping another Israelite, enslaving or selling the Israelite,

then that kidnaper shall die. So you shall purge the evil from your midst.

⁸ Guard against an outbreak of a leprous^a skin disease by being very careful; you shall carefully observe whatever the levitical priests instruct you, just as I have commanded them. ⁹ Remember what the LORD your God did to Miriam on your journey out of Egypt.

¹⁰ When you make your neighbor a loan of any kind, you shall not go into the house to take the pledge. ¹¹ You shall wait outside, while the person to whom you are making the loan brings the pledge out to you. ¹² If the person is poor, you shall not sleep in the garment given you as^b the pledge. ¹³ You shall give the pledge back by sunset, so that your neighbor may sleep in the cloak and bless you; and it will be to your credit before the LORD your God.

¹⁴ You shall not withhold the wages of poor and needy laborers, whether other Israelites or aliens who reside in your land in one of your towns. ¹⁵ You shall pay them their wages daily before sunset, because they are poor and their livelihood depends on them; other-

---

ᵃ A term for several skin diseases; precise meaning uncertain

ᵇ Heb lacks *the garment given you as*

---

the needy (14.28–29; 24.19–22; 25.4). **25:** *Pluck . . . hand,* to address immediate hunger (Lk 6.1; cf. Mt 12.1; Mk 2.23).

Chs 24–25: Laws promoting social harmony. 24.1–22: The chapter, like the previous one, begins with a restriction on marriage and concludes stipulating care for those in need (note 22.30 = 23.1 Heb). **1–4:** This complex law, theologically applied by two prophets (Isa 50.1; Jer 3.1,8), addresses only remarriage after divorce to a wife who subsequently married another; it does not prohibit remarriage in general. Biblical law includes no general laws of either marriage or divorce, only special cases that raise particular ethical or religious issues. **1:** Male-initiated divorce was the norm, though there is some evidence in the Near East and in the Jewish papyri from Elephantine in Egypt (fifth century BCE) of contracts permitting either party to initiate proceedings. *He finds . . . about her,* formula for disloyal action or betrayal of trust (1 Sam 29.3,6,8; 2 Kings 17.4; cf. 1 Sam 12.5). *Objectionable,* "indecent" (23.14). It is unclear from the term used what valid criteria for divorce were. *Certificate of divorce,* legally freeing her to remarry. **4:** *After she has been defiled,* not in general, since she is permitted to remarry, but specifically as regards relations with her first husband. **5:** Another of the rules for holy war (20.1–20; 21.10–14; 23.9–14). *Newly married,* contrast the premarital deferral from service in 20.7. *Be happy with,* better, "give happiness to," including conjugal joy. **6:** The law prohibits oppression in economic relations (like vv. 10–15). *Take . . . in pledge,* accept as collateral for a loan. *Mill or an upper millstone,* like the "garment" of v. 12, they are essential to survival, and thus may not be taken. **7:** Restricts the application of Ex 21.16 to kidnapers of fellow Israelites; perhaps also an interpretation of Deut 5.19. **8–9:** *Leprous skin disease,* not leprosy but an unidentified inflammation; see Lev 13.1–14.57. *Remember . . . Miriam,* see Num 12.1–15. **10–13:** Expands upon Ex 22.26–27 (cf. Am 2.8; Prov 20.16; 22.27; 27.13; Job 22.6). The Yavneh Yam inscription (late seventh century BCE) deals with a similar case. **14–15:** See Ex 22.21–24; Lev 19.13. Israel's ethics are based upon the conviction that God identifies with and vindicates the oppressed. **14:** The prohibition against economic exploitation is not contingent upon

wise they might cry to the LORD against you, and you would incur guilt.

[16] Parents shall not be put to death for their children, nor shall children be put to death for their parents; only for their own crimes may persons be put to death.

[17] You shall not deprive a resident alien or an orphan of justice; you shall not take a widow's garment in pledge. [18] Remember that you were a slave in Egypt and the LORD your God redeemed you from there; therefore I command you to do this.

[19] When you reap your harvest in your field and forget a sheaf in the field, you shall not go back to get it; it shall be left for the alien, the orphan, and the widow, so that the LORD your God may bless you in all your undertakings. [20] When you beat your olive trees, do not strip what is left; it shall be for the alien, the orphan, and the widow.

[21] When you gather the grapes of your vineyard, do not glean what is left; it shall be for the alien, the orphan, and the widow. [22] Remember that you were a slave in the land of Egypt; therefore I am commanding you to do this.

25 Suppose two persons have a dispute and enter into litigation, and the judges decide between them, declaring one to be in the right and the other to be in the wrong. [2] If the one in the wrong deserves to be flogged, the judge shall make that person lie down and be beaten in his presence with the number of lashes proportionate to the offense. [3] Forty lashes may be given but not more; if more lashes than these are given, your neighbor will be degraded in your sight.

[4] You shall not muzzle an ox while it is treading out the grain.

[5] When brothers reside together, and one of them dies and has no son, the wife of the deceased shall not be married outside the family to a stranger. Her husband's brother shall go in to her, taking her in marriage, and performing the duty of a husband's brother to her, [6] and the firstborn whom she bears shall succeed to the name of the deceased brother, so that his name may not be blotted out of Israel. [7] But if the man has no desire to marry his brother's widow, then his brother's widow shall go up to the elders at the gate and say, "My husband's brother refuses to perpetuate his brother's name in Israel; he will not perform the duty of a husband's brother to me." [8] Then the elders of his town shall summon him and speak to him. If he persists, saying, "I have no desire to marry her," [9] then his brother's wife shall go up to him in the presence of

---

ethnicity or nationality; see 1.16n. **15:** See 15.9n. **16:** This law restricting punishment to the responsible individual, cited in 2 Kings 14.6, applies to both civil and criminal law. Collective responsibility applies to offenses against God (5.9–10; Ex 34.7; Num 16.31–33; Josh 7.24–25; 2 Sam 21.1–9), a theological principle subsequently brought into conformity with the law of individual liability (7.10; Jer 31.29–30; Ezek 18). **17:** *You shall not deprive . . . of justice,* in Hebrew, identical to the comprehensive "You shall not distort justice" (16.19). This law, therefore, ensures protection of the most vulnerable, the *resident alien* or the *orphan. Take . . . in pledge,* better, "seize" to force payment (see Job 24.3). This accords the *widow* special protection; for day laborers, see vv. 10–13. **18:** See 15.15. **19–22:** Lev 19.9–10; 23.22. The story of Ruth, both a widow and an alien, presupposes such laws, which assign harvest gleanings to the needy, allowing them to eat without begging for food. **20:** *Beat,* with poles, so as to harvest the olives (Isa 17.6). **25.1–3:** A double restriction upon judicial flogging, also employed for discipline in nonjudicial contexts (Ex 21.20; Prov 10.13; 26.3; 1 Kings 12.14). **2:** *In his presence,* under the judge's direct supervision, "by [his] count" (the more likely rendering of NRSV *number of lashes*). **3:** *Forty lashes,* a definitive restriction for which there is no parallel in Near Eastern law; the *Middle Assyrian Laws* stipulate floggings of five to one hundred lashes. *Your neighbor,* the criminal, despite his judicial status, retains human dignity. **4:** For similar humane treatment of animals, see 22.6–7; Prov 12.10. **5–10:** Biblical, Near Eastern, and Roman inheritance law assigned special responsibilities to the "husband's brother" (vv. 5–7), for which Hebrew had a special term (cf. Latin "levir," hence "levirate marriage"). See Gen 38.8 and Ruth 4.5–6, which reflect variations of this law. **5:** *Outside the family,* NRSV has added *the family;* more likely, the frame of reference is the larger clan. The widow's marriage outside of the clan would diminish the landholding of her clan and add it to the new husband's, affecting the original equitable division of land among the tribes (Josh 13–21). *Her husband's brother shall go in to her,* possibly the brother's death provided an exception to the incest prohibition of marrying a sister-in-law (Lev 18.16; 20.21); alternatively, the Holiness Collection's incest laws might intend to prohibit levirate marriage

the elders, pull his sandal off his foot, spit in his face, and declare, "This is what is done to the man who does not build up his brother's house." [10] Throughout Israel his family shall be known as "the house of him whose sandal was pulled off."

[11] If men get into a fight with one another, and the wife of one intervenes to rescue her husband from the grip of his opponent by reaching out and seizing his genitals, [12] you shall cut off her hand; show no pity.

[13] You shall not have in your bag two kinds of weights, large and small. [14] You shall not have in your house two kinds of measures, large and small. [15] You shall have only a full and honest weight; you shall have only a full and honest measure, so that your days may be long in the land that the LORD your God is giving you. [16] For all who do such things, all who act dishonestly, are abhorrent to the LORD your God.

[17] Remember what Amalek did to you on your journey out of Egypt, [18] how he attacked you on the way, when you were faint and weary, and struck down all who lagged behind you; he did not fear God. [19] Therefore when the LORD your God has given you rest from all your enemies on every hand, in the land that the LORD your God is giving you as an inheritance to possess, you shall blot out the remembrance of Amalek from under heaven; do not forget.

26 When you have come into the land that the LORD your God is giving you as an inheritance to possess, and you possess it, and settle in it, [2] you shall take some of the first of all the fruit of the ground, which you harvest from the land that the LORD your God is giving you, and you shall put it in a basket and go to the place that the LORD your God will choose as a dwelling for his name. [3] You shall go to the priest who is in office at that time, and say to him, "Today I declare to the LORD your God that I have come into the land that the LORD swore to our ancestors to give us." [4] When the priest takes the basket from your hand and sets it down before the altar of the LORD your God, [5] you shall make this response before the LORD your God: "A wandering Aramean was my ancestor; he went down into Egypt and lived there as an alien, few in number, and there he became a great nation, mighty and populous. [6] When the Egyptians treated us harshly and afflicted us, by imposing hard labor on us, [7] we cried to the LORD, the God of our ancestors; the LORD heard our voice and saw our affliction, our toil, and our oppression. [8] The LORD brought

altogether. **6**: *Firstborn* alone here counts to the brother; cf. Gen 38.8. **9**: Legal title was symbolically claimed by walking over the land (see 11.24n.). Thus, transfer of title entailed passing the *sandal* (Ruth 4.7), while renunciation of title, as here, was symbolized by removal of the *sandal*. The intent of the ceremony is public shaming, since the dereliction of duty makes the brother's wife a widow, abandoning her to the class of the impoverished: "the resident aliens, the orphans, and the widows" (14.29n.). **10**: *Known as*, lit. "called by the name of," thus explicitly applying a form of retributive justice (19.19n.). For refusing to build up the deceased's "name" (vv. 6–7) and "house" (v. 9), the brother's own *house* is stigmatized by its new name. **11–12**: An additional law dealing with threats to reproduction (cf. Ex 21.22–25). Physical mutilation (characteristic in the *Middle Assyrian Laws*) is nowhere else prescribed in the Bible, except in the general formula for talion (19.21; Ex 21.23–24; Lev 24.19–20). That rationale does not apply here, however, since there is no symmetry between injury and punishment. The issue may rather be the perceived insult to dignity (cf. *Laws of Hammurabi* §195). **13–16**: Cf. *Laws of Hammurabi* §108; Lev 19.35–36; Am 8.5. **14**: By fraudulently using two different sets of counterweights—small ones to sell grain but large ones to purchase it—a merchant could turn a tidy profit. **17–19**: The tradition presupposes Ex 17.8–16, in which the Amalekites, a fierce desert tribe, attacked Israel (cf. Ps 83.4–8). **18**: These details are not reflected in Ex 17.8–16; they may have been supplied by the Deuteronomic author in order to justify the extirpation of Amalek (v. 19; cf. Ex 17.14; 1 Sam 15.2–3). **19**: *Rest*, see 3.20; 12.9n.

26.1–15: Concluding liturgies. Two already prescribed laws (14.22–29) are given a historical and theological foundation (similarly, 16.12, for the festival of weeks). **1–11**: The context is the festival of weeks (16.9–12), when the Israelite was to make an annual pilgrimage to the central sanctuary, bringing the first fruits of the harvest, to thank God for the land's bounty. **4**: *When the priest*, contrast v. 10. Vv. 3–4 may be a later addition intended to emphasize the role of priests in the ceremony. Thus, v. 5 may have originally continued v. 2. **5**: *Wandering Aramean* suggests the Jacob tradition (Gen 25.20). **6**: *Afflicted . . . hard labor*, see Ex 1.11–14. **8–9**: It is striking that the

us out of Egypt with a mighty hand and an outstretched arm, with a terrifying display of power, and with signs and wonders; [9] and he brought us into this place and gave us this land, a land flowing with milk and honey. [10] So now I bring the first of the fruit of the ground that you, O LORD, have given me." You shall set it down before the LORD your God and bow down before the LORD your God. [11] Then you, together with the Levites and the aliens who reside among you, shall celebrate with all the bounty that the LORD your God has given to you and to your house.

[12] When you have finished paying all the tithe of your produce in the third year (which is the year of the tithe), giving it to the Levites, the aliens, the orphans, and the widows, so that they may eat their fill within your towns, [13] then you shall say before the LORD your God: "I have removed the sacred portion from the house, and I have given it to the Levites, the resident aliens, the orphans,

and the widows, in accordance with your entire commandment that you commanded me; I have neither transgressed nor forgotten any of your commandments: [14] I have not eaten of it while in mourning; I have not removed any of it while I was unclean; and I have not offered any of it to the dead. I have obeyed the LORD my God, doing just as you commanded me. [15] Look down from your holy habitation, from heaven, and bless your people Israel and the ground that you have given us, as you swore to our ancestors—a land flowing with milk and honey."

[16] This very day the LORD your God is commanding you to observe these statutes and ordinances; so observe them diligently with all your heart and with all your soul. [17] Today you have obtained the LORD's agreement: to be your God; and for you to walk in his ways, to keep his statutes, his commandments, and his ordinances, and to obey him. [18] Today the LORD has obtained your agreement: to be his

giving of the law on Horeb is missing here. Perhaps this ancient liturgy did not know of this event. Alternatively, the giving of the law might not be thematically appropriate to a unit that emphasizes God's role as liberator. **11:** *Celebrate,* or "rejoice" (16.11,14–15), specifically in a festive meal consumed at the central sanctuary (12.7,18), which must include *the Levites and the aliens.* The mention of these marginal groups provides a transition to the following law. **12–15:** Produce was tithed annually and consumed by the farmer and his household at the central sanctuary (14.22–27); every third year that tithe was used locally to support the poor (14.28–29). **12:** *Aliens . . . widows,* see 1.16n.; 14.29; 23.3–8,20n. **14:** The formula, containing a triple confession of the donor's ritual purity, probably originated in donations of produce to God at a sanctuary, where purity would be expected. That formula has now been reused for the donation of food to the poor "within your towns" (v. 12). *Offered any of it to the dead,* the duty of the living to care for dead ancestors through food offerings at their place of burial was widely assumed in the ancient Near East (see the Ugaritic Aqhat epic), and continued to be carried out in Second Temple times (Tob 4.17). This practice is not in itself condemned; it is viewed as improper only in relation to sacred donations, because of the impurity associated with death (Lev 22.2–4). **15:** *From your holy habitation, from heaven,* as in 1 Kings 8.30. The double proposition may point to the correction of an older theology in light of a newer one, following Deuteronomy's normal view that only God's name resides in the Temple (12.11; 16.11; 26.2). For the earlier idea, that God himself inhabits the Temple, see 1 Kings 8.13; cf. Deut 12.5. *Bless your people Israel and the ground,* the farmer prays for the blessing of the community and of the land, not directly for fertility or the abundance of his own crops.

26.16–19: Formal conclusion, which presents the legal corpus as a mutually binding relationship between God and Israel. Having just read the law to the people, Moses presents it to them in a formal ratification ceremony (vv. 17–18; cf. 2 Kings 23.1–3). **16:** *Statutes and ordinances . . . observe . . . diligently* forms an inclusio with 12.1, thus providing the laws of chs 12–26 with an elegant frame to mark their conclusion. **17–18:** *Obtained,* the past tense points to a prior action or speech, no record of which survives, in which each party has proclaimed what is here described. Deuteronomy emphasizes that both Israel and God have explicitly assented to the covenant and have affirmed the mutuality of the obligations that each undertakes. This reciprocal model contrasts with the Sinai covenant, which was unilaterally offered by God (Ex 19.3–6) and unilaterally agreed to by Israel (Ex 19.8; 24.3,7). Deuteronomy invokes the language of the Sinai covenant as a model while revising it in the process. **18:** *His treasured people,* see 7.6n. *In praise . . . fame and . . . honor,* NRSV implies that the accolades will be given to Israel. The Hebrew also allows for the possibility that the honors will go to God because of his ac-

treasured people, as he promised you, and to keep his commandments; [19] for him to set you high above all nations that he has made, in praise and in fame and in honor; and for you to be a people holy to the LORD your God, as he promised.

27 Then Moses and the elders of Israel charged all the people as follows: Keep the entire commandment that I am commanding you today. [2] On the day that you cross over the Jordan into the land that the LORD your God is giving you, you shall set up large stones and cover them with plaster. [3] You shall write on them all the words of this law when you have crossed over, to enter the land that the LORD your God is giving you, a land flowing with milk and honey, as the LORD, the God of your ancestors, promised you. [4] So when you have crossed over the Jordan, you shall set up these stones, about which I am commanding you today, on Mount Ebal, and

you shall cover them with plaster. [5] And you shall build an altar there to the LORD your God, an altar of stones on which you have not used an iron tool. [6] You must build the altar of the LORD your God of unhewn[a] stones. Then offer up burnt offerings on it to the LORD your God, [7] make sacrifices of well-being, and eat them there, rejoicing before the LORD your God. [8] You shall write on the stones all the words of this law very clearly.

[9] Then Moses and the levitical priests spoke to all Israel, saying: Keep silence and hear, O Israel! This very day you have become the people of the LORD your God. [10] Therefore obey the LORD your God, observing his commandments and his statutes that I am commanding you today.

[11] The same day Moses charged the people as follows: [12] When you have crossed over the

a   Heb *whole*

tion on Israel's behalf (see Jer 13.11; 33.9). *As he promised you,* Ex 19.5–6. **19:** *High above all nations,* see 28.13–14n. *That he has made,* see Ex 19.5b. *A people holy to the LORD* continues the reference to Ex 19.5–6, while substituting *people* for "nation," which Deuteronomy uses for non-Israelites (12.29).

27.1–26: The ceremonies at Shechem. The injunctions of 11.29–32 are here reiterated and detailed. The laws of chs 12–26 are thus framed with ceremonies that connect entry into the land with obedience to the teaching of Moses. The chapter joins four separate sections that are only loosely connected to one another and to the rest of Deuteronomy. A later editor has aligned the sections with one another, while breaking up the continuity of the speech of chs 26 and 28. The resulting digression preserves several competing traditions about how and where the covenant between God and Israel was concluded: at Sinai; or on the plains of Moab; or at Gilgal immediately upon entering the land; or at the important northern shrine of Shechem (see 11.29n.). **1–8:** This section combines two separate requirements: the raising of plastered stones inscribed with the teaching (vv. 1–4,8) and the construction of a stone altar for sacrifice (vv. 5–7). **1:** Moses is here referred to in the third person, interrupting his first-person address (chs 5–26; 28). *And the elders,* nowhere else in Deuteronomy do they join Moses in addressing the people; this plural subject does not easily fit the following singular *I.* **2:** *On the day . . . large stones,* the Deuteronomistic Historian understands this command to have been fulfilled at Gilgal, just across the Jordan and less than a mile from Jericho (see Josh 4). *Cover them with plaster,* to serve as a surface for inscription. Archaeology attests the use of plaster-covered wall or stele inscriptions. **4:** *Mount Ebal,* at over 1,000 m (3,000 ft), the tallest mountain in the region. It lies in central Canaan, adjacent to the city of Shechem. But that site is inconsistent with v. 2 and the beginning of this verse, which each anticipate that the ceremony will take place immediately upon crossing the river. It would be impossible to reach Shechem in a day. The most logical explanation is that Josh 4 points to the original form of these verses, with Gilgal as the site where Israel complied with this command. That older tradition was then replaced here by the reference to the mountains around Shechem, the chief town of the northern tribes (Josh 24.1,32). **5–7:** These verses are an insertion that reinterprets the plastered stones on which the teaching is to be inscribed as an altar of *unhewn stones,* following Ex 20.25. Such an altar, outside of Jerusalem, conflicts with the centralization requirement of ch 12, and further suggests the antiquity and the independence of this tradition from the rest of Deuteronomy. The fulfillment of this law is narrated in Josh 8.30–35. **9–10:** This is a new paragraph, independent of what precedes it. **9:** *And the levitical priests,* see v. 1n.; here too the plural subject is continued by "I" (v. 10). *This very day,* contrast statements that define the bond as previously formed, either at the time of the Exodus (Ex 6.6–7) or at Sinai (4.20; Ex 19.5–6). **11–13:** A fragment that refers to an ancient covenant ceremony at Shechem, instituted at the

Jordan, these shall stand on Mount Gerizim for the blessing of the people: Simeon, Levi, Judah, Issachar, Joseph, and Benjamin. [13] And these shall stand on Mount Ebal for the curse: Reuben, Gad, Asher, Zebulun, Dan, and Naphtali. [14] Then the Levites shall declare in a loud voice to all the Israelites:

[15] "Cursed be anyone who makes an idol or casts an image, anything abhorrent to the LORD, the work of an artisan, and sets it up in secret." All the people shall respond, saying, "Amen!"

[16] "Cursed be anyone who dishonors father or mother." All the people shall say, "Amen!"

[17] "Cursed be anyone who moves a neighbor's boundary marker." All the people shall say, "Amen!"

[18] "Cursed be anyone who misleads a blind person on the road." All the people shall say, "Amen!"

[19] "Cursed be anyone who deprives the alien, the orphan, and the widow of justice." All the people shall say, "Amen!"

[20] "Cursed be anyone who lies with his father's wife, because he has violated his father's rights."[a] All the people shall say, "Amen!"

[21] "Cursed be anyone who lies with any animal." All the people shall say, "Amen!"

[22] "Cursed be anyone who lies with his sister, whether the daughter of his father or the daughter of his mother." All the people shall say, "Amen!"

[23] "Cursed be anyone who lies with his mother-in-law." All the people shall say, "Amen!"

[24] "Cursed be anyone who strikes down a neighbor in secret." All the people shall say, "Amen!"

[25] "Cursed be anyone who takes a bribe to shed innocent blood." All the people shall say, "Amen!"

[26] "Cursed be anyone who does not uphold the words of this law by observing them." All the people shall say, "Amen!"

28 If you will only obey the LORD your God, by diligently observing all his commandments that I am commanding you

---

[a] Heb *uncovered his father's skirt*

command of Moses (Josh 8.30–35). The antiquity of the tribal list is seen in the facts that Levi is listed as a tribe (Gen 49.5–7) and that the division of the house of Joseph into Manasseh and Ephraim has not yet occurred (Gen 49.22–26; contrast Deut 33.17). The division of the tribes into two groups of six is attested only here. **11:** *The same day,* lit. "on that day," without further specification. **12–13:** *Mount Gerizim for the blessing . . . Mount Ebal for the curse,* see 11.29n. One group of tribes, on Gerizim, proclaims a set of blessings (see 28.1–14); the other, on Ebal, a set of curses (see 28.15–68). **14–26:** Despite the paragraphing in NRSV, v. 14 more likely begins a new section, with a very different conception of the ceremony: The tribe of Levi alone proclaims a set of prohibited actions and *all the people*—acting in unison and not divided into tribes—respond, *Amen* (see Jer 11.3–5). There is no list of blessings (cf. v. 12). Nor is the "curse" intended by v. 13 (a description of divine punishment for wrongful action, as in 28.15–68) provided. The "cursed be" proclamations here stigmatize a summary list of rejected actions while making no references to the consequences of the transgressions. **14:** *Levites,* Deuteronomy's normal term is "levitical priests" (v. 9; 18.1). **15–26:** The twelve curses correspond to the twelve tribes, although this section makes no reference to the tribal division and the people function as a single entity (v. 14). The resulting incongruence points to the many editorial revisions that this chapter has undergone. **15:** See 4.15–31n. **16:** See 5.16. **17:** See 19.14n.

28.1–68: The consequences of obedience or disobedience: blessing or curse. The covenant specifies a series of blessings and curses that follow upon national obedience or disobedience to the law. These are modeled after ancient Near Eastern state treaties, in which the consequences of breach of the treaty are spelled out at its conclusion; this chapter has several close parallels to the *Vassal Treaty of Esarhaddon* (*VTE*), a Neo-Assyrian treaty dating to 672 BCE. The disproportion between the sections devoted to blessing (vv. 1–14) and to curse (vv. 15–68) may be a reaction to the Babylonian conquest, deportation, and exile of Judah (597 and 586 BCE), here recast as a prophetic warning. Two appendixes, vv. 47–57 and 58–68, each seek to make theological sense of that catastrophe. The two other legal collections of the Pentateuch (the Covenant Collection of Ex 21–23; the Holiness Collection of Lev 17–26) similarly end with exhortations to obedience, accompanied by blessings and curses (Ex 23.20–33; Lev 26). Here an inclusio frames and defines the blessings section: *if you . . . obey . . . by diligently observing* (vv. 1,13). **1–2:** The proem emphasizes the conditionality of the exalted status of Israel, perhaps

today, the LORD your God will set you high above all the nations of the earth; [2] all these blessings shall come upon you and overtake you, if you obey the LORD your God:

[3] Blessed shall you be in the city, and blessed shall you be in the field.

[4] Blessed shall be the fruit of your womb, the fruit of your ground, and the fruit of your livestock, both the increase of your cattle and the issue of your flock.

[5] Blessed shall be your basket and your kneading bowl.

[6] Blessed shall you be when you come in, and blessed shall you be when you go out.

[7] The LORD will cause your enemies who rise against you to be defeated before you; they shall come out against you one way, and flee before you seven ways. [8] The LORD will command the blessing upon you in your barns, and in all that you undertake; he will bless you in the land that the LORD your God is giving you. [9] The LORD will establish you as his holy people, as he has sworn to you, if you keep the commandments of the LORD your God and walk in his ways. [10] All the peoples of the earth shall see that you are called by the name of the LORD, and they shall be afraid of you. [11] The LORD will make you abound in prosperity, in the fruit of your womb, in the fruit of your livestock, and in the fruit of your ground in the land that the LORD swore to your ancestors to give

you. [12] The LORD will open for you his rich storehouse, the heavens, to give the rain of your land in its season and to bless all your undertakings. You will lend to many nations, but you will not borrow. [13] The LORD will make you the head, and not the tail; you shall be only at the top, and not at the bottom—if you obey the commandments of the LORD your God, which I am commanding you today, by diligently observing them, [14] and if you do not turn aside from any of the words that I am commanding you today, either to the right or to the left, following other gods to serve them.

[15] But if you will not obey the LORD your God by diligently observing all his commandments and decrees, which I am commanding you today, then all these curses shall come upon you and overtake you:

[16] Cursed shall you be in the city, and cursed shall you be in the field.

[17] Cursed shall be your basket and your kneading bowl.

[18] Cursed shall be the fruit of your womb, the fruit of your ground, the increase of your cattle and the issue of your flock.

[19] Cursed shall you be when you come in, and cursed shall you be when you go out.

[20] The LORD will send upon you disaster, panic, and frustration in everything you attempt to do, until you are destroyed and perish quickly, on account of the evil of your

because of the exile. *High above all the nations* (see also v. 13), a metaphor for the nation's election, also applied to the Davidic dynasty (Ps 89.27). (Contrast 26.19, where this affirmation is unconditional, fulfilling God's past promises.) **3–6:** The six benedictions have their malediction counterpart at vv. 16–19. The two antonym pairs (vv. 3,6) provide a frame to the unit. The opposites form a merism to stress totality (like "night and day"); see 6.7n. **3:** *City* and *field,* "everywhere," urban and rural. **4:** *Fruit . . . livestock,* fecundity is contingent upon obedience to God; see 7.12–14n. **7:** Military success is conditional upon covenantal obedience, rather than strength of arms (9.1–3; Josh 1.6–8). **9:** *The LORD will establish . . . if you keep,* holiness is conditional upon obedience, a shift from other passages where Israel's holiness is not future but present, and not conditional but unconditional (7.6; 14.2; cf. 26.19). **10:** *Called by the name of the LORD,* relationship with God includes accountability and corresponding divine oversight. The formula can apply to either the nation (here; 2 Chr 7.14; Isa 63.19; Jer 14.9) or an individual (Ex 33.12; Jer 15.16). **12:** *Storehouse,* in Israelite and Near Eastern cosmology, primordial waters above the dome of the sky were released as rain (Gen 1.7; 7.11). *Lend . . . borrow,* see 15.6.

28.15–68: Consequences of disobedience. A broad range of misfortunes, from infertility to military defeat (vv. 15–46), precede a second section (vv. 47–68) on foreign invasion, siege, national defeat, and exile, a reversal of the covenantal promises and of the nation's history of salvation: By disobeying the covenant, the nation undoes its own history. **15–46:** A chiastic inclusio frames the section: the initial sequence AB (*not obey . . . observing . . . curses . . . overtake,* v. 15) is repeated at the end as B´A´ (*curses . . . overtaking . . . not obey . . . observing,* v. 45). **15:** A negation of v. 1. **16–19:** Negating vv. 3–6. **20:** Corresponding to the tripartite blessing for obedience (v. 8) stands the triple threat of *disaster* [better, "curse"], *panic, and frustration.* The threats are spelled out in

deeds, because you have forsaken me. [21] The LORD will make the pestilence cling to you until it has consumed you off the land that you are entering to possess. [22] The LORD will afflict you with consumption, fever, inflammation, with fiery heat and drought, and with blight and mildew; they shall pursue you until you perish. [23] The sky over your head shall be bronze, and the earth under you iron. [24] The LORD will change the rain of your land into powder, and only dust shall come down upon you from the sky until you are destroyed.

[25] The LORD will cause you to be defeated before your enemies; you shall go out against them one way and flee before them seven ways. You shall become an object of horror to all the kingdoms of the earth. [26] Your corpses shall be food for every bird of the air and animal of the earth, and there shall be no one to frighten them away. [27] The LORD will afflict you with the boils of Egypt, with ulcers, scurvy, and itch, of which you cannot be healed. [28] The LORD will afflict you with madness, blindness, and confusion of mind; [29] you shall grope about at noon as blind people grope in darkness, but you shall be unable to find your way; and you shall be continually abused and robbed, without anyone to help. [30] You shall become engaged to a woman, but another man shall lie with her. You shall build a house, but not live in it. You shall plant a vineyard, but not enjoy its fruit. [31] Your ox shall be butchered before your eyes, but you shall not eat of it. Your donkey shall be stolen in front of you, and shall not be restored to you. Your sheep shall be given to your enemies, without anyone to help you. [32] Your sons and daughters shall be given to another people, while you look on; you will strain your eyes looking for them all day but be powerless to do anything. [33] A people whom you do not know shall eat up the fruit of your ground and of all your labors; you shall be continually abused and crushed, [34] and driven mad by the sight that your eyes shall see. [35] The LORD will strike you on the knees and on the legs with grievous boils of which you cannot be healed, from the sole of your foot to the crown of your head. [36] The LORD will bring you, and the king whom you set over you, to a nation that neither you nor your ancestors have known, where you shall serve other gods, of wood and stone. [37] You shall become an object of horror, a proverb, and a byword among all the peoples where the LORD will lead you.

[38] You shall carry much seed into the field but shall gather little in, for the locust shall consume it. [39] You shall plant vineyards and dress them, but you shall neither drink the wine nor gather the grapes, for the worm shall eat them. [40] You shall have olive trees throughout all your territory, but you shall not anoint yourself with the oil, for your olives shall drop off. [41] You shall have sons and daughters, but

---

vv. 21–44. *Me,* the first-person reference shifts from Moses to God, as at 7.4; 17.3. **21–44:** This section echoes treaties that the Neo-Assyrian empire imposed on its vassal states, suggesting that the curse section of these state treaties, perhaps in Aramaic translation, provided a model for this chapter. Judah was a vassal to the Assyrian empire (2 Kings 18.13–18) and both Neo-Assyrian and Judean officials spoke Aramaic (2 Kings 18.26–27). **23:** *Bronze . . . iron,* see *VTE* §§63–64: "May [the gods] make your ground like iron . . . Just as rain does not fall from a bronze sky . . ." **25:** Negates v. 7. **26:** Even executed criminals must be buried by sundown, lest the corpse become carrion (21.22–23); abrogation of that law underscores the punishment's horror (Jer 7.33). **27–35:** The apparently arbitrary sequence of punishments closely resembles *VTE* §§39–43, where each curse is associated with a particular Neo-Assyrian god: the moon god Sin with leprosy; the sun god Shamash, blindness; and Dilipat (the planet Venus), rape, dispossession, and pillage. **27:** *Boils of Egypt,* inversion of 7.15. See Ex 9.9–11. **28–29:** *Blindness,* Shamash, the Mesopotamian sun god, the god of justice, punishes disobedience by withholding light and vision; this punishment entails the breakdown of civil order and legal standards. **30:** *Woman . . . house . . . vineyard,* contrast 20.7, which provides the same conditions for exemption from conscription, in different order. **32:** The sale of the children to foreigners as slaves guarantees their non-return (Gen 37.25–38). **36:** Both the Neo-Assyrian army (2 Kings 17) and the Neo-Babylonian invaders (2 Kings 24–25) practiced deportation. **37:** *Byword,* the opposite idea was central to God's covenant with Abraham, whose people were to become the paradigm of divine providence (Gen 12.3). **38–42:** Futility curses. The frustration of human labor through infertility of the harvest (caused by invasion from insects or other natural enemies) is punishment for infringement

they shall not remain yours, for they shall go into captivity. ⁴²All your trees and the fruit of your ground the cicada shall take over. ⁴³Aliens residing among you shall ascend above you higher and higher, while you shall descend lower and lower. ⁴⁴They shall lend to you but you shall not lend to them; they shall be the head and you shall be the tail.

⁴⁵All these curses shall come upon you, pursuing and overtaking you until you are destroyed, because you did not obey the LORD your God, by observing the commandments and the decrees that he commanded you. ⁴⁶They shall be among you and your descendants as a sign and a portent forever.

⁴⁷Because you did not serve the LORD your God joyfully and with gladness of heart for the abundance of everything, ⁴⁸therefore you shall serve your enemies whom the LORD will send against you, in hunger and thirst, in nakedness and lack of everything. He will put an iron yoke on your neck until he has destroyed you. ⁴⁹The LORD will bring a nation from far away, from the end of the earth, to swoop down on you like an eagle, a nation whose language you do not understand, ⁵⁰a grim-faced nation showing no respect to the old or favor to the young. ⁵¹It shall consume the fruit of your livestock and the fruit of your ground until you are destroyed, leaving you neither grain, wine, and oil, nor the increase of your cattle and the issue of your flock, until it has made you perish. ⁵²It shall besiege you in all your towns until your high and fortified walls, in which you trusted, come down throughout your land; it shall besiege you in all your towns throughout the land that the LORD your God has given you. ⁵³In the desperate straits to which the enemy siege reduces you, you will eat the fruit of your womb, the flesh of your own sons and daughters whom the LORD your God has given you. ⁵⁴Even the most refined and gentle of men among you will begrudge food to his own brother, to the wife whom he embraces, and to the last of his remaining children, ⁵⁵giving to none of them any of the flesh of his children whom he is eating, because nothing else remains to him, in the desperate straits to which the enemy siege will reduce you in all your towns. ⁵⁶She who is the most refined and gentle among you, so gentle and refined that she does not venture to set the sole of her foot on the ground, will begrudge food to the husband whom she embraces, to her own son, and to her own daughter, ⁵⁷begrudging even the afterbirth that comes out from between her thighs, and the children that she bears, because she is eating them in secret for lack of anything else, in the desperate straits to which the enemy siege will reduce you in your towns.

of the covenant (Lev 26.20; Am 4.7–12), reversing the blessings of vv. 7–15. **43–44:** Reversing vv. 12b–13. **46:** *A sign and a portent,* the normal phrase for miracles God performed on behalf of Israel at the time of the Exodus, "signs and wonders" (4.34; 6.22; 7.19; 29.3; 34.11; Ex 7.3; 8.23; 10.1–2; 11.9–10), in the singular here designates the divine punishment of Israel.

28.47–57: Scenario of foreign invasion. A later appendix, outside the frame provided by vv. 45–46. **47:** *Because you did not serve,* the future curse is based upon wrongdoing in the past, in contrast to the conditional, future formulation of v. 15, which presents disobedience as a future possibility. *Abundance,* prosperity in the land will cause Israel to forget its source (see 6.11–12; 8.11–20; 33.15,18). **48:** The punishment corresponds precisely to the offense: *Serve* means both sacrificial worship of God (13.5) and labor as a servant or slave (5.13; 13.12). *Iron yoke,* symbolizing vassal status, as in Jer 27–28. **49–57:** Systematic presentation of foreign conquest, proceeding from invasion (vv. 48–50), to the invaders' plunder and despoiling of the land (v. 51), to crippling siege (v. 52), and culminating in the horrors of starvation that arise from the siege (vv. 53–57). These descriptions of the invader and of the consequences of the siege are based upon the literary model of the *Vassal Treaty of Esarhaddon.* **49–52:** Closely parallels Jer 5.15–19. **49:** *Like an eagle,* cf. Ezek 17.3,7; Hab 1.8. **51:** Contrast the idealist war laws of 20.19–20, which prohibit occupiers from despoiling the land. **52:** *It shall besiege you . . . until your . . . walls . . . come down,* the Neo-Assyrian (2 Kings 17.5) and Babylonian armies (2 Kings 24.3; 25.1–7) employed advanced engineering to mount a siege campaign involving ramparts, battering rams, and catapults. **53–57:** The starvation resulting from the siege causes a complete breakdown of the normal social order, as parents become predators of their children and family members compete for food. For cannibalism under siege conditions, see Lev 26.29; 2 Kings 6.28–32; Jer 19.9; Lam 4.10; Ezek 5.10; and *VTE* §§ 47,69,71,75.

58 If you do not diligently observe all the words of this law that are written in this book, fearing this glorious and awesome name, the LORD your God, 59 then the LORD will overwhelm both you and your offspring with severe and lasting afflictions and grievous and lasting maladies. 60 He will bring back upon you all the diseases of Egypt, of which you were in dread, and they shall cling to you. 61 Every other malady and affliction, even though not recorded in the book of this law, the LORD will inflict on you until you are destroyed. 62 Although once you were as numerous as the stars in heaven, you shall be left few in number, because you did not obey the LORD your God. 63 And just as the LORD took delight in making you prosperous and numerous, so the LORD will take delight in bringing you to ruin and destruction; you shall be plucked off the land that you are entering to possess. 64 The LORD will scatter you among all peoples, from one end of the earth to the other; and there you shall serve other gods, of wood and stone, which neither you nor your ancestors have known. 65 Among those nations you shall find no ease, no resting place for the sole of your foot. There the LORD will give you a trembling heart, failing eyes, and a languishing spirit. 66 Your life shall hang in doubt before you; night and day you shall be in dread, with no assurance of your life. 67 In the morning you shall say, "If only it were evening!" and at evening you shall say, "If only it were morning!"—because of the dread that your heart shall feel and the sights that your eyes shall see. 68 The LORD will bring you back in ships to Egypt, by a route that I promised you would never see again; and there you shall offer yourselves for sale to your enemies as male and female slaves, but there will be no buyer.

29 a These are the words of the covenant that the LORD commanded Moses to make with the Israelites in the land of Moab, in addition to the covenant that he had made with them at Horeb.

a   Ch 28.69 in Heb

28.58–68: Undoing the Exodus. This seems to represent a third layer to the chapter. 58: *This book,* how the commandments have become transformed from oral proclamation to written text is unexplained, since it is not until 31.9,24 that Moses commands that his teaching be put into writing. Moreover, hitherto the required obedience was to the plural "commandments" (vv. 1,9,13,15,45). Here, for the first time in the chapter, Israel must obey a codified, single *law* (Heb "torah" or "teaching"). *This . . . name,* NRSV should have capitalized "Name" to clarify its distinctive use; it stands directly for God (elsewhere in the Pentateuch only Lev 24.11). 59–68: Consistent with the "book" perspective, the consequences for breach of the written teaching have a different focus: a systematic reversal of the national history, covenantal promises, and theology included in that teaching. The punishment amounts to an anti-Torah that will dissolve the national identity. 59–61: After the miracle of the Exodus, God had promised, if the people obeyed, "I will not bring upon you any of the diseases that I brought upon the Egyptians" (Ex 15.26). 62: *Stars . . . heaven,* God will cancel the promise made to Abraham that his people shall be as numerous as the stars of heaven (Gen 15.5–6). 63: Dispossession and exile (as in 4.26; Lev 26.33–39) rescind the covenantal promise of the land, contravening even the unconditional divine promises of Gen 12.7; 13.17. 64: The double loss of Israel's identity: Dispersion of the population dissolves its political identity, and idol worship dissolves its religious identity. 65–67: In the absence of the national destiny provided by the covenant, historical existence has no meaning. 68: Forced return to Egypt, where the former taskmasters now spurn Israel's desperate bid to sell itself back into slavery and thus to undo its own history. For selling oneself into slavery under financial hardship to pay off debts or gain support ("indenture"), see Lev 25.39. *Route . . . never see again* (cf. 17.16), reverses the unconditional promise at the time of the Exodus: "the Egyptians whom you see today you shall never see again" (Ex 14.13).

29.1–30.20: Third discourse of Moses. The ratification ceremony for the covenant of the plains of Moab. Israel is formally adjured to enter the covenant: To swear to obey the laws of chs 12–26 under penalty of the sanctions of ch 28. 29.1–29: A didactic review of Israel's history (vv. 2–9) precedes an imprecation to ensure loyal adherence to the covenant (vv. 10–29). 1: Editorial heading. The laws, hitherto plural ("statutes and ordinances," 5.1; 12.1; cf. 4.45), are now a coherent, single tradition: *the covenant. In addition to,* presentation of the laws as a supplement to the Decalogue, in contrast to 4.44–45; 12.1, which mention neither the Decalogue nor the laws' supplementary status. This may be an effort to explain addition of the Decalogue to an earlier form

2 ªMoses summoned all Israel and said to them: You have seen all that the LORD did before your eyes in the land of Egypt, to Pharaoh and to all his servants and to all his land, ³ the great trials that your eyes saw, the signs, and those great wonders. ⁴ But to this day the LORD has not given you a mind to understand, or eyes to see, or ears to hear. ⁵ I have led you forty years in the wilderness. The clothes on your back have not worn out, and the sandals on your feet have not worn out; ⁶ you have not eaten bread, and you have not drunk wine or strong drink—so that you may know that I am the LORD your God. ⁷ When you came to this place, King Sihon of Heshbon and King Og of Bashan came out against us for battle, but we defeated them. ⁸ We took their land and gave it as an inheritance to the Reubenites, the Gadites, and the half-tribe of Manasseh. ⁹ Therefore diligently observe the words of this covenant, in order that you may succeedᵇ in everything that you do.

¹⁰ You stand assembled today, all of you, before the LORD your God—the leaders of your tribes,ᶜ your elders, and your officials, all the men of Israel, ¹¹ your children, your women, and the aliens who are in your camp, both those who cut your wood and those who draw your water— ¹² to enter into the covenant of the LORD your God, sworn by an oath, which the LORD your God is making with you today; ¹³ in order that he may establish you today as his people, and that he may be your God, as he promised you and as he swore to your ancestors, to Abraham, to Isaac, and to Jacob. ¹⁴ I am making this covenant, sworn by an oath, not only with you who stand here with us today before the LORD our God, ¹⁵ but also with those who are not here with us today. ¹⁶ You know how we lived in the land of Egypt, and how we came through the midst of the nations through which you passed. ¹⁷ You have seen their detestable things, the filthy idols of wood and stone, of silver and gold, that were among them. ¹⁸ It may be that there is among you a man or woman, or a family or tribe, whose heart is already turning away from the LORD our God to serve the gods of those nations. It may be that there is among you a root sprouting poisonous and bitter growth. ¹⁹ All who hear the words of this oath and bless themselves, thinking in their hearts, "We are safe even though we go our own stubborn ways" (thus bringing

a Ch 29.1 in Heb

b Or *deal wisely*

c Gk Syr: Heb *your leaders, your tribes*

of Deuteronomy. **2**: *You have seen*, as at 5.2–4, the present generation is in reality one generation removed from the miraculous events. **3**: *Signs . . . wonders*, see 28.46n. **4**: *But to this day*, more accurately: "The LORD has not given you . . . until today." The admonition creates a tension with the preceding two verses: The addressees who "have seen" the miraculous events (v. 2), which their own "eyes saw" (v. 3), are accused of having lacked *eyes to see*. The castigation reflects the episodes of rebellion (9.7–24). **5–6**: The speech reinterprets the wilderness wandering, originally intended as divine punishment of Israel (Num 14.13–35), and presents it positively, in didactic terms. **5**: *I*, see 7.4; 17.3; 28.20,68. *Clothes . . . feet*, see 8.4. **6**: *You have not eaten bread . . . not drunk wine*, the sense is, "It was not bread that you ate . . . nor wine that you drank." The manna, quails, and water that Israel consumed were supplied by divine providence (8.2–5; Ex 16; Num 11.4–9,31–33). *Know*, not abstract speculation but the recognition of God's historical actions on behalf of the nation. *I am the LORD your God*, better, "I, Yahweh, am your God" (6.4; Ex 20.2). **7–8**: See 1.4; 2.26–3.22; Num 21.21–35. **10**: *Stand assembled* in formal array for a public legal ceremony (cf. Ps 82.1). *Today*, transition from historical review (vv. 1–8) to present adjuration (similarly, *VTE* § 33). **12**: *Covenant . . . sworn by an oath*, the formula recurs at v. 14, thus framing the central idea, the binding relationship between God and Israel. *Oath*, more accurately, "its imprecation" or "its curse." Neo-Assyrian treaties were validated by means of a concluding imprecation (*VTE* §§37–56,58–106). The partner accepts the consequences of noncompliance. The laws of chs 12–26 represent the stipulations; ch 28, the sanctions; and ch 29, the imprecation. **14–15**: The covenant binds even future generations (as in *VTE* §§ 25,33,34,57); consequently, punishment for infraction extends to the third and fourth generation (5.9; Ex 20.5; 34.7). **17–27**: A stark, two-part warning, showing how the attempt of even a single individual secretly to withdraw from the covenant (vv. 17–19) jeopardizes the entire nation (vv. 20–28). **18**: *Turning away*, transferring loyalty to other gods (13.6–11; 17.2–7). *Poisonous and bitter growth*, Hos 10.4; Am 5.7; 6.12. **19**: *Bless themselves*, rather than proclaim the imprecation, hoping to escape the sanctions of the covenant. *Moist and dry*, probably

disaster on moist and dry alike) ª— [20] the Lord will be unwilling to pardon them, for the Lord's anger and passion will smoke against them. All the curses written in this book will descend on them, and the Lord will blot out their names from under heaven. [21] The Lord will single them out from all the tribes of Israel for calamity, in accordance with all the curses of the covenant written in this book of the law. [22] The next generation, your children who rise up after you, as well as the foreigner who comes from a distant country, will see the devastation of that land and the afflictions with which the Lord has afflicted it— [23] all its soil burned out by sulfur and salt, nothing planted, nothing sprouting, unable to support any vegetation, like the destruction of Sodom and Gomorrah, Admah and Zeboiim, which the Lord destroyed in his fierce anger— [24] they and indeed all the nations will wonder, "Why has the Lord done thus to this land? What caused this great display of anger?" [25] They will conclude, "It is because they abandoned the covenant of the Lord, the God of their ancestors, which he made with them when he brought them out of the land of Egypt. [26] They turned and served other gods, worshiping them, gods whom they had not known and whom he had not allotted to them; [27] so the anger of the Lord was kindled against that land, bringing on it every curse written in this book. [28] The Lord uprooted them from their land in anger, fury, and great wrath, and cast them into another land, as is now the case." [29] The secret things belong to the Lord our God, but the revealed things belong to us and to our children forever, to observe all the words of this law.

30

When all these things have happened to you, the blessings and the curses that I have set before you, if you call them to mind among all the nations where the Lord your God has driven you, [2] and return to the Lord your God, and you and your children obey him with all your heart and with all your soul, just as I am commanding you today, [3] then the Lord your God will restore your fortunes and have compassion on you, gathering you again from all the peoples among whom the Lord your God has scattered you. [4] Even if you are exiled to the ends of the world,ᵇ from there the Lord your God

ª Meaning of Heb uncertain
ᵇ Heb *of heaven*

paired antonyms designating totality (see 28.3–6n.). **20:** *Passion,* God's zeal to defend the mutual exclusivity of the covenant relation (5.9; Ex 34.14). *Descend on them,* more literally, "crouch down upon them" (cf. Gen 4.7), an animate image. *Blot out,* the erasure of a tablet or scroll (Num 5.23), given a theological cast: Following Mesopotamian models, the divine decree of human fate is recorded in a heavenly book, with erasure symbolizing punishment (9.14; Gen 6.7; Ex 17.14; 32.32; 2 Kings 14.27; Ps 9.6). **22–28:** The negative instruction. As the wilderness wandering provided an instructional lesson for the nation (vv. 5–6), so will Israel, transformed into a devastation, provide an object lesson. Vv. 24–28 provide a reversal of the Israelite child's inquiry about God's redemptive acts (4.32–38; Ex 12.25–27; 13.8–10). **23:** *Sulfur and salt* were used in antiquity as defoliants by invading armies. *Sodom . . . Zeboiim,* proverbial wicked cities in the arid area around the Dead Sea (cf. Gen 19.24–25; Isa 1.9–10). **25:** *The covenant,* conflating the covenants of Horeb and Moab (29.1). **26:** *Gods . . . not allotted to them,* as at 32.8–9, each nation is allocated its own god, and the Lord is the God of Israel. As at 5.8–9, the existence of other deities is here conceded. Contrast 4.19, where it is rather only inanimate "stars . . . that God has allotted," which reinterprets the polytheistic image from the later perspective of monotheism. **28:** *As is now the case,* reference to the present implies that the chapter was composed subsequent to the Babylonian exile of 586 bce. **29:** *Secret,* concealed acts that God will punish (vv. 18–19), or future events. More likely, the antithesis with *revealed* rejects religions of esoteric speculation that restrict access to truth to a learned few. This law (Heb "torah"), based upon a public revelation (ch 5) and Moses' instruction (chs 12–26), is accessible to all.

30.1–10: Reassurance of restoration. This section, with its emphasis on restoration, does not logically follow ch 29, and is most likely an insertion that serves the religious needs of a community different from that of the book's original audience (see v. 5n.). The unit employs the Heb word "shub," translated "return," "repent," or "restore," in seven different ways to establish the close bond between human repentance and divine forgiveness: (v. 1) "If you *call* them to mind . . . (v. 2) and *return* . . . (v. 3) then the Lord will *restore your fortunes* . . . and gathering you *again* . . . (v. 8) Then you shall *again* obey . . . (v. 9) For the Lord will *again* take delight . . . (v. 10) because you

will gather you, and from there he will bring you back. [5] The LORD your God will bring you into the land that your ancestors possessed, and you will possess it; he will make you more prosperous and numerous than your ancestors.

[6] Moreover, the LORD your God will circumcise your heart and the heart of your descendants, so that you will love the LORD your God with all your heart and with all your soul, in order that you may live. [7] The LORD your God will put all these curses on your enemies and on the adversaries who took advantage of you. [8] Then you shall again obey the LORD, observing all his commandments that I am commanding you today, [9] and the LORD your God will make you abundantly prosperous in all your undertakings, in the fruit of your body, in the fruit of your livestock, and in the fruit of your soil. For the LORD will again take delight in prospering you, just as he delighted in prospering your ancestors, [10] when you obey the LORD your God by observing his commandments and decrees that are written in this book of the law, because you turn to the LORD your God with all your heart and with all your soul.

[11] Surely, this commandment that I am commanding you today is not too hard

for you, nor is it too far away. [12] It is not in heaven, that you should say, "Who will go up to heaven for us, and get it for us so that we may hear it and observe it?" [13] Neither is it beyond the sea, that you should say, "Who will cross to the other side of the sea for us, and get it for us so that we may hear it and observe it?" [14] No, the word is very near to you; it is in your mouth and in your heart for you to observe.

[15] See, I have set before you today life and prosperity, death and adversity. [16] If you obey the commandments of the LORD your God[a] that I am commanding you today, by loving the LORD your God, walking in his ways, and observing his commandments, decrees, and ordinances, then you shall live and become numerous, and the LORD your God will bless you in the land that you are entering to possess. [17] But if your heart turns away and you do not hear, but are led astray to bow down to other gods and serve them, [18] I declare to you today that you shall perish; you shall not live long in the land that you are crossing the Jordan to enter and possess. [19] I call heaven and earth to witness against you today that I

[a] Gk: Heb lacks *If you obey the commandments of the LORD your God*

turn." 1: *Call them to mind,* lit. "take [them] to heart." 4: Cf. Am 9.2–3. 5: *Bring you into the land that your ancestors possessed,* the "you" explicitly refers to the Judean exiles in Babylon, rather than the desert generation whom Moses addresses on the plains of Transjordan. *More . . . numerous,* the covenantal promise (Gen 17.2; 22.17). For similar claims that the future will repeat the past while also surpassing it, see Isa 42.9; 43.6–20; 51.9–11. 6: *The LORD . . . will circumcise your heart,* God is the agent; previously Israel itself was to "circumcise . . . the foreskin of your heart" (see 10.16n.). The change suggests skepticism about the people's ability to effect such a change of heart independently (see Jer 31.31–34; Ezek 11.19–20; 36.26–27). 7: The curses are deflected from Israel to the adversary; contrast 28.47,49, where the foreign nation is God's agent to punish Israel. 9: *Fruit,* blessings upon return conforming to those promised upon initial entry (28.4). 10: *Obey the LORD . . . by observing . . . this book of the law,* or, more precisely, "this book of the teaching." The reference is to the text of Deuteronomy itself, which replaces the live speech of Moses (12.28,32) or prophetic speech (18.18–9) as revealer of God's word.

30.11–20: The original continuation of ch 29 is composed of two sections, vv. 11–14,15–20. 11–14: Turning their own imagery against them, the passage challenges the assumptions of Near Eastern wisdom schools about the inaccessibility of divine wisdom and the limits of human knowledge (cf. Job 28). 11: The accessibility of Moses' teaching. *Surely,* better, "because," logically continuing 29.29 and emphasizing the ready accessibility of the divinely given teaching. (The NRSV translation is an accommodation to the insertion of vv. 1–10.) *This commandment,* the teaching as a whole (as at 6.1). 12: See Prov 30.4. *That we may hear it,* lit. "so that he may proclaim it to us." 14: *In your mouth,* in antiquity, texts were normally read, taught, and recited aloud (6.7; 31.19, 21; Josh 1.8). 15–20: The necessity of choice. Life outside the covenant is *death.* 16: *Loving . . . walking in his ways,* in Near Eastern treaties, "love" means to act loyally and to honor the commitments of the treaty (6.5n.). 19: *Heaven and earth to witness,* see 4.26n.; 32.1n. *Choose life,* the didactic use of life and death suggests the influence of wisdom teachings upon the authors (Prov 11.19; 14.27; 18.21; cf. Jer 8.3; 21.8).

have set before you life and death, blessings and curses. Choose life so that you and your descendants may live, [20] loving the LORD your God, obeying him, and holding fast to him; for that means life to you and length of days, so that you may live in the land that the LORD swore to give to your ancestors, to Abraham, to Isaac, and to Jacob.

31

When Moses had finished speaking all[a] these words to all Israel, [2] he said to them: "I am now one hundred twenty years old. I am no longer able to get about, and the LORD has told me, 'You shall not cross over this Jordan.' [3] The LORD your God himself will cross over before you. He will destroy these nations before you, and you shall dispossess them. Joshua also will cross over before you, as the LORD promised. [4] The LORD will do to them as he did to Sihon and Og, the kings of the Amorites, and to their land, when he destroyed them. [5] The LORD will give them over to you and you shall deal with them in full accord with the command that I have given to you. [6] Be strong and bold; have no fear or dread of them, because it is the LORD your God who goes with you; he will not fail you or forsake you."

[7] Then Moses summoned Joshua and said to him in the sight of all Israel: "Be strong and bold, for you are the one who will go with this

---

[a] Q Ms Gk: MT *Moses went and spoke*

31.1–34.14: The death of Moses and the formation of the Torah. With the imprecation of ch 30 concluding the treaty between God and Israel, Deuteronomy now returns to Moses, the mediator of the treaty. His life is ending, and the question of succession is given a two-fold answer, since Moses was both political and religious leader of Israel. Joshua will be his political and military successor (31.1–8,14–15,23; 32.44,48–52; 34.9) and "a book . . . of this law" (31.24) will instruct the nation in religion. Deuteronomy thus ends in paradox: Moses, ostensibly the book's narrator, narrates his own death (ch 34), and the book of the teaching, already presupposed (29.27), nevertheless provides an account of its own formation (31.9–13,24–29). The conclusion of Deuteronomy also ends the Pentateuch. In incorporating Deuteronomy into that larger work, editors with the background of the exile added perspectives on the function of the entire Torah in the people's life. Finally, the Pentateuch's literary precedent of a patriarch's death-bed bequest and blessing (Gen 27; 48–49) led to the incorporation of "The Song of Moses" (32.1–43) and of "The Blessing of Moses" (ch 33), each of which may originally have circulated independently. The resulting text thus blends several viewpoints. Themes like the appointment of Joshua begin, then begin again from a different perspective, and then are continued only after an apparent digression, which marks the insertion of new material.

31.1–29: Moses makes arrangements for his death. Publicly announcing his imminent death, Moses invests Joshua with leadership and initiates the writing of the book of the teaching, which is to be taught regularly to the entire people. These two legacies seem independent of each other and suggest that an earlier narrative about leadership has been expanded with an account of the formation of Deuteronomy. Each tradition, furthermore, is doubled; the chapter thus contains many layers of tradition. First is a double announcement of Moses' imminent death: v. 2 (at his own initiative, citing previous divine commandment, in which he appoints Joshua directly) and vv. 14–15 (with no reference to a previous announcement, and with divine appointment of Joshua). Second is a double tradition of transfer of leadership: Although Moses begins a public ceremony in order himself to appoint the new leader (vv. 7–8), a variant tradition has God commission Joshua directly (vv. 14–15,23). Third is a double tradition of Moses' writing: one of "the book . . . of this law" (v. 24) and one of "this song" (v. 19). Each is a "witness" (vv. 21,26). The first tradition, which refers to Deuteronomy, was supplemented by the second in order to integrate the following "Song of Moses" (32.1–43). Fourth, in the "Song" tradition, Israel's future apostasy is already a foregone conclusion (vv. 16–22,28–29); in the covenant-making tradition, there is yet hope that, by taking the law to heart, Israel might avoid catastrophe (vv. 9–13,24–27). 2: *One hundred twenty years old,* the Hebrew places the age first, thus immediately announcing the key issue: Moses has reached the maximum age for humans (Gen 6.3), making it urgent to assure continuity of leadership. *I am no longer able to get about,* lit. "to go out and come in," i.e., lead the nation in military campaigns (28.6; Num 27.17; 1 Kings 3.7; cf. 2 Sam 11.1). 2–3: Resumes 1.37–38; 3.27–28. The death of a key leader and the transfer of his authority mark important turning points within the larger context of the Deuteronomistic History and partially follow a common model (cf. Josh 23.2; 1 Sam 12.2; 1 Kings 2.1–2). 4: The successful military campaigns in Transjordan provide assurance in the conquest of Canaan; Moses aims to counter Israel's intimidation (1.27–28;

people into the land that the Lord has sworn to their ancestors to give them; and you will put them in possession of it. [8] It is the Lord who goes before you. He will be with you; he will not fail you or forsake you. Do not fear or be dismayed."

[9] Then Moses wrote down this law, and gave it to the priests, the sons of Levi, who carried the ark of the covenant of the Lord, and to all the elders of Israel. [10] Moses commanded them: "Every seventh year, in the scheduled year of remission, during the festival of booths,[a] [11] when all Israel comes to appear before the Lord your God at the place that he will choose, you shall read this law before all Israel in their hearing. [12] Assemble the people—men, women, and children, as well as the aliens residing in your towns so that they may hear and learn to fear the Lord your God and to observe diligently all the words of this law, [13] and so that their children, who have not known it, may hear and learn to fear the Lord your God, as long as you live in the land that you are crossing over the Jordan to possess."

[14] The Lord said to Moses, "Your time to die is near; call Joshua and present yourselves in the tent of meeting, so that I may commission him." So Moses and Joshua went and presented themselves in the tent of meeting, [15] and the Lord appeared at the tent in a pillar of cloud; the pillar of cloud stood at the entrance to the tent.

[16] The Lord said to Moses, "Soon you will lie down with your ancestors. Then this people will begin to prostitute themselves to the foreign gods in their midst, the gods of the land into which they are going; they will forsake me, breaking my covenant that I have made with them. [17] My anger will be kindled against them in that day. I will forsake them and hide my face from them; they will become easy prey, and many terrible troubles will come upon them. In that day they will say, 'Have not these troubles come upon us because our God is not in our midst?' [18] On that day I will surely hide my face on account of all the evil they have done by turning to other gods. [19] Now therefore write this song, and teach it to the Israelites; put it in their mouths, in order that this song may be a witness for me against the Israelites. [20] For when I have brought them into the land flowing with milk and honey, which I promised on oath to their ancestors, and they have eaten their fill and grown fat, they will turn to other gods and serve them, despising me and breaking my covenant. [21] And when many terrible troubles come upon them, this song will confront them as a witness, because it will not be lost from the mouths of their descendants. For I know what they are inclined to do even now, before I have brought them into the land that I promised them on oath." [22] That very day Moses wrote this song and taught it to the Israelites.

[23] Then the Lord commissioned Joshua son of Nun and said, "Be strong and bold, for

---

a   Or *tabernacles*; Heb *succoth*

Num 13–14). **5:** *Command,* the ban (7.1–7; 12.29–31; 20.16–18). **9–13:** The institution of a covenant ceremony to be held in the sabbatical year (15.1–11), during the *festival of booths* (16.13–15). **12:** Stipulating that the teaching (NRSV "law"; Heb "torah") is taught to women, minors, and aliens, the law does not restrict the responsibility to observe the covenant to males (contrast Ex 19.15). **14:** *Tent of meeting,* in the Yahwistic source (J), the site outside camp where God speaks to Moses, with Joshua in attendance (Ex 33.7–11); contrast the Priestly literature's tabernacle, located in the center of the Israelite encampment, which houses the ark of the covenant and the altar (Ex 26–27; Num 7.1–3; 18.1–7). *So that I may commission him,* the standard tradition involves direct commission by Moses at God's command (3.27–28; 34.9; Num 27.18–23). **15:** The double reference to the *pillar of cloud,* located both *at* [or, "in"] *the tent* (cf. Ex 30.36; 40.34–35; Lev 16.2) and *at the entrance to the tent* (cf. Ex 33.9–10; Num 12.5) blends the traditions associated with each of the two tents (see v. 14n.). **17–18:** *Our God,* better, "our gods": The people will have strayed so far from the covenant that they attribute the resulting divine punishment to other gods, leading to God's angry response. **22–23:** The sequence of *Moses wrote* (v. 22) and . . . *commissioned* (v. 23) uses the same key terms as "When Moses finished writing . . . Moses commanded" (vv. 24–25). The repetition of the paired terms provided a means for editors to insert the section on the song (vv. 16–22). **23:** *The Lord commissioned,* lit. "he commanded," with no subject identified. NRSV has added the divine reference to clarify that the verse does not continue v. 22, but directly resumes vv. 14–15.

you shall bring the Israelites into the land that I promised them; I will be with you."

24 When Moses had finished writing down in a book the words of this law to the very end, 25 Moses commanded the Levites who carried the ark of the covenant of the LORD, saying, 26 "Take this book of the law and put it beside the ark of the covenant of the LORD your God; let it remain there as a witness against you. 27 For I know well how rebellious and stubborn you are. If you already have been so rebellious toward the LORD while I am still alive among you, how much more after my death! 28 Assemble to me all the elders of your tribes and your officials, so that I may recite these words in their hearing and call heaven and earth to witness against them. 29 For I know that after my death you will surely act corruptly, turning aside from the way that I have commanded you. In time to come trouble will befall you, because you will do what is evil in the sight of the LORD, provoking him to anger through the work of your hands."

30 Then Moses recited the words of this song, to the very end, in the hearing of the whole assembly of Israel:

32 Give ear, O heavens, and I will speak;
let the earth hear the words of my
mouth.
2 May my teaching drop like the rain,
my speech condense like the dew;
like gentle rain on grass,
like showers on new growth.

3 For I will proclaim the name of the LORD;
ascribe greatness to our God!

4 The Rock, his work is perfect,
and all his ways are just.
A faithful God, without deceit,
just and upright is he;
5 yet his degenerate children have dealt
falsely with him,[a]
a perverse and crooked generation.
6 Do you thus repay the LORD,
O foolish and senseless people?
Is not he your father, who created you,
who made you and established you?
7 Remember the days of old,
consider the years long past;
ask your father, and he will inform you;
your elders, and they will tell you.
8 When the Most High[b] apportioned the
nations,
when he divided humankind,
he fixed the boundaries of the peoples
according to the number of the gods;[c]
9 the LORD's own portion was his people,
Jacob his allotted share.

10 He sustained[d] him in a desert land,
in a howling wilderness waste;

a   Meaning of Heb uncertain
b   Traditional rendering of Heb *Elyon*
c   Q Ms Compare Gk Tg: MT *the Israelites*
d   Sam Gk Compare Tg: MT *found*

31.30–32.43: The Song of Moses. The Song is a late insertion that reflects upon Israel's history, probably presupposing the exile. In form it is a revised and expanded prophetic lawsuit (cf. Isa 1; Jer 2; Mic 6; Ps 50) with this structure: introduction and summoning of witnesses (vv. 1–3); accusation (vv. 4–6); recital of God's loving actions (vv. 7–14); indictment (vv. 15–18); declaration of punishment (vv. 19–25). Yet God interrupts his own judicial sentence to recognize a risk to his honor: Other nations might conclude that Israel's God was weak should they see Israel destroyed (vv. 26–27). God reverses himself, cancels the punishment, and decides instead to punish Israel's enemies so as to vindicate Israel (vv. 28–42). The Song concludes with a call for the divine council to praise God for his actions; the call may originate from within the divine council itself (v. 43; similarly Ps 29.1). A prose frame links the Song to Deuteronomy, identifying Moses, otherwise unmentioned, as its speaker (31.30; 32.44). **32.2:** *Teaching,* the original prophetic lawsuit has been combined with wisdom themes (Prov 1.5; 4.2; 17.21). **4:** *Rock,* more accurately, "Mountain," a title applied to the high god of ancient Canaan (see v. 8n.) and to the biblical God (vv. 15,18,30–31,37; Isa 44.8; Ps 78.35). **6:** *Created you,* when God redeemed Israel from Egypt (Ex 15.16, correcting NRSV "acquired"). **8:** *Most High,* or *Elyon* (text note b), is the title of El, the senior god who sat at the head of the divine council in the Ugaritic literature of ancient Canaan. The Bible applies El's title to Israel's God (Gen 14.18–22; Num 24.16; Ps 46.4; 47.2; esp. 78.35, where it is parallel to Rock). *Gods,* the lesser gods who make up the divine council (Ps 82.1; 89.6–7), to each of whom Elyon here assigns a foreign nation. **9:** *The LORD's own portion,* NRSV has added *own* in order to identify Yahweh with Elyon and avoid the impression that Yahweh is merely a member of the pantheon; see also 4.19n. **10:** *Sustained,* more

he shielded him, cared for him,
  guarded him as the apple of his eye.
[11] As an eagle stirs up its nest,
  and hovers over its young;
as it spreads its wings, takes them up,
  and bears them aloft on its pinions,
[12] the LORD alone guided him;
  no foreign god was with him.
[13] He set him atop the heights of the land,
  and fed him with[a] produce of the field;
he nursed him with honey from the
  crags,
  with oil from flinty rock;
[14] curds from the herd, and milk from the
  flock,
  with fat of lambs and rams;
Bashan bulls and goats,
  together with the choicest wheat—
  you drank fine wine from the blood of
  grapes.
[15] Jacob ate his fill;[b]
  Jeshurun grew fat, and kicked.
  You grew fat, bloated, and gorged!
He abandoned God who made him,
  and scoffed at the Rock of his salvation.
[16] They made him jealous with strange
  gods,
  with abhorrent things they provoked
  him.
[17] They sacrificed to demons, not God,
  to deities they had never known,
to new ones recently arrived,
  whom your ancestors had not feared.
[18] You were unmindful of the Rock that
  bore you;[c]
  you forgot the God who gave you birth.

[19] The LORD saw it, and was jealous;[d]
  he spurned[e] his sons and
  daughters.
[20] He said: I will hide my face from
  them,
  I will see what their end will be;
for they are a perverse generation,
  children in whom there is no
  faithfulness.
[21] They made me jealous with what is no
  god,
  provoked me with their idols.
So I will make them jealous with what is
  no people,
  provoke them with a foolish nation.
[22] For a fire is kindled by my anger,
  and burns to the depths of Sheol;
it devours the earth and its increase,
  and sets on fire the foundations of the
  mountains.
[23] I will heap disasters upon them,
  spend my arrows against them:
[24] wasting hunger,
  burning consumption,
  bitter pestilence.
The teeth of beasts I will send against
  them,
  with venom of things crawling in the
  dust.
[25] In the street the sword shall bereave,
  and in the chambers terror,

a Sam Gk Syr Tg: MT *he ate*
b Q Mss Sam Gk: MT lacks *Jacob ate his fill*
c Or *that begot you*
d Q Mss Gk: MT lacks *was jealous*
e Cn: Heb *he spurned because of provocation*

likely "found" (Hos 9.10). Overlooking the Egypt traditions, the Song here traces the beginnings of Israel to the wilderness period, romanticizing its ideal purity (similarly Hos 2.14–15; Jer 2.2–3; contrast Deut 9.6–7,22–27; Ezek 20). *Apple of his eye*, lit. the aperture or pupil of the eye. **11:** Israel as God's fledgling; see Ex 19.4. **13:** *Heights*, see Ex 15.17. **14:** *Curds*, symbolic of extravagant hospitality offered to special guests (Gen 18.8; Judg 5.25). *Bashan*, in northern Transjordan, was famous for its cattle. **15:** *Jeshurun*, probably meaning "upright," is a poetic term for Israel (33.5,26; Isa 44.2). **17:** *Demons*, better, "protective spirits" (also Ps 106.37). *Not God*, the language is sarcastic: "a non-god" (see v. 21). *To deities*, better, "to gods." **18:** God is depicted as a woman; *gave you birth* refers specifically to labor pain (Isa 51.2; cf. Isa 42.14). **21:** *Jealous* refers to the covenant's demand for exclusive loyalty to God (5.8; 6.15; Num 25.11). Accordingly, the punishment for breach of the covenant metes out precise retributive justice (see 19.19n.). The Hebrew emphasizes the sarcasm: thus, *with what is no god* and *what is no people*, lit. "with a non-god," "with a non-people." *Their idols*, lit. "their vapors" or "their vanities," even "their vapidities" (Jer 8.19; 10.15; 16.19; Eccl 1.2). **22:** *Sheol*, the underworld (Gen 37.35; 1 Sam 2.6; Ps 139.8); the abode of all the dead, not a place of damnation like the later idea of hell. **23:** *Arrows*, divine punishments (v. 42; Ezek 5.16; Ps 7.13; 18.14; 38.2). **24:** *Burning consumption*, the name of the Ugaritic god of pestilence; thus better, "devoured

for young man and woman alike,
    nursing child and old gray head.
26 I thought to scatter them[a]
    and blot out the memory of them from
       humankind;
27 but I feared provocation by the enemy,
    for their adversaries might
       misunderstand
and say, "Our hand is triumphant;
    it was not the LORD who did all this."

28 They are a nation void of sense;
    there is no understanding in them.
29 If they were wise, they would
      understand this;
    they would discern what the end
      would be.
30 How could one have routed a thousand,
    and two put a myriad to flight,
unless their Rock had sold them,
    the LORD had given them up?
31 Indeed their rock is not like our Rock;
    our enemies are fools.[a]
32 Their vine comes from the vinestock of
      Sodom,
    from the vineyards of Gomorrah;
their grapes are grapes of poison,
    their clusters are bitter;
33 their wine is the poison of serpents,
    the cruel venom of asps.

34 Is not this laid up in store with me,
    sealed up in my treasuries?
35 Vengeance is mine, and recompense,
    for the time when their foot shall slip;

because the day of their calamity is at
      hand,
    their doom comes swiftly.

36 Indeed the LORD will vindicate his
      people,
    have compassion on his servants,
when he sees that their power is gone,
    neither bond nor free remaining.
37 Then he will say: Where are their gods,
    the rock in which they took refuge,
38 who ate the fat of their sacrifices,
    and drank the wine of their libations?
Let them rise up and help you,
    let them be your protection!

39 See now that I, even I, am he;
    there is no god besides me.
I kill and I make alive;
    I wound and I heal;
    and no one can deliver from my hand.
40 For I lift up my hand to heaven,
    and swear: As I live forever,
41 when I whet my flashing sword,
    and my hand takes hold on judgment;
I will take vengeance on my adversaries,
    and will repay those who hate me.
42 I will make my arrows drunk with blood,
    and my sword shall devour flesh—
with the blood of the slain and the
      captives,
    from the long-haired enemy.

a   Gk: Meaning of Heb uncertain

by Plague." **25:** *Woman,* better, "young woman," to emphasize the double merism (28.3–6n.), which symbolizes the totality of the slaughter. **26–27:** The Song here pivots from judgment of Israel to her vindication at the expense of the foreign invaders. **27:** *I feared,* God has feelings and vulnerabilities (as at Gen 6.6). **28–33:** God's soliloquy is interrupted by another voice, who refers to God in the third person and speaks on behalf of Israel (vv. 30–31). **28–29:** The foreign nation, like Israel, has failed in wisdom, justifying God's judgment (see v. 6). **30:** Ironically inverts the holy war idea (3.22; 20.1): The enemy is reproached for failing to understand that it owes its triumph over Israel to God rather than force of arms. God will thus punish Israel's conquerors to preserve his honor (see 9.25–29; Num 14.13–16). **32:** *Sodom . . . Gomorrah,* here symbolizing moral corruption more than ruinous devastation (cf. 29.23n.). **34:** *This,* the punishment of the foreign nation, which is about to be announced (vv. 35–42). *Laid up . . . sealed up,* the formal legal procedures for rolling and then sealing a witnessed deed or contract with wax, so that the unaltered document can subsequently be introduced into court as evidence (Isa 8.16; Jer 32.9–15). **35:** *Vengeance,* better, "vindication," since the idea is not revenge but justice. **36:** *Their power is gone, neither bond nor free,* God will act when no one survives who can take charge or provide assistance (2 Kings 14.26; cf. 1 Kings 14.10; 21.21; 2 Kings 9.8). **39:** Similar to exilic Second Isaiah (Isa 41.4; 43.10,13; 44.6; 45.6–7,22; 48.12). **41:** *Takes,* lit. "returns," in retributive justice. Thus, *vengeance* gives the wrong idea (see v. 35n.). *Those who hate me,* treaty language that refers to disloyal action that violates the covenant; thus better

⁴³ Praise, O heavens,ᵃ his people,
  worship him, all you gods!ᵇ
For he will avenge the blood of his children,ᶜ
  and take vengeance on his adversaries;
he will repay those who hate him,ᵇ
  and cleanse the land for his people.ᵈ

⁴⁴ Moses came and recited all the words of this song in the hearing of the people, he and Joshuaᵉ son of Nun. ⁴⁵ When Moses had finished reciting all these words to all Israel, ⁴⁶ he said to them: "Take to heart all the words that I am giving in witness against you today; give them as a command to your children, so that they may diligently observe all the words of this law. ⁴⁷ This is no trifling matter for you, but rather your very life; through it you may live long in the land that you are crossing over the Jordan to possess."

⁴⁸ On that very day the LORD addressed Moses as follows: ⁴⁹ "Ascend this mountain of the Abarim, Mount Nebo, which is in the land of Moab, across from Jericho, and view the land of Canaan, which I am giving to the Israelites for a possession; ⁵⁰ you shall die there on the mountain that you ascend and shall be gathered to your kin, as your brother Aaron died on Mount Hor and was gathered to his kin; ⁵¹ because both of you broke faith with me among the Israelites at the waters of Meribath-kadesh in the wilderness of Zin, by failing to maintain my holiness among the Israelites. ⁵² Although you may view the land from a distance, you shall not enter it—the land that I am giving to the Israelites."

33 This is the blessing with which Moses, the man of God, blessed the Israelites before his death. ² He said:

The LORD came from Sinai,
  and dawned from Seir upon us;ᶠ
he shone forth from Mount Paran.
With him were myriads of holy ones;ᵍ

ᵃ Q Ms Gk: MT *nations*
ᵇ Q Ms Gk: MT lacks this line
ᶜ Q Ms Gk: MT *his servants*
ᵈ Q Ms Sam Gk Vg: MT *his land his people*
ᵉ Sam Gk Syr Vg: MT *Hoshea*
ᶠ Gk Syr Vg Compare Tg: Heb *upon them*
ᵍ Cn Compare Gk Sam Syr Vg: MT *He came from Ribeboth-kodesh,*

translated, "those who reject me" (5.9). **43:** The second, fourth, and fifth lines have been restored in light of the Dead Sea Scrolls. With *heavens* and *land,* the verse forms an inclusio to "heavens . . . earth" (v. 1), thus framing the poem and returning the focus to Israel's impending entry into the promised land. His people, instead, referring to God: "O heavens, rejoice with him!" *All you gods,* the divine council (v. 8n.; Ps 29.1), probably removed from the received Heb text because of the conflict with monotheism (see vv. 8–9n.). *Avenge the blood,* God as divine blood avenger (cf. 19.6), who removes the stain of Israel's blood from the land by requiting the aggressor for having spilled it (19.11–13). *Cleanse,* since the moral stain on the land can only be "wiped clean" (the word's literal meaning) with the blood of the murderer (Num 35.33–34; cf. Deut 21.8): here, the foreign nation. God's position is nonetheless morally ambiguous, since it was he who had sanctioned the foreign invasion as punishment for Israel's wrongdoing (vv. 19–26). *His people,* instead, referring to God: "O heavens, rejoice with him!"

32.44–47: Double conclusion to the Song. Two originally separate conclusions joined by Deuteronomy's editors. **44:** *All the words . . . ,* an inclusio (see 31.30). **45–47:** A separate section, the original continuation of 31.29 prior to the insertion of the Song. **46:** *All the words,* the laws of Deuteronomy (31.24); now, following the insertion of the Song, reinterpreted to refer to both.

32.48–52: Moses commanded to die. This section repeats the announcement of Moses' death (Num 27.12–14) and thus joins it to its logical continuation, the narrative of that death (Deut 34). The original connection between these two Priestly sections was broken by Deuteronomy's insertion into the Pentateuch. **49:** *This mountain of the Abarim, Mount Nebo,* as in the Priestly narrative (Num 27.12; 33.47); but, according to the Deuteronomistic tradition, Pisgah (3.27). The two traditions are joined at 34.1. **50:** *You shall die,* lit. "Die . . . !" This unusual imperative establishes that Moses both lives and dies at God's command (34.5n.). *Gathered to your kin,* burial in a family tomb, where the bones of the generations would be gathered together (2 Kings 8.24; 22.20; cf. 1 Kings 13.31); here used metaphorically, since Moses' burial place is unknown (34.6). *Mount Hor,* consistent with the Priestly tradition (Num 20.22–29; 33.37–39); but, in the Deuteronomistic tradition, "Moserah" (10.6). **51:** *You broke faith,* see Num 20.1–13; cf. 1.37n.; 4.21.

33.1–29: The Blessing of Moses. In form a father's blessing of his progeny when death is imminent (Gen 27.27–29; 48.15–16; 49.1–28; cf. 1 Kings 2.1–4), Moses' address to the tribes arrayed before him (29.2,10; 31.7,30)

at his right, a host of his own.[a]
[3] Indeed, O favorite among[b] peoples,
all his holy ones were in your charge;
they marched at your heels,
accepted direction from you.
[4] Moses charged us with the law,
as a possession for the assembly of
Jacob.
[5] There arose a king in Jeshurun,
when the leaders of the people
assembled—
the united tribes of Israel.

[6] May Reuben live, and not die out,
even though his numbers are few.

[7] And this he said of Judah:
O LORD, give heed to Judah,
and bring him to his people;

strengthen his hands for him,[c]
and be a help against his adversaries.

[8] And of Levi he said:
Give to Levi[d] your Thummim,
and your Urim to your loyal one,
whom you tested at Massah,
with whom you contended at the waters
of Meribah;
[9] who said of his father and mother,
"I regard them not";
he ignored his kin,
and did not acknowledge his
children.

a   Cn Compare Gk: meaning of Heb uncertain
b   Or O lover of the
c   Cn: Heb with his hands he contended
d   Q Ms Gk: MT lacks Give to Levi

treats all Israel as his own progeny, gathered before the deathbed (Gen 48.2; 49.33). Following the model of other blessings, the speaker addresses the tribes in the singular, as if they were individual sons (contrast v. 19). This poem is clearly an insertion, intruding between God's command to Moses to ascend Nebo to prepare for his death (32.49–50) and Moses' compliance (34.1–5). The literary model of the patriarchal blessing of the twelve tribes (vv. 6–25) has been consciously embedded in a framing poem addressed to a united Israel (vv. 1–5,26–29) that imitates victory hymns to the divine warrior (Judg 5; Ps 18.7–15; Hab 3; cf. Ex 15). That older model has been significantly transformed, however. In vv. 1–4, the expected climax of the divine theophany in the military defeat of the enemy has been totally eclipsed (cf. vv. 26–29), although it is the logical precondition for the proclamation of God as king (v. 5). The new climax is instead Moses' proclamation of Torah (v. 4n.). The reference here to Sinai instead of Deuteronomy's usual Horeb (see 1.2n.) is an attempt to integrate Deuteronomy with the other literary sources of the Pentateuch (Ex 19–20; Lev 25.1; Num 10.12). The editors have used an inclusio pattern to embed the blessing (with its focus upon the individual tribes) into the framing hymn to the divine warrior (where united Israel is the focus). Thus the word symmetry LORD:Jacob:Jeshurun::Jeshurun´ :Jacob´:LORD´ (A:B:C::C´:B´:A´; vv. 2,4,5,26,28,29) brackets the inserted blessing. Older hymns to the divine warrior sometimes list the tribes' contributions to the battle (Judg 5.14–18), which facilitates the combination of the two models. Although it draws upon older textual traditions, the poem in its present form is almost certainly exilic or postexilic. The combination of two separate literary models and the emphasis of divinely revealed Torah rather than the divine warrior's manifestation in battle suggest the later literary setting. **1:** *Man of God,* a type of prophet (Josh 14.6; 1 Sam 9.6; 1 Kings 13.1–32; 17.18,24; 2 Kings 4.7–41); this term is not used earlier of Moses in Deuteronomy. **2:** *The LORD . . . dawned,* God's departure from his distant mountain stronghold, dramatically coming to the rescue of his people, closely follows the model of Judg 5.4; Hab 3.3. *Myriads of holy ones,* the divine council who accompany God into battle (32.8n.; Ps 68.17; 89.7). *Sinai . . . Seir,* the parallelism locates *Sinai* near *Seir,* associated with Edom (Judg 5.4), in southern Transjordan. This tradition diverges from the one placing the mountain in the Sinai Peninsula, far to the southwest. **3:** *His holy ones,* originally, the divine council of v. 2, reinterpreted to refer to Israel (7.6; 14.2,21; 26.19; 28.9; Lev 19.2; Num 16.3) to provide a transition to v. 4. **4:** *Moses charged us,* since Moses is himself the speaker (v. 1), this verse is an insertion that presents the promulgation of the Torah (NRSV "law") as the climax of the divine warrior's theophany. **5:** *A king,* almost certainly God as divine king of Israel (Ex 15.18; Num 23.21; Judg 8.22–23; 1 Sam 8.7; Isa 33.22; Ps 29.10). *Jeshurun,* see 32.15n. **6:** *Reuben,* who once had the leadership of the firstborn (see Gen 49.3–4), is apparently threatened with extinction. (Simeon, Jacob's second born, is entirely missing.) **7:** *Judah,* in sore trouble because of an unnamed adversary, should be helped by other tribes. **8–11:** *Levi,* once a warlike tribe (Gen 49.5–7), is to receive the prerogatives of the priesthood: to teach *law,* or Torah (v. 10), and to officiate at the altar. **8:** *Thummim* and

For they observed your word,
  and kept your covenant.
[10] They teach Jacob your ordinances,
  and Israel your law;
they place incense before you,
  and whole burnt offerings on your
    altar.
[11] Bless, O LORD, his substance,
  and accept the work of his hands;
crush the loins of his adversaries,
  of those that hate him, so that they do
    not rise again.

[12] Of Benjamin he said:
  The beloved of the LORD rests in
    safety—
  the High God[a] surrounds him all day
    long—
  the beloved[b] rests between his
    shoulders.

[13] And of Joseph he said:
  Blessed by the LORD be his land,
    with the choice gifts of heaven
      above,
    and of the deep that lies beneath;
[14] with the choice fruits of the sun,
    and the rich yield of the months;
[15] with the finest produce of the ancient
      mountains,
    and the abundance of the everlasting
      hills;
[16] with the choice gifts of the earth and its
      fullness,
    and the favor of the one who dwells on
      Sinai.[c]
  Let these come on the head of Joseph,
    on the brow of the prince among his
      brothers.
[17] A firstborn[d] bull—majesty is his!
    His horns are the horns of a wild ox;

with them he gores the peoples,
  driving them to[e] the ends of the
    earth;
such are the myriads of Ephraim,
  such the thousands of Manasseh.

[18] And of Zebulun he said:
  Rejoice, Zebulun, in your going out;
    and Issachar, in your tents.
[19] They call peoples to the mountain;
    there they offer the right sacrifices;
  for they suck the affluence of the
      seas
    and the hidden treasures of the
      sand.

[20] And of Gad he said:
  Blessed be the enlargement of Gad!
    Gad lives like a lion;
    he tears at arm and scalp.
[21] He chose the best for himself,
    for there a commander's allotment was
      reserved;
  he came at the head of the people,
    he executed the justice of the LORD,
    and his ordinances for Israel.

[22] And of Dan he said:
  Dan is a lion's whelp
    that leaps forth from Bashan.

[a] Heb *above him*
[b] Heb *he*
[c] Cn: Heb *in the bush*
[d] Q Ms Gk Syr Vg: MT *His firstborn*
[e] Cn: Heb *the peoples, together*

Urim, the priestly divination devices (Ex 28.30; Ezra 2.63). *Massah* and *Meribah*, see Ex 17.1–7; Num 20.2–13. **9:** On Levi's zealous loyalty to the covenant, at the expense of *father and mother . . . kin, and . . . his children*, thus complying with 13.7, see Ex 32.25–29. **13–17:** See Gen 49.25–26. **16–17:** By ascribing primacy of rule and the status of *firstborn* to Joseph, this blessing conflicts with the law affirming the norm of primogeniture (21.15–17). **16:** *Who dwells on Sinai* refers to Ex 3.1–6 (see text note c); 19.1–20.21. *Prince*, Joseph (the Northern Kingdom, destroyed in 722 BCE) enjoyed greater prestige than Judah (v. 7). **17:** *Ephraim* and *Manasseh*, the two tribes making up "the house of Joseph" (Gen 48.13–14). **18–19:** *Zebulun* and *Issachar* will enjoy great influence owing to the resources of the Mediterranean and Lake Chinnereth, later known as the Sea of Galilee (Gen 49.13). **20–21:** *Gad* occupied the *best* tableland in Transjordan but aided the other tribes in the occupation of Canaan (Num 32). **22:** *Dan*, vigorous as a *lion's whelp*, must here already have migrated from its original tribal allotment on the coastal

²³ And of Naphtali he said:
　O Naphtali, sated with favor,
　　full of the blessing of the Lord,
　　possess the west and the south.

²⁴ And of Asher he said:
　Most blessed of sons be Asher;
　　may he be the favorite of his brothers,
　　and may he dip his foot in oil.
²⁵ Your bars are iron and bronze;
　　and as your days, so is your strength.

²⁶ There is none like God, O Jeshurun,
　who rides through the heavens to your
　　help,
　majestic through the skies.
²⁷ He subdues the ancient gods,ᵃ
　shattersᵇ the forces of old;ᶜ
he drove out the enemy before you,
　and said, "Destroy!"
²⁸ So Israel lives in safety,
　untroubled is Jacob's abodeᵈ
in a land of grain and wine,
　where the heavens drop down dew.
²⁹ Happy are you, O Israel! Who is like
　　you,
　a people saved by the Lord,

the shield of your help,
　and the sword of your triumph!
Your enemies shall come fawning to you,
　and you shall tread on their backs.

34 Then Moses went up from the plains of Moab to Mount Nebo, to the top of Pisgah, which is opposite Jericho, and the Lord showed him the whole land: Gilead as far as Dan, ² all Naphtali, the land of Ephraim and Manasseh, all the land of Judah as far as the Western Sea, ³ the Negeb, and the Plain— that is, the valley of Jericho, the city of palm trees—as far as Zoar. ⁴ The Lord said to him, "This is the land of which I swore to Abraham, to Isaac, and to Jacob, saying, 'I will give it to your descendants'; I have let you see it with your eyes, but you shall not cross over there." ⁵ Then Moses, the servant of the Lord, died there in the land of Moab, at the Lord's command. ⁶ He was buried in a valley in the land of Moab, opposite Beth-peor, but no one knows his burial place to this day.

ᵃ Or *The eternal God is a dwelling place*
ᵇ Cn: Heb *from underneath*
ᶜ Or *the everlasting arms*
ᵈ Or *fountain*

plain to the far north at the base of Mount Hermon (Judg 18). *Bashan,* see 32.14n. **23:** *Naphtali,* located in the region of the Sea of Galilee *west* and *south* of Dan. **24–25:** *Asher,* located below Phoenicia, is to be strong and prosperous. **26–29:** The resumption of the hymn to the divine warrior (vv. 2–5), and a return to the focus upon *Jeshurun* (v. 26), meaning all *Israel* (v. 28). **26:** Much like the Canaanite storm god Baal, Israel's divine warrior rides upon the clouds (Ps 18.10; 68.33; Isa 19.1). **27:** NRSV justifiably reinterprets the Hebrew (see text notes *a, b*) in order to continue the mythic imagery of v. 26. **28:** As in Ugaritic epic, the theophany of the divine warrior and his proclamation as king results in the fertility of the land. **29:** *Tread on their backs,* a standard symbol of military triumph (Josh 10.24; Ps 110.1; also attested in Neo-Assyrian reliefs).

　　34.1–12: The death of Moses. This chapter, the original continuation of ch 31 and 32.48–52, highlights the absence of access to Moses; since his burial site is unknown, it cannot become a venerated shrine. The Torah alone is his enduring bequest. At another level, however, it also continues Num 27, where God had commanded Moses to "go up this mountain" to survey the promised land before his death, and to "lay your hand" upon Joshua, to transfer the mantle of authority to him (vv. 12,18), bracketing Deuteronomy and suggesting that editors interrupted the narrative in order to include Deuteronomy in the Pentateuch. **1:** *Went up,* responding to the command of 32.49; Num 27.12. The verse joins two different traditions about the site of Moses' death: *Mount Nebo,* which is in Transjordan, east of Jericho; and Mount *Pisgah,* which is slightly to its west, and unmentioned in 32.49. Seeking to preserve both traditions, the editor presents them as if they were the same. **2–3:** The lofty vantage point allows Moses to look northward to the Sea of Galilee (area of the tribal allotment of Dan and *Naphtali*), to the *Western Sea* (the Mediterranean), south to the *Negeb* desert and along the Jordan rift valley as far south as *Zoar* (once located at the southern end of the Dead Sea as one of the "cities of the Plain"; Gen 14.2,8; 19.29). **5:** *At the Lord's command,* see 32.50n. The unusual formulation greatly honors Moses, who, despite advanced age, does not die of old age nor succumb to physical or intellectual infirmity. **6:** *He was buried,* the Heb states, "He buried him," a clear indication that God himself buried Moses, as he himself sealed Noah into the ark (Gen 7.16). Instead of Moses' progeny assuming the responsibility of caring for the dead, God

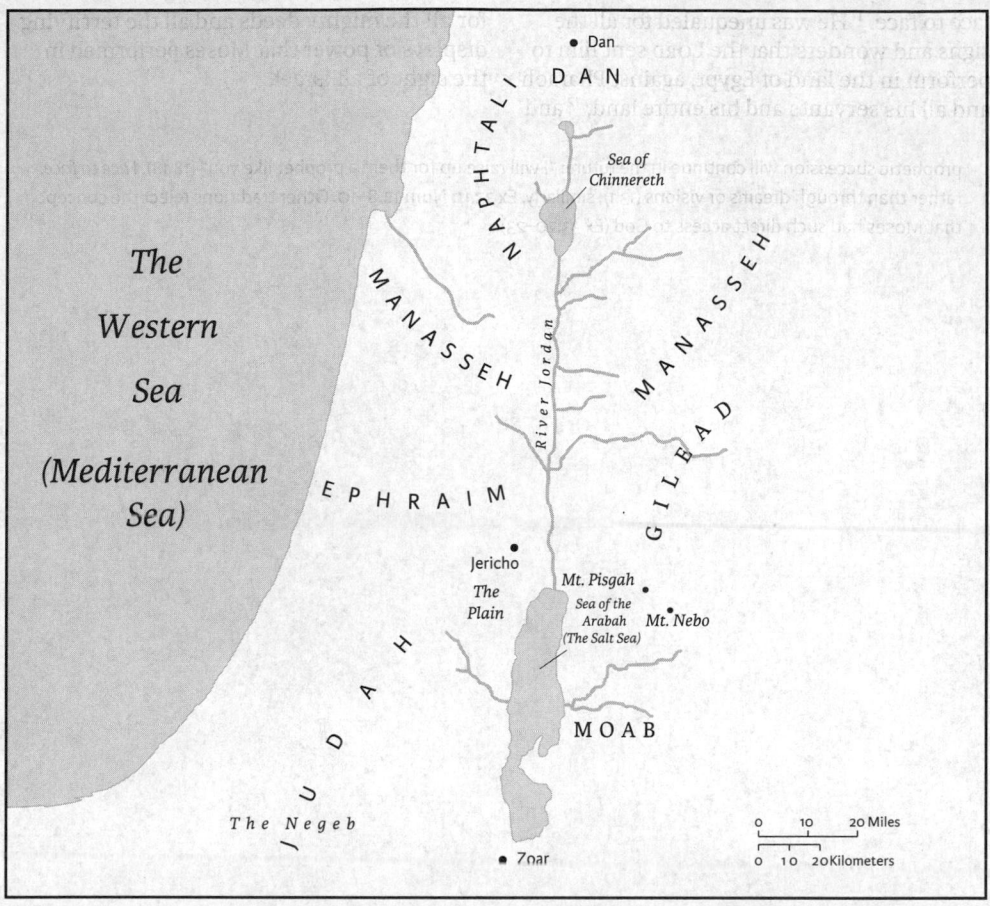

DAN

• Dan

NAPHTALI

Sea of
Chinnereth

MANASSEH

MANASSEH

River Jordan

GILEAD

The

Western

Sea

(Mediterranean
Sea)

EPHRAIM

• Jericho

The
Plain

Mt. Pisgah •

Sea of the
Arabah   Mt. Nebo
(The Salt Sea)

JUDAH

MOAB

The Negeb

• Zoar

| 0 | 10 | 20 Miles |
| 0 | 10 | 20 Kilometers |

What Moses saw from Mt. Nebo.

---

[7] Moses was one hundred twenty years old when he died; his sight was unimpaired and his vigor had not abated. [8] The Israelites wept for Moses in the plains of Moab thirty days; then the period of mourning for Moses was ended.

[9] Joshua son of Nun was full of the spirit of wisdom, because Moses had laid his hands on him; and the Israelites obeyed him, doing as the LORD had commanded Moses.

[10] Never since has there arisen a prophet in Israel like Moses, whom the LORD knew

undertook it personally. *Beth-peor,* 3.29; 4.46; Josh 13.20. *No one knows his burial place,* thus precluding pilgrimages to the site as a shrine. **7:** *One hundred twenty,* see 31.2n. **8:** *Thirty days,* so also for Aaron (Num 20.29), the full mourning period stipulated for a parent (21.13). **9:** *Full of the spirit of wisdom,* as at 1.13 and 16.18–20, Deuteronomy revises earlier traditions to stress wisdom as the essential qualification of office, and thus what Joshua receives from Moses. In Num 27.18, Joshua already possessed an undefined "spirit" (often associated with prophecy or possession), while Moses was to transfer his "authority" to him. *Laid his hands on him,* as at Num 27.22–23, a means of transfer of attributes (Lev 16.21; Num 8.10–13), here used for investiture into office. **10–12:** Moses as the greatest exemplar of prophecy both in direct access to divine revelation and in power to work miracles. The double elevation, which differs from his more human representation elsewhere in the book, suggests an editor's later, idealizing retrospective, with Deuteronomy now worked into the Pentateuch as a whole. **10:** *Never since,* more correctly, "But there never again arose in Israel a prophet like Moses." NRSV obscures the discrepancy between the perspective of this verse and the divine promise to Moses that the line of

face to face. [11] He was unequaled for all the signs and wonders that the LORD sent him to perform in the land of Egypt, against Pharaoh and all his servants and his entire land, [12] and for all the mighty deeds and all the terrifying displays of power that Moses performed in the sight of all Israel.

prophetic succession will continue in the future: "I will raise up for them a prophet like you" (18.18). *Face to face*, rather than through dreams or visions (13.1); similarly, Ex 33.11; Num 12.8–10. Other traditions reject the concept that Moses had such direct access to God (Ex 33.20–23).

INTRODUCTION TO THE HISTORICAL BOOKS

THE HISTORICAL BOOKS AND HISTORIOGRAPHY

The Christian bishop Athanasius, in the fourth century CE, first used the term "histories" for this section of the Bible, which now comprises the books of Joshua, Judges, Ruth, Samuel, Kings, Chronicles, Ezra, Nehemiah, and Esther. It is a misleading title, since these books cover a wide range of genres and often are not historical in modern senses of the word. Furthermore, there are several books that are similar to some of these "historical books," yet they are found in different sections of the Bible.

Large sections of the preceding books of Genesis, Exodus, and Numbers, and much of the opening section of Deuteronomy, contain narratives about the past. Similarly, there are several psalms that survey the past (e.g., Pss 78, 105, 106, 107). Yet, this material is not incorporated into the Historical Books. Thus, this section does not represent the collection of all works of the same genre, and its development as a canonical division is best understood in relation to the broader development of the biblical canon. Moreover, in the traditional Jewish arrangement of the books of the Bible, the books of Joshua, Judges, Samuel, and Kings are called the Former Prophets, thus beginning the second major division of the Hebrew Bible, the Prophets, which follows the Torah, the first five books of the Bible. The books of Ruth, Chronicles, Ezra, Nehemiah, and Esther, however, are found in the third major division, the Writings. Given this somewhat artificial nature of the canonical section the Historical Books, the rest of this introduction examines the nature of biblical historical texts, broadly construed, with a focus on the books Joshua through Esther, which now comprise the section of the Bible called Historical Books.

The idea that historical writing should capture the events "as they really were," that historians should attempt to write an objective account of the events of the past, is a notion that developed in European universities in modern times. Before that, history was typically didactic in nature, teaching the readers how to be good citizens or how to lead proper religious lives. Sometimes histories were produced in the royal court, in which case they were apologetic, showing how the king fulfilled his royal duties; elsewhere they were written by religious officials who aimed to show that their particular religious practices were correct. Surviving historical documents from the ancient Near East show similar religious and ideological goals. Thus, it should not be surprising that the biblical writers are not necessarily interested in the accurate recording of real events; rather, they use narratives about the past to illustrate various issues of significance to their audience, the ancient Israelite community.

It is easiest to understand the biblical notion of history by first focusing on works that are outside this canonical division. Exodus 13.3 begins: "Moses said to the people, 'Remember this day on which you came out of Egypt, out of the house of slavery.'" This would seem to suggest the importance of history for its own sake. However, this unit continues with a set of commandments that directly result from this event: "no leavened bread shall be eaten" (v. 3); "Seven days you shall eat unleavened bread, and on the seventh day there shall be a festival to the Lord" (v. 6); "no leavened bread shall be seen in your possession, and no leaven shall be seen among you in all your territory" (v. 7); "You shall tell your child on that day" (v. 8); "It shall serve for you as a sign on your hand and as a reminder on your forehead" (v. 9); "you shall set apart to the Lord all that first opens the womb. All the firstborn of your livestock that are males shall be the Lord's" (v. 12). These laws suggest the Exodus is to be remembered not as a disembodied historical event, as the beginning of v. 3 might suggest; rather, the Exodus is key because it serves as the basis for the observance of a central set of laws or norms.

The use of historical material in Psalms is even more instructive, since in them traditions about the past are typically found in a context that explicitly highlights their theological significance or purpose. For example, in Psalm 78 a particular set of traditions is chosen and shaped so

> "that the next generation might know them,
> the children yet unborn,

and rise up and tell them to their children,
    so that they should set their hope in God,
and not forget the works of God,
    but keep his commandments;
and that they should not be like their ancestors,
    a stubborn and rebellious generation,
a generation whose heart was not steadfast,
    whose spirit was not faithful to God" (vv. 6–8).

Psalm 106 uses "history" quite differently. It tells how God saved Israel time after time, despite their covenant violations, forming an argument to God that they should be rescued again:

"Save us, O Lord our God,
    and gather us from among the nations,
that we may give thanks to your holy name
    and glory in your praise" (v. 47).

Unfortunately, the Historical Books are usually not as explicit about their purposes as these psalms or Exodus 13; for this reason, the Historical Books need to be subjected to internal analysis, in order to see what motivations and interests shaped them.

ORGANIZATION INTO BOOKS AND LARGER UNITS

In pursuing this task, we must be mindful that the division of some biblical writings into separate books is just as arbitrary as the designation of a particular set of books as a single canonical unit, such as Historical Books. The division of Samuel, Kings, and Chronicles into two separate books is not original and was first done in the Greek Bible (the Septuagint [LXX]) so that each book would be of more reasonable size. In the formation of the canon, the books of Ezra and Nehemiah were originally considered a single work, and it is possible that the books of Joshua and Judges, which blend together well (see especially Josh 24.29–31 and Judg 2.8–10), were also perceived as a single work at an earlier period. Even the divisions between these larger works are not always certain; the first two chapters of Kings, for example, which narrate events at the end of David's life, fit the book of Samuel better than their current place.

In fact, it has been proposed that since the books of Joshua, Judges, Samuel, and Kings, along with the preceding book of Deuteronomy, fit so well together, these five books were edited together as a single work. This work is typically called the Deuteronomistic History, meaning the history written under the influence of ideas found in the book of Deuteronomy. This theory has much to commend it: These five books do read as a unified whole from a chronological perspective, narrating a continuous history from the end of the life of Moses through the Babylonian exile in the early sixth century BCE, and they share many phrases and ideological notions, such as an insistence on exclusive worship of God and the tragic consequences of idolatry, a concern with the centrality of Jerusalem, and a belief in the eternal supremacy of the dynasty founded by King David. If this theory is correct, the size of the Deuteronomistic History, and the long period that it covers, is quite remarkable, especially for an ancient historical work.

Many details of this theory remain debated; some scholars suggest that these books are not unified enough to be the work of a single individual, intellectual school, or movement. For example, the book of Samuel shows remarkably few contacts with the language of Deuteronomy, and the book of Kings contains narratives in which the great prophets Elijah and Elisha are legitimately active outside the Jerusalem Temple (see especially 1 Kings 18, concerning Elijah on Mount Carmel). Thus, various theories have been suggested concerning successive editions of the Deuteronomistic History, which many believe was begun in the seventh century under the Judean King Josiah (640–609 BCE), but completed only in the Babylonian exile (586–538 BCE) or later. Some suggest that the lack of unity is due to non-Deuteronomistic material that has been added at a late stage to an earlier Deuteronomistic History. There have also been attempts to isolate narratives that might have preceded the Deuteronomistic History and other sources used by the Deuteronomistic Historians, and to discern their original purposes before these narratives and sources became integrated into the larger literary work. In the last decade, some scholars have felt that the many differences outweigh the similarities, and the hypothesis of a Deuteronomistic history should be discarded. All agree that this collection has a long and complicated history, so it is impossible to speak of a unified purpose or interest in the compilation of the books of Joshua, Judges, Samuel, and Kings. They reflect at the minimum different interests at the stages of their development, pre-Deuteronomic, Deuteronomistic, and postexilic. The interests of each individual book of the Deuteronomistic History are discussed in the Introductions to those particular books.

Scholars have also found many similarities between Chronicles and Ezra-Nehemiah and have posited that these works belong to a single large history composed by the Chronicler, which parallels the Deuteronomistic History. A closer look at Chronicles and Ezra-Nehemiah, however, shows that they differ from each other in outlook and vocabulary, and that the general similarities between them are best attributed not to common authorship, but to the common time in which they were written, most likely the fourth century BCE.

Chronicles is a retelling with significant variations of the books of Genesis through Kings. It is likely that its author had some access to many external sources not found in our canonical Bibles, but the main feature of Chronicles is the remarkable way in which its author deals with sources, rewriting them to fit a particular notion of historical probability, namely, what really could have happened based on notions of how the world worked. For example, in the book of Kings, which does not have a clear retribution theory (a theory concerning punishment and reward), the Judean King Manasseh (698/687–642 BCE) is depicted as the most evil king of Judah, who is ultimately responsible for the destruction of the Temple in 586 (2 Kings 21). The same source, however, indicates that Manasseh reigned for fifty-five years, longer than any other king. For many biblical writers, a long life was a sign of divine favor. The contradiction between the behavior of Manasseh and his long reign did not bother the Deuteronomistic Historians, who did not believe that each individual king needed to be punished or rewarded for his behavior. The Chronicler, however, did believe in this type of retribution theology, and the Deuteronomistic Historians' depiction of Manasseh in Kings was clearly troublesome. For this reason, the Chronicler rewrote the life of Manasseh, adding 2 Chronicles 33.10–13:

> The LORD spoke to Manasseh and to his people, but they gave no heed. Therefore the LORD brought against them the commanders of the army of the king of Assyria, who took Manasseh captive in manacles, bound him with fetters, and brought him to Babylon. While he was in distress he entreated the favor of the LORD his God and humbled himself greatly before the God of his ancestors. He prayed to him, and God received his entreaty, heard his plea, and restored him again to Jerusalem and to his kingdom. Then Manasseh knew that the LORD indeed was God.

Thus, Manasseh fits the paradigms that the author of Chronicles believed to be true: All people need to be warned before they are punished; repentance is extremely effective; and individuals may succeed only if their behavior is meritorious. These beliefs forced a revision of the source's account so that Manasseh's life could be properly illustrative. Other examples of this type of revisionism are found throughout Chronicles and are discussed in the Introductions to 1 and 2 Chronicles; since, in the case of Samuel and Kings, we no longer have the sources on which they are based, we can only wonder if this type of radical reworking characterizes all the Historical Books.

SMALLER WORKS

The books of Ruth and Esther are both short stories, historical fictions, which are quite different in nature from the works discussed above, but very similar to the books of Tobit and Judith in the Apocrypha. They are more literary than the larger works of the Deuteronomistic Historians and the Chronicler; that is, their authors self-consciously manipulated their prose for esthetic as well as ideological purposes. For example, part of the structuring of Ruth involves symmetry: an 'eshet hayil ("a worthy woman" [3.11]), meets and marries a gibbor hayil ("a worthy man"; NRSV "a prominent rich man" [2.1]), and they live happily ever after. The book also opens with an ironic statement that is only apparent in Hebrew: There is a famine in "the house of bread" (Bethlehem). Esther as well is tightly structured, for example, using dinner parties as a major plot device for the book's progress. Despite the literary artistry of these books, however, they are also history in the sense outlined earlier—they narrate a past in order to convey lessons relevant to the community. The particular characteristics of these two very different books, each set in a distinct country and time, and each reflecting remarkably different ideologies, may be found in the Introduction to each.

The book of Ezra differs from these other Historical Books in its use of extensive quotations of official Persian documents (e.g., 7.12–26), which many scholars believe to be authentic. The book of Nehemiah lacks these documents but is exceptional in its own way: It is the only book in this collection to narrate history extensively from a first-person perspective, as a type of memoir, as in 13.15: "In those days I saw in Judah people treading wine presses on the sabbath, and bringing in heaps of grain and loading them on donkeys; and also wine, grapes, figs, and all kinds of burdens, which they brought into Jerusalem on the sabbath day; and I warned them at that time against selling food." In general, Ezra-Nehemiah is closer to the events that it narrates than any other biblical book, and thus it may reflect those events with greater accuracy than other biblical works, which are typically removed by centuries from the events being described. Nevertheless, we must also recognize the strong biases of this book, which is interested in fostering the importance of the Torah as the central document for the postexilic community (see especially Neh 8–9), and in emphasizing the grave dangers of intermarriage (Ezra 9–10; Neh 13). Thus, even Ezra-Nehemiah, which contains archival material and first-person accounts, and is among the latest of the books in this canonical division, should not be seen as straightforward, representative, and accurate history.

THE HISTORICAL BOOKS AND HISTORICITY

The problematic nature of all of these texts as historical documents does not mean that we have no idea of the historical periods that they cover, or that they are entirely useless as historical sources. Each text needs to be weighed individually in terms of its date of composition and its likely goals. Using these criteria, there are reasons to accept the veracity of, for example, the dry notice in 1 Kings 14.25–26 ("In the fifth year of King Rehoboam, King Shishak of Egypt came up against Jerusalem; he took away the treasures of the house of the Lord and the treasures of the king's house; he took everything. He also took away all the shields of gold that Solomon had made"), which might even come from an archival source. In contrast, there are good reasons to be suspicious of the historicity of the long, detailed, and embellished story of David slaying Goliath in 1 Sam 17; this story uses late biblical Hebrew language, comes from a different source than the surrounding material in Samuel, and is structured like a fairy-tale, in that the poor, short, unexpected hero gets to marry the tall king's daughter by killing the giant who had vilified God. Additionally, 2 Sam 21.19 reads: "Then there was another battle with the Philistines at Gob; and Elhanan son of Jaare-oregim, the Bethlehemite, killed Goliath the Gittite, the shaft of whose spear was like a weaver's beam." It is much more likely that a short tradition in which Goliath is killed by a relatively unknown figure (Elhanan) would be the source for the long, elaborate tale attributing the same event to the well-known David, rather than vice versa. Thus, the modern historian must subject each text in these Historical Books to the type of internal analysis used on nonbiblical historical texts.

There are a number of cases where we do have external, ancient Near Eastern written evidence that deals with events depicted in these Historical Books. For example, the events surrounding the siege of Jerusalem by the Assyrian King Sennacherib in 701 BCE are narrated in several Assyrian sources and are also depicted in the palace reliefs of that king. These sources suggest that part of the terse account in 2 Kings 18.13–16 is quite accurate, while the highly developed continuation of the story in chs 19 and 20, especially the note in 19.35, that the angel of the Lord killed 185,000 Assyrian soldiers in a single night, is most likely imaginative. Similarly, from various Mesopotamian sources, we know of a "house of Omri," and Omri's name is also mentioned on the Moabite Mesha Stele. This confirms the existence of the king of the Northern Kingdom of Israel mentioned in 1 Kings 16.23–28. However, Kings tells little of Omri's achievements during his twelve years as monarch, other than his building of Samaria and the notice that: "Omri did what was evil in the sight of the Lord; he did more evil than all who were before him. For he walked in all the way of Jeroboam son of Nebat, and in the sins that he caused Israel to commit, provoking the Lord, the God of Israel, to anger by their idols" (vv. 25–26). The external sources, however, suggest that Omri was a powerful king who established a significant name for himself through his military activities, information that the Bible lacks. This highlights the extreme selectivity of the biblical sources.

Archaeological evidence confirms the picture suggested above: There may be some truth (or kernel of truth) to some of the biblical stories, but in their current form, they lack historical veracity, because that is not their prime concern. Recent decades, for example, have seen a remarkable re-evaluation of the evidence concerning the conquest of the land of Canaan by Joshua. As more sites have been excavated, there is a growing consensus that the main story of Joshua, that of a speedy and complete conquest (e.g., Josh 11.23: "So Joshua took the whole land, according to all that the LORD had spoken to Moses"), cannot be upheld by the archaeological record, though there are indications of some destruction and conquest at the appropriate time. Various events and traditions have been reworked very substantially over time and ultimately included in the Bible in order to convey a particular picture of God.

In sum, the title Historical Books must not frame the way we read the following texts; if we read them as we read modern historical accounts, we will misunderstand these texts in the most fundamental way. Many of these texts do contain raw material for a modern historian researching the history of ancient Israel from the late second millennium through the fourth century BCE, but this material can only be teased out using sophisticated and complex tools—and even then, our reconstructions are often extremely tentative. This is because the various biblical historians wrote their accounts, sometimes using sources, to illustrate particular perspectives concerning the relationship between God and Israel. It is these religious and religio-political perspectives that we must try to appreciate as we study these books.

Marc Brettler

JOSHUA

NAME AND LOCATION IN CANON

The book is named after Joshua, depicted as the apprentice and successor to Moses, who was the military commander in the conquest of Canaan and the administrator of the allotment of that land to the Israelite tribes. According to Num 13.16, Moses renamed Hoshea (Heb *hoshe'a*, "salvation") Joshua (Heb *yehoshu'a*, "the Lord is salvation/help"), using a variant form of the divine name Yahweh.

The book of Joshua is the sixth book in both the Jewish and Christian canons, the first book of the Former Prophets or the first book of the so-called Historical Books, respectively (see Introduction to Historical Books, pp. 313–317).

AUTHORSHIP AND DATE OF COMPOSITION

The authorship of the book of Joshua is unknown. Some types of sources for the book's composition are identifiable (for example, the border descriptions and city lists in chs 14-19), though their origin and date are often disputed. The historiographic materials used in the book of Joshua correspond to those found in the ancient Near East as a whole. Thus there are traditional stories, etiologies, boundary and town lists, summary accounts and lists, and accounts patterned after redundant annalistic documents. These have been woven together with ritual and covenantal materials and other matters of priestly interest to communicate the book's messages.

Connections between the book of Joshua and the preceding books led earlier scholars to posit a "Hexateuch" (six books), with the book of Joshua completing the first five books of the Bible, the Pentateuch—the Hexateuch having as its main theme the promise of the land and its eventual conquest. More recently scholars have viewed Deuteronomy as the introduction to a larger historical work, the Deuteronomistic History, from the books of Deuteronomy through 2 Kings. Some scholars now treat Joshua as a middle book in a still larger composition from Genesis through 2 Kings. The final date of composition of the book of Joshua is unknown; it may be dependent upon the dating of the various editions of the Deuteronomistic History, of which it is now a part. One major edition of the larger work is generally dated to the late seventh century BCE.

STRUCTURE AND CONTENTS

The book of Joshua describes a conquest of Canaan and its allotment to the Israelite tribes. Through well-known traditional stories (e.g., Rahab and the spies, the crossing of the Jordan River, the capture of Jericho) as well as nonnarrative lists and ritual texts, the book portrays the fulfillment of God's covenantal promise to Israel's ancestors that their descendants would possess the land. Moreover, these stories challenge the book's readers to live in obedience to the Deuteronomic covenant so that they also will receive God's blessings in the land.

The book may be outlined as follows:

I. The Conquest	(1.1–12.24)
A. Preparation for the conquest	(1.1–5.12)
Commission of Joshua	(1.1–18)
Story of the spies and Rahab	(2.1–24)
The crossing of the Jordan	(3.1–5.1)
Final preparatory events at Gilgal	(5.2–12)
B. Conquest of the land	(5.13–12.24)
Central campaign	(5.13–8.35)
Jericho	(5.13–6.27)
Achan and Ai	(7.1–8.29)
Covenant renewal as land grant: Shechem	(8.30–35)

The southern and northern campaigns	(9.1–11.15)
Introductory statement	(9.1–2)
Southern campaign	(9.3–10.43)
Northern campaign	(11.1–15)
Summary of total conquest	(11.16–23)
A selective list of defeated cities' kings	(12.1–24)
II. The allotment of the land	(13.1–24.33)
B.' Division of the land	(13.1–21.45)
Land remaining	(13.1–7)
Transjordanian tribal allotment	(13.8–33)
Cisjordanian tribal allotment	(14.1–19.51)
Introduction to the process of allotment	(14.1–5)
Judah and Joseph allotments	(14.6–17.18)
Seven other tribal allotments	(18.1–19.51)
Summary of the process of allotment	(19.51)
Allotments to persons of marginal status	(20.1–21.42)
Cities of refuge	(20.1–9)
Levitical cities	(21.1–42)
Ironic conclusion	(21.43–45)
A.' Epilogue to the conquest and allotment	(22.1–24.33)
Misunderstanding with the Transjordanian tribes	(22.1–34)
Concluding charges	(23.1–24.28)
Appendixes	(24.29–33)

INTERPRETATION

The book should not be read as straightforward history—it telescopes and simplifies what was a long and complex process of occupation of the land by the Israelite tribes. Some details are lacking (e.g., how the Israelites came into possession of Shechem, 8.30-35), while the other events narrated in the book are selectively arranged to heighten the book's message. Thus the book's presentation of reality does not necessarily reflect the course of events. For example, a main theme of the book is a swift and complete conquest of the land, while most archaeological evidence suggests its gradual settlement. Consequently, archaeological excavations, together with sociological and anthropological analyses, must be used to understand the early history of Israel in the land.

Several literary devices and themes characterize the book. First, the structure of the book (see outline) has two main divisions: the conquest (1.1–12.24) and the allotment of the land (13.1–24.33). Within each main division, there are two subdivisions: A: preparations for the conquest (1.1–5.12) and B: the conquest's campaigns (5.13–12.24); B': the allotment of the conquered land (13.1–21.45) and A'; epilogue to the conquest and allotment (22.1–24.33). The body of the book (5.13–21.45) is bracketed by specially chosen introductory and concluding materials (1.1–5.12; 22.1–24.33). Each subdivision contains a number of units that contribute to the development of the plot and message of the book.

Second, the book follows a logical geographic arrangement. An east-to-west crossing into Canaan (chs 2-5) is followed by military campaigns directed at the center (chs 6-8), south (chs 9-10), and north (ch 11), concluded by a summary list (ch 12). The division of the land first covers the Transjordanian tribes (ch 13), then the south and central tribes (chs 14-17), then the northern and peripheral tribes (chs 18-19), and finally entities of marginal status (chs 20-21). At times, however, the story backtracks or repeats previously narrated details in a type of flashback. This is especially noticeable in chs 3-4 (the crossing of the Jordan) and ch 10 (the conquest of the south).

Third, typology, representing one character or event as an echo or foreshadowing of another, is utilized to portray Joshua as parallel to Moses. A few examples will illustrate: Moses leads the Israelites out of Egypt, Joshua leads the Israelites into Canaan; Moses leads Israel in a miraculous crossing of the Reed Sea, Joshua leads Israel in a miraculous crossing of the Jordan River; Moses sends out spies, Joshua sends out spies; Moses allots land to the tribes east of the Jordan, Joshua allots land to the tribes west of the Jordan. This typology, which depicts Joshua as a new Moses, assures the legitimacy of Joshua.

Fourth, the law or teaching (Heb "torah") of Moses plays a normative role in strategic parts of the book, and Israel's obedience or disobedience to the law determines success or failure. This law, especially prominent in chs 1 and 23, is further specified as "the law of Moses" and refers to some form of the law or teaching of Moses extant at the time that the book of Joshua was written, especially as found in Deuteronomy.

Fifth, ritual concerns dictate some of the narration. For example, the crossing of the Jordan River (chs 3-4), circumcision and Passover (ch 5), the conquest of Jericho (ch 6), and the implementations of the "ḥerem" (chs 6-8) all reflect ritual concerns that undergird the book's land claims.

A subset of these ritual concerns is the concept of the "ḥerem," which plays a significant role in the book (see 5.13–6.27; 7.6–26; 8.1–29; 10.28–39). This noun is usually translated "devoted thing" (7.1) and the related verb "utterly destroy" (10.28). The term is used primarily in contexts of warfare and destruction where the "ḥerem" stories are connected with the notion of obedience or disobedience to the LORD (cf. Deut 7; 20). Its purpose was to "drive out" or "dispossess" the Canaanites in order to carry out divine judgment on them, to protect the Israelites from Canaanite religious influence, and to fulfill the promises concerning the land. This kind of warfare is part of the political ideology that Israel shared with other nations in the ancient Near East, in which wars were dedicated to the glorification of the deity and the extension of the deity's land and reign. While it was considered a ritual category (similar to a concept of interdict or taboo), its use appears to have been linked to the administration of the distribution of war booty. Understanding the "ḥerem" has posed a significant problem throughout the history of interpretation.

Finally, the book utilizes a number of different land ideologies. Some of these may be anchored in historical geography, others are purely idealistic, and some are a mixture of the two. In the book's final form, these produce an abstract, idealized concept of the land, create tensions, and set the stage for irony. The dominant land ideology is the territory of the twelve tribes (both west and east of the Jordan) who completely fill up the land (chs 15-19; cf. Deut 4.45-49). In this view, the two-and-a-half Transjordanian tribes (those settled east of the Jordan) are an integral and vital part of "all Israel." A second, contrasting ideology restricts the true land of inheritance to the territory west of the Jordan (Cisjordan, the land of Canaan) (cf. Deut 12.10). It is this image of the land that lies behind the belief that crossing the Jordan was a step of outstanding significance (chs 3-4). This view also creates ironic tensions in 22.10-34, where the two-and-a-half tribes set up an altar in Transjordan. A third ideology presents the land as claimed but not fully conquered, noting "the land that remains" (13.2-6); and a fourth ideology is an expansionistic, utopian Israel, which claims the distant Euphrates as the northern boundary of Israel's inheritance (1.4; cf. Gen 15.18; Deut 1.7; 11.24). These last two notions instill the book with the flavor of unredeemed promise. The text develops two understandings of Israel's unfulfilled expectations. On the one hand, the incomplete conquest is judged to be the result of Israel's disobedience or military inability (15.63; 16.10; 17.12-13; 19.47); this serves as the basis for future threats to Israel's well-being (7.12; 23.12-13). On the other hand, the last two land ideologies function as hopeful indications of greater land blessings to Israel in the future (13.6b; 17.18; 23.5).

Thus the book of Joshua plays an important role not only in the story of the early history of Israel in the land, but also in the development of the theology of the Hebrew Bible. In many ways, it serves as the prologue for the remainder of the Deuteronomistic Historians' account of Israel's struggles in the land.

GUIDE TO READING

Considering the various literary devices described above, it is clear that reading the book of Joshua demands close attention to its literary complexity. Recognizing the different genres that the book employs is essential to a proper reading. Perhaps the most difficult section of the book for the modern reader is the allotment section (chs 14–19), where border descriptions and city lists overwhelm the reader with geographic detail. At this point, paying close attention to the narrative framework (e.g. 13.1–7; 14.1–15; 15.13–19; 16.1–4; 17.1–6; 17.14–18; 18.1–10; 19.49–51) is helpful in discerning its message and function in the book. Thus it is evident that the allocation of the land proceeds even before its total occupation and that a tension develops within the text between the land conquered and the land promised but not possessed (thus juxtaposing the different land ideologies mentioned earlier). Theologically, the section stresses the LORD's faithfulness in contrast to Israel's wavering obedience. This tension and contrast reaches a climax in the final concluding charges of Joshua (chs 23–24).

K. Lawson Younger, Jr.

1 After the death of Moses the servant of the LORD, the LORD spoke to Joshua son of Nun, Moses' assistant, saying, ² "My servant Moses is dead. Now proceed to cross the Jordan, you and all this people, into the land that I am giving to them, to the Israelites. ³ Every place that the sole of your foot will tread upon I have given to you, as I promised to Moses. ⁴ From the wilderness and the Lebanon as far as the great river, the river Euphrates, all the land of the Hittites, to the Great Sea in the west shall be your territory. ⁵ No one shall be able to stand against you all the days of your life. As I was with Moses, so I will be with you; I will not fail you or forsake you. ⁶ Be strong and courageous; for you shall put this people in possession of the land that I swore to their ancestors to give them. ⁷ Only be strong and very courageous, being careful to act in accordance with all the law that my servant Moses commanded you; do not turn from it to the right hand or to the left, so that you may be successful wherever you go. ⁸ This book of the law shall not depart out of your mouth; you shall meditate on it day and night, so that you may be careful to act in accordance with all that is written in it. For then you shall make your way prosperous, and then you shall be successful. ⁹ I hereby command you: Be strong and courageous; do not be frightened or dismayed, for the LORD your God is with you wherever you go."

¹⁰ Then Joshua commanded the officers of the people, ¹¹ "Pass through the camp, and command the people: 'Prepare your provisions; for in three days you are to cross over the Jordan, to go in to take possession of the land that the LORD your God gives you to possess.'"

¹² To the Reubenites, the Gadites, and the half-tribe of Manasseh Joshua said, ¹³ "Remember the word that Moses the servant of the LORD commanded you, saying, 'The LORD your God is providing you a place of rest, and will give you this land.' ¹⁴ Your wives, your little ones, and your livestock shall remain in the land that Moses gave you beyond the Jordan. But all the warriors among you shall cross over armed before your kindred and shall help them, ¹⁵ until the LORD gives rest to your kindred as well as to you, and they too take possession of the land that the LORD your God is giving them. Then you shall return to your own land and take possession of it, the land that Moses the servant of the LORD gave you beyond the Jordan to the east."

¹⁶ They answered Joshua: "All that you have commanded us we will do, and wherever you send us we will go. ¹⁷ Just as we obeyed Moses in all things, so we will obey you. Only may the LORD your God be with you, as he was with Moses! ¹⁸ Whoever rebels against your orders and disobeys your words, whatever you command, shall be put to death. Only be strong and courageous."

1.1–12.24: The Conquest. 1.1–5.12: Preparation for the conquest. 1.1–18: The commission of Joshua. 1: Moses' death (Deut 34) provides the setting for the commission. God did not allow Moses to enter the land (Deut 13.37n.; 32.48–52). 2–18: The commission contains four speeches (vv. 2–9, 10–11, 12–15, 16–18). 2–9: The Lord's speech outlines the means of success for Joshua and the Israelites: obedience to the book of the law (Heb "torah"). The Lord's speech also anticipates the main themes of the book: the crossing of the Jordan (1.1–5.12), the conquest (5.13–12.24), the division of the land (13.1–22.34), and obedience to the law of Moses (23.1–24.33). 2–5: The idealized boundaries of the land, given with the assurance of God's presence, were the *Jordan* River to the east, *the wilderness* or semidesert to the south and east, the *Lebanon* mountain range to the northwest, the *river Euphrates* in the far north, and the *Great Sea,* the Mediterranean Sea, to the west (cf. Deut 11.24–25; Num 34.1–12). 4: *All the land of the Hittites* is likely a later gloss, probably referring to northern Syria. The Hittite empire was no longer in existence at this time. 5: An explicit recognition that Joshua is the new Moses; cf. Ex 3.12. 6–9: As currently formulated, the text emphasizes that military success comes from the law's internalization, spoken of in 1.8 in terms of meditation with consequent obedience (cf. Deut 31.7–8; Ps 1.2–3). 11: *In three days* reflects ritual concerns (cf. Ex 3.18; 19.11). 12–15: Joshua's speech to the Transjordanian tribes is suffused with vocabulary that typifies Deuteronomy. Since the other tribes had helped Reuben, Gad, and the half-tribe of Manasseh conquer their land, they were to help the other Israelites acquire their land west of the Jordan. *The half-tribe of Manasseh,* according to territorial lists (see 13.29–31; 17) part of Manasseh occupied land east of the Jordan and part west. 13: See Deut 3.12–20. 16–18: The reply of the Transjordanian tribes rounds out the chapter by echoing the Lord's assurances of 1.1–9 (cf. Deut 9–10).

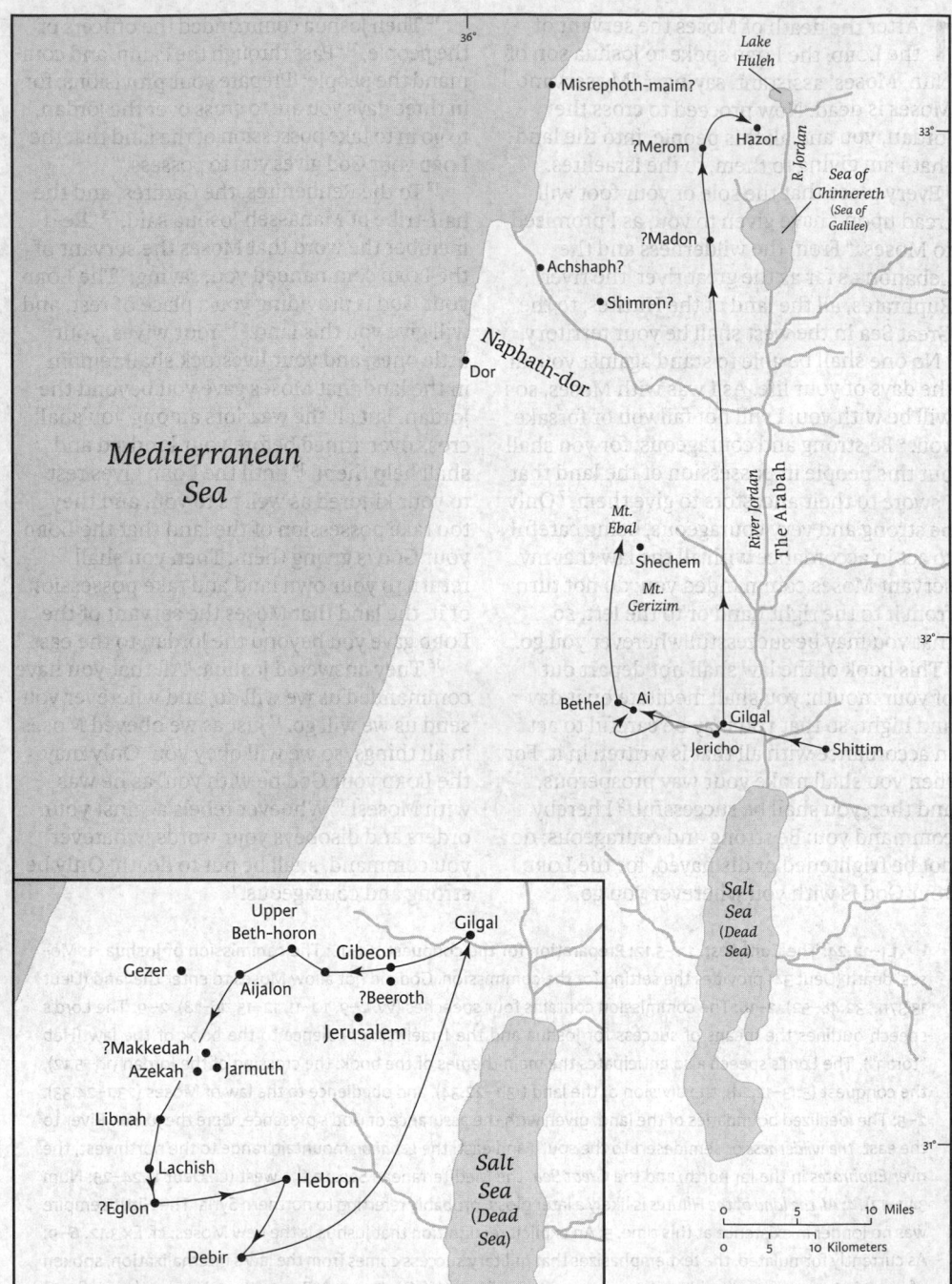

The conquest of Canaan according to the book of Joshua.

Map labels:

Mediterranean Sea

Lake Huleh
Misrephoth-maim?
?Merom
Hazor
R. Jordan
Sea of Chinnereth (Sea of Galilee)
?Madon
Achshaph?
Shimron?
Dor
Naphath-dor
The Arabah
River Jordan
Mt. Ebal
Shechem
Mt. Gerizim
Bethel
Ai
Gilgal
Jericho
Shittim
Salt Sea (Dead Sea)

Upper Beth-horon
Gilgal
Gibeon
Gezer
Aijalon
?Beeroth
?Makkedah
Jerusalem
Azekah
Jarmuth
Libnah
Lachish
Hebron
?Eglon
Debir
Salt Sea (Dead Sea)

0   5   10 Miles
0   5   10 Kilometers

2 Then Joshua son of Nun sent two men secretly from Shittim as spies, saying, "Go, view the land, especially Jericho." So they went, and entered the house of a prostitute whose name was Rahab, and spent the night there. [2] The king of Jericho was told, "Some Israelites have come here tonight to search out the land." [3] Then the king of Jericho sent orders to Rahab, "Bring out the men who have come to you, who entered your house, for they have come only to search out the whole land." [4] But the woman took the two men and hid them. Then she said, "True, the men came to me, but I did not know where they came from. [5] And when it was time to close the gate at dark, the men went out. Where the men went I do not know. Pursue them quickly, for you can overtake them." [6] She had, however, brought them up to the roof and hidden them with the stalks of flax that she had laid out on the roof. [7] So the men pursued them on the way to the Jordan as far as the fords. As soon as the pursuers had gone out, the gate was shut.

[8] Before they went to sleep, she came up to them on the roof [9] and said to the men: "I know that the LORD has given you the land, and that dread of you has fallen on us, and that all the inhabitants of the land melt in fear before you. [10] For we have heard how the LORD dried up the water of the Red Sea[a] before you when you came out of Egypt, and what you did to the two kings of the Amorites that were beyond the Jordan, to Sihon and Og, whom you utterly destroyed. [11] As soon as we heard it, our hearts melted, and there was no courage left in any of us because of you. The LORD your God is indeed God in heaven above and on earth below. [12] Now then, since I have dealt kindly with you, swear to me by the LORD that you in turn will deal kindly with my family. Give me a sign of good faith [13] that you will spare my father and mother, my brothers and sisters, and all who belong to them, and deliver our lives from death." [14] The men said to her, "Our life for yours! If you do not tell this business of ours, then we will deal kindly and faithfully with you when the LORD gives us the land."

[15] Then she let them down by a rope through the window, for her house was on the outer side of the city wall and she resided within the wall itself. [16] She said to them, "Go toward the hill country, so that the pursuers may not come upon you. Hide yourselves there three days, until the pursuers have returned; then afterward you may go your way." [17] The men said to her, "We will be released from this oath that you have made us swear to you [18] if we invade the land and you do not tie this crimson cord in the window through which you let us down, and you do not gather into your house your father and mother,

---

[a] Or *Sea of Reeds*

2.1–24: The story of the spies and Rahab. Interrupting the narrative (cf. 1.11 and 3.12), ch 2 functions as a type of parenthesis introducing important items that will form the background to the stories of the crossing of the Jordan and the conquest of Jericho. **1:** Joshua commissions two unnamed spies to go and investigate the land (cf. Num 13; Deut 1.21–23; Josh 7.2–3). The spies go to Jericho, west of the Jordan River, but surprisingly enter the house of a prostitute. While the text does not explicitly state that there was a sexual liaison between the spies and their hostess, it provides an undercurrent of ambiguous sexual innuendo. *Shittim* was the site of the Israelite camp, but also was the infamous place where the men of Israel had sexual relations with the women of Moab (Num 25.1). **2–13:** *Rahab* is at the center of the narrative. She is the only character with a name, and without her the spies would have had no success. She protects and delivers the spies and provides them with the information they seek. In Mt 1.5 Rahab is reckoned among the ancestors of Jesus, and in Heb 11.31 Rahab is counted as one of the heroes of faith. Rahab's confession in vv. 9–11 anticipates the "hearing and fearing" expressed in 5.1; 6.1; 9.1–3; 10.1–2; 11.1–5. **6:** *To the roof,* the just harvested (see 3.15n) flax had been laid on the flat roof to dry. **10:** *Dried up . . . the Red Sea,* language used only here and in 4.23; cf. Ex 14.21–29. *Sihon and Og,* see Num 21.21–35; Deut 2.26–3.11. *Utterly destroyed,* the first use of the "ḥerem" terminology (see Introduction, p. 320). **11:** The acknowledgment of the Lord as the God of *heaven* and *earth* is relatively unusual in the Hebrew Bible, but here anticipates the Divine Warrior's mighty actions once at the Jordan (chs 3–4), once at Jericho (ch 6), and twice in the skies over Gibeon (ch 10). **12:** *Family,* lit., "father's house." **14–21:** Ironically, Rahab, the Canaanite prostitute, shows unconditional loyalty toward the spies, risking everything; but the spies show conditioned loyalty to

your brothers, and all your family. [19] If any of you go out of the doors of your house into the street, they shall be responsible for their own death, and we shall be innocent; but if a hand is laid upon any who are with you in the house, we shall bear the responsibility for their death. [20] But if you tell this business of ours, then we shall be released from this oath that you made us swear to you." [21] She said, "According to your words, so be it." She sent them away and they departed. Then she tied the crimson cord in the window.

[22] They departed and went into the hill country and stayed there three days, until the pursuers returned. The pursuers had searched all along the way and found nothing. [23] Then the two men came down again from the hill country. They crossed over, came to Joshua son of Nun, and told him all that had happened to them. [24] They said to Joshua, "Truly the LORD has given all the land into our hands; moreover all the inhabitants of the land melt in fear before us."

3 Early in the morning Joshua rose and set out from Shittim with all the Israelites, and they came to the Jordan. They camped there before crossing over. [2] At the end of three days the officers went through the camp [3] and commanded the people, "When you see the ark of the covenant of the LORD your God being carried by the levitical priests, then you shall set out from your place. Follow it, [4] so that you may know the way you should go, for you have not passed this way before. Yet there shall be a space between you and it, a distance of about two thousand cubits; do not come any nearer to it." [5] Then Joshua said to the people, "Sanctify yourselves; for tomorrow the LORD will do wonders among you." [6] To the priests Joshua said, "Take up the ark of the covenant, and pass on in front of the people." So they took up the ark of the covenant and went in front of the people.

[7] The LORD said to Joshua, "This day I will begin to exalt you in the sight of all Israel, so that they may know that I will be with you as I was with Moses. [8] You are the one who shall command the priests who bear the ark of the covenant, 'When you come to the edge of the waters of the Jordan, you shall stand still in the Jordan.'" [9] Joshua then said to the Israelites, "Draw near and hear the words of the LORD your God." [10] Joshua said, "By this you shall know that among you is the living God who without fail will drive out from be-

Rahab, minimizing their risks. **16:** *Toward the hill country,* to the west. **22–24:** The report of the spies to Joshua is based on Rahab's words. In contrast to the spies of Num 13, they did not "view the land" as they were told (v. 1). Without Rahab these men would not have returned to give a report on the Canaanite disposition.

3.1–5.1: The crossing of the Jordan. The crossing of the Jordan is narrated in five units (3.1–17; 4.1–10; 4.11–14; 4.15–18; 4.19–5.1) that backtrack and overlap so that a number of events are recounted more than once. The use of anticipatory statements and resumptive repetitions provides a means of linking the units together (e.g., the anticipatory statement in 3.12 is tied to the resumptive repetition in 4.2). In this way a redactor has attempted to meld together different sources.

3.1–17: The initial story of the crossing. This unit notes that the Jordan is in flood (v. 15) because otherwise it is a relatively narrow river. The Jordan functions primarily as a ritual and ideological symbol representing the boundary between landlessness and settled peoplehood. It anticipates the importance of all boundaries in the book, particularly those of the allotments (chs 13–21) and the tribal dispute of ch 22. The fact that the procession begins and ends at early Israelite religious centers ([Abel]-Shittim and Gilgal) reinforces the ritual significance. **2:** Resumptive of 1.11. **3:** *The ark of the covenant* was the container for the text of the law; see Deut 31.26. It also symbolized God's presence among the tribes; it could be carried only by priests. It could be brought into battle, assuring the deity's presence among the nation (see 1 Sam 4.6–7). **4:** The people were to keep their distance because of the presence of God. *Two thousand cubits,* about 885 m (2,900 ft). **5:** *Sanctify yourselves* reflects the ritual background of the story. The Israelites were to purify themselves in preparation for the divine presence (cf. Ex 19.10–15). **10:** A stereotypical listing of the pre-Israelite population of Canaan; it is difficult to identify the individual groups specifically. *Hittites,* apparently a group in the land of Canaan (see Gen 23; Judg 3.5; contrast 1.4n.). The *Jebusites* are associated with Jerusalem (see 15.63). If the chronological setting for these events is approximately the thirteenth century BCE, the Canaan that the Israelite tribes entered was in a state of economic, social, and political turmoil, due in large measure to the collapsing of the Egyptian empire and

fore you the Canaanites, Hittites, Hivites, Per-izzites, Girgashites, Amorites, and Jebusites: [11] the ark of the covenant of the Lord of all the earth is going to pass before you into the Jordan. [12] So now select twelve men from the tribes of Israel, one from each tribe. [13] When the soles of the feet of the priests who bear the ark of the LORD, the Lord of all the earth, rest in the waters of the Jordan, the waters of the Jordan flowing from above shall be cut off; they shall stand in a single heap."

[14] When the people set out from their tents to cross over the Jordan, the priests bearing the ark of the covenant were in front of the people. [15] Now the Jordan overflows all its banks throughout the time of harvest. So when those who bore the ark had come to the Jordan, and the feet of the priests bearing the ark were dipped in the edge of the water, [16] the waters flowing from above stood still, rising up in a single heap far off at Adam, the city that is beside Zarethan, while those flowing toward the sea of the Arabah, the Dead Sea,[a] were wholly cut off. Then the people crossed over opposite Jericho. [17] While all Israel were crossing over on dry ground, the priests who bore the ark of the covenant of the LORD stood on dry ground in the middle of the Jordan, until the entire nation finished crossing over the Jordan.

4 When the entire nation had finished crossing over the Jordan, the LORD said to Joshua: [2] "Select twelve men from the people, one from each tribe, [3] and command them, 'Take twelve stones from here out of the middle of the Jordan, from the place where the priests' feet stood, carry them over with you, and lay them down in the place where you camp tonight.'" [4] Then Joshua summoned the twelve men from the Israelites, whom he had appointed, one from each tribe. [5] Joshua said to them, "Pass on before the ark of the LORD your God into the middle of the Jordan, and each of you take up a stone on his shoulder, one for each of the tribes of the Israelites, [6] so that this may be a sign among you. When your children ask in time to come, 'What do those stones mean to you?' [7] then you shall tell them that the waters of the Jordan were cut off in front of the ark of the covenant of the LORD. When it crossed over the Jordan, the waters of the Jordan were cut off. So these stones shall be to the Israelites a memorial forever."

[8] The Israelites did as Joshua commanded. They took up twelve stones out of the middle of the Jordan, according to the number of the tribes of the Israelites, as the LORD told Joshua, carried them over with them to the place where they camped, and laid them down there. [9] (Joshua set up twelve stones in the middle of the Jordan, in the place where the feet of the priests bearing the ark of the covenant had stood; and they are there to this day.)

[10] The priests who bore the ark remained standing in the middle of the Jordan, until everything was finished that the LORD commanded Joshua to tell the people, according to all that Moses had commanded Joshua. The people crossed over in haste. [11] As soon as all the people had finished crossing over, the ark of the LORD, and the priests, crossed over in front of the people. [12] The Reubenites, the Gadites, and the half-tribe of Manasseh crossed over armed before the Israelites, as Moses had ordered them. [13] About forty thousand armed for war crossed over before the LORD to the plains of Jericho for battle.

[a] Heb *Salt Sea*

many Canaanite city-state structures. **12:** Anticipates 4.2. **13:** *Stand*, cf. 10.13, where the moon is commanded to "stand still." *Heap*, a rare word used elsewhere only of the splitting of the Red Sea (Ex 15.8; Ps 78.13). **15:** *Harvest*, the spring harvest (March-April). **16:** *Adam*, 18 km (12 mi) north of Jericho, is probably Tell ed-Damiyeh. *Zarethan* is farther north. **17:** The continued presence of the priests with the ark in the midst of the dry riverbed anticipates 4.10.

4.1–10: The erecting of the twelve-stone memorial. This unit is repetitive (e.g., cf. vv. 6 and 21), and pre-serves different traditions. **9:** Another, perhaps later, tradition that locates a memorial of twelve stones in the bed of the Jordan itself; v. 8 narrates the removal of stones from the river bed to the shore, where they are part of the sanctuary of Gilgal (see v. 20). **10:** *In haste*, cf. Ex 12.33–34. **11–14:** The unit backtracks and again narrates again the crossing, emphasizing the role of the Transjordanian tribes and the exaltation of Joshua. **12–13:** A flashback reports that the eastern tribes have done what Moses commanded and Joshua reiterated (1.14; Deut

[14] On that day the LORD exalted Joshua in the sight of all Israel; and they stood in awe of him, as they had stood in awe of Moses, all the days of his life.

[15] The LORD said to Joshua, [16] "Command the priests who bear the ark of the covenant,[a] to come up out of the Jordan." [17] Joshua therefore commanded the priests, "Come up out of the Jordan." [18] When the priests bearing the ark of the covenant of the LORD came up from the middle of the Jordan, and the soles of the priests' feet touched dry ground, the waters of the Jordan returned to their place and overflowed all its banks, as before.

[19] The people came up out of the Jordan on the tenth day of the first month, and they camped in Gilgal on the east border of Jericho. [20] Those twelve stones, which they had taken out of the Jordan, Joshua set up in Gilgal, [21] saying to the Israelites, "When your children ask their parents in time to come, 'What do these stones mean?' [22] then you shall let your children know, 'Israel crossed over the Jordan here on dry ground.' [23] For the LORD your God dried up the waters of the Jordan for you until you crossed over, as the LORD your God did to the Red Sea,[b] which he dried up for us until we crossed over, [24] so that all the peoples of the earth may know that the hand of the LORD is mighty, and so that you may fear the LORD your God forever."

5 When all the kings of the Amorites beyond the Jordan to the west, and all the kings of the Canaanites by the sea, heard that the LORD had dried up the waters of the Jordan for the Israelites until they had crossed over, their hearts melted, and there was no longer any spirit in them, because of the Israelites.

[2] At that time the LORD said to Joshua, "Make flint knives and circumcise the Israelites a second time." [3] So Joshua made flint knives, and circumcised the Israelites at Gibeath-haaraloth.[c] [4] This is the reason why Joshua circumcised them: all the males of the people who came out of Egypt, all the warriors, had died during the journey through the wilderness after they had come out of Egypt. [5] Although all the people who came out had been circumcised, yet all the people born on the journey through the wilderness after they had come out of Egypt had not been circumcised. [6] For the Israelites traveled forty years in the wilderness, until all the nation, the warriors who came out of Egypt, perished, not having listened to the voice of the LORD. To them the LORD swore that he would not let them see the land that he had sworn to their ancestors to give us, a land flowing with

---

a   Or *treaty*, or *testimony*; Heb *eduth*
b   Or *Sea of Reeds*
c   That is *the Hill of the Foreskins*

3.18). **14:** Resumptive repetition stresses again the fulfillment of the Lord's exaltation of Joshua as with Moses. **15–18:** This unit backtracks and retells the ark's crossing and the unstopping of the river. **18:** An item-by-item reversal of what happened in 3.15–16. In fact, the verse backtracks to *the middle of the Jordan* before reporting that the priests actually leave the water.

4.19–5.1: The final unit emphasizes the instructional value of the memorial through comparison with the Red Sea crossing. **19:** The focus turns from the priests to the people. *The first month* was Abib (March–April), later called Nisan. The preparations for the first Passover began on the tenth day of the first month (Ex 12.3). *Gilgal*, whose precise location is disputed, was an important Israelite shrine. Its name means "circle," perhaps referring to the stone configuration; there are several locations with this name in the Bible. **23:** The connection of this event to the Exodus from Egypt is made explicit. **24:** As with the Exodus, both foreigner and Israelite (v. 22) must learn from this event (Ex 10.1–2). **5.1:** Resuming 2.9–11 and anticipating 9.1; 10.1; 11.1.

5.2–12: Final preparatory events at Gilgal. Three connected rituals are recounted: circumcision (vv. 2–9), Passover (v. 10), and the first consumption of the produce of the land at Gilgal (vv. 11–12). **2–9:** The disobedience of the older generation (those of the first circumcision who came out of Egypt and died in the wilderness) is contrasted to the obedience of the new generation (those participating in this circumcision). Circumcision was a ritual required of all males who were to celebrate the Passover (Ex 12.48). **2:** At one time circumcision was a fairly common practice in the ancient Near East; it became a sign of Israel's relationship with God. *A second time*, probably a later addition to mitigate the failure (see v. 5) to observe the obligation of Gen 17.9–14 or to emphasize Joshua as a parallel to Moses. **6:** To *give us*, an unusual authorial inclusion. The formula *a land flowing with*

milk and honey. [7] So it was their children, whom he raised up in their place, that Joshua circumcised; for they were uncircumcised, because they had not been circumcised on the way.

[8] When the circumcising of all the nation was done, they remained in their places in the camp until they were healed. [9] The LORD said to Joshua, "Today I have rolled away from you the disgrace of Egypt." And so that place is called Gilgal[a] to this day.

[10] While the Israelites were camped in Gilgal they kept the passover in the evening on the fourteenth day of the month in the plains of Jericho. [11] On the day after the passover, on that very day, they ate the produce of the land, unleavened cakes and parched grain. [12] The manna ceased on the day they ate the produce of the land, and the Israelites no longer had manna; they ate the crops of the land of Canaan that year.

[13] Once when Joshua was by Jericho, he looked up and saw a man standing before him with a drawn sword in his hand. Joshua went to him and said to him, "Are you one of us, or one of our adversaries?" [14] He replied, "Neither; but as commander of the army of the LORD I have now come." And Joshua fell on his face to the earth and worshiped, and he said to him, "What do you command your servant, my lord?" [15] The commander of the army of the LORD said to Joshua, "Remove the sandals from your feet, for the place where you stand is holy." And Joshua did so.

6 Now Jericho was shut up inside and out because of the Israelites; no one came out and no one went in. [2] The LORD said to Joshua, "See, I have handed Jericho over to you, along with its king and soldiers. [3] You shall march around the city, all the warriors circling the city once. Thus you shall do for six days, [4] with seven priests bearing seven trumpets of rams' horns before the ark. On the seventh day you shall march around the city seven times, the priests blowing the trumpets. [5] When they make a long blast with the ram's horn, as soon as you hear the sound of the trumpet, then all the people shall shout with a great shout; and the wall of the city will fall down flat, and all the people shall charge straight ahead." [6] So Joshua son of Nun summoned the priests and said to

[a] Related to Heb *galal* to roll

milk and honey (see Ex 3.8; Deut 6.3; etc.) anticipates the consumption of the land's produce (vv. 10–12). **9:** This is a folk-etymology of *Gilgal*, "the circle" (see 4.19n.). The precise nature of the *disgrace* is unclear; it may refer to Deut 9.28, demonstrating that the crossing and the circumcision are God's graciousness toward Israel in spite of Israel's lack of faithfulness in the wilderness. **10:** The celebration of the Passover reinforces the portrayal of Joshua as parallel to Moses (cf. Ex 12). **11–12:** Land claims are usually presented as a matter of conquests (chs 6–12) and geographic lists (chs 13–21), but here they are set forth in terms of ritual events and diet. The change from manna to the produce of the land signifies Israel's relocation from wilderness to land. Unleavened bread and roasted grain are used in rituals connected to Passover and first fruits (Lev 23.9–14).

5.13–12.24: Conquest of the land. The conquest of the land is recounted as three major campaigns: central (5.13–8.35), southern (9.1–10.43), and northern (11.1–15).

5.13–8.35: Central campaign. The central campaign, which is described in the greatest detail, has three sections: 5.13–6.27; 7.1–8.29; and 8.30–35.

5.13–6.27: Jericho: first application of "ḥerem" (see Introduction, p. 320). Jericho's capture is important because it is the first implementation of the "ḥerem" by the Israelites in the conquest. The interpretation of the archaeological evidence from Tell es-Sultan (ancient Jericho) is disputed, but in the thirteenth century BCE there was at best an unfortified village on the site. Like Moses (see Ex 3.1–4.17), Joshua receives a theophany followed by detailed instructions; 6.2–5 thus continues the scene of 5.13–15, with 6.1 being a parenthetical aside. **5.13–15:** The appearance of the *commander of the army of the LORD* is probably a fragment of a fuller tradition. He is not mentioned in the rest of the book. **14:** The commander is not part of a human army, but rather the commander of the heavenly forces (see Deut 33.2; Judg 5.20; Zech 9.14). **15:** A direct quotation from Ex 3.5, again showing that Joshua was the divinely appointed successor of Moses.

6.6–27: Jericho is captured by following the LORD's instructions. Ritual ceremony plays an important symbolic function, overcoming the walls of Jericho: seven priests, seven trumpets, seven days, seven encirclements on the seventh day, and a seventh-day climactic victory. The preponderance of "sevens" may recall the seven

them, "Take up the ark of the covenant, and have seven priests carry seven trumpets of rams' horns in front of the ark of the LORD." [7] To the people he said, "Go forward and march around the city; have the armed men pass on before the ark of the LORD."

[8] As Joshua had commanded the people, the seven priests carrying the seven trumpets of rams' horns before the LORD went forward, blowing the trumpets, with the ark of the covenant of the LORD following them. [9] And the armed men went before the priests who blew the trumpets; the rear guard came after the ark, while the trumpets blew continually. [10] To the people Joshua gave this command: "You shall not shout or let your voice be heard, nor shall you utter a word, until the day I tell you to shout. Then you shall shout." [11] So the ark of the LORD went around the city, circling it once; and they came into the camp, and spent the night in the camp.

[12] Then Joshua rose early in the morning, and the priests took up the ark of the LORD. [13] The seven priests carrying the seven trumpets of rams' horns before the ark of the LORD passed on, blowing the trumpets continually. The armed men went before them, and the rear guard came after the ark of the LORD, while the trumpets blew continually. [14] On the second day they marched around the city once and then returned to the camp. They did this for six days.

[15] On the seventh day they rose early, at dawn, and marched around the city in the same manner seven times. It was only on that day that they marched around the city seven times. [16] And at the seventh time, when the priests had blown the trumpets, Joshua said to the people, "Shout! For the LORD has given you the city. [17] The city and all that is in it shall be devoted to the LORD for destruction. Only Rahab the prostitute

and all who are with her in her house shall live because she hid the messengers we sent. [18] As for you, keep away from the things devoted to destruction, so as not to covet[a] and take any of the devoted things and make the camp of Israel an object for destruction, bringing trouble upon it. [19] But all silver and gold, and vessels of bronze and iron, are sacred to the LORD; they shall go into the treasury of the LORD." [20] So the people shouted, and the trumpets were blown. As soon as the people heard the sound of the trumpets, they raised a great shout, and the wall fell down flat; so the people charged straight ahead into the city and captured it. [21] Then they devoted to destruction by the edge of the sword all in the city, both men and women, young and old, oxen, sheep, and donkeys.

[22] Joshua said to the two men who had spied out the land, "Go into the prostitute's house, and bring the woman out of it and all who belong to her, as you swore to her." [23] So the young men who had been spies went in and brought Rahab out, along with her father, her mother, her brothers, and all who belonged to her—they brought all her kindred out—and set them outside the camp of Israel. [24] They burned down the city, and everything in it; only the silver and gold, and the vessels of bronze and iron, they put into the treasury of the house of the LORD. [25] But Rahab the prostitute, with her family and all who belonged to her, Joshua spared. Her family[b] has lived in Israel ever since. For she hid the messengers whom Joshua sent to spy out Jericho.

[26] Joshua then pronounced this oath, saying, "Cursed before the LORD be anyone who tries to build this city—this Jericho!

a Gk: Heb *devote to destruction* Compare 7.21
b Heb *She*

days of creation (Gen 1), implying the creation of a new order in the land and continuing the ritual land claim of 3.1–5.12. This is the first implementation of the "ḥerem," a ritual act. The Canaanite prostitute Rahab and her family are exempted from the "ḥerem" (v. 17, see ch 2). The account of the fall of Jericho is more ritually symbolic than military in its significance, though as a victory in the first battle, it prefigures success in the campaigns that will follow. **18:** *Bringing trouble upon it* anticipates the next story (7.25). **19–24:** Israel's faithfulness in the implementation of the "ḥerem" is emphasized and Achan's unfaithfulness is anticipated. Jericho represents a paradigm for the entire enterprise of conquest (8.2; 10.1; 24.11). **25:** *Ever since* indicates that the descendants of Rahab (i.e., Canaanites) survived and lived among the Israelites. **26:** The fulfillment of this enigmatic curse is

At the cost of his firstborn he shall lay its
foundation,
and at the cost of his youngest he shall
set up its gates!"
²⁷ So the LORD was with Joshua; and his
fame was in all the land.

7 But the Israelites broke faith in regard to
the devoted things: Achan son of Carmi
son of Zabdi son of Zerah, of the tribe of
Judah, took some of the devoted things; and
the anger of the LORD burned against the
Israelites.

² Joshua sent men from Jericho to Ai,
which is near Beth-aven, east of Bethel, and
said to them, "Go up and spy out the land."
And the men went up and spied out Ai.
³ Then they returned to Joshua and said to
him, "Not all the people need go up; about
two or three thousand men should go up and
attack Ai. Since they are so few, do not make
the whole people toil up there." ⁴ So about
three thousand of the people went up there;
and they fled before the men of Ai. ⁵ The men
of Ai killed about thirty-six of them, chasing
them from outside the gate as far as Sheba-
rim and killing them on the slope. The hearts
of the people melted and turned to water.

⁶ Then Joshua tore his clothes, and fell to
the ground on his face before the ark of the
LORD until the evening, he and the elders
of Israel; and they put dust on their heads.
⁷ Joshua said, "Ah, Lord GOD! Why have you
brought this people across the Jordan at
all, to hand us over to the Amorites so as to
destroy us? Would that we had been content
to settle beyond the Jordan! ⁸ O Lord, what
can I say, now that Israel has turned their
backs to their enemies! ⁹ The Canaanites and
all the inhabitants of the land will hear of it,
and surround us, and cut off our name from
the earth. Then what will you do for your
great name?"

¹⁰ The LORD said to Joshua, "Stand up! Why
have you fallen upon your face? ¹¹ Israel has
sinned; they have transgressed my covenant
that I imposed on them. They have taken
some of the devoted things; they have stolen,
they have acted deceitfully, and they have put
them among their own belongings. ¹² Therefore the Israelites are unable to stand before
their enemies; they turn their backs to their
enemies, because they have become a thing
devoted for destruction themselves. I will
be with you no more, unless you destroy the
devoted things from among you. ¹³ Proceed to
sanctify the people, and say, 'Sanctify yourselves for tomorrow; for thus says the LORD,
the God of Israel, "There are devoted things
among you, O Israel; you will be unable to
stand before your enemies until you take
away the devoted things from among you."
¹⁴ In the morning therefore you shall come
forward tribe by tribe. The tribe that the LORD
takes shall come near by clans, the clan that
the LORD takes shall come near by households, and the household that the LORD takes
shall come near one by one. ¹⁵ And the one
who is taken as having the devoted things
shall be burned with fire, together with all
that he has, for having transgressed the
covenant of the LORD, and for having done an
outrageous thing in Israel.'"

recorded in 1 Kings 16.34. **27**: The climactic conclusion: The Lord was with Joshua (see 1.5) and his fame was in all the land.

7.1–8.29: Achan and Ai. 7.1–5: First battle of Ai and Achan's sin. In contrast to the climactic conclusion in which Joshua is exalted (6.27), Achan's sin is described. Although only one person was unfaithful, all Israel was liable because the state of being devoted ("ḥerem") is contagious, and the booty would contaminate Israel's camp and put it into a state of devotion ("ḥerem"). **2:** The name *Ai* (modern et-Tell) means "the ruin." The site, 3 km (2 mi) east of Bethel, was uninhabited during the Late Bronze Age. **3–5:** The spies believe that Israel is too strong to worry about such a small fortress (contrast Num 13–14). Overconfidence spells a lack of consultation and of dependence on the Lord. The men of Ai thoroughly repulsed the Israelite contingent (cf. Num 14.42–45).

7.6–26: Second application of "ḥerem": Achan's execution. 6–9: Joshua's prayer of intercession recalls prayers of Moses (e.g., Ex 32.11–13; Num 11.11–15; 14.13–19; Deut 9.26–29). **6:** *Tore his clothes . . . dust on their heads,* traditional expressions of grief. **7:** *Amorites,* here a generic designation of the inhabitants of the land (see 24.15). **10–15:** God's answer to Joshua is a rebuke. **11–13:** There has been a covenant violation: a theft of God's property, the *devoted things* ("ḥerem") from Jericho. Only sanctifying themselves and removing the *devoted things* can prevent Israel from being a *devoted thing.* **14:** *The LORD takes,* by the casting of lots (a device that

[16] So Joshua rose early in the morning, and brought Israel near tribe by tribe, and the tribe of Judah was taken. [17] He brought near the clans of Judah, and the clan of the Zerahites was taken; and he brought near the clan of the Zerahites, family by family,[a] and Zabdi was taken. [18] And he brought near his household one by one, and Achan son of Carmi son of Zabdi son of Zerah, of the tribe of Judah, was taken. [19] Then Joshua said to Achan, "My son, give glory to the LORD God of Israel and make confession to him. Tell me now what you have done; do not hide it from me." [20] And Achan answered Joshua, "It is true; I am the one who sinned against the LORD God of Israel. This is what I did: [21] when I saw among the spoil a beautiful mantle from Shinar, and two hundred shekels of silver, and a bar of gold weighing fifty shekels, then I coveted them and took them. They now lie hidden in the ground inside my tent, with the silver underneath."

[22] So Joshua sent messengers, and they ran to the tent; and there it was, hidden in his tent with the silver underneath. [23] They took them out of the tent and brought them to Joshua and all the Israelites; and they spread them out before the LORD. [24] Then Joshua and all Israel with him took Achan son of Zerah, with the silver, the mantle, and the bar of gold, with his sons and daughters, with his oxen, donkeys, and sheep, and his tent and all that he had; and they brought them up to the Valley of Achor. [25] Joshua said, "Why did you bring trouble on us? The LORD is bringing trouble on you today." And all Israel stoned him to death; they burned them with fire, cast stones on them, [26] and raised over him a great heap of stones that remains to this day. Then the LORD turned from his burning anger. Therefore that place to this day is called the Valley of Achor.[b]

8 Then the LORD said to Joshua, "Do not fear or be dismayed; take all the fighting men with you, and go up now to Ai. See, I have handed over to you the king of Ai with his people, his city, and his land. [2] You shall do to Ai and its king as you did to Jericho and its king; only its spoil and its livestock you may take as booty for yourselves. Set an ambush against the city, behind it."

[3] So Joshua and all the fighting men set out to go up against Ai. Joshua chose thirty thousand warriors and sent them out by night [4] with the command, "You shall lie in ambush against the city, behind it; do not go very far from the city, but all of you stay alert. [5] I and all the people who are with me will approach the city. When they come out against us, as before, we shall flee from them. [6] They will come out after us until we have drawn them away from the city; for they will say, 'They are fleeing from us, as before.' While we flee from them, [7] you shall rise up from the ambush and seize the city; for the LORD your God will give it into your hand. [8] And when you have taken the city, you shall set the city on fire, doing as the LORD has ordered; see, I have commanded you." [9] So Joshua sent them out;

a   Mss Syr: MT *man by man*
b   That is *Trouble*

when thrown yields the proper yes-or-no answer through divine assistance). **16–21:** The process of selection successfully narrows down the guilty group, finding the guilty party. It also reinforces Achan's guilt. **20–21:** The actual "ḥerem" objects are listed in Achan's admission: a beautiful mantle from Shinar (Babylon), two hundred shekels of silver (about 5 lbs [2.3 kg]), and a fifty-shekel bar of gold (about 1.24 lbs [570 gm]). **22–26:** The resolution of the problem is found in the "ḥerem" of Achan and his family. **25:** This refers to 6.18. *Trouble* (Heb "'akar") is removed from Israel and ritually placed on Achan. **26:** *Valley of Achor,* a name derived from a wordplay on Achan's final state of "trouble" ("'akar"). The valley is probably the Buqeiah, just west of the northern end of the Dead Sea; in 15.7 it is on the border between Benjamin and Judah. The outcome for Achan and his family is an ironic reversal of that for Rahab and her family (6.25).

8.1–29: Third application of "ḥerem": second battle of Ai and Ai's destruction. 1–2: The Lord gives assurance and instructions, making clear that Achan's sin has been removed so that God can once again give Israel the land. Note also the modification of the "ḥerem": They may have the plunder of Ai. **3–8:** Joshua relates the Lord's instructions to the Israelites. The repetitions build suspense. **9–29:** Ai is captured and put under the "ḥerem." **9:** *Bethel,* the modern village of Beitin, is 17 km (11 mi) north of Jerusalem and 3 mi (5 km) northwest of Ai. Later it became one of the principal shrines of the Northern Kingdom (1 Kings 12.28–30; Gen 12.8; 28.11–22). **14–15:**

and they went to the place of ambush, and lay between Bethel and Ai, to the west of Ai; but Joshua spent that night in the camp.[a]

[10] In the morning Joshua rose early and mustered the people, and went up, with the elders of Israel, before the people to Ai. [11] All the fighting men who were with him went up, and drew near before the city, and camped on the north side of Ai, with a ravine between them and Ai. [12] Taking about five thousand men, he set them in ambush between Bethel and Ai, to the west of the city. [13] So they stationed the forces, the main encampment that was north of the city and its rear guard west of the city. But Joshua spent that night in the valley. [14] When the king of Ai saw this, he and all his people, the inhabitants of the city, hurried out early in the morning to the meeting place facing the Arabah to meet Israel in battle; but he did not know that there was an ambush against him behind the city. [15] And Joshua and all Israel made a pretense of being beaten before them, and fled in the direction of the wilderness. [16] So all the people who were in the city were called together to pursue them, and as they pursued Joshua they were drawn away from the city. [17] There was not a man left in Ai or Bethel who did not go out after Israel; they left the city open, and pursued Israel.

[18] Then the LORD said to Joshua, "Stretch out the sword that is in your hand toward Ai; for I will give it into your hand." And Joshua stretched out the sword that was in his hand toward the city. [19] As soon as he stretched out his hand, the troops in ambush rose quickly out of their place and rushed forward. They entered the city, took it, and at once set the city on fire. [20] So when the men of Ai looked back, the smoke of the city was rising to the sky. They had no power to flee this way or that, for the people who fled to the wilderness turned back against the pursuers. [21] When Joshua and all Israel saw that the ambush had taken the city and that the smoke of the city was rising, then they turned back and struck down the men of Ai. [22] And the others came out from the city against them; so they were surrounded by Israelites, some on one side, and some on the other; and Israel struck them down until no one was left who survived or escaped. [23] But the king of Ai was taken alive and brought to Joshua.

[24] When Israel had finished slaughtering all the inhabitants of Ai in the open wilderness where they pursued them, and when all of them to the very last had fallen by the edge of the sword, all Israel returned to Ai, and attacked it with the edge of the sword. [25] The total of those who fell that day, both men and women, was twelve thousand—all the people of Ai. [26] For Joshua did not draw back his hand, with which he stretched out the sword, until he had utterly destroyed all the inhabitants of Ai. [27] Only the livestock and the spoil of that city Israel took as their booty, according to the word of the LORD that he had issued to Joshua. [28] So Joshua burned Ai, and made it forever a heap of ruins, as it is to this day. [29] And he hanged the king of Ai on a tree until evening; and at sunset Joshua commanded, and they took his body down from the tree, threw it down at the entrance of the gate of the city, and raised over it a great heap of stones, which stands there to this day.

[30] Then Joshua built on Mount Ebal an altar to the LORD, the God of Israel, [31] just as

---

[a] Heb *among the people*

Facing the Arabah . . . in the direction of the wilderness, toward the Rift Valley, to the east. **18–29:** Joshua's stretching out his sword is similar to Moses' actions in Ex 14.15–21,26–27; 17.9–12, again suggesting the continuity between these two leaders, and Joshua's legitimacy. The third implementation of the "ḥerem" is the Canaanite city of Ai, which is depicted as a sacrificial burnt offering. Ironically, God allowed the Israelites to take some of the plunder from Ai that was under the "ḥerem" (v. 27), perhaps to avoid a repeat of the action of Achan. **28:** *Forever a heap of ruins,* lit. "an eternal tell, a devastation," cf. 11.13n.; Deut 13.16. **29:** The hanging of the king of Ai and his stone memorial in the gate of the city are common actions in ancient Near Eastern warfare. This also anticipates the execution of the five kings in 10.26–27 and follows the Deuteronomic injunction (Deut 21.22–23). It also contrasts to 1 Sam 15, where Saul does not put Agag, the Amalekite king, to death, thereby disqualifying himself from leadership.

8.30–35: Covenant renewal as land grant: Shechem. The events narrated in ch 9 are the natural sequel to the story about the fall of Ai (note that 8.29 flows into 9.3). Hence this account of covenant renewal is par-

Moses the servant of the LORD had commanded the Israelites, as it is written in the book of the law of Moses, "an altar of unhewn[a] stones, on which no iron tool has been used"; and they offered on it burnt offerings to the LORD, and sacrificed offerings of well-being. [32] And there, in the presence of the Israelites, Joshua[b] wrote on the stones a copy of the law of Moses, which he had written. [33] All Israel, alien as well as citizen, with their elders and officers and their judges, stood on opposite sides of the ark in front of the levitical priests who carried the ark of the covenant of the LORD, half of them in front of Mount Gerizim and half of them in front of Mount Ebal, as Moses the servant of the LORD had commanded at the first, that they should bless the people of Israel. [34] And afterward he read all the words of the law, blessings and curses, according to all that is written in the book of the law. [35] There was not a word of all that Moses commanded that Joshua did not read before all the assembly of Israel, and the women, and the little ones, and the aliens who resided among them.

9 Now when all the kings who were beyond the Jordan in the hill country and in the lowland all along the coast of the Great Sea toward Lebanon—the Hittites, the Amorites, the Canaanites, the Perizzites, the Hivites, and the Jebusites—heard of this, [2] they gathered together with one accord to fight Joshua and Israel.

[3] But when the inhabitants of Gibeon heard what Joshua had done to Jericho and to Ai, [4] they on their part acted with cunning: they went and prepared provisions,[c] and took worn-out sacks for their donkeys, and wineskins, worn-out and torn and mended, [5] with worn-out, patched sandals on their feet, and worn-out clothes; and all their provisions were dry and moldy. [6] They went to Joshua in the camp at Gilgal, and said to him and to the Israelites, "We have come from a far country; so now make a treaty with us." [7] But the Israelites said to the Hivites, "Perhaps you live among us; then how can we make a treaty with you?" [8] They said to Joshua, "We are your servants." And Joshua said to them, "Who are you? And where do you come from?" [9] They said to him, "Your servants have come from a very far country,

a   Heb *whole*
b   Heb *he*
c   Cn: Meaning of Heb uncertain

enthetical to the main action and is connected by many scholars with 24.1–28. Traveling to Ebal would have required the tribes to make a trip of about 50 km (30 mi) by road from Ai to Ebal and then to retrace their steps to encamp at Gilgal (9.6). This narrative serves to portray Joshua as carrying out the command given to Moses in Deut 27.4–7 (cf. Deut 11.29–30). Joshua, who obeyed, is the foil to Achan, who did not (cf. 6.27 and 7.1). The connections between this section and Deuteronomy are especially strong. **30:** *Mount Ebal* is one of the two mountains (Gerizim being the other) that flank the pass of Shechem in central Canaan. **31:** Quoting Deut 27.5. **32:** *On the stones*, not the stones of the altar, but those Moses had commanded to be used; see Deut 27.2–3; cf. Josh 24.26–27. *A copy of the law*, see Deut 17.18. **34:** *Blessings and curses*, see Deut 27.11–13; 28; cf. Lev 26.3–39. **35:** Patterned after the ritual of Deut 31.9–13.

9.1–11.15: The southern and northern campaigns. The conquests of southern and northern Canaan share the same geographic pattern: center to periphery. However, the account of the southern campaign is a much more developed narrative than that of the northern campaign, which can be observed in a comparison of the basic components of 9.3–10.43 and 11.1–15. Thus the region that became Judah's tribal allotment receives the greater emphasis (a pattern also found in chs 13–19 and Judg 1).

9.1–2: Introductory statement. The section recalls the motif of the inhabitants hearing and fearing (2.10 and 5.1; see also 10.1; 11.1), but in this case the reaction is not fear, but aggressive hostility. The exception is Gibeon, narrated first for contrastive reasons.

9.3–10.43: Southern campaign. 9.3–27: Gibeon. Ironically, Israel has just defeated Ai by means of a ruse; now Israel is the victim of a ruse. The Israelites do not turn to God to discern the Gibeonite strategy. As in the case of the first battle of Ai, the Israelites' overconfidence in their ability to discern the situation leads to a lack of dependence on the Lord. **3–15:** The Gibeonites are apparently Hivites. Fearing Israel, they pretend to be *from a far country* so as to take advantage of the more lenient treatment afforded to such people (Deut 20.15). **3:** *Gibeon* is the modern el-Jib, about 4 km (7 mi) southwest of Ai (see map on p. 322). **6:** *Treaty*, Heb "berit," also

because of the name of the LORD your God; for we have heard a report of him, of all that he did in Egypt, [10] and of all that he did to the two kings of the Amorites who were beyond the Jordan, King Sihon of Heshbon, and King Og of Bashan who lived in Ashtaroth. [11] So our elders and all the inhabitants of our country said to us, 'Take provisions in your hand for the journey; go to meet them, and say to them, "We are your servants; come now, make a treaty with us."' [12] Here is our bread; it was still warm when we took it from our houses as our food for the journey, on the day we set out to come to you, but now, see, it is dry and moldy; [13] these wineskins were new when we filled them, and see, they are burst; and these garments and sandals of ours are worn out from the very long journey." [14] So the leaders[a] partook of their provisions, and did not ask direction from the LORD. [15] And Joshua made peace with them, guaranteeing their lives by a treaty; and the leaders of the congregation swore an oath to them.

[16] But when three days had passed after they had made a treaty with them, they heard that they were their neighbors and were living among them. [17] So the Israelites set out and reached their cities on the third day. Now their cities were Gibeon, Chephirah, Beeroth, and Kiriath-jearim. [18] But the Israelites did not attack them, because the leaders of the congregation had sworn to them by the LORD, the God of Israel. Then all the congregation murmured against the leaders. [19] But all the leaders said to all the congregation, "We have sworn to them by the LORD, the God of Israel,

and now we must not touch them. [20] This is what we will do to them: We will let them live, so that wrath may not come upon us, because of the oath that we swore to them." [21] The leaders said to them, "Let them live." So they became hewers of wood and drawers of water for all the congregation, as the leaders had decided concerning them.

[22] Joshua summoned them, and said to them, "Why did you deceive us, saying, 'We are very far from you,' while in fact you are living among us? [23] Now therefore you are cursed, and some of you shall always be slaves, hewers of wood and drawers of water for the house of my God." [24] They answered Joshua, "Because it was told to your servants for a certainty that the LORD your God had commanded his servant Moses to give you all the land, and to destroy all the inhabitants of the land before you; so we were in great fear for our lives because of you, and did this thing. [25] And now we are in your hand: do as it seems good and right in your sight to do to us." [26] This is what he did for them: he saved them from the Israelites; and they did not kill them. [27] But on that day Joshua made them hewers of wood and drawers of water for the congregation and for the altar of the LORD, to continue to this day, in the place that he should choose.

10 When King Adoni-zedek of Jerusalem heard how Joshua had taken Ai, and had utterly destroyed it, doing to Ai and its king as he had done to Jericho and its king,

---

a Gk: Heb *men*

translated "covenant." **10:** See 2.10n. **14:** Although *the leaders* (lit. "the men") of Israel are specifically blamed for not consulting the Lord, Joshua is apparently included. None of Israel's leadership was exempt from blame. **16–27:** Discovery of the ruse and reaction. The Israelites discover the ruse of the Gibeonites, who readily admit their deception (vv. 24–25) because they know that Israel has to honor the pact between them (v. 20). The subservience of the Gibeonites is narrated twice in parallel: The leaders of the people save them and conclude their slave status, and so does Joshua (vv. 18–21 and vv. 22–27). **21:** *Hewers of wood and drawers of water,* according to Deut 29.10–13, the covenant was to erase distinctions between such lower class occupations and others. This designation thus suggests that the Gibeonites are outside the covenantal community. **24:** See Deut 20.16–18. Tensions with the Gibeonites persist into the monarchy (2 Sam 21.1–14). **27:** *The place that he should choose* is Deuteronomy's term for the central place of worship, later identified as Jerusalem (e.g., Deut 12.5–18).

10.1–43: The defeat of the Amorite alliance. This passage contains two scenes (vv. 1–15, vv. 16–43), both of which end with identical statements (vv. 15,43). Both scenes utilize temporal panels that back-track and overlap: Each subsequent panel takes a part of the previous panel and further develops it.

10.1–15: Scene one contains three panels (vv. 1–10,11,12–15). **1–10: The initial circumstances of the battle.** This panel is composed of two parts: the formation of the Amorite alliance headed by Adoni zedek of Jerusalem

and how the inhabitants of Gibeon had made peace with Israel and were among them, [2] he[a] became greatly frightened, because Gibeon was a large city, like one of the royal cities, and was larger than Ai, and all its men were warriors. [3] So King Adoni-zedek of Jerusalem sent a message to King Hoham of Hebron, to King Piram of Jarmuth, to King Japhia of Lachish, and to King Debir of Eglon, saying, [4] "Come up and help me, and let us attack Gibeon; for it has made peace with Joshua and with the Israelites." [5] Then the five kings of the Amorites—the king of Jerusalem, the king of Hebron, the king of Jarmuth, the king of Lachish, and the king of Eglon—gathered their forces, and went up with all their armies and camped against Gibeon, and made war against it.

[6] And the Gibeonites sent to Joshua at the camp in Gilgal, saying, "Do not abandon your servants; come up to us quickly, and save us, and help us; for all the kings of the Amorites who live in the hill country are gathered against us." [7] So Joshua went up from Gilgal, he and all the fighting force with him, all the mighty warriors. [8] The LORD said to Joshua, "Do not fear them, for I have handed them over to you; not one of them shall stand before you." [9] So Joshua came upon them suddenly, having marched up all night from Gilgal. [10] And the LORD threw them into a panic before

Israel, who inflicted a great slaughter on them at Gibeon, chased them by the way of the ascent of Beth-horon, and struck them down as far as Azekah and Makkedah. [11] As they fled before Israel, while they were going down the slope of Beth-horon, the LORD threw down huge stones from heaven on them as far as Azekah, and they died; there were more who died because of the hailstones than the Israelites killed with the sword.

[12] On the day when the LORD gave the Amorites over to the Israelites, Joshua spoke to the LORD; and he said in the sight of Israel,
"Sun, stand still at Gibeon,
    and Moon, in the valley of Aijalon."
[13] And the sun stood still, and the moon stopped,
    until the nation took vengeance on
        their enemies.
Is this not written in the Book of Jashar? The sun stopped in midheaven, and did not hurry to set for about a whole day. [14] There has been no day like it before or since, when the LORD heeded a human voice; for the LORD fought for Israel.

[15] Then Joshua returned, and all Israel with him, to the camp at Gilgal.

[16] Meanwhile, these five kings fled and hid themselves in the cave at Makkedah. [17] And

a Heb *they*

(vv. 1–5), and the initial open-field battle between the Israelites and the Amorite alliance with the slaughter and pursuit to Azekah (vv. 6–10). **1–2:** The treaty between Gibeon and Israel incited the kings of five Amorite city-states to attack Gibeon. Jerusalem, an important Bronze Age city-state, and later the capital of Judah, is the driving force in the alliance. **3:** See inset in map on p. 322 HB. **10:** The reference to *Azekah* and *Makkedah* anticipates the second panel of scene one as well as the first panel of scene two. *Azekah* is identified with Tell Zakariya; *Makkedah* is perhaps Khirbet el-Qom.

10.11: Divine intervention with hailstones. The second panel of scene one backtracks and overlaps the first panel, describing the enemy flight again to Azekah with the further development of the divine intervention with deadly *hailstones* (lit. "large stones from heaven"). Divine interventions are common motifs in ancient war accounts. These large hailstones (Heb "abanim gedolot") anticipate the large stones (Heb "abanim gedolot") that seal the kings in the caves (10.18,27; cf. 7.26).

10.12–15: Joshua's request to the LORD and the divine intervention. The third panel of scene one also backtracks and overlaps, describing Joshua's request to the Lord at the beginning of the battle with the further development of the divine intervention concerning the sun and moon (cf. Heb 3.11; Judg 5.20). The exact meaning of the divine intervention is difficult to ascertain because it is described only in poetry. **13:** *The Book of Jashar*, no longer extant, appears to have been a collection of poetry that extolled Israel's military victories and heroes (see 2 Sam 1.18). **15:** Scene one concludes with Joshua and Israel's return to Gilgal, which is repeated at the chapter's conclusion (v. 43) and need not be taken literally.

10.16–43: Scene two contains two panels (vv. 16–27; 28–39) and a summary (vv. 40–43). **16–27: The capture**

it was told Joshua, "The five kings have been found, hidden in the cave at Makkedah." [18] Joshua said, "Roll large stones against the mouth of the cave, and set men by it to guard them; [19] but do not stay there yourselves; pursue your enemies, and attack them from the rear. Do not let them enter their towns, for the LORD your God has given them into your hand." [20] When Joshua and the Israelites had finished inflicting a very great slaughter on them, until they were wiped out, and when the survivors had entered into the fortified towns, [21] all the people returned safe to Joshua in the camp at Makkedah; no one dared to speak[a] against any of the Israelites.

[22] Then Joshua said, "Open the mouth of the cave, and bring those five kings out to me from the cave." [23] They did so, and brought the five kings out to him from the cave, the king of Jerusalem, the king of Hebron, the king of Jarmuth, the king of Lachish, and the king of Eglon. [24] When they brought the kings out to Joshua, Joshua summoned all the Israelites, and said to the chiefs of the warriors who had gone with him, "Come near, put your feet on the necks of these kings." Then they came near and put their feet on their necks. [25] And Joshua said to them, "Do not be afraid or dismayed; be strong and courageous; for thus the LORD will do to all the enemies against whom you fight." [26] Afterward Joshua struck them down and put them to death, and he hung them on five trees. And they hung on the trees until evening. [27] At sunset Joshua commanded, and they took them down from the trees and threw them into the cave where they had hidden themselves; they set large stones against the mouth of the cave, which remain to this very day.

[28] Joshua took Makkedah on that day, and struck it and its king with the edge of the sword; he utterly destroyed every person in it; he left no one remaining. And he did to the king of Makkedah as he had done to the king of Jericho.

[29] Then Joshua passed on from Makkedah, and all Israel with him, to Libnah, and fought against Libnah. [30] The LORD gave it also and its king into the hand of Israel; and he struck it with the edge of the sword, and every person in it; he left no one remaining in it; and he did to its king as he had done to the king of Jericho.

[31] Next Joshua passed on from Libnah, and all Israel with him, to Lachish, and laid siege to it, and assaulted it. [32] The LORD gave Lachish into the hand of Israel, and he took it on the second day, and struck it with the edge of the sword, and every person in it, as he had done to Libnah.

[33] Then King Horam of Gezer came up to help Lachish; and Joshua struck him and his people, leaving him no survivors.

[34] From Lachish Joshua passed on with all Israel to Eglon; and they laid siege to it, and assaulted it; [35] and they took it that day, and struck it with the edge of the sword; and every person in it he utterly destroyed that day, as he had done to Lachish.

[36] Then Joshua went up with all Israel from Eglon to Hebron; they assaulted it, [37] and took

a Heb *moved his tongue*

and execution of the kings. The first panel backtracks and overlaps the pursuit, developing the capture and execution of the Amorite kings. The mention of *Makkedah* in v. 16 is resumptive (see v. 10). Ironically, the cave that the kings choose as their hiding place becomes first their prison, then their tomb. 24: *Feet on their necks*, symbolizing subjugation, as in 1 Kings 5.3; Ps 110.1. 26–27: In the ancient world, corpses of vanquished enemies were displayed for psychological effect; see 8.29n.

10.28–39: The capture and "ḥerem" of the cities. The second panel backtracks to the pursuit and develops the capture and "ḥerem" of the cities in a stereotyped and redundant manner. (A verbal form of "ḥerem" is translated "utterly destroyed" in vv. 28,35,37,39,40). This typical ancient Near Eastern war account uses hyperbole to emphasize the success of Israel and its God. The king of Gezer, at the center of the seven short episodes, emphasizes that city's importance. While the city is not captured, the defeat of its king and army in open battle crowns the southern campaign. 31–32: *Lachish* (Tell ed-Duweir) was one of the more important southern cities. 33: According to other passages, *Gezer* becomes an Israelite city only in the time of Solomon (see 1 Kings 9.16). The Ephraimites had failed to capture it (16.10; Judg 1.29). 34–35: *Eglon* may be identified with Tell Aitun. 36–39: *Hebron* and *Debir* (probably Khirbet Rabud) fall to "all" Israel. In 14.6–15 Caleb is credited

it, and struck it with the edge of the sword, and its king and its towns, and every person in it; he left no one remaining, just as he had done to Eglon, and utterly destroyed it with every person in it. [38] Then Joshua, with all Israel, turned back to Debir and assaulted it, [39] and he took it with its king and all its towns; they struck them with the edge of the sword, and utterly destroyed every person in it; he left no one remaining; just as he had done to Hebron, and, as he had done to Libnah and its king, so he did to Debir and its king. [40] So Joshua defeated the whole land, the hill country and the Negeb and the lowland and the slopes, and all their kings; he left no one remaining, but utterly destroyed all that breathed, as the LORD God of Israel commanded. [41] And Joshua defeated them from Kadesh-barnea to Gaza, and all the country of Goshen, as far as Gibeon. [42] Joshua took all these kings and their land at one time, because the LORD God of Israel fought for Israel. [43] Then Joshua returned, and all Israel with him, to the camp at Gilgal.

11 When King Jabin of Hazor heard of this, he sent to King Jobab of Madon, to the king of Shimron, to the king of Achshaph, [2] and to the kings who were in the northern hill country, and in the Arabah south of Chin-neroth, and in the lowland, and in Naphoth-dor on the west, [3] to the Canaanites in the east and the west, the Amorites, the Hittites, the Perizzites, and the Jebusites in the hill country, and the Hivites under Hermon in the land of Mizpah. [4] They came out, with all their troops, a great army, in number like the sand on the seashore, with very many horses and chariots. [5] All these kings joined their forces, and came and camped together at the waters of Merom, to fight with Israel.

[6] And the LORD said to Joshua, "Do not be afraid of them, for tomorrow at this time I will hand over all of them, slain, to Israel; you shall hamstring their horses, and burn their chariots with fire." [7] So Joshua came suddenly upon them with all his fighting force, by the waters of Merom, and fell upon them. [8] And the LORD handed them over to Israel, who attacked them and chased them as far as Great Sidon and Misrephoth-maim, and eastward as far as the valley of Mizpeh. They struck them down, until they had left no one remaining. [9] And Joshua did to them as the LORD commanded him; he hamstrung their horses, and burned their chariots with fire.

[10] Joshua turned back at that time, and took Hazor, and struck its king down with the sword. Before that time Hazor was the head of all those kingdoms. [11] And they put to the

with victory at Hebron (see 15.13–14), but Judah in general gets credit in Judg 1.10. In 15.15–17 and Judg 1.11–13 Othniel is credited with the capture of Debir. These conflicting accounts highlight the perspective of chs 1–12, a conquest by "all Israel."

10.40–43: Summary of the southern campaign. Overstatement emphasizes the greatness of the Israelite victory. Scene two concludes (like scene one) with Joshua and Israel returning to Gilgal (10.43). 40: *Negeb,* the semidesert region in the south. 41: *Kadesh-barnea,* Num 13.1–14.45n. and map [OBA, p. 79, D-3]; see Deut 1.19; 9.23. *Goshen,* a designation of the region north of the Negeb (see also 11.16); not the region with the same name in the Egyptian Delta (Gen 45.10; etc.).

11.1–15: Northern campaign. A literary mirror of 10.1–43 both in general structure and vocabulary, though less developed.

11.1–11: Defeat of the Canaanite coalition. A large and powerful Canaanite coalition is organized and headed by Jabin, the king of Hazor. The name *Jabin* occurs here and in Judg 4 and Ps 83.10. Scholars generally see Judg 4–5 as the source for this story. 1: The final occurrence of the "hearing" motif, see 5.1n. The locations of *Madon, Shimron,* and *Achshaph* are not certain. 2: The *Arabah* is the Jordan Valley; *Chinneroth,* the Sea of Galilee. 3–5: This enemy is superior to the Israelite army, both numerically and technologically (they have dreaded horses and chariots). This coalition presents the most significant threat to Israel's success in conquering the land. *Hermon,* the high mountain in the extreme north of Israel. *Merom* is a city in Galilee known from extrabiblical sources; its precise location is not certain. 6: The Lord's oracle of assurance precedes the victory (cf. 8.1; 10.8). *Hamstring their horses* means cutting a tendon of a rear leg to make them useless (see 2 Sam 8.4). 10–11: Hazor, the most important northern city, is totally destroyed by burning just like Jericho and Ai (cf. 6.24; 8.8,19). Jericho and Hazor frame the "conquest" of the land of Canaan.

sword all who were in it, utterly destroying them; there was no one left who breathed, and he burned Hazor with fire. [12] And all the towns of those kings, and all their kings, Joshua took, and struck them with the edge of the sword, utterly destroying them, as Moses the servant of the LORD had commanded. [13] But Israel burned none of the towns that stood on mounds except Hazor, which Joshua did burn. [14] All the spoil of these towns, and the livestock, the Israelites took for their booty; but all the people they struck down with the edge of the sword, until they had destroyed them, and they did not leave any who breathed. [15] As the LORD had commanded his servant Moses, so Moses commanded Joshua, and so Joshua did; he left nothing undone of all that the LORD had commanded Moses.

[16] So Joshua took all that land: the hill country and all the Negeb and all the land of Goshen and the lowland and the Arabah and the hill country of Israel and its lowland, [17] from Mount Halak, which rises toward Seir, as far as Baal-gad in the valley of Lebanon below Mount Hermon. He took all their kings, struck them down, and put them to death. [18] Joshua made war a long time with all those kings. [19] There was not a town that made peace with the Israelites, except the Hivites, the inhabitants of Gibeon; all were taken in battle. [20] For it was the LORD's doing to harden their hearts so that they would come against Israel in battle, in order that they might be utterly destroyed, and might receive no mercy, but be exterminated, just as the LORD had commanded Moses.

[21] At that time Joshua came and wiped out the Anakim from the hill country, from Hebron, from Debir, from Anab, and from all the hill country of Judah, and from all the hill country of Israel; Joshua utterly destroyed them with their towns. [22] None of the Anakim was left in the land of the Israelites; some remained only in Gaza, in Gath, and in Ashdod. [23] So Joshua took the whole land, according to all that the LORD had spoken to Moses; and Joshua gave it for an inheritance to Israel according to their tribal allotments. And the land had rest from war.

12 Now these are the kings of the land, whom the Israelites defeated, whose land they occupied beyond the Jordan toward the east, from the Wadi Arnon to Mount Hermon, with all the Arabah eastward: [2] King Sihon of the Amorites who lived at Heshbon, and ruled from Aroer, which is on the edge of the Wadi Arnon, and from the middle of the valley as far as the river Jabbok, the boundary of the Ammonites, that is, half of Gilead, [3] and the Arabah to the Sea of Chinneroth eastward, and in the direction of Beth-jeshimoth, to the sea of the Arabah, the Dead Sea,[a] southward to the foot of the slopes of Pisgah; [4] and King Og[b] of Bashan, one of the last of the Rephaim, who lived at Ashtaroth and at Edrei [5] and ruled over Mount Hermon and Salecah and all Bashan to the boundary of the Geshurites and the

a   Heb *Salt Sea*
b   Gk: Heb *the boundary of King Og*

11.12–15: Summary of northern campaign. The Israelite conquest in the north is summarized by noting several times that "all" was conquered by Joshua, the worthy successor to Moses, who fulfilled the requirements of Deut 20.16–17. **13:** *Mounds,* translating the Hebrew word for "tells," cf. 8.28n.

11.16–23: Summary of total conquest. 16–19: The word *all* characterizes these verses, emphasizing the totality of the conquest. **18–20:** The depiction here somewhat conflicts with the earlier accounts, suggesting that a protracted war was necessary. **20:** *Harden their hearts,* this phrase is elsewhere used of Pharaoh in Egypt (Ex 4.21; etc.), and suggests that, for the Lord and for the author, the inhabitants of the land were enemies comparable to the Egyptians. **21:** *The Anakim,* a term for pre-Israelite inhabitants of Canaan renowned for their size and strength (Deut 9.2). **23:** *And the land had rest from war,* a conclusion formula, moving toward a transition from the conquest to the division of land. This declaration recurs in 14.15, forming a literary link between the defeat of the Anakim by Joshua (ch 11) and their defeat by Caleb (ch 14).

12.1–24: A selective list of defeated cities' kings. An additional conclusion to the first section of the book. **1–6: Moses' exploits in Transjordan.** This summary draws from Deut 2–3; (see map on p. 252 in Deut). **2:** The story of *King Sihon* is narrated in Num 21.21–31 and Deut 2.26–37. **4:** The defeat of *Og* is narrated in Num 21.33–35 and Deut 3.1–17. *Bashan,* northern Transjordan. *Rephaim,* here another term for pre-Israelite inhabitants of Canaan.

Maacathites, and over half of Gilead to the boundary of King Sihon of Heshbon. [6] Moses, the servant of the LORD, and the Israelites defeated them; and Moses the servant of the LORD gave their land for a possession to the Reubenites and the Gadites and the half-tribe of Manasseh.

[7] The following are the kings of the land whom Joshua and the Israelites defeated on the west side of the Jordan, from Baal-gad in the valley of Lebanon to Mount Halak, that rises toward Seir (and Joshua gave their land to the tribes of Israel as a possession according to their allotments, [8] in the hill country, in the lowland, in the Arabah, in the slopes, in the wilderness, and in the Negeb, the land of the Hittites, Amorites, Canaanites, Perizzites, Hivites, and Jebusites):

[9] the king of Jericho	one
the king of Ai, which is next to Bethel	one
[10] the king of Jerusalem	one
the king of Hebron	one
[11] the king of Jarmuth	one
the king of Lachish	one
[12] the king of Eglon	one
the king of Gezer	one
[13] the king of Debir	one
the king of Geder	one
[14] the king of Hormah	one
the king of Arad	one
[15] the king of Libnah	one
the king of Adullam	one
[16] the king of Makkedah	one
the king of Bethel	one
[17] the king of Tappuah	one
the king of Hepher	one
[18] the king of Aphek	one
the king of Lasharon	one
[19] the king of Madon	one
the king of Hazor	one
[20] the king of Shimron-meron	one
the king of Achshaph	one
[21] the king of Taanach	one
the king of Megiddo	one
[22] the king of Kedesh	one
the king of Jokneam in Carmel	one
[23] the king of Dor in Naphath-dor	one
the king of Goiim in Galilee,[a]	one
[24] the king of Tirzah	one

thirty-one kings in all.

13 Now Joshua was old and advanced in years; and the LORD said to him, "You are old and advanced in years, and very much of the land still remains to be possessed. [2] This is the land that still remains: all the regions of the Philistines, and all those of

a   Gk: Heb *Gilgal*

12.7–24: Joshua's victories west of the Jordan. Previous narratives mention fewer than half of these cities. Vv. 9–13a follow the order of chs 6–10, but after that there is no clear pattern. This section thus seems to be adapted from a different source than the previous chapters. Moreover, the length of this list shows that previous narratives are selective, highlighting particular stories for ideological and theological purposes. For the location of the places, see map 4 at the end of this volume.

13.1–24.33: The allotment of land. Having completed his first task, the conquest (1.2–5), Joshua turns his attention to his second task (1.6): "Put this people in possession of the land" (cf. Deut 4.21; 15.4; 19.10). The concern over allotment or inheritance ("naḥalah") unifies this section (13.6; 14.3,13; 17.4,6,14; 19.49). The section emphasizes that the division follows the divine will, as mediated by Joshua and Eleazar the priest. It utilizes four types of sources: boundary descriptions; town lists integrated into boundary descriptions; town lists; and short narratives that relate incidents of importance within the allotments, providing didactic significance to the division of the land. The cities of refuge and Levitical cities are attached at the end of the section since it is necessary for the tribes to receive their inheritance before they can allocate parts of it to others. For this entire section, see map on p. 347.

13.1–7: Land remaining. The land remaining is defined by those towns and regions inside the borders of Canaan (cf. Num 34.1–12) that are not under Israelite control. This foreshadows other passages in chs 13–21 that contrast with the first half of the book, by documenting Israel's failure to capture all of the land, or by noting that foreigners live among the Israelites. These contrast ironically with the idealistic reports given in the text (cf. 15.63; 16.10; 17.11–13; 18.2; 19.47). The particular areas designated as outside Israelite possession are *the regions of the Philistines* (the southwestern coastal area), *and all those of the Geshurites* (east of the Sea of Galilee) (cf. 13.13), and the land of Phoenicia (northern coastal areas). Philistia and Geshur came under Israelite control during the period of David and Solomon (2 Sam 8.1–2; 3.3).

the Geshurites ³ (from the Shihor, which is east of Egypt, northward to the boundary of Ekron, it is reckoned as Canaanite; there are five rulers of the Philistines, those of Gaza, Ashdod, Ashkelon, Gath, and Ekron), and those of the Avvim ⁴ in the south; all the land of the Canaanites, and Mearah that belongs to the Sidonians, to Aphek, to the boundary of the Amorites, ⁵ and the land of the Gebalites, and all Lebanon, toward the east, from Baal-gad below Mount Hermon to Lebo-hamath, ⁶ all the inhabitants of the hill country from Lebanon to Misrephoth-maim, even all the Sidonians. I will myself drive them out from before the Israelites; only allot the land to Israel for an inheritance, as I have commanded you. ⁷ Now therefore divide this land for an inheritance to the nine tribes and the half-tribe of Manasseh."

⁸ With the other half-tribe of Manasseh[a] the Reubenites and the Gadites received their inheritance, which Moses gave them, beyond the Jordan eastward, as Moses the servant of the LORD gave them: ⁹ from Aroer, which is on the edge of the Wadi Arnon, and the town that is in the middle of the valley, and all the tableland from[b] Medeba as far as Dibon; ¹⁰ and all the cities of King Sihon of the Amorites, who reigned in Heshbon, as far as the boundary of the Ammonites; ¹¹ and Gilead, and the region of the Geshurites and Maacathites, and all Mount Hermon, and all Bashan to Salecah; ¹² all the kingdom of Og in Bashan, who reigned in Ashtaroth and in Edrei (he alone was left of the survivors of the Rephaim); these Moses had defeated and driven out. ¹³ Yet the Israelites did not drive out the Geshurites or the Maacathites; but Geshur and Maacath live within Israel to this day.

¹⁴ To the tribe of Levi alone Moses gave no inheritance; the offerings by fire to the LORD God of Israel are their inheritance, as he said to them.

¹⁵ Moses gave an inheritance to the tribe of the Reubenites according to their clans. ¹⁶ Their territory was from Aroer, which is on the edge of the Wadi Arnon, and the town that is in the middle of the valley, and all the tableland by Medeba; ¹⁷ with Heshbon, and all its towns that are in the tableland; Dibon, and Bamoth-baal, and Beth-baal-meon, ¹⁸ and Jahaz, and Kedemoth, and Mephaath, ¹⁹ and Kiriathaim, and Sibmah, and Zereth-shahar on the hill of the valley, ²⁰ and Beth-peor, and the slopes of Pisgah, and Beth-jeshimoth, ²¹ that is, all the towns of the tableland, and all the kingdom of King Sihon of the Amorites, who reigned in Heshbon, whom Moses defeated with the leaders of Midian, Evi and Rekem and Zur and Hur and Reba, as princes of Sihon, who lived in the land. ²² Along with the rest of those they put to death, the Israelites also put to the sword Balaam son of Beor, who practiced divination. ²³ And the border of the Reubenites was the Jordan and its banks. This was the inheritance of the Reubenites according to their families with their towns and villages.

²⁴ Moses gave an inheritance also to the tribe of the Gadites, according to their families. ²⁵ Their territory was Jazer, and all the towns of Gilead, and half the land of the Ammonites, to Aroer, which is east of Rabbah, ²⁶ and from Heshbon to Ramath-mizpeh and Betonim, and from Mahanaim to the territory of Debir,[c] ²⁷ and in the valley Beth-haram,

a Cn: Heb *With it*
b Compare Gk: Heb lacks *from*
c Gk Syr Vg: Heb *Lidebir*

13.8–33: Transjordanian tribal allotment. Before the allotments west of the Jordan can be described, the Transjordanian allotments that Moses made are recounted: a general description of the extent of the Transjordanian lands (13.8–13), a declaration that the Levites received no inheritance (13.14), a specific description of the Transjordanian territories (13.15–32), and again a declaration that the Levites received no inheritance (13.33). Israel had great difficulties controlling this territory throughout its history, though Deuteronomy considered it part of Israel (see Deut 3.12–17). See map on p. 237 [Num map #3] and map 2 at the end of this volume. 12: *Rephaim,* see 12.4n. 13: The first of a number of qualifications about Israelite success in possessing the land. 14: *Offerings by fire,* as the priestly tribe, the Levites were in charge of worship and shared the offerings; cf. Lev 7.29–36; etc. See also v. 33n. 21: *Midian,* see Num 31.1–12. 22: *Balaam,* in contrast to the narrative about him in Num 22–24, here this non-Israelite prophet is presented in a negative light, and only here and in Num 31.8 are the Israelites said to have killed him.

Beth-nimrah, Succoth, and Zaphon, the rest of the kingdom of King Sihon of Heshbon, the Jordan and its banks, as far as the lower end of the Sea of Chinnereth, eastward beyond the Jordan. [28] This is the inheritance of the Gadites according to their clans, with their towns and villages.

[29] Moses gave an inheritance to the half-tribe of Manasseh; it was allotted to the half-tribe of the Manassites according to their families. [30] Their territory extended from Mahanaim, through all Bashan, the whole kingdom of King Og of Bashan, and all the settlements of Jair, which are in Bashan, sixty towns, [31] and half of Gilead, and Ashtaroth, and Edrei, the towns of the kingdom of Og in Bashan; these were allotted to the people of Machir son of Manasseh according to their clans—for half the Machirites.

[32] These are the inheritances that Moses distributed in the plains of Moab, beyond the Jordan east of Jericho. [33] But to the tribe of Levi Moses gave no inheritance; the LORD God of Israel is their inheritance, as he said to them.

14 These are the inheritances that the Israelites received in the land of Canaan, which the priest Eleazar, and Joshua son of Nun, and the heads of the families of the tribes of the Israelites distributed to them. [2] Their inheritance was by lot, as the LORD had commanded Moses for the nine and one-half tribes. [3] For Moses had given an inheritance to the two and one-half tribes beyond the Jordan; but to the Levites he gave no inheritance among them. [4] For the people of Joseph were two tribes, Manasseh and Ephraim; and no portion was given to the Levites in the land, but only towns to live in, with their pasture lands for their flocks and herds. [5] The Israelites did as the LORD commanded Moses; they allotted the land.

[6] Then the people of Judah came to Joshua at Gilgal; and Caleb son of Jephunneh the Kenizzite said to him, "You know what the LORD said to Moses the man of God in Kadesh-barnea concerning you and me. [7] I was forty years old when Moses the servant of the LORD sent me from Kadesh-barnea to spy out the land; and I brought him an honest report. [8] But my companions who went up with me made the heart of the people melt; yet I wholeheartedly followed the LORD my God. [9] And Moses swore on that day, saying, 'Surely the land on which your foot has trodden shall be an inheritance for you and your children forever, because you have wholeheartedly followed the LORD my God.' [10] And now, as you see, the LORD has kept me alive, as he said, these forty-five years since the time that the LORD spoke this word to Moses, while Israel was journeying through the wilderness; and here I am today, eighty-five years old. [11] I am still as strong today as I was on the day that Moses sent me; my strength now is as my strength was then, for war, and for going and coming. [12] So now give me

14.1–19.51: Cisjordanian tribal allotment. The story of the allotments to the tribes west of the Jordan is framed by an introduction (14.1–5) and a summary (19.51). The main text is divided into two major sections: the Judah and Joseph allotments (14.6–17.18) and the seven other tribal allotments (18.1–19.51). 33: A somewhat different formulation from v. 14; cf. Deut 10.9; 18.2; 18.7.

14.1–5: Introduction to the process of allotment. Eleazar (the chief priest, son of Aaron), Joshua, and the heads of the tribal families oversaw this allotment, which was performed by lot (see 7.14n.). 4–5: See Num 34.13–15; 35.3. To maintain the number of tribes at twelve, the people of Joseph were counted as two tribes, Manasseh and Ephraim, to make up for Levi's lack of inheritance.

14.6–17.18: Judah and Joseph allotments. Parallel structures are used to describe the allotments to these tribes: narrative frames, boundary descriptions, and town lists, with vignettes in the center.

14.6–15.63: Judah. The tribe to which King David belonged is first.

14.6–15: Caleb's conquest. The success of Judah is specifically illustrated in the narrative frame story of Caleb's conquest of Hebron. Caleb was one of the original twelve spies sent into the land of Canaan (Num 13.30; 14.24). Caleb and his clan conquer Hebron, the home of the Anakim. The repetition in v. 15 of the statement and the land had rest from war connects this story to 11.21–23. Ironically, it was the fear of these very Anakim that caused Israel's disobedience and failure at Kadesh-barnea, according to Num 13.28 and Deut 1.28. 10: According to Deut 2.14, thirty-eight years elapsed from the events at Kadesh to the entry into the land; the events of the

this hill country of which the LORD spoke on that day; for you heard on that day how the Anakim were there, with great fortified cities; it may be that the LORD will be with me, and I shall drive them out, as the LORD said." ¹³ Then Joshua blessed him, and gave Hebron to Caleb son of Jephunneh for an inheritance. ¹⁴ So Hebron became the inheritance of Caleb son of Jephunneh the Kenizzite to this day, because he wholeheartedly followed the LORD, the God of Israel. ¹⁵ Now the name of Hebron formerly was Kiriath-arba;ᵃ this Arba wasᵇ the greatest man among the Anakim. And the land had rest from war.

15 The lot for the tribe of the people of Judah according to their families reached southward to the boundary of Edom, to the wilderness of Zin at the farthest south. ² And their south boundary ran from the end of the Dead Sea,ᶜ from the bay that faces southward; ³ it goes out southward of the ascent of Akrabbim, passes along to Zin, and goes up south of Kadesh-barnea, along by Hezron, up to Addar, makes a turn to Karka, ⁴ passes along to Azmon, goes out by the Wadi of Egypt, and comes to its end at the sea. This shall be your south boundary. ⁵ And the east boundary is the Dead Sea,ᶜ to the mouth of the Jordan. And the boundary on the north side runs from the bay of the sea at the mouth of the Jordan; ⁶ and the boundary goes up to Beth-hoglah, and passes along north of Beth-arabah; and the boundary goes up to the Stone of Bohan, Reuben's son; ⁷ and the boundary goes up to Debir from the

Valley of Achor, and so northward, turning toward Gilgal, which is opposite the ascent of Adummim, which is on the south side of the valley; and the boundary passes along to the waters of En-shemesh, and ends at En-rogel; ⁸ then the boundary goes up by the valley of the son of Hinnom at the southern slope of the Jebusites (that is, Jerusalem); and the boundary goes up to the top of the mountain that lies over against the valley of Hinnom, on the west, at the northern end of the valley of Rephaim; ⁹ then the boundary extends from the top of the mountain to the spring of the Waters of Nephtoah, and from there to the towns of Mount Ephron; then the boundary bends around to Baalah (that is, Kiriath-jearim); ¹⁰ and the boundary circles west of Baalah to Mount Seir, passes along to the northern slope of Mount Jearim (that is, Chesalon), and goes down to Beth-shemesh, and passes along by Timnah; ¹¹ the boundary goes out to the slope of the hill north of Ekron, then the boundary bends around to Shikkeron, and passes along to Mount Baalah, and goes out to Jabneel; then the boundary comes to an end at the sea. ¹² And the west boundary was the Mediterranean with its coast. This is the boundary surrounding the people of Judah according to their families.

¹³ According to the commandment of the LORD to Joshua, he gave to Caleb son of Jep-

ᵃ That is *the city of Arba*
ᵇ Heb lacks *this Arba was*
ᶜ Heb *Salt Sea*

preceding chapters thus took seven years. **13:** *Hebron* (Tell Rumeideh) is 31 km (19 mi) south of Jerusalem. **14:** This prime example of Judahite success is accomplished by a non-Israelite: Caleb is a Kenizzite (14.6,14) who is, however, ultimately incorporated into Judah's genealogy (1 Chr 2.9,18). **15:** See 15.13; Gen 23.2.

15.1–12: Judah's boundary description is given in a counterclockwise arrangement: south (vv. 2–4), east (v. 5), north (vv. 6–11), west (v. 12a; cf. 11.21–22; Judg 1.18–19; Josh 15.63), with a concluding boundary description (v. 12b). See map on p. 347 and map 4 at the end of this volume. **1:** *Wilderness of Zin,* the locale of Kadesh-barnea, in the southern Negeb (see 10.41n.; Num 20.1; Deut 32.51). **4:** *Wadi of Egypt,* either the Wadi Besor or the Wadi el-Arish, both south of Gaza. **6:** *Bohan,* means "thumb"; see 18.17. No son of Reuben with this name is mentioned elsewhere, and the location of part of the tribe of Reuben west of the Jordan is unusual. **7–8:** For the geography of Jerusalem, see map 4 at the end of this volume.

15.13–19: Vignettes about Judah's heroes (cf. 10.36–39; Judg 1.9–15): male, Caleb and Othniel (15.13–17), and female, Achsah (15.18–19). In the first vignette, Caleb conquers Hebron (see 14.6–15) and attacks the city of Debir. After recording Caleb's challenge and offer of his daughter in marriage (cf. 1 Sam 17.25), Othniel steps forward as the conquering hero of Debir. In the second, Achsah takes the initiative, urging her husband to ask for a field and then requesting her father to give her springs or pools since land without water is land without

hunneh a portion among the people of Judah, Kiriath-arba,[a] that is, Hebron (Arba was the father of Anak). [14] And Caleb drove out from there the three sons of Anak: Sheshai, Ahiman, and Talmai, the descendants of Anak. [15] From there he went up against the inhabitants of Debir; now the name of Debir formerly was Kiriath-sepher. [16] And Caleb said, "Whoever attacks Kiriath-sepher and takes it, to him I will give my daughter Achsah as wife." [17] Othniel son of Kenaz, the brother of Caleb, took it; and he gave him his daughter Achsah as wife. [18] When she came to him, she urged him to ask her father for a field. As she dismounted from her donkey, Caleb said to her, "What do you wish?" [19] She said to him, "Give me a present; since you have set me in the land of the Negeb, give me springs of water as well." So Caleb gave her the upper springs and the lower springs.

[20] This is the inheritance of the tribe of the people of Judah according to their families. [21] The towns belonging to the tribe of the people of Judah in the extreme south, toward the boundary of Edom, were Kabzeel, Eder, Jagur, [22] Kinah, Dimonah, Adadah, [23] Kedesh, Hazor, Ithnan, [24] Ziph, Telem, Bealoth, [25] Hazor-hadattah, Kerioth-hezron (that is, Hazor), [26] Amam, Shema, Moladah, [27] Hazar-gaddah, Heshmon, Beth-pelet, [28] Hazar-shual, Beer-sheba, Biziothiah, [29] Baalah, Iim, Ezem, [30] Eltolad, Chesil, Hormah, [31] Ziklag, Madmannah, Sansannah, [32] Lebaoth, Shilhim, Ain, and Rimmon: in all, twenty-nine towns, with their villages.

[33] And in the lowland, Eshtaol, Zorah, Ashnah, [34] Zanoah, En-gannim, Tappuah, Enam, [35] Jarmuth, Adullam, Socoh, Azekah, [36] Shaaraim, Adithaim, Gederah, Gederothaim: fourteen towns with their villages.

[37] Zenan, Hadashah, Migdal-gad, [38] Dilan, Mizpeh, Jokthe-el, [39] Lachish, Bozkath, Eglon, [40] Cabbon, Lahmam, Chitlish, [41] Gederoth, Beth-dagon, Naamah, and Makkedah: sixteen towns with their villages.

[42] Libnah, Ether, Ashan, [43] Iphtah, Ashnah, Nezib, [44] Keilah, Achzib, and Mareshah: nine towns with their villages.

[45] Ekron, with its dependencies and its villages; [46] from Ekron to the sea, all that were near Ashdod, with their villages.

[47] Ashdod, its towns and its villages; Gaza, its towns and its villages; to the Wadi of Egypt, and the Great Sea with its coast.

[48] And in the hill country, Shamir, Jattir, Socoh, [49] Dannah, Kiriath-sannah (that is, Debir), [50] Anab, Eshtemoh, Anim, [51] Goshen, Holon, and Giloh: eleven towns with their villages.

[52] Arab, Dumah, Eshan, [53] Janim, Beth-tappuah, Aphekah, [54] Humtah, Kiriath-arba (that is, Hebron), and Zior: nine towns with their villages.

[55] Maon, Carmel, Ziph, Juttah, [56] Jezreel, Jokdeam, Zanoah, [57] Kain, Gibeah, and Timnah: ten towns with their villages.

[58] Halhul, Beth-zur, Gedor, [59] Maarath, Beth-anoth, and Eltekon: six towns with their villages.

[60] Kiriath-baal (that is, Kiriath-jearim) and Rabbah: two towns with their villages.

[61] In the wilderness, Beth-arabah, Middin, Secacah, [62] Nibshan, the City of Salt, and En-gedi: six towns with their villages.

[63] But the people of Judah could not drive out the Jebusites, the inhabitants of Jerusalem; so the Jebusites live with the people of Judah in Jerusalem to this day.

16

The allotment of the Josephites went from the Jordan by Jericho, east of the waters of Jericho, into the wilderness, going

[a] That is the city of Arba

life. She seeks a sufficient blessing in the land.

15.20–62: A list of Judah's towns according to districts that is generally considered to have originated in the monarchic period. A similar list is found in 1 Kings 4.7–19.

15.63: A narrative postscript noting Judah's failure to conquer Jerusalem. This failure contrasts with Caleb's success in the initial narrative of Judah's allotment (14.6–15). David captures this city (2 Sam 5.6–9). *Jebusites*, Jebus, the name by which Jerusalem was known before its conquest by David.

16.1–17.18: Joseph (Ephraim and Half-Manasseh). As the primary power in the Northern Kingdom, Joseph is mentioned next. See map on p. 347.

16.1–4: A narrative frame that gives the general outline of the southern borders of the Joseph tribes (i.e., the southern boundary of Ephraim). There is ambiguity concerning the people of Joseph. They receive one

up from Jericho into the hill country to Bethel; [2] then going from Bethel to Luz, it passes along to Ataroth, the territory of the Archites; [3] then it goes down westward to the territory of the Japhletites, as far as the territory of Lower Beth-horon, then to Gezer, and it ends at the sea.

[4] The Josephites—Manasseh and Ephraim—received their inheritance.

[5] The territory of the Ephraimites by their families was as follows: the boundary of their inheritance on the east was Ataroth-addar as far as Upper Beth-horon, [6] and the boundary goes from there to the sea; on the north is Michmethath; then on the east the boundary makes a turn toward Taanath-shiloh, and passes along beyond it on the east to Janoah, [7] then it goes down from Janoah to Ataroth and to Naarah, and touches Jericho, ending at the Jordan. [8] From Tappuah the boundary goes westward to the Wadi Kanah, and ends at the sea. Such is the inheritance of the tribe of the Ephraimites by their families, [9] together with the towns that were set apart for the Ephraimites within the inheritance of the Manassites, all those towns with their villages. [10] They did not, however, drive out the Canaanites who lived in Gezer: so the Canaanites have lived within Ephraim to this day but have been made to do forced labor.

17 Then allotment was made to the tribe of Manasseh, for he was the firstborn of Joseph. To Machir the firstborn of Manasseh, the father of Gilead, were allotted Gilead and Bashan, because he was a warrior. [2] And allotments were made to the rest of the tribe of Manasseh, by their families, Abiezer, Helek, Asriel, Shechem, Hepher, and Shemida; these were the male descendants of Manasseh son of Joseph, by their families.

[3] Now Zelophehad son of Hepher son of Gilead son of Machir son of Manasseh had no sons, but only daughters; and these are the names of his daughters: Mahlah, Noah, Hoglah, Milcah, and Tirzah. [4] They came before the priest Eleazar and Joshua son of Nun and the leaders, and said, "The LORD commanded Moses to give us an inheritance along with our male kin." So according to the commandment of the LORD he gave them an inheritance among the kinsmen of their father. [5] Thus there fell to Manasseh ten portions, besides the land of Gilead and Bashan, which is on the other side of the Jordan, [6] because the daughters of Manasseh received an inheritance along with his sons. The land of Gilead was allotted to the rest of the Manassites.

[7] The territory of Manasseh reached from Asher to Michmethath, which is east of Shechem; then the boundary goes along southward to the inhabitants of En-tappuah. [8] The land of Tappuah belonged to Manasseh, but the town of Tappuah on the boundary

allotment (16.1), as if they constitute one tribe, yet they are recognized as two distinct tribal units (Manasseh and Ephraim; 14.4a). In addition, one of the tribes, Manasseh, is further divided. Part of the tribe has already received an allotment in Transjordan, while the remainder receives its allotment in Cisjordan.

16.5–10: Ephraim's boundary description is delineated. The fragmentary description here contrasts with that devoted to Judah (15.1–12). **10:** The Ephraimites failed to dispossess the Canaanites, though putting them under forced labor; cf. 15.63; Judg 1.29.

17.1–6: Ephraim's heroes. This somewhat disjointed section corresponds to Judah's vignettes of heroes. **1–2:** The mighty *warrior* (parallel to Caleb and Othniel in 15.13–17) is Machir, Manasseh's firstborn (cf. Num 32.39–40), who is given Gilead and Bashan, in Transjordan (see map on p. 347). Yet the allotment for *the rest of the tribe of Manasseh* west of the Jordan is given in the form of a town list without any connection to the ancestral hero. Although Ephraim's territory was listed first, Manasseh is considered the firstborn, as in Gen 48.13–20. **3–6:** The tribes' heroic women (corresponding to Achsah in 15.18–19) are the daughters of Zelophehad (see Num 27.1–11; 36.1–12).

17.7–13: Manasseh's boundary description is given. It includes a list of towns that the tribe had within the tribal allotments of Issachar and Asher (v. 11). As in the case of Ephraim, the Canaanites were not driven out, but were put to forced labor (vv. 12–13, cf. Judg 1.27–28). While the description of Judah's borders is related with precision and detail, those of Ephraim and Manasseh are fragmentary, take up much less textual space, and present numerous topographical difficulties. The integrity of Judah's territory is thus contrasted with the broken borders of the Joseph tribes.

of Manasseh belonged to the Ephraimites. [9] Then the boundary went down to the Wadi Kanah. The towns here, to the south of the wadi, among the towns of Manasseh, belong to Ephraim. Then the boundary of Manasseh goes along the north side of the wadi and ends at the sea. [10] The land to the south is Ephraim's and that to the north is Manasseh's, with the sea forming its boundary; on the north Asher is reached, and on the east Issachar. [11] Within Issachar and Asher, Manasseh had Beth-shean and its villages, Ibleam and its villages, the inhabitants of Dor and its villages, the inhabitants of En-dor and its villages, the inhabitants of Taanach and its villages, and the inhabitants of Megiddo and its villages (the third is Naphath).[a] [12] Yet the Manassites could not take possession of those towns; but the Canaanites continued to live in that land. [13] But when the Israelites grew strong, they put the Canaanites to forced labor, but did not utterly drive them out.

[14] The tribe of Joseph spoke to Joshua, saying, "Why have you given me but one lot and one portion as an inheritance, since we are a numerous people, whom all along the LORD has blessed?" [15] And Joshua said to them, "If you are a numerous people, go up to the forest, and clear ground there for yourselves in the land of the Perizzites and the Rephaim, since the hill country of Ephraim is too narrow for you." [16] The tribe of Joseph said, "The hill country is not enough for us; yet all the Canaanites who live in the plain have chariots of iron, both those in Beth-shean and its villages and those in the Valley of Jezreel." [17] Then Joshua said to the house of Joseph, to Ephraim and Manasseh, "You are indeed a numerous people, and have great power; you shall

not have one lot only, [18] but the hill country shall be yours, for though it is a forest, you shall clear it and possess it to its farthest borders; for you shall drive out the Canaanites, though they have chariots of iron, and though they are strong."

18 Then the whole congregation of the Israelites assembled at Shiloh, and set up the tent of meeting there. The land lay subdued before them.

[2] There remained among the Israelites seven tribes whose inheritance had not yet been apportioned. [3] So Joshua said to the Israelites, "How long will you be slack about going in and taking possession of the land that the LORD, the God of your ancestors, has given you? [4] Provide three men from each tribe, and I will send them out that they may begin to go throughout the land, writing a description of it with a view to their inheritances. Then come back to me. [5] They shall divide it into seven portions, Judah continuing in its territory on the south, and the house of Joseph in their territory on the north. [6] You shall describe the land in seven divisions and bring the description here to me; and I will cast lots for you here before the LORD our God. [7] The Levites have no portion among you, for the priesthood of the LORD is their heritage; and Gad and Reuben and the half-tribe of Manasseh have received their inheritance beyond the Jordan eastward, which Moses the servant of the LORD gave them."

[8] So the men started on their way; and Joshua charged those who went to write the description of the land, saying, "Go throughout the land and write a description of it, and come back to me; and I will cast lots for you

[a] Meaning of Heb uncertain

17.14–18: Joseph's portion. This narrative frame describes the demand of the people of Joseph and the double portion that they receive. This story is an ironic counterbalance to the quest for land by Caleb (14.6–15), and perhaps also by Achsah (15.18–19). The Josephites convey trepidation, contentiousness, and failure.

18.1–19.51: Seven other tribal allotments. The narration of the allotments to the remaining seven tribes. See map on p. 347 and map 4 at the end of this volume.

18.1–10: Assembly of Shiloh. General introduction to the allotments. The boundaries of the tribes in the land are asserted to be the result of the Lord's will and of Israel's obedience, not human will or historical contingency. 1: Shiloh, an important Israelite sanctuary in the period before the monarchy (Judg 18.31; 1 Sam 4.3–4). It is 31 km (19 mi) north of Jerusalem.

6: Lots, see 7.14n. 7: The Levites, see 13.14n., 33n.

here before the Lord in Shiloh." [9] So the men went and traversed the land and set down in a book a description of it by towns in seven divisions; then they came back to Joshua in the camp at Shiloh, [10] and Joshua cast lots for them in Shiloh before the Lord; and there Joshua apportioned the land to the Israelites, to each a portion.

[11] The lot of the tribe of Benjamin according to its families came up, and the territory allotted to it fell between the tribe of Judah and the tribe of Joseph. [12] On the north side their boundary began at the Jordan; then the boundary goes up to the slope of Jericho on the north, then up through the hill country westward; and it ends at the wilderness of Beth-aven. [13] From there the boundary passes along southward in the direction of Luz, to the slope of Luz (that is, Bethel), then the boundary goes down to Ataroth-addar, on the mountain that lies south of Lower Beth-horon. [14] Then the boundary goes in another direction, turning on the western side southward from the mountain that lies to the south, opposite Beth-horon, and it ends at Kiriath-baal (that is, Kiriath-jearim), a town belonging to the tribe of Judah. This forms the western side. [15] The southern side begins at the outskirts of Kiriath-jearim; and the boundary goes from there to Ephron,[a] to the spring of the Waters of Nephtoah; [16] then the boundary goes down to the border of the mountain that overlooks the valley of the son of Hinnom, which is at the north end of the valley of Rephaim; and it then goes down the valley of Hinnom, south of the slope of the Jebusites, and downward to En-rogel; [17] then it bends in a northerly direction going on to En-shemesh, and from there goes to Geliloth, which is opposite the ascent of Adummim; then it goes down to the Stone of Bohan, Reuben's son; [18] and passing on to the north of the slope of Beth-arabah[b] it goes down to the Arabah; [19] then the boundary passes on to the north of the slope of

Beth-hoglah; and the boundary ends at the northern bay of the Dead Sea,[c] at the south end of the Jordan: this is the southern border. [20] The Jordan forms its boundary on the eastern side. This is the inheritance of the tribe of Benjamin, according to its families, boundary by boundary all around.

[21] Now the towns of the tribe of Benjamin according to their families were Jericho, Beth-hoglah, Emek-keziz, [22] Beth-arabah, Zemaraim, Bethel, [23] Avvim, Parah, Ophrah, [24] Chephar-ammoni, Ophni, and Geba— twelve towns with their villages: [25] Gibeon, Ramah, Beeroth, [26] Mizpeh, Chephirah, Mozah, [27] Rekem, Irpeel, Taralah, [28] Zela, Haeleph, Jebus[d] (that is, Jerusalem), Gibeah[e] and Kiriath-jearim[f]—fourteen towns with their villages. This is the inheritance of the tribe of Benjamin according to its families.

19 The second lot came out for Simeon, for the tribe of Simeon, according to its families; its inheritance lay within the inheritance of the tribe of Judah. [2] It had for its inheritance Beer-sheba, Sheba, Moladah, [3] Hazar-shual, Balah, Ezem, [4] Eltolad, Bethul, Hormah, [5] Ziklag, Beth-marcaboth, Hazar-susah, [6] Beth-lebaoth, and Sharuhen—thirteen towns with their villages; [7] Ain, Rimmon, Ether, and Ashan—four towns with their villages; [8] together with all the villages all around these towns as far as Baalath-beer, Ramah of the Negeb. This was the inheritance of the tribe of Simeon according to its families. [9] The inheritance of the tribe of Simeon formed part of the territory of Judah; because the portion of the tribe of Judah was too large for them, the tribe of Simeon obtained an inheritance within their inheritance.

a   Cn See 15.9. Heb *westward*
b   Gk: Heb *to the slope over against the Arabah*
c   Heb *Salt Sea*
d   Gk Syr Vg: Heb *the Jebusite*
e   Heb *Gibeath*
f   Gk: Heb *Kiriath*

18.11–28: Benjamin. The territory of Benjamin is immediately north of Judah. **12–20:** A counter-clockwise boundary description is given. **17:** Bohan, see 15.6n. **21–28:** Benjamin's town list follows. Two districts of towns (vv. 21–24 and vv. 25–28) are presented in the same format as those for Judah (many scholars assume from the same source). **28:** *Jerusalem*, assigned to Judah in 15.63.

19.1–9: Simeon. The allotment is described only in terms of a town list (cf. 1 Chr 4.28–33). **9:** A gloss explaining why these do not follow a boundary description. A conjoining of Judah and Simeon is also found in Judg 1.3.

[10] The third lot came up for the tribe of Zebulun, according to its families. The boundary of its inheritance reached as far as Sarid; [11] then its boundary goes up westward, and on to Maralah, and touches Dabbesheth, then the wadi that is east of Jokneam; [12] from Sarid it goes in the other direction eastward toward the sunrise to the boundary of Chisloth-tabor; from there it goes to Daberath, then up to Japhia; [13] from there it passes along on the east toward the sunrise to Gath-hepher, to Eth-kazin, and going on to Rimmon it bends toward Neah; [14] then on the north the boundary makes a turn to Hannathon, and it ends at the valley of Iphtah-el; [15] and Kattath, Nahalal, Shimron, Idalah, and Bethlehem—twelve towns with their villages. [16] This is the inheritance of the tribe of Zebulun, according to its families—these towns with their villages.

[17] The fourth lot came out for Issachar, for the tribe of Issachar, according to its families. [18] Its territory included Jezreel, Chesulloth, Shunem, [19] Hapharaim, Shion, Anaharath, [20] Rabbith, Kishion, Ebez, [21] Remeth, Engannim, En-haddah, Beth-pazzez; [22] the boundary also touches Tabor, Shahazumah, and Beth-shemesh, and its boundary ends at the Jordan—sixteen towns with their villages. [23] This is the inheritance of the tribe of Issachar, according to its families—the towns with their villages.

[24] The fifth lot came out for the tribe of Asher according to its families. [25] Its boundary included Helkath, Hali, Beten, Achshaph, [26] Allammelech, Amad, and Mishal; on the west it touches Carmel and Shihor-libnath, [27] then it turns eastward, goes to Beth-dagon, and touches Zebulun and the valley of Iphtah-el northward to Beth-emek and Neiel; then it continues in the north to Cabul, [28] Ebron, Rehob, Hammon, Kanah, as far as Great Sidon; [29] then the boundary turns to Ramah, reaching to the fortified city of Tyre; then the boundary turns to Hosah, and it ends at the sea; Mahalab,[a] Achzib, [30] Ummah, Aphek, and Rehob—twenty-two towns with their villages. [31] This is the inheritance of the tribe of Asher according to its families—these towns with their villages.

[32] The sixth lot came out for the tribe of Naphtali, for the tribe of Naphtali, according to its families. [33] And its boundary ran from Heleph, from the oak in Zaanannim, and Adami-nekeb, and Jabneel, as far as Lakkum; and it ended at the Jordan; [34] then the boundary turns westward to Aznoth-tabor, and goes from there to Hukkok, touching Zebulun at the south, and Asher on the west, and Judah on the east at the Jordan. [35] The fortified towns are Ziddim, Zer, Hammath, Rakkath, Chinnereth, [36] Adamah, Ramah, Hazor, [37] Kedesh, Edrei, En-hazor, [38] Iron, Migdal-el, Horem, Beth-anath, and Beth-shemesh—nineteen towns with their villages. [39] This is the inheritance of the tribe of Naphtali according to its families—the towns with their villages.

[40] The seventh lot came out for the tribe of Dan, according to its families. [41] The territory of its inheritance included Zorah, Eshtaol, Ir-shemesh, [42] Shaalabbin, Aijalon, Ithlah, [43] Elon, Timnah, Ekron, [44] Eltekeh, Gibbethon, Baalath, [45] Jehud, Bene-berak, Gath-rimmon, [46] Me-jarkon, and Rakkon at the

---

[a] Cn Compare Gk: Heb *Mehebel*

19.10–16: Zebulun. 10–14: Zebulun's boundary description is given. 15: A town list integrated into a boundary description follows.

19.17–23: Issachar. 18–21: Issachar's town list. 22: A boundary fragment with v. 17 providing a formulaic introduction. Issachar's boundaries correspond to Solomon's tenth district (1 Kings 4.17). Consequently, there may be some relationship between this data and that administrative unit. Issachar is missing in the outline of Judg 1.

19.24–31: Asher. Asher's allotment is fragmentary, with a boundary description (vv. 26–30) and a town list integrated into a boundary description (vv. 25–26,28,30). The list includes some Phoenician cities such as Tyre (v. 29) that were never under Israelite control, suggesting that idealized elements are found in these lists.

19.32–39: Naphtali. Naphtali's allotment has a boundary description (vv. 33–34) and a town list (vv. 35–38). Vv. 32 and 39 provide the framework. The allotment is missing a northern border.

19.40–48: Dan. Like Simeon (vv. 1–9), the allotment is given only in the form of a town list (vv. 41–47), with

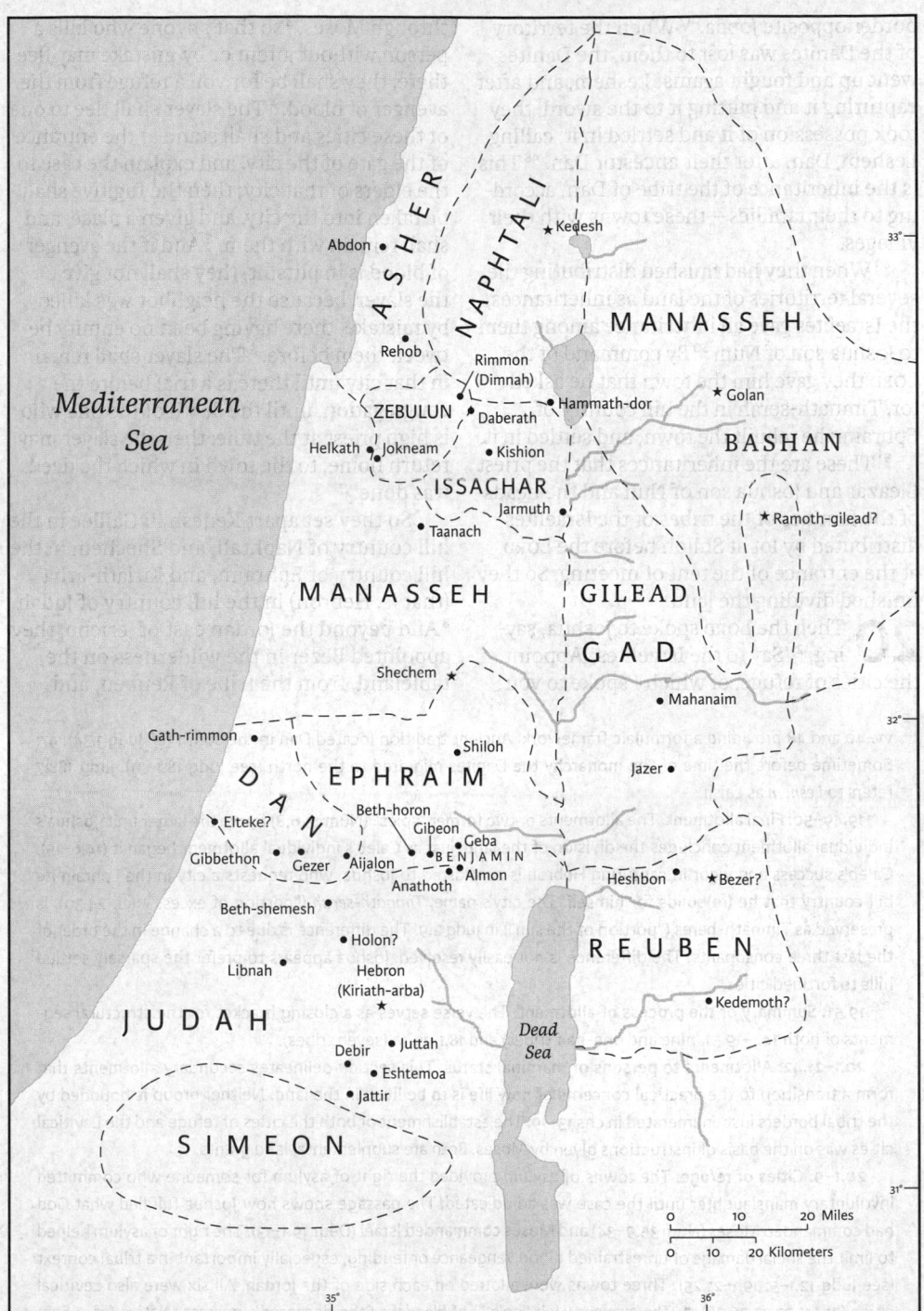

The Levitical cities. Cities of refuge are highlighted with a star. The tribal boundaries are shown by a dashed line.

Map labels:
Mediterranean Sea

ASHER
NAPHTALI
MANASSEH
BASHAN
ZEBULUN
ISSACHAR
GILEAD
GAD
DAN
EPHRAIM
BENJAMIN
REUBEN
JUDAH
SIMEON

Kedesh ★
Abdon
Rehob
Rimmon (Dimnah)
Hammath-dor
Golan ★
Daberath
Helkath   Jokneam
Kishion
Ramoth-gilead? ★
Jarmuth
Taanach
Shechem ★
Mahanaim
Shiloh
Gath-rimmon
Jazer
Elteke?
Beth-horon
Gibeon
Geba
Gibbethon   Gezer   Aijalon
Almon
Heshbon
Bezer? ★
Anathoth
Beth-shemesh
Holon?
REUBEN
Libnah
Hebron (Kiriath-arba) ★
Kedemoth?
Debir   Juttah
Eshtemoa
Jattir
Dead Sea

0   10   20 Miles
0   10   20 Kilometers

33°
32°
31°
35°
36°

border opposite Joppa. [47] When the territory of the Danites was lost to them, the Danites went up and fought against Leshem, and after capturing it and putting it to the sword, they took possession of it and settled in it, calling Leshem, Dan, after their ancestor Dan. [48] This is the inheritance of the tribe of Dan, according to their families—these towns with their villages.

[49] When they had finished distributing the several territories of the land as inheritances, the Israelites gave an inheritance among them to Joshua son of Nun. [50] By command of the LORD they gave him the town that he asked for, Timnath-serah in the hill country of Ephraim; he rebuilt the town, and settled in it.

[51] These are the inheritances that the priest Eleazar and Joshua son of Nun and the heads of the families of the tribes of the Israelites distributed by lot at Shiloh before the LORD, at the entrance of the tent of meeting. So they finished dividing the land.

20 Then the LORD spoke to Joshua, saying, [2] "Say to the Israelites, 'Appoint the cities of refuge, of which I spoke to you through Moses, [3] so that anyone who kills a person without intent or by mistake may flee there; they shall be for you a refuge from the avenger of blood. [4] The slayer shall flee to one of these cities and shall stand at the entrance of the gate of the city, and explain the case to the elders of that city; then the fugitive shall be taken into the city, and given a place, and shall remain with them. [5] And if the avenger of blood is in pursuit, they shall not give up the slayer, because the neighbor was killed by mistake, there having been no enmity between them before. [6] The slayer shall remain in that city until there is a trial before the congregation, until the death of the one who is high priest at the time: then the slayer may return home, to the town in which the deed was done.'"

[7] So they set apart Kedesh in Galilee in the hill country of Naphtali, and Shechem in the hill country of Ephraim, and Kiriath-arba (that is, Hebron) in the hill country of Judah. [8] And beyond the Jordan east of Jericho, they appointed Bezer in the wilderness on the tableland, from the tribe of Reuben, and

---

vv. 40 and 48 providing a formulaic framework. Ancient tradition located Dan in the south (cf. Judg 1.34). **47:** Sometime before the time of the monarchy the Danites migrated to the north (see Judg 18.1–31). Judg 18.27 refers to *Leshem* as Laish.

19.49–50: Final allotment. The allotments of two former "spies" (Num 13.6,8) frame the larger unit: Joshua's individual allotment concludes the division of the land, just as Caleb's individual allotment began it (14.6–15). Caleb's success and vigor in capturing Hebron is contrasted to Joshua, who requests a city in the Ephraimite hill country that he (re)builds for himself. The city's name, *Timnath-serah* ("portion of excess") (cf. 24.30), is preserved as Timnath-heres ("portion of the sun") in Judg 2.9. The difference is due to a change in the order of the last three consonants. The difference is not easily resolved. Joshua appears to prefer the sparsely settled hills to fortified cities.

19.51: Summary of the process of allotment. The verse serves as a closing bracket for the structural segments of both 14.1–19.51 (nine and one-half tribes) and 18.1–19.51 (seven tribes).

20.1–21.42: Allotments to persons of marginal status. This section delineates secondary allotments that form a transition to the practical concerns of how life is to be lived in the land. Neither group is bounded by the tribal borders just enumerated in chs 13–19. The establishment of both the cities of refuge and the Levitical cities was on the basis of instructions given by Moses. Both are supplemental land grants.

20.1–9: Cities of refuge. The towns of asylum provided the right of asylum for someone who committed involuntary manslaughter until the case was adjudicated. The passage shows how Joshua fulfilled what God had commanded Moses (Num 35.9–34) and Moses commanded Israel (Deut 19.1–13). The right of asylum helped to limit the social damage of unrestrained blood vengeance or feuding, especially important in a tribal context (see Judg 12.1–5; 19.1–21.25). Three towns were allotted on each side of the Jordan. All six were also Levitical cities (21.1,11,27,32,36,38). **3:** *The avenger* (Heb "go'el") *of blood* was the deceased's nearest relative (cf. 2 Sam 14.2–17). **4:** *The gate of the city* was where *the elders* of the city met to adjudicate disputes (cf. Ruth 4.1–12). **6:** Probably a later addition, incorporating the Priestly perspective of Num 35.25, with trial by the *congregation* (rather than the elders of v. 4), and implying that *the death of the . . . high priest* expiated the victim's death. **7–10:** See map on p. 347.

Ramoth in Gilead, from the tribe of Gad, and Golan in Bashan, from the tribe of Manasseh. [9] These were the cities designated for all the Israelites, and for the aliens residing among them, that anyone who killed a person without intent could flee there, so as not to die by the hand of the avenger of blood, until there was a trial before the congregation.

21 Then the heads of the families of the Levites came to the priest Eleazar and to Joshua son of Nun and to the heads of the families of the tribes of the Israelites; [2] they said to them at Shiloh in the land of Canaan, "The LORD commanded through Moses that we be given towns to live in, along with their pasture lands for our livestock." [3] So by command of the LORD the Israelites gave to the Levites the following towns and pasture lands out of their inheritance.

[4] The lot came out for the families of the Kohathites. So those Levites who were descendants of Aaron the priest received by lot thirteen towns from the tribes of Judah, Simeon, and Benjamin.

[5] The rest of the Kohathites received by lot ten towns from the families of the tribe of Ephraim, from the tribe of Dan, and the half-tribe of Manasseh.

[6] The Gershonites received by lot thirteen towns from the families of the tribe of Issachar, from the tribe of Asher, from the tribe of Naphtali, and from the half-tribe of Manasseh in Bashan.

[7] The Merarites according to their families received twelve towns from the tribe of Reuben, the tribe of Gad, and the tribe of Zebulun.

[8] These towns and their pasture lands the Israelites gave by lot to the Levites, as the LORD had commanded through Moses.

[9] Out of the tribe of Judah and the tribe of Simeon they gave the following towns mentioned by name, [10] which went to the descendants of Aaron, one of the families of the Kohathites who belonged to the Levites,

since the lot fell to them first. [11] They gave them Kiriath-arba (Arba being the father of Anak), that is Hebron, in the hill country of Judah, along with the pasture lands around it. [12] But the fields of the town and its villages had been given to Caleb son of Jephunneh as his holding.

[13] To the descendants of Aaron the priest they gave Hebron, the city of refuge for the slayer, with its pasture lands, Libnah with its pasture lands, [14] Jattir with its pasture lands, Eshtemoa with its pasture lands, [15] Holon with its pasture lands, Debir with its pasture lands, [16] Ain with its pasture lands, Juttah with its pasture lands, and Beth-shemesh with its pasture lands—nine towns out of these two tribes. [17] Out of the tribe of Benjamin: Gibeon with its pasture lands, Geba with its pasture lands, [18] Anathoth with its pasture lands, and Almon with its pasture lands—four towns. [19] The towns of the descendants of Aaron—the priests—were thirteen in all, with their pasture lands.

[20] As to the rest of the Kohathites belonging to the Kohathite families of the Levites, the towns allotted to them were out of the tribe of Ephraim. [21] To them were given Shechem, the city of refuge for the slayer, with its pasture lands in the hill country of Ephraim, Gezer with its pasture lands, [22] Kibzaim with its pasture lands, and Beth-horon with its pasture lands—four towns. [23] Out of the tribe of Dan: Elteke with its pasture lands, Gibbethon with its pasture lands, [24] Aijalon with its pasture lands, Gath-rimmon with its pasture lands—four towns. [25] Out of the half-tribe of Manasseh: Taanach with its pasture lands, and Gath-rimmon with its pasture lands—two towns. [26] The towns of the families of the rest of the Kohathites were ten in all, with their pasture lands.

[27] To the Gershonites, one of the families of the Levites, were given out of the half-tribe of Manasseh, Golan in Bashan with its pasture lands, the city of refuge for the slayer, and Beeshterah with its pasture

---

21.1–42: Levitical cities. Elsewhere the Levites have no inheritance (13.14,33; 18.7; Deut 10.8–9); nevertheless, they are integrated into the unity of Israel. As in the delineation of the tribal boundaries, there is some idealization. The total number of Levitical cities (forty-eight) as a multiple of twelve is likely symbolic. But the towns are not equally divided among the tribes. They are allotted to the three clans of the Levites: the Kohathites, Gershonites, and Merarites. 11–12: See 14.13–15n.; 15.13–19n. 13–40: See map on p. 347.

lands—two towns. ²⁸ Out of the tribe of Issachar: Kishion with its pasture lands, Daberath with its pasture lands, ²⁹ Jarmuth with its pasture lands, En-gannim with its pasture lands—four towns. ³⁰ Out of the tribe of Asher: Mishal with its pasture lands, Abdon with its pasture lands, ³¹ Helkath with its pasture lands, and Rehob with its pasture lands—four towns. ³² Out of the tribe of Naphtali: Kedesh in Galilee with its pasture lands, the city of refuge for the slayer, Hammoth-dor with its pasture lands, and Kartan with its pasture lands—three towns. ³³ The towns of the several families of the Gershonites were in all thirteen, with their pasture lands.

³⁴ To the rest of the Levites—the Merarite families—were given out of the tribe of Zebulun: Jokneam with its pasture lands, Kartah with its pasture lands, ³⁵ Dimnah with its pasture lands, Nahalal with its pasture lands—four towns. ³⁶ Out of the tribe of Reuben: Bezer with its pasture lands, Jahzah with its pasture lands, ³⁷ Kedemoth with its pasture lands, and Mephaath with its pasture lands—four towns. ³⁸ Out of the tribe of Gad: Ramoth in Gilead with its pasture lands, the city of refuge for the slayer, Mahanaim with its pasture lands, ³⁹ Heshbon with its pasture lands, Jazer with its pasture lands—four towns in all. ⁴⁰ As for the towns of the several Merarite families, that is, the remainder of the families of the Levites, those allotted to them were twelve in all.

⁴¹ The towns of the Levites within the holdings of the Israelites were in all forty-eight towns with their pasture lands. ⁴² Each of these towns had its pasture lands around it; so it was with all these towns.

⁴³ Thus the LORD gave to Israel all the land that he swore to their ancestors that he would give them; and having taken possession of it, they settled there. ⁴⁴ And the LORD gave them rest on every side just as he had sworn to their ancestors; not one of all their enemies had withstood them, for the LORD had given all their enemies into their hands. ⁴⁵ Not one of all the good promises that the LORD had made to the house of Israel had failed; all came to pass.

22 Then Joshua summoned the Reubenites, the Gadites, and the half-tribe of Manasseh, ² and said to them, "You have observed all that Moses the servant of the LORD commanded you, and have obeyed me in all that I have commanded you; ³ you have not forsaken your kindred these many days, down to this day, but have been careful to keep the charge of the LORD your God. ⁴ And now the LORD your God has given rest to your kindred, as he promised them; therefore turn and go to your tents in the land where your possession lies, which Moses the servant of the LORD gave you on the other side of the Jordan. ⁵ Take good care to observe the commandment and instruction that Moses the servant of the LORD commanded you, to love the LORD your God, to walk in all his ways, to keep his commandments, and to hold fast to him, and to serve him with all your heart and with all your soul." ⁶ So Joshua blessed them and sent them away, and they went to their tents.

⁷ Now to the one half of the tribe of Manasseh Moses had given a possession

21.43–45: Ironic conclusion. This is an ironic conclusion to the conquest and allotment sections of the book. The overstated claims of unmitigated success (note the use of Heb "kol" ["all" or "every"] six times) in these verses seem incongruent with the subtle statements given throughout 13.1–21.42 that there were failures among the tribes—some quite significant—as each attempted to secure its allotment. Nevertheless, the stress on the Lord's faithfulness contrasts with the squabbling over the Transjordanian altar in the next section (22.10–34).

22.1–24.33: Epilogue to the conquest and allotment. Three concluding sections are used to foster Israel's fidelity in the land. These take the form of a warning narrative (22.1–34) and a pair of exhorting addresses (23.1–16; 24.1–28) in which commitments to the covenant are renewed. Originally disparate materials have been selected and arranged to frame the book. In particular, participants and motifs from 1.1–18 recur in this section.

22.1–34: Misunderstanding with the Transjordanian tribes. The ties binding the tribes together were not firm, and conflicts were a continuing problem. The issue here is the place of legitimate worship, a central concern of Deuteronomy. 1–9: The Transjordanian tribes return to their homes on the east bank. 1–5: Joshua's farewell to the Transjordanian tribes structurally balances the introduction to them in 1.12–18. 5: To love the LORD

in Bashan; but to the other half Joshua had given a possession beside their fellow Israelites in the land west of the Jordan. And when Joshua sent them away to their tents and blessed them, [8] he said to them, "Go back to your tents with much wealth, and with very much livestock, with silver, gold, bronze, and iron, and with a great quantity of clothing; divide the spoil of your enemies with your kindred." [9] So the Reubenites and the Gadites and the half-tribe of Manasseh returned home, parting from the Israelites at Shiloh, which is in the land of Canaan, to go to the land of Gilead, their own land of which they had taken possession by command of the LORD through Moses.

[10] When they came to the region[a] near the Jordan that lies in the land of Canaan, the Reubenites and the Gadites and the half-tribe of Manasseh built there an altar by the Jordan, an altar of great size. [11] The Israelites heard that the Reubenites and the Gadites and the half-tribe of Manasseh had built an altar at the frontier of the land of Canaan, in the region[b] near the Jordan, on the side that belongs to the Israelites. [12] And when the people of Israel heard of it, the whole assembly of the Israelites gathered at Shiloh, to make war against them.

[13] Then the Israelites sent the priest Phinehas son of Eleazar to the Reubenites and the Gadites and the half-tribe of Manasseh, in the land of Gilead, [14] and with him ten chiefs, one from each of the tribal families of Israel, every one of them the head of a family among the clans of Israel. [15] They came to the Reubenites, the Gadites, and the half-tribe of Manasseh, in the land of Gilead, and they said to them, [16] "Thus says the whole congregation of the LORD, 'What is this treachery that you have committed against the God of Israel in turning away today from following the LORD, by building yourselves an altar today in rebellion against the LORD? [17] Have we not had enough of the sin at Peor from which even yet we have not cleansed ourselves, and for which a plague came upon the congregation of the LORD, [18] that you must turn away today from following the LORD! If you rebel against the LORD today, he will be angry with the whole congregation of Israel tomorrow. [19] But now, if your land is unclean, cross over into the LORD's land where the LORD's tabernacle now stands, and take for yourselves a possession among us; only do not rebel against the LORD, or rebel against us[c] by building yourselves an altar other than the altar of the LORD our God. [20] Did not Achan son of Zerah break faith in the matter of the devoted things, and wrath fell upon all the congregation of Israel? And he did not perish alone for his iniquity!'"

[21] Then the Reubenites, the Gadites, and the half-tribe of Manasseh said in answer to the heads of the families of Israel, [22] "The LORD, God of gods! The LORD, God of gods! He knows; and let Israel itself know! If it was in rebellion or in breach of faith toward the LORD, do not spare us today [23] for building an altar to turn away from following the LORD; or if we did so to offer burnt offerings or grain offerings or offerings of well-being on it, may the LORD himself take vengeance. [24] No! We did it from fear that in time to come your children might say to our children, 'What have you to do with the LORD, the God of Israel? [25] For the LORD has made the Jordan a boundary between us and you,

a   Or to Geliloth
b   Or at Geliloth
c   Or make rebels of us

anticipates 23.11; the language is Deuteronomic (see Deut 6.5; 10.12–13; 30.16; etc.). 7: See Deut 3.13; Josh 17.

22.10–34: The debate over the altar built by the Transjordanian tribes. The central role of *Phinehas* (see Ex 6.25; Num 25) in dealing with this conflict leads some scholars to conclude that priestly circles edited this story. 12: Holding strictly to the Deuteronomic law that forbade the offering of sacrifice anywhere except in the one central sanctuary (Deut 12.13–14), the other tribes apparently interpret the building of the altar as an act of disloyalty to Israel and to its God, and therefore prepare *to make war against them.* The extent to which the tribal settlement east of the Jordan is or is not part of Israel also stands behind this narrative. 17: *The sin at Peor,* Num 25.3–5. 19: Highly charged theological language suggests the superiority of the Cisjordanian tribes. 20: *Achan,* see ch 7. 24–25: The motive of the Transjordanian tribes was honorable; they built the altar as a witness to their loyalty to the Lord. They feared that in the future the Israelites west of the Jordan might discriminate against

you Reubenites and Gadites; you have no portion in the LORD.' So your children might make our children cease to worship the LORD. [26] Therefore we said, 'Let us now build an altar, not for burnt offering, nor for sacrifice, [27] but to be a witness between us and you, and between the generations after us, that we do perform the service of the LORD in his presence with our burnt offerings and sacrifices and offerings of well-being; so that your children may never say to our children in time to come, "You have no portion in the LORD."' [28] And we thought, If this should be said to us or to our descendants in time to come, we could say, 'Look at this copy of the altar of the LORD, which our ancestors made, not for burnt offerings, nor for sacrifice, but to be a witness between us and you.' [29] Far be it from us that we should rebel against the LORD, and turn away this day from following the LORD by building an altar for burnt offering, grain offering, or sacrifice, other than the altar of the LORD our God that stands before his tabernacle!"

[30] When the priest Phinehas and the chiefs of the congregation, the heads of the families of Israel who were with him, heard the words that the Reubenites and the Gadites and the Manassites spoke, they were satisfied. [31] The priest Phinehas son of Eleazar said to the Reubenites and the Gadites and the Manassites, "Today we know that the LORD is among us, because you have not committed this treachery against the LORD; now you have saved the Israelites from the hand of the LORD."

[32] Then the priest Phinehas son of Eleazar and the chiefs returned from the Reubenites and the Gadites in the land of Gilead to the land of Canaan, to the Israelites, and brought back word to them. [33] The report pleased the Israelites; and the Israelites blessed God and spoke no more of making war against them,

to destroy the land where the Reubenites and the Gadites were settled. [34] The Reubenites and the Gadites called the altar Witness;[a] "For," said they, "it is a witness between us that the LORD is God."

23 A long time afterward, when the LORD had given rest to Israel from all their enemies all around, and Joshua was old and well advanced in years, [2] Joshua summoned all Israel, their elders and heads, their judges and officers, and said to them, "I am now old and well advanced in years; [3] and you have seen all that the LORD your God has done to all these nations for your sake, for it is the LORD your God who has fought for you. [4] I have allotted to you as an inheritance for your tribes those nations that remain, along with all the nations that I have already cut off, from the Jordan to the Great Sea in the west. [5] The LORD your God will push them back before you, and drive them out of your sight; and you shall possess their land, as the LORD your God promised you. [6] Therefore be very steadfast to observe and do all that is written in the book of the law of Moses, turning aside from it neither to the right nor to the left, [7] so that you may not be mixed with these nations left here among you, or make mention of the names of their gods, or swear by them, or serve them, or bow yourselves down to them, [8] but hold fast to the LORD your God, as you have done to this day. [9] For the LORD has driven out before you great and strong nations; and as for you, no one has been able to withstand you to this day. [10] One of you puts to flight a thousand, since it is the LORD your God who fights for you, as he promised you. [11] Be very careful, therefore, to love the LORD your God. [12] For if you turn back, and join the survivors of these nations

a   Cn Compare Syr: Heb lacks *Witness*

them—a well-founded fear in light of this story (see Judg 12.1–5). **26–27:** It was not a real sacrificial altar, they claimed, but merely a memorial, *a witness* (cf. Gen 31.47–48; Josh 24.27).

23.1–24.28: Concluding charges. There are a number of similarities between Joshua's speech to the leaders (23.1–16) and his charge to the people (24.1–28). Both resemble the testaments of prior Israelite leaders: Jacob (Gen 48–49), Joseph (Gen 50.22–26), and especially Moses (Deut 32–33). Additionally, both have framing links with 1.2–9.

23.1–16: Covenantal charge to the leaders. Joshua's address to the leaders consists almost entirely of Deuteronomistic reflections. **1–5:** God's mighty acts of conquest. **6–11:** An exhortation to remain faithful to the Lord and his covenant so that the remaining land can be conquered. **12–16:** Warnings of judgments if Israel is

left here among you, and intermarry with them, so that you marry their women and they yours, [13] know assuredly that the LORD your God will not continue to drive out these nations before you; but they shall be a snare and a trap for you, a scourge on your sides, and thorns in your eyes, until you perish from this good land that the LORD your God has given you.

[14] "And now I am about to go the way of all the earth, and you know in your hearts and souls, all of you, that not one thing has failed of all the good things that the LORD your God promised concerning you; all have come to pass for you, not one of them has failed. [15] But just as all the good things that the LORD your God promised concerning you have been fulfilled for you, so the LORD will bring upon you all the bad things, until he has destroyed you from this good land that the LORD your God has given you. [16] If you transgress the covenant of the LORD your God, which he enjoined on you, and go and serve other gods and bow down to them, then the anger of the LORD will be kindled against you, and you shall perish quickly from the good land that he has given to you."

24 Then Joshua gathered all the tribes of Israel to Shechem, and summoned the elders, the heads, the judges, and the officers of Israel; and they presented themselves before God. [2] And Joshua said to all the people, "Thus says the LORD, the God of Israel: Long ago your ancestors—Terah and his sons Abraham and Nahor—lived beyond the Euphrates and served other gods. [3] Then I took your father Abraham from beyond the River and led him through all the land of Canaan and made his offspring many. I gave him Isaac; [4] and to Isaac I gave Jacob and Esau. I gave Esau the hill country of Seir to possess, but Jacob and his children went down to Egypt. [5] Then I sent Moses and Aaron, and I plagued Egypt with what I did in its midst; and afterwards I brought you out. [6] When I brought your ancestors out of Egypt, you came to the sea; and the Egyptians pursued your ancestors with chariots and horsemen to the Red Sea.[a] [7] When they cried out to the LORD, he put darkness between you and the Egyptians, and made the sea come upon them and cover them; and your eyes saw what I did to Egypt. Afterwards you lived in the wilderness a long time. [8] Then I brought you to the land of the Amorites, who lived on the other side of the Jordan; they fought with you, and I handed them over to you, and you took possession of their land, and I destroyed them before you. [9] Then King Balak son of Zippor of Moab, set out to fight against Israel. He sent and invited Balaam son of Beor to curse you, [10] but I would not listen to Balaam; therefore he blessed you; so I rescued you out of his hand. [11] When you went over the Jordan and came to Jericho, the citizens of Jericho fought against you, and also the Amorites, the Perizzites, the Canaanites, the Hittites, the Girgashites, the Hivites, and the Jebusites; and I handed them over to you. [12] I sent the hornet[b] ahead of you, which drove out before you the two kings of the Amorites; it was not by your sword or by your bow. [13] I gave you a land on which you had not labored, and towns that you had not built, and you live in them; you eat the fruit of vineyards and oliveyards that you did not plant.

[a] Or *Sea of Reeds*
[b] Meaning of Heb uncertain

unfaithful to the covenant, worshiping foreign gods. **14:** *Way of all the earth,* i.e., to die; see 1 Kings 2.2.
24.1–28: Covenant renewal of the people. Joshua fulfills the commands of Moses in Deut 11; 27; 31. All Israel unites under Joshua's leadership in the service of the Lord. Joshua's final meeting with the people takes place at Shechem (cf. 8.30–35). **1:** *Shechem* (Tell Balata) became an important Israelite religious and political center, and was already important in Genesis. The setting of Shechem thus frames the Hexateuch. **2–13:** A historical summary analogous to the prologues of ancient Near Eastern suzerainty treaties divides into three subdivisions: the ancestral period (vv. 2–4), the Egyptian period (vv. 5–7), and the conquest period (vv. 8–13). **2–4:** A summary of Gen 11.26–46.27. **5–10:** A summary of Exodus and Numbers, omitting any reference to the events at Mount Sinai. **9:** *Balak* and *Balaam,* see Num 22–24; Josh 13.22n. **11:** Perhaps a different tradition about Jericho from that found in ch 6. **12:** *The hornet,* a vivid image; see Ex 23.28; Deut 7.20. **13:** See Deut 6.10–11. **14–24:** A dialogue between Joshua and the people in which the issue of serving the Lord, not other gods, is weighed. The Israelites'

[14] "Now therefore revere the Lord, and serve him in sincerity and in faithfulness; put away the gods that your ancestors served beyond the River and in Egypt, and serve the Lord. [15] Now if you are unwilling to serve the Lord, choose this day whom you will serve, whether the gods your ancestors served in the region beyond the River or the gods of the Amorites in whose land you are living; but as for me and my household, we will serve the Lord."

[16] Then the people answered, "Far be it from us that we should forsake the Lord to serve other gods; [17] for it is the Lord our God who brought us and our ancestors up from the land of Egypt, out of the house of slavery, and who did those great signs in our sight. He protected us along all the way that we went, and among all the peoples through whom we passed; [18] and the Lord drove out before us all the peoples, the Amorites who lived in the land. Therefore we also will serve the Lord, for he is our God."

[19] But Joshua said to the people, "You cannot serve the Lord, for he is a holy God. He is a jealous God; he will not forgive your transgressions or your sins. [20] If you forsake the Lord and serve foreign gods, then he will turn and do you harm, and consume you, after having done you good." [21] And the people said to Joshua, "No, we will serve the Lord!" [22] Then Joshua said to the people, "You are witnesses against yourselves that you have chosen the Lord, to serve him." And they said, "We are witnesses." [23] He said, "Then put away the foreign gods that are among you, and incline your hearts to the Lord, the God of Israel." [24] The people said to Joshua, "The Lord our God we will serve, and him we will obey." [25] So Joshua made a covenant with the people that day, and made statutes and ordinances for them at Shechem. [26] Joshua wrote these words in the book of the law of God; and he took a large stone, and set it up there under the oak in the sanctuary of the Lord. [27] Joshua said to all the people, "See, this stone shall be a witness against us; for it has heard all the words of the Lord that he spoke to us; therefore it shall be a witness against you, if you deal falsely with your God." [28] So Joshua sent the people away to their inheritances.

[29] After these things Joshua son of Nun, the servant of the Lord, died, being one hundred ten years old. [30] They buried him in his own inheritance at Timnath-serah, which is in the hill country of Ephraim, north of Mount Gaash.

[31] Israel served the Lord all the days of Joshua, and all the days of the elders who outlived Joshua and had known all the work that the Lord did for Israel.

[32] The bones of Joseph, which the Israelites had brought up from Egypt, were buried at Shechem, in the portion of ground that Jacob had bought from the children of Hamor, the father of Shechem, for one hundred pieces of money;[a] it became an inheritance of the descendants of Joseph.

[33] Eleazar son of Aaron died; and they buried him at Gibeah, the town of his son Phinehas, which had been given him in the hill country of Ephraim.

[a] Heb *one hundred qesitah*

---

commitment to the covenant with the Lord is formalized. **14:** *The River,* the Euphrates. *In Egypt,* cf. Ezek 20.5–8; 23.3,8. **23:** See Gen 35.2–4. **26:** *A large stone,* cf. 8.32. *The oak,* see Gen 12.6; 35.4; Deut 11.30; Judg 9.6.

24.29–33: Appendixes. Appendixes are found in several biblical books; here three short notices are given. **29–31:** The death and burial of Joshua, with a comment concerning Israel's faithfulness to the Lord; cf. Judg 2.6–9. **32:** The reburial of the bones of Joseph in Shechem in the patriarchal plot (see Gen 50.25; Ex 13.19). Here again our attention is returned to Genesis. **33:** The death and burial of the priest Eleazar (see 13.1). This is a surprising ending, but it indicates the strength of the priestly interests in the book.

JUDGES

LOCATION IN CANON AND NAME

The book of Judges is the second book of the Former Prophets in the Jewish canon, and in Christian Bibles the second of the Historical Books. Its place was determined chronologically, as it covers the period after Joshua's death and before the establishment of kingship recounted in 1 Samuel.

The book is named after its principal characters, who are called only in the beginning of the book "judges" (2.16-19), meaning chieftains or rulers. The use of this term points to diverse leaders who acted in this period. Some are depicted as military leaders (Othniel, Ehud, Barak, Gideon and Jephthah); some as lone warriors (Shamgar and Samson); others had a religious mission (prophets: Deborah and Samuel; Nazirite: Samson; and priests: Eli and Samuel). Only a few are mentioned as sitting in judgment in the juridical sense (Deborah and Samuel), while there are some whose activities are not specified (Tola, Jair, Ibzan, Elon and Abdon). The Hebrew word *shaphat* ("to judge") and its derivative *shophet* ("a judge") can mean "adjudicate" but also "rule" (2 Chr 1.10; Is 51.5) and "vindicate, provide justice for" (Pss 10.18; 82.3). The range of leaders over the entire period produced the sweeping editorial rubric "Judges" (see also Ruth 1.1; 2 Sam 7.11; 2 Kings 23.22; 1 Chr 17.6, 10; Sir 46.11).

AUTHORSHIP AND LITERARY HISTORY

The early rabbis (*b. B. Bat.* 14b) assumed that the book of Judges was written by the prophet Samuel, who lived not long after the events described. Most modern biblical scholars maintain that, like other historiographic books of the Former Prophets, Judges was a compilation of materials edited by Deuteronomistic editors in the late seventh and sixth centuries BCE, with other materials, such as the story of Gibeah (chs 19–21), added later. Other scholars think that, because of stylistic and ideological considerations, the main redaction was completed in a pre-Deuteronomistic stage, in the late eighth or early seventh century BCE, and that it reflected the shocked mood in Judah after the downfall of the kingdom of Israel in 722 (see 18.30). All critical scholars agree, however, that the book was written long after the events depicted, and reflects later Judean goals and perspectives. Thus, even though some of the episodes may contain historical memories of the premonarchic period, it is difficult to speak of "the period of the judges" and to use the stories to reconstruct the history of early Israel.

STRUCTURE AND CONTENTS

The book has three parts: an introduction that explains the background of the judges' rise (1.1–3.6); a central section describing the activities of the judges (3.7–16.31); and a conclusion composed of two episodes: that of Micah and the conquest of Dan (chs 17–18), and the story of the rape in Gibeah with its subsequent civil war (chs 19–21). These last episodes create the impression that monarchy alone could end the chaotic period of the judges, and thus serves, along with the book as a whole, a fitting introduction to the book of Samuel that follows it in the Jewish canon.

The book of Judges does not cover the entire period of the judges, nor is its narrative chronological. It opens in the time of the elders who survived Joshua and concludes with events that took place in the third generation from the Exodus (18.30, 20.28). Moreover, the last two individuals designated as judges—Eli and Samuel—appear in the book of Samuel (1 Sam 4.18; 7.15-17). By closing the book with events from the beginning of the period and creating a circular structure, the author-editor exposes the inefficacy of the judges, who could only save and influence their people for a limited time. As the book states several times, after the death of the delivering judges, the people relapsed, were punished, and cried to the LORD to save them. This recurrent pattern of sin, punishment, appeal to God, rescue and peace results in a series of cyclical narratives of the book, gives the period its cyclic quality and the book its circular structure. Its non-chronological order shows that the author-editors' main purpose was not to record history, but to draw lessons from it.

INTERPRETATION

The book's two principal lessons are the role of God in history, and kingship, especially Judean kingship, as the preferred kind of leadership. The book describes the course of history as an interaction between God and his people, and its cyclical nature shows how extensively God directs history. But although the judges are the LORD's emissaries, their leadership ultimately fails. Thus, since they were unable to break the cyclical pattern, their rule created an expectation of monarchy, as a consecutive, continuous, and stable leadership, which could prevent anarchy. On the other hand, the book warns that a king may also be a villain, as in the case of Abimelech, symbolized by the bramble (ch 9). Thus, although the book prepares the ground for kingship, it does not depict it as ideal. In particular, by the way it depicts the tribe of Benjamin, it suggests that the kingdom of Saul, who was a Benjaminite, as well as the later Northern Kingdom of Israel, who was the origin of most of the judges (except Othniel from Judah), are not the future solution. The expectations are for a Judean king.

Yairah Amit

1 After the death of Joshua, the Israelites inquired of the LORD, "Who shall go up first for us against the Canaanites, to fight against them?" ² The LORD said, "Judah shall go up. I hereby give the land into his hand." ³ Judah said to his brother Simeon, "Come up with me into the territory allotted to me, that we may fight against the Canaanites; then I too will go with you into the territory allotted to you." So Simeon went with him. ⁴ Then Judah went up and the LORD gave the Canaanites and the Perizzites into their hand; and they defeated ten thousand of them at Bezek. ⁵ They came upon Adoni-bezek at Bezek, and fought against him, and defeated the Canaanites and the Perizzites. ⁶ Adoni-bezek fled; but they pursued him, and caught him, and cut off his thumbs and big toes. ⁷ Adoni-bezek said, "Seventy kings with their thumbs and big toes cut off used to pick up scraps under my table; as

I have done, so God has paid me back." They brought him to Jerusalem, and he died there.
⁸ Then the people of Judah fought against Jerusalem and took it. They put it to the sword and set the city on fire. ⁹ Afterward the people of Judah went down to fight against the Canaanites who lived in the hill country, in the Negeb, and in the lowland. ¹⁰ Judah went against the Canaanites who lived in Hebron (the name of Hebron was formerly Kiriath-arba); and they defeated Sheshai and Ahiman and Talmai.
¹¹ From there they went against the inhabitants of Debir (the name of Debir was formerly Kiriath-sepher). ¹² Then Caleb said, "Whoever attacks Kiriath-sepher and takes it, I will give him my daughter Achsah as wife." ¹³ And Othniel son of Kenaz, Caleb's younger brother, took it; and he gave him his daughter Achsah as wife. ¹⁴ When she came to him, she

1.1–3.6: Double introduction. The book of Judges opens with two introductions: the first (1.1–2.5) depicts "the days of the elders" (2.7), the second (2.6–3.6) the era of the judges.

1.1–2.5: The days of the elders. A brief period, less than a generation, passes between the death of Joshua and the beginning of the era of the judges. This first introduction explains how the people, who were loyal to the LORD in the days of Joshua (2.7), repeatedly did evil in his eyes; and how most of the tribes, though not Judah and Simeon, preferred to subjugate the nations who remained in the land after Joshua's death rather than to exterminate them; this caused Israel to sin.

1.1–20: The conquests of Judah. The tribe of Judah, accompanied by Simeon, is described as destroying all the Canaanites except the inhabitants of the valley, who had iron chariots. **3:** *His brother*, the connection between Judah and Simeon reflects the historical situation of the tribe of Simeon being part of Judah's inheritance (compare Josh 19.1–9 with 15.26–32). **4:** The *Perizzites* were one of the groups who inhabited Canaan (see Gen 15.20; Deut 7.1; Josh 3.11). *Bezek*, probably Khirbet Ibzik, about 15 mi (24 km) northeast of Shechem. **5–7:** *Adoni-bezek*, the king's name may be a corruption of Adoni-zedek, king of Jerusalem (see Josh 10.1); his burial in Jerusalem (v. 7 below) supports this. **8:** Here Judah conquered Jerusalem, but contrast v. 21; 19.10–12; and Josh 15.63. According to 2 Sam 5.6–9, Jerusalem remained a Jebusite enclave until the period of David. **9:** Judah's conquests south of Jerusalem. **10:** *Hebron,* only here is its conquest attributed to Judah; contrast Josh 10.36–37; 14.6–14; and v. 20 below. **13:** The representation of Othniel as younger than Caleb means that his clan is less important than Caleb's. The families of Caleb and Kenaz appear here as part of Judah; in Gen 36.15,42 Kenaz is an Edomite descended from Esau, which means that Edomites integrated into the tribe of Judah. **14:** Here Achsah addresses

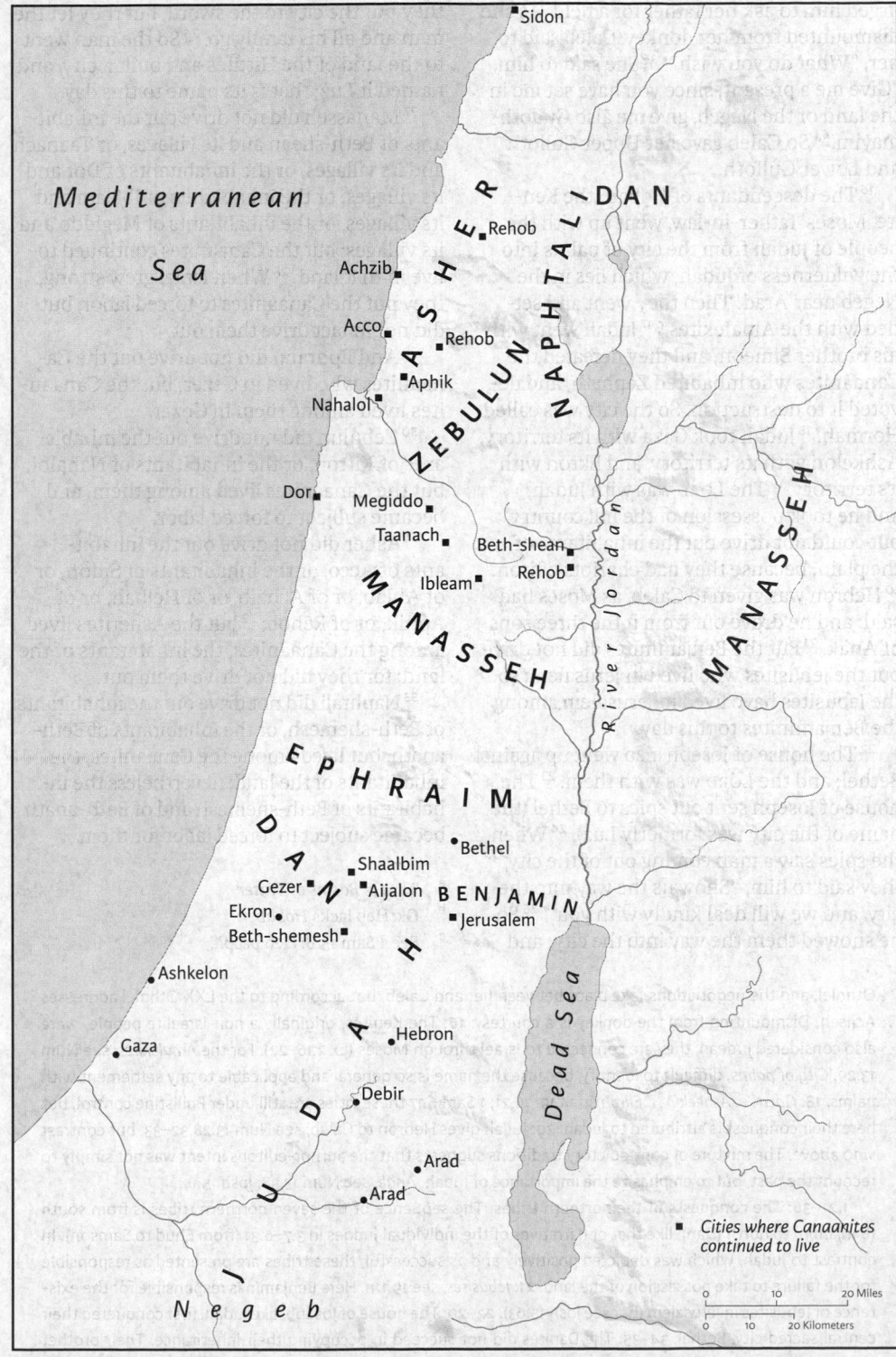

Tribal conquests in chapter 1. Starred cities are locales where Canaanites continued to live.

Within the image:

Mediterranean

Sea

Sidon

ASHER

NAPHTALI

DAN

Rehob

Achzib

Acco

Rehob

ZEBULUN

Aphik

Nahalol

Dor

Megiddo

Taanach

Beth-shean

Ibleam

Rehob

MANASSEH

MANASSEH

River Jordan

EPHRAIM

DAN

Bethel

Shaalbim

Gezer

Aijalon

BENJAMIN

Ekron

Jerusalem

Beth-shemesh

Ashkelon

Dead Sea

Gaza

Hebron

JUDAH

Debir

Arad

Arad

Negeb

■ Cities where Canaanites
continued to live

0   10   20 Miles

0   10   20 Kilometers

urged him to ask her father for a field. As she dismounted from her donkey, Caleb said to her, "What do you wish?" [15] She said to him, "Give me a present; since you have set me in the land of the Negeb, give me also Gulloth-mayim."[a] So Caleb gave her Upper Gulloth and Lower Gulloth.

[16] The descendants of Hobab[b] the Kenite, Moses' father-in-law, went up with the people of Judah from the city of palms into the wilderness of Judah, which lies in the Negeb near Arad. Then they went and settled with the Amalekites.[c] [17] Judah went with his brother Simeon, and they defeated the Canaanites who inhabited Zephath, and devoted it to destruction. So the city was called Hormah. [18] Judah took Gaza with its territory, Ashkelon with its territory, and Ekron with its territory. [19] The LORD was with Judah, and he took possession of the hill country, but could not drive out the inhabitants of the plain, because they had chariots of iron. [20] Hebron was given to Caleb, as Moses had said; and he drove out from it the three sons of Anak. [21] But the Benjaminites did not drive out the Jebusites who lived in Jerusalem; so the Jebusites have lived in Jerusalem among the Benjaminites to this day.

[22] The house of Joseph also went up against Bethel; and the LORD was with them. [23] The house of Joseph sent out spies to Bethel (the name of the city was formerly Luz). [24] When the spies saw a man coming out of the city, they said to him, "Show us the way into the city, and we will deal kindly with you." [25] So he showed them the way into the city; and they put the city to the sword, but they let the man and all his family go. [26] So the man went to the land of the Hittites and built a city, and named it Luz; that is its name to this day.

[27] Manasseh did not drive out the inhabitants of Beth-shean and its villages, or Taanach and its villages, or the inhabitants of Dor and its villages, or the inhabitants of Ibleam and its villages, or the inhabitants of Megiddo and its villages; but the Canaanites continued to live in that land. [28] When Israel grew strong, they put the Canaanites to forced labor, but did not in fact drive them out.

[29] And Ephraim did not drive out the Canaanites who lived in Gezer; but the Canaanites lived among them in Gezer.

[30] Zebulun did not drive out the inhabitants of Kitron, or the inhabitants of Nahalol; but the Canaanites lived among them, and became subject to forced labor.

[31] Asher did not drive out the inhabitants of Acco, or the inhabitants of Sidon, or of Ahlab, or of Achzib, or of Helbah, or of Aphik, or of Rehob; [32] but the Asherites lived among the Canaanites, the inhabitants of the land; for they did not drive them out.

[33] Naphtali did not drive out the inhabitants of Beth-shemesh, or the inhabitants of Beth-anath, but lived among the Canaanites, the inhabitants of the land; nevertheless the inhabitants of Beth-shemesh and of Beth-anath became subject to forced labor for them.

[a] That is *Basins of Water*
[b] Gk: Heb lacks *Hobab*
[c] See 1 Sam 15.6: Heb *people*

Othniel, and the negotiations take place between her and Caleb, but according to the LXX Othniel addresses Achsah. Dismounting from the donkey is a courtesy. **16**: The Kenites, originally a non-Israelite people, were also considered Judean; they are connected to Israel through Moses (Ex 2.16–22). For the *Amalekites,* see Num 13.29. *City of palms,* difficult to identify, because the name is so general and applicable to any settlement with palms. **18**: *Gaza . . . Ashkelon . . .Ekron,* in 14.19; 16.21; 1 Sam 6.17 these cities are still under Philistine control, but here their conquest is attributed to Judah. **20**: Judah gives Hebron to Caleb; see Num 13.28,32–33, but contrast v. 10 above. The mixture of contradictory traditions suggests that the author-editor's intent was not simply to recount the past, but to emphasize the importance of Judah. *Anak,* see Num 13.38; Josh 15.14.

1.21–36: The conquests of the northern tribes. The sequence of the seven northern tribes is from south (Benjamin) to north (Dan), like that of narratives of the individual judges in 3.7–6.31 (from Ehud to Samson). In contrast to Judah, which was depicted positively and as successful, these tribes are presented as responsible for the failure to take possession of the land. **21**: *Jebusites,* see 19.11n. Here Benjamin is responsible for the existence of Jebusites in Jerusalem (but see Josh 15.63). **22–29**: The house of Joseph, like Judah, first conquered their central sacred city, Bethel. **34–35**: The Danites did not succeed in occupying their inheritance. Their brother Joseph, unlike Judah who cooperated with Simeon, did not help them and preferred to subjugate the indig-

[34] The Amorites pressed the Danites back into the hill country; they did not allow them to come down to the plain. [35] The Amorites continued to live in Har-heres, in Aijalon, and in Shaalbim, but the hand of the house of Joseph rested heavily on them, and they became subject to forced labor. [36] The border of the Amorites ran from the ascent of Akrabbim, from Sela and upward.

2 Now the angel of the LORD went up from Gilgal to Bochim, and said, "I brought you up from Egypt, and brought you into the land that I had promised to your ancestors. I said, 'I will never break my covenant with you. [2] For your part, do not make a covenant with the inhabitants of this land; tear down their altars.' But you have not obeyed my command. See what you have done! [3] So now I say, I will not drive them out before you; but they shall become adversaries[a] to you, and their gods shall be a snare to you." [4] When the angel of the LORD spoke these words to all the Israelites, the people lifted up their voices and wept. [5] So they named that place Bochim,[b] and there they sacrificed to the LORD.

[6] When Joshua dismissed the people, the Israelites all went to their own inheritances to take possession of the land. [7] The people worshiped the LORD all the days of Joshua, and all the days of the elders who outlived Joshua, who had seen all the great work that the LORD had done for Israel. [8] Joshua son of Nun, the servant of the LORD, died at the age of one hundred ten years. [9] So they buried him within the bounds of his inheritance in Timnath-heres, in the hill country of Ephraim, north of Mount Gaash. [10] Moreover, that whole generation was gathered to their ancestors, and another generation grew up after them, who did not know the LORD or the work that he had done for Israel.

[11] Then the Israelites did what was evil in the sight of the LORD and worshiped the Baals; [12] and they abandoned the LORD, the God of their ancestors, who had brought them out of the land of Egypt; they followed other gods, from among the gods of the peoples who were all around them, and bowed down to them; and they provoked the LORD to anger. [13] They abandoned the LORD, and worshiped Baal and the Astartes. [14] So the anger of the LORD was kindled against Israel, and he gave them over to plunderers who plundered them, and he sold them into the power of their enemies all around, so that they could no longer withstand their enemies. [15] Whenever they marched out, the hand of the LORD was against them to bring misfortune, as the LORD had warned them and sworn to them; and they were in great distress.

[16] Then the LORD raised up judges, who delivered them out of the power of those who plundered them. [17] Yet they did not listen even to their judges; for they lusted after other gods and bowed down to them. They soon turned aside from the way in which their ancestors had walked, who had obeyed the commandments of the LORD; they did not follow their example. [18] Whenever the LORD raised up judges for them, the LORD was with the judge, and he delivered them from the hand of their enemies

---

a OL Vg Compare Gk: Heb *sides*
b That is *Weepers*

enous Amorites as forced laborers.

2.1–5: The assembly in Bochim. A divine messenger (*angel*) came to Bochim (lit. "Weepers"; see vv. 4–5) to rebuke the northern tribes, who had violated the covenant and sinned by not dispossessing the Canaanites. Bochim is often identified with Bethel (so LXX), as well as the connection of Bethel with weeping (20.23,26; 21.2 and Gen 35.8), and the connection between Gilgal (v.1) and Bethel (Hos 4.15; Am 4.4).

2.11–3.6: Summary characterization of the era of the judges. 2.11–19: A paradigm for the period, comprised of four repeated stages: doing evil (vv. 11–13); punishment by subjugation (vv. 14–15); deliverance by judges (v. 16); and days of calm, during which the judges ruled (vv. 17–19). The people always returned to sin, either during the judge's lifetime or after his death. The stage of crying to the LORD is absent here (cf. 3.9), further emphasizing the negative depiction of the period. This unit is rich in repetitions and Deuteronomistic expressions, suggesting late editing. **11:** *Baals*, Baal, whose name means "master," was one of the heads of the Canaanite pantheon. The use of the plural may indicate multiplicity of shrines, various manifestations of Baal or various idolatries, and is meant to emphasize the polytheistic nature of Israel's worship. **13:** *Astartes*, singular "Ashtoreth," the goddess of love and fertility, and Baal's consort.

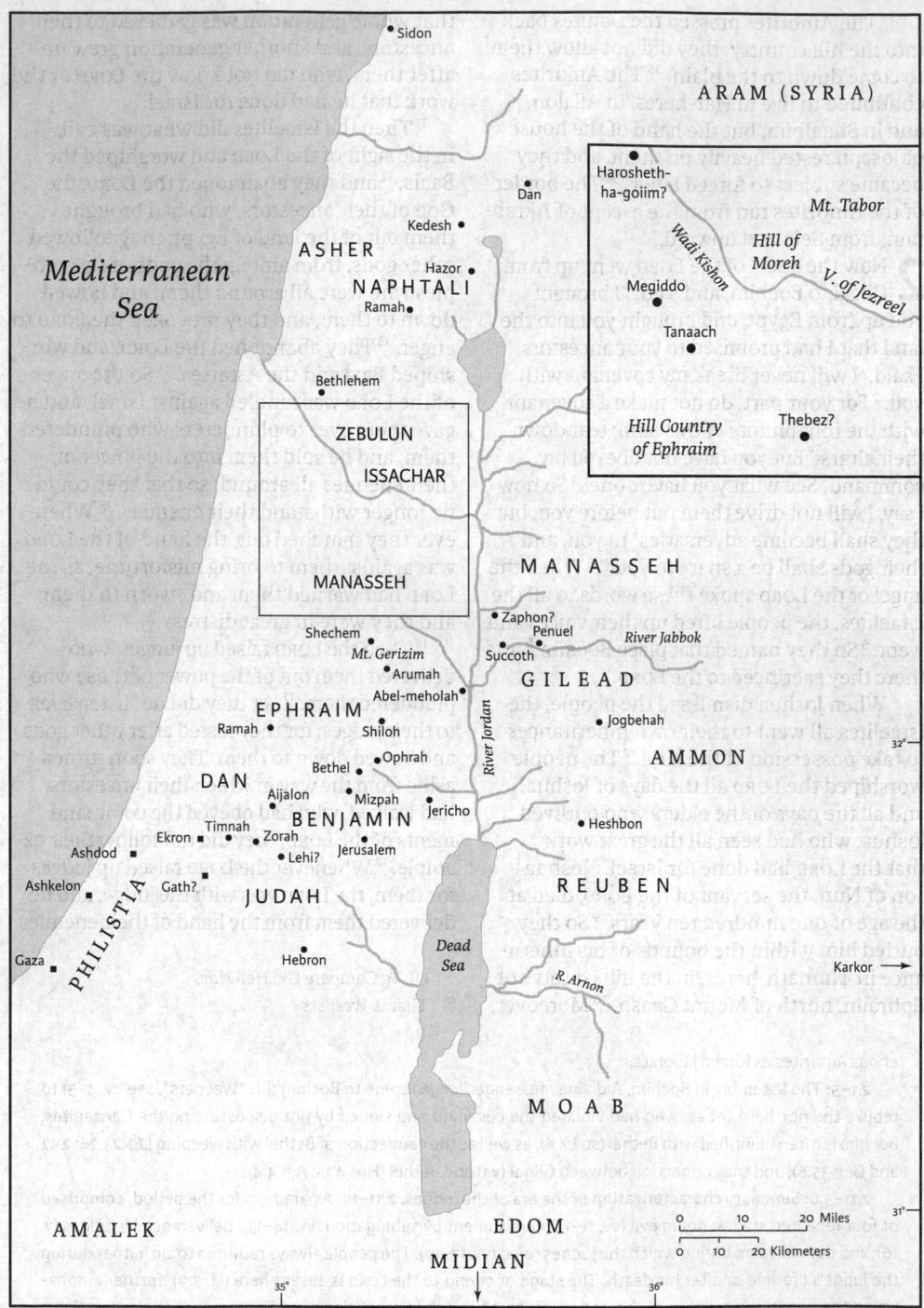

The geography of the book of Judges. Square boxes indicate Philistine cities.

all the days of the judge; for the LORD would be moved to pity by their groaning because of those who persecuted and oppressed them. [19] But whenever the judge died, they would relapse and behave worse than their ancestors, following other gods, worshiping them and bowing down to them. They would not drop any of their practices or their stubborn ways. [20] So the anger of the LORD was kindled against Israel; and he said, "Because this people have transgressed my covenant that I commanded their ancestors, and have not obeyed my voice, [21] I will no longer drive out before them any of the nations that Joshua left when he died." [22] In order to test Israel, whether or not they would take care to walk in the way of the LORD as their ancestors did, [23] the LORD had left those nations, not driving them out at once, and had not handed them over to Joshua.

3 Now these are the nations that the LORD left to test all those in Israel who had no experience of any war in Canaan [2] (it was only that successive generations of Israelites might know war, to teach those who had no experience of it before): [3] the five lords of the Philistines, and all the Canaanites, and the Sidonians, and the Hivites who lived on Mount Lebanon, from Mount Baal-hermon as far as Lebo-hamath. [4] They were for the testing of Israel, to know whether Israel would obey the commandments of the LORD, which he commanded their ancestors by Moses. [5] So the Israelites lived among the Canaanites, the Hittites, the Amorites, the Perizzites, the Hivites, and the Jebusites; [6] and they took their daughters as wives for themselves, and their own daughters they gave to their sons; and they worshiped their gods.

[7] The Israelites did what was evil in the sight of the LORD, forgetting the LORD their God, and worshiping the Baals and the Asherahs. [8] Therefore the anger of the LORD was kindled against Israel, and he sold them into the hand of King Cushan-rishathaim of Aram-naharaim; and the Israelites served Cushan-rishathaim eight years. [9] But when the Israelites cried out to the LORD, the LORD raised up a deliverer for the Israelites, who delivered them, Othniel son of Kenaz, Caleb's younger brother. [10] The spirit of the LORD came upon him, and he judged Israel; he went out to war, and the LORD gave King Cushan-rishathaim of Aram into his hand; and his hand prevailed over Cushan-rishathaim. [11] So the land had rest forty years. Then Othniel son of Kenaz died.

[12] The Israelites again did what was evil in the sight of the LORD; and the LORD strengthened King Eglon of Moab against Israel, because they had done what was evil in the sight of the LORD. [13] In alliance with the Ammonites and the Amalekites, he went and defeated Israel; and they took possession of the city of palms. [14] So the Israelites served King Eglon of Moab eighteen years.

[15] But when the Israelites cried out to the LORD, the LORD raised up for them a deliverer, Ehud son of Gera, the Benjaminite, a left-handed man. The Israelites sent tribute by him

---

2.20–3.6: Three answers regarding why the nations remained. The multiple perspectives here suggest that this section is a composite. **2.20–21:** The first answer: God's punishment for the sins of the people in the period of the judges. **2.22–23; 3.4:** The second answer: God intended to let the nations remain in order to test Israel's loyalty to him. **3.1–3:** The third answer: God planned to leave the nations in order to train Israel in fighting. **5–6:** Not dispossessing the Canaanites resulted in Israel's becoming assimilated among them.

3.7–16.31: Cycles of the judges. 3.7–11: Othniel the Kenizzite. The account of the first judge has typical formulas but no detailed deliverance story. Thus it serves as a transition from the introduction to the specific narratives. Othniel from Judah (see 1.13n.), who fought against an enemy from the far north, is depicted as a national leader and highlights the preeminence of Judah. **7:** *Asherahs,* the plural of Asherah, the consort of El, the chief god in the older Canaanite pantheon; on the plural, see 2.11n. Her name refers also to wooden symbols, trees or poles, which are prohibited in Deuteronomy (e.g., 16.21–22). **8:** *Cushan-rishathaim,* this strange, rhyming name means: "dark double-wickedness." *Aram-naharaim,* a distant place in northeast Syria (cf. Gen 24.10), which rhymes with its king's name. The use of a distant place attributes to the Judahite Othniel not just local but national prominence. **10:** *The spirit of the LORD,* charisma, allowing him to do activities he could not otherwise accomplish.

3.12–30: Ehud. The deliverance story of Ehud is not only the result of human tactics, planned and improvised, but also the result of divine providence. **13:** For the *Amalekites,* see 1.16n. *City of palms,* here as in Dt 34.3

to King Eglon of Moab. [16] Ehud made for himself a sword with two edges, a cubit in length; and he fastened it on his right thigh under his clothes. [17] Then he presented the tribute to King Eglon of Moab. Now Eglon was a very fat man. [18] When Ehud had finished presenting the tribute, he sent the people who carried the tribute on their way. [19] But he himself turned back at the sculptured stones near Gilgal, and said, "I have a secret message for you, O king." So the king said,[a] "Silence!" and all his attendants went out from his presence. [20] Ehud came to him, while he was sitting alone in his cool roof chamber, and said, "I have a message from God for you." So he rose from his seat. [21] Then Ehud reached with his left hand, took the sword from his right thigh, and thrust it into Eglon's[b] belly; [22] the hilt also went in after the blade, and the fat closed over the blade, for he did not draw the sword out of his belly; and the dirt came out.[c] [23] Then Ehud went out into the vestibule,[d] and closed the doors of the roof chamber on him, and locked them.

[24] After he had gone, the servants came. When they saw that the doors of the roof chamber were locked, they thought, "He must be relieving himself[e] in the cool chamber." [25] So they waited until they were embarrassed. When he still did not open the doors of the roof chamber, they took the key and opened them. There was their lord lying dead on the floor.

[26] Ehud escaped while they delayed, and passed beyond the sculptured stones, and escaped to Seirah. [27] When he arrived, he sounded the trumpet in the hill country of Ephraim; and the Israelites went down with him from the hill country, having him at their head. [28] He said to them, "Follow after me; for the LORD has given your enemies the Moabites into your hand." So they went down after him, and seized the fords of the Jordan against the Moabites, and allowed no one to cross over. [29] At that time they killed about ten thousand of the Moabites, all strong, able-bodied men; no one escaped. [30] So Moab was subdued that day under the hand of Israel. And the land had rest eighty years.

[31] After him came Shamgar son of Anath, who killed six hundred of the Philistines with an oxgoad. He too delivered Israel.

4 The Israelites again did what was evil in the sight of the LORD, after Ehud died. [2] So the LORD sold them into the hand of King Jabin of Canaan, who reigned in Hazor; the commander of his army was Sisera, who lived in Harosheth-ha-goiim. [3] Then the Israelites cried out to the LORD for help; for he had nine

---

a   Heb *he said*
b   Heb *his*
c   With Tg Vg: Meaning of Heb uncertain
d   Meaning of Heb uncertain
e   Heb *covering his feet*

---

and 2 Chr 28.15: Jericho. **16:** *A sword . . . a cubit*, Ehud's weapon was a dagger, shorter than ordinary swords (the word translated "cubit" occurs only here), about 12 inches and thus easy to hide, but sharpened on both *edges* in order to efficiently kill this portly king. **18:** This verse creates the impression of an elaborate and long gift-offering ceremony, which enabled Ehud to become familiar with the palace and its tenants. At the end, Ehud sent his people away and remained alone. **19:** Ehud arrived at Eglon's residency after previously visiting a sacred site with statues (Heb "pesilim," "idols") near Gilgal. **20:** *From God*, Ehud mentions God because he wants the stout king to stand up and thus to stretch himself. **25:** *Lying dead*, the servants were unaware of the murder and did not suspect Ehud, who then had time to escape. **26:** *Seirah*, location unknown. **28:** *The fords of the Jordan*, shallow places in the river that served for crossing. **29:** *No one escaped*, unlike a normal war, which usually has survivors; this is also an allusion to divine providence.

3.31: Shamgar. The report about Shamgar is reminiscent of stories of heroism (e.g., 15.15–16 and cf. 2 Sam 23.8). His name is mentioned in 5.6.

4.1–5.31: Deborah. The prose narrative in ch 4 complements the older poetic account in ch 5.

4.1–24: The prose narrative. Deborah the prophetess, Barak the army commander, and Jael wife of Heber the Kenite all contributed to achieving victory over the Canaanites. None of them is called a "deliverer," because in practice the true deliverer was God (vv. 14–15,23). **2:** *King Jabin of Canaan* (lit. "Jabin, king of Canaan"). Canaan, comprised of many city-states with their own rulers, did not have a single king. The use of the term "king of Canaan" reflects the desire to magnify the enemy and thus the deliverance. *Hazor,* a major city in the upper Galilee (see Josh 11.9). The origin of the name of *Sisera,* Jabin's general, is unknown, as is the precise location

hundred chariots of iron, and had oppressed the Israelites cruelly twenty years.

⁴ At that time Deborah, a prophetess, wife of Lappidoth, was judging Israel. ⁵ She used to sit under the palm of Deborah between Ramah and Bethel in the hill country of Ephraim; and the Israelites came up to her for judgment. ⁶ She sent and summoned Barak son of Abinoam from Kedesh in Naphtali, and said to him, "The LORD, the God of Israel, commands you, 'Go, take position at Mount Tabor, bringing ten thousand from the tribe of Naphtali and the tribe of Zebulun. ⁷ I will draw out Sisera, the general of Jabin's army, to meet you by the Wadi Kishon with his chariots and his troops; and I will give him into your hand.' " ⁸ Barak said to her, "If you will go with me, I will go; but if you will not go with me, I will not go." ⁹ And she said, "I will surely go with you; nevertheless, the road on which you are going will not lead to your glory, for the LORD will sell Sisera into the hand of a woman." Then Deborah got up and went with Barak to Kedesh. ¹⁰ Barak summoned Zebulun and Naphtali to Kedesh; and ten thousand warriors went up behind him; and Deborah went up with him.

¹¹ Now Heber the Kenite had separated from the other Kenites,ᵃ that is, the descendants of Hobab the father-in-law of Moses, and had encamped as far away as Elon-bezaanannim, which is near Kedesh.

¹² When Sisera was told that Barak son of Abinoam had gone up to Mount Tabor, ¹³ Sisera called out all his chariots, nine hundred chariots of iron, and all the troops who were with him, from Harosheth-ha-goiim to the Wadi Kishon. ¹⁴ Then Deborah said to Barak, "Up! For this is the day on which the LORD has given Sisera into your hand. The LORD is indeed going out before you." So Barak went down from Mount Tabor with ten thousand warriors following him. ¹⁵ And the LORD threw Sisera and all his chariots and all his army into a panicᵇ before Barak; Sisera got down from his chariot and fled away on foot, ¹⁶ while Barak pursued the chariots and the army to Harosheth-ha-goiim. All the army of Sisera fell by the sword; no one was left.

¹⁷ Now Sisera had fled away on foot to the tent of Jael wife of Heber the Kenite; for there was peace between King Jabin of Hazor and the clan of Heber the Kenite. ¹⁸ Jael came out to meet Sisera, and said to him, "Turn aside, my lord, turn aside to me; have no fear." So he turned aside to her into the tent, and she covered him with a rug. ¹⁹ Then he said to her, "Please give me a little water to drink; for I am thirsty." So she opened a skin of milk and gave him a drink and covered him. ²⁰ He said to her, "Stand at the entrance of the tent, and if anybody comes and asks you, 'Is anyone here?' say, 'No.' " ²¹ But Jael wife of Heber took a tent peg, and took a hammer in her hand, and went softly to him and drove the peg into his temple, until it went down into the ground—he was lying fast asleep from weariness—and he died. ²² Then, as Barak came in pursuit of Sisera, Jael went out to meet him, and said to him, "Come, and I will show you the man whom you are seeking." So he went into her tent; and there was Sisera lying dead, with the tent peg in his temple.

²³ So on that day God subdued King Jabin of Canaan before the Israelites. ²⁴ Then the hand of the Israelites bore harder and harder

ᵃ Heb *from the Kain*
ᵇ Heb adds *to the sword*; compare verse 16

of *Harosheth-ha-goiim.* Harosheth seems to be derived from harish, i.e., a plowed area, referring to the flat area near Taanach and Megiddo, where Sisera's chariots encamped. 4: *Deborah,* whose name means "bee," was a prophetess (compare Ex 15.20; 2 Kings 22.14; Neh 6.14; Isa 8.3. 5). She is the only woman who is a judge too. Deborah's location is in Mount Ephraim. 6: *Kedesh in Naphtali,* identified with Khirbet Kadish at the foot of today's Poriyah, above Tiberia. *Mount Tabor,* overlooking the Valley of Jezreel from the north. 7: The *Wadi Kishon,* a branch of Kishon, which flows close to Taanach and Megiddo (see 5.19). 8: The military leader needs the prophetess at his side, somewhat diminishing his heroic status. 9: *A woman,* the reader assumes that the woman is Deborah, but at the end will realize that Jael is meant. 11: The Kenites were a group associated with Judah (see 1.16n.). 14: Deborah predicts the LORD's direct participation in the battle; *before you,* the Hebrew has double meaning: before Barak's arrival or in front of him. 16: *No one was left,* this unrealistic detail also indicates divine intervention (cf. 3.29). 17: Sisera prefers the Kenites' encampment, due to the friendship between them and Jabin. 19: Although Sisera asked for *water,* Jael gave him *milk,* which has soothing qualities, because she

on King Jabin of Canaan, until they destroyed King Jabin of Canaan.

5 Then Deborah and Barak son of Abinoam sang on that day, saying:

2 "When locks are long in Israel,
　　when the people offer themselves
　　　willingly—
　　blessa the LORD!

3 "Hear, O kings; give ear, O princes;
　　to the LORD I will sing,
　　I will make melody to the LORD, the God
　　　of Israel.

4 "LORD, when you went out from Seir,
　　when you marched from the region of
　　　Edom,
the earth trembled,
　　and the heavens poured,
　　the clouds indeed poured water.
5 The mountains quaked before the LORD,
　　the One of Sinai,
　　before the LORD, the God of Israel.

6 "In the days of Shamgar son of Anath,
　　in the days of Jael, caravans ceased
　　and travelers kept to the byways.
7 The peasantry prospered in Israel,
　　they grew fat on plunder,
because you arose, Deborah,
　　arose as a mother in Israel.
8 When new gods were chosen,
　　then war was in the gates.
Was shield or spear to be seen
　　among forty thousand in Israel?
9 My heart goes out to the commanders of
　　Israel
who offered themselves willingly
　　　among the people.
　　Bless the LORD.

10 "Tell of it, you who ride on white donkeys,
　　you who sit on rich carpetsb
　　and you who walk by the way.

a Or *You who offer yourselves willingly among the
   people, bless*
b Meaning of Heb uncertain

wanted him to sleep deeply. **23–24:** The conclusion emphasizes that the victory was achieved mainly due to God's intervention; the role of the human heroes was secondary.

5.1–31: The poetic account: the song of Deborah. This is a hymn of praise thanking and extolling God for overcoming the enemies that threatened his people. The "people" here refers only to the northern tribes (Judah, Simon and Levi are not mentioned), which suggest that the poem was composed in the north. Notwithstanding the similarities between the song and the prose story (ch 4) with respect to the main characters and various details, there are also significant differences, such as the names of the tribes who participated in the battle and the absence of Jabin in the song. The prose narrative was likely composed after the song, attempting to resolve some unclear matters. The poem is written in the first person, expressing spontaneous enthusiasm (e.g., vv. 3,12) and using contrasts and extreme transitions (as from Jael to Sisera's mother). Although the text is often unclear, the song reflects the atmosphere of the northern kingdom, which means that it was written before its fall (722 BCE). Between the opening (vv. 2–3) and the closing (v. 31a) the song has three sections that feature contrasts: God's power versus his oppressed people (vv. 4–11c), the Israelites' army versus the Canaanites' (vv. 11d–23), and Jael who killed Sisera versus his expecting mother (vv. 24–30). **1:** According to the editor, the song is the immediate joyous reaction of Deborah and Barak to the victory. **2–3:** An opening that explains the circumstances of reciting the song. **2:** *When locks are long,* the Hebrew is difficult; if this translation is correct, it may refer to Nazirites who dedicated themselves to warfare wearing long hair. Alternatively, the Hebrew may mean "disasters" that confronted Israel. **3:** *I will sing . . . I will make melody,* the poetic parallelism emphasizes the involvement of the speaker, Deborah.

5.4–11c: The strength of God's epiphany versus the difficult situation of his people. 4: *Seir . . . Edom,* synonyms referring to God's epiphany in the southeast of Judah (cf. Deut 33.2), with accompanying manifestations of earthquake and storms. **5:** *Quaked,* lit. "flowed,"as if melted; cf. Am 9.5. **6:** *Shamgar,* see 3.31. **7:** *Peasantry,* the Heb probably means "open (unwalled) cities." People were afraid to live in such places, and fled to fortified cities. **8:** *New gods,* the abandonment of the LORD for the gods of Canaan is the cause of the war and of the lack of weapons. *Then,* repeated five times (vv. 8,11,13,19,22), indicating five stages in the course of the war: danger, gathering together, arrival at the battlefield, war, retreat. *Forty thousand,* an exaggerated typological number, which suggests a comprehensive war. **10:** Riding on donkeys, especially light-haired ones, was a symbol of

¹¹ To the sound of musicians^a at the
  watering places,
  there they repeat the triumphs of the
  LORD,
  the triumphs of his peasantry in Israel.

"Then down to the gates marched the
  people of the LORD.

¹² "Awake, awake, Deborah!
  Awake, awake, utter a song!
Arise, Barak, lead away your captives,
  O son of Abinoam.
¹³ Then down marched the remnant of the
  noble;
  the people of the LORD marched down
  for him^b against the mighty.
¹⁴ From Ephraim they set out^c into the
  valley,^d
  following you, Benjamin, with your kin;
from Machir marched down the
  commanders,
  and from Zebulun those who bear the
  marshal's staff;
¹⁵ the chiefs of Issachar came with Deborah,
  and Issachar faithful to Barak;
  into the valley they rushed out at his
  heels.

Among the clans of Reuben
  there were great searchings of heart.
¹⁶ Why did you tarry among the
  sheepfolds,
  to hear the piping for the flocks?
Among the clans of Reuben
  there were great searchings of heart.
¹⁷ Gilead stayed beyond the Jordan;
  and Dan, why did he abide with the
  ships?
Asher sat still at the coast of the sea,
  settling down by his landings.
¹⁸ Zebulun is a people that scorned death;
  Naphtali too, on the heights of
  the field.

¹⁹ "The kings came, they fought;
  then fought the kings of Canaan,
at Taanach, by the waters of Megiddo;
  they got no spoils of silver.
²⁰ The stars fought from heaven,
  from their courses they fought against
  Sisera.

a   Meaning of Heb uncertain
b   Gk: Heb me
c   Cn: Heb From Ephraim their root
d   Gk: Heb in Amalek

wealth (see 10.4). **11**: *Sound of musicians*, the Hebrew may refer to the noise made by the shepherds while driving their flocks to water; the sound of those who tell of God's victories will be louder than this. *His peasantry*, see v.6n. The LORD's deliverance restored confidence.

5.11d–23: The Israelite warriors versus the Canaanite kings. 11: The city gate served as a gathering place. **12:** The *song* here is a prophecy. **13:** The Hebrew is difficult; a preferable translation is: "Then they [the LORD's people] went down to Sarid [a city in the Jezreel Valley] against the mighty ones [the Canaanite kings], the LORD's people with its warriors." **14–18:** Description of the Israelite side. Most commentators think that only six tribes went to war (Ephraim, Benjamin, Machir [= Manasseh], Zebulun, Issachar, and Naphtali), while the other four (Reuben, Gilead [= Gad and the other half of Manasseh], Dan, and Asher) refused to join. According to the interpretation suggested here, all ten northern tribes participated. **14:** *Set out*, unclear; a better translation is: "From Ephraim chieftains [went down] to the valley." *Kin*, the collective noun here may be interpreted as "kinfolk," thus strengthening the forces of Benjamin. *Machir*, the firstborn son of Manasseh; cf. Josh 17.1. *Marshal's staff*, i.e., commanders who recorded the number of those going to war. **15:** *And Issachar*, Issachar is repeated twice, while Naphtali is absent; probably the second "Issachar" should be emended to "Naphtali." *Heart*, the center of thinking and wisdom (e.g., 1 Kings 3.12). **16:** *Why did you tarry*, here the Hebrew "lamah" is a term of negation with an emphatic "mem": "You did not tarry" (see v. 17). **17:** The depiction of *Gilead* is rhetorical, emphasizing that although they dwelled (NRSV: "stayed") far away, they participated in the war. *And Dan*, "Dan did not abide with the ships.." The tribe of *Asher*, who lived on the northern coastal plain, also joined the war. **18:** Only the tribes of *Zebulun* and *Naphtali* are described as bold warriors; perhaps that is why they alone are mentioned in the prose narrative (4.6,10). *On the heights*, an allusion to Naphtali's inheritance, as the war was in the valley in its territory. **19:** *Taanach*, in the Valley of Jezreel, near the ancient international highway connecting Egypt and Mesopotamia. **20:** Here Sisera rather than Jabin heads the alliance (see 4.2,23). **21:** *The onrushing torrent*, the Hebrew is obscure; a better translation is "the brook Kishon came in front of them." *March on, my soul*, a

²¹ The torrent Kishon swept them away,
the onrushing torrent, the torrent Kishon.
March on, my soul, with might!

²² "Then loud beat the horses' hoofs
with the galloping, galloping of his steeds.

²³ "Curse Meroz, says the angel of the LORD,
curse bitterly its inhabitants,
because they did not come to the help of
the LORD,
to the help of the LORD against the mighty.

²⁴ "Most blessed of women be Jael,
the wife of Heber the Kenite,
of tent-dwelling women most blessed.
²⁵ He asked water and she gave him milk,
she brought him curds in a lordly bowl.
²⁶ She put her hand to the tent peg
and her right hand to the workmen's
mallet;
she struck Sisera a blow,
she crushed his head,
she shattered and pierced his temple.
²⁷ He sank, he fell,
he lay still at her feet;
at her feet he sank, he fell;
where he sank, there he fell dead.

²⁸ "Out of the window she peered,
the mother of Sisera gazed^a through the
lattice:

'Why is his chariot so long in coming?
Why tarry the hoofbeats of his
chariots?'
²⁹ Her wisest ladies make answer,
indeed, she answers the question
herself:
³⁰ 'Are they not finding and dividing the
spoil?—
A girl or two for every man;
spoil of dyed stuffs for Sisera,
spoil of dyed stuffs embroidered,
two pieces of dyed work embroidered
for my neck as spoil?'

³¹ "So perish all your enemies, O LORD!
But may your friends be like the sun as
it rises in its might."

And the land had rest forty years.

6 The Israelites did what was evil in the sight of the LORD, and the LORD gave them into the hand of Midian seven years. ² The hand of Midian prevailed over Israel; and because of Midian the Israelites provided for themselves hiding places in the mountains, caves and strongholds. ³ For whenever the Israelites put in seed, the Midianites and the Amalekites and the people of the east would come up against them. ⁴ They would encamp against them and destroy the

---

^a   Gk Compare Tg: Heb *exclaimed*

self-address by the speaker because of the joy of victory. **22:** The noise of the feet of the enemy's horses fleeing from the confusion of the battle. **23:** Only the people of *Meroz*, which has not been identified, are cursed for not joining God and his warriors.

5.24–30: The victory of Jael, who is contrasted with the mother of defeated Sisera.

24–27: Death at the hands of a woman was considered shameful (cf. 9.54). **27:** *At her feet*, lit. "between her feet". Since "feet" can be a euphemism for genitals, there is a suggestion that Jael used her sexuality to entice Sisera, who *lay* with her. **28:** The picture of a woman looking through the window is found elsewhere in the Bible (e.g., 2 Sam 6.16; 2 Kings 9.30) and in the ancient Near East. **30:** *A girl or two*, taking women as captives (cf. Deut 21.10–11), another sexual connotation. *Dyed* and colored clothing were expensive luxury items. *My neck as spoil*, better "the necks of those who took the spoil." **31a:** Conclusion to the Song. *Your friends*, the people of the LORD are compared to the sun, rising with great intensity. **31b:** *And the land had rest forty years*, these words, using the formula for calm, are not part of the song, but the closing frame of Deborah's cycle.

6.1–8.28: Gideon. Gideon's cycle has two parts. The first (6.1–7.23) abounds with miracles, while Gideon is portrayed as excessively fearful and requiring divine support. In contrast, in the second (7.24–8.28), which is concerned with problems of leadership, there are no miracles and Gideon is presented as a charismatic leader. The two sections illustrate the central problem of the book of Judges: what is the preferred type of leadership: divine leadership with abundant miracles, or human rule?

6.1–10: Beginning of the first part of the Gideon cycle. 1–3: Nomadic tribes destroyed all the crops of the land, and the Israelites were forced to hide their grain in the hills. *Midian*, see Num 31.1–12. For the *Amalekites*,

produce of the land, as far as the neighborhood of Gaza, and leave no sustenance in Israel, and no sheep or ox or donkey. [5] For they and their livestock would come up, and they would even bring their tents, as thick as locusts; neither they nor their camels could be counted; so they wasted the land as they came in. [6] Thus Israel was greatly impoverished because of Midian; and the Israelites cried out to the LORD for help.

[7] When the Israelites cried to the LORD on account of the Midianites, [8] the LORD sent a prophet to the Israelites; and he said to them, "Thus says the LORD, the God of Israel: I led you up from Egypt, and brought you out of the house of slavery; [9] and I delivered you from the hand of the Egyptians, and from the hand of all who oppressed you, and drove them out before you, and gave you their land; [10] and I said to you, 'I am the LORD your God; you shall not pay reverence to the gods of the Amorites, in whose land you live.' But you have not given heed to my voice."

[11] Now the angel of the LORD came and sat under the oak at Ophrah, which belonged to Joash the Abiezrite, as his son Gideon was beating out wheat in the wine press, to hide it from the Midianites. [12] The angel of the LORD appeared to him and said to him, "The LORD is with you, you mighty warrior." [13] Gideon answered him, "But sir, if the LORD is with us, why then has all this happened to us? And where are all his wonderful deeds that our ancestors recounted to us, saying, 'Did not the LORD bring us up from Egypt?' But now the LORD has cast us off, and given us into the hand of Midian." [14] Then the LORD turned to him and said, "Go in this might of yours and deliver Israel from the hand of Midian; I hereby commission you." [15] He responded, "But sir, how can I deliver Israel? My clan is the weakest in Manasseh, and I am the least in my family." [16] The LORD said to him, "But I will be with you, and you shall strike down the Midianites, every one of them." [17] Then he said to him, "If now I have found favor with you, then show me a sign that it is you who speak with me. [18] Do not depart from here until I come to you, and bring out my present, and set it before you." And he said, "I will stay until you return."

[19] So Gideon went into his house and prepared a kid, and unleavened cakes from an ephah of flour; the meat he put in a basket, and the broth he put in a pot, and brought them to him under the oak and presented them. [20] The angel of God said to him, "Take the meat and the unleavened cakes, and put them on this rock, and pour out the broth." And he did so. [21] Then the angel of the LORD reached out the tip of the staff that was in his hand, and touched the meat and the unleavened cakes, and fire sprang up from the rock and consumed the meat and the unleavened cakes; and the angel of the LORD vanished from his sight. [22] Then Gideon perceived that it was the angel of the LORD; and Gideon said,

see 1.16n. 4: *Gaza*, marks the boundary of the entire land (see 1 Kgs 5.4). 5: *As locusts*, an image emphasizing large numbers. 7–10: *The Israelites cried out to the LORD*, but this time he sent a prophet to rebuke them rather than a deliverer to rescue them. These verses are absent in 4Q Judg a, a manuscript of the book of Judges in the Dead Sea Scrolls, and are likely a late addition.

6.11–24: **Gideon's appointment.** This is a stereotypical appointment or call scene composed of seven stages: meeting (vv. 11–13), presentation of the mission (v. 14), refusal (v. 15), encouragement (v. 16), request for a sign (vv. 17–22), acknowledgment and fear (v. 23), and further encouragement (v. 24). The appointment of some prophets has similar elements (e.g., Ex 3–4). 11: *Ophrah*, location unknown. *Abiezrite*, Abiezer is one of the important families in Manasseh (Josh 17.2), mentioned in the Samaria Ostraca from the mid-eighth century BCE. *Gideon*, his name, which means "hacker," anticipates his cutting down of sacred poles (cf. vv. 25, 30; the same Heb root is used in Deut 7.5 and elsewhere). See also v. 32n. *Wine press*, here a hiding place; see vv. 2–3. 12: *Angel*, (lit. "messenger"); Gideon is initially unaware of his divine identity (see v. 22). *You mighty warrior*, the angel hints to Gideon's future role, but the hiding Gideon understands it ironically and responds furiously. 15: *Weakest . . . least* (lit. "smallest, youngest"), although Gideon's family is prosperous (vv. 19,25,27), the choice of an unlikely hero (often the youngest son) is a repeated motif in the Bible (e.g., 1 Sam 9.21; 16.6–13). 18–21: This assumes that angels do not usually eat (cf. 13.15); the meal is transformed into a burnt offering. 19: *Ephah*, a large quantity of flour, ca. 21 qts (23 liters). 21: The appearance of fire from the rock (cf. 13.20; 1 Kings 18.38; etc.) and the sudden disappearance are also signs that this is an angel. 22: Gideon was afraid to see the divine presence (cf. 13,22; Gen

"Help me, Lord GOD! For I have seen the angel of the LORD face to face." [23] But the LORD said to him, "Peace be to you; do not fear, you shall not die." [24] Then Gideon built an altar there to the LORD, and called it, The LORD is peace. To this day it still stands at Ophrah, which belongs to the Abiezrites.

[25] That night the LORD said to him, "Take your father's bull, the second bull seven years old, and pull down the altar of Baal that belongs to your father, and cut down the sacred pole[a] that is beside it; [26] and build an altar to the LORD your God on the top of the stronghold here, in proper order; then take the second bull, and offer it as a burnt offering with the wood of the sacred pole[a] that you shall cut down." [27] So Gideon took ten of his servants, and did as the LORD had told him; but because he was too afraid of his family and the townspeople to do it by day, he did it by night.

[28] When the townspeople rose early in the morning, the altar of Baal was broken down, and the sacred pole[a] beside it was cut down, and the second bull was offered on the altar that had been built. [29] So they said to one another, "Who has done this?" After searching and inquiring, they were told, "Gideon son of Joash did it." [30] Then the townspeople said to Joash, "Bring out your son, so that he may die, for he has pulled down the altar of Baal and cut down the sacred pole[a] beside it." [31] But Joash said to all who were arrayed against him, "Will you contend for Baal? Or will you defend his cause? Whoever contends for him shall be put to death by morning. If he is a god, let him contend for himself, because his altar has been pulled down." [32] Therefore on that day Gideon[b] was called Jerubbaal, that is to say, "Let Baal contend against him," because he pulled down his altar.

[33] Then all the Midianites and the Amalekites and the people of the east came together, and crossing the Jordan they encamped in the Valley of Jezreel. [34] But the spirit of the LORD took possession of Gideon; and he sounded the trumpet, and the Abiezrites were called out to follow him. [35] He sent messengers throughout all Manasseh, and they too were called out to follow him. He also sent messengers to Asher, Zebulun, and Naphtali, and they went up to meet them.

[36] Then Gideon said to God, "In order to see whether you will deliver Israel by my hand, as you have said, [37] I am going to lay a fleece of wool on the threshing floor; if there is dew on the fleece alone, and it is dry on all the ground, then I shall know that you will deliver Israel by my hand, as you have said." [38] And it was so. When he rose early next morning and squeezed the fleece, he wrung enough dew from the fleece to fill a bowl with water. [39] Then Gideon said to God, "Do not let your anger burn against me, let me speak one more time; let me, please, make trial with the fleece just once more; let it be dry only on the fleece, and on all the ground let there be dew." [40] And God did so that night. It was dry on the fleece only, and on all the ground there was dew.

7 Then Jerubbaal (that is, Gideon) and all the troops that were with him rose early and encamped beside the spring of Harod;

---

a Heb *Asherah*
b Heb *he*

32.30; Ex 20.19). **24:** The altar's name is related to God's comforting words in v. 23.

6.25–32: Gideon destroys the altar and sacred pillar of Baal. This story indicates the proliferation of Baal worship and explains Gideon's other name, Jerubbaal, which might be the original name (see v. 11b). **25:** *Second bull*, the reference to two bulls (also vv. 26,28) is problematic; a better reading, found in some textual sources, is "the bull that had been fattened for seven years." *Sacred pole*, a symbol of the goddess Asherah (see 3.7n.). **31:** Joash puts Baal to the test in the eyes of his believers (cf. 1 Kings 18.20–40). *By morning* of the next day. Joash left time for Baal to prove himself. **32:** *Jerubbaal*, the original meaning of this name was probably "Baal makes great" or "Baal is a founder", the component "Jeru" appears in the name Jerusalem too; here a folk etymology suggests that it means to content or fight against Baal, referring to Gideon's battle with the worship of Baal.

6.33–7.25: The battle with the Midianites. 6.33–35: The military mustering. Gideon called to his assistance his own tribe and the neighboring tribes. **36–40:** The signs of the fleece. In order to be certain that God is with him, Gideon requested two additional and contradictory signs. **7.1–8:** Another test. In order to convince the people that deliverance comes from God, Gideon's army was gradually reduced from a force of 32,000 warriors

and the camp of Midian was north of them, below[a] the hill of Moreh, in the valley.

² The LORD said to Gideon, "The troops with you are too many for me to give the Midianites into their hand. Israel would only take the credit away from me, saying, 'My own hand has delivered me.' ³ Now therefore proclaim this in the hearing of the troops, 'Whoever is fearful and trembling, let him return home.'" Thus Gideon sifted them out;[b] twenty-two thousand returned, and ten thousand remained.

⁴ Then the LORD said to Gideon, "The troops are still too many; take them down to the water and I will sift them out for you there. When I say, 'This one shall go with you,' he shall go with you; and when I say, 'This one shall not go with you,' he shall not go." ⁵ So he brought the troops down to the water; and the LORD said to Gideon, "All those who lap the water with their tongues, as a dog laps, you shall put to one side; all those who kneel down to drink, putting their hands to their mouths,[c] you shall put to the other side." ⁶ The number of those that lapped was three hundred; but all the rest of the troops knelt down to drink water. ⁷ Then the LORD said to Gideon, "With the three hundred that lapped I will deliver you, and give the Midianites into your hand. Let all the others go to their homes." ⁸ So he took the jars of the troops from their hands,[d] and their trumpets; and he sent all the rest of Israel back to their own tents, but retained the three hundred. The camp of Midian was below him in the valley.

⁹ That same night the LORD said to him, "Get up, attack the camp; for I have given it into your hand. ¹⁰ But if you fear to attack, go down to the camp with your servant Purah; ¹¹ and you shall hear what they say, and afterward your hands shall be strengthened to attack the camp." Then he went down with his servant Purah to the outposts of the armed men that were in the camp. ¹² The Midianites and the Amalekites and all the people of the east lay along the valley as thick as locusts; and their camels were without number, countless as the sand on the seashore. ¹³ When Gideon arrived, there was a man telling a dream to his comrade; and he said, "I had a dream, and in it a cake of barley bread tumbled into the camp of Midian, and came to the tent, and struck it so that it fell; it turned upside down, and the tent collapsed." ¹⁴ And his comrade answered, "This is no other than the sword of Gideon son of Joash, a man of Israel; into his hand God has given Midian and all the army."

¹⁵ When Gideon heard the telling of the dream and its interpretation, he worshiped; and he returned to the camp of Israel, and said, "Get up; for the LORD has given the army of Midian into your hand." ¹⁶ After he divided the three hundred men into three companies, and put trumpets into the hands of all of them, and empty jars, with torches inside the jars, ¹⁷ he said to them, "Look at me, and do the same; when I come to the outskirts of the camp, do as I do. ¹⁸ When I blow the trumpet, I and all who are with me, then you also blow the trumpets around the whole camp, and shout, 'For the LORD and for Gideon!'"

¹⁹ So Gideon and the hundred who were with him came to the outskirts of the camp at the beginning of the middle watch, when they had just set the watch; and they blew the trumpets and smashed the jars that were in their hands. ²⁰ So the three companies blew the trumpets and broke the jars, holding

a   Heb *from*
b   Cn: Heb *home, and depart from Mount Gilead'*
c   Heb places the words *putting their hands to their mouths* after the word *lapped* in verse 6
d   Cn: Heb *So the people took provisions in their hands*

to a band of 300 who lapped water, thus highlighting God's intervention. **1:** *In the valley,* at the base of Gibeath-moreh, south of modern Afula. **9–15a:** The dream of the Midianite soldier. In order to encourage Gideon, God commanded him to approach the Midianite camp, where he heard a Midianite soldier recounting his dream to his friend about Gideon's victory. **13:** A dream was understood by the ancients as a divine message. The *cake* symbolizes Gideon the farmer, and the *tent* the nomadic Midianites. **15b–23:** The battle. The story emphasizes the passivity of Gideon's army, whose task was to blow the horns, to shout, and mainly to witness God's deliverance. **16:** *Three companies,* in order to surround the camp. **19:** The night is divided into three watches. During *the middle watch,* from approximately 10 p.m. to 2 a.m., sleep is strongest and the soldiers may panic at every sound. **20–23:** Both hands of the soldiers were occupied with horns to blow and jars with torches, so all they could do was to shout. God interfered and the soldiers simply watched how some of the Midianites killed one

in their left hands the torches, and in their right hands the trumpets to blow; and they cried, "A sword for the LORD and for Gideon!" [21] Every man stood in his place all around the camp, and all the men in camp ran; they cried out and fled. [22] When they blew the three hundred trumpets, the LORD set every man's sword against his fellow and against all the army; and the army fled as far as Beth-shittah toward Zererah,[a] as far as the border of Abel-meholah, by Tabbath. [23] And the men of Israel were called out from Naphtali and from Asher and from all Manasseh, and they pursued after the Midianites.

[24] Then Gideon sent messengers throughout all the hill country of Ephraim, saying, "Come down against the Midianites and seize the waters against them, as far as Beth-barah, and also the Jordan." So all the men of Ephraim were called out, and they seized the waters as far as Beth-barah, and also the Jordan. [25] They captured the two captains of Midian, Oreb and Zeeb; they killed Oreb at the rock of Oreb, and Zeeb they killed at the wine press of Zeeb, as they pursued the Midianites. They brought the heads of Oreb and Zeeb to Gideon beyond the Jordan.

8 Then the Ephraimites said to him, "What have you done to us, not to call us when you went to fight against the Midianites?" And they upbraided him violently. [2] So he said to them, "What have I done now in comparison with you? Is not the gleaning of the grapes of Ephraim better than the vintage of Abiezer? [3] God has given into your hands the captains of Midian, Oreb and Zeeb; what have I been

able to do in comparison with you?" When he said this, their anger against him subsided.

[4] Then Gideon came to the Jordan and crossed over, he and the three hundred who were with him, exhausted and famished.[b] [5] So he said to the people of Succoth, "Please give some loaves of bread to my followers, for they are exhausted, and I am pursuing Zebah and Zalmunna, the kings of Midian." [6] But the officials of Succoth said, "Do you already have in your possession the hands of Zebah and Zalmunna, that we should give bread to your army?" [7] Gideon replied, "Well then, when the LORD has given Zebah and Zalmunna into my hand, I will trample your flesh on the thorns of the wilderness and on briers." [8] From there he went up to Penuel, and made the same request of them; and the people of Penuel answered him as the people of Succoth had answered. [9] So he said to the people of Penuel, "When I come back victorious, I will break down this tower."

[10] Now Zebah and Zalmunna were in Karkor with their army, about fifteen thousand men, all who were left of all the army of the people of the east; for one hundred twenty thousand men bearing arms had fallen. [11] So Gideon went up by the caravan route east of Nobah and Jogbehah, and attacked the army; for the army was off its guard. [12] Zebah and Zalmunna fled; and he pursued them and took the two kings of Midian, Zebah and Zalmunna, and threw all the army into a panic.

---

a   Another reading is *Zeredah*
b   Gk: Heb *pursuing*

---

another and others escaped. Most of the places mentioned are not identifiable. **23:** More fighting units of Israel joined in the chase.

7.24–8.3: The confrontation with Ephraim (beginning of the second part of the Gideon cycle). Gideon prevented a civil war by calming Ephraim's warriors. He is characterized here not as a coward but as a responsible leader with diplomatic talent. **24–25:** Simultaneously or even before the chase : Gideon called on Ephraim's warriors to pursue the Midianites, adjacent to their territory. *Beth-barah,* precise location unknown. **8.1:** Ephraim's warriors were angry that Gideon did not involve them in the battle from the beginning (see 6.35). **2:** *Gleaning of the grapes,* the grapes that remain after the main part of a crop has been harvested. Gideon convinced them that their part, the killing of the two generals, was even more important than the battle itself.

8.4–21: Confrontation with Succoth and Penuel. Gideon's purpose was to smite the camp of the Midianites east of the Jordan River and to capture their leaders. Two Israelite cities in Transjordan refused to give bread to Gideon's exhausted three hundred warriors, so after his victory he acted as a decisive leader, punishing them severely. **5:** *Succoth,* probably Tell Deir 'Alla in the Transjordan Valley. *Kings,* here heads of tribes. **8:** *Penuel* is probably Tell edh-Dhahab esh-Sherqiyeh, east of Succoth (see Gen 32.23-31, 1 Kings 12.25). **10:** *Karkor,* probably a desert oasis in eastern Transjordan. The numbers are exaggerated. **11:** A nomadic route east of Amman.

¹³ When Gideon son of Joash returned from the battle by the ascent of Heres, ¹⁴ he caught a young man, one of the people of Succoth, and questioned him; and he listed for him the officials and elders of Succoth, seventy-seven people. ¹⁵ Then he came to the people of Succoth, and said, "Here are Zebah and Zalmunna, about whom you taunted me, saying, 'Do you already have in your possession the hands of Zebah and Zalmunna, that we should give bread to your troops who are exhausted?' " ¹⁶ So he took the elders of the city and he took thorns of the wilderness and briers and with them he trampledª the people of Succoth. ¹⁷ He also broke down the tower of Penuel, and killed the men of the city.

¹⁸ Then he said to Zebah and Zalmunna, "What about the men whom you killed at Tabor?" They answered, "As you are, so were they, every one of them; they resembled the sons of a king." ¹⁹ And he replied, "They were my brothers, the sons of my mother; as the LORD lives, if you had saved them alive, I would not kill you." ²⁰ So he said to Jether his firstborn, "Go kill them!" But the boy did not draw his sword, for he was afraid, because he was still a boy. ²¹ Then Zebah and Zalmunna said, "You come and kill us; for as the man is, so is his strength." So Gideon proceeded to kill Zebah and Zalmunna; and he took the crescents that were on the necks of their camels.

²² Then the Israelites said to Gideon, "Rule over us, you and your son and your grand-son also; for you have delivered us out of the hand of Midian." ²³ Gideon said to them, "I will not rule over you, and my son will not rule over you; the LORD will rule over you." ²⁴ Then Gideon said to them, "Let me make a request of you; each of you give me an earring he has taken as booty." (For the enemyᵇ had golden earrings, because they were Ishmaelites.) ²⁵ "We will willingly give them," they answered. So they spread a garment, and each threw into it an earring he had taken as booty. ²⁶ The weight of the golden earrings that he requested was one thousand seven hundred shekels of gold (apart from the crescents and the pendants and the purple garments worn by the kings of Midian, and the collars that were on the necks of their camels). ²⁷ Gideon made an ephod of it and put it in his town, in Ophrah; and all Israel prostituted themselves to it there, and it became a snare to Gideon and to his family. ²⁸ So Midian was subdued before the Israelites, and they lifted up their heads no more. So the land had rest forty years in the days of Gideon.

²⁹ Jerubbaal son of Joash went to live in his own house. ³⁰ Now Gideon had seventy sons, his own offspring, for he had many wives. ³¹ His concubine who was in Shechem also bore him a son, and he named him Abimelech. ³² Then Gideon son of Joash died at a

ª With verse 7, Compare Gk: Heb *he taught*
ᵇ Heb *they*

18: If this is the familiar *Tabor* (see 4.6n.), no battle between the Midianites and Gibeon's forces there has been reported. *Sons of a king*, they relate to Gideon as to a king. 21: The Midianite leaders preferred that Gideon, an experienced warrior, and not his young son, should kill them, because of honor and their wish to die quickly.

8.22–27: The offer of kingship to Gideon. Gideon's refusal to rule as king is interpreted in different ways: as connected to the ancient ideology that God alone is king; as a later anti-monarchical interpolation; or as a polite refusal even though he actually acted as a king. It may also reflect the editor's view that Israelite society was not yet ripe for a monarch, because the armies of only some tribes supported Gideon and the results could lead to a civil war (as in ch 9). The establishing of the ephod (a statue) is reminiscent of the calf in Ex 32:2–4. 22: *The Israelites*, i.e., Gideon's troops. *You and your son . . .* , indicating a dynasty. *You have delivered us*, the army sees Gideon and not the LORD as their deliverer. 24: *Ishmaelites*, instead of Midianites; the same substitution occurs in Gen 37.25–36. The two groups were likely related. 27: *Ephod,* usually part of the priestly vestments used in divination, but here apparently a statue intended to commemorate the deliverance that became a ritual object. 27b: A Deuteronomistic addition, contrasting the view that "he did good for Israel" (8.35; 9.16ff.) and highlighting the dangers of Gideon's actions.

8.29–9.57: Abimelech. Gideon had a concubine at Shechem, perhaps reflecting a political alliance. Their son was Abimelech, who wanted to become king. His brief and bloody reign marks the failure of the first attempt to establish a monarchy. 8.30: *Seventy*, a typological number signifying multiplicity. 31: *Concubine*, a woman with a status lower than that of a primary wife. *Shechem*, see 9.1n. *Abimelech*, his name, which means "My (divine)

good old age, and was buried in the tomb of his father Joash at Ophrah of the Abiezrites. [33] As soon as Gideon died, the Israelites relapsed and prostituted themselves with the Baals, making Baal-berith their god. [34] The Israelites did not remember the LORD their God, who had rescued them from the hand of all their enemies on every side; [35] and they did not exhibit loyalty to the house of Jerubbaal (that is, Gideon) in return for all the good that he had done to Israel.

9 Now Abimelech son of Jerubbaal went to Shechem to his mother's kinsfolk and said to them and to the whole clan of his mother's family, [2] "Say in the hearing of all the lords of Shechem, 'Which is better for you, that all seventy of the sons of Jerubbaal rule over you, or that one rule over you?' Remember also that I am your bone and your flesh." [3] So his mother's kinsfolk spoke all these words on his behalf in the hearing of all the lords of Shechem; and their hearts inclined to follow Abimelech, for they said, "He is our brother." [4] They gave him seventy pieces of silver out of the temple of Baal-berith with which Abimelech hired worthless and reckless fellows, who followed him. [5] He went to his father's house at Ophrah, and killed his brothers the sons of Jerubbaal, seventy men, on one stone; but Jotham, the youngest son of Jerubbaal, survived, for he hid himself. [6] Then all the lords of Shechem and all Beth-millo came together, and they went and made Abimelech king, by the oak of the pillar[a] at Shechem.

[7] When it was told to Jotham, he went and stood on the top of Mount Gerizim, and cried aloud and said to them, "Listen to me, you lords of Shechem, so that God may listen to you.
[8] The trees once went out
    to anoint a king over themselves.
So they said to the olive tree,
    'Reign over us.'
[9] The olive tree answered them,
    'Shall I stop producing my rich oil
        by which gods and mortals are
            honored,
        and go to sway over the trees?'
[10] Then the trees said to the fig tree,
    'You come and reign over us.'
[11] But the fig tree answered them,
    'Shall I stop producing my sweetness
        and my delicious fruit,
        and go to sway over the trees?'
[12] Then the trees said to the vine,
    'You come and reign over us.'
[13] But the vine said to them,
    'Shall I stop producing my wine
        that cheers gods and mortals,
        and go to sway over the trees?'
[14] So all the trees said to the bramble,
    'You come and reign over us.'

---

a   Cn: Meaning of Heb uncertain

---

father is king," hints at the tension between divine and human kingship. **32:** *Ophrah,* see 6.11. **33:** *Baal-berith,* meaning "Baal (or lord) of the covenant" (also called "El-berith" in 9.46), is a title not mentioned elsewhere. **9.1–6:** Abimelech's enthronement at his own initiative. **1:** *Shechem,* one of the most important political and religious centers in northern Israel; see Gen 12.6, 33.18–35.4; Josh 24.1; 1 Kings 12.1,25. **2:** *All seventy,* Abimelech's first argument for enthronement was false: Gideon's seventy sons could not rule over one city, Shechem. The second argument was family ties. **4:** *Seventy pieces,* corresponding to the number of Gideon's sons (8.30). A *temple* could also function as a treasury (cf. 1 Kings 7.51). *Worthless . . . fellows,* Jephthah (11.3) also utilized such people at the beginning of his road to rule; see also 1 Sam 22.2. **5:** *One stone,* against seventy people. The contrast is intended to shock the reader. *Jotham,* his name means "God acts with integrity." It is likely that some of the names in Gideon-Abimelech episodes are symbolic. **6:** *Beth-millo,* perhaps a quarter in the city built upon a filling of earth (Heb "millo'" means "fill"). *The oak of the pillar,* probably a holy place; see Gen 12.6; 35.4; Josh 24.23–27.

9.7–21: **Jotham's fable.** The fable (vv. 7–15) and its explication (vv. 16–20) are not consistent with the narrative surrounding it; e.g., Abimelech was not offered the monarchy. The fable was thus probably an independent anti-monarchic text, used here to criticize Abimelech and to emphasize the responsibility of choosing a king. The fable uses the pattern of "three and four," in which the final element is climactic: three refusals of the useful trees and one acceptance by the bramble, which leads to harm. **7:** Uttering from a high place is a literary model (cf. Num 23.14). Actually the Shechemites could not hear Jotham, because *the top of Mount Gerizim* was several hundred feet above Shechem. **9:** *Gods and mortals are honored,* oil and wine (v. 13) were used in worship as well

¹⁵ And the bramble said to the trees,
    'If in good faith you are anointing me
        king over you,
      then come and take refuge in my
        shade;
    but if not, let fire come out of the
        bramble
      and devour the cedars of Lebanon.'

¹⁶ "Now therefore, if you acted in good faith and honor when you made Abimelech king, and if you have dealt well with Jerubbaal and his house, and have done to him as his actions deserved— ¹⁷ for my father fought for you, and risked his life, and rescued you from the hand of Midian; ¹⁸ but you have risen up against my father's house this day, and have killed his sons, seventy men on one stone, and have made Abimelech, the son of his slave woman, king over the lords of Shechem, because he is your kinsman— ¹⁹ if, I say, you have acted in good faith and honor with Jerubbaal and with his house this day, then rejoice in Abimelech, and let him also rejoice in you; ²⁰ but if not, let fire come out from Abimelech, and devour the lords of Shechem, and Beth-millo; and let fire come out from the lords of Shechem, and from Beth-millo, and devour Abimelech." ²¹ Then Jotham ran away and fled, going to Beer, where he remained for fear of his brother Abimelech.

²² Abimelech ruled over Israel three years. ²³ But God sent an evil spirit between Abimelech and the lords of Shechem; and the lords of Shechem dealt treacherously with Abimelech. ²⁴ This happened so that the violence done to the seventy sons of Jerubbaal might be avenged[a] and their blood be laid on their brother Abimelech, who killed them, and on the lords of Shechem, who strengthened his hands to kill his brothers. ²⁵ So, out of hostility to him, the lords of Shechem set ambushes on the mountain tops. They robbed all who passed by them along that way; and it was reported to Abimelech.

²⁶ When Gaal son of Ebed moved into Shechem with his kinsfolk, the lords of Shechem put confidence in him. ²⁷ They went out into the field and gathered the grapes from their vineyards, trod them, and celebrated. Then they went into the temple of their god, ate and drank, and ridiculed Abimelech. ²⁸ Gaal son of Ebed said, "Who is Abimelech, and who are we of Shechem, that we should serve him? Did not the son of Jerubbaal and Zebul his officer serve the men of Hamor father of Shechem? Why then should we serve him? ²⁹ If only this people were under my command! Then I would remove Abimelech; I would say[b] to him, 'Increase your army, and come out.' "

³⁰ When Zebul the ruler of the city heard the words of Gaal son of Ebed, his anger was kindled. ³¹ He sent messengers to Abimelech at Arumah,[c] saying, "Look, Gaal son of Ebed and his kinsfolk have come to Shechem, and they are stirring up[d] the city against you. ³² Now therefore, go by night, you and the troops that are with you, and lie in wait in the fields. ³³ Then early in the morning, as soon as the sun rises, get up and rush on the city; and when he and the troops that are with him come out against you, you may deal with them as best you can."

³⁴ So Abimelech and all the troops with him got up by night and lay in wait against Shechem in four companies. ³⁵ When Gaal son of Ebed went out and stood in the entrance of the gate of the city, Abimelech and the troops with him rose from the ambush.

a Heb *might come*
b Gk: Heb *and he said*
c Cn See 9.41. Heb *Tormah*
d Cn: Heb *are besieging*

as in nonreligious activities. **14:** *Bramble,* a useless shrub which offers little shade and whose fruit is inedible. **16:** *Now therefore,* a transitional formula that introduces the explanation. **21:** *Beer,* which means "well," is an unidentified locale.

    9.22–57: The end of Abimelech's rule. 22: *Ruled over,* the Hebrew root ("s-r-r") means arbitrary rule (see Num 16.13). *Israel,* in reality, only Shechem and its environs. *Three years,* a typological number indicating a brief reign. **23–41:** The first battle at Shechem. **23–24:** Abimelech's fall and the war in Shechem are explained as a divine punishment, measure for measure (see also vv. 56–57). **25:** Social and economic causes are also mentioned. **26:** *Ebed* may be a name, or a title meaning the status of a "slave." *Kinsfolk,* perhaps not family but mercenaries; cf. 9.4. **28:** Gaal incites the citizens by rhetorical questions, identifying himself as a native Shechemite commit-

36 And when Gaal saw them, he said to Zebul, "Look, people are coming down from the mountain tops!" And Zebul said to him, "The shadows on the mountains look like people to you." 37 Gaal spoke again and said, "Look, people are coming down from Tabbur-erez, and one company is coming from the direction of Elon-meonenim."[a] 38 Then Zebul said to him, "Where is your boast[b] now, you who said, 'Who is Abimelech, that we should serve him?' Are not these the troops you made light of? Go out now and fight with them." 39 So Gaal went out at the head of the lords of Shechem, and fought with Abimelech. 40 Abimelech chased him, and he fled before him. Many fell wounded, up to the entrance of the gate. 41 So Abimelech resided at Arumah; and Zebul drove out Gaal and his kinsfolk, so that they could not live on at Shechem.

42 On the following day the people went out into the fields. When Abimelech was told, 43 he took his troops and divided them into three companies, and lay in wait in the fields. When he looked and saw the people coming out of the city, he rose against them and killed them. 44 Abimelech and the company that was[c] with him rushed forward and stood at the entrance of the gate of the city, while the two companies rushed on all who were in the fields and killed them. 45 Abimelech fought against the city all that day; he took the city, and killed the people that were in it; and he razed the city and sowed it with salt.

46 When all the lords of the Tower of Shechem heard of it, they entered the stronghold of the temple of El-berith. 47 Abimelech was told that all the lords of the Tower of Shechem were gathered together. 48 So Abimelech went up to Mount Zalmon, he and all the troops that were with him. Abimelech took an ax in his hand, cut down a bundle of brushwood, and took it up and laid it on his shoulder. Then he said to the troops with him, "What you have seen me do, do quickly, as I have done." 49 So every one of the troops cut down a bundle and following Abimelech put it against the stronghold, and they set the stronghold on fire over them, so that all the people of the Tower of Shechem also died, about a thousand men and women.

50 Then Abimelech went to Thebez, and encamped against Thebez, and took it. 51 But there was a strong tower within the city, and all the men and women and all the lords of the city fled to it and shut themselves in; and they went to the roof of the tower. 52 Abimelech came to the tower, and fought against it, and came near to the entrance of the tower to burn it with fire. 53 But a certain woman threw an upper millstone on Abimelech's head, and crushed his skull. 54 Immediately he called to the young man who carried his armor and said to him, "Draw your sword and kill me, so people will not say about me, 'A woman killed him.'" So the young man thrust him through, and he died. 55 When the Israelites saw that Abimelech was dead, they all went home. 56 Thus God repaid Abimelech for the crime he committed against his father in killing his seventy brothers; 57 and God also made all the wickedness of the people of Shechem fall

a   That is *Diviners' Oak*
b   Heb *mouth*
c   Vg and some Gk Mss: Heb *companies that were*

ted to the family of Hamor (Gen 34.2), and portraying Abimelech as a foreigner. **37:** *Tabbur-erez*, (lit. "the navel of the earth"); cf. Ezek 38.12. *Elon-meonenim*, (lit. "oak of the diviners"). The route is named after a holy tree. **42–45:** The second battle at Shechem; its cause is unexplained. **45:** *Sowed it with salt*, a symbolic action signifying a final destruction. **46–49:** The battle at the tower of Shechem; again, no reason for the battle is given. Abimelech is depicted here like the harmful fire in the fable; the image of fire connects this battle with the next one. **46:** *Tower of Shechem*, probably a fortified section of the city, but perhaps a settlement near it. *El-berith*, see 8.33n. **48:** *Zalmon*, a mountain near Shechem; some scholars identify it as Mount Ebal, opposite Mount Gerizim (see v. 7n.). **50–54:** The battle at Thebez and Abimelech's death. This time the fire is stopped, because Abimelech himself died in this war (see the reference to this battle in 2 Sam 11.20–21). **50:** *Thebez*, perhaps a corruption of Tirzah, located seven miles northeast of Shechem. **54:** Even at the point of death Abimelech was concerned for his honor and did not want to be killed by a woman. **55-57:** The Dispersion of the Army and the Cyclical End. **55:** Upon Abimelech's death, his army was dispersed. Gideon's refusal to reign was justified: the situation was not yet ripe for a monarch.

back on their heads, and on them came the curse of Jotham son of Jerubbaal.

10 After Abimelech, Tola son of Puah son of Dodo, a man of Issachar, who lived at Shamir in the hill country of Ephraim, rose to deliver Israel. ² He judged Israel twenty-three years. Then he died, and was buried at Shamir.

³ After him came Jair the Gileadite, who judged Israel twenty-two years. ⁴ He had thirty sons who rode on thirty donkeys; and they had thirty towns, which are in the land of Gilead, and are called Havvoth-jair to this day. ⁵ Jair died, and was buried in Kamon.

⁶ The Israelites again did what was evil in the sight of the LORD, worshiping the Baals and the Astartes, the gods of Aram, the gods of Sidon, the gods of Moab, the gods of the Ammonites, and the gods of the Philistines. Thus they abandoned the LORD, and did not worship him. ⁷ So the anger of the LORD was kindled against Israel, and he sold them into the hand of the Philistines and into the hand of the Ammonites, ⁸ and they crushed and oppressed the Israelites that year. For eighteen years they oppressed all the Israelites that were beyond the Jordan in the land of the Amorites, which is in Gilead. ⁹ The Ammonites also crossed the Jordan to fight against Judah and against Benjamin and against the house of Ephraim; so that Israel was greatly distressed.

¹⁰ So the Israelites cried to the LORD, saying, "We have sinned against you, because we have abandoned our God and have worshiped the Baals." ¹¹ And the LORD said to the Israelites, "Did I not deliver youᵃ from the Egyptians and from the Amorites, from the Ammonites and from the Philistines? ¹² The Sidonians also, and the Amalekites, and the Maonites, oppressed you; and you cried to me, and I delivered you out of their hand. ¹³ Yet you have abandoned me and worshiped other gods; therefore I will deliver you no more. ¹⁴ Go and cry to the gods whom you have chosen; let them deliver you in the time of your distress." ¹⁵ And the Israelites said to the LORD, "We have sinned; do to us whatever seems good to you; but deliver us this day!" ¹⁶ So they put away the foreign gods from among them and worshiped the LORD; and he could no longer bear to see Israel suffer.

¹⁷ Then the Ammonites were called to arms, and they encamped in Gilead; and the Israelites came together, and they encamped at Mizpah. ¹⁸ The commanders of the people

ᵃ Heb lacks *Did I not deliver you*

10.1–5: First list of consecutive judges. The two judges after Abimelech appear one after another, without the usual pattern of sin and punishment. Their brief and consecutive mention hints that continuity of leadership may prevent return to sin and thus points to the advantages of monarchy in spite of Abimelech's kingship. The descriptions of these judges are short reports: they do not narrate acts of deliverance, but merely list details such as where they lived and were buried, how long they judged, their property and numbers of descendants. For this reason many scholars call these individuals along with those in 12.8–15 "minor judges." 1: *To deliver*, but the story of deliverance is missing. *Tola* is from the tribe of Issachar, one of whose sons had the same name according to Gen 43.13. *Shamir*, location unknown, situated in Mount Ephraim. 3: According to Num 32.41; Deut 3.14; and 1 Chr 2.22–23, Jair conquered territory in Gilead. 4: *Thirty sons . . . thirty donkeys*, the large number of offspring and burros indicates his high status (cf. 8.30; 12.14; see 5.10n.). *Havvoth-jair* means "villages of Jair." 5: *Kamon*, location unknown.

10.6–12.15: Jephthah. A sense of disappointment accompanies most of the Jephthah stories, suggesting that even as the cycle continues, the judges are getting worse and worse.

10.6–16: Introduction to the Jephthah cycle. The stages of sin (here seven types of idolatry), punishment (Philistines and Ammonites), and crying out (repentance and direct rebuke by God) that precede the Jephthah cycle point to the increased severity of the situation, and suggest the need for a very able leader. 12: *The Maonites*, a nomadic tribe in southern Judah (1 Chr 4.41; 2 Chr 26.7).

10.17–11.11: Jephthah's appointment. The elders of Gilead could not find someone to lead the army against the Ammonites, so they offered it to Jephthah. As the son of a prostitute, he had been disinherited by his brothers, and he moved to the eastern border area, where he gained military experience as a bandit leader. Jephthah made his appointment conditional: if he led them to victory, he would be appointed their leader after the war too. 17: *Mizpah* (also 11.11), location unknown. 18: A situation of despair. The leadership is promised to whoever will dare to go to war. *Head*, a leader whose authority was not only military but also judicial and administrative.

of Gilead said to one another, "Who will begin the fight against the Ammonites? He shall be head over all the inhabitants of Gilead."

11 Now Jephthah the Gileadite, the son of a prostitute, was a mighty warrior. Gilead was the father of Jephthah. ² Gilead's wife also bore him sons; and when his wife's sons grew up, they drove Jephthah away, saying to him, "You shall not inherit anything in our father's house; for you are the son of another woman." ³ Then Jephthah fled from his brothers and lived in the land of Tob. Outlaws collected around Jephthah and went raiding with him.

⁴ After a time the Ammonites made war against Israel. ⁵ And when the Ammonites made war against Israel, the elders of Gilead went to bring Jephthah from the land of Tob. ⁶ They said to Jephthah, "Come and be our commander, so that we may fight with the Ammonites." ⁷ But Jephthah said to the elders of Gilead, "Are you not the very ones who rejected me and drove me out of my father's house? So why do you come to me now when you are in trouble?" ⁸ The elders of Gilead said to Jephthah, "Nevertheless, we have now turned back to you, so that you may go with us and fight with the Ammonites, and become head over us, over all the inhabitants of Gilead." ⁹ Jephthah said to the elders of Gilead, "If you bring me home again to fight with the Ammonites, and the Lord gives them over to me, I will be your head." ¹⁰ And the elders of Gilead said to Jephthah, "The Lord will be witness between us; we will surely do as you say." ¹¹ So Jephthah went with the elders of Gilead, and the people made him head and

commander over them; and Jephthah spoke all his words before the Lord at Mizpah.

¹² Then Jephthah sent messengers to the king of the Ammonites and said, "What is there between you and me, that you have come to me to fight against my land?" ¹³ The king of the Ammonites answered the messengers of Jephthah, "Because Israel, on coming from Egypt, took away my land from the Arnon to the Jabbok and to the Jordan; now therefore restore it peaceably." ¹⁴ Once again Jephthah sent messengers to the king of the Ammonites ¹⁵ and said to him: "Thus says Jephthah: Israel did not take away the land of Moab or the land of the Ammonites, ¹⁶ but when they came up from Egypt, Israel went through the wilderness to the Red Sea[a] and came to Kadesh. ¹⁷ Israel then sent messengers to the king of Edom, saying, 'Let us pass through your land'; but the king of Edom would not listen. They also sent to the king of Moab, but he would not consent. So Israel remained at Kadesh. ¹⁸ Then they journeyed through the wilderness, went around the land of Edom and the land of Moab, arrived on the east side of the land of Moab, and camped on the other side of the Arnon. They did not enter the territory of Moab, for the Arnon was the boundary of Moab. ¹⁹ Israel then sent messengers to King Sihon of the Amorites, king of Heshbon; and Israel said to him, 'Let us pass through your land to our country.' ²⁰ But Sihon did not trust Israel to pass through his territory; so Sihon gath-

[a] Or *Sea of Reeds*

11.2: Gilead's wife apparently bore him sons after Jephthah's birth. According to some ancient laws, Jephthah was also entitled to an inheritance. 3: *Tob*, in northeast Gilead. *Outlaws*, see 9.4n. 4: This verse logically belongs before 10.17. 5: *The elders* themselves, not emissaries from them. 6: *Commander*, a military officer whose authority was less than that of a "head" (cf. 10.18). Jephthah begins negotiations in order to be their head (v.9). 11: *Before the Lord*, at a temple or an altar.

11.12–28: Negotiations with the Ammonite king. Jephthah attempted to prevent war on Israelite territory "from the Arnon to the Jabbok and to the Jordan" (v. 13) by negotiation. His arguments were historical: the area had never belonged to Ammon, but to Sihon king of the Amorites (vv. 14–19); when Sihon did not allow the Israelites to pass through his land after the Exodus, they were forced to wage war against him (v. 20); their victory was God's will (vv. 21–24); for the past three hundred years the Ammonites had not claimed this area (vv. 25–26). Once the Ammonite king rejected Jephthah's arguments, war was inevitable (cf. Num 20.14–21; 33.37–49; Deut 2–3). Scholars think that this text is a late document concerning Israelite-Moabite relations, since throughout the negotiation Moab rather than Ammon is mentioned. 13: The borders of Sihon's land are the river *Arnon* in the south, the river *Jabbok* in the north, the river *Jordan* in the west, and the desert in the east. Reuben and Gad settled there. 16: *Kadesh*, i.e., Kadesh-barnea, a desert oasis in northern Sinai; see Num 13.25; 20.1. 19: *Heshbon*,

ered all his people together, and encamped at Jahaz, and fought with Israel. [21] Then the LORD, the God of Israel, gave Sihon and all his people into the hand of Israel, and they defeated them; so Israel occupied all the land of the Amorites, who inhabited that country. [22] They occupied all the territory of the Amorites from the Arnon to the Jabbok and from the wilderness to the Jordan. [23] So now the LORD, the God of Israel, has conquered the Amorites for the benefit of his people Israel. Do you intend to take their place? [24] Should you not possess what your god Chemosh gives you to possess? And should we not be the ones to possess everything that the LORD our God has conquered for our benefit? [25] Now are you any better than King Balak son of Zippor of Moab? Did he ever enter into conflict with Israel, or did he ever go to war with them? [26] While Israel lived in Heshbon and its villages, and in Aroer and its villages, and in all the towns that are along the Arnon, three hundred years, why did you not recover them within that time? [27] It is not I who have sinned against you, but you are the one who does me wrong by making war on me. Let the LORD, who is judge, decide today for the Israelites or for the Ammonites." [28] But the king of the Ammonites did not heed the message that Jephthah sent him.

[29] Then the spirit of the LORD came upon Jephthah, and he passed through Gilead and Manasseh. He passed on to Mizpah of Gilead, and from Mizpah of Gilead he passed on to the Ammonites. [30] And Jephthah made a vow to the LORD, and said, "If you will give the Ammonites into my hand, [31] then whoever comes out of the doors of my house to meet me, when I return victorious from the Ammonites, shall be the LORD's, to be offered up by me as a burnt offering." [32] So Jephthah crossed over to the Ammonites to fight against them; and the LORD gave them into his hand. [33] He inflicted a massive defeat on them from Aroer to the neighborhood of Minnith, twenty towns, and as far as Abel-keramim. So the Ammonites were subdued before the people of Israel.

[34] Then Jephthah came to his home at Mizpah; and there was his daughter coming out to meet him with timbrels and with dancing. She was his only child; he had no son or daughter except her. [35] When he saw her, he tore his clothes, and said, "Alas, my daughter! You have brought me very low; you have become the cause of great trouble to me. For I have opened my mouth to the LORD, and I cannot take back my vow." [36] She said to him, "My father, if you have opened your mouth to the LORD, do to me according to what has gone out of your mouth, now that the LORD has given you vengeance against your enemies, the Ammonites." [37] And she said to her father, "Let this thing be done for me: Grant me two months, so that I may go and wander[a] on the mountains, and bewail my virginity, my companions and I." [38] "Go," he said and sent her away for two months. So she departed, she and her companions, and bewailed her virginity on the mountains. [39] At the end of two months, she returned to her father, who did with her according to the vow he had made. She had never slept with a man. So there arose an Israelite custom that [40] for four days every year the daughters of Israel would go out to lament the daughter of Jephthah the Gileadite.

[a] Cn: Heb *go down*

Sihon's royal city, about 14 mi (23 km) southwest of Amman. **20:** *Jahaz*, location uncertain. **24:** *Chemosh,* the national god of Moab; the reference to him, and not to Milcom the god of Ammon, indicates the Moabite context of this document. Chemosh is mentioned in the Mesha inscription. **25:** *Balak,* see Num 22.2–24.5. **26:** *Aroer,* just north of the Arnon. *Three hundred,* a round and inexact number for the time from Joshua's conquest until Jephthah.

11.29–40: The war and the vow. Before the war Jephthah vowed that if the LORD granted him victory, he would offer up to him the first coming out of his house. When he returned home victorious, his only daughter came out to greet him, and he was obliged to fulfill his vow. This story shows Jephthah in a clear negative light, because of human sacrifice. **29:** Jephthah advanced in a northeasterly direction. **31:** The oath suggests a human sacrifice; 2 Kings 3:27 illustrates such a sacrifice at the time of war. **35:** Both Jephthah and his unnamed daughter understand the oath as an unconditional obligation; see Deut 23.21–23. **37:** *Virginity,* see v. 39. **40:** The etiological conclusion explains a preexisting custom.

12 The men of Ephraim were called to arms, and they crossed to Zaphon and said to Jephthah, "Why did you cross over to fight against the Ammonites, and did not call us to go with you? We will burn your house down over you!" [2] Jephthah said to them, "My people and I were engaged in conflict with the Ammonites who oppressed us[a] severely. But when I called you, you did not deliver me from their hand. [3] When I saw that you would not deliver me, I took my life in my hand, and crossed over against the Ammonites, and the LORD gave them into my hand. Why then have you come up to me this day, to fight against me?" [4] Then Jephthah gathered all the men of Gilead and fought with Ephraim; and the men of Gilead defeated Ephraim, because they said, "You are fugitives from Ephraim, you Gileadites—in the heart of Ephraim and Manasseh."[b] [5] Then the Gileadites took the fords of the Jordan against the Ephraimites. Whenever one of the fugitives of Ephraim said, "Let me go over," the men of Gilead would say to him, "Are you an Ephraimite?" When he said, "No," [6] they said to him, "Then say Shibboleth," and he said, "Sibboleth," for he could not pronounce it right. Then they seized him and killed him at the fords of the Jordan. Forty-two thousand of the Ephraimites fell at that time.

[7] Jephthah judged Israel six years. Then Jephthah the Gileadite died, and was buried in his town in Gilead.[c]

[8] After him Ibzan of Bethlehem judged Israel. [9] He had thirty sons. He gave his thirty daughters in marriage outside his clan and brought in thirty young women from outside for his sons. He judged Israel seven years. [10] Then Ibzan died, and was buried at Bethlehem.

[11] After him Elon the Zebulunite judged Israel; and he judged Israel ten years. [12] Then Elon the Zebulunite died, and was buried at Aijalon in the land of Zebulun.

[13] After him Abdon son of Hillel the Pirathonite judged Israel. [14] He had forty sons and thirty grandsons, who rode on seventy donkeys; he judged Israel eight years. [15] Then Abdon son of Hillel the Pirathonite died, and was buried at Pirathon in the land of Ephraim, in the hill country of the Amalekites.

13 The Israelites again did what was evil in the sight of the LORD, and the LORD gave them into the hand of the Philistines forty years.

a   Gk OL, Syr H: Heb lacks *who oppressed us*
b   Meaning of Heb uncertain: Gk omits *because . . . Manasseh*
c   Gk: Heb *in the towns of Gilead*

12.1–7: Jephthah's battle with Ephraim and the conclusion of the Jephthah cycle. This conflict, like Gideon's (8.1–3), is a struggle for intertribal hegemony, but since it ends with the death of forty-two thousand Ephraimites, it emphasizes Jephthah's negative characteristics. Another example of his negative behavior is the blocking of the Jordan crossings, a tactic used by Ehud against the Moabites (3.28); Jephthah used it against his own people. 1: *Zaphon*, in the central Jordan valley, perhaps near Succoth (Josh 13.27). 4: *Fugitives from Ephraim*, the men of Gilead were insulted by the Ephraimites. Perhaps this phrase relates to the inhabitants of Gilead in Transjordan as refugees who had left the region of Ephraim and Manasseh west of the Jordan River. 5: The Gileadites prevented the men of Ephraim from escaping westward to the Jordan. 6: *Shibboleth . . . sibboleth*, the difference in pronunciation shows variation in dialects. *Shibboleth* may mean river currents (Ps 69.3) or sheaves of grain (Gen 41.5–7).

12.8–15: Second list of consecutive judges. Three consecutive judges appear after Jephthah, and therefore there was no room for sin, punishment or deliverance (see 10.1–5n.). 8: *Bethlehem*, here a city in the territory of Zebulun (Josh 19.15). 9: Marriage was one of the means of creating foreign alliances (cf. 8.31). 13: Pirathon is located in the land of Ephraim, see 2 Sam 23.30; 1 Chr 27.14. 14: See 10.4n.

Chs 13–16: The Samson cycle. Samson differs from the other judges: he fought as an individual rather than a commander, and his miraculous heroic acts were the result of personal involvement with Philistine women. He did not deliver his people but only began the process and then died in enemy captivity. Like Jephthah he is also disappointing and his appearance as the last judge in the book leads toward the conclusion that monarchy is preferable to judges. The stories concerning Samson are filled with remnants of myth, legends, and folk traditions.

13.1–25: Samson's birth. This story is reminiscent of other annunciation stories (Gen 18.1–15; Judg 6.11–24; 1 Sam 1; 2 Kings 4.8–37). 1: *Forty years* is the longest period of subjugation in the book. There is no statement

[2] There was a certain man of Zorah, of the tribe of the Danites, whose name was Manoah. His wife was barren, having borne no children. [3] And the angel of the LORD appeared to the woman and said to her, "Although you are barren, having borne no children, you shall conceive and bear a son. [4] Now be careful not to drink wine or strong drink, or to eat anything unclean, [5] for you shall conceive and bear a son. No razor is to come on his head, for the boy shall be a nazirite[a] to God from birth. It is he who shall begin to deliver Israel from the hand of the Philistines." [6] Then the woman came and told her husband, "A man of God came to me, and his appearance was like that of an angel[b] of God, most awe-inspiring; I did not ask him where he came from, and he did not tell me his name; [7] but he said to me, 'You shall conceive and bear a son. So then drink no wine or strong drink, and eat nothing unclean, for the boy shall be a nazirite[a] to God from birth to the day of his death.'"

[8] Then Manoah entreated the LORD, and said, "O LORD, I pray, let the man of God whom you sent come to us again and teach us what we are to do concerning the boy who will be born." [9] God listened to Manoah, and the angel of God came again to the woman as she sat in the field; but her husband Manoah was not with her. [10] So the woman ran quickly and told her husband, "The man who came to me the other day has appeared to me." [11] Manoah got up and followed his wife, and came to the man and said to him, "Are you the man who spoke to this woman?" And he said, "I am." [12] Then Manoah said, "Now when your words come true, what is to be the boy's rule of life; what is he to do?" [13] The angel of the LORD said to Manoah, "Let the woman give heed to all that I said to her. [14] She may not eat of anything that comes from the vine. She is not to drink wine or strong drink, or eat any unclean thing. She is to observe everything that I commanded her."

[15] Manoah said to the angel of the LORD, "Allow us to detain you, and prepare a kid for you." [16] The angel of the LORD said to Manoah, "If you detain me, I will not eat your food; but if you want to prepare a burnt offering, then offer it to the LORD." (For Manoah did not know that he was the angel of the LORD.) [17] Then Manoah said to the angel of the LORD, "What is your name, so that we may honor you when your words come true?" [18] But the angel of the LORD said to him, "Why do you ask my name? It is too wonderful."

[19] So Manoah took the kid with the grain offering, and offered it on the rock to the LORD, to him who works[c] wonders.[d] [20] When the flame went up toward heaven from the altar, the angel of the LORD ascended in the flame of the altar while Manoah and his wife looked on; and they fell on their faces to the ground. [21] The an-

a   That is one separated or one consecrated
b   Or the angel
c   Gk Vg: Heb and working
d   Heb wonders, while Manoah and his wife looked on

that the Israelites cried out, strengthening the impression of distance from the LORD. 2: Zorah is in the territory of Dan, about 16 mi (25 km) west of Jerusalem. 5: Samson's status as a nazirite is exceptional. It is connected only to his hair, while other prohibitions apply to his mother; see Num 6.1–5. Begin, i.e., his deliverance will be partial. 7: To the day of his death, the woman does not repeat the angel's words exactly. She focuses upon her prohibitions and interprets the partial deliverance as alluding to the death of the child. Thus Manoah has a reason to ask for another visit of the messenger for further clarification. 8: Us, Manoah wants to be a full partner in the additional visit. 9: Due to women's preferred status in birth stories (compare 2 Kings 4.8–17), the angel appears to the woman again, and thereafter Manoah follows his wife. 13–14: The angel's answer relates to the woman and not to the child. 15: Like Gideon in 6.18, Manoah invites the angel to a meal in order to ascertain whether he is an angel. 16: The angel, behaving properly, refuses to eat. The second half of this verse (For Manoah . . .) may belong at the end of v. 15. 17–18: Manoah continues to question the angel and asks for his name, but the angel refuses to disclose it. 19–20: The angel behaves in a miraculous way and disappears in the flame while the sacrifice is offered. 20: Altar, i.e., the rock. 21–22: In contrast to his wife who understood early on that the visitor was an angel, Manoah realizes who the visitor was only after the angel disappeared, and he begins to be afraid (cf. 6.22). 23: Manoah's wife calms him with logical arguments. 24a: Many scholars connect the name of Samson (Heb "Shimshon") with the word for sun ("shemesh"), finding in it a mythological allusion. 24b–25: These verses summarize Samson's unique growth and development under divine protection. Eshtaol, near Zo-

gel of the LORD did not appear again to Manoah and his wife. Then Manoah realized that it was the angel of the LORD. ²² And Manoah said to his wife, "We shall surely die, for we have seen God." ²³ But his wife said to him, "If the LORD had meant to kill us, he would not have accepted a burnt offering and a grain offering at our hands, or shown us all these things, or now announced to us such things as these."

²⁴ The woman bore a son, and named him Samson. The boy grew, and the LORD blessed him. ²⁵ The spirit of the LORD began to stir him in Mahaneh-dan, between Zorah and Eshtaol.

14 Once Samson went down to Timnah, and at Timnah he saw a Philistine woman. ² Then he came up, and told his father and mother, "I saw a Philistine woman at Timnah; now get her for me as my wife." ³ But his father and mother said to him, "Is there not a woman among your kin, or among all ourᵃ people, that you must go to take a wife from the uncircumcised Philistines?" But Samson said to his father, "Get her for me, because she pleases me." ⁴ His father and mother did not know that this was from the LORD; for he was seeking a pretext to act against the Philistines. At that time the Philistines had dominion over Israel.

⁵ Then Samson went down with his father and mother to Timnah. When he came to the vineyards of Timnah, suddenly a young lion roared at him. ⁶ The spirit of the LORD rushed on him, and he tore the lion apart barehanded as one might tear apart a kid. But he did not tell his father or his mother what he had done. ⁷ Then he went down and talked with the woman, and she pleased Samson. ⁸ After a while he returned to marry her, and he turned aside to see the carcass of the lion, and there was a swarm of bees in the body of the lion, and honey. ⁹ He scraped it out into

his hands, and went on, eating as he went. When he came to his father and mother, he gave some to them, and they ate it. But he did not tell them that he had taken the honey from the carcass of the lion.

¹⁰ His father went down to the woman, and Samson made a feast there as the young men were accustomed to do. ¹¹ When the people saw him, they brought thirty companions to be with him. ¹² Samson said to them, "Let me now put a riddle to you. If you can explain it to me within the seven days of the feast, and find it out, then I will give you thirty linen garments and thirty festal garments. ¹³ But if you cannot explain it to me, then you shall give me thirty linen garments and thirty festal garments." So they said to him, "Ask your riddle; let us hear it." ¹⁴ He said to them,

"Out of the eater came something to eat.
Out of the strong came something sweet."

But for three days they could not explain the riddle.

¹⁵ On the fourthᵇ day they said to Samson's wife, "Coax your husband to explain the riddle to us, or we will burn you and your father's house with fire. Have you invited us here to impoverish us?" ¹⁶ So Samson's wife wept before him, saying, "You hate me; you do not really love me. You have asked a riddle of my people, but you have not explained it to me." He said to her, "Look, I have not told my father or my mother. Why should I tell you?" ¹⁷ She wept before him the seven days that their feast lasted; and because she nagged him, on the seventh day he told her. Then she explained the riddle to her people. ¹⁸ The men of the town said to him on the seventh day before the sun went down,

ᵃ Cn: Heb *my*
ᵇ Gk Syr: Heb *seventh*

rah (see v. 1n.).

14.1–15.20: Samson's marriage to the Timnite woman and its consequences. Samson's marriage to a Philistine woman was part of a deliberate divine strategy so that he would have justification for harming the Philistines (see 14.4). **14.1:** *Timnah,* between Beth-shemesh and Ekron, about 18 mi (30 km) west of Jerusalem. **5:** Samson leaves the main road, so his parents do not know of his struggle with the lion (v. 6; also v. 9). Several ancient heroes, such as Babylonian Gilgamesh and Greek Herakles or Hercules, are described as fighting with lions. **8:** The removal of honey from the skeleton of a lion has parallels in other ancient literature. **10:** The mention of the father by himself is difficult; a possible emendation is: "He went down to the woman." **12:** Proposing riddles accompanied by betting was an aspect of the entertainment at a feast. **14:** Samson's riddle is based on chance and personal experience, and is unsolvable without knowledge of his earlier acts. **16:** *My people,* phrasing that

"What is sweeter than honey?
What is stronger than a lion?"
And he said to them,
"If you had not plowed with my heifer,
you would not have found out my riddle."
¹⁹ Then the spirit of the LORD rushed on him, and he went down to Ashkelon. He killed thirty men of the town, took their spoil, and gave the festal garments to those who had explained the riddle. In hot anger he went back to his father's house. ²⁰ And Samson's wife was given to his companion, who had been his best man.

15 After a while, at the time of the wheat harvest, Samson went to visit his wife, bringing along a kid. He said, "I want to go into my wife's room." But her father would not allow him to go in. ² Her father said, "I was sure that you had rejected her; so I gave her to your companion. Is not her younger sister prettier than she? Why not take her instead?" ³ Samson said to them, "This time, when I do mischief to the Philistines, I will be without blame." ⁴ So Samson went and caught three hundred foxes, and took some torches; and he turned the foxesᵃ tail to tail, and put a torch between each pair of tails. ⁵ When he had set fire to the torches, he let the foxes go into the standing grain of the Philistines, and burned up the shocks and the standing grain, as well as the vineyards andᵇ olive groves. ⁶ Then the Philistines asked, "Who has done this?" And they said, "Samson, the son-in-law of the Timnite, because he has taken Samson's wife and given her to his companion." So the Philistines came up, and burned her and her father. ⁷ Samson said to them, "If this is what you do, I swear I will not stop until I have taken revenge on you." ⁸ He struck them down hip and thigh with great slaughter; and he went down and stayed in the cleft of the rock of Etam.

⁹ Then the Philistines came up and encamped in Judah, and made a raid on Lehi. ¹⁰ The men of Judah said, "Why have you come up against us?" They said, "We have come up to bind Samson, to do to him as he did to us." ¹¹ Then three thousand men of Judah went down to the cleft of the rock of Etam, and they said to Samson, "Do you not know that the Philistines are rulers over us? What then have you done to us?" He replied, "As they did to me, so I have done to them." ¹² They said to him, "We have come down to bind you, so that we may give you into the hands of the Philistines." Samson answered them, "Swear to me that you yourselves will not attack me." ¹³ They said to him, "No, we will only bind you and give you into their hands; we will not kill you." So they bound him with two new ropes, and brought him up from the rock.

¹⁴ When he came to Lehi, the Philistines came shouting to meet him; and the spirit of the LORD rushed on him, and the ropes that were on his arms became like flax that has caught fire, and his bonds melted off his hands. ¹⁵ Then he found a fresh jawbone of a donkey, reached down and took it, and with it he killed a thousand men. ¹⁶ And Samson said,

"With the jawbone of a donkey,
    heaps upon heaps,
with the jawbone of a donkey
    I have slain a thousand men."

¹⁷ When he had finished speaking, he threw away the jawbone; and that place was called Ramath-lehi.ᶜ

¹⁸ By then he was very thirsty, and he called on the LORD, saying, "You have granted this great victory by the hand of your servant. Am I now to die of thirst, and fall into the

ᵃ Heb *them*
ᵇ Gk Tg Vg: Heb lacks *and*
ᶜ That is *The Hill of the Jawbone*

emphasizes the national confrontation. **18:** Samson responds with another riddle, comparing the woman to a heifer and the method of solution to plowing. Samson hints that he knows how they arrived at the solution. **19:** *Ashkelon*, a Philistine city 25 mi (40 km) west-southwest of Timnah.

15.1–8: Samson continues his acts of violence against the Philistines. **4:** The motif of using foxes to damage fields is also known from ancient literature **8:** *Hip and thigh*, an idiom probably meaning a severe beating. *Etam*, a rock in Judah, near Zorah (see 1 Chr 4.3). **9:** Samson's presence in Judah leads the Philistines to apply further pressure on Judah. *Lehi*, not identified location. **15:** This act is reminiscent of the heroic acts of Shamgar (3.31). **16:** Samson does not mention God in his song of victory. **18:** Samson's thirst teaches him that his might and life

hands of the uncircumcised?" [19] So God split open the hollow place that is at Lehi, and water came from it. When he drank, his spirit returned, and he revived. Therefore it was named En-hakkore,[a] which is at Lehi to this day. [20] And he judged Israel in the days of the Philistines twenty years.

16 Once Samson went to Gaza, where he saw a prostitute and went in to her. [2] The Gazites were told,[b] "Samson has come here." So they circled around and lay in wait for him all night at the city gate. They kept quiet all night, thinking, "Let us wait until the light of the morning; then we will kill him." [3] But Samson lay only until midnight. Then at midnight he rose up, took hold of the doors of the city gate and the two posts, pulled them up, bar and all, put them on his shoulders, and carried them to the top of the hill that is in front of Hebron.

[4] After this he fell in love with a woman in the valley of Sorek, whose name was Delilah. [5] The lords of the Philistines came to her and said to her, "Coax him, and find out what makes his strength so great, and how we may overpower him, so that we may bind him in order to subdue him; and we will each give you eleven hundred pieces of silver." [6] So Delilah said to Samson, "Please tell me what makes your strength so great, and how you could be bound, so that one could subdue you." [7] Samson said to her, "If they bind me with seven fresh bowstrings that are not dried out, then I shall become weak, and be

like anyone else." [8] Then the lords of the Philistines brought her seven fresh bowstrings that had not dried out, and she bound him with them. [9] While men were lying in wait in an inner chamber, she said to him, "The Philistines are upon you, Samson!" But he snapped the bowstrings, as a strand of fiber snaps when it touches the fire. So the secret of his strength was not known.

[10] Then Delilah said to Samson, "You have mocked me and told me lies; please tell me how you could be bound." [11] He said to her, "If they bind me with new ropes that have not been used, then I shall become weak, and be like anyone else." [12] So Delilah took new ropes and bound him with them, and said to him, "The Philistines are upon you, Samson!" (The men lying in wait were in an inner chamber.) But he snapped the ropes off his arms like a thread.

[13] Then Delilah said to Samson, "Until now you have mocked me and told me lies; tell me how you could be bound." He said to her, "If you weave the seven locks of my head with the web and make it tight with the pin, then I shall become weak, and be like anyone else." [14] So while he slept, Delilah took the seven locks of his head and wove them into the web,[c] and made them tight with the pin. Then she said to him, "The Philistines are upon you,

---

a   That is *The Spring of the One who Called*
b   Gk: Heb lacks *were told*
c   Compare Gk: in verses 13-14, Heb lacks *and make it tight ... into the web*

---

are dependent upon God. **19:** The etymology connects the spring's name (see textual note *b*) with Samson's calling on God (v. 18). **20:** The position of the closing formula here indicates that the period of his being judge takes place after his marriage but before the events in ch 16 that will lead to his death.

16.1–21: Samson's downfall. Samson's final acts, which begin and end in the city of Gaza, lead to his death in Philistine captivity. Here too a woman plays a prominent role. **1–3:** *Gaza,* a Philistine city on the southeast coast of the Mediterranean. This story explains the Philistines' readiness to pay Delilah any price in order to catch Samson. **2:** *City gate,* a fortified structure with several rooms. **3:** Against the preparations of the townspeople "all night" (v. 2, twice), the author informs us twice that already *at midnight* Samson had left. *To the top of the hill that is in front of Hebron,* the geographical details emphasize the miracle. Samson walks more than 35 mi (56 km), from the seacoast to the mountains in front of Hebron, carrying on his shoulders the massive structure comprised of the doors, the gateposts, and the bar. **4–21:** Delilah's attempts to uncover the source of Samson's strength are based upon the model of ascending numbers (cf. 9.8–15). Three times she fails (vv. 6–9,10–12,13–14), but at the fourth (vv. 15–21) he reveals her his secret. In so doing he betrays his destiny and is punished. **4:** For the first time we are told that Samson was in love. *Delilah* is not explicitly identified as a Philistine; her name may refer to woven braids of hair, anticipating vv. 13–14 (see Song 7.6). *Valley of Sorek,* near Zorah (see 13.2n.). **5:** As there were five Philistine lords (see 3.3), Delilah was offered the enormous sum of 5,500 shekels. **7:** *Fresh bowstrings,* their freshness assures their flexibility and makes them more difficult to tear. **13:** *The web* and *the pin*

Samson!" But he awoke from his sleep, and pulled away the pin, the loom, and the web.

[15] Then she said to him, "How can you say, 'I love you,' when your heart is not with me? You have mocked me three times now and have not told me what makes your strength so great." [16] Finally, after she had nagged him with her words day after day, and pestered him, he was tired to death. [17] So he told her his whole secret, and said to her, "A razor has never come upon my head; for I have been a nazirite[a] to God from my mother's womb. If my head were shaved, then my strength would leave me; I would become weak, and be like anyone else."

[18] When Delilah realized that he had told her his whole secret, she sent and called the lords of the Philistines, saying, "This time come up, for he has told his whole secret to me." Then the lords of the Philistines came up to her, and brought the money in their hands. [19] She let him fall asleep on her lap; and she called a man, and had him shave off the seven locks of his head. He began to weaken,[b] and his strength left him. [20] Then she said, "The Philistines are upon you, Samson!" When he awoke from his sleep, he thought, "I will go out as at other times, and shake myself free." But he did not know that the LORD had left him. [21] So the Philistines seized him and gouged out his eyes. They brought him down to Gaza and bound him with bronze shackles; and he ground at the mill in the prison. [22] But the hair of his head began to grow again after it had been shaved.

[23] Now the lords of the Philistines gathered to offer a great sacrifice to their god Dagon, and to rejoice; for they said, "Our god has given Samson our enemy into our hand."

[24] When the people saw him, they praised their god; for they said, "Our god has given our enemy into our hand, the ravager of our country, who has killed many of us." [25] And when their hearts were merry, they said, "Call Samson, and let him entertain us." So they called Samson out of the prison, and he performed for them. They made him stand between the pillars; [26] and Samson said to the attendant who held him by the hand, "Let me feel the pillars on which the house rests, so that I may lean against them." [27] Now the house was full of men and women; all the lords of the Philistines were there, and on the roof there were about three thousand men and women, who looked on while Samson performed.

[28] Then Samson called to the LORD and said, "Lord GOD, remember me and strengthen me only this once, O God, so that with this one act of revenge I may pay back the Philistines for my two eyes."[c] [29] And Samson grasped the two middle pillars on which the house rested, and he leaned his weight against them, his right hand on the one and his left hand on the other. [30] Then Samson said, "Let me die with the Philistines." He strained with all his might; and the house fell on the lords and all the people who were in it. So those he killed at his death were more than those he had killed during his life. [31] Then his brothers and all his family came down and took him and brought him up and buried him between Zorah and Eshtaol in the tomb of his father Manoah. He had judged Israel twenty years.

a   That is one separated or one consecrated
b   Gk: Heb She began to torment him
c   Or so that I may be avenged upon the Philistines for one of my two eyes

were parts of a loom. **17:** See 13.5. **19:** *She called a man* to assist her in cutting his hair.

16.22–31: Samson's death and burial. The Philistines gather at the temple of the god Dagon (cf. 1 Sam 5.1) in Gaza to offer him sacrifices and to thank him for catching Samson. **22:** His hair growing back alludes to the connection with the LORD through the nazirite vow (see v. 17) and the renewal of his strength. **25:** The Philistines wish to enjoy the sight of Samson humiliated. **29:** It seems that the pillars were placed close together. **31:** *His brothers,* his compatriots. **31:** *He had judged Israel twenty years* returns to 15.20, to the period before the events of ch 16, and it ends the whole cycle.

17.1–18.31: Micah's house of God and the temple of Dan. This story criticizes the time of the judges by representing it as one of social and religious anarchy. Chronologically, it belongs to the beginning of the period (see 18.30). Its appearance at the end of the book emphasizes the limited influence of the judges' rule and the need for monarchy. Scholars think that Micah's temple is an allusion to Bethel, which is often mentioned along with Dan as one of the central shrines of the northern kingdom of Israel whose worship the narrative is criticizing.

17 There was a man in the hill country of Ephraim whose name was Micah. [2] He said to his mother, "The eleven hundred pieces of silver that were taken from you, about which you uttered a curse, and even spoke it in my hearing,—that silver is in my possession; I took it; but now I will return it to you."[a] And his mother said, "May my son be blessed by the LORD!" [3] Then he returned the eleven hundred pieces of silver to his mother; and his mother said, "I consecrate the silver to the LORD from my hand for my son, to make an idol of cast metal." [4] So when he returned the money to his mother, his mother took two hundred pieces of silver, and gave it to the silversmith, who made it into an idol of cast metal; and it was in the house of Micah. [5] This man Micah had a shrine, and he made an ephod and teraphim, and installed one of his sons, who became his priest. [6] In those days there was no king in Israel; all the people did what was right in their own eyes.

[7] Now there was a young man of Bethlehem in Judah, of the clan of Judah. He was a Levite residing there. [8] This man left the town of Bethlehem in Judah, to live wherever he could find a place. He came to the house of Micah in the hill country of Ephraim to carry on his work.[b] [9] Micah said to him, "From where do you come?" He replied, "I am a Levite of Bethlehem in Judah, and I am going to live wherever I can find a place." [10] Then Micah said to him, "Stay with me, and be to me a father and a priest, and I will give you ten pieces of silver a year, a set of clothes, and your living."[c]

[11] The Levite agreed to stay with the man; and the young man became to him like one of his sons. [12] So Micah installed the Levite, and the young man became his priest, and was in the house of Micah. [13] Then Micah said, "Now I know that the LORD will prosper me, because the Levite has become my priest."

18 In those days there was no king in Israel. And in those days the tribe of the Danites was seeking for itself a territory to live in; for until then no territory among the tribes of Israel had been allotted to them. [2] So the Danites sent five valiant men from the whole number of their clan, from Zorah and from Eshtaol, to spy out the land and to explore it; and they said to them, "Go, explore the land." When they came to the hill country of Ephraim, to the house of Micah, they stayed there. [3] While they were at Micah's house, they recognized the voice of the young Levite; so they went over and asked him, "Who brought you here? What are you doing in this place? What is your business here?" [4] He said to them, "Micah did such and such for me, and he hired me, and I have become his priest." [5] Then they said to him, "Inquire of God that we may know whether the mission we are undertaking will succeed." [6] The priest replied, "Go in peace. The mission you are on is under the eye of the LORD."

---

a The words *but now I will return it to you* are transposed from the end of verse 3 in Heb
b Or *Ephraim, continuing his journey*
c Heb *living, and the Levite went*

17.1–13: Micah's shrine and its idol. The story reveals how God was worshiped during the period of the judges: a statue could be made by means of stolen silver, and priests were appointed by people like Micah. **1:** *Hill country of Ephraim*, the name of Micah's town is not given. **3–4:** The mother says that she consecrated the silver to God, but in practice she set aside only two hundred of the eleven hundred pieces. *Cast metal*, a reference to a prohibited form of worship (Deut 27.15; Ex 20.3; 34.17; etc.). **5:** *Shrine*, (lit. "house of God"). *Ephod and teraphim*, part of priestly paraphernalia used in divination; see 8.27n. *One of his sons*, an illegitimate appointment, as he was not a Levite. **6:** A criticism of what precedes and what follows. **7:** *Of the clan of Judah*, a Levite could be only a temporary sojourner in Judah. **8:** *A place* to earn a livelihood. **10:** *A father*, Micah promises the Levite a respected position (cf. Gen 45.8).

18.1–31: The conquest of Dan and the establishment of its temple. The Danites' wandering may reflect intertribal relations during the premonarchical period, the difficult situation of the individual, and the character of the worship sites. **1:** On the tribe of Dan, which was forced to leave its territory, see 1.34–35; Josh 19.47. **5:** *Inquire of God*, before carrying out significant tasks, it was customary to inquire of God. **7:** *Laish*, the former name of Dan (v. 29; cf. Josh 19.47 where it is mentioned as Leshem). It was located in the northern Galilee, which is the extreme north of Israel, therefore described as an isolated location. *Sidonians*, Phoenicians, on the Mediterranean coast north of Israel. *Aram*, a common name to the Western Semitic tribes, who settled in Syria and western Mesopotamia, when the Israeli trible settled in Canaan, and established separate kingdoms

[7] The five men went on, and when they came to Laish, they observed the people who were there living securely, after the manner of the Sidonians, quiet and unsuspecting, lacking[a] nothing on earth, and possessing wealth.[b] Furthermore, they were far from the Sidonians and had no dealings with Aram.[c] [8] When they came to their kinsfolk at Zorah and Eshtaol, they said to them, "What do you report?" [9] They said, "Come, let us go up against them; for we have seen the land, and it is very good. Will you do nothing? Do not be slow to go, but enter in and possess the land. [10] When you go, you will come to an unsuspecting people. The land is broad—God has indeed given it into your hands—a place where there is no lack of anything on earth."

[11] Six hundred men of the Danite clan, armed with weapons of war, set out from Zorah and Eshtaol, [12] and went up and encamped at Kiriath-jearim in Judah. On this account that place is called Mahaneh-dan[d] to this day; it is west of Kiriath-jearim. [13] From there they passed on to the hill country of Ephraim, and came to the house of Micah.

[14] Then the five men who had gone to spy out the land (that is, Laish) said to their comrades, "Do you know that in these buildings there are an ephod, teraphim, and an idol of cast metal? Now therefore consider what you will do." [15] So they turned in that direction and came to the house of the young Levite, at the home of Micah, and greeted him. [16] While the six hundred men of the Danites, armed with their weapons of war, stood by the entrance of the gate, [17] the five men who had gone to spy out the land proceeded to enter and take the idol of cast metal, the ephod, and the teraphim.[e] The priest was standing by the entrance of the gate with the six hundred men armed with weapons of war. [18] When the men went into Micah's house and took the idol of cast metal, the ephod, and the teraphim, the priest said to them, "What are you doing?" [19] They said to him, "Keep quiet! Put your hand over your mouth, and come with us, and be to us a father and a priest. Is it better for you to be priest to the house of one person, or to be priest to a tribe and clan in Israel?" [20] Then the priest accepted the offer. He took the ephod, the teraphim, and the idol, and went along with the people.

[21] So they resumed their journey, putting the little ones, the livestock, and the goods in front of them. [22] When they were some distance from the home of Micah, the men who were in the houses near Micah's house were called out, and they overtook the Danites. [23] They shouted to the Danites, who turned around and said to Micah, "What is the matter that you come with such a company?" [24] He replied, "You take my gods that I made, and the priest, and go away, and what have I left? How then can you ask me, 'What is the matter?'" [25] And the Danites said to him, "You had better not let your voice be heard among us or else hot-tempered fellows will attack you, and you will lose your life and the lives of your household." [26] Then the Danites went their way. When Micah saw that they were too strong for him, he turned and went back to his home.

[27] The Danites, having taken what Micah had made, and the priest who belonged to him, came to Laish, to a people quiet and unsuspecting, put them to the sword, and burned down the city. [28] There was no deliverer, because it was far from Sidon and they had no dealings with Aram.[f] It was in the valley that belongs to Beth-rehob. They rebuilt the city, and lived in it. [29] They named the city Dan, after their ancestor Dan, who was born to Israel; but the name of the city was formerly Laish. [30] Then the Danites set up the idol for themselves. Jonathan son of

a   Cn Compare 18.10: Meaning of Heb uncertain
b   Meaning of Heb uncertain
c   Symmachus: Heb *with anyone*
d   That is *Camp of Dan*
e   Compare 17.4, 5; 18.14: Heb *teraphim and the cast metal*

like Aram Damascus, Aram Zoba and others (see v. 28). **9:** Cf. Num 14.7–9. **11:** *Six hundred* probably indicates a military unit (see 1 Sam 30.9). **12:** *Kiriath-jearim*, on the border between Judah and Benjamin, west of Jerusalem. *Mahaneh-dan,* (lit. "the camp of Dan"); location unknown. *To this day*, the time of the author. **21:** In order to protect their property and the weak, they placed them *in front*, so that the fighting men would serve as a buffer against pursuers coming from behind. **23:** The Danites are sarcastic, as they knew the real reason. **24:** Micah's answer indicates the depth of improper worship. **28:** *Beth-rehob*, elsewhere an Aramean kingdom (2 Sam 10.6)

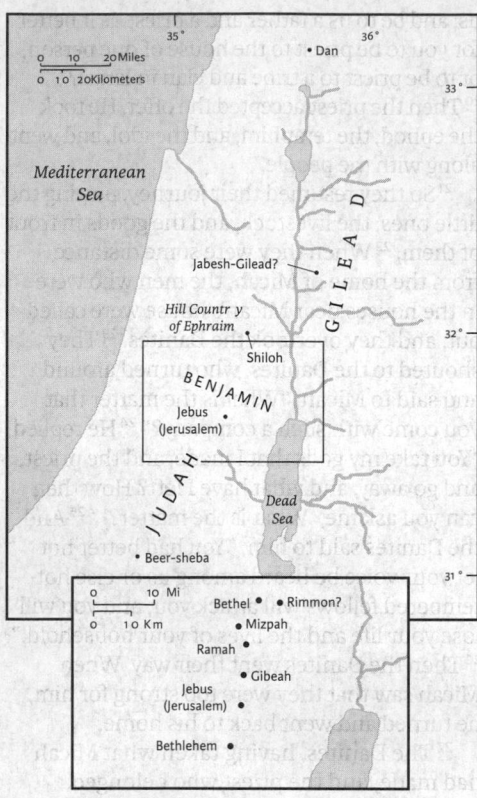

Chs 19–21: The Benjaminite War.

19

In those days, when there was no king in Israel, a certain Levite, residing in the remote parts of the hill country of Ephraim, took to himself a concubine from Bethlehem in Judah. [2] But his concubine became angry with[b] him, and she went away from him to her father's house at Bethlehem in Judah, and was there some four months. [3] Then her husband set out after her, to speak tenderly to her and bring her back. He had with him his servant and a couple of donkeys. When he reached[c] her father's house, the girl's father saw him and came with joy to meet him. [4] His father-in-law, the girl's father, made him stay, and he remained with him three days; so they ate and drank, and he[d] stayed there. [5] On the fourth day they got up early in the morning, and he prepared to go; but the girl's father said to his son-in-law, "Fortify yourself with a bit of food, and after that you may go." [6] So the two men sat and ate and drank together; and the girl's father said to the man, "Why not spend the night and enjoy yourself?" [7] When the man got up to go, his father-in-law kept urging him until he spent the night there again. [8] On the fifth day he got up early in the morning to leave; and the girl's father said, "Fortify yourself." So they lingered[e] until the day declined, and

Gershom, son of Moses,[a] and his sons were priests to the tribe of the Danites until the time the land went into captivity. [31] So they maintained as their own Micah's idol that he had made, as long as the house of God was at Shiloh.

[a] Another reading is *son of Manasseh*
[b] Gk OL: Heb *prostituted herself against*
[c] Gk: Heb *she brought him to*
[d] Compare verse 7 and Gk: Heb *they*
[e] Cn: Heb *Linger*

whose precise location is unclear. **30:** *Jonathan* the Levite was the grandson of Moses, belonging to the third generation after the Exodus. To disassociate the name of Moses ("Mosheh") from his grandson's misdeeds, his Hebrew name is turned by the Masoretic scribes into Manasseh by inserting a hanging letter N ("nun"). *Captivity*, when the Galileans were exiled by Assyria, 732 BCE (see 2 Kings 15.29). **31:** This verse is an editorial addition, introduced to connect the story with the book of Samuel (1 Sam 1). Shiloh was destroyed more than three centuries before the Assyrian invasion (see 1 Sam 4–5).

Chs 19–21: The events with Gibeah and Benjamin. A brutal rape in the town Gibeah of Benjamin (ch 19) led to a war between all the tribes of Israel and Benjamin, resulting in Benjamin's near extermination (ch 20). Subsequently the other tribes arranged for the surviving Benjaminites to marry women from Jabesh-gilead (21.1–14) and Shiloh (21.15–24). This exceptional story is dependent on other biblical stories and contains many unclear details. It focuses upon place names; all the individuals involved are anonymous. Through place names and what occurred in those places, the author expresses his preference for David's birthplace, Bethlehem in Judah, a place of hospitality, over Saul's birthplace, Gibeah in Benjamin, a place of rape, and thus hints at the later divine preference of David over Saul (see 1 Sam 15–16).

19.1–30: Between two cities. Gibeah is portrayed by means of plot and style as Sodom (cf. Gen 19). **1:** *Concubine:* A woman with a status lower than that of a primary wife. **3–9:** The generous hospitality offered in Beth-

the two of them ate and drank.[a] [9] When the man with his concubine and his servant got up to leave, his father-in-law, the girl's father, said to him, "Look, the day has worn on until it is almost evening. Spend the night. See, the day has drawn to a close. Spend the night here and enjoy yourself. Tomorrow you can get up early in the morning for your journey, and go home."

[10] But the man would not spend the night; he got up and departed, and arrived opposite Jebus (that is, Jerusalem). He had with him a couple of saddled donkeys, and his concubine was with him. [11] When they were near Jebus, the day was far spent, and the servant said to his master, "Come now, let us turn aside to this city of the Jebusites, and spend the night in it." [12] But his master said to him, "We will not turn aside into a city of foreigners, who do not belong to the people of Israel; but we will continue on to Gibeah." [13] Then he said to his servant, "Come, let us try to reach one of these places, and spend the night at Gibeah or at Ramah." [14] So they passed on and went their way; and the sun went down on them near Gibeah, which belongs to Benjamin. [15] They turned aside there, to go in and spend the night at Gibeah. He went in and sat down in the open square of the city, but no one took them in to spend the night.

[16] Then at evening there was an old man coming from his work in the field. The man was from the hill country of Ephraim, and he was residing in Gibeah. (The people of the place were Benjaminites.) [17] When the old man looked up and saw the wayfarer in the open square of the city, he said, "Where are you going and where do you come from?" [18] He answered him, "We are passing from Bethlehem in Judah to the remote parts of the hill country of Ephraim, from which I come. I went to Bethlehem in Judah; and I am going to my home.[b] Nobody has offered to take me in. [19] We your servants have straw and fodder for our donkeys, with bread and wine for me and the woman and the young man along with us. We need nothing more." [20] The old man said, "Peace be to you. I will care for all your wants; only do not spend the night in the square." [21] So he brought him into his house, and fed the donkeys; they washed their feet, and ate and drank.

[22] While they were enjoying themselves, the men of the city, a perverse lot, surrounded the house, and started pounding on the door. They said to the old man, the master of the house, "Bring out the man who came into your house, so that we may have intercourse with him." [23] And the man, the master of the house, went out to them and said to them, "No, my brothers, do not act so wickedly. Since this man is my guest, do not do this vile thing. [24] Here are my virgin daughter and his concubine; let me bring them out now. Ravish them and do whatever you want to them; but against this man do not do such a vile thing." [25] But the men would not listen to him. So the man seized his concubine, and put her out to them. They wantonly raped her, and abused her all through the night until the morning. And as the dawn began to break, they let her go. [26] As morning appeared, the woman came and fell down at the door of the man's house where her master was, until it was light.

[27] In the morning her master got up, opened the doors of the house, and when he went out to go on his way, there was his concubine lying at the door of the house, with her hands on the threshold. [28] "Get up," he said to her, "we are going." But there was no answer. Then he put her on the donkey; and the man

---

[a]   Gk: Heb lacks and drank

[b]   Gk Compare 19.29. Heb to the house of the LORD

---

lehem of Judah. **10:** *Jebus*, there is no nonbiblical evidence that Jebus was the previous name of Jerusalem; in the fourteenth-century BCE Amarna letters, it is already called Jerusalem. **12:** Ironically, seeking to avoid the potential inhospitality of a non-Israelite city, the Levite and his party suffer that very fate in an Israelite city. **13:** The mention of Ramah, located 6 mi (10 km) north of Jerusalem, alludes to the birthplace of Samuel (see 1 Sam 1.1), who anointed Saul and David as the first kings of Israel. **14–21:** Like Lot (Gen 19.2–3), the man who was host to the Levite and to those who accompanied him was a stranger in the city. **22–26:** There are many points of similarity between this incident and that of Sodom. The story in Judges is likely based on Genesis, and intends to portray the Israelite inhabitants of Gibeah as being as evil as the inhabitants of Sodom. **25:** The numerous descriptions of time (*all through the night until the morning, as the dawn began*) emphasize the brutality. **27:** The Levite's behavior was strange too: upon seeing the concubine's body, he called her to get up and go, as though

set out for his home. ²⁹ When he had entered his house, he took a knife, and grasping his concubine he cut her into twelve pieces, limb by limb, and sent her throughout all the territory of Israel. ³⁰ Then he commanded the men whom he sent, saying, "Thus shall you say to all the Israelites, 'Has such a thing ever happened[a] since the day that the Israelites came up from the land of Egypt until this day? Consider it, take counsel, and speak out.' "

20 Then all the Israelites came out, from Dan to Beer-sheba, including the land of Gilead, and the congregation assembled in one body before the LORD at Mizpah. ² The chiefs of all the people, of all the tribes of Israel, presented themselves in the assembly of the people of God, four hundred thousand foot-soldiers bearing arms. ³ (Now the Benjaminites heard that the people of Israel had gone up to Mizpah.) And the Israelites said, "Tell us, how did this criminal act come about?" ⁴ The Levite, the husband of the woman who was murdered, answered, "I came to Gibeah that belongs to Benjamin, I and my concubine, to spend the night. ⁵ The lords of Gibeah rose up against me, and surrounded the house at night. They intended to kill me, and they raped my concubine until she died. ⁶ Then I took my concubine and cut her into pieces, and sent her throughout the whole extent of Israel's territory; for they have committed a vile outrage in Israel. ⁷ So now, you Israelites, all of you, give your advice and counsel here."

⁸ All the people got up as one, saying, "We will not any of us go to our tents, nor will any of us return to our houses. ⁹ But now this is what we will do to Gibeah: we will go up[b] against it by lot. ¹⁰ We will take ten men of a hundred throughout all the tribes of Israel, and a hundred of a thousand, and a thousand of ten thousand, to bring provisions for the troops, who are going to repay[c] Gibeah of Benjamin for all the disgrace that they have done in Israel." ¹¹ So all the men of Israel gathered against the city, united as one.

¹² The tribes of Israel sent men through all the tribe of Benjamin, saying, "What crime is this that has been committed among you? ¹³ Now then, hand over those scoundrels in Gibeah, so that we may put them to death, and purge the evil from Israel." But the Benjaminites would not listen to their kinsfolk, the Israelites. ¹⁴ The Benjaminites came together out of the towns to Gibeah, to go out to battle against the Israelites. ¹⁵ On that day the Benjaminites mustered twenty-six thousand armed men from their towns, besides the inhabitants of Gibeah. ¹⁶ Of all this force, there were seven hundred picked men who were left-handed; every one could sling a stone at a hair, and not miss. ¹⁷ And the Israelites, apart from Benjamin, mustered four hundred thousand armed men, all of them warriors.

¹⁸ The Israelites proceeded to go up to Bethel, where they inquired of God, "Which of us shall go up first to battle against the

a Compare Gk: Heb ³⁰ And all who saw it said, "Such a thing has not happened or been seen
b Gk: Heb lacks *we will go up*
c Compare Gk: Meaning of Heb uncertain

nothing had happened. It is even unclear whether or not she was dead. **29:** The cutting up of the concubine's body and sending of the pieces throughout the land are also bizarre. It is based on an episode where Saul cut up a pair of oxen (see 1 Sam 11.7). There, the purpose was to dramatize what would happen to the oxen of those who refused to join the war, but what is its purpose here, and what is someone who receives a piece of human body supposed to think of it? This episode is meant to prefigure Saul, setting his later actions in a negative light.

20.1–48: The war against Benjamin. Benjamin's refusal to turn over the guilty people of Gibeah led to a bloody civil war. **1:** *From Dan to Beersheba,* the traditional northern and southern limits of Israelite territory. *Gilead,* Israelite territory in northern Transjordan. There is no other unified action like this elsewhere in the book of Judges. **2:** The numbers here and elsewhere in chs 20–21 are exaggerated. **3:** It is strange that the examination of the Levite is only performed once the army has been mustered. **4–11:** The Levite's report is brief and not investigated. **9:** The casting of lots determines when to go to war and which of the tribes will go first (v. 18); this also returns us to the beginning of the book (1.2). **10:** Ten percent are responsible for supplying the combatants. **15–17:** The numbers here are inconsistent with those in vv. 35,44–47. **16:** *Left-handed,* see 3.15. 1 Chr 12.2 mentions Benjaminite warriors who were ambidextrous. **18:** *Judah . . . first.* It is strange, but this is

Benjaminites?" And the LORD answered, "Judah shall go up first."

¹⁹ Then the Israelites got up in the morning, and encamped against Gibeah. ²⁰ The Israelites went out to battle against Benjamin; and the Israelites drew up the battle line against them at Gibeah. ²¹ The Benjaminites came out of Gibeah, and struck down on that day twenty-two thousand of the Israelites. ^{23 a} The Israelites went up and wept before the LORD until the evening; and they inquired of the LORD, "Shall we again draw near to battle against our kinsfolk the Benjaminites?" And the LORD said, "Go up against them." ²² The Israelites took courage, and again formed the battle line in the same place where they had formed it on the first day.

²⁴ So the Israelites advanced against the Benjaminites the second day. ²⁵ Benjamin moved out against them from Gibeah the second day, and struck down eighteen thousand of the Israelites, all of them armed men. ²⁶ Then all the Israelites, the whole army, went back to Bethel and wept, sitting there before the LORD; they fasted that day until evening. Then they offered burnt offerings and sacrifices of well-being before the LORD. ²⁷ And the Israelites inquired of the LORD (for the ark of the covenant of God was there in those days, ²⁸ and Phinehas son of Eleazar, son of Aaron, ministered before it in those days), saying, "Shall we go out once more to battle against our kinsfolk the Benjaminites, or shall we desist?" The LORD answered, "Go up, for tomorrow I will give them into your hand." ²⁹ So Israel stationed men in ambush around Gibeah. ³⁰ Then the Israelites went up against the Benjaminites on the third day, and set themselves in array against Gibeah, as before. ³¹ When the Benjaminites went out against the army, they were drawn away from the city. As before they began to inflict casualties on the troops, along the main roads, one of which goes up to Bethel and the other to Gibeah, as well as in the open country, killing about thirty men of Israel. ³² The Benjaminites thought, "They are being routed before us, as previously." But the Israelites said, "Let us retreat and draw them away from the city toward the roads." ³³ The main body of the Israelites drew back its battle line to Baal-tamar, while those Israelites who were in ambush rushed out of their place west^b of Geba. ³⁴ There came against Gibeah ten thousand picked men out of all Israel, and the battle was fierce. But the Benjaminites did not realize that disaster was close upon them.

³⁵ The LORD defeated Benjamin before Israel; and the Israelites destroyed twenty-five thousand one hundred men of Benjamin that day, all of them armed.

³⁶ Then the Benjaminites saw that they were defeated.^c

The Israelites gave ground to Benjamin, because they trusted to the troops in ambush that they had stationed against Gibeah. ³⁷ The troops in ambush rushed quickly upon Gibeah. Then they put the whole city to the sword. ³⁸ Now the agreement between the main body of Israel and the men in ambush

---

^a Verses 22 and 23 are transposed
^b Gk Vg: Heb *in the plain*
^c This sentence is continued by verse 45.

---

not mentioned in what follows. **19–25:** It is odd that although Israel went twice to war after asking the LORD and getting his approval, so many of them were killed by the Benjaminites. **26–28:** The army of Israel went up the third time to Bethel, where Phinehas, also belonging to the third generation after the Exodus (see Num 25.7–13; Josh 22), served as priest. God promised that this time he would help them. **29–47:** According to most scholars the description of this war is a combination of two versions, whose reworking into a single text is not smooth. Both versions tell of a strategy of ambush and decoy (cf. Josh 7–8). **29:** According to vv. 33–34, the main force was east of Gibeah, the ambush west of the city, while the decoy force was opposite the city. **30:** This refers to the decoy force alone; see v. 34. **31:** *To Gibeah,* a textual corruption, as they were fleeing from Gibeah. It most likely refers to Geba, located east of Gibeah. The choice of two directions of flight causes the pursuers to divide their forces. *About thirty men,* the small number of the fallen, in comparison to the first two wars, is probably influenced by the story of Ai, where exactly thirty fell (Josh 7.5). **33:** The main Israelite force had been mustered before in Baal-tamar, whose location has not been identified. **35:** See vv. 15–17n. **36b:** The second version begins here. This one emphasizes that the Israelite army, which had relied upon the ambush located to the west of Gibeah, waited for a sign indicating when to enter into battle, thus giving the decoy time to lead the

was that when they sent up a cloud of smoke out of the city [39] the main body of Israel should turn in battle. But Benjamin had begun to inflict casualties on the Israelites, killing about thirty of them; so they thought, "Surely they are defeated before us, as in the first battle." [40] But when the cloud, a column of smoke, began to rise out of the city, the Benjaminites looked behind them—and there was the whole city going up in smoke toward the sky! [41] Then the main body of Israel turned, and the Benjaminites were dismayed, for they saw that disaster was close upon them. [42] Therefore they turned away from the Israelites in the direction of the wilderness; but the battle overtook them, and those who came out of the city[a] were slaughtering them in between.[b] [43] Cutting down[c] the Benjaminites, they pursued them from Nohah[d] and trod them down as far as a place east of Gibeah. [44] Eighteen thousand Benjaminites fell, all of them courageous fighters. [45] When they turned and fled toward the wilderness to the rock of Rimmon, five thousand of them were cut down on the main roads, and they were pursued as far as Gidom, and two thousand of them were slain. [46] So all who fell that day of Benjamin were twenty-five thousand arms-bearing men, all of them courageous fighters. [47] But six hundred turned and fled toward the wilderness to the rock of Rimmon, and remained at the rock of Rimmon for four months. [48] Meanwhile, the Israelites turned back against the Benjaminites, and put them to the sword—the city, the people, the animals, and all that remained. Also the remaining towns they set on fire.

21 Now the Israelites had sworn at Mizpah, "No one of us shall give his daughter in marriage to Benjamin." [2] And the people came to Bethel, and sat there until evening before God, and they lifted up their voices and wept bitterly. [3] They said, "O LORD, the God of Israel, why has it come to pass that today there should be one tribe lacking in Israel?" [4] On the next day, the people got up early, and built an altar there, and offered burnt offerings and sacrifices of well-being. [5] Then the Israelites said, "Which of all the tribes of Israel did not come up in the assembly to the LORD?" For a solemn oath had been taken concerning whoever did not come up to the LORD to Mizpah, saying, "That one shall be put to death." [6] But the Israelites had compassion for Benjamin their kin, and said, "One tribe is cut off from Israel this day. [7] What shall we do for wives for those who are left, since we have sworn by the LORD that we will not give them any of our daughters as wives?"

[8] Then they said, "Is there anyone from the tribes of Israel who did not come up to the LORD to Mizpah?" It turned out that no one from Jabesh-gilead had come to the camp, to the assembly. [9] For when the roll was called among the people, not one of the inhabitants of Jabesh-gilead was there. [10] So the congregation sent twelve thousand soldiers there and commanded them, "Go, put the inhabitants of Jabesh-gilead to the sword, including the

a   Compare Vg and some Gk Mss: Heb *cities*
b   Compare Syr: Meaning of Heb uncertain
c   Gk: Heb *Surrounding*
d   Gk: Heb *pursued them at their resting place*

inhabitants of Gibeah away from their city. **38–39a:** The sign was a great cloud of smoke rising from the city. **43:** The Hebrew is poetic, perhaps a remnant of an epic centered on the victory over Benjamin. *Nohah*, Israel surrounded Benjamin and pursued them from a settlement called Nohah (see 1 Chr 8.2) until Geba, east of Gibeah (v. 31). **47:** Six hundred men of Benjamin found shelter for four months *at the Rock of Rimmon* on the edge of the wilderness to the east. **48:** The Israelites treated Benjamin like an apostate city (cf. Deut 13.13–19), destroying its population, property, and towns.

21.1–14: The war against Jabesh-gilead. This narrative is reminiscent of the story of the war against the Midianites at the time of the wilderness wanderings after the Exodus (Num 31). It is motivated by a desire to denounce Jabesh-gilead, which supported Saul (see 1 Sam 11; 31.11–13; 2 Sam 2.4–7; etc.). **1:** At the gathering in Mizpah (see 20.1) the Israelites took two oaths: not to marry their daughters to the Benjaminites (20.3; 21.1), and to put to death those who did not join the war (21.5). **2:** *Bethel* once again serves as a place for weeping (cf. 2.1–5; 20.23,26). **5:** Those who did not join the war were not committed to the oath. They were subject to the death penalty and their daughters could be given to the Benjaminites. **9:** *Jabesh-gilead* is located east of the Jordan in northern Gilead, but has not been definitively identified. **10–12:** Use of the number *twelve thousand* as well

women and the little ones. [11] This is what you shall do; every male and every woman that has lain with a male you shall devote to destruction." [12] And they found among the inhabitants of Jabesh-gilead four hundred young virgins who had never slept with a man and brought them to the camp at Shiloh, which is in the land of Canaan.

[13] Then the whole congregation sent word to the Benjaminites who were at the rock of Rimmon, and proclaimed peace to them. [14] Benjamin returned at that time; and they gave them the women whom they had saved alive of the women of Jabesh-gilead; but they did not suffice for them.

[15] The people had compassion on Benjamin because the LORD had made a breach in the tribes of Israel. [16] So the elders of the congregation said, "What shall we do for wives for those who are left, since there are no women left in Benjamin?" [17] And they said, "There must be heirs for the survivors of Benjamin, in order that a tribe may not be blotted out from Israel. [18] Yet we cannot give any of our daughters to them as wives." For the Israelites had sworn, "Cursed be anyone who gives a wife to Benjamin." [19] So they said, "Look,

the yearly festival of the LORD is taking place at Shiloh, which is north of Bethel, on the east of the highway that goes up from Bethel to Shechem, and south of Lebonah." [20] And they instructed the Benjaminites, saying, "Go and lie in wait in the vineyards, [21] and watch; when the young women of Shiloh come out to dance in the dances, then come out of the vineyards and each of you carry off a wife for himself from the young women of Shiloh, and go to the land of Benjamin. [22] Then if their fathers or their brothers come to complain to us, we will say to them, 'Be generous and allow us to have them; because we did not capture in battle a wife for each man. But neither did you incur guilt by giving your daughters to them.' " [23] The Benjaminites did so; they took wives for each of them from the dancers whom they abducted. Then they went and returned to their territory, and rebuilt the towns, and lived in them. [24] So the Israelites departed from there at that time by tribes and families, and they went out from there to their own territories.

[25] In those days there was no king in Israel; all the people did what was right in their own eyes.

as of the phrase *virgins who had never slept with a man* recalls Num 31. **14:** The six hundred surviving men from Benjamin *returned* from the rock of Rimmon (see 20.47).

21.15–24: The abduction at Shiloh. Killing the people of Jabesh-gilead provided wives for most of the Benjaminites, but there were still two hundred without wives. The motif of stealing women on a festival day is known from Greek and Roman literature. The connection between Benjamin and Shiloh prepares the ground for the decline of the town's status in the book of Samuel. **15:** *A breach,* the blow struck to the Benjaminites harmed the overall structure of the Israelite tribes. **19:** *The yearly festival,* it is not clear what feast this refers to: one of the three pilgrimage festivals, or to the fifteenth of Av (the fifth month) or the Day of Atonement. The two last were auspicious days for finding brides in later rabbinic times (*m. Ta'anit* 4.8). It may also refer to a local grape harvest festival (see 9.27). *Shiloh,* about 9 mi (15 km) north of Bethel.

21.25: Conclusion to the book of Judges. The book concludes with the last occurrence (see 17.6; 18.1; 19.1) of the motto that expresses disappointment in the judges and hope in the monarchy. Coming after the negative depiction of Gibeah, Saul's city, it is clear that the book hints at a monarchy whose roots are not in Benjamin, Saul's tribe. The book thus looks forward to the dynasty founded by David, who was from Bethlehem in Judah. This fits with other positive descriptions of Judah in the beginning of the book: it is Judah who leads the conquest in ch 1.1-20, and the Judean judge Othniel in ch 3.7-11 is idealized as a national leader.

RUTH

NAME AND LOCATION IN CANON

The book is named after its heroine, a young Moabite widow who leaves her land and family to follow her mother-in-law to Bethlehem in Judah, where she will become the great-grandmother of King David.

The book of Ruth is in the third division of the Hebrew Bible, the Writings; it is one of the Megillot, the five scrolls read on different Jewish holidays, with Ruth traditionally read at the late spring harvest festival of Weeks (Shavuot). In the Septuagint, and consequently in Christian Bibles, it comes between the books of Judges and Samuel. That is apparently where the writer of the book of Ruth intended it to be placed, since it begins "In the days when the judges ruled" (1.1), and ends with a list of ten generations from Perez to David, preparing us for David's arrival onto the stage of history in 1 Samuel and supplying the genealogy lacking there. The author's attempt to place Ruth after Judges and before Samuel in the Hebrew Bible was unsuccessful, however, presumably because that division of the Bible, the Prophets, had been closed before the book of Ruth was accepted as canonical, and it was placed in the final division.

AUTHORSHIP AND DATE

The book of Ruth was written by an unknown author, probably in the Second Temple period, when there was opposition to marriage by Jews with foreign women, particularly Ammonites and Moabites (see Ezra 9–10; Neh 10.29–31; 13.24–27). Nehemiah 13.1 cites Deut 23.4 as the basis for its demand to exclude all foreigners from Israel. Our book voices an alternate view: its heroine is an ideal Moabite woman, a model of righteousness, who altruistically follows her mother-in-law. Formal conversion to Judaism did not exist in this period, but Ruth clings to the God of Israel, and God blesses her and provides her with posterity: David. Boaz is also blessed, like the young Moabite woman whom he redeems.

The language of the book of Ruth supports a Second Temple period dating: its words and expressions, and their spelling, attest to a substantial Aramaic influence. Moreover, it shows no sign of the Deuteronomistic redaction that characterizes the earlier historical books (Joshua–Kings), suggesting that it was written by a later author to be inserted between Judges and Samuel, and not by the main preexilic authors of those books. An alternate view is that the book was written during the period of the monarchy, because of its interest in the ancestry of King David.

STRUCTURE

While Ruth is one of the shortest of the Bible's books, it comprises one of the Bible's longest stories, one of an idyllic-romantic character. Great misfortunes, both national (famine) and personal-familial (the death of Naomi's husband and sons) occur at the outset and propel the narrative forward. The former is resolved at the end of the exposition (1.6), and the bitter pessimism caused by the latter is limited to the first chapter—from here on, the story is bathed in an optimistic light, full of hope for a better future.

The book has no villains, and the protagonists almost compete with their exemplary behavior: all are helpful, considerate, and well intentioned. The absence of conflict also characterizes the relations with God. Apart from Naomi's defiant words in 1.20–21, the book depicts a wonder of harmonious relations with God. Pentateuchal laws also play a role in this harmony: the protagonists are fond of fulfilling the commandments, noticeable in their willingness to go above and beyond what the law requires, and they are rewarded accordingly.

The book is structured symmetrically. The family's history before their return from Moab and following the act of redemption are concentrated at the book's beginning (1.1–6) and end (4.18–22), framing the narrative. Chapters 1 and 4 are parallel, as are chs 2 and 3. Chapter 1 opens with the genealogy of Elimelech, an unknown Ephrathite; ch 4 ends with the genealogy from Perez to David. Chapter 1 opens with an allusion to the period of the judges; ch 4 ends with an allusion to the monarchic period—David. Chapter 1 mentions a direct act of God ending the famine (v. 6); ch 4 mentions God's second intervention, which resolves the personal-familial crisis (v. 13). These are the only direct acts of God in the book, and neither crisis is attributed to God (only Naomi in her suffering interprets her tragedies as God's actions; 1.13, 20–21). A female chorus explains Naomi's circumstances in both chapters: in ch 1 their reaction is sad astonishment at Naomi's return to Bethlehem (v. 19), in ch 4 their speech is prolonged and buoyant (vv. 14–15). A striking structural parallel is also developed in the conduct of the secondary characters Orpah, who ultimately decides against following Naomi (1.14), and the next-of-kin, who recants his willingness to redeem the field (4.6). Both serve to highlight the exceptional goodness of Ruth and Boaz.

Chapters 2 and 3 are also parallel. Chapter 2 depicts one day in Boaz's field; ch 3 describes a night. The day scene involves many secondary figures working in Boaz's field; the night scene is unobserved—Ruth and Boaz are alone on the threshing floor. Both chapters open with conversations between Naomi and Ruth, but here we are presented with clear oppositions: in ch 2 Ruth initiates, asking Naomi's permission to go to the fields to glean; Naomi is passive and her answer succinct, "Go, my daughter" (v. 2). In ch 3, Naomi initiates, asking Ruth to go to Boaz's field, and Ruth is the passive one who accepts Naomi's proposition, her answer brief: "All that you tell me I will do" (v. 5). The next locale in both chapters—which is the main locale in both—is Boaz's field. In ch 2, Ruth reaches the field before Boaz, whose arrival is marked by the word *wehinneh*, "just then" (v. 4). In ch 3, Boaz arrives before Ruth, whose appearance is also marked by *wehinneh* (v. 8 [NRSV] "and there"). In 2.5, Boaz asks about Ruth's identity; in 3.9 he asks Ruth, "Who are you?" Ruth's answer alludes to the difference between the characters' functioning in the two chapters: in ch 3 Ruth instructs Boaz what he must do (v. 9); in ch 2 she is passive, astonished at Boaz's graciousness toward her. In both chapters Boaz is careful to protect Ruth's honor: in ch 2 he takes care that she will stay with the young women (and not the men; v. 8), and that the men will neither reproach nor rebuke her (vv. 15, 16); in ch 3 he makes sure that no one will see her with him (v. 14). In 2.18 Ruth brings Naomi what was left after she had been satisfied, a sign of her good character, and in 3.17 she delivers barley to Naomi as Boaz had instructed, a sign of his good character. The final locale in both chapters is Naomi's home (2.18–23; 3.16–18).

INTERPRETATION AND GUIDE TO READING

The author of the book knows Pentateuchal law. The heroine's gleaning of the grain fields alludes both to the law of gleanings (Lev 19.9–10) and that concerning overlooking a sheaf in the field (Deut 24.19), laws that are here blended harmoniously. To redeem Ruth (3.9, 12–13) and the field (4.3–4), and to bind them together (4.5, 9–10), the book boldly combines the laws of redeeming a field (Lev 25.25–28) with that of levirate marriage (Deut 25.5–10), a law that does not correspond exactly to the legal situation here. In Ruth, the law regarding the redemption of a woman becomes a logical extension of the law of levirate marriage, as in later rabbinic interpretation in which different laws are combined and their discrepancies reconciled.

Other than laws, Ruth quotes or makes extensive use of earlier, First Temple period texts of all types. Clear ties to the Pentateuch are discernible in Ruth's actions on Boaz's threshing floor (ch 3), where her conduct is implicitly contrasted to that of Lot's daughters (Gen 19.30–38) and she is presented as being even more dignified than Tamar (Gen 38.14–15). The matriarchs Rachel and Leah are mentioned explicitly (4.11; cf. also Gen 12.1 with Ruth 2.11). The influence of the historical books is similarly evident: 1 Sam 1.8 leaves its imprint on Ruth 4.15; 1 Sam 9.9 is reflected in Ruth 4.7. The genealogy in 4.8–22 is constructed from the genealogy of Judah in 1 Chr 2.

This highly skilled narrative should be understood in its historical context, within the debates of the Second Temple period concerning intermarriage. The stance of Ruth is clear and unambiguous: *ḥesed*, kindness and loyalty, are more important than ethnicity.

Yair Zakovitch

1 In the days when the judges ruled, there was a famine in the land, and a certain man of Bethlehem in Judah went to live in the country of Moab, he and his wife and two sons. [2] The name of the man was Elimelech and the name of his wife Naomi, and the names of his two sons were Mahlon and Chilion; they were Ephrathites from Bethlehem in Judah. They went into the country of Moab and remained there. [3] But Elimelech, the husband of Naomi, died, and she was left with her two sons. [4] These took Moabite wives; the name of the one was Orpah and the name of the other Ruth. When they had lived there about ten years, [5] both Mahlon and Chilion also died, so that the woman was left without her two sons and her husband.

[6] Then she started to return with her daughters-in-law from the country of Moab, for she had heard in the country of Moab that the LORD had considered his people and given them food. [7] So she set out from the place where she had been living, she and her two daughters-in-law, and they went on their way to go back to the land of Judah. [8] But Naomi said to her two daughters-in-law, "Go back each of you to your mother's house. May the LORD deal kindly with you, as you have dealt with the dead and with me. [9] The LORD grant that you may find security, each of you in the house of your husband." Then she kissed them, and they wept aloud. [10] They said to her, "No, we will return with you to your people." [11] But Naomi said, "Turn back, my daughters, why will you go with me? Do I still have sons in my womb that they may become your husbands? [12] Turn back, my daughters, go your way, for I am too old to have a husband. Even if I thought there was hope for me, even if I should have a husband tonight and bear sons, [13] would you then wait until they were grown? Would you then refrain from marrying? No, my daughters, it has been far more bitter for me than for you, because the hand of the LORD has turned against me." [14] Then they wept aloud again. Orpah kissed her mother-in-law, but Ruth clung to her.

[15] So she said, "See, your sister-in-law has gone back to her people and to her gods; return after your sister-in-law." [16] But Ruth said,
"Do not press me to leave you
   or to turn back from following you!
Where you go, I will go;
   where you lodge, I will lodge;
your people shall be my people,
   and your God my God.
[17] Where you die, I will die—
   there will I be buried.
May the LORD do thus and so to me,
   and more as well,
if even death parts me from you!"
[18] When Naomi saw that she was determined to go with her, she said no more to her.

[19] So the two of them went on until they came to Bethlehem. When they came to Bethlehem, the whole town was stirred because of them; and the women said, "Is this Naomi?" [20] She said to them,
"Call me no longer Naomi,[a]

---

[a] That is *Pleasant*

1.1–5: Famine. These verses provide the background for the entire story. The family's prolonged absence from Israel and a string of misfortunes have left Naomi and her daughters-in-law in desperate straits. **1:** *Bethlehem*, 5 mi (8 km) south of Jerusalem, the home of David's family (1 Sam 16.1–5). It means "house of bread," and thus opens the book on an ironic note. *Moab*, the region east of the Dead Sea. According Gen 19.36–37, the Moabites are related to the Israelites: their patriarch, Lot, was Abraham's nephew. **2:** *Mahlon and Chilion*, the names are symbolic in an escalating order of gravity: Mahlon is related to the word for "sickness" (Heb "maḥalah"), and Chilion to the word for "destruction" (Heb "killayon"). *Ephrathites*, the family is from Bethlehem, also called Ephrathah (4.11; see Gen 35.19; 48.7). **3–5:** The legal status of women is determined to some extent by the men they are connected to—a father, husband, or male children. The status of these three women is thus dire.

1.6–19a: The return to Bethlehem. No description of the journey is given. Instead, we find a dialogue between Naomi and her daughters-in-law, during which Naomi fails to convince Ruth to leave her and return to Moab; Orpah returns to Moab, persuaded by the bleak picture Naomi describes. Ruth reveals her noble-mindedness, electing to remain with Naomi and follow Naomi's God, without expectation of reward or hope for a better life.

1.19b–22: The arrival at Bethlehem. The narrative focuses on Naomi. **19:** The chorus of women expresses wonder at the change in Naomi and ignores Ruth. In her grief, Naomi blames God for her sorrows. **20:** *Mara*,

call me Mara,[a]

    for the Almighty[b] has dealt bitterly with
    me.

[21] I went away full,

    but the LORD has brought me back
    empty;

why call me Naomi

    when the LORD has dealt harshly with[c]
    me,

    and the Almighty[b] has brought calamity
    upon me?"

[22] So Naomi returned together with Ruth the Moabite, her daughter-in-law, who came back with her from the country of Moab. They came to Bethlehem at the beginning of the barley harvest.

2 Now Naomi had a kinsman on her husband's side, a prominent rich man, of the family of Elimelech, whose name was Boaz. [2] And Ruth the Moabite said to Naomi, "Let me go to the field and glean among the ears of grain, behind someone in whose sight I may find favor." She said to her, "Go, my daughter." [3] So she went. She came and gleaned in the field behind the reapers. As it happened, she came to the part of the field belonging to Boaz, who was of the family of Elimelech. [4] Just then Boaz came from Bethlehem. He said to the reapers, "The LORD be with you." They answered, "The LORD bless you." [5] Then Boaz said to his servant who was in charge of the reapers, "To whom does this young woman belong?" [6] The servant who was in charge of the reapers answered, "She is the Moabite who came back with Naomi from the country of Moab. [7] She said, 'Please, let me glean and gather among the sheaves behind the reapers.' So she came, and she has been on her feet from early this morning until now, without resting even for a moment."[d]

[8] Then Boaz said to Ruth, "Now listen, my daughter, do not go to glean in another field or leave this one, but keep close to my young women. [9] Keep your eyes on the field that is being reaped, and follow behind them. I have ordered the young men not to bother you. If you get thirsty, go to the vessels and drink from what the young men have drawn." [10] Then she fell prostrate, with her face to the ground, and said to him, "Why have I found favor in your sight, that you should take notice of me, when I am a foreigner?" [11] But Boaz answered her, "All that you have done for your mother-in-law since the death of your husband has been fully told me, and how you left your father and mother and your native land and came to a people that you did not know before. [12] May the LORD reward you for your deeds, and may you have a full reward from the LORD, the God of Israel, under whose wings you have come for refuge!" [13] Then she said, "May I continue to find favor in your sight, my lord, for you have comforted me and spoken kindly to your servant, even though I am not one of your servants."

[14] At mealtime Boaz said to her, "Come here, and eat some of this bread, and dip your morsel in the sour wine." So she sat beside the reapers, and he heaped up for her some parched grain. She ate until she was satisfied, and she had some left over. [15] When she

---

a   That is *Bitter*

b   Traditional rendering of Heb *Shaddai*

c   Or *has testified against*

d   Compare Gk Vg: Meaning of Heb uncertain

"bitter," is the opposite of *Naomi*, "pleasant." **22:** The *barley harvest* was the earliest harvest.

    2.1–23: Ruth and Boaz's first encounter. 1–7: Ruth, who insisted on remaining with Naomi, again takes the initiative—now on foreign soil—and sets out to glean in order to provide for her mother-in-law and herself. The scene introduces the prosperous Boaz, a member of Elimelech's family. Chance events bring Ruth and Boaz together: Ruth happens to reach Boaz's field, and he happens to arrive while she gleans there. The Bible often suggests that the divine hand is behind such "chance." **8–14:** Boaz and Ruth speak. Boaz guides and dominates the exchange. The conversation secures their connection. He exhibits genuine concern for Ruth, for her food, honor, and drink. Ruth prostrates herself and wonders at his solicitude, since she is a foreigner. In his answer—the heart of the exchange—Boaz expresses admiration for her self-sacrifice and devotion to her mother-in-law, and his hope that God will reward her. Ruth continues to belittle herself, and Boaz proves his interest in her welfare by granting her more than she needs. **15–17:** Ruth returns to glean in Boaz's field, unaware of Boaz's efforts on her behalf. The section ends with an account of Boaz's generosity; the amount of barley Ruth gleaned

got up to glean, Boaz instructed his young men, "Let her glean even among the standing sheaves, and do not reproach her. [16] You must also pull out some handfuls for her from the bundles, and leave them for her to glean, and do not rebuke her."

[17] So she gleaned in the field until evening. Then she beat out what she had gleaned, and it was about an ephah of barley. [18] She picked it up and came into the town, and her mother-in-law saw how much she had gleaned. Then she took out and gave her what was left over after she herself had been satisfied. [19] Her mother-in-law said to her, "Where did you glean today? And where have you worked? Blessed be the man who took notice of you." So she told her mother-in-law with whom she had worked, and said, "The name of the man with whom I worked today is Boaz." [20] Then Naomi said to her daughter-in-law, "Blessed be he by the LORD, whose kindness has not forsaken the living or the dead!" Naomi also said to her, "The man is a relative of ours, one of our nearest kin."[a] [21] Then Ruth the Moabite said, "He even said to me, 'Stay close by my servants, until they have finished all my harvest.'" [22] Naomi said to Ruth, her daughter-in-law, "It is better, my daughter, that you go out with his young women, otherwise you might be bothered in another field." [23] So she stayed close to the young women of Boaz, gleaning until the end of the barley and wheat harvests; and she lived with her mother-in-law.

3 Naomi her mother-in-law said to her, "My daughter, I need to seek some security for you, so that it may be well with you. [2] Now here is our kinsman Boaz, with whose young women you have been working. See, he is winnowing barley tonight at the threshing floor. [3] Now wash and anoint yourself, and put on your best clothes and go down to the threshing floor; but do not make yourself known to the man until he has finished eating and drinking. [4] When he lies down, observe the place where he lies; then, go and uncover his feet and lie down; and he will tell you what to do." [5] She said to her, "All that you tell me I will do."

[6] So she went down to the threshing floor and did just as her mother-in-law had instructed her. [7] When Boaz had eaten and drunk, and he was in a contented mood, he went to lie down at the end of the heap of grain. Then she came stealthily and uncovered his feet, and lay down. [8] At midnight the man was startled, and turned over, and there, lying at his feet, was a woman! [9] He said, "Who are you?" And she answered, "I am Ruth, your servant; spread your cloak over your servant, for you are next-of-kin."[a]

---

[a] Or *one with the right to redeem*

---

that day (an *ephah* was about 2/3 bushel or 22 l) would have been sufficient for many days. **18–23**: Naomi and Ruth in Naomi's house. Boaz's opening words in the previous section supply Naomi's closing words here: concern that Ruth will stay with Boaz's young women and so avoid dishonor (vv. 8–9; 22). In the middle of each dialogue, the speaker (Boaz, Naomi) voices esteem for Ruth and a blessing (vv. 11–12; 20). Gaps are filled in the course of the conversation: to the amazed Naomi's question regarding the kindness shown Ruth, Ruth reveals the identity of the field-owner (v. 19). Naomi learns of Boaz's kindness toward Ruth, and Ruth learns that Boaz is one of the redeeming kinsmen (v. 20), a person related to the deceased Elimelech; he can thus allow the women to have access to the field of Elimelech. Ruth does not respond to Naomi's words, but speaks of her intention to glean until the end of the harvest (v. 21). Naomi agrees, remaining hopeful. The *wheat harvest,* in late spring, followed the barley harvest.

3.1–18: Ruth and Boaz's nighttime encounter. 1–5: As in 2.2, Naomi and Ruth again discuss matters in Naomi's home, though the roles are reversed: Naomi is the initiator who slowly intimates her objective. Naomi's instructions suggest that marriage is the aim (cf. Ezek 16.8–10). She expects Boaz to know what to do. **6–15:** Ruth reaches the field unnoticed; she needs to be seen by Boaz, alone. She follows Naomi's instructions but goes even further, making clear to Boaz that her actions refer to the law of redemption. Ruth's discretion as she proceeds to the threshing floor also characterizes her dialogue with Boaz and their subsequent actions. Ruth continues to lie at Boaz's feet until morning. Although "feet" is often a euphemism in the Bible for genitals (e.g., Isaiah 7.20), nothing explicit occurs between them. Both Ruth and Boaz are cautious for her reputation, as were Boaz and Naomi in the previous chapter. With Ruth's return from the threshing floor at dawn, hope reigns: Ruth

[10] He said, "May you be blessed by the LORD, my daughter; this last instance of your loyalty is better than the first; you have not gone after young men, whether poor or rich. [11] And now, my daughter, do not be afraid, I will do for you all that you ask, for all the assembly of my people know that you are a worthy woman. [12] But now, though it is true that I am a near kinsman, there is another kinsman more closely related than I. [13] Remain this night, and in the morning, if he will act as next-of-kin[a] for you, good; let him do it. If he is not willing to act as next-of-kin[a] for you, then, as the LORD lives, I will act as next-of-kin[a] for you. Lie down until the morning."

[14] So she lay at his feet until morning, but got up before one person could recognize another; for he said, "It must not be known that the woman came to the threshing floor." [15] Then he said, "Bring the cloak you are wearing and hold it out." So she held it, and he measured out six measures of barley, and put it on her back; then he went into the city. [16] She came to her mother-in-law, who said, "How did things go with you,[b] my daughter?" Then she told her all that the man had done for her, [17] saying, "He gave me these six measures of barley, for he said, 'Do not go back to your mother-in-law empty-handed.'" [18] She replied, "Wait, my daughter, until you learn how the matter turns out, for the man will not rest, but will settle the matter today."

4 No sooner had Boaz gone up to the gate and sat down there than the next-of-kin,[a] of whom Boaz had spoken, came passing by. So Boaz said, "Come over, friend; sit down here." And he went over and sat down. [2] Then Boaz took ten men of the elders of the city, and said, "Sit down here"; so they sat down. [3] He then said to the next-of-kin,[a] "Naomi, who has come back from the country of Moab, is selling the parcel of land that belonged to our kinsman Elimelech. [4] So I thought I would tell you of it, and say: Buy it in the presence of those sitting here, and in the presence of the elders of my people. If you will redeem it, redeem it; but if you will not, tell me, so that I may know; for there is no one prior to you to redeem it, and I come after you." So he said, "I will redeem it." [5] Then Boaz said, "The day you acquire the field from the hand of Naomi, you are also acquiring Ruth[c] the Moabite, the widow of the dead man, to maintain the dead man's name on his inheritance." [6] At this, the next-of-kin[a] said, "I cannot redeem it for myself without damaging my own inheritance. Take my right of redemption yourself, for I cannot redeem it."

[7] Now this was the custom in former times in Israel concerning redeeming and exchanging: to confirm a transaction, the one took off a sandal and gave it to the other; this was the manner of attesting in Israel. [8] So when the next-of-kin[a] said to Boaz, "Acquire it for yourself," he took off his sandal. [9] Then Boaz said to the elders and all the people, "Today you are witnesses that I have acquired from the

a Or one with the right to redeem
b Or "Who are you,
c OL Vg: Heb from the hand of Naomi and from Ruth

knows that she will be redeemed and she carries much barley, a sign of Boaz's favorable intentions. **10**: *Loyalty*, Heb "ḥesed", a key term in the Hebrew Bible, where God is expected to show "ḥesed" to Israel, and those with more power are expected to show "ḥesed" to those who are disadvantaged. **16–18**: Ruth reports to Naomi, and Naomi trusts Boaz that the identity of the redeemer will be known that very day. Here Ruth and Naomi conclude their active role. From now on they are passive, dependent upon the efforts of others.

4.1–22: Ruth is redeemed, Obed is born: the family's name continues. 1–12: Redemption at the city gate. The *gate* was where legal issues were settled (e.g., Deut 25.7). Boaz's authority at the city gate it is as great as it was with his young men: here also Boaz commands, and the city elders follow his instructions. Nevertheless, he does not take advantage of his position, and treats the closest kinsman fairly, allowing him to exercise his legal rights if he so desires. Awareness of the Pentateuch is evident by the rigor with which the law is kept and by repeated allusions to the laws of redeeming and that of levirate marriage (Lev 25.25–28; Deut 25.5–10), and also in the greetings of the people to Boaz and his household, where Ruth is depicted as one of the matriarchs, along with Rachel and Leah, the wives of Jacob (v. 11). **6**: The exact meaning of *damaging my own inheritance* is uncertain, but likely refers to a requirement that the current field of this redeemer would have to be shared

hand of Naomi all that belonged to Elimelech and all that belonged to Chilion and Mahlon. [10] I have also acquired Ruth the Moabite, the wife of Mahlon, to be my wife, to maintain the dead man's name on his inheritance, in order that the name of the dead may not be cut off from his kindred and from the gate of his native place; today you are witnesses." [11] Then all the people who were at the gate, along with the elders, said, "We are witnesses. May the LORD make the woman who is coming into your house like Rachel and Leah, who together built up the house of Israel. May you produce children in Ephrathah and bestow a name in Bethlehem; [12] and, through the children that the LORD will give you by this young woman, may your house be like the house of Perez, whom Tamar bore to Judah." [13] So Boaz took Ruth and she became his wife. When they came together, the LORD made her conceive, and she bore a son.

[14] Then the women said to Naomi, "Blessed be the LORD, who has not left you this day without next-of-kin;[a] and may his name be renowned in Israel! [15] He shall be to you a restorer of life and a nourisher of your old age; for your daughter-in-law who loves you, who is more to you than seven sons, has borne him." [16] Then Naomi took the child and laid him in her bosom, and became his nurse. [17] The women of the neighborhood gave him a name, saying, "A son has been born to Naomi." They named him Obed; he became the father of Jesse, the father of David.

[18] Now these are the descendants of Perez: Perez became the father of Hezron, [19] Hezron of Ram, Ram of Amminadab, [20] Amminadab of Nahshon, Nahshon of Salmon, [21] Salmon of Boaz, Boaz of Obed, [22] Obed of Jesse, and Jesse of David.

a Or *one with the right to redeem*

with heirs of Ruth as well as with his current heirs. **12:** By comparing Boaz's house to Perez's house, the most important clan in Judah, Ruth is compared to Tamar, the mother of Perez (Gen 38.29), another foreign woman who although a childless widow was granted illustrious progeny. **13–17:** The marriage of Ruth and Boaz and the birth of Obed. **13:** Just as God intervened to resolve the national crisis at the end of the introduction (1.6), so he intervenes in this final scene to resolve the family's misfortune. **14–15:** The chorus of women reappears, too, and in a change of tone blesses Naomi's good fortune. Whereas they previously ignored Ruth (1.19), now they glorify her. **16–17:** The meaning of the actions here is uncertain; it may reflect her adoption of this baby as her own. **17:** The section ends, illuminating the family's magnificent future.

18–22: The line of Perez. Once the narrative has named Obed as the grandfather of David (v. 17), it recounts the entire genealogy from Perez to David, as in Genesis, combining story with genealogy. Ten is the number of generations from Adam until Noah (Gen 5), and from Noah's son Shem until Abraham (Gen 11.10–26), indicating that the tenth generation, David, is the chosen one. It would appear that Obed has two fathers. Boaz is his biological father (and thus he appears in the list; v. 21), but he will be counted as the seed of Mahlon (4.5, 10).

1 SAMUEL

NAME

First and Second Samuel were originally a single work named after the prophet Samuel, who is the focal character of the first eight chapters of 1 Samuel. The name is not entirely appropriate, however, since Samuel dies before 1 Samuel ends (25.1).

LOCATION IN CANON

The original, single book of Samuel was divided into two books in the Greek translation of the Hebrew Bible (the Septuagint, abbreviated LXX) and grouped together with the book of Kings (also divided in two) to form 1–4 Reigns or 1–4 Kingdoms. These divisions were later introduced into Hebrew Bibles and subsequently became standard. The books of Samuel are part of the section of the Hebrew Bible known as the Former Prophets. The LXX and most English Bibles place 1 and 2 Samuel in the category of the Historical Books.

AUTHORSHIP

In the Babylonian Talmud (*b. B. Bat.* 14b, ca. sixth century CE) the prophet Samuel is identified as the author of those parts of the book that treat events before his death, with the rest being attributed to the prophets Nathan and Gad based on 1 Chr 29.29. Modern scholars consider 1 and 2 Samuel to have been written by several anonymous authors, and generally view it as part of a larger composition called the Deuteronomistic History. The Deuteronomistic History, encompassing the books of Deuteronomy, Joshua, Judges, 1 and 2 Samuel, and 1 and 2 Kings, relates Israel's history in the Promised Land, from the conquest under Joshua to the end of the kingdoms of Israel and Judah. It was written by one or more nameless authors and editors known as "Deuteronomists," abbreviated "Dtr(s)."

DATE AND CONTEXT OF COMPOSITION

The Deuteronomistic History was probably completed shortly after the Babylonian exile in 586 BCE and sought to offer a theological reason for the demise of Israel and Judah. Some scholars posit an earlier edition that promoted King Josiah (640–609 BCE) as a new David. Others argue for multiple preexilic, exilic, or postexilic editions.

LITERARY HISTORY

The Deuteronomist(s) edited various traditions into a single, running historical account. In 1 Samuel some scholars have posited source documents behind 4.1–7.1 (the "Ark Narrative"), chs 8–15 (the "Saul Cycle"), and chs 16–31 (the "Story of David's Rise"). These documents are theoretical, and the nature of the sources used by the Dtr(s) remains hypothetical. The Dtr(s) also occasionally inserted speeches or commentary in their own distinctive Deuteronomistic style into the narrative. Examples of Deuteronomistic style in 1 Samuel are 8.8 (the Exodus), 8.12 (the people crying out), and 12.14–15 (the review of Israel's history and the command to "heed the voice of the LORD").

STRUCTURE AND CONTENTS

First Samuel falls readily into three parts, each with a different central character: Samuel as a transitional figure—prophet, priest, and judge (chs 1–7), the emergence of Saul as Israel's first king (chs 8–15), and David's ascent (chs 16–31). David is the main hero not only of 1 and 2 Samuel but of the Deuteronomistic History as well. The pro-Davidic tone of 1 Samuel is evident in the fact that while Saul falters repeatedly, David can do no wrong. God eventually abandons Saul but is constantly with David. God's presence with David, first in Saul's court and then while hiding from Saul, is a major theme in the book.

INTERPRETATION

First Samuel is a literary masterpiece, full of wordplays, intricate plots with subtle twists, and portraits of complex characters. Some parts may also contain or reflect genuine history. While the book was written centuries after the events it describes, it is based on older source materials. At some stage in its development, the section dealing with David's rise seems to have been designed as an apology or defense of David and his kingship. The charge that David usurped the throne to which he had no hereditary right is effectively addressed in 1 Samuel by the contention that David was the LORD's anointed, who came to prominence as a result of divine election rather than personal ambition. First Samuel thus presents David as the innocent victim of Saul's jealousy, beloved by Israel's public and leading citizens including Saul's own children, and even by Saul at the beginning of their relationship, such that David became a member of the royal family through marriage.

GUIDE TO READING

Since 1 Samuel is a continuous narrative, it is best read from start to finish. This reading will be enriched by attention to details that cultivate an appreciation of the work as literature. For instance, the story is told by an "omniscient narrator" using techniques such as reporting private conversations and personal thoughts. Characters are rarely described, so that descriptions are particularly noteworthy. More often, their inner qualities and motives are revealed by their actions or words, leaving room for ambiguity. Further appreciation will result from recognizing the apologetic, especially pro-Davidic nature of the material. Was Saul really as bad and David as innocent as their portraits in this book indicate? What ulterior motives might David (and other characters) have had for their actions? How might a modern historian reconstruct the events related in 1 Samuel by setting aside the "spin" of the apologist? Some instances of "protesting too much" suggest that the historical reality was quite different, as when all of chs 24–31 seem dedicated to showing that David would not and could not have been involved in any attempt on Saul's life.

Steven L. McKenzie

1 There was a certain man of Ramathaim, a Zuphite[a] from the hill country of Ephraim, whose name was Elkanah son of Jeroham son of Elihu son of Tohu son of Zuph, an Ephraimite. [2] He had two wives; the name of the one was Hannah, and the name of the other Peninnah. Peninnah had children, but Hannah had no children.

[3] Now this man used to go up year by year from his town to worship and to sacrifice to the LORD of hosts at Shiloh, where the two sons of Eli, Hophni and Phinehas, were priests of the LORD. [4] On the day when Elkanah sacrificed, he would give portions to his wife Peninnah and to all her sons and daughters; [5] but to Hannah he gave a double portion,[b] because he loved her, though the LORD had closed her womb. [6] Her rival used to provoke her severely, to irritate her, because the LORD had closed her womb. [7] So it went on year by year; as often as she went up to the house of the LORD, she used to provoke her. Therefore Hannah wept and would not eat. [8] Her husband Elkanah said to her, "Hannah, why do you weep? Why do you not eat? Why is your heart sad? Am I not more to you than ten sons?"

a Compare Gk and 1 Chr 6.35-36: Heb *Ramathaim-zophim*

b Syr: Meaning of Heb uncertain

1.1–28: The birth and consecration of Samuel. The story of a barren woman who bears a child as a favor from God appears several other times in the Bible: Sarah (Gen 17.16–19), Rebekah (Gen 25.21–26), Rachel (Gen 29.31; 30.22–24), the mother of Samson (Judg 13.2–5), and Elizabeth (Lk 1.5–17). Such a child is designated by God for a special purpose. **1:** *Ramathaim,* a town in Ephraim, is called Ramah later in this chapter (v. 19). But in later chapters the Ramah that was Samuel's home seems to be located in Benjamin (7.16–17). **2:** *Peninnah* is "the second" (translated *the other* in the NRSV) wife; *Hannah* is obviously the favored one. Elkanah may have married Peninnah because of Hannah's failure to produce an heir (see Gen 16.1–2). Elkanah, therefore, was probably prosperous. **3:** Elkanah's annual pilgrimage to worship in Shiloh shows him to be a righteous man. The LORD *of hosts* or "armies" (Heb "tseba'ot") is a title describing Yahweh's leadership in war on Israel's behalf. *Hophni and Phinehas* are Egyptian names. **7:** The *house of the LORD* usually refers to a temple (Jer 7.12). But Josh 18.1; Ps 78.60 mention a tent of meeting or tabernacle in Shiloh, and 2 Sam 7.6–7 denies that the LORD dwelt in a "house" before Solomon's Temple. See 2.22. **9:** Eli's *seat beside the doorpost of the temple* (or "sanctuary," Heb "hekal")

⁹ After they had eaten and drunk at Shiloh, Hannah rose and presented herself before the LORD.ᵃ Now Eli the priest was sitting on the seat beside the doorpost of the temple of the LORD. ¹⁰ She was deeply distressed and prayed to the LORD, and wept bitterly. ¹¹ She made this vow: "O LORD of hosts, if only you will look on the misery of your servant, and remember me, and not forget your servant, but will give to your servant a male child, then I will set him before you as a naziriteᵇ until the day of his death. He shall drink neither wine nor intoxicants,ᶜ and no razor shall touch his head."

¹² As she continued praying before the LORD, Eli observed her mouth. ¹³ Hannah was praying silently; only her lips moved, but her voice was not heard; therefore Eli thought she was drunk. ¹⁴ So Eli said to her, "How long will you make a drunken spectacle of yourself? Put away your wine." ¹⁵ But Hannah answered, "No, my lord, I am a woman deeply troubled; I have drunk neither wine nor strong drink, but I have been pouring out my soul before the LORD. ¹⁶ Do not regard your servant as a worthless woman, for I have been speaking out of my great anxiety and vexation all this time." ¹⁷ Then Eli answered, "Go in peace; the God of Israel grant the petition you have made to him." ¹⁸ And she said, "Let your servant find favor in your sight." Then the woman went to her quarters,ᵈ ate and drank with her husband,ᵉ and her countenance was sad no longer.ᶠ

¹⁹ They rose early in the morning and worshiped before the LORD; then they went back to their house at Ramah. Elkanah knew his wife Hannah, and the LORD remembered her. ²⁰ In due time Hannah conceived and bore a son. She named him Samuel, for she said, "I have asked him of the LORD."

²¹ The man Elkanah and all his household went up to offer to the LORD the yearly sacrifice, and to pay his vow. ²² But Hannah did not go up, for she said to her husband, "As soon as the child is weaned, I will bring him, that he may appear in the presence of the LORD, and remain there forever; I will offer him as a naziriteᵇ for all time."ᵍ ²³ Her husband Elkanah said to her, "Do what seems best to you, wait until you have weaned him; only—may the LORD establish his word."ʰ So the woman remained and nursed her son, until she weaned him. ²⁴ When she had weaned him, she took him up with her, along with a three-year-old bull,ⁱ an ephah of flour, and a skin of wine. She brought him to the house of the LORD at Shiloh; and the child was young. ²⁵ Then they slaughtered the bull, and they brought the child to Eli. ²⁶ And she said, "Oh, my lord! As you live, my lord, I am the woman who was standing here in your presence, praying to the LORD. ²⁷ For this child I prayed; and the LORD has granted me the petition that I made to him. ²⁸ Therefore I have lent him to the LORD; as long as he lives, he is given to the LORD."

ᵃ Gk: Heb lacks *and presented herself before the* LORD
ᵇ That is *one separated* or *one consecrated*
ᶜ Cn Compare Gk Q Ms 1.22: MT *then I will give him to the* LORD *all the days of his life*
ᵈ Gk: Heb *went her way*
ᵉ Gk: Heb lacks *and drank with her husband*
ᶠ Gk: Meaning of Heb uncertain
ᵍ Cn Compare Q Ms: MT lacks *I will offer him as a nazirite for all time*
ʰ MT: Q Ms Gk Compare Syr *that which goes out of your mouth*
ⁱ Q Ms Gk Syr: MT *three bulls*

allowed him to see Hannah praying outside of the temple proper (see also 4.18). **11:** *Nazirites* were "devoted" to the LORD for a set period of time and were prohibited from drinking alcohol or eating grapes, cutting their hair or beards, and approaching a dead body (Num 6.1–21). *Intoxicants*, probably distilled wine or beer. **13:** *Eli thought she was drunk* because prayers were not usually silent. **17:** *The petition you have made*, the first of several wordplays in this chapter on the name of Saul, which sounds like the Hebrew verb for "ask, petition." **19:** *Elkanah knew his wife*, an idiom for sexual relations. **20:** *I have asked him of the LORD*, "asked" (Heb "sha'al") is another pun on the name Saul. **22–24:** *Weaned*, taken off breast milk. Samuel's age is not given, but he is older than an infant or toddler. *An ephah of flour* (v. 24), ca. .6 bu (23 l). **27:** *The petition that I made*, another pun on Saul's name. **28:** *Lent . . . given*, the Heb word for both is yet another pun on Saul's name. *He is given* is exactly the same as Saul's name in Hebrew ("sha'ul") and could be translated, "he is Saul to the LORD." Some scholars think, based on these puns, that this story was originally about Saul's birth rather than Samuel's. Other scholars think they are simply allusions to Saul as Israel's first king.

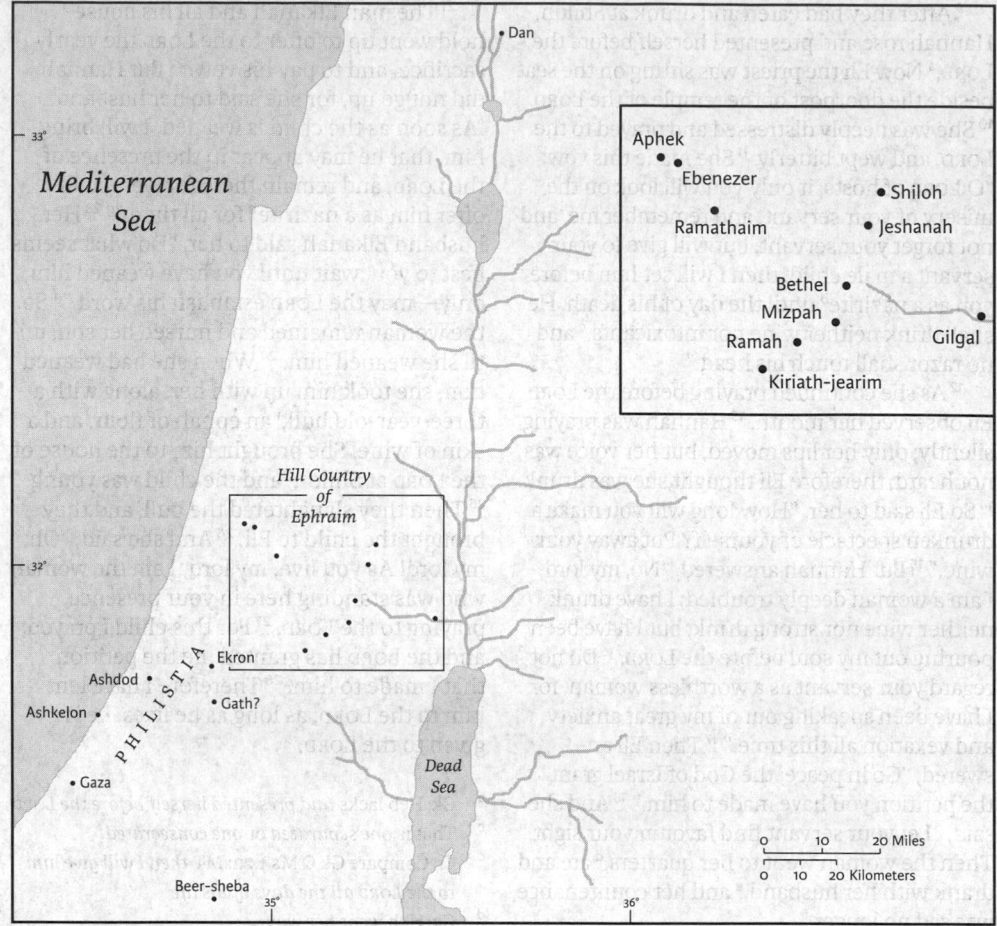

Chs 1–6: The activity of Samuel.

She left him there for[a] the LORD.

2 Hannah prayed and said,
"My heart exults in the LORD;
  my strength is exalted in my God.[b]
My mouth derides my enemies,
  because I rejoice in my[c] victory.

[2] "There is no Holy One like the LORD,
  no one besides you;
  there is no Rock like our God.
[3] Talk no more so very proudly,

let not arrogance come from your
  mouth;
for the LORD is a God of knowledge,
  and by him actions are weighed.
[4] The bows of the mighty are broken,
  but the feeble gird on strength.

a   Gk (Compare Q Ms) and Gk at 2.11: MT *And he* (that
    is, Elkanah) *worshiped there before*
b   Gk: Heb *the* LORD
c   Q Ms: MT *your*

2.1–10: The Song of Hannah. Biblical writers sometimes inserted poems into prose books where they seemed appropriate. In this case the poem seems to be considerably later than the surrounding context. It is a psalm of national thanksgiving, but its thankful tone appropriately reflects Hannah's sentiments. It was later used as a model for Lk 1.46–55. **1:** *Strength*, lit. "horn," draws on the image of a proud animal. **2:** *Rock*, a common metaphor for God (2 Sam 22.2–3; Ps 18.2; 28.1; 62.2,6). **3:** The enemies of Israel are addressed. **4:** The reversal of fortune for the downtrodden and oppressed. **5:** *The barren has borne seven*, this line probably suggested

[5] Those who were full have hired
    themselves out for bread,
  but those who were hungry are fat with
    spoil.
The barren has borne seven,
  but she who has many children is forlorn.
[6] The LORD kills and brings to life;
  he brings down to Sheol and raises up.
[7] The LORD makes poor and makes rich;
  he brings low, he also exalts.
[8] He raises up the poor from the dust;
  he lifts the needy from the ash heap,
to make them sit with princes
  and inherit a seat of honor.[a]
For the pillars of the earth are the LORD's,
  and on them he has set the world.

[9] "He will guard the feet of his faithful ones,
  but the wicked shall be cut off in
    darkness;
  for not by might does one prevail.
[10] The LORD! His adversaries shall be
    shattered;
  the Most High[b] will thunder in heaven.
The LORD will judge the ends of the earth;
  he will give strength to his king,
  and exalt the power of his anointed."

[11] Then Elkanah went home to Ramah, while the boy remained to minister to the LORD, in the presence of the priest Eli.

[12] Now the sons of Eli were scoundrels; they had no regard for the LORD [13] or for the duties of the priests to the people. When anyone offered sacrifice, the priest's serv-ant would come, while the meat was boiling, with a three-pronged fork in his hand, [14] and he would thrust it into the pan, or kettle, or caldron, or pot; all that the fork brought up the priest would take for himself.[c] This is what they did at Shiloh to all the Israelites who came there. [15] Moreover, before the fat was burned, the priest's servant would come and say to the one who was sacrificing, "Give meat for the priest to roast; for he will not accept boiled meat from you, but only raw." [16] And if the man said to him, "Let them burn the fat first, and then take whatever you wish," he would say, "No, you must give it now; if not, I will take it by force." [17] Thus the sin of the young men was very great in the sight of the LORD; for they treated the offer-ings of the LORD with contempt.

[18] Samuel was ministering before the LORD, a boy wearing a linen ephod. [19] His mother used to make for him a little robe and take it to him each year, when she went up with her husband to offer the yearly sacrifice. [20] Then Eli would bless Elkanah and his wife, and say, "May the LORD repay[d] you with children by this woman for the gift that she made to[e] the LORD"; and then they would return to their home.

[d] Gk (Compare Q Ms) adds *He grants the vow of the one who vows, and blesses the years of the just*
[b] Cn Heb *against him he*
[c] Gk Syr Vg: Heb *with it*
[d] Q Ms Gk: MT *give*
[e] Q Ms Gk: MT *for the petition that she asked of*

the insertion of the poem at this place. *Seven* is symbolic of a sizable family; Hannah will eventually have six children (2.21). **6–7:** *Brings to life* refers to birth, not resurrection from the dead. *Sheol* was the underworld (Isa 14.9–21), where all people were believed to go after death. (The idea of heaven and hell does not exist yet in the Bible.) Sheol may be metaphorical for conditions near death (Ps 86.13; 88.3–7), injuries, or serious trouble. **8:** *He raises up the poor . . . he lifts the needy,* God's concern for the poor and oppressed is a common theme in the Bible. *Pillars of the earth,* the earth is conceived of as a platform resting upon great pillars. **10:** *His king* shows that the psalm was written later than Hannah since there was no king of Israel yet in her time. *Anointed* (Heb "mashiaḥ") was a title for the king and the source of the postbiblical term "messiah," which never means future Davidic ruler in the Hebrew Bible.

2.12–26: The wicked sons of Eli. Samuel's faithful service, in contrast to the evil deeds of Eli's sons, hints that he will replace Eli. **12:** *They had no regard for,* lit. "they did not know." Its meaning here may be that Eli's sons did not have a personal relationship with the LORD. **13–17:** Priests made their living by receiving a portion of the sacrifices. The custom in Shiloh (vv. 13–14) was for the priest to get whatever the fork brought up while the meat was boiling, which is different from that prescribed elsewhere (contrast Lev 7.28–36; Deut 18.3). By de-manding the fat portion, which properly belonged to God, and taking it before the sacrifice was made, Eli's sons were sinning against the LORD (v. 25) and treating him with contempt (vv. 12,17). They also threatened violence against worshipers who tried to do right (v. 16). **18:** This *linen ephod* was a kind of apron worn by priests. **20:** *The*

²¹ And^a the LORD took note of Hannah; she conceived and bore three sons and two daughters. And the boy Samuel grew up in the presence of the LORD.

²² Now Eli was very old. He heard all that his sons were doing to all Israel, and how they lay with the women who served at the entrance to the tent of meeting. ²³ He said to them, "Why do you do such things? For I hear of your evil dealings from all these people. ²⁴ No, my sons; it is not a good report that I hear the people of the LORD spreading abroad. ²⁵ If one person sins against another, someone can intercede for the sinner with the LORD;^b but if someone sins against the LORD, who can make intercession?" But they would not listen to the voice of their father; for it was the will of the LORD to kill them.

²⁶ Now the boy Samuel continued to grow both in stature and in favor with the LORD and with the people.

²⁷ A man of God came to Eli and said to him, "Thus the LORD has said, 'I revealed^c myself to the family of your ancestor in Egypt when they were slaves^d to the house of Pharaoh. ²⁸ I chose him out of all the tribes of Israel to be my priest, to go up to my altar, to offer incense, to wear an ephod before me; and I gave to the family of your ancestor all my offerings by fire from the people of Israel. ²⁹ Why then look with greedy eye^e at my sacrifices and my offerings that I commanded, and honor your sons more than me by

fattening yourselves on the choicest parts of every offering of my people Israel?' ³⁰ Therefore the LORD the God of Israel declares: 'I promised that your family and the family of your ancestor should go in and out before me forever'; but now the LORD declares: 'Far be it from me; for those who honor me I will honor, and those who despise me shall be treated with contempt. ³¹ See, a time is coming when I will cut off your strength and the strength of your ancestor's family, so that no one in your family will live to old age. ³² Then in distress you will look with greedy eye^f on all the prosperity that shall be bestowed upon Israel; and no one in your family shall ever live to old age. ³³ The only one of you whom I shall not cut off from my altar shall be spared to weep out his^g eyes and grieve his^h heart; all the members of your household shall die by the sword.ⁱ ³⁴ The fate of your two sons, Hophni and Phinehas, shall be the sign to you—both of them shall die

a Q Ms Gk: MT *When*
b Gk Compare Q Ms: MT *another, God will mediate for him*
c Gk Tg Syr: Heb *Did I reveal*
d Q Ms Gk: MT lacks *slaves*
e Q Ms Gk: MT *then kick*
f Q Ms Gk: MT *will kick*
g Q Ms Gk: MT *your*
h Q Ms Gk: Heb *your*
i Q Ms See Gk: MT *die like mortals*

gift that she made, another pun on Saul's name. **22:** *And how they lay with the women who served at the entrance to the tent of meeting,* this line, if original, indicates that the shrine at Shiloh was a portable tent or tabernacle (see 1.7n.). However, this line is not in some of the best witnesses to the text of Samuel and may be borrowed from Ex 38.8. It is unknown exactly how these women *served at the entrance to the tent of meeting.* **25:** *It was the will of the LORD to kill them,* compare God's hardening of Pharaoh's heart in Ex 4–12.

2.27–36: The oracle against Eli. This passage was probably written by the Deuteronomistic author to justify the exclusion of Abiathar and his descendants from the priesthood in favor of Zadok and his descendants (1 Kings 2.27,35), which occurred due to Josiah's centralization of worship in Jerusalem (2 Kings 23.9). **27–28:** *Your ancestor* may refer to Moses, to whom Eli's family traced their ancestry. But the statement that he was chosen *out of all the tribes of Israel* seems to indicate Levi, and Moses was a Levite (Ex 2.1). **28:** *To go up to my altar, to offer incense, to wear an ephod,* three principal duties of priests. Going up to the altar refers to offering sacrifices. **30:** The promise mentioned here is not explicitly found in the Bible but resembles Ex 28.43, which is directed to Aaron. **31–33:** The cutting off of Eli's household probably refers not to the death of Eli and his sons in 4.11,18 but to Saul's annihilation of the priests of Nob in ch 22. *The only one of you* is Abiathar, who alone escaped the slaughter (22.18–23; 1 Kings 2.26–27). The Hebrew of v. 32a is obscure. **35:** The *faithful priest* is Zadok, who came to prominence when Abiathar was banished by Solomon (1 Kings 1–2). The language of this verse is very similar to that of 2 Sam 7.11–16, which promises a dynasty to David. Both were probably written by the Deuteronomistic Historian. See also 1 Sam 25.28; 1 Kings 11.38. *Anointed one,* see 2.10n.

on the same day. [35] I will raise up for myself a faithful priest, who shall do according to what is in my heart and in my mind. I will build him a sure house, and he shall go in and out before my anointed one forever. [36] Everyone who is left in your family shall come to implore him for a piece of silver or a loaf of bread, and shall say, Please put me in one of the priest's places, that I may eat a morsel of bread.'"

3 Now the boy Samuel was ministering to the LORD under Eli. The word of the LORD was rare in those days; visions were not widespread.

[2] At that time Eli, whose eyesight had begun to grow dim so that he could not see, was lying down in his room; [3] the lamp of God had not yet gone out, and Samuel was lying down in the temple of the LORD, where the ark of God was. [4] Then the LORD called, "Samuel! Samuel!"[a] and he said, "Here I am!" [5] and ran to Eli, and said, "Here I am, for you called me." But he said, "I did not call; lie down again." So he went and lay down. [6] The LORD called again, "Samuel!" Samuel got up and went to Eli, and said, "Here I am, for you called me." But he said, "I did not call, my son; lie down again." [7] Now Samuel did not yet know the LORD, and the word of the LORD had not yet been revealed to him. [8] The LORD called Samuel again, a third time. And he got up and went to Eli, and said, "Here I am, for you called me." Then Eli perceived that the LORD was calling the boy. [9] Therefore Eli said to Samuel, "Go, lie down; and if he calls you, you shall say, 'Speak, LORD, for your servant is listening.'" So Samuel went and lay down in his place.

[10] Now the LORD came and stood there, calling as before, "Samuel! Samuel!" And Samuel said, "Speak, for your servant is listening." [11] Then the LORD said to Samuel, "See, I am about to do something in Israel that will make both ears of anyone who hears of it tingle. [12] On that day I will fulfill against Eli all that I have spoken concerning his house, from beginning to end. [13] For I have told him that I am about to punish his house forever, for the iniquity that he knew, because his sons were blaspheming God,[b] and he did not restrain them. [14] Therefore I swear to the house of Eli that the iniquity of Eli's house shall not be expiated by sacrifice or offering forever."

[15] Samuel lay there until morning; then he opened the doors of the house of the LORD. Samuel was afraid to tell the vision to Eli. [16] But Eli called Samuel and said, "Samuel, my son." He said, "Here I am." [17] Eli said, "What was it that he told you? Do not hide it from me. May God do so to you and more also, if you hide anything from me of all that he told you." [18] So Samuel told him everything and hid nothing from him. Then he said, "It is the LORD; let him do what seems good to him."

[19] As Samuel grew up, the LORD was with him and let none of his words fall to the ground. [20] And all Israel from Dan to Beer-sheba knew that Samuel was a trustworthy prophet of the LORD. [21] The LORD continued to appear at Shiloh, for the LORD revealed himself to Samuel at Shiloh by the word of

---

a Q Ms Gk See 3.10: MT *the LORD called Samuel*
b Another reading is *for themselves*

3.1–4.1a: Samuel's call. 3.1: *Word of the LORD . . . visions* are means of prophetic revelation. **3:** The lamp in the temple burned at night (see Ex 27.21). *The lamp of God had not yet gone out,* hence it was just before dawn. Samuel's bed was inside the temple near the inner sanctuary where the *ark of God* was kept. The ark was a portable shrine or chest representing God's presence; see 4.4n. **7:** *Samuel did not yet know the LORD,* Samuel's role as a prophet had not yet been established since *the word of the LORD had not yet been revealed to him.* In this story Samuel comes to "know" the LORD by learning to recognize God's revelations. **9–10:** *Your servant,* a polite way of referring to oneself. **14:** Eli's sons profaned the sacrifices that might otherwise have *expiated* or atoned for their sins (2.12–17). **17:** *May God do so to you and more also,* a typical oath formula. Eli places Samuel under oath, forcing him to reveal his conversation with the LORD. **19:** All of Samuel's prophecies come true (none *fall to the ground*). **20:** *Dan to Beer-sheba,* the traditional northern and southern limits of Israel.

4.1b–22: The capture of the ark. Many scholars believe that 4.1–7.1 and possibly 2 Sam 6 are based on an old document called the "Ark Narrative" that described the capture and return of the ark. The ark is the focus of

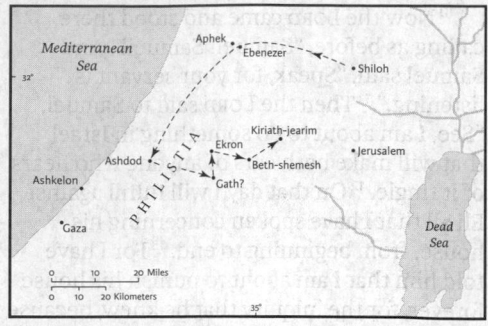

Chs 4–6: Wanderings of the ark of the covenant.

the LORD. ¹ And the word of Samuel came to all Israel.

In those days the Philistines mustered for war against Israel,ᵃ and Israel went out to

4 battle against them;ᵇ they encamped at Ebenezer, and the Philistines encamped at Aphek. ² The Philistines drew up in line against Israel, and when the battle was joined,ᶜ Israel was defeated by the Philistines, who killed about four thousand men on the field of battle. ³ When the troops came to the camp, the elders of Israel said, "Why has the LORD put us to rout today before the Philistines? Let us bring the ark of the covenant of the LORD here from Shiloh, so that he may come among us and save us from the power of our enemies." ⁴ So the people sent to Shiloh, and brought from there the ark of the covenant of the LORD of hosts, who is enthroned on the cherubim. The two sons of Eli, Hophni and Phinehas, were there with the ark of the covenant of God.

⁵ When the ark of the covenant of the LORD came into the camp, all Israel gave a mighty shout, so that the earth resounded. ⁶ When the Philistines heard the noise of the shouting, they said, "What does this great shouting in the camp of the Hebrews mean?" When they learned that the ark of the LORD had come to the camp, ⁷ the Philistines were afraid; for they said, "Gods haveᵈ come into the camp." They also said, "Woe to us! For nothing like this has happened before. ⁸ Woe to us! Who can deliver us from the power of these mighty gods? These are the gods who struck the Egyptians with every sort of plague in the wilderness. ⁹ Take courage, and be men, O Philistines, in order not to become slaves to the Hebrews as they have been to you; be men and fight."

¹⁰ So the Philistines fought; Israel was defeated, and they fled, everyone to his home. There was a very great slaughter, for there fell of Israel thirty thousand foot soldiers. ¹¹ The ark of God was captured; and the two sons of Eli, Hophni and Phinehas, died.

¹² A man of Benjamin ran from the battle line, and came to Shiloh the same day, with his clothes torn and with earth upon his head. ¹³ When he arrived, Eli was sitting upon his seat by the road watching, for his heart trem-

ᵃ Gk: Heb lacks *In those days the Philistines mustered for war against Israel*
ᵇ Gk: Heb *against the Philistines*
ᶜ Meaning of Heb uncertain
ᵈ Or *A god has*

this section rather than Samuel, who is not mentioned. **1b:** The *Philistines* came from the northeastern Mediterranean area (including the island of Crete; see Am 9.7) and entered Palestine (which is derived from "Philistine") in approximately 1200 BCE, about the same time the Israelites were emerging in the central highlands. In this period they were Israel's great enemy. **2:** *Four thousand men,* the numbers throughout this account are exaggerated, although some scholars think that the Hebrew word translated "thousand" refers to a military unit of far fewer than a thousand men. **4:** *Cherubim* were mythical griffin-like creatures with body parts from different creatures, especially human heads and wings. They were commonly depicted in palaces and temples. As the throne of "the LORD of hosts who sits *enthroned on the cherubim*" (cf. 3.3), the ark represented the LORD's presence in battle. In some passages the ark is described as simple in form and lacking cherubim (Deut 10.2–3) while in others it is depicted as ornate (Ex 25.10–22; 37.1–9) **6:** *Hebrews* is commonly used to distinguish Israelites ethnically from foreigners (Gen 14.13; Ex 1.15; 2.11,13; 3.18; 1 Sam 14.21; Jon 1.9). Sometimes, however, it seems to designate a broader socioeconomic group (Gen 39.14; 43.32). **8:** *Gods* implies that the Philistines had no conception that the Israelites worshiped only one god (but cf. 5.7–8,10–11). The Philistines also locate the plagues in the *wilderness* rather than in Egypt. In both cases the Israelite writer may be mocking the Philistines. See also 6.6n. **10:** *Thirty thousand,* see v. 2n. **12:** *With his clothes torn and with earth upon his head,* conventional signs of

bled for the ark of God. When the man came into the city and told the news, all the city cried out. [14] When Eli heard the sound of the outcry, he said, "What is this uproar?" Then the man came quickly and told Eli. [15] Now Eli was ninety-eight years old and his eyes were set, so that he could not see. [16] The man said to Eli, "I have just come from the battle; I fled from the battle today." He said, "How did it go, my son?" [17] The messenger replied, "Israel has fled before the Philistines, and there has also been a great slaughter among the troops; your two sons also, Hophni and Phinehas, are dead, and the ark of God has been captured." [18] When he mentioned the ark of God, Eli[a] fell over backward from his seat by the side of the gate; and his neck was broken and he died, for he was an old man, and heavy. He had judged Israel forty years.

[19] Now his daughter-in-law, the wife of Phinehas, was pregnant, about to give birth. When she heard the news that the ark of God was captured, and that her father-in-law and her husband were dead, she bowed and gave birth; for her labor pains overwhelmed her. [20] As she was about to die, the women attending her said to her, "Do not be afraid, for you have borne a son." But she did not answer or give heed. [21] She named the child Ichabod, meaning, "The glory has departed from Israel," because the ark of God had been captured and because of her father-in-law and her husband. [22] She said, "The glory has departed from Israel, for the ark of God has been captured."

5 When the Philistines captured the ark of God, they brought it from Ebenezer to Ashdod; [2] then the Philistines took the ark of God and brought it into the house of Dagon and placed it beside Dagon. [3] When the people of Ashdod rose early the next day, there was Dagon, fallen on his face to the ground before the ark of the LORD. So they took Dagon and put him back in his place. [4] But when they rose early on the next morning, Dagon had fallen on his face to the ground before the ark of the LORD, and the head of Dagon and both his hands were lying cut off upon the threshold; only the trunk of[b] Dagon was left to him. [5] This is why the priests of Dagon and all who enter the house of Dagon do not step on the threshold of Dagon in Ashdod to this day.

[6] The hand of the LORD was heavy upon the people of Ashdod, and he terrified and struck them with tumors, both in Ashdod and in its territory. [7] And when the inhabitants of Ashdod saw how things were, they said, "The ark of the God of Israel must not remain with us; for his hand is heavy on us and on our god Dagon." [8] So they sent and gathered together all the lords of the Philistines, and said, "What shall we do with the ark of the God of Israel?" The inhabitants of Gath replied, "Let the ark of God be moved on to us."[c] So they moved the ark of the God of Israel to Gath.[d] [9] But after they had brought it to Gath,[e] the hand of the LORD was against the city, causing a very great panic; he struck the inhabitants of the city,

a Heb *he*
b Heb lacks *the trunk of*
c Gk Compare Q Ms: MT *They answered, "Let the ark of the God of Israel be brought around to Gath."*
d Gk: Heb lacks *to Gath*
e Q Ms: MT lacks *to Gath*

mourning. **18:** Pious *Eli* is moved by the loss of the ark more than the loss of his wicked sons. *Forty years,* a round number for a generation. **21–22:** *Ichabod,* "Where is the glory?" or "Alas for the glory." "Glory" alludes to the ark.

5.1–12: The ark troubles the Philistines. In the ancient Near East, wars between nations were interpreted as contests between their respective gods. This story explains that although the Philistines defeated Israel, the LORD was superior to Dagon, a Philistine god. Similar ancient Near Eastern battle accounts explain defeat as punishment from the god of the vanquished. **1:** *Ashdod,* one of five principal Philistine cities along with Ashkelon, Ekron, Gath, and Gaza. **2:** *Beside Dagon* means beside the statue of Dagon in his temple. Dagon was a Canaanite god of grain whom the Philistines adopted as a major deity. **3:** *There was Dagon, fallen on his face to the ground before the ark of the LORD,* bowing prostrate was a sign of subservience. **4–5:** This is an etiology (a story that explains a custom, name, etc.) for the practice of jumping over thresholds in order to avoid offending the spirits of a particular building or space (see Zeph 1.9). **6–12:** The tumors and mice (in the next chapter) suggest that this outbreak was bubonic plague, which was common in coastlands. According to this story, however, the plague is the LORD's doing. **8:** The *lords of the Philistines* are the rulers of the Philistine pentapolis. The word "lord" ("seren") is Philistine and cognate with Gk "tyrannos" ("tyrant").

both young and old, so that tumors broke out on them. ¹⁰ So they sent the ark of the God of Israelª to Ekron. But when the ark of God came to Ekron, the people of Ekron cried out, "Whyᵇ have they brought around to usᶜ the ark of the God of Israel to kill usᶜ and ourᵈ people?" ¹¹ They sent therefore and gathered together all the lords of the Philistines, and said, "Send away the ark of the God of Israel, and let it return to its own place, that it may not kill us and our people." For there was a deathly panicᵉ throughout the whole city. The hand of God was very heavy there; ¹² those who did not die were stricken with tumors, and the cry of the city went up to heaven.

6 The ark of the LORD was in the country of the Philistines seven months. ² Then the Philistines called for the priests and the diviners and said, "What shall we do with the ark of the LORD? Tell us what we should send with it to its place." ³ They said, "If you send away the ark of the God of Israel, do not send it empty, but by all means return him a guilt offering. Then you will be healed and will be ransomed;ᶠ will not his hand then turn from you?" ⁴ And they said, "What is the guilt offering that we shall return to him?" They answered, "Five gold tumors and five gold mice, according to the number of the lords of the Philistines; for the same plague was upon all of you and upon your lords. ⁵ So you must make images of your tumors and images of your mice that ravage the land, and give glory to the God of Israel; perhaps he will lighten his hand on you and your gods and your land. ⁶ Why should you harden your hearts as the Egyptians and Pharaoh hardened their hearts? After he had made fools of them, did they not let the people go, and they departed? ⁷ Now then, get ready a new cart and two milch

cows that have never borne a yoke, and yoke the cows to the cart, but take their calves home, away from them. ⁸ Take the ark of the LORD and place it on the cart, and put in a box at its side the figures of gold, which you are returning to him as a guilt offering. Then send it off, and let it go its way. ⁹ And watch; if it goes up on the way to its own land, to Beth-shemesh, then it is he who has done us this great harm; but if not, then we shall know that it is not his hand that struck us; it happened to us by chance."

¹⁰ The men did so; they took two milch cows and yoked them to the cart, and shut up their calves at home. ¹¹ They put the ark of the LORD on the cart, and the box with the gold mice and the images of their tumors. ¹² The cows went straight in the direction of Beth-shemesh along one highway, lowing as they went; they turned neither to the right nor to the left, and the lords of the Philistines went after them as far as the border of Beth-shemesh.

¹³ Now the people of Beth-shemesh were reaping their wheat harvest in the valley. When they looked up and saw the ark, they went with rejoicing to meet it.ᵍ ¹⁴ The cart came into the field of Joshua of Beth-shemesh, and stopped there. A large stone was there; so they split up the wood of the cart and offered the cows as a burnt offering to the LORD. ¹⁵ The Levites took down the ark of the LORD and the box that was beside

ª QMs Gk: MT lacks *of Israel*
ᵇ QMs Gk: MT lacks *Why*
ᶜ Heb *me*
ᵈ Heb *my*
ᵉ QMs reads *a panic from the LORD*
ᶠ QMs Gk: MT *and it will be known to you*
ᵍ Gk: Heb *rejoiced to see it*

6.1–7.1: **The return of the ark. 6.3:** *Guilt offering,* not a sacrifice but compensation for taking the ark and appeasement of the Lord in hopes of avoiding further punishment. **4–5:** There is one gold tumor and one gold mouse for each of the five Philistine rulers (vv. 4,17–18). The images serve as substitutes for the rulers and their cities in order to carry the plague away by magic. **6:** Cf. Ex 8.19,32. A creative enhancement by the author, since the Philistines would not have known the story of the Exodus. **7:** A new cart is ritually pure. The two cows have never been yoked and are therefore fit to be sacrificed (cf. Num 19.2; Deut 21.3). *Milch cows* means that they have young calves. **9:** Unaccustomed to pulling a cart, these two cows would be expected to wander aimlessly in search of their calves. If instead they headed for Israelite territory, the Philistines would know that their sufferings had indeed been sent by the LORD. **12:** The cows take the most direct route into Israelite territory. **15:** This verse is likely a later addition by an editor concerned to have the Levites, the priestly tribe, handle the

it, in which were the gold objects, and set them upon the large stone. Then the people of Beth-shemesh offered burnt offerings and presented sacrifices on that day to the LORD. ¹⁶ When the five lords of the Philistines saw it, they returned that day to Ekron.

¹⁷ These are the gold tumors, which the Philistines returned as a guilt offering to the LORD: one for Ashdod, one for Gaza, one for Ashkelon, one for Gath, one for Ekron; ¹⁸ also the gold mice, according to the number of all the cities of the Philistines belonging to the five lords, both fortified cities and unwalled villages. The great stone, beside which they set down the ark of the LORD, is a witness to this day in the field of Joshua of Beth-shemesh.

¹⁹ The descendants of Jeconiah did not rejoice with the people of Beth-shemesh when they greeted[a] the ark of the LORD; and he killed seventy men of them.[b] The people mourned because the LORD had made a great slaughter among the people. ²⁰ Then the people of Beth-shemesh said, "Who is able to stand before the LORD, this holy God? To whom shall he go so that we may be rid of him?" ²¹ So they sent messengers to the inhabitants of Kiriath-jearim, saying, "The Philistines have returned the ark of the LORD. Come down and take it up to you." ¹ And the people of Kiriath-jearim came and took up the ark of the LORD, and brought it to the house of Abinadab on the hill. They consecrated his son, Eleazar, to have charge of the ark of the LORD.

7

² From the day that the ark was lodged at Kiriath-jearim, a long time passed, some twenty years, and all the house of Israel lamented[c] after the LORD.

³ Then Samuel said to all the house of Israel, "If you are returning to the LORD with all your heart, then put away the foreign gods and the Astartes from among you. Direct your heart to the LORD, and serve him only, and he will deliver you out of the hand of the Philistines." ⁴ So Israel put away the Baals and the Astartes, and they served the LORD only.

⁵ Then Samuel said, "Gather all Israel at Mizpah, and I will pray to the LORD for you." ⁶ So they gathered at Mizpah, and drew water and poured it out before the LORD. They fasted that day, and said, "We have sinned against the LORD." And Samuel judged the people of Israel at Mizpah.

⁷ When the Philistines heard that the people of Israel had gathered at Mizpah, the lords of the Philistines went up against Israel. And when the people of Israel heard of it they were afraid of the Philistines. ⁸ The people of Israel said to Samuel, "Do not cease to cry out to the LORD our God for us, and pray that he may save us from the hand of the Philistines." ⁹ So Samuel took a sucking lamb and offered it as a whole burnt offering to the LORD; Sam-

a Gk: Heb *And he killed some of the people of Beth-shemesh, because they looked into*
b Heb *killed seventy men, fifty thousand men*
c Meaning of Heb uncertain

ark. **17:** See 5.1n. **19:** It was *seventy* of the people of Beth-shemesh, not seventy of the *descendants of Jeconiah,* who were killed. The reason is uncertain, since nothing else is known about Jeconiah or his family. **20:** *To stand before the LORD* is a technical expression for priestly service, suggesting that the people are asking for a priest to handle the ark. It remains unclear how the absence of a priest relates to Jeconiah. **21:** *Kiriath-jearim* is located ca. 8 mi (13 km) northwest of Jerusalem. **7.1:** *Abinadab* is the father of several important priests (2 Sam 6.3–4,6–8; 1 Chr 13.7,9–11).

7.2–17: Samuel judges Israel. Samuel is depicted as a transitional figure between the judges and the monarchy. He embodies the roles of priest, prophet, and now judge (cf. Judg 10.6–16). **2:** *Twenty years* is a way of designating half a generation. This notice fits Samuel into the structure of the book of Judges where a period of foreign oppression precedes Israel's repentance. **3–4:** *Returning to the LORD with all your heart* is Deuteronomistic language (cf. Deut 30.10; Josh 22.5; 23.14; 24.23; Judg 10.16; 1 Sam 12.20,24; 1 Kings 8.23,48; 14.8; 2 Kings 10.31; 23.25). *Baals* and *Astartes,* the leading male and female gods of Canaan. **5:** *Mizpah,* located ca. 8 mi (13 km) north of Jerusalem, became the administrative and religious capital of Judah after Jerusalem's destruction in 586 BCE (2 Kings 25.23). Hence, the setting of this story in Mizpah may indicate a date of composition after 586 (similarly Judg 19–21). **6:** The elements of this ritual—prayer, libation, fasting, and confession—do not occur together anywhere else in the Bible. Since fasting suggests contrition and pouring out water suggests cleansing, a community purification ritual may be envisioned, perhaps in preparation for war. **8–9:** Samuel is

uel cried out to the LORD for Israel, and the LORD answered him. [10] As Samuel was offering up the burnt offering, the Philistines drew near to attack Israel; but the LORD thundered with a mighty voice that day against the Philistines and threw them into confusion; and they were routed before Israel. [11] And the men of Israel went out of Mizpah and pursued the Philistines, and struck them down as far as beyond Beth-car.

[12] Then Samuel took a stone and set it up between Mizpah and Jeshanah,[a] and named it Ebenezer;[b] for he said, "Thus far the LORD has helped us." [13] So the Philistines were subdued and did not again enter the territory of Israel; the hand of the LORD was against the Philistines all the days of Samuel. [14] The towns that the Philistines had taken from Israel were restored to Israel, from Ekron to Gath; and Israel recovered their territory from the hand of the Philistines. There was peace also between Israel and the Amorites.

[15] Samuel judged Israel all the days of his life. [16] He went on a circuit year by year to Bethel, Gilgal, and Mizpah; and he judged Israel in all these places. [17] Then he would come back to Ramah, for his home was there; he administered justice there to Israel, and built there an altar to the LORD.

8 When Samuel became old, he made his sons judges over Israel. [2] The name of his firstborn son was Joel, and the name of his second, Abijah; they were judges in Beersheba. [3] Yet his sons did not follow in his ways, but turned aside after gain; they took bribes and perverted justice.

[4] Then all the elders of Israel gathered together and came to Samuel at Ramah, [5] and said to him, "You are old and your sons do not follow in your ways; appoint for us, then, a king to govern us, like other nations." [6] But the thing displeased Samuel when they said, "Give us a king to govern us." Samuel prayed to the LORD, [7] and the LORD said to Samuel, "Listen to the voice of the people in all that they say to you; for they have not rejected you, but they have rejected me from being king over them. [8] Just as they have done to me,[c] from the day I brought them up out of Egypt to this day, forsaking me and serving

a Gk Syr: Heb *Shen*
b That is *Stone of Help*
c Gk: Heb lacks *to me*

an intercessor for the people in the tradition of Moses and Jeremiah. *A whole burnt offering,* one that is entirely consumed (Ex 29.18; Lev 8.21; Deut 13.16; 33.10). **10:** Thunder is considered the *voice* of God. **12:** An etiology for the name *Ebenezer,* which means "stone of the helper/warrior (God)." **13–14:** The statement that the Philistines *did not again enter the territory of Israel* is contradicted later in 1 Samuel. It may refer only to Samuel's lifetime. It serves the author's effort to cast Samuel as a judge; compare the Deuteronomistic formulas in Judg 3.30; 8.28; 11.33. *Amorites,* in Deuteronomy and Deuteronomistic literature the pre-Israelite inhabitants of Canaan. Contrast, e.g., Gen 14.7; 15.20, where "Amorites" refers to one pre-Israelite group. **15–17:** Scholars often identify two types of judges in the book of Judges: military leaders and legal functionaries. This chapter ascribes both roles to Samuel: His intercession brings victory over the Philistines (vv. 10–11), and he rides a circuit judging Israel (vv. 15–17). **16:** *Bethel, Gilgal, Mizpah,* and *Ramah* were all within traditional Benjaminite territory. See map on p. 411.

Chs 8–12: The beginning of kingship in Israel. These chapters recount the events in five distinct episodes: the people's request for a king and Samuel's response (ch 8); Saul's search for his father's asses and his anointing (9.1–10.16); the designation of Saul by lot (10.17–27a); Saul's victory over the Ammonites (10.27b–11.15); and Samuel's farewell address (ch 12). The stories in 9.1–10.16 and 10.27b–11.15 are generally recognized as older and neutral or positive in their attitude toward monarchy, while the other three episodes view kingship with suspicion and depict the people's request as a sin. The latter three texts are also widely recognized as Deuteronomistic. In the end, God allows a king but also warns the people against letting their king lead them astray.

8.1–22: The people request a king. 2: *Beer-sheba,* the southernmost city in Judah and far outside Samuel's jurisdiction in 7.15–17. It became an administrative center during Judah's monarchy. **3:** Samuel's sons, like Eli's, are corrupt (Deut 16.19 denounces taking bribes). Their unfitness to rule impels the elders to ask for a king. **4:** The *elders* were the leading and usually senior citizens. **6–7:** Samuel and the LORD are displeased by the request and consider it a rejection of the LORD. But is kingship regarded as inherently evil? Or does the request demonstrate a lack of faith in the LORD? **8:** The review of Israel's history is in typical Deuteronomistic style (cf.

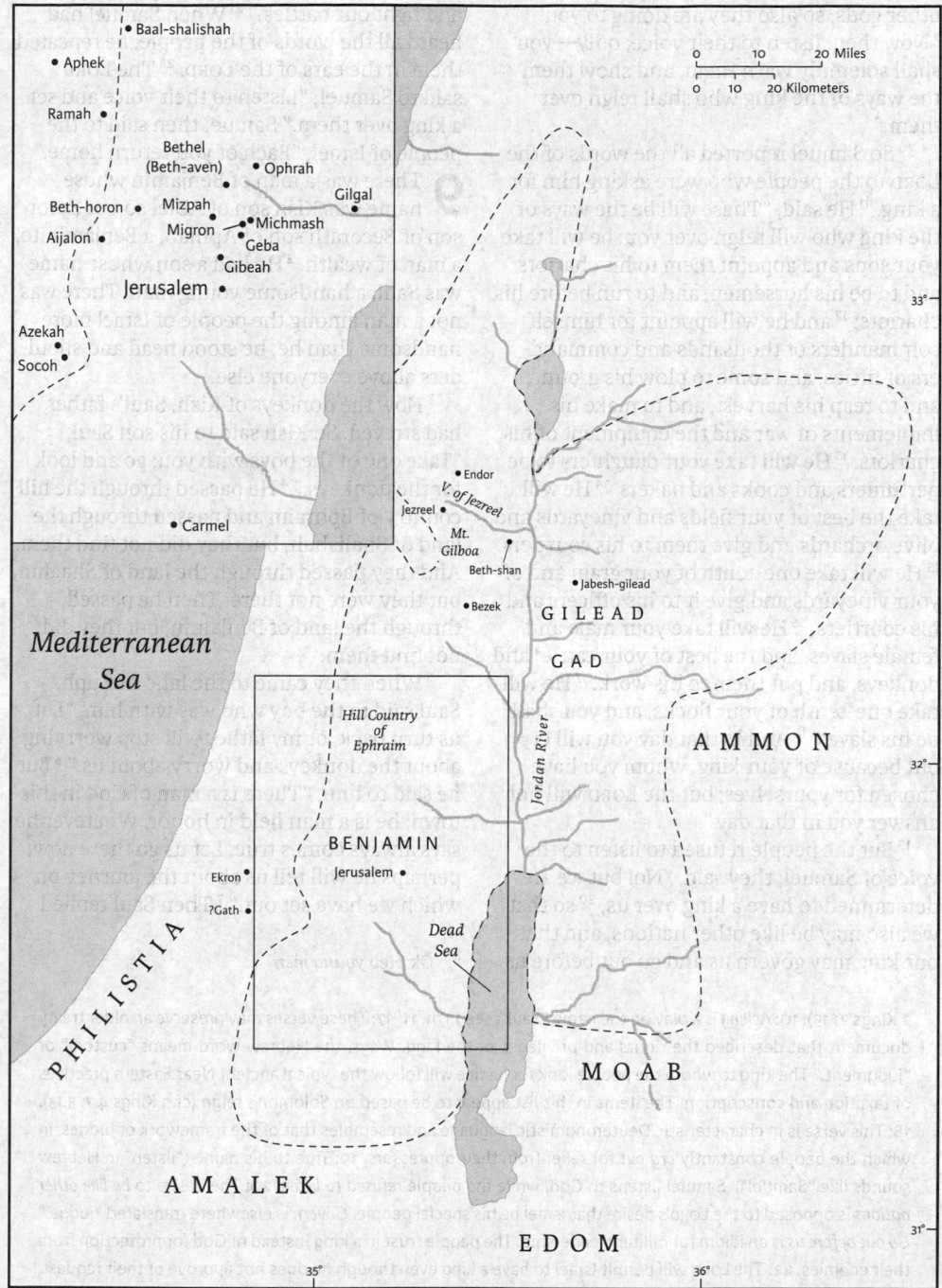

The kingdom of Saul according to the book of Samuel. The dashed line shows the approximate outer boundary of his kingdom.

Map labels:
- Baal-shalishah
- Aphek
- Ramah
- Bethel (Beth-aven)
- Ophrah
- Gilgal
- Beth-horon
- Mizpah
- Michmash
- Migron
- Geba
- Aijalon
- Gibeah
- Jerusalem
- Azekah
- Socoh
- Carmel
- Endor
- V. of Jezreel
- Jezreel
- Mt. Gilboa
- Beth-shan
- Bezek
- Jabesh-gilead
- GILEAD
- GAD
- AMMON
- Mediterranean Sea
- Hill Country of Ephraim
- Jordan River
- BENJAMIN
- Jerusalem
- Ekron
- ?Gath
- Dead Sea
- PHILISTIA
- MOAB
- AMALEK
- EDOM

other gods, so also they are doing to you. [9] Now then, listen to their voice; only—you shall solemnly warn them, and show them the ways of the king who shall reign over them."

[10] So Samuel reported all the words of the LORD to the people who were asking him for a king. [11] He said, "These will be the ways of the king who will reign over you: he will take your sons and appoint them to his chariots and to be his horsemen, and to run before his chariots; [12] and he will appoint for himself commanders of thousands and commanders of fifties, and some to plow his ground and to reap his harvest, and to make his implements of war and the equipment of his chariots. [13] He will take your daughters to be perfumers and cooks and bakers. [14] He will take the best of your fields and vineyards and olive orchards and give them to his courtiers. [15] He will take one-tenth of your grain and of your vineyards and give it to his officers and his courtiers. [16] He will take your male and female slaves, and the best of your cattle[a] and donkeys, and put them to his work. [17] He will take one-tenth of your flocks, and you shall be his slaves. [18] And in that day you will cry out because of your king, whom you have chosen for yourselves; but the LORD will not answer you in that day."

[19] But the people refused to listen to the voice of Samuel; they said, "No! but we are determined to have a king over us, [20] so that we also may be like other nations, and that our king may govern us and go out before us and fight our battles." [21] When Samuel had heard all the words of the people, he repeated them in the ears of the LORD. [22] The LORD said to Samuel, "Listen to their voice and set a king over them." Samuel then said to the people of Israel, "Each of you return home."

9 There was a man of Benjamin whose name was Kish son of Abiel son of Zeror son of Becorath son of Aphiah, a Benjaminite, a man of wealth. [2] He had a son whose name was Saul, a handsome young man. There was not a man among the people of Israel more handsome than he; he stood head and shoulders above everyone else.

[3] Now the donkeys of Kish, Saul's father, had strayed. So Kish said to his son Saul, "Take one of the boys with you; go and look for the donkeys." [4] He passed through the hill country of Ephraim and passed through the land of Shalishah, but they did not find them. And they passed through the land of Shaalim, but they were not there. Then he passed through the land of Benjamin, but they did not find them.

[5] When they came to the land of Zuph, Saul said to the boy who was with him, "Let us turn back, or my father will stop worrying about the donkeys and worry about us." [6] But he said to him, "There is a man of God in this town; he is a man held in honor. Whatever he says always comes true. Let us go there now; perhaps he will tell us about the journey on which we have set out." [7] Then Saul replied

---

[a] Gk: Heb *young men*

---

2 Kings 21.15). **10**: *Asking* is a play on the name "Saul"; see 1.17n. **11–17**: These verses may preserve an older treaty document that described the rights and privileges of the king. *Ways,* the Hebrew word means "custom" or "judgment." The king to whom the people look for justice will follow the typical ancient Near Eastern practices of taxation and conscription. The items in this list appear to be based on Solomon's reign (cf. 1 Kings 4.7; 5.13). **18**: This verse is in characteristic Deuteronomistic language and resembles that of the framework of Judges, in which the people constantly *cry out* for relief from their oppressors. **19**: True to his name ("listen" in Hebrew sounds like "Samuel"), Samuel listens to God, while the people *refused to listen*. **20**: The desire to *be like other nations* is opposed to the LORD's desire that Israel be his special people. *Govern* is elsewhere translated "judge." *Go out before us* is an idiom for military leadership. The people trust in a king instead of God for protection from their enemies. **22**: The LORD will permit Israel to have a king even though he does not approve of their request. *Each of you return home* is editorial and sets the stage for Samuel to call another assembly in 10.17.

9.1–10.16: **Saul's anointing.** This is an old story that has been edited by the Deuteronomist. Samuel appears not as a judge but as a "man of God." Both Saul and kingship are depicted positively. **9.2**: *Handsome* (lit. "good"), a description often attributed to leaders (Joseph, Gen 39.6; baby Moses, Ex 2.2; David, 1 Sam 16.12). Saul's height is also an important theme in 1 Samuel, especially for its contrast with David. **3**: *Boys* (better: "servants") need not have been young. **4**: *Shalishah* and *Shaalim* may both be puns on Saul's name. **6–7**: *What can we bring,* a

to the boy, "But if we go, what can we bring the man? For the bread in our sacks is gone, and there is no present to bring to the man of God. What have we?" [8] The boy answered Saul again, "Here, I have with me a quarter shekel of silver; I will give it to the man of God, to tell us our way." [9] (Formerly in Israel, anyone who went to inquire of God would say, "Come, let us go to the seer"; for the one who is now called a prophet was formerly called a seer.) [10] Saul said to the boy, "Good; come, let us go." So they went to the town where the man of God was.

[11] As they went up the hill to the town, they met some girls coming out to draw water, and said to them, "Is the seer here?" [12] They answered, "Yes, there he is just ahead of you. Hurry; he has come just now to the town, because the people have a sacrifice today at the shrine. [13] As soon as you enter the town, you will find him, before he goes up to the shrine to eat. For the people will not eat until he comes, since he must bless the sacrifice; afterward those eat who are invited. Now go up, for you will meet him immediately." [14] So they went up to the town. As they were entering the town, they saw Samuel coming out toward them on his way up to the shrine.

[15] Now the day before Saul came, the LORD had revealed to Samuel: [16] "Tomorrow about this time I will send to you a man from the land of Benjamin, and you shall anoint him to be ruler over my people Israel. He shall save my people from the hand of the Philistines;

for I have seen the suffering of[a] my people, because their outcry has come to me." [17] When Samuel saw Saul, the LORD told him, "Here is the man of whom I spoke to you. He it is who shall rule over my people." [18] Then Saul approached Samuel inside the gate, and said, "Tell me, please, where is the house of the seer?" [19] Samuel answered Saul, "I am the seer; go up before me to the shrine, for today you shall eat with me, and in the morning I will let you go and will tell you all that is on your mind. [20] As for your donkeys that were lost three days ago, give no further thought to them, for they have been found. And on whom is all Israel's desire fixed, if not on you and on all your ancestral house?" [21] Saul answered, "I am only a Benjaminite, from the least of the tribes of Israel, and my family is the humblest of all the families of the tribe of Benjamin. Why then have you spoken to me in this way?"

[22] Then Samuel took Saul and his servant-boy and brought them into the hall, and gave them a place at the head of those who had been invited, of whom there were about thirty. [23] And Samuel said to the cook, "Bring the portion I gave you, the one I asked you to put aside." [24] The cook took up the thigh and what went with it[b] and set them before Saul. Samuel said, "See, what was kept is set before you. Eat; for it is set[c] before you at the

a Gk: Heb lacks the suffering of
b Meaning of Heb uncertain
c Q Ms Gk: MT it was kept

single word in Hebrew, spelled exactly like the word "prophet." The man of God, a title for a prophet, turns out to be Samuel (v. 14). But the identification is secondary, since Saul and his servant do not initially know who Samuel is. In the original tale, Saul's encounter was with an anonymous seer. The town, probably Ramah, Samuel's home. The present was a payment to the man of God for divining the whereabouts of the donkeys. 8: A quarter shekel was a measure of weight (ca. .10 oz [3 gm]). 9: A note by an editor indicating that the word seer had gone out of use. 11: Drawing water was done by women, usually in the morning or evening when it was cooler. Hence, it was around sundown. 12: The shrine ("high place") was a hill or raised platform where worship, especially sacrifices, took place. Deuteronomistic literature condemns the high places once the Jerusalem Temple is built. 13: Sacrifices provided occasions for feasting after the portions of the animal designated for God were burned. 16: Ruler, a special term meaning "king designate." Their outcry has come to me, cf. Ex 3.9. 18: The gate, a fortified entryway into a walled city. It was the site of commerce and judicial proceedings. 19–20: In the original tale, the seer consulted God overnight in order to address Saul's need (v. 19). But in the present, edited version, Samuel has been told to expect Saul (vv. 15–17) and now goes ahead and tells him all that is on his mind, assuring him that the donkeys have been found (v. 20). The next morning is reserved for Saul's anointing. 21: Like others called by God (Moses, Ex 3–4; Jeremiah, Jer 1), Saul objects that he is unworthy. 22–24: Saul is the honored guest. The thigh is usually reserved for the deity or priests. These verses are likely editorial, since they

appointed time, so that you might eat with the guests."[a]

So Saul ate with Samuel that day. [25] When they came down from the shrine into the town, a bed was spread for Saul[b] on the roof, and he lay down to sleep.[c] [26] Then at the break of dawn[d] Samuel called to Saul upon the roof, "Get up, so that I may send you on your way." Saul got up, and both he and Samuel went out into the street.

[27] As they were going down to the outskirts of the town, Samuel said to Saul, "Tell the boy to go on before us, and when he has passed on, stop here yourself for a while, that I may make known to you the word of God."

10 [1] Samuel took a vial of oil and poured it on his head, and kissed him; he said, "The LORD has anointed you ruler over his people Israel. You shall reign over the people of the LORD and you will save them from the hand of their enemies all around. Now this shall be the sign to you that the LORD has anointed you ruler[e] over his heritage: [2] When you depart from me today you will meet two men by Rachel's tomb in the territory of Benjamin at Zelzah; they will say to you, 'The donkeys that you went to seek are found, and now your father has stopped worrying about them and is worrying about you, saying: What shall I do about my son?' [3] Then you shall go on from there further and come to the oak of Tabor; three men going up to God at Bethel will meet you there, one carrying three kids, another carrying three loaves of bread, and another carrying a skin of wine. [4] They will greet you and give you two loaves of bread, which you shall accept from them. [5] After that you shall come to Gibeath-elohim,[f] at the place where the Philistine garrison is; there, as you come to the town, you will meet a band

of prophets coming down from the shrine with harp, tambourine, flute, and lyre playing in front of them; they will be in a prophetic frenzy. [6] Then the spirit of the LORD will possess you, and you will be in a prophetic frenzy along with them and be turned into a different person. [7] Now when these signs meet you, do whatever you see fit to do, for God is with you. [8] And you shall go down to Gilgal ahead of me; then I will come down to you to present burnt offerings and offer sacrifices of well-being. Seven days you shall wait, until I come to you and show you what you shall do."

[9] As he turned away to leave Samuel, God gave him another heart; and all these signs were fulfilled that day. [10] When they were going from there[g] to Gibeah,[h] a band of prophets met him; and the spirit of God possessed him, and he fell into a prophetic frenzy along with them. [11] When all who knew him before saw how he prophesied with the prophets, the people said to one another, "What has come over the son of Kish? Is Saul also among the prophets?" [12] A man of the place answered, "And who is their father?" Therefore it became a proverb, "Is Saul also among the prophets?" [13] When his prophetic frenzy had ended, he went home.[i]

a Cn: Heb *it was kept for you, saying, I have invited the people*
b Gk: Heb *and he spoke with Saul*
c Gk: Heb lacks *and he lay down to sleep*
d Gk: Heb *and they arose early and at break of dawn*
e Gk: Heb lacks *over his people Israel. You shall… anointed you ruler*
f Or *the Hill of God*
g Gk: Heb *they came there*
h Or *the hill*
i Cn: Heb *he came to the shrine*

presuppose Samuel's foreknowledge of Saul's arrival. **10.1:** The LORD's *heritage* is the land of Israel. Every nation is understood as the inheritance of the god it worships. The LORD, creator of the world, is envisioned as having chosen Israel as his people (Deut 10.14–15; 32.8–9). **2:** *Zelzah*, location unknown. **3:** The *three men going up to God at Bethel* are carrying items for sacrifice. Tabor is a different place than that in Judg 4.6. **4:** *Greet* is a pun on Saul's name. The men give *two loaves of bread,* one for Saul and one for his servant. The Greek (LXX) reading, "two offerings of bread," suggests that Saul again receives the portion of a priest. **5–7:** Music was used to induce an ecstatic condition in which prophets uttered their oracles (2 Kings 3.15–16); *frenzy* (vv. 5–6,10,13) is a misleadingly pejorative translation. Like the judges, Saul will be moved to action by the spirit of the LORD (see Judg 3.10; 6.34; 11.29; 13.24; etc.). The instruction to *do whatever you see fit to do* is a military commission. **8:** This verse connects this story to 13.7b–15a. **10–13:** An etiology for the proverb, *Is Saul also among the prophets?* Here the proverb has a positive sense, showing that the LORD's spirit empowers Saul to prophesy and rule. A different

¹⁴ Saul's uncle said to him and to the boy, "Where did you go?" And he replied, "To seek the donkeys; and when we saw they were not to be found, we went to Samuel." ¹⁵ Saul's uncle said, "Tell me what Samuel said to you." ¹⁶ Saul said to his uncle, "He told us that the donkeys had been found." But about the matter of the kingship, of which Samuel had spoken, he did not tell him anything.

¹⁷ Samuel summoned the people to the LORD at Mizpah ¹⁸ and said to them,ᵃ "Thus says the LORD, the God of Israel, 'I brought up Israel out of Egypt, and I rescued you from the hand of the Egyptians and from the hand of all the kingdoms that were oppressing you.' ¹⁹ But to-day you have rejected your God, who saves you from all your calamities and your distresses; and you have said, 'No! but set a king over us.' Now therefore present yourselves before the LORD by your tribes and by your clans."

²⁰ Then Samuel brought all the tribes of Israel near, and the tribe of Benjamin was taken by lot. ²¹ He brought the tribe of Benjamin near by its families, and the family of the Matrites was taken by lot. Finally he brought the family of the Matrites near man by man,ᵇ and Saul the son of Kish was taken by lot. But when they sought him, he could not be found. ²² So they inquired again of the LORD, "Did the man come here?"ᶜ and the LORD said, "See, he has hidden himself among the baggage." ²³ Then they ran and brought him from there. When he took his stand among the people, he was head and shoulders taller than any of them. ²⁴ Samuel said to all the people, "Do you see the one whom the LORD has chosen? There is no one like him among all the people." And all the people shouted, "Long live the king!"

²⁵ Samuel told the people the rights and duties of the kingship; and he wrote them in a book and laid it up before the LORD. Then Samuel sent all the people back to their homes. ²⁶ Saul also went to his home at Gibeah, and with him went warriors whose hearts God had touched. ²⁷ But some worthless fellows said, "How can this man save us?" They despised him and brought him no present. But he held his peace.

Now Nahash, king of the Ammonites, had been grievously oppressing the Gadites and the Reubenites. He would gouge out the right eye of each of them and would not grant Israel a deliverer. No one was left of the Israelites across the Jordan whose right eye Nahash, king of the Ammonites, had not gouged out. But there were seven thousand men who had escaped from the Ammonites and had entered Jabesh-gilead.ᵈ

11 About a month later,ᵉ Nahash the Ammonite went up and besieged Jabesh-gilead; and all the men of Jabesh said

ᵃ Heb *to the people of Israel*

ᵇ Gk: Heb lacks *Finally … man by man*

ᶜ Gk: Heb *Is there yet a man to come here?*

ᵈ Q Ms Compare Josephus, *Antiquities* VI.v.1 (68-71): MT lacks *Now Nahash … entered Jabesh-gilead.*

ᵉ Q Ms Gk: MT lacks *About a month later*

explanation of the proverb occurs in 19.19–24. The *father* of a group of prophets (v. 12) is their leader. **14–16:** It is surprising that Saul's uncle rather than his father questions him, since the uncle has not been mentioned before in the story. These verses are an editorial addition that prepares for the following story (10.17–27a) by pointing out that since Saul's anointing was private, a public proclamation of his kingship is needed.

10.17–27a: Saul chosen by lot. 17: *Mizpah,* see 7.5n. **18–19:** The language of these verses is Deuteronomistic, especially the references to bringing up *Israel out of Egypt* and the accusation that they have *rejected* their God. **20–21:** Israelite society was structured in a descending hierarchy of tribe, clan, family ("house of the father"), and individual. In the Bible (Josh 7.14; 1 Sam 14.41) the lot is used to find by divine assistance a person guilty of breaking a law or vow. Some scholars believe that two stories are combined at this point, one in which Saul was present and chosen by lot and another in which he was chosen by oracle or because of his height. **22:** *Inquired,* another pun on Saul's name. **25:** *The rights and duties of the kingship* probably set out the responsibilities of king and people to each other. The expression here is nearly identical to "the ways of the king" in 8.9,11, although they may not refer to the same document. **26–27a:** Saul's return to Gibeah and the doubts of the *worthless fellows* prepare for the subsequent story in which Saul proves his ability to save Israel. By bringing him *no present* these people refuse to accept him as king.

10.27b–11.15: Saul proves himself able to lead in battle and is publicly made king. 10.27b: This paragraph was lost from the Hebrew text and has been restored from a Dead Sea Scroll fragment of Samuel, as the transla-tors' note indicates. The paragraph explains the reason for the conflict in ch 11. *The Gadites and the Reubenites*

to Nahash, "Make a treaty with us, and we will serve you." ² But Nahash the Ammonite said to them, "On this condition I will make a treaty with you, namely that I gouge out everyone's right eye, and thus put disgrace upon all Israel." ³ The elders of Jabesh said to him, "Give us seven days' respite that we may send messengers through all the territory of Israel. Then, if there is no one to save us, we will give ourselves up to you." ⁴ When the messengers came to Gibeah of Saul, they reported the matter in the hearing of the people; and all the people wept aloud.

⁵ Now Saul was coming from the field behind the oxen; and Saul said, "What is the matter with the people, that they are weeping?" So they told him the message from the inhabitants of Jabesh. ⁶ And the spirit of God came upon Saul in power when he heard these words, and his anger was greatly kindled. ⁷ He took a yoke of oxen, and cut them in pieces and sent them throughout all the territory of Israel by messengers, saying, "Whoever does not come out after Saul and Samuel, so shall it be done to his oxen!" Then the dread of the LORD fell upon the people, and they came out as one. ⁸ When he mustered them at Bezek, those from Israel were three hundred thousand, and those

from Judah seventy^a thousand. ⁹ They said to the messengers who had come, "Thus shall you say to the inhabitants of Jabesh-gilead: 'Tomorrow, by the time the sun is hot, you shall have deliverance.'" When the messengers came and told the inhabitants of Jabesh, they rejoiced. ¹⁰ So the inhabitants of Jabesh said, "Tomorrow we will give ourselves up to you, and you may do to us whatever seems good to you." ¹¹ The next day Saul put the people in three companies. At the morning watch they came into the camp and cut down the Ammonites until the heat of the day; and those who survived were scattered, so that no two of them were left together.

¹² The people said to Samuel, "Who is it that said, 'Shall Saul reign over us?' Give them to us so that we may put them to death." ¹³ But Saul said, "No one shall be put to death this day, for today the LORD has brought deliverance to Israel."

¹⁴ Samuel said to the people, "Come, let us go to Gilgal and there renew the kingship." ¹⁵ So all the people went to Gilgal, and there they made Saul king before the LORD in Gilgal. There they sacrificed offerings of well-

a   Q Ms Gk: MT *thirty*

were Israelites living east of the Jordan in territory that the Ammonite king, Nahash, considered his. The city of Jabesh in Gilead was farther north, outside the disputed area, but Nahash threatened it because some of the Israelites from Gad and Reuben had fled there. **2:** As a visible sign of their subjugation and a punishment for encroaching on his land, *Nahash* had been gouging out *everyone's right eye* among the Gadites and Reubenites (10.27b). **3:** The *elders of Jabesh* are willing to accept Nahash as their overlord. But he insists on the same measure against them as a punishment for their harboring those who fled from him and as a sign of *disgrace upon all Israel.* **3:** The messengers are not sent directly to Saul but *through all the territory of Israel,* thus indicating that this story was independent of preceding ones. **4–5:** Even in Gibeah the messengers do not seek out Saul; he learns of their mission because of the weeping of the people as he returns from the field. The story, then, does not assume that Saul is king. **6:** The *spirit of God* spurs Saul to military action as in the book of Judges (see 1 Sam 10.7n). **7:** Saul's dismembering the oxen represents a threat against those who do not join in the war. Dismemberment was a common curse for breaking a treaty, so that Saul's actions assume a treaty or covenant among the tribes. **8:** The distinction between Israel and Judah either is an anachronism or reflects a differentiation that was always felt if not institutionalized until after Solomon's reign. **10:** *We will give ourselves up to you,* lit. "we will come out to you" as in v. 3, could also be understood as "we will fight against you." **11:** Their day began at sundown, hence *the next day* would be "that evening" in our reckoning. *The morning watch* was in the early hours before sunrise. The Israelites marched all night to attack by surprise before dawn. **12–14:** An editorial addition that links 10.17–27a with 10.27b–11.15. *Samuel* plays no role in the preceding battle account; his name was probably added secondarily to the story. The editor also speaks of *renewing the kingship.* These verses, and the story as a whole, show how Saul succeeded in delivering Israel and thus answering his critics, and thereby present him in a positive light. **15:** The original story did not assume that Saul was already king but explained that the people *made Saul king* as a result of his victory on this occasion.

being before the LORD, and there Saul and all the Israelites rejoiced greatly.

12 Samuel said to all Israel, "I have listened to you in all that you have said to me, and have set a king over you. ² See, it is the king who leads you now; I am old and gray, but my sons are with you. I have led you from my youth until this day. ³ Here I am; testify against me before the LORD and before his anointed. Whose ox have I taken? Or whose donkey have I taken? Or whom have I defrauded? Whom have I oppressed? Or from whose hand have I taken a bribe to blind my eyes with it? Testify against me[a] and I will restore it to you." ⁴ They said, "You have not defrauded us or oppressed us or taken anything from the hand of anyone." ⁵ He said to them, "The LORD is witness against you, and his anointed is witness this day, that you have not found anything in my hand." And they said, "He is witness."

⁶ Samuel said to the people, "The LORD is witness, who[b] appointed Moses and Aaron and brought your ancestors up out of the land of Egypt. ⁷ Now therefore take your stand, so that I may enter into judgment with you before the LORD, and I will declare to you[c] all the saving deeds of the LORD that he performed for you and for your ancestors. ⁸ When Jacob went into Egypt and the Egyptians oppressed them,[d] then your ancestors cried to the LORD and the LORD sent Moses and Aaron, who brought forth your ancestors out of Egypt, and settled them in this place. ⁹ But they forgot the LORD their God; and he sold them into the hand of Sisera, commander of the army of King Jabin of[e] Hazor, and into the hand of the Philistines, and

into the hand of the king of Moab; and they fought against them. ¹⁰ Then they cried to the LORD, and said, 'We have sinned, because we have forsaken the LORD, and have served the Baals and the Astartes; but now rescue us out of the hand of our enemies, and we will serve you.' ¹¹ And the LORD sent Jerubbaal and Barak,[f] and Jephthah, and Samson,[g] and rescued you out of the hand of your enemies on every side; and you lived in safety. ¹² But when you saw that King Nahash of the Ammonites came against you, you said to me, 'No, but a king shall reign over us,' though the LORD your God was your king. ¹³ See, here is the king whom you have chosen, for whom you have asked; see, the LORD has set a king over you. ¹⁴ If you will fear the LORD and serve him and heed his voice and not rebel against the commandment of the LORD, and if both you and the king who reigns over you will follow the LORD your God, it will be well; ¹⁵ but if you will not heed the voice of the LORD, but rebel against the commandment of the LORD, then the hand of the LORD will be against you and your king.[h] ¹⁶ Now therefore take your stand and see this great thing that the LORD will do before your eyes. ¹⁷ Is it not the wheat harvest today? I will call upon the LORD, that he may send thunder and rain; and you shall

a Gk: Heb lacks *Testify against me*
b Gk: Heb lacks *is witness, who*
c Gk: Heb lacks *and I will declare to you*
d Gk: Heb lacks *and the Egyptians oppressed them*
e Gk: Heb lacks *King Jabin of*
f Gk Syr: Heb *Bedan*
g Gk: Heb *Samuel*
h Gk: Heb *and your ancestors*

12.1–25: Samuel's address. This chapter is a Deuteronomistic composition. Ancient historians often placed speeches, which they themselves composed and considered appropriate to the occasion, into the mouths of their characters. See, e.g., Josh 23–24 and 1 Kings 8. Most of Deuteronomy is cast as a speech of Moses. **2:** *My sons are with you,* Samuel is not putting his sons forward as leaders but mentions them as illustrating his old age; they are fully grown. **3:** Samuel's actions contrast with the "ways of the king" in 8.11–18; cf. Moses' words in Num 16.15. **6–12:** This retrospective on Israel's history is Deuteronomistic in language and orientation. **9:** *Sisera,* see Judg 4.2. *Philistines,* see Judg 13.1. *Moab,* see Judg 3.12. **10:** *Baals and the Astartes,* see 7.3–4. **11:** *Barak,* see Judg 4.6. The Hebrew text reads "Bedan." There is no story about Bedan in the book of Judges. Some scholars think Bedan reflects a distinct tradition; others think it is another name for Jephthah. If Barak is correct, the order here differs from Judges. *Jerubbaal,* see Judg 6.32. *Jephthah,* see Judg 11. *Samson,* see Judg 13–16. The Hebrew has "Samuel"; in either case, the reference is to the last judge. **12:** The mention of *Nahash* differs from ch 8, in which the Philistine threat leads the Israelites to request a king. **13:** *For whom you have asked,* a pun on Saul's name. **16–18:** The *wheat harvest* was in early summer, when rain would be very rare and a threat to the crops.

know and see that the wickedness that you have done in the sight of the LORD is great in demanding a king for yourselves." [18] So Samuel called upon the LORD, and the LORD sent thunder and rain that day; and all the people greatly feared the LORD and Samuel.

[19] All the people said to Samuel, "Pray to the LORD your God for your servants, so that we may not die; for we have added to all our sins the evil of demanding a king for ourselves." [20] And Samuel said to the people, "Do not be afraid; you have done all this evil, yet do not turn aside from following the LORD, but serve the LORD with all your heart; [21] and do not turn aside after useless things that cannot profit or save, for they are useless. [22] For the LORD will not cast away his people, for his great name's sake, because it has pleased the LORD to make you a people for himself. [23] Moreover as for me, far be it from me that I should sin against the LORD by ceasing to pray for you; and I will instruct you in the good and the right way. [24] Only fear the LORD, and serve him faithfully with all your heart; for consider what great things he has done for you. [25] But if you still do wickedly, you shall be swept away, both you and your king."

13 Saul was...[a] years old when he began to reign; and he reigned... and two[b] years over Israel.

[2] Saul chose three thousand out of Israel; two thousand were with Saul in Michmash and the hill country of Bethel, and a thousand were with Jonathan in Gibeah of Benjamin; the rest of the people he sent home to their tents. [3] Jonathan defeated the garrison of the Philistines that was at Geba; and the Philistines heard of it. And Saul blew the trumpet throughout all the land, saying, "Let the Hebrews hear!" [4] When all Israel heard that Saul had defeated the garrison of the

Philistines, and also that Israel had become odious to the Philistines, the people were called out to join Saul at Gilgal.

[5] The Philistines mustered to fight with Israel, thirty thousand chariots, and six thousand horsemen, and troops like the sand on the seashore in multitude; they came up and encamped at Michmash, to the east of Beth-aven. [6] When the Israelites saw that they were in distress (for the troops were hard pressed), the people hid themselves in caves and in holes and in rocks and in tombs and in cisterns. [7] Some Hebrews crossed the Jordan to the land of Gad and Gilead. Saul was still at Gilgal, and all the people followed him trembling.

[8] He waited seven days, the time appointed by Samuel; but Samuel did not come to Gilgal, and the people began to slip away from Saul.[c] [9] So Saul said, "Bring the burnt offering here to me, and the offerings of well-being." And he offered the burnt offering. [10] As soon as he had finished offering the burnt offering, Samuel arrived; and Saul went out to meet him and salute him. [11] Samuel said, "What have you done?" Saul replied, "When I saw that the people were slipping away from me, and that you did not come within the days appointed, and that the Philistines were mustering at Michmash, [12] I said, 'Now the Philistines will come down upon me at Gilgal, and I have not entreated the favor of the LORD'; so I forced myself, and offered the burnt offering." [13] Samuel said to Saul, "You have done foolishly; you have not kept the commandment of the LORD your God, which

a The number is lacking in the Heb text (the verse is lacking in the Septuagint).
b *Two* is not the entire number; something has dropped out.
c Heb *him*

Thus, it shows the LORD's response to Samuel and hints at his displeasure with the people. *Demanding* (vv. 17,19) is another pun on "Saul." **22:** *For his great name's sake*, the LORD's reputation might be damaged if he destroyed them too readily; see Num 14.13–16. **24–25:** The theology of divine reward and punishment is Deuteronomistic.

13.1–7a: Saul begins the war with the Philistines. 1: Saul's age and length of reign are uncertain. The Hebrew literally says that he was a year old when he began to reign and reigned two years; see the translators' notes. **3:** *Jonathan,* Saul's son, appears here for the first time, and as a grown man, indicating that this story is much later than 9.1–10.16, in which Saul is a young man. *Geba* and Gibeah are very similar in Hebrew and may be confused here. **4:** Saul, as king, is apparently given credit for his son's victory. **5:** *Beth-aven,* probably an alternative name for Bethel (v. 2). **7:** *Gad and Gilead,* east of the Jordan.

13.7b–15a: Saul's sin and rejection by God. 8: *The time appointed by Samuel* was *seven days* (10.8), but the

he commanded you. The LORD would have established your kingdom over Israel forever, [14] but now your kingdom will not continue; the LORD has sought out a man after his own heart; and the LORD has appointed him to be ruler over his people, because you have not kept what the LORD commanded you." [15] And Samuel left and went on his way from Gilgal.[a] The rest of the people followed Saul to join the army; they went up from Gilgal toward Gibeah of Benjamin.[b]

Saul counted the people who were present with him, about six hundred men. [16] Saul, his son Jonathan, and the people who were present with them stayed in Geba of Benjamin; but the Philistines encamped at Michmash. [17] And raiders came out of the camp of the Philistines in three companies; one company turned toward Ophrah, to the land of Shual, [18] another company turned toward Beth-horon, and another company turned toward the mountain[c] that looks down upon the valley of Zeboim toward the wilderness.

[19] Now there was no smith to be found throughout all the land of Israel; for the Philistines said, "The Hebrews must not make swords or spears for themselves"; [20] so all the Israelites went down to the Philistines to sharpen their plowshares, mattocks, axes, or sickles;[d] [21] The charge was two-thirds of a shekel[e] for the plowshares and for the mattocks, and one-third of a shekel for sharpening the axes and for setting the goads.[f] [22] So on the day of the battle neither sword nor

spear was to be found in the possession of any of the people with Saul and Jonathan; but Saul and his son Jonathan had them.

[23] Now a garrison of the Philistines had gone out to the pass of Michmash.

14 [1] One day Jonathan son of Saul said to the young man who carried his armor, "Come, let us go over to the Philistine garrison on the other side." But he did not tell his father. [2] Saul was staying in the outskirts of Gibeah under the pomegranate tree that is at Migron; the troops that were with him were about six hundred men, [3] along with Ahijah son of Ahitub, Ichabod's brother, son of Phinehas son of Eli, the priest of the LORD in Shiloh, carrying an ephod. Now the people did not know that Jonathan had gone. [4] In the pass,[g] by which Jonathan tried to go over to the Philistine garrison, there was a rocky crag on one side and a rocky crag on the other; the name of the one was Bozez, and the name of the other Seneh. [5] One crag rose on the north in front of Michmash, and the other on the south in front of Geba.

[6] Jonathan said to the young man who carried his armor, "Come, let us go over to

a   Gk: Heb *went up from Gilgal to Gibeah of Benjamin*
b   Gk: Heb lacks *The rest … of Benjamin*
c   Cn Compare Gk: Heb *toward the border*
d   Gk: Heb *plowshare*
e   Heb *was a pim*
f   Cn: Meaning of Heb uncertain
g   Heb *Between the passes*

intervening events in chs 10–12 require a much longer time. **13–14:** The nature of Saul's sin is not clear; perhaps he tried to usurp Samuel's role of religious leadership. But cf. 14.35, where Saul builds an altar to the LORD without being criticized. *Your kingdom,* like David (2 Sam 7.13–16), Saul had a chance to establish a long-lasting dynasty, but his sin prevented this. Another rejection, perhaps of Saul's individual kingship, occurs in ch 15. The *man after* the LORD's *own heart,* an allusion to David, is a way of saying he is chosen by the LORD and does not necessarily imply any special quality on David's part.

13.15b–14.52: Continuation of the Philistine war. 13.15b–23: These verses set the stage for the battle account in the next chapter. *Geba* and *Michmash* (v. 16) were across from each other on opposite sides of a valley. The Philistine domination took two forms: *Raiders* customarily went out from Michmash to attack Israelite settlements (vv. 17–18), and the Philistines controlled metalworking and hence the manufacture of weapons (vv. 19–22). **21:** A shekel (of silver) weighed ca. .4 oz (11.4 gr). **23:** The battle begins with the Philistines moving to the pass on their side of the valley. **14.1:** *The Philistine garrison on the other side* was the one sent as reinforcements (13.23). The Israelites and Philistines were camped on opposite sides of the ravine at Geba and Michmash, respectively (14.5). Jonathan's plan is to defeat this garrison and then perhaps to rally the Israelites who were hiding (vv. 11,22) into joining in and driving the Philistines back. **3:** For *Ichabod* and *Phinehas,* see 4.4,19. *Carrying an ephod,* not the linen ephod of 2.18, but a box whose contents were used to divine the will of God (v. 41; Ex 28.30). It was carried in priestly garments, which may be why the same word was used for both. *The people* often

the garrison of these uncircumcised; it may be that the LORD will act for us; for nothing can hinder the LORD from saving by many or by few." [7] His armor-bearer said to him, "Do all that your mind inclines to.[a] I am with you; as your mind is, so is mine."[b] [8] Then Jonathan said, "Now we will cross over to those men and will show ourselves to them. [9] If they say to us, 'Wait until we come to you,' then we will stand still in our place, and we will not go up to them. [10] But if they say, 'Come up to us,' then we will go up; for the LORD has given them into our hand. That will be the sign for us." [11] So both of them showed themselves to the garrison of the Philistines; and the Philistines said, "Look, Hebrews are coming out of the holes where they have hidden themselves." [12] The men of the garrison hailed Jonathan and his armor-bearer, saying, "Come up to us, and we will show you something." Jonathan said to his armor-bearer, "Come up after me; for the LORD has given them into the hand of Israel." [13] Then Jonathan climbed up on his hands and feet, with his armor-bearer following after him. The Philistines[c] fell before Jonathan, and his armor-bearer, coming after him, killed them. [14] In that first slaughter Jonathan and his armor-bearer killed about twenty men within an area about half a furrow long in an acre[d] of land. [15] There was a panic in the camp, in the field, and among all the people; the garrison and even the raiders trembled; the earth quaked; and it became a very great panic.

[16] Saul's lookouts in Gibeah of Benjamin were watching as the multitude was surging back and forth.[e] [17] Then Saul said to the troops that were with him, "Call the roll and see who has gone from us." When they had called the roll, Jonathan and his armor-bearer were not there. [18] Saul said to Ahijah, "Bring the ark[f] of God here." For at that time the ark[f] of God went with the Israelites. [19] While Saul was talking to the priest, the tumult in the camp of the Philistines increased more and more; and Saul said to the

priest, "Withdraw your hand." [20] Then Saul and all the people who were with him rallied and went into the battle; and every sword was against the other, so that there was very great confusion. [21] Now the Hebrews who previously had been with the Philistines and had gone up with them into the camp turned and joined the Israelites who were with Saul and Jonathan. [22] Likewise, when all the Israelites who had gone into hiding in the hill country of Ephraim heard that the Philistines were fleeing, they too followed closely after them in the battle. [23] So the LORD gave Israel the victory that day.

The battle passed beyond Beth-aven, and the troops with Saul numbered altogether about ten thousand men. The battle spread out over the hill country of Ephraim.

[24] Now Saul committed a very rash act on that day.[g] He had laid an oath on the troops, saying, "Cursed be anyone who eats food before it is evening and I have been avenged on my enemies." So none of the troops tasted food. [25] All the troops[h] came upon a honeycomb; and there was honey on the ground. [26] When the troops came upon the honeycomb, the honey was dripping out; but they did not put their hands to their mouths, for they feared the oath. [27] But Jonathan had not heard his father charge the troops with the oath; so he extended the staff that was in his hand, and dipped the tip of it in the honeycomb, and put his hand to his mouth; and his eyes brightened. [28] Then one of the soldiers said, "Your father strictly charged the troops with an oath, saying, 'Cursed be anyone who eats food this day.' And so the troops

a   Gk: Heb *Do all that is in your mind. Turn*
b   Gk: Heb lacks *so is mine*
c   Heb *They*
d   Heb *yoke*
e   Gk: Heb *they went and there*
f   Gk *the ephod*
g   Gk: Heb *The Israelites were distressed that day*
h   Heb *land*

means the army. **6:** *These uncircumcised,* a derogatory term for the Philistines, who, in contrast to the Israelites and Egyptians, did not practice male circumcision. **11:** *Hebrews,* see 4.6n. **18:** *The ark of God,* the Greek reading, "the ephod," is probably better (see v. 3). **19:** *Withdraw your hand,* Saul had called Ahijah the priest in order to consult the LORD through him, but the growing sound of battle made him decide to attack before finishing his inquiry. **21:** The *Hebrews* here are distinguished from the *Israelites.* They are first allied with the Philistines and

are faint." [29] Then Jonathan said, "My father has troubled the land; see how my eyes have brightened because I tasted a little of this honey. [30] How much better if today the troops had eaten freely of the spoil taken from their enemies; for now the slaughter among the Philistines has not been great."

[31] After they had struck down the Philistines that day from Michmash to Aijalon, the troops were very faint; [32] so the troops flew upon the spoil, and took sheep and oxen and calves, and slaughtered them on the ground; and the troops ate them with the blood. [33] Then it was reported to Saul, "Look, the troops are sinning against the LORD by eating with the blood." And he said, "You have dealt treacherously; roll a large stone before me here."[a] [34] Saul said, "Disperse yourselves among the troops, and say to them, 'Let all bring their oxen or their sheep, and slaughter them here, and eat; and do not sin against the LORD by eating with the blood.'" So all of the troops brought their oxen with them that night, and slaughtered them there. [35] And Saul built an altar to the LORD; it was the first altar that he built to the LORD.

[36] Then Saul said, "Let us go down after the Philistines by night and despoil them until the morning light; let us not leave one of them." They said, "Do whatever seems good to you." But the priest said, "Let us draw near to God here." [37] So Saul inquired of God, "Shall I go down after the Philistines? Will you give them into the hand of Israel?" But he did not answer him that day. [38] Saul said, "Come here, all you leaders of the people; and let us find out how this sin has arisen today. [39] For as the LORD lives who saves Israel, even if it is in my son Jonathan, he shall surely die!" But there was no one among all the people who answered him. [40] He said to all Israel, "You shall

be on one side, and I and my son Jonathan will be on the other side." The people said to Saul, "Do what seems good to you." [41] Then Saul said, "O LORD God of Israel, why have you not answered your servant today? If this guilt is in me or in my son Jonathan, O LORD God of Israel, give Urim; but if this guilt is in your people Israel,[b] give Thummim." And Jonathan and Saul were indicated by the lot, but the people were cleared. [42] Then Saul said, "Cast the lot between me and my son Jonathan." And Jonathan was taken.

[43] Then Saul said to Jonathan, "Tell me what you have done." Jonathan told him, "I tasted a little honey with the tip of the staff that was in my hand; here I am, I will die." [44] Saul said, "God do so to me and more also; you shall surely die, Jonathan!" [45] Then the people said to Saul, "Shall Jonathan die, who has accomplished this great victory in Israel? Far from it! As the LORD lives, not one hair of his head shall fall to the ground; for he has worked with God today." So the people ransomed Jonathan, and he did not die. [46] Then Saul withdrew from pursuing the Philistines; and the Philistines went to their own place.

[47] When Saul had taken the kingship over Israel, he fought against all his enemies on every side—against Moab, against the Ammonites, against Edom, against the kings of Zobah, and against the Philistines; wherever he turned he routed them. [48] He did valiantly, and struck down the Amalekites, and rescued Israel out of the hands of those who plundered them.

[49] Now the sons of Saul were Jonathan, Ishvi, and Malchishua; and the names of his

---

a   Gk: Heb *me this day*
b   Vg Compare Gk: Heb [41]*Saul said to the LORD*, the God of Israel

---

then turn against them; they may have been mercenaries (cf. 4.6). **24–30:** Saul's oath was an expression of piety to attract God's aid in the battle. It was foolish because his troops became faint from hunger. Most *honey* was made from dates; Jonathan has found a true delicacy (cf. Prov 25.16). **31–35:** The soldiers commit a ritual offense by slaughtering animals *on the ground* so that the blood does not drain out and eating meat cooked *with the blood,* contrary to laws such as Lev 19.26; Deut 12.16. Animals slaughtered on the *large stone* could be propped up to allow their blood to drain before cooking. **37:** *Inquired,* a pun on Saul's name. The lack of response indicates divine disfavor and may hint at God's future displeasure with Saul (see 28.6) **41–42:** The *Urim* and *Thummim* (Ex 28.30) answered yes-or-no questions and decided between two alternatives. **45:** It is not clear exactly how *the people ransomed Jonathan.* Perhaps an animal was substituted (Gen 22.13; Ex 13.13; 34.20). The story may foreshadow Jonathan's death in 31.2. **47–48:** This summary of Saul's military successes contrast (see map on p.

two daughters were these: the name of the firstborn was Merab, and the name of the younger, Michal. [50] The name of Saul's wife was Ahinoam daughter of Ahimaaz. And the name of the commander of his army was Abner son of Ner, Saul's uncle; [51] Kish was the father of Saul, and Ner the father of Abner was the son of Abiel.

[52] There was hard fighting against the Philistines all the days of Saul; and when Saul saw any strong or valiant warrior, he took him into his service.

15 Samuel said to Saul, "The LORD sent me to anoint you king over his people Israel; now therefore listen to the words of the LORD. [2] Thus says the LORD of hosts, 'I will punish the Amalekites for what they did in opposing the Israelites when they came up out of Egypt. [3] Now go and attack Amalek, and utterly destroy all that they have; do not spare them, but kill both man and woman, child and infant, ox and sheep, camel and donkey.'"

[4] So Saul summoned the people, and numbered them in Telaim, two hundred thousand foot soldiers, and ten thousand soldiers of Judah. [5] Saul came to the city of the Amalekites and lay in wait in the valley. [6] Saul said to the Kenites, "Go! Leave! Withdraw from among the Amalekites, or I will destroy you with them; for you showed kindness to all the people of Israel when they came up out of Egypt." So the Kenites withdrew from the Amalekites. [7] Saul defeated the Amalekites, from Havilah as far as Shur, which is east of Egypt. [8] He took King Agag of the Amalekites alive, but utterly destroyed all the people with the edge of the sword. [9] Saul and the people spared Agag, and the best of the sheep and of the cattle and of the fatlings, and the lambs, and all that was valuable, and would not utterly destroy them; all that was despised and worthless they utterly destroyed.

[10] The word of the LORD came to Samuel: [11] "I regret that I made Saul king, for he has turned back from following me, and has not carried out my commands." Samuel was angry; and he cried out to the LORD all night. [12] Samuel rose early in the morning to meet Saul, and Samuel was told, "Saul went to Carmel, where he set up a monument for himself, and on returning he passed on down to Gilgal." [13] When Samuel came to Saul, Saul said to him, "May you be blessed by the LORD; I have carried out the command of the LORD." [14] But Samuel said, "What then is this bleating of sheep in my ears, and the lowing of cattle that I hear?" [15] Saul said, "They have brought them from the Amalekites; for the people spared the best of the sheep and the cattle, to sacrifice to the LORD your God; but the rest we have utterly destroyed." [16] Then Samuel said to Saul, "Stop! I will tell you what the LORD said to me last night." He replied, "Speak."

[17] Samuel said, "Though you are little in your own eyes, are you not the head of the tribes of Israel? The LORD anointed you king over Israel. [18] And the LORD sent you on a mission, and said, 'Go, utterly destroy the sinners, the Amalekites, and fight against them until they are consumed.' [19] Why then did you

411) with the surrounding negative portrait of Saul. **48:** *Amalekites,* see 15.2n. **49:** *Ishvi,* perhaps another spelling of Ishbaal (2 Sam 2.8). **52:** *Any strong or valiant warrior,* an allusion to David (cf. 16.14–23).

15.1–35: Another story of Saul's rejection. Compare 13.7b–15a. **2:** *Amalekites,* a nomadic people south of Judah. The story mentioned here is recounted in Ex 17.8–16 and Deut 25.17–19. **3:** *Utterly destroy,* the "ban" or "devotion to destruction" (Heb "ḥerem") used by Israel (see Josh 6.17) and other peoples in the ancient Near East. The enemy and their property were exterminated as a kind of sacrifice to the deity. The instructions are given explicitly here in anticipation of Saul's disobedience. **4:** The numbers may be exaggerated or the word "thousand" may refer to a military unit much smaller than a thousand men (see 4.2n). **6:** *Kenites,* a clan in southern Judah; this verse indicates that they had settled with the Amalekites. Their name means "metalworkers." Their *kindness* to the Israelites is unknown. **9:** *Spared,* a direct violation of the order in v. 3. However, Saul claims (v. 15) that his intent was to kill them in sacrifice to the LORD. He may also have intended to execute Agag in some official or ritual way (vv. 32–33). **12:** Carmel, not the famous mount, but a town in Judah (Josh 15.55). **15:** Saul says his troops (*the people*) *spared the best of the sheep and the cattle,* though he is implicated in v. 9. His claim that the animals were spared for sacrifice provides the ground for Samuel's rebuke. *Your God* suggests that Saul has abandoned the LORD. **17–19:** The pronouns and verbs are singular and directed at Saul alone as *the head of*

not obey the voice of the LORD? Why did you swoop down on the spoil, and do what was evil in the sight of the LORD?" [20] Saul said to Samuel, "I have obeyed the voice of the LORD, I have gone on the mission on which the LORD sent me, I have brought Agag the king of Amalek, and I have utterly destroyed the Amalekites. [21] But from the spoil the people took sheep and cattle, the best of the things devoted to destruction, to sacrifice to the LORD your God in Gilgal." [22] And Samuel said,

"Has the LORD as great delight in burnt offerings and sacrifices,
    as in obedience to the voice of the LORD?
Surely, to obey is better than sacrifice,
    and to heed than the fat of rams.
[23] For rebellion is no less a sin than divination,
    and stubbornness is like iniquity and idolatry.
Because you have rejected the word of the LORD,
    he has also rejected you from being king."

[24] Saul said to Samuel, "I have sinned; for I have transgressed the commandment of the LORD and your words, because I feared the people and obeyed their voice. [25] Now therefore, I pray, pardon my sin, and return with me, so that I may worship the LORD." [26] Samuel said to Saul, "I will not return with you; for you have rejected the word of the LORD, and the LORD has rejected you from being king over Israel." [27] As Samuel turned to go away, Saul caught hold of the hem of his robe, and it tore. [28] And Samuel said to him, "The LORD has torn the kingdom of Israel from you

this very day, and has given it to a neighbor of yours, who is better than you. [29] Moreover the Glory of Israel will not recant[a] or change his mind; for he is not a mortal, that he should change his mind." [30] Then Saul[b] said, "I have sinned; yet honor me now before the elders of my people and before Israel, and return with me, so that I may worship the LORD your God." [31] So Samuel turned back after Saul; and Saul worshiped the LORD.

[32] Then Samuel said, "Bring Agag king of the Amalekites here to me." And Agag came to him haltingly.[c] Agag said, "Surely this is the bitterness of death."[d] [33] But Samuel said,

"As your sword has made women childless,
    so your mother shall be childless among women."

And Samuel hewed Agag in pieces before the LORD in Gilgal.

[34] Then Samuel went to Ramah; and Saul went up to his house in Gibeah of Saul. [35] Samuel did not see Saul again until the day of his death, but Samuel grieved over Saul. And the LORD was sorry that he had made Saul king over Israel.

16 The LORD said to Samuel, "How long will you grieve over Saul? I have rejected him from being king over Israel. Fill your horn with oil and set out; I will send you to Jesse the Bethlehemite, for I have provided for myself a king among his sons." [2] Samuel said, "How can I go? If Saul hears of it, he will kill me." And the LORD said, "Take a heifer

[a] Q Ms Gk: MT *deceive*
[b] Heb *he*
[c] Cn Compare Gk: Meaning of Heb uncertain
[d] Q Ms Gk: MT *Surely the bitterness of death is past*

the tribes of Israel (v. 17). **22:** *The fat of rams,* the part of the animal burned in sacrifices. The poetic form of this verse and the next recalls the oracles of the "writing" prophets (see Hos 6.6; Am 5.21–24; Mic 6.6–8). **23:** The *divination* condemned here is often related to foreign idolatry (see Deut 18.9–14). *Rebellion* and *stubbornness,* like *divination,* involve turning away from the LORD. **26:** This verse illustrates a narrative technique known to later rabbinic writers as "measure for measure"; Saul's punishment corresponds to his sin (both labeled "rejection"). See also v. 33. **27–28:** Grasping the *hem* of a person's garment was a way of submitting or pleading. Samuel uses the torn hem as an object lesson. The *neighbor* is David. Saul's robe is symbolic of his kingdom and becomes a literary motif in 1 Samuel (see ch 24). **29:** *The Glory of Israel,* an epithet for the LORD. The message of the verse seems to contradict the larger context in which the LORD has changed his mind about Saul being king. Some scholars address this contradiction by positing v. 29 as a late pious gloss. **33:** Samuel's dismemberment of Agag *before the LORD* was a ritual execution, perhaps for war crimes or violation of a treaty. **35:** *Samuel did not see Saul again until the day of his death,* anticipating ch 28 but in tension with 19.18–24.

16.1–13: The anointing of David. **1:** *Fill your horn with oil,* fine olive oil carried in a ram's horn was used for

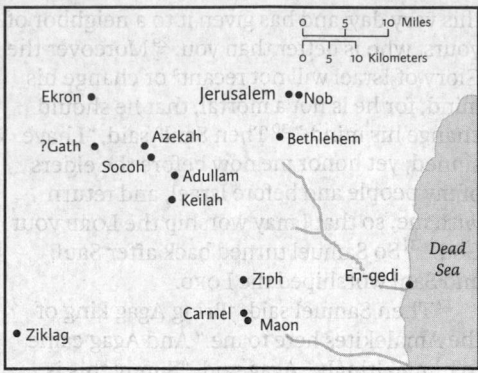

Chs 16–28: David's early career and his flight from Saul.

with you, and say, 'I have come to sacrifice to the LORD.' ³ Invite Jesse to the sacrifice, and I will show you what you shall do; and you shall anoint for me the one whom I name to you." ⁴ Samuel did what the LORD commanded, and came to Bethlehem. The elders of the city came to meet him trembling, and said, "Do you come peaceably?" ⁵ He said, "Peaceably; I have come to sacrifice to the LORD; sanctify yourselves and come with me to the sacrifice." And he sanctified Jesse and his sons and invited them to the sacrifice.

⁶ When they came, he looked on Eliab and thought, "Surely the LORD's anointed is now before the LORD."ᵃ ⁷ But the LORD said to Samuel, "Do not look on his appearance or on the height of his stature, because I have rejected him; for the LORD does not see as mortals see; they look on the outward appearance, but the

LORD looks on the heart." ⁸ Then Jesse called Abinadab, and made him pass before Samuel. He said, "Neither has the LORD chosen this one." ⁹ Then Jesse made Shammah pass by. And he said, "Neither has the LORD chosen this one." ¹⁰ Jesse made seven of his sons pass before Samuel, and Samuel said to Jesse, "The LORD has not chosen any of these." ¹¹ Samuel said to Jesse, "Are all your sons here?" And he said, "There remains yet the youngest, but he is keeping the sheep." And Samuel said to Jesse, "Send and bring him; for we will not sit down until he comes here." ¹² He sent and brought him in. Now he was ruddy, and had beautiful eyes, and was handsome. The LORD said, "Rise and anoint him; for this is the one." ¹³ Then Samuel took the horn of oil, and anointed him in the presence of his brothers; and the spirit of the LORD came mightily upon David from that day forward. Samuel then set out and went to Ramah.

¹⁴ Now the spirit of the LORD departed from Saul, and an evil spirit from the LORD tormented him. ¹⁵ And Saul's servants said to him, "See now, an evil spirit from God is tormenting you. ¹⁶ Let our lord now command the servants who attend you to look for someone who is skillful in playing the lyre; and when the evil spirit from God is upon you, he will play it, and you will feel better." ¹⁷ So Saul said to his servants, "Provide for me someone who can play well, and bring him to me." ¹⁸ One of the young men answered,

ᵃ Heb *him*

anointing a new king. **4–5:** Jesse seems to be among the *elders* or civic leaders of Bethlehem. Their *trembling* is perhaps because they suspect the nature of Samuel's mission and fear that his visit will bring consequences from Saul. Or perhaps they are afraid that he has come to condemn them for some wrongdoing. **6–7:** Eliab's height and good looks are reminiscent of Saul, whom the LORD has rejected as king. God is more impressed with inner qualities or the *heart*, which Samuel cannot know. **8–9:** Samuel is likely using some device like the Urim and Thummim to determine whether each of Jesse's sons is the chosen one. **10:** This verse and 17.12 credit Jesse with eight sons, while 1 Chr 2.13–15 mentions only seven. As the seventh son David would have been seen as specially blessed. His description as the eighth son may highlight his humble origins. **11:** *Youngest* may also mean "the smallest" and contrasts David with Saul. *Keeping the sheep*, shepherd was a common metaphor for a king (e.g., 2 Sam 5.2). **12:** *Ruddy* means "reddish" of hair and complexion (see Gen 25.25). *Handsome*, see 9.2n. **13:** *Spirit of the LORD*, see 10.5–7.

16.14–23: David wins a position at Saul's court. 14: The departure of *the spirit of the LORD* from Saul (cf. 10.5–7n) and its replacement by an *evil spirit from the LORD* further contrasts Saul and David (v. 13). The evil spirit may describe mental illness. The theological point is that the LORD abandoned Saul. **16:** *Lyre*, a hand-held stringed instrument. Musicians were thought to ward off evil spirits. **18:** *A man of valor*, a "nobleman" or "man of wealth" (9.1). *Prudent in speech* implies both eloquence and cleverness. *The LORD is with him*, a central theme

"I have seen a son of Jesse the Bethlehemite who is skillful in playing, a man of valor, a warrior, prudent in speech, and a man of good presence; and the LORD is with him." [19] So Saul sent messengers to Jesse, and said, "Send me your son David who is with the sheep." [20] Jesse took a donkey loaded with bread, a skin of wine, and a kid, and sent them by his son David to Saul. [21] And David came to Saul, and entered his service. Saul loved him greatly, and he became his armor-bearer. [22] Saul sent to Jesse, saying, "Let David remain in my service, for he has found favor in my sight." [23] And whenever the evil spirit from God came upon Saul, David took the lyre and played it with his hand, and Saul would be relieved and feel better, and the evil spirit would depart from him.

17 Now the Philistines gathered their armies for battle; they were gathered at Socoh, which belongs to Judah, and encamped between Socoh and Azekah, in Ephes-dammim. [2] Saul and the Israelites gathered and encamped in the valley of Elah, and formed ranks against the Philistines. [3] The Philistines stood on the mountain on the one side, and Israel stood on the mountain on the other side, with a valley between them. [4] And there came out from the camp of the Philistines a champion named Goliath, of Gath, whose height was six[a] cubits and a span. [5] He had a helmet of bronze on his head, and he was armed with a coat of mail; the weight of the coat was five thousand

shekels of bronze. [6] He had greaves of bronze on his legs and a javelin of bronze slung between his shoulders. [7] The shaft of his spear was like a weaver's beam, and his spear's head weighed six hundred shekels of iron; and his shield-bearer went before him. [8] He stood and shouted to the ranks of Israel, "Why have you come out to draw up for battle? Am I not a Philistine, and are you not servants of Saul? Choose a man for yourselves, and let him come down to me. [9] If he is able to fight with me and kill me, then we will be your servants; but if I prevail against him and kill him, then you shall be our servants and serve us." [10] And the Philistine said, "Today I defy the ranks of Israel! Give me a man, that we may fight together." [11] When Saul and all Israel heard these words of the Philistine, they were dismayed and greatly afraid.

[12] Now David was the son of an Ephrathite of Bethlehem in Judah, named Jesse, who had eight sons. In the days of Saul the man was already old and advanced in years.[b] [13] The three eldest sons of Jesse had followed Saul to the battle; the names of his three sons who went to the battle were Eliab the firstborn, and next to him Abinadab, and the third Shammah. [14] David was the youngest; the three eldest followed Saul, [15] but David went back and forth from Saul to feed his father's sheep at Bethlehem. [16] For forty days the

[a] MT: Q Ms Gk *four*
[b] Gk Syr: Heb *among men*

of the David story. **19:** David's role as a shepherd (see v. 11n) again hints at his future as king. **21:** *Armor-bearer* indicates David's skill as a warrior and his closeness to Saul.

17.1–58: David defeats the Philistine champion. An initial version of this story in vv. 1–11,32–49,51–54 has been extensively supplemented in the Hebrew text by vv. 12–31,50,55–58; 18.1–5. The supplementary material is absent from the Greek translation (the Septuagint, or LXX). Its addition has caused inconsistencies relating to David's presence in Saul's army, the way in which the Philistine died, and Saul's acquaintance with David. **4:** *Goliath*, a Philistine name, occurs only here and in v. 23, which is supplemental. Otherwise, David's opponent is called "the Philistine." The name has come into the story from 2 Sam 21.19, which says that a certain Elhanan killed Goliath. *Six cubits and a span*, about 9.5 ft (3 m). The Greek reading, "four cubits and a span," (6.6 ft [2 m]) is more realistic and probably original. The number "six" was mistakenly imported here (in place of "four") from v. 7. David's small stature contrasts with Goliath's as with Saul's. **5–7:** The armor described here reflects items from different armies at different times and is designed to give an imposing picture of the Philistine. **5:** *Five thousand shekels*, ca. 125 lb (57 kg). **6:** *Greaves*, armor for the shins. *Javelin*, better: "scimitar." **7:** The spear's description is borrowed from 2 Sam 21.19. *A weaver's beam* may refer to size or to a leather thong attached to some spears to facilitate hurling. *Six hundred shekels of iron*, ca. 15 lb (7 kg). **12:** *Ephrathites*, a subgroup within the Calebite clan, which was part of the tribe of Judah. The introduction of David suggests the beginning of a once independent version of the story. **14–15:** Here, David is a shepherd boy running errands rather than a

Philistine came forward and took his stand, morning and evening.

¹⁷ Jesse said to his son David, "Take for your brothers an ephah of this parched grain and these ten loaves, and carry them quickly to the camp to your brothers; ¹⁸ also take these ten cheeses to the commander of their thousand. See how your brothers fare, and bring some token from them."

¹⁹ Now Saul, and they, and all the men of Israel, were in the valley of Elah, fighting with the Philistines. ²⁰ David rose early in the morning, left the sheep with a keeper, took the provisions, and went as Jesse had commanded him. He came to the encampment as the army was going forth to the battle line, shouting the war cry. ²¹ Israel and the Philistines drew up for battle, army against army. ²² David left the things in charge of the keeper of the baggage, ran to the ranks, and went and greeted his brothers. ²³ As he talked with them, the champion, the Philistine of Gath, Goliath by name, came up out of the ranks of the Philistines, and spoke the same words as before. And David heard him.

²⁴ All the Israelites, when they saw the man, fled from him and were very much afraid. ²⁵ The Israelites said, "Have you seen this who has come up? Surely he has come up to defy Israel. The king will greatly enrich the man who kills him, and will give him his daughter and make his family free in Israel." ²⁶ David said to the men who stood by him, "What shall be done for the man who kills this Philistine, and takes away the reproach from Israel? For who is this uncircumcised Philistine that he should defy the armies of the living God?" ²⁷ The people answered him in the same way, "So shall it be done for the man who kills him."

²⁸ His eldest brother Eliab heard him talking to the men; and Eliab's anger was kindled against David. He said, "Why have you come down? With whom have you left those few sheep in the wilderness? I know your presumption and the evil of your heart; for you have come down just to see the battle." ²⁹ David said, "What have I done now? It was only a question." ³⁰ He turned away from him toward another and spoke in the same way; and the people answered him again as before.

³¹ When the words that David spoke were heard, they repeated them before Saul; and he sent for him. ³² David said to Saul, "Let no one's heart fail because of him; your servant will go and fight with this Philistine." ³³ Saul said to David, "You are not able to go against this Philistine to fight with him; for you are just a boy, and he has been a warrior from his youth." ³⁴ But David said to Saul, "Your servant used to keep sheep for his father; and whenever a lion or a bear came, and took a lamb from the flock, ³⁵ I went after it and struck it down, rescuing the lamb from its mouth; and if it turned against me, I would catch it by the jaw, strike it down, and kill it. ³⁶ Your servant has killed both lions and bears; and this uncircumcised Philistine shall be like one of them, since he has defied the armies of the living God." ³⁷ David said, "The LORD, who saved me from the paw of the lion and from the paw of the bear, will save me from the hand of this Philistine." So Saul said to David, "Go, and may the LORD be with you!"

³⁸ Saul clothed David with his armor; he put a bronze helmet on his head and clothed him with a coat of mail. ³⁹ David strapped Saul's sword over the armor, and he tried in vain to walk, for he was not used to them. Then David said to Saul, "I cannot walk with these; for I am not used to them." So David removed them. ⁴⁰ Then he took his staff in his hand, and chose five smooth stones from the

warrior as in 16.14–23. **16:** In this supplementary version of the story, the Philistine had been challenging the Israelites *for forty days*, while the initial version had David fight him the first time he comes out. **17:** *An ephah*, ca. .6 bu (23 l). **18:** *Some token*, a personal effect showing that the brothers were well. **25:** *Free in Israel* means exempt from slavery and from taxes and compulsory military service. **31:** *Saul* appears for the first time in the story here. Though king of Israel, he is eclipsed by David. **32:** *Your servant*, a polite term for oneself before a superior. **38–39:** David's inability to move in Saul's armor emphasizes his lack of experience as a soldier. It also shows Saul's failure to understand that David's advantage lay in his mobility. **40:** *His staff*, a shepherd's staff, not a weapon. The Philistine sees it as a stick (v. 43). *Wadi*, a dry streambed. The *sling* was not a toy but a standard weapon of ancient warfare. It consisted of two cords attached to a pouch from which a stone could be hurled a

wadi, and put them in his shepherd's bag, in the pouch; his sling was in his hand, and he drew near to the Philistine. ⁴¹ The Philistine came on and drew near to David, with his shield-bearer in front of him. ⁴² When the Philistine looked and saw David, he disdained him, for he was only a youth, ruddy and handsome in appearance. ⁴³ The Philistine said to David, "Am I a dog, that you come to me with sticks?" And the Philistine cursed David by his gods. ⁴⁴ The Philistine said to David, "Come to me, and I will give your flesh to the birds of the air and to the wild animals of the field." ⁴⁵ But David said to the Philistine, "You come to me with sword and spear and javelin; but I come to you in the name of the Lord of hosts, the God of the armies of Israel, whom you have defied. ⁴⁶ This very day the Lord will deliver you into my hand, and I will strike you down and cut off your head; and I will give the dead bodies of the Philistine army this very day to the birds of the air and to the wild animals of the earth, so that all the earth may know that there is a God in Israel, ⁴⁷ and that all this assembly may know that the Lord does not save by sword and spear; for the battle is the Lord's and he will give you into our hand." ⁴⁸ When the Philistine drew nearer to meet David, David ran quickly toward the battle line to meet the Philistine. ⁴⁹ David put his hand in his bag, took out a stone, slung it, and struck the Philistine on his forehead; the stone sank into his forehead, and he fell face down on the ground.

⁵⁰ So David prevailed over the Philistine with a sling and a stone, striking down the Philistine and killing him; there was no sword in David's hand. ⁵¹ Then David ran and stood over the Philistine; he grasped his sword, drew it out of its sheath, and killed him; then he cut off his head with it.

When the Philistines saw that their champion was dead, they fled. ⁵² The troops of Israel and Judah rose up with a shout and pursued the Philistines as far as Gathᵃ and the gates of Ekron, so that the wounded Philistines fell on the way from Shaaraim as far as Gath and Ekron. ⁵³ The Israelites came back from chasing the Philistines, and they plundered their camp. ⁵⁴ David took the head of the Philistine and brought it to Jerusalem; but he put his armor in his tent.

⁵⁵ When Saul saw David go out against the Philistine, he said to Abner, the commander of the army, "Abner, whose son is this young man?" Abner said, "As your soul lives, O king, I do not know." ⁵⁶ The king said, "Inquire whose son the stripling is." ⁵⁷ On David's return from killing the Philistine, Abner took him and brought him before Saul, with the head of the Philistine in his hand. ⁵⁸ Saul said to him, "Whose son are you, young man?" And David answered, "I am the son of your servant Jesse the Bethlehemite."

18

When Davidᵇ had finished speaking to Saul, the soul of Jonathan was bound to the soul of David, and Jonathan loved him as his own soul. ² Saul took him that day and would not let him return to his father's house. ³ Then Jonathan made a covenant with David, because he loved him as his own soul. ⁴ Jonathan stripped himself of the robe that

ᵃ Gk Syr: Heb *Gai*
ᵇ Heb *he*

considerable distance with great force and accuracy (Judg 20.16). **41–47:** Ancient warfare included taunting and trying to demoralize one's enemy. David's speech (vv. 45–47) is religious in nature and promises retribution for the Philistine's defiance of the Lord. David says he does not need the Philistine's arms because the Lord fights for him. The Philistine is distracted by David's staff (v. 43) and overlooks his real weapon, the sling. **49:** David's stone strikes the Philistine in the spot where he is vulnerable. David's speech shows that this is understood as God's doing. **50–51:** These verses make it appear as though David killed the Philistine twice, once with the sling stone (v. 50) and once by beheading him with his own sword (v. 51). The repetition results from the combination of two versions of the story, but v. 50 can be read as an overview of the entire episode. **54:** *Jerusalem*, an anachronism, since Jerusalem was conquered after David became king of Israel (2 Sam 5.6–9). *His tent*, perhaps read "the tent (shrine) of Yahweh." Goliath's sword later surfaces with the priests at Nob (21.9). **55:** *Whose son is this young man?*, idiomatic for "Who is this?" It indicates the story's originally independent nature, since according to 16.14–23 Saul and David already had a close relationship.

18.1–30: Saul becomes jealous of David. 1–3: *Loved* implies political loyalty in addition to personal affec-

he was wearing, and gave it to David, and his armor, and even his sword and his bow and his belt. [5] David went out and was successful wherever Saul sent him; as a result, Saul set him over the army. And all the people, even the servants of Saul, approved.

[6] As they were coming home, when David returned from killing the Philistine, the women came out of all the towns of Israel, singing and dancing, to meet King Saul, with tambourines, with songs of joy, and with musical instruments.[a] [7] And the women sang to one another as they made merry,

"Saul has killed his thousands,
      and David his ten thousands."
[8] Saul was very angry, for this saying displeased him. He said, "They have ascribed to David ten thousands, and to me they have ascribed thousands; what more can he have but the kingdom?" [9] So Saul eyed David from that day on.

[10] The next day an evil spirit from God rushed upon Saul, and he raved within his house, while David was playing the lyre, as he did day by day. Saul had his spear in his hand; [11] and Saul threw the spear, for he thought, "I will pin David to the wall." But David eluded him twice.

[12] Saul was afraid of David, because the LORD was with him but had departed from Saul. [13] So Saul removed him from his presence, and made him a commander of a thousand; and David marched out and came in,

leading the army. [14] David had success in all his undertakings; for the LORD was with him. [15] When Saul saw that he had great success, he stood in awe of him. [16] But all Israel and Judah loved David; for it was he who marched out and came in leading them.

[17] Then Saul said to David, "Here is my elder daughter Merab; I will give her to you as a wife; only be valiant for me and fight the LORD's battles." For Saul thought, "I will not raise a hand against him; let the Philistines deal with him." [18] David said to Saul, "Who am I and who are my kinsfolk, my father's family in Israel, that I should be son-in-law to the king?" [19] But at the time when Saul's daughter Merab should have been given to David, she was given to Adriel the Meholathite as a wife.

[20] Now Saul's daughter Michal loved David. Saul was told, and the thing pleased him. [21] Saul thought, "Let me give her to him that she may be a snare for him and that the hand of the Philistines may be against him." Therefore Saul said to David a second time,[b] "You shall now be my son-in-law." [22] Saul commanded his servants, "Speak to David in private and say, 'See, the king is delighted with you, and all his servants love you; now then, become the king's son-in-law.'" [23] So Saul's servants reported these words to David in private. And David said, "Does it seem to you a little thing to

a   Or *triangles,* or *three-stringed instruments*
b   Heb *by two*

tion. 4: Jonathan's royal robe and armor represent his status as crown prince. David is thus depicted as Saul's true successor, by the initiative of Jonathan himself. But David does not usurp the throne (see 17.38–39 where he does not wear Saul's armor). 6: *As they were coming home, when David returned from killing the Philistine,* the continuation of ch 17, showing that vv. 1–5 are an interruption of the initial narrative and part of the supplemental material in ch 17 (not found in the LXX). 7: *David* has slain *his ten thousands,* but David has killed only the single Philistine, Goliath. This is another indication of the interpolation of ch 17's portrait of David as a young shepherd rather than a warrior. 9: *Saul eyed David* means that Saul was suspicious of David. 10–11: These verses are also supplemental (and lacking in the LXX); initially, Saul's attempt to kill David with his spear (19.8–10) provided the climax to a series of subtle moves against David. *He raved,* lit. "he prophesied," referring to ecstatic behavior. 13–14: Saul promotes David because he is afraid to have David nearby and hopes that David will be killed in battle. *Marched out and came in,* an idiom for "went to war." 16: *All Israel and Judah loved David* expresses political loyalty and anticipates David's rule over both north and south (2 Sam 5.5). The army was devoted to David because of his military success. 17–19: These verses are supplemental; they are not found in the LXX. If these verses are related to 17.25, Saul has changed the conditions of his promise. David's response in v. 18 shows his humility and lack of ambition to be king. *Son-in-law to the king* was an important political position as a potential heir to the throne. In the end (v. 19), Saul reneges on his promise despite David's heroic deeds. 20: *Michal,* Saul's younger daughter. 21: This plan of Saul's is slightly more direct than his hope that David's promotion over the army would lead to his death. *Therefore Saul said to David a second time, "You shall now be my son-in-law,"* an

become the king's son-in-law, seeing that I am a poor man and of no repute?" ²⁴ The servants of Saul told him, "This is what David said." ²⁵ Then Saul said, "Thus shall you say to David, 'The king desires no marriage present except a hundred foreskins of the Philistines, that he may be avenged on the king's enemies.'" Now Saul planned to make David fall by the hand of the Philistines. ²⁶ When his servants told David these words, David was well pleased to be the king's son-in-law. Before the time had expired, ²⁷ David rose and went, along with his men, and killed one hundredᵃ of the Philistines; and David brought their foreskins, which were given in full number to the king, that he might become the king's son-in-law. Saul gave him his daughter Michal as a wife. ²⁸ But when Saul realized that the LORD was with David, and that Saul's daughter Michal loved him, ²⁹ Saul was still more afraid of David. So Saul was David's enemy from that time forward.

³⁰ Then the commanders of the Philistines came out to battle; and as often as they came out, David had more success than all the servants of Saul, so that his fame became very great.

19 Saul spoke with his son Jonathan and with all his servants about killing David. But Saul's son Jonathan took great delight in David. ² Jonathan told David, "My father Saul is trying to kill you; therefore be on guard tomorrow morning; stay in a secret place and hide yourself. ³ I will go out and stand beside my father in the field where you are, and I will speak to my father about you; if I learn anything I will tell you." ⁴ Jonathan spoke well of David to his father Saul, saying to him, "The king should not sin against his servant David, because he has not sinned against you, and because his deeds have been of good service to you; ⁵ for

he took his life in his hand when he attacked the Philistine, and the LORD brought about a great victory for all Israel. You saw it, and rejoiced; why then will you sin against an innocent person by killing David without cause?" ⁶ Saul heeded the voice of Jonathan; Saul swore, "As the LORD lives, he shall not be put to death." ⁷ So Jonathan called David and related all these things to him. Jonathan then brought David to Saul, and he was in his presence as before.

⁸ Again there was war, and David went out to fight the Philistines. He launched a heavy attack on them, so that they fled before him. ⁹ Then an evil spirit from the LORD came upon Saul, as he sat in his house with his spear in his hand, while David was playing music. ¹⁰ Saul sought to pin David to the wall with the spear; but he eluded Saul, so that he struck the spear into the wall. David fled and escaped that night.

¹¹ Saul sent messengers to David's house to keep watch over him, planning to kill him in the morning. David's wife Michal told him, "If you do not save your life tonight, tomorrow you will be killed." ¹² So Michal let David down through the window; he fled away and escaped. ¹³ Michal took an idolᵇ and laid it on the bed; she put a netᶜ of goats' hair on its head, and covered it with the clothes. ¹⁴ When Saul sent messengers to take David, she said, "He is sick." ¹⁵ Then Saul sent the messengers to see David for themselves. He said, "Bring him up to me in the bed, that I may kill him." ¹⁶ When the messengers came in, the idolᵈ was in the bed, with the coveringᶜ of goats'

ᵃ Gk Compare 2 Sam 3.14: Heb *two hundred*
ᵇ Heb *took the teraphim*
ᶜ Meaning of Heb uncertain
ᵈ Heb *the teraphim*

editorial addition explaining vv. 17–19. **23–25:** The *marriage present* ("bride-price") was set by the bride's father and paid by the groom. The use of foreskins as a bride-price plays on the references to the Philistines as uncircumcised (14.6; 31.4). **26:** *David was well pleased to be the king's son-in-law,* despite his claim to lack of ambition. **28:** *Michal loved him,* Michal's affection also entailed political loyalty.

19.1–24: Saul actively seeks David's life. 5: Killing an innocent person could bring God's wrath . Jonathan emphasizes that David is *innocent,* and Saul has no cause to kill him. **6:** *Saul swore,* an oath was a serious matter as it often involved the deity. In 1 Samuel, however, Saul consistently breaks his oaths. **9–10:** Cf. 16.23. **11–17:** This incident follows naturally upon the marriage in 18.20–29. **12:** The house was evidently built into the city wall (see Josh 2.15), so that David went *through the window* and escaped from the city. **13:** *An idol* (lit. "teraphim"), household gods (see Gen. 31.19–35n.; Judg 17.5.). The one used by Michal seems to have been close to life-size.

hair on its head. [17] Saul said to Michal, "Why have you deceived me like this, and let my enemy go, so that he has escaped?" Michal answered Saul, "He said to me, 'Let me go; why should I kill you?'"

[18] Now David fled and escaped; he came to Samuel at Ramah, and told him all that Saul had done to him. He and Samuel went and settled at Naioth. [19] Saul was told, "David is at Naioth in Ramah." [20] Then Saul sent messengers to take David. When they saw the company of the prophets in a frenzy, with Samuel standing in charge of[a] them, the spirit of God came upon the messengers of Saul, and they also fell into a prophetic frenzy. [21] When Saul was told, he sent other messengers, and they also fell into a frenzy. Saul sent messengers again the third time, and they also fell into a frenzy. [22] Then he himself went to Ramah. He came to the great well that is in Secu;[b] he asked, "Where are Samuel and David?" And someone said, "They are at Naioth in Ramah." [23] He went there, toward Naioth in Ramah; and the spirit of God came upon him. As he was going, he fell into a prophetic frenzy, until he came to Naioth in Ramah. [24] He too stripped off his clothes, and he too fell into a frenzy before Samuel. He lay naked all that day and all that night. Therefore it is said, "Is Saul also among the prophets?"

20 David fled from Naioth in Ramah. He came before Jonathan and said, "What have I done? What is my guilt? And what is my sin against your father that he is trying to take my life?" [2] He said to him, "Far from it! You shall not die. My father does nothing either great or small without disclosing it to me; and why should my father hide this from me? Never!" [3] But David also swore,

"Your father knows well that you like me; and he thinks, 'Do not let Jonathan know this, or he will be grieved.' But truly, as the LORD lives and as you yourself live, there is but a step between me and death." [4] Then Jonathan said to David, "Whatever you say, I will do for you." [5] David said to Jonathan, "Tomorrow is the new moon, and I should not fail to sit with the king at the meal; but let me go, so that I may hide in the field until the third evening. [6] If your father misses me at all, then say, 'David earnestly asked leave of me to run to Bethlehem his city; for there is a yearly sacrifice there for all the family.' [7] If he says, 'Good!' it will be well with your servant; but if he is angry, then know that evil has been determined by him. [8] Therefore deal kindly with your servant, for you have brought your servant into a sacred covenant[c] with you. But if there is guilt in me, kill me yourself; why should you bring me to your father?" [9] Jonathan said, "Far be it from you! If I knew that it was decided by my father that evil should come upon you, would I not tell you?" [10] Then David said to Jonathan, "Who will tell me if your father answers you harshly?" [11] Jonathan replied to David, "Come, let us go out into the field." So they both went out into the field.

[12] Jonathan said to David, "By the LORD, the God of Israel! When I have sounded out my father, about this time tomorrow, or on the third day, if he is well disposed toward David, shall I not then send and disclose it to you?

a   Meaning of Heb uncertain
b   Gk reads *to the well of the threshing floor on the bare height*
c   Heb *a covenant of the LORD*

17: Michal lies to protect herself. A threat from David does not explain her trick with the bed after his departure. 18: *Ramah,* Samuel's hometown, was about 2 mi (3 km) north of Gibeah. It is unlikely that David would have fled there rather than south to his home in Bethlehem; the story is included for literary and theological reasons; it shows that the prophets—and God through them—are on David's side. *Naioth* may be not a proper name but a word meaning "camps" or "huts" where the prophets lived near Ramah. 20–24: Frenzy, see 10.5–7n. 23: *Spirit of God,* cf. 10.5–7n; 11.6; 16.14–16. 23–24: *Is Saul also among the prophets?* here has a negative explanation (contrast 10.10–12). His loss of self-control and his nakedness are degrading. If Saul is among the prophets it is only because God is using prophecy to prevent him from harming David. 24: *Samuel,* cf. 15.35.

20.1–42: The covenant between David and Jonathan. 2: Jonathan is unaware that Saul has tried to kill David and still believes that his father would not act without first consulting him. 3: *You like me,* lit. "I have favor in your eyes" (see v. 29). 5: *New moon,* a day of sacrificing and feasting; see Num 28.11–15; Am 8.5. 8: David asks Jonathan to *deal kindly* with him. The term implies loyalty to a treaty, and David goes on to mention the cov-

¹³ But if my father intends to do you harm, the LORD do so to Jonathan, and more also, if I do not disclose it to you, and send you away, so that you may go in safety. May the LORD be with you, as he has been with my father. ¹⁴ If I am still alive, show me the faithful love of the LORD; but if I die,ᵃ ¹⁵ never cut off your faithful love from my house, even if the LORD were to cut off every one of the enemies of David from the face of the earth." ¹⁶ Thus Jonathan made a covenant with the house of David, saying, "May the LORD seek out the enemies of David." ¹⁷ Jonathan made David swear again by his love for him; for he loved him as he loved his own life.

¹⁸ Jonathan said to him, "Tomorrow is the new moon; you will be missed, because your place will be empty. ¹⁹ On the day after tomorrow, you shall go a long way down; go to the place where you hid yourself earlier, and remain beside the stone there.ᵃ ²⁰ I will shoot three arrows to the side of it, as though I shot at a mark. ²¹ Then I will send the boy, saying, 'Go, find the arrows.' If I say to the boy, 'Look, the arrows are on this side of you, collect them,' then you are to come, for, as the LORD lives, it is safe for you and there is no danger. ²² But if I say to the young man, 'Look, the arrows are beyond you,' then go; for the LORD has sent you away. ²³ As for the matter about which you and I have spoken, the LORD is witnessᵇ between you and me forever."

²⁴ So David hid himself in the field. When the new moon came, the king sat at the feast to eat. ²⁵ The king sat upon his seat, as at other times, upon the seat by the wall. Jonathan stood, while Abner sat by Saul's side; but David's place was empty.

²⁶ Saul did not say anything that day; for he thought, "Something has befallen him; he is not clean, surely he is not clean." ²⁷ But on the second day, the day after the new moon, David's place was empty. And Saul said to his son Jonathan, "Why has the son of Jesse not come to the feast, either yesterday or today?" ²⁸ Jonathan answered Saul, "David earnestly asked leave of me to go to Bethlehem; ²⁹ he said, 'Let me go; for our family is holding a sacrifice in the city, and my brother has commanded me to be there. So now, if I have found favor in your sight, let me get away, and see my brothers.' For this reason he has not come to the king's table."

³⁰ Then Saul's anger was kindled against Jonathan. He said to him, "You son of a perverse, rebellious woman! Do I not know that you have chosen the son of Jesse to your own shame, and to the shame of your mother's nakedness? ³¹ For as long as the son of Jesse lives upon the earth, neither you nor your kingdom shall be established. Now send and bring him to me, for he shall surely die." ³² Then Jonathan answered his father Saul, "Why should he be put to death? What has he done?" ³³ But Saul threw his spear at him to strike him; so Jonathan knew that it was the decision of his father to put David to death. ³⁴ Jonathan rose from the table in fierce anger and ate no food on the second day of the month, for he was grieved for David, and because his father had disgraced him.

³⁵ In the morning Jonathan went out into the field to the appointment with David, and

---

ᵃ Meaning of Heb uncertain
ᵇ Gk: Heb lacks witness

---

enant between them. **13**: *The LORD do so to Jonathan and more also,* an oath formula. Jonathan swears that he will warn David. Jonathan's wish that the LORD be with David as he was with Saul hints that David will be king. **14–15**: *Faithful love,* "loyalty" (Heb "ḥesed")" the same word as in v. 8. *My house* means Jonathan's descendants. David's oath of loyalty to Jonathan's house explains his treatment of Mephibosheth in 2 Sam 9. **16**: *The enemies of David* include Saul! **17**: *Love* again expresses political loyalty. **18–22**: Jonathan will signal David secretly during his target practice. If Jonathan tells his servant retrieving the arrows that they are back toward Jonathan, it is safe for David to come out of hiding. But if Jonathan tells the servant to go farther, David should flee immediately. **26**: *He is not clean,* ritual impurity, which could be caused by a variety of factors, disqualified a person from participation in some religious ceremonies (Lev 11–15). **27**: *The son of Jesse,* a disdainful reference to David. **30**: *Chosen the son of Jesse,* Saul accuses Jonathan of treason. *Nakedness,* a euphemism for the genitals. **33**: Saul tries to kill Jonathan with his spear, exactly as he had tried to kill David (18.10–11; 19.8–10). **41–42a**: An addition reiterating the affection and loyalty between David and Jonathan. If they could have met openly like this, the previous signal would have been unnecessary.

with him was a little boy. [36] He said to the boy, "Run and find the arrows that I shoot." As the boy ran, he shot an arrow beyond him. [37] When the boy came to the place where Jonathan's arrow had fallen, Jonathan called after the boy and said, "Is the arrow not beyond you?" [38] Jonathan called after the boy, "Hurry, be quick, do not linger." So Jonathan's boy gathered up the arrows and came to his master. [39] But the boy knew nothing; only Jonathan and David knew the arrangement. [40] Jonathan gave his weapons to the boy and said to him, "Go and carry them to the city." [41] As soon as the boy had gone, David rose from beside the stone heap[a] and prostrated himself with his face to the ground. He bowed three times, and they kissed each other, and wept with each other; David wept the more.[b] [42] Then Jonathan said to David, "Go in peace, since both of us have sworn in the name of the LORD, saying, 'The LORD shall be between me and you, and between my descendants and your descendants, forever.'" He got up and left; and Jonathan went into the city.[c]

21 [d] David came to Nob to the priest Ahimelech. Ahimelech came trembling to meet David, and said to him, "Why are you alone, and no one with you?" [2] David said to the priest Ahimelech, "The king has charged me with a matter, and said to me, 'No one must know anything of the matter about which I send you, and with which I have charged you.' I have made an appointment[e] with the young men for such and such a place. [3] Now then, what have you at hand? Give me five loaves of bread, or whatever is here." [4] The priest answered David, "I have no ordinary bread at hand, only holy bread—provided that the young men have kept themselves from women." [5] David answered the priest, "Indeed women have

been kept from us as always when I go on an expedition; the vessels of the young men are holy even when it is a common journey; how much more today will their vessels be holy?" [6] So the priest gave him the holy bread; for there was no bread there except the bread of the Presence, which is removed from before the LORD, to be replaced by hot bread on the day it is taken away.

[7] Now a certain man of the servants of Saul was there that day, detained before the LORD; his name was Doeg the Edomite, the chief of Saul's shepherds.

[8] David said to Ahimelech, "Is there no spear or sword here with you? I did not bring my sword or my weapons with me, because the king's business required haste." [9] The priest said, "The sword of Goliath the Philistine, whom you killed in the valley of Elah, is here wrapped in a cloth behind the ephod; if you will take that, take it, for there is none here except that one." David said, "There is none like it; give it to me."

[10] David rose and fled that day from Saul; he went to King Achish of Gath. [11] The servants of Achish said to him, "Is this not David the king of the land? Did they not sing to one another of him in dances,

'Saul has killed his thousands,
and David his ten thousands'?"

[12] David took these words to heart and was very much afraid of King Achish of Gath. [13] So he changed his behavior before them; he pretended to be mad when in their presence.[f] He

---

a   Gk: Heb *from beside the south*
b   Vg: Meaning of Heb uncertain
c   This sentence is 21.1 in Heb
d   Ch 21.2 in Heb
e   Q Ms Vg Compare Gk: Meaning of MT uncertain
f   Heb *in their hands*

21.1–15: David escapes to Nob. 1: *Nob* was between Gibeah and Jerusalem. *Ahimelech,* the great-grandson of Eli, *came trembling to meet David* apparently because David was alone, suggesting his fugitive status. **4:** *Provided that the young men have kept themselves from women,* those involved in sacred activities, such as worship and preparing for holy war, were prohibited from engaging in sexual relations (see Ex 19.15). **5:** *Vessels,* probably a euphemism for the sexual organs. **6:** *Bread of the Presence,* see Ex 25.30. **7:** *Detained before the LORD* probably means *Doeg* had a vow to fulfill. The fact that he is an *Edomite* is ominous, because Edomites are often depicted as Israel's hated enemies. **9:** *The sword of Goliath,* see 17.54n. The *ephod* mentioned here seems to be an idol (Judg 8.27) rather than a priestly garment. **10:** *Achish,* a Philistine name. In chs 27–29, David is his trusted vassal. **11:** *The king of the land,* if it is not an anachronism, indicates that the Philistines already recognize David as a

scratched marks on the doors of the gate, and let his spittle run down his beard. ¹⁴ Achish said to his servants, "Look, you see the man is mad; why then have you brought him to me? ¹⁵ Do I lack madmen, that you have brought this fellow to play the madman in my presence? Shall this fellow come into my house?"

22 David left there and escaped to the cave of Adullam; when his brothers and all his father's house heard of it, they went down there to him. ² Everyone who was in distress, and everyone who was in debt, and everyone who was discontented gathered to him; and he became captain over them. Those who were with him numbered about four hundred.

³ David went from there to Mizpeh of Moab. He said to the king of Moab, "Please let my father and mother come[a] to you, until I know what God will do for me." ⁴ He left them with the king of Moab, and they stayed with him all the time that David was in the stronghold. ⁵ Then the prophet Gad said to David, "Do not remain in the stronghold; leave, and go into the land of Judah." So David left, and went into the forest of Hereth.

⁶ Saul heard that David and those who were with him had been located. Saul was sitting at Gibeah, under the tamarisk tree on the height, with his spear in his hand, and all his servants were standing around him. ⁷ Saul said to his servants who stood around him, "Hear now, you Benjaminites; will the son of Jesse give every one of you fields and vineyards, will he make you all commanders of thousands and commanders of hundreds? ⁸ Is that why all of you have conspired against me? No one discloses to me when my son makes a league with the son of Jesse, none of you is sorry for me or discloses to me that

my son has stirred up my servant against me, to lie in wait, as he is doing today." ⁹ Doeg the Edomite, who was in charge of Saul's servants, answered, "I saw the son of Jesse coming to Nob, to Ahimelech son of Ahitub; ¹⁰ he inquired of the LORD for him, gave him provisions, and gave him the sword of Goliath the Philistine."

¹¹ The king sent for the priest Ahimelech son of Ahitub and for all his father's house, the priests who were at Nob; and all of them came to the king. ¹² Saul said, "Listen now, son of Ahitub." He answered, "Here I am, my lord." ¹³ Saul said to him, "Why have you conspired against me, you and the son of Jesse, by giving him bread and a sword, and by inquiring of God for him, so that he has risen against me, to lie in wait, as he is doing today?"

¹⁴ Then Ahimelech answered the king, "Who among all your servants is so faithful as David? He is the king's son-in-law, and is quick[b] to do your bidding, and is honored in your house. ¹⁵ Is today the first time that I have inquired of God for him? By no means! Do not let the king impute anything to his servant or to any member of my father's house; for your servant has known nothing of all this, much or little." ¹⁶ The king said, "You shall surely die, Ahimelech, you and all your father's house." ¹⁷ The king said to the guard who stood around him, "Turn and kill the priests of the LORD, because their hand also is with David; they knew that he fled, and did not disclose it to me." But the servants of the king would not raise their hand to attack the priests of the LORD. ¹⁸ Then

---

a   Syr Vg: Heb *come out*
b   Heb *and turns aside*

---

ruler. The Philistines quote the song in 18.7. **13–15**: *To be mad* was to be divinely "touched" (see the references to Saul prophesying in 18.10–11; 19.23–24). Thus, the Philistines, fearing divine wrath, leave David alone. The story ridicules the Philistines, who cannot tell madness from sanity and who admit to having plenty of *madmen*.

22.1–23: David at Adullam; massacre of the priests of Nob. 1: *Cave,* possibly an error for "stronghold" (v. 4). *Adullam* served as David's headquarters. **2:** The wilderness of Judah around Adullam had long been a hideout of fugitives. **3–4:** The book of Ruth indicates that David had a Moabite ancestry. *Stronghold,* probably Adullam. **5:** *The prophet Gad,* see 2 Sam 24.11. **7:** *Son of Jesse,* a disparaging reference to David. Kings commonly rewarded their servants with *fields and vineyards* and military appointments. The *Benjaminites* can expect no such rewards if David becomes king because his native tribe is Judah. **10:** Ch 21 does not mention that Ahimelech *inquired of the LORD for* David, but the accusation (whether true or not) plays an important role in the confrontation to follow. **18:** Only *Doeg* (see 21.7) dares to attack the LORD's priests, because he is an *Edomite. Linen ephod,* a gar-

the king said to Doeg, "You, Doeg, turn and attack the priests." Doeg the Edomite turned and attacked the priests; on that day he killed eighty-five who wore the linen ephod. [19] Nob, the city of the priests, he put to the sword; men and women, children and infants, oxen, donkeys, and sheep, he put to the sword.

[20] But one of the sons of Ahimelech son of Ahitub, named Abiathar, escaped and fled after David. [21] Abiathar told David that Saul had killed the priests of the LORD. [22] David said to Abiathar, "I knew on that day, when Doeg the Edomite was there, that he would surely tell Saul. I am responsible[a] for the lives of all your father's house. [23] Stay with me, and do not be afraid; for the one who seeks my life seeks your life; you will be safe with me."

23 Now they told David, "The Philistines are fighting against Keilah, and are robbing the threshing floors." [2] David inquired of the LORD, "Shall I go and attack these Philistines?" The LORD said to David, "Go and attack the Philistines and save Keilah." [3] But David's men said to him, "Look, we are afraid here in Judah; how much more then if we go to Keilah against the armies of the Philistines?" [4] Then David inquired of the LORD again. The LORD answered him, "Yes, go down to Keilah; for I will give the Philistines into your hand." [5] So David and his men went to Keilah, fought with the Philistines, brought away their livestock, and dealt them a heavy defeat. Thus David rescued the inhabitants of Keilah.

[6] When Abiathar son of Ahimelech fled to David at Keilah, he came down with an ephod in his hand. [7] Now it was told Saul that David had come to Keilah. And Saul said, "God has given[b] him into my hand; for he has shut himself in by entering a town that has gates and bars." [8] Saul summoned all the people to war, to go down to Keilah, to besiege David and his men. [9] When David learned that Saul was plotting evil against him, he said to

the priest Abiathar, "Bring the ephod here." [10] David said, "O LORD, the God of Israel, your servant has heard that Saul seeks to come to Keilah, to destroy the city on my account. [11] And now, will[c] Saul come down as your servant has heard? O LORD, the God of Israel, I beseech you, tell your servant." The LORD said, "He will come down." [12] Then David said, "Will the men of Keilah surrender me and my men into the hand of Saul?" The LORD said, "They will surrender you." [13] Then David and his men, who were about six hundred, set out and left Keilah; they wandered wherever they could go. When Saul was told that David had escaped from Keilah, he gave up the expedition. [14] David remained in the strongholds in the wilderness, in the hill country of the Wilderness of Ziph. Saul sought him every day, but the LORD[d] did not give him into his hand.

[15] David was in the Wilderness of Ziph at Horesh when he learned that[e] Saul had come out to seek his life. [16] Saul's son Jonathan set out and came to David at Horesh; there he strengthened his hand through the LORD.[f] [17] He said to him, "Do not be afraid; for the hand of my father Saul shall not find you; you shall be king over Israel, and I shall be second to you; my father Saul also knows that this is so." [18] Then the two of them made a covenant before the LORD; David remained at Horesh, and Jonathan went home.

[19] Then some Ziphites went up to Saul at Gibeah and said, "David is hiding among us in the strongholds of Horesh, on the hill of Hachilah, which is south of Jeshimon. [20] Now,

---

a   Gk Vg: Meaning of Heb uncertain
b   Gk Tg: Heb *made a stranger of*
c   Q Ms Compare Gk: MT *Will the men of Keilah surrender me into his hand? Will*
d   Q Ms Gk: MT *God*
e   Or *saw that*
f   Compare Q Ms Gk: MT *God*

---

ment worn by priests (2.18) **19:** Saul devotes the LORD's priests to destruction. Ironically, this is what he failed to do against the Amalekites in ch 15 (see vv. 8–9,14,19). **20–23:** The one escapee is Abiathar in fulfillment of the oracle in 2.27–36.

23.1–13: David's relief of Keilah. 1: *Keilah,* an independent city within Philistine territory. *Threshing floors,* open-air surfaces where grain was separated from chaff. **2–5:** This episode illustrates the importance of Abiathar's ability to divine. David's inquiries require a yes-or-no answer, which could be determined through the *ephod* (v. 6). **7–13:** David receives forewarning from the ephod, which allows him to escape Saul. Saul, in contrast, has no ephod, and later his efforts to consult the LORD go unanswered (28.6) **17:** It is extraordinary and

O king, whenever you wish to come down, do so; and our part will be to surrender him into the king's hand." [21] Saul said, "May you be blessed by the LORD for showing me compassion! [22] Go and make sure once more; find out exactly where he is, and who has seen him there; for I am told that he is very cunning. [23] Look around and learn all the hiding places where he lurks, and come back to me with sure information. Then I will go with you; and if he is in the land, I will search him out among all the thousands of Judah." [24] So they set out and went to Ziph ahead of Saul.

David and his men were in the wilderness of Maon, in the Arabah to the south of Jeshimon. [25] Saul and his men went to search for him. When David was told, he went down to the rock and stayed in the wilderness of Maon. When Saul heard that, he pursued David into the wilderness of Maon. [26] Saul went on one side of the mountain, and David and his men on the other side of the mountain. David was hurrying to get away from Saul, while Saul and his men were closing in on David and his men to capture them. [27] Then a messenger came to Saul, saying, "Hurry and come; for the Philistines have made a raid on the land." [28] So Saul stopped pursuing David, and went against the Philistines; therefore that place was called the Rock of Escape.[a] [29] [b]David then went up from there, and lived in the strongholds of En-gedi.

24

When Saul returned from following the Philistines, he was told, "David is in the wilderness of En-gedi." [2] Then Saul took three thousand chosen men out of all Israel, and went to look for David and his men in the direction of the Rocks of the Wild Goats. [3] He came to the sheepfolds beside the road, where there was a cave; and Saul went in to relieve himself.[c] Now David and

his men were sitting in the innermost parts of the cave. [4] The men of David said to him, "Here is the day of which the LORD said to you, 'I will give your enemy into your hand, and you shall do to him as it seems good to you.'" Then David went and stealthily cut off a corner of Saul's cloak. [5] Afterward David was stricken to the heart because he had cut off a corner of Saul's cloak. [6] He said to his men, "The LORD forbid that I should do this thing to my lord, the LORD's anointed, to raise my hand against him; for he is the LORD's anointed." [7] So David scolded his men severely and did not permit them to attack Saul. Then Saul got up and left the cave, and went on his way.

[8] Afterwards David also rose up and went out of the cave and called after Saul, "My lord the king!" When Saul looked behind him, David bowed with his face to the ground, and did obeisance. [9] David said to Saul, "Why do you listen to the words of those who say, 'David seeks to do you harm'? [10] This very day your eyes have seen how the LORD gave you into my hand in the cave; and some urged me to kill you, but I spared[d] you. I said, 'I will not raise my hand against my lord; for he is the LORD's anointed.' [11] See, my father, see the corner of your cloak in my hand; for by the fact that I cut off the corner of your cloak, and did not kill you, you may know for certain that there is no wrong or treason in my hands. I have not sinned against you, though you are hunting me to take my life. [12] May the LORD judge between me and you! May the LORD avenge me on you; but my hand shall not be against

a   Or *Rock of Division*; meaning of Heb uncertain
b   Ch 24.1 in Heb
c   Heb *to cover his feet*
d   Gk Syr Tg Vg: Heb *it* (my eye) *spared*

unbelievable that Jonathan would admit that David would be king in his place. **18:** Cf. 20.16. **25–29:** This story illustrates the LORD's protection of David, even though the LORD is not mentioned. Saul's withdrawal just at the moment he has David trapped hints at divine intervention. The name of this place (v. 28) means either "rock of escape" or "rock of division." Both are appropriate to the story.

24.1–22: David spares Saul's life (cf. ch. 25). **2:** *Three thousand,* see 4.2n. **3:** *To relieve himself,* lit. "to cover his feet," a denigrating portrayal of a king. **4a:** The prophecy cited by David's men is not recorded and could be their own invention. **4b–5:** These verses originally may have belonged after v. 7a. David's cutting off Saul's hem is symbolic for emasculation or usurpation of Saul's kingdom, which is why David's conscience bothers him. **6:** To attack *the Lord's anointed* (Saul) was to attack the LORD. **8:** *David bowed with his face to the ground, and did obeisance,* David thus shows the proper respect toward Saul as the LORD's anointed. **11:** *My father* is a respectful

you. [13] As the ancient proverb says, 'Out of the wicked comes forth wickedness'; but my hand shall not be against you. [14] Against whom has the king of Israel come out? Whom do you pursue? A dead dog? A single flea? [15] May the LORD therefore be judge, and give sentence between me and you. May he see to it, and plead my cause, and vindicate me against you."

[16] When David had finished speaking these words to Saul, Saul said, "Is this your voice, my son David?" Saul lifted up his voice and wept. [17] He said to David, "You are more righteous than I; for you have repaid me good, whereas I have repaid you evil. [18] Today you have explained how you have dealt well with me, in that you did not kill me when the LORD put me into your hands. [19] For who has ever found an enemy, and sent the enemy safely away? So may the LORD reward you with good for what you have done to me this day. [20] Now I know that you shall surely be king, and that the kingdom of Israel shall be established in your hand. [21] Swear to me therefore by the LORD that you will not cut off my descendants after me, and that you will not wipe out my name from my father's house." [22] So David swore this to Saul. Then Saul went home; but David and his men went up to the stronghold.

25 Now Samuel died; and all Israel assembled and mourned for him. They buried him at his home in Ramah.

Then David got up and went down to the wilderness of Paran.

[2] There was a man in Maon, whose property was in Carmel. The man was very rich; he had three thousand sheep and a thousand goats. He was shearing his sheep in Carmel. [3] Now the name of the man was Nabal, and the name of his wife Abigail. The woman was clever and beautiful, but the man was surly and mean; he was a Calebite. [4] David heard in the wilderness that Nabal was shearing his sheep. [5] So David sent ten young men; and David said to the young men, "Go up to Carmel, and go to Nabal, and greet him in my name. [6] Thus you shall salute him: 'Peace be to you, and peace be to your house, and peace be to all that you have. [7] I hear that you have shearers; now your shepherds have been with us, and we did them no harm, and they missed nothing, all the time they were in Carmel. [8] Ask your young men, and they will tell you. Therefore let my young men find favor in your sight; for we have come on a feast day. Please give whatever you have at hand to your servants and to your son David.'"

[9] When David's young men came, they said all this to Nabal in the name of David; and then they waited. [10] But Nabal answered David's servants, "Who is David? Who is the son of Jesse? There are many servants today

address from the younger David; it may also imply David's right to inherit Saul's kingdom. **14:** *A dead dog? A single flea?* Deliberately ambiguous. David could be disparaging himself as insignificant, or he could be saying that Saul is mistaken if he thinks David is insignificant. **16:** Saul's reference to David as *my son* recalls their once close relationship and hints that David will be Saul's successor. **20:** Saul recognizes that David will succeed him. **21–22:** A new king commonly killed all the descendants of the previous king in order to be rid of potential rivals. David's oath not to wipe out Saul's descendants anticipates his treatment of Mephibosheth (2 Sam 9); see further 20.14–15n.

25.1a: The death of Samuel. An editor's note that prepares for ch 28.

25.1b–43: Nabal and Abigail. In chs 24 and 26 David refuses to kill Saul, but in ch 25 he is almost guilty of killing many innocent people in Nabal's household. **2:** Carmel, see 15.12n. Nabal, like Saul, is a rich and powerful man. **3:** *Calebite,* lit. "as his heart," possibly an allusion to vv. 36–37. The Calebites were the leading clan of Judah. "Calebite" is also very similar to the word for "dog," which may be significant in view of the idiom for males in v. 22 as those who urinate on walls. *Nabal,* meaning "fool" (v. 25), is an unlikely name for parents to give to a child. Either the name "Nabal" was invented as appropriate to this man's character, or it originally meant something different (there are several other possible meanings). Nabal is also similar to the Heb words for "wine bottle" and "corpse," and so may allude to Nabal's later death following his drunkenness (vv. 36–38). Nabal's wife, *Abigail,* is his complete opposite. The only other Abigail in the Bible is David's sister (1 Chr 2.16). **4–8:** *Shearing his sheep,* a time of celebration. David hopes that Nabal, in the spirit of the festival, will give a generous gift. This gift is more or less obligatory as payment for not harming Nabal's shepherds. Hence, David's request can be read as a kind of extortion. The *ten young men* give Nabal an idea of the size of gift David is ex-

who are breaking away from their masters. [11] Shall I take my bread and my water and the meat that I have butchered for my shearers, and give it to men who come from I do not know where?" [12] So David's young men turned away, and came back and told him all this. [13] David said to his men, "Every man strap on his sword!" And every one of them strapped on his sword; David also strapped on his sword; and about four hundred men went up after David, while two hundred remained with the baggage.

[14] But one of the young men told Abigail, Nabal's wife, "David sent messengers out of the wilderness to salute our master; and he shouted insults at them. [15] Yet the men were very good to us, and we suffered no harm, and we never missed anything when we were in the fields, as long as we were with them; [16] they were a wall to us both by night and by day, all the while we were with them keeping the sheep. [17] Now therefore know this and consider what you should do; for evil has been decided against our master and against all his house; he is so ill-natured that no one can speak to him."

[18] Then Abigail hurried and took two hundred loaves, two skins of wine, five sheep ready dressed, five measures of parched grain, one hundred clusters of raisins, and two hundred cakes of figs. She loaded them on donkeys [19] and said to her young men, "Go on ahead of me; I am coming after you." But she did not tell her husband Nabal. [20] As she rode on the donkey and came down under cover of the mountain, David and his men came down toward her; and she met them. [21] Now David had said, "Surely it was in vain that I protected all that this fellow has in the wilderness, so that nothing was missed of all that belonged to him; but he has returned me evil for good. [22] God do so to David[a] and more also, if by morning I leave so much as one male of all who belong to him."

[23] When Abigail saw David, she hurried and alighted from the donkey, and fell before David on her face, bowing to the ground. [24] She fell at his feet and said, "Upon me alone, my lord, be the guilt; please let your servant speak in your ears, and hear the words of your servant. [25] My lord, do not take seriously this ill-natured fellow, Nabal; for as his name is, so is he; Nabal[b] is his name, and folly is with him; but I, your servant, did not see the young men of my lord, whom you sent.

[26] "Now then, my lord, as the LORD lives, and as you yourself live, since the LORD has restrained you from bloodguilt and from taking vengeance with your own hand, now let your enemies and those who seek to do evil to my lord be like Nabal. [27] And now let this present that your servant has brought to my lord be given to the young men who follow my lord. [28] Please forgive the trespass of your servant; for the LORD will certainly make my lord a sure house, because my lord is fighting the battles of the LORD; and evil shall not be found in you so long as you live. [29] If anyone should rise up to pursue you and to seek your life, the life of my lord shall be bound in the bundle of the living under the care of the LORD your God; but the lives of your enemies he shall sling out as from the hollow of a sling. [30] When the LORD has done to my

---

[a] Gk Compare Syr: Heb the enemies of David
[b] That is Fool

---

pecting—whatever ten men can carry; they may also be meant to intimidate Nabal. **10–11:** *Who is David? Who is the son of Jesse?* demean David as insignificant. Nabal goes on to call David a runaway slave and a vagabond. **14:** Nabal's own servants go to Abigail because they recognize him as ill-natured and untrustworthy. **18:** *Five measures* (Heb "se'ah"), about 1 bu (38 l). *Cakes,* clumps of dried *figs* rather than a baked product. **22:** David vows to annihilate every *male* (see v. 3n) in Nabal's household. Only the woman, Abigail, can prevent the tragedy. **23:** Abigail bows to David as before a king. **24:** Abigail is eloquent and tactful, calling herself David's *servant* (v. 24). **26:** This verse anticipates the conclusion of the story, according to which Nabal dies but not by David's hand. It may be out of place. **27:** Abigail diplomatically refers to the supplies she brings as a *present* for David's men. **28:** *Sure house* (see 2.35n.) suggests that Abigail knows David will be king. **29:** *If anyone should rise up to pursue you and to seek your life* alludes to Saul. The *bundle of the living,* the list of those who are alive. *Sling out* recalls David's victory in ch 17 and anticipates Nabal's death in 25.37. **30–31:** Abigail points out that shedding innocent blood would be an obstacle to David's kingship. *Prince,* the one designated as king. *When the LORD has dealt well with*

lord according to all the good that he has spoken concerning you, and has appointed you prince over Israel, [31] my lord shall have no cause of grief, or pangs of conscience, for having shed blood without cause or for having saved himself. And when the LORD has dealt well with my lord, then remember your servant."

[32] David said to Abigail, "Blessed be the LORD, the God of Israel, who sent you to meet me today! [33] Blessed be your good sense, and blessed be you, who have kept me today from bloodguilt and from avenging myself by my own hand! [34] For as surely as the LORD the God of Israel lives, who has restrained me from hurting you, unless you had hurried and come to meet me, truly by morning there would not have been left to Nabal so much as one male." [35] Then David received from her hand what she had brought him; he said to her, "Go up to your house in peace; see, I have heeded your voice, and I have granted your petition."

[36] Abigail came to Nabal; he was holding a feast in his house, like the feast of a king. Nabal's heart was merry within him, for he was very drunk; so she told him nothing at all until the morning light. [37] In the morning, when the wine had gone out of Nabal, his wife told him these things, and his heart died within him; he became like a stone. [38] About ten days later the LORD struck Nabal, and he died.

[39] When David heard that Nabal was dead, he said, "Blessed be the LORD who has judged the case of Nabal's insult to me, and has kept back his servant from evil; the LORD has returned the evildoing of Nabal upon his own head." Then David sent and wooed Abigail, to make her his wife. [40] When David's servants came to Abigail at Carmel, they said to her, "David has sent us to you to take you to him as his wife." [41] She rose and bowed down, with her face to the ground, and said, "Your servant is a slave to wash the feet of the servants of my lord." [42] Abigail got up hurriedly and rode away on a donkey; her five maids attended her. She went after the messengers of David and became his wife.

[43] David also married Ahinoam of Jezreel; both of them became his wives. [44] Saul had given his daughter Michal, David's wife, to Palti son of Laish, who was from Gallim.

26

Then the Ziphites came to Saul at Gibeah, saying, "David is in hiding on the hill of Hachilah, which is opposite Jeshimon."[a] [2] So Saul rose and went down to the Wilderness of Ziph, with three thousand chosen men of Israel, to seek David in the Wilderness of Ziph. [3] Saul encamped on the hill of Hachilah, which is opposite Jeshimon[a] beside the road. But David remained in the wilderness. When he learned that Saul had come after him into the wilderness, [4] David sent out spies, and learned that Saul had indeed arrived. [5] Then David set out and came to the place where Saul had encamped; and David saw the place where Saul lay, with Abner son of Ner, the commander of his army. Saul was lying within the encampment, while the army was encamped around him.

[6] Then David said to Ahimelech the Hittite, and to Joab's brother Abishai son of Zeruiah,

---

a   Or *opposite the wasteland*

my lord may refer to David's becoming king or ironically to Nabal's death. *Remember your servant* is a marriage proposal. **32–33:** David praises *the* LORD for sending Abigail because she saved him from committing murder and thus incurring *bloodguilt*. **35:** *I have granted your petition,* David already speaks as a king. **36:** The Heb word for *feast* is related to the root for "to drink," suggesting that drinking was the primary activity. *Like the feast of a king,* Nabal is again compared to a king. **37:** *When the wine had gone out of Nabal,* the name "Nabal" is similar to the word for wineskin in v. 18. *He became like a stone,* perhaps a coma, and another allusion to David's sling (ch 17). **43:** Saul's wife was also named *Ahinoam* (14.50). *Jezreel,* apparently a town near Carmel (Josh 15.56) rather than the northern valley of that name. **44:** *Saul had given his daughter Michal, David's wife, to Palti son of Laish,* this notice illustrates Saul's enmity toward David and prepares for the story of Michal's return in 2 Sam 3.13–16.

   26.1–25: David spares Saul's life again. This story is similar to the one in ch 24, and the two may be variants of a single original. In both, Saul is unknowingly defenseless before David, who is urged by his men to kill Saul but refuses because of Saul's status as the LORD's anointed. David then reveals to Saul that he could have killed him, and Saul expresses remorse for persecuting David and hints or states that David will succeed him as king.

"Who will go down with me into the camp to Saul?" Abishai said, "I will go down with you." [7] So David and Abishai went to the army by night; there Saul lay sleeping within the encampment, with his spear stuck in the ground at his head; and Abner and the army lay around him. [8] Abishai said to David, "God has given your enemy into your hand today; now therefore let me pin him to the ground with one stroke of the spear; I will not strike him twice." [9] But David said to Abishai, "Do not destroy him; for who can raise his hand against the LORD's anointed, and be guiltless?" [10] David said, "As the LORD lives, the LORD will strike him down; or his day will come to die; or he will go down into battle and perish. [11] The LORD forbid that I should raise my hand against the LORD's anointed; but now take the spear that is at his head, and the water jar, and let us go." [12] So David took the spear that was at Saul's head and the water jar, and they went away. No one saw it, or knew it, nor did anyone awake; for they were all asleep, because a deep sleep from the LORD had fallen upon them.

[13] Then David went over to the other side, and stood on top of a hill far away, with a great distance between them. [14] David called to the army and to Abner son of Ner, saying, "Abner! Will you not answer?" Then Abner replied, "Who are you that calls to the king?" [15] David said to Abner, "Are you not a man? Who is like you in Israel? Why then have you not kept watch over your lord the king? For one of the people came in to destroy your lord the king. [16] This thing that you have done is not good. As the LORD lives, you deserve to die, because you have not kept watch over your lord, the LORD's anointed. See now, where is the king's spear, or the water jar that was at his head?"

[17] Saul recognized David's voice, and said, "Is this your voice, my son David?" David said, "It is my voice, my lord, O king." [18] And he added, "Why does my lord pursue his servant? For what have I done? What guilt is on my hands? [19] Now therefore let my lord the king hear the words of his servant. If it is the LORD who has stirred you up against me, may he accept an offering; but if it is mortals, may they be cursed before the LORD, for they have driven me out today from my share in the heritage of the LORD, saying, 'Go, serve other gods.' [20] Now therefore, do not let my blood fall to the ground, away from the presence of the LORD; for the king of Israel has come out to seek a single flea, like one who hunts a partridge in the mountains."

[21] Then Saul said, "I have done wrong; come back, my son David, for I will never harm you again, because my life was precious in your sight today; I have been a fool, and have made a great mistake." [22] David replied, "Here is the spear, O king! Let one of the young men come over and get it. [23] The LORD rewards everyone for his righteousness and his faithfulness; for the LORD gave you into my hand today, but I would not raise my hand against the LORD's anointed. [24] As your life was precious today in my sight, so may my life be precious in the sight of the LORD, and may he rescue me from all tribulation." [25] Then Saul said to David, "Blessed be you, my son David! You will do many things and will succeed in them." So David went his way, and Saul returned to his place.

27 David said in his heart, "I shall now perish one day by the hand of Saul; there is nothing better for me than to escape to the land of the Philistines; then Saul will despair of seeking me any longer within the borders of Israel, and I shall escape out of his hand." [2] So David set out and went over, he and the six hundred men who were with

---

5: The army sleeps around the king in order to protect him. 6: *Joab,* David's nephew (1 Chr 2.16), later the commander of his army. 8: Ironically, the same *spear* that Saul used to try to kill David is now available for David to use against Saul. 9: See 24.6n. 13: *David went over to the other side,* if Saul pursues him he can lead Saul's army away from his own men. 19: David curses anyone who caused Saul to pursue him, because this has driven him from the land of Israel, which is the LORD's *heritage.* Each god was believed to have his own nation and each nation its god. *Other gods,* the gods of countries outside Israel where David says he has been driven. 20: *A partridge,* lit. "the caller." David calls to Saul from a mountain; cf. 24.14n. 25: Saul's blessing hints that David will be king (cf. 24.20).

27.1–28.2: **David becomes a vassal of the Philistines.** This chapter is in tension with 21.10–15, in which

him, to King Achish son of Maoch of Gath. [3] David stayed with Achish at Gath, he and his troops, every man with his household, and David with his two wives, Ahinoam of Jezreel, and Abigail of Carmel, Nabal's widow. [4] When Saul was told that David had fled to Gath, he no longer sought for him.

[5] Then David said to Achish, "If I have found favor in your sight, let a place be given me in one of the country towns, so that I may live there; for why should your servant live in the royal city with you?" [6] So that day Achish gave him Ziklag; therefore Ziklag has belonged to the kings of Judah to this day. [7] The length of time that David lived in the country of the Philistines was one year and four months.

[8] Now David and his men went up and made raids on the Geshurites, the Girzites, and the Amalekites; for these were the landed settlements from Telam[a] on the way to Shur and on to the land of Egypt. [9] David struck the land, leaving neither man nor woman alive, but took away the sheep, the oxen, the donkeys, the camels, and the clothing, and came back to Achish. [10] When Achish asked, "Against whom[b] have you made a raid today?" David would say, "Against the Negeb of Judah," or "Against the Negeb of the Jerahmeelites," or, "Against the Negeb of the Kenites." [11] David left neither man nor woman alive to be brought back to Gath, thinking, "They might tell about us, and say, 'David has done so and so.'" Such was his practice

all the time he lived in the country of the Philistines. [12] Achish trusted David, thinking, "He has made himself utterly abhorrent to his people Israel; therefore he shall always be my servant."

28 In those days the Philistines gathered their forces for war, to fight against Israel. Achish said to David, "You know, of course, that you and your men are to go out with me in the army." [2] David said to Achish, "Very well, then you shall know what your servant can do." Achish said to David, "Very well, I will make you my bodyguard for life."

[3] Now Samuel had died, and all Israel had mourned for him and buried him in Ramah, his own city. Saul had expelled the mediums and the wizards from the land. [4] The Philistines assembled, and came and encamped at Shunem. Saul gathered all Israel, and they encamped at Gilboa. [5] When Saul saw the army of the Philistines, he was afraid, and his heart trembled greatly. [6] When Saul inquired of the LORD, the LORD did not answer him, not by dreams, or by Urim, or by prophets. [7] Then Saul said to his servants, "Seek out for me a woman who is a medium, so that I may go to her and inquire of her." His servants said to him, "There is a medium at Endor."

[8] So Saul disguised himself and put on other clothes and went there, he and two men with him. They came to the woman by

a Compare Gk 15.4: Heb *from of old*
b Q Ms Gk Vg: MT lacks *whom*

David escapes from *Achish* by pretending to be mad. **27.3:** *Gath,* Goliath's home (17.4). **6:** Kings commonly gave land grants to faithful servants. *Ziklag* also guarded the southern frontier of Achish's territory. **8–12:** *The Negeb,* the southern wilderness area of Palestine. David conducts raids against non-Israelite peoples (v. 8). The mention of *Amalekites* is inconsistent with ch 15, in which they are all killed. David fools Achish by claiming to attack clans within Judah such as the "Kenizzites" (a better reading than *Kenites*) and *Jerahmeelites.* Thus, while Achish felt confident of David's loyalty because he thought David had betrayed his own people, the writer asserts that David's loyalty remained with Israel. **28.2:** *Then you shall know what your servant can do,* the statement is ambiguous. Achish thinks David is saying that he will show his potential against Israel. The reader knows that David is actually saying that in the heat of battle Achish will find out how David remains loyal to Israel.

28.3–25: Saul consults a spirit. 3: *Mediums* and *wizards* refer to persons who communicated with the dead; this is forbidden in Lev 19.31; 20.6,27; Deut 18.10. Ironically, Saul, who had *expelled* them, now seeks one out. **4:** *Shunem* and *Gilboa,* near the Jezreel Valley, far north of the Negeb where the previous stories were set. **6:** Three means of divining were *dreams,* or incubation, in which one slept at a holy place anticipating the answer to an inquiry; *Urim* or lots, used earlier in 14.41; and *prophets* like the man of God in 9.1–10.16. **7:** *A woman who is a medium,* lit. "a woman of spirits," using the word translated "medium" in v. 3. **11–12a:** An insertion identifying Samuel as the ghost. Originally, the woman recognized Saul because of his oath not to punish her in v. 10, a

night. And he said, "Consult a spirit for me, and bring up for me the one whom I name to you." ⁹ The woman said to him, "Surely you know what Saul has done, how he has cut off the mediums and the wizards from the land. Why then are you laying a snare for my life to bring about my death?" ¹⁰ But Saul swore to her by the LORD, "As the LORD lives, no punishment shall come upon you for this thing." ¹¹ Then the woman said, "Whom shall I bring up for you?" He answered, "Bring up Samuel for me." ¹² When the woman saw Samuel, she cried out with a loud voice; and the woman said to Saul, "Why have you deceived me? You are Saul!" ¹³ The king said to her, "Have no fear; what do you see?" The woman said to Saul, "I see a divine being^a coming up out of the ground." ¹⁴ He said to her, "What is his appearance?" She said, "An old man is coming up; he is wrapped in a robe." So Saul knew that it was Samuel, and he bowed with his face to the ground, and did obeisance.

¹⁵ Then Samuel said to Saul, "Why have you disturbed me by bringing me up?" Saul answered, "I am in great distress, for the Philistines are warring against me, and God has turned away from me and answers me no more, either by prophets or by dreams; so I have summoned you to tell me what I should do." ¹⁶ Samuel said, "Why then do you ask me, since the LORD has turned from you and become your enemy? ¹⁷ The LORD has done to you just as he spoke by me; for the LORD has torn the kingdom out of your hand, and given it to your neighbor, David. ¹⁸ Because you did not obey the voice of the LORD, and did not carry out his fierce wrath against Amalek, therefore the LORD has done this thing to you today. ¹⁹ Moreover the LORD will give Israel along with you into the hands of the Philistines; and tomorrow you and your sons shall be with me; the LORD will also give the army of Israel into the hands of the Philistines."

²⁰ Immediately Saul fell full length on the ground, filled with fear because of the words of Samuel; and there was no strength in him, for he had eaten nothing all day and all night. ²¹ The woman came to Saul, and when she saw that he was terrified, she said to him, "Your servant has listened to you; I have taken my life in my hand, and have listened to what you have said to me. ²² Now therefore, you also listen to your servant; let me set a morsel of bread before you. Eat, that you may have strength when you go on your way." ²³ He refused, and said, "I will not eat." But his servants, together with the woman, urged him; and he listened to their words. So he got up from the ground and sat on the bed. ²⁴ Now the woman had a fatted calf in the house. She quickly slaughtered it, and she took flour, kneaded it, and baked unleavened cakes. ²⁵ She put them before Saul and his servants, and they ate. Then they rose and went away that night.

29 Now the Philistines gathered all their forces at Aphek, while the Israelites were encamped by the fountain that is in Jezreel. ² As the lords of the Philistines were passing on by hundreds and by thousands, and David and his men were passing on in the rear with Achish, ³ the commanders of the Philistines said, "What are these Hebrews doing here?" Achish said to the commanders of the Philistines, "Is this not David, the servant of King Saul of Israel, who has been with me now for days and years? Since he deserted to me I have found no fault in him to this day." ⁴ But the commanders of the Philistines were angry with him; and the commanders of the Philistines said to him, "Send the man back, so that he may return to the place that you have assigned to him; he shall not go down with us to battle, or else he may become an

^a Or *a god*; or *gods*

promise that could only have been made by Saul. **13:** *Divine being*, a god or a ghost or spirit. *The ground*, better: "the underworld." **14:** *Robe*, Samuel's characteristic garment by which Saul recognizes him. **15:** *Disturbed me*, the spirits in the underworld were viewed as sleeping. **17–18:** See ch 15. **19:** *Tomorrow you and your sons shall be with me*, they will be dead. **20:** Saul's being *filled with fear* is unbecoming of the king and suggests that he is unfit for the role. **21:** *The woman* who is the medium is calmer and stronger than the *terrified* Saul. **24:** *A fatted calf in the house*, livestock were kept on the ground floor of houses with people's sleeping quarters on a second story.

29.1–11: The Philistines reject David. 2: *The lords of the Philistines*, the rulers of the five main Philistine cities. **3:** It is the *commanders* of the Philistine army who will actually be in battle, rather than the Philistine lords, who

adversary to us in the battle. For how could this fellow reconcile himself to his lord? Would it not be with the heads of the men here? [5] Is this not David, of whom they sing to one another in dances,

'Saul has killed his thousands,
and David his ten thousands'?"

[6] Then Achish called David and said to him, "As the LORD lives, you have been honest, and to me it seems right that you should march out and in with me in the campaign; for I have found nothing wrong in you from the day of your coming to me until today. Nevertheless the lords do not approve of you. [7] So go back now; and go peaceably; do nothing to displease the lords of the Philistines." [8] David said to Achish, "But what have I done? What have you found in your servant from the day I entered your service until now, that I should not go and fight against the enemies of my lord the king?" [9] Achish replied to David, "I know that you are as blameless in my sight as an angel of God; nevertheless, the commanders of the Philistines have said, 'He shall not go up with us to the battle.' [10] Now then rise early in the morning, you and the servants of your lord who came with you, and go to the place that I appointed for you. As for the evil report, do not take it to heart, for you have done well before me.[a] Start early in the morning, and leave as soon as you have light." [11] So David set out with his men early in the morning, to return to the land of the Philistines. But the Philistines went up to Jezreel.

30 Now when David and his men came to Ziklag on the third day, the Amalekites had made a raid on the Negeb and on Ziklag.

They had attacked Ziklag, burned it down, [2] and taken captive the women and all[b] who were in it, both small and great; they killed none of them, but carried them off, and went their way. [3] When David and his men came to the city, they found it burned down, and their wives and sons and daughters taken captive. [4] Then David and the people who were with him raised their voices and wept, until they had no more strength to weep. [5] David's two wives also had been taken captive, Ahinoam of Jezreel, and Abigail the widow of Nabal of Carmel. [6] David was in great danger; for the people spoke of stoning him, because all the people were bitter in spirit for their sons and daughters. But David strengthened himself in the LORD his God.

[7] David said to the priest Abiathar son of Ahimelech, "Bring me the ephod." So Abiathar brought the ephod to David. [8] David inquired of the LORD, "Shall I pursue this band? Shall I overtake them?" He answered him, "Pursue; for you shall surely overtake and shall surely rescue." [9] So David set out, he and the six hundred men who were with him. They came to the Wadi Besor, where those stayed who were left behind. [10] But David went on with the pursuit, he and four hundred men; two hundred stayed behind, too exhausted to cross the Wadi Besor.

[11] In the open country they found an Egyptian, and brought him to David. They gave him bread and he ate; they gave him water to drink; [12] they also gave him a piece of

---

a   Gk: Heb lacks *and go to the place … done well before me*
b   Gk: Heb lacks *and all*

---

object to the presence of David and his men. *Hebrews,* see 4.6n. **5:** The same song as in 18.7. **6:** *As the LORD lives,* Achish, the Philistine, swears by Yahweh, the God of Israel! **8:** *The enemies of my lord the king,* Achish takes this as a reference to himself, but David means Saul. **10:** *The place that I appointed for you,* Ziklag. **11:** David and the Philistines separate and go in opposite directions. Thus the writer shows that David is far away from the battle and had nothing to do with Saul's death.

30.1–31: The burning of Ziklag and David's pursuit of the Amalekites. 1: *On the third day.* Ziklag was about 50 mi (80 km) south of Aphek (v. 1). Again the writer emphasizes David's distance from the battle where Saul was killed. The Amalekite *raid* on Ziklag may have been in retaliation for David's raids against them (27.8). This story is inconsistent with ch 15, in which the Amalekites were all destroyed. **2:** *Both small and great,* poor or unimportant and wealthy or socially prominent, a figure of speech (a merism) meaning "everyone." **6:** *Strengthened himself* may mean summoning courage as well as gathering support within the army. David is here depicted as an ideal ruler. **7–8:** *Ephod,* a device (see 23.2–5n) used by priests to divine the answers to yes-or-no questions. David's access to God through the ephod contrasts with Saul's lack of response from God in 28.6 and highlights the theme: "the LORD was with him (David)." **9:** *Wadi Besor,* a major watercourse south of Gaza,

fig cake and two clusters of raisins. When he had eaten, his spirit revived; for he had not eaten bread or drunk water for three days and three nights. ¹³ Then David said to him, "To whom do you belong? Where are you from?" He said, "I am a young man of Egypt, servant to an Amalekite. My master left me behind because I fell sick three days ago. ¹⁴ We had made a raid on the Negeb of the Cherethites and on that which belongs to Judah and on the Negeb of Caleb; and we burned Ziklag down." ¹⁵ David said to him, "Will you take me down to this raiding party?" He said, "Swear to me by God that you will not kill me, or hand me over to my master, and I will take you down to them."

¹⁶ When he had taken him down, they were spread out all over the ground, eating and drinking and dancing, because of the great amount of spoil they had taken from the land of the Philistines and from the land of Judah. ¹⁷ David attacked them from twilight until the evening of the next day. Not one of them escaped, except four hundred young men, who mounted camels and fled. ¹⁸ David recovered all that the Amalekites had taken; and David rescued his two wives. ¹⁹ Nothing was missing, whether small or great, sons or daughters, spoil or anything that had been taken; David brought back everything. ²⁰ David also captured all the flocks and herds, which were driven ahead of the other cattle; people said, "This is David's spoil."

²¹ Then David came to the two hundred men who had been too exhausted to follow David, and who had been left at the Wadi Besor. They went out to meet David and to meet the people who were with him. When David drew near to the people he saluted them. ²² Then all the corrupt and worthless fellows among the men who had gone with David said, "Because they did not go with us, we will not give them any of the spoil that we have recovered, except that each man

may take his wife and children, and leave." ²³ But David said, "You shall not do so, my brothers, with what the Lord has given us; he has preserved us and handed over to us the raiding party that attacked us. ²⁴ Who would listen to you in this matter? For the share of the one who goes down into the battle shall be the same as the share of the one who stays by the baggage; they shall share alike." ²⁵ From that day forward he made it a statute and an ordinance for Israel; it continues to the present day.

²⁶ When David came to Ziklag, he sent part of the spoil to his friends, the elders of Judah, saying, "Here is a present for you from the spoil of the enemies of the Lord"; ²⁷ it was for those in Bethel, in Ramoth of the Negeb, in Jattir, ²⁸ in Aroer, in Siphmoth, in Eshtemoa, ²⁹ in Racal, in the towns of the Jerahmeelites, in the towns of the Kenites, ³⁰ in Hormah, in Bor-ashan, in Athach, ³¹ in Hebron, all the places where David and his men had roamed.

31 Now the Philistines fought against Israel; and the men of Israel fled before the Philistines, and many fell[a] on Mount Gilboa. ² The Philistines overtook Saul and his sons; and the Philistines killed Jonathan and Abinadab and Malchishua, the sons of Saul. ³ The battle pressed hard upon Saul; the archers found him, and he was badly wounded by them. ⁴ Then Saul said to his armor-bearer, "Draw your sword and thrust me through with it, so that these uncircumcised may not come and thrust me through, and make sport of me." But his armor-bearer was unwilling; for he was terrified. So Saul took his own sword and fell upon it. ⁵ When his armor-bearer saw that Saul was dead, he also fell upon his sword and died with him. ⁶ So Saul and his three sons and his armor-bearer and all his men died together on the same day.

[a] Heb *and they fell slain*

not far north of Egypt. **12:** *Fig cake,* see 25.18n. **14:** *Cherethites,* probably "Cretans," mercenaries from Crete, associated with the Philistines. **19:** *Small or great,* see v. 2n. **23–25:** An etiology for a custom in the writer's day. *A statute and an ordinance for Israel,* an illustration of David's kingly decisiveness and authority. **26–31:** David's gifts to the *elders* of these cities, all in southern Judah, would cause them to look favorably upon him when the time came to choose a king over Judah (2 Sam 2.4).

31.1–13: Saul's death. Compare 1 Chr 10 and 2 Sam 1. For the locations, see map on p. 452. **4:** *These uncircumcised,* a deprecating term for the Philistines. **5:** Although not condemned, suicide is rare in the Bible; see 2 Sam

⁷ When the men of Israel who were on the other side of the valley and those beyond the Jordan saw that the men of Israel had fled and that Saul and his sons were dead, they forsook their towns and fled; and the Philistines came and occupied them.

⁸ The next day, when the Philistines came to strip the dead, they found Saul and his three sons fallen on Mount Gilboa. ⁹ They cut off his head, stripped off his armor, and sent messengers throughout the land of the Philistines to carry the good news to the houses of their idols and to the people. ¹⁰ They put his armor in the temple of Astarte;ᵃ and they fastened his body to the wall of Beth-shan. ¹¹ But when the inhabitants of Jabesh-gilead heard what the Philistines had done to Saul, ¹² all the valiant men set out, traveled all night long, and took the body of Saul and the bodies of his sons from the wall of Beth-shan. They came to Jabesh and burned them there. ¹³ Then they took their bones and buried them under the tamarisk tree in Jabesh, and fasted seven days.

ᵃ Heb plural

17.23; 1 Kings 16.18; Mt 27.5. **9–10:** The Philistines humiliate Saul's corpse and credit their gods with the victory. *Astarte,* a Canaanite goddess. **11–13:** The men of Jabesh are likely moved to rescue Saul's body because of his rescue of their city at the beginning of his reign (10.27b–11.15). Cremation (vv. 12–13) was not practiced by the Israelites. They may have burned the bodies in this case to avoid further desecration of them by the Philistines. They *fasted seven days* apparently in mourning for Saul and his sons.

2 SAMUEL

NAME AND LOCATION IN CANON

First and Second Samuel were originally a single work, so that much of the information in the Introduction to 1 Samuel (pp. 399–400) pertains to 2 Samuel as well. The name of the book (as relating to the prophet Samuel) is even less appropriate for 2 Samuel, since Samuel dies before 1 Samuel ends and is never mentioned in 2 Samuel.

The division between 1 and 2 Samuel is artificial and was apparently based on considerations of length when it was first made in the LXX, where 2 Samuel bears the title 2 Kingdoms or 2 Reigns.

AUTHORSHIP AND DATE OF COMPOSITION

Since Samuel dies in 1 Sam 25.1, 2 Samuel was traditionally ascribed to Nathan and Gad based on the mention in 1 Chr 29.29 of the "records" of these two prophets. Modern scholars typically regard the Former Prophets in the Hebrew Bible (Joshua through 2 Kings, without Ruth) as the work of the Deuteronomistic Historian(s) or Dtr(s).

Scholars disagree about the number of editions and their dates for the Deuteronomistic History, though it is clear that the work was not completed before the Babylonian exile (586 BCE).

LITERARY HISTORY

The major critical issues in 2 Samuel revolve around chs 9–20. These chapters (or in some views chs 13–20), together with 1 Kings 1–2, have been dubbed the "Court History" or "Succession Narrative" (after their perceived intention of dealing with the question of who would succeed David as king). Many scholars have viewed this proposed source document as almost contemporaneous with the events it narrates. However, the extent and early date of this hypothetical source have been called into question because it is impossible to extract these chapters cleanly from the surrounding narrative and to see them as a separate source; there are, for example, ties between chs 9–20 and chs 2–4, such as the description of Mephibosheth's injury in 4.4 and 9.3 and the importance of the "sons of Zeruiah," Joab and his brothers. Questions of literary history also loom large in the consideration of ch 7, with its unconditional promise of a dynasty made to David. While scholars generally recognize this as a Deuteronomistic composition as it now stands, many of them think that underlying it is an older version of God's promise to David.

STRUCTURE AND CONTENTS

Second Samuel can be divided into four sections.

Section one (1.1–5.5) describes how, after Saul's death (ch 1), David becomes king first of Judah (2.1–4a) and then, after a civil war that included the assassinations of Abner (ch 3) and Ishbaal (ch 4), of all Israel (5.1–5).

Section two (5.6–12.31) tells of David's annexation of Jerusalem (5.5–6.23), his interest in building a temple there resulting in the divine promise of a dynasty (ch 7), and his victories over surrounding peoples (chs 8–12), which are interrupted by the story of his affair with Bathsheba (11.2–12.25).

Section three (chs 13–20) recounts Absalom's revolt and that led by Sheba (ch 20).

Section four (chs 21–24), often considered an appendix, is a miscellaneous collection of narratives, military lists, and poems.

INTERPRETATION

Scholars and other readers disagree about the perspective on David in these chapters. Some contend that the pro-Davidic, apologetic character of 1 Samuel continues, as those who stand in David's way perish, though never by his own hand or order. Joab and the "sons of Zeruiah" are often blamed for the murders of David's enemies—Abner (3.26–30), Absalom (18.1–15), and Amasa (20.4–10)—while David is too tender for such deeds (3.39; 16.10; 19.22) and is deeply grieved by their deaths (3.31–37; 18.22–19.8). In this reading, the annihilation of Saul's line (recounted apologetically in 21.1–14, which once preceded ch 9) secures David's hold on the throne. Only Mephibosheth, Jonathan's crippled son, remains alive, and David keeps a watchful eye on him by bringing him to the royal court (ch 9). Even when David commits adultery with Bathsheba and arranges for the death of her husband, it has been argued, David's repentance is exemplary and is immediately accepted (12.13). However, other readers point precisely to David's adultery and his inability to control his children as evidence that the Court History paints both David and the monarchy in a very negative light. It is fair to say that 2 Samuel in its current form depicts David as a complex, highly ambiguous character who is blessed by the LORD.

GUIDE TO READING

As with 1 Samuel, the story in 2 Samuel is best read sequentially. Characterization exemplified by deeds and speeches is even more significant in 2 Samuel than in 1 Samuel. The array of characters can bewilder new readers, so that keeping tabs on the identities of characters and their relationship to David can be useful. Minute, seemingly insignificant details in the narrative are worthy of note as they often signal points of historical or literary significance beneath the surface. Readers do well to ask which characters—especially David—benefit from events that are reported and whether those characters may have been responsible for bringing them about. As in 1 Samuel, a narrative that "protests too much" may lead the critical reader to question whether apologetic interest has replaced historical accuracy. For example, David benefits from Abner's death (3.20–39), and the narrative's repeated assertion that David dismissed Abner in peace and knew nothing about Joab's plan to murder him may lead one to suspect that the narrator is trying to counter just such a charge and even to speculate that David had some role in Abner's death.

The final four chapters of 2 Samuel contain six passages arranged in symmetrical order: narrative, list, poem, poem, list, narrative. The list (23.1–7) provides David's "last words," in the tradition of other leading biblical characters.

Steven L. McKenzie

1 After the death of Saul, when David had returned from defeating the Amalekites, David remained two days in Ziklag. [2] On the third day, a man came from Saul's camp, with his clothes torn and dirt on his head. When he came to David, he fell to the ground and did obeisance. [3] David said to him, "Where have you come from?" He said to him, "I have escaped from the camp of Israel." [4] David said to him, "How did things go? Tell me!" He answered, "The army fled from the battle, but also many of the army fell and died; and Saul and his son Jonathan also died." [5] Then David asked the young man who was reporting to him, "How do you know that Saul and his son Jonathan died?" [6] The young man reporting to him said, "I happened to be on Mount Gilboa; and there was Saul leaning on his spear, while the chariots and the horsemen drew close to him. [7] When he looked behind him, he saw me, and called to me. I answered, 'Here sir.' [8] And he said to me, 'Who are you?' I answered him, 'I am an Amalekite.' [9] He said to me, 'Come, stand over me and kill me; for convulsions have seized me, and yet my life still lingers.' [10] So I stood over him, and killed him, for I knew that he could not live after he had fallen. I took the crown that was on his head and the armlet that was on his arm, and I have brought them here to my lord."

[11] Then David took hold of his clothes and tore them; and all the men who were with him did the same. [12] They mourned and wept, and fasted until evening for Saul and for his son Jonathan, and for the army of the LORD and for the house of Israel, because they had fallen by the sword. [13] David said to the young man who had reported to him, "Where do you come from?" He answered, "I am the son of a resident alien, an Amalekite." [14] David

1.1–16: David learns of the death of Saul and Jonathan. Some scholars think this is a separate tradition of the account in 1 Sam 31, with which it disagrees. Another possibility is that the man who brings the news to David changes the story for his own benefit. 1.2: Tearing clothes and scattering dust on the head were conventional signs of mourning. 6: *The young man's* claim that he *happened to be on Mount Gilboa* in the heat of battle is probably a lie (see v. 10). 8: *Amalekite,* David has just come from successfully pursuing Amalekites (1 Sam 30), who are depicted as scavengers. It is ironic that an Amalekite killed Saul, who (according to 1 Sam 15) lost his kingship because he did not kill off the Amalekites. 10: The Amalekite stripped Saul's corpse and brought the *crown* and

said to him, "Were you not afraid to lift your hand to destroy the LORD's anointed?" [15] Then David called one of the young men and said, "Come here and strike him down." So he struck him down and he died. [16] David said to him, "Your blood be on your head; for your own mouth has testified against you, saying, 'I have killed the LORD's anointed.'"

[17] David intoned this lamentation over Saul and his son Jonathan. [18] (He ordered that The Song of the Bow[a] be taught to the people of Judah; it is written in the Book of Jashar.) He said:

[19] Your glory, O Israel, lies slain upon your
  high places!
  How the mighty have fallen!
[20] Tell it not in Gath,
  proclaim it not in the streets of
  Ashkelon;
or the daughters of the Philistines will
  rejoice,
  the daughters of the uncircumcised will
  exult.

[21] You mountains of Gilboa,
  let there be no dew or rain upon you,
  nor bounteous fields![b]
For there the shield of the mighty was
  defiled,
  the shield of Saul, anointed with oil no
  more.

[22] From the blood of the slain,
  from the fat of the mighty,
the bow of Jonathan did not turn back,
  nor the sword of Saul return empty.

[23] Saul and Jonathan, beloved and lovely!
  In life and in death they were not
  divided;
they were swifter than eagles,
  they were stronger than lions.

[24] O daughters of Israel, weep over Saul,
  who clothed you with crimson, in
  luxury,
  who put ornaments of gold on your
  apparel.

[25] How the mighty have fallen
  in the midst of the battle!

Jonathan lies slain upon your high
  places.
[26] I am distressed for you, my brother
  Jonathan;
greatly beloved were you to me;
  your love to me was wonderful,
  passing the love of women.

[27] How the mighty have fallen,
  and the weapons of war perished!

2 After this David inquired of the LORD, "Shall I go up into any of the cities of Judah?" The LORD said to him, "Go up." David said, "To which shall I go up?" He said, "To Hebron." [2] So David went up there, along with his two wives, Ahinoam of Jezreel, and Abigail the widow of Nabal of Carmel. [3] David brought up the men who were with

---

a   Heb *that The Bow*
b   Meaning of Heb uncertain

---

armlet, symbols of kingship, to David hoping for a reward. **12**: Fasting was another sign of mourning. **13–16**: As a *resident alien*, the Amalekite was subject to the same laws as an Israelite citizen, and therefore David holds him responsible for killing *the LORD's anointed*.

1.17–27: David's elegy over Saul and Jonathan. Many scholars consider plausible the text's attribution of authorship to David himself. **18**: *Song of the Bow,* the Hebrew has simply "bow." If not a copyist's mistake, this may refer to a type of song or a title. *Book of Jashar,* a lost collection of poems (see Josh 10.13). **19**: *Your glory,* an allusion to Saul and Jonathan. **20**: *Gath, Ashkelon,* Philistine cities. *Uncircumcised,* a disparaging term for the Philistines. **21**: *Mountains of Gilboa,* the site of the battle where Saul and Jonathan were killed. *Shields* were made of leather and were *anointed with oil* to keep them battle-ready. **24**: Saul's reign brought prosperity to Israel. **26**: *Passing the love of women* expresses the closeness of David's relationship to Jonathan but does not necessarily imply a sexual relationship.

2.1–11: David becomes king of Judah. 1: *Inquired,* probably by means of the ephod and Urim and Thummim (1 Sam 14.3,41; 28.6; 30.7–8). *Hebron,* principal city of the Calebites (see Josh 14.13; Judg 1.20), the leading clan in Judah and also the traditional site of the tombs of Israel's ancestors (Gen 23.19; 25.9; 49.29–32). **2**: *Ahinoam of Jezreel, Abigail the widow of Nabal of Carmel,* see 1 Sam 25, esp. v. 43. Both women were from the Calebite region.

him, every one with his household; and they settled in the towns of Hebron. [4] Then the people of Judah came, and there they anointed David king over the house of Judah.

When they told David, "It was the people of Jabesh-gilead who buried Saul," [5] David sent messengers to the people of Jabesh-gilead, and said to them, "May you be blessed by the LORD, because you showed this loyalty to Saul your lord, and buried him! [6] Now may the LORD show steadfast love and faithfulness to you! And I too will reward you because you have done this thing. [7] Therefore let your hands be strong, and be valiant; for Saul your lord is dead, and the house of Judah has anointed me king over them."

[8] But Abner son of Ner, commander of Saul's army, had taken Ishbaal[a] son of Saul, and brought him over to Mahanaim. [9] He made him king over Gilead, the Ashurites, Jezreel, Ephraim, Benjamin, and over all Israel. [10] Ishbaal,[a] Saul's son, was forty years old when he began to reign over Israel, and he reigned two years. But the house of Judah followed David. [11] The time that David was king in Hebron over the house of Judah was seven years and six months.

[12] Abner son of Ner, and the servants of Ishbaal[a] son of Saul, went out from Mahanaim to Gibeon. [13] Joab son of Zeruiah, and the servants of David, went out and met them at the pool of Gibeon. One group sat on one side of the pool, while the other sat on the other side of the pool. [14] Abner said to Joab, "Let the young men come forward and have a contest before us." Joab said, "Let them come forward." [15] So they came forward and were counted as they passed by, twelve for Benjamin and Ishbaal[a] son of Saul, and twelve of the servants of David. [16] Each grasped his opponent by the head, and thrust his sword in his opponent's side; so they fell down together. Therefore that place was called Helkath-hazzurim,[b] which is at Gibeon. [17] The battle was very fierce that day; and Abner and the men of Israel were beaten by the servants of David.

[18] The three sons of Zeruiah were there, Joab, Abishai, and Asahel. Now Asahel was as swift of foot as a wild gazelle. [19] Asahel pursued Abner, turning neither to the right nor to the left as he followed him. [20] Then Abner looked back and said, "Is it you, Asahel?" He answered, "Yes, it is." [21] Abner said to him, "Turn to your right or to your left, and seize one of the young men, and take his spoil." But Asahel would not turn away from following him. [22] Abner said again to Asahel, "Turn away from following me; why should I strike you to the ground? How then could I show my face to your brother Joab?" [23] But he refused to turn away. So Abner struck him in the stomach with the butt of his spear, so that the spear came out at his back. He fell there, and died where he lay. And all those who came to the place where Asahel had fallen and died, stood still.

a Gk Compare 1 Chr 8.33; 9.39: Heb *Ish-bosheth*, "man of shame"

b That is *Field of Sword-edges*

Nabal had been a leading Calebite, and marriage to his wife strengthened David's claims to the throne of Judah. **4:** David's gifts to the elders of Judah (1 Sam 30.26–31) further helped his bid to be their king. *Jabesh-gilead,* see 1 Sam 11; 31.11–13. **5–7:** In wooing Jabesh-gilead, David is seeking to win over the strongest enclave of support for Saul. His overture to Jabesh is likely what sparked the military response by Abner (v. 12). **8:** *Ishbaal* (Heb "Ish-bosheth"), pious scribes substituted the word "boshet," meaning "shame," for the name of the Canaanite god Baal. But Heb "ba'al" can also simply mean "lord" and might have been an epithet for Yahweh. The original form of the name, Ishbaal (a difference of a single letter in Heb), is preserved in 1 Chr 8.33; 9.39 and in some early Greek translations. *Mahanaim* was east of the Jordan in Gilead. Abner was forced to go there because the Philistines controlled the territory west of the Jordan. **9:** This list of Ishbaal's domains is idealistic at best considering the Philistine domination. "Ashurites" should probably read "Geshurites." Geshur was the region north of Gilead.

2.12–32: War between Israel and Judah. 14–17: This contest, the exact nature of which is unclear, quickly turned to war. **18:** *Zeruiah,* David's sister, according to 1 Chr 2.16. **19–23:** Asahel's death provides the motive for

²⁴ But Joab and Abishai pursued Abner. As the sun was going down they came to the hill of Ammah, which lies before Giah on the way to the wilderness of Gibeon. ²⁵ The Benjaminites rallied around Abner and formed a single band; they took their stand on the top of a hill. ²⁶ Then Abner called to Joab, "Is the sword to keep devouring forever? Do you not know that the end will be bitter? How long will it be before you order your people to turn from the pursuit of their kinsmen?" ²⁷ Joab said, "As God lives, if you had not spoken, the people would have continued to pursue their kinsmen, not stopping until morning." ²⁸ Joab sounded the trumpet and all the people stopped; they no longer pursued Israel or engaged in battle any further.

²⁹ Abner and his men traveled all that night through the Arabah; they crossed the Jordan, and, marching the whole forenoon,ᵃ they came to Mahanaim. ³⁰ Joab returned from the pursuit of Abner; and when he had gathered all the people together, there were missing of David's servants nineteen men besides Asahel. ³¹ But the servants of David had killed of Benjamin three hundred sixty of Abner's men. ³² They took up Asahel and buried him in the tomb of his father, which was at Bethlehem. Joab and his men marched all night, and the day broke upon them at Hebron.

3 There was a long war between the house of Saul and the house of David; David grew stronger and stronger, while the house of Saul became weaker and weaker.

² Sons were born to David at Hebron: his firstborn was Amnon, of Ahinoam of Jezreel; ³ his second, Chileab, of Abigail the widow of Nabal of Carmel; the third, Absalom son of Maacah, daughter of King Talmai of Geshur; ⁴ the fourth, Adonijah son of Haggith; the fifth, Shephatiah son of Abital; ⁵ and the sixth, Ithream, of David's wife Eglah. These were born to David in Hebron.

⁶ While there was war between the house of Saul and the house of David, Abner was making himself strong in the house of Saul. ⁷ Now Saul had a concubine whose name was Rizpah daughter of Aiah. And Ishbaalᵇ said to Abner, "Why have you gone in to my father's concubine?" ⁸ The words of Ishbaalᶜ made Abner very angry; he said, "Am I a dog's head for Judah? Today I keep showing loyalty to the house of your father Saul, to his brothers, and to his friends, and have not given you into the hand of David; and yet you charge me now with a crime concerning this woman. ⁹ So may God do to Abner and so may he add to it! For just what the LORD has sworn to David, that will I accomplish for him, ¹⁰ to transfer the kingdom from the house of Saul, and set up the throne of David over Israel and over Judah, from Dan to Beer-sheba." ¹¹ And Ishbaalᵇ could not answer Abner another word, because he feared him.

¹² Abner sent messengers to David at Hebron,ᵈ saying, "To whom does the land be-

ᵃ Meaning of Heb uncertain
ᵇ Heb And he
ᶜ Gk Compare 1 Chr 8.33; 9.39: Heb Ish-bosheth, "man of shame"
ᵈ Gk: Heb where he was

Joab's murder of Abner in 3.26–30. 29: *Arabah,* the rift valley of which the Jordan valley is a part.

3.1–5: **David's sons.** 1: The suggestion that there was *a long war* indicates that Saul and his family received more popular support than the book of 1 Samuel might imply. 2: *Amnon,* see ch 13. *Ahinoam,* see 1 Sam 25.43; 2 Sam 2.2. 3: Nothing more is known of *Chileab,* who apparently died young; in the LXX his name is Dalouia, and in 1 Chr 3.1 he is called Daniel. *Abigail,* see 1 Sam 25. *Absalom,* see chs 13–18. *Geshur,* see 2.9n. David's marriage to *Maacah* indicates that he had a political alliance with her father, *King Talmai.* 4–5: *Adonijah,* see 1 Kings 1. *Shephatiah* and *Ithream* are mentioned only here and in 1 Chr 3.3.

3.6–39: **Abner's death.** 7: *Concubine,* a woman (usually a slave) acquired for sexual purposes. To sleep with a member of the royal harem was to claim the throne (see 16.21–22; 1 Kings 2.13–25). Hence, Ishbaal's question is tantamount to an accusation of treason. 8: *Dog's head,* used only here in the Bible, this expression is obviously reproachful, but its origin is unknown, although comparison to a dog or a dead dog is a frequent form of self-deprecation (see 9.8; 2 Kings 18.3). Abner does not deny Ishbaal's accusation but is contemptuous. Although the power is his (2.8–9), he has been loyal to Ishbaal. 10: *From Dan to Beer-sheba,* the traditional northern and southern limits of Israel. 12: Abner offers to join David and bring the army with him. The author thereby shows that David had no motive for killing Abner. 13: David demands the return of *Saul's daughter Michal* because

long? Make your covenant with me, and I will give you my support to bring all Israel over to you." [13] He said, "Good; I will make a covenant with you. But one thing I require of you: you shall never appear in my presence unless you bring Saul's daughter Michal when you come to see me." [14] Then David sent messengers to Saul's son Ishbaal,[a] saying, "Give me my wife Michal, to whom I became engaged at the price of one hundred foreskins of the Philistines." [15] Ishbaal[a] sent and took her from her husband Paltiel the son of Laish. [16] But her husband went with her, weeping as he walked behind her all the way to Bahurim. Then Abner said to him, "Go back home!" So he went back.

[17] Abner sent word to the elders of Israel, saying, "For some time past you have been seeking David as king over you. [18] Now then bring it about; for the LORD has promised David: Through my servant David I will save my people Israel from the hand of the Philistines, and from all their enemies." [19] Abner also spoke directly to the Benjaminites; then Abner went to tell David at Hebron all that Israel and the whole house of Benjamin were ready to do.

[20] When Abner came with twenty men to David at Hebron, David made a feast for Abner and the men who were with him. [21] Abner said to David, "Let me go and rally all Israel to my lord the king, in order that they may make a covenant with you, and that you may reign over all that your heart desires." So David dismissed Abner, and he went away in peace.

[22] Just then the servants of David arrived with Joab from a raid, bringing much spoil with them. But Abner was not with David at Hebron, for David[b] had dismissed him, and he had gone away in peace. [23] When Joab and all the army that was with him came, it was told

Joab, "Abner son of Ner came to the king, and he has dismissed him, and he has gone away in peace." [24] Then Joab went to the king and said, "What have you done? Abner came to you; why did you dismiss him, so that he got away? [25] You know that Abner son of Ner came to deceive you, and to learn your comings and goings and to learn all that you are doing."

[26] When Joab came out from David's presence, he sent messengers after Abner, and they brought him back from the cistern of Sirah; but David did not know about it. [27] When Abner returned to Hebron, Joab took him aside in the gateway to speak with him privately, and there he stabbed him in the stomach. So he died for shedding[c] the blood of Asahel, Joab's[d] brother. [28] Afterward, when David heard of it, he said, "I and my kingdom are forever guiltless before the LORD for the blood of Abner son of Ner. [29] May the guilt[e] fall on the head of Joab, and on all his father's house; and may the house of Joab never be without one who has a discharge, or who is leprous,[f] or who holds a spindle, or who falls by the sword, or who lacks food!" [30] So Joab and his brother Abishai murdered Abner because he had killed their brother Asahel in the battle at Gibeon.

[31] Then David said to Joab and to all the people who were with him, "Tear your clothes, and put on sackcloth, and mourn over Abner." And King David followed the

a Heb Ish-bosheth
b Heb he
c Heb lacks shedding
d Heb his
e Heb May it
f A term for several skin diseases; precise meaning uncertain

it is through her that he claims a right to Saul's kingdom. 14: See 1 Sam 18.20–29. 15: It is not clear why Ishbaal returns Michal to David. Some scholars have suggested that he was under legal obligation. Paltiel, or Palti (1 Sam 25.44). 17: The elders of Israel, the tribal leaders. 18: The Philistines, Israel's principal enemy in 1 Samuel, whose defeat of Saul (1 Sam 31) meant that they were still a problem for David, which he will resolve in 5.17–25; cf. 21.15–22. 19: Benjamin, the tribe of both Saul and Abner; they would be the most reluctant to make David, a non-Benjaminite, king. 21: In peace, repeated in the following verses; the writer emphasizes (perhaps too much) David's noninvolvement in Abner's death. 25: Comings and goings, military maneuvers. Joab accuses Abner of spying. 26–27: The writer stresses that Joab, seeking to avenge his brother (2.18–23), acted alone. Some have suggested that Joab also feared losing his position as army commander to Abner (see 19.13; 20.8–10). 29: While David curses Joab, he does not now punish him (but see 1 Kings 2.5–6). Spindle, better: "crutch." 30: Abishai is not mentioned in the story but may have helped Joab plan Abner's murder. 31: Sackcloth, material worn by

bier. [32] They buried Abner at Hebron. The king lifted up his voice and wept at the grave of Abner, and all the people wept. [33] The king lamented for Abner, saying,

"Should Abner die as a fool dies?
[34] Your hands were not bound,
 your feet were not fettered;
as one falls before the wicked
 you have fallen."

And all the people wept over him again. [35] Then all the people came to persuade David to eat something while it was still day; but David swore, saying, "So may God do to me, and more, if I taste bread or anything else before the sun goes down!" [36] All the people took notice of it, and it pleased them; just as everything the king did pleased all the people. [37] So all the people and all Israel understood that day that the king had no part in the killing of Abner son of Ner. [38] And the king said to his servants, "Do you not know that a prince and a great man has fallen this day in Israel? [39] Today I am powerless, even though anointed king; these men, the sons of Zeruiah, are too violent for me. The LORD pay back the one who does wickedly in accordance with his wickedness!"

4 When Saul's son Ishbaal[a] heard that Abner had died at Hebron, his courage failed, and all Israel was dismayed. [2] Saul's son had two captains of raiding bands; the name of the one was Baanah, and the name of the other Rechab. They were sons of Rimmon a Benjaminite from Beeroth—for Beeroth is considered to belong to Benjamin. [3] (Now the people of Beeroth had fled to Gittaim and are there as resident aliens to this day).

[4] Saul's son Jonathan had a son who was crippled in his feet. He was five years old when the news about Saul and Jonathan came from Jezreel. His nurse picked him up and fled; and, in her haste to flee, it happened that he fell and became lame. His name was Mephibosheth.[b]

[5] Now the sons of Rimmon the Beerothite, Rechab and Baanah, set out, and about the heat of the day they came to the house of Ishbaal,[c] while he was taking his noonday rest. [6] They came inside the house as though to take wheat, and they struck him in the stomach; then Rechab and his brother Baanah escaped.[d] [7] Now they had come into the house while he was lying on his couch in his bedchamber; they attacked him, killed him, and beheaded him. Then they took his head and traveled by way of the Arabah all night long. [8] They brought the head of Ishbaal[c] to David at Hebron and said to the king, "Here is the head of Ishbaal,[c] son of Saul, your enemy, who sought your life; the LORD has avenged my lord the king this day on Saul and on his offspring."

[9] David answered Rechab and his brother Baanah, the sons of Rimmon the Beerothite, "As the LORD lives, who has redeemed my life out of every adversity, [10] when the one who told me, 'See, Saul is dead,' thought he was bringing good news, I seized him and killed him at Ziklag—this was the reward I gave him for his news. [11] How much more then, when wicked men have killed a righteous man on his bed in his own house! And now shall I not require his blood at your hand, and destroy you from the earth?" [12] So David commanded the young men, and they killed them; they cut off their hands and feet, and hung their bodies beside the pool at Hebron. But the head of Ishbaal[c] they took and buried in the tomb of Abner at Hebron.

a Heb lacks *Ishbaal*
b In 1 Chr 8.34 and 9.40, *Merib-baal*
c Heb *Ish-bosheth*
d Meaning of Heb of verse 6 uncertain

mourners. **33:** *Fool* (Heb "nabal") recalls the story in 1 Sam 25. **35–39:** These verses continue to stress (perhaps too strongly) David's lack of involvement in Abner's death.

4.1–12: The assassination of Ishbaal. Here too the author stresses that David was in no way involved in the death of his enemy. **3:** An explanation of how *Beeroth* came to be considered a Benjaminite city; the event referred to here is otherwise unknown. **4:** *Mephibosheth*, the original form of the name was Merib-baal (1 Chr 8.34; 9.40), cf. 2.8n. **7:** *Arabah*, see 2.29n. **8:** The assassins bring Ishbaal's head to David, expecting a reward for killing his enemy. **9–10:** See 1.1–16. **11:** *A righteous man*, David does not recognize Ishbaal's kingship and therefore does not call him the LORD's anointed. **12:** Execution of this nature was reserved for traitors.

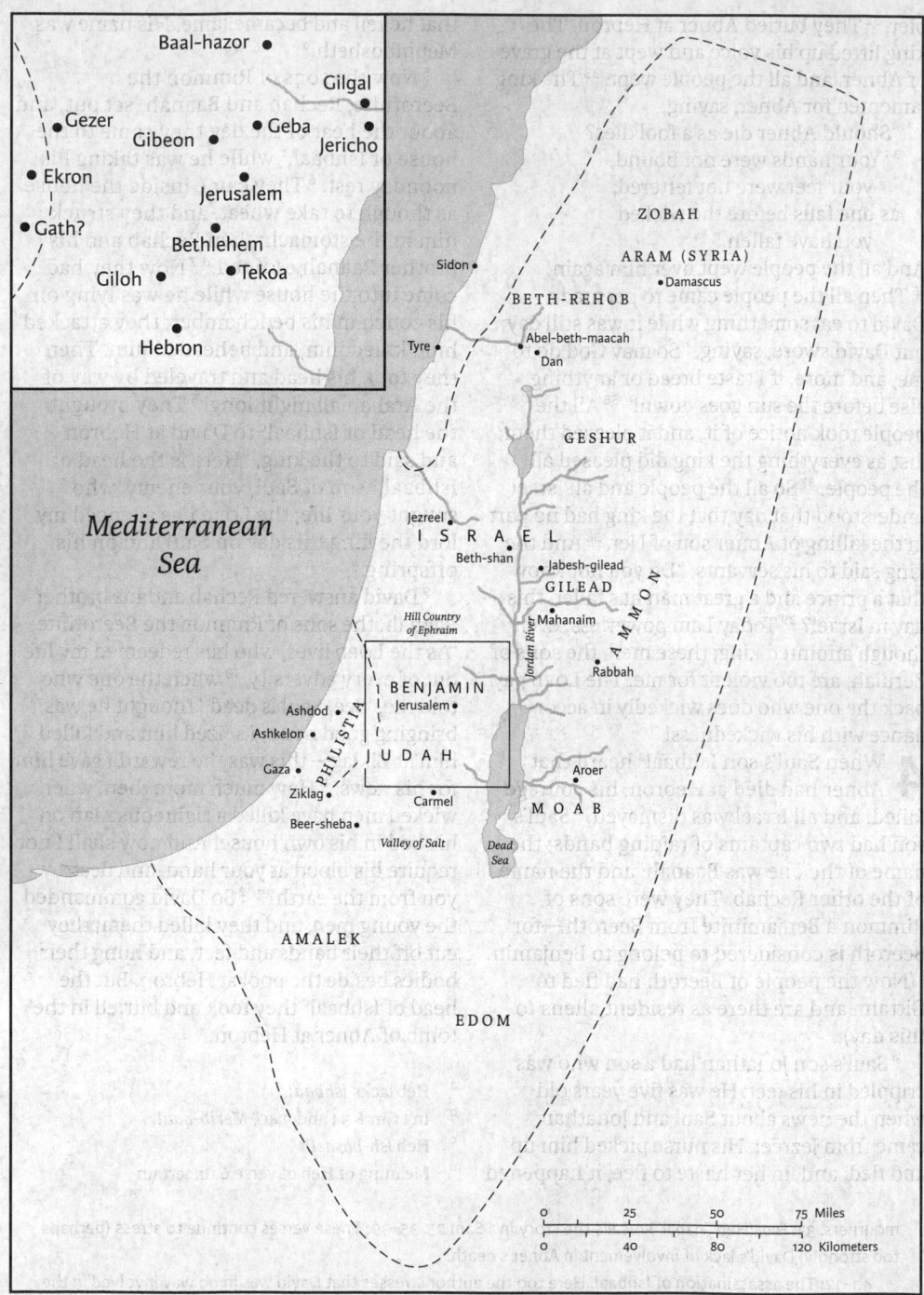

Mediterranean
Sea

Baal-hazor

Gilgal

Gezer
Gibeon   Geba
                        Jericho
Ekron
                Jerusalem
Gath?
        Bethlehem
Giloh   Tekoa

        Hebron

Sidon

Tyre

ZOBAH

ARAM (SYRIA)
        Damascus

BETH-REHOB

Abel-beth-maacah
        Dan

GESHUR

Jezreel
        ISRAEL
        Beth-shan   Jabesh-gilead
                GILEAD   A
        Hill Country   Mahanaim   M
        of Ephraim   M
                                                        O
        BENJAMIN   Rabbah   N
        Jerusalem

Ashdod
Ashkelon
        JUDAH
Gaza
Ziklag   Aroer
        Carmel
Beer-sheba   M O A B
        Valley of Salt
                Dead
                Sea

AMALEK

        EDOM

Jordan River

0   25   50   75   Miles
0   40   80   120   Kilometers

The kingdom of David according to Second Samuel. The dashed line shows the approximate boundary of
the kingdom at its greatest extent.

5 Then all the tribes of Israel came to David at Hebron, and said, "Look, we are your bone and flesh. [2] For some time, while Saul was king over us, it was you who led out Israel and brought it in. The LORD said to you: It is you who shall be shepherd of my people Israel, you who shall be ruler over Israel." [3] So all the elders of Israel came to the king at Hebron; and King David made a covenant with them at Hebron before the LORD, and they anointed David king over Israel. [4] David was thirty years old when he began to reign, and he reigned forty years. [5] At Hebron he reigned over Judah seven years and six months; and at Jerusalem he reigned over all Israel and Judah thirty-three years.

[6] The king and his men marched to Jerusalem against the Jebusites, the inhabitants of the land, who said to David, "You will not come in here, even the blind and the lame will turn you back"—thinking, "David cannot come in here." [7] Nevertheless David took the stronghold of Zion, which is now the city of David. [8] David had said on that day, "Whoever would strike down the Jebusites, let him get up the water shaft to attack the lame and the blind, those whom David hates." [a] Therefore it is said, "The blind and the lame shall not come into the house." [9] David occupied the stronghold, and named it the city of David. David built the city all around from the Millo

inward. [10] And David became greater and greater, for the LORD, the God of hosts, was with him.

[11] King Hiram of Tyre sent messengers to David, along with cedar trees, and carpenters and masons who built David a house. [12] David then perceived that the LORD had established him king over Israel, and that he had exalted his kingdom for the sake of his people Israel.

[13] In Jerusalem, after he came from Hebron, David took more concubines and wives; and more sons and daughters were born to David. [14] These are the names of those who were born to him in Jerusalem: Shammua, Shobab, Nathan, Solomon, [15] Ibhar, Elishua, Nepheg, Japhia, [16] Elishama, Eliada, and Eliphelet.

[17] When the Philistines heard that David had been anointed king over Israel, all the Philistines went up in search of David; but David heard about it and went down to the stronghold. [18] Now the Philistines had come and spread out in the valley of Rephaim. [19] David inquired of the LORD, "Shall I go up against the Philistines? Will you give them into my hand?" The LORD said to David, "Go up; for I will certainly give the Philistines into your hand." [20] So David came to Baal-perazim, and David defeated them there. He

[a] Another reading is *those who hate David*

5.1–16: David becomes king of all Israel and conquers Jerusalem. 1: *All the tribes of Israel,* the northern tribes, excluding Judah where David is already king (2.4). 2: *Led out* and *brought . . . in* are idioms for military leadership. *Shepherd,* a common metaphor for kings. *Ruler,* "king designate" (translated "prince" in 7.8). 3: *Elders,* senior tribal leaders. 4: *Forty years,* a round number for a generation. The actual length of David's reign is not certain, but scholars have proposed ca. 1005–965 BCE as likely dates. 6–8: Exactly how David conquered Jerusalem is not clear. The parallel in 1 Chr 11.5–6 leaves out these verses, perhaps indicating that the Chronicler found them confusing. The account may be an etiology for the saying in v. 8. 6: *Jebusites,* one group of pre-Israelite inhabitants of the land; see Gen 15.21; Ex 3.8; etc. 7: *Zion,* one of the hills on which Jerusalem stood; it becomes a name for the city as a whole. 8: One scholar has argued that *get up the water shaft* means "strike at the wind pipe" so as to kill the enemy rather than leaving any wounded (blind and lame). The saying may refer to the prohibition in Lev 21.18. 9: *City of David,* Jerusalem's location between Israel and Judah was ideal for a neutral capital in David's effort to unite the two. *Millo,* meaning "fill," apparently refers to a landfill or artificial platform created near the *stronghold.* 11: *Tyre,* the capital of Phoenicia, the country north of Israel. *Cedar,* a luxury item for which Lebanon in Phoenician territory was renowned. 13–16: A large harem was a sign of royal prestige. Marriages were also a way of sealing treaties with foreign powers. *Solomon* is born later (12.24); these verses are an anticipatory summary. Alternatively, the mention of Solomon here may suggest that the material has been organized thematically rather than chronologically. A list of sons born to David in Hebron was given in 2 Sam 3.2–5.

5.17–25: War with the Philistines. 17: David's defeat of the Philistines (see 3.18n.) probably preceded his conquest of Jerusalem, since they stood between Hebron and Jerusalem and would have resisted the unification of Israel and Judah. *The stronghold,* probably Adullam (see 1 Sam 22.1), not Jerusalem. 18: *The valley of Rephaim,*

said, "The LORD has burst forth against[a] my enemies before me, like a bursting flood." Therefore that place is called Baal-perazim.[b] [21] The Philistines abandoned their idols there, and David and his men carried them away.

[22] Once again the Philistines came up, and were spread out in the valley of Rephaim. [23] When David inquired of the LORD, he said, "You shall not go up; go around to their rear, and come upon them opposite the balsam trees. [24] When you hear the sound of marching in the tops of the balsam trees, then be on the alert; for then the LORD has gone out before you to strike down the army of the Philistines." [25] David did just as the LORD had commanded him; and he struck down the Philistines from Geba all the way to Gezer.

6 David again gathered all the chosen men of Israel, thirty thousand. [2] David and all the people with him set out and went from Baale-judah, to bring up from there the ark of God, which is called by the name of the LORD of hosts who is enthroned on the cherubim. [3] They carried the ark of God on a new cart, and brought it out of the house of Abinadab, which was on the hill. Uzzah and Ahio,[c] the sons of Abinadab, were driving the new cart [4] with the ark of God;[d] and Ahio[c] went in front of the ark. [5] David and all the house of Israel were dancing before the LORD with all their might, with songs[e] and lyres and harps and tambourines and castanets and cymbals.

[6] When they came to the threshing floor of Nacon, Uzzah reached out his hand to the ark of God and took hold of it, for the oxen shook it. [7] The anger of the LORD was kindled against Uzzah; and God struck him there be-

cause he reached out his hand to the ark;[f] and he died there beside the ark of God. [8] David was angry because the LORD had burst forth with an outburst upon Uzzah; so that place is called Perez-uzzah,[g] to this day. [9] David was afraid of the LORD that day; he said, "How can the ark of the LORD come into my care?" [10] So David was unwilling to take the ark of the LORD into his care in the city of David; instead David took it to the house of Obed-edom the Gittite. [11] The ark of the LORD remained in the house of Obed-edom the Gittite three months; and the LORD blessed Obed-edom and all his household.

[12] It was told King David, "The LORD has blessed the household of Obed-edom and all that belongs to him, because of the ark of God." So David went and brought up the ark of God from the house of Obed-edom to the city of David with rejoicing; [13] and when those who bore the ark of the LORD had gone six paces, he sacrificed an ox and a fatling. [14] David danced before the LORD with all his might; David was girded with a linen ephod. [15] So David and all the house of Israel brought up the ark of the LORD with shouting, and with the sound of the trumpet.

a   Heb *paraz*
b   That is *Lord of Bursting Forth*
c   Or *and his brother*
d   Compare Gk: Heb *and brought it out of the house of Abinadab, which was on the hill with the ark of God*
e   Q Ms Gk 1 Chr 13.8: Heb *fir trees*
f   1 Chr 13.10 Compare Q Ms: Meaning of Heb uncertain
g   That is *Bursting Out Against Uzzah*

probably located southwest of Jerusalem. **19:** *David inquired,* see 2.1n. **20:** An etiology explaining the name *Baal-perazim* (see note *b*); Yahweh and Baal are here equated. **21:** A victorious army typically captured the religious symbols that its opponent brought to the battlefield to show the superiority of its own gods; this is an ironic reversal of 1 Sam 4.5–11. **24:** The one *marching* is the Divine Warrior—the LORD—coming out to fight on Israel's behalf. **25:** *From Geba* near Jerusalem *all the way to Gezer* near the border of Philistine territory.

6.1–23: David brings the ark to Jerusalem. 1: *Thousand* probably designates a military unit of much smaller size. **2:** *Baale-judah,* another name for Kiriath-jearim, according to Josh 15.9, where the ark was left in 1 Sam 7.1. The *ark of God* was viewed as the throne of the LORD. Having it in Jerusalem would make the city the religious as well as the political capital. *Cherubim,* mythical griffins that often guarded temples and palaces (see 1 Sam 4.4n.). **6–8:** *Uzzah's* death shows the awesome holiness of the ark, which was not to be touched, even with the best intentions. The story is also an etiology explaining the name *Perez-uzzah* ("Uzzah's breach"). **10:** *Obed-edom the Gittite* (i.e., from Gath) was apparently among the Philistines who followed David from his days with Achish (1 Sam 27; 29). **13–14:** *He sacrificed,* David officiates as a priest here, which was not unusual for kings in the ancient Near East (8.18; 1 Kings 3.15; 9.25; Gen 14.18). *Linen ephod,* an apron typically worn by priests (1 Sam

[16] As the ark of the LORD came into the city of David, Michal daughter of Saul looked out of the window, and saw King David leaping and dancing before the LORD; and she despised him in her heart.

[17] They brought in the ark of the LORD, and set it in its place, inside the tent that David had pitched for it; and David offered burnt offerings and offerings of well-being before the LORD. [18] When David had finished offering the burnt offerings and the offerings of well-being, he blessed the people in the name of the LORD of hosts, [19] and distributed food among all the people, the whole multitude of Israel, both men and women, to each a cake of bread, a portion of meat,[a] and a cake of raisins. Then all the people went back to their homes.

[20] David returned to bless his household. But Michal the daughter of Saul came out to meet David, and said, "How the king of Israel honored himself today, uncovering himself today before the eyes of his servants' maids, as any vulgar fellow might shamelessly uncover himself!" [21] David said to Michal, "It was before the LORD, who chose me in place of your father and all his household, to appoint me as prince over Israel, the people of the LORD, that I have danced before the LORD. [22] I will make myself yet more contemptible than this, and I will be abased in my own eyes; but by the maids of whom you have spoken, by them I shall be held in honor." [23] And Michal the daughter of Saul had no child to the day of her death.

7 Now when the king was settled in his house, and the LORD had given him rest from all his enemies around him, [2] the king said to the prophet Nathan, "See now, I am living in a house of cedar, but the ark of God stays in a tent." [3] Nathan said to the king, "Go, do all that you have in mind; for the LORD is with you."

[4] But that same night the word of the LORD came to Nathan: [5] Go and tell my servant David: Thus says the LORD: Are you the one to build me a house to live in? [6] I have not lived in a house since the day I brought up the people of Israel from Egypt to this day, but I have been moving about in a tent and a tabernacle. [7] Wherever I have moved about among all the people of Israel, did I ever speak a word with any of the tribal leaders[b] of Israel, whom I commanded to shepherd my people Israel, saying, "Why have you not built me a house of cedar?" [8] Now therefore thus you shall say to my servant David: Thus says the LORD of hosts: I took you from the pasture, from following the sheep to be prince over my people Israel; [9] and I have been with you wherever you went, and have cut off all your enemies from before you; and I will make for

---

a   Vg: Meaning of Heb uncertain
b   Or *any of the tribes*

2.18). Apparently David is wearing little else (see v. 20). **20:** Michal accuses David of fraternizing with the lowest element of society, implying that he is not dignified enough to be king. **21–22:** David replies that he has been humbling himself before the LORD and that the LORD was pleased enough with him to make him king in place of her father, Saul. **23:** *Michal . . . had no child,* probably because David had no relations with her since her children would have been Saul's heirs and a threat to David's rule.

7.1–29: A dynasty for David. This chapter with the LORD's promise to David of an eternal dynasty is a key passage in the Deuteronomistic History. It combines the themes of Jerusalem as the divinely chosen center for worship and the Davidic line as the chosen dynasty in Judah. God's promise of an eternal dynasty (vv. 13–16) explains Judah's survival beyond the destruction of the Northern Kingdom of Israel in 722 BCE. The language and style of the chapter are thoroughly Deuteronomistic, although many scholars believe one or more older oracles underlie vv. 1–7. This promise is reflected in various forms in the Deuteronomistic History and in Pss 89 and 132, as well as in Chronicles. Some of these texts temper the unconditional, eternal nature of the promise. **1:** *The LORD had given him rest from all his enemies around him,* this statement is inconsistent with the accounts of David's wars in chs 8–20 and with 1 Kings 5.3–4, which says that rest came only to Solomon. It is also inconsistent with v. 11, which indicates that the "rest" lies in the future. It is not in the parallel in 1 Chr 17.1. **2:** *In a tent,* the tabernacle. **4–17:** The LORD's promise to David. **5–7:** The *house* ("bayit") David proposes to build is a temple. The LORD says instead (v. 11) that he will build David a house ("bayit"), that is, a dynasty. The claim in vv. 6–7 that the LORD has never had a *house* (i.e., temple) seems to overlook the temple in Shiloh (1 Sam 1–3). **8:** *Following the sheep,* see 1 Sam 17.15, 34. Kings in the ancient Near East were often described as shepherds; see 24.17;

you a great name, like the name of the great ones of the earth. [10] And I will appoint a place for my people Israel and will plant them, so that they may live in their own place, and be disturbed no more; and evildoers shall afflict them no more, as formerly, [11] from the time that I appointed judges over my people Israel; and I will give you rest from all your enemies. Moreover the LORD declares to you that the LORD will make you a house. [12] When your days are fulfilled and you lie down with your ancestors, I will raise up your offspring after you, who shall come forth from your body, and I will establish his kingdom. [13] He shall build a house for my name, and I will establish the throne of his kingdom forever. [14] I will be a father to him, and he shall be a son to me. When he commits iniquity, I will punish him with a rod such as mortals use, with blows inflicted by human beings. [15] But I will not take[a] my steadfast love from him, as I took it from Saul, whom I put away from before you. [16] Your house and your kingdom shall be made sure forever before me;[b] your throne shall be established forever. [17] In accordance with all these words and with all this vision, Nathan spoke to David.

[18] Then King David went in and sat before the LORD, and said, "Who am I, O Lord GOD, and what is my house, that you have brought me thus far? [19] And yet this was a small thing in your eyes, O Lord GOD; you have spoken also of your servant's house for a great while to come. May this be instruction for the people,[c] O Lord GOD! [20] And what more can David say to you? For you know your servant, O Lord GOD! [21] Because of your promise, and according to your own heart, you have wrought all this greatness, so that your servant may know it. [22] Therefore you are great, O LORD God; for there is no one like you, and there is no God besides you, according to all

that we have heard with our ears. [23] Who is like your people, like Israel? Is there another[d] nation on earth whose God went to redeem it as a people, and to make a name for himself, doing great and awesome things for them,[e] by driving out[f] before his people nations and their gods?[g] [24] And you established your people Israel for yourself to be your people forever; and you, O LORD, became their God. [25] And now, O LORD God, as for the word that you have spoken concerning your servant and concerning his house, confirm it forever; do as you have promised. [26] Thus your name will be magnified forever in the saying, 'The LORD of hosts is God over Israel'; and the house of your servant David will be established before you. [27] For you, O LORD of hosts, the God of Israel, have made this revelation to your servant, saying, 'I will build you a house'; therefore your servant has found courage to pray this prayer to you. [28] And now, O Lord GOD, you are God, and your words are true, and you have promised this good thing to your servant; [29] now therefore may it please you to bless the house of your servant, so that it may continue forever before you; for you, O Lord GOD, have spoken, and with your blessing shall the house of your servant be blessed forever."

8 Some time afterward, David attacked the Philistines and subdued them; David took Metheg-ammah out of the hand of the Philistines.

---

a   Gk Syr Vg 1 Chr 17.13: Heb *shall not depart*
b   Gk Heb Mss: MT *before you*; Compare 2 Sam 7.26, 29
c   Meaning of Heb uncertain
d   Gk: Heb *one*
e   Heb *you*
f   Gk 1 Chr 17.21: Heb *for your land*
g   Cn: Heb *before your people, whom you redeemed for yourself from Egypt, nations and its gods*

---

1 Chr 11.2; Ps 78.70; Isa 44.28. *Prince,* "king designate" (translated "ruler" in 5.2). **10:** *Place* in Hebrew may mean a shrine or place of worship. Here it refers to the Jerusalem Temple. **11–12:** See vv. 5–7n. **13:** David's son, Solomon, will build the temple. *Forever* here (and in v. 16) characterizes the dynasty as enduring but does not necessarily mean for all eternity. **14:** *Father . . . son,* a king was often described as the (adopted) "son" of God; see, e.g., Pss 2.7; 89.26–27. **15:** *Steadfast love,* another form of the promise; see Ps 89.1,24. **16:** Cf. 1 Sam 25.28. **18–29:** David's prayer to the LORD. Compare Solomon's prayers in 1 Kings 3.6–9 and 8.22–53. **23:** *Redeem . . . driving out* refer to the Exodus from Egypt and the conquest of Canaan. The language is Deuteronomistic. **24:** Cf. Ex 6.7; Deut 29.10–15. **27–29:** *Your servant,* a way of referring to oneself before a superior.

8.1–18: David's wars. 1: This verse represents David's decisive defeat of the Philistines, the archenemies of

² He also defeated the Moabites and, making them lie down on the ground, measured them off with a cord; he measured two lengths of cord for those who were to be put to death, and one length[a] for those who were to be spared. And the Moabites became servants to David and brought tribute. ³ David also struck down King Hadadezer son of Rehob of Zobah, as he went to restore his monument[b] at the river Euphrates. ⁴ David took from him one thousand seven hundred horsemen, and twenty thousand foot soldiers. David hamstrung all the chariot horses, but left enough for a hundred chariots. ⁵ When the Arameans of Damascus came to help King Hadadezer of Zobah, David killed twenty-two thousand men of the Arameans. ⁶ Then David put garrisons among the Arameans of Damascus; and the Arameans became servants to David and brought tribute. The LORD gave victory to David wherever he went. ⁷ David took the gold shields that were carried by the servants of Hadadezer, and brought them to Jerusalem. ⁸ From Betah and from Berothai, towns of Hadadezer, King David took a great amount of bronze. ⁹ When King Toi of Hamath heard that David had defeated the whole army of Hadadezer, ¹⁰ Toi sent his son Joram to King David, to greet him and to congratulate him because he had fought against Hadadezer and defeated him. Now Hadadezer had often been at war with Toi. Joram brought with him articles of silver,

gold, and bronze; ¹¹ these also King David dedicated to the LORD, together with the silver and gold that he dedicated from all the nations he subdued, ¹² from Edom, Moab, the Ammonites, the Philistines, Amalek, and from the spoil of King Hadadezer son of Rehob of Zobah.

¹³ David won a name for himself. When he returned, he killed eighteen thousand Edomites[c] in the Valley of Salt. ¹⁴ He put garrisons in Edom; throughout all Edom he put garrisons, and all the Edomites became David's servants. And the LORD gave victory to David wherever he went.

¹⁵ So David reigned over all Israel; and David administered justice and equity to all his people. ¹⁶ Joab son of Zeruiah was over the army; Jehoshaphat son of Ahilud was recorder; ¹⁷ Zadok son of Ahitub and Ahimelech son of Abiathar were priests; Seraiah was secretary; ¹⁸ Benaiah son of Jehoiada was over[d] the Cherethites and the Pelethites; and David's sons were priests.

9 David asked, "Is there still anyone left of the house of Saul to whom I may show kindness for Jonathan's sake?" ² Now there was a servant of the house of Saul whose name was Ziba, and he was summoned to David. The king said to him, "Are

[a] Heb *one full length*
[b] Compare 1 Sam 15.12 and 2 Sam 18.18
[c] Gk: Heb *returned from striking down eighteen thousand Arameans*
[d] Syr Tg Vg 20.23; 1 Chr 18.17: Heb lacks *was over*

Saul. They never surface again as enemies during his reign. 2: The *Moabites* lived on the other side of the Dead Sea from Israel. 3: *Zobah* was an Aramean (Syrian) city-state. *Restore* may also mean "leave," so that David, rather than Hadadezer, was traveling to the Euphrates to erect a monument. 4: *Hamstrung*, David crippled the hind legs of the horses he could not use to keep someone else from using them against him (see Josh 11.6). Thus the Israelites probably did not yet make extensive use of chariots. 5: *Twenty-two thousand* probably means twenty-two military units (see 6.1n.). 9: *Hamath*, modern Hama, an important city-state in central Syria north of Zobah. 10: *Joram* is an Israelite (Yahwistic) name; 1 Chr 18.18 calls him "Hadoram," an Aramaic name. 12: *Edom* was the country east of the Jordan, south of Moab and, at times, Judah. *Ammonites*, the ancient residents in the vicinity of the modern city of Amman, Jordan. 13: *Eighteen thousand*, see v. 5n. 15: It was viewed as the responsibility of kings in the ancient Near East to ensure the just and equitable treatment of all subjects, especially the poor and disadvantaged. 16–18: Cf. the similar list of David's cabinet in 20.23–26. *Cherethites and the Pelethites*, perhaps "Cretans" and "Philistines" who composed the royal bodyguard (23.23), probably mercenaries. *David's sons were priests*, the restriction of priesthood to the Levites had apparently not yet arisen. 17: *Ahimelech son of Abiathar* should probably be changed to "Abiathar son of Ahimelech" as indicated in 20.25 and also throughout 2 Sam.

9.1–13: Jonathan's son. 1: *Is there still anyone left of the house of Saul?* David's execution of Saul's sons and grandsons in 21.1–14 provides background to this question, and the story in 21.1–14 probably originally preceded ch 9. *Kindness* is covenant faithfulness. David wants to keep the promise of loyalty he made to Jonathan

you Ziba?" And he said, "At your service!" [3] The king said, "Is there anyone remaining of the house of Saul to whom I may show the kindness of God?" Ziba said to the king, "There remains a son of Jonathan; he is crippled in his feet." [4] The king said to him, "Where is he?" Ziba said to the king, "He is in the house of Machir son of Ammiel, at Lo-debar." [5] Then King David sent and brought him from the house of Machir son of Ammiel, at Lo-debar. [6] Mephibosheth[a] son of Jonathan son of Saul came to David, and fell on his face and did obeisance. David said, "Mephibosheth!"[a] He answered, "I am your servant." [7] David said to him, "Do not be afraid, for I will show you kindness for the sake of your father Jonathan; I will restore to you all the land of your grandfather Saul, and you yourself shall eat at my table always." [8] He did obeisance and said, "What is your servant, that you should look upon a dead dog such as I?"

[9] Then the king summoned Saul's servant Ziba, and said to him, "All that belonged to Saul and to all his house I have given to your master's grandson. [10] You and your sons and your servants shall till the land for him, and shall bring in the produce, so that your master's grandson may have food to eat; but your master's grandson Mephibosheth[a] shall always eat at my table." Now Ziba had fifteen sons and twenty servants. [11] Then Ziba said to the king, "According to all that my lord the king commands his servant, so your servant will do." Mephibosheth[a] ate at David's[b] table, like one of the king's sons. [12] Mephibosheth[a]

had a young son whose name was Mica. And all who lived in Ziba's house became Mephibosheth's[c] servants. [13] Mephibosheth[a] lived in Jerusalem, for he always ate at the king's table. Now he was lame in both his feet.

10 Some time afterward, the king of the Ammonites died, and his son Hanun succeeded him. [2] David said, "I will deal loyally with Hanun son of Nahash, just as his father dealt loyally with me." So David sent envoys to console him concerning his father. When David's envoys came into the land of the Ammonites, [3] the princes of the Ammonites said to their lord Hanun, "Do you really think that David is honoring your father just because he has sent messengers with condolences to you? Has not David sent his envoys to you to search the city, to spy it out, and to overthrow it?" [4] So Hanun seized David's envoys, shaved off half the beard of each, cut off their garments in the middle at their hips, and sent them away. [5] When David was told, he sent to meet them, for the men were greatly ashamed. The king said, "Remain at Jericho until your beards have grown, and then return."

[6] When the Ammonites saw that they had become odious to David, the Ammonites sent and hired the Arameans of Beth-rehob and the Arameans of Zobah, twenty thousand foot soldiers, as well as the king of Maacah,

a Or *Merib-baal*: See 4.4 note
b Gk: Heb *my*
c Or *Merib-baal's*: See 4.4 note

(1 Sam 18.1–4; 20.14–17). **3:** *Crippled in his feet,* see 4.4. This handicap made Mephibosheth unable to go to war and therefore unsuitable to be king. **4:** *Machir* became a loyal supporter of David (17.27). *Lo-debar,* a northern Israelite city east of the Jordan. **6:** *Fell on his face and did obeisance,* prostrating oneself was a sign of submission to God or the king. *Mephibosheth,* the name was originally Merib-baal; see 4.4n. **7:** Eating at the king's *table* was a sign of favor. In this case it allowed David to keep a close watch on Merib-baal, who was still heir to Saul's kingdom and therefore a potential rival (see 16.1–4; 19.24–30). **8:** *Dead dog,* a term of self-reproach (see 3.8n.). **9–13:** Merib-baal was to receive the income from Saul's lands, which Ziba and his family would work.

10.1–19: David defeats the Ammonites and Arameans. **2:** *Nahash,* Saul's enemy in 1 Sam 10.27b–11.15. *Ammonites,* see 8.12n. *Deal loyally . . . dealt loyally,* indicate that David and Nahash had a treaty. *Hanun's* actions in the following verses indicate that Israel was the superior partner in the treaty or that David was trying to make Israel the superior partner, and Hanun resisted. **4:** *The beard* was a symbol of masculinity, and cutting off half of it was symbolic emasculation. According to the Lachish reliefs, ancient Israelite and Judean men were typically bearded. Cutting off *their garments* below the waist was symbolic castration. **5:** *Jericho,* the closest Israelite city west of the Jordan opposite Ammon. **6:** *Beth-rehob, Zobah,* Aramean (Syrian) city-states. *Thousand,* probably

one thousand men, and the men of Tob, twelve thousand men. [7] When David heard of it, he sent Joab and all the army with the warriors. [8] The Ammonites came out and drew up in battle array at the entrance of the gate; but the Arameans of Zobah and of Rehob, and the men of Tob and Maacah, were by themselves in the open country.

[9] When Joab saw that the battle was set against him both in front and in the rear, he chose some of the picked men of Israel, and arrayed them against the Arameans; [10] the rest of his men he put in the charge of his brother Abishai, and he arrayed them against the Ammonites. [11] He said, "If the Arameans are too strong for me, then you shall help me; but if the Ammonites are too strong for you, then I will come and help you. [12] Be strong, and let us be courageous for the sake of our people, and for the cities of our God; and may the LORD do what seems good to him." [13] So Joab and the people who were with him moved forward into battle against the Arameans; and they fled before him. [14] When the Ammonites saw that the Arameans fled, they likewise fled before Abishai, and entered the city. Then Joab returned from fighting against the Ammonites, and came to Jerusalem.

[15] But when the Arameans saw that they had been defeated by Israel, they gathered themselves together. [16] Hadadezer sent and brought out the Arameans who were beyond the Euphrates; and they came to Helam, with Shobach the commander of the army

of Hadadezer at their head. [17] When it was told David, he gathered all Israel together, and crossed the Jordan, and came to Helam. The Arameans arrayed themselves against David and fought with him. [18] The Arameans fled before Israel; and David killed of the Arameans seven hundred chariot teams, and forty thousand horsemen,[a] and wounded Shobach the commander of their army, so that he died there. [19] When all the kings who were servants of Hadadezer saw that they had been defeated by Israel, they made peace with Israel, and became subject to them. So the Arameans were afraid to help the Ammonites any more.

11 In the spring of the year, the time when kings go out to battle, David sent Joab with his officers and all Israel with him; they ravaged the Ammonites, and besieged Rabbah. But David remained at Jerusalem.

[2] It happened, late one afternoon, when David rose from his couch and was walking about on the roof of the king's house, that he saw from the roof a woman bathing; the woman was very beautiful. [3] David sent someone to inquire about the woman. It was reported, "This is Bathsheba daughter of Eliam, the wife of Uriah the Hittite." [4] So David sent messengers to get her, and she came to him, and he lay with her. (Now she was purifying herself after her period.) Then she returned to her house. [5] The woman conceived; and she sent and told David, "I am pregnant."

---

[a] 1 Chr 19.18 and some Gk Mss read *foot soldiers*

used for a military unit of far fewer than 1,000 men. *Maacah, Tob,* small states in northern Transjordan. **8:** *The gate,* the city in question is Rabbah, capital of the Ammonites (see 12.26). *Rehob,* another Aramean city-state. **12:** *The cities of our God* were the cities Israel claimed east of the Jordan. Joab is rousing the army for "holy war." **18:** *Forty thousand,* see v. 6.

11.1–27: David and Bathsheba. 1: *In the spring of the year, the time when kings go out to battle,* an alternate translation is: "A year after the kings had gone out to battle." The story is set a year after the events in ch 10 and does not necessarily imply that kings were supposed to go to war each spring. *David remained at Jerusalem,* perhaps at the insistence of his army to avoid danger to himself (see 21.15–17), although here this may be a possible disparagement of David. **2:** *The roof of the king's house* was breezy and cool in the late afternoon, the ideal place for a nap. From there he was able to look down into the courtyard of surrounding houses, where he saw the *woman bathing.* **3:** *Inquire about the woman,* David wants to know whether she is married; if not, he can add her to his harem. *Eliam,* perhaps the son of Ahithophel, David's adviser (see 23.34; 16.15–17.23). *Uriah,* one of the "thirty" best soldiers of David, according to 23.39. Thus, Bathsheba was well-married and came from a distinguished family. The name "Uriah" is Israelite, but his epithet "the Hittite" indicated his non-Israelite heritage. He may have been a resident alien, a class whose rights kings were especially charged to guard. **4:** *Bathsheba was purifying herself after her period;* hence her bath (see Lev 15.19–28). She was at the most fertile time of her

[6] So David sent word to Joab, "Send me Uriah the Hittite." And Joab sent Uriah to David. [7] When Uriah came to him, David asked how Joab and the people fared, and how the war was going. [8] Then David said to Uriah, "Go down to your house, and wash your feet." Uriah went out of the king's house, and there followed him a present from the king. [9] But Uriah slept at the entrance of the king's house with all the servants of his lord, and did not go down to his house. [10] When they told David, "Uriah did not go down to his house," David said to Uriah, "You have just come from a journey. Why did you not go down to your house?" [11] Uriah said to David, "The ark and Israel and Judah remain in booths;[a] and my lord Joab and the servants of my lord are camping in the open field; shall I then go to my house, to eat and to drink, and to lie with my wife? As you live, and as your soul lives, I will not do such a thing." [12] Then David said to Uriah, "Remain here today also, and tomorrow I will send you back." So Uriah remained in Jerusalem that day. On the next day, [13] David invited him to eat and drink in his presence and made him drunk; and in the evening he went out to lie on his couch with the servants of his lord, but he did not go down to his house.

[14] In the morning David wrote a letter to Joab, and sent it by the hand of Uriah. [15] In the letter he wrote, "Set Uriah in the forefront of the hardest fighting, and then draw back from him, so that he may be struck down and die." [16] As Joab was besieging the city, he assigned Uriah to the place where he knew there were valiant warriors. [17] The men of the city came out and fought with Joab; and some of the servants of David among the people fell. Uriah the Hittite was killed as well. [18] Then Joab sent and told David all the news about the fighting; [19] and he instructed the messenger, "When you have finished telling the king all the news about the fighting, [20] then, if the king's anger rises, and if he says to you, 'Why did you go so near the city to fight? Did you not know that they would shoot from the wall? [21] Who killed Abimelech son of Jerubbaal?[b] Did not a woman throw an upper millstone on him from the wall, so that he died at Thebez? Why did you go so near the wall?' then you shall say, 'Your servant Uriah the Hittite is dead too.'"

[22] So the messenger went, and came and told David all that Joab had sent him to tell. [23] The messenger said to David, "The men gained an advantage over us, and came out against us in the field; but we drove them back to the entrance of the gate. [24] Then the archers shot at your servants from the wall; some of the king's servants are dead; and your servant Uriah the Hittite is dead also." [25] David said to the messenger, "Thus you shall say to Joab, 'Do not let this matter trouble you, for the sword devours now one and now another; press your attack on the city, and overthrow it.' And encourage him."

[26] When the wife of Uriah heard that her husband was dead, she made lamentation for him. [27] When the mourning was over, David sent and brought her to his house, and she became his wife, and bore him a son.

[a] Or at Succoth
[b] Gk Syr Judg 7.1: Heb Jerubbesheth

cycle when she slept with David. It is clear that David must be her child's father. 6–7: It was unusual for a soldier to be called back from battle for a personal audience. Since David asked Uriah only the most general questions, Uriah may have thought he was being tested, which in turn motivated him to demonstrate his loyalty to David and the army in the following verses. The *people*, the army. 8: *Wash your feet*, a euphemism for sexual intercourse. *Feet* can refer to the genitals (see Isa 6.2; 7.20). 9–13: As a pious soldier consecrated for war (see 1 Sam 21.4), Uriah refuses to have sexual relations with his wife, even when David gets him drunk. 14: David trusts Uriah's loyalty enough to send his death warrant by his own hand, knowing that Uriah, if he could read, would not open it. 16–17: Joab places Uriah in a dangerous place but does not have time to implement David's order fully. Uriah is killed along with other soldiers because of a tactical error by Joab. 18–21: Joab uses Uriah's death to cover up his mistake in allowing the troops to come too close to the city wall. The story of *Abimelech son of Jerubbaal* (v. 21) is in Judg 9. *An upper millstone*, a large stone used for grinding grain. 25: David's attitude toward Joab changes when he learns of Uriah's death. 27b: *David . . . displeased the LORD*, the author's moral condemnation links the account of David's offense in ch 11 with the judgment in ch 12.

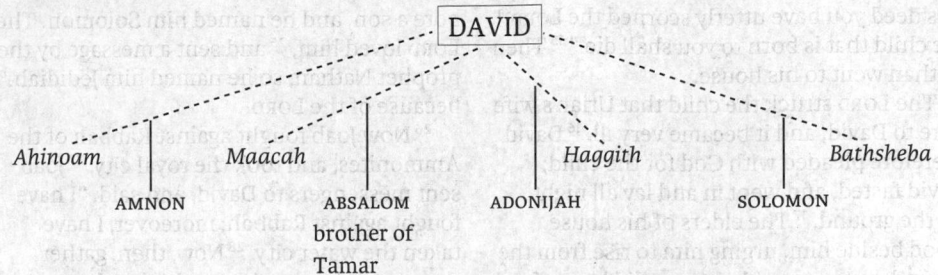

DAVID

Ahinoam | Maacah | Haggith | Bathsheba

AMNON | ABSALOM
brother of
Tamar | ADONIJAH | SOLOMON

The sons of David. According to 2 Sam 3.2–5 (see also 1 Chr 3.1–4) and 2 Sam 5.13–14 (1 Chr 3.5–9; 14.3–7), David had many children, at least twenty of whom are named. In the narrative of the struggle for succession in 2 Samuel 13–18 and 1 Kings 1–2, the principal sons in the order of their birth are: Amnon, Absalom, Adonijah, and Solomon. Dashed lines show wives; solid lines show sons.

12 But the thing that David had done displeased the LORD, [1] and the LORD sent Nathan to David. He came to him, and said to him, "There were two men in a certain city, the one rich and the other poor. [2] The rich man had very many flocks and herds; [3] but the poor man had nothing but one little ewe lamb, which he had bought. He brought it up, and it grew up with him and with his children; it used to eat of his meager fare, and drink from his cup, and lie in his bosom, and it was like a daughter to him. [4] Now there came a traveler to the rich man, and he was loath to take one of his own flock or herd to prepare for the wayfarer who had come to him, but he took the poor man's lamb, and prepared that for the guest who had come to him." [5] Then David's anger was greatly kindled against the man. He said to Nathan, "As the LORD lives, the man who has done this deserves to die; [6] he shall restore the lamb fourfold, because he did this thing, and because he had no pity."

[7] Nathan said to David, "You are the man! Thus says the LORD, the God of Israel: I anointed you king over Israel, and I rescued you from the hand of Saul; [8] I gave you your master's house, and your master's wives into your bosom, and gave you the house of Israel and of Judah; and if that had been too little, I would have added as much more. [9] Why have you despised the word of the LORD, to do what is evil in his sight? You have struck down Uriah the Hittite with the sword, and have taken his wife to be your wife, and have killed him with the sword of the Ammonites. [10] Now therefore the sword shall never depart from your house, for you have despised me, and have taken the wife of Uriah the Hittite to be your wife. [11] Thus says the LORD: I will raise up trouble against you from within your own house; and I will take your wives before your eyes, and give them to your neighbor, and he shall lie with your wives in the sight of this very sun. [12] For you did it secretly; but I will do this thing before all Israel, and before the sun." [13] David said to Nathan, "I have sinned against the LORD." Nathan said to David, "Now the LORD has put away your sin; you shall not die. [14] Nevertheless, because by

12.1–25: David's punishment. 1–6: The prophet Nathan couches his parable as a legal case to get David to pronounce judgment on himself. As king he was responsible for protecting the rights of the poor. However, the vagueness of the case ("*Two men in a certain city*") hints that it is contained by Nathan. *Fourfold* (v. 6), as prescribed in Ex 22.1; other textual witnesses have "sevenfold." **8:** There is some textual support for reading "daughter(s)" (Heb "bat") instead of *house* (Heb "bayit" or "beyt") both times in this verse. "Daughter(s)" would fit the point of the verse better — that David had many women as wives and concubines, including Saul's daughter Michal, but like the rich man in Nathan's parable, he stole what belonged to his poor neighbor. *Your master's wives,* David took over Saul's harem. **10:** *The sword,* a metaphor for violence, alluding to the events in chs 13–20. **11–12:** An allusion to Absalom's future revolt, specifically his deed in 16.20–23. **13–18:** David's sin is transferred (not *put away*) to his newborn son, who dies because of it. This is the clearest indication in the Hebrew Bible of the application of intergenerational punishment by God (see Ex 20.5; 34.7; Deut 5.9), where the

this deed you have utterly scorned the LORD,[a] the child that is born to you shall die." [15] Then Nathan went to his house.

The LORD struck the child that Uriah's wife bore to David, and it became very ill. [16] David therefore pleaded with God for the child; David fasted, and went in and lay all night on the ground. [17] The elders of his house stood beside him, urging him to rise from the ground; but he would not, nor did he eat food with them. [18] On the seventh day the child died. And the servants of David were afraid to tell him that the child was dead; for they said, "While the child was still alive, we spoke to him, and he did not listen to us; how then can we tell him the child is dead? He may do himself some harm." [19] But when David saw that his servants were whispering together, he perceived that the child was dead; and David said to his servants, "Is the child dead?" They said, "He is dead."

[20] Then David rose from the ground, washed, anointed himself, and changed his clothes. He went into the house of the LORD, and worshiped; he then went to his own house; and when he asked, they set food before him and he ate. [21] Then his servants said to him, "What is this thing that you have done? You fasted and wept for the child while it was alive; but when the child died, you rose and ate food." [22] He said, "While the child was still alive, I fasted and wept; for I said, 'Who knows? The LORD may be gracious to me, and the child may live.' [23] But now he is dead; why should I fast? Can I bring him back again? I shall go to him, but he will not return to me."

[24] Then David consoled his wife Bathsheba, and went to her, and lay with her; and she bore a son, and he named him Solomon. The LORD loved him, [25] and sent a message by the prophet Nathan; so he named him Jedidiah,[b] because of the LORD.

[26] Now Joab fought against Rabbah of the Ammonites, and took the royal city. [27] Joab sent messengers to David, and said, "I have fought against Rabbah; moreover, I have taken the water city. [28] Now, then, gather the rest of the people together, and encamp against the city, and take it; or I myself will take the city, and it will be called by my name." [29] So David gathered all the people together and went to Rabbah, and fought against it and took it. [30] He took the crown of Milcom[c] from his head; the weight of it was a talent of gold, and in it was a precious stone; and it was placed on David's head. He also brought forth the spoil of the city, a very great amount. [31] He brought out the people who were in it, and set them to work with saws and iron picks and iron axes, or sent them to the brickworks. Thus he did to all the cities of the Ammonites. Then David and all the people returned to Jerusalem.

13 Some time passed. David's son Absalom had a beautiful sister whose name was Tamar; and David's son Amnon fell in love with her. [2] Amnon was so tormented that he made himself ill because of his sister Tamar, for she was a virgin and it seemed impossible to Amnon to do anything to her. [3] But Amnon had a friend whose name was

---

a Ancient scribal tradition: Compare 1 Sam 25.22 note: Heb *scorned the enemies of the LORD*

b That is *Beloved of the LORD*

c Gk See 1 Kings 11.5, 33: Heb *their kings*

---

sin is perceived as property that may be inherited. **20**: *House of the LORD,* an anachronism, since the Temple in Jerusalem had not yet been built. **24–25**: *Solomon* means "his replacement"; he was a replacement for the dead child. *Jedidiah* ("beloved of Yahweh"), which does not occur elsewhere for Solomon, hints that he will replace David (whose name means "beloved") as king.

12.26–31: The conclusion of the Ammonite war. 26–29: Joab captured the citadel and the water supply of Rabbah, the Ammonite capital, so that conquering the rest of the city was fairly simple. This Joab left for David, as the king, to complete. **30**: *Milcom,* the national Ammonite god. *A talent,* about 75 lb (34 kg).

13.1–39: The rape of Tamar and the murder of Amnon. In its current context, this and the following chapter reflect a measure-for-measure punishment of David. He appropriated Bathsheba and arranged for Uriah's death, so rape and death are unleashed against his house. Originally, though, this story may have been unconnected to the Bathsheba event and served to introduce Absalom's revolt. **1**: Tamar was Absalom's full *sister,* Amnon's half-sister. *Amnon* was David's oldest son and the crown prince. The next oldest had apparently died (perhaps as a child), leaving Absalom as second in line of succession to the throne (cf. 3.2–3). **2**: *It seemed impos-*

Jonadab, the son of David's brother Shimeah; and Jonadab was a very crafty man. [4] He said to him, "O son of the king, why are you so haggard morning after morning? Will you not tell me?" Amnon said to him, "I love Tamar, my brother Absalom's sister." [5] Jonadab said to him, "Lie down on your bed, and pretend to be ill; and when your father comes to see you, say to him, 'Let my sister Tamar come and give me something to eat, and prepare the food in my sight, so that I may see it and eat it from her hand.'" [6] So Amnon lay down, and pretended to be ill; and when the king came to see him, Amnon said to the king, "Please let my sister Tamar come and make a couple of cakes in my sight, so that I may eat from her hand."

[7] Then David sent home to Tamar, saying, "Go to your brother Amnon's house, and prepare food for him." [8] So Tamar went to her brother Amnon's house, where he was lying down. She took dough, kneaded it, made cakes in his sight, and baked the cakes. [9] Then she took the pan and set them[a] out before him, but he refused to eat. Amnon said, "Send out everyone from me." So everyone went out from him. [10] Then Amnon said to Tamar, "Bring the food into the chamber, so that I may eat from your hand." So Tamar took the cakes she had made, and brought them into the chamber to Amnon her brother. [11] But when she brought them near him to eat, he took hold of her, and said to her, "Come, lie with me, my sister." [12] She answered him, "No, my brother, do not force me; for such a thing is not done in Israel; do not do anything so vile! [13] As for me, where

could I carry my shame? And as for you, you would be as one of the scoundrels in Israel. Now therefore, I beg you, speak to the king; for he will not withhold me from you." [14] But he would not listen to her; and being stronger than she, he forced her and lay with her.

[15] Then Amnon was seized with a very great loathing for her; indeed, his loathing was even greater than the lust he had felt for her. Amnon said to her, "Get out!" [16] But she said to him, "No, my brother;[b] for this wrong in sending me away is greater than the other that you did to me." But he would not listen to her. [17] He called the young man who served him and said, "Put this woman out of my presence, and bolt the door after her." [18] (Now she was wearing a long robe with sleeves; for this is how the virgin daughters of the king were clothed in earlier times.[c]) So his servant put her out, and bolted the door after her. [19] But Tamar put ashes on her head, and tore the long robe that she was wearing; she put her hand on her head, and went away, crying aloud as she went.

[20] Her brother Absalom said to her, "Has Amnon your brother been with you? Be quiet for now, my sister; he is your brother; do not take this to heart." So Tamar remained, a desolate woman, in her brother Absalom's house. [21] When King David heard of all these things, he became very angry, but he would not punish his son Amnon, because he loved

a Heb *and poured*
b Cn Compare Gk Vg: Meaning of Heb uncertain
c Cn: Heb *were clothed in robes*

sible to Amnon to do anything to her, as the king's virgin daughter Tamar may have been guarded. However, the verb translated "seemed impossible" might be translated "seemed wonderful." **6**: *Cakes,* the Hebrew word is similar to the word for "heart" and may indicate their shape and hints at the erotic nature of the story. **10**: *The chamber,* Amnon's bedroom where he is feigning illness. **11**: *My sister* not only reflects the kinship of Amnon to Tamar but is also a term of endearment and sexual desire in ancient love poetry (i.e., Song 4.9–10; 5.1). **12**: *Such a thing* may refer to incest or rape or both. **13**: *He will not withhold me from you,* Tamar suggests that David would allow their marriage despite its incestuous nature. Perhaps she is just trying to buy time. **16**: Ex 22.16 and Deut 22.28–29 required marriage in such cases. Tamar may have such laws in mind when she says that in sending her away Amnon is committing a *greater* wrong than the rape itself. **17**: *This woman,* a contemptuous reference. The word "woman" is not in the Heb, so that it might be translated "this thing." Having robbed Tamar of her virginity, Amnon takes her identity as well. **18**: *A long robe with sleeves,* used also for Joseph's garment in Gen 37.3; the exact nature of this garment is unknown. **19**: Putting ashes on the head and tearing clothes were signs of grief, though Tamar may also have torn *the long robe* worn by the king's virgin daughters because it was no longer appropriate. **20**: *Desolate,* because she is unmarried and childless. **21**: *Because he loved him* may be the

him, for he was his firstborn.[a] [22] But Absalom spoke to Amnon neither good nor bad; for Absalom hated Amnon, because he had raped his sister Tamar.

[23] After two full years Absalom had sheepshearers at Baal-hazor, which is near Ephraim, and Absalom invited all the king's sons. [24] Absalom came to the king, and said, "Your servant has sheepshearers; will the king and his servants please go with your servant?" [25] But the king said to Absalom, "No, my son, let us not all go, or else we will be burdensome to you." He pressed him, but he would not go but gave him his blessing. [26] Then Absalom said, "If not, please let my brother Amnon go with us." The king said to him, "Why should he go with you?" [27] But Absalom pressed him until he let Amnon and all the king's sons go with him. Absalom made a feast like a king's feast.[b] [28] Then Absalom commanded his servants, "Watch when Amnon's heart is merry with wine, and when I say to you, 'Strike Amnon,' then kill him. Do not be afraid; have I not myself commanded you? Be courageous and valiant." [29] So the servants of Absalom did to Amnon as Absalom had commanded. Then all the king's sons rose, and each mounted his mule and fled.

[30] While they were on the way, the report came to David that Absalom had killed all the king's sons, and not one of them was left. [31] The king rose, tore his garments, and lay on the ground; and all his servants who were standing by tore their garments. [32] But Jonadab, the son of David's brother Shimeah, said, "Let not my lord suppose that they have killed all the young men the king's sons; Am-

non alone is dead. This has been determined by Absalom from the day Amnon[c] raped his sister Tamar. [33] Now therefore, do not let my lord the king take it to heart, as if all the king's sons were dead; for Amnon alone is dead."

[34] But Absalom fled. When the young man who kept watch looked up, he saw many people coming from the Horonaim road[d] by the side of the mountain. [35] Jonadab said to the king, "See, the king's sons have come; as your servant said, so it has come about." [36] As soon as he had finished speaking, the king's sons arrived, and raised their voices and wept; and the king and all his servants also wept very bitterly.

[37] But Absalom fled, and went to Talmai son of Ammihud, king of Geshur. David mourned for his son day after day. [38] Absalom, having fled to Geshur, stayed there three years. [39] And the heart of[e] the king went out, yearning for Absalom; for he was now consoled over the death of Amnon.

14 Now Joab son of Zeruiah perceived that the king's mind was on Absalom. [2] Joab sent to Tekoa and brought from there a wise woman. He said to her, "Pretend to be a mourner; put on mourning garments, do not anoint yourself with oil, but behave like a woman who has been mourning many days for the dead. [3] Go to the king and speak to

a   Q Ms Gk: MT lacks *but he would not punish . . . firstborn*
b   Gk Compare Q Ms: MT lacks *Absalom made a feast like a king's feast*
c   Heb *he*
d   Cn Compare Gk: Heb *the road behind him*
e   Q Ms Gk: MT *And David*

writer's way of assuring the reader that David had nothing to do with Amnon's death. **22:** *Neither good nor bad* means not at all. **23:** Sheepshearing was a time of celebration. **24–25:** In light of what follows, Absalom's invitation to David makes the reader wonder whether he already intended to kill his father and assume the throne. **27:** The *feast* was a drinking bout, as indicated by the word's etymology and the next verse. **29:** David and his sons rode on *mules* (18.9; 1 Kings 1.33). **30–33:** David initially thought that Absalom had killed all the king's sons, which would make sense if he were attempting a coup. But his intention at this point is purely revenge against Amnon. *Jonadab* appears as a false friend to Amnon (cf. vv. 3–5). **36:** *The king . . . wept very bitterly,* David's great love for Amnon and his noninvolvement in Amnon's death are stressed. **37:** *Talmai . . . king of Geshur,* Absalom's maternal grandfather with whom David apparently has a treaty (see 2.9n.). **39:** *And the heart of the king went out, yearning for Absalom,* better: "The king's spirit for marching out against Absalom was exhausted." David did not yearn for Absalom but was tired of going out after him; hence David's reluctance in the next chapter to allow Absalom back into his presence.

14.1–33: Absalom's return. **1:** *The king's mind was on Absalom* does not mean that David was now favorably inclined toward Absalom, as this story makes clear. **2:** *Tekoa,* a village south of Bethlehem where the prophet

him as follows." And Joab put the words into her mouth.

⁴ When the woman of Tekoa came to the king, she fell on her face to the ground and did obeisance, and said, "Help, O king!" ⁵ The king asked her, "What is your trouble?" She answered, "Alas, I am a widow; my husband is dead. ⁶ Your servant had two sons, and they fought with one another in the field; there was no one to part them, and one struck the other and killed him. ⁷ Now the whole family has risen against your servant. They say, 'Give up the man who struck his brother, so that we may kill him for the life of his brother whom he murdered, even if we destroy the heir as well.' Thus they would quench my one remaining ember, and leave to my husband neither name nor remnant on the face of the earth."

⁸ Then the king said to the woman, "Go to your house, and I will give orders concerning you." ⁹ The woman of Tekoa said to the king, "On me be the guilt, my lord the king, and on my father's house; let the king and his throne be guiltless." ¹⁰ The king said, "If anyone says anything to you, bring him to me, and he shall never touch you again." ¹¹ Then she said, "Please, may the king keep the Lord your God in mind, so that the avenger of blood may kill no more, and my son not be destroyed." He said, "As the Lord lives, not one hair of your son shall fall to the ground."

¹² Then the woman said, "Please let your servant speak a word to my lord the king." He said, "Speak." ¹³ The woman said, "Why then have you planned such a thing against the people of God? For in giving this decision the king convicts himself, inasmuch as the king does not bring his banished one home again. ¹⁴ We must all die; we are like water spilled on the ground, which cannot be gathered up. But God will not take away a life; he will devise plans so as not to keep an outcast banished forever from his presence.ᵃ ¹⁵ Now I have come to say this to my lord the king because the people have made me afraid; your servant thought, 'I will speak to the king; it may be that the king will perform the request of his servant. ¹⁶ For the king will hear, and deliver his servant from the hand of the man who would cut both me and my son off from the heritage of God.' ¹⁷ Your servant thought, 'The word of my lord the king will set me at rest'; for my lord the king is like the angel of God, discerning good and evil. The Lord your God be with you!"

¹⁸ Then the king answered the woman, "Do not withhold from me anything I ask you." The woman said, "Let my lord the king speak." ¹⁹ The king said, "Is the hand of Joab with you in all this?" The woman answered and said, "As surely as you live, my lord the king, one cannot turn right or left from anything that my lord the king has said. For it was your servant Joab who commanded me; it was he who put all these words into the mouth of your servant. ²⁰ In order to change the course of affairs your servant Joab did this. But my lord has wisdom like the wisdom

ᵃ Meaning of Heb uncertain

Amos was from (see Am 1.1). Perhaps David took an interest in this case because the woman was from his home territory. *Wise* in the Hebrew Bible often means skilled as well as clever (see Ex 28.3). This woman was a skilled actress. **4:** *Fell . . . to the ground and did obeisance,* prostration was the proper way of bowing before a king. **5–7:** As in ch 12, a fictional legal case is presented to David in order to get him to pronounce judgment on a matter concerning himself. *Two sons* (v. 6), one of whom kills the other, like Amnon and Absalom. *Leave to my husband neither name nor remnant* (v. 7). This part of the woman's case is not paralleled in David's family since he has many other sons. It is crucial to the woman's place, yet does not figure into David's decision or the outcome of the story. **8–11:** David grants the woman's request and swears by the Lord that her one remaining son will not be harmed. The woman will urge David to apply this oath to his situation with Absalom. Since David's ruling is contrary to the customary punishment, the woman accepts any guilt that David may incur (v. 9). *Avenger of blood,* one charged with taking vengeance for the death of a relative. **13:** *The woman* now applies David's decree to the situation with Absalom. It is not clear how David's refusal to bring Absalom back is *a thing against the people of God.* **14:** Amnon is dead and cannot be brought to life again, but David can accept Absalom, who is still alive. **15–17:** These verses seem out of place and may originally have gone after v. 7. The woman continues to plead for her son, but David has already rendered his decision. *The man who would cut both me and my son off,* the avenger of blood (see v. 11). *The heritage of God,* the land of Israel and its people. **19:** *Your servant,* a polite

of the angel of God to know all things that are on the earth."

²¹ Then the king said to Joab, "Very well, I grant this; go, bring back the young man Absalom." ²² Joab prostrated himself with his face to the ground and did obeisance, and blessed the king; and Joab said, "Today your servant knows that I have found favor in your sight, my lord the king, in that the king has granted the request of his servant." ²³ So Joab set off, went to Geshur, and brought Absalom to Jerusalem. ²⁴ The king said, "Let him go to his own house; he is not to come into my presence." So Absalom went to his own house, and did not come into the king's presence.

²⁵ Now in all Israel there was no one to be praised so much for his beauty as Absalom; from the sole of his foot to the crown of his head there was no blemish in him. ²⁶ When he cut the hair of his head (for at the end of every year he used to cut it; when it was heavy on him, he cut it), he weighed the hair of his head, two hundred shekels by the king's weight. ²⁷ There were born to Absalom three sons, and one daughter whose name was Tamar; she was a beautiful woman.

²⁸ So Absalom lived two full years in Jerusalem, without coming into the king's presence. ²⁹ Then Absalom sent for Joab to send him to the king; but Joab would not come to him. He sent a second time, but Joab would not come. ³⁰ Then he said to his servants, "Look, Joab's field is next to mine, and he has barley there; go and set it on fire." So Absalom's servants set the field on fire. ³¹ Then Joab rose and went to Absalom at his house, and said to him, "Why have your servants set my field on fire?" ³² Absalom answered Joab, "Look, I sent word to you: Come here, that I

may send you to the king with the question, 'Why have I come from Geshur? It would be better for me to be there still.' Now let me go into the king's presence; if there is guilt in me, let him kill me!" ³³ Then Joab went to the king and told him; and he summoned Absalom. So he came to the king and prostrated himself with his face to the ground before the king; and the king kissed Absalom.

15 After this Absalom got himself a chariot and horses, and fifty men to run ahead of him. ² Absalom used to rise early and stand beside the road into the gate; and when anyone brought a suit before the king for judgment, Absalom would call out and say, "From what city are you?" When the person said, "Your servant is of such and such a tribe in Israel," ³ Absalom would say, "See, your claims are good and right; but there is no one deputed by the king to hear you." ⁴ Absalom said moreover, "If only I were judge in the land! Then all who had a suit or cause might come to me, and I would give them justice." ⁵ Whenever people came near to do obeisance to him, he would put out his hand and take hold of them, and kiss them. ⁶ Thus Absalom did to every Israelite who came to the king for judgment; so Absalom stole the hearts of the people of Israel.

⁷ At the end of fourᵃ years Absalom said to the king, "Please let me go to Hebron and pay the vow that I have made to the LORD. ⁸ For your servant made a vow while I lived at Geshur in Aram: If the LORD will indeed bring me back to Jerusalem, then I will worship the LORD in Hebron."ᵇ ⁹ The king said to him, "Go

ᵃ Gk Syr: Heb *forty*
ᵇ Gk Mss: Heb lacks *in Hebron*

form of self-reference. **21–24:** David allows Absalom to return but refuses to see him personally. **26:** *Two hundred shekels,* ca. 5 lb (2.3 kg), an extraordinary amount of hair. The reference to his hair foreshadows Absalom's mode of death (18.9–15). **27:** Absalom named his daughter after his sister, *Tamar* (ch 13). The reference to his three sons is contradicted in 18.18, where he says he had no son. **28–33:** This episode further shows Absalom's violent nature and suggests that Joab may have held a grudge against him. *The king kissed Absalom,* a gesture of recognition and reconciliation, performed only after Absalom did his obeisance to David. This subservience, however, did not last long.

15.1–12: Absalom revolts. 1: *Chariot and horses, and fifty men to run ahead,* parts of the king's entourage (1 Kings 1.5). The fifty men were probably a royal bodyguard. Absalom is making a claim to be king. **2:** *When anyone brought a suit before the king for judgment,* one of the king's roles in the ancient world was to serve as a judge in special cases. David may have been weak in this role, and Absalom took advantage. **5:** *Do obeisance to him,* the proper attitude before a king, but Absalom presented himself as a man of the people. **6:** *Stole the*

in peace." So he got up, and went to Hebron. [10] But Absalom sent secret messengers throughout all the tribes of Israel, saying, "As soon as you hear the sound of the trumpet, then shout: Absalom has become king at Hebron!" [11] Two hundred men from Jerusalem went with Absalom; they were invited guests, and they went in their innocence, knowing nothing of the matter. [12] While Absalom was offering the sacrifices, he sent for[a] Ahithophel the Gilonite, David's counselor, from his city Giloh. The conspiracy grew in strength, and the people with Absalom kept increasing.

[13] A messenger came to David, saying, "The hearts of the Israelites have gone after Absalom." [14] Then David said to all his officials who were with him at Jerusalem, "Get up! Let us flee, or there will be no escape for us from Absalom. Hurry, or he will soon overtake us, and bring disaster down upon us, and attack the city with the edge of the sword." [15] The king's officials said to the king, "Your servants are ready to do whatever our lord the king decides." [16] So the king left, followed by all his household, except ten concubines whom he left behind to look after the house. [17] The king left, followed by all the people; and they stopped at the last house. [18] All his officials passed by him; and all the Cherethites, and all the Pelethites, and all the six hundred Gittites who had followed him from Gath, passed on before the king.

[19] Then the king said to Ittai the Gittite, "Why are you also coming with us? Go back,

and stay with the king; for you are a foreigner, and also an exile from your home. [20] You came only yesterday, and shall I today make you wander about with us, while I go wherever I can? Go back, and take your kinsfolk with you; and may the LORD show[b] steadfast love and faithfulness to you." [21] But Ittai answered the king, "As the LORD lives, and as my lord the king lives, wherever my lord the king may be, whether for death or for life, there also your servant will be." [22] David said to Ittai, "Go then, march on." So Ittai the Gittite marched on, with all his men and all the little ones who were with him. [23] The whole country wept aloud as all the people passed by; the king crossed the Wadi Kidron, and all the people moved on toward the wilderness.

[24] Abiathar came up, and Zadok also, with all the Levites, carrying the ark of the covenant of God. They set down the ark of God, until the people had all passed out of the city. [25] Then the king said to Zadok, "Carry the ark of God back into the city. If I find favor in the eyes of the LORD, he will bring me back and let me see both it and the place where it stays. [26] But if he says, 'I take no pleasure in you,' here I am, let him do to me what seems good to him." [27] The king also said to the priest Zadok, "Look,[c] go back to the city in peace, you and Abiathar,[d] with your two

a   Or *he sent*
b   Gk Compare 2.6: Heb lacks *may the LORD show*
c   Gk: Heb *Are you a seer* or *Do you see?*
d   Cn: Heb lacks *and Abiathar*

---

hearts or "deceived" (cf. Gen 31.20). **7–10:** Absalom has made a vow to worship at the local shrine of *the LORD in Hebron* (v. 8) and must go there to fulfill it. But he has ulterior motives for choosing Hebron. He is deliberately recalling his father's rise by declaring himself king in Hebron, the capital of Judah, where David had been made king of both Judah and Israel and had ruled Judah for seven years (5.1–7). Absalom probably found supporters in Hebron among those discontented that David had moved the capital. His revolt, however, spread *throughout all the tribes of Israel* (v. 10). *Geshur in Aram* (v. 8), where Absalom fled after killing Amnon (13.37–39). **12:** *Ahithophel* was renowned as *David's counselor* (see 16.15–23). His presence with Absalom meant that *the conspiracy grew in strength.*

15.13–16.14: David flees Jerusalem. 15.13: *Israelites,* perhaps only the residents of the north. But since Absalom began the revolt in Hebron, it has now spread through the entire country. **16:** *Concubines,* see 3.7n. **17:** *The last house,* on the outskirts of Jerusalem. **18:** *Cherethites* and *Pelethites,* see 8.18n. *Gittites,* Philistines from Gath. All these groups had followed David from his days with the Philistines (1 Sam 27; 29). **19:** *Ittai,* commander of the Gittites. **20:** *Yesterday,* an idiom for "recently." David is amazed that these Philistines who only recently joined him are more loyal than his own people. **21:** It is striking that Ittai, the Philistine, swears by the LORD (Yahweh) the God of Israel. **23:** *The Wadi Kidron,* the valley between Jerusalem and the Mount of Olives. David heads east toward the Jordan River. **24:** *Abiathar* and *Zadok,* David's two priests. **25–29:** Caring for the ark properly would

sons, Ahimaaz your son, and Jonathan son of Abiathar. [28] See, I will wait at the fords of the wilderness until word comes from you to inform me." [29] So Zadok and Abiathar carried the ark of God back to Jerusalem, and they remained there.

[30] But David went up the ascent of the Mount of Olives, weeping as he went, with his head covered and walking barefoot; and all the people who were with him covered their heads and went up, weeping as they went. [31] David was told that Ahithophel was among the conspirators with Absalom. And David said, "O LORD, I pray you, turn the counsel of Ahithophel into foolishness."

[32] When David came to the summit, where God was worshiped, Hushai the Archite came to meet him with his coat torn and earth on his head. [33] David said to him, "If you go on with me, you will be a burden to me. [34] But if you return to the city and say to Absalom, 'I will be your servant, O king; as I have been your father's servant in time past, so now I will be your servant,' then you will defeat for me the counsel of Ahithophel. [35] The priests Zadok and Abiathar will be with you there. So whatever you hear from the king's house, tell it to the priests Zadok and Abiathar. [36] Their two sons are with them there, Zadok's son Ahimaaz and Abiathar's son Jonathan; and by them you shall report to me everything you hear." [37] So Hushai, David's friend, came into the city, just as Absalom was entering Jerusalem.

16 When David had passed a little beyond the summit, Ziba the servant of Mephibosheth[a] met him, with a couple of donkeys saddled, carrying two hundred loaves of bread, one hundred bunches of raisins, one hundred of summer fruits, and one skin of wine. [2] The king said to Ziba, "Why have you brought these?" Ziba answered, "The donkeys are for the king's household to ride, the bread and summer fruit for the young men to eat, and the wine is for those to drink who faint in the wilderness." [3] The king said, "And where is your master's son?" Ziba said to the king, "He remains in Jerusalem; for he said, 'Today the house of Israel will give me back my grandfather's kingdom.'" [4] Then the king said to Ziba, "All that belonged to Mephibosheth[a] is now yours." Ziba said, "I do obeisance; let me find favor in your sight, my lord the king."

[5] When King David came to Bahurim, a man of the family of the house of Saul came out whose name was Shimei son of Gera; he came out cursing. [6] He threw stones at David and at all the servants of King David; now all the people and all the warriors were on his right and on his left. [7] Shimei shouted while he cursed, "Out! Out! Murderer! Scoundrel! [8] The LORD has avenged on all of you the blood of the house of Saul, in whose place you have reigned; and the LORD has given the kingdom into the hand of your son Absalom. See, disaster has overtaken you; for you are a man of blood."

[9] Then Abishai son of Zeruiah said to the king, "Why should this dead dog curse my lord the king? Let me go over and take off his head." [10] But the king said, "What have I to do with you, you sons of Zeruiah? If he

a Or *Merib-baal*: See 4.4 note

---

slow David's retreat (see 6.1–11). Besides, the priests could serve as David's spies in Jerusalem. **30:** *His head covered and walking barefoot,* conventional signs of mourning. **31–37:** David was disheartened to learn that his wise adviser, Ahithophel (see 16.23), had joined Absalom. As he walked up the Mount of Olives (v. 31), he prayed for help against Ahithophel. His prayer was answered at the *summit* when he met Hushai, who would help him defeat Ahithophel's advice. *Where God was worshiped* (v. 32), a shrine at the top of the Mount of Olives; such "high places" are outlawed in the Deuteronomistic History once the Temple is built. **37:** *David's friend* (v. 37), perhaps a title for an intimate adviser. **16.2:** *Young men,* soldiers. **3–4:** *Your master's son,* Merib-baal (Mephibosheth), Saul's grandson (see ch 9). Ziba claims that Merib-baal is planning to take over his grandfather's place as king. But Ziba may be lying (19.24–30). David rewards Ziba by giving him Saul's property. There is some question about whether David has the legal right to do this. **5:** *Shimei* belonged not only to Saul's tribe (Benjamin) but also to his *family* or clan. **6–8:** Shimei accused David of murdering members of Saul's family and usurping the throne. This indicates that David's execution of Saul's sons and grandsons (21.1–14) preceded Absalom's revolt. **9–10:** *Abishai,* the brother of Joab and Asahel (see 2.18–23). Called the *sons of Zeruiah* (David's sister) in 2 Samuel and

is cursing because the LORD has said to him, 'Curse David,' who then shall say, 'Why have you done so?'" [11] David said to Abishai and to all his servants, "My own son seeks my life; how much more now may this Benjaminite! Let him alone, and let him curse; for the LORD has bidden him. [12] It may be that the LORD will look on my distress,[a] and the LORD will repay me with good for this cursing of me today." [13] So David and his men went on the road, while Shimei went along on the hillside opposite him and cursed as he went, throwing stones and flinging dust at him. [14] The king and all the people who were with him arrived weary at the Jordan;[b] and there he refreshed himself.

[15] Now Absalom and all the Israelites[c] came to Jerusalem; Ahithophel was with him. [16] When Hushai the Archite, David's friend, came to Absalom, Hushai said to Absalom, "Long live the king! Long live the king!" [17] Absalom said to Hushai, "Is this your loyalty to your friend? Why did you not go with your friend?" [18] Hushai said to Absalom, "No; but the one whom the LORD and this people and all the Israelites have chosen, his I will be, and with him I will remain. [19] Moreover, whom should I serve? Should it not be his son? Just as I have served your father, so I will serve you."

[20] Then Absalom said to Ahithophel, "Give us your counsel; what shall we do?" [21] Ahithophel said to Absalom, "Go in to your father's concubines, the ones he has left to look after the house; and all Israel will hear that you have made yourself odious to your father, and the hands of all who are with you will be strengthened." [22] So they pitched a tent for Absalom upon the roof; and Absalom went in to his father's concubines in the sight of all Israel. [23] Now in those days the counsel that Ahithophel gave was as if one consulted the oracle[d] of God; so all the counsel of Ahithophel was esteemed, both by David and by Absalom.

17 Moreover Ahithophel said to Absalom, "Let me choose twelve thousand men, and I will set out and pursue David tonight. [2] I will come upon him while he is weary and discouraged, and throw him into a panic; and all the people who are with him will flee. I will strike down only the king, [3] and I will bring all the people back to you as a bride comes home to her husband. You seek the life of only one man,[e] and all the people will be at peace." [4] The advice pleased Absalom and all the elders of Israel.

[5] Then Absalom said, "Call Hushai the Archite also, and let us hear too what he has to say." [6] When Hushai came to Absalom, Absalom said to him, "This is what Ahithophel

a   Gk Vg: Heb *iniquity*
b   Gk: Heb lacks *at the Jordan*
c   Gk: Heb *all the people, the men of Israel*
d   Heb *word*
e   Gk: Heb *like the return of the whole (is) the man whom you seek*

portrayed as violent men in contrast to gentle David. *Dead dog,* see 3.8n.; 9.8n. **11:** *This Benjaminite,* a demeaning reference to Shimei.

16.15–17.29: Overcoming Ahithophel. 16.16: *David's friend,* see 15.37n. *Long live the king,* the utterance is duplicitous; for Hushai, David is still king. **18:** *The one whom the LORD and this people and all the Israelites have chosen,* again, Hushai means David. **19:** Hushai's duplicity continues. *Should it not be his son?* For Hushai, the answer is no. *Just as I have served your father, so I will serve you,* Hushai is saying that by serving Absalom he is actually serving David. In all cases (vv. 16–19), Absalom is unaware of Hushai's true meaning. **20–22:** To sleep with a member of the harem is to claim the throne. Hence, by having relations with David's concubines, Absalom makes his claim to kingship emphatic. He also fulfills Nathan's prophecy (12.12), which was likely written with Absalom's act in view. **23:** *Ahithophel* may have been Bathsheba's grandfather (cf. 11.3 and 23.34) and may have held a grudge against David for his treatment of Bathsheba and Uriah. **17.1–4:** *Ahithophel's* sensible advice is to attack while David's forces are weak from fleeing. Once David is dead, he says, all who followed him will turn to Absalom. **5–14:** *Hushai* says that David will not be so easy to find or his troops so easy to defeat (vv. 8–10). He advises Absalom to wait, gather the full force of Israel, then attack (vv. 11–13). Hushai is trying to buy time for David to reorganize his forces. Hushai also plays on Absalom's ego, saying that all the people will follow him, and he can lead them into battle (v. 12). Even though Ahithophel's advice is better than Hushai's *the LORD had ordained* that Absalom would be persuaded to follow Hushai. **15:** *Hushai* sends word to

has said; shall we do as he advises? If not, you tell us." [7] Then Hushai said to Absalom, "This time the counsel that Ahithophel has given is not good." [8] Hushai continued, "You know that your father and his men are warriors, and that they are enraged, like a bear robbed of her cubs in the field. Besides, your father is expert in war; he will not spend the night with the troops. [9] Even now he has hidden himself in one of the pits, or in some other place. And when some of our troops[a] fall at the first attack, whoever hears it will say, 'There has been a slaughter among the troops who follow Absalom.' [10] Then even the valiant warrior, whose heart is like the heart of a lion, will utterly melt with fear; for all Israel knows that your father is a warrior, and that those who are with him are valiant warriors. [11] But my counsel is that all Israel be gathered to you, from Dan to Beer-sheba, like the sand by the sea for multitude, and that you go to battle in person. [12] So we shall come upon him in whatever place he may be found, and we shall light on him as the dew falls on the ground; and he will not survive, nor will any of those with him. [13] If he withdraws into a city, then all Israel will bring ropes to that city, and we shall drag it into the valley, until not even a pebble is to be found there." [14] Absalom and all the men of Israel said, "The counsel of Hushai the Archite is better than the counsel of Ahithophel." For the LORD had ordained to defeat the good counsel of Ahithophel, so that the LORD might bring ruin on Absalom.

[15] Then Hushai said to the priests Zadok and Abiathar, "Thus and so did Ahithophel counsel Absalom and the elders of Israel; and thus and so I have counseled. [16] Therefore send quickly and tell David, 'Do not lodge tonight at the fords of the wilderness, but by all means cross over; otherwise the king

and all the people who are with him will be swallowed up.'" [17] Jonathan and Ahimaaz were waiting at En-rogel; a servant-girl used to go and tell them, and they would go and tell King David; for they could not risk being seen entering the city. [18] But a boy saw them, and told Absalom; so both of them went away quickly, and came to the house of a man at Bahurim, who had a well in his courtyard; and they went down into it. [19] The man's wife took a covering, stretched it over the well's mouth, and spread out grain on it; and nothing was known of it. [20] When Absalom's servants came to the woman at the house, they said, "Where are Ahimaaz and Jonathan?" The woman said to them, "They have crossed over the brook[b] of water." And when they had searched and could not find them, they returned to Jerusalem.

[21] After they had gone, the men came up out of the well, and went and told King David. They said to David, "Go and cross the water quickly; for thus and so has Ahithophel counseled against you." [22] So David and all the people who were with him set out and crossed the Jordan; by daybreak not one was left who had not crossed the Jordan.

[23] When Ahithophel saw that his counsel was not followed, he saddled his donkey and went off home to his own city. He set his house in order, and hanged himself; he died and was buried in the tomb of his father.

[24] Then David came to Mahanaim, while Absalom crossed the Jordan with all the men of Israel. [25] Now Absalom had set Amasa over the army in the place of Joab. Amasa was the son of a man named Ithra the Ishmaelite,[c] who had married Abigal daughter of Na-

---

a   Gk Mss: Heb some of them
b   Meaning of Heb uncertain
c   1 Chr 2.17: Heb Israelite

David through the priests Zadok and Abiathar and their sons (see 15:24–29). **16:** Hushai has bought David some time but urges him to cross the Jordan quickly and escape. **17:** Jonathan and Ahimaaz, the sons of Zadok and Abiathar. En-rogel, "the spring of the fuller," in the Kidron Valley south of Jerusalem. **18–19:** Well, a simple pit whose opening could be covered with a blanket and grain spread over it for camouflage. **23:** Ahithophel . . . hanged himself, perhaps because he knew that the end of Absalom's reign was imminent. There is no stigma associated with suicide in the Bible; see 1 Sam 31.5n. **24:** Mahanaim, the site east of the Jordan where Abner had conducted Ishbaal after making him king (2.8); it was easily defensible. **25:** Amasa, David's nephew, the son of his sister Zeruiah (see 1 Chr 2.16). Zeruiah is called the daughter of Nahash here rather than the daughter of Jesse. This may be a scribal error (note that Nahash occurs in v. 27), or Abigal may have been David's half sister.

hash, sister of Zeruiah, Joab's mother. [26] The Israelites and Absalom encamped in the land of Gilead.

[27] When David came to Mahanaim, Shobi son of Nahash from Rabbah of the Ammonites, and Machir son of Ammiel from Lo-debar, and Barzillai the Gileadite from Rogelim, [28] brought beds, basins, and earthen vessels, wheat, barley, meal, parched grain, beans and lentils,[a] [29] honey and curds, sheep, and cheese from the herd, for David and the people with him to eat; for they said, "The troops are hungry and weary and thirsty in the wilderness."

18 Then David mustered the men who were with him, and set over them commanders of thousands and commanders of hundreds. [2] And David divided the army into three groups:[b] one third under the command of Joab, one third under the command of Abishai son of Zeruiah, Joab's brother, and one third under the command of Ittai the Gittite. The king said to the men, "I myself will also go out with you." [3] But the men said, "You shall not go out. For if we flee, they will not care about us. If half of us die, they will not care about us. But you are worth ten thousand of us;[c] therefore it is better that you send us help from the city." [4] The king said to them, "Whatever seems best to you I will do." So the king stood at the side of the gate, while all the army marched out by hundreds and by thousands. [5] The king ordered Joab and Abishai and Ittai, saying, "Deal gently for my sake with the young man Absalom." And all the people heard when the king gave orders to all the commanders concerning Absalom.

[6] So the army went out into the field against Israel; and the battle was fought in the forest of Ephraim. [7] The men of Israel were defeated there by the servants of David,

and the slaughter there was great on that day, twenty thousand men. [8] The battle spread over the face of all the country; and the forest claimed more victims that day than the sword.

[9] Absalom happened to meet the servants of David. Absalom was riding on his mule, and the mule went under the thick branches of a great oak. His head caught fast in the oak, and he was left hanging[d] between heaven and earth, while the mule that was under him went on. [10] A man saw it, and told Joab, "I saw Absalom hanging in an oak." [11] Joab said to the man who told him, "What, you saw him! Why then did you not strike him there to the ground? I would have been glad to give you ten pieces of silver and a belt." [12] But the man said to Joab, "Even if I felt in my hand the weight of a thousand pieces of silver, I would not raise my hand against the king's son; for in our hearing the king commanded you and Abishai and Ittai, saying: For my sake protect the young man Absalom! [13] On the other hand, if I had dealt treacherously against his life[e] (and there is nothing hidden from the king), then you yourself would have stood aloof." [14] Joab said, "I will not waste time like this with you." He took three spears in his hand, and thrust them into the heart of Absalom, while he was still alive in the oak. [15] And ten young men, Joab's armor-bearers, surrounded Absalom and struck him, and killed him.

[16] Then Joab sounded the trumpet, and the troops came back from pursuing Israel,

a Heb *and lentils and parched grain*
b Gk: Heb *sent forth the army*
c Gk Vg Symmachus: Heb *for now there are ten thousand such as we*
d Gk Syr Tg: Heb *was put*
e Another reading is *at the risk of my life*

27: *Nahash*, the Ammonite king with whom David had a treaty (10.1–2). His son, *Shobi*, loyal to the treaty, now helps David in exile. *Machir*, see 9.4.

18.1–19.10: The defeat and death of Absalom. 18.3: *You shall not go out,* cf. the story in 21.15–17. 5: Through David's order concerning Absalom, the writer shows that David was not responsible for Absalom's death. 6–8: David chooses the rugged *forest of Ephraim* as the battle site, thereby countering the larger numbers of Absalom's army. This is another benefit afforded him by the delay that Hushai achieved. 9: *Mule,* the royal mount for King David and his sons (see 13.29; 1 Kings 1.38). Thus, Absalom's unseating from the mule symbolizes his loss of the kingdom. His being caught by the head recalls his glorious hair (14.26) and suggests that his pride was his downfall. 12: *In our hearing the king commanded,* see v. 5. 14: *Spears* may also be translated "sticks." Apparently, Joab stabbed or struck Absalom with them in order to dislodge him from the tree and finish him off

for Joab restrained the troops. [17] They took Absalom, threw him into a great pit in the forest, and raised over him a very great heap of stones. Meanwhile all the Israelites fled to their homes. [18] Now Absalom in his lifetime had taken and set up for himself a pillar that is in the King's Valley, for he said, "I have no son to keep my name in remembrance"; he called the pillar by his own name. It is called Absalom's Monument to this day.

[19] Then Ahimaaz son of Zadok said, "Let me run, and carry tidings to the king that the LORD has delivered him from the power of his enemies." [20] Joab said to him, "You are not to carry tidings today; you may carry tidings another day, but today you shall not do so, because the king's son is dead." [21] Then Joab said to a Cushite, "Go, tell the king what you have seen." The Cushite bowed before Joab, and ran. [22] Then Ahimaaz son of Zadok said again to Joab, "Come what may, let me also run after the Cushite." And Joab said, "Why will you run, my son, seeing that you have no reward[a] for the tidings?" [23] "Come what may," he said, "I will run." So he said to him, "Run." Then Ahimaaz ran by the way of the Plain, and outran the Cushite.

[24] Now David was sitting between the two gates. The sentinel went up to the roof of the gate by the wall, and when he looked up, he saw a man running alone. [25] The sentinel shouted and told the king. The king said, "If he is alone, there are tidings in his mouth." He kept coming, and drew near. [26] Then the sentinel saw another man running; and the sentinel called to the gatekeeper and said, "See, another man running alone!" The king said, "He also is bringing tidings." [27] The sentinel said, "I think the running of the first one is like the running of Ahimaaz son of Zadok."

The king said, "He is a good man, and comes with good tidings."

[28] Then Ahimaaz cried out to the king, "All is well!" He prostrated himself before the king with his face to the ground, and said, "Blessed be the LORD your God, who has delivered up the men who raised their hand against my lord the king." [29] The king said, "Is it well with the young man Absalom?" Ahimaaz answered, "When Joab sent your servant,[b] I saw a great tumult, but I do not know what it was." [30] The king said, "Turn aside, and stand here." So he turned aside, and stood still.

[31] Then the Cushite came; and the Cushite said, "Good tidings for my lord the king! For the LORD has vindicated you this day, delivering you from the power of all who rose up against you." [32] The king said to the Cushite, "Is it well with the young man Absalom?" The Cushite answered, "May the enemies of my lord the king, and all who rise up to do you harm, be like that young man."

[33][c] The king was deeply moved, and went up to the chamber over the gate, and wept; and as he went, he said, "O my son Absalom, my son, my son Absalom! Would I had died instead of you, O Absalom, my son, my son!"

19 It was told Joab, "The king is weeping and mourning for Absalom." [2] So the victory that day was turned into mourning for all the troops; for the troops heard that day, "The king is grieving for his son." [3] The troops stole into the city that day as soldiers steal in who are ashamed when they flee in battle. [4] The king covered his face, and the king cried with a loud voice, "O my son Absalom, O Absalom, my son, my son!" [5] Then

---

[a] Meaning of Heb uncertain
[b] Heb the king's servant, your servant
[c] Ch 19.1 in Heb

(v. 15). **15:** *Ten young men,* hence, no individual could be blamed for the actual killing. **17:** *A very great heap of stones,* this kind of burial was reserved for a cursed person (Josh 7.26). **18:** *No son,* cf. 14.27. *Absalom's Monument,* later identified with the late Hellenistic or Roman-period tomb in the Kidron valley. **19–20:** *Ahimaaz* wants to deliver the good news of the victory to David, but Joab refuses because he knows that Absalom's death will not be welcome news to David. *Because the king's son* was *dead* may be the narrator's words rather than Joab's (see v. 29). **21:** *Cushite,* a Nubian or Ethiopian. **27:** *Good tidings,* victory usually constitutes good news. But the writer goes on to depict David as focused on Absalom, whose death will be bad news to David despite the victory. **29:** *Ahimaaz* apparently does not know that Absalom is dead. **32:** The *Cushite* thinks that Absalom's death is also good news. **18.33–19.8:** David is portrayed as very distraught at his son's death, despite the political gain it means for him. Compare David's laments over Saul and Jonathan (1.11–27) and Abner (3.31–39), whose deaths

Joab came into the house to the king, and said, "Today you have covered with shame the faces of all your officers who have saved your life today, and the lives of your sons and your daughters, and the lives of your wives and your concubines, [6] for love of those who hate you and for hatred of those who love you. You have made it clear today that commanders and officers are nothing to you; for I perceive that if Absalom were alive and all of us were dead today, then you would be pleased. [7] So go out at once and speak kindly to your servants; for I swear by the LORD, if you do not go, not a man will stay with you this night; and this will be worse for you than any disaster that has come upon you from your youth until now." [8] Then the king got up and took his seat in the gate. The troops were all told, "See, the king is sitting in the gate"; and all the troops came before the king.

Meanwhile, all the Israelites had fled to their homes. [9] All the people were disputing throughout all the tribes of Israel, saying, "The king delivered us from the hand of our enemies, and saved us from the hand of the Philistines; and now he has fled out of the land because of Absalom. [10] But Absalom, whom we anointed over us, is dead in battle. Now therefore why do you say nothing about bringing the king back?"

[11] King David sent this message to the priests Zadok and Abiathar, "Say to the elders of Judah, 'Why should you be the last to bring the king back to his house? The talk of all Israel has come to the king.[a] [12] You are my kin, you are my bone and my flesh; why then should you be the last to bring back the king?' [13] And say to Amasa, 'Are you not my bone and my flesh? So may God do to me,

and more, if you are not the commander of my army from now on, in place of Joab.'" [14] Amasa[b] swayed the hearts of all the people of Judah as one, and they sent word to the king, "Return, both you and all your servants." [15] So the king came back to the Jordan; and Judah came to Gilgal to meet the king and to bring him over the Jordan.

[16] Shimei son of Gera, the Benjaminite, from Bahurim, hurried to come down with the people of Judah to meet King David; [17] with him were a thousand people from Benjamin. And Ziba, the servant of the house of Saul, with his fifteen sons and his twenty servants, rushed down to the Jordan ahead of the king, [18] while the crossing was taking place,[c] to bring over the king's household, and to do his pleasure.

Shimei son of Gera fell down before the king, as he was about to cross the Jordan, [19] and said to the king, "May my lord not hold me guilty or remember how your servant did wrong on the day my lord the king left Jerusalem; may the king not bear it in mind. [20] For your servant knows that I have sinned; therefore, see, I have come this day, the first of all the house of Joseph to come down to meet my lord the king." [21] Abishai son of Zeruiah answered, "Shall not Shimei be put to death for this, because he cursed the LORD's anointed?" [22] But David said, "What have I to do with you, you sons of Zeruiah, that you should today become an adversary to me? Shall anyone be put to death in Israel this day? For do I not know that I am this day

a   Gk: Heb *to the king, to his house*

b   Heb *He*

c   Cn: Heb *the ford crossed*

also benefited him. **19.6:** *Love* and *hate* can be political terms for loyalty and disloyalty. Joab's point is that David shows love to those who are disloyal to him (Absalom) while failing to show love or appreciation toward his loyal subjects. **9:** *All the tribes of Israel* may refer to the northern tribes, not Judah, which is the focus of the subsequent narrative.

19.11–43: David returns to Jerusalem. 11–12: David contacts the tribal leaders or *elders* of Judah to encourage them to welcome him back as king before *all Israel* (i.e., the northern tribes) does so. **13:** David appoints *Amasa* as his army commander in place of Joab because of Amasa's influence in Judah's army (see 17.25), and perhaps also because David shrewdly calculated that this would gain favor with the troops who had been loyal to Absalom, since Amasa was Absalom's commander. It may also be intended to express David's anger at Joab for having disobeyed his instructions regarding Absalom. All of these factors may provide motivation for Joab's murder of Amasa (20.10). *My bone and my flesh*, David was Amasa's uncle (see 17.25). **14:** Amasa, in turn, persuades the *people* (i.e., army) of Judah to return to David. **15:** *Gilgal*, west of the Jordan River, was an ancient Israelite shrine

king over Israel?" [23] The king said to Shimei, "You shall not die." And the king gave him his oath.

[24] Mephibosheth[a] grandson of Saul came down to meet the king; he had not taken care of his feet, or trimmed his beard, or washed his clothes, from the day the king left until the day he came back in safety. [25] When he came from Jerusalem to meet the king, the king said to him, "Why did you not go with me, Mephibosheth?"[a] [26] He answered, "My lord, O king, my servant deceived me; for your servant said to him, 'Saddle a donkey for me,[b] so that I may ride on it and go with the king.' For your servant is lame. [27] He has slandered your servant to my lord the king. But my lord the king is like the angel of God; do therefore what seems good to you. [28] For all my father's house were doomed to death before my lord the king; but you set your servant among those who eat at your table. What further right have I, then, to appeal to the king?" [29] The king said to him, "Why speak any more of your affairs? I have decided: you and Ziba shall divide the land." [30] Mephibosheth[a] said to the king, "Let him take it all, since my lord the king has arrived home safely."

[31] Now Barzillai the Gileadite had come down from Rogelim; he went on with the king to the Jordan, to escort him over the Jordan. [32] Barzillai was a very aged man, eighty years old. He had provided the king with food while he stayed at Mahanaim, for he was a very wealthy man. [33] The king said to Barzillai, "Come over with me, and I will provide for you in Jerusalem at my side." [34] But Barzillai said to the king, "How many years have I still to live, that I should go up with the king to Jerusalem? [35] Today I am eighty years old; can I discern what is pleasant and what is not? Can your servant taste what he eats or what he drinks? Can I still listen to the voice of singing men and singing women? Why then should your servant be an added burden to my lord the king? [36] Your servant will go a little way over the Jordan with the king. Why should the king recompense me with such a reward? [37] Please let your servant return, so that I may die in my own town, near the graves of my father and my mother. But here is your servant Chimham; let him go over with my lord the king; and do for him whatever seems good to you." [38] The king answered, "Chimham shall go over with me, and I will do for him whatever seems good to you; and all that you desire of me I will do for you." [39] Then all the people crossed over the Jordan, and the king crossed over; the king kissed Barzillai and blessed him, and he returned to his own home. [40] The king went on to Gilgal, and Chimham went on with him; all the people of Judah, and also half the people of Israel, brought the king on his way.

---

a   Or *Merib-baal*: See 4.4 note
b   Gk Syr Vg: Heb *said, 'I will saddle a donkey for myself*

---

where Saul had been made king (1 Sam 11.15). **16–23:** *Shimei* and those with him were from the tribe of *Benjamin*, Saul's tribe. Shimei had ridiculed David when he fled from Jerusalem (16.5–13). Now that David is victorious, he asks forgiveness. David grants it, perhaps in part because of the *thousand people* (soldiers) *from Benjamin* with Shimei. *House of Joseph* (v. 20), the northern tribes, Israel as opposed to Judah. *Abishai* still wants to kill Shimei (16.9), but David refuses. This is part of the author's portrayal of David as gentle, in contrast to the violent *sons of Zeruiah* (v. 22). It may also have been customary for a new king to pardon criminals on the day of his coronation (see 1 Sam 11.13). **24:** *Taken care of his feet* may mean trimmed his toenails, since the writer cites it as evidence that Merib-baal (*Mephibosheth*) had been mourning David's exile. **25–30:** *Ziba* had accused Merib-baal of plotting to take the throne (16.1–4). Merib-baal here defends himself, saying that Ziba refused to help him to flee with David, and he could not leave on his own accord because of his physical condition. David's decision (v. 29) indicates that he does not know which of them is telling the truth. *All my father's house were doomed to death before my lord the king,* a new king often executed all the heirs of his predecessor in order to have no rival for the throne. **31–40:** *Barzillai* had helped to provide for David in exile (17.27). David now invites him to come live in his palace in Jerusalem. Barzillai replies that he is too old to enjoy it, but he arranges for the king to take his son Chimham instead. **35:** *Can I discern . . .* , lit. "Can I know between good and evil?" likely a reference to sexual pleasure. Cf. Gen 2.9; Isa 7.15. **41:** Barzillai says that he is too old to enjoy the pleasures of taste, music,

[41] Then all the people of Israel came to the king, and said to him, "Why have our kindred the people of Judah stolen you away, and brought the king and his household over the Jordan, and all David's men with him?" [42] All the people of Judah answered the people of Israel, "Because the king is near of kin to us. Why then are you angry over this matter? Have we eaten at all at the king's expense? Or has he given us any gift?" [43] But the people of Israel answered the people of Judah, "We have ten shares in the king, and in David also we have more than you. Why then did you despise us? Were we not the first to speak of bringing back our king?" But the words of the people of Judah were fiercer than the words of the people of Israel.

20 Now a scoundrel named Sheba son of Bichri, a Benjaminite, happened to be there. He sounded the trumpet and cried out,

"We have no portion in David,
no share in the son of Jesse!
Everyone to your tents, O Israel!"

[2] So all the people of Israel withdrew from David and followed Sheba son of Bichri; but the people of Judah followed their king steadfastly from the Jordan to Jerusalem.

[3] David came to his house at Jerusalem; and the king took the ten concubines whom he had left to look after the house, and put them in a house under guard, and provided for them, but did not go in to them. So they were shut up until the day of their death, living as if in widowhood.

[4] Then the king said to Amasa, "Call the men of Judah together to me within three days, and be here yourself." [5] So Amasa went to summon Judah; but he delayed beyond the set time that had been appointed him. [6] David

said to Abishai, "Now Sheba son of Bichri will do us more harm than Absalom; take your lord's servants and pursue him, or he will find fortified cities for himself, and escape from us." [7] Joab's men went out after him, along with the Cherethites, the Pelethites, and all the warriors; they went out from Jerusalem to pursue Sheba son of Bichri. [8] When they were at the large stone that is in Gibeon, Amasa came to meet them. Now Joab was wearing a soldier's garment and over it was a belt with a sword in its sheath fastened at his waist; as he went forward it fell out. [9] Joab said to Amasa, "Is it well with you, my brother?" And Joab took Amasa by the beard with his right hand to kiss him. [10] But Amasa did not notice the sword in Joab's hand; Joab struck him in the belly so that his entrails poured out on the ground, and he died. He did not strike a second blow.

Then Joab and his brother Abishai pursued Sheba son of Bichri. [11] And one of Joab's men took his stand by Amasa, and said, "Whoever favors Joab, and whoever is for David, let him follow Joab." [12] Amasa lay wallowing in his blood on the highway, and the man saw that all the people were stopping. Since he saw that all who came by him were stopping, he carried Amasa from the highway into a field, and threw a garment over him. [13] Once he was removed from the highway, all the people went on after Joab to pursue Sheba son of Bichri.

[14] Sheba[a] passed through all the tribes of Israel to Abel of Beth-maacah;[b] and all the Bichrites[c] assembled, and followed him

a Heb *He*
b Compare 20.15: Heb *and Beth-maacah*
c Compare Gk Vg: Heb *Berites*

or sex that are available at David's court. But his son is not too old. The army (*people*) of Judah welcomes David back before the army of Israel. **42:** The army of Judah denies that it has received any special favors or bribes from David. **43:** *Ten shares*, the ten northern tribes of Israel.

20.1–26: Sheba's revolt. 1: *Happened to be there*, at the scene in Gilgal described in 19.41–43. Ch 20 continues that story. *Everyone to your tents*, an idiom for military demobilization; Sheba is calling for the army of Israel to withdraw from David; cf. 1 Kings 12.16. **2:** *All the people of Israel*, the northern tribes. The phrase exaggerates the extent of the northern disaffection with David (see v. 21). **3:** David no longer had sexual relations with the *ten concubines* he had left behind, because Absalom had slept with them (16.20–22). **7:** *The Cherethites* and *Pelethites*, perhaps "Cretans" and "Philistines," who composed the royal bodyguard (8.19). **8–10:** *Joab*'s assassination of *Amasa* is similar to his murder of Abner (3.26–39). His implied motive had to do with the fact that Amasa had taken Joab's place as army commander (19.13). His actual motive was more likely political: to rid David of a powerful rival for the leadership of Judah. **13:** *The people*, the army. **14:** *Abel of Beth-maacah* is in the extreme

inside. [15] Joab's forces[a] came and besieged him in Abel of Beth-maacah; they threw up a siege ramp against the city, and it stood against the rampart. Joab's forces were battering the wall to break it down. [16] Then a wise woman called from the city, "Listen! Listen! Tell Joab, 'Come here, I want to speak to you.'" [17] He came near her; and the woman said, "Are you Joab?" He answered, "I am." Then she said to him, "Listen to the words of your servant." He answered, "I am listening." [18] Then she said, "They used to say in the old days, 'Let them inquire at Abel'; and so they would settle a matter. [19] I am one of those who are peaceable and faithful in Israel; you seek to destroy a city that is a mother in Israel; why will you swallow up the heritage of the LORD?" [20] Joab answered, "Far be it from me, far be it, that I should swallow up or destroy! [21] That is not the case! But a man of the hill country of Ephraim, called Sheba son of Bichri, has lifted up his hand against King David; give him up alone, and I will withdraw from the city." The woman said to Joab, "His head shall be thrown over the wall to you." [22] Then the woman went to all the people with her wise plan. And they cut off the head of Sheba son of Bichri, and threw it out to Joab. So he blew the trumpet, and they dispersed from the city, and all went to their homes, while Joab returned to Jerusalem to the king.

[23] Now Joab was in command of all the army of Israel;[b] Benaiah son of Jehoiada was in command of the Cherethites and the Pelethites; [24] Adoram was in charge of the forced labor; Jehoshaphat son of Ahilud was the recorder; [25] Sheva was secretary; Zadok and Abiathar were priests; [26] and Ira the Jairite was also David's priest.

21 Now there was a famine in the days of David for three years, year after year; and David inquired of the LORD. The LORD said, "There is bloodguilt on Saul and on his house, because he put the Gibeonites to death." [2] So the king called the Gibeonites and spoke to them. (Now the Gibeonites were not of the people of Israel, but of the remnant

---

a   Heb *They*
b   Cn: Heb *Joab to all the army, Israel*

northern part of Israel. **15:** Ancient Israelite cities were surrounded by thick walls that had to be broken through with battering rams. **16:** *Wise woman* (cf. ch 14) in this case could be a title for a city official. She is certainly intelligent and eloquent and acts on behalf of her city. **18:** *Let them inquire at Abel* implies that Abel was a central city for settling legal disputes or for divination. **19:** *A mother in Israel,* a large city, a metropolis. *The heritage of the LORD,* the land and people of Israel; see 1 Sam 10.1. **20:** The woman pleads for her city based on its antiquity and historical value to Israel. **21:** The woman apparently does not know about Sheba, indicating that his revolt did not reach to all Israel but included only part of Benjamin and *the hill country of Ephraim.* **23–26:** This cabinet list is similar to the one in 8.16–18. It probably came to this location by attachment to 21.1–14, which originally stood directly before 9.1. Alternatively, the two lists are used to frame the section, sometimes called "David under the curse." The two lists are probably variants, although according to some scholars they reflect different periods in David's reign. *The Cherethites and the Pelethites,* see v. 7n. *Forced labor,* conscripted from the northern tribes by David and Solomon. *Adoram* or Adoniram (1 Kings 4.6) was later stoned when the Israelites rebelled against the Davidic dynasty (1 Kings 12.18).

Chs 21–24: An appendix of miscellaneous stories and poems. The final four chapters of 2 Samuel contain six passages arranged in chiastic order: narrative (21.1–14), list (21.15–22), poem (22.1–51), poem (23.1–7), list (23.8–38), narrative (24.1–25). The accumulation of these passages may have come about as follows. 21.1–14 was moved from its original place before ch 9. The motive was likely to lessen the impression that David had Saul's heirs killed for political reasons. The story in 24.1–25 was added to 21.1–14 (see 24.1) and placed as the final episode in David's life before the account of his death in 1 Kings 1–2 because it anticipated the founding of the Temple under Solomon. The lists may have been added next, separating the two narratives. The two psalms were then inserted. Ch 22 is a song of deliverance and praise for victory. It is appropriate following the list of victories in 21.15–22. Then 23.1–7 provides David's "last words," in the tradition of other leading biblical characters.

21.1–14: The execution of Saul's heirs. 1–2: The *Gibeonites* had a special treaty with Israel (Josh 9). This story assumes that the violation of that treaty brought divine wrath. The Bible nowhere recounts Saul's attempted extermination of the Gibeonites. *Amorites,* one of several groups of pre-Israelite residents of the land of Ca-

of the Amorites; although the people of Israel had sworn to spare them, Saul had tried to wipe them out in his zeal for the people of Israel and Judah.) ³ David said to the Gibeonites, "What shall I do for you? How shall I make expiation, that you may bless the heritage of the LORD?" ⁴ The Gibeonites said to him, "It is not a matter of silver or gold between us and Saul or his house; neither is it for us to put anyone to death in Israel." He said, "What do you say that I should do for you?" ⁵ They said to the king, "The man who consumed us and planned to destroy us, so that we should have no place in all the territory of Israel— ⁶ let seven of his sons be handed over to us, and we will impale them before the LORD at Gibeon on the mountain of the LORD."ᵃ The king said, "I will hand them over."

⁷ But the king spared Mephibosheth,ᵇ the son of Saul's son Jonathan, because of the oath of the LORD that was between them, between David and Jonathan son of Saul. ⁸ The king took the two sons of Rizpah daughter of Aiah, whom she bore to Saul, Armoni and Mephibosheth;ᵇ and the five sons of Merabᶜ daughter of Saul, whom she bore to Adriel son of Barzillai the Meholathite; ⁹ he gave them into the hands of the Gibeonites, and they impaled them on the mountain before the LORD. The seven of them perished together. They were put to death in the first days of harvest, at the beginning of barley harvest.

¹⁰ Then Rizpah the daughter of Aiah took sackcloth, and spread it on a rock for herself, from the beginning of harvest until rain fell on them from the heavens; she did not allow the birds of the air to come on the bodiesᵈ by day, or the wild animals by night. ¹¹ When David was told what Rizpah daughter of Aiah, the concubine of Saul, had done, ¹² David went and took the bones of Saul and the bones of his son Jonathan from the people of Jabesh-gilead, who had stolen them from the public square of Beth-shan, where the Philistines had hung them up, on the day the Philistines killed Saul on Gilboa. ¹³ He brought up from there the bones of Saul and the bones of his son Jonathan; and they gathered the bones of those who had been impaled. ¹⁴ They buried the bones of Saul and of his son Jonathan in the land of Benjamin in Zela, in the tomb of his father Kish; they did all that the king commanded. After that, God heeded supplications for the land.

¹⁵ The Philistines went to war again with Israel, and David went down together with his servants. They fought against the Philistines, and David grew weary. ¹⁶ Ishbi-benob, one of the descendants of the giants, whose spear weighed three hundred shekels of bronze, and who was fitted out with new weapons,ᵉ said he would kill David. ¹⁷ But Abishai son of Zeruiah came to his aid, and attacked the Philistine and killed him. Then David's men swore to him, "You shall not go out with us to battle any longer, so that you do not quench the lamp of Israel."

ᵃ Cn Compare Gk and 21.9: Heb *at Gibeah of Saul, the chosen of the* LORD
ᵇ Or *Merib-baal:* See 4.4 note
ᶜ Two Heb Mss Syr Compare Gk: MT *Michal*
ᵈ Heb *them*
ᵉ Heb *was belted anew*

naan, often used in the Deuteronomistic History for all of them. **3:** *The heritage of the* LORD, the land and people of Israel; see 1 Sam 10.1n. **4:** The Gibeonites regard this as a matter for blood vengeance, but as resident aliens in Israel they do not have that right. **5–9:** Typically, the founder of a new dynasty annihilated the potential claimants from the previous dynasty as David does here. Saul's alleged offense provides a religious legitimation for this political act. Only Merib-baal is spared (v. 7), probably because he is crippled and therefore cannot be king, though this may also reflect David's relationship with Jonathan (see 1 Sam 18.1–3; 20.17,41–42). On the other hand, the theme of David's affection for and covenant with Jonathan may have been developed by the author from the historical fact of David's preservation of Merib-baal. This event took place early in David's reign over Israel and originally came before 9.1, where David asks if anyone is left in Saul's house. *Sons* (v. 6) also includes grandsons. *Mephibosheth* (v. 8), not Jonathan's son, Merib-baal, who was spared. The *barley harvest* was in April-May. **10:** *Rizpah* was Saul's concubine (3.7–11). **11–14:** As a result of Rizpah's courageous action, David tries to honor the memory of Saul and Jonathan; see 1 Sam 31.12–13.

21.15–22: Stories from the Philistine wars. The stories recounted here come from the battles with the Philistines earlier in David's reign. **16:** *Three hundred shekels* was about 8 lb (3.5 kg). **17:** The insistence of David's men

[18] After this a battle took place with the Philistines, at Gob; then Sibbecai the Hushathite killed Saph, who was one of the descendants of the giants. [19] Then there was another battle with the Philistines at Gob; and Elhanan son of Jaare-oregim, the Bethlehemite, killed Goliath the Gittite, the shaft of whose spear was like a weaver's beam. [20] There was again war at Gath, where there was a man of great size, who had six fingers on each hand, and six toes on each foot, twenty-four in number; he too was descended from the giants. [21] When he taunted Israel, Jonathan son of David's brother Shimei, killed him. [22] These four were descended from the giants in Gath; they fell by the hands of David and his servants.

22

David spoke to the Lord the words of this song on the day when the Lord delivered him from the hand of all his enemies, and from the hand of Saul. [2] He said:

The Lord is my rock, my fortress, and my
    deliverer,
    [3] my God, my rock, in whom I take refuge,
my shield and the horn of my salvation,
    my stronghold and my refuge,
    my savior; you save me from violence.
[4] I call upon the Lord, who is worthy to be
    praised,
    and I am saved from my enemies.

[5] For the waves of death encompassed me,
    the torrents of perdition assailed me;
[6] the cords of Sheol entangled me,
    the snares of death confronted me.

[7] In my distress I called upon the Lord;
    to my God I called.
From his temple he heard my voice,
    and my cry came to his ears.

[8] Then the earth reeled and rocked;
    the foundations of the heavens
        trembled
    and quaked, because he was angry.
[9] Smoke went up from his nostrils,
    and devouring fire from his mouth;
    glowing coals flamed forth from him.
[10] He bowed the heavens, and came down;
    thick darkness was under his feet.
[11] He rode on a cherub, and flew;
    he was seen upon the wings of the
        wind.
[12] He made darkness around him a canopy,
    thick clouds, a gathering of water.
[13] Out of the brightness before him
    coals of fire flamed forth.
[14] The Lord thundered from heaven;
    the Most High uttered his voice.
[15] He sent out arrows, and scattered them
    —lightning, and routed them.
[16] Then the channels of the sea were seen,
    the foundations of the world were laid
        bare
at the rebuke of the Lord,
    at the blast of the breath of his nostrils.

[17] He reached from on high, he took me,
    he drew me out of mighty waters.
[18] He delivered me from my strong enemy,
    from those who hated me;
    for they were too mighty for me.

that he not go to battle may lie behind 11.1; 18.3. **19:** This represents an earlier tradition than 1 Sam 17 concerning the death of Goliath; the otherwise unknown Elhanan, rather than David, slays him. The story in 1 Sam 17 is an elaboration and reworking of this tradition, attributing the victory to the better-known David, cf. 1 Chr 20.5.

22.1–51: A psalm of praise. This psalm, which is essentially the same as Psalm 18, was written long after David's time but is inserted here as appropriate to his sentiments. The psalm praises the Lord for appearing to rescue the psalmist (vv. 1–20) and for continued support of the psalmist's military activities (vv. 21–51). Its placement following the exploits of David's heroes in 21.15–22 and David's own rescue (vv. 15–17) is appropriate. **2–3:** *Rock,* a metaphor for the Lord as protector. **5–6:** *Perdition,* the underworld, the abode of the dead, known in the Bible as *Sheol.* **7:** *Temple* suggests that this psalm was written after David, since the Temple was built by Solomon, although it may refer to God's heavenly abode (see Ps 11.4). **8:** The Lord's appearance is accompanied by earthquake. **9:** The Lord is pictured here as a fire-breathing dragon. **11–16:** The Lord is depicted here as a storm god. **11:** *Cherub,* a mythical, griffinlike creature. **14–15:** God's *voice* is thunder (Job 40.9; Ps 29.3), and he throws *lightning* bolts at his enemies. *Most High,* a title of El, head of the Canaanite pantheon. The title is later appropriated for the Lord. **16:** The psalmist envisions the world as flat; he is trapped in the underworld beneath *the foundations of the world,* which the Lord's roar uncovers. **32:** This is a monotheistic claim; the Lord (Yahweh)

[19] They came upon me in the day of my
calamity,
but the Lord was my stay.
[20] He brought me out into a broad place;
he delivered me, because he delighted
in me.

[21] The Lord rewarded me according to my
righteousness;
according to the cleanness of my hands
he recompensed me.
[22] For I have kept the ways of the Lord,
and have not wickedly departed from
my God.
[23] For all his ordinances were before me,
and from his statutes I did not turn
aside.
[24] I was blameless before him,
and I kept myself from guilt.
[25] Therefore the Lord has recompensed me
according to my righteousness,
according to my cleanness in his
sight.

[26] With the loyal you show yourself loyal;
with the blameless you show yourself
blameless;
[27] with the pure you show yourself pure,
and with the crooked you show yourself
perverse.
[28] You deliver a humble people,
but your eyes are upon the haughty to
bring them down.
[29] Indeed, you are my lamp, O Lord,
the Lord lightens my darkness.
[30] By you I can crush a troop,
and by my God I can leap over a wall.
[31] This God—his way is perfect;
the promise of the Lord proves true;
he is a shield for all who take refuge in
him.

[32] For who is God, but the Lord?
And who is a rock, except our God?
[33] The God who has girded me with
strength[a]
has opened wide my path.[b]
[34] He made my[c] feet like the feet of deer,
and set me secure on the heights.
[35] He trains my hands for war,
so that my arms can bend a bow of
bronze.

[36] You have given me the shield of your
salvation,
and your help[d] has made me great.
[37] You have made me stride freely,
and my feet do not slip;
[38] I pursued my enemies and destroyed
them,
and did not turn back until they were
consumed.
[39] I consumed them; I struck them down,
so that they did not rise;
they fell under my feet.
[40] For you girded me with strength for the
battle;
you made my assailants sink
under me.
[41] You made my enemies turn their backs
to me,
those who hated me, and I destroyed
them.
[42] They looked, but there was no one to
save them;
they cried to the Lord, but he did not
answer them.
[43] I beat them fine like the dust of the
earth,
I crushed them and stamped them
down like the mire of the streets.

[44] You delivered me from strife with the
peoples;[e]
you kept me as the head of the
nations;
people whom I had not known served
me.
[45] Foreigners came cringing to me;
as soon as they heard of me, they
obeyed me.
[46] Foreigners lost heart,
and came trembling out of their
strongholds.

[47] The Lord lives! Blessed be my rock,
and exalted be my God, the rock of my
salvation,

[a]   Q Ms Gk Syr Vg Compare Ps 18.32: MT *God is my
strong refuge*
[b]   Meaning of Heb uncertain
[c]   Another reading is *his*
[d]   Q Ms: MT *your answering*
[e]   Gk: Heb *from strife with my people*

48 the God who gave me vengeance
and brought down peoples under me,
49 who brought me out from my enemies;
you exalted me above my adversaries,
you delivered me from the violent.

50 For this I will extol you, O LORD, among
the nations,
and sing praises to your name.
51 He is a tower of salvation for his king,
and shows steadfast love to his
anointed,
to David and his descendants forever.

23 Now these are the last words of David:
The oracle of David, son of Jesse,
the oracle of the man whom God
exalted,[a]
the anointed of the God of Jacob,
the favorite of the Strong One of Israel:

2 The spirit of the LORD speaks through me,
his word is upon my tongue.
3 The God of Israel has spoken,
the Rock of Israel has said to me:
One who rules over people justly,
ruling in the fear of God,
4 is like the light of morning,
like the sun rising on a cloudless
morning,
gleaming from the rain on the grassy
land.

5 Is not my house like this with God?
For he has made with me an everlasting
covenant,
ordered in all things and secure.

Will he not cause to prosper
all my help and my desire?
6 But the godless are[b] all like thorns that
are thrown away;
for they cannot be picked up with the
hand;
7 to touch them one uses an iron bar
or the shaft of a spear.
And they are entirely consumed in fire
on the spot.[c]

8 These are the names of the warriors
whom David had: Josheb-basshebeth a
Tahchemonite; he was chief of the Three;[d]
he wielded his spear[e] against eight hundred
whom he killed at one time.
9 Next to him among the three warriors
was Eleazar son of Dodo son of Ahohi. He
was with David when they defied the Philistines who were gathered there for battle.
The Israelites withdrew, 10 but he stood his
ground. He struck down the Philistines until
his arm grew weary, though his hand clung
to the sword. The LORD brought about a great
victory that day. Then the people came back
to him—but only to strip the dead.
11 Next to him was Shammah son of
Agee, the Hararite. The Philistines gathered
together at Lehi, where there was a plot of
ground full of lentils; and the army fled from

a Q Ms: MT *who was raised on high*
b Heb *But worthlessness*
c Heb *in sitting*
d Gk Vg Compare 1 Chr 11.11: Meaning of Heb
uncertain
e 1 Chr 11.11: Meaning of Heb uncertain

alone is God. **33–43:** The LORD equips the psalmist for battle. **47:** *Rock,* see vv. 2–3n. **51:** *Steadfast love,* loyalty. This verse alludes to the LORD's promise to David of an enduring dynasty (2 Sam 7). *Anointed,* Heb "mashiaḥ" ("messiah"), a royal title appropriate for any king (see 1 Sam 2.10n). *David and his descendants,* if original, sug- gests that the psalm comes from royal circles in Judah.

23.1–7: The last words of David. There may have been a literary tradition in the Bible of ascribing poems to leading characters as their "last words." Compare the poems attributed to Jacob in Gen 49 and to Moses in Deut 32–33. David's last words, though, do not consist of a blessing of Israel. Like Moses, however, David is portrayed as a prophet pronouncing an oracle (23.1–2). The actual date of David's "last words" is uncertain. In contrast to ch 22, 23.1–7 has no parallel in Psalms. **1:** *Anointed,* a royal title, here referring to David, echoing the end of ch 22. *Strong One of Israel,* an epithet for the LORD. **3:** *Rock,* see 22.3,47. **4:** The image of the king as the sun was common in the ancient Near East, especially in Egypt, although less so in Israel. **5:** *House,* the king's (David's) dy- nasty. *Everlasting covenant,* the LORD's promise of a dynasty for David in 7.16; cf. Ps 89.28–29. **6–7:** These verses continue the image of vv. 3–4. The *godless* are like *thorns* consumed by the sun's heat.

23.8–39: David's heroes. 8–12: Nothing more is known about *the Three* greatest warriors in David's army.

the Philistines. [12] But he took his stand in the middle of the plot, defended it, and killed the Philistines; and the LORD brought about a great victory.

[13] Towards the beginning of harvest three of the thirty[a] chiefs went down to join David at the cave of Adullam, while a band of Philistines was encamped in the valley of Rephaim. [14] David was then in the stronghold; and the garrison of the Philistines was then at Bethlehem. [15] David said longingly, "O that someone would give me water to drink from the well of Bethlehem that is by the gate!" [16] Then the three warriors broke through the camp of the Philistines, drew water from the well of Bethlehem that was by the gate, and brought it to David. But he would not drink of it; he poured it out to the LORD, [17] for he said, "The LORD forbid that I should do this. Can I drink the blood of the men who went at the risk of their lives?" Therefore he would not drink it. The three warriors did these things.

[18] Now Abishai son of Zeruiah, the brother of Joab, was chief of the Thirty.[b] With his spear he fought against three hundred men and killed them, and won a name beside the Three. [19] He was the most renowned of the Thirty,[c] and became their commander; but he did not attain to the Three.

[20] Benaiah son of Jehoiada was a valiant warrior[d] from Kabzeel, a doer of great deeds; he struck down two sons of Ariel[e] of Moab. He also went down and killed a lion in a pit on a day when snow had fallen. [21] And he killed an Egyptian, a handsome man. The Egyptian had a spear in his hand; but Benaiah went against him with a staff, snatched the spear out of the Egyptian's hand, and killed him with his own spear. [22] Such were the things Benaiah son of Jehoiada did, and won a name beside the three warriors. [23] He was renowned among the Thirty, but he did not attain to the Three. And David put him in charge of his bodyguard.

[24] Among the Thirty were Asahel brother of Joab; Elhanan son of Dodo of Bethlehem; [25] Shammah of Harod; Elika of Harod; [26] Helez the Paltite; Ira son of Ikkesh of Tekoa; [27] Abiezer of Anathoth; Mebunnai the Hushathite; [28] Zalmon the Ahohite; Maharai of Netophah; [29] Heleb son of Baanah of Netophah; Ittai son of Ribai of Gibeah of the Benjaminites; [30] Benaiah of Pirathon; Hiddai of the torrents of Gaash; [31] Abi-albon the Arbathite; Azmaveth of Bahurim; [32] Eliahba of Shaalbon; the sons of Jashen: Jonathan [33] son of [f]Shammah the Hararite; Ahiam son of Sharar the Hararite; [34] Eliphelet son of Ahasbai of Maacah; Eliam son of Ahithophel the Gilonite; [35] Hezro[g] of Carmel; Paarai the Arbite; [36] Igal son of Nathan of Zobah; Bani the Gadite; [37] Zelek the Ammonite; Naharai of Beeroth, the armor-bearer of Joab son of Zeruiah; [38] Ira the Ithrite; Gareb the Ithrite; [39] Uriah the Hittite—thirty-seven in all.

---

a   Heb adds *head*
b   Two Heb Mss Syr: MT *Three*
c   Syr Compare 1 Chr 11.25: Heb *Was he the most renowned of the Three?*
d   Another reading is *the son of Ish-hai*
e   Gk: Heb lacks *sons of*
f   Gk: Heb lacks *son of*
g   Another reading is *Hezrai*

13–17: This story is not about the three warriors just listed but about three anonymous members of the honor guard of *the thirty*. **13:** *The beginning of harvest*, the weather was hot and dry, which is why David became thirsty. *The cave of Adullam*, "cave" may be an error for "stronghold"; the two words differ by one letter in Hebrew. *Adullam* was David's headquarters and hideout when he fled from Saul (cf. 1 Sam 22.1–4). **14:** *Stronghold*, the fortress at Adullam. Since a *garrison of the Philistines was then at Bethlehem*, this must have been early in David's reign or even before he became king. *Bethlehem*, David's hometown, hence his fond remembrance of the water there. **16–17:** *He poured it out to the LORD*, there are different interpretations of David's actions here. Some think he is angry that the men risked their lives foolishly. Others suggest that this was a libation or sacrifice to God, a great honor to the three men. **20–23:** *Benaiah*, the commander of David's bodyguard and later of the army under Solomon. **24:** *Asahel* seems to be a young warrior aspiring to greatness in the story of his death (2.18–23). It is surprising to find his name in this list of soldiers who distinguished themselves in David's army. This may indicate that the story in 2 Sam 2 was invented to give Joab a personal motive, rather than the political one of following David's order, for killing Abner. *Elhanan* killed Goliath (21.19). **30:** *Benaiah*, a different man from the Benaiah in vv. 20–23. **39:** *Uriah*, Bathsheba's husband (ch 11). It is uncertain how the count of *thirty-seven*

24

Again the anger of the Lord was kindled against Israel, and he incited David against them, saying, "Go, count the people of Israel and Judah." [2] So the king said to Joab and the commanders of the army,[a] who were with him, "Go through all the tribes of Israel, from Dan to Beer-sheba, and take a census of the people, so that I may know how many there are." [3] But Joab said to the king, "May the Lord your God increase the number of the people a hundredfold, while the eyes of my lord the king can still see it! But why does my lord the king want to do this?" [4] But the king's word prevailed against Joab and the commanders of the army. So Joab and the commanders of the army went out from the presence of the king to take a census of the people of Israel. [5] They crossed the Jordan, and began from[b] Aroer and from the city that is in the middle of the valley, toward Gad and on to Jazer. [6] Then they came to Gilead, and to Kadesh in the land of the Hittites;[c] and they came to Dan, and from Dan[d] they went around to Sidon, [7] and came to the fortress of Tyre and to all the cities of the Hivites and Canaanites; and they went out to the Negeb of Judah at Beer-sheba. [8] So when they had gone through all the land, they came back to Jerusalem at the end of nine months and twenty days. [9] Joab reported to the king the number of those who had been recorded: in Israel there were eight hundred thousand soldiers able to draw the sword, and those of Judah were five hundred thousand.

[10] But afterward, David was stricken to the heart because he had numbered the people. David said to the Lord, "I have sinned greatly in what I have done. But now, O Lord, I pray you, take away the guilt of your servant; for I have done very foolishly." [11] When David rose in the morning, the word of the Lord came to the prophet Gad, David's seer, saying, [12] "Go and say to David: Thus says the Lord: Three things I offer[e] you; choose one of them, and I will do it to you." [13] So Gad came to David and told him; he asked him, "Shall three[f] years of famine come to you on your land? Or will you flee three months before your foes while they pursue you? Or shall there be three days' pestilence in your land? Now consider, and decide what answer I shall return to the one who sent me." [14] Then David said to Gad, "I

---

a 1 Chr 21.2 Gk: Heb *to Joab the commander of the army*
b Gk Mss: Heb *encamped in Aroer south of*
c Gk: Heb *to the land of Tahtim-hodshi*
d Cn Compare Gk: Heb *they came to Dan-jaan and*
e Or *hold over*
f 1 Chr 21.12 Gk: Heb *seven*

---

is achieved. The list in vv. 24–39 has thirty names in it. The addition of the "Three" plus Abishai and Benaiah brings the number to thirty-five. Joab may have been counted as a member of this elite group, though his name is not specifically mentioned. There are textual variations in vv. 24–39 where an additional name may have been read.

24.1–25: David's census. The final narrative in 2 Samuel. It must be remembered that 2 Samuel and 1 Kings were originally part of a larger work and not separate books. This chapter, then, was not written as a conclusion to 2 Samuel. Rather, it anticipates the building of the Temple under Solomon (vv. 18–25; see 1 Kings chs 5–6; 8) and thus looks forward to the important results of David's reign. **1:** *Again* implies that this story is the sequel to an earlier one, perhaps 21.1–14. This same story is found in 1 Chr 21, which says that Satan rather than the anger of the Lord *incited* David. It is only in postexilic texts that (the) Satan becomes important in biblical literature. Both reflect the belief that natural calamity is the result of human sin. It is not clear why taking a census was sinful; some scholars suggest it was a sign of David's inordinate pride or that the census was meant to bring about unacceptable changes in Israelite society. (A census usually provided the basis for conscription and taxation.) Another possibility is that all men enrolled in the census were required to be ritually pure as when they went to battle, and this requirement was easily broken. **2:** *From Dan to Beer-sheba*, the traditional northern and southern limits of Israel. **3–4:** These potential dangers may explain Joab's reluctance to carry out the census. **5–7:** The census takers began at *Aroer* east of the Dead Sea and moved north as far as *Dan*, then crossed over the Jordan and went south through traditional Israel until they reached *Beer-sheba*. **9:** The count is limited to men of military age. *Thousand* may refer to a much smaller military unit. Israel and Judah are numbered separately because Judah, as David's native tribe, was exempted from taxation. **10–14:** *Stricken to the heart*, conscience-stricken; the language David uses is similar to 2 Sam 12.13. David is given a choice of three punishments. He chooses *the*

am in great distress; let us fall into the hand of the LORD, for his mercy is great; but let me not fall into human hands."

[15] So the LORD sent a pestilence on Israel from that morning until the appointed time; and seventy thousand of the people died, from Dan to Beer-sheba. [16] But when the angel stretched out his hand toward Jerusalem to destroy it, the LORD relented concerning the evil, and said to the angel who was bringing destruction among the people, "It is enough; now stay your hand." The angel of the LORD was then by the threshing floor of Araunah the Jebusite. [17] When David saw the angel who was destroying the people, he said to the LORD, "I alone have sinned, and I alone have done wickedly; but these sheep, what have they done? Let your hand, I pray, be against me and against my father's house."

[18] That day Gad came to David and said to him, "Go up and erect an altar to the LORD on the threshing floor of Araunah the Jebusite." [19] Following Gad's instructions, David went up, as the LORD had commanded. [20] When Araunah looked down, he saw the king and his servants coming toward him; and Araunah went out and prostrated himself before the king with his face to the ground. [21] Araunah said, "Why has my lord the king come to his servant?" David said, "To buy the threshing floor from you in order to build an altar to the LORD, so that the plague may be averted from the people." [22] Then Araunah said to David, "Let my lord the king take and offer up what seems good to him; here are the oxen for the burnt offering, and the threshing sledges and the yokes of the oxen for the wood. [23] All this, O king, Araunah gives to the king." And Araunah said to the king, "May the LORD your God respond favorably to you."

[24] But the king said to Araunah, "No, but I will buy them from you for a price; I will not offer burnt offerings to the LORD my God that cost me nothing." So David bought the threshing floor and the oxen for fifty shekels of silver. [25] David built there an altar to the LORD, and offered burnt offerings and offerings of well-being. So the LORD answered his supplication for the land, and the plague was averted from Israel.

hand of the LORD, an idiom for plague, trusting in the LORD's mercy. 15–16: David's strategy works. The plague is stopped after only one day and Jerusalem is spared. *The appointed time* (v. 15) may be the time of the evening meal. *Thousand* may be a military unit of much fewer than 1,000. *Evil* (v. 16), not moral evil but destruction. *Araunah*, called Ornan in 1 Chr 21. *Jebusite*, a pre-Israelite native of Jerusalem (5.6–10). *Threshing floor*, a flat, high area where grain was separated from the chaff. God also appears to people at threshing floors elsewhere in the Bible (Judg 6.11–12). 17: *Sheep*, the people of Jerusalem with David, as king, imagined as their shepherd; see 7.8n. 18–25: These verses indicate that the plague was stopped after David built his altar and made his offerings rather than by the LORD's free will as in v. 16. The site of David's altar is the location of the later altar of burnt offering of Solomon's Temple. *Fifty shekels* was about 1.25 lb (.57 kg).

1 KINGS

NAME

In the Greek Bible, the Septuagint (LXX), this book is called *Basileion 3* ("reigns" or "dynasties"). The Greek translators linked the two books of Samuel with the two books of Kings (the books of Samuel are labeled *Basileion 1* and *2*) because they narrate the story of the Israelite and Judean monarchy from its beginning until its end; indeed, 1 Kings opens with the death of David, the main character of the book of Samuel. In the Hebrew Bible, 1 and 2 Kings were originally a single book called Kings; it was divided into two, in the fifteenth century, under the influence of the Greek and Latin translations. This division originated in the Greek Bible for practical reasons: one long scroll of Kings was difficult to handle. This division artificially splits up the stories of the Israelite king Ahaziah and those of the prophet Elijah. It is probably based on a view of 2 Kings 1.1 ("after the death of Ahab") as patterned on the opening of the books of Joshua ("after the death of Moses"), Judges ("after the death of Joshua"), and 2 Samuel ("after the death of Saul").

CANONICAL STATUS AND LOCATION

In the Christian canon, 1 and 2 Kings belong to the "Historical Books" and are followed by the books of Chronicles, which offer an alternative account of the period of the monarchy. In the Jewish canon, the books of Kings close the first part of the Prophets, the "Former Prophets" comprised of Joshua, Judges, Samuel, and Kings. The exact meaning of this term is unclear since although prophets play some role in these books, it is not a major one. The Former Prophets do, however, provide the necessary background for the oracles of doom and of restoration that follow in the books of the "Latter Prophets."

AUTHORSHIP

Jewish tradition (*b. B. Bat.* 14b–15a) regards the prophet Jeremiah, a contemporary of the last kings of Judah, as the author of the book of Kings, perhaps because of the stylistic similarities between the books of Kings and Jeremiah. Kings and Jeremiah are both written in a style, which contemporary scholars call "Deuteronomistic"; they also share with Deuteronomy and the other books of the Former Prophets key vocabulary and theological concepts. For this reason, most scholars call the books of Deuteronomy through Kings the "Deuteronomistic History." In fact, the last episodes in the Former Prophets, the destruction of Jerusalem and the deportation of the people, related at the end of 2 Kings, are already alluded to in Deuteronomy (see Deut 6.15 and 28.47–68). For these reasons, modern scholars posit that scribes who belonged to the same social and ideological group edited the books from Deuteronomy to Kings.

DATES OF COMPOSITION AND LITERARY HISTORY

There are some indications that the first Deuteronomistic edition of the book of Kings as well as of the book of Deuteronomy was written in approximately 620 BCE, during the reign of the Judean king Josiah. According to 2 Kings 22–23, Josiah undertook a religious reform aimed at making Jerusalem the only legitimate sanctuary for the worship of the Lord. This reform follows the main theological ideas expressed in Deuteronomy, namely the centralization of worship and the exclusive veneration of the Lord, the God who had chosen Israel as his special property. The Josianic edition's conclusion was probably 2 Kings 23.25: "Before him there was no king like him, who turned to the Lord with all his heart, with all his soul, and with all his might." This ideal description of Josiah corresponds exactly to the central exhortation of the book of Deuteronomy: "You shall love the Lord your God with all your heart, and with all your soul, and with all your might" (Deut 6.5). The aim of the Josianic edition of Kings would then have been to demonstrate that Josiah fulfilled God's will by his religious and political acts. This quite optimistic work was revised anew after the destruction of Jerusalem in 586 BCE; it attempted to explain the reasons for the end of the Judean monarchy and the exile to Babylon. The last event related in 2 Kings is the alleviation of the status of king Jehoiachin, which occurred under the Babylonian king Evil-merodach (Amel-Marduk) who reigned briefly in 562–561 BCE. Therefore many scholars think that the book of Kings in its present form was written shortly after this date. Scholars have more recently pointed to evidence suggesting that the books underwent further revision during the Persian period.

The Deuteronomistic authors and editors integrated several older sources or independent documents into their work. The "Book of the Acts of Solomon" (1 Kings 11.41) may have been one such work. Later, Kings refers to "the Book of the Annals of the Kings of Israel" (e.g., 1 Kings 14.19) and "the Book of the Annals of the Kings of Judah" (e.g., 1 Kings 14.29). Such annals probably existed in the courts of Samaria and Jerusalem and were known by the authors and editors of Kings. Most of the prophetic stories about Elijah and Elisha, as well as other prophetic stories, may have existed as independent scrolls before they were incorporated at a late stage into the book of Kings. We can thus say that much of the book of Kings was produced by authors and editors that we can label as "Deuteronomists," though they incorporated some earlier sources, and the editing of the book continued into the first half of the Persian period, the late sixth and fifth centuries BCE.

STRUCTURE AND CONTENTS

The book of Kings tells the story of the Judean and Israelite monarchies from the "United Monarchy" under Solomon (1 Kings 1–11) and its division after his death into the Northern Kingdom of Israel and the Southern Kingdom of Judah (1 Kings 12), until the end of Israel (2 Kings 17) and of Judah (2 Kings 24–25). First Kings covers the time from Solomon until King Jehoshaphat of Judah and King Ahaziah of Israel. The story of Solomon can be divided into three parts: chs 1–2; 3.1–9.9; and 9.10–11.43. Chapters 1–2 relate his rise to power. The narrative of his reign is bookmarked by two divine manifestations in chs 3 and 9. Chapters 3–8 present the positive part of Solomon's activity: his wisdom and especially the construction of the Jerusalem Temple, followed by a long prayer. God's second speech to Solomon is forward-looking, evoking the possibility of his downfall, and ultimately the destruction of the Temple and the exile. First Kings 9.10–11.43 reviews Solomon negatively: he imposes forced labor upon the people, loves many foreign women, and worships their divinities. The last chapter prepares the reader for ch 12, where the kingdom is divided, and Jeroboam becomes the first king of Israel, and Rehoboam the first king of Judah. After the account of Jeroboam's reign the story of both kingdoms is narrated (until 2 Kings 17) in a synchronistic way, where the reign of each king is framed by introductory and final formulas. The information about Judean kings is more extensive, indicating that the Judean scribes likely had more information about their own kings. The formulas have the following pattern:

JUDEAN KINGS	ISRAELITE KINGS
Introductory synchronism	Introductory synchronism
The king's age at his enthronement	–
Length of reign	Length of reign
Name of his mother	–
Theological judgment	Theological judgment
Final reference to the annals of the kings of Judah	Final reference to the annals of the kings of Israel
Death of the king	Death of the king
Burial	–
Name of the successor	Name of the successor

After the story of Jeroboam and Rehoboam (chs 12–14), the narrative continues with two Judean kings (Abijam and Asa in 15.1–24) before describing the chaotic situation in the Northern Kingdom, which after several coups sees the rise of King Omri, the founder of Samaria, the capital of the Northern Kingdom (15.25–16.28). The last quarter of 1 Kings is devoted to the story of Omri's son Ahab and his Phoenician wife Jezebel (16.29–22.40). Their worship of the god Baal provokes a dramatic conflict with the LORD's prophet Elijah, which culminates in a public competition between the many prophets of Baal and the lone prophet Elijah on Mount Carmel (ch 18). First Kings concludes with short notices about Jehoshaphat of Judah and Ahaziah of Israel (22.41–53); the final verse reporting the ongoing veneration of Baal in the Northern Kingdom, which provoked the LORD's anger (22.53) hints at the end of Israel (2 Kings 17) and Judah (2 Kings 24–25).

INTERPRETATION

The book of Kings is historiography in the sense that it presents a chronological succession from the beginning of the Israelite monarchy until its end, covering roughly a time span from 970 to 560 BCE, but it is not historiography in the ancient Greek or modern meaning of the term. First of all, the book of King is an anonymous work; in contrast to the ancient Greek historians Herodotus and Thucydides, there is no author who speaks in the first person and who presents sources and evaluates information. There is no inquiry at all about "how things really happened." For the author(s) of Kings, the LORD is the major actor in the history of the Judean and Israelite kings. The kings whose reigns are positively evaluated are monarchs who conform themselves to God's will, whereas the unfaithful kings provoke God's punishment and in some cases, are ultimately responsible for the fall of Samaria and Jerusalem. There is no interest in an objective comprehensive and complete recounting of the past. Kings such as Josiah, whose hazardous geopolitical policies may appear strange to modern readers, are presented very positively, whereas kings with a long, apparently peaceful reign, such as Manasseh, are judged very negatively. The main interest of the authors of Kings is not the political, economical, and military achievements of kings, but their religious attitude, especially as expressed through exclusive worship of the LORD in the Temple of Jerusalem, the only legitimate sanctuary, which plays a central role throughout the book of Kings. Jeroboam, the first king of the Northern Kingdom after its separation from Judah, is described as the founder of two sanctuaries in Dan and Bethel, which appear as illegitimate competitors with the Temple of Jerusalem (1 Kings 12). Consequently, all subsequent northern kings are systematically blamed for "Jeroboam's sin." The southern kings are compared to their "father" David (1 Kings 15.3,11; 2 Kings 14.3; 16.2; 18.3; 22.2) and are evaluated based on their loyalty to the Jerusalem Temple and their condemnation of the other places of worship (the "high places").

Several narratives describe attempts by kings of Judah to reform the Jerusalem Temple (Joash, 2 Kings 12; Hezekiah, 2 Kings 18; Josiah, 2 Kings 23); these are generally followed by a return to previous idolatry (Ahaz, 2 Kings 16:10–18; Manasseh, 2 Kings 21). Only Josiah accomplishes a full restoration of the Temple, establishing an implicit parallel between Josiah, the reformer king, and Solomon, the founder of the Temple. This suggests that the first edition of Kings was an attempt to glorify Josiah as the ideal descendant of David and Solomon. The destruction of Jerusalem and its Temple in 586 BCE caused a thoroughgoing revision of Kings, which was transformed into an explanation of that exile. These editors, working during the Babylonian exile or during the first decades of the Persian period, offered a "theodicy," an explanation of how a good God could cause such evil: the fall of Jerusalem and the destruction of the Temple are not due to the LORD's inability to defend his nation against its enemies; on the contrary, the LORD himself had ordered the Babylonians to invade Judah in order to punish it because it did not conform to divine law as expressed in the book of Deuteronomy.

Kings concludes with the release of King Jehoiachin from Babylonian prison (2 Kings 25.27–30). The purpose of these verses is debated: Are they a theological justification of the end of monarchy and the exile or do they express hope for the renewal of the Davidic dynasty? It is difficult to decide, and the following book of Isaiah, where oracles of doom alternate with oracles of restoration and the announcement of an ideal king, has the same ambivalence.

An early form of the books of Samuel and Kings triggered an interpretative rewriting, namely the books of Chronicles. Chronicles offers an alternative, less ambiguous account of the Judean monarchy. It omits almost all of the story of the Northern Kingdom, and ends with the decree of the Persian king allowing the Judeans to return from exile and to rebuild the Jerusalem Temple.

GUIDE TO READING

The best way to understand the meaning of Kings is to read the whole story starting with Solomon (or even better with David in the books of Samuel) until its end. The reader should pay attention to the way in which the different kings are presented and also to the importance of the prophets and the prophetic stories, which alternate with the narratives about good and bad kings. It is worth asking questions concerning the theology of Kings, specifically the manner in which it attempts to give sense to a national disaster and to affirm that the LORD is the God of Israel and of Judah and also the master of all other nations.

Thomas Römer

1

King David was old and advanced in years; and although they covered him with clothes, he could not get warm. ² So his servants said to him, "Let a young virgin be sought for my lord the king, and let her wait on the king, and be his attendant; let her lie in your bosom, so that my lord the king may be warm." ³ So they searched for a beautiful girl throughout all the territory of Israel, and found Abishag the Shunammite, and brought her to the king. ⁴ The girl was very beautiful. She became the king's attendant and served him, but the king did not know her sexually.

⁵ Now Adonijah son of Haggith exalted himself, saying, "I will be king"; he prepared for himself chariots and horsemen, and fifty men to run before him. ⁶ His father had never at any time displeased him by asking, "Why have you done thus and so?" He was also a very handsome man, and he was born next after Absalom. ⁷ He conferred with Joab son of Zeruiah and with the priest Abiathar, and they supported Adonijah. ⁸ But the priest Zadok, and Benaiah son of Jehoiada, and the prophet Nathan, and Shimei, and Rei, and David's own warriors did not side with Adonijah.

⁹ Adonijah sacrificed sheep, oxen, and fatted cattle by the stone Zoheleth, which is beside En-rogel, and he invited all his broth-ers, the king's sons, and all the royal officials of Judah, ¹⁰ but he did not invite the prophet Nathan or Benaiah or the warriors or his brother Solomon.

¹¹ Then Nathan said to Bathsheba, Solomon's mother, "Have you not heard that Adonijah son of Haggith has become king and our lord David does not know it? ¹² Now therefore come, let me give you advice, so that you may save your own life and the life of your son Solomon. ¹³ Go in at once to King David, and say to him, 'Did you not, my lord the king, swear to your servant, saying: Your son Solomon shall succeed me as king, and he shall sit on my throne? Why then is Adonijah king?' ¹⁴ Then while you are still there speaking with the king, I will come in after you and confirm your words."

¹⁵ So Bathsheba went to the king in his room. The king was very old; Abishag the Shunammite was attending the king. ¹⁶ Bathsheba bowed and did obeisance to the king, and the king said, "What do you wish?" ¹⁷ She said to him, "My lord, you swore to your servant by the LORD your God, saying: Your son Solomon shall succeed me as king, and he shall sit on my throne. ¹⁸ But now suddenly Adonijah has become king, though you, my lord the king, do not know it. ¹⁹ He has sacrificed oxen, fatted cattle, and sheep

1.1–53: **Solomon's rise to the throne.** The opening chapters of 1 Kings continue the account of the succession to David, which begins in 2 Samuel (see Introduction to 2 Samuel). The first chapter of Kings shows that Solomon was not the expected successor, but became king after a court intrigue, a well-attested motif in Assyrian and Babylonian literature. **1–4:** Virility and the ability to govern were connected in antiquity (see 1 Sam 16.22 where Absalom sleeps in public with David's wives to show that he is the new king). The strategy of David's servants to revive his vigor fails. The question of his successor has thus become unavoidable. **3:** *Abishag* is from Shunem, a town in the Jezreel valley in northern Israel. **4:** Despite Abishag's integration into David's harem, the old king is unable to have sexual relations with her. **5–8:** After the deaths of Amnon and Absalom (Chileab is mentioned only in 2 Sam 3.4), Adonijah, the next oldest son, thinks he should succeed his father to the throne. The narrator also suggests his suitability because he is *very handsome*, a royal attribute. Adonijah tries to gain support for his claim, and two important members of the court are on his side: *Joab*, David's nephew (his sister's son, according to 1 Chr 2.16) and head of the army, and *Abiathar*, David's priest, who had escaped Saul's slaughter of the priests of Nob (1 Sam 22.20–23). The opposing group (v. 8) includes members of the Jerusalemite aristocracy: the priest *Zadok* and the prophet *Nathan*, *Benaiah*, a chief of foreign mercenaries, and *Shimei*, whose identity is not clear. Perhaps one may identify him with the one mentioned in 2 Sam 16.5–14. The Zadok-Nathan party is also supported by *David's own warriors*, David's bodyguard. **9–10:** Adonijah's abundant sacrifices by the stone *Zoheleth* (the "snake stone") at *En-rogel* (the "fuller's spring," in the Kidron Valley southeast of Jerusalem) are meant to foster unity among his party. **11–14:** There is no mention in the previous story of an oath sworn by David in favor of Solomon, so it may be an invention of Nathan and Bathsheba to manipulate the ailing king. **15–31:** Bathsheba and Nathan's strategy is successful in convincing David to proclaim Solomon his successor. According to v. 22 Bathsheba is present while Nathan is speaking to David, whereas according to v. 28 she

in abundance, and has invited all the children of the king, the priest Abiathar, and Joab the commander of the army; but your servant Solomon he has not invited. 20 But you, my lord the king—the eyes of all Israel are on you to tell them who shall sit on the throne of my lord the king after him. 21 Otherwise it will come to pass, when my lord the king sleeps with his ancestors, that my son Solomon and I will be counted offenders."

22 While she was still speaking with the king, the prophet Nathan came in. 23 The king was told, "Here is the prophet Nathan." When he came in before the king, he did obeisance to the king, with his face to the ground. 24 Nathan said, "My lord the king, have you said, 'Adonijah shall succeed me as king, and he shall sit on my throne'? 25 For today he has gone down and has sacrificed oxen, fatted cattle, and sheep in abundance, and has invited all the king's children, Joab the commander[a] of the army, and the priest Abiathar, who are now eating and drinking before him, and saying, 'Long live King Adonijah!' 26 But he did not invite me, your servant, and the priest Zadok, and Benaiah son of Jehoiada, and your servant Solomon. 27 Has this thing been brought about by my lord the king and you have not let your servants know who should sit on the throne of my lord the king after him?"

28 King David answered, "Summon Bathsheba to me." So she came into the king's presence, and stood before the king. 29 The king swore, saying, "As the LORD lives, who has saved my life from every adversity, 30 as I swore to you by the LORD, the God of Israel, 'Your son Solomon shall succeed me as king, and he shall sit on my throne in my place,' so will I do this day." 31 Then Bathsheba bowed with her face to the ground, and did obeisance to the king, and said, "May my lord King David live forever!"

32 King David said, "Summon to me the priest Zadok, the prophet Nathan, and Benaiah son of Jehoiada." When they came before the king, 33 the king said to them, "Take with you the servants of your lord, and have my son Solomon ride on my own mule, and bring him down to Gihon. 34 There let the priest Zadok and the prophet Nathan anoint him king over Israel; then blow the trumpet, and say, 'Long live King Solomon!' 35 You shall go up following him. Let him enter and sit on my throne; he shall be king in my place; for I have appointed him to be ruler over Israel and over Judah." 36 Benaiah son of Jehoiada answered the king, "Amen! May the LORD, the God of my lord the king, so ordain. 37 As the LORD has been with my lord the king, so may he be with Solomon, and make his throne greater than the throne of my lord King David."

38 So the priest Zadok, the prophet Nathan, and Benaiah son of Jehoiada, and the Cherethites and the Pelethites, went down and had Solomon ride on King David's mule, and led him to Gihon. 39 There the priest Zadok took the horn of oil from the tent and anointed Solomon. Then they blew the trumpet, and all the people said, "Long live King Solomon!" 40 And all the people went up following him, playing on pipes and rejoicing with great joy, so that the earth quaked at their noise.

41 Adonijah and all the guests who were with him heard it as they finished feasting. When Joab heard the sound of the trumpet, he said, "Why is the city in an uproar?" 42 While he was still speaking, Jonathan son of the priest Abiathar arrived. Adonijah said, "Come in, for you are a worthy man and surely you bring good news." 43 Jonathan answered Adonijah, "No, for our lord King David has made Solomon king; 44 the king has sent with him the priest Zadok, the prophet Nathan,

a Gk: Heb *the commanders*

seems to have left the audience, suggesting that the story has undergone revision. 32–40: The anointing of Solomon takes place at *Gihon*, the main spring of Jerusalem located in the Kidron Valley. 38: Whereas Saul and David were anointed only by the prophet Samuel, but following the LORD's instructions, Solomon is anointed by a prophet and by a priest, but without explicit divine authorization. The *Cherethites* and *Pelethites*, who participate in the ritual, are David's personal troops; the names may allude to their Cretan and Philistine origin. 39: *Tent*, the mobile sanctuary, which David transferred to Jerusalem, will be replaced by the Temple built by Solomon. 40: After the anointing a solemn procession to the throne begins the new king's rule. 41–53: *Jonathan*, son of Abiathar, who supported David during Absalom's revolt (2 Sam 15.36; 17.17) informs Adonijah that he will

and Benaiah son of Jehoiada, and the Cherethites and the Pelethites; and they had him ride on the king's mule; ⁴⁵ the priest Zadok and the prophet Nathan have anointed him king at Gihon; and they have gone up from there rejoicing, so that the city is in an uproar. This is the noise that you heard. ⁴⁶ Solomon now sits on the royal throne. ⁴⁷ Moreover the king's servants came to congratulate our lord King David, saying, 'May God make the name of Solomon more famous than yours, and make his throne greater than your throne.' The king bowed in worship on the bed ⁴⁸ and went on to pray thus, 'Blessed be the LORD, the God of Israel, who today has granted one of my offspringᵃ to sit on my throne and permitted me to witness it.'"

⁴⁹ Then all the guests of Adonijah got up trembling and went their own ways. ⁵⁰ Adonijah, fearing Solomon, got up and went to grasp the horns of the altar. ⁵¹ Solomon was informed, "Adonijah is afraid of King Solomon; see, he has laid hold of the horns of the altar, saying, 'Let King Solomon swear to me first that he will not kill his servant with the sword.'" ⁵² So Solomon responded, "If he proves to be a worthy man, not one of his hairs shall fall to the ground; but if wickedness is found in him, he shall die." ⁵³ Then King Solomon sent to have him brought down from the altar. He came to do obeisance to King Solomon; and Solomon said to him, "Go home."

2 When David's time to die drew near, he charged his son Solomon, saying: ² "I am about to go the way of all the earth. Be strong, be courageous, ³ and keep the charge of the LORD your God, walking in his ways and keeping his statutes, his commandments, his ordinances, and his testimonies, as it is written in the law of Moses, so that you may prosper in all that you do and wherever you turn. ⁴ Then the LORD will establish his word that he spoke concerning me: 'If your heirs take heed to their way, to walk before me in faithfulness with all their heart and with all their soul, there shall not fail you a successor on the throne of Israel.'

⁵ "Moreover you know also what Joab son of Zeruiah did to me, how he dealt with the two commanders of the armies of Israel, Abner son of Ner, and Amasa son of Jether, whom he murdered, retaliating in time of peace for blood that had been shed in war, and putting the blood of war on the belt around his waist, and on the sandals on his feet. ⁶ Act therefore according to your wisdom, but do not let his gray head go down to Sheol in peace. ⁷ Deal loyally, however, with the sons of Barzillai the Gileadite, and let them be among those who eat at your table; for with such loyalty they met me when I fled from your brother Absalom. ⁸ There is also with you Shimei son of Gera, the Benjaminite

ᵃ   Gk: Heb *one*

not become king over Israel. **50:** Adonijah fears revenge and grasps *the horns of the altar*. The altar with four horns (see Ex 29.12; 30,3; Lev 4.7), quarter-round stones on each corner, was understood in some traditions as offering a place of asylum. **52:** Solomon promises that he will not harm Adonijah if he proves to be a *worthy man*, behaving loyally to the new king (but see 2.29–30).

2.1–12: David's last words and his death. 1–4: David's exhortations recall God's words to Joshua, Israel's leader after Moses' death (Josh 1.2–9). Solomon, like every king in Israel, must abide by God's commandments as written in the *law of Moses* (see Deut 17.18–20), particularly Deuteronomy; many of David's exhortations are taken from that book (see Deut 4.29,40; 8.6; 10.12; 11.1; 29.9). **4:** A summary and interpretation of the dynastic promise of 2 Sam 7.12–16. The unconditional promise of an eternal dynasty in 2 Sam 7 is here transformed into a conditional promise, stating that the Davidic dynasty will last only if his successors respect God's will as expressed in Deuteronomy. **5–9:** David's order legitimates Solomon's killing of *Joab* and *Shimei* (vv. 28–46). **5–6:** *Joab*, a supporter of Adonijah, was formerly a loyal follower of David, who had carried out several murders, some at David's request. David accuses him of killing Abner (2 Sam 3.6–39) and Amasa (2 Sam 20.9–10). **8–9:** *Shimei*, who did not support Adonijah (1.8), has to die because he cursed David; David had sworn to him that he would not harm him (2 Sam 19.23), but David now asks Solomon to kill his former antagonist. **6:** Solomon's wisdom, which will be a main feature of his reign, is first alluded to here. *Sheol*, the underworld where all the dead go. David asks Solomon to hasten Joab's and Shimei's descent there. **7:** In contrast, Barzillai is a model of dutiful service to the king (2 Sam 17.27–29; 19.32–39). He is therefore to be allowed to eat at the king's

from Bahurim, who cursed me with a terrible curse on the day when I went to Mahanaim; but when he came down to meet me at the Jordan, I swore to him by the LORD, 'I will not put you to death with the sword.' ⁹ Therefore do not hold him guiltless, for you are a wise man; you will know what you ought to do to him, and you must bring his gray head down with blood to Sheol."

¹⁰ Then David slept with his ancestors, and was buried in the city of David. ¹¹ The time that David reigned over Israel was forty years; he reigned seven years in Hebron, and thirty-three years in Jerusalem. ¹² So Solomon sat on the throne of his father David; and his kingdom was firmly established.

¹³ Then Adonijah son of Haggith came to Bathsheba, Solomon's mother. She asked, "Do you come peaceably?" He said, "Peaceably." ¹⁴ Then he said, "May I have a word with you?" She said, "Go on." ¹⁵ He said, "You know that the kingdom was mine, and that all Israel expected me to reign; however, the kingdom has turned about and become my brother's, for it was his from the LORD. ¹⁶ And now I have one request to make of you; do not refuse me." She said to him, "Go on." ¹⁷ He said, "Please ask King Solomon—he will not refuse you—to give me Abishag the Shunammite as my wife." ¹⁸ Bathsheba said, "Very well; I will speak to the king on your behalf."

¹⁹ So Bathsheba went to King Solomon, to speak to him on behalf of Adonijah. The king rose to meet her, and bowed down to her; then he sat on his throne, and had a throne brought for the king's mother, and she sat on his right. ²⁰ Then she said, "I have one small request to make of you; do not refuse me." And the king said to her, "Make your request, my mother; for I will not refuse you." ²¹ She said, "Let Abishag the Shunammite be given to your brother Adonijah as his wife." ²² King Solomon answered his mother, "And why do you ask Abishag the Shunammite for Adonijah? Ask for him the kingdom as well! For he is my elder brother; ask not only for him but also for the priest Abiathar and for Joab son of Zeruiah!" ²³ Then King Solomon swore by the LORD, "So may God do to me, and more also, for Adonijah has devised this scheme at the risk of his life! ²⁴ Now therefore as the LORD lives, who has established me and placed me on the throne of my father David, and who has made me a house as he promised, today Adonijah shall be put to death." ²⁵ So King Solomon sent Benaiah son of Jehoiada; he struck him down, and he died.

²⁶ The king said to the priest Abiathar, "Go to Anathoth, to your estate; for you deserve death. But I will not at this time put you to death, because you carried the ark of the Lord GOD before my father David, and because you shared in all the hardships my father endured." ²⁷ So Solomon banished Abiathar from being priest to the LORD, thus fulfilling the word of the LORD that he had spoken concerning the house of Eli in Shiloh.

²⁸ When the news came to Joab—for Joab had supported Adonijah though he had not supported Absalom—Joab fled to the tent of the LORD and grasped the horns of the altar. ²⁹ When it was told King Solomon, "Joab has fled to the tent of the LORD and now is

table, a high distinction. 10: *David slept with his ancestors,* this standard formula occurs for kings who died a natural death and expresses the idea of being united with one's ancestors in Sheol, as well as being buried in the family tomb. 11: The *forty-year* reign of David should be understood symbolically as a reign of a complete, perfect period. In general, it is difficult to reconstruct historical dates for this period, but the first half of the tenth century BCE is probably correct; see Chronological Table of Rulers on p. 486. 12: The notice about the establishment of Solomon's kingdom is repeated in v. 46. Between these two verses the narrator tells us how this was accomplished.

2.13–46: Solomon's elimination of his enemies and consolidation of his kingship. The fates of Adonijah, Abiathar, Joab, and Shimei. 13–25: *Adonijah's* request, which is relayed by Bathsheba, to marry David's last concubine Abishag is ambiguous since it can be understood as legitimating a claim to the throne (see 2 Sam 16.20–22). In Solomon's eyes Adonijah is still a rival who has to die. 26–27: Adonijah's death is followed by the banishing of his supporter, the priest *Abiathar.* Abiathar's exile to *Anathoth* (ca. 4 mi [6 km] northeast of Jerusalem), the hometown of the prophet Jeremiah, fulfils the divine oracle against the descendants of the priest Eli in 1 Sam 2.27–36. 28–35: The death of *Joab* may cast a negative light on

beside the altar," Solomon sent Benaiah son of Jehoiada, saying, "Go, strike him down." [30] So Benaiah came to the tent of the LORD and said to him, "The king commands, 'Come out.'" But he said, "No, I will die here." Then Benaiah brought the king word again, saying, "Thus said Joab, and thus he answered me." [31] The king replied to him, "Do as he has said, strike him down and bury him; and thus take away from me and from my father's house the guilt for the blood that Joab shed without cause. [32] The LORD will bring back his bloody deeds on his own head, because, without the knowledge of my father David, he attacked and killed with the sword two men more righteous and better than himself, Abner son of Ner, commander of the army of Israel, and Amasa son of Jether, commander of the army of Judah. [33] So shall their blood come back on the head of Joab and on the head of his descendants forever; but to David, and to his descendants, and to his house, and to his throne, there shall be peace from the LORD forevermore." [34] Then Benaiah son of Jehoiada went up and struck him down and killed him; and he was buried at his own house near the wilderness. [35] The king put Benaiah son of Jehoiada over the army in his place, and the king put the priest Zadok in the place of Abiathar.

[36] Then the king sent and summoned Shimei, and said to him, "Build yourself a house in Jerusalem, and live there, and do not go out from there to any place whatever. [37] For on the day you go out, and cross the Wadi Kidron, know for certain that you shall die; your blood shall be on your own head." [38] And Shimei said to the king, "The sentence is fair; as my lord the king has said, so will your servant do." So Shimei lived in Jerusalem many days.

[39] But it happened at the end of three years that two of Shimei's slaves ran away to King Achish son of Maacah of Gath. When it was told Shimei, "Your slaves are in Gath," [40] Shimei arose and saddled a donkey, and went to Achish in Gath, to search for his slaves; Shimei went and brought his slaves from Gath. [41] When Solomon was told that Shimei had gone from Jerusalem to Gath and returned, [42] the king sent and summoned Shimei, and said to him, "Did I not make you swear by the LORD, and solemnly adjure you, saying, 'Know for certain that on the day you go out and go to any place whatever, you shall die'? And you said to me, 'The sentence is fair; I accept.' [43] Why then have you not kept your oath to the LORD and the commandment with which I charged you?" [44] The king also said to Shimei, "You know in your own heart all the evil that you did to my father David; so the LORD will bring back your evil on your own head. [45] But King Solomon shall be blessed, and the throne of David shall be established before the LORD forever." [46] Then the king commanded Benaiah son of Jehoiada; and he went out and struck him down, and he died.

So the kingdom was established in the hand of Solomon.

3 Solomon made a marriage alliance with Pharaoh king of Egypt; he took Pharaoh's daughter and brought her into the city of David, until he had finished building his own house and the house of the LORD and the wall around Jerusalem. [2] The people were sacrificing at the high places, however, because no

---

Solomon since he has Benaiah (who also killed Adonijah) kill him inside the holy tent where Joab grasped the horns of the altar (see 1.50). **36–46:** *Shimei* is first put under house arrest in Jerusalem in order to prevent him from crossing the *Wadi Kidron* (to enter the territory of Benjamin, King Saul's home) in order to instigate a revolt from his power base. But when three of his slaves run away, Shimei goes westward to the Philistine town of Gath. Solomon takes this opportunity to have him executed. In this passage the murders of Joab and Shimei are not related as fulfillment of David's order; they are presented as Solomon's own initiative. His kingdom is therefore established by violence, but this need not be seen as a negative value-judgment by our author: Assyrian, Babylonian, and Persian texts tell similar stories about the rise to power of important kings.

3.1–28: Solomon's wisdom. 1: The story of Solomon's reign starts with a note about his marriage with *Pharaoh's daughter*. This marriage is also mentioned in the Masoretic Text (MT) in 7.8 and 9.16–17,24, while the LXX reports it in different places (2.35c.f.; 5.14; 7.45). The Pharaoh's name is not noted, and the historicity of this information is difficult to establish. Deut 17.16; 26.28 warns against too-close relations with Egypt, so this text

house had yet been built for the name of the LORD.

³ Solomon loved the LORD, walking in the statutes of his father David; only, he sacrificed and offered incense at the high places. ⁴ The king went to Gibeon to sacrifice there, for that was the principal high place; Solomon used to offer a thousand burnt offerings on that altar. ⁵ At Gibeon the LORD appeared to Solomon in a dream by night; and God said, "Ask what I should give you." ⁶ And Solomon said, "You have shown great and steadfast love to your servant my father David, because he walked before you in faithfulness, in righteousness, and in uprightness of heart toward you; and you have kept for him this great and steadfast love, and have given him a son to sit on his throne today. ⁷ And now, O LORD my God, you have made your servant king in place of my father David, although I am only a little child; I do not know how to go out or come in. ⁸ And your servant is in the midst of the people whom you have chosen, a great people, so numerous they cannot be numbered or counted. ⁹ Give your servant therefore an understanding mind to govern your people, able to discern between good and evil; for who can govern this your great people?"

¹⁰ It pleased the Lord that Solomon had asked this. ¹¹ God said to him, "Because you have asked this, and have not asked for yourself long life or riches, or for the life of your enemies, but have asked for yourself understanding to discern what is right, ¹² I now do according to your word. Indeed I give you a wise and discerning mind; no one like you has been before you and no one like you shall arise after you. ¹³ I give you also what you have not asked, both riches and honor all your life; no other king shall compare with you. ¹⁴ If you will walk in my ways, keeping my statutes and my commandments, as your father David walked, then I will lengthen your life."

¹⁵ Then Solomon awoke; it had been a dream. He came to Jerusalem where he stood before the ark of the covenant of the LORD. He offered up burnt offerings and offerings of well-being, and provided a feast for all his servants.

¹⁶ Later, two women who were prostitutes came to the king and stood before him. ¹⁷ The one woman said, "Please, my lord, this woman and I live in the same house; and I gave birth while she was in the house. ¹⁸ Then on the third day after I gave birth, this woman also gave birth. We were together; there was no one else with us in the house, only the two of us were in the house. ¹⁹ Then this woman's son died in the night, because she lay on him. ²⁰ She got up in the middle of the night and took my son from beside me while your servant slept. She laid him at her breast, and laid her dead son

may hint that Solomon was not an ideal king. **2–3:** In a description of other less-than-ideal behavior, the people and Solomon, in contradiction to Deuteronomic law (Deut 12) worship at the *high places*, local open-air sanctuaries, which are often condemned as idolatrous. They are regularly mentioned in the accusations against the "bad kings." Here, however, Solomon is somewhat exonerated, since the Temple for the God of Israel, the only legitimate sanctuary, has not yet been built. **4–15:** The divine vision organizes the story of Solomon's rule in two parts (see also 9.1–9). 3.4–8.66 relate mostly the positive aspects of his reign, which culminates with the building of the Temple; chs 9.10–11.43 underline Solomon's problematic behavior, which led to disaster. **4:** *Gibeon*, 5.6 mi (9 km) northwest of Jerusalem, was an important religious and political center during the monarchy. Solomon honors the place by seeking there, through sacrifices and an incubation dream, a divine oracle at the beginning of his reign. **5–9:** God tests Solomon and he behaves rightly in asking for wisdom in order to accomplish his royal task. **7:** Solomon's self-presentation as a *little child* or a young boy is not a reference to his age, but a conventional expression that expresses incapacity to accomplish an important task (see Judg 6.15; Jer 1.6). *To go out or come in* concerns military experience (see Num 27.15–17). **12–13:** God is pleased by Solomon's quest for wisdom and also promises him outstanding wealth. Both themes are developed in the following account of Solomon's reign. **14:** The divine promise is offered conditionally. **15:** The correct place for the LORD's worship is Jerusalem and not Gibeon. **16–28:** The "judgment of Solomon" is the first illustration of the king's newly acquired wisdom, since administration of justice is an important royal function. The name of Solomon is not mentioned in this story, which may have been originally an independent folktale. Its incorporation in the Solomon narrative contrasts with ch 2 where Solomon uses his wisdom to kill his enemies by the sword.

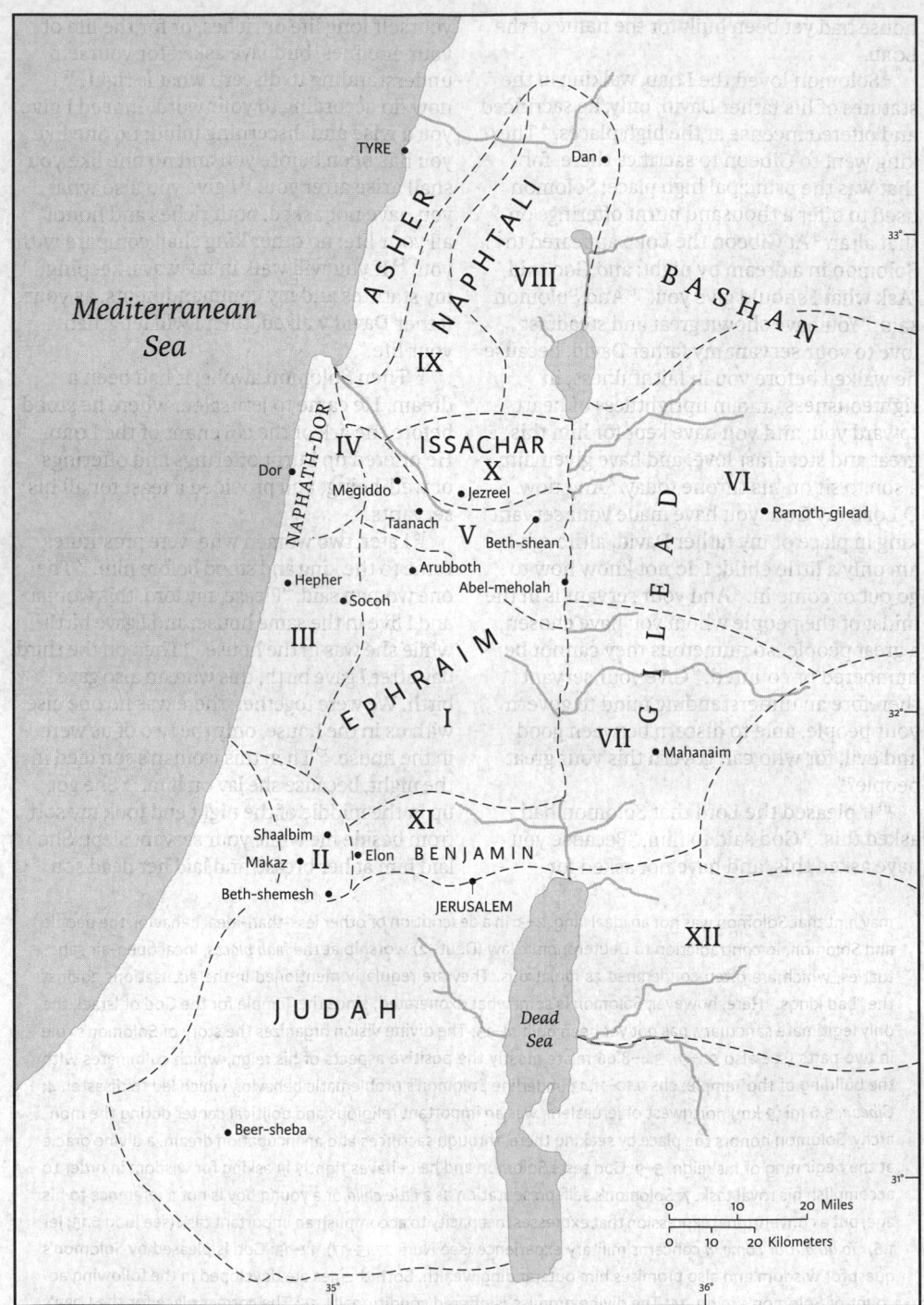

Mediterranean
Sea

TYRE

Dan

ASHER

NAPHTALI

VIII

BASHAN

IX

33°

NAPHATH-DOR

IV

ISSACHAR

X

Dor

Megiddo

Jezreel

VI

Taanach

V

Beth-shean

Ramoth-gilead

Arubboth

Abel-meholah

Hepher

Socoh

III

EPHRAIM

I

G I L E A D

32°

Mahanaim

VII

Shaalbim

XI

Makaz

Elon

BENJAMIN

Beth-shemesh

JERUSALEM

XII

JUDAH

Dead
Sea

31°

Beer-sheba

0   10   20 Miles

0   10   20 Kilometers

35°

36°

4.7–19: Solomon's twelve administrative districts.

at my breast. ²¹ When I rose in the morning to nurse my son, I saw that he was dead; but when I looked at him closely in the morning, clearly it was not the son I had borne." ²² But the other woman said, "No, the living son is mine, and the dead son is yours." The first said, "No, the dead son is yours, and the living son is mine." So they argued before the king.

²³ Then the king said, "The one says, 'This is my son that is alive, and your son is dead'; while the other says, 'Not so! Your son is dead, and my son is the living one.'" ²⁴ So the king said, "Bring me a sword," and they brought a sword before the king. ²⁵ The king said, "Divide the living boy in two; then give half to the one, and half to the other." ²⁶ But the woman whose son was alive said to the king—because compassion for her son burned within her—"Please, my lord, give her the living boy; certainly do not kill him!" The other said, "It shall be neither mine nor yours; divide it." ²⁷ Then the king responded: "Give the first woman the living boy; do not kill him. She is his mother." ²⁸ All Israel heard of the judgment that the king had rendered; and they stood in awe of the king, because they perceived that the wisdom of God was in him, to execute justice.

4 King Solomon was king over all Israel, ² and these were his high officials: Azariah son of Zadok was the priest; ³ Elihoreph and Ahijah sons of Shisha were secretaries; Jehoshaphat son of Ahilud was recorder; ⁴ Benaiah son of Jehoiada was in command of the army; Zadok and Abiathar were priests; ⁵ Azariah son of Nathan was over the officials; Zabud son of Nathan was priest and king's

friend; ⁶ Ahishar was in charge of the palace; and Adoniram son of Abda was in charge of the forced labor.

⁷ Solomon had twelve officials over all Israel, who provided food for the king and his household; each one had to make provision for one month in the year. ⁸ These were their names: Ben-hur, in the hill country of Ephraim; ⁹ Ben-deker, in Makaz, Shaalbim, Beth-shemesh, and Elon-beth-hanan; ¹⁰ Ben-hesed, in Arubboth (to him belonged Socoh and all the land of Hepher); ¹¹ Ben-abinadab, in all Naphath-dor (he had Taphath, Solomon's daughter, as his wife); ¹² Baana son of Ahilud, in Taanach, Megiddo, and all Beth-shean, which is beside Zarethan below Jezreel, and from Beth-shean to Abel-meholah, as far as the other side of Jokmeam; ¹³ Ben-geber, in Ramoth-gilead (he had the villages of Jair son of Manasseh, which are in Gilead, and he had the region of Argob, which is in Bashan, sixty great cities with walls and bronze bars); ¹⁴ Ahinadab son of Iddo, in Mahanaim; ¹⁵ Ahimaaz, in Naphtali (he had taken Basemath, Solomon's daughter, as his wife); ¹⁶ Baana son of Hushai, in Asher and Bealoth; ¹⁷ Jehoshaphat son of Paruah, in Issachar; ¹⁸ Shimei son of Ela, in Benjamin; ¹⁹ Geber son of Uri, in the land of Gilead, the country of King Sihon of the Amorites and of King Og of Bashan. And there was one official in the land of Judah.

²⁰ Judah and Israel were as numerous as the sand by the sea; they ate and drank and were happy. ²¹ ^a Solomon was sovereign over

---

^a Ch 5.1 in Heb

24–27: The royal sword is used in order to preserve life and establish justice.

4.1–34: **The organization of Solomon's kingdom. 1–6:** A list of Solomon's high officials. The most important positions at the royal court were the priest (surprisingly v. 4 mentions Abiathar, who according to 2.27 had been banished); the state-secretary or "scribe" and spokesman; the chief commander of the army; the chief of the officials (see vv. 7–19); the king's friend, a title for the king's confidant; the prime minister, called the one who *was in charge of the palace*; and the supervisor of the forced labor, a new institution that will play an important role during Solomon's reign. **7–19:** Twelve officials who functioned as governors in charge of twelve regions in northern Israel, only partially based on traditional tribal areas (see map on p. 494). They organized taxes and provisions for the king and the Jerusalem court, with each region responsible for the provision for one month of the year. **19:** The text is uncertain here. The NRSV reference to *Judah* is found in some Greek manuscripts but not in the Hebrew. A later copyist probably missed a reference to Judah and inserted it here. The Hebrew reads: "there was one official in the land," probably the governor mentioned in v. 5 to whom the twelve officials were responsible. **20:** The concluding remark suggests that under Solomon's reign God's promise to the patriarchs (Gen 22.17; 32.12) that Israel would be *as numerous as the sand by the sea* had been fulfilled. **21–28:** Solomon is

all the kingdoms from the Euphrates to the land of the Philistines, even to the border of Egypt; they brought tribute and served Solomon all the days of his life.

²² Solomon's provision for one day was thirty cors of choice flour, and sixty cors of meal, ²³ ten fat oxen, and twenty pasture-fed cattle, one hundred sheep, besides deer, gazelles, roebucks, and fatted fowl. ²⁴ For he had dominion over all the region west of the Euphrates from Tiphsah to Gaza, over all the kings west of the Euphrates; and he had peace on all sides. ²⁵ During Solomon's lifetime Judah and Israel lived in safety, from Dan even to Beer-sheba, all of them under their vines and fig trees. ²⁶ Solomon also had forty thousand stalls of horses for his chariots, and twelve thousand horsemen. ²⁷ Those officials supplied provisions for King Solomon and for all who came to King Solomon's table, each one in his month; they let nothing be lacking. ²⁸ They also brought to the required place barley and straw for the horses and swift steeds, each according to his charge.

²⁹ God gave Solomon very great wisdom, discernment, and breadth of understanding as vast as the sand on the seashore, ³⁰ so that Solomon's wisdom surpassed the wisdom of all the people of the east, and all the wisdom of Egypt. ³¹ He was wiser than anyone else, wiser than Ethan the Ezrahite, and Heman, Calcol, and Darda, children of Mahol; his fame spread throughout all the surrounding nations. ³² He composed three thousand proverbs, and his songs numbered a thousand

and five. ³³ He would speak of trees, from the cedar that is in the Lebanon to the hyssop that grows in the wall; he would speak of animals, and birds, and reptiles, and fish. ³⁴ People came from all the nations to hear the wisdom of Solomon; they came from all the kings of the earth who had heard of his wisdom.

5ᵃ Now King Hiram of Tyre sent his servants to Solomon, when he heard that they had anointed him king in place of his father; for Hiram had always been a friend to David. ² Solomon sent word to Hiram, saying, ³ "You know that my father David could not build a house for the name of the LORD his God because of the warfare with which his enemies surrounded him, until the LORD put them under the soles of his feet.ᵇ ⁴ But now the LORD my God has given me rest on every side; there is neither adversary nor misfortune. ⁵ So I intend to build a house for the name of the LORD my God, as the LORD said to my father David, 'Your son, whom I will set on your throne in your place, shall build the house for my name.' ⁶ Therefore command that cedars from the Lebanon be cut for me. My servants will join your servants, and I will give you whatever wages you set for your servants; for you know that there is no one among us who knows how to cut timber like the Sidonians."

⁷ When Hiram heard the words of Solomon, he rejoiced greatly, and said, "Blessed be

ᵃ Ch 5.15 in Heb
ᵇ Gk Tg Vg: Heb *my feet* or *his feet*

described as dominating all kingdoms in the ancient Near East, an idealized description based on the borders of the land promised to Abraham in Gen 15.18. More realistic boundaries of Israel are found in v. 25, *from Dan . . . to Beer-sheba* (the traditional northern and southern limits of Israel and Judah). **22–23,27–28:** Additional information (see 4.7) about the royal provisions, which are incredibly high. **26:** For Solomon's *horses* see 10.26–29. **29–34:** Solomon surpasses the other nations also in wisdom. He is wiser than the great nations of wisdom, *Egypt* and *the people of the east* (probably Assyria and Babylon) and wiser than the great men known for their wisdom: *Ethan, Heman, Calcol,* and *Darda* (mentioned in 1 Chr 2.6; 6.18–28). **32:** Solomon's reputation as a maker of *proverbs* is reflected in Prov 1.1; 10.1; 25.1, where he is considered to be the author of different collections of proverbs. For the attribution of *songs* to Solomon, see Pss 72; 127; Song 1.1.

5.1–18: Solomon's relation with Hiram of Tyre and the preparations for building the Temple. According to 2 Sam 5.11, King *Hiram of Tyre* was an ally of David. After Solomon's rise to the throne he sends a goodwill embassy to him, to show that he wanted to continue the good relationship between the two kingdoms. **2–6:** Solomon's request to Hiram. **3–4:** The divine gift of *rest* from all enemies is a prominent theme in the Deuteronomistic History (e.g., Deut 12.10; Josh 21.44; 23.1; 2 Sam 7.1). Here this rest is a necessary condition for the building of the Temple. **6:** The Phoenicians were famous for their *cedars*, one of their chief exports. *Sidonians,* here probably a general term for the Phoenicians. Sidon, like Tyre, is a city on the

the LORD today, who has given to David a wise son to be over this great people." [8] Hiram sent word to Solomon, "I have heard the message that you have sent to me; I will fulfill all your needs in the matter of cedar and cypress timber. [9] My servants shall bring it down to the sea from the Lebanon; I will make it into rafts to go by sea to the place you indicate. I will have them broken up there for you to take away. And you shall meet my needs by providing food for my household." [10] So Hiram supplied Solomon's every need for timber of cedar and cypress. [11] Solomon in turn gave Hiram twenty thousand cors of wheat as food for his household, and twenty cors of fine oil. Solomon gave this to Hiram year by year. [12] So the LORD gave Solomon wisdom, as he promised him. There was peace between Hiram and Solomon; and the two of them made a treaty.

[13] King Solomon conscripted forced labor out of all Israel; the levy numbered thirty thousand men. [14] He sent them to the Lebanon, ten thousand a month in shifts; they would be a month in the Lebanon and two months at home; Adoniram was in charge of the forced labor. [15] Solomon also had seventy thousand laborers and eighty thousand stonecutters in the hill country, [16] besides Solomon's three thousand three hundred supervisors who were over the work, having charge of the people who did the work. [17] At the king's command, they quarried out great, costly stones in order to lay the foundation of the house with dressed stones. [18] So Solomon's builders and Hiram's builders and the Gebalites did the stonecutting and prepared the timber and the stone to build the house.

6 In the four hundred eightieth year after the Israelites came out of the land of Egypt, in the fourth year of Solomon's reign over Israel, in the month of Ziv, which is the second month, he began to build the house of the LORD. [2] The house that King Solomon built for the LORD was sixty cubits long, twenty cubits wide, and thirty cubits high. [3] The vestibule in front of the nave of the house was twenty cubits wide, across the width of the house. Its depth was ten cubits in front of the house. [4] For the house he made windows with recessed frames.[a] [5] He also built a structure against the wall of the house, running around the walls of the house, both the nave and the inner sanctuary; and he made side chambers all around. [6] The lowest story[b] was five cubits wide, the middle one was six cubits wide, and the third was seven cubits wide; for around the outside of the house he made offsets on the wall in order that the supporting beams should not be inserted into the walls of the house.

[7] The house was built with stone finished at the quarry, so that neither hammer nor ax nor any tool of iron was heard in the temple while it was being built.

a Gk: Meaning of Heb uncertain
b Gk: Heb *structure*

Phoenician cost, south of Beirut. **7–12:** Hiram transports the wood in *rafts* and Solomon pays with very large amounts of *wheat* and *oil*. **12:** There is a wordplay in Hebrew between *peace* (Heb "shalom") and the name of Solomon ("shelomoh"). **13–18:** Contrary to 9.20–22, this passage states that Solomon compelled the Israelites to *forced labor* in order to build the Temple. **18:** The *Gebalites*, the inhabitants of Byblos, a Phoenician city north of Tyre, are mentioned here as a separate group. From early times Byblos was an important timber port, and later was a major shipping center of papyrus; the term "Bible" is derived from the city's name.

6.1–38: The building of the Temple. The Temple and its fittings are described in detail, whereas the palace complex is described more briefly (7.1–12), suggesting that the writer was more interested in the Temple than the palace. The Temple is foreshadowed in Ex 25–31; 35–40, and is similar in design to sanctuaries found in Assyria, Syria, and Israel. The closest parallels can be found at Hazor in Israel, Tell Tayinat in southeastern Turkey, and Ain Dara in Syria. **1:** The *four hundred eightieth year* after the Exodus is not historical fact and likely belongs to a late, typological chronological system. The Hebrew month *Ziv*, which is numbered second according to the Babylonian system from the spring New Year, falls in April-May. **2–10:** A *cubit* is the distance from the tip of the elbow to the tip of the middle finger (ca. 17.5 in [45 cm]). The Temple's form is tripartite, comprising the *vestibule* or entrance hall, the *nave* or main hall, and the *inner sanctuary*, the "most holy place" (v. 16) of the sanctuary, to which access was severely restricted. A complex structure is built around the Temple. **7:** No iron tools were used

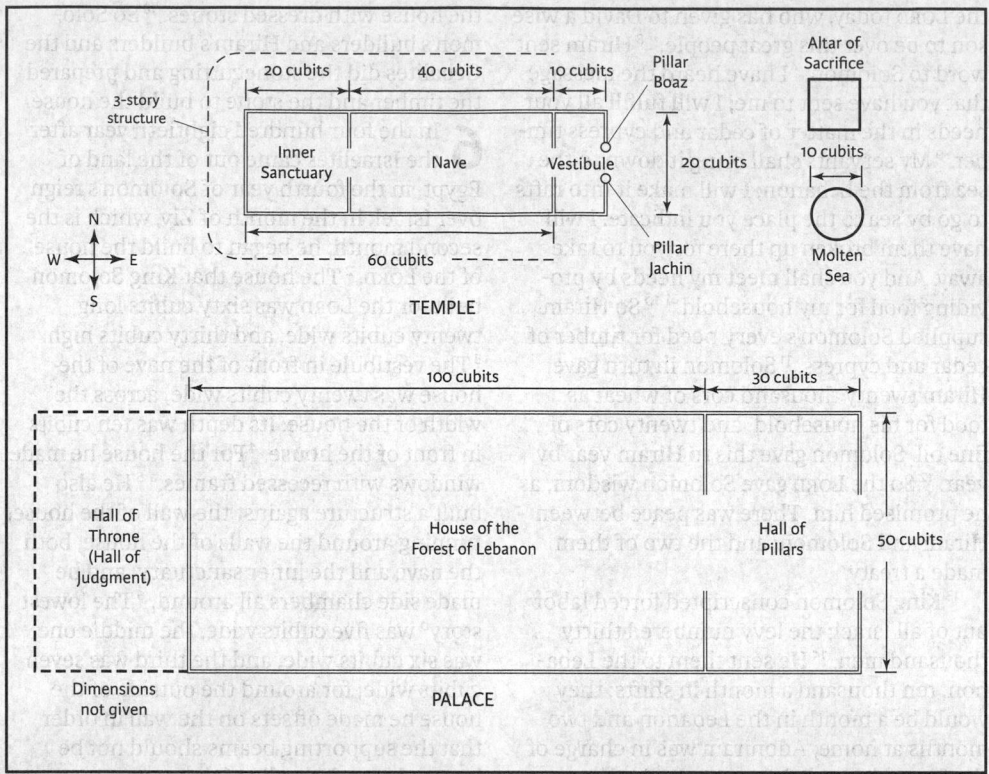

The Temple and palace of Solomon according to First Kings.

8 The entrance for the middle story was on the south side of the house: one went up by winding stairs to the middle story, and from the middle story to the third. **9** So he built the house, and finished it; he roofed the house with beams and planks of cedar. **10** He built the structure against the whole house, each story[a] five cubits high, and it was joined to the house with timbers of cedar.

11 Now the word of the LORD came to Solomon, **12** "Concerning this house that you are building, if you will walk in my statutes, obey my ordinances, and keep all my commandments by walking in them, then I will establish my promise with you, which I made to your father David. **13** I will dwell among the children of Israel, and will not forsake my people Israel."

14 So Solomon built the house, and finished it. **15** He lined the walls of the house on the inside with boards of cedar; from the floor of the house to the rafters of the ceiling, he covered them on the inside with wood; and he covered the floor of the house with boards of cypress. **16** He built twenty cubits of the rear of the house with boards of cedar from the floor to the rafters, and he built this within as an inner sanctuary, as the most holy place. **17** The house, that is, the nave in front of the inner sanctuary, was forty cubits long. **18** The cedar within the house had carvings of gourds and open flowers; all was cedar, no stone was seen. **19** The inner sanctuary he prepared in the innermost part of the

---

a   Heb lacks *each story*

at the Temple site; cf. Ex 20.25; Deut 27.5. **11–13**: God's speech to Solomon interrupts the building report and insists that the divine presence will inhabit the sanctuary only if Solomon observes the divine *commandments* (see also Jer 7.1–15). **14–36**: After the building of the external structure is concluded, the construction of the inside of the Temple is described. **15–18**: The interior walls, floors, and ceilings are covered with wood, so that all stones are covered. **19–28**: Particular attention is paid to the inner sanctuary, the holiest part of the Temple

house, to set there the ark of the covenant of the LORD. ²⁰ The interior of the inner sanctuary was twenty cubits long, twenty cubits wide, and twenty cubits high; he overlaid it with pure gold. He also overlaid the altar with cedar.ᵃ ²¹ Solomon overlaid the inside of the house with pure gold, then he drew chains of gold across, in front of the inner sanctuary, and overlaid it with gold. ²² Next he overlaid the whole house with gold, in order that the whole house might be perfect; even the whole altar that belonged to the inner sanctuary he overlaid with gold.

²³ In the inner sanctuary he made two cherubim of olivewood, each ten cubits high. ²⁴ Five cubits was the length of one wing of the cherub, and five cubits the length of the other wing of the cherub; it was ten cubits from the tip of one wing to the tip of the other. ²⁵ The other cherub also measured ten cubits; both cherubim had the same measure and the same form. ²⁶ The height of one cherub was ten cubits, and so was that of the other cherub. ²⁷ He put the cherubim in the innermost part of the house; the wings of the cherubim were spread out so that a wing of one was touching the one wall, and a wing of the other cherub was touching the other wall; their other wings toward the center of the house were touching wing to wing. ²⁸ He also overlaid the cherubim with gold.

²⁹ He carved the walls of the house all around about with carved engravings of cherubim, palm trees, and open flowers, in the inner and outer rooms. ³⁰ The floor of the house he overlaid with gold, in the inner and outer rooms.

³¹ For the entrance to the inner sanctuary he made doors of olivewood; the lintel and the doorposts were five-sided.ᵃ ³² He covered the two doors of olivewood with carvings of cherubim, palm trees, and open flowers; he overlaid them with gold, and spread gold on the cherubim and on the palm trees.

³³ So also he made for the entrance to the nave doorposts of olivewood, four-sided each, ³⁴ and two doors of cypress wood; the two leaves of the one door were folding, and the two leaves of the other door were folding. ³⁵ He carved cherubim, palm trees, and open flowers, overlaying them with gold evenly applied upon the carved work. ³⁶ He built the inner court with three courses of dressed stone to one course of cedar beams.

³⁷ In the fourth year the foundation of the house of the LORD was laid, in the month of Ziv. ³⁸ In the eleventh year, in the month of Bul, which is the eighth month, the house was finished in all its parts, and according to all its specifications. He was seven years in building it.

7 Solomon was building his own house thirteen years, and he finished his entire house. ² He built the House of the Forest of the Lebanon one hundred cubits long, fifty cubits wide, and thirty cubits high, built on four rows of cedar pillars, with cedar beams on the pillars. ³ It was roofed with cedar on the forty-five rafters, fifteen in each row, which were on the pillars. ⁴ There were window frames in the three rows, facing each other in the

---

ᵃ Meaning of Heb uncertain

where the *ark of the covenant*, a component of God's throne, is placed. **23–28:** The *cherubim* are winged, composite creatures well known in the ancient Near East. They may be guardians of the ark (see Gen 3.24, where they are guardians of the garden of Eden). In Assyria and Babylon winged sphinxes stood at the entrance of temples and palaces. In Phoenician art, winged human-faced creatures support the throne of a king, a function they likely had in the Temple here (see Ps 99.1; 2 Kings 19.15). **29–36:** The authors highlight the splendor of the decoration: everything was overlaid with gold, and there were special carvings, with the *cherubim* symbolizing divine protection, and *open flowers* and *palm trees* for fertility. The different, richly decorated *doors* separate the three parts of the Temple. **36–38:** Building the Temple took seven years and six months.

7.1–12: Building the palace. In the ancient Near East the palace and the (royal) sanctuary often belong to the same complex. Here the Temple is relatively modest compared to the palace. **1:** Therefore it is not astonishing that Solomon spent thirteen years, almost twice as long on his palace as he did on the Temple. This remark can also be understood as a discreet criticism of Solomon's priorities. **2–5:** *House of the Forest of the Lebanon,* the rows of cedar pillars suggest the idea of a forest. Such a structure may show Egyptian influence. It was perhaps a treasury and armory (see 1 Kings 10.17 and Isa 22.8). For the author, this was the most important building of

three rows. ⁵ All the doorways and doorposts had four-sided frames, opposite, facing each other in the three rows.

⁶ He made the Hall of Pillars fifty cubits long and thirty cubits wide. There was a porch in front with pillars, and a canopy in front of them.

⁷ He made the Hall of the Throne where he was to pronounce judgment, the Hall of Justice, covered with cedar from floor to floor.

⁸ His own house where he would reside, in the other court back of the hall, was of the same construction. Solomon also made a house like this hall for Pharaoh's daughter, whom he had taken in marriage.

⁹ All these were made of costly stones, cut according to measure, sawed with saws, back and front, from the foundation to the coping, and from outside to the great court. ¹⁰ The foundation was of costly stones, huge stones, stones of eight and ten cubits. ¹¹ There were costly stones above, cut to measure, and cedarwood. ¹² The great court had three courses of dressed stone to one layer of cedar beams all around; so had the inner court of the house of the Lᴏʀᴅ, and the vestibule of the house.

¹³ Now King Solomon invited and received Hiram from Tyre. ¹⁴ He was the son of a widow of the tribe of Naphtali, whose father, a man of Tyre, had been an artisan in bronze; he was full of skill, intelligence, and knowledge in working bronze. He came to King Solomon, and did all his work.

¹⁵ He cast two pillars of bronze. Eighteen cubits was the height of the one, and a cord of twelve cubits would encircle it; the second pillar was the same.ᵃ ¹⁶ He also made two capitals of molten bronze, to set on the tops of the pillars; the height of the one capital was five cubits, and the height of the other capital was five cubits. ¹⁷ There were nets of checker work with wreaths of chain work for the capitals on the tops of the pillars; sevenᵇ for the one capital, and sevenᵇ for the other capital. ¹⁸ He made the columns with two rows around each latticework to cover the capitals that were above the pomegranates; he did the same with the other capital. ¹⁹ Now the capitals that were on the tops of the pillars in the vestibule were of lily-work, four cubits high. ²⁰ The capitals were on the two pillars and also above the rounded projection that was beside the latticework; there were two hundred pomegranates in rows all around; and so with the other capital. ²¹ He set up the pillars at the vestibule of the temple; he set up the pillar on the south and called it Jachin; and he set up the pillar on the north and called it Boaz. ²² On the tops of the pillars was lily-work. Thus the work of the pillars was finished.

²³ Then he made the molten sea; it was round, ten cubits from brim to brim, and

ᵃ Cn: Heb and a cord of twelve cubits encircled the second pillar; Compare Jer 52.21
ᵇ Heb: Gk a net

the palace complex. 6–7: The Hall of Pillars could have been the waiting hall for the Hall of the Throne, where the king dispensed justice. 8: The private quarters comprise Solomon's residence and a residence for the daughter of Pharaoh (see 3.1 and 9.24). The author does not tell us about the harem for Solomon's other wives. 9–12: The foundations were built with huge quarry blocks.

7.13–51: Hiram and the furnishings of the Temple. 13–14: The Hiram who appears here as craftsman is called Huram-abi in 2 Chr 2.12–13 and should not be confused with King Hiram of ch 5. The detail about his Israelite mother (according to 2 Chr 2.12, his mother is not from the tribe of Naphtali but from Dan) was provided to reassure the reader that the main craftsman of the Temple was not a foreigner (cf. Ezra 4.1–3 for a similar sensitivity to the question of involvement in the Temple building). His skills are like those of Bezalel, who constructed the Tabernacle (Ex 31.3; 35.31). 15–22: The two huge pillars (more than 26 ft [8 m] high) at the entry of the vestibule symbolize the Lᴏʀᴅ's presence in the Temple and his protection of the royal dynasty. This is also symbolized in their names: Jachin (which also occurs in the name of King Jehoiachin) means "he will establish" and refers to God's initiative to establish the throne of the king (2 Sam 7.13); Boaz ("by him he is mighty") expresses the king's dependence on the divine favor. 23–26: Molten, molded or cast. The molten sea was a large metal basin filled with water (two thousand baths: a bath equals ca. 6 gal [23 l]) representing the primeval watery chaos subdued by the Lᴏʀᴅ, creator of the world (see Ps 74). The twelve oxen or bulls that supported the basin represented divine strength (see 1 Kings 12.28). According to 2 Chr 4.6 the molten sea was used for

five cubits high. A line of thirty cubits would encircle it completely. [24] Under its brim were panels all around it, each of ten cubits, surrounding the sea; there were two rows of panels, cast when it was cast. [25] It stood on twelve oxen, three facing north, three facing west, three facing south, and three facing east; the sea was set on them. The hindquarters of each were toward the inside. [26] Its thickness was a handbreadth; its brim was made like the brim of a cup, like the flower of a lily; it held two thousand baths.[a]

[27] He also made the ten stands of bronze; each stand was four cubits long, four cubits wide, and three cubits high. [28] This was the construction of the stands: they had borders; the borders were within the frames; [29] on the borders that were set in the frames were lions, oxen, and cherubim. On the frames, both above and below the lions and oxen, there were wreaths of beveled work. [30] Each stand had four bronze wheels and axles of bronze; at the four corners were supports for a basin. The supports were cast with wreaths at the side of each. [31] Its opening was within the crown whose height was one cubit; its opening was round, as a pedestal is made; it was a cubit and a half wide. At its opening there were carvings; its borders were four-sided, not round. [32] The four wheels were underneath the borders; the axles of the wheels were in the stands; and the height of a wheel was a cubit and a half. [33] The wheels were made like a chariot wheel; their axles, their rims, their spokes, and their hubs were all cast. [34] There were four supports at the four corners of each stand; the supports were of one piece with the stands. [35] On the top of the stand there was a round band half a cubit high; on the top of the stand, its stays and its borders were of one piece with it. [36] On the surfaces of its stays and on its borders he carved cherubim, lions, and palm trees, where each had space, with wreaths all around. [37] In this way he made the ten stands; all of them were cast alike, with the same size and the same form.

[38] He made ten basins of bronze; each basin held forty baths,[a] each basin measured four cubits; there was a basin for each of the ten stands. [39] He set five of the stands on the south side of the house, and five on the north side of the house; he set the sea on the southeast corner of the house.

[40] Hiram also made the pots, the shovels, and the basins. So Hiram finished all the work that he did for King Solomon on the house of the LORD: [41] the two pillars, the two bowls of the capitals that were on the tops of the pillars, the two latticeworks to cover the two bowls of the capitals that were on the tops of the pillars; [42] the four hundred pomegranates for the two latticeworks, two rows of pomegranates for each latticework, to cover the two bowls of the capitals that were on the pillars; [43] the ten stands, the ten basins on the stands; [44] the one sea, and the twelve oxen underneath the sea.

[45] The pots, the shovels, and the basins, all these vessels that Hiram made for King Solomon for the house of the LORD were of burnished bronze. [46] In the plain of the Jordan the king cast them, in the clay ground between Succoth and Zarethan. [47] Solomon left all the vessels unweighed, because there were so many of them; the weight of the bronze was not determined.

[48] So Solomon made all the vessels that were in the house of the LORD: the golden altar, the golden table for the bread of the Presence, [49] the lampstands of pure gold, five on the south side and five on the north, in front of the inner sanctuary; the flowers, the lamps, and the tongs, of gold; [50] the cups, snuffers, basins, dishes for incense, and firepans, of pure gold; the sockets for the

[a]   A Heb measure of volume

the ritual washings of the priest. **27–39:** The wheeled stands and their bases may have originally symbolized God's power to provide water and rain, but later they were understood to provide the water necessary for the performance of sacrificial worship. **40–51:** The division of work between Hiram and Solomon: Hiram made the objects of *bronze*, whereas Solomon made the more prestigious vessels of *gold*. **46:** Hiram did his work in the *Jordan* valley, where appropriate clay is to be found. *Succoth*, probably Deir Alla, and *Zarethan*, were in Transjordan near the Jabbok River. **48–50:** Solomon himself is responsible for all objects related directly to

doors of the innermost part of the house, the most holy place, and for the doors of the nave of the temple, of gold.

[51] Thus all the work that King Solomon did on the house of the LORD was finished. Solomon brought in the things that his father David had dedicated, the silver, the gold, and the vessels, and stored them in the treasuries of the house of the LORD.

8 Then Solomon assembled the elders of Israel and all the heads of the tribes, the leaders of the ancestral houses of the Israelites, before King Solomon in Jerusalem, to bring up the ark of the covenant of the LORD out of the city of David, which is Zion. [2] All the people of Israel assembled to King Solomon at the festival in the month Ethanim, which is the seventh month. [3] And all the elders of Israel came, and the priests carried the ark. [4] So they brought up the ark of the LORD, the tent of meeting, and all the holy vessels that were in the tent; the priests and the Levites brought them up. [5] King Solomon and all the congregation of Israel, who had assembled before him, were with him before the ark, sacrificing so many sheep and oxen that they could not be counted or numbered. [6] Then the priests brought the ark of the covenant of the LORD to its place, in the inner sanctuary of the house, in the most holy place, underneath the wings of the cherubim. [7] For the cherubim spread out their wings over the place of the ark, so that the cherubim made a covering above the ark and its poles. [8] The poles were so long that the ends of the poles were seen from the holy place in front of the inner sanctuary; but they could

not be seen from outside; they are there to this day. [9] There was nothing in the ark except the two tablets of stone that Moses had placed there at Horeb, where the LORD made a covenant with the Israelites, when they came out of the land of Egypt. [10] And when the priests came out of the holy place, a cloud filled the house of the LORD, [11] so that the priests could not stand to minister because of the cloud; for the glory of the LORD filled the house of the LORD.

[12] Then Solomon said,

"The LORD has said that he would dwell in
thick darkness.
[13] I have built you an exalted house,
a place for you to dwell in forever."

[14] Then the king turned around and blessed all the assembly of Israel, while all the assembly of Israel stood. [15] He said, "Blessed be the LORD, the God of Israel, who with his hand has fulfilled what he promised with his mouth to my father David, saying, [16] 'Since the day that I brought my people Israel out of Egypt, I have not chosen a city from any of the tribes of Israel in which to build a house, that my name might be there; but I chose David to be over my people Israel.' [17] My father David had it in mind to build a house for the name of the LORD, the God of Israel. [18] But the LORD said to my father David, 'You did well to consider building a house for my name; [19] nevertheless you shall not build the house, but your son who shall be born to you shall build the house for my name.' [20] Now the LORD has upheld the promise that he made; for I have risen in the place of my father David; I sit on the throne of Israel, as

sacrificial worship. *Bread of the Presence,* see Ex 25.30; Lev 24.5–9. **51:** See 2 Sam 8.9–12, where David *dedicates* his booty to the LORD.

8.1–66: The inauguration of the Temple. 1–13: The ark is now transferred from the tent sanctuary into the inner sanctuary of the Temple. **2:** The Temple was finished in the eighth month (6.38), so the inauguration took place in the following year in the *seventh month* (September-October), after the end of the harvest seasons, at the festival of booths (tabernacles); see v. 66. **3–4:** As in Josh 3–4, the ark is carried by the *priests* and *Levites,* because touching it is dangerous for lay people. **9:** The statement that nothing was in the ark but the *tablets of stone that Moses had placed* (see Deut 10.1–5) is meant to counter the popular idea that God is present in the ark. **10–11:** A cloud is often associated with divine appearances (e.g., Ex 13.21–22; 16.10; 19.9) and covers the earlier tent sanctuary upon its completion in Ex 40.34–38. **12–13:** An independent poetic statement, which in the LXX has different wording and follows v. 53. It suggests that the God of Israel was considered to be a weather-god who wants to dwell in *darkness,* in a cloud. **14–66:** Solomon pronounces three prayers that provide important clues to the later authors' theological understanding of the Temple. **14–21:** The first prayer, in front of the assembly, builds on the promise to David of an eternal dynasty in 2 Sam 7 and highlights that Solomon is David's

the LORD promised, and have built the house for the name of the LORD, the God of Israel. 21 There I have provided a place for the ark, in which is the covenant of the LORD that he made with our ancestors when he brought them out of the land of Egypt."

22 Then Solomon stood before the altar of the LORD in the presence of all the assembly of Israel, and spread out his hands to heaven. 23 He said, "O LORD, God of Israel, there is no God like you in heaven above or on earth beneath, keeping covenant and steadfast love for your servants who walk before you with all their heart, 24 the covenant that you kept for your servant my father David as you declared to him; you promised with your mouth and have this day fulfilled with your hand. 25 Therefore, O LORD, God of Israel, keep for your servant my father David that which you promised him, saying, 'There shall never fail you a successor before me to sit on the throne of Israel, if only your children look to their way, to walk before me as you have walked before me.' 26 Therefore, O God of Israel, let your word be confirmed, which you promised to your servant my father David.

27 "But will God indeed dwell on the earth? Even heaven and the highest heaven cannot contain you, much less this house that I have built! 28 Regard your servant's prayer and his plea, O LORD my God, heeding the cry and the prayer that your servant prays to you today; 29 that your eyes may be open night and day toward this house, the place of which you said, 'My name shall be there,' that you may heed the prayer that your servant prays toward this place. 30 Hear the plea of your servant and of your people Israel when they pray toward this place; O hear in heaven your dwelling place; heed and forgive.

31 "If someone sins against a neighbor and is given an oath to swear, and comes and swears before your altar in this house, 32 then

hear in heaven, and act, and judge your servants, condemning the guilty by bringing their conduct on their own head, and vindicating the righteous by rewarding them according to their righteousness.

33 "When your people Israel, having sinned against you, are defeated before an enemy but turn again to you, confess your name, pray and plead with you in this house, 34 then hear in heaven, forgive the sin of your people Israel, and bring them again to the land that you gave to their ancestors.

35 "When heaven is shut up and there is no rain because they have sinned against you, and then they pray toward this place, confess your name, and turn from their sin, because you punish[a] them, 36 then hear in heaven, and forgive the sin of your servants, your people Israel, when you teach them the good way in which they should walk; and grant rain on your land, which you have given to your people as an inheritance.

37 "If there is famine in the land, if there is plague, blight, mildew, locust, or caterpillar; if their enemy besieges them in any[b] of their cities; whatever plague, whatever sickness there is; 38 whatever prayer, whatever plea there is from any individual or from all your people Israel, all knowing the afflictions of their own hearts so that they stretch out their hands toward this house; 39 then hear in heaven your dwelling place, forgive, act, and render to all whose hearts you know—according to all their ways, for only you know what is in every human heart— 40 so that they may fear you all the days that they live in the land that you gave to our ancestors.

41 "Likewise when a foreigner, who is not of your people Israel, comes from a distant land because of your name 42 —for they shall hear

a Or when you answer
b Gk Syr: Heb in the land

legitimate successor and the proper Temple builder. **22–53:** The second prayer, in front of the altar, is the central piece of the dedication. The authors reassert seven times that the LORD does not *dwell* in the Temple (contrast v. 13), but in *heaven* (vv. 32,34,36,39,43,45,49). The Temple is the place to pray to God. But as Solomon enumerates seven different occasions for prayer—sin of an individual (vv. 31–32); defeat in battle (vv. 33–34); drought (vv. 35–36); famine and plagues (vv. 37–40); a foreigner who comes to pray (vv. 41–43); war (vv. 44–45); sin of the people and deportation (vv. 46–51)—the scene changes. Prayer is initially located in the Temple, then it is in the direction of the sanctuary, and finally, the praying individuals are in another country and pray *toward* the city and the Temple. This presupposes the situation after the Babylonian exile. **33–40,46–51:** These occasions

of your great name, your mighty hand, and your outstretched arm—when a foreigner comes and prays toward this house, ⁴³ then hear in heaven your dwelling place, and do according to all that the foreigner calls to you, so that all the peoples of the earth may know your name and fear you, as do your people Israel, and so that they may know that your name has been invoked on this house that I have built.

⁴⁴ "If your people go out to battle against their enemy, by whatever way you shall send them, and they pray to the LORD toward the city that you have chosen and the house that I have built for your name, ⁴⁵ then hear in heaven their prayer and their plea, and maintain their cause.

⁴⁶ "If they sin against you—for there is no one who does not sin—and you are angry with them and give them to an enemy, so that they are carried away captive to the land of the enemy, far off or near; ⁴⁷ yet if they come to their senses in the land to which they have been taken captive, and repent, and plead with you in the land of their captors, saying, 'We have sinned, and have done wrong; we have acted wickedly'; ⁴⁸ if they repent with all their heart and soul in the land of their enemies, who took them captive, and pray to you toward their land, which you gave to their ancestors, the city that you have chosen, and the house that I have built for your name; ⁴⁹ then hear in heaven your dwelling place their prayer and their plea, maintain their cause ⁵⁰ and forgive your people who have sinned against you, and all their transgressions that they have committed against you; and grant them compassion in the sight of their captors, so that they may have compassion on them ⁵¹ (for they are your people and heritage, which you brought out of Egypt, from the midst of the iron-smelter). ⁵² Let your eyes be open to the plea of your servant, and to the plea of your people Israel, listening to them whenever they call to you. ⁵³ For you have separated them from among all the peoples of the earth, to be your heritage, just as

you promised through Moses, your servant, when you brought our ancestors out of Egypt, O Lord GOD."

⁵⁴ Now when Solomon finished offering all this prayer and this plea to the LORD, he arose from facing the altar of the LORD, where he had knelt with hands outstretched toward heaven; ⁵⁵ he stood and blessed all the assembly of Israel with a loud voice:

⁵⁶ "Blessed be the LORD, who has given rest to his people Israel according to all that he promised; not one word has failed of all his good promise, which he spoke through his servant Moses. ⁵⁷ The LORD our God be with us, as he was with our ancestors; may he not leave us or abandon us, ⁵⁸ but incline our hearts to him, to walk in all his ways, and to keep his commandments, his statutes, and his ordinances, which he commanded our ancestors. ⁵⁹ Let these words of mine, with which I pleaded before the LORD, be near to the LORD our God day and night, and may he maintain the cause of his servant and the cause of his people Israel, as each day requires; ⁶⁰ so that all the peoples of the earth may know that the LORD is God; there is no other. ⁶¹ Therefore devote yourselves completely to the LORD our God, walking in his statutes and keeping his commandments, as at this day."

⁶² Then the king, and all Israel with him, offered sacrifice before the LORD. ⁶³ Solomon offered as sacrifices of well-being to the LORD twenty-two thousand oxen and one hundred twenty thousand sheep. So the king and all the people of Israel dedicated the house of the LORD. ⁶⁴ The same day the king consecrated the middle of the court that was in front of the house of the LORD; for there he offered the burnt offerings and the grain offerings and the fat pieces of the sacrifices of well-being, because the bronze altar that was before the LORD was too small to receive the burnt offerings and the grain offerings and the fat pieces of the sacrifices of well-being.

⁶⁵ So Solomon held the festival at that time, and all Israel with him—a great assem-

for prayer are parallel to the curses in Deut 28.21–25,38,64–65. **51:** *Iron-smelter,* see Deut 4.20. **54–61:** The last prayer, spoken again in front of the people, reasserts, like Josh 21.43–45, that the LORD has fulfilled all his promises. It repeats the Deuteronomistic exhortation to respond to this gift by the observance of the divine commandments. **62–64:** The number of the *sacrifices* is highly exaggerated, symbolizing Solomon's and the peo-

bly, people from Lebo-hamath to the Wadi of Egypt—before the LORD our God, seven days.[a] [66] On the eighth day he sent the people away; and they blessed the king, and went to their tents, joyful and in good spirits because of all the goodness that the LORD had shown to his servant David and to his people Israel.

9 When Solomon had finished building the house of the LORD and the king's house and all that Solomon desired to build, [2] the LORD appeared to Solomon a second time, as he had appeared to him at Gibeon. [3] The LORD said to him, "I have heard your prayer and your plea, which you made before me; I have consecrated this house that you have built, and put my name there forever; my eyes and my heart will be there for all time. [4] As for you, if you will walk before me, as David your father walked, with integrity of heart and uprightness, doing according to all that I have commanded you, and keeping my statutes and my ordinances, [5] then I will establish your royal throne over Israel forever, as I promised your father David, saying, 'There shall not fail you a successor on the throne of Israel.'

[6] "If you turn aside from following me, you or your children, and do not keep my commandments and my statutes that I have set before you, but go and serve other gods and worship them, [7] then I will cut Israel off from the land that I have given them; and the house that I have consecrated for my name I will cast out of my sight; and Israel will become a proverb and a taunt among all peoples. [8] This house will become a heap

of ruins;[b] everyone passing by it will be astonished, and will hiss; and they will say, 'Why has the LORD done such a thing to this land and to this house?' [9] Then they will say, 'Because they have forsaken the LORD their God, who brought their ancestors out of the land of Egypt, and embraced other gods, worshiping them and serving them; therefore the LORD has brought this disaster upon them.'"

[10] At the end of twenty years, in which Solomon had built the two houses, the house of the LORD and the king's house, [11] King Hiram of Tyre having supplied Solomon with cedar and cypress timber and gold, as much as he desired, King Solomon gave to Hiram twenty cities in the land of Galilee. [12] But when Hiram came from Tyre to see the cities that Solomon had given him, they did not please him. [13] Therefore he said, "What kind of cities are these that you have given me, my brother?" So they are called the land of Cabul[c] to this day. [14] But Hiram had sent to the king one hundred twenty talents of gold.

[15] This is the account of the forced labor that King Solomon conscripted to build the house of the LORD and his own house, the Millo and the wall of Jerusalem, Hazor, Megiddo, Gezer [16] (Pharaoh king of Egypt had gone up and captured Gezer and burned it down, had killed the Canaanites who lived

a Compare Gk: Heb *seven days and seven days, fourteen days*
b Syr Old Latin: Heb *will become high*
c Perhaps meaning *a land good for nothing*

ple's attachment to the new sanctuary. **65–66:** The dedication of the Temple took place during the festival of Tabernacles. According to Deut 16.13–15 the participants are sent home on the eighth day. The limits of the land are defined here (less extensively than in 4.21,24) in the north by *Lebo-hamath* (in the southern Orontes valley in Lebanon) and in the south by the *Wadi of Egypt* (the Wadi el-Arish or the Wadi Besor, both south of Gaza).

9.1–9: God's second appearance to Solomon. This text recalls 3.4–15 and hints at the king's dark side, which will appear more and more clearly. **3–5:** God's loyalty to Solomon depends on his behavior regarding the divine law. **6–9:** The disobedience of Solomon and his successor is suggested; this disobedience will lead to the exile. **8–9:** Cf. Deut 29.23–24.

9.10–28: The ambiguity of Solomon's wealth (see also 10.14–29). **10–14:** The text reports that Solomon paid a heavy price to the king of Tyre, *twenty cities*; this almost makes Solomon into Hiram's vassal. In order to correct this idea, the text states that Hiram had paid Solomon 120 talents of gold (a *talent* is ca. 75 lb [34 kg]). **13:** The name of the town of *Cabul* (8 mi [14 km] southeast of Acco) is explained with a play on the Heb verb "to waste away." **15–24:** The many building projects attributed to Solomon are executed through *forced labor*. **15:** *Millo* (lit. "fill") refers to terraces to stabilize the wall and the official buildings of Jerusalem. **15–19:** The *cities* that Solomon built are located in strategic places, and are enumerated from north to south. The note about *Gezer* interrupts the list. This town is presented as Pharaoh's dowry to Solomon: see also 3.1; 9.24;

in the city, and had given it as dowry to his daughter, Solomon's wife; [17] so Solomon rebuilt Gezer), Lower Beth-horon, [18] Baalath, Tamar in the wilderness, within the land, [19] as well as all of Solomon's storage cities, the cities for his chariots, the cities for his cavalry, and whatever Solomon desired to build, in Jerusalem, in Lebanon, and in all the land of his dominion. [20] All the people who were left of the Amorites, the Hittites, the Perizzites, the Hivites, and the Jebusites, who were not of the people of Israel— [21] their descendants who were still left in the land, whom the Israelites were unable to destroy completely—these Solomon conscripted for slave labor, and so they are to this day. [22] But of the Israelites Solomon made no slaves; they were the soldiers, they were his officials, his commanders, his captains, and the commanders of his chariotry and cavalry.

[23] These were the chief officers who were over Solomon's work: five hundred fifty, who had charge of the people who carried on the work.

[24] But Pharaoh's daughter went up from the city of David to her own house that Solomon had built for her; then he built the Millo.

[25] Three times a year Solomon used to offer up burnt offerings and sacrifices of well-being on the altar that he built for the LORD, offering incense[a] before the LORD. So he completed the house.

[26] King Solomon built a fleet of ships at Ezion-geber, which is near Eloth on the shore of the Red Sea,[b] in the land of Edom. [27] Hiram sent his servants with the fleet, sailors who were familiar with the sea, together with the servants of Solomon. [28] They went to Ophir, and imported from there four hundred twenty talents of gold, which they delivered to King Solomon.

10 When the queen of Sheba heard of the fame of Solomon (fame due to[c] the name of the LORD), she came to test him with hard questions. [2] She came to Jerusalem with a very great retinue, with camels bearing spices, and very much gold, and precious stones; and when she came to Solomon, she told him all that was on her mind. [3] Solomon answered all her questions; there was nothing hidden from the king that he could not explain to her. [4] When the queen of Sheba had observed all the wisdom of Solomon, the house that he had built, [5] the food of his table, the seating of his officials, and the attendance of his servants, their clothing, his valets, and his burnt offerings that he offered at the house of the LORD, there was no more spirit in her.

[6] So she said to the king, "The report was true that I heard in my own land of your accomplishments and of your wisdom, [7] but I did not believe the reports until I came and my own eyes had seen it. Not even half had been told me; your wisdom and prosperity far surpass the report that I had heard. [8] Happy are your wives![d] Happy are these your servants, who continually attend you and hear your wisdom! [9] Blessed be the LORD your God, who has delighted in you and set you on the throne of Israel! Because the LORD loved Israel forever, he has made you king to execute justice and righteousness." [10] Then she gave the king one hundred twenty talents of gold, a great quantity of spices, and precious stones; never again did spices come in such quantity as that which the queen of Sheba gave to King Solomon.

---

a   Gk: Heb *offering incense with it that was*
b   Or *Sea of Reeds*
c   Meaning of Heb uncertain
d   Gk Syr: Heb *men*

11.1. **20–23:** This passage modifies 5.13 and 11.26–28, stating that only the former inhabitants of the land were conscripted for forced labor. **24–28:** In this summary of Solomon's wealth we are told of his naval enterprises. **26:** *Ezion-geber,* perhaps a small island in the Gulf of Aqaba. *Eloth,* also spelled "Elath," is at the northern tip of the same body of water. **28:** The location of *Ophir* is uncertain. For the biblical writers it probably designated southern Arabia (Gen 10.29; Isa 13.12; Job 28.16).

10.1–13: **The visit of the queen of Sheba.** This story, which resembles a tale from *A Thousand and One Nights,* interrupts the enumeration of Solomon's wealth. *Sheba* is in Arabia. **4–5:** The queen of Sheba is overwhelmed by Solomon's wealth and wisdom. **6–13:** According to an Ethiopian tradition, all Ethiopian emperors descended from the union between Solomon and the queen of Sheba. **10:** The queen offers more than two tons of gold.

¹¹ Moreover, the fleet of Hiram, which carried gold from Ophir, brought from Ophir a great quantity of almug wood and precious stones. ¹² From the almug wood the king made supports for the house of the LORD, and for the king's house, lyres also and harps for the singers; no such almug wood has come or been seen to this day.

¹³ Meanwhile King Solomon gave to the queen of Sheba every desire that she expressed, as well as what he gave her out of Solomon's royal bounty. Then she returned to her own land, with her servants.

¹⁴ The weight of gold that came to Solomon in one year was six hundred sixty-six talents of gold, ¹⁵ besides that which came from the traders and from the business of the merchants, and from all the kings of Arabia and the governors of the land. ¹⁶ King Solomon made two hundred large shields of beaten gold; six hundred shekels of gold went into each large shield. ¹⁷ He made three hundred shields of beaten gold; three minas of gold went into each shield; and the king put them in the House of the Forest of Lebanon. ¹⁸ The king also made a great ivory throne, and overlaid it with the finest gold. ¹⁹ The throne had six steps. The top of the throne was rounded in the back, and on each side of the seat were arm rests and two lions standing beside the arm rests, ²⁰ while twelve lions were standing, one on each end of a step on the six steps. Nothing like it was ever made in any kingdom. ²¹ All King Solomon's drinking vessels were of gold, and all the vessels of the House of the Forest of Lebanon were of pure gold; none were of silver—it was not con-

sidered as anything in the days of Solomon. ²² For the king had a fleet of ships of Tarshish at sea with the fleet of Hiram. Once every three years the fleet of ships of Tarshish used to come bringing gold, silver, ivory, apes, and peacocks.ᵃ

²³ Thus King Solomon excelled all the kings of the earth in riches and in wisdom. ²⁴ The whole earth sought the presence of Solomon to hear his wisdom, which God had put into his mind. ²⁵ Every one of them brought a present, objects of silver and gold, garments, weaponry, spices, horses, and mules, so much year by year.

²⁶ Solomon gathered together chariots and horses; he had fourteen hundred chariots and twelve thousand horses, which he stationed in the chariot cities and with the king in Jerusalem. ²⁷ The king made silver as common in Jerusalem as stones, and he made cedars as numerous as the sycamores of the Shephelah. ²⁸ Solomon's import of horses was from Egypt and Kue, and the king's traders received them from Kue at a price. ²⁹ A chariot could be imported from Egypt for six hundred shekels of silver, and a horse for one hundred fifty; so through the king's traders they were exported to all the kings of the Hittites and the kings of Aram.

11 King Solomon loved many foreign women along with the daughter of Pharaoh: Moabite, Ammonite, Edomite, Sidonian, and Hittite women, ² from the nations concerning which the LORD had said to the Israelites, "You shall not enter into marriage

ᵃ Or *baboons*

11–12: The verses belong to 9.26–28. *Almug wood*, a precious wood of uncertain species (traditionally sandalwood).

10.14–29: The ambiguity of Solomon's wealth, continued (see also 9.10–28). 14–22: Contrary to Deut 17.17, Solomon has almost an obsession for *gold*. 14–15: A *talent* is ca. 75 lb (34 kg). The number of *six hundred sixty-six*, Solomon's income, symbolizes totality (see also Ezra 2.13; contrast Rev 13.18). 16: A *shekel* is ca. .4 oz (11.5 g). 17: A *mina* is ca. 20 oz (570 g). 18–20: Solomon's *throne*, which symbolizes the divine cosmos of which the king was the guarantor, has many parallels in ancient Near Eastern art. 21–22: The location of *Tarshish* is uncertain; it may be Tarsus in southern Turkey or Tartessus in southern Spain. 23–29: Contrary to Deut 17.16, Solomon accumulates many *horses*. 27: *The Shephelah*, the foothills between the Mediterranean coastal plain and the Judean hill country. 28–29: According to this translation, Solomon was the intermediary in horse-trading between Egypt and Asia Minor. 28: *Kue*, Cilicia, in southern Asia Minor. 29: *Hittites*, a non-Semitic population in northern Syria and southern Turkey; *Aram*, southern Syria.

11.1–43: The troublesome end of Solomon's reign. 1–8: Contrary to Deut 17.17, Solomon introduces a thousand foreign wives and concubines into his harem. 2: A quotation from Deut 7.3–4, which prohibited intermar-

with them, neither shall they with you; for they will surely incline your heart to follow their gods"; Solomon clung to these in love. ³ Among his wives were seven hundred princesses and three hundred concubines; and his wives turned away his heart. ⁴ For when Solomon was old, his wives turned away his heart after other gods; and his heart was not true to the LORD his God, as was the heart of his father David. ⁵ For Solomon followed Astarte the goddess of the Sidonians, and Milcom the abomination of the Ammonites. ⁶ So Solomon did what was evil in the sight of the LORD, and did not completely follow the LORD, as his father David had done. ⁷ Then Solomon built a high place for Chemosh the abomination of Moab, and for Molech the abomination of the Ammonites, on the mountain east of Jerusalem. ⁸ He did the same for all his foreign wives, who offered incense and sacrificed to their gods.

⁹ Then the LORD was angry with Solomon, because his heart had turned away from the LORD, the God of Israel, who had appeared to him twice, ¹⁰ and had commanded him concerning this matter, that he should not follow other gods; but he did not observe what the LORD commanded. ¹¹ Therefore the LORD said to Solomon, "Since this has been your mind and you have not kept my covenant and my statutes that I have commanded you, I will surely tear the kingdom from you and give it to your servant. ¹² Yet for the sake of your father David I will not do it in your lifetime; I will tear it out of the hand of your son. ¹³ I will not, however, tear away the entire kingdom; I will give one tribe to your son, for the sake of my servant David and for the sake of Jerusalem, which I have chosen."

¹⁴ Then the LORD raised up an adversary against Solomon, Hadad the Edomite; he was of the royal house in Edom. ¹⁵ For when David was in Edom, and Joab the commander of the army went up to bury the dead, he killed every male in Edom ¹⁶ (for Joab and all Israel remained there six months, until he had eliminated every male in Edom); ¹⁷ but Hadad fled to Egypt with some Edomites who were servants of his father. He was a young boy at that time. ¹⁸ They set out from Midian and came to Paran; they took people with them from Paran and came to Egypt, to Pharaoh king of Egypt, who gave him a house, assigned him an allowance of food, and gave him land. ¹⁹ Hadad found great favor in the sight of Pharaoh, so that he gave him his sister-in-law for a wife, the sister of Queen Tahpenes. ²⁰ The sister of Tahpenes gave birth by him to his son Genubath, whom Tahpenes weaned in Pharaoh's house; Genubath was in Pharaoh's house among the children of Pharaoh. ²¹ When Hadad heard in Egypt that David slept with his ancestors and that Joab the commander of the army was dead, Hadad said to Pharaoh, "Let me depart, that I may go to my own country." ²² But Pharaoh said to him, "What do you lack with me that you now seek to go to your own country?" And he said, "No, do let me go."

²³ God raised up another adversary against Solomon,ᵃ Rezon son of Eliada, who had fled from his master, King Hadadezer of Zobah. ²⁴ He gathered followers around him and became leader of a marauding band, after the slaughter by David; they went to Damascus, settled there, and made him king in Damascus. ²⁵ He was an adversary of Israel all the days of Solomon, making trouble as Hadad did; he despised Israel and reigned over Aram.

ᵃ Heb *him*

riage with the Canaanite population. 4: The note about Solomon's old age recalls the aging David, who was manipulated by his wife Bathsheba. Now the foreign wives lead Solomon to worship their foreign deities. 5–8: *Astarte* was a popular Canaanite goddess and was especially venerated in Sidon; *Milcom* was the national god of the Ammonites. The *mountain east of Jerusalem* is the Mount of Olives. 9–13: In his last speech to Solomon, the LORD announces the splitting up of the kingdom during the reign of Solomon's son. 14–40: Solomon is also punished during his own lifetime by three enemies that God raises up. 14–22: *Hadad*, an Edomite prince who fled to Egypt during David's campaign against Edom (2 Sam 8.14). 19–22: His integration into Pharaoh's house recalls the story of the young Moses. Pharaoh, whom Solomon considered an ally, offers asylum to his enemies. 19: *Tahpenes*, not a proper name, but a transcription of the Egyptian title "wife of the king." 20: *Genubath*, perhaps an Arabic word meaning "guest." 23–25: *Rezon son of Eliada*, a mercenary who served king *Hadadezer of Zobah*, an Aramean city-state northeast of Israel. After a revolt he became king of *Damascus*, the capital of

²⁶ Jeroboam son of Nebat, an Ephraimite of Zeredah, a servant of Solomon, whose mother's name was Zeruah, a widow, rebelled against the king. ²⁷ The following was the reason he rebelled against the king. Solomon built the Millo, and closed up the gap in the wall^a of the city of his father David. ²⁸ The man Jeroboam was very able, and when Solomon saw that the young man was industrious he gave him charge over all the forced labor of the house of Joseph. ²⁹ About that time, when Jeroboam was leaving Jerusalem, the prophet Ahijah the Shilonite found him on the road. Ahijah had clothed himself with a new garment. The two of them were alone in the open country ³⁰ when Ahijah laid hold of the new garment he was wearing and tore it into twelve pieces. ³¹ He then said to Jeroboam: Take for yourself ten pieces; for thus says the LORD, the God of Israel, "See, I am about to tear the kingdom from the hand of Solomon, and will give you ten tribes. ³² One tribe will remain his, for the sake of my servant David and for the sake of Jerusalem, the city that I have chosen out of all the tribes of Israel. ³³ This is because he has^b forsaken me, worshiped Astarte the goddess of the Sidonians, Chemosh the god of Moab, and Milcom the god of the Ammonites, and has^b not walked in my ways, doing what is right in my sight and keeping my statutes and my ordinances, as his father David did. ³⁴ Nevertheless I will not take the whole kingdom away from him but will make him ruler all the days of his life, for the sake of my servant David whom I chose and who did keep my commandments and my statutes; ³⁵ but I will take the kingdom away from his son and give it to you—that is, the ten tribes. ³⁶ Yet to his son I will give one tribe, so that my servant David may always have a lamp before me in Jerusalem, the city where I have chosen to put my name. ³⁷ I will take you, and you shall reign over all that your soul desires; you shall be king over Israel. ³⁸ If you will listen to all that I command you, walk in my ways, and do what is right in my sight by keeping my statutes and my commandments, as David my servant did, I will be with you, and will build you an enduring house, as I built for David, and I will give Israel to you. ³⁹ For this reason I will punish the descendants of David, but not forever." ⁴⁰ Solomon sought therefore to kill Jeroboam; but Jeroboam promptly fled to Egypt, to King Shishak of Egypt, and remained in Egypt until the death of Solomon.

⁴¹ Now the rest of the acts of Solomon, all that he did as well as his wisdom, are they not written in the Book of the Acts of Solomon? ⁴² The time that Solomon reigned in Jerusalem over all Israel was forty years. ⁴³ Solomon slept with his ancestors and was buried in the city of his father David; and his son Rehoboam succeeded him.

12 Rehoboam went to Shechem, for all Israel had come to Shechem to make him king. ² When Jeroboam son of Nebat heard of it (for he was still in Egypt, where he had fled from King Solomon), then Jeroboam returned

---

a Heb lacks *in the wall*
b Gk Syr Vg: Heb *they have*

southern Syria. **26–40:** *Jeroboam son of Nebat*, an Ephraimite; *Zeredah* is an important town in the hill country of Ephraim. He had been a supervisor of the labor force of the *house of Joseph*, which designates northern tribes, especially Ephraim and Manasseh. The name of the queen mother is typically mentioned only for Judean kings. *Zeruah* means "leper"; scribes may have modified her original name to vilify the first ruler of the Northern Kingdom of Israel. **29–39:** The encounter between Jeroboam and the prophet *Ahijah* from Shiloh, an important sanctuary in Ephraim (see 1 Sam 1.3), has many parallels with the scene of Saul's rejection in 1 Sam 15.27–28. **29–33:** After the prophet tore his mantle into twelve pieces, it is surprising that ten parts (symbolizing ten tribes) are given to Jeroboam and only one tribe (Judah) is given to the Davidic dynasty. The missing tribe may be Benjamin (see 12.21), sometimes belonging to the Northern Kingdom, and finally, perhaps under King Josiah, annexed by Judah. **34–39:** Because of the promise related in 2 Sam 7.11–16, God will not bring David's dynasty to a total end. **40:** Like Hadad, Jeroboam seeks asylum in *Egypt*. The Pharaoh *Shishak* is Shoshenq I, who ruled Egypt ca. 945–924 BCE; he is the first Pharaoh named in the Bible. **41–43:** The concluding formula for Solomon, who like David reigned for forty years, a typological number. The *Book of the Acts of Solomon* may have been a source for the authors of 1 Kings 1–11. Solomon's son *Rehoboam* succeeded him in Jerusalem, and ruled ca. 928–911 BCE.

12.1–33: The disruption of Solomon's kingdom. 1–5: In order to rally the northern tribes, Rehoboam goes

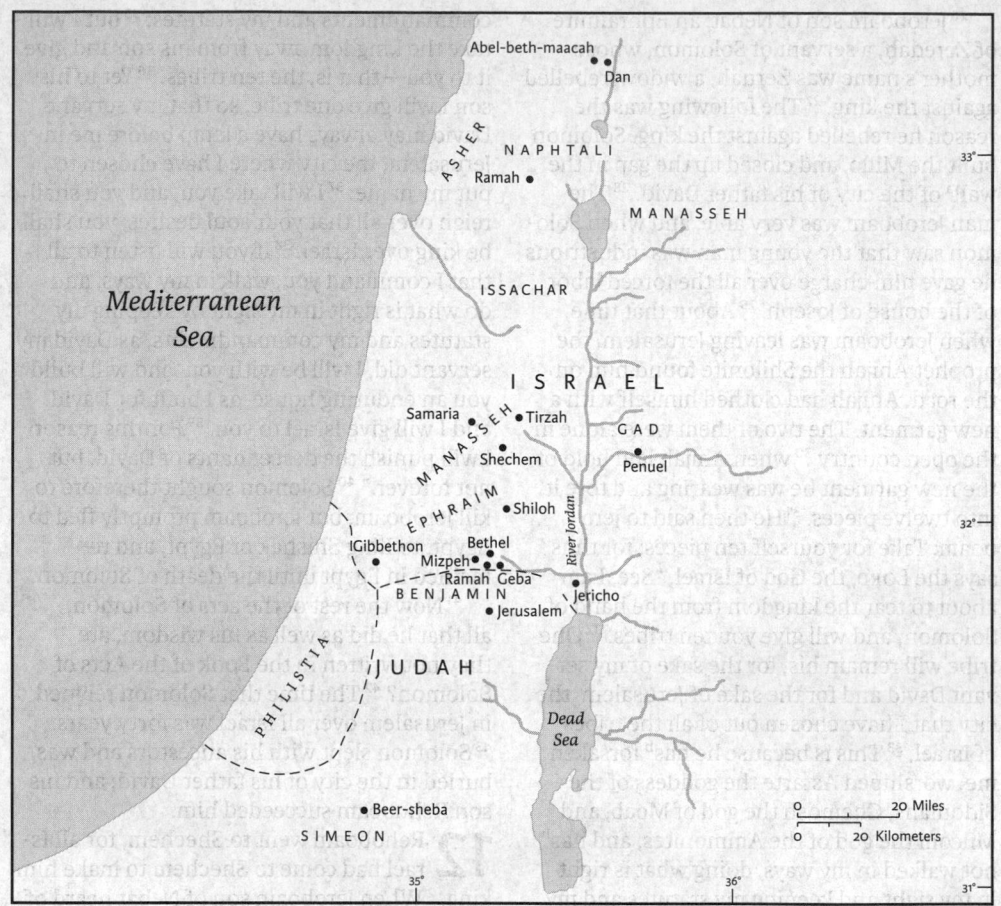

The geography of chs. 12–16. The dashed line shows the approximate boundaries between Israel, Judah and Philistia.

from[a] Egypt. [3] And they sent and called him; and Jeroboam and all the assembly of Israel came and said to Rehoboam, [4] "Your father made our yoke heavy. Now therefore lighten the hard service of your father and his heavy yoke that he placed on us, and we will serve you." [5] He said to them, "Go away for three days, then come again to me." So the people went away.

[6] Then King Rehoboam took counsel with the older men who had attended his father Solomon while he was still alive,

saying, "How do you advise me to answer this people?" [7] They answered him, "If you will be a servant to this people today and serve them, and speak good words to them when you answer them, then they will be your servants forever." [8] But he disregarded the advice that the older men gave him, and consulted with the young men who had grown up with him and now attended him. [9] He said to them, "What do you advise that

a   Gk Vg Compare 2 Chr 10.2: Heb *lived in*

to *Shechem*, located at the end of the pass between Mount Ebal and Mount Gerizim (near modern Nablus). Shechem was one of the most important places in the north (see Deut 27; Josh 24). For David, the northern tribes had come to Hebron in the south (2 Sam 5.3); now Solomon's successor Rehoboam is obliged to go north. 2–5: His rival *Jeroboam* is depicted as a second Moses who has come back from Egypt to liberate the people, who suffer under forced labor. 6–15: Rehoboam is patterned after the Pharaoh of the Exodus story,

we answer this people who have said to me, 'Lighten the yoke that your father put on us'?" [10] The young men who had grown up with him said to him, "Thus you should say to this people who spoke to you, 'Your father made our yoke heavy, but you must lighten it for us'; thus you should say to them, 'My little finger is thicker than my father's loins. [11] Now, whereas my father laid on you a heavy yoke, I will add to your yoke. My father disciplined you with whips, but I will discipline you with scorpions.'"

[12] So Jeroboam and all the people came to Rehoboam the third day, as the king had said, "Come to me again the third day." [13] The king answered the people harshly. He disregarded the advice that the older men had given him [14] and spoke to them according to the advice of the young men, "My father made your yoke heavy, but I will add to your yoke; my father disciplined you with whips, but I will discipline you with scorpions." [15] So the king did not listen to the people, because it was a turn of affairs brought about by the LORD that he might fulfill his word, which the LORD had spoken by Ahijah the Shilonite to Jeroboam son of Nebat.

[16] When all Israel saw that the king would not listen to them, the people answered the king,

"What share do we have in David?
    We have no inheritance in the son of
        Jesse.
To your tents, O Israel!
    Look now to your own house, O David."

So Israel went away to their tents. [17] But Rehoboam reigned over the Israelites who were living in the towns of Judah. [18] When King Rehoboam sent Adoram, who was taskmaster over the forced labor, all Israel stoned him to death. King Rehoboam then hurriedly mounted his chariot to flee to Jerusalem. [19] So Israel has been in rebellion against the house of David to this day.

[20] When all Israel heard that Jeroboam had returned, they sent and called him to the assembly and made him king over all Israel. There was no one who followed the house of David, except the tribe of Judah alone.

[21] When Rehoboam came to Jerusalem, he assembled all the house of Judah and the tribe of Benjamin, one hundred eighty thousand chosen troops to fight against the house of Israel, to restore the kingdom to Rehoboam son of Solomon. [22] But the word of God came to Shemaiah the man of God: [23] Say to King Rehoboam of Judah, son of Solomon, and to all the house of Judah and Benjamin, and to the rest of the people, [24] "Thus says the LORD, You shall not go up or fight against your kindred the people of Israel. Let everyone go home, for this thing is from me." So they heeded the word of the LORD and went home again, according to the word of the LORD.

[25] Then Jeroboam built Shechem in the hill country of Ephraim, and resided there; he went out from there and built Penuel. [26] Then Jeroboam said to himself, "Now the kingdom may well revert to the house of David. [27] If this people continues to go up to offer sacrifices in the house of the LORD at Jerusalem, the heart of this people will turn again to their master, King Rehoboam of Judah; they will kill me and return to King Rehoboam of Judah." [28] So the king took counsel, and made two calves of gold. He said to the people,[a] "You have gone up to Jerusalem long enough. Here are your gods, O Israel, who brought you

[a] Gk: Heb to them

---

increasing oppression (the *yoke*) in response to complaints and hardening his heart. **10:** NRSV *my little finger* follows LXX; MT has "my small one," probably an expression for the penis. Rehoboam and his young counselors think that they are much more manly than their ancestors. **11:** *Scorpions,* perhaps a whip embedded with thorns. **16–20:** The tribes of the north refuse to follow Rehoboam. **16:** The cry *"To your tents, O Israel!"* was a traditional exclamation (see 2 Sam 20.1) of the northern tribes, perhaps used as an appeal to return home after a battle. **18:** *Adoram,* see 4.6. **20:** Jeroboam ruled ca. 928–907 BCE. **21–24:** Rehoboam, who wants to wage war against the northern tribes, is forbidden to do so by the otherwise unknown prophet *Shemaiah.* LXX has a second (shorter and different) version of 12.1–33, labeled 12.24.a–z. **25–33:** Jeroboam constructs national sanctuaries at northern and southern cities in his kingdom, *Dan* and *Bethel.* This act is referred to as a refrain throughout Kings as "the sin of Jeroboam." **28–29:** According to the Deuteronomistic Historians, Jeroboam worshiped the LORD there in the form of a calf; the plural in v. 28 refers to the two statues at Dan and Bethel.

up out of the land of Egypt." [29] He set one in Bethel, and the other he put in Dan. [30] And this thing became a sin, for the people went to worship before the one at Bethel and before the other as far as Dan.[a] [31] He also made houses[b] on high places, and appointed priests from among all the people, who were not Levites. [32] Jeroboam appointed a festival on the fifteenth day of the eighth month like the festival that was in Judah, and he offered sacrifices on the altar; so he did in Bethel, sacrificing to the calves that he had made. And he placed in Bethel the priests of the high places that he had made. [33] He went up to the altar that he had made in Bethel on the fifteenth day in the eighth month, in the month that he alone had devised; he appointed a festival for the people of Israel, and he went up to the altar to offer incense.

13 While Jeroboam was standing by the altar to offer incense, a man of God came out of Judah by the word of the LORD to Bethel [2] and proclaimed against the altar by the word of the LORD, and said, "O altar, altar, thus says the LORD: 'A son shall be born to the house of David, Josiah by name; and he shall sacrifice on you the priests of the high places who offer incense on you, and human bones shall be burned on you.'" [3] He gave a sign the same day, saying, "This is the sign that the LORD has spoken: 'The altar shall be torn down, and the ashes that are on it shall be poured out.'" [4] When the king heard what the man of God cried out against the altar at Bethel, Jeroboam stretched out his hand from the altar, saying, "Seize him!" But the hand that he stretched out against him withered so that he could not draw it back to himself. [5] The altar also was torn down, and the ashes poured out from the altar, according to the sign that the man of God had given by the

word of the LORD. [6] The king said to the man of God, "Entreat now the favor of the LORD your God, and pray for me, so that my hand may be restored to me." So the man of God entreated the LORD; and the king's hand was restored to him, and became as it was before. [7] Then the king said to the man of God, "Come home with me and dine, and I will give you a gift." [8] But the man of God said to the king, "If you give me half your kingdom, I will not go in with you; nor will I eat food or drink water in this place. [9] For thus I was commanded by the word of the LORD: You shall not eat food, or drink water, or return by the way that you came." [10] So he went another way, and did not return by the way that he had come to Bethel.

[11] Now there lived an old prophet in Bethel. One of his sons came and told him all that the man of God had done that day in Bethel; the words also that he had spoken to the king, they told to their father. [12] Their father said to them, "Which way did he go?" And his sons showed him the way that the man of God who came from Judah had gone. [13] Then he said to his sons, "Saddle a donkey for me." So they saddled a donkey for him, and he mounted it. [14] He went after the man of God, and found him sitting under an oak tree. He said to him, "Are you the man of God who came from Judah?" He answered, "I am." [15] Then he said to him, "Come home with me and eat some food." [16] But he said, "I cannot return with you, or go in with you; nor will I eat food or drink water with you in this place; [17] for it was said to me by the word of the LORD: You shall not eat food or drink water there, or return by the way that

---

a   Compare Gk: Heb *went to the one as far as Dan*
b   Gk Vg Compare 13.32: Heb *a house*

The wording is almost identical to the people's comment when Aaron made the golden calf in the desert (Ex 32.4). **31–33:** The Judean authors relate further transgressions of Jeroboam: high places, illegitimate priests, and a different festival calendar.

13.1–34: Jeroboam and the man of God from Judah. 1–10: As Jeroboam stands *by the altar*, that is, on the steps leading to it, he is confronted by an anonymous *man of God*, a prophet, who announces the end of the kingdom of Israel and the profanation of the sanctuary of Bethel by the Judean king *Josiah* (see 2 Kings 23.15–19). Such prophecies that connect distant parts of this work are typical of the Deuteronomistic History. **4:** The *withered* (lit. "dried") *hand* of Jeroboam demonstrates the prophet's power over the king. **6–10:** Having restored the king's hand, the prophet obeys the LORD's order and refuses any compensation. **11–32:** But in the following story the man of God acts differently and follows a prophet from Bethel who claims that God has spoken to him

you came." [18] Then the other[a] said to him, "I also am a prophet as you are, and an angel spoke to me by the word of the LORD: Bring him back with you into your house so that he may eat food and drink water." But he was deceiving him. [19] Then the man of God[a] went back with him, and ate food and drank water in his house.

[20] As they were sitting at the table, the word of the LORD came to the prophet who had brought him back; [21] and he proclaimed to the man of God who came from Judah, "Thus says the LORD: Because you have disobeyed the word of the LORD, and have not kept the commandment that the LORD your God commanded you, [22] but have come back and have eaten food and drunk water in the place of which he said to you, 'Eat no food, and drink no water,' your body shall not come to your ancestral tomb." [23] After the man of God[a] had eaten food and had drunk, they saddled for him a donkey belonging to the prophet who had brought him back. [24] Then as he went away, a lion met him on the road and killed him. His body was thrown in the road, and the donkey stood beside it; the lion also stood beside the body. [25] People passed by and saw the body thrown in the road, with the lion standing by the body. And they came and told it in the town where the old prophet lived. [26] When the prophet who had brought him back from the way heard of it, he said, "It is the man of God who disobeyed the word of the LORD; therefore the LORD has given him to the lion, which has torn him and killed him according to the word that the LORD spoke to him." [27] Then he said to his sons, "Saddle a donkey for me." So they saddled one, [28] and he went and found the body thrown in the road, with the donkey and the lion standing beside the body. The lion had not eaten the body or attacked the donkey. [29] The prophet took up the body of the man of God, laid it on the donkey, and brought it back to the city,[b] to mourn and to bury him. [30] He laid the body in his own grave; and they mourned over him, saying, "Alas, my brother!" [31] After he had buried him, he said to his sons, "When I die, bury me in the grave in which the man of God is buried; lay my bones beside his bones. [32] For the saying that he proclaimed by the word of the LORD against the altar in Bethel, and against all the houses of the high places that are in the cities of Samaria, shall surely come to pass."

[33] Even after this event Jeroboam did not turn from his evil way, but made priests for the high places again from among all the people; any who wanted to be priests he consecrated for the high places. [34] This matter became sin to the house of Jeroboam, so as to cut it off and to destroy it from the face of the earth.

14 At that time Abijah son of Jeroboam fell sick. [2] Jeroboam said to his wife, "Go, disguise yourself, so that it will not be known that you are the wife of Jeroboam, and go to Shiloh; for the prophet Ahijah is there, who said of me that I should be king over this people. [3] Take with you ten loaves, some cakes, and a jar of honey, and go to him; he will tell you what shall happen to the child."

[4] Jeroboam's wife did so; she set out and went to Shiloh, and came to the house of Ahijah. Now Ahijah could not see, for his eyes were dim because of his age. [5] But the LORD said to Ahijah, "The wife of Jeroboam is coming to inquire of you concerning her son; for he is sick. Thus and thus you shall say to her."

When she came, she pretended to be another woman. [6] But when Ahijah heard the sound of her feet, as she came in at the door, he said, "Come in, wife of Jeroboam;

---

a Heb *he*

b Gk: Heb *he came to the town of the old prophet*

---

in another way; together, the stories illustrate that God's word must be heeded precisely. **24–28:** A *lion* would not normally be expected to kill a man and then simply stand over the body beside an uneaten donkey. This stresses the holiness of the man of God, which was acknowledged even by the lion. **32:** *Samaria* became the capital of the Northern Kingdom under Omri (16.24); here it means the entire Northern Kingdom. **33–34:** The concluding passage about Jeroboam's ongoing sin also introduces the following story.

14.1–31: The deaths of Jeroboam of Israel and Rehoboam of Judah. 1–18: The story of the illness of Jeroboam's son leads to an encounter between Jeroboam's wife and the prophet Ahijah, who had invested Jeroboam

why do you pretend to be another? For I am charged with heavy tidings for you. [7] Go, tell Jeroboam, 'Thus says the LORD, the God of Israel: Because I exalted you from among the people, made you leader over my people Israel, [8] and tore the kingdom away from the house of David to give it to you; yet you have not been like my servant David, who kept my commandments and followed me with all his heart, doing only that which was right in my sight, [9] but you have done evil above all those who were before you and have gone and made for yourself other gods, and cast images, provoking me to anger, and have thrust me behind your back; [10] therefore, I will bring evil upon the house of Jeroboam. I will cut off from Jeroboam every male, both bond and free in Israel, and will consume the house of Jeroboam, just as one burns up dung until it is all gone. [11] Anyone belonging to Jeroboam who dies in the city, the dogs shall eat; and anyone who dies in the open country, the birds of the air shall eat; for the LORD has spoken.' [12] Therefore set out, go to your house. When your feet enter the city, the child shall die. [13] All Israel shall mourn for him and bury him; for he alone of Jeroboam's family shall come to the grave, because in him there is found something pleasing to the LORD, the God of Israel, in the house of Jeroboam. [14] Moreover the LORD will raise up for himself a king over Israel, who shall cut off the house of Jeroboam today, even right now![a]

[15] "The LORD will strike Israel, as a reed is shaken in the water; he will root up Israel out of this good land that he gave to their ancestors, and scatter them beyond the Euphrates, because they have made their sacred poles,[b] provoking the LORD to anger. [16] He will give

Israel up because of the sins of Jeroboam, which he sinned and which he caused Israel to commit."

[17] Then Jeroboam's wife got up and went away, and she came to Tirzah. As she came to the threshold of the house, the child died. [18] All Israel buried him and mourned for him, according to the word of the LORD, which he spoke by his servant the prophet Ahijah.

[19] Now the rest of the acts of Jeroboam, how he warred and how he reigned, are written in the Book of the Annals of the Kings of Israel. [20] The time that Jeroboam reigned was twenty-two years; then he slept with his ancestors, and his son Nadab succeeded him.

[21] Now Rehoboam son of Solomon reigned in Judah. Rehoboam was forty-one years old when he began to reign, and he reigned seventeen years in Jerusalem, the city that the LORD had chosen out of all the tribes of Israel, to put his name there. His mother's name was Naamah the Ammonite. [22] Judah did what was evil in the sight of the LORD; they provoked him to jealousy with their sins that they committed, more than all that their ancestors had done. [23] For they also built for themselves high places, pillars, and sacred poles[b] on every high hill and under every green tree; [24] there were also male temple prostitutes in the land. They committed all the abominations of the nations that the LORD drove out before the people of Israel.

[25] In the fifth year of King Rehoboam, King Shishak of Egypt came up against Jerusalem; [26] he took away the treasures of the house

a Meaning of Heb uncertain
b Heb *Asherim*

as ruler over Israel (11.29–31). **6–11:** Ahijah first delivers an oracle about the fall of Jeroboam's dynasty. **14:** An allusion to the conspiracy of Baasha (15.27–30). **15–16:** A prophecy of the fall of the Northern Kingdom. **15:** *Ancestors*, lit. "fathers," the generation of the entry into the land; *beyond the Euphrates*, allusion to the Assyrian empire, which annexed the Northern Kingdom and deported parts of its population in 722 BCE. The *sacred poles* are symbols of the goddess Asherah, who may have also been venerated as the consort of the God of Israel. **16:** The *sins* of Jeroboam, see 12.25–33n. **17–18:** The mention of *Tirzah* (probably Tell el-Far'ah, ca. 6 mi [10 km] north-northeast of Shechem) suggests that it had become Jeroboam's city of residence. According to 15.21 it became Israel's capital (for a short time) under Baasha. **19–20:** A standard conclusion for the reign of each king (see Introduction). **21–31:** The reign of *Rehoboam* is not much better than that of Jeroboam; the description of the disorder in worship is very close to what is reported from the north. **23:** *Pillars* are phallus-shaped standing stones, used in fertility rituals. These rituals were celebrated on *high hills* and under *green trees* (see also Jer 2.20), which also symbolized fertility. **24:** *Temple prostitutes,* "lit. "holy person." The term is probably a

of the LORD and the treasures of the king's house; he took everything. He also took away all the shields of gold that Solomon had made; [27] so King Rehoboam made shields of bronze instead, and committed them to the hands of the officers of the guard, who kept the door of the king's house. [28] As often as the king went into the house of the LORD, the guard carried them and brought them back to the guardroom.

[29] Now the rest of the acts of Rehoboam, and all that he did, are they not written in the Book of the Annals of the Kings of Judah? [30] There was war between Rehoboam and Jeroboam continually. [31] Rehoboam slept with his ancestors and was buried with his ancestors in the city of David. His mother's name was Naamah the Ammonite. His son Abijam succeeded him.

15 Now in the eighteenth year of King Jeroboam son of Nebat, Abijam began to reign over Judah. [2] He reigned for three years in Jerusalem. His mother's name was Maacah daughter of Abishalom. [3] He committed all the sins that his father did before him; his heart was not true to the LORD his God, like the heart of his father David. [4] Nevertheless for David's sake the LORD his God gave him a lamp in Jerusalem, setting up his son after him, and establishing Jerusalem; [5] because David did what was right in the sight of the LORD, and did not turn aside from anything that he commanded him all the days of his

life, except in the matter of Uriah the Hittite. [6] The war begun between Rehoboam and Jeroboam continued all the days of his life. [7] The rest of the acts of Abijam, and all that he did, are they not written in the Book of the Annals of the Kings of Judah? There was war between Abijam and Jeroboam. [8] Abijam slept with his ancestors, and they buried him in the city of David. Then his son Asa succeeded him.

[9] In the twentieth year of King Jeroboam of Israel, Asa began to reign over Judah; [10] he reigned forty-one years in Jerusalem. His mother's name was Maacah daughter of Abishalom. [11] Asa did what was right in the sight of the LORD, as his father David had done. [12] He put away the male temple prostitutes out of the land, and removed all the idols that his ancestors had made. [13] He also removed his mother Maacah from being queen mother, because she had made an abominable image for Asherah; Asa cut down her image and burned it at the Wadi Kidron. [14] But the high places were not taken away. Nevertheless the heart of Asa was true to the LORD all his days. [15] He brought into the house of the LORD the votive gifts of his father and his own votive gifts—silver, gold, and utensils.

[16] There was war between Asa and King Baasha of Israel all their days. [17] King Baasha of Israel went up against Judah, and built Ramah, to prevent anyone from going out or

euphemism for a prostitute; scholars debate whether some form of ritual prostitution is meant. **25–28:** Pharaoh *Shishak's* (see 11.40) campaign to the north is also attested in Egyptian sources that mention many locations in the Northern Kingdom but not Jerusalem. **30:** *Wars* will frequently occur between Israel and Judah.

15.1–24: Abijam and Asa, kings of Judah. From this point until the fall of the Northern Kingdom, the accession year of each Judean king is dated with respect to the year of reign of the northern king. **1–8:** *Abijam* (called Abijah in the books of Chronicles), a king who reigned for a short time (ca. 911–908 BCE) is said to be as bad as Rehoboam. **2:** His mother was probably the daughter or granddaughter of David's son Absalom, whose mother's name was Maacah. (See 2 Sam 3.3; 2 Chr 11.20. 2 Chr 13.2 gives a different name). **4:** The LORD maintains the dynasty only because of David; the *lamp* (see 11.36) or "light" symbolizes the living representative of the house of David. **5:** *The matter of Uriah the Hittite,* see 2 Sam 11–12. **9–24:** In contrast to Abijam, *Asa* is depicted as a good king with one of the longest reigns (ca. 907–867 BCE). **10–15:** If the *Maacah* here is identical with the one mentioned in 15.2, then Asa would be Abijam's brother, and not his son (v. 8). Perhaps *mother* is a title for queen mother, who would remain in power as long as she lived; Maacah's removal from that office strengthens this hypothesis. According to the Deuteronomistic authors of Kings, *Asa* is the first reforming king, who acts against the syncretistic and idolatrous worship in Jerusalem. **12:** *Male temple prostitutes,* see 14.24n. **14:** Nevertheless he does not remove the *high places,* although he favored the Jerusalem Temple by transferring to it votive gifts presumably offered at other sanctuaries. **16–22:** Military hostilities between Asa and the northern usurper *Baasha,* whose reign is related later in 15.27–30 and 15.33–16.7. **17:** Baasha conquered *Ramah* (6 mi [10

coming in to King Asa of Judah. [18] Then Asa took all the silver and the gold that were left in the treasures of the house of the LORD and the treasures of the king's house, and gave them into the hands of his servants. King Asa sent them to King Ben-hadad son of Tabrimmon son of Hezion of Aram, who resided in Damascus, saying, [19] "Let there be an alliance between me and you, like that between my father and your father: I am sending you a present of silver and gold; go, break your alliance with King Baasha of Israel, so that he may withdraw from me." [20] Ben-hadad listened to King Asa, and sent the commanders of his armies against the cities of Israel. He conquered Ijon, Dan, Abel-beth-maacah, and all Chinneroth, with all the land of Naphtali. [21] When Baasha heard of it, he stopped building Ramah and lived in Tirzah. [22] Then King Asa made a proclamation to all Judah, none was exempt: they carried away the stones of Ramah and its timber, with which Baasha had been building; with them King Asa built Geba of Benjamin and Mizpah. [23] Now the rest of all the acts of Asa, all his power, all that he did, and the cities that he built, are they not written in the Book of the Annals of the Kings of Judah? But in his old age he was diseased in his feet. [24] Then Asa slept with his ancestors, and was buried with his ancestors in the city of his father David; his son Jehoshaphat succeeded him.

[25] Nadab son of Jeroboam began to reign over Israel in the second year of King Asa of Judah; he reigned over Israel two years. [26] He did what was evil in the sight of the LORD, walking in the way of his ancestor and in the sin that he caused Israel to commit.

[27] Baasha son of Ahijah, of the house of Issachar, conspired against him; and Baasha struck him down at Gibbethon, which belonged to the Philistines; for Nadab and all Israel were laying siege to Gibbethon. [28] So Baasha killed Nadab[a] in the third year of King Asa of Judah, and succeeded him. [29] As soon as he was king, he killed all the house of Jeroboam; he left to the house of Jeroboam not one that breathed, until he had destroyed it, according to the word of the LORD that he spoke by his servant Ahijah the Shilonite— [30] because of the sins of Jeroboam that he committed and that he caused Israel to commit, and because of the anger to which he provoked the LORD, the God of Israel.

[31] Now the rest of the acts of Nadab, and all that he did, are they not written in the Book of the Annals of the Kings of Israel? [32] There was war between Asa and King Baasha of Israel all their days.

[33] In the third year of King Asa of Judah, Baasha son of Ahijah began to reign over all Israel at Tirzah; he reigned twenty-four years. [34] He did what was evil in the sight of the LORD, walking in the way of Jeroboam and in the sin that he caused Israel to commit.

16 The word of the LORD came to Jehu son of Hanani against Baasha, saying, [2] "Since I exalted you out of the dust and

---

[a] Heb *him*

km] north of Jerusalem) located in the territory of Benjamin and fortified it in order to use it as a border citadel against Judah. **18–19:** Asa is forced to make an alliance against Baasha with *King Ben-hadad* of *Damascus*. **20–21:** Ben-hadad is convinced by the important gifts and conquers important locations in the north of Israel. *Ijon, Dan*, at the headwaters of Jordan; *Abel-beth-maacah*, 5 mi (8 km) west of Dan. *Chinneroth*, the land between the mountains and the lake of Galilee. All these territories belonged to *Naphtali*. **22–24:** Asa uses the material that Baasha had brought to Ramah and builds two border fortresses in the north of Benjamin because he wants to stress that it belongs to Judah: *Geba* and *Mizpah*. The latter means "look-out post"; it designates a town 8 mi (13 km) north of Jerusalem, which became an important administrative center after the fall of Jerusalem in 586 BCE (see 2 Kings 25.22). **23–24:** The note about the king's disease of the *feet*, perhaps a euphemism for the genitals, may come from the royal archives. This could mean that his son Jehoshaphat (22.41) governed during the last years of Asa's life.

15.25–16.34: The northern kings from Nadab to Ahab. 15.25–32: The authors provide little precise information about *Nadab* (ca. 907–906 BCE) and make him as evil as Jeroboam. **27–28:** He is killed by *Baasha*, an officer from the tribe of *Issachar*, during the siege of the Philistine town *Gibbethon*, just west of Gezer. **29–30:** The extermination of the whole family of Jeroboam fulfills the prophetic oracle against the house of Jeroboam in 14.7–14. **15.33–16.7:** *Baasha* (ca. 906–883 BCE) established *Tirzah* (see 14.17) as the capital of the Northern King-

made you leader over my people Israel, and you have walked in the way of Jeroboam, and have caused my people Israel to sin, provoking me to anger with their sins, ³ therefore, I will consume Baasha and his house, and I will make your house like the house of Jeroboam son of Nebat. ⁴ Anyone belonging to Baasha who dies in the city the dogs shall eat; and anyone of his who dies in the field the birds of the air shall eat."

⁵ Now the rest of the acts of Baasha, what he did, and his power, are they not written in the Book of the Annals of the Kings of Israel? ⁶ Baasha slept with his ancestors, and was buried at Tirzah; and his son Elah succeeded him. ⁷ Moreover the word of the LORD came by the prophet Jehu son of Hanani against Baasha and his house, both because of all the evil that he did in the sight of the LORD, provoking him to anger with the work of his hands, in being like the house of Jeroboam, and also because he destroyed it.

⁸ In the twenty-sixth year of King Asa of Judah, Elah son of Baasha began to reign over Israel in Tirzah; he reigned two years. ⁹ But his servant Zimri, commander of half his chariots, conspired against him. When he was at Tirzah, drinking himself drunk in the house of Arza, who was in charge of the palace at Tirzah, ¹⁰ Zimri came in and struck him down and killed him, in the twenty-seventh year of King Asa of Judah, and succeeded him.

¹¹ When he began to reign, as soon as he had seated himself on his throne, he killed all the house of Baasha; he did not leave him a single male of his kindred or his friends. ¹² Thus Zimri destroyed all the house of Baa-sha, according to the word of the LORD, which he spoke against Baasha by the prophet Jehu— ¹³ because of all the sins of Baasha and the sins of his son Elah that they committed, and that they caused Israel to commit, provoking the LORD God of Israel to anger with their idols. ¹⁴ Now the rest of the acts of Elah, and all that he did, are they not written in the Book of the Annals of the Kings of Israel?

¹⁵ In the twenty-seventh year of King Asa of Judah, Zimri reigned seven days in Tirzah. Now the troops were encamped against Gibbethon, which belonged to the Philistines, ¹⁶ and the troops who were encamped heard it said, "Zimri has conspired, and he has killed the king"; therefore all Israel made Omri, the commander of the army, king over Israel that day in the camp. ¹⁷ So Omri went up from Gibbethon, and all Israel with him, and they besieged Tirzah. ¹⁸ When Zimri saw that the city was taken, he went into the citadel of the king's house; he burned down the king's house over himself with fire, and died— ¹⁹ because of the sins that he committed, doing evil in the sight of the LORD, walking in the way of Jeroboam, and for the sin that he committed, causing Israel to sin. ²⁰ Now the rest of the acts of Zimri, and the conspiracy that he made, are they not written in the Book of the Annals of the Kings of Israel?

²¹ Then the people of Israel were divided into two parts; half of the people followed Tibni son of Ginath, to make him king, and half followed Omri. ²² But the people who followed Omri overcame the people who followed Tibni son of Ginath; so Tibni died, and Omri became king. ²³ In the thirty-first year of King Asa of Judah, Omri began to reign over

dom, until Omri moved it to Samaria (16.24). **16.1–4:** The divine oracle by the otherwise unknown prophet *Jehu* (not to be confused with the later King Jehu) announces to Baasha, who *walked in the way of Jeroboam* (15.34), the end of his dynasty, as did the prophet Ahijah to Jeroboam (14.7–14). **8–14:** Baasha's son Elah (ca. 883–882 BCE) has a very short reign since he is murdered by his officer Zimri during a banquet in the house of Arza, the royal chamberlain (for the title, see 4.6), who participated in the conspiracy. Like Nadab (15.29–30), Zimri exterminates all the descendants of the murdered king. **15–22:** The chaotic and anarchic situation in the Northern Kingdom culminates with the reign of Zimri, which lasted only a week. During the siege of Gibbethon (see 15.27–28n.), Omri, supported by an important part of the army ("all Israel" in v. 17 is a rhetorical exaggeration) besieged Tirzah, and Zimri committed suicide to avoid the humiliation of being killed by his enemy. This section emphasizes the instability of the northern kingship, in contrast to that of Judah. **21–22:** For five years there is a civil war. Omri's claim to kingship is challenged by *Tibni*, who finally *died*—in all likelihood, he was killed. There were apparently two competing factions in the Israelite army. **23–28:** The biblical authors describe *Omri's* reign (ca. 882–871) briefly. The Assyrians considered Omri as one of Israel's most important kings, referring to

Israel; he reigned for twelve years, six of them in Tirzah.

²⁴ He bought the hill of Samaria from Shemer for two talents of silver; he fortified the hill, and called the city that he built, Samaria, after the name of Shemer, the owner of the hill.

²⁵ Omri did what was evil in the sight of the Lord; he did more evil than all who were before him. ²⁶ For he walked in all the way of Jeroboam son of Nebat, and in the sins that he caused Israel to commit, provoking the Lord, the God of Israel, to anger by their idols. ²⁷ Now the rest of the acts of Omri that he did, and the power that he showed, are they not written in the Book of the Annals of the Kings of Israel? ²⁸ Omri slept with his ancestors, and was buried in Samaria; his son Ahab succeeded him.

²⁹ In the thirty-eighth year of King Asa of Judah, Ahab son of Omri began to reign over Israel; Ahab son of Omri reigned over Israel in Samaria twenty-two years. ³⁰ Ahab son of Omri did evil in the sight of the Lord more than all who were before him.

³¹ And as if it had been a light thing for him to walk in the sins of Jeroboam son of Nebat, he took as his wife Jezebel daughter of King Ethbaal of the Sidonians, and went and served Baal, and worshiped him. ³² He erected an altar for Baal in the house of Baal, which he built in Samaria. ³³ Ahab also made a sacred pole.ᵃ Ahab did more to provoke the anger of the Lord, the God of Israel, than had all the kings of Israel who were before him. ³⁴ In his days Hiel of Bethel built Jericho; he laid its foundation at the cost of Abiram his firstborn, and set up its gates at the cost of his youngest son Segub, according to the word of the Lord, which he spoke by Joshua son of Nun.

17 Now Elijah the Tishbite, of Tishbeᵇ in Gilead, said to Ahab, "As the Lord the God of Israel lives, before whom I stand, there shall be neither dew nor rain these years, except by my word." ² The word of the Lord came to him, saying, ³ "Go from here and turn eastward, and hide yourself by the Wadi Cherith, which is east of the Jordan. ⁴ You shall drink from the wadi, and I have commanded the ravens to feed you there." ⁵ So he went and did according to the word of the Lord; he went and lived by the Wadi

ᵃ Heb *Asherah*
ᵇ Gk: Heb *of the settlers*

Israel as "the land of the house of Omri" long after Omri's descendants had ceased to rule. The name Omri is unique in Israel and may be of Amorite or Arabic origin (like Omar). **24:** The only reported event of his reign is his purchase of the hill of *Samaria*, which became the capital of the Northern Kingdom until its fall in 722 (cf. David's purchase of Araunah's threshing floor in 2 Sam 24.18–25). **25–28:** The rest consists of stereotypical expressions, presenting Omri as a sinner, worse than his predecessors. **29–34:** The sinfulness of Israel's kings culminates with *Ahab* (ca. 873–852 BCE). His name may signify "the brother of the father"; it is perhaps a throne–name indicating a coregency of the prince with his father. **31:** The authors sharply condemn his marriage with Jezebel, a Phoenician princess. Her name includes a title of the Canaanite god Baal ("zebul"), revocalized to hint at dung ("zebel"). Her father *Ethbaal* is documented by nonbiblical sources as king of Tyre (for *Sidon* as a general term, see 6.6n.). **32–33:** Ahab introduces the worship of Baal into the Northern Kingdom. *Baal* is not a proper name but a title ("lord, master") given in the Levant to the weather-god who brought rain and fertility to the land. Nevertheless the names of his children all contain the name of the god of Israel. **34:** See Josh 6.26. Archeological evidence for an occupation of *Jericho* during the monarchic period points to the seventh century BCE. *At the cost of . . . his firstborn . . . his youngest son* may mean human sacrifices at the occasion of the foundation of an important building. Another possibility is to see the death of *Hiel*'s children as the consequence of Joshua's curse upon the rebuilding of the ruins of Jericho.

17.1–21. Elijah. Most of the narratives about the prophet Elijah (1 Kings 17–21) are inserted in account of the reign of Ahab, whose death is related in 22.37–40. The final Elijah narratives take place during the reign of Ahaziah (2 Kings 1–2).

17.1–18.46: The prophet Elijah and the drought. 17.1–6: *Elijah* comes from *Tishbe*, a town north of the Jabbok River in *Gilead* in Transjordan. Elijah's name (which means "My god is the Lord") may reflect his theological program, since he will fight against the worship of Baal. **1:** The Lord's bringing a drought upon the land shows that he is the real weather-god instead of Baal. **2–5:** Following a divine order Elijah escapes the famine and dwells

Places associated with the Elijah narratives. The dashed line shows the approximate boundaries between Israel, Judah and Philistia.

Cherith, which is east of the Jordan. [6] The ravens brought him bread and meat in the morning, and bread and meat in the evening; and he drank from the wadi. [7] But after a while the wadi dried up, because there was no rain in the land.

[8] Then the word of the LORD came to him, saying, [9] "Go now to Zarephath, which belongs to Sidon, and live there; for I have commanded a widow there to feed you." [10] So he set out and went to Zarephath. When he came to the gate of the town, a widow was there gathering sticks; he called to her and said, "Bring me a little water in a vessel, so that I may drink." [11] As she was going to bring it, he called to her and said, "Bring me a morsel of bread in your hand." [12] But she said, "As the LORD your God lives, I have nothing baked, only a handful of meal in a jar, and a little oil in a jug; I am now gathering a couple of sticks, so that I may go home and prepare it for myself and my son, that we may eat it, and die." [13] Elijah said to her,

at the *Wadi Cherith*, an unidentified brook *east of the Jordan*. 6: The feeding of the hero by animals is a frequent motif in folktales. *Ravens* are known as always hungry and eating rotten flesh. Paradoxically, they provide meat for Elijah. 7–16: Elijah has to go north. 9: *Zarephath* (10 mi [16 km] south of Sidon) is in Phoenician territory, the heartland of Baal-worship. Elijah's miracle shows that the God of Israel alone can provide food and life. 12: *Meal*

"Do not be afraid; go and do as you have said; but first make me a little cake of it and bring it to me, and afterwards make something for yourself and your son. ¹⁴ For thus says the LORD the God of Israel: The jar of meal will not be emptied and the jug of oil will not fail until the day that the LORD sends rain on the earth." ¹⁵ She went and did as Elijah said, so that she as well as he and her household ate for many days. ¹⁶ The jar of meal was not emptied, neither did the jug of oil fail, according to the word of the LORD that he spoke by Elijah.

¹⁷ After this the son of the woman, the mistress of the house, became ill; his illness was so severe that there was no breath left in him. ¹⁸ She then said to Elijah, "What have you against me, O man of God? You have come to me to bring my sin to remembrance, and to cause the death of my son!" ¹⁹ But he said to her, "Give me your son." He took him from her bosom, carried him up into the upper chamber where he was lodging, and laid him on his own bed. ²⁰ He cried out to the LORD, "O LORD my God, have you brought calamity even upon the widow with whom I am staying, by killing her son?" ²¹ Then he stretched himself upon the child three times, and cried out to the LORD, "O LORD my God, let this child's life come into him again." ²² The LORD listened to the voice of Elijah; the life of the child came into him again, and he revived. ²³ Elijah took the child, brought him down from the upper chamber into the house, and gave him to his mother; then Elijah said, "See, your son is alive." ²⁴ So the woman said to Elijah, "Now I know that you are a man of God, and that the word of the LORD in your mouth is truth."

18 After many days the word of the LORD came to Elijah, in the third year of the drought,ᵃ saying, "Go, present yourself to Ahab; I will send rain on the earth." ² So Elijah went to present himself to Ahab. The famine was severe in Samaria. ³ Ahab summoned Obadiah, who was in charge of the palace. (Now Obadiah revered the LORD greatly; ⁴ when Jezebel was killing off the prophets of the LORD, Obadiah took a hundred prophets, hid them fifty to a cave, and provided them with bread and water.) ⁵ Then Ahab said to Obadiah, "Go through the land to all the springs of water and to all the wadis; perhaps we may find grass to keep the horses and mules alive, and not lose some of the animals." ⁶ So they divided the land between them to pass through it; Ahab went in one direction by himself, and Obadiah went in another direction by himself.

⁷ As Obadiah was on the way, Elijah met him; Obadiah recognized him, fell on his face, and said, "Is it you, my lord Elijah?" ⁸ He answered him, "It is I. Go, tell your lord that Elijah is here." ⁹ And he said, "How have I sinned, that you would hand your servant over to Ahab, to kill me? ¹⁰ As the LORD your God lives, there is no nation or kingdom to which my lord has not sent to seek you; and when they would say, 'He is not here,' he would require an oath of the kingdom or nation, that they had not found you. ¹¹ But now you say, 'Go, tell your lord that Elijah is here.' ¹² As soon as I have gone from you, the spirit of the LORD will carry you I know not where; so, when I come and tell Ahab and he cannot find you, he will kill me, although I your servant have revered the LORD from my youth. ¹³ Has it not been told my lord what I did when Jezebel killed the prophets of the LORD, how I hid a hundred of the LORD's prophets fifty to a cave, and provided them

ᵃ Heb lacks *of the drought*

and *oil* are the basic ingredients for bread. **17–24:** Elijah's revival of the widow's son manifests again the LORD's power. The Ugaritic Baal epic tells that during the dry summer Baal dies and comes back to life in autumn by the help of his sister. The God of Israel is not a dying God; on the contrary, his prophet is able to bring the dead back to life. **18:** The woman understands the death of her son as punishment for some obscure *sin*. **19–23:** Elijah's lying on the dead boy has a parallel in a similar story about Elisha in 2 Kings 4.34. It reflects a magical conception of transferring life into a dead body. The story emphasizes that this magic can work only if God pays attention to the *voice* of his prophet. **24:** A foreign woman acknowledges the power of the God of Israel. **18.1–46:** Now Elijah, the prophet of the LORD, directly confronts the prophets of Baal. **1–16:** This confrontation is introduced by an encounter between Elijah and *Obadiah*, Ahab's chamberlain. This encounter prepares the meeting between Elijah and Ahab. As Obadiah's name ("servant of the LORD") indicates, he is a faithful worshiper of the

with bread and water? ¹⁴ Yet now you say, 'Go, tell your lord that Elijah is here'; he will surely kill me." ¹⁵ Elijah said, "As the LORD of hosts lives, before whom I stand, I will surely show myself to him today." ¹⁶ So Obadiah went to meet Ahab, and told him; and Ahab went to meet Elijah.

¹⁷ When Ahab saw Elijah, Ahab said to him, "Is it you, you troubler of Israel?" ¹⁸ He answered, "I have not troubled Israel; but you have, and your father's house, because you have forsaken the commandments of the LORD and followed the Baals. ¹⁹ Now therefore have all Israel assemble for me at Mount Carmel, with the four hundred fifty prophets of Baal and the four hundred prophets of Asherah, who eat at Jezebel's table."

²⁰ So Ahab sent to all the Israelites, and assembled the prophets at Mount Carmel. ²¹ Elijah then came near to all the people, and said, "How long will you go limping with two different opinions? If the LORD is God, follow him; but if Baal, then follow him." The people did not answer him a word. ²² Then Elijah said to the people, "I, even I only, am left a prophet of the LORD; but Baal's prophets number four hundred fifty. ²³ Let two bulls be given to us; let them choose one bull for themselves, cut it in pieces, and lay it on the wood, but put no fire to it; I will prepare the other bull and lay it on the wood, but put no fire to it. ²⁴ Then you call on the name of your god and I will call on the name of the LORD; the god who answers by fire is indeed God." All the people answered, "Well spoken!" ²⁵ Then Elijah said to the prophets of Baal, "Choose for yourselves one bull and prepare it first,

for you are many; then call on the name of your god, but put no fire to it." ²⁶ So they took the bull that was given them, prepared it, and called on the name of Baal from morning until noon, crying, "O Baal, answer us!" But there was no voice, and no answer. They limped about the altar that they had made. ²⁷ At noon Elijah mocked them, saying, "Cry aloud! Surely he is a god; either he is meditating, or he has wandered away, or he is on a journey, or perhaps he is asleep and must be awakened." ²⁸ Then they cried aloud and, as was their custom, they cut themselves with swords and lances until the blood gushed out over them. ²⁹ As midday passed, they raved on until the time of the offering of the oblation, but there was no voice, no answer, and no response.

³⁰ Then Elijah said to all the people, "Come closer to me"; and all the people came closer to him. First he repaired the altar of the LORD that had been thrown down; ³¹ Elijah took twelve stones, according to the number of the tribes of the sons of Jacob, to whom the word of the LORD came, saying, "Israel shall be your name"; ³² with the stones he built an altar in the name of the LORD. Then he made a trench around the altar, large enough to contain two measures of seed. ³³ Next he put the wood in order, cut the bull in pieces, and laid it on the wood. He said, "Fill four jars with water and pour it on the burnt offering and on the wood." ³⁴ Then he said, "Do it a second time"; and they did it a second time. Again he said, "Do it a third time"; and they did it a third time, ³⁵ so that the water ran all around the altar, and filled the trench also with water.

God of Israel and protects God's prophets from Ahab's vengeful wife Jezebel. 17–20: The encounter between Ahab and Elijah prepares the way for the competition between the many prophets of Baal and the one prophet of the LORD. 17: *Troubler*, this word may also mean "sorcerer." 19: The high number of the prophets of Baal (*four hundred fifty*) emphasizes the disproportion of forces. The *four hundred prophets of Asherah*, who do not appear again in the following story, have been inserted here to emphasize Ahab's and Jezebel's Canaanite religion. The competition is on *Mount Carmel*, on the coast above modern Haifa. 20: *All the Israelites*, a rhetorical expression, meaning the people as represented by its elders and other dignitaries. 20–24: In his harangue Elijah pretends to be the only prophet of the LORD; but see 18.4. 24: The LORD's association with *fire* and lightning is well attested (Ex 19; Lev 9.24); Baal was also venerated as a god of fire and lightning. 25–29: Baal's prophets are unsuccessful, in spite of engaging in self-laceration until the evening (*the time of the offering of the oblation*). Elijah's mockery recalls the critique of idols in Deutero-Isaiah (Isa 40–55). 27: *He has wandered away*, a disrespectful euphemism meaning that Baal has to relieve himself. 29: *They raved*, lit. "they prophesied." 30–40: Elijah prepares the revelation of the LORD by restoring or building an altar. 30–32: A sacrifice to the LORD needs to be offered on an *altar*. The author of these verses knows the Jacob story in Genesis and quotes Gen 35.10. 32–35: The large *trench*

³⁶ At the time of the offering of the oblation, the prophet Elijah came near and said, "O LORD, God of Abraham, Isaac, and Israel, let it be known this day that you are God in Israel, that I am your servant, and that I have done all these things at your bidding. ³⁷ Answer me, O LORD, answer me, so that this people may know that you, O LORD, are God, and that you have turned their hearts back." ³⁸ Then the fire of the LORD fell and consumed the burnt offering, the wood, the stones, and the dust, and even licked up the water that was in the trench. ³⁹ When all the people saw it, they fell on their faces and said, "The LORD indeed is God; the LORD indeed is God." ⁴⁰ Elijah said to them, "Seize the prophets of Baal; do not let one of them escape." Then they seized them; and Elijah brought them down to the Wadi Kishon, and killed them there.

⁴¹ Elijah said to Ahab, "Go up, eat and drink; for there is a sound of rushing rain." ⁴² So Ahab went up to eat and to drink. Elijah went up to the top of Carmel; there he bowed himself down upon the earth and put his face between his knees. ⁴³ He said to his servant, "Go up now, look toward the sea." He went up and looked, and said, "There is nothing." Then he said, "Go again seven times." ⁴⁴ At the seventh time he said, "Look, a little cloud no bigger than a person's hand is rising out of the sea." Then he said, "Go say to Ahab, 'Harness your chariot and go down before the rain stops you.'" ⁴⁵ In a little while the heavens grew black with clouds and wind; there was a heavy rain. Ahab rode off and went to Jezreel. ⁴⁶ But the hand of the LORD was on Elijah; he girded up his loins and ran in front of Ahab to the entrance of Jezreel.

19 Ahab told Jezebel all that Elijah had done, and how he had killed all the prophets with the sword. ² Then Jezebel sent a messenger to Elijah, saying, "So may the gods do to me, and more also, if I do not make your life like the life of one of them by this time tomorrow." ³ Then he was afraid; he got up and fled for his life, and came to Beer-sheba, which belongs to Judah; he left his servant there.

⁴ But he himself went a day's journey into the wilderness, and came and sat down under a solitary broom tree. He asked that he might die: "It is enough; now, O LORD, take away my life, for I am no better than my ancestors." ⁵ Then he lay down under the broom tree and fell asleep. Suddenly an angel touched him and said to him, "Get up and eat." ⁶ He looked, and there at his head was a cake baked on hot stones, and a jar of water. He ate and drank, and lay down again. ⁷ The angel of the LORD came a second time, touched him, and said, "Get up and eat, otherwise the journey will be too much for you." ⁸ He got up, and ate and drank; then he went in the strength of that food forty days and forty nights to Horeb the mount of God. ⁹ At that place he came to a cave, and spent the night there.

filled with water prevents any human manipulation. **36–37:** Elijah's prayer contrasts with the ecstatic behavior of the prophets of Baal. **38–39:** The LORD's manifestation through fire leads to the people's recognition that he is the only god. The cry "*The LORD indeed is God*" echoes the name of Elijah (see 17.1–6n.). **40:** The killing of the prophets of Baal at *Wadi Kishon*, a seasonal stream at the eastern base of Mount Carmel, is shocking to modern readers (cf. the Levites killing the idolatrous people in Ex 32.27–28). **41–46:** These verses conclude the drought narrative. **45:** *Jezreel*, located in a valley ca. 25 mi (40 km) southeast of Mount Carmel, was where Ahab and Jezebel had a palace (21.1). **46:** The LORD orders Elijah to go there, for the next confrontation. Miraculously, Elijah *ran* as fast as Ahab's chariot.

19.1–18: Elijah at the mountain of God. **1–3:** Elijah's violence against the prophets of Baal provokes Jezebel's violence against him, and he flees until he reaches Beer-sheba, in the very south, at the border of the Judean desert. **4–8:** He goes to the *wilderness*, the place of death, because he wishes to *die*, but again the LORD nourishes him miraculously (see 17.5–6) and orders him on a long journey to Mount *Horeb*, an alternate name, especially in Deuteronomy, for Mount Sinai. In the following narrative Elijah is depicted as a new Moses. This is already indicated by the mention of the *forty days and forty nights*, which recall Moses' sojourn on the mountain of God. **9–14:** Elijah's encounter with the LORD takes place at the cave where Moses had stood to meet the God of Israel (Ex 33.21–23). The encounter is framed by Elijah's statement that he has been *zealous* for the LORD, that is, enthusiastic and exclusive in devotion to the LORD. The same word (sometimes translated "jealous") is used

Then the word of the LORD came to him, saying, "What are you doing here, Elijah?" [10] He answered, "I have been very zealous for the LORD, the God of hosts; for the Israelites have forsaken your covenant, thrown down your altars, and killed your prophets with the sword. I alone am left, and they are seeking my life, to take it away."

[11] He said, "Go out and stand on the mountain before the LORD, for the LORD is about to pass by." Now there was a great wind, so strong that it was splitting mountains and breaking rocks in pieces before the LORD, but the LORD was not in the wind; and after the wind an earthquake, but the LORD was not in the earthquake; [12] and after the earthquake a fire, but the LORD was not in the fire; and after the fire a sound of sheer silence. [13] When Elijah heard it, he wrapped his face in his mantle and went out and stood at the entrance of the cave. Then there came a voice to him that said, "What are you doing here, Elijah?" [14] He answered, "I have been very zealous for the LORD, the God of hosts; for the Israelites have forsaken your covenant, thrown down your altars, and killed your prophets with the sword. I alone am left, and they are seeking my life, to take it away." [15] Then the LORD said to him, "Go, return on your way to the wilderness of Damascus; when you arrive, you shall anoint Hazael as king over Aram. [16] Also you shall anoint Jehu son of Nimshi as king over Israel; and you shall anoint Elisha son of Shaphat of Abel-meholah as prophet in your place. [17] Whoever

escapes from the sword of Hazael, Jehu shall kill; and whoever escapes from the sword of Jehu, Elisha shall kill. [18] Yet I will leave seven thousand in Israel, all the knees that have not bowed to Baal, and every mouth that has not kissed him."

[19] So he set out from there, and found Elisha son of Shaphat, who was plowing. There were twelve yoke of oxen ahead of him, and he was with the twelfth. Elijah passed by him and threw his mantle over him. [20] He left the oxen, ran after Elijah, and said, "Let me kiss my father and my mother, and then I will follow you." Then Elijah[a] said to him, "Go back again; for what have I done to you?" [21] He returned from following him, took the yoke of oxen, and slaughtered them; using the equipment from the oxen, he boiled their flesh, and gave it to the people, and they ate. Then he set out and followed Elijah, and became his servant.

20 King Ben-hadad of Aram gathered all his army together; thirty-two kings were with him, along with horses and chariots. He marched against Samaria, laid siege to it, and attacked it. [2] Then he sent messengers into the city to King Ahab of Israel, and said to him: "Thus says Ben-hadad: [3] Your silver and gold are mine; your fairest wives and children also are mine." [4] The king of Israel answered, "As you say, my lord, O king, I am yours, and all that I have." [5] The messengers came again and said: "Thus says Ben-hadad: I

a Heb *he*

---

to describe God. **10–13:** This unexpected divine manifestation can be understood as a critique of the common idea that God has to reveal himself spectacularly by *wind, earthquake,* and *fire* (see Ex 19.16–18; Deut 4.36 and also 1 Kings 18). Here God comes to Elijah in *sheer silence,* in a barely audible whisper. The author of this narrative was probably polemicizing against the previous Carmel narrative. **15–18:** The order given to Elijah to *anoint Hazael as king over Aram* (see 2 Kings 8.7–15), *Jehu as king over Israel* (2 Kings 9–10), and the prophet *Elisha* as his successor hints ahead to the narratives about the time after Ahab, which will also be characterized by violence. Anointing of kings by a prophet is common; a prophet anointing another prophet is unique. **15:** *Wilderness of Damascus,* missing in the LXX, probably means the desert east of the Lake of Tiberias.

19.19–21: Elisha becomes Elijah's servant and successor. Elisha is the first of the three persons mentioned in vv. 15–18 to enter the scene. In fact, he and not Elijah will anoint Hazael and Jehu. **19:** *Twelve yoke of oxen:* likely an allusion to the twelve tribes of Israel. *Threw his mantle over him,* a symbolic act, transferring Elijah's power and abilities to his successor. **21:** The burning of the yoke symbolizes Elisha's break with his former life.

20.1–43: Wars between the Israelites and the Arameans. Elijah does not appear in this narrative. Ahab is hardly mentioned (see vv. 2,13–14), suggesting to some scholars that this story originally belonged to a later time of Israel's history. **1–12:** *Ben-hadad,* head of an impressive alliance (thirty-two kings, or chiefs of various tribes), besieges Samaria and tries to convince the king of Israel to become his vassal and to surrender.

sent to you, saying, 'Deliver to me your silver and gold, your wives and children'; [6] nevertheless I will send my servants to you tomorrow about this time, and they shall search your house and the houses of your servants, and lay hands on whatever pleases them,[a] and take it away."

[7] Then the king of Israel called all the elders of the land, and said, "Look now! See how this man is seeking trouble; for he sent to me for my wives, my children, my silver, and my gold; and I did not refuse him." [8] Then all the elders and all the people said to him, "Do not listen or consent." [9] So he said to the messengers of Ben-hadad, "Tell my lord the king: All that you first demanded of your servant I will do; but this thing I cannot do." The messengers left and brought him word again. [10] Ben-hadad sent to him and said, "The gods do so to me, and more also, if the dust of Samaria will provide a handful for each of the people who follow me." [11] The king of Israel answered, "Tell him: One who puts on armor should not brag like one who takes it off." [12] When Ben-hadad heard this message—now he had been drinking with the kings in the booths—he said to his men, "Take your positions!" And they took their positions against the city.

[13] Then a certain prophet came up to King Ahab of Israel and said, "Thus says the LORD, Have you seen all this great multitude? Look, I will give it into your hand today; and you shall know that I am the LORD." [14] Ahab said, "By whom?" He said, "Thus says the LORD, By the young men who serve the district governors." Then he said, "Who shall begin the battle?" He answered, "You." [15] Then he mustered the young men who served the district governors, two hundred thirty-two; after them he mustered all the people of Israel, seven thousand.

[16] They went out at noon, while Ben-hadad was drinking himself drunk in the booths, he and the thirty-two kings allied with him. [17] The young men who served the district governors went out first. Ben-hadad had sent out scouts,[b] and they reported to him, "Men have come out from Samaria." [18] He said, "If they have come out for peace, take them alive; if they have come out for war, take them alive."

[19] But these had already come out of the city: the young men who served the district governors, and the army that followed them. [20] Each killed his man; the Arameans fled and Israel pursued them, but King Ben-hadad of Aram escaped on a horse with the cavalry. [21] The king of Israel went out, attacked the horses and chariots, and defeated the Arameans with a great slaughter.

[22] Then the prophet approached the king of Israel and said to him, "Come, strengthen yourself, and consider well what you have to do; for in the spring the king of Aram will come up against you."

[23] The servants of the king of Aram said to him, "Their gods are gods of the hills, and so they were stronger than we; but let us fight against them in the plain, and surely we shall be stronger than they. [24] Also do this: remove the kings, each from his post, and put commanders in place of them; [25] and muster an army like the army that you have lost, horse for horse, and chariot for chariot; then we will fight against them in the plain, and surely we shall be stronger than they." He heeded their voice, and did so.

[26] In the spring Ben-hadad mustered the Arameans and went up to Aphek to fight against Israel. [27] After the Israelites had been mustered

a   Gk Syr Vg: Heb *you*
b   Heb lacks *scouts*

11: Ahab quotes a popular aphorism, warning Ben-hadad against too much confidence about his power. **13–15:** Through an anonymous prophet, the LORD announces to the king of Israel that he will provide for the victory against the Arameans. **13:** *I will give it into your hand,* a common expression to express divine assistance in war. **14–15:** *Young men,* unmarried soldiers. *District,* a word normally used of the provinces of the Persian Empire (e.g., Ezra 2.1; Dan 8.2). **16–21:** Attacking at an unexpected time, at *noon,* when the besiegers were relaxing and even *drunk,* the Israelite army defeats the Arameans. **22–34:** Ben-hadad does not give up. **22–25:** He reorganizes his army in order to attack Israel in the *spring* (after his autumn defeat). **23:** *Their gods are gods of the hills,* or "their god is a god of the hills." It is not clear if the Arameans think that the Israelites worship several mountain gods, or only the LORD. The origin of the Israelites is indeed in the mountains of Israel. **26–30:** The battle takes place at *Aphek,* probably situated east of the Lake of Galilee. **28:** An anony-

and provisioned, they went out to engage them; the people of Israel encamped opposite them like two little flocks of goats, while the Arameans filled the country. [28] A man of God approached and said to the king of Israel, "Thus says the LORD: Because the Arameans have said, 'The LORD is a god of the hills but he is not a god of the valleys,' therefore I will give all this great multitude into your hand, and you shall know that I am the LORD." [29] They encamped opposite one another seven days. Then on the seventh day the battle began; the Israelites killed one hundred thousand Aramean foot soldiers in one day. [30] The rest fled into the city of Aphek; and the wall fell on twenty-seven thousand men that were left.

Ben-hadad also fled, and entered the city to hide. [31] His servants said to him, "Look, we have heard that the kings of the house of Israel are merciful kings; let us put sackcloth around our waists and ropes on our heads, and go out to the king of Israel; perhaps he will spare your life." [32] So they tied sackcloth around their waists, put ropes on their heads, went to the king of Israel, and said, "Your servant Ben-hadad says, 'Please let me live.'" And he said, "Is he still alive? He is my brother." [33] Now the men were watching for an omen; they quickly took it up from him and said, "Yes, Ben-hadad is your brother." Then he said, "Go and bring him." So Ben-hadad came out to him; and he had him come up into the chariot. [34] Ben-hadad[a] said to him, "I will restore the towns that my father took from your father; and you may establish bazaars for yourself in Damascus, as my father did in Samaria." The king of Israel responded,[b] "I will let you go on those terms." So he made a treaty with him and let him go.

[35] At the command of the LORD a certain member of a company of prophets[c] said to another, "Strike me!" But the man refused to strike him. [36] Then he said to him, "Because you have not obeyed the voice of the LORD, as soon as you have left me, a lion will kill you." And when he had left him, a lion met him and killed him. [37] Then he found another man and said, "Strike me!" So the man hit him, striking and wounding him. [38] Then the prophet departed, and waited for the king along the road, disguising himself with a bandage over his eyes. [39] As the king passed by, he cried to the king and said, "Your servant went out into the thick of the battle; then a soldier turned and brought a man to me, and said, 'Guard this man; if he is missing, your life shall be given for his life, or else you shall pay a talent of silver.' [40] While your servant was busy here and there, he was gone." The king of Israel said to him, "So shall your judgment be; you yourself have decided it." [41] Then he quickly took the bandage away from his eyes. The king of Israel recognized him as one of the prophets. [42] Then he said to him, "Thus says the LORD, 'Because you have let the man go whom I had devoted to destruction, therefore your life shall be for his life, and your people for his people.'" [43] The king of Israel set out toward home, resentful and sullen, and came to Samaria.

21 Later the following events took place: Naboth the Jezreelite had a vineyard in Jezreel, beside the palace of King Ahab of Samaria. [2] And Ahab said to Naboth, "Give me your vineyard, so that I may have it for a vegetable garden, because it is near my

a Heb *He*
b Heb lacks *The king of Israel responded*
c Heb *of the sons of the prophets*

mous prophet confirms the saying of the Arameans: the LORD is a god of the hills (see v. 23). **29–30:** The outcome recalls the battle of Jericho in Josh 6: on the *seventh* day the Israelites win the battle, and the *wall* of Aphek, where the Arameans have fled, *falls* down. **30–34:** Ben-hadad has no other choice than to offer a treaty to the king of Israel. **32–33:** *Brother* here connotes an equal treaty partner. **34:** *Bazaars* allow the Israelites free trade in Damascus. **35–43:** This story criticizes the treaty that the king of Israel concluded with Ben-hadad. A member of a prophetic guild, who pretends to have been wounded during the war, confounds the king with an invented case (like Nathan in 2 Sam 12.1–7) in order to denounce the king's action as contrary to God's will. **36:** *A lion . . . killed him,* recalling the prophetic story in 13.24. **39:** *A talent of silver* (about 75 lb [34 kg]) was an exorbitant price and impossible to pay unless one was very wealthy. **42:** Cf. 1 Sam 15.

21.1–29: Naboth's vineyard. **1–4:** *Naboth* of *Jezreel,* where Ahab had a winter palace, refuses to sell his land to the king, because he does not want to alienate the property of his clan (cf. Lev 25.8–34). The story shows how

house; I will give you a better vineyard for it; or, if it seems good to you, I will give you its value in money." [3] But Naboth said to Ahab, "The LORD forbid that I should give you my ancestral inheritance." [4] Ahab went home resentful and sullen because of what Naboth the Jezreelite had said to him; for he had said, "I will not give you my ancestral inheritance." He lay down on his bed, turned away his face, and would not eat.

[5] His wife Jezebel came to him and said, "Why are you so depressed that you will not eat?" [6] He said to her, "Because I spoke to Naboth the Jezreelite and said to him, 'Give me your vineyard for money; or else, if you prefer, I will give you another vineyard for it'; but he answered, 'I will not give you my vineyard.'" [7] His wife Jezebel said to him, "Do you now govern Israel? Get up, eat some food, and be cheerful; I will give you the vineyard of Naboth the Jezreelite."

[8] So she wrote letters in Ahab's name and sealed them with his seal; she sent the letters to the elders and the nobles who lived with Naboth in his city. [9] She wrote in the letters, "Proclaim a fast, and seat Naboth at the head of the assembly; [10] seat two scoundrels opposite him, and have them bring a charge against him, saying, 'You have cursed God and the king.' Then take him out, and stone him to death." [11] The men of his city, the elders and the nobles who lived in his city, did as Jezebel had sent word to them. Just as it was written in the letters that she had sent to them, [12] they proclaimed a fast and seated Naboth at the head of the assembly. [13] The two scoundrels came in and sat opposite him; and the scoundrels brought a charge against Naboth, in the presence of the people, saying, "Naboth cursed God and the king." So they took him outside the city, and stoned him to death. [14] Then they sent to Jezebel, saying, "Naboth has been stoned; he is dead."

[15] As soon as Jezebel heard that Naboth had been stoned and was dead, Jezebel said to Ahab, "Go, take possession of the vineyard of Naboth the Jezreelite, which he refused to give you for money; for Naboth is not alive, but dead." [16] As soon as Ahab heard that Naboth was dead, Ahab set out to go down to the vineyard of Naboth the Jezreelite, to take possession of it.

[17] Then the word of the LORD came to Elijah the Tishbite, saying: [18] Go down to meet King Ahab of Israel, who rules[a] in Samaria; he is now in the vineyard of Naboth, where he has gone to take possession. [19] You shall say to him, "Thus says the LORD: Have you killed, and also taken possession?" You shall say to him, "Thus says the LORD: In the place where dogs licked up the blood of Naboth, dogs will also lick up your blood."

[20] Ahab said to Elijah, "Have you found me, O my enemy?" He answered, "I have found you. Because you have sold yourself to do what is evil in the sight of the LORD, [21] I will bring disaster on you; I will consume you, and will cut off from Ahab every male, bond or free, in Israel; [22] and I will make your house like the house of Jeroboam son of Nebat, and like the house of Baasha son of Ahijah, because you have provoked me to anger and have caused Israel to sin. [23] Also concerning Jezebel the LORD said, 'The dogs shall eat Jezebel within the bounds of Jezreel.' [24] Anyone belonging to Ahab who dies in the city the dogs shall eat; and anyone of his who dies in the open country the birds of the air shall eat."

[25] (Indeed, there was no one like Ahab, who sold himself to do what was evil in the sight of the LORD, urged on by his wife Jezebel. [26] He acted most abominably in going after idols, as the Amorites had

[a] Heb *who is*

---

a free man is able to resist the king. **5–14:** Like David, who sent a letter to his commander in order to get rid of Uriah (2 Sam 11.14–15), Jezebel sends *letters* to the *elders* and *nobles* in order to have Naboth executed with a false accusation. **10:** *Scoundrels,* lit. "sons of worthlessness." **15–16:** Apparently the king could claim the possessions of a man who had been condemned to death. **17–29:** Despite the fact that it was Jezebel who took the initiative to kill Naboth, the LORD sends Elijah to confront Ahab. **18:** According to this verse the incident transpired in *Samaria* and not in Jezreel. **23–24:** *The dogs shall eat . . . ,* dogs were considered unclean animals. The absence of a proper burial place is one of the worst curses in the Bible (e.g., Deut 28.26; Jer 34.20) and other ancient

done, whom the LORD drove out before the Israelites.)

²⁷ When Ahab heard those words, he tore his clothes and put sackcloth over his bare flesh; he fasted, lay in the sackcloth, and went about dejectedly. ²⁸ Then the word of the LORD came to Elijah the Tishbite: ²⁹ "Have you seen how Ahab has humbled himself before me? Because he has humbled himself before me, I will not bring the disaster in his days; but in his son's days I will bring the disaster on his house."

22 For three years Aram and Israel continued without war. ² But in the third year King Jehoshaphat of Judah came down to the king of Israel. ³ The king of Israel said to his servants, "Do you know that Ramoth-gilead belongs to us, yet we are doing nothing to take it out of the hand of the king of Aram?" ⁴ He said to Jehoshaphat, "Will you go with me to battle at Ramoth-gilead?" Jehoshaphat replied to the king of Israel, "I am as you are; my people are your people, my horses are your horses."

⁵ But Jehoshaphat also said to the king of Israel, "Inquire first for the word of the LORD." ⁶ Then the king of Israel gathered the prophets together, about four hundred of them, and said to them, "Shall I go to battle against Ramoth-gilead, or shall I refrain?" They said, "Go up; for the LORD will give it into the hand of the king." ⁷ But Jehoshaphat said, "Is there no other prophet of the LORD here of whom we may inquire?" ⁸ The king of Israel said to Jehoshaphat, "There is still one other by

whom we may inquire of the LORD, Micaiah son of Imlah; but I hate him, for he never prophesies anything favorable about me, but only disaster." Jehoshaphat said, "Let the king not say such a thing." ⁹ Then the king of Israel summoned an officer and said, "Bring quickly Micaiah son of Imlah." ¹⁰ Now the king of Israel and King Jehoshaphat of Judah were sitting on their thrones, arrayed in their robes, at the threshing floor at the entrance of the gate of Samaria; and all the prophets were prophesying before them. ¹¹ Zedekiah son of Chenaanah made for himself horns of iron, and he said, "Thus says the LORD: With these you shall gore the Arameans until they are destroyed." ¹² All the prophets were prophesying the same and saying, "Go up to Ramoth-gilead and triumph; the LORD will give it into the hand of the king."

¹³ The messenger who had gone to summon Micaiah said to him, "Look, the words of the prophets with one accord are favorable to the king; let your word be like the word of one of them, and speak favorably." ¹⁴ But Micaiah said, "As the LORD lives, whatever the LORD says to me, that I will speak."

¹⁵ When he had come to the king, the king said to him, "Micaiah, shall we go to Ramoth-gilead to battle, or shall we refrain?" He answered him, "Go up and triumph; the LORD will give it into the hand of the king." ¹⁶ But the king said to him, "How many times must I make you swear to tell me nothing but the truth in the name of the LORD?" ¹⁷ Then Mi-

---

texts. **27–29:** In reaction to the prophetic word Ahab adopts the traditional mourning rites so the punishment is transferred to his son Joram.

    22.1–40: The campaign of Ramoth-gilead and the death of Ahab. 1–36: In this battle story, continuing ch 20, Ahab is mentioned by name only in v. 20 (see 20.1–43n.). **1–4:** The beginning of the story suggests that king *Jehoshaphat* of Judah (see vv. 41–50) is a vassal of the Israelite king, since he has to participate in a war against the *king of Aram* to retrieve the fortress of *Ramoth-gilead* in Transjordan. **5–28:** The story about the prophetic counsel interrupts the battle report that is continued in v. 29. **6:** The *four hundred* prophets are part of the royal entourage. **7–9:** Jehoshaphat asks for an independent prophet of the LORD. *Micaiah son of Imlah*, a prophet of doom, is not the same as the prophet Micah of the book of that name in the Twelve Minor Prophets. 1 Kings 22 (and its parallel in 2 Chr 18) is the only biblical story in which he is mentioned. It is surprising that the king of Israel does not mention the prophet Elijah in this context. **10–16:** *Zedekiah* is the chief of the official court prophets. His symbolic action (*horns of iron*) is meant to bring about the king's victory. *Horns* are symbols of power and strength (cf. the similar narrative in Jer 28). Micaiah's first answer, repeating the favorable oracle, reflects either irony or that he is afraid of punishment in case of a negative oracle (see v. 24). **17–18:** The second oracle describes a vision of a flock without a *shepherd*, namely the king, who in the ancient Near East was the shepherd of his people. **19–23:** Micaiah's second vision describes the heavenly court (see also Job

caiah[a] said, "I saw all Israel scattered on the mountains, like sheep that have no shepherd; and the LORD said, 'These have no master; let each one go home in peace.'" [18] The king of Israel said to Jehoshaphat, "Did I not tell you that he would not prophesy anything favorable about me, but only disaster?"

[19] Then Micaiah[a] said, "Therefore hear the word of the LORD: I saw the LORD sitting on his throne, with all the host of heaven standing beside him to the right and to the left of him. [20] And the LORD said, 'Who will entice Ahab, so that he may go up and fall at Ramoth-gilead?' Then one said one thing, and another said another, [21] until a spirit came forward and stood before the LORD, saying, 'I will entice him.' [22] 'How?' the LORD asked him. He replied, 'I will go out and be a lying spirit in the mouth of all his prophets.' Then the LORD[a] said, 'You are to entice him, and you shall succeed; go out and do it.' [23] So you see, the LORD has put a lying spirit in the mouth of all these your prophets; the LORD has decreed disaster for you."

[24] Then Zedekiah son of Chenaanah came up to Micaiah, slapped him on the cheek, and said, "Which way did the spirit of the LORD pass from me to speak to you?" [25] Micaiah replied, "You will find out on that day when you go in to hide in an inner chamber." [26] The king of Israel then ordered, "Take Micaiah, and return him to Amon the governor of the city and to Joash the king's son, [27] and say, 'Thus says the king: Put this fellow in prison, and feed him on reduced rations of bread and water until I come in peace.'" [28] Micaiah said, "If you return in peace, the LORD has not spoken by me." And he said, "Hear, you peoples, all of you!"

[29] So the king of Israel and King Jehoshaphat of Judah went up to Ramoth-gilead. [30] The king of Israel said to Jehoshaphat, "I will disguise myself and go into battle, but you wear your robes." So the king of Israel disguised himself and went into battle. [31] Now the king of Aram had commanded the thirty-two captains of his chariots, "Fight with no one small or great, but only with the king of Israel." [32] When the captains of the chariots saw Jehoshaphat, they said, "It is surely the king of Israel." So they turned to fight against him; and Jehoshaphat cried out. [33] When the captains of the chariots saw that it was not the king of Israel, they turned back from pursuing him. [34] But a certain man drew his bow and unknowingly struck the king of Israel between the scale armor and the breastplate; so he said to the driver of his chariot, "Turn around, and carry me out of the battle, for I am wounded." [35] The battle grew hot that day, and the king was propped up in his chariot facing the Arameans, until at evening he died; the blood from the wound had flowed into the bottom of the chariot. [36] Then about sunset a shout went through the army, "Every man to his city, and every man to his country!"

[37] So the king died, and was brought to Samaria; they buried the king in Samaria. [38] They washed the chariot by the pool of Samaria; the dogs licked up his blood, and the prostitutes washed themselves in it,[b] according to the word of the LORD that he had spoken. [39] Now the rest of the acts of Ahab, and all that he did, and the ivory house that he built, and all the cities that he built, are they not written in the Book of the Annals of the Kings of Israel? [40] So Ahab slept with his ancestors; and his son Ahaziah succeeded him.

[41] Jehoshaphat son of Asa began to reign over Judah in the fourth year of King Ahab of Israel. [42] Jehoshaphat was thirty-five years old when he began to reign, and he reigned

a Heb he
b Heb lacks in it

1–2). 22: The *lying spirit* is a member of the divine council. 24–28: The king prefers the majority view. 26: Like Jeremiah (Jer 37.15), Micaiah is kept in prison, in the house of the *king's son*. 29–36: The *disguise* of the king of Israel indicates that he is lacking faith in the victory and that he tries to avert the first vision of Micaiah. 34: But he cannot oppose God's decision and is killed in spite of his disguise. 37–40: The conclusion of Ahab's reign is described in stereotypical expressions known from other kings, except for v. 38, which alludes to Elijah's prophecy in 21.19 in which *the dogs licked up his blood*. The reference to the *prostitutes* exceeds what Elijah announced. Their obscene action makes Ahab's death even more infamous.

22.41–53: Jehoshaphat of Judah and Ahaziah of Israel. 41–50: For the redactors of the book of Kings *Je-*

twenty-five years in Jerusalem. His mother's name was Azubah daughter of Shilhi. ⁴³ He walked in all the way of his father Asa; he did not turn aside from it, doing what was right in the sight of the Lord; yet the high places were not taken away, and the people still sacrificed and offered incense on the high places. ⁴⁴ Jehoshaphat also made peace with the king of Israel.

⁴⁵ Now the rest of the acts of Jehoshaphat, and his power that he showed, and how he waged war, are they not written in the Book of the Annals of the Kings of Judah? ⁴⁶ The remnant of the male temple prostitutes who were still in the land in the days of his father Asa, he exterminated.

⁴⁷ There was no king in Edom; a deputy was king. ⁴⁸ Jehoshaphat made ships of the Tarshish type to go to Ophir for gold; but they did not go, for the ships were wrecked at Ezion-geber. ⁴⁹ Then Ahaziah son of Ahab said to Jehoshaphat, "Let my servants go with your servants in the ships," but Jehoshaphat was not willing. ⁵⁰ Jehoshaphat slept with his ancestors and was buried with his ancestors in the city of his father David; his son Jehoram succeeded him.

⁵¹ Ahaziah son of Ahab began to reign over Israel in Samaria in the seventeenth year of King Jehoshaphat of Judah; he reigned two years over Israel. ⁵² He did what was evil in the sight of the Lord, and walked in the way of his father and mother, and in the way of Jeroboam son of Nebat, who caused Israel to sin. ⁵³ He served Baal and worshiped him; he provoked the Lord, the God of Israel, to anger, just as his father had done.

hoshaphat (ca. 870–846 BCE) was a good king, except that he tolerated sanctuaries outside the Jerusalem Temple. 46: *Male temple prostitutes,* see 14.24n. 47–50: Like Solomon, Jehoshaphat built *ships of the Tarshish type* in order to continue his ancestor's exotic expeditions, but he did not succeed; see 10.22n. 51–53: This introduces the reign of the Israelite king *Ahaziah* (ca. 852–851 BCE), which is continued in 2 Kings 1. Originally, the two books of Kings were a single book (see Introduction).

2 KINGS

For a discussion of the composition and character of 1–2 Kings, see the Introduction to 1 Kings (pp. 485–486).

NAME

In the Hebrew Bible the book of 2 Kings is called *Kings 2*, in the Greek Bible *Basileion 4* ("reigns" or "dynasties"). Originally 2 Kings was joined with 1 Kings as a single book.

CANONICAL STATUS AND LOCATION

In the Hebrew Bible, *Kings 2* is the last book of the "Former Prophets" (Josh, Judg, 1–2 Sam, 1–2 Kings). This book, which ends with the destruction of Jerusalem and the deportation of the Judeans to Babylon (others flee to Egypt), is followed by the book of Isaiah, which opens the "Latter Prophets." Thus 2 Kings offers background to the prophetic oracles of doom and restoration in the following prophetic books. In Christian Bibles 2 Kings is followed by 1–2 Chronicles, which has an alternate history of the period of the monarchy.

AUTHORSHIP AND DATE OF COMPOSITION

The authors and redactors of 2 Kings are the same as those of 1 Kings. Scholars often label them "Deuteronomists," because their language, style, and theological perspective are largely inspired by the book of Deuteronomy. The final episode in 2 Kings mentions the Babylonian king Evil-merodach, who ruled around 562 BCE, so the last redactor of the books must have lived after that.

STRUCTURE AND CONTENTS

Second Kings starts during the short reign of Ahaziah king of Israel, with a formula ("after the death of Ahab") that recalls the beginnings of the preceding books of Joshua, Judges, and 2 Samuel. The book is divided thematically into two parts: chs 1–17 continue the synchronic history of the two kingdoms of Judah and Israel until the fall of Samaria in the late eighth century; and chs 18–25 relate the last century and a half of the Judean kingdom until the Babylonian exile of 586. The first part contains several stories about the prophet Elisha (chs 2–8). After he is installed as Elijah's successor, he performs many miracles, several of which parallel tales told about Elijah: restoration of a spring in Jericho (Elisha provides water); punishment of jeering boys (Elisha provokes death); the everlasting oil; the purifying of a stew; the feeding of a hundred men (Elisha provides food); the revival of the Shunamite woman's son (Elisha provides life). Elisha also heals a leprous Aramean officer and recovers an ax head from the Jordan. But he appears also involved in high politics when he legitimates two coups d'état: he anoints the Aramean Hazael, and Jehu, who will exterminate the house of Ahab; the story of Jehu's revolution is told in chs 9–10.

The reign of queen Athaliah over Judah in ch 11 interrupts the Davidic dynasty, and is presented as illegitimate. The Davidic line continues with King Joash (ch 12), who escaped from Athaliah's massacre. Chapters 13–17 continue the parallel history of the two kingdoms, which is told from a clearly Judean perspective: the northern kings Jehoahaz, Jehoash, Jeroboam II, Zechariah, Shallum, Menachem, Pekahiah, Pekah, and Hoshea are altogether bad kings, since they continue the "sins of Jeroboam" (see 1 Kings 12), venerating the LORD outside Jerusalem and worshiping other deities. Among the Judean kings Jehoash, Amaziah, Azariah, and Jotham are considered good kings, although they are criticized for tolerating the high places outside Jerusalem. The Judean king Ahaz, however, is presented as walking in the way of the kings of Israel. Throughout this presentation parallels are drawn between Israel and Judah. The fall of Israel related in 2 Kings 17 does not mean that Judah will be safe forever. Chapter 17 provides a long commentary in typical Deuteronomistic style, which indicates the reasons that led to the end of the Northern Kingdom and its transformation into an Assyrian province; it also hints ahead at the destruction of Judah (vv. 19–20).

In the second part of 2 Kings (chs 18–25), which relates the story of the kingdom of Judah until its end, two kings, Hezekiah and Josiah, are presented in a very positive way. Hezekiah (chs 18–20) abolishes the illegitimate religious practices; under his reign the Assyrian siege of Jerusalem fails because of the LORD's intervention. His son Manasseh (ch 21) is presented as the worst of all kings of Judah, although he reigned for fifty-five years. He is explicitly compared to the worst Israelite king, Ahab, reintroducing forbidden religious practices; the redactor presents him as responsible for the later destruction of Jerusalem. He is succeeded by the wicked Amon, who is followed by Josiah, who undertakes a sweeping religious reform, making Jerusalem the only legitimate sanctuary for the worship of the LORD and destroying all symbols of unorthodox worship (chs 22–23). But Josiah is killed by the Egyptian king, and his four successors Jeoahaz, Jehoiakim, Jehoiachin, and Zedekiah (chs 23–24), act in a jarring contrast to him. The Deuteronomistic redactors judge them each with the same formula: "he did what was evil in the sight of the LORD, just as his father(s) had done." They hasten the destruction of Jerusalem by the Babylonians, who are presented as the tool of divine punishment (chs 24–25). The story ends with a short note about the release of the Judean king Jehoiachin from his Babylonian prison: he stays in Babylon but becomes a privileged guest at the table of the king of Babylon (25.27–30).

INTERPRETATION

Because 2 Kings is part of a single composition with 1 Kings, it is not surprising that it shares the same view of history that is presented there, offering not necessarily complete and accurate history but a theological explanation of the double failure of the northern and southern monarchies. For the authors of Kings, the north had been condemned from its very beginnings. For the Judean, Davidic kings the issue was more complicated. The LORD had promised to David an eternal dynasty (2 Sam 7), but Jerusalem had been destroyed and Judah had come under Babylonian domination. Did this mean that God did not stand by his word? The authors of Kings gave a double answer. First, they understood the promise as conditional: only if the kings behave according to God's commandments, as written down in the book of Deuteronomy, would there be always a Davidic king in Jerusalem (see, e.g., 1 Kings 9.4–7). Second, the mention of Jehoiachin's release out of his prison (2 Kings 25.27–30) may indicate hope for the future restoration of the Davidic monarchy. But the end of 2 Kings may also be understood otherwise (see 25.27–30n.).

GUIDE FOR READING

Since 2 Kings is not a self-contained book, the reader should start with 1 Kings or, even better, with the books of Samuel. The role played by the "good kings" Hezekiah and Josiah, and how their deeds cannot prevent the fall of Jerusalem and the Babylonian exile, deserve particular attention, as do the parallels between the miracles of Elisha and Elijah.

Thomas Römer

1

After the death of Ahab, Moab rebelled against Israel.

[2] Ahaziah had fallen through the lattice in his upper chamber in Samaria, and lay injured; so he sent messengers, telling them, "Go, inquire of Baal-zebub, the god of Ekron, whether I shall recover from this injury." [3] But the angel of the LORD said to Elijah the Tishbite, "Get up, go to meet the messengers of the king of Samaria, and say to them, 'Is it because there is no God in Israel that you are going to inquire of Baal-zebub, the god of Ekron?' [4] Now therefore thus says the LORD, 'You shall not leave the bed to which you have gone, but you shall surely die.'" So Elijah went.

[5] The messengers returned to the king, who said to them, "Why have you returned?" [6] They answered him, "There came a man to meet us, who said to us, 'Go back to the king who sent you, and say to him: Thus says the LORD: Is it because there is no God in Israel that you are sending to inquire of Baal-zebub, the god of Ekron? Therefore you shall not leave the bed to which you have gone, but shall surely die.'" [7] He said to them, "What sort of man was he who came to meet you and told you these things?" [8] They answered him, "A hairy man, with a leather belt around his waist." He said, "It is Elijah the Tishbite."

[9] Then the king sent to him a captain of fifty with his fifty men. He went up to Elijah, who was sitting on the top of a hill, and said to him, "O man of God, the king says, 'Come down.'" [10] But Elijah answered the captain of fifty, "If I am a man of God, let fire come down from heaven and consume you and your fifty." Then fire came down from heaven, and consumed him and his fifty.

[11] Again the king sent to him another captain of fifty with his fifty. He went up[a] and said to him, "O man of God, this is the king's order: Come down quickly!" [12] But Elijah answered them, "If I am a man of God, let fire come down from heaven and consume you and your fifty." Then the fire of God came down from heaven and consumed him and his fifty.

[13] Again the king sent the captain of a third fifty with his fifty. So the third captain of fifty went up, and came and fell on his knees before Elijah, and entreated him, "O man of God, please let my life, and the life of these fifty servants of yours, be precious in your sight. [14] Look, fire came down from heaven and consumed the two former captains of fifty men with their fifties; but now let my life be precious in your sight." [15] Then the angel of the LORD said to Elijah, "Go down with him; do not be afraid of him." So he set out and went down with him to the king, [16] and said to him, "Thus says the LORD: Because you have sent messengers to inquire of Baal-zebub, the god of Ekron,—is it because there is no God in Israel to inquire of his word?—therefore you shall not leave the bed to which you have gone, but you shall surely die."

---

[a] Gk Compare verses 9, 13: Heb *He answered*

1.1–17: The encounter between King Ahaziah and the prophet Elijah. 1: The notice *After the death of Ahab, Moab rebelled against Israel* also appears in 3.5 where it stands at a better place. **2–9:** Ahaziah, who falls through the *lattice* on the flat roof of his house, on part of which was built the *upper chamber*, perhaps a bedroom, wants to consult a local manifestation of the god Baal and is confronted by the prophet Elijah. **2:** *Baal-zebub* means "lord of the flies"; the second word is probably a parody by the biblical writers on a more original "zebul" ("prince"; cf. 1 Kings 16.31n.; Mk 3.22). *Ekron* is the northernmost of the Philistine cities, ca. 25 mi (40 km) west of Jerusalem. **3:** The *angel* (Heb "mal'ak," lit. "messenger") *of the LORD* is juxtaposed to Ahaziah's messengers. The word "mal'ak" may denote a human person or a supernatural being. **4–6:** The king's messengers receive their oracle not from Baal of Ekron but from Elijah, who speaks in the name of the LORD. **7–8:** The king identifies Elijah through his description as a *hairy man, with a leather belt*. This outfit may have been typical of prophetic groups that were hostile to urban culture (cf. Mk 1.6). **9–16:** This scene, where the king sends other messengers, contains a play on words: when the officer harshly asks the *man of God* (Heb "'ish 'elohim") to descend, Elijah instead sends down the *fire of God* ("'esh 'elohim"). **10:** *Fire* is often a tool of divine punishment (e.g., Gen 19.24; Lev 10.2; Num 16.35). **13–16:** The third officer behaves respectfully and Elijah comes down, but his oracle of death for the king is not altered. **17–18:** The notice that *Jehoram* of Israel becomes Ahaziah's successor in the second year of Jehoram of Judah disagrees with 3.1, where Jehoram of Israel becomes king in the eighteenth

The geography of chs. 1–14. The dashed line shows the approximate boundaries between Israel, Judah and Philistia.

---

[17] So he died according to the word of the LORD that Elijah had spoken. His brother,[a] Jehoram succeeded him as king in the second year of King Jehoram son of Jehoshaphat of Judah, because Ahaziah had no son. [18] Now the rest of the acts of Ahaziah that he did, are they not written in the Book of the Annals of the Kings of Israel?

2 Now when the LORD was about to take Elijah up to heaven by a whirlwind, Elijah and Elisha were on their way from Gilgal. [2] Elijah said to Elisha, "Stay here; for the LORD has sent me as far as Bethel." But Elisha said, "As the LORD lives, and as you yourself live,

a Gk Syr: Heb lacks *His brother*

year of Jehoshaphat of Judah. There may have been a coregency in Judah between Jehoshaphat and his son Jehoram, or there may be some textual or historical confusion because both kings in Judah and Israel had the same name.

2.1–18: Elisha succeeds Elijah. This narrative marks the transition between the narratives about Elijah and those about Elisha. **1:** This verse anticipates v. 11. *Gilgal*, located between Jericho and the Jordan, is Elisha's home, according to 4.38. **2–6:** The *company of prophets* designates a prophetic community near Bethel that has been informed about Elijah's imminent ascension. The supposed journey from Gilgal to Bethel and then

I will not leave you." So they went down to Bethel. [3] The company of prophets[a] who were in Bethel came out to Elisha, and said to him, "Do you know that today the LORD will take your master away from you?" And he said, "Yes, I know; keep silent."

[4] Elijah said to him, "Elisha, stay here; for the LORD has sent me to Jericho." But he said, "As the LORD lives, and as you yourself live, I will not leave you." So they came to Jericho. [5] The company of prophets[a] who were at Jericho drew near to Elisha, and said to him, "Do you know that today the LORD will take your master away from you?" And he answered, "Yes, I know; be silent."

[6] Then Elijah said to him, "Stay here; for the LORD has sent me to the Jordan." But he said, "As the LORD lives, and as you yourself live, I will not leave you." So the two of them went on. [7] Fifty men of the company of prophets[a] also went, and stood at some distance from them, as they both were standing by the Jordan. [8] Then Elijah took his mantle and rolled it up, and struck the water; the water was parted to the one side and to the other, until the two of them crossed on dry ground.

[9] When they had crossed, Elijah said to Elisha, "Tell me what I may do for you, before I am taken from you." Elisha said, "Please let me inherit a double share of your spirit." [10] He responded, "You have asked a hard thing; yet, if you see me as I am being taken from you, it will be granted you; if not, it will not." [11] As they continued walking and talking, a chariot of fire and horses of fire separated the two

of them, and Elijah ascended in a whirlwind into heaven. [12] Elisha kept watching and crying out, "Father, father! The chariots of Israel and its horsemen!" But when he could no longer see him, he grasped his own clothes and tore them in two pieces.

[13] He picked up the mantle of Elijah that had fallen from him, and went back and stood on the bank of the Jordan. [14] He took the mantle of Elijah that had fallen from him, and struck the water, saying, "Where is the LORD, the God of Elijah?" When he had struck the water, the water was parted to the one side and to the other, and Elisha went over.

[15] When the company of prophets[a] who were at Jericho saw him at a distance, they declared, "The spirit of Elijah rests on Elisha." They came to meet him and bowed to the ground before him. [16] They said to him, "See now, we have fifty strong men among your servants; please let them go and seek your master; it may be that the spirit of the LORD has caught him up and thrown him down on some mountain or into some valley." He responded, "No, do not send them." [17] But when they urged him until he was ashamed, he said, "Send them." So they sent fifty men who searched for three days but did not find him. [18] When they came back to him (he had remained at Jericho), he said to them, "Did I not say to you, Do not go?"

[19] Now the people of the city said to Elisha, "The location of this city is good, as my lord

---

[a] Heb *sons of the prophets*

back to Jericho is confusing, and may be a later element in the story. **7–8:** Elijah's *mantle,* already mentioned in 1 Kings 19.19. The parting of the waters of the Jordan recalls the crossing of that river by the Israelites under Joshua (Josh 3–4) and Moses' parting of the Sea of Reeds (Ex 14). **9–10:** Elisha is asking Elijah for a *double share of your spirit,* which according to Deut 21.17 was the share of the eldest son, who received twice as much as his brothers. With his request Elisha appears as Elijah's "eldest son" and successor. **11–12:** The *chariot of fire and horses* symbolize the divine army. Elijah goes to heaven in a *whirlwind,* or in a storm, which is one of the LORD's manifestations (Nah 1.3; Job 38.1; Ps 50.3) thereby integrating Elijah into the divine sphere. Such ascension is unique to Elijah in the Bible and explains Elijah's importance in Jewish tradition (see Mal 4.5–6). The phrase *the chariots of Israel and its horsemen* suggests that prophetic power equals the strength of cavalry; see also 13.14. **13–14:** Elisha's ability to repeat Elijah's parting of the water shows that he has received his master's spirit. **15–18:** The prophetic community (the "sons of the prophets"; see textual note *a*) near Jericho is aware that Elisha has become Elijah's successor, but they do not know that Elijah has been taken to heaven. Only Elisha has seen what happened in the whirlwind.

2.19–25: Elisha's first miracles. These miracles demonstrate that Elisha can either bless or curse in the name of God. **19–22:** He purifies an infected *spring* near Jericho, throwing salt in it. *Salt* was considered to have cleans-

sees; but the water is bad, and the land is unfruitful." ²⁰ He said, "Bring me a new bowl, and put salt in it." So they brought it to him. ²¹ Then he went to the spring of water and threw the salt into it, and said, "Thus says the LORD, I have made this water wholesome; from now on neither death nor miscarriage shall come from it." ²² So the water has been wholesome to this day, according to the word that Elisha spoke.

²³ He went up from there to Bethel; and while he was going up on the way, some small boys came out of the city and jeered at him, saying, "Go away, baldhead! Go away, baldhead!" ²⁴ When he turned around and saw them, he cursed them in the name of the LORD. Then two she-bears came out of the woods and mauled forty-two of the boys. ²⁵ From there he went on to Mount Carmel, and then returned to Samaria.

3 In the eighteenth year of King Jehoshaphat of Judah, Jehoram son of Ahab became king over Israel in Samaria; he reigned twelve years. ² He did what was evil in the sight of the LORD, though not like his father and mother, for he removed the pillar of Baal that his father had made. ³ Nevertheless he clung to the sin of Jeroboam son of Nebat, which he caused Israel to commit; he did not depart from it.

⁴ Now King Mesha of Moab was a sheep breeder, who used to deliver to the king of Israel one hundred thousand lambs, and the wool of one hundred thousand rams. ⁵ But when Ahab died, the king of Moab rebelled against the king of Israel. ⁶ So King Jehoram marched out of Samaria at that time and mustered all Israel. ⁷ As he went he sent word to King Jehoshaphat of Judah, "The king of Moab has rebelled against me; will you go with me to battle against Moab?" He answered, "I will; I am with you, my people are your people, my horses are your horses." ⁸ Then he asked, "By which way shall we march?" Jehoram answered, "By the way of the wilderness of Edom."

⁹ So the king of Israel, the king of Judah, and the king of Edom set out; and when they had made a roundabout march of seven days, there was no water for the army or for the animals that were with them. ¹⁰ Then the king of Israel said, "Alas! The LORD has summoned us, three kings, only to be handed over to Moab." ¹¹ But Jehoshaphat said, "Is there no prophet of the LORD here, through whom we may inquire of the LORD?" Then one of the servants of the king of Israel answered, "Elisha son of Shaphat, who used to pour water on the hands of Elijah, is here." ¹² Jehoshaphat said, "The word of the LORD is with him." So the king of Israel and Jehoshaphat and the king of Edom went down to him.

¹³ Elisha said to the king of Israel, "What have I to do with you? Go to your father's

---

ing and protective capacities. **23–25:** The episode of the cursing of the boys of Bethel who jeered at the prophet seems shocking to modern readers. For the ancient reader it demonstrated that it was dangerous to behave disrespectfully toward a man of God. **24:** The narrator does not tell the content of Elisha's *curse*, and whether or not he intended to kill the boys. *Forty-two boys*, "forty-two" is a number sometimes associated with death: Jehu kills forty-two victims (10.14), and the Egyptian Book of the Dead mentions forty-two judges of the dead. **25:** Elisha's travel to *Mount Carmel* recalls Elijah's victory against the prophets of Baal, and helps establish Elisha as a new Elijah.

3.1–27: Jehoram of Israel, Elisha and the war against Moab. 1–3: *Jehoram's* behavior is less wicked that that of his father *Ahab*. For the chronological problem see 1.17–18n. **3:** The *sin of Jeroboam* designates illicit worship outside of Jerusalem (see 1 Kings 12). **4–8:** The campaign against Moab echoes the war report of 1 Kings 22. *Jehoshaphat*, previously allied to Ahab, is now an ally, or even vassal, of Ahab's son (cf. v. 7 and 1 Kings 22.4). **4–5:** King *Mesha* of Moab is also known from the Moabite Stone discovered in 1868, a stela with an inscription celebrating Mesha's victory over Israel, which may allude to the revolt mentioned in v. 5. **8:** The descent to *Edom* in the south is necessary because of the Moabite fortifications in the north. **9:** The mention of *the king of Edom* may be inaccurate (see 1 Kings 22.47). **10–12:** Unlike the Israelite king, who is afraid that the LORD may have gathered the allies for their demise, the pious Judean king asks for a prophet of the LORD. **11:** Elisha pouring *water on the hands of Elijah* recalls his relationship to his prophetic predecessor; this is a gesture of deference, as of a servant to his master or of a son to his father. The mention of *water* also alludes to the water miracle that follows. **13–14:** Elisha represents the position of the Judean redactors of the book of Kings that only

prophets or to your mother's." But the king of Israel said to him, "No; it is the Lord who has summoned us, three kings, only to be handed over to Moab." ¹⁴ Elisha said, "As the Lord of hosts lives, whom I serve, were it not that I have regard for King Jehoshaphat of Judah, I would give you neither a look nor a glance. ¹⁵ But get me a musician." And then, while the musician was playing, the power of the Lord came on him. ¹⁶ And he said, "Thus says the Lord, 'I will make this wadi full of pools.' ¹⁷ For thus says the Lord, 'You shall see neither wind nor rain, but the wadi shall be filled with water, so that you shall drink, you, your cattle, and your animals.' ¹⁸ This is only a trifle in the sight of the Lord, for he will also hand Moab over to you. ¹⁹ You shall conquer every fortified city and every choice city; every good tree you shall fell, all springs of water you shall stop up, and every good piece of land you shall ruin with stones." ²⁰ The next day, about the time of the morning offering, suddenly water began to flow from the direction of Edom, until the country was filled with water.

²¹ When all the Moabites heard that the kings had come up to fight against them, all who were able to put on armor, from the youngest to the oldest, were called out and were drawn up at the frontier. ²² When they rose early in the morning, and the sun shone upon the water, the Moabites saw the water opposite them as red as blood. ²³ They said, "This is blood; the kings must have fought together, and killed one another. Now then, Moab, to the spoil!" ²⁴ But when they came

to the camp of Israel, the Israelites rose up and attacked the Moabites, who fled before them; as they entered Moab they continued the attack.ᵃ ²⁵ The cities they overturned, and on every good piece of land everyone threw a stone, until it was covered; every spring of water they stopped up, and every good tree they felled. Only at Kir-hareseth did the stone walls remain, until the slingers surrounded and attacked it. ²⁶ When the king of Moab saw that the battle was going against him, he took with him seven hundred swordsmen to break through, opposite the king of Edom; but they could not. ²⁷ Then he took his firstborn son who was to succeed him, and offered him as a burnt offering on the wall. And great wrath came upon Israel, so they withdrew from him and returned to their own land.

4 Now the wife of a member of the company of prophetsᵇ cried to Elisha, "Your servant my husband is dead; and you know that your servant feared the Lord, but a creditor has come to take my two children as slaves." ² Elisha said to her, "What shall I do for you? Tell me, what do you have in the house?" She answered, "Your servant has nothing in the house, except a jar of oil." ³ He said, "Go outside, borrow vessels from all your neighbors, empty vessels and not just a few. ⁴ Then go in, and shut the door behind you and your children, and start pouring into all these vessels; when each is full, set it aside." ⁵ So she left him and shut the

ᵃ Compare Gk Syr: Meaning of Heb uncertain
ᵇ Heb the sons of the prophets

Judean kings are worthy of divine help. **15:** Music induced ecstasy through which the prophet prophesied (cf. 1 Sam 10.5–6). *The power of the Lord*, lit. "the hand of the Lord." **16–19:** Elisha predicts water and a (first) victory over Moab. **16:** *Pools*, or ditches. Groundwater can be obtained in a desert terrain by tapping the water table, but according to Elisha's oracle the gift of water is a miracle. **20–25:** After the fulfillment of the water miracle (v. 20), the allies are successful in their war against Moab. **22–23:** The red light of the rising sun on the water deceives the Moabites, who think it is the *blood* of the allies' armies. **24–25:** Large parts of the Moabite territory were destroyed, but not *Kir-hareseth* ("Fortress of the guard," modern Kerak). **26–27:** The king of Moab, seeing no chance to escape, sacrifices his *firstborn son* to his god Chemosh. The *great wrath* originally referred to the wrath of Chemosh, who responded positively to this human offering by decimating the Israelite army. The biblical redactors probably understood it as a kind of disgust that repelled the Israelites.

4.1–44: Further miracles by Elisha. Elisha is more of a miracle worker than Elijah; some miracles that are told of both belonged originally to the Elisha traditions. **1–7:** The oil miracle is similar to the story in 1 Kings 17.7–16. **1:** A widow of one of the prophetic groups over which Elisha apparently exercises leadership (the dead prophet is called *servant* of Elisha) is obliged to sell her *children as slaves* in order to pay her debts (see Ex 21.7; Neh 5.5). **2–7:** Elisha does not play an active role in the production of abundant oil; he only tells the woman what she has

door behind her and her children; they kept bringing vessels to her, and she kept pouring. ⁶ When the vessels were full, she said to her son, "Bring me another vessel." But he said to her, "There are no more." Then the oil stopped flowing. ⁷ She came and told the man of God, and he said, "Go sell the oil and pay your debts, and you and your children can live on the rest."

⁸ One day Elisha was passing through Shunem, where a wealthy woman lived, who urged him to have a meal. So whenever he passed that way, he would stop there for a meal. ⁹ She said to her husband, "Look, I am sure that this man who regularly passes our way is a holy man of God. ¹⁰ Let us make a small roof chamber with walls, and put there for him a bed, a table, a chair, and a lamp, so that he can stay there whenever he comes to us."

¹¹ One day when he came there, he went up to the chamber and lay down there. ¹² He said to his servant Gehazi, "Call the Shunammite woman." When he had called her, she stood before him. ¹³ He said to him, "Say to her, Since you have taken all this trouble for us, what may be done for you? Would you have a word spoken on your behalf to the king or to the commander of the army?" She answered, "I live among my own people." ¹⁴ He said, "What then may be done for her?" Gehazi answered, "Well, she has no son, and her husband is old." ¹⁵ He said, "Call her." When he had called her, she stood at the door. ¹⁶ He said, "At this season, in due time, you shall embrace a son." She replied, "No, my lord, O man of God; do not deceive your servant."

¹⁷ The woman conceived and bore a son at that season, in due time, as Elisha had declared to her.

¹⁸ When the child was older, he went out one day to his father among the reapers. ¹⁹ He complained to his father, "Oh, my head, my head!" The father said to his servant, "Carry him to his mother." ²⁰ He carried him and brought him to his mother; the child sat on her lap until noon, and he died. ²¹ She went up and laid him on the bed of the man of God, closed the door on him, and left. ²² Then she called to her husband, and said, "Send me one of the servants and one of the donkeys, so that I may quickly go to the man of God and come back again." ²³ He said, "Why go to him today? It is neither new moon nor sabbath." She said, "It will be all right." ²⁴ Then she saddled the donkey and said to her servant, "Urge the animal on; do not hold back for me unless I tell you." ²⁵ So she set out, and came to the man of God at Mount Carmel.

When the man of God saw her coming, he said to Gehazi his servant, "Look, there is the Shunammite woman; ²⁶ run at once to meet her, and say to her, Are you all right? Is your husband all right? Is the child all right?" She answered, "It is all right." ²⁷ When she came to the man of God at the mountain, she caught hold of his feet. Gehazi approached to push her away. But the man of God said, "Let her alone, for she is in bitter distress; the LORD has hidden it from me and has not told me." ²⁸ Then she said, "Did I ask my lord for a son? Did I not say, Do not mislead me?" ²⁹ He said to Gehazi, "Gird up your loins, and take my staff in your hand, and go. If you meet anyone, give no greeting, and if anyone greets you, do not answer; and lay my staff on the face of the child." ³⁰ Then the mother of the child said, "As the LORD lives, and as you yourself live, I will not leave without you." So he rose up and followed her. ³¹ Gehazi went

to do. **8–37:** The boy's revival is reminiscent of 1 Kings 17.17–24. **8:** *Shunem*, a town in the Jezreel Valley ca. 10 mi (16 km) east of Megiddo. **9–17:** Elisha's visit to the house of a childless and aged couple and his promise of a son that shall be born to them because of their hospitality recalls Gen 18.1–15. **12:** *Gehazi* is Elisha's personal servant and mediator between him and the hosts. **18–31:** After her son dies unexpectedly the mother travels to *Mount Carmel*, where Elisha resides (see v. 25). **21:** The placing of the dead son in the chamber that was reserved for Elisha can be understood either as a reproach to Elisha (see also v. 28) or as an attempt to retain the "soul," the life-essence of the boy. **23:** *It is neither new moon nor Sabbath*, it was apparently the custom to consult prophets on such holy days. **24–25:** The story highlights the woman's initiative (she *saddled* and rode *the donkey*), whereas her husband appears to be passive and resigned. **29–31:** The dispatch of Gehazi with Elisha's *staff* (see Moses' staff in Ex 4.1–4; 17.8–13) was meant to allay the mother's impatience, since Gehazi is able to reach Shunem quicker than Elisha. In other ancient Near Eastern texts, prophets also send items that belong to them

on ahead and laid the staff on the face of the child, but there was no sound or sign of life. He came back to meet him and told him, "The child has not awakened."

[32] When Elisha came into the house, he saw the child lying dead on his bed. [33] So he went in and closed the door on the two of them, and prayed to the LORD. [34] Then he got up on the bed[a] and lay upon the child, putting his mouth upon his mouth, his eyes upon his eyes, and his hands upon his hands; and while he lay bent over him, the flesh of the child became warm. [35] He got down, walked once to and fro in the room, then got up again and bent over him; the child sneezed seven times, and the child opened his eyes. [36] Elisha[b] summoned Gehazi and said, "Call the Shunammite woman." So he called her. When she came to him, he said, "Take your son." [37] She came and fell at his feet, bowing to the ground; then she took her son and left.

[38] When Elisha returned to Gilgal, there was a famine in the land. As the company of prophets was[c] sitting before him, he said to his servant, "Put the large pot on, and make some stew for the company of prophets."[d] [39] One of them went out into the field to gather herbs; he found a wild vine and gathered from it a lapful of wild gourds, and came and cut them up into the pot of stew, not knowing what they were. [40] They served some for the men to eat. But while they were eating the stew, they cried out, "O man of God, there is death in the pot!" They could not eat it. [41] He said, "Then bring some flour." He threw it into the pot, and said, "Serve the people and let them eat." And there was nothing harmful in the pot.

[42] A man came from Baal-shalishah, bringing food from the first fruits to the man of God: twenty loaves of barley and fresh ears of grain in his sack. Elisha said, "Give it to the people and let them eat." [43] But his servant said, "How can I set this before a hundred people?" So he repeated, "Give it to the people and let them eat, for thus says the LORD, 'They shall eat and have some left.'" [44] He set it before them, they ate, and had some left, according to the word of the LORD.

5 Naaman, commander of the army of the king of Aram, was a great man and in high favor with his master, because by him the LORD had given victory to Aram. The man, though a mighty warrior, suffered from leprosy.[e] [2] Now the Arameans on one of their raids had taken a young girl captive from the land of Israel, and she served Naaman's wife. [3] She said to her mistress, "If only my lord were with the prophet who is in Samaria! He would cure him of his leprosy."[e] [4] So Naaman[b] went in and told his lord just what the girl from the land of Israel had said. [5] And the king of Aram said, "Go then, and I will send along a letter to the king of Israel."

a   Heb lacks *on the bed*
b   Heb *he*
c   Heb *sons of the prophets were*
d   Heb *sons of the prophets*
e   A term for several skin diseases; precise meaning uncertain

in order to accomplish a miracle. **32–37:** Gehazi's failure highlights the effect of Elisha's personal appearance and success. **33:** Elisha's prayer to the LORD precedes his mysterious actions. **34–35:** Crouching over the boy's body suggests a magic ritual in which the properties of the living party were transferred to the dead. *The child sneezed seven times*, the sneezing signifies that life has returned. Seven is the number of perfection. **38–41:** Elisha appears again as providing food. He makes a poisoned meal edible by adding some *flour*. **42–44:** Elisha's multiplication of food provides the pattern for the stories about Jesus doing the same in the Gospels. **42:** *Baal-shalishah*, located in the hills of Ephraim ca. 11 mi (18 km) southwest of Samaria.

5.1–27: Elisha heals an Aramean officer. This story teaches that the LORD is not only the god of the Israelites but also the god of the foreigners. **1:** *Naaman*, a name meaning "gracious," which is attested in the ancient Near East as a proper name as well as an epithet of royal personages. His *leprosy* (see textual note e) was not contagious and did not exclude him from society. **2–7:** Informed by an Israelite maidservant about Elisha's power, the contact is established by a *letter* of the Aramean king to the king of Israel. **3:** *The prophet who is in Samaria* refers to Elisha, who in this story is not associated with a prophetic community but lives alone in Samaria, the capital of the Northern Kingdom. **5–7:** Despite the excessive gifts (*ten talents*, ca. 340 kg [755 lb], *of silver* and *six thousand shekels*, ca. 70 kg [150 lb] *of gold*), the Israelite king suspects that the Aramean king is seeking an occasion

He went, taking with him ten talents of silver, six thousand shekels of gold, and ten sets of garments. [6] He brought the letter to the king of Israel, which read, "When this letter reaches you, know that I have sent to you my servant Naaman, that you may cure him of his leprosy."[a] [7] When the king of Israel read the letter, he tore his clothes and said, "Am I God, to give death or life, that this man sends word to me to cure a man of his leprosy?[a] Just look and see how he is trying to pick a quarrel with me."

[8] But when Elisha the man of God heard that the king of Israel had torn his clothes, he sent a message to the king, "Why have you torn your clothes? Let him come to me, that he may learn that there is a prophet in Israel." [9] So Naaman came with his horses and chariots, and halted at the entrance of Elisha's house. [10] Elisha sent a messenger to him, saying, "Go, wash in the Jordan seven times, and your flesh shall be restored and you shall be clean." [11] But Naaman became angry and went away, saying, "I thought that for me he would surely come out, and stand and call on the name of the LORD his God, and would wave his hand over the spot, and cure the leprosy![a] [12] Are not Abana[b] and Pharpar, the rivers of Damascus, better than all the waters of Israel? Could I not wash in them, and be clean?" He turned and went away in a rage. [13] But his servants approached and said to him, "Father, if the prophet had commanded you to do something difficult, would you not have done it? How much more, when all he said to you was, 'Wash, and be clean'?" [14] So he went down and immersed himself seven times in the Jordan, according to the word of the man of God; his flesh was restored like the flesh of a young boy, and he was clean.

[15] Then he returned to the man of God, he and all his company; he came and stood before him and said, "Now I know that there is no God in all the earth except in Israel; please accept a present from your servant." [16] But he said, "As the LORD lives, whom I serve, I will accept nothing!" He urged him to accept, but he refused. [17] Then Naaman said, "If not, please let two mule-loads of earth be given to your servant; for your servant will no longer offer burnt offering or sacrifice to any god except the LORD. [18] But may the LORD pardon your servant on one count: when my master goes into the house of Rimmon to worship there, leaning on my arm, and I bow down in the house of Rimmon, when I do bow down in the house of Rimmon, may the LORD pardon your servant on this one count." [19] He said to him, "Go in peace."

But when Naaman had gone from him a short distance, [20] Gehazi, the servant of Elisha the man of God, thought, "My master has let that Aramean Naaman off too lightly by not accepting from him what he offered. As the LORD lives, I will run after him and get something out of him." [21] So Gehazi went after Naaman. When Naaman saw someone running after him, he jumped down from the chariot to meet him and said, "Is everything all right?" [22] He replied, "Yes, but my master has sent me to say, 'Two members of a company of prophets[c] have just come to me from the hill country of Ephraim; please give them a talent of silver and two changes of clothing.'" [23] Naaman said, "Please accept two talents." He urged him, and tied up two talents of silver in two bags, with two changes of clothing, and gave them to two of his servants, who carried them in front of Gehazi.[d]

---

[a] A term for several skin diseases; precise meaning uncertain
[b] Another reading is *Amana*
[c] Heb *sons of the prophets*
[d] Heb *him*

---

for war. **8–13:** Elisha's laconic advice to Naaman to *wash seven times* (see 4.35n.) *in the Jordan* is taken by Naaman as insulting. **13:** His servants persuade him to reconsider his hasty interpretation of Elisha's words. *Father*, a title of respect referring to a superior. **14–15:** After his healing, Naaman proclaims a monotheistic confession, which recalls Rahab's confession (Josh 2.11): the LORD is not only the God of Israel, but of *all the earth*. **16–17:** In order to worship the LORD outside of Israel, Naaman wants to take with him Israelite *earth*, i.e., "soil." **18:** After Naaman's conversion, he cannot offend his king who venerates *Rimmon*, so he will only pretend to worship this "false" god. The vocalization Rimmon (which means "pomegranate") may be a parody of the name of the Aramean weather-god Hadad Ramanu ("the Thunderer"). **19–27:** Whereas Elisha had refused any payment (v.

24 When he came to the citadel, he took the bags[a] from them, and stored them inside; he dismissed the men, and they left.

25 He went in and stood before his master; and Elisha said to him, "Where have you been, Gehazi?" He answered, "Your servant has not gone anywhere at all." 26 But he said to him, "Did I not go with you in spirit when someone left his chariot to meet you? Is this a time to accept money and to accept clothing, olive orchards and vineyards, sheep and oxen, and male and female slaves? 27 Therefore the leprosy[b] of Naaman shall cling to you, and to your descendants forever." So he left his presence leprous,[b] as white as snow.

6 Now the company of prophets[c] said to Elisha, "As you see, the place where we live under your charge is too small for us. 2 Let us go to the Jordan, and let us collect logs there, one for each of us, and build a place there for us to live." He answered, "Do so." 3 Then one of them said, "Please come with your servants." And he answered, "I will." 4 So he went with them. When they came to the Jordan, they cut down trees. 5 But as one was felling a log, his ax head fell into the water; he cried out, "Alas, master! It was borrowed." 6 Then the man of God said, "Where did it fall?" When he showed him the place, he cut off a stick, and threw it in there, and made the iron float. 7 He said, "Pick it up." So he reached out his hand and took it.

8 Once when the king of Aram was at war with Israel, he took counsel with his officers. He said, "At such and such a place shall be my camp." 9 But the man of God sent word to the king of Israel, "Take care not to pass this place, because the Arameans are going down there." 10 The king of Israel sent word to the place of which the man of God spoke. More than once or twice he warned such a place[d] so that it was on the alert.

11 The mind of the king of Aram was greatly perturbed because of this; he called his officers and said to them, "Now tell me who among us sides with the king of Israel?" 12 Then one of his officers said, "No one, my lord king. It is Elisha, the prophet in Israel, who tells the king of Israel the words that you speak in your bedchamber." 13 He said, "Go and find where he is; I will send and seize him." He was told, "He is in Dothan." 14 So he sent horses and chariots there and a great army; they came by night, and surrounded the city.

15 When an attendant of the man of God rose early in the morning and went out, an army with horses and chariots was all around the city. His servant said, "Alas, master! What shall we do?" 16 He replied, "Do not be afraid, for there are more with us than there are with them." 17 Then Elisha prayed: "O LORD, please open his eyes that he may see." So the LORD opened the eyes of the servant, and he saw; the mountain was full of horses and chariots of fire all around Elisha. 18 When the Arameans[e] came down against him, Elisha prayed to the LORD, and said, "Strike this people, please, with blindness." So he struck them with blindness as Elisha had asked.

a   Heb lacks the bags
b   A term for several skin diseases; precise meaning uncertain
c   Heb sons of the prophets
d   Heb warned it
e   Heb they

16) his servant Gehazi is eager for profit and is punished for that. 27: Gehazi, who pursued profit from the healed Naaman, is now afflicted with his disease. Leprous, as white as snow, the same punishment happened to Miriam, who had criticized Moses (Num 12.10).

6.1–7: Elisha makes iron float. Another miracle story that illustrates the prophetic community's dependence on its master. 5: It was borrowed, the community could not afford to have its own ax, so Elisha's help is vital.

6.8–23: Elisha and the Aramean invasion. 8–10: Elisha forewarns the king of Israel about an Aramean attack. 8: At war, refers probably to border raids as in 5.2. The king of Aram, his name is not mentioned, which may indicate the episode's legendary character. 11–14: The Aramean king suspects betrayal, but he is told that Elisha knows everything, even the words spoken in the king's bedchamber (v. 12), the most intimate part of the royal palace. 13: Now Elisha is in Dothan (see Gen 37.17), located ca. 11 mi (18 km) north of Samaria. 15–23: The two scenes are connected by the motif of blindness. 15–17: When the LORD opens the eyes of Elisha's servant, he sees the celestial army, horses and chariots of fire (see 2.11–12n.). 18–23: When the LORD opens the eyes of

¹⁹ Elisha said to them, "This is not the way, and this is not the city; follow me, and I will bring you to the man whom you seek." And he led them to Samaria.

²⁰ As soon as they entered Samaria, Elisha said, "O LORD, open the eyes of these men so that they may see." The LORD opened their eyes, and they saw that they were inside Samaria. ²¹ When the king of Israel saw them he said to Elisha, "Father, shall I kill them? Shall I kill them?" ²² He answered, "No! Did you capture with your sword and your bow those whom you want to kill? Set food and water before them so that they may eat and drink; and let them go to their master." ²³ So he prepared for them a great feast; after they ate and drank, he sent them on their way, and they went to their master. And the Arameans no longer came raiding into the land of Israel.

²⁴ Some time later King Ben-hadad of Aram mustered his entire army; he marched against Samaria and laid siege to it. ²⁵ As the siege continued, famine in Samaria became so great that a donkey's head was sold for eighty shekels of silver, and one-fourth of a kab of dove's dung for five shekels of silver. ²⁶ Now as the king of Israel was walking on the city wall, a woman cried out to him, "Help, my lord king!" ²⁷ He said, "No! Let the LORD help you. How can I help you? From the threshing floor or from the wine press?" ²⁸ But then the king asked her, "What is your complaint?" She answered, "This woman said to me, 'Give up your son; we will eat him today, and we will eat my son tomorrow.' ²⁹ So we cooked my son and ate him. The next day I said to her, 'Give up your son and we will eat him.' But she has hidden her son." ³⁰ When the

king heard the words of the woman he tore his clothes—now since he was walking on the city wall, the people could see that he had sackcloth on his body underneath— ³¹ and he said, "So may God do to me, and more, if the head of Elisha son of Shaphat stays on his shoulders today." ³² So he dispatched a man from his presence.

Now Elisha was sitting in his house, and the elders were sitting with him. Before the messenger arrived, Elisha said to the elders, "Are you aware that this murderer has sent someone to take off my head? When the messenger comes, see that you shut the door and hold it closed against him. Is not the sound of his master's feet behind him?" ³³ While he was still speaking with them, the king[a] came down to him and said, "This trouble is from the LORD! Why should I hope in the LORD any longer?"

7 ¹ But Elisha said, "Hear the word of the LORD: thus says the LORD, Tomorrow about this time a measure of choice meal shall be sold for a shekel, and two measures of barley for a shekel, at the gate of Samaria." ² Then the captain on whose hand the king leaned said to the man of God, "Even if the LORD were to make windows in the sky, could such a thing happen?" But he said, "You shall see it with your own eyes, but you shall not eat from it."

³ Now there were four leprous[b] men outside the city gate, who said to one another, "Why should we sit here until we die? ⁴ If we say, 'Let us enter the city,' the famine is in the

[a] See 7.2: Heb messenger
[b] A term for several skin diseases; precise meaning uncertain

the Arameans they discover that they have been captured. 21–23: Elisha prevents the Israelite king from killing them so that they can report the power of the God of Israel to their king. 21: Father, see 5.13n. 6.24–7.20: Elisha and the siege of Samaria. This story, which relates a second siege of the capital of the Northern Kingdom (for the first, see 1 Kings 20.1) by Ben-hadad of Aram, incorporates several originally independent anecdotes. 24–30: Two examples are given in order to illustrate the severity of the famine during the siege. 25: First, the exorbitant prices for the little remaining barely edible food: eighty shekels of silver (2 lb [900 gr]) for a donkey's head; five shekels (ca. 2 oz [57 gr]) for a kab (ca 1.1 qt [1.3 liters] of dove's dung. 26–29: Second, an episode about women eating their children. Cannibalism is mentioned as a consequence of siege elsewhere in the Hebrew Bible (Deut 28.53–57; Ezek 5.10; Lam 2.20; 4.10) and in nonbiblical texts. 30–31: The Israelite king, who has been wearing sackcloth, as a sign of humiliation and repentance, sees no way to help his people and irrationally seeks vengeance on the prophet Elisha. 6.32–7.2: Elisha however is under the protection of the local elders (v. 32) and announces that the following day food will be available in Samaria at normal prices. 7.1: A measure (Heb "se'ah"), ca. 7.7 liters (7 qt). 3–5: The four leprous men are ritually impure so they have to reside

city, and we shall die there; but if we sit here, we shall also die. Therefore, let us desert to the Aramean camp; if they spare our lives, we shall live; and if they kill us, we shall but die." [5] So they arose at twilight to go to the Aramean camp; but when they came to the edge of the Aramean camp, there was no one there at all. [6] For the Lord had caused the Aramean army to hear the sound of chariots, and of horses, the sound of a great army, so that they said to one another, "The king of Israel has hired the kings of the Hittites and the kings of Egypt to fight against us." [7] So they fled away in the twilight and abandoned their tents, their horses, and their donkeys leaving the camp just as it was, and fled for their lives. [8] When these leprous[a] men had come to the edge of the camp, they went into a tent, ate and drank, carried off silver, gold, and clothing, and went and hid them. Then they came back, entered another tent, carried off things from it, and went and hid them.

[9] Then they said to one another, "What we are doing is wrong. This is a day of good news; if we are silent and wait until the morning light, we will be found guilty; therefore let us go and tell the king's household." [10] So they came and called to the gatekeepers of the city, and told them, "We went to the Aramean camp, but there was no one to be seen or heard there, nothing but the horses tied, the donkeys tied, and the tents as they were." [11] Then the gatekeepers called out and proclaimed it to the king's household. [12] The king got up in the night, and said to his servants, "I will tell you what the Arameans have prepared against us. They know that we are starving; so they have left the camp to hide themselves in the open country, thinking, 'When they come out of the city, we shall

take them alive and get into the city.'" [13] One of his servants said, "Let some men take five of the remaining horses, since those left here will suffer the fate of the whole multitude of Israel that have perished already;[b] let us send and find out." [14] So they took two mounted men, and the king sent them after the Aramean army, saying, "Go and find out." [15] So they went after them as far as the Jordan; the whole way was littered with garments and equipment that the Arameans had thrown away in their haste. So the messengers returned, and told the king.

[16] Then the people went out, and plundered the camp of the Arameans. So a measure of choice meal was sold for a shekel, and two measures of barley for a shekel, according to the word of the LORD. [17] Now the king had appointed the captain on whose hand he leaned to have charge of the gate; the people trampled him to death in the gate, just as the man of God had said when the king came down to him. [18] For when the man of God had said to the king, "Two measures of barley shall be sold for a shekel, and a measure of choice meal for a shekel, about this time tomorrow in the gate of Samaria," [19] the captain had answered the man of God, "Even if the LORD were to make windows in the sky, could such a thing happen?" And he had answered, "You shall see it with your own eyes, but you shall not eat from it." [20] It did indeed happen to him; the people trampled him to death in the gate.

8 Now Elisha had said to the woman whose son he had restored to life, "Get up and go with your household, and settle wherever

---

[a] A term for several skin diseases; precise meaning uncertain

[b] Compare Gk Syr Vg: Meaning of Heb uncertain

---

outside the city (see Lev 13.46). Deserting to the Arameans, they find their camp empty. **6–7:** The narrator tells why the camp was abandoned: the LORD has made the Arameans hear the sound of a great army, which they interpreted as the army of the *Hittites* and the *Egyptians*, frequent rivals for control of the Levant. **8–20:** The Israelite king interprets the emptiness of the Aramean camp as military strategy; he is finally convinced that the LORD has intervened in favor of Israel. **14:** *Two mounted men,* better "two chariot teams." **18–19:** This verbatim repetition of Elisha's oracle and the answer of the skeptical officer in vv. 1–2 shows that the prophetic word has been fulfilled. **17,20:** Standing at the gate of Samaria where he had asserted that there would be no food available (vv. 1–2), the officer is trampled to death in the scramble to acquire food.

8.1–6: Elisha saves the life of the Shunammite woman. This story is related to the preceding one by the theme of *famine.* **1–3:** Warned by the prophet, the woman, whose son Elisha has brought back to life (4.32–37), escapes a famine with her son (see v. 5) by sojourning as an immigrant in the land of the Philistines. Her long

you can; for the LORD has called for a famine, and it will come on the land for seven years." [2] So the woman got up and did according to the word of the man of God; she went with her household and settled in the land of the Philistines seven years. [3] At the end of the seven years, when the woman returned from the land of the Philistines, she set out to appeal to the king for her house and her land. [4] Now the king was talking with Gehazi the servant of the man of God, saying, "Tell me all the great things that Elisha has done." [5] While he was telling the king how Elisha had restored a dead person to life, the woman whose son he had restored to life appealed to the king for her house and her land. Gehazi said, "My lord king, here is the woman, and here is her son whom Elisha restored to life." [6] When the king questioned the woman, she told him. So the king appointed an official for her, saying, "Restore all that was hers, together with all the revenue of the fields from the day that she left the land until now."

[7] Elisha went to Damascus while King Ben-hadad of Aram was ill. When it was told him, "The man of God has come here," [8] the king said to Hazael, "Take a present with you and go to meet the man of God. Inquire of the LORD through him, whether I shall recover from this illness." [9] So Hazael went to meet him, taking a present with him, all kinds of goods of Damascus, forty camel loads. When he entered and stood before him, he said, "Your son King Ben-hadad of Aram has sent me to you, saying, 'Shall I recover from this illness?'" [10] Elisha said to him, "Go, say to him, 'You shall certainly recover'; but the LORD has shown me that he shall certainly die." [11] He fixed his gaze and stared at him, until he was ashamed. Then the man of God wept. [12] Hazael asked, "Why does my lord weep?" He answered, "Because I know the evil that you will do to the people of Israel; you will set their fortresses on fire, you will kill their young men with the sword, dash in pieces their little ones, and rip up their pregnant women." [13] Hazael said, "What is your servant, who is a mere dog, that he should do this great thing?" Elisha answered, "The LORD has shown me that you are to be king over Aram." [14] Then he left Elisha, and went to his master Ben-hadad,[a] who said to him, "What did Elisha say to you?" And he answered, "He told me that you would certainly recover." [15] But the next day he took the bed-cover and dipped it in water and spread it over the king's face, until he died. And Hazael succeeded him.

[16] In the fifth year of King Joram son of Ahab of Israel,[b] Jehoram son of King Jehoshaphat of Judah began to reign. [17] He was thirty-two years old when he became king, and he reigned eight years in Jerusalem. [18] He walked in the way of the kings of Israel, as the house of Ahab had done, for the daughter of

a   Heb lacks *Ben-hadad*
b   Gk Syr: Heb adds *Jehoshaphat being king of Judah,*

absence (*seven years*) makes her lose her estate; it may have become crown property. **4–6:** Her appeal to the king succeeds because of her close relationship with Elisha.

8.7–15: Elisha and the Aramean kings Ben-hadad and Hazael. This story is difficult to understand, in part because of later redactors who connected it to 1 Kings 19.15, where Elijah is told to anoint Hazael king of Aram. **7–10:** Elisha's response to Hazael, who has been sent by Ben-hadad to *inquire of the LORD* about his illness, appears as a deliberate misleading of the Aramean king. Hazael should tell the king that he will recover (see v. 14), but in fact he will die through Hazael's hands (v. 15). Elisha's behavior was absent in the older story, which reported only an oracle of healing. The killing of the king was Hazael's own initiative. **9:** *Your son*, an expression of deference. **11–15:** Elisha foresees the sufferings and cruelties that Hazael will inflict on Israel, which are not explicitly related in the Bible (see however 10.32; 13.3,22; 15.16n.; Am 1.3–4). **13:** *A mere dog*, self-designation of deference. Elisha does not anoint Hazael but only reveals that he will be king. **15:** *Bed-cover*, the translation of this word is uncertain (perhaps "grating"). In Assyrian inscriptions Hazael is designated as a "son of a nobody," a standard expression for usurpers. Verse 15 may be understood as referring to Hazael's murdering Ben-hadad by suffocation, but the sense of *spread it over the king's face* is not absolutely clear. It could also refer to an attempt to lower the king's fever with a cold blanket.

8.16–29: Jehoram and Ahaziah of Judah. Both these Judean kings are evaluated negatively. **16–24:** *Jehoram* or *Joram* (see vv. 21,23–24), who reigned ca. 851–843 BCE, had to face revolts from *Edom* and *Libnah* (vv. 20–22),

Ahab was his wife. He did what was evil in the sight of the Lord. ¹⁹ Yet the Lord would not destroy Judah, for the sake of his servant David, since he had promised to give a lamp to him and to his descendants forever.

²⁰ In his days Edom revolted against the rule of Judah, and set up a king of their own. ²¹ Then Joram crossed over to Zair with all his chariots. He set out by night and attacked the Edomites and their chariot commanders who had surrounded him;ᵃ but his army fled home. ²² So Edom has been in revolt against the rule of Judah to this day. Libnah also revolted at the same time. ²³ Now the rest of the acts of Joram, and all that he did, are they not written in the Book of the Annals of the Kings of Judah? ²⁴ So Joram slept with his ancestors, and was buried with them in the city of David; his son Ahaziah succeeded him.

²⁵ In the twelfth year of King Joram son of Ahab of Israel, Ahaziah son of King Jehoram of Judah began to reign. ²⁶ Ahaziah was twenty-two years old when he began to reign; he reigned one year in Jerusalem. His mother's name was Athaliah, a granddaughter of King Omri of Israel. ²⁷ He also walked in the way of the house of Ahab, doing what was evil in the sight of the Lord, as the house of Ahab had done, for he was son-in-law to the house of Ahab.

²⁸ He went with Joram son of Ahab to wage war against King Hazael of Aram at Ramoth-gilead, where the Arameans wounded Joram. ²⁹ King Joram returned to be healed in Jezreel of the wounds that the Arameans had inflicted on him at Ramah, when he fought against King Hazael of Aram. King Ahaziah son of

Jehoram of Judah went down to see Joram son of Ahab in Jezreel, because he was wounded.

9 Then the prophet Elisha called a member of the company of prophetsᵇ and said to him, "Gird up your loins; take this flask of oil in your hand, and go to Ramoth-gilead. ² When you arrive, look there for Jehu son of Jehoshaphat, son of Nimshi; go in and get him to leave his companions, and take him into an inner chamber. ³ Then take the flask of oil, pour it on his head, and say, 'Thus says the Lord: I anoint you king over Israel.' Then open the door and flee; do not linger."

⁴ So the young man, the young prophet, went to Ramoth-gilead. ⁵ He arrived while the commanders of the army were in council, and he announced, "I have a message for you, commander." "For which one of us?" asked Jehu. "For you, commander." ⁶ So Jehuᶜ got up and went inside; the young man poured the oil on his head, saying to him, "Thus says the Lord the God of Israel: I anoint you king over the people of the Lord, over Israel. ⁷ You shall strike down the house of your master Ahab, so that I may avenge on Jezebel the blood of my servants the prophets, and the blood of all the servants of the Lord. ⁸ For the whole house of Ahab shall perish; I will cut off from Ahab every male, bond or free, in Israel. ⁹ I will make the house of Ahab like the house of Jeroboam son of Nebat, and like the house of Baasha son of Ahijah. ¹⁰ The dogs shall eat Jezebel in the territory of Jezreel, and no one shall bury her." Then he opened the door and fled.

ᵃ Meaning of Heb uncertain
ᵇ Heb *sons of the prophets*
ᶜ Heb *he*

which was a border town next to Philistine territory and perhaps never really part of Judah. **25–29:** *Ahaziah* (ca. 843–842 BCE) was murdered by Jehu after one year of reign. **26:** *Athaliah, a granddaughter of King Omri*, lit. "daughter of Omri." Scholars disagree about whether this illegitimate queen of Judah (ch 11) was the daughter of Ahab and Jezebel (1 Kings 17.31) or of Omri, Ahab's father. **28–29:** *Ramoth-gilead* was already the site of a military confrontation between Israel and Aram in 1 Kings 22.29–36. The report about the wounded Joram of Israel who needs to recover from his battle-wounds provides the introduction for the following account of Jehu's revolt.

9.1–10.36: Jehu's revolt and reign. The long account of Jehu's revolt describes the end of Omri's dynasty. The redactors of Kings have a mixed opinion of Jehu: they appreciate him because he tries to eradicate Baal worship in the Northern Kingdom, but since he is a northern king they are obliged to condemn him. **9.1–9:** The anointing of Jehu (fulfilling the divine order given to Elijah in 1 Kings 19.16) is performed by a young member of Elisha's prophetic group. **2:** *Jehu son of Jehoshaphat, son of Nimshi*, the name of Jehu (in 1 Kings 16.1 a prophet's name) corresponds to Jehu's religious conviction; it means: "The Lord is God." His father's name also refers to the god of Israel ("The Lord will judge"); *Nimshi* means "weasel." **7–10:** These words recall 1 Kings 14.10–11

[11] When Jehu came back to his master's officers, they said to him, "Is everything all right? Why did that madman come to you?" He answered them, "You know the sort and how they babble." [12] They said, "Liar! Come on, tell us!" So he said, "This is just what he said to me: 'Thus says the LORD, I anoint you king over Israel.'" [13] Then hurriedly they all took their cloaks and spread them for him on the bare[a] steps; and they blew the trumpet, and proclaimed, "Jehu is king."

[14] Thus Jehu son of Jehoshaphat son of Nimshi conspired against Joram. Joram with all Israel had been on guard at Ramoth-gilead against King Hazael of Aram; [15] but King Joram had returned to be healed in Jezreel of the wounds that the Arameans had inflicted on him, when he fought against King Hazael of Aram. So Jehu said, "If this is your wish, then let no one slip out of the city to go and tell the news in Jezreel." [16] Then Jehu mounted his chariot and went to Jezreel, where Joram was lying ill. King Ahaziah of Judah had come down to visit Joram.

[17] In Jezreel, the sentinel standing on the tower spied the company of Jehu arriving, and said, "I see a company." Joram said, "Take a horseman; send him to meet them, and let him say, 'Is it peace?'" [18] So the horseman went to meet him; he said, "Thus says the king, 'Is it peace?'" Jehu responded, "What have you to do with peace? Fall in behind me." The sentinel reported, saying, "The messenger reached them, but he is not coming back." [19] Then he sent out a second horseman, who came to them and said, "Thus says the king, 'Is it peace?'" Jehu answered, "What have you to do with peace? Fall in behind me." [20] Again the sentinel reported, "He reached them, but he is not coming back. It looks like the driving of Jehu son of Nimshi; for he drives like a maniac."

[21] Joram said, "Get ready." And they got his chariot ready. Then King Joram of Israel and King Ahaziah of Judah set out, each in his chariot, and went to meet Jehu; they met him at the property of Naboth the Jezreelite. [22] When Joram saw Jehu, he said, "Is it peace, Jehu?" He answered, "What peace can there be, so long as the many whoredoms and sorceries of your mother Jezebel continue?" [23] Then Joram reined about and fled, saying to Ahaziah, "Treason, Ahaziah!" [24] Jehu drew his bow with all his strength, and shot Joram between the shoulders, so that the arrow pierced his heart; and he sank in his chariot. [25] Jehu said to his aide Bidkar, "Lift him out, and throw him on the plot of ground belonging to Naboth the Jezreelite; for remember, when you and I rode side by side behind his father Ahab how the LORD uttered this oracle against him: [26] 'For the blood of Naboth and for the blood of his children that I saw yesterday, says the LORD, I swear I will repay you on this very plot of ground.' Now therefore lift him out and throw him on the plot of ground, in accordance with the word of the LORD."

[27] When King Ahaziah of Judah saw this, he fled in the direction of Beth-haggan. Jehu pursued him, saying, "Shoot him also!" And they shot him[b] in the chariot at the ascent to Gur, which is by Ibleam. Then he fled to Megiddo, and died there. [28] His officers carried him in a chariot to Jerusalem, and buried him in his tomb with his ancestors in the city of David.

a   Meaning of Heb uncertain
b   Syr Vg Compare Gk: Heb lacks *and they shot him*

and 21.21–24. 7: *Jezebel*, see 1 Kings 16.31n. 11–13: Jehu's anointing was secret (as was Saul's in 1 Sam 9.27–10.1), but it becomes immediately public. 11: *Madman*, a demeaning reference to the apparently well-known young prophet, perhaps referring to his ecstatic behavior. 13: *They blew the trumpet*, see 1 Kings 1.34. 14–28: The report of Jehu's coup sums up the situation described in 8.28–29. Joram of Israel and Ahaziah are together in Jezreel, so Jehu kills them both. 20: *Like a maniac*, better "with madness." Jehu's chariot driving is described with a word from the same root as the "madman" in v. 11. 21: The kings meet Jehu at the former *property of Naboth*. They belong to Ahab's family, and their end will start at the site of Ahab and Jezebel's hideous act (see 1 Kings 21). 22: *Whoredoms and sorceries* of Jezebel, both terms refer to the worship of Baal and his female counterpart, in which religious prostitution and magic activities may have occurred. 27: Ahaziah's death was motivated by his relation to Joram (he was either his nephew or his cousin, see 8.26n.). *Beth-haggan* is identified with Engannin (Josh 19.21), modern Jenin. *Ibleam* is nearby, at the southern end of the Jezreel valley. 28: Ahaziah is killed in *Megiddo*, as King Josiah will be (see 23.29–30); both kings are *carried in a chariot to Jerusalem* to be buried there.

²⁹ In the eleventh year of Joram son of Ahab, Ahaziah began to reign over Judah. ³⁰ When Jehu came to Jezreel, Jezebel heard of it; she painted her eyes, and adorned her head, and looked out of the window. ³¹ As Jehu entered the gate, she said, "Is it peace, Zimri, murderer of your master?" ³² He looked up to the window and said, "Who is on my side? Who?" Two or three eunuchs looked out at him. ³³ He said, "Throw her down." So they threw her down; some of her blood spattered on the wall and on the horses, which trampled on her. ³⁴ Then he went in and ate and drank; he said, "See to that cursed woman and bury her; for she is a king's daughter." ³⁵ But when they went to bury her, they found no more of her than the skull and the feet and the palms of her hands. ³⁶ When they came back and told him, he said, "This is the word of the Lord, which he spoke by his servant Elijah the Tishbite, 'In the territory of Jezreel the dogs shall eat the flesh of Jezebel; ³⁷ the corpse of Jezebel shall be like dung on the field in the territory of Jezreel, so that no one can say, This is Jezebel.'"

10 Now Ahab had seventy sons in Samaria. So Jehu wrote letters and sent them to Samaria, to the rulers of Jezreel,^a to the elders, and to the guardians of the sons of^b Ahab, saying, ² "Since your master's sons are with you and you have at your disposal chariots and horses, a fortified city, and weapons, ³ select the son of your master who is the best qualified, set him on his father's throne, and fight for your master's house." ⁴ But they were utterly terrified and said, "Look, two kings could not withstand him; how then can we stand?" ⁵ So the steward of the palace, and the governor of the city, along with the elders and the guardians, sent word to Jehu: "We are your servants; we will do anything you say. We will not make anyone king; do whatever you think right." ⁶ Then he wrote them a second letter, saying, "If you are on my side, and if you are ready to obey me, take the heads of your master's sons and come to me at Jezreel tomorrow at this time." Now the king's sons, seventy persons, were with the leaders of the city, who were charged with their upbringing. ⁷ When the letter reached them, they took the king's sons and killed them, seventy persons; they put their heads in baskets and sent them to him at Jezreel. ⁸ When the messenger came and told him, "They have brought the heads of the king's sons," he said, "Lay them in two heaps at the entrance of the gate until the morning." ⁹ Then in the morning when he went out, he stood and said to all the people, "You are innocent. It was I who conspired against my master and killed him; but who struck down all these? ¹⁰ Know then that there shall fall to the earth nothing of the word of the Lord, which the Lord spoke concerning the house of Ahab; for the Lord has done what he said through his servant Elijah." ¹¹ So Jehu killed all who were left of the house of Ahab in Jezreel, all his leaders, close friends, and priests, until he left him no survivor.

¹² Then he set out and went to Samaria. On the way, when he was at Beth-eked of the Shepherds, ¹³ Jehu met relatives of King Ahaziah of Judah and said, "Who are you?" They answered, "We are kin of Ahaziah; we have come down to visit the royal princes and the sons of the queen mother." ¹⁴ He said,

^a Or *of the city*; Vg Compare Gk
^b Gk: Heb lacks *of the sons of*

29: The report about the beginning of Ahaziah's reign, with a chronology that differs from previous notes (8.25), is probably a correction placed at an odd place. **30–37:** The murder of *Jezebel* is presented as the accomplishment of Elijah's oracle (compare vv. 36–37 with 1 Kings 21.23). **30:** Jezebel appears as "woman at the window," a frequent motif in ancient Near Eastern art, representing prostitutes or fertility goddesses and suggesting sexual availability. **31:** She identifies Jehu with *Zimri*, who killed King Baasha (1 Kings 16.9–20), but reigned only a week. **33:** Jezebel is killed by the *eunuchs* who were at her service. **10.1–11:** Jehu massacres the remnant of the house of Ahab. **1:** *Seventy sons*, seventy is a round number in the Bible (see Judg 8.30; Deut 10.22) and in many other texts from the ancient Near East. It is unclear why Jehu should write letters to the governors or *rulers of Jezreel*, since he is already in the city (9.30). LXX suggests "Samaria" instead of Jezreel (see textual note a). **10:** Such a reference to a former prophetic oracle (1 Kings 21.21–24) is typical for the Deuteronomistic redactors of Kings (see also v. 17). **12–14:** Jehu's slaughtering continues with the relatives of the Judean king. **12:** *Beth-eked*,

"Take them alive." They took them alive, and slaughtered them at the pit of Beth-eked, forty-two in all; he spared none of them.

[15] When he left there, he met Jehonadab son of Rechab coming to meet him; he greeted him, and said to him, "Is your heart as true to mine as mine is to yours?"[a] Jehonadab answered, "It is." Jehu said,[b] "If it is, give me your hand." So he gave him his hand. Jehu took him up with him into the chariot. [16] He said, "Come with me, and see my zeal for the LORD." So he[c] had him ride in his chariot. [17] When he came to Samaria, he killed all who were left to Ahab in Samaria, until he had wiped them out, according to the word of the LORD that he spoke to Elijah.

[18] Then Jehu assembled all the people and said to them, "Ahab offered Baal small service; but Jehu will offer much more. [19] Now therefore summon to me all the prophets of Baal, all his worshipers, and all his priests; let none be missing, for I have a great sacrifice to offer to Baal; whoever is missing shall not live." But Jehu was acting with cunning in order to destroy the worshipers of Baal. [20] Jehu decreed, "Sanctify a solemn assembly for Baal." So they proclaimed it. [21] Jehu sent word throughout all Israel; all the worshipers of Baal came, so that there was no one left who did not come. They entered the temple of Baal, until the temple of Baal was filled from wall to wall. [22] He said to the keeper of the wardrobe, "Bring out the vestments for all the worshipers of Baal." So he brought out the vestments for them. [23] Then Jehu entered the temple of Baal with Jehonadab son of Rechab; he said to the worshipers of Baal, "Search and see that there is no worshiper of the LORD here among you, but only worshipers of Baal." [24] Then they proceeded to offer sacrifices and burnt offerings.

Now Jehu had stationed eighty men outside, saying, "Whoever allows any of those to escape whom I deliver into your hands shall forfeit his life." [25] As soon as he had finished presenting the burnt offering, Jehu said to the guards and to the officers, "Come in and kill them; let no one escape." So they put them to the sword. The guards and the officers threw them out, and then went into the citadel of the temple of Baal. [26] They brought out the pillar[d] that was in the temple of Baal, and burned it. [27] Then they demolished the pillar of Baal, and destroyed the temple of Baal, and made it a latrine to this day.

[28] Thus Jehu wiped out Baal from Israel. [29] But Jehu did not turn aside from the sins of Jeroboam son of Nebat, which he caused Israel to commit—the golden calves that were in Bethel and in Dan. [30] The LORD said to Jehu, "Because you have done well in carrying out what I consider right, and in accordance with all that was in my heart have dealt with the house of Ahab, your sons of the fourth generation shall sit on the throne of Israel." [31] But Jehu was not careful to follow the law of the LORD the God of Israel with all his heart; he did not turn from the sins of Jeroboam, which he caused Israel to commit.

[32] In those days the LORD began to trim off parts of Israel. Hazael defeated them throughout the territory of Israel: [33] from the Jordan eastward, all the land of Gilead, the Gadites, the Reubenites, and the Manassites,

a   Gk: Heb *Is it right with your heart, as my heart is with your heart?*
b   Gk: Heb lacks *Jehu said*
c   Gk Syr Tg: Heb *they*
d   Gk Vg Syr Tg: Heb *pillars*

an unidentified place, apparently a gathering-place for shepherds. **14:** *Forty-two*, see 2.24n. **15–17:** *Jehonadab son of Rechab* is mentioned in Jer 35 as the founder of a small religious group committed to a life-style that rejected urban culture. Here he is portrayed as an ally of Jehu. **16:** *Chariot*, Heb "rekeb," recalling the name Rechab ("rekab"). Jehonadab was perhaps a rider, like Jehu (see 9.25). **18–27:** To a modern reader Jehu's massacre of all worshipers of Baal appears as religious fanaticism, surpassing even Elijah's killing of the prophets of Baal in 1 Kings 18.40. The narrator was absolutely hostile to the worship of Baal, so that he did not have such reservations. **28–31:** Nevertheless, the evaluation of Jehu is ambivalent. **30:** Like David, he receives a dynastic promise, which is however limited to the fourth generation. **29, 31:** For the redactors of Kings, Jehu's worship of the LORD was wrong, because he venerated him outside of Jerusalem, continuing *the sins of Jeroboam* (see 1 Kings 12). **32–33:** During Jehu's reign, the Northern Kingdom declined and Jehu eventually lost its Transjordanian territory to the Arameans. An Assyrian stele reports that Jehu had become a vassal of King Shalmaneser III (ruled ca.

from Aroer, which is by the Wadi Arnon, that is, Gilead and Bashan. ³⁴ Now the rest of the acts of Jehu, all that he did, and all his power, are they not written in the Book of the Annals of the Kings of Israel? ³⁵ So Jehu slept with his ancestors, and they buried him in Samaria. His son Jehoahaz succeeded him. ³⁶ The time that Jehu reigned over Israel in Samaria was twenty-eight years.

11 Now when Athaliah, Ahaziah's mother, saw that her son was dead, she set about to destroy all the royal family. ² But Jehosheba, King Joram's daughter, Ahaziah's sister, took Joash son of Ahaziah, and stole him away from among the king's children who were about to be killed; she put[a] him and his nurse in a bedroom. Thus she[b] hid him from Athaliah, so that he was not killed; ³ he remained with her six years, hidden in the house of the LORD, while Athaliah reigned over the land.

⁴ But in the seventh year Jehoiada summoned the captains of the Carites and of the guards and had them come to him in the house of the LORD. He made a covenant with them and put them under oath in the house of the LORD; then he showed them the king's son. ⁵ He commanded them, "This is what you are to do. one-third of you, those who go off duty on the sabbath and guard the king's house ⁶ (another third being at the gate Sur and a third at the gate behind the guards), shall guard the palace; ⁷ and your two divisions that come on duty in force on the sabbath and guard the house of the LORD[c] ⁸ shall surround the king, each with weapons in hand; and whoever approaches the ranks is to be killed. Be with the king in his comings and goings."

⁹ The captains did according to all that the priest Jehoiada commanded; each brought his men who were to go off duty on the sabbath, with those who were to come on duty on the sabbath, and came to the priest Jehoiada. ¹⁰ The priest delivered to the captains the spears and shields that had been King David's, which were in the house of the LORD; ¹¹ the guards stood, every man with his weapons in his hand, from the south side of the house to the north side of the house, around the altar and the house, to guard the king on every side. ¹² Then he brought out the king's son, put the crown on him, and gave him the covenant;[d] they proclaimed him king, and anointed him; they clapped their hands and shouted, "Long live the king!"

¹³ When Athaliah heard the noise of the guard and of the people, she went into the house of the LORD to the people; ¹⁴ when she

---

a With 2 Chr 22.11: Heb lacks *she put*
b Gk Syr Vg Compare 2 Chr 22.11: Heb *they*
c Heb *the LORD to the king*
d Or *treaty* or *testimony*; Heb *eduth*

859–824 BCE), a fact not mentioned in the Bible. **34–36:** Very little of the *twenty-eight years* of Jehu's reign (ca. 842–814 BCE) is recorded.

11.1–21: The reign of Athaliah in Judah. The reign of *Athaliah* (ca. 842–836 BCE), *Ahaziah's* mother, interrupts the Davidic line, since she is from the north (see 8.26n.). For the redactors of the book of Kings, she was considered an illegitimate ruler; therefore her reign lacks the typical introductory and concluding formulas. Athaliah's name means "the LORD is exalted," but she seems to have sponsored Baal worship (see v. 18). **1–3:** Like Jehu in the north, Athaliah tries to massacre all potential heirs to the throne, but one member of the royal family escapes (for the same literary motif see Judg 9.5): *Joash* is hidden by Ahaziah's sister *Jehosheba*. **4–12:** The priest *Jehoiada*, who according to 2 Chr 22.11 was Jehosheba's husband, organizes the rebellion in the *seventh year* (the number may be typological or symbolic). **4:** The *Carites* (Carians) are either a bodyguard from Cilicia or the same as the Cherethites (1 Kings 1.38). **5–11:** The details of the deployment of the troops are unclear. Apparently three companies should stand on different strategic positions (the location of the *gate Sur* is unknown), and two other groups (or two of the three previous ones?) should protect the new king. **12:** *Crown*, cf. 2 Sam 1.10; Ex 28.36–38. The *covenant* may refer to the divine promise to the Davidic dynasty (2 Sam 7) or to a list of regulations for the conduct of kingship (like Deut 17.18–20). *Long live the king*, the same exclamation as in 1 Kings 1.25. **13–16:** The story moves now to the end of Athaliah, who will be executed along with her followers outside the Temple. **14:** *Pillar*, or podium, a place of royal appearance (see 23.3). The parallel account in 2 Chr 23.13 interprets this as the pillars Jachin and Boaz (see 1 Kings 7.21) at the Temple entrance. The *people of the land* designates here, as elsewhere in the book of Kings, the rural aristocracy that intervened in critical situations in order to

looked, there was the king standing by the pillar, according to custom, with the captains and the trumpeters beside the king, and all the people of the land rejoicing and blowing trumpets. Athaliah tore her clothes and cried, "Treason! Treason!" [15] Then the priest Jehoiada commanded the captains who were set over the army, "Bring her out between the ranks, and kill with the sword anyone who follows her." For the priest said, "Let her not be killed in the house of the Lord." [16] So they laid hands on her; she went through the horses' entrance to the king's house, and there she was put to death.

[17] Jehoiada made a covenant between the Lord and the king and people, that they should be the Lord's people; also between the king and the people. [18] Then all the people of the land went to the house of Baal, and tore it down; his altars and his images they broke in pieces, and they killed Mattan, the priest of Baal, before the altars. The priest posted guards over the house of the Lord. [19] He took the captains, the Carites, the guards, and all the people of the land; then they brought the king down from the house of the Lord, marching through the gate of the guards to the king's house. He took his seat on the throne of the kings. [20] So all the people of the land rejoiced; and the city was quiet after Athaliah had been killed with the sword at the king's house.

[21] [a]Jehoash[b] was seven years old when he began to reign.

12 In the seventh year of Jehu, Jehoash began to reign; he reigned forty years in Jerusalem. His mother's name was Zibiah of Beer-sheba. [2] Jehoash did what was right in the sight of the Lord all his days, because the priest Jehoiada instructed him. [3] Nevertheless the high places were not taken away; the people continued to sacrifice and make offerings on the high places.

[4] Jehoash said to the priests, "All the money offered as sacred donations that is brought into the house of the Lord, the money for which each person is assessed—the money from the assessment of persons—and the money from the voluntary offerings brought into the house of the Lord, [5] let the priests receive from each of the donors; and let them repair the house wherever any need of repairs is discovered." [6] But by the twenty-third year of King Jehoash the priests had made no repairs on the house. [7] Therefore King Jehoash summoned the priest Jehoiada with the other priests and said to them, "Why are you not repairing the house? Now therefore do not accept any more money from your donors but hand it over for the repair of the house." [8] So the priests agreed that they would neither accept more money from the people nor repair the house.

[9] Then the priest Jehoiada took a chest, made a hole in its lid, and set it beside the altar on the right side as one entered the house of the Lord; the priests who guarded the threshold put in it all the money that was brought into the house of the Lord. [10] Whenever they saw that there was a great deal of

a Ch 12.1 in Heb
b Another spelling is *Joash*; see verse 19

defend the traditional worship of the God of Israel. **16:** *The horses' entrance,* perhaps the Horse Gate mentioned in Jer 31.40 and Neh 3.28. **17–20:** The unusual threefold *covenant between the Lord and the king and people* mediated by a priest has become necessary because Athaliah's reign had interrupted the Davidic succession. The covenant would then be the renewal of the Davidic dynasty as chosen by God and accepted by the people (see 2 Sam 5.3). **18:** There is no other mention of Athaliah being a fervent worshiper of Baal. The Baal priest *Mattan* appears only here and in the parallel account in 2 Chr 23.17.

12.1–21: The reign of Jehoash (or Joash), king of Judah (ca. 836–798 bce). **1–3:** In the Deuteronomistic introduction, Jehoash is said to have ruled *forty* years. This may well be a symbolic number, and may include the six years of Athaliah. **2–3:** For the redactors Jehoash was a good king, although he tolerated worship of the Lord in places other than the Temple in Jerusalem. **4–16:** The repair of the Temple foreshadows King Josiah's repairs (see 22.3–7). But unlike Josiah's reform, Jehoash's will fail. **4:** *Money . . . sacred donations,* money that replaced the traditional sacrifices (see Lev 27.1–8). **6–8:** The priests were unwilling to spend the money they received to repair the Temple. **6:** *The twenty-third year,* this is the year Jehoahaz of Israel acceded to the throne (13.1). **9–12:** The priest Jehoiada is centralizing and supervising the money for the restoration, as does the priest Hilkiah in 22.4–6. **10:** *High priest,* this title is used only from the Persian period onward, when this episode may have been

money in the chest, the king's secretary and the high priest went up, counted the money that was found in the house of the LORD, and tied it up in bags. [11] They would give the money that was weighed out into the hands of the workers who had the oversight of the house of the LORD; then they paid it out to the carpenters and the builders who worked on the house of the LORD, [12] to the masons and the stonecutters, as well as to buy timber and quarried stone for making repairs on the house of the LORD, as well as for any outlay for repairs of the house. [13] But for the house of the LORD no basins of silver, snuffers, bowls, trumpets, or any vessels of gold, or of silver, were made from the money that was brought into the house of the LORD, [14] for that was given to the workers who were repairing the house of the LORD with it. [15] They did not ask an accounting from those into whose hand they delivered the money to pay out to the workers, for they dealt honestly. [16] The money from the guilt offerings and the money from the sin offerings was not brought into the house of the LORD; it belonged to the priests.

[17] At that time King Hazael of Aram went up, fought against Gath, and took it. But when Hazael set his face to go up against Jerusalem, [18] King Jehoash of Judah took all the votive gifts that Jehoshaphat, Jehoram, and Ahaziah, his ancestors, the kings of Judah, had dedicated, as well as his own votive gifts, all the gold that was found in the treasuries of the house of the LORD and of the king's house, and sent these to King Hazael of Aram. Then Hazael withdrew from Jerusalem.

[19] Now the rest of the acts of Joash, and all that he did, are they not written in the Book of the Annals of the Kings of Judah? [20] His servants arose, devised a conspiracy, and killed Joash in the house of Millo, on the way that goes down to Silla. [21] It was Jozacar son of Shimeath and Jehozabad son of Shomer, his servants, who struck him down, so that he died. He was buried with his ancestors in the city of David; then his son Amaziah succeeded him.

13 In the twenty-third year of King Joash son of Ahaziah of Judah, Jehoahaz son of Jehu began to reign over Israel in Samaria; he reigned seventeen years. [2] He did what was evil in the sight of the LORD, and followed the sins of Jeroboam son of Nebat, which he caused Israel to sin; he did not depart from them. [3] The anger of the LORD was kindled against Israel, so that he gave them repeatedly into the hand of King Hazael of Aram, then into the hand of Ben-hadad son of Hazael. [4] But Jehoahaz entreated the LORD, and the LORD heeded him; for he saw the oppression of Israel, how the king of Aram oppressed them. [5] Therefore the LORD gave Israel a savior, so that they escaped from the hand of the Arameans; and the people of Israel lived in their homes as formerly. [6] Nevertheless they did not depart from the sins of the house of Jeroboam, which he caused Israel to sin, but walked[a] in them; the sacred pole[b] also remained in Samaria. [7] So Jehoahaz was left with an army of not more than fifty horse-

---

[a] Gk Syr Tg Vg: Heb *he walked*

[b] Heb *Asherah*

---

composed. **13:** The meaning of the verse is unclear. It may refer to lack of adequate silver, causing a very modest restoration, or that the priests were not allowed to use the money for their Temple vessels. **16:** There was apparently some dispute about the silver, which belonged directly to the priests (see Lev 7.7–10). **17–18:** After Israel (see 10.32–33), Hazael of Aram is now attacking the Philistine coast (the city of *Gath*) and *Jerusalem*. He was more interested in controlling the trade routes in the south than in occupying the capital of Judah. Therefore he accepts the tribute that Jehoash is immediately willing to pay. **19–21:** The parallel account in 2 Chr 24.24–27 gives a different explanation of the death of Joash. **20:** *Millo*, see 1 Kings 9.15n. **21:** *Jozacar . . .* and *Jehozabad*, NRSV follows the LXX. In the MT both murderers are named Jehozabad.

13.1–25: Jehoahaz and Jehoash (Joash) of Israel and the death of Elisha. The chronological data offered in chs 13–15 are confusing and do not allow for a reconstruction of a coherent chronological system. All dates given in parentheses are hypothetical. **1–9:** *Jehoahaz* (ca. 817–800 BCE), evaluated as a bad king who nevertheless has the LORD on his side, faces renewed Aramean oppression. **5:** The identity of the *savior* sent by God is not specified, and some think he was the Assyrian king, who fought the Arameans, and others suggest an Israelite general (the term *savior* is sometimes used in Judges for a judge functioning as a military leader). **6:** *Sacred pole*

men, ten chariots and ten thousand footmen; for the king of Aram had destroyed them and made them like the dust at threshing. ⁸ Now the rest of the acts of Jehoahaz and all that he did, including his might, are they not written in the Book of the Annals of the Kings of Israel? ⁹ So Jehoahaz slept with his ancestors, and they buried him in Samaria; then his son Joash succeeded him.

¹⁰ In the thirty-seventh year of King Joash of Judah, Jehoash son of Jehoahaz began to reign over Israel in Samaria; he reigned sixteen years. ¹¹ He also did what was evil in the sight of the LORD; he did not depart from all the sins of Jeroboam son of Nebat, which he caused Israel to sin, but he walked in them. ¹² Now the rest of the acts of Joash, and all that he did, as well as the might with which he fought against King Amaziah of Judah, are they not written in the Book of the Annals of the Kings of Israel? ¹³ So Joash slept with his ancestors, and Jeroboam sat upon his throne; Joash was buried in Samaria with the kings of Israel.

¹⁴ Now when Elisha had fallen sick with the illness of which he was to die, King Joash of Israel went down to him, and wept before him, crying, "My father, my father! The chariots of Israel and its horsemen!" ¹⁵ Elisha said to him, "Take a bow and arrows"; so he took a bow and arrows. ¹⁶ Then he said to the king of Israel, "Draw the bow"; and he drew it. Elisha laid his hands on the king's hands. ¹⁷ Then he said, "Open the window eastward"; and he opened it. Elisha said, "Shoot"; and he shot. Then he said, "The LORD's arrow of victory,

the arrow of victory over Aram! For you shall fight the Arameans in Aphek until you have made an end of them." ¹⁸ He continued, "Take the arrows"; and he took them. He said to the king of Israel, "Strike the ground with them"; he struck three times, and stopped. ¹⁹ Then the man of God was angry with him, and said, "You should have struck five or six times; then you would have struck down Aram until you had made an end of it, but now you will strike down Aram only three times."

²⁰ So Elisha died, and they buried him. Now bands of Moabites used to invade the land in the spring of the year. ²¹ As a man was being buried, a marauding band was seen and the man was thrown into the grave of Elisha; as soon as the man touched the bones of Elisha, he came to life and stood on his feet.

²² Now King Hazael of Aram oppressed Israel all the days of Jehoahaz. ²³ But the LORD was gracious to them and had compassion on them; he turned toward them, because of his covenant with Abraham, Isaac, and Jacob, and would not destroy them; nor has he banished them from his presence until now.

²⁴ When King Hazael of Aram died, his son Ben-hadad succeeded him. ²⁵ Then Jehoash son of Jehoahaz took again from Ben-hadad son of Hazael the towns that he had taken from his father Jehoahaz in war. Three times Joash defeated him and recovered the towns of Israel.

14 In the second year of King Joash son of Joahaz of Israel, King Amaziah son of Joash of Judah, began to reign. ² He was twenty-five years old when he began to reign,

(Heb "'asherah"), a symbol of the goddess Asherah. **7–8:** As in the book of Judges (e.g., 2.18; 3.9,15), the sending of a savior does not provoke a return to the LORD; therefore the Israelite *army* is drastically reduced. **10–21:** The redactors do not tell much about the wicked *Jehoash*, whose name is identical to that of his Judean colleague. His reign (ca. 800–784 BCE) provides the context for the story about Elisha's death. **11–13:** The concluding formula of his reign already appears here and is repeated in 14.15–16. **14:** *Elisha* has not been mentioned since the anointing of Jehu, some fifty years before (9.1–3). He is now an old man about to die. *Chariots of Israel . . .*, see 2.11–12n. **15–19:** Elisha has the king perform two symbolic actions, which foretell his incomplete victory against the Arameans. *Arrows* were used in the ancient Near East as tools of divination. **17:** *Aphek*, see 1 Kings 20.26n. **20–21:** Even after his death, Elisha is still able to perform a miracle. **22–23:** These verses return to the reign of Jehoahaz; they were inserted by a later redactor to connect with vv. 4–5, and they give another reason for God's help against the Arameans: his *covenant* with the patriarchs. **24–25:** A reference to the encounter between Elisha and Jehoahaz, stating that his son Jehoash defeated the Arameans *three times* (see v. 19).

14.1–29: Amaziah of Judah and Jeroboam (II) of Israel. **1–22:** *Amaziah* (ca. 798–769 BCE) waged war against Edom and Israel and was severely defeated by the Israelite king. **1–6:** At the beginning of his reign he executes the conspirators who had murdered his father. Described as a bad king, he nevertheless follows the Deutero-

and he reigned twenty-nine years in Jerusalem. His mother's name was Jehoaddin of Jerusalem. ³ He did what was right in the sight of the LORD, yet not like his ancestor David; in all things he did as his father Joash had done. ⁴ But the high places were not removed; the people still sacrificed and made offerings on the high places. ⁵ As soon as the royal power was firmly in his hand he killed his servants who had murdered his father the king. ⁶ But he did not put to death the children of the murderers; according to what is written in the book of the law of Moses, where the LORD commanded, "The parents shall not be put to death for the children, or the children be put to death for the parents; but all shall be put to death for their own sins."

⁷ He killed ten thousand Edomites in the Valley of Salt and took Sela by storm; he called it Jokthe-el, which is its name to this day.

⁸ Then Amaziah sent messengers to King Jehoash son of Jehoahaz, son of Jehu, of Israel, saying, "Come, let us look one another in the face." ⁹ King Jehoash of Israel sent word to King Amaziah of Judah, "A thornbush on Lebanon sent to a cedar on Lebanon, saying, 'Give your daughter to my son for a wife'; but a wild animal of Lebanon passed by and trampled down the thornbush. ¹⁰ You have indeed defeated Edom, and your heart has lifted you up. Be content with your glory, and stay at home; for why should you provoke trouble so that you fall, you and Judah with you?"

¹¹ But Amaziah would not listen. So King Jehoash of Israel went up; he and King Amaziah of Judah faced one another in battle at Beth-shemesh, which belongs to Judah. ¹² Judah was defeated by Israel; everyone fled home. ¹³ King Jehoash of Israel captured King Amaziah of Judah son of Jehoash, son of Ahaziah, at Beth-shemesh; he came to Jerusalem, and broke down the wall of Jerusalem from the Ephraim Gate to the Corner Gate, a distance of four hundred cubits. ¹⁴ He seized all the gold and silver, and all the vessels that were found in the house of the LORD and in the treasuries of the king's house, as well as hostages; then he returned to Samaria.

¹⁵ Now the rest of the acts that Jehoash did, his might, and how he fought with King Amaziah of Judah, are they not written in the Book of the Annals of the Kings of Israel? ¹⁶ Jehoash slept with his ancestors, and was buried in Samaria with the kings of Israel; then his son Jeroboam succeeded him.

¹⁷ King Amaziah son of Joash of Judah lived fifteen years after the death of King Jehoash son of Jehoahaz of Israel. ¹⁸ Now the rest of the deeds of Amaziah, are they not written in the Book of the Annals of the Kings of Judah? ¹⁹ They made a conspiracy against him in Jerusalem, and he fled to Lachish. But they sent after him to Lachish, and killed him there. ²⁰ They brought him on horses; he was buried in Jerusalem with his ancestors in the city of David. ²¹ All the people of Judah took Azariah, who was sixteen years old, and made him king to succeed his father Amaziah. ²² He rebuilt Elath and restored it to Judah, after King Amaziah[a] slept with his ancestors.

²³ In the fifteenth year of King Amaziah son of Joash of Judah, King Jeroboam son of

---

a Heb the king

---

nomic law. **6**: See Deut 24.16. **7–14**: After a successful campaign against the Edomites he defeats the much stronger king of Israel. **7**: The *Valley of Salt* (see 2 Sam 8.13) probably refers to the area south of the Dead Sea. *Sela* ("rock") is a common noun, which is also employed as a proper name to designate several rocky places, including the capital of Edom. **9**: The Israelite king compares Amaziah of Judah to a *thornbush* easily trampled down by any *wild animal* (for another fable about trees and the thornbush, see Judg 9.7–15). **11**: *Beth-shemesh*, ca. 16 mi (25 km) west of Jerusalem, a city that Israel and Judah both claimed as belonging to their territory. **13**: *Four hundred cubits*, ca. 583 ft (177 m). **14**: The deportation of the *vessels* from the Temple foreshadows its destruction and the deportation of its precious objects by the Babylonians in 25.14–15. **15–16**: see 13.10–13. **17–22**: The names and the motives of the movers of the conspiracy against Amaziah are not mentioned. **19**: The king's unsuccessful flight to *Lachish*, Judah's second city, ca. 28 mi (45 km) southwest of Jerusalem, suggests that the conspirators controlled the capital. **21–22**: *The people of Judah* may also be translated as the "army of Judah," which would suggest that the king's young son *Azariah* (see 15.1–7) was brought to the throne by the military. **22**: Azariah continues to exercise control over Edom by reintegrating the port of *Elath* (1 Kings 9.26) into Judean

Joash of Israel began to reign in Samaria; he reigned forty-one years. [24] He did what was evil in the sight of the LORD; he did not depart from all the sins of Jeroboam son of Nebat, which he caused Israel to sin. [25] He restored the border of Israel from Lebo-hamath as far as the Sea of the Arabah, according to the word of the LORD, the God of Israel, which he spoke by his servant Jonah son of Amittai, the prophet, who was from Gath-hepher. [26] For the LORD saw that the distress of Israel was very bitter; there was no one left, bond or free, and no one to help Israel. [27] But the LORD had not said that he would blot out the name of Israel from under heaven, so he saved them by the hand of Jeroboam son of Joash.

[28] Now the rest of the acts of Jeroboam, and all that he did, and his might, how he fought, and how he recovered for Israel Damascus and Hamath, which had belonged to Judah, are they not written in the Book of the Annals of the Kings of Israel? [29] Jeroboam slept with his ancestors, the kings of Israel; his son Zechariah succeeded him.

15 In the twenty-seventh year of King Jeroboam of Israel King Azariah son of Amaziah of Judah began to reign. [2] He was sixteen years old when he began to reign, and he reigned fifty-two years in Jerusalem. His mother's name was Jecoliah of Jerusalem. [3] He did what was right in the sight of the LORD, just as his father Amaziah had done. [4] Nevertheless the high places were not taken away; the people still sacrificed and made offerings on the high places. [5] The LORD struck the king, so that

he was leprous[a] to the day of his death, and lived in a separate house. Jotham the king's son was in charge of the palace, governing the people of the land. [6] Now the rest of the acts of Azariah, and all that he did, are they not written in the Book of the Annals of the Kings of Judah? [7] Azariah slept with his ancestors; they buried him with his ancestors in the city of David; his son Jotham succeeded him.

[8] In the thirty-eighth year of King Azariah of Judah, Zechariah son of Jeroboam reigned over Israel in Samaria six months. [9] He did what was evil in the sight of the LORD, as his ancestors had done. He did not depart from the sins of Jeroboam son of Nebat, which he caused Israel to sin. [10] Shallum son of Jabesh conspired against him, and struck him down in public and killed him, and reigned in place of him. [11] Now the rest of the deeds of Zechariah are written in the Book of the Annals of the Kings of Israel. [12] This was the promise of the LORD that he gave to Jehu, "Your sons shall sit on the throne of Israel to the fourth generation." And so it happened.

[13] Shallum son of Jabesh began to reign in the thirty-ninth year of King Uzziah of Judah; he reigned one month in Samaria. [14] Then Menahem son of Gadi came up from Tirzah and came to Samaria; he struck down Shallum son of Jabesh in Samaria and killed him; he reigned in place of him. [15] Now the rest of the deeds of Shallum, including the con-

---

a   A term for several skin diseases; precise meaning uncertain

---

territory. **23–29:** *Jeroboam* II, who had an exceptionally long reign (ca. 788–747 BCE, probably including a coregency with his father), and who brought Israel to power and wealth, is treated very briefly in the book of Kings; the books of Hosea and Amos also refer to his rule. **25:** *Lebo-hamath*, see 1 Kings 8.65n. The prophecy to which this verse refers is not found elsewhere in the Bible and is attributed to a nationalistic prophet named *Jonah son of Amittai*, whose name is given to the protagonist of the book of Jonah (see Jon 1.1). *Gath-hepher* is in southern Galilee about 14 mi (23 km) northeast of Megiddo. **26:** That the LORD sees Israel's *distress* recalls 13.4 as well as Ex 3.7 and Deut 26.7. God cares for Israel in spite of its bad kings. **28:** Jeroboam *recovered . . . Damascus and Hamath*, this assertion of territorial expansion is puzzling, since neither city ever belonged to Israel.

15.1–7: Azariah of Judah. Also called Uzziah, which may be his throne name, this Judean king is presented positively but very briefly. Many scholars think that some of his long reign of *fifty-two years* (ca. 792–740) included a coregency with his son. **5:** He was struck with a skin disease (leprosy; see textual note *a*) and due to his ritual impurity had to live in a *separate house*, in quarantine, and had to hand over regency to his son *Jotham* during his lifetime. **5:** *People of the land*, see 11.14n.

15.8–31: Israel's last kings. 8–12: The assassination of *Zechariah* after a brief reign (ca. 747 BCE) is presented as the fulfillment of God's oracle that Jehu's dynasty would last four generations (compare v. 12 with 10.30). **13–16:** *Shallum*, Zechariah's murderer, holds power for only *one month* (747 BCE), when he is killed by *Menahem*.

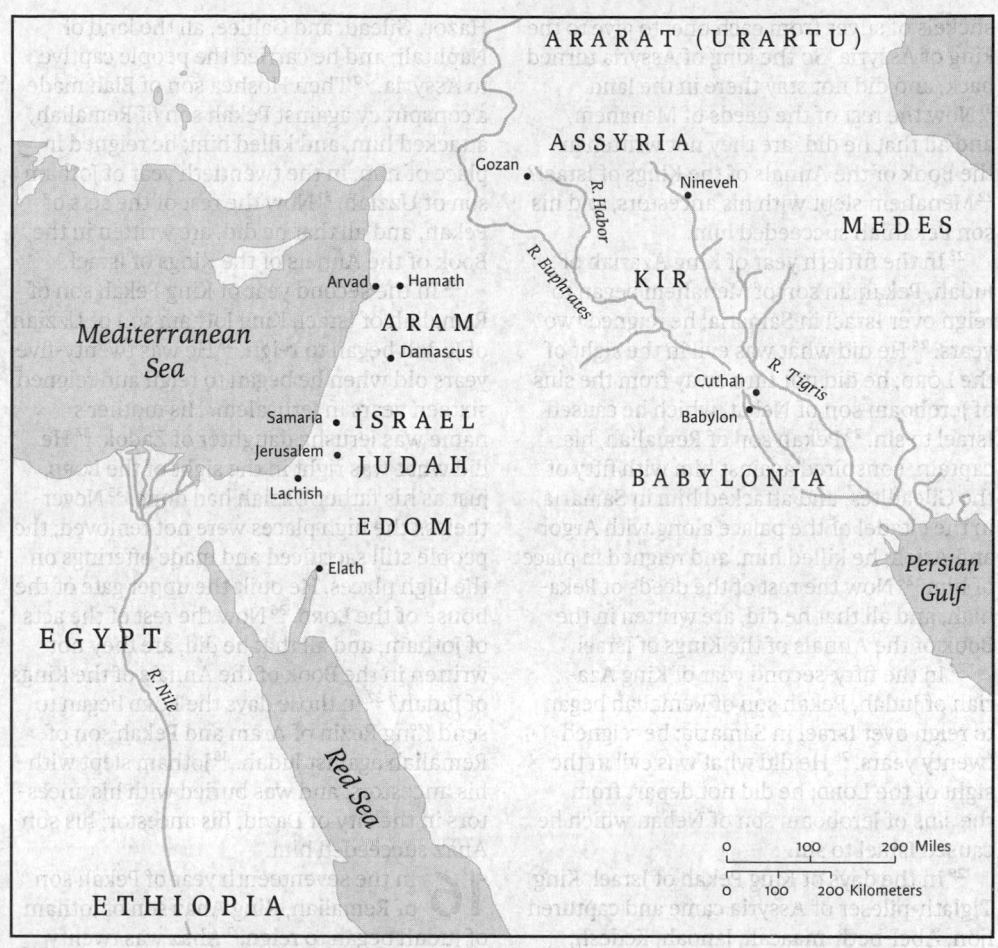

Chs 15–21: Assyria and Israel and Judah.

spiracy that he made, are written in the Book of the Annals of the Kings of Israel. [16] At that time Menahem sacked Tiphsah, all who were in it and its territory from Tirzah on; because they did not open it to him, he sacked it. He ripped open all the pregnant women in it.

[17] In the thirty-ninth year of King Azariah of Judah, Menahem son of Gadi began to reign over Israel; he reigned ten years in Sa-maria. [18] He did what was evil in the sight of the LORD; he did not depart all his days from any of the sins of Jeroboam son of Nebat, which he caused Israel to sin. [19] King Pul of Assyria came against the land; Menahem gave Pul a thousand talents of silver, so that he might help him confirm his hold on the royal power. [20] Menahem exacted the money from Israel, that is, from all the wealthy, fifty

14: *Tirzah* was the former capital of the Northern Kingdom; see 1 Kings 14.17–18n. 16: This verse, which stands between the concluding formula of Shallum's reign and the beginning of Menahem's rule, reports the new king's atrocities. *Tiphsah* is probably to be identified, as suggested by the LXX, with Tappuah, ca. 9 mi (15 km) south of Shechem. The only Tiphsah known otherwise is located on the Euphrates (see 1 Kings 4.24). *He ripped open all the pregnant women*, such horrific action was a common feature of warfare in the ancient Near East (see 8.12; Am 1.13). 17–22: *Menahem* (ca. 747–737 BCE) had to submit to the Assyrians. 19: *King Pul*, another name for the Assyrian king Tiglath-pileser III (see v. 29); with the reign of this king (ca. 745–727 BCE) Assyrian domination in the west was firmly established. *A thousand talents of silver*, ca. 75,000 lb (34,000 kg). 20: In order to pay this

shekels of silver from each one, to give to the king of Assyria. So the king of Assyria turned back, and did not stay there in the land. [21] Now the rest of the deeds of Menahem, and all that he did, are they not written in the Book of the Annals of the Kings of Israel? [22] Menahem slept with his ancestors, and his son Pekahiah succeeded him.

[23] In the fiftieth year of King Azariah of Judah, Pekahiah son of Menahem began to reign over Israel in Samaria; he reigned two years. [24] He did what was evil in the sight of the LORD; he did not turn away from the sins of Jeroboam son of Nebat, which he caused Israel to sin. [25] Pekah son of Remaliah, his captain, conspired against him with fifty of the Gileadites, and attacked him in Samaria, in the citadel of the palace along with Argob and Arieh; he killed him, and reigned in place of him. [26] Now the rest of the deeds of Pekahiah, and all that he did, are written in the Book of the Annals of the Kings of Israel.

[27] In the fifty-second year of King Azariah of Judah, Pekah son of Remaliah began to reign over Israel in Samaria; he reigned twenty years. [28] He did what was evil in the sight of the LORD; he did not depart from the sins of Jeroboam son of Nebat, which he caused Israel to sin.

[29] In the days of King Pekah of Israel, King Tiglath-pileser of Assyria came and captured Ijon, Abel-beth-maacah, Janoah, Kedesh,

Hazor, Gilead, and Galilee, all the land of Naphtali; and he carried the people captive to Assyria. [30] Then Hoshea son of Elah made a conspiracy against Pekah son of Remaliah, attacked him, and killed him; he reigned in place of him, in the twentieth year of Jotham son of Uzziah. [31] Now the rest of the acts of Pekah, and all that he did, are written in the Book of the Annals of the Kings of Israel.

[32] In the second year of King Pekah son of Remaliah of Israel, King Jotham son of Uzziah of Judah began to reign. [33] He was twenty-five years old when he began to reign and reigned sixteen years in Jerusalem. His mother's name was Jerusha daughter of Zadok. [34] He did what was right in the sight of the LORD, just as his father Uzziah had done. [35] Nevertheless the high places were not removed; the people still sacrificed and made offerings on the high places. He built the upper gate of the house of the LORD. [36] Now the rest of the acts of Jotham, and all that he did, are they not written in the Book of the Annals of the Kings of Judah? [37] In those days the LORD began to send King Rezin of Aram and Pekah son of Remaliah against Judah. [38] Jotham slept with his ancestors, and was buried with his ancestors in the city of David, his ancestor; his son Ahaz succeeded him.

16 In the seventeenth year of Pekah son of Remaliah, King Ahaz son of Jotham of Judah began to reign. [2] Ahaz was twenty

tribute and to prevent the annexation of his kingdom, Menahem raises special taxes. *Fifty shekels,* ca. 20 oz (570 gr). **23–26:** *Pekahiah* (737–735 BCE), too, is the victim of conspiracy, which illustrates the chaotic situation. His murderer, *Pekah,* has a shortened form of the same name. **25:** The usurper is supported by fifty *Gileadites,* which suggests intertribal rivalry. *Argob and Arieh* ("lion") may be place names transferred from v. 29; another view is that these are the names of two sphinxlike statues at the entrance of the palace. **27–31:** There are several problems concerning Pekah's reign, and some scholars wonder if this king really existed (see also the lack of chronological precision in v. 29). If so, his reign must have been much shorter (ca. 735–732). **29:** The localities mentioned here probably refer to different campaigns of *Tiglath-pileser* III. Important territories in the north and the east of Israel were transformed into Assyrian provinces, and deportation of some of the population also took place. **30:** According to Assyrian sources, Hoshea conspired against Pekah with Assyrian support. *In the twentieth year of Jotham,* this indication for Pekah's assassination is clumsy. According to 16.1 it was during Pekah's reign that Jotham's son acceded to the throne.

15.32–16.20: Jotham and Ahaz, kings of Judah. 15.32–38: *Jotham* (ca. 759–743 BCE) had already been exercising power in Judah during his father's illness (15.5); the *sixteen years* of reign include this coregency. **33:** His mother was a *daughter of Zadok,* which may indicate a priestly lineage; see 1 Kings 1.38–39; 2 Sam 8.17. **35:** *He built the upper gate,* it is not clear if this is a new construction or a rebuilding of a formerly damaged gate (see 14.13–14; the upper gate is also mentioned in Ezek 9.2). 2 Chr 27 adds much more building activity during Jotham's reign. **37:** The attacks by the kings *Rezin of Aram and Pekah* of Israel (see 16.5–9) are the context of Isa 7–9. **16.1–20:** *Ahaz* (ca. 743/735–727/715 BCE; the exact chronology of his reign is much debated) is described as

years old when he began to reign; he reigned sixteen years in Jerusalem. He did not do what was right in the sight of the LORD his God, as his ancestor David had done, ³ but he walked in the way of the kings of Israel. He even made his son pass through fire, according to the abominable practices of the nations whom the LORD drove out before the people of Israel. ⁴ He sacrificed and made offerings on the high places, on the hills, and under every green tree.

⁵ Then King Rezin of Aram and King Pekah son of Remaliah of Israel came up to wage war on Jerusalem; they besieged Ahaz but could not conquer him. ⁶ At that time the king of Edom^a recovered Elath for Edom,^b and drove the Judeans from Elath; and the Edomites came to Elath, where they live to this day. ⁷ Ahaz sent messengers to King Tiglath-pileser of Assyria, saying, "I am your servant and your son. Come up, and rescue me from the hand of the king of Aram and from the hand of the king of Israel, who are attacking me." ⁸ Ahaz also took the silver and gold found in the house of the LORD and in the treasures of the king's house, and sent a present to the king of Assyria. ⁹ The king of Assyria listened to him; the king of Assyria marched up against Damascus, and took it, carrying its people captive to Kir; then he killed Rezin.

¹⁰ When King Ahaz went to Damascus to meet King Tiglath-pileser of Assyria, he saw the altar that was at Damascus. King Ahaz sent to the priest Uriah a model of the altar, and its pattern, exact in all its details. ¹¹ The priest Uriah built the altar; in accor-

dance with all that King Ahaz had sent from Damascus, just so did the priest Uriah build it, before King Ahaz arrived from Damascus. ¹² When the king came from Damascus, the king viewed the altar. Then the king drew near to the altar, went up on it, ¹³ and offered his burnt offering and his grain offering, poured his drink offering, and dashed the blood of his offerings of well-being against the altar. ¹⁴ The bronze altar that was before the LORD he removed from the front of the house, from the place between his altar and the house of the LORD, and put it on the north side of his altar. ¹⁵ King Ahaz commanded the priest Uriah, saying, "Upon the great altar offer the morning burnt offering, and the evening grain offering, and the king's burnt offering, and his grain offering, with the burnt offering of all the people of the land, their grain offering, and their drink offering; then dash against it all the blood of the burnt offering, and all the blood of the sacrifice; but the bronze altar shall be for me to inquire by." ¹⁶ The priest Uriah did everything that King Ahaz commanded.

¹⁷ Then King Ahaz cut off the frames of the stands, and removed the laver from them; he removed the sea from the bronze oxen that were under it, and put it on a pediment of stone. ¹⁸ The covered portal for use on the sabbath that had been built inside the palace, and the outer entrance for the king he removed from^c the house of the LORD. He did

a   Cn: Heb *King Rezin of Aram*

b   Cn: Heb *Aram*

c   Cn: Heb lacks *from*

one of Judah's worst kings. **3**: He is compared to the northern kings and accused of making *his son pass through fire*, which may allude to human sacrifice (see 3.27; Jer. 7.31; 19.5). According to Lev 18.21 and Jer 32.35 such sacrifices were offered to a god Molech, whose identity is unclear. **5–9**: The reason for the attack of *Rezin* and *Pekah* was to force Ahaz to join an anti-Assyrian coalition. **6**: During this military crisis Ahaz loses *Elath* (see 14.22) to the *Edomites*. **7–8**: Ahaz's behavior is similar to that of Menahem of Israel (15.20); he becomes a vassal of the Assyrian king *Tiglath-pileser*. **9**: Tiglath-pileser deports the population of *Damascus* to *Kir* (its location is unknown; in Aramaic it can also mean "city"), which according to Am 9.7 is the original Aramean homeland. **10–16**: This episode reports the introduction of a new Aramean-style altar to replace the former altar of the Jerusalemite Temple (see 1 Kings 8.64). **10–11**: The altar is built by the *priest Uriah*, also mentioned in Isa 8.2, according to a model of an altar that Ahaz had seen in Damascus. **15**: The old bronze altar will serve from now on *to inquire by*, perhaps by divination (such as reading the entrails of animals sacrificed); see also 2 Chr 28.23. **17**: Ahaz apparently removes precious elements of the Temple furnishings, like the *bronze oxen* supporting the *sea* (1 Kings 7.23–29). **18**: *Because of the king of Assyria* suggests that Ahaz needed these objects in order to pay tribute to his suzerain.

this because of the king of Assyria. [19] Now the rest of the acts of Ahaz that he did, are they not written in the Book of the Annals of the Kings of Judah? [20] Ahaz slept with his ancestors, and was buried with his ancestors in the city of David; his son Hezekiah succeeded him.

17 In the twelfth year of King Ahaz of Judah, Hoshea son of Elah began to reign in Samaria over Israel; he reigned nine years. [2] He did what was evil in the sight of the LORD, yet not like the kings of Israel who were before him. [3] King Shalmaneser of Assyria came up against him; Hoshea became his vassal, and paid him tribute. [4] But the king of Assyria found treachery in Hoshea; for he had sent messengers to King So of Egypt, and offered no tribute to the king of Assyria, as he had done year by year; therefore the king of Assyria confined him and imprisoned him.

[5] Then the king of Assyria invaded all the land and came to Samaria; for three years he besieged it. [6] In the ninth year of Hoshea the king of Assyria captured Samaria; he carried the Israelites away to Assyria. He placed them in Halah, on the Habor, the river of Gozan, and in the cities of the Medes.

[7] This occurred because the people of Israel had sinned against the LORD their God, who had brought them up out of the land of Egypt from under the hand of Pharaoh king of Egypt. They had worshiped other gods [8] and walked in the customs of the nations whom the LORD drove out before the people of Israel, and in the customs that the kings of Israel had introduced.[a] [9] The people of Israel secretly did things that were not right against the LORD their God. They built for themselves high places at all their towns, from watchtower to fortified city; [10] they set up for themselves

pillars and sacred poles[b] on every high hill and under every green tree; [11] there they made offerings on all the high places, as the nations did whom the LORD carried away before them. They did wicked things, provoking the LORD to anger; [12] they served idols, of which the LORD had said to them, "You shall not do this." [13] Yet the LORD warned Israel and Judah by every prophet and every seer, saying, "Turn from your evil ways and keep my commandments and my statutes, in accordance with all the law that I commanded your ancestors and that I sent to you by my servants the prophets." [14] They would not listen but were stubborn, as their ancestors had been, who did not believe in the LORD their God. [15] They despised his statutes, and his covenant that he made with their ancestors, and the warnings that he gave them. They went after false idols and became false; they followed the nations that were around them, concerning whom the LORD had commanded them that they should not do as they did. [16] They rejected all the commandments of the LORD their God and made for themselves cast images of two calves; they made a sacred pole,[c] worshiped all the host of heaven, and served Baal. [17] They made their sons and their daughters pass through fire; they used divination and augury; and they sold themselves to do evil in the sight of the LORD, provoking him to anger. [18] Therefore the LORD was very angry with Israel and removed them out of his sight; none was left but the tribe of Judah alone.

[19] Judah also did not keep the commandments of the LORD their God but walked in

---

a Meaning of Heb uncertain
b Heb *Asherim*
c Heb *Asherah*

17.1–41: The end of the kingdom of Israel. 1–4: *Hoshea*, the last king of Israel (ca. 732–722 BCE) is not considered as bad as his predecessors (see v. 2), probably because of his anti-Assyrian politics. **3–4:** Although at the beginning of his reign he is a loyal vassal of the Assyrian king Shalmaneser V (ca. 727–722 BCE), later he tries to find Egyptian support against the Assyrians. **4:** *King So of Egypt*: no Pharaoh with this name is known. *So* could be a reference to the Egyptian town of Sais, or an incorrect transcription of the Egyptian word for "king." **5–6:** Samaria was taken in 722 BCE, and parts of the population deported to *Halah* and *Habor* in northwestern Mesopotamia and to *the cities of the Medes* farther east. **7–23:** This passage is a theological commentary from the Deuteronomistic perspective explaining the reasons for the collapse of Israel. The main reason for the catastrophe is the worship of other gods and the rejection of the LORD and his messengers, the prophets. **16–17:** For the *two calves*, see 1 Kings 12.28–30; *sacred pole*, see 13.6n. The veneration of the *host of heaven* (the planets and stars) and the practice of *divination and augury* will reappear under the reign of the Judean king Manasseh

the customs that Israel had introduced. [20] The LORD rejected all the descendants of Israel; he punished them and gave them into the hand of plunderers, until he had banished them from his presence.

[21] When he had torn Israel from the house of David, they made Jeroboam son of Nebat king. Jeroboam drove Israel from following the LORD and made them commit great sin. [22] The people of Israel continued in all the sins that Jeroboam committed; they did not depart from them [23] until the LORD removed Israel out of his sight, as he had foretold through all his servants the prophets. So Israel was exiled from their own land to Assyria until this day.

[24] The king of Assyria brought people from Babylon, Cuthah, Avva, Hamath, and Sepharvaim, and placed them in the cities of Samaria in place of the people of Israel; they took possession of Samaria, and settled in its cities. [25] When they first settled there, they did not worship the LORD; therefore the LORD sent lions among them, which killed some of them. [26] So the king of Assyria was told, "The nations that you have carried away and placed in the cities of Samaria do not know the law of the god of the land; therefore he has sent lions among them; they are killing them, because they do not know the law of the god of the land." [27] Then the king of Assyria commanded, "Send there one of the priests whom you carried away from there; let him[a] go and live there, and teach them the law of the god of the land." [28] So one of the priests whom they had carried away from Samaria came and lived in Bethel; he taught them how they should worship the LORD.

[29] But every nation still made gods of its own and put them in the shrines of the high places that the people of Samaria had made, every nation in the cities in which they lived; [30] the people of Babylon made Succoth-benoth, the people of Cuth made Nergal, the people of Hamath made Ashima; [31] the Avvites made Nibhaz and Tartak; the Sepharvites burned their children in the fire to Adrammelech and Anammelech, the gods of Sepharvaim. [32] They also worshiped the LORD and appointed from among themselves all sorts of people as priests of the high places, who sacrificed for them in the shrines of the high places. [33] So they worshiped the LORD but also served their own gods, after the manner of the nations from among whom they had been carried away. [34] To this day they continue to practice their former customs.

They do not worship the LORD and they do not follow the statutes or the ordinances or the law or the commandment that the LORD commanded the children of Jacob, whom he named Israel. [35] The LORD had made a covenant with them and commanded them, "You shall not worship other gods or bow yourselves to them or serve them or sacrifice to them, [36] but you shall worship the LORD, who brought you out of the land of Egypt with great power and with an outstretched arm; you shall bow yourselves to him, and to him you shall sacrifice. [37] The statutes and the ordinances and the law and the commandment that he wrote for you, you shall always be careful to observe. You shall not

a   Syr Vg: Heb them

(21.3–6). *Pass through fire*, see 16.3n. **19**: *Judah also did not keep the commandments of the LORD*, a later addition informing the reader that Judah will finally have the same destiny as Israel. **21–23**: A summary of the history of the Northern Kingdom of Israel from the Deuteronomistic perspective. **23**: *So Israel was exiled . . . until this day*, probably the original conclusion to the chapter. **24–28**: Assyrian policy was to mix conquered populations. **24**: These populations are said to come from *Babylon*; *Cuthah*, ca. 12 mi (20 km) northeast of Babylon; *Avva*, probably close to *Hamath* on the Orontes; and *Sepharvaim*, probably also in Syria. (See also 18.34; 19.13.) **25**: *The LORD sent lions*, this may either refer to a lion plague (such plagues are also attested in an Assyrian document) or is perhaps a narrative motif (see 1 Kings 13.24; 20.36), which explains how the non-Israelite population adopted the worship of the LORD. **28**: After the destruction of Samaria, *Bethel* continued to be an important religious center for the inhabitants of the former kingdom of Israel (see 1 Kings 12.29–30). **29–40**: This passage denounces a syncretistic religion of the "people of Samaria" (now the name of the Assyrian province that replaced the former Northern Kingdom) and is an origin of the Judean polemics against its inhabitants, who will later be called "Samaritans." **30–31**: *Nergal* was the Babylonian god of the underworld; little is known about the other

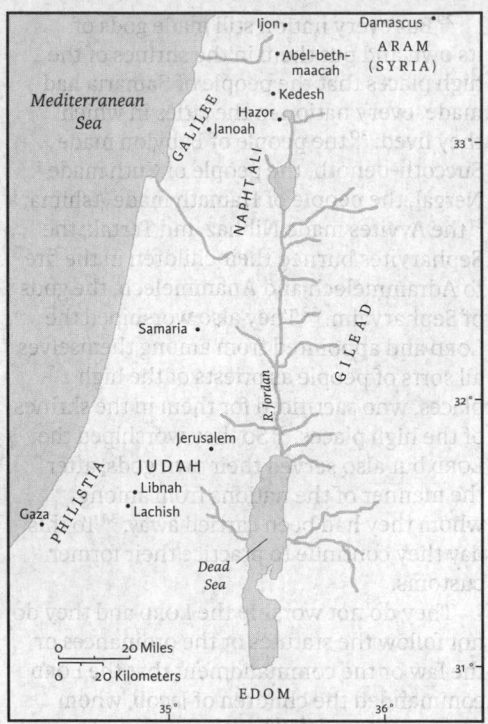

Chs 18–20: Places associated with Sennacherib's invasion of Judah.

worship other gods; ³⁸ you shall not forget the covenant that I have made with you. You shall not worship other gods, ³⁹ but you shall worship the LORD your God; he will deliver you out of the hand of all your enemies." ⁴⁰ They would not listen, however, but they continued to practice their former custom.

⁴¹ So these nations worshiped the LORD, but also served their carved images; to this day their children and their children's children continue to do as their ancestors did.

18 In the third year of King Hoshea son of Elah of Israel, Hezekiah son of King Ahaz of Judah began to reign. ² He was twenty-five years old when he began to reign; he reigned twenty-nine years in Jerusalem. His mother's name was Abi daughter of Zechariah. ³ He did what was right in the sight of the LORD just as his ancestor David had done. ⁴ He removed the high places, broke down the pillars, and cut down the sacred pole.ᵃ He broke in pieces the bronze serpent that Moses had made, for until those days the people of Israel had made offerings to it; it was called Nehushtan. ⁵ He trusted in the LORD the God of Israel; so that there was no one like him among all the kings of Judah after him, or among those who were before him. ⁶ For he held fast to the LORD; he did not depart from following him but kept the commandments that the LORD commanded Moses. ⁷ The LORD was with him; wherever he went, he prospered. He rebelled against the king of Assyria and would not serve him. ⁸ He attacked the Philistines as far as Gaza and its territory, from watchtower to fortified city.

⁹ In the fourth year of King Hezekiah, which was the seventh year of King Hoshea son of Elah of Israel, King Shalmaneser of Assyria came up against Samaria, besieged it, ¹⁰ and at the end of three years, took it. In the sixth year of Hezekiah, which was the ninth year of King Hoshea of Israel, Samaria was taken. ¹¹ The king of Assyria carried the Israelites away to Assyria, settled them in Halah, on the Habor, the river of Gozan, and in the cities of the Medes, ¹² because

ᵃ Heb *Asherah*

deities mentioned. **41**: This concluding verse resumes v. 33 and introduces the anti-Samaritan polemics into the reader's present (*to this day*).

18.1–19.37: King Hezekiah and the siege of Jerusalem. Together with David and Josiah, *Hezekiah* is one of the most praised kings. The exact chronology of his reign is unclear (ca. 727/715–698/687 BCE are the most widely accepted possibilities; perhaps he began as coregent in 729, and reigned alone in 715). The decisive event of his reign is the Assyrian siege of Jerusalem in 701 BCE, an event also described in Assyrian sources. **1–6**: In the introduction, Hezekiah is described as a religious reformer. **4**: He is the first Judean king to remove the *high places*, which had existed in Judah since the beginnings of the monarchy. He also removed from the Temple the *sacred pole* (Heb "'asherah"), a symbol of the goddess Asherah, who had been venerated as a consort of the LORD. *Nehushtan*, a bronze serpent associated with Moses (see Num 21.1–9), which may be linked either to the veneration of Asherah or to the Egyptian worship of a snake goddess. **5**: This verse ranks Hezekiah even higher than Josiah (but see 23.25) and David. **7–18**: Hezekiah's revolt against the Assyrians provokes the siege of Jerusalem by King Sennacherib (ruled ca. 705–681 BCE). The narrative in 18.13–20.19 also appears with some differences in

they did not obey the voice of the LORD their God but transgressed his covenant— all that Moses the servant of the LORD had commanded; they neither listened nor obeyed.

[13] In the fourteenth year of King Hezekiah, King Sennacherib of Assyria came up against all the fortified cities of Judah and captured them. [14] King Hezekiah of Judah sent to the king of Assyria at Lachish, saying, "I have done wrong; withdraw from me; whatever you impose on me I will bear." The king of Assyria demanded of King Hezekiah of Judah three hundred talents of silver and thirty talents of gold. [15] Hezekiah gave him all the silver that was found in the house of the LORD and in the treasuries of the king's house. [16] At that time Hezekiah stripped the gold from the doors of the temple of the LORD, and from the doorposts that King Hezekiah of Judah had overlaid and gave it to the king of Assyria. [17] The king of Assyria sent the Tartan, the Rabsaris, and the Rabshakeh with a great army from Lachish to King Hezekiah at Jerusalem. They went up and came to Jerusalem. When they arrived, they came and stood by the conduit of the upper pool, which is on the highway to the Fuller's Field. [18] When they called for the king, there came out to them Eliakim son of Hilkiah, who was in charge of the palace, and Shebnah the secretary, and Joah son of Asaph, the recorder.

[19] The Rabshakeh said to them, "Say to Hezekiah: Thus says the great king, the king of Assyria: On what do you base this confidence of yours? [20] Do you think that mere words are strategy and power for war?

On whom do you now rely, that you have rebelled against me? [21] See, you are relying now on Egypt, that broken reed of a staff, which will pierce the hand of anyone who leans on it. Such is Pharaoh king of Egypt to all who rely on him. [22] But if you say to me, 'We rely on the LORD our God,' is it not he whose high places and altars Hezekiah has removed, saying to Judah and to Jerusalem, 'You shall worship before this altar in Jerusalem'? [23] Come now, make a wager with my master the king of Assyria: I will give you two thousand horses, if you are able on your part to set riders on them. [24] How then can you repulse a single captain among the least of my master's servants, when you rely on Egypt for chariots and for horsemen? [25] Moreover, is it without the LORD that I have come up against this place to destroy it? The LORD said to me, Go up against this land, and destroy it."

[26] Then Eliakim son of Hilkiah, and Shebnah, and Joah said to the Rabshakeh, "Please speak to your servants in the Aramaic language, for we understand it; do not speak to us in the language of Judah within the hearing of the people who are on the wall." [27] But the Rabshakeh said to them, "Has my master sent me to speak these words to your master and to you, and not to the people sitting on the wall, who are doomed with you to eat their own dung and to drink their own urine?"

[28] Then the Rabshakeh stood and called out in a loud voice in the language of Judah, "Hear the word of the great king, the king of Assyria! [29] Thus says the king: 'Do not let Hezekiah deceive you, for he will not be

Isa 36–39. 9–12: The summary of the fall of Samaria (see 17.1–6) is background to the siege of Jerusalem. 13–16: Astonishingly Hezekiah submits immediately to the Assyrian king, promising that he would be a loyal vassal, and paying a tribute for which he has to plunder the Temple. 14: *Lachish* (see 14.19) had become the Assyrian headquarters. 17: In spite of the payment of tribute the Assyrian king wants to take on Jerusalem. This discrepancy with vv. 13–16 may indicate that this verse starts an alternative version of the Assyrian siege. The *Tartan* (chief commander), the *Rabsaris* (lit. "chief eunuch"), and the *Rabshakeh* (lit. "chief butler") are high Assyrian officials. Only the *Rabshakeh* plays a role in the following narrative. *The upper pool*, for the problem of its location see Isa 7.3n. 18: The three Assyrians are faced by three high Judean officials (for the titles see 1 Kings 4.2–6). 19–25: The Rabshakeh's speech is an example of psychological warfare in the first millennium BCE. In the first part of this speech he alludes to Hezekiah's reform (v. 22) and claims that the LORD is on the Assyrian side (v. 25). 26–27: These verses provide a transition between the two parts of the Rabshakeh's speech. The Judean officials do not want him to speak in Hebrew (*the language of Judah*), but in *Aramaic*, the principal language of diplomacy in the Assyrian empire, which was not understood by the ordinary people. 27: *Eat their own dung*, a crude description of the consequences of a long siege. 28–35: Now the Rabshakeh insists on the impotence of Hezekiah

able to deliver you out of my hand. [30] Do not let Hezekiah make you rely on the LORD by saying, The LORD will surely deliver us, and this city will not be given into the hand of the king of Assyria.' [31] Do not listen to Hezekiah; for thus says the king of Assyria: 'Make your peace with me and come out to me; then every one of you will eat from your own vine and your own fig tree, and drink water from your own cistern, [32] until I come and take you away to a land like your own land, a land of grain and wine, a land of bread and vineyards, a land of olive oil and honey, that you may live and not die. Do not listen to Hezekiah when he misleads you by saying, The LORD will deliver us. [33] Has any of the gods of the nations ever delivered its land out of the hand of the king of Assyria? [34] Where are the gods of Hamath and Arpad? Where are the gods of Sepharvaim, Hena, and Ivvah? Have they delivered Samaria out of my hand? [35] Who among all the gods of the countries have delivered their countries out of my hand, that the LORD should deliver Jerusalem out of my hand?'"

[36] But the people were silent and answered him not a word, for the king's command was, "Do not answer him." [37] Then Eliakim son of Hilkiah, who was in charge of the palace, and Shebna the secretary, and Joah son of Asaph, the recorder, came to Hezekiah with their clothes torn and told him the words of the Rabshakeh.

19 When King Hezekiah heard it, he tore his clothes, covered himself with sackcloth, and went into the house of the LORD. [2] And he sent Eliakim, who was in charge of the palace, and Shebna the secretary, and the senior priests, covered with sackcloth, to the prophet Isaiah son of Amoz. [3] They said to him, "Thus says Hezekiah, This day is a day of distress, of rebuke, and of disgrace;

children have come to the birth, and there is no strength to bring them forth. [4] It may be that the LORD your God heard all the words of the Rabshakeh, whom his master the king of Assyria has sent to mock the living God, and will rebuke the words that the LORD your God has heard; therefore lift up your prayer for the remnant that is left." [5] When the servants of King Hezekiah came to Isaiah, [6] Isaiah said to them, "Say to your master, 'Thus says the LORD: Do not be afraid because of the words that you have heard, with which the servants of the king of Assyria have reviled me. [7] I myself will put a spirit in him, so that he shall hear a rumor and return to his own land; I will cause him to fall by the sword in his own land.'"

[8] The Rabshakeh returned, and found the king of Assyria fighting against Libnah; for he had heard that the king had left Lachish. [9] When the king[a] heard concerning King Tirhakah of Ethiopia,[b] "See, he has set out to fight against you," he sent messengers again to Hezekiah, saying, [10] "Thus shall you speak to King Hezekiah of Judah: Do not let your God on whom you rely deceive you by promising that Jerusalem will not be given into the hand of the king of Assyria. [11] See, you have heard what the kings of Assyria have done to all lands, destroying them utterly. Shall you be delivered? [12] Have the gods of the nations delivered them, the nations that my predecessors destroyed, Gozan, Haran, Rezeph, and the people of Eden who were in Telassar? [13] Where is the king of Hamath, the king of Arpad, the king of the city of Sepharvaim, the king of Hena, or the king of Ivvah?"

[14] Hezekiah received the letter from the hand of the messengers and read it; then

---

a Heb *he*

b Or *Nubia*; Heb *Cush*

---

and the LORD, claiming that no god of any country was able to resist the Assyrians and their gods (v. 33). **32:** Cf. Deut 8.7–9. **34:** A list of cities conquered by the Assyrians; see 17.24. *Arpad*, the capital of an Aramean state, which had joined an anti-Assyrian coalition. **36–37:** The people and the officials do not react to these words. The action now moves to Hezekiah. **37:** *Clothes torn* (see also 19.1), an act of remorse. **19.1–7:** Hezekiah consults the prophet *Isaiah* who announces to the king's messengers an oracle of salvation. **7:** The LORD will put a *spirit* into the mind of the Assyrian king in order to entice him, ultimately to his death (cf. 1 Kings 22.20–23). **8–13:** The withdrawal of the Assyrian army at this stage seems odd. Verses 8–9 may belong to a source older than the surrounding verses. **8:** *Libnah*, see 8.22n. **9:** *Tirhakah of Ethiopia* became the ruler of Egypt in 689 BCE and was only a young boy during the siege of Jerusalem in 701—this suggests that this section is not historically accurate but

Hezekiah went up to the house of the LORD and spread it before the LORD. ¹⁵ And Hezekiah prayed before the LORD, and said: "O LORD the God of Israel, who are enthroned above the cherubim, you are God, you alone, of all the kingdoms of the earth; you have made heaven and earth. ¹⁶ Incline your ear, O LORD, and hear; open your eyes, O LORD, and see; hear the words of Sennacherib, which he has sent to mock the living God. ¹⁷ Truly, O LORD, the kings of Assyria have laid waste the nations and their lands, ¹⁸ and have hurled their gods into the fire, though they were no gods but the work of human hands—wood and stone— and so they were destroyed. ¹⁹ So now, O LORD our God, save us, I pray you, from his hand, so that all the kingdoms of the earth may know that you, O LORD, are God alone."

²⁰ Then Isaiah son of Amoz sent to Hezekiah, saying, "Thus says the LORD, the God of Israel: I have heard your prayer to me about King Sennacherib of Assyria. ²¹ This is the word that the LORD has spoken concerning him:

She despises you, she scorns you—
　virgin daughter Zion;
she tosses her head—behind your back,
　daughter Jerusalem.

²² "Whom have you mocked and reviled?
　Against whom have you raised your
　　voice
and haughtily lifted your eyes?
　Against the Holy One of Israel!
²³ By your messengers you have mocked
　the Lord,
　and you have said, 'With my many
　　chariots
I have gone up the heights of the
　mountains,
　to the far recesses of Lebanon;

I felled its tallest cedars,
　its choicest cypresses;
I entered its farthest retreat,
　its densest forest.
²⁴ I dug wells
　and drank foreign waters,
I dried up with the sole of my foot
　all the streams of Egypt.'

²⁵ "Have you not heard
　that I determined it long ago?
I planned from days of old
　what now I bring to pass,
that you should make fortified cities
　crash into heaps of ruins,
²⁶ while their inhabitants, shorn of
　strength,
　are dismayed and confounded;
they have become like plants of the field
　and like tender grass,
like grass on the housetops,
　blighted before it is grown.

²⁷ "But I know your risingª and your sitting,
　your going out and coming in,
　and your raging against me.
²⁸ Because you have raged against me
　and your arrogance has come to my
　　ears,
I will put my hook in your nose
　and my bit in your mouth;
I will turn you back on the way
　by which you came.

²⁹ "And this shall be the sign for you: This year you shall eat what grows of itself, and in the second year what springs from that; then in the third year sow, reap, plant vineyards, and eat their fruit. ³⁰ The surviving remnant

ª Gk Compare Isa 37.27 Q Ms: MT lacks *rising*

is legendary. **10–13:** This new Assyrian propaganda repeats the arguments of 18.32–35. **14:** Hezekiah is informed of this by a *letter*, a small scroll that he could *spread* out. **15–19:** Hezekiah's prayer depicts him as a pious king who affirms that the LORD is the only true God. **15:** *Cherubim*: see 1 Kings 6.23–28. **18:** *Have hurled their gods into fire*, the Assyrians did indeed capture and sometimes destroy divine statues, not by burning them however, but by breaking them into pieces. **20–34:** A second prophecy of Isaiah brings God's response to Hezekiah's prayer. **21–28:** These verses contain an oracle against the Assyrian king Sennacherib, whose word (vv. 10–13) is now opposed to the LORD's word. **21:** *Virgin daughter Zion*, both Israelite and foreign cities are often represented as female, especially in poetry. **28:** *I will put my hook in your nose*, it was Assyrian practice to humiliate vassals and prisoners; here the LORD does this to Assyria. **29–31:** The second response is directed to Hezekiah. The theme of a *sign* is often linked with the prophet Isaiah (20.9; Isa 7.11; 8.1), as is the theme of a surviving *remnant* (Isa

of the house of Judah shall again take root downward, and bear fruit upward; ³¹ for from Jerusalem a remnant shall go out, and from Mount Zion a band of survivors. The zeal of the LORD of hosts will do this.

³² "Therefore thus says the LORD concerning the king of Assyria: He shall not come into this city, shoot an arrow there, come before it with a shield, or cast up a siege ramp against it. ³³ By the way that he came, by the same he shall return; he shall not come into this city, says the LORD. ³⁴ For I will defend this city to save it, for my own sake and for the sake of my servant David."

³⁵ That very night the angel of the LORD set out and struck down one hundred eighty-five thousand in the camp of the Assyrians; when morning dawned, they were all dead bodies. ³⁶ Then King Sennacherib of Assyria left, went home, and lived at Nineveh. ³⁷ As he was worshiping in the house of his god Nisroch, his sons Adrammelech and Sharezer killed him with the sword, and they escaped into the land of Ararat. His son Esar-haddon succeeded him.

20
In those days Hezekiah became sick and was at the point of death. The prophet Isaiah son of Amoz came to him, and said to him, "Thus says the LORD: Set your house in order, for you shall die; you shall not recover." ² Then Hezekiah turned his face to the wall and prayed to the LORD: ³ "Remember now, O LORD, I implore you, how I have walked before you in faithfulness with a whole heart, and have done what is good in your sight." Hezekiah wept bitterly. ⁴ Before Isaiah had gone out of the middle court, the word of the LORD came to him: ⁵ "Turn back, and say to Hezekiah prince of my people, Thus says the LORD, the God of your ancestor David: I have heard your prayer, I have seen your tears; indeed, I will heal you; on the third day you shall go up to the house of the LORD. ⁶ I will add fifteen years to your life. I will deliver you and this city out of the hand of the king of Assyria; I will defend this city for my own sake and for my servant David's sake." ⁷ Then Isaiah said, "Bring a lump of figs. Let them take it and apply it to the boil, so that he may recover."

⁸ Hezekiah said to Isaiah, "What shall be the sign that the LORD will heal me, and that I shall go up to the house of the LORD on the third day?" ⁹ Isaiah said, "This is the sign to you from the LORD, that the LORD will do the thing that he has promised: the shadow has now advanced ten intervals; shall it retreat ten intervals?" ¹⁰ Hezekiah answered, "It is normal for the shadow to lengthen ten intervals; rather let the shadow retreat ten intervals." ¹¹ The prophet Isaiah cried to the LORD; and he brought the shadow back the ten intervals, by which the sun[a] had declined on the dial of Ahaz.

¹² At that time King Merodach-baladan son of Baladan of Babylon sent envoys with letters and a present to Hezekiah, for he had

---

a   Syr See Isa 38.8 and Tg: Heb *it*

10.21–22). **32–34:** The LORD reaffirms that he will *defend* Jerusalem, which is his home and the capital city of the kingdom ruled by the dynasty founded by David, his *servant*; see 38.6; Ps 132.11,13–18. **35–37:** The prophetic word is fulfilled, and the Assyrian army abandons the siege. **35:** The LORD's *angel* striking Israel's enemies recalls Ex 12. *One hundred eighty-five thousand*, an exaggerated number emphasizing the strength of the Assyrian army and the LORD's great power. **36:** Assyrian records are silent about the circumstances under which the assault of Jerusalem concluded. **37:** The assassination of Sennacherib (in approximately 681 BCE, twenty years later) is corroborated by Assyrian documents, which, however, do not give clear details. His successor *Esar-haddon* ruled ca. 681–669 BCE. *Ararat* is in Armenia.

   20.1–21: Isaiah heals Hezekiah and announces the Babylonian exile. The last story about Hezekiah brings some ambiguity to his portrait because his actions appear to hasten the end of Judah. **1–7:** Struck with a life-threatening illness, Hezekiah's prayer receives a favorable response through Isaiah. **6:** *I will add fifteen years*, this oracle led the redactors to date the siege of Jerusalem in the fourteenth year (18.13) of Hezekiah's twenty-nine year reign (18.2). The verse also suggests that Hezekiah's illness happened during the Assyrian siege. **7:** Isaiah also has medical skills and heals the king's disease with a *fig*-poultice. **8–11:** Hezekiah seems to doubt that he will recover complete health. He is given a *sign*: a *shadow*'s movement is reversed. **11:** *The dial of Ahaz*, lit. "the steps of Ahaz." The expression may allude to an otherwise unknown construction with steps, perhaps used as

heard that Hezekiah had been sick. [13] Hezekiah welcomed them;[a] he showed them all his treasure house, the silver, the gold, the spices, the precious oil, his armory, all that was found in his storehouses; there was nothing in his house or in all his realm that Hezekiah did not show them. [14] Then the prophet Isaiah came to King Hezekiah, and said to him, "What did these men say? From where did they come to you?" Hezekiah answered, "They have come from a far country, from Babylon." [15] He said, "What have they seen in your house?" Hezekiah answered, "They have seen all that is in my house; there is nothing in my storehouses that I did not show them."

[16] Then Isaiah said to Hezekiah, "Hear the word of the LORD: [17] Days are coming when all that is in your house, and that which your ancestors have stored up until this day, shall be carried to Babylon; nothing shall be left, says the LORD. [18] Some of your own sons who are born to you shall be taken away; they shall be eunuchs in the palace of the king of Babylon." [19] Then Hezekiah said to Isaiah, "The word of the LORD that you have spoken is good." For he thought, "Why not, if there will be peace and security in my days?"

[20] The rest of the deeds of Hezekiah, all his power, how he made the pool and the conduit and brought water into the city, are they not written in the Book of the Annals of the Kings of Judah? [21] Hezekiah slept with his ancestors; and his son Manasseh succeeded him.

21

Manasseh was twelve years old when he began to reign; he reigned fifty-five years in Jerusalem. His mother's name was Hephzibah. [2] He did what was evil in the sight of the LORD, following the abominable practices of the nations that the LORD drove out before the people of Israel. [3] For he rebuilt the high places that his father Hezekiah had destroyed; he erected altars for Baal, made a sacred pole,[b] as King Ahab of Israel had done, worshiped all the host of heaven, and served them. [4] He built altars in the house of the LORD, of which the LORD had said, "In Jerusalem I will put my name." [5] He built altars for all the host of heaven in the two courts of the house of the LORD. [6] He made his son pass through fire; he practiced soothsaying and augury, and dealt with mediums and with wizards. He did much evil in the sight of the LORD, provoking him to anger. [7] The carved image of Asherah that he had made he set in the house of which the LORD said to David and to his son Solomon, "In this house, and in Jerusalem, which I have chosen out of all the tribes of Israel, I will put my name forever; [8] I will not cause the feet of Israel to wander any more out of the land that I gave to their ancestors, if only they will be careful to do according to all that I have commanded them, and according to all the law that my servant Moses commanded them." [9] But they did not listen; Manasseh misled them to do more evil than the nations had done that the LORD destroyed before the people of Israel.

[10] The LORD said by his servants the prophets, [11] "Because King Manasseh of Judah has committed these abominations,

a Gk Vg Syr: Heb *When Hezekiah heard about them*
b Heb *Asherah*

a sanctuary for the sun-god and as a sundial. **12–15:** The strange episode about a Babylonian embassy recalls the visit of the queen of Sheba to Solomon and thus establishes a parallel between Hezekiah and Solomon. **12:** *Merodach-baladan,* a Babylonian king who ruled 721–710 BCE, and then briefly in 703 (see Isa 39.1). **16–19:** Isaiah's oracle attributes to this embassy a negative meaning, since he predicts the deportation of the Temple's treasures to Babylon, anticipating chs 24–25. **19:** *Why not,* Hezekiah receives the oracle ambiguously. **20–21:** The short conclusion of Hezekiah's reign mentions a pool and a conduit. The so-called "Hezekiah's Tunnel" (the Siloam Tunnel) is still extant under the city of David in Jerusalem.

21.1–26: The reigns of Manasseh and Amon. 1–18: For the redactors of the book of Kings, *Manasseh* is the worst of all Judean kings and is explicitly compared to the northern king Ahab (v. 3). **1:** His reign is said to have lasted fifty-five years, which does not exactly fit the probable dates of his reign (698/687–642 BCE). **2–16:** Although he had a long reign, the only thing we are told about him is his religious counterreform. He reintroduces the worship of other deities into the Temple, as well as the "sacred pole" (see v. 7; 18.4n.). The long enumeration of his religious failures shows that Manasseh contravened all the important laws of the book of Deuteronomy (v. 2=Deut 18.9; vv. 3,7=Deut 16.21; v. 5=Deut 17.3; v. 6=Deut 18.10–11; v. 16=Deut 19.10). **10–15:** In this anony-

has done things more wicked than all that the Amorites did, who were before him, and has caused Judah also to sin with his idols; [12] therefore thus says the LORD, the God of Israel, I am bringing upon Jerusalem and Judah such evil that the ears of everyone who hears of it will tingle. [13] I will stretch over Jerusalem the measuring line for Samaria, and the plummet for the house of Ahab; I will wipe Jerusalem as one wipes a dish, wiping it and turning it upside down. [14] I will cast off the remnant of my heritage, and give them into the hand of their enemies; they shall become a prey and a spoil to all their enemies, [15] because they have done what is evil in my sight and have provoked me to anger, since the day their ancestors came out of Egypt, even to this day."

[16] Moreover Manasseh shed very much innocent blood, until he had filled Jerusalem from one end to another, besides the sin that he caused Judah to sin so that they did what was evil in the sight of the LORD.

[17] Now the rest of the acts of Manasseh, all that he did, and the sin that he committed, are they not written in the Book of the Annals of the Kings of Judah? [18] Manasseh slept with his ancestors, and was buried in the garden of his house, in the garden of Uzza. His son Amon succeeded him.

[19] Amon was twenty-two years old when he began to reign; he reigned two years in Jerusalem. His mother's name was Meshullemeth daughter of Haruz of Jotbah. [20] He did what was evil in the sight of the LORD, as his father Manasseh had done. [21] He walked in all the way in which his father walked, served the idols that his father served, and worshiped them; [22] he abandoned the LORD, the God of his ancestors, and did not walk in the way of the LORD. [23] The servants of Amon conspired against him, and killed the king in his house. [24] But the people of the land killed all those who had conspired against King Amon, and the people of the land made his son Josiah king in place of him. [25] Now the rest of the acts of Amon that he did, are they not written in the Book of the Annals of the Kings of Judah? [26] He was buried in his tomb in the garden of Uzza; then his son Josiah succeeded him.

22 Josiah was eight years old when he began to reign; he reigned thirty-one years in Jerusalem. His mother's name was Jedidah daughter of Adaiah of Bozkath. [2] He did what was right in the sight of the LORD, and walked in all the way of his father David; he did not turn aside to the right or to the left.

[3] In the eighteenth year of King Josiah, the king sent Shaphan son of Azaliah, son

mous prophetic oracle, Manasseh is presented as the main culprit responsible for the fall of Jerusalem and the exile. **11:** *Amorites,* traditional inhabitants of the land of Canaan before the Israelites' arrival. **13:** Jerusalem will therefore be assessed by the divine architect (cf. Isa 34.11; Lam 2.8; Am 7.7–9), and, like a dangerous building, condemned. It will be emptied of all that is in it, wiped clean like a dish after a meal. This divine judgment parallels that on Samaria (ch 17; Am 7.7–9) and *the house of Ahab* (1 Kings 21.21–22; 2 Kings 9–10). **17–18:** One may reasonably guess that during Manasseh's long reign some important events took place and that his reign was a peaceful time. But the redactors of the book of Kings are not interested in these aspects. **18:** *Garden of Uzza,* see also v. 26; its precise location and significance are debated. **19–26:** *Amon*'s short reign (ca. 641–640 BCE) ended with his murder by his court officials. **23:** The only other information about his reign has to do with his religious activities: he continued the syncretism of his father. **24:** *The people of the land* (see 11.14n.), probably some of the free landowners, opposed the rebellion and put Amon's son Josiah on the throne.

22.1–23.30: Josiah's reign and reform. For the authors of the book of Kings *Josiah* (ca. 640–609 BCE) is the perfect king, a new David, but also a new Moses and a new Joshua. In contrast to Hezekiah, Josiah is presented entirely positively. He launches a religious, political, and economic reform and declares the Temple in Jerusalem to be the only legitimate place to worship the LORD. The story contains two different narratives, which are intermingled: the discovery of the "book of the law," and the religious reform. **22.1:** Josiah was *eight years old* when he came to the throne, which means that Judah was then governed by high officials, probably those mentioned in the following narrative. **2:** *He did not turn aside to the right or to the left,* see Deut 5.32; 17.20; Josh 1.7; etc. **3–10:** The report about Josiah repairing the Temple recalls 12.10–16. **3–4:** *Shaphan* and *Hilkiah* are the main actors in the discovery of the book. *Shaphan* was a high official, ancestor of an important family of civil servants at the Judean court (see Jer 36). *Hilkiah* (probably not to be identified with the father of the prophet Jeremiah)

of Meshullam, the secretary, to the house of the LORD, saying, 4 "Go up to the high priest Hilkiah, and have him count the entire sum of the money that has been brought into the house of the LORD, which the keepers of the threshold have collected from the people; 5 let it be given into the hand of the workers who have the oversight of the house of the LORD; let them give it to the workers who are at the house of the LORD, repairing the house, 6 that is, to the carpenters, to the builders, to the masons; and let them use it to buy timber and quarried stone to repair the house. 7 But no accounting shall be asked from them for the money that is delivered into their hand, for they deal honestly."

8 The high priest Hilkiah said to Shaphan the secretary, "I have found the book of the law in the house of the LORD." When Hilkiah gave the book to Shaphan, he read it. 9 Then Shaphan the secretary came to the king, and reported to the king, "Your servants have emptied out the money that was found in the house, and have delivered it into the hand of the workers who have oversight of the house of the LORD." 10 Shaphan the secretary informed the king, "The priest Hilkiah has given me a book." Shaphan then read it aloud to the king.

11 When the king heard the words of the book of the law, he tore his clothes. 12 Then the king commanded the priest Hilkiah, Ahikam son of Shaphan, Achbor son of Micaiah, Shaphan the secretary, and the king's servant Asaiah, saying, 13 "Go, inquire of the LORD for me, for the people, and for all Judah, concerning the words of this book that has been found; for great is the wrath of the LORD that is kindled against us, because our ances-

tors did not obey the words of this book, to do according to all that is written concerning us."

14 So the priest Hilkiah, Ahikam, Achbor, Shaphan, and Asaiah went to the prophetess Huldah the wife of Shallum son of Tikvah, son of Harhas, keeper of the wardrobe; she resided in Jerusalem in the Second Quarter, where they consulted her. 15 She declared to them, "Thus says the LORD, the God of Israel: Tell the man who sent you to me, 16 Thus says the LORD, I will indeed bring disaster on this place and on its inhabitants—all the words of the book that the king of Judah has read. 17 Because they have abandoned me and have made offerings to other gods, so that they have provoked me to anger with all the work of their hands, therefore my wrath will be kindled against this place, and it will not be quenched. 18 But as to the king of Judah, who sent you to inquire of the LORD, thus shall you say to him, Thus says the LORD, the God of Israel: Regarding the words that you have heard, 19 because your heart was penitent, and you humbled yourself before the LORD, when you heard how I spoke against this place, and against its inhabitants, that they should become a desolation and a curse, and because you have torn your clothes and wept before me, I also have heard you, says the LORD. 20 Therefore, I will gather you to your ancestors, and you shall be gathered to your grave in peace; your eyes shall not see all the disaster that I will bring on this place." They took the message back to the king.

23 Then the king directed that all the elders of Judah and Jerusalem should be gathered to him. 2 The king went up to the house of the LORD, and with him went

is the *high priest*, an anachronistic expression (see 12.10n.). **8–10:** The *book*, which reaches the king through Shaphan and Hilkiah is meant to be some form of the book of Deuteronomy. **11:** This becomes clear in the king's reaction of despair and repentance (*he tore his clothes*), which is provoked by curses like Deut 28.61 and 29.21. **12–20:** The king's consultation of a prophetess through high officials (v. 12) may seem surprising, since he had understood already what the book was about (v. 13). **14:** *The prophetess Huldah* was married to a Temple or court officer, the *keeper of the wardrobe* (see 10.22) and she lived in the *Second Quarter*, which refers to a new quarter in the north, built when Jerusalem expanded at the end of the eighth or during the seventh century BCE. **15–18:** Huldah's word confirms the oracle of the unnamed prophets in 21.10–15 (see also Jer 19.14–15). **19–20:** Her oracle concerning Josiah is inconsistent with what is reported later, since he did not die *in peace* but was killed by the Egyptian king (23.29). Perhaps her prophecy meant that Josiah would be spared the agony of Judah's destruction and exile. **23.1–3:** The king himself reads the book to *all the people* and renews the covenant with the LORD. The "book of the law" can therefore also be called *the book of the covenant*. This ceremony begins the religious

all the people of Judah, all the inhabitants of Jerusalem, the priests, the prophets, and all the people, both small and great; he read in their hearing all the words of the book of the covenant that had been found in the house of the LORD. ³ The king stood by the pillar and made a covenant before the LORD, to follow the LORD, keeping his commandments, his decrees, and his statutes, with all his heart and all his soul, to perform the words of this covenant that were written in this book. All the people joined in the covenant.

⁴ The king commanded the high priest Hilkiah, the priests of the second order, and the guardians of the threshold, to bring out of the temple of the LORD all the vessels made for Baal, for Asherah, and for all the host of heaven; he burned them outside Jerusalem in the fields of the Kidron, and carried their ashes to Bethel. ⁵ He deposed the idolatrous priests whom the kings of Judah had ordained to make offerings in the high places at the cities of Judah and around Jerusalem; those also who made offerings to Baal, to the sun, the moon, the constellations, and all the host of the heavens. ⁶ He brought out the image ofª Asherah from the house of the LORD, outside Jerusalem, to the Wadi Kidron, burned it at the Wadi Kidron, beat it to dust and threw the dust of it upon the graves of the common people. ⁷ He broke down the houses of the male temple prostitutes that were in the house of the LORD, where the women did weaving for Asherah. ⁸ He brought all the priests out of the towns of Judah, and defiled the high places where the priests had made offerings, from Geba to Beer-sheba; he broke down the high places of the gates that were at the entrance of the gate of Joshua the governor of the city, which were on the left at the gate of the city. ⁹ The priests of the high places, however, did not come up to the altar of the LORD in Jerusalem, but ate unleavened bread among their kindred. ¹⁰ He defiled Topheth, which is in the valley of Ben-hinnom, so that no one would make a son or a daughter pass through fire as an offering to Molech. ¹¹ He removed the horses that the kings of Judah had dedicated to the sun, at the entrance to the house of the LORD, by the chamber of the eunuch Nathan-melech, which was in the precincts;ᵇ then he burned the chariots of the sun with fire. ¹² The altars on the roof of the upper chamber of Ahaz, which the kings of Judah had made, and the altars that Manasseh had made in the two courts of the house of the LORD, he pulled down from there and broke in pieces, and threw the rubble into the Wadi Kidron. ¹³ The king defiled the high places that were east of Jerusalem, to the south of the Mount of Destruction, which King Solomon of Israel had built for Astarte the abomination of the Sidonians, for Chemosh the abomination of Moab, and for Milcom the abomination of the Ammonites. ¹⁴ He broke the pillars in pieces, cut down the sacred poles,ᶜ and covered the sites with human bones.

¹⁵ Moreover, the altar at Bethel, the high place erected by Jeroboam son of Nebat, who

ª Heb lacks *image of*
ᵇ Meaning of Heb uncertain
ᶜ Heb *Asherim*

reforms, which are described in vv. 4–20. **4–6:** All symbols and statues of other deities are removed from the Temple and destroyed. **4:** The *Kidron* area, which is the valley to the east of the city of David, was used as a burial and burning place (v. 6; see 1 Kings 15.13). **5:** *Idolatrous priests,* a term borrowed from Assyrian where it designates a special type of priests. *Host of the heavens,* see 17.16–17n. **7–9:** This passage relates actions against the religious personnel. **7:** *Male temple prostitutes,* see 1 Kings 22.46n. **8:** The *priests* of the local sanctuaries outside Jerusalem (*the towns of Judah*) were expelled and the sanctuaries were defiled, so that they could no longer be used for the worship of the LORD. *Geba,* ca. 6 mi (10 km) north of Jerusalem, in Benjamin, which may indicate that the Benjaminite territory had become part of the kingdom of Judah. **9:** The priests of the *high places* (1 Kings 3.2–4) were not integrated into the personnel of the Temple in Jerusalem. **10–14:** Further destructions are reported. **10:** *Topheth,* a place used for human sacrifices (see Jer 7.31). *Molech,* see 16.3n. **11:** *Horses,* see 2.11n. *Precincts* (see textual note b), perhaps a Persian word, which indicates that this passage was written during the Persian period. **13:** See 1 Kings 11.5–8n. *Mount of Destruction,* probably a sarcastic wordplay on "mount of oil," since it refers to the Mount of Olives, where the worship of other deities was practiced. **14:** The sites were covered *with human bones* (see also vv. 16 and 20) in order to make them ritually impure. **15–20:** The destruc-

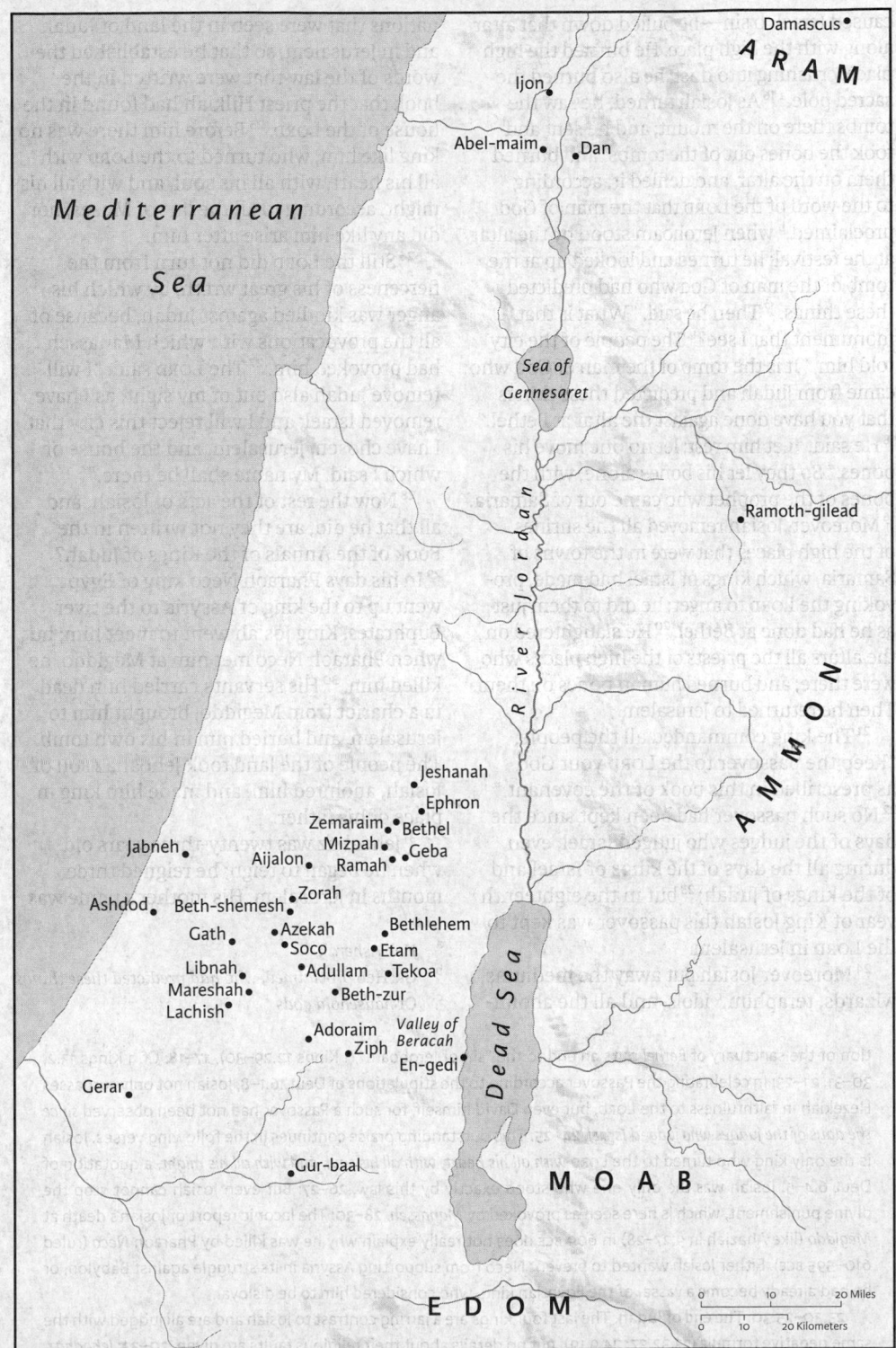

Mediterranean Sea

Damascus

A R A M

Ijon

Abel-maim   Dan

Sea of Gennesaret

Ramoth-gilead

River Jordan

A M M O N

Jeshanah
Ephron
Zemaraim   Bethel
Mizpah   Geba
Jabneh
Aijalon   Ramah
Zorah
Ashdod   Beth-shemesh
Bethlehem
Gath   Azekah
Soco   Etam
Libnah   Adullam   Tekoa
Mareshah   Beth-zur
Lachish

Adoraim   *Valley of Beracah*
Ziph
En-gedi

Dead Sea

Gerar

M O A B

Gur-baal

E D O M

0   10   20 Miles
0   10   20 Kilometers

Important cities in Judah in the late seventh and early sixth centuries BCE.

caused Israel to sin—he pulled down that altar along with the high place. He burned the high place, crushing it to dust; he also burned the sacred pole.[a] 16 As Josiah turned, he saw the tombs there on the mount; and he sent and took the bones out of the tombs, and burned them on the altar, and defiled it, according to the word of the LORD that the man of God proclaimed,[b] when Jeroboam stood by the altar at the festival; he turned and looked up at the tomb of the man of God who had predicted these things. 17 Then he said, "What is that monument that I see?" The people of the city told him, "It is the tomb of the man of God who came from Judah and predicted these things that you have done against the altar at Bethel." 18 He said, "Let him rest; let no one move his bones." So they let his bones alone, with the bones of the prophet who came out of Samaria. 19 Moreover, Josiah removed all the shrines of the high places that were in the towns of Samaria, which kings of Israel had made, provoking the LORD to anger; he did to them just as he had done at Bethel. 20 He slaughtered on the altars all the priests of the high places who were there, and burned human bones on them. Then he returned to Jerusalem.

21 The king commanded all the people, "Keep the passover to the LORD your God as prescribed in this book of the covenant." 22 No such passover had been kept since the days of the judges who judged Israel, even during all the days of the kings of Israel and of the kings of Judah; 23 but in the eighteenth year of King Josiah this passover was kept to the LORD in Jerusalem.

24 Moreover Josiah put away the mediums, wizards, teraphim,[c] idols, and all the abomi-

nations that were seen in the land of Judah and in Jerusalem, so that he established the words of the law that were written in the book that the priest Hilkiah had found in the house of the LORD. 25 Before him there was no king like him, who turned to the LORD with all his heart, with all his soul, and with all his might, according to all the law of Moses; nor did any like him arise after him.

26 Still the LORD did not turn from the fierceness of his great wrath, by which his anger was kindled against Judah, because of all the provocations with which Manasseh had provoked him. 27 The LORD said, "I will remove Judah also out of my sight, as I have removed Israel; and I will reject this city that I have chosen, Jerusalem, and the house of which I said, My name shall be there."

28 Now the rest of the acts of Josiah, and all that he did, are they not written in the Book of the Annals of the Kings of Judah? 29 In his days Pharaoh Neco king of Egypt went up to the king of Assyria to the river Euphrates. King Josiah went to meet him; but when Pharaoh Neco met him at Megiddo, he killed him. 30 His servants carried him dead in a chariot from Megiddo, brought him to Jerusalem, and buried him in his own tomb. The people of the land took Jehoahaz son of Josiah, anointed him, and made him king in place of his father.

31 Jehoahaz was twenty-three years old when he began to reign; he reigned three months in Jerusalem. His mother's name was

a Heb *Asherah*
b Gk: Heb *proclaimed, who had predicted these things*
c Or *household gods*

tion of the sanctuary of *Bethel* puts an end to the "sin of Jeroboam" (1 Kings 12.29–30). **17–18:** Cf. 1 Kings 13.2, 30–31. **21–23:** In celebrating the Passover according to the stipulations of Deut 16.1–8, Josiah not only surpasses Hezekiah in faithfulness to the LORD, but even David himself, for such a Passover had not been observed *since the days of the judges who judged Israel*. **24–25:** This outstanding praise continues in the following verses. Josiah is the only king who turned to the LORD *with all his heart, with all his soul, and with all his might,* a quotation of Deut 6.4–5: Josiah was the only one who stood exactly by this law. **26–27:** But even Josiah cannot stop the divine punishment, which is here seen as provoked by *Manasseh*. **28–30:** The laconic report of Josiah's death at *Megiddo* (like Ahaziah in 9.27–28) in 609 BCE does not really explain why he was killed by Pharaoh *Neco* (ruled 610–595 BCE). Either Josiah wanted to prevent Neco from supporting Assyria in its struggle against Babylon, or he had already become a vassal of the Egyptian king, who considered him to be disloyal.

23.30–25.30: The end of Judah. The last four kings are a jarring contrast to Josiah and are all judged with the same negative formula (23.32,37; 24.9,19), but no details about their religious faults are given. **30–33:** *Jehoahaz*, anointed by *the people of the land* (see 11.14n.), ruled for *three* months in 609 BCE. He was unacceptable to *Neco*,

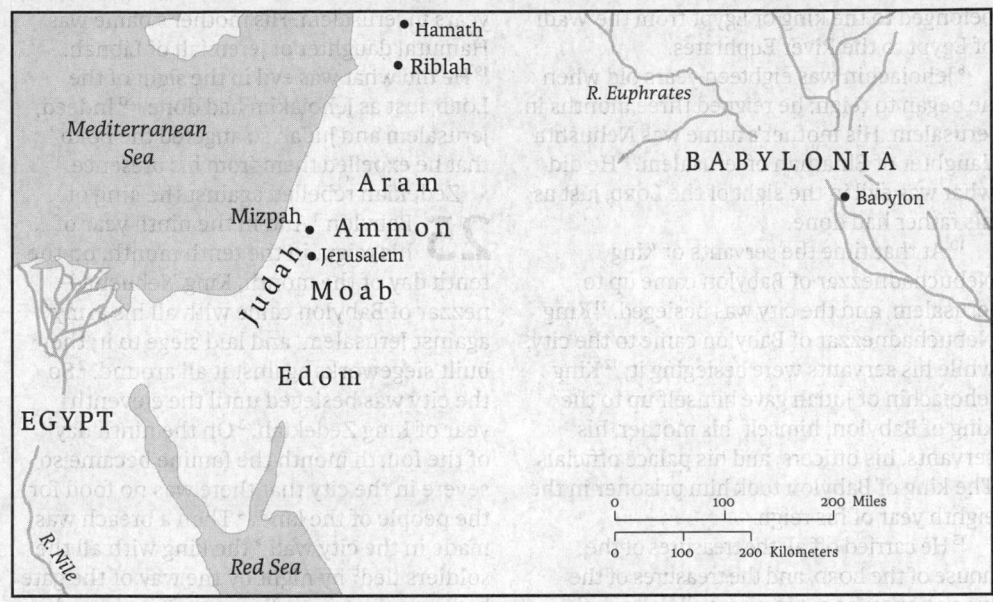

Chs 24–25: Babylon and Judah in the early sixth century BCE.

Hamutal daughter of Jeremiah of Libnah. ³²He did what was evil in the sight of the LORD, just as his ancestors had done. ³³Pharaoh Neco confined him at Riblah in the land of Hamath, so that he might not reign in Jerusalem, and imposed tribute on the land of one hundred talents of silver and a talent of gold. ³⁴Pharaoh Neco made Eliakim son of Josiah king in place of his father Josiah, and changed his name to Jehoiakim. But he took Jehoahaz away; he came to Egypt, and died there. ³⁵Jehoiakim gave the silver and the gold to Pharaoh, but he taxed the land in order to meet Pharaoh's demand for money. He exacted the silver and the gold from the people of the land, from all according to their assessment, to give it to Pharaoh Neco.

³⁶Jehoiakim was twenty-five years old when he began to reign; he reigned eleven years in Jerusalem. His mother's name was Zebidah daughter of Pedaiah of Rumah. ³⁷He did what was evil in the sight of the LORD, just as all his ancestors had done.

24 In his days King Nebuchadnezzar of Babylon came up; Jehoiakim became his servant for three years; then he turned and rebelled against him. ²The LORD sent against him bands of the Chaldeans, bands of the Arameans, bands of the Moabites, and bands of the Ammonites; he sent them against Judah to destroy it, according to the word of the LORD that he spoke by his servants the prophets. ³Surely this came upon Judah at the command of the LORD, to remove them out of his sight, for the sins of Manasseh, for all that he had committed, ⁴and also for the innocent blood that he had shed; for he filled Jerusalem with innocent blood, and the LORD was not willing to pardon.

⁵Now the rest of the deeds of Jehoiakim, and all that he did, are they not written in the Book of the Annals of the Kings of Judah? ⁶So Jehoiakim slept with his ancestors; then his son Jehoiachin succeeded him. ⁷The king of Egypt did not come again out of his land, for the king of Babylon had taken over all that

for a short time Judah's new overlord, who deported him temporarily to *Riblah*, an important town in northern Syria, which later became headquarters of the Babylonian king Nebuchadnezzar (25.6). **34–35:** When making *Eliakim* the new king, Neco changes his name to *Jehoiakim*. **36–37:** *Jehoiakim* reigned ca. 608–597 BCE. **24.1:** He initially submits to King Nebuchadnezzar of Babylon (ruled 605–562 BCE), who had defeated the Assyrians in 605, but then he rebels. **2–7:** This rebellion provoked even more military pressure from the neighbors of Judah. **3–4:** *Sins of Manasseh*, see 23.26–27. **7:** There is no escape from the king of Babylon who controls the Levant

belonged to the king of Egypt from the Wadi of Egypt to the River Euphrates.

[8] Jehoiachin was eighteen years old when he began to reign; he reigned three months in Jerusalem. His mother's name was Nehushta daughter of Elnathan of Jerusalem. [9] He did what was evil in the sight of the LORD, just as his father had done.

[10] At that time the servants of King Nebuchadnezzar of Babylon came up to Jerusalem, and the city was besieged. [11] King Nebuchadnezzar of Babylon came to the city, while his servants were besieging it; [12] King Jehoiachin of Judah gave himself up to the king of Babylon, himself, his mother, his servants, his officers, and his palace officials. The king of Babylon took him prisoner in the eighth year of his reign.

[13] He carried off all the treasures of the house of the LORD, and the treasures of the king's house; he cut in pieces all the vessels of gold in the temple of the LORD, which King Solomon of Israel had made, all this as the LORD had foretold. [14] He carried away all Jerusalem, all the officials, all the warriors, ten thousand captives, all the artisans and the smiths; no one remained, except the poorest people of the land. [15] He carried away Jehoiachin to Babylon; the king's mother, the king's wives, his officials, and the elite of the land, he took into captivity from Jerusalem to Babylon. [16] The king of Babylon brought captive to Babylon all the men of valor, seven thousand, the artisans and the smiths, one thousand, all of them strong and fit for war. [17] The king of Babylon made Mattaniah, Jehoiachin's uncle, king in his place, and changed his name to Zedekiah.

[18] Zedekiah was twenty-one years old when he began to reign; he reigned eleven years in Jerusalem. His mother's name was Hamutal daughter of Jeremiah of Libnah. [19] He did what was evil in the sight of the LORD, just as Jehoiakim had done. [20] Indeed, Jerusalem and Judah so angered the LORD that he expelled them from his presence.

Zedekiah rebelled against the king of

25

Babylon. [1] And in the ninth year of his reign, in the tenth month, on the tenth day of the month, King Nebuchadnezzar of Babylon came with all his army against Jerusalem, and laid siege to it; they built siegeworks against it all around. [2] So the city was besieged until the eleventh year of King Zedekiah. [3] On the ninth day of the fourth month the famine became so severe in the city that there was no food for the people of the land. [4] Then a breach was made in the city wall;[a] the king with all the soldiers fled[b] by night by the way of the gate between the two walls, by the king's garden, though the Chaldeans were all around the city. They went in the direction of the Arabah. [5] But the army of the Chaldeans pursued the king, and overtook him in the plains of Jericho; all his army was scattered, deserting him. [6] Then they captured the king and brought him up to the king of Babylon at Riblah, who passed sentence on him. [7] They slaughtered the sons of Zedekiah before his eyes, then put out the eyes of Zedekiah; they bound him in fetters and took him to Babylon.

[8] In the fifth month, on the seventh day of the month—which was the nineteenth year

a Heb lacks wall
b Gk Compare Jer 39.4; 52.7: Heb lacks the king and lacks fled

and Mesopotamia (from the Wadi of Egypt to the River Euphrates). 8–17: Jehoiachin has to pay the price for his father's rebellion, a siege of Jerusalem in 597 BCE and his and the court's exile to Babylon. 12: Jehoiachin's quick surrender avoids the destruction of Jerusalem. 13: The Temple and the palace treasures are usually the primary target for booty. 14–16: The numbers of the deported population are probably not based on historical records. Instead of ten thousand, Jer 52.28 has 3,023. 17: The Babylonian king establishes Mattaniah, Jehoiachin's uncle, as king and changes his name to Zedekiah. 18–20: Zedekiah is the last Judean ruler (597–586 BCE). His rebellion provokes the destruction of Jerusalem and the end of the Judean kingdom. Chapter 25: Most of ch 25 is also found, with variations, in Jer 52. 1–7: The result of Zedekiah's disloyal behavior, most likely an alliance with Egypt, was another siege of Jerusalem. 4–5: The king tries to flee with the soldiers (his bodyguard) and is captured in the plains of Jericho. The place of Israel's first victory when conquering the land becomes now a place of defeat. 6–7: His breaking of the loyalty oath is sanctioned with harsh punishment. His sons are killed in order to exterminate the Davidic dynasty. Riblah, see 23.33n. 8–12: Nebuzaradan, a high Babylonian officer, whose

of King Nebuchadnezzar, king of Babylon—Nebuzaradan, the captain of the bodyguard, a servant of the king of Babylon, came to Jerusalem. [9] He burned the house of the LORD, the king's house, and all the houses of Jerusalem; every great house he burned down. [10] All the army of the Chaldeans who were with the captain of the guard broke down the walls around Jerusalem. [11] Nebuzaradan the captain of the guard carried into exile the rest of the people who were left in the city and the deserters who had defected to the king of Babylon—all the rest of the population. [12] But the captain of the guard left some of the poorest people of the land to be vinedressers and tillers of the soil.

[13] The bronze pillars that were in the house of the LORD, as well as the stands and the bronze sea that were in the house of the LORD, the Chaldeans broke in pieces, and carried the bronze to Babylon. [14] They took away the pots, the shovels, the snuffers, the dishes for incense, and all the bronze vessels used in the temple service, [15] as well as the firepans and the basins. What was made of gold the captain of the guard took away for the gold, and what was made of silver, for the silver. [16] As for the two pillars, the one sea, and the stands, which Solomon had made for the house of the LORD, the bronze of all these vessels was beyond weighing. [17] The height of the one pillar was eighteen cubits, and on it was a bronze capital; the height of the capital was three cubits; latticework and pomegranates, all of bronze, were on the capital all around. The second pillar had the same, with the latticework.

[18] The captain of the guard took the chief priest Seraiah, the second priest Zephaniah, and the three guardians of the threshold; [19] from the city he took an officer who had been in command of the soldiers, and five men of the king's council who were found in the city; the secretary who was the commander of the army who mustered the people of the land; and sixty men of the people of the land who were found in the city. [20] Nebuzaradan the captain of the guard took them, and brought them to the king of Babylon at Riblah. [21] The king of Babylon struck them down and put them to death at Riblah in the land of Hamath. So Judah went into exile out of its land.

[22] He appointed Gedaliah son of Ahikam son of Shaphan as governor over the people who remained in the land of Judah, whom King Nebuchadnezzar of Babylon had left. [23] Now when all the captains of the forces and their men heard that the king of Babylon had appointed Gedaliah as governor, they came with their men to Gedaliah at Mizpah, namely, Ishmael son of Nethaniah, Johanan son of Kareah, Seraiah son of Tanhumeth the Netophathite, and Jaazaniah son of the Maacathite. [24] Gedaliah swore to them and their men, saying, "Do not be afraid because of the Chaldean officials; live in the land, serve the king of Babylon, and it shall be well with you." [25] But in the seventh month, Ishmael son of Nethaniah son of Elishama, of the royal family, came with ten men; they struck down Gedaliah so that he died, along with the Judeans and Chaldeans who were with him at Mizpah. [26] Then all the people, high and low,[a] and the captains of the forces set out and went to Egypt; for they were afraid of the Chaldeans.

[27] In the thirty-seventh year of the exile of King Jehoiachin of Judah, in the twelfth

[a] Or young and old

title means literally "chief of the butchers," destroys the Temple, the palace, and the city and its walls. He also organizes a second deportation to Babylon, which does not affect the whole population. **13–17:** The authors take great interest in the detailed description of the deported Temple furnishings (see 1 Kings 7.15–51). **18–21:** Some of the royal officials are executed at *Riblah*, probably because they belonged to the anti-Babylonian party. **21:** *So Judah went into exile out of its land*, this was perhaps the original conclusion of the edition of the book of Kings in the Babylonian period. **22–26:** The episode of Gedaliah's appointment as a governor and his assassination by the nationalistic party is related in greater detail in Jer 40–43. **22:** *Gedaliah*, the grandson of Josiah's secretary Shaphan (23.12). **23:** *Mizpah*, ca. 7 mi (2 km) north of Jerusalem become the administrative center during Babylonian occupation. **25:** *Ishmael*, who kills Gedaliah, is said to be member of *the royal family*. He fails however to reestablish the Davidic dynasty. **26:** The remaining people fled to *Egypt*. This conclusion seems to wipe out Israel's whole history, which started with the Exodus out of Egypt and now ends with a return to

month, on the twenty-seventh day of the month, King Evil-merodach of Babylon, in the year that he began to reign, released King Jehoiachin of Judah from prison; [28] he spoke kindly to him, and gave him a seat above the other seats of the kings who were with him in Babylon. [29] So Jehoiachin put aside his prison clothes. Every day of his life he dined regularly in the king's presence. [30] For his allowance, a regular allowance was given him by the king, a portion every day, as long as he lived.

Egypt. **27–30:** This epilogue relates the rehabilitation of Jehoiachin under the Babylonian king *Evil-merodach* (Amel-marduk, 562–560 BCE), which may be understood as a faint hope for the renewal of the Davidic dynasty. What happens to Jehoiachin also recalls such heroes of Diaspora narratives as Joseph, Mordecai, and Daniel: all are exiles who are liberated from prison (see Gen 41.40: Dan 2.48; Esth 10.3) and become part of the court of the foreign king. The accession to new status is symbolized by the changing of clothes (see Gen 41.24; Dan 5.29; Esth 6.10–11). Jehoiachin could therefore symbolize all the Jews who accepted that their "exile" had become "Diaspora," a place outside the land of Israel, where they could live their lives.

1 CHRONICLES

NAME AND LOCATION IN CANON

Like other books in the Bible, Chronicles was originally untitled. The title given to it by the early rabbis, "the book of the events of the days" (*seper dibre hayyamim*), suggests that the book is a history, addressing past events in chronological order; the same phrase is used often in Kings (e.g., 1 Kings 14.19) for one of the sources of the books of Kings. The name of Chronicles in the ancient Greek translation of the Jewish scriptures, the Septuagint, is *Paraleipomena*, meaning "the things left out"; this name suggests that Chronicles records the events left out of earlier biblical history. These understandings of Chronicles are contested by most modern scholars. It was the church father Jerome's description of the book as a "chronicle," a summary of divine history, that has proven to be most influential in the history of modern interpretation.

Like the books of Samuel and Kings, Chronicles was originally one book. It was probably divided by the Greek translators, perhaps because of its length. The break between the two books, however, comes at a natural point, with the notice of the death of King David at the end of 1 Chronicles, and the account of the reign of his successor Solomon at the beginning of 2 Chronicles.

In printed Jewish Bibles, Chronicles is the last book in the third and final division of the canon, the Writings ("Ketubim"), although in some manuscripts it occurs earlier, either as the first of the Writings, or before Ezra-Nehemiah, that is, in chronological order. In Christian Bibles, Chronicles is one of the Historical Books and follows the books of Kings.

AUTHORSHIP AND DATE OF COMPOSITION

Most likely the anonymous author lived in Jerusalem and had great familiarity with the Temple and its assorted traditions. Since the book of Ezra begins where Chronicles ends, with the decree of the Persian king Cyrus the Great that allowed the exiled Jews to return home and rebuild the Temple (538 BCE), some scholars have suggested that Chronicles, Ezra, and its continuation in Nehemiah, had a single author or editor. Other scholars think that the linguistic, thematic, and historiographic differences between Chronicles and Ezra-Nehemiah are too great to posit a common author. In this view, which is followed here, the Chronicler's history, which begins with the first person (Adam) and ends with the Babylonian exile in 586 BCE and Cyrus's summons to the exiled Jews to return home (2 Chr 36.21–23), should be separated from the postexilic history of Ezra-Nehemiah. Although there are significant similarities between the Chronicles, Ezra, and Nehemiah, the differences outweigh the similarities, and one individual is unlikely to have written all three works. Hence, in the following pages, "the Chronicler" designates the author of Chronicles.

The Chronicler wrote after much of the Hebrew Bible had already been written, and he draws extensively upon this rich literary tradition. The dependence of Chronicles upon Genesis is evident in the genealogies (1 Chr 1–9); the dependence upon Samuel is clear in the narration of Saul's demise and David's reign (1 Chr 10–29); and the dependence upon Kings is unmistakable in the narration of Solomon and the Judahite kingdom (2 Chr 1–36). The Chronicler's work is also informed by a variety of other biblical texts. Citations from or allusions to the Torah and the books of Joshua, Isaiah, Jeremiah, Ezekiel, Psalms, and Ruth all appear in Chronicles. Scholars generally agree that the Chronicler also had access to sources that did not become part of the Bible, but their nature and extent are disputed.

It is difficult to date Chronicles precisely, beyond noting that it must be postexilic, since it begins with Cyrus's decree. A range of over three hundred and fifty years, from the late sixth to the mid-second century BCE, has been suggested for its time of composition. A date in the fourth century seems most plausible, because it would account both for the author's references to other biblical writings and for literary features within the work that anticipate similar features in Jewish Hellenistic writings. But there are no specific references, no absolute synchronisms, and no extrabiblical citations that definitively date the book to a given decade or quarter-century.

STRUCTURE, CONTENTS, AND INTERPRETATION

Chronicles has three major sections: the genealogies (1 Chr 1–9), the history of the United Monarchy (1 Chr 10–2 Chr 9), and the history of the Judahite monarchy (2 Chr 10–36). The first section, which forms the introduction to the work, begins with Adam (1 Chr 1), but focuses upon the identity, interrelationships, and location of Israel's many tribes (1 Chr 2–9). In traditional societies such genealogies explain and justify the place and function of various individuals, people, and institutions. In the case of 1 Chr 1–8, the Chronicler stresses the ties between Israel and the land. The very scope and structure of the Chronicler's genealogical system underscore the indivisibility of Israel. Within this larger structure, Judah, Levi, and Benjamin receive by far the most extensive genealogies. In the Chronicler's view, these three tribes are critical to preserving Israel's distinctive legacy. The list of those Jews who returned from exile (1 Chr 9) concludes these chapters by highlighting the continuity between earlier Israel and postexilic Judah (the Persian province of Yehud). In the second section, after briefly addressing and condemning the reign of Saul (1 Chr 10), the Chronicler devotes most of his attention to the highly successful reigns of David (1 Chr 11–29) and Solomon (2 Chr 1–9), which clearly represent a high point of the history. The rest of the book relates the emergence, continuation, and fall of the kingdom of Judah (2 Chr 10–36). Because Chronicles begins with the first person (Adam) and ends with the aftermath of the Babylonian exile (2 Chr 36), it forms a parallel story of Israel's past—albeit much shorter and later—to the story of Israel's past found in Genesis through Kings.

It is no accident that the Chronicler places David and Solomon's achievements at the center of Israelite history. The author thereby underscores the prominence of those Israelite institutions he believed developed, were consolidated, or were transformed during this period—the priesthood, descended from Aaron; the Levites in all their responsibilities as singers, teachers, administrators, and ancillaries to the priests; the Davidic dynasty; and, last but not least, the Temple itself. Having set the establishment of Israel's normative political and religious institutions in the time of David and Solomon, the Chronicler never reneges on their pertinence to the lives of all Israelites in later centuries.

Following the death of Solomon and the ascension of his son Rehoboam, the ten northern tribes secede from southern rule (2 Chr 11.1–17). Whereas the author of Kings follows the course of both the Northern and the Southern Kingdoms, the Chronicler concentrates on the tribes of Judah, Benjamin, and Levi, who make up the Southern Kingdom of Judah (2 Chr 11.5–6,12,13–17,23). In Chronicles the course of the Judahite monarchy is characterized by both defeats and successes. The Chronicler consistently documents the achievements of Judah's best kings—Abijah (2 Chr 13.2–21), Asa (2 Chr 14.1–6; 15.8–15), Jehoshaphat (2 Chr 17.1–9; 19.4–11), Hezekiah (2 Chr 29–31), and Josiah (2 Chr 34.1–7)—to institute reforms, reunite the people, and recover lost territories. Major regressions occur in the reigns of Ahaz (2 Chr 28), Manasseh (2 Chr 33.1–11), and the final kings of Judah (2 Chr 36.1–13). In depicting their history, the Chronicler is largely dependent on Kings, but as the episode concerning Manasseh's repentance and restoration (2 Chr 33.12–19; cf. 2 Kings 21.1–16) demonstrates, he may revise these sources to fit his theology, making both major and minor changes, additions, and deletions.

Throughout the work, God sends prophets to warn monarchs, leaders, and people alike about the consequences of their actions, imploring them to repent. Whereas in Kings, prophets are most often a fixture of life in the Northern Kingdom (e.g., Elijah and Elisha) and are rare in the life of the Southern Kingdom (Isaiah being a notable exception), in Chronicles prophets and prophetic figures, such as Shemaiah (2 Chr 12.5–6), Azariah (2 Chr 15.1–7), Hanani (2 Chr 16.7–9), Jehu (2 Chr 19.2–3) and Zechariah (2 Chr 24.20), appear in the reign of virtually every significant southern king. In this way, the Chronicler stresses that Moses' promise that the LORD would create a prophetic succession, patterned after the prophetic ministry of Moses himself (Deut 18.15–22), was fulfilled in the history of Judah. In his commentary on the defeat and exile of the Southern Kingdom, the Chronicler adds that Judah was exiled only after the LORD sent a steady supply of prophets to stir the people and priestly leaders to reform, but their warnings went unheeded (2 Chr 36.14–16).

Both Kings and Chronicles end by describing the Babylonian invasion and exile in the sixth century BCE, but Chronicles also includes Cyrus's decree allowing the exiles to return to Judah (2 Chr 36.22–23), offering a clearer hope for the future than does the conclusion of Kings. In this way Chronicles contains and relativizes the tremendous tragedy of the Babylonian deportations soberly depicted in 2 Kings 24–25. Thus Chronicles, with its positive ending and emphasis on the power of repentance, may be seen as more optimistic than the history of Samuel-Kings, which it has rewritten. As the beginning of Chronicles introduces the people of Israel and charts their emergence in the land, the ending of the book anticipates their return.

GUIDE TO READING CHRONICLES

If one begins to read Chronicles as one would any other book from beginning to end, one encounters some formidable challenges. Because the first nine chapters comprise lists and genealogies, they make for difficult reading. In order to keep the overall structure in mind, note how the work starts with a universal genealogy beginning with the first person (Adam) and ending with the ancestor of Israel (Jacob) and his twelve sons (1 Chr 1.1–2.1). The rest of the genealogies deal with the descendants of Jacob's sons, giving pride of place to Judah, Levi, and Benjamin, the three tribes that dominated life in postexilic Judah. The rest of the book contains mostly narratives about the history of the Davidic monarchy. Note also how much space the biblical author devotes to the united monarchy of David and Solomon (1 Chr 11.1–2 Chr 9.31), presenting this period as the apex of Israelite history. Because this material and that dealing with the history of the Judahite kingdom (2 Chr 10.1–36:23) both draw upon and differ from Samuel-Kings (with many deletions and additions), readers may find it helpful not only to read Chronicles on its own terms as a distinct literary work, but also to compare its presentation of the past with that found in the older writing of Samuel-Kings.

Gary N. Knoppers

1 Adam, Seth, Enosh; [2] Kenan, Mahalalel, Jared; [3] Enoch, Methuselah, Lamech; [4] Noah, Shem, Ham, and Japheth.

[5] The descendants of Japheth: Gomer, Magog, Madai, Javan, Tubal, Meshech, and Tiras. [6] The descendants of Gomer: Ashkenaz, Diphath,[a] and Togarmah. [7] The descendants of Javan: Elishah, Tarshish, Kittim, and Rodanim.[b]

[8] The descendants of Ham: Cush, Egypt, Put, and Canaan. [9] The descendants of Cush: Seba, Havilah, Sabta, Raama, and Sabteca. The descendants of Raamah: Sheba and Dedan. [10] Cush became the father of Nimrod; he was the first to be a mighty one on the earth.

[11] Egypt became the father of Ludim, Anamim, Lehabim, Naphtuhim, [12] Pathrusim, Casluhim, and Caphtorim, from whom the Philistines come.[c]

[13] Canaan became the father of Sidon his firstborn, and Heth, [14] and the Jebusites, the Amorites, the Girgashites, [15] the Hivites, the Arkites, the Sinites, [16] the Arvadites, the Zemarites, and the Hamathites.

[17] The descendants of Shem: Elam, Asshur, Arpachshad, Lud, Aram, Uz, Hul, Gether, and Meshech.[d] [18] Arpachshad became the father

a Gen 10.3 *Riphath*; See Gk Vg
b Gen 10.4 *Dodanim*; See Syr Vg
c Heb *Casluhim, from which the Philistines come, Caphtorim*; See Am 9.7, Jer 47.4
d *Mash* in Gen 10.23

1.1–22: From the first person to Israel: a universal genealogy. Drawing upon numerous lineages in Genesis, the author traces the development of and interrelationships among a variety of nations, ending with Israel—the focal point of his interest. **1–4:** The ten names represent ten generations, beginning with Adam and ending with Noah. The Chronicler's tally is a marvel of condensation, having been culled from the much longer and more detailed narrative lineage of Adam in Gen 5.1–32. **4:** Each of Noah's three sons can be associated with a relatively large geographic area: Shem (peoples to the east of ancient Israel); Ham (peoples to the south and southwest); Japheth (peoples to the north and west). Although most modern scholars believe that Canaan was ethnically and linguistically Semitic, and thus should be descended from Shem, in the Bible Canaan is descended from Ham, perhaps because of Canaan's long political relationship to Egypt.

1.5–23: Descendants of Noah. These verses are largely drawn from Gen 10.1–29, the "Table of Nations," which enumerates some seventy descendants of Noah's sons, symbolizing seventy peoples of the world. This creates both a genealogical tree and map by which all the world's nations are related to each other through a common ancestor, Noah. See map on p. 23. **5–7:** The sons of Japheth represent Anatolia (e.g., Togarmah, Tubal, Meshech), including Greek settlements (Javan) and islands in the Mediterranean Sea, such as Elishah (Cyprus), Kittim (Caphtor and other isles), and Rodanim (Rhodes). **5:** Ham's children represent peoples and areas in the Egyptian political sphere: Cush to the south of Egypt (Sudan or Ethiopia), Egypt, Put to the west (Libya), and Canaan to the north. **11–16:** These lists of Egypt's and Canaan's descendants closely follow Gen 10.13–18. **11:** *Philistines,* see Jer 47.4; Am 9.7. **13–15:** The sons of Canaan inhabit Sidon (the Phoenician coast) and include the traditional inhabitants of the land of Canaan (*Heth* [the Hittites] and those in v. 14), and those of coastal (*Arkites, Sinites, Arvadites, Zemarites*) and inland (*Hamathites*) Syria. **17:** Located in Mesopotamia (*Elam, Asshur, Arpachshad*), Asia Minor (*Lud* and *Meshech*), Syria (*Aram*); others cannot be identified. **17–18:** Although in v. 8

of Shelah; and Shelah became the father of Eber. [19] To Eber were born two sons: the name of the one was Peleg (for in his days the earth was divided), and the name of his brother Joktan. [20] Joktan became the father of Almodad, Sheleph, Hazarmaveth, Jerah, [21] Hadoram, Uzal, Diklah, [22] Ebal, Abimael, Sheba, [23] Ophir, Havilah, and Jobab; all these were the descendants of Joktan.

[24] Shem, Arpachshad, Shelah; [25] Eber, Peleg, Reu; [26] Serug, Nahor, Terah; [27] Abram, that is, Abraham.

[28] The sons of Abraham: Isaac and Ishmael. [29] These are their genealogies: the firstborn of Ishmael, Nebaioth; and Kedar, Adbeel, Mibsam, [30] Mishma, Dumah, Massa, Hadad, Tema, [31] Jetur, Naphish, and Kedemah. These are the sons of Ishmael. [32] The sons of Keturah, Abraham's concubine: she bore Zimran, Jokshan, Medan, Midian, Ishbak, and Shuah. The sons of Jokshan: Sheba and Dedan. [33] The sons of Midian: Ephah, Epher, Hanoch, Abida, and Eldaah. All these were the descendants of Keturah.

[34] Abraham became the father of Isaac. The sons of Isaac: Esau and Israel. [35] The sons of Esau: Eliphaz, Reuel, Jeush, Jalam, and Korah. [36] The sons of Eliphaz: Teman, Omar, Zephi, Gatam, Kenaz, Timna, and Amalek. [37] The sons of Reuel: Nahath, Zerah, Shammah, and Mizzah.

[38] The sons of Seir: Lotan, Shobal, Zibeon, Anah, Dishon, Ezer, and Dishan. [39] The sons of Lotan: Hori and Homam; and Lotan's sister was Timna. [40] The sons of Shobal: Alian, Manahath, Ebal, Shephi, and

Onam. The sons of Zibeon: Aiah and Anah. [41] The sons of Anah: Dishon. The sons of Dishon: Hamran, Eshban, Ithran, and Cheran. [42] The sons of Ezer: Bilhan, Zaavan, and Jaakan.[a] The sons of Dishan:[b] Uz and Aran.

[43] These are the kings who reigned in the land of Edom before any king reigned over the Israelites: Bela son of Beor, whose city was called Dinhabah. [44] When Bela died, Jobab son of Zerah of Bozrah succeeded him. [45] When Jobab died, Husham of the land of the Temanites succeeded him. [46] When Husham died, Hadad son of Bedad, who defeated Midian in the country of Moab, succeeded him; and the name of his city was Avith. [47] When Hadad died, Samlah of Masrekah succeeded him. [48] When Samlah died, Shaul[c] of Rehoboth on the Euphrates succeeded him. [49] When Shaul[c] died, Baal-hanan son of Achbor succeeded him. [50] When Baal-hanan died, Hadad succeeded him; the name of his city was Pai, and his wife's name Mehetabel daughter of Matred, daughter of Me-zahab. [51] And Hadad died.

The clans[d] of Edom were: clans[d] Timna, Aliah,[e] Jetheth, [52] Oholibamah, Elah, Pinon, [53] Kenaz, Teman, Mibzar, [54] Magdiel, and Iram; these are the clans[d] of Edom.

[a] Or and Akan; See Gen 36.27
[b] See 1.38: Heb Dishon
[c] Or Saul
[d] Or chiefs
[e] Or Alvah; See Gen 36.40

Canaan is descended from Ham, Eber, after whom the Hebrews (gentilic "'ibri") are named, is a descendant of Shem, indicating Israelite feelings of kinship to the Semitic peoples of the east. 19: *The earth was divided,* the Hebrew puns on Peleg's name, which is derived from a verb meaning "to divide, split." 20: *Joktan's* descendants inhabit the Arabian peninsula.

1.24–27: Shem's genealogy is extracted from Gen 11.10–26. 27: *Abram,* this begins the second major unit in the Chronicler's universal genealogy; the first was dominated by the descendants of Noah (1 Chr 1.4b–23). 28: For *Isaac and Ishmael,* the Chronicler fashions a very brief genealogy from narrative materials in Genesis (16.11; 17.18–19; 25.9); their mothers, Sarah and Hagar, are not mentioned. Ishmael is associated with the northern part of the Sinai peninsula and northwestern Arabia (Gen 16.10–12; 17.20; 21.13), as are the descendants of Keturah (vv. 32–33). 29–31: Drawn from the Ishmaelite genealogy in Gen 25.12–18. 32–33: In the source text (Gen 25.1–13), *Keturah* appears as Abraham's second wife, taken sometime after the death of Sarah (Gen 25.1–3). The Chronicler's reference to her as a concubine may be based on his reading of Gen 25.1–2 in light of Gen 25.5–6. 34–37: The genealogy of Sarah and Abraham draws upon Gen 25.19–26 and Gen 36.2–14. The Chronicler always refers to Jacob as *Israel* (see Gen 32.22–32). 38–42: *The sons of Seir,* abridged and adapted from Gen 36.20–28. 43–54: The lists of Edomite monarchs (1.43–51a) and Edomite chieftains (1.51b–54) are adapted and slightly abridged

2 These are the sons of Israel: Reuben, Simeon, Levi, Judah, Issachar, Zebulun, ²Dan, Joseph, Benjamin, Naphtali, Gad, and Asher. ³The sons of Judah: Er, Onan, and Shelah; these three the Canaanite woman Bath-shua bore to him. Now Er, Judah's firstborn, was wicked in the sight of the LORD, and he put him to death. ⁴His daughter-in-law Tamar also bore him Perez and Zerah. Judah had five sons in all.

⁵The sons of Perez: Hezron and Hamul. ⁶The sons of Zerah: Zimri, Ethan, Heman, Calcol, and Dara,ᵃ five in all. ⁷The sons of Carmi: Achar, the troubler of Israel, who transgressed in the matter of the devoted thing; ⁸and Ethan's son was Azariah.

⁹The sons of Hezron, who were born to him: Jerahmeel, Ram, and Chelubai. ¹⁰Ram became the father of Amminadab, and Amminadab became the father of Nahshon, prince of the sons of Judah. ¹¹Nahshon became the father of Salma, Salma of Boaz, ¹²Boaz of Obed, Obed of Jesse. ¹³Jesse became the father of Eliab his firstborn, Abinadab the second, Shimea the third, ¹⁴Nethanel the fourth, Raddai the fifth, ¹⁵Ozem the sixth, David the seventh; ¹⁶and their sisters were Zeruiah and Abigail. The sons of Zeruiah: Abishai, Joab, and Asahel, three. ¹⁷Abigail bore Amasa, and the father of Amasa was Jether the Ishmaelite.

¹⁸Caleb son of Hezron had children by his wife Azubah, and by Jerioth; these were her sons: Jesher, Shobab, and Ardon. ¹⁹When Azubah died, Caleb married Ephrath, who bore him Hur. ²⁰Hur became the father of Uri, and Uri became the father of Bezalel.

²¹Afterward Hezron went in to the daughter of Machir father of Gilead, whom he married when he was sixty years old; and she bore him Segub; ²²and Segub became the father of Jair, who had twenty-three towns in the land of Gilead. ²³But Geshur and Aram took from them Havvoth-jair, Kenath and its villages, sixty towns. All these were descendants of Machir, father of Gilead. ²⁴After the death of Hezron, in Caleb-ephrathah, Abijah wife of Hezron bore him Ashhur, father of Tekoa.

²⁵The sons of Jerahmeel, the firstborn of Hezron: Ram his firstborn, Bunah, Oren, Ozem, and Ahijah. ²⁶Jerahmeel also had another wife, whose name was Atarah; she was the mother of Onam. ²⁷The sons of Ram, the firstborn of Jerahmeel: Maaz, Jamin, and Eker. ²⁸The sons of Onam: Shammai and Jada. The sons of Shammai: Nadab and Abishur. ²⁹The name of

ᵃ Or *Darda*; Compare Syr Tg some Gk Mss; See 1 Kings 4.31

from Gen 36.31–39 and Gen 36.40–43, respectively. The Chronicler presents the history of Edom, Israel's neighbor to the southeast, in capsule form up to the time of the inception of the Israelite monarchy, the beginning of his own narrative history (ch 10). **2.1–2:** This list of Israel's descendants is the natural continuation of the progeny of Abraham (1.28–33) and Isaac (1.34–37) and serves as the introduction to the lineages of Israel's many sons, which follows in 2.3–9.1. The order of the sons is largely arranged according to mother—Leah (Reuben, Simeon, Levi, Judah, Issachar, Zebulun); Rachel (Joseph, Benjamin); Bilhah (Dan, Naphtali); and Zilpah (Gad, Asher).

2.3–4.23: The descendants of Judah. The Chronicler first offers a long genealogy of Judah, demonstrating Judah's importance to the Chronicler's History. **2.4:** *Daughter-in-law,* an allusion to the sexual relationship between Judah and Tamar (Gen 38.12–26). Having earlier referred to the Canaanite status of Bath-shua (v. 3; cf. Gen 38.1–5), the Chronicler presents another unusual feature of Judah's lineage, which did not disqualify it from preeminence. **6–8:** Drawn from two sources: Josh 7.1 (2.6a,7) and 1 Kings 5.11 (2.6b). **7:** *Achar,* called Achan in Josh 7, but cf. Josh 7.24–25. **10:** *Amminadab,* as the father of Nahshon, see Num 2.3. **11:** Taken from Ruth 4.20–21. **13–17:** The lineages of Jesse's sons and daughters have been drawn, in part, from 1 Sam 16.1–23; 17.1–51; 2 Sam 2.18. **18–20:** The descendants of Caleb are a major interest of the Chronicler, taking up a sizable portion of Judah's lineages (2.18–20,42–50a,50b–55; 4.1–7). This may be because some earlier sources suggest that he was a Kenizzite (e.g., Num 32.12), and thus not part of Israel (the Chronicler is correcting this tradition). **21:** *Machir* is sometimes associated with Manasseh, most often as Manasseh's son (Gen 50.23; Num 32.39–40; Deut 3.14–15; cf. Judg 5.14). The connection with Manasseh is affirmed in 7.14–17. **22–23:** The subject shifts back to Hezron, last mentioned in v. 9. **22:** *Jair* is a son of Manasseh in Num 32.41 and Deut 3.14, but he appears here as the grandson of Hezron. **24:** *Father of Tekoa,* Tekoa in earlier books is the name of a Judean city, but in genealogies,

Abishur's wife was Abihail, and she bore him Ahban and Molid. [30] The sons of Nadab: Seled and Appaim; and Seled died childless. [31] The son[a] of Appaim: Ishi. The son[a] of Ishi: Sheshan. The son[a] of Sheshan: Ahlai. [32] The sons of Jada, Shammai's brother: Jether and Jonathan; and Jether died childless. [33] The sons of Jonathan: Peleth and Zaza. These were the descendants of Jerahmeel. [34] Now Sheshan had no sons, only daughters; but Sheshan had an Egyptian slave, whose name was Jarha. [35] So Sheshan gave his daughter in marriage to his slave Jarha; and she bore him Attai. [36] Attai became the father of Nathan, and Nathan of Zabad. [37] Zabad became the father of Ephlal, and Ephlal of Obed. [38] Obed became the father of Jehu, and Jehu of Azariah. [39] Azariah became the father of Helez, and Helez of Eleasah. [40] Eleasah became the father of Sismai, and Sismai of Shallum. [41] Shallum became the father of Jekamiah, and Jekamiah of Elishama.

[42] The sons of Caleb brother of Jerahmeel: Mesha[b] his firstborn, who was father of Ziph. The sons of Mareshah father of Hebron. [43] The sons of Hebron: Korah, Tappuah, Rekem, and Shema. [44] Shema became father of Raham, father of Jorkeam; and Rekem became the father of Shammai. [45] The son of Shammai: Maon; and Maon was the father of Beth-zur. [46] Ephah also, Caleb's concubine, bore Haran, Moza, and Gazez; and Haran became the father of Gazez. [47] The sons of Jahdai: Regem, Jotham, Geshan, Pelet, Ephah, and Shaaph. [48] Maacah, Caleb's concubine, bore Sheber and Tirhanah. [49] She also bore Shaaph father of Madmannah, Sheva father of Machbenah and father of Gibea; and the daughter of Caleb was Achsah. [50] These were the descendants of Caleb.

The sons[c] of Hur the firstborn of Ephrathah: Shobal father of Kiriath-jearim, [51] Salma father of Bethlehem, and Hareph father of Beth-gader. [52] Shobal father of Kiriath-jearim had other sons: Haroeh, half of the Menuhoth. [53] And the families of Kiriath-jearim: the Ithrites, the Puthites, the Shumathites, and the Mishraites; from these came the Zorathites and the Eshtaolites. [54] The sons of Salma: Bethlehem, the Netophathites, Atroth-beth-joab, and half of the Manahathites, the Zorites. [55] The families also of the scribes that lived at Jabez: the Tirathites, the Shimeathites, and the Sucathites. These are the Kenites who came from Hammath, father of the house of Rechab.

3 These are the sons of David who were born to him in Hebron: the firstborn Amnon, by Ahinoam the Jezreelite; the second Daniel, by Abigail the Carmelite; [2] the third Absalom, son of Maacah, daughter of King Talmai of Geshur; the fourth Adonijah, son of Haggith; [3] the fifth Shephatiah, by Abital; the sixth Ithream, by his wife Eglah; [4] six were born to him in Hebron, where he reigned for seven years and six months. And he reigned thirty-three years in Jerusalem. [5] These were born to him in Jerusalem: Shimea, Shobab, Nathan, and Solomon, four by Bath-shua, daughter of Ammiel; [6] then Ibhar, Elishama, Eliphelet, [7] Nogah, Nepheg, Japhia, [8] Elishama, Eliada, and Eliphelet, nine. [9] All these were David's sons, besides the sons of the concubines; and Tamar was their sister.

a Heb *sons*
b Gk reads *Mareshah*
c Gk Vg: Heb *son*

ethnic and geographic dimensions of names can overlap. **25–41:** Both the genealogy of Jerahmeel (vv. 25–33), the first-born of Hezron (vv. 9,25) and the genealogy of Sheshan (vv. 34–41) are unique to Chronicles. **42–50:** The second of the genealogies for Caleb's descendants (see vv. 18–20n.). Many of the names listed also occur in the Judahite town list of Josh 15. **50b–55:** Largely without parallel, this genealogy reverts to the line of Hur (v. 19). Each of Hur's three sons is depicted as a founder (lit. "father") of a town. The *Kenites* (Num 24.20–22; Judg 4.11,17–21; 5.24–27; 1 Sam 15.6; 30.29) ultimately descend from their eponymous ancestor, Cain (Gen 4.1–25).

3.1–24: The descendants of David. 1–9: Some names of David's sons, and their order, are different in the present text of 2 Samuel. **1–3:** These verses are based on 2 Sam 3.2–4. David's lineage follows naturally 2.9–17, which enumerates the descendants of Ram, including David and the children of David's two sisters Zeruiah and Abigail. **4:** This verse draws upon and reworks 2 Sam 5.5. Consistent with David's rule over all Israel in chs 11–29, the writer avoids the distinction between Israel and Judah found in his source. **5–9:** These verses are

¹⁰ The descendants of Solomon: Rehoboam, Abijah his son, Asa his son, Jehoshaphat his son, ¹¹ Joram his son, Ahaziah his son, Joash his son, ¹² Amaziah his son, Azariah his son, Jotham his son, ¹³ Ahaz his son, Hezekiah his son, Manasseh his son, ¹⁴ Amon his son, Josiah his son. ¹⁵ The sons of Josiah: Johanan the firstborn, the second Jehoiakim, the third Zedekiah, the fourth Shallum. ¹⁶ The descendants of Jehoiakim: Jeconiah his son, Zedekiah his son; ¹⁷ and the sons of Jeconiah, the captive: Shealtiel his son, ¹⁸ Malchiram, Pedaiah, Shenazzar, Jekamiah, Hoshama, and Nedabiah; ¹⁹ The sons of Pedaiah: Zerubbabel and Shimei; and the sons of Zerubbabel: Meshullam and Hananiah, and Shelomith was their sister; ²⁰ and Hashubah, Ohel, Berechiah, Hasadiah, and Jushab-hesed, five. ²¹ The sons of Hananiah: Pelatiah and Jeshaiah, his son*a* Rephaiah, his son*a* Arnan, his son*a* Obadiah, his son*a* Shecaniah. ²² The son*b* of Shecaniah: Shemaiah. And the sons of Shemaiah: Hattush, Igal, Bariah, Neariah, and Shaphat, six. ²³ The sons of Neariah: Elioenai, Hizkiah, and Azrikam, three. ²⁴ The sons of Elioenai: Hodaviah, Eliashib, Pelaiah, Akkub, Johanan, Delaiah, and Anani, seven.

4 The sons of Judah: Perez, Hezron, Carmi, Hur, and Shobal. ² Reaiah son of Shobal became the father of Jahath, and Jahath became the father of Ahumai and Lahad. These were the families of the Zorathites. ³ These were the sons*c* of Etam: Jezreel, Ishma, and Idbash; and the name of their sister was Hazzelelponi, ⁴ and Penuel was the father of Gedor, and Ezer the father of Hushah. These were the sons of Hur, the firstborn of Ephrathah, the father of Bethlehem. ⁵ Ashhur father of Tekoa had two wives, Helah and Naarah; ⁶ Naarah bore him Ahuzzam, Hepher, Temeni, and Haahashtari.*d* These were the sons of Naarah. ⁷ The sons of Helah: Zereth, Izhar,*e* and Ethnan. ⁸ Koz became the father of Anub, Zobebah, and the families of Aharhel son of Harum. ⁹ Jabez was honored more than his brothers; and his mother named him Jabez, saying, "Because I bore him in pain." ¹⁰ Jabez called on the God of Israel, saying, "Oh that you would bless me and enlarge my border, and that your hand might be with me, and that you would keep me from hurt and harm!" And God granted what he asked. ¹¹ Chelub the brother of Shuhah became the father of Mehir, who was the father of Eshton. ¹² Eshton became the father of Beth-rapha, Paseah, and Tehinnah the father of Ir-nahash. These are the men of Recah. ¹³ The sons of Kenaz: Othniel and Seraiah; and the sons of Othniel: Hathath and Meonothai.*f* ¹⁴ Meonothai became the father of Ophrah; and Seraiah became the father of Joab father of Ge-harashim,*g* so-called because they were artisans. ¹⁵ The sons of Caleb son of Jephunneh: Iru, Elah, and Naam; and the son*b* of Elah: Kenaz. ¹⁶ The sons of Jehallelel: Ziph, Ziphah, Tiria, and Asarel. ¹⁷ The sons of Ezrah: Jether, Mered, Epher, and Jalon. These are the sons of Bithiah, daughter of Pharaoh, whom

a Gk Compare Syr Vg: Heb *sons of*
b Heb *sons*
c Gk Compare Vg: Heb *the father*
d Or *Ahashtari*
e Another reading is *Zohar*
f Gk Vg: Heb lacks *and Meonothai*
g That is *Valley of artisans*

largely dependent upon 2 Sam 5.13–16. **10–14:** A fifteen-generation genealogy from Solomon to Josiah, noting only the Davidic king in each generation. **15–18:** A largely unparalleled genealogy from Josiah to Pedaiah. The second half of ch 3 gives special attention to Josiah and his various offspring. **18:** *Shenazzar,* some identify him with Sheshbazzar of Ezra 1.8, who led a group of early returnees from exile. **19–24:** The list of Davidic descendants from *Pedaiah* to *the sons of Elioenai* is unique to the Chronicler and likely reflects aspirations for a renewed Davidic monarchy in the postexilic period. **19:** *Zerubbabel* was a leader of the postexilic Judean community in the late sixth century BCE; see Ezra 3.2; Hag 1.1. **22:** *Hattush* returned from exile in Babylon (Ezra 8.2).

4.1–23: Descendants of Judah. *The sons of Judah,* in contrast to the largely linear genealogy of David (ch 3), this chapter describes several unconnected branches of Judeans. It also narrates several short anecdotes about individual Judeans (e.g., vv. 9–10,23). As in other genealogies, names of individuals here occur as place names elsewhere. **1:** The sequence *Perez . . . Shobal* signifies a line of descent; these persons are not brothers. **4b–7:** Return to the genealogy of Caleb; see 2.18–20n. **9–10:** There is a wordplay in Hebrew: "ya'bets" (Jabez), "'otseb"

Mered married;[a] and she conceived and bore[b] Miriam, Shammai, and Ishbah father of Eshtemoa. [18] And his Judean wife bore Jered father of Gedor, Heber father of Soco, and Jekuthiel father of Zanoah. [19] The sons of the wife of Hodiah, the sister of Naham, were the fathers of Keilah the Garmite and Eshtemoa the Maacathite. [20] The sons of Shimon: Amnon, Rinnah, Ben-hanan, and Tilon. The sons of Ishi: Zoheth and Ben-zoheth. [21] The sons of Shelah son of Judah: Er father of Lecah, Laadah father of Mareshah, and the families of the guild of linen workers at Beth-ashbea; [22] and Jokim, and the men of Cozeba, and Joash, and Saraph, who married into Moab but returned to Lehem[c] (now the records[d] are ancient). [23] These were the potters and inhabitants of Netaim and Gederah; they lived there with the king in his service.

[24] The sons of Simeon: Nemuel, Jamin, Jarib, Zerah, Shaul;[e] [25] Shallum was his son, Mibsam his son, Mishma his son. [26] The sons of Mishma: Hammuel his son, Zaccur his son, Shimei his son. [27] Shimei had sixteen sons and six daughters; but his brothers did not have many children, nor did all their family multiply like the Judeans. [28] They lived in Beer-sheba, Moladah, Hazar-shual, [29] Bilhah, Ezem, Tolad, [30] Bethuel, Hormah, Ziklag, [31] Beth-marcaboth, Hazar-susim, Beth-biri, and Shaaraim. These were their towns until David became king. [32] And their villages were Etam, Ain, Rimmon, Tochen, and Ashan, five towns, [33] along with all their villages that were around these towns as far as Baal. These were their settlements. And they kept a genealogical record.

[34] Meshobab, Jamlech, Joshah son of Amaziah, [35] Joel, Jehu son of Joshibiah son of Seraiah son of Asiel, [36] Elioenai, Jaakobah, Jeshohaiah, Asaiah, Adiel, Jesimiel, Benaiah, [37] Ziza son of Shiphi son of Allon son of Jedaiah son of Shimri son of Shemaiah— [38] these mentioned by name were leaders in their families, and their clans increased greatly. [39] They journeyed to the entrance of Gedor, to the east side of the valley, to seek pasture for their flocks, [40] where they found rich, good pasture, and the land was very broad, quiet, and peaceful; for the former inhabitants there belonged to Ham. [41] These, registered by name, came in the days of King Hezekiah of Judah, and attacked their tents and the Meunim who were found there, and exterminated them to this day, and settled in their place, because there was pasture there for their flocks. [42] And some of them, five hundred men of the Simeonites, went to Mount Seir, having as their leaders Pelatiah, Neariah, Rephaiah, and Uzziel, sons of Ishi; [43] they destroyed the remnant of the Amalekites that had escaped, and they have lived there to this day.

5 The sons of Reuben the firstborn of Israel. (He was the firstborn, but because he defiled his father's bed his birthright was

---

a   The clause: *These are . . . married* is transposed from verse 18
b   Heb lacks *and bore*
c   Vg Compare Gk: Heb *and Jashubi-lahem*
d   Or *matters*
e   Or *Saul*

(pain), and "'otsbi" (harm). **21:** In referring to Shelah, the text returns to the original sons of Judah (2.3–4). **22:** *Married into Moab*, the Chronicler again posits some close links between Judah and its neighbors. Possible links may be hinted at in Ezra 2.6; 8.4; 10.30. Intermarriage with Moabites in the postexilic period is also attested (Ezra 9.1; Neh 13.23; Ruth), but in contrast to Chronicles, in Ezra and Nehemiah such marriages are banned.

4.24–43: The descendants of Simeon. Here too, the Chronicler punctuates his genealogical prologue with anecdotes about geography, migrations, and wars (vv. 27–33,38–43). The genealogy of Simeon immediately follows that of its neighbor, Judah. **24–27:** The lineage of Simeon is traced through his son Shaul. The names listed in v. 24 (Nemuel, Jamin, Jarib, Zerah, and Shaul) are derived from Gen 46.10; Ex 6.15; and esp. Num 26.12–14. The rest of the genealogy (vv. 26–27) is unique to the Chronicler. **28–33:** Taken, with some changes, from Josh 19.2–8. **33–43:** A list of Simeonite leaders (v. 38) is followed by a description of the expansion of the tribe demographically and geographically. The ruthlessness displayed by the Simeonites recalls the intemperate behavior of their eponymous ancestor (Gen 34.25–29; 49.5–7). **41:** *Hezekiah*, see 2 Chr 29–32.

5.1–10: The descendants of Reuben. Reuben was firstborn (Gen 29.31–30.21; 35.23–26; 46.8–9; Ex 1.2; 6.14; Num 26.5; Ezek 48.31–35), but he does not appear first in the Chronicler's genealogies. **1:** Joseph, firstborn of Rachel, rather than Reuben, firstborn of Leah, attained to the birthright because Reuben had sexual relations

given to the sons of Joseph son of Israel, so that he is not enrolled in the genealogy according to the birthright; [2] though Judah became prominent among his brothers and a ruler came from him, yet the birthright belonged to Joseph.) [3] The sons of Reuben, the firstborn of Israel: Hanoch, Pallu, Hezron, and Carmi. [4] The sons of Joel: Shemaiah his son, Gog his son, Shimei his son, [5] Micah his son, Reaiah his son, Baal his son, [6] Beerah his son, whom King Tilgath-pilneser of Assyria carried away into exile; he was a chieftain of the Reubenites. [7] And his kindred by their families, when the genealogy of their generations was reckoned: the chief, Jeiel, and Zechariah, [8] and Bela son of Azaz, son of Shema, son of Joel, who lived in Aroer, as far as Nebo and Baal-meon. [9] He also lived to the east as far as the beginning of the desert this side of the Euphrates, because their cattle had multiplied in the land of Gilead. [10] And in the days of Saul they made war on the Hagrites, who fell by their hand; and they lived in their tents throughout all the region east of Gilead.

[11] The sons of Gad lived beside them in the land of Bashan as far as Salecah: [12] Joel the chief, Shapham the second, Janai, and Shaphat in Bashan. [13] And their kindred according to their clans: Michael, Meshullam, Sheba, Jorai, Jacan, Zia, and Eber, seven. [14] These were the sons of Abihail son of Huri, son of Jaroah, son of Gilead, son of Michael, son of Jeshishai, son of Jahdo, son of Buz; [15] Ahi son of Abdiel, son of Guni, was chief in their clan; [16] and they lived in Gilead, in Bashan and in its towns, and in all the pasture lands of Sharon to their limits. [17] All of these were enrolled by genealogies in the days of King Jotham of Judah, and in the days of King Jeroboam of Israel.

[18] The Reubenites, the Gadites, and the half-tribe of Manasseh had valiant warriors, who carried shield and sword, and drew the bow, expert in war, forty-four thousand seven hundred sixty, ready for service. [19] They made war on the Hagrites, Jetur, Naphish, and Nodab; [20] and when they received help against them, the Hagrites and all who were with them were given into their hands, for they cried to God in the battle, and he granted their entreaty because they trusted in him. [21] They captured their livestock: fifty thousand of their camels, two hundred fifty thousand sheep, two thousand donkeys, and one hundred thousand captives. [22] Many fell slain, because the war was of God. And they lived in their territory until the exile.

[23] The members of the half-tribe of Manasseh lived in the land; they were very

with Jacob's concubine Bilhah (Gen 35.22; 49.4). **2:** *A ruler came from him,* the writer alludes to David's kingship, which eventually encompassed all twelve tribes (28.4; 1 Sam 13.14; 25.30; Mic 5.2). **3:** The Chronicler derives this list from Num 26.5–6. *Carmi* is one of the Reubenite clans with possible ties to Judah (Gen 46.9; Ex 6.14; Num 26.6; Josh 7.1,18,24,26; 1 Chr 2.7; 4.1). **6:** In contrast to Kings, which largely loses its concentration upon individual tribes in its coverage of the dual monarchies, the Chronicler's history maintains a continuous interest in the fate of individual tribes. *Tilgath-pilneser,* the Chronicler's spelling (5.26; 2 Chr 28.20) of Tiglath-pileser (III), King of Assyria (745–727 BCE); cf. 2 Kings 15.29. **9:** In this case, *Gilead* refers to the territory east of the Jordan, which is south of the Jabbok and north of the Arnon. There is some overlap with Gad's territorial holdings in Josh 13. **10:** *The days of Saul,* who was the first king of Israel, in the late eleventh century BCE.

5.11–17: The descendants of Gad. Like the Reubenites, the Gadites were located east of the Jordan River. **16:** Rather than signifying a *pasture land,* Heb "migrash" means the belt of land or open space outside a town or a sanctuary. *Sharon* refers here not to the (coastal) Sharon plain, the common designation of Sharon in the Bible, but to the town of Sharon in Transjordan, a place also mentioned in the Moabite Mesha inscription (line 13). **17:** *King Jotham of Judah* (759–743 BCE) and *King Jeroboam* (II) *of Israel* (788–747 BCE).

5.18–22: The wars of the Transjordan tribes. In some traditions (Num 32.1–42; Deut 3.12–16; 29.6–7; Josh 13.8–31) and once elsewhere in Chronicles (1 Chr 12.38), Reuben, Gad, and East Manasseh are treated as a larger entity. These two and a half tribes join forces, share a common muster, partake in the spoils gained by fighting a collective enemy, and experience a common fate (vv. 22,25–26). The number *forty-four thousand seven hundred sixty* (v. 18) is notable for its specificity, not for its magnitude.

5.23–24: The descendants of Half-Manasseh. This part of the tribe of Manasseh was located east of the Jordan River, to the north of Gad.

numerous from Bashan to Baal-hermon, Senir, and Mount Hermon. [24] These were the heads of their clans: Epher,[a] Ishi, Eliel, Azriel, Jeremiah, Hodaviah, and Jahdiel, mighty warriors, famous men, heads of their clans. [25] But they transgressed against the God of their ancestors, and prostituted themselves to the gods of the peoples of the land, whom God had destroyed before them. [26] So the God of Israel stirred up the spirit of King Pul of Assyria, the spirit of King Tilgath-pilneser of Assyria, and he carried them away, namely, the Reubenites, the Gadites, and the half-tribe of Manasseh, and brought them to Halah, Habor, Hara, and the river Gozan, to this day.

6 [b] The sons of Levi: Gershom,[c] Kohath, and Merari. [2] The sons of Kohath: Amram, Izhar, Hebron, and Uzziel. [3] The children of Amram: Aaron, Moses, and Miriam. The sons of Aaron: Nadab, Abihu, Eleazar, and Ithamar. [4] Eleazar became the father of Phinehas, Phinehas of Abishua, [5] Abishua of Bukki, Bukki of Uzzi, [6] Uzzi of Zerahiah, Zerahiah of Meraioth, [7] Meraioth of Amariah, Amariah of Ahitub, [8] Ahitub of Zadok, Zadok of Ahimaaz, [9] Ahimaaz of Azariah, Azariah of Johanan, [10] and Johanan of Azariah (it was he who served as priest in the house that Solomon built in Jerusalem). [11] Azariah became the father of Amariah, Amariah of Ahitub, [12] Ahitub of Zadok, Zadok of Shallum, [13] Shallum of Hilkiah, Hilkiah of Azariah, [14] Azariah of Seraiah, Seraiah of Jehozadak;

[15] and Jehozadak went into exile when the LORD sent Judah and Jerusalem into exile by the hand of Nebuchadnezzar.

[16] [d] The sons of Levi: Gershom, Kohath, and Merari. [17] These are the names of the sons of Gershom: Libni and Shimei. [18] The sons of Kohath: Amram, Izhar, Hebron, and Uzziel. [19] The sons of Merari: Mahli and Mushi. These are the clans of the Levites according to their ancestry. [20] Of Gershom: Libni his son, Jahath his son, Zimmah his son, [21] Joah his son, Iddo his son, Zerah his son, Jeatherai his son. [22] The sons of Kohath: Amminadab his son, Korah his son, Assir his son, [23] Elkanah his son, Ebiasaph his son, Assir his son, [24] Tahath his son, Uriel his son, Uzziah his son, and Shaul his son. [25] The sons of Elkanah: Amasai and Ahimoth, [26] Elkanah his son, Zophai his son, Nahath his son, [27] Eliab his son, Jeroham his son, Elkanah his son. [28] The sons of Samuel: Joel[e] his firstborn, the second Abijah.[f] [29] The sons of Merari: Mahli, Libni his son, Shimei his son, Uzzah his son, [30] Shimea his son, Haggiah his son, and Asaiah his son.

[31] These are the men whom David put in charge of the service of song in the house

a   Gk Vg: Heb *and Epher*
b   Ch 5.27 in Heb
c   Heb *Gershon*, variant of *Gershom*; See 6.16
d   Ch 6.1 in Heb
e   Gk Syr Compare verse 33 and 1 Sam 8.2: Heb lacks *Joel*
f   Heb reads *Vashni, and Abijah* for *the second Abijah*, taking *the second* as a proper name

---

5.25–26: The exile of the Transjordanian tribes. The campaigns of 733–732 BCE by *Tilgath-pilneser* III (also known as *Pul*), were primarily directed against King Rezin of Damascus, but also resulted in the capture of Gilead and Galilee (2 Kings 15.29). The list of sites in v. 26 is borrowed, however, from 2 Kings 17.6 (parallel 2 Kings 18.11), which details the destinations of the later Samarian deportees in the Assyrian exile of 722 BCE.

6.1–81: The descendants of Levi take center stage in the genealogies of Chronicles. For the Chronicler, the Levites are second in importance only to the Judeans, so their genealogy is especially long and detailed. As with other tribes, attention is paid to issues of identity and location: who the Levites are (vv. 1–53) and where they live (vv. 54–81). **1–15:** A priestly line is traced from Levi in the ancestral period (cf. Gen 46.11; Ex 6.16–25; Num 3.17–20) all the way to Jehozadak (v. 15), who was taken to Babylon in the exile of 586 BCE. **8:** Scholars debate the origin of David's main priest Zadok with some suggesting that he was originally Canaanite; this genealogy in Chronicles is the first source to explicitly connect him to the line of Aaron and Levi. Twelve generations of priests precede Zadok and twelve generations of priests succeed him, hence the era of Zadok, which coincides with the construction of the Temple, marks the halfway point between the ancestral era and the exile. **10:** *Azariah,* cf. 1 Kings 4.2. **14:** *Seraiah,* see 2 Kings 25.18. **16–48:** Lineages for three major groups within the Levites—the Gershonites, the Kohathites, and the Merarites (vv. 16–30)—preface lineages of levitical singers from the same three groups (vv. 31–48). Levitical choirs are an intrinsic component of the Chronicler's system of worship, appearing some thirty times in his history. The genealogies thus are not purely antiquarian, but in places justify the institutions of postexilic Judah. **28:** *Samuel,* cf. 1 Sam 1.1; 8.2. **31–32:** Referring back to the three levitical clans, the writer

The Levitical towns. Cities of refuge are highlighted with a star. The tribal boundaries are shown by a dashed line.

of the LORD, after the ark came to rest there. [32] They ministered with song before the tabernacle of the tent of meeting, until Solomon had built the house of the LORD in Jerusalem; and they performed their service in due order. [33] These are the men who served; and their sons were: Of the Kohathites: Heman, the singer, son of Joel, son of Samuel, [34] son of Elkanah, son of Jeroham, son of Eliel, son of Toah, [35] son of Zuph, son of Elkanah, son of Mahath, son of Amasai, [36] son of Elkanah, son of Joel, son of Azariah, son of Zephaniah, [37] son of Tahath, son of Assir, son of Ebiasaph, son of Korah, [38] son of Izhar, son of Kohath, son of Levi, son of Israel; [39] and his brother Asaph, who stood on his right, namely, Asaph son of Berechiah, son of Shimea, [40] son of Michael, son of Baaseiah, son of Malchijah, [41] son of Ethni, son of Zerah, son of Adaiah, [42] son of Ethan, son of Zimmah, son of Shimei, [43] son of Jahath, son of Gershom, son of Levi. [44] On the left were their kindred the sons of Merari: Ethan son of Kishi, son of Abdi, son of Malluch, [45] son of Hashabiah, son of Amaziah, son of Hilkiah, [46] son of Amzi, son of Bani, son of Shemer, [47] son of Mahli, son of Mushi, son of Merari, son of Levi; [48] and their kindred the Levites were appointed for all the service of the tabernacle of the house of God.

[49] But Aaron and his sons made offerings on the altar of burnt offering and on the altar of incense, doing all the work of the most holy place, to make atonement for Israel,

according to all that Moses the servant of God had commanded. [50] These are the sons of Aaron: Eleazar his son, Phinehas his son, Abishua his son, [51] Bukki his son, Uzzi his son, Zerahiah his son, [52] Meraioth his son, Amariah his son, Ahitub his son, [53] Zadok his son, Ahimaaz his son.

[54] These are their dwelling places according to their settlements within their borders: to the sons of Aaron of the families of Kohathites—for the lot fell to them first— [55] to them they gave Hebron in the land of Judah and its surrounding pasture lands, [56] but the fields of the city and its villages they gave to Caleb son of Jephunneh. [57] To the sons of Aaron they gave the cities of refuge: Hebron, Libnah with its pasture lands, Jattir, Eshtemoa with its pasture lands, [58] Hilen[a] with its pasture lands, Debir with its pasture lands, [59] Ashan with its pasture lands, and Beth-shemesh with its pasture lands. [60] From the tribe of Benjamin, Geba with its pasture lands, Alemeth with its pasture lands, and Anathoth with its pasture lands. All their towns throughout their families were thirteen.

[61] To the rest of the Kohathites were given by lot out of the family of the tribe, out of the half-tribe, the half of Manasseh, ten towns. [62] To the Gershomites according to their families were allotted thirteen towns out of the tribes of Issachar, Asher, Naphtali, and

[a] Other readings *Hilez, Holon*; See Josh 21.15

summarizes the duties of the Gershonites, Kohathites, and Merarites adopted during the United Monarchy of David and Solomon, the time in which the Temple was built. Three specific descendants—Asaph from Gershon (vv. 39–43), Heman from Kohath (vv. 33–38), and Ethan from Merari (vv. 44–47)—took on official roles in the state religion. **33:** *Heman,* "Asaph" (v. 39), and "Ethan" (v. 42) represent three classes or guilds of singers. Because David's reign is definitive for the levitical singers, the patronyms Asaph, Heman, and Ethan serve as organizing principles for them (2 Chr 5.12; 29.14; 35.15). **44:** *Ethan* represents the Merarites (6.18,29; 15.17), but in many other instances Jeduthun serves this role (16.41; 25.1,3,6; 2 Chr 5.12; 29.14; 35.15). **49–53:** The Aaronic priests officiate within the sanctuary and make offerings (23.30–32; Ex 38–42; 30.1–10; Lev 8.1–9.24; 18.8–20; Ezek 44.13). **49:** *The most holy place* (lit. "holy of holies") is the exclusive domain of the priests (Ex 26.33–34; Num 18.1–5; Ezek 44.15–16; 2 Chr 5.11; 29.7). Other members of the tribe of Levi may serve as Temple staff, but the priests alone officiate at the inner sanctuary. *To make atonement for Israel* refers to the Day of Atonement ritual of Lev 16. This festival, mentioned only in Priestly sources in the Torah, probably became especially significant during the time of the Chronicler. **54–81:** The list of levitical towns is drawn from an earlier version of Josh 21.3–42. **55–60:** The location of Aaronide settlements is limited to the traditional domains of three tribes: Judah, Simeon, and Benjamin. On *pasture lands,* see 5.16n. **57:** The creation of *cities of refuge* or asylum was demanded in Deuteronomic (Deut 4.41–43; 19.1–13) and Priestly law (Num 35.6–15,25–28,32). Most, if not all, of the towns designated for asylum (Josh 20.7–8) doubled as levitical settlements.

Manasseh in Bashan. ⁶³ To the Merarites according to their families were allotted twelve towns out of the tribes of Reuben, Gad, and Zebulun. ⁶⁴ So the people of Israel gave the Levites the towns with their pasture lands. ⁶⁵ They also gave them by lot out of the tribes of Judah, Simeon, and Benjamin these towns that are mentioned by name.

⁶⁶ And some of the families of the sons of Kohath had towns of their territory out of the tribe of Ephraim. ⁶⁷ They were given the cities of refuge: Shechem with its pasture lands in the hill country of Ephraim, Gezer with its pasture lands, ⁶⁸ Jokmeam with its pasture lands, Beth-horon with its pasture lands, ⁶⁹ Aijalon with its pasture lands, Gath-rimmon with its pasture lands; ⁷⁰ and out of the half-tribe of Manasseh, Aner with its pasture lands, and Bileam with its pasture lands, for the rest of the families of the Kohathites.

⁷¹ To the Gershomites: out of the half-tribe of Manasseh: Golan in Bashan with its pasture lands and Ashtaroth with its pasture lands; ⁷² and out of the tribe of Issachar: Kedesh with its pasture lands, Daberathᵃ with its pasture lands, ⁷³ Ramoth with its pasture lands, and Anem with its pasture lands; ⁷⁴ out of the tribe of Asher: Mashal with its pasture lands, Abdon with its pasture lands, ⁷⁵ Hukok with its pasture lands, and Rehob with its pasture lands; ⁷⁶ and out of the tribe of Naphtali: Kedesh in Galilee with its pasture lands, Hammon with its pasture lands, and Kiriathaim with its pasture lands. ⁷⁷ To the rest of the Merarites out of the tribe of Zebulun: Rimmono with its pasture lands, Tabor with its pasture lands, ⁷⁸ and across the Jordan from Jericho, on the east side of the Jordan, out of the tribe of Reuben: Bezer in the steppe with its pasture lands, Jahzah with its pasture lands, ⁷⁹ Kedemoth with its pasture lands, and Mephaath with its pasture lands; ⁸⁰ and out of the tribe of Gad: Ramoth in Gilead with its pasture lands, Mahanaim

with its pasture lands, ⁸¹ Heshbon with its pasture lands, and Jazer with its pasture lands.

7 The sonsᵇ of Issachar: Tola, Puah, Jashub, and Shimron, four. ² The sons of Tola: Uzzi, Rephaiah, Jeriel, Jahmai, Ibsam, and Shemuel, heads of their ancestral houses, namely of Tola, mighty warriors of their generations, their number in the days of David being twenty-two thousand six hundred. ³ The sonᶜ of Uzzi: Izrahiah. And the sons of Izrahiah: Michael, Obadiah, Joel, and Isshiah, five, all of them chiefs; ⁴ and along with them, by their generations, according to their ancestral houses, were units of the fighting force, thirty-six thousand, for they had many wives and sons. ⁵ Their kindred belonging to all the families of Issachar were in all eighty-seven thousand mighty warriors, enrolled by genealogy.

⁶ The sons of Benjamin: Bela, Becher, and Jediael, three. ⁷ The sons of Bela: Ezbon, Uzzi, Uzziel, Jerimoth, and Iri, five, heads of ancestral houses, mighty warriors; and their enrollment by genealogies was twenty-two thousand thirty-four. ⁸ The sons of Becher: Zemirah, Joash, Eliezer, Elioenai, Omri, Jeremoth, Abijah, Anathoth, and Alemeth. All these were the sons of Becher; ⁹ and their enrollment by genealogies, according to their generations, as heads of their ancestral houses, mighty warriors, was twenty thousand two hundred. ¹⁰ The sons of Jediael: Bilhan. And the sons of Bilhan: Jeush, Benjamin, Ehud, Chenaanah, Zethan, Tarshish, and Ahishahar. ¹¹ All these were the sons of Jediael according to the heads of their ancestral houses, mighty warriors, seventeen thousand two hundred, ready for service in war. ¹² And Shuppim and Hup-

ᵃ Or *Dobrath*
ᵇ Syr Compare Vg: Heb *And to the sons*
ᶜ Heb *sons*

7.1–5: **The descendants of Issachar.** Issachar's progeny are traced through his eldest son Tola (Gen 46.13; Num 26.23–25; Judg 5.15). As in some other genealogies (4.42–43; 5.7–10,18–22; 7.9–12,40), large numbers, growth, and military prowess are stressed.

7.6–12: **The descendants of Benjamin.** A genealogy of Zebulun may be missing here (Gen 46.17–27; Num 26.23–50), as another genealogy of Benjamin is found in 8.1–40. **12:** Some commentators emend *sons of Ir* to "sons of Dan" on the supposition that this verse contains a fragment of the apparently missing genealogy of Dan (Gen 46.13; Num 26.42; Judg 5.17).

pim were the sons of Ir, Hushim the son[a] of Aher.

[13] The descendants of Naphtali: Jahziel, Guni, Jezer, and Shallum, the descendants of Bilhah.

[14] The sons of Manasseh: Asriel, whom his Aramean concubine bore; she bore Machir the father of Gilead. [15] And Machir took a wife for Huppim and for Shuppim. The name of his sister was Maacah. And the name of the second was Zelophehad; and Zelophehad had daughters. [16] Maacah the wife of Machir bore a son, and she named him Peresh; the name of his brother was Sheresh; and his sons were Ulam and Rekem. [17] The son[a] of Ulam: Bedan. These were the sons of Gilead son of Machir, son of Manasseh. [18] And his sister Hammolecheth bore Ishhod, Abiezer, and Mahlah.

[19] The sons of Shemida were Ahian, Shechem, Likhi, and Aniam.

[20] The sons of Ephraim: Shuthelah, and Bered his son, Tahath his son, Eleadah his son, Tahath his son, [21] Zabad his son, Shuthelah his son, and Ezer and Elead. Now the people of Gath, who were born in the land, killed them, because they came down to raid their cattle. [22] And their father Ephraim mourned many days, and his brothers came to comfort him. [23] Ephraim[b] went in to his wife, and she conceived and bore a son; and he named him Beriah, because disaster[c] had befallen his house. [24] His daughter was Sheerah, who built both Lower and Upper Beth-horon, and Uzzen-sheerah. [25] Rephah was his son, Resheph his son, Telah his son, Tahan his son, [26] Ladan his son, Ammihud his son, Elishama his son, [27] Nun[d] his son, Joshua his

son. [28] Their possessions and settlements were Bethel and its towns, and eastward Naaran, and westward Gezer and its towns, Shechem and its towns, as far as Ayyah and its towns; [29] also along the borders of the Manassites, Beth-shean and its towns, Taanach and its towns, Megiddo and its towns, Dor and its towns. In these lived the sons of Joseph son of Israel.

[30] The sons of Asher: Imnah, Ishvah, Ishvi, Beriah, and their sister Serah. [31] The sons of Beriah: Heber and Malchiel, who was the father of Birzaith. [32] Heber became the father of Japhlet, Shomer, Hotham, and their sister Shua. [33] The sons of Japhlet: Pasach, Bimhal, and Ashvath. These are the sons of Japhlet. [34] The sons of Shemer: Ahi, Rohgah, Hubbah, and Aram. [35] The sons of Helem[e] his brother: Zophah, Imna, Shelesh, and Amal. [36] The sons of Zophah: Suah, Harnepher, Shual, Beri, Imrah, [37] Bezer, Hod, Shamma, Shilshah, Ithran, and Beera. [38] The sons of Jether: Jephunneh, Pispa, and Ara. [39] The sons of Ulla: Arah, Hanniel, and Rizia. [40] All of these were men of Asher, heads of ancestral houses, select mighty warriors, chief of the princes. Their number enrolled by genealogies, for service in war, was twenty-six thousand men.

8 Benjamin became the father of Bela his firstborn, Ashbel the second, Aharah the third, [2] Nohah the fourth, and Rapha the fifth.

a Heb *sons*
b Heb *He*
c Heb *beraah*
d Here spelled *Non*; see Ex 33.11
e Or *Hotham*; see 7.32

7.13: The descendants of Naphtali. As in Gen 46.23–25, *Bilhah* is the mother of *Naphtali* (where she is also the mother of Dan).

7.14–19: The descendants of Manasseh (cf. Num 26.29–34). For the progeny of Manasseh east of the Jordan, see 5.23–24. **15:** On the daughters of *Zelophehad,* see Num 27.1–11; 36.1–12; Josh 17.3.

7.20–29: The descendants of Ephraim. Tradition (Gen 48.8–22; Deut 33.17) posits a close relationship between the two sons of Joseph—Manasseh and Ephraim. This is why the Chronicler treats them sequentially and considers their settlements (vv. 28–29; cf. Josh 16–18) together. **21–24:** In depicting Ephraim, his wife, and his sons living in the land, this short tale conflicts with Genesis (chs 41–50; cf. Ex 12.40) in which Ephraim is born in Egypt and never enters the land. Here too the Chronicler emphasizes Israel's long-term connection to the land. **27:** *Joshua,* the hero of the book of Joshua; see Josh 1.1; 24.29–30.

7.30–40: The descendants of Asher. The genealogy may be compared with Gen 46.17 and Num 26.44–47, but much of its information is unparalleled elsewhere in the Bible.

8.1–9.1: The descendants of Benjamin. Another genealogy, fuller than that in 7.6–12. Along with Judah and Levi, Benjamin receives substantial attention from the Chronicler. The great coverage these three tribes receive

³ And Bela had sons: Addar, Gera, Abihud,ᵃ ⁴ Abishua, Naaman, Ahoah, ⁵ Gera, Shephuphan, and Huram. ⁶ These are the sons of Ehud (they were heads of ancestral houses of the inhabitants of Geba, and they were carried into exile to Manahath): ⁷ Naaman,ᵇ Ahijah, and Gera, that is, Heglam,ᶜ who became the father of Uzza and Ahihud. ⁸ And Shaharaim had sons in the country of Moab after he had sent away his wives Hushim and Baara. ⁹ He had sons by his wife Hodesh: Jobab, Zibia, Mesha, Malcam, ¹⁰ Jeuz, Sachia, and Mirmah. These were his sons, heads of ancestral houses. ¹¹ He also had sons by Hushim: Abitub and Elpaal. ¹² The sons of Elpaal: Eber, Misham, and Shemed, who built Ono and Lod with its towns, ¹³ and Beriah and Shema (they were heads of ancestral houses of the inhabitants of Aijalon, who put to flight the inhabitants of Gath); ¹⁴ and Ahio, Shashak, and Jeremoth. ¹⁵ Zebadiah, Arad, Eder, ¹⁶ Michael, Ishpah, and Joha were sons of Beriah. ¹⁷ Zebadiah, Meshullam, Hizki, Heber, ¹⁸ Ishmerai, Izliah, and Jobab were the sons of Elpaal. ¹⁹ Jakim, Zichri, Zabdi, ²⁰ Elienai, Zillethai, Eliel, ²¹ Adaiah, Beraiah, and Shimrath were the sons of Shimei. ²² Ishpan, Eber, Eliel, ²³ Abdon, Zichri, Hanan, ²⁴ Hananiah, Elam, Anthothijah, ²⁵ Iphdeiah, and Penuel were the sons of Shashak. ²⁶ Shamsherai, Sheariah, Athaliah, ²⁷ Jaareshiah, Elijah, and Zichri were the sons of Jeroham. ²⁸ These were the heads of ancestral houses, according to their generations, chiefs. These lived in Jerusalem.

²⁹ Jeielᵈ the father of Gibeon lived in Gibeon, and the name of his wife was Maacah. ³⁰ His firstborn son: Abdon, then Zur, Kish, Baal,ᵉ Nadab, ³¹ Gedor, Ahio, Zecher,

³² and Mikloth, who became the father of Shimeah. Now these also lived opposite their kindred in Jerusalem, with their kindred. ³³ Ner became the father of Kish, Kish of Saul,ᶠ Saulᶠ of Jonathan, Malchishua, Abinadab, and Esh-baal; ³⁴ and the son of Jonathan was Merib-baal; and Merib-baal became the father of Micah. ³⁵ The sons of Micah: Pithon, Melech, Tarea, and Ahaz. ³⁶ Ahaz became the father of Jehoaddah; and Jehoaddah became the father of Alemeth, Azmaveth, and Zimri; Zimri became the father of Moza. ³⁷ Moza became the father of Binea; Raphah was his son, Eleasah his son, Azel his son. ³⁸ Azel had six sons, and these are their names: Azrikam, Bocheru, Ishmael, Sheariah, Obadiah, and Hanan; all these were the sons of Azel. ³⁹ The sons of his brother Eshek: Ulam his firstborn, Jeush the second, and Eliphelet the third. ⁴⁰ The sons of Ulam were mighty warriors, archers, having many children and grandchildren, one hundred fifty. All these were Benjaminites.

9 So all Israel was enrolled by genealogies; and these are written in the Book of the Kings of Israel. And Judah was taken into exile in Babylon because of their unfaithfulness. ² Now the first to live again in their possessions in their towns were Israelites, priests, Levites, and temple servants.

³ And some of the people of Judah, Benjamin, Ephraim, and Manasseh lived in

ᵃ Or *father of Ehud*; see 8.6
ᵇ Heb *and Naaman*
ᶜ Or *he carried them into exile*
ᵈ Compare 9.35: Heb lacks *Jeiel*
ᵉ Gk Ms adds *Ner*; Compare 8.33 and 9.36
ᶠ Or *Shaul*

reflects both the author's interests and circumstances in postexilic Judah, into which sections of Benjamin were incorporated. The author's interest in Benjamin is also reflected in the narrative portions of the Chronicler's work (2 Chr 11.1,3,12,23). **8.33–40:** Saul's genealogy is followed for eleven generations (cf. 10.1–14). **33–34:** *Eshbaal* and *Merib-baal* are probably earlier forms of "Ishbosheth" (2 Sam 2.8) and "Mephibosheth" (2 Sam 4.4). **9.1:** The reference to genealogical registrations concludes the Chronicler's introductions to Israel's twelve tribes, begun in 2.1–2. In the Chronicler's theology, the exile marks an important dividing line between monarchic Israel and Judah in the Persian period. *Unfaithfulness* is a Priestly term. Its use here, as the cause for exile, reflects the significance of Priestly material to this author. The same term is also used in 1 Chr 10.13 (the death of Saul) and 2 Chr 36.14 (the exile of Judah).

9.2–34: The genealogies of Jerusalem families in postexilic Judah. This first section of this passage (vv. 2–18) is partially paralleled in Neh 11.3–19. By mentioning these families, officials, and their interrelationships, the author establishes links between the Israel of old (outlined in chs 2–8) and the Jerusalem community of

Jerusalem: [4] Uthai son of Ammihud, son of Omri, son of Imri, son of Bani, from the sons of Perez son of Judah. [5] And of the Shilonites: Asaiah the firstborn, and his sons. [6] Of the sons of Zerah: Jeuel and their kin, six hundred ninety. [7] Of the Benjaminites: Sallu son of Meshullam, son of Hodaviah, son of Hassenuah, [8] Ibneiah son of Jeroham, Elah son of Uzzi, son of Michri, and Meshullam son of Shephatiah, son of Reuel, son of Ibnijah; [9] and their kindred according to their generations, nine hundred fifty-six. All these were heads of families according to their ancestral houses.

[10] Of the priests: Jedaiah, Jehoiarib, Jachin, [11] and Azariah son of Hilkiah, son of Meshullam, son of Zadok, son of Meraioth, son of Ahitub, the chief officer of the house of God; [12] and Adaiah son of Jeroham, son of Pashhur, son of Malchijah, and Maasai son of Adiel, son of Jahzerah, son of Meshullam, son of Meshillemith, son of Immer; [13] besides their kindred, heads of their ancestral houses, one thousand seven hundred sixty, qualified for the work of the service of the house of God.

[14] Of the Levites: Shemaiah son of Hasshub, son of Azrikam, son of Hashabiah, of the sons of Merari; [15] and Bakbakkar, Heresh, Galal, and Mattaniah son of Mica, son of Zichri, son of Asaph; [16] and Obadiah son of Shemaiah, son of Galal, son of Jeduthun, and Berechiah son of Asa, son of Elkanah, who lived in the villages of the Netophathites.

[17] The gatekeepers were: Shallum, Akkub, Talmon, Ahiman; and their kindred Shallum was the chief, [18] stationed previously in the king's gate on the east side. These were the gatekeepers of the camp of the Levites. [19] Shallum son of Kore, son of Ebiasaph, son of Korah, and his kindred of his ancestral house, the Korahites, were in charge of the work of the service, guardians of the thresholds of the tent, as their ancestors had been in charge of the camp of the LORD, guard-

ians of the entrance. [20] And Phinehas son of Eleazar was chief over them in former times; the LORD was with him. [21] Zechariah son of Meshelemiah was gatekeeper at the entrance of the tent of meeting. [22] All these, who were chosen as gatekeepers at the thresholds, were two hundred twelve. They were enrolled by genealogies in their villages. David and the seer Samuel established them in their office of trust. [23] So they and their descendants were in charge of the gates of the house of the LORD, that is, the house of the tent, as guards. [24] The gatekeepers were on the four sides, east, west, north, and south; [25] and their kindred who were in their villages were obliged to come in every seven days, in turn, to be with them; [26] for the four chief gatekeepers, who were Levites, were in charge of the chambers and the treasures of the house of God. [27] And they would spend the night near the house of God; for on them lay the duty of watching, and they had charge of opening it every morning.

[28] Some of them had charge of the utensils of service, for they were required to count them when they were brought in and taken out. [29] Others of them were appointed over the furniture, and over all the holy utensils, also over the choice flour, the wine, the oil, the incense, and the spices. [30] Others, of the sons of the priests, prepared the mixing of the spices, [31] and Mattithiah, one of the Levites, the firstborn of Shallum the Korahite, was in charge of making the flat cakes. [32] Also some of their kindred of the Kohathites had charge of the rows of bread, to prepare them for each sabbath.

[33] Now these are the singers, the heads of ancestral houses of the Levites, living in the chambers of the temple free from other service, for they were on duty day and night. [34] These were heads of ancestral houses of the Levites, according to their generations; these leaders lived in Jerusalem.

his own time. **3:** The detail of people of *Ephraim and Manasseh* living in Jerusalem is not found in Nehemiah, and reflects the Chronicler's interest in all of Israel. **10–11:** The list of priests should be read in light of the pre-exilic succession of priests found in 6.1–15. **17–34:** The list of levitical gatekeepers and singers, as well as the description of their duties, is unparalleled in the list of Neh 11. The passage illustrates the Chronicler's interest in continuity by insisting that the arrangements David (and here Samuel, v. 22) made on their behalf (chs 15–17; 26) were followed when the Jewish exiles returned from Babylon. The gatekeepers perform multiple functions: not only guard duty, but also administration and even baking. **20:** *Phinehas*, cf. Num 25.11–13. **32:** *Rows of bread,*

³⁵ In Gibeon lived the father of Gibeon, Jeiel, and the name of his wife was Maacah. ³⁶ His firstborn son was Abdon, then Zur, Kish, Baal, Ner, Nadab, ³⁷ Gedor, Ahio, Zechariah, and Mikloth; ³⁸ and Mikloth became the father of Shimeam; and these also lived opposite their kindred in Jerusalem, with their kindred. ³⁹ Ner became the father of Kish, Kish of Saul, Saul of Jonathan, Malchishua, Abinadab, and Esh-baal; ⁴⁰ and the son of Jonathan was Merib-baal; and Merib-baal became the father of Micah. ⁴¹ The sons of Micah: Pithon, Melech, Tahrea, and Ahaz;ᵃ ⁴² and Ahaz became the father of Jarah, and Jarah of Alemeth, Azmaveth, and Zimri; and Zimri became the father of Moza. ⁴³ Moza became the father of Binea; and Rephaiah was his son, Eleasah his son, Azel his son. ⁴⁴ Azel had six sons, and these are their names: Azrikam, Bocheru, Ishmael, Sheariah, Obadiah, and Hanan; these were the sons of Azel.

10 Now the Philistines fought against Israel; and the men of Israel fled before the Philistines, and fell slain on Mount Gilboa. ² The Philistines overtook Saul and his sons; and the Philistines killed Jonathan and Abinadab and Malchishua, sons of Saul. ³ The battle pressed hard on Saul; and the archers found him, and he was wounded by the archers. ⁴ Then Saul said to his armor-bearer, "Draw your sword, and thrust me through with it, so that these uncircumcised may not come and make sport of me." But his armor-bearer was unwilling, for he was terrified. So Saul took his own sword and fell on it. ⁵ When his armor-bearer saw that Saul was dead, he also fell on his sword and died. ⁶ Thus Saul died; he and his three sons and all his house died together. ⁷ When all the men of Israel who were in the valley saw that the armyᵇ had fled and that Saul and his sons were dead, they abandoned their towns and fled; and the Philistines came and occupied them.

⁸ The next day when the Philistines came to strip the dead, they found Saul and his sons fallen on Mount Gilboa. ⁹ They stripped him and took his head and his armor, and sent messengers throughout the land of the Philistines to carry the good news to their idols and to the people. ¹⁰ They put his armor in the temple of their gods, and fastened his head in the temple of Dagon. ¹¹ But when all Jabesh-gilead heard everything that the Philistines had done to Saul, ¹² all the valiant warriors got up and took away the body of Saul and the bodies of his sons, and brought them to Jabesh. Then they buried their bones under the oak in Jabesh, and fasted seven days.

¹³ So Saul died for his unfaithfulness; he was unfaithful to the Lord in that he did not keep the command of the Lord; moreover, he had consulted a medium, seeking guidance, ¹⁴ and did not seek guidance from the Lord. Therefore the Lordᶜ put him to death

ᵃ Compare 8.35: Heb lacks *and Ahaz*
ᵇ Heb *they*
ᶜ Heb *he*

cf. Lev 24.5–9. **35–44:** A transition, repeating the genealogy of Saul from 8.29–38 to introduce the first king of the United Monarchy (10.1–14).

10.1–14: The demise of Saul. Verses 1–12 are parallel to 1 Sam 31.1–13. Of the many incidents in Saul's career, the Chronicler presents only the last—the story of Saul's death, assuming that the reader is generally familiar with the earlier part of the story from 1 Samuel. The evaluation of Saul's reign—the Chronicler's own addition—plays on both the Heb roots "m'l" ("to be unfaithful, disobedient"; see 1.9) and "drš" ("to seek out, consult"), which are key terms in Chronicles. Saul dies because of his infidelity, even consulting a necromancer (1 Sam 28.3,7–25). Consultation with mediums to obtain contact with the dead is forbidden in legal texts (Lev 19.31; 20.6,27; Deut 18.11) and condemned in at least one prophetic text (Isa 8.18–19). This addition typifies the work of the Chronicler, who often searches his sources to find a clear theological cause for national disaster. **4–5:** *Uncircumcised,* unlike most of their contemporaries in the Near East, the Philistines did not practice circumcision. *Fell on his sword,* suicide is infrequent, but not condemned, in the Bible; see 2 Sam 17.23; 1 Kings 16.18; and, in the New Testament, Mt 27.5. **6:** *All his house died,* a generalization, ignoring the continuing genealogy of Saul (cf. 8.33–40; 9.35–44). **10:** *Dagon,* a Canaanite god of grain, adopted by the Philistines as one of their principal deities. **11–12:** *Jabesh-gilead,* in 1 Sam 11, Saul is acclaimed king after his rescue of this city east of the Jordan from Ammonite oppression. **14:** As elsewhere in Chronicles, the choice of kings belongs to God (e.g., 28.2–5; 29.10–12).

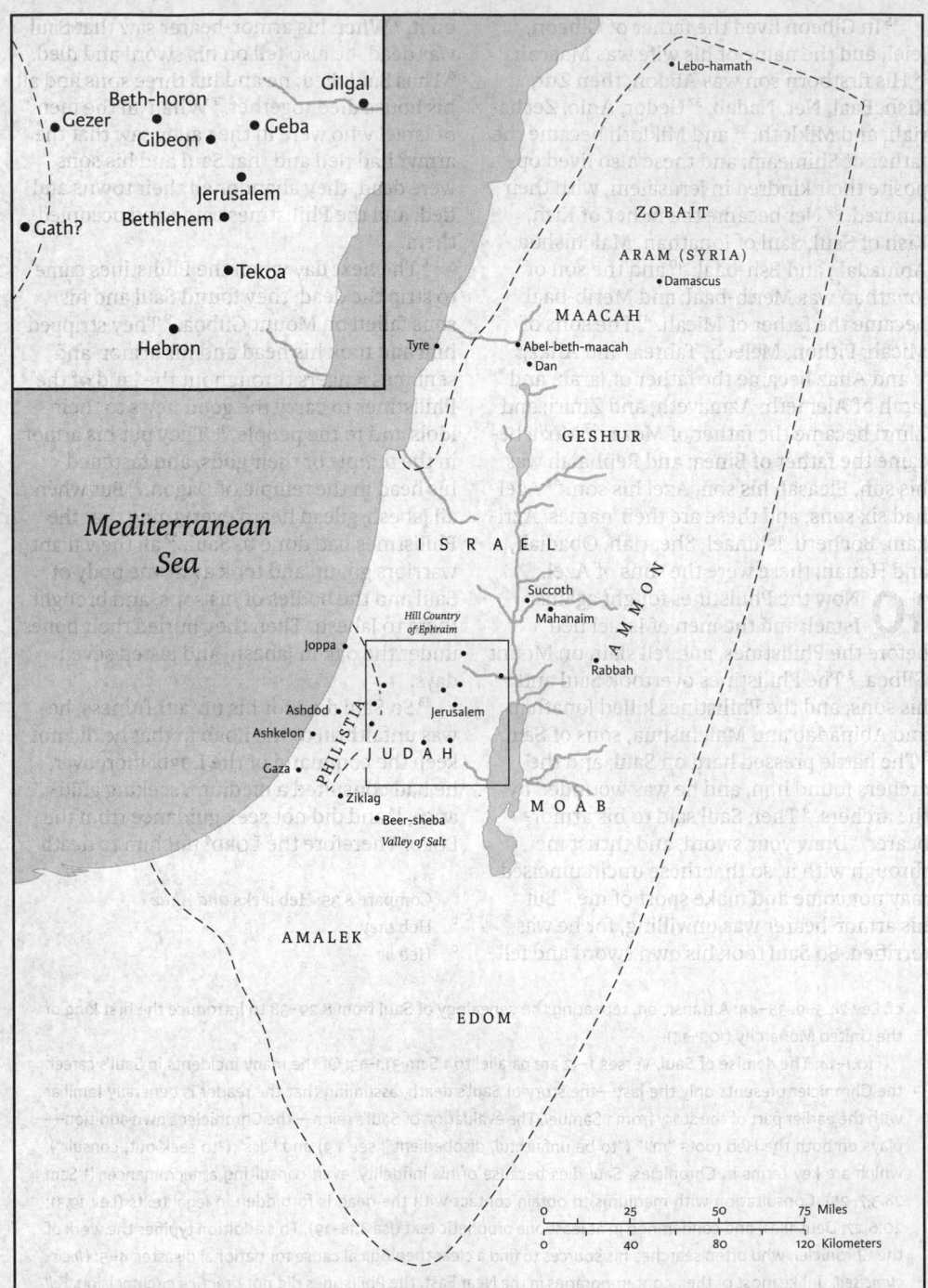

The kingdom of David according to Firsth Chronicles. The dashed line shows the approximate boundary of the kingdom at its greatest extent.

and turned the kingdom over to David son of Jesse.

11 Then all Israel gathered together to David at Hebron and said, "See, we are your bone and flesh. ² For some time now, even while Saul was king, it was you who commanded the army of Israel. The LORD your God said to you: It is you who shall be shepherd of my people Israel, you who shall be ruler over my people Israel." ³ So all the elders of Israel came to the king at Hebron, and David made a covenant with them at Hebron before the LORD. And they anointed David king over Israel, according to the word of the LORD by Samuel.

⁴ David and all Israel marched to Jerusalem, that is Jebus, where the Jebusites were, the inhabitants of the land. ⁵ The inhabitants of Jebus said to David, "You will not come in here." Nevertheless David took the stronghold of Zion, now the city of David. ⁶ David had said, "Whoever attacks the Jebusites first shall be chief and commander." And Joab son of Zeruiah went up first, so he became chief. ⁷ David resided in the stronghold; therefore it was called the city of David. ⁸ He built the city all around, from the Millo in complete circuit; and Joab repaired the rest of the city. ⁹ And David became greater and greater, for the LORD of hosts was with him.

¹⁰ Now these are the chiefs of David's warriors, who gave him strong support in his kingdom, together with all Israel, to make him king, according to the word of the LORD concerning Israel. ¹¹ This is an account of David's mighty warriors: Jashobeam, son of Hachmoni,ᵃ was chief of the Three;ᵇ he wielded his spear against three hundred whom he killed at one time.

¹² And next to him among the three warriors was Eleazar son of Dodo, the Ahohite. ¹³ He was with David at Pas-dammim when the Philistines were gathered there for battle. There was a plot of ground full of barley. Now the people had fled from the Philistines, ¹⁴ but he and David took their stand in the middle of the plot, defended it, and killed the Philistines; and the LORD saved them by a great victory.

¹⁵ Three of the thirty chiefs went down to the rock to David at the cave of Adullam, while the army of Philistines was encamped in the valley of Rephaim. ¹⁶ David was then in the stronghold; and the garrison of the Philistines was then at Bethlehem. ¹⁷ David said longingly, "O that someone would give me water to drink from the well of Bethlehem that is by the gate!" ¹⁸ Then the Three broke through the camp of the Philistines, and drew water from the well of Bethlehem that was by the gate, and they brought it to David.

ᵃ Or a Hachmonite
ᵇ Compare 2 Sam 23.8: Heb Thirty or captains

11.1–47: The impressive beginnings of David's reign. David does not seek out the kingship; the Israelites *gathered together to David* to make him king (v. 1). Pan-Israelite assemblies are regular occurrences in Chronicles (13.2; 2 Chr 15.9; 20.4; 23.2; 24.5; 25.5; 32.4,6). In this case, the consequences are clear. David immediately becomes king over all of Israel's tribes. In 2 Samuel David first becomes king over two tribes and only after considerable struggle becomes king over the northern tribes as well (2 Sam 2–5), but this information, which casts doubt on the greatness of David, is omitted by the Chronicler. **4–9:** David, leading *all Israel* (v. 4; cf. 2 Sam 5.6), captures Jerusalem as his first public act upon being made king. Such reorganizing of chronology typifies the Chronicler. By situating the capture of Jerusalem (borrowed from 2 Sam 5.6–10) at this point in the narrative, the author underscores the primacy of Jerusalem. **6:** *Joab* became the head of the army (see 18.15); his role in the capture of Jerusalem is not reported in 2 Sam 5 (cf. v. 8, another mention of Joab not in 2 Sam). **8:** David's building projects consisted essentially of a palace and fortifications in Jerusalem. The Chronicler attributes more building activity to David than do the authors of 2 Samuel (2 Sam 5.9,11; 7.2; 1 Chr 17.1; 2 Chr 2.2). *Millo*, probably "fill" for artificial terraces. **10–47:** The list of *the chiefs of David's warriors* largely follows an appendix to 2 Samuel (23.8–39). It is moved here, early in David's reign, to illustrate the consolidation of David's kingship. Israel's call to David to serve as king is followed by a visible demonstration of military support from various commanders, *together with all Israel* (v. 10). Little is otherwise known about these heroes. **18:** *He poured it out to the LORD* as a libation (1 Sam 7.6; Jer 44.16–18); such water libations became especially important in the later Second Temple period, especially in connection with the festival of

But David would not drink of it; he poured it out to the LORD, [19] and said, "My God forbid that I should do this. Can I drink the blood of these men? For at the risk of their lives they brought it." Therefore he would not drink it. The three warriors did these things.

[20] Now Abishai,[a] the brother of Joab, was chief of the Thirty.[b] With his spear he fought against three hundred and killed them, and won a name beside the Three. [21] He was the most renowned[c] of the Thirty,[b] and became their commander; but he did not attain to the Three.

[22] Benaiah son of Jehoiada was a valiant man[d] of Kabzeel, a doer of great deeds; he struck down two sons of[e] Ariel of Moab. He also went down and killed a lion in a pit on a day when snow had fallen. [23] And he killed an Egyptian, a man of great stature, five cubits tall. The Egyptian had in his hand a spear like a weaver's beam; but Benaiah went against him with a staff, snatched the spear out of the Egyptian's hand, and killed him with his own spear. [24] Such were the things Benaiah son of Jehoiada did, and he won a name beside the three warriors. [25] He was renowned among the Thirty, but he did not attain to the Three. And David put him in charge of his bodyguard.

[26] The warriors of the armies were Asahel brother of Joab, Elhanan son of Dodo of Bethlehem, [27] Shammoth of Harod,[f] Helez the Pelonite, [28] Ira son of Ikkesh of Tekoa, Abiezer of Anathoth, [29] Sibbecai the Hushathite, Ilai the Ahohite, [30] Maharai of Netophah, Heled son of Baanah of Netophah, [31] Ithai son of Ribai of Gibeah of the Benjaminites, Benaiah of Pirathon, [32] Hurai of the wadis of Gaash, Abiel the Arbathite, [33] Azmaveth of Baharum, Eliahba of Shaalbon, [34] Hashem[g] the Gizonite, Jonathan son of Shagee the Hararite, [35] Ahiam son of Sachar the Hararite, Eliphal son of Ur, [36] Hepher the Mecherathite, Ahijah the Pelonite, [37] Hezro of Carmel, Naarai son of Ezbai, [38] Joel the brother of Nathan, Mibhar

son of Hagri, [39] Zelek the Ammonite, Naharai of Beeroth, the armor-bearer of Joab son of Zeruiah, [40] Ira the Ithrite, Gareb the Ithrite, [41] Uriah the Hittite, Zabad son of Ahlai, [42] Adina son of Shiza the Reubenite, a leader of the Reubenites, and thirty with him, [43] Hanan son of Maacah, and Joshaphat the Mithnite, [44] Uzzia the Ashterathite, Shama and Jeiel sons of Hotham the Aroerite, [45] Jediael son of Shimri, and his brother Joha the Tizite, [46] Eliel the Mahavite, and Jeribai and Joshaviah sons of Elnaam, and Ithmah the Moabite, [47] Eliel, and Obed, and Jaasiel the Mezobaite.

12 The following are those who came to David at Ziklag, while he could not move about freely because of Saul son of Kish; they were among the mighty warriors who helped him in war. [2] They were archers, and could shoot arrows and sling stones with either the right hand or the left; they were Benjaminites, Saul's kindred. [3] The chief was Ahiezer, then Joash, both sons of Shemaah of Gibeah; also Jeziel and Pelet sons of Azmaveth; Beracah, Jehu of Anathoth, [4] Ishmaiah of Gibeon, a warrior among the Thirty and a leader over the Thirty; Jeremiah,[h] Jahaziel, Johanan, Jozabad of Gederah, [5] Eluzai,[i] Jerimoth, Bealiah, Shemariah, Shephatiah the Haruphite; [6] Elkanah, Isshiah, Azarel, Joezer, and Jashobeam, the Korahites; [7] and Joelah and Zebadiah, sons of Jeroham of Gedor.

[8] From the Gadites there went over to David at the stronghold in the wilderness

---

a   Gk Vg Tg Compare 2 Sam 23.18: Heb *Abshai*
b   Syr: Heb *Three*
c   Compare 2 Sam 23.19: Heb *more renowned among the two*
d   Syr: Heb *the son of a valiant man*
e   See 2 Sam 23.20: Heb lacks *sons of*
f   Compare 2 Sam 23.25: Heb *the Harorite*
g   Compare Gk and 2 Sam 23.32: Heb *the sons of Hashem*
h   Heb verse 5
i   Heb verse 6

---

booths (Sukkot). **41a:** *Uriah*, the only reference in Chronicles to the man known in 2 Sam 11–12 as the husband of Bathsheba before David. **41b–47:** These verses are unparalleled in 2 Sam 23.8–39.

12.1–40: David's national prestige and power grow. Warriors from Benjamin (vv. 1–8), Gad (vv. 9–16), Benjamin and Judah (vv. 17–19), and Manasseh (vv. 20–23) rally to David, consolidating his rule. This is set during an early stage of David's career (v. 1), suggesting that the Benjaminites defected to David while Saul was still alive (cf. 2 Sam 2.12–32). This material has few parallels in 2 Samuel, and scholars debate whether it is based on

mighty and experienced warriors, expert with shield and spear, whose faces were like the faces of lions, and who were swift as gazelles on the mountains: [9] Ezer the chief, Obadiah second, Eliab third, [10] Mishmannah fourth, Jeremiah fifth, [11] Attai sixth, Eliel seventh, [12] Johanan eighth, Elzabad ninth, [13] Jeremiah tenth, Machbannai eleventh. [14] These Gadites were officers of the army, the least equal to a hundred and the greatest to a thousand. [15] These are the men who crossed the Jordan in the first month, when it was overflowing all its banks, and put to flight all those in the valleys, to the east and to the west.

[16] Some Benjaminites and Judahites came to the stronghold to David. [17] David went out to meet them and said to them, "If you have come to me in friendship, to help me, then my heart will be knit to you; but if you have come to betray me to my adversaries, though my hands have done no wrong, then may the God of our ancestors see and give judgment." [18] Then the spirit came upon Amasai, chief of the Thirty, and he said,

> "We are yours, O David;
>   and with you, O son of Jesse!
> Peace, peace to you,
>   and peace to the one who helps you!
>   For your God is the one who helps you."

Then David received them, and made them officers of his troops.

[19] Some of the Manassites deserted to David when he came with the Philistines for the battle against Saul. (Yet he did not help them, for the rulers of the Philistines took counsel and sent him away, saying, "He will desert to his master Saul at the cost of our heads.") [20] As he went to Ziklag these Manassites deserted to him: Adnah, Jozabad, Jediael, Michael, Jozabad, Elihu, and Zillethai, chiefs of the thousands in Manasseh. [21] They helped David against the band of raiders,[a] for they were all warriors and commanders in the army. [22] Indeed from day to day people kept coming to David to help him, until there was a great army, like an army of God.

[23] These are the numbers of the divisions of the armed troops who came to David in Hebron to turn the kingdom of Saul over to him, according to the word of the LORD. [24] The people of Judah bearing shield and spear numbered six thousand eight hundred armed troops. [25] Of the Simeonites, mighty warriors, seven thousand one hundred. [26] Of the Levites four thousand six hundred. [27] Jehoiada, leader of the house of Aaron, and with him three thousand seven hundred. [28] Zadok, a young warrior, and twenty-two commanders from his own ancestral house. [29] Of the Benjaminites, the kindred of Saul, three thousand, of whom the majority had continued to keep their allegiance to the house of Saul. [30] Of the Ephraimites, twenty thousand eight hundred, mighty warriors, notables in their ancestral houses. [31] Of the half-tribe of Manasseh, eighteen thousand, who were expressly named to come and make David king. [32] Of Issachar, those who had understanding of the times, to know what Israel ought to do, two hundred chiefs, and all their kindred

---

[a] Or *as officers of his troops*

other sources or is an imaginative composition of the Chronicler. **1:** *Ziklag,* see 1 Sam 27.6; 30. **2:** Cf. Judg 20.16. **8:** *Like . . . lions,* cf. Deut 33.20. **15:** *The first month,* in the spring. **18:** *The spirit came upon,* lit. "a spirit clothed"; cf. Judg 6.34; 2 Chr 24.20. The acclamation of Amasai, *peace, peace to you,* contrasts with the anti-David sentiment sometimes found in 2 Samuel (e.g., 2 Sam 20.1). Because of the divine support for David, those who support David may also be blessed. The language is reminiscent of the blessing bestowed on Abram (Gen 12.3) except that there is no curse. **19–20:** *The battle against Saul,* this is the battle referred to in ch 10. The Chronicler here summarizes 1 Sam 29.1–30.1. **22:** *An army* (lit. "camp") *of God,* either expressing the superlative (i.e., "a very great army"), or referring to the heavenly armies (e.g., see Deut 33.2; Josh 5.14). **23:** *In Hebron,* see 11.1. **23–39a:** The beginning of v. 23, *these are the numbers,* introduces a long stylized list (vv. 25–38) of David's armed forces. The tribal muster, totaling thirteen, is the most complete tally of the Israelite tribes in the Bible. The active allegiance shown by Israelite military officials to David accords with divine will and results in a smooth transfer of power (10.14; 11.3,10). The heroic portrayal of intertribal solidarity (v. 38) contrasts with the tribal disorganization and civil strife found in Judges. **28:** *Zadok, a young warrior,* probably to be identified as the priest who served with Abiathar at the court of David (15.11; 2 Sam 8.17) and who subsequently enjoyed Solomon's exclu-

under their command. [33] Of Zebulun, fifty thousand seasoned troops, equipped for battle with all the weapons of war, to help David[a] with singleness of purpose. [34] Of Naphtali, a thousand commanders, with whom there were thirty-seven thousand armed with shield and spear. [35] Of the Danites, twenty-eight thousand six hundred equipped for battle. [36] Of Asher, forty thousand seasoned troops ready for battle. [37] Of the Reubenites and Gadites and the half-tribe of Manasseh from beyond the Jordan, one hundred twenty thousand armed with all the weapons of war.

[38] All these, warriors arrayed in battle order, came to Hebron with full intent to make David king over all Israel; likewise all the rest of Israel were of a single mind to make David king. [39] They were there with David for three days, eating and drinking, for their kindred had provided for them. [40] And also their neighbors, from as far away as Issachar and Zebulun and Naphtali, came bringing food on donkeys, camels, mules, and oxen—abundant provisions of meal, cakes of figs, clusters of raisins, wine, oil, oxen, and sheep, for there was joy in Israel.

13 David consulted with the commanders of the thousands and of the hundreds, with every leader. [2] David said to the whole assembly of Israel, "If it seems good to you, and if it is the will of the LORD our God, let us send abroad to our kindred who remain in all the land of Israel, including the priests and Levites in the cities that have pasture lands, that they may come together to us. [3] Then let

us bring again the ark of our God to us; for we did not turn to it in the days of Saul." [4] The whole assembly agreed to do so, for the thing pleased all the people.

[5] So David assembled all Israel from the Shihor of Egypt to Lebo-hamath, to bring the ark of God from Kiriath-jearim. [6] And David and all Israel went up to Baalah, that is, to Kiriath-jearim, which belongs to Judah, to bring up from there the ark of God, the LORD, who is enthroned on the cherubim, which is called by his[b] name. [7] They carried the ark of God on a new cart, from the house of Abinadab, and Uzzah and Ahio[c] were driving the cart. [8] David and all Israel were dancing before God with all their might, with song and lyres and harps and tambourines and cymbals and trumpets.

[9] When they came to the threshing floor of Chidon, Uzzah put out his hand to hold the ark, for the oxen shook it. [10] The anger of the LORD was kindled against Uzzah; he struck him down because he put out his hand to the ark; and he died there before God. [11] David was angry because the LORD had burst out against Uzzah; so that place is called Perez-uzzah[d] to this day. [12] David was afraid of God that day; he said, "How can I bring the ark of God into my care?" [13] So David did not take the ark into his care into the city of David; he

a   Gk: Heb lacks *David*
b   Heb lacks *his*
c   Or *and his brother*
d   That is *Bursting Out Against Uzzah*

sive patronage following Solomon's purge of Abiathar (1 Kings 2.35; cf. 29.22). **39–40:** Elaborate feasts, like the one celebrated by David and representatives from the various Israelite tribes, punctuate high points in Israelite and Judean history (15.25–16.3; 29.20–22; 2 Chr 7.8–10; 20.27–28; 29.30–36; 30.21–27) and also play a crucial role in Esther, also from the Persian period. This nationwide celebration concludes the initial phase of David's reign.

13.1–14: David and the ark, Part 1. Having been firmly and unanimously established as king, David leads all Israel in the attempt to retrieve a national symbol of Israel's religion and bring it to the new capital. **2:** The Chronicler's Levites live at various sites within Israel's tribal territories (6.54–81). Because this priestly tribe is an essential component of Israel and Israel's most sacred symbol to Jerusalem must be transferred properly to Jerusalem, the Chronicler adds to his source participation of the priests and Levites, along with an emphasis on all Israel. **3:** No reference is made to the capture of the ark by the Philistines (cf. 1 Sam 4.11–7.1); here its neglect is implicitly another example of Saul's unfaithfulness (see 10.13–14). **5:** *From the Shihor of Egypt* (probably the easternmost branch of the Nile) *to Lebo-hamath* (in Syria), the northern and southern limits of Israel (cf. 2 Chr 7.8). **6–14:** This material is largely drawn from 2 Sam 6.2–11. **6:** *The ark,* a portable box, was a unifying religious symbol in the premonarchic period (Josh 3.1–17; 4.1–18; 1 Sam 4.1–7.1). According to Ex 25.10–21; 37.1–9, its construction was ordained by God and implemented by Moses. *Enthroned on the cherubim,* see 1 Sam 4.4n. **11:** *Burst out,* see note *d.* **13:** The *city of David* refers to Mount Zion, the section of Jerusalem fortified by David

took it instead to the house of Obed-edom the Gittite. [14] The ark of God remained with the household of Obed-edom in his house three months, and the LORD blessed the household of Obed-edom and all that he had.

14 King Hiram of Tyre sent messengers to David, along with cedar logs, and masons and carpenters to build a house for him. [2] David then perceived that the LORD had established him as king over Israel, and that his kingdom was highly exalted for the sake of his people Israel.

[3] David took more wives in Jerusalem, and David became the father of more sons and daughters. [4] These are the names of the children whom he had in Jerusalem: Shammua, Shobab, and Nathan; Solomon, [5] Ibhar, Elishua, and Elpelet; [6] Nogah, Nepheg, and Japhia; [7] Elishama, Beeliada, and Eliphelet.

[8] When the Philistines heard that David had been anointed king over all Israel, all the Philistines went up in search of David; and David heard of it and went out against them. [9] Now the Philistines had come and made a raid in the valley of Rephaim. [10] David inquired of God, "Shall I go up against the Philistines? Will you give them into my hand?" The LORD said to him, "Go up, and I will give them into your hand." [11] So he went up to Baal-perazim, and David defeated them there. David said, "God has burst out[a] against my enemies by my hand, like a bursting flood." Therefore that place is called Baal-perazim.[b] [12] They abandoned their gods there, and at David's command they were burned.

[13] Once again the Philistines made a raid in the valley. [14] When David again inquired of God, God said to him, "You shall not go up after them; go around and come on them opposite the balsam trees. [15] When you hear the sound of marching in the tops of the balsam trees, then go out to battle; for God has gone out before you to strike down the army of the Philistines." [16] David did as God had commanded him, and they struck down the Philistine army from Gibeon to Gezer. [17] The fame of David went out into all lands, and the LORD brought the fear of him on all nations.

15 David[c] built houses for himself in the city of David, and he prepared a place for the ark of God and pitched a tent for it. [2] Then David commanded that no one but the Levites were to carry the ark of God, for the LORD had chosen them to carry the ark

a Heb *paraz*
b That is *Lord of Bursting Out*
c Heb *He*

---

and renamed in his honor (11.7). In Chronicles *Obed-edom* is a Levite, who functions as a gatekeeper (15.18,24) and a musician (15.21; 16.5; 26.4–8). **14:** The blessing on Obed-edom's house hints that the setback suffered by David is only temporary.

14.1–7: David's success in Jerusalem (cf. 2 Sam 5.11–16). According to 1 Kings 5.15–26 (cf. 2 Chr 2.2–15), Hiram (called Huram in Chronicles) had very good relations with David. The link between blessings for David and blessings for Israel anticipates Nathan's dynastic oracle (17.1–17). **3:** Accumulating wives and progeny is consistently a positive sign of stature in Chronicles (25.5; 26.4–5; 2 Chr 11.18–23; 13.21; 14.3–7). For David's sons, see 3.1–9.

14.8–17: Philistine attacks (cf. 2 Sam 5.17–25). If the mishandling of the ark (13.9–11) represented an internal challenge to the establishment of Jerusalem's worship, the Philistine aggressions were an external threat to the viability of David's rule. The two narratives detailing David's exploits against the Philistines are replete with "holy-war" phraseology, reflecting the notion that the LORD fights on behalf of his people and secures victory for them (Ex 14.4,18; Josh 11.2,24; Judg 3.28; 4.7,17; 18.10; 20.28; 1 Sam 14.12,23; 23.4). **12:** In 2 Sam 5.21, David carries these images home. In having the images consigned to fire, the Chronicler has David act in accordance with Deuteronomic law (Deut 7.25; 12.3). **16:** *From Gibeon to Gezer*, about 28 km (18 mi), a limited area. **17:** International respect denotes divine blessing (2 Chr 9.5–8,23; 17.10; 26.8,15; 32.23).

15.1–16.3: David and the ark, Part 2. Having been successful in war and blessed by God, David turns his attention again to the matter of the ark. In the ancient Near East successful kings were expected to honor the deities who led them by supporting and endowing places of worship. Much of chs 15–16, which supplements material from 2 Sam 6 with original material concerning the Levites, elaborates on this very point. **15.1:** The houses David builds for himself most likely refer to domiciles in addition to the palace built by Huram of Tyre (14.1). David's construction activity establishes a positive pattern for other kings to follow (2 Chr 11.5–12; 14.6;

of the LORD and to minister to him forever. ³ David assembled all Israel in Jerusalem to bring up the ark of the LORD to its place, which he had prepared for it. ⁴ Then David gathered together the descendants of Aaron and the Levites: ⁵ of the sons of Kohath, Uriel the chief, with one hundred twenty of his kindred; ⁶ of the sons of Merari, Asaiah the chief, with two hundred twenty of his kindred; ⁷ of the sons of Gershom, Joel the chief, with one hundred thirty of his kindred; ⁸ of the sons of Elizaphan, Shemaiah the chief, with two hundred of his kindred; ⁹ of the sons of Hebron, Eliel the chief, with eighty of his kindred; ¹⁰ of the sons of Uzziel, Amminadab the chief, with one hundred twelve of his kindred.

¹¹ David summoned the priests Zadok and Abiathar, and the Levites Uriel, Asaiah, Joel, Shemaiah, Eliel, and Amminadab. ¹² He said to them, "You are the heads of families of the Levites; sanctify yourselves, you and your kindred, so that you may bring up the ark of the LORD, the God of Israel, to the place that I have prepared for it. ¹³ Because you did not carry it the first time,ᵃ the LORD our God burst out against us, because we did not give it proper care." ¹⁴ So the priests and the Levites sanctified themselves to bring up the ark of the LORD, the God of Israel. ¹⁵ And the Levites carried the ark of God on their shoulders with the poles, as

Moses had commanded according to the word of the LORD.

¹⁶ David also commanded the chiefs of the Levites to appoint their kindred as the singers to play on musical instruments, on harps and lyres and cymbals, to raise loud sounds of joy. ¹⁷ So the Levites appointed Heman son of Joel; and of his kindred Asaph son of Berechiah; and of the sons of Merari, their kindred, Ethan son of Kushaiah; ¹⁸ and with them their kindred of the second order, Zechariah, Jaaziel, Shemiramoth, Jehiel, Unni, Eliab, Benaiah, Maaseiah, Mattithiah, Eliphelehu, and Mikneiah, and the gatekeepers Obed-edom and Jeiel. ¹⁹ The singers Heman, Asaph, and Ethan were to sound bronze cymbals; ²⁰ Zechariah, Aziel, Shemiramoth, Jehiel, Unni, Eliab, Maaseiah, and Benaiah were to play harps according to Alamoth; ²¹ but Mattithiah, Eliphelehu, Mikneiah, Obed-edom, Jeiel, and Azaziah were to lead with lyres according to the Sheminith. ²² Chenaniah, leader of the Levites in music, was to direct the music, for he understood it. ²³ Berechiah and Elkanah were to be gatekeepers for the ark. ²⁴ Shebaniah, Joshaphat, Nethanel, Amasai, Zechariah, Benaiah, and Eliezer, the priests, were to blow the trumpets before the ark of God. Obed-edom and Jehiah also were to be gatekeepers for the ark.

ᵃ Meaning of Heb uncertain

26.2; 32.27–30). **2:** David's command that *no one but the Levites* carry the ark responds to Uzzah's unfortunate death (13.10) through the lens of the Priestly material (Num 4.4–15; 7.9), the implication being that the proper personnel had not been involved in the first attempt to bring the ark into the City of David (v. 13). The following verses detail what personnel and actions David deems necessary to install the ark successfully. **3:** The reference to a *place* for the ark of God implies a sacred precinct or sanctuary (Deut 12.5,11; 14.23–25; 15.20; Josh 9.27; 1 Chr 21.22,25; 2 Chr 3.1). **11:** The two priests *Zadok and Abiathar* appear together during the first part of the reign of David (15.29,35; 18.16; 19.11; 20.25). Each of these priests headed or represented major priestly houses. See further 6.8n. **13:** The Chronicler plays on Hebrew roots "prṣ," "to break out" (13.3,11; 14.11; 15.13) and "drš," "to seek." The earlier attempt to redress neglect of the ark—"for we did not seek (drš) it in the days of Saul" (13.3)—was brought to a swift end by the divine outbreak (burst out, Heb "prṣ"; 13.10–11) against Uzzah. As later events made clear, the problem was not Israel's communal decision "to seek" the ark, but the manner in which the people involved handled the arrangements. In the new attempt David insists on the intimate involvement of the priests and Levites to rectify the deficiency. **15:** *On their shoulders with the poles,* the Chronicler asserts that the law of Moses was followed (Num 7.9). **16:** *Musical instruments* figure prominently in the Chronicler's ritual liturgies (16.42; 2 Chr 5.13; 7.6; 23.13; 34.12). In some texts the instruments are associated with David himself (2 Chr 29.24,26–27; Neh 12.36; cf. Am 6.5). Though David could not build the Temple (ch 17, 2 Sam 7), the Chronicler emphasizes here and elsewhere that David initiated the project, in their case by establishing the guilds of levitical Temple singers. **18:** Many of these singers are mentioned again in vv. 20–21 and 16.5–6. **20–21:** *Alamoth* and *Sheminith* are obscure musical terms found in Psalms (6.1; 12.1; 46.1). **25–28:** The Chronicler re-

²⁵ So David and the elders of Israel, and the commanders of the thousands, went to bring up the ark of the covenant of the LORD from the house of Obed-edom with rejoicing. ²⁶ And because God helped the Levites who were carrying the ark of the covenant of the LORD, they sacrificed seven bulls and seven rams. ²⁷ David was clothed with a robe of fine linen, as also were all the Levites who were carrying the ark, and the singers, and Chenaniah the leader of the music of the singers; and David wore a linen ephod. ²⁸ So all Israel brought up the ark of the covenant of the LORD with shouting, to the sound of the horn, trumpets, and cymbals, and made loud music on harps and lyres.

²⁹ As the ark of the covenant of the LORD came to the city of David, Michal daughter of Saul looked out of the window, and saw King David leaping and dancing; and she despised him in her heart.

16 They brought in the ark of God, and set it inside the tent that David had pitched for it; and they offered burnt offerings and offerings of well-being before God. ² When David had finished offering the burnt offerings and the offerings of well-being, he blessed the people in the name of the LORD; ³ and he distributed to every person in Israel—man and woman alike—to each a loaf of bread, a portion of meat,ᵃ and a cake of raisins.

⁴ He appointed certain of the Levites as ministers before the ark of the LORD, to invoke, to thank, and to praise the LORD, the God of Israel. ⁵ Asaph was the chief, and second to him Zechariah, Jeiel, Shemiramoth, Jehiel, Mattithiah, Eliab, Benaiah, Obededom, and Jeiel, with harps and lyres; Asaph was to sound the cymbals, ⁶ and the priests Benaiah and Jahaziel were to blow trumpets

regularly, before the ark of the covenant of God.

⁷ Then on that day David first appointed the singing of praises to the LORD by Asaph and his kindred.

⁸ O give thanks to the LORD, call on his
   name,
   make known his deeds among the
      peoples.
⁹ Sing to him, sing praises to him,
   tell of all his wonderful works.
¹⁰ Glory in his holy name;
   let the hearts of those who seek the
      LORD rejoice.
¹¹ Seek the LORD and his strength,
   seek his presence continually.
¹² Remember the wonderful works he has
      done,
   his miracles, and the judgments he
      uttered,
¹³ O offspring of his servant Israel,ᵇ
   children of Jacob, his chosen ones.

¹⁴ He is the LORD our God;
   his judgments are in all the earth.
¹⁵ Remember his covenant forever,
   the word that he commanded, for a
      thousand generations,
¹⁶ the covenant that he made with
      Abraham,
   his sworn promise to Isaac,
¹⁷ which he confirmed to Jacob as a statute,
   to Israel as an everlasting covenant,
¹⁸ saying, "To you I will give the land of
      Canaan
   as your portion for an inheritance."

ᵃ Compare Gk Syr Vg: Meaning of Heb uncertain
ᵇ Another reading is *Abraham* (compare Ps 105.6)

writes 2 Sam 6.12–15 to underscore the broad support for David's campaign to complete the transfer of the ark. The elaborate apparel worn by the Levites in Chronicles contrasts markedly with that depicted in Samuel (see Ex 28.6–14,39–43; Sir 45.8).

15.29–16.3: Michal and all Israel. A significant abridgment of 2 Sam 6.16–23, omitting the details of how Michal mocked David.

16.4–43: Staffing the national sanctuaries. With the ark successfully elevated to the place David prepared for it, David designates certain Levites and priests to officiate there. He also staffs the tabernacle at the *high place* in Gibeon (vv. 39–42). **7–36:** The *praises* David instructs the Levites to sing are a medley of extracts, with some variations, from the Psalms: vv. 8–22, cf. Ps 105.1–15; vv. 23–33, cf. Ps 96; vv. 34–36, cf. Ps 106.1,47–48. By the period of the Chronicler, some form of the book of Psalms probably already existed as a liturgical collec-

[19] When they were few in number,
of little account, and strangers in the
land,[a]
[20] wandering from nation to nation,
from one kingdom to another people,
[21] he allowed no one to oppress them;
he rebuked kings on their account,
[22] saying, "Do not touch my anointed ones;
do my prophets no harm."

[23] Sing to the LORD, all the earth.
Tell of his salvation from day to day.
[24] Declare his glory among the nations,
his marvelous works among all the
peoples.
[25] For great is the LORD, and greatly to be
praised;
he is to be revered above all gods.
[26] For all the gods of the peoples are idols,
but the LORD made the heavens.
[27] Honor and majesty are before him;
strength and joy are in his place.

[28] Ascribe to the LORD, O families of the
peoples,
ascribe to the LORD glory and strength.
[29] Ascribe to the LORD the glory due his
name;
bring an offering, and come before him.
Worship the LORD in holy splendor;
[30] tremble before him, all the earth.
The world is firmly established; it shall
never be moved.
[31] Let the heavens be glad, and let the earth
rejoice,
and let them say among the nations,
"The LORD is king!"
[32] Let the sea roar, and all that fills it;
let the field exult, and everything in it.
[33] Then shall the trees of the forest sing for joy
before the LORD, for he comes to judge
the earth.

[34] O give thanks to the LORD, for he is good;
for his steadfast love endures forever.
[35] Say also:
"Save us, O God of our salvation,
and gather and rescue us from among
the nations,
that we may give thanks to your holy name,
and glory in your praise.
[36] Blessed be the LORD, the God of Israel,
from everlasting to everlasting."
Then all the people said "Amen!" and praised
the LORD.

[37] David left Asaph and his kinsfolk there
before the ark of the covenant of the LORD
to minister regularly before the ark as each
day required, [38] and also Obed-edom and his[b]
sixty-eight kinsfolk; while Obed-edom son
of Jeduthun and Hosah were to be gatekeepers. [39] And he left the priest Zadok and his
kindred the priests before the tabernacle of
the LORD in the high place that was at Gibeon,
[40] to offer burnt offerings to the LORD on the
altar of burnt offering regularly, morning and
evening, according to all that is written in the
law of the LORD that he commanded Israel.
[41] With them were Heman and Jeduthun, and
the rest of those chosen and expressly named
to render thanks to the LORD, for his steadfast
love endures forever. [42] Heman and Jeduthun
had with them trumpets and cymbals for the
music, and instruments for sacred song. The
sons of Jeduthun were appointed to the gate.
[43] Then all the people departed to their
homes, and David went home to bless his
household.

17 Now when David settled in his house,
David said to the prophet Nathan, "I
am living in a house of cedar, but the ark of

---

a Heb *in it*
b Gk Syr Vg: Heb *their*

---

tion, and possibly was already attributed to David. **37–43:** David provides for both the ark in Jerusalem and the
tabernacle at Gibeon. The Chronicler does not deem the Gibeon shrine to be inherently illicit. The sacrifices
performed there by Zadok and his priests accorded with *all that is written in the law of the LORD* (v. 40). Like the
newly dedicated ministry of praise associated with the ark in Jerusalem, the Gibeon precinct has its own singers and musicians, authorized to praise God (v. 42). Two guilds of singers, represented by Heman and Jeduthun,
serve at Gibeon, while the third guild of singers, represented by Asaph (v. 37) serves in Jerusalem. Only after the
construction of the long-awaited Temple will worship outside Jerusalem be prohibited (2 Chr 1.3–6; 5.5). **43:**
Taken from 2 Sam 6.19–20, a continuation of v. 3.

17.1–15: The promises to David. The narration largely follows 2 Sam 7.1–16. *Under a tent,* see Ex 26.1–2,7; Num

the covenant of the Lord is under a tent." [2] Nathan said to David, "Do all that you have in mind, for God is with you."

[3] But that same night the word of the Lord came to Nathan, saying: [4] Go and tell my servant David: Thus says the Lord: You shall not build me a house to live in. [5] For I have not lived in a house since the day I brought out Israel to this very day, but I have lived in a tent and a tabernacle.[a] [6] Wherever I have moved about among all Israel, did I ever speak a word with any of the judges of Israel, whom I commanded to shepherd my people, saying, Why have you not built me a house of cedar? [7] Now therefore thus you shall say to my servant David: Thus says the Lord of hosts: I took you from the pasture, from following the sheep, to be ruler over my people Israel; [8] and I have been with you wherever you went, and have cut off all your enemies before you; and I will make for you a name, like the name of the great ones of the earth. [9] I will appoint a place for my people Israel, and will plant them, so that they may live in their own place, and be disturbed no more; and evildoers shall wear them down no more, as they did formerly, [10] from the time that I appointed judges over my people Israel; and I will subdue all your enemies.

Moreover I declare to you that the Lord will build you a house. [11] When your days are fulfilled to go to be with your ancestors, I will raise up your offspring after you, one of your own sons, and I will establish his kingdom. [12] He shall build a house for me, and I will es-

tablish his throne forever. [13] I will be a father to him, and he shall be a son to me. I will not take my steadfast love from him, as I took it from him who was before you, [14] but I will confirm him in my house and in my kingdom forever, and his throne shall be established forever. [15] In accordance with all these words and all this vision, Nathan spoke to David.

[16] Then King David went in and sat before the Lord, and said, "Who am I, O Lord God, and what is my house, that you have brought me thus far? [17] And even this was a small thing in your sight, O God; you have also spoken of your servant's house for a great while to come. You regard me as someone of high rank,[b] O Lord God! [18] And what more can David say to you for honoring your servant? You know your servant. [19] For your servant's sake, O Lord, and according to your own heart, you have done all these great deeds, making known all these great things. [20] There is no one like you, O Lord, and there is no God besides you, according to all that we have heard with our ears. [21] Who is like your people Israel, one nation on the earth whom God went to redeem to be his people, making for yourself a name for great and terrible things, in driving out nations before your people whom you redeemed from Egypt? [22] And you made your people Israel to be your people forever; and you, O Lord, became their God.

[a] Gk 2 Sam 7.6: Heb *but I have been from tent to tent and from tabernacle*
[b] Meaning of Heb uncertain

4.21–28. 2: Nathan here is offering his personal opinion, which is corrected by God in the revelation that follows. David's lack of suitability for this project is explained later in 22.7–10. 5: After the Exodus, Israel's system of worship was mobile. The roving nature of God's presence with Israel was consistent with the mobility of Israel itself. 8–9: The Chronicler, like the Deuteronomist (1 Kings 5.17–18), associates national stability and peace with the establishment of a permanent sanctuary in the land. In this manner, Nathan's oracle points forward to the reign of Solomon, which according to biblical text is an unprecedented age of peace, prosperity, and international prestige (1 Kings 4.20; 5.4; 8.66; 1 Chr 22.9,18; 2 Chr 1.7–18; 8.1–9,31). 10: In speaking of the Lord building a house for David, the text develops a wordplay on the different connotations of Heb "bayit" ("house," "temple," "dynasty"). 13: *I will be a father to him,* a formula of adoption (2 Sam 7.14; Ps 2.7–8; Isa 9.6; cf. Ps 89.26). *I will not take my steadfast love from him,* the guarantee of succession is not predicated upon the loyalty of the sons. In fact, the second part of 2 Sam 7.14, which stresses that the individual Davidic king may be punished, is lacking here, further highlighting the Chronicler's positive vision of Davidic kingship. 14: *In my kingdom forever,* God manifests his kingship through the kingdom of David and his heirs (17.14; 28.5; 29.11; 2 Chr 13.8; cf. 2 Sam 7.16).

17.16–27: David's prayer. The narration largely follows 2 Sam 7.17–29. 21: God's incomparability and unique status are linked to Israel's unique status. 23–24: David's only petitions focus on the promises directed toward his dynasty (cf. vv. 8b–14).

23 "And now, O LORD, as for the word that you have spoken concerning your servant and concerning his house, let it be established forever, and do as you have promised. 24 Thus your name will be established and magnified forever in the saying, 'The LORD of hosts, the God of Israel, is Israel's God'; and the house of your servant David will be established in your presence. 25 For you, my God, have revealed to your servant that you will build a house for him; therefore your servant has found it possible to pray before you. 26 And now, O LORD, you are God, and you have promised this good thing to your servant; 27 therefore may it please you to bless the house of your servant, that it may continue forever before you. For you, O LORD, have blessed and are blessed[a] forever."

18 Some time afterward, David attacked the Philistines and subdued them; he took Gath and its villages from the Philistines.

2 He defeated Moab, and the Moabites became subject to David and brought tribute.

3 David also struck down King Hadadezer of Zobah, toward Hamath,[b] as he went to set up a monument at the river Euphrates. 4 David took from him one thousand chariots, seven thousand cavalry, and twenty thousand foot soldiers. David hamstrung all the chariot horses, but left one hundred of them. 5 When the Arameans of Damascus came to help King Hadadezer of Zobah, David killed twenty-two thousand Arameans. 6 Then David put garrisons[c] in Aram of Damascus; and the Arameans became

subject to David, and brought tribute. The LORD gave victory to David wherever he went. 7 David took the gold shields that were carried by the servants of Hadadezer, and brought them to Jerusalem. 8 From Tibhath and from Cun, cities of Hadadezer, David took a vast quantity of bronze; with it Solomon made the bronze sea and the pillars and the vessels of bronze.

9 When King Tou of Hamath heard that David had defeated the whole army of King Hadadezer of Zobah, 10 he sent his son Hadoram to King David, to greet him and to congratulate him, because he had fought against Hadadezer and defeated him. Now Hadadezer had often been at war with Tou. He sent all sorts of articles of gold, of silver, and of bronze; 11 these also King David dedicated to the LORD, together with the silver and gold that he had carried off from all the nations, from Edom, Moab, the Ammonites, the Philistines, and Amalek.

12 Abishai son of Zeruiah killed eighteen thousand Edomites in the Valley of Salt. 13 He put garrisons in Edom; and all the Edomites became subject to David. And the LORD gave victory to David wherever he went.

14 So David reigned over all Israel; and he administered justice and equity to all his people. 15 Joab son of Zeruiah was over the army; Jehoshaphat son of Ahilud was recorder;

a Or *and it is blessed*
b Meaning of Heb uncertain
c Gk Vg 2 Sam 8.6 Compare Syr: Heb lacks *garrisons*

18.1–20.8: The kingdom expanded. A new phase in David's reign begins, one dominated by foreign military campaigns. David's success in war is evident in all directions: to the west against the Philistines (18.1; 20.4–8), to the southeast against Edom (18.12–13), to the east against Moab (18.2) and Ammon (19.1–19; 20.1–3), and to the northeast against a variety of Aramean states (18.3–8; 19.6–19). (See map on p. 585.) In this way, David uses the fulfillment of one of Nathan's promises—the subjugation of all his enemies—to lay the foundations for the fulfillment of another—the construction of a temple by David's son. The juxtaposition suggests that David's hands were bloodied by war, so he could not build the Temple (22.7–10). **18.1–13:** Drawn from 2 Sam 8.1–14. **5:** *The Arameans of Damascus,* the defeat of one state by an invading power could upset the balance of power in the entire region, especially affecting neighboring states of the defeated kingdom. **7–11:** It was customary for pious kings in the ancient world to dedicate war spoils to the temples of the deities who granted them victory. In this instance, David's plunder, which according to 2 Sam 8.7 was merely brought to Jerusalem, is incorporated into the Temple built by Solomon (1 Kings 7.13–47; 2 Chr 3.15–4.22; Josephus, *Ant.* 7.106). **8:** *Tibhath* and *Cun* occur only here in the Bible; their exact locations are uncertain. **9:** *Tou,* Toi in 2 Sam 8.9. **12:** In 2 Sam 8.13 this victory is attributed to David himself. **14–17:** Taken from 2 Sam 8.15–18, the list of officials reflects the growth of the bureaucracy as the kingdom expanded. **16:** *Ahimelech* probably became one of David's priests as the replace-

¹⁶ Zadok son of Ahitub and Ahimelech son of Abiathar were priests; Shavsha was secretary; ¹⁷ Benaiah son of Jehoiada was over the Cherethites and the Pelethites; and David's sons were the chief officials in the service of the king.

19 Some time afterward, King Nahash of the Ammonites died, and his son succeeded him. ² David said, "I will deal loyally with Hanun son of Nahash, for his father dealt loyally with me." So David sent messengers to console him concerning his father. When David's servants came to Hanun in the land of the Ammonites, to console him, ³ the officials of the Ammonites said to Hanun, "Do you think, because David has sent consolers to you, that he is honoring your father? Have not his servants come to you to search and to overthrow and to spy out the land?" ⁴ So Hanun seized David's servants, shaved them, cut off their garments in the middle at their hips, and sent them away; ⁵ and they departed. When David was told about the men, he sent messengers to them, for they felt greatly humiliated. The king said, "Remain at Jericho until your beards have grown, and then return."

⁶ When the Ammonites saw that they had made themselves odious to David, Hanun and the Ammonites sent a thousand talents of silver to hire chariots and cavalry from Mesopotamia, from Aram-maacah and from Zobah. ⁷ They hired thirty-two thousand chariots and the king of Maacah with his army, who came and camped before Medeba. And the Ammonites were mustered from their cities and came to battle. ⁸ When David heard of it, he sent Joab and all the army of the warriors. ⁹ The Ammonites came out and drew up in battle array at the entrance of the city, and the kings who had come were by themselves in the open country.

¹⁰ When Joab saw that the line of battle was set against him both in front and in the rear, he chose some of the picked men of Israel and arrayed them against the Arameans; ¹¹ the rest of his troops he put in the charge of his brother Abishai, and they were arrayed against the Ammonites. ¹² He said, "If the Arameans are too strong for me, then you shall help me; but if the Ammonites are too strong for you, then I will help you. ¹³ Be strong, and let us be courageous for our people and for the cities of our God; and may the LORD do what seems good to him." ¹⁴ So Joab and the troops who were with him advanced toward the Arameans for battle; and they fled before him. ¹⁵ When the Ammonites saw that the Arameans fled, they likewise fled before Abishai, Joab's brother, and entered the city. Then Joab came to Jerusalem.

¹⁶ But when the Arameans saw that they had been defeated by Israel, they sent messengers and brought out the Arameans who were beyond the Euphrates, with Shophach the commander of the army of Hadadezer at their head. ¹⁷ When David was informed, he gathered all Israel together, crossed the Jordan, came to them, and drew up his forces against them. When David set the battle in array against the Arameans, they fought with him. ¹⁸ The Arameans fled before Israel; and David killed seven thousand Aramean charioteers and forty thousand foot soldiers, and also killed Shophach the commander of their army. ¹⁹ When the servants of Hadadezer saw that they had been defeated by Israel, they made peace with David, and became subject

ment for his father Abiathar (15.11). **17:** David employs his sons as high-ranking officials in his cabinet instead of as priests (2 Sam 8.18); two other kings make use of princes in managing state affairs (2 Chr 11.22–23; 21.3). **19.1:** The death of a king could usher in a period of instability and uncertainty for his people. Because international arrangements were made between the leaders of nations, and not between the nations themselves, the death of a leader could signal the end of such agreements. **3:** *To spy out the land,* to Hanun's counselors, David's string of victories against the Philistines, Moabites, Edomites, and Arameans establish an imperialistic pattern that they could ignore only at their own peril. **5:** The quarantine furnishes David's aides with the requisite time to recover and regain their dignity. **7:** *Medeba,* ca. 20 mi (30 km) south-southwest of the Ammonite capital of Rabbah; not mentioned in 2 Sam 10, the source for this chapter. **16:** *The Euphrates,* lit. "the river." In biblical narratives, "the river" usually designates the Euphrates (e.g., Gen 2.14; 15.18; Deut 1.7; 2 Kings 23.29; 24.7; 1 Chr 5.9), but the Jordan and the Yarmuk are also possibilities. **19:** The new balance of power in the region, tilted in Israel's favor, leaves the Ammonites isolated from their former allies. The victories of Joab and David succeed

to him. So the Arameans were not willing to help the Ammonites any more.

20 In the spring of the year, the time when kings go out to battle, Joab led out the army, ravaged the country of the Ammonites, and came and besieged Rabbah. But David remained at Jerusalem. Joab attacked Rabbah, and overthrew it. [2] David took the crown of Milcom[a] from his head; he found that it weighed a talent of gold, and in it was a precious stone; and it was placed on David's head. He also brought out the booty of the city, a very great amount. [3] He brought out the people who were in it, and set them to work[b] with saws and iron picks and axes.[c] Thus David did to all the cities of the Ammonites. Then David and all the people returned to Jerusalem.

[4] After this, war broke out with the Philistines at Gezer; then Sibbecai the Hushathite killed Sippai, who was one of the descendants of the giants; and the Philistines were subdued. [5] Again there was war with the Philistines; and Elhanan son of Jair killed Lahmi the brother of Goliath the Gittite, the shaft of whose spear was like a weaver's beam. [6] Again there was war at Gath, where there was a man of great size, who had six fingers on each hand, and six toes on each foot, twenty-four in number; he also was descended from the giants. [7] When he taunted Israel, Jonathan son of Shimea, David's brother, killed him. [8] These were descended from the giants in Gath; they fell by the hand of David and his servants.

21 Satan stood up against Israel, and incited David to count the people of Israel. [2] So David said to Joab and the commanders of the army, "Go, number Israel, from Beer-sheba to Dan, and bring me a report, so that I may know their number." [3] But Joab said, "May the LORD increase the number of his people a hundredfold! Are they not, my lord the king, all of them my lord's servants? Why then should my lord require this? Why should he bring guilt on Israel?" [4] But the king's word prevailed against Joab. So Joab departed and went throughout all Israel, and came back to Jerusalem. [5] Joab gave the total count of the people to David. In all Israel there were one million one hundred thousand men who drew the sword, and in Judah four hundred seventy thousand who drew the sword. [6] But he did not include Levi and Benjamin in the numbering, for the king's command was abhorrent to Joab.

a Gk Vg See 1 Kings 11.5, 33: MT *of their king*
b Compare 2 Sam 12.31: Heb *and he sawed*
c Compare 2 Sam 12.31: Heb *saws*

in disrupting the traditional military ties between the Ammonites and the Arameans. **20.1–3:** Verse 1 is taken from 2 Sam 11.1, while vv. 2–3 are taken from 2 Sam 12.26a,30–31. In Samuel the reference to David's staying in Jerusalem provides the background to the troubling story of David's affair with Bathsheba. But in Chronicles, the same notice is incidental, providing the reader an explanation as to David's whereabouts. The Chronicler omits completely the story of David's liaison with Bathsheba and its aftermath (2 Sam 11.2–12.25), which casts David in a negative light. *Milcom* was the national deity of the Ammonites (1 Kings 11.5,7,33; 2 Kings 23.13). **4–8:** The final exploits of David and his soldiers are taken from 2 Sam 21.18–22. The stories in 2 Samuel about the rape of Tamar, Absalom's rebellion, the execution of Saul's descendants, and the disaffection of the northern tribes, which cast David in a negative light, do not appear in Chronicles. **5:** The text may harmonize two different claims found in Samuel: In 1 Sam 17.50 David kills the Philistine giant, identified earlier as Goliath of Gath (1 Sam 17.4), but in 2 Sam 21.19 Elhanan kills Goliath the Gittite. By having Elhanan kill the brother of Goliath the Gittite, and not Goliath himself, the Chronicler accommodates both claims.

21.1–22.1: David the repentant sinner. The Chronicler recasts and supplements a story also found in 2 Sam 24. The guilt of David is pronounced in Chronicles (vv. 1–7), in which Joab warns David that it is sinful to count Israel in a casual fashion (cf. Ex 31.11–16); but so are his repentance and his efforts to intercede on behalf of Israel (vv. 8–17). David is thus forewarned before he is punished, reflecting a major tendency of the Chronicler. **21.1:** *Satan,* Heb "satan" should be translated as "an adversary" rather than "Satan" (cf. 2 Sam 24.1; see Job 1.6n.; Zech 3.1n.). Significantly, it replaces "the anger of the LORD" of 2 Sam 24.1. Having just experienced a string of impressive military victories against the Ammonites, Syrians, and Philistines (chs 18–20), David uncritically falls prey to the designs of one of his opponents. **2:** *From Beer-sheba to Dan,* the southern and northern limits of Israel proper. **5:** The total is lower in 2 Sam 24.9, but the number for Judah is higher there. In both cases the figures are improb-

⁷ But God was displeased with this thing, and he struck Israel. ⁸ David said to God, "I have sinned greatly in that I have done this thing. But now, I pray you, take away the guilt of your servant; for I have done very foolishly." ⁹ The LORD spoke to Gad, David's seer, saying, ¹⁰ "Go and say to David, 'Thus says the LORD: Three things I offer you; choose one of them, so that I may do it to you.'" ¹¹ So Gad came to David and said to him, "Thus says the LORD, 'Take your choice: ¹² either three years of famine; or three months of devastation by your foes, while the sword of your enemies overtakes you; or three days of the sword of the LORD, pestilence on the land, and the angel of the LORD destroying throughout all the territory of Israel.' Now decide what answer I shall return to the one who sent me." ¹³ Then David said to Gad, "I am in great distress; let me fall into the hand of the LORD, for his mercy is very great; but let me not fall into human hands."

¹⁴ So the LORD sent a pestilence on Israel; and seventy thousand persons fell in Israel. ¹⁵ And God sent an angel to Jerusalem to destroy it; but when he was about to destroy it, the LORD took note and relented concerning the calamity; he said to the destroying angel, "Enough! Stay your hand." The angel of the LORD was then standing by the threshing floor of Ornan the Jebusite. ¹⁶ David looked up and saw the angel of the LORD standing between earth and heaven, and in his hand a drawn sword stretched out over Jerusalem. Then David and the elders, clothed in sackcloth, fell on their faces. ¹⁷ And David said to God, "Was it not I who gave the command to count the people? It is I who have sinned and done very wickedly. But these sheep, what have they done? Let your hand, I pray, O LORD my God, be against me and against my father's house; but do not let your people be plagued!"

¹⁸ Then the angel of the LORD commanded Gad to tell David that he should go up and erect an altar to the LORD on the threshing floor of Ornan the Jebusite. ¹⁹ So David went up following Gad's instructions, which he had spoken in the name of the LORD. ²⁰ Ornan turned and saw the angel; and while his four sons who were with him hid themselves, Ornan continued to thresh wheat. ²¹ As David came to Ornan, Ornan looked and saw David; he went out from the threshing floor, and did obeisance to David with his face to the ground. ²² David said to Ornan, "Give me the site of the threshing floor that I may build on it an altar to the LORD—give it to me at its full price—so that the plague may be averted from the people." ²³ Then Ornan said to David, "Take it; and let my lord the king do what seems good to him; see, I present the oxen for burnt offerings, and the threshing sledges for the wood, and the wheat for a grain offering. I give it all." ²⁴ But King David said to Ornan, "No; I will buy them for the full price. I will not take for the LORD what is yours, nor offer burnt offerings that cost me nothing." ²⁵ So David paid Ornan six hundred shekels of gold by weight for the site. ²⁶ David built there an altar to the LORD and presented burnt offerings and offerings of well-being. He called upon the LORD, and he answered him with fire from heaven on the altar of burnt offering. ²⁷ Then the LORD commanded the angel, and he put his sword back into its sheath.

²⁸ At that time, when David saw that the LORD had answered him at the threshing floor of Ornan the Jebusite, he made his sacrifices there. ²⁹ For the tabernacle of the LORD, which Moses had made in the wilderness, and the altar of burnt offering were at that time in the high place at Gibeon; ³⁰ but David could not go before it to inquire of God, for he was afraid of the sword of the angel of the LORD.

22 ¹ Then David said, "Here shall be the house of the LORD God and here the altar of burnt offering for Israel."

able. 8: *Take away*, better "transfer," as in 2 Sam 12.13. In both cases, the sin of David is transferred elsewhere. 15: *Ornan*, called Araunah in 2 Sam 24. 17: Along with the authors of Deut 7.9–10; 24.16; Jer 31.28–30; Ezek 18; 33.12–20, David argues for limiting the scope of divinely administered punishment of humans to the guilty parties themselves. 26: The addition of a divine confirmation of David's sacrifices by fire, following the pattern of Lev 9.24 and 1 Kings 18.36–39, establishes David's altar as an enduring fixture in Israelite worship. 22.1: David ratifies the divine action (21.26–27) by declaring the site to be the home of the future Temple. Here and elsewhere (2 Chr 3.1), the Chronicler shows unusual interest in offering explanations why the Temple was built on its current site.

² David gave orders to gather together the aliens who were residing in the land of Israel, and he set stonecutters to prepare dressed stones for building the house of God. ³ David also provided great stores of iron for nails for the doors of the gates and for clamps, as well as bronze in quantities beyond weighing, ⁴ and cedar logs without number—for the Sidonians and Tyrians brought great quantities of cedar to David. ⁵ For David said, "My son Solomon is young and inexperienced, and the house that is to be built for the LORD must be exceedingly magnificent, famous and glorified throughout all lands; I will therefore make preparation for it." So David provided materials in great quantity before his death.

⁶ Then he called for his son Solomon and charged him to build a house for the LORD, the God of Israel. ⁷ David said to Solomon, "My son, I had planned to build a house to the name of the LORD my God. ⁸ But the word of the LORD came to me, saying, 'You have shed much blood and have waged great wars; you shall not build a house to my name, because you have shed so much blood in my sight on the earth. ⁹ See, a son shall be born to you; he shall be a man of peace. I will give him peace from all his enemies on every side; for his name shall be Solomon,ᵃ and I will give peaceᵇ and quiet to Israel in his days. ¹⁰ He shall build a house for my name. He shall be a son to me, and I will be a father to him, and I will establish his royal throne in Israel forever.' ¹¹ Now, my son, the LORD be with you, so that you may succeed in building the house of the LORD your God, as he has spoken

concerning you. ¹² Only, may the LORD grant you discretion and understanding, so that when he gives you charge over Israel you may keep the law of the LORD your God. ¹³ Then you will prosper if you are careful to observe the statutes and the ordinances that the LORD commanded Moses for Israel. Be strong and of good courage. Do not be afraid or dismayed. ¹⁴ With great pains I have provided for the house of the LORD one hundred thousand talents of gold, one million talents of silver, and bronze and iron beyond weighing, for there is so much of it; timber and stone too I have provided. To these you must add more. ¹⁵ You have an abundance of workers: stonecutters, masons, carpenters, and all kinds of artisans without number, skilled in working ¹⁶ gold, silver, bronze, and iron. Now begin the work, and the LORD be with you."

¹⁷ David also commanded all the leaders of Israel to help his son Solomon, saying, ¹⁸ "Is not the LORD your God with you? Has he not given you peace on every side? For he has delivered the inhabitants of the land into my hand; and the land is subdued before the LORD and his people. ¹⁹ Now set your mind and heart to seek the LORD your God. Go and build the sanctuary of the LORD God so that the ark of the covenant of the LORD and the holy vessels of God may be brought into a house built for the name of the LORD."

23 When David was old and full of days, he made his son Solomon king over Israel.

ᵃ Heb *Shelomoh*
ᵇ Heb *shalom*

22.2–19: David prepares for the construction of the Temple. David wants the future Temple to be *famous and glorified throughout all the lands;* palace-temple complexes communicated the power of a god and his king to the god(s), populace, vassals, and foreign emissaries. But Solomon is *young and inexperienced,* so David undertakes the preparations himself. Of David's many sons (see 3.1–4; 14.3–7), Solomon was one of the youngest (1 Sam 20.31; 2 Sam 13.21b [LXX; 4QSama]; 1 Kings 1.12,17; 2.22). **7–16:** This learned passage, which quotes from the dynastic promise (ch 17; cf. 2 Sam 7) and other texts, explains David's inability to build the Temple, suggesting that only Solomon (Heb "shelomoh"), understood as a man of peace ("shalom"), may build it, an issue not addressed by the books of Samuel and Kings. David, however, both here and in the following chapters, does much preparation for the project. **8:** *Much blood,* referring either to the plague (1 Chr 21.11–14) or to David's various wars. **14:** *One hundred thousand talents of gold* and *one million talents of silver,* the point is not realism but extravagance; a talent weighed ca. 75 lb (34 kg). David's gifts are deliberately excessive. **17–19:** Following the norms of Deut 12.8–14, only when peace is established may the Temple be built. **18:** *Inhabitants of the land,* the Canaanites are in view (Num 32.22,29; Josh 2.24; 18.1; 23.3–5,9–13; 24.11,18).

23.1–32: Establishing a national administration. David attains a venerable stage in his life (v. 1), *full of days,*

² David assembled all the leaders of Israel and the priests and the Levites. ³ The Levites, thirty years old and upward, were counted, and the total was thirty-eight thousand. ⁴ "Twenty-four thousand of these," David said, "shall have charge of the work in the house of the LORD, six thousand shall be officers and judges, ⁵ four thousand gatekeepers, and four thousand shall offer praises to the LORD with the instruments that I have made for praise." ⁶ And David organized them in divisions corresponding to the sons of Levi: Gershon,ᵃ Kohath, and Merari.

⁷ The sons of Gershonᵇ were Ladan and Shimei. ⁸ The sons of Ladan: Jehiel the chief, Zetham, and Joel, three. ⁹ The sons of Shimei: Shelomoth, Haziel, and Haran, three. These were the heads of families of Ladan. ¹⁰ And the sons of Shimei: Jahath, Zina, Jeush, and Beriah. These four were the sons of Shimei. ¹¹ Jahath was the chief, and Zizah the second; but Jeush and Beriah did not have many sons, so they were enrolled as a single family.

¹² The sons of Kohath: Amram, Izhar, Hebron, and Uzziel, four. ¹³ The sons of Amram: Aaron and Moses. Aaron was set apart to consecrate the most holy things, so that he and his sons forever should make offerings before the LORD, and minister to him and pronounce blessings in his name forever; ¹⁴ but as for Moses the man of God, his sons were to be reckoned among the tribe of Levi. ¹⁵ The sons of Moses: Gershom and Eliezer. ¹⁶ The

sons of Gershom: Shebuel the chief. ¹⁷ The sons of Eliezer: Rehabiah the chief; Eliezer had no other sons, but the sons of Rehabiah were very numerous. ¹⁸ The sons of Izhar: Shelomith the chief. ¹⁹ The sons of Hebron: Jeriah the chief, Amariah the second, Jahaziel the third, and Jekameam the fourth. ²⁰ The sons of Uzziel: Micah the chief and Isshiah the second.

²¹ The sons of Merari: Mahli and Mushi. The sons of Mahli: Eleazar and Kish. ²² Eleazar died having no sons, but only daughters; their kindred, the sons of Kish, married them. ²³ The sons of Mushi: Mahli, Eder, and Jeremoth, three.

²⁴ These were the sons of Levi by their ancestral houses, the heads of families as they were enrolled according to the number of the names of the individuals from twenty years old and upward who were to do the work for the service of the house of the LORD. ²⁵ For David said, "The LORD, the God of Israel, has given rest to his people; and he resides in Jerusalem forever. ²⁶ And so the Levites no longer need to carry the tabernacle or any of the things for its service"— ²⁷ for according to the last words of David these were the number of the Levites from twenty years old and upward— ²⁸ "but their duty shall be to assist the descendants of Aaron for the service

ᵃ Or Gershom; See 1 Chr 6.1, note, and 23.15
ᵇ Vg Compare Gk Syr: Heb to the Gershonite

much like Abraham (Gen 25.8), Isaac (Gen 35.29), and Job (42.17) before him. He begins preparing for his death and the reign of his son by convening his administrative leadership. This transition is smooth, in contrast to 2 Sam 15–1 Kings 2, much of which the Chronicler omits. The Chronicler will eventually return to the issue of Solomon's accession, but his first priority is to detail David's appointment of and instructions to *the leaders of Israel, the priests, and the Levites* (v. 2), who will help Solomon to succeed in his various tasks, especially completing the Temple. The summit of select leaders forms the background of David's major administrative initiatives, outlined in the narratives and the lists of 23.3–27.34. **5:** The divisions and responsibilities of the gatekeepers are outlined in ch 26. **6:** The tripartite segmentation of the Levites in vv. 6–23 resembles that of earlier Priestly sources (Ex 6.16–19; Num 3.17–39; cf. 1 Chr 6.1,16–47). **7–23:** The advent of the Temple, and the centralized worship that it represents, leads to the establishment of a system of divisions or courses among the Levites and priests. Each division was to work its appointed turn in rotation until a round was completed and a new round was begun. Although attributed to David's initiative, this development, unattested in preexilic texts, is known only in the Second Temple period. It persists to the Roman period (see Lk 1.5). Thus, here the Chronicler is legitimating worship as he knew it by attributing it to David. **13:** The mandate for the sons of Aaron to *make offerings before the LORD* is detailed in a number of contexts (Ex 29.38–42; 30.1–10; Lev 8.1–9.24; 18.8–20). **18:** Although included in the earlier genealogy (6.37), the line of Korah is not mentioned here; this is probably connected with the tradition of Korah's rebellion narrated in Num 16. **25–32:** The levitical job description is revised in light of the move toward one permanent, stationary sanctuary. **28:** The Heb means "stand at the side of," rather than

of the house of the LORD, having the care of the courts and the chambers, the cleansing of all that is holy, and any work for the service of the house of God; [29] to assist also with the rows of bread, the choice flour for the grain offering, the wafers of unleavened bread, the baked offering, the offering mixed with oil, and all measures of quantity or size. [30] And they shall stand every morning, thanking and praising the LORD, and likewise at evening, [31] and whenever burnt offerings are offered to the LORD on sabbaths, new moons, and appointed festivals, according to the number required of them, regularly before the LORD. [32] Thus they shall keep charge of the tent of meeting and the sanctuary, and shall attend the descendants of Aaron, their kindred, for the service of the house of the LORD."

24

The divisions of the descendants of Aaron were these. The sons of Aaron: Nadab, Abihu, Eleazar, and Ithamar. [2] But Nadab and Abihu died before their father, and had no sons; so Eleazar and Ithamar became the priests. [3] Along with Zadok of the sons of Eleazar, and Ahimelech of the sons of Ithamar, David organized them according to the appointed duties in their service. [4] Since more chief men were found among the sons of Eleazar than among the sons of Ithamar, they organized them under sixteen heads of ancestral houses of the sons of Eleazar, and eight of the sons of Ithamar. [5] They organized them by lot, all alike, for there were officers of the sanctuary and officers of God among both the sons of Eleazar and the sons of Ithamar. [6] The scribe Shemaiah son of Nethanel, a Levite, recorded them in the presence of the king, and the officers, and Zadok the priest, and Ahimelech son of Abiathar, and the heads of ancestral houses of the priests and of the Levites; one ancestral house being chosen for Eleazar and one chosen for Ithamar.

[7] The first lot fell to Jehoiarib, the second to Jedaiah, [8] the third to Harim, the fourth to Seorim, [9] the fifth to Malchijah, the sixth to Mijamin, [10] the seventh to Hakkoz, the eighth to Abijah, [11] the ninth to Jeshua, the tenth to Shecaniah, [12] the eleventh to Eliashib, the twelfth to Jakim, [13] the thirteenth to Huppah, the fourteenth to Jeshebeab, [14] the fifteenth to Bilgah, the sixteenth to Immer, [15] the seventeenth to Hezir, the eighteenth to Happizzez, [16] the nineteenth to Pethahiah, the twentieth to Jehezkel, [17] the twenty-first to Jachin, the twenty-second to Gamul, [18] the twenty-third to Delaiah, the twenty-fourth to Maaziah. [19] These had as their appointed duty in their service to enter the house of the LORD according to the procedure established for them by their ancestor Aaron, as the LORD God of Israel had commanded him.

[20] And of the rest of the sons of Levi: of the sons of Amram, Shubael; of the sons of Shubael, Jehdeiah. [21] Of Rehabiah: of the sons of Rehabiah, Isshiah the chief. [22] Of the Izharites, Shelomoth; of the sons of Shelomoth, Jahath. [23] The sons of Hebron:[a] Jeriah the chief,[b] Amariah the second, Jahaziel the third, Jekameam the fourth. [24] The sons of Uzziel, Micah; of the sons of Micah, Shamir. [25] The brother of Micah, Isshiah; of the sons of Isshiah, Zechariah. [26] The sons of Merari: Mahli and Mushi. The sons of Jaaziah: Beno.[c] [27] The sons of Merari: of Jaaziah, Beno,[c] Shoham, Zaccur, and Ibri. [28] Of Mahli: Eleazar, who had no sons. [29] Of Kish, the sons of Kish: Jerahmeel. [30] The sons of Mushi: Mahli, Eder, and Jerimoth. These were the sons of the Levites according to their ancestral houses. [31] These also cast lots corresponding to their kindred, the descendants of Aaron, in the

---

a   See 23.19: Heb lacks *Hebron*
b   See 23.19: Heb lacks *the chief*
c   Or *his son*: Meaning of Heb uncertain

---

to assist the descendants of Aaron. In Chronicles the Levites and the priests have different but complementary responsibilities (see also Neh 12.45). **29**: *Rows of bread*, cf. Lev 25.4–9; 2 Chr 13.11. **30–31**: The Levites are to praise the LORD *whenever burnt offerings are offered* by the priests (16.4,7–38; 23.5). This contrasts with descriptions of Tabernacle worship in the Torah, which depict a sanctuary of silence.

24.1–19: David's priestly appointments. David organizes the priests into twenty-four divisions, which cast lots for places. **3**: *The sons of Eleazar, and . . . Ithamar* represent the two major priestly families (15.11; 18.16–17; 25.1; cf. 2 Sam 8.16–18). **20–31**: This list of Levites overlaps with that of 23.7–23. **31**: The Levites rotate by courses just as the priests do.

presence of King David, Zadok, Ahimelech, and the heads of ancestral houses of the priests and of the Levites, the chief as well as the youngest brother.

25 David and the officers of the army also set apart for the service the sons of Asaph, and of Heman, and of Jeduthun, who should prophesy with lyres, harps, and cymbals. The list of those who did the work and of their duties was: [2] Of the sons of Asaph: Zaccur, Joseph, Nethaniah, and Asarelah, sons of Asaph, under the direction of Asaph, who prophesied under the direction of the king. [3] Of Jeduthun, the sons of Jeduthun: Gedaliah, Zeri, Jeshaiah, Shimei,[a] Hashabiah, and Mattithiah, six, under the direction of their father Jeduthun, who prophesied with the lyre in thanksgiving and praise to the LORD. [4] Of Heman, the sons of Heman: Bukkiah, Mattaniah, Uzziel, Shebuel, and Jerimoth, Hananiah, Hanani, Eliathah, Giddalti, and Romamti-ezer, Joshbekashah, Mallothi, Hothir, Mahazioth. [5] All these were the sons of Heman the king's seer, according to the promise of God to exalt him; for God had given Heman fourteen sons and three daughters. [6] They were all under the direction of their father for the music in the house of the LORD with cymbals, harps, and lyres for the service of the house of God. Asaph, Jeduthun, and Heman were under the order of the king. [7] They and their kindred, who were trained in singing to the LORD, all of whom were skillful, numbered two hundred eighty-eight. [8] And they cast lots for their duties, small and great, teacher and pupil alike.

[9] The first lot fell for Asaph to Joseph; the second to Gedaliah, to him and his brothers and his sons, twelve; [10] the third to Zaccur, his sons and his brothers, twelve; [11] the fourth to Izri, his sons and his brothers, twelve; [12] the fifth to Nethaniah, his sons and his brothers, twelve; [13] the sixth to Bukkiah, his sons and his brothers, twelve; [14] the seventh to Jesarelah,[b] his sons and his brothers, twelve; [15] the eighth to Jeshaiah, his sons and his brothers, twelve; [16] the ninth to Mattaniah, his sons and his brothers, twelve; [17] the tenth to Shimei, his sons and his brothers, twelve; [18] the eleventh to Azarel, his sons and his brothers, twelve; [19] the twelfth to Hashabiah, his sons and his brothers, twelve; [20] to the thirteenth, Shubael, his sons and his brothers, twelve; [21] to the fourteenth, Mattithiah, his sons and his brothers, twelve; [22] to the fifteenth, to Jeremoth, his sons and his brothers, twelve; [23] to the sixteenth, to Hananiah, his sons and his brothers, twelve; [24] to the seventeenth, to Joshbekashah, his sons and his brothers, twelve; [25] to the eighteenth, to Hanani, his sons and his brothers, twelve; [26] to the nineteenth, to Mallothi, his sons and his brothers, twelve; [27] to the twentieth, to Eliathah, his sons and his brothers, twelve; [28] to the twenty-first, to Hothir, his sons and his brothers, twelve; [29] to the twenty-second, to Giddalti, his sons and his brothers, twelve; [30] to the twenty-third, to Mahazioth, his sons and his brothers, twelve; [31] to the twenty-fourth, to Romamti-ezer, his sons and his brothers, twelve.

26 As for the divisions of the gatekeepers: of the Korahites, Meshelemiah son of Kore, of the sons of Asaph. [2] Meshelemiah had sons: Zechariah the firstborn, Jediael

a One Ms: Gk: MT lacks *Shimei*
b Or *Asarelah*; see 25.2

25.1–31: The singers. Speaking of the singers as being *set apart* (v. 1) establishes a parallelism between David's choice and investiture of the singers, the Levites, and the priests (cf. 23.13; Num 8.14; 16.9,21; Deut 10.8; Ezra 10.8,16). On *the sons of Asaph, Heman,* and *Jeduthun,* see 6.33,44n. The allusion to music and song as a kind of prophecy (vv. 1–3; cf. 2 Chr 24.19–22) is striking and may be connected to the later tradition of David as a prophet who composed the psalms through divine inspiration; cf. 2 Kings 3.15. **1:** The *officers of the army,* as part of David's governmental apparatus, have a say in the establishment of courses for the singers. **8:** As with the priests (24.5) and other Levites (24.31), a lottery is held to determine the twenty-four divisions for the singers.

26.1–19: The gatekeepers. Part of David's administrative organization involves the gatekeepers, whom the Chronicler counts as Levites (cf. Ezra 2.42,70; Neh 11.19). Sanctuary guards were active in David's earlier reign when David transported the ark (15.18,23–24; 16.38,42; 23.5). Along with performing guard duty, the gatekeepers open the Temple in the morning; administer the use of the vessels, including the holy utensils; take charge of the flour, wine, spices, and oil (9.17–32); and perform administrative service on behalf of the king (2 Chr 31.14;

the second, Zebadiah the third, Jathniel the fourth, [3] Elam the fifth, Jehohanan the sixth, Eliehoenai the seventh. [4] Obed-edom had sons: Shemaiah the firstborn, Jehozabad the second, Joah the third, Sachar the fourth, Nethanel the fifth, [5] Ammiel the sixth, Issachar the seventh, Peullethai the eighth; for God blessed him. [6] Also to his son Shemaiah sons were born who exercised authority in their ancestral houses, for they were men of great ability. [7] The sons of Shemaiah: Othni, Rephael, Obed, and Elzabad, whose brothers were able men, Elihu and Semachiah. [8] All these, sons of Obed-edom with their sons and brothers, were able men qualified for the service; sixty-two of Obed-edom. [9] Meshelemiah had sons and brothers, able men, eighteen. [10] Hosah, of the sons of Merari, had sons: Shimri the chief (for though he was not the firstborn, his father made him chief), [11] Hilkiah the second, Tebaliah the third, Zechariah the fourth: all the sons and brothers of Hosah totaled thirteen.

[12] These divisions of the gatekeepers, corresponding to their leaders, had duties, just as their kindred did, ministering in the house of the Lord; [13] and they cast lots by ancestral houses, small and great alike, for their gates. [14] The lot for the east fell to Shelemiah. They cast lots also for his son Zechariah, a prudent counselor, and his lot came out for the north. [15] Obed-edom's came out for the south, and to his sons was allotted the storehouse. [16] For Shuppim and Hosah it came out for the west, at the gate of Shallecheth on the ascending road. Guard corresponded to guard. [17] On the east there were six Levites each day,[a] on the north four each day, on the south four each day, as well as two and two at the storehouse; [18] and for the colonnade[b] on the west there were four at the road and two at the colonnade.[b] [19] These were the divisions of the gatekeepers among the Korahites and the sons of Merari.

[20] And of the Levites, Ahijah had charge of the treasuries of the house of God and the treasuries of the dedicated gifts. [21] The sons of Ladan, the sons of the Gershonites belonging to Ladan, the heads of families belonging to Ladan the Gershonite: Jehieli.[c] [22] The sons of Jehieli, Zetham and his brother Joel, were in charge of the treasuries of the house of the Lord. [23] Of the Amramites, the Izharites, the Hebronites, and the Uzzielites: [24] Shebuel son of Gershom, son of Moses, was chief officer in charge of the treasuries. [25] His brothers: from Eliezer were his son Rehabiah, his son Jeshaiah, his son Joram, his son Zichri, and his son Shelomoth. [26] This Shelomoth and his brothers were in charge of all the treasuries of the dedicated gifts that King David, and the heads of families, and the officers of the thousands and the hundreds, and the commanders of the army, had dedicated. [27] From booty won in battles they dedicated gifts for the maintenance of the house of the Lord. [28] Also all that Samuel the seer, and Saul son of Kish, and Abner son of Ner, and Joab son of Zeruiah had dedicated—all dedicated gifts were in the care of Shelomoth[d] and his brothers.

[29] Of the Izharites, Chenaniah and his sons were appointed to outside duties for Israel, as officers and judges. [30] Of the Hebronites, Hashabiah and his brothers, one thousand seven hundred men of ability, had the oversight of Israel west of the Jordan for all the work of the Lord and for the service of the king. [31] Of the Hebronites, Jerijah was chief of the Hebronites. (In the fortieth year of David's reign search was made, of whatever genealogy or family, and men of great ability

---

a Gk: Heb lacks *each day*
b Heb *parbar*: meaning uncertain
c The Hebrew text of verse 21 is confused
d Gk Compare 26.28: Heb *Shelomith*

34.13). **13:** Because the lottery was held to determine which family was to serve at which gate, the number of members within a particular family did not determine or affect the process of selection. **16:** *Shuppim,* perhaps a scribal error, repeating the previous word. *Gate of Shallecheth,* the name occurs only here, and may also be a scribal error.

26.20–32: Treasurers, regional officials, and judges. Israel's leadership makes the task of Solomon easier by endowing the Temple and organizing its finances. The Levites also take on broad responsibilities, such as *oversight of Israel west of the Jordan* as *officers and judges* (vv. 29–30; cf. 23.3–5; 2 Chr 17.2; 19.5). **31:** *Fortieth year,* i.e.,

among them were found at Jazer in Gilead.)
[32] King David appointed him and his brothers, two thousand seven hundred men of ability, heads of families, to have the oversight of the Reubenites, the Gadites, and the half-tribe of the Manassites for everything pertaining to God and for the affairs of the king.

27 This is the list of the people of Israel, the heads of families, the commanders of the thousands and the hundreds, and their officers who served the king in all matters concerning the divisions that came and went, month after month throughout the year, each division numbering twenty-four thousand:

[2] Jashobeam son of Zabdiel was in charge of the first division in the first month; in his division were twenty-four thousand. [3] He was a descendant of Perez, and was chief of all the commanders of the army for the first month. [4] Dodai the Ahohite was in charge of the division of the second month; Mikloth was the chief officer of his division. In his division were twenty-four thousand. [5] The third commander, for the third month, was Benaiah son of the priest Jehoiada, as chief; in his division were twenty-four thousand. [6] This is the Benaiah who was a mighty man of the Thirty and in command of the Thirty; his son Ammizabad was in charge of his division.[a] [7] Asahel brother of Joab was fourth, for the fourth month, and his son Zebadiah after him; in his division were twenty-four thousand. [8] The fifth commander, for the fifth month, was Shamhuth, the Izrahite; in his division were twenty-four thousand. [9] Sixth, for the sixth month, was Ira son of Ikkesh the Tekoite; in his division were twenty-four thousand. [10] Seventh, for the seventh month, was Helez the Pelonite, of the Ephraimites; in his division were twenty-four thousand.

[11] Eighth, for the eighth month, was Sibbecai the Hushathite, of the Zerahites; in his division were twenty-four thousand. [12] Ninth, for the ninth month, was Abiezer of Anathoth, a Benjaminite; in his division were twenty-four thousand. [13] Tenth, for the tenth month, was Maharai of Netophah, of the Zerahites; in his division were twenty-four thousand. [14] Eleventh, for the eleventh month, was Benaiah of Pirathon, of the Ephraimites; in his division were twenty-four thousand. [15] Twelfth, for the twelfth month, was Heldai the Netophathite, of Othniel; in his division were twenty-four thousand.

[16] Over the tribes of Israel, for the Reubenites, Eliezer son of Zichri was chief officer; for the Simeonites, Shephatiah son of Maacah; [17] for Levi, Hashabiah son of Kemuel; for Aaron, Zadok; [18] for Judah, Elihu, one of David's brothers; for Issachar, Omri son of Michael; [19] for Zebulun, Ishmaiah son of Obadiah; for Naphtali, Jerimoth son of Azriel; [20] for the Ephraimites, Hoshea son of Azaziah; for the half-tribe of Manasseh, Joel son of Pedaiah; [21] for the half-tribe of Manasseh in Gilead, Iddo son of Zechariah; for Benjamin, Jaasiel son of Abner; [22] for Dan, Azarel son of Jeroham. These were the leaders of the tribes of Israel. [23] David did not count those below twenty years of age, for the LORD had promised to make Israel as numerous as the stars of heaven. [24] Joab son of Zeruiah began to count them, but did not finish; yet wrath came upon Israel for this, and the number was not entered into the account of the Annals of King David.

[25] Over the king's treasuries was Azmaveth son of Adiel. Over the treasuries in

---

a Gk Vg: Heb *Ammizabad was his division*

David's last; see 29.27. **32:** The Persian-period distinction between matters pertaining to the king and matters pertaining to God is found only in Chronicles (26.30,32; 2 Chr 19.11) and Ezra (7.26).

27.1–24: Military leaders. The orderly organization of the military, no less than the organization of the priests and the Levites, is part of David's legacy in Chronicles. The system established—twelve monthly relays of 24,000, each headed by a divisional leader (vv. 2–16)—reflects his standard administrative procedure (23.6–23; 24.1–19; 25.8–31; 26.1–12). **1:** The noun "mispar" may be translated as "census" (rather than as *list*) both here and in vv. 23–24 (cf. 23.3). **2–15:** Many of the names in this list are also found in 11.11–47; 2 Sam 23.8–39. **16–22:** Each of the tribes has its own "chief officer" participate in the national government. See 5.6n. **23:** The enumeration of twelve military divisions (288,000) leads the writer to explain why no general census of Israel is included (cf. Num 1.3,45). By counting Israelite males who were less than twenty years of age, David would be casting aspersions on the validity of one of God's solemn promises to Abraham (Gen 22.17). **24:** See ch 21.

the country, in the cities, in the villages and in the towers, was Jonathan son of Uzziah. ²⁶ Over those who did the work of the field, tilling the soil, was Ezri son of Chelub. ²⁷ Over the vineyards was Shimei the Ramathite. Over the produce of the vineyards for the wine cellars was Zabdi the Shiphmite. ²⁸ Over the olive and sycamore trees in the Shephelah was Baal-hanan the Gederite. Over the stores of oil was Joash. ²⁹ Over the herds that pastured in Sharon was Shitrai the Sharonite. Over the herds in the valleys was Shaphat son of Adlai. ³⁰ Over the camels was Obil the Ishmaelite. Over the donkeys was Jehdeiah the Meronothite. Over the flocks was Jaziz the Hagrite. ³¹ All these were stewards of King David's property.

³² Jonathan, David's uncle, was a counselor, being a man of understanding and a scribe; Jehiel son of Hachmoni attended the king's sons. ³³ Ahithophel was the king's counselor, and Hushai the Archite was the king's friend. ³⁴ After Ahithophel came Jehoiada son of Benaiah, and Abiathar. Joab was commander of the king's army.

28

David assembled at Jerusalem all the officials of Israel, the officials of the tribes, the officers of the divisions that served the king, the commanders of the thousands, the commanders of the hundreds, the stewards of all the property and cattle of the king and his sons, together with the palace officials, the mighty warriors, and all the warriors. ² Then King David rose to his feet and said: "Hear me, my brothers and my people. I had planned to build a house of rest for the ark of the covenant of the LORD, for the footstool of our God; and I made preparations for building. ³ But God said to me, 'You shall not build a house for my name, for you are a warrior and have shed blood.' ⁴ Yet the LORD God of Israel chose me from all my ancestral house to be king over Israel forever; for he chose Judah as leader, and in the house of Judah my father's house, and among my father's sons he took delight in making me king over all Israel. ⁵ And of all my sons, for the LORD has given me many, he has chosen my son Solomon to sit upon the throne of the kingdom of the LORD over Israel. ⁶ He said to me, 'It is your son Solomon who shall build my house and my courts, for I have chosen him to be a son to me, and I will be a father to him. ⁷ I will establish his kingdom forever if he continues resolute in keeping my commandments and my ordinances, as he is today.' ⁸ Now therefore in the sight of all Israel, the assembly of the LORD, and in the hearing of our God, observe and search out all the commandments of the LORD your God; that you may possess this good land, and leave it for an inheritance to your children after you forever.

⁹ "And you, my son Solomon, know the God of your father, and serve him with single mind and willing heart; for the LORD searches

27.25–32: Other administrators. The Davidic state is multifaceted. The king owns agricultural estates (v. 27), operates storehouses in both urban and rural areas for agricultural produce (vv. 27–28), and has an investment in, if not some control over, trade (v. 30). The king employs a variety of high officials who supervise his estates, fieldworkers, and storage facilities. The king also has advisers and officers (vv. 32–34) at his disposal. Some aspects of this complicated system may be anachronistic, but they are consistent with ancient Near Eastern royal practice. 30: The *camels* and *donkeys* (or she-asses) are related directly not to agriculture, but to trade. Because the major trade routes of the ancient Near East passed through the region, trade was an important sector of the Israelite economy. 33: On *Ahithophel* and *Hushai*, see 2 Sam 15.12,23–37.

28.1–10: All Israel ratifies accession. Having concluded his administrative organization, David assembles a large national convocation to prepare the way for Solomon's rule. 1: Assemblies are common in the Chronicler's history (13.5; 15.3; 2 Chr 5.2–3; 11.1; 20.26). In this case, David convokes all of his nation's dignitaries to Jerusalem to witness his charge to Solomon and to enlist their support for Solomon. 2: On the ark as God's footstool, cf. Pss 99.5; 132.7. 3: See 22.6–8. 4: *Chose me,* in Chronicles the Levites (15.2; 2 Chr 29.11), the tribe of Judah, and more specifically David and Solomon are all elect of God. Emphasis on Solomon's election contrasts sharply with 1 Kings 1–2. 6–7: Cf. 17.11–14; 22.9–10. 7: The perdurability of Davidic kingship is contingent on Solomon's obedience (cf. 17.11; 1 Kings 3.14; 8.61; 9.4), which the duty to build the Temple exemplifies (v. 10). 8: The addressee is Israel. Much like the authors of Deuteronomy (4.23–28; 28.58–64; 30.18), the Chronicler conditions Israel's possession of the land upon its obedience to God.

every mind, and understands every plan and thought. If you seek him, he will be found by you; but if you forsake him, he will abandon you forever. [10] Take heed now, for the LORD has chosen you to build a house as the sanctuary; be strong, and act."

[11] Then David gave his son Solomon the plan of the vestibule of the temple, and of its houses, its treasuries, its upper rooms, and its inner chambers, and of the room for the mercy seat;[a] [12] and the plan of all that he had in mind: for the courts of the house of the LORD, all the surrounding chambers, the treasuries of the house of God, and the treasuries for dedicated gifts; [13] for the divisions of the priests and of the Levites, and all the work of the service in the house of the LORD; for all the vessels for the service in the house of the LORD, [14] the weight of gold for all golden vessels for each service, the weight of silver vessels for each service, [15] the weight of the golden lampstands and their lamps, the weight of gold for each lampstand and its lamps, the weight of silver for a lampstand and its lamps, according to the use of each in the service, [16] the weight of gold for each table for the rows of bread, the silver for the silver tables, [17] and pure gold for the forks, the basins, and the cups; for the golden bowls and the weight of each; for the silver bowls and the weight of each; [18] for the altar of incense made of refined gold, and its weight; also his plan for the golden chariot of the cherubim that spread their wings and covered the ark of the covenant of the LORD.

[19] "All this, in writing at the LORD's direction, he made clear to me—the plan of all the works."

[20] David said further to his son Solomon, "Be strong and of good courage, and act. Do not be afraid or dismayed; for the LORD God, my God, is with you. He will not fail you or forsake you, until all the work for the service of the house of the LORD is finished. [21] Here are the divisions of the priests and the Levites for all the service of the house of God; and with you in all the work will be every volunteer who has skill for any kind of service; also the officers and all the people will be wholly at your command."

29 King David said to the whole assembly, "My son Solomon, whom alone God has chosen, is young and inexperienced, and the work is great; for the temple[b] will not be for mortals but for the LORD God. [2] So I have provided for the house of my God, so far as I was able, the gold for the things of gold, the silver for the things of silver, and the bronze for the things of bronze, the iron for the things of iron, and wood for the things of wood, besides great quantities of onyx and stones for setting, antimony, colored stones, all sorts of precious stones, and marble in abundance. [3] Moreover, in addition to all that I have provided for the holy house, I have a treasure of my own of gold and silver, and because of my devotion to the house of my God I give it to the house of my God: [4] three thousand talents of gold, of the gold of Ophir, and seven thousand talents of refined silver, for overlaying the walls of the house, [5] and for all the work to be done by artisans, gold for the things of gold and silver for the things of silver. Who then will offer willingly, consecrating themselves today to the LORD?"

[6] Then the leaders of ancestral houses made their freewill offerings, as did also the leaders of the tribes, the commanders of the thousands and of the hundreds, and the officers over the king's work. [7] They gave for the service of the house of God five thousand

a Or the cover
b Heb fortress

28.11–21: A plan for the Temple. Much as Moses received plans for the tabernacle (Ex 25.9), David has a divinely composed written plan for the Temple (v. 19), which he presents to Solomon. 20: The transition from David to Solomon is patterned after Moses and Joshua; note especially *Be strong and of good courage* (Deut 31.7; 31.23; Josh 1.6–18).
29.1–9: Endowments for the Temple. To explain his own copious preparations, David contrasts young Solomon's youthful vulnerability with the tremendous task that lies ahead (cf. 22.5). David's generosity sets the stage for Israel's leadership to show similar benevolence (vv. 6–9). There are parallels with Israel's gifts to the tabernacle (Ex 25.1–7; 35.4–9,20–29). 4: *Ophir*, probably in southern Arabia, was famous for its gold; see Isa 13.12. On the quantities, see 22.14n. 7: The *daric* was a Persian coin, generally thought to be 8.4 gr, minted

talents and ten thousand darics of gold, ten thousand talents of silver, eighteen thousand talents of bronze, and one hundred thousand talents of iron. [8] Whoever had precious stones gave them to the treasury of the house of the LORD, into the care of Jehiel the Gershonite. [9] Then the people rejoiced because these had given willingly, for with single mind they had offered freely to the LORD; King David also rejoiced greatly.

[10] Then David blessed the LORD in the presence of all the assembly; David said: "Blessed are you, O LORD, the God of our ancestor Israel, forever and ever. [11] Yours, O LORD, are the greatness, the power, the glory, the victory, and the majesty; for all that is in the heavens and on the earth is yours; yours is the kingdom, O LORD, and you are exalted as head above all. [12] Riches and honor come from you, and you rule over all. In your hand are power and might; and it is in your hand to make great and to give strength to all. [13] And now, our God, we give thanks to you and praise your glorious name.

[14] "But who am I, and what is my people, that we should be able to make this freewill offering? For all things come from you, and of your own have we given you. [15] For we are aliens and transients before you, as were all our ancestors; our days on the earth are like a shadow, and there is no hope. [16] O LORD our God, all this abundance that we have provided for building you a house for your holy name comes from your hand and is all your own. [17] I know, my God, that you search the heart, and take pleasure in uprightness; in the uprightness of my heart I have freely offered all these things, and now I have seen

your people, who are present here, offering freely and joyously to you. [18] O LORD, the God of Abraham, Isaac, and Israel, our ancestors, keep forever such purposes and thoughts in the hearts of your people, and direct their hearts toward you. [19] Grant to my son Solomon that with single mind he may keep your commandments, your decrees, and your statutes, performing all of them, and that he may build the temple[a] for which I have made provision."

[20] Then David said to the whole assembly, "Bless the LORD your God." And all the assembly blessed the LORD, the God of their ancestors, and bowed their heads and prostrated themselves before the LORD and the king. [21] On the next day they offered sacrifices and burnt offerings to the LORD, a thousand bulls, a thousand rams, and a thousand lambs, with their libations, and sacrifices in abundance for all Israel; [22] and they ate and drank before the LORD on that day with great joy.

They made David's son Solomon king a second time; they anointed him as the LORD's prince, and Zadok as priest. [23] Then Solomon sat on the throne of the LORD, succeeding his father David as king; he prospered, and all Israel obeyed him. [24] All the leaders and the mighty warriors, and also all the sons of King David, pledged their allegiance to King Solomon. [25] The LORD highly exalted Solomon in the sight of all Israel, and bestowed upon him such royal majesty as had not been on any king before him in Israel.

[26] Thus David son of Jesse reigned over all Israel. [27] The period that he reigned over

---

[a] Heb fortress

sometime after 515 BCE (cf. Ezra 8.27).

29.10–19: David's farewell prayer. The Chronicler follows a paradigm in which final addresses are made by great leaders—Jacob (Gen 49.1–28), Moses (Deut 32.1–44,45–47; 33.1–29), Joshua (23.1–16; 24.1–28), Samuel (1 Sam 12.1–25), and David (2 Sam 23.1–7; 1 Kings 2.1–10). David's acclamation of the LORD's sovereignty (vv. 10–13) resonates with sentiments expressed earlier in the Psalm anthology (16.24–26) and with the prayer that he offered following Nathan's dynastic oracle (17.16–27). From David's point of view, all that he and the people donate to God ultimately stems from God himself (v. 14). Thus, following earlier biblical norms, these gifts serve as acknowledgments of God's sovereignty. **15:** *Aliens and transients,* cf. Lev 25.23.

29.20–30: David's death and the transition to Solomon. David's final blessing of Israel is coupled with the anointing of Solomon as his chosen successor. In contrast to Samuel and Kings, the transition is smooth and without incident. **22:** Another all-Israelite feast (see 12.39n.). *A second time,* whereas David earlier designated Solomon king over Israel (23.1), all of Israel's leaders now publicly endorse Solomon's enthronement. **24:** Even *all the sons of King David* acclaim Solomon, a clear polemic against the account in Samuel-Kings (2 Sam 15.1–

Israel was forty years; he reigned seven years in Hebron, and thirty-three years in Jerusalem. 28 He died in a good old age, full of days, riches, and honor; and his son Solomon succeeded him. 29 Now the acts of King David, from first to last, are written in the records of the seer Samuel, and in the records of the prophet Nathan, and in the records of the seer Gad, 30 with accounts of all his rule and his might and of the events that befell him and Israel and all the kingdoms of the earth.

16.14; 1 Kings 1.9–10,25–26; 2.15). **25:** In *royal majesty* Solomon's reign is unparalleled. **27:** David's reign is dated to ca. 1005–965 BCE. **28:** David enjoys a long, productive, and respected life. Security and longevity are marks of divine blessing (2 Chr 24.15; Deut 4.40; 5.16; Isa 52.10; 65.17–19). *Full of days,* see 23.1n. **29:** In the Chronicler's time, Judeans thought of the prophets not only as great figures from Israel's past but also authors of historical writings about that past. That David's reign is the subject of these three otherwise unknown accounts written by prophets during his reign, is one more indication of the Chronicler's desire to enhance David's legacy.

2 CHRONICLES

Second Chronicles is a continuation of First Chronicles, and the two originally formed one book, as they still do in the traditional Hebrew text. (For an introduction to this work, see the Introduction to 1 Chronicles.)

The organization of 2 Chronicles falls into two major parts: the reign of Solomon (chs 1–9) and the kingdom of Judah (chs 10–36). In Chronicles the tenure of Solomon represents the apex of Israelite history, a time of unprecedented glory, prosperity, and peace. If David's reign was highly successful because David consolidated Israel's international position and prepared for the long-awaited Temple, Solomon's reign was even more successful because he brought these plans to fruition. Accordingly, much space is devoted in chs 2–7 to the construction, furnishings, and dedication of this national edifice. As the home of the ark of the covenant and the tabernacle, the Temple represents the continuation and fulfillment of earlier Israelite religious institutions. The careful attention given to the Temple and its worship reflects the importance that the Chronicler ascribed to this institution in the postexilic era. For the author, the Temple is the divinely sanctioned place for both sacrifice and prayer (6.1–7.22), a view also present in the book of Kings.

The Chronicler's account of the divided monarchy differs in many respects from that found in 1 and 2 Kings, even though he draws heavily from Kings to write his own work. The writer excludes the independent history of the Northern Kingdom because he regards both the kingship and the sanctuaries of this new state as an affront to God (13.4–12). The choice not to recount the record of northern Israel also means that the stories of northern prophets such as Elijah and Elisha are not found in Chronicles. The author does add, however, much coverage to the Southern Kingdom of Judah, including a letter from Elijah to a southern king (2 Chr 21.12–15). Some of the material unique to Chronicles reflects well on the reigns of major Judahite monarchs, such as Asa (chs 14–16), Jehoshaphat (chs 17–20), and Hezekiah (chs 29–32). Throughout his presentation, the Chronicler exhibits a keen concern for all Israelite tribes. The Chronicler criticizes the Northern Kingdom and its monarchs, but he still considers the northern tribes as Israelite and shows a sustained interest in their contacts with Judah. In the latter part of its history, Judah lost ground to its enemies and was exiled from its land to Babylon (586 BCE). A major concern of the Chronicler is not only to trace this decline, but also to explain it and to commend the reforms aimed at reversing it. On the whole, he presents a more optimistic version of this period than do the authors of Kings. (See further the Introduction to 1 Chronicles, pp. 575-577 HB.)

Gary N. Knoppers

1 Solomon son of David established himself in his kingdom; the LORD his God was with him and made him exceedingly great.

² Solomon summoned all Israel, the commanders of the thousands and of the hundreds, the judges, and all the leaders of all Israel, the heads of families. ³ Then Solomon, and the whole assembly with him, went to the high place that was at Gibeon; for God's tent of meeting, which Moses the servant of the LORD had made in the wilderness, was there. ⁴ (But David had brought the ark of God up from Kiriath-jearim to the place that David had prepared for it; for he had pitched a tent for it in Jerusalem.) ⁵ Moreover the bronze altar that Bezalel son of Uri, son of Hur, had made, was there in front of the tabernacle of the LORD. And Solomon and the assembly inquired at it. ⁶ Solomon went up there to the bronze altar before the LORD, which was at the tent of meeting, and offered a thousand burnt offerings on it.

⁷ That night God appeared to Solomon, and said to him, "Ask what I should give you." ⁸ Solomon said to God, "You have shown great and steadfast love to my father David, and have made me succeed him as king. ⁹ O LORD God, let your promise to my father David now be fulfilled, for you have made me king over a people as numerous as the dust of the earth.

¹⁰ Give me now wisdom and knowledge to go out and come in before this people, for who can rule this great people of yours?" ¹¹ God answered Solomon, "Because this was in your heart, and you have not asked for possessions, wealth, honor, or the life of those who hate you, and have not even asked for long life, but have asked for wisdom and knowledge for yourself that you may rule my people over whom I have made you king, ¹² wisdom and knowledge are granted to you. I will also give you riches, possessions, and honor, such as none of the kings had who were before you, and none after you shall have the like." ¹³ So Solomon came from[a] the high place at Gibeon, from the tent of meeting, to Jerusalem. And he reigned over Israel.

¹⁴ Solomon gathered together chariots and horses; he had fourteen hundred chariots and twelve thousand horses, which he stationed in the chariot cities and with the king in Jerusalem. ¹⁵ The king made silver and gold as common in Jerusalem as stone, and he made cedar as plentiful as the sycamore of the Shephelah. ¹⁶ Solomon's horses were imported from Egypt and Kue; the king's traders received them from Kue at the prevailing price. ¹⁷ They imported from Egypt, and then

a   Gk Vg: Heb *to*

1.1–17: Solomon takes charge, journeys to Gibeon, and prospers. Solomon rules an Israel unified and unhampered by internal factions or strife. Solomon's legitimacy is stressed by repeated references to him as David's rightful successor and king by divine choice (1 Chr 17.11; 23.1; 28.6; 29.23–25; 2 Chr 1.1; 6.10; 7.17–18). The Chronicler presents the United Monarchy as the time when Israel's authoritative institutions took shape. The idealized presentation of David and Solomon effectively establishes a model by which later periods are judged. **1:** Solomon ruled ca. 968–928 BCE. When Solomon took office, he immediately *established himself in his kingdom* and enjoyed the LORD's blessings (v. 1). There was no need to pacify, eliminate, or exile his domestic foes (1 Kings 1–2) because David had already consolidated support for Solomon (1 Chr 23–29). **2–13:** The support of military, local, and civil officials enables the nation to embark on major new initiatives in a harmonious fashion (1 Chr 11.1–3; 13.1–4; 23.1–2; 28.1; 29.1–25). In this case, the author transforms a story about Solomon's private pilgrimage to the high place at Gibeon (1 Kings 3.3–15) into a national pilgrimage, adding that the tent of meeting (see Ex 38–39) was located at Gibeon (1 Chr 16.39–42). This type of addition, which harmonizes a variety of earlier texts, typifies Chronicles. **4:** See 1 Chr 13; 15. **5:** On *Bezalel* and the *bronze altar,* cf. Ex 27.1–2; 31.1; 1 Chr 2.20. The emphasis here is on continuity. **11–12:** The divine gifts of unprecedented *wisdom and knowledge,* as well as *possessions, wealth* and *honor* set the tone and tenor of Solomon's reign. Nevertheless, the theme of Solomon's wisdom is not as pronounced in Chronicles as it is in Kings. **14–17:** These verses, drawn from 1 Kings 10.26–29, illustrate that God's promises to Solomon at Gibeon are being realized. The rearrangement of earlier sources is typical of the Chronicler. **15:** *The Shephelah,* the foothills between the coastal plain and the Judean hill country. **16:** *Kue,* in Cilicia, in southern Asia Minor. **17:** A *shekel* weighed about 11.5 gr (.4 oz). The *kings of the Hittites* ruled over northern Syria; *Aram* was southern Syria.

2.1–18: Solomon prepares to build the Temple. As David's appointed successor, Solomon brings his father's

exported, a chariot for six hundred shekels of silver, and a horse for one hundred fifty; so through them these were exported to all the kings of the Hittites and the kings of Aram.

2 [a] Solomon decided to build a temple for the name of the LORD, and a royal palace for himself. [2] [b] Solomon conscripted seventy thousand laborers and eighty thousand stonecutters in the hill country, with three thousand six hundred to oversee them.

[3] Solomon sent word to King Huram of Tyre: "Once you dealt with my father David and sent him cedar to build himself a house to live in. [4] I am now about to build a house for the name of the LORD my God and dedicate it to him for offering fragrant incense before him, and for the regular offering of the rows of bread, and for burnt offerings morning and evening, on the sabbaths and the new moons and the appointed festivals of the LORD our God, as ordained forever for Israel. [5] The house that I am about to build will be great, for our God is greater than other gods. [6] But who is able to build him a house, since heaven, even highest heaven, cannot contain him? Who am I to build a house for him, except as a place to make offerings before him? [7] So now send me an artisan skilled to work in gold, silver, bronze, and iron, and in purple, crimson, and blue fabrics, trained also in engraving, to join the skilled workers who are with me in Judah and Jerusalem, whom my father David provided. [8] Send me also cedar, cypress, and algum timber from Lebanon, for I know that your servants are skilled in cutting Lebanon timber. My servants will work with your servants [9] to prepare timber for me in abundance, for the house I am about to build will be great and wonderful. [10] I will provide for your servants, those who cut the timber, twenty thousand cors of crushed wheat, twenty thousand cors of barley, twenty thousand baths[c] of wine, and twenty thousand baths of oil."

[11] Then King Huram of Tyre answered in a letter that he sent to Solomon, "Because the LORD loves his people he has made you king over them." [12] Huram also said, "Blessed be the LORD God of Israel, who made heaven and earth, who has given King David a wise son, endowed with discretion and understanding, who will build a temple for the LORD, and a royal palace for himself.

[13] "I have dispatched Huram-abi, a skilled artisan, endowed with understanding, [14] the son of one of the Danite women, his father a Tyrian. He is trained to work in gold, silver, bronze, iron, stone, and wood, and in purple, blue, and crimson fabrics and fine linen, and to do all sorts of engraving and execute any design that may be assigned him, with your artisans, the artisans of my lord, your father David. [15] Now, as for the wheat, barley, oil, and wine, of which my lord has spoken, let him send them to his servants. [16] We will cut whatever timber you need from Lebanon, and bring it to you as rafts by sea to Joppa; you will take it up to Jerusalem."

[17] Then Solomon took a census of all the aliens who were residing in the land of Israel, after the census that his father David had taken; and there were found to be one hundred fifty-three thousand six hundred. [18] Seventy thousand of them he assigned as laborers, eighty thousand as stonecutters in the hill

a Ch 1.18 in Heb
b Ch 2.1 in Heb
c A Hebrew measure of volume

hopes and designs to fruition by focusing much of his energy on constructing, equipping, and staffing the Temple. Like David, Solomon is a devoted patron of his nation's worship and makes this the first priority of his reign. **1–10:** These verses, largely drawn from 1 Kings 5.1–6,11, provide external confirmation of both Solomon's gifts and the plan to build a temple. Vv. 4–5, however, have no source in Kings, and reflect later theological notions. **3:** *Huram* (called Hiram in 1 Kings) had been an ally of David (see 2 Sam 5.11), sending him materials to build his palace. **4:** *Rows of bread,* see 1 Chr 9.32; Lev 24.5–9. *Burnt offerings,* see 1 Chr 16.40; Ex 29.38–42; Lev 6.20. **8:** *Algum* ("almug" in 1 Kings), an unidentified species of tree. **10:** A *cor* was about 230 l (6.5 bu); a *bath* about 23 l (6 gal). **11–12:** An elaborated version of 1 Kings 5.7. **13–16:** Cf. 1 Kings 7.13–14. There *Huram-abi* is called Hiram and hails from Naphtali. **17–18:** The census of *aliens* is a prelude to conscription for the Temple's construction (1 Kings 9.22). In Chronicles Solomon does not conscript Israelites to build the Temple and other public buildings as he does in Kings (1 Kings 5.13–18; 12.4).

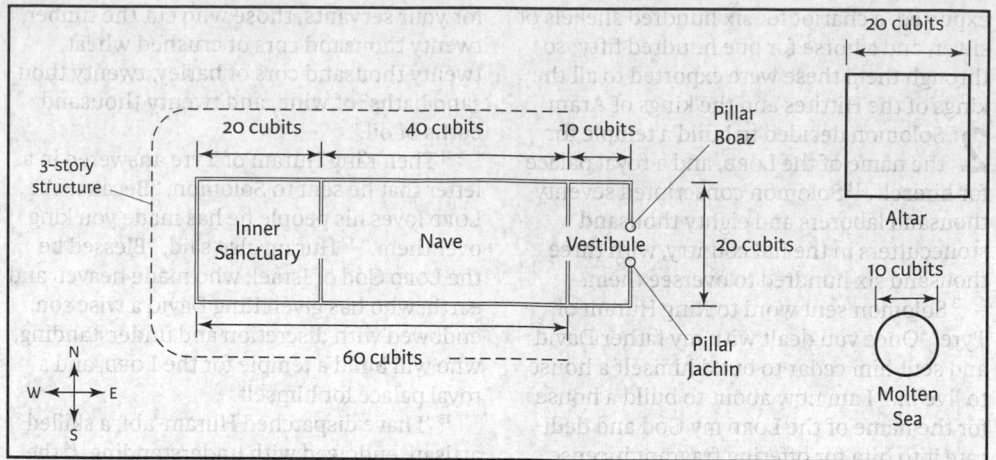

The Temple of Solomon according to Second Chronicles.

country, and three thousand six hundred as overseers to make the people work.

3 Solomon began to build the house of the LORD in Jerusalem on Mount Moriah, where the LORD had appeared to his father David, at the place that David had designated, on the threshing floor of Ornan the Jebusite. [2] He began to build on the second day of the second month of the fourth year of his reign. [3] These are Solomon's measurements[a] for building the house of God: the length, in cubits of the old standard, was sixty cubits, and the width twenty cubits. [4] The vestibule in front of the nave of the house was twenty cubits long, across the width of the house;[b] and its height was one hundred twenty cubits. He overlaid it on the inside with pure gold.

[5] The nave he lined with cypress, covered it with fine gold, and made palms and chains on it. [6] He adorned the house with settings of precious stones. The gold was gold from Parvaim. [7] So he lined the house with gold—its beams, its thresholds, its walls, and its doors; and he carved cherubim on the walls.

[8] He made the most holy place; its length, corresponding to the width of the house, was twenty cubits, and its width was twenty cubits; he overlaid it with six hundred talents of fine gold. [9] The weight of the nails was fifty shekels of gold. He overlaid the upper chambers with gold.

a Syr: Heb *foundations*
b Compare 1 Kings 6.3: Meaning of Heb uncertain

3.1–17: Temple construction (see map above). A condensed and rewritten version of 1 Kings 6; 7.15–22 (see also the notes there). 1: Only here is *Mount Moriah*, the site of the binding of Isaac (Gen 22.2), explicitly identified with the Temple site. According to the Chronicler, it is also the location where David was instructed to build an altar to God (1 Chr 21.15–22.1) following his calamitous census (1 Chr 21.1–14). 3: *House of God*, like the Tabernacle described in Exodus, Solomon's Temple had three major sections, though some of these sections have different names: a "vestibule" (v. 4), a "nave" (vv. 4–5), and a "most holy place" (v. 8). Of these "the most holy place" was the most exclusive and sacred, but the "nave" (or sanctuary) was the largest and contained an incense altar, the "ten golden lampstands" (v. 7), and the "ten tables" (v. 8). Archaeology has revealed a variety of ancient Near Eastern parallels to the tripartite design depicted here. A *cubit* was about 45 cm (18 in); the cubit of *the old standard* may have been slightly longer. 4: The measurement of *one hundred twenty cubits* for the height of the main part of the building dwarfs the thirty cubits measurement of Solomon's Temple in 1 Kings 6.2. 6: The location of *Parvaim* is unknown. 8–9: The Chronicler portrays Solomon, like David (1 Chr 29.1–5), as deliberately excessive in providing for the Temple. The *six hundred talents of fine gold* is the equivalent of over 20,000 kg (45,000 lbs). 1 Kings 6.19–22 simply speaks of "pure gold." 10–14: Largely abridged from 1 Kings 6.23–28. 10: *Cherubim* were winged, sphinxlike creatures with human faces (cf. Gen 3.24; 1 Kings 6.23; Ezek 41.18–19). In the ancient Near East, kings were sometimes represented as sitting on a throne supported by

¹⁰ In the most holy place he made two carved cherubim and overlaid[a] them with gold. ¹¹ The wings of the cherubim together extended twenty cubits: one wing of the one, five cubits long, touched the wall of the house, and its other wing, five cubits long, touched the wing of the other cherub; ¹² and of this cherub, one wing, five cubits long, touched the wall of the house, and the other wing, also five cubits long, was joined to the wing of the first cherub. ¹³ The wings of these cherubim extended twenty cubits; the cherubim[b] stood on their feet, facing the nave. ¹⁴ And Solomon[c] made the curtain of blue and purple and crimson fabrics and fine linen, and worked cherubim into it.

¹⁵ In front of the house he made two pillars thirty-five cubits high, with a capital of five cubits on the top of each. ¹⁶ He made encircling[d] chains and put them on the tops of the pillars; and he made one hundred pomegranates, and put them on the chains. ¹⁷ He set up the pillars in front of the temple, one on the right, the other on the left; the one on the right he called Jachin, and the one on the left, Boaz.

4 He made an altar of bronze, twenty cubits long, twenty cubits wide, and ten cubits high. ² Then he made the molten sea; it was round, ten cubits from rim to rim, and five cubits high. A line of thirty cubits would encircle it completely. ³ Under it were panels all around, each of ten cubits, surrounding the sea; there were two rows of panels, cast when it was cast. ⁴ It stood on twelve oxen, three facing north, three facing west, three facing south, and three facing east; the sea was set on them. The hindquarters of each were toward the inside. ⁵ Its thickness was a handbreadth; its rim was made like the rim of a cup, like the flower of a lily; it held three thousand baths.[e] ⁶ He also made ten basins in which to wash, and set five on the right side, and five on the left. In these they were to rinse what was used for the burnt offering. The sea was for the priests to wash in.

⁷ He made ten golden lampstands as prescribed, and set them in the temple, five on the south side and five on the north. ⁸ He also made ten tables and placed them in the temple, five on the right side and five on the left. And he made one hundred basins of gold. ⁹ He made the court of the priests, and

a   Heb *they overlaid*
b   Heb *they*
c   Heb *he*
d   Cn: Heb *in the inner sanctuary*
e   A Hebrew measure of volume

cherubim. In this case, however, the "cherubim" symbolized the invisible LORD's enthronement in *the most holy place*. **14:** The reference to the *curtain* draws a parallel between the tabernacle (Ex 26.31) and the Temple. 1 Kings 6.31 instead mentions doors. The Chronicler often buttresses the antiquity of the Jerusalem Temple by stressing the continuity between it and older religious institutions such as the tabernacle. **15–17:** On *Jachin* and *Boaz*, see 1 Kings 7.15–22n. **15:** *Pillars*, one pillar stood on each side of the Temple's entrance. Their height of *thirty-five cubits* is nearly double that registered in 1 Kings 7.15.

4.1–22: The Temple furnishings. Largely taken from 1 Kings 7.23–51 (excepting vv. 27–37). **1:** The reference to the *altar of bronze* may have been drawn from 1 Kings 8.64 (cf. 2 Kings 16.14). See also 2 Chr 1.5 and Ezek 43.13–17. **2–6:** *The molten sea*, made from cast bronze, rested upon a foundation of twelve oxen or bulls, which were traditionally associated with strength and fertility in ancient Canaan. Given that one bath measured approximately 6 gal (23 l), this Temple furnishing was of monumental size. 1 Kings 7.23–26 also describes the *molten sea*, but does not mention that it was used for priestly ablutions. **4:** The *twelve oxen* supporting the molten sea are grouped in threes and face outward in each of the four directions of the compass. **6:** *Ten basins*, see 1 Kings 7.38–39. The tabernacle had only one basin (Ex 30.17). *To wash*, the explanation is not found in Kings. It has been drawn from the Priestly description of the tent of meeting (Ex 30.17–21). **7:** *Ten golden lampstands*, Chronicles, in conformity with Kings, mentions multiple lampstands in the Temple (1 Chr 28.15; 2 Chr 4.20 || 1 Kings 7.49). In contrast, the tabernacle has one lampstand (Ex 25.31–40; 31.8; Lev 24.1–4; Num 8.2–4). As "a statute forever throughout your generations" (Lev 24.3), the candelabrum's lamps were to burn every evening (Ex 25.37; 30.7–8; Lev 24.3; Num 8.2; 2 Chr 13.11). **8:** *Ten tables*, in contrast with the one table in the tabernacle (Ex 25.23–30; 26.35; Lev 24.5–9; 2 Chr 13.11) and the one table in the Temple described by 1 Kings 7.48, the Chronicler's Temple had ten. On these tables the "bread of the Presence" would be laid. **9:** The reference to the *court of the priests* likely reflects the Temple of the Chronicler's own day in which the inner court (1 Kings 6.36; 7.12) was reserved for priests and the outer

the great court, and doors for the court; he overlaid their doors with bronze. ¹⁰ He set the sea at the southeast corner of the house.

¹¹ And Huram made the pots, the shovels, and the basins. Thus Huram finished the work that he did for King Solomon on the house of God: ¹² the two pillars, the bowls, and the two capitals on the top of the pillars; and the two latticeworks to cover the two bowls of the capitals that were on the top of the pillars; ¹³ the four hundred pomegranates for the two latticeworks, two rows of pomegranates for each latticework, to cover the two bowls of the capitals that were on the pillars. ¹⁴ He made the stands, the basins on the stands, ¹⁵ the one sea, and the twelve oxen underneath it. ¹⁶ The pots, the shovels, the forks, and all the equipment for these Huram-abi made of burnished bronze for King Solomon for the house of the LORD. ¹⁷ In the plain of the Jordan the king cast them, in the clay ground between Succoth and Zeredah. ¹⁸ Solomon made all these things in great quantities, so that the weight of the bronze was not determined.

¹⁹ So Solomon made all the things that were in the house of God: the golden altar, the tables for the bread of the Presence, ²⁰ the lampstands and their lamps of pure gold to burn before the inner sanctuary, as prescribed; ²¹ the flowers, the lamps, and the tongs, of purest gold; ²² the snuffers, basins, ladles, and firepans, of pure gold. As for the entrance to the temple: the inner doors to the most holy place and the doors of the nave of the temple were of gold.

5 Thus all the work that Solomon did for the house of the LORD was finished. Solomon brought in the things that his father David had dedicated, and stored the silver, the gold, and all the vessels in the treasuries of the house of God.

² Then Solomon assembled the elders of Israel and all the heads of the tribes, the leaders of the ancestral houses of the people of Israel, in Jerusalem, to bring up the ark of the covenant of the LORD out of the city of David, which is Zion. ³ And all the Israelites assembled before the king at the festival that is in the seventh month. ⁴ And all the elders of Israel came, and the Levites carried the ark. ⁵ So they brought up the ark, the tent of meeting, and all the holy vessels that were in the tent; the priests and the Levites brought them up. ⁶ King Solomon and all the congregation of Israel, who had assembled before him, were before the ark, sacrificing so many sheep and oxen that they could not be numbered or counted. ⁷ Then the priests brought the ark of the covenant of the LORD to its place, in the inner sanctuary of the house, in the most holy place, underneath the wings of the cherubim. ⁸ For the cherubim spread out their wings over the place of the ark, so that the cherubim made a covering above the ark and its poles. ⁹ The poles were so long that the ends of the poles were seen from the holy place in front of the inner sanctuary; but they could not be seen from outside; they are there to this day. ¹⁰ There was nothing in the ark except the two tablets that Moses put there at Horeb, where the LORD made a covenantᵃ with the people of Israel after they came out of Egypt.

¹¹ Now when the priests came out of the holy place (for all the priests who were

ᵃ Heb lacks a covenant

court was for laity, at least on some occasions (1 Chr 28.12; 2 Chr 7.7; 29.16; Neh 8.16). See also Ezekiel's restored temple (Ezek 41.15; 42.7–14; 44.19; 45.19; 46.1). **11:** *Huram,* see 2.13–16n. The *pots, the shovels, and the basins* were employed in sacrificial rituals (Ex 27.3; 1 Kings 7.40). **17:** *Succoth and Zeredah* (Zarethan in 1 Kings 7.46) were towns situated east of the Jordan River. **19:** *Bread of the Presence,* see Ex 25.30; Lev 24.5–9.

5.1–14: The ark and the tent of meeting ascend into the Temple. These verses, except vv. 11b–13a, are largely drawn from 1 Kings 8.1–13. The incorporation of both the tabernacle and the ark into the Temple means that both of these older religious institutions find their fulfillment in the Jerusalem sanctuary. Like the authors of Deuteronomy (ch 12) and the Deuteronomistic History (Joshua–2 Kings), the Chronicler commends the centralization of Yahwistic worship and the abolition of all other sanctuaries. Sacrifices are to be carried out only at the Jerusalem Temple and prayers are to be offered at or toward this site (5.5–6.42), making the Temple the focal point of national life. **2:** On the importance of assemblies in Chronicles, see 1.2–13n. **4:** That the Levites carry the ark conforms to David's instructions (1 Chr 15.2) and Deuteronomic law (Deut 10.8). In 1 Kings 8.3, the

present had sanctified themselves, without regard to their divisions), [12] all the levitical singers, Asaph, Heman, and Jeduthun, their sons and kindred, arrayed in fine linen, with cymbals, harps, and lyres, stood east of the altar with one hundred twenty priests who were trumpeters. [13] It was the duty of the trumpeters and singers to make themselves heard in unison in praise and thanksgiving to the Lord, and when the song was raised, with trumpets and cymbals and other musical instruments, in praise to the Lord,

"For he is good,

for his steadfast love endures forever,"
the house, the house of the Lord, was filled with a cloud, [14] so that the priests could not stand to minister because of the cloud; for the glory of the Lord filled the house of God.

6 Then Solomon said, "The Lord has said that he would reside in thick darkness. [2] I have built you an exalted house, a place for you to reside in forever."

[3] Then the king turned around and blessed all the assembly of Israel, while all the assembly of Israel stood. [4] And he said, "Blessed be the Lord, the God of Israel, who with his hand has fulfilled what he promised with his mouth to my father David, saying, [5] 'Since the day that I brought my people out of the land of Egypt, I have not chosen a city from any of the tribes of Israel in which to build a house, so that my name might be there, and I chose no one as ruler over my people Israel; [6] but I have chosen Jerusalem in order that my name may be there, and I have chosen

David to be over my people Israel.' [7] My father David had it in mind to build a house for the name of the Lord, the God of Israel. [8] But the Lord said to my father David, 'You did well to consider building a house for my name; [9] nevertheless you shall not build the house, but your son who shall be born to you shall build the house for my name.' [10] Now the Lord has fulfilled his promise that he made; for I have succeeded my father David, and sit on the throne of Israel, as the Lord promised, and have built the house for the name of the Lord, the God of Israel. [11] There I have set the ark, in which is the covenant of the Lord that he made with the people of Israel."

[12] Then Solomon[a] stood before the altar of the Lord in the presence of the whole assembly of Israel, and spread out his hands. [13] Solomon had made a bronze platform five cubits long, five cubits wide, and three cubits high, and had set it in the court; and he stood on it. Then he knelt on his knees in the presence of the whole assembly of Israel, and spread out his hands toward heaven. [14] He said, "O Lord, God of Israel, there is no God like you, in heaven or on earth, keeping covenant in steadfast love with your servants who walk before you with all their heart— [15] you who have kept for your servant, my father David, what you promised to him. Indeed, you promised with your mouth and this day have fulfilled with your hand. [16] Therefore, O Lord, God of Israel, keep for your servant, my father David, that which you promised

---

[a] Heb *he*

"priests" do so. **10**: *Two tablets,* see Deut 10.1–5. *Horeb* is another name for Sinai. **11–13**: The Chronicler's addition to the Kings narrative points out that David's levitical and priestly arrangements (1 Chr 15–16; 25–26) were broadly implemented. *Asaph, Heman, and Jeduthun,* see 1 Chr 6.33n.,44n. **13**: For the hymnic excerpt, see 7.3n. *Cloud,* see 1 Kings 8.10–11n.

6.1–42: Solomon's blessing and Temple dedication prayer. With the exception of vv. 13 and 41–42, this entire chapter is reproduced, with some significant modifications, from the author's version of 1 Kings 8.12–52. Solomon's public speeches situate the Temple's construction in Israel's national life—past, present, and future. **4–11**: In his blessing, Solomon praises God that a number of the promises to David (1 Chr 17.1–15) have been fulfilled. **12–40**: The pattern of divine fidelity recounted in Solomon's blessing becomes the occasion for Solomon to request that other divine promises be realized (vv. 14–17). The heart of the prayer of dedication (vv. 22–40) consists of seven petitions detailing a variety of predicaments in which the nation may find itself, including defeat by the enemy (vv. 24–25), drought (vv. 26–27), open pitched battles (vv. 34–35), and even exile (vv. 36–39). In each case Solomon prays that God might listen from his heavenly dwelling and be attentive to the prayers of his people. **13**: The *bronze platform* is found only here. **16**: *My law* (Heb "torah"), replacing "before me" of 1 Kings 8.25. This small change likely reflects the new importance of the Torah-book in the postexilic commu-

him, saying, 'There shall never fail you a successor before me to sit on the throne of Israel, if only your children keep to their way, to walk in my law as you have walked before me.' [17] Therefore, O LORD, God of Israel, let your word be confirmed, which you promised to your servant David.

[18] "But will God indeed reside with mortals on earth? Even heaven and the highest heaven cannot contain you, how much less this house that I have built! [19] Regard your servant's prayer and his plea, O LORD my God, heeding the cry and the prayer that your servant prays to you. [20] May your eyes be open day and night toward this house, the place where you promised to set your name, and may you heed the prayer that your servant prays toward this place. [21] And hear the plea of your servant and of your people Israel, when they pray toward this place; may you hear from heaven your dwelling place; hear and forgive.

[22] "If someone sins against another and is required to take an oath and comes and swears before your altar in this house, [23] may you hear from heaven, and act, and judge your servants, repaying the guilty by bringing their conduct on their own head, and vindicating those who are in the right by rewarding them in accordance with their righteousness.

[24] "When your people Israel, having sinned against you, are defeated before an enemy but turn again to you, confess your name, pray and plead with you in this house, [25] may you hear from heaven, and forgive the sin of your people Israel, and bring them again to the land that you gave to them and to their ancestors.

[26] "When heaven is shut up and there is no rain because they have sinned against you, and then they pray toward this place, confess your name, and turn from their sin, because you punish them, [27] may you hear in heaven, forgive the sin of your servants, your people Israel, when you teach them the good way in which they should walk; and send down rain upon your land, which you have given to your people as an inheritance.

[28] "If there is famine in the land, if there is plague, blight, mildew, locust, or caterpillar; if their enemies besiege them in any of the settlements of the lands; whatever suffering, whatever sickness there is; [29] whatever prayer, whatever plea from any individual or from all your people Israel, all knowing their own suffering and their own sorrows so that they stretch out their hands toward this house; [30] may you hear from heaven, your dwelling place, forgive, and render to all whose heart you know, according to all their ways, for only you know the human heart. [31] Thus may they fear you and walk in your ways all the days that they live in the land that you gave to our ancestors.

[32] "Likewise when foreigners, who are not of your people Israel, come from a distant land because of your great name, and your mighty hand, and your outstretched arm, when they come and pray toward this house, [33] may you hear from heaven your dwelling place, and do whatever the foreigners ask of you, in order that all the peoples of the earth may know your name and fear you, as do your people Israel, and that they may know that your name has been invoked on this house that I have built.

[34] "If your people go out to battle against their enemies, by whatever way you shall send them, and they pray to you toward this city that you have chosen and the house that I have built for your name, [35] then hear from heaven their prayer and their plea, and maintain their cause.

[36] "If they sin against you—for there is no one who does not sin—and you are angry with them and give them to an enemy, so that they are carried away captive to a land far or near; [37] then if they come to their senses in the land to which they have been taken captive, and repent, and plead with you in the land of their captivity, saying, 'We have sinned, and have done wrong; we have acted wickedly'; [38] if they repent with all their heart and soul in the land of their captivity, to which they were taken captive, and pray toward their land, which you gave to their ancestors, the city that you have chosen, and the house that I have built for your name, [39] then hear from heaven your dwelling place their prayer and their pleas, maintain their cause and forgive your people who have sinned against you. [40] Now, O my God, let your eyes be open and your ears attentive to prayer from this place.

41 "Now rise up, O LORD God, and go to
  your resting place,
  you and the ark of your might.
Let your priests, O LORD God, be clothed
  with salvation,
  and let your faithful rejoice in your
  goodness.
42 O LORD God, do not reject your anointed
  one.
  Remember your steadfast love for your
  servant David."

7 When Solomon had ended his prayer, fire
came down from heaven and consumed
the burnt offering and the sacrifices; and
the glory of the LORD filled the temple. 2 The
priests could not enter the house of the
LORD, because the glory of the LORD filled the
LORD's house. 3 When all the people of Israel
saw the fire come down and the glory of the
LORD on the temple, they bowed down on
the pavement with their faces to the ground,
and worshiped and gave thanks to the LORD,
saying,
  "For he is good,
    for his steadfast love endures forever."
4 Then the king and all the people offered sacrifice before the LORD. 5 King Solomon offered
as a sacrifice twenty-two thousand oxen and
one hundred twenty thousand sheep. So the
king and all the people dedicated the house
of God. 6 The priests stood at their posts; the
Levites also, with the instruments for music
to the LORD that King David had made for giving thanks to the LORD—for his steadfast love
endures forever—whenever David offered

praises by their ministry. Opposite them
the priests sounded trumpets; and all Israel
stood.
7 Solomon consecrated the middle of the
court that was in front of the house of the
LORD; for there he offered the burnt offerings and the fat of the offerings of well-being
because the bronze altar Solomon had made
could not hold the burnt offering and the
grain offering and the fat parts.
8 At that time Solomon held the festival
for seven days, and all Israel with him, a very
great congregation, from Lebo-hamath to the
Wadi of Egypt. 9 On the eighth day they held
a solemn assembly; for they had observed
the dedication of the altar seven days and
the festival seven days. 10 On the twenty-third
day of the seventh month he sent the people
away to their homes, joyful and in good
spirits because of the goodness that the LORD
had shown to David and to Solomon and to
his people Israel.
11 Thus Solomon finished the house of the
LORD and the king's house; all that Solomon
had planned to do in the house of the LORD
and in his own house he successfully accomplished.
12 Then the LORD appeared to Solomon
in the night and said to him: "I have heard
your prayer, and have chosen this place for
myself as a house of sacrifice. 13 When I shut
up the heavens so that there is no rain, or
command the locust to devour the land, or
send pestilence among my people, 14 if my
people who are called by my name humble

nity. **41–42:** Solomon's prayer of 1 Kings 8 is given a new conclusion from Ps 132.8–10.

7.1–22: Divine consecration, national thanksgiving, and a warning. Both the Deuteronomist (1 Kings 9.1–9) and the Chronicler mention a divine response to Solomon's prayer (vv. 16–22), but the Chronicler also includes other material affirming both the Temple (vv. 1–3,11) and King Solomon's petitions (vv. 13–15). The divine response to Solomon therefore explicitly validates Jerusalem as the site of Israel's central sanctuary. **1:** The divine consecration of *the burnt offering and the sacrifices* by *fire*, not found in 1 Kings 8–9, dramatically legitimates the Jerusalem Temple as an enduring fixture of Israelite life (Lev 9.24; 1 Kings 18.36–39; 1 Chr 21.26). **3:** The people's liturgical refrain—*"For he is good, for his steadfast love endures forever"*—also found in Ps 136 (and 1 Chr 16.34; 2 Chr 5.13; 7.6; 20.21; Ezra 3.11), was likely a significant element of the postexilic Temple liturgy. **7–8:** Taken in part from 1 Kings 8.65–66. *From Lebo-hamath to the Wadi of Egypt,* the northern and southern limits of Solomon's rule. *Lebo-hamath* is probably in the southern Orontes valley in Lebanon. *The Wadi of Egypt,* either the Wadi Besor or the Wadi el-Arish, both south of Gaza. See map on p. 592 HB. **9–10:** The festivities last far longer than in 1 Kings 8.66, in which the Priestly legislation is not a consideration (cf. Lev 23.36; Num 29.35–38; Neh 8.18). **13–14:** The Temple is approved as an appropriate means of divine-human communications. Should king or people find themselves in duress, they may respond in four ways: *humble themselves, pray, seek my face, and turn from their wicked ways.* For his part, the LORD will *hear from heaven, and will forgive their sin and heal their land*

Chs 8–9. The kingdom of Solomon.

themselves, pray, seek my face, and turn from their wicked ways, then I will hear from heaven, and will forgive their sin and heal their land. [15] Now my eyes will be open and my ears attentive to the prayer that is made in this place. [16] For now I have chosen and consecrated this house so that my name may be there forever; my eyes and my heart will be there for all time. [17] As for you, if you walk before me, as your father David walked, doing according to all that I have commanded you and keeping my statutes and my ordinances, [18] then I will establish your royal throne, as I made covenant with your father David saying, 'You shall never lack a successor to rule over Israel.'

[19] "But if you[a] turn aside and forsake my statutes and my commandments that I have set before you, and go and serve other gods and worship them, [20] then I will pluck you[b] up from the land that I have given you;[b] and this house, which I have consecrated for my name, I will cast out of my sight, and will make it a proverb and a byword among all peoples. [21] And regarding this house, now exalted, everyone passing by will be astonished, and say, 'Why has the LORD done such a thing to this land and to this house?' [22] Then they will say, 'Because they abandoned the LORD the God of their ancestors who brought them out of the land of Egypt, and they adopted other gods, and worshiped them and served them; therefore he has brought all this calamity upon them.'"

8 At the end of twenty years, during which Solomon had built the house of the LORD and his own house, [2] Solomon rebuilt the cit-

ies that Huram had given to him, and settled the people of Israel in them.

[3] Solomon went to Hamath-zobah, and captured it. [4] He built Tadmor in the wilderness and all the storage towns that he built in Hamath. [5] He also built Upper Beth-horon and Lower Beth-horon, fortified cities, with walls, gates, and bars, [6] and Baalath, as well as all Solomon's storage towns, and all the towns for his chariots, the towns for his cavalry, and whatever Solomon desired to build, in Jerusalem, in Lebanon, and in all the land of his dominion. [7] All the people who were left of the Hittites, the Amorites, the Perizzites, the Hivites, and the Jebusites, who were not of Israel, [8] from their descendants who were still left in the land, whom the people of Israel had not destroyed—these Solomon conscripted for forced labor, as is still the case today. [9] But of the people of Israel Solomon made no slaves for his work; they were soldiers, and his officers, the commanders of his chariotry and cavalry. [10] These were the chief officers of King Solomon, two hundred fifty of them, who exercised authority over the people.

[11] Solomon brought Pharaoh's daughter from the city of David to the house that he had built for her, for he said, "My wife shall not live in the house of King David of Israel, for the places to which the ark of the LORD has come are holy."

a   The word *you* in this verse is plural
b   Heb *them*

(v. 14). **19–22**: Israel's possession of the land, as well as the longevity of the Temple itself, are keyed to national obedience (cf. 1 Chr 28.7).

8.1–18: Solomon the successful king. Following the Temple's dedication, Solomon advances his program of public works (vv. 3–6,11), continues his patronage of the nation's worship (vv. 12–15), employs the tribute from a foreign king to good advantage (v. 2; cf. 1 Kings 9.10–14), and engages in international trade (vv. 17–18). **2**: This reflects a remarkable reversal of the tradition recorded in 1 Kings 9.11–13. **3**: An otherwise unattested campaign. Although in Chronicles Solomon (Heb "shelomoh") is a man of peace ("shalom"; 1 Chr 22.9), he here expands his kingdom through military means. No place named *Hamath-zobah* is known; elsewhere Hamath and Zobah are separate kingdoms in Syria. **4**: Solomon's control reaches to Syria (see map on p. 626 HB). The system of twelve prefects and the districts they governed (1 Kings 4.7–19) is not found in Chronicles, possibly because these districts did not follow traditional tribal boundaries. *Tadmor* is later Palmyra, an important oasis in the desert ca. 225 km (140 mi) northeast of Damascus. Some Hebrew texts of 1 Kings 9.18 read "Tamar," a small place in Judah, while others read "Tadmor," as in Chronicles. **7–10**: Largely derived from 1 Kings 9.20–23. **7**: These are some of the traditional inhabitants of the land of Canaan; see Gen 15.20; Deut 20.17. **11**: Compare 1 Kings 3.1;

[12] Then Solomon offered up burnt offerings to the LORD on the altar of the LORD that he had built in front of the vestibule, [13] as the duty of each day required, offering according to the commandment of Moses for the sabbaths, the new moons, and the three annual festivals—the festival of unleavened bread, the festival of weeks, and the festival of booths. [14] According to the ordinance of his father David, he appointed the divisions of the priests for their service, and the Levites for their offices of praise and ministry alongside the priests as the duty of each day required, and the gatekeepers in their divisions for the several gates; for so David the man of God had commanded. [15] They did not turn away from what the king had commanded the priests and Levites regarding anything at all, or regarding the treasuries.

[16] Thus all the work of Solomon was accomplished from[a] the day the foundation of the house of the LORD was laid until the house of the LORD was finished completely.

[17] Then Solomon went to Ezion-geber and Eloth on the shore of the sea, in the land of Edom. [18] Huram sent him, in the care of his servants, ships and servants familiar with the sea. They went to Ophir, together with the servants of Solomon, and imported from there four hundred fifty talents of gold and brought it to King Solomon.

9 When the queen of Sheba heard of the fame of Solomon, she came to Jerusalem to test him with hard questions, having a very great retinue and camels bearing spices and very much gold and precious stones. When she came to Solomon, she discussed with him all that was on her mind. [2] Solomon answered all her questions; there was nothing hidden from Solomon that he could not explain to her. [3] When the queen of Sheba had observed the wisdom of Solomon, the house that he had built, [4] the food of his table, the seating of his officials, and the attendance of his servants, and their clothing, his valets, and their clothing, and his burnt offerings[b] that he offered at the house of the LORD, there was no more spirit left in her.

[5] So she said to the king, "The report was true that I heard in my own land of your accomplishments and of your wisdom, [6] but I did not believe the[c] reports until I came and my own eyes saw it. Not even half of the greatness of your wisdom had been told to me; you far surpass the report that I had heard. [7] Happy are your people! Happy are these your servants, who continually attend you and hear your wisdom! [8] Blessed be the LORD your God, who has delighted in you and set you on his throne as king for the LORD your God. Because your God loved Israel and would establish them forever, he has made you king over them, that you may execute justice and righteousness." [9] Then she gave the king one hundred twenty talents of gold, a very great quantity of spices, and precious stones: there were no spices such as those that the queen of Sheba gave to King Solomon.

[10] Moreover the servants of Huram and the servants of Solomon who brought gold from

a Gk Syr Vg: Heb *to*
b Gk Syr Vg 1 Kings 10.5: Heb *ascent*
c Heb *their*

7.8; 9.24; Ezek 44.9. **12–15:** Solomon keeps the commandments of Moses in his offerings and keeps all of the ordinances of his father David in his appointments of priests and Levites (1 Chr 22.7–16; 28.6–10,20–21). **17–18:** Largely taken from 1 Kings 9.26–28. **17:** *Ezion-geber* and *Eloth* (Eliat) are at the northern tip of the west arm of *the sea* (the Red Sea). **18:** *Ophir*, see 1 Chr 29.4n.

9.1–31: Solomon in all of his glory. The earlier divine promise of unmatched wealth and wisdom (1.11–12) is realized. Solomon receives unprecedented international recognition (vv. 1–8,23–24), continues his endowments of palace and Temple (vv. 15–20), enjoys unsurpassed riches (vv. 22,27), shares in the benefits of international trade (vv. 10–11,13–14,21,28), and presides over a substantial kingdom (vv. 25–26). In Chronicles, the era of David and Solomon (the United Monarchy) is the epitome in the history of Israel, the model of unity and orthodoxy by which both earlier and later leaders, officials, and people will be judged (7.10; 11.17; 30.26; 35.3–4). **1–12:** Taken from 1 Kings 10.1–13. **1:** *Sheba* is in Arabia. **4:** *No more spirit left,* that is, she was breathless. **8:** Solomon sits on *his throne,* that is, the LORD's throne. The Chronicler draws a close link between God's kingdom, kingship, and throne and those of the two major kings of the United Monarchy—David and Solomon, who discharge their responsibilities well as the LORD's appointees (1 Chr 17.14; 28.5; 29.11; 2 Chr 13.8). **9:** A *talent*

Ophir brought algum wood and precious stones. [11] From the algum wood, the king made steps[a] for the house of the LORD and for the king's house, lyres also and harps for the singers; there never was seen the like of them before in the land of Judah.

[12] Meanwhile King Solomon granted the queen of Sheba every desire that she expressed, well beyond what she had brought to the king. Then she returned to her own land, with her servants.

[13] The weight of gold that came to Solomon in one year was six hundred sixty-six talents of gold, [14] besides that which the traders and merchants brought; and all the kings of Arabia and the governors of the land brought gold and silver to Solomon. [15] King Solomon made two hundred large shields of beaten gold; six hundred shekels of beaten gold went into each large shield. [16] He made three hundred shields of beaten gold; three hundred shekels of gold went into each shield; and the king put them in the House of the Forest of Lebanon. [17] The king also made a great ivory throne, and overlaid it with pure gold. [18] The throne had six steps and a footstool of gold, which were attached to the throne, and on each side of the seat were arm rests and two lions standing beside the arm rests, [19] while twelve lions were standing, one on each end of a step on the six steps. The like of it was never made in any kingdom.

[20] All King Solomon's drinking vessels were of gold, and all the vessels of the House of the Forest of Lebanon were of pure gold; silver was not considered as anything in the days of Solomon. [21] For the king's ships went to Tarshish with the servants of Huram; once every three years the ships of Tarshish used to come bringing gold, silver, ivory, apes, and peacocks.[b]

[22] Thus King Solomon excelled all the kings of the earth in riches and in wisdom. [23] All the kings of the earth sought the presence of Solomon to hear his wisdom, which God had put into his mind. [24] Every one of them brought a present, objects of silver and gold, garments, weaponry, spices, horses, and mules, so much year by year. [25] Solomon had four thousand stalls for horses and chariots, and twelve thousand horses, which he stationed in the chariot cities and with the king in Jerusalem. [26] He ruled over all the kings from the Euphrates to the land of the Philistines, and to the border of Egypt. [27] The king made silver as common in Jerusalem as stone, and cedar as plentiful as the sycamore of the Shephelah. [28] Horses were imported for Solomon from Egypt and from all lands.

[29] Now the rest of the acts of Solomon, from first to last, are they not written in the

[a] Gk Vg: Meaning of Heb uncertain
[b] Or baboons

weighed about 75 lb (34 kg). **11:** *Algum,* see 2.8n. **13–28:** Largely drawn from 1 Kings 10.14–28a. **15:** *Large shields,* these ornamental objects of great value were later taken by King Shishak of Egypt during his campaign through parts of Canaan (12.9–11). **16:** *The House of the Forest of Lebanon,* perhaps named because of the extensive use of Lebanon cedar inside. This complex, which was probably located south of the Temple, actually contained five buildings. Being most interested in the Temple, the Chronicler does not elaborate on the description and functions of this building (cf. 1 Kings 7.1–12). **17:** *Great ivory throne,* both Solomon's official seat and a symbol of his prestige, wealth, and power (cf. Ex 11.5; 2 Sam 3.10). **18:** *Footstool,* another royal symbol (cf. 1 Kings 10.18–20). The term is also used to represent defeated enemies (Ps 110.1), the ark (1 Chr 28.2), Zion (Lam 2.1), and the earth itself (Isa 66.1). **21:** *Tarshish,* probably the city of Tarsus on the southern coast of Turkey, or perhaps Tartessus in southern Spain. **25–29:** Cf. 1.14–16n. Verse 26 is drawn from 1 Kings 4.21; Solomon is the dominant ruler of the region from northern Syria to the border of Egypt (cf. 7.8). **29:** *Nathan,* see 1 Chr 17.1–15; *Ahijah,* see 1 Kings 11.29–39; *Iddo* is not known apart from notices such as this (see 12.15; 13.22). **29–31:** Solomon's reign ends as it began with a unified nation under an exemplary king. Israel is unhampered by internal factions or strife. The nation enjoys unparalleled glory. Solomon's tenure is untainted by sin or misadventure. Any information found in Kings that would potentially tarnish Solomon's reputation has been omitted (1 Kings 9.11–16; 11.1–38). Solomon is not blamed for the later division of the kingdom (cf. 1 Kings 11.1–13,31–38). Because the Chronicler heightens the great benefit of Davidic-Solomonic leadership for the people, those who might deviate from this norm (10.3) will be suspect. It is unclear if the sources mentioned in v. 29 and elsewhere are nonbiblical sources, refer to other sections of the Bible, or never existed. Some scholars believe that they are cited here as a way of justi-

Chs 10–12: The divided monarchy. The dashed line shows the approximate boundaries between Israel, Judah, and Philistia.

history of the prophet Nathan, and in the prophecy of Ahijah the Shilonite, and in the visions of the seer Iddo concerning Jeroboam son of Nebat? [30] Solomon reigned in Jerusalem over all Israel forty years. [31] Solomon slept with his ancestors and was buried in the city of his father David; and his son Rehoboam succeeded him.

10 Rehoboam went to Shechem, for all Israel had come to Shechem to make him king. [2] When Jeroboam son of Nebat heard of it (for he was in Egypt, where he

fying the Chronicler's history, which differs in such significant ways from Kings. In any case, it is a credit to Solomon that his reign is the subject of no less than three prophetic works. This is one indication of the high esteem in which prophets and writings associated with prophets were held in the postexilic period (cf. 1 Chr 29.29n.).

10.1–18: The difficult beginning to Rehoboam's reign (928–911 BCE). Compared with 1 Kings 12.1–24; 14.21–31, Chronicles almost doubles the amount of coverage devoted to *Rehoboam* and presents a much more complex narration of his reign (10.1–12.16). Rehoboam's accession is not characterized by the unanimity that both David (1 Chr 11) and Solomon (2 Chr 1) enjoyed. 1: Rehoboam ascends to the throne and immediately finds himself thrust into a national assembly at *Shechem* bargaining for the future of his nation with disaffected representatives of the northern tribes (cf. 1 Kings 12.1–24). *Shechem,* in the later Northern Kingdom, was located in the hill country of Ephraim between Mounts Ebal and Gerizim. The national convocation was likely held here because Shechem was an important and historic town in ancient Israel (Josh 8.30–35; 20.7; 17.7; 21.21; 24.1–28; 1 Kings

had fled from King Solomon), then Jeroboam returned from Egypt. [3] They sent and called him; and Jeroboam and all Israel came and said to Rehoboam, [4] "Your father made our yoke heavy. Now therefore lighten the hard service of your father and his heavy yoke that he placed on us, and we will serve you." [5] He said to them, "Come to me again in three days." So the people went away.

[6] Then King Rehoboam took counsel with the older men who had attended his father Solomon while he was still alive, saying, "How do you advise me to answer this people?" [7] They answered him, "If you will be kind to this people and please them, and speak good words to them, then they will be your servants forever." [8] But he rejected the advice that the older men gave him, and consulted the young men who had grown up with him and now attended him. [9] He said to them, "What do you advise that we answer this people who have said to me, 'Lighten the yoke that your father put on us'?" [10] The young men who had grown up with him said to him, "Thus should you speak to the people who said to you, 'Your father made our yoke heavy, but you must lighten it for us'; tell them, 'My little finger is thicker than my father's loins. [11] Now, whereas my father laid on you a heavy yoke, I will add to your yoke. My father disciplined you with whips, but I will discipline you with scorpions.'"

[12] So Jeroboam and all the people came to Rehoboam the third day, as the king had said, "Come to me again the third day." [13] The king answered them harshly. King Rehoboam rejected the advice of the older men; [14] he spoke to them in accordance with the advice of the young men, "My father made your yoke heavy, but I will add to it; my father disciplined you with whips, but I will discipline you with scorpions." [15] So the king did not listen to the people, because it was a turn of affairs brought about by God so that the LORD might fulfill his word, which he had spoken by Ahijah the Shilonite to Jeroboam son of Nebat.

[16] When all Israel saw that the king would not listen to them, the people answered the king,

"What share do we have in David?
    We have no inheritance in the son of Jesse.
Each of you to your tents, O Israel!
    Look now to your own house, O David."

So all Israel departed to their tents. [17] But Rehoboam reigned over the people of Israel who were living in the cities of Judah. [18] When King Rehoboam sent Hadoram, who was taskmaster over the forced labor, the people of Israel stoned him to death. King Rehoboam hurriedly mounted his chariot to flee to Jerusalem. [19] So Israel has been in rebellion against the house of David to this day.

11 When Rehoboam came to Jerusalem, he assembled one hundred eighty thousand chosen troops of the house of Judah and Benjamin to fight against Israel, to restore the kingdom to Rehoboam. [2] But the word of the LORD came to Shemaiah the man of God: [3] Say to King Rehoboam of Judah, son of Solomon, and to all Israel in Judah and Benjamin, [4] "Thus says the LORD: You shall not go up or

12.1–17; 1 Chr 6.52; 7.28). **2–3:** Jeroboam, the head of the northern tribes (1 Kings 11.26–43), is both present and an active protagonist in the proceedings (also v. 12). In Chronicles both Jeroboam and Rehoboam are personally responsible for the events of the secession (13.4–12). **15:** *His word . . . by Ahijah,* see 1 Kings 11.29–39. Ultimately, the division is a *turn of affairs* that could not have occurred without divine assent. This verse assumes familiarity on the part of the reader with 1 Kings 11.29–39, even though the Chronicler, by means of omissions, allusions, rearrangements, and additions, creates his own distinctive version of the division. **16:** In Chronicles, the northern Israelites' cry of secession (1 Kings 12.16) constitutes an abrupt about-face from the allegiance they had displayed since early in David's reign (1 Chr 12.1–40). Because the Chronicler views both the kingship and the worship of the northern realm as illegitimate, he—unlike the author of Kings—does not recount the independent history of the Northern Kingdom.

11.1–23: Rehoboam's recovery. The Chronicler enumerates in great detail the fidelity he ascribes to the first three years of Rehoboam's reign (11.17). The obedience before a prophet (11.1–4) and the fortification of various cities (vv. 5–12) are two steps in this process of renewal. **1–4:** Drawn from 1 Kings 12.21–24. **3:** The Chronicler does not restrict the use of *Israel* strictly to the northern tribes (cf. 2 Sam 2.9; 1 Kings 12.18,20). He also regularly

fight against your kindred. Let everyone return home, for this thing is from me." So they heeded the word of the LORD and turned back from the expedition against Jeroboam.

[5] Rehoboam resided in Jerusalem, and he built cities for defense in Judah. [6] He built up Bethlehem, Etam, Tekoa, [7] Beth-zur, Soco, Adullam, [8] Gath, Mareshah, Ziph, [9] Adoraim, Lachish, Azekah, [10] Zorah, Aijalon, and Hebron, fortified cities that are in Judah and in Benjamin. [11] He made the fortresses strong, and put commanders in them, and stores of food, oil, and wine. [12] He also put large shields and spears in all the cities, and made them very strong. So he held Judah and Benjamin.

[13] The priests and the Levites who were in all Israel presented themselves to him from all their territories. [14] The Levites had left their common lands and their holdings and had come to Judah and Jerusalem, because Jeroboam and his sons had prevented them from serving as priests of the LORD, [15] and had appointed his own priests for the high places, and for the goat-demons, and for the calves that he had made. [16] Those who had set their hearts to seek the LORD God of Israel came after them from all the tribes of Israel to Jerusalem to sacrifice to the LORD, the God of their ancestors. [17] They strengthened the kingdom of Judah, and for three years they made Rehoboam son of Solomon secure, for they walked for three years in the way of David and Solomon.

[18] Rehoboam took as his wife Mahalath daughter of Jerimoth son of David, and of Abihail daughter of Eliab son of Jesse. [19] She bore him sons: Jeush, Shemariah, and Zaham. [20] After her he took Maacah daughter of Absalom, who bore him Abijah, Attai, Ziza, and Shelomith. [21] Rehoboam loved Maacah daughter of Absalom more than all his other wives and concubines (he took eighteen wives and sixty concubines, and became the father of twenty-eight sons and sixty daughters). [22] Rehoboam appointed Abijah son of Maacah as chief prince among his brothers, for he intended to make him king. [23] He dealt wisely, and distributed some of his sons through all the districts of Judah and Benjamin, in all the fortified cities; he gave them abundant provisions, and found many wives for them.

12 When the rule of Rehoboam was established and he grew strong, he abandoned the law of the LORD, he and all Israel with him. [2] In the fifth year of King Rehoboam, because they had been unfaithful to the LORD, King Shishak of Egypt came up against Jerusalem [3] with twelve hundred chariots and sixty thousand cavalry. A countless army came with him from Egypt—Libyans, Sukkiim, and Ethiopians.[a] [4] He took the fortified cities of Judah and came as far as Jerusalem. [5] Then the prophet Shemaiah came to Rehoboam and to the officers of Judah, who had gathered at Jerusalem because of Shishak, and said to them, "Thus says the LORD: You abandoned me, so I have abandoned you to the hand of Shishak." [6] Then the officers of Israel and the king humbled themselves and

[a] Or *Nubians*; Heb *Cushites*

uses *Israel* to refer to those Israelites who reside in *Judah and Benjamin*. 5–12: These verses likely draw upon an unknown source. See map on p. 630 HB. 13–17: The wholesale exodus of priests and Levites from Israel to Judah simultaneously strengthens Judah and indicts Jeroboam, who *prevented them from serving as priests of the LORD*. On Jeroboam's religious innovations, see 1 Kings 12.28; 13.33; 14.8–9. 15: *Goat-demons*, an obscure and polemical reference not found in the source text depicting Jeroboam's religious innovations (1 Kings 12.28). Worship of goat-demons is outlawed in Priestly legislation (Lev 17.7). 18–21: Large families signify stature in Chronicles (1 Chr 14.3; 2 Chr 11.18–23; 13.21; 14.3–7; cf. Gen 1.28). 22–23: Like his grandfather David, Rehoboam appoints his sons to positions in his administration (1 Chr 18.17).

12.1–16: National decline and a reprieve. After a short recovery (11.1–23), Rehoboam and Judah abandon *the law of the LORD* and therefore Egypt invades (cf. 1 Kings 14.25). The outlines of the Egyptian invasion are found in 1 Kings 14.25–28, but the Chronicler has elaborated them significantly, especially in his addition of v. 1, which suggests that the invasion was punishment for apostasy. 2: *Shishak* (Shoshenq I) ruled Egypt 945–924 BCE. 3: *Sukkiim*, unknown. 5: The prophet's speech, like many other biblical texts, invokes the principle of measure for measure: Those who abandon God will be abandoned by God. 6–8: Because of their repentance (cf. 11.1–4), Rehoboam and the people stave off complete disaster. Hence, Rehoboam is the first of many kings to benefit

said, "The LORD is in the right." [7] When the LORD saw that they humbled themselves, the word of the LORD came to Shemaiah, saying: "They have humbled themselves; I will not destroy them, but I will grant them some deliverance, and my wrath shall not be poured out on Jerusalem by the hand of Shishak. [8] Nevertheless they shall be his servants, so that they may know the difference between serving me and serving the kingdoms of other lands."

[9] So King Shishak of Egypt came up against Jerusalem; he took away the treasures of the house of the LORD and the treasures of the king's house; he took everything. He also took away the shields of gold that Solomon had made; [10] but King Rehoboam made in place of them shields of bronze, and committed them to the hands of the officers of the guard, who kept the door of the king's house. [11] Whenever the king went into the house of the LORD, the guard would come along bearing them, and would then bring them back to the guardroom. [12] Because he humbled himself the wrath of the LORD turned from him, so as not to destroy them completely; moreover, conditions were good in Judah.

[13] So King Rehoboam established himself in Jerusalem and reigned. Rehoboam was forty-one years old when he began to reign; he reigned seventeen years in Jerusalem, the city that the LORD had chosen out of all the tribes of Israel to put his name there. His mother's name was Naamah the Ammonite. [14] He did evil, for he did not set his heart to seek the LORD.

[15] Now the acts of Rehoboam, from first to last, are they not written in the records of the prophet Shemaiah and of the seer Iddo, recorded by genealogy? There were continual wars between Rehoboam and Jeroboam. [16] Rehoboam slept with his ancestors and was buried in the city of David; and his son Abijah succeeded him.

13 In the eighteenth year of King Jeroboam, Abijah began to reign over Judah. [2] He reigned for three years in Jerusalem. His mother's name was Micaiah daughter of Uriel of Gibeah.

Now there was war between Abijah and Jeroboam. [3] Abijah engaged in battle, having an army of valiant warriors, four hundred thousand picked men; and Jeroboam drew up his line of battle against him with eight hundred thousand picked mighty warriors. [4] Then Abijah stood on the slope of Mount Zemaraim that is in the hill country of Ephraim, and said, "Listen to me, Jeroboam and all Israel! [5] Do you not know that the LORD God of Israel gave the kingship over Israel forever to David and his sons by a covenant of salt? [6] Yet Jeroboam son of Nebat,

from God's promises in response to Solomon's Temple prayer (7.12–15). **13–16:** Cf. 1 Kings 14.21–24,29–31. **15:** *Iddo,* see 9.29n.

13.1–22: The successful reign of Abijah (911–908 BCE). In Chronicles, as opposed to 1 Kings 15.1–8, Abijah (called Abijam in 1 Kings) is one of Judah's better monarchs. In a war against *Jeroboam and all Israel,* he defends the standards established by David and Solomon as normative for all Israelites. Much of the chapter is an original composition of the Chronicler, elaborating on 1 Kings 15.6. The fundamental principle illustrated through this narrative is "the people of Judah prevailed, because they relied on the LORD, the God of their ancestors" (v. 8). **2:** *Micaiah,* there is a text-critical issue here. The Hebrew gives Abijah's mother a Yahwistic name (meaning "Who is like the LORD"), whereas the ancient versions name her "Maacah" in conformity with 1 Kings 15.2 and 2 Chr 11.20. **3:** Developing a theme of earlier holy-war narratives (Judg 7.2–8; 1 Sam 14.6; 17.45–47), the Chronicler here and elsewhere stresses that great numbers do not guarantee victory (14.7–14; 20.1–30; 24.24; cf. Zech 4.6). *Eight hundred thousand,* the Chronicler's numbers here and elsewhere are sometimes stupendous (e.g., 1 Chr 5.18; 23.3–5; 27.1–15; 2 Chr 14.8–9; 17.14–18; 25.5–6; 26.12–13; 28.6–8). Some scholars have thought that the Hebrew word for "thousand" refers simply to one military unit, meaning that the actual numbers involved would be far less. But it is more likely that the incredible numbers are a literary convention or scribal embellishment to mark off (what is for the Chronicler) Israel's classical past. The use of large, round numbers is also sometimes found in earlier biblical sources (e.g., 1 Kings 8.5,62–64). **5:** In speaking to *Jeroboam and all Israel* (v. 4) of *the kingship over Israel* as belonging to the Davidic dynasty, Abijah plays on the different connotations of Israel. *Covenant of salt,* the reference to "salt" indicates that the kingship that has been covenanted to David will be enduring (Lev 2.13; Num 18.19). In v. 8, the kingdom of the LORD is itself said to be in the hands of David

a servant of Solomon son of David, rose up and rebelled against his lord; [7] and certain worthless scoundrels gathered around him and defied Rehoboam son of Solomon, when Rehoboam was young and irresolute and could not withstand them.

[8] "And now you think that you can withstand the kingdom of the LORD in the hand of the sons of David, because you are a great multitude and have with you the golden calves that Jeroboam made as gods for you. [9] Have you not driven out the priests of the LORD, the descendants of Aaron, and the Levites, and made priests for yourselves like the peoples of other lands? Whoever comes to be consecrated with a young bull or seven rams becomes a priest of what are no gods. [10] But as for us, the LORD is our God, and we have not abandoned him. We have priests ministering to the LORD who are descendants of Aaron, and Levites for their service. [11] They offer to the LORD every morning and every evening burnt offerings and fragrant incense, set out the rows of bread on the table of pure gold, and care for the golden lampstand so that its lamps may burn every evening; for we keep the charge of the LORD our God, but you have abandoned him. [12] See, God is with us at our head, and his priests have their battle trumpets to sound the call to battle against you. O Israelites, do not fight against the LORD, the God of your ancestors; for you cannot succeed."

[13] Jeroboam had sent an ambush around to come on them from behind; thus his troops[a] were in front of Judah, and the ambush was behind them. [14] When Judah turned, the battle was in front of them and behind them. They cried out to the LORD, and the priests blew the trumpets. [15] Then the people of Judah raised the battle shout. And when the people of Judah shouted, God defeated Jeroboam and all Israel before Abijah and Judah. [16] The Israelites fled before Judah, and God gave them into their hands. [17] Abijah and his army defeated them with great slaughter; five hundred thousand picked men of Israel fell slain. [18] Thus the Israelites were subdued at that time, and the people of Judah prevailed, because they relied on the LORD, the God of their ancestors. [19] Abijah pursued Jeroboam, and took cities from him: Bethel with its villages and Jeshanah with its villages and Ephron[b] with its villages. [20] Jeroboam did not recover his power in the days of Abijah; the LORD struck him down, and he died. [21] But Abijah grew strong. He took fourteen wives, and became the father of twenty-two sons and sixteen daughters. [22] The rest of the acts of Abijah, his behavior and his deeds, are written in the story of the prophet Iddo.

[a] Heb *they*
[b] Another reading is *Ephrain*

and his descendants (cf. 1 Chr 17.14; 28.5; 2 Chr 9.8n). **6–7:** Disunion occurred when Jeroboam and *worthless scoundrels* exploited a young and inexperienced Rehoboam. This polemicizes against 1 Kings 11.11–13,29–38. **8–11:** Abijah's enumeration of the proper religious practices of Judah is heavily indebted to the descriptions of Temple worship during the United Monarchy (1 Chr 15–16; 23–29; 2 Chr 2–4) and the descriptions of tabernacle worship during the era of Moses (Ex 25.30–40; 29.1–9,38–42; 30.7–10; Lev 24.3–9; Num 8.2–4; 28.3–8). **19:** Judah recaptures some of the territory it presumably lost in the secession. The Chronicler commends Judean kings who exercise influence in the northern realm (15.8–9; 17.2; 30.5–12; 34.6–7,33). **20:** Here God himself struck Jeroboam *and he died;* cf. 1 Kings 14.19–20. **21:** See 11.18–21n. **22:** The Hebrew word for *story* ("midrash") can also be translated as exposition, study, or "commentary" (24.27; cf. Sir 51.23). The reference thus designates a writing or commentary of *Iddo* (rather than an annalistic account) on the early monarchy. See also 9.29n.; 12.15.

14.1–15.19: Reforms, victory, and expansion: the first period of Asa's reign (908–867 BCE). The Chronicler's treatment of Asa (14.1–16.14), almost three times longer than that of 1 Kings 15.9–24, presents two distinct phases in Asa's reign: a long thirty-four-year period of fidelity and a short seven-year period of infidelity (16.1–12). The shorter text of Kings is supplemented significantly. Kings has a pattern of piety followed by lack of trust in God. The Chronicler subsumes elements of Kings to his retribution theology, creating a pattern of piety and its reward, then impiety and its punishment. Prophetic figures play a significant role in these elaborations. **14.1:** In Chronicles *rest* from war is a sign of divine blessing (1 Chr 17.8–9; 22.9; 2 Chr 14.6; 32.22). **2–8:** At the beginning of his reign Asa takes advantage of peaceful conditions to institute religious reforms (cf. 1 Kings 15.12–15) and

14

^a So Abijah slept with his ancestors, and they buried him in the city of David. His son Asa succeeded him. In his days the land had rest for ten years. ² ^bAsa did what was good and right in the sight of the LORD his God. ³ He took away the foreign altars and the high places, broke down the pillars, hewed down the sacred poles,^c ⁴ and commanded Judah to seek the LORD, the God of their ancestors, and to keep the law and the commandment. ⁵ He also removed from all the cities of Judah the high places and the incense altars. And the kingdom had rest under him. ⁶ He built fortified cities in Judah while the land had rest. He had no war in those years, for the LORD gave him peace. ⁷ He said to Judah, "Let us build these cities, and surround them with walls and towers, gates and bars; the land is still ours because we have sought the LORD our God; we have sought him, and he has given us peace on every side." So they built and prospered. ⁸ Asa had an army of three hundred thousand from Judah, armed with large shields and spears, and two hundred eighty thousand troops from Benjamin who carried shields and drew bows; all these were mighty warriors.

⁹ Zerah the Ethiopian^d came out against them with an army of a million men and three hundred chariots, and came as far as Mareshah. ¹⁰ Asa went out to meet him, and they drew up their lines of battle in the valley of Zephathah at Mareshah. ¹¹ Asa cried to the LORD his God, "O LORD, there is no difference for you between helping the mighty and the weak. Help us, O LORD our God, for we rely on you, and in your name we have come against this multitude. O LORD, you are our God; let no mortal prevail against you." ¹² So the LORD defeated the Ethiopians^e before Asa and before Judah, and the Ethiopians^e fled. ¹³ Asa and the army with him pursued them as far as Gerar, and the Ethiopians^e fell until no one remained alive; for they were broken before the LORD and his army. The people of Judah^f carried away a great quantity of booty. ¹⁴ They defeated all the cities around Gerar, for the fear of the LORD was on them. They plundered all the cities; for there was much plunder in them. ¹⁵ They also attacked the tents of those who had livestock,^g and carried away sheep and goats in abundance, and camels. Then they returned to Jerusalem.

15

The spirit of God came upon Azariah son of Oded. ² He went out to meet Asa and said to him, "Hear me, Asa, and all Judah and Benjamin: The LORD is with you, while you are with him. If you seek him, he will be found by you, but if you abandon him, he will abandon you. ³ For a long time Israel was without the true God, and without a teaching priest, and without law; ⁴ but when in their distress they turned to the LORD, the God of Israel, and sought him, he was found by them. ⁵ In those times it was not safe for anyone to go or come, for great disturbances afflicted all the inhabitants of the lands. ⁶ They were broken in pieces, nation against nation and city against city, for God troubled them with every sort of distress. ⁷ But you, take courage! Do not let your hands be weak, for your work shall be rewarded."

⁸ When Asa heard these words, the prophecy of Azariah son of Oded,^h he took

---

^a Ch 13.23 in Heb
^b Ch 14.1 in Heb
^c Heb *Asherim*
^d Or *Nubian*; Heb *Cushite*
^e Or *Nubians*; Heb *Cushites*
^f Heb *They*
^g Meaning of Heb uncertain
^h Compare Syr Vg: Heb *the prophecy, the prophet Obed*

---

embark on a series of public works. **8–9:** On the large numbers, see 13.3n. **9–15:** Another holy-war narrative (cf. 13.2–20) in which an outnumbered Judah confronts a much more powerful foe (Zerah, who is otherwise unknown). In the midst of battle, Asa calls out to the LORD for deliverance in accordance with the petitions of Solomon's prayer (6.34–35). When king and people rely on God, they are able to achieve a major victory and take enormous booty (vv. 12–15). **9:** *Ethiopian*, the Hebrew speaks of a Cushite. Cush was an area to the south of Egypt. Sudan, Nubia, and Ethiopia are all possibilities. **10:** *Mareshah*, ca. 40 km (25 mi) southwest of Jerusalem, one of the southern cities fortified by Rehoboam (see 11.5–10). See map on p. 630 HB. **15.1–7:** The prophet Azariah (whose name means "the LORD has helped") appears only in this chapter. His oracle speaks of reciprocity in divine-human relations. *The LORD is with you, while you are with him* (15.2), the corollary of the measure-for-measure principle articulated earlier by Shemaiah (12.5). Pointing to the chaos of the distant past, the prophet

courage, and put away the abominable idols from all the land of Judah and Benjamin and from the towns that he had taken in the hill country of Ephraim. He repaired the altar of the LORD that was in front of the vestibule of the house of the LORD.[a] [9] He gathered all Judah and Benjamin, and those from Ephraim, Manasseh, and Simeon who were residing as aliens with them, for great numbers had deserted to him from Israel when they saw that the LORD his God was with him. [10] They were gathered at Jerusalem in the third month of the fifteenth year of the reign of Asa. [11] They sacrificed to the LORD on that day, from the booty that they had brought, seven hundred oxen and seven thousand sheep. [12] They entered into a covenant to seek the LORD, the God of their ancestors, with all their heart and with all their soul. [13] Whoever would not seek the LORD, the God of Israel, should be put to death, whether young or old, man or woman. [14] They took an oath to the LORD with a loud voice, and with shouting, and with trumpets, and with horns. [15] All Judah rejoiced over the oath; for they had sworn with all their heart, and had sought him with their whole desire, and he was found by them, and the LORD gave them rest all around.

[16] King Asa even removed his mother Maacah from being queen mother because she had made an abominable image for Asherah. Asa cut down her image, crushed it, and burned it at the Wadi Kidron. [17] But the high places were not taken out of Israel. Nevertheless the heart of Asa was true all his days. [18] He brought into the house of God the votive gifts of his father and his own votive gifts—silver, gold, and utensils. [19] And there was no more war until the thirty-fifth year of the reign of Asa.

16 In the thirty-sixth year of the reign of Asa, King Baasha of Israel went up against Judah, and built Ramah, to prevent anyone from going out or coming into the territory of[b] King Asa of Judah. [2] Then Asa took silver and gold from the treasures of the house of the LORD and the king's house, and sent them to King Ben-hadad of Aram, who resided in Damascus, saying, [3] "Let there be an alliance between me and you, like that between my father and your father; I am sending to you silver and gold; go, break your alliance with King Baasha of Israel, so that he may withdraw from me." [4] Ben-hadad listened to King Asa, and sent the commanders of his armies against the cities of Israel. They conquered Ijon, Dan, Abel-maim, and all the store-cities of Naphtali. [5] When Baasha heard of it, he stopped building Ramah, and let his work cease. [6] Then King Asa brought all Judah, and they carried away the stones of Ramah and its timber, with which Baasha had been building, and with them he built up Geba and Mizpah.

[7] At that time the seer Hanani came to King Asa of Judah, and said to him, "Because you relied on the king of Aram, and did not rely on the LORD your God, the army of the king of Aram has escaped you. [8] Were not

---

a   Heb *the vestibule of the LORD*
b   Heb lacks *the territory of*

---

warns Asa about the perils of abandoning God. **8–19:** In response to Azariah's admonitions, Asa initiates a covenant renewal (vv. 8–15; cf. Ex 19.3–8) and institutes further religious reforms (vv. 16–18; cf. 1 Kings 15.13–15). **9:** *From Ephriam, Manasseh, and Simeon.* Even though Simeon is located south of Judah, it is often counted among the northern tribes in earlier biblical literature (Gen 29.33; 34.25,30; 35.23; 46.10). That members of these tribes had defected to Asa is an indication of diving blessing.

16.1–14: Asa's decline. The war with Baasha (cf. 1 Kings 15.16–22) marks a turning point in Asa's tenure because he enters an alliance with *Ben-hadad of Aram* to counter an invasion by *Baasha of Israel.* Even though Asa enters this treaty in self-defense, the Chronicler considers such alliances as compromising Judah's commitment to God, who can defend the powerless from the mighty. Opposition to pacts with foreign powers is also found in earlier biblical literature (Deut 7.2; Hos 7.10–13; 8.9–10; Isa 20; 28.14–28; 30.1–5; Jer 2.14–19,33–37). **1:** *Ramah* was located just 9 km (6 mi) north of Jerusalem. **7–9:** The judgment oracle of *the seer Hanani* (apparently the father of the prophet Jehu; 19.2) heightens the disparity between the two periods of Asa's rule. Whereas Asa formerly relied on God and was able to defeat the vast armies of *Ethiopia* and *Libya* (14.7–14; 15.8), Asa's reliance on Ben-hadad is tantamount to nonreliance on the LORD (16.7). Ironically, Asa will now always be plagued by

the Ethiopians[a] and the Libyans a huge army with exceedingly many chariots and cavalry? Yet because you relied on the LORD, he gave them into your hand. [9] For the eyes of the LORD range throughout the entire earth, to strengthen those whose heart is true to him. You have done foolishly in this; for from now on you will have wars." [10] Then Asa was angry with the seer, and put him in the stocks, in prison, for he was in a rage with him because of this. And Asa inflicted cruelties on some of the people at the same time.

[11] The acts of Asa, from first to last, are written in the Book of the Kings of Judah and Israel. [12] In the thirty-ninth year of his reign Asa was diseased in his feet, and his disease became severe; yet even in his disease he did not seek the LORD, but sought help from physicians. [13] Then Asa slept with his ancestors, dying in the forty-first year of his reign. [14] They buried him in the tomb that he had hewn out for himself in the city of David. They laid him on a bier that had been filled with various kinds of spices prepared by the perfumer's art; and they made a very great fire in his honor.

17 His son Jehoshaphat succeeded him, and strengthened himself against Israel. [2] He placed forces in all the fortified cities of Judah, and set garrisons in the land of Judah, and in the cities of Ephraim that his father Asa had taken. [3] The LORD was with Jehoshaphat, because he walked in the earlier ways of his father;[b] he did not seek the Baals, [4] but sought the God of his father and walked in his commandments, and not according to the ways of Israel. [5] Therefore the LORD established the kingdom in his hand. All Judah brought tribute to Jehoshaphat, and he had great riches and honor. [6] His heart was courageous in the ways of the LORD; and furthermore he removed the high places and the sacred poles[c] from Judah.

[7] In the third year of his reign he sent his officials, Ben-hail, Obadiah, Zechariah, Nethanel, and Micaiah, to teach in the cities of Judah. [8] With them were the Levites, Shemaiah, Nethaniah, Zebadiah, Asahel, Shemiramoth, Jehonathan, Adonijah, Tobijah, and Tob-adonijah; and with these Levites, the priests Elishama and Jehoram. [9] They taught in Judah, having the book of the law of the LORD with them; they went around through all the cities of Judah and taught among the people.

[10] The fear of the LORD fell on all the kingdoms of the lands around Judah, and they did not make war against Jehoshaphat. [11] Some of the Philistines brought Jehoshaphat presents, and silver for tribute; and the Arabs also brought him seven thousand seven hundred rams and seven thousand seven hundred male goats. [12] Jehoshaphat grew steadily greater. He built fortresses and storage cities in Judah. [13] He carried out great works in the cities of Judah. He had soldiers, mighty warriors, in Jerusalem. [14] This was the muster of them by ancestral houses: Of Judah, the

a Or *Nubians*; Heb *Cushites*
b Another reading is *his father David*
c Heb *Asherim*

wars (cf. 1 Kings 15.16). **12:** The infirmity in Asa's feet (1 Kings 15.23) becomes another indication of Asa's unfaithfulness, because *in his disease he did not seek the LORD*. The comment that he relied on physicians reflects an ironic pun on Asa's name, which the Chronicler likely construed (based on Aramaic) as "healer" or "physician."

17.1–19: The promising beginning to the reign of Jehoshaphat (870–846 BCE). Both Kings and Chronicles commend Jehoshaphat (1 Kings 22.43–44; 2 Chr 17.3–4; 20.32–33), but the Chronicler's depiction of Jehoshaphat's reign is much more extensive and includes major events not recorded in Kings. Scholars continue to debate whether these events were based on the additional sources that the Chronicler had, or were freely composed. Most of the new material, such as Jehoshaphat's civil, military, and judicial reforms (17.1–19; 19.4–11) and his war against the eastern coalition (20.1–30), reflects well on Jehoshaphat. Upon taking office, Jehoshaphat immediately takes charge of his kingdom. As he institutes reforms, deploys troops, and fortifies cities, Jehoshaphat only grows stronger and more widely respected. Prophetic material concerning the northern prophet Elijah, which is embedded in Jehoshaphat's reign in Kings, is absent here. **2:** *Cities of Ephraim,* probably referring to 13.19. **7–9:** Jehoshaphat initiates a campaign to educate the Judean people in *the book of the law of the LORD* (cf. Deut 17.18–20; 2 Kings 22.8–13) by sending officers, Levites, and priests throughout the cities of Judah. This addition reflects the growing importance in the postexilic era of the Torah-book, and of the Levites as teachers (see esp. Neh 8). **11:** Tribute from the nations is a sign of divine favor (1 Chr 18.6; 2 Chr 8.2; 9.1–9;

commanders of the thousands: Adnah the commander, with three hundred thousand mighty warriors, [15] and next to him Jehohanan the commander, with two hundred eighty thousand, [16] and next to him Amasiah son of Zichri, a volunteer for the service of the LORD, with two hundred thousand mighty warriors. [17] Of Benjamin: Eliada, a mighty warrior, with two hundred thousand armed with bow and shield, [18] and next to him Jehozabad with one hundred eighty thousand armed for war. [19] These were in the service of the king, besides those whom the king had placed in the fortified cities throughout all Judah.

18 Now Jehoshaphat had great riches and honor; and he made a marriage alliance with Ahab. [2] After some years he went down to Ahab in Samaria. Ahab slaughtered an abundance of sheep and oxen for him and for the people who were with him, and induced him to go up against Ramoth-gilead. [3] King Ahab of Israel said to King Jehoshaphat of Judah, "Will you go with me to Ramoth-gilead?" He answered him, "I am with you, my people are your people. We will be with you in the war."

[4] But Jehoshaphat also said to the king of Israel, "Inquire first for the word of the LORD." [5] Then the king of Israel gathered the prophets together, four hundred of them, and said to them, "Shall we go to battle against Ramoth-gilead, or shall I refrain?" They said, "Go up; for God will give it into the hand of the king." [6] But Jehoshaphat said, "Is there no other prophet of the LORD here of whom we may inquire?" [7] The king of Israel said to Jehoshaphat, "There is still one other by whom we may inquire of the LORD, Micaiah son of Imlah; but I hate him, for he never prophesies anything favorable about me, but

only disaster." Jehoshaphat said, "Let the king not say such a thing." [8] Then the king of Israel summoned an officer and said, "Bring quickly Micaiah son of Imlah." [9] Now the king of Israel and King Jehoshaphat of Judah were sitting on their thrones, arrayed in their robes; and they were sitting at the threshing floor at the entrance of the gate of Samaria; and all the prophets were prophesying before them. [10] Zedekiah son of Chenaanah made for himself horns of iron, and he said, "Thus says the LORD: With these you shall gore the Arameans until they are destroyed." [11] All the prophets were prophesying the same and saying, "Go up to Ramoth-gilead and triumph; the LORD will give it into the hand of the king."

[12] The messenger who had gone to summon Micaiah said to him, "Look, the words of the prophets with one accord are favorable to the king; let your word be like the word of one of them, and speak favorably." [13] But Micaiah said, "As the LORD lives, whatever my God says, that I will speak."

[14] When he had come to the king, the king said to him, "Micaiah, shall we go to Ramoth-gilead to battle, or shall I refrain?" He answered, "Go up and triumph; they will be given into your hand." [15] But the king said to him, "How many times must I make you swear to tell me nothing but the truth in the name of the LORD?" [16] Then Micaiah[a] said, "I saw all Israel scattered on the mountains, like sheep without a shepherd; and the LORD said, 'These have no master; let each one go home in peace.'" [17] The king of Israel said to Jehoshaphat, "Did I not tell you that he would not prophesy anything favorable about me, but only disaster?"

---

[a] Heb *he*

26.8). **14–18:** On the large numbers, see 13.3n.

18.1–19.3: Jehoshaphat's first misstep. The Chronicler relates two shortcomings of Jehoshaphat, both involving his relations with northern Israel. The first involves Jehoshaphat's ill-fated treaty with the king of Israel, Ahab, in 1 Kings 22.1–40, which is reproduced with very few changes. **18.1:** Presumably this *marriage alliance* involved Jehoshaphat's son, Jehoram, and Ahab's daughter, Athaliah (21.6; 22.2; cf. 2 Kings 8.18). In the reign of Jehoshaphat's successors, the relationship with Ahab's dynasty becomes the conduit for Judah's royalty to adopt ill-advised and iniquitous policies (21.6; 22.3–5). **2:** The lavish feast, during which Ahab incites his Judean counterpart, does not appear in 1 Kings 22. **2–3:** *Ramoth-gilead* was an Israelite city in northern Jordan that had apparently been captured by the Arameans. **3:** *I am with you*, the Chronicler depicts Jehoshaphat as a willing and equal partner to his northern counterpart, Ahab. In Kings, Jehoshaphat appears as the junior partner in the coa-

[18] Then Micaiah[a] said, "Therefore hear the word of the LORD: I saw the LORD sitting on his throne, with all the host of heaven standing to the right and to the left of him. [19] And the LORD said, 'Who will entice King Ahab of Israel, so that he may go up and fall at Ramoth-gilead?' Then one said one thing, and another said another, [20] until a spirit came forward and stood before the LORD, saying, 'I will entice him.' The LORD asked him, 'How?' [21] He replied, 'I will go out and be a lying spirit in the mouth of all his prophets.' Then the LORD[a] said, 'You are to entice him, and you shall succeed; go out and do it.' [22] So you see, the LORD has put a lying spirit in the mouth of these your prophets; the LORD has decreed disaster for you."

[23] Then Zedekiah son of Chenaanah came up to Micaiah, slapped him on the cheek, and said, "Which way did the spirit of the LORD pass from me to speak to you?" [24] Micaiah replied, "You will find out on that day when you go in to hide in an inner chamber." [25] The king of Israel then ordered, "Take Micaiah, and return him to Amon the governor of the city and to Joash the king's son; [26] and say, 'Thus says the king: Put this fellow in prison, and feed him on reduced rations of bread and water until I return in peace.'" [27] Micaiah said, "If you return in peace, the LORD has not spoken by me." And he said, "Hear, you peoples, all of you!"

[28] So the king of Israel and King Jehoshaphat of Judah went up to Ramoth-gilead. [29] The king of Israel said to Jehoshaphat, "I will disguise myself and go into battle, but you wear your robes." So the king of Israel disguised himself, and they went into battle. [30] Now the king of Aram had commanded the captains of his chariots, "Fight with no one small or great, but only with the king of Israel." [31] When the captains of the chariots saw Jehoshaphat, they said, "It is the king of Israel." So they turned to fight against him; and Jehoshaphat cried out, and the LORD helped him. God drew them away from him, [32] for when the captains of the chariots saw that it was not the king of Israel, they turned back from pursuing him. [33] But a certain man drew his bow and unknowingly struck the king of Israel between the scale armor and the breastplate; so he said to the driver of his chariot, "Turn around, and carry me out of the battle, for I am wounded." [34] The battle grew hot that day, and the king of Israel propped himself up in his chariot facing the Arameans until evening; then at sunset he died.

19 King Jehoshaphat of Judah returned in safety to his house in Jerusalem. [2] Jehu son of Hanani the seer went out to meet him and said to King Jehoshaphat, "Should you help the wicked and love those who hate the LORD? Because of this, wrath has gone out against you from the LORD. [3] Nevertheless, some good is found in you, for you destroyed the sacred poles[b] out of the land, and have set your heart to seek God."

[4] Jehoshaphat resided at Jerusalem; then he went out again among the people, from Beer-sheba to the hill country of Ephraim,

a   Heb *he*

b   Heb *Asheroth*

---

lition. **10:** A symbolic action, as elsewhere in the prophetic repertoire. **18:** The LORD is meeting with his heavenly council (see Job 1.6; 2.1; Ps 82.1), and the prophet is a witness to the proceedings (see Jer 23.18,22). **21–22:** The revelation that the prophets have received is itself false; cf. Deut 13.3. **31:** *The LORD helped him,* this phrase, which does not appear in 1 Kings 22, resonates with the divine promises of 7.12–15. The Chronicler adds this phrase to reinforce his theology: God, who is fair and compassionate, is in control of events.

19.1–20.30: In contrast to the previous Jehoshaphat material, this has no parallel in Kings. **19.1–3:** This rebuke by the prophet *Jehu son of Hanani* (see 16.7–9n.) chastises Jehoshaphat for entering into a coalition with Ahab of Israel (see ch 18). Jehoshaphat was disloyal to God in that he proposed to *help the wicked* and was loyal to *those who hate the LORD.* Fidelity to one precludes fidelity to the other.

19.4–11: Recovery and further reforms. Jehoshaphat returns to and develops policies he instituted at the beginning of his reign (17.1–19). The geographic scope of the restoration (v. 4) is extensive, reclaiming Jehoshaphat's entire realm, including sections of the Northern Kingdom over which he held sway (17.1–2). Other texts depict the juridical responsibilities of monarchs (e.g., 2 Sam 8.15–18; 1 Kings 3.16–28), but only with Jehoshaphat in Chronicles do we find a full-blown judicial reform. He appoints *judges . . . in all the fortified cities of*

and brought them back to the Lord, the God of their ancestors. ⁵ He appointed judges in the land in all the fortified cities of Judah, city by city, ⁶ and said to the judges, "Consider what you are doing, for you judge not on behalf of human beings but on the Lord's behalf; he is with you in giving judgment. ⁷ Now, let the fear of the Lord be upon you; take care what you do, for there is no perversion of justice with the Lord our God, or partiality, or taking of bribes."

⁸ Moreover in Jerusalem Jehoshaphat appointed certain Levites and priests and heads of families of Israel, to give judgment for the Lord and to decide disputed cases. They had their seat at Jerusalem. ⁹ He charged them: "This is how you shall act: in the fear of the Lord, in faithfulness, and with your whole heart; ¹⁰ whenever a case comes to you from your kindred who live in their cities, concerning bloodshed, law or commandment, statutes or ordinances, then you shall instruct them, so that they may not incur guilt before the Lord and wrath may not come on you and your kindred. Do so, and you will not incur guilt. ¹¹ See, Amariah the chief priest is over you in all matters of the Lord; and Zebadiah son of Ishmael, the governor of the house of Judah, in all the king's matters; and the Levites will serve you as officers. Deal courageously, and may the Lord be with the good!"

20 After this the Moabites and Ammonites, and with them some of the Meunites,ᵃ came against Jehoshaphat for battle. ² Messengersᵇ came and told Jehoshaphat, "A great multitude is coming against you from Edom,ᶜ from beyond the sea; already they are at Hazazon-tamar" (that is, En-gedi). ³ Jehoshaphat was afraid; he set himself to seek the Lord, and proclaimed a fast throughout all Judah. ⁴ Judah assembled to seek help from the Lord; from all the towns of Judah they came to seek the Lord.

⁵ Jehoshaphat stood in the assembly of Judah and Jerusalem, in the house of the Lord, before the new court, ⁶ and said, "O Lord, God of our ancestors, are you not God in heaven? Do you not rule over all the kingdoms of the nations? In your hand are power and might, so that no one is able to withstand you. ⁷ Did you not, O our God, drive out the inhabitants of this land before your people Israel, and give it forever to the descendants of your friend Abraham? ⁸ They have lived in it, and in it have built you a sanctuary for your name, saying, ⁹ 'If disaster comes upon us, the sword, judgment,ᵈ or pestilence, or famine, we will stand before this house, and before

ᵃ Compare 26.7: Heb *Ammonites*
ᵇ Heb *They*
ᶜ One Ms: MT *Aram*
ᵈ Or *the sword of judgment*

Judah and established a court of appeals in the capital city of Jerusalem. Some see this as reflecting the creativity of the Chronicler, who derived this reform from the Heb word "shaphat," "to judge," in the king's name (cf. 16.12n.). **11:** The distinction between *matters of the Lord* and *the king's matters* is found only in Chronicles (1 Chr 26.30,32; 2 Chr 19.11) and Ezra (7.26), suggesting that the contours of this reform reflect Persian-period realities during which the Judeans were subject to a foreign king.

20.1–30: Dramatic triumph in holy war. Sometime after his judicial reformation, Jehoshaphat is confronted with an international crisis that threatens to overwhelm his people, the invasion of Judah (see v. 2) by a southeastern coalition of powers. **1:** *Meunites,* a textually difficult term. The Meunites are a group of disputed origin, who are mentioned only in late biblical texts (1 Chr 4.41; 2 Chr 20.2; 26.7). In one theory the Meunites were a Transjordanian or Arabian group, while in another the Meunites were from one of several sites or areas called Maon—most likely either Maon 12 mi (20 km) south of Gaza or the Maon region of southwestern Edom. Given the existence of another Maon in Judah (e.g., 1 Chr 2.45), more than one entity with the name "Meunites" may be meant (see Ezra 2.50 || Neh 7.52). **3–4:** Afraid, Jehoshaphat *set himself to seek the Lord* and proclaimed a national *fast* (cf. Judg 20.26 and 1 Sam 7.6; Jer 36.6,9; Zech 8.19; Joel 2.12; 2 Chr 1.5; 25.20). In resorting to Jerusalem, the people honor the divine directive given at Solomon's Temple dedication to seek the Lord in times of need (7.14). **6–12:** Jehoshaphat's prayer, which laments Judah's plight and solicits a divine response, recalls specific features of previous royal prayers (1 Chr 14.9,14; 29.10–19; 2 Chr 14.10–11). By contrasting divine omnipotence with human helplessness, the king lays the foundation for the petition that follows (v. 12). **8–9:** Echoing Solomon's prayer (see 6.28,34), Jehoshaphat's appeal is based on the existence of the Temple, because

you, for your name is in this house, and cry to you in our distress, and you will hear and save.' [10] See now, the people of Ammon, Moab, and Mount Seir, whom you would not let Israel invade when they came from the land of Egypt, and whom they avoided and did not destroy— [11] they reward us by coming to drive us out of your possession that you have given us to inherit. [12] O our God, will you not execute judgment upon them? For we are powerless against this great multitude that is coming against us. We do not know what to do, but our eyes are on you."

[13] Meanwhile all Judah stood before the LORD, with their little ones, their wives, and their children. [14] Then the spirit of the LORD came upon Jahaziel son of Zechariah, son of Benaiah, son of Jeiel, son of Mattaniah, a Levite of the sons of Asaph, in the middle of the assembly. [15] He said, "Listen, all Judah and inhabitants of Jerusalem, and King Jehoshaphat: Thus says the LORD to you: 'Do not fear or be dismayed at this great multitude; for the battle is not yours but God's. [16] Tomorrow go down against them; they will come up by the ascent of Ziz; you will find them at the end of the valley, before the wilderness of Jeruel. [17] This battle is not for you to fight; take your position, stand still, and see the victory of the LORD on your behalf, O Judah and Jerusalem.' Do not fear or be dismayed; tomorrow go out against them, and the LORD will be with you."

[18] Then Jehoshaphat bowed down with his face to the ground, and all Judah and the inhabitants of Jerusalem fell down before the LORD, worshiping the LORD. [19] And the Levites, of the Kohathites and the Korahites, stood up to praise the LORD, the God of Israel, with a very loud voice.

[20] They rose early in the morning and went out into the wilderness of Tekoa; and as they went out, Jehoshaphat stood and said, "Listen to me, O Judah and inhabitants of Jerusalem! Believe in the LORD your God and you will be established; believe his prophets." [21] When he had taken counsel with the people, he appointed those who were to sing to the LORD and praise him in holy splendor, as they went before the army, saying,

"Give thanks to the LORD,
    for his steadfast love endures forever."

[22] As they began to sing and praise, the LORD set an ambush against the Ammonites, Moab, and Mount Seir, who had come against Judah, so that they were routed. [23] For the Ammonites and Moab attacked the inhabitants of Mount Seir, destroying them utterly; and when they had made an end of the inhabitants of Seir, they all helped to destroy one another.

[24] When Judah came to the watchtower of the wilderness, they looked toward the multitude; they were corpses lying on the ground; no one had escaped. [25] When Jehoshaphat and his people came to take the booty from them, they found livestock[a] in great numbers, goods, clothing, and precious things, which they took for themselves until they could carry no more. They spent three days taking the booty, because of its abundance. [26] On the fourth day they assembled in the Valley of Beracah, for there they blessed the LORD; therefore that place has been called the Valley of Beracah[b] to this day. [27] Then all the people of Judah and Jerusalem, with Jehoshaphat at their head, returned to Jerusalem with joy, for the LORD had enabled them to rejoice over their enemies. [28] They came to Jerusalem, with harps and lyres and trumpets, to the house of the LORD. [29] The fear of God came on all the kingdoms of the countries when

a Gk: Heb *among them*
b That is *Blessing*

this sanctuary was accepted by God as the place where efficacious prayers could be offered (7.1–2,14). **11–12:** The very nations spared by the LORD when the Israelites entered the land (Deut 2.1–22) are now threatening Judah's existence within it. **14–15:** The levitical singer *Jahaziel* serves as a prophet and as the designate priest, as in other sacral wars (cf. Deut 20.2–4; 1 Chr 25.1–8). His assurance of victory, evoked as elsewhere by faith in God, quotes both Moses (Ex 14.13–14) and David (1 Sam 17.47). **16:** *Ziz . . . Jeruel,* occurring only here and precise location unknown. **17:** The residents of Jerusalem and Judah are to play the role of onlookers. **20:** Cf. Isa 7.9. **22–23:** The divine warrior throws Israel's enemies into a panic (cf. Judg 7.22; 1 Sam 14.20) so that they attack each other. **29:** As in other holy wars, *the fear of God* descends upon *all the kingdoms of the countries* (Ex 15.14–16; Deut 2.25;

they heard that the LORD had fought against the enemies of Israel. [30] And the realm of Jehoshaphat was quiet, for his God gave him rest all around.

[31] So Jehoshaphat reigned over Judah. He was thirty-five years old when he began to reign; he reigned twenty-five years in Jerusalem. His mother's name was Azubah daughter of Shilhi. [32] He walked in the way of his father Asa and did not turn aside from it, doing what was right in the sight of the LORD. [33] Yet the high places were not removed; the people had not yet set their hearts upon the God of their ancestors.

[34] Now the rest of the acts of Jehoshaphat, from first to last, are written in the Annals of Jehu son of Hanani, which are recorded in the Book of the Kings of Israel.

[35] After this King Jehoshaphat of Judah joined with King Ahaziah of Israel, who did wickedly. [36] He joined him in building ships to go to Tarshish; they built the ships in Ezion-geber. [37] Then Eliezer son of Dodavahu of Mareshah prophesied against Jehoshaphat, saying, "Because you have joined with Ahaziah, the LORD will destroy what you have made." And the ships were wrecked and were not able to go to Tarshish.

21

Jehoshaphat slept with his ancestors and was buried with his ancestors in the city of David; his son Jehoram succeeded him. [2] He had brothers, the sons of Jehoshaphat: Azariah, Jehiel, Zechariah, Azariah, Michael, and Shephatiah; all these were the sons of King Jehoshaphat of Judah.[a]

[3] Their father gave them many gifts, of silver, gold, and valuable possessions, together with fortified cities in Judah; but he gave the kingdom to Jehoram, because he was the firstborn. [4] When Jehoram had ascended the throne of his father and was established, he put all his brothers to the sword, and also some of the officials of Israel. [5] Jehoram was thirty-two years old when he began to reign; he reigned eight years in Jerusalem. [6] He walked in the way of the kings of Israel, as the house of Ahab had done; for the daughter of Ahab was his wife. He did what was evil in the sight of the LORD. [7] Yet the LORD would not destroy the house of David because of the covenant that he had made with David, and since he had promised to give a lamp to him and to his descendants forever.

[8] In his days Edom revolted against the rule of Judah and set up a king of their own. [9] Then Jehoram crossed over with his commanders and all his chariots. He set out by night and attacked the Edomites, who had surrounded him and his chariot commanders. [10] So Edom has been in revolt against the rule of Judah to this day. At that time Libnah also revolted against his rule, because he had forsaken the LORD, the God of his ancestors.

[11] Moreover he made high places in the hill country of Judah, and led the inhabitants of Jerusalem into unfaithfulness, and made Judah go astray. [12] A letter came to him from the prophet Elijah, saying: "Thus says the LORD, the

a   Gk Syr: Heb *Israel*

11.25; Josh 2.9,11,24; 5.1; 10.1–2; 1 Sam 4.7–8; 14.15; 1 Chr 14.7; 2 Chr 14.13).

20.31–37: Jehoshaphat's second misstep. Following the concluding notices to Jehoshaphat's reign (vv. 31–34; on *Jehu* see 16.7n.; cf. 1 Kings 22.41–45), the author narrates a failure. Again (18.1–19.3), a pact with Israel (vv. 35–37) marks a regression in Jehoshaphat's rule. Here, after the covenant is condemned by a prophet, *the ships were wrecked* (cf. 1 Kings 22.48–49). **36:** *Tarshish,* see 9.21n. *Ezion-geber* was a port city on the Red Sea.

21.1–20: Decline under Jehoram (851–843 BCE). Like the Elijah material, the Elisha material, found in Kings as part of the account of Jehoram's reign, is lacking in Chronicles. Jehoram appears as a more wicked king in Chronicles than in the briefer, but also negative, account of 2 Kings 8.16–24. Jehoram intensifies the pattern of close cooperation with the Northern Kingdom begun by his father (21.6; cf. 18.1–34; 20.35–37). **2–4:** Jehoram's *brothers,* who had possessions and administrative responsibilities in their own right (cf. 11.22–23n.), are eliminated by the new king. **5–7:** The divine promises (1 Chr 17.1–15) restrain the exercise of divine wrath against *the house of David* (cf. 2 Kings 8.17–19). **7:** *Lamp,* fief or territorial dominion might be a better translation of the Hebrew. The promises are interpreted as involving continued rule for David's descendants in Jerusalem. **8–10:** Largely taken from 2 Kings 8.20–22. **10:** The revolt of Libnah (see 2 Kings 8.22) is explained by the Chronicler as another divine punishment. **12–15:** Elijah's letter, unparalleled in Kings, is remarkable. Elijah has not previously been mentioned in Chronicles and, according to the chronology in Kings, may have already ascended at this

God of your father David: Because you have not walked in the ways of your father Jehoshaphat or in the ways of King Asa of Judah, [13] but have walked in the way of the kings of Israel, and have led Judah and the inhabitants of Jerusalem into unfaithfulness, as the house of Ahab led Israel into unfaithfulness, and because you also have killed your brothers, members of your father's house, who were better than yourself, [14] see, the LORD will bring a great plague on your people, your children, your wives, and all your possessions, [15] and you yourself will have a severe sickness with a disease of your bowels, until your bowels come out, day after day, because of the disease."

[16] The LORD aroused against Jehoram the anger of the Philistines and of the Arabs who are near the Ethiopians.[a] [17] They came up against Judah, invaded it, and carried away all the possessions they found that belonged to the king's house, along with his sons and his wives, so that no son was left to him except Jehoahaz, his youngest son.

[18] After all this the LORD struck him in his bowels with an incurable disease. [19] In course of time, at the end of two years, his bowels came out because of the disease, and he died in great agony. His people made no fire in his honor, like the fires made for his ancestors. [20] He was thirty-two years old when he began to reign; he reigned eight years in Jerusalem. He departed with no one's regret. They buried him in the city of David, but not in the tombs of the kings.

22 The inhabitants of Jerusalem made his youngest son Ahaziah king as his successor; for the troops who came with the Arabs to the camp had killed all the older sons. So Ahaziah son of Jehoram reigned as king of Judah. [2] Ahaziah was forty-two years old when he began to reign; he reigned one year in Jerusalem. His mother's name was Athaliah, a granddaughter of Omri. [3] He also walked in the ways of the house of Ahab, for his mother was his counselor in doing wickedly. [4] He did what was evil in the sight of the LORD, as the house of Ahab had done; for after the death of his father they were his counselors, to his ruin. [5] He even followed their advice, and went with Jehoram son of King Ahab of Israel to make war against King Hazael of Aram at Ramoth-gilead. The Arameans wounded Joram, [6] and he returned to be healed in Jezreel of the wounds that he had received at Ramah, when he fought King Hazael of Aram. And Ahaziah son of King Jehoram of Judah went down to see Joram son of Ahab in Jezreel, because he was sick.

[7] But it was ordained by God that the downfall of Ahaziah should come about through his going to visit Joram. For when he came there he went out with Jehoram to meet Jehu son of Nimshi, whom the LORD had anointed to destroy the house of Ahab. [8] When Jehu was executing judgment on the

a Or *Nubians*; Heb *Cushites*

point. Furthermore, early prophecy was primarily oral. The letter might be used as a way for a northern prophet to communicate with a southern king, but it also reflects the increasing significance of a written book-culture in the Chronicler's time. **16–17:** A foreign invasion plunders Judah and leaves Jehoram with only his youngest son still living in Jerusalem (cf. v. 14). On the *Ethiopians*, see 14.9n. **17:** *Jehoahaz*, see 22.1–9n. **18–19:** A fulfillment of Elijah's prediction (v. 15). *Disease*, cf. 16.12. *Fire*, cf. 16.14. **20:** Cf. 2 Kings 8.23–24.

22.1–9: The brief and ill-fated reign of Ahaziah (843–842 BCE). Following the premature death of Jehoram (21.18–20), the inhabitants of Jerusalem install young Ahaziah (also called Jehoahaz in 21.17) as king (v. 1), but this effort at restoration soon fails. The effects of Ahaziah's collaboration with the Northern Kingdom and emulation of northern practices threaten to topple both the Davidic dynasty and the traditional pattern of Temple worship in Jerusalem (23.18; 24.7). **2:** *Forty-two years*, there is a text-critical issue here. The more likely figure is "twenty-two years," as in 2 Kings 8.26. Ahaziah's father died at age forty (21.20). **3–4:** The expansion of Ahaziah's evaluation in 2 Kings 8.27 draws attention to the intimate involvement of *the house of Ahab* from the Northern Kingdom in Judean royal affairs. Athaliah was the daughter of Ahab (18.1n.), son of Omri. Here too the Chronicler assumes familiarity with the book of Kings. **5–9:** The failure of the alliance with Joram (2 Kings 8.28–29), the death of Ahaziah's kinsmen (2 Kings 10.12–14), and the death of Ahaziah himself (2 Kings 9.27) leaves a vacuum in Davidic leadership (v. 9). In Chronicles Ahaziah's demise is attributed to divine purpose (v. 7a). On the anointing of Jehu and the assassination of Joram, see 2 Kings 9.1–26.

house of Ahab, he met the officials of Judah and the sons of Ahaziah's brothers, who attended Ahaziah, and he killed them. [9] He searched for Ahaziah, who was captured while hiding in Samaria and was brought to Jehu, and put to death. They buried him, for they said, "He is the grandson of Jehoshaphat, who sought the LORD with all his heart." And the house of Ahaziah had no one able to rule the kingdom.

[10] Now when Athaliah, Ahaziah's mother, saw that her son was dead, she set about to destroy all the royal family of the house of Judah. [11] But Jehoshabeath, the king's daughter, took Joash son of Ahaziah, and stole him away from among the king's children who were about to be killed; she put him and his nurse in a bedroom. Thus Jehoshabeath, daughter of King Jehoram and wife of the priest Jehoiada—because she was a sister of Ahaziah—hid him from Athaliah, so that she did not kill him; [12] he remained with them six years, hidden in the house of God, while Athaliah reigned over the land.

23 But in the seventh year Jehoiada took courage, and entered into a compact with the commanders of the hundreds, Azariah son of Jeroham, Ishmael son of Jehohanan, Azariah son of Obed, Maaseiah son of Adaiah, and Elishaphat son of Zichri. [2] They went around through Judah and gathered the Levites from all the towns of Judah, and the heads of families of Israel, and they came to Jerusalem. [3] Then the whole assembly made a covenant with the king in the house of God. Jehoiada[a] said to them, "Here is the king's son! Let him reign, as the LORD promised concerning the sons of David. [4] This is what you are to do: one-third of you, priests and Levites, who come on duty on the sabbath, shall be gatekeepers, [5] one-third shall be at the king's house, and one-third at the Gate of the Foundation; and all the people shall be in the courts of the house of the LORD. [6] Do not let anyone enter the house of the LORD except the priests and ministering Levites; they may enter, for they are holy, but all the other[b] people shall observe the instructions of the LORD. [7] The Levites shall surround the king, each with his weapons in his hand; and whoever enters the house shall be killed. Stay with the king in his comings and goings."

[8] The Levites and all Judah did according to all that the priest Jehoiada commanded; each brought his men, who were to come on duty on the sabbath, with those who were to go off duty on the sabbath; for the priest Jehoiada did not dismiss the divisions. [9] The priest Jehoiada delivered to the captains the spears and the large and small shields that had been King David's, which were in the house of God; [10] and he set all the people as a guard for the king, everyone with weapon in hand, from the south side of the house to the north side of the house, around the altar and the house. [11] Then he brought out the king's son, put the crown on him, and gave him the covenant;[c] they proclaimed him king, and Jehoiada and his sons anointed him; and they shouted, "Long live the king!"

[12] When Athaliah heard the noise of the people running and praising the king, she went into the house of the LORD to the people; [13] and when she looked, there was the king standing by his pillar at the entrance, and the captains and the trumpeters beside

---

a   Heb *He*
b   Heb lacks *other*
c   Or *treaty*, or *testimony*; Heb *eduth*

22.10–23.15: The tenure and fall of Athaliah. Athaliah's reign (842–836 BCE; cf. 2 Kings 11.1–16) marks the point of gravest threat in a long sequence of repeated blows to the Davidic dynasty. Her plan to eliminate all potential heirs is thwarted, however, by *Jehoshabeath, daughter of King Jehoram* (vv. 11–12; called Jehosheba in Kings). **23.1–7:** The first steps in the plot against Athaliah (2 Kings 11.4–8) are rewritten according to the Chronicler's characteristic interests in the Levites, priests, gatekeepers, *the heads of* the *families of Israel,* and the people at large (cf. 1 Chr 15–16; 23–27). From the outset, the coup is the work of all the people, not just select military officers. **1:** *Compact,* Heb "berit," usually translated "covenant." **3:** The restoration honors the enduring political standards bequeathed to Israel during the United Monarchy. A return to normalcy after a period of apostasy or upheaval includes the restoration of the Davidic dynasty (22.1; 23.20–21; 26.1; 33.25; 36.1). **7:** On the military dimension of levitical duties, see 1 Chr 26.1–19n. **11:** *The covenant,* Heb "'edut", probably a list of divinely given laws. **13:** The *pillar,* probably Jachin or Boaz; see 3.15–17. On *the people of the land* see 2 Kings 11.14n.

the king, and all the people of the land rejoicing and blowing trumpets, and the singers with their musical instruments leading in the celebration. Athaliah tore her clothes, and cried, "Treason! Treason!" ¹⁴ Then the priest Jehoiada brought out the captains who were set over the army, saying to them, "Bring her out between the ranks; anyone who follows her is to be put to the sword." For the priest said, "Do not put her to death in the house of the LORD." ¹⁵ So they laid hands on her; she went into the entrance of the Horse Gate of the king's house, and there they put her to death.

¹⁶ Jehoiada made a covenant between himself and all the people and the king that they should be the LORD's people. ¹⁷ Then all the people went to the house of Baal, and tore it down; his altars and his images they broke in pieces, and they killed Mattan, the priest of Baal, in front of the altars. ¹⁸ Jehoiada assigned the care of the house of the LORD to the levitical priests whom David had organized to be in charge of the house of the LORD, to offer burnt offerings to the LORD, as it is written in the law of Moses, with rejoicing and with singing, according to the order of David. ¹⁹ He stationed the gatekeepers at the gates of the house of the LORD so that no one should enter who was in any way unclean. ²⁰ And he took the captains, the nobles, the governors of the people, and all the people of the land, and they brought the king down from the house of the LORD, marching through the upper gate to the king's house. They set the king on the royal throne. ²¹ So all

the people of the land rejoiced, and the city was quiet after Athaliah had been killed with the sword.

24 Joash was seven years old when he began to reign; he reigned forty years in Jerusalem; his mother's name was Zibiah of Beer-sheba. ² Joash did what was right in the sight of the LORD all the days of the priest Jehoiada. ³ Jehoiada got two wives for him, and he became the father of sons and daughters.

⁴ Some time afterward Joash decided to restore the house of the LORD. ⁵ He assembled the priests and the Levites and said to them, "Go out to the cities of Judah and gather money from all Israel to repair the house of your God, year by year; and see that you act quickly." But the Levites did not act quickly. ⁶ So the king summoned Jehoiada the chief, and said to him, "Why have you not required the Levites to bring in from Judah and Jerusalem the tax levied by Moses, the servant of the LORD, onª the congregation of Israel for the tent of the covenant?"ᵇ ⁷ For the children of Athaliah, that wicked woman, had broken into the house of God, and had even used all the dedicated things of the house of the LORD for the Baals.

⁸ So the king gave command, and they made a chest, and set it outside the gate of the house of the LORD. ⁹ A proclamation was made throughout Judah and Jerusalem to bring in for the LORD the tax that Moses the servant of God laid on Israel in the wilder-

ª Compare Vg: Heb *and*
ᵇ Or *treaty*, or *testimony*; Heb *eduth*

23.16–21: The reformation of Jehoiada. This priest leads *the people* in undoing the damage inflicted by Athaliah and her predecessors (cf. 2 Kings 11.17–20). His efforts result in the destruction of the temple of Baal, the reinstitution of proper personnel at the Temple, and the enthronement of young Joah. 16: As in Asa's reign, a national covenant (Heb "berit") is made or renewed (15.8–19). 18–19: These verses are an addition by the Chronicler in the middle of a narrative that otherwise largely follows Kings. They emphasize two issues that are key to the Chronicler: the role of *the law of Moses* and the role of *David* in organizing the Temple service. 21: The *quiet* that descends on Jerusalem is a sign of divine blessing (1 Chr 4.40; 22.9; 2 Chr 14.1,6; 20.30).

24.1–27: The Temple restoration of Joash (836–798 BCE) and his later regression. Following Kings, where the king's name is Jehoash, the Chronicler devotes considerable attention to Joash's restoration of the Temple, but in contrast to his source, limits it to the life of Jehoiada (cf. 2 Kings 12). After the good priest dies (vv. 15–16), Joash falls under the influence of his officers and backslides (vv. 17–22). He subsequently confronts a disastrous foreign invasion (vv. 23–24) and a successful conspiracy (vv. 25–26). 3: On large families, see 11.18–21n. 4–14: Joash expends great effort to rebuild the neglected Temple. He displays strong leadership in ensuring that the renovations proceed rapidly (vv. 5–6). The Chronicler, in an attempt to bolster the significance of the Temple, adds to his source, insisting that all donated funds were given with great enthusiasm (v. 10). 6: *The tax levied by*

ness. [10] All the leaders and all the people rejoiced and brought their tax and dropped it into the chest until it was full. [11] Whenever the chest was brought to the king's officers by the Levites, when they saw that there was a large amount of money in it, the king's secretary and the officer of the chief priest would come and empty the chest and take it and return it to its place. So they did day after day, and collected money in abundance. [12] The king and Jehoiada gave it to those who had charge of the work of the house of the LORD, and they hired masons and carpenters to restore the house of the LORD, and also workers in iron and bronze to repair the house of the LORD. [13] So those who were engaged in the work labored, and the repairing went forward at their hands, and they restored the house of God to its proper condition and strengthened it. [14] When they had finished, they brought the rest of the money to the king and Jehoiada, and with it were made utensils for the house of the LORD, utensils for the service and for the burnt offerings, and ladles, and vessels of gold and silver. They offered burnt offerings in the house of the LORD regularly all the days of Jehoiada.

[15] But Jehoiada grew old and full of days, and died; he was one hundred thirty years old at his death. [16] And they buried him in the city of David among the kings, because he had done good in Israel, and for God and his house.

[17] Now after the death of Jehoiada the officials of Judah came and did obeisance to the king; then the king listened to them. [18] They abandoned the house of the LORD, the God of their ancestors, and served the sacred poles[a] and the idols. And wrath came upon Judah and Jerusalem for this guilt of theirs. [19] Yet he sent prophets among them to bring them back to the LORD; they testified against them, but they would not listen.

[20] Then the spirit of God took possession of[b] Zechariah son of the priest Jehoiada; he stood above the people and said to them, "Thus says God: Why do you transgress the commandments of the LORD, so that you cannot prosper? Because you have forsaken the LORD, he has also forsaken you." [21] But they conspired against him, and by command of the king they stoned him to death in the court of the house of the LORD. [22] King Joash did not remember the kindness that Jehoiada, Zechariah's father, had shown him, but killed his son. As he was dying, he said, "May the LORD see and avenge!"

[23] At the end of the year the army of Aram came up against Joash. They came to Judah and Jerusalem, and destroyed all the officials of the people from among them, and sent all the booty they took to the king of Damascus. [24] Although the army of Aram had come with few men, the LORD delivered into their hand a very great army, because they had abandoned the LORD, the God of their ancestors. Thus they executed judgment on Joash.

[25] When they had withdrawn, leaving him severely wounded, his servants conspired against him because of the blood of the son[c] of the priest Jehoiada, and they killed him on his bed. So he died; and they buried him in the city of David, but they did not bury him in the tombs of the kings. [26] Those who conspired against him were Zabad son of Shimeath the Ammonite, and Jehozabad son of Shimrith the Moabite. [27] Accounts of his sons, and of the many oracles against him, and of the rebuilding[d] of the house of God are written in the Commentary on the Book of the Kings. And his son Amaziah succeeded him.

a Heb *Asherim*
b Heb *clothed itself with*
c Gk Vg: Heb *sons*
d Heb *founding*

Moses, see Ex 30.11–16; Lev 27.1–8. **13–14:** The collections for Temple renovation are so successful that funds are left to fashion new *utensils, ladles,* and *vessels.* In this respect, the peoples' generosity recalls that displayed in the reign of David (1 Chr 29.11–19). **15–16:** The highly positive evaluation of the priest Jehoiada's tenure resembles those written about Judah's better kings. **17–22:** These episodes, not found in Kings, detail the extent of Joash's regression. They follow typical patterns of the Chronicler: apostasy, prophet's warning, lack of repentance, (a second warning,) and punishment. **20–21:** The assassination of the prophet *Zechariah* is the work of both Joash and his officials. **25–26:** Joash himself falls victim to assassination in retaliation for the murder of Jehoiada's son(s) (v. 22; cf. 2 Kings 12.19–21). **27:** *Commentary,* see 13.22n.

25 Amaziah was twenty-five years old when he began to reign, and he reigned twenty-nine years in Jerusalem. His mother's name was Jehoaddan of Jerusalem. [2] He did what was right in the sight of the LORD, yet not with a true heart. [3] As soon as the royal power was firmly in his hand he killed his servants who had murdered his father the king. [4] But he did not put their children to death, according to what is written in the law, in the book of Moses, where the LORD commanded, "The parents shall not be put to death for the children, or the children be put to death for the parents; but all shall be put to death for their own sins."

[5] Amaziah assembled the people of Judah, and set them by ancestral houses under commanders of the thousands and of the hundreds for all Judah and Benjamin. He mustered those twenty years old and upward, and found that they were three hundred thousand picked troops fit for war, able to handle spear and shield. [6] He also hired one hundred thousand mighty warriors from Israel for one hundred talents of silver. [7] But a man of God came to him and said, "O king, do not let the army of Israel go with you, for the LORD is not with Israel—all these Ephraimites. [8] Rather, go by yourself and act; be strong in battle, or God will fling you down before the enemy; for God has power to help or to overthrow." [9] Amaziah said to the man of God, "But what shall we do about the hundred talents that I have given to the army of Israel?" The man of God answered, "The LORD is able to give you much more than this." [10] Then Amaziah discharged the army that had come to him from Ephraim, letting them go home again. But they became very angry with Judah, and returned home in fierce anger.

[11] Amaziah took courage, and led out his people; he went to the Valley of Salt, and struck down ten thousand men of Seir. [12] The people of Judah captured another ten thousand alive, took them to the top of Sela, and threw them down from the top of Sela, so that all of them were dashed to pieces. [13] But the men of the army whom Amaziah sent back, not letting them go with him to battle, fell on the cities of Judah from Samaria to Beth-horon; they killed three thousand people in them, and took much booty.

[14] Now after Amaziah came from the slaughter of the Edomites, he brought the gods of the people of Seir, set them up as his gods, and worshiped them, making offerings to them. [15] The LORD was angry with Amaziah and sent to him a prophet, who said to him, "Why have you resorted to a people's gods who could not deliver their own people from your hand?" [16] But as he was speaking the king[a] said to him, "Have we made you a royal counselor? Stop! Why should you be put to death?" So the prophet stopped, but said, "I know that God has determined to destroy you, because you have done this and have not listened to my advice."

[17] Then King Amaziah of Judah took counsel and sent to King Joash son of Jehoahaz son of Jehu of Israel, saying, "Come, let us look one another in the face." [18] King Joash of Israel sent word to King Amaziah of Judah, "A thornbush on Lebanon sent to a cedar on Lebanon, saying, 'Give your daughter to my son for a wife'; but a wild animal of Lebanon passed by and trampled down the thornbush. [19] You say, 'See, I have defeated Edom,' and your heart has lifted you up in boastfulness. Now stay at home; why should you provoke

a Heb *he*

25.1–28: The mixed record of Amaziah (789–769 BCE). The Chronicler expands the coverage devoted to Amaziah (2 Kings 14.2–14,17–20) through the addition of two sections (vv. 5–10 and vv. 12–16), each of which contains a prophetic figure. His reign is divided into two periods similar to other kings: In the first half of his tenure (vv. 1–13) Amaziah proves obedient to the prophetic word and enjoys success, while in the second half of his reign Amaziah engages in idolatry and suffers defeat (vv. 14–28). 3–4: Amaziah avenges his father's death but does not violate Deut 24.16. 5–10: The king's attempt to supplement his country's muster by hiring Israelite mercenaries encounters a prophetic reprimand. 5–6: On the large numbers, see 13.3n. A *hundred talents* weighed about 3,400 kg (7,000 lb). The Chronicler regards any military alliance, whether with foreign powers or with northern Israel, as illicit (see 16.1–14n.). 11–13: The prophet's counsel of complete reliance on God results in Judah's victory (cf. 13.13–21; 14.7–14; 20.1–30), but the alienated mercenaries wreak some havoc in Judah and

trouble so that you fall, you and Judah with you?"

[20] But Amaziah would not listen—it was God's doing, in order to hand them over, because they had sought the gods of Edom. [21] So King Joash of Israel went up; he and King Amaziah of Judah faced one another in battle at Beth-shemesh, which belongs to Judah. [22] Judah was defeated by Israel; everyone fled home. [23] King Joash of Israel captured King Amaziah of Judah, son of Joash, son of Ahaziah, at Beth-shemesh; he brought him to Jerusalem, and broke down the wall of Jerusalem from the Ephraim Gate to the Corner Gate, a distance of four hundred cubits. [24] He seized all the gold and silver, and all the vessels that were found in the house of God, and Obed-edom with them; he seized also the treasuries of the king's house, also hostages; then he returned to Samaria.

[25] King Amaziah son of Joash of Judah, lived fifteen years after the death of King Joash son of Jehoahaz of Israel. [26] Now the rest of the deeds of Amaziah, from first to last, are they not written in the Book of the Kings of Judah and Israel? [27] From the time that Amaziah turned away from the LORD they made a conspiracy against him in Jerusalem, and he fled to Lachish. But they sent after him to Lachish, and killed him there. [28] They brought him back on horses; he was buried with his ancestors in the city of David.

26 Then all the people of Judah took Uzziah, who was sixteen years old, and made him king to succeed his father Amaziah. [2] He rebuilt Eloth and restored it to Judah, after the king slept with his ancestors. [3] Uzziah was sixteen years old when he began to reign, and he reigned fifty-two years in Jerusalem. His mother's name was Jecoliah of Jerusalem. [4] He did what was right in the sight of the LORD, just as his father Amaziah had done. [5] He set himself to seek God in the days of Zechariah, who instructed him in the fear of God; and as long as he sought the LORD, God made him prosper.

[6] He went out and made war against the Philistines, and broke down the wall of Gath and the wall of Jabneh and the wall of Ashdod; he built cities in the territory of Ashdod and elsewhere among the Philistines. [7] God helped him against the Philistines, against the Arabs who lived in Gur-baal, and against the Meunites. [8] The Ammonites paid tribute to Uzziah, and his fame spread even to the border of Egypt, for he became very strong. [9] Moreover Uzziah built towers in Jerusalem at the Corner Gate, at the Valley Gate, and at the Angle, and fortified them. [10] He built towers in the wilderness and hewed out many cisterns, for he had large herds, both in the Shephelah and in the plain, and he had farmers and vinedressers in the hills and in the fertile lands, for he loved the soil. [11] Moreover Uzziah had an army of soldiers, fit for war, in divisions according to the numbers in the muster made by the secretary Jeiel and the officer Maaseiah, under the direction of Hananiah, one of the king's commanders. [12] The whole number of the heads of ancestral houses of mighty warriors was two thousand six hundred. [13] Under their command was an army of three hundred seven thousand five hundred, who could make war with mighty power, to help the king against the enemy. [14] Uzziah provided for all the army the

---

Samaria. **20**: The second part of the verse is an expansion of the Chronicler's source (2 Kings 14.11), emphasizing that this was not a whim, but the fair punishment of God. **22–24**: Amaziah and his kingdom suffer further defeat and humiliation. As the people experience military loss, some destruction to Jerusalem, the plunder of the temples and royal palace, and the capture of some of their soldiers as prisoners of war, they enter into a type of exilic situation (cf. 36.1–21) from which they need to be restored.

26.1–15: The builder and reformer, Uzziah (785–733 BCE). In Kings Uzziah (Azariah) is a minor figure (2 Kings 14.21–22; 15.1–7), but the much longer account in Chronicles presents this monarch as a major reformer whose fame extended all the way to Egypt (26.8). The additional material is of various types; some may be based on sources, while other pieces are likely composed by the Chronicler. **1–4:** Cf. 2 Kings 14.21–22; 15.2–3. **5:** The Chronicler links Uzziah's good conduct to the influence of Zechariah, an otherwise unattested prophet; cf. 24.22. **6–15:** Uzziah's achievements include territorial expansion, victory in war, rebuilding towns, and amassing a large, well-equipped army. Like David (1 Chr 27.25–31), Uzziah also enhances the condition of his royal estates. **7:** *Meunites*, see 20.2n. **12–13:** On the large numbers, see 13.3n.

shields, spears, helmets, coats of mail, bows, and stones for slinging. [15] In Jerusalem he set up machines, invented by skilled workers, on the towers and the corners for shooting arrows and large stones. And his fame spread far, for he was marvelously helped until he became strong.

[16] But when he had become strong he grew proud, to his destruction. For he was false to the LORD his God, and entered the temple of the LORD to make offering on the altar of incense. [17] But the priest Azariah went in after him, with eighty priests of the LORD who were men of valor; [18] they withstood King Uzziah, and said to him, "It is not for you, Uzziah, to make offering to the LORD, but for the priests the descendants of Aaron, who are consecrated to make offering. Go out of the sanctuary; for you have done wrong, and it will bring you no honor from the LORD God." [19] Then Uzziah was angry. Now he had a censer in his hand to make offering, and when he became angry with the priests a leprous[a] disease broke out on his forehead, in the presence of the priests in the house of the LORD, by the altar of incense. [20] When the chief priest Azariah, and all the priests, looked at him, he was leprous[a] in his forehead. They hurried him out, and he himself hurried to get out, because the LORD had struck him. [21] King Uzziah was leprous[a] to the day of his death, and being leprous[a] lived in a separate house, for he was excluded from the house of the LORD. His son Jotham was in charge of the palace of the king, governing the people of the land.

[22] Now the rest of the acts of Uzziah, from first to last, the prophet Isaiah son of Amoz wrote. [23] Uzziah slept with his ancestors; they buried him near his ancestors in the burial field that belonged to the kings, for they said, "He is leprous."[a] His son Jotham succeeded him.

27 Jotham was twenty-five years old when he began to reign; he reigned sixteen years in Jerusalem. His mother's name was Jerushah daughter of Zadok. [2] He did what was right in the sight of the LORD just as his father Uzziah had done—only he did not invade the temple of the LORD. But the people still followed corrupt practices. [3] He built the upper gate of the house of the LORD, and did extensive building on the wall of Ophel. [4] Moreover he built cities in the hill country of Judah, and forts and towers on the wooded hills. [5] He fought with the king of the Ammonites and prevailed against them. The Ammonites gave him that year one hundred talents of silver, ten thousand cors of wheat and ten thousand of barley. The Ammonites paid him the same amount in the second and the third years. [6] So Jotham became strong because he ordered his ways before the LORD his God. [7] Now the rest of the acts of Jotham, and all his wars and his ways, are written in the Book of the Kings of Israel and Judah. [8] He was twenty-five years old when he began to reign; he reigned sixteen years in Jerusalem.

[a] A term for several skin diseases; precise meaning uncertain

26.16–23: **Uzziah's hubris.** Having consolidated his rule and realm (1.1; 11.12; 17.1), Uzziah overreaches by turning against God and encroaching on the sacrificial duties of the priests. Most of this material is lacking in Kings, and it is likely a clever composition of the Chronicler, who imagined that the leprosy resulted from assuming priestly prerogatives and entering the sanctuary with incense. Leprosy caused serious impurity (Lev 13–14), and thus Uzziah could never enter the Temple again. **16:** *False to the LORD*, lit. "acted faithlessly (Heb "m'l") against the LORD." **21–23:** Except for the reference to Isaiah, this material is taken from 2 Kings 15.5–7. The attribution to Isaiah means that the Chronicler can lay claim to prophetic authority for at least some of the material in his narration of Uzziah's reign (cf. 1 Chr 29.29; 2 Chr 9.29; 13.22). **22:** *Isaiah*, on the prophets as ancestors of written works, see 1 Chr 29.29n.

27.1–9: **The accomplishments of Jotham (759–743 BCE).** As in Kings, Jotham is rated positively (2 Kings 15.32–38), but the Chronicler adds more material about his reign, especially about his public works and military might. **4:** Like Uzziah (26.6–10), Jotham does not confine his building initiatives to Jerusalem. He establishes towns in the hill country of Judah, and he builds fortresses and towers in the wooded areas. **5:** *Ammonites*, some scholars emend to "Meunites" (20.1n), but no king of the Meunites is mentioned in other biblical texts. A *talent* weighed about 75 lb (34 kg), and a *cor* was about 6.5 bu (230 l).

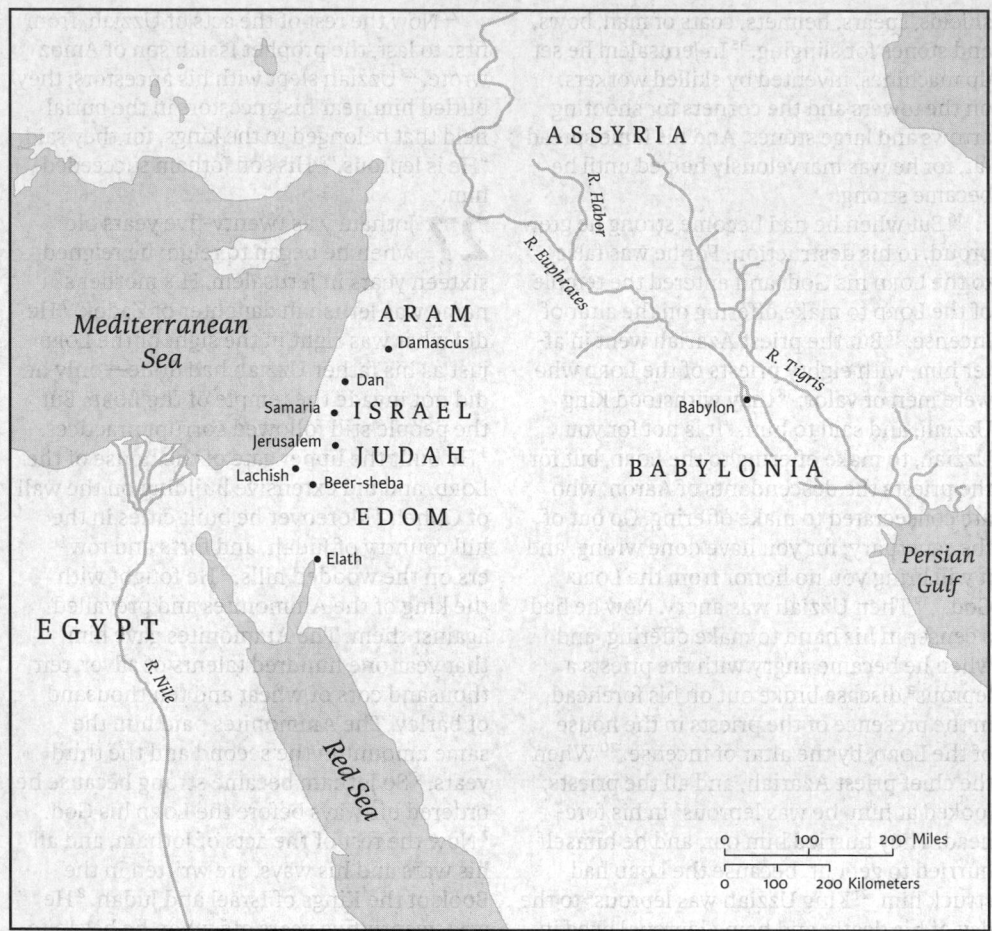

Chs 28–33: Assyria and Israel and Judah.

9 Jotham slept with his ancestors, and they buried him in the city of David; and his son Ahaz succeeded him.

28 Ahaz was twenty years old when he began to reign; he reigned sixteen years in Jerusalem. He did not do what was right in the sight of the LORD, as his ancestor David had done, 2 but he walked in the ways of the kings of Israel. He even made cast images for the Baals; 3 and he made offerings in the valley of the son of Hinnom, and made his sons pass through fire, according to the abominable practices of the nations whom the LORD drove out before the people of Israel. 4 He sacrificed and made offerings on the high places, on the hills, and under every green tree.

5 Therefore the LORD his God gave him into the hand of the king of Aram, who defeated him and took captive a great number of his people and brought them to Damascus. He was also given into the hand of the

28.1–27: Unending failure under Ahaz (743/753–727/715 BCE; the data are inconsistent). Unlike the reigns of almost all monarchs in Chronicles, the reign of Ahaz is one of unmitigated disaster. The author draws on 2 Kings 16, but his own presentation is substantially longer and different. Ahaz's refusal to turn from his wicked ways affords him the dubious distinction of being Judah's worst king (cf. 33.12–17). 3: *Pass through fire*, see 2 Kings 16.1–4n. 5–7: The Chronicler directly attributes the onslaughts by Assyria and Israel (2 Kings 16.5) to divine retribution for Ahaz's religious transgressions (2 Kings 16.2–4; 2 Chr 28.2–4). Chronicles depicts two

king of Israel, who defeated him with great slaughter. [6] Pekah son of Remaliah killed one hundred twenty thousand in Judah in one day, all of them valiant warriors, because they had abandoned the LORD, the God of their ancestors. [7] And Zichri, a mighty warrior of Ephraim, killed the king's son Maaseiah, Azrikam the commander of the palace, and Elkanah the next in authority to the king.

[8] The people of Israel took captive two hundred thousand of their kin, women, sons, and daughters; they also took much booty from them and brought the booty to Samaria. [9] But a prophet of the LORD was there, whose name was Oded; he went out to meet the army that came to Samaria, and said to them, "Because the LORD, the God of your ancestors, was angry with Judah, he gave them into your hand, but you have killed them in a rage that has reached up to heaven. [10] Now you intend to subjugate the people of Judah and Jerusalem, male and female, as your slaves. But what have you except sins against the LORD your God? [11] Now hear me, and send back the captives whom you have taken from your kindred, for the fierce wrath of the LORD is upon you." [12] Moreover, certain chiefs of the Ephraimites, Azariah son of Johanan, Berechiah son of Meshillemoth, Jehizkiah son of Shallum, and Amasa son of Hadlai, stood up against those who were coming from the war, [13] and said to them, "You shall not bring the captives in here, for you propose to bring on us guilt against the LORD in addition to our present sins and guilt. For our guilt is already great, and there is fierce wrath against Israel." [14] So the warriors left the captives and the booty before the officials and all the assembly. [15] Then those who were mentioned by name got up and took the captives, and with the booty they clothed all that were naked among them; they clothed them, gave them sandals, provided them with food and drink, and anointed them; and carrying all the feeble among them on donkeys, they brought them to their kindred at Jericho, the city of palm trees. Then they returned to Samaria.

[16] At that time King Ahaz sent to the king[a] of Assyria for help. [17] For the Edomites had again invaded and defeated Judah, and carried away captives. [18] And the Philistines had made raids on the cities in the Shephelah and the Negeb of Judah, and had taken Beth-shemesh, Aijalon, Gederoth, Soco with its villages, Timnah with its villages, and Gimzo with its villages; and they settled there. [19] For the LORD brought Judah low because of King Ahaz of Israel, for he had behaved without restraint in Judah and had been faithless to the LORD. [20] So King Tilgath-pilneser of Assyria came against him, and oppressed him instead of strengthening him. [21] For Ahaz plundered the house of the LORD and the houses of the king and of the officials, and gave tribute to the king of Assyria; but it did not help him.

[22] In the time of his distress he became yet more faithless to the LORD—this same King Ahaz. [23] For he sacrificed to the gods of Damascus, which had defeated him, and said, "Because the gods of the kings of Aram helped them, I will sacrifice to them so that they may help me." But they were the ruin of him, and of all Israel. [24] Ahaz gathered togeth-

---

[a] Gk Syr Vg Compare 2 Kings 16.7: Heb *kings*

separate and distinct invasions, whereas Kings presents Syria and Israel as acting in consort (2 Kings 16.5–6). **8–15:** The people of Israel seize a vast number of captives, but this act brings a strong prophetic censure and the prisoners are compassionately released. This section, most likely a free composition of the Chronicler, illustrates some of his basic concerns, including the need for prophetic warning before punishment, and the complete efficacy of repentance. That the prophet was a northern Israelite and the Israelites themselves repented indicates that the Northern and Southern Kingdoms still had an essential unity as "kin" (vv. 8,11). **16–20:** Invasions by the Edomites and the Philistines prompted Ahaz to send Temple tribute to the king of Assyria (Tiglath-pileser III, 745–727 BCE; here called *Tilgath-pilneser*) for *help* (cf. 2 Kings 16.7–8), but the Assyrian king *oppressed him* instead. On the opposition to alliances, see 16.1–14n. **21:** One more sign of Ahaz's desperate state—he plunders his own temple, palace, and official residences in an unsuccessful campaign to win relief from the pressure exerted by the Assyrian king. **22–25:** Ahaz's foreign policy disasters lead him to abandon his own religious institutions and worship the gods of the lands who defeated him. In Chronicles this is but one more indication of the ignominy that characterizes Ahaz's rule.

er the utensils of the house of God, and cut in pieces the utensils of the house of God. He shut up the doors of the house of the LORD and made himself altars in every corner of Jerusalem. ²⁵ In every city of Judah he made high places to make offerings to other gods, provoking to anger the LORD, the God of his ancestors. ²⁶ Now the rest of his acts and all his ways, from first to last, are written in the Book of the Kings of Judah and Israel. ²⁷ Ahaz slept with his ancestors, and they buried him in the city, in Jerusalem; but they did not bring him into the tombs of the kings of Israel. His son Hezekiah succeeded him.

29 Hezekiah began to reign when he was twenty-five years old; he reigned twenty-nine years in Jerusalem. His mother's name was Abijah daughter of Zechariah. ² He did what was right in the sight of the LORD, just as his ancestor David had done.

³ In the first year of his reign, in the first month, he opened the doors of the house of the LORD and repaired them. ⁴ He brought in the priests and the Levites and assembled them in the square on the east. ⁵ He said to them, "Listen to me, Levites! Sanctify yourselves, and sanctify the house of the LORD, the God of your ancestors, and carry out the filth from the holy place. ⁶ For our ancestors have been unfaithful and have done what was evil in the sight of the LORD our God; they have forsaken him, and have turned away their faces from the dwelling of the LORD, and turned their backs. ⁷ They also shut the doors of the vestibule and put out the lamps, and have not offered incense or made burnt offerings in the holy place to the God of Israel. ⁸ Therefore the wrath of the LORD came upon Judah and Jerusalem, and he has made them an object of horror, of astonishment,

and of hissing, as you see with your own eyes. ⁹ Our fathers have fallen by the sword and our sons and our daughters and our wives are in captivity for this. ¹⁰ Now it is in my heart to make a covenant with the LORD, the God of Israel, so that his fierce anger may turn away from us. ¹¹ My sons, do not now be negligent, for the LORD has chosen you to stand in his presence to minister to him, and to be his ministers and make offerings to him."

¹² Then the Levites arose, Mahath son of Amasai, and Joel son of Azariah, of the sons of the Kohathites; and of the sons of Merari, Kish son of Abdi, and Azariah son of Jehallelel; and of the Gershonites, Joah son of Zimmah, and Eden son of Joah; ¹³ and of the sons of Elizaphan, Shimri and Jeuel; and of the sons of Asaph, Zechariah and Mattaniah; ¹⁴ and of the sons of Heman, Jehuel and Shimei; and of the sons of Jeduthun, Shemaiah and Uzziel. ¹⁵ They gathered their brothers, sanctified themselves, and went in as the king had commanded, by the words of the LORD, to cleanse the house of the LORD. ¹⁶ The priests went into the inner part of the house of the LORD to cleanse it, and they brought out all the unclean things that they found in the temple of the LORD into the court of the house of the LORD; and the Levites took them and carried them out to the Wadi Kidron. ¹⁷ They began to sanctify on the first day of the first month, and on the eighth day of the month they came to the vestibule of the LORD; then for eight days they sanctified the house of the LORD, and on the sixteenth day of the first month they finished. ¹⁸ Then they went inside to King Hezekiah and said, "We have cleansed all the house of the LORD, the altar of burnt offering and all its utensils, and the table for the rows of bread and all

29.1–36: Restoring the Temple: the beginning of Hezekiah's rule. The Chronicler devotes more attention to Hezekiah (ruled 727/715–698/687 BCE; the data are inconsistent) than to any other king except David and Solomon (29.1–32.33); the Chronicler views Hezekiah as an "ideal" king of the post Davidic-Solomonic era, much like Josiah in Kings. Sennacherib's invasion, which dominates the coverage of Hezekiah in 2 Kings 18.9–19.37, thus appears in condensed form (32.1–23). Instead, the Chronicler focuses on Hezekiah's reforms and restoration of the Temple, which are described in much greater detail than in his sources (29.1–31.21; cf. 2 Kings 18.4,16,22). 3–11: Hezekiah begins by engaging a domestic policy crisis—the sorry legacy left by his predecessor (28.24). He oversees the repair of the Temple (vv. 3–4) and encourages the Levites to resume their traditional tasks (vv. 5–11). He makes a covenant with the LORD (v. 10; cf. 15.8–19) to move the nation from a state of wrath (v. 8) to one of blessing. He does this immediately upon assuming the throne (v. 3), reflecting his great righteousness. 12–19: The priests and Levites complete the Temple purification (cf. 13.10–11). 18: *Rows of bread*, see 2.4n.

its utensils. ¹⁹ All the utensils that King Ahaz repudiated during his reign when he was faithless, we have made ready and sanctified; see, they are in front of the altar of the LORD."

²⁰ Then King Hezekiah rose early, assembled the officials of the city, and went up to the house of the LORD. ²¹ They brought seven bulls, seven rams, seven lambs, and seven male goats for a sin offering for the kingdom and for the sanctuary and for Judah. He commanded the priests the descendants of Aaron to offer them on the altar of the LORD. ²² So they slaughtered the bulls, and the priests received the blood and dashed it against the altar; they slaughtered the rams and their blood was dashed against the altar; they also slaughtered the lambs and their blood was dashed against the altar. ²³ Then the male goats for the sin offering were brought to the king and the assembly; they laid their hands on them, ²⁴ and the priests slaughtered them and made a sin offering with their blood at the altar, to make atonement for all Israel. For the king commanded that the burnt offering and the sin offering should be made for all Israel.

²⁵ He stationed the Levites in the house of the LORD with cymbals, harps, and lyres, according to the commandment of David and of Gad the king's seer and of the prophet Nathan, for the commandment was from the LORD through his prophets. ²⁶ The Levites stood with the instruments of David, and the priests with the trumpets. ²⁷ Then Hezekiah commanded that the burnt offering be offered on the altar. When the burnt offering began, the song to the LORD began also, and the trumpets, accompanied by the instruments of King David of Israel. ²⁸ The whole assembly worshiped, the singers sang, and the trumpeters sounded; all this continued until the burnt offering was finished. ²⁹ When the offering was finished, the king and all who were present with him bowed down and worshiped. ³⁰ King Hezekiah and the officials commanded the Levites to sing praises to the LORD with the words of David and of the seer Asaph. They sang praises with gladness, and they bowed down and worshiped.

³¹ Then Hezekiah said, "You have now consecrated yourselves to the LORD; come near, bring sacrifices and thank offerings to the house of the LORD." The assembly brought sacrifices and thank offerings; and all who were of a willing heart brought burnt offerings. ³² The number of the burnt offerings that the assembly brought was seventy bulls, one hundred rams, and two hundred lambs; all these were for a burnt offering to the LORD. ³³ The consecrated offerings were six hundred bulls and three thousand sheep. ³⁴ But the priests were too few and could not skin all the burnt offerings, so, until other priests had sanctified themselves, their kindred, the Levites, helped them until the work was finished—for the Levites were more conscientious[a] than the priests in sanctifying themselves. ³⁵ Besides the great number of burnt offerings there was the fat of the offerings of well being, and there were the drink offerings for the burnt offerings. Thus the service of the house of the LORD was restored. ³⁶ And Hezekiah and all the people rejoiced because of what God had done for the people; for the thing had come about suddenly.

30 Hezekiah sent word to all Israel and Judah, and wrote letters also to Ephraim and Manasseh, that they should

---

[a] Heb *upright in heart*

20–36: As in the time of Solomon's Temple dedication (5.2–7.6), the praises of the Levites follow the offering of sacrifices. The swift (re)establishment of *the service of the house of the LORD* (vv. 35–36) effectively reverses the neglect of the Temple in Ahaz's reign. The restoration of the proper Temple service results in great joy (cf. 30.25–26). **22:** Cf. Num 18.17; Lev 17.6. **27:** The coordination of Temple hymns and Temple sacrifices is a consistent theme in Chronicles (1 Chr 23.30–31n.). **34:** *Levites*, the Chronicler has a special sympathy for the plight of the Levites, even though he normally maintains a distinction between their roles and responsibilities and those of the priests. The Chronicler stresses cooperation and complimentarity between the priests and Levites, not competition and hierarchy (1 Chr 23.28–32; 28.12–13,21; 2 Chr 5.4–14; 13.9–12; 23.1–11; 35.3). In Chronicles, the priests and Levites share a common genealogy (1 Chr 6.1–81).

30.1–31.1: National Passover and further religious reforms. The consecration and rededication of the Temple complete, Hezekiah leads the people in celebrating a national Passover. The restoration of proper worship

come to the house of the LORD at Jerusalem, to keep the passover to the LORD the God of Israel. [2] For the king and his officials and all the assembly in Jerusalem had taken counsel to keep the passover in the second month [3] (for they could not keep it at its proper time because the priests had not sanctified themselves in sufficient number, nor had the people assembled in Jerusalem). [4] The plan seemed right to the king and all the assembly. [5] So they decreed to make a proclamation throughout all Israel, from Beer-sheba to Dan, that the people should come and keep the passover to the LORD the God of Israel, at Jerusalem; for they had not kept it in great numbers as prescribed. [6] So couriers went throughout all Israel and Judah with letters from the king and his officials, as the king had commanded, saying, "O people of Israel, return to the LORD, the God of Abraham, Isaac, and Israel, so that he may turn again to the remnant of you who have escaped from the hand of the kings of Assyria. [7] Do not be like your ancestors and your kindred, who were faithless to the LORD God of their ancestors, so that he made them a desolation, as you see. [8] Do not now be stiff-necked as your ancestors were, but yield yourselves to the LORD and come to his sanctuary, which he has sanctified forever, and serve the LORD your God, so that his fierce anger may turn away from you. [9] For as you return to the LORD, your kindred and your children

will find compassion with their captors, and return to this land. For the LORD your God is gracious and merciful, and will not turn away his face from you, if you return to him."

[10] So the couriers went from city to city through the country of Ephraim and Manasseh, and as far as Zebulun; but they laughed them to scorn, and mocked them. [11] Only a few from Asher, Manasseh, and Zebulun humbled themselves and came to Jerusalem. [12] The hand of God was also on Judah to give them one heart to do what the king and the officials commanded by the word of the LORD.

[13] Many people came together in Jerusalem to keep the festival of unleavened bread in the second month, a very large assembly. [14] They set to work and removed the altars that were in Jerusalem, and all the altars for offering incense they took away and threw into the Wadi Kidron. [15] They slaughtered the passover lamb on the fourteenth day of the second month. The priests and the Levites were ashamed, and they sanctified themselves and brought burnt offerings into the house of the LORD. [16] They took their accustomed posts according to the law of Moses the man of God; the priests dashed the blood that they received[a] from the hands of the Levites. [17] For there were many in the assembly who had not sanctified themselves;

[a] Heb lacks *that they received*

moves from the Passover offering, to destroying illicit altars in Jerusalem (vv. 13–14), to celebrating the Festival of Unleavened Bread (vv. 13,21; cf. Ex 23.14–17; Deut 16.16–17), to shattering *the pillars*, hacking apart *the sacred poles*, and tearing down *the high places and the altars throughout all Judah and Benjamin, and in Ephraim and Manasseh* (31.1). The alternation in Hezekiah's reforms is significant—from reestablishing ritual purity at the Temple to enforcing ritual unity in both Judah and the former Northern Kingdom. **30.1**: *Wrote letters*. The distribution of royal declarations by missives was common in the Persian period. The Persian empire was renowned for its international postal system. **2**: A somewhat similar delay in observing the Passover is legislated in Num 9.9–13. **5–9**: Hezekiah appeals to the remnant of the northern tribes and invites them to participate in the Passover. In spite of the Assyrian exile (v. 6; cf. 2 Kings 18.9–12), the northerners are still Israelites, and their positive response may elicit compassion for their relatives in exile (v. 9). **5**: *From Beer-sheba to Dan*, the traditional southern and northern limits of Israel; see 1 Chr 21.2. **10–14**: Hezekiah's offer meets with an enthusiastic response from Judah and a mixed response from the northern tribes. **15–27**: The national celebration is reminiscent of the heady days of the United Monarchy. **18–20**: These verses suggest that the stereotypical view of postexilic Judaism as legalistic and inflexible is incorrect. **25**: *Resident aliens*, cf. Num 9.14.

31.2–19: The priestly and levitical divisions reestablished. Hezekiah continues his reforms by reinstituting the priestly and levitical divisions first set out by David (1 Chr 23–26; 28.13,21) and implemented by Solomon (2 Chr 8.14). **4–10**: Like David (1 Chr 22.14–16; 29.2–5), the king contributes toward the support of the Temple and its staff. As in David's time (1 Chr 29.6–9), the people respond with their own generous gifts. **11–20**: Heze-

therefore the Levites had to slaughter the passover lamb for everyone who was not clean, to make it holy to the LORD. [18] For a multitude of the people, many of them from Ephraim, Manasseh, Issachar, and Zebulun, had not cleansed themselves, yet they ate the passover otherwise than as prescribed. But Hezekiah prayed for them, saying, "The good LORD pardon all [19] who set their hearts to seek God, the LORD the God of their ancestors, even though not in accordance with the sanctuary's rules of cleanness." [20] The LORD heard Hezekiah, and healed the people. [21] The people of Israel who were present at Jerusalem kept the festival of unleavened bread seven days with great gladness; and the Levites and the priests praised the LORD day by day, accompanied by loud instruments for the LORD. [22] Hezekiah spoke encouragingly to all the Levites who showed good skill in the service of the LORD. So the people ate the food of the festival for seven days, sacrificing offerings of well-being and giving thanks to the LORD the God of their ancestors.

[23] Then the whole assembly agreed together to keep the festival for another seven days; so they kept it for another seven days with gladness. [24] For King Hezekiah of Judah gave the assembly a thousand bulls and seven thousand sheep for offerings, and the officials gave the assembly a thousand bulls and ten thousand sheep. The priests sanctified themselves in great numbers. [25] The whole assembly of Judah, the priests and the Levites, and the whole assembly that came out of Israel, and the resident aliens who came out of the land of Israel, and the resident aliens who lived in Judah, rejoiced. [26] There was great joy in Jerusalem, for since the time of Solomon son of King David of Israel there had been nothing like this in Jerusalem. [27] Then the priests and the Levites stood up and blessed the people, and their voice was heard; their prayer came to his holy dwelling in heaven.

31

Now when all this was finished, all Israel who were present went out to the cities of Judah and broke down the pillars, hewed down the sacred poles,[a] and pulled down the high places and the altars throughout all Judah and Benjamin, and in Ephraim and Manasseh, until they had destroyed them all. Then all the people of Israel returned to their cities, all to their individual properties.

[2] Hezekiah appointed the divisions of the priests and of the Levites, division by division, everyone according to his service, the priests and the Levites, for burnt offerings and offerings of well-being, to minister in the gates of the camp of the LORD and to give thanks and praise. [3] The contribution of the king from his own possessions was for the burnt offerings: the burnt offerings of morning and evening, and the burnt offerings for the sabbaths, the new moons, and the appointed festivals, as it is written in the law of the LORD. [4] He commanded the people who lived in Jerusalem to give the portion due to the priests and the Levites, so that they might devote themselves to the law of the LORD. [5] As soon as the word spread, the people of Israel gave in abundance the first fruits of grain, wine, oil, honey, and of all the produce of the field; and they brought in abundantly the tithe of everything. [6] The people of Israel and Judah who lived in the cities of Judah also brought in the tithe of cattle and sheep, and the tithe of the dedicated things that had been consecrated to the LORD their God, and laid them in heaps. [7] In the third month they began to pile up the heaps, and finished them in the seventh month. [8] When Hezekiah and the officials came and saw the heaps, they blessed the LORD and his people Israel. [9] Hezekiah questioned the priests and the Levites about the heaps. [10] The chief priest Azariah, who was of the house of Zadok, answered him, "Since they began to bring the contributions into the house of the LORD, we have had enough to eat and have plenty to spare; for the LORD has blessed his people, so that we have this great supply left over."

[11] Then Hezekiah commanded them to prepare store-chambers in the house of the LORD; and they prepared them. [12] Faithfully they brought in the contributions, the tithes and the dedicated things. The chief officer in charge of them was Conaniah the Levite, with his brother Shimei as second; [13] while Jehiel, Azaziah, Nahath, Asahel, Jerimoth, Jozabad, Eliel, Ismachiah, Mahath, and Benaiah were overseers assisting Conaniah and his brother

[a] Heb *Asherim*

Shimei, by the appointment of King Hezekiah and of Azariah the chief officer of the house of God. ¹⁴ Kore son of Imnah the Levite, keeper of the east gate, was in charge of the freewill offerings to God, to apportion the contribution reserved for the Lord and the most holy offerings. ¹⁵ Eden, Miniamin, Jeshua, Shemaiah, Amariah, and Shecaniah were faithfully assisting him in the cities of the priests, to distribute the portions to their kindred, old and young alike, by divisions, ¹⁶ except those enrolled by genealogy, males from three years old and upwards, all who entered the house of the Lord as the duty of each day required, for their service according to their offices, by their divisions. ¹⁷ The enrollment of the priests was according to their ancestral houses; that of the Levites from twenty years old and upwards was according to their offices, by their divisions. ¹⁸ The priests were enrolled with all their little children, their wives, their sons, and their daughters, the whole multitude; for they were faithful in keeping themselves holy. ¹⁹ And for the descendants of Aaron, the priests, who were in the fields of common land belonging to their towns, town by town, the people designated by name were to distribute portions to every male among the priests and to everyone among the Levites who was enrolled.

²⁰ Hezekiah did this throughout all Judah; he did what was good and right and faithful before the Lord his God. ²¹ And every work that he undertook in the service of the house of God, and in accordance with the law and the commandments, to seek his God, he did with all his heart; and he prospered.

32 After these things and these acts of faithfulness, King Sennacherib of Assyria came and invaded Judah and encamped against the fortified cities, thinking to win them for himself. ² When Hezekiah saw that Sennacherib had come and intended to fight against Jerusalem, ³ he planned with his officers and his warriors to stop the flow of the springs that were outside the city; and they helped him. ⁴ A great many people were gathered, and they stopped all the springs and the wadi that flowed through the land, saying, "Why should the Assyrian kings come and find water in abundance?" ⁵ Hezekiah[a] set to work resolutely and built up the entire wall that was broken down, and raised towers on it,[b] and outside it he built another wall; he also strengthened the Millo in the city of David, and made weapons and shields in abundance. ⁶ He appointed combat commanders over the people, and gathered them together to him in the square at the gate of the city and spoke encouragingly to them, saying, ⁷ "Be strong and of good courage. Do not be afraid or dismayed before the king of Assyria and all the horde that is with him; for there is one greater with us than with him. ⁸ With him is an arm of flesh; but with us is the Lord our God, to help us and to fight our battles." The people were encouraged by the words of King Hezekiah of Judah.

⁹ After this, while King Sennacherib of Assyria was at Lachish with all his forces, he sent his servants to Jerusalem to King Hezeki-

---

a Heb *He*
b Vg: Heb *and raised on the towers*

---

kiah ensures that the contributions and tithes will be properly cared for and stored. **20–21:** A summation and commendation of Hezekiah's reforms, which emphasize that anyone who serves God *in accordance with the law and the commandments . . . with all his heart* will *prosper*.

32.1–23: Sennacherib's invasion of Judah and threat to Jerusalem. The Chronicler borrows from and abbreviates 2 Kings 18.13–19.13, omitting Hezekiah's stripping of the Temple and his tribute to Sennacherib (2 Kings 18.13–16), which might reflect negatively on Hezekiah. The complex account of Kings is simplified, and some parallel texts from the source have been conflated to create a smoother depiction of the events. **1:** *After these . . . acts of faithfulness*, in Chronicles, Sennacherib's invasion is a complete shock. Some scholars explain this massive foreign invasion as a divinely administered test of Hezekiah (cf. Gen 22.1). It is a test of Hezekiah and Judah, but the Chronicler never maintains that the Lord initiated this war (contrast 12.2; 21.16; 28.5; 33.11–36.17). **2–8:** Sennacherib's campaign took place in 701 BCE. Repairs to Jerusalem's infrastructure, including the construction of the Siloam water tunnel (see 32.30), are made to prepare for the eventuality of an attack by Sennacherib. To this end, Hezekiah also initiates a program of urban mobilization. **5:** *Millo*, see 1 Chr 11.8n. **9–19:** As in Kings, the Assyrians try to convince the Jerusalemites that their God is no different from the defeated deities of other

ah of Judah and to all the people of Judah that were in Jerusalem, saying, [10] "Thus says King Sennacherib of Assyria: On what are you relying, that you undergo the siege of Jerusalem? [11] Is not Hezekiah misleading you, handing you over to die by famine and by thirst, when he tells you, 'The LORD our God will save us from the hand of the king of Assyria'? [12] Was it not this same Hezekiah who took away his high places and his altars and commanded Judah and Jerusalem, saying, 'Before one altar you shall worship, and upon it you shall make your offerings'? [13] Do you not know what I and my ancestors have done to all the peoples of other lands? Were the gods of the nations of those lands at all able to save their lands out of my hand? [14] Who among all the gods of those nations that my ancestors utterly destroyed was able to save his people from my hand, that your God should be able to save you from my hand? [15] Now therefore do not let Hezekiah deceive you or mislead you in this fashion, and do not believe him, for no god of any nation or kingdom has been able to save his people from my hand or from the hand of my ancestors. How much less will your God save you out of my hand!"

[16] His servants said still more against the Lord GOD and against his servant Hezekiah. [17] He also wrote letters to throw contempt on the LORD the God of Israel and to speak against him, saying, "Just as the gods of the nations in other lands did not rescue their people from my hands, so the God of Hezekiah will not rescue his people from my hand." [18] They shouted it with a loud voice in the language of Judah to the people of Jerusalem who were on the wall, to frighten and terrify them, in order that they might take the city. [19] They spoke of the God of Jerusalem as if he were like the gods of the peoples of the earth, which are the work of human hands. [20] Then King Hezekiah and the prophet Isaiah son of Amoz prayed because of this

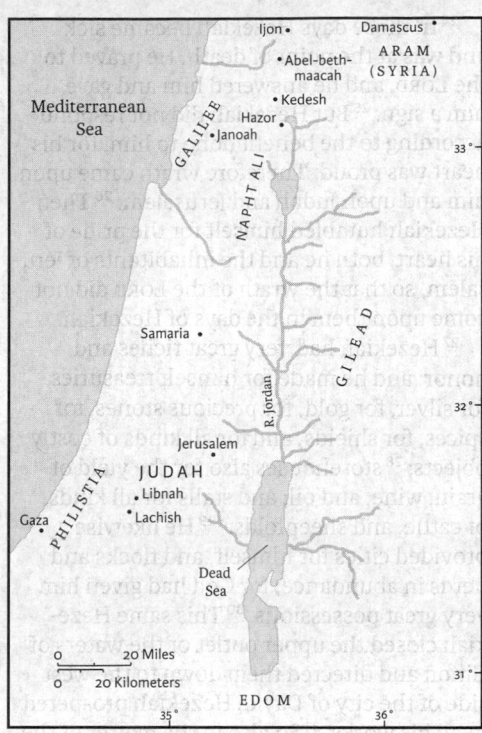

Ch 32: Places associated with Sennacherib's invasion of Judah.

and cried to heaven. [21] And the LORD sent an angel who cut off all the mighty warriors and commanders and officers in the camp of the king of Assyria. So he returned in disgrace to his own land. When he came into the house of his god, some of his own sons struck him down there with the sword. [22] So the LORD saved Hezekiah and the inhabitants of Jerusalem from the hand of King Sennacherib of Assyria and from the hand of all his enemies; he gave them rest[a] on every side. [23] Many brought gifts to the LORD in Jerusalem and precious things to King Hezekiah of Judah, so that he was exalted in the sight of all nations from that time onward.

a Gk Vg: Heb *guided them*

peoples. From the perspective of the Chronicler, this is blasphemy because the deities of other nations are *the work of human hands* (cf. 2 Kings 18.17–35). **18:** *The language of Judah,* later called Hebrew. **20:** Like other pious kings before him, Hezekiah appeals to God in conformity with the precedent established by David (1 Chr 17.16–27; 29.10–19) and Solomon (2 Chr 5.13–6.42); cf. 2 Kings 19.1–34. **21:** The LORD's dramatic deliverance of Hezekiah and Jerusalem responds directly to the prayer uttered by Hezekiah and Isaiah (v. 20; cf. 2 Kings 19.1–14) and accords with the LORD's earlier promises to Solomon (7.12–15; cf. 6.28–30). **22–23:** *Rest on every side* is a sign of divine favor (14.1n.), as is tribute from the nations (1 Chr 18.6; 2 Chr 8.2; 17.5,11).

²⁴ In those days Hezekiah became sick and was at the point of death. He prayed to the Lord, and he answered him and gave him a sign. ²⁵ But Hezekiah did not respond according to the benefit done to him, for his heart was proud. Therefore wrath came upon him and upon Judah and Jerusalem. ²⁶ Then Hezekiah humbled himself for the pride of his heart, both he and the inhabitants of Jerusalem, so that the wrath of the Lord did not come upon them in the days of Hezekiah.

²⁷ Hezekiah had very great riches and honor; and he made for himself treasuries for silver, for gold, for precious stones, for spices, for shields, and for all kinds of costly objects; ²⁸ storehouses also for the yield of grain, wine, and oil; and stalls for all kinds of cattle, and sheepfolds.ᵃ ²⁹ He likewise provided cities for himself, and flocks and herds in abundance; for God had given him very great possessions. ³⁰ This same Hezekiah closed the upper outlet of the waters of Gihon and directed them down to the west side of the city of David. Hezekiah prospered in all his works. ³¹ So also in the matter of the envoys of the officials of Babylon, who had been sent to him to inquire about the sign that had been done in the land, God left him to himself, in order to test him and to know all that was in his heart.

³² Now the rest of the acts of Hezekiah, and his good deeds, are written in the vision of the prophet Isaiah son of Amoz in the Book of the Kings of Judah and Israel. ³³ Hezekiah slept with his ancestors, and they buried him on the ascent to the tombs of the descendants of David; and all Judah and the inhabitants of Jerusalem did him honor at his death. His son Manasseh succeeded him.

33 Manasseh was twelve years old when he began to reign; he reigned fifty-five years in Jerusalem. ² He did what was evil in the sight of the Lord, according to the abominable practices of the nations whom the Lord drove out before the people of Israel. ³ For he rebuilt the high places that his father Hezekiah had pulled down, and erected altars to the Baals, made sacred poles,ᵇ worshiped all the host of heaven, and served them. ⁴ He built altars in the house of the Lord, of which the Lord had said, "In Jerusalem shall my name be forever." ⁵ He built altars for all the host of heaven in the two courts of the house of the Lord. ⁶ He made his son pass through fire in the valley of the son of Hinnom, practiced soothsaying and augury and sorcery, and dealt with mediums and with wizards. He did much evil in the sight of the Lord, provoking him to anger. ⁷ The carved image of the idol that he had made he set in the house of God, of which God said to David and to his son Solomon, "In this house, and in Jerusalem, which I have chosen out of all the tribes of Israel, I will put my name forever; ⁸ I will never again remove the feet of Israel from the land that I appointed for your ancestors, if only they will be careful to do all that I have commanded them, all the law, the statutes, and the ordinances given through Moses." ⁹ Manasseh misled Judah and the inhabitants of Jerusalem, so that they did more evil than the nations whom the Lord had destroyed before the people of Israel.

¹⁰ The Lord spoke to Manasseh and to his people, but they gave no heed. ¹¹ Therefore

ᵃ Gk Vg: Heb *flocks for folds*
ᵇ Heb *Asheroth*

32.24–33: Hezekiah's sickness, recovery, and wealth. Even this pious king was not without his faults (32.24–26; cf. 2 Kings 20.1–19; Isa 38–39); see 2 Chr 6.36. But like David (1 Chr 21.8,17) and Rehoboam (2 Chr 12.7) before him, Hezekiah *humbled himself* before God (see 7.14). 27–30: Most of these economic and political initiatives are focused outside Jerusalem (cf. vv. 2–8). 27: Royal wealth indicates divine blessing in Chronicles, and Hezekiah's assets rival those of Solomon (1.11–12,14–17; 9.1–8,23–24). 31: Cf. 2 Kings 20.12–19.

33.1–20: Manasseh: regression and repentance. As in Kings, for the Chronicler, Manasseh (ruled 698/687–642 BCE; the data are inconsistent) is a wicked king (vv. 2–9). Nevertheless, after Manasseh suffers divine punishment in the form of exile (v. 11), he repents, changes course, and is forgiven (vv. 12–19). In so doing, Manasseh is presented as a model for Judean deportees living in other lands. These events have no source in Kings. 2–9: Drawn from 2 Kings 21.2–9. 6: *Pass through fire*, see 2 Kings 16.3n. 10: The long-range prophecy of terrible disaster in 2 Kings 21.10–15 becomes a summons to repent, which temporarily goes unheeded. 11–13: The exile of Manasseh, which does not appear in Kings, leads the Judean king to entreat the favor of the Lord and humble

the Lord brought against them the commanders of the army of the king of Assyria, who took Manasseh captive in manacles, bound him with fetters, and brought him to Babylon. [12] While he was in distress he entreated the favor of the Lord his God and humbled himself greatly before the God of his ancestors. [13] He prayed to him, and God received his entreaty, heard his plea, and restored him again to Jerusalem and to his kingdom. Then Manasseh knew that the Lord indeed was God.

[14] Afterward he built an outer wall for the city of David west of Gihon, in the valley, reaching the entrance at the Fish Gate; he carried it around Ophel, and raised it to a very great height. He also put commanders of the army in all the fortified cities in Judah. [15] He took away the foreign gods and the idol from the house of the Lord, and all the altars that he had built on the mountain of the house of the Lord and in Jerusalem, and he threw them out of the city. [16] He also restored the altar of the Lord and offered on it sacrifices of well-being and of thanksgiving; and he commanded Judah to serve the Lord the God of Israel. [17] The people, however, still sacrificed at the high places, but only to the Lord their God.

[18] Now the rest of the acts of Manasseh, his prayer to his God, and the words of the seers who spoke to him in the name of the Lord God of Israel, these are in the Annals of the Kings of Israel. [19] His prayer, and how God received his entreaty, all his sin and his faithlessness, the sites on which he built high places and set up the sacred poles[a] and the images, before he humbled himself, these are written in the records of the seers.[b] [20] So Manasseh slept with his ancestors, and they buried him in his house. His son Amon succeeded him.

[21] Amon was twenty-two years old when he began to reign; he reigned two years in Jerusalem. [22] He did what was evil in the sight of the Lord, as his father Manasseh had done. Amon sacrificed to all the images that his father Manasseh had made, and served them. [23] He did not humble himself before the Lord, as his father Manasseh had humbled himself, but this Amon incurred more and more guilt. [24] His servants conspired against him and killed him in his house. [25] But the people of the land killed all those who had conspired against King Amon; and the people of the land made his son Josiah king to succeed him.

34 Josiah was eight years old when he began to reign; he reigned thirty-one years in Jerusalem. [2] He did what was right in the sight of the Lord, and walked in the ways of his ancestor David; he did not turn aside to the right or to the left. [3] For in the eighth year of his reign, while he was still a boy, he began

a   Heb *Asherim*
b   One Ms Gk: MT *of Hozai*

himself. 11: *Babylon,* the reference is not impossible, because the Assyrians maintained a major presence in Babylon at this time. Nevertheless, Assyrian records mention that Manasseh was a loyal vassal. Whether historical or not, the story demonstrates how even one of Judah's worst kings, with God's help, could reverse course in exile, be brought back to his land, institute reforms, and make a new beginning. In this respect, the entire episode offered hope and confirmation to members of the Judean postexilic community, some of whom had ancestors who returned from the Babylonian exile. 13: Going beyond his earlier pledge to Solomon (7.14), God restores Manasseh to his land. Manasseh becomes a model of how to deal with self-made adversity (6.36–39). 14–17: Like other reformer kings (11.5–12; 14.3–7; 17.1–19; 32.27–30), Manasseh constructs fortifications and enforces religious centralization. 18–20: Cf. 2 Kings 21.17–18. 18–19: *His prayer,* this is the basis for the later composition "The Prayer of Manasseh," now a book of the Apocrypha and a similar psalm in the Dead Sea Scrolls.

33.21–25: Degeneracy under Amon (641–640 BCE). This monarch follows the model of the earlier, rather than the later, Manasseh, who *humbled himself* (33.2–9). The account is adapted from 2 Kings 21.19–26. 23–25: In refusing to correct his policies, Amon follows the obstinate course set by Ahaz (28.1–27), worsens Judah's plight, and is punished. 25: *People of the land,* see 2 Kings 11.14n.

34.1–33: Josiah (640–609 BCE): the champion of centralization. Both Kings (2 Kings 22.1–23.30) and Chronicles (34.1–35.27) acclaim Josiah's many reforms throughout Jerusalem and the land of Israel and Judah, but the Chronicler makes these reforms the work of all the people and not simply Josiah himself. 3–7: The Chronicler restructures the account of the reform found in Kings in several ways, including the idea that Josiah began to

to seek the God of his ancestor David, and in the twelfth year he began to purge Judah and Jerusalem of the high places, the sacred poles,[a] and the carved and the cast images. [4] In his presence they pulled down the altars of the Baals; he demolished the incense altars that stood above them. He broke down the sacred poles[a] and the carved and the cast images; he made dust of them and scattered it over the graves of those who had sacrificed to them. [5] He also burned the bones of the priests on their altars, and purged Judah and Jerusalem. [6] In the towns of Manasseh, Ephraim, and Simeon, and as far as Naphtali, in their ruins[b] all around, [7] he broke down the altars, beat the sacred poles[a] and the images into powder, and demolished all the incense altars throughout all the land of Israel. Then he returned to Jerusalem.

[8] In the eighteenth year of his reign, when he had purged the land and the house, he sent Shaphan son of Azaliah, Maaseiah the governor of the city, and Joah son of Joahaz, the recorder, to repair the house of the LORD his God. [9] They came to the high priest Hilkiah and delivered the money that had been brought into the house of God, which the Levites, the keepers of the threshold, had collected from Manasseh and Ephraim and from all the remnant of Israel and from all Judah and Benjamin and from the inhabitants of Jerusalem. [10] They delivered it to the workers who had the oversight of the house of the LORD, and the workers who were working in the house of the LORD gave it for repairing and restoring the house. [11] They gave it to the carpenters and the builders to buy quarried stone, and timber for binders, and beams for the buildings that the kings of Judah had let go to ruin. [12] The people did the work faithfully. Over them were ap-

pointed the Levites Jahath and Obadiah, of the sons of Merari, along with Zechariah and Meshullam, of the sons of the Kohathites, to have oversight. Other Levites, all skillful with instruments of music, [13] were over the burden bearers and directed all who did work in every kind of service; and some of the Levites were scribes, and officials, and gatekeepers.

[14] While they were bringing out the money that had been brought into the house of the LORD, the priest Hilkiah found the book of the law of the LORD given through Moses. [15] Hilkiah said to the secretary Shaphan, "I have found the book of the law in the house of the LORD"; and Hilkiah gave the book to Shaphan. [16] Shaphan brought the book to the king, and further reported to the king, "All that was committed to your servants they are doing. [17] They have emptied out the money that was found in the house of the LORD and have delivered it into the hand of the overseers and the workers." [18] The secretary Shaphan informed the king, "The priest Hilkiah has given me a book." Shaphan then read it aloud to the king.

[19] When the king heard the words of the law he tore his clothes. [20] Then the king commanded Hilkiah, Ahikam son of Shaphan, Abdon son of Micah, the secretary Shaphan, and the king's servant Asaiah: [21] "Go, inquire of the LORD for me and for those who are left in Israel and in Judah, concerning the words of the book that has been found; for the wrath of the LORD that is poured out on us is great, because our ancestors did not keep the word of the LORD, to act in accordance with all that is written in this book."

a   Heb *Asherim*
b   Meaning of Heb uncertain

---

see the LORD in the eighth year of his reign, rather than later, as in Kings (2 Kings 22.3). In the twelfth year he initiates a number of national expeditions, which *purge Judah and Jerusalem* of all rival religious shrines to the Temple. **6:** The geographic extent of Josiah's interventions, from Simeon to Naphtali, are an addition to the Kings source material. Josiah restores proper religious observance throughout all Israel. **8–21:** Adapted in part from 2 Kings 22.3–13. The discovery of *the book of the law of the LORD*, while Temple repairs are underway (vv. 8–14), becomes a matter of grave concern to Josiah because its contents bode ill for Judah. **9:** Since Josiah has already implemented reforms in North and South, it is no great surprise that funds for the Temple restoration project do not merely stem from the people in Judah (2 Kings 22.4), but also from *Manasseh and Ephraim and from all the remnant of Israel*. **14:** Most scholars think that *the book of the law of the LORD* refers to Deuteronomy in 2 Kings 22, but in Chronicles it may refer to the entire Pentateuch (or an earlier version of it). The Passover

22 So Hilkiah and those whom the king had sent went to the prophet Huldah, the wife of Shallum son of Tokhath son of Hasrah, keeper of the wardrobe (who lived in Jerusalem in the Second Quarter) and spoke to her to that effect. 23 She declared to them, "Thus says the LORD, the God of Israel: Tell the man who sent you to me, 24 Thus says the LORD: I will indeed bring disaster upon this place and upon its inhabitants, all the curses that are written in the book that was read before the king of Judah. 25 Because they have forsaken me and have made offerings to other gods, so that they have provoked me to anger with all the works of their hands, my wrath will be poured out on this place and will not be quenched. 26 But as to the king of Judah, who sent you to inquire of the LORD, thus shall you say to him: Thus says the LORD, the God of Israel: Regarding the words that you have heard, 27 because your heart was penitent and you humbled yourself before God when you heard his words against this place and its inhabitants, and you have humbled yourself before me, and have torn your clothes and wept before me, I also have heard you, says the LORD. 28 I will gather you to your ancestors and you shall be gathered to your grave in peace; your eyes shall not see all the disaster that I will bring on this place and its inhabitants." They took the message back to the king.

29 Then the king sent word and gathered together all the elders of Judah and Jerusalem. 30 The king went up to the house of the LORD, with all the people of Judah, the inhabitants of Jerusalem, the priests and the Levites, all the people both great and small; he read in their hearing all the words of the book of the covenant that had been found in the house of the LORD. 31 The king stood in his place and made a covenant before the LORD, to follow the LORD, keeping his commandments, his decrees, and his statutes, with all his heart and all his soul, to perform the words of the covenant that were written in this book. 32 Then he made all who were present in Jerusalem and in Benjamin pledge themselves to it. And the inhabitants of Jerusalem acted according to the covenant of God, the God of their ancestors. 33 Josiah took away all the abominations from all the territory that belonged to the people of Israel, and made all who were in Israel worship the LORD their God. All his days they did not turn away from following the LORD the God of their ancestors.

35 Josiah kept a passover to the LORD in Jerusalem; they slaughtered the passover lamb on the fourteenth day of the first month. 2 He appointed the priests to their offices and encouraged them in the service of the house of the LORD. 3 He said to the Levites who taught all Israel and who were holy to the LORD, "Put the holy ark in the house that Solomon son of David, king of Israel, built; you need no longer carry it on your shoulders. Now serve the LORD your God and his people Israel. 4 Make preparations by your ancestral houses by your divisions, following the written directions of King David of Israel and the written directions of his son Solomon. 5 Take position in the holy place according to the groupings of the ancestral houses of your kindred the people, and let there be Levites for each division of an ancestral house.a 6 Slaughter the passover lamb, sanctify yourselves, and on behalf of your kindred make preparations, acting according to the word of the LORD by Moses."

a Meaning of Heb uncertain

celebration (35.1–19) draws on more than one collection of earlier biblical law. 22–28: Huldah's oracle, drawn from 2 Kings 22.14–20, portrays a bleak future for Judah. 29–33: Like other noted Judean leaders who wish to avoid or counter a period of decline (15.8–19; 23.16; 29.10), Josiah leads the nation in covenant renewal (cf. 2 Kings 23.1–3). The ratification of the covenant leads to the implementation of reforms throughout his land (cf. 2 Kings 23.4–10). The result is religious unity for the nation *all his days*.

35.1–19: Passover celebration. As in 2 Kings (23.4–20), national reforms (34.33) lead to a national Passover (2 Kings 23.21–23). Josiah's Passover offering is described in much more detail than in Kings. 3: The only reference to the ark during the Judahite monarchy (chs 10–36). The pedagogical responsibility of the Levites, who *taught all Israel,* is found elsewhere (Deut 33.8–11) but is more frequent in postexilic texts (e.g., 17.7–9; Neh 8.7–8). 4–6: The provisions made during the United Monarchy are the model for the levitical and priestly divisions (31.2–

[7] Then Josiah contributed to the people, as passover offerings for all that were present, lambs and kids from the flock to the number of thirty thousand, and three thousand bulls; these were from the king's possessions. [8] His officials contributed willingly to the people, to the priests, and to the Levites. Hilkiah, Zechariah, and Jehiel, the chief officers of the house of God, gave to the priests for the passover offerings two thousand six hundred lambs and kids and three hundred bulls. [9] Conaniah also, and his brothers Shemaiah and Nethanel, and Hashabiah and Jeiel and Jozabad, the chiefs of the Levites, gave to the Levites for the passover offerings five thousand lambs and kids and five hundred bulls.

[10] When the service had been prepared for, the priests stood in their place, and the Levites in their divisions according to the king's command. [11] They slaughtered the passover lamb, and the priests dashed the blood that they received[a] from them, while the Levites did the skinning. [12] They set aside the burnt offerings so that they might distribute them according to the groupings of the ancestral houses of the people, to offer to the LORD, as it is written in the book of Moses. And they did the same with the bulls. [13] They roasted the passover lamb with fire according to the ordinance; and they boiled the holy offerings in pots, in caldrons, and in pans, and carried them quickly to all the people. [14] Afterward they made preparations for themselves and for the priests, because the priests the descendants of Aaron were occupied in offering the burnt offerings and the fat parts until night; so the Levites made preparations for themselves and for the priests, the descen-

dants of Aaron. [15] The singers, the descendants of Asaph, were in their place according to the command of David, and Asaph, and Heman, and the king's seer Jeduthun. The gatekeepers were at each gate; they did not need to interrupt their service, for their kindred the Levites made preparations for them.

[16] So all the service of the LORD was prepared that day, to keep the passover and to offer burnt offerings on the altar of the LORD, according to the command of King Josiah. [17] The people of Israel who were present kept the passover at that time, and the festival of unleavened bread seven days. [18] No passover like it had been kept in Israel since the days of the prophet Samuel; none of the kings of Israel had kept such a passover as was kept by Josiah, by the priests and the Levites, by all Judah and Israel who were present, and by the inhabitants of Jerusalem. [19] In the eighteenth year of the reign of Josiah this passover was kept.

[20] After all this, when Josiah had set the temple in order, King Neco of Egypt went up to fight at Carchemish on the Euphrates, and Josiah went out against him. [21] But Neco[b] sent envoys to him, saying, "What have I to do with you, king of Judah? I am not coming against you today, but against the house with which I am at war; and God has commanded me to hurry. Cease opposing God, who is with me, so that he will not destroy you." [22] But Josiah would not turn away from him, but disguised himself in order to fight with him. He did not listen to the words of Neco

a   Heb lacks *that they received*
b   Heb *he*

19n.). **7–9:** The contributions of king, officials, and Levites (cf. 34.9) help make the Passover a civic event. **13:** The preparations of the Passover lamb are said to accord with the ordinance (cf. vv. 6,12). The beginning of the verse, properly translated, reads, "They boiled the Passover lamb with fire." This difficult idea reflects a combination of Ex 12.8, which prescribes that the lamb must be broiled on a fire, and Deut 16.7, which prescribes that it must be boiled. These reflect different customs, which ultimately came into conflict when the Torah was canonized. Chronicles and later rabbinic texts often dealt with such problems through harmonization, thus "boiling with fire." **18:** The national Passover is unparalleled since the days of Samuel (cf. 2 Kings 23.22). Chronicles, like 2 Kings 23.21–22, attributes to Josiah an incomparably successful Passover celebration. The Passover of Hezekiah (30.1–22) was also important, but enjoyed more limited participation than Josiah's Passover, which was attended by the *priests and the Levites, by all Judah and Israel,* and *the inhabitants of Jerusalem* (cf. 30.10–11).

35.20–27: Josiah's defeat and death by Pharaoh Neco. Unlike 2 Kings 23.29–30, in Chronicles Neco acts explicitly as a messenger and agent of God. The addition justifies the death of the otherwise righteous Josiah; he did not heed the prophetic voice. **20:** *Neco,* it is unclear why Josiah intervened against one of the superpow-

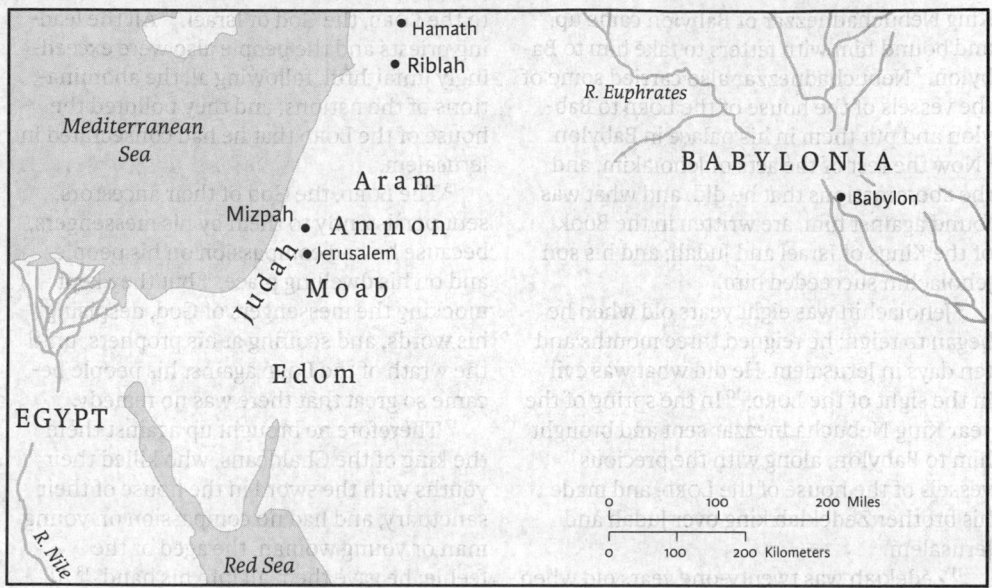

Ch 36: Babylon and Judah in the early sixth century BCE.

from the mouth of God, but joined battle in the plain of Megiddo. ²³ The archers shot King Josiah; and the king said to his servants, "Take me away, for I am badly wounded." ²⁴ So his servants took him out of the chariot and carried him in his second chariot[a] and brought him to Jerusalem. There he died, and was buried in the tombs of his ancestors. All Judah and Jerusalem mourned for Josiah. ²⁵ Jeremiah also uttered a lament for Josiah, and all the singing men and singing women have spoken of Josiah in their laments to this day. They made these a custom in Israel; they are recorded in the Laments. ²⁶ Now the rest of the acts of Josiah and his faithful deeds in accordance with what is written in the law of the LORD, ²⁷ and his acts, first and last, are written in the Book of the Kings of Israel and Judah.

36 The people of the land took Jehoahaz son of Josiah and made him king to succeed his father in Jerusalem. ² Jehoahaz was twenty-three years old when he began to reign; he reigned three months in Jerusalem. ³ Then the king of Egypt deposed him in Jerusalem and laid on the land a tribute of one hundred talents of silver and one talent of gold. ⁴ The king of Egypt made his brother Eliakim king over Judah and Jerusalem, and changed his name to Jehoiakim; but Neco took his brother Jehoahaz and carried him to Egypt.

⁵ Jehoiakim was twenty-five years old when he began to reign; he reigned eleven years in Jerusalem. He did what was evil in the sight of the LORD his God. ⁶ Against him

a   Or *the chariot of his deputy*

ers of his day. Josiah may have been in an alliance with Neco's enemies (cf. 2 Kings 23.29). **23:** *Archers shot,* in conformity with Huldah's prophecy (34.24–28), Josiah is gathered to his fathers (v. 24) and does not see great calamity come to Jerusalem (36.17–21). The Chronicler may understand Huldah's prophecy to mean that Josiah would die in a time of peace for Judah, rathen that to mean the type of death Josiah would suffer himself (cf. 2 Kings 22.20 || 2 Chr 34.28).

36.1–14: Judah's last four kings. The Chronicler's history of Judah's final decades is much briefer and less gruesome than that of 2 Kings 24–25. Either the Chronicler had a shorter version of our book of Kings, or living in the postexilic restoration community, he felt no need to dwell on the details of the disaster of the exile. **1–4:** The account of the reign of Jehoahaz (609 BCE) is largely taken from 2 Kings 23.30–34. In Chronicles Jehoahaz receives no evaluation. **5–8:** The reign of Jehoiakim (608–598) is much abridged and adapted from

King Nebuchadnezzar of Babylon came up, and bound him with fetters to take him to Babylon. [7] Nebuchadnezzar also carried some of the vessels of the house of the LORD to Babylon and put them in his palace in Babylon. [8] Now the rest of the acts of Jehoiakim, and the abominations that he did, and what was found against him, are written in the Book of the Kings of Israel and Judah; and his son Jehoiachin succeeded him.

[9] Jehoiachin was eight years old when he began to reign; he reigned three months and ten days in Jerusalem. He did what was evil in the sight of the LORD. [10] In the spring of the year King Nebuchadnezzar sent and brought him to Babylon, along with the precious vessels of the house of the LORD, and made his brother Zedekiah king over Judah and Jerusalem.

[11] Zedekiah was twenty-one years old when he began to reign; he reigned eleven years in Jerusalem. [12] He did what was evil in the sight of the LORD his God. He did not humble himself before the prophet Jeremiah who spoke from the mouth of the LORD. [13] He also rebelled against King Nebuchadnezzar, who had made him swear by God; he stiffened his neck and hardened his heart against turning to the LORD, the God of Israel. [14] All the leading priests and the people also were exceedingly unfaithful, following all the abominations of the nations; and they polluted the house of the LORD that he had consecrated in Jerusalem.

[15] The LORD, the God of their ancestors, sent persistently to them by his messengers, because he had compassion on his people and on his dwelling place; [16] but they kept mocking the messengers of God, despising his words, and scoffing at his prophets, until the wrath of the LORD against his people became so great that there was no remedy.

[17] Therefore he brought up against them the king of the Chaldeans, who killed their youths with the sword in the house of their sanctuary, and had no compassion on young man or young woman, the aged or the feeble; he gave them all into his hand. [18] All the vessels of the house of God, large and small, and the treasures of the house of the LORD, and the treasures of the king and of his officials, all these he brought to Babylon. [19] They burned the house of God, broke down the wall of Jerusalem, burned all its palaces with fire, and destroyed all its precious vessels. [20] He took into exile in Babylon those

2 Kings 23.36–24.6. See also Dan 1.1–2. **6:** *Nebuchadnezzar* II who ruled Babylon from 605 to 562 BCE, was one of its most powerful and successful kings. Among his foreign policy accomplishments were the conquest of Tyre (Ezek 27.12) and the invasion of Egypt (Ezek 29.19–21). Both Chronicles and 2 Kings 24.1–17 mention a Babylonian invasion, which affected both Jehoiakim and his son Jehoiachin (598/7 BCE). But only Chronicles claims that the Babylonian king came to Jerusalem to bring both *Jehoiakim* and later his son Jehoiachin, along with various precious Temple *vessels*, to Babylon (v. 10). **9–10:** Jehoiachin (597) was eighteen years old, not *eight years old* (see 2 Kings 24.8). He suffers a personal exile, along with *the precious vessels of the house of the LORD*, but in 2 Kings 24.8–17 the exile of 597 BCE is a much more widespread deportation. **11–14:** Taken in part from 2 Kings 25.18–20. Like Ahaz (ch 28) and Amon (33.23), Zedekiah (597–586) refused to *humble himself*. The Chronicler criticizes Zedekiah, *the leading priests*, and *the people* for being *exceedingly unfaithful* (see 1 Chr 10.1–14n.). Thus, the Chronicler, unlike the author of Kings, offers a specific reason for why the exile occurred under Zedekiah. **13:** *Rebelled*, the Babylonians under *Nebuchadnezzar* II took swift reprisal against vassals who chose to revolt. In this case, the Chronicler finds fault with Zedekiah himself for violating his oath to God and refusing to reverse his course. **14:** *The leading priests*, the Chronicler blames not only royalty but also higher echelon priests and *the people* themselves for the exile. **17–22:** The fall of Jerusalem took place in 586 BCE.

36.15–23: Exile and the call to return. The Deuteronomist places a great deal of blame for Judah's fall on the sins of Manasseh (2 Kings 21.10–15; 23.26–27; 24.3–4), but this is impossible for the Chronicler, who narrated Manasseh's repentance (33.12–13). Instead, the references to the gradual rise in divine wrath, the repeated lack of repentance, and the succession of unheeded messengers and prophets (cf. 15.1–8; 21.12–15; 25.15–17) suggest that the Chronicler attributes the exile to a preponderance of unrequited sins during the last generations of Judah's independence (cf. 2 Kings 24.20). **17–21:** The record of Judah's exile in 586 BCE is partially drawn from 2 Kings 25.1–21. This author does not depict an Egyptian exile of 582 BCE (2 Kings 25.22–26). **17:** *The Chaldeans*, the Babylonians. **20:** The *kingdom of Persia*, under Cyrus the Great (v. 22), defeated the kingdoms of Media,

who had escaped from the sword, and they became servants to him and to his sons until the establishment of the kingdom of Persia, ²¹ to fulfill the word of the LORD by the mouth of Jeremiah, until the land had made up for its sabbaths. All the days that it lay desolate it kept sabbath, to fulfill seventy years.

²² In the first year of King Cyrus of Persia, in fulfillment of the word of the LORD spoken by Jeremiah, the LORD stirred up the spirit of King Cyrus of Persia so that he sent a herald throughout all his kingdom and also declared in a written edict: ²³ "Thus says King Cyrus of Persia: The LORD, the God of heaven, has given me all the kingdoms of the earth, and he has charged me to build him a house at Jerusalem, which is in Judah. Whoever is among you of all his people, may the LORD his God be with him! Let him go up."

Lydia, and Babylon, thus becoming one of the ancient world's great empires. At the height of its power, Persia ruled a vast territory stretching from Greece in the west to India in the east. **21:** On the prophecies of Jeremiah, see Jer 25.11–12; 29.10, which are here conflated with Lev 26.34–35,43. **22–23:** Kings ends with the mercies shown to Jehoiachin in exile (2 Kings 25.27–30), but Chronicles offers a clearer hope for the future: King Cyrus's decree in 538 BCE of an end to exile. As Chronicles repeatedly demonstrates, exile need not be a final conclusion, but a condition from which it is possible to return (6.36–39; 7.12–15; 33.12–13). Indeed, from the perspective of the books of Ezra-Nehemiah, Cyrus's decree marks the beginning of Persian-period Judah (Ezra 1.1–3). The return is *in fulfillment of the word of the LORD spoken by Jeremiah,* emphasizing one last time, at the book's conclusion, the power of the prophetic word. Some manuscripts of the Hebrew Bible end with Chronicles, in which case the scriptures conclude with an optimistic note of anticipation.

EZRA

NAME AND LOCATION IN CANON

The books of Ezra and Nehemiah form a single book in early Hebrew and Greek manuscripts of the Bible, but are separated into two in later Christian tradition. The books are named for their principal characters, both Jewish leaders of the fifth century BCE. Ezra is featured in chs 7–10 of the book that bears his name, and in Neh 8–9; Nehemiah is prominent in the book that bears his name.

In the traditional order of books in the Hebrew Bible, Ezra-Nehemiah is found in the third division of the canon, the Writings. In modern printed Jewish Bibles, following some ancient manuscripts, Ezra-Nehemiah is near the end and comes just before the last book, Chronicles. In other ancient sources, Ezra-Nehemiah is the last book in the Writings. In most Christian canons, Ezra-Nehemiah is located among the historical books and immediately follows Chronicles. The Greek book of 1 Esdras, which includes sections of both Ezra and Nehemiah, is part of the Apocrypha; in Eastern Orthodox canons it precedes Ezra-Nehemiah. (See further Introduction to 1 Esdras.)

HISTORICAL BACKGROUND

The unified book of Ezra-Nehemiah (Esdras b in Greek manuscripts) describes the return of exiles from Babylonia in 538 BCE, and the reconstruction of Jewish life in Judah under Persian imperial rule between 538 and approximately 420. According to its account, the return, authorized by the edict of the Persian king Cyrus, marked the beginning of a lengthy process of rebuilding Jerusalem and the Temple. During this period Israel reconstituted itself as the "people of the Book," with scripture, specifically the first five books of the Bible (the Torah, also known as the Law of Moses, or as the Pentateuch), becoming authoritative for communal and personal life. These developments took place during the reign of several Persian kings and under the Jewish leadership of Zerubbabel, Joshua, Ezra, and Nehemiah. While the Temple and its personnel gained unprecedented powers, the community developed new criteria for identity and membership.

Cyrus's edict permitting the return to Judah sets the agenda for the entire book of Ezra-Nehemiah, launching a national and religious rebirth and reconstruction that includes rebuilding the Temple, the community, and Jerusalem. The edict also establishes official Persian legitimation of Jewish life in the Persian province of Yehud (the name for Judah in Aramaic and other sources), claiming harmony between Persian imperial policies and the will of Israel's God, a position that pervades Ezra-Nehemiah.

It is difficult to reconstruct the actual history of this period. Based on additional information from the books of Haggai and Zechariah, many scholars think that the return and rebuilding took place in four or more steps, though this is uncertain. First, the earliest returnees, led by Sheshbazzar in 538, began to rebuild the Temple but for some reason abandoned the project. Second, a later group of exiles, under the leadership of Zerubbabel and Jeshua, resumed rebuilding during the reign of the Persian king Darius I (522–486) and completed the Temple reconstruction in 515. Third, a group led by Ezra in 458 during the reign of Artaxerxes I (465–424) reestablished the Torah, the law of Moses, as the authority for Jews in Yehud. Finally, a group led by Nehemiah beginning in 445, later in the reign of Artaxerxes I, restored Jerusalem's walls and repopulated Jerusalem. Some scholars have suggested that Ezra's return, with its religious innovations, took place only after Nehemiah's political improvements. Most scholars favor the reconstruction given above, which follows the biblical sequence and which will be used in the annotations. Archaeological studies suggest only limited development in the province of Judah during the Persian period. This raises questions about the extent and effectiveness of the reconstruction that Ezra-Nehemiah describes.

DATE OF COMPOSITION, LITERARY HISTORY, AND STRUCTURE

Ezra-Nehemiah was probably composed in Judah after 400 BCE. It shares some themes and vocabulary with Chronicles, another Persian-period book, and Ezra 1.1–3 overlaps the end of Chronicles, 2 Chr 36.22–23. However, the books use different vocabulary and have different ideologies, and were most likely composed by different authors (see Introduction to 1 Chronicles, pp. 575-577). Ezra-Nehemiah also shares elements with several later books in antiquity under the name of Ezra that are preserved in the Apocrypha and Pseudepigrapha, including 1 Esdras, which contains all of Ezra 1–10 as well as Nehemiah 8, and 2 Esdras.

Ezra-Nehemiah has a complicated literary history. It incorporates what are presented as contemporary sources into its account. These include first-person memoirs of both Ezra (Ezra 7.27–9.15) and Nehemiah (Neh 1.1–7.5; 12.27–13.31); letters of various officials, often written in Aramaic, the lingua franca of the Persian empire; and assorted lists. Moreover, although most of Ezra-Nehemiah is written in Hebrew, Ezra 4.6–6.18 and 7.12–26 are in Aramaic, including not only official documents but also the narrative in which they are quoted.

Despite this composite appearance, however, the final form of Ezra-Nehemiah has a carefully developed structure. The work opens with God's promise and Cyrus's decree allowing the Temple to be rebuilt (Ezra 1.1–4), and continues with exiled Israel's response (Ezra 1.5–Neh 7.73), culminating in celebration of reconstruction (Neh 8–13). After an anticipatory summary of enthusiastic reaction (Ezra 1.5–11) and a framing section of the list of returnees (Ezra 2), the response takes place in three stages: Stage One describes the reconstruction of the Temple in 538–515 BCE (Ezra 3–6); Stage Two describes the mission of Ezra and the formation of the community according to Torah in 458 (Ezra 7–10); and Stage Three describes the rebuilding of Jerusalem under Nehemiah's leadership in 445–444 (Neh 1.1–7.5). These stages close with another framing section, the repeated list of returnees (Neh 7.6–73). The work concludes with celebration of renewal and reconstruction (Neh 8–13). This last section describes the reading and implementation of the Torah (Neh 8); the confession and commitment of the people (Neh 9–10); the repopulation of the city and review of the people (Neh 11.1–12.26); and a service of dedication, including celebration, purification, procession, and separation (Neh 12.27–13.3). The very end is a coda in which Nehemiah recounts some of his reforms and invokes God's remembrance (Neh 13.4–31).

INTERPRETATION AND GUIDE TO READING

Because it has a continuous chronology, Ezra-Nehemiah should be read from beginning to end as a unified narrative. According to this narrative, the returned exiles were not only concerned with restoring preexilic institutions, such as the altar and the Temple, and restoring the city. They also adapted to changed circumstances by establishing religious practices that conformed to their understanding of the book of the Torah, which likely reached its final form in the late postexilic period. To the author, the returned exiles were a godly remnant with a renewed commitment to perpetuate the covenantal teachings that kept them distinct. The returned exiles were also a minority within the vast, polytheistic, and multicultural Persian empire. Consequently, they sought to protect their ethnic and religious identity by establishing rigorous religious boundaries between themselves and their neighbors. The author was especially worried that the community might repeat the mistakes that caused the exile, such as intermarriage, and a new destruction would follow.

Through its structure and narrative, Ezra-Nehemiah emphasizes the role of the people themselves in rebuilding, as well as the power of authoritative documents.

Tamara Cohn Eskenazi

1 In the first year of King Cyrus of Persia, in order that the word of the LORD by the mouth of Jeremiah might be accomplished, the LORD stirred up the spirit of King Cyrus of Persia so that he sent a herald throughout all his kingdom, and also in a written edict declared:

2 "Thus says King Cyrus of Persia: The LORD, the God of heaven, has given me all the kingdoms of the earth, and he has charged me to build him a house at Jerusalem in Judah. 3 Any of those among you who are of his people—may their God be with them!—are now permitted to go up to Jerusalem in Judah, and rebuild the house of the LORD, the God of Israel—he is the God who is in Jerusalem; 4 and let all survivors, in whatever place they reside, be assisted by the people of their place with silver and gold, with goods and with animals, besides freewill offerings for the house of God in Jerusalem."

5 The heads of the families of Judah and Benjamin, and the priests and the Levites—everyone whose spirit God had stirred—got ready to go up and rebuild the house of the LORD in Jerusalem. 6 All their neighbors aided them with silver vessels, with gold, with goods, with animals, and with valuable gifts, besides all that was freely offered. 7 King Cyrus himself brought out the vessels of the house of the LORD that Nebuchadnezzar had carried away from Jerusalem and placed in the house of his gods. 8 King Cyrus of Persia had them released into the charge of Mithredath the treasurer, who counted them out to Sheshbazzar the prince of Judah. 9 And this was the inventory: gold basins, thirty; silver basins, one thousand; knives,[a] twenty-nine; 10 gold bowls, thirty; other silver bowls, four hundred ten; other vessels, one thousand; 11 the total of the gold and silver vessels was five thousand four hundred. All these Sheshbazzar brought up, when the exiles were brought up from Babylonia to Jerusalem.

2 Now these were the people of the province who came from those captive exiles whom King Nebuchadnezzar of Babylon had carried captive to Babylonia; they returned to

a   Vg: Meaning of Heb uncertain

1.1–4: God's promise and Cyrus's decree. The decree by the Persian king authorizes return to Judah and rebuilding God's house in Jerusalem, after its destruction by the Babylonians and the deportation to Babylonia in the early sixth century BCE. The rest of the book describes three stages of return and rebuilding. Most of this decree appears in 2 Chr 36.22–23, and in a different form in Ezra 6.2–5. 1: King Cyrus, the Persian king (559–530 BCE) who conquered Babylon in 539 BCE. This edict in 538 (the first year of the text) is consistent with Persian religious and political policy: ancient inscriptions depict Cyrus as restorer of several temples. Jeremiah, a sixth-century BCE prophet who lived through the destruction of Judah and repeatedly promised a restoration; see, e.g., Jer 29.10. 2: God of heaven, a typical postexilic title (e.g., Neh 1.5; Dan 2.18). 3: His people, i.e., worshipers of Israel's God. Are now permitted, better translated as a command to go up (see 2 Chr 36.23; 1 Esd 2.5). Rebuild the house of the LORD, the Temple had been destroyed by the Babylonians in 586 BCE (see 2 Kings 25). But in Ezra-Nehemiah, the notion of the house of the LORD encompasses more than the Temple and includes eventually the city itself and its dedicated inhabitants. 4: Survivors, primarily referring to Jews still in exile and perhaps those in the land who survived the crisis.

1.5–Neh 7.73: The three stages of return and reconstruction.

1.5–8: These verses sum up the enthusiastic response by the people to the decree, a response that leads to the reconstruction described in Ezra 2–Neh 7. 5: Judah and Benjamin formerly constituted the kingdom of Judah (destroyed by Babylon); the other tribes of the Northern Kingdom of Israel (destroyed and exiled by Assyria in 722 BCE; see 2 Kings 17) did not return. The Levites were religious functionaries; the priests were a subgroup of Levites who according to tradition were descended from Aaron, the first priest (see Ex 28.1) with unique responsibilities for the sanctuary. 7–11: The return of the sacred vessels symbolizes continuity with the destroyed Temple, whose looting is described in 2 Kings 25.13–17. The number of itemized vessels is smaller than the total given of 5,400. 7: Nebuchadnezzar, the Babylonian king who destroyed the first Temple in 586 BCE (see 2 Kings 25.1). 8: Sheshbazzar, a leader of the early return (see also 5.14–16); some scholars think that he was descended from King David.

2.1–70: The list of returnees. With its repetition in Neh 7.6–73a, the list frames the three stages of reconstruction. It also reflects combined waves of immigration, and is thus anachronistic here. It was expanded over

Jerusalem and Judah, all to their own towns. ² They came with Zerubbabel, Jeshua, Nehemiah, Seraiah, Reelaiah, Mordecai, Bilshan, Mispar, Bigvai, Rehum, and Baanah.

The number of the Israelite people: ³ the descendants of Parosh, two thousand one hundred seventy-two. ⁴ Of Shephatiah, three hundred seventy-two. ⁵ Of Arah, seven hundred seventy-five. ⁶ Of Pahath-moab, namely the descendants of Jeshua and Joab, two thousand eight hundred twelve. ⁷ Of Elam, one thousand two hundred fifty-four. ⁸ Of Zattu, nine hundred forty-five. ⁹ Of Zaccai, seven hundred sixty. ¹⁰ Of Bani, six hundred forty-two. ¹¹ Of Bebai, six hundred twenty-three. ¹² Of Azgad, one thousand two hundred twenty-two. ¹³ Of Adonikam, six hundred sixty-six. ¹⁴ Of Bigvai, two thousand fifty-six. ¹⁵ Of Adin, four hundred fifty-four. ¹⁶ Of Ater, namely of Hezekiah, ninety-eight. ¹⁷ Of Bezai, three hundred twenty-three. ¹⁸ Of Jorah, one hundred twelve. ¹⁹ Of Hashum, two hundred twenty-three. ²⁰ Of Gibbar, ninety-five. ²¹ Of Bethlehem, one hundred twenty-three. ²² The people of Netophah, fifty-six. ²³ Of Anathoth, one hundred twenty-eight. ²⁴ The descendants of Azmaveth, forty-two. ²⁵ Of Kiriatharim, Chephirah, and Beeroth, seven hundred forty-three. ²⁶ Of Ramah and Geba, six hundred twenty-one. ²⁷ The people of Michmas, one hundred twenty-two. ²⁸ Of Bethel and Ai, two hundred twenty-three. ²⁹ The descendants of Nebo, fifty-two. ³⁰ Of Magbish, one hundred fifty-six. ³¹ Of the other Elam, one thousand two hundred fifty-four. ³² Of Harim, three hundred twenty. ³³ Of Lod, Hadid, and Ono, seven hundred twenty-five. ³⁴ Of Jericho, three hundred forty-five. ³⁵ Of Senaah, three thousand six hundred thirty.

³⁶ The priests: the descendants of Jedaiah, of the house of Jeshua, nine hundred seventy-three. ³⁷ Of Immer, one thousand fifty-two. ³⁸ Of Pashhur, one thousand two hundred forty-seven. ³⁹ Of Harim, one thousand seventeen.

⁴⁰ The Levites: the descendants of Jeshua and Kadmiel, of the descendants of Hodaviah, seventy-four. ⁴¹ The singers: the descendants of Asaph, one hundred twenty-eight. ⁴² The descendants of the gatekeepers: of Shallum, of Ater, of Talmon, of Akkub, of Hatita, and of Shobai, in all one hundred thirty-nine.

⁴³ The temple servants: the descendants of Ziha, Hasupha, Tabbaoth, ⁴⁴ Keros, Siaha, Padon, ⁴⁵ Lebanah, Hagabah, Akkub, ⁴⁶ Hagab, Shamlai, Hanan, ⁴⁷ Giddel, Gahar, Reaiah, ⁴⁸ Rezin, Nekoda, Gazzam, ⁴⁹ Uzza, Paseah, Besai, ⁵⁰ Asnah, Meunim, Nephisim, ⁵¹ Bakbuk, Hakupha, Harhur, ⁵² Bazluth, Mehida, Harsha, ⁵³ Barkos, Sisera, Temah, ⁵⁴ Neziah, and Hatipha.

⁵⁵ The descendants of Solomon's servants: Sotai, Hassophereth, Peruda, ⁵⁶ Jaalah, Darkon, Giddel, ⁵⁷ Shephatiah, Hattil, Pochereth-hazzebaim, and Ami.

⁵⁸ All the temple servants and the descendants of Solomon's servants were three hundred ninety-two.

⁵⁹ The following were those who came up from Tel-melah, Tel-harsha, Cherub, Addan, and Immer, though they could not prove their families or their descent, whether they belonged to Israel: ⁶⁰ the descendants of Delaiah, Tobiah, and Nekoda, six hundred fifty-two. ⁶¹ Also, of the descendants of the priests: the descendants of Habaiah, Hak-

decades and includes other members of the restored Judean community between 538 and 444 BCE. The list is organized according to three groups: Israelites (laity), Levites, and priests. **1–2:** *Zerubbabel, Jeshua, Nehemiah,* of the list of leaders, only these three (if this Nehemiah is identical with the governor of Neh 1.1) will play a role in Ezra-Nehemiah. Zerubbabel is among the last known descendants of David in the Hebrew Bible (see 1 Chr 3.19) and is elsewhere called "governor" (e.g., Hag 1.1). He is one of the two major leaders of Stage One of the return and reconstruction. Jeshua the priest is elsewhere called "high priest" (e.g., Hag 1.1). He is the other major leader of Stage One. **2b–35:** Lay Israelites are listed by family ancestral names (vv. 2b–20) and towns of origin (vv. 21–35). Archaeology provides evidence of increased population during the Persian period at many of the sites mentioned here. **36–39:** *Priests* include four families claiming descent from Aaron (cf. 1 Chr 24). **40–42:** *Levites* are listed according to their Temple functions in the postexilic period. **43–58:** Other Temple personnel and miscellaneous groups. **59–63:** As a result of the book's concern with communal identity, uncertain genealogies jeopardize membership in the community. Several of these names, however, are later included as community members. Some of the listed towns (like Tel Melah in v. 59) are in Babylonia. **61–63:** Priestly legitimacy depends

koz, and Barzillai (who had married one of the daughters of Barzillai the Gileadite, and was called by their name). [62] These looked for their entries in the genealogical records, but they were not found there, and so they were excluded from the priesthood as unclean; [63] the governor told them that they were not to partake of the most holy food, until there should be a priest to consult Urim and Thummim.

[64] The whole assembly together was forty-two thousand three hundred sixty, [65] besides their male and female servants, of whom there were seven thousand three hundred thirty-seven; and they had two hundred male and female singers. [66] They had seven hundred thirty-six horses, two hundred forty-five mules, [67] four hundred thirty-five camels, and six thousand seven hundred twenty donkeys.

[68] As soon as they came to the house of the LORD in Jerusalem, some of the heads of families made freewill offerings for the house of God, to erect it on its site. [69] According to their resources they gave to the building fund sixty-one thousand darics of gold, five thousand minas of silver, and one hundred priestly robes.

[70] The priests, the Levites, and some of the people lived in Jerusalem and its vicinity;[a] and the singers, the gatekeepers, and the temple servants lived in their towns, and all Israel in their towns.

3 When the seventh month came, and the Israelites were in the towns, the people gathered together in Jerusalem. [2] Then Jeshua son of Jozadak, with his fellow priests, and Zerubbabel son of Shealtiel with his kin set out to build the altar of the God of Israel, to offer burnt offerings on it, as prescribed in the law of Moses the man of God. [3] They set up the altar on its foundation, because they were in dread of the neighboring peoples, and they offered burnt offerings upon it to the LORD, morning and evening. [4] And they kept the festival of booths,[b] as prescribed, and offered the daily burnt offerings by number according to the ordinance, as required for each day, [5] and after that the regular burnt offerings, the offerings at the new moon and at all the sacred festivals of the LORD, and the

a 1 Esdras 5.46: Heb lacks *lived in Jerusalem and its vicinity*
b Or *tabernacles*; Heb *succoth*

on descent from Aaron. Illegitimate priests threaten the sanctity of the Temple. **61:** *Barzillai the Gileadite,* see 2 Sam 17.27; 19.31. The adoption of the father-in-law's name suggests that Barzillai did not have a male heir. **63:** *Urim and Thummim* were a device, like casting lots, that priests used to ascertain divine guidance in certain situations (Ex 28.30; Lev 8.8; Deut 33.8). *Governor,* Heb "tirshata," a Persian title. **64:** The total listed, 42,360, exceeds the sum of the enumerated groups (around 30,000), one of several signs of the list's expansion or an indication that the total includes women. **65–67:** The number of servants, as well as of singers and livestock, suggests relatively modest economic means. **69:** The precise monetary value of this contribution to the Temple is uncertain because the value of the daric and the mina fluctuated. Nevertheless, the passage suggests that the community invested a great deal in restoring its Temple. The *priestly robes* are specialized garments for official service. **70:** *All Israel in their towns,* Ezra-Nehemiah emphasizes continuity, suggesting a return to pre-exilic settlements. In reality, however, the Persian province of Yehud was considerably smaller than the earlier kingdom of Judah.

3.1–6.22: Stage One of reconstruction: building the Temple. Ezra 3 emphasizes the determination of the returnees to rebuild the Temple as soon as possible.

3.1–7: First step: rebuilding the altar. The restoration of the altar and a functioning priesthood indicates the resumption of sacrificial worship, a central means of religious expression in the ancient world. **1:** *The seventh month,* Tishri (September-October). **2:** *Jeshua . . . and Zerubbabel,* Ezra-Nehemiah assumes a pattern of dual leadership by a priest and a secular leader. *The law* (Heb "torah") *of Moses,* most likely some form of the Pentateuch (see notes to Neh 8). Ezra-Nehemiah is keen on describing conformity to the "torah", or teaching, of Moses (hence to God's teachings) as the guiding principle in reconstruction. **3–6:** The detailed catalogue of sacrifices confirms the resumption of worship according to authoritative traditions. **3:** *Dread of the neighboring peoples,* tension with local inhabitants and neighboring peoples is a major theme in Ezra-Nehemiah. Some scholars see in this tension a debate between returning Judeans and those Judeans who remained in the land over who can represent postexilic "Israel"; others suggest that surrounding cultures saw Jewish renewal as a

offerings of everyone who made a freewill offering to the Lord. [6] From the first day of the
seventh month they began to offer burnt offerings to the Lord. But the foundation of the
temple of the Lord was not yet laid. [7] So they
gave money to the masons and the carpenters, and food, drink, and oil to the Sidonians
and the Tyrians to bring cedar trees from
Lebanon to the sea, to Joppa, according to the
grant that they had from King Cyrus of Persia.

[8] In the second year after their arrival at
the house of God at Jerusalem, in the second
month, Zerubbabel son of Shealtiel and Jeshua son of Jozadak made a beginning, together
with the rest of their people, the priests and
the Levites and all who had come to Jerusalem from the captivity. They appointed the
Levites, from twenty years old and upward, to
have the oversight of the work on the house
of the Lord. [9] And Jeshua with his sons and
his kin, and Kadmiel and his sons, Binnui and
Hodaviah[a] along with the sons of Henadad,
the Levites, their sons and kin, together took
charge of the workers in the house of God.

[10] When the builders laid the foundation of
the temple of the Lord, the priests in their vestments were stationed to praise the Lord with

trumpets, and the Levites, the sons of Asaph,
with cymbals, according to the directions of
King David of Israel; [11] and they sang respon-
sively, praising and giving thanks to the Lord,

"For he is good,
    for his steadfast love endures forever
        toward Israel."

And all the people responded with a great
shout when they praised the Lord, because
the foundation of the house of the Lord was
laid. [12] But many of the priests and Levites
and heads of families, old people who had
seen the first house on its foundations, wept
with a loud voice when they saw this house,
though many shouted aloud for joy, [13] so that
the people could not distinguish the sound
of the joyful shout from the sound of the
people's weeping, for the people shouted so
loudly that the sound was heard far away.

4 When the adversaries of Judah and
Benjamin heard that the returned exiles
were building a temple to the Lord, the God
of Israel, [2] they approached Zerubbabel and
the heads of families and said to them, "Let

---

[a] Compare 2.40; Neh 7.43; 1 Esdras 5.58: Heb *sons of
Judah*

---

threat, as Ezra 4 indicates. **4:** *The festival of booths,* see Lev 23.34. **5:** *Offerings at the new moon,* see Num 29.6. **7:**
Sidon and Tyre helped build Solomon's Temple (1 Kings 5–7).

3.8–13: Second step: founding the Second Temple. The laying of the foundation of the Temple provokes
opposition from the people in the land and causes a delay in building the Temple itself. According to Ezra-Nehemiah, this explains why the Temple was rebuilt only in the time of King Darius. The historical reality was likely
more complex; see the description of the people's loss of interest depicted in the books of Haggai and Zechariah. **8:** *Second year,* 537 or 536. Hag 2.18 dates the founding differently, to 520 BCE. Ezra 5.16 credits Sheshbazzar,
not Zerubbabel and Jeshua, with laying the foundations. Ezra-Nehemiah thus compresses various events in its
thematic presentation. **10–13:** Celebration of temple-foundings is a common ancient Near Eastern practice.
10: *David*'s crowning achievement for Ezra-Nehemiah (as for Chronicles) is the development of liturgy. **11:** The
quoted words are a frequently occurring refrain in late Psalms (e.g., 106.1; 107.1; 118.1; 136.1). **12:** *The first house,*
Solomon's Temple, destroyed in 586. *Old people ... wept,* postexilic sources contrast the splendor of Solomon's
Temple with the less glorious, postexilic Second Temple. King Herod renovated this Temple magnificently in
the first century BCE. **13:** *The sound was heard far away,* the rejoicing alerts the neighbors and triggers the opposition.

4.1–6.22: Opposition and support (including Aramaic documents). The edict of Cyrus authorized rebuilding the Temple, which according to several biblical sources was completed in 515 BCE, during the reign
of Darius I. Ezra 4–6 explains the delay in building by describing opposition from neighbors to the building
project.

4.1–24: Opposition from neighbors halts rebuilding. The opposition reflects competition for political and
perhaps economic privileges within the Persian empire, as well as the definition of religious legitimacy. This
section uses material out of chronological order to explain persistent hostilities and thus to account for the
delay in rebuilding. **1–6: Initial opposition.** Ezra 4 presents the would-be supporters, soon to become adversaries, as self-proclaimed foreigners, which accounts for their exclusion from this particular sacred project. **2:** *We*

us build with you, for we worship your God as you do, and we have been sacrificing to him ever since the days of King Esar-haddon of Assyria who brought us here." ³ But Zerubbabel, Jeshua, and the rest of the heads of families in Israel said to them, "You shall have no part with us in building a house to our God; but we alone will build to the Lᴏʀᴅ, the God of Israel, as King Cyrus of Persia has commanded us."

⁴ Then the people of the land discouraged the people of Judah, and made them afraid to build, ⁵ and they bribed officials to frustrate their plan throughout the reign of King Cyrus of Persia and until the reign of King Darius of Persia.

⁶ In the reign of Ahasuerus, in his accession year, they wrote an accusation against the inhabitants of Judah and Jerusalem.

⁷ And in the days of Artaxerxes, Bishlam and Mithredath and Tabeel and the rest of their associates wrote to King Artaxerxes of Persia; the letter was written in Aramaic and translated.ᵃ ⁸ Rehum the royal deputy and Shimshai the scribe wrote a letter against Jerusalem to King Artaxerxes as follows ⁹ (then Rehum the royal deputy, Shimshai the scribe, and the rest of their associates, the judges, the envoys, the officials, the Persians, the people of Erech, the Babylonians, the people of Susa, that is, the Elamites, ¹⁰ and the rest of the nations whom the great and noble Osnappar deported and settled in the cities of Samaria and in the rest of the province Beyond the River wrote—and now ¹¹ this is a copy of the letter that they sent):

"To King Artaxerxes: Your servants, the people of the province Beyond the River, send greeting. And now ¹² may it be known to the king that the Jews who came up from you to us have gone to Jerusalem. They are rebuilding that rebellious and wicked city; they are finishing the walls and repairing the foundations. ¹³ Now may it be known to the

ᵃ Heb adds *in Aramaic,* indicating that 4.8–6.18 is in Aramaic. Another interpretation is *The letter was written in the Aramaic script and set forth in the Aramaic language*

worship your God, according to 2 Kings 17, Assyria forcibly repopulated Samaria after deporting the Israelites, and these foreigners developed a syncretistic religion (2 Kings 17.41). *Esar-haddon,* king of Assyria (681–669). According to 2 Kings 17.3; 18.9, the king who resettled foreigners in northern Israel in 722 ʙᴄᴇ was Shalmaneser (727–722); see 2 Kings 17.24. 3: *We alone will build . . . as King Cyrus . . . commanded us,* the rebuilders claim that Cyrus's decree applies only to them, the sole legitimate remnant of Judah. Seeking to preserve ethnic and religious boundaries in the multicultural milieu of the Persian empire, as well as to protect the Temple's sanctity, the returnees initially refuse partnership with other groups. Once the Temple is built, however, Ezra-Nehemiah shows some readiness to include outsiders (see 6.21). 4: *The people of the land,* local inhabitants. Although Ezra-Nehemiah implies that these people were all of foreign descent, the groups may have included Judeans who had not been in exile and did not share the ideology or practices of those who repatriated. Tension with the people of the land is later expressed in the crisis of mixed marriages (Ezra 9–10). 5: *King Darius of Persia* ruled 522–486 ʙᴄᴇ. The Temple was rebuilt in his time (see 6.15). 6: *Ahasuerus,* or Xerxes I (486–465 ʙᴄᴇ), prominent in the book of Esther. This document is not preserved. 7–24: Further opposition during the reign of Artaxerxes, who reigned in the fifth century ʙᴄᴇ, after King Darius. The record of this opposition, which focuses on the rebuilding of Jerusalem's walls, is out of chronological order and serves to document how foreign adversaries (e.g., 4.10) repeatedly sabotaged Jewish rebuilding. 7a: *Artaxerxes* I, king of Persia (465–424). According to Ezra 7–Neh 2, the missions of Ezra and Nehemiah took place during his reign. 7b–11: The report to the king comes from Persian officials located around Judah and local inhabitants. 7b: *Aramaic,* the lingua franca of the Persian period. The text continues in Aramaic until 6:18, suggesting a distinct Aramaic source for this information. 8–10: Various explanatory material. The letter begins only in v. 11. 10: *Osnappar,* Ashurbanipal, king of Assyria (669–627). *Samaria,* a designation for the northern Israelite region, named after its capital. In the Persian period Samaria emerged as a center of provincial administration as well. *Province Beyond the River,* the Persian satrapy west of the Euphrates River, including Yehud (Judah) and Samaria. By the fifth century ʙᴄᴇ, Samaria and Yehud were separate provinces, each with its own governor.

4.11–16: The opponents' letter. 12: *Rebuilding that . . . city,* Neh 1–7 records the rebuilding of the city in the twentieth year of Artaxerxes (444 ʙᴄᴇ). 13–14: The opponents warn that Judean rebuilding will result in sedition and loss of income to the king. Ironically, however, their letter proves the antiquity of the city and of Jewish claims to it. *Share the salt of the palace,* an idiomatic expression of loyalty to the palace as well as of mutual

king that, if this city is rebuilt and the walls finished, they will not pay tribute, custom, or toll, and the royal revenue will be reduced. [14] Now because we share the salt of the palace and it is not fitting for us to witness the king's dishonor, therefore we send and inform the king, [15] so that a search may be made in the annals of your ancestors. You will discover in the annals that this is a rebellious city, hurtful to kings and provinces, and that sedition was stirred up in it from long ago. On that account this city was laid waste. [16] We make known to the king that, if this city is rebuilt and its walls finished, you will then have no possession in the province Beyond the River."

[17] The king sent an answer: "To Rehum the royal deputy and Shimshai the scribe and the rest of their associates who live in Samaria and in the rest of the province Beyond the River, greeting. And now [18] the letter that you sent to us has been read in translation before me. [19] So I made a decree, and someone searched and discovered that this city has risen against kings from long ago, and that rebellion and sedition have been made in it. [20] Jerusalem has had mighty kings who ruled over the whole province Beyond the River, to whom tribute, custom, and toll were paid. [21] Therefore issue an order that these people be made to cease, and that this city not be rebuilt, until I make a decree. [22] Moreover, take care not to be slack

in this matter; why should damage grow to the hurt of the king?"

[23] Then when the copy of King Artaxerxes' letter was read before Rehum and the scribe Shimshai and their associates, they hurried to the Jews in Jerusalem and by force and power made them cease. [24] At that time the work on the house of God in Jerusalem stopped and was discontinued until the second year of the reign of King Darius of Persia.

5 Now the prophets, Haggai[a] and Zechariah son of Iddo, prophesied to the Jews who were in Judah and Jerusalem, in the name of the God of Israel who was over them. [2] Then Zerubbabel son of Shealtiel and Jeshua son of Jozadak set out to rebuild the house of God in Jerusalem; and with them were the prophets of God, helping them.

[3] At the same time Tattenai the governor of the province Beyond the River and Shetharbozenai and their associates came to them and spoke to them thus, "Who gave you a decree to build this house and to finish this structure?" [4] They[b] also asked them this, "What are the names of the men who are building this building?" [5] But the eye of their God was upon the elders of the Jews, and they did not stop them until a report reached Darius and then answer was returned by letter in reply to it.

a Aram adds *the prophet*
b Gk Syr: Aram *We*

interests. **15:** *Annals of your ancestors,* the Assyrians and Babylonians kept careful records, and the Persians inherited and enlarged their bureaucracy. Here, as elsewhere in Ezra-Nehemiah, written records play a crucial role in establishing authority. **16:** *No possession,* revolt in Jerusalem will endanger Persian rule throughout the western region of the empire.

4.17–24: Royal response, prohibiting building. This correspondence in Artaxerxes' time in the fifth century BCE anachronistically explains the delay in rebuilding. **19:** *Rebellion and sedition,* presumably a reference to earlier rebellions against Assyria and Babylonia. **21:** *Until I make a decree,* this loophole will enable Nehemiah to secure a new decree. **24:** *At that time,* the narrative resumes the story about the Temple that was interrupted after 4.5. *The second year of . . . Darius,* i.e., 520 BCE, when rebuilding resumes, as also in the books of Haggai and Zechariah.

5.1–6.12: Third step: resumption of rebuilding of the Temple. The prophets Haggai and Zechariah inspire the people to resume rebuilding, and the Temple is finally completed at the time of Darius, in 515 BCE, after King Darius supports and extends King Cyrus's permission. **5.1–2:** Resumption of building begins with the urging of two prophets. **1:** *Haggai . . . and Zechariah,* in the books of Haggai and Zechariah, these prophets exhort leaders and community to build, starting in the second year of Darius (520 BCE). **2:** *Then Zerubbabel . . . and Jeshua,* see 2.1–2n.

5.3–17: New official Persian inquiry and correspondence lead to renewal of building permit. 3: *Tattenai,* a Persian official mentioned in nonbiblical sources as governor of the entire province Beyond the River, of which Yehud is a subunit (see 4.10n.).

⁶ The copy of the letter that Tattenai the governor of the province Beyond the River and Shethar-bozenai and his associates the envoys who were in the province Beyond the River sent to King Darius; ⁷ they sent him a report, in which was written as follows: "To Darius the king, all peace! ⁸ May it be known to the king that we went to the province of Judah, to the house of the great God. It is being built of hewn stone, and timber is laid in the walls; this work is being done diligently and prospers in their hands. ⁹ Then we spoke to those elders and asked them, 'Who gave you a decree to build this house and to finish this structure?' ¹⁰ We also asked them their names, for your information, so that we might write down the names of the men at their head. ¹¹ This was their reply to us: 'We are the servants of the God of heaven and earth, and we are rebuilding the house that was built many years ago, which a great king of Israel built and finished. ¹² But because our ancestors had angered the God of heaven, he gave them into the hand of King Nebuchadnezzar of Babylon, the Chaldean, who destroyed this house and carried away the people to Babylonia. ¹³ However, King Cyrus of Babylon, in the first year of his reign, made a decree that this house of God should be rebuilt. ¹⁴ Moreover, the gold and silver vessels of the house of God, which Nebuchadnezzar had taken out of the temple in Jerusalem and had brought into the temple of Babylon, these King Cyrus took out of the temple of Babylon, and they were delivered to a man named Sheshbazzar, whom he had made governor. ¹⁵ He said to him, "Take these vessels; go and put them in the temple in Jerusalem, and let the house of God be rebuilt on its site." ¹⁶ Then this Sheshbazzar came and laid the foundations of the house of God in Jerusalem; and from that time until now it has been under construction, and it is not yet finished.' ¹⁷ And now, if it seems good to the king, have a search made in the royal archives there in Babylon, to see whether a decree was issued by King Cyrus for the rebuilding of this house of God in Jerusalem. Let the king send us his pleasure in this matter."

6 Then King Darius made a decree, and they searched the archives where the documents were stored in Babylon. ² But it was in Ecbatana, the capital in the province of Media, that a scroll was found on which this was written: "A record. ³ In the first year of his reign, King Cyrus issued a decree: Concerning the house of God at Jerusalem, let the house be rebuilt, the place where sacrifices are offered and burnt offerings are brought;ᵃ its height shall be sixty cubits and its width sixty cubits, ⁴ with three courses of hewn stones and one course of timber; let the cost be paid from the royal treasury. ⁵ Moreover, let the gold and silver vessels of the house of God, which Nebuchadnezzar took out of the temple in Jerusalem and brought to Babylon, be restored and brought back to the temple in Jerusalem, each to its place; you shall put them in the house of God."

ᵃ Meaning of Aram uncertain

5.6–17: New correspondence from sympathetic officials reverses the letters of 4.7–16. Tattenai the governor does not stop the builders while waiting for further instructions from King Darius. 8: *Judah,* Yehud in the Aramaic text, is the name of the province in the Persian period, as is evident in extant seals and seal impressions. Tattenai's report indicates building activities well in progress. 11–16: This report generally parallels Ezra 1, but emphasizes Sheshbazzar's role as governor and does not mention Zerubbabel. 11: *A great king,* Solomon; see 2 Chr 3–4. 12: *Nebuchadnezzar,* see 1.7n. *Chaldean,* a late biblical term for the Babylonians. 13: *King Cyrus of Babylon,* the Persian king who controlled Babylon, where the Temple treasures were stored; see Ezra 1. 14: *Sheshbazzar,* see 1.7n. 1 Esdras 6.18, which parallels this account, also mentions Zerubbabel. 17: Tattenai seeks to ascertain both whether Cyrus authorized building, and if Darius wishes it to continue.

6.1–12: Darius's edict in support of the Temple. A discovery of Cyrus's memorandum confirms the legitimacy of the Temple in Jerusalem and brings additional support from King Darius. 2: *Ecbatana,* the summer residence of Persian kings, now Hamadan in Iran. 3–5: This archival version of Cyrus's decree emphasizes building size and funding; it is more generous than the public version (Ezra 1.1–4), explicitly offering royal financial support (v. 4). The relation between the two versions is uncertain. 3: *Sixty cubits,* a cubit is about 18 in (45 cm). The measurements are incomplete, not mentioning length (unless a square building is intended). 6–12: Darius's support of

⁶"Now you, Tattenai, governor of the province Beyond the River, Shethar-bozenai, and you, their associates, the envoys in the province Beyond the River, keep away; ⁷ let the work on this house of God alone; let the governor of the Jews and the elders of the Jews rebuild this house of God on its site. ⁸ Moreover I make a decree regarding what you shall do for these elders of the Jews for the rebuilding of this house of God: the cost is to be paid to these people, in full and without delay, from the royal revenue, the tribute of the province Beyond the River. ⁹ Whatever is needed—young bulls, rams, or sheep for burnt offerings to the God of heaven, wheat, salt, wine, or oil, as the priests in Jerusalem require—let that be given to them day by day without fail, ¹⁰ so that they may offer pleasing sacrifices to the God of heaven, and pray for the life of the king and his children. ¹¹ Furthermore I decree that if anyone alters this edict, a beam shall be pulled out of the house of the perpetrator, who then shall be impaled on it. The house shall be made a dunghill. ¹² May the God who has established his name there overthrow any king or people that shall put forth a hand to alter this, or to destroy this house of God in Jerusalem. I, Darius, make a decree; let it be done with all diligence."

¹³ Then, according to the word sent by King Darius, Tattenai, the governor of the province Beyond the River, Shethar-bozenai, and their associates did with all diligence what King Darius had ordered. ¹⁴ So the elders of the Jews built and prospered, through the prophesying of the prophet Haggai and Zechariah son of Iddo. They finished their building by command of the God of Israel and by decree of Cyrus, Darius, and King Artaxerxes of Persia; ¹⁵ and this house was finished on the third day of the month of Adar, in the sixth year of the reign of King Darius.

¹⁶ The people of Israel, the priests and the Levites, and the rest of the returned exiles, celebrated the dedication of this house of God with joy. ¹⁷ They offered at the dedication of this house of God one hundred bulls, two hundred rams, four hundred lambs, and as a sin offering for all Israel, twelve male goats, according to the number of the tribes of Israel. ¹⁸ Then they set the priests in their divisions and the Levites in their courses for the service of God at Jerusalem, as it is written in the book of Moses.

the Temple is extremely generous. If the information is reliable, it might indicate Persia's attempt to stabilize its hold in the Mediterranean area by securing the goodwill of the people of Yehud. Nonbiblical sources show that Darius also supported Egypt's religious institutions. **7:** *Governor,* Tattenai does not name a contemporary governor of Yehud itself (presumably Zerubbabel). **8:** *The cost,* Darius designates provincial revenue for the Temple, although this may antagonize other local, taxpaying districts.

6.13–18: The completion of the Temple. The Temple is finally completed, an accomplishment credited to the Judeans guided by God and authorized by three Persian kings. This concludes Stage One of the return and reconstruction. It will be followed by Stage Two, reconstructing the community in Ezra 7–10, and by Stage Three, rebuilding Jerusalem's walls in Neh 1–7. **14:** The conclusion highlights the elders and prophetic inspiration. *Cyrus, Darius, and King Artaxerxes,* according to Ezra 1–6, the Temple itself was rebuilt during Cyrus's and Darius's reigns, and completed in 515 BCE, before the time of Artaxerxes (464–424 BCE); hence his name in the list is at first puzzling. It can be explained in terms of Ezra-Nehemiah's larger understanding that the fuller restoration of the house of God goes beyond the Temple to include the rebuilding of the community by Ezra and the city by Nehemiah, culminating in Neh 7 under Artaxerxes. Ezra 6.14 thus suggests the unity of Ezra-Nehemiah. The joint authorization, first by God and then by kings, is crucial to Ezra-Nehemiah's historical and theological understanding. **15:** *Finished on the third day . . . of Adar . . . sixth year,* March 12, 515 BCE.

6.16–22: The concluding dedication. The dedication of the Temple is described briefly. A more extensive celebration in Ezra-Nehemiah will follow the rebuilding of the city's walls as the completion of the entire "house of God" (Neh 8–13). **16:** *People of Israel,* i.e., *the returned exiles* (lit. "sons of exile") who now represent the fullness of Israel. **17:** *Sin offering,* or purification offering; see Num 7. *Twelve male goats . . . the number of the tribes,* the remnant that includes only Judah, Benjamin, and the Levites nevertheless worships on behalf of the full house of Israel, which it now represents. **18:** *Written in the book of Moses,* Ex 29; Lev 8; and Num 3; 4; and 8 designate priestly and levitical tasks. Ezra-Nehemiah stresses the religious legitimacy of the Temple, which

¹⁹ On the fourteenth day of the first month the returned exiles kept the passover. ²⁰ For both the priests and the Levites had purified themselves; all of them were clean. So they killed the passover lamb for all the returned exiles, for their fellow priests, and for themselves. ²¹ It was eaten by the people of Israel who had returned from exile, and also by all who had joined them and separated themselves from the pollutions of the nations of the land to worship the LORD, the God of Israel. ²² With joy they celebrated the festival of unleavened bread seven days; for the LORD had made them joyful, and had turned the heart of the king of Assyria to them, so that he aided them in the work on the house of God, the God of Israel.

7 After this, in the reign of King Artaxerxes of Persia, Ezra son of Seraiah, son of Azariah, son of Hilkiah, ² son of Shallum, son of Zadok, son of Ahitub, ³ son of Amariah, son of Azariah, son of Meraioth, ⁴ son of Zerahiah, son of Uzzi, son of Bukki, ⁵ son of Abishua, son of Phinehas, son of Eleazar, son of the chief priest Aaron— ⁶ this Ezra went up from Babylonia. He was a scribe skilled in the law of Moses that the LORD the God of Israel had given; and the king granted him all that he asked, for the hand of the LORD his God was upon him.

⁷ Some of the people of Israel, and some of the priests and Levites, the singers and gatekeepers, and the temple servants also went up to Jerusalem, in the seventh year of King Artaxerxes. ⁸ They came to Jerusalem in the fifth month, which was in the seventh year of the king. ⁹ On the first day of the first month the journey up from Babylon was begun, and on the first day of the fifth month he came to Jerusalem, for the gracious hand of his God was upon him. ¹⁰ For Ezra had set his heart to study the law of the LORD, and to do it, and to teach the statutes and ordinances in Israel.

¹¹ This is a copy of the letter that King Artaxerxes gave to the priest Ezra, the scribe, a scholar of the text of the commandments of the LORD and his statutes for Israel: ¹² "Arta-

complements the political legitimacy granted by Cyrus and Darius. **19–22:** Celebrating the passover and the festival of unleavened bread (some five weeks after the Temple's dedication) has special significance for the reconstruction because the return from exile was viewed by some as a second Exodus (cf. Isa 52.11–12). **20:** *They killed,* the priestly laws of Lev 23.4–6 are followed here. **21:** *All who had joined them,* whereas the returnees excluded others from the act of rebuilding, reserving the task to "God's people" explicitly commissioned by Cyrus (Ezra 1:2–4 and 4:3), others may join once the Temple is rebuilt, following Ex 12.48, which notes that circumcised non-Israelites may participate in the Passover offering. **22:** *King of Assyria,* an anachronistic reference to the Persian king, alluding to the earliest exile by Assyria, which is now reversed.

7.1–10.44: Stage Two of reconstruction: the mission of Ezra and the reformation of the community according to the Torah. Ezra's mission focuses on the processes by which the community restructures itself to conform to an interpretation of the law that requires a separation from the people of the land. The implicit chronology in Ezra-Nehemiah places this event in 458 BCE, during the reign of Artaxerxes I, though some scholars believe that the date should be 398 BCE, during the reign of Artaxerxes II.

7.1–10: The narrator's introduction of Ezra. 1–6: Ezra's long pedigree establishes his impeccable credentials both as priest of the most distinguished line and as scribe—the two roles that will account for his stature and acceptance within the Jewish community. **1:** *Artaxerxes,* probably Artaxerxes I (465–424 BCE); see Introduction. **5:** *Chief priest,* Ezra is identified as one qualified to serve as a chief or high priest, even though he never undertakes this role in Ezra-Nehemiah. **6:** *Scribe,* a highly educated person, often in an important advisory position to kings. *Skilled in the law of Moses,* knowledgeable about the Torah. **7:** *Israel . . . priests . . . Levites,* Ezra's caravan includes the same basic groups as Ezra 2. *The seventh year of king Artaxerxes,* 458 BCE. **8:** *The fifth month,* Ab (July–August). **9:** *The first day of the first month,* i.e., Nisan (March-April), two weeks before Passover. The dates may be symbolic, reflecting the Exodus from Egypt in the first month (Ex 12.2; Num 33.3) and the destruction of the Temple in the fifth (2 Kings 25.8). However, five months would be a reasonable time for a journey from Babylon to Jerusalem. **10:** Ezra's goals of studying, teaching, and practicing God's law account for his subsequent actions and model Jewish aspirations. These add to his credentials as priest and establish his qualifications as an authoritative teacher of God's law.

7.11–26: Royal introduction of Ezra and his mission. This Aramaic royal letter establishes Ezra's credentials within the Persian bureaucracy. It reauthorizes immigration to Judah (v. 13) and royal subsidy for the Temple (vv.

xerxes, king of kings, to the priest Ezra, the scribe of the law of the God of heaven: Peace.[a] And now [13] I decree that any of the people of Israel or their priests or Levites in my kingdom who freely offers to go to Jerusalem may go with you. [14] For you are sent by the king and his seven counselors to make inquiries about Judah and Jerusalem according to the law of your God, which is in your hand, [15] and also to convey the silver and gold that the king and his counselors have freely offered to the God of Israel, whose dwelling is in Jerusalem, [16] with all the silver and gold that you shall find in the whole province of Babylonia, and with the freewill offerings of the people and the priests, given willingly for the house of their God in Jerusalem. [17] With this money, then, you shall with all diligence buy bulls, rams, and lambs, and their grain offerings and their drink offerings, and you shall offer them on the altar of the house of your God in Jerusalem. [18] Whatever seems good to you and your colleagues to do with the rest of the silver and gold, you may do, according to the will of your God. [19] The vessels that have been given you for the service of the house of your God, you shall deliver before the God of Jerusalem. [20] And whatever else is required for the house of your God, which you are responsible for providing, you may provide out of the king's treasury.

[21] "I, King Artaxerxes, decree to all the treasurers in the province Beyond the River: Whatever the priest Ezra, the scribe of the law of the God of heaven, requires of you, let it be done with all diligence, [22] up to one hundred talents of silver, one hundred cors of wheat, one hundred baths[b] of wine, one hundred baths[b] of oil, and unlimited salt. [23] Whatever is commanded by the God of heaven, let it be done with zeal for the house of the God of heaven, or wrath will come upon the realm of the king and his heirs. [24] We also notify you that it shall not be lawful to impose tribute, custom, or toll on any of the priests, the Levites, the singers, the doorkeepers, the temple servants, or other servants of this house of God.

[25] "And you, Ezra, according to the God-given wisdom you possess, appoint magistrates and judges who may judge all the people in the province Beyond the River who know the laws of your God; and you shall teach those who do not know them. [26] All who will not obey the law of your God and the law of the king, let judgment be strictly executed on them, whether for death or for banishment or for confiscation of their goods or for imprisonment."

[27] Blessed be the LORD, the God of our ancestors, who put such a thing as this into the heart of the king to glorify the house of the LORD in Jerusalem, [28] and who extended to me steadfast love before the king and his counselors, and before all the king's mighty officers. I took courage, for the hand of the LORD my God was upon me, and I gathered leaders from Israel to go up with me.

---

a   Syr Vg 1 Esdras 8.9: Aram *Perfect*
b   A Heb measure of volume

14–24). It seems to place the Torah on equal footing with royal law (v. 26). **14:** *Seven counselors*, Persian royal advisers (see Esth 1.14 and Herodotus, *Histories* 3.84). *The law of your God,* referring in Ezra-Nehemiah to the book of the Torah. **15–19:** The royal privileges include financial support for the Temple by the king himself, voluntary contributions from Babylonian Jews for the Temple, and a free hand to use the surplus. **20:** Artaxerxes virtually gives Ezra a blank check, showing great trust in Ezra. **21–24:** Artaxerxes assures a generous year's supply of provisions for the Temple. **21:** Additional support is to come from local officials. **22:** A *talent* was 75 lb (34 kg); a *cor* 6.5 bushels (230 l); and a *bath* about 6 gal (23 l). **24:** Tax exemption for Temple personnel is unusual. **25:** *All the people* probably means Jews in the province. **26:** The king affirms Ezra's comprehensive authority, as well as the Torah's. *The law of your God and the law of the king,* this crucial phrase sets the Torah as legally authoritative for the Jewish community in Yehud. It implies something akin to autonomy and self-rule in matters of religion and the Temple. For some scholars, it suggests that the Torah was compiled by Ezra as a result of Persian authorization and encouragement, but this is not stated.

7.27–9.15: Ezra's memoirs. The text resumes in Hebrew, with Ezra as narrator. He will describe the journey and the crisis of mixed marriages.

7.27–8.36: Ezra's journey and arrival. 7.27–28: Ezra expresses gratitude to God, rather than to the king.

8 These are their family heads, and this is the genealogy of those who went up with me from Babylonia, in the reign of King Artaxerxes: [2] Of the descendants of Phinehas, Gershom. Of Ithamar, Daniel. Of David, Hattush, [3] of the descendants of Shecaniah. Of Parosh, Zechariah, with whom were registered one hundred fifty males. [4] Of the descendants of Pahath-moab, Eliehoenai son of Zerahiah, and with him two hundred males. [5] Of the descendants of Zattu,[a] Shecaniah son of Jahaziel, and with him three hundred males. [6] Of the descendants of Adin, Ebed son of Jonathan, and with him fifty males. [7] Of the descendants of Elam, Jeshaiah son of Athaliah, and with him seventy males. [8] Of the descendants of Shephatiah, Zebadiah son of Michael, and with him eighty males. [9] Of the descendants of Joab, Obadiah son of Jehiel, and with him two hundred eighteen males. [10] Of the descendants of Bani,[b] Shelomith son of Josiphiah, and with him one hundred sixty males. [11] Of the descendants of Bebai, Zechariah son of Bebai, and with him twenty-eight males. [12] Of the descendants of Azgad, Johanan son of Hakkatan, and with him one hundred ten males. [13] Of the descendants of Adonikam, those who came later, their names being Eliphelet, Jeuel, and Shemaiah, and with them sixty males. [14] Of the descendants of Bigvai, Uthai and Zaccur, and with them seventy males.

[15] I gathered them by the river that runs to Ahava, and there we camped three days. As I reviewed the people and the priests, I found there none of the descendants of Levi. [16] Then I sent for Eliezer, Ariel, Shemaiah, Elnathan, Jarib, Elnathan, Nathan, Zechariah, and Meshullam, who were leaders, and for Joiarib and Elnathan, who were wise, [17] and

sent them to Iddo, the leader at the place called Casiphia, telling them what to say to Iddo and his colleagues the temple servants at Casiphia, namely, to send us ministers for the house of our God. [18] Since the gracious hand of our God was upon us, they brought us a man of discretion, of the descendants of Mahli son of Levi son of Israel, namely Sherebiah, with his sons and kin, eighteen; [19] also Hashabiah and with him Jeshaiah of the descendants of Merari, with his kin and their sons, twenty; [20] besides two hundred twenty of the temple servants, whom David and his officials had set apart to attend the Levites. These were all mentioned by name.

[21] Then I proclaimed a fast there, at the river Ahava, that we might deny ourselves[c] before our God, to seek from him a safe journey for ourselves, our children, and all our possessions. [22] For I was ashamed to ask the king for a band of soldiers and cavalry to protect us against the enemy on our way, since we had told the king that the hand of our God is gracious to all who seek him, but his power and his wrath are against all who forsake him. [23] So we fasted and petitioned our God for this, and he listened to our entreaty.

[24] Then I set apart twelve of the leading priests: Sherebiah, Hashabiah, and ten of their kin with them. [25] And I weighed out to them the silver and the gold and the vessels, the offering for the house of our God that the king, his counselors, his lords, and all Israel there present had offered; [26] I weighed out into their hand six hundred fifty talents of silver, and one hundred silver vessels worth . . .

---

[a] Gk 1 Esdras 8.32: Heb lacks *of Zattu*
[b] Gk 1 Esdras 8.36: Heb lacks *Bani*
[c] Or *might fast*

8.1–20: Ezra's caravan numbers about 1,500 men (women are not mentioned); like Ezra 2, the list mingles clan names and place names, although some important individuals are also singled out. 2: *Hattush*, 1 Chr 3.22 mentions a descendant of David with this name, although nothing further is reported about him. Apparently some Davidic descendants remained in Babylonia after the return to Judah had begun. 4–20: The additional members and clans in Ezra's caravan include names that already appeared in Ezra 2 (e.g., Pahath-moab in Ezra 2.6 and 8.4). 15: *Ahava*, an unknown location along one of the canals of the river Euphrates. *None of . . . Levi*, Ezra demonstrates concern for the proper maintenance of the Temple and broadens the scope of its personnel to include the lesser officials. 21–30: Ezra requires of the community spiritual as well as physical preparations. 21: *Fast*, a common preparation for beseeching God. *All our possessions*, even with the well-guarded royal roads, a long journey was hazardous, especially when transporting gold and silver. 22: *I was ashamed*, Ezra's timidity and trust indicate that God's power is ultimately greater than that of the Persian king's army. 24–30: Further

talents,[a] and one hundred talents of gold, [27] twenty gold bowls worth a thousand darics, and two vessels of fine polished bronze as precious as gold. [28] And I said to them, "You are holy to the LORD, and the vessels are holy; and the silver and the gold are a freewill offering to the LORD, the God of your ancestors. [29] Guard them and keep them until you weigh them before the chief priests and the Levites and the heads of families in Israel at Jerusalem, within the chambers of the house of the LORD." [30] So the priests and the Levites took over the silver, the gold, and the vessels as they were weighed out, to bring them to Jerusalem, to the house of our God.

[31] Then we left the river Ahava on the twelfth day of the first month, to go to Jerusalem; the hand of our God was upon us, and he delivered us from the hand of the enemy and from ambushes along the way. [32] We came to Jerusalem and remained there three days. [33] On the fourth day, within the house of our God, the silver, the gold, and the vessels were weighed into the hands of the priest Meremoth son of Uriah, and with him was Eleazar son of Phinehas, and with them were the Levites, Jozabad son of Jeshua and Noadiah son of Binnui. [34] The total was counted and weighed, and the weight of everything was recorded.

[35] At that time those who had come from captivity, the returned exiles, offered burnt offerings to the God of Israel, twelve bulls for all Israel, ninety-six rams, seventy-seven lambs, and as a sin offering twelve male goats; all this was a burnt offering to the LORD. [36] They also delivered the king's commissions to the king's satraps and to the governors of the province Beyond the River; and they supported the people and the house of God.

9 After these things had been done, the officials approached me and said, "The people of Israel, the priests, and the Levites have not separated themselves from the peoples of the lands with their abominations, from the Canaanites, the Hittites, the Perizzites, the Jebusites, the Ammonites, the Moabites, the Egyptians, and the Amorites. [2] For they have taken some of their daughters as wives for themselves and for their sons. Thus the holy seed has mixed itself with the peoples of the lands, and in this faithlessness the officials and leaders have led the way." [3] When I heard this, I tore my garment and

---

[a] The number of talents is lacking

preparations that empower the clergy. **26:** *Talents* weigh about 75 lbs (34 kg) each. **27:** *Darics,* see 2.69n. **28:** *The vessels are holy,* holiness is derived from their dedication to God; these are not vessels from the First Temple. **31–36:** Arrival and celebration. **31:** *Twelfth day of the first month* (Nisan [March–April]), two days before the Passover commemorating the Exodus. A new Exodus may be implicit; however, for reasons of weather, spring was the season for expeditions (see 2 Sam 11.1). **33:** Ezra ensures that the gifts are transferred to both priests and Levites. **35:** *Returned exiles,* the restored community. **36:** *Satraps,* high officials in the Persian government, usually provincial governors.

9.1–15: The crisis of mixed marriages. The crisis in Stage Two of the reconstruction comes when men, including Jewish leaders, marry foreign women. To ensure survival as a small (see Ezra 9.8) minority in the midst of surrounding cultures, Ezra-Nehemiah advocates separatist policies. In this section, it calls for excluding foreign wives and their children from the community. The concern with intermarriages resembles the Athenian laws of 451 BCE, which demanded that both parents be Athenian if a person was to be considered a citizen. The similar concern in Ezra-Nehemiah may, therefore, be also related to the greater power bestowed upon community members. **1:** *Have not separated,* Deut 7.1–5 prohibits any relation with the people of Canaan, and Deut 20.15-18 further demands their annihilation on the ground that they lead to religious defection. Ezra-Nehemiah substitutes separation for destruction. *Their abominations, from the Canaanites,* more accurately, "their abominations like the Canaanites." The informants equate the religious practices of the present inhabitants with those of the earlier nations at the time of Joshua. *Canaanites . . . Amorites,* Deut 7 specifically prohibits relations with Canaanites, Perizzites, Hittites, Jebusites, and Amorites. Deut 23.3–8 specifically excludes Ammonites and Moabites from the congregation, but permits the incorporation of Egyptians at some point. This verse has thus extended the range of the earlier prohibition. The targeted prohibited families probably include Judeans who had not gone into exile. **2:** *Holy seed* is progeny dedicated through birth to God. The term probably reflects Isa 6.13, in reference to the purified remnant.

my mantle, and pulled hair from my head and beard, and sat appalled. ⁴ Then all who trembled at the words of the God of Israel, because of the faithlessness of the returned exiles, gathered around me while I sat appalled until the evening sacrifice.

⁵ At the evening sacrifice I got up from my fasting, with my garments and my mantle torn, and fell on my knees, spread out my hands to the LORD my God, ⁶ and said,

"O my God, I am too ashamed and embarrassed to lift my face to you, my God, for our iniquities have risen higher than our heads, and our guilt has mounted up to the heavens. ⁷ From the days of our ancestors to this day we have been deep in guilt, and for our iniquities we, our kings, and our priests have been handed over to the kings of the lands, to the sword, to captivity, to plundering, and to utter shame, as is now the case. ⁸ But now for a brief moment favor has been shown by the LORD our God, who has left us a remnant, and given us a stake in his holy place, in order that heᵃ may brighten our eyes and grant us a little sustenance in our slavery. ⁹ For we are slaves; yet our God has not forsaken us in our slavery, but has extended to us his steadfast love before the kings of Persia, to give us new life to set up the house of our God, to repair its ruins, and to give us a wall in Judea and Jerusalem.

¹⁰ "And now, our God, what shall we say after this? For we have forsaken your commandments, ¹¹ which you commanded by your servants the prophets, saying, 'The land that you are entering to possess is a land unclean with the pollutions of the peoples of the lands, with their abominations. They have filled it from end to end with their uncleanness. ¹² Therefore do not give your daughters to their sons, neither take their daughters for your sons, and never seek their peace or prosperity, so that you may be strong and eat the good of the land and leave it for an inheritance to your children forever.' ¹³ After all that has come upon us for our evil deeds and for our great guilt, seeing that you, our God, have punished us less than our iniquities deserved and have given us such a remnant as this, ¹⁴ shall we break your commandments again and intermarry with the peoples who practice these abominations? Would you not be angry with us until you destroy us without remnant or survivor? ¹⁵ O LORD, God of Israel, you are just, but we have escaped as a remnant, as is now the case. Here we are before you in our guilt, though no one can face you because of this."

10 While Ezra prayed and made confession, weeping and throwing himself down before the house of God, a very great assembly of men, women, and children gathered to him out of Israel; the people also wept bitterly. ² Shecaniah son of Jehiel, of the

---

ᵃ Heb *our God*

9.3–4: Ezra reacts with mourning and prayer. His penitence produces remorse and generates communal action.

9.5–15: Ezra's prayer. More a sermon than a confession, the prayer rehearses events of the past in order to alter community behavior. Like the prophets and the Deuteronomistic History, Ezra interprets Israel's political devastation as the consequence of religious and moral failings by Israel, and uses the fear of a recurrence to motivate the community to separate from the other inhabitants of the land. **7:** *As is now the case*, the end of exile is understood as a result of divine forgiveness, not Israel's changed behavior. **8:** *Little sustenance*, Ezra's confession expresses the vulnerability of a small remnant. **9:** *For we are slaves*, i.e., a colonized people under Persian control. *Repair its ruins*, i.e., physical and spiritual reconstruction. *A wall*, actually "a fence," a metaphor for a weak protective barrier. **11–12:** This paraphrase and blending of Priestly (Lev 18.24–30) and Deuteronomic (Deut 7.3–4) material is characteristic of this period, when the Torah as a book became authoritative.

10.1–44: Resolution of crisis. The crisis is resolved through communal consensus to reinterpret earlier laws and apply them to present circumstances, and therefore to oppose mixed marriages within the covenant community.

10.1–6: The impact of Ezra's prayer. Ezra's prayer (see the similar later prayer in Dan 9) attracts a crowd and inspires remorse and repentance. **2:** *Have married*, (lit. "have settled"), i.e., established on the land. Inheritance of land is a concern (see Ezra 9.12; Deut 7). The proposal to exclude foreign wives comes from Shecaniah, a community member (his father's name, Jehiel, appears in 10.26 among the transgressors). The resolution will be

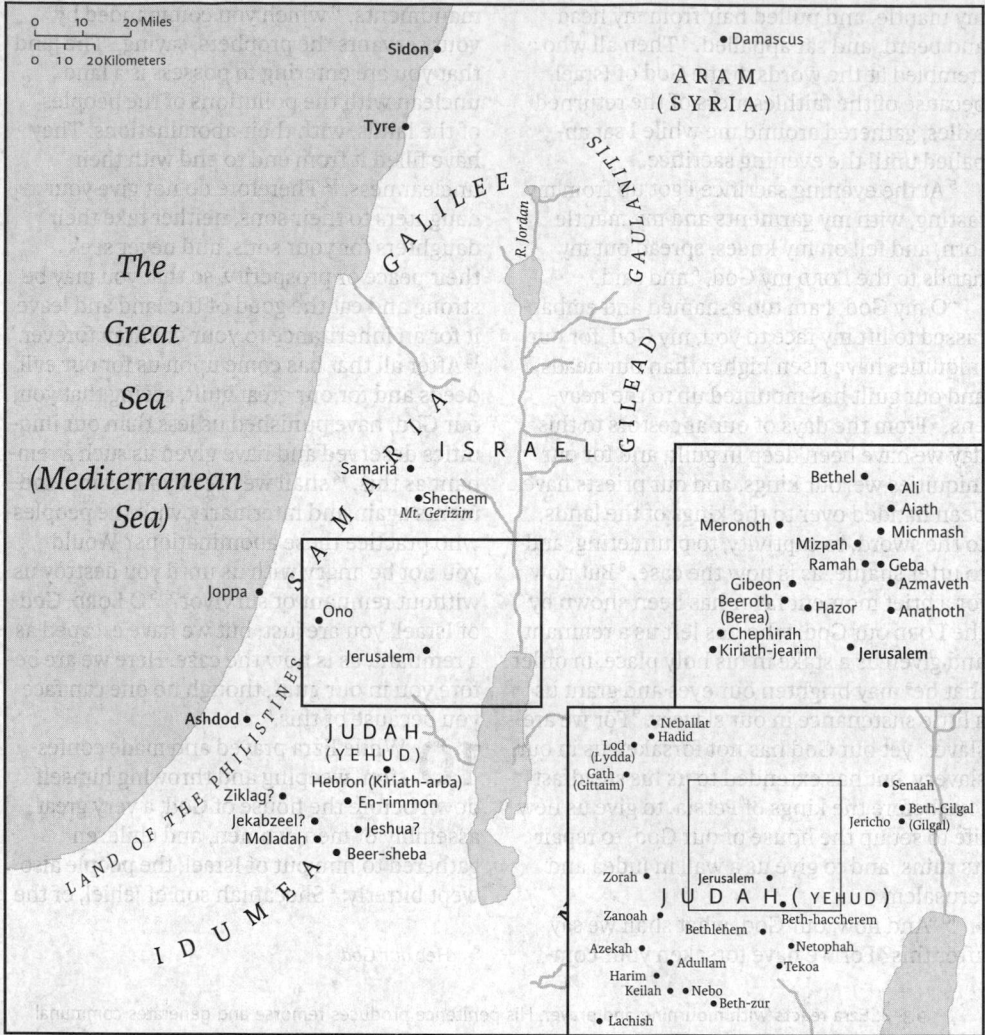

Judah and its neighbors in Ezra-Nehemia.

descendants of Elam, addressed Ezra, saying, "We have broken faith with our God and have married foreign women from the peoples of the land, but even now there is hope for Israel in spite of this. ³ So now let us make a covenant with our God to send away all these wives and their children, according to the counsel of my lord and of those who tremble at the commandment of our God; and let it be done according to the law. ⁴ Take action, for it is your duty, and we are with you; be strong, and do it." ⁵ Then Ezra stood up and made the leading priests, the Levites, and all Israel swear that they would do as had been said. So they swore.

⁶ Then Ezra withdrew from before the house of God, and went to the chamber of Jehohanan son of Eliashib, where he spent the

determined by consensus. 3: The children of such marriages are to be sent away as well, thereby not separated from their mothers. *Let it be done according to the law,* the Pentateuch does not include a law that demands dissolving mixed marriages. The reference implies an interpretation, applying a prohibition against such marriages to these new circumstances. 4–5: The people authorize Ezra to act. Although authorized by the Persian king, Ezra only assumes a leadership role when the community invites him to do so. 6: *The chamber,* an office

night.[a] He did not eat bread or drink water, for he was mourning over the faithlessness of the exiles. [7] They made a proclamation throughout Judah and Jerusalem to all the returned exiles that they should assemble at Jerusalem, [8] and that if any did not come within three days, by order of the officials and the elders all their property should be forfeited, and they themselves banned from the congregation of the exiles.

[9] Then all the people of Judah and Benjamin assembled at Jerusalem within the three days; it was the ninth month, on the twentieth day of the month. All the people sat in the open square before the house of God, trembling because of this matter and because of the heavy rain. [10] Then Ezra the priest stood up and said to them, "You have trespassed and married foreign women, and so increased the guilt of Israel. [11] Now make confession to the LORD the God of your ancestors, and do his will; separate yourselves from the peoples of the land and from the foreign wives." [12] Then all the assembly answered with a loud voice, "It is so; we must do as you have said. [13] But the people are many, and it is a time of heavy rain; we cannot stand in the open. Nor is this a task for one day or for two, for many of us have transgressed in this matter. [14] Let our officials represent the whole assembly, and let all in our towns who have taken foreign wives come at appointed times, and with them the elders and judges of every town, until the fierce wrath of our God on this account is averted from us." [15] Only Jonathan son of Asahel and Jahzeiah son of Tikvah opposed this, and Meshullam and Shabbethai the Levites supported them.

[16] Then the returned exiles did so. Ezra the priest selected men,[b] heads of families, according to their families, each of them designated by name. On the first day of the tenth month they sat down to examine the matter. [17] By the first day of the first month they had come to the end of all the men who had married foreign women.

[18] There were found of the descendants of the priests who had married foreign women, of the descendants of Jeshua son of Jozadak and his brothers: Maaseiah, Eliezer, Jarib, and Gedaliah. [19] They pledged themselves to send away their wives, and their guilt offering

a 1 Esdras 9.2: Heb *where he went*
b 1 Esdras 9.16: Syr: Heb *And there were selected Ezra,*

within the Temple complex that as a priest, Ezra may use. *Jehohanan son of Eliashib* appears in the priestly lists (Neh 12.23), although both names are common in the postexilic period.

10.7–8: Steps toward resolution. These include an invitation to an assembly for the purpose of communal decision, and a threat in case of noncompliance. Although Artaxerxes' letter authorizes Ezra to issue decrees, Ezra resorts to a communal process instead (see 10.5,16). Threats of confiscation apply to those who refuse to participate in the general assembly, not those who offer a different opinion as to what should be done.

10.9–15: A communal process for resolution. The report focuses on the process in which the entire community participates in deciding and enforcing criteria for membership. **9:** *Heavy rain*s are typical of the cold ninth month, Chislev (November-December). **10–11:** *Married* (lit. "settled"); see 10.2n. This is Ezra's first directive; he commands only at the invitation of the community. **12–14:** The community assents and offers the mechanism for resolution. **14:** *Have taken* (lit. "have settled"); see 10.2n. Again, the community is responsible for action, devising a representative form ("our officials") of government. **15:** A minority opposition is registered, establishing that majority decision carries even without unanimity. *Meshullam* could be Ezra's companion in 8.16.

10.16–44: Results: compliance with communal decision. The issue of mixed marriages constitutes the first test of the new, legal status of the Torah, illustrating how an ancient book may shape the present and future through communal interpretive process. **16:** *The returned exiles did so* on the basis of a democratic process. *Ezra ... selected men,* the Hebrew text states that the community selects the committee, with Ezra serving as a member. This is consistent with the rest of Ezra-Nehemiah where the broader community plays a crucial role. **17:** *By the first day of the first month,* the commission's deliberations began in December 458 (v. 16) and concluded three months later in March 457 BCE, about one year after Ezra's caravan first set out for Jerusalem (7.9). **18:** *Had married* (lit. "had settled"); see 10.2n. *Jeshua son of Jozadak,* the high priest in the early return. See 2.1–2n. **18–19:** The explicit report that the high priest's family fully complied with the communal decision is crucial to the book's reforms. It affirms the ultimate status of the Torah, as the priests, who have the most power, submit

was a ram of the flock for their guilt. [20] Of the descendants of Immer: Hanani and Zebadiah. [21] Of the descendants of Harim: Maaseiah, Elijah, Shemaiah, Jehiel, and Uzziah. [22] Of the descendants of Pashhur: Elioenai, Maaseiah, Ishmael, Nethanel, Jozabad, and Elasah.

[23] Of the Levites: Jozabad, Shimei, Kelaiah (that is, Kelita), Pethahiah, Judah, and Eliezer. [24] Of the singers: Eliashib. Of the gatekeepers: Shallum, Telem, and Uri.

[25] And of Israel: of the descendants of Parosh: Ramiah, Izziah, Malchijah, Mijamin, Eleazar, Hashabiah,[a] and Benaiah. [26] Of the descendants of Elam: Mattaniah, Zechariah, Jehiel, Abdi, Jeremoth, and Elijah. [27] Of the descendants of Zattu: Elioenai, Eliashib, Mattaniah, Jeremoth, Zabad, and Aziza. [28] Of the descendants of Bebai: Jehohanan, Hananiah, Zabbai, and Athlai. [29] Of the descendants of Bani: Meshullam, Malluch, Adaiah, Jashub, Sheal, and Jeremoth. [30] Of the descendants of Pahath-moab: Adna, Chelal, Benaiah, Maaseiah, Mattaniah, Bezalel, Binnui, and Manasseh. [31] Of the descendants of Harim: Eliezer, Isshijah, Malchijah, Shemaiah, Shimeon, [32] Benjamin, Malluch, and Shemariah. [33] Of the descendants of Hashum: Mattenai, Mattattah, Zabad, Eliphelet, Jeremai, Manasseh, and Shimei. [34] Of the descendants of Bani: Maadai, Amram, Uel, [35] Benaiah, Bedeiah, Cheluhi, [36] Vaniah, Meremoth, Eliashib, [37] Mattaniah, Mattenai, and Jaasu. [38] Of the descendants of Binnui:[b] Shimei, [39] Shelemiah, Nathan, Adaiah, [40] Machnadebai, Shashai, Sharai, [41] Azarel, Shelemiah, Shemariah, [42] Shallum, Amariah, and Joseph. [43] Of the descendants of Nebo: Jeiel, Mattithiah, Zabad, Zebina, Jaddai, Joel, and Benaiah. [44] All these had married foreign women, and they sent them away with their children.[c]

a 1 Esdras 9.26 Gk: Heb *Malchijah*
b Gk: Heb *Bani, Binnui*
c 1 Esdras 9.36; meaning of Heb uncertain

to its teachings. **20–44:** List of other offenders. There are more than a hundred offenders (the names are not always distinct), including members of the high priest's family (v. 18). **44:** *They sent them away with their children,* this sentence does not appear in Ezra 10, which ends abruptly, but comes from the later 1 Esdras. The Hebrew in Ezra 10.44 states: "Some had wives with whom they had sons." Ezra 10.44 thus does not report that the women and children of nonpriestly families were expelled. The conclusion of Stage Two (Ezra 7–10) focuses, rather, on establishing boundaries based on the Torah without resorting to military force (with emotional casualties that are not reported).

NEHEMIAH

The book of Nehemiah was originally the second section of a single book (Ezra-Nehemiah, preserved as Esdras b in the ancient Greek versions of the Bible); see further the Introduction to Ezra (pp. 667–668).

The Nehemiah section of Ezra-Nehemiah depicts the final stage of Jewish reconstruction after exile, featuring Nehemiah as the Jewish governor under Persian rule, who rebuilds Jerusalem's walls (1.1–7.5) and oversees many reforms. Large portions of this book are called the Nehemiah memoir, a first-person account of his activities. The book's structure continues the narrative that began with Ezra 1. Nehemiah 1 begins with Stage Three of the return from exile, when Nehemiah rebuilds Jerusalem's walls (Neh 1.1–7.5). This is followed by the repetition of the list of returnees (7.6–73; see Ezra 2) that frames the three stages of return and reconstruction. The book concludes with the grand celebration of the reconstruction by the rededicated community, now organized according to the Torah, the "law of Moses" (chs 8–13), with rebuilt Jerusalem as its holy city.

Nehemiah is presented as a dynamic, enterprising man who achieves his goal of rebuilding despite repeated interference from other leaders such as the governor of Samaria (see 2.9–10). Although he does not appear elsewhere in the Hebrew Bible, Nehemiah is mentioned in 2 Macc 1.19–36 and Sirach 49.13.

Tamara Cohn Eskenazi

1 The words of Nehemiah son of Hacaliah. In the month of Chislev, in the twentieth year, while I was in Susa the capital, [2] one of my brothers, Hanani, came with certain men from Judah; and I asked them about the Jews that survived, those who had escaped the captivity, and about Jerusalem. [3] They replied, "The survivors there in the province who escaped captivity are in great trouble and shame; the wall of Jerusalem is broken down, and its gates have been destroyed by fire."

[4] When I heard these words I sat down and wept, and mourned for days, fasting and praying before the God of heaven. [5] I said, "O Lord God of heaven, the great and awesome God who keeps covenant and steadfast love with those who love him and keep his commandments; [6] let your ear be attentive and your eyes open to hear the prayer of your servant that I now pray before you day and night for your servants, the people of Israel, confessing the sins of the people of Israel, which we have sinned against you. Both I and my family have sinned. [7] We have offended you deeply, failing to keep the commandments, the statutes, and the ordinances that you commanded your servant Moses. [8] Remember the word that you commanded your servant Moses, 'If you are unfaithful, I will scatter you among the peoples; [9] but if you

1.1–7.5: Stage Three of reconstruction: rebuilding Jerusalem under Nehemiah's leadership. These chapters come from what scholars call "the Nehemiah memoir," first-person material in the name of Nehemiah (also found in chs 12–13). This section describes how Nehemiah, the king's cupbearer, becomes the governor of Judah and rebuilds Jerusalem's walls.

1:1–2:10: Nehemiah's commission. While serving the Persian king in Persia, Nehemiah learns about his people's plight in Judah and asks permission to go and help them. 1.1: *Nehemiah,* a cupbearer (see 1.11n.) to King Artaxerxes I (465–424 BCE). *Words of Nehemiah son of Hacaliah,* this is the beginning of the Nehemiah Memoir. His father's name and his family are otherwise unknown. *Chislev* (November-December). *In the twentieth year,* most likely of Artaxerxes I (2.1), namely 445 BCE. *Susa,* the winter residence of Persian kings in Persia (modern Iran). Excavations have uncovered a magnificent palace there. 2–3: *Jews that survived,* this includes those who remained in the land after 586 BCE, as well as those who had returned since (see Ezra 1.1–4). *The wall of Jerusalem* was *broken down* by the Babylonians in 586 BCE, and apparently suffered further deterioration, possibly due to later unrecorded conflicts.

1.4–11: Nehemiah's prayer. The prayer incorporates themes from Deuteronomy about reasons for the dispersion and the possibility of restoration. It reflects Nehemiah's piety and expresses postexilic hope for restoration. 5: *God of heaven,* a typical postexilic title (e.g., Ezra 1.2; Dan 2.18). 8–9: A paraphrase of ideas about God

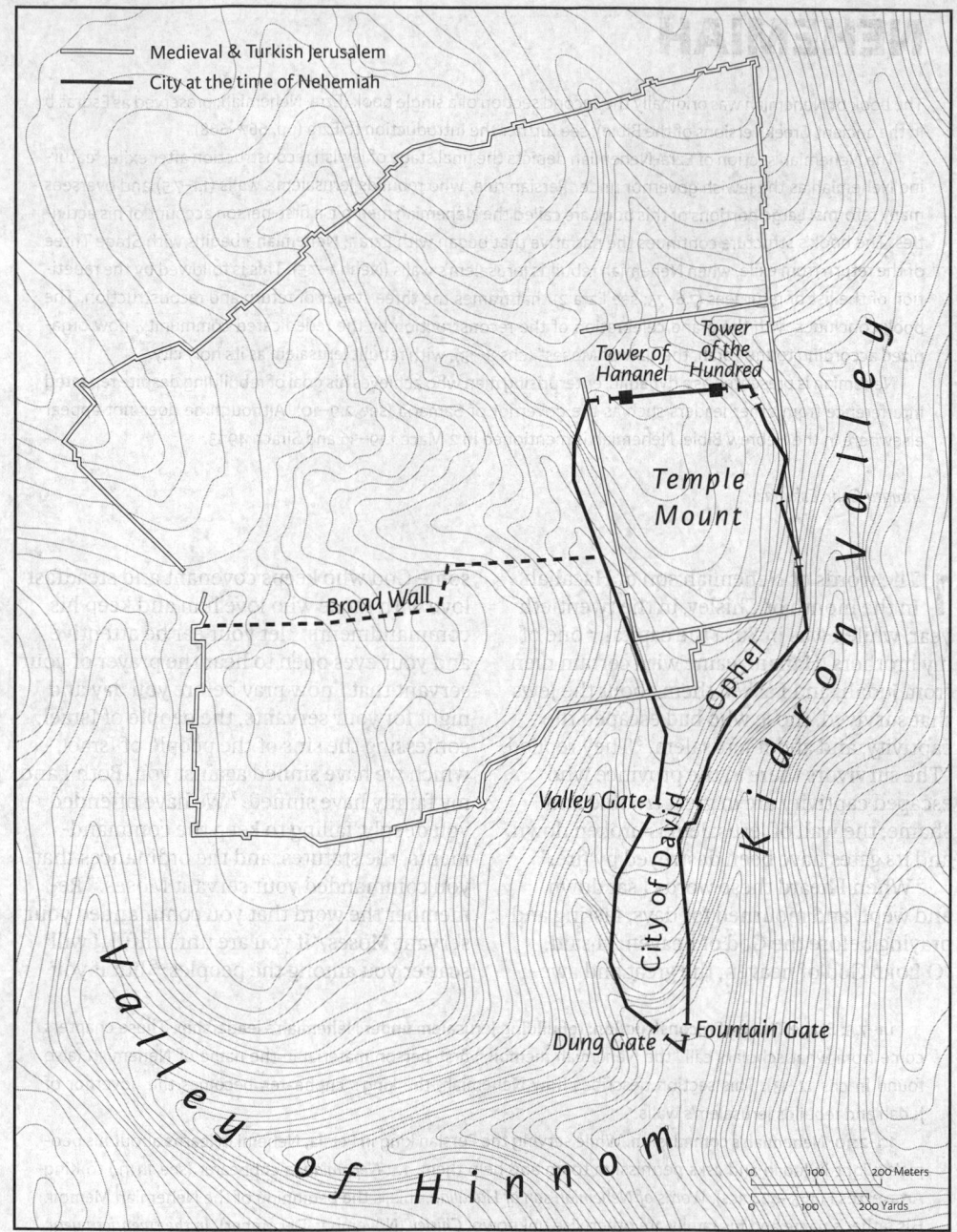

Jerusalem in the time of Nehemiah.

return to me and keep my commandments and do them, though your outcasts are under the farthest skies, I will gather them from there and bring them to the place at which I have chosen to establish my name.' [10] They are your servants and your people, whom you redeemed by your great power and your strong hand. [11] O Lord, let your ear be attentive to the prayer of your servant, and to the prayer of your servants who delight in revering your name. Give success to your servant today, and grant him mercy in the sight of this man!"

At the time, I was cupbearer to the king.

2 In the month of Nisan, in the twentieth year of King Artaxerxes, when wine was served him, I carried the wine and gave it to the king. Now, I had never been sad in his presence before. [2] So the king said to me, "Why is your face sad, since you are not sick? This can only be sadness of the heart." Then I was very much afraid. [3] I said to the king, "May the king live forever! Why should my face not be sad, when the city, the place of my ancestors' graves, lies waste, and its gates have been destroyed by fire?" [4] Then the king said to me, "What do you request?" So I prayed to the God of heaven. [5] Then I said to the king, "If it pleases the king, and if your servant has found favor with you, I ask that you send me to Judah, to the city of my ancestors' graves, so that I may rebuild it." [6] The king said to me (the queen also was sitting beside him), "How long will you be gone, and when will you return?" So it pleased the king to send me, and I set him a date. [7] Then I said to the king, "If it pleases the king, let letters be given me to the governors of the province Beyond the River, that they may grant me passage until I arrive in Judah; [8] and a letter to Asaph, the keeper of the king's forest, directing him to give me timber to make beams for the gates of the temple fortress, and for the wall of the city, and for the house that I shall occupy." And the king granted me what I asked, for the gracious hand of my God was upon me.

[9] Then I came to the governors of the province Beyond the River, and gave them the king's letters. Now the king had sent officers of the army and cavalry with me. [10] When Sanballat the Horonite and Tobiah the Ammonite official heard this, it displeased them greatly that someone had come to seek the welfare of the people of Israel.

[11] So I came to Jerusalem and was there for three days. [12] Then I got up during the night,

from Deuteronomy (e.g., Deut 30.1–5). **11**: *This man*, Artaxerxes I. *Cupbearer*, a trusted high royal courtier who sampled wine for quality and safety (see 2.1).

2.1–8: Nehemiah's commission. Nehemiah uses an opportunity to propose a daring request, risking the king's disapproval. **1**: *Nisan*, March-April, the month of the Exodus from Egypt. The chronology of 1.1 (November-December) and 2.1 (March-April), both in the twentieth year, makes sense if Nehemiah's reckoning begins the year in the fall. (Both a spring and a fall new year are found in the Bible.) **2**: *I was... afraid*, because his request could imply divided loyalties, even treason. **3**: *My ancestors' graves*, depicting Jerusalem as graveyard dramatizes the importance of honoring ancestors and minimizes the threat that rebuilding Jerusalem might otherwise suggest. Ezra 4.21 indicates that this king had prohibited rebuilding of Jerusalem's walls until further notice. **6**: The *queen*'s presence may indicate an intimate setting of the conversation, perhaps accounting for the king's benevolence. She is not named; according to Greek sources, Artaxerxes' queen was Damaspia. *I set him a date*, 5.14 and 13.6 indicate that Nehemiah's mission as governor lasted twelve years. **8**: *Temple fortress*, Nehemiah explicitly mentions plans for the Temple's gates and fortifications, including the city's walls, only after securing the king's consent.

2.9–10: Journey and opposition. Nehemiah's military escort visibly testifies to royal support for his mission. His arrival is met with opposition perhaps because it unsettles the political and economic equilibrium, such as control by Samaria or members of the aristocracy. Sanballat and Tobiah head the opposition against Nehemiah's renewal efforts. **10**: *Sanballat* is mentioned in the Aramaic Elephantine documents from fifth-century BCE Egypt as a governor of Samaria, Judah's northern neighbor, the former Israelite state now a province named after its chief city; see Ezra 4.10. He was apparently also related by marriage to Jerusalem's high priest (see 13.28n). *Tobiah the Ammonite official*, probably a Jew. Nehemiah discredits him because of a connection to Ammon, Judah's eastern neighbor and a group excluded from membership in Israel according to Deut 23.4–7. His name is a compound Hebrew word for "good" ("tob") and "Yah", a reference to Israel's God (see also 6.18 and 13.4–9n).

a few men with me; I told no one what God had put into my heart to do for Jerusalem. The only animal I took was the animal I rode. [13] I went out by night by the Valley Gate past the Dragon's Spring and to the Dung Gate, and I inspected the walls of Jerusalem that had been broken down and its gates that had been destroyed by fire. [14] Then I went on to the Fountain Gate and to the King's Pool; but there was no place for the animal I was riding to continue. [15] So I went up by way of the valley by night and inspected the wall. Then I turned back and entered by the Valley Gate, and so returned. [16] The officials did not know where I had gone or what I was doing; I had not yet told the Jews, the priests, the nobles, the officials, and the rest that were to do the work.

[17] Then I said to them, "You see the trouble we are in, how Jerusalem lies in ruins with its gates burned. Come, let us rebuild the wall of Jerusalem, so that we may no longer suffer disgrace." [18] I told them that the hand of my God had been gracious upon me, and also the words that the king had spoken to me. Then they said, "Let us start building!" So they committed themselves to the common good. [19] But when Sanballat the Horonite and Tobiah the Ammonite official, and Geshem the Arab heard of it, they mocked and ridiculed us, saying, "What is this that you are doing? Are you rebelling against the king?" [20] Then I replied to them, "The God of heaven is the one who will give us success, and we his servants are going to start building; but you have no share or claim or historic right in Jerusalem."

3 Then the high priest Eliashib set to work with his fellow priests and rebuilt the Sheep Gate. They consecrated it and set up its doors; they consecrated it as far as the Tower of the Hundred and as far as the Tower of Hananel. [2] And the men of Jericho built next to him. And next to them[a] Zaccur son of Imri built.

[3] The sons of Hassenaah built the Fish Gate; they laid its beams and set up its

[a] Heb *him*

2.11–18: Nehemiah's initial work in Jerusalem. Nehemiah undertakes a nighttime inspection of the walls, assessing the damage. **12:** *I told no one* (see v. 16), to avoid interference with his plans, Nehemiah keeps his initial inspection secret. **13–15:** Nehemiah's circuit of the walls confirms their dilapidated condition. Many of the landmarks can no longer be identified. **13:** *The Valley Gate* is in the western wall, the *Dragon's Spring* is unknown, and the *Dung Gate* is at the southern end of the wall (in a different location from the present Dung Gate in Jerusalem). **14:** The location of the *Fountain Gate* is uncertain; the *King's Pool* is probably the Pool of Siloam (3.15). *No place... to continue,* earlier structures and pathways of the eastern slope have collapsed beyond repair, making passage difficult. The damage on this side of the city seems beyond repair, which accounts for why the rebuilt Jerusalem will be smaller. **17–18:** Nehemiah galvanizes the Jews of Judah to rebuild by appealing to communal pride and disclosing divine and royal support.

2.19–20: Opposition. Sanballat and his associates attempt to stop Nehemiah by implying that he is a rebel, a charge that would antagonize Persian authorities. **19:** *Sanballat... and Tobiah,* see 2.10n. *Geshem,* known from nonbiblical sources as king of Qedar in Arabia, controlled territory south-southeast of Judah. *Rebelling,* a trumped-up charge to arouse Persian authorities' suspicion; cf. Ezra 4. **20:** *You have no share ... in Jerusalem,* Nehemiah seeks to protect Judah from Samaria's control and interference. At stake may be the status of Yehud as a separate Persian province under Judean control. Like Zerubbabel earlier (Ezra 4), Nehemiah restricts non-Jewish participation in rebuilding.

3.1–32: Building the walls despite opposition. Rebuilding Jerusalem's walls reinforces the religious, political, and commercial power of Jerusalem. The list of participants offers important information for discerning the scope of Jerusalem, showing that it was considerably smaller than it had been before its destruction. The list of builders (some of whom probably subsidized the project rather than physically participating in the building) indicates strong communal support. In Ezra-Nehemiah, the rebuilding of the walls is presented as an extension of rebuilding the Temple in accordance with King Cyrus's edict in Ezra 1.

3.1–5: Restoring Jerusalem's northern boundary. 1: *The high priest Eliashib,* grandson of the priest Jeshua (12.10; Ezra 3.2). *They consecrated it,* consecrating the gates marks the project as a holy task: The city as a whole is by extension as holy as a house of God (see Neh 11:1). *The Tower of Hananel,* a boundary in Zech 14.10 for a

doors, its bolts, and its bars. ⁴ Next to them Meremoth son of Uriah son of Hakkoz made repairs. Next to them Meshullam son of Berechiah son of Meshezabel made repairs. Next to them Zadok son of Baana made repairs. ⁵ Next to them the Tekoites made repairs; but their nobles would not put their shoulders to the work of their Lord.ᵃ

⁶ Joiada son of Paseah and Meshullam son of Besodeiah repaired the Old Gate; they laid its beams and set up its doors, its bolts, and its bars. ⁷ Next to them repairs were made by Melatiah the Gibeonite and Jadon the Meronothite—the men of Gibeon and of Mizpah—who were under the jurisdiction ofᵇ the governor of the province Beyond the River. ⁸ Next to them Uzziel son of Harhaiah, one of the goldsmiths, made repairs. Next to him Hananiah, one of the perfumers, made repairs; and they restored Jerusalem as far as the Broad Wall. ⁹ Next to them Rephaiah son of Hur, ruler of half the district ofᶜ Jerusalem, made repairs. ¹⁰ Next to them Jedaiah son of Harumaph made repairs opposite his house; and next to him Hattush son of Hashabneiah made repairs. ¹¹ Malchijah son of Harim and Hasshub son of Pahath-moab repaired another section and the Tower of the Ovens. ¹² Next to him Shallum son of Hallohesh, ruler of half the district ofᶜ Jerusalem, made repairs, he and his daughters.

¹³ Hanun and the inhabitants of Zanoah repaired the Valley Gate; they rebuilt it and set up its doors, its bolts, and its bars, and repaired a thousand cubits of the wall, as far as the Dung Gate.

¹⁴ Malchijah son of Rechab, ruler of the district ofᵈ Beth-haccherem, repaired the Dung Gate; he rebuilt it and set up its doors, its bolts, and its bars.

¹⁵ And Shallum son of Col-hozeh, ruler of the district ofᵈ Mizpah, repaired the Fountain Gate; he rebuilt it and covered it and set up its doors, its bolts, and its bars; and he built the wall of the Pool of Shelah of the king's garden, as far as the stairs that go down from the City of David. ¹⁶ After him Nehemiah son of Azbuk, ruler of half the district ofᶜ Beth-zur, repaired from a point opposite the graves of David, as far as the artificial pool and the house of the warriors. ¹⁷ After him the Levites made repairs: Rehum son of Bani; next to him Hashabiah, ruler of half the district ofᶜ Keilah, made repairs for his district. ¹⁸ After him their kin made repairs: Binnui,ᵉ son of Henadad, ruler of half the district ofᶜ Keilah; ¹⁹ next to him Ezer son of Jeshua, rulerᶠ of Mizpah, repaired another section opposite the ascent to the armory at the Angle. ²⁰ After him Baruch son of Zabbai repaired another section from the Angle to the door of the

ᵃ Or *lords*
ᵇ Meaning of Heb uncertain
ᶜ Or *supervisor of half the portion assigned to*
ᵈ Or *supervisor of the portion assigned to*
ᵉ Gk Syr Compare verse 24, 10.9: Heb *Bavvai*
ᶠ Or *supervisor*

newly sanctified Jerusalem. Most of the gates and other places named in the chapter cannot be located with certainty; see 2.13–14n. **2:** *Men of Jericho,* here and in vv. 9–11 volunteers from various districts of Yehud take responsibility for specific segments of the wall. **4:** *Hakkoz,* one of the families whose genealogy had been suspect initially (Ezra 2.61; Neh 7:63), but which has now been integrated. **5:** *The Tekoites,* residents of Tekoa, 10 mi (16 km) south of Jerusalem. Their efforts, despite abstention by leaders, underscore the popular nature of rebuilding.

3.6–14: Restoring Jerusalem's western boundary. The individuals named here are otherwise unknown. **8:** *Goldsmiths . . . perfumers,* traders in luxury items offer evidence of growing commerce and urbanization. *They restored,* more accurately "they left out," suggesting that the rebuilt city was smaller than earlier Jerusalem. *The Broad Wall* was probably originally built by King Hezekiah in the late eighth century BCE (see 2 Chr 32.5) to enlarge the city's defenses. An excavated portion of it can be seen in today's Jerusalem. **9–12:** The task is divided among leaders of five districts, some outside Jerusalem. **12:** *His daughters,* their role, like the men's, may have entailed physical participation and financial sponsorship.

3.15–32: Restoring Jerusalem's southern and eastern boundaries. 16: *Graves of David,* see 2 Chr 33.33. **23–24:** Jerusalemites take charge of areas adjacent to their dwellings.

…of the high priest Eliashib. [21] After …Meremoth son of Uriah son of Hakkoz …paired another section from the door of the house of Eliashib to the end of the house of Eliashib. [22] After him the priests, the men of the surrounding area, made repairs. [23] After them Benjamin and Hasshub made repairs opposite their house. After them Azariah son of Maaseiah son of Ananiah made repairs beside his own house. [24] After him Binnui son of Henadad repaired another section, from the house of Azariah to the Angle and to the corner. [25] Palal son of Uzai repaired opposite the Angle and the tower projecting from the upper house of the king at the court of the guard. After him Pedaiah son of Parosh [26] and the temple servants living[a] on Ophel made repairs up to a point opposite the Water Gate on the east and the projecting tower. [27] After him the Tekoites repaired another section opposite the great projecting tower as far as the wall of Ophel.

[28] Above the Horse Gate the priests made repairs, each one opposite his own house. [29] After them Zadok son of Immer made repairs opposite his own house. After him Shemaiah son of Shecaniah, the keeper of the East Gate, made repairs. [30] After him Hananiah son of Shelemiah and Hanun sixth son of Zalaph repaired another section. After him Meshullam son of Berechiah made repairs opposite his living quarters. [31] After him Malchijah, one of the goldsmiths, made repairs as far as the house of the temple servants and of the merchants, opposite the Muster Gate,[b] and to the upper room of the corner. [32] And between the upper room of the corner and the Sheep Gate the goldsmiths and the merchants made repairs.

4 [c] Now when Sanballat heard that we were building the wall, he was angry and greatly enraged, and he mocked the Jews. [2] He said in the presence of his associates and of the army of Samaria, "What are these feeble Jews doing? Will they restore things? Will they sacrifice? Will they finish it in a day? Will they revive the stones out of the heaps of rubbish—and burned ones at that?" [3] Tobiah the Ammonite was beside him, and he said, "That stone wall they are building—any fox going up on it would break it down!" [4] Hear, O our God, for we are despised; turn their taunt back on their own heads, and give them over as plunder in a land of captivity. [5] Do not cover their guilt, and do not let their sin be blotted out from your sight; for they have hurled insults in the face of the builders.

[6] So we rebuilt the wall, and all the wall was joined together to half its height; for the people had a mind to work.

[7] [d] But when Sanballat and Tobiah and the Arabs and the Ammonites and the Ashdodites heard that the repairing of the walls of Jerusalem was going forward and the gaps were beginning to be closed, they were very angry, [8] and all plotted together to come and fight against Jerusalem and to cause confusion in it. [9] So we prayed to our God, and set a guard as a protection against them day and night.

[10] But Judah said, "The strength of the burden bearers is failing, and there is too much rubbish so that we are unable to work on the wall." [11] And our enemies said, "They will not know or see anything before we come upon them and kill them and stop the work." [12] When the Jews who lived near them came, they said to us ten times, "From all the places where they live[e] they will come up against

a Cn: Heb *were living*
b Or *Hammiphkad Gate*
c Ch 3.33 in Heb
d Ch 4.1 in Heb
e Cn: Heb *you return*

4.1–6.14: Obstacles to reconstruction. Nehemiah's memoir about Sanballat's opposition (2.19) resumes. Nehemiah, like the earlier returnees (Ezra 3–6 and Ezra 7–10), encounters problems that hamper progress. Three types of threats to building activities are mentioned: intimidation by outsiders (4.1–23), economic hardships (5.1–19), and plots against Nehemiah (6.1–14).
4.1–23: First obstacle: intimidation. The neighboring people under Sanballat of Samaria (see 2.10n.) use taunts and threats. The tension with Samaria reproduces ancient competition between the two preexilic capital cities, Samaria of the Northern Kingdom of Israel and Jerusalem, of the Southern Kingdom of Judah, both now under Persian control. 4–5: Nehemiah punctuates his report with several invocations of God, often with a formulaic "remember me" (see 5.19n.). 10–12: The builders temporarily succumb to the difficulties of the work

us."[a] [13] So in the lowest parts of the space behind the wall, in open places, I stationed the people according to their families,[b] with their swords, their spears, and their bows. [14] After I looked these things over, I stood up and said to the nobles and the officials and the rest of the people, "Do not be afraid of them. Remember the Lord, who is great and awesome, and fight for your kin, your sons, your daughters, your wives, and your homes."

[15] When our enemies heard that their plot was known to us, and that God had frustrated it, we all returned to the wall, each to his work. [16] From that day on, half of my servants worked on construction, and half held the spears, shields, bows, and body-armor; and the leaders posted themselves behind the whole house of Judah, [17] who were building the wall. The burden bearers carried their loads in such a way that each labored on the work with one hand and with the other held a weapon. [18] And each of the builders had his sword strapped at his side while he built. The man who sounded the trumpet was beside me. [19] And I said to the nobles, the officials, and the rest of the people, "The work is great and widely spread out, and we are separated far from one another on the wall. [20] Rally to us wherever you hear the sound of the trumpet. Our God will fight for us."

[21] So we labored at the work, and half of them held the spears from break of dawn until the stars came out. [22] I also said to the people at that time, "Let every man and his servant pass the night inside Jerusalem, so that they may be a guard for us by night and may labor by day." [23] So neither I nor my brothers nor my servants nor the men of the guard who followed me ever took off our clothes; each kept his weapon in his right hand.[c]

5 Now there was a great outcry of the people and of their wives against their Jewish kin. [2] For there were those who said, "With our sons and our daughters, we are many; we must get grain, so that we may eat and stay alive." [3] There were also those who said, "We are having to pledge our fields, our vineyards, and our houses in order to get grain during the famine." [4] And there were those who said, "We are having to borrow money on our fields and vineyards to pay the king's tax. [5] Now our flesh is the same as that of our kindred; our children are the same as their children; and yet we are forcing our sons and daughters to be slaves, and some of our daughters have been ravished; we are powerless, and our fields and vineyards now belong to others."

[6] I was very angry when I heard their outcry and these complaints. [7] After thinking

a   Compare Gk Syr: Meaning of Heb uncertain
b   Meaning of Heb uncertain
c   Cn: Heb *each his weapon the water*

and their opponents' intimidation. **10:** *Judah,* the Jewish community. **13–14:** Nehemiah reorganizes the builders and provides them with military protection; he demonstrates readiness for physical combat, confident in God's help. **15–23:** Nehemiah attributes successful rallying of the Jewish builders to improved security measures as well as to God's support.

5.1–19: Second obstacle: economic hardships. The people's burden of heavy taxes to the Persian king (5.4) is aggravated by the wealthier Jews who exploit the situation for their own profit. To redress the balance, Nehemiah initiates economic reforms. He attempts to convince the wealthy that their Judean poor are also their kin, thus creating a community despite class and economic differences (see further at 6:17–19n). The poor Judeans describe their decline into slavery. Biblical laws about slavery are inconsistent (compare Ex 21.2–10 and Deut 15.12–18 with Lev 25.35–43) although they all provide for the release of Israelite slaves at some point. **2:** *We are many,* better emended to "we pledge" (see v. 3), suggesting that sons and daughters are pledged as security for loans and become slaves when loans are defaulted. **3:** The problem is the default on loans during famine and the consequent loss of property and family. **4:** *The king's tax,* the heavy levy from the provinces extracted by the Persian government. **5:** Results: Farmers are reduced to indentured slavery and lose their land and home (the basic necessity for economic survival) to wealthier compatriots. *Ravished,* daughters were particularly vulnerable at times of economic hardship. Moreover, unlike males, daughters (according to Ex 21:7–10) cannot be redeemed when they become sexually attached to the master's household.

5.6–19: Nehemiah's response. Nehemiah combats economic hardships by reforming the practices of the

it over, I brought charges against the nobles and the officials; I said to them, "You are all taking interest from your own people." And I called a great assembly to deal with them, [8] and said to them, "As far as we were able, we have bought back our Jewish kindred who had been sold to other nations; but now you are selling your own kin, who must then be bought back by us!" They were silent, and could not find a word to say. [9] So I said, "The thing that you are doing is not good. Should you not walk in the fear of our God, to prevent the taunts of the nations our enemies? [10] Moreover I and my brothers and my servants are lending them money and grain. Let us stop this taking of interest. [11] Restore to them, this very day, their fields, their vineyards, their olive orchards, and their houses, and the interest on money, grain, wine, and oil that you have been exacting from them." [12] Then they said, "We will restore everything and demand nothing more from them. We will do as you say." And I called the priests, and made them take an oath to do as they had promised. [13] I also shook out the fold of my garment and said, "So may God shake out everyone from house and from property who does not perform this promise. Thus may they be shaken out and emptied." And all the assembly said, "Amen," and praised the LORD. And the people did as they had promised.

[14] Moreover from the time that I was appointed to be their governor in the land of Judah, from the twentieth year to the thirty-second year of King Artaxerxes, twelve years, neither I nor my brothers ate the food allowance of the governor. [15] The former governors who were before me laid heavy burdens on the people, and took food and wine from them, besides forty shekels of silver. Even their servants lorded it over the people. But I did not do so, because of the fear of God. [16] Indeed, I devoted myself to the work on this wall, and acquired no land; and all my servants were gathered there for the work. [17] Moreover there were at my table one hundred fifty people, Jews and officials, besides those who came to us from the nations around us. [18] Now that which was prepared for one day was one ox and six choice sheep; also fowls were prepared for me, and every ten days skins of wine in abundance; yet with all this I did not demand the food allowance of the governor, because of the heavy burden of labor on the people. [19] Remember for my good, O my God, all that I have done for this people.

6 Now when it was reported to Sanballat and Tobiah and to Geshem the Arab and to the rest of our enemies that I had built the wall and that there was no gap left in it (though up to that time I had not set up the doors in the gates), [2] Sanballat and Geshem

wealthy and contributing personally to the economy from his own funds. **7:** *The nobles and the officials,* upper-class members exploiting the economic instability. *Taking interest,* more accurately, "taking pledges," i.e., keeping items used as pledges (family members, fields, and houses); this practice is prohibited in Ex 22.24–26; Deut 24.10. **8:** *We have bought back,* the reference is to redeeming Israelite sold as slaves to foreigners (as in Lev 25:47–48). **10:** Nehemiah shows some sympathy for the nobles by admitting a measure of his own culpability at an earlier stage but urges that the time has come for reform, and leads them by example. Nehemiah's measures resemble the remission of debts in the jubilee year (Lev 25). **12:** Like Ezra (see Ezra 10), Nehemiah extracts a public oath from leaders. The priests administer a religiously binding oath to ensure the efficacy of the appended curses. **13:** Symbolic actions could accompany curses in the ancient Near East. *Fold,* the equivalent of a pocket. The gesture connotes removing all excessive matter (including wealth). **14–19:** The Persian government expected local populations to support the governors. Nehemiah foregoes such privileges and subsidizes the office with his own personal funds. He uses this generosity as model for the Jewish aristocracy. **14:** *Governor,* this is the first we hear about Nehemiah's official position as governor, a title for several different ranks of officials. *Twentieth year,* see 1.1n. **15:** The Bible does not preserve names of other governors after Zerubbabel, although some, possibly from the intervening period, have been found in archaeological discoveries. *Forty shekels,* about 1 lb (456 gr). **17:** *Those who to us came from the nations,* the reference is to officials and guests from the rest of the empire. **19:** *Remember for my good,* such prayers are typical of Nehemiah (e.g., 4.4–5; 6.14; 13.14,31).

6.1–14: Third obstacle: plots against Nehemiah. Nehemiah describes several attempts to harm him personally. **1–4:** Attempts to harm Nehemiah in an unprotected place. **1:** *Sanballat and Tobiah and . . . Geshem,* see

sent to me, saying, "Come and let us meet together in one of the villages in the plain of Ono." But they intended to do me harm. ³ So I sent messengers to them, saying, "I am doing a great work and I cannot come down. Why should the work stop while I leave it to come down to you?" ⁴ They sent to me four times in this way, and I answered them in the same manner. ⁵ In the same way Sanballat for the fifth time sent his servant to me with an open letter in his hand. ⁶ In it was written, "It is reported among the nations—and Geshem[a] also says it—that you and the Jews intend to rebel; that is why you are building the wall; and according to this report you wish to become their king. ⁷ You have also set up prophets to proclaim in Jerusalem concerning you, 'There is a king in Judah!' And now it will be reported to the king according to these words. So come, therefore, and let us confer together." ⁸ Then I sent to him, saying, "No such things as you say have been done; you are inventing them out of your own mind" ⁹ —for they all wanted to frighten us, thinking, "Their hands will drop from the work, and it will not be done." But now, O God, strengthen my hands.

¹⁰ One day when I went into the house of Shemaiah son of Delaiah son of Mehetabel, who was confined to his house, he said, "Let us meet together in the house of God, within the temple, and let us close the doors of the temple, for they are coming to kill you; indeed, tonight they are coming to kill you."

¹¹ But I said, "Should a man like me run away? Would a man like me go into the temple to save his life? I will not go in!" ¹² Then I perceived and saw that God had not sent him at all, but he had pronounced the prophecy against me because Tobiah and Sanballat had hired him. ¹³ He was hired for this purpose, to intimidate me and make me sin by acting in this way, and so they could give me a bad name, in order to taunt me. ¹⁴ Remember Tobiah and Sanballat, O my God, according to these things that they did, and also the prophetess Noadiah and the rest of the prophets who wanted to make me afraid.

¹⁵ So the wall was finished on the twenty-fifth day of the month Elul, in fifty-two days. ¹⁶ And when all our enemies heard of it, all the nations around us were afraid[b] and fell greatly in their own esteem; for they perceived that this work had been accomplished with the help of our God. ¹⁷ Moreover in those days the nobles of Judah sent many letters to Tobiah, and Tobiah's letters came to them. ¹⁸ For many in Judah were bound by oath to him, because he was the son-in-law of Shecaniah son of Arah: and his son Jehohanan had married the daughter of Meshullam son of Berechiah. ¹⁹ Also they spoke of his good deeds in my presence, and reported my words to him. And Tobiah sent letters to intimidate me.

a Heb *Gashmu*
b Another reading is *saw*

2.10n.,19n. The opposition comes from several different groups. 2: *Plain of Ono,* in the northwest of the province of Yehud, far from the safety of Jerusalem. 5–7: Attempts to frighten Nehemiah by threatening to report his alleged rebellion to the king. 7: *Prophets* in Israel anointed kings (e.g., 1 Kings 1.34; 19.15–16); such an act could imply sedition on Nehemiah's part. 10–13: Attempts to entice Nehemiah to discredit himself with religious authorities by entering the inner part of the Temple. 10: *Shemaiah* is a suspected enemy within the community. 13: Entering sections of the Temple reserved for priests would cast Nehemiah as a sinful usurper violating the priestly domain and the Temple's sanctity. 14: Nehemiah's repeated plea for divine remembrance (cf. 5.19). *The prophetess Noadiah,* otherwise unknown, she is one of four named prophetesses in the Hebrew Bible (the others are Miriam, Deborah, and Huldah).

6.15–19: The completion of the walls. The extraordinarily short time ("fifty-two days") it took to restore the wall reflects the zeal of the community and Nehemiah's leadership abilities. 15: *Elul,* August-September. *Fifty-two days,* excavated remnants of Nehemiah's wall reflect the haste of the builders. 17–19: The opposition does not fall silent, but only changes its tactics, unsuccessfully. Tobiah's family ties with distinguished Jerusalemites, like Sanballat's (see Neh 13.28n.) suggest a conflict in Judah about the nature of the restored community. Nehemiah envisions a community based on Jewish kinship regardless of class; his opponents seek alliances along economic position, with the upper classes uniting across ethnic boundaries. 17: *Tobiah,* see 2.10n. 19: Some Jerusalemites seek rapprochement or compromise between Nehemiah and Tobiah.

7 Now when the wall had been built and I had set up the doors, and the gate-keepers, the singers, and the Levites had been appointed, [2] I gave my brother Hanani charge over Jerusalem, along with Hananiah the commander of the citadel—for he was a faithful man and feared God more than many. [3] And I said to them, "The gates of Jerusalem are not to be opened until the sun is hot; while the gatekeepers[a] are still standing guard, let them shut and bar the doors. Appoint guards from among the inhabitants of Jerusalem, some at their watch posts, and others before their own houses." [4] The city was wide and large, but the people within it were few and no houses had been built.

[5] Then my God put it into my mind to assemble the nobles and the officials and the people to be enrolled by genealogy. And I found the book of the genealogy of those who were the first to come back, and I found the following written in it:

[6] These are the people of the province who came up out of the captivity of those exiles whom King Nebuchadnezzar of Babylon had carried into exile; they returned to Jerusalem and Judah, each to his town. [7] They came with Zerubbabel, Jeshua, Nehemiah, Azariah, Raamiah, Nahamani, Mordecai, Bilshan, Mispereth, Bigvai, Nehum, Baanah.

The number of the Israelite people: [8] the descendants of Parosh, two thousand one hundred seventy-two. [9] Of Shephatiah, three hundred seventy-two. [10] Of Arah, six hundred fifty-two. [11] Of Pahath-moab, namely the descendants of Jeshua and Joab, two thousand eight hundred eighteen. [12] Of Elam, one thousand two hundred fifty-four. [13] Of Zattu, eight hundred forty-five. [14] Of Zaccai, seven hundred sixty. [15] Of Binnui, six hundred forty-eight. [16] Of Bebai, six hundred twenty-eight. [17] Of Azgad, two thousand three hundred twenty-two. [18] Of Adonikam, six hundred sixty-seven. [19] Of Bigvai, two thousand sixty-seven. [20] Of Adin, six hundred fifty-five. [21] Of Ater, namely of Hezekiah, ninety-eight. [22] Of Hashum, three hundred twenty-eight. [23] Of Bezai, three hundred twenty-four. [24] Of Hariph, one hundred twelve. [25] Of Gibeon, ninety-five. [26] The people of Bethlehem and Netophah, one hundred eighty-eight. [27] Of Anathoth, one hundred twenty-eight. [28] Of Beth-azmaveth, forty-two. [29] Of Kiriath-jearim, Chephirah, and Beeroth, seven hundred forty-three. [30] Of Ramah and Geba, six hundred twenty-one. [31] Of Michmas, one hundred twenty-two. [32] Of Bethel and Ai, one hundred twenty-three. [33] Of the other Nebo, fifty-two. [34] The descendants of the other Elam, one thousand two hundred fifty-four. [35] Of Harim, three hundred twenty. [36] Of Jericho, three hundred forty-five. [37] Of Lod, Hadid, and Ono, seven hundred twenty-one. [38] Of Senaah, three thousand nine hundred thirty.

[39] The priests: the descendants of Jedaiah, namely the house of Jeshua, nine hundred seventy-three. [40] Of Immer, one thousand fifty-two. [41] Of Pashhur, one thousand two hundred forty-seven. [42] Of Harim, one thousand seventeen.

---

[a] Heb *while they*

7.1–5: **Setting up guards.** Nehemiah places religious functionaries to guard the city gates, thereby establishing Jewish control as well as indicating that the city, like the Temple, is now under religious supervision. **1:** *Gatekeepers . . . singers . . . Levites* ordinarily officiated at the Temple. As guards of the city's gates, they symbolize the new sanctity of the city as a whole (see 11.1). **2:** *Hanani,* see 1.2. *Citadel,* fortress (see 2.8). **3:** For reasons of safety, the gates are to be open only during broad daylight. Although foreigners are not thereby excluded, their coming and going is subject to Jewish control. **4:** *The people within it were few,* most returnees had resumed a largely agrarian life in the surrounding countryside. Nehemiah's measures encourage greater urbanization, which is facilitated further in ch 11. **5:** The sparse population of Jerusalem is used as an editorial device to repeat this list from Ezra 2.

7.6–73: **Frame: repeated list of returnees.** Reproducing Ezra 2.1–70 with insignificant variations, the list serves a twofold purpose here. First, it connects the last stage of reconstruction with the successful efforts of the previous generations, as a continuous response to Cyrus's original decree (Ezra 1). By repeating the list from Ezra 2, Ezra-Nehemiah melds the three stages of return and reconstruction (Temple, community, city) into a single, unified event, spanning nearly a century (538–444 BCE). Second, it identifies who now legitimately belongs to the restored community and is subject to the legal and religious practices, privileges, and respon-

[43] The Levites: the descendants of Jeshua, namely of Kadmiel of the descendants of Hodevah, seventy-four. [44] The singers: the descendants of Asaph, one hundred forty-eight. [45] The gatekeepers: the descendants of Shallum, of Ater, of Talmon, of Akkub, of Hatita, of Shobai, one hundred thirty-eight.

[46] The temple servants: the descendants of Ziha, of Hasupha, of Tabbaoth, [47] of Keros, of Sia, of Padon, [48] of Lebana, of Hagaba, of Shalmai, [49] of Hanan, of Giddel, of Gahar, [50] of Reaiah, of Rezin, of Nekoda, [51] of Gazzam, of Uzza, of Paseah, [52] of Besai, of Meunim, of Nephushesim, [53] of Bakbuk, of Hakupha, of Harhur, [54] of Bazlith, of Mehida, of Harsha, [55] of Barkos, of Sisera, of Temah, [56] of Neziah, of Hatipha.

[57] The descendants of Solomon's servants: of Sotai, of Sophereth, of Perida, [58] of Jaala, of Darkon, of Giddel, [59] of Shephatiah, of Hattil, of Pochereth-hazzebaim, of Amon.

[60] All the temple servants and the descendants of Solomon's servants were three hundred ninety-two.

[61] The following were those who came up from Tel-melah, Tel-harsha, Cherub, Addon, and Immer, but they could not prove their ancestral houses or their descent, whether they belonged to Israel: [62] the descendants of Delaiah, of Tobiah, of Nekoda, six hundred forty-two. [63] Also, of the priests: the descendants of Hobaiah, of Hakkoz, of Barzillai (who had married one of the daughters of Barzillai the Gileadite and was called by their name). [64] These sought their registration among those enrolled in the genealogies, but it was not found there, so they were excluded from the priesthood as unclean; [65] the governor told them that they were not to partake of the most holy food, until a priest with Urim and Thummim should come.

[66] The whole assembly together was forty-two thousand three hundred sixty, [67] besides their male and female slaves, of whom there were seven thousand three hundred thirty-seven; and they had two hundred forty-five singers, male and female. [68] They had seven hundred thirty-six horses, two hundred forty-five mules,[a] [69] four hundred thirty-five camels, and six thousand seven hundred twenty donkeys.

[70] Now some of the heads of ancestral houses contributed to the work. The governor gave to the treasury one thousand darics of gold, fifty basins, and five hundred thirty priestly robes. [71] And some of the heads of ancestral houses gave into the building fund twenty thousand darics of gold and two thousand two hundred minas of silver. [72] And what the rest of the people gave was twenty thousand darics of gold, two thousand minas of silver, and sixty-seven priestly robes.

[73] So the priests, the Levites, the gatekeepers, the singers, some of the people, the temple servants, and all Israel settled in their towns.

When the seventh month came—the people of Israel being settled in their towns—

[a] Ezra 2.66 and the margins of some Hebrew Mss: MT lacks *They had ... forty-five mules*

sibilities that follow. On the list itself, see the notes to Ezra 2. **66**: *Forty-two thousand three hundred sixty,* same total for the population as Ezra 2.64, although some numbers within the two lists do not match. **70–72**: The parallel in Ezra 2.68–69 differs. For the value of such contributions, see note there. **73**: *The seventh month,* Tishri (September-October; see Ezra 3.1), designated as a beginning of the new year in later Judaism. Lev 23.23–24 and Num 29.1–6 specify practices for this date without mention of reading the Torah (see ch 8).

8.1–13.31: Celebration of renewal and reconstruction. The celebration represents the completion of the restoration that began in the time of King Cyrus nearly a century before. The reconstructed "house of God" encompasses the rebuilt Temple (Ezra 3–6), the reformed community (Ezra 7–10), and Jerusalem as a holy city (11.1), surrounded by a wall (Nehemiah 1–7). The rededication and celebration that this chapter inaugurates extend over several weeks, at least from the first day of the seventh month (8.2) to the twenty-fourth (9.1), longer than any other celebration in the Bible.

8.1–18: Celebrating by reading and implementing the Torah. The reconstruction culminates when the community summons Ezra to bring "the book of the law of Moses" (8.1), i.e., the Torah. Neh 8 signals the historical moment when the Torah, probably most of the Pentateuch, is publicly (re)introduced and receives communal sanction. Thus the ceremony in Neh 8 recalls Sinai as the receiving of God's teachings by the entire people,

8 [1] all the people gathered together into the square before the Water Gate. They told the scribe Ezra to bring the book of the law of Moses, which the LORD had given to Israel. [2] Accordingly, the priest Ezra brought the law before the assembly, both men and women and all who could hear with understanding. This was on the first day of the seventh month. [3] He read from it facing the square before the Water Gate from early morning until midday, in the presence of the men and the women and those who could understand; and the ears of all the people were attentive to the book of the law. [4] The scribe Ezra stood on a wooden platform that had been made for the purpose; and beside him stood Mattithiah, Shema, Anaiah, Uriah, Hilkiah, and Maaseiah on his right hand; and Pedaiah, Mishael, Malchijah, Hashum, Hash-baddanah, Zechariah, and Meshullam on his left hand. [5] And Ezra opened the book in the sight of all the people, for he was standing above all the people; and when he opened it, all the people stood up. [6] Then Ezra blessed the LORD, the great God, and all the people answered, "Amen, Amen," lifting up their hands. Then they bowed their heads and worshiped the LORD with their faces to the ground. [7] Also Jeshua, Bani, Shere-

biah, Jamin, Akkub, Shabbethai, Hodiah, Maaseiah, Kelita, Azariah, Jozabad, Hanan, Pelaiah, the Levites,[a] helped the people to understand the law, while the people remained in their places. [8] So they read from the book, from the law of God, with interpretation. They gave the sense, so that the people understood the reading.

[9] And Nehemiah, who was the governor, and Ezra the priest and scribe, and the Levites who taught the people said to all the people, "This day is holy to the LORD your God; do not mourn or weep." For all the people wept when they heard the words of the law. [10] Then he said to them, "Go your way, eat the fat and drink sweet wine and send portions of them to those for whom nothing is prepared, for this day is holy to our LORD; and do not be grieved, for the joy of the LORD is your strength." [11] So the Levites stilled all the people, saying, "Be quiet, for this day is holy; do not be grieved." [12] And all the people went their way to eat and drink and to send portions and to make great rejoicing, because they had understood the words that were declared to them.

---

a   1 Esdras 9.48 Vg: Heb *and the Levites*

---

transforming them into "the people of the Book." The account is no longer Nehemiah's memoir but an anonymous, third-person report. Some scholars argue that this section was originally attached to the Ezra material, either before or after Ezra 9–10.

8.1–12: The first public reading of the book of Torah. This public reading of scriptures initiates a practice that will continue in Jewish and Christian traditions. The narrative emphasizes through repetition the special bond between the people and the "book." Only in this and in the following section does Ezra appear as a contemporary of Nehemiah. **1:** *The water gate,* this area is outside the Temple. Neither the Temple nor the priests (except for Ezra) are mentioned in these celebrations until ch. 10. *They told the scribe Ezra,* the people, not Ezra, initiate the ceremony. *The book of the law of Moses,* i.e., the Torah. From the people's reaction and other details in Ezra-Nehemiah, scholars conclude that some form of today's Pentateuch, especially Deuteronomy, is being used. **2:** Both men and women participate in this ceremony of hearing and receiving the Torah (see Deut 31.12). The implicit date for the reading is September 444 (or perhaps 443). **4:** *Beside him stood . . .,* Ezra's assistants include laity, as well as Levites, who are elsewhere connected to the study of the law. Their participation expresses broadened access to the authoritative teachings, a move away from exclusive control by priests (see Jer 18.18). **5:** *When he opened it,* i.e., unrolled the scroll. *All the people stood up,* in veneration of God's presence reflected in the book. This signals a dramatic relocation of divine presence authority away from the Temple. **7:** *Helped the people to understand,* they either translate the Hebrew into the more familiar Aramaic or explain the content for greater clarity. **9:** *Nehemiah . . . and Ezra,* representing political and religious leadership, working harmoniously. This is the only verse that mentions both together. *The people wept,* either because of the warnings in the Torah or because they were overwhelmed by the moment. Ezra and Nehemiah emphasize that God's law is ultimately a source of joy.

8.13–18: Implementing Torah: the festival of booths. The people now take initiative to study and implement the Torah, in this case celebrating the festival commanded in Leviticus, Numbers, and Deuteronomy (see

¹³ On the second day the heads of ancestral houses of all the people, with the priests and the Levites, came together to the scribe Ezra in order to study the words of the law. ¹⁴ And they found it written in the law, which the LORD had commanded by Moses, that the people of Israel should live in booths[a] during the festival of the seventh month, ¹⁵ and that they should publish and proclaim in all their towns and in Jerusalem as follows, "Go out to the hills and bring branches of olive, wild olive, myrtle, palm, and other leafy trees to make booths,[a] as it is written." ¹⁶ So the people went out and brought them, and made booths[a] for themselves, each on the roofs of their houses, and in their courts and in the courts of the house of God, and in the square at the Water Gate and in the square at the Gate of Ephraim. ¹⁷ And all the assembly of those who had returned from the captivity made booths[a] and lived in them; for from the days of Jeshua son of Nun to that day the people of Israel had not done so. And there was very great rejoicing. ¹⁸ And day by day, from the first day to the last day, he read from the book of the law of God. They kept the festival seven days; and on the eighth day there was a solemn assembly, according to the ordinance.

9 Now on the twenty-fourth day of this month the people of Israel were assembled with fasting and in sackcloth, and with earth on their heads.[b] ² Then those of Israelite descent separated themselves from all foreigners, and stood and confessed their sins and the iniquities of their ancestors. ³ They stood up in their place and read from the book of the law of the LORD their God for a fourth part of the day, and for another fourth they made confession and worshiped the LORD their God. ⁴ Then Jeshua, Bani, Kadmiel, Shebaniah, Bunni, Sherebiah, Bani, and Chenani stood on the stairs of the Levites and cried out with a loud voice to the LORD their God. ⁵ Then the Levites, Jeshua, Kadmiel, Bani, Hashabneiah, Sherebiah, Hodiah, Shebaniah, and Pethahiah, said, "Stand up and bless the LORD your God from everlasting to everlasting. Blessed be your glorious name, which is exalted above all blessing and praise."

ᵃ Or *tabernacles*; Heb *succoth*
ᵇ Heb *on them*

v. 18). **14:** *They found it written*, reading the Torah made them aware of the regulations for the festival. *They . . . should live in booths* (Heb "sukkot"), see Lev 23.42–43. The fast of the Day of Atonement (set for the tenth of the month in Lev 23.26–32) is not mentioned. **15:** Lev 23.40 specifies types of tree branches, though it is not clear that these were to be used for building booths. **17:** Ezra-Nehemiah identifies the community as those who had returned from the captivity and links it with the first settlement of the land. *Jeshua son of Nun*, the leader of conquest of the land after the Exodus, and the hero of the book of Joshua. Josh 1.7–8 attributes ultimate successful survival to the study of the Torah, a practice that the restored community seeks to emulate. **18:** Deut 31.10–13 demands public readings of the Torah on the feast of booths (Sukkot) only every seventh year. As a result of rabbinic interpretation of chs 8–9, public reading became a weekly feature of Jewish worship. *The ordinance*, in Lev 23.36.

9.1–10.39: Celebration through confession and commitment. The lengthy prayer that follows restates Israelite history as a tale of divine faithfulness and Israelite faithlessness (Neh 9). To show their difference from their disloyal ancestors and in the hope of reversing the current plight, the postexilic community binds itself to God's Torah in oath and undertakes additional responsibilities to keep God's teachings (Neh 10).

9.1–37: The great communal confession rehearses Israel's history. The people's prayer illustrates their awareness of their tradition and their commitment to repair damage done to Israel's relationship with God by earlier generations. The historical review also functions as a pedagogical tool for a new generation, emphasizing important moments in that history. The Temple is never mentioned. **1–5:** The preparations for prayer. **1:** Fasting as spiritual preparation is undertaken *on the twenty-fourth day*, a date elsewhere not specified for special worship. **2:** The recitation of shared history and confession of ancestral sins apply only to the Israelites. This may account for the separation; alternatively, this separation may be part of retaining ethnic boundaries and excluding foreigners from participating in any joint worship. **3:** The combination of prayer and Torah reading will later characterize synagogue worship. **4–5:** Some of the Levites who shared the platform with Ezra earlier (8.4,7) now lead the congregation without him.

[6] And Ezra said:[a] "You are the LORD, you alone; you have made heaven, the heaven of heavens, with all their host, the earth and all that is on it, the seas and all that is in them. To all of them you give life, and the host of heaven worships you. [7] You are the LORD, the God who chose Abram and brought him out of Ur of the Chaldeans and gave him the name Abraham; [8] and you found his heart faithful before you, and made with him a covenant to give to his descendants the land of the Canaanite, the Hittite, the Amorite, the Perizzite, the Jebusite, and the Girgashite; and you have fulfilled your promise, for you are righteous.

[9] "And you saw the distress of our ancestors in Egypt and heard their cry at the Red Sea.[b] [10] You performed signs and wonders against Pharaoh and all his servants and all the people of his land, for you knew that they acted insolently against our ancestors. You made a name for yourself, which remains to this day. [11] And you divided the sea before them, so that they passed through the sea on dry land, but you threw their pursuers into the depths, like a stone into mighty waters. [12] Moreover, you led them by day with a pillar of cloud, and by night with a pillar of fire, to give them light on the way in which they should go. [13] You came down also upon Mount Sinai, and spoke with them from heaven, and gave them right ordinances and true laws, good statutes and commandments, [14] and you made known your holy sabbath to them and gave them commandments and statutes and a law through your servant Moses. [15] For their hunger you gave them bread from heaven, and for their thirst you brought water for them out of the rock, and you told them to go in to possess the land that you swore to give them.

[16] "But they and our ancestors acted presumptuously and stiffened their necks and did not obey your commandments; [17] they refused to obey, and were not mindful of the wonders that you performed among them; but they stiffened their necks and determined to return to their slavery in Egypt. But you are a God ready to forgive, gracious and merciful, slow to anger and abounding in steadfast love, and you did not forsake them. [18] Even when they had cast an image of a calf for themselves and said, 'This is your God who brought you up out of Egypt,' and had committed great blasphemies, [19] you in your great mercies did not forsake them in the wilderness; the pillar of cloud that led them in the way did not leave them by day, nor the pillar of fire by night that gave them light on the way by which they should go. [20] You gave your good spirit to instruct them, and did not withhold your manna from their mouths, and gave them water for their thirst. [21] Forty years you sustained them in the wilderness so that they lacked nothing; their clothes did not wear out and their feet did not swell. [22] And you gave them kingdoms and peoples, and allotted to them every corner,[c] so they took possession of the land of King Sihon of Heshbon and the

a   Gk: Heb lacks *And Ezra said*
b   Or *Sea of Reeds*
c   Meaning of Heb uncertain

9.6–37: The communal prayer. This communal profession of faith articulates shared history and leads to renewed formal commitment to God's teaching (in ch 10). The community recalls the cycles of God's forbearance despite Israel's earlier infidelities (vv. 6–31) and hopes to be worthy of it in the present dire circumstances (vv. 32–37). As in the historical psalms, history is not invoked for its own sake (e.g., Pss 105–106). **6:** *And Ezra said*, Ezra's name does not appear in the Hebrew text but is inserted into the early Greek versions. Ezra's role in the Hebrew Bible concluded when he placed the Torah into the care of the community and trained others to guide the community accordingly (8:13). The great prayer in the Hebrew Bible is thus assigned to the community and its representatives.

9.7–31: Recitation of historical experience. A summary of traditions preserved in Genesis–2 Kings in which the Israelites repeatedly fail to honor God. **7–8:** See Gen 12–26. **8:** *Made with him a covenant*, Abraham appears as the paradigm of faithfulness.

9–23: Highlights of events in Exodus–Deuteronomy describing God's actions on behalf of Israel. **13:** Unlike some of the earlier historical summaries (e.g., Deut 26.5–9; Josh 24.2–13), this one mentions the revelation at Sinai. **19:** *Pillar*, see Ex 13.21. **20:** *Good spirit*, perhaps a reference to the appointment of elders (Num 11.17–29).

land of King Og of Bashan. ²³ You multiplied their descendants like the stars of heaven, and brought them into the land that you had told their ancestors to enter and possess. ²⁴ So the descendants went in and possessed the land, and you subdued before them the inhabitants of the land, the Canaanites, and gave them into their hands, with their kings and the peoples of the land, to do with them as they pleased. ²⁵ And they captured fortress cities and a rich land, and took possession of houses filled with all sorts of goods, hewn cisterns, vineyards, olive orchards, and fruit trees in abundance; so they ate, and were filled and became fat, and delighted themselves in your great goodness.

²⁶ "Nevertheless they were disobedient and rebelled against you and cast your law behind their backs and killed your prophets, who had warned them in order to turn them back to you, and they committed great blasphemies. ²⁷ Therefore you gave them into the hands of their enemies, who made them suffer. Then in the time of their suffering they cried out to you and you heard them from heaven, and according to your great mercies you gave them saviors who saved them from the hands of their enemies. ²⁸ But after they had rest, they again did evil before you, and you abandoned them to the hands of their enemies, so that they had dominion over them; yet when they turned and cried to you, you heard from heaven, and many times you rescued them according to your mercies. ²⁹ And you warned them in order to turn them back to your law. Yet they acted presumptuously and did not obey your commandments, but sinned against your ordinances, by the observance of which a person

shall live. They turned a stubborn shoulder and stiffened their neck and would not obey. ³⁰ Many years you were patient with them, and warned them by your spirit through your prophets; yet they would not listen. Therefore you handed them over to the peoples of the lands. ³¹ Nevertheless, in your great mercies you did not make an end of them or forsake them, for you are a gracious and merciful God.

³² "Now therefore, our God—the great and mighty and awesome God, keeping covenant and steadfast love—do not treat lightly all the hardship that has come upon us, upon our kings, our officials, our priests, our prophets, our ancestors, and all your people, since the time of the kings of Assyria until today. ³³ You have been just in all that has come upon us, for you have dealt faithfully and we have acted wickedly; ³⁴ our kings, our officials, our priests, and our ancestors have not kept your law or heeded the commandments and the warnings that you gave them. ³⁵ Even in their own kingdom, and in the great goodness you bestowed on them, and in the large and rich land that you set before them, they did not serve you and did not turn from their wicked works. ³⁶ Here we are, slaves to this day— slaves in the land that you gave to our ancestors to enjoy its fruit and its good gifts. ³⁷ Its rich yield goes to the kings whom you have set over us because of our sins; they have power also over our bodies and over our livestock at their pleasure, and we are in great distress."

³⁸ ᵃBecause of all this we make a firm agreement in writing, and on that sealed

ᵃ Ch 10.1 in Heb

22: *Sihon . . . Og,* kings defeated in the battles for the land of Canaan (Num 21.21–35). 24–25: This conquest is described in Joshua. 26–31: A summary interpretation of the period from Joshua to the destruction of Jerusalem (see Judges–2 Kings) in which Israelites repeatedly spurned God when they were prosperous. 27: *Saviors,* the same Heb word is translated "deliverer" in Judg 3.9,15.

9.32–37: **The present distress.** The community now contrasts its circumstances with those of past generations, hoping for God's compassion. 32: *Now therefore,* after reciting a history of God's loyalty and Israel's disobedience, the community affirms God's righteousness. *The time of the kings of Assyria,* Assyria controlled the land from the mid-eighth to the late seventh centuries BCE, destroying the northern kingdom of Israel in 722 BCE. 36: *Here we are, slaves to this day,* still subject to foreign rulers. In Ezra-Nehemiah, this criticism of Persian rule is unique; elsewhere the book presents Persian rulers as benevolent.

9.38–10.39: **Commitment: the communal pledge.** Notwithstanding its plight, the community pledges loyalty to Israel's God and to God's teachings, namely the Torah. 9.38: *Because of all this,* because of this history

document are inscribed the names of our officials, our Levites, and our priests.

10 [a] Upon the sealed document are the names of Nehemiah the governor, son of Hacaliah, and Zedekiah; [2] Seraiah, Azariah, Jeremiah, [3] Pashhur, Amariah, Malchijah, [4] Hattush, Shebaniah, Malluch, [5] Harim, Meremoth, Obadiah, [6] Daniel, Ginnethon, Baruch, [7] Meshullam, Abijah, Mijamin, [8] Maaziah, Bilgai, Shemaiah; these are the priests. [9] And the Levites: Jeshua son of Azaniah, Binnui of the sons of Henadad, Kadmiel; [10] and their associates, Shebaniah, Hodiah, Kelita, Pelaiah, Hanan, [11] Mica, Rehob, Hashabiah, [12] Zaccur, Sherebiah, Shebaniah, [13] Hodiah, Bani, Beninu. [14] The leaders of the people: Parosh, Pahath-moab, Elam, Zattu, Bani, [15] Bunni, Azgad, Bebai, [16] Adonijah, Bigvai, Adin, [17] Ater, Hezekiah, Azzur, [18] Hodiah, Hashum, Bezai, [19] Hariph, Anathoth, Nebai, [20] Magpiash, Meshullam, Hezir, [21] Meshezabel, Zadok, Jaddua, [22] Pelatiah, Hanan, Anaiah, [23] Hoshea, Hananiah, Hasshub, [24] Hallohesh, Pilha, Shobek, [25] Rehum, Hashabnah, Maaseiah, [26] Ahiah, Hanan, Anan, [27] Malluch, Harim, and Baanah.

[28] The rest of the people, the priests, the Levites, the gatekeepers, the singers, the temple servants, and all who have separated themselves from the peoples of the lands to adhere to the law of God, their wives, their sons, their daughters, all who have knowledge and understanding, [29] join with their kin, their nobles, and enter into a curse and an oath to walk in God's law, which was given by Moses the servant of God, and to observe and do all the commandments of the LORD our Lord and his ordinances and his statutes. [30] We will not give our daughters to the peoples of the land or take their daughters for our sons; [31] and if the peoples of the land bring in merchandise or any grain on the sabbath day to sell, we will not buy it from them on the sabbath or on a holy day; and we will forego the crops of the seventh year and the exaction of every debt.

[32] We also lay on ourselves the obligation to charge ourselves yearly one-third of a shekel for the service of the house of our God: [33] for the rows of bread, the regular grain offering, the regular burnt offering, the sabbaths, the new moons, the appointed festivals, the sacred donations, and the sin offerings to make atonement for Israel, and for all the work of the house of our God. [34] We have also cast lots among the priests, the Levites, and the people, for the wood offering, to bring it into the house of our God, by ancestral houses, at appointed times, year by year, to burn on the altar of the LORD our God, as it is written in the law. [35] We obligate

[a] Ch 10.2 in Heb

the community commits itself unilaterally by a binding pledge to obedience. **10.1–27:** Signatories on behalf of the entire community include persons and clan names from several previous lists (Ezra 2–Neh 7; Ezra 8), but also reflects a broader religious and social participation. **28:** *The rest of the people,* the entire people affirm their voluntary commitment to the pledge. *Separated themselves,* see 9.2; 13.3. **29:** The purpose of the pledge is to have all members bind themselves to God's Torah. **30–39:** This section lists voluntarily assumed obligations that reflect practices important for Jewish identity in the fifth century BCE. They express the seriousness with which the community vows to uphold the Torah, and they combine various laws from the Pentateuch/Torah as it now exists.

10.30–31: Protecting religious and ethnic boundaries, an important theme throughout Ezra-Nehemiah. **30:** *We will not give our daughters,* see Ezra 9–10. **31:** *Buy . . . on the sabbath,* sabbath laws prohibit work on this day (e.g., Ex 31.12–17); the pledge classifies buying as work. The sabbath may have become especially important during the Babylonian exile. *Forego the crops,* see Ex 23.11. *Debt,* see Deut 15.1–3 (although the vocabulary differs).

10.32–39: Securing religious and social institutions. 32: *We also lay on ourselves the obligation,* the voluntary Temple tax reflects the commitment to undertake support of the Temple. *One-third of a shekel,* the Torah does not require annual Temple tax (Ex 30.13 is a one-time requirement). This self-imposed tax endures throughout the Second Temple period (see Mt 17.24). **33–38:** Provisions for regular Temple sacrifices and worship. **33:** *Rows of bread* are placed on a special table at the sanctuary on the sabbath (Ex 25.29; Lev 24.5–9). *Sin offerings,* or purification offerings, regular sacrifices in the Temple for public or personal transgression (Lev 4.13–21). **34:** *Wood,* for the altar's fires. This obligation is also not prescribed by the Pentateuch/Torah. **35:** *First fruits,* see Ex 22.29;

ourselves to bring the first fruits of our soil and the first fruits of all fruit of every tree, year by year, to the house of the LORD; [36] also to bring to the house of our God, to the priests who minister in the house of our God, the firstborn of our sons and of our livestock, as it is written in the law, and the firstlings of our herds and of our flocks; [37] and to bring the first of our dough, and our contributions, the fruit of every tree, the wine and the oil, to the priests, to the chambers of the house of our God; and to bring to the Levites the tithes from our soil, for it is the Levites who collect the tithes in all our rural towns. [38] And the priest, the descendant of Aaron, shall be with the Levites when the Levites receive the tithes; and the Levites shall bring up a tithe of the tithes to the house of our God, to the chambers of the storehouse. [39] For the people of Israel and the sons of Levi shall bring the contribution of grain, wine, and oil to the storerooms where the vessels of the sanctuary are, and where the priests that minister, and the gatekeepers and the singers are. We will not neglect the house of our God.

11 Now the leaders of the people lived in Jerusalem; and the rest of the people cast lots to bring one out of ten to live in the holy city Jerusalem, while nine-tenths remained in the other towns. [2] And the people blessed all those who willingly offered to live in Jerusalem.

[3] These are the leaders of the province who lived in Jerusalem; but in the towns of Judah all lived on their property in their towns:

Israel, the priests, the Levites, the temple servants, and the descendants of Solomon's servants. [4] And in Jerusalem lived some of the Judahites and of the Benjaminites. Of the Judahites: Athaiah son of Uzziah son of Zechariah son of Amariah son of Shephatiah son of Mahalalel, of the descendants of Perez; [5] and Maaseiah son of Baruch son of Colhozeh son of Hazaiah son of Adaiah son of Joiarib son of Zechariah son of the Shilonite. [6] All the descendants of Perez who lived in Jerusalem were four hundred sixty-eight valiant warriors.

[7] And these are the Benjaminites: Sallu son of Meshullam son of Joed son of Pedaiah son of Kolaiah son of Maaseiah son of Ithiel son of Jeshaiah. [8] And his brothers[a] Gabbai, Sallai: nine hundred twenty-eight. [9] Joel son of Zichri was their overseer; and Judah son of Hassenuah was second in charge of the city.

[10] Of the priests: Jedaiah son of Joiarib, Jachin, [11] Seraiah son of Hilkiah son of Meshullam son of Zadok son of Meraioth son of Ahitub, officer of the house of God, [12] and their associates who did the work of the house, eight hundred twenty-two; and Adaiah son of Jeroham son of Pelaliah son of Amzi son of Zechariah son of Pashhur son of Malchijah, [13] and his associates, heads of ancestral houses, two hundred forty-two; and Amashsai son of Azarel son of Ahzai son of Meshillemoth son of Immer, [14] and their associates, valiant warriors, one hundred

[a] Gk Mss: Heb *And after him*

23.19; Num 18.15–18. **36:** *Firstborn*, see Ex 22.29. **37:** *Tithes*, see Lev 27.30; Num 18.25–32. *The chambers* were the Temple storerooms (13.13; Ezra 8.29; 10.6). **38:** The Levites and priests depended on contributions.

11.1–12.26: The repopulation of Jerusalem and a review. This section reviews the genealogical and geographical extent of the community as part of repopulating Jerusalem.

11.1–36: Repopulation. After identifying the various groups, the restored community requires ten percent of its members to dwell in Jerusalem. The lists of chs 11–12 are compiled from different sources. **1:** *Holy city*, for Ezra-Nehemiah, the entire city, not only the Temple, is now holy (see also Ezek 48.35). *Nine-tenths remained*, see 11.3–24n.

11.3–24: Census of repopulated Jerusalem. The total of enumerated residents of Jerusalem's population in 11.1–24 is slightly over 3,000. Taking this to represent 10 percent of the population indicates about 30,000 residents for the entire province. This number is considerably smaller than the number of returnees (42,360) in Ezra 2.64 and Neh 7.66, but conforms to estimates reached by archaeologists on the basis of nonbiblical data. It also roughly corresponds to the sum total of numbers in the lists of Ezra 2 and Neh 7. See Ezra 2:64n. **4–6:** *Judahites* are traced back to their ancestor Judah through his three sons: *Perez* (11.4; cf. Gen 38.29); the *Shilonite* (11.5), probably Shelah (Gen 38.4); and Zerah (11.24; Gen 38.30). **7–9:** *Benjaminites.* The individual names are otherwise unknown. **10–14:** *Priests.* The group includes three families. Some of these names appear also in Ezra's pedigree

twenty-eight; their overseer was Zabdiel son of Haggedolim.

¹⁵ And of the Levites: Shemaiah son of Hasshub son of Azrikam son of Hashabiah son of Bunni; ¹⁶ and Shabbethai and Jozabad, of the leaders of the Levites, who were over the outside work of the house of God; ¹⁷ and Mattaniah son of Mica son of Zabdi son of Asaph, who was the leader to begin the thanksgiving in prayer, and Bakbukiah, the second among his associates; and Abda son of Shammua son of Galal son of Jeduthun. ¹⁸ All the Levites in the holy city were two hundred eighty-four.

¹⁹ The gatekeepers, Akkub, Talmon and their associates, who kept watch at the gates, were one hundred seventy-two. ²⁰ And the rest of Israel, and of the priests and the Levites, were in all the towns of Judah, all of them in their inheritance. ²¹ But the temple servants lived on Ophel; and Ziha and Gishpa were over the temple servants.

²² The overseer of the Levites in Jerusalem was Uzzi son of Bani son of Hashabiah son of Mattaniah son of Mica, of the descendants of Asaph, the singers, in charge of the work of the house of God. ²³ For there was a command from the king concerning them, and a settled provision for the singers, as was required every day. ²⁴ And Pethahiah son of Meshezabel, of the descendants of Zerah son of Judah, was at the king's hand in all matters concerning the people.

²⁵ And as for the villages, with their fields, some of the people of Judah lived in Kiriatharba and its villages, and in Dibon and its villages, and in Jekabzeel and its villages, ²⁶ and in Jeshua and in Moladah and Beth-pelet, ²⁷ in Hazar-shual, in Beer-sheba and its villages, ²⁸ in Ziklag, in Meconah and its villages, ²⁹ in En-rimmon, in Zorah, in Jarmuth, ³⁰ Zanoah,

Adullam, and their villages, Lachish and its fields, and Azekah and its villages. So they camped from Beer-sheba to the valley of Hinnom. ³¹ The people of Benjamin also lived from Geba onward, at Michmash, Aija, Bethel and its villages, ³² Anathoth, Nob, Ananiah, ³³ Hazor, Ramah, Gittaim, ³⁴ Hadid, Zeboim, Neballat, ³⁵ Lod, and Ono, the valley of artisans. ³⁶ And certain divisions of the Levites in Judah were joined to Benjamin.

12 These are the priests and the Levites who came up with Zerubbabel son of Shealtiel, and Jeshua: Seraiah, Jeremiah, Ezra, ² Amariah, Malluch, Hattush, ³ Shecaniah, Rehum, Meremoth, ⁴ Iddo, Ginnethoi, Abijah, ⁵ Mijamin, Maadiah, Bilgah, ⁶ Shemaiah, Joiarib, Jedaiah, ⁷ Sallu, Amok, Hilkiah, Jedaiah. These were the leaders of the priests and of their associates in the days of Jeshua.

⁸ And the Levites: Jeshua, Binnui, Kadmiel, Sherebiah, Judah, and Mattaniah, who with his associates was in charge of the songs of thanksgiving. ⁹ And Bakbukiah and Unno their associates stood opposite them in the service. ¹⁰ Jeshua was the father of Joiakim, Joiakim the father of Eliashib, Eliashib the father of Joiada, ¹¹ Joiada the father of Jonathan, and Jonathan the father of Jaddua.

¹² In the days of Joiakim the priests, heads of ancestral houses, were: of Seraiah, Meraiah; of Jeremiah, Hananiah; ¹³ of Ezra, Meshullam; of Amariah, Jehohanan; ¹⁴ of Malluchi, Jonathan; of Shebaniah, Joseph; ¹⁵ of Harim, Adna; of Meraioth, Helkai; ¹⁶ of Iddo, Zechariah; of Ginnethon, Meshullam; ¹⁷ of Abijah, Zichri; of Miniamin, of Moadiah, Piltai; ¹⁸ of Bilgah, Shammua; of Shemaiah, Jehonathan; ¹⁹ of Joiarib, Mattenai; of Jedaiah, Uzzi; ²⁰ of Sallai, Kallai; of Amok, Eber; ²¹ of Hilkiah, Hashabiah; of Jedaiah, Nethanel.

(Ezra 7.1–5). **19:** *Gatekeepers,* see Ezra 2.42 Neh 7.45. **24:** *At the king's hand,* i.e., directly accountable to the king.

11.25–36: Census of other Jewish settlements. The geographical area spanned by the villages extends beyond the known boundaries of the Persian province of Yehud (Judah). The list, then, is either an ideal echoing Josh 15, envisioning a greater province, or (more likely) a register of Jews also in towns outside Yehud proper or an expanded list from a considerably later time. (For the location of sites that can be identified, see the map on p. 686.)

12.1–26: Review of priestly and levitical genealogies. The reconstituted community again (cf. ch 7) reviews its Temple personnel, spanning the entire era of reconstruction (520–444 BCE). The list is artificial and problematic, but its existence reflects the importance of priests and Levites in this period, a concern also reflected in the books of Chronicles. Although many names are familiar from other lists, the information resists clear chronological schematization. **1:** *Came up with Zerubbabel . . . and Jeshua,* i.e., the governor and priest leading Stage

[22] As for the Levites, in the days of Eliashib, Joiada, Johanan, and Jaddua, there were recorded the heads of ancestral houses; also the priests until the reign of Darius the Persian. [23] The Levites, heads of ancestral houses, were recorded in the Book of the Annals until the days of Johanan son of Eliashib. [24] And the leaders of the Levites: Hashabiah, Sherebiah, and Jeshua son of Kadmiel, with their associates over against them, to praise and to give thanks, according to the commandment of David the man of God, section opposite to section. [25] Mattaniah, Bakbukiah, Obadiah, Meshullam, Talmon, and Akkub were gatekeepers standing guard at the storehouses of the gates. [26] These were in the days of Joiakim son of Jeshua son of Jozadak, and in the days of the governor Nehemiah and of the priest Ezra, the scribe.

[27] Now at the dedication of the wall of Jerusalem they sought out the Levites in all their places, to bring them to Jerusalem to celebrate the dedication with rejoicing, with thanksgivings and with singing, with cymbals, harps, and lyres. [28] The companies of the singers gathered together from the circuit around Jerusalem and from the villages of the Netophathites; [29] also from Beth-gilgal and from the region of Geba and Azmaveth; for the singers had built for themselves villages around Jerusalem. [30] And the priests and the Levites purified themselves; and they purified the people and the gates and the wall.

[31] Then I brought the leaders of Judah up onto the wall, and appointed two great companies that gave thanks and went in procession. One went to the right on the wall to the Dung Gate; [32] and after them went Hoshaiah and half the officials of Judah, [33] and Aza-riah, Ezra, Meshullam, [34] Judah, Benjamin, Shemaiah, and Jeremiah, [35] and some of the young priests with trumpets: Zechariah son of Jonathan son of Shemaiah son of Mattaniah son of Micaiah son of Zaccur son of Asaph; [36] and his kindred, Shemaiah, Azarel, Milalai, Gilalai, Maai, Nethanel, Judah, and Hanani, with the musical instruments of David the man of God; and the scribe Ezra went in front of them. [37] At the Fountain Gate, in front of them, they went straight up by the stairs of the city of David, at the ascent of the wall, above the house of David, to the Water Gate on the east.

[38] The other company of those who gave thanks went to the left,[a] and I followed them with half of the people on the wall, above the Tower of the Ovens, to the Broad Wall, [39] and above the Gate of Ephraim, and by the Old Gate, and by the Fish Gate and the Tower of Hananel and the Tower of the Hundred, to the Sheep Gate; and they came to a halt at the Gate of the Guard. [40] So both companies of those who gave thanks stood in the house of God, and I and half of the officials with me; [41] and the priests Eliakim, Maaseiah, Miniamin, Micaiah, Elioenai, Zechariah, and Hananiah, with trumpets; [42] and Maaseiah, Shemaiah, Eleazar, Uzzi, Jehohanan, Malchijah, Elam, and Ezer. And the singers sang with Jezrahiah as their leader. [43] They offered great sacrifices that day and rejoiced, for God had made them rejoice with great joy; the women and children also rejoiced. The joy of Jerusalem was heard far away.

[44] On that day men were appointed over the chambers for the stores, the contribu-

---

[a] Cn: Heb opposite

One of the return (see Ezra 2.1–2n.). **22:** *Until the reign of Darius the Persian,* Darius I (522–486). Some scholars suggest that the reference is to Darius II (423–404 BCE). **24:** *David,* see Ezra 3.10n. **26:** *Joiakim . . . Nehemiah . . . Ezra,* the three figures—the officiating priest, the governor, and the priest Ezra in his capacity as scribe—mark the period of completion of the task. Now all is ready for the grand finale.

12.27–13.3: Grand finale: a service of dedication: celebration, purification, procession, and separation. 12.27: The initiative again comes from the community (cf. 8.1). **30:** This unique ceremony of purification signals that the people are sanctified and Jerusalem is "the holy city" (11.1).

12.31–42: The procession. Two groups circled the city on the wall and alongside it. On the gates named, see 2.13–14n.; 3.1n. **31:** *Then I,* Nehemiah. *Two great companies,* the groups marched in opposite directions and met at the Temple. **36:** *The scribe Ezra,* this final appearance by Ezra is striking; as a priest (Ezra 7.1–5), he leads the priests. **42:** Antiphonal singing by the professional liturgical singers.

12.43–13.3: Final communal actions on the day of dedication. These include sacrifices and separation in

tions, the first fruits, and the tithes, to gather into them the portions required by the law for the priests and for the Levites from the fields belonging to the towns; for Judah rejoiced over the priests and the Levites who ministered. ⁴⁵ They performed the service of their God and the service of purification, as did the singers and the gatekeepers, according to the command of David and his son Solomon. ⁴⁶ For in the days of David and Asaph long ago there was a leader of the singers, and there were songs of praise and thanksgiving to God. ⁴⁷ In the days of Zerubbabel and in the days of Nehemiah all Israel gave the daily portions for the singers and the gatekeepers. They set apart that which was for the Levites; and the Levites set apart that which was for the descendants of Aaron.

13 On that day they read from the book of Moses in the hearing of the people; and in it was found written that no Ammonite or Moabite should ever enter the assembly of God, ² because they did not meet the Israelites with bread and water, but hired Balaam against them to curse them—yet our God turned the curse into a blessing. ³ When the people heard the law, they separated from Israel all those of foreign descent.

⁴ Now before this, the priest Eliashib, who was appointed over the chambers of the house of our God, and who was related to Tobiah, ⁵ prepared for Tobiah a large room where they had previously put the grain offering, the frankincense, the vessels, and the tithes of grain, wine, and oil, which were given by commandment to the Levites, singers, and gatekeepers, and the contributions for the priests. ⁶ While this was taking place I was not in Jerusalem, for in the thirty-second year of King Artaxerxes of Babylon I went to the king. After some time I asked leave of the king ⁷ and returned to Jerusalem. I then discovered the wrong that Eliashib had done on behalf of Tobiah, preparing a room for him in the courts of the house of God. ⁸ And I was very angry, and I threw all the household furniture of Tobiah out of the room. ⁹ Then I gave orders and they cleansed the chambers, and I brought back the vessels of the house of God, with the grain offering and the frankincense.

¹⁰ I also found out that the portions of the Levites had not been given to them; so that the Levites and the singers, who had conducted the service, had gone back to their fields. ¹¹ So I remonstrated with the officials and said, "Why is the house of God

accordance with the Torah. **12.46:** *Asaph,* see 7.44; 1 Chr 16.5. **47:** *The days of Zerubbabel and . . . Nehemiah,* the description of the celebration reckons from the beginning of the return (Ezra 2) to Nehemiah, the period covered by the unified Ezra-Nehemiah. **13.1–3:** The final action on that day implements the Torah by separating from foreigners. Although distinct from the issues of intermarriage (Ezra 9–10 and Neh 13.23–28), the separation is part of the social and religious boundaries that the restored community seeks to maintain within the multicultural setting of the Persian empire. The virtual quotation from Deut 23.4–7 indicates that Deuteronomy was available to the postexilic community as part of its Torah or "law of Moses." **1.** *No Ammonite or Moabite should ever enter,* see Deut 23.3. **2:** *Balaam,* see Num 22–24 and Deut 23.5-6.

13.4–31: Coda. Nehemiah's memoir (interrupted in 7.5) resumes with a retrospective from a time after 433 BCE, after Nehemiah had served twelve years as governor (13.6; 5.14). At some point after returning to King Artaxerxes, Nehemiah came back to Jerusalem, discovered violations of the communal pledge of ch 10, and took steps to restore order. These violations pertain to the purity of the Temple, observance of the sabbath, and intermarriage. **4–9:** Nehemiah evicts Tobiah from the desecrated Temple precinct. Nehemiah first referred to Tobiah as an "Ammonite official" (2.10), a national connection that may justify his expulsion (see 13.1–3). Apparently other Judeans considered Tobiah (whose name refers to Israel's God; see 2.10n) a legitimate member of the community. His connection with the priests and installation at the Temple support this conclusion. On Tobiah's priestly relations, see 6.18. **4:** *The priest Eliashib,* possibly, but not necessarily the high priest (of 3.1 and 13.28); the name was common in this era. *Appointed over the chambers,* hence controlling the storage and distribution of Temple resources). **6:** *The thirty-second year,* 433 BCE. **9:** *Cleansed,* for Nehemiah, Tobiah's illegitimate presence ritually contaminated the room.

13.10–13: Nehemiah rectifies violations regarding Levites and singers (cf. 10.37–39). **10:** *Levites . . . had gone,* Nehemiah may imply that Tobiah's presence hastened the departure of Levites who had not been paid. **11:**

forsaken?" And I gathered them together and set them in their stations. [12] Then all Judah brought the tithe of the grain, wine, and oil into the storehouses. [13] And I appointed as treasurers over the storehouses the priest Shelemiah, the scribe Zadok, and Pedaiah of the Levites, and as their assistant Hanan son of Zaccur son of Mattaniah, for they were considered faithful; and their duty was to distribute to their associates. [14] Remember me, O my God, concerning this, and do not wipe out my good deeds that I have done for the house of my God and for his service.

[15] In those days I saw in Judah people treading wine presses on the sabbath, and bringing in heaps of grain and loading them on donkeys; and also wine, grapes, figs, and all kinds of burdens, which they brought into Jerusalem on the sabbath day; and I warned them at that time against selling food. [16] Tyrians also, who lived in the city, brought in fish and all kinds of merchandise and sold them on the sabbath to the people of Judah, and in Jerusalem. [17] Then I remonstrated with the nobles of Judah and said to them, "What is this evil thing that you are doing, profaning the sabbath day? [18] Did not your ancestors act in this way, and did not our God bring all this disaster on us and on this city? Yet you bring more wrath on Israel by profaning the sabbath."

[19] When it began to be dark at the gates of Jerusalem before the sabbath, I commanded that the doors should be shut and gave orders that they should not be opened until after the sabbath. And I set some of my servants over the gates, to prevent any burden from being brought in on the sabbath day. [20] Then the merchants and sellers of all kinds of merchandise spent the night outside Jerusalem once or twice. [21] But I warned them and said to them, "Why do you spend the night in front of the wall? If you do so again, I will lay hands on you." From that time on they did not come on the sabbath. [22] And I commanded the Levites that they should purify themselves and come and guard the gates, to keep the sabbath day holy. Remember this also in my favor, O my God, and spare me according to the greatness of your steadfast love.

[23] In those days also I saw Jews who had married women of Ashdod, Ammon, and Moab; [24] and half of their children spoke the language of Ashdod, and they could not speak the language of Judah, but spoke the language of various peoples. [25] And I contended with them and cursed them and beat some of them and pulled out their hair; and I made them take an oath in the name of God, saying, "You shall not give your daughters to their sons, or take their daughters for your sons or for yourselves. [26] Did not King Solomon of Israel sin on account of such women? Among the many nations there was no king like him, and he was beloved by his God, and God made him king over all Israel; nevertheless, foreign women made even him to sin. [27] Shall we then listen to you and do all this great evil and act treacherously against our God by marrying foreign women?"

Gathered them, i.e., the dispersed Levites. **12:** The opening words should be translated "All Judah had brought." Nehemiah alleges that the desertion of Levites resulted less from lack of contributions than from mismanagement, possibly by Tobiah. **13:** *And I appointed,* Nehemiah's chooses new supervisors. *Considered faithful,* an important trait because of previous corruption under Tobiah and Eliashib. **14:** Conclusion: Nehemiah's plea for remembrance for these restoration efforts.

13.15–22: Nehemiah rectifies sabbath violations (cf. 10.31). The sabbath constitutes another cultural and religious boundary, one that gains importance in the postexilic period. **15:** *In those days,* when Nehemiah returned to Jerusalem for the second time, after 433 BCE. **16:** *Tyrians,* merchants from Tyre, in modern Lebanon. **19–22:** Shutting the gates during the sabbath prevented foreign trading in the city during the sabbath. **22:** *They should purify themselves,* purified Levites guard the gates (7.1–3; 11.1) to secure sanctity, especially on the holy sabbath. Such measures are unique to the book of Ezra-Nehemiah, underscoring the holiness of the entire city.

13.23–29: Intermarriage problems (cf. 10.30). On marriage with foreigners in Ezra-Nehemiah, see Ezra 9–10, especially Ezra 9.1–15n. The problem, as Nehemiah presents it, is different from Ezra 9.2; it concerns loss of Jewish identity exemplified by the disappearance of Hebrew among children of mixed marriages. Intermarriage also signals for him turning away from Israel's God. **23:** *Ashdod,* a Philistine city on the southeast coast of the Mediterranean. **26:** *King Solomon*'s marriages corrupted his relations with God (1 Kings 11.1–8) and thus

²⁸ And one of the sons of Jehoiada, son of the high priest Eliashib, was the son-in-law of Sanballat the Horonite; I chased him away from me. ²⁹ Remember them, O my God, because they have defiled the priesthood, the covenant of the priests and the Levites.

³⁰ Thus I cleansed them from everything foreign, and I established the duties of the priests and Levites, each in his work; ³¹ and I provided for the wood offering, at appointed times, and for the first fruits. Remember me, O my God, for good.

exemplify the danger to the present community. **28:** *Son of the high priest Eliashib, was the son-in-law of Sanballat,* evidently, some Jews, including the high priest's family, considered contracting marriage with Sanballat's family as appropriate. Eliashib consecrated the gates in 3.1. *Sanballat,* the family of Sanballat, the governor of Samaria (see 2.10n.). His sons had Hebrew names. 2 Kings 17 describes the residents of Samaria as foreigners who accepted some aspects of Yahwistic worship. Samarians, like the later Samaritans, may have claimed, instead, that they were a remnant of the northern kingdom of Israel and true offspring of Abraham through Jacob. Like Ezra, Nehemiah vehemently objects to what he construes as intermarriage. *I chased him away,* Nehemiah acts firmly to protect the Temple's purity from illegitimate behavior by a priest. The Jewish historian Josephus reports that the Samaritan Temple near Shechem was built in the fourth century BCE for a priest expelled from Jerusalem *Ant.* 11.8.2).

13.30–31: Conclusion. The purification of the priesthood and Temple administration was difficult because of the status of the opposing priests. Therefore, Nehemiah presents restoring order and sanctity to the worship system as the crown of his achievement. **31:** *I provided for the wood offering . . . and for the first fruits,* see 10.34–35, in which the community pledges to provide these. *For good,* with "good" as the last word, Nehemiah invokes a final blessing.

ESTHER

NAME

The book of Esther takes its name from its heroine, the Jewish woman of the Diaspora who becomes queen of Persia, saves her people from genocide, and with her guardian, Mordecai, inaugurates the new Jewish festival of Purim. This title first appears in the Greek translation (the Septuagint, LXX) of the story and thus may not belong to the Hebrew original. According to 2.7, Esther has a Hebrew name, Hadassah, but is otherwise called Esther, a name that is cognate with Ishtar, the Babylonian goddess of love and war, or with the Persian word *stara*, "star." The Latin (Vulgate) translation calls her Hester.

CANONICAL STATUS

Esther is the only book of the Hebrew Bible unattested among the Dead Sea Scrolls (third century BCE to first century CE), nor does the New Testament ever allude to it. Like The Song of Solomon (on which the New Testament is similarly mute), the book of Esther provoked debate among rabbis and church fathers over its scriptural status for reasons that were not always spelled out. Neither book so much as mentions God or such key Jewish concepts as covenant, temple, sacrifice, or prayer. Furthermore, both Esther and Song of Solomon celebrate, albeit in different contexts, the power of feminine sexuality. Another factor in its late admission to the biblical canon may have been the book's enthusiastic account of the Jewish communities' slaughter of their enemies, an aspect of Esther that continues to trouble readers today.

Only by the third or fourth centuries CE does the scroll appear to have successfully overcome all rabbinical reservations about its canonicity. Early Christians harbored similar doubts; as late as the fourth century when the Western church had accepted Esther in its Bible, some Eastern Church authorities continued to question it. The sixteenth-century Protestant reformer Martin Luther wished it had never been written.

In the Jewish scriptures ("Tanakh"), the book of Esther appears in the third section, the Writings ("Ketubim"); coming after Ecclesiastes, it is the last of the five festal scrolls ("Megillot"). Esther is read twice through on the Jewish festival Purim. In Christian Bibles the book is grouped with the Historical Books, after Ezra and Nehemiah, in recognition of the story's setting in the Persian period (550–333 BCE).

Complicating Esther's place in the biblical canon are more than a hundred additional verses in the Greek (Septuagint) version that do not appear in surviving Hebrew manuscripts. These verses are excluded from their Bibles by Jews and Protestants, while Roman Catholic and Orthodox Christians accept them. A translation of the full Greek text of Esther, including these additions, is part of the Apocryphal/Deuterocanonical Books in most editions of this Bible.

AUTHORSHIP, DATE, AND LITERARY HISTORY

Esther contains some folktale motifs, but its many allusions to other biblical texts, most notably the Joseph story (Gen 37–48), suggest a literate and cultured author, probably from a socially prominent Jewish family in Persia. The anonymous author makes a case for living a full Jewish life within the strictures imposed by the alien Diaspora environment. The version of Esther contained in the Hebrew Bible was probably composed in the early Hellenistic period (late fourth or early third century BCE).

In light of the extra Greek verses mentioned above, as well as a slightly different version of Esther preserved in a few Greek manuscripts, the existing biblical (canonical) version of Esther clearly evolved over time; many scholars, for example, doubt that the Purim festival figured in earlier versions of the Esther story.

CONTENTS AND INTERPRETATION

Although the action of Esther takes place over a period of ten years in the reign of the Persian King Ahasuerus, the ten chapters of the story progress swiftly. The narrative relates how Esther came to be queen (in place of the disgraced Vashti) and how a rivalry between her uncle Mordecai and his enemy Haman threatened the entire Jewish community. Through Esther's cleverness and boldness the plot was foiled, and the Jews were given permission to defend themselves. The story serves, perhaps secondarily, as the background for the Jewish holiday of Purim.

Despite the setting and the author's familiarity with Persian customs, vocabulary, and names, Esther is not a work of history but a historical novella, that is, a fictional story within a historical framework. Ahasuerus is probably meant to be Xerxes I of Persia (486–465 BCE), but there is no historical evidence for a Queen Vashti or for a Jewish queen, much less a Queen Esther. The concept of immutable "laws of the Persians and the Medes" (1.19) appears only in Esther. The story's purpose is to entertain, but more importantly to demonstrate the inevitability of retributive justice and, paradoxically, the need for oppressed minorities to act shrewdly and boldly for that justice to prevail. In addition, the book's historical tone legitimates the festival of Purim, which was probably a Babylonian or Persian holiday adopted by Diaspora Jews. Purim is not mentioned in the rest of the Bible.

As a woman, Esther herself mirrors the marginal and sometimes precarious status of Diaspora Jews. The author, in fact, may be advocating a measure of accommodation with the larger Gentile world by ignoring the question of how a good Jew like Esther can justify marrying a Gentile and inevitably violating Jewish dietary rules.

The most intractable interpretive problem of Esther centers on God. Because God is never explicitly named in Esther, scholars are divided as to whether the author excluded divine participation altogether or intended to imply that God was active behind the scenes. The ambiguous reference in 4.14 to help "from another quarter" has been invoked to argue both positions. The Greek additions to Esther took care to mention God frequently, thereby resolving this interpretive dilemma and, incidentally, providing an instance of early Jewish biblical interpretation at work.

GUIDE TO READING

For the fullest appreciation of the story, readers should keep in mind that Esther's narrative style overflows with exaggeration and hyperbole: the duration of royal feasts, the silliness of the king's first decree, Esther's excessive beauty regimen, and the body count of the Jews' victims. Furthermore, in Esther one encounters a surprisingly modern tension between various forms of comedy—such as satire, irony, and farce—and tragedy. The author has adroitly bound these together and balanced them within the narrative by complex patterns of symmetries, reversals, foreshadowing, and recurring motifs. For example, the story begins and ends with a feast, while additional banquets punctuate the narrative at key moments. Royal edicts, often highly ironic, similarly mark the course of the action. At different moments leading characters mirror each other directly or in reverse. The disobedient queen Vashti is deposed, but new queen Esther triumphantly defies royal law. Esther successfully begs the king for the lives of her people whom Haman has doomed; Haman in vain supplicates Esther for his own life. The most cleverly constructed moment of the story occurs in ch 6 when Haman suddenly finds himself in the humiliating position of presenting the royal reward he expected himself to his nemesis, Mordecai, instead.

While the main characters in Esther are essentially stereotypes without distinctive personalities, one character does change over the course of the story. Esther begins as a passive figure, notable only for her beauty and obedient nature. Since all the women in the harem are beautiful, presumably it is her exceptional sexual skills that win her the crown. However, after Mordecai's challenge to Esther in 4.13–14, Esther seems to embrace her Jewishness; with this self-recognition, Esther becomes the decisive actor in the story, risking her life, issuing orders to Mordecai, and, later, to the king himself. Ultimately, it is on Esther's authority, albeit in concert with Mordecai, that Purim is established, making Esther the only woman to authorize a Jewish religious tradition.

Mary Joan Winn Leith

1 This happened in the days of Ahasuerus, the same Ahasuerus who ruled over one hundred twenty-seven provinces from India to Ethiopia.[a] [2] In those days when King Ahasuerus sat on his royal throne in the citadel of Susa, [3] in the third year of his reign, he gave a banquet for all his officials and ministers. The army of Persia and Media and the nobles and governors of the provinces were present, [4] while he displayed the great wealth of his kingdom and the splendor and pomp of his majesty for many days, one hundred eighty days in all.

[5] When these days were completed, the king gave for all the people present in the citadel of Susa, both great and small, a banquet lasting for seven days, in the court of the garden of the king's palace. [6] There were white cotton curtains and blue hangings tied with cords of fine linen and purple to silver rings[b] and marble pillars. There were couches of gold and silver on a mosaic pavement of porphyry, marble, mother-of-pearl, and colored stones. [7] Drinks were served in golden goblets, goblets of different kinds, and the royal wine was lavished according to the bounty of the king. [8] Drinking was by flagons, without restraint; for the king had given orders to all the officials of his palace to do as each one desired. [9] Furthermore, Queen Vashti gave a banquet for the women in the palace of King Ahasuerus.

[10] On the seventh day, when the king was merry with wine, he commanded Mehuman, Biztha, Harbona, Bigtha and Abagtha, Zethar and Carkas, the seven eunuchs who attended him, [11] to bring Queen Vashti before the king, wearing the royal crown, in order to show the peoples and the officials her beauty; for she was fair to behold. [12] But Queen Vashti refused to come at the king's command conveyed by the eunuchs. At this the king was enraged, and his anger burned within him.

[13] Then the king consulted the sages who knew the laws[c] (for this was the king's procedure toward all who were versed in law and custom, [14] and those next to him were Carshena, Shethar, Admatha, Tarshish, Meres, Marsena, and Memucan, the seven officials of Persia and Media, who had access to the king, and sat first in the kingdom): [15] "According to the law, what is to be done to Queen Vashti because she has not performed the command of King Ahasuerus conveyed by the eunuchs?" [16] Then Memucan said in the presence of the king and the officials, "Not only has Queen Vashti done wrong to the king, but also to all the officials and all the peoples who are in all the provinces of King Ahasuerus. [17] For this deed of the queen will

a Or *Nubia*; Heb *Cush*
b Or *rods*
c Cn: Heb *times*

1.1–9: King Ahasuerus holds a feast. 1: *Ahasuerus* (Ezra 4.6; not the same as in Dan 9.1 or Tob 14.15) is probably Xerxes I (486–465 BCE) whose Persian Empire from *India* (Indus Valley) to *Ethiopia* (Heb "Cush," modern Sudan and Ethiopia) included some twenty satrapies (Herodotus 3.89) subdivided into *provinces*. **2:** *Susa*, Ahasuerus's winter capital in northwestern Iran, 180 mi (400 km) east of ancient Babylon. The *citadel* was a fortified section of the palace. **3–4:** Greek writers mention sumptuous feasts held by Persian kings. The *banquet*, with its exaggerated length of *one hundred and eighty days* (see Jdt 1.16), is the first of several that occur at key moments in the story. **5–6:** *Garden . . . curtains . . . couches*, the extravagance emphasizes power and wealth. **8:** *Drinking was . . . without restraint*, demonstrating the king's characteristic permissiveness, excess, and lack of control over his court (cf. 3.11; 5.6; 7.2), which foreshadows his later inability to control Queen Vashti. **9:** *Vashti*, a Persian name meaning "beloved." Xerxes I's queen was Amestris (Herodotus 7.61); no *Vashti* appears in any ancient records. Vashti's *banquet for the women* emphasizes the separate, gendered spheres of king and queen, a factor in Esther's later bravery.

1.10–22: Queen Vashti's downfall. 10: A person *merry with wine* (Prov 15.15) may come to grief (see 5.9; 1 Sam 25.36; 2 Sam 13.28; Dan 5.2). *Eunuchs* were castrated males who served in the Persian court. The list of their names lends the story an air of authenticity. **12:** This episode occurs in reverse in 5.2 when Esther comes uninvited into the king's presence. **13-18:** A satirical moment: the king's *sages who knew the laws* inflate a domestic dispute into a national crisis. **14:** Only the closest royal advisers enjoyed free *access to the king* (see 4.11). The seven *officials* have Persian names. The fear of a feminine insurrection against patriarchal order lies just below the surface of many ancient myths and legends. Contrary to Memucan's dire imaginings, the real danger will

be made known to all women, causing them to look with contempt on their husbands, since they will say, 'King Ahasuerus commanded Queen Vashti to be brought before him, and she did not come.' [18] This very day the noble ladies of Persia and Media who have heard of the queen's behavior will rebel against[a] the king's officials, and there will be no end of contempt and wrath! [19] If it pleases the king, let a royal order go out from him, and let it be written among the laws of the Persians and the Medes so that it may not be altered, that Vashti is never again to come before King Ahasuerus; and let the king give her royal position to another who is better than she. [20] So when the decree made by the king is proclaimed throughout all his kingdom, vast as it is, all women will give honor to their husbands, high and low alike."

[21] This advice pleased the king and the officials, and the king did as Memucan proposed; [22] he sent letters to all the royal provinces, to every province in its own script and to every people in its own language, declaring that every man should be master in his own house.[b]

2 After these things, when the anger of King Ahasuerus had abated, he remembered Vashti and what she had done and what had been decreed against her. [2] Then the king's servants who attended him said, "Let beautiful young virgins be sought out for the king. [3] And let the king appoint commissioners in all the provinces of his kingdom to gather all the beautiful young virgins to the harem in the citadel of Susa under custody of Hegai, the king's eunuch, who is in charge of the women; let their cosmetic treatments be given them. [4] And let the girl who pleases the king be queen instead of Vashti." This pleased the king, and he did so.

[5] Now there was a Jew in the citadel of Susa whose name was Mordecai son of Jair son of Shimei son of Kish, a Benjaminite. [6] Kish[c] had been carried away from Jerusalem among the captives carried away with King Jeconiah of Judah, whom King Nebuchadnezzar of

a   Cn: Heb *will tell*
b   Heb adds *and speak according to the language of his people*
c   Heb *a Benjaminite [c]who*

come in the form of a conspiracy by palace bodyguards (2.21). **19**: *To another who is better than she* uses the same words as Samuel's rejection of Saul in favor of David (1 Sam 15.28). No sources outside the Bible indicate that the *laws of the Persians and the Medes* could *not be altered* (8.8; Dan 6.8,12), but here the phrase subtly contrasts excessive legalism with true justice. This *royal order* is the first in a series of edicts by the king. **20**: An instance of narrative irony: by decreeing that *all women* must *give honor to their husbands*, the king draws attention to his own failure to control his wife. **22**: Persian royal pronouncements were issued in Aramaic, the official language of Persian diplomacy, as well as in the *languages* of subject peoples (see Ezra 4.7,17). *Letters*, the Persian postal system was renowned (Herodotus 8.98).

2.1–18: Esther becomes queen. 1–4: The king agrees to seek a new queen. 1: *Remembered* (i.e., positively; see Gen 40.14); the king may be regretting his treatment of Vashti but cannot risk losing face by reversing his earlier decision (1.19). **2:** Patriarchal societies insist on a *virgin* bride to ensure the paternity of children within the marriage (see Ex 22.16; Lev 21.13). In fact, Persian kings could marry women only from certain noble Persian families. **3:** *Let the king appoint commissioners* echoes the Joseph story (see Gen 41.34–35), a biblical text to which the book of Esther often alludes. *Eunuch*, see 1.10n. Eunuchs were especially needed as overseers of the king's *harem* (lit. "house of women"). *Cosmetic treatments* (see vv. 9,12).

2.5–11: Introducing two Jewish heroes: Mordecai and Esther. 5–6: *Mordecai*, a name derived from the Babylonian god Marduk. Mordecai's Benjaminite ancestry includes King Saul (1 Sam 9.1–2), while Haman's genealogy (3.1) connects him to Saul's enemy, the Amalekite King Agag (1 Sam 15). *Jew* (Heb "yehudi"), originally anyone from the kingdom of Judah (2 Kings 16.6), is used here in its usual later sense of an adherent to Judaism. Mordecai's presence *in the citadel* (see 1.2n.) probably means he was a minor court official (see 2.19). The Hebrew wording implies it was Mordecai who was exiled with *Judah*'s last king, Jehoiachin (here called *Jeconiah*), when the Babylonian king *Nebuchadnezzar* conquered Judah in 597 BCE (2 Kings 24), over a hundred years earlier. To avoid an unlikely century-old Mordecai, translators have often emended the text to make Mordecai's great-grandfather, Kish, part of the original exile. *Susa*, see 1.2n. **7:** Esther's Hebrew name *Hadassah* means "myrtle." Her Gentile name, *Esther*, derives from Ishtar, Babylonian goddess of sexual allure and war, or from the Persian

Babylon had carried away. [7] Mordecai[a] had brought up Hadassah, that is Esther, his cousin, for she had neither father nor mother; the girl was fair and beautiful, and when her father and her mother died, Mordecai adopted her as his own daughter. [8] So when the king's order and his edict were proclaimed, and when many young women were gathered in the citadel of Susa in custody of Hegai, Esther also was taken into the king's palace and put in custody of Hegai, who had charge of the women. [9] The girl pleased him and won his favor, and he quickly provided her with her cosmetic treatments and her portion of food, and with seven chosen maids from the king's palace, and advanced her and her maids to the best place in the harem. [10] Esther did not reveal her people or kindred, for Mordecai had charged her not to tell. [11] Every day Mordecai would walk around in front of the court of the harem, to learn how Esther was and how she fared.

[12] The turn came for each girl to go in to King Ahasuerus, after being twelve months under the regulations for the women, since this was the regular period of their cosmetic treatment, six months with oil of myrrh and six months with perfumes and cosmetics for women. [13] When the girl went in to the king she was given whatever she asked for to take with her from the harem to the king's palace. [14] In the evening she went in; then in the morning she came back to the second harem in custody of Shaashgaz, the king's eunuch, who was in charge of the concubines; she did not go in to the king again, unless the king

delighted in her and she was summoned by name. [15] When the turn came for Esther daughter of Abihail the uncle of Mordecai, who had adopted her as his own daughter, to go in to the king, she asked for nothing except what Hegai the king's eunuch, who had charge of the women, advised. Now Esther was admired by all who saw her. [16] When Esther was taken to King Ahasuerus in his royal palace in the tenth month, which is the month of Tebeth, in the seventh year of his reign, [17] the king loved Esther more than all the other women; of all the virgins she won his favor and devotion, so that he set the royal crown on her head and made her queen instead of Vashti. [18] Then the king gave a great banquet to all his officials and ministers—"Esther's banquet." He also granted a holiday[b] to the provinces, and gave gifts with royal liberality.

[19] When the virgins were being gathered together,[c] Mordecai was sitting at the king's gate. [20] Now Esther had not revealed her kindred or her people, as Mordecai had charged her; for Esther obeyed Mordecai just as when she was brought up by him. [21] In those days, while Mordecai was sitting at the king's gate, Bigthan and Teresh, two of the king's eunuchs, who guarded the threshold, became angry and conspired to assassinate[d] King Ahasuerus. [22] But the matter came to

a Heb *He*
b Or *an amnesty*
c Heb adds *a second time*
d Heb *to lay hands on*

---

word for "star," or both. Like other Jewish exiles (Dan 1.6–7) Esther has both a Hebrew and a Babylonian name. **9:** In winning the *favor* of Hegai, Esther resembles Joseph in the house of Potiphar (Gen 39.2–6) and Daniel at the Babylonian court (Dan 1.9). Unlike Daniel (1.8), Esther appears unconcerned with Jewish dietary rules.

2.12–18: Esther becomes queen. 14: The impossibility of seeing the king again unless *summoned by name* foreshadows Esther's dilemma in 4.11–16. **15:** As Esther takes her fateful step toward queenship, her father's name (*Abihail*) is supplied in the manner of preexilic queens of Judah (see 1 Kings 15.2; 22.42; 2 Kings 15.33). In asking only for what Hegai *advised*, Esther demonstrates the characteristic prudence that will continue to serve her well. **16:** *Tebeth*, December-January. *In the seventh year of his reign*, Ahasuerus has been testing queen candidates now for about four years. **17:** Cf. Gen 37.3. **18:** *Esther's banquet*, probably a wedding feast, foreshadows the two she gives later (5.5; 6.14–7.1), as well as the feast of Purim (9.22). A *holiday*, declared by a king on special occasions, was primarily economic (see Jer 34.8–11), often involving relief from tribute obligations, taxes, debt-slavery, and military service (see Lev 25.10–11). *Gifts* foreshadows 9.22.

2.19–23: Mordecai and Esther save the king's life. 19: *The king's gate*, the gathering place for royal officials. **20:** Esther's silence about *her kindred or her people* indicates her compliant nature and heightens suspense. **21:** Some interpreters of Esther have seen divine intervention in this and later mysterious coincidences (see

the knowledge of Mordecai, and he told it to Queen Esther, and Esther told the king in the name of Mordecai. [23] When the affair was investigated and found to be so, both the men were hanged on the gallows. It was recorded in the book of the annals in the presence of the king.

3 After these things King Ahasuerus promoted Haman son of Hammedatha the Agagite, and advanced him and set his seat above all the officials who were with him. [2] And all the king's servants who were at the king's gate bowed down and did obeisance to Haman; for the king had so commanded concerning him. But Mordecai did not bow down or do obeisance. [3] Then the king's servants who were at the king's gate said to Mordecai, "Why do you disobey the king's command?" [4] When they spoke to him day after day and he would not listen to them, they told Haman, in order to see whether Mordecai's words would avail; for he had told them that he was a Jew. [5] When Haman saw that Mordecai did not bow down or do obeisance to him, Haman was infuriated. [6] But he thought it beneath him to lay hands on Mordecai alone. So, having been told who Mordecai's people were, Haman plotted to destroy all the Jews, the people of Mordecai, throughout the whole kingdom of Ahasuerus.

[7] In the first month, which is the month of Nisan, in the twelfth year of King Ahasuerus, they cast Pur—which means "the lot"—before Haman for the day and for the month, and the lot fell on the thirteenth day[a] of the twelfth month, which is the month of Adar. [8] Then Haman said to King Ahasuerus, "There is a certain people scattered and separated among the peoples in all the provinces of your kingdom; their laws are different from those of every other people, and they do not keep the king's laws, so that it is not appropriate for the king to tolerate them. [9] If it pleases the king, let a decree be issued for their destruction, and I will pay ten thousand talents of silver into the hands of those who have charge of the king's business, so that they may put it into the king's treasuries." [10] So the king took his signet ring from his hand and gave it to Haman son of Hammedatha the Agagite, the enemy of the Jews. [11] The king said to Haman, "The money is given to you, and the people as well, to do with them as it seems good to you."

[12] Then the king's secretaries were summoned on the thirteenth day of the first month, and an edict, according to all that Haman commanded, was written to the king's satraps and to the governors over all the provinces and to the officials of all the peoples, to every province in its own script and every people in its own language; it was written in the name of King Ahasuerus and sealed with the king's ring. [13] Letters were sent by couri-

---

a   Cn Compare Gk and verse 13 below: Heb *the twelfth month*

4.14; 6.1–3). *Conspired to assassinate*, see 3.6n. 23: *Hanged on the gallows* (lit. "on a tree"), i.e., by impalement, a disgraceful death, a foreshadowing of 5.14; 7.9–10; 9.13–14. *The book of the annals*, an official record of royal acts (cf. 10.2; 1 Kings 14.19,29; 2 Chr 25.26; 32.32).

3.1–15: Haman plots to annihilate the Jews. 1: *Agagite*, descended from King Agag the Amalekite (see 2.5n.). 2: Suggestions for why *Mordecai did not bow down* include ancestral enmity between Mordecai and Haman (see 2.5n.) or that Mordecai, like contemporary Greeks, abhorred as dishonorable the Persian custom of abasing oneself on the ground to superiors. 4: *Day after day* echoes Joseph's rejection of Potiphar's wife (Gen 39.10). 6: In 2.21 the Heb verb *to destroy* is translated "assassinate" and *plotted* as "conspired." The identical wording sets up a parallel between Haman's plot and that of the conspirators in 2.21–23. 7: *The twelfth year*, Esther has been queen for five years. The reference to *pur*, a Babylonian loanword for "lot," may have been inserted by a later editor to connect the plot of Esther more closely with the Purim festival (see 9.20–32n.). Passover occurs in *Nisan* (March-April), the first month of the Babylonian and Jewish year. Traditional Jewish interpretation drew elaborate parallels between the Esther story and Passover. *Adar*, February-March. 8: Haman begins with the truth: the Jews were indeed *scattered and separated* (Zech 7.14) and, like other subject peoples, their statutes (Deut 4.5–6) were different. He slides into falsehood in asserting that Jews *do not keep the king's laws*. 9: *Ten thousand talents of silver* is an astronomical sum, the equivalent of hundreds of millions of US dollars. 10: The *signet ring* authorizes Haman to sign documents in the king's name (3.12; 8.2,8; cf. Gen 41.41–42; 1 Kings 21.8–9). The first appearance of Haman's epithet, *enemy of the Jews* (8.1; 9.10,24). 12: Another irony: the deadly *edict* goes

ers to all the king's provinces, giving orders to destroy, to kill, and to annihilate all Jews, young and old, women and children, in one day, the thirteenth day of the twelfth month, which is the month of Adar, and to plunder their goods. ¹⁴ A copy of the document was to be issued as a decree in every province by proclamation, calling on all the peoples to be ready for that day. ¹⁵ The couriers went quickly by order of the king, and the decree was issued in the citadel of Susa. The king and Haman sat down to drink; but the city of Susa was thrown into confusion.

4 When Mordecai learned all that had been done, Mordecai tore his clothes and put on sackcloth and ashes, and went through the city, wailing with a loud and bitter cry; ² he went up to the entrance of the king's gate, for no one might enter the king's gate clothed with sackcloth. ³ In every province, wherever the king's command and his decree came, there was great mourning among the Jews, with fasting and weeping and lamenting, and most of them lay in sackcloth and ashes.

⁴ When Esther's maids and her eunuchs came and told her, the queen was deeply distressed; she sent garments to clothe Mordecai, so that he might take off his sackcloth; but he would not accept them. ⁵ Then Esther called for Hathach, one of the king's eunuchs, who had been appointed to attend her, and ordered him to go to Mordecai to learn what was happening and why. ⁶ Hathach went out to Mordecai in the open square of the city in front of the king's gate, ⁷ and Mordecai told him all that had happened to him, and the exact sum of money that Haman had promised to pay into the king's treasuries for the destruction of the Jews. ⁸ Mordecai also gave him a copy of the written decree issued in Susa for their destruction, that he might show it to Esther, explain it to her, and charge her to go to the king to make supplication to him and entreat him for her people.

⁹ Hathach went and told Esther what Mordecai had said. ¹⁰ Then Esther spoke to Hathach and gave him a message for Mordecai, saying, ¹¹ "All the king's servants and the people of the king's provinces know that if any man or woman goes to the king inside the inner court without being called, there is but one law—all alike are to be put to death. Only if the king holds out the golden scepter to someone, may that person live. I myself have not been called to come in to the king for thirty days." ¹² When they told Mordecai what Esther had said, ¹³ Mordecai told them to reply to Esther, "Do not think that in the king's palace you will escape any more than all the other Jews. ¹⁴ For if you keep silence at such a time as this, relief and deliverance will rise for the Jews from another quarter, but you and your father's family will perish. Who knows? Perhaps you have come to royal dignity for just such a time as this." ¹⁵ Then Esther said in reply to Mordecai, ¹⁶ "Go, gather all the Jews to be found in Susa, and hold a fast on my behalf, and neither eat nor drink for three days, night or day. I and my maids will also fast as you do. After that I will go to the king, though it is against the law; and if I perish, I perish." ¹⁷ Mordecai then went away and did everything as Esther had ordered him.

5 On the third day Esther put on her royal robes and stood in the inner court of the king's palace, opposite the king's hall. The

---

out on the day before Passover (v. 7n.; Ex 12.6; Lev 23.5). It is issued in various *languages*; see 1.22n. **13**: *Couriers*, see 1.22n. **15**: *Citadel of Susa*, see 1.2n.

4.1–17: Mordecai persuades Esther to risk her life to save her people. **1**: *Sackcloth and ashes* and torn clothing were traditional signs of mourning and repentance (2 Sam 3.31; Job 42.6; Dan 9.3; Jon 3.6). **2**: No one rendered ritually unclean by mourning could *enter the king's gate*. **3**: *Fasting* was believed to influence the deity (Lev 16.29–31; Judg 20.26; 2 Sam 12.16; 1 Kings 21.27; Jon 3.5,8; Ezra 8.21–23; Joel 1.14; 2.12–14; 1 Macc 3.47). **4–10**: Esther, her Jewish identity still secret, is unaware of the edict. **6**: The city *square* is a traditional place of public mourning (Amos 5.16; Isa 15.3; Jer 48.38). **8**: *Susa*, see 1.2n. **11**: Like other biblical heroes called upon to save their people (Ex 3.11; 4.10; Judg 6.15; Jer 1.6), Esther initially objects. *I myself have not been called to come in to the king*, see 2.14. **14**: *From another quarter*, perhaps a reference to divine providence (see 2.21n.). *Who knows?* Often precedes an expression of hope for divine mercy (2 Sam 12.22; Joel 2.14; Jon 3.9). **16-17**: Esther's request for a community fast foreshadows her religious authority in 9.29. *If I perish*, Esther voices resignation or selfless dedication (see Gen 43.14).

king was sitting on his royal throne inside the palace opposite the entrance to the palace. [2] As soon as the king saw Queen Esther standing in the court, she won his favor and he held out to her the golden scepter that was in his hand. Then Esther approached and touched the top of the scepter. [3] The king said to her, "What is it, Queen Esther? What is your request? It shall be given you, even to the half of my kingdom." [4] Then Esther said, "If it pleases the king, let the king and Haman come today to a banquet that I have prepared for the king." [5] Then the king said, "Bring Haman quickly, so that we may do as Esther desires." So the king and Haman came to the banquet that Esther had prepared. [6] While they were drinking wine, the king said to Esther, "What is your petition? It shall be granted you. And what is your request? Even to the half of my kingdom, it shall be fulfilled." [7] Then Esther said, "This is my petition and request: [8] If I have won the king's favor, and if it pleases the king to grant my petition and fulfill my request, let the king and Haman come tomorrow to the banquet that I will prepare for them, and then I will do as the king has said."

[9] Haman went out that day happy and in good spirits. But when Haman saw Mordecai in the king's gate, and observed that he neither rose nor trembled before him, he was infuriated with Mordecai; [10] nevertheless Haman restrained himself and went home. Then he sent and called for his friends and his wife Zeresh, [11] and Haman recounted to them the splendor of his riches, the number of his sons, all the promotions with which the king had honored him, and how he had advanced him above the officials and the ministers of the king. [12] Haman added, "Even Queen Esther let no one but myself come with the king to the banquet that she prepared. Tomorrow also I am invited by her, together with the king. [13] Yet all this does me no good so long as I see the Jew Mordecai sitting at the king's gate." [14] Then his wife Zeresh and all his friends said to him, "Let a gallows fifty cubits high be made, and in the morning tell the king to have Mordecai hanged on it; then go with the king to the banquet in good spirits." This advice pleased Haman, and he had the gallows made.

6 On that night the king could not sleep, and he gave orders to bring the book of records, the annals, and they were read to the king. [2] It was found written how Mordecai had told about Bigthana and Teresh, two of the king's eunuchs, who guarded the threshold, and who had conspired to assassinate[a] King Ahasuerus. [3] Then the king said, "What honor or distinction has been bestowed on Mordecai for this?" The king's servants who attended him said, "Nothing has been done for him." [4] The king said, "Who is in the court?" Now Haman had just entered the outer court of the king's palace to speak to the king about having Mordecai hanged on the gallows that he had prepared for him. [5] So the king's servants told him, "Haman is there, standing in the court." The king said, "Let him come in." [6] So Haman

---

a   Heb *to lay hands on*

5.1–8: Esther before the king. 2: Esther resembles women who plead on another's behalf (1 Sam 25.24–31; 2 Sam 14.4–17). *Favor*, see 2.9,17 (Ex 12.36). **3:** Three times the king will offer *half of my kingdom* (v. 6; 7.2), exaggeration for emphasis. Typical of folktales, the third offer (7.2) succeeds. **4:** *Banquet*, see 1.3–4n. Food, reassuring and nurturing, is a common motif in stories of women confronting powerful men; Esther works indirectly to achieve her goal (Judg 5.25; Prov 9.1–5; see Jdt 10.5; 12.1,17–20).

5.9–14: Haman's happiness is spoiled. 9: *Good spirits*, the same term is used of Ahasuerus ("merry") in 1.10. **10–14:** *Zeresh* is an exemplary son-bearing wife (5.11; 9.7–10); as Esther's negative counterpart, Zeresh loyally counsels her husband. Haman's boasting sets him up as an arrogant fool ripe for a fall, a theme also found in wisdom literature (Prov 11.28; 13.3; 16.5,18; 27.1; 29.20). *Gallows*, see 2.23n. *Fifty cubits*, ca. 72 ft (22 m), an exaggerated height. Only *the king* can order an execution.

6.1–13: Mordecai's triumph. This masterpiece of ironic narrative uses alliteration, repetition, understatement, and reversal. **1–2:** The king's insomnia, a traditional folktale device (Dan 6.18; 1 Esd 3.3), is not explained and is another instance of opportune fate in Esther (see 2.9,15,17,21; 3.7; 4.14; 5.2; 6.13). *Annals*, see 2.23n. Herodotus (8.85,90) notes that Persian kings kept records of courtiers' noble deeds. **6:** *Whom the king wishes to*

came in, and the king said to him, "What shall be done for the man whom the king wishes to honor?" Haman said to himself, "Whom would the king wish to honor more than me?" [7] So Haman said to the king, "For the man whom the king wishes to honor, [8] let royal robes be brought, which the king has worn, and a horse that the king has ridden, with a royal crown on its head. [9] Let the robes and the horse be handed over to one of the king's most noble officials; let him[a] robe the man whom the king wishes to honor, and let him[a] conduct the man on horseback through the open square of the city, proclaiming before him: 'Thus shall it be done for the man whom the king wishes to honor.'" [10] Then the king said to Haman, "Quickly, take the robes and the horse, as you have said, and do so to the Jew Mordecai who sits at the king's gate. Leave out nothing that you have mentioned." [11] So Haman took the robes and the horse and robed Mordecai and led him riding through the open square of the city, proclaiming, "Thus shall it be done for the man whom the king wishes to honor."

[12] Then Mordecai returned to the king's gate, but Haman hurried to his house, mourning and with his head covered. [13] When Haman told his wife Zeresh and all his friends everything that had happened to him, his advisers and his wife Zeresh said to him, "If Mordecai, before whom your downfall has begun, is of the Jewish people, you will not prevail against him, but will surely fall before him."

[14] While they were still talking with him, the king's eunuchs arrived and hurried Haman off to the banquet that Esther had prepared. [1] So the king and Haman went in to **7** feast with Queen Esther. [2] On the second day, as they were drinking wine, the king again said to Esther, "What is your petition, Queen Esther? It shall be granted you. And what is your request? Even to the half of my kingdom, it shall be fulfilled." [3] Then Queen Esther answered, "If I have won your favor, O king, and if it pleases the king, let my life be given me—that is my petition—and the lives of my people—that is my request. [4] For we have been sold, I and my people, to be destroyed, to be killed, and to be annihilated. If we had been sold merely as slaves, men and women, I would have held my peace; but no enemy can compensate for this damage to the king."[b] [5] Then King Ahasuerus said to Queen Esther, "Who is he, and where is he, who has presumed to do this?" [6] Esther said, "A foe and enemy, this wicked Haman!" Then Haman was terrified before the king and the queen. [7] The king rose from the feast in wrath and went into the palace garden, but Haman stayed to beg his life from Queen Esther, for he saw that the king had determined to destroy him. [8] When the king returned from the palace garden to the banquet hall, Haman had thrown himself on the couch where Esther was reclining; and the king said, "Will he even assault the queen in my presence, in my

a Heb *them*
b Meaning of Heb uncertain

honor, the phrase is repeated six times in vv. 6–11. The king's omission of the name parallels Haman's concealment of the identity of those he intended to annihilate (3.8). **8:** *Royal robes*, a gesture of favor (Gen 37.3; 41.42; 1 Sam 18.4; 1 Kings 1.33). *Crown*, an ornament for the horse's head depicted on Mesopotamian and Persian reliefs. **11:** The *open square*, previously the site of Mordecai's mourning (4.6), now witnesses his honor. **12:** *Head covered*, a sign of grief (2 Sam 15.30; 19.4; Jer 14.4), which foreshadows Haman's own downfall.

   6.14–7.10: Esther's second banquet and Haman's fall. 7.2: *Half of my kingdom*, see 5.3n. **3:** No longer self-effacing (see 2.20n.; 5.4n.) Esther seizes the right moment to speak directly of herself and of her people. **4:** *Sold*, probably a reference to Haman's bribe in 3.11 (see 4.7; but note the metaphorical use of the verb in Deut 32.30; Judg 2.14; 3.8; 4.2,9; 10.7). *To be destroyed*, etc., Esther quotes from the royal edict (3.13). *Damage to the king*, perhaps the king would be shamed if his queen were dishonored. **6:** Like Esther before the king in 15.5, now Haman is *terrified before the king and the queen*. **8:** Following common custom (8.3; 1 Sam 25.23–24; 2 Kings 4.27), Haman tries to supplicate the queen by falling at her feet. His gesture contrasts with Mordecai's in 3.2. *Assault the queen*, Ahasuerus mistakes Haman's posture as a sexual assault, an unpardonable affront to both male and royal honor and, as such, a capital offense. *They covered Haman's face* probably to protect the king from ritual pollution by association with a condemned criminal; access to the Persian king (1.14; 4.11) was restricted for

own house?" As the words left the mouth of the king, they covered Haman's face. [9] Then Harbona, one of the eunuchs in attendance on the king, said, "Look, the very gallows that Haman has prepared for Mordecai, whose word saved the king, stands at Haman's house, fifty cubits high." And the king said, "Hang him on that." [10] So they hanged Haman on the gallows that he had prepared for Mordecai. Then the anger of the king abated.

8 On that day King Ahasuerus gave to Queen Esther the house of Haman, the enemy of the Jews; and Mordecai came before the king, for Esther had told what he was to her. [2] Then the king took off his signet ring, which he had taken from Haman, and gave it to Mordecai. So Esther set Mordecai over the house of Haman.

[3] Then Esther spoke again to the king; she fell at his feet, weeping and pleading with him to avert the evil design of Haman the Agagite and the plot that he had devised against the Jews. [4] The king held out the golden scepter to Esther, [5] and Esther rose and stood before the king. She said, "If it pleases the king, and if I have won his favor, and if the thing seems right before the king, and I have his approval, let an order be written to revoke the letters devised by Haman son of Hammedatha the Agagite, which he wrote giving orders to destroy the Jews who are in all the provinces of the king. [6] For how can I bear to see the calamity that is coming on my people? Or how can I bear to see the destruction of my kindred?" [7] Then King Ahasuerus said to Queen Esther and to the Jew Mordecai, "See, I have given Esther the house of Haman, and they have hanged him on the gallows, because he plotted to lay hands on the Jews. [8] You may write as you please with regard to the Jews, in the name of the king, and seal it with the king's ring; for an edict written in the name of the king and sealed with the king's ring cannot be revoked."

[9] The king's secretaries were summoned at that time, in the third month, which is the month of Sivan, on the twenty-third day; and an edict was written, according to all that Mordecai commanded, to the Jews and to the satraps and the governors and the officials of the provinces from India to Ethiopia,[a] one hundred twenty-seven provinces, to every province in its own script and to every people in its own language, and also to the Jews in their script and their language. [10] He wrote letters in the name of King Ahasuerus, sealed them with the king's ring, and sent them by mounted couriers riding on fast steeds bred from the royal herd.[b] [11] By these letters the king allowed the Jews who were in every city to assemble and defend their lives, to destroy, to kill, and to annihilate any armed force of any people or province that might attack them, with their children and women, and to plunder their goods [12] on a single day throughout all the provinces of King Ahasuerus, on the thirteenth day of the twelfth month, which is the month of Adar. [13] A copy of the writ was to be issued as a decree in every province and published to all peoples, and the Jews were to be ready on that day to take revenge on their enemies. [14] So the couriers, mounted on their swift royal steeds, hurried out, urged by the king's command. The decree was issued in the citadel of Susa.

[15] Then Mordecai went out from the presence of the king, wearing royal robes of blue

---

a   Or *Nubia*; Heb *Cush*

b   Meaning of Heb uncertain

---

religious as well as political reasons. **9–10:** *Gallows*, see 2.23n. Poetic justice prevails (cf. Prov 26.27).

8.1–17: Mordecai rises to power and counteracts the anti-Jewish edict. Reversals abound in this chapter (see 1 Sam 2.1–10). **1:** In 3.9, Haman offered the king money; now the king gives Haman's wealth to Esther. **2:** Haman's exalted position becomes Mordecai's with the transfer of the king's signet ring (see v. 8; 3.10n). **3:** The edict against the Jews still stands. **5:** *Devised by Haman*, Esther diplomatically dissociates the king from the royal edict. **8:** The king's earlier edict *cannot be revoked* (see 1.19n.), but a new edict can neutralize the former's intent. **9:** The verse follows the same general structure as 3.12–13 (see 1.19–22) while reversing the effect. *Sivan*, May-June. *Language*, see 1.22n. **11:** *Allowed*, not commanded. *Destroy . . . annihilate* (the same wording appears in 3.13). The hyperbolic style and the pattern of reversals and retribution, rather than any real historical event, account for the excess of bloodshed to come (9.5–16). **12:** The date of the intended extermination (3.7,13) becomes a day of triumph and relates to the Purim festival (see 9.21). *Adar*, February-March. **14:** See 1.22n. *Citadel*

and white, with a great golden crown and a mantle of fine linen and purple, while the city of Susa shouted and rejoiced. [16] For the Jews there was light and gladness, joy and honor. [17] In every province and in every city, wherever the king's command and his edict came, there was gladness and joy among the Jews, a festival and a holiday. Furthermore, many of the peoples of the country professed to be Jews, because the fear of the Jews had fallen upon them.

9 Now in the twelfth month, which is the month of Adar, on the thirteenth day, when the king's command and edict were about to be executed, on the very day when the enemies of the Jews hoped to gain power over them, but which had been changed to a day when the Jews would gain power over their foes, [2] the Jews gathered in their cities throughout all the provinces of King Ahasuerus to lay hands on those who had sought their ruin; and no one could withstand them, because the fear of them had fallen upon all peoples. [3] All the officials of the provinces, the satraps and the governors, and the royal officials were supporting the Jews, because the fear of Mordecai had fallen upon them. [4] For Mordecai was powerful in the king's house, and his fame spread throughout all the provinces as the man Mordecai grew more and more powerful. [5] So the Jews struck down all their enemies with the sword, slaughtering, and destroying them, and did as they pleased to those who hated them. [6] In the citadel of Susa the Jews killed and destroyed five hundred people. [7] They killed Parshandatha, Dalphon, Aspatha, [8] Poratha, Adalia, Aridatha, [9] Parmashta, Arisai, Aridai, Vaizatha, [10] the ten sons of Haman son of Hammedatha, the enemy of the Jews; but they did not touch the plunder.

[11] That very day the number of those killed in the citadel of Susa was reported to the king. [12] The king said to Queen Esther, "In the citadel of Susa the Jews have killed five hundred people and also the ten sons of Haman. What have they done in the rest of the king's provinces? Now what is your petition? It shall be granted you. And what further is your request? It shall be fulfilled." [13] Esther said, "If it pleases the king, let the Jews who are in Susa be allowed tomorrow also to do according to this day's edict, and let the ten sons of Haman be hanged on the gallows." [14] So the king commanded this to be done; a decree was issued in Susa, and the ten sons of Haman were hanged. [15] The Jews who were in Susa gathered also on the fourteenth day of the month of Adar and they killed three hundred persons in Susa; but they did not touch the plunder.

[16] Now the other Jews who were in the king's provinces also gathered to defend their lives, and gained relief from their enemies, and killed seventy-five thousand of those who hated them; but they laid no hands on the plunder. [17] This was on the thirteenth day of the month of Adar, and on the fourteenth day they rested and made that a day of feasting and gladness.

of Susa, see 1.2n. **15–17:** Mordecai's attire contrasts with 4.1, as the Jews' mourning in 4.1–4 turns to joy. **16:** *Light and gladness, joy and honor* contrast with 4.3. **17:** *Professed to be Jews*, this translation is possible, but the Heb may simply mean that Gentiles joined the Jews in their resistance (see 9.3), not that they converted to Judaism. An earlier version of the book may have ended here with no mention of the festival.

9.1–10.3: The origins of Purim. 9.1–19: The Jews triumph over their enemies. 1: A reminder that the king's edict against the Jews still stands; the terms of the second edict allow the Jews to defend themselves. *Adar,* February-March. **2–4:** The Jews' victory is described in language reminiscent of holy war, the Exodus, and the conquest of Canaan. Opposition to the Jews is implied by *no one could withstand them* (Josh 23.9). *The fear of them,* a supernatural terror common in holy war (Ex 15.14–16; Josh 2.8–12; Ps 105.38). **4:** Mordecai's power resembles that of Moses (Ex 11.3). **6:** *Citadel of Susa,* see 1.2n. **7-10:** Haman boasted unwisely about his many sons (5.11). Hebrew manuscripts arrange the names of Haman's ten sons in unusual formations. The names are recited in a single breath during Purim synagogue services. **10:** The note that the Jews did not *plunder* (as in vv. 15,16; contrast 3.13 and 8.11) is a reminder of the Agag story (see 2.5; 3.1) where the Jews plundered to their own hurt (1 Sam 15.9). **12-15:** At Esther's *request* (5.3,6; 7.2) the king grants the Jews of Susa (as distinct from the *citadel of Susa*) a second day of revenge and allows them to dishonor Haman further by hanging (impaling, see 2.23n.) the corpses of his sons in public (Josh 8.29; 10.26; 1 Sam 17.54; 31.10). Notice of the extra day is probably

[18] But the Jews who were in Susa gathered on the thirteenth day and on the fourteenth, and rested on the fifteenth day, making that a day of feasting and gladness. [19] Therefore the Jews of the villages, who live in the open towns, hold the fourteenth day of the month of Adar as a day for gladness and feasting, a holiday on which they send gifts of food to one another.

[20] Mordecai recorded these things, and sent letters to all the Jews who were in all the provinces of King Ahasuerus, both near and far, [21] enjoining them that they should keep the fourteenth day of the month Adar and also the fifteenth day of the same month, year by year, [22] as the days on which the Jews gained relief from their enemies, and as the month that had been turned for them from sorrow into gladness and from mourning into a holiday; that they should make them days of feasting and gladness, days for sending gifts of food to one another and presents to the poor. [23] So the Jews adopted as a custom what they had begun to do, as Mordecai had written to them.

[24] Haman son of Hammedatha the Agagite, the enemy of all the Jews, had plotted against the Jews to destroy them, and had cast Pur—that is "the lot"—to crush and destroy them; [25] but when Esther came before the king, he gave orders in writing that the wicked plot that he had devised against the Jews should come upon his own head, and that he and his sons should be hanged on the gallows.

[26] Therefore these days are called Purim, from the word Pur. Thus because of all that was written in this letter, and of what they had faced in this matter, and of what had happened to them, [27] the Jews established and accepted as a custom for themselves and their descendants and all who joined them, that without fail they would continue to observe these two days every year, as it was written and at the time appointed. [28] These days should be remembered and kept throughout every generation, in every family, province, and city; and these days of Purim should never fall into disuse among the Jews, nor should the commemoration of these days cease among their descendants.

[29] Queen Esther daughter of Abihail, along with the Jew Mordecai, gave full written authority, confirming this second letter about Purim. [30] Letters were sent wishing peace and security to all the Jews, to the one hundred twenty-seven provinces of the kingdom of Ahasuerus, [31] and giving orders that these days of Purim should be observed at their appointed seasons, as the Jew Mordecai and Queen Esther enjoined on the Jews, just as they had laid down for themselves and for their descendants regulations concerning their fasts and their lamentations. [32] The command of Queen Esther fixed these practices of Purim, and it was recorded in writing.

10 King Ahasuerus laid tribute on the land and on the islands of the sea. [2] All the acts of his power and might, and the full ac-

a device to explain why city Jews celebrated Purim for two days and country Jews only one (see vv. 18–19). **18–19:** Jews today observe Purim with *feasting* and *gifts of food* (see 2.9, "portion of food"; Neh 8.10).

9.20–32: The inauguration of the feast of Purim. The emphasis upon the written word, a particular concern in postexilic Judaism, was probably intended to legitimize a festival not mentioned in the Torah (cf. the origin of Hanukkah: 1 Macc 4.56–59; 2 Macc 1.1–2.28; 10.1–8). **20:** *Near and far*, Isa 57.19. **22:** Purim occurs not on the day of the Jews' military triumph but on the day they obtained their *relief*. *Sorrow into gladness*, Isa 61.3; Jer 31.13. **23:** Ex 24.3. **24–26:** A plot summary that differs slightly from the book. Esther's name does not appear in the Heb text of v. 25 and has been added by the translator. The festival came to be called Purim for the lot, Heb "pur" (pl. "purim"), which Haman cast (see 3.7n.). **24:** *Crush* (Heb "hummam"), a wordplay on Haman's name. **28:** *Remembered; commemoration*, see Ex 13.3; 20.8. **29–32:** Probably added later. The Heb text is extremely corrupt and the verses do not appear in some ancient versions. **30:** *Peace and security*, the wording suggests Purim fulfills the prophecy of Zech 8.19 (see Isa 39.8; Jer 33.6) and therefore the humanly inaugurated festival is legitimate. **31:** *Fasts*, not the Jewish Fast of Esther, which came to be universally observed on the thirteenth of Adar only beginning in the ninth century CE. **32:** Queen Esther is the only woman in the Bible credited with establishing a religious observance.

10.1–3: Postscript: the greatness of Ahasuerus and Mordecai. 1: This seemingly irrelevant comment may imply that the king prospered with Mordecai's assistance (see Gen 47.1–26). **2:** *Written in the annals*, a standard

count of the high honor of Mordecai, to which the king advanced him, are they not written in the annals of the kings of Media and Persia? ³ For Mordecai the Jew was next in rank to King Ahasuerus, and he was powerful among the Jews and popular with his many kindred, for he sought the good of his people and interceded for the welfare of all his descendants.

formula for historical reports in Kings and Chronicles (1 Kings 14.19,29; 2 Chr 25.26; 32.32). 3: The book ends without reference to Esther. Rather, Mordecai is the model of a successful Diaspora Jew and of Jews living harmoniously in the Gentile world.

INTRODUCTION TO THE POETICAL AND WISDOM BOOKS

PLACEMENT AND CONTENTS

The poetical and wisdom books are Job, Psalms, Proverbs, Ecclesiastes, and the Song of Solomon. The creation of a canonical division called the "Poetical Books" is a relatively late development. In Jewish tradition these five books are included in the Writings, the third division of the canon; their order varies in different sources. The earliest evidence for seeing these five books as a unit comes from the second century CE, though it took many centuries for these five books, in the arrangement found here, to be recognized as the third section of the Bible. The order of these books was variable, and some traditions placed them at the end of the Christian Old Testament, while others put them as the second part of that book immediately following the Torah or Pentateuch, the first five books of the Bible. Its current placement in English Bibles follows some manuscript traditions, which most likely sought to organize the first section of the Bible by placing the Torah, the most authoritative section, first, followed by works about the past (the Historical Books), books about the present (the Poetical Books), and books about the future (the Prophetic Books). This arrangement, which places the prophets last, would be especially significant once the Hebrew Bible became the Old Testament and was seen as an introduction to the New Testament. The Prophetic Books would then immediately precede the Gospels as prophecy followed by fulfillment.

The five Poetical Books were written or collected at widely different times and consist of a number of literary types: love poetry (the Song of Solomon), Temple liturgy (most of Psalms), and wisdom literature (Job, Proverbs, and Ecclesiastes). It is also likely that they entered the canon for quite different reasons: Psalms was used for prayers; the Song of Solomon was probably first canonized as an ancient love poem used in wedding ceremonies; while Job, Proverbs, and Ecclesiastes may have been placed together in the canon because all three belong to a category of writings known as wisdom literature. These books thus do not form a coherent unit, especially when compared to other canonical divisions, such as the Historical Books or the Prophetic Books.

"Wisdom literature" describes works that share, as their focus, reflection on universal human concerns, especially the understanding of individual experiences and the maintenance of ordered relationships that lead both to success on the human plane and to divine approval. Books classified by scholars as "wisdom literature" are thus in some ways a departure from the concerns of other biblical books. They do not focus primarily on the nation of Israel and on its great formative historical memories, such as the Exodus from Egypt, on Jerusalem and the Temple. They do not mention covenant, as the central theological notion that elsewhere in the Bible binds together God, the people of Israel, and the land of Israel. In more recent scholarship, the concept of "wisdom" has been criticized as too elastic and amorphous. Indeed, the three wisdom books in this collection are remarkably different from one another: Proverbs suggests that the righteous are rewarded and do not suffer; the book of Job profoundly challenges this view; while Ecclesiastes, in contrast to both Job and Proverbs, is deeply skeptical of the utility of wisdom. We must recognize that "wisdom" is a modern category, deriving from the beginning of the twentieth century, and thus Job, Proverbs, and Ecclesiastes were not originally grouped together on generic grounds. On the other hand, they share a thematic interdependence. Proverbs is representative of a type of ancient Near Eastern thought that looked for pattern and repetition in nature and in the moral life. In this tradition, the regular recurrence of natural phenomena could provide an analogy to guide human beings in their social interactions:

> As charcoal is to hot embers and wood to fire,
> so is a quarrelsome person for kindling strife (Prov 26.21).

The inevitability of the natural occurrence is mirrored in the inevitability of the social one. This kind of thinking then was extended to moral behavior, with the argument that good behavior, like good farming practice, will be rewarded:

> Anyone who tends a fig tree will eat its fruit,
>> and anyone who takes care of a master will be honored (Prov 27.18).

Job and Ecclesiastes relate to this widespread ancient Near Eastern tradition in different ways. Job denies the inevitability of rewards for living an upright life and decisively refutes the idea that human suffering is always deserved. Ecclesiastes treats the idea of inevitability in a different way: The natural repetitions of seasons, tasks, and occupations become an image of futility, in which people are "like fish taken in a cruel net, and like birds caught in a snare" (9.12), powerless to understand their own destiny. The themes of the wisdom tradition are continued in the Apocryphal/Deuterocanonical books of the Wisdom of Solomon and Sirach (Ecclesiasticus), both of which combine didactic themes and style familiar especially from the book of Proverbs with retrospective summaries of Israel's history.

Although these five books are loosely described as Poetical Books, they are not all poetry, nor are all biblical poetic works found in this canonical section. Although Ecclesiastes contains some poetical sections, such as the poem of 3.1–8 ("For everything there is a season"), or quoted poetic proverbs (e.g., 7.1–6), the book is predominantly prose. Additionally, the nature of the poetry in these books is very different, ranging from the highly structured, largely static poetry of Proverbs, to the intensely erotic, more free-flowing poetry of Song of Solomon.

THE CHARACTERISTICS OF BIBLICAL POETRY

These books do, as noted above, incorporate a large amount of poetry, so it is appropriate to here examine the basic structures of biblical poetry. Poetry is a cross-cultural phenomenon: Most cultures distinguish between an everyday type of discourse (prose), and heightened discourse (poetry). This heightening may be accomplished in a number of different ways, including the use of figuration (e.g., metaphor, simile), meter, and certain types of sound patterning, such as alliteration and rhyme. Yet there is no cross-cultural pattern for poetry. Thus Hebrew poetry, unlike its classical English counterpart, has neither (true) rhythm nor rhyme; nevertheless, it is poetic in that it uses certain devices in significant enough concentration to distinguish it from everyday speech, or prose. The prose-poetry distinction is relative rather than absolute; as in English, we may speak of poetic prose and prosaic poetry. Thus, "pure prose" and "pure poetry" should be seen as opposites on a continuum, within which a large variety of possibilities occur in the Bible as in other literary traditions.

The main shared characteristic between typical English poetry and biblical poetry is the use of figuration. This may be seen, for example, in Ps 23. The central image of this psalm is introduced by the metaphor, "The LORD is my shepherd" (v. 1). The following verses unpack or detail the meaning of this metaphor, noting in vv. 2–3 how God, the ideal shepherd, tends his people/sheep:

> He makes me lie down in green pastures;
>> he leads me beside still waters;
>> he restores my soul.
> He leads me in right paths
>> for his name's sake.

Psalm 1 is characterized by a set of two contrasting similes: the righteous

> . . . are like trees
>> planted by streams of water,
> which yield their fruit in its season,
>> and their leaves do not wither (v. 3),

while the wicked "are like chaff that the wind drives away" (v. 4). The Song of Solomon is especially rich in similes and metaphors, as in the beginning of ch 2:

> I am a rose of Sharon,
>> a lily of the valleys.

> As a lily among brambles,
> so is my love among maidens.
> As an apple tree among the trees of the wood,
> so is my beloved among young men.
> With great delight I sat in his shadow,
> and his fruit was sweet to my taste.

The main characteristic of biblical poetry, nevertheless, is not figuration, but parallelism, in which most poetic lines may be divided into two (or sometimes three) parts; the second part of the line is intimately connected to the first part, and typically seconds it in some way. For example, Ps 6.2 reads:

> Be gracious to me, O LORD, for I am languishing;
> O LORD, heal me, for my bones are shaking with terror.

The verse clearly divides into two more or less equal sections, and each element in the first part is mirrored, seconded, or paralleled in the second: Be gracious to me || heal me; O LORD || O LORD; for I am languishing || for my bones are shaking with terror. This parallelism, which is not typical of biblical prose, serves as the backbone of biblical poetry.

Since the eighteenth century, it has been customary to see three main types of parallelism in the Bible: synonymous, antithetical, and synthetic. The quotation above from Ps 6.2 is an example of synonymous parallelism. Antithetical parallelism can be seen in Prov 10.1:

> A wise child makes a glad father,
> but a foolish child is a mother's grief.

In this balanced, two-part line, "a wise child" is antithetical, or opposite, to "a foolish child," and "makes a glad father" is antithetical to "is a mother's grief." In synthetic parallelism, the second part of the line completes the thought of the first part, and is neither the same nor the opposite—both parts are needed to complete the thought. For example, Song 1.9 reads:

> I compare you, my love,
> to a mare among Pharaoh's chariots.

Here the second part concludes the idea of the first.

The appropriateness of the three labels—synonymous, antithetical, and synthetic—which were accepted in biblical scholarship for two centuries, has been called into question on several grounds. First, some have noted that languages have no true synonyms; thus "synonymous parallelism" is a misleading term. Furthermore, very often two parallel words can be similar, but are not truly synonymous, as may be seen in the example from Ps 6.2: "I am languishing" || "my bones are shaking with terror." The term antithetical parallelism has been questioned because not all elements of part B are the antithesis of part A. This may be seen in the example from Prov 10.1, where "child" is used in both parts A and B; a true antithesis might contrast a "wise child" with a "foolish parent." Finally, "synthetic" has been criticized as too vague a term. These criticisms are fair. Nevertheless, the three terms, if understood as ideal types from which actual lines may deviate to a greater or lesser extent, remain useful.

A much more serious criticism of the classical model emerged in the middle 1980s. Before that, many scholars believed that parallelism is formulaic, and the second half of the poetic line typically adds little to the line, but merely seconds it. Several scholars have suggested just the opposite, that the second part heightens or extends the first. Thus, the typical biblical verse should be read "A, and even more so, B." According to this model, which has gained substantial support in the last three decades, we would not read Ps 6.2b, "O LORD, heal me, for my bones are shaking with terror" as a type of filler that merely restates "Be gracious to me, O LORD, for I am languishing." Rather we would understand the verse as a whole as: "Be gracious to me, O LORD, for I am languishing," and moreover, "O LORD, heal me, for my bones are shaking with terror," where the claim "for my bones are shaking with terror" is a more vivid description that intensifies the verse's opening "for I am languishing." Sometimes it is quite clear that the second part of the verse does not merely parallel the first but does go beyond it in some significant fashion, and thus justifies this newer model. Yet there are cases in which the second part actually does seem to function as a filler, carrying little if any semantic weight, let alone intensifying the first. For example, the major image of Ps 121 is the ability of God to protect the individual. This is expressed at the psalm's center, where God is imagined metaphorically as a "shade" (v. 5) from the intense Mediterranean sun. The psalm continues (v. 6): "The sun shall not strike you by day, nor the moon by night." Clearly, the second part, "nor the moon by night" is not an intensification; in fact, it makes no sense, since no one in ancient Israel was afflicted with moonburn or moonstroke. The second part here is a(n antithetical) filler and carries no semantic weight. It should be seen as part of an ancient Near Eastern and biblical pattern of word pairs, where a particular word (e.g., "sun" or "father") automatically evokes a related ("synonymous" or "antithetical") word (e.g., "moon" or "mother").

Thus, parallelism is much more complicated than would appear on the surface. Clearly it is characterized by sets of lines, each of which may be divided into two parts, typically of the same length and mirroring each other on the semantic, syntactic, and phonological levels. It is unclear if the second should typically be read as an intensification of the first, or as a filler that carries little or no semantic value. This uncertainty is extremely frustrating, not only because it leaves us unsure how to read much of biblical poetry, especially the extent to which we do or do not need to pay close attention to the second half of the line, but also because our understanding of biblical poetry will affect our reconstruction of many Israelite institutions. To return to Prov 10.1—"A wise child makes a glad father, but a foolish child is a mother's grief"—if we follow the older understanding of parallelism, the second half is largely a filler, indicating that the father had the major role in the child's upbringing in ancient Israel, while if we follow the newer understanding, where the second intensifies the first, the mother was primarily responsible for the child.

Another area that has engendered significant controversy over the last few decades concerns the extent to which meter or rhythm existed in biblical poetry. Much of this debate concerns the definition of meter. In English and other modern Western languages, meter is generally understood as a pattern of stressed and unstressed syllables; if this is how we should understand it in biblical poetic texts, these texts in their current form lack meter or rhythm. Metrical patterns can only be found in biblical texts if they are emended or reconstructed extensively. There is, however, a tendency for the parts of each line, in most poetic works, to be approximately the same length. There is some possibility that this reflects the remnant of some metrical system, and that at an earlier time, each part had not only the same length, but the same meter, but this pattern of stressed and unstressed syllables has been lost as a result of changes in the pronunciation of ancient Hebrew over time. More likely, the similarity of length is part of the larger system of parallelism, which encouraged each part to mirror its counterpart in length, as well as in semantic, syntactic, and phonological structure.

Scholars have until recently been primarily concerned with the line as the main unit of biblical poetry. This is not really surprising, given how foreign biblical parallelism is to the modern Western (but not the ancient Near Eastern) ear. This interest in the line has obscured the significance of the strophe or stanza and of the poem as a whole. But the last few decades have seen a legitimate return to these larger units. For example, it had become a habit when studying passages like Job 3 to concentrate solely on the parallelism of lines like v. 5:

> Let gloom and deep darkness claim it.
> Let clouds settle upon it;
> let the blackness of the day terrify it.

Now, in addition to this type of analysis, scholars study how the poet uses images of day and night, light and darkness, throughout the chapter, in order to create this exquisite poem. This is not, however, an either/or proposition: By studying how the individual line functions as poetry and how these lines join together (sometimes) into stanzas, which combine into complete poems, we gain a much fuller appreciation and understanding of these Poetical Books.

AUTHORSHIP

At least four of the five Poetical Books cohere in terms of their traditional authorship. Many of the Psalms contain superscriptions or titles incorporating "of David," and many early Jewish and Christian traditions attribute all 150 of the Psalms to David. Proverbs 1.1 ("The proverbs of Solomon son of David, king of Israel"), 10.1, and 25.1 explicitly attribute (sections of) that book to Solomon. Ecclesiastes, in its opening chapter, presents itself as the work of "the Teacher, when king over Israel in Jerusalem" (1.12; cf. 1.1); premodern Jewish and Christian tradition understood this royal teacher to be Solomon, who is described in 1 Kings as being exceedingly rich, just like the protagonist of Ecclesiastes. Finally, the Song of Solomon opens with an explicit (but secondary) note concerning its author: "the Song of Songs, which is Solomon's." Given the clear connection of Psalms, Proverbs, Ecclesiastes, and Song of Solomon to David and Solomon, it is not surprising that some early Christian interpreters connected Job as well to the period of Solomon. This canonical division of five books thus likely came into being as the compilations connected to the early kings David and his son Solomon, and was only secondarily labeled the "Poetical Books." The traditional attributions of authorship, however, have been rejected by modern scholars; see the Introduction to each book for a detailed discussion.

JOB

NAME AND LOCATION IN CANON

The book bears the name of its principal character, Job, a righteous man who is afflicted by God, apparently unjustly, and who demands restitution. In Jewish tradition the book of Job belongs with the poetical books in the division called the Writings (Ketubim). Printed Hebrew Bibles place Job after Psalms and Proverbs, although other positions are found in earlier Hebrew manuscripts and lists. In older Christian Bibles, Job was sometimes placed with the historical books and sometimes with the poetical books; but its consistent place now is as the first of the poetical books, preceding Psalms.

AUTHORSHIP, DATE OF COMPOSITION, AND HISTORICAL CONTEXT

The book is anonymous, and it offers few clues to its historical context or date of composition. Most scholars would date it between the seventh and fourth centuries BCE, but its story is set in much older times.

LITERARY HISTORY, STRUCTURE, AND CONTENTS

Many scholars have proposed that the prose prologue and epilogue reflect a tale about Job older than the poetic dialogues. In the sixth century BCE the prophet Ezekiel mentions Job, along with Noah, the hero of the Flood story (Gen 6–9), and Dan'el, as heroes who saved others by their righteousness (Ezek 14.14,20).

The frame of the book is the prose prologue and epilogue (chs 1–2; 42.7–17). Within that frame are the poetic dialogues: first, three cycles of speeches by Job and his friends (chs 3–31) plus the Elihu speeches (chs 32–37), and second, two speeches by the LORD, each followed by a response from Job (38.1–42.6). The third cycle of speeches by Job and his friends presents many problems, and it is possible that the original order of the book is no longer correctly preserved. It has also commonly been thought that the speeches of Elihu (chs 32–37) and the poem on wisdom (ch 28) are later additions to the book's first edition, but a tendency among scholars to regard the book as a unified whole is becoming noticeable.

INTERPRETATION

The book of Job is perhaps the most sustained piece of theological writing in the Hebrew Bible, and it is unique in the Bible for its sympathetic portrayal of differing theological points of view. The theme of the book is often described as the problem of suffering, but it is rather that of the injustice of undeserved suffering. By the standards of his day, Job's suffering can only be a sign that he is a great sinner; resisting that implication, he demands that God explain why he, a righteous man, is being so badly treated. More than that, he reasons that his case shows that God is not governing the world in justice, and he argues that the prosperity of the wicked and the suffering of the righteous in general are further evidence of God's neglect of justice. When he replies to Job, God speaks only of his designs in creating the universe and does not mention the issue of justice, no doubt implying that Job is right, that justice is not a primary divine concern.

Among the books of the Bible, Job is highly unusual, and, unsurprisingly, its force has often been misunderstood or evaded. In the older history of interpretation, the book was commonly viewed as a repository of wise sayings, and its overall theme was little appreciated. In our own time, it is recognized as a major work of world literature, capable of diverse interpretations.

GUIDE TO READING

The chapters most essential for understanding the narrative and the argument are: chs 1–2 (the prologue); 3–11 (the first cycle of dialogues between Job and the friends); 29–31 (Job's final speech); 38.1–42.6 (the divine speeches, with Job's responses); 42.7–17 (the epilogue).

David J. A. Clines

1 There was once a man in the land of Uz whose name was Job. That man was blameless and upright, one who feared God and turned away from evil. [2] There were born to him seven sons and three daughters. [3] He had seven thousand sheep, three thousand camels, five hundred yoke of oxen, five hundred donkeys, and very many servants; so that this man was the greatest of all the people of the east. [4] His sons used to go and hold feasts in one another's houses in turn; and they would send and invite their three sisters to eat and drink with them. [5] And when the feast days had run their course, Job would send and sanctify them, and he would rise early in the morning and offer burnt offerings according to the number of them all; for Job said, "It may be that my children have sinned, and cursed God in their hearts." This is what Job always did.

[6] One day the heavenly beings[a] came to present themselves before the LORD, and Satan[b] also came among them. [7] The LORD said to Satan,[b] "Where have you come from?" Satan[b] answered the LORD, "From going to and fro on the earth, and from walking up and down on it." [8] The LORD said to Satan,[b] "Have you considered my servant Job? There is no one like him on the earth, a blameless and upright man who fears God and turns away from evil." [9] Then Satan[b] answered the LORD, "Does Job fear God for nothing? [10] Have you not put a fence around him and his house and all that he has, on every side? You have blessed the work of his hands, and his possessions have increased in the land. [11] But stretch out your hand now, and touch all that he has, and he will curse you to your face." [12] The LORD said to Satan,[b] "Very well, all that he has is in your power; only do not stretch out your hand against him!" So Satan[b] went out from the presence of the LORD.

[13] One day when his sons and daughters were eating and drinking wine in the eldest brother's house, [14] a messenger came to Job and said, "The oxen were plowing and the donkeys were feeding beside them, [15] and the Sabeans fell on them and carried them off, and killed the servants with the edge of the sword; I alone have escaped to tell you." [16] While he was still speaking, another came and said, "The fire of God fell from heaven and burned up the sheep and the servants, and consumed them; I alone have escaped to tell you." [17] While he was still speaking, another came and said, "The Chaldeans formed three columns, made a raid on the camels and carried them off, and killed the servants with the edge of the sword; I alone have escaped to tell you." [18] While he was still speaking, another came and said, "Your sons and daughters were eating and drinking wine in their eldest brother's house, [19] and suddenly a great wind came across the desert, struck the four corners of the house, and it fell on the young people,

[a] Heb *sons of God*
[b] Or *the Accuser*; Heb *ha-satan*

1.1–2.13: Prologue. The prose prologue contains five scenes, artistically arranged: the first, third, and fifth scenes (1.1–5,13–22; 2.7–13) take place on earth, the second and fourth (1.6–12; 2.1–6) in heaven. All the earthly characters, including Job, remain ignorant throughout the book of what takes place on the heavenly plane. **1.1–5:** The naïve language, in the style of a folktale, evokes a distant past. *The land of Uz* is Edom, southeast of Israel (cf. Jer 25.20; Lam 4.21). Job is not an Israelite; but he is a worshiper of the true God, although he, along with his friends, calls him "El," "Eloah," and "Elohim" (all meaning "God"), and "Shadday" ("the Almighty"), not "Yahweh" ("the LORD"). **2:** *Seven sons*, a perfect number. **4:** *Hold feasts . . . in turn*, lit. "each on his day," presumably on birthdays. **5:** *Cursed*, the Heb text has the word "blessed" here, apparently as a euphemism or pious scribal correction (so also in 1.11; 2.5,9; see also 1 Kings 21.13). **6–12:** The gathering of the divine council in heaven (cf. 1 Kings 22.19–22; Ps 82.1) includes "the Satan," i.e., "the adversary" of Job and other humans (cf. Zech 3.1), not of God; he is not the "devil" of later Jewish and Christian literature (see textual note b). Here he acts as God's eyes and ears on earth. He questions whether Job's righteousness is for its own sake or for the sake of its reward. **13–22:** Four messengers announce four disasters, from all directions: *Sabeans* come from the south (Sheba), *Chaldeans* from the north, the lightning (*fire of God*) from the west, with storms sweeping

and they are dead; I alone have escaped to tell you."

²⁰ Then Job arose, tore his robe, shaved his head, and fell on the ground and worshiped. ²¹ He said, "Naked I came from my mother's womb, and naked shall I return there; the LORD gave, and the LORD has taken away; blessed be the name of the LORD."

²² In all this Job did not sin or charge God with wrongdoing.

2 One day the heavenly beings[a] came to present themselves before the LORD, and Satan[b] also came among them to present himself before the LORD. ² The LORD said to Satan,[b] "Where have you come from?" Satan[c] answered the LORD, "From going to and fro on the earth, and from walking up and down on it." ³ The LORD said to Satan,[b] "Have you considered my servant Job? There is no one like him on the earth, a blameless and upright man who fears God and turns away from evil. He still persists in his integrity, although you incited me against him, to destroy him for no reason." ⁴ Then Satan[b] answered the LORD, "Skin for skin! All that people have they will give to save their lives.[d] ⁵ But stretch out your hand now and touch his bone and his flesh, and he will curse you to your face." ⁶ The LORD said to Satan,[b] "Very well, he is in your power; only spare his life."

⁷ So Satan[b] went out from the presence of the LORD, and inflicted loathsome sores on Job from the sole of his foot to the crown of his head. ⁸ Job[e] took a potsherd with which to scrape himself, and sat among the ashes.

⁹ Then his wife said to him, "Do you still persist in your integrity? Curse[f] God, and die." ¹⁰ But he said to her, "You speak as any foolish woman would speak. Shall we receive the good at the hand of God, and not receive the bad?" In all this Job did not sin with his lips.

¹¹ Now when Job's three friends heard of all these troubles that had come upon him, each of them set out from his home—Eliphaz the Temanite, Bildad the Shuhite, and Zophar the Naamathite. They met together to go and console and comfort him. ¹² When they saw him from a distance, they did not recognize him, and they raised their voices and wept aloud; they tore their robes and threw dust in the air upon their heads. ¹³ They sat with him on the ground seven days and seven nights, and no one spoke a word to him, for they saw that his suffering was very great.

---

a Heb *sons of God*
b Or *the Accuser*; Heb *ha-satan*
c Or *The Accuser*; Heb *ha-satan*
d Or *All that the man has he will give for his life*
e Heb *He*
f Heb *Bless*

---

in from the Mediterranean, the *great wind* from the eastern desert. **21:** Job praises the LORD for both good and evil, proving God's confidence in him justified. The *mother's womb* to which Job will return is that of mother earth (cf. Gen 3.19). **2.1–6:** Now again in the heavenly council, the LORD remarks that Job *still persists in his integrity*, i.e., continues blameless as ever. **4:** *Skin for skin!* Job has saved his own skin by piously accepting the death of his children; if God now attacks Job himself, Job will attack God, by cursing him (see 1.5n.). **7–13:** The fourth scene dissolves into the fifth: God authorizes the suffering, and immediately the Satan afflicts Job. **7:** *Loathsome sores*, some unspecified skin disease (cf. 7.5; 30.30). **8:** To express his sense of desolation and isolation, Job removes himself from society and sits on the rubbish heap outside his city, performing rituals of mourning (cf. Ezek 27.30; Jon 3.6). He uses broken pieces of pottery he finds there to scratch himself to relieve the itchiness. **9:** The outcome of all Job's piety has been to rob his wife of her ten children, her social standing, and her livelihood. When she urges him to *curse God* (see 1.5n.), and so bring his misery to an end with death, he mildly replies that she is speaking like *any foolish woman*, i.e., low-class, irreligious women, abandoning their family's standards of formal and proper behavior. *Job did not sin with his lips*, it is not implied that he sinned in what he thought. Job has disproved the Satan's claim that Job would sin with his lips by cursing God. **11–13:** Job, being a chieftain of great importance (1.3), has other high-ranking friends. These three, all apparently from other towns in Edom, have kindly intentions toward him, but when they see how badly he is suffering they do not offer him any consolation, but treat him as if he were already dead, throwing *dust . . . upon their heads*, a mourning ritual (see Josh 7.6; Lam 2.10), and silently mourning him *seven days and seven nights* (see Gen 50.10; Sir 22.12).

3 After this Job opened his mouth and cursed the day of his birth. [2] Job said:
[3] "Let the day perish in which I was born,
  and the night that said,
    'A man-child is conceived.'
[4] Let that day be darkness!
  May God above not seek it,
  or light shine on it.
[5] Let gloom and deep darkness claim it.
  Let clouds settle upon it;
  let the blackness of the day terrify it.
[6] That night—let thick darkness seize it!
  let it not rejoice among the days of the year;
  let it not come into the number of the months.
[7] Yes, let that night be barren;
  let no joyful cry be heard[a] in it.
[8] Let those curse it who curse the Sea,[b]
  those who are skilled to rouse up Leviathan.
[9] Let the stars of its dawn be dark;
  let it hope for light, but have none;
  may it not see the eyelids of the morning—
[10] because it did not shut the doors of my mother's womb,
  and hide trouble from my eyes.

[11] "Why did I not die at birth,
  come forth from the womb and expire?
[12] Why were there knees to receive me,

or breasts for me to suck?
[13] Now I would be lying down and quiet;
  I would be asleep; then I would be at rest
[14] with kings and counselors of the earth
  who rebuild ruins for themselves,
[15] or with princes who have gold,
  who fill their houses with silver.
[16] Or why was I not buried like a stillborn child,
  like an infant that never sees the light?
[17] There the wicked cease from troubling,
  and there the weary are at rest.
[18] There the prisoners are at ease together;
  they do not hear the voice of the taskmaster.
[19] The small and the great are there,
  and the slaves are free from their masters.

[20] "Why is light given to one in misery,
  and life to the bitter in soul,
[21] who long for death, but it does not come,
  and dig for it more than for hidden treasures;
[22] who rejoice exceedingly,
  and are glad when they find the grave?
[23] Why is light given to one who cannot see the way,

[a] Heb *come*
[b] Cn: Heb *day*

3.1–42.6: The dialogues.

3.1–11.20: First cycle of speeches.

3.1–26: Job's first speech. After the grandeur and deliberateness of the prologue (chs 1–2), the reader is suddenly plunged into the dramatic turmoil of the poem (3.1–42.6); the external description of suffering gives way to Job's inner experience. Its three strophes express a wish he had never been born (vv. 3–10); failing that, a wish he had died at birth (vv. 11–19); failing that, a wish that he, and people suffering as he does, could simply die when they are ready (vv. 20–26). **3–10:** A curse naturally concerns the future, and a curse on the day of his birth (cf. Jer 20.14–18) is a futile curse, for the past cannot be changed. Job wishes that the day of his birth and conception (viewed poetically as one event) could have been blacked out (vv. 4–6a) so that it would not have entered into the calendar of the year (vv. 6b,c); he wishes that the sorcerers who put a curse on days could have made it one of the unlucky days, in which it would have been impossible for his parents to have conceived him or for his mother to have given birth to him (vv. 8a,10a). **8:** Some ancient magicians obviously believed they could *rouse up Leviathan*, the sea-monster (cf. Ps 104.26; Isa 27.1) and dragon of chaos (see 7.12; Ps 74.13–14), who would perhaps swallow up the sun, so causing the darkness of eclipse. **11–19:** If he had to be born, why could he not have died at birth (v. 11a) or, at least, have been stillborn (v. 16)? Death has for him now become sweeter than life, and he compares the quiet peacefulness of the underworld (Sheol; cf. Eccl 6.3–5; Sir 30.3) to his present troubled and anxious lot (vv. 13–19). **14.** Near Eastern kings frequently boasted that they had rebuilt famous ruined cities. **20–26:** Now Job not only asks why he himself has to go on living, but why people in general cannot simply die when they want to (vv. 20–23). **23:** Previously, God's hedge of protection about his life (cf.

whom God has fenced in?

²⁴ For my sighing comes like[a] my bread,
and my groanings are poured out like
water.

²⁵ Truly the thing that I fear comes upon
me,
and what I dread befalls me.

²⁶ I am not at ease, nor am I quiet;
I have no rest; but trouble comes."

4 Then Eliphaz the Temanite answered:
² "If one ventures a word with you, will
you be offended?
But who can keep from speaking?

³ See, you have instructed many;
you have strengthened the weak hands.

⁴ Your words have supported those who
were stumbling,
and you have made firm the feeble
knees.

⁵ But now it has come to you, and you are
impatient;
it touches you, and you are dismayed.

⁶ Is not your fear of God your confidence,
and the integrity of your ways your
hope?

⁷ "Think now, who that was innocent ever
perished?
Or where were the upright cut off?

⁸ As I have seen, those who plow iniquity
and sow trouble reap the same.

⁹ By the breath of God they perish,
and by the blast of his anger they are
consumed.

¹⁰ The roar of the lion, the voice of the
fierce lion,
and the teeth of the young lions are
broken.

¹¹ The strong lion perishes for lack of prey,
and the whelps of the lioness are
scattered.

¹² "Now a word came stealing to me,
my ear received the whisper of it.

¹³ Amid thoughts from visions of the
night,
when deep sleep falls on mortals,

¹⁴ dread came upon me, and trembling,
which made all my bones shake.

¹⁵ A spirit glided past my face;
the hair of my flesh bristled.

¹⁶ It stood still,
but I could not discern its appearance.
A form was before my eyes;
there was silence, then I heard a voice:

¹⁷ 'Can mortals be righteous before[b] God?
Can human beings be pure before[b] their
Maker?

¹⁸ Even in his servants he puts no trust,
and his angels he charges with error;

¹⁹ how much more those who live in
houses of clay,
whose foundation is in the dust,
who are crushed like a moth.

²⁰ Between morning and evening they are
destroyed;
they perish forever without any
regarding it.

²¹ Their tent-cord is plucked up within
them,
and they die devoid of wisdom.'

a Heb *before*
b Or *more than*

1.10) had ensured his well-being; but now that he wants to die, God's preservation of his life seems an artificial prolongation of his misery, and the hedge has become a prison wall rather than a wall of defense. **26:** Unlike the restfulness of the underworld, which is what he desires, his life has no *rest*, but only *trouble*.

4.1–5.27: Eliphaz's first speech. Eliphaz regards Job as a pious man and urges him not to lose heart, since the innocent never finally suffer. Even the pious are not perfect, however, and may experience reproof and discipline (5.17); but they will soon come to an end (4.6). **4.2–6:** Eliphaz is not scornful in reminding Job how he has comforted others; he believes that Job's good deeds are a reason why God will soon restore him. **7–11:** Eliphaz describes the fate of the wicked, as a contrast to what Job can expect since he is not one of them. **8:** Cf. Hos 10.13; Gal 6.7. **10:** Cf. Ps 58.6. **12–21:** However, not even the angels are perfect (v. 18), still less the righteous (v. 17; cf. 15.14–16; 25.4–6). They are mere mortals, who, unlike the angels, can expire within a single day (v. 20a) and be so insignificant that they can die without anyone noticing (v. 20b) and without their ever attaining wisdom (v. 21b). Eliphaz's dream or waking vision terrified him because of its supernatural source, but the message it

5 "Call now; is there anyone who will
answer you?
To which of the holy ones will you turn?
[2] Surely vexation kills the fool,
and jealousy slays the simple.
[3] I have seen fools taking root,
but suddenly I cursed their dwelling.
[4] Their children are far from safety,
they are crushed in the gate,
and there is no one to deliver them.
[5] The hungry eat their harvest,
and they take it even out of the thorns;[a]
and the thirsty[b] pant after their wealth.
[6] For misery does not come from the earth,
nor does trouble sprout from the
ground;
[7] but human beings are born to trouble
just as sparks[c] fly upward.

[8] "As for me, I would seek God,
and to God I would commit my cause.
[9] He does great things and unsearchable,
marvelous things without number.
[10] He gives rain on the earth
and sends waters on the fields;
[11] he sets on high those who are lowly,
and those who mourn are lifted to
safety.
[12] He frustrates the devices of the crafty,
so that their hands achieve no success.
[13] He takes the wise in their own craftiness;
and the schemes of the wily are brought
to a quick end.
[14] They meet with darkness in the daytime,
and grope at noonday as in the night.
[15] But he saves the needy from the sword of
their mouth,
from the hand of the mighty.

[16] So the poor have hope,
and injustice shuts its mouth.
[17] "How happy is the one whom God
reproves;
therefore do not despise the discipline
of the Almighty.[d]
[18] For he wounds, but he binds up;
he strikes, but his hands heal.
[19] He will deliver you from six troubles;
in seven no harm shall touch you.
[20] In famine he will redeem you from
death,
and in war from the power of the
sword.
[21] You shall be hidden from the scourge of
the tongue,
and shall not fear destruction when it
comes.
[22] At destruction and famine you shall
laugh,
and shall not fear the wild animals of
the earth.
[23] For you shall be in league with the
stones of the field,
and the wild animals shall be at peace
with you.
[24] You shall know that your tent is safe,
you shall inspect your fold and miss
nothing.
[25] You shall know that your descendants
will be many,

a   Meaning of Heb uncertain
b   Aquila Symmachus Syr Vg: Heb *snare*
c   Or *birds*; Heb *sons of Resheph*
d   Traditional rendering of Heb *Shaddai*

brought was obvious. Appeals to revelatory experience are unusual in wisdom books, but see 33.15–18. **5.1–7:** Suffering, in fact, has to be expected. Not believing that Job really wants to die (as in ch 3), Eliphaz assumes Job is hoping to escape his suffering. But that is wishful thinking, for suffering is natural for humans; they always bring trouble upon themselves (v. 7 may be better translated "Humans beget suffering for themselves"). Even the angels (*the holy ones*, v. 1) cannot prevent the cycle of cause and effect when humans sin and bring punishment upon themselves. The fools whose *vexation* or resentment and *jealousy* bring them to ruin are a case in point (cf. Prov 12.16; 14.30; Sir 30.24). **8–16:** As in 4.2–6, Eliphaz regards Job as an essentially pious man, who should patiently leave his *cause*, or case, in divine hands (v. 8), since God is a great reverser of fortunes (vv. 11–16). **10–15:** The destructive acts of God (vv. 12–14) are enclosed within the frame of his saving acts (vv. 10–11,15), so the chief effect of this picture of God's working is to give *hope* to the poor (v. 16; contrast Lk 1.51–53). **17–27:** Eliphaz interprets Job's suffering as God's disciplining (cf. Ps 94.12; Prov 3.11–12; Hos 6.1), which is a blessing in itself (v. 17) and that "he who wounds is he who soothes the sore" (v. 18, JB). Job must only recognize and not reject (*despise*, v. 17) God's discipline, and "apply it to yourself" (v. 27, NIV).

and your offspring like the grass of the
earth.

26 You shall come to your grave in ripe old
age,
as a shock of grain comes up to the
threshing floor in its season.

27 See, we have searched this out; it is true.
Hear, and know it for yourself."

6 Then Job answered:
2 "O that my vexation were weighed,
and all my calamity laid in the
balances!

3 For then it would be heavier than the
sand of the sea;
therefore my words have been rash.

4 For the arrows of the Almighty[a] are in me;
my spirit drinks their poison;
the terrors of God are arrayed against
me.

5 Does the wild ass bray over its grass,
or the ox low over its fodder?

6 Can that which is tasteless be eaten
without salt,
or is there any flavor in the juice of
mallows?[b]

7 My appetite refuses to touch them;
they are like food that is loathsome to
me.[b]

8 "O that I might have my request,
and that God would grant my
desire;

9 that it would please God to crush me,
that he would let loose his hand and cut
me off!

10 This would be my consolation;
I would even exult[b] in unrelenting pain;
for I have not denied the words of the
Holy One.

11 What is my strength, that I should wait?

And what is my end, that I should be
patient?

12 Is my strength the strength of stones,
or is my flesh bronze?

13 In truth I have no help in me,
and any resource is driven from me.

14 "Those who withhold[c] kindness from a
friend
forsake the fear of the Almighty.[a]

15 My companions are treacherous like a
torrent-bed,
like freshets that pass away,

16 that run dark with ice,
turbid with melting snow.

17 In time of heat they disappear;
when it is hot, they vanish from their
place.

18 The caravans turn aside from their
course;
they go up into the waste, and perish.

19 The caravans of Tema look,
the travelers of Sheba hope.

20 They are disappointed because they
were confident;
they come there and are confounded.

21 Such you have now become to me;[d]
you see my calamity, and are afraid.

22 Have I said, 'Make me a gift'?
Or, 'From your wealth offer a bribe for
me'?

23 Or, 'Save me from an opponent's hand'?
Or, 'Ransom me from the hand of
oppressors'?

a   Traditional rendering of Heb *Shaddai*
b   Meaning of Heb uncertain
c   Syr Vg Compare Tg: Meaning of Heb uncertain
d   Cn Compare Gk Syr: Meaning of Heb uncertain

6.1–7.21: Job's second speech. 6.1–13: A soliloquy, addressed to no one. In ch 3 Job had only asked why sufferers like him must go on living; but here he actively yearns for immediate death (vv. 8–9). If he could die
now, before his suffering leads him into blasphemy, he could at least have the *consolation* of not having *denied
the words*, the commandments, of the *Holy One*. Eliphaz has called on Job to be *patient*, but patience needs a
strength that Job does not have (vv. 11–13). He begins to think of God as his enemy, armed with poisoned *arrows* and with *terrors* as his army (v. 4; cf. Deut 32.23; Lam 2.4). 14–30: Turning now to the friends, Job accuses
them of defrauding him of friendship's debt of *kindness* or, rather, "loyalty" (v. 14), *afraid* that if they identify
themselves too closely with Job they too will come under God's judgment (v. 21). 15–17: The *torrent-bed* and
freshets are the wadis that are full of water during the rainy seasons but are dry during the summer when water
is most needed (cf. Jer 15.18). 18–20: *Tema* and *Sheba*, areas in northern and southwestern Arabia, respectively.

24 "Teach me, and I will be silent;
  make me understand how I have gone
    wrong.
25 How forceful are honest words!
  But your reproof, what does it reprove?
26 Do you think that you can reprove
    words,
  as if the speech of the desperate were
    wind?
27 You would even cast lots over the
    orphan,
  and bargain over your friend.

28 "But now, be pleased to look at me;
  for I will not lie to your face.
29 Turn, I pray, let no wrong be done.
  Turn now, my vindication is at stake.
30 Is there any wrong on my tongue?
  Cannot my taste discern calamity?

7 "Do not human beings have a hard
    service on earth,
  and are not their days like the days of a
    laborer?
2 Like a slave who longs for the shadow,
  and like laborers who look for their
    wages,
3 so I am allotted months of emptiness,
  and nights of misery are apportioned
    to me.
4 When I lie down I say, 'When shall I
    rise?'
  But the night is long,
  and I am full of tossing until dawn.
5 My flesh is clothed with worms and dirt;
  my skin hardens, then breaks out
    again.
6 My days are swifter than a weaver's
    shuttle,
  and come to their end without hope.ᵃ

7 "Remember that my life is a breath;
  my eye will never again see good.
8 The eye that beholds me will see me no

more;
  while your eyes are upon me, I shall be
    gone.
9 As the cloud fades and vanishes,
  so those who go down to Sheol do not
    come up;
10 they return no more to their houses,
  nor do their places know them any
    more.

11 "Therefore I will not restrain my mouth;
  I will speak in the anguish of my spirit;
  I will complain in the bitterness of my
    soul.
12 Am I the Sea, or the Dragon,
  that you set a guard over me?
13 When I say, 'My bed will comfort me,
  my couch will ease my complaint,'
14 then you scare me with dreams
  and terrify me with visions,
15 so that I would choose strangling
  and death rather than this body.
16 I loathe my life; I would not live forever.
  Let me alone, for my days are a breath.
17 What are human beings, that you make
    so much of them,
  that you set your mind on them,
18 visit them every morning,
  test them every moment?
19 Will you not look away from me for a
    while,
  let me alone until I swallow my
    spittle?
20 If I sin, what do I do to you, you watcher
    of humanity?
  Why have you made me your target?
  Why have I become a burden to you?
21 Why do you not pardon my
    transgression
  and take away my iniquity?

ᵃ Or as the thread runs out

7.1–21: Turning now to God, Job interweaves his own death-wish with his experience of the futility and misery of human life generally. 9: *Sheol,* the abode of the dead. 12: God, far from letting him alone, treats him like one of the legendary monsters of the deep, Yam (*the Sea*) or Tannin (*the Dragon*), who had to be muzzled by God at creation (cf. 3.8n.; 38.8–11; Isa 51.9). 17–18: A bitter parody of Ps 8.4. The psalm expresses wonder at the high status humans have been given as rulers of the earth despite their apparent insignificance on the cosmic scale. Job's language is a reproof of God for the disproportionate attention God gives to mortals, subjecting them to perpetual hostile scrutiny.

For now I shall lie in the earth;
    you will seek me, but I shall not be."

8 Then Bildad the Shuhite answered:
2 "How long will you say these things,
    and the words of your mouth be a great
        wind?
3 Does God pervert justice?
    Or does the Almighty[a] pervert the
        right?
4 If your children sinned against him,
    he delivered them into the power of
        their transgression.
5 If you will seek God
    and make supplication to the Almighty,[a]
6 if you are pure and upright,
    surely then he will rouse himself for
        you
    and restore to you your rightful place.
7 Though your beginning was small,
    your latter days will be very great.

8 "For inquire now of bygone generations,
    and consider what their ancestors have
        found;
9 for we are but of yesterday, and we know
        nothing,
    for our days on earth are but a shadow.
10 Will they not teach you and tell you
    and utter words out of their
        understanding?

11 "Can papyrus grow where there is no
        marsh?
    Can reeds flourish where there is no
        water?
12 While yet in flower and not cut down,
    they wither before any other plant.

13 Such are the paths of all who forget God;
    the hope of the godless shall perish.
14 Their confidence is gossamer,
    a spider's house their trust.
15 If one leans against its house, it will not
        stand;
    if one lays hold of it, it will not endure.
16 The wicked thrive[b] before the sun,
    and their shoots spread over the garden.
17 Their roots twine around the stoneheap;
    they live among the rocks.[c]
18 If they are destroyed from their place,
    then it will deny them, saying, 'I have
        never seen you.'
19 See, these are their happy ways,[d]
    and out of the earth still others will
        spring.

20 "See, God will not reject a blameless
        person,
    nor take the hand of evildoers.
21 He will yet fill your mouth with laughter,
    and your lips with shouts of joy.
22 Those who hate you will be clothed with
        shame,
    and the tent of the wicked will be no
        more."

9 Then Job answered:
2 "Indeed I know that this is so;
    but how can a mortal be just before
        God?

a   Traditional rendering of Heb *Shaddai*
b   Heb *He thrives*
c   Gk Vg: Meaning of Heb uncertain
d   Meaning of Heb uncertain

8.1–22: Bildad's first speech. Like all the friends, Bildad believes that suffering is punishment, and that the death of Job's children is proof of their sin. Bildad has less confidence in Job's righteousness than Eliphaz did, and his encouragement to Job depends on a condition, *if you are pure and upright* (v. 6). **2–7:** Job's children are dead, so they must have sinned (v. 4). By contrast, Job himself is not dead, so he must be innocent of anything deserving of death. He has only to *seek God* in prayer (v. 5), and if he is *pure and upright* his prayer will be heard. **8–19:** No effect without a cause, as the case of the wicked shows. **8–10:** Bildad's trust in the wisdom of *bygone generations* instead of *we [who] know nothing* is contrasted with Job's reliance on his own experience (6.4–7,30). **20–22:** Bildad believes Job may yet prove to be a *blameless person* (v. 20).

    9.1–10.22: Job's third speech. Here is Job's strongest statement so far of his feeling of powerlessness (e.g. 9.3–4,14–20,30–31), his sense of being trapped (9.15,20,27–31), and his belief that God's apparent concern for him throughout his life has not really been for his benefit, but in order to fasten guilt upon him (10.13–14). Novel in this speech is the question of how Job is to be vindicated, that is, shown publicly to be in the right after all. It is a hopeless task to make God declare him innocent (9.2), which eventually throws Job into despair (10.15–16).

3 If one wished to contend with him,
  one could not answer him once in a
    thousand.
4 He is wise in heart, and mighty in
    strength
—who has resisted him, and succeeded?—
5 he who removes mountains, and they do
    not know it,
  when he overturns them in his anger;
6 who shakes the earth out of its place,
  and its pillars tremble;
7 who commands the sun, and it does not
    rise;
  who seals up the stars;
8 who alone stretched out the heavens
  and trampled the waves of the Sea;a
9 who made the Bear and Orion,
  the Pleiades and the chambers of the
    south;
10 who does great things beyond
    understanding,
  and marvelous things without number.
11 Look, he passes by me, and I do not see
    him;
  he moves on, but I do not perceive him.
12 He snatches away; who can stop him?
  Who will say to him, 'What are you
    doing?'

13 "God will not turn back his anger;
  the helpers of Rahab bowed beneath
    him.
14 How then can I answer him,
  choosing my words with him?
15 Though I am innocent, I cannot answer
    him;
  I must appeal for mercy to my accuser.b
16 If I summoned him and he answered me,

I do not believe that he would listen to
    my voice.
17 For he crushes me with a tempest,
  and multiplies my wounds without
    cause;
18 he will not let me get my breath,
  but fills me with bitterness.
19 If it is a contest of strength, he is the
    strong one!
  If it is a matter of justice, who can
    summon him?c
20 Though I am innocent, my own mouth
    would condemn me;
  though I am blameless, he would prove
    me perverse.
21 I am blameless; I do not know myself;
  I loathe my life.
22 It is all one; therefore I say,
  he destroys both the blameless and the
    wicked.
23 When disaster brings sudden death,
  he mocks at the calamityd of the
    innocent.
24 The earth is given into the hand of the
    wicked;
  he covers the eyes of its judges—
  if it is not he, who then is it?

25 "My days are swifter than a runner;
  they flee away, they see no good.

a Or trampled the back of the sea dragon
b Or for my right
c Compare Gk: Heb me
d Meaning of Heb uncertain

But it has become an ambition that will only grow in attraction for him as the book progresses (cf. 13.13–23; 16.18–21; 19.23–27; 23.2–14). **9.2:** Job is not saying that no one can actually be *just* in the sight of God, but complaining that because God has such power and wisdom he can defeat any human's attempt to be declared righteous or "win his case" (REB) against God; God will not give humans the satisfaction of hearing their innocence affirmed. **5–13:** Job focuses upon the more negative aspects of God's power (vv. 5–7) not in order to picture him as a God of chaos but to emphasize his freedom to act, whether for good or ill. His freedom makes him incomprehensible (v. 10), unaccountable (v. 12), and uncontrollable (v. 13). **9:** Bear, Orion, Pleiades, in the translation the familiar names of the star groups in Greek tradition are substituted for the Heb terms; cf. 38.31–33; Am 5.8. **13:** *Rahab*, the legendary sea-monster of chaos, similar to or identical with Leviathan, with whom God did battle at creation (see also 26.12; Ps 89.10; Isa 51.9). **14–24:** Job believes that even if he could bring God to court he would not get vindication. **15:** Job is not going to *appeal for mercy* for that might sound like an admission of guilt. What he wants is vindication, not relief from his sufferings. **17:** *Tempest*, better "storm." **22:** God *destroys both the blameless and the wicked* because he is determined upon hostility to humans. **25–35:** The monologue has turned

26 They go by like skiffs of reed,
   like an eagle swooping on the prey.
27 If I say, 'I will forget my complaint;
   I will put off my sad countenance and
      be of good cheer,'
28 I become afraid of all my suffering,
   for I know you will not hold me
      innocent.
29 I shall be condemned;
   why then do I labor in vain?
30 If I wash myself with soap
   and cleanse my hands with lye,
31 yet you will plunge me into filth,
   and my own clothes will abhor me.
32 For he is not a mortal, as I am, that I
      might answer him,
   that we should come to trial together.
33 There is no umpire[a] between us,
   who might lay his hand on us both.
34 If he would take his rod away from me,
   and not let dread of him terrify me,
35 then I would speak without fear of him,
   for I know I am not what I am thought
      to be.[b]

10 "I loathe my life;
   I will give free utterance to my
      complaint;
   I will speak in the bitterness of my soul.
2 I will say to God, Do not condemn me;
   let me know why you contend against me.
3 Does it seem good to you to oppress,
   to despise the work of your hands
   and favor the schemes of the wicked?
4 Do you have eyes of flesh?
   Do you see as humans see?
5 Are your days like the days of mortals,
   or your years like human years,
6 that you seek out my iniquity
   and search for my sin,
7 although you know that I am not guilty,
   and there is no one to deliver out of
      your hand?

8 Your hands fashioned and made me;
   and now you turn and destroy me.[c]
9 Remember that you fashioned me like
      clay;
   and will you turn me to dust again?
10 Did you not pour me out like milk
   and curdle me like cheese?
11 You clothed me with skin and flesh,
   and knit me together with bones and
      sinews.
12 You have granted me life and steadfast
      love,
   and your care has preserved my
      spirit.
13 Yet these things you hid in your heart;
   I know that this was your purpose.
14 If I sin, you watch me,
   and do not acquit me of my iniquity.
15 If I am wicked, woe to me!
   If I am righteous, I cannot lift up my
      head,
for I am filled with disgrace
   and look upon my affliction.
16 Bold as a lion you hunt me;
   you repeat your exploits against me.
17 You renew your witnesses against me,
   and increase your vexation toward me;
   you bring fresh troops against me.[d]

18 "Why did you bring me forth from the
      womb?
   Would that I had died before any eye
      had seen me,
19 and were as though I had not been,
   carried from the womb to the grave.

a   Another reading is *Would that there were an*
    umpire
b   Cn: Heb *for I am not so in myself*
c   Cn Compare Gk Syr: Heb *made me together all*
    around, and you destroy me
d   Cn Compare Gk: Heb *toward me; changes and a*
    troop are with me

into an address to God. **32–35:** A legal confrontation with God is doomed because the two parties cannot be on
the same level (v. 32). Job needs an *umpire* or arbitrator, one who would *lay his hand* upon both parties as a gesture of reconciliation. Since there is no such umpire, Job will have to conduct his lawsuit himself. **10.1–2:** Job's
intention to begin a legal controversy with God. **3–7:** Speculation about God's motives for his treatment of Job.
8–17: The contradiction between God's real and apparent purposes in creating Job and keeping him alive. **9:** Cf.
33.6; Gen 2.7; 3.19; Isa 64.8. **10:** Human conception is pictured as cheese-making: semen, a milk-like substance,
is poured into the womb, where, like cheese, it coagulates into the embryo (cf. Ps 139.13–16; Wis 7.2). **18–22:** An
appeal for release from God's oppressive presence.

²⁰ Are not the days of my life few?^a
Let me alone, that I may find a little
comfort^b
²¹ before I go, never to return,
to the land of gloom and deep darkness,
²² the land of gloom^c and chaos,
where light is like darkness."

11 Then Zophar the Naamathite answered:
² "Should a multitude of words go
unanswered,
and should one full of talk be
vindicated?
³ Should your babble put others to silence,
and when you mock, shall no one
shame you?
⁴ For you say, 'My conduct^d is pure,
and I am clean in God's^e sight.'
⁵ But O that God would speak,
and open his lips to you,
⁶ and that he would tell you the secrets of
wisdom!
For wisdom is many-sided.^f
Know then that God exacts of you less
than your guilt deserves.

⁷ "Can you find out the deep things of
God?
Can you find out the limit of the
Almighty?^g
⁸ It is higher than heaven^h—what can you
do?
Deeper than Sheol—what can you
know?
⁹ Its measure is longer than the earth,
and broader than the sea.
¹⁰ If he passes through, and imprisons,
and assembles for judgment, who can
hinder him?
¹¹ For he knows those who are worthless;
when he sees iniquity, will he not
consider it?

¹² But a stupid person will get understanding,
when a wild ass is born human.^f
¹³ "If you direct your heart rightly,
you will stretch out your hands toward
him.
¹⁴ If iniquity is in your hand, put it far away,
and do not let wickedness reside in
your tents.
¹⁵ Surely then you will lift up your face
without blemish;
you will be secure, and will not fear.
¹⁶ You will forget your misery;
you will remember it as waters that
have passed away.
¹⁷ And your life will be brighter than the
noonday;
its darkness will be like the morning.
¹⁸ And you will have confidence, because
there is hope;
you will be protectedⁱ and take your rest
in safety.
¹⁹ You will lie down, and no one will make
you afraid;
many will entreat your favor.
²⁰ But the eyes of the wicked will fail;
all way of escape will be lost to them,
and their hope is to breathe their last."

12 Then Job answered:
² "No doubt you are the people,
and wisdom will die with you.

^a Cn Compare Gk Syr: Heb *Are not my days few? Let him cease!*
^b Heb *that I may brighten up a little*
^c Heb *gloom as darkness, deep darkness*
^d Gk: Heb *teaching*
^e Heb *your*
^f Meaning of Heb uncertain
^g Traditional rendering of Heb *Shaddai*
^h Heb *The heights of heaven*
ⁱ Or *you will look around*

11.1–20: Zophar's first speech. Zophar is the least sympathetic of the three friends. His message to Job is simple: you are suffering because God knows that you are a secret sinner (v. 6); therefore repent (vv. 13–14)! **4–6:** Zophar agrees with Job that the real issue is the question of sin. Since it is not obvious that Job is a sinner, his sin must be secret. So bad a sinner is Job that even with all his punishment God is letting Job off lightly (v. 6). **7–12:** God's wisdom is focused on the detection of wrongdoing. **8:** *Sheol*, the abode of the dead. **13–20:** Restoration depends entirely on Job's complete repentance. He must *stretch out* his *hands* in prayer and renounce his present sinfulness. The result will be a clear conscience (*you will lift up your face*) and a sense of security (v. 15).

12.1–20.29: Second cycle of speeches.

³ But I have understanding as well as you;
　　I am not inferior to you.
　　Who does not know such things as
　　　these?
⁴ I am a laughingstock to my friends;
　　I, who called upon God and he
　　　answered me,
　　a just and blameless man, I am a
　　　laughingstock.
⁵ Those at ease have contempt for
　　misfortune,^a
　　but it is ready for those whose feet are
　　　unstable.
⁶ The tents of robbers are at peace,
　　and those who provoke God are secure,
　　who bring their god in their hands.^b

⁷ "But ask the animals, and they will teach
　　you;
　　the birds of the air, and they will tell
　　　you;
⁸ ask the plants of the earth,^c and they will
　　teach you;
　　and the fish of the sea will declare to
　　　you.
⁹ Who among all these does not know
　　that the hand of the Lord has done
　　　this?
¹⁰ In his hand is the life of every living
　　thing
　　and the breath of every human being.
¹¹ Does not the ear test words
　　as the palate tastes food?
¹² Is wisdom with the aged,
　　and understanding in length of days?

¹³ "With God^d are wisdom and strength;
　　he has counsel and understanding.
¹⁴ If he tears down, no one can rebuild;
　　if he shuts someone in, no one can
　　　open up.

¹⁵ If he withholds the waters, they dry up;
　　if he sends them out, they overwhelm
　　　the land.
¹⁶ With him are strength and wisdom;
　　the deceived and the deceiver are his.
¹⁷ He leads counselors away stripped,
　　and makes fools of judges.
¹⁸ He looses the sash of kings,
　　and binds a waistcloth on their loins.
¹⁹ He leads priests away stripped,
　　and overthrows the mighty.
²⁰ He deprives of speech those who are
　　trusted,
　　and takes away the discernment of the
　　　elders.
²¹ He pours contempt on princes,
　　and looses the belt of the strong.
²² He uncovers the deeps out of darkness,
　　and brings deep darkness to light.
²³ He makes nations great, then destroys
　　them;
　　he enlarges nations, then leads them
　　　away.
²⁴ He strips understanding from the
　　leaders^e of the earth,
　　and makes them wander in a pathless
　　　waste.
²⁵ They grope in the dark without light;
　　he makes them stagger like a drunkard.

13 ¹ "Look, my eye has seen all this,
　　my ear has heard and understood it.
² What you know, I also know;
　　I am not inferior to you.

^a Meaning of Heb uncertain
^b Or *whom God brought forth by his hand*; Meaning of Heb uncertain
^c Or *speak to the earth*
^d Heb *him*
^e Heb adds *of the people*

12.1–14.22: Job's fourth speech. In the first part, Job addresses his friends (12.2–13.19) and in the second, God (13.20–14.22). The essence of the whole speech is: I want nothing to do with you *worthless physicians* (13.4); I desire to *speak to the Almighty* (13.3). 12.2–13.19: For the first time Job shows himself contemptuous of the friends. He believes his wisdom is superior to theirs (12.2), for he knows something they do not: that it is possible for a right-eous person to be afflicted and, equally, that the deeds of the wicked can go unpunished (vv. 4–6). 7–12: Job is not addressing the friends, but ironically imagining what they might say to him. 13–25: This hymn to the destructive power of the Almighty presents Job's new wisdom: God is no calm governor of a well-ordered universe, but an eccentric deity who cannot be comprehended or tamed. His chief characteristic is his upsetting of stable order. 13.1–3: Nevertheless, Job is determined to argue a lawsuit with God. 4–12: The friends have been speaking as false witnesses on behalf of God. Although Job has many doubts about God's justice, he does not doubt that God will

³ But I would speak to the Almighty,ᵃ
  and I desire to argue my case with God.
⁴ As for you, you whitewash with lies;
  all of you are worthless physicians.
⁵ If you would only keep silent,
  that would be your wisdom!
⁶ Hear now my reasoning,
  and listen to the pleadings of my lips.
⁷ Will you speak falsely for God,
  and speak deceitfully for him?
⁸ Will you show partiality toward him,
  will you plead the case for God?
⁹ Will it be well with you when he searches
  you out?
  Or can you deceive him, as one person
  deceives another?
¹⁰ He will surely rebuke you
  if in secret you show partiality.
¹¹ Will not his majesty terrify you,
  and the dread of him fall upon you?
¹² Your maxims are proverbs of ashes,
  your defenses are defenses of clay.

¹³ "Let me have silence, and I will speak,
  and let come on me what may.
¹⁴ I will take my flesh in my teeth,
  and put my life in my hand.ᵇ
¹⁵ See, he will kill me; I have no hope;ᶜ
  but I will defend my ways to his face.
¹⁶ This will be my salvation,
  that the godless shall not come before
  him.
¹⁷ Listen carefully to my words,
  and let my declaration be in your ears.
¹⁸ I have indeed prepared my case;
  I know that I shall be vindicated.
¹⁹ Who is there that will contend with me?
  For then I would be silent and die.
²⁰ Only grant two things to me,
  then I will not hide myself from your
  face:

²¹ withdraw your hand far from me,
  and do not let dread of you terrify me.
²² Then call, and I will answer;
  or let me speak, and you reply to me.
²³ How many are my iniquities and my
  sins?
  Make me know my transgression and
  my sin.
²⁴ Why do you hide your face,
  and count me as your enemy?
²⁵ Will you frighten a windblown leaf
  and pursue dry chaff?
²⁶ For you write bitter things against me,
  and make me reapᵈ the iniquities of my
  youth.
²⁷ You put my feet in the stocks,
  and watch all my paths;
  you set a bound to the soles of my feet.
²⁸ One wastes away like a rotten thing,
  like a garment that is moth-eaten.

14 "A mortal, born of woman, few of days
  and full of trouble,
² comes up like a flower and withers,
  flees like a shadow and does not last.
³ Do you fix your eyes on such a one?
  Do you bring me into judgment with
  you?
⁴ Who can bring a clean thing out of an
  unclean?
  No one can.
⁵ Since their days are determined,
  and the number of their months is
  known to you,
  and you have appointed the bounds
  that they cannot pass,

ᵃ Traditional rendering of Heb *Shaddai*
ᵇ Gk: Heb *Why should I take … in my hand?*
ᶜ Or *Though he kill me, yet I will trust in him*
ᵈ Heb *inherit*

punish the friends for their *partiality* toward himself (v. 10) and their lack of objectivity. 13–19: Ending his address to the friends, Job explains what he will ask of God. Unlike chs 7 and 9–10, where he asked God to stop paying attention to him, he now deliberately calls God into disputation with him (v. 22). It is dangerous (v. 14), suicidal in fact (v. 15); but Job is sure that right is on his side (v. 18). 15: The traditional translation of the verse (see textual note c) is based on an alternate reading of the Hebrew. 20–27: Job first insists that God bring out in the open what he has against Job, but with two conditions for fairness (v. 20): God must *withdraw* his *hand* of punishment from him, and he must not *terrify* him (v. 21). 24: *Enemy* (Heb "'oyeb," possibly a wordplay on Job's name ("'iyyob"). 14.1–22: The focus changes from Job himself to the lot of humanity. Humans are too unimportant for God to scrutinize them as he does Job; he could reasonably overlook their sins. 1: The expression *born of woman* is simply a synonym for any human being (see 15.14). 7–12: The hopes of a tree and of humankind are contrasted. A tree that is cut down can

⁶ look away from them, and desist,ᵃ
    that they may enjoy, like laborers, their
      days.

⁷ "For there is hope for a tree,
    if it is cut down, that it will sprout
      again,
    and that its shoots will not cease.
⁸ Though its root grows old in the earth,
    and its stump dies in the ground,
⁹ yet at the scent of water it will bud
    and put forth branches like a young
      plant.
¹⁰ But mortals die, and are laid low;
    humans expire, and where are they?
¹¹ As waters fail from a lake,
    and a river wastes away and dries up,
¹² so mortals lie down and do not rise
      again;
    until the heavens are no more, they will
      not awake
    or be roused out of their sleep.
¹³ O that you would hide me in Sheol,
    that you would conceal me until your
      wrath is past,
    that you would appoint me a set time,
      and remember me!
¹⁴ If mortals die, will they live again?
    All the days of my service I would wait
    until my release should come.
¹⁵ You would call, and I would answer you;
    you would long for the work of your
      hands.
¹⁶ For then you would notᵇ number my
      steps,
    you would not keep watch over my sin;
¹⁷ my transgression would be sealed up in
      a bag,
    and you would cover over my iniquity.

¹⁸ "But the mountain falls and crumbles
      away,
    and the rock is removed from its place;
¹⁹ the waters wear away the stones;
    the torrents wash away the soil of the
      earth;
    so you destroy the hope of mortals.
²⁰ You prevail forever against them, and
    they pass away;
    you change their countenance, and
      send them away.
²¹ Their children come to honor, and they
    do not know it;
    they are brought low, and it goes
      unnoticed.
²² They feel only the pain of their own
      bodies,
    and mourn only for themselves."

15 Then Eliphaz the Temanite answered:
² "Should the wise answer with windy
    knowledge,
    and fill themselves with the east wind?
³ Should they argue in unprofitable talk,
    or in words with which they can do no
      good?
⁴ But you are doing away with the fear of
    God,
    and hindering meditation before God.
⁵ For your iniquity teaches your mouth,
    and you choose the tongue of the crafty.
⁶ Your own mouth condemns you, and
    not I;
    your own lips testify against you.

⁷ "Are you the firstborn of the human race?
    Were you brought forth before the hills?

ᵃ Cn: Heb *that they may desist*
ᵇ Syr: Heb lacks *not*

hope for new life; for humans there is none *until the heavens are no more*, i.e., never. If only Sheol, the underworld, could be, not a final resting place without an exit, but a temporary hiding-place from God's scrutiny and anger (v. 13). **14:** A rhetorical question, expecting the answer No! **18–19:** The only expectation humans can have is that God will final. **18–19:** The only expectation humans can have is that God will finally *prevail against them*.

    15.1–35: Eliphaz's second speech. **2–16:** Eliphaz regards Job's faults as both intellectual and moral. His intellectual mistake is not to realize that even the most perfect human is tainted in God's sight (vv. 14–16). His moral fault is not to bear his suffering with bravery and patience. Whatever Job's original fault, it was minor compared with the sin of his present behavior; it is a sin against himself (v. 6) and against God (v. 13) to speak so one-sidedly and bitterly about God. The very passion of Job's speech is proof that he is in the wrong (vv. 12–13). **2:** *East wind*, the oppressively hot wind from the desert. **4:** *Fear of God* is the emotion of fear proper to a human being in the presence of God. Job's charges against God imply he has lost his due sense of creatureliness. **7:**

8 Have you listened in the council of God?
And do you limit wisdom to yourself?
9 What do you know that we do not know?
What do you understand that is not
clear to us?
10 The gray-haired and the aged are on our
side,
those older than your father.
11 Are the consolations of God too small
for you,
or the word that deals gently with you?
12 Why does your heart carry you away,
and why do your eyes flash,a
13 so that you turn your spirit against God,
and let such words go out of your
mouth?
14 What are mortals, that they can be
clean?
Or those born of woman, that they can
be righteous?
15 God puts no trust even in his holy ones,
and the heavens are not clean in his
sight;
16 how much less one who is abominable
and corrupt,
one who drinks iniquity like water!

17 "I will show you; listen to me;
what I have seen I will declare—
18 what sages have told,
and their ancestors have not hidden,
19 to whom alone the land was given,
and no stranger passed among
them.
20 The wicked writhe in pain all their days,
through all the years that are laid up for
the ruthless.
21 Terrifying sounds are in their ears;
in prosperity the destroyer will come
upon them.
22 They despair of returning from
darkness,
and they are destined for the sword.
23 They wander abroad for bread, saying,
'Where is it?'

They know that a day of darkness is
ready at hand;
24 distress and anguish terrify them;
they prevail against them, like a king
prepared for battle.
25 Because they stretched out their hands
against God,
and bid defiance to the Almighty,b
26 running stubbornly against him
with a thick-bossed shield;
27 because they have covered their faces
with their fat,
and gathered fat upon their loins,
28 they will live in desolate cities,
in houses that no one should inhabit,
houses destined to become heaps of
ruins;
29 they will not be rich, and their wealth
will not endure,
nor will they strike root in the earth;c
30 they will not escape from darkness;
the flame will dry up their shoots,
and their blossomd will be swept awaye
by the wind.
31 Let them not trust in emptiness,
deceiving themselves;
for emptiness will be their recompense.
32 It will be paid in full before their time,
and their branch will not be green.
33 They will shake off their unripe grape,
like the vine,
and cast off their blossoms, like the
olive tree.
34 For the company of the godless is barren,
and fire consumes the tents of bribery.
35 They conceive mischief and bring forth
evil
and their heart prepares deceit."

a Meaning of Heb uncertain
b Traditional rendering of Heb *Shaddai*
c Vg: Meaning of Heb uncertain
d Gk: Heb *mouth*
e Cn: Heb *will depart*

Council of God, see 1.6–12n. **14:** *Born of woman*, see 14.1n. **16:** An extreme generalization about humans as compared with God's purity (cf. 25.4–6). **17–35:** This depiction of the miserable life and fearsome fate of the wicked (cf. 18.5–21; 20.4–29) concerns, first, their life-long fear of death (vv. 20–26), and, second, their final destiny (vv. 27–35), that they will die prematurely (vv. 31–33). As always, Eliphaz believes Job is not one of the truly wicked, so this is a depiction of what does not apply to him. But he had better take care that he does not join them in his hostility toward God (v. 25).

16

Then Job answered:
2 "I have heard many such things;
miserable comforters are you all.
3 Have windy words no limit?
Or what provokes you that you keep on
talking?
4 I also could talk as you do,
if you were in my place;
I could join words together against you,
and shake my head at you.
5 I could encourage you with my mouth,
and the solace of my lips would assuage
your pain.

6 "If I speak, my pain is not assuaged,
and if I forbear, how much of it leaves
me?
7 Surely now God has worn me out;
he hasª made desolate all my
company.
8 And he hasª shriveled me up,
which is a witness against me;
my leanness has risen up against me,
and it testifies to my face.
9 He has torn me in his wrath, and hated
me;
he has gnashed his teeth at me;
my adversary sharpens his eyes against
me.
10 They have gaped at me with their
mouths;
they have struck me insolently on the
cheek;
they mass themselves together against
me.
11 God gives me up to the ungodly,
and casts me into the hands of the
wicked.
12 I was at ease, and he broke me in two;

he seized me by the neck and dashed
me to pieces;
he set me up as his target;
13 his archers surround me.
He slashes open my kidneys, and shows no
mercy;
he pours out my gall on the ground.
14 He bursts upon me again and again;
he rushes at me like a warrior.
15 I have sewed sackcloth upon my skin,
and have laid my strength in the dust.
16 My face is red with weeping,
and deep darkness is on my eyelids,
17 though there is no violence in my hands,
and my prayer is pure.

18 "O earth, do not cover my blood;
let my outcry find no resting place.
19 Even now, in fact, my witness is in
heaven,
and he that vouches for me is on high.
20 My friends scorn me;
my eye pours out tears to God,
21 that he would maintain the right of a
mortal with God,
asᵇ one does for a neighbor.
22 For when a few years have come,
I shall go the way from which I shall not
return.

17

My spirit is broken, my days are extinct,
the grave is ready for me.
2 Surely there are mockers around me,
and my eye dwells on their provocation.

ª Heb *you have*
ᵇ Syr Vg Tg: Heb *and*

16.1–17.16: Job's fifth speech. This is the most disjointed of Job's speeches so far. Several earlier themes recur: he criticizes the friends (16.2–6); he then soliloquizes, lamenting the attacks of God (vv. 7–17); he imagines his possible vindication (vv. 18–22); he makes a lament about the friends (17.1–10); he fears that he will die without being vindicated (vv. 11–16). Unlike his previous speech (chs 12–14), the subject here is always Job himself and not humanity in general. **16.7–17:** Job depicts God's assaults as if they were the attacks by various kinds of opponents, a wild animal (vv. 9–10), a traitor (v. 11), a wrestler (v. 12), an archer (vv. 12c–13a), a swordsman (vv. 13b–14). Cf. Lam 3.1–20. **18–22:** God's wrongful attack on Job will probably lead to Job's death. So he appeals to the earth to take blood revenge for him once he is dead—upon God! **18:** *O earth, do not cover my blood,* is the same kind of cry as Abel's who was unlawfully killed (Gen 4.10). **19:** Even now, while he is still alive, he has a *witness . . . in heaven,* which cannot be God, since God has been nothing but his enemy (vv. 7–14). His witness is his own innocence. **20:** *My friends scorn me,* better translated "It is my cry that is my spokesman." **17.1–16:** Job is confident that he is in the right, but he does not expect he will live to see his innocence vindicated. **1:** He is

³ "Lay down a pledge for me with yourself;
    who is there that will give surety for
        me?
⁴ Since you have closed their minds to
        understanding,
    therefore you will not let them triumph.
⁵ Those who denounce friends for
        reward—
    the eyes of their children will fail.

⁶ "He has made me a byword of the
        peoples,
    and I am one before whom people spit.
⁷ My eye has grown dim from grief,
    and all my members are like a shadow.
⁸ The upright are appalled at this,
    and the innocent stir themselves up
        against the godless.
⁹ Yet the righteous hold to their way,
    and they that have clean hands grow
        stronger and stronger.
¹⁰ But you, come back now, all of you,
    and I shall not find a sensible person
        among you.
¹¹ My days are past, my plans are broken
        off,
    the desires of my heart.
¹² They make night into day;
    'The light,' they say, 'is near to the
        darkness.'ᵃ
¹³ If I look for Sheol as my house,
    if I spread my couch in darkness,
¹⁴ if I say to the Pit, 'You are my father,'
    and to the worm, 'My mother,' or
        'My sister,'
¹⁵ where then is my hope?
    Who will see my hope?
¹⁶ Will it go down to the bars of Sheol?

Shall we descend together into the
        dust?"

18 Then Bildad the Shuhite answered:
    ² "How long will you hunt for words?
    Consider, and then we shall speak.
³ Why are we counted as cattle?
    Why are we stupid in your sight?
⁴ You who tear yourself in your anger—
    shall the earth be forsaken because of
        you,
    or the rock be removed out of its place?

⁵ "Surely the light of the wicked is put out,
    and the flame of their fire does not shine.
⁶ The light is dark in their tent,
    and the lamp above them is put out.
⁷ Their strong steps are shortened,
    and their own schemes throw them
        down.
⁸ For they are thrust into a net by their own
        feet,
    and they walk into a pitfall.
⁹ A trap seizes them by the heel;
    a snare lays hold of them.
¹⁰ A rope is hid for them in the ground,
    a trap for them in the path.
¹¹ Terrors frighten them on every side,
    and chase them at their heels.
¹² Their strength is consumed by hunger,ᵇ
    and calamity is ready for their
        stumbling.
¹³ By disease their skin is consumed,ᶜ

ᵃ Meaning of Heb uncertain
ᵇ Or *Disaster is hungry for them*
ᶜ Cn: Heb *It consumes the limbs of his skin*

not literally at death's door (cf. 16:22) but psychologically he is already in the grip of death. **3:** Since no one will guarantee his innocence, he must ask God to accept his own person as his *pledge*. **8–9:** Job adopts the point of view of the friends. **11–16:** Job falls again into despair, not a despair that robs him of his belief in his own innocence; but a despair that he can ever be shown to be innocent. **13–14:** *The Pit*, another term for Sheol. Job has lost his family and can only expect to join the family of worms in the underworld.

18.1–21: Bildad's second speech. After an opening address to Job (vv. 2–4), this speech contains nothing but a description of the fate of the wicked. This is probably not Bildad's prediction of Job's future but a description of the kind of fate that does not await him (as in his first speech, Bildad does not think Job one of the wicked). Yet he does see in Job, who is fighting a battle between doctrine and experience, someone who is tearing himself to pieces. And he finds Job's demand for a new theology deeply disturbing: *shall . . . the rock be removed out of its place?* (v. 4). **5–21:** Eliphaz's picture of the fate of the wicked in ch 15 focused on how they experience terror and insecurity all their life; but Bildad concentrates on the final days of the wicked, describing how they are trapped by death (vv. 8–10), torn from their dwellings (v. 14), and brought before the lord of the underworld (v.

the firstborn of Death consumes their
limbs.

¹⁴ They are torn from the tent in which
they trusted,
and are brought to the king of terrors.

¹⁵ In their tents nothing remains;
sulfur is scattered upon their
habitations.

¹⁶ Their roots dry up beneath,
and their branches wither above.

¹⁷ Their memory perishes from the earth,
and they have no name in the street.

¹⁸ They are thrust from light into darkness,
and driven out of the world.

¹⁹ They have no offspring or descendant
among their people,
and no survivor where they used to live.

²⁰ They of the west are appalled at their
fate,
and horror seizes those of the east.

²¹ Surely such are the dwellings of the
ungodly,
such is the place of those who do not
know God."

19 Then Job answered:
² "How long will you torment me,
and break me in pieces with words?

³ These ten times you have cast reproach
upon me;
are you not ashamed to wrong me?

⁴ And even if it is true that I have erred,
my error remains with me.

⁵ If indeed you magnify yourselves against
me,
and make my humiliation an argument
against me,

⁶ know then that God has put me in the
wrong,

and closed his net around me.

⁷ Even when I cry out, 'Violence!' I am not
answered;
I call aloud, but there is no justice.

⁸ He has walled up my way so that I cannot
pass,
and he has set darkness upon my paths.

⁹ He has stripped my glory from me,
and taken the crown from my head.

¹⁰ He breaks me down on every side, and I
am gone,
he has uprooted my hope like a tree.

¹¹ He has kindled his wrath against me,
and counts me as his adversary.

¹² His troops come on together;
they have thrown up siegeworksᵃ
against me,
and encamp around my tent.

¹³ "He has put my family far from me,
and my acquaintances are wholly
estranged from me.

¹⁴ My relatives and my close friends have
failed me;

¹⁵ the guests in my house have forgotten
me;
my serving girls count me as a stranger;
I have become an alien in their eyes.

¹⁶ I call to my servant, but he gives me no
answer;
I must myself plead with him.

¹⁷ My breath is repulsive to my wife;
I am loathsome to my own family.

¹⁸ Even young children despise me;

ᵃ Cn: Heb *their way*

---

14). **13–14:** *Death* was represented in ancient mythology as a king ruling over the underworld; Death's *firstborn* will be one of his offspring, such as disease, and the *terrors* are his agents who drag people from life down into his kingdom.

19.1–29: Job's sixth speech. In this speech there is an address to the friends at beginning, middle, and end (vv. 2–6,21–22,28–29). Between these addresses there is a complaint (vv. 7–20) and an expression of wish, knowledge, and desire (vv. 23–27). **2–6:** Job begins to recognize the friends as his enemies. **3:** *Ten times*, i.e., many times. **4:** Job does not admit to any sin. But if he had sinned, it would not have been a sin against the friends; so it is unfair of them to attack him. **7–12:** To depict the wrongs God has done him, Job deploys a range of images of assault (cf. 16.9,12–14): he is like a townsman who has been robbed (v. 7), a traveler who finds his path blocked and nightfall overtaking him (v. 8), a prince humiliated by a foreign ruler (v. 9), a tree pulled out of the ground (v. 10), a person who finds his friend has become his enemy (v. 11), a city besieged by enemies (v. 12). **13–20:** Here is the literal truth of what Job is experiencing, as distinct from the feelings his experience provoked

when I rise, they talk against me.

19 All my intimate friends abhor me,
and those whom I loved have turned
against me.
20 My bones cling to my skin and to my
flesh,
and I have escaped by the skin of my
teeth.
21 Have pity on me, have pity on me, O you
my friends,
for the hand of God has touched me!
22 Why do you, like God, pursue me,
never satisfied with my flesh?

23 "O that my words were written down!
O that they were inscribed in a book!
24 O that with an iron pen and with lead
they were engraved on a rock forever!
25 For I know that my Redeemer[a] lives,
and that at the last he[b] will stand upon
the earth;[c]
26 and after my skin has been thus
destroyed,
then in[d] my flesh I shall see God,[e]
27 whom I shall see on my side,[f]
and my eyes shall behold, and not
another.
My heart faints within me!
28 If you say, 'How we will persecute him!'
and, 'The root of the matter is found in
him';
29 be afraid of the sword,
for wrath brings the punishment of the
sword,

so that you may know there is a
judgment."

20 Then Zophar the Naamathite answered:
2 "Pay attention! My thoughts urge me to
answer,
because of the agitation within me.
3 I hear censure that insults me,
and a spirit beyond my understanding
answers me.
4 Do you not know this from of old,
ever since mortals were placed on
earth,
5 that the exulting of the wicked is short,
and the joy of the godless is but for a
moment?
6 Even though they mount up high as the
heavens,
and their head reaches to the clouds,
7 they will perish forever like their own
dung;
those who have seen them will say,
'Where are they?'
8 They will fly away like a dream, and not
be found;

a Or *Vindicator*
b Or *that he the Last*
c Heb *dust*
d Or *without*
e Meaning of Heb of this verse uncertain
f Or *for myself*

in vv. 7–12. He is isolated and alienated, because his suffering is understood as punishment for sin. **20:** Normally bones are the body's framework, and the flesh and skin cling to them; Job feels so weak that it seems his bones need support. *Escaped by the skin of my teeth*, or rather, with the skin of my teeth, means that Job feels he has been flayed alive, his skin being stripped from every part of his body except his teeth, which of course have no skin. **21:** *Have pity on me*, i.e., stop persecuting me. **23–27:** If his *words*, his claim to innocence, could be chiseled in stone in an inscription (not a *book*, v. 23), God would eventually rise last (rather than *at the last*, v. 25) in the court case to deliver his verdict that would clear Job, even after his death (v. 26a). Nevertheless, what Job really desires is to see his name cleared while he is still alive (v. 26b should probably be translated "Yet, to behold God while still in my flesh—that is my desire, to see him with my own eyes"). **25:** The word *Redeemer* or *Vindicator* should not be capitalized, since the kinsman or champion (as the Heb "go'el" means) is not God (God is his enemy). The only champion Job has is his own innocence, which he has spoken of in 16.18–21 as his witness, his advocate ("he that vouches for me"), and his spokesman. **28–29:** Job turns to the friends again. They say *the root of the matter is found in him*, i.e., he is the author of his own misfortunes; he says they should *be afraid of the sword*, since they have accused him unjustly, and that is a crime.

20.1–29: Zophar's second speech. It is mostly devoted to the theme of the doom of the wicked. But unlike Eliphaz (ch 15), for whom the fate of the wicked is a picture of what Job is not, or Bildad (ch 18), for whom it is a picture of what Job may become, for Zophar it is a picture of what Job will not avoid unless he changes radically.

they will be chased away like a vision of
the night.

9 The eye that saw them will see them no
more,
nor will their place behold them any
longer.

10 Their children will seek the favor of the
poor,
and their hands will give back their
wealth.

11 Their bodies, once full of youth,
will lie down in the dust with them.

12 "Though wickedness is sweet in their
mouth,
though they hide it under their tongues,

13 though they are loath to let it go,
and hold it in their mouths,

14 yet their food is turned in their
stomachs;
it is the venom of asps within them.

15 They swallow down riches and vomit
them up again;
God casts them out of their bellies.

16 They will suck the poison of asps;
the tongue of a viper will kill them.

17 They will not look on the rivers,
the streams flowing with honey and
curds.

18 They will give back the fruit of their toil,
and will not swallow it down;
from the profit of their trading
they will get no enjoyment.

19 For they have crushed and abandoned
the poor,
they have seized a house that they did
not build.

20 "They knew no quiet in their bellies;
in their greed they let nothing escape.

21 There was nothing left after they had
eaten;
therefore their prosperity will not
endure.

22 In full sufficiency they will be in distress;

all the force of misery will come upon
them.

23 To fill their belly to the full
God[a] will send his fierce anger into
them,
and rain it upon them as their food.[b]

24 They will flee from an iron weapon;
a bronze arrow will strike them
through.

25 It is drawn forth and comes out of their
body,
and the glittering point comes out of
their gall;
terrors come upon them.

26 Utter darkness is laid up for their
treasures;
a fire fanned by no one will devour
them;
what is left in their tent will be
consumed.

27 The heavens will reveal their iniquity,
and the earth will rise up against them.

28 The possessions of their house will be
carried away,
dragged off in the day of God's[c] wrath.

29 This is the portion of the wicked from
God,
the heritage decreed for them by God."

21 Then Job answered:
2 "Listen carefully to my words,
and let this be your consolation.

3 Bear with me, and I will speak;
then after I have spoken, mock on.

4 As for me, is my complaint addressed to
mortals?
Why should I not be impatient?

5 Look at me, and be appalled,
and lay your hand upon your mouth.

6 When I think of it I am dismayed,

---

a Heb *he*
b Cn: Meaning of Heb uncertain
c Heb *his*

4–11: The key image here is the disappearance of the wicked. **12–23:** The key image here is eating: nothing the wicked eat brings them lasting benefit. **24–29:** A nightmarish collection of images (weapons, law court, fire, flood) of how inescapable is the final doom of the wicked.

21.1–27.23: Third cycle of speeches.

21.1–34: Job's seventh speech. Job denies the friends' belief that the wicked do not prosper but come to an early grave. **6–16:** The wicked prosper; why is that so? Within three verses Job contradicts Zophar (v. 7; cf. 20.11),

and shuddering seizes my flesh.
7 Why do the wicked live on,
　reach old age, and grow mighty in
　　power?
8 Their children are established in their
　presence,
　and their offspring before their eyes.
9 Their houses are safe from fear,
　and no rod of God is upon them.
10 Their bull breeds without fail;
　their cow calves and never miscarries.
11 They send out their little ones like a
　flock,
　and their children dance around.
12 They sing to the tambourine and the
　lyre,
　and rejoice to the sound of the pipe.
13 They spend their days in prosperity,
　and in peace they go down to Sheol.
14 They say to God, 'Leave us alone!
　We do not desire to know your ways.
15 What is the Almighty,[a] that we should
　serve him?
　And what profit do we get if we pray to
　　him?'
16 Is not their prosperity indeed their own
　achievement?[b]
　The plans of the wicked are repugnant
　　to me.

17 "How often is the lamp of the wicked put
　out?
　How often does calamity come upon
　　them?
　How often does God[c] distribute pains in
　　his anger?
18 How often are they like straw before the
　wind,
　and like chaff that the storm carries away?
19 You say, 'God stores up their iniquity for
　their children.'

Let it be paid back to them, so that they
　may know it.
20 Let their own eyes see their destruction,
　and let them drink of the wrath of the
　　Almighty.[a]
21 For what do they care for their
　household after them,
　when the number of their months is
　　cut off?
22 Will any teach God knowledge,
　seeing that he judges those that are on
　　high?
23 One dies in full prosperity,
　being wholly at ease and secure,
24 his loins full of milk
　and the marrow of his bones moist.
25 Another dies in bitterness of soul,
　never having tasted of good.
26 They lie down alike in the dust,
　and the worms cover them.

27 "Oh, I know your thoughts,
　and your schemes to wrong me.
28 For you say, 'Where is the house of the
　prince?
　Where is the tent in which the wicked
　　lived?'
29 Have you not asked those who travel the
　roads,
　and do you not accept their testimony,
30 that the wicked are spared in the day of
　calamity,
　and are rescued in the day of wrath?
31 Who declares their way to their face,
　and who repays them for what they
　　have done?

a Traditional rendering of Heb *Shaddai*
b Heb *in their hand*
c Heb *he*

Bildad (v. 8; cf. 18.19), and Eliphaz (v. 9; cf. 5.24). **13:** *Sheol,* the abode of the dead. **17–21:** Only rarely do the wicked suffer. If the friends say, Well, their children suffer (v. 19), Job replies: Retribution should strike the people who deserve it! **17:** Job challenges the notion that the wicked do not live long (cf. 18.5; Prov 13.9; 24.20). **18:** Job disputes the axiom that the wicked are *straw before the wind* (cf. Ps 35.5) or *like chaff that the storm carries away* (cf. Ps 1.4). **19–21:** *You say* is not in the Hebrew; alternatively, the sentence may be translated, "Is God storing up punishment for their children?" **22–26:** Being good or bad makes no difference; the same fate happens to all. **27–34:** *I know your thoughts,* the friends have been thinking: the wicked suffer, Job is suffering, therefore Job belongs with the wicked. But the wicked do not suffer, says Job; ask any traveler, who will tell tales of famous wicked persons who are spared retribution (v. 30), are never denounced (v. 31), and whose tombs are watched over to protect them from grave robbers (v. 32).

³² When they are carried to the grave,
　a watch is kept over their tomb.
³³ The clods of the valley are sweet to
　them;
　everyone will follow after,
　and those who went before are
　innumerable.
³⁴ How then will you comfort me with
　empty nothings?
　There is nothing left of your answers
　but falsehood.”

22

Then Eliphaz the Temanite answered:
² “Can a mortal be of use to God?
　Can even the wisest be of service to
　him?
³ Is it any pleasure to the Almighty[a] if you
　are righteous,
　or is it gain to him if you make your
　ways blameless?
⁴ Is it for your piety that he reproves you,
　and enters into judgment with you?
⁵ Is not your wickedness great?
　There is no end to your iniquities.
⁶ For you have exacted pledges from your
　family for no reason,
　and stripped the naked of their
　clothing.
⁷ You have given no water to the weary to
　drink,
　and you have withheld bread from the
　hungry.
⁸ The powerful possess the land,
　and the favored live in it.
⁹ You have sent widows away empty-
　handed,
　and the arms of the orphans you have
　crushed.[b]
¹⁰ Therefore snares are around you,
　and sudden terror overwhelms you,
¹¹ or darkness so that you cannot see;
　a flood of water covers you.

¹² “Is not God high in the heavens?
　See the highest stars, how lofty they
　are!
¹³ Therefore you say, ‘What does God
　know?
　Can he judge through the deep
　darkness?
¹⁴ Thick clouds enwrap him, so that he
　does not see,
　and he walks on the dome of heaven.’
¹⁵ Will you keep to the old way
　that the wicked have trod?
¹⁶ They were snatched away before their
　time;
　their foundation was washed away by
　a flood.
¹⁷ They said to God, ‘Leave us alone,’
　and ‘What can the Almighty[a] do to us?’[c]
¹⁸ Yet he filled their houses with good
　things—
　but the plans of the wicked are
　repugnant to me.
¹⁹ The righteous see it and are glad;
　the innocent laugh them to scorn,
²⁰ saying, ‘Surely our adversaries are cut
　off,
　and what they left, the fire has
　consumed.’

²¹ “Agree with God,[d] and be at peace;
　in this way good will come to you.
²² Receive instruction from his
　mouth,
　and lay up his words in your heart.

---

a　Traditional rendering of Heb *Shaddai*
b　Gk Syr Tg Vg: Heb *were crushed*
c　Gk Syr: Heb *them*
d　Heb *him*

22.1–30: Eliphaz's third speech. **2–11:** As in his first speech (chs 4–5), Eliphaz believes that Job will be delivered *because of the cleanness of your hands* (v. 30). Surprisingly, however, he here apparently accuses Job of untold wickedness (v. 5), mainly social injustice (vv. 6–9). But he cannot believe that Job has actually *exacted pledges . . . for no reason, and stripped the naked of their clothing* (v. 6), withheld *water* and bread, i.e., food, *from the hungry* (v. 7), and rejected the pleas of *widows* and *orphans* (v. 9). He must mean that, since Job is suffering for some cause, and since the cause cannot be found in any wrong that Job has done, his sin must lie in what he has failed to do. **12–20:** God can see Job's secret sins; they are sins of omission. **21–30:** How Job can be delivered. The speech ends on an uplifting note: Job has only to *return* to God (v. 23), *pray* and fulfil his vows (v. 27); then

²³ If you return to the Almighty,ᵃ you will
    be restored,
  if you remove unrighteousness from
      your tents,
²⁴ if you treat gold like dust,
  and gold of Ophir like the stones of the
      torrent-bed,
²⁵ and if the Almightyᵃ is your gold
  and your precious silver,
²⁶ then you will delight yourself in the
    Almighty,ᵃ
  and lift up your face to God.
²⁷ You will pray to him, and he will hear
    you,
  and you will pay your vows.
²⁸ You will decide on a matter, and it will be
    established for you,
  and light will shine on your ways.
²⁹ When others are humiliated, you say it
    is pride;
  for he saves the humble.
³⁰ He will deliver even those who are
    guilty;
  they will escape because of the
      cleanness of your hands."ᵇ

23 Then Job answered:
² "Today also my complaint is bitter;ᶜ
  hisᵈ hand is heavy despite my groaning.
³ Oh, that I knew where I might find him,
  that I might come even to his dwelling!
⁴ I would lay my case before him,
  and fill my mouth with arguments.
⁵ I would learn what he would answer me,
  and understand what he would say to me.

⁶ Would he contend with me in the
    greatness of his power?
  No; but he would give heed to me.
⁷ There an upright person could reason
    with him,
  and I should be acquitted forever by my
      judge.

⁸ "If I go forward, he is not there;
  or backward, I cannot perceive him;
⁹ on the left he hides, and I cannot behold
    him;
  I turnᵉ to the right, but I cannot see
      him.
¹⁰ But he knows the way that I take;
  when he has tested me, I shall come out
      like gold.
¹¹ My foot has held fast to his steps;
  I have kept his way and have not turned
      aside.
¹² I have not departed from the
    commandment of his lips;
  I have treasured inᶠ my bosom the
      words of his mouth.
¹³ But he stands alone and who can
    dissuade him?

ᵃ Traditional rendering of Heb *Shaddai*
ᵇ Meaning of Heb uncertain
ᶜ Syr Vg Tg: Heb *rebellious*
ᵈ Gk Syr: Heb *my*
ᵉ Syr Vg: Heb *he turns*
ᶠ Gk Vg: Heb *from*

everything he does will prosper (v. 28). Cf. Zophar's advice in 11:13–20. **24:** There is a pun involving the words for *gold* (Heb "batser") and *like the stones* (Heb "betsur") and the words *dust* (Heb "'apar") and *Ophir* (Heb "'opir"). *Ophir* was an Arabian city famous for its high-quality gold (Gen 10.29; 1 Kings 9.28; 1 Chr 29.4).

23.1–24.25: Job's eighth speech. This speech is a soliloquy, addressed neither to the friends nor to God. In ch 23 Job is concerned mainly with himself and his sense of how inaccessible God is to him. In ch 24 his concern is with others, especially the innocent poor, who seem to be neglected by God. If he could gain access to God, he would be vindicated; but he despairs of ever receiving such vindication, since God plainly does not hold regular *times* for judgment when wrongs are righted (24.1). **23.3–17:** *Oh, that I knew where I might find him . . . !* God is plainly not entering into the lawsuit that Job desires (cf. 19.26), so Job must search him out. But his quest is a failure (vv. 8–9). God is not acting fairly or legally; *what he desires, that he does* (v. 13), and that is only to harm Job. **4–7:** When Job first imagined a lawsuit with God (9.3–4), he immediately recognized that he could not succeed. But the more he considers the idea, the more it becomes a reality. In a later speech, even though he has no hope of success (13.15), he craves to enter into dispute with him (13.3). In his next speech he announces that he already has a "witness" stationed in heaven, his "cry" that is his spokesman (16.19–20). Still later, he expresses his conviction that his case will be heard, even if after his death (19.27). Now he believes that he would get justice from God if only he could locate him. **8–9:** *Forward, backward, left,* and *right* designate the four cardinal

What he desires, that he does.
¹⁴ For he will complete what he appoints for me;
and many such things are in his mind.
¹⁵ Therefore I am terrified at his presence;
when I consider, I am in dread of him.
¹⁶ God has made my heart faint;
the Almighty[a] has terrified me;
¹⁷ If only I could vanish in darkness,
and thick darkness would cover my face![b]

24 ¹ "Why are times not kept by the Almighty,[a]
and why do those who know him never see his days?
² The wicked[c] remove landmarks;
they seize flocks and pasture them.
³ They drive away the donkey of the orphan;
they take the widow's ox for a pledge.
⁴ They thrust the needy off the road;
the poor of the earth all hide themselves.
⁵ Like wild asses in the desert
they go out to their toil,
scavenging in the wasteland
food for their young.
⁶ They reap in a field not their own
and they glean in the vineyard of the wicked.
⁷ They lie all night naked, without clothing,
and have no covering in the cold.
⁸ They are wet with the rain of the mountains,
and cling to the rock for want of shelter.

⁹ "There are those who snatch the orphan child from the breast,
and take as a pledge the infant of the poor.

¹⁰ They go about naked, without clothing;
though hungry, they carry the sheaves;
¹¹ between their terraces[d] they press out oil;
they tread the wine presses, but suffer thirst.
¹² From the city the dying groan,
and the throat of the wounded cries for help;
yet God pays no attention to their prayer.

¹³ "There are those who rebel against the light,
who are not acquainted with its ways,
and do not stay in its paths.
¹⁴ The murderer rises at dusk
to kill the poor and needy,
and in the night is like a thief.
¹⁵ The eye of the adulterer also waits for the twilight,
saying, 'No eye will see me';
and he disguises his face.
¹⁶ In the dark they dig through houses;
by day they shut themselves up;
they do not know the light.
¹⁷ For deep darkness is morning to all of them;
for they are friends with the terrors of deep darkness.

¹⁸ "Swift are they on the face of the waters;
their portion in the land is cursed;

---

a   Traditional rendering of Heb *Shaddai*
b   Or *But I am not destroyed by the darkness; he has concealed the thick darkness from me*
c   Gk: Heb *they*
d   Meaning of Heb uncertain

---

directions: east, west, south, and north. **24.1–25:** Why does God not hold regular assize days, i.e., judicial proceedings (*times*, v. 1), during which the injustices in the world's government could be cleared up? **2–12:** Why is the injustice of the suffering of the innocent poor allowed to go on for so long? God *pays no attention to their prayer* (v. 12). **2:** *Landmarks*, i.e., boundary stones; removing a neighbor's landmarks in order to increase the size of one's own property is prohibited (cf. Deut 9.14; 27.17; Prov 22.28; 23.10; Hos 5.10). **3:** The orphan, i.e., the fatherless, and the widow are examples of the poor and underprivileged. Those pictured here are not as poor as the homeless daylaborers of vv. 5–6. **6:** *Glean*, those who owned fields and vineyards were supposed to leave some produce for the poor to gather (Lev 19.9–10; 23.22; Deut 24.1; Ruth 2.1–10). **9:** Children could be taken as slaves until parents paid debts to creditors (2 Kings 4:1–7; Neh 5.1–5). **10–11:** See v.6n. **13–17:** Why is the injustice of the successful evildoer allowed to continue? Three typical rebels *against the light* (v. 13)—the murderer, the adulterer, and the thief—are allowed to live, though their friends are *the terrors of deep darkness* (v. 17) and they

no treader turns toward their vineyards.
¹⁹ Drought and heat snatch away the snow
     waters;
   so does Sheol those who have sinned.
²⁰ The womb forgets them;
   the worm finds them sweet;
they are no longer remembered;
   so wickedness is broken like a tree.

²¹ "They harmᵃ the childless woman,
   and do no good to the widow.
²² Yet Godᵇ prolongs the life of the mighty
     by his power;
   they rise up when they despair of life.
²³ He gives them security, and they are
     supported;
   his eyes are upon their ways.
²⁴ They are exalted a little while, and then
     are gone;
   they wither and fade like the mallow;ᶜ
   they are cut off like the heads of grain.
²⁵ If it is not so, who will prove me a liar,
   and show that there is nothing in what
     I say?"

25 Then Bildad the Shuhite answered:
     ² "Dominion and fear are with God;ᵈ
   he makes peace in his high heaven.
³ Is there any number to his armies?
   Upon whom does his light not arise?
⁴ How then can a mortal be righteous
     before God?
   How can one born of woman be pure?
⁵ If even the moon is not bright
   and the stars are not pure in his
     sight,

⁶ how much less a mortal, who is a maggot,
   and a human being, who is a worm!"

26 Then Job answered:
     ² "How you have helped one who has
       no power!
   How you have assisted the arm that has
     no strength!
³ How you have counseled one who has no
     wisdom,
   and given much good advice!
⁴ With whose help have you uttered words,
   and whose spirit has come forth from
     you?
⁵ The shades below tremble,
   the waters and their inhabitants.
⁶ Sheol is naked before God,
   and Abaddon has no covering.
⁷ He stretches out Zaphonᵉ over the void,
   and hangs the earth upon nothing.
⁸ He binds up the waters in his thick
     clouds,
   and the cloud is not torn open by them.
⁹ He covers the face of the full moon,
   and spreads over it his cloud.
¹⁰ He has described a circle on the face of
     the waters,

ᵃ Gk Tg: Heb *feed on* or *associate with*
ᵇ Heb *he*
ᶜ Gk: Heb *like all others*
ᵈ Heb *him*
ᵉ Or *the North*

should by rights be with them in the underworld. **18–25:** These verses about the early death of the wicked are so unlike Job's views that they must be either a quotation by Job of the friends (rsv adds "You say" at the beginning of v. 16), or, possibly part of the missing third speech of Zophar. See also 27.7–10n.

25.1–26.14: Bildad's third speech. As it stands, Bildad's speech is uncommonly short (25.2–6) but although 26.1–14 is now assigned to Job, it was probably originally part of Bildad's speech. Such a rearrangement would help remove the problem of having three speeches of Job in a row (chaps. 26, 27–28, 29–31) without any intervening words from the friends. The theme of Bildad's speech would then be the power of God, in three spheres: in the heavens (25.2–6), in the underworld (26.5–6), and in creation (26.7–13). The speech is an address to Job (cf. 25.4,6; 26.14), belittling him (26.2–4), denying his claim to innocence (25.2–6), and putting him in his place by focusing exclusively on God's untrammeled power (26.5–14). **25.2–3:** *He makes peace in his high heaven*, probably an allusion to God's defeat at creation of the powers of chaos (cf. 9.13; 26.11–13; Isa 51.9). Peace through terror is God's style, according to Bildad. **26.5:** *Shades*, i.e., the inhabitants of the underworld. **6:** *Abaddon* (meaning "destruction"), another name for Sheol, the abode of the dead. **7:** At creation, God stretched out the heavens (here called *Zaphon*, "the north") like a tent without a center pole and suspended the earth from *nothing*. **8:** The *clouds* are conceived as waterskins (cf. 38.37). **10:** The *circle on the face of the waters* appears to be both the

at the boundary between light and
darkness.
[11] The pillars of heaven tremble,
and are astounded at his rebuke.
[12] By his power he stilled the Sea;
by his understanding he struck down
Rahab.
[13] By his wind the heavens were made fair;
his hand pierced the fleeing serpent.
[14] These are indeed but the outskirts of his
ways;
and how small a whisper do we hear of
him!
But the thunder of his power who can
understand?"

27 Job again took up his discourse and
said:
[2] "As God lives, who has taken away my
right,
and the Almighty,[a] who has made my
soul bitter,
[3] as long as my breath is in me
and the spirit of God is in my nostrils,
[4] my lips will not speak falsehood,
and my tongue will not utter deceit.
[5] Far be it from me to say that you are right;
until I die I will not put away my
integrity from me.
[6] I hold fast my righteousness, and will not
let it go;

my heart does not reproach me for any
of my days.

[7] "May my enemy be like the wicked,
and may my opponent be like the
unrighteous.
[8] For what is the hope of the godless when
God cuts them off,
when God takes away their lives?
[9] Will God hear their cry
when trouble comes upon them?
[10] Will they take delight in the Almighty?[a]
Will they call upon God at all times?
[11] I will teach you concerning the hand of
God;
that which is with the Almighty[a] I will
not conceal.
[12] All of you have seen it yourselves;
why then have you become altogether
vain?

[13] "This is the portion of the wicked with
God,
and the heritage that oppressors receive
from the Almighty:[a]
[14] If their children are multiplied, it is for
the sword;

[a] Traditional rendering of Heb *Shaddai*

horizon where the sky meets the earth and the boundary between day and night. **11**: The *pillars of heaven* are envisaged as supporting the solid canopy of heaven; they are the same as the "foundations of the heavens" (2 Sam 22.8). **12**: The depiction is still of the creation of the world, when according to some biblical myths God waged a battle against a monster known as *Sea* or *Rahab* (cf. 9.13n.; Ps 89.11; Isa 51.9). **13**: The *fleeing serpent* is another of God's primordial enemies, called Leviathan in 3.8 and Isa 27.1. **14**: These visible and reputed proofs of God's greatness are but the *outskirts of his ways*, and convey only a faint *whisper* of the *thunder* of his actual power. Humans cannot hope to comprehend the real God, but can catch only a glimpse of him.

27.1–6,11–12: Job's ninth speech. Although chs 27–28 are traditionally ascribed to Job, some of their contents seem more natural in the mouths of other speakers. Chs 27.7–10,11–23 should probably be assigned to Zophar (who otherwise does not have a third speech), and ch 28 may well be the conclusion of Elihu's speeches displaced from this point (see notes on 32.1–37.24), although many think it is an independent poem, not spoken by any of the characters in the book of Job. **1–6**: Job's speech here is short and to the point: for the first time, he swears an oath to his innocence. **2**: Job swears by the life of God—a bold move, for to do so is effectively a curse upon God if the oath is not true. **5**: If he were to accept the friends' reproaches, he would be denying what he knows to be true about himself. **11–12**: Job himself, not the stories of the slaying of the dragon at creation, is the best testimony to the power of God and to his intentions.

27.7–10,13–17; 24.18–24; 27.18–23: Zophar's third speech. The remainder of ch 27 is similar to Zophar's second speech in ch 20, except that here the focus is on the fact of the destiny of the wicked, whereas there it had been on the behavior that marks them out as wicked. He does not mean that Job is one of the wicked; rather, he paints this picture of their destiny to frighten Job into amendment of life so as to avoid the fate of the wicked.

and their offspring have not enough to
eat.

[15] Those who survive them the pestilence
buries,
and their widows make no lamentation.

[16] Though they heap up silver like dust,
and pile up clothing like clay—

[17] they may pile it up, but the just will
wear it,
and the innocent will divide the silver.

[18] They build their houses like nests,
like booths made by sentinels of the
vineyard.

[19] They go to bed with wealth, but will do
so no more;
they open their eyes, and it is gone.

[20] Terrors overtake them like a flood;
in the night a whirlwind carries them
off.

[21] The east wind lifts them up and they are
gone;
it sweeps them out of their place.

[22] It[a] hurls at them without pity;
they flee from its[b] power in headlong
flight.

[23] It[a] claps its[b] hands at them,
and hisses at them from its[b] place.

28 "Surely there is a mine for silver,
and a place for gold to be refined.

[2] Iron is taken out of the earth,
and copper is smelted from ore.

[3] Miners put[c] an end to darkness,
and search out to the farthest
bound
the ore in gloom and deep
darkness.

[4] They open shafts in a valley away from
human habitation;
they are forgotten by travelers,
they sway suspended, remote from
people.

[5] As for the earth, out of it comes bread;
but underneath it is turned up as by
fire.

[6] Its stones are the place of sapphires,[d]
and its dust contains gold.

[7] "That path no bird of prey knows,
and the falcon's eye has not seen it.

[8] The proud wild animals have not trodden
it;
the lion has not passed over it.

[9] "They put their hand to the flinty rock,
and overturn mountains by the
roots.

[10] They cut out channels in the rocks,
and their eyes see every precious
thing.

[11] The sources of the rivers they probe;[e]
hidden things they bring to light.

[12] "But where shall wisdom be found?
And where is the place of
understanding?

a Or *He* (that is God)
b Or *his*
c Heb *He puts*
d Or *lapis lazuli*
e Gk Vg: Heb *bind*

Ironically, much of the fate of the wicked has already befallen Job. **27.18:** *Nests* and *booths* are fragile, temporary structures. **21:** *The east wind* is the sirocco, the hot, violent wind that blew down the house of Job's children (1.19).

28.1–28: A poem on wisdom, or conclusion of Elihu's speeches. Although as it stands ch 28 is part of a speech of Job, it is hard to see why Job, who is focused on the question of justice, should be interested in the issue of how wisdom is to be acquired. Most scholars therefore regard the chapter as an independent poem, not spoken by any of the characters in the book of Job, which has found its way into it. Alternatively, its theme of the desirability of wisdom might be seen as most suitable in the mouth of Elihu (and its final sentence is very like 37.24, the final sentence of Elihu's other speeches). Quite possibly, the speeches of Elihu, now in chs 32–37, originally preceded this poem in ch 28. **1–11:** The poem begins, in the fashion of a riddle, with a topic far different from the actual subject of the poem, which is the acquisition of wisdom. The opening topic is that of mining minerals, its theme being the extreme efforts humans will go to in order to acquire things that are precious. In remote places (*forgotten by travelers*, v. 4) miners dig *shafts* where they dangle from ropes (*sway suspended*). Their lamps *put an end to darkness* underground (v. 3). Their tunnels are a *path no bird of prey knows*

¹³ Mortals do not know the way to it,ᵃ
and it is not found in the land of the
living.
¹⁴ The deep says, 'It is not in me,'
and the sea says, 'It is not with me.'
¹⁵ It cannot be gotten for gold,
and silver cannot be weighed out as its
price.
¹⁶ It cannot be valued in the gold of Ophir,
in precious onyx or sapphire.ᵇ
¹⁷ Gold and glass cannot equal it,
nor can it be exchanged for jewels of
fine gold.
¹⁸ No mention shall be made of coral or of
crystal;
the price of wisdom is above pearls.
¹⁹ The chrysolite of Ethiopiaᶜ cannot
compare with it,
nor can it be valued in pure gold.

²⁰ "Where then does wisdom come from?
And where is the place of
understanding?
²¹ It is hidden from the eyes of all living,
and concealed from the birds of the air.
²² Abaddon and Death say,
'We have heard a rumor of it with our
ears.'

²³ "God understands the way to it,
and he knows its place.
²⁴ For he looks to the ends of the earth,
and sees everything under the heavens.
²⁵ When he gave to the wind its weight,
and apportioned out the waters by
measure;
²⁶ when he made a decree for the rain,
and a way for the thunderbolt;
²⁷ then he saw it and declared it;
he established it, and searched it out.
²⁸ And he said to humankind,
'Truly, the fear of the Lord, that is wisdom;
and to depart from evil is
understanding.'"

29 Job again took up his discourse and said:
² "O that I were as in the months of old,
as in the days when God watched over
me;
³ when his lamp shone over my head,
and by his light I walked through
darkness;
⁴ when I was in my prime,
when the friendship of God was upon
my tent;
⁵ when the Almightyᵈ was still with me,
when my children were around me;
⁶ when my steps were washed with milk,
and the rock poured out for me streams
of oil!

ᵃ Gk: Heb *its price*
ᵇ Or *lapis lazuli*
ᶜ Or *Nubia*; Heb *Cush*
ᵈ Traditional rendering of Heb *Shaddai*

(v. 7). **12:** Wisdom is even more desirable, but harder to get at than the precious metals. **13–19:** Wisdom is apparently impossible to find or to buy (but see v. 28!). **14:** The Deep and the Sea are, unusually, personified, as ancient powers that might know the location of valuable objects like wisdom. **15–19:** Even if it could be found, wisdom could not be bought, being more valuable than the most expensive items, gold, silver, precious stones, and glass. **16:** *Ophir*, known as a source of gold; see 22.24n. **17:** *Glass* in pre-Roman times was as expensive as precious stones; it was used in jewelry and inlays. **20–27:** Wisdom is apparently inaccessible to humans, its place being known only to God (v. 23), who determined its nature at creation (vv. 24–27). **20–22:** *Abaddon and Death*, see 26.6n. **28:** Surprisingly, it turns out, although wisdom is desirable and precious, and cannot be found in any place or bought for any price, there is no secret about its essence. It consists of *the fear of the Lord*, i.e., the emotion of fear in the presence of God, and of shunning evil—that is, a proper attitude both to religion and to ethics. It is the attitude of Job in 1.1.

29.1–31.40: Job's tenth speech. The speech consists of three sections: in the first Job surveys, in nostalgic mood, his happy former life (ch 29); in the second he portrays, in pathetic mood, his present isolation and degradation (ch 30); in the third, he utters, in defiant mood, a series of self-curses that climax with a desperate appeal to be heard and vindicated (ch 31). The presence of the friends is ignored completely, and, except for 30.20–23, God is not addressed: the focus is entirely on Job's own experience. **29.2–25:** Job wishes he were still living his former life. **2–6:** A picture of his domestic bliss, realistic description mingling with metaphors like *my*

7 When I went out to the gate of the city,
  when I took my seat in the square,
8 the young men saw me and withdrew,
  and the aged rose up and stood;
9 the nobles refrained from talking,
  and laid their hands on their mouths;
10 the voices of princes were hushed,
  and their tongues stuck to the roof of
  their mouths.
11 When the ear heard, it commended me,
  and when the eye saw, it approved;
12 because I delivered the poor who cried,
  and the orphan who had no helper.
13 The blessing of the wretched came upon
  me,
  and I caused the widow's heart to sing
  for joy.
14 I put on righteousness, and it clothed
  me;
  my justice was like a robe and a turban.
15 I was eyes to the blind,
  and feet to the lame.
16 I was a father to the needy,
  and I championed the cause of the
  stranger.
17 I broke the fangs of the unrighteous,
  and made them drop their prey from
  their teeth.
18 Then I thought, 'I shall die in my nest,
  and I shall multiply my days like the
  phoenix;[a]
19 my roots spread out to the waters,
  with the dew all night on my branches;
20 my glory was fresh with me,
  and my bow ever new in my hand.'

21 "They listened to me, and waited,
  and kept silence for my counsel.
22 After I spoke they did not speak again,
  and my word dropped upon them like
  dew.[b]
23 They waited for me as for the rain;
  they opened their mouths as for the
  spring rain.
24 I smiled on them when they had no
  confidence;
  and the light of my countenance they
  did not extinguish.[c]
25 I chose their way, and sat as chief,
  and I lived like a king among his troops,
  like one who comforts mourners.

30 "But now they make sport of me,
  those who are younger than I,
  whose fathers I would have disdained
  to set with the dogs of my flock.
2 What could I gain from the strength of
  their hands?
  All their vigor is gone.
3 Through want and hard hunger
  they gnaw the dry and desolate ground,
4 they pick mallow and the leaves of
  bushes,
  and to warm themselves the roots of
  broom.
5 They are driven out from society;
  people shout after them as after a thief.
6 In the gullies of wadis they must live,
  in holes in the ground, and in the rocks.
7 Among the bushes they bray;
  under the nettles they huddle together.
8 A senseless, disreputable brood,
  they have been whipped out of the land.

a Or like sand
b Heb lacks like dew
c Meaning of Heb uncertain

steps were washed with milk (v. 6), signifying a superabundance of wealth. 7–25: A picture of his social worth, its principal ingredient being the honor accorded by his fellow citizens. 7: The town square at the gate of the city was the place where men would transact business and settle matters of law (cf. Ruth 4.1–12). 8: Young men saw me and withdrew as a mark of deference. 12–17: Job remembers his main role as protector of the underprivileged: the poor, orphans, the dying, widows, the blind, the lame, strangers. 14: Righteousness adorned him, bringing him honor as a costly garment would. 17: Enemies of the underprivileged, the unrighteous, are pictured as wild animals. 18: Phoenix, a mythical bird that lives for 500 years or more and thought to be reborn from its ashes. 25: Job claims to have held an almost royal status. 30.1–31: Job depicts his present situation—his dishonor (vv. 1–15) and his inner suffering (vv. 16–23)—and concludes with an address to God (vv. 20–23), and a lament (vv. 24–31). 1: The young men who despise him are scorned as low-born. Contrast Job's words in 24.1–12. 2–8: Their fathers are imagined by Job as without honor (disreputable, v. 8), excluded from ordinary society (v. 5) and living rough in the wild (v. 6), and with only leaves and roots to eat (v. 4). 4: Mallow, or "saltwort," a leafy plant eaten by the

9 "And now they mock me in song;
   I am a byword to them.
10 They abhor me, they keep aloof from
   me;
   they do not hesitate to spit at the sight
   of me.
11 Because God has loosed my bowstring
   and humbled me,
   they have cast off restraint in my
   presence.
12 On my right hand the rabble rise up;
   they send me sprawling,
   and build roads for my ruin.
13 They break up my path,
   they promote my calamity;
   no one restrains[a] them.
14 As through a wide breach they come;
   amid the crash they roll on.
15 Terrors are turned upon me;
   my honor is pursued as by the wind,
   and my prosperity has passed away like
   a cloud.

16 "And now my soul is poured out within
   me;
   days of affliction have taken hold of me.
17 The night racks my bones,
   and the pain that gnaws me takes no rest.
18 With violence he seizes my garment;[b]
   he grasps me by[c] the collar of my tunic.
19 He has cast me into the mire,
   and I have become like dust and ashes.
20 I cry to you and you do not answer me;
   I stand, and you merely look at me.
21 You have turned cruel to me;
   with the might of your hand you
   persecute me.
22 You lift me up on the wind, you make me
   ride on it,
   and you toss me about in the roar of the
   storm.

23 I know that you will bring me to death,
   and to the house appointed for all
   living.

24 "Surely one does not turn against the
   needy,[d]
   when in disaster they cry for help.[e]
25 Did I not weep for those whose day was
   hard?
   Was not my soul grieved for the poor?
26 But when I looked for good, evil came;
   and when I waited for light, darkness
   came.
27 My inward parts are in turmoil, and are
   never still;
   days of affliction come to meet me.
28 I go about in sunless gloom;
   I stand up in the assembly and cry for
   help.
29 I am a brother of jackals,
   and a companion of ostriches.
30 My skin turns black and falls from me,
   and my bones burn with heat.
31 My lyre is turned to mourning,
   and my pipe to the voice of those who
   weep.

31

"I have made a covenant with my eyes;
how then could I look upon a virgin?
2 What would be my portion from God
   above,
   and my heritage from the Almighty[f] on
   high?

a Cn: Heb *helps*
b Gk: Heb *my garment is disfigured*
c Heb *like*
d Heb *ruin*
e Cn: Meaning of Heb uncertain
f Traditional rendering of Heb *Shaddai*

very poor. *Broom*, the largest bush in the desert; its roots made good charcoal. **9–15:** The same young men as in v. 1, who in happier days would have deferred to him (29.6), now scorn Job as a sinner suffering God's punishment. **11–14:** He depicts them as military enemies, attacking him like a besieged city (cf. 16.12–14; 19.12). **16–23:** Worse even than his loss of honor is his sense that God has become his torturer, who intends his death (v. 23). **16:** *My soul is poured out within me*, i.e., his life force is running away like liquid from a vessel. **24–31:** Job's misery is a compound of his loss of former dignity, inner turmoil, physical pain. He is in *mourning* for the loss of what he once had. **29:** Job's miserable cries are like those of *jackals* and *ostriches*, creatures that inhabit desolate places. **31.1–40:** For the last time, Job summons God to a lawsuit, demanding he state what the charges against him are (v. 35). He imagines himself composing a document affirming his innocence, an oath of clearance, in the form of a curse upon himself that is meant to come into effect if he is lying. He declares his innocence against seven

3 Does not calamity befall the
  unrighteous,
  and disaster the workers of iniquity?
4 Does he not see my ways,
  and number all my steps?

5 "If I have walked with falsehood,
  and my foot has hurried to
    deceit—
6 let me be weighed in a just balance,
  and let God know my
    integrity!—
7 if my step has turned aside from the way,
  and my heart has followed my eyes,
  and if any spot has clung to my hands;
8 then let me sow, and another eat;
  and let what grows for me be rooted
    out.

9 "If my heart has been enticed by a
    woman,
  and I have lain in wait at my neighbor's
    door;
10 then let my wife grind for another,
  and let other men kneel over her.
11 For that would be a heinous crime;
  that would be a criminal
    offense;
12 for that would be a fire consuming down
    to Abaddon,
  and it would burn to the root all my
    harvest.

13 "If I have rejected the cause of my male
    or female slaves,
  when they brought a complaint against
    me;
14 what then shall I do when God rises up?
  When he makes inquiry, what shall I
    answer him?
15 Did not he who made me in the womb
  make them?

And did not one fashion us in the
  womb?

16 "If I have withheld anything that the
    poor desired,
  or have caused the eyes of the widow
    to fail,
17 or have eaten my morsel alone,
  and the orphan has not eaten from it—
18 for from my youth I reared the orphan[a]
  like a father,
  and from my mother's womb I guided
    the widow[b]—
19 if I have seen anyone perish for lack of
    clothing,
  or a poor person without covering,
20 whose loins have not blessed me,
  and who was not warmed with the
    fleece of my sheep;
21 if I have raised my hand against the
    orphan,
  because I saw I had supporters at the
    gate;
22 then let my shoulder blade fall from my
    shoulder,
  and let my arm be broken from its
    socket.
23 For I was in terror of calamity from God,
  and I could not have faced his
    majesty.

24 "If I have made gold my trust,
  or called fine gold my confidence;
25 if I have rejoiced because my wealth was
    great,
  or because my hand had gotten much;
26 if I have looked at the sun[c] when it
    shone,

a Heb him
b Heb her
c Heb the light

possible charges: deceit (vv. 5–8), adultery (vv. 9–12), disregard of servants (vv. 13–15), disregard of the poor (vv. 16–23), trust in wealth (vv. 24–28), rejoicing at the misfortune of others (vv. 29–34), and assault on the land (vv. 38–40b). 1: He has kept himself so far from sexual misconduct that he has even forbidden his desires. 9–10: In Job's world, a man's adultery with a married woman is an offense against the woman's husband, so the punishment he would deserve is to suffer the multiple adultery of other men with his wife after she had become a prostitute. The verb *kneel* has a sexual overtone. 12: *Abaddon*, the abode of the dead (see 26.6n). 13–15: Job goes far beyond the obligations of his time in admitting that slaves have any rights and in affirming their common humanity with him. 16–23: Job's humanitarian deeds are implicitly a rebuttal of Eliphaz's claims (24.6–9). Cf. 29.12–17. 21: *At the gate*, see 29.7n. 24–28: Confidence in one's wealth and the devotion paid to heavenly bodies

or the moon moving in splendor,
27 and my heart has been secretly enticed,
and my mouth has kissed my hand;
28 this also would be an iniquity to be
punished by the judges,
for I should have been false to God
above.

29 "If I have rejoiced at the ruin of those
who hated me,
or exulted when evil overtook them—
30 I have not let my mouth sin
by asking for their lives with a curse—
31 if those of my tent ever said,
'O that we might be sated with his
flesh!'a—
32 the stranger has not lodged in the street;
I have opened my doors to the
traveler—
33 if I have concealed my transgressions as
others do,b
by hiding my iniquity in my bosom,
34 because I stood in great fear of the
multitude,
and the contempt of families terrified
me,
so that I kept silence, and did not go out
of doors—
35 O that I had one to hear me!
(Here is my signature! Let the Almightyc
answer me!)
O that I had the indictment written by
my adversary!

36 Surely I would carry it on my shoulder;
I would bind it on me like a crown;
37 I would give him an account of all my
steps;
like a prince I would approach him.

38 "If my land has cried out against me,
and its furrows have wept together;
39 if I have eaten its yield without payment,
and caused the death of its owners;
40 let thorns grow instead of wheat,
and foul weeds instead of barley."

The words of Job are ended.

32 So these three men ceased to answer
Job, because he was righteous in his
own eyes. 2 Then Elihu son of Barachel the
Buzite, of the family of Ram, became angry. He
was angry at Job because he justified himself
rather than God; 3 he was angry also at Job's
three friends because they had found no answer, though they had declared Job to be in the
wrong.d 4 Now Elihu had waited to speak to Job,
because they were older than he. 5 But when
Elihu saw that there was no answer in the
mouths of these three men, he became angry.

a   Meaning of Heb uncertain
b   Or as Adam did
c   Traditional rendering of Heb Shaddai
d   Another ancient tradition reads answer, and had
put God in the wrong

are two forms of false worship. **27**: *My mouth has kissed my hand*, to throw a kiss as a gesture of worship. **31**: *O
that we might be sated with his flesh!*, or better, "O that there were someone not yet satisfied with his meat!"
There is no chance of finding anyone who has not benefited from Job's hospitality. **35–37**: These verses are the
climax to the speech, and it is strange that they are not at the end; perhaps vv. 38–40 have been misplaced and
should follow v. 34. **35**: *One to hear me*, i.e., God. **36**: Job would be proud to display the sheet of charges God has
against him, for it would be blank (or else filled with falsehoods).

32.1–37.24: Elihu's speeches. Many scholars think that the Elihu speeches (chs. 32–37) are a later addition to the
book, partly because Elihu is not mentioned in the prologue or epilogue. It may be, however, that the Elihu speeches originally followed directly after the last of the friends' third speeches, i.e., after chap. 27, and that chap. 28 was
the last of Elihu's speeches. This rearrangement would make better sense of the phrase *these three men* in 32.1, and it
would also mean that the LORD addresses Job immediately after Job's last speech (chaps. 29–31) is concluded. In any
case, the Elihu speeches are part of the book we now have, and Elihu has a distinctive contribution to make to its
argument. Elihu, who professes himself opposed both to Job and to his friends (32.2–3,10–12; 33.1–12) is offering a
middle way between them. Against the friends, he argues that suffering is not necessarily the penalty for sin already
committed, but may be a warning, to keep a person back from sin; it is better understood as discipline or education.

32.1–33.33: Elihu's first speech. 32.6–14: Elihu has hitherto deferred to the other friends on account of their
greater age, but he realizes that all humans have an equal access to wisdom, since all have in them the *breath of
the Almighty* (v. 8; cf. Gen 2.7). He feels he must speak because the friends have not answered Job adequately (vv.

⁶ Elihu son of Barachel the Buzite answered:
"I am young in years,
and you are aged;
therefore I was timid and afraid
to declare my opinion to you.
⁷ I said, 'Let days speak,
and many years teach wisdom.'
⁸ But truly it is the spirit in a mortal,
the breath of the Almighty,^a that makes
for understanding.
⁹ It is not the old^b that are wise,
nor the aged that understand what is
right.
¹⁰ Therefore I say, 'Listen to me;
let me also declare my opinion.'

¹¹ "See, I waited for your words,
I listened for your wise sayings,
while you searched out what to say.
¹² I gave you my attention,
but there was in fact no one that
confuted Job,
no one among you that answered his
words.
¹³ Yet do not say, 'We have found wisdom;
God may vanquish him, not a
human.'
¹⁴ He has not directed his words against
me,
and I will not answer him with your
speeches.

¹⁵ "They are dismayed, they answer no
more;
they have not a word to say.
¹⁶ And am I to wait, because they do not
speak,
because they stand there, and answer
no more?
¹⁷ I also will give my answer;
I also will declare my opinion.
¹⁸ For I am full of words;
the spirit within me constrains me.

¹⁹ My heart is indeed like wine that has no
vent;
like new wineskins, it is ready to burst.
²⁰ I must speak, so that I may find relief;
I must open my lips and answer.
²¹ I will not show partiality to any person
or use flattery toward anyone.
²² For I do not know how to flatter—
or my Maker would soon put an end to
me!

33 "But now, hear my speech, O Job,
and listen to all my words.
² See, I open my mouth;
the tongue in my mouth speaks.
³ My words declare the uprightness of my
heart,
and what my lips know they speak
sincerely.
⁴ The spirit of God has made me,
and the breath of the Almighty^a gives
me life.
⁵ Answer me, if you can;
set your words in order before me; take
your stand.
⁶ See, before God I am as you are;
I too was formed from a piece of clay.
⁷ No fear of me need terrify you;
my pressure will not be heavy on you.

⁸ "Surely, you have spoken in my hearing,
and I have heard the sound of your
words.
⁹ You say, 'I am clean, without
transgression;
I am pure, and there is no iniquity in
me.
¹⁰ Look, he finds occasions against me,
he counts me as his enemy;
¹¹ he puts my feet in the stocks,
and watches all my paths.'

^a Traditional rendering of Heb *Shaddai*
^b Gk Syr Vg: Heb *many*

11–14). **7:** *I said*, i.e., to myself. **9:** *It is not the old that are wise*, he must mean that it is not always the old who have wisdom. **15:** From here to the end of ch 33 Elihu addresses Job, referring to the friends as "they." **17–22:** Elihu's third reason for speaking is that he feels he will explode with frustration if he does not. **19:** It is not his *heart* but his "belly" that is like a wineskin that the new fermenting wine will burst if it is not vented. **33.1–7:** Elihu challenges Job to prepare for debate. **8–33:** Job believes, says Elihu, that he is faultless (v. 9), that God's treatment of him is pure malice (vv. 10–11), and that God refuses to answer his complaints of injustice (v. 13). Elihu's response is that God has various ways of speaking to humans, e.g., dreams (vv. 15–17) and suffering (vv. 19–28). In both

¹² "But in this you are not right. I will
answer you:
God is greater than any mortal.
¹³ Why do you contend against him,
saying, 'He will answer none of my[a]
words'?
¹⁴ For God speaks in one way,
and in two, though people do not
perceive it.
¹⁵ In a dream, in a vision of the night,
when deep sleep falls on mortals,
while they slumber on their beds,
¹⁶ then he opens their ears,
and terrifies them with warnings,
¹⁷ that he may turn them aside from their
deeds,
and keep them from pride,
¹⁸ to spare their souls from the Pit,
their lives from traversing the River.
¹⁹ They are also chastened with pain upon
their beds,
and with continual strife in their bones,
²⁰ so that their lives loathe bread,
and their appetites dainty food.
²¹ Their flesh is so wasted away that it
cannot be seen;
and their bones, once invisible, now
stick out.
²² Their souls draw near the Pit,
and their lives to those who bring
death.
²³ Then, if there should be for one of them
an angel,
a mediator, one of a thousand,
one who declares a person upright,
²⁴ and he is gracious to that person, and
says,
'Deliver him from going down into the
Pit;
I have found a ransom;

²⁵ let his flesh become fresh with youth;
let him return to the days of his
youthful vigor';
²⁶ then he prays to God, and is accepted by
him,
he comes into his presence with joy,
and God[b] repays him for his
righteousness.
²⁷ That person sings to others and says,
'I sinned, and perverted what was right,
and it was not paid back to me.
²⁸ He has redeemed my soul from going
down to the Pit,
and my life shall see the light.'

²⁹ "God indeed does all these things,
twice, three times, with mortals,
³⁰ to bring back their souls from the Pit,
so that they may see the light of life.[c]
³¹ Pay heed, Job, listen to me;
be silent, and I will speak.
³² If you have anything to say, answer me;
speak, for I desire to justify you.
³³ If not, listen to me;
be silent, and I will teach you wisdom."

34

Then Elihu continued and said:
² "Hear my words, you wise men,
and give ear to me, you who know;
³ for the ear tests words
as the palate tastes food.
⁴ Let us choose what is right;
let us determine among ourselves what
is good.
⁵ For Job has said, 'I am innocent,
and God has taken away my right;

a Compare Gk: Heb his
b Heb he
c Syr: Heb to be lighted with the light of life

cases, God's purpose is not to punish but to rescue humans from their sin (vv. 29–30). **18:** *The Pit*, another term for Sheol, the abode of the dead. *The River*, the underworld stream the dead must cross before they reach Sheol, like the Greek river Styx. **23:** *An angel, a mediator, one of a thousand*, probably "the thousand" were a group of supportive angels (unlike the accusatory angel the Satan), who would take up the cause of humans in the divine court (cf. 5.1, where Eliphaz denies that Job can expect any help from such angels). **24:** *Ransom* is usually money paid to release a guilty person from punishment, but here some unspecified ground for forgiveness. **32:** Elihu's ultimate purpose, to *justify* Job, is like that of the supportive angels.

34.1–37: Elihu's second speech. In vv. 2–15 Elihu addresses the friends, in vv. 16–37 Job. God, he argues, cannot do wrong by failing to execute retribution; but Job is doing wrong by claiming that God has acted unjustly toward him. All of Elihu's criticism of Job concerns Job's speeches; he does not hold against him anything he may have said or done before the book opened. His focus is not on what Job deserves but on the infamy of his

⁶ in spite of being right I am counted a liar;
my wound is incurable, though I am
without transgression.'
⁷ Who is there like Job,
who drinks up scoffing like water,
⁸ who goes in company with evildoers
and walks with the wicked?
⁹ For he has said, 'It profits one nothing
to take delight in God.'

¹⁰ "Therefore, hear me, you who have
sense,
far be it from God that he should do
wickedness,
and from the Almightyᵃ that he should
do wrong.
¹¹ For according to their deeds he will repay
them,
and according to their ways he will
make it befall them.
¹² Of a truth, God will not do wickedly,
and the Almightyᵃ will not pervert
justice.
¹³ Who gave him charge over the earth
and who laid on himᵇ the whole world?
¹⁴ If he should take back his spiritᶜ to
himself,
and gather to himself his breath,
¹⁵ all flesh would perish together,
and all mortals return to dust.

¹⁶ "If you have understanding, hear this;
listen to what I say.
¹⁷ Shall one who hates justice govern?
Will you condemn one who is righteous
and mighty,
¹⁸ who says to a king, 'You scoundrel!'
and to princes, 'You wicked men!';
¹⁹ who shows no partiality to nobles,
nor regards the rich more than the poor,
for they are all the work of his hands?

²⁰ In a moment they die;
at midnight the people are shaken and
pass away,
and the mighty are taken away by no
human hand.

²¹ "For his eyes are upon the ways of
mortals,
and he sees all their steps.
²² There is no gloom or deep darkness
where evildoers may hide themselves.
²³ For he has not appointed a timeᵈ for
anyone
to go before God in judgment.
²⁴ He shatters the mighty without
investigation,
and sets others in their place.
²⁵ Thus, knowing their works,
he overturns them in the night, and
they are crushed.
²⁶ He strikes them for their wickedness
while others look on,
²⁷ because they turned aside from
following him,
and had no regard for any of his ways,
²⁸ so that they caused the cry of the poor to
come to him,
and he heard the cry of the afflicted—
²⁹ When he is quiet, who can condemn?
When he hides his face, who can behold
him,
whether it be a nation or an
individual?—

ᵃ Traditional rendering of Heb *Shaddai*
ᵇ Heb lacks *on him*
ᶜ Heb *his heart his spirit*
ᵈ Cn: Heb *yet*

complaints against God. **7:** *Scoffing* is blasphemy against God, which is how Elihu regards Job's criticism of God. **8:** *Goes in company with evildoers*, metaphorically, by questioning the divine justice, Job puts himself in bad company. **9:** According to Job in 21.15, it is the wicked who say that there is no profit in religion, but Elihu asserts that Job's words, such as those in 9.22 and 21.7, amount to the same thing. Yet if Job were to say that religion is indeed profitable, he would deny that his piety is disinterested and he would accept the calumny of the Satan! **10–15:** God acts justly, for the righteous remain alive; if he did not, they might well be dead, for he has only to *gather to himself his breath* and mortals die. **16–37:** Turning to Job, Elihu makes the same argument: God, as the universal ruler, cannot act wrongly, and Job's suggestion that he can is itself a wickedness. **21:** Although Elihu speaks of *mortals* generally, his concern is purely with rulers. **24–28:** Elihu does not refer to all rulers, only to those who have behaved unjustly.

30 so that the godless should not reign,
   or those who ensnare the people.

31 "For has anyone said to God,
   'I have endured punishment; I will not
      offend any more;
32 teach me what I do not see;
   if I have done iniquity, I will do it no
      more'?
33 Will he then pay back to suit you,
   because you reject it?
For you must choose, and not I;
   therefore declare what you know.ᵃ
34 Those who have sense will say to me,
   and the wise who hear me will say,
35 'Job speaks without knowledge,
   his words are without insight.'
36 Would that Job were tried to the limit,
   because his answers are those of the
      wicked.
37 For he adds rebellion to his sin;
   he claps his hands among us,
   and multiplies his words against God."

35 Elihu continued and said:
   2 "Do you think this to be just?
You say, 'I am in the right before God.'
3 If you ask, 'What advantage have I?
   How am I better off than if I had sinned?'
4 I will answer you
   and your friends with you.
5 Look at the heavens and see;
   observe the clouds, which are higher
      than you.
6 If you have sinned, what do you
      accomplish against him?
   And if your transgressions are
      multiplied, what do you do to him?
7 If you are righteous, what do you give to
      him;
   or what does he receive from your
      hand?

8 Your wickedness affects others like you,
   and your righteousness, other human
      beings.

9 "Because of the multitude of oppressions
      people cry out;
   they call for help because of the arm of
      the mighty.
10 But no one says, 'Where is God my
      Maker,
   who gives strength in the night,
11 who teaches us more than the animals of
      the earth,
   and makes us wiser than the birds of
      the air?'
12 There they cry out, but he does not
      answer,
   because of the pride of evildoers.
13 Surely God does not hear an empty cry,
   nor does the Almightyᵇ regard it.
14 How much less when you say that you do
      not see him,
   that the case is before him, and you are
      waiting for him!
15 And now, because his anger does not
      punish,
   and he does not greatly heed
      transgression,ᶜ
16 Job opens his mouth in empty talk,
   he multiplies words without
      knowledge."

36 Elihu continued and said:
   2 "Bear with me a little, and I will show
      you,

ᵃ Meaning of Heb of verses 29-33 uncertain
ᵇ Traditional rendering of Heb *Shaddai*
ᶜ Theodotion Symmachus Compare Vg: Meaning of
   Heb uncertain

35.1–16: Elihu's third speech. 2–8: Elihu takes up Job's complaints, that he is no better off than if he had sinned (v. 3b), and that there is no benefit in righteousness (v. 3a). Elihu responds that piety should be assessed in terms of benefit, and that justice is not a matter of one's own rights and deserts, but of others benefiting from one's virtue. 6: Reminiscent of Job in 7.20; but whereas Job meant that any sin he may have done is hardly worth retribution since he himself will soon be dead, Elihu means that the important thing is the effect of sin or righteousness upon humans rather than upon God. 9–16: The absence of a response from God does not mean that God cares nothing about humans, as Job claimed (24.12). God responds to the cries of the oppressed only if they deserve justice, for being oppressed is no proof of innocence, and crying out in pain is not the same as crying to God for deliverance.

for I have yet something to say on God's behalf.

³ I will bring my knowledge from far away,
and ascribe righteousness to my Maker.
⁴ For truly my words are not false;
one who is perfect in knowledge is with you.

⁵ "Surely God is mighty and does not despise any;
he is mighty in strength of understanding.
⁶ He does not keep the wicked alive,
but gives the afflicted their right.
⁷ He does not withdraw his eyes from the righteous,
but with kings on the throne
he sets them forever, and they are exalted.
⁸ And if they are bound in fetters
and caught in the cords of affliction,
⁹ then he declares to them their work
and their transgressions, that they are behaving arrogantly.
¹⁰ He opens their ears to instruction,
and commands that they return from iniquity.
¹¹ If they listen, and serve him,
they complete their days in prosperity,
and their years in pleasantness.
¹² But if they do not listen, they shall perish by the sword,
and die without knowledge.

¹³ "The godless in heart cherish anger;
they do not cry for help when he binds them.
¹⁴ They die in their youth,
and their life ends in shame.ᵃ
¹⁵ He delivers the afflicted by their affliction,
and opens their ear by adversity.

¹⁶ He also allured you out of distress
into a broad place where there was no constraint,
and what was set on your table was full of fatness.

¹⁷ "But you are obsessed with the case of the wicked;
judgment and justice seize you.
¹⁸ Beware that wrath does not entice you into scoffing,
and do not let the greatness of the ransom turn you aside.
¹⁹ Will your cry avail to keep you from distress,
or will all the force of your strength?
²⁰ Do not long for the night,
when peoples are cut off in their place.
²¹ Beware! Do not turn to iniquity;
because of that you have been tried by affliction.
²² See, God is exalted in his power;
who is a teacher like him?
²³ Who has prescribed for him his way,
or who can say, 'You have done wrong'?

²⁴ "Remember to extol his work,
of which mortals have sung.
²⁵ All people have looked on it;
everyone watches it from far away.
²⁶ Surely God is great, and we do not know him;
the number of his years is unsearchable.
²⁷ For he draws up the drops of water;
he distillsᵇ his mist in rain,
²⁸ which the skies pour down
and drop upon mortals abundantly.
²⁹ Can anyone understand the spreading of the clouds,

ᵃ Heb *ends among the temple prostitutes*
ᵇ Cn: Heb *they distill*

36.1–37.24: Elihu's fourth speech. It has two parts: 36.2–25, continuing the theme of the justice of God, and 36.26–37.24, an instruction on the theme of the God of nature, its subtext being that God's energies in creation and world governance are vehicles of his righteous judgments. 36.5–15: The topic is how God treats those righteous people who fall into sin (vv. 7–12,15) in comparison with how he treats the truly wicked (vv. 6,14). By allowing that the righteous are sometimes sinful, Elihu transcends the traditional dogma that drew a firm line between righteous and wicked. 16–25: Now Elihu offers his personal advice to Job. Finding himself subject to God's punishment, what he should do is not to complain about the injustice of it, but to discover in it God's instruction. 36.26–37.24: Suffering is education, says Elihu, and God is the great Teacher. He has built into the order of creation lessons for the improvement of humans. Rain, for example, is a means of exhibiting divine

the thunderings of his pavilion?
30 See, he scatters his lightning around him
and covers the roots of the sea.
31 For by these he governs peoples;
he gives food in abundance.
32 He covers his hands with the lightning,
and commands it to strike the mark.
33 Its crashing[a] tells about him;
he is jealous[a] with anger against
iniquity.

37
"At this also my heart trembles,
and leaps out of its place.
2 Listen, listen to the thunder of his voice
and the rumbling that comes from his
mouth.
3 Under the whole heaven he lets it loose,
and his lightning to the corners of the
earth.
4 After it his voice roars;
he thunders with his majestic voice
and he does not restrain the lightnings[b]
when his voice is heard.
5 God thunders wondrously with his voice;
he does great things that we cannot
comprehend.
6 For to the snow he says, 'Fall on the
earth';
and the shower of rain, his heavy
shower of rain,
7 serves as a sign on everyone's hand,
so that all whom he has made may
know it.[c]
8 Then the animals go into their lairs
and remain in their dens.
9 From its chamber comes the whirlwind,
and cold from the scattering winds.
10 By the breath of God ice is given,
and the broad waters are frozen fast.
11 He loads the thick cloud with moisture;
the clouds scatter his lightning.

12 They turn round and round by his
guidance,
to accomplish all that he commands
them
on the face of the habitable world.
13 Whether for correction, or for his land,
or for love, he causes it to happen.

14 "Hear this, O Job;
stop and consider the wondrous works
of God.
15 Do you know how God lays his command
upon them,
and causes the lightning of his cloud to
shine?
16 Do you know the balancings of the
clouds,
the wondrous works of the one whose
knowledge is perfect,
17 you whose garments are hot
when the earth is still because of the
south wind?
18 Can you, like him, spread out the skies,
hard as a molten mirror?
19 Teach us what we shall say to him;
we cannot draw up our case because of
darkness.
20 Should he be told that I want to speak?
Did anyone ever wish to be swallowed
up?
21 Now, no one can look on the light
when it is bright in the skies,
when the wind has passed and cleared
them.
22 Out of the north comes golden splendor;
around God is awesome majesty.

a   Meaning of Heb uncertain
b   Heb *them*
c   Meaning of Heb of verse 7 uncertain

munificence toward humans. **29**: *Pavilion,* God's heavenly dwelling (cf. 2 Sam 22.12). **30**: *Covers the roots of the sea,* the verb should rather mean "uncovers." **32**: It is here bolt lightning, as distinct from sheet lightning in v. 30. **36.33–37.5**: Thunder and lightning are further examples of how God teaches humans. **37.6–8**: The snows and rains of winter are both mysterious (v. 5b) and a further communication of the divine, "so that all may recognize that he is at work" (as v. 7b should probably be translated). **9–13**: Other meteorological phenomena. **9**: The winds are stored in heavenly chambers. *Whirlwind,* or rather "tempest" (a whirlwind is properly a tornado). **13**: Rain can have various significances: it may be a punishment (a *correction*), a sign of God's *love* (or rather, "loyalty"), or a token of his care for his world (as when it falls on uninhabited land; cf. 38.26). In any case, it tells humans something about God's workings. **14–24**: Some of the most obscure verses in the whole book. **22**: The *north* sometimes means the heavens (as in 26.7), and the *golden splendor* may be simply the sun. For the

23 The Almighty[a]—we cannot find him;
    he is great in power and justice,
    and abundant righteousness he will not
        violate.
24 Therefore mortals fear him;
    he does not regard any who are wise in
        their own conceit."

38

Then the LORD answered Job out of the whirlwind:

2 "Who is this that darkens counsel by
    words without knowledge?
3 Gird up your loins like a man,
    I will question you, and you shall
        declare to me.

4 "Where were you when I laid the
    foundation of the earth?
    Tell me, if you have understanding.
5 Who determined its measurements—
    surely you know!
    Or who stretched the line upon it?
6 On what were its bases sunk,
    or who laid its cornerstone
7 when the morning stars sang together
    and all the heavenly beings[b] shouted
        for joy?

8 "Or who shut in the sea with doors
    when it burst out from the womb?—
9 when I made the clouds its garment,
    and thick darkness its swaddling band,

10 and prescribed bounds for it,
    and set bars and doors,
11 and said, 'Thus far shall you come, and
    no farther,
    and here shall your proud waves be
        stopped'?

12 "Have you commanded the morning
    since your days began,
    and caused the dawn to know its place,
13 so that it might take hold of the skirts of
    the earth,
    and the wicked be shaken out of it?
14 It is changed like clay under the seal,
    and it is dyed[c] like a garment.
15 Light is withheld from the wicked,
    and their uplifted arm is broken.

16 "Have you entered into the springs of
    the sea,
    or walked in the recesses of the deep?
17 Have the gates of death been revealed to
    you,
    or have you seen the gates of deep
        darkness?
18 Have you comprehended the expanse of
    the earth?
    Declare, if you know all this.

---

a   Traditional rendering of Heb *Shaddai*
b   Heb *sons of God*
c   Cn: Heb *and they stand forth*

---

possibility that the speeches of Elihu originally ended with the poem about wisdom, see 32.1–37.24n; 28.1–28n.

38.1–42.6: The LORD's speeches and Job's responses.

38.1–40.2: The LORD's first speech. Between the proem in 38.2–3 and the peroration in 40.1–2, the speech is divided into two almost equal halves: 38.4–38 concerning the physical universe, and 38.39–39.30 concerning the world of animals. The divine speeches are notable for their silence over Job's complaint of injustice, as if God means to say that administering justice is not part of his cosmic plan. **38.1:** *Whirlwind*, better "storm," see 37.9. **2:** *Counsel*, or rather "the plan," the set of divine principles according to which the creation is run. Job *darkens*, or "obscures," them by focusing on his quest for justice, which is not included in the divine plan. **3:** *Gird up your loins like a man*, as a warrior does in preparation for combat. Job had better understand that summoning God to trial will not lead to a calm, rational, orderly legal process. **4–38:** In ten strophes, the LORD sketches his design, or plan, for the universe. **4–7:** Creation is conceived as the erection of a building. For the creator as architect, see Prov 8.27–30. The earth was built on foundations (vv. 4–6; see Pss 78.69; 102.25; 104.5; Isa 48.13), and strict limits were set for the primeval waters of chaos (vv. 8–11; 26.10; Pss 104.9; 148.6). **5:** *The line*, the measuring line for its foundations. **6:** *Cornerstone* should properly be "capstone," the last and topmost stone laid. Sinking the bases and laying the capstone mark the beginning and end of the work. **7:** The *stars* are regarded as *heavenly beings*. **8–11:** The separation of sea and land at creation. There is allusion to the ancient myth of a primordial divine struggle with the sea (cf. 7.12; 9.13), although the imagery uncharacteristically treats the sea as a newborn baby. **12–15:** The daily renewal of creation as each day is created afresh. As in 24.13–17, it is assumed that the wicked prefer the cover of darkness for their activities. **16–18:** The extent of the world, together with

¹⁹ "Where is the way to the dwelling of
   light,
   and where is the place of darkness,
²⁰ that you may take it to its territory
   and that you may discern the paths to
      its home?
²¹ Surely you know, for you were born then,
   and the number of your days is great!

²² "Have you entered the storehouses of
   the snow,
   or have you seen the storehouses of the
      hail,
²³ which I have reserved for the time of
   trouble,
   for the day of battle and war?
²⁴ What is the way to the place where the
   light is distributed,
   or where the east wind is scattered
      upon the earth?

²⁵ "Who has cut a channel for the torrents
   of rain,
   and a way for the thunderbolt,
²⁶ to bring rain on a land where no one
   lives,
   on the desert, which is empty of human
      life,
²⁷ to satisfy the waste and desolate land,
   and to make the ground put forth grass?

²⁸ "Has the rain a father,
   or who has begotten the drops of dew?
²⁹ From whose womb did the ice come
   forth,
   and who has given birth to the
      hoarfrost of heaven?

³⁰ The waters become hard like stone,
   and the face of the deep is frozen.

³¹ "Can you bind the chains of the
   Pleiades,
   or loose the cords of Orion?
³² Can you lead forth the Mazzaroth in
   their season,
   or can you guide the Bear with its
      children?
³³ Do you know the ordinances of the
   heavens?
   Can you establish their rule on the
      earth?

³⁴ "Can you lift up your voice to the
   clouds,
   so that a flood of waters may cover you?
³⁵ Can you send forth lightnings, so that
   they may go
   and say to you, 'Here we are'?
³⁶ Who has put wisdom in the inward
   parts,[a]
   or given understanding to the mind?[a]
³⁷ Who has the wisdom to number the
   clouds?
   Or who can tilt the waterskins of the
      heavens,
³⁸ when the dust runs into a mass
   and the clods cling together?

³⁹ "Can you hunt the prey for the lion,
   or satisfy the appetite of the young
      lions,

[a] Meaning of Heb uncertain

the underworld, *death* being regarded as a city with *gates*. **19–21:** *Light* and *darkness* are thought of as dwelling in the same home, using it each day in turns. **22–24:** *Snow, hail*, and heat are kept in heavenly storehouses. **24:** It is probably "heat," rather than *light* that is distributed over the earth, often by the hot, violent *east wind* or sirocco. **25–27:** Rainstorms travel via an unseen channel through the air from the clouds to the earth. **28–30:** *Rain, dew, ice, hoarfrost* are more placid forms of moisture than torrents (v. 25). **28:** *Has the rain a father?* No, it has no mythological ancestry, it is not supernatural. **29:** *Ice* is properly "rime" formed when water droplets in fog freeze, as on trees, as distinct from *hoarfrost* formed when water vapor settles, as on the ground. **31–33:** The four constellations, the *Pleiades, Orion, Mazzaroth* (perhaps the Hyades), and the *Bear* (or better, Aldebaran), were all regarded as bringers of rain; see 9.9n. *Binding* and *loosing* would be interfering with their rain-making. **34–38:** The clouds and lightning do not fall of their own accord, but in obedience to their master's voice. **36:** The verse should be translated: "Who gave the ibis its wisdom or endowed the rooster with its intelligence?" Both birds were regarded as foretellers of rain, which is depicted as stored in great jars (v. 37; not *waterskins*) in the clouds. **38.39–39.30:** In seven strophes, nine animals are depicted. They are all undomesticated animals, which live independently of humans. **38.39–41:** The lion and the raven—one huge, the other small—both need

⁴⁰ when they crouch in their dens,
  or lie in wait in their covert?
⁴¹ Who provides for the raven its prey,
  when its young ones cry to God,
  and wander about for lack of food?

39 "Do you know when the mountain
  goats give birth?
  Do you observe the calving of the deer?
² Can you number the months that they
  fulfill,
  and do you know the time when they
  give birth,
³ when they crouch to give birth to their
  offspring,
  and are delivered of their young?
⁴ Their young ones become strong, they
  grow up in the open;
  they go forth, and do not return to
  them.

⁵ "Who has let the wild ass go free?
  Who has loosed the bonds of the swift
  ass,
⁶ to which I have given the steppe for its
  home,
  the salt land for its dwelling place?
⁷ It scorns the tumult of the city;
  it does not hear the shouts of the driver.
⁸ It ranges the mountains as its pasture,
  and it searches after every green thing.

⁹ "Is the wild ox willing to serve you?
  Will it spend the night at your crib?
¹⁰ Can you tie it in the furrow with ropes,
  or will it harrow the valleys after you?
¹¹ Will you depend on it because its
  strength is great,
  and will you hand over your labor to it?
¹² Do you have faith in it that it will return,
  and bring your grain to your threshing
  floor?ᵃ

¹³ "The ostrich's wings flap wildly,
  though its pinions lack plumage.ᵇ

¹⁴ For it leaves its eggs to the earth,
  and lets them be warmed on the
  ground,
¹⁵ forgetting that a foot may crush them,
  and that a wild animal may trample
  them.
¹⁶ It deals cruelly with its young, as if they
  were not its own;
  though its labor should be in vain, yet it
  has no fear;
¹⁷ because God has made it forget wisdom,
  and given it no share in understanding.
¹⁸ When it spreads its plumes aloft,ᵇ
  it laughs at the horse and its rider.

¹⁹ "Do you give the horse its might?
  Do you clothe its neck with mane?
²⁰ Do you make it leap like the locust?
  Its majestic snorting is terrible.
²¹ It pawsᶜ violently, exults mightily;
  it goes out to meet the weapons.
²² It laughs at fear, and is not dismayed;
  it does not turn back from the sword.
²³ Upon it rattle the quiver,
  the flashing spear, and the javelin.
²⁴ With fierceness and rage it swallows the
  ground;
  it cannot stand still at the sound of the
  trumpet.
²⁵ When the trumpet sounds, it says 'Aha!'
  From a distance it smells the battle,
  the thunder of the captains, and the
  shouting.

²⁶ "Is it by your wisdom that the hawk
  soars,
  and spreads its wings toward the south?
²⁷ Is it at your command that the eagle
  mounts up

ᵃ Heb *your grain and your threshing floor*
ᵇ Meaning of Heb uncertain
ᶜ Gk Syr Vg: Heb *they dig*

to hunt to feed their young. **39.1–4:** *Mountain goats* or ibexes, unlike lions and ravens, are shy and elusive. **5–8:** The *wild ass* or onager was famous for its independence and freedom, in contrast to its domesticated cousin the ass. **9–12:** The *wild ox* or aurochs was a massive animal with long thick horns; it too is contrasted with its obedient and hard-working domesticated counterpart. **13–18:** The *ostrich* is a paradoxical creature: it is a bird that cannot fly, and while reputedly foolish, it is clever enough to escape its predators. **19–25:** The war *horse* is not exactly wild, but it has a will of its own and is not a servant of humans. **26–30:** The *hawk* and the *eagle* are

and makes its nest on high?

²⁸ It lives on the rock and makes its home
in the fastness of the rocky crag.

²⁹ From there it spies the prey;
its eyes see it from far away.

³⁰ Its young ones suck up blood;
and where the slain are, there it is."

40 And the LORD said to Job:
² "Shall a faultfinder contend with the
Almighty?ᵃ
Anyone who argues with God must
respond."

³ Then Job answered the LORD:

⁴ "See, I am of small account; what shall I
answer you?
I lay my hand on my mouth.

⁵ I have spoken once, and I will not answer;
twice, but will proceed no further."

⁶ Then the LORD answered Job out of the
whirlwind:

⁷ "Gird up your loins like a man;
I will question you, and you declare to
me.

⁸ Will you even put me in the wrong?
Will you condemn me that you may be
justified?

⁹ Have you an arm like God,
and can you thunder with a voice like
his?

¹⁰ "Deck yourself with majesty and dignity;
clothe yourself with glory and splendor.

¹¹ Pour out the overflowings of your anger,
and look on all who are proud, and
abase them.

¹² Look on all who are proud, and bring
them low;
tread down the wicked where they
stand.

¹³ Hide them all in the dust together;
bind their faces in the world below.ᵇ

¹⁴ Then I will also acknowledge to you
that your own right hand can give you
victory.

¹⁵ "Look at Behemoth,
which I made just as I made you;
it eats grass like an ox.

¹⁶ Its strength is in its loins,
and its power in the muscles of its belly.

¹⁷ It makes its tail stiff like a cedar;
the sinews of its thighs are knit
together.

¹⁸ Its bones are tubes of bronze,
its limbs like bars of iron.

¹⁹ "It is the first of the great acts of God—
only its Maker can approach it with the
sword.

²⁰ For the mountains yield food for it
where all the wild animals play.

ᵃ Traditional rendering of Heb *Shaddai*
ᵇ Heb *the hidden place*

birds of prey. **26:** The *wisdom* of the hawk is its instinct for its seasonal migration. **27:** *Eagle*, probably vulture. **30:** Vultures feed on the dead *slain* in battle. **40.1–2:** Despite the didactic language of the divine speech, this challenge shows that the ruling metaphor is still that of the lawsuit, in which Job must now either concede the case or offer new arguments.

40.3–5: Job's first response. Strikingly, Job does not capitulate; he says only that he will not repeat what he has already said. He defers his response until he speaks again in 42.2–6.

40.6–41.34: The LORD's second speech. 40.7–14: God's question *Will you even put me in the wrong?* (v. 8) means that he has correctly heard Job's speeches as not merely a demand for personal vindication but as a far-reaching critique of God's government of the world and as a demand for an alternative world order. God is obviously not going to change his world order, so his ironic response is: let Job re-order the world to his own taste by crushing the wicked (vv. 11–13); then he will have nothing to complain about. **15–24:** *Behemoth* is an ambiguous figure. It is dangerous, and yet to try capturing it is so absurd that it is beyond being a danger. It is powerful but actually does little except sleep, eat, and procreate. Unlike the animals of the first divine speech, it is a beast without qualities. Yet it is God's showpiece (v. 19a). Is it because it so well represents God's freedom to refuse rules and rationality and principles of utility? *Behemoth* is literally the plural of the common Heb term for "animal." Scholarly opinion is divided as to whether it is a primeval monster (v. 19) or is to be identified with

21 Under the lotus plants it lies,
  in the covert of the reeds and in the
      marsh.
22 The lotus trees cover it for shade;
  the willows of the wadi surround it.
23 Even if the river is turbulent, it is not
      frightened;
  it is confident though Jordan rushes
      against its mouth.
24 Can one take it with hooks[a]
  or pierce its nose with a snare?

41 [b] "Can you draw out Leviathan[c] with a
      fishhook,
  or press down its tongue with a cord?
2 Can you put a rope in its nose,
  or pierce its jaw with a hook?
3 Will it make many supplications to you?
  Will it speak soft words to you?
4 Will it make a covenant with you
  to be taken as your servant forever?
5 Will you play with it as with a bird,
  or will you put it on leash for your girls?
6 Will traders bargain over it?
  Will they divide it up among the
      merchants?
7 Can you fill its skin with harpoons,
  or its head with fishing spears?
8 Lay hands on it;
  think of the battle; you will not do it
      again!
9 [d] Any hope of capturing it[e] will be
      disappointed;
  were not even the gods[f] overwhelmed
      at the sight of it?
10 No one is so fierce as to dare to stir it up.
  Who can stand before it?[g]
11 Who can confront it[g] and be safe?[h]
  —under the whole heaven, who?[i]

12 "I will not keep silence concerning its
      limbs,
  or its mighty strength, or its splendid
      frame.
13 Who can strip off its outer garment?
  Who can penetrate its double coat of
      mail?[j]

14 Who can open the doors of its face?
  There is terror all around its teeth.
15 Its back[k] is made of shields in rows,
  shut up closely as with a seal.
16 One is so near to another
  that no air can come between them.
17 They are joined one to another;
  they clasp each other and cannot be
      separated.
18 Its sneezes flash forth light,
  and its eyes are like the eyelids of the
      dawn.
19 From its mouth go flaming torches;
  sparks of fire leap out.
20 Out of its nostrils comes smoke,
  as from a boiling pot and burning
      rushes.
21 Its breath kindles coals,
  and a flame comes out of its mouth.
22 In its neck abides strength,
  and terror dances before it.
23 The folds of its flesh cling together;
  it is firmly cast and immovable.
24 Its heart is as hard as stone,
  as hard as the lower millstone.
25 When it raises itself up the gods are
      afraid;
  at the crashing they are beside
      themselves.
26 Though the sword reaches it, it does not
      avail,
  nor does the spear, the dart, or the
      javelin.

a Cn: Heb *in his eyes*
b Ch 40.25 in Heb
c Or *the crocodile*
d Ch 41.1 in Heb
e Heb *of it*
f Cn Compare Symmachus Syr: Heb *one is*
g Heb *me*
h Gk: Heb *that I shall repay*
i Heb *to me*
j Gk: Heb *bridle*
k Cn Compare Gk Vg: Heb *pride*

the hippopotamus. It is otherwise not mentioned in the Hebrew Bible; see 2 Esd 6.49,51. **41.1–34:** The depiction of *Leviathan* treats, first, the impossibility of capturing it (vv. 1–11), second, its physical characteristics (vv. 12–24), and third, the creature in motion (vv. 25–32). Unlike Behemoth, who was indolent and unthreatening, Leviathan is nothing but violence and turmoil. Leviathan is described in terms that evoke the crocodile; some

²⁷ It counts iron as straw,
  and bronze as rotten wood.
²⁸ The arrow cannot make it flee;
  slingstones, for it, are turned to chaff.
²⁹ Clubs are counted as chaff;
  it laughs at the rattle of javelins.
³⁰ Its underparts are like sharp potsherds;
  it spreads itself like a threshing sledge
    on the mire.
³¹ It makes the deep boil like a pot;
  it makes the sea like a pot of ointment.
³² It leaves a shining wake behind it;
  one would think the deep to be white-
    haired.
³³ On earth it has no equal,
  a creature without fear.
³⁴ It surveys everything that is lofty;
  it is king over all that are proud."

42 Then Job answered the LORD:
² "I know that you can do all things,
  and that no purpose of yours can be
    thwarted.
³ 'Who is this that hides counsel without
    knowledge?'
Therefore I have uttered what I did not
    understand,
  things too wonderful for me, which I
    did not know.

⁴ 'Hear, and I will speak;
  I will question you, and you declare to
    me.'
⁵ I had heard of you by the hearing of the
    ear,
  but now my eye sees you;
⁶ therefore I despise myself,
  and repent in dust and ashes."

⁷ After the LORD had spoken these words to Job, the LORD said to Eliphaz the Temanite: "My wrath is kindled against you and against your two friends; for you have not spoken of me what is right, as my servant Job has. ⁸ Now therefore take seven bulls and seven rams, and go to my servant Job, and offer up for yourselves a burnt offering; and my servant Job shall pray for you, for I will accept his prayer not to deal with you according to your folly; for you have not spoken of me what is right, as my servant Job has done." ⁹ So Eliphaz the Temanite and Bildad the Shuhite and Zophar the Naamathite went and did what the LORD had told them; and the LORD accepted Job's prayer.

¹⁰ And the LORD restored the fortunes of Job when he had prayed for his friends; and the LORD gave Job twice as much as he had before. ¹¹ Then there came to him all his

---

scholars understand it as the mythical chaos monster. (See 3.8n.) **34:** As *king* of beasts, Leviathan is a source of pleasure and pride for its maker.

42.1–6: Job's second response. Job abandons his lawsuit against God, but his charges have not been answered. He says: (1) *I know that you can do all things* (v. 2). He has always known that, but he means that he now recognizes that for God questions of justice are collapsed into the issue of his power. Job can only ever confront God's power, a sphere where he will inevitably be a loser. (2) *I have uttered . . . things too wonderful for me* (v. 3), Job means that he now realizes that cosmic justice is a marvel beyond human comprehension, like the structure of the universe. Justice is not a principle or value to which God is subject. (3) Now that he has *heard* God for himself and his *eye sees* him (a metaphor for his experience of God), he "submits" and "accepts consolation." *I despise myself*, no object of the verb is expressed, and the verb is probably not Heb "ma'as," "despise," but "masas," "melt, be discouraged," as in Josh 2.11 (REB rightly translates "I yield"). *Repent*, Job has never acknowledged any sin, so he cannot be repenting; the verb means rather "be comforted." Job means he will now end his period of mourning (in *dust and ashes*) and resume his normal life.

42.7–17: Epilogue. The naïve narrative of the folktale world of the prologue resumes, as Job is vindicated in the eyes of his friends (vv. 7–9) and his extended family (vv. 10–17). **7:** Surprisingly, the LORD is angry with the friends and their *folly* (v. 8), but says Job has *spoken of me what is right*. He must be referring to Job's conclusion that God does not execute justice in the realm of humans, which the friends always denied but which God himself has effectively admitted in his speeches. **10–17:** Job's lost possessions are restored to him twice over— perhaps an acknowledgment that what he had lost at the beginning of the story had actually been stolen from him by God (cf. Ex 22.4, where a thief must pay double restitution). He acquires a new family to replace his dead children, and he is feted by his family and friends. The pious man Job once again becomes the wealthiest man in all the east; so is the doctrine of retribution—which the book of Job has seemed so concerned to refute—here

brothers and sisters and all who had known him before, and they ate bread with him in his house; they showed him sympathy and comforted him for all the evil that the Lord had brought upon him; and each of them gave him a piece of money[a] and a gold ring. [12] The Lord blessed the latter days of Job more than his beginning; and he had fourteen thousand sheep, six thousand camels, a thousand yoke of oxen, and a thousand donkeys. [13] He also had seven sons and three daughters. [14] He named the first Jemimah, the second Keziah, and the third Keren-happuch. [15] In all the land there were no women so beautiful as Job's daughters; and their father gave them an inheritance along with their brothers. [16] After this Job lived one hundred and forty years, and saw his children, and his children's children, four generations. [17] And Job died, old and full of days.

[a] Heb *a qesitah*

affirmed? 11: *Bread* means "food." The *piece of money* is not a coin but a piece of silver of guaranteed weight. 14: *Jemimah* probably means "turtledove," *Keziah* "cassia" or cinnamon, *Keren-happuch* "antinomy," a black eye-cosmetic, the three names invoking the three senses of hearing, taste, and sight. 15: Along with his sons, Job's daughters are given an inheritance, an unusual practice.

PSALMS

NAME, LOCATION IN CANON, AND NUMBERING

The word "Psalms" derives from the Greek name of the book, *Psalmoi*, which means songs played on a stringed instrument. This title reflects the musical character of the Psalms as hymns that were sung, accompanied by strings. The book's name in Hebrew is *Tehillim*, "praises," which reflects the religious character of the psalms.

In Jewish Bibles today the book of Psalms is the first book of the Writings, the third part of the canon. In Christian Bibles it is one of the poetical books, coming after the book of Job. In older manuscripts these books often occur in a slightly different order.

There have been two systems of numbering the psalms, one dependent on the Hebrew text and the other on the Greek Septuagint (LXX). The LXX counted Pss 9–10 and 114–115 as single poems and divided Pss 116 and 148 into two poems, resulting in a discrepancy of one from the Hebrew numbering of Pss 8–147; in the case of Pss 9–10 the LXX is clearly correct: they form a single acrostic (alphabetic) psalm. The Latin Vulgate and older Roman Catholic translations follow the Septuagint numbering; all modern translations follow the Hebrew numbering. There are also two systems of numbering psalm verses. The most common system, used by the NRSV and several other translations, assigns no verse number to the superscription or title, so that "v. 1" is always the first line of the psalm poem. The other system follows printed Hebrew Bibles in assigning a verse number to the superscription and thus often is one verse behind the NRSV verse number.

DATE AND AUTHORSHIP

The book of Psalms is an anthology, or more properly an anthology of anthologies, comprising several collections of hymns that were composed at various times and places in ancient Israel, mostly in the first half of the first millennium BCE. Although many are attributed to King David, and some to other individuals, scholars agree that few if any were actually written by them. Rather, their authors, like those of many of the books of the Hebrew Bible, are anonymous.

STRUCTURE AND SUPERSCRIPTIONS

The book of Psalms is divided into five books, a deliberate parallel to the five books of the Torah or Pentateuch. Each of these five parts—Psalms 1–41; 42–72; 73–89; 90–106; 107–150—ends with a doxology or "word of praise." Psalm 1 introduces this collection by explicitly mentioning "the law (Heb *torah*) of the Lord." Psalm 150 serves as a megadoxology, concluding both the fifth part and the book of Psalms as a whole. In it "everything that breathes" praises the Lord in heaven and on earth, using a wide variety of musical instruments.

Both within the five parts, and sometimes ignoring that division, which occurred relatively late in the book's formation, we find evidence of other collections. A note at the end of Ps 72 states "The prayers of David son of Jesse are ended," but there follows another eighteen psalms attributed to David. Psalms 42–49; 84; 85; 87; and 88 are attributed to "the Korahites," members of a priestly family whose ancestor was Korah. Psalms 50 and 73–83 are attributed to Asaph, one of Korah's sons, and Ps 88 to Heman, another of his sons. Psalms 93–99, clustered together, share the theme of divine kingship. Each of Pss 120–134 is called "A Song of Ascents," apparently another collection, perhaps sung by pilgrims as they made their way up to Jerusalem or into the Temple precincts. There are repetitions in the psalms as well (e.g., Ps 14 = Ps 53), further showing that the book in its final form is an anthology of collections, some of which contained the same texts.

Scholars have also identified another collection. Psalms 43–83 are called the "Elohistic Psalter," because in these psalms there is a preference for the divine name "Elohim" ("God") over "Yahweh" ("the Lord"), which is much more frequent in the other psalms.

Many of the psalms have superscriptions—titles or prefatory verses that were added over the centuries. They are attempts to align the event to a biblical character, especially to David, or more often to inform the reader about the origin of the psalm or its melodies. Unfortunately, few of the technical terms can be identified with any certainty. The phrase "To the leader" occurs fifty-five times, usually with the ascription of the psalm

"Of David." Some terms may be the names of melodies, for example, "Do not Destroy" (Pss 57–59; 75), and "The Deer of the Dawn" (Ps 22). Other terms that occur are "Prayer" (Heb *tepillah*), "Maskil" ("instructive poem"?), "Psalm" (Heb *mizmor*), "Miktam," and "Song" (*shir*). Many of these and other terms in the superscriptions are obscure or uncertain, as is the term "Selah," a Hebrew word occurring seventy-one times in the body of thirty-nine psalms, perhaps to mark stanza divisions.

GENRES

More than eighty psalms fall into one of three main types or genres: hymn, petition (used in these notes for the customary "lament," that being only one component of the petition), and thanksgiving.

- *Hymn* (approximately twenty-eight psalms). The structure is simple: a call to worship, often with the subject named (e.g., "Praise the LORD, all you nations," Ps 117.1), sometimes with musical instruments mentioned (e.g., "Praise him with trumpet sound," Ps 150.3). The invitatory is often repeated in the final verse. The body of the poem is normally introduced by the preposition "for, because," giving the basis for the praise. This is typically something God has done, often the act by which Israel came into being as a people: the Exodus from Egypt and entry into Canaan. References to this one event can be in historical terms with human characters prominent (e.g., Ps 105) or in mythical terms with God portrayed as acting directly rather than through human agency (e.g., Ps 114).
- *Individual petition.* Petitionary psalms begin with an unadorned cry to the LORD (e.g., "Help, O LORD!" Ps 12.1). This is followed by a complaint, namely a description of a difficulty facing the psalmist such as sickness, unfair legal accusation, treachery of former friends, or ostracism from the community as a consequence of sin. Usually there is a statement of trust, uttered despite the trouble, which is often described hyperbolically (e.g., "I am not afraid of ten thousands of people," Ps 3:6). The worshiper prays for rescue and sometimes also for the downfall of the enemy. Some contain confessions of guilt, while others suggest that the psalmist is persecuted for unclear or unfair reasons. Each petition is a mini-drama with three actors: the psalmist, the enemies ("the wicked"), and God. Psalmists portray themselves as loyal followers of the LORD who are victims of a serious affliction (often personified) from which their LORD, their patron, should rescue them.
- *Community petitions* complain that the LORD has abandoned the nation to its enemies. They often "remember" or recite before God the event that brought Israel into existence in the hope that God will reactivate that event. Can the LORD allow that founding event to be annulled by an enemy? The foundational event can be described in various ways, for example, transplanting a vine from Egypt (Ps 80.8,14) or defeating Sea and installing the people in their land (Ps 77).
- *Individual thanksgiving.* Such psalms presume that the LORD has answered the petition and now give thanks to the LORD. In a sense they are a continuation of the individual petition, for they report to the community how God has heard the petition, a biblical way of giving thanks.

About thirty psalms are grouped together by scholars according to their subject: royal songs, Zion songs, festival songs, and liturgies. According to style or tone, others are reckoned "songs of trust" (e.g., Pss 23; 91; 121) and "instructions" (e.g., Pss 37; 49; 73). Three psalms have "torah" (law or instruction) as their subject (Pss 1; 19; 119).

INTERPRETATION

For nearly three thousand years the 150 Psalms have been a lovingly memorized and well-thumbed prayer book, transposing to the daily life of Jews and Christians the meeting of Israel and its LORD. Many were familiar to the prophet Isaiah and to other biblical writers and editors. They were prayed from antiquity onward, by the founders of rabbinic Judaism, the early Christians, the fathers of the church, and the medieval synagogue and church. They are today a treasure shared by Jews and Christians. The psalms' power lies not only in being sacred scripture but in reflecting human feelings before God and expressing them directly, concretely, and skillfully.

As prayers and schools of prayer, the psalms guide modern believers in their relationship to God. Their range and honesty encourage people to come before God in their weakness and need as well as in their strength. Against a modern tendency to make a relationship to God completely private, most of the poems are communal; even individual petitions and songs of trust display a vivid sense of belonging to a people chosen and blessed by God. Against self-centered worshipers, the psalms are unhesitatingly theocentric—the world is made for and by God—though they balance it with the conviction that the LORD loves the people of Israel and is passionate about their flourishing. Psalms is the most cited Old Testament book in the New Testament. Christians praying the psalms have traditionally linked their prayer with that of Jesus, whose prayer becomes the prayer of the church.

Despite the psalms' splendor and humanity, people often find it difficult to pray them, for many of the psalms seem violent and vindictive. We must remember, however, that the chief issue for biblical worshipers is God's power to save. Can God save from life's dangers and grant protection and prosperity? Since the arena in which power was displayed most vividly is the battlefield, it is not surprising that the LORD was often portrayed as a warrior, ruling with power. The war imagery is, however, secondary to the main point: God is a just ruler and judge, who upholds the faithful and righteous and puts down the wicked and rebellious.

So-called vindictive psalms are especially difficult for those who simplistically view Christianity as uniformly gentle and concerned primarily with the individual soul. Yet these psalms are not interested in punishment for its own sake but in redressing a wrong in the present. The psalmists think concretely rather than abstractly: they view evil as embodied in unjust people and pray for their elimination, including their potential for living on in their children. The psalms generally entrust the carrying out of these wishes into God's hands in the conviction that only God can make the world truly just and good. Sufferers can, however, cry out to God to take action, and even use words that appear extreme. Those who trust in God (see Ps 37.5–6) can pray these psalms by leaving everything—execution and timetable—in God's hands.

Richard J. Clifford

BOOK I PSALMS 1–41

Psalm 1

¹ Happy are those
   who do not follow the advice of the
      wicked,
or take the path that sinners tread,
   or sit in the seat of scoffers;
² but their delight is in the law of the
   LORD,
   and on his law they meditate day and
      night.
³ They are like trees
   planted by streams of water,
which yield their fruit in its season,
   and their leaves do not wither.
In all that they do, they prosper.

⁴ The wicked are not so,
   but are like chaff that the wind drives
      away.
⁵ Therefore the wicked will not stand in
      the judgment,
   nor sinners in the congregation of the
      righteous;
⁶ for the LORD watches over the way of the
      righteous,
   but the way of the wicked will perish.

Psalm 2

¹ Why do the nations conspire,
   and the peoples plot in vain?
² The kings of the earth set themselves,
   and the rulers take counsel together,
      against the LORD and his anointed, saying,

Ps 1: The two ways. A torah or instructional psalm serving as an introduction to the Psalms. Pss 1 and 2 are introductory to the book of Psalms in that both celebrate the saving presence of God—Ps 1 for the individual and Ps 2 for the Davidic king—who offers protection from the wicked. Unlike the following psalms, these introductory works lack a Davidic superscription, suggesting their secondary, editorial function. Using the metaphor of the two ways, one leading to life and the other to death, Psalm 1 declares that reciting God's saving torah or teaching (in this case, including the psalms) keeps one on the path of life. There are themes of wisdom literature in this psalm. 1–3: Any individual who adheres to the torah (*law*) and rejects the views of the wicked is fortunate. 1: *Scoffers,* like *the wicked* and *sinners,* they contemptuously dismiss God's capacity to rule of the world. 2: *Meditate,* lit. "recite"; ancients usually read aloud. 3: *Trees,* possibly the trees in the Temple garden (Pss 52.8; 92.12–15) on Mount Zion, abundantly watered, symbolizing life (Pss 46.4; 65.9; Ezek 47.12). 4–6: In contrast to the well-watered and deeply rooted tree (a vertical image; cf. Jer 17.7–8) is the dry and wind-driven *chaff* (a horizontal image).

³ "Let us burst their bonds asunder,
and cast their cords from us."

⁴ He who sits in the heavens laughs;
the LORD has them in derision.
⁵ Then he will speak to them in his wrath,
and terrify them in his fury, saying,
⁶ "I have set my king on Zion, my holy hill."

⁷ I will tell of the decree of the LORD:
He said to me, "You are my son;
today I have begotten you.
⁸ Ask of me, and I will make the nations
your heritage,
and the ends of the earth your
possession.
⁹ You shall break them with a rod of iron,
and dash them in pieces like a potter's
vessel."

¹⁰ Now therefore, O kings, be wise;
be warned, O rulers of the earth.
¹¹ Serve the LORD with fear,
with trembling ¹² kiss his feet,ᵃ
or he will be angry, and you will perish in
the way;
for his wrath is quickly kindled.

Happy are all who take refuge in him.

Psalm 3

A Psalm of David, when he fled from his son Absalom.

¹ O LORD, how many are my foes!
Many are rising against me;
² many are saying to me,
"There is no help for youᵇ in
God."   *Selah*

³ But you, O LORD, are a shield around me,
my glory, and the one who lifts up my
head.
⁴ I cry aloud to the LORD,
and he answers me from his
holy hill.   *Selah*

⁵ I lie down and sleep;
I wake again, for the LORD sustains me.
⁶ I am not afraid of ten thousands of
people
who have set themselves against me all
around.

⁷ Rise up, O LORD!
Deliver me, O my God!

ᵃ Cn: Meaning of Heb of verses 11b and 12a is
uncertain
ᵇ Syr: Heb *him*

Ps 2: The Israelite king, instrument of God's rule. In this royal psalm, a court poet asks incredulously why the nations dare to threaten the Davidic king (vv. 1–3) when the Most High has stated that the king is his son and representative, hence in principle the most high among earthly kings. Like Ps 1, Ps 2 is introductory, and there are links between the two psalms, which are considered a single unit in some traditions: Ps 2.11 ends with "happy," echoing the first word in Ps 1; "the way [of the wicked] will perish" in 1.6 is echoed in 2.11, "you will perish in the way"; thematically, the divine instruction of the psalms protects from evil just as the divine promise protects the Israelite king and people from evil kings. **1–3:** In describing hostile nations, the speaker quotes their deluded speech as in Pss 48.4–8; 76; and Ezek 38–39. **2:** *Anointed* (Heb "mashiaḥ"), is always used in the Hebrew Bible of an actual ruler rather than of a future king. **4–9:** Dismissing the vain posturing of the kings, the Davidic king cites God's adoption formula (see 2 Sam 7.14; Ps 89.26–27) and promise of universal sovereignty. **6:** *Zion, my holy hill,* Jerusalem, where the royal palace and the Temple were part of the same architectural complex. **10–11:** In the light of the divine promise, the poet warns the kings to end their rebellion and submit. **12:** The exact meaning of the words translated *kiss his feet* is debated.

Ps 3: Threatened by many but trusting still. An individual petition. Threatened by "many enemies" (v. 1) who deny that the LORD can provide "help" and "deliverance" (vv. 2,8), the psalmist calmly affirms God's presence. Each of the three sections (vv. 1–3; 4–6; 7–8) begins with a prayer and ends with a statement of confidence. **Superscription:** The superscription, secondarily inserted here, situates the psalm with David fleeing from his rebellious son Absalom (2 Sam 15–18). **1:** The psalmist responds to the enemies by addressing God as "you" (v. 3) and using divine titles expressing power to save. **2:** *Selah* (also vv. 4,8) is a musical notation, used a total of seventy-eight times in the Bible, only in Psalms and Hab 3. Its exact meaning is uncertain, but it is typically used after a section of a psalm, perhaps indicating an interlude. **3:** *My glory,* one who restores one's glory or dignity. **4:** *His holy hill,* Mount Zion, where some psalmists believed God was most present (but contrast, e.g., Ps 2.4,

For you strike all my enemies on the
cheek;
you break the teeth of the wicked.

[8] Deliverance belongs to the LORD;
may your blessing be on your people!
Selah

Psalm 4

*To the leader: with stringed instruments. A Psalm of
David.*

[1] Answer me when I call, O God of my
right!
You gave me room when I was in
distress.
Be gracious to me, and hear my prayer.

[2] How long, you people, shall my honor
suffer shame?
How long will you love vain words, and
seek after lies? Selah
[3] But know that the LORD has set apart the
faithful for himself;
the LORD hears when I call to him.

[4] When you are disturbed,[a] do not sin;
ponder it on your beds, and be silent.
Selah
[5] Offer right sacrifices,
and put your trust in the LORD.

[6] There are many who say, "O that we
might see some good!
Let the light of your face shine on us,
O LORD!"
[7] You have put gladness in my heart
more than when their grain and wine
abound.

[8] I will both lie down and sleep in peace;
for you alone, O LORD, make me lie
down in safety.

Psalm 5

To the leader: for the flutes. A Psalm of David.

[1] Give ear to my words, O LORD;
give heed to my sighing.
[2] Listen to the sound of my cry,
my King and my God,
for to you I pray.
[3] O LORD, in the morning you hear my
voice;
in the morning I plead my case to you,
and watch.

[4] For you are not a God who delights in
wickedness;
evil will not sojourn with you.
[5] The boastful will not stand before your
eyes;
you hate all evildoers.
[6] You destroy those who speak lies;
the LORD abhors the bloodthirsty and
deceitful.

[7] But I, through the abundance of your
steadfast love,
will enter your house,
I will bow down toward your holy temple
in awe of you.
[8] Lead me, O LORD, in your righteousness
because of my enemies;
make your way straight before me.

[9] For there is no truth in their mouths;
their hearts are destruction;

---

[a] Or *are angry*

"He who sits in the heavens"). **5:** *I lie down,* calmly sleeping as enemies lurk is an act of trust. **7:** God striking the enemies on the mouth for their words is poetic justice, punishment fitting the crime. The psalmist, however, leaves the actual punishment to God.

Ps 4: Rescue me so I can be an example to sinners. An individual petition, with a strong emphasis on trust. **1–3:** Confident in the care God lavishes on the faithful (vv. 1a, 3b), the psalmist boldly demands that the slanderers cease their lies. **2:** *Selah* (also v. 4), see Ps 3.2n. **4:** *Ponder it on your beds,* reflect in private in contrast to public worship, as in v. 5, "offer right sacrifices." **6:** Unlike *many* who demand divine gifts as a right, the psalmist quietly relies upon the LORD to grant joy and security. *Light . . . shine,* cf. Num 6.24–26.

Ps 5: Prayer for access to the Temple. An individual petition for protection from the wicked who seem to be keeping the psalmist away from the presence of God in the Temple. Two themes alternate: seeking and enjoying God's presence (vv. 1–3,7–8,11–12), and the threat of the wicked (vv. 4–6,9–10). **7:** *But I . . . will enter your house,* emphatically states the psalmist's intent to visit the Temple, and thus asks for God's help through

their throats are open graves;
    they flatter with their tongues.
[10] Make them bear their guilt, O God;
    let them fall by their own counsels;
because of their many transgressions cast
      them out,
    for they have rebelled against you.

[11] But let all who take refuge in you rejoice;
    let them ever sing for joy.
Spread your protection over them,
    so that those who love your name may
      exult in you.
[12] For you bless the righteous, O Lord;
    you cover them with favor as with a
      shield.

Psalm 6

*To the leader: with stringed instruments; according
to The Sheminith. A Psalm of David.*

[1] O Lord, do not rebuke me in your anger,
    or discipline me in your wrath.
[2] Be gracious to me, O Lord, for I am
      languishing;
    O Lord, heal me, for my bones are
      shaking with terror.
[3] My soul also is struck with terror,
    while you, O Lord—how long?

[4] Turn, O Lord, save my life;
    deliver me for the sake of your steadfast
      love.
[5] For in death there is no remembrance of
      you;
    in Sheol who can give you praise?

[6] I am weary with my moaning;
    every night I flood my bed with tears;
    I drench my couch with my weeping.
[7] My eyes waste away because of grief;
    they grow weak because of all my foes.

[8] Depart from me, all you workers of evil,
    for the Lord has heard the sound of my
      weeping.
[9] The Lord has heard my supplication;
    the Lord accepts my prayer.
[10] All my enemies shall be ashamed and
      struck with terror;
    they shall turn back, and in a moment
      be put to shame.

Psalm 7

*A Shiggaion of David, which he sang to the Lord
concerning Cush, a Benjaminite.*

[1] O Lord my God, in you I take refuge;
    save me from all my pursuers, and
      deliver me,

divine *steadfast love* (Heb "ḥesed," a major theme in the Psalms) to travel there safely (v. 8). **9:** *Mouths, hearts, throats, tongues,* the enemies are characterized by their perverted organs of speech and the inconsistency of their words and their intentions. **11–12:** The mixing of private longing and public celebration and joy shows that the psalmist hopes to join fellow Israelites in worshiping God.

    Ps 6: Plea for God's help in sickness. An individual petition consisting of petition (vv. 1–2,4–5), complaint (vv. 2–3,6–7), mention of enemies (v. 8), and statement of trust (vv. 9–10). Tightly structured in two major parts, vv. 1–5 address God, and vv. 6–10 address God and the enemies. The psalm is one of the seven penitential psalms in Christian tradition (Pss 6; 32; 38; 51; 102; 130; 143). **Superscription:** *Sheminith,* "the eighth" (cf. "octave"), a musical term of uncertain significance. **3:** The sufferer interprets physical illness and emotional exhaustion as divine abandonment and asks *how long* the estrangement will last. **4:** The opening imperative verb *turn* (to me), addressed to God, is matched by the imperative verb in v. 8, "depart from me," addressed to the enemies, whose exact nature is unclear here, as in many psalms. Separation from the God whom the psalmist delights in praising is intolerable. **5:** *Sheol* is the underworld, where all reside after death. The psalmist's death will diminish the praise due to God; cf. Pss 30.9; 88.10–12; 115.17. **8:** A sudden change of mood, caused by renewed confidence in God's help, which may have been intimated by a sign or oracle that the psalmist perceived.

    Ps 7: Prayer for deliverance from enemies and for justice. This individual petition begins with the psalmist seeking refuge, perhaps in the Temple, and taking an oath of innocence (vv. 1–8); it continues by a plea for justice for the entire world (vv. 9–16), and ends with a statement of trust (v. 17). **Superscription:** This incident in David's life is otherwise unknown, suggesting that these superscriptions are based on events beyond those narrated in the books of Samuel. *Shiggaion,* a musical term of unknown meaning, occurring only here. **1–5:** An innocent person could claim sanctuary at the altar (Ex 21.14; 1 Kings 2.28–35), though an oath of innocence involved risk if one did not tell the truth. Job 31 contains a much longer negative oath of self-imprecation, which

2 or like a lion they will tear me apart;
    they will drag me away, with no one to
        rescue.

3 O Lord my God, if I have done this,
    if there is wrong in my hands,
4 if I have repaid my ally with harm
    or plundered my foe without cause,
5 then let the enemy pursue and overtake
        me,
    trample my life to the ground,
    and lay my soul in the dust.   *Selah*

6 Rise up, O Lord, in your anger;
    lift yourself up against the fury of my
        enemies;
    awake, O my God;[a] you have appointed
        a judgment.
7 Let the assembly of the peoples be
        gathered around you,
    and over it take your seat[b] on high.
8 The Lord judges the peoples;
    judge me, O Lord, according to my
        righteousness
    and according to the integrity that is
        in me.

9 O let the evil of the wicked come to an end,
    but establish the righteous,
you who test the minds and hearts,
    O righteous God.
10 God is my shield,
    who saves the upright in heart.
11 God is a righteous judge,
    and a God who has indignation every
        day.

12 If one does not repent, God[c] will whet
        his sword;
    he has bent and strung his bow;

13 he has prepared his deadly weapons,
    making his arrows fiery shafts.
14 See how they conceive evil,
    and are pregnant with mischief,
    and bring forth lies.
15 They make a pit, digging it out,
    and fall into the hole that they have
        made.
16 Their mischief returns upon their own
        heads,
    and on their own heads their violence
        descends.

17 I will give to the Lord the thanks due to
        his righteousness,
    and sing praise to the name of the Lord,
        the Most High.

Psalm 8

To the leader: according to The Gittith. A Psalm of David.

1 O Lord, our Sovereign,
    how majestic is your name in all the
        earth!

You have set your glory above the
        heavens.
2 Out of the mouths of babes and
        infants
you have founded a bulwark because of
        your foes,
    to silence the enemy and the
        avenger.

3 When I look at your heavens, the work of
        your fingers,

---

a   Or *awake for me*
b   Cn: Heb *return*
c   Heb *he*

---

was used by ancients to protest their innocence. **5:** *Selah,* see Ps 3.2n. **6–8:** The psalmist urgently appeals for protection to the divine judge surrounded, it seems, by members of the heavenly court having responsibility over the nations. **15–16:** That the wicked are caught in the traps they set is a common idea in wisdom literature (e.g., Prov 26.27; see also Pss 9.15–16; 35.7–8; 141.10). **17:** Thanks given for the anticipated rescue.

Ps 8: Wonder at the Lord's creation of humans. This memorable hymn praises God who has given such honor and responsibility to humans. **Superscription:** *Gittith,* an unknown musical term, also in Pss 81; 84. **1:** *Name,* parallel to *glory* (of God). As often in hymns, the opening invitation is reprised in the final line (v. 9), forming an inclusio or envelope structure. **2:** The text is unclear; it may refer to the Lord's victory over chaotic forces (see Pss 89; 93). **3–8:** Looking at the vast universe, the poet is awed by the Lord's attentiveness to one small element in that universe: humans, who have been given the honor of ruling the three domains of sky, earth, and sea. The picture is much like Gen 1.26–28, where humans rule over the three domains and enjoy the dignity of being

the moon and the stars that you have
established;
[4] what are human beings that you are
mindful of them,
mortals[a] that you care for them?

[5] Yet you have made them a little lower
than God,[b]
and crowned them with glory and
honor.
[6] You have given them dominion over the
works of your hands;
you have put all things under their feet,
[7] all sheep and oxen,
and also the beasts of the field,
[8] the birds of the air, and the fish of the
sea,
whatever passes along the paths of the
seas.

[9] O Lord, our Sovereign,
how majestic is your name in all the
earth!

Psalm 9

*To the leader: according to Muth-labben. A Psalm
of David.*

[1] I will give thanks to the Lord with my
whole heart;
I will tell of all your wonderful deeds.
[2] I will be glad and exult in you;
I will sing praise to your name, O Most
High.

[3] When my enemies turned back,
they stumbled and perished before
you.

[4] For you have maintained my just cause;
you have sat on the throne giving
righteous judgment.

[5] You have rebuked the nations, you have
destroyed the wicked;
you have blotted out their name forever
and ever.
[6] The enemies have vanished in everlasting
ruins;
their cities you have rooted out;
the very memory of them has perished.

[7] But the Lord sits enthroned forever,
he has established his throne for
judgment.
[8] He judges the world with righteousness;
he judges the peoples with equity.

[9] The Lord is a stronghold for the oppressed,
a stronghold in times of trouble.
[10] And those who know your name put
their trust in you,
for you, O Lord, have not forsaken
those who seek you.

[11] Sing praises to the Lord, who dwells in
Zion.
Declare his deeds among the peoples.
[12] For he who avenges blood is mindful of
them;
he does not forget the cry of the
afflicted.

---

a Heb *ben adam*, lit. *son of man*
b Or *than the divine beings* or *angels*: Heb *elohim*

created in the image of God. **4:** Contrast Ps 144.3; Job 7.17. **5:** *God,* better, "heavenly beings" (Heb "elohim," [lit. "gods"]; see textual note *b*). As the heavenly world is ruled by heavenly beings, so the earthly world, parallel to it, is ruled by earthly beings.

Ps 9–10: Thanks, petition, and pain at God's delay in coming. Hebrew tradition handed down Pss 9–10 as two poems, but together they form one unit with an acrostic structure: Each section begins with a successive letter of the Hebrew alphabet, though this psalm is poorly transmitted and some of this structure is broken. The Greek text also shows it is a single poem. As in other acrostic poems (Pss 25; 34; 37; 111; 112; 119; 145; Lam 1–4; Prov 31.10–31), the alphabetic structure provides a formal unity, and the content is less systematically structured. The psalm records three successive experiences of God: joyous recognition of benefits to the singer (9.3–4) and the nation (9.5–8), a cry for help during an attack (9.13–14), and a deeply felt desire for justice (10.1–18). **Superscription:** *Muth-labben,* a musical term of unknown meaning; see also Ps 48.15n. **9.1:** A promise to tell others what God has done for the psalmist (vv. 3–4) and for the nation (vv. 5–8). **7–10:** The Lord as righteous judge and defender of the oppressed, a common theme in the Psalms (e.g., 98.9). **13–20:** Awareness of God's salvation inspires fresh petitions (vv. 13–14,19–20) and a serene statement that divine justice will

¹³ Be gracious to me, O Lord.
　See what I suffer from those who hate
　　me;
　you are the one who lifts me up from
　　the gates of death,
¹⁴ so that I may recount all your praises,
　and, in the gates of daughter Zion,
　rejoice in your deliverance.

¹⁵ The nations have sunk in the pit that
　　they made;
　in the net that they hid has their own
　　foot been caught.
¹⁶ The Lord has made himself known, he
　　has executed judgment;
　the wicked are snared in the work of
　　their own hands.　*Higgaion. Selah*

¹⁷ The wicked shall depart to Sheol,
　all the nations that forget God.

¹⁸ For the needy shall not always be
　　forgotten,
　nor the hope of the poor perish forever.

¹⁹ Rise up, O Lord! Do not let mortals
　　prevail;
　let the nations be judged before you.
²⁰ Put them in fear, O Lord;
　let the nations know that they are only
　　human.　　　　　　　　*Selah*

Psalm 10

¹ Why, O Lord, do you stand far off?
　Why do you hide yourself in times of
　　trouble?
² In arrogance the wicked persecute the
　　poor—
　let them be caught in the schemes they
　　have devised.

³ For the wicked boast of the desires of
　　their heart,
　those greedy for gain curse and
　　renounce the Lord.

⁴ In the pride of their countenance the
　　wicked say, "God will not seek it out";
　all their thoughts are, "There is no
　　God."

⁵ Their ways prosper at all times;
　your judgments are on high, out of their
　　sight;
　as for their foes, they scoff at them.
⁶ They think in their heart, "We shall not
　　be moved;
　throughout all generations we shall not
　　meet adversity."

⁷ Their mouths are filled with cursing and
　　deceit and oppression;
　under their tongues are mischief and
　　iniquity.
⁸ They sit in ambush in the villages;
　in hiding places they murder the
　　innocent.

Their eyes stealthily watch for the
　　helpless;
⁹ they lurk in secret like a lion in its
　　covert;
they lurk that they may seize the poor;
　they seize the poor and drag them off in
　　their net.

¹⁰ They stoop, they crouch,
　and the helpless fall by their might.
¹¹ They think in their heart, "God has
　　forgotten,
　he has hidden his face, he will never
　　see it."

¹² Rise up, O Lord; O God, lift up your
　　hand;
　do not forget the oppressed.
¹³ Why do the wicked renounce God,
　and say in their hearts, "You will not
　　call us to account"?

prevail (vv. 15–18). **14:** A significant theme of the Psalms is that God enjoys being praised; cf. 6.4–5. **15–16:** See Ps 7.15–16n. *Higgaion*, a musical term of unknown meaning, occurring only here. *Selah* (also v. 20), see Ps 3.2n. **17:** *Sheol*, the underworld, the abode of the dead. **10.1–18:** With the question *Why?* (v. 1), the psalmist complains of the effects of God's absence—the persecution of the poor by the wealthy (v. 2a)—and gives an unusually long description of the wicked who devote all their energy to evil (vv. 3–11). Rather than requesting only his help, the psalmist here offers a broader argument about the power of evildoers and the suffering of the righteous.

14 But you do see! Indeed you note trouble
and grief,
that you may take it into your hands;
the helpless commit themselves to you;
you have been the helper of the
orphan.

15 Break the arm of the wicked and
evildoers;
seek out their wickedness until you find
none.
16 The LORD is king forever and ever;
the nations shall perish from his land.

17 O LORD, you will hear the desire of the
meek;
you will strengthen their heart, you will
incline your ear
18 to do justice for the orphan and the
oppressed,
so that those from earth may strike
terror no more.[a]

Psalm 11

To the leader. Of David.

1 In the LORD I take refuge; how can you say
to me,
"Flee like a bird to the mountains;[b]
2 for look, the wicked bend the bow,
they have fitted their arrow to the
string,
to shoot in the dark at the upright in
heart.
3 If the foundations are destroyed,
what can the righteous do?"

4 The LORD is in his holy temple;
the LORD's throne is in heaven.
His eyes behold, his gaze examines
humankind.
5 The LORD tests the righteous and the
wicked,
and his soul hates the lover of violence.
6 On the wicked he will rain coals of fire
and sulfur;
a scorching wind shall be the portion of
their cup.
7 For the LORD is righteous;
he loves righteous deeds;
the upright shall behold his face.

Psalm 12

*To the leader: according to The Sheminith. A Psalm
of David.*

1 Help, O LORD, for there is no longer
anyone who is godly;
the faithful have disappeared from
humankind.
2 They utter lies to each other;
with flattering lips and a double heart
they speak.

3 May the LORD cut off all flattering lips,
the tongue that makes great boasts,
4 those who say, "With our tongues we will
prevail;
our lips are our own—who is our
master?"

a Meaning of Heb uncertain
b Gk Syr Jerome Tg: Heb *flee to your mountain, O bird*

Ps 11: Trust in the LORD and do not panic. A song of trust, which develops one aspect of the individual petition, the statement of trust in the LORD in the Temple (as in Pss 27.8–9,13; 42.2). **1:** *Flee like a bird to the mountains!*
Disaster in the form of invading armies and moral collapse has struck and people are urging flight. A fleeing
bird is a symbol of panic-stricken flight as in Isa 16.2; Prov 27.8. **4–7:** Rejecting the advice of others, the psalmist
chooses instead to trust in the LORD's protective presence in the Temple, confident that the LORD is a just judge
who scrutinizes human conduct, curbs the wicked, upholds the loyal. **4:** It is uncertain if the psalmist means
God's heavenly *temple*, in which case the initial ideas are synonymous, or if God is being depicted as present
both in *heaven* and in the earthly *temple* in Jerusalem. **6:** *Coals of fire and sulfur* and *a scorching wind*, divine
weapons (see Gen 19.24; Am 7.4). **7:** The *upright* see the LORD's *face*, i.e., experience the divine presence in the
Temple; see Pss 27.8–9; 42.2.

Ps 12: Prayer in a time of moral disorder and lawlessness. An individual petition provoked by the destructive
speech of the powerful (vv. 1–4); it is answered by a promise of divine intervention (v. 5) that invites the psalmist's trust (vv. 6–8). Like Ps 60.6–8, this psalm seems to preserve an oracle of salvation (v. 5), perhaps uttered by
a Temple official in response to a petition (cf. 1 Sam 1.11–18). **Superscription:** *Sheminith*, see Ps 6n. **3:** *Cut off all
flattering lips*, victimized by an ungodly group using lies to control the community (vv. 1–2), the psalmist begs

5 "Because the poor are despoiled, because
     the needy groan,
   I will now rise up," says the LORD;
   "I will place them in the safety for
     which they long."
6 The promises of the LORD are promises
     that are pure,
   silver refined in a furnace on the
     ground,
   purified seven times.

7 You, O LORD, will protect us;
   you will guard us from this generation
     forever.
8 On every side the wicked prowl,
   as vileness is exalted among
     humankind.

Psalm 13

To the leader. A Psalm of David.

1 How long, O LORD? Will you forget me
     forever?
   How long will you hide your face from
     me?
2 How long must I bear pain[a] in my soul,
   and have sorrow in my heart all day
     long?
   How long shall my enemy be exalted over
     me?

3 Consider and answer me, O LORD my
     God!
   Give light to my eyes, or I will sleep the
     sleep of death,
4 and my enemy will say, "I have prevailed";
   my foes will rejoice because I am
     shaken.

5 But I trusted in your steadfast love;
   my heart shall rejoice in your salvation.
6 I will sing to the LORD,
   because he has dealt bountifully
     with me.

Psalm 14

To the leader. Of David.

1 Fools say in their hearts, "There is no
     God."
   They are corrupt, they do abominable
     deeds;
   there is no one who does good.

2 The LORD looks down from heaven on
     humankind
   to see if there are any who are wise,
   who seek after God.

3 They have all gone astray, they are all
     alike perverse;
   there is no one who does good,
   no, not one.

4 Have they no knowledge, all the
     evildoers
   who eat up my people as they eat bread,
   and do not call upon the LORD?

5 There they shall be in great terror,
   for God is with the company of the
     righteous.
6 You would confound the plans of the
     poor,
   but the LORD is their refuge.

a Syr: Heb *hold counsels*

God to destroy their capacity to speak. **6–7:** The psalmist takes the *promises* as already operating.

Ps 13: How long will the enemy threaten my life? An individual petition. **1:** *How long?* A request to know exactly how much longer the suffering is destined to last, or perhaps a rhetorical complaint. *Hide your face,* God has refused to look beneficently at the psalmist, causing his grief. **2:** The psalmists blend internal anguish and external danger; often not distinguishing psychological, physical, and social suffering. **3:** *Consider and answer me,* a contemporary paraphrase might be, "Look at me! Talk to me!" *Give light to my eyes,* i.e., give me joy and vitality (see Prov 29.13). **5:** *But I trusted,* anxiety shifts to trust in the LORD, as is typical of individual petitions.

Ps 14: Refusal to be silenced by those who deny God's justice. A condemnation of those who deny that God is active in the world and a declaration of trust in the God who cares for the poor (among whom the psalmist wants to be counted). Psalm 53 is a near duplicate of this psalm. **1:** *There is no God,* denies God's ability to govern, not necessarily God's existence; see Ps 10.4. **2:** God's scrutiny lays bare the deniers' folly and malice. In the style of wisdom literature, the rebellious are contrasted with the *wise, who seek after God.* **4:** Evildoers will finally learn that God defends those whom they exploit. **5:** *There,* evidently a reference to Mount Zion as in Pss

⁷O that deliverance for Israel would come
from Zion!
When the LORD restores the fortunes of
his people,
Jacob will rejoice; Israel will be glad.

Psalm 15
A Psalm of David.

¹O LORD, who may abide in your tent?
Who may dwell on your holy hill?

²Those who walk blamelessly, and do
what is right,
and speak the truth from their heart;
³who do not slander with their
tongue,
and do no evil to their friends,
nor take up a reproach against their
neighbors;
⁴in whose eyes the wicked are despised,
but who honor those who fear the
LORD;
who stand by their oath even to their
hurt;
⁵who do not lend money at interest,
and do not take a bribe against the
innocent.

Those who do these things shall never be
moved.

Psalm 16
A Miktam of David.

¹Protect me, O God, for in you I take
refuge.
²I say to the LORD, "You are my Lord;
I have no good apart from you."[a]

³As for the holy ones in the land, they are
the noble,
in whom is all my delight.

⁴Those who choose another god multiply
their sorrows;[b]
their drink offerings of blood I will not
pour out
or take their names upon my lips.

⁵The LORD is my chosen portion and my cup;
you hold my lot.
⁶The boundary lines have fallen for me in
pleasant places;
I have a goodly heritage.

⁷I bless the LORD who gives me counsel;
in the night also my heart instructs me.
⁸I keep the LORD always before me;
because he is at my right hand, I shall
not be moved.

a Jerome Tg: Meaning of Heb uncertain
b Cn: Meaning of Heb uncertain

48.6; 76.3. **7:** A generalized conclusion, moving from the individual to the community, as Israel lives in the hope that salvation comes from *Zion*. *When the LORD restores* may refer to the destruction of Jerusalem in 586 BCE.

Ps 15: Who will be admitted into God's presence? The psalm seems to reflect a ritual admitting worshipers to the Temple (cf. Ps 24 and Isa 33.14b–16). Ten actions describe the righteousness expected of a genuine worshiper: the first two are positive (v. 2), the second three, negative (v. 3), the third three, negative and positive (v. 4), and the last two negative (v. 5b). **1:** *Tent*, a poetic designation for the Temple (Pss 27.5; 61.4). **2–5b:** The ten clauses describing the ideal worshiper overlap and make their effect cumulative. **2:** *Walk*, conduct oneself. *Speak the truth from their heart*, one does not say one thing while intending another. **4:** *In whose eyes the wicked are despised*, the righteous reject anyone rejected by God. **5:** *Do not lend money at interest*, forbidden by Ex 22.25 and Lev 25.37. Money (i.e., silver that was weighed out) was not regarded as a commodity. **5c:** After the confession, an officiant, perhaps a priest or Levite, presumably admitted worshipers to the security of the Temple.

Ps 16: The LORD dwells in the Temple. A declaration of trust in the one God of Israel, though others worship many gods: a daunting yet joyous commitment. **Superscription:** *Miktam*, a technical term of unknown meaning. **1–2:** Though seemingly a cry for rescue from an immediate danger, the verses are most probably a declaration of trust in a particular God—the LORD—in traditional client-patron language. **3:** NRSV interprets the unclear verse as referring to Israelites whose fellowship one gains when one professes faith in the LORD. **4:** *Drink offerings of blood*, blood offerings are not often attested in biblical religion; see Ps 50.13, and cf. Ex 24.6. **5–6:** *Portion, lot, boundary lines, heritage*, references to the distribution and possession of the land of Israel (Josh 13–19). Possibly the psalmist was a priest; see Num 18.20; Josh 18.7. **7–11:** The response of the individual

⁹ Therefore my heart is glad, and my soul rejoices;
  my body also rests secure.
¹⁰ For you do not give me up to Sheol,
  or let your faithful one see the Pit.

¹¹ You show me the path of life.
  In your presence there is fullness of joy;
  in your right hand are pleasures forevermore.

Psalm 17

A Prayer of David.

¹ Hear a just cause, O LORD; attend to my cry;
  give ear to my prayer from lips free of deceit.
² From you let my vindication come;
  let your eyes see the right.

³ If you try my heart, if you visit me by night,
  if you test me, you will find no wickedness in me;
  my mouth does not transgress.
⁴ As for what others do, by the word of your lips
  I have avoided the ways of the violent.
⁵ My steps have held fast to your paths;
  my feet have not slipped.

⁶ I call upon you, for you will answer me, O God;
  incline your ear to me, hear my words.
⁷ Wondrously show your steadfast love,
  O savior of those who seek refuge
  from their adversaries at your right hand.

⁸ Guard me as the apple of the eye;
  hide me in the shadow of your wings,
⁹ from the wicked who despoil me,
  my deadly enemies who surround me.
¹⁰ They close their hearts to pity;
  with their mouths they speak arrogantly.
¹¹ They track me down;[a] now they surround me;
  they set their eyes to cast me to the ground.
¹² They are like a lion eager to tear,
  like a young lion lurking in ambush.

¹³ Rise up, O LORD, confront them,
  overthrow them!
  By your sword deliver my life from the wicked,
¹⁴ from mortals—by your hand,
  O LORD—
  from mortals whose portion in life is in this world.
  May their bellies be filled with what you have stored up for them;
  may their children have more than enough;
  may they leave something over to their little ones.

¹⁵ As for me, I shall behold your face in righteousness;
  when I awake I shall be satisfied,
  beholding your likeness.

ᵃ One Ms Compare Syr: MT *Our steps*

whose God is now the LORD, giving praise (v. 8) and rejoicing in God's nearness (vv. 9–11). **10:** *Sheol . . . the Pit,* the abode of the dead.

Ps 17: Rescue me, your loyal client, and let me see your face. An individual petition stressing the psalmist's past loyalty (vv. 1–5), present need (vv. 6–14), and ardent hope to see God in the Temple (v. 15). **1–5:** Wishing to gain a fair hearing, the psalmist claims to have passed every testing and been proven loyal. **6:** *You will answer me,* the result of the long-established trust between divine patron and human client. The psalmist personalizes life's many dangers as human enemies. **7:** *Steadfast love* (Heb "ḥesed"), a covenantal term here, referring to the loving obligations assumed by each partner. **8:** *Apple of the eye,* the pupil. *Shadow of your wings* (Pss 36.7; 57.1; etc.), either disembodied wings representing divine protection as in Egyptian religion, or the wings of the composite animals guarding the deity's throne in the Temple, the cherubim. **13:** *Confront them* (lit. "come before their face"), anticipating the conclusion of the psalm where the supplicant wants to see God's face. **14:** Expresses the wish that the wicked and their families undergo what they have tried to inflict on others. **15:** Though presumably still in danger, the psalmist speaks with the certainty that the opening petition has been granted. Although the Priestly source of the Pentateuch depicts the Temple as aniconic, without statue or image, language such as *I shall behold your face* may suggest that at one point the Temple had an image of God.

Psalm 18

To the leader. A Psalm of David the servant of the
Lord, who addressed the words of this song to the
Lord on the day when the Lord delivered him from
the hand of all his enemies, and from the hand of
Saul. He said:

¹ I love you, O Lord, my strength.
² The Lord is my rock, my fortress, and my
    deliverer,
  my God, my rock in whom I take refuge,
  my shield, and the horn of my salvation,
    my stronghold.
³ I call upon the Lord, who is worthy to be
    praised,
  so I shall be saved from my enemies.

⁴ The cords of death encompassed me;
  the torrents of perdition assailed me;
⁵ the cords of Sheol entangled me;
  the snares of death confronted me.

⁶ In my distress I called upon the Lord;
  to my God I cried for help.
From his temple he heard my voice,
  and my cry to him reached his ears.

⁷ Then the earth reeled and rocked;
  the foundations also of the mountains
    trembled
  and quaked, because he was angry.
⁸ Smoke went up from his nostrils,
  and devouring fire from his mouth;
  glowing coals flamed forth from him.
⁹ He bowed the heavens, and came down;
  thick darkness was under his feet.
¹⁰ He rode on a cherub, and flew;
  he came swiftly upon the wings of the
    wind.
¹¹ He made darkness his covering around
    him,

his canopy thick clouds dark with
    water.
¹² Out of the brightness before him
  there broke through his clouds
  hailstones and coals of fire.
¹³ The Lord also thundered in the
    heavens,
  and the Most High uttered his voice.ᵃ
¹⁴ And he sent out his arrows, and
    scattered them;
  he flashed forth lightnings, and routed
    them.
¹⁵ Then the channels of the sea were seen,
  and the foundations of the world were
    laid bare
at your rebuke, O Lord,
  at the blast of the breath of your
    nostrils.

¹⁶ He reached down from on high, he took
    me;
  he drew me out of mighty waters.
¹⁷ He delivered me from my strong
    enemy,
  and from those who hated me;
  for they were too mighty for me.
¹⁸ They confronted me in the day of my
    calamity;
  but the Lord was my support.
¹⁹ He brought me out into a broad place;
  he delivered me, because he delighted
    in me.

²⁰ The Lord rewarded me according to my
    righteousness;
  according to the cleanness of my hands
    he recompensed me.

ᵃ Gk See 2 Sam 22.14: Heb adds *hailstones and coals*
of fire

Ps 18: A royal thanksgiving. A report of the king's rescue (vv. 1–19) is followed by reflections on his intimate relationship with the Lord and his primacy among earth's kings (vv. 20–45); the psalm ends with a fresh acknowledgment of the Lord's aid (vv. 46–50). Some scholars think that Ps 18 may have been sung at the coronation of the Davidic king to ground his authority in the Lord's creation victory (cf. Ps 89.5–28). An alternate version of the psalm appears in 2 Sam 22. **Superscription:** Rescues of David from foreign kings and domestic enemies including Saul (e.g., 1 Sam 18.10–30). **2:** An unusually long list of divine epithets. **4–5:** The enemies from which the Lord delivered the king are cosmic, both the chaotic *torrents* of the primordial sea, and the power of *death*, in *Sheol*, the underworld, the abode of the dead. **7–15:** Answering the appeal of the king was a divine appearance or theophany, with the Lord described as a storm god. **10:** *Cherub*, one of the bearers of the divine throne (see Ex 25.18–120; Ezek 1; Ps 17.8n.). **16–19:** Deliverance from a tight spot (v. 6) into a *broad*, unconfined *place* (see also v. 36). **20–24:** *According to my righteousness* (vv. 20,24), having fulfilled his covenant

²¹ For I have kept the ways of the LORD,
  and have not wickedly departed from
    my God.
²² For all his ordinances were before me,
  and his statutes I did not put away from
    me.
²³ I was blameless before him,
  and I kept myself from guilt.
²⁴ Therefore the LORD has recompensed me
    according to my righteousness,
  according to the cleanness of my hands
    in his sight.

²⁵ With the loyal you show yourself loyal;
  with the blameless you show yourself
    blameless;
²⁶ with the pure you show yourself pure;
  and with the crooked you show yourself
    perverse.
²⁷ For you deliver a humble people,
  but the haughty eyes you bring down.
²⁸ It is you who light my lamp;
  the LORD, my God, lights up my darkness.
²⁹ By you I can crush a troop,
  and by my God I can leap over a wall.
³⁰ This God—his way is perfect;
  the promise of the LORD proves true;
  he is a shield for all who take refuge in
    him.

³¹ For who is God except the LORD?
  And who is a rock besides our God?—
³² the God who girded me with strength,
  and made my way safe.
³³ He made my feet like the feet of a deer,
  and set me secure on the heights.
³⁴ He trains my hands for war,
  so that my arms can bend a bow of
    bronze.
³⁵ You have given me the shield of your
    salvation,
  and your right hand has supported me;
  your help[a] has made me great.
³⁶ You gave me a wide place for my steps
    under me,
  and my feet did not slip.
³⁷ I pursued my enemies and overtook
    them;

and did not turn back until they were
    consumed.
³⁸ I struck them down, so that they were
    not able to rise;
  they fell under my feet.
³⁹ For you girded me with strength for the
    battle;
  you made my assailants sink under me.
⁴⁰ You made my enemies turn their backs
    to me,
  and those who hated me I destroyed.
⁴¹ They cried for help, but there was no one
    to save them;
  they cried to the LORD, but he did not
    answer them.
⁴² I beat them fine, like dust before the
    wind;
  I cast them out like the mire of the
    streets.

⁴³ You delivered me from strife with the
    peoples;[b]
  you made me head of the nations;
  people whom I had not known served
    me.
⁴⁴ As soon as they heard of me they obeyed
    me;
  foreigners came cringing to me.
⁴⁵ Foreigners lost heart,
  and came trembling out of their
    strongholds.

⁴⁶ The LORD lives! Blessed be my rock,
  and exalted be the God of my
    salvation,
⁴⁷ the God who gave me vengeance
  and subdued peoples under me;
⁴⁸ who delivered me from my enemies;
  indeed, you exalted me above my
    adversaries;
  you delivered me from the violent.

⁴⁹ For this I will extol you, O LORD, among
    the nations,
  and sing praises to your name.

a Or *gentleness*
b Gk Tg: Heb *people*

responsibilities, the king counts on his patron's loyal response. **25–45**: A new section with fresh topics: the
LORD as loyal supporter (vv. 25–31), arming the king and granting him victory (vv. 32–42), and installing him as
head of the kings of the world (vv. 43–45). **46–48**: Repetition of the epithets of the LORD from vv. 1–3, *rock* and

⁵⁰ Great triumphs he gives to his king,
　and shows steadfast love to his anointed,
　to David and his descendants forever.

Psalm 19

To the leader. A Psalm of David.

¹ The heavens are telling the glory of God;
　and the firmament[a] proclaims his
　　handiwork.
² Day to day pours forth speech,
　and night to night declares knowledge.
³ There is no speech, nor are there words;
　their voice is not heard;
⁴ yet their voice[b] goes out through all the
　earth,
　and their words to the end of the world.

In the heavens[c] he has set a tent for the sun,
⁵ which comes out like a bridegroom from
　his wedding canopy,
　and like a strong man runs its course
　　with joy.
⁶ Its rising is from the end of the heavens,
　and its circuit to the end of them;
　and nothing is hid from its heat.

⁷ The law of the LORD is perfect,
　reviving the soul;
the decrees of the LORD are sure,
　making wise the simple;
⁸ the precepts of the LORD are right,
　rejoicing the heart;
the commandment of the LORD is clear,
　enlightening the eyes;

⁹ the fear of the LORD is pure,
　enduring forever;
the ordinances of the LORD are true
　and righteous altogether.
¹⁰ More to be desired are they than gold,
　even much fine gold;
sweeter also than honey,
　and drippings of the honeycomb.

¹¹ Moreover by them is your servant
　warned;
　in keeping them there is great reward.
¹² But who can detect their errors?
　Clear me from hidden faults.
¹³ Keep back your servant also from the
　insolent;[d]
　do not let them have dominion over me.
Then I shall be blameless,
　and innocent of great transgression.

¹⁴ Let the words of my mouth and the
　meditation of my heart
be acceptable to you,
　O LORD, my rock and my redeemer.

Psalm 20

To the leader. A Psalm of David.

¹ The LORD answer you in the day of trouble!
　The name of the God of Jacob protect you!

a　Or *dome*
b　Gk Jerome Compare Syr: Heb *line*
c　Heb *In them*
d　Or *from proud thoughts*

deliverer, bring the psalm to a close. **50:** The LORD's eternal commitment to the dynasty of David (see 2 Sam 7.13; Ps 89.27–37).

　Ps 19: Divine instruction gives light and life to humans. Like Pss 1 and 119, this psalm insists that divine instruction (Heb "torah") transforms humans. Though many scholars divide the psalm into two distinct parts, a hymn to the sun in vv. 1–6 and a meditation on wisdom in vv. 7–14, the poem is coherent. Divine wisdom, discernible in the daily movements of the heavens (vv. 1–4b), particularly in the sun's steady course (vv. 4c–6), is also visible in the teaching (vv. 7–9) to which humans have access; the psalm concludes with a prayer to fulfill these teachings (vv. 10–14). **1–4:** Without a word being said, the sun leads the day-night rhythm of the heavens that manifests divine control. **4:** *A tent for the sun,* God has given authority to the sun to lead the course of the heavens. In comparable religious literature, the head of the pantheon authorized lesser deities to build their tent dwellings. The sun symbolizes divine justice and wisdom because nothing is hid from its rays. **7–10:** There are six synonyms for instruction or law (Heb "torah") in vv. 7–9. The first four describe the law's beneficial effects on humans; the final two are instead concerned with the teaching itself (v. 9). **11–13:** May the wisdom contained in the law instruct the psalmist's heart. **12:** *Errors* and *hidden faults* may refer to inadvertent sins.

　Ps 20: Prayer for the king's victory. A communal petition for the king's victory, connected with Ps 21. The first part (vv. 1–5) prays that the king will be victorious in battle, and the second (vv. 6–9) gives an assurance that he will be successful. **1:** *The LORD answer you,* occurs as petition in v. 1, assurance in v. 6, and petition in v. 9.

² May he send you help from the
sanctuary,
and give you support from Zion.
³ May he remember all your offerings,
and regard with favor your burnt
sacrifices.   *Selah*

⁴ May he grant you your heart's desire,
and fulfill all your plans.
⁵ May we shout for joy over your victory,
and in the name of our God set up our
banners.
May the Lord fulfill all your petitions.

⁶ Now I know that the Lord will help his
anointed;
he will answer him from his holy
heaven
with mighty victories by his right hand.
⁷ Some take pride in chariots, and some in
horses;
but our pride is in the name of the Lord
our God.
⁸ They will collapse and fall,
but we shall rise and stand upright.

⁹ Give victory to the king, O Lord;
answer us when we call.ᵃ

Psalm 21
To the leader. A Psalm of David.

¹ In your strength the king rejoices, O Lord,
and in your help how greatly he exults!
² You have given him his heart's desire,
and have not withheld the request of
his lips.   *Selah*
³ For you meet him with rich blessings;
you set a crown of fine gold on his head.

⁴ He asked you for life; you gave it to him—
length of days forever and ever.
⁵ His glory is great through your help;
splendor and majesty you bestow on
him.
⁶ You bestow on him blessings forever;
you make him glad with the joy of your
presence.
⁷ For the king trusts in the Lord,
and through the steadfast love of the
Most High he shall not be moved.

⁸ Your hand will find out all your
enemies;
your right hand will find out those who
hate you.
⁹ You will make them like a fiery furnace
when you appear.
The Lord will swallow them up in his
wrath,
and fire will consume them.
¹⁰ You will destroy their offspring from the
earth,
and their children from among
humankind.
¹¹ If they plan evil against you,
if they devise mischief, they will not
succeed.
¹² For you will put them to flight;
you will aim at their faces with your
bows.

¹³ Be exalted, O Lord, in your strength!
We will sing and praise your power.

ᵃ Gk: Heb *give victory, O Lord; let the King answer us when we call*

Day of trouble, a military crisis requiring the king to act as military commander. 3: *Offerings* and *sacrifices* could be offered to gain divine favor. *Selah*, see Ps 3.2n. 6: *Now I know*, the phrase elsewhere expresses great confidence (Job 19.25; Pss 41.11; 56.9); it may reflect a positive oracle that the king received. 7–8: Victory lies with God rather than superior military technology; cf. Ps 44.3.

Ps 21: Thanksgiving for the king's victory. A royal thanksgiving, a companion piece to Ps 20, reporting a victory gained with the Lord's help (vv. 1–7); it is followed by an assurance of future help (vv. 8–12) and concluded by a prayer (v. 13). The king's military role was understood to implement divine justice in an often hostile world. 1: *Rejoices* and *exults*, refers not only to the inner feelings of the king but to the public celebration that would follow a major victory. 2: *Selah*, see Ps 3.2n. 4–7: The king's divine-like qualities are not intrinsic to him, but are bestowed by God. 4: *Life*, not only the king's life but the people's as well, for the victory has brought security and prosperity. 5: *Glory . . . splendor and majesty*, the nimbus of light surrounding gods and kings. 10: *Destroy their offspring*, no one should be left to carry on the enemies' nefarious work. 13: Such a victory is an occasion for the entire community to rejoice in God.

Psalm 22

To the leader: according to The Deer of the Dawn.
A Psalm of David.

¹ My God, my God, why have you forsaken
me?
Why are you so far from helping me,
from the words of my groaning?
² O my God, I cry by day, but you do not
answer;
and by night, but find no rest.

³ Yet you are holy,
enthroned on the praises of Israel.
⁴ In you our ancestors trusted;
they trusted, and you delivered them.
⁵ To you they cried, and were saved;
in you they trusted, and were not put to
shame.

⁶ But I am a worm, and not human;
scorned by others, and despised by the
people.
⁷ All who see me mock at me;
they make mouths at me, they shake
their heads;
⁸ "Commit your cause to the Lord; let him
deliver—
let him rescue the one in whom he
delights!"

⁹ Yet it was you who took me from the womb;
you kept me safe on my mother's breast.
¹⁰ On you I was cast from my birth,
and since my mother bore me you have
been my God.
¹¹ Do not be far from me,
for trouble is near
and there is no one to help.

¹² Many bulls encircle me,
strong bulls of Bashan surround
me;
¹³ they open wide their mouths at me,
like a ravening and roaring lion.

¹⁴ I am poured out like water,
and all my bones are out of joint;
my heart is like wax;
it is melted within my breast;
¹⁵ my mouthᵃ is dried up like a
potsherd,
and my tongue sticks to my jaws;
you lay me in the dust of death.

¹⁶ For dogs are all around me;
a company of evildoers encircles
me.
My hands and feet have shriveled;ᵇ
¹⁷ I can count all my bones.
They stare and gloat over me;
¹⁸ they divide my clothes among
themselves,
and for my clothing they cast lots.

¹⁹ But you, O Lord, do not be far away!
O my help, come quickly to my aid!
²⁰ Deliver my soul from the sword,
my lifeᶜ from the power of the dog!
²¹ Save me from the mouth of the
lion!

From the horns of the wild oxen you have
rescuedᵈ me.

ᵃ Cn: Heb *strength*
ᵇ Meaning of Heb uncertain
ᶜ Heb *my only one*
ᵈ Heb *answered*

Ps 22: Plea to be delivered from relentless enemies. An individual petition remarkable for its intense expressions of anguish (vv. 1–2,6–8,12–18), vivid recollections of God's healing presence (vv. 3–5,9–11), lively gratitude for rescue (vv. 22–26), and trust in God's universal sovereignty (vv. 27–31). **Superscription:** *According to the Deer of the Dawn,* a musical term, perhaps indicating the melody to which the words were sung. **1–21:** The complaint is that the Lord, the patron of Israel's ancestors (vv. 3–5) has not rescued one who suffers even though he has been faithful (vv. 9–11). **6:** The dehumanized psalmist is mocked by his enemies. **12–21:** The extensive and diverse metaphors for the supplicant's trouble express the great extent of his trouble. **12–13:** Enemies stalk the psalmist like wild beasts (Ps 7.2; Isa 56.9). The subhuman bestial world is contrasted with the human worshipers in the Temple (v. 22). **12:** *Bashan,* a fertile region in northern Transjordan famous for its cattle. **14:** *Poured out like water,* tears were conceived as welling up from the abdomen, that is, coming from the physical center of the person. **16:** *My hands and feet have shriveled,* textually obscure: (lit. "like a lion my hands and feet"); see textual note b. **17–18:** *I can count all my bones* (lit. "ribs"), robbers have stripped the psalmist of his clothes and he is

22 I will tell of your name to my brothers
and sisters;[a]
in the midst of the congregation I will
praise you:
23 You who fear the LORD, praise him!
All you offspring of Jacob, glorify him;
stand in awe of him, all you offspring of
Israel!
24 For he did not despise or abhor
the affliction of the afflicted;
he did not hide his face from me,[b]
but heard when I[c] cried to him.

25 From you comes my praise in the great
congregation;
my vows I will pay before those who
fear him.
26 The poor[d] shall eat and be satisfied;
those who seek him shall praise the
LORD.
May your hearts live forever!

27 All the ends of the earth shall
remember
and turn to the LORD;
and all the families of the nations
shall worship before him.[e]
28 For dominion belongs to the LORD,
and he rules over the nations.

29 To him,[f] indeed, shall all who sleep in[g]
the earth bow down;
before him shall bow all who go down
to the dust,
and I shall live for him.[h]
30 Posterity will serve him;
future generations will be told about
the Lord,

31 and[i] proclaim his deliverance to a people
yet unborn,
saying that he has done it.

Psalm 23

A Psalm of David.

1 The LORD is my shepherd, I shall not want.
2 He makes me lie down in green pastures;
he leads me beside still waters;[j]
3 he restores my soul.[k]
He leads me in right paths[l]
for his name's sake.

4 Even though I walk through the darkest
valley,[m]
I fear no evil;
for you are with me;
your rod and your staff—
they comfort me.

5 You prepare a table before me
in the presence of my enemies;

a   Or *kindred*
b   Heb *him*
c   Heb *he*
d   Or *afflicted*
e   Gk Syr Jerome: Heb *you*
f   Cn: Heb *They have eaten and*
g   Cn: Heb *all the fat ones*
h   Compare Gk Syr Vg: Heb *and he who cannot keep
    himself alive*
i   Compare Gk: Heb *it will be told about the Lord to
    the generation,* 31*they will come and*
j   Heb *waters of rest*
k   Or *life*
l   Or *paths of righteousness*
m   Or *the valley of the shadow of death*

emaciated. **22–31:** The psalmist attempts to motivate God to rescue him by promising that he will then give thanks among humans, in the *great congregation* (v. 25), likely the Temple in Jerusalem; the rescue of a single individual will then have larger, even universal (see v. 27) and future (vv. 30–31) ramifications. **22:** *Tell of your name,* declare to others what God has done, thereby encouraging them to praise God. **27:** On praise of God by the nations, see, e.g., Pss 67.2–4; 86.9; 117.1. **29:** On worship by the dead, contrast Pss 6.5; 30.9; 88.10–12; 115.17.

Ps 23: The LORD as shepherd and host. The most beloved of the psalms, a song of trust. Though seemingly idyllic, evil lurks at the margin (vv. 4a, 5b), and "nature" is sometimes dangerous (v. 4). The poem transposes to individual experience the Exodus traditions of the divine shepherd guiding Israel (e.g., Ps 78.43–55). There are two distinct images of God in the psalm: shepherd (vv. 1–4), and host of a banquet (v. 5); and two grammatical persons used of God: *he* in vv. 1–3, *you* in vv. 4–6. **1:** *Shepherd,* a favorite title of ancient Near Eastern kings, symbolizing especially the king's compassionate care for his people (Pss 80.1; 95.7; 100.3; Isa 40.11; Jer 10.21; Ezek 34.11–16). Verse 1 can be paraphrased: It is the LORD who is my shepherd; that is why I lack nothing. **2:** *Still waters,* not swiftly running, so the sheep can keep their footing as they drink from the pool. **5:** *Prepare a table,*

you anoint my head with oil;
  my cup overflows.
[6] Surely[a] goodness and mercy[b] shall follow
  me
  all the days of my life,
and I shall dwell in the house of the LORD
  my whole life long.[c]

Psalm 24

Of David. A Psalm.

[1] The earth is the LORD's and all that is
  in it,
  the world, and those who live in it;
[2] for he has founded it on the seas,
  and established it on the rivers.

[3] Who shall ascend the hill of the LORD?
  And who shall stand in his holy place?
[4] Those who have clean hands and pure
  hearts,
  who do not lift up their souls to what
  is false,
  and do not swear deceitfully.
[5] They will receive blessing from the LORD,
  and vindication from the God of their
  salvation.
[6] Such is the company of those who seek
  him,
  who seek the face of the God
  of Jacob.[d]   *Selah*

[7] Lift up your heads, O gates!
  and be lifted up, O ancient doors!
  that the King of glory may come in.
[8] Who is the King of glory?
  The LORD, strong and mighty,
  the LORD, mighty in battle.
[9] Lift up your heads, O gates!
  and be lifted up, O ancient doors!
  that the King of glory may come in.
[10] Who is this King of glory?
  The LORD of hosts,
  he is the King of glory.   *Selah*

Psalm 25

Of David.

[1] To you, O LORD, I lift up my soul.
[2] O my God, in you I trust;
  do not let me be put to shame;
  do not let my enemies exult over me.
[3] Do not let those who wait for you be put
  to shame;
  let them be ashamed who are wantonly
  treacherous.

[4] Make me to know your ways, O LORD;
  teach me your paths.

a Or *Only*
b Or *kindness*
c Heb *for length of days*
d Gk Syr: Heb *your face, O Jacob*

the image of shepherd changes to that of host of a meal; cf. Ps 78.19. *In the presence of my enemies,* the LORD's invitation to dine vindicates the psalmist as just, whereas the enemies are not invited. **6:** *My whole life long,* the Hebrew suggests simply long life, not "forever." Residing in the *house of the LORD* implies divine protection.

  Ps 24: The holiness of the house of the LORD. A hymn celebrating the LORD's enthronement that begins, like Ps 15, with a demand of right conduct. The psalm proceeds in three stages: the proclamation of the cosmic victory of the LORD (vv. 1–2), a scrutiny to make certain that only the loyal enter and welcome the Divine Warrior to his dwelling (vv. 3–6), and a call to the Temple gates to welcome God the king. **1–2:** Presupposed is the combat myth in which the storm god defeats chaotic Sea, creates the universe, and erects a palace (temple) to commemorate the victory. Israel likely borrowed and transformed this myth from its Canaanite predecessors. **3–6:** Only those loyal to the victorious LORD are fit to share the fruits of victory; the questions determine whether worshipers have been loyal. **4:** *Lift up their souls to what is false,* similar to the commandment of the Decalogue, "You shall have no other gods before you" (Ex 20.3; Deut 5.7). **5:** *Blessing from the LORD,* the deity shares the fruits of victory. **6:** *Selah* (also v. 10), see Ps 3.2n. **7:** *Lift up your heads, O gates!* Personified, the Temple *gates* are invited to lift up their heads in joy and join the chorus welcoming the triumphant warrior; some scholars emend "gates" to "gatekeepers."

  Ps 25: Prayer for forgiveness and guidance. An individual petition in acrostic form (see Ps 9–10n.), divided into three parts (vv. 1–7; 8–14; 15–22). The first and third parts are lengthy petitions in which "I" (the singer) addresses "you" (God); the middle part (with the exception of v. 11) is a hymn-lesson, speaking of God in the third person. **1:** *My soul,* Heb "nepesh," the throat, face, and breast area, often rendered "soul" or "life" because one's vital signs are palpable in that part of the body; the Hebrew Bible does not recognize a body-soul dichotomy.

⁵ Lead me in your truth, and teach me,
for you are the God of my salvation;
for you I wait all day long.

⁶ Be mindful of your mercy, O Lord, and of
your steadfast love,
for they have been from of old.
⁷ Do not remember the sins of my youth or
my transgressions;
according to your steadfast love
remember me,
for your goodness' sake, O Lord!

⁸ Good and upright is the Lord;
therefore he instructs sinners in the
way.
⁹ He leads the humble in what is right,
and teaches the humble his way.
¹⁰ All the paths of the Lord are steadfast
love and faithfulness,
for those who keep his covenant and his
decrees.

¹¹ For your name's sake, O Lord,
pardon my guilt, for it is great.
¹² Who are they that fear the Lord?
He will teach them the way that they
should choose.

¹³ They will abide in prosperity,
and their children shall possess the
land.
¹⁴ The friendship of the Lord is for those
who fear him,
and he makes his covenant known to
them.
¹⁵ My eyes are ever toward the Lord,
for he will pluck my feet out of the net.

¹⁶ Turn to me and be gracious to me,
for I am lonely and afflicted.

¹⁷ Relieve the troubles of my heart,
and bring me[a] out of my distress.
¹⁸ Consider my affliction and my
trouble,
and forgive all my sins.

¹⁹ Consider how many are my foes,
and with what violent hatred they hate
me.
²⁰ O guard my life, and deliver me;
do not let me be put to shame, for I take
refuge in you.
²¹ May integrity and uprightness preserve
me,
for I wait for you.

²² Redeem Israel, O God,
out of all its troubles.

Psalm 26
Of David.

¹ Vindicate me, O Lord,
for I have walked in my integrity,
and I have trusted in the Lord without
wavering.
² Prove me, O Lord, and try me;
test my heart and mind.
³ For your steadfast love is before my
eyes,
and I walk in faithfulness to you.[b]

⁴ I do not sit with the worthless,
nor do I consort with hypocrites;
⁵ I hate the company of evildoers,
and will not sit with the wicked.

⁶ I wash my hands in innocence,
and go around your altar, O Lord,

a Or *The troubles of my heart are enlarged; bring me*
b Or *in your faithfulness*

8–14: Apart from v. 11, the middle section is a hymn-lesson about divine guidance with allusions to the Exodus (*way, he leads, paths, covenant*). Even the petition for forgiveness in v. 11, *pardon my guilt*, cites Moses' plea in Ex 34.9. 15–22: As motives to move God to help, the psalmist simply says *I am lonely* (v. 16), my foes are many (v. 19), and *I wait for you* (v. 21). 22: At its conclusion, the psalm is generalized to the community.

Ps 26: Plea for salvation and for a declaration of righteousness. An individual petition, probably of a priest (presumably only a priest could *go around your altar*, v. 6) who is awed by the demands of his office. Since a priest represented all Israel (e.g., Ex 28.29–30) and Israel was a priestly people among the nations, a priest's psalm could be used by any individual. Walking occurs at the psalm's beginning and end, suggesting participation in sacred processions. 1: The priest asks God to *vindicate* his claims of right conduct, for no one's self-assessment is valid without God's acceptance. 4–5: As in Pss 1 and 101, the worshiper *hates* (rejects) the

⁷ singing aloud a song of thanksgiving,
    and telling all your wondrous deeds.

⁸ O LORD, I love the house in which you
        dwell,
    and the place where your glory abides.
⁹ Do not sweep me away with sinners,
    nor my life with the bloodthirsty,
¹⁰ those in whose hands are evil devices,
    and whose right hands are full of bribes.

¹¹ But as for me, I walk in my integrity;
    redeem me, and be gracious to me.
¹² My foot stands on level ground;
    in the great congregation I will bless the
        LORD.

Psalm 27

Of David.

¹ The LORD is my light and my salvation;
    whom shall I fear?
The LORD is the stronghold[a] of my life;
    of whom shall I be afraid?

² When evildoers assail me
    to devour my flesh—
my adversaries and foes—
    they shall stumble and fall.

³ Though an army encamp against me,
    my heart shall not fear;
though war rise up against me,
    yet I will be confident.

⁴ One thing I asked of the LORD,
    that will I seek after:

to live in the house of the LORD
    all the days of my life,
to behold the beauty of the LORD,
    and to inquire in his temple.

⁵ For he will hide me in his shelter
    in the day of trouble;
he will conceal me under the cover of his
        tent;
    he will set me high on a rock.

⁶ Now my head is lifted up
    above my enemies all around me,
and I will offer in his tent
    sacrifices with shouts of joy;
I will sing and make melody to the LORD.

⁷ Hear, O LORD, when I cry aloud,
    be gracious to me and answer me!
⁸ "Come," my heart says, "seek his face!"
    Your face, LORD, do I seek.
⁹ Do not hide your face from me.

Do not turn your servant away in
        anger,
    you who have been my help.
Do not cast me off, do not forsake me,
    O God of my salvation!
¹⁰ If my father and mother forsake me,
    the LORD will take me up.

¹¹ Teach me your way, O LORD,
    and lead me on a level path
    because of my enemies.

---

a Or *refuge*

---

company and the projects of the wicked. **4:** *Sit with,* implies partnering (1 Sam 2.8; Ps 101.6). **6:** *I wash my hands,* washing is commanded by priestly rituals (Ex 30.21). **8–10:** In contrast to "hating" the wicked in vv. 4–5, the psalmist "loves," in the sense of choosing, God's house and ways. **11:** Confident of God's acceptance, the psalmist resolves to continue walking the right path.

Ps 27: Longing to find the LORD in the Temple despite obstacles. Two psalm genres, song of trust (vv. 1–6) and individual petition (vv. 7–14), have been combined to express intense desire and courageous journeying. Mention of enemies and the desire to see God's face in the Temple unify these two parts. **1–3:** *Light* is associated with the sanctuary as in Pss 36.9; 43.3; 56.13; in antiquity kings and divinities were often depicted as emanating light. **2:** *Devour my flesh,* the enemies are compared to wild animals (Pss 7.2; 17.12). **4:** Three metaphors for desiring God: living in God's house (Ps 84.4), beholding God's beauty (Ex 24.11), and seeking (*inquire*) an oracle. **5:** There are three metaphors for hope; all refer to the Temple: *shelter, tent* (Am 9.11; Ps 18.11), and *rock* (Ps 61.2). **6:** *Now,* the psalmist can now look down from a secure place upon the enemies that once posed a threat. **7–10:** A sudden shift to petition/lament as the psalmist becomes aware that enemies still pose a threat. **8:** *My heart says,* a unique variant of the idiom "to say in one's heart," connoting utter sincerity. On God's *face,* see Ps 17.15n. **10:** The image of God as parent is rare in Psalms (see, e.g., 103.13). **11:** *Lead me on a level path,* the psalmist asks

¹²Do not give me up to the will of my
adversaries,
for false witnesses have risen against
me,
and they are breathing out violence.

¹³I believe that I shall see the goodness of
the LORD
in the land of the living.
¹⁴Wait for the LORD;
be strong, and let your heart take
courage;
wait for the LORD!

Psalm 28
Of David.

¹To you, O LORD, I call;
my rock, do not refuse to hear me,
for if you are silent to me,
I shall be like those who go down to the
Pit.
²Hear the voice of my supplication,
as I cry to you for help,
as I lift up my hands
toward your most holy sanctuary.ᵃ

³Do not drag me away with the wicked,
with those who are workers of evil,
who speak peace with their neighbors,
while mischief is in their hearts.
⁴Repay them according to their work,
and according to the evil of their deeds;
repay them according to the work of their
hands;
render them their due reward.

⁵Because they do not regard the works of
the LORD,
or the work of his hands,
he will break them down and build them
up no more.

⁶Blessed be the LORD,
for he has heard the sound of my
pleadings.
⁷The LORD is my strength and my shield;
in him my heart trusts;
so I am helped, and my heart exults,
and with my song I give thanks to him.

⁸The LORD is the strength of his people;
he is the saving refuge of his anointed.
⁹O save your people, and bless your
heritage;
be their shepherd, and carry them
forever.

Psalm 29
A Psalm of David.

¹Ascribe to the LORD, O heavenly beings,ᵇ
ascribe to the LORD glory and
strength.
²Ascribe to the LORD the glory of his name;
worship the LORD in holy splendor.

³The voice of the LORD is over the waters;
the God of glory thunders,
the LORD, over mighty waters.

ᵃ   Heb *your innermost sanctuary*
ᵇ   Heb *sons of gods*

to be protected on the journey. **13:** *In the land of the living,* better rendered "in the land of life," an idiom for the Temple as in Pss 52.5; 56.13. **14:** Perhaps recited in response, as encouragement to the psalmist.

Ps 28: Plea for the vindication of one falsely accused. An individual petition that asks God to indicate the innocence of a person in the absence of reliable witnesses. The psalmist prays that God not be silent (v. 1) and allow false accusers to win the day. **1:** *The Pit,* a synonym for Sheol, the abode of the dead. **2:** *Lift up my hands* was a posture of prayer. **3:** *Those . . . who speak peace,* false accusers. **6–8:** *Blessed be the LORD,* the LORD has spoken, perhaps through an oracle, and the psalmist responds with intense joy. **7:** *Strength* and *shield* complement "rock" (v. 1). **8–9:** As in other psalms (e.g., 14; 20; 25), the conclusion moves from the individual to the community, and to its leader, the *anointed* king. **9:** *Shepherd . . . carry,* the final prayer may evoke Isa 40.11, where God carries "[the lambs] in his bosom, and gently leads the mother sheep."

Ps 29: Acknowledging the LORD's might in the storm. A hymn in which heavenly beings praise the LORD of the storm who brings life-giving rain; many scholars think that this was a Canaanite psalm adapted by early Israel. **1:** The *heavenly beings* (lit. "sons of gods") are summoned to acknowledge the LORD returning victorious to the assembly (cf. Pss 82.1; 89.5–7). **2:** *In holy splendor,* perhaps "when the Holy One appears." **3–9:** The symbol of a cosmic event, a massive storm roars in from the Mediterranean and hits the coast with deafening thunderclaps (*the voice of the LORD,* used seven times in this section), drenching rain, and lightning flashes. The lumi-

⁴ The voice of the LORD is powerful;
    the voice of the LORD is full of majesty.

⁵ The voice of the LORD breaks the cedars;
    the LORD breaks the cedars of Lebanon.
⁶ He makes Lebanon skip like a calf,
    and Sirion like a young wild ox.

⁷ The voice of the LORD flashes forth flames
    of fire.
⁸ The voice of the LORD shakes the
    wilderness;
    the LORD shakes the wilderness of
        Kadesh.

⁹ The voice of the LORD causes the oaks to
    whirl,ᵃ
    and strips the forest bare;
    and in his temple all say, "Glory!"

¹⁰ The LORD sits enthroned over the flood;
    the LORD sits enthroned as king forever.
¹¹ May the LORD give strength to his people!
    May the LORD bless his people with peace!

Psalm 30

A Psalm. A Song at the dedication of the temple.
Of David.

¹ I will extol you, O LORD, for you have
    drawn me up,
    and did not let my foes rejoice over me.
² O LORD my God, I cried to you for help,
    and you have healed me.
³ O LORD, you brought up my soul from
    Sheol,

restored me to life from among those
    gone down to the Pit.ᵇ

⁴ Sing praises to the LORD, O you his
    faithful ones,
    and give thanks to his holy name.
⁵ For his anger is but for a moment;
    his favor is for a lifetime.
Weeping may linger for the night,
    but joy comes with the morning.

⁶ As for me, I said in my prosperity,
    "I shall never be moved."
⁷ By your favor, O LORD,
    you had established me as a strong
        mountain;
you hid your face;
    I was dismayed.

⁸ To you, O LORD, I cried,
    and to the LORD I made
        supplication:
⁹ "What profit is there in my death,
    if I go down to the Pit?
Will the dust praise you?
    Will it tell of your faithfulness?
¹⁰ Hear, O LORD, and be gracious
    to me!
    O LORD, be my helper!"

¹¹ You have turned my mourning into
    dancing;

ᵃ Or *causes the deer to calve*
ᵇ Or *that I should not go down to the Pit*

nous thundercloud is imagined as the LORD's chariot, and the thunder, rain, and lightning are his soldiers. They sweep across the trees and appear to shatter and shake the forested mountain; earthquake also accompanies a divine appearance or theophany (e.g., Pss 18.7; 114.7). **6**: *Sirion,* Mount Hermon (see Deut 3.9), at the southern border of *Lebanon.* **8**: *Wilderness of Kadesh,* the desert east of the city of Kadesh in central western Syria. **10**: *Enthroned over the flood,* ancient myths sometimes depicted the storm god defeating hostile Sea and building his palace upon its body. The heavenly beings pray that the divine king would extend the fruits of victory to Israel, the LORD's special people.

Ps 30: Praise for deliverance. A thanksgiving with a persistent metaphor system: going down, death, silence; and rising up, life, praise. God moves the psalmist from one state to the other. The divine names ("the LORD" and "God") add up to twelve, the number of the tribes of Israel, suggesting that the healing is a type of what God does for all the tribes. **Superscription:** The words *at the dedication of the temple* were added when this psalm was sung at the Feast of Dedication (Hanukkah) commemorating the cleansing of the Temple by Judas Maccabeus in 164 BCE. **3**: Language of death and recovery is used by people who were saved by God from life-threatening problems. *Sheol . . . the Pit,* the abode of the dead. **6**: *I shall never be moved,* the psalmist's smugness preceded the crisis. Withdrawal of divine support led to collapse (cf. Ps 104.27–30). **9**: The theme that God should save a psalmist because the dead do not praise God is common in the Psalms (see Ps 6.5n.). **11–12**: The

you have taken off my sackcloth
and clothed me with joy,
¹² so that my soul[a] may praise you and not
be silent.
O LORD my God, I will give thanks to
you forever.

Psalm 31
To the leader. A Psalm of David.

¹ In you, O LORD, I seek refuge;
do not let me ever be put to shame;
in your righteousness deliver me.
² Incline your ear to me;
rescue me speedily.
Be a rock of refuge for me,
a strong fortress to save me.

³ You are indeed my rock and my fortress;
for your name's sake lead me and guide
me,
⁴ take me out of the net that is hidden for
me,
for you are my refuge.
⁵ Into your hand I commit my spirit;
you have redeemed me, O LORD, faithful
God.

⁶ You hate[b] those who pay regard to
worthless idols,
but I trust in the LORD.
⁷ I will exult and rejoice in your steadfast
love,
because you have seen my affliction;
you have taken heed of my adversities,
⁸ and have not delivered me into the hand
of the enemy;
you have set my feet in a broad place.

⁹ Be gracious to me, O LORD, for I am in
distress;
my eye wastes away from grief,
my soul and body also.

¹⁰ For my life is spent with sorrow,
and my years with sighing;
my strength fails because of my misery,[c]
and my bones waste away.

¹¹ I am the scorn of all my adversaries,
a horror[d] to my neighbors,
an object of dread to my acquaintances;
those who see me in the street flee from
me.
¹² I have passed out of mind like one who
is dead;
I have become like a broken vessel.
¹³ For I hear the whispering of many—
terror all around!—
as they scheme together against me,
as they plot to take my life.

¹⁴ But I trust in you, O LORD;
I say, "You are my God."
¹⁵ My times are in your hand;
deliver me from the hand of my
enemies and persecutors.
¹⁶ Let your face shine upon your servant;
save me in your steadfast love.
¹⁷ Do not let me be put to shame, O LORD,
for I call on you;
let the wicked be put to shame;
let them go dumbfounded to Sheol.
¹⁸ Let the lying lips be stilled
that speak insolently against the
righteous
with pride and contempt.

¹⁹ O how abundant is your goodness
that you have laid up for those who fear
you,

a Heb *that glory*
b One Heb Ms Gk Syr Jerome: MT *I hate*
c Gk Syr: Heb *my iniquity*
d Cn: Heb *exceedingly*

psalmist casts off the mourning garments (*sackcloth*) to dance with joy.

Ps 31: Prayer for deliverance, and thanksgiving. An individual petition that combines features of a petition (vv. 1–4,9–18) and a thanksgiving (vv. 5–8,19–24). **2–4:** The metaphors for refuge are spatial: *rock, fortress* (lit. "safe house"), crag (v. 3, NRSV "rock"). The psalmist asks to be led to those places. **9–18:** The psalm returns to direct petition. Sickness, or perhaps old age, has cut off the sufferer from family and friends (vv. 9–13). **16:** *Let your face shine*, a likely reference to the Priestly blessing (Num 6.25), meaning to adopt an open countenance that looks directly at the other person (see also Pss 4.6; 80.3). **17:** *Sheol*, the underworld, the abode of the dead. **19:** A major change in mood: leaving behind complaints, the psalmist expresses thanks. God hides the loyal in a shelter (a reference to the Temple as in Am 9.11; Pss 18.11; 27.5). The quest for a "safe house" in v. 2 has been

and accomplished for those who take
  refuge in you,
    in the sight of everyone!
20 In the shelter of your presence you hide
  them
    from human plots;
you hold them safe under your shelter
    from contentious tongues.

21 Blessed be the LORD,
  for he has wondrously shown his
    steadfast love to me
  when I was beset as a city under siege.
22 I had said in my alarm,
  "I am driven far[a] from your sight."
But you heard my supplications
  when I cried out to you for help.

23 Love the LORD, all you his saints.
  The LORD preserves the faithful,
  but abundantly repays the one who acts
    haughtily.
24 Be strong, and let your heart take
    courage,
  all you who wait for the LORD.

Psalm 32
Of David. A Maskil.

1 Happy are those whose transgression is
    forgiven,
  whose sin is covered.
2 Happy are those to whom the LORD
    imputes no iniquity,
  and in whose spirit there is no
    deceit.

3 While I kept silence, my body wasted
    away
  through my groaning all day long.
4 For day and night your hand was heavy
    upon me;
  my strength was dried up[b] as by the
    heat of summer.   *Selah*

5 Then I acknowledged my sin to you,
  and I did not hide my iniquity;
I said, "I will confess my transgressions to
    the LORD,"
  and you forgave the guilt of
    my sin.   *Selah*

6 Therefore let all who are faithful
  offer prayer to you;
at a time of distress,[c] the rush of mighty
    waters
  shall not reach them.
7 You are a hiding place for me;
  you preserve me from trouble;
  you surround me with glad cries of
    deliverance.   *Selah*

8 I will instruct you and teach you the way
    you should go;
  I will counsel you with my eye upon
    you.
9 Do not be like a horse or a mule, without
    understanding,

a Another reading is *cut off*
b Meaning of Heb uncertain
c Cn: Heb *at a time of finding only*

answered by God's granting admission to the Temple. **23–24:** As is often the case in Psalms, at the end the petitioner moves from himself to the broader community. **23:** *Saints* is a misleading translation; it is elsewhere translated "faithful" or "loyal" ones.

Ps 32: Happy the one whose sin is forgiven. An individual thanksgiving, though in Christian tradition it is classed among the seven penitential psalms (Pss 6; 32; 38; 51; 102; 130; 143). The psalm has three mutually reinforcing metaphors for sin and three for forgiveness: sin is a burden one has to bear or carry, forgiveness occurring when God bears it away; sin is an act that God keeps on seeing (it is "in God's face"), forgiveness occurring when God covers it so it can no longer be seen; sin is "imputing iniquity," judging someone is a sinner and withholding blessing, and forgiveness consists in changing that judgment. **Superscription:** *Maskil,* a technical term of uncertain significance. **1:** *Whose transgression is forgiven,* an indirect way of expressing God's action. The psalmist's feverish attempts to *cover* (lit. "hide") the sin prevented God from *cover*ing it (looking away from it). **4:** *Your hand was heavy upon me* is an idiom for punishment (see 1 Sam 5.6). *Selah* (also vv. 5,7), see Ps 3.2n. **6–11:** Deeply moved by the experience of God's mercy, the singer tells the faithful what they may not realize: sin need not destroy you or separate you from God. **9:** *Like a horse or a mule,* people can turn away like work animals who do not understand human speech, but joy follows forgiveness.

whose temper must be curbed with bit
    and bridle,
else it will not stay near you.

¹⁰ Many are the torments of the wicked,
    but steadfast love surrounds those who
        trust in the LORD.
¹¹ Be glad in the LORD and rejoice,
    O righteous,
and shout for joy, all you upright in
    heart.

Psalm 33

¹ Rejoice in the LORD, O you righteous.
    Praise befits the upright.
² Praise the LORD with the lyre;
    make melody to him with the harp of
        ten strings.
³ Sing to him a new song;
    play skillfully on the strings, with loud
        shouts.

⁴ For the word of the LORD is upright,
    and all his work is done in faithfulness.
⁵ He loves righteousness and justice;
    the earth is full of the steadfast love of
        the LORD.

⁶ By the word of the LORD the heavens were
    made,
and all their host by the breath of his
    mouth.
⁷ He gathered the waters of the sea as in a
    bottle;
he put the deeps in storehouses.

⁸ Let all the earth fear the LORD;
    let all the inhabitants of the world
        stand in awe of him.
⁹ For he spoke, and it came to be;
    he commanded, and it stood firm.

¹⁰ The LORD brings the counsel of the
    nations to nothing;
he frustrates the plans of the
    peoples.
¹¹ The counsel of the LORD stands
    forever,
the thoughts of his heart to all
    generations.
¹² Happy is the nation whose God is the
    LORD,
the people whom he has chosen as his
    heritage.

¹³ The LORD looks down from heaven;
    he sees all humankind.
¹⁴ From where he sits enthroned he
    watches
all the inhabitants of the earth—
¹⁵ he who fashions the hearts of them all,
    and observes all their deeds.
¹⁶ A king is not saved by his great army;
    a warrior is not delivered by his great
        strength.
¹⁷ The war horse is a vain hope for
    victory,
and by its great might it cannot save.

¹⁸ Truly the eye of the LORD is on those
    who fear him,
on those who hope in his steadfast
    love,
¹⁹ to deliver their soul from death,
    and to keep them alive in famine.

²⁰ Our soul waits for the LORD;
    he is our help and shield.
²¹ Our heart is glad in him,
    because we trust in his holy name.
²² Let your steadfast love, O LORD, be
    upon us,
even as we hope in you.

Ps 33: Praise of the LORD who created the universe. A hymn praising the divine word that made the three-tiered universe and guides it even when humans try to pervert it to their ends. **1–11:** The conjunction *for* in vv. 4 and 9 introduces the motive for giving praise, in this case, God's *upright* and powerful *word* that has brought the universe into being (vv. 6–7; cf. Gen 1.6). That creative word determines the course of history, and no human word can contravene it (vv. 10–11). **7:** *Storehouses,* cf. Ps 135.7; Job 38.22. **12–22:** Though not mentioned by name, Israel is declared *happy* or fortunate (v. 12) simply by being chosen out of all the nations. When the LORD scrutinizes humanity, all purely human sources of strength are relativized (vv. 16–17; cf. v. 10; Ps 20.7). Israel's (and the nations') task is not to rely on human strength but to wait on the LORD's goodness and power. **20–22:** These verses are connected causally and suggest that God should save Israel because of Israel's trust in God.

Psalm 34

Of David, when he feigned madness before Abimelech, so that he drove him out, and he went away.

¹I will bless the LORD at all times;
  his praise shall continually be in my
    mouth.
²My soul makes its boast in the LORD;
  let the humble hear and be glad.
³O magnify the LORD with me,
  and let us exalt his name together.

⁴I sought the LORD, and he answered me,
  and delivered me from all my fears.
⁵Look to him, and be radiant;
  so your[a] faces shall never be ashamed.
⁶This poor soul cried, and was heard by
    the LORD,
  and was saved from every trouble.
⁷The angel of the LORD encamps
  around those who fear him, and
    delivers them.
⁸O taste and see that the LORD is good;
  happy are those who take refuge in him.
⁹O fear the LORD, you his holy ones,
  for those who fear him have no want.
¹⁰The young lions suffer want and
    hunger,
  but those who seek the LORD lack no
    good thing.

¹¹Come, O children, listen to me;
  I will teach you the fear of the LORD.
¹²Which of you desires life,
  and covets many days to enjoy good?
¹³Keep your tongue from evil,
  and your lips from speaking deceit.

¹⁴Depart from evil, and do good;
  seek peace, and pursue it.

¹⁵The eyes of the LORD are on the
    righteous,
  and his ears are open to their cry.
¹⁶The face of the LORD is against evildoers,
  to cut off the remembrance of them
    from the earth.
¹⁷When the righteous cry for help, the
    LORD hears,
  and rescues them from all their
    troubles.
¹⁸The LORD is near to the brokenhearted,
  and saves the crushed in spirit.

¹⁹Many are the afflictions of the righteous,
  but the LORD rescues them from them
    all.
²⁰He keeps all their bones;
  not one of them will be broken.
²¹Evil brings death to the wicked,
  and those who hate the righteous will
    be condemned.
²²The LORD redeems the life of his servants;
  none of those who take refuge in him
    will be condemned.

Psalm 35

Of David.

¹Contend, O LORD, with those who
    contend with me;
  fight against those who fight against me!
²Take hold of shield and buckler,
  and rise up to help me!

a   Gk Syr Jerome: Heb *their*

Ps 34: Praise and acknowledgment of deliverance from danger. An individual thanksgiving in acrostic form (see Ps 9–10n.). Individual thanksgivings publicize the deliverance to encourage others to remain loyal to God. The didactic element is underlined in this psalm. **Superscription:** According to 1 Sam 21.10–15, David feigned madness before Achish, not Abimelech. The ascription of this psalm to that particular historical situation is likely secondary. **8:** *Taste,* a metaphor for experience. **11–22:** Borrowing from the portrait of personified Wisdom (especially Prov 9), the healed psalmist teaches others how to gain life. "Life" here is long life resulting from righteous conduct, in contrast to the brief life of the wicked, who die prematurely. **11:** *Fear of the LORD,* best rendered "revering the LORD." **16–17:** The psalm reads better if this order of the two verses is reversed, following the order of the alphabet found in Lam 2; 3; 4.

Ps 35: Prayer for deliverance from enemies. An individual petition in three sections (vv. 1–10; 11–18; 19–28). It uses many metaphors for enemies—soldiers (vv. 1–3), hunters (v. 7), and lions (v. 17)—and the imagery of war, lawsuit, and conspiracy to show that the whole world is arrayed against a lone individual. Positive petitions (vv. 1–3,17,22–24,27) alternate with imprecations (vv. 4–6,8,19,25–26), promises of thanksgiving (vv. 9–10,18,28), and complaints (vv. 7,11–16). Each of the psalm's three sections concludes with a promise of praise

3 Draw the spear and javelin
  against my pursuers;
say to my soul,
  "I am your salvation."

4 Let them be put to shame and dishonor
  who seek after my life.
Let them be turned back and confounded
  who devise evil against me.
5 Let them be like chaff before the wind,
  with the angel of the LORD driving
    them on.
6 Let their way be dark and slippery,
  with the angel of the LORD pursuing
    them.

7 For without cause they hid their net[a] for
    me;
  without cause they dug a pit[b] for my life.
8 Let ruin come on them unawares.
And let the net that they hid ensnare
    them;
  let them fall in it—to their ruin.

9 Then my soul shall rejoice in the LORD,
  exulting in his deliverance.
10 All my bones shall say,
  "O LORD, who is like you?
You deliver the weak
  from those too strong for them,
  the weak and needy from those who
    despoil them."

11 Malicious witnesses rise up;
  they ask me about things I do not know.
12 They repay me evil for good;
  my soul is forlorn.
13 But as for me, when they were sick,
  I wore sackcloth;
  I afflicted myself with fasting.
I prayed with head bowed[c] on my bosom,
  14 as though I grieved for a friend or a
      brother;
I went about as one who laments for a
      mother,
  bowed down and in mourning.

15 But at my stumbling they gathered in
    glee,
  they gathered together against me;
ruffians whom I did not know
  tore at me without ceasing;
16 they impiously mocked more and more,[d]
  gnashing at me with their teeth.

17 How long, O LORD, will you look on?
  Rescue me from their ravages,
  my life from the lions!
18 Then I will thank you in the great
    congregation;
  in the mighty throng I will praise you.

19 Do not let my treacherous enemies
    rejoice over me,
  or those who hate me without cause
    wink the eye.
20 For they do not speak peace,
  but they conceive deceitful words
    against those who are quiet in the
      land.
21 They open wide their mouths against
    me;
  they say, "Aha, Aha,
  our eyes have seen it."

22 You have seen, O LORD; do not be silent!
  O Lord, do not be far from me!
23 Wake up! Bestir yourself for my defense,
  for my cause, my God and my Lord!
24 Vindicate me, O LORD, my God,
  according to your righteousness,
  and do not let them rejoice over me.
25 Do not let them say to themselves,
  "Aha, we have our heart's desire."
Do not let them say, "We have swallowed
    you[e] up."

a Heb a pit, their net
b The word pit is transposed from the preceding line
c Or My prayer turned back
d Cn Compare Gk: Heb like the profanest of mockers
   of a cake
e Heb him

(vv. 9–10,18,28). 4: Be put to shame and dishonor, God is asked to bring about the rescue in full view of others.
5–6: The angel of the LORD is God's emissary, effecting punishment. 7–8: See Ps 7.15–16n. 23: Wake up, the demand reflects the ancient Near Eastern view that God rested after a great deed (as in Gen 2.3) and required a
fresh summons (Pss 44.23; 59.5; Isa 51.9).

²⁶ Let all those who rejoice at my calamity
   be put to shame and confusion;
let those who exalt themselves against me
   be clothed with shame and dishonor.

²⁷ Let those who desire my vindication
   shout for joy and be glad,
   and say evermore,
"Great is the LORD,
   who delights in the welfare of his
      servant."
²⁸ Then my tongue shall tell of your
      righteousness
   and of your praise all day long.

Psalm 36

To the leader. Of David, the servant of the LORD.

¹ Transgression speaks to the wicked
   deep in their hearts;
there is no fear of God
   before their eyes.
² For they flatter themselves in their own
      eyes
   that their iniquity cannot be found out
      and hated.
³ The words of their mouths are mischief
      and deceit;
   they have ceased to act wisely and do
      good.
⁴ They plot mischief while on their beds;
   they are set on a way that is not good;
   they do not reject evil.

⁵ Your steadfast love, O LORD, extends to
      the heavens,
   your faithfulness to the clouds.
⁶ Your righteousness is like the mighty
      mountains,

your judgments are like the great deep;
you save humans and animals alike,
      O LORD.

⁷ How precious is your steadfast love,
      O God!
All people may take refuge in the
      shadow of your wings.
⁸ They feast on the abundance of your
      house,
   and you give them drink from the river
      of your delights.
⁹ For with you is the fountain of life;
   in your light we see light.

¹⁰ O continue your steadfast love to those
      who know you,
   and your salvation to the upright of heart!
¹¹ Do not let the foot of the arrogant tread
      on me,
   or the hand of the wicked drive me away.
¹² There the evildoers lie prostrate;
   they are thrust down, unable to rise.

Psalm 37

Of David.

¹ Do not fret because of the wicked;
   do not be envious of wrongdoers,
² for they will soon fade like the grass,
   and wither like the green herb.

³ Trust in the LORD, and do good;
   so you will live in the land, and enjoy
      security.
⁴ Take delight in the LORD,
   and he will give you the desires of your
      heart.

Ps 36: God sustains the faithful. An individual petition that develops the statement of trust to an unusual degree. Instead of complaining about the attacks of the wicked, the psalmist gives a vivid portrait of the wicked person (vv. 1–4). The statement of trust (vv. 5–9) enlarges on the LORD's saving power, and the petition is extended (vv. 10–12). **1–4:** The self-ruled individual is contrasted with the God-ruled world. **4:** *While on their beds,* i.e., privately, at night; cf. Mic 2.1. **5–9:** The wicked are unaware that God works in all parts of the universe—sky, mountains (earth), and sea (vv. 5–6)—and especially in the Temple (*your house*) from which flows the *river of your delights* (v. 8); cf. Ps 46.4; Ezek 47.1–2. **7:** *Shadow of your wings,* see Ps 17.8n. **9:** *In your light we see light,* enjoy life (Job 3.16; Ps 49.19), which is made possible by the luminous God present in the Temple. **12:** *There,* possibly a reference to Zion and its Temple as in Pss 48.6; 76.3; 87.4.

Ps 37: Exhortation to courage and endurance. An instructional poem in acrostic form (see Ps 9–10n.), using aphorisms and exhortations to encourage people to a faithful life (see Pss 49; 78; 127; 128). **1–11:** One should maintain one's equanimity when the wicked prosper and are admired. Retribution is inevitable, however, for the wicked will be shamed (their hopes will prove empty) and the righteous rewarded, typically with the pre-

⁵ Commit your way to the LORD;
  trust in him, and he will act.
⁶ He will make your vindication shine like
    the light,
  and the justice of your cause like the
    noonday.

⁷ Be still before the LORD, and wait
    patiently for him;
  do not fret over those who prosper in
    their way,
  over those who carry out evil devices.

⁸ Refrain from anger, and forsake wrath.
  Do not fret—it leads only to evil.
⁹ For the wicked shall be cut off,
  but those who wait for the LORD shall
    inherit the land.

¹⁰ Yet a little while, and the wicked will be
    no more;
  though you look diligently for their
    place, they will not be there.
¹¹ But the meek shall inherit the land,
  and delight themselves in abundant
    prosperity.

¹² The wicked plot against the righteous,
  and gnash their teeth at them;
¹³ but the LORD laughs at the wicked,
  for he sees that their day is coming.

¹⁴ The wicked draw the sword and bend
    their bows
  to bring down the poor and needy,
  to kill those who walk uprightly;
¹⁵ their sword shall enter their own heart,
  and their bows shall be broken.

¹⁶ Better is a little that the righteous person
    has
  than the abundance of many wicked.
¹⁷ For the arms of the wicked shall be
    broken,
  but the LORD upholds the righteous.

¹⁸ The LORD knows the days of the
    blameless,
  and their heritage will abide forever;
¹⁹ they are not put to shame in evil times,
  in the days of famine they have
    abundance.

²⁰ But the wicked perish,
  and the enemies of the LORD are like the
    glory of the pastures;
  they vanish—like smoke they vanish
    away.

²¹ The wicked borrow, and do not
    pay back,
  but the righteous are generous and keep
    giving;
²² for those blessed by the LORD shall
    inherit the land,
  but those cursed by him shall be
    cut off.

²³ Our steps[a] are made firm by the LORD,
  when he delights in our[b] way;
²⁴ though we stumble,[c] we[d] shall not fall
    headlong,
  for the LORD holds us[e] by the hand.

²⁵ I have been young, and now am old,
  yet I have not seen the righteous
    forsaken
  or their children begging bread.
²⁶ They are ever giving liberally and
    lending,
  and their children become a blessing.

²⁷ Depart from evil, and do good;
  so you shall abide forever.

---

a Heb *A man's steps*
b Heb *his*
c Heb *he stumbles*
d Heb *he*
e Heb *him*

cious gift of the land (vv. 3,9,11,22,29,34). **12–20:** The wicked try to attack the righteous, but the LORD defends them. **21–26:** The same Heb word in vv. 21 and 26 marks off the section (NRSV *borrow, lending*). To give to others is to show confidence in the LORD and eventually leads to a share in the LORD's land (vv. 21–22). **25:** *I have not seen the righteous forsaken,* a statement of how the universe runs under divine rule, not necessarily an empirical observation. **27–40:** Three imperative verbs dominate the section: *Depart* (v. 27), *Wait* (v. 34), and *Mark* (v. 37).

²⁸ For the Lᴏʀᴅ loves justice;
he will not forsake his faithful ones.

The righteous shall be kept safe forever,
but the children of the wicked shall be
cut off.
²⁹ The righteous shall inherit the land,
and live in it forever.

³⁰ The mouths of the righteous utter
wisdom,
and their tongues speak justice.
³¹ The law of their God is in their hearts;
their steps do not slip.

³² The wicked watch for the righteous,
and seek to kill them.
³³ The Lᴏʀᴅ will not abandon them to their
power,
or let them be condemned when they
are brought to trial.

³⁴ Wait for the Lᴏʀᴅ, and keep to his way,
and he will exalt you to inherit the land;
you will look on the destruction of the
wicked.

³⁵ I have seen the wicked oppressing,
and towering like a cedar of
Lebanon.ª
³⁶ Again Iᵇ passed by, and they were no
more;
though I sought them, they could not
be found.

³⁷ Mark the blameless, and behold the
upright,
for there is posterity for the peaceable.
³⁸ But transgressors shall be altogether
destroyed;
the posterity of the wicked shall be cut
off.

³⁹ The salvation of the righteous is from
the Lᴏʀᴅ;
he is their refuge in the time of trouble.
⁴⁰ The Lᴏʀᴅ helps them and rescues them;
he rescues them from the wicked, and
saves them,
because they take refuge in him.

Psalm 38

A Psalm of David, for the memorial offering.

¹ O Lᴏʀᴅ, do not rebuke me in your anger,
or discipline me in your wrath.
² For your arrows have sunk into me,
and your hand has come down
on me.

³ There is no soundness in my flesh
because of your indignation;
there is no health in my bones
because of my sin.
⁴ For my iniquities have gone over my
head;
they weigh like a burden too heavy
for me.

⁵ My wounds grow foul and fester
because of my foolishness;
⁶ I am utterly bowed down and prostrate;
all day long I go around mourning.
⁷ For my loins are filled with burning,
and there is no soundness in my flesh.
⁸ I am utterly spent and crushed;
I groan because of the tumult of my
heart.

⁹ O Lord, all my longing is known to you;
my sighing is not hidden from you.
¹⁰ My heart throbs, my strength fails me;
as for the light of my eyes—it also has
gone from me.

a Gk: Meaning of Heb uncertain
b Gk Syr Jerome: Heb *he*

35–36: Like wisdom literature, this psalm emphasizes experience and observation.
   Ps 38: Confession of sin and plea for forgiveness. An individual petition notable for its vivid portrayal of anguish resulting from sin and of patient waiting for healing. People have interpreted the psalmist's illness as divine rejection and therefore keep their distance. An individual lament in the Hebrew Bible, this psalm in Christian tradition is one of the seven penitential psalms (Pss 6; 32; 51; 102; 130; 143). **Superscription:** *For the memorial offering* (also Ps 70), meaning uncertain. 1: Compare 6.1, suggesting that this was a stereotypical way of beginning a petition psalm. Psalms 6 and 38 are quite different, however: the petitioner in Ps 6 assumes that he is being unjustly punished, while this psalmist confesses his guilt. 9–10: The verses echo the anguish

¹¹ My friends and companions stand aloof
 from my affliction,
  and my neighbors stand far off.

¹² Those who seek my life lay their
  snares;
  those who seek to hurt me speak of
  ruin,
  and meditate treachery all day long.

¹³ But I am like the deaf, I do not hear;
  like the mute, who cannot speak.
¹⁴ Truly, I am like one who does not hear,
  and in whose mouth is no retort.

¹⁵ But it is for you, O LORD, that I wait;
  it is you, O Lord my God, who will
  answer.
¹⁶ For I pray, "Only do not let them rejoice
  over me,
  those who boast against me when my
  foot slips."

¹⁷ For I am ready to fall,
  and my pain is ever with me.
¹⁸ I confess my iniquity;
  I am sorry for my sin.
¹⁹ Those who are my foes without causeᵃ
  are mighty,
  and many are those who hate me
  wrongfully.
²⁰ Those who render me evil for good
  are my adversaries because I follow
  after good.

²¹ Do not forsake me, O LORD;
  O my God, do not be far from me;
²² make haste to help me,
  O Lord, my salvation.

Psalm 39

To the leader: to Jeduthun. A Psalm of David.

¹ I said, "I will guard my ways
  that I may not sin with my tongue;
I will keep a muzzle on my mouth
  as long as the wicked are in my presence."
² I was silent and still;
  I held my peace to no avail;
my distress grew worse,
  ³ my heart became hot within me.
While I mused, the fire burned;
  then I spoke with my tongue:

⁴ "LORD, let me know my end,
  and what is the measure of my days;
  let me know how fleeting my life is.
⁵ You have made my days a few handbreadths,
  and my lifetime is as nothing in your
  sight.
Surely everyone stands as a mere
  breath.   *Selah*
  ⁶ Surely everyone goes about like a
  shadow.
Surely for nothing they are in turmoil;
  they heap up, and do not know who will
  gather.

⁷ "And now, O Lord, what do I wait for?
  My hope is in you.
⁸ Deliver me from all my transgressions.
  Do not make me the scorn of the fool.
⁹ I am silent; I do not open my mouth,
  for it is you who have done it.
¹⁰ Remove your stroke from me;
  I am worn down by the blowsᵇ of your
  hand.

ᵃ Q Ms: MT *my living foes*
ᵇ Heb *hostility*

described in vv. 3–8. **11:** Cf. Ps 31.9–18n. **15–16:** The verses echo the anguish in vv. 11–14. **15:** The psalmist trusts God rather than humans. **21–22:** The closing petitions are similar in syntax to the opening petitions (vv. 1–2). **21:** *Do not forsake me* is also a stereotypical expression in petitions, e.g., Ps 27.9.

Ps 39: Plea that suffering might end. An individual petition. Forced to remain silent because enemies misinterpret any utterance (vv. 1–3), the psalmist asks God how much longer the suffering will continue (vv. 4–6). Since the suffering comes from God, only God can end it (vv. 7–13). **Superscription:** *Jeduthun* (also in the superscriptions of Pss 62 and 77), a Temple singer (1 Chr 25.1; etc.). **1:** *Sin with my tongue*, better, "offend by my speech"; since one's words might convince others that the suffering is just retribution for rebellion, the psalmist resolves to complain only to God. **4:** *Let me know my end*, better , "Let me know the term (of my affliction), what the length of my days (of suffering) is," expressing the belief that afflictions lasted for a predetermined period. To the psalmist, it is unfair of God to burden an already short life span with a lengthy affliction. **5:** *Selah*

11 "You chastise mortals
  in punishment for sin,
consuming like a moth what is dear to
    them;
  surely everyone is a mere breath.   *Selah*

12 "Hear my prayer, O LORD,
  and give ear to my cry;
  do not hold your peace at my tears.
For I am your passing guest,
  an alien, like all my forebears.
13 Turn your gaze away from me, that I may
    smile again,
  before I depart and am no more."

Psalm 40

To the leader. Of David. A Psalm.

1 I waited patiently for the LORD;
  he inclined to me and heard my cry.
2 He drew me up from the desolate pit,[a]
  out of the miry bog,
and set my feet upon a rock,
  making my steps secure.
3 He put a new song in my mouth,
  a song of praise to our God.
Many will see and fear,
  and put their trust in the LORD.

4 Happy are those who make
  the LORD their trust,
who do not turn to the proud,
  to those who go astray after false
    gods.
5 You have multiplied, O LORD my God,
  your wondrous deeds and your
    thoughts toward us;
  none can compare with you.
Were I to proclaim and tell of them,
  they would be more than can be
    counted.

6 Sacrifice and offering you do not desire,
  but you have given me an open ear.[b]
Burnt offering and sin offering
  you have not required.
7 Then I said, "Here I am;
  in the scroll of the book it is written of
    me.[c]
8 I delight to do your will, O my God;
  your law is within my heart."

9 I have told the glad news of
    deliverance
  in the great congregation;
see, I have not restrained my lips,
  as you know, O LORD.
10 I have not hidden your saving help
    within my heart,
  I have spoken of your faithfulness and
    your salvation;
I have not concealed your steadfast love
    and your faithfulness
  from the great congregation.

11 Do not, O LORD, withhold
  your mercy from me;
let your steadfast love and your
    faithfulness
  keep me safe forever.
12 For evils have encompassed me
  without number;
my iniquities have overtaken me,
  until I cannot see;
they are more than the hairs of my head,
  and my heart fails me.

13 Be pleased, O LORD, to deliver me;
  O LORD, make haste to help me.

a   Cn: Heb *pit of tumult*
b   Heb *ears you have dug for me*
c   Meaning of Heb uncertain

(also v. 11), see Ps 3.2n. 7: *And now,* signals the shift from complaint to petition. 12: See Lev 25.23; 1 Chr 29.15. 13: A similar image is found in Job 7.19; in both cases, the sufferer asks God to look less closely, for if God scrutinizes people, they will surely be found guilty.

Ps 40: A thanksgiving with a plea for further help. A hybrid psalm of thanksgiving (vv. 1–10) and individual petition (vv. 11–17). After experiencing salvation, the psalmist faces further adversity. Vv. 13–17 are duplicated in Ps 70. 1–3b: Report of the rescue. 3: *New song,* "new" refers to the startling new action celebrated in the song. 6–8: Instead of the customary sacrifice offering, God asks for a self-offering through obedience; cf. 1 Sam 15.22; Ps 50.8–9; Mic 6.6–7. 7: *Here I am,* the psalmist is completely available for the task (cf. Isa 6.8), in this case, to tell of the deliverance and its significance (vv. 9–10). *The scroll of the book,* what is decreed from on high and immutable; cf. Pss 69.28; 139.16. 8: Observing God's word is internalized. 11–17: Acceptance of the task of proc-

¹⁴ Let all those be put to shame and
  confusion
  who seek to snatch away my life;
let those be turned back and brought to
  dishonor
  who desire my hurt.
¹⁵ Let those be appalled because of their
  shame
  who say to me, "Aha, Aha!"

¹⁶ But may all who seek you
  rejoice and be glad in you;
may those who love your salvation
  say continually, "Great is the LORD!"
¹⁷ As for me, I am poor and needy,
  but the Lord takes thought for me.
You are my help and my deliverer;
  do not delay, O my God.

Psalm 41
To the leader. A Psalm of David.

¹ Happy are those who consider the poor;ᵃ
  the LORD delivers them in the day of
  trouble.
² The LORD protects them and keeps them
  alive;
  they are called happy in the land.
You do not give them up to the will of
  their enemies.
³ The LORD sustains them on their sickbed;
  in their illness you heal all their
  infirmities.ᵇ

⁴ As for me, I said, "O LORD, be gracious to
  me;
  heal me, for I have sinned against you."
⁵ My enemies wonder in malice
  when I will die, and my name perish.

⁶ And when they come to see me, they
  utter empty words,
  while their hearts gather mischief;
  when they go out, they tell it abroad.
⁷ All who hate me whisper together about
  me;
  they imagine the worst for me.

⁸ They think that a deadly thing has
  fastened on me,
  that I will not rise again from where I lie.
⁹ Even my bosom friend in whom I trusted,
  who ate of my bread, has lifted the heel
  against me.
¹⁰ But you, O LORD, be gracious to me,
  and raise me up, that I may repay them.

¹¹ By this I know that you are pleased with
  me;
  because my enemy has not triumphed
  over me.
¹² But you have upheld me because of my
  integrity,
  and set me in your presence forever.

¹³ Blessed be the LORD, the God of Israel,
  from everlasting to everlasting.
    Amen and Amen.

BOOK II PSALMS 42–72

Psalm 42
To the leader. A Maskil of the Korahites.

¹ As a deer longs for flowing streams,
  so my soul longs for you, O God.

ᵃ Or *weak*
ᵇ Heb *you change all his bed*

lamation puts the psalmist in fresh danger and in need of God's help. **14:** *Shame*, violating accepted morality brought dishonor upon the violator. The prayer is that the enemies' schemes be publicly frustrated. **15:** *Aha, Aha*, malicious cries of triumph that the psalmist hopes will be proved foolish by God's judgment. **16:** God's help will encourage other righteous people. **17:** Psalms often depicts the supplicant as *poor* and *needy*.

  Ps 41: Thanksgiving for rescue. A thanksgiving in which the psalmist in vv. 4–10 cites an earlier prayer as a kind of verbal votive offering. **1:** *Happy are those who consider the poor* (i.e., those who are attentive to the poor) is the psalmist's conclusion after a profound deliverance (like Ps 32.1). Those who help the needy are themselves helped in their need. **4–10:** The psalmist's earlier prayer shows fear of enemies who wanted the psalmist to die and leave behind no name, i.e., no children to carry on the family. **4:** The psalmist believes that sin is the cause of illness. **10:** To be raised from the sickbed constitutes a declaration of the psalmist's innocence to the enemies who wish the psalmist dead. **12:** *Forever* is hyperbolic. **13:** Not a part of the psalm, but a doxology or blessing concluding Book I, the first of five editorial sections of the Psalms. The vast majority of the previous psalms were ascribed to David; the following nine are not.

[2] My soul thirsts for God,
   for the living God.
When shall I come and behold
   the face of God?
[3] My tears have been my food
   day and night,
while people say to me continually,
   "Where is your God?"

[4] These things I remember,
   as I pour out my soul:
how I went with the throng,[a]
   and led them in procession to the house
      of God,
with glad shouts and songs of
      thanksgiving,
   a multitude keeping festival.
[5] Why are you cast down, O my soul,
   and why are you disquieted within
      me?
Hope in God; for I shall again praise him,
   my help [6] and my God.

My soul is cast down within me;
   therefore I remember you
from the land of Jordan and of Hermon,
   from Mount Mizar.
[7] Deep calls to deep
   at the thunder of your cataracts;
all your waves and your billows
   have gone over me.
[8] By day the LORD commands his steadfast
      love,
   and at night his song is with me,
   a prayer to the God of my life.

[9] I say to God, my rock,
   "Why have you forgotten me?
Why must I walk about mournfully
   because the enemy oppresses me?"
[10] As with a deadly wound in my body,
   my adversaries taunt me,
while they say to me continually,
   "Where is your God?"

[11] Why are you cast down, O my soul,
   and why are you disquieted within me?
Hope in God; for I shall again praise him,
   my help and my God.

Psalm 43

[1] Vindicate me, O God, and defend my
      cause
   against an ungodly people;
from those who are deceitful and
      unjust
   deliver me!
[2] For you are the God in whom I take
      refuge;
   why have you cast me off?
Why must I walk about mournfully
   because of the oppression of the
      enemy?
[3] O send out your light and your truth;
   let them lead me;
let them bring me to your holy hill
   and to your dwelling.
[4] Then I will go to the altar of God,
   to God my exceeding joy;

[a]   Meaning of Heb uncertain

Ps 42–43: Longing to join the community in the Temple. Though handed down as two poems, the psalm is actually one poem (see the identical refrain in 42.6,11 and 43.5), an individual petition to be in the Temple (like Pss 27, 62, and 84). Here the sufferer, away from the protection of the Temple, complains of taunts by unbelievers (42.9–10) and pleads for a guide for the journey home. Distinctive is the psalmist's inner dialogue between discouragement and resolve, despair and hope. **Superscription:** *Maskil,* a technical term of uncertain significance. *Korahites,* lit. "sons of Korah," also in Pss 42–49; 84–85; and 87–88). Korah was a Levite priest (see Num 16) and his descendants were Temple singers (2 Chr 20.19) who favored phrases such as *the living God* (Pss 42.2; 84.2) *the face of God* (Pss 42.2; 44.24; 88.14) and *refuge* (Pss 43.2; 46.1,7; 48.3) **42.1–5:** The taunts of those who reject God depress the psalmist and awaken painful memories of past worship with believers. Verses 1–5 are unified by water imagery. **6–11:** Even in anger against God, the psalmist is able to hope (vv. 8,11b) and pray (vv. 8,9). **6:** *Land of Jordan and of Hermon,* northern sites, near the headwaters of the Jordan and far from Jerusalem. *Mizar,* precise location unknown. **7:** *Deep calls to deep,* the subterranean cosmic waters that symbolize chaos and death (cf. Jon 2.3–4; Ps 18.4–6). Being distant from the dwelling of the saving God is like being in the power of the chaotic sea. **43.1–5:** The tone changes and the prayer becomes more robust, asking God to send *your light and your truth,* qualities personified as heavenly beings able to lead the psalmist to God's shrine.

and I will praise you with the harp,
  O God, my God.

[5] Why are you cast down, O my soul,
  and why are you disquieted within
    me?
Hope in God; for I shall again praise him,
  my help and my God.

Psalm 44

To the leader. Of the Korahites. A Maskil.

[1] We have heard with our ears, O God,
  our ancestors have told us,
what deeds you performed in their days,
  in the days of old:
[2] you with your own hand drove out the
    nations,
  but them you planted;
you afflicted the peoples,
  but them you set free;
[3] for not by their own sword did they win
    the land,
  nor did their own arm give them
    victory;
but your right hand, and your arm,
  and the light of your countenance,
  for you delighted in them.

[4] You are my King and my God;
  you command[a] victories for Jacob.
[5] Through you we push down our foes;
  through your name we tread down our
    assailants.
[6] For not in my bow do I trust,
  nor can my sword save me.
[7] But you have saved us from our foes,
  and have put to confusion those who
    hate us.
[8] In God we have boasted continually,
  and we will give thanks to your name
    forever.   *Selah*

[9] Yet you have rejected us and abased us,
  and have not gone out with our armies.

[10] You made us turn back from the foe,
  and our enemies have gotten spoil.
[11] You have made us like sheep for
    slaughter,
  and have scattered us among the
    nations.
[12] You have sold your people for a trifle,
  demanding no high price for them.

[13] You have made us the taunt of our
    neighbors,
  the derision and scorn of those around
    us.
[14] You have made us a byword among the
    nations,
  a laughingstock[b] among the peoples.
[15] All day long my disgrace is before me,
  and shame has covered my face
[16] at the words of the taunters and revilers,
  at the sight of the enemy and the
    avenger.

[17] All this has come upon us,
  yet we have not forgotten you,
  or been false to your covenant.
[18] Our heart has not turned back,
  nor have our steps departed from your
    way,
[19] yet you have broken us in the haunt of
    jackals,
  and covered us with deep darkness.

[20] If we had forgotten the name of our God,
  or spread out our hands to a strange
    god,
[21] would not God discover this?
  For he knows the secrets of the heart.
[22] Because of you we are being killed all
    day long,
  and accounted as sheep for the slaughter.

a Gk Syr: Heb *You are my King, O God; command*
b Heb *a shaking of the head*

Ps 44: Prayer for recovery from national defeat. A communal petition on the occasion of a military defeat. Like similar communal petitions (Pss 77 and 89), it recalls the settling of the people in Canaan (vv. 1–3) to remind God to be faithful to that original moment. Not conscious of having sinned, the community asks why God let them fall into the hands of their enemies. **Superscription:** *Korahites,* see Ps 42–43n. *Maskil,* a technical term of uncertain significance. **1–8:** Israel's founding moment was the Exodus-Conquest, though the singer singles out the Conquest. Then, as now, the people trusted entirely in God's protection. **8:** *Selah,* see Ps 3.2n. **9–16:** The complaint: You have given us into the hand of our enemies. **17–22:** We have done nothing to warrant your

23 Rouse yourself! Why do you sleep,
   O Lord?
   Awake, do not cast us off forever!
24 Why do you hide your face?
   Why do you forget our affliction and
      oppression?
25 For we sink down to the dust;
   our bodies cling to the ground.
26 Rise up, come to our help.
   Redeem us for the sake of your
      steadfast love.

Psalm 45

To the leader: according to Lilies. Of the Korahites.
A Maskil. A love song.

1 My heart overflows with a goodly theme;
   I address my verses to the king;
   my tongue is like the pen of a ready
      scribe.

2 You are the most handsome of men;
   grace is poured upon your lips;
   therefore God has blessed you forever.
3 Gird your sword on your thigh, O mighty
      one,
   in your glory and majesty.

4 In your majesty ride on victoriously
   for the cause of truth and to defend[a] the
      right;
   let your right hand teach you dread
      deeds.

5 Your arrows are sharp
   in the heart of the king's enemies;
   the peoples fall under you.

6 Your throne, O God,[b] endures forever and
      ever.
   Your royal scepter is a scepter of
      equity;
7 you love righteousness and hate
      wickedness.
Therefore God, your God, has anointed
      you
   with the oil of gladness beyond your
      companions;
8 your robes are all fragrant with myrrh
      and aloes and cassia.
From ivory palaces stringed instruments
      make you glad;
9 daughters of kings are among your
      ladies of honor;
   at your right hand stands the queen in
      gold of Ophir.

10 Hear, O daughter, consider and incline
      your ear;
   forget your people and your father's
      house,
11 and the king will desire your beauty.

---

a   Cn: Heb *and the meekness of*
b   Or *Your throne is a throne of God, it*

---

abandoning us. **22:** The community struggles with being God's people when God is silent before their pain. **23:** As in Pss 35.23; 59.4; Isa 51.9, the psalmist expresses frustration at God's inaction using the ancient Near Eastern motif of the God who needs to be awakened. **26–27:** In conclusion, the psalmist offers two motivations for God: Israel's terrible state, and God's steadfast love (Heb "ḥesed") toward Israel.

Ps 45: Celebration of the king's wedding. A song for the king's wedding to a foreign princess, applied in later interpretation to the messianic king. Jewish tradition sees the singer as a model Torah scholar and the king as messiah. Christianity too sees a messianic reference; see Heb 1.8. **Superscription:** *According to Lilies,* probably refers to a melody (also Pss 69; 80; cf. 60). *Korahites,* see Ps 42–43n. *Maskil,* a technical term of uncertain significance. **1–6:** After an invocation (v. 1), the court poet praises the king's beauty (most *handsome of men,* v. 2), which implies divine favor (as in Gen 39.6; 1 Sam 16.12; 17.42). Similarly, *grace is poured upon your lips* in v. 2 means to utter decisions made by a wise heart (as in Prov 22.11). Verses 3–6 speak of the king's military prowess: by his wisdom and military skill, the king is an instrument of divine justice. **6:** *O God,* if a reference to the king, the only time in the Bible that the Davidic king is divinized in this fashion; see also textual note *b* and v. 17n. **7–16:** As vv. 2–6 focused on the king as defender of the land, vv. 7–16 emphasize the virility of the king to beget an heir, an ancient and modern concern. **7:** The anointing of the king was the central act of the coronation ritual. *Gladness,* elsewhere associated with marriage as in Jer 7.34; 16.9; 25.10; 33.11. **8:** *Myrrh and aloes and cassia,* evoke a sensuous and erotic mood (Prov 7.17–18; Song 1.13; 5.13). **9:** *The queen,* most likely the queen mother, since according to vv. 13–14 the bride is "in her chamber" from which she will be led to the king. According to 1 Kings 2.19, the queen mother sat on the king's right as in Ps 45.9, so it is she who addresses the

Since he is your lord, bow to him;
¹² the people[a] of Tyre will seek your
favor with gifts,
the richest of the people ¹³ with all kinds
of wealth.

The princess is decked in her chamber
with gold-woven robes;[b]
¹⁴ in many-colored robes she is led to
the king;
behind her the virgins, her companions,
follow.
¹⁵ With joy and gladness they are led along
as they enter the palace of the king.

¹⁶ In the place of ancestors you, O king,[c]
shall have sons;
you will make them princes in all the
earth.
¹⁷ I will cause your name to be celebrated
in all generations;
therefore the peoples will praise you
forever and ever.

Psalm 46

*To the leader. Of the Korahites. According to
Alamoth. A Song.*

¹ God is our refuge and strength,
a very present[d] help in trouble.
² Therefore we will not fear, though the
earth should change,
though the mountains shake in the
heart of the sea;
³ though its waters roar and foam,
though the mountains tremble with its
tumult.   *Selah*

⁴ There is a river whose streams make glad
the city of God,
the holy habitation of the Most
High.
⁵ God is in the midst of the city;[e] it shall
not be moved;
God will help it when the morning
dawns.
⁶ The nations are in an uproar, the
kingdoms totter;
he utters his voice, the earth melts.
⁷ The LORD of hosts is with us;
the God of Jacob is our refuge.[f]   *Selah*

⁸ Come, behold the works of the LORD;
see what desolations he has brought on
the earth.
⁹ He makes wars cease to the end of the
earth;
he breaks the bow, and shatters the
spear;
he burns the shields with fire.
¹⁰ "Be still, and know that I am God!
I am exalted among the nations,
I am exalted in the earth."
¹¹ The LORD of hosts is with us;
the God of Jacob is our refuge.[f]   *Selah*

a Heb *daughter*
b Or *people.* ¹³*All glorious is the princess within, gold
embroidery is her clothing*
c Heb lacks *O king*
d Or *well proved*
e Heb *of it*
f Or *fortress*

bride in vv. 10–12. *Ophir,* in southern Arabia (see Gen 10.29), a famous source of gold. **12:** *Tyre,* in Phoenicia, was known for its luxury items and fine craftsmanship. **17:** The court poet fulfills his task of making the king's name known, remarkably attributing to the king the type of praise elsewhere associated with God (e.g., Ps 145.21).

Ps 46: The glory of Mount Zion, residence of the LORD. A song of Zion, like Pss 48, 76, 84, and 122. The first of a cluster of three psalms about the LORD reigning in Jerusalem. Three refrains (vv. 1,7,11) structure the poem. **Superscription:** *Korahites,* see Ps 42–43n. *Alamoth,* probably a melody; see 1 Chr 15.20. **1–3:** The psalmist trusts in Zion, which many Israelites believed was the center of the world and residence of the LORD, which remains unshaken though the earth "totter" (NRSV *change*) and plunge into pre-creation chaos. **3:** *Selah* (also vv. 7,11), see Ps 3.2n. **4–7:** In contrast to the tumultuous and dangerous waters in vv. 2–3, the calm river of v. 4 is controlled by God to provide water and fertility for the holy city. The attacks of the rebellious nations in v. 6 function as a historical complement to the cosmic disaster in vv. 2–3. Yet God's *voice,* thunder, defeats them. **9:** Rather than just defeating the enemies, as in most psalms, God ends war. **10:** Stop what you are doing and embrace the peace the LORD has achieved. Zion is the place where God's victory is most visible and most appropriately praised.

Psalm 47

To the leader. Of the Korahites. A Psalm.

¹ Clap your hands, all you peoples;
　shout to God with loud songs of joy.
² For the LORD, the Most High, is awesome,
　a great king over all the earth.
³ He subdued peoples under us,
　and nations under our feet.
⁴ He chose our heritage for us,
　the pride of Jacob whom he loves.　*Selah*

⁵ God has gone up with a shout,
　the LORD with the sound of a trumpet.
⁶ Sing praises to God, sing praises;
　sing praises to our King, sing praises.
⁷ For God is the king of all the earth;
　sing praises with a psalm.ᵃ

⁸ God is king over the nations;
　God sits on his holy throne.
⁹ The princes of the peoples gather
　as the people of the God of Abraham.
For the shields of the earth belong to God;
　he is highly exalted.

Psalm 48

A Song. A Psalm of the Korahites.

¹ Great is the LORD and greatly to be praised
　in the city of our God.
His holy mountain, ² beautiful in elevation,
　is the joy of all the earth,

Mount Zion, in the far north,
　the city of the great King.
³ Within its citadels God
　has shown himself a sure defense.

⁴ Then the kings assembled,
　they came on together.
⁵ As soon as they saw it, they were
　astounded;
　they were in panic, they took to flight;
⁶ trembling took hold of them there,
　pains as of a woman in labor,
⁷ as when an east wind shatters
　the ships of Tarshish.
⁸ As we have heard, so have we seen
　in the city of the LORD of hosts,
in the city of our God,
　which God establishes forever.　*Selah*

⁹ We ponder your steadfast love, O God,
　in the midst of your temple.
¹⁰ Your name, O God, like your praise,
　reaches to the ends of the earth.
Your right hand is filled with victory.
　¹¹ Let Mount Zion be glad,
let the townsᵇ of Judah rejoice
　because of your judgments.

ᵃ Heb *Maskil*
ᵇ Heb *daughters*

Ps 47: Acclaim the LORD the king of heaven and earth! An enthronement hymn, like Pss 93; 95–99, celebrating the LORD reigning over heaven and earth. The occasion for the recitation of this psalm is uncertain. **Superscription:** *Korahites*, see Ps 42–43n. **1–4:** Presupposed is the LORD's universal victory also celebrated in Pss 2, 46, 48, 76, 93. Israel's task is to offer a suitable welcome and receive the territory (*our heritage*, v. 4) that the victorious LORD assigns. **2:** *A great king*, better "the Great King," a title of suzerains in Mesopotamia, Egypt, and the Hittite kingdom. **4:** *Selah*, see Ps 3.2n. **5:** *Gone up*, ascended the throne as in 2 Sam 6.15; Isa 14.13. The *shout* and *trumpet* were part of the ritual proclaiming the new king (see 1 Kings 1.39–49). **6–8:** The threefold repetition of *king* makes clear the psalm's theme. **9:** *Gather as the people of the God of Abraham*, a possible translation is "The princes of the people assemble with the people of the God of Abraham." *Shields*, i.e., rulers (by metonymy).

Ps 48: A hymn to Zion, the place of God's peace. A song of Zion, like Pss 46; 76; 84; 122. Comparable Near Eastern texts describe how a particular god became the most high god by defeating chaos and then, after receiving the acclaim of the other heavenly beings, constructed a palace to memorialize the victory. Ps 48 seems to see "the kings" (v. 4) as representing the same disorderly power. **Superscription:** *Korahites*, see Ps 42–43n. **1–3:** Seven epithets are applied to Zion. The description is highly idealized. *In the far north*, better "the heights of Zaphon," the mountain home of the storm god Baal (modern Jebel el-Aqra' on the coast of northern Syria). The LORD has taken over Baal's domain. **4–8:** Rather than referring to a specific historical battle, the verses probably refer to a symbolic gathering of rebellious kingdoms against the LORD's governance of the universe. But this is no normal military victory: the nations needed only to see the magnificent Jerusalem, and they capitulated. **7:** *East wind*, the weapon of the storm god. *Tarshish*, location uncertain; it may be Tarsus in southern Turkey or Tartessus in southern Spain. **8:** *Selah*, see Ps 3.2n. **9–14:** The Temple buildings memorialize the LORD's

¹² Walk about Zion, go all around it,
   count its towers,
¹³ consider well its ramparts;
   go through its citadels,
that you may tell the next generation
   ¹⁴ that this is God,
our God forever and ever.
   He will be our guide forever.

Psalm 49

To the leader. Of the Korahites. A Psalm.

¹ Hear this, all you peoples;
   give ear, all inhabitants of the world,
² both low and high,
   rich and poor together.
³ My mouth shall speak wisdom;
   the meditation of my heart shall be
      understanding.
⁴ I will incline my ear to a proverb;
   I will solve my riddle to the music of the
      harp.

⁵ Why should I fear in times of trouble,
   when the iniquity of my persecutors
      surrounds me,
⁶ those who trust in their wealth
   and boast of the abundance of their
      riches?
⁷ Truly, no ransom avails for one's life,[a]
   there is no price one can give to God
      for it.
⁸ For the ransom of life is costly,
   and can never suffice,
⁹ that one should live on forever
   and never see the grave.[b]

¹⁰ When we look at the wise, they die;
   fool and dolt perish together
   and leave their wealth to others.
¹¹ Their graves[c] are their homes forever,
   their dwelling places to all
      generations,
   though they named lands their own.
¹² Mortals cannot abide in their pomp;
   they are like the animals that perish.

¹³ Such is the fate of the foolhardy,
   the end of those[d] who are pleased with
      their lot.   *Selah*
¹⁴ Like sheep they are appointed for Sheol;
   Death shall be their shepherd;
straight to the grave they descend,[e]
   and their form shall waste away;
   Sheol shall be their home.[f]
¹⁵ But God will ransom my soul from the
      power of Sheol,
   for he will receive me.   *Selah*

¹⁶ Do not be afraid when some become
      rich,
   when the wealth of their houses
      increases.
¹⁷ For when they die they will carry
      nothing away;

a Another reading is *no one can ransom a brother*
b Heb *the pit*
c Gk Syr Compare Tg: Heb *their inward* (thought)
d Tg: Heb *after them*
e Cn: Heb *the upright shall have dominion over them
   in the morning*
f Meaning of Heb uncertain

steadfast love (Heb "ḥesed") manifested in the victory that brought order and justice to the world. Military might is a means to justice, the right governance of the world. The psalm begins and ends (vv. 1–3,12–14) with the mountains and the buildings that remind visitors of the mercy and grandeur of God. **12–13:** *Walk about Zion . . . consider well its ramparts,* a command to contemplate the result of the divine victory just won, perhaps referring to a ritual procession through the city. **14:** The final word, *forever* (Heb "'al-mut"), may be out of place here and belong with the superscription of the following psalm as "Alamot" (Heb "'alamot"; see Ps 46n.).

   Ps 49: An instruction on the limits of wealth. Though often classed as a wisdom psalm, instruction is a more apt term, in this case instruction about the folly of relying on wealth rather than God. Two sets of refrains tie the poem together and highlight its theme (vv. 7 and 15, 12 and 20). The text is often obscure, as the textual notes attest. **Superscription:** *Korahites,* see Ps 42–43n. **1–4:** A formal call for attention like Deut 32.1–3 and Ps 78.1–4. **5–12:** As in individual petitions, this psalmist has enemies (the arrogant wealthy), but instead of calling on God for rescue, reflects on the folly of relying on wealth. **12:** The psalmist's well-considered conclusion: wealth cannot stave off death. **13–20:** As the poem progresses, the tone grows bolder. **13:** *Selah* (also v. 15), see Ps 3.2n. **14:** *Sheol,* the abode of the dead. **15:** Though the wealthy seem to triumph, God will *ransom* and "take" (NRSV *receive*) the psalmist from the clutches of the underworld. The Hebrew word for "take" elsewhere describes

their wealth will not go down after
them.
18 Though in their lifetime they count
themselves happy
—for you are praised when you do well
for yourself—
19 they[a] will go to the company of their
ancestors,
who will never again see the light.
20 Mortals cannot abide in their pomp;
they are like the animals that perish.

Psalm 50

A Psalm of Asaph.

1 The mighty one, God the LORD,
speaks and summons the earth
from the rising of the sun to its setting.
2 Out of Zion, the perfection of beauty,
God shines forth.

3 Our God comes and does not keep
silence,
before him is a devouring fire,
and a mighty tempest all around him.
4 He calls to the heavens above
and to the earth, that he may judge his
people:
5 "Gather to me my faithful ones,
who made a covenant with me by
sacrifice!"
6 The heavens declare his righteousness,
for God himself is judge.   *Selah*

7 "Hear, O my people, and I will speak,
O Israel, I will testify against you.
I am God, your God.

8 Not for your sacrifices do I rebuke you;
your burnt offerings are continually
before me.
9 I will not accept a bull from your house,
or goats from your folds.
10 For every wild animal of the forest is
mine,
the cattle on a thousand hills.
11 I know all the birds of the air,[b]
and all that moves in the field is mine.

12 "If I were hungry, I would not tell you,
for the world and all that is in it is
mine.
13 Do I eat the flesh of bulls,
or drink the blood of goats?
14 Offer to God a sacrifice of thanksgiving,[c]
and pay your vows to the Most High.
15 Call on me in the day of trouble;
I will deliver you, and you shall glorify
me."

16 But to the wicked God says:
"What right have you to recite my
statutes,
or take my covenant on your lips?
17 For you hate discipline,
and you cast my words behind you.
18 You make friends with a thief when you
see one,
and you keep company with adulterers.

a   Cn: Heb *you*
b   Gk Syr Tg: Heb *mountains*
c   Or *make thanksgiving your sacrifice to God*

God's lifting loyal servants to the safety of heaven (see Ps 73.24; Gen 5.24; 2 Kings 2.10). **20:** Repeating v. 12.

Ps 50: A covenant renewal liturgy. A covenant liturgy like Pss 81 and 95. The poem is the first attributed to Asaph, one of David's musicians (1 Chr 6.39; 15.17; 16.5–7); the other Asaph psalms appear together as a collection in 73–83. **1–6:** Appearing in the storm at Mount Sinai (Ex 19), God made a covenant with Israel and now invites Israel to renew it on Mount Zion in Jerusalem. **4:** *Heavens . . . earth*, ancient treaties and covenants invoked such primal pairs as witnesses, and they are appropriately invoked here as the people are questioned about their fidelity to the covenant. **5:** *My faithful ones*, better, "consecrated ones," those who have become God's people by entering into the covenant. **6:** *Selah*, see Ps 3.2n. **7–15:** On God's rejection of animal sacrifice, see Isa 1.10–17; Jer 6.20; Am 5.21–24. Aggressive rebukes and questions often preceded renewal of vows, e.g., Ps 81; Josh 24; 1 Sam 12. The goal was positive: to encourage repentance. **7:** *I am God, your God*, a paraphrase of the beginning of the Decalogue (Ex 20.2); perhaps the entire Decalogue was meant to be repeated at this point in the ritual. **14:** *A sacrifice of thanksgiving* was mostly eaten by the worshiper, and thus would not be construed as feeding God in the same way as a burnt offering; contrast Ps 66.13–15. **16–23:** Though not everyone is guilty of the sins named in this section, the whole congregation must listen to the rebukes, for each is a member of the community. Verses 8–13 rebuked sacrifices that were a substitute for sincere calling unto God; vv. 16–21

¹⁹ "You give your mouth free rein for evil,
and your tongue frames deceit.
²⁰ You sit and speak against your kin;
you slander your own mother's child.
²¹ These things you have done and I have
been silent;
you thought that I was one just like
yourself.
But now I rebuke you, and lay the charge
before you.

²² "Mark this, then, you who forget God,
or I will tear you apart, and there will be
no one to deliver.
²³ Those who bring thanksgiving as their
sacrifice honor me;
to those who go the right wayª
I will show the salvation of God."

Psalm 51

*To the leader. A Psalm of David, when the prophet
Nathan came to him, after he had gone in to
Bathsheba.*

¹ Have mercy on me, O God,
according to your steadfast love;
according to your abundant mercy
blot out my transgressions.
² Wash me thoroughly from my
iniquity,
and cleanse me from my sin.

³ For I know my transgressions,
and my sin is ever before me.
⁴ Against you, you alone, have I sinned,
and done what is evil in your sight,
so that you are justified in your sentence
and blameless when you pass
judgment.

⁵ Indeed, I was born guilty,
a sinner when my mother conceived me.

⁶ You desire truth in the inward being;ᵇ
therefore teach me wisdom in my secret
heart.
⁷ Purge me with hyssop, and I shall be
clean;
wash me, and I shall be whiter than
snow.
⁸ Let me hear joy and gladness;
let the bones that you have crushed
rejoice.
⁹ Hide your face from my sins,
and blot out all my iniquities.

¹⁰ Create in me a clean heart, O God,
and put a new and rightᶜ spirit within
me.
¹¹ Do not cast me away from your presence,
and do not take your holy spirit from
me.
¹² Restore to me the joy of your salvation,
and sustain in me a willingᵈ spirit.

¹³ Then I will teach transgressors your
ways,
and sinners will return to you.
¹⁴ Deliver me from bloodshed, O God,
O God of my salvation,
and my tongue will sing aloud of your
deliverance.

ª Heb *who set a way*
ᵇ Meaning of Heb uncertain
ᶜ Or *steadfast*
ᵈ Or *generous*

---

condemns the sins themselves. **22–23:** A final warning and blessing.

Ps 51: Prayer of repentance and renewal. An individual petition, one of the most profound of the seven penitential psalms in Christian tradition (Pss 6; 32; 38; 51; 102; 130; 143). It is attributed to David after the prophet
Nathan confronted him over his adultery with Bathsheba and the murder of Uriah (2 Sam 12), a reminder that
all humans, even the most revered, must ask God for forgiveness. The first section (vv. 1–9) is marked by the
repetition of *blot out* in vv. 1 and 9, and *wash* in vv. 2 and 7. Repetition of *heart, God,* and *spirit* in vv. 10 and 17
frame the second section (vv. 10–19). As in Ps 50, contrition is considered more valuable than sacrifices. **1–8:**
The psalmist asks forgiveness "as befits your faithfulness" (NRSV *according to your abundant mercy,* v. 1), i.e.,
because of who God is. Since the metaphor here for sin is stain, the psalmist asks for cleansing and purifying
what is soiled or defiled. **5:** *I was born guilty,* the psalmist was never without sin (cf. Ps 88.15). The sense here,
as in some other psalms, is that people are inherently sinful and therefore deserve divine compassion. **7:** The
branches of *hyssop,* a wild shrub, were used for sprinkling liquids in purification rituals (Lev 14.4; Nu 19.6).
9–17: The effects of forgiveness—interior renewal, nearness to God, an enlivened spirit, joy—will inspire the

¹⁵ O Lord, open my lips,
    and my mouth will declare your praise.
¹⁶ For you have no delight in sacrifice;
    if I were to give a burnt offering, you
        would not be pleased.
¹⁷ The sacrifice acceptable to God[a] is a
        broken spirit;
    a broken and contrite heart, O God, you
        will not despise.

¹⁸ Do good to Zion in your good pleasure;
    rebuild the walls of Jerusalem,
¹⁹ then you will delight in right sacrifices,
    in burnt offerings and whole burnt
        offerings;
    then bulls will be offered on your altar.

Psalm 52

To the leader. A Maskil of David, when Doeg the
Edomite came to Saul and said to him, "David has
come to the house of Ahimelech."

¹ Why do you boast, O mighty one,
    of mischief done against the godly?[b]
    All day long ² you are plotting
        destruction.
Your tongue is like a sharp razor,
    you worker of treachery.
³ You love evil more than good,
    and lying more than speaking the truth.
                                        Selah
⁴ You love all words that devour,
    O deceitful tongue.

⁵ But God will break you down forever;
    he will snatch and tear you from your
        tent;
    he will uproot you from the land of the
        living.   *Selah*
⁶ The righteous will see, and fear,
    and will laugh at the evildoer,[c] saying,
⁷ "See the one who would not take
        refuge in God,
but trusted in abundant riches,
    and sought refuge in wealth!"[d]

⁸ But I am like a green olive tree
    in the house of God.
I trust in the steadfast love of God
    forever and ever.
⁹ I will thank you forever,
    because of what you have done.
In the presence of the faithful
    I will proclaim[e] your name, for it is
        good.

Psalm 53

To the leader: according to Mahalath. A Maskil of
David.

¹ Fools say in their hearts, "There is no
        God."

a Or *My sacrifice, O God,*
b Cn Compare Syr: Heb *the kindness of God*
c Heb *him*
d Syr Tg: Heb *in his destruction*
e Cn: Heb *wait for*

psalmist to teach sinners (vv. 13–15), which is of more value than sacrifice (v. 17). **18–19:** Apparently an addition inspired by the statement that *a broken spirit* is an acceptable sacrifice (v. 17): the Temple will be rebuilt and then there will be sacrifices again. As in other psalms, a personal petition is turned into a national psalm, here reflecting the destruction of Jerusalem in 586 BCE.

Ps 52: True confidence. A contrast between the self-confident, wicked warrior and the person who trusts God. The psalmist denounces the wicked (vv. 1–4) and confidently awaits God's punishment of them (vv. 5–7), and concludes with a declaration of trust in God (vv. 8–9). It is similar to Ps 36. **Superscription:** *Maskil,* a technical term of uncertain significance. On Doeg's betrayal of David, see 1 Sam 21.1–8; 22.6–19. **1–4:** The psalm uses types, typical ways of behaving (e.g., the wicked plot against the good person), common in wisdom literature. **1:** *O mighty one,* often applied to God (e.g., Ps 50.1), it is ironically applied to the self-important deceiver whose days are numbered. **3:** *Selah* (also v. 5), see Ps 3.2n. **5–7:** Justice must be seen to be done. **5:** *Land of the living,* better, "the land of life," i.e., the Temple, as in Pss 27.13; 116.9. The sinner will be excluded from the Temple, but the psalmist will be *like a green olive tree in the house of God* (v. 8). **6:** A common theme in Psalms: by applying justice in the world, God encourages people to act justly. **8:** *But I,* abruptly shifts attention to the psalmist who enjoys the protection of the Temple. Ancient temples had gardens that symbolized the life-giving capacity of the god worshiped there.

Ps 53: Refusal to be silenced by those who deny God's justice. A condemnation of those who deny that God is active in the world, and a declaration of trust in the God who cares for the poor (among whom the psalmist

They are corrupt, they commit
abominable acts;
there is no one who does good.

[2] God looks down from heaven on
humankind
to see if there are any who are wise,
who seek after God.

[3] They have all fallen away, they are all
alike perverse;
there is no one who does good,
no, not one.

[4] Have they no knowledge, those
evildoers,
who eat up my people as they eat
bread,
and do not call upon God?

[5] There they shall be in great terror,
in terror such as has not been.
For God will scatter the bones of the
ungodly;[a]
they will be put to shame,[b] for God has
rejected them.

[6] O that deliverance for Israel would come
from Zion!
When God restores the fortunes of his
people,
Jacob will rejoice; Israel will be glad.

Psalm 54

*To the leader: with stringed instruments. A Maskil of
David, when the Ziphites went and told Saul, "David
is in hiding among us."*

[1] Save me, O God, by your name,
and vindicate me by your might.
[2] Hear my prayer, O God;
give ear to the words of my mouth.

[3] For the insolent have risen against me,
the ruthless seek my life;
they do not set God before them.   *Selah*

[4] But surely, God is my helper;
the Lord is the upholder of[c] my life.
[5] He will repay my enemies for their evil.
In your faithfulness, put an end to
them.

[6] With a freewill offering I will sacrifice to
you;
I will give thanks to your name, O LORD,
for it is good.
[7] For he has delivered me from every
trouble,
and my eye has looked in triumph on
my enemies.

a   Cn Compare Gk Syr: Heb *him who encamps against
you*
b   Gk: Heb *you have put (them) to shame*
c   Gk Syr Jerome: Heb *is of those who uphold* or *is
with those who uphold*

wants to be counted). This psalm is a near duplicate of Ps 14. A major difference is that this psalm is part of the "Elohistic Psalter" (Pss 42–83), which prefers the divine name "Elohim," translated "God" rather than "the LORD," and thus replaces many of the "LORD"s of Ps 14 with "God." **Superscription:** *Mahalath, Maskil,* technical terms of uncertain significance. **1:** *There is no God,* denies God's ability to govern, not necessarily God's existence; see Ps 10.4. **2:** God's scrutiny lays bare the deniers' folly and malice. In the style of wisdom literature, the rebellious are contrasted with the *wise, who seek after God.* **4:** Evildoers will finally learn that God defends those whom they exploit. **5:** Divine judgment will scatter the bones of the wicked to the four winds and they will be deprived of proper burial. *There,* evidently a reference to Mount Zion as in Pss 48.6; 76.3. **6:** A generalized conclusion, moving from the individual to the community, as Israel lives in the hope that salvation comes from *Zion. When God restores* may refer to the destruction of Jerusalem in 586 BCE.

Ps 54: God's saving power. An individual petition that focuses on the power of God's name (vv. 1,6). **Superscription:** *Maskil,* a technical term of uncertain significance. On David's betrayal by the residents of Ziph, see 1 Sam 23.15–29. **1:** *Name,* when a person is presented to others, the name is a pledge, in this case that help is on the way. The psalmist wants to be vindicated, that is, shown to be in the right in a conflict with foes. In addition "name" is important in Psalms since the body of most psalms starts with a divine name or title, as here, where the Heb reads "O God, save me." **3:** *Selah,* see Ps 3.2n. **4:** A strong statement of trust in God as *helper* and *upholder* who will punish the enemies. **6:** The psalmist offers God two motivations to help: a *freewill offering,* and a promise to thank God publicly, thereby encouraging others.

Psalm 55

To the leader: with stringed instruments. A Maskil of David.

[1] Give ear to my prayer, O God;
  do not hide yourself from my
    supplication.
[2] Attend to me, and answer me;
  I am troubled in my complaint.
I am distraught [3] by the noise of the enemy,
  because of the clamor of the wicked.
For they bring[a] trouble upon me,
  and in anger they cherish enmity
    against me.

[4] My heart is in anguish within me,
  the terrors of death have fallen upon
    me.
[5] Fear and trembling come upon me,
  and horror overwhelms me.
[6] And I say, "O that I had wings like a dove!
  I would fly away and be at rest;
[7] truly, I would flee far away;
  I would lodge in the wilderness;   *Selah*
[8] I would hurry to find a shelter for myself
  from the raging wind and tempest."

[9] Confuse, O Lord, confound their speech;
  for I see violence and strife in the city.
[10] Day and night they go around it
  on its walls,
and iniquity and trouble are within it;
  [11] ruin is in its midst;
oppression and fraud
  do not depart from its marketplace.

[12] It is not enemies who taunt me—
  I could bear that;
it is not adversaries who deal insolently
    with me—
  I could hide from them.

[13] But it is you, my equal,
  my companion, my familiar friend,
[14] with whom I kept pleasant company;
  we walked in the house of God with the
    throng.
[15] Let death come upon them;
  let them go down alive to Sheol;
  for evil is in their homes and in their
    hearts.

[16] But I call upon God,
  and the LORD will save me.
[17] Evening and morning and at noon
  I utter my complaint and moan,
  and he will hear my voice.
[18] He will redeem me unharmed
  from the battle that I wage,
  for many are arrayed against me.
[19] God, who is enthroned from of old, *Selah*
  will hear, and will humble them—
because they do not change,
  and do not fear God.

[20] My companion laid hands on a
    friend
  and violated a covenant with me[b]
[21] with speech smoother than butter,
  but with a heart set on war;
with words that were softer than oil,
  but in fact were drawn swords.

[22] Cast your burden[c] on the LORD,
  and he will sustain you;
he will never permit
  the righteous to be moved.

a Cn Compare Gk: Heb *they cause to totter*
b Heb lacks *with me*
c Or *Cast what he has given you*

Ps 55: Plea to be delivered from violence and false friends. The petition of an individual emotionally distraught (vv. 4–8) by the violence of the community (*the city*, v. 9) and the deceit of a friend (vv. 12–15,22–23). In the second part (vv. 16–23), the psalmist finds solace in the hope that God will bring justice. **Superscription:** *Maskil*, a technical term of uncertain significance. **1–2:** The Hebrew words rendered *O God . . . I am troubled* are repeated in vv. 22–23 by *moved* and *O God*, which conclude the psalm. **6–7:** In contrast to most psalms, the supplicant does not feel he can find security in the Temple and wants to move far away. **7:** *Selah* (also v. 19), see Ps 3.2n. **12–15:** Harder to bear than societal corruption is the betrayal of a friend, a thought repeated in vv. 22–23. **12:** Not merely crying for revenge; the psalmist wants judgment on the wicked to be visible. **15:** *Alive,* in the prime of life (cf. Num 16.30; Ps 124.3). *Sheol*, the underworld, the abode of the dead. **17:** Either a reference to praying three times a day, as in later Judaism, or a figure of speech, meaning perpetual prayer. **22:** The psalmist is assured, perhaps by a priest or prophet, of divine protection.

23 But you, O God, will cast them down
   into the lowest pit;
the bloodthirsty and treacherous
   shall not live out half their days.
But I will trust in you.

Psalm 56

*To the leader: according to The Dove on Far-off
Terebinths. Of David. A Miktam, when the Philistines
seized him in Gath.*

1 Be gracious to me, O God, for people
      trample on me;
   all day long foes oppress me;
2 my enemies trample on me all day long,
   for many fight against me.
O Most High, 3 when I am afraid,
   I put my trust in you.
4 In God, whose word I praise,
   in God I trust; I am not afraid;
   what can flesh do to me?

5 All day long they seek to injure my
      cause;
   all their thoughts are against me for
      evil.
6 They stir up strife, they lurk,
   they watch my steps.
As they hoped to have my life,
   7 so repay[a] them for their crime;
   in wrath cast down the peoples, O God!

8 You have kept count of my tossings;
   put my tears in your bottle.
   Are they not in your record?
9 Then my enemies will retreat
   in the day when I call.
   This I know, that[b] God is for me.

10 In God, whose word I praise,
   in the LORD, whose word I praise,
11 in God I trust; I am not afraid.
   What can a mere mortal do to me?

12 My vows to you I must perform, O God;
   I will render thank offerings to you.
13 For you have delivered my soul from death,
   and my feet from falling,
so that I may walk before God
   in the light of life.

Psalm 57

*To the leader: Do Not Destroy. Of David. A Miktam,
when he fled from Saul, in the cave.*

1 Be merciful to me, O God, be merciful to
      me,
   for in you my soul takes refuge;
in the shadow of your wings I will take
      refuge,
   until the destroying storms pass by.
2 I cry to God Most High,
   to God who fulfills his purpose for me.
3 He will send from heaven and save me,
   he will put to shame those who trample
      on me.   *Selah*
God will send forth his steadfast love and
      his faithfulness.

4 I lie down among lions
   that greedily devour[c] human prey;
their teeth are spears and arrows,
   their tongues sharp swords.

a   Cn: Heb *rescue*
b   Or *because*
c   Cn: Heb *are aflame for*

Ps 56: Trust in the midst of oppression. Petition of a victim of oppression, notable for its assertions of trust (vv. 2c–4,8–13). The poem is structured by its two refrains, vv. 3–4 and 10–11, and is characterized by repetition. **Superscription:** *The Dove on Far-off Terebinths,* probably the name of a melody. *Miktam,* a technical term of unknown meaning. The psalm is associated with David when the Philistines seized him in Gath (1 Sam 21.11–15). **8:** *My tears in your bottle,* as a shepherd keeps track of his animals by putting pebbles in a bag. *Record,* the same Heb word is translated "book" elsewhere; see Ps 40.7n. With that statement, the tone changes to serene trust in God. **13:** *In the light of life,* in contrast to Sheol, the dark underworld.

Ps 57: A petition for God's faithfulness and a promise of praise. An individual petition divided by refrains (vv. 5,11) into two parts and unified by mention of God's steadfast love and faithfulness (vv. 3,10). **Superscription:** *Do Not Destroy,* perhaps a melody. *Miktam,* a technical term of unknown meaning. The psalm is related to David's being pursued by Saul (1 Sam 22–24). **1:** *The shadow of your wings,* either the wings of the cherubim, protectors of the throne of God in the Temple (1 Kings 6.27; 8.6; Ps 17.8n.) or possibly a comparison of the deity to a bird hovering protectively over its nestlings as in Deut 32.11 and some Egyptian divine images. **3:** *Steadfast love . . . faithfulness* (also v. 10), commonly paired, the two words express one concept, God's loving fidelity. *Selah* (also v. 6),

⁵ Be exalted, O God, above the heavens.
　　Let your glory be over all the earth.

⁶ They set a net for my steps;
　　my soul was bowed down.
They dug a pit in my path,
　　but they have fallen into it
　　　themselves.　　　　　　　　　Selah
⁷ My heart is steadfast, O God,
　　my heart is steadfast.
I will sing and make melody.
　　⁸ Awake, my soul!
Awake, O harp and lyre!
　　I will awake the dawn.
⁹ I will give thanks to you, O Lord, among
　　the peoples;
　　I will sing praises to you among the
　　　nations.
¹⁰ For your steadfast love is as high as the
　　heavens;
　　your faithfulness extends to the
　　　clouds.

¹¹ Be exalted, O God, above the heavens.
　　Let your glory be over all the earth.

Psalm 58

*To the leader: Do Not Destroy. Of David.
A Miktam.*

¹ Do you indeed decree what is right, you
　　gods?ᵃ
　　Do you judge people fairly?
² No, in your hearts you devise wrongs;
　　your hands deal out violence on earth.

³ The wicked go astray from the womb;
　　they err from their birth,
　　　speaking lies.

⁴ They have venom like the venom of a
　　serpent,
　　like the deaf adder that stops its ear,
⁵ so that it does not hear the voice of
　　charmers
　　or of the cunning enchanter.

⁶ O God, break the teeth in their
　　mouths;
　　tear out the fangs of the young lions,
　　　O Lord!
⁷ Let them vanish like water that runs
　　away;
　　like grass let them be trodden downᵇ
　　　and wither.
⁸ Let them be like the snail that dissolves
　　into slime;
　　like the untimely birth that never sees
　　　the sun.
⁹ Sooner than your pots can feel the heat
　　of thorns,
　　whether green or ablaze, may he sweep
　　　them away!

¹⁰ The righteous will rejoice when they see
　　vengeance done;
　　they will bathe their feet in the blood of
　　　the wicked.
¹¹ People will say, "Surely there is a reward
　　for the righteous;
　　surely there is a God who judges on
　　　earth."

ᵃ Or *mighty lords*
ᵇ Cn: Meaning of Heb uncertain

see Ps 3.2n. **4:** The images of *lions* and weapons combine to express great danger, as do those of hunters in v. 6.
6: See 7.15–16n. **7–10:** With the light of dawn, danger disappears, and the psalmist sings a song of thanksgiving
in anticipation of salvation. **9:** The psalmist's declaration of a desire to acknowledge God widely is meant to
motivate God to save him. **10–11:** The psalmist is asking God to act according to his character.

　　Ps 58: The importance of divine justice. Beginning with a contemptuous dismissal of evil "gods" who spon-
sor evil humans (vv. 1–5), the psalmist petitions God to break their power (vv. 6–9) and enable the just to enjoy
peace (vv. 10–11), encouraging people to recognize that a just deity controls the world. **Superscription:** *Do Not
Destroy,* see Ps 57n. *Miktam,* a technical term of unknown meaning. **1:** *You gods,* refers either to wicked humans
behaving arrogantly (as in 2 Kings 24.15; Ezek 17:13) or, more likely, to heavenly beings who rebelled against the
Lord's absolute authority to incite humans to act wickedly (vv. 3–5). Ps 82 is similar. **6–9:** *Break the teeth,* with
a wealth of images the psalmist asks for a divine intervention that will restore God's original intentions. **10–11:**
A successful intervention will let everyone know that there is a just god. *Bathe . . . in the blood,* the gory image
expresses the totality of God's victory; cf. Ps 68.23; Isa 63.1–6.

Psalm 59

To the leader: Do Not Destroy. Of David. A Miktam, when Saul ordered his house to be watched in order to kill him.

¹ Deliver me from my enemies, O my God;
  protect me from those who rise up
      against me.
² Deliver me from those who work evil;
  from the bloodthirsty save me.

³ Even now they lie in wait for my life;
  the mighty stir up strife against me.
For no transgression or sin of mine,
    O LORD,
⁴ for no fault of mine, they run and
      make ready.

Rouse yourself, come to my help and see!
⁵ You, LORD God of hosts, are God of
      Israel.
Awake to punish all the nations;
  spare none of those who treacherously
      plot evil. *Selah*

⁶ Each evening they come back,
  howling like dogs
  and prowling about the city.
⁷ There they are, bellowing with their
      mouths,
  with sharp words[a] on their lips—
  for "Who," they think,[b] "will hear us?"

⁸ But you laugh at them, O LORD;
  you hold all the nations in derision.
⁹ O my strength, I will watch for you;
  for you, O God, are my fortress.
¹⁰ My God in his steadfast love will
      meet me;

my God will let me look in triumph on
  my enemies.

¹¹ Do not kill them, or my people may
      forget;
  make them totter by your power, and
      bring them down,
  O Lord, our shield.
¹² For the sin of their mouths, the words of
      their lips,
  let them be trapped in their pride.
For the cursing and lies that they utter,
¹³ consume them in wrath;
  consume them until they are no
      more.
Then it will be known to the ends of the
      earth
  that God rules over Jacob. *Selah*

¹⁴ Each evening they come back,
  howling like dogs
  and prowling about the city.
¹⁵ They roam about for food,
  and growl if they do not get their fill.

¹⁶ But I will sing of your might;
  I will sing aloud of your steadfast love
      in the morning.
For you have been a fortress for me
  and a refuge in the day of my
      distress.
¹⁷ O my strength, I will sing praises to you,
  for you, O God, are my fortress,
  the God who shows me steadfast
      love.

a   Heb *with swords*
b   Heb lacks *they think*

Ps 59: Prayer against the enemies of the community. The designation of the enemies as "all the nations" (vv. 5,8), "the city" (vv. 6,14), and "known to the ends of the earth" (v. 13) suggests that the poem is a petition of the community, perhaps uttered by the king. The doubled structure of the poem (vv. 1–10,11–17; note the refrains in vv. 6,14 and 9,17) enables the sufferer to change from a simple desire for personal rescue to a passion for justice, hope, and eagerness to sing praise. **Superscription:** *Do Not Destroy,* see Ps 57n. *Miktam,* a technical term of unknown meaning. The episode is related in 1 Sam 19.11–17. **4:** *Rouse yourself,* God is imagined as a sleeping warrior needing to be awakened by his frightened people as in Pss 44.23; 78.65; 121.4; Isa 51.9. **5:** *Selah* (also v. 13), see Ps 3.2n. **6–7,14–15:** The enemies are like dogs, not attacking but constantly yelping, and their cry is *Who . . . will hear us?* i.e., God is unable to save the city. **8:** *But you* introduces the statement of praise in vv. 8–10 just as *but I* (v. 16) introduces the statement of praise in vv. 16–17. This verse is similar to Ps 2.4, in a similar context of God mocking the nations for believing that he is powerless to save Israel. **11–13:** The psalmist wants God to make an object lesson out of the enemies. **16–17:** As is appropriate to this psalm, God is depicted metaphorically as *fortress, refuge,* and *strength;* see Ps 18.1–2. **16:** *In the morning,* see Ps 57.9–10.

Psalm 60

To the leader: according to the Lily of the Covenant.
A Miktam of David; for instruction; when he
struggled with Aram-naharaim and with Aram-
zobah, and when Joab on his return killed twelve
thousand Edomites in the Valley of Salt.

[1] O God, you have rejected us, broken our
    defenses;
  you have been angry; now restore us!
[2] You have caused the land to quake; you
    have torn it open;
  repair the cracks in it, for it is tottering.
[3] You have made your people suffer hard
    things;
  you have given us wine to drink that
    made us reel.

[4] You have set up a banner for those who
    fear you,
  to rally to it out of bowshot.[a]   Selah
[5] Give victory with your right hand, and
    answer us,[b]
  so that those whom you love may be
    rescued.

[6] God has promised in his sanctuary:[c]
  "With exultation I will divide up
    Shechem,
  and portion out the Vale of Succoth.
[7] Gilead is mine, and Manasseh is mine;
  Ephraim is my helmet;
  Judah is my scepter.

[8] Moab is my washbasin;
  on Edom I hurl my shoe;
  over Philistia I shout in triumph."

[9] Who will bring me to the fortified city?
  Who will lead me to Edom?
[10] Have you not rejected us, O God?
  You do not go out, O God, with our
    armies.
[11] O grant us help against the foe,
  for human help is worthless.
[12] With God we shall do valiantly;
  it is he who will tread down our foes.

Psalm 61

To the leader: with stringed instruments.
Of David.

[1] Hear my cry, O God;
  listen to my prayer.
[2] From the end of the earth I call to you,
  when my heart is faint.

Lead me to the rock
  that is higher than I;
[3] for you are my refuge,
  a strong tower against the enemy.

a Gk Syr Jerome: Heb *because of the truth*
b Another reading is *me*
c Or *by his holiness*

Ps 60: **May God grant victory!** A community petition that God would be faithful to his ancient promise of protection (vv. 6–8) and support the beleaguered army (vv. 9–11). Verses 5–12 also appear in Ps 108.6–13. **Superscription:** *According to the Lily of the Covenant,* see Ps 45n.; cf. Ps 80. *Miktam,* a technical term of unknown meaning. Israel's struggles with Aram-naharaim (in northeastern Syria) and Aram-zobah (an Aramean city-state) are told in 2 Sam 8.3–8 and 10.6–13; Joab was David's general. **1–5:** Complaint and petition. **4:** *You have set up a banner,* best rendered as a petition: "Set up a banner so that we may rally to it." *Selah,* see Ps 3.2n. **6–8:** The psalmist cites an ancient oracle, probably uttered after a victory, in order to remind God to be faithful to it in the present crisis. *Shechem,* a major city in central Israel (*Ephraim,* the northern kingdom). *The Vale of Succoth,* in the east Jordan Valley. *Gilead* and *Manasseh,* Israelite territory in Transjordan. *Judah,* the southern kingdom. *Moab* and *Edom,* in southern Transjordan, and *Philistia,* on the southeastern Mediterranean coast, were areas subjected to Israel as vassals (see 2 Sam 8.11–12). *I hurl my shoe,* probably a reference to the legal gesture of claiming ownership attested in Ruth 4.7. **9–12:** Complaint and petition. **9:** *Who will bring me to the fortified city?* A prayer that God lead the commander of Israel's armies (perhaps the king) against their foes. *Fortified city,* a seemingly impregnable fort, probably referring to Bozrah, the capital of Edom. **10:** Reprises v. 1. *Go out . . . with our armies,* according to 1 Sam 4, the Israelites could carry the ark with them to bring God along in battle; in later times, divine support was imagined without the ark's presence. **11–12:** A common biblical theme, that victory depends on God alone, not on human might.

Ps 61: **Plea to be in God's Temple.** An individual, far away from the Temple, prays to be led there and enjoy its protection and nourishment. **2–4:** *From the end of the earth,* a remote place, far from the center in Jerusalem.

4 Let me abide in your tent forever,
      find refuge under the shelter of
            your wings.   *Selah*
5 For you, O God, have heard my vows;
      you have given me the heritage of those
            who fear your name.

6 Prolong the life of the king;
      may his years endure to all generations!
7 May he be enthroned forever before God;
      appoint steadfast love and faithfulness
            to watch over him!

8 So I will always sing praises to your name,
      as I pay my vows day after day.

Psalm 62

To the leader: according to Jeduthun. A Psalm of David.

1 For God alone my soul waits in
      silence;
      from him comes my salvation.
2 He alone is my rock and my salvation,
      my fortress; I shall never be shaken.

3 How long will you assail a person,
      will you batter your victim, all of you,
      as you would a leaning wall, a tottering
            fence?
4 Their only plan is to bring down a person
      of prominence.
      They take pleasure in falsehood;
they bless with their mouths,
      but inwardly they curse.   *Selah*

5 For God alone my soul waits in silence,
      for my hope is from him.
6 He alone is my rock and my salvation,
      my fortress; I shall not be shaken.
7 On God rests my deliverance and my
      honor;
      my mighty rock, my refuge is in God.

8 Trust in him at all times, O people;
      pour out your heart before him;
      God is a refuge for us.   *Selah*

9 Those of low estate are but a breath,
      those of high estate are a delusion;
in the balances they go up;
      they are together lighter than a
            breath.
10 Put no confidence in extortion,
      and set no vain hopes on robbery;
      if riches increase, do not set your heart
            on them.

11 Once God has spoken;
      twice have I heard this:
that power belongs to God,
      12 and steadfast love belongs to you,
            O Lord.
For you repay to all
      according to their work.

Psalm 63

A Psalm of David, when he was in the Wilderness of Judah.

1 O God, you are my God, I seek you,
      my soul thirsts for you;

Rock, refuge, tower, tent, shelter of your wings, all can refer to the Temple and its precincts; see also Ps 57.1n. **4:** *Selah,* see Ps 3.2n. **5–8:** *You . . . have heard my vows,* best understood as a prayer of one still far from the Temple, confident that God has heard his vows. **6:** The sudden mention of the king is surprising, but the king, as God's anointed, was closely associated with the Temple; he also represented the people and so the psalmist's request is to join the people in their worship as in Pss 42–43.

Ps 62: Trust in God the stronghold. A song of trust, recording the feelings of an individual beset by enemies. Various synonyms for salvation and for God as a fortress predominate. **Superscription:** *Jeduthun,* see Ps 39n. **3–4:** Instead of speaking about the enemies, the psalmist speaks to the enemies (as in Pss 2.10–11; 4.2; 75.4–7); this is likely a literary conceit. **4:** *Selah* (also v. 8), see Ps 3.2n. **5:** *For God alone my soul waits in silence,* reprises v. 1; the psalmist's attitude differs totally from that of the evildoers (v. 4). **8–10:** Lest others be intimidated and cease trusting, the psalmist shares the hard-won conviction that nothing but God suffices. **9:** The good deeds of the evildoers are so unsubstantial, they are weightless. **11:** *Once . . . twice,* numerical parallelism, where a number X is paralleled by X+1. This verse thus means that *I heard* the one thing that God spoke, *that power belongs to God.*

Ps 63: Longing for God. A song of desire to be protected from enemies (vv. 9–10) and be in God's house (vv. 2–5), like Pss 27; 42–43; 61; and 84. The superscription associates the poem with David hiding from Saul in the wilderness of Judah (1 Sam 23.14–15; 24.1). **1:** *My soul thirsts,* communion with God is expressed in metaphors of

my flesh faints for you,
  as in a dry and weary land where there
    is no water.
[2] So I have looked upon you in the
    sanctuary,
  beholding your power and glory.
[3] Because your steadfast love is better than
    life,
  my lips will praise you.
[4] So I will bless you as long as I live;
  I will lift up my hands and call on your
    name.

[5] My soul is satisfied as with a rich feast,[a]
  and my mouth praises you with joyful
    lips
[6] when I think of you on my bed,
  and meditate on you in the watches of
    the night;
[7] for you have been my help,
  and in the shadow of your wings I sing
    for joy.
[8] My soul clings to you;
  your right hand upholds me.

[9] But those who seek to destroy my life
  shall go down into the depths of the
    earth;
[10] they shall be given over to the power of
    the sword,
  they shall be prey for jackals.
[11] But the king shall rejoice in God;
  all who swear by him shall exult,
  for the mouths of liars will be
    stopped.

Psalm 64

To the leader. A Psalm of David.

[1] Hear my voice, O God, in my complaint;
  preserve my life from the dread enemy.
[2] Hide me from the secret plots of the
    wicked,
  from the scheming of evildoers,
[3] who whet their tongues like swords,
  who aim bitter words like arrows,
[4] shooting from ambush at the blameless;
  they shoot suddenly and without fear.
[5] They hold fast to their evil purpose;
  they talk of laying snares secretly,
  thinking, "Who can see us?[b]
  [6] Who can search out our crimes?[c]
  We have thought out a cunningly
    conceived plot."
  For the human heart and mind are
    deep.

[7] But God will shoot his arrow at them;
  they will be wounded suddenly.
[8] Because of their tongue he will bring
    them to ruin;[d]
  all who see them will shake with horror.
[9] Then everyone will fear;
  they will tell what God has brought about,
  and ponder what he has done.

---

a Heb *with fat and fatness*
b Syr: Heb *them*
c Cn: Heb *They search out crimes*
d Cn: Heb *They will bring him to ruin, their tongue being against them*

---

eating, seeing (v. 2), and praising (vv. 3–5). In Hebrew, the word for *soul* also means "throat," so the verse is punning. **2:** *I have looked*, the NRSV translation assumes the psalmist is already in the Temple, but in similar psalms being in the Temple is in the future. Thus one can translate, "I shall look upon." **3:** *Better than life*, experiencing God in the Temple is better than mere existence elsewhere. **6:** *On my bed*, spontaneous private prayer by the sleepless individual, in contrast to commanded ritual performance as in Pss 4:4b–5a; 149:5b,6–11. **6–11:** In contrast to the first part of the psalm (vv. 1–5), which expresses the hope of being in the Temple, the second part (vv. 6–11) acknowledges that God has never ceased being the psalmist's God. *Shadow of your wings*, see Ps 57.1n. **11:** For a similar concluding prayer mentioning the king, see Ps 61.6n.

Ps 64: **Protection from enemies' plots.** A carefully constructed individual petition to be protected from people who deny that God rules society. The second part (vv. 6–10), the statement of hope and trust, reverses the key words of the first part (vv. 1–5): *arrows/arrow* in vv. 3b and 7a; *tongues/tongue* in vv. 3a and 8a; *suddenly* in vv. 4b and 7b; *shoot* in vv. 4a, 4b, and 7a; *fear* in vv. 4b and 9a; and *see* in vv. 5c and 8b. God will *shoot his arrow* at those who have shot arrows at the righteous; those who use their *tongues* to attack the righteous and assert God's impotence will be ruined because of their tongue, that is, their words. The second part expresses the firm hope that God will undo each malicious act. **9:** *Then everyone will fear*, like many individual petitions, the conclusion moves from the single person to the community, here stating that people will be in awe as they

¹⁰ Let the righteous rejoice in the LORD
  and take refuge in him.
Let all the upright in heart glory.

Psalm 65

To the leader. A Psalm of David. A Song.

¹ Praise is due to you,
  O God, in Zion;
and to you shall vows be performed,
  ² O you who answer prayer!
To you all flesh shall come.
³ When deeds of iniquity overwhelm us,
  you forgive our transgressions.
⁴ Happy are those whom you choose and
    bring near
  to live in your courts.
We shall be satisfied with the goodness of
    your house,
  your holy temple.

⁵ By awesome deeds you answer us with
    deliverance,
  O God of our salvation;
you are the hope of all the ends of the earth
  and of the farthest seas.
⁶ By your^a strength you established the
    mountains;
  you are girded with might.
⁷ You silence the roaring of the seas,
  the roaring of their waves,
  the tumult of the peoples.
⁸ Those who live at earth's farthest bounds
  are awed by your signs;
you make the gateways of the morning and
  the evening shout for joy.

⁹ You visit the earth and water it,
  you greatly enrich it;

the river of God is full of water;
  you provide the people with grain,
  for so you have prepared it.
¹⁰ You water its furrows abundantly,
  settling its ridges,
softening it with showers,
  and blessing its growth.
¹¹ You crown the year with your bounty;
  your wagon tracks overflow with
    richness.
¹² The pastures of the wilderness overflow,
  the hills gird themselves with joy,
¹³ the meadows clothe themselves with
    flocks,
  the valleys deck themselves with grain,
  they shout and sing together for joy.

Psalm 66

To the leader. A Song. A Psalm.

¹ Make a joyful noise to God, all the earth;
  ² sing the glory of his name;
  give to him glorious praise.
³ Say to God, "How awesome are your deeds!
  Because of your great power, your
    enemies cringe before you.
⁴ All the earth worships you;
  they sing praises to you,
  sing praises to your name."   *Selah*

⁵ Come and see what God has done:
  he is awesome in his deeds among
    mortals.
⁶ He turned the sea into dry land;
  they passed through the river on foot.
There we rejoiced in him,
  ⁷ who rules by his might forever,

---

^a Gk Jerome: Heb *his*

recognize God's just action.
  Ps 65: Thanksgiving for God's enlivening the world. 1–4: In Hebrew, the opening lines begin with "to you,"
underlining the centrality of God, to whom every liturgical act performed on Mount Zion is directed. **2:** *All flesh
shall come,* see Pss 22.27n.; 100n. **3–4:** *Forgive . . . bring near,* liturgical vocabulary. **5:** *Awesome deeds,* deeds that
elicit wonder. In Ps 106.22 the phrase refers to the Exodus miracles, and in Isa 5.8 to creation victory. **6–7:** The
divine victory associated with creation: the *mountains* are placed in their bases (see Pss 89.12; 90.2) and the
chaotic primeval waters are defeated (see Ps 89.9–13). **9–13:** One benefit of God's creation victory is that the
once-dangerous waters now fertilize the earth. The psalmist focuses on the waters that make the earth bloom
and give nurture to humans. **9:** *River of God,* see Ps 36.5–9n. **12–13:** Implicitly compares the earth to human
beings, beautifully attired and singing joyous songs. The abundance of the harvest has a mythological quality.
  Ps 66: Thanksgiving to God for help in danger. In this community thanksgiving, an individual calls upon the
whole world (vv. 1–4,16–19) to acknowledge God's rescue of the people from danger (vv. 8–12) and promises to
fulfill a vow made in that time of danger (vv. 13–15). **4:** *Selah* (also vv. 7,15), see Ps 3.2n. **5–6:** *Come and see,* when

whose eyes keep watch on the nations—
  let the rebellious not exalt themselves.
                                        Selah

[8] Bless our God, O peoples,
  let the sound of his praise be heard,
[9] who has kept us among the living,
  and has not let our feet slip.
[10] For you, O God, have tested us;
  you have tried us as silver is tried.
[11] You brought us into the net;
  you laid burdens on our backs;
[12] you let people ride over our heads;
  we went through fire and through
    water;
yet you have brought us out to a spacious
    place.[a]

[13] I will come into your house with burnt
    offerings;
  I will pay you my vows,
[14] those that my lips uttered
  and my mouth promised when I was in
    trouble.
[15] I will offer to you burnt offerings of
    fatlings,
  with the smoke of the sacrifice of rams;
I will make an offering of bulls and goats.
                                        Selah

[16] Come and hear, all you who fear God,
  and I will tell what he has done for me.
[17] I cried aloud to him,
  and he was extolled with my tongue.
[18] If I had cherished iniquity in my heart,
  the Lord would not have listened.

[19] But truly God has listened;
  he has given heed to the words of my
    prayer.

[20] Blessed be God,
  because he has not rejected my prayer
  or removed his steadfast love from me.

Psalm 67

To the leader: with stringed instruments. A Psalm. A Song.

[1] May God be gracious to us and bless us
  and make his face to shine upon us,
                                        Selah
[2] that your way may be known upon earth,
  your saving power among all nations.
[3] Let the peoples praise you, O God;
  let all the peoples praise you.

[4] Let the nations be glad and sing for joy,
  for you judge the peoples with equity
  and guide the nations upon earth. *Selah*
[5] Let the peoples praise you, O God;
  let all the peoples praise you.

[6] The earth has yielded its increase;
  God, our God, has blessed us.
[7] May God continue to bless us;
  let all the ends of the earth revere him.

Psalm 68

To the leader. Of David. A Psalm. A Song.

[1] Let God rise up, let his enemies be scattered;
  let those who hate him flee before him.

a   Cn Compare Gk Syr Jerome Tg: Heb *to a saturation*

grave danger threatened, the psalmist called people to remember the great formative event of the Exodus (see Ex 14.21–22; Josh 4.23), assuming that God will be faithful to that past act. **10:** *Silver* ore was *tried* or refined by heat, which separated the pure silver from other minerals. **16–20:** Ritual thanksgiving is not enough; the psalmist must proclaim God's mighty works to the world.

  Ps 67: May the nations acknowledge God in our prosperity! In this communal petition, the psalmist prays that the nations may see how God has caused Israel to prosper, has protected the people, and will judge them equitably, and that the nations will therefore praise him. "Bless" and "praise" are key words, repeated several times, emphasizing the theme of the psalm. **1:** *Make his face to shine upon us,* a reworking of the priestly blessing in Num 6.24–26. Like the sun and moon, the face is a light shining in favor upon the people (Pss 31.16; 80.3,7,19). *Selah* (also v. 4), see Ps 3.2n. **3–5:** The center of the poem is v. 4, the only three-line verse: it is framed by vv. 3 and 5. **6:** *The earth has yielded,* best translated as a prayer, "May the earth yield its increase": the people pray for their prosperity so that their God might receive more honor.

  Ps 68: The victorious Lord comes to the aid of Israel. Psalm 68 is the most difficult psalm in the book, and scholars do not agree on what kind of poem Psalm 68 is, as well as what many of its words or phrases mean. It is perhaps best taken as a communal thanksgiving for defending the people against infertility and attack. The

2 As smoke is driven away, so drive them
away;
  as wax melts before the fire,
  let the wicked perish before God.
3 But let the righteous be joyful;
  let them exult before God;
  let them be jubilant with joy.

4 Sing to God, sing praises to his name;
  lift up a song to him who rides upon the
    clouds[a]—
his name is the LORD—
  be exultant before him.

5 Father of orphans and protector of
    widows
  is God in his holy habitation.
6 God gives the desolate a home to live in;
  he leads out the prisoners to prosperity,
  but the rebellious live in a parched land.

7 O God, when you went out before your
    people,
  when you marched through the
    wilderness,   Selah
8 the earth quaked, the heavens poured
    down rain
  at the presence of God, the God of Sinai,
  at the presence of God, the God of
    Israel.
9 Rain in abundance, O God, you showered
    abroad;
  you restored your heritage when it
    languished;
10 your flock found a dwelling in it;
  in your goodness, O God, you provided
    for the needy.

11 The Lord gives the command;
  great is the company of those[b] who bore
    the tidings:
12 "The kings of the armies, they flee,
    they flee!"
The women at home divide the spoil,
  13 though they stay among the
    sheepfolds—

the wings of a dove covered with silver,
  its pinions with green gold.
14 When the Almighty[c] scattered kings
    there,
  snow fell on Zalmon.

15 O mighty mountain, mountain of
    Bashan;
  O many-peaked mountain, mountain of
    Bashan!
16 Why do you look with envy, O many-
    peaked mountain,
  at the mount that God desired for his
    abode,
  where the LORD will reside forever?

17 With mighty chariotry, twice ten
    thousand,
  thousands upon thousands,
  the Lord came from Sinai into the holy
    place.[d]
18 You ascended the high mount,
  leading captives in your train
  and receiving gifts from people,
even from those who rebel against the
    LORD God's abiding there.
19 Blessed be the Lord,
  who daily bears us up;
  God is our salvation.   Selah
20 Our God is a God of salvation,
  and to GOD, the Lord, belongs escape
    from death.

21 But God will shatter the heads of his
    enemies,
  the hairy crown of those who walk in
    their guilty ways.
22 The Lord said,
  "I will bring them back from Bashan,

a Or cast up a highway for him who rides through the
   deserts
b Or company of the women
c Traditional rendering of Heb Shaddai
d Cn: Heb The Lord among them Sinai in the holy
   (place)

battle-victory is described in cosmic terms, waged against "the depths of the sea" (v. 22), "wild animals," and
"the herd of bulls" (v. 30), as well as "the kings of the armies" (v. 12). 1–3: A summons for God to act. 4–6: Invitation to sing to the God of justice. 4: Who rides upon the clouds, God's storm-cloud chariot; see also v. 33. 7–14:
God's victorious campaign to make the earth fertile and safe. 7: Selah (also vv. 19,32), see Ps 3.2n. 7–8: Cf. Judg
5.4–5. 15–23: The LORD returns to his holy mountain residence, Mount Zion, having earlier appeared at Sinai

I will bring them back from the depths of
the sea,
[23] so that you may bathe[a] your feet in blood,
so that the tongues of your dogs may
have their share from the foe."

[24] Your solemn processions are seen,[b]
O God,
the processions of my God, my King,
into the sanctuary—
[25] the singers in front, the musicians last,
between them girls playing
tambourines:
[26] "Bless God in the great congregation,
the LORD, O you who are of Israel's
fountain!"
[27] There is Benjamin, the least of them, in
the lead,
the princes of Judah in a body,
the princes of Zebulun, the princes of
Naphtali.

[28] Summon your might, O God;
show your strength, O God, as you have
done for us before.
[29] Because of your temple at Jerusalem
kings bear gifts to you.
[30] Rebuke the wild animals that live among
the reeds,
the herd of bulls with the calves of the
peoples.
Trample[c] under foot those who lust after
tribute;
scatter the peoples who delight in war.[d]
[31] Let bronze be brought from Egypt;
let Ethiopia[e] hasten to stretch out its
hands to God.

[32] Sing to God, O kingdoms of the earth;
sing praises to the Lord, *Selah*
[33] O rider in the heavens, the ancient
heavens;
listen, he sends out his voice, his
mighty voice.

[34] Ascribe power to God,
whose majesty is over Israel;
and whose power is in the skies.
[35] Awesome is God in his[f] sanctuary,
the God of Israel;
he gives power and strength to his
people.

Blessed be God!

Psalm 69

To the leader: according to Lilies. Of David.

[1] Save me, O God,
for the waters have come up to my neck.
[2] I sink in deep mire,
where there is no foothold;
I have come into deep waters,
and the flood sweeps over me.
[3] I am weary with my crying;
my throat is parched.
My eyes grow dim
with waiting for my God.

[4] More in number than the hairs of my
head
are those who hate me without cause;
many are those who would destroy me,
my enemies who accuse me falsely.
What I did not steal
must I now restore?
[5] O God, you know my folly;
the wrongs I have done are not hidden
from you.

[6] Do not let those who hope in you be put
to shame because of me,
O Lord GOD of hosts;

a Gk Syr Tg: Heb *shatter*
b Or *have been seen*
c Cn: Heb *Trampling*
d Meaning of Heb of verse 30 is uncertain
e Or *Nubia*; Heb *Cush*
f Gk: Heb *from your*

(v. 8). **14–15:** *Zalmon,* precise location unknown; perhaps a mountain in *Bashan,* in northern Transjordan. **23:** *Bathe
. . . in blood,* see 58.10n. **24–31:** The tribes of Israel follow in procession. **32–35.** The nations are to bring tribute to
the victorious LORD in the Temple and acknowledge God. **33–35:** Cf. Ps 29.1–3,11. *Rider in the heavens,* see v. 4n.

 Ps 69: A loyal servant's prayer for deliverance. An individual petition, marked by deep commitment to God's
cause. Verses 13d–29 repeat words occurring in vv. 1–13a, unifying the poem and lending it intensity. Another
stylistic feature of the poem is the alternation between *I* (the psalmist) and *you* (God). **Superscription:** *According to Lilies,* probably refers to a melody (also Pss 45; 80). **1–4:** References to waters unify vv. 1–3, and references

do not let those who seek you be
    dishonored because of me,
        O God of Israel.
⁷ It is for your sake that I have borne
    reproach,
    that shame has covered my face.
⁸ I have become a stranger to my kindred,
    an alien to my mother's children.

⁹ It is zeal for your house that has
    consumed me;
    the insults of those who insult you have
        fallen on me.
¹⁰ When I humbled my soul with fasting,^a
    they insulted me for doing so.
¹¹ When I made sackcloth my clothing,
    I became a byword to them.
¹² I am the subject of gossip for those who
    sit in the gate,
    and the drunkards make songs
        about me.

¹³ But as for me, my prayer is to you,
    O Lord.
    At an acceptable time, O God,
    in the abundance of your steadfast love,
        answer me.
With your faithful help ¹⁴ rescue me
    from sinking in the mire;
let me be delivered from my enemies
    and from the deep waters.
¹⁵ Do not let the flood sweep over me,
    or the deep swallow me up,
    or the Pit close its mouth over me.

¹⁶ Answer me, O Lord, for your steadfast
    love is good;
    according to your abundant mercy, turn
        to me.
¹⁷ Do not hide your face from your
    servant,
    for I am in distress—make haste to
        answer me.
¹⁸ Draw near to me, redeem me,
    set me free because of my enemies.

¹⁹ You know the insults I receive,
    and my shame and dishonor;
    my foes are all known to you.
²⁰ Insults have broken my heart,
    so that I am in despair.
I looked for pity, but there was none;
    and for comforters, but I found none.
²¹ They gave me poison for food,
    and for my thirst they gave me vinegar
        to drink.

²² Let their table be a trap for them,
    a snare for their allies.
²³ Let their eyes be darkened so that they
    cannot see,
    and make their loins tremble
        continually.
²⁴ Pour out your indignation upon them,
    and let your burning anger overtake
        them.
²⁵ May their camp be a desolation;
    let no one live in their tents.
²⁶ For they persecute those whom you have
    struck down,
    and those whom you have wounded,
        they attack still more.^b
²⁷ Add guilt to their guilt;
    may they have no acquittal from you.
²⁸ Let them be blotted out of the book of
    the living;
    let them not be enrolled among the
        righteous.
²⁹ But I am lowly and in pain;
    let your salvation, O God, protect me.

³⁰ I will praise the name of God with a
    song;
    I will magnify him with thanksgiving.
³¹ This will please the Lord more than an ox
    or a bull with horns and hoofs.
³² Let the oppressed see it and be glad;
    you who seek God, let your hearts revive.

---

a Gk Syr: Heb *I wept, with fasting my soul*, or *I made
my soul mourn with fasting*
b Gk Syr: Heb *recount the pain of*

to bodily organs (*throat, eyes, hairs of my head*) unify vv. 3–4. **5–12:** The psalmist asks for help promoting the
honor of God's house (v. 7), though freely conceding personal weakness and folly (v. 5). **8:** See Ps 38.11; Job
19.13–15. **22–29:** The psalmist is less interested in personal vengeance than in being publicly vindicated as God's
innocent and loyal servant. **28:** *The book of the living* was a scroll containing the fates of individuals. In postbiblical Judaism, the book was inscribed at the New Year, and sealed and finalized on Yom Kippur. **30–31:** A verbal

³³ For the LORD hears the needy,
  and does not despise his own that are
    in bonds.

³⁴ Let heaven and earth praise him,
  the seas and everything that moves in
    them.
³⁵ For God will save Zion
  and rebuild the cities of Judah;
and his servants shall live[a] there and
    possess it;
  ³⁶ the children of his servants shall
    inherit it,
  and those who love his name shall live
    in it.

Psalm 70

*To the leader. Of David, for the memorial
offering.*

¹ Be pleased, O God, to deliver me.
  O LORD, make haste to help me!
² Let those be put to shame and
    confusion
  who seek my life.
Let those be turned back and brought to
    dishonor
  who desire to hurt me.
³ Let those who say, "Aha, Aha!"
  turn back because of their shame.

⁴ Let all who seek you
  rejoice and be glad in you.
Let those who love your salvation
  say evermore, "God is great!"
⁵ But I am poor and needy;
  hasten to me, O God!
You are my help and my deliverer;
  O LORD, do not delay!

Psalm 71

¹ In you, O LORD, I take refuge;
  let me never be put to shame.
² In your righteousness deliver me and
    rescue me;
  incline your ear to me and save me.
³ Be to me a rock of refuge,
  a strong fortress,[b] to save me,
  for you are my rock and my fortress.

⁴ Rescue me, O my God, from the hand of
    the wicked,
  from the grasp of the unjust and cruel.
⁵ For you, O Lord, are my hope,
  my trust, O LORD, from my youth.
⁶ Upon you I have leaned from my birth;
  it was you who took me from my
    mother's womb.
My praise is continually of you.

⁷ I have been like a portent to many,
  but you are my strong refuge.
⁸ My mouth is filled with your praise,
  and with your glory all day long.
⁹ Do not cast me off in the time of old age;
  do not forsake me when my strength is
    spent.
¹⁰ For my enemies speak concerning me,
  and those who watch for my life consult
    together.
¹¹ They say, "Pursue and seize that person
  whom God has forsaken,
  for there is no one to deliver."

---

a Syr: Heb *and they shall live*
b Gk Compare 31.3: Heb *to come continually you have
    commanded*

offering is superior to an animal one; cf. Ps 51.16–17. **32–36:** The salvation of the supplicant is not for his own sake, but so others will praise God. **35:** Perhaps a reference to the attack of the Assyrian king Sennacherib in 701 BCE, or to the destruction of Jerusalem in 586 BCE.

Ps 70: A prayer that the psalmist's persecutors would be defeated. An individual petition, which is also found with a few variants in Ps 40.13–17. **Superscription:** *For the memorial offering* (also Ps 38), meaning uncertain. **1–3:** *God, help,* and *make haste,* the words are echoed in the final lines, bringing closure to the poem. **2:** *Shame,* violating accepted morality brought dishonor upon the violator. The prayer is that the enemies' schemes be publicly frustrated. **3:** *Aha, Aha,* malicious cries of triumph that the psalmist hopes will be proved foolish by God's judgment. **4:** God's help of this individual will encourage other righteous people. **5:** Psalms often depicts the supplicant as *poor* and *needy.*

Ps 71: An elderly person's plea for help. An individual petition that recycles material from Pss 22 and 31. Vv. 1–13 and 14–24 seem to constitute its two parts. **3:** *Rock of refuge,* a massive rock formation, a frequent metaphor

¹² O God, do not be far from me;
    O my God, make haste to help me!
¹³ Let my accusers be put to shame and
        consumed;
    let those who seek to hurt me
    be covered with scorn and disgrace.
¹⁴ But I will hope continually,
    and will praise you yet more and more.
¹⁵ My mouth will tell of your righteous acts,
    of your deeds of salvation all day long,
    though their number is past my
        knowledge.
¹⁶ I will come praising the mighty deeds of
        the Lord GOD,
    I will praise your righteousness, yours
        alone.

¹⁷ O God, from my youth you have taught me,
    and I still proclaim your wondrous
        deeds.
¹⁸ So even to old age and gray hairs,
    O God, do not forsake me,
until I proclaim your might
    to all the generations to come.ᵃ
Your power ¹⁹ and your righteousness, O God,
    reach the high heavens.

You who have done great things,
    O God, who is like you?
²⁰ You who have made me see many
        troubles and calamities
    will revive me again;
from the depths of the earth
    you will bring me up again.
²¹ You will increase my honor,
    and comfort me once again.

²² I will also praise you with the harp
    for your faithfulness, O my God;

I will sing praises to you with the lyre,
    O Holy One of Israel.
²³ My lips will shout for joy
    when I sing praises to you;
    my soul also, which you have rescued.
²⁴ All day long my tongue will talk of your
        righteous help,
for those who tried to do me harm
    have been put to shame, and disgraced.

Psalm 72
Of Solomon.

¹ Give the king your justice, O God,
    and your righteousness to a king's son.
² May he judge your people with
        righteousness,
    and your poor with justice.
³ May the mountains yield prosperity for
        the people,
    and the hills, in righteousness.
⁴ May he defend the cause of the poor of
        the people,
    give deliverance to the needy,
    and crush the oppressor.

⁵ May he liveᵇ while the sun endures,
    and as long as the moon, throughout all
        generations.
⁶ May he be like rain that falls on the
        mown grass,
    like showers that water the earth.
⁷ In his days may righteousness flourish
    and peace abound, until the moon is no
        more.

ᵃ Gk Compare Syr: Heb *to a generation, to all that*
    come
ᵇ Gk: Heb *may they fear you*

for God saving and helping someone. **7:** *A portent to many,* an example of God's merciful care for loyal servants.
14–16: The psalmist is unusually buoyant despite the troubles. **17–21:** The psalmist looks back at a long life,
finds that God has always been faithful, and is inspired by such fidelity. **24:** As in many petitions, the person
praying imagines that the prayer has already been heard and the problem rectified.

Ps 72: Prayer that the king may prosper and extend God's rule to all lands. A royal psalm that may have been
used at the king's coronation or anniversary. It views the Israelite king as the instrument of divine justice and
protector of the poor (vv. 1–4,12–14), ensuring that the riches of creation are available to all (vv. 5–7); and he is
the icon of God's universal rule (vv. 8–11). Nonetheless, he is still a human being in constant need of divine help
(vv. 1,15–17). It is one of two psalms attributed to King Solomon (see also Ps 127), probably because an editor
imagined that the land boundaries in v. 8 reflected the boundaries of Solomon's kingdom (see 1 Kings 4.24). **1–2:**
Justice, righteousness, conformity to the divine will, which leads to *prosperity* (v. 3). **2:** *Your poor,* the existence of
the poor (vv. 2, 4) is contrary to the divine will, so the king is to be an instrument of the more equitable distribu-

⁸ May he have dominion from sea to sea,
  and from the River to the ends of the
    earth.
⁹ May his foes[a] bow down before him,
  and his enemies lick the dust.
¹⁰ May the kings of Tarshish and of the
    isles
  render him tribute,
may the kings of Sheba and Seba
  bring gifts.
¹¹ May all kings fall down before him,
  all nations give him service.

¹² For he delivers the needy when they call,
  the poor and those who have no helper.
¹³ He has pity on the weak and the needy,
  and saves the lives of the needy.
¹⁴ From oppression and violence he
    redeems their life;
  and precious is their blood in his sight.

¹⁵ Long may he live!
  May gold of Sheba be given to him.
May prayer be made for him continually,
  and blessings invoked for him all day
    long.
¹⁶ May there be abundance of grain in the
    land;
  may it wave on the tops of the
    mountains;
  may its fruit be like Lebanon;
and may people blossom in the cities
  like the grass of the field.
¹⁷ May his name endure forever,
  his fame continue as long as the sun.
May all nations be blessed in him;[b]
  may they pronounce him happy.

¹⁸ Blessed be the LORD, the God of Israel,
  who alone does wondrous things.
¹⁹ Blessed be his glorious name forever;
  may his glory fill the whole earth.
    Amen and Amen.

²⁰ The prayers of David son of Jesse are
    ended.

BOOK III PSALMS 73–89

Psalm 73
A Psalm of Asaph.

¹ Truly God is good to the upright,[c]
  to those who are pure in heart.
² But as for me, my feet had almost
    stumbled;
  my steps had nearly slipped.
³ For I was envious of the arrogant;
  I saw the prosperity of the wicked.

⁴ For they have no pain;
  their bodies are sound and sleek.
⁵ They are not in trouble as others are;
  they are not plagued like other people.
⁶ Therefore pride is their necklace;
  violence covers them like a garment.
⁷ Their eyes swell out with fatness;
  their hearts overflow with follies.
⁸ They scoff and speak with malice;
  loftily they threaten oppression.
⁹ They set their mouths against heaven,
  and their tongues range over the earth.

a Cn: Heb *those who live in the wilderness*
b Or *bless themselves by him*
c Or *good to Israel*

tion of the world's goods. **8–11:** As representative of the Lord of the world, the Israelite king receives the tribute of all the kings of the world in God's name. **8:** *The River*, the Euphrates. **10:** *Tarshish*, location uncertain; it may be Tarsus in southern Turkey or Tartessus in southern Spain. *The isles*, the islands of the eastern Aegean Sea. *Sheba* and *Seba*, both in southwestern Arabia. **12–14:** A repetition of the royal responsibilities, emphasizing the poor, similar to 2–4. **15–17:** Another cycle of blessings, similar to 5–11. **18–19:** A doxology, not part of the psalm, which marks the conclusion of Book Two of the Psalter. **20:** This verse suggests that at one time the book of Psalms, or at least the psalms attributed to David, ended here. (Other psalms also attributed to David will follow; e.g., 86; 101; 103.) This is important evidence for the growth of the book of Psalms over time.

Ps 73: Declaration of trust. Though sometimes classed as a wisdom psalm because it explores the problem of evil, the psalm actually records the psalmist's passage from despair at the apparent triumph of the wicked (vv. 3–12), through various stratagems to solve the problem (vv. 13–17), to a final appreciation of God's justice, nearness, and care (vv. 18–28). The psalm suggests that the wicked may triumph, but only temporarily. It opens a collection of psalms attributed to Asaph (73–83; see Ps 50n.). **1:** A statement of faith, paraphrased in the final

¹⁰ Therefore the people turn and praise
    them,ᵃ
    and find no fault in them.ᵇ
¹¹ And they say, "How can God know?
    Is there knowledge in the Most High?"
¹² Such are the wicked;
    always at ease, they increase in riches.
¹³ All in vain I have kept my heart clean
    and washed my hands in innocence.
¹⁴ For all day long I have been plagued,
    and am punished every morning.

¹⁵ If I had said, "I will talk on in this way,"
    I would have been untrue to the circle
        of your children.
¹⁶ But when I thought how to understand
        this,
    it seemed to me a wearisome task,
¹⁷ until I went into the sanctuary of God;
    then I perceived their end.
¹⁸ Truly you set them in slippery places;
    you make them fall to ruin.
¹⁹ How they are destroyed in a moment,
    swept away utterly by terrors!
²⁰ They areᶜ like a dream when one awakes;
    on awaking you despise their phantoms.

²¹ When my soul was embittered,
    when I was pricked in heart,
²² I was stupid and ignorant;
    I was like a brute beast toward you.
²³ Nevertheless I am continually with you;
    you hold my right hand.
²⁴ You guide me with your counsel,
    and afterward you will receive me with
        honor.ᵈ
²⁵ Whom have I in heaven but you?
    And there is nothing on earth that I
        desire other than you.

²⁶ My flesh and my heart may fail,
    but God is the strengthᵉ of my heart and
        my portion forever.

²⁷ Indeed, those who are far from you will
        perish;
    you put an end to those who are false
        to you.
²⁸ But for me it is good to be near God;
    I have made the Lord GOD my refuge,
    to tell of all your works.

Psalm 74
A Maskil of Asaph.

¹ O God, why do you cast us off forever?
    Why does your anger smoke against the
        sheep of your pasture?
² Remember your congregation, which you
        acquired long ago,
    which you redeemed to be the tribe of
        your heritage.
    Remember Mount Zion, where you
        came to dwell.
³ Direct your steps to the perpetual ruins;
    the enemy has destroyed everything in
        the sanctuary.

⁴ Your foes have roared within your holy
        place;
    they set up their emblems there.
⁵ At the upper entrance they hacked
    the wooden trellis with axes.ᶠ

ᵃ Cn: Heb *his people return here*
ᵇ Cn: Heb *abundant waters are drained by them*
ᶜ Cn: Heb *Lord*
ᵈ Or *to glory*
ᵉ Heb *rock*
ᶠ Cn Compare Gk Syr: Meaning of Heb uncertain

verse (v. 28). The verses in between tell how the psalmist came to such trust. **3–11:** Verses 3–7 tell what the psalmist *sees* (evildoers' well-fed bodies) and vv. 8–11 tell what the psalmist *hears* (their arrogant words). **17:** *I went into the sanctuary*, rejecting such strategies as criticizing God's injustice like Job (v. 15) or trying to reason about it (v. 16), the psalmist resolves to confront God in the sanctuary (v. 17) and there comes to understand *their* (the wicked) *end*: they are eventually swept away suddenly (vv. 18–20). **21–22:** An admission of guilt and an encouragement for others not to entertain such *stupid* and *brutish* thoughts. **24:** *Receive me*, elevate to the security of God's domain, like Enoch (Gen 5.24), Elijah (2 Kings 2.11–12), and the psalmist in Ps 49.15.

Ps 74: **The community begs God to restore the devastated Temple.** A community petition that expresses pain over the immense punishment and abandonment symbolized by the ruined Temple (1–11), remembers in liturgical prayer God's primordial victory that created the world of which the Temple is a central part (vv. 12–17), and turns the experience into a triple prayer that God act now for his own sake (vv. 18–19,20–21,22–23). **Superscription:** *Maskil*, a technical term of uncertain significance. *Asaph*, see Ps 73n. **4:** *Emblems*, better, "signs," as

⁶ And then, with hatchets and hammers,
  they smashed all its carved work.
⁷ They set your sanctuary on fire;
  they desecrated the dwelling place of
    your name,
  bringing it to the ground.
⁸ They said to themselves, "We will utterly
    subdue them";
  they burned all the meeting places of
    God in the land.

⁹ We do not see our emblems;
  there is no longer any prophet,
  and there is no one among us who
    knows how long.
¹⁰ How long, O God, is the foe to scoff?
  Is the enemy to revile your name
    forever?
¹¹ Why do you hold back your hand;
  why do you keep your hand inᵃ your
    bosom?

¹² Yet God my King is from of old,
  working salvation in the earth.
¹³ You divided the sea by your might;
  you broke the heads of the dragons in
    the waters.
¹⁴ You crushed the heads of Leviathan;
  you gave him as foodᵇ for the creatures
    of the wilderness.
¹⁵ You cut openings for springs and
    torrents;
  you dried up ever-flowing streams.
¹⁶ Yours is the day, yours also the night;
  you established the luminariesᶜ and the
    sun.
¹⁷ You have fixed all the bounds of the
    earth;
  you made summer and winter.

¹⁸ Remember this, O Lᴏʀᴅ, how the enemy
    scoffs,
  and an impious people reviles your
    name.
¹⁹ Do not deliver the soul of your dove to
    the wild animals;
  do not forget the life of your poor
    forever.

²⁰ Have regard for yourᵈ covenant,
  for the dark places of the land are full of
    the haunts of violence.
²¹ Do not let the downtrodden be put to
    shame;
  let the poor and needy praise your
    name.
²² Rise up, O God, plead your cause;
  remember how the impious scoff at you
    all day long.
²³ Do not forget the clamor of your foes,
  the uproar of your adversaries that goes
    up continually.

Psalm 75

*To the leader: Do Not Destroy. A Psalm of Asaph.
A Song.*

¹ We give thanks to you, O God;
  we give thanks; your name is near.
People tell of your wondrous deeds.

² At the set time that I appoint
  I will judge with equity.
³ When the earth totters, with all its
    inhabitants,
  it is I who keep its pillars steady.   *Selah*

ᵃ Cn: Heb *do you consume your right hand from*
ᵇ Heb *food for the people*
ᶜ Or *moon*; Heb *light*
ᵈ Gk Syr: Heb *the*

also in v. 9, a prophetic word telling when divine rescue will come. The psalmist complains in v. 9 that there is no one to give such an assuring word. **12–17:** Since God created the Temple as part of the universe, its devastated state calls into question God's ability to rule the universe. The psalmist therefore reminds God of the triumphant act of creation, using a variant of a Canaanite creation story known from Ugarit about Baal defeating the watery chaos. **14:** The mythological creature *Leviathan*, known from Ugarit, is a manifestation of primeval watery chaos; see also Isa 27.1; Job 3.8; 26.12–13; 41.1). **19:** *Your dove*, unclear; it may be an affectionate term for the king, or the dove may be a symbol of vulnerability (Pss 11.1; 102.7; 124.7). **20:** The *covenant* assured Israel's perpetual existence. **22–23:** In order to motivate God, the psalmist calls Israel's enemies *your* [God's] *foes*.

  Ps 75: The community thanks God for putting down the wicked. A thanksgiving praising God (v. 1) for doing just deeds, in this case, punishing the wicked (vv. 2–5,6–8). The actual punishment is announced in an oracle of judgment with God speaking (vv. 2–5). **Superscription:** *Do Not Destroy*, see Ps 57n. *Asaph*, see Ps 73n. **3:** *The*

⁴I say to the boastful, "Do not boast,"
  and to the wicked, "Do not lift up your
    horn;
⁵do not lift up your horn on high,
  or speak with insolent neck."

⁶For not from the east or from the west
  and not from the wilderness comes
    lifting up;
⁷but it is God who executes judgment,
  putting down one and lifting up
    another.
⁸For in the hand of the Lord there is a cup
  with foaming wine, well mixed;
he will pour a draught from it,
  and all the wicked of the earth
  shall drain it down to the dregs.
⁹But I will rejoice[a] forever;
  I will sing praises to the God of Jacob.

¹⁰All the horns of the wicked I will cut off,
  but the horns of the righteous shall be
    exalted.

Psalm 76

*To the leader: with stringed instruments. A Psalm of
Asaph. A Song.*

¹In Judah God is known,
  his name is great in Israel.
²His abode has been established in Salem,
  his dwelling place in Zion.
³There he broke the flashing arrows,
  the shield, the sword, and the weapons
    of war.   *Selah*

⁴Glorious are you, more majestic
  than the everlasting mountains.[b]
⁵The stouthearted were stripped of their
    spoil;
  they sank into sleep;
none of the troops
  was able to lift a hand.
⁶At your rebuke, O God of Jacob,
  both rider and horse lay stunned.

⁷But you indeed are awesome!
  Who can stand before you
  when once your anger is roused?
⁸From the heavens you uttered
    judgment;
  the earth feared and was still
⁹when God rose up to establish
    judgment,
  to save all the oppressed of the
    earth.   *Selah*

¹⁰Human wrath serves only to praise you,
  when you bind the last bit of your[c]
    wrath around you.
¹¹Make vows to the Lord your God, and
    perform them;
  let all who are around him bring gifts
  to the one who is awesome,
¹²who cuts off the spirit of princes,
  who inspires fear in the kings of the
    earth.

a Gk: Heb *declare*
b Gk: Heb *the mountains of prey*
c Heb lacks *your*

earth *totters,* when God speaks, the earth trembles. *Selah,* see Ps 3.2n. **4:** *Lifting up* a *horn* represents pride, arrogance, and victory. **6–8:** Expansion of the divine command, spoken perhaps by the king, the envoy of God. **8:** The *cup* (of the Lord's wrath in Isa 51.17; Jer 25.15) is a metaphor for punishment. **9–10:** The speaker accepts with joy the divine task of implementing justice.

Ps 76: God is acknowledged as victorious in the holy city. A song of Zion, celebrating Zion as the site where God won the victory that established the world as just and prosperous. **Superscription:** *Asaph,* see Ps 73n. **1–3:** By the creation-victory described in vv. 4–10, God is now recognized by all Israel as supreme over all other powers, and dwelling in *Salem* (an alternate name for Jerusalem, as in Gen 14.18). **3:** *Selah* (also v. 9), see Ps 3.2n. **7–10:** The psalm presumes that the cosmic battle was fought at the base of Mount Zion; comparable religious texts also tell how the storm god defeated his enemies at the base of his holy mountain. After the battle, God established the rules or justice to which the universe must conform (8–9); even the typically noisy *rider and horse* (v. 6), and *the earth* (v. 8) were *still* and quiet. **10:** *Human wrath serves only to praise you,* better "Even wrathful Edom praises you, the remnant of Hamath keeps your feast," referring to frequent enemies of Israel to the southeast and to the north, respectively. **11–12:** Because Zion is the site of the Lord's victory and of his dwelling, all nations must come there to pay homage. The pilgrimage of the nations is a significant theme in the Bible (Isa 2.1–4 || Mic 4.1–3; Isa 60–62; 66.20–21).

Psalm 77

To the leader: according to Jeduthun. Of Asaph.
A Psalm.

¹ I cry aloud to God,
  aloud to God, that he may hear me.
² In the day of my trouble I seek the Lord;
  in the night my hand is stretched out
    without wearying;
  my soul refuses to be comforted.
³ I think of God, and I moan;
  I meditate, and my spirit faints.   *Selah*

⁴ You keep my eyelids from closing;
  I am so troubled that I cannot speak.
⁵ I consider the days of old,
  and remember the years of long ago.
⁶ I commune[a] with my heart in the night;
  I meditate and search my spirit:[b]
⁷ "Will the Lord spurn forever,
  and never again be favorable?
⁸ Has his steadfast love ceased forever?
  Are his promises at an end for all time?
⁹ Has God forgotten to be gracious?
  Has he in anger shut up his
    compassion?"   *Selah*
¹⁰ And I say, "It is my grief
  that the right hand of the Most High
    has changed."

¹¹ I will call to mind the deeds of the LORD;
  I will remember your wonders of old.
¹² I will meditate on all your work,
  and muse on your mighty deeds.

¹³ Your way, O God, is holy.
  What god is so great as our God?
¹⁴ You are the God who works wonders;
  you have displayed your might among
    the peoples.
¹⁵ With your strong arm you redeemed
    your people,
  the descendants of Jacob and Joseph. *Selah*

¹⁶ When the waters saw you, O God,
  when the waters saw you, they were afraid;
  the very deep trembled.
¹⁷ The clouds poured out water;
  the skies thundered;
  your arrows flashed on every side.
¹⁸ The crash of your thunder was in the
    whirlwind;
  your lightnings lit up the world;
  the earth trembled and shook.
¹⁹ Your way was through the sea,
  your path, through the mighty waters;
  yet your footprints were unseen.
²⁰ You led your people like a flock
  by the hand of Moses and Aaron.

Psalm 78

A Maskil of Asaph.

¹ Give ear, O my people, to my teaching;
  incline your ears to the words of my
    mouth.

a   Gk Syr: Heb *My music*
b   Syr Jerome: Heb *my spirit searches*

Ps 77: The mighty acts of God in national trouble. Though often classed as an individual lament or petition, the psalm is a community petition in which a speaker expresses the personal distress of all (vv. 1–10) and recalls God's past fidelity to the nation (vv. 11–20). **Superscription:** *Jeduthun,* see Ps 39n. *Asaph,* see Ps 73n. **3:** *Selah* (also vv. 9,15), see Ps 3.2n. **10:** *The right hand of the Most High has changed, right hand* connotes supreme power. That the LORD seems unable to save the people depresses the singer. **11–12:** *Call to mind, remember, meditate, muse,* the verbs here mean to recite aloud as in a ritual, as if the very recital in God's hearing would spur God to renew the acts that established the community. **11–20:** Combining historical and cosmic language, the psalmist describes the Exodus from Egypt, Israel's great founding event, noting that even then no visible trace of God's power was seen (v. 19c). **15:** *The descendants of Jacob and Joseph,* i.e., the Israelites. **16–19:** Cf. Pss 18.7–15; 114.3–6.

    Ps 78: A lesson from history. Ps 78 juxtaposes two series of events in Israel's history (vv. 12–39,40–72) to demonstrate that the people's sin has triggered divine punishment, but, even more important, the offer of a new beginning. The first series of events is limited to those that took place "in the wilderness . . . in the desert" (v. 40; cf. Ex 14–Num 11); the second set is broader, embracing the entire Exodus including the conquest of Canaan, the founding of the national shrine at Shiloh, its rejection, and the choice of Zion and of David. The psalmist's attempt to persuade the northern kingdom of Israel ("the Ephraimites," v. 9) to accept the Davidic king suggests a time of composition in the eighth or seventh century BCE when the Northern and Southern Kingdoms were separated. The psalm makes clear that history is not recalled for its own sake, but for didactic reasons (see vv. 6–8). **Superscription:** *Maskil,* a technical term of uncertain significance. *Asaph,* see Ps 73n. **1–11:**

²I will open my mouth in a parable;
   I will utter dark sayings from of old,
³things that we have heard and known,
   that our ancestors have told us.
⁴We will not hide them from their
      children;
   we will tell to the coming generation
the glorious deeds of the LORD, and his
      might,
   and the wonders that he has done.

⁵He established a decree in Jacob,
   and appointed a law in Israel,
which he commanded our ancestors
   to teach to their children;
⁶that the next generation might know
      them,
   the children yet unborn,
and rise up and tell them to their children,
   ⁷so that they should set their hope in
      God,
and not forget the works of God,
   but keep his commandments;
⁸and that they should not be like their
      ancestors,
   a stubborn and rebellious generation,
a generation whose heart was not
      steadfast,
   whose spirit was not faithful to God.

⁹The Ephraimites, armed withᵃ the bow,
   turned back on the day of battle.
¹⁰They did not keep God's covenant,
   but refused to walk according to
      his law.
¹¹They forgot what he had done,
   and the miracles that he had shown
      them.
¹²In the sight of their ancestors he worked
      marvels
   in the land of Egypt, in the fields of
      Zoan.
¹³He divided the sea and let them pass
      through it,
   and made the waters stand like a heap.

¹⁴In the daytime he led them with
      a cloud,
   and all night long with a fiery light.
¹⁵He split rocks open in the wilderness,
   and gave them drink abundantly as
      from the deep.
¹⁶He made streams come out of the
      rock,
   and caused waters to flow down like
      rivers.

¹⁷Yet they sinned still more against him,
   rebelling against the Most High in the
      desert.
¹⁸They tested God in their heart
   by demanding the food they craved.
¹⁹They spoke against God, saying,
   "Can God spread a table in the
      wilderness?
²⁰Even though he struck the rock so that
      water gushed out
   and torrents overflowed,
can he also give bread,
   or provide meat for his people?"

²¹Therefore, when the LORD heard, he was
      full of rage;
   a fire was kindled against Jacob,
   his anger mounted against Israel,
²²because they had no faith in God,
   and did not trust his saving power.
²³Yet he commanded the skies
      above,
   and opened the doors of heaven;
²⁴he rained down on them manna to
      eat,
   and gave them the grain of heaven.
²⁵Mortals ate of the bread of angels;
   he sent them food in abundance.
²⁶He caused the east wind to blow in the
      heavens,
   and by his power he led out the south
      wind;

ᵃ Heb *armed with shooting*

Like Moses in Deut 5 and 18.18–19, the psalmist promises to interpret the national tradition so that the hearers might respond properly to God's new gracious act: choosing David as king and Zion as the national shrine. **2:** *Parable*, better, "lessons." **12–40:** Casting the wilderness traditions in a different order from the Pentateuch, the psalm mentions gracious act (vv. 12–16), rebellion (vv. 17–20), divine anger and punishment (vv. 21–31), and then, surprisingly, God's forgiveness and fresh invitation (vv. 32–39). **12:** *Zoan*, a city in northern Egypt. **13:** Ex 14.21, 29; 15.8. **14:** Ex 13.21–22; 14.19–20. **15–16:** Ex 17.6; Num 20.11; Isa 48.21. *The deep*, the chaotic waters

27 he rained flesh upon them like dust,
    winged birds like the sand of the seas;
28 he let them fall within their camp,
    all around their dwellings.
29 And they ate and were well filled,
    for he gave them what they craved.
30 But before they had satisfied their
        craving,
    while the food was still in their mouths,
31 the anger of God rose against them
    and he killed the strongest of them,
    and laid low the flower of Israel.

32 In spite of all this they still sinned;
    they did not believe in his wonders.
33 So he made their days vanish like a
        breath,
    and their years in terror.
34 When he killed them, they sought for
        him;
    they repented and sought God
        earnestly.
35 They remembered that God was their
        rock,
    the Most High God their redeemer.
36 But they flattered him with their
        mouths;
    they lied to him with their tongues.
37 Their heart was not steadfast toward
        him;
    they were not true to his covenant.
38 Yet he, being compassionate,
    forgave their iniquity,
    and did not destroy them;
often he restrained his anger,
    and did not stir up all his wrath.
39 He remembered that they were but
        flesh,
    a wind that passes and does not come
        again.
40 How often they rebelled against him in
        the wilderness
    and grieved him in the desert!
41 They tested God again and again,
    and provoked the Holy One of Israel.
42 They did not keep in mind his power,
    or the day when he redeemed them
        from the foe;

43 when he displayed his signs in Egypt,
    and his miracles in the fields of Zoan.
44 He turned their rivers to blood,
    so that they could not drink of their
        streams.
45 He sent among them swarms of flies,
    which devoured them,
    and frogs, which destroyed them.
46 He gave their crops to the caterpillar,
    and the fruit of their labor to the
        locust.
47 He destroyed their vines with hail,
    and their sycamores with frost.
48 He gave over their cattle to the hail,
    and their flocks to thunderbolts.
49 He let loose on them his fierce anger,
    wrath, indignation, and distress,
    a company of destroying angels.
50 He made a path for his anger;
    he did not spare them from death,
    but gave their lives over to the plague.
51 He struck all the firstborn in Egypt,
    the first issue of their strength in the
        tents of Ham.
52 Then he led out his people like sheep,
    and guided them in the wilderness like
        a flock.
53 He led them in safety, so that they were
        not afraid;
    but the sea overwhelmed their enemies.
54 And he brought them to his holy hill,
    to the mountain that his right hand had
        won.
55 He drove out nations before them;
    he apportioned them for a possession
    and settled the tribes of Israel in their
        tents.

56 Yet they tested the Most High God,
    and rebelled against him.
    They did not observe his decrees,
57 but turned away and were faithless like
        their ancestors;
    they twisted like a treacherous bow.
58 For they provoked him to anger with
        their high places;
    they moved him to jealousy with their
        idols.

vanquished by God, which served Israel's need for water; cf. Ps 104.5–14. **18–31:** The provisioning of the people with food after the Exodus is drawn from Ex 16 and Num 11. **40–54:** Different traditions but the same order: gracious act (vv. 40–55), rebellion (vv. 56–58), divine anger and punishment (vv. 59–64), forgiveness and offer

⁵⁹ When God heard, he was full of wrath,
and he utterly rejected Israel.
⁶⁰ He abandoned his dwelling at Shiloh,
the tent where he dwelt among
mortals,
⁶¹ and delivered his power to captivity,
his glory to the hand of the foe.
⁶² He gave his people to the sword,
and vented his wrath on his heritage.
⁶³ Fire devoured their young men,
and their girls had no marriage song.
⁶⁴ Their priests fell by the sword,
and their widows made no
lamentation.
⁶⁵ Then the Lord awoke as from sleep,
like a warrior shouting because of wine.
⁶⁶ He put his adversaries to rout;
he put them to everlasting disgrace.

⁶⁷ He rejected the tent of Joseph,
he did not choose the tribe of Ephraim;
⁶⁸ but he chose the tribe of Judah,
Mount Zion, which he loves.
⁶⁹ He built his sanctuary like the high
heavens,
like the earth, which he has founded
forever.
⁷⁰ He chose his servant David,
and took him from the sheepfolds;
⁷¹ from tending the nursing ewes he
brought him
to be the shepherd of his people Jacob,
of Israel, his inheritance.
⁷² With upright heart he tended them,
and guided them with skillful hand.

Psalm 79
A Psalm of Asaph.

¹ O God, the nations have come into your
inheritance;
they have defiled your holy temple;
they have laid Jerusalem in ruins.
² They have given the bodies of your
servants
to the birds of the air for food,
the flesh of your faithful to the wild
animals of the earth.
³ They have poured out their blood like
water
all around Jerusalem,
and there was no one to bury them.
⁴ We have become a taunt to our
neighbors,
mocked and derided by those
around us.

⁵ How long, O LORD? Will you be angry
forever?
Will your jealous wrath burn like fire?
⁶ Pour out your anger on the nations
that do not know you,
and on the kingdoms
that do not call on your name.
⁷ For they have devoured Jacob
and laid waste his habitation.

⁸ Do not remember against us the
iniquities of our ancestors;
let your compassion come speedily to
meet us,
for we are brought very low.

(vv. 65–72). Here too the traditions are not identical to what is preserved in the books of Exodus and Numbers. **45–51:** The plagues (Ex 7–11; Ps 105.26–36). **51:** *Ham,* Egypt; see Gen 10.6. **52–55:** Cf. Ex 15.13; Ps 77.20. **60:** The ark of the covenant was in Shiloh according to 1 Sam 3–4 before it was brought to Jerusalem. It is uncertain when Shiloh was destroyed, even though Jeremiah also mentions this event (26.6,9). **61:** *His power . . . his glory,* referring to the ark, captured by the Philistines (1 Sam 4–6). **67–68:** God rejected the Northern Kingdom of Israel (*Joseph, Ephraim*) in favor of the Southern Kingdom of *Judah.* **71–72:** The image of the king as *shepherd* of the people is common in the ancient Near East.

Ps 79: A community petition for punishment for those dishonoring God. Though the prayer might seem concerned only with revenge, it actually seeks to maintain the community's relationship to God and uphold the divine honor. The initial verses suggest that it reflects the destruction of Jerusalem and the Temple by the Babylonian army in 586 BCE. **Superscription:** *Asaph,* see Ps 73n. **1:** *Your inheritance,* the land given by God. **2:** *The bodies . . . to the wild animals,* leaving bodies unburied shows the disrespect of victors and created grief for those defeated. **5:** *How long?* not necessarily a rhetorical question; people in antiquity sought to know how long an affliction would last. **8:** *Do not remember . . . the iniquities of our ancestors,* more accurately, "our past iniquities." The people do not deny they have sinned and deserve punishment, but object that their enemies have sinned

⁹ Help us, O God of our
　　salvation,
　for the glory of your name;
deliver us, and forgive our sins,
　for your name's sake.
¹⁰ Why should the nations say,
　　"Where is their God?"
Let the avenging of the outpoured blood of
　　your servants
　be known among the nations before our
　　eyes.

¹¹ Let the groans of the prisoners come
　　before you;
　according to your great power preserve
　　those doomed to die.
¹² Return sevenfold into the bosom of our
　　neighbors
　the taunts with which they taunted you,
　　O Lord!
¹³ Then we your people, the flock of your
　　pasture,
　will give thanks to you forever;
　from generation to generation we will
　　recount your praise.

Psalm 80

To the leader: on Lilies, a Covenant. Of Asaph.
A Psalm.

¹ Give ear, O Shepherd of Israel,
　you who lead Joseph like
　　a flock!
You who are enthroned upon the
　　cherubim, shine forth
² before Ephraim and Benjamin and
　　Manasseh.

Stir up your might,
　and come to save us!

³ Restore us, O God;
　let your face shine, that we may be
　　saved.

⁴ O Lord God of hosts,
　how long will you be angry with your
　　people's prayers?
⁵ You have fed them with the bread of tears,
　and given them tears to drink in full
　　measure.
⁶ You make us the scorn[a] of our neighbors;
　our enemies laugh among themselves.

⁷ Restore us, O God of hosts;
　let your face shine, that we may be saved.

⁸ You brought a vine out of Egypt;
　you drove out the nations and planted it.
⁹ You cleared the ground for it;
　it took deep root and filled the land.
¹⁰ The mountains were covered with its
　　shade,
　the mighty cedars with its branches;
¹¹ it sent out its branches to the sea,
　and its shoots to the River.
¹² Why then have you broken down its walls,
　so that all who pass along the way pluck
　　its fruit?
¹³ The boar from the forest ravages it,
　and all that move in the field feed on it.

a　Syr: Heb *strife*

much more by attacking the Lord's Temple and deserve immediate and severe punishment. **9–13**: A set of reasons why God should respond. **11–13**: Keep us as your people and defend your Temple and you are guaranteed praise forever! Like Pss 77 and 78, Ps 79 ends with—and Ps 80 begins with—the image of the divine shepherd, connecting these psalms "of Asaph."

Ps 80: Prayer that the shepherd of Israel would restore the people. A community petition: vv. 1–7 ask God to aid the northern tribes suffering from the effects of God's anger, vv. 8–13 recall Israel's founding event (the Exodus and settlement of Canaan) called into question by the enemies' triumph, and vv. 12–19 pray that God act now. The psalm imagines the founding event as the transplanting of a vine to Canaan; cf. Isa 5.1–7; Ezek 17.1–10. **Superscription:** *On Lilies,* probably refers to a melody (cf. Pss 45; 69). *Covenant,* cf. Ps 60. *Asaph,* see Ps 73n. **1:** *Ephraim and Benjamin and Manasseh,* northern tribes separated from Judah since the schism of ca. 922 BCE. In 722, Assyria defeated the Northern Kingdom and seized its territory. God is imagined as *enthroned upon the cherubim,* namely present above the ark of the covenant in the Temple. **4:** The epithet *God of hosts,* which refers to God with his heavenly army, is especially suitable here, since God is asked to fight on behalf of Israel. **8–13:** Ex 15.17; Ps 44.2; and Ezek 19.10–14 also speak of the founding of Israel as a planting. **11:** *The River,* the Euphrates. **14–19:** May God protect the vine and *the one at your right hand* (v. 17, the Davidic king). Then we will

¹⁴ Turn again, O God of hosts;
　　look down from heaven, and see;
have regard for this vine,
　　¹⁵ the stock that your right hand
　　　　planted.ᵃ
¹⁶ They have burned it with fire, they have
　　cut it down;ᵇ
　　may they perish at the rebuke of your
　　　　countenance.
¹⁷ But let your hand be upon the one at
　　your right hand,
　　the one whom you made strong for
　　　　yourself.
¹⁸ Then we will never turn back from you;
　　give us life, and we will call on your
　　　　name.

¹⁹ Restore us, O Lord God of hosts;
　　let your face shine, that we may be
　　　　saved.

Psalm 81

To the leader: according to The Gittith. Of Asaph.

¹ Sing aloud to God our strength;
　　shout for joy to the God of Jacob.
² Raise a song, sound the tambourine,
　　the sweet lyre with the harp.
³ Blow the trumpet at the new moon,
　　at the full moon, on our festal day.
⁴ For it is a statute for Israel,
　　an ordinance of the God of Jacob.
⁵ He made it a decree in Joseph,
　　when he went out overᶜ the land of
　　　　Egypt.

I hear a voice I had not known:
⁶ "I relieved yourᵈ shoulder of the burden;
　　yourᵈ hands were freed from the basket.

⁷ In distress you called, and I rescued you;
　　I answered you in the secret place of
　　　　thunder;
　　I tested you at the waters of
　　　　Meribah.　　　　　　　　　*Selah*
⁸ Hear, O my people, while I admonish you;
　　O Israel, if you would but listen to me!
⁹ There shall be no strange god among you;
　　you shall not bow down to a foreign god.
¹⁰ I am the Lord your God,
　　who brought you up out of the land of
　　　　Egypt.
　　Open your mouth wide and I will fill it.

¹¹ "But my people did not listen to my
　　voice;
　　Israel would not submit to me.
¹² So I gave them over to their stubborn
　　hearts,
　　to follow their own counsels.
¹³ O that my people would listen to me,
　　that Israel would walk in my ways!
¹⁴ Then I would quickly subdue their
　　enemies,
　　and turn my hand against their foes.
¹⁵ Those who hate the Lord would cringe
　　before him,
　　and their doom would last forever.
¹⁶ I would feed youᵉ with the finest of the
　　wheat,

ᵃ Heb adds from verse 17 *and upon the one whom you made strong for yourself*
ᵇ Cn: Heb *it is cut down*
ᶜ Or *against*
ᵈ Heb *his*
ᵉ Cn Compare verse 16b: Heb *he would feed him*

be restored and faithful to God.

Ps 81: Invitation to renew the covenant. A covenant renewal liturgy like Ps 50 in which the community is invited to renew the covenant (vv. 1–5b) and is confronted with the consequences of disobedience (vv. 5c–16). **Superscription:** *Gittith,* see Ps 8n. *Asaph,* see Ps 73n. **3:** *Festal day,* the exact reference is uncertain; little is known about the covenant renewal ceremony in ancient Israel. **5:** *Joseph,* referring to the tribes of Ephraim and Manasseh, the principal constituents of the Northern Kingdom of Israel. *I hear a voice I had not known,* introduces an oracle in which God, speaking in the first person (vv. 6–10), describes the people's liberation from Egyptian bondage, their encounter with the Lord at Sinai, and guidance in the wilderness (vv. 6–7), and reminds the people of the commandment of loving the Lord alone (vv. 8–10). **7:** *The secret place of thunder,* Mount Sinai where God appeared in thunder (Ex 19.16,18; 20.18). For *the waters of Meribah,* see Ex 17.17; Num 20.13. *Selah,* see Ps 3.2n. **9–10:** A restatement of the beginning of the Decalogue. **9:** *Foreign god,* see Deut 32.12. **10:** *Open your mouth wide and I will fill it,* to accept the Lord's food in the wilderness is equivalently to accept the Lord as their God. **11–16:** A similar harsh scrutiny is found in Josh 24.19–21. Such language is meant to explain why all is not well with Is-

and with honey from the rock I would
  satisfy you."

Psalm 82

A Psalm of Asaph.

[1] God has taken his place in the divine
  council;
  in the midst of the gods he holds
  judgment:
[2] "How long will you judge unjustly
  and show partiality to the wicked? *Selah*
[3] Give justice to the weak and the orphan;
  maintain the right of the lowly and the
  destitute.
[4] Rescue the weak and the needy;
  deliver them from the hand of the
  wicked."

[5] They have neither knowledge nor
  understanding,
  they walk around in darkness;
  all the foundations of the earth are
  shaken.

[6] I say, "You are gods,
  children of the Most High, all of you;
[7] nevertheless, you shall die like mortals,
  and fall like any prince."[a]

[8] Rise up, O God, judge the earth;
  for all the nations belong to you!

Psalm 83

A Song. A Psalm of Asaph.

[1] O God, do not keep silence;
  do not hold your peace or be still, O God!
[2] Even now your enemies are in tumult;
  those who hate you have raised their
  heads.
[3] They lay crafty plans against your people;
  they consult together against those you
  protect.
[4] They say, "Come, let us wipe them out as
  a nation;
  let the name of Israel be remembered
  no more."
[5] They conspire with one accord;
  against you they make a covenant—
[6] the tents of Edom and the Ishmaelites,
  Moab and the Hagrites,
[7] Gebal and Ammon and Amalek,
  Philistia with the inhabitants of Tyre;
[8] Assyria also has joined them;
  they are the strong arm of the children
  of Lot.   *Selah*

[a] Or *fall as one man, O princes*

rael in the psalmist's period. **16:** *Finest of the wheat,* see Deut 32.14; Ps 147.14. *Honey from the rock,* see Deut 32.13.

Ps 82: Petition for divine justice. As in Ps 29, and to a lesser extent Pss 58 and 75, the setting is the assembly of the heavenly beings, who were thought to rule the nations of the earth under God's supervision (cf. Deut 32.8–9). This psalm tells how these beings lost their authority by ruling unjustly, and how God took over their rule. The psalm shares mythic and historical material with Gen 6.1–2; Isa 14.12–21; and Ezek 28.1–19. A variant of this judgment scene is Ps 58. **Superscription:** *Asaph,* see Ps 73n. **1:** *Divine council,* in 1 Kings 22.19–22; Isa 6; 40.1–9, the assembly is thoroughly obedient to God. In Ps 82, the gods are summoned to trial, found guilty of misrule, and punished with mortality, i.e., loss of divine status and expulsion from heaven. **2–4:** Acting both as prosecuting attorney and judge, God accuses them of not giving *justice to the weak,* i.e., not aiding them. **2:** *Selah,* see Ps 3.2n. **5:** Either a comment of the psalmist or of the heavenly prosecutor. **6–7:** The verdict. **8:** The implication of what precedes: A call for *God,* now acting alone, to *judge* fairly.

Ps 83: A plea that God would protect the community. A community petition that God might protect the people from ten nations bent on annihilating Israel. Ten is symbolic for many as in Gen 5 (ten individuals before the Flood); Gen 31.7; Num 14.22; Job 19.3. The list reflects no single historical reality but is cumulative, like the listing of enemies in Ezek 38–39, designating all enemies of God's people. In structure, v. 1 is the opening plea, vv. 2–8 the complaint (a conspiracy against Israel), and vv. 9–18 the plea that God wipe out all enemies (vv. 9–12) using the weapons of storm (vv. 13–17), so God's holy name may be exalted on earth (v. 18). **Superscription:** *Asaph,* see Ps 73n. **4–8:** The psalmist cites the speech of conspirators (v. 4) as in Ex 1.10 and Ps 2.3. **6:** *The tents of Edom,* the territory south and east of the Dead Sea. *Ishmaelites,* nomads (Gen 37.25) related to the Edomites (Gen 36.3, 9–10). *Moab,* east of the Dead Sea. *Hagrites,* their territory was east of Gilead (1 Chr 5.10,19–20). **7:** *Gebal,* later known as Byblos, on the coast of Lebanon. *Ammon,* in central Transjordan. *Amalek,* a people dispossessed by Israel in Ex 17.8–16; they disappear from the Bible after the time of David (1 Sam 15 and 30:13–25). **8:** *Assyria*

⁹ Do to them as you did to Midian,
  as to Sisera and Jabin at the Wadi
    Kishon,
¹⁰ who were destroyed at En-dor,
  who became dung for the ground.
¹¹ Make their nobles like Oreb and Zeeb,
  all their princes like Zebah and
    Zalmunna,
¹² who said, "Let us take the pastures of
    God
  for our own possession."

¹³ O my God, make them like whirling
    dust,ᵃ
  like chaff before the wind.
¹⁴ As fire consumes the forest,
  as the flame sets the mountains ablaze,
¹⁵ so pursue them with your tempest
  and terrify them with your hurricane.
¹⁶ Fill their faces with shame,
  so that they may seek your name, O LORD.
¹⁷ Let them be put to shame and dismayed
    forever;
  let them perish in disgrace.
¹⁸ Let them know that you alone,
  whose name is the LORD,
  are the Most High over all the earth.

Psalm 84

*To the leader: according to The Gittith. Of the
Korahites. A Psalm.*

¹ How lovely is your dwelling place,
  O LORD of hosts!
² My soul longs, indeed it faints
  for the courts of the LORD;
my heart and my flesh sing for joy
  to the living God.

³ Even the sparrow finds a home,
  and the swallow a nest for herself,
  where she may lay her young,
at your altars, O LORD of hosts,
  my King and my God.
⁴ Happy are those who live in your house,
  ever singing your praise.   *Selah*

⁵ Happy are those whose strength is in
    you,
  in whose heart are the highways to
    Zion.ᵇ
⁶ As they go through the valley of Baca
  they make it a place of springs;
  the early rain also covers it with pools.
⁷ They go from strength to strength;
  the God of gods will be seen in Zion.

⁸ O LORD God of hosts, hear my prayer;
  give ear, O God of Jacob!   *Selah*
⁹ Behold our shield, O God;
  look on the face of your anointed.

¹⁰ For a day in your courts is better
  than a thousand elsewhere.
I would rather be a doorkeeper in the
    house of my God
  than live in the tents of wickedness.
¹¹ For the LORD God is a sun and shield;
  he bestows favor and honor.
No good thing does the LORD withhold
  from those who walk uprightly.
¹² O LORD of hosts,
  happy is everyone who trusts in you.

ᵃ Or *a tumbleweed*
ᵇ Heb lacks *to Zion*

---

conquered the northern kingdom of Israel in 722 BCE and thereafter harassed Judah. *The children of Lot* were
Moab and Ammon (Gen 19.36–38). *Selah,* see Ps 3.2n. **9–18:** May you show your enemies that you are supreme.
The events in vv. 10–12 are narrated in Judg 4–8. **9:** *Midian,* a confederation of desert tribes. **10:** *En-dor,* near
Mount Tabor in central Israel. **11:** *Oreb* and *Zeeb,* Midianite captains slain by Ephraimites (Judg 7.25; 8.3). *Zebah*
and *Zalmunna,* Midianite kings slain by Gideon (Judg 8.4–21). **13–14:** These verses may have been accompanied
by symbolic actions.

  Ps 84: Longing for the Temple and a prayer for the Davidic king. A song of Zion, with emphasis on the desire to participate in its worship (cf. Pss 42–43; 63). **Superscription:** *Gittith,* see Ps 8n. *Korahites,* see Ps 42–43n.
1: *Lovely,* better, "beloved" as in Isa 5.1 and Deut 33.12. **3:** *At your altars,* NRSV wrongly assumes birds' nests are
at the altar, where birds' nests would never be allowed. The comparison is to a homeless bird finding a home
for its young. It is unclear, however, if people could live on the Temple grounds, as suggested here and in Ps
23.6. **4:** *Selah* (also v. 8), see Ps 3.2n. **5–7:** The joyous final stage of the journey to Zion. **6:** *Baca,* precise location
unknown. **9:** *Our shield, your anointed,* the Davidic king played an important role in the ceremonies in Zion.

Psalm 85

To the leader. Of the Korahites. A Psalm.

[1] LORD, you were favorable to your land;
  you restored the fortunes of Jacob.
[2] You forgave the iniquity of your people;
  you pardoned all their sin. *Selah*
[3] You withdrew all your wrath;
  you turned from your hot anger.

[4] Restore us again, O God of our salvation,
  and put away your indignation toward
    us.
[5] Will you be angry with us forever?
  Will you prolong your anger to all
    generations?
[6] Will you not revive us again,
  so that your people may rejoice in you?
[7] Show us your steadfast love, O LORD,
  and grant us your salvation.

[8] Let me hear what God the LORD will
    speak,
  for he will speak peace to his people,
  to his faithful, to those who turn to him
    in their hearts.[a]
[9] Surely his salvation is at hand for those
    who fear him,
  that his glory may dwell in our land.

[10] Steadfast love and faithfulness will meet;
  righteousness and peace will kiss each
    other.
[11] Faithfulness will spring up from the
    ground,
  and righteousness will look down from
    the sky.
[12] The LORD will give what is good,
  and our land will yield its increase.
[13] Righteousness will go before him,
  and will make a path for his steps.

Psalm 86

A Prayer of David.

[1] Incline your ear, O LORD, and answer me,
  for I am poor and needy.
[2] Preserve my life, for I am devoted to you;
  save your servant who trusts in you.
You are my God; [3] be gracious to me, O Lord,
  for to you do I cry all day long.
[4] Gladden the soul of your servant,
  for to you, O Lord, I lift up my soul.
[5] For you, O Lord, are good and forgiving,
  abounding in steadfast love to all who
    call on you.
[6] Give ear, O LORD, to my prayer;
  listen to my cry of supplication.
[7] In the day of my trouble I call on you,
  for you will answer me.

[8] There is none like you among the gods,
    O Lord,
  nor are there any works like yours.
[9] All the nations you have made shall come
  and bow down before you, O Lord,
  and shall glorify your name.
[10] For you are great and do wondrous things;
  you alone are God.
[11] Teach me your way, O LORD,
  that I may walk in your truth;
  give me an undivided heart to revere
    your name.
[12] I give thanks to you, O Lord my God,
  with my whole heart,
  and I will glorify your name forever.
[13] For great is your steadfast love toward
    me;
  you have delivered my soul from the
    depths of Sheol.

[a] Gk: Heb *but let them not turn back to folly*

Ps 85: A prayer for forgiveness. A community petition that God would be merciful as in the past (vv. 1–3) and forgive this discouraged generation (vv. 4–13). **Superscription:** *Korahites*, see Ps 42–43n. **2:** *Pardoned*, lit. "covered." *Selah*, see Ps 3.2n. **8:** Though the exact mechanisms are unclear, worshipers expected to be able to discern the divine will, especially at the Temple. **10–13:** The effects of divine forgiveness on land and people are expressed in memorable metaphors and personifications: courtiers greeting each other with exquisite courtesy (v. 10), the land itself growing righteousness like a plant (vv. 11–12), and messengers preparing for the LORD's arrival (v. 13); cf. Ps 89.14.

Ps 86: Desire for God as helper. An individual petition that expresses the psalmist's desire to be God's loyal servant (vv. 1–7); it celebrates God's incomparability (vv. 8–13) prior to asking for help in a particular need (vv. 14–17). **1:** *Incline your ear . . . answer me*, repeated in v. 7 (NRSV *call . . . answer*), which concludes the section. The poet is proud to be the servant of so responsive a Lord. *Poor and needy*, to express one's poverty makes a claim

[14] O God, the insolent rise up against
 me;
a band of ruffians seeks my life,
and they do not set you before them.
[15] But you, O Lord, are a God merciful and
 gracious,
slow to anger and abounding in
 steadfast love and faithfulness.
[16] Turn to me and be gracious to me;
give your strength to your servant;
save the child of your serving girl.
[17] Show me a sign of your favor,
so that those who hate me may see it
 and be put to shame,
because you, Lord, have helped me and
 comforted me.

Psalm 87
Of the Korahites. A Psalm. A Song.

[1] On the holy mount stands the city he
 founded;
[2] the Lord loves the gates of Zion
more than all the dwellings of Jacob.
[3] Glorious things are spoken of you,
O city of God. *Selah*

[4] Among those who know me I mention
 Rahab and Babylon;
Philistia too, and Tyre, with Ethiopia[a]—
"This one was born there," they say.

[5] And of Zion it shall be said,
"This one and that one were born in it";

for the Most High himself will
 establish it.
[6] The Lord records, as he registers the
 peoples,
"This one was born there." *Selah*

[7] Singers and dancers alike say,
"All my springs are in you."

Psalm 88
*A Song. A Psalm of the Korahites. To the leader:
according to Mahalath Leannoth. A Maskil of
Heman the Ezrahite.*

[1] O Lord, God of my salvation,
when, at night, I cry out in your
 presence,
[2] let my prayer come before you;
incline your ear to my cry.

[3] For my soul is full of troubles,
and my life draws near to Sheol.
[4] I am counted among those who go down
 to the Pit;
I am like those who have no help,
[5] like those forsaken among the dead,
like the slain that lie in the grave,
like those whom you remember no
 more,
for they are cut off from your hand.
[6] You have put me in the depths of the Pit,
in the regions dark and deep.

[a] Or *Nubia*; Heb *Cush*

against God, for God wants the faithful to enjoy the goods of creation. **8:** Cf. Pss 71.19; 89.6–7; Ex 15.11. **9:** See Ps 22.27n. **14–17:** Having praised the Lord's graciousness in vv. 1–7 and 8–13, the psalmist now asks for the same compassion and justice in the present need. **13:** *Sheol*, the abode of the dead. **15:** Citing the attributes of God's compassionate nature from Ex 34.6.

 Ps 87: Zion, God's chosen city. A song of Zion, probably from the sixth or fifth century BCE, assuring exiled Israelites their true home is Zion and welcoming the nations who bring them home. **Superscription:** *Korahites*, see Ps 42–43n. **3:** *Glorious things*, hymns sung in the city of God, as in Pss 48.1; 76.1. *Selah* (also v. 6), see Ps 3.2n. **4:** *Rahab*, probably Egypt (see Isa 30.7). *Philistia*, on the southeastern Mediterranean coast. *Tyre*, an important coastal city north of Israel, standing for Phoenicia (modern Lebanon). *This one was born there*, either Zion or the country where the exiles dwell. In the similar phrases in vv. 5 and 6, the referent is clearly Zion. Birth in a foreign country does not prevent one from calling Zion mother; cf. Isa 40–55 where Zion regains her husband and children. **7:** *All my springs*, citation of a song celebrating Zion as a source of fertility as in Ps 46.4.

 Ps 88: The prayer of a near-hopeless individual. Perhaps the bleakest individual petition in the Psalms, with no expressions of trust and, strikingly, no mention of enemies; in a sense God is regarded as the enemy. The poem has three sections (vv. 1–9a, 9b–12, 13–18), each introduced by a verb of crying and a mention of the Lord (vv. 1a, 9b, 13a). The middle section develops the theme of God's withdrawal through six questions. **Superscription:** *Korahites*, see Ps 42–43n. *Mahalath Leannoth*, probably a melody. *Maskil*, a technical term of uncertain significance. *Heman the Ezrahite*, a legendary wise man (1 Kings 4.31) or Temple musician (see, e.g., 1 Chr 6.33); only

[7] Your wrath lies heavy upon me,
and you overwhelm me with all your
waves. *Selah*

[8] You have caused my companions to shun
me;
you have made me a thing of horror to
them.
I am shut in so that I cannot escape;
[9] my eye grows dim through sorrow.
Every day I call on you, O LORD;
I spread out my hands to you.
[10] Do you work wonders for the dead?
Do the shades rise up to praise you?
Selah

[11] Is your steadfast love declared in the
grave,
or your faithfulness in Abaddon?
[12] Are your wonders known in the darkness,
or your saving help in the land of
forgetfulness?

[13] But I, O LORD, cry out to you;
in the morning my prayer comes before
you.
[14] O LORD, why do you cast me off?
Why do you hide your face from me?
[15] Wretched and close to death from my
youth up,
I suffer your terrors; I am desperate.[a]
[16] Your wrath has swept over me;
your dread assaults destroy me.
[17] They surround me like a flood all day
long;
from all sides they close in on me.

[18] You have caused friend and neighbor to
shun me;
my companions are in darkness.

Psalm 89
A Maskil of Ethan the Ezrahite.

[1] I will sing of your steadfast love, O LORD,[b]
forever;
with my mouth I will proclaim your
faithfulness to all generations.
[2] I declare that your steadfast love is
established forever;
your faithfulness is as firm as the
heavens.

[3] You said, "I have made a covenant with
my chosen one,
I have sworn to my servant David:
[4] 'I will establish your descendants
forever,
and build your throne for all
generations.'" *Selah*

[5] Let the heavens praise your wonders,
O LORD,
your faithfulness in the assembly of the
holy ones.
[6] For who in the skies can be compared to
the LORD?
Who among the heavenly beings is like
the LORD,

---

a   Meaning of Heb uncertain
b   Gk: Heb *the steadfast love of the LORD*

---

this psalm is ascribed to him. **3–4:** *Sheol . . . the Pit*, the underworld where all go upon death; the psalmist is seeing that he is almost dead. **7:** *Your wrath*, more impersonal than in English, something like "away from your favor
and blessing." *Your waves*, Sheol was sometimes imagined as a watery place (e.g., Ps 42.7; Jon 2.3). *Selah* (also v.
10), see Ps 3.2n. **8:** The psalmist feels that God is the direct cause of all of his problems. **11–12:** If I die, the psalmist is saying, I will be in the underworld where you are not praised; see Ps 6.5n. *Abaddon* (lit. "destruction"),
another name for the abode of the dead. **13–18:** Extending the thought of the first section, these verses detail
the cruel behavior of God, asking *Why?* (v. 14). Yet the psalmist holds out the hope that God will return to him.

  Ps 89: A plea that God will remain faithful to the covenant with David. Written when the king was important to national life (the tenth to the sixth centuries BCE), the community petition asks God to honor the
ancient promise to give victory to the Davidic king (vv. 1–37) since that promise has been called into question
by an unspecified defeat (vv. 38–51). **Superscription:** *Maskil*, a technical term of uncertain significance. *Ethan
the Ezrahite*, according to 1 Kings 4.31 a sage, and according to 1 Chr 15.17,19, a Temple musician. Only this psalm
is ascribed to him. **1:** *Steadfast love*, occurring seven times, the Heb word "ḥesed" underscores God's close
relationship to the Davidic king. **1–4:** God's promise to David is no less rooted in creation than the never-failing
cycle of the heavens. **4:** *Selah* (also vv. 37,45,48), see Ps 3.2n. **5–14:** According to several biblical passages (e.g.,
Ps 74.12–17), at the time of the creation of the universe, the heavenly assembly acknowledges the supremacy

⁷ a God feared in the council of the holy
ones,
great and awesome[a] above all that are
around him?
⁸ O Lord God of hosts,
who is as mighty as you, O Lord?
Your faithfulness surrounds you.
⁹ You rule the raging of the sea;
when its waves rise, you still them.
¹⁰ You crushed Rahab like a carcass;
you scattered your enemies with your
mighty arm.
¹¹ The heavens are yours, the earth also is
yours;
the world and all that is in it—you have
founded them.
¹² The north and the south[b]—you created
them;
Tabor and Hermon joyously praise your
name.
¹³ You have a mighty arm;
strong is your hand, high your right
hand.
¹⁴ Righteousness and justice are the
foundation of your throne;
steadfast love and faithfulness go
before you.
¹⁵ Happy are the people who know the
festal shout,
who walk, O Lord, in the light of your
countenance;
¹⁶ they exult in your name all day long,
and extol[c] your righteousness.
¹⁷ For you are the glory of their strength;
by your favor our horn is exalted.
¹⁸ For our shield belongs to the Lord,
our king to the Holy One of Israel.

¹⁹ Then you spoke in a vision to your
faithful one, and said:
"I have set the crown[d] on one who is
mighty,
I have exalted one chosen from the
people.

²⁰ I have found my servant David;
with my holy oil I have anointed him;
²¹ my hand shall always remain with him;
my arm also shall strengthen him.
²² The enemy shall not outwit him,
the wicked shall not humble him.
²³ I will crush his foes before him
and strike down those who hate him.
²⁴ My faithfulness and steadfast love shall
be with him;
and in my name his horn shall be
exalted.
²⁵ I will set his hand on the sea
and his right hand on the rivers.
²⁶ He shall cry to me, 'You are my Father,
my God, and the Rock of my salvation!'
²⁷ I will make him the firstborn,
the highest of the kings of the earth.
²⁸ Forever I will keep my steadfast love for
him,
and my covenant with him will stand
firm.
²⁹ I will establish his line forever,
and his throne as long as the heavens
endure.
³⁰ If his children forsake my law
and do not walk according to my
ordinances,
³¹ if they violate my statutes
and do not keep my commandments,
³² then I will punish their transgression
with the rod
and their iniquity with scourges;
³³ but I will not remove from him my
steadfast love,
or be false to my faithfulness.
³⁴ I will not violate my covenant,
or alter the word that went forth from
my lips.

a Gk Syr: Heb *greatly awesome*
b Or *Zaphon and Yamin*
c Cn: Heb *are exalted in*
d Cn: Heb *help*

of the God who defeated Sea (vv. 9–10), arranged heaven and earth (vv. 11–12), and ascended to the throne (vv. 13–14). **6:** Cf. Pss 71.19; 86.8; Ex 15.11. **10:** *Rahab,* a name for the primeval chaos monster; Job 26.12; Isa 51.9. **12:** *Tabor and Hermon,* two prominent mountains, in southern and northern Galilee respectively. **14:** Cf. Ps 85.10–14. **15–18:** Paralleling the celebration in the heavens is the celebration of God's victory on earth. **19–37:** Time is collapsed, and David is chosen as king and anointed immediately after the conquest of chaos, as a human king who represents the divine. **25:** The king shares the divine task of controlling the primeval forces of watery chaos. **28–37:** The promise to David is unconditional: as in 2 Sam 7, on which this is based, if one of David's

35 Once and for all I have sworn by my
　　holiness;
　　I will not lie to David.
36 His line shall continue forever,
　　and his throne endure before me like
　　　the sun.
37 It shall be established forever like the
　　moon,
　　an enduring witness in the skies." *Selah*

38 But now you have spurned and rejected
　　him;
　　you are full of wrath against your
　　　anointed.
39 You have renounced the covenant with
　　your servant;
　　you have defiled his crown in the dust.
40 You have broken through all his walls;
　　you have laid his strongholds in ruins.
41 All who pass by plunder him;
　　he has become the scorn of his
　　　neighbors.
42 You have exalted the right hand of his
　　foes;
　　you have made all his enemies rejoice.
43 Moreover, you have turned back the
　　edge of his sword,
　　and you have not supported him in
　　　battle.
44 You have removed the scepter from his
　　hand,[a]
　　and hurled his throne to the ground.
45 You have cut short the days of his youth;
　　you have covered him with shame. *Selah*

46 How long, O LORD? Will you hide
　　yourself forever?
　　How long will your wrath burn like fire?
47 Remember how short my time is—[b]

for what vanity you have created all
　　mortals!
48 Who can live and never see death?
　　Who can escape the power of Sheol? *Selah*

49 Lord, where is your steadfast love of old,
　　which by your faithfulness you swore
　　　to David?
50 Remember, O Lord, how your servant is
　　taunted;
　　how I bear in my bosom the insults of
　　　the peoples,[c]
51 with which your enemies taunt, O LORD,
　　with which they taunted the footsteps
　　　of your anointed.

52 Blessed be the LORD forever.
　　Amen and Amen.

BOOK IV PSALMS 90–106

Psalm 90
A Prayer of Moses, the man of God.

1 Lord, you have been our dwelling place[d]
　　in all generations.
2 Before the mountains were brought forth,
　　or ever you had formed the earth and
　　　the world,
　　from everlasting to everlasting you are
　　　God.

3 You turn us[e] back to dust,
　　and say, "Turn back, you mortals."

a　Cn: Heb *removed his cleanness*
b　Meaning of Heb uncertain
c　Cn: Heb *bosom all of many peoples*
d　Another reading is *our refuge*
e　Heb *humankind*

descendants is unfaithful to the covenant, that king will be punished but the dynasty will not be rejected.
26–27: Language of (divine) adoption; see 2 Sam 7.14; Ps 2.9. **38–51:** A Davidic king has suffered defeat, and the
community speaker insists that God remember the promise of fidelity. **48:** *Sheol*, the abode of the dead. **52:** This
doxology or praise of God is not part of the psalm, but was inserted by an editor to mark the end of the third
book of psalms. It is possible that the book of Psalms at one point began with Psalm 2 and ended with this
psalm, focusing on Davidic kingship.

　　Ps 90: A prayer that God would rein in his wrath. Though scholars interpret the psalm as a meditation on
human frailty and God's eternity, it is best viewed as a community petition complaining that God's wrath has
lasted beyond the human life span and asking how much longer this unhappy state will continue (vv. 11–12).
This interpretation rests on two pieces of evidence: ancients sought to know exactly how long tribulations
were fated to last (Jer 25.11,12; 2 Sam 24.13; Pss 39.4; 74.9); and the proper translation of vv. 11–12: "Who knows
the [pre–determined] extent of your anger, . . . Teach us how to calculate our days [of affliction], let us bring that

4 For a thousand years in your sight
   are like yesterday when it is past,
   or like a watch in the night.

5 You sweep them away; they are like a
      dream,
   like grass that is renewed in the
      morning;
6 in the morning it flourishes and is
      renewed;
   in the evening it fades and withers.

7 For we are consumed by your anger;
   by your wrath we are overwhelmed.
8 You have set our iniquities before you,
   our secret sins in the light of your
      countenance.

9 For all our days pass away under your
      wrath;
   our years come to an end[a] like a sigh.
10 The days of our life are seventy
      years,
   or perhaps eighty, if we are strong;
even then their span[b] is only toil and
      trouble;
   they are soon gone, and we fly
      away.

11 Who considers the power of your
      anger?
   Your wrath is as great as the fear that is
      due you.
12 So teach us to count our days
   that we may gain a wise heart.

13 Turn, O Lord! How long?
   Have compassion on your servants!
14 Satisfy us in the morning with your
      steadfast love,

so that we may rejoice and be glad all
      our days.
15 Make us glad as many days as you have
      afflicted us,
   and as many years as we have seen evil.
16 Let your work be manifest to your
      servants,
   and your glorious power to their
      children.
17 Let the favor of the Lord our God be
      upon us,
   and prosper for us the work of our
      hands—
   O prosper the work of our hands!

Psalm 91

1 You who live in the shelter of the Most
      High,
   who abide in the shadow of the
      Almighty,[c]
2 will say to the Lord, "My refuge and my
      fortress;
   my God, in whom I trust."
3 For he will deliver you from the snare of
      the fowler
   and from the deadly pestilence;
4 he will cover you with his pinions,
   and under his wings you will find
      refuge;
   his faithfulness is a shield and buckler.
5 You will not fear the terror of the night,
   or the arrow that flies by day,
6 or the pestilence that stalks in darkness,
   or the destruction that wastes at
      noonday.

a Syr: Heb *we bring our years to an end*
b Cn Compare Gk Syr Jerome Tg: Heb *pride*
c Traditional rendering of Heb *Shaddai*

awareness into our minds." **Superscription:** Only this psalm is attributed to Moses, who often asked God to turn and have compassion (e.g., Ex 32.12) as in Ps 90.13. **1–6:** Divine eternity is contrasted with human mortality. **3:** *Turn back,* God decreed mortality and a short life span for humans. **5–6:** *Like grass,* cf. Ps 102.11; Isa 40.6–8. **7–12:** The psalmist complains that it is unfair to live one's entire life span in a period of divine wrath, i.e., withdrawal of divine blessing. *Seventy years . . . eighty,* even an exceptionally old person would never have enjoyed a period of blessing; an example of numerical parallelism (see Ps 62.11n.). **13–17:** May God turn from wrath so the community might experience God as being near and favorable.

Ps 91: Trust in God as protector. A song of trust that makes three promises of assistance, each of progressively decreasing length: vv. 1–8; 9–13; 14–16. Through v. 13, a person speaks in God's name; in vv. 14–16, God speaks in the first person. Striking imagery is used to show how the person who trusts God is protected, even when surrounded by death. **4:** *Pinions . . . wings,* possibly a reference to the winged cherubim guarding the Holy

7 A thousand may fall at your side,
  ten thousand at your right hand,
  but it will not come near you.
8 You will only look with your eyes
  and see the punishment of the wicked.

9 Because you have made the LORD your
    refuge,[a]
  the Most High your dwelling place,
10 no evil shall befall you,
  no scourge come near your tent.

11 For he will command his angels
    concerning you
  to guard you in all your ways.
12 On their hands they will bear you up,
  so that you will not dash your foot
    against a stone.
13 You will tread on the lion and the
    adder,
  the young lion and the serpent you will
    trample under foot.

14 Those who love me, I will deliver;
  I will protect those who know my name.
15 When they call to me, I will answer
    them;
  I will be with them in trouble,
  I will rescue them and honor them.
16 With long life I will satisfy them,
  and show them my salvation.

Psalm 92

A Psalm. A Song for the Sabbath Day.

1 It is good to give thanks to the LORD,
  to sing praises to your name, O Most
    High;

2 to declare your steadfast love in the
    morning,
  and your faithfulness by night,
3 to the music of the lute and the harp,
  to the melody of the lyre.
4 For you, O LORD, have made me glad by
    your work;
  at the works of your hands I sing for
    joy.

5 How great are your works, O LORD!
  Your thoughts are very deep!
6 The dullard cannot know,
  the stupid cannot understand this:
7 though the wicked sprout like grass
  and all evildoers flourish,
they are doomed to destruction forever,
  8 but you, O LORD, are on high forever.
9 For your enemies, O LORD,
  for your enemies shall perish;
  all evildoers shall be scattered.

10 But you have exalted my horn like that of
    the wild ox;
  you have poured over me[b] fresh oil.
11 My eyes have seen the downfall of my
    enemies;
  my ears have heard the doom of my evil
    assailants.

12 The righteous flourish like the palm
    tree,
  and grow like a cedar in Lebanon.

a Cn: Heb *Because you, LORD, are my refuge; you have
made*
b Syr: Meaning of Heb uncertain

of Holies in the Temple (Ex 25.20; 1 Kings 6.23–28,32; Ezek 1.4–9), but more likely a reference to a protecting bird as in Egyptian iconography and Ex 19.4; Deut 32.10–12. **7:** *Thousand . . . ten thousand,* an example of numerical parallelism; see Ps 62.11n. **9–13:** *His angels,* angels (divine messengers) lead one through perils, as in Ex 23.20,23 and 32.34. Here they serve to explain how the lone individual is saved from the surrounding destruction: God has appointed protective angels for him. **14–16:** The last assurance is the most intense, for God speaks in the first person; there are seven verbs depicting God's protection. It is striking that there is no demand for absolute righteousness in order to be saved, only love and trust of God.

Ps 92: Thanksgiving for God's governance of the world. A thanksgiving for God's governance has been developed into a hymn. which according to the superscription was recited on *the Sabbath Day,* perhaps because it deals with creation and uses the name of God seven times. **1:** *It is good to give thanks,* perhaps in the sense of "Come let us give thanks." **6–11:** God's just rule works in hidden ways that the foolish do not grasp. **8:** The exact center of the poem, asserting God's triumph in a short, indirect and reverential manner. **10:** *Horn,* a metaphor for strength. **12–15:** The righteous person is compared to a tree as in Pss 1.3; 52.8; Jer 17.8. The tree grows in the garden within the Jerusalem Temple. Ancient temples had orchards that symbolized the fertility that comes

¹³ They are planted in the house of the
  LORD;
  they flourish in the courts of our God.
¹⁴ In old age they still produce fruit;
  they are always green and full of sap,
¹⁵ showing that the LORD is upright;
  he is my rock, and there is no
  unrighteousness in him.

Psalm 93

¹ The LORD is king, he is robed in majesty;
  the LORD is robed, he is girded with
  strength.
He has established the world; it shall never
  be moved;
² your throne is established from of
  old;
  you are from everlasting.

³ The floods have lifted up, O LORD,
  the floods have lifted up their voice;
  the floods lift up their roaring.
⁴ More majestic than the thunders of
  mighty waters,
  more majestic than the waves[a] of the
  sea,
  majestic on high is the LORD!

⁵ Your decrees are very sure;
  holiness befits your house,
  O LORD, forevermore.

Psalm 94

¹ O LORD, you God of vengeance,
  you God of vengeance, shine forth!

² Rise up, O judge of the earth;
  give to the proud what they deserve!
³ O LORD, how long shall the wicked,
  how long shall the wicked exult?

⁴ They pour out their arrogant words;
  all the evildoers boast.
⁵ They crush your people, O LORD,
  and afflict your heritage.
⁶ They kill the widow and the stranger,
  they murder the orphan,
⁷ and they say, "The LORD does not see;
  the God of Jacob does not perceive."

⁸ Understand, O dullest of the people;
  fools, when will you be wise?
⁹ He who planted the ear, does he not
  hear?
He who formed the eye, does he not see?
¹⁰ He who disciplines the nations,
he who teaches knowledge to humankind,
  does he not chastise?
¹¹ The LORD knows our thoughts,[b]
  that they are but an empty breath.

¹² Happy are those whom you discipline,
  O LORD,
  and whom you teach out of your law,
¹³ giving them respite from days of trouble,
  until a pit is dug for the wicked.
¹⁴ For the LORD will not forsake his people;
  he will not abandon his heritage;

a Cn: Heb *majestic are the waves*
b Heb *the thoughts of humankind*

from God. The flourishing of the righteous, like creation, testifies to God's power and righteousness.

Ps 93: The LORD is enthroned as supreme. Like Pss 95–99, Ps 93 praises the LORD as sole king of the universe. Early Israel shared the ancient view that a deity became supreme by defeating chaos and creating a stable and fertile world. In hymns such as this, the LORD defeats chaos (vv. 3–4), and the victory brings an orderly world into being (v. 1c). It is unclear if these psalms celebrating God's kingship were recited at a particular festival commemorating these events. **1:** On his return a victorious warrior would be *robed* in magnificent garments symbolizing the victory. **3–4:** In the cosmic battle, the LORD, using the weapons of a storm (lightning, thunder, wind, rain), defeats Sea (referring to the Canaanite myth in which Baal, the storm god, defeats Sea) attempting to encroach upon the land; cf. Pss 29; 48; 76.12–14; 89.9–10; 104.1–6. **5:** The victorious king proclaims the *decrees* that will govern the new universe.

Ps 94: Rise up, O LORD, to bring justice. A community petition that God would directly rectify wrongs against Israel. The Hebrew word for such rectifying or vindication is "naqam" (v. 1), upholding the rights of the poor; NRSV *vengeance* is misleading. The poem has a petition (vv. 1–2), complaint (vv. 3–7), questioning of God (vv. 3,20), challenge to the wicked (vv. 9–10,16), and statements of trust (vv. 17–18,22). The psalmist models confidence in God (vv. 17–18), boldly addressing God (vv. 1–3,12–13) and the wicked (vv. 8–11). **6:** God is called upon here as "father of orphans and protector of widows" (Ps 68.5). **12:** As in Prov 3.12, a justification for the

¹⁵ for justice will return to the righteous,
 and all the upright in heart will
  follow it.

¹⁶ Who rises up for me against the wicked?
 Who stands up for me against
  evildoers?
¹⁷ If the LORD had not been my help,
 my soul would soon have lived in the
  land of silence.
¹⁸ When I thought, "My foot is slipping,"
 your steadfast love, O LORD, held me up.
¹⁹ When the cares of my heart are many,
 your consolations cheer my soul.
²⁰ Can wicked rulers be allied with you,
 those who contrive mischief by statute?
²¹ They band together against the life of the
  righteous,
 and condemn the innocent to death.
²² But the LORD has become my stronghold,
 and my God the rock of my refuge.
²³ He will repay them for their iniquity
 and wipe them out for their wickedness;
  the LORD our God will wipe them out.

Psalm 95

¹ O come, let us sing to the LORD;
 let us make a joyful noise to the rock of
  our salvation!
² Let us come into his presence with
  thanksgiving;
 let us make a joyful noise to him with
  songs of praise!
³ For the LORD is a great God,
 and a great King above all gods.
⁴ In his hand are the depths of the earth;
 the heights of the mountains are his
  also.
⁵ The sea is his, for he made it,
  and the dry land, which his hands have
   formed.

⁶ O come, let us worship and bow down,
 let us kneel before the LORD, our Maker!
⁷ For he is our God,
 and we are the people of his pasture,
 and the sheep of his hand.

O that today you would listen to his voice!
 ⁸ Do not harden your hearts, as at Meribah,
 as on the day at Massah in the wilderness,
⁹ when your ancestors tested me,
 and put me to the proof, though they
  had seen my work.
¹⁰ For forty years I loathed that generation
 and said, "They are a people whose
  hearts go astray,
 and they do not regard my ways."
¹¹ Therefore in my anger I swore,
 "They shall not enter my rest."

Psalm 96

¹ O sing to the LORD a new song;
 sing to the LORD, all the earth.
² Sing to the LORD, bless his name;
 tell of his salvation from day to day.
³ Declare his glory among the nations,
 his marvelous works among all the
  peoples.
⁴ For great is the LORD, and greatly to be
  praised;
 he is to be revered above all gods.
⁵ For all the gods of the peoples are idols,
 but the LORD made the heavens.
⁶ Honor and majesty are before him;
 strength and beauty are in his
  sanctuary.

suffering of the seemingly innocent.

Ps 95: Worship and obedience to the glorious LORD. A hymn celebrating the LORD enthroned as supreme (see Ps 93n.). It invites Israel to sing (vv. 1–5), bow down before the LORD (vv. 6–7c), and obey (vv. 7d–11). Themes and phrases of Pss 95–99 overlap and interchange. **1:** *The rock*, a common metaphor for God—a massive cliff or mesa that serves as a refuge (*salvation*). **3:** *A great King*, a title of suzerains in Mesopotamia, Egypt, and the Hittite kingdom. **7:** *The sheep of his hand*, connotes special love in that God does not delegate the care of Israel to hirelings. **7d–11:** The tone and speaker change, and the community is told that as the LORD's own flock, they are held to a high standard (cf. Pss 50; 81.8–9). **8:** *Meribah*, a place in the wilderness, related by popular etymology to "place of strife"; *Massah*, another place in the wilderness, in popular etymology, "place of testing"; for both see Ex 17.1–7; Num 21.1–9. **10–11:** God's refusal to allow the first generation to enter the land (*my rest*) is told in Num 14 and Deut 1.34–2.15; here it serves as a reminder for the community to obey God.

Ps 96: Praise of the LORD who comes to judge the world. A hymn celebrating the LORD's kingship (see Ps

⁷ Ascribe to the LORD, O families of the
    peoples,
  ascribe to the LORD glory and strength.
⁸ Ascribe to the LORD the glory due his
    name;
  bring an offering, and come into his
    courts.
⁹ Worship the LORD in holy splendor;
  tremble before him, all the earth.

¹⁰ Say among the nations, "The LORD is
    king!
  The world is firmly established; it shall
    never be moved.
  He will judge the peoples with equity."
¹¹ Let the heavens be glad, and let the earth
    rejoice;
  let the sea roar, and all that fills it;
¹² let the field exult, and everything in it.
  Then shall all the trees of the forest sing
    for joy
¹³ before the LORD; for he is coming,
  for he is coming to judge the earth.
  He will judge the world with
    righteousness,
  and the peoples with his truth.

Psalm 97

¹ The LORD is king! Let the earth rejoice;
  let the many coastlands be glad!
² Clouds and thick darkness are all around
    him;
  righteousness and justice are the
    foundation of his throne.
³ Fire goes before him,
  and consumes his adversaries on every
    side.

⁴ His lightnings light up the world;
  the earth sees and trembles.
⁵ The mountains melt like wax before the
    LORD,
  before the Lord of all the earth.

⁶ The heavens proclaim his righteousness;
  and all the peoples behold his glory.
⁷ All worshipers of images are put to
    shame,
  those who make their boast in
    worthless idols;
  all gods bow down before him.
⁸ Zion hears and is glad,
  and the towns[a] of Judah rejoice,
  because of your judgments, O God.
⁹ For you, O LORD, are most high over all
    the earth;
  you are exalted far above all gods.

¹⁰ The LORD loves those who hate[b] evil;
  he guards the lives of his faithful;
  he rescues them from the hand of the
    wicked.
¹¹ Light dawns[c] for the righteous,
  and joy for the upright in heart.
¹² Rejoice in the LORD, O you righteous,
  and give thanks to his holy name!

Psalm 98

A Psalm.

¹ O sing to the LORD a new song,
  for he has done marvelous things.

a Heb *daughters*
b Cn: Heb *You who love the LORD hate*
c Gk Syr Jerome: Heb *is sown*

93n.) in which vv. 1–6 invite the whole world to sing, vv. 7–10 the family of nations, and vv. 11–13 heaven and earth. **1:** *New song,* celebrating God's arrival as a just king. **7:** *O families of the peoples,* the nations are to turn from their own deities to worship the LORD who has become king (v. 10). How the nations are meant to know this is unclear, but many of these psalms address peoples who are not physically present. Verses 7–9 quote Ps 29.1–2, with changes in the groups addressed. **10:** The LORD has gained royal supremacy by his powerful deeds. **13:** Only God, rather than any human king can *judge the world with righteousness;* this is the cause of great rejoicing.

Ps 97: Rejoice in the LORD who reigns over heaven and earth! A hymn celebrating the LORD who comes to rule the earth (v. 1; see Ps 93n.). The LORD's triumph is manifested in storm and theophany imagery (vv. 2–5). Worshipers of other deities are shamed as they see the LORD triumphant (vv. 6–7). Zion and its surrounding towns rejoice at the coming of so exalted a God (vv. 8–9). The psalm ends with an exhortation to show reverence to the powerful LORD, who, as in the previous psalm, will be manifest in justice (vv. 10–12).

Ps 98: Praise of the LORD, just and victorious ruler of the world. A hymn celebrating the victory of the LORD over the forces of evil, a victory that brought peace and justice to the world; see Ps 93n. Verses 1–3 invite Israel

His right hand and his holy arm
  have gotten him victory.
2 The Lord has made known his
    victory;
  he has revealed his vindication in the
    sight of the nations.
3 He has remembered his steadfast love
    and faithfulness
  to the house of Israel.
All the ends of the earth have seen
  the victory of our God.

4 Make a joyful noise to the Lord, all the
    earth;
  break forth into joyous song and sing
    praises.
5 Sing praises to the Lord with the
    lyre,
  with the lyre and the sound of
    melody.
6 With trumpets and the sound of the
    horn
  make a joyful noise before the King,
    the Lord.

7 Let the sea roar, and all that fills it;
  the world and those who live in it.
8 Let the floods clap their hands;
  let the hills sing together for
    joy
9 at the presence of the Lord, for he is
    coming
  to judge the earth.
He will judge the world with
  righteousness,
  and the peoples with equity.

Psalm 99

1 The Lord is king; let the peoples tremble!
  He sits enthroned upon the cherubim;
    let the earth quake!
2 The Lord is great in Zion;
  he is exalted over all the peoples.
3 Let them praise your great and awesome
    name.
  Holy is he!
4 Mighty King,[a] lover of justice,
  you have established equity;
you have executed justice
  and righteousness in Jacob.
5 Extol the Lord our God;
  worship at his footstool.
  Holy is he!

6 Moses and Aaron were among his
    priests,
  Samuel also was among those who
    called on his name.
  They cried to the Lord, and he
    answered them.
7 He spoke to them in the pillar of cloud;
  they kept his decrees,
  and the statutes that he gave them.

8 O Lord our God, you answered them;
  you were a forgiving God to them,
  but an avenger of their wrongdoings.
9 Extol the Lord our God,
  and worship at his holy mountain;
  for the Lord our God is holy.

a   Cn: Heb *And a king's strength*

to sing praise, vv. 4–6 invite the inhabitants of the earth to join in the song, and vv. 7–9 invite the inanimate elements of the world. The poem begins by announcing that the Lord has won a great victory and ends by introducing the Lord to his new subjects. **1:** On *a new song,* see Ps 96.1. **4–8:** The noisy acclamation of God as king mimics the human coronation ceremony. **9:** *Judge,* not judgment at the end of time but judgment in the biblical sense of ruling justly now.

Ps 99: Announcement that the Lord the king rules with justice. The last of the enthronement hymns (Pss 93; 95–99) celebrates the Lord's victory, enthronement, and authoritative decrees. Verses 1–5 call on the nations to recognize the Lord who establishes justice in the world, and vv. 6–9 describe how divine justice is mediated by Israel's traditions. Each section is concluded by the exhortation "Extol the Lord our God." **1:** *The cherubim* form a throne, on which God is enthroned; cf. 1 Sam 4.4; Ps 17.8n. **3:** *Holy is he!* the phrase appears again in v. 5 and is repeated climactically in v. 9, *the Lord our God is holy.* **4:** As in the other psalms about God's kingship, the emphasis is on divine justice. Human kings served as a type of supreme court; here God the king takes over this role, but unlike human kings he adjudicates fairly and impartially. **5:** The *footstool* of the cherubim throne (see v. 1) was the ark of the covenant. **6:** *Moses and Aaron . . . Samuel,* these ancient leaders mediated God's decrees to Israel. **9:** A variant of v. 5, forming a refrain.

Psalm 100

A Psalm of thanksgiving.

¹ Make a joyful noise to the LORD, all the earth.
² Worship the LORD with gladness;
come into his presence with singing.

³ Know that the LORD is God.
It is he that made us, and we are his;ᵃ
we are his people, and the sheep of his
pasture.

⁴ Enter his gates with thanksgiving,
and his courts with praise.
Give thanks to him, bless his name.

⁵ For the LORD is good;
his steadfast love endures forever,
and his faithfulness to all generations.

Psalm 101

Of David. A Psalm.

¹ I will sing of loyalty and of justice;
to you, O LORD, I will sing.
² I will study the way that is blameless.
When shall I attain it?

I will walk with integrity of heart
within my house;
³ I will not set before my eyes
anything that is base.

I hate the work of those who fall away;
it shall not cling to me.

⁴ Perverseness of heart shall be far from
me;
I will know nothing of evil.

⁵ One who secretly slanders a neighbor
I will destroy.
A haughty look and an arrogant heart
I will not tolerate.

⁶ I will look with favor on the faithful in
the land,
so that they may live with me;
whoever walks in the way that is
blameless
shall minister to me.

⁷ No one who practices deceit
shall remain in my house;
no one who utters lies
shall continue in my presence.

⁸ Morning by morning I will destroy
all the wicked in the land,
cutting off all evildoers
from the city of the LORD.

Psalm 102

*A prayer of one afflicted, when faint and pleading
before the LORD.*

¹ Hear my prayer, O LORD;
let my cry come to you.

ᵃ Another reading is *and not we ourselves*

Ps 100: A call to the nations to worship the LORD. A hymn echoing the call to the nations in the enthronement psalms (Pss 93; 95–99). There are seven invitations to worship: *make a joyful noise, worship, come, know,
enter, give thanks,* and *bless.* The motives for giving praise are introduced by *that* in v. 3a and *for* in v. 5a. Vv. 1–3
and 4–5 are parallel sections, expressing a similar sentiment in different words. The pilgrimage of the nations
to Mount Zion is also found in Pss 22.27; 76.11–12; Isa 2.1–4; 60–62; 66.18–23. **3:** *Sheep of his pasture,* sheep that
the LORD personally pastures, not delegating it to anyone else, as in Pss 74.1; 79.13; 95.7; Jer 23.1; Ezek 34.31.

Ps 101: Commitment to executing justice. Although explicitly stated, the psalm was most likely recited by
the king, who proclaimed a commitment to rule in a manner befitting his divine patron. Acknowledging the
divine *loyalty and . . . justice* (v. 1) that brought him to his throne, the king prays for the strength to fulfill his
duties (v. 2ab). He makes twelve promises (*I will . . .*), being loyal (vv. 2c–4), forbidding abuses by members of
the court (v. 5), appointing only God-fearing administrators (v. 6), expelling the wicked (v. 7), and administering a fair judicial system (v. 8). Underlying the king's vows is the desire to be a good servant and ruler, blessed
by his divine patron. **8:** *Morning by morning,* that is, each morning. At night sin is rampant; justice comes with
the morning sun as in Job 38.12–13. Ps 19 also associates the law with the all-seeing sun. *The city of the LORD* is
Jerusalem, also the royal city.

Ps 102: A plea for the restoration of the psalmist and of Zion. This individual petition blends personal and
national complaints into a single prayer. It is one of the seven penitential psalms in Christian tradition (Pss 6;
32; 38; 51; 102; 130; 143). Drawing a contrast between fragile mortal humans (vv. 3–11,23–24b) and the eternal

2 Do not hide your face from me
  in the day of my distress.
Incline your ear to me;
    answer me speedily in the day when I
    call.

3 For my days pass away like smoke,
  and my bones burn like a furnace.
4 My heart is stricken and withered like
    grass;
  I am too wasted to eat my bread.
5 Because of my loud groaning
  my bones cling to my skin.
6 I am like an owl of the wilderness,
  like a little owl of the waste places.
7 I lie awake;
  I am like a lonely bird on the housetop.
8 All day long my enemies taunt me;
    those who deride me use my name for
    a curse.
9 For I eat ashes like bread,
  and mingle tears with my drink,
10 because of your indignation and anger;
    for you have lifted me up and thrown
    me aside.
11 My days are like an evening shadow;
  I wither away like grass.

12 But you, O LORD, are enthroned
    forever;
  your name endures to all generations.
13 You will rise up and have compassion on
    Zion,
  for it is time to favor it;
  the appointed time has come.
14 For your servants hold its stones dear,
  and have pity on its dust.
15 The nations will fear the name of the
    LORD,
  and all the kings of the earth your glory.
16 For the LORD will build up Zion;
  he will appear in his glory.

17 He will regard the prayer of the destitute,
  and will not despise their prayer.

18 Let this be recorded for a generation to
    come,
  so that a people yet unborn may praise
    the LORD:
19 that he looked down from his holy
    height,
  from heaven the LORD looked at the
    earth,
20 to hear the groans of the prisoners,
  to set free those who were doomed to
    die;
21 so that the name of the LORD may be
    declared in Zion,
  and his praise in Jerusalem,
22 when peoples gather together,
  and kingdoms, to worship the LORD.

23 He has broken my strength in
    midcourse;
  he has shortened my days.
24 "O my God," I say, "do not take me away
    at the midpoint of my life,
you whose years endure
  throughout all generations."

25 Long ago you laid the foundation of the
    earth,
  and the heavens are the work of your
    hands.
26 They will perish, but you endure;
  they will all wear out like a garment.
You change them like clothing, and they
    pass away;
27 but you are the same, and your years
    have no end.
28 The children of your servants shall live
    secure;
  their offspring shall be established in
    your presence.

LORD (vv. 12–22, 24c–27), the psalm begs for the healing that will win for the LORD the praise of the nations (vv. 15,18–22) and nurture a new generation of Israelite worshipers (v. 28). There are three parallel sections: vv. 1–11: Hear me, for my days swiftly *pass away*; vv. 12–22: When you show *compassion*, all will honor you in your Temple; vv. 23–28: Do not make my short life (*shorten my days*) even briefer, O Eternal One. The mixture of private petition and request for the restoration of Zion may suggest that private prayer is more efficacious if it includes broader, communal requests. The superscription, *A prayer of one afflicted, when faint and pleading before the LORD*, suggests that anyone beset with woes or afflicted may recite this prayer. 3–11: The diverse figures of speech combine to express the psalmist's desperation. 13: Implies that this is the *time* to rebuild the Temple, which would date the psalm in the early postexilic period (late fifth century BCE). 11: *Like grass*, cf. Ps 90.5–6; Isa

Psalm 103

Of David.

¹ Bless the LORD, O my soul,
  and all that is within me,
  bless his holy name.
² Bless the LORD, O my soul,
  and do not forget all his benefits—
³ who forgives all your iniquity,
  who heals all your diseases,
⁴ who redeems your life from the Pit,
  who crowns you with steadfast love and
    mercy,
⁵ who satisfies you with good as long as
    you live[a]
  so that your youth is renewed like the
    eagle's.

⁶ The LORD works vindication
  and justice for all who are oppressed.
⁷ He made known his ways to Moses,
  his acts to the people of Israel.
⁸ The LORD is merciful and gracious,
  slow to anger and abounding in
    steadfast love.
⁹ He will not always accuse,
  nor will he keep his anger forever.
¹⁰ He does not deal with us according to
    our sins,
  nor repay us according to our iniquities.
¹¹ For as the heavens are high above the earth,
  so great is his steadfast love toward
    those who fear him;
¹² as far as the east is from the west,
  so far he removes our transgressions
    from us.

¹³ As a father has compassion for his children,
  so the LORD has compassion for those
    who fear him.
¹⁴ For he knows how we were made;
  he remembers that we are dust.

¹⁵ As for mortals, their days are like grass;
  they flourish like a flower of the field;
¹⁶ for the wind passes over it, and it is gone,
  and its place knows it no more.
¹⁷ But the steadfast love of the LORD is from
    everlasting to everlasting
  on those who fear him,
  and his righteousness to children's
    children,
¹⁸ to those who keep his covenant
  and remember to do his commandments.

¹⁹ The LORD has established his throne in
    the heavens,
  and his kingdom rules over all.
²⁰ Bless the LORD, O you his angels,
  you mighty ones who do his bidding,
  obedient to his spoken word.
²¹ Bless the LORD, all his hosts,
  his ministers that do his will.
²² Bless the LORD, all his works,
  in all places of his dominion.
Bless the LORD, O my soul.

Psalm 104

¹ Bless the LORD, O my soul.
  O LORD my God, you are very great.

a   Meaning of Heb uncertain

40.6–8. 22: For the idea of all nations worshiping at the Temple, see Ps 100n.

Ps 103: Praise to the LORD for forgiveness. As Ps 102 combined national and personal complaints into one petition, so Ps 103 blends personal and national benefits into one hymn. The poem draws two distinct parallels: God heals individuals (vv. 1–5) and the nation (vv. 6–14); God summons earthly beings (vv. 15–18) and heavenly beings (vv. 19–22) to give praise. 1–5: The opening verses match the closing verses (19–22) in length and in the repeated *Bless!* 3–5: The six blessings are essentially one: the healing of life-threatening forces. The first blessing mentioned, *who forgives all your iniquity*, is the key: God is fundamentally forgiving. *The Pit*, the abode of the dead. Having been personally healed, the psalmist hopes that the nation will be similarly healed (vv. 6–14). 5: *Renewed like the eagle's*, like the vigor that seems to come with the annual molting of the eagle. 8: Echoes Ex 34.6, when God forgave Israel after their apostasy with the golden calf. The psalm views the Exodus more as the forgiveness of Israel rather than the defeat of Egypt. 14: As *dust* (see Gen 2.7), people cannot be judged too harshly, and deserve divine compassion. 15–18: Even though they are *grass* (see Ps 102.11n.), they receive God's *steadfast love* (Heb "ḥesed") and righteousness. 22: the psalm ends as it began, the words *Bless the LORD, O my soul* forming an inclusio.

Ps 104: Praise to the LORD who made the universe beautiful and life-giving. The hymn praises divine wisdom through a series of vignettes (vv. 1–9,10–12,13–18,19–23,24–26), a reflection (vv. 27–30) and a prayer (vv.

You are clothed with honor and majesty,
　²wrapped in light as with a garment.
You stretch out the heavens like a tent,
　³you set the beams of your[a] chambers
　　on the waters,
you make the clouds your[a] chariot,
　you ride on the wings of the wind,
⁴you make the winds your[a] messengers,
　fire and flame your[a] ministers.

⁵You set the earth on its foundations,
　so that it shall never be shaken.
⁶You cover it with the deep as with a
　　garment;
　the waters stood above the
　　mountains.
⁷At your rebuke they flee;
　at the sound of your thunder they take
　　to flight.
⁸They rose up to the mountains, ran down
　　to the valleys
　to the place that you appointed for
　　them.
⁹You set a boundary that they may not
　　pass,
　so that they might not again cover the
　　earth.

¹⁰You make springs gush forth in the
　　valleys;
　they flow between the hills,
¹¹giving drink to every wild animal;
　the wild asses quench their thirst.
¹²By the streams[b] the birds of the air have
　　their habitation;
　they sing among the branches.
¹³From your lofty abode you water the
　　mountains;
　the earth is satisfied with the fruit of
　　your work.

¹⁴You cause the grass to grow for the
　　cattle,
　and plants for people to use,[c]

to bring forth food from the earth,
　¹⁵and wine to gladden the human heart,
oil to make the face shine,
　and bread to strengthen the human heart.
¹⁶The trees of the LORD are watered
　　abundantly,
　the cedars of Lebanon that he planted.
¹⁷In them the birds build their nests;
　the stork has its home in the fir trees.
¹⁸The high mountains are for the wild
　　goats;
　the rocks are a refuge for the coneys.
¹⁹You have made the moon to mark the
　　seasons;
　the sun knows its time for setting.
²⁰You make darkness, and it is night,
　when all the animals of the forest come
　　creeping out.
²¹The young lions roar for their prey,
　seeking their food from God.
²²When the sun rises, they withdraw
　and lie down in their dens.
²³People go out to their work
　and to their labor until the evening.

²⁴O LORD, how manifold are your works!
　In wisdom you have made them all;
　the earth is full of your creatures.
²⁵Yonder is the sea, great and wide,
　creeping things innumerable are there,
　living things both small and great.
²⁶There go the ships,
　and Leviathan that you formed to sport
　　in it.

²⁷These all look to you
　to give them their food in due season;

a Heb *his*
b Heb *By them*
c Or *to cultivate*

31–35). God, luminous and triumphant (vv. 1–4), organizes the primordial waters (vv. 5–18,24–26) and darkness (vv. 19–23) into a harmonious whole that supports life (vv. 27–35). The depiction owes much to the mythology of neighboring cultures: the storm god who vanquishes Sea (vv. 1–18), and the Egyptian sun-disk Aten whose rays illuminate the world (vv. 19–30); it also shares language and themes with Job 38–39. Psalms 103 and 104 begin and end similarly, but are very different in theme and tone. **1:** *Honor and majesty* are royal qualities. God is depicted in the psalm as a king who has constructed the superlative building project: the world. **2:** *Stretch out the heavens,* cf. Job 9.8; Isa 40.22; 42.5; Zech 12.1. **4:** Cf. Ps 148.8. **9:** Cf. Job 38.8–11; Prov 8.29; Jer 5.22. **13:** See Pss

28 when you give to them, they gather it up;
   when you open your hand, they are
      filled with good things.
29 When you hide your face, they are
      dismayed;
   when you take away their breath, they
      die
   and return to their dust.
30 When you send forth your spirit,[a] they
      are created;
   and you renew the face of the ground.

31 May the glory of the LORD endure
      forever;
   may the LORD rejoice in his works—
32 who looks on the earth and it trembles,
   who touches the mountains and they
      smoke.
33 I will sing to the LORD as long as I live;
   I will sing praise to my God while I have
      being.
34 May my meditation be pleasing to him,
   for I rejoice in the LORD.
35 Let sinners be consumed from the earth,
   and let the wicked be no more.
Bless the LORD, O my soul.
Praise the LORD!

Psalm 105

1 O give thanks to the LORD, call on his
      name,
   make known his deeds among the
      peoples.
2 Sing to him, sing praises to him;
   tell of all his wonderful works.
3 Glory in his holy name;
   let the hearts of those who seek the
      LORD rejoice.
4 Seek the LORD and his strength;
   seek his presence continually.

5 Remember the wonderful works he has
      done,
   his miracles, and the judgments he has
      uttered,
6 O offspring of his servant Abraham,[b]
   children of Jacob, his chosen ones.

7 He is the LORD our God;
   his judgments are in all the earth.
8 He is mindful of his covenant forever,
   of the word that he commanded, for a
      thousand generations,
9 the covenant that he made with
      Abraham,
   his sworn promise to Isaac,
10 which he confirmed to Jacob as a statute,
   to Israel as an everlasting covenant,
11 saying, "To you I will give the land of
      Canaan
   as your portion for an inheritance."

12 When they were few in number,
   of little account, and strangers in it,
13 wandering from nation to nation,
   from one kingdom to another people,
14 he allowed no one to oppress them;
   he rebuked kings on their account,
15 saying, "Do not touch my anointed ones;
   do my prophets no harm."

16 When he summoned famine against the
      land,
   and broke every staff of bread,
17 he had sent a man ahead of them,
   Joseph, who was sold as a slave.
18 His feet were hurt with fetters,
   his neck was put in a collar of iron;

a   Or your breath
b   Another reading is Israel (compare 1 Chr 16.13)

36.8n.; 65.9. 21: See Job 38.39. 24: The psalm's key verse, summarizing the wonder of the world. 26: Leviathan,
see Ps 74.14n. 27–30: The world continues to depend on God. 29–30: Cf. Gen 1.30; 2.7; 3.19. 31–32: A prayer that
God will continue to act beneficently. Mountains . . . smoke, see Ps 144.5. 35: Sinners and the wicked destroy the
harmony of the world.

Ps 105: Praise of the LORD who has acted wonderfully toward Israel. A hymn to God's wondrous guidance
of Israel, like Pss 135 and 136. Ps 105 makes the land of Canaan a symbol of God's generosity and fidelity. The
promise is realized differently in each of the four historical periods selected. From v. 7 forward, a form of the key
words "word/promise," "land," and "servant" occurs in each section. After an invitation to praise (vv. 1–6) and
mention of the covenant promise of land (vv. 7–11; see Gen 15; 17; 28.13–14), the psalm follows the traditional
historical periods: Abraham in Canaan (vv. 12–15; Gen 12–26), Joseph in the land of Egypt (vv. 16–22; Gen 37–47);
Israel in Egypt (vv. 23–38; Ex 1–15); and Israel in the wilderness (vv. 39–45; Ex 16–17). 15: Abraham is called a

¹⁹ until what he had said came to pass,
the word of the LORD kept testing him.
²⁰ The king sent and released him;
the ruler of the peoples set him free.
²¹ He made him lord of his house,
and ruler of all his possessions,
²² to instruct^a his officials at his pleasure,
and to teach his elders wisdom.

²³ Then Israel came to Egypt;
Jacob lived as an alien in the land of
Ham.
²⁴ And the LORD made his people very
fruitful,
and made them stronger than their
foes,
²⁵ whose hearts he then turned to hate his
people,
to deal craftily with his servants.

²⁶ He sent his servant Moses,
and Aaron whom he had chosen.
²⁷ They performed his signs among them,
and miracles in the land of Ham.
²⁸ He sent darkness, and made the land
dark;
they rebelled^b against his words.
²⁹ He turned their waters into blood,
and caused their fish to die.
³⁰ Their land swarmed with frogs,
even in the chambers of their kings.
³¹ He spoke, and there came swarms of
flies,
and gnats throughout their country.
³² He gave them hail for rain,
and lightning that flashed through their
land.
³³ He struck their vines and fig trees,
and shattered the trees of their
country.
³⁴ He spoke, and the locusts came,
and young locusts without number;

³⁵ they devoured all the vegetation in their
land,
and ate up the fruit of their ground.
³⁶ He struck down all the firstborn in their
land,
the first issue of all their strength.

³⁷ Then he brought Israel^c out with silver
and gold,
and there was no one among their
tribes who stumbled.
³⁸ Egypt was glad when they departed,
for dread of them had fallen upon it.
³⁹ He spread a cloud for a covering,
and fire to give light by night.
⁴⁰ They asked, and he brought quails,
and gave them food from heaven in
abundance.
⁴¹ He opened the rock, and water gushed
out;
it flowed through the desert like a river.
⁴² For he remembered his holy promise,
and Abraham, his servant.

⁴³ So he brought his people out with joy,
his chosen ones with singing.
⁴⁴ He gave them the lands of the nations,
and they took possession of the wealth
of the peoples,
⁴⁵ that they might keep his statutes
and observe his laws.
Praise the LORD!

Psalm 106

¹ Praise the LORD!
O give thanks to the LORD, for he is
good;
for his steadfast love endures forever.

---

^a Gk Syr Jerome: Heb *to bind*
^b Cn Compare Gk Syr: Heb *they did not rebel*
^c Heb *them*

---

prophet in Gen 20.7; none of the patriarchs are ever called *anointed* (Heb "mashiah") elsewhere (except for 1 Chr 16.23, which quotes this psalm). **18:** This is one of many cases in this psalm where the retelling of the past differs in detail from the narratives in the Torah. **27–36:** In terms of number and order, this differs strikingly from the plague narrative in Exodus. **38:** This contrasts with the account in Ex 14–15 of the Egyptians chasing after the Israelites and drowning in the Reed Sea. **42:** The relation between Israel and its land is permanent and unalterable, predicated on *his holy promise*. **45:** But the gift of the land depends on obedience to God. If written in the exilic period, this psalm would remind the people to return to God so that they might return to the land, and to remind God of his absolute, unalterable promise.

Ps 106: A confession of sin and record of divine forgiveness. A storytelling poem, describing seven occa-

² Who can utter the mighty doings of the
  LORD,
    or declare all his praise?
³ Happy are those who observe justice,
    who do righteousness at all times.

⁴ Remember me, O LORD, when you show
    favor to your people;
    help me when you deliver them;
⁵ that I may see the prosperity of your
    chosen ones,
  that I may rejoice in the gladness of
    your nation,
  that I may glory in your heritage.

⁶ Both we and our ancestors have sinned;
    we have committed iniquity, have done
    wickedly.
⁷ Our ancestors, when they were in Egypt,
    did not consider your wonderful
    works;
  they did not remember the abundance of
    your steadfast love,
    but rebelled against the Most High[a] at
    the Red Sea.[b]
⁸ Yet he saved them for his name's sake,
    so that he might make known his
    mighty power.
⁹ He rebuked the Red Sea,[b] and it became
    dry;
  he led them through the deep as
    through a desert.
¹⁰ So he saved them from the hand of the
    foe,
  and delivered them from the hand of
    the enemy.
¹¹ The waters covered their adversaries;
    not one of them was left.
¹² Then they believed his words;
    they sang his praise.

¹³ But they soon forgot his works;
    they did not wait for his counsel.
¹⁴ But they had a wanton craving in the
    wilderness,
    and put God to the test in the desert;
¹⁵ he gave them what they asked,
    but sent a wasting disease among
    them.

¹⁶ They were jealous of Moses in the
    camp,
  and of Aaron, the holy one of the
    LORD.
¹⁷ The earth opened and swallowed up
    Dathan,
    and covered the faction of Abiram.
¹⁸ Fire also broke out in their
    company;
    the flame burned up the wicked.

¹⁹ They made a calf at Horeb
    and worshiped a cast image.
²⁰ They exchanged the glory of God[c]
    for the image of an ox that eats
    grass.
²¹ They forgot God, their Savior,
    who had done great things in
    Egypt,
²² wondrous works in the land of Ham,
    and awesome deeds by the Red Sea.[b]
²³ Therefore he said he would destroy
    them—
    had not Moses, his chosen one,
  stood in the breach before him,
    to turn away his wrath from destroying
    them.

a Cn Compare 78.17, 56: Heb *rebelled at the sea*
b Or *Sea of Reeds*
c Compare Gk Mss: Heb *exchanged their glory*

sions of sin and forgiveness (vv. 6–46). Seven seems to symbolize completeness. Each occasion is identified by a place name (noted in italics): Rebellion and rescue *at the Red Sea* (vv. 6–12; Ex 14–15); testing God *in the desert* (vv. 13–15; Ex 16–17); jealousy of Moses *in the camp* (vv. 16–18; Num 16); the calf *at Horeb* and Moses' intercession (vv. 19–23; Ex 32); refusal to attack from the south and divine threat (vv. 23–27; Num 14), the sin with Baal of *Peor* and Phinehas' intercession (vv. 28–31; Num 25); sin *at the waters of Meribah* (vv. 32–33; Num 20); sacrifice of children in *Canaan* (vv. 34–46). The seventh and climactic occasion is complex, for the sin is typical rather than a single act: the sacrifice of infants (vv. 34–39) representing the people's adoption of corrupt native ways. The punishment is also typical, a series of punishments (v. 41) and mercies. In terms of theme (history) and opening (*Praise the LORD*), it is connected to the previous psalm, although its theme and understanding of the Israelite past is quite different from it. The past, presented in cycles of Israelite sin and divine forgiveness, is recounted

24 Then they despised the pleasant land,
  having no faith in his promise.
25 They grumbled in their tents,
  and did not obey the voice of the LORD.
26 Therefore he raised his hand and swore
    to them
  that he would make them fall in the
    wilderness,
27 and would disperse[a] their descendants
    among the nations,
  scattering them over the lands.

28 Then they attached themselves to the
    Baal of Peor,
  and ate sacrifices offered to the dead;
29 they provoked the LORD to anger with
    their deeds,
  and a plague broke out among them.
30 Then Phinehas stood up and interceded,
  and the plague was stopped.
31 And that has been reckoned to him as
    righteousness
  from generation to generation forever.

32 They angered the LORD[b] at the waters of
    Meribah,
  and it went ill with Moses on their
    account;
33 for they made his spirit bitter,
  and he spoke words that were rash.

34 They did not destroy the peoples,
  as the LORD commanded them,
35 but they mingled with the nations
  and learned to do as they did.
36 They served their idols,
  which became a snare to them.
37 They sacrificed their sons
  and their daughters to the demons;
38 they poured out innocent blood,
  the blood of their sons and daughters,
whom they sacrificed to the idols of
    Canaan;
  and the land was polluted with blood.

39 Thus they became unclean by their acts,
  and prostituted themselves in their
    doings.

40 Then the anger of the LORD was kindled
    against his people,
  and he abhorred his heritage;
41 he gave them into the hand of the nations,
  so that those who hated them ruled
    over them.
42 Their enemies oppressed them,
  and they were brought into subjection
    under their power.
43 Many times he delivered them,
  but they were rebellious in their purposes,
  and were brought low through their
    iniquity.
44 Nevertheless he regarded their distress
  when he heard their cry.
45 For their sake he remembered his
    covenant,
  and showed compassion according to the
    abundance of his steadfast love.
46 He caused them to be pitied
  by all who held them captive.

47 Save us, O LORD our God,
  and gather us from among the nations,
that we may give thanks to your holy name
  and glory in your praise.

48 Blessed be the LORD, the God of Israel,
  from everlasting to everlasting.
And let all the people say, "Amen."
  Praise the LORD!

BOOK V PSALMS 107–150

Psalm 107

1 O give thanks to the LORD, for he is good;
  for his steadfast love endures forever.

a Syr Compare Ezek 20.23: Heb *cause to fall*
b Heb *him*

in order to call upon God to forgive again (v. 47). **19:** *Horeb,* an alternate name for Sinai. **22:** *Ham,* see Ps 78.51n. **24:** In other words, they heeded the spies who recommended against fighting against the Canaanites. **37–38:** Exile is blamed on child-sacrifice, which made the land ritually impure; see 2 Kings 16.3; 21.6; Jer 19.5; Ezek 20.31; 23.37. **47:** A reference to the exile to Babylon in the early sixth century BCE. **48:** The plea of v. 47 was the original end of the psalm; the doxology in v. 48 was inserted by an editor when the Psalms were divided into five books or sections.

  Ps 107: Thanksgiving for bringing back the people from exile. This community thanksgiving logically fol-

² Let the redeemed of the LORD say so,
  those he redeemed from trouble
³ and gathered in from the lands,
  from the east and from the west,
  from the north and from the south.ᵃ

⁴ Some wandered in desert wastes,
  finding no way to an inhabited town;
⁵ hungry and thirsty,
  their soul fainted within them.
⁶ Then they cried to the LORD in their
    trouble,
  and he delivered them from their
    distress;
⁷ he led them by a straight way,
  until they reached an inhabited town.
⁸ Let them thank the LORD for his steadfast
    love,
  for his wonderful works to humankind.
⁹ For he satisfies the thirsty,
  and the hungry he fills with good
    things.

¹⁰ Some sat in darkness and in gloom,
  prisoners in misery and in irons,
¹¹ for they had rebelled against the words
    of God,
  and spurned the counsel of the Most
    High.
¹² Their hearts were bowed down with hard
    labor;
  they fell down, with no one to help.
¹³ Then they cried to the LORD in their
    trouble,
  and he saved them from their distress;
¹⁴ he brought them out of darkness and
    gloom,
  and broke their bonds asunder.
¹⁵ Let them thank the LORD for his steadfast
    love,
  for his wonderful works to humankind.

¹⁶ For he shatters the doors of bronze,
  and cuts in two the bars of iron.

¹⁷ Some were sickᵇ through their sinful
    ways,
  and because of their iniquities endured
    affliction;
¹⁸ they loathed any kind of food,
  and they drew near to the gates of
    death.
¹⁹ Then they cried to the LORD in their
    trouble,
  and he saved them from their
    distress;
²⁰ he sent out his word and healed them,
  and delivered them from destruction.
²¹ Let them thank the LORD for his steadfast
    love,
  for his wonderful works to
    humankind.
²² And let them offer thanksgiving
    sacrifices,
  and tell of his deeds with songs of joy.

²³ Some went down to the sea in ships,
  doing business on the mighty waters;
²⁴ they saw the deeds of the LORD,
  his wondrous works in the deep.
²⁵ For he commanded and raised the
    stormy wind,
  which lifted up the waves of the sea.
²⁶ They mounted up to heaven, they went
    down to the depths;
  their courage melted away in their
    calamity;
²⁷ they reeled and staggered like
    drunkards,
  and were at their wits' end.

ᵃ Cn: Heb *sea*
ᵇ Cn: Heb *fools*

lows the two pleas for the exile to end in the previous Pss 105 and 106. Ps 107 provides four examples of divine deliverance (vv. 4–9; 10–16; 17–22; 23–32), followed by a final section (vv. 33–43) transposing the deliverance of vv. 4–32 into the daily governance of the land. The number four may suggest totality; cf. Isa 11.12. In each panel a danger occurs (vv. 4–5; 10–12; 17–18; 23–27), the afflicted cry out to the LORD (vv. 6; 13; 19; 28) who rescues them (vv. 6b–7; 13b–14; 19b–10; 28b–30), prompting them to respond with thanksgiving (vv. 8–9; 15–16; 21–22; 31–32). Verse 33 marks a new section with its initial verb (*he turns*). Vv. 1–3 invited the returned exiles to give praise; vv. 4–32 depict the four rescued groups: those hungering and thirsting in the wilderness (vv. 4–9); prisoners (vv. 10–16); the sick (vv. 17–22); those caught in an ocean storm (vv. 23–32); these are all metaphorical for the tribulations of the Babylonian exile of the sixth century BCE, and the difficulties of returning by foot from Babylon. Vv. 33–43 describe the LORD's rescue and governance of Israel. **2:** *The redeemed of the LORD*, in its

28 Then they cried to the LORD in their trouble,
  and he brought them out from their distress;
29 he made the storm be still,
  and the waves of the sea were hushed.
30 Then they were glad because they had quiet,
  and he brought them to their desired haven.
31 Let them thank the LORD for his steadfast love,
  for his wonderful works to humankind.
32 Let them extol him in the congregation of the people,
  and praise him in the assembly of the elders.

33 He turns rivers into a desert,
  springs of water into thirsty ground,
34 a fruitful land into a salty waste,
  because of the wickedness of its inhabitants.
35 He turns a desert into pools of water,
  a parched land into springs of water.
36 And there he lets the hungry live,
  and they establish a town to live in;
37 they sow fields, and plant vineyards,
  and get a fruitful yield.
38 By his blessing they multiply greatly,
  and he does not let their cattle decrease.

39 When they are diminished and brought low
  through oppression, trouble, and sorrow,
40 he pours contempt on princes
  and makes them wander in trackless wastes;
41 but he raises up the needy out of distress,
  and makes their families like flocks.
42 The upright see it and are glad;
  and all wickedness stops its mouth.

43 Let those who are wise give heed to these things,
  and consider the steadfast love of the LORD.

Psalm 108

A Song. A Psalm of David.

1 My heart is steadfast, O God, my heart is steadfast;[a]
  I will sing and make melody.
  Awake, my soul![b]
2 Awake, O harp and lyre!
  I will awake the dawn.
3 I will give thanks to you, O LORD, among the peoples,
  and I will sing praises to you among the nations.
4 For your steadfast love is higher than the heavens,
  and your faithfulness reaches to the clouds.

5 Be exalted, O God, above the heavens,
  and let your glory be over all the earth.
6 Give victory with your right hand, and answer me,
  so that those whom you love may be rescued.

7 God has promised in his sanctuary:[c]
  "With exultation I will divide up Shechem,
  and portion out the Vale of Succoth.
8 Gilead is mine; Manasseh is mine;
  Ephraim is my helmet;
  Judah is my scepter.
9 Moab is my washbasin;
  on Edom I hurl my shoe;
  over Philistia I shout in triumph."

a Heb Mss Gk Syr: MT lacks *my heart is steadfast*
b Compare 57.8: Heb *also my soul*
c Or *by his holiness*

one other biblical use, the inhabitants of restored Zion (Isa 62.12). **11:** The exile was a punishment for Israel's behavior. **35:** Cf. Isa 41.18; 43.19. **41–42:** Two main themes of psalms: the vindication of the needy, which leads to public recognition of God's greatness. **43:** The *wise* understand that the LORD's *steadfast love* (Heb "ḥesed") allows for periods of tribulation and defeat, but Israel will always be restored.

Ps 108: A prayer for victory. A community petition using material from other psalms; vv. 1–5 appear also in Ps 57.7–11 and vv. 6–13 appear in Ps 60.5–12. For detailed comments, see the annotations to those texts. In vv. 1–6, the psalmist resolves to praise God's love and faithfulness; vv. 7–9 cite an ancient oracle; and vv. 10–13

¹⁰ Who will bring me to the fortified city?
  Who will lead me to Edom?
¹¹ Have you not rejected us, O God?
  You do not go out, O God, with our
    armies.
¹² O grant us help against the foe,
  for human help is worthless.
¹³ With God we shall do valiantly;
  it is he who will tread down our foes.

Psalm 109

To the leader. Of David. A Psalm.

¹ Do not be silent, O God of my praise.
² For wicked and deceitful mouths are
    opened against me,
  speaking against me with lying tongues.
³ They beset me with words of hate,
  and attack me without cause.
⁴ In return for my love they accuse me,
  even while I make prayer for them.^a
⁵ So they reward me evil for good,
  and hatred for my love.

⁶ They say,^b "Appoint a wicked man against
    him;
  let an accuser stand on his right.
⁷ When he is tried, let him be found guilty;
  let his prayer be counted as sin.
⁸ May his days be few;
  may another seize his position.
⁹ May his children be orphans,
  and his wife a widow.
¹⁰ May his children wander about and beg;
  may they be driven out of^c the ruins
    they inhabit.
¹¹ May the creditor seize all that he has;
  may strangers plunder the fruits of his
    toil.
¹² May there be no one to do him a
    kindness,
  nor anyone to pity his orphaned
    children.

¹³ May his posterity be cut off;
  may his name be blotted out in the
    second generation.
¹⁴ May the iniquity of his father^d be
    remembered before the LORD,
  and do not let the sin of his mother be
    blotted out.
¹⁵ Let them be before the LORD
    continually,
  and may his^e memory be cut off from
    the earth.
¹⁶ For he did not remember to show
    kindness,
  but pursued the poor and needy
  and the brokenhearted to their
    death.
¹⁷ He loved to curse; let curses come on
    him.
  He did not like blessing; may it be far
    from him.
¹⁸ He clothed himself with cursing as his
    coat,
  may it soak into his body like water,
  like oil into his bones.
¹⁹ May it be like a garment that he wraps
    around himself,
  like a belt that he wears every day."

²⁰ May that be the reward of my accusers
    from the LORD,
  of those who speak evil against my
    life.
²¹ But you, O LORD my Lord,
  act on my behalf for your name's sake;
  because your steadfast love is good,
    deliver me.

a Syr: Heb *I prayer*
b Heb lacks *They say*
c Gk: Heb *and seek*
d Cn: Heb *fathers*
e Gk: Heb *their*

complain and pray.

Ps 109: Prayer for vindication. An urgent petition of an individual accused of exploiting the poor (v. 16) and who has therefore been cursed by enemies (vv. 6–19). Petitioners typically complain to God of their perilous plight; in this case the complaint is in the form of a quotation of the enemies' curses (twelve curses in vv. 6–19). NRSV adds *They* (the enemies) *say* in v. 6a to make clear the psalmist is citing the enemy's curses rather than personally cursing; other translations understand the curses to be those of the psalmist against his enemies. **6:** The word for accuser, Heb "satan," later means Satan, the devil. **14:** Following Ex 34.7 ("visiting the iniquity of the parents upon the children") and other texts, may he be subject to intergenerational punishment. **20:** *May that be the reward,* a prayer that the curses fall on the enemies so as to demonstrate to all that the LORD has

²² For I am poor and needy,
  and my heart is pierced within me.
²³ I am gone like a shadow at evening;
  I am shaken off like a locust.
²⁴ My knees are weak through fasting;
  my body has become gaunt.
²⁵ I am an object of scorn to my
    accusers;
  when they see me, they shake their
    heads.

²⁶ Help me, O LORD my God!
  Save me according to your steadfast
    love.
²⁷ Let them know that this is your hand;
  you, O LORD, have done it.
²⁸ Let them curse, but you will bless.
  Let my assailants be put to shame;^a may
    your servant be glad.
²⁹ May my accusers be clothed with
    dishonor;
  may they be wrapped in their own
    shame as in a mantle.
³⁰ With my mouth I will give great thanks
    to the LORD;
  I will praise him in the midst of the
    throng.
³¹ For he stands at the right hand of the
    needy,
  to save them from those who would
    condemn them to death.

Psalm 110

Of David. A Psalm.

¹ The LORD says to my lord,
  "Sit at my right hand
until I make your enemies your footstool."

² The LORD sends out from Zion
  your mighty scepter.
  Rule in the midst of your foes.
³ Your people will offer themselves
    willingly
  on the day you lead your forces
  on the holy mountains.^b
From the womb of the morning,
  like dew, your youth^c will come to you.
⁴ The LORD has sworn and will not change
    his mind,
  "You are a priest forever according to
    the order of Melchizedek."^d

⁵ The Lord is at your right hand;
  he will shatter kings on the day of his
    wrath.
⁶ He will execute judgment among the
    nations,
  filling them with corpses;
he will shatter heads
  over the wide earth.
⁷ He will drink from the stream by the
    path;
  therefore he will lift up his head.

Psalm 111

¹ Praise the LORD!
I will give thanks to the LORD with my
    whole heart,
  in the company of the upright, in the
    congregation.

a Gk: Heb *They have risen up and have been put to
   shame*
b Another reading is *in holy splendor*
c Cn: Heb *the dew of your youth*
d Or *forever, a rightful king by my edict*

vindicated the psalmist. Cf. also v. 29. **22:** *I am poor and needy,* far from persecuting the poor as the enemies have asserted (v. 16), the psalmist is himself poor and needy and thus has a claim on God's protection. **28:** For the psalmist, curses are not automatically effective but depend on God. **31:** The word for *right hand* links this psalm with the next (see 110.1).

Ps 110: Victory to the Davidic king. A royal psalm in which a court official cites promises of victory made to the Davidic king (vv. 1,4) and then elaborates them (vv. 2–3,5–7). Christian interpretation has understood the king's victory as prefiguring Jesus' resurrection and rule over the nations (Acts 2.34; 1 Cor 15.25; Heb 1.3,13). **1–3:** *Sit,* take your throne; *right hand* is the place of honor; *footstool,* victorious kings were depicted with their feet on their defeated foes' necks. **3:** Though very obscure, the general sense is clear: the king will lead the army and defeat the LORD's enemies. **4–7:** *Melchizedek,* priest-king of pre-Israelite Jerusalem who greeted Abraham in Gen 14.17–20; the tradition is applied only here to the Davidic king. As elsewhere in the ancient Near East, Israelite kings are sometimes described as exercising priestly duties (e.g., 2 Sam 6.13–14; 8.18; 1 Kings 3.4). **7:** Obscure, possibly referring to a ritual of the warrior returning from victory.

² Great are the works of the LORD,
  studied by all who delight in them.
³ Full of honor and majesty is his work,
  and his righteousness endures forever.
⁴ He has gained renown by his wonderful
  deeds;
  the LORD is gracious and merciful.
⁵ He provides food for those who fear him;
  he is ever mindful of his covenant.
⁶ He has shown his people the power of his
  works,
  in giving them the heritage of the nations.
⁷ The works of his hands are faithful and just;
  all his precepts are trustworthy.
⁸ They are established forever and ever,
  to be performed with faithfulness and
  uprightness.
⁹ He sent redemption to his people;
  he has commanded his covenant forever.
  Holy and awesome is his name.
¹⁰ The fear of the LORD is the beginning of
  wisdom;
  all those who practice itª have a good
  understanding.
  His praise endures forever.

Psalm 112

¹ Praise the LORD!
  Happy are those who fear the LORD,
  who greatly delight in his
  commandments.
² Their descendants will be mighty in the
  land;

the generation of the upright will be
  blessed.
³ Wealth and riches are in their houses,
  and their righteousness endures forever.
⁴ They rise in the darkness as a light for the
  upright;
  they are gracious, merciful, and
  righteous.
⁵ It is well with those who deal generously
  and lend,
  who conduct their affairs with justice.
⁶ For the righteous will never be moved;
  they will be remembered forever.
⁷ They are not afraid of evil tidings;
  their hearts are firm, secure in the LORD.
⁸ Their hearts are steady, they will not be
  afraid;
  in the end they will look in triumph on
  their foes.
⁹ They have distributed freely, they have
  given to the poor;
  their righteousness endures forever;
  their horn is exalted in honor.
¹⁰ The wicked see it and are angry;
  they gnash their teeth and melt away;
  the desire of the wicked comes to nothing.

Psalm 113

¹ Praise the LORD!
  Praise, O servants of the LORD;
  praise the name of the LORD.

ª Gk Syr: Heb *them*

Ps 111: Hymn to God's great deeds. A hymn in acrostic form (see Ps 9–10n.) celebrating the great deeds of the Exodus-Conquest. 5: Food may refer to the manna and quail that God provided in the wilderness (see Ex 16; Num 11; Ps 105.40). 7: The verse is the transition from admiring the divine deeds (v. 2b) to imitating the God who did them (*all his precepts*; *those who practice it*, v. 10). 10: *Fear of the LORD* (best rendered "revering the LORD"), pointing forward to v. 1 of Ps 112, its companion piece. See Ps 19.9; Prov 1.7; 9.10; etc.

Ps 112: Blessings on those who treasure God's acts and give to the poor. An instruction in acrostic form (see Ps 9–10n.) and companion piece to Psalm 111, depicting the righteous person as one who ponders God's works (cf. Ps 111.2) and puts into practice God's precepts (cf. Ps 111.7). The virtue singled out is mercy shown in giving to the poor (vv. 4,5,9). Paradoxically, generous givers do not deprive their children of an inheritance (vv. 2–3) nor suffer the shame that comes with poverty (vv. 6,8,10), for the LORD will recompense them. This psalm and Prov 19.17 influenced Jewish and Christian views of almsgiving (e.g., Dan 4.24; Matt 6.12). 1: *Fear the LORD*, see Ps 110.10n. 3: *And their righteousness endures forever* helps to join this psalm to Ps 111; see 111.3. 9: *Horn*, a metaphor for strength.

Ps 113: A hymn to the just God. Like other hymns, this one opens and closes with a call to praise, and specifically names those called to praise ("servants of the LORD," v. 1). Ps 113 concludes the three Hallelujah psalms (Pss 111–113) and begins the "Egyptian Hallel" (= Heb "praise") psalms (113–118) sung at major Jewish festivals even though the Bible does not suggest that they are a collection. Many scholars think that Pss 113–114 were sung before the Passover meal and Pss 115–118 after it. Images of "high" and "low" unify the psalm. 1: It is uncertain

2 Blessed be the name of the LORD
  from this time on and forevermore.
3 From the rising of the sun to its setting
  the name of the LORD is to be
    praised.
4 The LORD is high above all nations,
  and his glory above the heavens.

5 Who is like the LORD our God,
  who is seated on high,
6 who looks far down
  on the heavens and the earth?
7 He raises the poor from the dust,
  and lifts the needy from the ash
    heap,
8 to make them sit with princes,
  with the princes of his people.
9 He gives the barren woman a home,
  making her the joyous mother of
    children.
Praise the LORD!

Psalm 114

1 When Israel went out from Egypt,
  the house of Jacob from a people of
    strange language,
2 Judah became God'sª sanctuary,
  Israel his dominion.

3 The sea looked and fled;
  Jordan turned back.

4 The mountains skipped like rams,
  the hills like lambs.

5 Why is it, O sea, that you flee?
  O Jordan, that you turn back?
6 O mountains, that you skip like rams?
  O hills, like lambs?

7 Tremble, O earth, at the presence of the
    LORD,
  at the presence of the God of Jacob,
8 who turns the rock into a pool of
    water,
  the flint into a spring of water.

Psalm 115

1 Not to us, O LORD, not to us, but to your
    name give glory,
  for the sake of your steadfast love and
    your faithfulness.
2 Why should the nations say,
  "Where is their God?"

3 Our God is in the heavens;
  he does whatever he pleases.
4 Their idols are silver and gold,
  the work of human hands.
5 They have mouths, but do not speak;
  eyes, but do not see.

ª Heb *his*

if the *servants of the LORD* refer to all worshipers or is a technical term for a specific group in the Temple. *The name* represents the person, here the LORD who rules earth and heaven (vv. 2–4). In late biblical and in postbiblical texts, the *name* of God was used as a surrogate for God. 5–6: A rhetorical question expecting the answer "None." 6: *Who looks far down*, better "who rules over." 7–9: Two typical examples of divine ruling: enabling a poor man to sit with honor among the village elders, and giving the barren woman a child; cf. 1 Sam 2.4–8.

Ps 114: The wonder of the Exodus. A unique psalm with hymnlike features, celebrating the Exodus from Egypt and the Conquest, with the crossing of the sea and the Jordan River. An apt Hallel psalm (Pss 113–118) with standard synonymous parallelism and internal repetition (vv. 3–4 || 5–6). 1–4: Somewhat abruptly, the psalm describes Israel leaving Egypt through the sea (see Ex 14–15) to a safe land. Telescoping events, this poem has the people cross from Egypt directly into Canaan (*Judah, Israel*, v. 2, where the Southern and Northern kingdoms are meant). 2: Strikingly, it is at the Exodus, and not at Sinai, that Israel becomes God's holy people (a preferable translation to *sanctuary*). 3: *The sea* is parallel to *Jordan* and is personified as a defeated warrior (cf. Pss 77.16; 104.7). The LORD taunts sea and mountains as they tremble and flee (Ps 96.9; Deut 2.25). 8: A reference to God providing water in the wilderness from a *rock*; see Ps 78.15,20; Ex 17.6; Num 20.11.

Ps 115: Show forth your glory to the nations. A community petition that the LORD in the heavens (v. 3), too powerful to be contained in earthly statues (vv. 4–8), might display his glory on earth and enable Israel to live in trust (vv. 9–18). 1: *Not to us*, better, "Not for our sake, O LORD, not for our sake, but for the sake of your name display your glory." The Hebrew phrase, lit., "to give glory," actually means "display glory" as in Ezek 39.21. 2: *Where is their God?* a taunt that Israel's God is powerless. 3–8: There are two contrasts: between our God (singular) in the heavens and their gods (images, plural) on earth; between God who acts and the gods who cannot. 3:

⁶They have ears, but do not hear;
    noses, but do not smell.
⁷They have hands, but do not feel;
    feet, but do not walk;
    they make no sound in their
        throats.
⁸Those who make them are like them;
    so are all who trust in them.

⁹O Israel, trust in the LORD!
    He is their help and their shield.
¹⁰O house of Aaron, trust in the LORD!
    He is their help and their shield.
¹¹You who fear the LORD, trust in the
        LORD!
    He is their help and their shield.

¹²The LORD has been mindful of us; he will
        bless us;
    he will bless the house of Israel;
    he will bless the house of Aaron;
¹³he will bless those who fear the LORD,
    both small and great.

¹⁴May the LORD give you increase,
    both you and your children.
¹⁵May you be blessed by the LORD,
    who made heaven and earth.

¹⁶The heavens are the LORD's heavens,
    but the earth he has given to human
        beings.
¹⁷The dead do not praise the LORD,
    nor do any that go down into silence.
¹⁸But we will bless the LORD
    from this time on and forevermore.
Praise the LORD!

Psalm 116

¹I love the LORD, because he has heard
    my voice and my supplications.
²Because he inclined his ear to me,
    therefore I will call on him as long as I
        live.
³The snares of death encompassed me;
    the pangs of Sheol laid hold on me;
    I suffered distress and anguish.
⁴Then I called on the name of the LORD:
    "O LORD, I pray, save my life!"

⁵Gracious is the LORD, and righteous;
    our God is merciful.
⁶The LORD protects the simple;
    when I was brought low, he saved me.
⁷Return, O my soul, to your rest,
    for the LORD has dealt bountifully with
        you.

⁸For you have delivered my soul from
        death,
    my eyes from tears,
    my feet from stumbling.
⁹I walk before the LORD
    in the land of the living.
¹⁰I kept my faith, even when I said,
    "I am greatly afflicted";
¹¹I said in my consternation,
    "Everyone is a liar."

¹²What shall I return to the LORD
    for all his bounty to me?
¹³I will lift up the cup of salvation
    and call on the name of the LORD,
¹⁴I will pay my vows to the LORD
    in the presence of all his people.

Our God is in the heavens, a bold response to the taunt *Where is their God?* Ridicule of divine images is common in exilic texts and later (e.g., Jer 10.1–16; Isa 40.18–20; 41.6–7; Bel). **9**: *Trust in the LORD,* those who trust in images will be frustrated (v. 8) and those who trust in the LORD will find a *help* and *shield* (vv. 9–11). **10**: *House of Aaron,* the priests, who claimed Aaron as their ancestor. **12–13**: The psalmist turns to God, asking him to bless the same three groups who were just asked (vv. 10–11) to have trust in the LORD. **15**: *Who made heaven and earth,* see Ps 124.8n. **17**: According to the biblical worldview, all who died went down to Sheol, the underworld, where all was quiet; the dead could thus be called those *that go down into silence.* See also 6.5n.

Ps 116: Thanksgiving to a saving God. An individual thanksgiving for having found a saving God rather than for a particular rescue. God is attentive (vv. 1–2) and merciful (vv. 5–6), and the psalmist resolves to respond by acts of trust (vv. 7,9–11) and worship (vv. 12–19). There seem to be four sections: the rescue and the resulting relationship (vv. 1–4); the nature of God revealed by the rescue and the psalmist's response (vv. 5–8); resolve to live as a trusting client of the divine patron (vv. 9–11); resolve to offer appropriate ritual thanks (vv. 12–19). **1**: *I love the LORD,* in the sense of choose (Prov 12.1; 20.13; Isa 41.8); the Hebrew reads "I love that the LORD has heard." **3**: *Sheol,* the underworld, the abode of the dead. **7**: *Soul* refers to breathing or life-force.

¹⁵ Precious in the sight of the LORD
is the death of his faithful ones.
¹⁶ O LORD, I am your servant;
I am your servant, the child of your
serving girl.
You have loosed my bonds.
¹⁷ I will offer to you a thanksgiving sacrifice
and call on the name of the LORD.
¹⁸ I will pay my vows to the LORD
in the presence of all his people,
¹⁹ in the courts of the house of the LORD,
in your midst, O Jerusalem.
Praise the LORD!

Psalm 117

¹ Praise the LORD, all you nations!
Extol him, all you peoples!
² For great is his steadfast love toward us,
and the faithfulness of the LORD
endures forever.
Praise the LORD!

Psalm 118

¹ O give thanks to the LORD, for he is good;
his steadfast love endures forever!

² Let Israel say,
"His steadfast love endures forever."
³ Let the house of Aaron say,
"His steadfast love endures forever."
⁴ Let those who fear the LORD say,
"His steadfast love endures forever."

⁵ Out of my distress I called on the LORD;
the LORD answered me and set me in a
broad place.

⁶ With the LORD on my side I do not fear.
What can mortals do to me?
⁷ The LORD is on my side to help me;
I shall look in triumph on those who
hate me.
⁸ It is better to take refuge in the LORD
than to put confidence in mortals.
⁹ It is better to take refuge in the LORD
than to put confidence in princes.

¹⁰ All nations surrounded me;
in the name of the LORD I cut them off!
¹¹ They surrounded me, surrounded me on
every side;
in the name of the LORD I cut them off!
¹² They surrounded me like bees;
they blazed[a] like a fire of thorns;
in the name of the LORD I cut them off!
¹³ I was pushed hard,[b] so that I was
falling,
but the LORD helped me.
¹⁴ The LORD is my strength and my might;
he has become my salvation.

¹⁵ There are glad songs of victory in the
tents of the righteous:
"The right hand of the LORD does
valiantly;
¹⁶ the right hand of the LORD is exalted;
the right hand of the LORD does
valiantly."
¹⁷ I shall not die, but I shall live,
and recount the deeds of the LORD.

---

a Gk: Heb *were extinguished*
b Gk Syr Jerome: Heb *You pushed me hard*

13: *Cup of salvation,* a drink offering poured out in thanksgiving (e.g., Ex 25.29; Lev 23.37). **14:** A person in a precarious situation could make a vow that would be fulfilled upon being saved. **15:** *Precious,* in the sense of "*too* precious" as in Ps 72.14, i.e., grievous in the LORD's sight. **17–18:** When in distress, the psalmist *vowed* to offer *a thanksgiving sacrifice.*

Ps 117: Invitation to the nations to worship. In the Bible's shortest chapter, this psalm is a hymn with an invitatory, which is repeated in the last verse, and the motive for praise is introduced by *for* (v. 2a). Oddly, the motive for the nations to give praise is the LORD's steadfast love and faithfulness toward Israel. Perhaps for the psalmist Israel showcases the LORD's generosity and exemplifies what the LORD intends for all peoples.

Ps 118: Giving thanks in a solemn procession. A thanksgiving, spoken in the first person, possibly by the king speaking for the people. The salvation is described twice, in vv. 5–9 as a transfer from a tight spot to a broad place, and in vv. 10–18 as rescue from hostile nations. As the procession enters the Temple precincts, the leader asks for admittance (v. 19) and an officiant states the qualifications necessary for entering (v. 20). In v. 21, the speaker, now within the Temple, gives fresh thanks, and in vv. 22–27, the congregation takes up the praise. The final verse repeats the beginning, forming an inclusio. **1–4:** *His steadfast love,* a covenant term (Heb "ḥesed"); the speaker gives thanks for the LORD's fidelity to past promises of protection. **5:** *Distress,* lit. "restricted

¹⁸ The LORD has punished me severely,
  but he did not give me over to death.

¹⁹ Open to me the gates of righteousness,
  that I may enter through them
  and give thanks to the LORD.

²⁰ This is the gate of the LORD;
  the righteous shall enter through it.

²¹ I thank you that you have answered me
  and have become my salvation.
²² The stone that the builders rejected
  has become the chief cornerstone.
²³ This is the LORD's doing;
  it is marvelous in our eyes.
²⁴ This is the day that the LORD has made;
  let us rejoice and be glad in it.^a
²⁵ Save us, we beseech you, O LORD!
  O LORD, we beseech you, give us
  success!

²⁶ Blessed is the one who comes in the
  name of the LORD.^b
  We bless you from the house of the
  LORD.
²⁷ The LORD is God,
  and he has given us light.

Bind the festal procession with branches,
  up to the horns of the altar.^c

²⁸ You are my God, and I will give thanks
  to you;
  you are my God, I will extol you.

²⁹ O give thanks to the LORD, for he is
  good,
  for his steadfast love endures forever.

Psalm 119

¹ Happy are those whose way is
  blameless,
  who walk in the law of the LORD.
² Happy are those who keep his decrees,
  who seek him with their whole heart,
³ who also do no wrong,
  but walk in his ways.
⁴ You have commanded your precepts
  to be kept diligently.
⁵ O that my ways may be steadfast
  in keeping your statutes!

^a Or *in him*
^b Or *Blessed in the name of the* LORD *is the one who comes*
^c Meaning of Heb uncertain

place." **12:** *Bees,* a metaphor for enemies as in Deut 1.44. **14:** Copied from Ex 15.2. **22:** *The stone,* the unsuitable stone becomes the very cornerstone toward which all the building blocks are oriented; such a transformation from low to high is a sign of divine intervention (v. 23). **27:** *Bind the festal procession with branches, up to the horns of the altar* was probably a ritual instruction that accidentally became part of the psalm. The horns were four projections at the corners of the altar.

Ps 119: The grandeur and the necessity of divine teaching. An individual petition that the LORD's teaching (Heb "torah," NRSV "law") guide one's every moment: in danger and discouragement, in joy and exultation. The psalm is an elaborate acrostic (see Ps 9–10n.): Each of the twenty-two stanzas begins with a successive letter of the Hebrew alphabet, and each stanza has eight verses and (usually) eight synonyms of "law," more accurately "authoritative teaching": "law," "word," "promise(s)," "ordinances," "statutes," "commandments," "decrees," and "precepts." Though for the most part synonymous in this psalm, each term may retain its own shade of meaning: illumination ("law," "word"), moral demand ("ordinances," "statutes," "commandments"), guidance ("decrees, precepts"), and promise ("promise"). Life is regarded as warfare with the evil principle; definitive victory lies only in the future. The major weapon in the battle is the divine word, for its observance trains the passions, gives strength in temptation, and elevates the mind to God. The psalm is constructed as a petition, as seen in its multiple imperatives, as in v. 149. Often petitions and references to "torah" (the two main themes), are combined in a single verse, as in v. 173. Yet, even after reading the entire psalm, it is uncertain exactly what "torah" means: if it refers to the law of Moses, it is odd that there is no mention of him or of Sinai.

This is the longest psalm in the Bible and is innovative in the manner that it refers to the Torah with words typically used of God, such as "love" (e.g., vv. 47,97), "truth" (v. 142), and "true" (v. 151). This reflects the growing importance of the Torah in the postexilic period, and anticipates the idea that the Torah is a type of stand-in for God, who is no longer regarded as imminent. **1:** *Law,* teaching that is authoritative because of divine origin. "Law" is a less satisfactory rendering. **135:** *Shine,* see Num 6.24–26.

⁶ Then I shall not be put to shame,
  having my eyes fixed on all your
    commandments.
⁷ I will praise you with an upright heart,
  when I learn your righteous ordinances.
⁸ I will observe your statutes;
  do not utterly forsake me.

⁹ How can young people keep their way
    pure?
  By guarding it according to your word.
¹⁰ With my whole heart I seek you;
  do not let me stray from your
    commandments.
¹¹ I treasure your word in my heart,
  so that I may not sin against you.
¹² Blessed are you, O LORD;
  teach me your statutes.
¹³ With my lips I declare
  all the ordinances of your mouth.
¹⁴ I delight in the way of your decrees
  as much as in all riches.
¹⁵ I will meditate on your precepts,
  and fix my eyes on your ways.
¹⁶ I will delight in your statutes;
  I will not forget your word.

¹⁷ Deal bountifully with your servant,
  so that I may live and observe your
    word.
¹⁸ Open my eyes, so that I may behold
  wondrous things out of your law.
¹⁹ I live as an alien in the land;
  do not hide your commandments from
    me.
²⁰ My soul is consumed with longing
  for your ordinances at all times.
²¹ You rebuke the insolent, accursed ones,
  who wander from your
    commandments;
²² take away from me their scorn and
    contempt,
  for I have kept your decrees.
²³ Even though princes sit plotting against
    me,
  your servant will meditate on your
    statutes.
²⁴ Your decrees are my delight,
  they are my counselors.

²⁵ My soul clings to the dust;
  revive me according to your word.

²⁶ When I told of my ways, you answered
    me;
  teach me your statutes.
²⁷ Make me understand the way of your
    precepts,
  and I will meditate on your wondrous
    works.
²⁸ My soul melts away for sorrow;
  strengthen me according to your word.
²⁹ Put false ways far from me;
  and graciously teach me your law.
³⁰ I have chosen the way of faithfulness;
  I set your ordinances before me.
³¹ I cling to your decrees, O LORD;
  let me not be put to shame.
³² I run the way of your commandments,
  for you enlarge my understanding.

³³ Teach me, O LORD, the way of your
    statutes,
  and I will observe it to the end.
³⁴ Give me understanding, that I may keep
    your law
  and observe it with my whole heart.
³⁵ Lead me in the path of your
    commandments,
  for I delight in it.
³⁶ Turn my heart to your decrees,
  and not to selfish gain.
³⁷ Turn my eyes from looking at vanities;
  give me life in your ways.
³⁸ Confirm to your servant your promise,
  which is for those who fear you.
³⁹ Turn away the disgrace that I dread,
  for your ordinances are good.
⁴⁰ See, I have longed for your precepts;
  in your righteousness give me life.

⁴¹ Let your steadfast love come to me,
    O LORD,
  your salvation according to your
    promise.
⁴² Then I shall have an answer for those
    who taunt me,
  for I trust in your word.
⁴³ Do not take the word of truth utterly out
    of my mouth,
  for my hope is in your ordinances.
⁴⁴ I will keep your law continually,
  forever and ever.
⁴⁵ I shall walk at liberty,
  for I have sought your precepts.

46 I will also speak of your decrees before
  kings,
  and shall not be put to shame;
47 I find my delight in your
  commandments,
  because I love them.
48 I revere your commandments, which I
  love,
  and I will meditate on your statutes.

49 Remember your word to your servant,
  in which you have made me hope.
50 This is my comfort in my distress,
  that your promise gives me life.
51 The arrogant utterly deride me,
  but I do not turn away from your law.
52 When I think of your ordinances from
  of old,
  I take comfort, O Lord.
53 Hot indignation seizes me because of
  the wicked,
  those who forsake your law.
54 Your statutes have been my songs
  wherever I make my home.
55 I remember your name in the night,
    O Lord,
  and keep your law.
56 This blessing has fallen to me,
  for I have kept your precepts.

57 The Lord is my portion;
  I promise to keep your words.
58 I implore your favor with all my heart;
  be gracious to me according to your
    promise.
59 When I think of your ways,
  I turn my feet to your decrees;
60 I hurry and do not delay
  to keep your commandments.
61 Though the cords of the wicked ensnare
  me,
  I do not forget your law.
62 At midnight I rise to praise you,
  because of your righteous ordinances.
63 I am a companion of all who fear you,
  of those who keep your precepts.
64 The earth, O Lord, is full of your
    steadfast love;
  teach me your statutes.

65 You have dealt well with your servant,
  O Lord, according to your word.

66 Teach me good judgment and
    knowledge,
  for I believe in your commandments.
67 Before I was humbled I went astray,
  but now I keep your word.
68 You are good and do good;
  teach me your statutes.
69 The arrogant smear me with lies,
  but with my whole heart I keep your
    precepts.
70 Their hearts are fat and gross,
  but I delight in your law.
71 It is good for me that I was humbled,
  so that I might learn your statutes.
72 The law of your mouth is better to me
  than thousands of gold and silver
    pieces.

73 Your hands have made and fashioned
    me;
  give me understanding that I may learn
    your commandments.
74 Those who fear you shall see me and
    rejoice,
  because I have hoped in your word.
75 I know, O Lord, that your judgments are
    right,
  and that in faithfulness you have
    humbled me.
76 Let your steadfast love become my
    comfort
  according to your promise to your
    servant.
77 Let your mercy come to me, that I may
    live;
  for your law is my delight.
78 Let the arrogant be put to shame,
  because they have subverted me with
    guile;
  as for me, I will meditate on your
    precepts.
79 Let those who fear you turn to me,
  so that they may know your decrees.
80 May my heart be blameless in your
    statutes,
  so that I may not be put to shame.

81 My soul languishes for your salvation;
  I hope in your word.
82 My eyes fail with watching for your
    promise;
  I ask, "When will you comfort me?"

83 For I have become like a wineskin in the
    smoke,
    yet I have not forgotten your statutes.
84 How long must your servant endure?
    When will you judge those who
    persecute me?
85 The arrogant have dug pitfalls for me;
    they flout your law.
86 All your commandments are enduring;
    I am persecuted without cause; help me!
87 They have almost made an end of me on
    earth;
    but I have not forsaken your precepts.
88 In your steadfast love spare my life,
    so that I may keep the decrees of your
    mouth.

89 The LORD exists forever;
    your word is firmly fixed in heaven.
90 Your faithfulness endures to all
    generations;
    you have established the earth, and it
    stands fast.
91 By your appointment they stand today,
    for all things are your servants.
92 If your law had not been my delight,
    I would have perished in my misery.
93 I will never forget your precepts,
    for by them you have given me life.
94 I am yours; save me,
    for I have sought your precepts.
95 The wicked lie in wait to destroy me,
    but I consider your decrees.
96 I have seen a limit to all perfection,
    but your commandment is exceedingly
    broad.

97 Oh, how I love your law!
    It is my meditation all day long.
98 Your commandment makes me wiser
    than my enemies,
    for it is always with me.
99 I have more understanding than all my
    teachers,
    for your decrees are my meditation.
100 I understand more than the aged,
    for I keep your precepts.
101 I hold back my feet from every evil way,
    in order to keep your word.
102 I do not turn away from your
    ordinances,
    for you have taught me.

103 How sweet are your words to my taste,
    sweeter than honey to my mouth!
104 Through your precepts I get
    understanding;
    therefore I hate every false way.

105 Your word is a lamp to my feet
    and a light to my path.
106 I have sworn an oath and confirmed it,
    to observe your righteous ordinances.
107 I am severely afflicted;
    give me life, O LORD, according to your
    word.
108 Accept my offerings of praise, O LORD,
    and teach me your ordinances.
109 I hold my life in my hand continually,
    but I do not forget your law.
110 The wicked have laid a snare for me,
    but I do not stray from your precepts.
111 Your decrees are my heritage forever;
    they are the joy of my heart.
112 I incline my heart to perform your
    statutes
    forever, to the end.

113 I hate the double-minded,
    but I love your law.
114 You are my hiding place and my shield;
    I hope in your word.
115 Go away from me, you evildoers,
    that I may keep the commandments of
    my God.
116 Uphold me according to your promise,
    that I may live,
    and let me not be put to shame in my
    hope.
117 Hold me up, that I may be safe
    and have regard for your statutes
    continually.
118 You spurn all who go astray from your
    statutes;
    for their cunning is in vain.
119 All the wicked of the earth you count as
    dross;
    therefore I love your decrees.
120 My flesh trembles for fear of you,
    and I am afraid of your judgments.

121 I have done what is just and right;
    do not leave me to my oppressors.
122 Guarantee your servant's well-being;
    do not let the godless oppress me.

123 My eyes fail from watching for your
     salvation,
  and for the fulfillment of your righteous
     promise.
124 Deal with your servant according to
     your steadfast love,
  and teach me your statutes.
125 I am your servant; give me
     understanding,
  so that I may know your decrees.
126 It is time for the LORD to act,
  for your law has been broken.
127 Truly I love your commandments
  more than gold, more than fine gold.
128 Truly I direct my steps by all your
     precepts;[a]
  I hate every false way.

129 Your decrees are wonderful;
  therefore my soul keeps them.
130 The unfolding of your words gives light;
  it imparts understanding to the simple.
131 With open mouth I pant,
  because I long for your commandments.
132 Turn to me and be gracious to me,
  as is your custom toward those who
     love your name.
133 Keep my steps steady according to your
     promise,
  and never let iniquity have dominion
     over me.
134 Redeem me from human oppression,
  that I may keep your precepts.
135 Make your face shine upon your servant,
  and teach me your statutes.
136 My eyes shed streams of tears
  because your law is not kept.

137 You are righteous, O LORD,
  and your judgments are right.
138 You have appointed your decrees in
     righteousness
  and in all faithfulness.
139 My zeal consumes me
  because my foes forget your words.
140 Your promise is well tried,
  and your servant loves it.
141 I am small and despised,
  yet I do not forget your precepts.
142 Your righteousness is an everlasting
     righteousness,
  and your law is the truth.

143 Trouble and anguish have come upon me,
  but your commandments are my
     delight.
144 Your decrees are righteous forever;
  give me understanding that I may live.

145 With my whole heart I cry; answer me,
     O LORD.
  I will keep your statutes.
146 I cry to you; save me,
  that I may observe your decrees.
147 I rise before dawn and cry for help;
  I put my hope in your words.
148 My eyes are awake before each watch of
     the night,
  that I may meditate on your promise.
149 In your steadfast love hear my voice;
  O LORD, in your justice preserve my life.
150 Those who persecute me with evil
     purpose draw near;
  they are far from your law.
151 Yet you are near, O LORD,
  and all your commandments are true.
152 Long ago I learned from your decrees
  that you have established them forever.

153 Look on my misery and rescue me,
  for I do not forget your law.
154 Plead my cause and redeem me;
  give me life according to your promise.
155 Salvation is far from the wicked,
  for they do not seek your statutes.
156 Great is your mercy, O LORD;
  give me life according to your justice.
157 Many are my persecutors and my
     adversaries,
  yet I do not swerve from your decrees.
158 I look at the faithless with disgust,
  because they do not keep your
     commands.
159 Consider how I love your precepts;
  preserve my life according to your
     steadfast love.
160 The sum of your word is truth;
  and every one of your righteous
     ordinances endures forever.

161 Princes persecute me without cause,
  but my heart stands in awe of your
     words.

a Gk Jerome: Meaning of Heb uncertain

¹⁶² I rejoice at your word
 like one who finds great spoil.
¹⁶³ I hate and abhor falsehood,
 but I love your law.
¹⁶⁴ Seven times a day I praise you
 for your righteous ordinances.
¹⁶⁵ Great peace have those who love your
  law;
 nothing can make them stumble.
¹⁶⁶ I hope for your salvation, O Lord,
 and I fulfill your commandments.
¹⁶⁷ My soul keeps your decrees;
 I love them exceedingly.
¹⁶⁸ I keep your precepts and decrees,
 for all my ways are before you.

¹⁶⁹ Let my cry come before you, O Lord;
 give me understanding according to
  your word.
¹⁷⁰ Let my supplication come before you;
 deliver me according to your
  promise.
¹⁷¹ My lips will pour forth praise,
 because you teach me your statutes.
¹⁷² My tongue will sing of your promise,
 for all your commandments are right.
¹⁷³ Let your hand be ready to help me,
 for I have chosen your precepts.
¹⁷⁴ I long for your salvation, O Lord,
 and your law is my delight.
¹⁷⁵ Let me live that I may praise you,
 and let your ordinances help me.
¹⁷⁶ I have gone astray like a lost sheep; seek
 out your servant,

for I do not forget your
 commandments.

Psalm 120

A Song of Ascents.

¹ In my distress I cry to the Lord,
 that he may answer me:
² "Deliver me, O Lord,
 from lying lips,
 from a deceitful tongue."

³ What shall be given to you?
 And what more shall be done to you,
 you deceitful tongue?
⁴ A warrior's sharp arrows,
 with glowing coals of the broom tree!

⁵ Woe is me, that I am an alien in
  Meshech,
 that I must live among the tents of
  Kedar.
⁶ Too long have I had my dwelling
 among those who hate peace.
⁷ I am for peace;
 but when I speak,
 they are for war.

Psalm 121

A Song of Ascents.

¹ I lift up my eyes to the hills—
 from where will my help come?
² My help comes from the Lord,
 who made heaven and earth.

Ps 120: Prayer for rescue from slanderers. This is the first of the collection of Songs of Ascents, Pss 120–134. The meaning of this superscription is debated; it may refer to the steplike parallelism in many of the poems (e.g., Ps 127.1: "unless the Lord builds the house . . . unless the Lord guards the city"), or to songs sung while going up to Jerusalem for pilgrimage. This psalm is an individual petition with the expected petitions for the punishment of enemies (vv. 3–4) and complaints (vv. 2–3,5–7), though without a statement of hope. The two complaints—slanderous attacks (vv. 2–4) and unwilling exile in a hostile country far from Jerusalem (vv. 5–7)—tell the same story with two metaphor systems (tongues as weapons, being in a distant, hostile land). Reputation, a community, and a home—all these have been taken from the psalmist. Others' words have become weapons (vv. 2–3,7) and the only rescue the psalmist can imagine is retaliation in military terms (vv. 3–4). **4:** *Broom,* a desert shrub. **5:** *Meshech . . . Kedar,* places far from Jerusalem in the remote north (southern Asia Minor [see Ezek 38.2]), and remote south (northern Arabia [Isa 21.13–17]), symbolizing distance. **7:** *Peace* (Heb "shalom"), perhaps a play on the name of Jerusalem.

 Ps 121: Confidence in God's care. A declaration of trust shaped by tight, steplike parallelism: "not slumber" links vv. 3–4; "keep" links vv. 3–5 and 7–8. "Coming" in v. 8 echoes "come" in v. 1, concluding the poem. Perhaps this was recited by a traveler, even a pilgrim to Zion who asks the question, which he first answers (v. 2); the answer is then expanded upon by a priest conscious that the Lord dwells in Zion (vv. 3–8). God's careful protection is the dominant image; the Lord guides one's steps and does not slumber even when people sleep.

³ He will not let your foot be moved;
    he who keeps you will not slumber.
⁴ He who keeps Israel
    will neither slumber nor sleep.

⁵ The LORD is your keeper;
    the LORD is your shade at your right
      hand.
⁶ The sun shall not strike you by day,
    nor the moon by night.

⁷ The LORD will keep you from all evil;
    he will keep your life.
⁸ The LORD will keep
    your going out and your coming in
    from this time on and forevermore.

Psalm 122

A Song of Ascents. Of David.

¹ I was glad when they said to me,
    "Let us go to the house of the LORD!"
² Our feet are standing
    within your gates, O Jerusalem.

³ Jerusalem—built as a city
    that is bound firmly together.
⁴ To it the tribes go up,
    the tribes of the LORD,
as was decreed for Israel,
    to give thanks to the name of the LORD.

⁵ For there the thrones for judgment were
    set up,
    the thrones of the house of David.

⁶ Pray for the peace of Jerusalem:
    "May they prosper who love you.
⁷ Peace be within your walls,
    and security within your towers."
⁸ For the sake of my relatives and friends
    I will say, "Peace be within you."
⁹ For the sake of the house of the LORD our
    God,
    I will seek your good.

Psalm 123

A Song of Ascents.

¹ To you I lift up my eyes,
    O you who are enthroned in the
      heavens!
² As the eyes of servants
    look to the hand of their master,
as the eyes of a maid
    to the hand of her mistress,
so our eyes look to the LORD our God,
    until he has mercy upon us.

³ Have mercy upon us, O LORD, have mercy
    upon us,
    for we have had more than enough of
      contempt.

Superscription: *Song of Ascents,* see Ps 120n. **1:** *Hills,* probably those around Jerusalem. **2:** *Who made heaven and earth,* see Ps 124.8n. **5:** *The LORD is your keeper,* the exact center of the poem.

   Ps 122: Longing to go to Zion and a prayer for its peace. A song of Zion celebrating the sacred city for its beautiful buildings (v. 3), worship in common (v. 4), and just legal decisions (v. 5). One can imagine a pilgrim, awed by the holiness of the place, uttering the prayer for the welfare of the city (vv. 6–9). **Superscription:** *Song of Ascents,* see Ps 120n. **1:** *Let us go,* Passover, Weeks (Pentecost), and Tabernacles were pilgrimage festivals, requiring heads of households to travel to Jerusalem and ascend its hills (Ex 23.17; 34.23; Deut 16.16). *The house of the LORD,* the Temple (also v. 9). **5:** *Thrones for judgment,* Jerusalem was the city of the Davidic king; *judgment* can refer to legal decisions as well as to ordinary governance. **6–7:** The other pilgrims are probably being addressed here. **6:** *Pray for the peace of Jerusalem,* alliterative in Hebrew ("sha'alu shalom yerushalaim") **9:** The concluding reference to the Temple forms an inclusio with v. 1, emphasizing that it is the presence of God in the Temple that makes Jerusalem such a significant and holy city.

   Ps 123: A plea for divine mercy. A community petition, perhaps composed in the Second Temple period when the nation felt the indignity (v. 3) of being a small state in the vast Persian empire. Feeling like a power-less slave (NRSV "servant," v. 2), the community speaker ("I" in v. 1) feels constricted, repeating a plea for divine mercy three times. The psalmist's hope is not constricted, however, for the prayer is directed to the divine king "enthroned in the heavens" (v. 1). **Superscription:** *Song of Ascents,* see Ps 120n. **2:** *The eyes of servants,* the metaphor of looking expectantly to the LORD is developed through servants looking at their masters; contrasts are maximized—male and female, plural and singular—to express completeness: all look to you. Female images of God are very rare in the Bible (e.g., Isa 49.14–16), especially in Psalms, making the comparison of God to *mistress* noteworthy.

⁴Our soul has had more than its fill
of the scorn of those who are at ease,
of the contempt of the proud.

Psalm 124
A Song of Ascents. Of David.

¹If it had not been the LORD who was on
our side
—let Israel now say—
²if it had not been the LORD who was on
our side,
when our enemies attacked us,
³then they would have swallowed us up
alive,
when their anger was kindled against
us;
⁴then the flood would have swept us
away,
the torrent would have gone over us;
⁵then over us would have gone
the raging waters.

⁶Blessed be the LORD,
who has not given us
as prey to their teeth.
⁷We have escaped like a bird
from the snare of the fowlers;
the snare is broken,
and we have escaped.

⁸Our help is in the name of the LORD,
who made heaven and earth.

Psalm 125
A Song of Ascents.

¹Those who trust in the LORD are like
Mount Zion,
which cannot be moved, but abides
forever.
²As the mountains surround Jerusalem,
so the LORD surrounds his people,
from this time on and forevermore.
³For the scepter of wickedness shall not rest
on the land allotted to the righteous,
so that the righteous might not stretch out
their hands to do wrong.
⁴Do good, O LORD, to those who are good,
and to those who are upright in their
hearts.
⁵But those who turn aside to their own
crooked ways
the LORD will lead away with evildoers.
Peace be upon Israel!

Psalm 126
A Song of Ascents.

¹When the LORD restored the fortunes of
Zion,[a]

ᵃ Or *brought back those who returned to Zion*

Ps 124: **Giving thanks after a narrow escape.** A community thanksgiving notable for its simple theme: give thanks for we would have died if the LORD had not rescued us. The simple theme is mirrored by a simple structure: the first two verses begin "If it had not been the LORD who was on our side" and the next three begin with "then" followed by a complex step-parallelism. Such step-parallelism, common in the Songs of Ascents (see Ps 120n.), adds drama and movement. **1:** *Let Israel now say,* the singer provides the community with the proper words to express their intense relief and gratitude. **3–5:** The metaphors of devouring beasts and waters flooding the earth are used for the enemies. **7:** *Like a bird,* a totally different metaphor for the rescued nation: a little bird flying upward to freedom from a broken trap, a perfect symbol of miraculous deliverance. **8:** *Who made heaven and earth,* a frequent postexilic epithet for God (see also Pss 115.15; 121.2; 146.6); here it emphasizes that God the powerful creator can still help Israel.

Ps 125: **Prayer for Zion's purification from evildoers.** A Zion song that, unlike most other such songs, prays that sinners be removed from its midst so it might truly be worthy of the LORD (vv. 4–5). Examples of such purifying judgments are Isa 1.21–28; 65; Zeph 3.11–13. Like other Songs of Ascents (Pss 122; 123; 124; 126; see Ps 120n.), Ps 125 has an opening statement (vv. 1–3) followed by a prayer (vv. 4–5). **2:** *The mountains,* majestic pillars of the universe, the hills surrounding Jerusalem are an apt symbol of the powerful and ever-present LORD present in Zion. **3:** *Scepter of wickedness:* A scepter wielded by an unjust ruler cannot rest (figuratively) on the land given to the righteous lest they be led to do wrong. **4:** *Do good . . . to those who are upright,* justice means upholding the righteous as well as punishing the wicked. **5:** *Peace be upon Israel!* is repeated later in this collection, in 128.6.

Ps 126: **A prayer for the return of all the exiles.** A community prayer for the return of all exiles and the restoration of Israel. Like other Songs of Ascents (Pss 122–125; see 120n.), it has an opening statement (vv. 1–3) developed into a prayer (vv. 4–5). It also is characterized by step-parallelism: "restore the fortunes," "then,"

we were like those who dream.
² Then our mouth was filled with
laughter,
and our tongue with shouts of joy;
then it was said among the nations,
"The LORD has done great things for
them."
³ The LORD has done great things for us,
and we rejoiced.

⁴ Restore our fortunes, O LORD,
like the watercourses in the Negeb.
⁵ May those who sow in tears
reap with shouts of joy.
⁶ Those who go out weeping,
bearing the seed for sowing,
shall come home with shouts of joy,
carrying their sheaves.

Psalm 127
A Song of Ascents. Of Solomon.

¹ Unless the LORD builds the house,
those who build it labor in vain.
Unless the LORD guards the city,

the guard keeps watch in vain.
² It is in vain that you rise up early
and go late to rest,
eating the bread of anxious toil;
for he gives sleep to his beloved.ᵃ

³ Sons are indeed a heritage from the LORD,
the fruit of the womb a reward.
⁴ Like arrows in the hand of a warrior
are the sons of one's youth.
⁵ Happy is the man who has
his quiver full of them.
He shall not be put to shame
when he speaks with his enemies in the
gate.

Psalm 128
A Song of Ascents.

¹ Happy is everyone who fears the LORD,
who walks in his ways.
² You shall eat the fruit of the labor of your
hands;

ᵃ   Or *for he provides for his beloved during sleep*

"the LORD has done great things," "shouts of joy," and the verb "bearing/carrying." The psalmist regards the return of the exiles from Babylon, where they had been deported in the early sixth century BCE, as a past event, yet prays for the return of all in the spirit of grand promises such as Isa 60.10. The book of Ezra suggests that in fact few returned from Babylon, the return was a disappointment, and the hyperbolic prophecies of Isa 40–55 were not fulfilled. **4**: *Restore our fortunes*, picks up "restored the fortunes" (v. 1) and prays for its completion. *The watercourses in the Negeb*, riverbeds in the arid south, dry except when a rare rainstorm in an instant creates torrents sweeping away all in their path, a bold metaphor for sudden transformation of infertile land. The metaphor is ironic, since such watercourses are destructive, yet it sets the stage for the positive water and agricultural imagery in the following verses.

Ps 127: An instruction and prayer for the house. This psalm does not fit the usual categories. It is a declaration that one of God's greatest blessings is children (in that culture, sons), and is a companion piece to Ps 128. Step-parallelism highlights the words *unless, in vain*, and *sons*. Hebrew wordplay unites vv. 1–2 and 3–5: *builds* ("yibneh") and *those who build* ("bonayo") in v. 1, and *sons* ("banim") in vv. 3–4. Those same *sons* will protect the family head when he confronts enemies in the city gate, thereby linking v. 4 and v. 1cd (*guards the city*). **Superscription:** *Song of Ascents*, see Ps 120n. Since it deals with building, the psalm is ascribed to King Solomon (see Ps 72n.), who built the First Temple (see also v. 2n.). **1:** *House*, can refer both to the Temple and to the dynasty, as well as to a household. **2:** *Beloved* (Heb "yedid") recalls Solomon's birth name Jedidiah ("yedidyah," 2 Sam 12.25). **3–5:** Asserting the uselessness of human effort alone to build a house and protect the city (vv. 1–2), vv. 3–5 declare that it is through sons that the LORD builds a house(hold) and protects the community. *The gate* was the setting for legal and commercial transactions; see, e.g., Ruth 4.1–12; Prov 30.23,31.

Ps 128: The blessings of the man who fears God. A companion piece to Ps 127, declaring that he "who fears the LORD" (v. 1) will flourish in his family (v. 3), national, and religious life (vv. 5–6). The three spheres were closely related, for the father was paterfamilias of the house, the king was paterfamilias of the house of Israel, and the LORD functioned as the patrimonial lord to whom Israel was bound through covenant. Correspondingly, the blessings include family (fruitful wife, many children), nation (prosperity of Jerusalem, seat of the dynasty), and God (font of blessings). Like several Songs of Ascents (see Ps 120n.), the poem has two parts: a statement of trust (vv. 1–4) and a prayer that builds on the statement (vv. 5–6). **1:** *Happy*, fortunate because of a quality

you shall be happy, and it shall go well
   with you.

³ Your wife will be like a fruitful vine
   within your house;
your children will be like olive shoots
   around your table.
⁴ Thus shall the man be blessed
   who fears the LORD.

⁵ The LORD bless you from Zion.
   May you see the prosperity of Jerusalem
   all the days of your life.
⁶ May you see your children's children.
   Peace be upon Israel!

Psalm 129

A Song of Ascents.

¹ "Often have they attacked me from my
      youth"
   —let Israel now say—
² "often have they attacked me from my
      youth,
   yet they have not prevailed against me.
³ The plowers plowed on my back;
   they made their furrows long."
⁴ The LORD is righteous;
   he has cut the cords of the wicked.
⁵ May all who hate Zion
   be put to shame and turned backward.

⁶ Let them be like the grass on the
      housetops
   that withers before it grows up,
⁷ with which reapers do not fill their
      hands
   or binders of sheaves their arms,
⁸ while those who pass by do not say,
   "The blessing of the LORD be upon you!
   We bless you in the name of the LORD!"

Psalm 130

A Song of Ascents.

¹ Out of the depths I cry to you, O LORD.
   ² Lord, hear my voice!
Let your ears be attentive
   to the voice of my supplications!

³ If you, O LORD, should mark iniquities,
   Lord, who could stand?
⁴ But there is forgiveness with you,
   so that you may be revered.

⁵ I wait for the LORD, my soul waits,
   and in his word I hope;
⁶ my soul waits for the Lord
   more than those who watch for the
      morning,
   more than those who watch for the
      morning.

possessed or a choice made. **3:** The verse both expresses and reinforces the status of the father as head of the household. **6:** *Peace be upon Israel!* see Ps 125.5n.

Ps 129: Prayer against Zion's enemies. A community petition that the LORD punish those who have persecuted Israel. As often in Songs of Ascents (see Ps 120n.), step-parallelism highlights key phrases, "often have they attacked me from my youth" and "blessing/bless." The complaint is not so much of present suffering but of relentless, unending sufferings "from my youth" (vv. 1,2), perhaps referring to Egyptian bondage (cf. Hos 2.15; Jer 2.2; Ezek 23.3). **3:** *Plowed on my back,* perhaps echoing Isa 51.23, which quotes Israel's tormentors in the exile. Thus the psalmist complains about the sufferings of being the LORD's people in the world, selecting two typical instances of suffering, one from the Exodus (vv. 1,2) and the other from the sixth-century BCE exile (v. 3). **6:** *Grass on the housetops,* weeds growing on mud-plastered roofs; cf. 2 Kings 19.26; Isa 37.27. **9:** Likely a standard blessing formula used in the postexilic period.

Ps 130: Waiting for the LORD's redemption. One of the seven penitential psalms in Christian tradition (Pss 6; 32; 38; 51; 102; 130; 143), this individual petition seeks rescue "out of the depths" (v. 1), but seems even more intent on simply being heard by God. The usual statement of trust takes the form of resolutions to wait for the LORD (vv. 5–6) and the other common feature of petitions, teaching others to revere the LORD, appears in vv. 7–8. Verses 1–6 detail the psalmist's desire to be heard, and vv. 7–8 detail the psalmist's and Israel's waiting for the redeeming LORD (vv. 5–8). Its central theme is that humans are inherently sinful, and thus God must be inherently forgiving. **Superscription:** *Song of Ascents,* see Ps 120n. **1:** *Out of the depths,* Latin Vulgate, "de profundis"; God seems too distant to hear the psalmist's voice. **4:** At the middle of the psalm, the psalmist reminds God of his forgiving nature. **5–6:** *Wait,* repeated three times in step-parallelism; waiting expectantly is a form of prayer.

⁷O Israel, hope in the LORD!
  For with the LORD there is steadfast love,
    and with him is great power to redeem.
⁸It is he who will redeem Israel
    from all its iniquities.

Psalm 131

A Song of Ascents. Of David.

¹O LORD, my heart is not lifted up,
    my eyes are not raised too high;
I do not occupy myself with things
    too great and too marvelous for me.
²But I have calmed and quieted my soul,
    like a weaned child with its mother;
    my soul is like the weaned child that is
      with me.ᵃ

³O Israel, hope in the LORD
    from this time on and forevermore.

Psalm 132

A Song of Ascents.

¹O LORD, remember in David's favor
    all the hardships he endured;
²how he swore to the LORD
    and vowed to the Mighty One of Jacob,
³"I will not enter my house
    or get into my bed;

⁴I will not give sleep to my eyes
    or slumber to my eyelids,
⁵until I find a place for the LORD,
    a dwelling place for the Mighty One of
      Jacob."

⁶We heard of it in Ephrathah;
    we found it in the fields of Jaar.
⁷"Let us go to his dwelling place;
    let us worship at his footstool."

⁸Rise up, O LORD, and go to your resting
      place,
    you and the ark of your might.
⁹Let your priests be clothed with
      righteousness,
    and let your faithful shout for joy.
¹⁰For your servant David's sake
    do not turn away the face of your
      anointed one.

¹¹The LORD swore to David a sure
      oath
    from which he will not turn back:
"One of the sons of your body
    I will set on your throne.

ᵃ   Or *my soul within me is like a weaned child*

Ps 131: Waiting for the LORD like a child. A declaration of trust with an extraordinary central metaphor: a weaned child, in that culture a three- to five-year-old. The poem is framed by its opening and closing occurrences of "the LORD" and its opening and closing statements, the first put negatively ("my heart is not lifted up") and the second put positively ("I have calmed and quieted my soul"). The three-fold denial in v. 1 and the doubled affirmation in v. 2 show deep feeling. V. 3, as in many other psalms, moves from the individual to the community, here inviting all Israel to imitate the singer's calm and trust. **Superscription:** *Song of Ascents,* see Ps 120n. **2:** *Like a weaned child with its mother,* the singer, like the child, has been nurtured daily and would not doubt the mother's further care. The image of God as female is the second in the Songs of Ascents; cf. Ps 125.2.

Ps 132: Bringing the LORD to reign in Zion. A royal psalm narrating in four stanzas David's desire to be affirmed as king and to transfer the ark-throne of the LORD to Zion. In vv. 1–5, David swears to provide a dwelling place for the LORD; in vv. 6–10, the ark is found and taken solemnly to Jerusalem; in vv. 11–13, the LORD swears to give David an eternal dynasty and ratifies the choice of Zion; vv. 14–18 affirm and expand these choices. Each of the four stanzas has five couplets and each contains the name "David"; the last line of each stanza is linked to the first line of the following stanza by word repetition ("find/found" in vv. 5 and 6; "David" in vv. 10 and 11; "desired" in vv. 13 and 14). In both structure and content, it is quite atypical of the Songs of Ascents (see Ps 120n.). **2–5:** An extensive elaboration of 2 Sam 7.2. **2:** *The Mighty One of Jacob* (also v. 5), see Gen 49.24; Isa 1.24; 49.26. **6–10:** The singer asks that the LORD allow the ark to be transferred to Zion (vv. 6–9) and that he support David (v. 10; cf. v. 1). **6–7:** A poetic version of the discovery of the ark of the covenant, the visible symbol of God's presence, and its transfer to Jerusalem; cf. 2 Sam 6. **6:** *Ephrathah,* near Bethlehem, in Judah. *Jaar,* a variant of Kiriath-jearim (1 Sam 7.1–2). **7:** The ark was the *footstool* component of the divine cherubim throne; cf. Ps 99.5. **8:** Cf. Num 10.35–36. **11–14:** The first request is answered in vv. 11–12 and the second in vv. 13–14. This is a paraphrase of 1 Sam 7.5–17, though that passage (like Ps 89.28–37) makes an unconditional promise of dynasty to David, while in this psalm (v. 12: *If your sons*) it is conditional. The choice of Zion, however, is presented as uncondi-

¹² If your sons keep my covenant
    and my decrees that I shall teach them,
their sons also, forevermore,
    shall sit on your throne."

¹³ For the LORD has chosen Zion;
    he has desired it for his habitation:
¹⁴ "This is my resting place forever;
    here I will reside, for I have desired it.
¹⁵ I will abundantly bless its provisions;
    I will satisfy its poor with bread.
¹⁶ Its priests I will clothe with salvation,
    and its faithful will shout for joy.
¹⁷ There I will cause a horn to sprout up for
        David;
    I have prepared a lamp for my anointed
        one.
¹⁸ His enemies I will clothe with disgrace,
    but on him, his crown will gleam."

Psalm 133

A Song of Ascents.

¹ How very good and pleasant it is
    when kindred live together in unity!
² It is like the precious oil on the head,
    running down upon the beard,
on the beard of Aaron,
    running down over the collar of his
        robes.

³ It is like the dew of Hermon,
    which falls on the mountains of Zion.
For there the LORD ordained his blessing,
    life forevermore.

Psalm 134

A Song of Ascents.

¹ Come, bless the LORD, all you servants of
        the LORD,
    who stand by night in the house of the
        LORD!
² Lift up your hands to the holy place,
    and bless the LORD.

³ May the LORD, maker of heaven and
        earth,
    bless you from Zion.

Psalm 135

¹ Praise the LORD!
    Praise the name of the LORD;
    give praise, O servants of the LORD,
² you that stand in the house of the LORD,
    in the courts of the house of our God.
³ Praise the LORD, for the LORD is good;
    sing to his name, for he is gracious.
⁴ For the LORD has chosen Jacob for himself,
    Israel as his own possession.

tional and eternal (v. 14: *This is my resting place forever*). **17**: *Horn*, a symbol of strength. *Lamp*, cf. 2 Sam 21.17.

Ps 133: The divine gift of unity. A song of Zion like several Songs of Ascents (Pss 122; 125; 128; 129; 132; see Ps 120n.). Like them, it has step-parallelism: "running down" three times in vv. 2–3 (NRSV "falls down" in v. 3). Like Ps 122, it celebrates Jerusalem as the place where the tribes of Israel happily gather on holy days. The famous first line of Ps 133 recalls Ps 122.4. The references to Aaron and Zion, although somewhat obscure, connect it to the previous psalm. **2**: *Oil* was used for washing in antiquity, and in the ordination rite of priests (Lev 8.12) and thus stirs thoughts of joyous Temple celebrations that bring the community together. The abundance of oil in the ceremonies evokes the plentiful dew of Mount Herman in the north that was so important in the agricultural life of Israel, especially in the dry summer months.

Ps 134: Come, bless the LORD. The final Song of Ascents (see Ps 120n.) is a blessing, similar to the blessings concluding each of the five books of the Psalms. It mentions themes prominent in the collection such as the Temple in Zion and its ceremonies. It is also similar to the opening and closing of the following psalm. The repeated invitation "Bless the LORD" and the response to it in v. 3 provides structure. **1**: It is uncertain exactly which group is meant by *all you servants of the LORD, who stand by night in the house of the LORD!* **2**: *Lifting up . . . hands* was the position of prayer in antiquity.

Ps 135: Praise of the LORD who brought Israel to its land. A hymn praising the LORD the creator for defeating Pharaoh and the nations who held the land intended for Israel. It forms a pair with Ps 136. The psalm has drawn heavily on earlier tradition (e.g., v. 4 from Deut 7.6; v. 7 from Jer 10.13). These borrowings, late linguistic features, and the attack on images (vv. 15–18) were characteristic of postexilic times when the concept of authoritative scripture was developing. Ps 135 has a concentric or sandwich structure: "Praise the LORD / Blessed is the LORD" is the frame (vv. 1a, 21b), within which vv. 1b–4 match 19–20, and vv. 5–7 match 15–18; the center is vv. 8–14, which describe the LORD's great acts on behalf of Israel. **4**: *Possession*, Heb "segullah," something treasured and

5 For I know that the LORD is great;
  our Lord is above all gods.
6 Whatever the LORD pleases he does,
  in heaven and on earth,
  in the seas and all deeps.
7 He it is who makes the clouds rise at the
    end of the earth;
  he makes lightnings for the rain
  and brings out the wind from his
    storehouses.

8 He it was who struck down the firstborn
    of Egypt,
  both human beings and animals;
9 he sent signs and wonders
  into your midst, O Egypt,
  against Pharaoh and all his servants.
10 He struck down many nations
  and killed mighty kings—
11 Sihon, king of the Amorites,
  and Og, king of Bashan,
  and all the kingdoms of Canaan—
12 and gave their land as a heritage,
  a heritage to his people Israel.

13 Your name, O LORD, endures forever,
  your renown, O LORD, throughout all
    ages.
14 For the LORD will vindicate his people,
  and have compassion on his servants.

15 The idols of the nations are silver and gold,
  the work of human hands.

16 They have mouths, but they do not
    speak;
  they have eyes, but they do not see;
17 they have ears, but they do not hear,
  and there is no breath in their mouths.
18 Those who make them
  and all who trust them
  shall become like them.

19 O house of Israel, bless the LORD!
  O house of Aaron, bless the LORD!
20 O house of Levi, bless the LORD!
  You that fear the LORD, bless the LORD!
21 Blessed be the LORD from Zion,
  he who resides in Jerusalem.
Praise the LORD!

Psalm 136

1 O give thanks to the LORD, for he is good,
  for his steadfast love endures forever.
2 O give thanks to the God of gods,
  for his steadfast love endures forever.
3 O give thanks to the Lord of lords,
  for his steadfast love endures forever;

4 who alone does great wonders,
  for his steadfast love endures forever;
5 who by understanding made the heavens,
  for his steadfast love endures forever;
6 who spread out the earth on the waters,
  for his steadfast love endures forever;
7 who made the great lights,
  for his steadfast love endures forever;

set apart ("stashed") by a god or a king. 5: *I know,* a confession of faith like that in Ex 18.10–11. *Above all gods,* see Pss 29.1; 89.6–8. 6–7: God's actions in nature are a preface to his actions in history; both illustrate God's immense power. *Storehouses,* cf. Ps 33.11; Job 38.22. 8–14: The great founding act of Israel was the Exodus, here presented in two panels, as in Ps 114 linking Exodus and Conquest. The first concerns Egypt (i.e., the Exodus proper), and the second concerns the Transjordanian kings Sihon and Og, and the kingdoms of Canaan (i.e., the Conquest). 8: See Ex 12.29. 9: A reference to the plagues; see Ex 7.3; Deut 6.22. 11: *Sihon* (king of the Amorites, in central Transjordan) and *Og* (king of Bashan, in northern Transjordan), see Num 21.21–35; Deut 2.24–3.7. 12: *Heritage,* Canaan as a land that is to be inherited by successive generations of Israelites. 13: A restatement of Ex 3.15. 15–18: Cf. Ps 115.4–11. 19–20: Similar to and likely based on Ps 118.3–4.

Ps 136: Praise of the LORD who created the world and Israel. A hymn telling of the creation of the world and of the Exodus and Conquest, the holy people designed to motivate Israel to give praise, and perhaps for God to remember Israel in its "low estate" (v. 23), when it is persecuted and suffers from famine (vv. 24–25). Pss 135 and 136 share vocabulary and a similar view of sacred history, though Ps 136 uniquely preserves the antiphonal reply "for his steadfast love endures forever" (26 times), which was frequently used in ritual in the postexilic period (see Ezra 3.11; 1 Chr 16.34; Ps 118.1–4). 1–3: *Give thanks to the LORD/God* (vv. 1–3,26) opens and closes Ps 136 and also Ps 118 (vv. 1,29), suggesting that Pss 113–118 and 135–136 were meant to frame the Songs of Ascents (Pss 120–134). As the psalm progresses, each new stage of divine activity is introduced by the participle form of the verb (vv. 4a, 5a, 6a, 7a, 10a, 13a, 16a, and 17a). The psalm narrates a single series of divine actions, beginning

⁸ the sun to rule over the day,
  for his steadfast love endures forever;
⁹ the moon and stars to rule over the night,
  for his steadfast love endures forever;

¹⁰ who struck Egypt through their
    firstborn,
  for his steadfast love endures forever;
¹¹ and brought Israel out from among them,
  for his steadfast love endures forever;
¹² with a strong hand and an outstretched
    arm,
  for his steadfast love endures forever;
¹³ who divided the Red Sea^a in two,
  for his steadfast love endures forever;
¹⁴ and made Israel pass through the midst
    of it,
  for his steadfast love endures forever;
¹⁵ but overthrew Pharaoh and his army in
    the Red Sea,^a
  for his steadfast love endures forever;
¹⁶ who led his people through the wilderness,
  for his steadfast love endures forever;
¹⁷ who struck down great kings,
  for his steadfast love endures forever;
¹⁸ and killed famous kings,
  for his steadfast love endures forever;
¹⁹ Sihon, king of the Amorites,
  for his steadfast love endures forever;
²⁰ and Og, king of Bashan,
  for his steadfast love endures forever;
²¹ and gave their land as a heritage,
  for his steadfast love endures forever;
²² a heritage to his servant Israel,
  for his steadfast love endures forever.

²³ It is he who remembered us in our low
    estate,
  for his steadfast love endures forever;
²⁴ and rescued us from our foes,
  for his steadfast love endures forever;
²⁵ who gives food to all flesh,
  for his steadfast love endures forever.

²⁶ O give thanks to the God of heaven,
  for his steadfast love endures forever.

Psalm 137

¹ By the rivers of Babylon—
  there we sat down and there we wept
  when we remembered Zion.
² On the willows^b there
  we hung up our harps.
³ For there our captors
  asked us for songs,
and our tormentors asked for mirth, saying,
  "Sing us one of the songs of Zion!"

⁴ How could we sing the LORD's song
  in a foreign land?
⁵ If I forget you, O Jerusalem,
  let my right hand wither!
⁶ Let my tongue cling to the roof of my
    mouth,
  if I do not remember you,
if I do not set Jerusalem
  above my highest joy.

---

^a Or *Sea of Reeds*
^b Or *poplars*

with creation and ending with deliverance and guidance into the land. **7–9:** Cf. Gen 1.16. **10–14:** Like Ps 135, Ps 136 sees the Exodus primarily as two events: liberation through defeating Pharaoh in Egypt (vv. 10–14) and the giving of land through overcoming kings in Transjordan and Canaan (vv. 17–22). **19–20:** *Sihon . . . and Og,* see Ps 135.11n. **23–25:** Changes in syntax and grammatical person (from third to second person) indicate the shift from recital of the past to speaking of Israel dwelling in the land of Canaan. In Canaan, God still wondrously protects and feeds the people.

Ps 137: A lament over destroyed Jerusalem. A community petition that complains vigorously of the destruction of Jerusalem by the Babylonians in 586 BCE. The first stanza (vv. 1–3) is framed by "Zion," the second (vv. 4–6) by "Jerusalem," and the third, a cry for justice against Edom and Babylon, the enemies responsible for the destruction. Although the last stanza is repugnant to modern readers and is often omitted in modern uses of the psalm, one must understand it as the cry of one singer who feels acutely the dishonor inflicted by an arrogant empire and its helpers. **1:** *Rivers,* irrigation canals. **3:** *Mirth,* to be understood as "songs of joy," abstract for concrete. Such songs (e.g., Pss 46; 48; 76; 84; 122) told of the grandeur of Zion where the LORD defeated enemy kings and dwelled in the midst of Israel. It is humiliating to sing them now, especially to people who laugh at them. **5:** Wordplay: the Heb word "shakaḥ" is a homonym for two different verbs, "to forget" and "to wither."

⁷Remember, O Lᴏʀᴅ, against the Edomites
the day of Jerusalem's fall,
how they said, "Tear it down! Tear it down!
Down to its foundations!"
⁸O daughter Babylon, you devastator!ᵃ
Happy shall they be who pay you back
what you have done to us!
⁹Happy shall they be who take your little
ones
and dash them against the rock!

Psalm 138
Of David.

¹I give you thanks, O Lᴏʀᴅ, with my whole
heart;
before the gods I sing your praise;
²I bow down toward your holy temple
and give thanks to your name for your
steadfast love and your faithfulness;
for you have exalted your name and
your word
above everything.ᵇ
³On the day I called, you answered me,
you increased my strength of soul.ᶜ

⁴All the kings of the earth shall praise you,
O Lᴏʀᴅ,
for they have heard the words of your
mouth.
⁵They shall sing of the ways of the Lᴏʀᴅ,
for great is the glory of the Lᴏʀᴅ.
⁶For though the Lᴏʀᴅ is high, he regards
the lowly;
but the haughty he perceives from far
away.

⁷Though I walk in the midst of trouble,
you preserve me against the wrath of
my enemies;
you stretch out your hand,
and your right hand delivers me.
⁸The Lᴏʀᴅ will fulfill his purpose for me;
your steadfast love, O Lᴏʀᴅ, endures
forever.
Do not forsake the work of your hands.

Psalm 139
To the leader. Of David. A Psalm.

¹O Lᴏʀᴅ, you have searched me and
known me.
²You know when I sit down and when I
rise up;
you discern my thoughts from far away.
³You search out my path and my lying
down,
and are acquainted with all my ways.
⁴Even before a word is on my tongue,
O Lᴏʀᴅ, you know it completely.
⁵You hem me in, behind and before,
and lay your hand upon me.
⁶Such knowledge is too wonderful for me;
it is so high that I cannot attain it.

⁷Where can I go from your spirit?
Or where can I flee from your
presence?

ᵃ Or *you who are devastated*
ᵇ Cn: Heb *you have exalted your word above all your
name*
ᶜ Syr Compare Gk Tg: Heb *you made me arrogant in
my soul with strength*

5–6: *Hand* and *tongue* are the means of making music. 7: *Edom*, south of the Dead Sea, Edom was an ally in the Babylonian destruction of the city (Lam 4.21; Ezek 25.12–14; 36.5; Obad 8–14). 8: *Babylon*, by poetic justice, it will suffer what it forced others to suffer.

Ps 138: From personal to universal thanks. An individual thanksgiving that gives thanks for a rescue (vv. 1–3), invites the kings of the world to offer their praise (vv. 4–6), and asserts confidence in the Lᴏʀᴅ's future protection (vv. 7–8). The first in a collection of David psalms (Pss 138–145). 1: *Before the gods,* either the heavenly beings who serve in the court of the Most High God (see Ps 29.1n.), or the "gods" of the kings mentioned in vv. 4–6. 3: Going beyond a conventional thanksgiving; the psalmist seems to give thanks for protection throughout life. 4–5: So wonderful has been God's protection that kings, representing the nations, should offer praise (cf. Pss 67.3–5; 126.2). Exactly what is meant by *the words of your mouth* is unclear. 8: As v. 3 sums up the psalmist's past relationship, this verse sums up the psalmist's hope that the relationship will continue.

Ps 139: A request for guidance from a powerful God. Often classed as an individual petition, this poem is unique, recording an individual's experience of God, first as an intimidating outsider (vv. 1–12), and then as a nurturing insider (vv. 13–18). Only after experiencing the range of God's power and beauty does the psalmist comprehend his or her own place and the malice of sin (vv. 19–24). 2: *Sit down . . . rise up,* i.e., always; a merism,

8 If I ascend to heaven, you are there;
  if I make my bed in Sheol, you are there.
9 If I take the wings of the morning
  and settle at the farthest limits of the
    sea,
10 even there your hand shall lead me,
  and your right hand shall hold me fast.
11 If I say, "Surely the darkness shall cover
    me,
  and the light around me become
    night,"
12 even the darkness is not dark to you;
  the night is as bright as the day,
  for darkness is as light to you.

13 For it was you who formed my inward
    parts;
  you knit me together in my mother's
    womb.
14 I praise you, for I am fearfully and
    wonderfully made.
  Wonderful are your works;
that I know very well.
15 My frame was not hidden from you,
when I was being made in secret,
  intricately woven in the depths of the
    earth.
16 Your eyes beheld my unformed
    substance.
In your book were written
  all the days that were formed for me,
  when none of them as yet existed.
17 How weighty to me are your thoughts,
    O God!
  How vast is the sum of them!

18 I try to count them—they are more than
    the sand;
  I come to the end[a]—I am still with you.

19 O that you would kill the wicked, O God,
  and that the bloodthirsty would depart
    from me—
20 those who speak of you maliciously,
  and lift themselves up against you for
    evil![b]
21 Do I not hate those who hate you,
    O LORD?
  And do I not loathe those who rise up
    against you?
22 I hate them with perfect hatred;
  I count them my enemies.
23 Search me, O God, and know my heart;
  test me and know my thoughts.
24 See if there is any wicked[c] way in me,
  and lead me in the way everlasting.[d]

Psalm 140

To the leader. A Psalm of David.

1 Deliver me, O LORD, from evildoers;
  protect me from those who are violent,
2 who plan evil things in their minds
  and stir up wars continually.
3 They make their tongue sharp as a snake's,
  and under their lips is the venom of
    vipers.   *Selah*

a Or *I awake*
b Cn: Meaning of Heb uncertain
c Heb *hurtful*
d Or *the ancient way.* Compare Jer 6.16

in which the ends of a spectrum represent the entire spectrum. **9:** *The wings of the morning,* if I leave at dawn. **8:** *Sheol,* the underworld, the abode of the dead. **13:** *For it was you,* better "It was surely you." The perspective suddenly shifts from outside to inside as the psalmist realizes that the divine power that seemed to loom over life and constrict it (vv. 1–12) also gives life and shapes it in the maternal womb. Delicacy, growth, and "maternal" involvement are also God's work. **14:** *I am . . . wonderfully made,* the psalmist's own creation is as wondrous as the other great deeds of the LORD (e.g., Pss 65.5; 106.22; 145.6). **18:** *I am still with you,* no longer feeling alone and judged, the psalmist knows God is near and has been so from the beginning. God's great power and omnipresence (vv. 1–12) are complemented by nearness and personal care (vv. 13–18). **19–24:** The psalmist's solidarity with God, whom he asks for protection from his wicked enemies.

Ps 140: Petition, complaint, and hope. An individual petition that helps the sufferer move from pain to peaceful hope. NRSV correctly marks the stanzas: vv. 1–3,4–5,6–8,9–11,12–13 on the basis of their syntax, content, and word count. Vv. 1–3 and 4–5 are paired by their syntax, each beginning with similar petitions and descriptions of enemies ("Protect me from those who are violent, who plan . . ."), and each section ends with "Selah," which typically marks a disjunction (see Ps 3.2n.). Vv. 6–8 are distinct by their initial verb "I say" and assertions of loyalty to the LORD. Vv. 9–11 reverse the order of previous sections by beginning with a complaint (v. 9a) and ending with a petition (vv. 9b–11). The final section, vv. 12–13, the statement of trust, is marked by

⁴Guard me, O LORD, from the hands of the
      wicked;
   protect me from the violent
   who have planned my downfall.
⁵The arrogant have hidden a trap for me,
   and with cords they have spread
      a net,ᵃ
   along the road they have set snares
      for me.   Selah

⁶I say to the LORD, "You are my God;
   give ear, O LORD, to the voice of my
      supplications."
⁷O LORD, my Lord, my strong deliverer,
   you have covered my head in the day of
      battle.
⁸Do not grant, O LORD, the desires of the
      wicked;
   do not further their evil plot.ᵇ   Selah

⁹Those who surround me lift up their
      heads;ᶜ
   let the mischief of their lips overwhelm
      them!
¹⁰Let burning coals fall on them!
   Let them be flung into pits, no more to
      rise!
¹¹Do not let the slanderer be established in
      the land;
   let evil speedily hunt down the
      violent!

¹²I know that the LORD maintains the
      cause of the needy,
   and executes justice for the poor.
¹³Surely the righteous shall give thanks to
      your name;
   the upright shall live in your
      presence.

Psalm 141
A Psalm of David.

¹I call upon you, O LORD; come quickly to
      me;
   give ear to my voice when I call to you.
²Let my prayer be counted as incense
      before you,
   and the lifting up of my hands as an
      evening sacrifice.

³Set a guard over my mouth, O LORD;
   keep watch over the door of my lips.
⁴Do not turn my heart to any evil,
   to busy myself with wicked deeds
in company with those who work
      iniquity;
   do not let me eat of their delicacies.

⁵Let the righteous strike me;
   let the faithful correct me.
Never let the oil of the wicked anoint my
      head,ᵈ
   for my prayer is continuallyᵉ against
      their wicked deeds.
⁶When they are given over to those who
      shall condemn them,
   then they shall learn that my words
      were pleasant.
⁷Like a rock that one breaks apart and
      shatters on the land,

ᵃ Or *they have spread cords as a net*
ᵇ Heb adds *they are exalted*
ᶜ Cn Compare Gk: Heb *those who surround me are uplifted in head*; Heb divides verses 8 and 9 differently
ᵈ Gk: Meaning of Heb uncertain
ᵉ Cn: Heb *for continually and my prayer*

its initial verb *I know*. **6:** *I say,* shifts from petition to confession that the LORD has been loyal in the past. **7:** *You have covered my head*, you protected my head. **12:** *I know,* shifts back from petition to confession (as in v. 6), affirming God's fidelity as in Jon 4.2; Pss 20.6; 56.9; 135.5. The psalmist wants to be counted among the *needy* and *poor* whom the LORD always helps. **13:** *Surely* emphasizes the psalmist's triumphant hope that the righteous will be rescued.

Ps 141: Save me from my own evil impulses and from evil companions. An individual petition. Vv. 1–2 ask God to give special attention to the psalmist's plea, and vv. 3–4 beg to be kept from sin and evil companions (vv. 3–4). Vv. 5–7 are textually uncertain. Vv. 8–10 express total trust in God and hope of future protection. **2:** *As incense before you*, according to Ex 30.6, priests offered incense every morning, and according to Ex 29.38–42, the evening sacrifice was burned at the entrance of the tent of meeting. **3:** *My mouth,* in the Bible, the most expressive human organ is the mouth, for words reveal the inner self, the heart. Acknowledging the perversity of the human heart (cf. Jer 17.5; 23.17), the psalmist asks God to purify that vital organ (cf. Ps 51.10). **4:** *Eat of their*

so shall their bones be strewn at the
mouth of Sheol.[a]

[8] But my eyes are turned toward you,
O GOD, my Lord;
in you I seek refuge; do not leave me
defenseless.
[9] Keep me from the trap that they have laid
for me,
and from the snares of evildoers.
[10] Let the wicked fall into their own nets,
while I alone escape.

Psalm 142

*A Maskil of David. When he was in the cave.
A Prayer.*

[1] With my voice I cry to the LORD;
with my voice I make supplication to
the LORD.
[2] I pour out my complaint before him;
I tell my trouble before him.
[3] When my spirit is faint,
you know my way.

In the path where I walk
they have hidden a trap for me.
[4] Look on my right hand and see—
there is no one who takes notice
of me;

no refuge remains to me;
no one cares for me.

[5] I cry to you, O LORD;
I say, "You are my refuge,
my portion in the land of the living."
[6] Give heed to my cry,
for I am brought very low.

Save me from my persecutors,
for they are too strong for me.
[7] Bring me out of prison,
so that I may give thanks to your name.
The righteous will surround me,
for you will deal bountifully with me.

Psalm 143

A Psalm of David.

[1] Hear my prayer, O LORD;
give ear to my supplications in your
faithfulness;
answer me in your righteousness.
[2] Do not enter into judgment with your
servant,
for no one living is righteous before
you.

[a] Meaning of Heb of verses 5-7 is uncertain

delicacies, share their fellowship; cf. Ps 41.9. **7:** Some scholars suggest that the words *Like a rock that one breaks apart and shatters on the land* were accompanied with the ritual shattering of a rock. *Sheol,* the underworld, the abode of the dead. **10:** See Ps 7.15–16n.

Ps 142: Prayer of a friendless person for God's help. An individual petition that proceeds in two stages: the first stage (vv. 1–4) simply lists the peril and danger and declares there is no one else to turn to, and the second (vv. 5–7), with more confidence, calls God "my refuge, my portion in the land of the living" (v. 5) and promises praise. **Superscription:** *Maskil,* a technical term of uncertain significance. *In the cave,* most likely referring to the story of David fleeing from Saul (1 Sam 24). **4:** Loyal friends customarily stood at one's *right hand* (Ps 109.31), but no one is there for the psalmist. **5:** For the first time, the psalmist addresses God, using two impressive metaphors that illustrate God's ability to help at this time of crisis. *Refuge* is elsewhere parallel to mighty rock (Pss 62.7; 91.2; 94.22). *Portion* means a share in land (cf. Josh 18.5,6,9), which in that agrarian society was the source of food and clothing. *You are . . . my portion,* cf. Num 18.20. **7:** As a motivation for divine help, *so that I may give thanks to your name* is similar to Ps 86.12; these psalmists assume that God wants to be thanked, and this motivates divine behavior.

Ps 143: A plea that God would act out of fidelity to a loyal servant. An individual petition that requests divine attention and deliverance from enemies, insisting that no person is righteous before God. It is one of the seven penitential psalms in Christian tradition (Pss 6; 32; 38; 51; 102; 130; 143). Though old material has been re-cycled, Ps 143 is unique, establishing the idea that dealings with God must be based on divine faithfulness and righteousness (vv. 1–2, 10c–12), rather than on human actions. The poetic structure is not easy to determine. "I remember" in v. 5 changes the topic from petition to remembering past times. Verse 7 clearly begins a new section, for each verse in vv. 7–10a begins with a verb in the imperative mood. The final section, vv. 10b–12, is indicated by a shift in syntax: all the verbs except the last are placed at or near the end of the colon (unit). **5:**

³For the enemy has pursued me,
  crushing my life to the ground,
  making me sit in darkness like those
    long dead.
⁴Therefore my spirit faints within me;
  my heart within me is appalled.

⁵I remember the days of old,
  I think about all your deeds,
  I meditate on the works of your hands.
⁶I stretch out my hands to you;
  my soul thirsts for you like a parched
    land.   Selah

⁷Answer me quickly, O LORD;
  my spirit fails.
Do not hide your face from me,
  or I shall be like those who go down to
    the Pit.
⁸Let me hear of your steadfast love in the
    morning,
  for in you I put my trust.
Teach me the way I should go,
  for to you I lift up my soul.

⁹Save me, O LORD, from my enemies;
  I have fled to you for refuge.ᵃ
¹⁰Teach me to do your will,
  for you are my God.
Let your good spirit lead me
  on a level path.

¹¹For your name's sake, O LORD, preserve
    my life.
  In your righteousness bring me out of
    trouble.
¹²In your steadfast love cut off my enemies,
  and destroy all my adversaries,
  for I am your servant.

Psalm 144
Of David.

¹Blessed be the LORD, my rock,
  who trains my hands for war, and my
    fingers for battle;
²my rockᵇ and my fortress,
  my stronghold and my deliverer,
my shield, in whom I take refuge,
  who subdues the peoplesᶜ under
    me.

³O LORD, what are human beings that you
    regard them,
  or mortals that you think of them?
⁴They are like a breath;
  their days are like a passing shadow.

⁵Bow your heavens, O LORD, and come
    down;
  touch the mountains so that they
    smoke.
⁶Make the lightning flash and scatter
    them;
  send out your arrows and rout
    them.
⁷Stretch out your hand from on high;
  set me free and rescue me from the
    mighty waters,
  from the hand of aliens,
⁸whose mouths speak lies,
  and whose right hands are false.

⁹I will sing a new song to you, O God;
  upon a ten-stringed harp I will play
    to you,

ᵃ One Heb Ms Gk: MT *to you I have hidden*
ᵇ With 18.2 and 2 Sam 22.2: Heb *my steadfast love*
ᶜ Heb Mss Syr Aquila Jerome: MT *my people*

The days of old refers to God's great actions in creation and history; see Ps 77.11–12. 6: *Thirsts*, see Pss 42.1; 63.1. *Selah*, see Ps 3.2n. 7: *Do not hide your face from me* refers to the idea that God on occasion, for no reason, ignores innocent supplicants. *The Pit*, a synonym for Sheol, the abode of the dead. 8: *Morning* was an especially propitious time for a good judgment (see Ps 90.14). 11: Since the psalmist is assuming a relationship with God that depends on divine mercy rather than fair judgment of human actions, he evokes God's name (reputation), as in some prophetic literature (e.g., Ezek 20.9) and some psalms (e.g., 23.3).

Ps 144: A royal request for divine assistance. A psalm in which an individual, possibly the king, asks for divine assistance and general peace and security. The manner in which this late psalm quotes other psalms makes it especially difficult to interpret. 1: *Blessed be the LORD*, a formula for praising God for a beneficial act, in this case for equipping the supplicant, possibly to wage war. 3: Cf. Ps 8.4; Job 7.17. 4: Cf. Pss 102.11; 109.23. 5: The beginning of the verse is taken from 2 Sam 22.10=Ps 18.10. 7: *Mighty waters . . . the hand of aliens*, a mixture of cosmic language and historic language, the first referring to the waters of chaos and the second to the human

¹⁰ the one who gives victory to kings,
 who rescues his servant David.
¹¹ Rescue me from the cruel sword,
 and deliver me from the hand of aliens,
whose mouths speak lies,
 and whose right hands are false.

¹² May our sons in their youth
 be like plants full grown,
our daughters like corner pillars,
 cut for the building of a palace.
¹³ May our barns be filled,
 with produce of every kind;
may our sheep increase by thousands,
 by tens of thousands in our fields,
  ¹⁴ and may our cattle be heavy with
   young.
May there be no breach in the walls,ᵃ no exile,
 and no cry of distress in our streets.

¹⁵ Happy are the people to whom such
 blessings fall;
 happy are the people whose God is the
  LORD.

Psalm 145

Praise. Of David.

¹ I will extol you, my God and King,
 and bless your name forever and ever.
² Every day I will bless you,
 and praise your name forever and ever.
³ Great is the LORD, and greatly to be
 praised;
 his greatness is unsearchable.

⁴ One generation shall laud your works to
 another,
 and shall declare your mighty acts.
⁵ On the glorious splendor of your majesty,
 and on your wondrous works, I will
  meditate.
⁶ The might of your awesome deeds shall
 be proclaimed,
 and I will declare your greatness.
⁷ They shall celebrate the fame of your
 abundant goodness,
 and shall sing aloud of your
  righteousness.

⁸ The LORD is gracious and merciful,
 slow to anger and abounding in
  steadfast love.
⁹ The LORD is good to all,
 and his compassion is over all that he
  has made.

¹⁰ All your works shall give thanks to you,
 O LORD,
 and all your faithful shall bless you.
¹¹ They shall speak of the glory of your
 kingdom,
 and tell of your power,
¹² to make known to all people yourᵇ
 mighty deeds,
 and the glorious splendor of yourᶜ
 kingdom.

ᵃ Heb lacks *in the walls*
ᵇ Gk Jerome Syr: Heb *his*
ᶜ Heb *his*

agents of chaotic forces. **9–10:** King David was a famous poet and musician; see 1 Sam 16.18; 2 Sam 1.17. **12–15:** In an agrarian society, political peace and agricultural fertility go together; this psalm seems to assume a period of *distress*. This blessing that the psalmist requests would be suitable for a royal psalm since the king protects the land from invaders and blesses its fertility (cf. Ps 72.3–7).

 Ps 145: Praise of the goodness of the LORD the king. A hymn ending the Davidic collection (Pss 138–145) and preparing for the hymns (Pss 146–150) that conclude the Psalms in a symphony of praise. This psalm too is an acrostic (see Ps 9–10n.), although the fourteenth letter ("nun") is missing in the Hebrew text. The singer's own voice is prominent: "I will extol you, my God" (vv. 1–2) and "My mouth will speak the praise of the LORD" (v. 21). In vv. 3–7, one generation tells the next of the acts of the LORD. V. 8, "the LORD is gracious and merciful," emphasizes the loving governance behind those acts (vv. 11–13) and the generosity toward human beings (vv. 10–20). The final verse (v. 21) reprises the first. **1:** *My . . . King*, most of the attributes mentioned in the psalm are connected to royalty; this initial reference also points forward to the four occurrences of *kingdom* in vv. 11–13. **2:** *Your name*, your presence. **4:** *One generation shall laud your works to another*, like the process of education in Ps 78.4 (cf. Ex 13.8,14; Deut 6.20). The children experience the effects of the mighty deeds of old that are constantly renewed. **5:** Glory, *splendor* and *majesty* are royal qualities that God as king possesses. **8:** Citation of the divine attributes in Ex 34.6. **11:** *Your kingdom*, occurs four times at the psalm's center in vv. 11–13. The contexts

[13] Your kingdom is an everlasting kingdom,
and your dominion endures throughout
all generations.

The Lord is faithful in all his words,
and gracious in all his deeds.[a]
[14] The Lord upholds all who are falling,
and raises up all who are bowed down.
[15] The eyes of all look to you,
and you give them their food in due
season.
[16] You open your hand,
satisfying the desire of every living thing.
[17] The Lord is just in all his ways,
and kind in all his doings.
[18] The Lord is near to all who call on him,
to all who call on him in truth.
[19] He fulfills the desire of all who fear him;
he also hears their cry, and saves them.
[20] The Lord watches over all who love him,
but all the wicked he will destroy.

[21] My mouth will speak the praise of the Lord,
and all flesh will bless his holy name
forever and ever.

Psalm 146

[1] Praise the Lord!
Praise the Lord, O my soul!
[2] I will praise the Lord as long as I live;
I will sing praises to my God all my life
long.

[3] Do not put your trust in princes,
in mortals, in whom there is no help.

[4] When their breath departs, they return to
the earth;
on that very day their plans perish.

[5] Happy are those whose help is the God
of Jacob,
whose hope is in the Lord their God,
[6] who made heaven and earth,
the sea, and all that is in them;
who keeps faith forever;
[7] who executes justice for the
oppressed;
who gives food to the hungry.

The Lord sets the prisoners free;
[8] the Lord opens the eyes of the blind.
The Lord lifts up those who are bowed
down;
the Lord loves the righteous.
[9] The Lord watches over the strangers;
he upholds the orphan and the widow,
but the way of the wicked he brings to
ruin.

[10] The Lord will reign forever,
your God, O Zion, for all generations.
Praise the Lord!

Psalm 147

[1] Praise the Lord!
How good it is to sing praises to our God;
for he is gracious, and a song of praise
is fitting.

[a] These two lines supplied by Q Ms Gk Syr

make clear that the word means active rule, reigning, rather than static kingdom. **13:** Cf. Dan 4.3. **14–16:** Cf. Pss 104.27; 146.7–8. **17–18:** The word *all* appears twice in each of these verses, and another three times before the psalm concludes, for a total of seventeen times, emphasizing God's incomparability.

Ps 146: Praise of the Lord, savior of the downtrodden. A hymn, like Pss 147–150; together, these five psalms form the concluding doxology to the entire book of Psalms. Each of these hymns begins and ends with "Hallelujah" (traditionally translated "Praise the Lord"). The singer in Ps 146 engages in an inner dialogue ("O my soul!" v. 1b) before addressing the community in v. 3. Such reflection enables the singer to appreciate the vanity of human resources (vv. 3–4) and the compassion of the Lord's governance of the world (vv. 5–9). **5:** In contrast to placing one's hopes in human helpers, weak and mortal (vv. 3–4), the psalmist's hopes are in the Lord, already covenanted to Israel, the powerful and just creator and judge (vv. 6–7). **6:** *Who made heaven and earth,* see Ps 124.8n. **7–9:** All the Lord's actions here are rescues of beleaguered individuals, inspiring the psalmist to hope and praise for rescues in the future. **9:** God's justice is complete; *the way of the wicked he brings to ruin,* before their plans reach fruition. **10:** These aspects of God—creator, righteous judge—are related to his kingship, mentioned explicitly only in the final verse. This connects Pss 145 and 146.

Ps 147: Praise the Lord who restores Jerusalem. The second of the five hymns concluding the Psalms. Each of its three sections (vv. 1–6, 7–11, and 12–20) begins with an invitation in the imperative to praise the Lord and

² The LORD builds up Jerusalem;
   he gathers the outcasts of Israel.
³ He heals the brokenhearted,
   and binds up their wounds.
⁴ He determines the number of the stars;
   he gives to all of them their names.
⁵ Great is our Lord, and abundant in power;
   his understanding is beyond measure.
⁶ The LORD lifts up the downtrodden;
   he casts the wicked to the ground.

⁷ Sing to the LORD with thanksgiving;
   make melody to our God on the lyre.
⁸ He covers the heavens with clouds,
   prepares rain for the earth,
   makes grass grow on the hills.
⁹ He gives to the animals their food,
   and to the young ravens when they cry.
¹⁰ His delight is not in the strength of the
   horse,
   nor his pleasure in the speed of a
   runner;ᵃ
¹¹ but the LORD takes pleasure in those who
   fear him,
   in those who hope in his steadfast love.

¹² Praise the LORD, O Jerusalem!
   Praise your God, O Zion!
¹³ For he strengthens the bars of your gates;
   he blesses your children within you.
¹⁴ He grants peaceᵇ within your borders;
   he fills you with the finest of wheat.

¹⁵ He sends out his command to the
   earth;
   his word runs swiftly.
¹⁶ He gives snow like wool;
   he scatters frost like ashes.
¹⁷ He hurls down hail like crumbs—
   who can stand before his cold?
¹⁸ He sends out his word, and melts them;
   he makes his wind blow, and the waters
   flow.
¹⁹ He declares his word to Jacob,
   his statutes and ordinances to Israel.
²⁰ He has not dealt thus with any other
   nation;
   they do not know his ordinances.
Praise the LORD!

Psalm 148

¹ Praise the LORD!
Praise the LORD from the heavens;
   praise him in the heights!
² Praise him, all his angels;
   praise him, all his host!

³ Praise him, sun and moon;
   praise him, all you shining stars!
⁴ Praise him, you highest heavens,
   and you waters above the heavens!

ᵃ Heb *legs of a person*
ᵇ Or *prosperity*

lists the divine acts for which praise is to be given. Vv. 1–6 cite the LORD's restoration of Jerusalem and gathering of exiles; vv. 7–11 cite the LORD's control of fertility for the nurture of humans, and vv. 12–20 cite the LORD's gift to Israel of his powerful word. Written for a scattered, malnourished, and demoralized people, most likely in the exilic or postexilic period, the psalm teaches them how to see divine purpose and give thanks. **4:** *He determines the number of the stars*, creating the heavens and rebuilding Zion are parallel works as in Isa 51.16, for God ensures that the original creation continues. The psalm interprets creation in the manner of Isaiah 40–55. **7–11:** Again directing creation to benefit Israel, God promises to restore the devastated lands to provide food. **7:** It is unclear if *thanksgiving* is a sacrifice or verbal thanks. **15:** *His word*, vv. 15–20 have seven terms for the word of God, some repeated: *command, word, statutes, ordinances*. **19–20:** The LORD spoke *his word* at Sinai and afterward. It made Israel distinctive then (Deut 4.5–8) and does so now, for God *has not dealt thus with any other nation* (v. 20a). The Torah here is recognized as Israel's special gift (*his ordinances*) from God.

Ps 148: Let heaven and earth praise the LORD. The third of the hymns that make up the doxology concluding the Psalms. More formal than the two preceding psalms, it employs the verb "to praise" twelve times, "LORD" four times, and "the name (of the LORD)" three times; it is neatly composed of two almost equal panels, vv. 1–6, introduced by "Praise the LORD from the heavens," and vv. 7–14, introduced by "Praise the LORD from the earth." Unlike other hymns, it focuses on the groups invited to praise, the inhabitants of heaven (vv. 1–4), and the inhabitants of earth (vv. 7–12). The divine acts meriting praise are mentioned only briefly: for the first group (vv. 5–6), the motive for giving praise is that the LORD created them and assigned them all their tasks); for the second (v. 13), the motive is that the LORD's name and glory are exalted above heaven and earth. **3:** This may

⁵ Let them praise the name of the Lord,
　for he commanded and they were
　　created.
⁶ He established them forever and ever;
　he fixed their bounds, which cannot be
　　passed.ᵃ

⁷ Praise the Lord from the earth,
　you sea monsters and all deeps,
⁸ fire and hail, snow and frost,
　stormy wind fulfilling his command!

⁹ Mountains and all hills,
　fruit trees and all cedars!
¹⁰ Wild animals and all cattle,
　creeping things and flying birds!

¹¹ Kings of the earth and all peoples,
　princes and all rulers of the earth!
¹² Young men and women alike,
　old and young together!

¹³ Let them praise the name of the Lord,
　for his name alone is exalted;
　his glory is above earth and heaven.
¹⁴ He has raised up a horn for his
　　people,
　praise for all his faithful,
　for the people of Israel who are close
　　to him.
Praise the Lord!

Psalm 149

¹ Praise the Lord!
Sing to the Lord a new song,
　his praise in the assembly of the
　　faithful.
² Let Israel be glad in its Maker;
　let the children of Zion rejoice in their
　　King.
³ Let them praise his name with
　　dancing,
　making melody to him with tambourine
　　and lyre.
⁴ For the Lord takes pleasure in his
　　people;
　he adorns the humble with victory.
⁵ Let the faithful exult in glory;
　let them sing for joy on their couches.
⁶ Let the high praises of God be in their
　　throats
　and two-edged swords in their hands,
⁷ to execute vengeance on the nations
　and punishment on the peoples,
⁸ to bind their kings with fetters
　and their nobles with chains of iron,
⁹ to execute on them the judgment
　　decreed.
This is glory for all his faithful ones.
Praise the Lord!

ᵃ Or *he set a law that cannot pass away*

recall other ancient cultures, in which astral bodies were deities. **5:** *For he commanded and they were created*, the psalm recognizes here and elsewhere the orderly Priestly story of creation by word in Gen 1, emphasizing that God continues to have this role in the universe. **7–8:** Somewhat autonomous deities in surrounding cultures, but under God's strict control here. **14:** *A horn for his people,* a symbol of strength.

Ps 149: Praise for Israel's task in the world. This fourth hymn in the series of five concluding the Psalms may disturb readers with its apparent call to vengeance against foreigners. Ps 149 develops the ideas of two psalms, the immediately preceding Ps 148, which singles out Israel as having a mission to proclaim the supremacy of the Lord to the nations (Ps 148.14), and Ps 2 (second from the beginning as Ps 149 is second from the last) in which the Davidic king is given authority to subdue the nations. Ps 149 transposes the royal role of Ps 2 to the entire nation (as in Isa 55.3). Ps 149 has two stanzas, vv. 1–4 and 5–9, the first inviting praise for the Lord's victory and second equating that praise metaphorically with weapons of war against the rebellious kings. **1:** *New song,* as in Isa 42.10 and other psalms (e.g., 33.3; 96.1; 98.1); here in response to creation, for Israel is *glad in its Maker* (v. 2); the act establishes the kingship of the Lord. In the previous psalm, God as king is creating the universe, while here he creates Israel. **5:** *On their couches,* symbolizes private (in contrast to public) expression as in Pss 4.4; 6.6; 36.4; Hos 7.14. **6:** Wielding a *sword* (and the other military actions in vv. 7–9) is a metaphor for proclaiming the Lord's sovereignty over kings and nations. The conjunction *and* makes the statements of v. 6a and 6b into a comparison: praising God is like wielding a sword. Israel has the task of embodying divine sovereignty and rendering it visible in the world. This unmasks false gods and invites the nations to join in God's praise and recognition of Israel. **7:** *Vengeance,* best rendered "retribution" for the kings' refusal to recognize their true suzerain. **9:** *Judgment decreed,* the ultimate triumph of the Lord.

Psalm 150

[1] Praise the LORD!
Praise God in his sanctuary;
  praise him in his mighty firmament![a]
[2] Praise him for his mighty deeds;
  praise him according to his surpassing
    greatness!

[3] Praise him with trumpet sound;
  praise him with lute and harp!

[4] Praise him with tambourine and dance;
  praise him with strings and pipe!
[5] Praise him with clanging cymbals;
  praise him with loud clashing cymbals!
[6] Let everything that breathes praise the
    LORD!
Praise the LORD!

a   Or *dome*

Ps 150: Climactic praise for the LORD's total sovereignty. The last of the final five hymns ending the Psalms. All the verses except the final one (v. 6) begin with the same verb in the imperative mood: *Praise him* . . . ! The verb occurs thirteen times in this final outburst of praise. Each of the first four books of the Psalms ends with a one- or two-verse doxology (Pss 41.13; 72.18–19; 89.52; 106.48), and it is fitting that a whole poem be the final doxology that notes where (v. 1), why (v. 2), and how (vv. 3–5) God should be praised. The invitatory extends throughout the whole poem; the poem is one long invitation to give praise. The group summoned to give praise, whom most psalms name almost immediately, is not revealed until the end, and it is vast: "everything that breathes" (v. 6). It goes beyond Israel to the entire human race, even to animals. The vast reach of the poem is a reminder that the call of one people is made in view of God's commitment to all.

PROVERBS

NAME AND PLACE IN CANON

In Jewish tradition the Proverbs of Solomon (Heb *mishle shelomoh*), shortened to Proverbs (*mishle*), is found in the third division of the canon, the Writings, grouped with Psalms and Job. The order of the books varies in early manuscripts, with Proverbs either after Psalms and Job or sandwiched between them. In Christian Bibles, Proverbs is one of the poetical and wisdom books and is placed between Psalms and Ecclesiastes.

AUTHORSHIP

The book of Proverbs is traditionally attributed to King Solomon (1.1; 10.1; 25.1), who ruled in the mid-tenth century BCE. Although he had a reputation for wisdom (1 Kings 4.29–34), it is unlikely that this is more than a general attribution to lend authority to the collection. The proverbs in the main section (10.1–22.16) have the character of folk wisdom, generated in an oral culture and passed down over many generations. At some point in the preexilic period they were collected and written down, a process that may have taken place at the hands of sages or scribes at the court of a king such as Solomon or Hezekiah (715–687 BCE), who is mentioned in 25.1. Later sections, such as chs 1–9, were probably added by scribes in the attempt to bring the collection together.

LITERARY HISTORY AND DATING

The book of Proverbs is a composite, consisting of several different collections dating from different periods and most likely with different authors. Proverbs 10.1–22.16 ("The proverbs of Solomon") is the main sayings collection and probably the oldest. Proverbs 25–29 forms a distinct unit of further proverbial material, with some repeats from the main collection (e.g., 21.9 = 25.24) and is dated to the time of Hezekiah. Proverbs 22.17–24.34 ("The words of the wise") is also a separate collection, which has close connections with an Egyptian wisdom text "The Instruction of Amenemope." This Egyptian text, which dates to ca. 1100 BCE, was copied by schoolchildren learning to read and write. Proverbs 22.17–23.11 especially may contain evidence of copying from "Amenemope," suggesting a school context for at least part of the book of Proverbs. Proverbs 25–29 ("Proverbs of Solomon that the officials of King Hezekiah of Judah copied") is another distinct unit, with some repetitions from the main collection (e.g., 21.9 = 25.24). There are two attributions at the end of the book, to Agur (30.1) and Lemuel (31.1), confirming that Proverbs is essentially a collection of collections. Finally, Proverbs 1–9, which opens the book, is often regarded as its latest part, with a more advanced theology and reflection on the nature of the wisdom, although it no doubt contains older material.

The complex stages of oral and literary development make it difficult to situate the book historically. The major sayings collections are likely preexilic, written down in the ninth or eighth century BCE. Other sections, such as chs 1–9, are later, probably from the exilic or early postexilic period, the sixth and fifth centuries BCE. The book as a whole probably was shaped in the early postexilic period.

CONTENTS AND INTERPRETATION

In chs 1–9, Proverbs presents itself as a handbook of the experience of others designed to offer insight and guidance to any, but especially the young, who seek its advice. The purpose of the book is set out in the introduction (1.2–7), which mentions learning about "wisdom" and "instruction." Instruction refers both to the educational role of this teaching and to a genre of literature paralleled in Egypt and found in Proverbs 1–9, that of instruction from father and mother to child (1.8; 4.1–4; 6.20–21). There is a moral dimension to this teaching, which includes learning about "righteousness, justice, and equity" (1.3, terms familiar from elsewhere in the Bible), accompanied by a highly practical purpose which includes "shrewdness, knowledge, and prudence" (1.4).

At the climax of the introduction to Proverbs is the idea that "the fear of the LORD is the beginning of knowledge" (1.7; cf. 9.10; 15.33), a sentiment that introduces the divine dimension to the apparently human quest for wisdom. In this phrase is the recognition that at the beginning and end of the quest stands God, who is the author of all wisdom and understanding. Although only a part of this is accessible to human beings (16.1–2,9; 21.30), the person who seeks wisdom will truly gain insight by first fearing the Lord. Wisdom, personified as a woman in chs 1–9, is the mediator of that divine wisdom in her offer of its fruits to human beings (1.20–33;

8.4–5; 9.5–6), leading them on the path to "life" (3.16–18). The threat to the gaining of wisdom comes from her antithesis, the strange woman (chs 2; 5; 7; 9) whose path leads to death (2.18–19). Woman Wisdom is not just the embodiment of the kind of woman any young man might seek as a wife, but she is also described in cosmic terms as having been present with God during creation (8.22–31). This depiction underscores the underlying theological emphasis of the book of Proverbs on God as creator. God creates the world and sustains it; Woman Wisdom delights in all that he has made (8.30–31). God set up an order in the world and in society that can be known by human beings through wisdom, an order that helps them to lead a virtuous, moral, successful life. The rewards of wise living are longevity, offspring, wealth, the respect of others, and a fulfilled existence. This rather simplistic view of behaving well, and hence automatically reaping wisdom's rewards, was challenged by the later wisdom books of Job and Ecclesiastes, whose authors argue that experience teaches otherwise.

Although the NRSV translation "my child" opens up the audience to all seekers of wisdom, the Hebrew actually reads "my son," and the material is essentially addressed to men. They would have been the main recipients of education in the home and in schools. However, this orientation is balanced by reference to the mother's involvement in the teaching process (1.8; 6.20; cf. 31.1), by the figure of the ideal wife in 31.10–31, and by the two female figures of chs 1–9.

In the body of the book the main literary form for transmitting wisdom is the proverb (1.6), a pithy one- or two-line saying that conveys truth by the use of comparison between unlike phenomena or parallel thoughts that extend understanding. Proverbs occur in two main types: antithetical, and synonymous. Antithetical proverbs provide a contrast in the second line, while synonymous proverbs use the second line to extend the thought of the first. The former type predominates in chs 10–15, while the latter is more frequent from ch 16 on-ward. Interpreting proverbs is an intellectual discipline, not for the fool (26.7,9), and proverbs that are in tension or even contradictory are sometimes juxtaposed (e.g., 17.27–28; 26.4–5). For the most part the arrangement of proverbs seems random, however, although there are some small thematic clusters (e.g., 25.1–7), and there is some evidence of catchwords, plays on words, alliteration, and assonance in the Hebrew, which may have been aides to memorization. The binary form of proverbs and their perspective on the world are related. There is often a stress on opposite types: the righteous and the wicked, the rich and the poor, the diligent and the lazy, the patient person and the angry one, the restrained speaker and the gossip. This schematic organization of types is matched by the view of divine retribution, whereby the good are rewarded and the wicked punished.

The authors of texts such as Ecclesiasticus (Sirach; early second century BCE) and the Wisdom of Solomon (first century BCE or first century CE) were clearly familiar with Proverbs. For example, Sirach 24 rereads Proverbs 8 by identifying Wisdom with Torah; and the Wisdom of Solomon sees personified Wisdom as a hypostasis of the LORD (e.g., Wis 7.22; 8.2). Fragments of Proverbs were found at Qumran, and a few previously unknown wisdom texts seem to use its imagery (e.g., in 4Q185 the figure of Woman Folly from Prov 5; 7; 9 reappears). Proverbs seems to have influenced the rabbinic wisdom collection Pirqe Abot ("The sayings of the Fathers") in the Mishnah. Early Christians saw Jesus in part as a wisdom teacher (see especially the Q material in the Synoptic Gospels) and employed traditions about personified Wisdom to understand his identity and mission (e.g., Jn 1.1–18; Col 1.15–20). The letter of James in the New Testament contains wisdom instruction, and its author exalts "wisdom from above" (3.13–18), echoing portrayals of Woman Wisdom in Proverbs.

GUIDE TO READING

Despite its heterogeneous nature, the book of Proverbs can be read from beginning to end. The beginning and end of the book are formed by representations of two symbolically related women: personified wisdom (chs 1–9), and the "woman of substance" (31.10–31) who is a human embodiment of Woman Wisdom. Thus, the introductory chapters invite the reader to acquire wisdom. The body of the book provides sustained training in the perceptiveness and values needed to become wise. And the conclusion portrays the fulfillment of living in wisdom's household.

It is equally appropriate, however, to read each of the different collections independently, appreciating their distinct literary forms and tropes. Indeed, since there seldom seems to be an intentional order to the proverbial sayings, readers may also ponder them individually, thinking about life contexts to which they are applicable. The book of Proverbs invites multiple forms of reading.

Katharine Dell

1

The proverbs of Solomon son of David,
king of Israel:

[2] For learning about wisdom and instruction,
for understanding words of insight,
[3] for gaining instruction in wise dealing,
righteousness, justice, and equity;
[4] to teach shrewdness to the simple,
knowledge and prudence to the
young—
[5] let the wise also hear and gain in
learning,
and the discerning acquire skill,
[6] to understand a proverb and a figure,
the words of the wise and their riddles.

[7] The fear of the LORD is the beginning of
knowledge;
fools despise wisdom and instruction.

[8] Hear, my child, your father's instruction,
and do not reject your mother's teaching;
[9] for they are a fair garland for your head,
and pendants for your neck.

[10] My child, if sinners entice you,
do not consent.
[11] If they say, "Come with us, let us lie in
wait for blood;
let us wantonly ambush the innocent;
[12] like Sheol let us swallow them alive
and whole, like those who go down to
the Pit.
[13] We shall find all kinds of costly things;
we shall fill our houses with booty.
[14] Throw in your lot among us;
we will all have one purse"—
[15] my child, do not walk in their way,
keep your foot from their paths;
[16] for their feet run to evil,
and they hurry to shed blood.
[17] For in vain is the net baited
while the bird is looking on;
[18] yet they lie in wait—to kill themselves!
and set an ambush—for their own lives!
[19] Such is the end[a] of all who are greedy for
gain;

[a] Gk: Heb *are the ways*

1.1–7: **Introduction. 1:** *Solomon son of David, king of Israel,* King Solomon, successor to his father, David (see 1 Kings 1–11) ruled a united kingdom of Israel in the mid-tenth century BCE. He is famed for his wisdom (1 Kings 4) and his role as Temple builder (1 Kings 6). The latter role is not mentioned here, nor is there much mention of ritual activity in Proverbs. The attribution is probably pseudonymous, though Solomon may have coined some proverbs. His court is a possible setting for the collection of proverbial material and may have witnessed a time of cultural expansion and international connections. **2–6:** The instructional purpose of the book; see the Introduction. The address is to the *simple* and the *young,* but also to the *wise* who never cease the learning process. **6:** *A proverb* (see Introduction) . . . *figure,* an artistic saying or terse poem; *riddles,* enigmatic puzzles in brief, concentrated form that challenge the reader to find a solution. **7:** The divine dimension. *Fear of the LORD,* i.e., reverence and awe, is a prerequisite for wisdom (9.10; 15.33; 31.30b; Job 28.28; Ps 111.10; Sir 1.14). A contrast is made here between God-fearers and *fools,* unlike the usual contrast between wise person and fool. Fools have no desire to learn: they are not just unintelligent, but their conduct is unethical.

1.8–19: **Parental warning against the enticements of sinners. 8:** *My child* (lit. "my son") could reflect the home educational situation or represent a student in a teacher/pupil relationship in a school setting. *Father* and *mother* have parallel teaching roles within the family, at least in the child's early years. The term *teaching* (Heb "torah") refers here not to law specifically (as frequently elsewhere in the Hebrew Bible) but to wisdom instruction. It is significant that the same term can refer to covenant law, which also contains ethical instruction (as in Deuteronomy). Sirach 24 identifies the two. **9:** *Fair garland* and *pendants,* wisdom instruction is often associated with adornment (cf. the portrayal of Woman Wisdom as beautifully adorned and yet more valuable than costly jewels in ch 8). Here the metaphor means that the teaching should be an intimate part of one, as if worn on head and neck (cf. 3.22; 4.9; 6.21; 7.3; Job 31.35–36). **12:** *Sheol . . . the Pit,* the abode of the dead (see also 5.5; 7.27; 9.18; 23.27; 27.30; 30.16). Cf. the depiction in Ugaritic mythology of Mot, the god of death, with a vast throat stretching from earth to heaven into which he swallows his victims whole and alive. **15:** *Way . . . paths,* a frequently used image in Proverbs for a life course (e.g., 2.7–20; 3.6,17,23; 8.13,20; 11.5; 28.18). **16:** Cf. Isa 59.7. **17–18:** The citation of a popular proverb, using animal imagery: if a *bird* is watching, there is no use in setting a trap for it. Ironically, these wicked but stupid ambushers are both those who set the traps and those who fall into them.

it takes away the life of its
    possessors.

20 Wisdom cries out in the street;
    in the squares she raises her voice.
21 At the busiest corner she cries out;
    at the entrance of the city gates she
        speaks:
22 "How long, O simple ones, will you love
        being simple?
How long will scoffers delight in their
        scoffing
    and fools hate knowledge?
23 Give heed to my reproof;
I will pour out my thoughts to you;
    I will make my words known to you.
24 Because I have called and you refused,
    have stretched out my hand and no one
        heeded,
25 and because you have ignored all my
        counsel
    and would have none of my reproof,
26 I also will laugh at your calamity;
    I will mock when panic strikes you,
27 when panic strikes you like a storm,
    and your calamity comes like a whirlwind,
    when distress and anguish come upon
        you.
28 Then they will call upon me, but I will
        not answer;
    they will seek me diligently, but will not
        find me.
29 Because they hated knowledge
    and did not choose the fear of the LORD,

30 would have none of my counsel,
    and despised all my reproof,
31 therefore they shall eat the fruit of their
    way
    and be sated with their own devices.
32 For waywardness kills the simple,
    and the complacency of fools destroys
        them;
33 but those who listen to me will be secure
    and will live at ease, without dread of
        disaster."

2 My child, if you accept my words
    and treasure up my commandments
        within you,
2 making your ear attentive to wisdom
    and inclining your heart to
        understanding;
3 if you indeed cry out for insight,
    and raise your voice for
        understanding;
4 if you seek it like silver,
    and search for it as for hidden
        treasures—
5 then you will understand the fear of the
    LORD
    and find the knowledge of God.
6 For the LORD gives wisdom;
    from his mouth come knowledge and
        understanding;
7 he stores up sound wisdom for the
    upright;
    he is a shield to those who walk
        blamelessly,

1.20–33: **Wisdom personified as a prophet.** Wisdom speaks out in *the street, the squares, the busiest corner* and *the city gates*, i.e., the hub of city social life where legal decisions were often made (cf. Ruth 4.1). This portrayal has many similarities to the prophetic role (v. 22, cf. Jer 4.14,21; v. 24, cf. Isa 65.2,12; 66.4; Jer 7.13,24–27), and contains a strong, reproving tone (vv. 26–32). Listening and hearing are an important part of the pedagogical relationship in Proverbs. **22:** The *simple* (see 1.4) can learn if inclined to do so, but *scoffers* and *fools* are generally beyond hope of instruction (1.7; 15.12; 26.3). **23:** *Reproof* (Heb "tokaḥat"), also translated as "rebuke" and "admonition," is a central part of wisdom instruction (e.g., 1.23,30; 3.11; 5.12; 12.1; 15.5,31–32; 29.1). **32–33:** The contrast between not listening to Wisdom and heeding her is drawn sharply in these verses: life or death, security or disaster.

2.1–22: **The advantages of following wisdom.** This poem of 22 lines (the number of letters in the Hebrew alphabet) expresses the benefits of following wisdom in contrast to succumbing to the enticements of a "strange woman" (see v. 16n.) who is *loose.* The conditional aspect of reaping wisdom's rewards is stressed by the keyword "if" and a strong note of warning is sounded. **2:** *Heart* denotes not only the seat of the emotions but also the rational center of a person (i.e., the mind; see 4.23). **4:** Wisdom is often compared to *silver* or treasure or other precious metals (3.14–16; 8.10–11,19; Job 28.15–19); the inference is that both are hard to find (hence *hidden treasures*; contrast 8.1–5 where wisdom's treasures are openly offered). **5:** *Fear of the LORD*, see 1.7n. **6:** Wisdom comes directly from the mouth of God (cf. Sir 24.3). Wis 7.25 makes the close identification of wisdom with God

[8] guarding the paths of justice
  and preserving the way of his faithful
    ones.
[9] Then you will understand righteousness
    and justice
  and equity, every good path;
[10] for wisdom will come into your heart,
  and knowledge will be pleasant to your
    soul;
[11] prudence will watch over you;
  and understanding will guard you.
[12] It will save you from the way of evil,
  from those who speak perversely,
[13] who forsake the paths of uprightness
  to walk in the ways of darkness,
[14] who rejoice in doing evil
  and delight in the perverseness of evil;
[15] those whose paths are crooked,
  and who are devious in their ways.

[16] You will be saved from the loose[a] woman,
  from the adulteress with her smooth
    words,
[17] who forsakes the partner of her youth
  and forgets her sacred covenant;
[18] for her way[b] leads down to death,
  and her paths to the shades;
[19] those who go to her never come back,
  nor do they regain the paths of life.

[20] Therefore walk in the way of the good,
  and keep to the paths of the just.
[21] For the upright will abide in the land,
  and the innocent will remain in it;
[22] but the wicked will be cut off from the
    land,

and the treacherous will be rooted out
    of it.

3 My child, do not forget my teaching,
  but let your heart keep my
    commandments;
[2] for length of days and years of life
  and abundant welfare they will give
    you.

[3] Do not let loyalty and faithfulness forsake
    you;
  bind them around your neck,
  write them on the tablet of your heart.
[4] So you will find favor and good repute
  in the sight of God and of people.

[5] Trust in the LORD with all your heart,
  and do not rely on your own insight.
[6] In all your ways acknowledge him,
  and he will make straight your paths.
[7] Do not be wise in your own eyes;
  fear the LORD, and turn away from evil.
[8] It will be a healing for your flesh
  and a refreshment for your body.

[9] Honor the LORD with your substance
  and with the first fruits of all your
    produce;
[10] then your barns will be filled with
    plenty,
  and your vats will be bursting with
    wine.

---

a   Heb *strange*
b   Cn: Heb *house*

---

into a metaphysical claim. **8:** *Paths* and *way* (see 1.15n.), a major theme of chs 1–9 is the choice between the path of wisdom, and hence of life, or the path of the loose woman that leads to death (see final summary in vv. 20–22). *Paths of justice* denotes the righteous behavior God requires. **9:** Here the qualities listed in 1.3 are reiterated and associated with *every good path* (i.e., a range of moral options one might take). **16:** *Loose,* Heb "zarah" (lit. "strange, foreign"); see 5.1–23n.; 7.5; 22.14. *Adulteress,* Heb "nokriyyah" (lit. "alien" or possibly "foreign" woman); see 5.20; 6.24; 7.5; 23.27. These are parallel terms for the same woman who is essentially "other" and clearly threatens marital life. **17:** *Sacred covenant* (lit. "covenant of her God") refers to marriage (cf. Mal 2.10–16). **18:** *The shades,* the dead. **19:** *Never come back,* the route to death is a one-way ticket (Job 7.9).

3.1–12: Instruction in the fear of the LORD. 2: *Length of days and years of life,* longevity is a gift of wisdom (3.18; 8.25; 9.11). **3:** Wisdom's values are to be worn around the *neck* as an amulet or ornament (cf. Deut 6.6–9 in reference to the commandments of God), i.e., intimately and personally appropriated and written *on the tablet of your heart,* i.e., memorized and internalized; cf. 3.22; 6.20–21; 7.3. **5:** *Do not rely on your own insight,* not an anti-intellectual admonition but a warning against arrogance. **7b:** See 1.7n. **8:** In addition to being associated with life (3.2n.) wisdom is also linked with health and healing (4.22; 12.18). **9–10:** *First fruits,* see Ex 23.19; Deut 26.1–11. This is one of the few references in Proverbs to ritual practices (see also 7.14n.). Honoring God in this

¹¹ My child, do not despise the LORD's
　　discipline
　　or be weary of his reproof,
¹² for the LORD reproves the one he loves,
　　as a father the son in whom he delights.

¹³ Happy are those who find wisdom,
　　and those who get understanding,
¹⁴ for her income is better than silver,
　　and her revenue better than gold.
¹⁵ She is more precious than jewels,
　　and nothing you desire can compare
　　　with her.
¹⁶ Long life is in her right hand;
　　in her left hand are riches and honor.
¹⁷ Her ways are ways of pleasantness,
　　and all her paths are peace.
¹⁸ She is a tree of life to those who lay hold
　　　of her;
　　those who hold her fast are called
　　　happy.

¹⁹ The LORD by wisdom founded the earth;
　　by understanding he established the
　　　heavens;
²⁰ by his knowledge the deeps broke open,
　　and the clouds drop down the dew.
²¹ My child, do not let these escape from
　　　your sight:
　　keep sound wisdom and prudence,
²² and they will be life for your soul
　　and adornment for your neck.

²³ Then you will walk on your way securely
　　and your foot will not stumble.
²⁴ If you sit down,^a you will not be afraid;
　　when you lie down, your sleep will be
　　　sweet.
²⁵ Do not be afraid of sudden panic,
　　or of the storm that strikes the wicked;
²⁶ for the LORD will be your confidence
　　and will keep your foot from being
　　　caught.

²⁷ Do not withhold good from those to
　　　whom it is due,^b
　　when it is in your power to do it.
²⁸ Do not say to your neighbor, "Go, and
　　　come again,
　　tomorrow I will give it"—when you
　　　have it with you.
²⁹ Do not plan harm against your
　　　neighbor
　　who lives trustingly beside you.
³⁰ Do not quarrel with anyone without
　　　cause,
　　when no harm has been done to you.
³¹ Do not envy the violent
　　and do not choose any of their ways;
³² for the perverse are an abomination to
　　　the LORD,
　　but the upright are in his confidence.

a　Gk: Heb *lie down*
b　Heb *from its owners*

way leads to future plentiful harvests. **11–12:** Suffering is understood here as a sign of God's discipline (Deut 8.5; Ps 94.12–13), a sentiment echoed by the friends of Job (e.g., Job 5.17–18).

3.13–20: A description of Wisdom. 13: *Happy are those* is a characteristic wisdom formula (8.34; 20.7; 28.14; 29.18; 31.28; Ps 1.1) often called a beatitude (cf. Mt 5.3–11; Lk 6.20–23). Beatitudes extol a virtue or experience by exclaiming how fortunate its possessor is. **14–15:** Cf. Job 28.15–19 and see 2.4n. Wisdom transcends all attempts at comparison. **16:** The imagery echoes that of the Egyptian goddess Ma'at, who represents right order. She was portrayed with the symbols of life in one hand and of wealth and prestige in the other. **18:** *Tree of life*, a symbol of longevity and well-being, but also a source of eternal life in Gen 2.9; 3.22, from which humans are barred. It is also an Egyptian motif, associated with the sycamore tree. **19–20:** This is the first association of wisdom with creation, expanded in 8.22–31. It shows the integral part that wisdom played in the divine creative act. *The deeps* represent the subterranean waters of chaos over which God has ultimate control (cf. Ps 29.10); the *dew*, the moisture from above that continues to sustain the earth.

3.21–35: An admonition, six prohibitions and three aphorisms on the fate of righteous and wicked. 22: Cf. v. 3n. **23–26:** Along with life (v. 2n.) and health (v. 8n.), security is one of the benefits of wisdom (e.g., 2.11–12; 4.12; 10.25). **25:** *Do not* is the language of prohibition, used six times in succession here in short, proverbial-type sentences. *Sudden panic* is usually associated with unexpected disaster (cf. 1.26–27). **27–28:** The language suggests that the issue concerns loans and their repayment (cf. 6.1–5; 11.24). **31:** Envy of *the violent* may spring from their seeming prosperity. **32:** *Abomination to the LORD* has a special meaning in Proverbs in reference of moral offenses that God finds loathsome, often concerning falsity in speech, thought, or words.

33 The LORD's curse is on the house of the
    wicked,
    but he blesses the abode of the
       righteous.
34 Toward the scorners he is scornful,
    but to the humble he shows favor.
35 The wise will inherit honor,
    but stubborn fools, disgrace.

4 Listen, children, to a father's instruction,
    and be attentive, that you may gain[a]
       insight;
2 for I give you good precepts:
    do not forsake my teaching.
3 When I was a son with my father,
    tender, and my mother's favorite,
4 he taught me, and said to me,
    "Let your heart hold fast my words;
    keep my commandments, and live.
5 Get wisdom; get insight: do not forget,
    nor turn away
    from the words of my mouth.
6 Do not forsake her, and she will keep you;
    love her, and she will guard you.
7 The beginning of wisdom is this: Get
       wisdom,
    and whatever else you get, get insight.
8 Prize her highly, and she will exalt you;
    she will honor you if you embrace her.
9 She will place on your head a fair garland;
    she will bestow on you a beautiful
       crown."

10 Hear, my child, and accept my words,
    that the years of your life may be many.
11 I have taught you the way of wisdom;
    I have led you in the paths of
       uprightness.
12 When you walk, your step will not be
       hampered;

    and if you run, you will not stumble.
13 Keep hold of instruction; do not let go;
    guard her, for she is your life.
14 Do not enter the path of the wicked,
    and do not walk in the way of evildoers.
15 Avoid it; do not go on it;
    turn away from it and pass on.
16 For they cannot sleep unless they have
       done wrong;
    they are robbed of sleep unless they
       have made someone stumble.
17 For they eat the bread of wickedness
    and drink the wine of violence.
18 But the path of the righteous is like the
       light of dawn,
    which shines brighter and brighter until
       full day.
19 The way of the wicked is like deep
       darkness;
    they do not know what they stumble
       over.
20 My child, be attentive to my words;
    incline your ear to my sayings.
21 Do not let them escape from your sight;
    keep them within your heart.
22 For they are life to those who find them,
    and healing to all their flesh.
23 Keep your heart with all vigilance,
    for from it flow the springs of life.
24 Put away from you crooked speech,
    and put devious talk far from you.
25 Let your eyes look directly forward,
    and your gaze be straight before you.
26 Keep straight the path of your feet,
    and all your ways will be sure.
27 Do not swerve to the right or to the left;
    turn your foot away from evil.

a Heb *know*

4.1–9: Get wisdom, get insight. The father's instruction is now emphasized, and he recalls his instruction from his own father (v. 3). The message passed down from generation to generation remains the same: "Get wisdom, get insight" (vv. 5,7). **6–8:** *Love . . . embrace* suggests the metaphor of wisdom as the beloved wife (cf. 5.15–20; 7.4; 31.20–31). **9:** See 1.9n.

4.10–27: The two paths. The father's instruction continues with the image of two alternate paths: that of wisdom/righteousness or that of the wicked. It is a common image in the book (1.15–6; 2.7–20; 3.6,17,23; 5.5,21; 6.23; 7.25; 8.13,20,32; 9.6; 10.9; 11.5; 16.17; 28.6). **18–19:** In keeping with the binary way of understanding reality common in Proverbs, the ways of righteous and wicked are compared to light and dark. **24:** *Crooked speech* is the dark side of Proverbs' emphasis on proper speech and speech ethics. **25–27:** What is *straight* is an image of righteousness and correct conduct. The contrast between crooked and straight is a fundamental metaphor in the wisdom tradition (cf. 8.8–9).

5

My child, be attentive to my wisdom;
  incline your ear to my understanding,
[2] so that you may hold on to prudence,
  and your lips may guard knowledge.
[3] For the lips of a loose[a] woman drip honey,
  and her speech is smoother than oil;
[4] but in the end she is bitter as wormwood,
  sharp as a two-edged sword.
[5] Her feet go down to death;
  her steps follow the path to Sheol.
[6] She does not keep straight to the path of
    life;
  her ways wander, and she does not
    know it.

[7] And now, my child,[b] listen to me,
  and do not depart from the words of my
    mouth.
[8] Keep your way far from her,
  and do not go near the door of her
    house;
[9] or you will give your honor to others,
  and your years to the merciless,
[10] and strangers will take their fill of your
    wealth,
  and your labors will go to the house of
    an alien;
[11] and at the end of your life you will groan,
  when your flesh and body are
    consumed,
[12] and you say, "Oh, how I hated discipline,
  and my heart despised reproof!
[13] I did not listen to the voice of my
    teachers
  or incline my ear to my instructors.

[14] Now I am at the point of utter ruin
  in the public assembly."

[15] Drink water from your own cistern,
  flowing water from your own well.
[16] Should your springs be scattered abroad,
  streams of water in the streets?
[17] Let them be for yourself alone,
  and not for sharing with strangers.
[18] Let your fountain be blessed,
  and rejoice in the wife of your youth,
[19] a lovely deer, a graceful doe.
May her breasts satisfy you at all times;
  may you be intoxicated always by her
    love.
[20] Why should you be intoxicated, my son,
  by another woman
  and embrace the bosom of an
    adulteress?
[21] For human ways are under the eyes of
    the LORD,
  and he examines all their paths.
[22] The iniquities of the wicked ensnare them,
  and they are caught in the toils of their
    sin.
[23] They die for lack of discipline,
  and because of their great folly they are
    lost.

6

My child, if you have given your pledge
  to your neighbor,
  if you have bound yourself to another,[c]

[a] Heb *strange*
[b] Gk Vg: Heb *children*
[c] Or *a stranger*

5.1–23: Avoid the temptations of the loose woman. The antithesis to woman Wisdom is the loose or strange woman (Heb "zarah," vv. 3,20a) who is also described as an adulteress (Heb "nokriyyah," v. 20b; lit., "alien"). Since the Heb words literally mean "strange" and "foreign," the terminology may reflect the postexilic prohibition of marriage to foreign women (Ezra 9–10; Neh 13.23–30). See 2.16n. Probably a prostitute, she may also be another man's wife (7.19). She is aligned with the path of the wicked which is ultimately the path to death (v. 5). 3: *Smooth speech*, like crooked talk (4.24n.) is another dark side of speech. 4: *Wormwood*, an extremely bitter and poisonous herbal extract. 5: *Sheol*, the abode of the dead; see 1.12n. 9: Probably a reference to the young man's youthful, sexual vigor, wasted on a union that will bear no fruit. 10: Probably a reference to loss of earnings: prostitutes are expensive! 14: *Ruin in the public assembly*, public shame was a strong deterrent and was used for social control (cf. Ezra 10.8). 15–16: *Water* is a euphemism for sexual activity (cf. Song 4.12b,15). *Your own cistern* and *well* refer to "your wife" as the source of that water. *Springs* refer to male sexual activity, which is wasted in this context, with water in the streets possibly indicating offspring outside marriage. 18–19: Exhortation to rejoice in sexual intimacy with one's own wife. *Fountain* refers to her sexual organs, seen as the property of her husband, and possibly to the offspring that will ensue. Comparing a lover to *deer* or *doe*, cf. Song 2.9,17; 4.5. 22–23: The metaphor represents humans as game animals and *folly* and *sin* as hidden, fatal traps that require *discipline* (Heb "musar"; 1.23n.) to avoid. Cf. 1.17–18.

² you are snared by the utterance of your
    lips,ᵃ
  caught by the words of your mouth.
³ So do this, my child, and save yourself,
    for you have come into your neighbor's
      power:
  go, hurry,ᵇ and plead with your
    neighbor.
⁴ Give your eyes no sleep
  and your eyelids no slumber;
⁵ save yourself like a gazelle from the
    hunter,ᶜ
  like a bird from the hand of the fowler.

⁶ Go to the ant, you lazybones;
  consider its ways, and be wise.
⁷ Without having any chief
  or officer or ruler,
⁸ it prepares its food in summer,
  and gathers its sustenance in
    harvest.
⁹ How long will you lie there, O lazybones?
  When will you rise from your sleep?
¹⁰ A little sleep, a little slumber,
  a little folding of the hands to rest,
¹¹ and poverty will come upon you like a
    robber,
  and want, like an armed warrior.

¹² A scoundrel and a villain
  goes around with crooked speech,
¹³ winking the eyes, shuffling the feet,
  pointing the fingers,
¹⁴ with perverted mind devising evil,
  continually sowing discord;
¹⁵ on such a one calamity will descend
    suddenly;
  in a moment, damage beyond repair.

¹⁶ There are six things that the Lᴏʀᴅ
    hates,
  seven that are an abomination to
    him:
¹⁷ haughty eyes, a lying tongue,
  and hands that shed innocent blood,
¹⁸ a heart that devises wicked plans,
  feet that hurry to run to evil,
¹⁹ a lying witness who testifies falsely,
  and one who sows discord in a
    family.

²⁰ My child, keep your father's
    commandment,
  and do not forsake your mother's
    teaching.
²¹ Bind them upon your heart always;
  tie them around your neck.
²² When you walk, theyᵈ will lead you;
  when you lie down, theyᵈ will watch
    over you;
  and when you awake, theyᵈ will talk
    with you.
²³ For the commandment is a lamp and the
    teaching a light,
  and the reproofs of discipline are the
    way of life,
²⁴ to preserve you from the wife of
    another,ᵉ
  from the smooth tongue of the
    adulteress.
²⁵ Do not desire her beauty in your
    heart,

ᵃ Cn Compare Gk Syr: Heb *the words of your mouth*
ᵇ Or *humble yourself*
ᶜ Cn: Heb *from the hand*
ᵈ Heb *it*
ᵉ Gk: MT *the evil woman*

6.1–19: Practical admonitions. 1–5: The dangers of acting as a surety or guarantor for another who is borrowing money because he is in debt (cf. 11.15; 17.18; 20.16; 22.26–27). **5:** See 5.22–23n. Admonition to extricate
oneself, however debasing or difficult it may seem, suggests the seriousness of the danger. **6–11:** Didactic
comparison with plants or animals is a common technique in wisdom literature (cf. 30.15–19; 24–31; see also
Judg 9.5–8; 1 Kings 4.33–34). Laziness is a frequent topic in Proverbs (cf. 10.26; 18.9; 20.4,13; 22.13; 24.30–34;
26.13–16). **12–15:** Warnings against worthless and unsavory types. **12:** *Crooked speech* indicates deceitful talk. **13:**
Winking the eyes, shuffling the feet, and *pointing the fingers* are forms of body language that indicate character.
16–19: A numerical saying (cf. 30.18–21; Am 1.3–2.8) concerning seven vices disliked by the Lᴏʀᴅ. *Abomination*,
see 3.32n.
    6.20–35: The dangers of adultery. 20: *Father* and *mother*, see 1.8n. **21:** For the idea of binding and tying the
teachings to the body, cf. 3.3n.; Deut 6.6–8. **23:** The importance of *discipline* is a favorite theme of the wise.
24–29: The *wife of another*, i.e., an adulteress, is the subject here. A contrast is made (v. 26) between a mere

and do not let her capture you with her
eyelashes;
²⁶ for a prostitute's fee is only a loaf of
bread,ᵃ
but the wife of another stalks a man's
very life.
²⁷ Can fire be carried in the bosom
without burning one's clothes?
²⁸ Or can one walk on hot coals
without scorching the feet?
²⁹ So is he who sleeps with his neighbor's
wife;
no one who touches her will go
unpunished.
³⁰ Thieves are not despised who steal only
to satisfy their appetite when they are
hungry.
³¹ Yet if they are caught, they will pay
sevenfold;
they will forfeit all the goods of their
house.
³² But he who commits adultery has no
sense;
he who does it destroys himself.
³³ He will get wounds and dishonor,
and his disgrace will not be wiped away.
³⁴ For jealousy arouses a husband's fury,
and he shows no restraint when he
takes revenge.
³⁵ He will accept no compensation,
and refuses a bribe no matter how
great.

7 My child, keep my words
and store up my commandments with
you;
² keep my commandments and live,

keep my teachings as the apple of your
eye;
³ bind them on your fingers,
write them on the tablet of your heart.
⁴ Say to wisdom, "You are my sister,"
and call insight your intimate friend,
⁵ that they may keep you from the looseᵇ
woman,
from the adulteress with her smooth
words.

⁶ For at the window of my house
I looked out through my lattice,
⁷ and I saw among the simple ones,
I observed among the youths,
a young man without sense,
⁸ passing along the street near her corner,
taking the road to her house
⁹ in the twilight, in the evening,
at the time of night and darkness.

¹⁰ Then a woman comes toward him,
decked out like a prostitute, wily of
heart.ᶜ
¹¹ She is loud and wayward;
her feet do not stay at home;
¹² now in the street, now in the squares,
and at every corner she lies in wait.
¹³ She seizes him and kisses him,
and with impudent face she says to him:
¹⁴ "I had to offer sacrifices,
and today I have paid my vows;

ᵃ Cn Compare Gk Syr Vg Tg: Heb *for because of a
harlot to a piece of bread*
ᵇ Heb *strange*
ᶜ Meaning of Heb uncertain

prostitute and the social harm caused by succumbing to another man's wife. This suggests that the issue was not simply sexual conduct itself but the danger posed to the social system—including the system of inheritance—by adultery, which could result in uncertainty about paternity. **30–31:** The comparison is made with *thieves* for whom punishment for a seemingly minor crime is quite extensive, including forfeiture of property. **32–35:** For the adulterer retribution is worse and inescapable. In Lev 20.10 adultery is explicitly a capital crime; Proverbs seems to be aware of this (see v. 26), but focuses on the emotions and personal revenge of the cuckolded husband.

7.1–27: Another warning against the loose woman. 2–3: *Apple of your eye,* i.e., pupil. The triad of eye, fingers, and heart denotes the whole person. Binding on *fingers* and writing on the *tablet of your heart* recalls Deuteronomic exhortations about the law (Deut 6.8; 11.18); cf. 3.3n. **4:** *Sister* here does not imply kinship, but is a conventional term of endearment for the beloved (Song 4.9–12; 5.1). *Intimate friend* could be male or female, and the envisaged relationship is an egalitarian one. **6–23:** A seduction by the loose woman is described in narrative form. **10:** It is not clear whether the woman is a *prostitute* or simply dressed as one. Since she is married (vv. 19–20), the act is clearly one of adultery (cf. 6.24–35). **11:** *Loud,* also characteristic of folly in 9.13. **12:** *Street,*

¹⁵ so now I have come out to meet you,
  to seek you eagerly, and I have found
    you!
¹⁶ I have decked my couch with coverings,
  colored spreads of Egyptian linen;
¹⁷ I have perfumed my bed with myrrh,
  aloes, and cinnamon.
¹⁸ Come, let us take our fill of love until
    morning;
  let us delight ourselves with love.
¹⁹ For my husband is not at home;
  he has gone on a long journey.
²⁰ He took a bag of money with him;
  he will not come home until full moon."

²¹ With much seductive speech she
    persuades him;
  with her smooth talk she compels him.
²² Right away he follows her,
  and goes like an ox to the slaughter,
or bounds like a stag toward the trapᵃ
    ²³ until an arrow pierces its entrails.
He is like a bird rushing into a snare,
  not knowing that it will cost him his life.

²⁴ And now, my children, listen to me,
  and be attentive to the words of my
    mouth.
²⁵ Do not let your hearts turn aside to her
    ways;
  do not stray into her paths.
²⁶ For many are those she has laid low,
  and numerous are her victims.
²⁷ Her house is the way to Sheol,
  going down to the chambers of death.

8 Does not wisdom call,
  and does not understanding raise her
    voice?
² On the heights, beside the way,
  at the crossroads she takes her stand;
³ beside the gates in front of the town,
  at the entrance of the portals she cries
    out:
⁴ "To you, O people, I call,
  and my cry is to all that live.
⁵ O simple ones, learn prudence;
  acquire intelligence, you who lack it.
⁶ Hear, for I will speak noble things,
  and from my lips will come what is
    right;
⁷ for my mouth will utter truth;
  wickedness is an abomination to my
    lips.
⁸ All the words of my mouth are righteous;
  there is nothing twisted or crooked in
    them.
⁹ They are all straight to one who
    understands
  and right to those who find
    knowledge.
¹⁰ Take my instruction instead of silver,
  and knowledge rather than choice gold;
¹¹ for wisdom is better than jewels,
  and all that you may desire cannot
    compare with her.
¹² I, wisdom, live with prudence,ᵇ
  and I attain knowledge and discretion.
¹³ The fear of the Lord is hatred of evil.

ᵃ Cn Compare Gk: Meaning of Heb uncertain
ᵇ Meaning of Heb uncertain

squares, corner, also spaces where wisdom is found in 1.20. The seductive woman is her polar opposite. **14:** The act of offering *sacrifices* and *vows* could suggest that this woman was participating in a non-Israelite fertility ritual, although an Israelite worship situation is possible (cf. Lev 7.16). **17:** *Myrrh* is an aromatic resin; *aloes and cinnamon* are expensive aromatic spices imported from Arabia and South Asia. Their mention creates an atmosphere of expensive lushness (cf. Song 1.13; 3.6; 4.6,11,14–16; 5.5,13). **21:** *Seductive speech* and *smooth talk* (cf. 2.16) are part of the repertoire of negative and dangerous forms of speech Proverbs warns against (see 4.24n.). **22–27:** The emphasis on the "strange woman's" inexorable pull toward death heightens her stark opposition to Wisdom, personified as a woman who offers life (3.16; 8.35–36). **27:** *Sheol*, the abode of the dead. Sheol was thought to have many chambers (probably seven), of which the "depths" was the worst (cf. 9.18).

  8.1–36: Woman Wisdom calls (cf. Sir 24.1–34; Wis 7.22–8.1). This chapter contains the most profoundly developed depiction of Woman Wisdom in Proverbs, especially vv. 22–31 where she is aligned with God at creation. **1–5:** Public address of Wisdom to all people; cf. 1.20–33, and especially to those who need to learn *prudence* and *intelligence*. **6–9:** Woman Wisdom is the antithesis to the loose woman and her deceptively smooth speech (2.16; 5.3; 7.21): she utters *truth*, and *righteous* and *straight* words. **10–11:** See 2.4n. Wisdom is more valuable than any precious metals or jewels (cf. v. 19; 2.4; Job 28.15–19). **13:** *Fear of the Lord*, see 1.7n. The divine

Pride and arrogance and the way of evil
and perverted speech I hate.
14 I have good advice and sound wisdom;
I have insight, I have strength.
15 By me kings reign,
and rulers decree what is just;
16 by me rulers rule,
and nobles, all who govern rightly.
17 I love those who love me,
and those who seek me diligently find
me.
18 Riches and honor are with me,
enduring wealth and prosperity.
19 My fruit is better than gold, even fine
gold,
and my yield than choice silver.
20 I walk in the way of righteousness,
along the paths of justice,
21 endowing with wealth those who love
me,
and filling their treasuries.
22 The LORD created me at the beginning[a]
of his work,[b]
the first of his acts of long ago.
23 Ages ago I was set up,
at the first, before the beginning of the
earth.
24 When there were no depths I was
brought forth,
when there were no springs abounding
with water.
25 Before the mountains had been shaped,

before the hills, I was brought forth—
26 when he had not yet made earth and
fields,[c]
or the world's first bits of soil.
27 When he established the heavens, I was
there,
when he drew a circle on the face of the
deep,
28 when he made firm the skies above,
when he established the fountains of
the deep,
29 when he assigned to the sea its limit,
so that the waters might not transgress
his command,
when he marked out the foundations of
the earth,
30 then I was beside him, like a master
worker;[d]
and I was daily his[e] delight,
rejoicing before him always,
31 rejoicing in his inhabited world
and delighting in the human race.

32 "And now, my children, listen to me:
happy are those who keep my
ways.

a   Or me as the beginning
b   Heb way
c   Meaning of Heb uncertain
d   Another reading is little child
e   Gk: Heb lacks his

dimension is introduced and it is clear that this figure and God are at one in their opposition to *evil*. **15–16:** Her authority is that by which *kings reign*. For the close association between wisdom and just rule see also 16.10,13; 20.26,28; 25.1–7; 28.2–3,15–16; 29.2,12,14,16,26; 30.27–31; 31.1–9. Solomon's prayer for wisdom (1 Kings 3.7–9), his wise judgment (1 Kings 3.16–29), and administrative skill (1Kings 4) are narrative examples of this idea. **17:** In contrast to Job 28, which represents wisdom as hidden and elusive, Proverbs emphasizes the responsiveness and accessibility of wisdom to those who *love* and *seek* her; cf. Sir 4.14; Wis 6.12–13. The relationship is two-way: Wisdom will respond to *those who love me*. **18–21:** The word translated *prosperity* in v. 18 and *righteousness* in v. 20 is the same in Hebrew ("tsedaqah"). In general the wisdom tradition believed that moral well-being led to material well-being, though the "better than" sayings (e.g., 16.8) stress the superiority of moral values. **21:** Following Wisdom leads to material wealth; the wise are ever pragmatic. **22–31:** Wisdom recounts her origins as created by God before the physical world came into being and her role as God's helper in creation (cf. Sir 1.4; 24.9). God's ordered creation of the world is then described. **22:** *Created,* the proper translation of the Heb word ("qanah") is debated, but "acquired" (see 4.5,7) or "engendered, conceived" (Gen 4.1) are also possible. **23:** *Set up,* the same term used in Ps 2.6 for the Israelite king. **24–29:** An account of creation; cf. Gen 1; Job 28.25–27; 38.4–11; Ps 104.5–9. **30:** The word translated *master worker* or "little child" (see textual note d) suggests either an actual role for Wisdom in setting up the world or an image related to the sense of delight expressed in v. 30b. Comparisons have been made with the Egyptian goddess Ma'at, daughter of the creator god Amun Re, who is sometimes depicted as a little child playing on his lap. **32–36:** The *life . . . death* contrast is a fundamental trope in Proverbs. See 2.18–19; 3.2,16–18; 4.4,13; 5.5–6; 7.27; 9.11; 11.19; etc.

33 Hear instruction and be wise,
and do not neglect it.
34 Happy is the one who listens to me,
watching daily at my gates,
waiting beside my doors.
35 For whoever finds me finds life
and obtains favor from the LORD;
36 but those who miss me injure themselves;
all who hate me love death."

9 Wisdom has built her house,
she has hewn her seven pillars.
2 She has slaughtered her animals, she has
mixed her wine,
she has also set her table.
3 She has sent out her servant-girls, she
calls
from the highest places in the town,
4 "You that are simple, turn in here!"
To those without sense she says,
5 "Come, eat of my bread
and drink of the wine I have mixed.
6 Lay aside immaturity,[a] and live,
and walk in the way of insight."

7 Whoever corrects a scoffer wins abuse;
whoever rebukes the wicked gets hurt.
8 A scoffer who is rebuked will only hate
you;
the wise, when rebuked, will love you.
9 Give instruction[b] to the wise, and they
will become wiser still;
teach the righteous and they will gain in
learning.

10 The fear of the LORD is the beginning of
wisdom,
and the knowledge of the Holy One is
insight.
11 For by me your days will be multiplied,
and years will be added to your life.
12 If you are wise, you are wise for
yourself;
if you scoff, you alone will bear it.

13 The foolish woman is loud;
she is ignorant and knows nothing.
14 She sits at the door of her house,
on a seat at the high places of the
town,
15 calling to those who pass by,
who are going straight on their way,
16 "You who are simple, turn in here!"
And to those without sense she says,
17 "Stolen water is sweet,
and bread eaten in secret is pleasant."
18 But they do not know that the dead[c] are
there,
that her guests are in the depths of
Sheol.

10 The proverbs of Solomon.

A wise child makes a glad father,
but a foolish child is a mother's grief.

a Or *simpleness*
b Heb lacks *instruction*
c Heb *shades*

9.1–18: Wisdom's banquet. The tension between invitations to a banquet given by Wisdom and one given by the *foolish woman* (v. 13; Heb "'eshet kesilut," a variant on the loose woman), is developed here, with a section of aphorisms contrasting *scoffers* with *the wise* dividing the two calls (vv. 7–12). **1:** *Seven pillars* may allude simply to the pillars of Wisdom's house or may suggest the pillars on which the earth was founded (Job 9.6; 26.11; Ps 75.3; cf. 8.29–30). The number seven denotes completeness. **2:** *Slaughtered her animals* and *mixed her wine* suggests a feast. Wine was sometimes mixed with spices (cf. Song 8.2). **4:** Her call is to the *simple,* meaning the untutored rather than simpletons, and to *those without sense,* who are clearly susceptible to seduction (cf. v. 16 in reference to the foolish woman's charms). **7–9:** Proverbs uses several different terms to contrast with the wise. The *scoffer* is characterized by arrogance and self-absorption (21.24) and hence lacks the receptiveness to correction displayed by the wise (cf. 13.1; 15.12). **10:** *Fear of the LORD,* see 1.7n. **17:** *Stolen water* is probably a euphemism for illicit sex (see 5.15–16n.). **18:** This woman's banquet (like that of the loose woman, 2.18–19; 5.5; 7.27) entertains the dead in the deepest chamber of *Sheol* (see 7.27n.).

10.1–22.16: Proverbial sayings. A long series of separate two-line sayings, sometimes connected by catchwords and thematic associations or forming small clusters. Most probably originally circulated orally. Opposites such as wise and foolish, righteous and wicked are frequently juxtaposed. Antithetic parallelism, in which the second line restates the first line in an opposite way, is used more frequently in chs 10–15, while 16–22 favor synonymous or synthetic parallelism, in which the second line repeats or extends the thought of the first. **10.1:**

² Treasures gained by wickedness do not
profit,
but righteousness delivers from death.
³ The LORD does not let the righteous go
hungry,
but he thwarts the craving of the
wicked.
⁴ A slack hand causes poverty,
but the hand of the diligent makes rich.
⁵ A child who gathers in summer is
prudent,
but a child who sleeps in harvest brings
shame.
⁶ Blessings are on the head of the
righteous,
but the mouth of the wicked conceals
violence.
⁷ The memory of the righteous is a
blessing,
but the name of the wicked will rot.
⁸ The wise of heart will heed
commandments,
but a babbling fool will come to ruin.
⁹ Whoever walks in integrity walks
securely,
but whoever follows perverse ways will
be found out.
¹⁰ Whoever winks the eye causes trouble,
but the one who rebukes boldly makes
peace.ᵃ
¹¹ The mouth of the righteous is a fountain
of life,
but the mouth of the wicked conceals
violence.
¹² Hatred stirs up strife,
but love covers all offenses.

¹³ On the lips of one who has
understanding wisdom is found,
but a rod is for the back of one who
lacks sense.
¹⁴ The wise lay up knowledge,
but the babbling of a fool brings ruin
near.
¹⁵ The wealth of the rich is their fortress;
the poverty of the poor is their ruin.
¹⁶ The wage of the righteous leads to life,
the gain of the wicked to sin.
¹⁷ Whoever heeds instruction is on the
path to life,
but one who rejects a rebuke goes
astray.
¹⁸ Lying lips conceal hatred,
and whoever utters slander is a fool.
¹⁹ When words are many, transgression is
not lacking,
but the prudent are restrained in
speech.
²⁰ The tongue of the righteous is choice
silver;
the mind of the wicked is of little worth.
²¹ The lips of the righteous feed many,
but fools die for lack of sense.
²² The blessing of the LORD makes rich,
and he adds no sorrow with it.ᵇ
²³ Doing wrong is like sport to a fool,
but wise conduct is pleasure to a person
of understanding.
²⁴ What the wicked dread will come upon
them,

ᵃ Gk: Heb *but a babbling fool will come to ruin*
ᵇ Or *and toil adds nothing to it*

Proverbs of Solomon, see Introduction. This proverb (cf. 15.20) links with the parental instruction found in chs 1–9 (e.g., 1.8) and acts as a bridge between the two sections. The effects of wise and foolish children is a frequent topic; cf. v. 5; 13.1; 15.20; 17.21,25; 19.13,26. **2–3:** Affirmation of the doctrine of divine retribution whereby the righteous are rewarded and the wicked punished; cf. 3.2,16; 9.11; 10.27; 13.12. Other proverbs complicate this doctrine of divine reward and punishment (e.g., 15.16; 16.8), and the books of Job and Ecclesiastes challenge it profoundly. **4–5:** Laziness is a major theme of Proverbs: it leads directly to poverty, while diligence leads to material prosperity (cf. 6.6–11; 12.24,27; 13.4; 15.19). **7:** The remembering of one's *name* and deeds by children and community is a sign of blessing in biblical and Jewish tradition. **8:** Numerous proverbs in this chapter address the topic of the power of speech for good or ill. See vv. 11,13–14,18–21,31–32. The topic is prominent throughout Proverbs, e.g., 2.12; 12.13–14,17–19,22–23; 13.3; 22.14; 24.26; 25.15; 26.28; 31.26. **9:** *Walks . . . ways*, see 1.15n. **10:** He who *winks the eye* is not to be trusted as it suggests covert activity (cf. 6.13). **11:** Four things are said to be a fountain of life in this section: the teaching of the wise (13.14), revering the LORD (14.27), Wisdom (16.22), and here, the *mouth of the righteous*, i.e., their speech. **15–16:** Verse 15 is a neutral observation about the reality of *wealth* and *poverty*; v. 16 adds ethical comments on the *gain of the wicked*. Cf. 11.28 and 18.11, where the protection of wealth is declared to be illusory. **18–21:** See v. 8n. Different parts of the mouth are featured to reiter-

but the desire of the righteous will be
granted.
25 When the tempest passes, the wicked
are no more,
but the righteous are established
forever.
26 Like vinegar to the teeth, and smoke to
the eyes,
so are the lazy to their employers.
27 The fear of the LORD prolongs life,
but the years of the wicked will be short.
28 The hope of the righteous ends in gladness,
but the expectation of the wicked
comes to nothing.
29 The way of the LORD is a stronghold for
the upright,
but destruction for evildoers.
30 The righteous will never be removed,
but the wicked will not remain in the land.
31 The mouth of the righteous brings forth
wisdom,
but the perverse tongue will be cut off.
32 The lips of the righteous know what is
acceptable,
but the mouth of the wicked what is
perverse.

11 A false balance is an abomination to
the LORD,
but an accurate weight is his delight.
2 When pride comes, then comes disgrace;
but wisdom is with the humble.
3 The integrity of the upright guides them,
but the crookedness of the treacherous
destroys them.
4 Riches do not profit in the day of wrath,
but righteousness delivers from death.
5 The righteousness of the blameless keeps
their ways straight,
but the wicked fall by their own
wickedness.

6 The righteousness of the upright saves
them,
but the treacherous are taken captive by
their schemes.
7 When the wicked die, their hope
perishes,
and the expectation of the godless
comes to nothing.
8 The righteous are delivered from trouble,
and the wicked get into it instead.
9 With their mouths the godless would
destroy their neighbors,
but by knowledge the righteous are
delivered.
10 When it goes well with the righteous, the
city rejoices;
and when the wicked perish, there is
jubilation.
11 By the blessing of the upright a city is
exalted,
but it is overthrown by the mouth of the
wicked.
12 Whoever belittles another lacks sense,
but an intelligent person remains silent.
13 A gossip goes about telling secrets,
but one who is trustworthy in spirit
keeps a confidence.
14 Where there is no guidance, a nation[a]
falls,
but in an abundance of counselors
there is safety.
15 To guarantee loans for a stranger brings
trouble,
but there is safety in refusing to do so.
16 A gracious woman gets honor,
but she who hates virtue is covered
with shame.[b]

a Or an army
b Compare Gk Syr: Heb lacks but she ... shame

ate the need for restraint. **24**: See vv. 2–3n. **25**: *The tempest* may represent divine judgment (e.g., 1.27; Isa 21.2;
29.6; 66.15; Ps 83.16). **26**: See 6.6–11n. **27**: *The fear of the LORD*, see 1.7n and 3.2n. **28–30**: See vv. 2–3n. **31–32**: See
v. 8n. **11.1**: Weights and balances and their misuse is another recurring theme in Proverbs (see 16.11; 20.10,23; cf.
Lev 19.35–37; Deut 25.13–16). **2**: The *humble* are closely associated with the wise (15.33; 18.12; 22.4; Sir 3.17–24).
3: The wisdom tradition often observes how those who intend to harm others end up harming themselves; cf.
v. 6; 26.27; Job 18.7–8. **5–11**: Here, in vv. 18–21, and throughout chs 10–15 the primary contrast terms are the
righteous and the *wicked* rather than the wise and the foolish. Passages like 9.7–9 suggest that these terms are
roughly equivalent. **12–13**: The issue of speech ethics is prominent in Proverbs; see 4.24n. and 5.21n. For gossip
cf. 20.19; 25.9; Sir 27.16–17. **14**: *Counselors*, a possible role for the wise themselves. **15**: See 6.1–5n. **16–17**: In v. 16
the NRSV follows the Septuagint, which adds lines b and c. The original MT contrast may have been between
the *gracious woman* who gets honor versus *aggressive* men who gain temporary riches. Taken in parallel with v.

The timid become destitute,[a]
but the aggressive gain riches.

[17] Those who are kind reward themselves,
but the cruel do themselves harm.

[18] The wicked earn no real gain,
but those who sow righteousness get a
true reward.

[19] Whoever is steadfast in righteousness
will live,
but whoever pursues evil will die.

[20] Crooked minds are an abomination to
the LORD,
but those of blameless ways are his
delight.

[21] Be assured, the wicked will not go
unpunished,
but those who are righteous will escape.

[22] Like a gold ring in a pig's snout
is a beautiful woman without good
sense.

[23] The desire of the righteous ends only in
good;
the expectation of the wicked in
wrath.

[24] Some give freely, yet grow all the richer;
others withhold what is due, and only
suffer want.

[25] A generous person will be enriched,
and one who gives water will get water.

[26] The people curse those who hold back
grain,
but a blessing is on the head of those
who sell it.

[27] Whoever diligently seeks good seeks
favor,
but evil comes to the one who searches
for it.

[28] Those who trust in their riches will
wither,[b]

but the righteous will flourish like green
leaves.

[29] Those who trouble their households will
inherit wind,
and the fool will be servant to the wise.

[30] The fruit of the righteous is a tree of life,
but violence[c] takes lives away.

[31] If the righteous are repaid on earth,
how much more the wicked and the
sinner!

12 Whoever loves discipline loves
knowledge,
but those who hate to be rebuked are
stupid.

[2] The good obtain favor from the LORD,
but those who devise evil he condemns.

[3] No one finds security by wickedness,
but the root of the righteous will never
be moved.

[4] A good wife is the crown of her husband,
but she who brings shame is like
rottenness in his bones.

[5] The thoughts of the righteous are just;
the advice of the wicked is treacherous.

[6] The words of the wicked are a deadly
ambush,
but the speech of the upright delivers
them.

[7] The wicked are overthrown and are no
more,
but the house of the righteous will
stand.

[8] One is commended for good sense,
but a perverse mind is despised.

[9] Better to be despised and have a servant,

a Gk: Heb lacks *The timid . . . destitute*
b Cn: Heb *fall*
c Cn Compare Gk Syr: Heb *a wise man*

17 there is a pairing with the *kind* versus the *cruel.* **18–21:** See 10.2–3n. **22:** A single-line proverb containing a criticism of superficial esteem for beauty using an animal comparison. Ear and nose rings were common adornments of women. Such beauty is wasted on both a senseless woman and an unclean pig. **24–26:** These proverbs are linked thematically by the idea of generosity versus greed. The paradox of v. 24 is explained by v. 25: a *generous person* inspires others to reciprocate (cf. v. 17). In contrast, *those who hold back grain* in a time of scarcity, waiting for the price to rise, are cursed by the community. **27:** Seeking and finding that which you seek. Divine *favor* accompanies human favor (cf. 8.35; 12.2; 18.22). **28,30:** Plant imagery often describes the flourishing of *the righteous* (cf. v. 30; Pss 1.3; 92.12–14). **12.1:** The place of *discipline* (Heb "musar") is an important theme in Proverbs (cf. 3.11; 5.12; 13.1; 15.5) and is often paired with the concept of reproof. See 1.23n. **2–3:** See 10.2–3n. **4:** A preoccupation of the wise is the choice of a *good wife* for the young initiate in wisdom (cf. 18.22; 19.31–34; 31.10–31; Sir 26.1–3,13–18). **9:** The "better" saying conveys insight through paradox (cf. 15.16–17; 16.8,19,32; 17.1,12; 19.1,22; 21.9,19; 22.1; 25.24; 27.5,10c; 28.6; Eccl 4.6,13; 7.1–3; 9.4). *Despised* is a strong translation. The word can mean "of

than to be self-important and lack food.
[10] The righteous know the needs of their
  animals,
  but the mercy of the wicked is cruel.
[11] Those who till their land will have plenty
  of food,
  but those who follow worthless pursuits
    have no sense.
[12] The wicked covet the proceeds of
  wickedness,[a]
  but the root of the righteous bears fruit.
[13] The evil are ensnared by the
  transgression of their lips,
  but the righteous escape from trouble.
[14] From the fruit of the mouth one is filled
  with good things,
  and manual labor has its reward.
[15] Fools think their own way is right,
  but the wise listen to advice.
[16] Fools show their anger at once,
  but the prudent ignore an insult.
[17] Whoever speaks the truth gives honest
  evidence,
  but a false witness speaks deceitfully.
[18] Rash words are like sword thrusts,
  but the tongue of the wise brings
    healing.
[19] Truthful lips endure forever,
  but a lying tongue lasts only a moment.
[20] Deceit is in the mind of those who plan
  evil,
  but those who counsel peace have joy.
[21] No harm happens to the righteous,
  but the wicked are filled with trouble.
[22] Lying lips are an abomination to the
  LORD,
  but those who act faithfully are his
    delight.
[23] One who is clever conceals knowledge,
  but the mind of a fool[b] broadcasts folly.
[24] The hand of the diligent will rule,
  while the lazy will be put to forced
    labor.

[25] Anxiety weighs down the human heart,
  but a good word cheers it up.
[26] The righteous gives good advice to
  friends,[c]
  but the way of the wicked leads astray.
[27] The lazy do not roast[d] their game,
  but the diligent obtain precious
    wealth.[d]
[28] In the path of righteousness there is life,
  in walking its path there is no death.

13 A wise child loves discipline,[e]
  but a scoffer does not listen to
    rebuke.
[2] From the fruit of their words good
  persons eat good things,
  but the desire of the treacherous is for
    wrongdoing.
[3] Those who guard their mouths preserve
  their lives;
  those who open wide their lips come to
    ruin.
[4] The appetite of the lazy craves, and gets
  nothing,
  while the appetite of the diligent is
    richly supplied.
[5] The righteous hate falsehood,
  but the wicked act shamefully and
    disgracefully.
[6] Righteousness guards one whose way is
  upright,
  but sin overthrows the wicked.
[7] Some pretend to be rich, yet have
  nothing;
  others pretend to be poor, yet have
    great wealth.
[8] Wealth is a ransom for a person's life,
  but the poor get no threats.

a   Or *covet the catch of the wicked*
b   Heb *the heart of fools*
c   Syr: Meaning of Heb uncertain
d   Meaning of Heb uncertain
e   Cn: Heb *A wise child the discipline of his father*

little account." Cf. Sir 10.27. **10:** What passes for *mercy* with the *wicked* is in fact *cruel*. On the treatment of animals in the first half of the verse, cf. Deut 25.4. **11:** Cf. 28.19. **13–23:** A cluster of sayings on the theme of speech.
See 10.8n.,18–21. **17:** The setting is the law court (cf. 14.25; 25.18). **24:** See 6.6–11n. **25–26:** Internal worry versus
encouragement from outside (cf. 15.13; 17.22). **27:** Some are too *lazy* to cook their own food and so starve in the
midst of abundance (cf. 13.4; 19.24). The *diligent* do not waste such opportunities: an exhortation to good use of
resources. **13.1–3:** Care in listening and speaking is a frequent topic, e.g., vv. 13–14,18; see also 10.8n.,18–21n. **4:**
Cf. v. 25. **7–8,11:** Paradoxes of wealth and poverty. The wise were against excessive wealth, but in favor of a
moderate amount, enough to feel secure. Wealth can even put one in danger of criminal threats (v. 8). Get-rich-

⁹ The light of the righteous rejoices,
  but the lamp of the wicked goes out.
¹⁰ By insolence the heedless make strife,
  but wisdom is with those who take
    advice.
¹¹ Wealth hastily gotten[a] will dwindle,
  but those who gather little by little will
    increase it.
¹² Hope deferred makes the heart sick,
  but a desire fulfilled is a tree of life.
¹³ Those who despise the word bring
    destruction on themselves,
  but those who respect the
    commandment will be rewarded.
¹⁴ The teaching of the wise is a fountain of
    life,
  so that one may avoid the snares of
    death.
¹⁵ Good sense wins favor,
  but the way of the faithless is their
    ruin.[b]
¹⁶ The clever do all things intelligently,
  but the fool displays folly.
¹⁷ A bad messenger brings trouble,
  but a faithful envoy, healing.
¹⁸ Poverty and disgrace are for the one who
    ignores instruction,
  but one who heeds reproof is
    honored.
¹⁹ A desire realized is sweet to the soul,
  but to turn away from evil is an
    abomination to fools.
²⁰ Whoever walks with the wise becomes
    wise,
  but the companion of fools suffers
    harm.

²¹ Misfortune pursues sinners,
  but prosperity rewards the righteous.
²² The good leave an inheritance to their
    children's children,
  but the sinner's wealth is laid up for the
    righteous.
²³ The field of the poor may yield much
    food,
  but it is swept away through injustice.
²⁴ Those who spare the rod hate their
    children,
  but those who love them are diligent to
    discipline them.
²⁵ The righteous have enough to satisfy
    their appetite,
  but the belly of the wicked is empty.

14 The wise woman[c] builds her house,
  but the foolish tears it down with her
    own hands.
² Those who walk uprightly fear the Lord,
  but one who is devious in conduct
    despises him.
³ The talk of fools is a rod for their backs,[d]
  but the lips of the wise preserve them.
⁴ Where there are no oxen, there is no
    grain;
  abundant crops come by the strength
    of the ox.
⁵ A faithful witness does not lie,
  but a false witness breathes out lies.
⁶ A scoffer seeks wisdom in vain,

a Gk Vg: Heb *from vanity*
b Cn Compare Gk Syr Vg Tg: Heb *is enduring*
c Heb *Wisdom of women*
d Cn: Heb *a rod of pride*

quick schemes are not favored but rather careful saving (v. 11). **9:** *Light* and *lamp* are symbols of life (20.20; 24.20; Job 3.20; Ps 97.11). **12:** *Tree of life* is a symbol of the fullness of life, such as humans feel when a *desire* is *fulfilled* (cf. v. 19; 3.18n.; 11.30). **13:** *Word* and *commandment* refer to the advice of the sages, but came to be understood as references to the Torah (Deut 30.11–14; Sir 24.23; Bar 4.1). **14:** See 10.11n. **17:** The *messenger* played an important role (cf. 22.21; 25.13,25; 26.6). They were professionally trained to high standards and enjoyed a high status in society. **21–23:** *Prosperity* is the reward of the righteous according to the doctrine of retribution. This in turn enables those rewards to be passed down through the generations. That the wicked were sometimes prosperous troubled the sages, who resolved the contradiction by assuming that the sinner's wealth (only temporarily enjoyed) goes eventually to the righteous (cf. Job 27.13–17). **23:** Despite their belief in the doctrine of retribution, the sages recognized that not all poverty is caused by laziness or bad judgment but also by the *injustice* of the powerful. **24:** *Spare the rod* indicates the emphasis placed on necessary discipline (cf. 22.15; 23.13–14; 26.3; 29.15); the sages, however, were opposed to cruelty in any form. **14.1:** *The wise woman* could be Woman Wisdom who also *builds her house* (cf. 9.1) and the *foolish,* her antithesis (cf. 9.13–18), but the saying also alludes to the critical role of women in Israelite society; cf. 31.10–31. **2:** See 1.7n. Beginning with ch 14, proverbs that mention the Lord appear with increasing frequency. **4:** The ox was a highly valued work animal (cf. 12.10; Deut

but knowledge is easy for one who
understands.
7 Leave the presence of a fool,
for there you do not find words of
knowledge.
8 It is the wisdom of the clever to
understand where they go,
but the folly of fools misleads.
9 Fools mock at the guilt offering,[a]
but the upright enjoy God's favor.
10 The heart knows its own bitterness,
and no stranger shares its joy.
11 The house of the wicked is destroyed,
but the tent of the upright flourishes.
12 There is a way that seems right to a
person,
but its end is the way to death.[b]
13 Even in laughter the heart is sad,
and the end of joy is grief.
14 The perverse get what their ways
deserve,
and the good, what their deeds
deserve.[c]
15 The simple believe everything,
but the clever consider their steps.
16 The wise are cautious and turn away
from evil,
but the fool throws off restraint and is
careless.
17 One who is quick-tempered acts
foolishly,
and the schemer is hated.
18 The simple are adorned with[d] folly,
but the clever are crowned with
knowledge.
19 The evil bow down before the good,
the wicked at the gates of the righteous.
20 The poor are disliked even by their
neighbors,

but the rich have many friends.
21 Those who despise their neighbors are
sinners,
but happy are those who are kind to the
poor.
22 Do they not err that plan evil?
Those who plan good find loyalty and
faithfulness.
23 In all toil there is profit,
but mere talk leads only to poverty.
24 The crown of the wise is their
wisdom,[e]
but folly is the garland[f] of fools.
25 A truthful witness saves lives,
but one who utters lies is a betrayer.
26 In the fear of the LORD one has strong
confidence,
and one's children will have a
refuge.
27 The fear of the LORD is a fountain of
life,
so that one may avoid the snares of
death.
28 The glory of a king is a multitude of
people;
without people a prince is ruined.
29 Whoever is slow to anger has great
understanding,
but one who has a hasty temper exalts
folly.
30 A tranquil mind gives life to the flesh,
but passion makes the bones rot.

a Meaning of Heb uncertain
b Heb *ways of death*
c Cn: Heb *from upon him*
d Or *inherit*
e Cn Compare Gk: Heb *riches*
f Cn: Heb *is the folly*

22.10; 1 Kings 19.19). **6:** For the scoffer see 9.7–8a; 13.1; 15.12; 21.24; 22.10. **9:** *Guilt offering* (see Lev 5.14–19; 6.1–7) is an offering of reparation or compensation; cf. 3.9–10n. The *upright* have no need to do so as they already *enjoy God's favor*. **10:** *The heart* is the seat of the inner person and no one else can know its deepest emotions. **11:** See 10.2–3n. **12:** Choices can be misleading, and no one can predict the future (cf. 16.25). **13:** Cf. Eccl 7.2–4. **15–18:** A series of sayings about good and bad judgment. **17:** Anger, as an uncontrolled and anti–social expression of emotion, is often warned against; see v. 29; 16.32; 19.11; 27.4; 29.11,22. **19:** Righteousness is ultimately stronger than wickedness according to the doctrine of retribution. **20–21:** A social reality that connects wealth with popularity in v. 20 (cf. 19.4) is relativized by v. 21, which chastises the very *neighbors* who ignore the poor (cf. v. 31; 17.5). **24:** The image of the *crown* is also used to describe a good wife (12.4), knowledge (14.18), old age (16.31), and grandchildren (17.6). **26–27:** *Fear of the LORD*, see 1.7n. *Fountain of life*, see 10.11n. **28:** A king needs his people; his glory does not simply rest on himself. **29–30:** Self-control is a key virtue in Proverbs (cf. 12.16; 15.18; 19.19; 20.3; 25.28). Here "passion" refers not to sexual passion but to strong, unregulated emotion of any sort. *Flesh*

[31] Those who oppress the poor insult their
Maker,
but those who are kind to the needy
honor him.
[32] The wicked are overthrown by their
evildoing,
but the righteous find a refuge in their
integrity.[a]
[33] Wisdom is at home in the mind of one
who has understanding,
but it is not[b] known in the heart of
fools.
[34] Righteousness exalts a nation,
but sin is a reproach to any people.
[35] A servant who deals wisely has the
king's favor,
but his wrath falls on one who acts
shamefully.

15 A soft answer turns away wrath,
but a harsh word stirs up anger.
[2] The tongue of the wise dispenses
knowledge,[c]
but the mouths of fools pour out folly.
[3] The eyes of the LORD are in every place,
keeping watch on the evil and the good.
[4] A gentle tongue is a tree of life,
but perverseness in it breaks the spirit.
[5] A fool despises a parent's instruction,
but the one who heeds admonition is
prudent.
[6] In the house of the righteous there is
much treasure,
but trouble befalls the income of the
wicked.
[7] The lips of the wise spread knowledge;
not so the minds of fools.
[8] The sacrifice of the wicked is an
abomination to the LORD,
but the prayer of the upright is his delight.
[9] The way of the wicked is an abomination
to the LORD,
but he loves the one who pursues
righteousness.

[10] There is severe discipline for one who
forsakes the way,
but one who hates a rebuke will die.
[11] Sheol and Abaddon lie open before the
LORD,
how much more human hearts!
[12] Scoffers do not like to be rebuked;
they will not go to the wise.
[13] A glad heart makes a cheerful
countenance,
but by sorrow of heart the spirit is
broken.
[14] The mind of one who has understanding
seeks knowledge,
but the mouths of fools feed on folly.
[15] All the days of the poor are hard,
but a cheerful heart has a continual
feast.
[16] Better is a little with the fear of the
LORD
than great treasure and trouble with it.
[17] Better is a dinner of vegetables where
love is
than a fatted ox and hatred with it.
[18] Those who are hot-tempered stir up
strife,
but those who are slow to anger calm
contention.
[19] The way of the lazy is overgrown with
thorns,
but the path of the upright is a level
highway.
[20] A wise child makes a glad father,
but the foolish despise their mothers.
[21] Folly is a joy to one who has no sense,
but a person of understanding walks
straight ahead.
[22] Without counsel, plans go wrong,
but with many advisers they succeed.

a Gk Syr: Heb *in their death*
b Gk Syr: Heb lacks *not*
c Cn: Heb *makes knowledge good*

and *bones* is a frequent fixed pair in the Bible (cf. Gen 2.23; Judg. 9.2; Job 2.5). **31:** Concern for *the poor* is a theme in the wisdom literature (cf. 17.5; 19.17; 21.13; 22.16; 28.3), in the prophets (e.g., Ezek 22.29; Am 4.1; Zech 7.10), and in the law (e.g., Ex 22.25–27; Lev 25.36–37; Deut 14.28–29; 24.19–22). **35:** Cf. 16.14; 19.12. **15.1–2,4,7:** A series of sayings on proper and improper speech. See 10.8n.,18–21; 12.13–23. **4:** *Tree of life,* see 13.12n. **5:** Cf. vv. 31–33. **8:** Sincerity in worship is essential (v. 29; 21.3,27). **11:** *Sheol,* the underworld; *Abaddon* (lit. "Destruction") is an alternative abode for the place and state of the dead (cf. 1.13; for 11b, cf. 20.27; Sir 42.18). **16–17:** Two *better . . . than* sayings that put in question the value of prosperity (cf. 16.8; 17.1). A *dinner of vegetables* is simple fare in contrast to the luxury of eating a *fatted ox.* **20:** See 10.1n. **22:** The importance of *counsel* and planning is a favorite theme

²³ To make an apt answer is a joy to
anyone,
and a word in season, how good it is!
²⁴ For the wise the path of life leads
upward,
in order to avoid Sheol below.
²⁵ The Lord tears down the house of the
proud,
but maintains the widow's boundaries.
²⁶ Evil plans are an abomination to the Lord,
but gracious words are pure.
²⁷ Those who are greedy for unjust gain
make trouble for their households,
but those who hate bribes will live.
²⁸ The mind of the righteous ponders how
to answer,
but the mouth of the wicked pours out
evil.
²⁹ The Lord is far from the wicked,
but he hears the prayer of the righteous.
³⁰ The light of the eyes rejoices the heart,
and good news refreshes the body.
³¹ The ear that heeds wholesome
admonition
will lodge among the wise.
³² Those who ignore instruction despise
themselves,
but those who heed admonition gain
understanding.
³³ The fear of the Lord is instruction in
wisdom,
and humility goes before honor.

16 The plans of the mind belong to
mortals,
but the answer of the tongue is from
the Lord.

² All one's ways may be pure in one's own
eyes,
but the Lord weighs the spirit.
³ Commit your work to the Lord,
and your plans will be established.
⁴ The Lord has made everything for its
purpose,
even the wicked for the day of
trouble.
⁵ All those who are arrogant are an
abomination to the Lord;
be assured, they will not go
unpunished.
⁶ By loyalty and faithfulness iniquity is
atoned for,
and by the fear of the Lord one avoids
evil.
⁷ When the ways of people please the
Lord,
he causes even their enemies to be at
peace with them.
⁸ Better is a little with righteousness
than large income with injustice.
⁹ The human mind plans the way,
but the Lord directs the steps.
¹⁰ Inspired decisions are on the lips of a
king;
his mouth does not sin in judgment.
¹¹ Honest balances and scales are the
Lord's;
all the weights in the bag are his work.
¹² It is an abomination to kings to do evil,
for the throne is established by
righteousness.
¹³ Righteous lips are the delight of a king,
and he loves those who speak what is
right.

of the wise (cf. 11.14; 13.10; 19.20; 20.18); see v. 26 for its antithesis. **24:** Slight variant on the image of the path (see 1.15n.), this time leading *upward* (representing success) or downward (representing failure), because of Sheol's location *below* the earth's surface. **25:** Boundaries are the markers that indicate the extent of a field (see 22.28; Deut 19.4). Widows were lowly members of society and vulnerable to the encroachments of the powerful (cf. Job 24.2–3), hence the special divine protection (cf. 23.10–11). **27:** The wise oppose bribery in all its forms, cf. 17.23; Sir 20.29. **30:** *The light of the eyes* refers to the friendly looks of another person. A frequent theme in Proverbs is the effect others, and particularly their words, have upon a person (cf. 12.25). **31–33:** On the importance of *admonition* see 1.23n. The word translated *instruction* in vv. 5,32,33 (Heb "musar") is elsewhere often translated as discipline; see 12.1n. **33:** *Fear of the Lord*, see 1.7n. **16.1–7:** A string of proverbs that stress the role of the Lord in directing the lives both of individuals and of wider communities. **1:** Cf. vv. 9,33; 19.21; 20.24; 21.30–31. **2:** Cf. 17.3; 21.2; 24.12. **4:** *The day of trouble* is a day on which disaster strikes unexpectedly (cf. 11.4; Eccl 7.17). **6:** *Loyalty and faithfulness* indicate proper devotion (cf. 3.3; 14.22). *Fear of the Lord*, see 1.7n. **7:** God's pleasure leads not only to internal but also to external *peace* in relation to *enemies*. **8:** Cf. 15.16–17. **10–15:** A small group of sayings concerning the *king*. **10:** *Inspired decisions* indicate the king's wisdom and authority. Solomon embodies the

¹⁴ A king's wrath is a messenger of death,
    and whoever is wise will appease it.
¹⁵ In the light of a king's face there is life,
    and his favor is like the clouds that
        bring the spring rain.
¹⁶ How much better to get wisdom than
    gold!
    To get understanding is to be chosen
        rather than silver.
¹⁷ The highway of the upright avoids evil;
    those who guard their way preserve
        their lives.
¹⁸ Pride goes before destruction,
    and a haughty spirit before a fall.
¹⁹ It is better to be of a lowly spirit among
    the poor
    than to divide the spoil with the proud.
²⁰ Those who are attentive to a matter will
    prosper,
    and happy are those who trust in the
        LORD.
²¹ The wise of heart is called perceptive,
    and pleasant speech increases
        persuasiveness.
²² Wisdom is a fountain of life to one who
    has it,
    but folly is the punishment of fools.
²³ The mind of the wise makes their speech
    judicious,
    and adds persuasiveness to their lips.
²⁴ Pleasant words are like a honeycomb,
    sweetness to the soul and health to the
        body.
²⁵ Sometimes there is a way that seems to
    be right,
    but in the end it is the way to death.
²⁶ The appetite of workers works for them;
    their hunger urges them on.
²⁷ Scoundrels concoct evil,
    and their speech is like a scorching fire.
²⁸ A perverse person spreads strife,

and a whisperer separates close friends.
²⁹ The violent entice their neighbors,
    and lead them in a way that is not good.
³⁰ One who winks the eyes plans[a] perverse
    things;
    one who compresses the lips brings evil
        to pass.
³¹ Gray hair is a crown of glory;
    it is gained in a righteous life.
³² One who is slow to anger is better than
    the mighty,
    and one whose temper is controlled
        than one who captures a city.
³³ The lot is cast into the lap,
    but the decision is the LORD's alone.

17 Better is a dry morsel with quiet
    than a house full of feasting with strife.
² A slave who deals wisely will rule over a
    child who acts shamefully,
    and will share the inheritance as one of
        the family.
³ The crucible is for silver, and the furnace
    is for gold,
    but the LORD tests the heart.
⁴ An evildoer listens to wicked lips;
    and a liar gives heed to a mischievous
        tongue.
⁵ Those who mock the poor insult their
    Maker;
    those who are glad at calamity will not
        go unpunished.
⁶ Grandchildren are the crown of the aged,
    and the glory of children is their
        parents.
⁷ Fine speech is not becoming to a fool;
    still less is false speech to a ruler.[b]
⁸ A bribe is like a magic stone in the eyes of
    those who give it;

---

a Gk Syr Vg Tg: Heb *to plan*
b Or *a noble person*

ideal of the wise king (1 Kings 3.7–9,16–28). **11**: Cf. 11.1n. **14**: *A king's wrath* is more dangerous than that of most people because of the power he wields, hence it is worth appeasing (cf. 19.12; 20.2). **15**: Royal favor is compared to the clouds that precede the spring rains and water the first crop, valued as a great blessing (cf. Hos 6.3). **16**: Cf. 8.10–11. **18–19**: Cf. 11.2. **21**: Perception and eloquence are keynotes of the wise person who needs at times to employ powers of persuasion (cf. v. 23). Contrast the persuasive seductiveness of the loose woman in 2.16; 5.3; 7.5. **22**: Cf. 10.11. **25**: =14.12. **26**: *Hunger* is appreciated as a motive for diligence; cf. Eccl 6.7. **27–30**: Four sayings on different types of wicked people and their dangerous speech; see 10.8n. **31**: The *gray hair* of the elderly is related to *righteous* living, which was thought to produce longevity (cf. 20.29; Sir 25.3–6). **32**: See 14.17n. **33**: Casting lots was a common way of making decisions. All destinies are in God's hands, even the direction in which *the lot* falls (cf. 18.18). **17.1**: Cf. 15.16–17. **2**: Wisdom can trump even the norms of law and custom (cf.

wherever they turn they prosper.

9 One who forgives an affront fosters friendship,
but one who dwells on disputes will alienate a friend.

10 A rebuke strikes deeper into a discerning person
than a hundred blows into a fool.

11 Evil people seek only rebellion,
but a cruel messenger will be sent against them.

12 Better to meet a she-bear robbed of its cubs
than to confront a fool immersed in folly.

13 Evil will not depart from the house
of one who returns evil for good.

14 The beginning of strife is like letting out water;
so stop before the quarrel breaks out.

15 One who justifies the wicked and one who condemns the righteous
are both alike an abomination to the LORD.

16 Why should fools have a price in hand
to buy wisdom, when they have no mind to learn?

17 A friend loves at all times,
and kinsfolk are born to share adversity.

18 It is senseless to give a pledge,
to become surety for a neighbor.

19 One who loves transgression loves strife;
one who builds a high threshold invites broken bones.

20 The crooked of mind do not prosper,
and the perverse of tongue fall into calamity.

21 The one who begets a fool gets trouble;
the parent of a fool has no joy.

22 A cheerful heart is a good medicine,
but a downcast spirit dries up the bones.

23 The wicked accept a concealed bribe
to pervert the ways of justice.

24 The discerning person looks to wisdom,
but the eyes of a fool to the ends of the earth.

25 Foolish children are a grief to their father
and bitterness to her who bore them.

26 To impose a fine on the innocent is not right,
or to flog the noble for their integrity.

27 One who spares words is knowledgeable;
one who is cool in spirit has understanding.

28 Even fools who keep silent are considered wise;
when they close their lips, they are deemed intelligent.

18 The one who lives alone is self-indulgent,
showing contempt for all who have sound judgment.[a]

2 A fool takes no pleasure in understanding,
but only in expressing personal opinion.

a   Meaning of Heb uncertain

19.10b). **3:** A *crucible* tests for impurities in precious metal; cf. 27.21. **4:** See 14.7n. **5:** See 14.31n. **8:** An unusual observation that a bribe works. *In the eyes of,* however, indicates self-delusion. Gifts to curry favor were acceptable up to a point (cf. 18.16; 21.14), but elsewhere bribery is condemned (e.g., v. 23). **9:** Forgiveness in the context of friendship; cf. 10.12. **10:** *A hundred blows,* Deut 25.3 limits corporal punishment to forty blows. **12:** Meeting an angry *she-bear,* a popular image for great danger (cf. 2 Sam 17.8; 2 Kings 2.23–24; Hos 13.8). **14:** *Letting out water* from a dam, a process that is unstoppable once it is started. **15:** The abuse of judicial power was a serious concern; cf. v. 26; 19.5; Deut 25.1; Ex 23.2–3,6–8; Isa 5.23. **16:** *A price in hand* is probably a fee to the wise. Such fools think they can buy wisdom with no commitment to it. **17:** A true friend is supportive in good times and bad, while relatives are regarded as more of a safety net in adversity (cf. 18.24). **18:** Cf. 6.1–5; 11.15; 20.16. **19:** *Builds a high threshold,* a "cause and effect" proverb. Just as a badly built (and perhaps ostentatious) *threshold invites* problems, so deliberate provocation to transgression causes conflict. **20:** See 10.2–3n. **21:** See 10.1n. **22:** *Dries up the bones* indicates the withering effect of depression on the whole body. **23:** Cf. v. 8; 15.27. **24:** *The eyes of a fool* gaze on the distant horizon (and unattainable goals) when wisdom is actually close at hand and readily attainable to the *discerning person* (cf. Deut 30.11–15). **25:** See 10.1n. **26:** See v. 15n.; cf. 18.5; Deut 22.19; Am 2.8. **27–28:** A pair of proverbs on the ambiguity of silence, normally a virtue of the wise (cf. 10.19; 12.23; 13.3; 15.28), but paradoxically when fools keep silent they are *considered wise.* **18.1–2:** The loner and the *fool* have this in com-

³ When wickedness comes, contempt
comes also;
and with dishonor comes disgrace.
⁴ The words of the mouth are deep waters;
the fountain of wisdom is a gushing
stream.
⁵ It is not right to be partial to the guilty,
or to subvert the innocent in judgment.
⁶ A fool's lips bring strife,
and a fool's mouth invites a flogging.
⁷ The mouths of fools are their ruin,
and their lips a snare to themselves.
⁸ The words of a whisperer are like
delicious morsels;
they go down into the inner parts of the
body.
⁹ One who is slack in work
is close kin to a vandal.
¹⁰ The name of the LORD is a strong tower;
the righteous run into it and are safe.
¹¹ The wealth of the rich is their strong city;
in their imagination it is like a high
wall.
¹² Before destruction one's heart is
haughty,
but humility goes before honor.
¹³ If one gives answer before hearing,
it is folly and shame.
¹⁴ The human spirit will endure sickness;
but a broken spirit—who can bear?
¹⁵ An intelligent mind acquires knowledge,
and the ear of the wise seeks
knowledge.
¹⁶ A gift opens doors;
it gives access to the great.
¹⁷ The one who first states a case seems
right,

until the other comes and cross-
examines.
¹⁸ Casting the lot puts an end to disputes
and decides between powerful
contenders.
¹⁹ An ally offended is stronger than a city;[a]
such quarreling is like the bars of a
castle.
²⁰ From the fruit of the mouth one's
stomach is satisfied;
the yield of the lips brings satisfaction.
²¹ Death and life are in the power of the
tongue,
and those who love it will eat its fruits.
²² He who finds a wife finds a good thing,
and obtains favor from the LORD.
²³ The poor use entreaties,
but the rich answer roughly.
²⁴ Some[b] friends play at friendship[c]
but a true friend sticks closer than one's
nearest kin.

19 Better the poor walking in integrity
than one perverse of speech who is a
fool.
² Desire without knowledge is not good,
and one who moves too hurriedly
misses the way.
³ One's own folly leads to ruin,
yet the heart rages against the LORD.
⁴ Wealth brings many friends,
but the poor are left friendless.
⁵ A false witness will not go unpunished,
and a liar will not escape.

a   Gk Syr Vg Tg: Meaning of Heb uncertain
b   Syr Tg: Heb *A man of*
c   Cn Compare Syr Vg Tg: Meaning of Heb uncertain

mon: neither listens to the other (cf. v. 13). The proverbs are linked by a wordplay in Hebrew. **4**: The *deep waters* of speech are ambiguous: words can be life-giving as wisdom is, but they can also be dangerous (cf. v. 21; 10.11). By the first alternative, the two lines would be synonymous, otherwise antithetical. **5**: See 17.15n.,26. **6–7**: The danger of foolish speech is a common topic; cf. 10.13–14; 12.13; 13.3; 14.3. **8**: *A whisperer* indicates a gossip for whom scandal is as essential as food (= 26.22). **9**: See 6.6–11n. **10–11**: A proverb pair containing a subtle contrast: *the name of the LORD* (a phrase found only here in Proverbs) offers security (cf. Pss 61.4; 124.8), but the protection of wealth may prove to be imaginary (cf. 10.15–16; 11.4). **12**: Cf. 11.2; 15.33; 16.18; 18.3. **14**: The contrast here is between physical illness and psychological depression. **16**: See 17.8n. **17–18**: Legal language suggesting that both sides of a case must be argued for a fair airing of opposing views, and that intractable disputes can only be settled by *casting the lot*, i.e., seeking God's decision; cf. 16.33. **19**: *An ally offended* is likely to build up impenetrable barriers due to a strong sense of personal injury. **20–21**: See 10.8n. **22**: See 12.4n. **23**: The power-lessness of the poor leads to *entreaties* while the rich can answer as they please; cf. Sir 13.3. **19.1**: A "better than" saying; cf. 15.16–17; 16.8; 17; 28.6. **2**: *Desire* indicates intention, and hurried movement represents action; hasti-ness in both creates problems. **3**: The fool is self-deceived and misplaces blame; cf. Sir 15.11–20. **4**: *The poor are*

[6] Many seek the favor of the generous,
   and everyone is a friend to a giver of
      gifts.
[7] If the poor are hated even by their kin,
   how much more are they shunned by
      their friends!
When they call after them, they are not
      there.[a]
[8] To get wisdom is to love oneself;
   to keep understanding is to prosper.
[9] A false witness will not go unpunished,
   and the liar will perish.
[10] It is not fitting for a fool to live in luxury,
   much less for a slave to rule over
      princes.
[11] Those with good sense are slow to anger,
   and it is their glory to overlook an
      offense.
[12] A king's anger is like the growling of a
      lion,
   but his favor is like dew on the grass.
[13] A stupid child is ruin to a father,
   and a wife's quarreling is a continual
      dripping of rain.
[14] House and wealth are inherited from
      parents,
   but a prudent wife is from the LORD.
[15] Laziness brings on deep sleep;
   an idle person will suffer hunger.
[16] Those who keep the commandment will
      live;
   those who are heedless of their ways
      will die.
[17] Whoever is kind to the poor lends to the
      LORD,
   and will be repaid in full.
[18] Discipline your children while there is
      hope;
   do not set your heart on their destruction.
[19] A violent tempered person will pay the
      penalty;

if you effect a rescue, you will only have
      to do it again.[a]
[20] Listen to advice and accept instruction,
   that you may gain wisdom for the
      future.
[21] The human mind may devise many
      plans,
   but it is the purpose of the LORD that
      will be established.
[22] What is desirable in a person is loyalty,
   and it is better to be poor than a liar.
[23] The fear of the LORD is life indeed;
   filled with it one rests secure
   and suffers no harm.
[24] The lazy person buries a hand in the
      dish,
   and will not even bring it back to the
      mouth.
[25] Strike a scoffer, and the simple will learn
      prudence;
   reprove the intelligent, and they will
      gain knowledge.
[26] Those who do violence to their father
   and chase away their mother
   are children who cause shame and
      bring reproach.
[27] Cease straying, my child, from the words
   of knowledge,
   in order that you may hear
      instruction.
[28] A worthless witness mocks at justice,
   and the mouth of the wicked devours
      iniquity.
[29] Condemnation is ready for scoffers,
   and flogging for the backs of fools.

20 Wine is a mocker, strong drink a
      brawler,
   and whoever is led astray by it is not
      wise.

[a]   Meaning of Heb uncertain

left friendless, see vv. 6–7; see also 14.20n. 5: A court of law is envisaged; the false witness is a frequent topic (see v. 9; 6.19; 12.17; 14.5,25; 21.28; 25.7c–10,18; Ex 20.16; 23.1–3,7). 10: This proverb decries a situation that has gone topsy-turvy; cf. 30.21–22; Eccl 10.6–7. 11–12: Warnings against anger; see 14–17n. For the king's anger and favor see 16.14–15n. 13–14: A male perspective on domestic unhappiness contrasted with the advantages of a prudent wife; cf. 31.10–31. 16: The commandment is that of any legitimate authority such as parent, sage, or the LORD (cf. 13.13). 17: God's commitment to the poor, cf. 14.31n.; 17.5; 28.27. 18: While there is hope, during childhood, when there is potential for change and lasting formation can occur. 19: The violent tempered person will be punished. He is locked into a repeated pattern and cannot be helped. 20: The value of seeking advice and instruction is a frequent topic; cf. 1.8; 4.1,10; 23.12. 21: Cf. 16.1,9,33; 21.30–31. 22: Loyalty has overtones of covenant loyalty. 23: Fear of the LORD, see 1.7n. 24: See 6.6–11n. 25: See 9.7–9n.; 12.1n. 26: See 10.1n. 20.1: Warnings about the effects

² The dread anger of a king is like the
  growling of a lion;
  anyone who provokes him to anger
    forfeits life itself.
³ It is honorable to refrain from strife,
  but every fool is quick to quarrel.
⁴ The lazy person does not plow in season;
  harvest comes, and there is nothing to
    be found.
⁵ The purposes in the human mind are like
    deep water,
  but the intelligent will draw them out.
⁶ Many proclaim themselves loyal,
  but who can find one worthy of trust?
⁷ The righteous walk in integrity—
  happy are the children who follow
    them!
⁸ A king who sits on the throne of
    judgment
  winnows all evil with his eyes.
⁹ Who can say, "I have made my heart
    clean;
  I am pure from my sin"?
¹⁰ Diverse weights and diverse measures
  are both alike an abomination to the Lord.
¹¹ Even children make themselves known
    by their acts,
  by whether what they do is pure and
    right.
¹² The hearing ear and the seeing eye—
  the Lord has made them both.
¹³ Do not love sleep, or else you will come
    to poverty;
  open your eyes, and you will have
    plenty of bread.
¹⁴ "Bad, bad," says the buyer,
  then goes away and boasts.
¹⁵ There is gold, and abundance of costly
    stones;
  but the lips informed by knowledge are
    a precious jewel.

¹⁶ Take the garment of one who has given
    surety for a stranger;
  seize the pledge given as surety for
    foreigners.
¹⁷ Bread gained by deceit is sweet,
  but afterward the mouth will be full of
    gravel.
¹⁸ Plans are established by taking advice;
  wage war by following wise guidance.
¹⁹ A gossip reveals secrets;
  therefore do not associate with a
    babbler.
²⁰ If you curse father or mother,
  your lamp will go out in utter darkness.
²¹ An estate quickly acquired in the
    beginning
  will not be blessed in the end.
²² Do not say, "I will repay evil";
  wait for the Lord, and he will help you.
²³ Differing weights are an abomination to
    the Lord,
  and false scales are not good.
²⁴ All our steps are ordered by the Lord;
  how then can we understand our own
    ways?
²⁵ It is a snare for one to say rashly, "It is
    holy,"
  and begin to reflect only after making
    a vow.
²⁶ A wise king winnows the wicked,
  and drives the wheel over them.
²⁷ The human spirit is the lamp of the
    Lord,
  searching every inmost part.
²⁸ Loyalty and faithfulness preserve the
    king,
  and his throne is upheld by
    righteousness.ᵃ
²⁹ The glory of youths is their strength,

ᵃ Gk: Heb *loyalty*

of *wine* and *strong drink* (cf. 23.19–21,29–35; 31.4–5). **2:** See 16.14; 19.12. **3:** Cf. 17.14; 26.17. **4:** See 6.6–11n. **5:** The wise have good powers of expression of their deepest thoughts (see 18.4). **6:** *Many . . . but*, for similar contrasts see 18.24; 31.29. **8:** *Winnows* refers to spotting evil quickly, cf. v. 26. **9:** A rhetorical question anticipating the answer "no one." **10:** See. v. 23; 11.1n. **13:** See 6.6–11n. **14:** In the world of bartering, the *buyer* misleadingly downgrades the deal to get a good price and then is pleased with his deception. **15:** See 2.4n. **16:** See 6.1–5n.; 27.13. Giving *surety* for a stranger or foreigner, who has no ties to the community, is a high-risk strategy. **17:** The difference between initial appearance and later reality; cf. 9.17–18; Job 20.12–14. **18:** See 15.22n.; 24.5–6. **20:** *Lamp will go out*, see 13.9n. **21:** *Quickly acquired*, not properly inherited. On the insubstantiality of hastily or unjustly acquired wealth see 1.10–19; 10.2; 13.11; 15.6; 16.8; 28.8,20,22. **23:** See v. 10; 11.1n. **24:** On divine control see 16.1–7. **25:** See the reckless vow by Jephthah in Judg 11.29–40; cf. Eccl 5.4–6. **26:** *The wheel* is a threshing implement (v.

but the beauty of the aged is their gray
hair.

30 Blows that wound cleanse away evil;
beatings make clean the innermost
parts.

21 The king's heart is a stream of water in
the hand of the Lord;
he turns it wherever he will.

2 All deeds are right in the sight of the
doer,
but the Lord weighs the heart.

3 To do righteousness and justice
is more acceptable to the Lord than
sacrifice.

4 Haughty eyes and a proud heart—
the lamp of the wicked—are sin.

5 The plans of the diligent lead surely to
abundance,
but everyone who is hasty comes only
to want.

6 The getting of treasures by a lying tongue
is a fleeting vapor and a snare[a] of
death.

7 The violence of the wicked will sweep
them away,
because they refuse to do what is just.

8 The way of the guilty is crooked,
but the conduct of the pure is right.

9 It is better to live in a corner of the
housetop
than in a house shared with a
contentious wife.

10 The souls of the wicked desire evil;
their neighbors find no mercy in their
eyes.

11 When a scoffer is punished, the simple
become wiser;
when the wise are instructed, they
increase in knowledge.

12 The Righteous One observes the house
of the wicked;
he casts the wicked down to ruin.

13 If you close your ear to the cry of the
poor,
you will cry out and not be heard.

14 A gift in secret averts anger;
and a concealed bribe in the bosom,
strong wrath.

15 When justice is done, it is a joy to the
righteous,
but dismay to evildoers.

16 Whoever wanders from the way of
understanding
will rest in the assembly of the dead.

17 Whoever loves pleasure will suffer want;
whoever loves wine and oil will not be
rich.

18 The wicked is a ransom for the righteous,
and the faithless for the upright.

19 It is better to live in a desert land
than with a contentious and fretful wife.

20 Precious treasure remains[b] in the house
of the wise,
but the fool devours it.

21 Whoever pursues righteousness and
kindness
will find life[c] and honor.

22 One wise person went up against a city
of warriors
and brought down the stronghold in
which they trusted.

23 To watch over mouth and tongue
is to keep out of trouble.

24 The proud, haughty person, named
"Scoffer,"
acts with arrogant pride.

25 The craving of the lazy person is fatal,
for lazy hands refuse to labor.

26 All day long the wicked covet,[d]

a Gk: Heb *seekers*
b Gk: Heb *and oil*
c Gk: Heb *life and righteousness*
d Gk: Heb *all day long one covets covetously*

8; Isa 28.27). **27:** *Lamp,* cf. Zeph 1.12. See also 15.11; 16.2; 17.3. **29:** See 16.31. **30:** Corporal punishment as a component of pedagogical discipline (cf. 13.24; 22.15; 23.13–14). **21.1:** Even the mind of a king is controlled by God (cf.
vv. 30–31). **2:** Cf. 16.2. **3:** Cf. 15.8,29; 28.9,13. The fixed pair *righteousness and justice* is common, cf. 18.19; Ps 33.5;
and in the opposite order, Isa 56.1; Job 37.28; 2 Sam 8.15. **6:** See 20.21n. **9:** *Contentious wife,* cf. v. 19; 25.24; 27.15;
cf. also 19.13–14n. *In a corner of the housetop,* either an exposed roof or a small room constructed on top of the
house (2 Kings 4.10). **12:** *Righteous One,* i.e., God (cf. 13.6; 19.3) **13:** See 14.31n. **14:** See 17.8n. **16:** *Assembly of the
dead,* i.e., Sheol. **17:** Warnings against overindulgence and overspending; cf. v. 20. **18:** *Ransom* indicates compensation money. The righteous are rescued from danger and the wicked put in their place (cf. 11.8; 13.8). **19:** Cf.
19.13–14; 21.9. **22:** *One wise person* indicates a narrative about the superiority of wisdom to military strength; cf.

but the righteous give and do not hold
    back.
27 The sacrifice of the wicked is an
    abomination;
    how much more when brought with evil
    intent.
28 A false witness will perish,
    but a good listener will testify
    successfully.
29 The wicked put on a bold face,
    but the upright give thought to[a] their
    ways.
30 No wisdom, no understanding, no
    counsel,
    can avail against the LORD.
31 The horse is made ready for the day of
    battle,
    but the victory belongs to the LORD.

22 A good name is to be chosen rather
    than great riches,
    and favor is better than silver or gold.
2 The rich and the poor have this in
    common:
    the LORD is the maker of them all.
3 The clever see danger and hide;
    but the simple go on, and suffer for it.
4 The reward for humility and fear of the
    LORD
    is riches and honor and life.
5 Thorns and snares are in the way of the
    perverse;
    the cautious will keep far from them.
6 Train children in the right way,
    and when old, they will not stray.
7 The rich rule over the poor,
    and the borrower is the slave of the
    lender.
8 Whoever sows injustice will reap
    calamity,

and the rod of anger will fail.
9 Those who are generous are blessed,
    for they share their bread with the
    poor.
10 Drive out a scoffer, and strife goes out;
    quarreling and abuse will cease.
11 Those who love a pure heart and are
    gracious in speech
    will have the king as a friend.
12 The eyes of the LORD keep watch over
    knowledge,
    but he overthrows the words of the
    faithless.
13 The lazy person says, "There is a lion
    outside!
    I shall be killed in the streets!"
14 The mouth of a loose[b] woman is a deep
    pit;
    he with whom the LORD is angry falls
    into it.
15 Folly is bound up in the heart of a boy,
    but the rod of discipline drives it far
    away.
16 Oppressing the poor in order to enrich
    oneself,
    and giving to the rich, will lead only to
    loss.

17 The words of the wise:

Incline your ear and hear my words,[c]
    and apply your mind to my teaching;
18 for it will be pleasant if you keep them
    within you,

a   Another reading is *establish*
b   Heb *strange*
c   Cn Compare Gk: Heb *Incline your ear, and hear the
     words of the wise*

Eccl 9.13–16. **23:** See 10.8n. **24:** See 9.7–9n. **25:** See 6.6–11n. **27:** See v. 3n. **28:** See 19.5n. **30–31:** The limitations of
human wisdom in the light of the LORD's superior wisdom; cf. 16.1–7. **22.1:** A *good name*, cf. Sir 41.12–13. **2:** God as
creator of all, cf. 29.13; Job 31.13–15. **4–5:** See 10.2–3n. **7:** *The borrower is the slave*, debt slavery was a reality in
ancient Israel (Ex 21.2–7; 2 Kings 4.1; Neh 5.5). **9:** See 14.31n. **13:** The excuses of the lazy person become more and
more ridiculous; cf. 26.13. **14:** Cf. 2.16–17; 7.10–27. **15:** See 13.24n. **16:** *Giving to the rich* probably indicates attempting to bribe them.

22.17–24.22: The words of the wise. This section forms a separate collection. Its sayings are formulated as
longer units of second-person address, like the Egyptian "Instruction" genre and like Proverbs 1–9. The unit
22.17–23.11 has close similarities to the Egyptian "Instruction of Amenemope" (ca. 1100 BCE; see CoS 1.115–22), a
text widely copied in schools. 22.17–23.11 follows its topical order and hence could be a Hebrew adaptation of
the Egyptian text. **22.17–21:** A prologue, patterned after the introduction to "Amenemope." **20:** *Thirty sayings*
may correspond to the thirty sections of "Amenemope," though it is not clear how there are thirty units in this

if all of them are ready on your lips.
¹⁹ So that your trust may be in the Lord,
I have made them known to you
today—yes, to you.
²⁰ Have I not written for you thirty sayings
of admonition and knowledge,
²¹ to show you what is right and true,
so that you may give a true answer to
those who sent you?

²² Do not rob the poor because they are
poor,
or crush the afflicted at the gate;
²³ for the Lord pleads their cause
and despoils of life those who despoil
them.
²⁴ Make no friends with those given to
anger,
and do not associate with hotheads,
²⁵ or you may learn their ways
and entangle yourself in a snare.
²⁶ Do not be one of those who give pledges,
who become surety for debts.
²⁷ If you have nothing with which to pay,
why should your bed be taken from
under you?
²⁸ Do not remove the ancient landmark
that your ancestors set up.
²⁹ Do you see those who are skillful in their
work?
They will serve kings;
they will not serve common people.

23 When you sit down to eat with a ruler,
observe carefully whatᵃ is before you,
² and put a knife to your throat
if you have a big appetite.
³ Do not desire the ruler'sᵇ delicacies,
for they are deceptive food.
⁴ Do not wear yourself out to get rich;
be wise enough to desist.
⁵ When your eyes light upon it, it is gone;
for suddenly it takes wings to itself,

flying like an eagle toward heaven.
⁶ Do not eat the bread of the stingy;
do not desire their delicacies;
⁷ for like a hair in the throat, so are they.ᶜ
"Eat and drink!" they say to you;
but they do not mean it.
⁸ You will vomit up the little you have
eaten,
and you will waste your pleasant
words.
⁹ Do not speak in the hearing of a fool,
who will only despise the wisdom of
your words.
¹⁰ Do not remove an ancient landmark
or encroach on the fields of orphans,
¹¹ for their redeemer is strong;
he will plead their cause against you.
¹² Apply your mind to instruction
and your ear to words of knowledge.
¹³ Do not withhold discipline from your
children;
if you beat them with a rod, they will
not die.
¹⁴ If you beat them with the rod,
you will save their lives from Sheol.
¹⁵ My child, if your heart is wise,
my heart too will be glad.
¹⁶ My soul will rejoice
when your lips speak what is right.
¹⁷ Do not let your heart envy sinners,
but always continue in the fear of the
Lord.
¹⁸ Surely there is a future,
and your hope will not be cut off.

¹⁹ Hear, my child, and be wise,
and direct your mind in the way.
²⁰ Do not be among winebibbers,
or among gluttonous eaters of meat;

ᵃ Or *who*
ᵇ Heb *his*
ᶜ Meaning of Heb uncertain

---

section. **22–23:** As in "Amenemope," concern for *the poor* follows the prologue. The Lord replaces the Egyptian Ma'at here as the one who pleads their cause. **24–25:** See 14.7n. **26–27:** See 6.1–5n. **28:** *Ancient landmark* is a marker indicating a property boundary (cf. Deut 19.14; 27.17) which has ancestral authority. "Amenemope" contains a similar admonition. **29:** *Serve kings*, cf. the similar comment in "Amenemope." **23.1–3:** Etiquette at the table of the powerful is an important topic in "Amenemope" and in other Egyptian instructions. See also Sir 31.12–18. **2:** *Knife to your throat*, i.e., restrain your hunger. **4–5:** "Amenemope" has a corresponding image using geese instead of an eagle. **6–8:** "Amenemope" has a similar metaphor. **10–11:** See 15.25; 22.28; *redeemer* refers to God. **13–14:** See 13.24n. *Sheol*, the abode of the dead. **17–18:** Cautions against envy; cf. 3.31; 24.1,19–20; 27.4. **20–**

²¹ for the drunkard and the glutton will
    come to poverty,
and drowsiness will clothe them with
    rags.

²² Listen to your father who begot you,
    and do not despise your mother when
        she is old.
²³ Buy truth, and do not sell it;
    buy wisdom, instruction, and
        understanding.
²⁴ The father of the righteous will greatly
        rejoice;
    he who begets a wise son will be glad
        in him.
²⁵ Let your father and mother be glad;
    let her who bore you rejoice.

²⁶ My child, give me your heart,
    and let your eyes observe[a] my ways.
²⁷ For a prostitute is a deep pit;
    an adulteress[b] is a narrow well.
²⁸ She lies in wait like a robber
    and increases the number of the
        faithless.

²⁹ Who has woe? Who has sorrow?
    Who has strife? Who has
        complaining?
Who has wounds without cause?
    Who has redness of eyes?
³⁰ Those who linger late over wine,
    those who keep trying mixed wines.
³¹ Do not look at wine when it is red,
    when it sparkles in the cup
    and goes down smoothly.
³² At the last it bites like a serpent,
    and stings like an adder.
³³ Your eyes will see strange things,
    and your mind utter perverse things.
³⁴ You will be like one who lies down in the
        midst of the sea,
    like one who lies on the top of a mast.[c]
³⁵ "They struck me," you will say,[d] "but I
        was not hurt;
    they beat me, but I did not feel it."

When shall I awake?
    I will seek another drink."

24 Do not envy the wicked,
    nor desire to be with them;
² for their minds devise violence,
    and their lips talk of mischief.

³ By wisdom a house is built,
    and by understanding it is established;
⁴ by knowledge the rooms are filled
    with all precious and pleasant riches.
⁵ Wise warriors are mightier than strong
        ones,[e]
    and those who have knowledge than
        those who have strength;
⁶ for by wise guidance you can wage your
        war,
    and in abundance of counselors there
        is victory.
⁷ Wisdom is too high for fools;
    in the gate they do not open their
        mouths.

⁸ Whoever plans to do evil
    will be called a mischief-maker.
⁹ The devising of folly is sin,
    and the scoffer is an abomination to all.

¹⁰ If you faint in the day of adversity,
    your strength being small;
¹¹ if you hold back from rescuing those
        taken away to death,
    those who go staggering to the
        slaughter;
¹² if you say, "Look, we did not know
        this"—
    does not he who weighs the heart
        perceive it?
Does not he who keeps watch over your
        soul know it?

a Another reading is *delight in*
b Heb *an alien woman*
c Meaning of Heb uncertain
d Gk Syr Vg Tg: Heb lacks *you will say*
e Gk Compare Syr Tg: Heb *A wise man is strength*

21: Warning against excessive eating and drinking; cf. Deut 21.18–21. 22–25: Parental relationships; see 10.1n.
26–28: A briefer version of Prov 7. Cf. 2.16; 6.26; 7.10. 29–35: A humorous mocking of the ill effects of drunkenness (cf. vv. 20–21; 20.1; 31.4–5; cf. Isa 5.11) with a comparison to seasickness in v. 34 (cf. Ps 107.26–27). 24.3–4:
House indicates both building and household; cf. v. 27; 9.1; 14.1; 31.10–31. 5–6: Wise strategy outdoes might (cf.
21.22; but contrast 21.30–31.). 10–12: God sees through excuses for not helping victims of violence and *weighs*

And will he not repay all according to
their deeds?

[13] My child, eat honey, for it is good,
and the drippings of the honeycomb are
sweet to your taste.
[14] Know that wisdom is such to your soul;
if you find it, you will find a future,
and your hope will not be cut off.

[15] Do not lie in wait like an outlaw against
the home of the righteous;
do no violence to the place where the
righteous live;
[16] for though they fall seven times, they
will rise again;
but the wicked are overthrown by
calamity.

[17] Do not rejoice when your enemies fall,
and do not let your heart be glad when
they stumble,
[18] or else the LORD will see it and be
displeased,
and turn away his anger from them.

[19] Do not fret because of evildoers.
Do not envy the wicked;
[20] for the evil have no future;
the lamp of the wicked will go out.

[21] My child, fear the LORD and the king,
and do not disobey either of them;[a]
[22] for disaster comes from them suddenly,
and who knows the ruin that both can
bring?

[23] These also are sayings of the wise:

Partiality in judging is not good.
[24] Whoever says to the wicked, "You are
innocent,"
will be cursed by peoples, abhorred by
nations;
[25] but those who rebuke the wicked will
have delight,
and a good blessing will come upon
them.
[26] One who gives an honest answer
gives a kiss on the lips.

[27] Prepare your work outside,
get everything ready for you in the field;
and after that build your house.

[28] Do not be a witness against your
neighbor without cause,
and do not deceive with your lips.
[29] Do not say, "I will do to others as they
have done to me;
I will pay them back for what they have
done."

[30] I passed by the field of one who was
lazy,
by the vineyard of a stupid person;
[31] and see, it was all overgrown with
thorns;
the ground was covered with nettles,
and its stone wall was broken down.
[32] Then I saw and considered it;
I looked and received instruction.
[33] A little sleep, a little slumber,
a little folding of the hands to rest,
[34] and poverty will come upon you like a
robber,
and want, like an armed warrior.

25 These are other proverbs of Solomon
that the officials of King Hezekiah of
Judah copied.

---

[a] Gk: Heb *do not associate with those who change*

the heart (cf. 16.2; 21.2). **13–14:** *Honey* refers to wisdom here (cf. 16.24; Ps 19.10; Ezek 3.3; Ps 119.103). **16:** The doctrine of retribution is affirmed (see 10:2–3n.), though it is assumed that the righteous do encounter hardship. **17–18:** Cf. Ps 35.11–16,19; Job 31.29. Contrast Pss 37.10–13; 52.5–7; 58.10–11. **19–20:** See 10.2–3n.; cf. Job 18.5–6. **21–22:** *The LORD and the king* are often associated in authority and respect; cf. 16.10; 21.1; Ex 22.28; 1 Kings 21.13.

24.23–34: Further words of the wise. A short separate section, an appendix to the words of the wise in 22.17–24.22. **23b–25,28:** Legal language; cf. 17.15n.; 28.21; Lev 19.15; Deut 16.19. **26:** *Kiss on the lips*, a gesture of respect and affection that should accompany truth. **27:** The importance of correct priorities and advance preparation. **29:** Human beings should not take punishment into their own hands; cf. vv. 17–18. **30–34:** A short teaching-narrative about laziness; see 6.6–11n.

² It is the glory of God to conceal things,
  but the glory of kings is to search things
    out.
³ Like the heavens for height, like the earth
    for depth,
  so the mind of kings is unsearchable.
⁴ Take away the dross from the silver,
  and the smith has material for a
    vessel;
⁵ take away the wicked from the presence
    of the king,
  and his throne will be established in
    righteousness.
⁶ Do not put yourself forward in the king's
    presence
  or stand in the place of the great;
⁷ for it is better to be told, "Come up here,"
  than to be put lower in the presence of
    a noble.

What your eyes have seen
  ⁸ do not hastily bring into court;
for[a] what will you do in the end,
  when your neighbor puts you to
    shame?
⁹ Argue your case with your neighbor
    directly,
  and do not disclose another's secret;
¹⁰ or else someone who hears you will
    bring shame upon you,
  and your ill repute will have no end.

¹¹ A word fitly spoken
  is like apples of gold in a setting of
    silver.
¹² Like a gold ring or an ornament of gold
  is a wise rebuke to a listening ear.
¹³ Like the cold of snow in the time of
    harvest

are faithful messengers to those who
    send them;
  they refresh the spirit of their masters.
¹⁴ Like clouds and wind without rain
  is one who boasts of a gift never given.
¹⁵ With patience a ruler may be persuaded,
  and a soft tongue can break bones.
¹⁶ If you have found honey, eat only
    enough for you,
  or else, having too much, you will
    vomit it.
¹⁷ Let your foot be seldom in your
    neighbor's house,
  otherwise the neighbor will become
    weary of you and hate you.
¹⁸ Like a war club, a sword, or a sharp arrow
  is one who bears false witness against a
    neighbor.
¹⁹ Like a bad tooth or a lame foot
  is trust in a faithless person in time of
    trouble.
²⁰ Like vinegar on a wound[b]
  is one who sings songs to a heavy heart.
Like a moth in clothing or a worm in wood,
  sorrow gnaws at the human heart.[c]
²¹ If your enemies are hungry, give them
    bread to eat;
  and if they are thirsty, give them water
    to drink;
²² for you will heap coals of fire on their
    heads,
  and the LORD will reward you.
²³ The north wind produces rain,
  and a backbiting tongue, angry looks.

a Cn: Heb *or else*
b Gk: Heb *Like one who takes off a garment on a cold
   day, like vinegar on lye*
c Gk Syr Tg: Heb lacks *Like a moth … human heart*

25.1–29.27: Proverbial sayings copied by Hezekiah's officials. The heading refers not only to Solomon (cf. 1.1;
10.1), to whom the proverbial sayings are attributed, but also to the officials of King Hezekiah (king of Judah ca.
715–687 BCE) who were involved in their transmission. This note gives a rare indication of a historical context for
this collection. 25.1: *Copied* refers to the editing and arranging of older sayings. 2–3: God's world is mysterious,
but the king is endowed with the profound wisdom to seek to comprehend it. Cf. 1 Kings 4.29–34. *Glory* here
means "action worthy of glory." 4–5: For similar uses of the metaphor of refining metals, see 27.21–22; Job 33.10;
Isa 1.25; 48.10; Jer 6.29–30; Ezek 22.17–22. 6–7a: Proverb against self-promotion. 7c–10: Caution about haste in
going to court with a grievance, advising direct mediation where possible. 11–12: The comparison of wisdom
and its good practices to ornaments is a frequent motif; see 2.4n. On good speech cf. 15.23; 16.24; 20.15. 13–14:
Use of weather imagery to illuminate human behavior (cf. v. 23). 15: A positive view of the power of persuasion.
16–17: The merits of restraint; cf. Sir 37.27–31. 18: See 19.5n. 22: *Heap coals of fire on their heads,* undeserved kindness awakens remorse; cf. Rom 12.17–21. A similar Egyptian penitential ritual was possibly known to the sages

²⁴ It is better to live in a corner of the
    housetop
    than in a house shared with a
       contentious wife.
²⁵ Like cold water to a thirsty soul,
    so is good news from a far country.
²⁶ Like a muddied spring or a polluted
    fountain
    are the righteous who give way before
       the wicked.
²⁷ It is not good to eat much honey,
    or to seek honor on top of honor.
²⁸ Like a city breached, without walls,
    is one who lacks self-control.

26 Like snow in summer or rain in
    harvest,
    so honor is not fitting for a fool.
² Like a sparrow in its flitting, like a
    swallow in its flying,
    an undeserved curse goes nowhere.
³ A whip for the horse, a bridle for the
    donkey,
    and a rod for the back of fools.
⁴ Do not answer fools according to their folly,
    or you will be a fool yourself.
⁵ Answer fools according to their folly,
    or they will be wise in their own eyes.
⁶ It is like cutting off one's foot and
    drinking down violence,
    to send a message by a fool.
⁷ The legs of a disabled person hang limp;
    so does a proverb in the mouth of a fool.
⁸ It is like binding a stone in a sling
    to give honor to a fool.
⁹ Like a thornbush brandished by the hand
    of a drunkard
    is a proverb in the mouth of a fool.
¹⁰ Like an archer who wounds everybody
    is one who hires a passing fool or
      drunkard.ª
¹¹ Like a dog that returns to its vomit

is a fool who reverts to his folly.
¹² Do you see persons wise in their own
    eyes?
    There is more hope for fools than for
      them.
¹³ The lazy person says, "There is a lion in
    the road!
    There is a lion in the streets!"
¹⁴ As a door turns on its hinges,
    so does a lazy person in bed.
¹⁵ The lazy person buries a hand in the dish,
    and is too tired to bring it back to the
      mouth.
¹⁶ The lazy person is wiser in self-esteem
    than seven who can answer discreetly.
¹⁷ Like somebody who takes a passing dog
    by the ears
    is one who meddles in the quarrel of
      another.
¹⁸ Like a maniac who shoots deadly
    firebrands and arrows,
¹⁹ so is one who deceives a neighbor
    and says, "I am only joking!"
²⁰ For lack of wood the fire goes out,
    and where there is no whisperer,
      quarreling ceases.
²¹ As charcoal is to hot embers and wood
    to fire,
    so is a quarrelsome person for kindling
      strife.
²² The words of a whisperer are like
    delicious morsels;
    they go down into the inner parts of the
      body.
²³ Like the glazeᵇ covering an earthen
    vessel
    are smoothᶜ lips with an evil heart.

ª Meaning of Heb uncertain
ᵇ Cn: Heb *silver of dross*
ᶜ Gk: Heb *burning*

---

of Israel. **24**: Cf. 21.9n. **26**: *A muddied spring* refers to a befouled supply of fresh water, thus rendered useless (cf. Ezek. 34.18). **27–28**: Cf. vv. 16–17.

    26.1–12: A section on fools. The term used for fool here (Heb "kesil") refers to someone who is self-complacent to the point of obtuseness. **4–5**: Juxtaposing two proverbs provokes reflection on their competing claims. Answering fools *according to their folly* means speaking to them on their level. On the one hand, doing so likens you to them; on the other, not doing so means they will think they have outwitted you. **8**: *Binding a stone in a sling* is used as a metaphor for doing something that defeats the purpose; stones are meant to be thrown from a sling, not bound in it. **9**: The expression may indicate uselessness (cf. vv. 7–8) or the use of a proverb in a hurtful way. **13–16**: A section on lazy people; see 6.6–11n. **13**: A ridiculous excuse; a *lion* is not likely to appear in the *streets*. **15**: Such people are too lazy to eat (cf. 19.24). **17–28**: A section on the consequences of antisocial speech

24 An enemy dissembles in speaking
  while harboring deceit within;
25 when an enemy speaks graciously, do
    not believe it,
  for there are seven abominations
    concealed within;
26 though hatred is covered with guile,
  the enemy's wickedness will be exposed
    in the assembly.
27 Whoever digs a pit will fall into it,
  and a stone will come back on the one
    who starts it rolling.
28 A lying tongue hates its victims,
  and a flattering mouth works ruin.

27 Do not boast about tomorrow,
  for you do not know what a day may
    bring.
2 Let another praise you, and not your own
    mouth—
  a stranger, and not your own lips.
3 A stone is heavy, and sand is weighty,
  but a fool's provocation is heavier than
    both.
4 Wrath is cruel, anger is overwhelming,
  but who is able to stand before
    jealousy?
5 Better is open rebuke
  than hidden love.
6 Well meant are the wounds a friend
    inflicts,
  but profuse are the kisses of an
    enemy.
7 The sated appetite spurns honey,
  but to a ravenous appetite even the
    bitter is sweet.
8 Like a bird that strays from its nest
  is one who strays from home.
9 Perfume and incense make the heart
    glad,
  but the soul is torn by trouble.a
10 Do not forsake your friend or the friend
    of your parent;
  do not go to the house of your kindred
    in the day of your calamity.

Better is a neighbor who is nearby
  than kindred who are far away.
11 Be wise, my child, and make my heart glad,
  so that I may answer whoever
    reproaches me.
12 The clever see danger and hide;
  but the simple go on, and suffer for it.
13 Take the garment of one who has given
    surety for a stranger;
  seize the pledge given as surety for
    foreigners.b
14 Whoever blesses a neighbor with a loud
    voice,
  rising early in the morning,
  will be counted as cursing.
15 A continual dripping on a rainy day
  and a contentious wife are alike;
16 to restrain her is to restrain the wind
  or to grasp oil in the right hand.c
17 Iron sharpens iron,
  and one person sharpens the witsd of
    another.
18 Anyone who tends a fig tree will eat its
    fruit,
  and anyone who takes care of a master
    will be honored.
19 Just as water reflects the face,
  so one human heart reflects another.
20 Sheol and Abaddon are never satisfied,
  and human eyes are never satisfied.
21 The crucible is for silver, and the furnace
    is for gold,
  so a person is testede by being praised.
22 Crush a fool in a mortar with a pestle
    along with crushed grain,
  but the folly will not be driven out.

a Gk: Heb *the sweetness of a friend is better than
  one's own counsel*
b Vg and 20.16: Heb *for a foreign woman*
c Meaning of Heb uncertain
d Heb *face*
e Heb lacks *is tested*

and behavior. On concern for speech see 10.8n. **22:** See 18.18. **27:** A kind of "poetic justice" (cf. Ps 7.15; Eccl 10.8).
  27.1–22: A miscellaneous collection featuring proverb pairs. 1–2: The words *boast* and *praise* are the same
in Hebrew. **3–4:** The imagery of overwhelming weight or force links these proverbs. **5–6:** Two proverbs on the
paradoxes of true friendship. **7:** The same insight as expressed in Benjamin Franklin's proverb, "Hunger is a
good pickle." **10:** A tripartite proverb in which the main maxim is in the final part of the verse. **12:** Cf. 22.3. **13:**
See 20.16. Repetition of earlier proverbs occurs frequently in this section. **14:** A humorous proverb on untimely
behavior; cf. Eccl 3.1–8. **15–16:** See 19.13–14n. **17–19:** Proverbs on beneficial interpersonal relationships. **20:** *Sheol*

²³ Know well the condition of your flocks,
  and give attention to your herds;
²⁴ for riches do not last forever,
  nor a crown for all generations.
²⁵ When the grass is gone, and new growth
    appears,
  and the herbage of the mountains is
    gathered,
²⁶ the lambs will provide your clothing,
  and the goats the price of a field;
²⁷ there will be enough goats' milk for your
    food,
  for the food of your household
  and nourishment for your servant-
    girls.

28

The wicked flee when no one
  pursues,
  but the righteous are as bold as a lion.
² When a land rebels
  it has many rulers;
but with an intelligent ruler
  there is lasting order.ᵃ
³ A rulerᵇ who oppresses the poor
  is a beating rain that leaves no food.
⁴ Those who forsake the law praise the
    wicked,
  but those who keep the law struggle
    against them.
⁵ The evil do not understand justice,
  but those who seek the LORD
    understand it completely.
⁶ Better to be poor and walk in
    integrity
  than to be crooked in one's ways even
    though rich.
⁷ Those who keep the law are wise
    children,
  but companions of gluttons shame their
    parents.

⁸ One who augments wealth by exorbitant
    interest
  gathers it for another who is kind to the
    poor.
⁹ When one will not listen to the law,
  even one's prayers are an
    abomination.
¹⁰ Those who mislead the upright into evil
    ways
  will fall into pits of their own making,
  but the blameless will have a goodly
    inheritance.
¹¹ The rich is wise in self-esteem,
  but an intelligent poor person sees
    through the pose.
¹² When the righteous triumph, there is
    great glory,
  but when the wicked prevail, people go
    into hiding.
¹³ No one who conceals transgressions will
    prosper,
  but one who confesses and forsakes
    them will obtain mercy.
¹⁴ Happy is the one who is never without
    fear,
  but one who is hard-hearted will fall
    into calamity.
¹⁵ Like a roaring lion or a charging
    bear
  is a wicked ruler over a poor people.
¹⁶ A ruler who lacks understanding is a
    cruel oppressor;
  but one who hates unjust gain will
    enjoy a long life.
¹⁷ If someone is burdened with the blood
    of another,

ᵃ Meaning of Heb uncertain
ᵇ Cn: Heb A poor person

and Abaddon, see 15.11n. **21**: Cf. 17.3 where it is the LORD who tests. **22**: The Heb term for fool here is "'ewil," a person of obstinate disposition without proper moral orientation. **23–27**: A section of practical advice on tending flocks and herds (cf. 12.10; Sir 7.22). The reference to a *crown* in v. 24 and the traditional link of king and shepherd imagery (e.g., 1 Kings 22.17; Isa 44.28) means that it could be read as royal advice.

28.1–29.7: A distinct unit characterized by many antithetical proverbs and a concern for just government. 28.1 and 29.27 both contrast the righteous and the wicked. **28.2**: *Many rulers* may refer to factions in the reign of a weak king or to a period of political instability. **3**: *A beating rain that leaves no food* refers to the ruining of a ripe crop by heavy rain (cf. 26.1). **4**: *The law* (Heb "torah"; cf. vv. 7,9; 29.18) can mean either revealed law or teaching, as often in Proverbs (e.g., 3.1). **5**: Cf. 29.7. **8**: *Exorbitant interest* is forbidden in biblical law; see Ex 22.25; Lev 25.36; Deut 23.19. By the principle of retribution, the oppressor should not profit (cf. 13.22; 14.31; 19.17). **9**: Cf. 15.8,29. **11**: *In self-esteem*, (lit., "in his own eyes"), the characteristic of a fool (cf. 3.7; 14.12; 26.5,12; 28.26). **14**: *Fear*, a different word than in the phrase "the fear of the LORD." The wise understand danger; fools do not (cf.

let that killer be a fugitive until death;
let no one offer assistance.
[18] One who walks in integrity will be safe,
but whoever follows crooked ways will
fall into the Pit.[a]
[19] Anyone who tills the land will have
plenty of bread,
but one who follows worthless pursuits
will have plenty of poverty.
[20] The faithful will abound with blessings,
but one who is in a hurry to be rich will
not go unpunished.
[21] To show partiality is not good—
yet for a piece of bread a person may do
wrong.
[22] The miser is in a hurry to get rich
and does not know that loss is sure to
come.
[23] Whoever rebukes a person will
afterward find more favor
than one who flatters with the tongue.
[24] Anyone who robs father or mother
and says, "That is no crime,"
is partner to a thug.
[25] The greedy person stirs up strife,
but whoever trusts in the Lord will be
enriched.
[26] Those who trust in their own wits are
fools;
but those who walk in wisdom come
through safely.
[27] Whoever gives to the poor will lack
nothing,
but one who turns a blind eye will get
many a curse.
[28] When the wicked prevail, people go into
hiding;
but when they perish, the righteous
increase.

29 One who is often reproved, yet
remains stubborn,
will suddenly be broken beyond
healing.
[2] When the righteous are in authority, the
people rejoice;

but when the wicked rule, the people
groan.
[3] A child who loves wisdom makes a parent
glad,
but to keep company with prostitutes is
to squander one's substance.
[4] By justice a king gives stability to the
land,
but one who makes heavy exactions
ruins it.
[5] Whoever flatters a neighbor
is spreading a net for the neighbor's
feet.
[6] In the transgression of the evil there is a
snare,
but the righteous sing and rejoice.
[7] The righteous know the rights of the
poor;
the wicked have no such
understanding.
[8] Scoffers set a city aflame,
but the wise turn away wrath.
[9] If the wise go to law with fools,
there is ranting and ridicule without
relief.
[10] The bloodthirsty hate the blameless,
and they seek the life of the upright.
[11] A fool gives full vent to anger,
but the wise quietly holds it back.
[12] If a ruler listens to falsehood,
all his officials will be wicked.
[13] The poor and the oppressor have this in
common:
the Lord gives light to the eyes of both.
[14] If a king judges the poor with equity,
his throne will be established forever.
[15] The rod and reproof give wisdom,
but a mother is disgraced by a neglected
child.
[16] When the wicked are in authority,
transgression increases,
but the righteous will look upon their
downfall.

[a] Syr: Heb *fall all at once*

14.16; 27.12). **17:** Cf. Cain in Gen 4.12. **18:** *The Pit*, i.e., Sheol, the abode of the dead; see 1.12n. **19:** See 6.6–11n.; 20.21n. **21:** *For a piece of bread*, bribery (cf. 18.5; 24.23b), accompanied by greed. **23:** See 1.23n. **25–26:** Proper and misplaced trust connect these sayings. **27:** See 14.31n. **29.1:** See 1.23n. **3:** See 10.1n. **4:** Cf. 16.10–13; 20.28. **5–6:** Two proverbs linked by the imagery of a hidden trap. **7:** Cf. 28.5. Wisdom literature often associates evil with a failure to perceive the true nature of things. **8:** *Set a city aflame,* i.e., ignite anger. **9:** *With fools* it is impossible to conduct a reasonable dispute (cf. 26.4). **11–13:** On self-restraint see 12.16; 14.17. **12:** On the critical role of the

17 Discipline your children, and they will
give you rest;
they will give delight to your heart.
18 Where there is no prophecy, the people
cast off restraint,
but happy are those who keep the law.
19 By mere words servants are not disciplined,
for though they understand, they will
not give heed.
20 Do you see someone who is hasty in
speech?
There is more hope for a fool than for
anyone like that.
21 A slave pampered from childhood
will come to a bad end.ᵃ
22 One given to anger stirs up strife,
and the hothead causes much
transgression.
23 A person's pride will bring humiliation,
but one who is lowly in spirit will
obtain honor.
24 To be a partner of a thief is to hate one's
own life;
one hears the victim's curse, but
discloses nothing.ᵇ
25 The fear of othersᶜ lays a snare,
but one who trusts in the LORD is secure.
26 Many seek the favor of a ruler,
but it is from the LORD that one gets
justice.
27 The unjust are an abomination to the
righteous,
but the upright are an abomination to
the wicked.

30 The words of Agur son of Jakeh. An
oracle.
Thus says the man: I am weary, O God,
I am weary, O God. How can I prevail?ᵈ

2 Surely I am too stupid to be human;
I do not have human understanding.
3 I have not learned wisdom,
nor have I knowledge of the holy
ones.ᵉ
4 Who has ascended to heaven and come
down?
Who has gathered the wind in the
hollow of the hand?
Who has wrapped up the waters in a
garment?
Who has established all the ends of the
earth?
What is the person's name?
And what is the name of the person's
child?
Surely you know!

5 Every word of God proves true;
he is a shield to those who take refuge
in him.
6 Do not add to his words,
or else he will rebuke you, and you will
be found a liar.

7 Two things I ask of you;
do not deny them to me before I die:
8 Remove far from me falsehood and
lying;
give me neither poverty nor riches;
feed me with the food that I need,
9 or I shall be full, and deny you,
and say, "Who is the LORD?"

ᵃ Vg: Meaning of Heb uncertain
ᵇ Meaning of Heb uncertain
ᶜ Or *human fear*
ᵈ Or *I am spent.* Meaning of Heb uncertain
ᵉ Or *Holy One*

king see 14.25; 16.10,12–13; 25.5; 29.4. **13:** Cf. 22.2. The LORD gives life irrespective of a person's moral nature. **18:** *Prophecy,* lit. "vision." *Law,* cf. 28.4n. A society lacking guidance experiences chaos. **19,21:** The concern with servants suggests that the audience of Proverbs is the upper class. **23:** Cf. 15.33; 16.18–19; 18.12. **24:** *Partner of a thief,* not an actual accomplice, but someone with knowledge of the crime who *discloses nothing* (cf. Lev. 5.1). **25:** Anxious *fear of others* detracts from trusting the LORD.

30.1–14: The words of Agur. A separate section with its own attribution to "Agur son of Jakeh," an unknown figure. **1:** *An oracle* (Heb "massa'"); cf. Num 24.14–25 (the oracle of Balaam). Others understand the Heb to mean "from Massa," a region of northern Arabia with a tribal group of that name, attested in Assyrian sources as early as 734 BCE, indicating that Agur was a non-Israelite sage. **2–3:** The writer acknowledges his limitations in self-deprecating terms (cf. Ps 73.21–2; Job 25.4–6). **4:** Rhetorical questions implying the answer "God" and referring to his work in creation (cf. Job 38.4–41). **5–6:** A pious response to vv. 1–4; cf. Ps 18.30 (v. 5); Deut 4.2 (v. 6). **7–10:** A prayer to God to be kept from *falsehood* and to be given just enough. This is the only prayer in the book of

or I shall be poor, and steal,
and profane the name of my God.

[10] Do not slander a servant to a master,
or the servant will curse you, and you
will be held guilty.

[11] There are those who curse their fathers
and do not bless their mothers.
[12] There are those who are pure in their
own eyes
yet are not cleansed of their
filthiness.
[13] There are those—how lofty are their
eyes,
how high their eyelids lift!—
[14] there are those whose teeth are swords,
whose teeth are knives,
to devour the poor from off the earth,
the needy from among mortals.

[15] The leech[a] has two daughters;
"Give, give," they cry.
Three things are never satisfied;
four never say, "Enough":
[16] Sheol, the barren womb,
the earth ever thirsty for water,
and the fire that never says,
"Enough."[a]

[17] The eye that mocks a father
and scorns to obey a mother
will be pecked out by the ravens of the
valley
and eaten by the vultures.

[18] Three things are too wonderful for me;
four I do not understand:
[19] the way of an eagle in the sky,
the way of a snake on a rock,

the way of a ship on the high seas,
and the way of a man with a girl.

[20] This is the way of an adulteress:
she eats, and wipes her mouth,
and says, "I have done no wrong."

[21] Under three things the earth trembles;
under four it cannot bear up:
[22] a slave when he becomes king,
and a fool when glutted with food;
[23] an unloved woman when she gets a
husband,
and a maid when she succeeds her
mistress.

[24] Four things on earth are small,
yet they are exceedingly wise:
[25] the ants are a people without strength,
yet they provide their food in the summer;
[26] the badgers are a people without power,
yet they make their homes in the
rocks;
[27] the locusts have no king,
yet all of them march in rank;
[28] the lizard[b] can be grasped in the hand,
yet it is found in kings' palaces.

[29] Three things are stately in their stride;
four are stately in their gait:
[30] the lion, which is mightiest among wild
animals
and does not turn back before any;
[31] the strutting rooster,[c] the he-goat,
and a king striding before[a] his people.

a Meaning of Heb uncertain
b Or *spider*
c Gk Syr Tg Compare Vg: Meaning of Heb uncertain

Proverbs and could be a later addition (cf. Sir 31.1–4). **11–14:** Four types of sinners are described: the unfilial, the self-deluded, the arrogant, and those who exploit the poor. The sayings are linked by repetition of keywords.
30.15–31: Numerical sayings. 15: *The leech* is a bloodsucking worm, an image of the insatiable. *Two daughters,* the suckers by which the leech attaches. *Three . . . four,* a numerical saying. **16:** Four unlike phenomena are listed as insatiable: *Sheol,* the abode of the dead, never ceases claiming victims; the *barren womb* (cf. Gen 30.1) in that the woman's desire for a child does not go away; the thirst of the dry *earth* for water; and the consuming *fire* (cf. Amos 7.4). **18–19:** The catchword *way,* although used in different senses (course, manner, path, and sexual relations) unites the phenomena; cf. Wis 5.10–11. **20:** A moralizing comment on v. 19d in the context of adultery; *eats,* engages in illicit sex (cf. 5.15; 9.17). **21–23:** Four intolerable situations. *Maid . . . mistress;* cf. Sarah and Hagar in Gen 16.3–4. **24–28:** Four small yet instructive creatures. Wisdom is valued over size and power. **29–31:** Four examples of grandeur; cf. the association of lion and king in 19.12; 20.2.

³² If you have been foolish, exalting
  yourself,
  or if you have been devising evil,
  put your hand on your mouth.
³³ For as pressing milk produces curds,
  and pressing the nose produces blood,
  so pressing anger produces strife.

31 The words of King Lemuel. An oracle
  that his mother taught him:

² No, my son! No, son of my womb!
  No, son of my vows!
³ Do not give your strength to women,
  your ways to those who destroy kings.
⁴ It is not for kings, O Lemuel,
  it is not for kings to drink wine,
  or for rulers to desire[a] strong drink;
⁵ or else they will drink and forget what
  has been decreed,
  and will pervert the rights of all the
  afflicted.
⁶ Give strong drink to one who is perishing,
  and wine to those in bitter distress;
⁷ let them drink and forget their poverty,
  and remember their misery no more.
⁸ Speak out for those who cannot speak,
  for the rights of all the destitute.[b]
⁹ Speak out, judge righteously,
  defend the rights of the poor and
  needy.

¹⁰ A capable wife who can find?
  She is far more precious than jewels.
¹¹ The heart of her husband trusts in her,
  and he will have no lack of gain.
¹² She does him good, and not harm,
  all the days of her life.
¹³ She seeks wool and flax,
  and works with willing hands.

¹⁴ She is like the ships of the merchant,
  she brings her food from far away.
¹⁵ She rises while it is still night
  and provides food for her household
  and tasks for her servant-girls.
¹⁶ She considers a field and buys it;
  with the fruit of her hands she plants a
  vineyard.
¹⁷ She girds herself with strength,
  and makes her arms strong.
¹⁸ She perceives that her merchandise is
  profitable.
  Her lamp does not go out at night.
¹⁹ She puts her hands to the distaff,
  and her hands hold the spindle.
²⁰ She opens her hand to the poor,
  and reaches out her hands to the
  needy.
²¹ She is not afraid for her household when
  it snows,
  for all her household are clothed in
  crimson.
²² She makes herself coverings;
  her clothing is fine linen and purple.
²³ Her husband is known in the city gates,
  taking his seat among the elders of the
  land.
²⁴ She makes linen garments and sells
  them;
  she supplies the merchant with sashes.
²⁵ Strength and dignity are her clothing,
  and she laughs at the time to come.
²⁶ She opens her mouth with wisdom,
  and the teaching of kindness is on her
  tongue.
²⁷ She looks well to the ways of her
  household,

ᵃ Cn: Heb *where*
ᵇ Heb *all children of passing away*

31.1–9: **The words of Lemuel,** an unknown king who, like Agur (30.1), may have been a non-Israelite. **1:** *An oracle*, see 30.1n. *His mother*, cf. 1.8b; 6.20b. **2–9:** Warnings against women and wine (only to be used for those in distress), and stress on his duties as king, notably to protect the powerless.

31.10–31 **The capable wife.** An acrostic poem of 22 lines (in which each verse begins with a subsequent letter of the Hebrew alphabet) from the point of view of the *husband* (vv. 11,23,28) and *children* (v. 28) about the ideal *wife* (v. 10) whose virtues are listed in hymnic style. **10:** *Capable* (Heb "hayil"), variously rendered as "good," "perfect," "virtuous," "noble," "worthy," or "valiant" (cf. 12.4; Ruth 3.11). *Who can find?* suggests it is difficult to do so (cf. 18.22; 19.14). *More precious than jewels* echoes personified Wisdom in 3.15; 8.11. **11–19:** Her varied economic activities contribute to the well-being of the household. **19:** *Spindle, distaff,* tools used in spinning. **20:** *Opens her hand,* see Deut 15.7. **21–22:** *Crimson . . . purple,* luxury items. **23:** The *city gates,* where commercial and legal transactions took place (22.22; 24.7; Deut 21.19; 25.7; Ruth 4.1–12). **25:** She is independent and confident;

and does not eat the bread of
idleness.
²⁸ Her children rise up and call her happy;
her husband too, and he praises her:
²⁹ "Many women have done excellently,
but you surpass them all."

³⁰ Charm is deceitful, and beauty is vain,
but a woman who fears the LORD is to
be praised.
³¹ Give her a share in the fruit of her hands,
and let her works praise her in the city
gates.

cf. Job 5.22; 39.22. **26:** Cf. personified Wisdom in 8.6–10. **31:** Praise from both family and the community. As one
who *fears the LORD* (see 1.7n.) she is the embodiment of wisdom.

ECCLESIASTES

Ecclesiastes is the Latin transliteration of the Greek rendering of the pen-name of the author, known in Hebrew as *Qohelet* (also *Qoheleth*), which literally means "Gatherer" or "Acquirer" (of wisdom, wealth, pleasures). The Hebrew term indicates something of the acquisitive environment in which the author lived and taught. The Greek term, though, meant a member of an assembly and "Ecclesiastes" was soon interpreted, incorrectly, to mean "one who gathers the assembly," hence, "Preacher." Modern scholars noting that the author of the book is more like a philosopher than a preacher, sometimes prefer to translate the name as "Teacher" (cf. 12.9). The superscription of the book (1.2) presents Qohelet as "the son of David" who ruled in Jerusalem, evoking the memory of Solomon, king of Israel (968–928 BCE), the consummate sage and gatherer of wealth and wisdom (see 1 Kings 3–4; 10). Apart from the superscription and 1.12–2.11, however, the author never speaks as king, and the epilogue portrays the author as a teacher rather than as a king (12.9–14). Moreover, the perspective in most of the book is that of an outsider to the royal court (3.16; 4.13–16; 8.1–6; 10.16–20).

CANONICAL STATUS AND LOCATION IN THE CANON

Ecclesiastes is one of the poetical and wisdom books in the Christian canon. It shares many generic features of form and content with Proverbs and Job, the other books commonly referred to as wisdom literature. In the Jewish canon, it is placed in the third division of the canon, the Writings, as one of the Megillot or "five scrolls" (Ruth, Song of Solomon, Ecclesiastes, Lamentations, Esther). Perhaps because of its radical ideas, it was a controversial book in antiquity. In Jewish tradition the canonical status of Ecclesiastes was debated as late as the second century CE. Although Ecclesiastes is included on second-century Christian canonical lists, Bishop Theodore of Mopsuestia (fifth century) questioned its sacred status.

DATE OF COMPOSITION, HISTORICAL CONTEXT, AND INTERPRETATION

The date of the book is disputed, although most scholars argue on linguistic grounds that it should be dated to the postexilic period (after 539 BCE). The presence of two indisputable Persian loan words ("parks" in 2.5; "sentence" in 8.11) points to a date some time after 450 BCE, for there are no Persian loan words or Persian names in the Hebrew Bible that can be dated earlier. The abundance of Aramaisms (i.e., Aramaic loan words, forms, and constructions) also points to the postexilic period, when Aramaic became widely used in Palestine. A number of specific idioms regarding inheritance, grants, prisons, social abuses, judicial problems, and socioeconomic classes are attested in documents from the Persian period; in no other periods in history do we find such a coincidence of terminology. These features, together with the absence of Greek loan words or ideas with an indisputably Greek origin, suggest that the book should be probably dated sometime before the Hellenistic period, between 450 and 330 BCE, although many scholars date it a century later, based in part on putative links between Ecclesiastes and Greek philosophical ideas. The book is better understood, however, against the background of the ancient Near East.

The Persian period was characterized by tremendous economic activity, spurred on by the introduction of standardized coinage by the Persian central government beginning around 515 BCE. Money subsequently became a commodity, desired for its own sake (cf. 5.10; 7.12; 10.19). Standardized currency helped to democratize economic opportunities, so that it became possible for even the poorest people in society to become wealthy. As in any era of significant economic innovation, the Persian period brought both opportunities and risks to the average person in the empire.

The volatile economy led to widespread insecurity as people toiled to get ahead or simply to gain some control over their lives, and thus understand what was happening in their world. Qohelet uses the attitudes in that uncertain period as a trope to speak theologically about human attempts to control their lives and understand a world that is contradictory, if not altogether absurd. The sense of the individual as a small part of a large scene is evident in the political allusions (e.g., 4.1), which should be read against the background of the empire. Many descriptions of life and death emphasize the impotence of individuals to change their environment (8.8). The inevitability of one's fate (3.15; 6.10), the unavoidability of death (3.19), and the repetitions of life (3.1–8) all work together to create a vision of the remoteness, the inscrutability, and ultimately the indifference of the world to the individual. In a vision of bleak grandeur the author faces this indifference, acknowledges it, and admits an inability to transcend it, but nevertheless derives from it a hard-won wisdom: This is how the world is.

The author appears to have drawn lessons from the wider wisdom tradition, yet he often approached the preoccupation of his audience through socioeconomic idioms current in his generation. Despite the newness of their environment, the fundamental problems they faced about the possibility of coping with life in a world that is inconsistent, if not contradictory, were not new after all (see 1.10). Every generation must deal with the fact that mortals inevitably live in a world in which they do not have control ("all is vanity") and life can only be lived before a sovereign God who alone determines all that happens on earth.

LITERARY STRUCTURE AND GUIDE TO READING

Opinions as to the literary structure of Ecclesiastes have ranged from the claim that there is no structure at all to attempts to work out intricate patterns. Most readers, however, discern only a rough structure. Clearly marked is the superscription (1.1) and the epilogue (12.9–14), and the motto of the book ("vanity of vanities"), which appears first in 1.2 and for the last time in 12.8. The opening poem (1.3–11) is matched at the end by a concluding poem (12.1–7). Between them the book has two halves of approximately equal length (1.12–6.9; 6.10–11.10). Within each half the first part presents a problematic situation (1.12–4.16; 6.10–8.17), and the second part contains advice on how to cope with that situation (5.1–6.9; 9.1–11.10).

Because the book is relatively short, it should be read in a single sitting. Readers should be alert for the repeated phrases that underline the recurrent perceptions of the author (e.g., "vanity of vanities," "chasing after wind," "under the sun"). Also, the reader is likely to note certain tensions, if not contradictions, in the book. Whether these represent the author's quotation and refutation of current opinion or whether they represent the author's own internal sense of contradictory experience remains debated. But the different perspectives, as well as the ironic tone, give the book a lively quality and the reader the sense of having been plunged into the midst of a conversation about important ideas.

Choon-Leong Seow

1

The words of the Teacher,[a] the son of David, king in Jerusalem.

[2] Vanity of vanities, says the Teacher,[a]
    vanity of vanities! All is vanity.
[3] What do people gain from all the toil
    at which they toil under the sun?
[4] A generation goes, and a generation
      comes,
    but the earth remains forever.
[5] The sun rises and the sun goes
      down,
    and hurries to the place where it
      rises.
[6] The wind blows to the south,
    and goes around to the north;
round and round goes the wind,
    and on its circuits the wind returns.
[7] All streams run to the sea,
    but the sea is not full;
to the place where the streams flow,
    there they continue to flow.
[8] All things[b] are wearisome;
    more than one can express;

the eye is not satisfied with seeing,
    or the ear filled with hearing.
[9] What has been is what will be,
    and what has been done is what will be
      done;
    there is nothing new under the sun.
[10] Is there a thing of which it is said,
    "See, this is new"?
It has already been,
    in the ages before us.
[11] The people of long ago are not
      remembered,
    nor will there be any remembrance
of people yet to come
    by those who come after them.
[12] I, the Teacher,[a] when king over Israel in Jerusalem, [13] applied my mind to seek and to search out by wisdom all that is done under heaven; it is an unhappy business that God has given to human beings to be busy with.

a Heb *Qoheleth*, traditionally rendered *Preacher*
b Or *words*

1.1: Superscription. The author is identified by his pen-name, *Teacher* (Heb "Qohelet"; cf. 12.9), properly, "Gatherer"—one who is supposed to have accumulated plenty of everything, including wisdom, wealth, and pleasure. The description of the author as *the son of David, king in Jerusalem* evokes images of Solomon, the consummate gatherer of wealth, wisdom, and pleasure (see also 1.2–2.11; 1 Kings 3–4; 10).

1.2–11: Preface. Despite constant activity, the world seems always to remain the same. **2:** *Vanity,* Heb "hebel," which literally means "breath" or "vapor" (Isa 57.13; Ps 62.9). In Ecclesiastes, it is used as a metaphor for things that cannot be grasped either physically or intellectually, things that are ephemeral, insubstantial, enigmatic, or absurd. Elsewhere in the Bible, the human life span and human beings themselves are said to be "hebel" (see Pss 39.4–11; 62.9; 78.33; Job 7.16). *Vanity of vanities* is a way of expressing the superlative in Hebrew; hence the phrase means "utter vanity." Virtually identical words are found in 12.8, the last verse of the book before the epilogue (12.9–14); the epigram thus frames the book. **3:** The term *gain* does not mean just "benefit," but "excess," "advantage," or "surplus." *Toil* is not the same as "work." The normal Hebrew word for the latter is also the word for "worship," but the word for *toil* typically bears negative connotations. *From all the toil* may also be translated as "in exchange for all their toil." Here, as elsewhere in the book, *toil* refers not only to the process of toiling, but to the fruit of one's toiling (see 2.10). The phrase *under the sun* occurs in the Bible only in Ecclesiastes, but it is attested elsewhere in the ancient Near East. It is a near synonym of "under the heavens" (1.13; 2.3; 3.1). "Under the heavens," however, is a spatial designation (referring to what is happening "everywhere in the world"), whereas *under the sun* refers to the realm of the living as opposed to the realm of the dead (cf. 4.15; 9.6,9). **4:** *The earth remains forever,* better "the world always stays the same." Despite human toiling and the coming and going of human generations, the world remains as it was. **5–7:** The elements of nature—light, air, and water—are also engaged in daily activities, with no new results. *The sun . . . hurries* (lit. "stomps" or "pants") to its destination, only to have to recommence its routine. The winds blow every which way and streams flow endlessly, with no new results. **8–11:** As with nature, so with knowledge; human speculations and endless instructions produce nothing new. **11:** Cf. 2.16; 9.5.

1.12–2.11: The author's experiences and accomplishments. The style of this passage is similar to that of many royal inscriptions in the ancient Near East. The author, in his assumed role as king, has experienced it all and done it all, but even he has to admit that nothing is ultimately reliable. **1.12:** The author takes on the persona of Solomon (1.1n.; 2.9). **13:** *Unhappy business* or "terrible preoccupation" may refer to human anxiety

[14] I saw all the deeds that are done under the sun; and see, all is vanity and a chasing after wind.[a]

[15] What is crooked cannot be made straight,
and what is lacking cannot be counted.

[16] I said to myself, "I have acquired great wisdom, surpassing all who were over Jerusalem before me; and my mind has had great experience of wisdom and knowledge." [17] And I applied my mind to know wisdom and to know madness and folly. I perceived that this also is but a chasing after wind.[a]

[18] For in much wisdom is much vexation,
and those who increase knowledge
increase sorrow.

2 I said to myself, "Come now, I will make a test of pleasure; enjoy yourself." But again, this also was vanity. [2] I said of laughter, "It is mad," and of pleasure, "What use is it?" [3] I searched with my mind how to cheer my body with wine—my mind still guiding me with wisdom—and how to lay hold on folly, until I might see what was good for mortals to do under heaven during the few days of their life. [4] I made great works; I built houses and planted vineyards for myself; [5] I made myself gardens and parks, and planted in them all kinds of fruit trees. [6] I made myself pools from which to water the forest of growing trees. [7] I bought male and female slaves, and had slaves who were born in my house; I also had great possessions of herds and flocks, more than any who had been before me in Jerusalem. [8] I also gathered for myself silver and gold and the treasure of kings and of the provinces; I got singers, both men and women, and delights of the flesh, and many concubines.[b]

[9] So I became great and surpassed all who were before me in Jerusalem; also my wisdom remained with me. [10] Whatever my eyes desired I did not keep from them; I kept my heart from no pleasure, for my heart found pleasure in all my toil, and this was my reward for all my toil. [11] Then I considered all that my hands had done and the toil I had spent in doing it, and again, all was vanity and a chasing after wind,[a] and there was nothing to be gained under the sun.

[12] So I turned to consider wisdom and madness and folly; for what can the one do who comes after the king? Only what has already been done. [13] Then I saw that wisdom excels folly as light excels darkness.

[14] The wise have eyes in their head,
but fools walk in darkness.

Yet I perceived that the same fate befalls all of them. [15] Then I said to myself, "What happens to the fool will happen to me also; why then have I been so very wise?" And I said to myself that this also is vanity. [16] For there is no enduring remembrance of the wise or of fools, seeing that in the days to come all will have been long forgotten. How can the wise die just like fools? [17] So I hated life, because what is done under the sun was grievous to me; for all is vanity and a chasing after wind.[a]

[18] I hated all my toil in which I had toiled under the sun, seeing that I must leave it to those who come after me [19]—and who knows whether they will be wise or foolish? Yet they will be master of all for which I toiled and used my wisdom under the sun. This also is vanity. [20] So I turned and gave my heart up to despair concerning all the toil of my labors under the sun, [21] because sometimes one who has toiled with wisdom

---

[a] Or *a feeding on wind.* See Hos 12.1
[b] Meaning of Heb uncertain

---

over all that is happening in the world. **14:** *Under the sun,* see 1.3n. *Chasing after wind,* i.e., pursuit of futility (Hos 12.2; Prov 15.14; Sir 34.1–2). **15:** A proverb about humanly impossible tasks (cf. 7.13). **2.4–11:** A summary of accomplishments like those found in royal inscriptions. Despite his worldly successes, the author concludes that everything is but "vanity"—that is, beyond the grasp of mortals. **11:** *Nothing to be gained,* cf. 1.3n.

2.12–26: The leveling effect of death. Whatever advantage anyone might have in life is negated by death. **12–17:** Wisdom is better than folly (*as light excels darkness,* v. 13), yet the wise and fools face *the same fate* of death (v. 14; cf. 3.19–20; 9.2–3), and they are all *forgotten* after their death (cf. 1.11). **17:** *Chasing after wind,* see 1.14n. **18–23:** Toil does not give an advantage in the face of death. People cannot take the fruit of their toil with them when they die, and thus are discontented with it when they live. Even the possibility of passing an inheritance to heirs does not give enjoyment, for the heirs may not deserve the inheritance. **18:** *Under the sun,* see

and knowledge and skill must leave all to be enjoyed by another who did not toil for it. This also is vanity and a great evil. [22] What do mortals get from all the toil and strain with which they toil under the sun? [23] For all their days are full of pain, and their work is a vexation; even at night their minds do not rest. This also is vanity.

[24] There is nothing better for mortals than to eat and drink, and find enjoyment in their toil. This also, I saw, is from the hand of God; [25] for apart from him[a] who can eat or who can have enjoyment? [26] For to the one who pleases him God gives wisdom and knowledge and joy; but to the sinner he gives the work of gathering and heaping, only to give to one who pleases God. This also is vanity and a chasing after wind.[b]

3 For everything there is a season, and a time for every matter under heaven:
[2] a time to be born, and a time to die;
a time to plant, and a time to pluck up
    what is planted;
[3] a time to kill, and a time to heal;
a time to break down, and a time to build
    up;
[4] a time to weep, and a time to laugh;
a time to mourn, and a time to dance;
[5] a time to throw away stones, and a time
    to gather stones together;

a time to embrace, and a time to refrain
    from embracing;
[6] a time to seek, and a time to lose;
a time to keep, and a time to throw away;
[7] a time to tear, and a time to sew;
a time to keep silence, and a time to speak;
[8] a time to love, and a time to hate;
a time for war, and a time for peace.

[9] What gain have the workers from their toil? [10] I have seen the business that God has given to everyone to be busy with. [11] He has made everything suitable for its time; moreover he has put a sense of past and future into their minds, yet they cannot find out what God has done from the beginning to the end. [12] I know that there is nothing better for them than to be happy and enjoy themselves as long as they live; [13] moreover, it is God's gift that all should eat and drink and take pleasure in all their toil. [14] I know that whatever God does endures forever; nothing can be added to it, nor anything taken from it; God has done this, so that all should stand in awe before him. [15] That which is, already has been; that which is to be, already is; and God seeks out what has gone by.[c]

[a] Gk Syr: Heb *apart from me*
[b] Or *a feeding on wind.* See Hos 12.1
[c] Heb *what is pursued*

1.3n. **24–26:** People do not have control over their future; the only good is to partake of life fully in the present, for enjoyment is *from the hand of God* (v. 24). Cf. 3.13; 5.18; 9.7–10. The sovereign God arbitrarily gives the possibility of enjoyment to those who are somehow favored, but not to *the sinner*, a term that may simply mean "the one who misses out," the loser (cf. 7.26; 9.2,18; Prov 8.36; 13.22; 14.21; 19.2; 20.2).

3.1–15: The determination of events. God determines time and timing. **1–8:** A rhythmic series of contrary pairs (seven sets, each with two pairs of opposites) that together represent the totality and variety of the times and seasons humans encounter. These events include those that simply happen to people (like being born and dying) and occasions to which they must respond (like planting and plucking up what is planted). **9:** The rhetorical question is essentially the same as in 1.3; 2.22; 6.11, except that human beings are called *the workers* (lit. "the one who acts"), even though God is the one who acts effectively in the following verses. **10:** *Business,* see 1.13n. **11:** The same God who *made everything suitable for its time* ironically puts *a sense of past and future* (lit. "eternity") into human consciousness. Human beings must live with this paradox of knowing the reality that transcends the moment ("eternity") while being able to cope only with the moment. **12–13:** In view of human limitations, one should partake of good, for it is *God's gift* to do so; cf. 5.18. **14:** *Whatever God does endures forever,* the Hebrew should be taken to mean that God's deeds are "eternal," i.e., not bound by time (see 3.11n.). The timeless, eternal character of God's doing stands in stark contrast to the "eternity" that exists only in human hearts (v. 11). Human activity is always only "in its time" (v. 11), whereas God's activity is not bound by time. The language of adding and subtracting is used elsewhere for matters that are decisive, authoritative, and invariable (Deut 4.2; 12.32; cf. Jer 26.2; Prov 30.6). God establishes the difference so that human beings might know their place, that is, *stand in awe* of God. **15:** *What has gone by,* lit. "what is pursued."

[16] Moreover I saw under the sun that in the place of justice, wickedness was there, and in the place of righteousness, wickedness was there as well. [17] I said in my heart, God will judge the righteous and the wicked, for he has appointed a time for every matter, and for every work. [18] I said in my heart with regard to human beings that God is testing them to show that they are but animals. [19] For the fate of humans and the fate of animals is the same; as one dies, so dies the other. They all have the same breath, and humans have no advantage over the animals; for all is vanity. [20] All go to one place; all are from the dust, and all turn to dust again. [21] Who knows whether the human spirit goes upward and the spirit of animals goes downward to the earth? [22] So I saw that there is nothing better than that all should enjoy their work, for that is their lot; who can bring them to see what will be after them?

4 Again I saw all the oppressions that are practiced under the sun. Look, the tears of the oppressed—with no one to comfort them! On the side of their oppressors there was power—with no one to comfort them. [2] And I thought the dead, who have already died, more fortunate than the living, who are still alive; [3] but better than both is the one who has not yet been, and has not seen the evil deeds that are done under the sun.

[4] Then I saw that all toil and all skill in work come from one person's envy of another. This also is vanity and a chasing after wind.[a]

[5] Fools fold their hands
  and consume their own flesh.
[6] Better is a handful with quiet
  than two handfuls with toil,
  and a chasing after wind.[a]

[7] Again, I saw vanity under the sun: [8] the case of solitary individuals, without sons or brothers; yet there is no end to all their toil, and their eyes are never satisfied with riches. "For whom am I toiling," they ask, "and depriving myself of pleasure?" This also is vanity and an unhappy business.

[9] Two are better than one, because they have a good reward for their toil. [10] For if they fall, one will lift up the other; but woe to one who is alone and falls and does not have another to help. [11] Again, if two lie together, they keep warm; but how can one keep warm alone? [12] And though one might prevail against another, two will withstand one. A threefold cord is not quickly broken.

[13] Better is a poor but wise youth than an old but foolish king, who will no longer take advice. [14] One can indeed come out of prison to reign, even though born poor in the kingdom. [15] I saw all the living who, moving about under the sun, follow that[b] youth who replaced the king;[c] [16] there was no end to all those people whom he led. Yet those who come later will not rejoice in him. Surely this also is vanity and a chasing after wind.[a]

---

a Or *a feeding on wind*. See Hos 12.1
b Heb *the second*
c Heb *him*

3.16–22: **The determination of humanity's fate.** There are injustices in the world, even in places where one might expect justice; cf. 8.14. God will, however, adjudicate the situation in God's own time; cf. 12.14. **19:** As far as mortality is concerned, human beings have no advantage over animals: All must die. **20:** *One place,* Sheol, the abode of the dead (9.10). *Dust,* 12.7; Gen 3:19. **21:** *Who knows,* a rhetorical question. The author is apparently skeptical about the belief in survival after death, an idea which was beginning to be developed.

4.1–16: **Relative good.** In the light of the author's insistence that there is nothing better for humanity than to enjoy work (3.22), these verses make plain that everything thought by mortals to be good is only relatively so. **1–3:** The living still have to witness the injustices of life, whereas the dead no longer have to do so and those who have never been born never have to do so. **4–6:** On the one hand, human toil and strivings are driven by envy. On the other hand, the idleness of fools is self-destructive. The better alternative, even if only relatively good, is to have a little (material goods, enjoyment, or both), but to have it with peace. **6:** Sayings of the form "*better . . . than*" are common in Proverbs (12.9; 15.16–17; 16.8). **7–8:** People toil for no reason other than habit or obsessive compulsion. **7:** *Under the sun,* 1.3n. **9–12:** There is relative advantage in numbers, but no guarantee. A three-ply cord may still snap, although not as easily as a cord with only two strands or one. **13–16:** It is better to start out poorly and end up well. Every generation will have its new underdog-turned-hero, who will seem to have limitless support from populace, until the next hero comes along. **16:** *Vanity,* 1.2n. *Chasing after wind,* 1.14n.

5 [a] Guard your steps when you go to the house of God; to draw near to listen is better than the sacrifice offered by fools; for they do not know how to keep from doing evil.[b] 2 [c]Never be rash with your mouth, nor let your heart be quick to utter a word before God, for God is in heaven, and you upon earth; therefore let your words be few.

3 For dreams come with many cares, and a fool's voice with many words.

4 When you make a vow to God, do not delay fulfilling it; for he has no pleasure in fools. Fulfill what you vow. 5 It is better that you should not vow than that you should vow and not fulfill it. 6 Do not let your mouth lead you into sin, and do not say before the messenger that it was a mistake; why should God be angry at your words, and destroy the work of your hands?

7 With many dreams come vanities and a multitude of words;[d] but fear God.

8 If you see in a province the oppression of the poor and the violation of justice and right, do not be amazed at the matter; for the high official is watched by a higher, and there are yet higher ones over them. 9 But all things considered, this is an advantage for a land: a king for a plowed field.[d]

10 The lover of money will not be satisfied with money; nor the lover of wealth, with gain. This also is vanity.

11 When goods increase, those who eat them increase; and what gain has their owner but to see them with his eyes?

12 Sweet is the sleep of laborers, whether they eat little or much; but the surfeit of the rich will not let them sleep.

13 There is a grievous ill that I have seen under the sun: riches were kept by their owners to their hurt, 14 and those riches were lost in a bad venture; though they are parents of children, they have nothing in their hands. 15 As they came from their mother's womb, so they shall go again, naked as they came; they shall take nothing for their toil, which they may carry away with their hands. 16 This also is a grievous ill: just as they came, so shall they go; and what

a Ch 4.17 in Heb
b Cn: Heb *they do not know how to do evil*
c Ch 5.1 in Heb
d Meaning of Heb uncertain

5.1–7: **Attitude before God.** God and human beings do not belong to the same realm. It is necessary, therefore, to have the right attitude before God. **1:** It is more acceptable to obey God than to show off one's religiosity, as fools often do (cf. Prov 21.3; 1 Sam 15.22; Am 5.22–24; Hos 6.6). *They do not know how to keep from doing evil,* fools are often described as lacking perceptiveness (Prov 10.21,23; 14.8; 18.2). **3:** In the ancient Near East, *dreams* were often seen as foreshadowing the future, though in coded symbols (cf. the anxiety-producing dreams of Pharaoh in Gen 41 and Nebuchadnezzar in Dan 2; 4). **4–7:** Vows must be taken seriously; cf. Deut 23.21–22; Sir 18.2. The text warns against the lack of restraint in speech, for the mouth may bring condemnation to the entire person (cf. Lev 5.4; Prov 10.19). It is unclear who *the messenger* in v. 6 refers to; perhaps the Temple priest to whom people went to confess that they had erred (see Num 15.22–31; Lev 4.2,22,27–30). The confession would be useless, however, because God would still be angry at the foolish utterances. **7:** *Fear God,* respect and awe before God are central values in wisdom literature (Job 1.1,8; 2.3; 28.28; Prov 1.7).

5.8–6.9: **Enjoy, but do not be greedy.** The passage is arranged in such a way that the outer sections lead inward toward its center in 5.20, with its call for enjoyment. **5.8:** *High official* (lit. "high one"), a term elsewhere used of someone who is arrogant (Job 41.34; Ps 138.6; Isa 10.33; Ezek 21.26) and never of officials of any sort. This text does not refer to a government bureaucracy, but to ambitious people who strive to get ahead of one another and commit injustice in the process. No matter how high they get, however, there will always be people higher than they who look down upon them. **9:** The meaning of this verse is obscure. **10:** Wealth itself is not the problem here but greed—the insatiability of the rich (see Sir 31.5–7). *Vanity,* 1.2n. **11:** The rhetorical question presupposes a negative answer. *To see them with his eyes* implies that wealth is good only for present enjoyment. **12:** The contrast is not between one who works and one who is a sluggard, but between poor *laborers* (or "employees") and *the rich* who cannot stop worrying despite the plenty they already possess (Sir 31:1). *Surfeit,* overindulgence in food or perhaps possessions. The rich consume so much that they are unable to sleep either because of indigestion or worry, or both. **13–14:** The case of the rich person who accumulates much wealth, only to lose it all. **15:** When people are buried, they figuratively return to the womb of mother earth; cf. Job 1.21;

gain do they have from toiling for the wind? [17] Besides, all their days they eat in darkness, in much vexation and sickness and resentment.

[18] This is what I have seen to be good: it is fitting to eat and drink and find enjoyment in all the toil with which one toils under the sun the few days of the life God gives us; for this is our lot. [19] Likewise all to whom God gives wealth and possessions and whom he enables to enjoy them, and to accept their lot and find enjoyment in their toil—this is the gift of God. [20] For they will scarcely brood over the days of their lives, because God keeps them occupied with the joy of their hearts.

6 There is an evil that I have seen under the sun, and it lies heavy upon humankind: [2] those to whom God gives wealth, possessions, and honor, so that they lack nothing of all that they desire, yet God does not enable them to enjoy these things, but a stranger enjoys them. This is vanity; it is a grievous ill. [3] A man may beget a hundred children, and live many years; but however many are the days of his years, if he does not enjoy life's good things, or has no burial, I say that a still-born child is better off than he. [4] For it comes into vanity and goes into darkness, and in darkness its name is covered; [5] moreover it has not seen the sun or known anything; yet it finds rest rather than he. [6] Even though he should live a thousand years twice over, yet enjoy no good—do not all go to one place?

[7] All human toil is for the mouth, yet the appetite is not satisfied. [8] For what advantage have the wise over fools? And what do the poor have who know how to conduct themselves before the living? [9] Better is the sight of the eyes than the wandering of desire; this also is vanity and a chasing after wind.[a]

[10] Whatever has come to be has already been named, and it is known what human beings are, and that they are not able to dispute with those who are stronger. [11] The more words, the more vanity, so how is one the better? [12] For who knows what is good for mortals while they live the few days of their vain life, which they pass like a shadow? For who can tell them what will be after them under the sun?

---

[a]   Or *a feeding on wind*. See Hos 12.1

Sir 40.1. **17:** The preceding verses focus on the loss of possessions; this one highlights the complementary ill of not enjoying what one does possess. **18–19:** The right to enjoy life is, as a rule, given by God to all humanity. **18:** *Under the sun*, 1.3n. **19:** *Gift of God*, cf. 3.12–13n. **20:** *They will scarcely brood over the days of their lives*, perhaps better "they should not much call to mind the days of their lives." Rather than constantly thinking about their lives and their mortality they should enjoy the present because God has given them joy. The Hebrew word translated *keeps them occupied* is the same form for the word "answer" (Prov 15.1,23; 16.1; 29.19; Job 32.3,5). **6.1–2:** Whereas God has given some people the opportunity to enjoy (5.18–19), sometimes God does the contrary. **3:** *But however many are the days of his years*, perhaps better "and yet he complains that the days of his years will come to pass." Even though this person has everything that anyone might desire, including abundant wealth, progeny, and long life, he complains about the days ahead of him, dissatisfied with all that he has, and even worried about proper burial when he dies. In that case, he is no better off than *a stillborn child* (cf. Job 3.16–18). **4–6:** There is no point in having a long life if one cannot enjoy it. **7:** *The appetite is not satisfied,* the language here alludes to the insatiability of Death in Canaanite mythology (cf. Isa 5.14; Hab 2.5; Prov 27.20; 30.16). Compare the similar perspective on unending activity in 1.3–8. **8–9:** *Sight of the eyes . . . wandering of desire*, the contrast appears to be between what is present and the insatiable appetite for what is not. The answer lies in the enjoyment of what one has, i.e., in contentment. **9:** For the form of the saying, see 4.6n. *Vanity . . . chasing after wind*, 1.2n.; 1.14n.

6.10–7.14: The limits of knowledge. The passage begins (6.10–12) and ends (7.13–14) with statements that emphasize human ignorance and weakness, over against divine determination and the deity's incomprehensible activity. The "better . . . than" sayings in 7.1–12 are, therefore, quoted in mockery: they illustrate the sort of sayings proffered by those who believe that mortals know what is really good. **6.10–12:** Despite the passive verbs (v. 10), it is clear that the author means that God is the one who has *named* and *known*. **10:** *Dispute with those who are stronger*, a possible allusion to Job 9.1–4. **11–12:** The reference to abundant and empty words anticipates the sayings to follow (7.1–12). By using rhetorical questions, the author suggests that humans have no advantage, because no one *knows what is good for mortals*. Neither the foolish nor the wise can give others

7 A good name is better than precious
ointment,
and the day of death, than the day of
birth.
[2] It is better to go to the house of
mourning
than to go to the house of feasting;
for this is the end of everyone,
and the living will lay it to heart.
[3] Sorrow is better than laughter,
for by sadness of countenance the heart
is made glad.
[4] The heart of the wise is in the house of
mourning;
but the heart of fools is in the house of
mirth.
[5] It is better to hear the rebuke of the wise
than to hear the song of fools.
[6] For like the crackling of thorns under a
pot,
so is the laughter of fools;
this also is vanity.
[7] Surely oppression makes the wise foolish,
and a bribe corrupts the heart.
[8] Better is the end of a thing than its
beginning;
the patient in spirit are better than the
proud in spirit.
[9] Do not be quick to anger,
for anger lodges in the bosom of fools.
[10] Do not say, "Why were the former days
better than these?"
For it is not from wisdom that you ask
this.

[11] Wisdom is as good as an inheritance,
an advantage to those who see the sun.
[12] For the protection of wisdom is like the
protection of money,
and the advantage of knowledge is that
wisdom gives life to the one who
possesses it.
[13] Consider the work of God;
who can make straight what he has
made crooked?
[14] In the day of prosperity be joyful, and in
the day of adversity consider; God has made
the one as well as the other, so that mortals
may not find out anything that will come
after them.
[15] In my vain life I have seen everything;
there are righteous people who perish in their
righteousness, and there are wicked people
who prolong their life in their evildoing. [16] Do
not be too righteous, and do not act too wise;
why should you destroy yourself? [17] Do not be
too wicked, and do not be a fool; why should
you die before your time? [18] It is good that you
should take hold of the one, without letting
go of the other; for the one who fears God
shall succeed with both.
[19] Wisdom gives strength to the wise more
than ten rulers that are in a city.
[20] Surely there is no one on earth so righteous as to do good without ever sinning.
[21] Do not give heed to everything that people say, or you may hear your servant cursing
you; [22] your heart knows that many times you
have yourself cursed others.

advice on what is universally good. **7.1–12:** A series of "better . . . than" sayings imitating the style of traditional
proverbs (see 4.6n.), with their tendency to present issues in dialectical pairs: fame and luxury (v. 1a), birth and
death (v. 1b), funeral and wedding (v. 2), merriment and sadness (v. 3), mourning and pleasure (v. 4), rebuke and
praise (v. 5), the wise and the fool (vv. 6–7), beginning and end (v. 8), patience and arrogance (v. 8). The sayings
are all subverted and relativized, however. The effect of the overall presentation is to show that no one knows
what is universally good. Each saying may contain an element of truth, but the sum total of these many words
is, again, "vanity" (v. 6; see 1.2n.)—just so much empty talk (cf. 6.11). **13–14:** People should accept good when it
is accessible and face adversity when that is a reality; see 1.15; 3.14.

   7.15–29: Righteousness and wisdom are elusive. This passage consists of two parts: The first concerns the
dangers of extreme behavior, including excessive righteousness and wisdom (vv. 15–22); the second concerns
the elusiveness of wisdom (vv. 23–29). **15:** The traditional doctrine of retribution (e.g., Prov 11.3–11) is often
contradicted by experience. **16:** Those who aspire to extreme righteousness (also meaning "rightness") may destroy themselves. **17:** Those who are too wicked and foolish will suffer the consequences. The wisdom tradition
often advocates moderation (see Sir 7.4–5). **18:** *The one . . . the other* refers to the two ideas in vv. 16–17. Whoever
is religious (*fears God*) will follow both precepts. **19:** Perhaps a proverbial illustration of the value people place
on wisdom and power, although neither will avert death. **20:** Perfect righteousness ("rightness") is impossible,
for every mortal misses the mark (cf. 1 Kings 8.46; 2 Chr 6.26; Pss 14.1–3; 53.1–3; 143.2; Prov 20.9; Job 4.17).

23 All this I have tested by wisdom; I said, "I will be wise," but it was far from me. 24 That which is, is far off, and deep, very deep; who can find it out? 25 I turned my mind to know and to search out and to seek wisdom and the sum of things, and to know that wickedness is folly and that foolishness is madness. 26 I found more bitter than death the woman who is a trap, whose heart is snares and nets, whose hands are fetters; one who pleases God escapes her, but the sinner is taken by her. 27 See, this is what I found, says the Teacher,[a] adding one thing to another to find the sum, 28 which my mind has sought repeatedly, but I have not found. One man among a thousand I found, but a woman among all these I have not found. 29 See, this alone I found, that God made human beings straightforward, but they have devised many schemes.

8 Who is like the wise man?
   And who knows the interpretation of a
      thing?
Wisdom makes one's face shine,
   and the hardness of one's countenance
      is changed.

2 Keep[b] the king's command because of your sacred oath. 3 Do not be terrified; go from his presence, do not delay when the matter is unpleasant, for he does whatever he pleases. 4 For the word of the king is powerful, and who can say to him, "What are you doing?" 5 Whoever obeys a command will meet no harm, and the wise mind will know the time and way. 6 For every matter has its time and way, although the troubles of mortals lie heavy upon them. 7 Indeed, they do not know what is to be, for who can tell them how it will be? 8 No one has power over the wind[c] to restrain the wind,[c] or power over the day of death; there is no discharge from the battle, nor does wickedness deliver those who practice it. 9 All this I observed, applying my mind to all that is done under the sun, while one person exercises authority over another to the other's hurt.

10 Then I saw the wicked buried; they used to go in and out of the holy place, and were praised in the city where they had done such things.[d] This also is vanity. 11 Because sentence against an evil deed is not executed speedily, the human heart is fully set to do evil. 12 Though sinners do evil a hundred times and prolong their lives, yet I know

a   Qoheleth, traditionally rendered Preacher
b   Heb I keep
c   Or breath
d   Meaning of Heb uncertain

26: *The woman who is a trap*, this is not a polemic against women in general but echoes in allegorical fashion the warnings in other wisdom writings against Folly, personified as a seductive woman (Prov 2.16–19; 5.20; 6.24–35; 7.5–27; 23.27–28). Wisdom is elusive, but Folly is on a hunt to catch people unawares. 27: *Teacher*, see 1.1n. *Adding one thing to another*, an image of an accountant or merchant working on a ledger (cf. v. 25). 28: *One man among a thousand . . . a woman among all these*, this notoriously difficult sentence may be a gloss prompted by misinterpretation of v. 26 as referring to women in general. The first part of the verse refers to the elusiveness of wisdom (cf. Prov 1.28; 3.13–15; 31.10).

8.1–17: **Reflections on the limits of power. 1–5:** Traditional advice on how to react to arbitrary power only shows the limits of wisdom. **1:** *Makes one's face shine*, elsewhere it is always God who "makes one's face shine" (Num 6.25; Pss 31.16; 67.1; 80.3,7,19; 119.135; etc.). The idiom means "to be gracious" or "to be pleasant." Wisdom causes one to act pleasantly. **2:** *Because of*, perhaps "in the manner of." *Sacred oath*, an oath sworn in the name of God (Ex 22.11; 2 Sam 21.7; 1 Kings 2.43), hence, the most solemn oath. A *king's command* should be taken that seriously. **3:** *Do not delay when the matter is unpleasant*, or "do not persist in a harmful thing," possibly an allusion to sedition. In the face of overwhelming odds, one should not do anything dangerous. **5b–7:** *Time and way*, lit. "time and judgment" (cf. 3.1,16–17). There are a proper time and a proper judgment, although no one knows when and how until after the fact. **8:** *Power over the wind to restrain the wind*, or "power over the (life-)breath to hold back the (life-)breath." No one has the power to avert death. *No discharge from battle*, better "no substitution in battle." No one can send a substitute to take his or her place in the final battle that is death. **10:** The wicked are properly interred and honored upon their death (Job 21.32–33). *Vanity*,1.2n. **11:** The slow judicial process encourages the wicked to do even more evil (Job 21.19–21). **12–13:** The wicked may live long, but the human life span is finally limited: they will not *prolong their days* (that are) *like a shadow*, a transient and unreliable

that it will be well with those who fear God, because they stand in fear before him, ¹³ but it will not be well with the wicked, neither will they prolong their days like a shadow, because they do not stand in fear before God.

¹⁴ There is a vanity that takes place on earth, that there are righteous people who are treated according to the conduct of the wicked, and there are wicked people who are treated according to the conduct of the righteous. I said that this also is vanity. ¹⁵ So I commend enjoyment, for there is nothing better for people under the sun than to eat, and drink, and enjoy themselves, for this will go with them in their toil through the days of life that God gives them under the sun.

¹⁶ When I applied my mind to know wisdom, and to see the business that is done on earth, how one's eyes see sleep neither day nor night, ¹⁷ then I saw all the work of God, that no one can find out what is happening under the sun. However much they may toil in seeking, they will not find it out; even though those who are wise claim to know, they cannot find it out.

9 All this I laid to heart, examining it all, how the righteous and the wise and their deeds are in the hand of God; whether it is love or hate one does not know. Everything that confronts them ² is vanity,ᵃ since the same fate comes to all, to the righteous and the wicked, to the good and the evil,ᵇ to the clean and the unclean, to those who sacrifice and those who do not sacrifice. As are the good, so are the sinners; those who swear are like those who shun an oath. ³ This is an evil in all that happens under the sun, that the same fate comes to everyone. Moreover, the hearts of all are full of evil; madness is in their hearts while they live, and after that they go to the dead. ⁴ But whoever is joined with all the living has hope, for a living dog is better than a dead lion. ⁵ The living know that they will die, but the dead know nothing; they have no more reward, and even the memory of them is lost. ⁶ Their love and their hate and their envy have already perished; never again will they have any share in all that happens under the sun.

⁷ Go, eat your bread with enjoyment, and drink your wine with a merry heart; for God has long ago approved what you do. ⁸ Let your garments always be white; do not let oil be lacking on your head. ⁹ Enjoy life with the wife whom you love, all the days of your vain life that are given you under the sun, because that is your portion in life and in your toil at which you toil under the sun. ¹⁰ Whatever your hand finds to do, do with your might; for there is no work or thought or knowledge or wisdom in Sheol, to which you are going.

¹¹ Again I saw that under the sun the race is not to the swift, nor the battle to the strong,

ᵃ Syr Compare Gk: Heb *Everything that confronts them ²is everything*

ᵇ Gk Syr Vg: Heb lacks *and the evil*

thing (cf. 6.12; Pss 102.11; 109.23; 144.4; Job 8.9; 14.2; 17.7). **14:** *Vanity . . . vanity,* here means an incomprehensible situation (see 1.2n.). **15:** *To eat, and drink, and enjoy,* traditionally "to eat, and to drink, and to be merry" (KJV); cf. 2.24; 3.13; 5.18; 9.7. **16–17:** *One's eyes see sleep neither day nor night,* an idiom for constant effort. Even those who are so dedicated to understanding God's mysterious activity cannot find what they yearn to know.

9.1–10: Enjoy life. All people face the common fate of death, regardless of their character. Yet life is better than death and one should enjoy life whenever able to do so. **1–2:** *Love* and *hate* may refer to human emotions that accompany their *deeds,* or to divine favor and disfavor. Since death *comes to all* (cf. 2.14–15; 3.19), one cannot deduce God's attitude. *Vanity,*1.2n. **4–6:** For all its limitations, life is still better than death, for the dead will not have whatever life has to offer. For the living, there are still some possibilities, however uncertain and ephemeral those may be. **7–10:** Enjoy life while you can, for God has already *approved what you do;* when you die this will be impossible. A similar passage in the ancient Mesopotamian epic of Gilgamesh suggests that the advice to enjoy life in the full knowledge of certain death was a piece of folk wisdom. **8:** *Let your garments always be white,* clean garments indicate a happy, prosperous life. *Oil . . . on your head,* another indication of happiness and prosperity (cf. Ps 23.5). **9:** *Vain life,* lit. "days of vanity," here refers to the ephemeral nature of life (see 1.2n.). **10:** *Whatever your hand finds to do,* means one's ability to act (cf. Lev 12.8; 25.28; 1 Sam 10.7). *Sheol,* the abode of the dead.

9.11–10.15: The world is full of risks. 9.11–12: The author disputes the cause-and-effect or act-and-consequence logic that characterizes Proverbs' view of life. Outcomes are not predictable. *Time and chance,* i.e., death

nor bread to the wise, nor riches to the intelligent, nor favor to the skillful; but time and chance happen to them all. [12] For no one can anticipate the time of disaster. Like fish taken in a cruel net, and like birds caught in a snare, so mortals are snared at a time of calamity, when it suddenly falls upon them.

[13] I have also seen this example of wisdom under the sun, and it seemed great to me. [14] There was a little city with few people in it. A great king came against it and besieged it, building great siegeworks against it. [15] Now there was found in it a poor wise man, and he by his wisdom delivered the city. Yet no one remembered that poor man. [16] So I said, "Wisdom is better than might; yet the poor man's wisdom is despised, and his words are not heeded."

[17] The quiet words of the wise are more to be heeded
than the shouting of a ruler among fools.
[18] Wisdom is better than weapons of war,
but one bungler destroys much good.

10 Dead flies make the perfumer's ointment give off a foul odor;
so a little folly outweighs wisdom and honor.
[2] The heart of the wise inclines to the right,
but the heart of a fool to the left.
[3] Even when fools walk on the road, they lack sense,
and show to everyone that they are fools.
[4] If the anger of the ruler rises against you,
do not leave your post,
for calmness will undo great offenses.
[5] There is an evil that I have seen under the sun, as great an error as if it proceeded from

the ruler: [6] folly is set in many high places, and the rich sit in a low place. [7] I have seen slaves on horseback, and princes walking on foot like slaves.

[8] Whoever digs a pit will fall into it;
and whoever breaks through a wall will be bitten by a snake.
[9] Whoever quarries stones will be hurt by them;
and whoever splits logs will be endangered by them.
[10] If the iron is blunt, and one does not whet the edge,
then more strength must be exerted;
but wisdom helps one to succeed.
[11] If the snake bites before it is charmed,
there is no advantage in a charmer.

[12] Words spoken by the wise bring them favor,
but the lips of fools consume them.
[13] The words of their mouths begin in foolishness,
and their talk ends in wicked madness;
[14] yet fools talk on and on.
No one knows what is to happen,
and who can tell anyone what the future holds?
[15] The toil of fools wears them out,
for they do not even know the way to town.

[16] Alas for you, O land, when your king is a servant,[a]
and your princes feast in the morning!

[a] Or a child

as an unpredictable event. **13–16:** An illustration that wisdom provides no guarantee. *Wisdom* may be *better than might,* but wisdom may not be heeded because of issues of social class. **15:** *Delivered,* better "might have delivered." The text concerns lost opportunity. This wise man might have saved the city, but no one thought of him because of his lowly status. **17:** A proverb that can only be understood ironically in light of v. 16. **18:** The relative virtue of wisdom is negated by a single fool. **10.1:** With a slight emendation, the text reads "a fly that dies" instead of *dead flies.* Just as a single fool might negate the value of wisdom, so a single dead fly could ruin a pot of precious ointment. **2:** *Right . . . left,* indicate opposite sides, but may also carry ethical connotations of what is good and right on the one hand, and what is bad and sinister on the other. **5–7:** A world turned topsy-turvy (see Prov 26.1; 30.21–23; Isa 3.4–5). **8:** The hunter who *digs a pit* to trap animals is most vulnerable to his own trap. A farmer who breaks down old walls to build new ones is susceptible to dangers that come with that task. **9:** *Whoever quarries stones* or *splits logs* is vulnerable to occupational hazards. **10–11:** Just as precautionary measures might help avert accidents, so wisdom is desirable. Yet, sometimes the precautionary measure may come too late or where there may be no advantage in taking the measure at all (as with snakes that cannot be charmed).

10.16–11.6: Living with risks. First political risks are discussed (10.16–20), then economic risks (11.1–6).

[17] Happy are you, O land, when your king is
a nobleman,
and your princes feast at the proper
time—
for strength, and not for drunkenness!
[18] Through sloth the roof sinks in,
and through indolence the house leaks.
[19] Feasts are made for laughter;
wine gladdens life,
and money meets every need.
[20] Do not curse the king, even in your
thoughts,
or curse the rich, even in your
bedroom;
for a bird of the air may carry your voice,
or some winged creature tell the matter.

11 Send out your bread upon the waters,
for after many days you will get it back.
[2] Divide your means seven ways, or even
eight,
for you do not know what disaster may
happen on earth.
[3] When clouds are full,
they empty rain on the earth;

whether a tree falls to the south or to the
north,
in the place where the tree falls, there it
will lie.
[4] Whoever observes the wind will not sow;
and whoever regards the clouds will not
reap.
[5] Just as you do not know how the breath
comes to the bones in the mother's womb,
so you do not know the work of God, who
makes everything.
[6] In the morning sow your seed, and at
evening do not let your hands be idle; for you
do not know which will prosper, this or that,
or whether both alike will be good.
[7] Light is sweet, and it is pleasant for the
eyes to see the sun.
[8] Even those who live many years should
rejoice in them all; yet let them remember
that the days of darkness will be many. All
that comes is vanity.
[9] Rejoice, young man, while you are young,
and let your heart cheer you in the days of
your youth. Follow the inclination of your

10.16–17: *Your king is a servant,* or "your king is a boy" (the Heb word has both meanings). The point is that incompetent people have gained power (cf. 9.17–18; 10.5–6), and other leaders, too, have proven themselves unqualified because of their indiscretion. 18–19: *The house leaks,* or, "the house collapses": subversive political commentary in the guise of an innocuous proverb. The saying appears to be about the ruin of a house because of the owner's laziness, but *the house* may have political overtones, suggesting the incompetence and indiscretion of the leaders. Similarly, v. 19 may be read as a proverb affirming life's pleasures and rewards, or as a critique of the irresponsible lifestyle of the elite. 20: The Heb verb for *curse* used here simply means "to denigrate" or "to vilify." The author warns against the kinds of subversive activity suggested by the "inside jokes" of vv. 18–19. Even cryptic and private criticisms will become known to those in power. 11.1: *Send out your bread upon the waters,* a parallel from an Egyptian wisdom text suggests that this is about spontaneous good deeds. Generosity is expressed by the image of bread that is voluntarily given up, released upon the waters, where it will either float downstream or sink. One may do something without thinking much about it, yet one may not lose all in such an action. 2: *Divide your means seven ways, or even eight,* lit. "Give a portion to seven or even to eight." This is a numerical saying (Prov 6.16; 30.15–33; Am 1–2); *seven* and *eight* together signify a large, though indefinite, amount (cf. Mic 5.5). The point is to be generous "although" (instead of *for*) one does not know what the future may bring. 3–4: *Clouds* and *wind* are mysterious things that mortals do not control. When clouds are saturated it will rain, and when a tree is blown by a north wind or a south wind it will fall accordingly. People are powerless either to cause these natural phenomena or to prevent them from happening. The farmer who waits for the perfect weather conditions to *sow* or to *reap* will never do so. 5: The Heb word for *breath* is the same word used for "wind" in v. 4. The word used for *mother* (lit. "full one") echoes the reference to the clouds being "full" (v. 3). Just as the movement of the wind is a mystery, so too the way the life-breath enters a body is a mystery. Likewise, the activity of God is a mystery beyond human understanding (cf. Ps 139.13–16). 6: Instead of waiting for the perfect timing, one should be willing to work at any time—*in the morning* or *at evening*.

11.7–12.8: Conclusion: enjoy life while there is still time to do so. 8: *All that comes is vanity* (see 1.2n.), i.e., nothing is permanent. 9: *But know that . . . God will bring you into judgment*: the translation implies that enjoyment is contrary to the will of God. For the author, however, enjoyment is a divine gift (2.24–26; 3.10–15; 5.18–20; 9.7,9). A better translation is: "and know that . . . God will bring you into judgment" for failure to accept

heart and the desire of your eyes, but know that for all these things God will bring you into judgment.

[10] Banish anxiety from your mind, and put away pain from your body; for youth and the dawn of life are vanity.

12 Remember your creator in the days of your youth, before the days of trouble come, and the years draw near when you will say, "I have no pleasure in them"; [2] before the sun and the light and the moon and the stars are darkened and the clouds return with[a] the rain; [3] in the day when the guards of the house tremble, and the strong men are bent, and the women who grind cease working because they are few, and those who look through the windows see dimly; [4] when the doors on the street are shut, and the sound of the grinding is low, and one rises up at the sound of a bird, and all the daughters of song are brought low; [5] when one is afraid of heights, and terrors are in the road; the almond tree blossoms, the grasshopper drags itself along[b] and desire fails; because all must go to their eternal home, and the mourners will go about the streets; [6] before the silver cord is snapped,[c] and the golden bowl is broken, and the pitcher is broken at the fountain, and the wheel broken at the cistern, [7] and the dust returns to the earth as it was, and the breath[d] returns to God who gave it. [8] Vanity of vanities, says the Teacher;[e] all is vanity.

[9] Besides being wise, the Teacher[e] also taught the people knowledge, weighing and studying and arranging many proverbs. [10] The Teacher[e] sought to find pleasing words, and he wrote words of truth plainly.

[11] The sayings of the wise are like goads, and like nails firmly fixed are the collected sayings that are given by one shepherd.[f] [12] Of anything beyond these, my child, beware.

a Or *after*; Heb *'ahar*
b Or *is a burden*
c Syr Vg Compare Gk: Heb *is removed*
d Or *the spirit*
e *Qoheleth*, traditionally rendered *Preacher*
f Meaning of Heb uncertain

the gift of enjoyment. **12.1:** The mention of the *creator* anticipates v. 7. The Heb for *your creator* ("bore'eka") sounds like the word "cistern" ("bor") in v. 6. The call to *remember* points back to the injunction to enjoy while one is able (11.7–10), but it also points forward to the scene of death at the end of the passage and to the creator who gave and will receive the human life-breath (v. 7.) **2–7:** In a poem that uses eschatological language, the author takes poetic license in arguing that mortals should enjoy what they can while they still have a chance, for a time may come when no one can enjoy. With poetic exaggeration, the author depicts the end of human life in terms of the end of the world. **2:** The language of the darkening sky is reminiscent of prophetic eschatology (cf. Isa 5.30; 13.10; Ezek 32.7–8; Am 5.8; 8.9; Mic 3.6). The Heb text says that rain clouds return "after" (not *with*) the rain, a sign of disaster, perhaps implying the return of the Flood (Gen 7.11–12; 8.2). **3:** *In the day when* (cf. Mal 3.1–3). Even the strong and valiant are terrified of what is happening (cf. Rev 6.12–17). The women who work the mills suddenly stop work (cf. Mt 24.40–41; Lk 17.34–35). Women look out the windows in despair (cf. Judg 5.28). The domestic routines are interrupted. **4:** *The doors* of the street-bazaar *are shut*; the mills that produce meals are silenced. *One rises up at the sound of a bird*, better "the sound of the birds rises," a reference to the cacophony of birds of prey descending. Thus, while the salutary sound of the mill drops, the unsavory sound of the birds rises. Moreover, the birds actually descend when they see the terror on the ground (v. 5). **5:** The translation of this difficult text depends on the interpretation of the scenario. The consonantal text of the Hebrew suggests the decline and dying of several types of trees. Thus, it is not the blossoming of *the almond tree*, but the tree becoming "hideous." The "locust" tree, too, "droops" (NRSV: *the grasshopper drags itself along*), while the caper-berry tree defoliates (NRSV: *desire fails*). In short, nature languishes (Am 1.2; Joel 2.12; Hab 3.17; Rev 6.12–14), as humanity marches toward the grave, *their eternal home* and an imaginary funeral takes place. **6:** Symbols of the permanent end of life. **7:** See Gen 2.7; 3.19. **8:** *Vanity of vanities*, the words echo 1.2, which together with this verse frame the body of the book.

12.9–14: Epilogue. An assessment and apology for the author and the book. **9:** The author is a typical sage: He teaches, gathers wisdom sayings, and works with them. **10:** Like a sage, the author's words have been deliberately chosen and rightly presented. **11:** The words of the wise are hard to hear but, like goads and nails, they have been deliberately applied as by a shepherd to his flock. **12:** A formulaic conclusion to establish the

Of making many books there is no end, and much study is a weariness of the flesh. [13] The end of the matter; all has been heard. Fear God, and keep his commandments; for that is the whole duty of everyone.

[14] For God will bring every deed into judgment, including[a] every secret thing, whether good or evil.

[a] Or *into the judgment on*

authority of the text. Everything intended by the author has been laid out. **13:** *The end of the matter*, these words originally ended the epilogue and, hence, the book. The words beyond this point are later additions. The call to *fear God* is found elsewhere in the book (3.14; 5.7; 8.12–13), but the call to obey God's *commandments* is not.

THE SONG OF SOLOMON

NAME OF BOOK AND LOCATION IN CANON

The Song of Solomon (Heb "Song of Songs"), also known as Canticles, appears in the Megillot, or "five scrolls" (Ruth, Song of Songs, Ecclesiastes, Lamentations, Esther), in the third part of the Jewish canon, the Writings. In the Christian canon it is among the Poetical and Wisdom books.

AUTHORSHIP, DATE OF COMPOSITION, LITERARY AND HISTORICAL CONTEXT

The Song of Solomon, the Bible's only love poem, offers no clues about when, where, or under what circumstances it was composed. Its author is unknown. The traditional attribution of the book to Solomon probably derives from references to Solomon in the poem (1.5; 3.7,9,11; 8.11,12) and his reputation as the composer of songs (1 Kings 4.32) and owner of a large harem (1 Kings 11.3).

Speculation about the date of composition ranges from the time of Solomon (tenth century BCE) to the Hellenistic period (fourth to second centuries BCE). Some scholars see the Song as a collection, in which case the various love poems would come from different authors and different times.

Similarities to Mesopotamian (3000–1000 BCE) and, in particular, Egyptian love poetry (thirteenth to eleventh centuries BCE), indicate that the poet drew upon a rich cultural tradition of love poetry. Shared features include wishing, desiring, praising the beloved, metaphoric descriptions of the body, double entendre, nature imagery, and the appeal to the senses. Sometimes a dialogue format is used; frequently the lovers address each other as "sister" and "brother." Many of the Mesopotamian love poems deal with the marriage of the goddess and her consort and were used in ritual contexts. In contrast, the Song, like the Egyptian love poems, is not about gods nor does it appear to have had anything to do with worship.

STRUCTURE AND CONTENTS

The Song is about how glorious it is to be in love. It looks at love from both a woman's and a man's point of view, and it consists entirely of dialogue, so that we learn about love through what lovers say about it. The dialogue format creates the impression that we are overhearing the lovers as they speak, and observing their love unfold. The poet seeks to immortalize a vision of love as strong as death by portraying the lovers as forever seeking and finding gratification of their mutual desire. They delight in each other and in the sights, sounds, smells, tastes, and tangibility of the world around them, making the Song a feast for the senses.

A third speaking voice belongs to the women of Jerusalem, a kind of chorus functioning as an audience within the poem and whose presence, because the lovers are aware of and encourage it, facilitates the reader's entry into the lovers' seemingly private world of erotic intimacy.

The poem begins and ends with short speeches in which the speakers change frequently, and the voices of the woman, the man, and, occasionally, the women of Jerusalem intermingle (1.2–2.7; 8.1–14). In between—although the structure is not rigid—are two cycles of long speeches, in which the woman speaks, then the man, with the woman interrupting his speeches at the end (2.8–3.11 and 4.1–5.1; 5.2–6.3 and 6.4–7.13).

INTERPRETATION

Allegory was the dominant mode of interpretation from the early centuries of the Common Era until the rise of critical biblical scholarship in the nineteenth century. Jewish interpreters typically read the Song as an account of the relationship between God and Israel, while Christians saw it as about the love between Christ and the church, or Christ (or the divine logos) and the individual believer. Modern scholars recognize its subject as human love, though some have argued that it originated as a liturgical text whose speakers are a god and goddess. Whether the Song was included in the canon because it had been allegorized or was allegorized because it had been included in the canon has long been debated. Allegorization alone cannot have been the reason the Song was included, since the text must have already achieved a certain status—perhaps as national religious literature—for anyone to have taken the trouble to develop an allegorical interpretation of it.

GUIDE TO READING

The Song is a lyric poem, not a record of events in the lives of two lovers. This means that unusual events or sudden transitions do not require explanation to make them seem more realistic or more intelligible. When we read lyric poetry, which is essentially a discontinuous form, we should not expect to find the kind of linear unfolding of events that produces a plot. The Song meanders, repeating themes, images, phrases, and sometimes whole sections. As we read the poem, we may feel that we get to know the lovers, for they each have their own distinctive way of talking about their love and its effect on them. She is lovesick (2.5; 5.8), and she tells stories in which he comes to court her and she searches for him (2.8–17; 3.1–5; 5.2–8). He is overwhelmed by her (4.9; 6.5), and praises her charms in detail (4.1–15; 6.4–10; 7.1–9). Yet even as we build a picture of them, we need to recognize that the woman and the man are personae created by the poet to represent all lovers. They appear in various guises—shepherds, vineyard keepers, royal figures—as well as appearing as themselves. Because they are not real lovers, their movements are not restricted. They effortlessly traverse the poetic landscape—vineyards, gardens, palaces, houses, rocky cliffs, the wilderness, Lebanon—finding pleasure wherever their fancy takes them.

Readers are meant to revel in the poem's sonorousness, rich vocabulary, and exotic images. Its dense metaphoric language and extravagant images are not reducible to simple prose paraphrase, and typically the metaphors the lovers use to describe each other's bodies hide as much as they reveal.

This is no private poem, intended for a lover's ears only. It invites its readers to participate in the wonder of love, along with the women of Jerusalem, whose presence serves as a reminder that what seems to be a closed dialogue between lovers is indeed addressed to the reader.

J. Cheryl Exum

1

The Song of Songs, which is Solomon's.

² Let him kiss me with the kisses of his
    mouth!
For your love is better than wine,
  ³ your anointing oils are fragrant,
your name is perfume poured out;
  therefore the maidens love you.
⁴ Draw me after you, let us make haste.
  The king has brought me into his
    chambers.
We will exult and rejoice in you;

we will extol your love more than wine;
  rightly do they love you.

⁵ I am black and beautiful,
  O daughters of Jerusalem,
like the tents of Kedar,
  like the curtains of Solomon.
⁶ Do not gaze at me because I am dark,
  because the sun has gazed on me.
My mother's sons were angry with me;
  they made me keeper of the vineyards,
but my own vineyard I have not kept!

1.1: Title. *Song of Songs*, a superlative, "the best song," like "king of kings" (Ezek 26.7), the king above all kings; "holy of holies" (Ex 26.33), the most holy place; "vanity of vanities" (Eccl 1.2), the height of absurdity. Hebrew "shir" is a generic term for "song" or "poem." *Which is Solomon's* could indicate authorship, or that Solomon is the dedicatee, or that the Song is connected with him in some way (compare the use of "of David" as an editorial superscription to many psalms).

1.2–2.7: A montage of short speeches. 1.2: The poem begins with a romantic relationship already in progress. The woman speaks about her lover as "him," as though he were not there, then suddenly he materializes and she speaks to him of *your love*. *Love*, a plural form referring to physical lovemaking (4.10; 7.12; cf. Prov 7.18). Like *wine*, love is intoxicating (cf. Judg 9.13). **4:** *The king*, i.e., the lover in his royal or Solomonic guise. Here too she speaks of him in the third person, as the king, and then in the second person "you," as in v. 2. *We*, the lovers, or, more likely, the woman and the *maidens* mentioned in v. 3, who are probably also the "they" at the end of v. 4. She is besotted with him and imagines that other women are similarly affected. **5–6:** *Black and beautiful*, her dark skin, she explains, is due to exposure to the sun while working in the vineyards. **5:** *Daughters of Jerusalem*, the female inhabitants of Jerusalem (cf. "sons of Israel" for Israelites). *Kedar*, a northern Arabian tribe whose name means "dark." **6:** No reason is given for the brothers' anger nor is any further reference made to it. *My*

⁷ Tell me, you whom my soul loves,
　　where you pasture your flock,
　　where you make it lie down at noon;
for why should I be like one who is veiled
　　beside the flocks of your companions?

⁸ If you do not know,
　　O fairest among women,
follow the tracks of the flock,
　　and pasture your kids
　　beside the shepherds' tents.

⁹ I compare you, my love,
　　to a mare among Pharaoh's chariots.
¹⁰ Your cheeks are comely with ornaments,
　　your neck with strings of jewels.
¹¹ We will make you ornaments of gold,
　　studded with silver.

¹² While the king was on his couch,
　　my nard gave forth its fragrance.
¹³ My beloved is to me a bag of myrrh
　　that lies between my breasts.
¹⁴ My beloved is to me a cluster of henna
　　blossoms
　　in the vineyards of En-gedi.

¹⁵ Ah, you are beautiful, my love;
　　ah, you are beautiful;
　　your eyes are doves.
¹⁶ Ah, you are beautiful, my beloved,

truly lovely.
Our couch is green;
¹⁷ the beams of our house are cedar,
　　our rafters^a are pine.

2 I am a rose^b of Sharon,
　　a lily of the valleys.

² As a lily among brambles,
　　so is my love among maidens.

³ As an apple tree among the trees of the
　　wood,
　　so is my beloved among young men.
With great delight I sat in his shadow,
　　and his fruit was sweet to my taste.
⁴ He brought me to the banqueting house,
　　and his intention toward me was love.
⁵ Sustain me with raisins,
　　refresh me with apples;
　　for I am faint with love.
⁶ O that his left hand were under my head,
　　and that his right hand embraced me!
⁷ I adjure you, O daughters of Jerusalem,
　　by the gazelles or the wild does:
do not stir up or awaken love
　　until it is ready!

a　Meaning of Heb uncertain
b　Heb *crocus*

own vineyard refers to the woman herself, probably with a sexual meaning, as also in 8.12. **7–8:** The lovers appear in the guise of shepherds. **7:** *Pasture your flock*, there is no term for flock in the Hebrew, which reads, "Where do you graze?" This is one of many instances of double entendre in the Song: the man grazes or feeds among the lilies and in the gardens, figures for the woman herself (2.1–2; 4.12–5.1; see also 2.16 and 6.2–3, where NRSV also inserts "flock"). *Veiled* could refer to a disguise, or, better, read "one who wanders," with some ancient versions. **8:** Spoken either by the man or by the women of Jerusalem, who elsewhere address the woman as "fairest among women" (5.9; 6.1). **9–11:** The man compares his beloved to a fine horse, a common form of praise in antiquity. **11:** He will have the work done, without specifying who will do it (though possibly "we" could be the lovers or the man and the women of Jerusalem). **12–14:** The woman speaks of her beloved as *the king*, as in 1.4. The fragrance of *nard* and *myrrh*, costly aromatics, blend with the natural scent of *henna blossoms*, which are strongly scented and grow in dense clusters. *En-gedi*, an oasis on the western shore of the Dead Sea. **1.15–2.3:** Mutual adoration. The man (v. 15) and the woman (vv. 16–17) praise each other in similar terms. She compares herself to flowers we cannot identify with any certainty (2.1). He turns her self-description into a compliment (v. 2), which she returns in a way that echoes his words (v. 3). *Sharon*, either the coastal plain between Jaffa and Mount Carmel or simply "the plain." **2.4:** *Banqueting house*, lit. "house of wine," where the lovers dwell in their mutual intoxication. **5–7:** The woman addresses the women of Jerusalem. *Faint with love*, lovesickness, for which the cause, love, is also the cure. **6:** Either a wish or a statement of fact; see 8.3. **7:** See 3.5; 8.4. This resembles a conventional way of swearing an oath but lacks the solemnity: the word for "gazelles" looks and sounds like the word for "hosts" in the name "Lord of Hosts," and Hebrew "'aylot hassadeh" ("wild does") recalls the divine name El Shaddai. *Love* is personified as something that has a will of its own.

[8] The voice of my beloved!
  Look, he comes,
leaping upon the mountains,
  bounding over the hills.
[9] My beloved is like a gazelle
  or a young stag.
Look, there he stands
  behind our wall,
gazing in at the windows,
  looking through the lattice.
[10] My beloved speaks and says to me:
"Arise, my love, my fair one,
  and come away;
[11] for now the winter is past,
  the rain is over and gone.
[12] The flowers appear on the earth;
  the time of singing has come,
and the voice of the turtledove
  is heard in our land.
[13] The fig tree puts forth its figs,
  and the vines are in blossom;
  they give forth fragrance.
Arise, my love, my fair one,
  and come away.
[14] O my dove, in the clefts of the rock,
  in the covert of the cliff,
let me see your face,
  let me hear your voice;
for your voice is sweet,
  and your face is lovely.
[15] Catch us the foxes,
  the little foxes,
that ruin the vineyards—
  for our vineyards are in blossom."

[16] My beloved is mine and I am his;
  he pastures his flock among the lilies.
[17] Until the day breathes
  and the shadows flee,
turn, my beloved, be like a gazelle
  or a young stag on the cleft mountains.[a]

3 Upon my bed at night
  I sought him whom my soul loves;
I sought him, but found him not;
  I called him, but he gave no answer.[b]
[2] "I will rise now and go about the city,
  in the streets and in the squares;
I will seek him whom my soul loves."
  I sought him, but found him not.
[3] The sentinels found me,
  as they went about in the city.
"Have you seen him whom my soul loves?"
[4] Scarcely had I passed them,
  when I found him whom my soul loves.
I held him, and would not let him go
  until I brought him into my mother's
    house,
  and into the chamber of her that
    conceived me.
[5] I adjure you, O daughters of Jerusalem,
  by the gazelles or the wild does:
do not stir up or awaken love
  until it is ready!

[6] What is that coming up from the wilderness,
  like a column of smoke,

a Or *on the mountains of Bether*; meaning of Heb uncertain
b Gk: Heb lacks this line

2.8–3.11: The woman's first long speech. The woman's primary mode of speaking about love is to tell stories in which she and her lover are characters. As stories, these parts of the Song, unlike the poem as a whole, have plots. Here she tells three. **2.8–17:** The first describes the man's visit to her house and his invitation to her to join him outdoors to enjoy the springtime. *The voice of my beloved*, better, "Listen! My lover!" "Listen" and *look* create the impression of immediacy. His movements are captured in process as he draws closer: *leaping* and *bounding*, then *standing* and *gazing*. **11:** *Winter*, the rainy season. **12:** *Time of singing* may also be read as "time of pruning." **14:** She seems inaccessible, perhaps also shy and hesitant. **15–17:** She answers his request to hear her voice. *Foxes* and *vineyards*, young men and young women. In v. 15 she speaks for women in general; in v. 16, about her relationship with her lover, which is exclusive and mutual. **17:** *Until the day breathes and the shadows flee* could refer to either evening or morning. Whereas she seems to be saying that the time has come for her lover to return, over the mountains, from which he came (v. 8), *cleft mountains* (or emend to "mountains of spices" as in 8.14) alludes to the woman herself and the various pleasures her body offers, perhaps her breasts (see 4.5–6). **3.1–5:** In her second story, she describes her nocturnal search for her beloved and its resolution when she finds him. **5:** See 2.7; 8.4. **3.6–11:** Her third story. A luxurious conveyance approaches, bearing her lover, whom she casts in the role of King Solomon on his wedding day. **6:** *Coming up*, the procession is in motion. First

perfumed with myrrh and frankincense,
  with all the fragrant powders of the
    merchant?
[7] Look, it is the litter of Solomon!
Around it are sixty mighty men
  of the mighty men of Israel,
[8] all equipped with swords
  and expert in war,
each with his sword at his thigh
  because of alarms by night.
[9] King Solomon made himself a palanquin
  from the wood of Lebanon.
[10] He made its posts of silver,
  its back of gold, its seat of purple;
its interior was inlaid with love.[a]
  Daughters of Jerusalem,
  [11] come out.
Look, O daughters of Zion,
  at King Solomon,
at the crown with which his mother
    crowned him
  on the day of his wedding,
  on the day of the gladness of his heart.

4 How beautiful you are, my love,
  how very beautiful!
Your eyes are doves
  behind your veil.
Your hair is like a flock of goats,
  moving down the slopes of Gilead.
[2] Your teeth are like a flock of shorn ewes
  that have come up from the washing,
all of which bear twins,

and not one among them is bereaved.
[3] Your lips are like a crimson thread,
  and your mouth is lovely.
Your cheeks are like halves of a
    pomegranate
  behind your veil.
[4] Your neck is like the tower of David,
  built in courses;
on it hang a thousand bucklers,
  all of them shields of warriors.
[5] Your two breasts are like two fawns,
  twins of a gazelle,
  that feed among the lilies.
[6] Until the day breathes
  and the shadows flee,
I will hasten to the mountain of myrrh
  and the hill of frankincense.
[7] You are altogether beautiful, my love;
  there is no flaw in you.
[8] Come with me from Lebanon, my bride;
  come with me from Lebanon.
Depart[b] from the peak of Amana,
  from the peak of Senir and Hermon,
from the dens of lions,
  from the mountains of leopards.

[9] You have ravished my heart, my sister, my
    bride,
  you have ravished my heart with a
    glance of your eyes,

---

a Meaning of Heb uncertain
b Or *Look*

it looks *like a column of smoke.* Next comes an appeal to the sense of smell created by the fragrant aromas of *myrrh* and *frankincense,* suggesting that what is approaching from the distance might be a caravan laden with *fragrant powders of the merchant.* **7–8:** *Look,* now the source of the smoke and the fragrance can be seen, a *litter* or *palanquin* (v. 9), an enclosed chair or couch carried by bearers, surrounded by an armed escort. **9–10:** The trappings of the magnificent *palanquin* progressively come into view. *Love* is not a material for decorating, like *wood, silver, gold,* and *purple,* and should be emended to "precious stones" or "ebony."

4.1–5.1: The man's first long speech. The man's mode of speaking about love is to look at his lover, tell her what he sees and how it affects him. **4.1–5:** He describes parts of her body, using similes and metaphors. **1:** *Goats, moving down the slopes,* flowing tresses of wavy black hair (goats were commonly black or dark colored). *Gilead,* a hilly region in northern Jordan. **2:** *Teeth,* white and evenly paired, with none missing. **3:** *Cheeks, halves of a pomegranate,* perhaps rosy cheeks glimpsed through a white mesh *veil.* **4:** The image suggests a *neck* adorned with a necklace made up of several rows of beads. *Tower of David* evokes her regal quality; no such tower is known. **5:** Elsewhere the man is described as *feeding among the lilies,* an erotically suggestive image in which the lilies signify the woman (2.16; 6.2–3). **6:** He responds to her exhortation of 2.17. *Mountain of myrrh, hill of frankincense,* the woman's breasts, the woman herself, and the place where the lovers enjoy love's pleasures. **8:** *Bride,* here and v. 11, and "my sister, my bride" (4.9,10,12; 5.1) are terms of endearment. *Amana, Senir,* and *Hermon,* peaks in the Anti-Lebanon mountain range, north of Israel, where lions and leopards make their dens, create a contrast to the accessible mountains of v. 6 and symbolize the woman's inaccessibility and the awe she inspires

with one jewel of your necklace.
¹⁰ How sweet is your love, my sister, my
      bride!
  how much better is your love than
      wine,
  and the fragrance of your oils than any
      spice!
¹¹ Your lips distill nectar, my bride;
  honey and milk are under your tongue;
  the scent of your garments is like the
      scent of Lebanon.
¹² A garden locked is my sister, my bride,
  a garden locked, a fountain sealed.
¹³ Your channelᵃ is an orchard of
      pomegranates
  with all choicest fruits,
  henna with nard,
¹⁴ nard and saffron, calamus and
      cinnamon,
  with all trees of frankincense,
myrrh and aloes,
  with all chief spices—
¹⁵ a garden fountain, a well of living water,
  and flowing streams from Lebanon.

¹⁶ Awake, O north wind,
  and come, O south wind!
Blow upon my garden
  that its fragrance may be wafted abroad.
Let my beloved come to his garden,
  and eat its choicest fruits.

5 I come to my garden, my sister, my bride;
  I gather my myrrh with my spice,

I eat my honeycomb with my honey,
  I drink my wine with my milk.

Eat, friends, drink,
  and be drunk with love.

² I slept, but my heart was awake.
Listen! my beloved is knocking.
"Open to me, my sister, my love,
  my dove, my perfect one;
for my head is wet with dew,
  my locks with the drops of the night."
³ I had put off my garment;
  how could I put it on again?
I had bathed my feet;
  how could I soil them?
⁴ My beloved thrust his hand into the
      opening,
  and my inmost being yearned for him.
⁵ I arose to open to my beloved,
  and my hands dripped with myrrh,
my fingers with liquid myrrh,
  upon the handles of the bolt.
⁶ I opened to my beloved,
  but my beloved had turned and was
      gone.
My soul failed me when he spoke.
I sought him, but did not find him;
  I called him, but he gave no answer.
⁷ Making their rounds in the city
  the sentinels found me;
they beat me, they wounded me,

ᵃ Meaning of Heb uncertain

in him. **9:** *Ravished*, either "stirred my heart" or "captured my heart." He speaks of love in terms of conquest, describing his feeling of being overwhelmed by her as something she has done to him. **11:** *The scent of Lebanon*, i.e., the fragrant cedars. **4.12–5.1:** A cluster of metaphors create a picture of his lover as a fragrant garden, full of edible delights. **4.12:** *Garden locked*, his private garden for his exclusive pleasure. **13–15:** She is a paradisiacal garden, where exotic spice-bearing plants and trees from such faraway places as Arabia, Africa, and India grow side by side. **16:** The woman interrupts him, first inviting the winds into her garden to whet the man's appetite by stirring up its sweet smells, then inviting her lover to an erotic banquet. **5.1:** Eating and drinking are symbols of sexual intimacy. *Eat, friends*, the women of Jerusalem encourage the lovers in their mutual intoxication.

  5.2–6.3: The woman's second long speech. Again the woman tells of a visit by the man followed by her search for him in the city streets at night. A dialogue with the women of Jerusalem enables her story to reach the desired outcome, union with her lover. **5.2–8:** See 3.1–5. Her story is replete with sexual allusions. **5.2:** *I slept, but my heart was awake*, a light sleep, in which the woman, desiring or anticipating her lover's visit, is half-listening for his voice. **3:** Either an explanation for her delay, addressed to the women of Jerusalem, or a playful reply to her lover ("I have put off my garment"). **5.** *Myrrh*, with which the woman had anointed herself, or perfumed her bed (Prov 7.17), or both. **6:** *My soul failed me* (lit. "went forth") may refer to swooning or fainting (cf. the similar expression used of dying, Gen 35.18; Ps 146.4). *When he spoke*, better translated, "because of him" or "when he left." **7:** A forceful reminder of the perils of love, or of the willingness of love to suffer. No justification

they took away my mantle,
 those sentinels of the walls.
[8] I adjure you, O daughters of Jerusalem,
 if you find my beloved,
tell him this:
 I am faint with love.

[9] What is your beloved more than another
  beloved,
 O fairest among women?
What is your beloved more than another
  beloved,
 that you thus adjure us?

[10] My beloved is all radiant and ruddy,
 distinguished among ten thousand.
[11] His head is the finest gold;
 his locks are wavy,
 black as a raven.
[12] His eyes are like doves
 beside springs of water,
bathed in milk,
 fitly set.[a]
[13] His cheeks are like beds of spices,
 yielding fragrance.
His lips are lilies,
 distilling liquid myrrh.
[14] His arms are rounded gold,
 set with jewels.
His body is ivory work,[a]
 encrusted with sapphires.[b]
[15] His legs are alabaster columns,
 set upon bases of gold.
His appearance is like Lebanon,
 choice as the cedars.

[16] His speech is most sweet,
 and he is altogether desirable.
This is my beloved and this is my friend,
 O daughters of Jerusalem.

6 Where has your beloved gone,
 O fairest among women?
Which way has your beloved turned,
 that we may seek him with you?

[2] My beloved has gone down to his garden,
 to the beds of spices,
to pasture his flock in the gardens,
 and to gather lilies.
[3] I am my beloved's and my beloved is mine;
 he pastures his flock among the lilies.

[4] You are beautiful as Tirzah, my love,
 comely as Jerusalem,
 terrible as an army with banners.
[5] Turn away your eyes from me,
 for they overwhelm me!
Your hair is like a flock of goats,
 moving down the slopes of Gilead.
[6] Your teeth are like a flock of ewes,
 that have come up from the washing;
all of them bear twins,
 and not one among them is bereaved.
[7] Your cheeks are like halves of a
  pomegranate
 behind your veil.

***

a Meaning of Heb uncertain
b Heb *lapis lazuli*

***

is given for the woman's harsh treatment at the hands of the *sentinels*, and the verse is ambiguous regarding the severity of their attack. **5.9–6.3:** The women of Jerusalem's questions and the woman's answers reveal that they are not taking the search too seriously. **9:** They ask what is so special about him. **10–16:** She answers by praising him, thereby evoking his presence. The images are intimate and erotically suggestive. **10:** *Radiant and ruddy*, a sign of health, youthfulness, and beauty (Ps 104.15; 1 Sam 16.12; 17.42; Lam 4.7). **12:** *Doves* in pellucid pools, as though *bathed in milk*, evoke the pupil and iris surrounded by the wet milky whiteness of the eye. **14–16:** Her description of his statuesque body made of strong and precious materials expresses his value to her. **16:** *His speech* (lit. "his palate"), better, "his mouth," since she is describing his physical attributes. *My friend*, her only use of a term of endearment he uses frequently of her (1.9,15; 2.2,10,13; 4.1,7; 5.2; 6.4, where NRSV translates, "my love"). **6.1:** The playfulness of the dialogue is obvious, since they ask her where he has gone in order to help her find him. **2–3:** She knows where he is. The *garden* represents both the woman and the setting for lovemaking. Grazing *in the gardens* and *among the lilies* are double entendres for erotic play (see 1.7n.).

 6.4–7.9: The man's second long speech. Again the man describes the woman's charms in similes and metaphors. **6.4:** *Tirzah*, capital of the Northern Kingdom of Israel ca. 920–880 BCE. *Terrible as an army with banners*, more likely the Hebrew means "as awesome in splendor as they," i.e., Jerusalem and Tirzah in this verse; the moon and the sun in v. 10. **5a:** *They overwhelm me*, he describes the way he feels as something she has done to

8 There are sixty queens and eighty
   concubines,
  and maidens without number.
9 My dove, my perfect one, is the only one,
  the darling of her mother,
  flawless to her that bore her.
The maidens saw her and called her
   happy;
  the queens and concubines also, and
   they praised her.
10 "Who is this that looks forth like the
   dawn,
  fair as the moon, bright as the sun,
  terrible as an army with banners?"

11 I went down to the nut orchard,
  to look at the blossoms of the
   valley,
to see whether the vines had budded,
  whether the pomegranates were in
   bloom.
12 Before I was aware, my fancy set me
  in a chariot beside my prince.ᵃ

13 ᵇReturn, return, O Shulammite!
  Return, return, that we may look upon
   you.

Why should you look upon the
   Shulammite,
  as upon a dance before two armies?ᶜ

7 How graceful are your feet in sandals,
   O queenly maiden!
Your rounded thighs are like jewels,
  the work of a master hand.
2 Your navel is a rounded bowl
  that never lacks mixed wine.
Your belly is a heap of wheat,
  encircled with lilies.
3 Your two breasts are like two fawns,
  twins of a gazelle.
4 Your neck is like an ivory tower.
Your eyes are pools in Heshbon,
  by the gate of Bath-rabbim.
Your nose is like a tower of Lebanon,
  overlooking Damascus.
5 Your head crowns you like Carmel,
  and your flowing locks are like purple;
  a king is held captive in the tresses.ᵈ

6 How fair and pleasant you are,
   O loved one, delectable maiden!ᵉ
7 You are statelyᶠ as a palm tree,
  and your breasts are like its clusters.
8 I say I will climb the palm tree
  and lay hold of its branches.

ᵃ Cn: Meaning of Heb uncertain
ᵇ Ch 7.1 in Heb
ᶜ Or *dance of Mahanaim*
ᵈ Meaning of Heb uncertain
ᵉ Syr: Heb *in delights*
ᶠ Heb *This your stature is*

him (cf. 4.9). **5b–7:** See 4.1–3n. **9–10:** A royal fantasy (cf. 1.2–4,12; 3.6–11). **10:** The man's words or words he puts in the mouth of the queens and other royal wives (here translated "concubines"). **11–12:** *I went down to the nut orchard*, either the man's words or a short interruption of his speech by the woman, since in v. 13 she is asked to return. **12:** The verse is corrupt and untranslatable. **13:** *Shulammite*, not a proper name; possibly meaning "the perfect one," it evokes the name "Solomon." *We*, the man and the women of Jerusalem. *A dance before two armies*, the meaning of the phrase is obscure. **7.1:** *Your rounded thighs are like jewels* probably refers to the curves of hips or thighs as resembling ornaments of some type. **2:** Parts of the body not normally exposed to view are described in metaphors that are not transparent. Perhaps *navel* is a euphemism for "vulva." *Heap of wheat* suggests the softness and gentle curve of the woman's stomach. **4:** The image evokes the gracefulness of a long neck. *Your eyes are pools*, the same Hebrew word, "'ayin," means both "eye" and "spring." *Heshbon*, east of Jerusalem in Transjordan, where excavations have revealed the remains of a large reservoir, dating from the ninth to eighth centuries BCE. The location of *Bath-rabbim*, meaning "daughter of many," is unknown. Perhaps the significance of *Lebanon* has to do with its scent; cf. 4.11n. **5:** The comparison to Mount Carmel, which overlooks the Mediterranean Sea at Haifa, suggests the stately way she holds her head. *Locks are like purple*, shiny black hair has a purple sheen. Purple, the color of royalty, evokes rich and luxurious hair, suitable for capturing a *king*. **7–9:** *I say I will climb*, i.e., "I intend to climb." The man puts himself in the picture (cf. 5.1), and, through a series of images, moves closer to the object of his desire. First he must climb the tall *palm tree* to reach *its clusters* that represent his lover's breasts (v. 7). Then, envisioned as grape clusters (v. 8), her breasts become more accessible.

O may your breasts be like clusters of the
      vine,
   and the scent of your breath like apples,
[9] and your kisses[a] like the best wine
      that goes down[b] smoothly,
   gliding over lips and teeth.[c]

[10] I am my beloved's,
   and his desire is for me.
[11] Come, my beloved,
   let us go forth into the fields,
   and lodge in the villages;
[12] let us go out early to the vineyards,
   and see whether the vines have
      budded,
whether the grape blossoms have
      opened
   and the pomegranates are in bloom.
There I will give you my love.
[13] The mandrakes give forth fragrance,
   and over our doors are all choice fruits,
new as well as old,
   which I have laid up for you, O my
      beloved.

8 O that you were like a brother to me,
   who nursed at my mother's breast!
If I met you outside, I would kiss you,
   and no one would despise me.
[2] I would lead you and bring you
   into the house of my mother,
   and into the chamber of the one who
      bore me.[d]
I would give you spiced wine to drink,
   the juice of my pomegranates.
[3] O that his left hand were under my head,
   and that his right hand embraced me!
[4] I adjure you, O daughters of Jerusalem,

do not stir up or awaken love
   until it is ready!

[5] Who is that coming up from the
      wilderness,
   leaning upon her beloved?

Under the apple tree I awakened you.
There your mother was in labor with
      you;
   there she who bore you was in labor.

[6] Set me as a seal upon your heart,
   as a seal upon your arm;
for love is strong as death,
   passion fierce as the grave.
Its flashes are flashes of fire,
   a raging flame.
[7] Many waters cannot quench love,
   neither can floods drown it.
If one offered for love
   all the wealth of one's house,
   it would be utterly scorned.

[8] We have a little sister,
   and she has no breasts.
What shall we do for our sister,
   on the day when she is spoken for?
[9] If she is a wall,
   we will build upon her a battlement of
      silver;
but if she is a door,

a   Heb *palate*
b   Heb *down for my lover*
c   Gk Syr Vg: Heb *lips of sleepers*
d   Gk Syr: Heb *my mother; she* (or *you*) *will teach me*

7.10–13: **The woman's reply.** The man's second long speech, like his first, gives rise to the woman's invitation to love (cf. 4.16). 11: *Villages*, the same Hebrew word also means "henna bushes," preferable here because of the outdoor setting. 13: *Mandrakes* were thought by some to be an aphrodisiac.

8.1–14: **A montage of short speeches.** 1–4: The woman speaks of her desire. 3–4: Cf. 2.6–7. 5a: The women of Jerusalem speak about the lovers. 5b: *In labor*, better, "conceived you." The woman aroused her lover in a setting where his mother also enjoyed sexual intimacy. 6–7: The only statement in the Song about the nature of love in general. The poet places these words in the mouth of the woman, who speaks to the man not, as she has until now, about their love, but about love itself. 6: She wants to be intimately and permanently close to him, like a seal he might wear. Seals made of precious or semiprecious metal or stone could be worn on a necklace or a bracelet for the wrist or upper arm, or a signet ring. *Love is strong as death*, not stronger. Their struggle to possess the same object (the loved one) is illustrated in the rivalry between their counterparts, *passion* (more precisely, "jealousy") and *the grave* (Heb "Sheol," the abode of the dead). 8–12: The lovers speak in similitudes about themselves and their beloved. 8–10: Unlike the girl in her example, for whom preparations will be made when she reaches marriageable age, the woman asserts that she needs no such arrangements, since she has

we will enclose her with boards of
cedar.

¹⁰ I was a wall,
and my breasts were like towers;
then I was in his eyes
as one who brings[a] peace.

¹¹ Solomon had a vineyard at Baal-hamon;
he entrusted the vineyard to keepers;
each one was to bring for its fruit a
thousand pieces of silver.

¹² My vineyard, my very own, is for
myself;
you, O Solomon, may have the
thousand,

and the keepers of the fruit two
hundred!

¹³ O you who dwell in the gardens,
my companions are listening for your
voice;
let me hear it.

¹⁴ Make haste, my beloved,
and be like a gazelle
or a young stag
upon the mountains of spices!

[a] Or *finds*

already surrendered to her lover. **10:** In the context of a city under siege (v. 9), to *bring peace* signifies surrender, and to find peace is to have the offer of surrender accepted (Deut 20.10–11; Josh 9.15; 11.19). **11–12:** The man compares his vineyard (the woman; see 1.6n.) to Solomon's: it is more valuable and he alone will tend it. *Baal-hamon*, no such place is known; meanings of the name, "owner of wealth" or "husband of a multitude," suggest that it was chosen to emphasize Solomon's privileged status. **13–14:** The poet does not bring the Song to a proper close, so that the love it celebrates can remain unending. **13:** *Let me hear it*, the man's words send us back to the beginning of the Song, where we hear the woman's voice, speaking of her desire. **14:** *Make haste*, the Hebrew word indicates movement away from the speaker. *Mountains of spices*, an erotic image for the woman herself; see 2.17; 4.6. As in 2.17, the woman appears to be sending her lover away and calling him to her at the same time. The effect is to leave love forever in progress, for only when the woman seems to send her lover away can the poem begin again with longing and the quest to gratify desire.

INTRODUCTION
TO THE PROPHETIC BOOKS

CANONICAL PLACEMENT AND CONTENTS

In both the Jewish and the Christian canons the prophetic books form a distinct section of the Bible. The two traditions differ, however, with respect to the number, sequence, and placement of the prophetic books. Jewish tradition divides the canon into three parts: the Torah (i.e., Genesis–Deuteronomy), the Prophets, and the Writings. The term "Former Prophets" is used to designate the historical books Joshua–2 Kings (excluding Ruth), perhaps reflecting a tradition that these books were written by prophets, and the term "Latter Prophets" is used for those books that bear the name of a particular prophet (i.e., Isaiah, Jeremiah, Ezekiel, and the twelve Minor Prophets). In Christian Bibles the prophetic books form the last section of the Old Testament canon, following the Pentateuch, the Historical Books, and the Poetical Books. Christian tradition includes Daniel among the prophetic books, in contrast to Judaism, which groups Daniel with the Writings. Also, Christian Bibles place Lamentations, which is not a book of prophecy, immediately after the book of Jeremiah, reflecting the tradition of the Septuagint (the ancient Greek translation [LXX] of the Hebrew Bible) that Jeremiah was the author of Lamentations. Likewise, in some Christian canons, the Apocryphal/Deuterocanonical book of Baruch comes after Lamentations, because of the connection between the prophet Jeremiah and his scribe, Baruch.

THE NATURE AND COMPOSITION OF THE PROPHETIC BOOKS

The prophetic books are unusual and complex compositions. With the exception of Jonah, which is a story about a prophet, these books all contain extended sayings and speeches that purport to come from the prophet whose name the book bears. While the books undoubtedly do preserve authentic words of the prophets in question, one should not think of the prophetic books simply as transcriptions of the words of prophets. Although much remains unknown about the composition of the prophetic books, it is possible to reconstruct a general picture. Scholars generally agree that the poetic materials in the prophetic books originated as oral pronouncements by the prophet to a public audience. These oracles were subsequently written down, perhaps by the prophet or an associate. The circumstances that led to these original written collections were undoubtedly different. A reference in the book of Isaiah suggests that oracles might be written down as a form of authentication (Isa 30.8). The book of Jeremiah describes how Jeremiah, having been banned from speaking publicly in the Temple, had his assistant Baruch write down a selection of his prophetic words so that they could be taken into the Temple and read to the people (Jer 36.5–6). When King Jehoiakim destroyed the scroll, Jeremiah had Baruch write out another copy, to which they added additional material (Jer 36.27–32). This collection may have formed the nucleus of the book of Jeremiah. On the other hand, unlike most of the other prophetic books, Ezekiel may have been composed as a written document from the beginning. Elsewhere in the Bible there is further evidence of prophetic collections; see 1 Chr 29.29; 2 Chr 9.29.

Once small collections of prophetic oracles and pronouncements were made, they were subject to further editing, rearranging, annotating, and expansion. In some cases narratives about the prophet were added; these are both autobiographical (e.g., Isa 6; 8; Jer 1.4–19; 13.1–11; Hos 1–2; Am 7.1–7) and biographical (e.g., Isa 7; 36–39; Jer 26; 36–44; Hos 3; Am 7.10–17). The occasions for such editorial activity would have differed, but national crises may have prompted some of this process. Most likely, written collections of the oracles of the prophets Amos and Hosea, which were originally addressed to the Northern Kingdom of Israel, were brought to the Southern Kingdom of Judah after the fall of the Northern Kingdom in 722 BCE, and edited and circulated there. Isaiah of Jerusalem seems to have knowledge of Amos's oracles, and Jeremiah is unquestionably influenced by Hosea. Many of the prophetic books originating before the fall of Judah to the Babylonians and the exile of most Judeans to Babylon in 586 BCE show evidence of editorial additions and reorganizations that reflect the circumstances of exilic and postexilic times, that is, from later in the sixth century BCE and beyond. The book of Amos, for example, now includes material that presupposes the fall of Judah (9.11–15). The most dramatic example of the expansion and reworking of prophetic materials is the book of Isaiah. Although it contains extensive material from the eighth-century prophet, chs 40–55 clearly reflect the situation of the Babylonian exile, and chs 56–66 the period of the restoration of the Judean community in the late sixth century BCE. Yet even though the book contains materials dating from several centuries, it is unified by a number of motifs, themes, and topics that recur throughout the work.

The complex activity of preserving and developing the prophetic oracle collections reflects a conviction that the prophet's words were not only significant for the circumstance in which they were originally pronounced but potentially relevant for later ones as well. At the same time, the freedom with which later generations could rework the prophetic oracles indicates that the prophets' words did not at first possess the kind of fixed authority that is later associated with the concept of "scripture." Although the processes by which the prophetic books came to assume a relatively final form and canonical status are difficult to trace, this probably occurred during the Persian and early Hellenistic periods (the fifth through the third centuries BCE). Most likely, during this time scribal editors added the superscriptions that introduce most of the books, indicating the identity of the prophet (name, father's name, and occasionally other information) and often the kings of Israel or Judah during whose reigns the prophets were active (e.g., Isa 1.1; Jer 1.1–3; Hos 1.1). In addition to editorial additions to the individual prophetic books, the smaller prophetic books (Hosea–Malachi) were arranged and edited to form a group known as "the Book of the Twelve," which was copied on a single scroll. By the beginning of the second century BCE Ben Sira refers to these prophets as "the twelve" (Sir 49.10). The number twelve is symbolic of the twelve sons of Jacob and the twelve tribes of Israel, and considerable editorial work was required to organize these prophetic materials into a grouping of twelve. In fact, the book of Zechariah consists of three separate collections (chs 1–8, 9–11, 12–14) grouped together editorially. Only the first of these comes from the prophet Zechariah, whereas the other two are anonymous. The final book in the collection, Malachi, is also an anonymous piece, since "Malachi" is not a personal name but a phrase meaning "my messenger," picked up from 3.1 to serve as the name of the prophet in the superscription.

THE PHENOMENON OF PROPHECY

The phenomenon of prophecy was widespread in the ancient Near East, and many important themes and genres familiar from biblical prophecy have parallels there. Moreover, many more prophets were active in ancient Israel and Judah than those whose work is represented in the prophetic books of the Bible, and their activities were more varied than these writings suggest. The books of Samuel and Kings provide important additional information. Since our sources are limited, it is difficult to reconstruct the history of prophecy. Some of the features are clear, however. The prophet was essentially an intermediary between God and the people, and one of the major functions was that of messenger. Often prophets introduced their communications with a version of the formula typically used by messengers, "Thus says the LORD." But prophets might also bring inquiries from the people to God or make intercession on behalf of the people. In contrast to priesthood, which was exclusively male, both women and men could be prophets. Women prophets included Deborah (Judg 4.4), Huldah (2 Kings 22.14), and Noadiah (Neh 6.10); see also Joel 2.28. Additional aspects of the prophetic role are suggested by the various terms used to identify them. In addition to "prophet" (Heb nabi', perhaps meaning "one who is called"), a prophet could be called a seer (Heb ro'eh, e.g. 1 Sam 9.9; and ḥozeh, e.g., Am 7.12), and a holy man (Heb 'ish ha'elohim, literally "man of God"; e.g., 2 Kings 1.9).

The history of prophecy in ancient Israel can be traced for more than a thousand years, from the premonarchical period to the turn of the era. As one would expect, over such a long time the nature and function of prophecy altered in response to changing historical, social, and religious circumstances. Four periods define the major epochs of prophecy: the early monarchical period (eleventh through ninth centuries), the Assyrian crisis (eighth century), the Babylonian crisis (late seventh through early sixth centuries), and the postexilic restoration (mid-sixth through mid-fifth centuries).

The extant evidence suggests that in the earliest period prophets may have been local or itinerant holy men and women who were revered for their special religious powers and who might be consulted for a variety of private inquiries, from locating lost property (1 Sam 9.1–10) to learning whether a sick child would live or die (1 Kings 14.1–18). Some lived in prophetic communities that cultivated ecstatic forms of religious experience (1 Sam 19.18–24; 2 Kings 6.1–7). Prophets also had the public function of declaring God's will concerning whether the people should go to war (Judg 4.4–10). The emergence of monarchy in ancient Israel may have changed aspects of the prophets' role. Prophets appear as king-makers and king-breakers, as they announce that God has designated an individual to become king or has rejected a reigning king (1 Sam 10.1; 15.23; 1 Kings 11.29–39; 14.1–18). Though prophets continued their role in advising about matters of war (1 Kings 22), they also served as critics of the king in religious and social affairs. The consolidation of royal power and the foreign religious practices introduced through royal marriages often threatened older tribal institutions and values. The conflict between Elijah, the prophet, and Ahab and Jezebel, the king and queen, illustrates these tensions between prophet and king (1 Kings 18–21).

Prophecy appears to have undergone a dramatic change during the eighth century, although this impression may be affected by the change in the nature of the sources of information. From the eighth century on, collections of prophetic oracles are preserved; yet, with the exceptions of Jeremiah and Ezekiel, few extended narratives about prophets exist. It does appear that in this period prophets began to function less as private counselors and critics of kings and more as public figures who influenced opinion through their pronouncements in the Temple courts and in other public places. Prophets of the eighth century (Amos, Hosea, Isaiah, Micah) interpreted international affairs, critiqued complacent religious practices, and condemned the abuses of social justice that accompanied the increasing urbanization and centralization of state power characteristic of the eighth century. The prophetic careers of Hosea, Micah, and Isaiah took place in the shadow of the expansionist Assyrian empire, which eventually put an end to the Northern Kingdom of Israel in 722 and subjected the Southern Kingdom of Judah to the status of a vassal. The prophets interpreted these events, however, in terms of the judgment of the LORD, not simply as the success of the powerful Assyrians. This perspective allowed Isaiah, for example, to anticipate the ultimate downfall of Assyria because of its overweening arrogance.

The third major period of prophecy occurred during the Babylonian crisis. The prophet Nahum celebrated the defeat of Assyria (612–609 BCE), but when Babylon succeeded Assyria as the dominant empire the excitement he expressed soon turned to confusion, as expressed in Hab 1–2. Jeremiah's prophetic career spanned the time from the decline of Assyria through the Babylonian overlordship of Judah, to the revolt and destruction of Judah in 586 and the exile of a significant portion of its population. Although it is difficult to correlate many of his poetic oracles with specific events in this period, the narratives about Jeremiah give a vivid picture of a nation and its leadership deeply conflicted about what political course to follow and the religious significance of the choices that were forced upon it. Even the prophetic community was bitterly divided and gave contradictory advice to the king concerning the will of the LORD (Jer 26–29; 36–44). Overlapping the career of Jeremiah, the prophet Ezekiel (active 593–ca. 571 BCE) was among the Judeans exiled to Babylon after the revolt of 597 BCE, a decade before the final revolt and the destruction of Jerusalem. Ezekiel's prophetic work was first to persuade the exiled Judeans of the inevitability of Jerusalem's destruction, and, following the fall of the city, to begin to articulate the theological grounds for conceiving a possible future, including a return of the exiles and a rebuilding of the destroyed Temple. In contrast to the prophets who preceded him, Ezekiel drew strongly on priestly traditions for his categories of thought, forms of speech, and evocative symbols.

The defeat of the Babylonian empire by the Persian king Cyrus altered political conditions dramatically. Although Judah did not regain its independence but became a part of the Persian empire, Cyrus and his successors authorized the rebuilding of the Temple and of Jerusalem, allowing members of the exiled community in Babylon who so desired to return to Judah. Thus the prophetic task during this period largely concerned issues of the restoration of the community and its institutions in a context significantly different from that which prevailed during the Israelite and Judean monarchies. The anonymous prophet whose work is found in Isa 40–55 (often called "Second Isaiah") addressed the Babylonian exiles just at the time that Cyrus was engaged in the conquest of Babylon. Second Isaiah's message to the exilic community was that unfolding events represented God's action in history. He thus interpreted the significance of Cyrus as God's "anointed" who would rebuild Jerusalem, and he encouraged the exiles to return to Jerusalem. The process of rebuilding the Temple (520–515 BCE) provides the context for the prophets Haggai and Zechariah. Zechariah in particular suggests this was a time of expectation that perhaps the monarchy might be restored, an event that did not occur. Issues concerning reorganization of the Judean community and tensions regarding economic justice, institutional corruption, and the boundaries of the community are variously reflected in Zechariah, Isa 56–66, and Malachi, prophets who were active in roughly the period 525–475 BCE.

Although prophets in all periods might speak of the dramatic intervention of God in historical events and the consequent transformation of the conditions of life, this type of language seems to have become more common and more vivid in the postexilic prophets (e.g., Isa 56–66, Zechariah, Malachi, Joel, and postexilic additions to earlier prophetic books, such as Isa 24–27). Some of the passages anticipate a war or other cataclysmic event of cosmic proportions that will precede a time of deliverance, peace, and virtual re-creation of the world. Such imagery and the expectations it expresses suggest to some scholars that apocalyptic literature, with its focus on the details of the end time as revealed by a heavenly messenger, was an outgrowth of the phenomenon of prophecy.

The book of Daniel, the only book in the Hebrew Bible that could be called an apocalypse, illustrates the complexity of the matter. Although Christian tradition groups Daniel with the prophetic books, Jewish tradition places it in the Writings (as noted earlier). The first part of the book consists of a cycle of narratives in which Daniel and his friends are portrayed as sages trained in the technical skills of Babylonian scribal wisdom. Like Joseph, Daniel is able to interpret dreams sent by God. He is not presented as a prophet. In the latter part of the book, however, Daniel is the recipient of visions that disclose the future. These vision reports do bear significant similarities to those found in Ezekiel and especially in Zechariah, though their almost allegorical style is quite different. Similarly, although general claims about God's foreknowledge of historical events can be found in Second Isaiah, Daniel's representation of history as predetermined both with respect to its epochal structure and its specific events is strikingly different from the representation of history by the prophets. A clue to the relationship of apocalyptic writing to prophecy may be found in Daniel 9, where Daniel is presented as studying the book of Jeremiah and receiving an angelic interpretation of its significance. As suggested by the presentation of Daniel as a technically trained sage, the authors of apocalyptic books were perhaps themselves learned scribes who studied and appropriated aspects of the prophetic tradition and combined them with other influences in their attempts to understand the nature of the cosmos and the course of history.

Marvin A. Sweeney

ISAIAH

NAME AND CANONICAL STATUS

The book of Isaiah (Heb "yesha'yah(u)," "the LORD saves") is named for the prophet Isaiah ben Amoz who lived during the latter half of the eighth century BCE at the time of the Assyrian invasions of Israel and Judah. Isaiah is included among the Latter Prophets in the Jewish Bible and among the Prophets of the Old Testament in the Christian Bible. Jewish manuscripts and traditions frequently place Isaiah first because he lived before Jeremiah and Ezekiel, although the book sometimes appears after Jeremiah and Ezekiel because of its concern with comfort or restoration (b. B. Bat. 14b). In Christian Bibles, Isaiah is usually first among the Prophets because he lived before Jeremiah and Ezekiel, although the Minor Prophets sometimes appear first in some manuscripts of the Greek Septuagint (LXX) versions, probably because the prophet Hosea was thought to have lived before Isaiah.

AUTHORSHIP, COMPOSITION, AND LITERARY HISTORY

Traditional interpreters In both Judaism and Christianity attribute the book of Isaiah to the prophet Isaiah, but interpreters as early as the Middle Ages observed that the second portion of the book, beginning in ch 40, presupposes the conclusion of the Babylonian exile and the rise of King Cyrus of Persia in 545–539 BCE (see 44.28; 45.1). Modern scholars generally attribute the book to three major stages of composition: (1) the works of Isaiah ben Amoz, which appear generally in chs 1–39; (2) the work of an anonymous prophet known as Second Isaiah from the conclusion of the Babylonian exile in chs 40–55; and (3) the work of Third Isaiah, a collection of materials from a number of prophetic hands who wrote during the early Persian-period restoration of Jerusalem (late sixth through fifth or early fourth centuries BCE) in chs 56–66. Some interpreters maintain that chs 56–66 should be included with Second Isaiah, and others maintain that chs 1–39 have been heavily edited in the seventh, sixth, and fifth centuries BCE as well. Altogether, the book appears to have gone through at least four stages of composition: first, during the lifetime of Isaiah ben Amoz, who witnessed the period of the Assyrian invasions of Israel and Judah in 742–701 BCE; second, during the late seventh-century BCE restoration of King Josiah of Judah (640–609 BCE), when Isaiah was edited to support the king's reforms; third, during the late sixth-century BCE collapse of Babylon and the rise of King Cyrus of Persia (559–530 BCE), who authorized the return of exiled Jews to Jerusalem to rebuild the Temple; and fourth, during the late fifth and early fourth centuries BCE when Nehemiah and Ezra attempted to consolidate the Jerusalem Temple's status as holy center of Judaism in keeping with their understandings of the Torah and the Isaian tradition. The writers of each stage of Isaiah's composition edited and expanded the book in order to demonstrate that the prophet addressed events of their own times. Whereas Isaiah ben Amoz spoke about divine judgment and restoration in his own day, each of the subsequent editions of the book presupposes that Isaiah's visions of restoration would be realized in their own time.

HISTORICAL CONTEXTS

Four pivotal moments in the history of the Israelite people form the background of the various parts of Isaiah.

1. *The Syro-Ephraimite war and its aftermath*. After a period of relative peace between Israel (the Northern Kingdom, often called "Ephraim" in Isaiah after its most important tribe) and Judah (the Southern Kingdom), international tensions rose when Tiglath-pileser III became king of the Assyrian empire in 745 BCE and began an effort to conquer the lands to the west of Assyria, including Syria, Israel, and Judah. Uzziah, the king of Judah whose reign began during the peaceful era, died in 733 (6.1), but because he was quarantined due to an illness, his son Jotham became king in 759, followed by Jotham's son Ahaz in 743 or 735 (the chronology is disputed). Pekah, king of Israel, and Rezin, king of Syria (Damascus or Aram) tried, beginning in 735, to enlist Ahaz in an alliance against Assyria, and when that effort failed, they attacked Judah to replace Ahaz with a king more amenable to their policies (ch 7). This conflict is known as the Syro-Ephraimite war, since it was a war of Syria and Ephraim against Judah. Ahaz successfully turned to Assyria for help in fending off Israel and Syria. The price he paid was steep: Judah became a vassal of Assyria.

2. *The Assyrian invasion.* During the decades following the Syro-Ephraimite war, the Assyrians expanded their influence in the area, taking over Syria and then attacking the Northern Kingdom, which fell in 722. When the Assyrian ruler at the time, Sargon II, died in 705, Hezekiah, the king of Judah and son of Ahaz, rebelled against Assyria. Hezekiah had thought to take advantage of the confusion at the change of rulers, and in addition sought support from Egypt that was not forthcoming (36.6). The new Assyrian king, Sennacherib, retaliated and conquered the cities surrounding Jerusalem in 701. Hezekiah was able to avert the conquest of Jerusalem itself only by paying tribute.

3. *The conquest of Jerusalem and the exile.* During the century following these events, the Assyrian empire gradually weakened. In 612, the rising Babylonian empire conquered the Assyrian capital, Nineveh, and the international power struggle became one between Babylon and Egypt, with Judah caught between. In 605 the Babylonian king, Nebuchadnezzar, defeated the Egyptian pharaoh, Neco, at the battle of Carchemish, and Babylon became the leading empire of the day. Judah came under Babylon's control, and when the last king of Judah, Zedekiah, rebelled against Babylon, the result was an invasion by Nebuchadnezzar. In 586 he destroyed Jerusalem and its Temple and deported a good deal of the population to Babylon, an event referred to as the exile.

4. *The return.* During the sixth century BCE, the Babylonians were increasingly challenged by the rise of another great empire, the Persians. In 539 Cyrus, the Persian king, defeated the Babylonians at the battle of Opis. Cyrus allowed the Jews to return to Judah, and many (though not all) eventually did so. The returning exiles rebuilt Jerusalem and the Temple.

CONTENTS AND STRUCTURE

Although the book of Isaiah was composed in stages, the final form of Isaiah is designed to be read as a single work ascribed to the prophet Isaiah ben Amoz. Its different sections are unified partly by common themes, such as the Davidic/Zion tradition that presumes the ultimate rule of Jerusalem and the restored Israel by the house of David, under the sovereignty of the LORD. The various sections are also linked through common vocabulary, such as the divine title "the Holy One of Israel" (for example, 1.4; 29.19; 40.25; 60.9). The literary structure of Isaiah consists of two major parts, both of which are concerned with reading Isaiah as a witness to Jerusalem as the seat of the LORD's sovereignty throughout all of creation. Chapters 1–33 address the period of punishment and anticipate the period of restoration through which the LORD's sovereignty will be recognized throughout the world, and chs 34–66 presuppose that the time of restoration and the recognition of the LORD's sovereignty are at hand. A more detailed outline of the formal literary structure of the book is as follows:

THE VISION OF ISAIAH BEN AMOZ:	
PROPHETIC EXHORTATION TO JERUSALEM AND JUDAH TO ADHERE TO THE LORD	
I. The LORD's plans to reveal worldwide sovereignty at Zion	1.1–33.24
A. Prologue to the book: Introductory oracles concerning the LORD's plans to purify Jerusalem	1.1–31
B. Prophetic instruction concerning the LORD's plans to reveal worldwide sovereignty at Zion: Announcement of the Day of the LORD	2.1–33.24
1. prophetic announcement concerning the purging of Zion for its role as the center for the LORD's world rule	2.1–4.6
2. prophetic instruction concerning Assyrian judgment against Israel and the restoration of the Davidic kingdom	5.1–12.6
3. prophetic announcement concerning the preparation of the nations for the LORD's world rule	13.1–27.13
a. announcements concerning the nations	13.1–23.18
b. restoration for Zion at the center of the nations	24.1–27.13
4. prophetic instruction concerning the LORD's plans for the new king in Jerusalem	28.1–33.24

INTERPRETATION

The book of Isaiah serves as a theological reflection upon Jerusalem's experience of threat, exile, and restoration. It takes up fundamental questions of divine involvement in human history. To what extent is the LORD sovereign over Israel and Judah on the one hand, and the nations and all creation on the other? To what extent does the LORD bring both judgment and restoration to Jerusalem, Israel, and the world at large? To what extent is the LORD hidden in times of suffering and to what extent will the LORD deliberately bring suffering on one generation to achieve divine purpose in another? To what extent does the LORD's promise of security to Jerusalem/Zion and the royal house of David hold true? To what extent should human beings respond to the LORD's intervention in the human world with faithfulness? Such questions have occupied the readers of the book of Isaiah from ancient through modern times. Jewish interpreters have looked to Isaiah to understand the time when the LORD would restore Jerusalem, and Christian interpreters have looked to Isaiah to understand when the LORD would reveal the Messiah. Indeed, two major copies of the book of Isaiah and a number of shorter Isaian texts were found among the Dead Sea Scrolls at Qumran. The command "in the wilderness prepare the way of the LORD" apparently motivated the Qumran sect to move to the wilderness of the Dead Sea to await the time that God would destroy the Romans and all others considered evil in the world. Citations from Isaiah play a major role in presenting the life and significance of Jesus in the New Testament, and readings from Isaiah play an especially important role in Jewish liturgy where Isaian texts are frequently read to complete and interpret the reading of the Torah.

Marvin A. Sweeney

1

The vision of Isaiah son of Amoz, which he saw concerning Judah and Jerusalem in the days of Uzziah, Jotham, Ahaz, and Hezekiah, kings of Judah.

2 Hear, O heavens, and listen, O earth;
    for the LORD has spoken:
I reared children and brought them up,
    but they have rebelled against me.
3 The ox knows its owner,
    and the donkey its master's crib;
but Israel does not know,
    my people do not understand.

4 Ah, sinful nation,
    people laden with iniquity,
offspring who do evil,
    children who deal corruptly,
who have forsaken the LORD,
    who have despised the Holy One of Israel,
    who are utterly estranged!

5 Why do you seek further beatings?
    Why do you continue to rebel?
The whole head is sick,
    and the whole heart faint.
6 From the sole of the foot even to the
        head,
    there is no soundness in it,
but bruises and sores
    and bleeding wounds;
they have not been drained,
    or bound up,
    or softened with oil.

7 Your country lies desolate,
    your cities are burned with fire;
in your very presence
    aliens devour your land;
    it is desolate, as overthrown by
        foreigners.
8 And daughter Zion is left
    like a booth in a vineyard,

1.1–33.24: The LORD's plans to reveal worldwide sovereignty at Zion. The first half of the book focuses especially on the punishment of Zion and its anticipation of future restoration in an effort to demonstrate the LORD's plans to reveal sovereignty over Israel, the nations, and creation at large. The second half of the book (chs 34–66) presupposes that the time of the restoration and the LORD's revelation are at hand.

1.1–31: Prologue to the book of Isaiah: Introductory oracles concerning divine plans to purge Jerusalem. The prologue in ch 1 is an introduction both to the entire book of Isaiah and to the first portion of the book in chs 1–33. It is designed to convince its audience that Jerusalem's suffering during the late eighth century BCE and beyond was due to the LORD's plans to purge Jerusalem in preparation for its role as the seat for the LORD's rule over all of creation. In keeping with his understanding of the David/Zion tradition, Isaiah presumes the LORD's sovereignty, righteousness, and power to defend the royal house of David and the city of Jerusalem. The prophet therefore contends that Jerusalem's suffering is due to human wrongdoing and that the city must be purged to enable it to serve as the LORD's capital for all of creation. Such a position is theologically problematic, presuming the guilt of those who suffer.

1.1: Superscription. The prophetic books typically begin with a superscription that provides the reader with essential information concerning the prophet (cf. Jer 1.1–3; Ezek 1.1–3; Hos 1.1; Joel 1.1; Am 1.1; Obad 1; Mic 1.1; Nah 1.1; Hab 1.1; Zeph 1.1). This superscription introduces both the entire book and 1.2–31. Subsequent superscriptions in 2.1; 13.1; 14.28; 15.1; 17.1; 19.1; 21.1,11,13; 22.1; 23.1; and 30.6 introduce smaller subunits. Isaiah's *vision* (both visual and auditory communication from the LORD) reveals divine plans concerning Judah and Jerusalem during the reigns of the Judean monarchs, Uzziah (783–742 BCE); Jotham (742–735 BCE); Ahaz (735–715 BCE); and Hezekiah (715–687 BCE). Although the superscription identifies the setting of the book in relation to the eighth-century BCE Assyrian invasions of the Northern Kingdom of Israel and the Southern Kingdom of Judah, the book as a whole takes up Jerusalem's experiences through the time of the Babylonian exile and the early Persian period restoration in the sixth century BCE.

1.2–20: The speech of the accuser. The prophet employs the language of the courtroom, beginning with the LORD's accusation speech that charges Israel with wrongdoing, to explain Jerusalem's suffering. 2–3: Appeal to all creation, namely, heaven and earth, to witness the divine complaints against Israel (cf. Deut 32.1; Mic 6.1–8). The passage metaphorically portrays Israel as the LORD's rebellious children who do not even have the understanding of animals. 4–9: Rhetorical questions designed to motivate the listeners to return to God. The suffering of the people is presented as the result of their own wrongdoing rather than any lapse on the LORD's part. The imagery shifts from personal illness and injury to the suffering of the entire land during the Assyrian invasions, when Jerusalem was left standing alone surrounded by the forces of the Assyrian king Sennacherib 701 BCE (2 Kings 18–20; Isa 36–39). 4: *The Holy One of Israel*, a divine title that occurs throughout the book.

like a shelter in a cucumber field,
 like a besieged city.
⁹ If the LORD of hosts
 had not left us a few survivors,
we would have been like Sodom,
 and become like Gomorrah.

¹⁰ Hear the word of the LORD,
 you rulers of Sodom!
Listen to the teaching of our God,
 you people of Gomorrah!
¹¹ What to me is the multitude of your
 sacrifices?
 says the LORD;
I have had enough of burnt offerings of
 rams
 and the fat of fed beasts;
I do not delight in the blood of bulls,
 or of lambs, or of goats.

¹² When you come to appear before me,ᵃ
 who asked this from your hand?
 Trample my courts no more;
¹³ bringing offerings is futile;
 incense is an abomination to me.
New moon and sabbath and calling of
 convocation—
 I cannot endure solemn assemblies
 with iniquity.
¹⁴ Your new moons and your appointed
 festivals
 my soul hates;
they have become a burden to me,
 I am weary of bearing them.
¹⁵ When you stretch out your hands,
 I will hide my eyes from you;

even though you make many prayers,
 I will not listen;
 your hands are full of blood.
¹⁶ Wash yourselves; make yourselves
 clean;
 remove the evil of your doings
 from before my eyes;
cease to do evil,
¹⁷ learn to do good;
seek justice,
 rescue the oppressed,
defend the orphan,
 plead for the widow.

¹⁸ Come now, let us argue it out,
 says the LORD:
though your sins are like scarlet,
 they shall be like snow;
though they are red like crimson,
 they shall become like wool.
¹⁹ If you are willing and obedient,
 you shall eat the good of the
 land;
²⁰ but if you refuse and rebel,
 you shall be devoured by the
 sword;
 for the mouth of the LORD has
 spoken.

²¹ How the faithful city
 has become a whore!
 She that was full of justice,
righteousness lodged in her—

ᵃ Or *see my face*

8: Jerusalem is frequently personified as *daughter Zion* in Isaiah (10.32; 16.1; 37.22; 52.2; 62.11) and elsewhere (e.g., Zeph 3.14–20; Lam 1.6; 2; 4.22). 9: *Sodom* and *Gomorrah*, the evil cities destroyed by the LORD (Gen 18–19). 10–17: The prophet continues to characterize the people as Sodom and Gomorrah in an effort to accuse them of insincere worship. Although many interpreters maintain that Isaiah opposes ritual and sacrificial worship in principle, the LORD's instructions call for moral action to accompany Temple worship (see 1 Sam 15.22; Ps 50.7–15). The LORD threatens to ignore the people's prayers, a disturbing claim in the face of foreign invasion and a frequent concern of both Isaiah (e.g., 8.17; 54.8; 59.2; 64.6) and the Psalms (e.g., 10.11; 13.2; 22.25; 27.9; 51.11; 104.29). 13: Sacrifices were offered at *sabbath* (weekly) and *new moon* (monthly) festivals. 18–20: The accusation speech employs legal language and sacrificial imagery to conclude with an appeal to return to the LORD.

 1.21–31: The speech of the judge. The courtroom metaphor continues as the LORD now speaks as the judge who announces Zion's ultimate redemption and restoration. Jerusalem suffered greatly under the Assyrians and the Babylonians from the late eighth through the sixth centuries BCE, but the book of Isaiah understands these events in relation to Jerusalem's restoration in the early Persian period. 21–26: The prophet's announcement of Jerusalem's rehabilitation combines metaphorical charges that the city is a *whore* and that it must be purified much as metal is refined by the removal of impurities known as *dross*. The principal accusation is the corruption

but now murderers!
²² Your silver has become dross,
   your wine is mixed with water.
²³ Your princes are rebels
   and companions of thieves.
Everyone loves a bribe
   and runs after gifts.
They do not defend the orphan,
   and the widow's cause does not come
      before them.

²⁴ Therefore says the Sovereign, the LORD
      of hosts, the Mighty One of Israel:
Ah, I will pour out my wrath on my
      enemies,
   and avenge myself on my foes!
²⁵ I will turn my hand against you;
   I will smelt away your dross as with lye
   and remove all your alloy.
²⁶ And I will restore your judges as at the first,
   and your counselors as at the
      beginning.
Afterward you shall be called the city of
      righteousness,
   the faithful city.

²⁷ Zion shall be redeemed by justice,
   and those in her who repent, by
      righteousness.

²⁸ But rebels and sinners shall be destroyed
      together,
   and those who forsake the LORD shall
      be consumed.
²⁹ For you shall be ashamed of the oaks
   in which you delighted;
and you shall blush for the gardens
   that you have chosen.
³⁰ For you shall be like an oak
   whose leaf withers,
   and like a garden without water.
³¹ The strong shall become like tinder,
   and their work[a] like a spark;
they and their work shall burn
      together,
   with no one to quench them.

2 The word that Isaiah son of Amoz saw
concerning Judah and Jerusalem.

² In days to come
   the mountain of the LORD's house
shall be established as the highest of the
      mountains,
   and shall be raised above the hills;
all the nations shall stream to it.
   ³ Many peoples shall come and say,

a   Or *its makers*

of the judicial process (cf. 5.23; 33.15; Am 5.10,12; Mic 3.9,11). **27–28:** The prophet distinguishes the fate of the righteous from the wicked (see chs 65–66). **29–31:** The metaphor of the tree portrays the restoration of Zion. Trees and gardens were frequently associated with Canaanite fertility rites and goddesses. The prophet maintains that the dead branches must be trimmed and the tree burned. Later oracles will stress the new growth of the tree (6.12–13; 11.1–9).

2.1–4.6: Prophetic announcement concerning the purging of Zion for its role as the center for the LORD's world rule. This unit begins with its own superscription (see 1.1n.). Ideal portrayals of Jerusalem as a center for the pilgrimage of the nations appear at the beginning (2.2–4) and as a holy center for the remnant of Israel at the end (4.2–6) of the unit. The material in 2.5–4.1 focuses in detail on the LORD's plans for purging Zion in preparation for its divine role.

2.1: Superscription. A shorter version of the superscription in 1.1, specifying the concern with Judah and Jerusalem.

2.2–4: Announcement concerning the establishment of Zion as the center for the LORD's worldwide sovereignty. This oracle portrays a future time when the nations will make pilgrimage to Zion, the site of the Jerusalem Temple. The ideal of the nations at peace in Zion is a primary tenet of Davidic/Zion theology, which maintains that the LORD protects Zion as the seat of divine sovereignty in creation (Pss 2; 46; 48; cf. Ps 47). A parallel version of this passage appears in Mic 4.1–5, and it is also cited in Joel 3.10 and Zech 8.20–23. **2:** *In days to come*, past interpreters, including the Septuagint (LXX), have understood the Heb eschatologically as "in the ~~la~~tter days," but it simply means "in the future." *The mountain of the LORD's house*, throughout the ancient Near ~~East~~ temples were described as the houses in which gods dwelt. In common with this ancient motif, Jerusalem ~~is r~~epresented as the cosmic mountain (10.12,32; 11.9; 16.1; 29.8; 30.29; 40.9; 57.13; 65.26; Ps 48.1–2; Ezek ~~40.2~~). **3:** *Instruction*, Heb "torah." Although "torah" is frequently translated as "law," the term means

"Come, let us go up to the mountain of the
    LORD,
    to the house of the God of Jacob;
that he may teach us his ways
    and that we may walk in his paths."
For out of Zion shall go forth instruction,
    and the word of the LORD from
        Jerusalem.
⁴ He shall judge between the nations,
    and shall arbitrate for many peoples;
they shall beat their swords into
    plowshares,
    and their spears into pruning hooks;
nation shall not lift up sword against
    nation,
    neither shall they learn war any more.

⁵ O house of Jacob,
    come, let us walk
    in the light of the LORD!
⁶ For you have forsaken the ways of ᵃ your
    people,
    O house of Jacob.
Indeed they are full of diviners ᵇ from the
    east
    and of soothsayers like the Philistines,
    and they clasp hands with
        foreigners.
⁷ Their land is filled with silver and gold,
    and there is no end to their treasures;
their land is filled with horses,
    and there is no end to their chariots.
⁸ Their land is filled with idols;
    they bow down to the work of their
        hands,

to what their own fingers have made.
⁹ And so people are humbled,
    and everyone is brought low—
    do not forgive them!
¹⁰ Enter into the rock,
    and hide in the dust
from the terror of the LORD,
    and from the glory of his majesty.
¹¹ The haughty eyes of people shall be
        brought low,
    and the pride of everyone shall be
        humbled;
and the LORD alone will be exalted on that
    day.
¹² For the LORD of hosts has a day
    against all that is proud and lofty,
    against all that is lifted up and high; ᶜ
¹³ against all the cedars of Lebanon,
    lofty and lifted up;
    and against all the oaks of Bashan;
¹⁴ against all the high mountains,
    and against all the lofty hills;
¹⁵ against every high tower,
    and against every fortified wall;
¹⁶ against all the ships of Tarshish,
    and against all the beautiful craft. ᵈ
¹⁷ The haughtiness of people shall be
        humbled,
    and the pride of everyone shall be
        brought low;

a Heb lacks *the ways of*
b Cn: Heb lacks *of diviners*
c Cn Compare Gk: Heb *low*
d Compare Gk: Meaning of Heb uncertain

"teaching, instruction."

2.5–4.6: The prophet's address concerning the purging of Zion. The prophet outlines in three addresses how the ideal portrayal of the nations' recognition of the LORD at Zion expressed in 2.2–4 is to be achieved. **2.5–9:** The first oracular address begins with an invitation to the *house of Jacob*, a term frequently employed to characterize Israel (see Gen 32.28; Ex 19.3; Ps 114.1; Isa 46.3), to join the nations in their pilgrimage to Zion. The passage quickly turns to assertions that the LORD has forsaken the people because of their alleged wrongdoing in dealing with foreigners. The passage points to a source of tension: while it posits an ideal scenario of world peace and cooperation among the nations, it also points to the nations as a source of corruption and evil because of their associations with divinatory practices (cf. Deut 18.9–14); wealth in the form of *silver, gold, horses,* and *chariots* (cf. 1 Kings 10.26); and *idols* (cf. Isa 44.9–20). In the view of the prophet, such practices render the nations unholy and their association with Jacob renders Israel unholy as well. **10–21:** In the second oracular address, the prophet announces the future Day of the LORD as a time when the LORD will appear to punish and bring down all who are arrogant, high, proud, and uplifted in the world so that the LORD alone will be recognized as the true sovereign. The Day of the LORD tradition is well known among the prophets (see Isa 13.6,9; Ezek 13.5; Joel 1.15; 2.11,31; 3.14; Am 5.18–20; Obad 15; Zeph 1.7,14; Mal 4.5). **13:** *Lebanon,* the mountainous area north of Israel famous for its cedars; *Bashan,* the high plateau in northern Transjordan known for its timber (Ezek 27.6).

and the LORD alone will be exalted on
   that day.
¹⁸ The idols shall utterly pass away.
¹⁹ Enter the caves of the rocks
   and the holes of the ground,
from the terror of the LORD,
   and from the glory of his majesty,
   when he rises to terrify the earth.
²⁰ On that day people will throw away
   to the moles and to the bats
their idols of silver and their idols of gold,
   which they made for themselves to
      worship,
²¹ to enter the caverns of the rocks
   and the clefts in the crags,
from the terror of the LORD,
   and from the glory of his majesty,
   when he rises to terrify the earth.
²² Turn away from mortals,
   who have only breath in their nostrils,
   for of what account are they?

3 For now the Sovereign, the LORD of hosts,
   is taking away from Jerusalem and from
      Judah
support and staff—
   all support of bread,
   and all support of water—
² warrior and soldier,
   judge and prophet,
   diviner and elder,
³ captain of fifty
   and dignitary,
counselor and skillful magician
   and expert enchanter.
⁴ And I will make boys their princes,
   and babes shall rule over them.
⁵ The people will be oppressed,
   everyone by another
   and everyone by a neighbor;

the youth will be insolent to the
   elder,
   and the base to the honorable.

⁶ Someone will even seize a relative,
   a member of the clan, saying,
"You have a cloak;
   you shall be our leader,
and this heap of ruins
   shall be under your rule."
⁷ But the other will cry out on that day,
   saying,
"I will not be a healer;
   in my house there is neither bread nor
      cloak;
you shall not make me
   leader of the people."
⁸ For Jerusalem has stumbled
   and Judah has fallen,
because their speech and their deeds are
      against the LORD,
   defying his glorious presence.

⁹ The look on their faces bears witness
      against them;
   they proclaim their sin like Sodom,
   they do not hide it.
Woe to them!
   For they have brought evil on
      themselves.
¹⁰ Tell the innocent how fortunate they are,
   for they shall eat the fruit of their
      labors.
¹¹ Woe to the guilty! How unfortunate they
      are,
   for what their hands have done shall be
      done to them.
¹² My people—children are their
      oppressors,

16: *Tarshish*, either in southern Turkey (later Tarsus) or in southern Spain. **2.22–4.6**: The third oracular address focuses specifically on the purging of Jerusalem and Judah. **2.22**: The introductory wisdom saying pleads with the audience to desist from human self-reliance. **3.1–11**: The prophet elaborates the purging of Jerusalem and Judah by focusing on the punishment of the male leaders of the city and the nation. The Assyrians were well known for deporting the leading figures and skilled craftspeople of a conquered society in order to exploit their talents elsewhere in the empire and to destabilize the conquered society to prevent further revolt. The prophet once again characterizes the people as Sodom (see 1.10; Gen 18–19) in order to press home his point that the suffering of the people must be the result of their own wrongdoing. **3.12–4.1**: The prophet portrays a courtroom scene in which the LORD charges the leaders of the nation with exploitation of the poor (by enclosure and confiscation of lands, indentured service, etc.), a frequent topic of eighth-century BCE prophetic polemic (Am 2.6–11; 6.4–7; 8.4–6; Mic 2.1–3; 3.1–4,9–12). He accuses the women of Jerusalem of arrogance and being more concerned with fashion than with the fate of their city and nation. When Jerusalem is conquered, the

and women rule over them.
O my people, your leaders mislead you,
   and confuse the course of your paths.

[13] The LORD rises to argue his case;
   he stands to judge the peoples.
[14] The LORD enters into judgment
   with the elders and princes of his
      people:
It is you who have devoured the vineyard;
   the spoil of the poor is in your houses.
[15] What do you mean by crushing my
      people,
   by grinding the face of the poor? says
      the Lord GOD of hosts.

[16] The LORD said:
Because the daughters of Zion are haughty
   and walk with outstretched necks,
   glancing wantonly with their eyes,
mincing along as they go,
   tinkling with their feet;
[17] the Lord will afflict with scabs
   the heads of the daughters of Zion,
   and the LORD will lay bare their secret
      parts.

[18] In that day the Lord will take away the finery of the anklets, the headbands, and the crescents; [19] the pendants, the bracelets, and the scarfs; [20] the headdresses, the armlets, the sashes, the perfume boxes, and the amulets; [21] the signet rings and nose rings; [22] the festal robes, the mantles, the cloaks, and the handbags; [23] the garments of gauze, the linen garments, the turbans, and the veils.
[24] Instead of perfume there will be a
      stench;

and instead of a sash, a rope;
and instead of well-set hair, baldness;
   and instead of a rich robe, a binding of
      sackcloth;
   instead of beauty, shame.[a]
[25] Your men shall fall by the sword
   and your warriors in battle.
[26] And her gates shall lament and mourn;
   ravaged, she shall sit upon the ground.

4 Seven women shall take hold of one man
   in that day, saying,
"We will eat our own bread and wear our
      own clothes;
just let us be called by your name;
   take away our disgrace."

[2] On that day the branch of the LORD shall be beautiful and glorious, and the fruit of the land shall be the pride and glory of the survivors of Israel. [3] Whoever is left in Zion and remains in Jerusalem will be called holy, everyone who has been recorded for life in Jerusalem, [4] once the Lord has washed away the filth of the daughters of Zion and cleansed the bloodstains of Jerusalem from its midst by a spirit of judgment and by a spirit of burning. [5] Then the LORD will create over the whole site of Mount Zion and over its places of assembly a cloud by day and smoke and the shining of a flaming fire by night. Indeed over all the glory there will be a canopy. [6] It will serve as a pavilion, a shade by day from the heat, and a refuge and a shelter from the storm and rain.

[a] Q Ms: MT lacks *shame*

women will be stripped, humiliated, and desperate to find a husband in the devastation, even willing to forego the financial support mandated by law (Ex 21.10). **4.2–6:** An idyllic portrayal of the restored Jerusalem following its period of purging begins with the formula, *on that day*. The passage combines the metaphor of the *branch* that will grow again after it is cut (cf. 6.12–13; 11.1–9) with the imagery of the daughters of Zion, washing and purifying themselves after their menstrual periods (see Lev 15.19–24). *Cloud by day* and *flaming fire by night* over the sacred site of Mount Zion recalls the LORD leading Israel at the time of the Exodus and Wilderness wandering (e.g., Ex 13.21–22; 14.19–20; 24.15–18; 40.34–38; Num 10.11–36; cf. 1 Kings 8.10–12). Such imagery also refers to the column of smoke and fire that rises from the Temple altar during sacrifice to signify the LORD's presence. Here the smoke and fire forms a protective canopy for the restored city.

   5.1–12.6: Prophetic instruction concerning Assyrian judgment against Israel and the restoration of the Davidic kingdom. Although chs 5–12 lack a superscription, the interest in both Israel and Judah is clear throughout the unit. The passage begins (5.3) with an announcement of divine judgment against Israel and Judah in 5.1–30, and a lengthy elaboration concerning the significance of that judgment and the restoration to follow

5

Let me sing for my beloved
  my love-song concerning his vineyard:
My beloved had a vineyard
  on a very fertile hill.
[2] He dug it and cleared it of stones,
  and planted it with choice vines;
he built a watchtower in the midst of it,
  and hewed out a wine vat in it;
he expected it to yield grapes,
  but it yielded wild grapes.

[3] And now, inhabitants of Jerusalem
  and people of Judah,
judge between me
  and my vineyard.
[4] What more was there to do for my
  vineyard
  that I have not done in it?
When I expected it to yield grapes,
  why did it yield wild grapes?

[5] And now I will tell you
  what I will do to my vineyard.
I will remove its hedge,
  and it shall be devoured;
I will break down its wall,
  and it shall be trampled down.
[6] I will make it a waste;
  it shall not be pruned or hoed,
  and it shall be overgrown with briers
    and thorns;
I will also command the clouds
  that they rain no rain upon it.

[7] For the vineyard of the LORD of hosts
  is the house of Israel,
and the people of Judah
  are his pleasant planting;
he expected justice,
  but saw bloodshed;
righteousness,
  but heard a cry!
[8] Ah, you who join house to house,
  who add field to field,
until there is room for no one but you,
  and you are left to live alone
    in the midst of the land!
[9] The LORD of hosts has sworn in my
  hearing:
Surely many houses shall be desolate,
  large and beautiful houses, without
    inhabitant.
[10] For ten acres of vineyard shall yield but
  one bath,
  and a homer of seed shall yield a mere
    ephah.[a]

[11] Ah, you who rise early in the morning
  in pursuit of strong drink,
who linger in the evening
  to be inflamed by wine,
[12] whose feasts consist of lyre and harp,
  tambourine and flute and wine,
but who do not regard the deeds of the
  LORD,

a The Heb *bath*, *homer*, and *ephah* are measures of
   quantity

in 6.1–12.6.

5.1–30: Announcement of judgment against Israel and Judah. This block of oracles combines the prophet's accusations of social wrongdoing in Israel with a vivid portrayal of the approach of the Assyrian army in an effort to argue that the LORD has brought the Assyrians to punish Israel. **1–7:** Isaiah's song of the vineyard (see also 27.2–6) allegorically portrays the LORD as Isaiah's friend (*beloved* does not adequately convey the Hebrew here) who worked so hard to ensure a productive vineyard only to be disappointed when it yielded sour grapes. The allegory, which is explained only at the end, draws in the audience, as many in ancient Judah would have had extensive experience in vineyards. Its conclusion uses puns to make its point, viz., the LORD expects *justice* (Heb "mishpat"), but sees only *bloodshed* (Heb "mispaḥ"), and hopes for *righteousness* (Heb "tsedaqah") only to hear a *cry* (Heb "tse aqah"). **8–24:** A series of "woe" (NRSV "*Ah*") oracles (see also 28.1; 29.1,15; 30.1; 31.1; 33.1; Hab 2.6–19), each introduced by the Heb exclamation "hoy" ("woe!") warns the people of coming punishment due to the failure of the leadership of Israel to ensure justice as called for in Israel's law codes, particularly Ex 20–23. **8–10:** The first oracle criticizes seizure of property, a frequent concern of eighth-century BCE prophets (see 3.12–4.1n.). *bath* is a liquid measure of ca. 6 gal (23 liters), a poor yield for ten acres. A *homer* is ca. 6.5 bu (230 liters), and ⟨ep⟩*hah* is only one-tenth of a *homer*. **11–17:** The prophet charges Israel's leadership with drunken incompe-⟨tence.⟩ Drunkenness is frequently denounced in the prophets (Isa 28.7–8; Hos 4.11; 7.5; Am 4.1; Mic 2.11). **12:** ⟨the⟩ ⟨wor⟩d *work*, or plan and agenda, of God is a central motif in Isaiah (5.19; 10.12; 14.24–27; 19.12,17; 23.9;

or see the work of his hands!
¹³ Therefore my people go into exile
    without knowledge;
their nobles are dying of hunger,
    and their multitude is parched with
        thirst.

¹⁴ Therefore Sheol has enlarged its appetite
    and opened its mouth beyond measure;
the nobility of Jerusalemᵃ and her
        multitude go down,
    her throng and all who exult in her.
¹⁵ People are bowed down, everyone is
        brought low,
    and the eyes of the haughty are
        humbled.
¹⁶ But the LORD of hosts is exalted by
        justice,
    and the Holy God shows himself holy
        by righteousness.
¹⁷ Then the lambs shall graze as in their
        pasture,
    fatlingsᵇ and kids shall feed among the
        ruins.

¹⁸ Ah, you who drag iniquity along with
        cords of falsehood,
    who drag sin along as with cart ropes,
¹⁹ who say, "Let him make haste,
    let him speed his work
    that we may see it;
let the plan of the Holy One of Israel
        hasten to fulfillment,
    that we may know it!"
²⁰ Ah, you who call evil good
    and good evil,

who put darkness for light
    and light for darkness,
who put bitter for sweet
    and sweet for bitter!
²¹ Ah, you who are wise in your own eyes,
    and shrewd in your own sight!
²² Ah, you who are heroes in drinking wine
    and valiant at mixing drink,
²³ who acquit the guilty for a bribe,
    and deprive the innocent of their rights!
²⁴ Therefore, as the tongue of fire devours
        the stubble,
    and as dry grass sinks down in the
        flame,
so their root will become rotten,
    and their blossom go up like dust;
for they have rejected the instruction of
        the LORD of hosts,
    and have despised the word of the Holy
        One of Israel.

²⁵ Therefore the anger of the LORD was
        kindled against his people,
    and he stretched out his hand against
        them and struck them;
    the mountains quaked,
and their corpses were like refuse
    in the streets.
For all this his anger has not turned away,
    and his hand is stretched out still.

²⁶ He will raise a signal for a nation far
        away,

ᵃ Heb *her nobility*
ᵇ Cn Compare Gk: Heb *aliens*

28.21; 30.1). **14:** The threat of exile and death is personified as *Sheol*, the underworld abode of the dead, which opens its mouth to swallow up the leadership of the people, much as they swallowed wine and food at their feasts. Such abasement of the people highlights the LORD's power, holiness, and righteousness in the eyes of the prophet. **20–24:** The prophet charges that the people can no longer distinguish between right and wrong, perverting the judicial system (1.23; Mic 3.11; cf. Ex 23.8; Deut 16.19) in their own narcissism and drunkenness. Returning to the vineyard allegory of 5.1–7, the prophet charges that the people will be utterly consumed by *fire* for neglecting divine instruction. **25–30:** The final subunit shifts from the metaphor of a burning vineyard to a chilling portrayal of the approaching Assyrian army summoned by the LORD. The outstretched hand of the LORD appears throughout 9.7–10.5 as well, and builds upon the imagery of Moses' outstretched hand throughout the plagues of the Exodus narratives (see Ex 7–10), the crossing of the sea (Ex 14.26–29), the provision of water from the rock (Ex 17.1–7), and the defeat of Amalek in the wilderness (Ex 17.8–16). The *signal* (Heb "nes") raised to summon the nations likewise recalls the LORD's "banner" ("nes") in Ex 17.15–16. The roaring of the Assyrian army like lions recalls the lion as the symbol of the tribe of Judah and the house of David (Gen 49.9), now turned against the people. The darkening cloud over the land recalls the pillar of cloud and smoke, identified with the LORD's presence during the Exodus and in the Holy of Holies in the Temple (see 4.2–6n.), but now absent.

and whistle for a people at the ends of
the earth;
Here they come, swiftly, speedily!
[27] None of them is weary, none stumbles,
none slumbers or sleeps,
not a loincloth is loose,
not a sandal-thong broken;
[28] their arrows are sharp,
all their bows bent,
their horses' hoofs seem like flint,
and their wheels like the whirlwind.
[29] Their roaring is like a lion,
like young lions they roar;
they growl and seize their prey,
they carry it off, and no one can rescue.
[30] They will roar over it on that day,
like the roaring of the sea.
And if one look to the land—
only darkness and distress;
and the light grows dark with
clouds.

6 In the year that King Uzziah died, I saw
the Lord sitting on a throne, high and
lofty; and the hem of his robe filled the temple. [2] Seraphs were in attendance above him;
each had six wings: with two they covered
their faces, and with two they covered their
feet, and with two they flew. [3] And one called
to another and said:
"Holy, holy, holy is the LORD of hosts;
the whole earth is full of his glory."
[4] The pivots[a] on the thresholds shook at the
voices of those who called, and the house
filled with smoke. [5] And I said: "Woe is me! I
am lost, for I am a man of unclean lips, and
I live among a people of unclean lips; yet my
eyes have seen the King, the LORD of hosts!"
[6] Then one of the seraphs flew to me,
holding a live coal that had been taken from
the altar with a pair of tongs. [7] The seraph[b]

[a] Meaning of Heb uncertain
[b] Heb *He*

6.1–13: Isaiah's commission. Isaiah's lengthy explanation of divine judgment and restoration in 6.1–12.6 begins with a first-person visionary account of his commission as a prophet. Prophetic visions are common in the
Bible (Ex 33; 1 Sam 3; 1 Kings 19; Jer 1.11–19; 24; Ezek 1–3; 8–11; 40–48; Am 7–9; Hab 2.2; Zech 1.7–6.15) and in the
larger ancient Near Eastern world (cf. Balaam's visions in Num 22–24). Although they are commonly associated with temples, priests (e.g., Moses; Samuel; Jeremiah; Ezekiel; Zechariah) and non-priests (Elijah; Amos;
Habakkuk) alike may experience visions. Although Isaiah is not a priest, his vision portrays the LORD enthroned
in the Holy of Holies of the Jerusalem Temple. As a royal adviser, Isaiah would stand with the king by the column
at the entrance of the Temple where he could see the interior of the Temple (2 Kings 11.14; 23.3). Such a vision
of the LORD's royal court corresponds to the visions of Micaiah ben Imlah (1 Kings 22.19–23) and Ezekiel (Ezek
1). Given the emphasis on purging the people from sin, it is possible that the vision takes place on Yom Kippur,
the Day of Atonement, when the priest beholds the LORD in the Holy of Holies to atone on behalf of the people
(Lev 16; 23.26–32). **1–2:** *King Uzziah* of Judah, also known as Azariah, died in 742 or 733 BCE (2 Kings 15.1–7,32);
the chronology is uncertain for this period. The reigns of his son, Jotham, and grandson, Ahaz, saw the first attempts by the Syro-Ephraimite alliance, i.e., the Northern Kingdom of Israel and Aram, to invade Judah, thereby
initiating Assyria's attempts to take control of the region (2 Kings 15.32–16.20; Isa 7.1–9.6). Because Isaiah is
heavily influenced by the royal Davidic/Zion theology, he sees the LORD enthroned as a king in the Holy of
Holies of the Temple. The ark of the covenant, which was housed in the Holy of Holies (1 Kings 8.6–9), was
believed to serve as the footstool for the LORD's throne (see 1 Sam 4.4; 6.2; Isa 37.16; 66.1; Pss 80.2; 99.1). The
seraphs are heavenly beings who serve as attendants to the divine king. The Hebrew word "serap" (lit. "fiery
one") also refers to fiery snakes in the wilderness (Num 21.6–9; Deut 8.15; cf. Isa 14.29; 30.6). Here, they are
comparable to the cherubim, winged creatures of composite animal and human form, that are guardians of the
ark (Ex 25.10–22). Isaiah's vision of the seraphs is apparently influenced by the imagery of the flickering lights of
the lamp stands in the thick incense smoke that fills the Temple during worship. *Feet,* probably a euphemism for
genitals. **3–4:** The hymn of the seraphs, well known in both Jewish and Christian worship, recounts the LORD's
holiness as sovereign of all creation, and points to the liturgical setting of Isaiah's vision. The shaking of the
resholds likely represents the movement of the Temple doors as they are opened. *Smoke* accompanies the
presence (4.5; 30.27; Ex 19.18; Ps 18.8), in this case also from the fire on the altar (v. 6). **5:** Isaiah recognizes
not sufficiently pure to stand before the LORD in the Temple (cf. Ex 33.18–20). **6–7:** The cleansing of
h with a hot coal from the altar presupposes the mouth purification rituals of oracular priests

touched my mouth with it and said: "Now that this has touched your lips, your guilt has departed and your sin is blotted out." [8] Then I heard the voice of the Lord saying, "Whom shall I send, and who will go for us?" And I said, "Here am I; send me!" [9] And he said, "Go and say to this people:

'Keep listening, but do not comprehend; keep looking, but do not understand.'
[10] Make the mind of this people dull, and stop their ears, and shut their eyes, so that they may not look with their eyes, and listen with their ears, and comprehend with their minds, and turn and be healed."
[11] Then I said, "How long, O Lord?" And he said:
"Until cities lie waste without inhabitant, and houses without people,

and the land is utterly desolate;
[12] until the LORD sends everyone far away, and vast is the emptiness in the midst of the land.
[13] Even if a tenth part remain in it, it will be burned again, like a terebinth or an oak whose stump remains standing when it is felled."[a]
The holy seed is its stump.

7 In the days of Ahaz son of Jotham son of Uzziah, king of Judah, King Rezin of Aram and King Pekah son of Remaliah of Israel went up to attack Jerusalem, but could not mount an attack against it. [2] When the house of David heard that Aram had allied itself with Ephraim, the heart of Ahaz[b] and the

a Meaning of Heb uncertain
b Heb *his heart*

in ancient Mesopotamia so that they could speak on behalf of their gods. **8:** The LORD's question and Isaiah's response recalls the experience of Micaiah (1 Kings 22.20–21). *Us*, the plural refers to the entire divine assembly. **9–10:** The LORD's commission to Isaiah is one of the most disturbing elements of the book, insofar as Isaiah's task is to ensure that the people will not see, hear, or understand so that they cannot repent and thereby avoid the punishment of the LORD (cf. the LORD's hardening the heart of Pharaoh; Ex 7.3–5; 10.1). **11–13:** Isaiah's response *How long?* is often understood to be a sign of his resignation to the divine will and his empathy for his people, although other figures, such as Abraham (Gen 18), Moses (Ex 33; Num 14), Amos (Am 7.1–6), and Job were not afraid to challenge the LORD when they thought a divine act was questionable. The concluding images of judgment against the land culminate in a portrayal of a tree stump that must be burned after the tree is cut down. Despite the horrific imagery of a mere 10 percent survival rate, the account concludes with a hopeful image of new growth from the ravaged stump that will constitute the holy seed of restoration (see Ezra 9.2).

7.1–8.15: Narrative concerning the LORD's judgment against Judah. The explanation of divine judgment shifts to a third-person narrative concerning Isaiah's confrontation with King Ahaz of Judah (743/735–727/715 BCE) at the time of the Syro-Ephraimite invasion of Judah (see 1 Kings 16) in 7.1–25, followed by a return to Isaiah's first-person narrative in 8.1–15 concerning the significance of the Maher-shalal-hash-baz sign (see textual note *a* on 8.1). The passage has a complex history of revision in response to changing circumstances. Thus many images are alternately used with positive and negative significance.

7.1–25: Dialogue between King Ahaz and Isaiah. The narrative begins with reference to the Syro-Ephraimite War of 735–732 BCE. In an attempt to oppose advances into western Asia by the Assyrian King Tiglath-pileser III (745–727), King Rezin of Damascus (Aram; ca. 750–732) and King Pekah of Israel (735–732) formed the Syro-Ephraimite alliance. Pekah came to the throne of Israel in a coup engineered by Aram that saw the assassination of his predecessor, Pekahiah (737–735), the son of the pro-Assyrian Menahem (747–737; 2 Kings 15.17–26). Rezin and Menahem attempted to assemble all of the smaller states in the region into a united force that would face the Assyrians. King Jotham of Judah (759–743), who likely knew all too well the animosity between Israel and Aram over the past century (King Ahab of Israel was killed at Ramoth-gilead while fighting the Arameans; see 1 Kings 22), refused to join such an unstable alliance. Jotham died of unknown causes before the combined forces of the northern kingdom of Israel and Aram arrived at Jerusalem, leaving his twenty-year-old son Ahaz to face the threat (1 Kings 16). The goal of the assault was to force Judah into the Syro-Ephraimite alliance by removing the Davidic king and replacing him with a presumably more pliable figure named "son of Tabeel" (v. 6). **2:** *Ephraim*, the northern kingdom of Israel. **3–9:** *The end of the conduit of the upper pool on the highway to the*

heart of his people shook as the trees of the forest shake before the wind.

[3] Then the LORD said to Isaiah, Go out to meet Ahaz, you and your son Shear-jashub,[a] at the end of the conduit of the upper pool on the highway to the Fuller's Field, [4] and say to him, Take heed, be quiet, do not fear, and do not let your heart be faint because of these two smoldering stumps of firebrands, because of the fierce anger of Rezin and Aram and the son of Remaliah. [5] Because Aram—with Ephraim and the son of Remaliah—has plotted evil against you, saying, [6] Let us go up against Judah and cut off Jerusalem[b] and conquer it for ourselves and make the son of Tabeel king in it; [7] therefore thus says the Lord GOD:

It shall not stand,
    and it shall not come to pass.
[8] For the head of Aram is Damascus,
    and the head of Damascus is Rezin.
(Within sixty-five years Ephraim will be shattered, no longer a people.)
[9] The head of Ephraim is Samaria,
    and the head of Samaria is the son of
        Remaliah.

If you do not stand firm in faith,
    you shall not stand at all.

[10] Again the LORD spoke to Ahaz, saying, [11] Ask a sign of the LORD your God; let it be deep as Sheol or high as heaven. [12] But Ahaz said, I will not ask, and I will not put the LORD to the test. [13] Then Isaiah[c] said: "Hear then, O house of David! Is it too little for you to weary mortals, that you weary my God also? [14] Therefore the Lord himself will give you a sign. Look, the young woman[d] is with child and shall bear a son, and shall name him Immanuel.[e] [15] He shall eat curds and honey by the time he knows how to refuse the evil and choose the good. [16] For before the child knows how to refuse the evil and choose the good, the land before whose two kings you are in dread will be deserted. [17] The LORD will bring on you and on your people and on your ancestral house such days as have not come

a   That is *A remnant shall return*
b   Heb *cut it off*
c   Heb *he*
d   Gk *the virgin*
e   That is *God is with us*

Fuller's Field. A *fuller* is a person who processes wool. The location refers to the Gihon spring, Jerusalem's water source, which was located beyond the fortified wall of the city in the Kidron Valley immediately east of the city of David. All ancient cities faced the problem of access to water in times of siege. Like several ancient Israelite cities, Jerusalem had a tunnel that would allow protected access to the Gihon from inside the walls of the city. Ahaz was inspecting Jerusalem's defenses when Isaiah arrived with his son, symbolically named *Shear-jashub* ("a remnant will return"). The symbolic name is both a reassurance that the LORD would defend Jerusalem in keeping with the Davidic/Zion tradition, and also an acknowledgment of Judah's losses. **4**: Isaiah's advice to trust in the LORD makes some practical military sense, since the Israelite and Aramean armies would hardly have time to lay a protracted siege of Jerusalem, leaving their own borders open to Assyrian attack. **9**: *If you do not stand firm in faith* (Heb "'im lo' ta'aminu"), *you shall not stand at all* ("lo' te'amenu," lit. "you will not be secure"), a wordplay between two forms of the Heb verb, "'amen," "to stand firm." **10–25**: The narrative suggests that Ahaz is skeptical, prompting the prophet to demand that the king ask a "sign" of the LORD. **11**: *Sheol*, the underworld. Although Ahaz rejects Isaiah's advice, his response to the prophet is a model of piety insofar as he will not put the LORD to the test. **14**: Isaiah's reply emphasizes the LORD's own *sign*, i.e., the birth of the child *Immanuel* ("God is with us") to express the LORD's commitment to defend Jerusalem. The *young woman* is not identified; she may be either the wife of Isaiah (cf. 8.3) or of King Ahaz. Although 7.14 is cited in Mt 1.23 as a proof text for the virgin birth of Jesus, based on the LXX translation "parthenos" (virgin), the Heb word "'almah" simply means *young woman*, not virgin. **15–17**: *Curds and honey*, choice fare, difficult to obtain during a siege; by the time the child is weaned (two to three years) the northern allies will have been totally defeated and the land (of milk and honey) will return to the prosperity it enjoyed under David and Solomon. **18–19**: A negative oracle describing dire consequences, particularly the subjugation of Judah by the Assyrian empire, that will befall Jerusalem [Ju]dah as a result of Ahaz's refusal to accept Isaiah's promises. The Isaiah narrative presumes Ahaz's decision [to seek] help to the Assyrian King Tiglath-pileser (2 Kings 16.7–18). Ahaz's appeal to Assyria put him and his [subjec]t to the Assyrians. Had he followed Isaiah's advice to wait out the siege, Tiglath-pileser, needing [to in]vade Aram and Israel, would have come anyway, and Ahaz would not have been so indebted.

since the day that Ephraim departed from Judah—the king of Assyria."

[18] On that day the LORD will whistle for the fly that is at the sources of the streams of Egypt, and for the bee that is in the land of Assyria. [19] And they will all come and settle in the steep ravines, and in the clefts of the rocks, and on all the thornbushes, and on all the pastures.

[20] On that day the Lord will shave with a razor hired beyond the River—with the king of Assyria—the head and the hair of the feet, and it will take off the beard as well.

[21] On that day one will keep alive a young cow and two sheep, [22] and will eat curds because of the abundance of milk that they give; for everyone that is left in the land shall eat curds and honey.

[23] On that day every place where there used to be a thousand vines, worth a thousand shekels of silver, will become briers and thorns. [24] With bow and arrows one will go there, for all the land will be briers and thorns; [25] and as for all the hills that used to be hoed with a hoe, you will not go there for fear of briers and thorns; but they will become a place where cattle are let loose and where sheep tread.

8 Then the LORD said to me, Take a large tablet and write on it in common characters, "Belonging to Maher-shalal-hash-baz,"[a] [2] and have it attested[b] for me by reliable witnesses, the priest Uriah and Zechariah son of Jeberechiah. [3] And I went to the prophetess, and she conceived and bore a son. Then the LORD said to me, Name him Maher-shalal-hash-baz; [4] for before the child knows how to call "My father" or "My mother," the wealth of Damascus and the spoil of Samaria will be carried away by the king of Assyria.

[5] The LORD spoke to me again: [6] Because this people has refused the waters of Shiloah that flow gently, and melt in fear before[c] Rezin and the son of Remaliah; [7] therefore, the Lord is bringing up against it the mighty flood waters of the River, the king of Assyria and all his glory; it will rise above all its channels and overflow all its banks; [8] it will sweep on into Judah as a flood, and, pouring over, it will reach up to the neck; and its outspread wings will fill the breadth of your land, O Immanuel.

[9] Band together, you peoples, and be
dismayed;
listen, all you far countries;
gird yourselves and be dismayed;
gird yourselves and be dismayed!
[10] Take counsel together, but it shall be
brought to naught;
speak a word, but it will not stand,
for God is with us.[d]

a That is *The spoil speeds, the prey hastens*
b Q Ms Gk Syr: MT *and I caused to be attested*
c Cn: Meaning of Heb uncertain
d Heb *immanu el*

20: For the shaming of prisoners by the removal of facial and body hair, see 2 Sam 10.1–5. *Feet*, genitals. **21–22:** A reuse of the curds-and-honey motif signifying that the land will go back to pasture as a result of invasion. **23–25:** Reuse of the motif of the reversion of the vineyards to briers and thorns, as in 5.6. **23:** *A thousand shekels*, ca. 25 lb (55 kg).

8.1–15: Autobiographical account concerning the Maher-shalal-hash-baz sign. The narrative abruptly shifts to Isaiah's first-person account concerning the birth of his son, Maher-shalal-hash-baz , who serves as a sign concerning the impending judgment to be suffered by Judah when the Assyrian king takes control of Judah. **1–4:** The prophet recounts how he secured witnesses concerning the future birth of his son, *Maher-shalal-hash-baz*, whose name means "the spoil speeds, the prey hastens," symbolically conveying the speed with which the Assyrians will act against the Syro-Ephraimite coalition and establish their authority over Judah. **2:** *Uriah and Zechariah*, the former may be the chief priest of the Jerusalem Temple (2 Kings 16.10–16) and the latter the father-in-law of Ahaz (2 Kings 18.2). **3:** *The prophetess*, Isaiah's wife, perhaps in the service of the Temple or court. **5–8:** The prophet makes clear the LORD's dissatisfaction with Ahaz's refusal to accept the divine offer of protection. *The waters of Shiloah*, the stream fed by the Gihon spring that symbolizes the LORD's sustenance of Jerusalem and the house of David (Neh 2.14; 3.15). The oracle plays on the imagery of the protective stream that now becomes a threatening force as it overflows its banks to flood the land. **7:** *The River*, the Euphrates, in western Assyria. **8:** Whereas *Immanuel*, "God is with us," earlier signified God's protection of Judah, the name now symbolizes the LORD's punishment of the land. **9–10:** A brief hymn expands on the Immanuel theme with

[11] For the LORD spoke thus to me while his hand was strong upon me, and warned me not to walk in the way of this people, saying: [12] Do not call conspiracy all that this people calls conspiracy, and do not fear what it fears, or be in dread. [13] But the LORD of hosts, him you shall regard as holy; let him be your fear, and let him be your dread. [14] He will become a sanctuary, a stone one strikes against; for both houses of Israel he will become a rock one stumbles over—a trap and a snare for the inhabitants of Jerusalem. [15] And many among them shall stumble; they shall fall and be broken; they shall be snared and taken.

[16] Bind up the testimony, seal the teaching among my disciples. [17] I will wait for the LORD, who is hiding his face from the house of Jacob, and I will hope in him. [18] See, I and the children whom the LORD has given me are signs and portents in Israel from the LORD of hosts, who dwells on Mount Zion. [19] Now if people say to you, "Consult the ghosts and the familiar spirits that chirp and mutter; should not a people consult their gods, the dead on behalf of the living, [20] for teaching and for instruction?" surely, those who speak like this will have no dawn! [21] They will pass through the land,[a] greatly distressed and hungry; when they are hungry, they will be enraged and will curse[b] their king and their gods. They will turn their faces upward, [22] or they will look to the earth, but will see only distress and darkness, the gloom of anguish; and they will be thrust into thick darkness.[c]

9[d] But there will be no gloom for those who were in anguish. In the former time he brought into contempt the land of Zebulun and the land of Naphtali, but in the latter time he will make glorious the way of the sea, the land beyond the Jordan, Galilee of the nations.

[2] [e] The people who walked in darkness
    have seen a great light;
those who lived in a land of deep darkness—
    on them light has shined.
[3] You have multiplied the nation,
    you have increased its joy;

a Heb *it*
b Or *curse by*
c Meaning of Heb uncertain
d Ch 8.23 in Heb
e Ch 9.1 in Heb

reference to the victorious Jerusalem of the future (anticipating 8.16–12.6). **11–15:** The *hand* of the Lord signifies possession by the spirit of God, resulting in transformed prophetic consciousness (e.g., 1 Kings 18.46; 2 Kings 3.15; Ezek 1.3; 3.22; 8.1; 33.22). Isaiah's opposition to Ahaz and his circle has apparently led to accusations of conspiracy directed against him and his followers.

8.16–12.6: Announcement concerning the fall of Assyria and the restoration of the Davidic kingdom. Having laid out the scenario for Jerusalem's and Judah's judgment at the hands of Assyria in 7.1–8.15, the prophet's oracles then turn to a scenario of divine judgment against Assyria for its own arrogance (cf. 2.10–21) and the restoration of righteous Davidic rule over a reunited Israel and Judah.

8.16–9.7: Prophetic instruction concerning the LORD's signs to Israel and the house of David. Isaiah now expresses frustration as he decides to wait for the LORD to act. Isaiah maintains that the LORD is hiding from the nation, a disturbing proposition that is meant to overcome suggestions of divine impotence or maliciousness in the face of crisis, but nevertheless points to the LORD as an important cause of Judah's suffering. **8.16:** The commands to *bind up the testimony* and *seal the teaching* (Heb "torah") among *my disciples* is an ambiguous statement. Heb "limmuday," translated here as "my disciples," may also refer to "my teachings," since "limmud" means "taught," whether the content is the teaching or the person taught. The phrase may have played a role in motivating the expansion of the book of Isaiah in the exilic and postexilic periods as later interpreters reflected upon the meaning of the prophet's oracles in relation to their own times. **8.18–9.7:** The prophet anticipates a period of gloom and darkness until a new Davidic monarch arises to replace Ahaz. **18:** *I and the children*, Shear-jashub and Maher-shalal-hash-baz, are portents for the future; the name Isaiah ("The LORD saves") connotes the hope of salvation. **19:** Recourse to *ghosts and the familiar spirits* (i.e., necromancy) was a practice in ancient Israel and Judah, though often condemned (19.3; Lev 19.31; Deut 18.10–11). Here Isaiah threatens that only lead to greater distress and darkness. **9.1:** *Zebulun* and *Naphtali* refer to the Assyrian annexation of tribal territories in Galilee following Tiglath-pileser's defeat of northern Israel in 732 BCE. The Assyrian Dur (Dor, *the way of the sea*), Gal'azu (Gilead, *the land beyond the Jordan*), and Magidu (Megiddo, *ions*), areas just south and west of Zebulun and Naphtali, were also carved out of Israel at this

they rejoice before you
> as with joy at the harvest,
> as people exult when dividing plunder.

⁴ For the yoke of their burden,
> and the bar across their shoulders,
> the rod of their oppressor,
> you have broken as on the day of Midian.

⁵ For all the boots of the tramping warriors
> and all the garments rolled in blood
> shall be burned as fuel for the fire.

⁶ For a child has been born for us,
> a son given to us;

authority rests upon his shoulders;
> and he is named

Wonderful Counselor, Mighty God,
> Everlasting Father, Prince of Peace.

⁷ His authority shall grow continually,
> and there shall be endless peace

for the throne of David and his kingdom.
> He will establish and uphold it

with justice and with righteousness
> from this time onward and forevermore.

The zeal of the LORD of hosts will do this.

⁸ The Lord sent a word against Jacob,
> and it fell on Israel;

⁹ and all the people knew it—
> Ephraim and the inhabitants of
> > Samaria—
> but in pride and arrogance of heart they
> > said:

¹⁰ "The bricks have fallen,
> but we will build with dressed stones;

the sycamores have been cut down,
> but we will put cedars in their place."

¹¹ So the LORD raised adversaries[a] against
> > them,
> and stirred up their enemies,

¹² the Arameans on the east and the
> > Philistines on the west,
> and they devoured Israel with open
> > mouth.

For all this his anger has not turned away;
> his hand is stretched out still.

¹³ The people did not turn to him who
> > struck them,
> or seek the LORD of hosts.

¹⁴ So the LORD cut off from Israel head and
> > tail,
> palm branch and reed in one day—

¹⁵ elders and dignitaries are the head,
> and prophets who teach lies are the tail;

¹⁶ for those who led this people led them
> > astray,
> and those who were led by them were
> > left in confusion.

¹⁷ That is why the Lord did not have pity
> on[b] their young people,

a Cn: Heb *the adversaries of Rezin*
b Q Ms: MT *rejoice over*

time. **2–7:** The royal song of thanksgiving answers the hopes of those who wait for the LORD to act to restore righteous Davidic rule in Israel. **4–5:** Military oppression is symbolized by the yoke (10.27; 14.25), the bar (10.24), the rod (10.24; 14.5; Gen 49.10), and the trampling boot. **4:** *The day of Midian* refers to Gideon's defeat of Midian and deliverance of Israel in Judg 7.15–25. **6–7:** The birth of a new king, perhaps Hezekiah, the son and successor of Ahaz, signals a new period of *peace, justice,* and *righteousness* in which Davidic rule will be reestablished in Israel. See also Ps 2.7. *For us,* see 6.8n.

9.8–10.4: Prophetic warning of judgment to Israel's leaders. The prophet returns to a focus on northern Israel. The oracles in this passage all conclude with the formulaic statement, "for all this, his (the LORD's) anger has not turned away; his hand is stretched out still" (9.12b, 17b, 21b; 10.4b). The occurrence of this formula in 5.25 indicates that 5.1–30 and 9.8–10.4 form a literary envelope around 6.1–9.7. The oracles presuppose Israel's experience in the Syro-Ephraimite alliance, and point to Israel's leadership as the cause of its problems. **9.8–12:** This oracle presupposes Aram's (and Philistia's) aggression against Israel in the ninth century BCE when King Ahab was killed in battle (1 Kings 22). Later Israelite kings and their Judean vassals were contained by the Aramean push into Philistia (2 Kings 10.32; 12.17–18; 13.7). **8:** *Jacob* is the eponymous ancestor of Israel (Gen 32.22–32; 35.9–15) and is especially associated with northern Israelite locations. **9:** *Ephraim* is the dominant tribe of northern Israel, and Samaria is the capital of the Northern Kingdom (1 Kings 16.24). **13–17:** Isaiah decries Israel's failure to recognize that the LORD was the party responsible for striking against Israel's leaders. Although the Jehu dynasty eventually achieved security for Israel during the reigns of Jehoash (800–784) and Jeroboam II (788–747; 2 Kings 13.24–25; 14.23–29), ancient Near Eastern sources indicate that Jehu (842–814) and Jehoash did so by forming an alliance with Assyria to contain Aram. King Zechariah (747), the last king of

or compassion on their orphans and
widows;
for everyone was godless and an evildoer,
and every mouth spoke folly.
For all this his anger has not turned away;
his hand is stretched out still.

18 For wickedness burned like a fire,
consuming briers and thorns;
it kindled the thickets of the forest,
and they swirled upward in a column of
smoke.
19 Through the wrath of the LORD of hosts
the land was burned,
and the people became like fuel for the
fire;
no one spared another.
20 They gorged on the right, but still were
hungry,
and they devoured on the left, but were
not satisfied;
they devoured the flesh of their own
kindred;[a]
21 Manasseh devoured Ephraim, and
Ephraim Manasseh,
and together they were against Judah.
For all this his anger has not turned away;
his hand is stretched out still.

10 Ah, you who make iniquitous decrees,
who write oppressive statutes,
2 to turn aside the needy from justice
and to rob the poor of my people of
their right,
that widows may be your spoil,

and that you may make the orphans
your prey!
3 What will you do on the day of punishment,
in the calamity that will come from far
away?
To whom will you flee for help,
and where will you leave your wealth,
4 so as not to crouch among the prisoners
or fall among the slain?
For all this his anger has not turned away;
his hand is stretched out still.

5 Ah, Assyria, the rod of my anger—
the club in their hands is my fury!
6 Against a godless nation I send him,
and against the people of my wrath I
command him,
to take spoil and seize plunder,
and to tread them down like the mire of
the streets.
7 But this is not what he intends,
nor does he have this in mind;
but it is in his heart to destroy,
and to cut off nations not a few.
8 For he says:
"Are not my commanders all kings?
9 Is not Calno like Carchemish?
Is not Hamath like Arpad?
Is not Samaria like Damascus?
10 As my hand has reached to the kingdoms
of the idols
whose images were greater than those
of Jerusalem and Samaria,

a Or *arm*

the house of Jehu, was ultimately assassinated by pro-Aramean elements in Israel (2 Kings 8–12). **18–21:** The last
years of the kingdom of Israel were marked by a series of royal assassinations as pro-Assyrian and pro-Aramean
elements struggled for control of the nation. King Pekah (see 7.1–25n.), who joined Israel with Aram to form the
Syro-Ephraimite alliance, gained his throne by assassinating Pekahiah, the son of the pro-Assyrian King Menahem (2 Kings 15.17–26; cf. 2 Kings 15.25). **21:** *Ephraim* and *Manasseh* were the two largest tribes in the Northern
Kingdom of Israel. **10.1–4:** The last oracle of the sequence begins with "woe" (*Ah*) to signal the prophet's judgment against Israel's leadership for its oppression of the poor and manipulation of the judicial system (see
5.20–24n.). Ultimately the Assyrian King Tiglath-pileser (745–727) stripped away much of Israel's outlying territory, which prompted Hoshea (732–722) to assassinate Pekah and submit to Assyria (2 Kings 15.29–30).

10.5–12.6: Prophetic announcement of Assyrian downfall and Davidic restoration. The final oracular sequence in chs 5–12 takes up divine judgment against the Assyrian monarch for his arrogance and the coming
restoration of righteous Davidic rule over a reunified Israel and Judah. **10.5–11:** The sequence begins with a
"[Ah]" (*Ah*) oracle directed against the Assyrian king. Although the LORD sent the Assyrians to punish Israel, the
[Assyrian] king arrogantly sees himself and not the LORD as the true power in the world. The Assyrian monarch
[he]re is Sargon II (721–705 BCE). **9:** The cities named are all Aramean cities conquered by Tiglath-pile-
[ser or] Sargon. *Calno* (Calneh) in 740 and 738; *Carchemish* in 717; *Hamath* in 738 and again in 720; *Arpad*

¹¹ shall I not do to Jerusalem and her idols
what I have done to Samaria and her
images?"

¹² When the Lord has finished all his work
on Mount Zion and on Jerusalem, he^a will
punish the arrogant boasting of the king of
Assyria and his haughty pride. ¹³ For he says:
"By the strength of my hand I have
done it,
and by my wisdom, for I have
understanding;
I have removed the boundaries of peoples,
and have plundered their treasures;
like a bull I have brought down those
who sat on thrones.
¹⁴ My hand has found, like a nest,
the wealth of the peoples;
and as one gathers eggs that have been
forsaken,
so I have gathered all the earth;
and there was none that moved a wing,
or opened its mouth, or chirped."

¹⁵ Shall the ax vaunt itself over the one
who wields it,
or the saw magnify itself against the
one who handles it?
As if a rod should raise the one who lifts
it up,
or as if a staff should lift the one who is
not wood!
¹⁶ Therefore the Sovereign, the LORD of
hosts,
will send wasting sickness among his
stout warriors,

and under his glory a burning will be
kindled,
like the burning of fire.
¹⁷ The light of Israel will become a fire,
and his Holy One a flame;
and it will burn and devour
his thorns and briers in one day.
¹⁸ The glory of his forest and his fruitful
land
the LORD will destroy, both soul and
body,
and it will be as when an invalid wastes
away.
¹⁹ The remnant of the trees of his forest
will be so few
that a child can write them down.

²⁰ On that day the remnant of Israel and
the survivors of the house of Jacob will no
more lean on the one who struck them,
but will lean on the LORD, the Holy One of
Israel, in truth. ²¹ A remnant will return, the
remnant of Jacob, to the mighty God. ²² For
though your people Israel were like the
sand of the sea, only a remnant of them will
return. Destruction is decreed, overflowing
with righteousness. ²³ For the Lord GOD of
hosts will make a full end, as decreed, in all
the earth.^b
²⁴ Therefore thus says the Lord GOD of
hosts: O my people, who live in Zion, do not
be afraid of the Assyrians when they beat
you with a rod and lift up their staff against

^a   Heb *I*
^b   Or *land*

in 740; and *Damascus* in 732. **10–11:** To the Assyrian king, *Samaria* and *Jerusalem* are ruled by idols and will fall
to him just like the others. **12–19:** Once the LORD completes the punishment of Jerusalem, divine attention will
turn to the punishment of the Assyrian king for his arrogant and self-aggrandizing boasting. **15:** The imagery
of *ax* and *saw* presupposes the Assyrian practice of cutting down trees in the land of their enemies to provide
wood for siege engines and to destroy the agricultural base of the economy (cf. Deut 20.19–20). The LORD will
become a raging fire that will burn Assyria, symbolically portrayed as felled trees. **20–27a:** The prophet returns
to the theme of the remnant that will survive the Syro-Aramean and Assyrian onslaughts (cf. 1.9; 4.2–6; 6.12–13;
7.1–15) to see the final overthrow of the Assyrians. **24:** Assyria has become an oppressor of Israel much like the
pharaoh of Egypt at the time of the Exodus. The oracle plays on the image of Assyria's *rod* (cf. 10.5), first to be
used to punish Israel, then as an instrument of oppression, and finally used against Assyria, much as the rods of
Moses and Aaron were used against Egypt during the plagues and at the parting of the sea (Ex 6–11; 13–15). **26:**
A reference to Gideon's defeat of *Midian* at the rock of *Oreb* (Judg 7.25). **10.27b–11.9:** The advance of the Assyrian
king against Jerusalem generally follows the route from northern Israel through Benjamin south into Jerusalem.
The Assyrian king who threatens Jerusalem is likely Sargon II, who passed through Jerusalem in 720 BCE and
put on a show of force to intimidate the city on his way to confront the Egyptians and Philistines at Raphia.

you as the Egyptians did. [25] For in a very little while my indignation will come to an end, and my anger will be directed to their destruction. [26] The LORD of hosts will wield a whip against them, as when he struck Midian at the rock of Oreb; his staff will be over the sea, and he will lift it as he did in Egypt. [27] On that day his burden will be removed from your shoulder, and his yoke will be destroyed from your neck.

He has gone up from Rimmon,[a]
[28] he has come to Aiath;
he has passed through Migron,
    at Michmash he stores his baggage;
[29] they have crossed over the pass,
    at Geba they lodge for the night;
Ramah trembles,
    Gibeah of Saul has fled.
[30] Cry aloud, O daughter Gallim!
    Listen, O Laishah!
    Answer her, O Anathoth!
[31] Madmenah is in flight,
    the inhabitants of Gebim flee for safety.
[32] This very day he will halt at Nob,
    he will shake his fist
    at the mount of daughter Zion,
    the hill of Jerusalem.

[33] Look, the Sovereign, the LORD of hosts,
    will lop the boughs with terrifying
        power;
the tallest trees will be cut down,
    and the lofty will be brought low.
[34] He will hack down the thickets of the
        forest with an ax,
    and Lebanon with its majestic trees[b]
        will fall.

11 A shoot shall come out from the stump
    of Jesse,
    and a branch shall grow out of his roots.
[2] The spirit of the LORD shall rest on him,
    the spirit of wisdom and
        understanding,
    the spirit of counsel and might,
    the spirit of knowledge and the fear of
        the LORD.
[3] His delight shall be in the fear of the
        LORD.

He shall not judge by what his eyes see,
    or decide by what his ears hear;
[4] but with righteousness he shall judge the
        poor,
    and decide with equity for the meek of
        the earth;
he shall strike the earth with the rod of his
        mouth,
    and with the breath of his lips he shall
        kill the wicked.
[5] Righteousness shall be the belt around
        his waist,
    and faithfulness the belt around his
        loins.

[6] The wolf shall live with the lamb,
    the leopard shall lie down with the kid,
the calf and the lion and the fatling
        together,
    and a little child shall lead them.
[7] The cow and the bear shall graze,
    their young shall lie down together;
    and the lion shall eat straw like the ox.
[8] The nursing child shall play over the hole
        of the asp,
    and the weaned child shall put its hand
        on the adder's den.
[9] They will not hurt or destroy
    on all my holy mountain;
for the earth will be full of the knowledge
        of the LORD
    as the waters cover the sea.

[10] On that day the root of Jesse shall stand

a   Cn: Heb *and his yoke from your neck, and a yoke*
     will be destroyed because of fatness
b   Cn Compare Gk Vg: Heb *with a majestic one*

10.27b–32: Some of the cities named cannot be identified with certainty, but all are presumably not far north of Jerusalem. 33: Isaiah's use of tree imagery appears once again (see 10.15–19). 34: *Lebanon,* see 2.13n. 11.1–9: In place of the felled Assyrian tree, the stump will produce a new branch that will grow into the new and righteous Davidic monarch who will preside over Jerusalem in peace (cf. 6.12–13; 9.1–7). 1: *Jesse,* the father of David (1 Sam 16.1–20). 2: *The spirit of the LORD,* the charismatic endowment of the future ruler is expressed in three pairs of attributes; LXX adds "the spirit of piety," providing the basis for the seven gifts of the Holy Spirit in Christian theology. 6–8: The idyllic scenario in which the animals live in peace and even a baby is safe recalls the garden

as a signal to the peoples; the nations shall inquire of him, and his dwelling shall be glorious.

¹¹ On that day the Lord will extend his hand yet a second time to recover the remnant that is left of his people, from Assyria, from Egypt, from Pathros, from Ethiopia,ᵃ from Elam, from Shinar, from Hamath, and from the coastlands of the sea.

¹² He will raise a signal for the nations,
   and will assemble the outcasts of Israel,
and gather the dispersed of Judah
   from the four corners of the earth.
¹³ The jealousy of Ephraim shall depart,
   the hostility of Judah shall be cut off;
Ephraim shall not be jealous of Judah,
   and Judah shall not be hostile towards
      Ephraim.
¹⁴ But they shall swoop down on the backs
      of the Philistines in the west,
   together they shall plunder the people
      of the east.
They shall put forth their hand against
      Edom and Moab,
   and the Ammonites shall obey them.
¹⁵ And the Lord will utterly destroy
   the tongue of the sea of Egypt;
and will wave his hand over the River
   with his scorching wind;
and will split it into seven channels,
   and make a way to cross on foot;
¹⁶ so there shall be a highway from Assyria

for the remnant that is left of his
      people,
as there was for Israel
   when they came up from the land of
      Egypt.

12 You will say in that day:
   I will give thanks to you, O Lord,
   for though you were angry with me,
your anger turned away,
   and you comforted me.

² Surely God is my salvation;
   I will trust, and will not be afraid,
for the Lord Godᵇ is my strength and my
      might;
   he has become my salvation.

³ With joy you will draw water from the wells of salvation. ⁴ And you will say in that day:
Give thanks to the Lord,
   call on his name;
make known his deeds among the nations;
   proclaim that his name is exalted.

⁵ Sing praises to the Lord, for he has done
      gloriously;
   let this be knownᶜ in all the earth.

ᵃ Or *Nubia;* Heb *Cush*
ᵇ Heb *for Yah, the* Lord
ᶜ Or *this is made known*

of Eden (Gen 2). **9:** *My holy mountain,* see 2.2n. **10:** The *signal* (Heb "nes," "banner") that summons the nations recalls the banner of the Lord that summoned the Assyrians in 5.26 and that symbolized the defeat of Amalek in Ex 17.15–16. **11–16:** The restoration of righteous Davidic rule in Jerusalem prompts the return of Israel's exiles and the restoration of the united Davidic empire. Israelites were exiled to Assyria and others had fled to Egypt during the course of the Assyrian invasions in the late eighth century. **11:** *Pathros,* in southern Egypt; *Ethiopia* (Heb "Cush"), south of Egypt; *Elam,* in southern Iran, east of Babylonia; *Shinar,* the plain of Babylon; *Hamath,* in north central Aram (Syria); *the coastlands of the sea,* the Phoenician littoral on the eastern Mediterranean coast, or the islands of the eastern Aegean. **12–14:** With the exiles recovered, Israel and Judah will reunite under the rule of the Davidic king as in the days of David and Solomon, to conquer Philistia and Transjordan (*Edom, Moab,* and *the Ammonites*), regions that had once been part of the kingdom of David and Solomon (2 Sam 8). **15:** The Lord's defeat of the sea of Egypt recalls the parting of the sea at the time of the Exodus (Ex 14–15). The *scorching wind* is a dry sirocco or east wind that plays a role in the parting of the sea and other acts of the Lord (Ex 10.13; 14.21). *The River,* the Euphrates. *Seven channels* evokes mythological traditions about the dragon Leviathan (cf. 27.1), who has seven heads in Canaanite mythology. The *highway from Assyria* is compared to the King's Highway, a trade route through Transjordan, that Israel followed on its way through Moab to the promised land (Num 20.17; 21.22; Deut 2.17). **12.1–6:** The concluding song of thanksgiving quotes from the Song of the Sea in Ex 15 (see esp. Ex 15.1–3) and various Psalms (e.g., 105.1; 118.14,21). The drawing of water suggests a setting in the celebration of Sukkot (Tabernacles; Lev 23.33–44), when water libations were poured at the Temple to celebrate the end of the fruit harvest and the onset of the rainy season as well as Israel's journey through the wilderness.

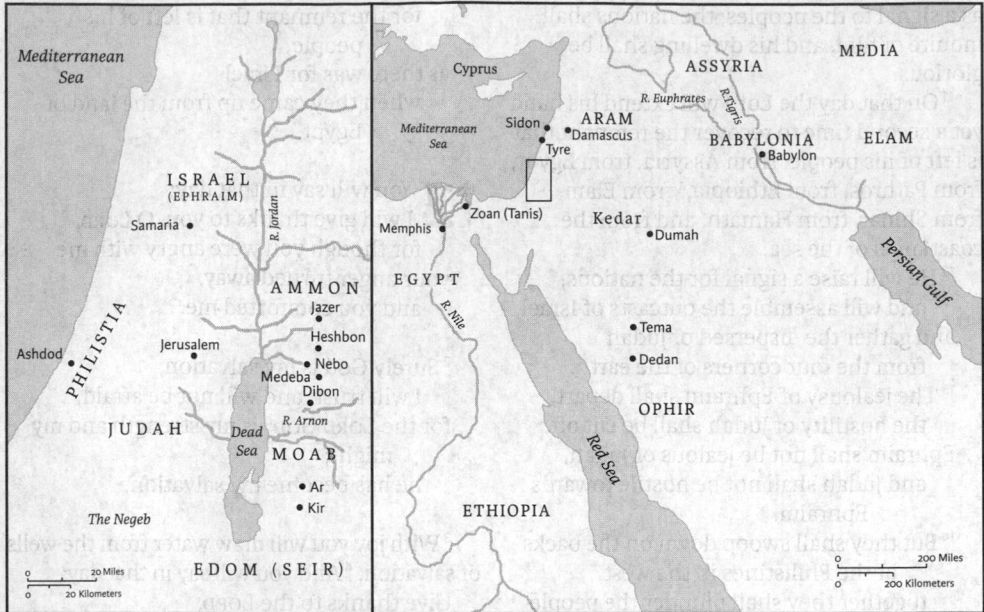

Places mentioned in the oracles against the nations.

---

⁶ Shout aloud and sing for joy, O royalᵃ
  Zion,
    for great in your midst is the Holy One
      of Israel.

13 The oracle concerning Babylon that
  Isaiah son of Amoz saw.

² On a bare hill raise a signal,
    cry aloud to them;
  wave the hand for them to enter
    the gates of the nobles.
³ I myself have commanded my
    consecrated ones,

ᵃ Or *O inhabitant of*

13.1–27.13: Prophetic announcement concerning the preparation of the nations for the LORD's world rule. The oracles concerning the nations in chs 13–23 together with prophecies of restoration for Zion and Israel in chs 24–27 constitute a major unit that anticipates the LORD's actions and sovereignty from throughout the entire world. The superscription in 13.1 that introduces this section is styled much like that in 2.1. Major blocks of oracles concerning the nations are a common feature of prophetic books (see Jer 46–51; Ezek 25–32; Am 1–2; Ob; Nah; Zeph 2.4–15). Isaiah's oracles are each marked with a superscription that identifies it as an oracle or pronouncement (Heb "massa'") concerning the nation in question. The prophet's pronouncements include nations that were ultimately conquered by the Persian empire, beginning with the Persian King Cyrus's conquest of Babylon in 539 BCE, which prompted his decree to end the Babylonian exile and allow Jews to return to their own land (2 Chr 36.22–23; Ezra 1.1–4). Insofar as the latter portions of Isaiah designate Cyrus as the LORD's "messiah" and "temple builder" (44.28; 45.1), the final form of the book of Isaiah views Cyrus and the Persian empire as the means by which the LORD exercises worldwide sovereignty.

13.1–14.32: Isaiah's pronouncement concerning Babylon. The prophet's oracle concerning Babylon includes a summation in 14.24–27 that applies the oracles concerning Assyria to Babylon, and an appendix in 14.28–32 that takes up Philistia. **13.1:** The superscription both introduces the oracle concerning Babylon and the oracles concerning the nations throughout Isaiah 13–23. **13.2–14.27:** The lengthy oracle concerning Babylon is unexpected immediately following the earlier concerns with Assyria and its threat to Israel and Judah in the eighth century. Nevertheless, the book as a whole also addresses the Babylonian exile and the Persian-period restoration in the sixth century BCE. It therefore portrays Babylon as the natural successor to Assyria as the LORD's agent of punishment who must in turn be brought down to realize Jerusalem's restoration. **13.2–5:** The sum-

have summoned my warriors, my
proudly exulting ones,
to execute my anger.

4 Listen, a tumult on the mountains
as of a great multitude!
Listen, an uproar of kingdoms,
of nations gathering together!
The LORD of hosts is mustering
an army for battle.
5 They come from a distant land,
from the end of the heavens,
the LORD and the weapons of his
indignation,
to destroy the whole earth.

6 Wail, for the day of the LORD is near;
it will come like destruction from the
Almighty!a
7 Therefore all hands will be feeble,
and every human heart will melt,
8 and they will be dismayed.
Pangs and agony will seize them;
they will be in anguish like a woman in
labor.
They will look aghast at one another;
their faces will be aflame.
9 See, the day of the LORD comes,
cruel, with wrath and fierce anger,
to make the earth a desolation,
and to destroy its sinners from it.
10 For the stars of the heavens and their
constellations
will not give their light;
the sun will be dark at its rising,
and the moon will not shed its light.
11 I will punish the world for its evil,
and the wicked for their iniquity;
I will put an end to the pride of the
arrogant,

and lay low the insolence of tyrants.
12 I will make mortals more rare than fine
gold,
and humans than the gold of Ophir.
13 Therefore I will make the heavens
tremble,
and the earth will be shaken out of its
place,
at the wrath of the LORD of hosts
in the day of his fierce anger.
14 Like a hunted gazelle,
or like sheep with no one to gather
them,
all will turn to their own people,
and all will flee to their own lands.
15 Whoever is found will be thrust through,
and whoever is caught will fall by the
sword.
16 Their infants will be dashed to pieces
before their eyes;
their houses will be plundered,
and their wives ravished.
17 See, I am stirring up the Medes against
them,
who have no regard for silver
and do not delight in gold.
18 Their bows will slaughter the young
men;
they will have no mercy on the fruit of
the womb;
their eyes will not pity children.
19 And Babylon, the glory of kingdoms,
the splendor and pride of the
Chaldeans,
will be like Sodom and Gomorrah
when God overthrew them.
20 It will never be inhabited
or lived in for all generations;

a Traditional rendering of Heb *Shaddai*

mons to war presupposes Israel's holy war traditions (cf. Deut 20; Josh 1–11) in which the LORD fights on behalf of Israel and employs a heavenly army (see Ex 23.20–33; Josh 5.13–15; 2 Kings 6.15–19; 7.3–8). **6–8:** *The day of the LORD*, see 2.10–21n. The imagery of wailing together with *pangs* and *agony* evokes the imagery of childbirth. Such imagery builds on the role that the birth of Isaiah's own symbolically named sons play in communicating his oracles (7.1–9; 8.1–15,18). **9–16:** Because the LORD is the sovereign of all creation, elements of creation such as the stars, moon, and sun, all play roles in the assault against the arrogant and evil on the Day of the LORD. **12:** *Ophir*, in Arabia, was known for its gold (1 Kings 9.26–28). **17–22:** The *Medes* are a nation northwest of Persia, which allied with the Babylonians in 627–609 BCE to bring down the Assyrian empire. Later, under the rule of Cyrus, they united with Persia to form the Persian empire, which in turn conquered Babylonia in 539 BCE. **19:** *Chaldeans*, the Babylonians. *Sodom and Gomorrah*, see 1.9n. **20–22:** The reversion of cities to a primitive condition is a common theme in Isaiah; see 14.22; 17.23; 18.6; 25.2; 27.10–11; 32.13–14; 34.8–15. Although Cyrus

Arabs will not pitch their tents there,
  shepherds will not make their flocks lie
    down there.
21 But wild animals will lie down there,
  and its houses will be full of howling
    creatures;
there ostriches will live,
  and there goat-demons will dance.
22 Hyenas will cry in its towers,
  and jackals in the pleasant palaces;
its time is close at hand,
  and its days will not be prolonged.

14 But the Lord will have compassion on Jacob and will again choose Israel, and will set them in their own land; and aliens will join them and attach themselves to the house of Jacob. 2 And the nations will take them and bring them to their place, and the house of Israel will possess the nations[a] as male and female slaves in the Lord's land; they will take captive those who were their captors, and rule over those who oppressed them.

3 When the Lord has given you rest from your pain and turmoil and the hard service with which you were made to serve, 4 you will take up this taunt against the king of Babylon:

How the oppressor has ceased!
  How his insolence[b] has ceased!
5 The Lord has broken the staff of the
    wicked,
  the scepter of rulers,
6 that struck down the peoples in wrath
  with unceasing blows,
that ruled the nations in anger
  with unrelenting persecution.
7 The whole earth is at rest and quiet;
  they break forth into singing.

8 The cypresses exult over you,
  the cedars of Lebanon, saying,
"Since you were laid low,
  no one comes to cut us down."
9 Sheol beneath is stirred up
  to meet you when you come;
it rouses the shades to greet you,
  all who were leaders of the earth;
it raises from their thrones
  all who were kings of the nations.
10 All of them will speak
  and say to you:
"You too have become as weak as we!
  You have become like us!"
11 Your pomp is brought down to Sheol,
  and the sound of your harps;
maggots are the bed beneath you,
  and worms are your covering.

12 How you are fallen from heaven,
  O Day Star, son of Dawn!
How you are cut down to the ground,
  you who laid the nations low!
13 You said in your heart,
  "I will ascend to heaven;
I will raise my throne
  above the stars of God;
I will sit on the mount of assembly
  on the heights of Zaphon;[c]
14 I will ascend to the tops of the clouds,
  I will make myself like the Most High."
15 But you are brought down to Sheol,
  to the depths of the Pit.

a Heb *them*
b Q Ms Compare Gk Syr Vg: Meaning of MT uncertain
c Or *assembly in the far north*

defeated the Babylonian army in the field, Babylon surrendered to him peacefully and was not destroyed. **21:** *Goat-demons*, satyrs and demons, including Lilith (34.14), are at home in the wilderness. **14.1–2:** With the defeat and destruction of Babylon, the Lord turns to the restoration of Israel to its own land. **3–23:** The Lord instructs Isaiah to sing a taunt song at the downfall of the king of Babylon. **7–8:** Both Assyrian and Babylonian kings were known for cutting down the cypresses and *cedars* of Lebanon (2.13n), as the wood was prized for building luxurious palaces (see 37.24). The trees therefore rejoice at the king's death. **9–11:** *Sheol*, the underworld, prepares to welcome the dead king. Despite his arrogance (cf. 10.5–32), the king must recognize that no one, not even kings, escapes death and its consequences. **12–14:** The names *Day Star* and *son of Dawn* draw on divine names known from Canaanite mythology. The name was translated as Lucifer in Latin, and the passage was later understood to refer to Satan's fall from heaven. The taunt song apparently reflects mythological references to failed attempts by gods to challenge the rule of the chief god (see also Ezek 28; Ps 82). **15:** The king's descent to *Sheol* (also called *the Pit*) draws on mythic patterns such as the Mesopotamian "Descent of Ishtar/Inanna to the Underworld," in which a goddess descends to the netherworld in an attempt to recover her dead consort. *Zaphon* ("north") is the mythological northern mountain of Baal in Canaanite mythology; it is identified with

¹⁶ Those who see you will stare at you,
  and ponder over you:
"Is this the man who made the earth
    tremble,
  who shook kingdoms,
¹⁷ who made the world like a desert
  and overthrew its cities,
  who would not let his prisoners go
    home?"
¹⁸ All the kings of the nations lie in glory,
  each in his own tomb;
¹⁹ but you are cast out, away from your
    grave,
  like loathsome carrion,ᵃ
clothed with the dead, those pierced by
    the sword,
  who go down to the stones of the Pit,
  like a corpse trampled underfoot.
²⁰ You will not be joined with them in
    burial,
  because you have destroyed your land,
  you have killed your people.

May the descendants of evildoers
  nevermore be named!
²¹ Prepare slaughter for his sons
  because of the guilt of their father.ᵇ
Let them never rise to possess the earth
  or cover the face of the world with cities.

²² I will rise up against them, says the LORD
of hosts, and will cut off from Babylon name
and remnant, offspring and posterity, says
the LORD. ²³ And I will make it a possession of
the hedgehog, and pools of water, and I will
sweep it with the broom of destruction, says
the LORD of hosts.

²⁴ The LORD of hosts has sworn:
As I have designed,
  so shall it be;
and as I have planned,
  so shall it come to pass:
²⁵ I will break the Assyrian in my land,
  and on my mountains trample him
    under foot;
his yoke shall be removed from them,
  and his burden from their
    shoulders.
²⁶ This is the plan that is planned
  concerning the whole earth;
and this is the hand that is stretched out
  over all the nations.
²⁷ For the LORD of hosts has planned,
  and who will annul it?
His hand is stretched out,
  and who will turn it back?

²⁸ In the year that King Ahaz died this
    oracle came:

²⁹ Do not rejoice, all you Philistines,
  that the rod that struck you is broken,
for from the root of the snake will come
    forth an adder,
  and its fruit will be a flying fiery
    serpent.
³⁰ The firstborn of the poor will graze,
  and the needy lie down in safety;
but I will make your root die of famine,
  and your remnant Iᶜ will kill.
³¹ Wail, O gate; cry, O city;

ᵃ Cn Compare Gk: Heb *like a loathed branch*
ᵇ Syr Compare Gk: Heb *fathers*
ᶜ Q Ms Vg: MT *he*

Mount Zion in Ps 48.2. **18–21:** Allusion to the body of the king lying unburied in vv. 19–20 indicate that the passage originally presupposed the Assyrian King Sargon II, whose body was reportedly left on the battlefield in 705 BCE. **22–23:** A prose conclusion repeating the motif of reversion to primitive conditions (see 13.20–22n.). **24–27:** The reference to the LORD's plan to defeat Assyria in the land of Israel draws an analogy between Assyria and Babylon as nations that must be punished for their arrogance following their roles as agents for divine punishment of Israel. The similarities with 10.5–34 suggest that the two passages may once have formed a unit in an earlier edition of Isaiah's oracles. Babylon succeeds Assyria as the major enemy in chs 40–55. The reference to the LORD's plan also anticipates statements that concerning the LORD's word in 40.8 and the realization of divine plans in 55.11.

14.28–32: Appendix concerning Isaiah's pronouncement against Philistia. Following the death of King Ahaz (715 BCE), Philistia attempted to revolt against Assyria, and likely approached Ahaz's son, King Hezekiah (727/715–698/687) for support. Isaiah was opposed to military alliances against Assyria due to his belief in the Davidic/Zion theology that posited the LORD's protection of Jerusalem (cf. 7.1–25). Sargon put down the Philis-

melt in fear, O Philistia, all of you!
For smoke comes out of the north,
    and there is no straggler in its ranks.

32 What will one answer the messengers of
    the nation?
"The LORD has founded Zion,
    and the needy among his people
    will find refuge in her."

15 An oracle concerning Moab.

Because Ar is laid waste in a night,
    Moab is undone;
because Kir is laid waste in a night,
    Moab is undone.
2 Dibon[a] has gone up to the temple,
    to the high places to weep;
over Nebo and over Medeba
    Moab wails.
On every head is baldness,
    every beard is shorn;
3 in the streets they bind on sackcloth;
    on the housetops and in the squares
    everyone wails and melts in tears.
4 Heshbon and Elealeh cry out,
    their voices are heard as far as Jahaz;
therefore the loins of Moab quiver;[b]
    his soul trembles.
5 My heart cries out for Moab;
    his fugitives flee to Zoar,
    to Eglath-shelishiyah.
For at the ascent of Luhith
    they go up weeping;

on the road to Horonaim
    they raise a cry of destruction;
6 the waters of Nimrim
    are a desolation;
the grass is withered, the new growth fails,
    the verdure is no more.
7 Therefore the abundance they have
    gained
    and what they have laid up
they carry away
    over the Wadi of the Willows.
8 For a cry has gone
    around the land of Moab;
the wailing reaches to Eglaim,
    the wailing reaches to Beer-elim.
9 For the waters of Dibon[c] are full of
    blood;
    yet I will bring upon Dibon[c] even
    more—
a lion for those of Moab who escape,
    for the remnant of the land.

16 Send lambs
    to the ruler of the land,
from Sela, by way of the desert,
    to the mount of daughter Zion.
2 Like fluttering birds,
    like scattered nestlings,
so are the daughters of Moab
    at the fords of the Arnon.

a Cn: Heb *the house and Dibon*
b Cn Compare Gk Syr: Heb *the armed men of Moab
cry aloud*
c Q Ms Vg Compare Syr: MT *Dimon*

tine revolt in 713 BCE.

15.1–16.14: Isaiah's pronouncement concerning Moab. The superscription introduces a lamentation concerning the downfall of Moab, a nation east of the Dead Sea that was often on unfriendly terms with Israel and Judah (cf. Gen 19.30–37). The poem employs the poetic meter typical of dirges in ancient Hebrew poetry (cf. Lam 1–2). Elements of the oracle also appear in Jer 48.29–38, which employs the Isaian oracle to comment on Moab's fate at the hands of Babylon in Jeremiah's time. Although the setting of this oracle is disputed, a likely setting is Tiglath-pileser's invasion of Israel during the Syro-Ephraimite War of 735–732 BCE. Moabite territory north of the Arnon had once been the tribal territory of Reuben and perhaps Gad (see Num 32). In the Moabite Stone (Mesha Stele, ninth century BCE), the Moabite King Mesha boasts of having defeated Israel—and the men of Gad in particular—and taking their land. The Assyrians would have considered this territory to be Israelite and therefore fair game for their own plans for taking control of the region. Moab's appeal for assistance to Jerusalem makes sense in the Syro-Ephraimite War, because Ahaz summons the Assyrians for assistance and maintains his loyalty as an Assyrian vassal (see 7.1–25) **15.1–9:** The Moabite towns mentioned in the oracle indicate an invasion that targeted Moabite territory north of the Wadi Arnon, the Wadi el-Mujib that flows into the Dead Sea. **1–4:** The cities of *Ar, Kir*(-hareseth), *Nebo, Medeba, Heshbon,* and *Elealeh,* are all located in the north and subject to attack. *Dibon* and *Jahaz,* on the old border of Moab just north of the Arnon, only serve as witnesses. *Baldness . . . sackcloth,* signs of mourning. **5–8:** The southern cities and locations, none of which can be conclusively identified,

3 "Give counsel,
   grant justice;
make your shade like night
   at the height of noon;
hide the outcasts,
   do not betray the fugitive;
4 let the outcasts of Moab
   settle among you;
be a refuge to them
   from the destroyer."

When the oppressor is no more,
   and destruction has ceased,
and marauders have vanished from the
   land,
5 then a throne shall be established in
   steadfast love
   in the tent of David,
   and on it shall sit in faithfulness
a ruler who seeks justice
   and is swift to do what is right.

6 We have heard of the pride of Moab
   —how proud he is!—
of his arrogance, his pride, and his
   insolence;
   his boasts are false.
7 Therefore let Moab wail,
   let everyone wail for Moab.
Mourn, utterly stricken,
   for the raisin cakes of Kir-hareseth.

8 For the fields of Heshbon languish,
   and the vines of Sibmah,
whose clusters once made drunk
   the lords of the nations,
reached to Jazer
   and strayed to the desert;
their shoots once spread abroad
   and crossed over the sea.
9 Therefore I weep with the weeping of Jazer
   for the vines of Sibmah;

I drench you with my tears,
   O Heshbon and Elealeh;
for the shout over your fruit harvest
   and your grain harvest has ceased.
10 Joy and gladness are taken away
   from the fruitful field;
and in the vineyards no songs are sung,
   no shouts are raised;
no treader treads out wine in the presses;
   the vintage-shout is hushed.ᵃ
11 Therefore my heart throbs like a harp for
      Moab,
   and my very soul for Kir-heres.
12 When Moab presents himself, when he
wearies himself upon the high place, when
he comes to his sanctuary to pray, he will not
prevail.
13 This was the word that the LORD spoke
concerning Moab in the past. 14 But now the
LORD says, In three years, like the years of
a hired worker, the glory of Moab will be
brought into contempt, in spite of all its great
multitude; and those who survive will be very
few and feeble.

17 An oracle concerning Damascus.

See, Damascus will cease to be a city,
   and will become a heap of ruins.
2 Her towns will be deserted forever;ᵇ
   they will be places for flocks,
   which will lie down, and no one will
      make them afraid.
3 The fortress will disappear from Ephraim,
   and the kingdom from Damascus;
and the remnant of Aram will be
   like the glory of the children of Israel,
         says the LORD of hosts.

ᵃ Gk: Heb *I have hushed*
ᵇ Cn Compare Gk: Heb *the cities of Aroer are deserted*

are places to which refugees flee from the assault in the north. **16.1:** *Sela*, unidentified, perhaps modern Petra.
8–11: Lament for the destruction of the vineyards of *Sibmah*, apparently the wine-producing region of Moab.

17.1–18.7: Isaiah's pronouncement concerning Damascus. The superscription identifies this unit as the prophet's pronouncement concerning Damascus, but the contents of the oracle include material concerning Israel and the LORD's recognition by Cush (i.e., Ethiopia). This suggests that the oracle is concerned with the Syro-Ephraimite coalition of Aram-Damascus and Israel, and Israel's efforts to convince Cush to join in opposition to Assyria. **17.1b–6:** The initial segment of the oracle targets both *Damascus*, the capital of Aram, and *Ephraim*, the tribal name identified with the Northern Kingdom of Israel. Isaiah's favored images of harvest and gleaning then portray the decimation of Israel at the hands of the Assyrians. The *Valley of Rephaim* (lit. the Valley

⁴ On that day
the glory of Jacob will be brought low,
and the fat of his flesh will grow lean.
⁵ And it shall be as when reapers gather
standing grain
and their arms harvest the ears,
and as when one gleans the ears of grain
in the Valley of Rephaim.
⁶ Gleanings will be left in it,
as when an olive tree is beaten—
two or three berries
in the top of the highest bough,
four or five
on the branches of a fruit tree,
says the LORD God of Israel.

⁷ On that day people will regard their
Maker, and their eyes will look to the Holy
One of Israel; ⁸ they will not have regard for
the altars, the work of their hands, and they
will not look to what their own fingers have
made, either the sacred poles[a] or the altars of
incense.
⁹ On that day their strong cities will be
like the deserted places of the Hivites and
the Amorites,[b] which they deserted because
of the children of Israel, and there will be
desolation.

¹⁰ For you have forgotten the God of your
salvation,
and have not remembered the Rock of
your refuge;
therefore, though you plant pleasant
plants
and set out slips of an alien god,
¹¹ though you make them grow on the day
that you plant them,

and make them blossom in the morning
that you sow;
yet the harvest will flee away
in a day of grief and incurable pain.

¹² Ah, the thunder of many peoples,
they thunder like the thundering of the
sea!
Ah, the roar of nations,
they roar like the roaring of mighty
waters!
¹³ The nations roar like the roaring of many
waters,
but he will rebuke them, and they will
flee far away,
chased like chaff on the mountains before
the wind
and whirling dust before the
storm.
¹⁴ At evening time, lo, terror!
Before morning, they are no more.
This is the fate of those who despoil
us,
and the lot of those who plunder us.

18 Ah, land of whirring wings
beyond the rivers of Ethiopia,[c]
² sending ambassadors by the Nile
in vessels of papyrus on the
waters!
Go, you swift messengers,
to a nation tall and smooth,
to a people feared near and far,

a Heb *Asherim*
b Cn Compare Gk: Heb *places of the wood and the highest bough*
c Or *Nubia*; Heb *Cush*

of the Shades), is located south of Jerusalem (2 Sam 5.18). The beating of *olive trees* appears also in 10.5–33. **7–8:** The LORD's actions against Israel will prompt the people to reconsider their adherence to other gods. *Sacred poles* were tree trunks or monoliths dedicated to the goddess Asherah (2 Kings 17.7–18; 10.16). **9–11:** *Hivites* and *Amorites*, pre-Israelite inhabitants of the land displaced because of their idolatry and evil practices (Deut 7.1–6). *Slips of an alien god*, i.e., veneration of a vegetation deity, perhaps the Mesopotamian Tammuz (see Ezek 8.14–18), also known as Adonis. **12–14:** The prophet employs the mythological motif of the combat with the sea to portray the LORD's defeat of the nations (Pss 46; 74; 93; Ex 15). In Isaiah's understanding of the Davidic/Zion tradition, the LORD alone defends Jerusalem (cf. Ps 2). **18.1–7:** The appended "woe" (*Ah*) oracle focuses on Cush (*Ethiopia*) to whom Israel sent messengers in 724 BCE during the reign of King Hoshea in an effort to gain support for its revolt against Assyria (2 Kings 17.4). Isaiah is consistently opposed to such alliances, and looks to the natural world to illustrate his view. When grapes are cut and harvested, the vines are left to the mercy of birds and animals. When nations see how the LORD trims these shoots and leaves the remnant to be picked over, they will bring offerings to Zion to recognize the LORD's sovereignty.

a nation mighty and conquering,
   whose land the rivers divide.

³ All you inhabitants of the world,
   you who live on the earth,
when a signal is raised on the mountains,
   look!
   When a trumpet is blown, listen!
⁴ For thus the LORD said to me:
I will quietly look from my dwelling
   like clear heat in sunshine,
   like a cloud of dew in the heat of
      harvest.
⁵ For before the harvest, when the blossom
      is over
   and the flower becomes a ripening
      grape,
he will cut off the shoots with pruning
      hooks,
   and the spreading branches he will hew
      away.
⁶ They shall all be left
   to the birds of prey of the mountains
   and to the animals of the earth.
And the birds of prey will summer on them,
   and all the animals of the earth will
      winter on them.

⁷ At that time gifts will be brought to the
LORD of hosts fromᵃ a people tall and smooth,
from a people feared near and far, a nation
mighty and conquering, whose land the
rivers divide, to Mount Zion, the place of the
name of the LORD of hosts.

19 An oracle concerning Egypt.

See, the LORD is riding on a swift cloud
   and comes to Egypt;
the idols of Egypt will tremble at his
      presence,

and the heart of the Egyptians will melt
      within them.
² I will stir up Egyptians against Egyptians,
   and they will fight, one against the
      other,
   neighbor against neighbor,
   city against city, kingdom against
      kingdom;
³ the spirit of the Egyptians within them
      will be emptied out,
   and I will confound their plans;
they will consult the idols and the spirits
      of the dead
   and the ghosts and the familiar spirits;
⁴ I will deliver the Egyptians
   into the hand of a hard master;
a fierce king will rule over them,
   says the Sovereign, the LORD of
      hosts.

⁵ The waters of the Nile will be dried up,
   and the river will be parched and dry;
⁶ its canals will become foul,
   and the branches of Egypt's Nile will
      diminish and dry up,
   reeds and rushes will rot away.
⁷ There will be bare places by the Nile,
   on the brink of the Nile;
and all that is sown by the Nile will dry up,
   be driven away, and be no more.
⁸ Those who fish will mourn;
   all who cast hooks in the Nile will
      lament,
   and those who spread nets on the water
      will languish.
⁹ The workers in flax will be in despair,
   and the carders and those at the loom
      will grow pale.
¹⁰ Its weavers will be dismayed,

ᵃ   Q Ms Gk Vg: MT *of*

19.1–20.6: Isaiah's pronouncement concerning Egypt. Isaiah's pronouncement concerning Egypt includes
both the oracle against Egypt in 19.1b–25 and a narrative concerning Isaiah's symbolic actions at the time of
the fall of Ashdod that legitimizes the oracle concerning Egypt. 19.1–25: Egypt played an important role in attempting to foment revolt against the Assyrians by Israel, Judah, and the other small states in the Syro-Israelite
region. Such moves would help to defend them from Assyrian invasion through the Sinai and enable them to
extend their own influence into western Asia. 1a: The superscription follows the standard form for Isaiah's
pronouncements (13.1a; 15.1a; 17.1a; 23.1a). 1b–10: The LORD is portrayed as riding on a cloud (cf. Pss 18.10; 68.33),
which is also how the Canaanite god Baal and the Assyrian god Assur were sometimes portrayed. The conflict
among the Egyptians presupposes the internal struggle that took place in Egypt during the late eighth century,
resulting finally in the emergence of the Twenty-fifth Ethiopian Dynasty, ca. 715 BCE. The Nile River provides

and all who work for wages will be grieved.

[11] The princes of Zoan are utterly foolish; the wise counselors of Pharaoh give stupid counsel.
How can you say to Pharaoh,
"I am one of the sages,
a descendant of ancient kings"?
[12] Where now are your sages?
Let them tell you and make known what the LORD of hosts has planned against Egypt.
[13] The princes of Zoan have become fools, and the princes of Memphis are deluded;
those who are the cornerstones of its tribes
have led Egypt astray.
[14] The LORD has poured into them[a]
a spirit of confusion;
and they have made Egypt stagger in all its doings
as a drunkard staggers around in vomit.
[15] Neither head nor tail, palm branch or reed,
will be able to do anything for Egypt.

[16] On that day the Egyptians will be like women, and tremble with fear before the hand that the LORD of hosts raises against them. [17] And the land of Judah will become a terror to the Egyptians; everyone to whom it is mentioned will fear because of the plan that the LORD of hosts is planning against them.

[18] On that day there will be five cities in the land of Egypt that speak the language of Canaan and swear allegiance to the LORD of hosts. One of these will be called the City of the Sun.

[19] On that day there will be an altar to the LORD in the center of the land of Egypt, and a pillar to the LORD at its border. [20] It will be a sign and a witness to the LORD of hosts in the land of Egypt; when they cry to the LORD because of oppressors, he will send them a savior, and will defend and deliver them. [21] The LORD will make himself known to the Egyptians; and the Egyptians will know the LORD on that day, and will worship with sacrifice and burnt offering, and they will make vows to the LORD and perform them. [22] The LORD will strike Egypt, striking and healing; they will return to the LORD, and he will listen to their supplications and heal them.

[23] On that day there will be a highway from Egypt to Assyria, and the Assyrian will come into Egypt, and the Egyptian into Assyria, and the Egyptians will worship with the Assyrians.

[24] On that day Israel will be the third with Egypt and Assyria, a blessing in the midst of the earth, [25] whom the LORD of hosts has blessed, saying, "Blessed be Egypt my people, and Assyria the work of my hands, and Israel my heritage."

20 In the year that the commander-in-chief, who was sent by King Sargon of Assyria, came to Ashdod and fought against it

[a] Gk Compare Tg: Heb *it*

the agricultural foundations for Egypt; the loss of its waters would devastate Egypt. **11–15:** Isaiah returns to his critique of Jerusalem's efforts to establish an alliance with Egypt against Assyria. *Zoan* is another name for the Egyptian city of Rameses or Tanis in the Delta region. The site is associated with the Exodus tradition (Ps 78.12,43; cf. Ex 1.11). *Memphis* is the capital of Lower (Northern) Egypt. *Head, tail, palm branch*, and *reed* refer to the leadership and people of Israel (see 9.14–15). **16–25:** The oracle concerning the course of future punishment and restoration for Egypt may include some later expansions of the text that presuppose Assyria's conquest of Egypt in 671 BCE and the rise of the Twenty-sixth Saite Egyptian Dynasty that began as an Assyrian vassal but ultimately served as an autonomous Assyrian ally as Assyrian power declined. The five "on that day" statements posit that Egypt will ultimately recognize the LORD together with Israel and the Assyrians. Such a sentiment builds on images of the nations' recognition of the LORD in 2.2–4; 60.10–12; 61.5–10; 66.18–24. **18:** *The City of the Sun*, the Egyptian city Heliopolis (Jer 43.13). *The language of Canaan*, Hebrew. The passage may refer to the Judean diaspora in Egypt. *Five cities* in which Judeans were settled are mentioned in Jer 2.16; 43.7; 44.1. **20.1–6:** King Sargon II of Assyria (722–705) put down a revolt by the Philistine city of Ashdod in 711 BCE. The revolt was instigated by Egypt. In order to illustrate his view that alliance with the Egyptians and Ethiopians is useless, Isaiah walks about Jerusalem naked for three years to symbolize the fate of the Egyptians and Ethiopians taken

and took it—² at that time the LORD had spoken to Isaiah son of Amoz, saying, "Go, and loose the sackcloth from your loins and take your sandals off your feet," and he had done so, walking naked and barefoot. ³ Then the LORD said, "Just as my servant Isaiah has walked naked and barefoot for three years as a sign and a portent against Egypt and Ethiopia,ᵃ ⁴ so shall the king of Assyria lead away the Egyptians as captives and the Ethiopiansᵇ as exiles, both the young and the old, naked and barefoot, with buttocks uncovered, to the shame of Egypt. ⁵ And they shall be dismayed and confounded because of Ethiopiaᵃ their hope and of Egypt their boast. ⁶ In that day the inhabitants of this coastland will say, 'See, this is what has happened to those in whom we hoped and to whom we fled for help and deliverance from the king of Assyria! And we, how shall we escape?'"

21
The oracle concerning the wilderness of the sea.

As whirlwinds in the Negeb sweep on,
   it comes from the desert,
   from a terrible land.
² A stern vision is told to me;
   the betrayer betrays,
   and the destroyer destroys.
Go up, O Elam,
   lay siege, O Media;
all the sighing she has caused
   I bring to an end.
³ Therefore my loins are filled with
      anguish;
   pangs have seized me,
   like the pangs of a woman in labor;

I am bowed down so that I cannot hear,
   I am dismayed so that I cannot see.
⁴ My mind reels, horror has appalled me;
   the twilight I longed for
   has been turned for me into trembling.
⁵ They prepare the table,
   they spread the rugs,
   they eat, they drink.
Rise up, commanders,
   oil the shield!
⁶ For thus the Lord said to me:
"Go, post a lookout,
   let him announce what he sees.
⁷ When he sees riders, horsemen in pairs,
   riders on donkeys, riders on camels,
let him listen diligently,
   very diligently."
⁸ Then the watcherᶜ called out:
"Upon a watchtower I stand, O Lord,
   continually by day,
and at my post I am stationed
   throughout the night.
⁹ Look, there they come, riders,
   horsemen in pairs!"
Then he responded,
   "Fallen, fallen is Babylon;
and all the images of her gods
   lie shattered on the ground."
¹⁰ O my threshed and winnowed one,
   what I have heard from the LORD of
      hosts,
   the God of Israel, I announce to you.

ᵃ Or *Nubia*; Heb *Cush*
ᵇ Or *Nubians*; Heb *Cushites*
ᶜ Q Ms: MT *a lion*

---

prisoner by the Assyrians. Prophets frequently engaged in symbolic actions that were meant to symbolize and realize their prophetic messages (see Jer 27–28; Ezek 5; Hos 1–3).

21.1–10: Isaiah's pronouncement concerning the wilderness of the sea. The reference to Babylon's fall in v. 9 indicates that *the wilderness of the sea* refers to Babylon. The oracle expresses Isaiah's view that Babylon would be defeated by Assyria. The term likely refers to the marshlands of southern Babylonia where the Tigris and Euphrates Rivers join and flow into the Persian Gulf. The Babylonian prince Merodach-baladan, who allied with Hezekiah to revolt against Assyria in 705–701 BCE (cf. ch 39), hid from Sennacherib in this region through 689 BCE. The watchman waits for word concerning Babylon only to learn of its defeat. The references to *Elam* and *Media* in v. 2 suggest the possibility of a later setting. Media, northeast of Babylon, allied with it to defeat Assyria in 627–609 BCE. Elam, directly east of Babylon, had been conquered by the Assyrians in the mid-seventh century, but was allied with Merodach-baladan in the late eighth century. Perhaps they later joined with Media against Assyria. Elam and Media formed part of the Persian empire that defeated Babylon in 539 BCE. Isaiah's original oracle was either updated or later read to account for that event. 1: *Negeb*, the desert region south of Judah.

¹¹ The oracle concerning Dumah.

One is calling to me from Seir,
"Sentinel, what of the night?
Sentinel, what of the night?"
¹² The sentinel says:
"Morning comes, and also the night.
If you will inquire, inquire;
come back again."

¹³ The oracle concerning the desert plain.

In the scrub of the desert plain you will
lodge,
O caravans of Dedanites.
¹⁴ Bring water to the thirsty,
meet the fugitive with bread,
O inhabitants of the land of Tema.
¹⁵ For they have fled from the swords,
from the drawn sword,
from the bent bow,
and from the stress of battle.
¹⁶ For thus the Lord said to me: Within a
year, according to the years of a hired worker,
all the glory of Kedar will come to an end;
¹⁷ and the remaining bows of Kedar's warriors
will be few; for the LORD, the God of Israel,
has spoken.

22 The oracle concerning the valley of
vision.

What do you mean that you have gone up,
all of you, to the housetops,
² you that are full of shoutings,
tumultuous city, exultant town?
Your slain are not slain by the sword,
nor are they dead in battle.
³ Your rulers have all fled together;
they were captured without the use of
a bow.ᵃ
All of you who were found were captured,
though they had fled far away.ᵇ
⁴ Therefore I said:
Look away from me,
let me weep bitter tears;
do not try to comfort me
for the destruction of my beloved
people.

⁵ For the Lord GOD of hosts has a day
of tumult and trampling and confusion
in the valley of vision,
a battering down of walls
and a cry for help to the mountains.
⁶ Elam bore the quiver
with chariots and cavalry,ᶜ
and Kir uncovered the shield.
⁷ Your choicest valleys were full of
chariots,

ᵃ Or *without their bows*
ᵇ Gk Syr Vg: Heb *fled from far away*
ᶜ Meaning of Heb uncertain

21.11–12: Isaiah's pronouncement concerning Dumah. *Dumah,* a major oasis in the Arabian Desert conquered by the Assyrian King Sennacherib in 689 BCE. *Seir* is a name for Edom, located southeast of the Dead Sea.

21.13–17: Isaiah's pronouncement concerning Arabia. Although the NRSV refers to the *desert plain*, the Hebrew text refers to Arabia, including the Arabian Desert situated to the east of Transjordan, to the west of Babylon, and south into the Arabian peninsula. The Assyrians conducted a number of campaigns in this region from the late eighth through the seventh centuries BCE. The most likely scenario is Sennacherib's defeat of *Kedar* in the northern Arabian desert in 689 BCE. The cities of *Dedan* and *Tema* were located in the northwestern Arabian peninsula south of Edom or Seir.

22.1–22: Isaiah's pronouncement concerning the valley of vision. The contents of this oracle indicate that *the valley of vision* refers to Jerusalem. No such name is known. The term is meant as a pun on the name of the Kidron Valley that defines the eastern boundary of biblical Jerusalem. Kidron means "darkness" or "gloom," and Isaiah's use of the term *valley of vision* to refer to the site is a play that reverses the meaning of the valley's name to designate it as a site of vision or revelation concerning the LORD's intentions for the city of Jerusalem. **1b–14:** The oracle begins with Isaiah's observations concerning the rejoicing of the city at the deliverance of the city of Jerusalem from an enemy, most likely the lifting of Sennacherib's siege of Jerusalem in 701 BCE. Although Isaiah 36–37 indicates that Sennacherib withdrew following the LORD's defeat of his army, Assyrian records indicate that no such defeat took place and that Sennacherib withdrew after accepting Hezekiah's surrender. Isaiah points out the cost of the siege: although Jerusalem was spared, the land of Judah was devastated by the Assyrians. The prophet Micah from Moresheth-gath along Judah's border with Philistia was forced to flee for his life

and the cavalry took their stand at the gates.

⁸ He has taken away the covering of Judah.

On that day you looked to the weapons of the House of the Forest, ⁹ and you saw that there were many breaches in the city of David, and you collected the waters of the lower pool. ¹⁰ You counted the houses of Jerusalem, and you broke down the houses to fortify the wall. ¹¹ You made a reservoir between the two walls for the water of the old pool. But you did not look to him who did it, or have regard for him who planned it long ago.

¹² In that day the Lord God of hosts
  called to weeping and mourning,
  to baldness and putting on sackcloth;
¹³ but instead there was joy and festivity,
  killing oxen and slaughtering sheep,
  eating meat and drinking wine.
"Let us eat and drink,
  for tomorrow we die."
¹⁴ The Lord of hosts has revealed himself
  in my ears:
Surely this iniquity will not be forgiven
    you until you die,
  says the Lord God of hosts.

¹⁵ Thus says the Lord God of hosts: Come, go to this steward, to Shebna, who is master of the household, and say to him: ¹⁶ What right do you have here? Who are your relatives here, that you have cut out a tomb here for yourself, cutting a tomb on the height, and carving a habitation for yourself in the rock? ¹⁷ The Lord is about to hurl you away violently, my fellow. He will seize firm hold on you, ¹⁸ whirl you round and round, and throw you like a ball into a wide land; there you shall die, and there your splendid chariots shall lie, O you disgrace to your master's house! ¹⁹ I will thrust you from your office, and you will be pulled down from your post.

²⁰ On that day I will call my servant Eliakim son of Hilkiah, ²¹ and will clothe him with your robe and bind your sash on him. I will commit your authority to his hand, and he shall be a father to the inhabitants of Jerusalem and to the house of Judah. ²² I will place on his shoulder the key of the house of David; he shall open, and no one shall shut; he shall shut, and no one shall open. ²³ I will fasten him like a peg in a secure place, and he will become a throne of honor to his ancestral house. ²⁴ And they will hang on him the whole weight of his ancestral house, the offspring and issue, every small vessel, from the cups to all the flagons. ²⁵ On that day, says the Lord of hosts, the peg that was fastened in a secure place will give way; it will be cut down and fall, and the load that was on it will perish, for the Lord has spoken.

23

The oracle concerning Tyre.

Wail, O ships of Tarshish,
  for your fortress is destroyed.ᵃ

ᵃ Cn Compare verse 14: Heb *for it is destroyed, without houses*

to Jerusalem to escape the Assyrian attack (Mic 1–2; see also 36.1; 37.8). **6:** *Elam* and *Kir* refer to elements of the Assyrian army. Elam was located in southern Iran and allied with Merodach-baladan against Assyria, although Assyria was known for incorporating military units of its vassals into its own army. Kir was an Aramean city subjugated by Assyria. **8b–11:** Prose expansion describing preparations for the siege. *The waters of the lower pool*, the prophet refers to King Hezekiah's attempts to fortify the city, including his digging of the Siloam Tunnel under *the city of David* to channel the waters of the Gihon Spring into Jerusalem where they would form the Siloam pool protected by Jerusalem's walls at the southern tip of the city. Such a move eliminated the problem that Ahaz faced: protecting the water source (7.1–9). The famed Siloam Inscription commemorates the digging of the tunnel. **12–14:** Bitter, fatalistic rejoicing in a time of disaster. **15–25:** Isaiah condemns the *steward Shebna*, a major administrative official in charge of the royal palace (*household*); his tomb has been found in the Kidron Valley east of Jerusalem. The prophet condemns Shebna for building his tomb when the Lord plans to remove him from office and replace him with *Eliakim son of Hilkiah*. In 36.2 Eliakim ben Hilkiah is called the officer "in charge of the palace" and Shebna the "secretary" or "recorder." The secretary may have worked under the supervision of the officer "over the house." In Isaiah's view, Eliakim will ultimately lose his job as well.

23.1–18: Isaiah's pronouncement concerning Tyre. *Tyre* was the dominant Phoenician city located along the sea coast north of Akko and south of *Sidon*. It was the major sea power of the day with a large navy that de-

When they came in from Cyprus
    they learned of it.
[2] Be still, O inhabitants of the coast,
    O merchants of Sidon,
your messengers crossed over the sea[a]
    [3] and were on the mighty waters;
your revenue was the grain of Shihor,
    the harvest of the Nile;
    you were the merchant of the nations.
[4] Be ashamed, O Sidon, for the sea has
    spoken,
    the fortress of the sea, saying:
"I have neither labored nor given birth,
    I have neither reared young men
    nor brought up young women."
[5] When the report comes to Egypt,
    they will be in anguish over the report
        about Tyre.
[6] Cross over to Tarshish—
    wail, O inhabitants of the coast!
[7] Is this your exultant city
    whose origin is from days of old,
whose feet carried her
    to settle far away?
[8] Who has planned this
    against Tyre, the bestower of crowns,
whose merchants were princes,
    whose traders were the honored of the
        earth?
[9] The LORD of hosts has planned it—
    to defile the pride of all glory,
    to shame all the honored of the earth.
[10] Cross over to your own land,
    O ships of[b] Tarshish;
    this is a harbor[c] no more.
[11] He has stretched out his hand over the
    sea,
    he has shaken the kingdoms;
the LORD has given command concerning
    Canaan
    to destroy its fortresses.

[12] He said:
You will exult no longer,
    O oppressed virgin daughter Sidon;
rise, cross over to Cyprus—
    even there you will have no rest.

[13] Look at the land of the Chaldeans!
This is the people; it was not Assyria. They
destined Tyre for wild animals. They erected
their siege towers, they tore down her palaces, they made her a ruin.[d]
    [14] Wail, O ships of Tarshish,
    for your fortress is destroyed.
[15] From that day Tyre will be forgotten for
seventy years, the lifetime of one king. At the
end of seventy years, it will happen to Tyre as
in the song about the prostitute:
    [16] Take a harp,
    go about the city,
    you forgotten prostitute!
Make sweet melody,
    sing many songs,
    that you may be remembered.
[17] At the end of seventy years, the LORD will
visit Tyre, and she will return to her trade,
and will prostitute herself with all the kingdoms of the world on the face of the earth.
[18] Her merchandise and her wages will be
dedicated to the LORD; her profits[e] will not
be stored or hoarded, but her merchandise
will supply abundant food and fine clothing for those who live in the presence of the
LORD.

---

a Q Ms: MT *crossing over the sea, they replenished you*
b Cn Compare Gk: Heb *like the Nile, daughter*
c Cn: Heb *restraint*
d Meaning of Heb uncertain
e Heb *it*

fended the island city from attack and engaged in trade throughout the Mediterranean (see Ezek 27). Tyre was allied with Hezekiah in the revolt against Assyria in 705–701 BCE, but Sennacherib's assault against Phoenicia in 701 quickly forced Tyre and its Phoenician dependents to submit. With Tyre out of the picture, Hezekiah's allies in western Asia quickly capitulated, leaving him to face Assyria alone. **1:** *Tarshish*, see 2.16n. **3:** *Shihor*, Lower (northern) Egypt. **13–18:** The oracle has been updated by a reference to the *Chaldeans*, the Neo-Babylonian empire founded by Nabo-polassar in 625 BCE. His son Nebuchadnezzar (605–562 BCE) conquered Tyre—but did not destroy it—following a thirteen year siege that ended in 572 BCE (cf. Ezek 26–28). The *seventy-year* period of Tyre's decline corresponds to Jeremiah's claims of a seventy-year period for Jerusalem's exile (Jer 25.11–12; 29.10). Because Tyre trades with many nations, she is disparaged as a *prostitute*, but ultimately her merchandise will be dedicated to the LORD (cf. 19.16–25).

24 Now the LORD is about to lay waste
the earth and make it desolate,
and he will twist its surface and scatter
its inhabitants.
[2] And it shall be, as with the people, so
with the priest;
as with the slave, so with his master;
as with the maid, so with her mistress;
as with the buyer, so with the seller;
as with the lender, so with the
borrower;
as with the creditor, so with the debtor.
[3] The earth shall be utterly laid waste and
utterly despoiled;
for the LORD has spoken this word.

[4] The earth dries up and withers,
the world languishes and withers;
the heavens languish together with the
earth.
[5] The earth lies polluted
under its inhabitants;
for they have transgressed laws,
violated the statutes,
broken the everlasting covenant.
[6] Therefore a curse devours the earth,
and its inhabitants suffer for their guilt;

therefore the inhabitants of the earth
dwindled,
and few people are left.
[7] The wine dries up,
the vine languishes,
all the merry-hearted sigh.
[8] The mirth of the timbrels is stilled,
the noise of the jubilant has ceased,
the mirth of the lyre is stilled.
[9] No longer do they drink wine with singing;
strong drink is bitter to those who
drink it.
[10] The city of chaos is broken down,
every house is shut up so that no one
can enter.
[11] There is an outcry in the streets for lack
of wine;
all joy has reached its eventide;
the gladness of the earth is banished.
[12] Desolation is left in the city,
the gates are battered into ruins.
[13] For thus it shall be on the earth
and among the nations,
as when an olive tree is beaten,
as at the gleaning when the grape
harvest is ended.

24.1–27.13: Prophetic announcement of the LORD's new world order based in Zion. Chapters 24–27 form a distinct block of material at the conclusion of Isaiah's oracles concerning the nations. This material posits the future withering of creation (24.1–13), the downfall of an unnamed exalted city (24.10,12; 25.2,3; 26.5), the recognition of the LORD by the nations at Zion (25.6–8), and the ultimate restoration of Zion itself as the seat of the LORD's sovereignty throughout the world of both creation and the nations. Although these chapters are sometimes called "the Isaiah apocalypse," the themes of cosmic chaos and restoration, the resurrection of the dead (26.14,19), and the view that the future constitutes the end of time need not indicate that these chapters are an apocalyptic work; the formula "in that day" may serve as a simple reference to the future. Similarly, mythological perspectives can be used to identify divine action in the world. Rather than pointing to the end of time, chs 24–27 point to the restoration of Jerusalem in chs 25–27 following the portrayal of its period of punishment in ch 24. The frequent citation of earlier prophetic literature indicates that this material was composed at a later time, probably in the sixth century BCE when the Babylonian exile was coming to an end and Jerusalem's restoration was at hand.

24.1–23: Prophetic announcement of the LORD's punishment of the earth. The depiction of a devastated land appears frequently in ancient Near Eastern treaty curses, the covenant curses of the biblical law codes (e.g., Lev 26; Deut 28–29), and the judgment scenarios of the prophets (e.g., Isa 34.11–17; Jer 5.6; 19.7–9; Hos 4; 13.7–8; Zeph 2.9). The background of such scenarios is the withdrawal or death of fertility gods such as the Canaanite Baal or the Mesopotamian Tammuz. Likewise, biblical literature, particularly Deuteronomy and many of the prophets, maintains that the LORD also ensures the fertility of the land in conjunction with human behavior. 5: *The everlasting covenant* is the foundation for all creation, including Israel (Gen 9.16; 17.7; Ex 31.16; Lev 24.8; Isa 55.3; 61.8; Jer 32.40; Ezek 37.26). 10: *The city of chaos* is not named, although the context suggests that it represents the enemy of the LORD, such as the Assyrian capital Nineveh, Babylon, or the capital of any empire that might threaten Israel or the LORD. Chaos (Heb "tohu") describes the state of the earth before creation commenced (Gen 1.2). The defeat of human enemies is frequently portrayed in cosmic terms (e.g., Ex 15). 13: The beating of the *olive tree*

¹⁴ They lift up their voices, they sing for
joy;
they shout from the west over the
majesty of the Lord.
¹⁵ Therefore in the east give glory to the
Lord;
in the coastlands of the sea glorify the
name of the Lord, the God of Israel.
¹⁶ From the ends of the earth we hear songs
of praise,
of glory to the Righteous One.
But I say, I pine away,
I pine away. Woe is me!
For the treacherous deal treacherously,
the treacherous deal very
treacherously.

¹⁷ Terror, and the pit, and the snare
are upon you, O inhabitant of the earth!
¹⁸ Whoever flees at the sound of the terror
shall fall into the pit;
and whoever climbs out of the pit
shall be caught in the snare.
For the windows of heaven are opened,
and the foundations of the earth
tremble.
¹⁹ The earth is utterly broken,
the earth is torn asunder,
the earth is violently shaken.
²⁰ The earth staggers like a drunkard,
it sways like a hut;
its transgression lies heavy upon it,
and it falls, and will not rise again.

²¹ On that day the Lord will punish
the host of heaven in heaven,
and on earth the kings of the earth.
²² They will be gathered together
like prisoners in a pit;
they will be shut up in a prison,

and after many days they will be
punished.
²³ Then the moon will be abashed,
and the sun ashamed;
for the Lord of hosts will reign
on Mount Zion and in Jerusalem,
and before his elders he will manifest his
glory.

25 O Lord, you are my God;
I will exalt you, I will praise your
name;
for you have done wonderful things,
plans formed of old, faithful and sure.
² For you have made the city a heap,
the fortified city a ruin;
the palace of aliens is a city no more,
it will never be rebuilt.
³ Therefore strong peoples will glorify you;
cities of ruthless nations will fear you.
⁴ For you have been a refuge to the poor,
a refuge to the needy in their distress,
a shelter from the rainstorm and a
shade from the heat.
When the blast of the ruthless was like a
winter rainstorm,
⁵ the noise of aliens like heat in a dry
place,
you subdued the heat with the shade of
clouds;
the song of the ruthless was stilled.

⁶ On this mountain the Lord of hosts will
make for all peoples
a feast of rich food, a feast of well-aged
wines,
of rich food filled with marrow, of well-
aged wines strained clear.
⁷ And he will destroy on this mountain
the shroud that is cast over all peoples,

alludes to 17.6 (cf. 10.33–34). **14–16:** The downfall of the city of chaos prompts the recognition of the Lord from throughout the world. *The coastlands of the sea*, the Aegean island, i.e., the far west. The treachery of *the treacherous* is a citation of 21.2 (cf. 33.1), which portrays the downfall of Babylon. **17–20:** There was no escape when *the windows of heaven* opened at the time of the flood (Gen 7.11), and there is no escape from the Lord's judgment now. **21–23:** *The host of heaven . . . kings of the earth*, the gods and rulers of the nations.

25.1–12: The Lord's blessing of the earth at Zion. With the downfall of the enemy city, the time of restoration may begin. **1–5:** A communal psalm of thanksgiving greets the Lord following the downfall of the oppressive city, much like the hymn of praise sung by Moses, Miriam, and the people at the Sea in Ex 15. **4–5:** Citation of language from 4.5b–6 and 32.1–2. **6–12:** A banquet for all the nations is held on Mount Zion in the aftermath of the Lord's victory over the city of chaos. Such a banquet symbolizes worship at the Jerusalem Temple, particularly since the sacrifice of offering at the Temple altar was conceived as a meal or banquet shared by the

the sheet that is spread over all nations;
⁸ he will swallow up death forever.
Then the Lord GOD will wipe away the
tears from all faces,
and the disgrace of his people he will
take away from all the earth,
for the LORD has spoken.
⁹ It will be said on that day,
Lo, this is our God; we have waited for
him, so that he might save us.
This is the LORD for whom we have
waited;
let us be glad and rejoice in his
salvation.
¹⁰ For the hand of the LORD will rest on this
mountain.

The Moabites shall be trodden down in
their place
as straw is trodden down in a dung-pit.
¹¹ Though they spread out their hands in
the midst of it,
as swimmers spread out their hands to
swim,
their pride will be laid low despite the
struggleᵃ of their hands.
¹² The high fortifications of his walls will
be brought down,
laid low, cast to the ground, even to the
dust.

26 On that day this song will be sung in
the land of Judah:
We have a strong city;
he sets up victory
like walls and bulwarks.
² Open the gates,
so that the righteous nation that keeps
faith

may enter in.
³ Those of steadfast mind you keep in
peace—
in peace because they trust in you.
⁴ Trust in the LORD forever,
for in the LORD GODᵇ
you have an everlasting rock.
⁵ For he has brought low
the inhabitants of the height;
the lofty city he lays low.
He lays it low to the ground,
casts it to the dust.
⁶ The foot tramples it,
the feet of the poor,
the steps of the needy.

⁷ The way of the righteous is level;
O Just One, you make smooth the path
of the righteous.
⁸ In the path of your judgments,
O LORD, we wait for you;
your name and your renown
are the soul's desire.
⁹ My soul yearns for you in the night,
my spirit within me earnestly seeks you.
For when your judgments are in the earth,
the inhabitants of the world learn
righteousness.
¹⁰ If favor is shown to the wicked,
they do not learn righteousness;
in the land of uprightness they deal
perversely
and do not see the majesty of the LORD.
¹¹ O LORD, your hand is lifted up,
but they do not see it.
Let them see your zeal for your people,

ᵃ Meaning of Heb uncertain
ᵇ Heb *in Yah, the* LORD

people with their God. **7:** *Shroud, sheet,* garments worn in time of mourning. **8:** *Swallow up death,* in ancient Near Eastern mythological traditions the fertility god, e.g., the Canaanite Baal or the Mesopotamian Tammuz, is rescued from the underworld to bring fertility and life back to the world of creation. As sovereign of creation, the LORD now brings life to creation. **8b–12:** *Wipe away the tears,* cf. Rev 7.1; 21.4. The demise of Moab refers to the defeat of Moab by Babylon in the sixth century BCE, and cites 2.9–17 to portray the downfall of the arrogant.
  26.1–21: Judah's petition to the LORD for deliverance. The liturgical setting of the thanksgiving hymn and the banquet in ch 25 prompts the liturgical hymns in ch 26 that praise the LORD and call for deliverance from the wicked. **1b–6:** The initial song of praise celebrates the victory of the LORD over the oppressive city of chaos mentioned in 24.10. **4:** *Trust in the* LORD, a common feature of complaint psalms that petition the LORD for deliverance in a time of threat or need (e.g., Pss 6; 7). **5a:** *The inhabitants of the height,* cf. 2.6–21 concerning the LORD's capacity to bring down the arrogant. **7–10:** Confidence in the LORD. The LORD's righteousness becomes a factor in teaching righteousness to the wicked of the world. **11–19:** Petitions for action on the part of the LORD.

and be ashamed.
Let the fire for your adversaries
consume them.
[12] O LORD, you will ordain peace for us,
for indeed, all that we have done, you
have done for us.
[13] O LORD our God,
other lords besides you have ruled
over us,
but we acknowledge your name alone.
[14] The dead do not live;
shades do not rise—
because you have punished and destroyed
them,
and wiped out all memory of them.
[15] But you have increased the nation,
O LORD,
you have increased the nation; you are
glorified;
you have enlarged all the borders of the
land.

[16] O LORD, in distress they sought you,
they poured out a prayer[a]
when your chastening was on them.
[17] Like a woman with child,
who writhes and cries out in her pangs
when she is near her time,
so were we because of you, O LORD;
[18] we were with child, we writhed,
but we gave birth only to wind.
We have won no victories on earth,
and no one is born to inhabit the world.
[19] Your dead shall live, their corpses[b] shall
rise.
O dwellers in the dust, awake and sing
for joy!
For your dew is a radiant dew,
and the earth will give birth to those
long dead.[c]

[20] Come, my people, enter your
chambers,
and shut your doors behind you;
hide yourselves for a little while
until the wrath is past.
[21] For the LORD comes out from his place
to punish the inhabitants of the earth
for their iniquity;
the earth will disclose the blood shed on it,
and will no longer cover its slain.

27 On that day the LORD with his cruel
and great and strong sword will punish
Leviathan the fleeing serpent, Leviathan the
twisting serpent, and he will kill the dragon
that is in the sea.

[2] On that day:
A pleasant vineyard, sing about it!
[3] I, the LORD, am its keeper;
every moment I water it.
I guard it night and day
so that no one can harm it;
[4] I have no wrath.
If it gives me thorns and briers,
I will march to battle against it.
I will burn it up.
[5] Or else let it cling to me for protection,
let it make peace with me,
let it make peace with me.

[6] In days to come[d] Jacob shall take root,
Israel shall blossom and put forth
shoots,
and fill the whole world with fruit.

a   Meaning of Heb uncertain
b   Cn Compare Syr Tg: Heb *my corpse*
c   Heb *to the shades*
d   Heb *Those to come*

13: *Other lords,* perhaps an allusion to the oppressor city of chaos (24.10), whose downfall will come in response to the people's petition. **14:** *The dead do not live,* a common theme in the psalms; only the living can praise God (Pss 6.5; 30.9; 49.10–20); see 39.18–19. **17–18:** Childbirth is a common image for an immanent event (see 13.8; 66.7–9). **19:** *Your dead shall live,* the response to v. 14, expressing an intuition of a meaningful survival of death; cf. Ezek 37.1–14; Dan 12.2. **20–21:** Exhortation to wait for the LORD (cf. 2.10,19,21).

27.1: The LORD's defeat of Leviathan. *Leviathan,* the seven-headed serpent known from Ugaritic and biblical tradition as a chaos monster whose defeat by the LORD aids in bringing about order in creation (Ps 74.13–14; cf. Isa 11.15–16).

27.2–13: The new vineyard allegory plays upon the earlier allegory in 5.1–7 that accused the people of Israel and Judah of wrongdoing before the LORD. Now the LORD stands ready to resume care for the vineyard. **6:** *Jacob*

[7] Has he struck them down as he struck
     down those who struck them?
   Or have they been killed as their killers
     were killed?
[8] By expulsion,[a] by exile you struggled
     against them;
   with his fierce blast he removed them in
     the day of the east wind.
[9] Therefore by this the guilt of Jacob will be
     expiated,
   and this will be the full fruit of the
     removal of his sin:
when he makes all the stones of the altars
   like chalkstones crushed to pieces,
   no sacred poles[b] or incense altars will
     remain standing.
[10] For the fortified city is solitary,
   a habitation deserted and forsaken, like
     the wilderness;
the calves graze there,
   there they lie down, and strip its
     branches.
[11] When its boughs are dry, they are
     broken;
   women come and make a fire of them.
For this is a people without understanding;
   therefore he that made them will not
     have compassion on them,
   he that formed them will show them no
     favor.

[12] On that day the LORD will thresh from
the channel of the Euphrates to the Wadi
of Egypt, and you will be gathered one by
one, O people of Israel. [13] And on that day a
great trumpet will be blown, and those who
were lost in the land of Assyria and those
who were driven out to the land of Egypt

will come and worship the LORD on the holy
mountain at Jerusalem.

28 Ah, the proud garland of the
        drunkards of Ephraim,
   and the fading flower of its glorious
     beauty,
   which is on the head of those bloated
     with rich food, of those overcome
     with wine!
[2] See, the Lord has one who is mighty and
     strong;
   like a storm of hail, a destroying
     tempest,
like a storm of mighty, overflowing waters;
   with his hand he will hurl them down
     to the earth.
[3] Trampled under foot will be
   the proud garland of the drunkards of
     Ephraim.
[4] And the fading flower of its glorious
     beauty,
   which is on the head of those bloated
     with rich food,
will be like a first-ripe fig before the
     summer;
   whoever sees it, eats it up
   as soon as it comes to hand.

[5] In that day the LORD of hosts will be a
     garland of glory,
   and a diadem of beauty, to the remnant
     of his people;
[6] and a spirit of justice to the one who sits
     in judgment,

---

[a] Meaning of Heb uncertain
[b] Heb *Asherim*

---

shall take root, cf. 11.1–9. **7–13:** A justification of the LORD. The suffering of the people constitutes the LORD's efforts to purge the nation of sins and idolatry. **10:** *The fortified city*, referring to the unnamed city of 24.10; 25.2; 26.5. **11:** *Without understanding*, cf. 1.2–3. **12–13:** With the downfall of the oppressor, the time to gather the exiles from Assyria and Egypt has now arrived (cf. 11.15–16).

28.1–33.24: Prophetic instruction concerning the LORD's plans for the new king in Jerusalem. This block of material is defined by its introductory "Woe" (NRSV "Ah," "Ha," "Oh," "Alas,") oracle forms (28.1; 29.1,15; 30.1; 31.1; 33.1); its overall concern for the deliverance of Jerusalem from Assyria; and its culminating concern for the establishment of a righteous king in Jerusalem.

28.1–29: Prophetic instruction concerning the LORD's purpose in bringing Assyrian rule. This oracle condemns both Israelite and Judean leadership as an explanation for Assyrian rule of Israel and Judah. **1–4:** The introductory "woe" ("Ah") oracle condemns the leadership of northern Israel (*Ephraim* was the dominant tribe of northern Israel) for self-indulgence in food and wine (cf. 5.8–24). *Proud garland* and *glorious beauty* designate the royal crown. **5–6:** The LORD's promise to support a future monarch who rules in justice and defends the na-

and strength to those who turn back
    the battle at the gate.

[7] These also reel with wine
    and stagger with strong drink;
the priest and the prophet reel with strong
    drink,
    they are confused with wine,
    they stagger with strong drink;
they err in vision,
    they stumble in giving judgment.
[8] All tables are covered with filthy vomit;
    no place is clean.

[9] "Whom will he teach knowledge,
    and to whom will he explain the
        message?
Those who are weaned from milk,
    those taken from the breast?
[10] For it is precept upon precept, precept
    upon precept,
    line upon line, line upon line,
    here a little, there a little."[a]

[11] Truly, with stammering lip
    and with alien tongue
he will speak to this people,
    [12] to whom he has said,
"This is rest;
    give rest to the weary;
and this is repose";
    yet they would not hear.
[13] Therefore the word of the LORD will be
    to them,
    "Precept upon precept, precept upon
        precept,
    line upon line, line upon line,
    here a little, there a little;"[a]
in order that they may go, and fall
    backward,
    and be broken, and snared, and taken.

[14] Therefore hear the word of the LORD, you
    scoffers

who rule this people in Jerusalem.
[15] Because you have said, "We have made a
    covenant with death,
    and with Sheol we have an agreement;
when the overwhelming scourge passes
    through
    it will not come to us;
for we have made lies our refuge,
    and in falsehood we have taken
        shelter";
[16] therefore thus says the Lord GOD,
See, I am laying in Zion a foundation
    stone,
    a tested stone,
a precious cornerstone, a sure foundation:
    "One who trusts will not panic."
[17] And I will make justice the line,
    and righteousness the plummet;
hail will sweep away the refuge of lies,
    and waters will overwhelm the
        shelter.
[18] Then your covenant with death will be
    annulled,
    and your agreement with Sheol will not
        stand;
when the overwhelming scourge passes
    through
    you will be beaten down by it.
[19] As often as it passes through, it will take
    you;
    for morning by morning it will pass
        through,
    by day and by night;
and it will be sheer terror to understand
    the message.
[20] For the bed is too short to stretch
    oneself on it,
    and the covering too narrow to wrap
    oneself in it.
[21] For the LORD will rise up as on Mount
    Perazim,
    he will rage as in the valley of Gibeon

---

a Meaning of Heb of this verse uncertain

tion (cf. 9.1–7; 11.1–9). **7–13**: The oracle presupposes the Canaanite "marzeaḥ" ritual, associated with funerary rites that called for all-night drinking and feasting. This ritual has also been associated with the conclusion of treaties. **14–22**: An indictment of Jerusalem's leadership. The covenant with Sheol, the abode of the dead, plays upon the previously noted "marzeaḥ" ritual. It may also refer to an alliance with Egypt. **16**: The *foundation stone* in Jerusalem symbolizes both the foundation for a major building, such as the Jerusalem Temple, and the Davidic/Zion tradition of the LORD's promise of security for Jerusalem and the house of David. **21**: *Perazim* refers to the LORD's victory over the Philistines at Baal-perazim (2 Sam 5.17–21) and *Gibeon* to the victory over the Canaanites

to do his deed—strange is his deed!—
and to work his work—alien is his work!

²² Now therefore do not scoff,
or your bonds will be made stronger;
for I have heard a decree of destruction
from the Lord God of hosts upon the whole land.

²³ Listen, and hear my voice;
Pay attention, and hear my speech.
²⁴ Do those who plow for sowing plow continually?
Do they continually open and harrow their ground?
²⁵ When they have leveled its surface,
do they not scatter dill, sow cummin,
and plant wheat in rows
and barley in its proper place,
and spelt as the border?
²⁶ For they are well instructed;
their God teaches them.

²⁷ Dill is not threshed with a threshing sledge,
nor is a cart wheel rolled over cummin;
but dill is beaten out with a stick,
and cummin with a rod.
²⁸ Grain is crushed for bread,
but one does not thresh it forever;
one drives the cart wheel and horses over it,
but does not pulverize it.
²⁹ This also comes from the Lord of hosts;
he is wonderful in counsel,
and excellent in wisdom.

29 Ah, Ariel, Ariel,
the city where David encamped!
Add year to year;
let the festivals run their round.
² Yet I will distress Ariel,

and there shall be moaning and lamentation,
and Jerusalem[a] shall be to me like an Ariel.[b]
³ And like David[c] I will encamp against you;
I will besiege you with towers
and raise siegeworks against you.
⁴ Then deep from the earth you shall speak,
from low in the dust your words shall come;
your voice shall come from the ground like the voice of a ghost,
and your speech shall whisper out of the dust.

⁵ But the multitude of your foes[d] shall be like small dust,
and the multitude of tyrants like flying chaff.
And in an instant, suddenly,
⁶ you will be visited by the Lord of hosts
with thunder and earthquake and great noise,
with whirlwind and tempest, and the flame of a devouring fire.
⁷ And the multitude of all the nations that fight against Ariel,
all that fight against her and her stronghold, and who distress her,
shall be like a dream, a vision of the night.
⁸ Just as when a hungry person dreams of eating
and wakes up still hungry,
or a thirsty person dreams of drinking

a Heb *she*
b Probable meaning, *altar hearth*; compare Ezek 43.15
c Gk: Meaning of Heb uncertain
d Cn: Heb *strangers*

(Josh 10.10). But now, the Lord will punish Jerusalem's leaders. **23–29:** The concluding allegory illustrates the duration of the punishment. Just as a farmer must plow the ground and then thresh, beat, and crush the crops to prepare them for human use, so the Lord will plow and thresh the people in preparation for their restoration.

29.1–24: Prophetic instruction concerning the Lord's purpose in assaulting Ariel/Zion. **1–4:** The first portion of this "woe" ("*Ah*") oracle begins with a portrayal of an assault against the city of Jerusalem, apparently presupposing or anticipating an Assyrian attack. Just as *David* once conquered Jerusalem (2 Sam 5.6–9), the Lord will do the same with a foreign army. **1:** The Heb term *Ariel* means "lion of God," recalling the lion as the symbol for Judah (Gen 49.8–11). It is related to a Heb word that designates the hearth of the altar (Ezek 43.15–16). **6–7:** God will appear with all the elements of a theophany as a divine warrior to fight against those attacking

and wakes up faint, still thirsty,
so shall the multitude of all the nations be
    that fight against Mount Zion.

9 Stupefy yourselves and be in a stupor,
    blind yourselves and be blind!
Be drunk, but not from wine;
    stagger, but not from strong drink!
10 For the LORD has poured out upon you
    a spirit of deep sleep;
he has closed your eyes, you prophets,
    and covered your heads, you seers.
11 The vision of all this has become for you
like the words of a sealed document. If it is
given to those who can read, with the command, "Read this," they say, "We cannot, for
it is sealed." 12 And if it is given to those who
cannot read, saying, "Read this," they say,
"We cannot read."

13 The Lord said:
Because these people draw near with their
    mouths
    and honor me with their lips,
    while their hearts are far from me,
and their worship of me is a human
    commandment learned by rote;
14 so I will again do
    amazing things with this people,
    shocking and amazing.
The wisdom of their wise shall perish,
    and the discernment of the discerning
        shall be hidden.

15 Ha! You who hide a plan too deep for the
    LORD,
    whose deeds are in the dark,
    and who say, "Who sees us? Who
        knows us?"
16 You turn things upside down!

Shall the potter be regarded as the clay?
Shall the thing made say of its maker,
    "He did not make me";
or the thing formed say of the one who
    formed it,
    "He has no understanding"?

17 Shall not Lebanon in a very little while
    become a fruitful field,
    and the fruitful field be regarded as a
        forest?
18 On that day the deaf shall hear
    the words of a scroll,
and out of their gloom and darkness
    the eyes of the blind shall see.
19 The meek shall obtain fresh joy in the
    LORD,
    and the neediest people shall exult in
        the Holy One of Israel.
20 For the tyrant shall be no more,
    and the scoffer shall cease to be;
    all those alert to do evil shall be cut
        off—
21 those who cause a person to lose a
    lawsuit,
    who set a trap for the arbiter in the gate,
    and without grounds deny justice to the
        one in the right.

22 Therefore thus says the LORD, who
redeemed Abraham, concerning the house of
Jacob:
No longer shall Jacob be ashamed,
    no longer shall his face grow pale.
23 For when he sees his children,
    the work of my hands, in his midst,
    they will sanctify my name;
they will sanctify the Holy One of Jacob,
    and will stand in awe of the God of
        Israel.

Jerusalem. **9–10:** *Stupefy . . . blind yourselves* recalls the prophet's commission in 6.9–10 to render the people blind, deaf, and ignorant so that they will not repent and be saved. The *deep sleep* poured on the people is like that of the first human when the woman was created (Gen 2.21) and of Abraham when he had a vision of Israel's deliverance from Egypt at the Exodus (Gen 15.12–16). **11–12:** The *sealed document*, cf. 8.16–17. Ultimately, the significance of Isaiah's prophecies will be understood only when later generations read them, perhaps in the time of the Babylonian exile (chs 40–55) or the Persian-period restoration (chs 56–66). **13–14:** Cf. 1.10–17. **15–24:** The second portion of this "woe" (*Ha!*) oracle focuses on the future realization of the LORD's purposes for Zion. The LORD is the *potter* and not the *clay*; cf. 45.9; Jer 18.1–6. **17:** *Lebanon*, 2.13n; see also 10.34. The deaf and the blind (cf. 6.9–10) will understand when they read the scroll of Isaiah's prophecies (cf. 8.16–23). **22:** *Abraham*, cf. 41.8; 51.2. Abraham, redeemed by God's call to journey into the promised land, becomes the model for those who returned to Judah in the post–disaster period.

24 And those who err in spirit will come to
understanding,
and those who grumble will accept
instruction.

30

Oh, rebellious children, says the
Lord,
who carry out a plan, but not mine;
who make an alliance, but against my will,
adding sin to sin;
2 who set out to go down to Egypt
without asking for my counsel,
to take refuge in the protection of Pharaoh,
and to seek shelter in the shadow of
Egypt;
3 Therefore the protection of Pharaoh shall
become your shame,
and the shelter in the shadow of Egypt
your humiliation.
4 For though his officials are at Zoan
and his envoys reach Hanes,
5 everyone comes to shame
through a people that cannot profit
them,
that brings neither help nor profit,
but shame and disgrace.

6 An oracle concerning the animals of the
Negeb.
Through a land of trouble and distress,
of lioness and roaring[a] lion,
of viper and flying serpent,
they carry their riches on the backs of
donkeys,
and their treasures on the humps of
camels,
to a people that cannot profit them.
7 For Egypt's help is worthless and empty,
therefore I have called her,
"Rahab who sits still."[b]

8 Go now, write it before them on a tablet,
and inscribe it in a book,
so that it may be for the time to come
as a witness forever.
9 For they are a rebellious people,
faithless children,
children who will not hear
the instruction of the Lord;
10 who say to the seers, "Do not see";
and to the prophets, "Do not prophesy
to us what is right;
speak to us smooth things,
prophesy illusions,
11 leave the way, turn aside from the path,
let us hear no more about the Holy One
of Israel."
12 Therefore thus says the Holy One of
Israel:
Because you reject this word,
and put your trust in oppression and
deceit,
and rely on them;
13 therefore this iniquity shall become for
you
like a break in a high wall, bulging out,
and about to collapse,
whose crash comes suddenly, in an
instant;
14 its breaking is like that of a potter's
vessel
that is smashed so ruthlessly
that among its fragments not a sherd is
found
for taking fire from the hearth,
or dipping water out of the cistern.
15 For thus said the Lord God, the Holy One
of Israel:

a Cn: Heb *from them*
b Meaning of Heb uncertain

30.1–33: Prophetic instruction concerning the Lord's delay in delivering the people from Assyria. This
lengthy "woe" oracle-complex expresses Isaiah's dissatisfaction with Hezekiah's embassies to Egypt in order to
enlist support for his revolt against Assyria in 701 BCE. 1–11: Isaiah opposes attempts to ally with other nations
for Jerusalem's protection because his understanding of Davidic/Zion theology holds that the Lord alone will
protect Jerusalem and the house of David. 4: *Zoan*, see 19.11–15n. *Hanes* is south of Memphis. 6–7: The *oracle*
condemns Judah for sending a caravan of goods to Egypt to enlist Egyptian aid. *Negeb*, see 20.1n. *Rahab* is a
mythological sea dragon that sometimes symbolizes Egypt (51.9–11; Ps 89.9; Job 9.13). 8–11: The prophet records
his oracle because the people are not ready to hear him but only want to hear *smooth* or comforting things.
The significance of the Lord's actions will only be understood at a later time (cf. 8.16–23; 29.11–12). 12–17: The
prophet argues that the Lord will delay deliverance from Assyria because the people do not trust the prophet's

In returning and rest you shall be saved;
 in quietness and in trust shall be your
  strength.
But you refused [16] and said,
"No! We will flee upon horses"—
 therefore you shall flee!
and, "We will ride upon swift steeds"—
 therefore your pursuers shall be swift!
[17] A thousand shall flee at the threat of one,
 at the threat of five you shall flee,
until you are left
 like a flagstaff on the top of a mountain,
 like a signal on a hill.

[18] Therefore the LORD waits to be gracious
 to you;
 therefore he will rise up to show mercy
  to you.
For the LORD is a God of justice;
 blessed are all those who wait for him.
[19] Truly, O people in Zion, inhabitants of Jerusalem, you shall weep no more. He will surely be gracious to you at the sound of your cry; when he hears it, he will answer you. [20] Though the Lord may give you the bread of adversity and the water of affliction, yet your Teacher will not hide himself any more, but your eyes shall see your Teacher. [21] And when you turn to the right or when you turn to the left, your ears shall hear a word behind you, saying, "This is the way; walk in it." [22] Then you will defile your silver-covered idols and your gold-plated images. You will scatter them like filthy rags; you will say to them, "Away with you!"

[23] He will give rain for the seed with which you sow the ground, and grain, the produce of the ground, which will be rich and plenteous. On that day your cattle will graze in broad pastures; [24] and the oxen and donkeys that till the ground will eat silage, which has been winnowed with shovel and fork. [25] On every lofty mountain and every high hill there will be brooks running with water—on a day of the great slaughter, when the towers fall. [26] Moreover the light of the moon will be like the light of the sun, and the light of the sun will be sevenfold, like the light of seven days, on the day when the LORD binds up the injuries of his people, and heals the wounds inflicted by his blow.

[27] See, the name of the LORD comes from
 far away,
 burning with his anger, and in thick
  rising smoke;[a]
his lips are full of indignation,
 and his tongue is like a devouring fire;
[28] his breath is like an overflowing stream
 that reaches up to the neck—
to sift the nations with the sieve of
 destruction,
 and to place on the jaws of the peoples a
  bridle that leads them astray.

[29] You shall have a song as in the night when a holy festival is kept; and gladness of heart, as when one sets out to the sound of the flute to go to the mountain of the LORD, to the Rock of Israel. [30] And the LORD will cause his majestic voice to be heard and the descending blow of his arm to be seen, in furious anger and a flame of devouring fire, with a cloudburst and tempest and hailstones. [31] The Assyrian will be terror-stricken at the voice of the LORD, when he strikes with his rod. [32] And every stroke of the staff of punishment that the LORD lays upon him will be to the sound of timbrels and lyres; battling with brandished arm he will fight with him. [33] For his burning place[b] has long been prepared; truly it is made ready for the king,[c] its pyre made deep and wide, with fire and wood in abundance; the breath of the LORD, like a stream of sulfur, kindles it.

[a] Meaning of Heb uncertain
[b] Or *Topheth*
[c] Or *Molech*

message. 17: *A thousand shall flee*, see Lev 26.36–37; Deut 32.30. 18–26: The LORD will ultimately show mercy to Jerusalem. A *Teacher*, perhaps someone who would interpret the prophecies that were bound up. Such a statement might motivate the writings of later prophets in chs 40–66. 27–33: Ultimately, the LORD will strike down the Assyrian oppressor (cf. 10.5–33; 14.24–27). The oracle invokes the imagery of a Temple festival when the LORD is revealed in the smoke and flame of the incense burners and lamp stands of the Jerusalem Temple, perhaps at Rosh ha-Shanah (New Year) or Yom Kippur (Day of Atonement), when the LORD judges the wicked.

31

Alas for those who go down to Egypt
      for help
and who rely on horses,
who trust in chariots because they are
      many
      and in horsemen because they are very
            strong,
but do not look to the Holy One of Israel
      or consult the LORD!
[2] Yet he too is wise and brings disaster;
      he does not call back his words,
but will rise against the house of the
            evildoers,
      and against the helpers of those who
            work iniquity.
[3] The Egyptians are human, and not God;
      their horses are flesh, and not spirit.
When the LORD stretches out his hand,
      the helper will stumble, and the one
            helped will fall,
      and they will all perish together.

[4] For thus the LORD said to me,
As a lion or a young lion growls over its
            prey,
      and—when a band of shepherds is
            called out against it—
is not terrified by their shouting
      or daunted at their noise,
so the LORD of hosts will come down
      to fight upon Mount Zion and upon its
            hill.
[5] Like birds hovering overhead, so the
            LORD of hosts
      will protect Jerusalem;
he will protect and deliver it,
      he will spare and rescue it.

[6] Turn back to him whom you[a] have deeply
betrayed, O people of Israel. [7] For on that day
all of you shall throw away your idols of silver
and idols of gold, which your hands have sin-
fully made for you.
[8] "Then the Assyrian shall fall by a sword,
            not of mortals;

and a sword, not of humans, shall
            devour him;
he shall flee from the sword,
      and his young men shall be put to
            forced labor.
[9] His rock shall pass away in terror,
      and his officers desert the standard in
            panic,"
says the LORD, whose fire is in Zion,
      and whose furnace is in
            Jerusalem.

32

See, a king will reign in
      righteousness,
      and princes will rule with justice.
[2] Each will be like a hiding place from the
            wind,
      a covert from the tempest,
like streams of water in a dry place,
      like the shade of a great rock in a weary
            land.
[3] Then the eyes of those who have sight
      will not be closed,
      and the ears of those who have hearing
            will listen.
[4] The minds of the rash will have good
            judgment,
      and the tongues of stammerers will
            speak readily and distinctly.
[5] A fool will no longer be called noble,
      nor a villain said to be honorable.
[6] For fools speak folly,
      and their minds plot iniquity:
to practice ungodliness,
      to utter error concerning the LORD,
to leave the craving of the hungry
            unsatisfied,
      and to deprive the thirsty of drink.
[7] The villainies of villains are evil;
      they devise wicked devices
to ruin the poor with lying words,
      even when the plea of the needy is
            right.

---

[a] Heb *they*

31.1–9: The prophet's warning concerning reliance on Egyptian aid against Assyria. Isaiah again condemns
attempts to ally with Egypt in preparation for Hezekiah's revolt against Assyria in 701 BCE. The prophet employs
the allegories of a lion over its prey and a bird protecting its young to illustrate his point. 1: Cf. Ps 20.7. 8–9: The
final defeat of Assyria (14.24–27). *Fire, furnace*, a reference to the temple altar.

32.1–33.24: Prophetic instruction concerning the righteous king. 32.1–8: When the king rules over Jerusalem in righteousness (cf. 9.1–7; 11.1–16), the blind will see, the deaf will hear, the people will understand (revers-

⁸ But those who are noble plan noble things,
and by noble things they stand.

⁹ Rise up, you women who are at ease, hear
my voice;
you complacent daughters, listen to my
speech.
¹⁰ In little more than a year
you will shudder, you complacent ones;
for the vintage will fail,
the fruit harvest will not come.
¹¹ Tremble, you women who are at ease,
shudder, you complacent ones;
strip, and make yourselves bare,
and put sackcloth on your loins.
¹² Beat your breasts for the pleasant fields,
for the fruitful vine,
¹³ for the soil of my people
growing up in thorns and briers;
yes, for all the joyous houses
in the jubilant city.
¹⁴ For the palace will be forsaken,
the populous city deserted;
the hill and the watchtower
will become dens forever,
the joy of wild asses,
a pasture for flocks;
¹⁵ until a spirit from on high is poured out
on us,
and the wilderness becomes a fruitful
field,
and the fruitful field is deemed a forest.
¹⁶ Then justice will dwell in the wilderness,
and righteousness abide in the fruitful
field.
¹⁷ The effect of righteousness will be
peace,
and the result of righteousness,
quietness and trust forever.
¹⁸ My people will abide in a peaceful
habitation,
in secure dwellings, and in quiet resting
places.

¹⁹ The forest will disappear completely,[a]
and the city will be utterly laid low.
²⁰ Happy will you be who sow beside every
stream,
who let the ox and the donkey range
freely.

33 Ah, you destroyer,
who yourself have not been destroyed;
you treacherous one,
with whom no one has dealt
treacherously!
When you have ceased to destroy,
you will be destroyed;
and when you have stopped dealing
treacherously,
you will be dealt with treacherously.

² O Lord, be gracious to us; we wait for
you.
Be our arm every morning,
our salvation in the time of trouble.
³ At the sound of tumult, peoples fled;
before your majesty, nations
scattered.
⁴ Spoil was gathered as the caterpillar
gathers;
as locusts leap, they leaped[b] upon it.
⁵ The Lord is exalted, he dwells on high;
he filled Zion with justice and
righteousness;
⁶ he will be the stability of your times,
abundance of salvation, wisdom, and
knowledge;
the fear of the Lord is Zion's treasure.[c]

⁷ Listen! the valiant[b] cry in the streets;
the envoys of peace weep bitterly.

a Cn: Heb *And it will hail when the forest comes down*
b Meaning of Heb uncertain
c Heb *his treasure*; meaning of Heb uncertain

ing 6.9–10). **9–20:** The prophet summarizes the themes of his prophecies by describing the reversal from crop failure to a transformation of the natural and moral environment through a spirit from on high (cf. 5.6; 11.1–9). **33.1–24:** The prophet's announcement of the righteous king is formulated as a liturgical cycle that combines elements of the complaint songs with the announcement of the king. **1:** The liturgy begins with a "woe" (*Ah*) oracle that proclaims the downfall of the oppressor. **2–4:** An address to the Lord petitions for relief from the oppressor. **5–6:** An address to the audience reiterates Isaiah's view that the Lord is exalted (cf. 2.9–21). **7–9:** The prophet summarizes the suffering and withering of the land that precede the rise of the righteous king. *Lebanon*, 2.13n. *Sharon*, the fertile coastal plain extending south from Akko/Acre and Dor nearly to Jaffa/Joppa.

8 The highways are deserted,
  travelers have quit the road.
The treaty is broken,
  its oaths[a] are despised,
  its obligation[b] is disregarded.
9 The land mourns and languishes;
  Lebanon is confounded and withers
    away;
Sharon is like a desert;
  and Bashan and Carmel shake off their
    leaves.

10 "Now I will arise," says the Lord,
  "now I will lift myself up;
  now I will be exalted.
11 You conceive chaff, you bring forth
    stubble;
  your breath is a fire that will consume
    you.
12 And the peoples will be as if burned to
    lime,
  like thorns cut down, that are burned in
    the fire."

13 Hear, you who are far away, what I have
    done;
  and you who are near, acknowledge my
    might.
14 The sinners in Zion are afraid,
  trembling has seized the godless:
"Who among us can live with the
    devouring fire?
  Who among us can live with everlasting
    flames?"
15 Those who walk righteously and speak
    uprightly,
  who despise the gain of
    oppression,
who wave away a bribe instead of
    accepting it,
  who stop their ears from hearing of
    bloodshed
  and shut their eyes from looking on
    evil,
16 they will live on the heights;

their refuge will be the fortresses of
    rocks;
  their food will be supplied, their water
    assured.

17 Your eyes will see the king in his beauty;
  they will behold a land that stretches
    far away.
18 Your mind will muse on the terror:
  "Where is the one who counted?
  Where is the one who weighed the
    tribute?
  Where is the one who counted the
    towers?"
19 No longer will you see the insolent
    people,
  the people of an obscure speech that
    you cannot comprehend,
  stammering in a language that you
    cannot understand.
20 Look on Zion, the city of our appointed
    festivals!
  Your eyes will see Jerusalem,
  a quiet habitation, an immovable tent,
whose stakes will never be pulled up,
  and none of whose ropes will be broken.
21 But there the Lord in majesty will be
    for us
  a place of broad rivers and streams,
where no galley with oars can go,
  nor stately ship can pass.
22 For the Lord is our judge, the Lord is our
    ruler,
  the Lord is our king; he will save us.

23 Your rigging hangs loose;
  it cannot hold the mast firm in its
    place,
  or keep the sail spread out.

Then prey and spoil in abundance will be
    divided;

a   Q Ms: MT cities
b   Or everyone

Bashan, the fertile plain south of Aram (Syria) and east of the Kinneret (Sea of Galilee). Carmel, the fertile mountain range that extends from Akko/Acre south along the eastern edge of the Sharon coastal plain. 10–12: A response in which the God of Israel threatens to arise and burn the enemy like thorns; cf. 10.16–17; 30.27–33. 13–16: Those in Zion who do not trust in the Lord will also suffer. 17–24: Those who had been blind, deaf, and ignorant (32.1–3; cf. 6.9–10) will finally see the righteous king in Jerusalem. 19: Obscure speech, the Assyrian oppressors, who speak a foreign language, will be gone, and Zion will again see its Temple festivals.

even the lame will fall to plundering.
²⁴ And no inhabitant will say, "I am sick";
the people who live there will be
forgiven their iniquity.

34 Draw near, O nations, to hear;
O peoples, give heed!
Let the earth hear, and all that fills it;
the world, and all that comes from it.
² For the LORD is enraged against all the
nations,
and furious against all their hordes;
he has doomed them, has given them
over for slaughter.
³ Their slain shall be cast out,
and the stench of their corpses shall
rise;
the mountains shall flow with their
blood.
⁴ All the host of heaven shall rot away,
and the skies roll up like a scroll.
All their host shall wither
like a leaf withering on a vine,
or fruit withering on a fig tree.

⁵ When my sword has drunk its fill in the
heavens,
lo, it will descend upon Edom,
upon the people I have doomed to
judgment.
⁶ The LORD has a sword; it is sated with
blood,
it is gorged with fat,

with the blood of lambs and goats,
with the fat of the kidneys of rams.
For the LORD has a sacrifice in Bozrah,
a great slaughter in the land of
Edom.
⁷ Wild oxen shall fall with them,
and young steers with the mighty
bulls.
Their land shall be soaked with blood,
and their soil made rich with fat.

⁸ For the LORD has a day of vengeance,
a year of vindication by Zion's cause.ᵃ
⁹ And the streams of Edomᵇ shall be turned
into pitch,
and her soil into sulfur;
her land shall become burning pitch.
¹⁰ Night and day it shall not be quenched;
its smoke shall go up forever.
From generation to generation it shall lie
waste;
no one shall pass through it forever and
ever.
¹¹ But the hawkᶜ and the hedgehogᶜ shall
possess it;
the owlᶜ and the raven shall live in it.
He shall stretch the line of confusion
over it,

a   Or *of recompense by Zion's defender*
b   Heb *her streams*
c   Identification uncertain

34.1–66.24: Concerning the realization of the LORD's plans for revealing worldwide sovereignty from Zion.
Whereas chs 1–33 anticipate the revelation of the LORD's worldwide sovereignty at Zion, the second half of the
book in chs 34–66 presupposes that the time is at hand.

34.1–35.10: Prophetic instruction concerning the LORD's power to return the redeemed exiles to Zion. Chs
34–35 introduce the second half of the book of Zion with an emphasis on the judgment of the nations, represented by Edom, and the return of the exiles to Zion.

34.1–17: Prophetic instruction concerning the LORD's power over the nations. Chapter 34 emphasizes the
LORD's power over the nations by focusing especially on the fate of Edom, Israel's neighbor to the southeast
(cf. 63.1–6). Edom, which is condemned in biblical literature for its role in the destruction of Jerusalem (Jer
49.7–22; Ezek 25.12–17; Ob; Ps 137.7; Lam 4.21–22), began to decline in the sixth century BCE as Arab tribes began to encroach upon Edomite territory. This decline provides a counterpart for the judgment leveled against
Israel and Jerusalem in ch 1. Links between chs 34 and 1 include parallel calls to attention (34.1; 1.2); the LORD's
vengeance (34.8; 1.24); unquenchable burning (34.10; 1.24); the mouth of the LORD that has spoken (34.16; 1.20);
the sword of punishment (34.5,6; 1.20); the sacrificial blood and fat of cattle (34.6–7; 1.11–15); Sodom and Gomorrah (34.9–10; 1.7–9,10); and wilting leaves (34.4; 1.30). **1–15:** The address to the nations calls their attention
to Edom's punishment. The portrayal of destruction employs the images of sacrifice. **6:** *Bozrah:* a major city in
Edom. **8:** The passage takes up the "Day of the LORD" theme (cf. 2.10–21; 13.6–16). **9–10:** The fate of Edom will
resemble that of Sodom and Gomorrah (Gen 19.24–28), located at the southern end of the Dead Sea by Edom.
11: Confusion (Heb "tohu") and chaos (Heb "bohu") are terms employed to describe primeval chaos prior to

and the plummet of chaos over[a] its
    nobles.
[12] They shall name it No Kingdom There,
    and all its princes shall be nothing.
[13] Thorns shall grow over its strongholds,
    nettles and thistles in its fortresses.
It shall be the haunt of jackals,
    an abode for ostriches.
[14] Wildcats shall meet with hyenas,
    goat-demons shall call to each other;
there too Lilith shall repose,
    and find a place to rest.
[15] There shall the owl nest
    and lay and hatch and brood in its
      shadow;
there too the buzzards shall gather,
    each one with its mate.
[16] Seek and read from the book of the
    Lord:
Not one of these shall be missing;
    none shall be without its mate.
For the mouth of the Lord has
    commanded,
    and his spirit has gathered them.
[17] He has cast the lot for them,
    his hand has portioned it out to them
      with the line;
they shall possess it forever,
    from generation to generation they
      shall live in it.

35 The wilderness and the dry land shall
    be glad,
    the desert shall rejoice and blossom;
like the crocus [2] it shall blossom
    abundantly,
    and rejoice with joy and singing.

The glory of Lebanon shall be given to it,
    the majesty of Carmel and Sharon.
They shall see the glory of the Lord,
    the majesty of our God.

[3] Strengthen the weak hands,
    and make firm the feeble knees.
[4] Say to those who are of a fearful heart,
    "Be strong, do not fear!
Here is your God.
    He will come with vengeance,
with terrible recompense.
    He will come and save you."

[5] Then the eyes of the blind shall be
    opened,
    and the ears of the deaf unstopped;
[6] then the lame shall leap like a deer,
    and the tongue of the speechless sing
      for joy.
For waters shall break forth in the
    wilderness,
    and streams in the desert;
[7] the burning sand shall become a
    pool,
    and the thirsty ground springs of
      water;
the haunt of jackals shall become a
    swamp,[b]
    the grass shall become reeds and
      rushes.

[8] A highway shall be there,
    and it shall be called the Holy Way;

a Heb lacks *over*
b Cn: Heb *in the haunt of jackals is her resting place*

creation (Gen 1.2). **14:** *Lilith* is a hostile goddess associated with the night in Sumerian mythology. In later Jewish folklore, she is known as Adam's first wife who gives birth to demons. **16–17:** *Book of the Lord,* perhaps the book of Isaiah as it then existed. The second address asks the reader to search the book for confirmation of the Lord's purpose concerning the nations.

35.1–10: Prophetic oracle of salvation concerning the return of the redeemed to Zion. The return of the exiles to Zion is portrayed here as a second Exodus in which the people return to Zion through the wilderness. **1–2:** The announcement of the return emphasizes the rejoicing and blooming of the wilderness as the Lord is sovereign of all creation. *Lebanon* is the mountain range north of Israel, *Carmel* is the fertile mountain range running south of Akko/Acre, and *Sharon* is the coastal plain to the west of Carmel; contrast 33.9. **4:** *Do not fear* is the reassurance formula addressed by the prophet to King Ahaz in 7.4 and to Hezekiah in 37.6. **5–6:** A reversal of 6.9–10. The open eyes of the blind and the unstopped ears of the deaf indicate that the Lord's commands that Isaiah render the people blind and deaf so that they cannot repent and be saved are now at an end (cf. 29.18; 32.3; 42.16,18–19; 43.8; 44.18). **8–10:** The highway through the wilderness is a motif of both the Exodus/Wilderness tradition (Num 20.17; 21.22; Deut 2.8) and the second exodus of the book of Isaiah (40.3; 42.16; 43.19). The

the unclean shall not travel on it,[a]
  but it shall be for God's people;[b]
  no traveler, not even fools, shall go
    astray.
[9] No lion shall be there,
  nor shall any ravenous beast come up
    on it;
they shall not be found there,
  but the redeemed shall walk there.
[10] And the ransomed of the LORD shall
    return,
  and come to Zion with singing;
everlasting joy shall be upon their heads;
  they shall obtain joy and gladness,
  and sorrow and sighing shall flee away.

36

In the fourteenth year of King Hezekiah, King Sennacherib of Assyria came up against all the fortified cities of Judah and captured them. [2] The king of Assyria sent the Rabshakeh from Lachish to King Hezekiah at Jerusalem, with a great army. He stood by the conduit of the upper pool on the highway to the Fuller's Field. [3] And there came out to him Eliakim son of Hilkiah, who was in charge of the palace, and Shebna the secretary, and Joah son of Asaph, the recorder.

[4] The Rabshakeh said to them, "Say to Hezekiah: Thus says the great king, the

a Or *pass it by*
b Cn: Heb *for them*

return of exiles from Egypt and Assyria appears in 11.16; 27.12–13.

36.1–39.8: Historical narratives concerning Hezekiah. These narratives also appear in 2 Kings 18–20. Because the prophet Isaiah makes his last appearance here in the book of Isaiah, many interpreters consider chs 36–39 to be drawn from 2 Kings 18–20 in order to form a historical appendix to First Isaiah (chs 1–39). Although chs 36–39 may originally have been intended as an appendix in an early edition of the book, the reference to the exile of Hezekiah's sons to Babylon in 39.1–8 indicates that they now are transitional chapters that prepare the reader for the downfall of Babylon and the return of the exiles to Zion beginning in ch 40. The figure of Hezekiah is contrasted with that of Ahaz in 7.1–9.6 to demonstrate that Hezekiah's return to the LORD results in the deliverance of his people whereas Ahaz's refusal to turn to the LORD resulted in the subjugation of his people to Assyria. Such a portrayal also facilitates Second Isaiah's call to turn to the LORD in chs 40–55 at the time of the restoration. Although chs 36–39 are largely parallel to 2 Kings 18–20, subtle differences in the text indicate an effort to whitewash Hezekiah's character in Isa 36–39 in order to present him as a pure figure who places his trust entirely in the LORD.

36.1–37.38: Confrontation story concerning the LORD's defeat of Sennacherib at Jerusalem. This narrative presents an account of the siege of Jerusalem by the Assyrian King Sennacherib in 701 BCE. King Hezekiah allied with Babylon and assembled a coalition to revolt against Assyria following the death of Sargon II in 705 BCE. Sargon's successor, Sennacherib, attacked western Asia including Judah in 701 BCE. As Hezekiah's allies quickly submitted to Assyria, Hezekiah found himself alone against the Assyrians. Sennacherib's records indicate that he concentrated his attack in southwestern Judah along the border with Philistia, that he devastated the land of Judah, that he besieged Jerusalem, and that he ultimately forced Hezekiah to submit, taking away captives, a great deal of booty, and even Hezekiah's own daughters. Hezekiah nevertheless retained his throne. Sennacherib was assassinated by his own sons in 681 BCE. Most interpreters maintain that chs 36–37 are an idealized account of the siege designed to celebrate the LORD's victory over Sennacherib as the Assyrian empire began to decline in the seventh century BCE. **36.1:** *The fourteenth year,* 701 BCE, the year Sennacherib invaded western Asia. The narrative of Hezekiah's initial capitulation to Sennacherib in 2 Kings 18.14–16 does not appear here. **2–22:** The Assyrian Rabshakeh, "Cup-bearer" or "Chief Steward" of the Assyrian king, presents the terms of surrender to Hezekiah and the besieged defenders of Jerusalem. **2:** *Lachish,* the major royal city in southwestern Judah. Excavations indicate that it was conquered by the Assyrians, who forced Jewish prisoners of war to build a ramp up the side of the city's fortifications. A pit with 1,500 human skeletons on the site indicates the extent of the Judean casualties. Wall reliefs at Sennacherib's palace in Nineveh portray the defeat of Lachish in order to impress visitors with his power. *Conduit of the upper pool,* the same location where Isaiah confronted Ahaz (see 7.3–9n.). **3:** The Judean officers negotiate with the Rabshakeh on behalf of Hezekiah. *Shebna,* here described as the secretary, appears as the King's chief administrator "over the house" in 22.15–25. Shebna has now been replaced by *Eliakim.* **4–10:** The Rabshakeh's speech is meant to intimidate the Judean defenders and weaken their morale. At this point, the Egyptians, with whom Hezekiah had allied, had already been turned back by the

king of Assyria: On what do you base this confidence of yours? [5] Do you think that mere words are strategy and power for war? On whom do you now rely, that you have rebelled against me? [6] See, you are relying on Egypt, that broken reed of a staff, which will pierce the hand of anyone who leans on it. Such is Pharaoh king of Egypt to all who rely on him. [7] But if you say to me, 'We rely on the LORD our God,' is it not he whose high places and altars Hezekiah has removed, saying to Judah and to Jerusalem, 'You shall worship before this altar'? [8] Come now, make a wager with my master the king of Assyria: I will give you two thousand horses, if you are able on your part to set riders on them. [9] How then can you repulse a single captain among the least of my master's servants, when you rely on Egypt for chariots and for horsemen? [10] Moreover, is it without the LORD that I have come up against this land to destroy it? The LORD said to me, Go up against this land, and destroy it."

[11] Then Eliakim, Shebna, and Joah said to the Rabshakeh, "Please speak to your servants in Aramaic, for we understand it; do not speak to us in the language of Judah within the hearing of the people who are on the wall." [12] But the Rabshakeh said, "Has my master sent me to speak these words to your master and to you, and not to the people sitting on the wall, who are doomed with you to eat their own dung and drink their own urine?"

[13] Then the Rabshakeh stood and called out in a loud voice in the language of Judah, "Hear the words of the great king, the king of Assyria! [14] Thus says the king: 'Do not let Hezekiah deceive you, for he will not be able to deliver you. [15] Do not let Hezekiah make you rely on the LORD by saying, The LORD will surely deliver us; this city will not be given into the hand of the king of Assyria.' [16] Do not listen to Hezekiah; for thus says the king of Assyria: 'Make your peace with me and come out to me; then every one of you will eat from your own vine and your own fig tree and drink water from your own cistern, [17] until I come and take you away to a land like your own land, a land of grain and wine, a land of bread and vineyards. [18] Do not let Hezekiah mislead you by saying, The LORD will save us. Has any of the gods of the nations saved their land out of the hand of the king of Assyria? [19] Where are the gods of Hamath and Arpad? Where are the gods of Sepharvaim? Have they delivered Samaria out of my hand? [20] Who among all the gods of these countries have saved their countries out of my hand, that the LORD should save Jerusalem out of my hand?'"

[21] But they were silent and answered him not a word, for the king's command was, "Do not answer him." [22] Then Eliakim son of Hilkiah, who was in charge of the palace, and Shebna the secretary, and Joah son of Asaph, the recorder, came to Hezekiah with their clothes torn, and told him the words of the Rabshakeh.

37 When King Hezekiah heard it, he tore his clothes, covered himself with sackcloth, and went into the house of the LORD. [2] And he sent Eliakim, who was in charge of the palace, and Shebna the secretary, and the senior priests, covered with sackcloth, to the prophet Isaiah son of Amoz. [3] They said to him, "Thus says Hezekiah, This day is a day of distress, of rebuke, and

---

Assyrians. The Rabshakeh's boastful speech may have represented Assyrian views but has drawn on 10.8–11,13–14. **6:** Cf. the sayings on the Egyptian alliance (18.1–19.15; 30.1–7; 31.1–3). **7:** On Hezekiah's removal of the high places, see 2 Kings 18.3–6. **10:** Appeal to the anger of the national deity reflects Isaiah's sayings about Assyria as the LORD's agent for the punishment of Israel. **11:** *Aramaic* was the language of diplomacy from the late Neo-Assyrian period onward. *The language of Judah* is Hebrew. **12–20:** The Rabshakeh speaks in Hebrew in order to address the Judean troops directly and appeal for their surrender. His description of their circumstances reveals the desperate conditions in a besieged city (cf. 2 Kings 6.24–32). Deportation of soldiers and skilled persons from subjugated lands was a standard Assyrian practice. **19:** *Hamath* and *Arpad* were cities conquered by the Assyrians (see 10.9n.). *Samaria,* the capital of northern Israel conquered by the Assyrians in 722 BCE (2 Kings 17). *Sepharvaim,* located in Aram between Hamath and Damascus, was a city under Assyrian control to which northern Israelites were deported (2 Kings 17.24,31). **37.1–7:** The delegation to Isaiah recalls the consultation of prophets by earlier and later kings (1 Kings 22.5–28; 2 Kings 1.9–17; 3.11–17; 22.11–14; Jer 21.1–4). The prophet's

of disgrace; children have come to the birth, and there is no strength to bring them forth. [4] It may be that the LORD your God heard the words of the Rabshakeh, whom his master the king of Assyria has sent to mock the living God, and will rebuke the words that the LORD your God has heard; therefore lift up your prayer for the remnant that is left."

[5] When the servants of King Hezekiah came to Isaiah, [6] Isaiah said to them, "Say to your master, 'Thus says the LORD: Do not be afraid because of the words that you have heard, with which the servants of the king of Assyria have reviled me. [7] I myself will put a spirit in him, so that he shall hear a rumor, and return to his own land; I will cause him to fall by the sword in his own land.'"

[8] The Rabshakeh returned, and found the king of Assyria fighting against Libnah; for he had heard that the king had left Lachish. [9] Now the king[a] heard concerning King Tirhakah of Ethiopia,[b] "He has set out to fight against you." When he heard it, he sent messengers to Hezekiah, saying, [10] "Thus shall you speak to King Hezekiah of Judah: Do not let your God on whom you rely deceive you by promising that Jerusalem will not be given into the hand of the king of Assyria. [11] See, you have heard what the kings of Assyria have done to all lands, destroying them utterly. Shall you be delivered? [12] Have the gods of the nations delivered them, the nations that my predecessors destroyed, Gozan, Haran, Rezeph, and the people of Eden who were in Telassar? [13] Where is the king of Hamath, the king of Arpad, the king of the city of Sepharvaim, the king of Hena, or the king of Ivvah?"

[14] Hezekiah received the letter from the hand of the messengers and read it; then Hezekiah went up to the house of the LORD and spread it before the LORD. [15] And Hezekiah prayed to the LORD, saying: [16] "O LORD of hosts, God of Israel, who are enthroned above the cherubim, you are God, you alone, of all the kingdoms of the earth; you have made heaven and earth. [17] Incline your ear, O LORD, and hear; open your eyes, O LORD, and see; hear all the words of Sennacherib, which he has sent to mock the living God. [18] Truly, O LORD, the kings of Assyria have laid waste all the nations and their lands, [19] and have hurled their gods into the fire, though they were no gods, but the work of human hands—wood and stone—and so they were destroyed. [20] So now, O LORD our God, save us from his hand, so that all the kingdoms of the earth may know that you alone are the LORD."

[21] Then Isaiah son of Amoz sent to Hezekiah, saying: "Thus says the LORD, the God of Israel: Because you have prayed to me concerning King Sennacherib of Assyria, [22] this is the word that the LORD has spoken concerning him:

She despises you, she scorns you—
    virgin daughter Zion;
she tosses her head—behind your back,
    daughter Jerusalem.

[23] "Whom have you mocked and reviled?
    Against whom have you raised your
        voice
and haughtily lifted your eyes?
    Against the Holy One of Israel!
[24] By your servants you have mocked the
        Lord,
    and you have said, 'With my many
        chariots

a Heb *he*
b Or *Nubia*; Heb *Cush*

immediate response reassures Hezekiah with the classic formula "do not fear" (cf. 7.4). **8–13:** The Rabshakeh delivers a second message to Hezekiah from Sennacherib. Having taken Lachish, Sennacherib is besieging *Libnah*, located near Lachish although the precise site is disputed. **9:** *King Tirhakah of Ethiopia* may have been a general in the army since he came to the throne of Egypt only in 690. **12:** Northern Mesopotamian sites taken by the Assyrians: *Gozan*, on the Habur River in Mesopotamia (2 Kings 17.6); *Haran*, on the Balikh River (Gen 11.27–32); *Rezeph*, near the west end of the Jebel Singar; *Eden*, between the Euphrates and the Balikh Rivers (Am 1.5; Ezek 27.23); and *Telassar*, located near Eden in Aram. **13:** See 36.19n. *Hena* and *Ivvah* are unknown. **14–20:** Unlike Ahaz in 7.1–25, Hezekiah turns to the LORD in this time of distress. **16:** *Enthroned above the cherubim*, the ark of the covenant and its cherubim (66.1; 1 Sam 4.4; 2 Sam 6.2), which served as the LORD's throne in the Holy of Holies in the Jerusalem Temple (1 Kings 8.6–7). **21–35:** Isaiah conveys the LORD's oracle of reassurance to Hezekiah. The LORD repeats claims of greatness made by Sennacherib to illustrate his arrogance (cf. 2.10–21). Mesopotamian

I have gone up the heights of the
  mountains,
    to the far recesses of Lebanon;
I felled its tallest cedars,
    its choicest cypresses;
I came to its remotest height,
    its densest forest.
²⁵ I dug wells
    and drank waters,
I dried up with the sole of my foot
    all the streams of Egypt.'

²⁶ "Have you not heard
    that I determined it long ago?
I planned from days of old
    what now I bring to pass,
that you should make fortified cities
    crash into heaps of ruins,
²⁷ while their inhabitants, shorn of
    strength,
    are dismayed and confounded;
they have become like plants of the field
    and like tender grass,
like grass on the housetops,
    blighted[a] before it is grown.

²⁸ "I know your rising up[b] and your sitting
    down,
    your going out and coming in,
    and your raging against me.
²⁹ Because you have raged against me
    and your arrogance has come to my
      ears,
I will put my hook in your nose
    and my bit in your mouth;
I will turn you back on the way
    by which you came.

³⁰ "And this shall be the sign for you:
This year eat what grows of itself, and in
the second year what springs from that;
then in the third year sow, reap, plant
vineyards, and eat their fruit. ³¹ The surviving remnant of the house of Judah shall
again take root downward, and bear fruit
upward; ³² for from Jerusalem a remnant
shall go out, and from Mount Zion a band
of survivors. The zeal of the LORD of hosts
will do this.

³³ "Therefore thus says the LORD concerning the king of Assyria: He shall not come
into this city, shoot an arrow there, come
before it with a shield, or cast up a siege ramp
against it. ³⁴ By the way that he came, by the
same he shall return; he shall not come into
this city, says the LORD. ³⁵ For I will defend
this city to save it, for my own sake and for
the sake of my servant David."

³⁶ Then the angel of the LORD set out
and struck down one hundred eighty-five
thousand in the camp of the Assyrians;
when morning dawned, they were all dead
bodies. ³⁷ Then King Sennacherib of Assyria
left, went home, and lived at Nineveh. ³⁸ As
he was worshiping in the house of his god
Nisroch, his sons Adrammelech and Sharezer
killed him with the sword, and they escaped
into the land of Ararat. His son Esar-haddon
succeeded him.

38 In those days Hezekiah became sick
    and was at the point of death. The
prophet Isaiah son of Amoz came to him,
and said to him, "Thus says the LORD: Set
your house in order, for you shall die; you
shall not recover." ² Then Hezekiah turned
his face to the wall, and prayed to the LORD:

---

a   With 2 Kings 19.26: Heb *field*
b   Q Ms Gk: MT lacks *your rising up*

---

kings frequently felled trees in *Lebanon* (see 2.13n). **22**: *Virgin daughter Zion,* see 1.8n. **26**: Whereas the Assyrian
king claims great accomplishments, the LORD had planned long ago to bring the Assyrians as a tool of punishment (cf. 5.8–30; 10.5–34). **30–35**: The surviving remnant of Judah, like the ruined Judean wheat crop, will
continue to grow each season in the aftermath of the Assyrian invasion, i.e., the LORD will defend Jerusalem in
keeping with the Davidic/Zion tradition. **36–38**: The angel of death that killed the Assyrian troops recalls the
tenth plague of the Exodus that saw the deaths of the firstborn of Egypt (Ex 11; 12.29–32). Sennacherib was assassinated by his own sons in 681 BCE as part of a coup. The coup was put down, and another son, Esarhaddon,
succeeded his father. **38**: The name *Nisroch* is elsewhere unattested. *Ararat* is Armenia.

38.1–22: Royal narrative concerning Hezekiah's recovery from illness. This narrative complements the earlier narrative in chs 36–37 concerning the deliverance of Jerusalem (cf. 2 Kings 20.1–11). **1–8**: *In those days* coordinates this account with chs 36–37, although the contents of the narrative indicate an event well before the

³ "Remember now, O LORD, I implore you, how I have walked before you in faithfulness with a whole heart, and have done what is good in your sight." And Hezekiah wept bitterly.

⁴ Then the word of the LORD came to Isaiah: ⁵ "Go and say to Hezekiah, Thus says the LORD, the God of your ancestor David: I have heard your prayer, I have seen your tears; I will add fifteen years to your life. ⁶ I will deliver you and this city out of the hand of the king of Assyria, and defend this city.

⁷ "This is the sign to you from the LORD, that the LORD will do this thing that he has promised: ⁸ See, I will make the shadow cast by the declining sun on the dial of Ahaz turn back ten steps." So the sun turned back on the dial the ten steps by which it had declined.ᵃ

⁹ A writing of King Hezekiah of Judah, after he had been sick and had recovered from his sickness:

¹⁰ I said: In the noontide of my days
    I must depart;
I am consigned to the gates of Sheol
    for the rest of my years.
¹¹ I said, I shall not see the LORD
    in the land of the living;
I shall look upon mortals no more
    among the inhabitants of the
        world.
¹² My dwelling is plucked up and removed
        from me
    like a shepherd's tent;
like a weaver I have rolled up my life;
    he cuts me off from the loom;
from day to night you bring me to an end;ᵃ
    ¹³ I cry for helpᵇ until morning;
like a lion he breaks all my bones;
    from day to night you bring me to an
        end.ᵃ

¹⁴ Like a swallow or a craneᵃ I clamor,
    I moan like a dove.
My eyes are weary with looking
        upward.
    O Lord, I am oppressed; be my
        security!
¹⁵ But what can I say? For he has spoken
        to me,
    and he himself has done it.
All my sleep has fledᶜ
    because of the bitterness of my soul.

¹⁶ O Lord, by these things people live,
    and in all these is the life of my
        spirit.ᵃ
    Oh, restore me to health and make me
        live!
¹⁷ Surely it was for my welfare
    that I had great bitterness;
but you have held backᵈ my life
    from the pit of destruction,
for you have cast all my sins
    behind your back.
¹⁸ For Sheol cannot thank you,
    death cannot praise you;
those who go down to the Pit cannot hope
    for your faithfulness.
¹⁹ The living, the living, they thank you,
    as I do this day;
fathers make known to children
    your faithfulness.

²⁰ The LORD will save me,
    and we will sing to stringed
        instrumentsᵉ
all the days of our lives,
    at the house of the LORD.

ᵃ Meaning of Heb uncertain
ᵇ Cn: Meaning of Heb uncertain
ᶜ Cn Compare Syr: Heb *I will walk slowly all my years*
ᵈ Cn Compare Gk Vg: Heb *loved*
ᵉ Heb *my stringed instruments*

siege of Jerusalem. **3:** Hezekiah's petition to the LORD resembles Ps 26. The LORD's promise to deliver Hezekiah and his city out of the hand of the king of Assyria indicates that this account is meant to be read with chs 36–37. **4–8:** The miraculous reversal of *ten steps* on the sundial of Ahaz both confirms the LORD's oracle and reminds the reader of Hezekiah's contrasting portrayal with that of Ahaz in 7.1–9.6. **5:** *Fifteen years*, calculated on the basis of 2 Kings 18.2,13. **9–22:** A song of thanksgiving attributed to Hezekiah (cf. Pss 30; 32; 92; Jon 2). The song does not appear in 2 Kings 20.1–11. It functions here to highlight Hezekiah's piety. **10–13:** Elements of complaint introduce the song, conveying Hezekiah's distress. **10:** *Sheol*, the underworld. **14–16:** Petition for security and

²¹ Now Isaiah had said, "Let them take a lump of figs, and apply it to the boil, so that he may recover." ²² Hezekiah also had said, "What is the sign that I shall go up to the house of the LORD?"

39 At that time King Merodach-baladan son of Baladan of Babylon sent envoys with letters and a present to Hezekiah, for he heard that he had been sick and had recovered. ² Hezekiah welcomed them; he showed them his treasure house, the silver, the gold, the spices, the precious oil, his whole armory, all that was found in his storehouses. There was nothing in his house or in all his realm that Hezekiah did not show them. ³ Then the prophet Isaiah came to King Hezekiah and said to him, "What did these men say? From where did they come to you?" Hezekiah answered, "They have come to me from a far country, from Babylon." ⁴ He said, "What have they seen in your house?" Hezekiah answered, "They have seen all that is in my house; there is nothing in my storehouses that I did not show them."

⁵ Then Isaiah said to Hezekiah, "Hear the word of the LORD of hosts: ⁶ Days are coming when all that is in your house, and that which your ancestors have stored up until this day, shall be carried to Babylon; nothing shall be left, says the LORD. ⁷ Some of your own sons who are born to you shall be taken away; they shall be eunuchs in the palace of the king of Babylon." ⁸ Then Hezekiah said to Isaiah, "The word of the LORD that you have spoken is good." For he thought, "There will be peace and security in my days."

40 Comfort, O comfort my people,
    says your God.
² Speak tenderly to Jerusalem,
    and cry to her
that she has served her term,
    that her penalty is paid,
that she has received from the LORD's hand
    double for all her sins.

³ A voice cries out:
"In the wilderness prepare the way of the
    LORD,

health. **17–20:** Thanksgiving for restoration to health. *The Pit,* a poetic synonym for *Sheol.* **21–22:** Isaiah acts as a healer in prescribing a compress for Hezekiah's boil; cf. 2 Kings 20.8.

39.1–8: Narrative concerning Isaiah's condemnation of Hezekiah for allying with Merodach-baladan of Babylon. Hezekiah entered into an alliance with Prince *Merodach-baladan* (Marduk-apal-Iddina) of Babylon to mount a revolt against Assyria in 705–701 BCE. Babylon was also an Assyrian vassal at this time. The strategy was to hit Assyria simultaneously from both east and west, and thereby force Sennacherib to divide his forces, but it failed when Hezekiah was forced to capitulate in 701 BCE. Merodach-baladan was never caught, although Sennacherib was still hunting him as late as 689 BCE. A parallel narrative appears in 2 Kings 20.12–19. **1–2:** The phrase *at that time* coordinates the narrative with both chs 36–37 and 38. The display of wealth and provisions demonstrates to Merodach-baladan's envoys that Hezekiah is prepared for revolt. **3–8:** Isaiah, based on his adherence to Davidic/Zion theology, objects to the alliance on the grounds that the LORD will protect Jerusalem and the king. Isaiah's statements that Hezekiah's wealth and sons will be carried off to Babylon corresponds to Sennacherib's account of the siege. In the context of the book of Isaiah, it foreshadows the Babylonian exile presupposed from ch 40 on. Hezekiah's concluding question reemphasizes his piety. In 2 Kings 20.19, the formulation of the question highlights his self-interest.

40.1–54.17: Prophetic instruction that the LORD maintains covenant and restores Zion. Chapter 40 begins the portion of the book (chs 40–55) attributed to an anonymous prophet of the latter years of the Babylonian exile when King Cyrus of Persia conquered Babylonia and decreed that Jews could return to their homeland (ca. 545–539 BCE). Although these chapters are clearly written long after the time of the eighth-century prophet Isaiah, they nevertheless share his basic theological perspective rooted in the Zion/Davidic tradition, i.e., that the LORD protects Zion, although the Davidic covenant is now applied to the people rather than to the Davidic king (55.3). These chapters therefore function within the book to describe the realization of the LORD's plans to restore Zion as articulated throughout chs 1–33.

40.1–11: Renewed prophetic commission to announce the LORD's restoration of Zion. This segment renews the prophet's commission to speak (cf. ch 6) and announces that the time of the restoration is at hand. **1–2:** A message of comfort to Jerusalem. *Double* restitution of stolen property is the penalty in the case of theft (Ex 22.7). **3–5:** The voices are those of the attendants in the heavenly court of the LORD (cf. 1 Kings 22.19–23; Isa 6;

make straight in the desert a highway
  for our God.
⁴ Every valley shall be lifted up,
  and every mountain and hill be made
    low;
the uneven ground shall become level,
  and the rough places a plain.
⁵ Then the glory of the LORD shall be
    revealed,
  and all people shall see it together,
  for the mouth of the LORD has spoken."

⁶ A voice says, "Cry out!"
  And I said, "What shall I cry?"
All people are grass,
  their constancy is like the flower of the
    field.
⁷ The grass withers, the flower fades,
  when the breath of the LORD blows
    upon it;
  surely the people are grass.
⁸ The grass withers, the flower fades;
  but the word of our God will stand
    forever.
⁹ Get you up to a high mountain,
  O Zion, herald of good tidings;ᵃ
lift up your voice with strength,
  O Jerusalem, herald of good tidings,ᵇ
  lift it up, do not fear;
say to the cities of Judah,
  "Here is your God!"
¹⁰ See, the Lord GOD comes with might,
  and his arm rules for him;
his reward is with him,
  and his recompense before him.
¹¹ He will feed his flock like a shepherd;
  he will gather the lambs in his arms,

and carry them in his bosom,
  and gently lead the mother sheep.

¹² Who has measured the waters in the
    hollow of his hand
  and marked off the heavens with a
    span,
enclosed the dust of the earth in a
    measure,
  and weighed the mountains in scales
  and the hills in a balance?
¹³ Who has directed the spirit of the LORD,
  or as his counselor has instructed him?
¹⁴ Whom did he consult for his
    enlightenment,
  and who taught him the path of justice?
Who taught him knowledge,
  and showed him the way of
    understanding?
¹⁵ Even the nations are like a drop from a
    bucket,
  and are accounted as dust on the
    scales;
  see, he takes up the isles like fine dust.
¹⁶ Lebanon would not provide fuel enough,
  nor are its animals enough for a burnt
    offering.
¹⁷ All the nations are as nothing before
    him;
  they are accounted by him as less than
    nothing and emptiness.

¹⁸ To whom then will you liken God,
  or what likeness compare with him?

ᵃ Or *O herald of good tidings to Zion*
ᵇ Or *O herald of good tidings to Jerusalem*

Ps 82). The passage evokes the tradition of the journey through the wilderness in which the people traveled along the King's Highway in Transjordan on their way to the land of Israel (Num 20.17; 21.22; Deut 2.8). *The glory of the LORD* refers to the divine presence, often symbolized by a cloud of smoke and flickering flame, such as was seen at Sinai, upon the wilderness Tabernacle, and in the Holy of Holies of the Temple (see Ex 19.16; 40.34–38; 1 Kings 8.10–13). 6–8: The prophet's message emphasizes the permanence of God's word. Just as Isaiah said that the LORD would restore Jerusalem (e.g., 2.1–4; 31.4–5; 33.20), now it comes to pass (cf. 55.10–11). 9–11: *Zion* or *Jerusalem* functions as the *herald* of the LORD to announce the news of God's return and Zion's restoration. Using the typical image of Mesopotamian and Judean kings, the LORD appears as a *shepherd* who cares for the *flock* (cf. 1 Sam 16.11,19; 17.1,20,34–37).

40.12–31: The LORD is the master of creation. This is the first of a series of sections (40.12–31; 41.1–42.13; 42.14–44.23) that are designed to demonstrate that the LORD is indeed acting to restore Zion. The first focuses on the LORD's role as the creator. 12–14: The argumentative style of the passage employs rhetorical questions to make its basic points. 15–17: *Lebanon*'s fuel (see 2.13n) refers to its tall trees that, like the animals of its forests, are insufficient to provide a suitable sacrifice before the LORD. 18–20: The beginning of this prophet's polemic

19 An idol? —A workman casts it,
  and a goldsmith overlays it with gold,
  and casts for it silver chains.
20 As a gift one chooses mulberry wood[a]
  —wood that will not rot—
then seeks out a skilled artisan
  to set up an image that will not topple.

21 Have you not known? Have you not
    heard?
  Has it not been told you from the
    beginning?
  Have you not understood from the
    foundations of the earth?
22 It is he who sits above the circle of the
    earth,
  and its inhabitants are like
    grasshoppers;
who stretches out the heavens like a
    curtain,
  and spreads them like a tent to live in;
23 who brings princes to naught,
  and makes the rulers of the earth as
    nothing.

24 Scarcely are they planted, scarcely sown,
  scarcely has their stem taken root in the
    earth,
when he blows upon them, and they
    wither,
  and the tempest carries them off like
    stubble.

25 To whom then will you compare me,
  or who is my equal? says the Holy One.
26 Lift up your eyes on high and see:
  Who created these?
He who brings out their host and numbers
    them,

  calling them all by name;
because he is great in strength,
  mighty in power,
  not one is missing.

27 Why do you say, O Jacob,
  and speak, O Israel,
"My way is hidden from the LORD,
  and my right is disregarded by my
    God"?
28 Have you not known? Have you not
    heard?
The LORD is the everlasting God,
  the Creator of the ends of the earth.
He does not faint or grow weary;
  his understanding is unsearchable.
29 He gives power to the faint,
  and strengthens the powerless.
30 Even youths will faint and be weary,
  and the young will fall exhausted;
31 but those who wait for the LORD shall
    renew their strength,
  they shall mount up with wings like
    eagles,
they shall run and not be weary,
  they shall walk and not faint.

41 Listen to me in silence, O coastlands;
  let the peoples renew their
    strength;
let them approach, then let them speak;
  let us together draw near for
    judgment.

2 Who has roused a victor from the east,
  summoned him to his service?
He delivers up nations to him,
  and tramples kings under foot;

a Meaning of Heb uncertain

against idolatry, which also targets aspects of the religious and intellectual tradition of the Babylonians (also 41.6–7,29; 42.17; 43.10; 44.9–20; 45.16,20; 46.1–7; Jer 10.1–10). **21–24**: A rhetorical recapitulation of vv. 12–20. The language in which the cosmos is here described should be compared with Gen 1.1–31. **25–26**: The passage returns to the key question of v. 18. The Heb verb "bara'" ("create") is for the most part restricted to Gen 1 and these chapters (40.28; 41.26; 42.5; 43.1,7,15; 45.7,8,12,18; 48.7; 54.16). **27–31**: An attempt to answer the crisis of faith that political disaster provoked by presenting the LORD as a cosmic rather than a purely national deity. Waiting for God, implying trust, is frequently advocated in the book (8.17; 30.18; 49.23; 64.4).

41.1–42.13: The LORD is the master of human events. The second contention in the series is the power of the LORD to play a decisive role in human events. **41.1–4**: The passage is formulated as a courtroom scene in which the LORD cross-examines witnesses. The LORD demands the attention of the *coastlands* (the islands of the Aegean) and the nations. **2**: The first point is that the LORD has summoned *a victor from the east*, King Cyrus II of Persia (559–530), who would conquer the Babylonian empire in 539 BCE. He is called to emerge as the LORD's

he makes them like dust with his sword,
  like driven stubble with his bow.
[3] He pursues them and passes on safely,
  scarcely touching the path with his feet.
[4] Who has performed and done this,
  calling the generations from the
    beginning?
I, the LORD, am first,
  and will be with the last.
[5] The coastlands have seen and are afraid,
  the ends of the earth tremble;
  they have drawn near and come.
[6] Each one helps the other,
  saying to one another, "Take courage!"
[7] The artisan encourages the goldsmith,
  and the one who smooths with the
    hammer encourages the one who
    strikes the anvil,
saying of the soldering, "It is good";
  and they fasten it with nails so that it
    cannot be moved.
[8] But you, Israel, my servant,
  Jacob, whom I have chosen,
  the offspring of Abraham, my friend;
[9] you whom I took from the ends of the
    earth,
  and called from its farthest corners,
saying to you, "You are my servant,
  I have chosen you and not cast you off";
[10] do not fear, for I am with you,
  do not be afraid, for I am your God;
I will strengthen you, I will help you,
  I will uphold you with my victorious
    right hand.

[11] Yes, all who are incensed against you
  shall be ashamed and disgraced;

those who strive against you
  shall be as nothing and shall perish.
[12] You shall seek those who contend with
    you,
  but you shall not find them;
those who war against you
  shall be as nothing at all.
[13] For I, the LORD your God,
  hold your right hand;
it is I who say to you, "Do not fear,
  I will help you."

[14] Do not fear, you worm Jacob,
  you insect[a] Israel!
I will help you, says the LORD;
  your Redeemer is the Holy One of Israel.
[15] Now, I will make of you a threshing
    sledge,
  sharp, new, and having teeth;
you shall thresh the mountains and crush
    them,
  and you shall make the hills like chaff.
[16] You shall winnow them and the wind
    shall carry them away,
  and the tempest shall scatter them.
Then you shall rejoice in the LORD;
  in the Holy One of Israel you shall glory.

[17] When the poor and needy seek water,
  and there is none,
  and their tongue is parched with thirst,
I the LORD will answer them,
  I the God of Israel will not forsake them.
[18] I will open rivers on the bare heights,[b]

[a] Syr: Heb men of
[b] Or trails

anointed king and Temple builder in 44.28; 45.1. 4: By claiming to be *first* and *last* (see 44.6; 48.12), the LORD asserts control over all events in human history from beginning to end. 5–20: The LORD maintains that just as the coastlands and nations have granted recognition, Jacob/Israel must do likewise. 5–7: The nations fear the approach of the LORD, and build idols in a futile attempt to protect themselves (cf. 44.9–20). 8–20: Israel must recognize the LORD's power to act in the human world just as the nations have done. 8: *Israel* is the LORD's servant much like Moses (Ex 14.31) and David (2 Sam 7.5). The mention of *Abraham* recalls the origins of Israel's covenant with the LORD (Gen 15). In exilic texts the people of Israel are often referred to as *Jacob*, whose story of exile and return (Gen 28–32) is similar to that of the exiles in Babylon. Based on the perspective of the Zion/Davidic covenant tradition, the LORD has chosen Israel and will uphold the covenant to protect the nation. 10: The reassurance formula *do not fear* supports the assertions of the LORD. 11–17: The LORD reiterates the reassurance theme in an effort to convince the audience of the LORD's absolute fidelity to the divine promise. 14: The LORD as *Redeemer* (43.14; 44.6; 47.4; see Ex 6.6; 15.13) is the first of many echoes of the Exodus tradition in these chapters. 15–16: A *threshing sledge* was employed to crush grain stalks so that the chaff could be removed from the grain. 17–20: As creator, the LORD is able to provide for the needs of the poor as in the time of the wilderness

and fountains in the midst of the
valleys;
I will make the wilderness a pool of
water,
and the dry land springs of water.
[19] I will put in the wilderness the cedar,
the acacia, the myrtle, and the olive;
I will set in the desert the cypress,
the plane and the pine together,
[20] so that all may see and know,
all may consider and understand,
that the hand of the LORD has done this,
the Holy One of Israel has created it.

[21] Set forth your case, says the LORD;
bring your proofs, says the King of
Jacob.
[22] Let them bring them, and tell us
what is to happen.
Tell us the former things, what they are,
so that we may consider them,
and that we may know their outcome;
or declare to us the things to come.
[23] Tell us what is to come hereafter,
that we may know that you are gods;
do good, or do harm,
that we may be afraid and terrified.
[24] You, indeed, are nothing
and your work is nothing at all;
whoever chooses you is an
abomination.

[25] I stirred up one from the north, and he
has come,
from the rising of the sun he was
summoned by name.[a]
He shall trample[b] on rulers as on mortar,
as the potter treads clay.
[26] Who declared it from the beginning, so
that we might know,

and beforehand, so that we might say,
"He is right"?
There was no one who declared it, none
who proclaimed,
none who heard your words.
[27] I first have declared it to Zion,[c]
and I give to Jerusalem a herald of good
tidings.
[28] But when I look there is no one;
among these there is no counselor
who, when I ask, gives an answer.
[29] No, they are all a delusion;
their works are nothing;
their images are empty wind.

42

Here is my servant, whom I uphold,
my chosen, in whom my soul delights;
I have put my spirit upon him;
he will bring forth justice to the nations.
[2] He will not cry or lift up his voice,
or make it heard in the street;
[3] a bruised reed he will not break,
and a dimly burning wick he will not
quench;
he will faithfully bring forth justice.
[4] He will not grow faint or be crushed
until he has established justice in the
earth;
and the coastlands wait for his teaching.

[5] Thus says God, the LORD,
who created the heavens and stretched
them out,
who spread out the earth and what
comes from it,

a   Cn Compare Q Ms Gk: MT *and he shall call on my name*
b   Cn: Heb *come*
c   Cn: Heb *First to Zion—Behold, behold them*

wandering (Ex 17.1–7; Num 20.2–13; Pss 78.15–16; 105.41). **21–29:** The passage returns to the courtroom imagery (cf. vv. 1–5) in which the LORD demands counterarguments from the gods of the nations. The LORD presumes that they cannot explain the past or the future and therefore do not have the capacity to act like the LORD, much less to challenge the LORD's power to act in the human world. **25:** *One from the north* and from the east, the LORD once again claims to have brought a deliverer, i.e., Cyrus (41.2; 44.28; 45.1), which demonstrates once again the LORD's capacity to act in human affairs. Having claimed to have announced these events long ago, the LORD observes that there is no one to answer. **42.1–4:** The first of the four so-called "servant songs" of Isaiah (see 49.1–6; 50.4–11; 52.13–53.12). The servant represents Israel. **5–9:** As a covenant to the peoples and a light to the nations, Israel's experience of punishment and restoration becomes the means by which all the nations will recognize the LORD's sovereignty in the world. By opening the eyes of the blind and the ears of the deaf, the servant brings to an end the period of blindness and deafness called for in Isaiah's commission (6.9–10).

who gives breath to the people upon it
and spirit to those who walk in it:
⁶ I am the LORD, I have called you in
righteousness,
I have taken you by the hand and kept
you;
I have given you as a covenant to the
people,ᵃ
a light to the nations,
⁷ to open the eyes that are blind,
to bring out the prisoners from the
dungeon,
from the prison those who sit in
darkness.
⁸ I am the LORD, that is my name;
my glory I give to no other,
nor my praise to idols.
⁹ See, the former things have come to pass,
and new things I now declare;
before they spring forth,
I tell you of them.

¹⁰ Sing to the LORD a new song,
his praise from the end of the earth!
Let the sea roarᵇ and all that fills it,
the coastlands and their inhabitants.
¹¹ Let the desert and its towns lift up their
voice,
the villages that Kedar inhabits;
let the inhabitants of Sela sing for joy,
let them shout from the tops of the
mountains.
¹² Let them give glory to the LORD,
and declare his praise in the coastlands.
¹³ The LORD goes forth like a soldier,
like a warrior he stirs up his fury;

he cries out, he shouts aloud,
he shows himself mighty against his
foes.

¹⁴ For a long time I have held my peace,
I have kept still and restrained myself;
now I will cry out like a woman in labor,
I will gasp and pant.
¹⁵ I will lay waste mountains and hills,
and dry up all their herbage;
I will turn the rivers into islands,
and dry up the pools.
¹⁶ I will lead the blind
by a road they do not know,
by paths they have not known
I will guide them.
I will turn the darkness before them into
light,
the rough places into level ground.
These are the things I will do,
and I will not forsake them.
¹⁷ They shall be turned back and utterly
put to shame—
those who trust in carved images,
who say to cast images,
"You are our gods."

¹⁸ Listen, you that are deaf;
and you that are blind, look up and see!
¹⁹ Who is blind but my servant,
or deaf like my messenger whom I
send?

ᵃ Meaning of Heb uncertain
ᵇ Cn Compare Ps 96.11; 98.7: Heb *Those who go down to the sea*

That the former things have come to pass, i.e., those things foretold earlier in the book of Isaiah, serves as an argument that the things now declared will also happen. **10–13:** A hymn of praise for the LORD closes the section devoted to demonstrating the LORD's mastery of human events. Now creation itself rejoices like worshipers in the Temple (cf. Pss 96; 98). *Kedar* is located in the Arabian desert (see 21.16), and *Sela* is located in Edom.

42.14–44.23: The LORD is the redeemer of Israel. The third contention in the series is that the LORD redeems Israel. Insofar as Israel had suffered punishment and exile at the hands of the Assyrians and the Babylonians, acting as agents of the LORD, such a contention is designed to answer claims that the LORD is an enemy to Israel or that the LORD is powerless to redeem Israel. **42.14–17:** The LORD's silence and inaction during the period of Israel's punishment has come to an end. The image of a woman in childbirth (cf. 13.8; 26.1–18) indicates that the time for action has come. The passage evokes the wilderness tradition (see 40.3–5n.) to portray the LORD's guidance of Israel. The *blind* are now given light (cf. 6.9–10; 8.23). **18–25:** The passage addresses Israel as the *blind* and the *deaf*, a recurrent image (6.9–10; 29.9,18; 32.3; 35.5; 42.16; 43.8) denoting spiritual imperception and obtuseness. In fact, however, the LORD has controlled the fate of the nation all along. Now the time has come for Israel to recognize the LORD as their redeemer. Although the LORD had revealed divine "torah" ("teaching," v. 21) to the people, they were punished for having failed to observe the LORD's instruction, improperly translated

Who is blind like my dedicated one,
   or blind like the servant of the Lord?
20 He sees many things, but does[a] not
      observe them;
   his ears are open, but he does not hear.
21 The Lord was pleased, for the sake of his
      righteousness,
   to magnify his teaching and make it
      glorious.
22 But this is a people robbed and
      plundered,
   all of them are trapped in holes
   and hidden in prisons;
they have become a prey with no one to
      rescue,
   a spoil with no one to say, "Restore!"
23 Who among you will give heed to this,
   who will attend and listen for the time
      to come?
24 Who gave up Jacob to the spoiler,
   and Israel to the robbers?
Was it not the Lord, against whom we
      have sinned,
   in whose ways they would not walk,
   and whose law they would not obey?
25 So he poured upon him the heat of his
      anger
   and the fury of war;
it set him on fire all around, but he did not
      understand;
   it burned him, but he did not take it to
      heart.

43 But now thus says the Lord,
   he who created you, O Jacob,
   he who formed you, O Israel:
Do not fear, for I have redeemed you;
   I have called you by name, you are
      mine.
2 When you pass through the waters, I will
      be with you;

and through the rivers, they shall not
      overwhelm you;
when you walk through fire you shall not
      be burned,
   and the flame shall not consume you.
3 For I am the Lord your God,
   the Holy One of Israel, your Savior.
I give Egypt as your ransom,
   Ethiopia[b] and Seba in exchange for
      you.
4 Because you are precious in my sight,
   and honored, and I love you,
I give people in return for you,
   nations in exchange for your life.
5 Do not fear, for I am with you;
   I will bring your offspring from the
      east,
   and from the west I will gather you;
6 I will say to the north, "Give them up,"
   and to the south, "Do not withhold;
bring my sons from far away
   and my daughters from the end of the
      earth—
7 everyone who is called by my name,
   whom I created for my glory,
   whom I formed and made."

8 Bring forth the people who are blind, yet
      have eyes,
   who are deaf, yet have ears!
9 Let all the nations gather together,
   and let the peoples assemble.
Who among them declared this,
   and foretold to us the former things?
Let them bring their witnesses to justify
      them,
   and let them hear and say, "It is true."
10 You are my witnesses, says the Lord,

a   Heb *You see many things but do*
b   Or *Nubia*; Heb *Cush*

in v. 24 as "law" (cf. 2.2–4; 5.24). **43.1–7:** The reassurance formula *do not fear* (cf. 7.4; 37.6; 41.10,14) emphasizes that Israel's punishment is now over and redemption is at hand. **2:** The passage evokes the Exodus and wilderness tradition as Israel passes through waters (see, e.g., Ex 14–15) as it returns from exile to its homeland. *Through fire*, cf. Ps 66.12. **3:** *Egypt, Ethiopia*, and *Seba* (or Sheba, a kingdom in southwestern Arabia), all of which Cyrus was expected to conquer, serve as a ransom for the redemption of Israel from its exile. The return of the exiles from throughout the world is a frequent theme in Isaiah (11.15–16; 27.12–13; 35.1–10; 49.22; 60.9).

   43.8–44.23: The setting returns to the courtroom as the Lord substantiates the claims to redeem Israel (see 41.1–5,21–29). **43.8–13:** The Lord calls both blind and deaf Israel (6.9–10; 42.19–20; cf. 42.7) and the nations to witness to the Lord's claims. **9:** *The former things*, the statements of the Lord's plans found in the Isaian tradition. Only the Lord can carry out Israel's redemption; no idols can possibly manifest such planning and

and my servant whom I have chosen,
so that you may know and believe me
and understand that I am he.
Before me no god was formed,
nor shall there be any after me.
[11] I, I am the LORD,
and besides me there is no savior.
[12] I declared and saved and proclaimed,
when there was no strange god among
you;
and you are my witnesses, says the
LORD.
[13] I am God, and also henceforth I am He;
there is no one who can deliver from
my hand;
I work and who can hinder it?

[14] Thus says the LORD,
your Redeemer, the Holy One of Israel:
For your sake I will send to Babylon
and break down all the bars,
and the shouting of the Chaldeans will
be turned to lamentation.[a]
[15] I am the LORD, your Holy One,
the Creator of Israel, your King.
[16] Thus says the LORD,
who makes a way in the sea,
a path in the mighty waters,
[17] who brings out chariot and horse,
army and warrior;
they lie down, they cannot rise,
they are extinguished, quenched like a
wick:
[18] Do not remember the former
things,
or consider the things of old.
[19] I am about to do a new thing;
now it springs forth, do you not
perceive it?
I will make a way in the wilderness
and rivers in the desert.

[20] The wild animals will honor me,
the jackals and the ostriches;
for I give water in the wilderness,
rivers in the desert,
to give drink to my chosen people,
[21] the people whom I formed for myself
so that they might declare my praise.

[22] Yet you did not call upon me, O Jacob;
but you have been weary of me,
O Israel!
[23] You have not brought me your sheep for
burnt offerings,
or honored me with your sacrifices.
I have not burdened you with offerings,
or wearied you with frankincense.
[24] You have not bought me sweet cane with
money,
or satisfied me with the fat of your
sacrifices.
But you have burdened me with your sins;
you have wearied me with your
iniquities.
[25] I, I am He
who blots out your transgressions for
my own sake,
and I will not remember your sins.
[26] Accuse me, let us go to trial;
set forth your case, so that you may be
proved right.
[27] Your first ancestor sinned,
and your interpreters transgressed
against me.
[28] Therefore I profaned the princes of the
sanctuary,
I delivered Jacob to utter destruction,
and Israel to reviling.

a   Meaning of Heb uncertain

power. 14–15: *Redeemer* and *Holy One* are frequent designations for the LORD in this section of Isaiah (41.14; 47.4; 48.17;49.7; 54.5). *Chaldea*, a term for the Neo-Babylonian empire of Nebuchadnezzar. 16–21: The LORD is identified as the one who led Israel through the sea at the time of the Exodus (Ex 14–15), the *former things* of v. 18 which provide the foundation for understanding the *new thing*, i.e., the exodus from Babylon. Once again, the LORD provides a highway in the wilderness for the people to return home (11.15–16; 27.12–13; 35.1–10; 40.3–5). Water in the wilderness recalls the wilderness tradition (Ex 15.22–27; 17.17; Num 20.2–13). 22–28: The LORD justifies past punishment of Israel, charging that the people did not honor the LORD appropriately with sacrifices, but sinned instead. Nevertheless, the LORD will not remember those sins now that the punishment is over. 27: *First ancestor*, Jacob (cf. Hos 12.2–4). *Interpreters transgressed*, translation and meaning are uncertain; perhaps it is a denunciation of optimistic prophets during the time of the monarchy who led the people astray.

44 But now hear, O Jacob my servant,
Israel whom I have chosen!
2 Thus says the LORD who made you,
who formed you in the womb and will
help you:
Do not fear, O Jacob my servant,
Jeshurun whom I have chosen.
3 For I will pour water on the thirsty land,
and streams on the dry ground;
I will pour my spirit upon your
descendants,
and my blessing on your offspring.
4 They shall spring up like a green tamarisk,
like willows by flowing streams.
5 This one will say, "I am the LORD's,"
another will be called by the name of
Jacob,
yet another will write on the hand, "The
LORD's,"
and adopt the name of Israel.

6 Thus says the LORD, the King of Israel,
and his Redeemer, the LORD of hosts:
I am the first and I am the last;
besides me there is no god.
7 Who is like me? Let them proclaim it,
let them declare and set it forth before
me.
Who has announced from of old the
things to come?[a]
Let them tell us[b] what is yet to be.
8 Do not fear, or be afraid;
have I not told you from of old and
declared it?
You are my witnesses!
Is there any god besides me?
There is no other rock; I know not one.

9 All who make idols are nothing, and the
things they delight in do not profit; their
witnesses neither see nor know. And so they
will be put to shame. 10 Who would fashion
a god or cast an image that can do no good?
11 Look, all its devotees shall be put to shame;

the artisans too are merely human. Let them
all assemble, let them stand up; they shall be
terrified, they shall all be put to shame.
12 The ironsmith fashions it[c] and works it
over the coals, shaping it with hammers, and
forging it with his strong arm; he becomes
hungry and his strength fails, he drinks no
water and is faint. 13 The carpenter stretches
a line, marks it out with a stylus, fashions it
with planes, and marks it with a compass; he
makes it in human form, with human beauty,
to be set up in a shrine. 14 He cuts down
cedars or chooses a holm tree or an oak and
lets it grow strong among the trees of the forest. He plants a cedar and the rain nourishes
it. 15 Then it can be used as fuel. Part of it he
takes and warms himself; he kindles a fire
and bakes bread. Then he makes a god and
worships it, makes it a carved image and
bows down before it. 16 Half of it he burns in
the fire; over this half he roasts meat, eats
it and is satisfied. He also warms himself
and says, "Ah, I am warm, I can feel the fire!"
17 The rest of it he makes into a god, his idol,
bows down to it and worships it; he prays to it
and says, "Save me, for you are my god!"
18 They do not know, nor do they comprehend; for their eyes are shut, so that they cannot see, and their minds as well, so that they
cannot understand. 19 No one considers, nor is
there knowledge or discernment to say, "Half
of it I burned in the fire; I also baked bread on
its coals, I roasted meat and have eaten. Now
shall I make the rest of it an abomination?
Shall I fall down before a block of wood?"
20 He feeds on ashes; a deluded mind has led
him astray, and he cannot save himself or say,
"Is not this thing in my right hand a fraud?"

a Cn: Heb *from my placing an eternal people and*
things to come
b Tg: Heb *them*
c Cn: Heb *an ax*

44.1–5: An oracle of salvation for Israel. **2:** *Jeshurun,* "one who is upright," is a poetic name for Israel (Deut 32.15; 33.5,26). **3:** The passage employs the imagery of libation offerings poured out at the Temple at the festival of Sukkot, "Tabernacles," to celebrate the onset of the rainy season and fertility in the land. **6–8:** A recapitulation of earlier arguments for the incomparability of the LORD who has declared the divine plans for Israel from the beginning (see 41.21–29; 43.10–13). **9–20:** A lengthy and satirical prose polemic against idolatry, describing how artisans meticulously fashion idols out of metal and wood and then declare the idol to be a god (cf. Wis 13–15; Let Jer). The blindness and deafness motif is here applied to the idols who can neither see nor hear (cf. 6.9–10;

²¹ Remember these things, O Jacob,
  and Israel, for you are my servant;
I formed you, you are my servant;
  O Israel, you will not be forgotten
    by me.
²² I have swept away your transgressions
    like a cloud,
  and your sins like mist;
return to me, for I have redeemed you.

²³ Sing, O heavens, for the LORD has
    done it;
  shout, O depths of the earth;
break forth into singing, O mountains,
  O forest, and every tree in it!
For the LORD has redeemed Jacob,
  and will be glorified in Israel.

²⁴ Thus says the LORD, your Redeemer,
  who formed you in the womb:
I am the LORD, who made all things,
  who alone stretched out the
    heavens,
  who by myself spread out the earth;
²⁵ who frustrates the omens of liars,
  and makes fools of diviners;
who turns back the wise,
  and makes their knowledge foolish;
²⁶ who confirms the word of his servant,
  and fulfills the prediction of his
    messengers;

who says of Jerusalem, "It shall be
    inhabited,"
  and of the cities of Judah, "They shall
    be rebuilt,
  and I will raise up their ruins";
²⁷ who says to the deep, "Be dry—
  I will dry up your rivers";
²⁸ who says of Cyrus, "He is my shepherd,
  and he shall carry out all my purpose";
and who says of Jerusalem, "It shall be
    rebuilt,"
  and of the temple, "Your foundation
    shall be laid."

45 Thus says the LORD to his anointed,
  to Cyrus,
  whose right hand I have grasped
to subdue nations before him
  and strip kings of their robes,
to open doors before him—
  and the gates shall not be closed:
² I will go before you
  and level the mountains,ᵃ
I will break in pieces the doors of bronze
  and cut through the bars of iron,
³ I will give you the treasures of
    darkness
  and riches hidden in secret places,
so that you may know that it is I, the LORD,

ᵃ Q Ms Gk: MT *the swellings*

42.18–20). **21–22:** Conclusion of the oracle in vv. 6–8. **23:** Hymnic conclusion in which all creation celebrates the redemption of Israel.

44.24–48.22: The LORD will use Cyrus for the restoration of Zion. This lengthy unit constitutes the fourth contention in the series. The claim that the LORD uses Cyrus to restore Zion is particularly controversial because the Persian king is a foreign monarch who displaces the role traditionally assigned to the Davidic king as anointed one and Temple builder. Nevertheless, Cyrus's conquest of Babylon in 539 BCE opened the way for his declaration that exiled Jews could return to their homeland to rebuild the Temple (2 Chr 36.22–23; Ezra 1.1–4). Since Cyrus does not restore Davidic kingship, the prophet determines that the LORD has declared Cyrus to be the righteous king of Isaian tradition (9.1–7; 11.1–16; 32.1–8).

44.24–45.8: The LORD's announcement concerning Cyrus. The LORD announces the plan to use Cyrus as the redeemer of Zion. **44.24–28:** Reiterations of the divine qualities and roles previously articulated. **25:** *Omens . . . diviners*, Babylonian religion was renowned for its use of techniques for determining the future. **28:** *Shepherd*, a common metaphor for ruler (56.11; Jer 23.4). Cyrus II (558–530 BCE), founder of the Persian Empire, is identified with the LORD's long established plans, including the rebuilding of Jerusalem and the Temple, a role formerly accomplished by David and Solomon. **45.1–7:** Cyrus is commissioned to act as the LORD's agent for restoration, and is identified as the LORD's messiah or *anointed* one to signify that the Persian king now occupies the role once held by the Davidic kings. The imagery presupposes elements of the Babylonian Akitu or New Year Festival in which the Babylonian king's right to rule is renewed for the coming year. The king grasps the hand of Marduk, the god of Babylon, and is granted the tablets of destiny as part of his authorization to rule. Cyrus was authorized to serve as king of Babylon when he participated in the Akitu festival in 539 BCE. The LORD here takes

the God of Israel, who call you by your
name.
4 For the sake of my servant Jacob,
and Israel my chosen,
I call you by your name,
I surname you, though you do not know
me.
5 I am the LORD, and there is no other;
besides me there is no god.
I arm you, though you do not know
me,
6 so that they may know, from the rising of
the sun
and from the west, that there is no one
besides me;
I am the LORD, and there is no other.
7 I form light and create darkness,
I make weal and create woe;
I the LORD do all these things.

8 Shower, O heavens, from above,
and let the skies rain down
righteousness;
let the earth open, that salvation may
spring up,[a]
and let it cause righteousness to sprout
up also;
I the LORD have created it.

9 Woe to you who strive with your Maker,
earthen vessels with the potter![b]
Does the clay say to the one who fashions
it, "What are you making"?
or "Your work has no handles"?
10 Woe to anyone who says to a father,
"What are you begetting?"
or to a woman, "With what are you in
labor?"
11 Thus says the LORD,
the Holy One of Israel, and its Maker:
Will you question me[c] about my children,
or command me concerning the work
of my hands?
12 I made the earth,

and created humankind upon it;
it was my hands that stretched out the
heavens,
and I commanded all their host.
13 I have aroused Cyrus[d] in
righteousness,
and I will make all his paths straight;
he shall build my city
and set my exiles free,
not for price or reward,
says the LORD of hosts.
14 Thus says the LORD:
The wealth of Egypt and the merchandise
of Ethiopia,[e]
and the Sabeans, tall of stature,
shall come over to you and be yours,
they shall follow you;
they shall come over in chains and bow
down to you.
They will make supplication to you,
saying,
"God is with you alone, and there is no
other;
there is no god besides him."
15 Truly, you are a God who hides
himself,
O God of Israel, the Savior.
16 All of them are put to shame and
confounded,
the makers of idols go in confusion
together.
17 But Israel is saved by the LORD
with everlasting salvation;
you shall not be put to shame or
confounded
to all eternity.

18 For thus says the LORD,

a Q Ms: MT *that they may bring forth salvation*
b Cn: Heb *with the potsherds*, or *with the potters*
c Cn: Heb *Ask me of things to come*
d Heb *him*
e Or *Nubia*; Heb *Cush*

on the role of Marduk, is declared to be the only God, and authorizes Cyrus to rule. **8:** The heavens celebrate Cyrus's role with showers and a hymn of praise.

45.9–48.19: Trial scene concerning the LORD's use of Cyrus as redeemer. The contention that the LORD had chosen Cyrus as king was no doubt controversial. Once again, the LORD appears in court to support such claims. **45.9–19:** An introductory court speech disputes any challenge to the LORD's decision. For the metaphor of the potter and the clay see 29.16; Jer 18.1–6. **14:** *Egypt, Ethiopia*, and *Seba*. In contrast to 43.3 where these nations are given to Cyrus as a ransom, here their wealth will come to Israel when they are conquered by Cyrus. **20–25:**

who created the heavens
  (he is God!),
who formed the earth and made it
  (he established it;
he did not create it a chaos,
  he formed it to be inhabited!):
I am the Lord, and there is no other.
19 I did not speak in secret,
  in a land of darkness;
I did not say to the offspring of Jacob,
  "Seek me in chaos."
I the Lord speak the truth,
  I declare what is right.

20 Assemble yourselves and come together,
  draw near, you survivors of the nations!
They have no knowledge—
  those who carry about their wooden
    idols,
and keep on praying to a god
  that cannot save.
21 Declare and present your case;
  let them take counsel together!
Who told this long ago?
  Who declared it of old?
Was it not I, the Lord?
  There is no other god besides me,
a righteous God and a Savior;
  there is no one besides me.

22 Turn to me and be saved,
  all the ends of the earth!
For I am God, and there is no other.
23 By myself I have sworn,
  from my mouth has gone forth in
    righteousness
  a word that shall not return:
"To me every knee shall bow,
  every tongue shall swear."

24 Only in the Lord, it shall be said of me,
  are righteousness and strength;

all who were incensed against him
  shall come to him and be ashamed.
25 In the Lord all the offspring of Israel
  shall triumph and glory.

46 Bel bows down, Nebo stoops,
  their idols are on beasts and cattle;
these things you carry are loaded
  as burdens on weary animals.
2 They stoop, they bow down together;
  they cannot save the burden,
  but themselves go into captivity.

3 Listen to me, O house of Jacob,
  all the remnant of the house of Israel,
who have been borne by me from your birth,
  carried from the womb;
4 even to your old age I am he,
  even when you turn gray I will carry you.
I have made, and I will bear;
  I will carry and will save.

5 To whom will you liken me and make me
    equal,
  and compare me, as though we were
    alike?
6 Those who lavish gold from the purse,
  and weigh out silver in the scales—
they hire a goldsmith, who makes it into
    a god;
  then they fall down and worship!
7 They lift it to their shoulders, they carry it,
  they set it in its place, and it stands
    there;
  it cannot move from its place.
If one cries out to it, it does not
    answer
  or save anyone from trouble.

8 Remember this and consider,a

a   Meaning of Heb uncertain

An offer of salvation and a demand for Lord to be recognized as sovereign of all creation by the nations and by Israel.

46.1–47.15: Presentation of evidence concerning the Lord's power. Two major sections (46.1–13 and 47.1–15) demonstrate the powerlessness of Babylon's gods before the Lord. **46.1–4:** This section draws on the imagery of the Babylonian Akitu or New Year festival, when the gods are paraded through the streets of Babylon in procession to the temple of Marduk, city god of Babylon, at the center of the city. Bel and Nebo appear as burdens to those who carry them through the streets rather than as powerful gods who can act on behalf of their people. *Bel*, meaning "lord," is a title of Marduk, and *Nebo* is the city god of Borsippa and son of Marduk. In contrast to their weakness, the Lord asserts the capacity to carry Israel as well as to redeem. **5–7:** A satirical

recall it to mind, you transgressors,
⁹ remember the former things of old;
for I am God, and there is no other;
   I am God, and there is no one like me,
¹⁰ declaring the end from the beginning
   and from ancient times things not yet
      done,
saying, "My purpose shall stand,
   and I will fulfill my intention,"
¹¹ calling a bird of prey from the east,
   the man for my purpose from a far
      country.
I have spoken, and I will bring it to pass;
   I have planned, and I will do it.

¹² Listen to me, you stubborn of heart,
   you who are far from deliverance:
¹³ I bring near my deliverance, it is not far
      off,
   and my salvation will not tarry;
I will put salvation in Zion,
   for Israel my glory.

47 Come down and sit in the dust,
      virgin daughter Babylon!
Sit on the ground without a throne,
   daughter Chaldea!
For you shall no more be called
   tender and delicate.
² Take the millstones and grind meal,
   remove your veil,
strip off your robe, uncover your legs,
   pass through the rivers.
³ Your nakedness shall be uncovered,
   and your shame shall be seen.
I will take vengeance,
   and I will spare no one.
⁴ Our Redeemer—the Lord of hosts is his
      name—
   is the Holy One of Israel.

⁵ Sit in silence, and go into darkness,
   daughter Chaldea!

For you shall no more be called
   the mistress of kingdoms.
⁶ I was angry with my people,
   I profaned my heritage;
I gave them into your hand,
   you showed them no mercy;
on the aged you made your yoke
   exceedingly heavy.
⁷ You said, "I shall be mistress forever,"
   so that you did not lay these things to
      heart
   or remember their end.

⁸ Now therefore hear this, you lover of
      pleasures,
   who sit securely,
who say in your heart,
   "I am, and there is no one besides me;
I shall not sit as a widow
   or know the loss of children"—
⁹ both these things shall come upon you
   in a moment, in one day:
the loss of children and widowhood
   shall come upon you in full measure,
in spite of your many sorceries
   and the great power of your
      enchantments.

¹⁰ You felt secure in your wickedness;
   you said, "No one sees me."
Your wisdom and your knowledge
   led you astray,
and you said in your heart,
   "I am, and there is no one besides me."
¹¹ But evil shall come upon you,
   which you cannot charm away;
disaster shall fall upon you,
   which you will not be able to ward
      off;
and ruin shall come on you suddenly,
   of which you know nothing.

¹² Stand fast in your enchantments

polemic against idols; see 40.18–20; 44.9–20. **8–11:** A reiteration of the incomparability of the Lord who predicts events and brings them to pass; see 40.2–5; 41.25–29; 43.10–13; 44.6–8. **11:** The *bird of prey* from the east is Cyrus. **47.1–15:** Babylon is portrayed as a once magnificent princess who has been thrown to the dirt and humiliated before her conquerors. It was common for cities in the ancient Near Eastern world to be portrayed as women or goddesses; cf. Jerusalem's designation as "daughter Zion" (see 1.8n.; 37.22; 52.2). **5–7:** Babylon, much like the Assyrian king earlier (see 10.5–34; 14.24–27), overstepped its bounds in oppressing Israel and failing to recognize that it acted as the Lord's agent. **8–11:** Babylon's boast of uniqueness is countered by the claim of the God of Israel's incomparability. **12–15:** Babylonian diviners and astrologers developed mathematics and other

and your many sorceries,
   with which you have labored from your
      youth;
perhaps you may be able to succeed,
   perhaps you may inspire terror.
¹³ You are wearied with your many
     consultations;
   let those who study[a] the heavens
stand up and save you,
   those who gaze at the stars,
and at each new moon predict
   what[b] shall befall you.

¹⁴ See, they are like stubble,
   the fire consumes them;
they cannot deliver themselves
   from the power of the flame.
No coal for warming oneself is this,
   no fire to sit before!
¹⁵ Such to you are those with whom you
     have labored,
who have trafficked with you from your
     youth;
they all wander about in their own paths;
   there is no one to save you.

48 Hear this, O house of Jacob,
   who are called by the name of Israel,
and who came forth from the loins[c] of
     Judah;
who swear by the name of the Lord,
   and invoke the God of Israel,
   but not in truth or right.
² For they call themselves after the holy
     city,
   and lean on the God of Israel;
   the Lord of hosts is his name.

³ The former things I declared long ago,
   they went out from my mouth and I
     made them known;
   then suddenly I did them and they
     came to pass.
⁴ Because I know that you are obstinate,

and your neck is an iron sinew
   and your forehead brass,
⁵ I declared them to you from long ago,
   before they came to pass I announced
     them to you,
so that you would not say, "My idol did
     them,
   my carved image and my cast image
     commanded them."

⁶ You have heard; now see all this;
   and will you not declare it?
From this time forward I make you hear
     new things,
   hidden things that you have not known.
⁷ They are created now, not long ago;
   before today you have never heard of
     them,
   so that you could not say, "I already
     knew them."
⁸ You have never heard, you have never
     known,
   from of old your ear has not been
     opened.
For I knew that you would deal very
     treacherously,
   and that from birth you were called a
     rebel.

⁹ For my name's sake I defer my anger,
   for the sake of my praise I restrain it for
     you,
   so that I may not cut you off.
¹⁰ See, I have refined you, but not like[d]
     silver;
   I have tested you in the furnace of
     adversity.
¹¹ For my own sake, for my own sake, I do
     it,

---

a   Meaning of Heb uncertain
b   Gk Syr Compare Vg: Heb *from what*
c   Cn: Heb *waters*
d   Cn: Heb *with*

sciences in their attempts to track the movements of the planets and the stars to determine the will of the gods. Despite such expertise, Babylon's efforts are useless before the Lord.

   48.1–22: A series of courtroom summary speeches and concluding hymn reiterates the Lord's right to use Cyrus as the redeemer of Israel. **1–5:** The fulfillment of prophecies should have persuaded the people to recognize the truth of the Lord's claims. **6–8:** The *new things* are the conquests of Cyrus, which are destined to lead to a change of fortune for Judah; cf. 43.18–19. Proof is necessary because of Israel's history of religious infidelity. **9–11:** The concern for the divine name or reputation and divine sanctity is also a prominent theme in Ezekiel

for why should my name[a] be profaned?
My glory I will not give to another.

¹² Listen to me, O Jacob,
and Israel, whom I called:
I am He; I am the first,
and I am the last.
¹³ My hand laid the foundation of the
earth,
and my right hand spread out the
heavens;
when I summon them,
they stand at attention.

¹⁴ Assemble, all of you, and hear!
Who among them has declared these
things?
The LORD loves him;
he shall perform his purpose on
Babylon,
and his arm shall be against the
Chaldeans.
¹⁵ I, even I, have spoken and called him,
I have brought him, and he will prosper
in his way.
¹⁶ Draw near to me, hear this!
From the beginning I have not spoken
in secret,
from the time it came to be I have been
there.
And now the Lord GOD has sent me and
his spirit.

¹⁷ Thus says the LORD,
your Redeemer, the Holy One of Israel:
I am the LORD your God,
who teaches you for your own good,
who leads you in the way you should go.

¹⁸ O that you had paid attention to my
commandments!
Then your prosperity would have been
like a river,
and your success like the waves of the
sea;
¹⁹ your offspring would have been like the
sand,
and your descendants like its grains;
their name would never be cut off
or destroyed from before me.

²⁰ Go out from Babylon, flee from Chaldea,
declare this with a shout of joy,
proclaim it,
send it forth to the end of the earth;
say, "The LORD has redeemed his
servant Jacob!"
²¹ They did not thirst when he led them
through the deserts;
he made water flow for them from the
rock;
he split open the rock and the water
gushed out.

²² "There is no peace," says the LORD, "for
the wicked."

49

Listen to me, O coastlands,
pay attention, you peoples from far
away!
The LORD called me before I was born,
while I was in my mother's womb he
named me.
² He made my mouth like a sharp sword,
in the shadow of his hand he hid me;

a   Gk Old Latin: Heb *for why should it*

(e.g., 36.11,21–23). The imagery of refined silver is drawn from 1.24–25. **12–16:** *First* and *last*; see also 41.4; 43.10; 44.6. **14:** *Chaldeans*, the Neo-Babylonian kingdom. **17–19:** The LORD reiterates the terms of the ancestral covenant with Abraham (Gen 15.5; 17.1–8; 22.16–18) and with Jacob (Gen 28.13–14; 35.9–15) to emphasize the cost to Israel of its failure to observe the LORD's commandments. **20–22:** The concluding hymn calls upon the exiles to flee from Babylon and Chaldea and to journey through the wilderness as they make their way home. The theme of water in the wilderness (Ex 17.1–7; Num 20.2–13) demonstrates the LORD's sustenance on this new exodus from Babylon. **22:** See also 57.21.

49.1–54.17: The LORD is restoring Zion. The fifth and concluding contention in the series is the prophet's announcement that the LORD is restoring Zion. This lengthy unit focuses especially on the role of the servant figure, earlier identified as Israel, in the divine plan.

49.1–13: Announcement concerning the role of the servant. The servant is defined both in relation to the restoration of Israel and as a light to the nations. **1–6:** The second of the "servant songs" (see 42.1n.) presents the servant as an individual figure who is also identified as Israel. He is called from the womb much like Jeremiah

he made me a polished arrow,
    in his quiver he hid me away.
[3] And he said to me, "You are my servant,
    Israel, in whom I will be glorified."
[4] But I said, "I have labored in vain,
    I have spent my strength for nothing
        and vanity;
yet surely my cause is with the LORD,
    and my reward with my God."

[5] And now the LORD says,
    who formed me in the womb to be his
        servant,
to bring Jacob back to him,
    and that Israel might be gathered to
        him,
for I am honored in the sight of the LORD,
    and my God has become my strength—
[6] he says,
"It is too light a thing that you should be
    my servant
    to raise up the tribes of Jacob
    and to restore the survivors of Israel;
I will give you as a light to the nations,
    that my salvation may reach to the end
        of the earth."

[7] Thus says the LORD,
    the Redeemer of Israel and his Holy
        One,
to one deeply despised, abhorred by the
    nations,
    the slave of rulers,
"Kings shall see and stand up,
    princes, and they shall prostrate
        themselves,
because of the LORD, who is faithful,
    the Holy One of Israel, who has chosen
        you."

[8] Thus says the LORD:

In a time of favor I have answered you,
    on a day of salvation I have helped you;
I have kept you and given you
    as a covenant to the people,[a]
to establish the land,
    to apportion the desolate heritages;
[9] saying to the prisoners, "Come out,"
    to those who are in darkness, "Show
        yourselves."
They shall feed along the ways,
    on all the bare heights[b] shall be their
        pasture;
[10] they shall not hunger or thirst,
    neither scorching wind nor sun shall
        strike them down,
for he who has pity on them will lead
    them,
    and by springs of water will guide them.
[11] And I will turn all my mountains into a
    road,
    and my highways shall be raised up.
[12] Lo, these shall come from far away,
    and lo, these from the north and from
        the west,
    and these from the land of Syene.[c]

[13] Sing for joy, O heavens, and exult,
        O earth;
    break forth, O mountains, into singing!
For the LORD has comforted his people,
    and will have compassion on his
        suffering ones.

[14] But Zion said, "The LORD has forsaken
    me,
    my Lord has forgotten me."
[15] Can a woman forget her nursing child,

a   Meaning of Heb uncertain
b   Or the trails
c   Q Ms: MT Sinim

(Jer 1.5). 3: The servant is here specifically identified as Israel, although his task in v. 5 is to bring Israel/Jacob to the LORD. 6: *A light to the nations,* see 42.5–9n. 7–12: An oracle of restoration. 7: The servant's restoration demonstrates the sovereignty of the LORD in the world; cf. 52.13–15. 8–12: *Covenant to the people,* here the role of the servant in relation to the people Israel who will be released from prison to return through the wilderness to their homeland in a second exodus (see also 40.3–5; 41.17–20; 43.19; 48.20–22). 12: *Syene,* Aswan in Upper (southern) Egypt at the first cataract of the Nile, where a Jewish settlement existed prior to the Persian conquest of Egypt in 525 BCE. 13: The concluding hymn portrays the celebration of all creation at the restoration of Israel (cf. 44.23; 45.8).

49.14–52.12: The LORD's announcement of the restoration of Zion. The LORD attempts to convince Israel that despite her experience of exile the LORD will now return the nation to Zion. 49.14–18: Many Jews in Babylonian

or show no compassion for the child of
her womb?
Even these may forget,
yet I will not forget you.
16 See, I have inscribed you on the palms of
my hands;
your walls are continually before me.
17 Your builders outdo your destroyers,[a]
and those who laid you waste go away
from you.
18 Lift up your eyes all around and see;
they all gather, they come to you.
As I live, says the LORD,
you shall put all of them on like an
ornament,
and like a bride you shall bind them on.

19 Surely your waste and your desolate
places
and your devastated land—
surely now you will be too crowded for
your inhabitants,
and those who swallowed you up will
be far away.
20 The children born in the time of your
bereavement
will yet say in your hearing:
"The place is too crowded for me;
make room for me to settle."
21 Then you will say in your heart,
"Who has borne me these?
I was bereaved and barren,
exiled and put away—
so who has reared these?
I was left all alone—
where then have these come from?"

22 Thus says the Lord GOD:
I will soon lift up my hand to the
nations,
and raise my signal to the
peoples;

and they shall bring your sons in their
bosom,
and your daughters shall be carried on
their shoulders.
23 Kings shall be your foster fathers,
and their queens your nursing
mothers.
With their faces to the ground they shall
bow down to you,
and lick the dust of your feet.
Then you will know that I am the LORD;
those who wait for me shall not be put
to shame.

24 Can the prey be taken from the
mighty,
or the captives of a tyrant[b] be rescued?
25 But thus says the LORD:
Even the captives of the mighty shall be
taken,
and the prey of the tyrant be rescued;
for I will contend with those who contend
with you,
and I will save your children.
26 I will make your oppressors eat their
own flesh,
and they shall be drunk with their own
blood as with wine.
Then all flesh shall know
that I am the LORD your Savior,
and your Redeemer, the Mighty One of
Jacob.

50

Thus says the LORD:
Where is your mother's bill of divorce
with which I put her away?
Or which of my creditors is it
to whom I have sold you?
No, because of your sins you were sold,

---

a Or *Your children come swiftly; your destroyers*
b Q Ms Syr Vg: MT *of a righteous person*

exile would have questioned the power of the LORD to protect the nation. In this section Zion is personified as a
woman (49.14; 50.1; 51.17–52.2; 54.1–14; see 1.8n.). The LORD similarly is compared to a mother with her child and
claims not to have forgotten or abandoned the people (cf. 66.13). **18:** This verse is echoed and developed in Bar
5.5–9. **22–23:** The raised hand of the LORD reverses the hand of judgment extended against Israel (9.7–10.4) and
recalls the banner that signals restoration (11.1–16). **24–26:** The rhetorical questions function here as assertions
of divine power insofar as the LORD can make these things happen. **50.1–11:** The language of the courtroom appears once again as the LORD explains the divine role in Israel's experience. **1–3:** Rhetorical questions are used
to make the LORD's case. Zion is portrayed as a mother, who was neither divorced nor sold to creditors to pay
the LORD's bill. Instead, the LORD contends that she was sold for the sins of the nation. Nevertheless, the LORD

and for your transgressions your
mother was put away.
² Why was no one there when I came?
Why did no one answer when I called?
Is my hand shortened, that it cannot
redeem?
Or have I no power to deliver?
By my rebuke I dry up the sea,
I make the rivers a desert;
their fish stink for lack of water,
and die of thirst.ª
³ I clothe the heavens with blackness,
and make sackcloth their covering.

⁴ The Lord GOD has given me
the tongue of a teacher,ᵇ
that I may know how to sustain
the weary with a word.
Morning by morning he wakens—
wakens my ear
to listen as those who are taught.
⁵ The Lord GOD has opened my ear,
and I was not rebellious,
I did not turn backward.
⁶ I gave my back to those who struck me,
and my cheeks to those who pulled out
the beard;
I did not hide my face
from insult and spitting.

⁷ The Lord GOD helps me;
therefore I have not been disgraced;
therefore I have set my face like flint,
and I know that I shall not be put to
shame;
⁸ he who vindicates me is near.
Who will contend with me?
Let us stand up together.
Who are my adversaries?
Let them confront me.
⁹ It is the Lord GOD who helps me;

who will declare me guilty?
All of them will wear out like a garment;
the moth will eat them up.

¹⁰ Who among you fears the LORD
and obeys the voice of his servant,
who walks in darkness
and has no light,
yet trusts in the name of the LORD
and relies upon his God?
¹¹ But all of you are kindlers of fire,
lighters of firebrands.ᶜ
Walk in the flame of your fire,
and among the brands that you have
kindled!
This is what you shall have from my hand:
you shall lie down in torment.

51 Listen to me, you that pursue
righteousness,
you that seek the LORD.
Look to the rock from which you were
hewn,
and to the quarry from which you were
dug.
² Look to Abraham your father
and to Sarah who bore you;
for he was but one when I called him,
but I blessed him and made him
many.
³ For the LORD will comfort Zion;
he will comfort all her waste places,
and will make her wilderness like Eden,
her desert like the garden of the LORD;
joy and gladness will be found in her,
thanksgiving and the voice of song.

ª Or *die on the thirsty ground*
ᵇ Cn: Heb *of those who are taught*
ᶜ Syr: Heb *you gird yourselves with firebrands*

asserts divine power as creator of the universe to redeem. **4–9:** The third servant song (see 42.1n.) appears in vv. 4–11, although vv. 10–11 presuppose a different speaker. **4:** The servant links himself with Isaiah's disciples (see 8.16n.). **6:** Obedience to God entailed suffering (cf. 6.9–10, which calls for the suffering of the people as part of the divine plan). The persecution of the servant recalls that of Jeremiah (Jer 11.9; 20.1–2; 26.7–24). **10–11:** The LORD maintains that those who refuse to fear the LORD and honor the servant kindle the fire of their own suffering (cf. 1.29–31). **51.1–52.12:** Proof for the restoration for Zion. **51.1–8:** The LORD addresses the righteous who seek the LORD. The argument proceeds from the basis of the LORD's promises to make Abraham and Sarah into a great nation by which all nations will be blessed (Gen 12.2–3; cf. Gen 15.1–6,17–21; 17.15–22; 22.15–18). To fulfill the ancestral promise, the LORD will comfort and restore Zion. Israel will then emerge as a basis for sending the LORD's teaching (Heb "torah") and *justice* to the entire world (cf. 2.2–4). Even if the world changes, the

4 Listen to me, my people,
  and give heed to me, my nation;
for a teaching will go out from me,
  and my justice for a light to the
    peoples.
5 I will bring near my deliverance swiftly,
  my salvation has gone out
  and my arms will rule the peoples;
the coastlands wait for me,
  and for my arm they hope.
6 Lift up your eyes to the heavens,
  and look at the earth beneath;
for the heavens will vanish like smoke,
  the earth will wear out like a garment,
  and those who live on it will die like
    gnats;[a]
but my salvation will be forever,
  and my deliverance will never be ended.

7 Listen to me, you who know righteousness,
  you people who have my teaching in
    your hearts;
do not fear the reproach of others,
  and do not be dismayed when they
    revile you.
8 For the moth will eat them up like a
    garment,
  and the worm will eat them like wool;
but my deliverance will be forever,
  and my salvation to all generations.

9 Awake, awake, put on strength,
  O arm of the Lord!
Awake, as in days of old,
  the generations of long ago!
Was it not you who cut Rahab in pieces,
  who pierced the dragon?
10 Was it not you who dried up the sea,
  the waters of the great deep;
who made the depths of the sea a way
  for the redeemed to cross over?
11 So the ransomed of the Lord shall
    return,

and come to Zion with singing;
everlasting joy shall be upon their heads;
  they shall obtain joy and gladness,
  and sorrow and sighing shall flee away.

12 I, I am he who comforts you;
  why then are you afraid of a mere
    mortal who must die,
  a human being who fades like grass?
13 You have forgotten the Lord, your
    Maker,
  who stretched out the heavens
  and laid the foundations of the earth.
You fear continually all day long
  because of the fury of the oppressor,
who is bent on destruction.
  But where is the fury of the oppressor?
14 The oppressed shall speedily be
    released;
  they shall not die and go down to the
    Pit,
  nor shall they lack bread.
15 For I am the Lord your God,
  who stirs up the sea so that its waves
    roar—
  the Lord of hosts is his name.
16 I have put my words in your mouth,
  and hidden you in the shadow of my
    hand,
stretching out[b] the heavens
  and laying the foundations of the earth,
  and saying to Zion, "You are my
    people."

17 Rouse yourself, rouse yourself!
  Stand up, O Jerusalem,
you who have drunk at the hand of the
    Lord
  the cup of his wrath,
who have drunk to the dregs

a Or in like manner
b Syr: Heb planting

promises of the Lord never change. 9–11: The prophet calls upon the arm of the Lord to act (cf. Ps 44.23) and
recounts past actions. Rahab is a mythological sea monster who is defeated by God before creation (Ps 89.10;
Job 26.12; cf. Ps 74.12–17; Isa 27.1). Again, the Exodus from Egypt and the crossing of the sea illustrate the power
of the Lord to redeem Israel (Ex 14–15; cf. Isa 11.15–16; 27.12–13). 12–16: Israel should not fear human opponents
when the Lord, creator of heaven and earth, acts on their behalf. 14: The Pit, Sheol, the underworld (cf. 14.9–11).
17–23: The prophet addresses Jerusalem, here portrayed as a woman who has suffered at the hands of the Lord.
The metaphorical cup of divine wrath appears elsewhere (e.g., Jer 25.15–29; Hab 2.15–16). As a result of the devastation, Jerusalem's children lie dead leaving no one to help her. The Lord announces the end of Jerusalem's

the bowl of staggering.
¹⁸ There is no one to guide her
among all the children she has borne;
there is no one to take her by the hand
among all the children she has brought
up.
¹⁹ These two things have befallen you
—who will grieve with you?—
devastation and destruction, famine and
sword—
who will comfort you?ᵃ
²⁰ Your children have fainted,
they lie at the head of every street
like an antelope in a net;
they are full of the wrath of the LORD,
the rebuke of your God.

²¹ Therefore hear this, you who are
wounded,ᵇ
who are drunk, but not with wine:
²² Thus says your Sovereign, the LORD,
your God who pleads the cause of his
people:
See, I have taken from your hand the cup
of staggering;
you shall drink no more
from the bowl of my wrath.
²³ And I will put it into the hand of your
tormentors,
who have said to you,
"Bow down, that we may walk on you";
and you have made your back like the
ground
and like the street for them to walk on.

52 Awake, awake,
put on your strength, O Zion!
Put on your beautiful garments,
O Jerusalem, the holy city;
for the uncircumcised and the unclean
shall enter you no more.

² Shake yourself from the dust, rise up,
O captiveᶜ Jerusalem;
loose the bonds from your neck,
O captive daughter Zion!

³ For thus says the LORD: You were sold for
nothing, and you shall be redeemed without
money. ⁴ For thus says the Lord GOD: Long ago,
my people went down into Egypt to reside there
as aliens; the Assyrian, too, has oppressed them
without cause. ⁵ Now therefore what am I doing
here, says the LORD, seeing that my people are
taken away without cause? Their rulers howl,
says the LORD, and continually, all day long, my
name is despised. ⁶ Therefore my people shall
know my name; therefore in that day they shall
know that it is I who speak; here am I.

⁷ How beautiful upon the mountains
are the feet of the messenger who
announces peace,
who brings good news,
who announces salvation,
who says to Zion, "Your God reigns."
⁸ Listen! Your sentinels lift up their voices,
together they sing for joy;
for in plain sight they see
the return of the LORD to Zion.
⁹ Break forth together into singing,
you ruins of Jerusalem;
for the LORD has comforted his people,
he has redeemed Jerusalem.
¹⁰ The LORD has bared his holy arm
before the eyes of all the nations;
and all the ends of the earth shall see
the salvation of our God.

ᵃ Q Ms Gk Syr Vg: MT *how may I comfort you?*
ᵇ Or *humbled*
ᶜ Cn: Heb *rise up, sit*

suffering and declares that the cup of divine wrath will now be drunk by her oppressors. **52.1–6**: The imagery of restoration reverses many of the miseries described in Lamentations (cf. Lam 1.9–10,14,17; 2.10). The prophet addresses Jerusalem as a woman once again (see 1.8n.; 37.22), and calls upon her to awake and to put on her beautiful clothing because her suffering is over. Foreign enemies will no longer enter or rape her and subject her to captivity. **3–6**: The LORD explains how Israel was oppressed both by Egypt (Ex 1–15) during the Exodus and Assyria in more recent times. The LORD will therefore act to redeem the people and to put an end to the derision of the divine name among Israel's oppressors. When the LORD acts, the people will know their God. **7–10**: As in 40.9, the prophet once again describes the messenger who brings good news that the LORD is returning to Zion (cf. Isa 40.9; Nah 1.15 [Heb 2.1]). **11–12**: In response to the LORD's return to Zion, the exiles are called upon to leave Babylon and to form a holy procession bearing the Temple vessels (see Ezra 1.7–11) as they return to their

[11] Depart, depart, go out from there!
  Touch no unclean thing;
go out from the midst of it, purify
    yourselves,
  you who carry the vessels of the LORD.
[12] For you shall not go out in haste,
  and you shall not go in flight;
for the LORD will go before you,
  and the God of Israel will be your rear
    guard.

[13] See, my servant shall prosper;
  he shall be exalted and lifted up,
  and shall be very high.
[14] Just as there were many who were
    astonished at him[a]
  —so marred was his appearance,
    beyond human semblance,
  and his form beyond that of mortals—
[15] so he shall startle[b] many nations;
  kings shall shut their mouths because
    of him;
for that which had not been told them
    they shall see,
  and that which they had not heard they
    shall contemplate.

53

Who has believed what we have heard?
  And to whom has the arm of the LORD
    been revealed?
[2] For he grew up before him like a young
    plant,
  and like a root out of dry ground;
he had no form or majesty that we should
    look at him,
  nothing in his appearance that we
    should desire him.
[3] He was despised and rejected by others;
  a man of suffering[c] and acquainted with
    infirmity;

and as one from whom others hide their
    faces[d]
  he was despised, and we held him of no
    account.

[4] Surely he has borne our infirmities
  and carried our diseases;
yet we accounted him stricken,
  struck down by God, and afflicted.
[5] But he was wounded for our
    transgressions,
  crushed for our iniquities;
upon him was the punishment that made
    us whole,
  and by his bruises we are healed.
[6] All we like sheep have gone astray;
  we have all turned to our own way,
and the LORD has laid on him
  the iniquity of us all.

[7] He was oppressed, and he was afflicted,
  yet he did not open his mouth;
like a lamb that is led to the slaughter,
  and like a sheep that before its shearers
    is silent,
  so he did not open his mouth.
[8] By a perversion of justice he was taken
    away.
  Who could have imagined his future?
For he was cut off from the land of the
    living,
  stricken for the transgression of my
    people.

[a] Syr Tg: Heb you
[b] Meaning of Heb uncertain
[c] Or a man of sorrows
[d] Or as one who hides his face from us

homeland. Not . . . in haste, the exodus from Babylon will be different from the first Exodus; cf. Ex 12.11; 13.21–22.
  52.13–53.12: Announcement of the exaltation of the servant of the LORD. The fourth and final servant song (see 42.1n.) portrays the suffering of the servant and his ultimate exaltation. Talmudic tradition identifies the servant with Moses, who suffered throughout the wilderness journey (b. Sotah 14a), and early Christian tradition identifies the servant with Jesus (Acts 8.32–35). Second Isaiah identifies the servant with Israel (49.3), although the servant's mission is to restore Israel and Jacob to the LORD (49.5). Other figures identified with the servant include the prophet Jeremiah, who was persecuted throughout his life; King Josiah, who was killed by Pharaoh Neco at Megiddo (2 Kings 23.29–30); and King Jehoiachin, who was exiled to Babylon (2 Kings 24.10–16). 52.13–15: The disfigurement and suffering of the servant, but also his exaltation elicit astonishment from foreign nations and rulers (cf. 49.7). 53.1–12: The intense suffering of the servant is defined vicariously; just as the LORD calls for Israel to be blind and deaf so that they will suffer punishment (6.9–10), so the servant now exemplifies that role. His suffering serves as a means to atone for the sins of the nation, much like a lamb

9 They made his grave with the wicked
  and his tomb[a] with the rich,[b]
although he had done no violence,
  and there was no deceit in his mouth.

10 Yet it was the will of the LORD to crush
  him with pain.[c]
When you make his life an offering for
  sin,[d]
  he shall see his offspring, and shall
    prolong his days;
through him the will of the LORD shall
  prosper.
11 Out of his anguish he shall see light;[e]
he shall find satisfaction through his
  knowledge.
  The righteous one,[f] my servant, shall
    make many righteous,
  and he shall bear their iniquities.
12 Therefore I will allot him a portion with
  the great,
  and he shall divide the spoil with the
    strong;
because he poured out himself to death,
  and was numbered with the
    transgressors;
yet he bore the sin of many,
  and made intercession for the
    transgressors.

54 Sing, O barren one who did not bear;
  burst into song and shout,
  you who have not been in labor!
For the children of the desolate woman
  will be more
  than the children of her that is married,
    says the LORD.
2 Enlarge the site of your tent,
  and let the curtains of your habitations
    be stretched out;
do not hold back; lengthen your cords
  and strengthen your stakes.

3 For you will spread out to the right and to
  the left,
  and your descendants will possess the
    nations
  and will settle the desolate towns.

4 Do not fear, for you will not be ashamed;
  do not be discouraged, for you will not
    suffer disgrace;
for you will forget the shame of your
  youth,
  and the disgrace of your widowhood
    you will remember no more.
5 For your Maker is your husband,
  the LORD of hosts is his name;
the Holy One of Israel is your Redeemer,
  the God of the whole earth he is called.
6 For the LORD has called you
  like a wife forsaken and grieved in
    spirit,
like the wife of a man's youth when she is
  cast off,
  says your God.
7 For a brief moment I abandoned you,
  but with great compassion I will gather
    you.
8 In overflowing wrath for a moment
  I hid my face from you,
but with everlasting love I will have
  compassion on you,
  says the LORD, your Redeemer.

9 This is like the days of Noah to me:
  Just as I swore that the waters of Noah

a Q Ms: MT *and in his death*
b Cn: Heb *with a rich person*
c Or *by disease*; meaning of Heb uncertain
d Meaning of Heb uncertain
e Q Mss: MT lacks *light*
f Or *and he shall find satisfaction. Through his
  knowledge, the righteous one*

sacrificed at the Temple altar. **10:** The servant's *offspring* refer to those who follow his example and teaching
after his death rather than indicating that he survived and was rehabilitated.

54.1–17: Restoration of the covenant between the LORD and Zion. Like other major sections of Second
Isaiah, 49.1–54.17 closes with a hymn (cf. 42.13; 44.23; 48.20–22). **1–3:** Zion is addressed once again as a woman
(cf. 49.14; 50.1; 51.17–52.2). Much like Sarah (Gen 16.1), she is described as a barren woman. In keeping with the
promises to Abraham and Sarah, Zion will soon have so many children that her home will not be able to contain
them (Gen 12.2–3; cf. Gen 15.1–6,17–21; 17.15–22; 22.15–18). **4–10:** The reassurance formula (cf. 7.4; 37.6) informs
Zion that her time as an abandoned woman is at an end. The passage metaphorically identifies the LORD as
Zion's husband in keeping with Israelite tradition that posited a marriage relationship between the LORD and

would never again go over the earth,
so I have sworn that I will not be angry
     with you
     and will not rebuke you.
[10] For the mountains may depart
     and the hills be removed,
but my steadfast love shall not depart from
     you,
     and my covenant of peace shall not be
          removed,
     says the LORD, who has compassion on
          you.

[11] O afflicted one, storm-tossed, and not
          comforted,
     I am about to set your stones in
          antimony,
     and lay your foundations with
          sapphires.[a]
[12] I will make your pinnacles of rubies,
     your gates of jewels,
     and all your wall of precious stones.
[13] All your children shall be taught by the
          LORD,
     and great shall be the prosperity of your
          children.
[14] In righteousness you shall be
          established;
     you shall be far from oppression, for
          you shall not fear;
     and from terror, for it shall not come
          near you.
[15] If anyone stirs up strife,

it is not from me;
whoever stirs up strife with you
     shall fall because of you.
[16] See it is I who have created the smith
     who blows the fire of coals,
     and produces a weapon fit for its
          purpose;
I have also created the ravager to destroy.
     [17] No weapon that is fashioned against
          you shall prosper,
     and you shall confute every tongue that
          rises against you in judgment.
This is the heritage of the servants of the
     LORD
     and their vindication from me, says the
          LORD.

55 Ho, everyone who thirsts,
     come to the waters;
and you that have no money,
     come, buy and eat!
Come, buy wine and milk
     without money and without price.
[2] Why do you spend your money for that
     which is not bread,
     and your labor for that which does not
          satisfy?
Listen carefully to me, and eat what is
     good,
     and delight yourselves in rich food.
[3] Incline your ear, and come to me;

[a]   Or *lapis lazuli*

Israel (cf. Jer 2; Ezek 16; Hos 1–3; Zeph 3.14–20). **8**: *Hid my face*, cf. 8.16–17. **9**: *Days of Noah*, an allusion to the eternal covenant made with Noah never again to destroy the earth by flood (Gen 9.8–17), invoked to illustrate the permanence and validity of this new divine promise. **10**: The *covenant of peace* signifies God's lasting commitment to be present with *steadfast love* (Heb "ḥesed"); cf. 55.3; Num 25.10–13; Ezek 34.25. **11–17**: The LORD addresses Jerusalem as a bride about to be decked out in jewels before her wedding. **11–13a**: The new Jerusalem is adorned with precious stones and gems by builders supernaturally instructed; cf. Ezek 28.13–19. Christian apocalyptic literature draws on this imagery to describe the new Jerusalem (Rev 21.18–21). **17b**: The future Jerusalem will be given to the servants of the LORD. The mention of this faithful segment of the people serves as a point of transition to the last section of the book (cf. 56.6; 63.17; 65.8–9,13–16; 66.14). Scholars are divided as to whether the second part of the book (Second Isaiah) ends with ch 54 or ch 55.

55.1–66.24: Prophetic exhortation to adhere to the LORD's covenant. The final block of the book of Isaiah calls upon the audience of the book to adhere to the LORD as the period of restoration is at hand. Although most of this material is attributed to Third Isaiah, generally recognized as a collective designation for anonymous prophets of the early Persian period, the block is introduced by the final chapter of Second Isaiah in ch 55.

55.1–13: Exhortation to adhere to the LORD. 1–5: The prophet employs the metaphors of thirst and hunger to invite the audience of the book to partake of what the LORD has to offer. The invitation is formulated in the language of wisdom literature, which often employs the metaphor of food to portray the pursuit of wisdom (cf. Prov 9.1–6). **3–5**: The prophet reiterates the Davidic covenant tradition with its promise of eternal kingship for

listen, so that you may live.
I will make with you an everlasting
covenant,
my steadfast, sure love for David.
⁴ See, I made him a witness to the peoples,
a leader and commander for the
peoples.
⁵ See, you shall call nations that you do not
know,
and nations that do not know you shall
run to you,
because of the LORD your God, the Holy
One of Israel,
for he has glorified you.

⁶ Seek the LORD while he may be found,
call upon him while he is near;
⁷ let the wicked forsake their way,
and the unrighteous their thoughts;
let them return to the LORD, that he may
have mercy on them,
and to our God, for he will abundantly
pardon.
⁸ For my thoughts are not your thoughts,
nor are your ways my ways, says the
LORD.
⁹ For as the heavens are higher than the
earth,
so are my ways higher than your
ways
and my thoughts than your thoughts.

¹⁰ For as the rain and the snow come down
from heaven,
and do not return there until they have
watered the earth,
making it bring forth and sprout,
giving seed to the sower and bread to
the eater,
¹¹ so shall my word be that goes out from
my mouth;
it shall not return to me empty,
but it shall accomplish that which I
purpose,
and succeed in the thing for which I
sent it.

¹² For you shall go out in joy,
and be led back in peace;
the mountains and the hills before you
shall burst into song,
and all the trees of the field shall clap
their hands.
¹³ Instead of the thorn shall come up the
cypress;
instead of the brier shall come up the
myrtle;
and it shall be to the LORD for a memorial,
for an everlasting sign that shall not be
cut off.

56

Thus says the LORD:
Maintain justice, and do what
is right,

the house of David (2 Sam 7). Because no Davidic king would ascend the throne under Persian rule, however, the prophet applies the Davidic covenant to the people of Israel at large. Just as David established an empire over surrounding nations (2 Sam 8), Israel will now serve as a means to call nations to recognize the LORD (cf. 2.2–4). **6–13:** The exhortation to follow the LORD addresses the audience directly (cf. 1.17; Am 5.6,14). The distinction between the righteous and the wicked in this passage is a rhetorical device to persuade the audience to choose to be included among the righteous rather than to suffer punishment with the wicked. **8–9:** The distinction between the ways and thoughts of the LORD and those of the audience builds the case that the LORD planned for punishment to culminate in restoration. **10–11:** The passage reiterates the permanence of the LORD's word (cf. 40.8), and that it will accomplish the divine purpose (cf. 14.27). **12–13:** In contrast to the thorns and thistles produced by Israel in the vineyard song (5.1–7), Israel will grow into *cypress* and *myrtle* as an everlasting sign of its relationship with the LORD (cf. 11.1–16). The imagery also recapitulates the theme of glorious return in 40.3–5 and 48.20–22, the beginning and end of chs 40–48. It therefore indicates a point of closure at a stage in the formation of the book. **13:** *Memorial,* lit. "name."

56.1–66.24: Portrayal of the restored covenant community. The collection of writings in chs 56–66 is generally ascribed to Third Isaiah, a name for various anonymous prophets from the time of the early Persian period restoration in the late sixth through the fifth centuries BCE.

56.1–59.21: Instruction concerning proper observance of the covenant. The various subunits of this section of Isaiah offer instruction concerning the observance of the covenant with the LORD as the restoration comes to fruition. **56.1–8:** The passage begins with a general statement of principles concerning the LORD's

for soon my salvation will come,
and my deliverance be revealed.

[2] Happy is the mortal who does this,
the one who holds it fast,
who keeps the sabbath, not profaning it,
and refrains from doing any evil.

[3] Do not let the foreigner joined to the
LORD say,
"The LORD will surely separate me from
his people";
and do not let the eunuch say,
"I am just a dry tree."
[4] For thus says the LORD:
To the eunuchs who keep my sabbaths,
who choose the things that please me
and hold fast my covenant,
[5] I will give, in my house and within my walls,
a monument and a name
better than sons and daughters;
I will give them an everlasting name
that shall not be cut off.

[6] And the foreigners who join themselves
to the LORD,
to minister to him, to love the name of
the LORD,
and to be his servants,
all who keep the sabbath, and do not
profane it,
and hold fast my covenant—
[7] these I will bring to my holy mountain,
and make them joyful in my house of
prayer;

their burnt offerings and their sacrifices
will be accepted on my altar;
for my house shall be called a house of
prayer
for all peoples.
[8] Thus says the Lord GOD,
who gathers the outcasts of Israel,
I will gather others to them
besides those already gathered.[a]

[9] All you wild animals,
all you wild animals in the forest, come
to devour!
[10] Israel's[b] sentinels are blind,
they are all without knowledge;
they are all silent dogs
that cannot bark;
dreaming, lying down,
loving to slumber.
[11] The dogs have a mighty appetite;
they never have enough.
The shepherds also have no
understanding;
they have all turned to their own way,
to their own gain, one and all.
[12] "Come," they say, "let us[c] get wine;
let us fill ourselves with strong drink.
And tomorrow will be like today,
great beyond measure."

a Heb *besides his gathered ones*
b Heb *His*
c Q Ms Syr Vg Tg: MT *me*

expectations. Justice and righteousness are the basis of biblical law and subsequent Jewish tradition. **2:** *The sabbath* is the foundational observance of Jewish tradition, having been founded as the LORD's day of rest from the time of creation (Gen 2.1–3; cf. Ex 20.8–11; 31.12–17; 20.8–11; Lev 19.30; 23.3; Deut 5.12–15). **3–8:** Foreigners joined to the LORD refers to those who have converted to Judaism, much as Jethro (Ex 18) and Ruth (Ruth 1) were viewed. Although Ezra and Nehemiah expelled foreign women from Jerusalem, those expelled maintained their native languages and religious traditions without having converted (Neh 13.23–30; Ezra 9–10; cf. Deut 7.1–6). Deut 21.10–14 defines the procedure for marriage to a foreign woman captured in war, and biblical laws constantly stress that foreigners may join Israel if they observe the LORD's instructions (cf. Ex 12.48–49; Lev 24.22; Num 9.14; 15.27–31). *Eunuch,* castrated, e.g., for service in a foreign court or harem. Deut 23.1–8 bans eunuchs, Ammonites and Moabites, and those born of an illicit marriage from membership in the community, but the present passage makes provision for eunuchs and foreigners if they observe the sabbath as the foundation of the covenant with the LORD.

56.9–57.21: The LORD's willingness to forgive those who repent and return to the LORD. **56.9–12:** The prophet metaphorically compares Israel's sentinels or leaders to wild animals and silent dogs, who lack understanding and serve only their own immediate interests (cf. 1.2–3; cf. Jer 12.8–9; Ezek 39.17). Alternatively, they are drunks (see 5.11–12; 28.1,7–13). Such characterization is designed to motivate the audience to accept the proph-

57

The righteous perish,
and no one takes it to heart;
the devout are taken away,
while no one understands.
For the righteous are taken away from
calamity,
[2] and they enter into peace;
those who walk uprightly
will rest on their couches.
[3] But as for you, come here,
you children of a sorceress,
you offspring of an adulterer and a
whore.[a]
[4] Whom are you mocking?
Against whom do you open your mouth
wide
and stick out your tongue?
Are you not children of transgression,
the offspring of deceit—
[5] you that burn with lust among the oaks,
under every green tree;
you that slaughter your children in the
valleys,
under the clefts of the rocks?
[6] Among the smooth stones of the valley is
your portion;
they, they, are your lot;
to them you have poured out a drink
offering,
you have brought a grain offering.
Shall I be appeased for these things?
[7] Upon a high and lofty mountain
you have set your bed,
and there you went up to offer sacrifice.
[8] Behind the door and the doorpost
you have set up your symbol;
for, in deserting me,[b] you have uncovered
your bed,
you have gone up to it,
you have made it wide;

and you have made a bargain for yourself
with them,
you have loved their bed,
you have gazed on their nakedness.[c]
[9] You journeyed to Molech[d] with oil,
and multiplied your perfumes;
you sent your envoys far away,
and sent down even to Sheol.
[10] You grew weary from your many
wanderings,
but you did not say, "It is useless."
You found your desire rekindled,
and so you did not weaken.
[11] Whom did you dread and fear
so that you lied,
and did not remember me
or give me a thought?
Have I not kept silent and closed my eyes,[e]
and so you do not fear me?
[12] I will concede your righteousness and
your works,
but they will not help you.
[13] When you cry out, let your collection of
idols deliver you!
The wind will carry them off,
a breath will take them away.
But whoever takes refuge in me shall
possess the land
and inherit my holy mountain.

[14] It shall be said,
"Build up, build up, prepare the
way,

---

a   Heb *an adulterer and she plays the whore*
b   Meaning of Heb uncertain
c   Or *their phallus*; Heb *the hand*
d   Or *the king*
e   Gk Vg: Heb *silent even for a long time*

---

et's teachings concerning observance of the LORD's covenant. **57.1–13:** The prophet chastises Israel for idolatrous and immoral behavior. **1–2:** A complaint that the probably violent death of the righteous goes unnoticed
and unlamented; cf. Ps 12.1; Mic 7.2. Placed here as a contrast with the polemic that follows. The righteous die in
peace, but their fate is ignored. **3–10:** The prophet portrays non-Israelite fertility worship, often associated with
sexual rites in the Bible (e.g., Num 25; Lev 18.24–39). The language in these verses has much sexual innuendo.
6: Streams would be an appropriate place to pour out libations to the gods. **7:** High mountains or hills are often
sanctuary sites because they symbolize the majesty of the gods and more practically because grain is more
readily threshed in the winds that blow across hilltops. **9:** *Molech* is a Canaanite god to whom children were
apparently sacrificed (Lev 18.21; 20.2–5; 2 Kings 3.27; 23.10; Jer 7.31; 32.35); the spelling of his name is uncertain
because the vowels employed in it are taken from Heb "boshet" ("shame"). *Sheol* is the underworld. **11–12:** The
LORD's rhetorical questions assert that the people feared their idols. The LORD claims to have remained silent

remove every obstruction from my
people's way."
[15] For thus says the high and lofty one
who inhabits eternity, whose name is
Holy:
I dwell in the high and holy place,
and also with those who are contrite
and humble in spirit,
to revive the spirit of the humble,
and to revive the heart of the contrite.
[16] For I will not continually accuse,
nor will I always be angry;
for then the spirits would grow faint
before me,
even the souls that I have made.
[17] Because of their wicked covetousness I
was angry;
I struck them, I hid and was angry;
but they kept turning back to their own
ways.
[18] I have seen their ways, but I will heal them;
I will lead them and repay them with
comfort,
creating for their mourners the fruit of
the lips.[a]
[19] Peace, peace, to the far and the near, says
the LORD;
and I will heal them.
[20] But the wicked are like the tossing sea
that cannot keep still;
its waters toss up mire and mud.
[21] There is no peace, says my God, for the
wicked.

58 Shout out, do not hold back!
Lift up your voice like a trumpet!
Announce to my people their rebellion,

to the house of Jacob their sins.
[2] Yet day after day they seek me
and delight to know my ways,
as if they were a nation that practiced
righteousness
and did not forsake the ordinance of
their God;
they ask of me righteous judgments,
they delight to draw near to God.
[3] "Why do we fast, but you do not see?
Why humble ourselves, but you do not
notice?"
Look, you serve your own interest on your
fast day,
and oppress all your workers.
[4] Look, you fast only to quarrel and to
fight
and to strike with a wicked fist.
Such fasting as you do today
will not make your voice heard on
high.
[5] Is such the fast that I choose,
a day to humble oneself?
Is it to bow down the head like a bulrush,
and to lie in sackcloth and ashes?
Will you call this a fast,
a day acceptable to the LORD?

[6] Is not this the fast that I choose:
to loose the bonds of injustice,
to undo the thongs of the yoke,
to let the oppressed go free,
and to break every yoke?
[7] Is it not to share your bread with the
hungry,

a   Meaning of Heb uncertain

through the period of Israel's oppression and exile, but now the LORD has returned. **14–21:** The prophet now turns to themes of restoration and a concluding diatribe. **14–15:** The motif of the highway that leads the exiles home, as in the Exodus tradition (cf. 11.15–16; 27.12–13; 35.1–10; 40.3–5) is now applied metaphorically. The LORD emphasizes that the time of judgment is now past and that the time of healing and peace has begun. **18:** *The fruit of the lips,* praise and joyful prayer in the place of mourning, as an accompaniment or substitute for sacrifice (cf. Hos 14.2). **21:** A concluding diatribe condemns the wicked who will have no peace (cf. 48.22).

58.1–14: A call to repentance and promise of restoration. The LORD calls upon the people to repent and defines the criteria by which they may observe the covenant. **1–2:** The celebratory tone evokes festival observance in the Temple, but the LORD's first demand is for righteous moral action to accompany holy ritual action. **3–5:** The questions of the people presuppose a time of distress that would have continued throughout the Babylonian exile as the people waited for a divine response that was long in coming. Fasting was a means to humble oneself before the LORD in such a time of distress (cf. Zech 7.1–14; 8.18–19; Joel 1.14; 2.15). **6–14:** A definition of genuine fasting. The LORD then spells out the means by which one should practice righteousness before the LORD. Concern for the poor is a hallmark of biblical tradition, including both biblical law and the prophets (Ex

and bring the homeless poor into your
house;
when you see the naked, to cover them,
and not to hide yourself from your own
kin?
[8] Then your light shall break forth like the
dawn,
and your healing shall spring up
quickly;
your vindicator[a] shall go before you,
the glory of the LORD shall be your rear
guard.
[9] Then you shall call, and the LORD will
answer;
you shall cry for help, and he will say,
Here I am.

If you remove the yoke from among you,
the pointing of the finger, the speaking
of evil,
[10] if you offer your food to the hungry
and satisfy the needs of the afflicted,
then your light shall rise in the
darkness
and your gloom be like the
noonday.
[11] The LORD will guide you continually,
and satisfy your needs in parched
places,
and make your bones strong;
and you shall be like a watered garden,
like a spring of water,
whose waters never fail.
[12] Your ancient ruins shall be rebuilt;
you shall raise up the foundations of
many generations;
you shall be called the repairer of the
breach,
the restorer of streets to live in.

[13] If you refrain from trampling the sabbath,
from pursuing your own interests on
my holy day;
if you call the sabbath a delight

and the holy day of the LORD honorable;
if you honor it, not going your own ways,
serving your own interests, or pursuing
your own affairs;[b]
[14] then you shall take delight in the LORD,
and I will make you ride upon the
heights of the earth;
I will feed you with the heritage of your
ancestor Jacob,
for the mouth of the LORD has spoken.

59 See, the LORD's hand is not too short
to save,
nor his ear too dull to hear.
[2] Rather, your iniquities have been barriers
between you and your God,
and your sins have hidden his face from you
so that he does not hear.
[3] For your hands are defiled with blood,
and your fingers with iniquity;
your lips have spoken lies,
your tongue mutters wickedness.
[4] No one brings suit justly,
no one goes to law honestly;
they rely on empty pleas, they speak lies,
conceiving mischief and begetting
iniquity.
[5] They hatch adders' eggs,
and weave the spider's web;
whoever eats their eggs dies,
and the crushed egg hatches out a viper.
[6] Their webs cannot serve as clothing;
they cannot cover themselves with
what they make.
Their works are works of iniquity,
and deeds of violence are in their hands.
[7] Their feet run to evil,
and they rush to shed innocent blood;
their thoughts are thoughts of iniquity,
desolation and destruction are in their
highways.

[a] Or *vindication*
[b] Heb *or speaking words*

22.21–27; 23.10–11; Lev 19.9–10; Deut 14.28–29; Isa 1.10–17; Am 2.6–8). **9:** When the people are righteous, the
LORD answers the prayers of the nation (cf. 1.10–17, esp. v. 15) and rebuilds its ruins. **12:** *Ruins . . . foundations*, a
reinterpretation of earlier promises of restoration (44.26–28). **13–14:** The LORD's instruction culminates in observance of the *sabbath* (cf. 56.1–8). For the final formula see 40.5.

59.1–21: The lament of the nation will be answered when the LORD comes to restore those who repent. **1–8:**
The prophet argues that the LORD has the power and the will to restore the nation, but the people have not
yet begun to practice righteousness. **2:** *Hidden his face*, cf. 8.16–17. **3:** *Hands . . . defiled with blood*, cf. 1.18–20. **5:**

⁸ The way of peace they do not know,
  and there is no justice in their paths.
Their roads they have made crooked;
  no one who walks in them knows peace.

⁹ Therefore justice is far from us,
  and righteousness does not reach us;
we wait for light, and lo! there is darkness;
  and for brightness, but we walk in
    gloom.
¹⁰ We grope like the blind along a wall,
  groping like those who have no eyes;
we stumble at noon as in the twilight,
  among the vigorousᵃ as though we were
    dead.
¹¹ We all growl like bears;
  like doves we moan mournfully.
We wait for justice, but there is none;
  for salvation, but it is far from us.
¹² For our transgressions before you are
    many,
  and our sins testify against us.
Our transgressions indeed are with us,
  and we know our iniquities:
¹³ transgressing, and denying the Lord,
  and turning away from following our
    God,
talking oppression and revolt,
  conceiving lying words and uttering
    them from the heart.
¹⁴ Justice is turned back,
  and righteousness stands at a distance;
for truth stumbles in the public square,
  and uprightness cannot enter.
¹⁵ Truth is lacking,
  and whoever turns from evil is
    despoiled.

The Lord saw it, and it displeased him
  that there was no justice.
¹⁶ He saw that there was no one,

and was appalled that there was no one
    to intervene;
so his own arm brought him victory,
  and his righteousness upheld him.
¹⁷ He put on righteousness like a
    breastplate,
  and a helmet of salvation on his
    head;
he put on garments of vengeance for
    clothing,
  and wrapped himself in fury as in a
    mantle.
¹⁸ According to their deeds, so will he
    repay;
  wrath to his adversaries, requital to his
    enemies;
to the coastlands he will render
    requital.
¹⁹ So those in the west shall fear the name
    of the Lord,
  and those in the east, his glory;
for he will come like a pent-up stream
  that the wind of the Lord drives on.

²⁰ And he will come to Zion as Redeemer,
  to those in Jacob who turn from
    transgression, says the Lord.
²¹ And as for me, this is my covenant with
them, says the Lord: my spirit that is upon
you, and my words that I have put in your
mouth, shall not depart out of your mouth,
or out of the mouths of your children,
or out of the mouths of your children's
children, says the Lord, from now on and
forever.

60 Arise, shine; for your light has come,
and the glory of the Lord has risen
upon you.

ᵃ Meaning of Heb uncertain

Adders and *spiders* are poisonous and represent sins that destroy the wicked (cf. Pss 58.3–4; 140.1–3). **9–15a**: A communal confession of sin, though only v. 12 is addressed to God (cf. Pss 51.5; 90.8). The passage appears to be a meditation on 8.16–23, which portrays divine absence and the people groping in darkness. **15b–21**: The Lord prepares to come in judgment on seeing that there is no justice. **17**: The Lord's justice is described metaphorically as armor that a warrior puts on for battle. **18–20**: When the wicked are punished, Zion will be redeemed (cf. 1.27–28). **21**: A promise of prophetic guidance (cf. 53.10; 61.1–4).

60.1–62.12: Proclamation of restoration for the nation. These chapters have strong similarities of content and style with chs 40–55. **60.1–9**: Zion's restoration, the return of the glory of the Lord, and the approach of the nations bearing gifts. As before, Zion is imaged as a woman (cf. 49.4; 52.1–2,7–12; 54.1–17). **1**: *Arise, shine,* see 51.17; 52.1–2; and cf. 2.2–4; 8.23. **1b–2**: *The glory of the Lord* is described as it was in the wilderness tabernacle (Ex

² For darkness shall cover the earth,
   and thick darkness the peoples;
but the LORD will arise upon you,
   and his glory will appear over you.
³ Nations shall come to your light,
   and kings to the brightness of your
      dawn.

⁴ Lift up your eyes and look around;
   they all gather together, they come to
      you;
your sons shall come from far away,
   and your daughters shall be carried on
      their nurses' arms.
⁵ Then you shall see and be radiant;
   your heart shall thrill and rejoice,ᵃ
because the abundance of the sea shall be
   brought to you,
   the wealth of the nations shall come to
      you.
⁶ A multitude of camels shall cover you,
   the young camels of Midian and Ephah;
   all those from Sheba shall come.
They shall bring gold and frankincense,
   and shall proclaim the praise of the
      LORD.
⁷ All the flocks of Kedar shall be gathered
   to you,
   the rams of Nebaioth shall minister to
      you;
they shall be acceptable on my altar,
   and I will glorify my glorious house.

⁸ Who are these that fly like a cloud,
   and like doves to their windows?
⁹ For the coastlands shall wait for me,
   the ships of Tarshish first,
to bring your children from far away,
   their silver and gold with them,
for the name of the LORD your God,
   and for the Holy One of Israel,

because he has glorified you.
¹⁰ Foreigners shall build up your walls,
   and their kings shall minister to you;
for in my wrath I struck you down,
   but in my favor I have had mercy on
      you.
¹¹ Your gates shall always be open;
   day and night they shall not be shut,
so that nations shall bring you their
   wealth,
   with their kings led in procession.
¹² For the nation and kingdom
   that will not serve you shall perish;
   those nations shall be utterly laid waste.
¹³ The glory of Lebanon shall come to you,
   the cypress, the plane, and the pine,
to beautify the place of my sanctuary;
   and I will glorify where my feet rest.
¹⁴ The descendants of those who oppressed
   you
shall come bending low to you,
and all who despised you
   shall bow down at your feet;
they shall call you the City of the LORD,
   the Zion of the Holy One of Israel.
¹⁵ Whereas you have been forsaken and
   hated,
   with no one passing through,
I will make you majestic forever,
   a joy from age to age.
¹⁶ You shall suck the milk of nations,
   you shall suck the breasts of kings;
and you shall know that I, the LORD, am
   your Savior
   and your Redeemer, the Mighty One of
      Jacob.

¹⁷ Instead of bronze I will bring gold,
   instead of iron I will bring silver;

ᵃ   Heb *be enlarged*

40.34–38), the Jerusalem Temple (1 Kings 8.1–13), and the restored Zion (4.2–5). **3**: The approach of the nations echoes the procession to Zion in 2.2–4. **4**: Dispersed Judeans will return, assisted by Gentiles (also 49.12; 51.9–11; 60.8–9; 66.20). **5–9**: Foreigners will bring gifts to honor the LORD (cf. 45.14,22–23; 60.11,16; Zeph 3.9–10; Hag 2.1–9). **6–7**: The Arabian kingdoms *Midian* (Ex 2.15), *Ephah* (Gen 25.4), *Sheba* (Gen 10.17; 1 Kings 10.1–13), *Kedar* (Isa 21.13–17; Jer 49.28–29), and *Nebaioth* (Gen 25.13). **9**: *Coastlands,* the islands of the Aegean. *Tarshish,* either in southern Turkey (later Tarsus) or in southern Spain. **10–22**: Whereas the nations in the past were brought by the LORD for Zion's punishment, now they will come to submit to her and to sustain her. **13**: *Lebanon* was known for its tall trees that were prized throughout the ancient Near East for splendid building projects, including the Jerusalem Temple (2.13; 1 Kings 5.8–10). The place where the LORD's feet rest is the Holy of Holies of the Temple where the ark of the covenant served as the footstool for the LORD's throne (cf. 66.1). **16**: *The breasts of kings,* a

instead of wood, bronze,
  instead of stones, iron.
I will appoint Peace as your overseer
  and Righteousness as your taskmaster.
¹⁸ Violence shall no more be heard in your
      land,
  devastation or destruction within your
      borders;
you shall call your walls Salvation,
  and your gates Praise.
¹⁹ The sun shall no longer be
  your light by day,
nor for brightness shall the moon
  give light to you by night;ª
but the LORD will be your everlasting
      light,
  and your God will be your glory.
²⁰ Your sun shall no more go down,
  or your moon withdraw itself;
for the LORD will be your everlasting light,
  and your days of mourning shall be
      ended.
²¹ Your people shall all be righteous;
  they shall possess the land forever.
They are the shoot that I planted, the work
      of my hands,
  so that I might be glorified.
²² The least of them shall become a clan,
  and the smallest one a mighty nation;
I am the LORD;
  in its time I will accomplish it quickly.

61

The spirit of the Lord GOD is upon me,
  because the LORD has anointed me;
he has sent me to bring good news to the
      oppressed,
  to bind up the brokenhearted,
to proclaim liberty to the captives,
  and release to the prisoners;
² to proclaim the year of the LORD's
      favor,
  and the day of vengeance of our God;
  to comfort all who mourn;

³ to provide for those who mourn in
      Zion—
  to give them a garland instead of ashes,
the oil of gladness instead of mourning,
  the mantle of praise instead of a faint
      spirit.
They will be called oaks of righteousness,
  the planting of the LORD, to display his
      glory.
⁴ They shall build up the ancient ruins,
  they shall raise up the former
      devastations;
they shall repair the ruined cities,
  the devastations of many generations.

⁵ Strangers shall stand and feed your
      flocks,
  foreigners shall till your land and dress
      your vines;
⁶ but you shall be called priests of the
      LORD,
  you shall be named ministers of our
      God;
you shall enjoy the wealth of the
      nations,
  and in their riches you shall glory.
⁷ Because theirᵇ shame was double,
  and dishonor was proclaimed as their
      lot,
therefore they shall possess a double
      portion;
  everlasting joy shall be theirs.

⁸ For I the LORD love justice,
  I hate robbery and wrongdoing;ᶜ
I will faithfully give them their
      recompense,
  and I will make an everlasting covenant
      with them.

ª QMs Gk Old Latin Tg: MT lacks *by night*
ᵇ Heb *your*
ᶜ Or *robbery with a burnt offering*

metaphor for the nations' sustenance of Zion. **21:** *The shoot that I planted,* cf. 6.12–13; 11.1–16. **22:** The concluding statements recall the promise of both land and a numerous posterity to the ancestors (Gen 12.1–3; 15.5–6,17–21; 17.1–8; 28.10–15; 35.9–15). **61.1–7:** This passage presupposes the persona of the servant from Second Isaiah (cf. 42.1–4; 49.1–6; 50.4–11; 52.13–53.12). **1–2:** The imagery evokes the priestly proclamation of a year of jubilee or re-lease from debt (Lev 25.8–17). The year of jubilee was observed every fiftieth year as a means to forgive debt and to return land and property to its ancestral owners. It is applied here to the return of Zion to its exiled people. **3b:** *Oaks of righteousness, the planting of the LORD,* see 6.12–13; 11.1–9; cf. 5.1–7; 27.2–6. **6:** The people of Israel will serve as priests to the nations (cf. Ex 19.6). Their double portion recalls Zion's double punishment (40.2). **8–9:**

9 Their descendants shall be known among
the nations,
and their offspring among the peoples;
all who see them shall acknowledge
that they are a people whom the LORD
has blessed.
10 I will greatly rejoice in the LORD,
my whole being shall exult in my God;
for he has clothed me with the garments of
salvation,
he has covered me with the robe of
righteousness,
as a bridegroom decks himself with a
garland,
and as a bride adorns herself with her
jewels.
11 For as the earth brings forth its shoots,
and as a garden causes what is sown in
it to spring up,
so the Lord GOD will cause righteousness
and praise
to spring up before all the nations.

62 For Zion's sake I will not keep silent,
and for Jerusalem's sake I will not rest,
until her vindication shines out like the
dawn,
and her salvation like a burning torch.
2 The nations shall see your vindication,
and all the kings your glory;
and you shall be called by a new name
that the mouth of the LORD will give.
3 You shall be a crown of beauty in the
hand of the LORD,
and a royal diadem in the hand of your
God.
4 You shall no more be termed Forsaken,a
and your land shall no more be termed
Desolate;b
but you shall be called My Delight Is in Her,c

and your land Married;d
for the LORD delights in you,
and your land shall be married.
5 For as a young man marries a young
woman,
so shall your buildere marry you,
and as the bridegroom rejoices over the
bride,
so shall your God rejoice over you.
6 Upon your walls, O Jerusalem,
I have posted sentinels;
all day and all night
they shall never be silent.
You who remind the LORD,
take no rest,
7 and give him no rest
until he establishes Jerusalem
and makes it renowned throughout the
earth.
8 The LORD has sworn by his right hand
and by his mighty arm:
I will not again give your grain
to be food for your enemies,
and foreigners shall not drink the wine
for which you have labored;
9 but those who garner it shall eat it
and praise the LORD,
and those who gather it shall drink it
in my holy courts.

10 Go through, go through the gates,
prepare the way for the people;
build up, build up the highway,
clear it of stones,

a Heb *Azubah*
b Heb *Shemamah*
c Heb *Hephzibah*
d Heb *Beulah*
e Cn: Heb *your sons*

An everlasting covenant with the restored people of Zion (cf. 54.9–10). **61.10–62.12:** Joy at the LORD's restoration of Zion (61.10–11). Just as Zion is dressed as a bride (52.12; 54.11–14) and the LORD is dressed in the armor of righteousness to redeem Zion (59.16–21), so the prophet now dresses for the wedding that will celebrate the reunion of the LORD and Zion. The imagery of growing shoots symbolizes the restoration (cf. 6.12–13; 11.1–9). **62.1–12:** The bridal imagery confirms Zion's restored status. Whereas the nations were appalled at the sight of the servant (52.13–53.12), now they will witness the emergence of a beautiful Zion. **3:** The *crown of beauty* also symbolizes the restored walls of the city (4.2; 28.5–6). **4:** *No more be termed Forsaken . . . Desolate*, cf. 54.1,6. **5:** The builder is now the LORD in contrast to 44.28 where it was Cyrus acting on behalf of the LORD. **6–9:** The task of the sentinels or watchers is to ensure that the LORD keeps the divine promise to restore Zion. The image is based in part on the armed guards of a city, but it also presupposes the role of the priestly gatekeepers who ensured the sanctity of the Temple and its holy courts (1 Chr 9.17–27; 26.1–19; cf. 2 Kings 11.4–8). **10–12:** Once again

lift up an ensign over the peoples.
¹¹ The LORD has proclaimed
    to the end of the earth:
Say to daughter Zion,
    "See, your salvation comes;
his reward is with him,
    and his recompense before him."
¹² They shall be called, "The Holy People,
    The Redeemed of the LORD";
and you shall be called, "Sought Out,
    A City Not Forsaken."

63 "Who is this that comes from Edom,
    from Bozrah in garments stained
        crimson?
Who is this so splendidly robed,
    marching in his great might?"

"It is I, announcing vindication,
    mighty to save."

² "Why are your robes red,
    and your garments like theirs who tread
        the wine press?"

³ "I have trodden the wine press alone,
    and from the peoples no one was with
        me;
I trod them in my anger
    and trampled them in my wrath;
their juice spattered on my garments,
    and stained all my robes.
⁴ For the day of vengeance was in my heart,
    and the year for my redeeming work
        had come.

⁵ I looked, but there was no helper;
    I stared, but there was no one to sustain
        me;
so my own arm brought me victory,
    and my wrath sustained me.
⁶ I trampled down peoples in my anger,
    I crushed them in my wrath,
    and I poured out their lifeblood on the
        earth."

⁷ I will recount the gracious deeds of the
        LORD,
    the praiseworthy acts of the LORD,
because of all that the LORD has done
    for us,
    and the great favor to the house of
        Israel
that he has shown them according to his
        mercy,
    according to the abundance of his
        steadfast love.
⁸ For he said, "Surely they are my people,
    children who will not deal falsely";
and he became their savior
⁹ in all their distress.
It was no messengerᵃ or angel
    but his presence that saved them;ᵇ
in his love and in his pity he redeemed them;
    he lifted them up and carried them all
        the days of old.

ᵃ Gk: Heb *anguish*
ᵇ Or *savior. ⁹In all their distress he was distressed; the*
    angel of his presence saved them;

the prophet calls for the people to go out (48.20–22), to prepare the *highway* (11.15; 27.12–13; 35.1–10; 40.3–5), and to raise the *ensign* (Heb "nes"; cf. 11.10; 49.22) to proclaim Zion's restoration.

63.1–66.24: The prophet's instruction concerning the process of Zion's restoration. The final unit of Third Isaiah and the book as a whole focuses on the means by which the LORD will judge the wicked before the ideal restoration can be achieved. Such a view attempts to explain why the ideals of the book have not yet been achieved (e.g., 2.2–4; 9.1–7; 11.1–16) by charging that some among the people are wicked rather than by raising questions about the LORD's ability to bring about the restoration.

63.1–6: Vengeance on Edom. During the sixth through the fourth centuries BCE, Edom disintegrated as it was displaced by Arabian tribal groups that formed the Nabatean kingdom. The Isaian oracle explains the Edomite decline as a deliberate act of the LORD (cf. ch 34). **1:** *Edom* is located southeast of the Dead Sea and the Negeb regions of Judah. *Bozrah*, a key city in Edom. **2–3:** The prophet employs the imagery of treading wine to depict the LORD's blood-splattered clothing. Now that the vineyard has been restored (27.2–6), the harvest metaphorically begins. **4–6:** The LORD's day of vengeance builds upon the Day of the LORD tradition in Isaiah when evil is defeated (2.10–21; 13.6–22; 34.8–17; 61.2).

63.7–64.12: A psalm of communal lamentation. 7–9: Recollection of Israel's deliverance from Egypt. See Ex 23.20, which asserts that an angel would lead Israel through the wilderness. In Ex 13.17–21, however, the LORD,

¹⁰ But they rebelled
  and grieved his holy spirit;
therefore he became their enemy;
  he himself fought against them.
¹¹ Then they^a remembered the days of old,
  of Moses his servant.^b
Where is the one who brought them up
  out of the sea
  with the shepherds of his flock?
Where is the one who put within them
  his holy spirit,
¹² who caused his glorious arm
  to march at the right hand of Moses,
who divided the waters before them
  to make for himself an everlasting name,
  ¹³ who led them through the depths?
Like a horse in the desert,
  they did not stumble.
¹⁴ Like cattle that go down into the valley,
  the spirit of the LORD gave them rest.
Thus you led your people,
  to make for yourself a glorious name.
¹⁵ Look down from heaven and see,
  from your holy and glorious habitation.
Where are your zeal and your might?
  The yearning of your heart and your
    compassion?
  They are withheld from me.
¹⁶ For you are our father,
  though Abraham does not know us
  and Israel does not acknowledge us;
you, O LORD, are our father;
  our Redeemer from of old is your name.
¹⁷ Why, O LORD, do you make us stray from
    your ways
  and harden our heart, so that we do not
    fear you?
Turn back for the sake of your servants,
  for the sake of the tribes that are your
    heritage.
¹⁸ Your holy people took possession for a
    little while;
  but now our adversaries have trampled
    down your sanctuary.

¹⁹ We have long been like those whom you
    do not rule,
  like those not called by your name.

64 O that you would tear open the
  heavens and come down,
  so that the mountains would quake at
    your presence—
² ^cas when fire kindles brushwood
  and the fire causes water to boil—
to make your name known to your
    adversaries,
  so that the nations might tremble at
    your presence!
³ When you did awesome deeds that we
    did not expect,
  you came down, the mountains quaked
    at your presence.
⁴ From ages past no one has heard,
  no ear has perceived,
no eye has seen any God besides you,
  who works for those who wait for
    him.
⁵ You meet those who gladly do right,
  those who remember you in your
    ways.
But you were angry, and we sinned;
  because you hid yourself we
    transgressed.^d
⁶ We have all become like one who is
    unclean,
  and all our righteous deeds are like a
    filthy cloth.
We all fade like a leaf,
  and our iniquities, like the wind, take
    us away.
⁷ There is no one who calls on your name,
  or attempts to take hold of you;

---

^a Heb *he*
^b Cn: Heb *his people*
^c Ch 64.1 in Heb
^d Meaning of Heb uncertain

---

symbolized as the pillar of smoke and fire, leads the nation. **10**: *But they rebelled*, i.e., in the wilderness; see Ex 32–34; Num 11–25. **15–19**: Direct appeal for the LORD to *look down* and *see*. **17**: The prophet takes up the motif of the hardened heart, applied to Pharaoh in the Exodus tradition (Ex 7.3–5; cf. Isa 6.9–10) to demand that the LORD cease afflicting Israel. **18**: The trampling of the sanctuary would refer to the Babylonian destruction of the Jerusalem Temple. **64.1–3**: A direct appeal to God, characteristic of the lament psalms, to intervene, to appear in power as in the days of old (cf. Ex 19.16–18; Judg 5.4–5; Ps 68.7–8; Hab 3.3–15). **5b–7**: The prophet reiterates the LORD's anger and hidden face from the people (cf. 8.16–17). Having been ravaged, the nation has now become

for you have hidden your face from us,
    and have delivered[a] us into the hand of
        our iniquity.
⁸ Yet, O Lord, you are our Father;
    we are the clay, and you are our potter;
    we are all the work of your hand.
⁹ Do not be exceedingly angry, O Lord,
    and do not remember iniquity forever.
    Now consider, we are all your people.
¹⁰ Your holy cities have become a
        wilderness,
    Zion has become a wilderness,
    Jerusalem a desolation.
¹¹ Our holy and beautiful house,
    where our ancestors praised you,
has been burned by fire,
    and all our pleasant places have become
        ruins.
¹² After all this, will you restrain yourself,
        O Lord?
    Will you keep silent, and punish us so
        severely?

65 I was ready to be sought out by those
        who did not ask,
    to be found by those who did not seek
        me.
I said, "Here I am, here I am,"
    to a nation that did not call on my
        name.
² I held out my hands all day long
    to a rebellious people,
who walk in a way that is not good,
    following their own devices;
³ a people who provoke me
    to my face continually,
sacrificing in gardens
    and offering incense on bricks;
⁴ who sit inside tombs,
    and spend the night in secret places;
who eat swine's flesh,

with broth of abominable things in
        their vessels;
⁵ who say, "Keep to yourself,
    do not come near me, for I am too holy
        for you."
These are a smoke in my nostrils,
    a fire that burns all day long.
⁶ See, it is written before me:
    I will not keep silent, but I will repay;
I will indeed repay into their laps
    ⁷ their[b] iniquities and their[b] ancestors'
        iniquities together,
                    says the Lord;
because they offered incense on the
        mountains
    and reviled me on the hills,
I will measure into their laps
    full payment for their actions.
⁸ Thus says the Lord:
As the wine is found in the cluster,
    and they say, "Do not destroy it,
    for there is a blessing in it,"
so I will do for my servants' sake,
    and not destroy them all.
⁹ I will bring forth descendants[c] from
        Jacob,
    and from Judah inheritors[d] of my
        mountains;
my chosen shall inherit it,
    and my servants shall settle there.
¹⁰ Sharon shall become a pasture for flocks,
    and the Valley of Achor a place for
        herds to lie down,
    for my people who have sought me.
¹¹ But you who forsake the Lord,
    who forget my holy mountain,

a Gk Syr Old Latin Tg: Heb *melted*
b Gk Syr: Heb *your*
c Or *a descendant*
d Or *an inheritor*

impure. No one calls upon the Lord because the Lord is the source of Israel's punishment. **8–12:** A final appeal for the Lord to cease the divine silence and the punishment of the nation. Now that the Temple is destroyed, the Lord's relationship with the nation is in jeopardy. **8:** *Clay . . . potter,* cf. 29.16; 45.9.

65.1–66.24: The Lord's answer. The passage attempts to explain the failure of the nation to attain the ideals stated in the book by charging that evil still exists among the people. **1–7:** The people rejected the Lord despite the Lord's readiness to be sought. **3–4:** *Sacrificing in gardens,* non-Israelite fertility rituals practiced in gardens (cf. 1.28–31; 66.17). A list of abominations follows, such as tomb rituals to worship or consult the dead (Deut 18.11–12) and the eating of swine's flesh (66.17; Deut 14.8). **8–25:** The seed of Jacob will be restored in the new creation on Zion, but the wicked will be destroyed. **9:** The descendants of both *Jacob* (northern Israel) and *Judah* will be restored in keeping with the Lord's covenant. **10:** *Sharon,*

who set a table for Fortune
  and fill cups of mixed wine for Destiny;
¹² I will destine you to the sword,
  and all of you shall bow down to the
    slaughter;
because, when I called, you did not
    answer,
  when I spoke, you did not listen,
but you did what was evil in my sight,
  and chose what I did not delight in.
¹³ Therefore thus says the Lord GOD:
My servants shall eat,
  but you shall be hungry;
my servants shall drink,
  but you shall be thirsty;
my servants shall rejoice,
  but you shall be put to shame;
¹⁴ my servants shall sing for gladness of
    heart,
  but you shall cry out for pain of heart,
  and shall wail for anguish of spirit.
¹⁵ You shall leave your name to my chosen
    to use as a curse,
  and the Lord GOD will put you to death;
  but to his servants he will give a
    different name.
¹⁶ Then whoever invokes a blessing in the
    land
  shall bless by the God of faithfulness,
and whoever takes an oath in the land
  shall swear by the God of faithfulness;
because the former troubles are
    forgotten
  and are hidden from my sight.

¹⁷ For I am about to create new heavens
  and a new earth;
the former things shall not be remembered
  or come to mind.

¹⁸ But be glad and rejoice forever
  in what I am creating;
for I am about to create Jerusalem as a joy,
  and its people as a delight.
¹⁹ I will rejoice in Jerusalem,
  and delight in my people;
no more shall the sound of weeping be
    heard in it,
  or the cry of distress.
²⁰ No more shall there be in it
  an infant that lives but a few days,
  or an old person who does not live out
    a lifetime;
for one who dies at a hundred years will be
    considered a youth,
  and one who falls short of a hundred
    will be considered accursed.
²¹ They shall build houses and inhabit
    them;
  they shall plant vineyards and eat their
    fruit.
²² They shall not build and another
    inhabit;
  they shall not plant and another eat;
for like the days of a tree shall the days of
    my people be,
  and my chosen shall long enjoy the
    work of their hands.
²³ They shall not labor in vain,
  or bear children for calamity;[a]
for they shall be offspring blessed by the
    LORD—
  and their descendants as well.
²⁴ Before they call I will answer,
  while they are yet speaking I will hear.
²⁵ The wolf and the lamb shall feed
    together,

---

a Or *sudden terror*

---

the coastal plain south of Akko and the Carmel, formerly desolate (33.9), and *Achor*, the barren valley south of Jericho and west of the Dead Sea (Josh 7.24; Hos 2.15), will both become fertile pastureland. The border regions of Israel will be secure. **11–12:** *Fortune* and *Destiny*, Heb "Gad" and "Meni," deities of fate and good luck venerated among Syrians, Arabs, and Nabateans. **13–16:** The contrasting fates of the wicked and the LORD's servants, i.e., those who are righteous. **15–16:** The names of the reprobate will serve as a curse, like the names of the prophets Ahab and Zedekiah executed by the Babylonians (Jer 29.22). The giving of a new name signifies a new status (43.1,7; 44.1–5; 62.2). **17–25:** The new heavens and earth essentially constitutes a new creation. Insofar as the Temple was the holy center of creation, its destruction and rebuilding entailed a new creation. Life in the restored land will be idyllic. **17b:** *Former things,* 43.18. **20:** The prediction of vastly increased life expectancy connotes a return to the original creation (cf. Gen 5). **21–23:** The future Israel will witness the reversal of familiar curses attached to treaties and covenants; see 62.8–9; Deut 28.30. **22:** *Days of a tree,* cf. 6.12–13; Job 14.7–9. **23:** The imagery of successful childbirth reverses that employed to describe

the lion shall eat straw like the ox;
    but the serpent—its food shall be dust!
They shall not hurt or destroy
    on all my holy mountain,
                says the Lord.

66 Thus says the Lord:
    Heaven is my throne
    and the earth is my footstool;
what is the house that you would build
    for me,
    and what is my resting place?
² All these things my hand has made,
    and so all these things are mine,ᵃ
                says the Lord.
But this is the one to whom I will look,
    to the humble and contrite in spirit,
    who trembles at my word.

³ Whoever slaughters an ox is like one who
    kills a human being;
    whoever sacrifices a lamb, like one who
    breaks a dog's neck;
whoever presents a grain offering, like one
    who offers swine's blood;ᵇ
    whoever makes a memorial offering
        of frankincense, like one who
        blesses an idol.
These have chosen their own ways,
    and in their abominations they take
        delight;
⁴ I also will choose to mockᶜ them,
    and bring upon them what they fear;
because, when I called, no one answered,
    when I spoke, they did not listen;
but they did what was evil in my sight,
    and chose what did not please me.
⁵ Hear the word of the Lord,
    you who tremble at his word:
Your own people who hate you
    and reject you for my name's sake

have said, "Let the Lord be glorified,
    so that we may see your joy";
    but it is they who shall be put to
        shame.

⁶ Listen, an uproar from the city!
    A voice from the temple!
The voice of the Lord,
    dealing retribution to his enemies!

⁷ Before she was in labor
    she gave birth;
before her pain came upon her
    she delivered a son.
⁸ Who has heard of such a thing?
    Who has seen such things?
Shall a land be born in one day?
    Shall a nation be delivered in one
        moment?
Yet as soon as Zion was in labor
    she delivered her children.
⁹ Shall I open the womb and not deliver?
    says the Lord;
shall I, the one who delivers, shut the
    womb?
    says your God.

¹⁰ Rejoice with Jerusalem, and be glad for
    her,
    all you who love her;
rejoice with her in joy,
    all you who mourn over her—
¹¹ that you may nurse and be satisfied
    from her consoling breast;
that you may drink deeply with delight
    from her glorious bosom.

ᵃ Gk Syr: Heb *these things came to be*
ᵇ Meaning of Heb uncertain
ᶜ Or *to punish*

the Day of the Lord (13.8; cf. 26.17–18). **24–25:** The idyllic portrayal of predators at peace with prey is drawn from 11.6–9.

66.1–24: Restoration for the righteous. **1–4:** The Temple (*house*) only symbolizes the divine reality of the Lord's sovereignty (see 1 Kings 8.27). A saying directed against false understandings and expectations associated with the Jerusalem Temple and its sacrificial worship, rather than against the Temple as such or the project of rebuilding. Without an attitude of humility, sacrifice and offerings are of no use (cf. 1.10–17); see also 65.3–4n. **6:** The judgment to come has its source in the Temple; cf. Joel 3.16; Am 1.2. **7–9:** Here miraculously easy childbirth symbolizes the downfall of the old world and the rise of the new (contrast 13.8; 26.17–18; 37.3). **10–14:** The imagery of the rejoicing Jerusalem extends the metaphor of childbirth to the portrayal of a nursing mother (cf. 54.1–17). *River . . . overflowing stream*, now an image of prosperity; contrast 8.6–8, which portrays the Assyrian

[12] For thus says the LORD:
I will extend prosperity to her like a river,
and the wealth of the nations like an
overflowing stream;
and you shall nurse and be carried on her
arm,
and dandled on her knees.
[13] As a mother comforts her child,
so I will comfort you;
you shall be comforted in Jerusalem.
[14] You shall see, and your heart shall
rejoice;
your bodies[a] shall flourish like the
grass;
and it shall be known that the hand of the
LORD is with his servants,
and his indignation is against his
enemies.
[15] For the LORD will come in fire,
and his chariots like the whirlwind,
to pay back his anger in fury,
and his rebuke in flames of fire.
[16] For by fire will the LORD execute
judgment,
and by his sword, on all flesh;
and those slain by the LORD shall be
many.

[17] Those who sanctify and purify themselves to go into the gardens, following the
one in the center, eating the flesh of pigs,
vermin, and rodents, shall come to an end
together, says the LORD.

[18] For I know[b] their works and their
thoughts, and I am[c] coming to gather all nations and tongues; and they shall come and
shall see my glory, [19] and I will set a sign among
them. From them I will send survivors to the
nations, to Tarshish, Put,[d] and Lud—which
draw the bow—to Tubal and Javan, to the
coastlands far away that have not heard of my
fame or seen my glory; and they shall declare
my glory among the nations. [20] They shall
bring all your kindred from all the nations
as an offering to the LORD, on horses, and in
chariots, and in litters, and on mules, and on
dromedaries, to my holy mountain Jerusalem,
says the LORD, just as the Israelites bring a
grain offering in a clean vessel to the house of
the LORD. [21] And I will also take some of them
as priests and as Levites, says the LORD.

[22] For as the new heavens and the new
earth,
which I will make,
shall remain before me, says the LORD;
so shall your descendants and your
name remain.
[23] From new moon to new moon,
and from sabbath to sabbath,
all flesh shall come to worship before me,
says the LORD.

[24] And they shall go out and look at the
dead bodies of the people who have rebelled
against me; for their worm shall not die, their
fire shall not be quenched, and they shall be
an abhorrence to all flesh.

a   Heb *bones*
b   Gk Syr: Heb lacks *know*
c   Gk Syr Vg Tg: Heb *it is*
d   Gk: Heb *Pul*

onslaught as a flood that will inundate the land. **15–24**: Judgment and new creation at Zion. **15–16**: Theophanies
and scenarios of judgment often feature fire (26.11; 29.5–6; 30.27,33; 31.9; 33.12,14; 34.10) and the LORD's sword
(27.1; 31.8; 34.5–7). **17**: See 65.3–4n. **18–21**: The gathering of the nations at Zion recalls 2.2–4. *Tarshish*, either
later Tarsus in southern Turkey, or Tartessus in Spain; *Put*, in Libya; *Lud*, Lydia in Asia Minor; *Tubal*, also in Asia
Minor; *Javan*, Greece or Ionia. Those taken to be *priests* and *Levites* are drawn from the returned exiles, not from
the nations. **22–23**: The new creation (cf. 65.15–16) is declared permanent, like the old creation (Gen 9.8–17). **24**:
The book closes with a portrayal of the fate of the wicked, designed to motivate the audience to identify with
the righteous.

JEREMIAH

NAME AND CANONICAL STATUS

The book of Jeremiah, the second scroll among the major prophets alongside Isaiah and Ezekiel, is a compilation of prophetic oracles edited by members of the Deuteronomistic school and attributed to the prophet by that name. For the different placement of the prophets in Hebrew and Christian Bibles see the essay on "The Canons of the Bible."

HISTORICAL CONTEXT

Jeremiah lived during the critical years spanning the "golden age" of the Judean king Josiah (640–609 BCE) and the subsequent fall and destruction of Jerusalem and the deportations of the Judean population into captivity (597–586 BCE), all at the hand of Nebuchadrezzar II of Babylon. Some scholars think that Jeremiah was born in 627 BCE and began his prophetic ministry only in 609 BCE following the death of King Josiah. The traditional assumption, however, suggested by the text itself and followed here, is that he began his ministry in 627 BCE (Jer 25.3) and prophesied until well after the deportation of 586 BCE and the subsequent murder of Gedaliah and flight of a major group of Judeans to Egypt. Jeremiah, along with his friend and scribal colleague Baruch, was forcibly taken by this group as a hostage to Egypt, where he is last heard speaking judgment oracles against the community in the years following 586 BCE.

Jeremiah was born during the final years of the reign of King Manasseh (ca. 645 BCE) and began his ministry during the initial period of Josiah's reform movement. At this time the youthful king Josiah was rejecting the "accommodationist" pro-Assyrian policies of his early advisers and beginning to flex his ambitious nationalistic policies directed against his Assyrian overlords and toward the reunification of Israel and Judah (2 Chr 34.1–7). As a part of these ambitious political goals, Josiah's thoroughgoing religious reform movement attempted to remove the syncretistic elements of the accommodationist rituals, purge worship of non-Yahwistic practices and elements, and reunify the country around the central power-base of Jerusalem, similar to the goals of the reform movement of his great-grandfather, Hezekiah (2 Kings 18.1–8). Jeremiah, deeply steeped in the Deuteronomistic tradition of many of the prophets, was likely an early advocate of Josiah's reform, and Jeremiah held Josiah in esteem as an exemplar of the righteous king (Jer 22.15–16), a view shared with the Deuteronomistic Historians (2 Kings 22.2; 23.25).

Josiah was killed in an adventurous and risky military move against Egypt in 609 BCE (see 22.10n.), and the reform almost certainly collapsed. By 605 Babylon was clearly in control of Palestine and the last kings of Judah—Jehoiakim, Jehoiachin, and Zedekiah—were unable to avoid the awful results of Babylonian expansionism. Jehoiakim joined in a revolt against the Babylonians in 601 BCE, which led to a Babylonian invasion and the first deportation of 597 BCE. His uncle, Zedekiah, tried to walk a narrow line between the various political factions demanding attention at the Jerusalem court, but he too eventually joined a revolt, leading to the final destruction of Jerusalem at the hand of the Babylonians in 586 and the second deportation of its population.

Jeremiah was from the town of Anathoth in Benjamin. He may therefore have belonged to the disaffected priestly clan of Abiathar, which had lost its Temple privileges centuries earlier when King Solomon consolidated his power and had his potential adversaries—who had supported his brother Adonijah's claims to the throne—either eliminated or exiled (1 Kings 1.5–2.46). As part of this consolidation, Solomon promoted the priestly family of Zadok, who supported him in the succession. With the Temple firmly in Zadokite priestly hands, the descendents of Abiathar languished in rural sites, which themselves were eventually shut down during the reforms of Hezekiah and Josiah. As one of those descendents, Jeremiah may have been heir to sentiments that ran deeply in favor of the old tribal traditions and values and in opposition to the "Jerusalemite" policies predominant since the reign of Solomon.

JOSIAH (640–609 BCE)

SHALLUM (609; elsewhere usually called Jehoahaz)

JEHOIAKIM (608–598; elsewhere also called Eliakim)

JEHOIACHIN (597; also called Jeconiah and Coniah)

First Babylonian Siege of Jerusalem (597)

ZEDEKIAH (597–586; elsewhere also called Mattaniah)

Fall of Jerusalem (586)

NOTE: Dates are for reigns, not life spans. Dashed lines indicate genealogy.

The last kings of Judah in the book of Jeremiah.

STRUCTURE AND CONTENTS OF THE BOOK

The book of Jeremiah was edited into three major cycles of oracles and traditions. Each cycle is more-or-less chronologically ordered, and each is concluded by a reference to the creation of the scroll of 605 BCE, written at the dictation of Jeremiah by his scribal colleague, Baruch. References to this scroll are found in chs 25, 36, and 45, and these references divide the book into its constitutive cycles. It is often assumed that the scroll produced at this time (the second scroll, Jer 36.32) formed the core of oracles now found in the first cycle, chs 1–24. The book concludes with a compilation of "oracles against the nations" in chs 46–51. The book of Jeremiah is unique in many regards, but especially because the Greek tradition differs from the Hebrew tradition in this book more than in any other. A major difference is that the Greek tradition (the Septuagint) locates the "oracles against the nations" not at the end of the book but rather immediately following an appropriate reference to "this book" at 25.13. This and other differences between the Hebrew and Greek traditions has convinced many scholars that the Greek tradition preserves earlier and better traditions concerning the oracles, the language of the text, and the character of Jeremiah. Both of these textual traditions are attested among the Hebrew biblical texts found at Qumran (the Dead Sea Scrolls), indicating that the book of Jeremiah had a fluid editorial history.

INTERPRETATION

Jeremiah's message was closely related to the core values of the Deuteronomic tradition. A virulent antipathy toward "foreign gods," especially the Canaanite Baal, is combined with a fierce devotion to the ethics and mores of Deuteronomy's humanitarian program. Jeremiah shares the basic commitments and outlook of the Deuteronomistic History, even though the prophet is never mentioned in that history. Central to this outlook is the conviction that the disastrous political events leading to the destruction of Jerusalem and the exile of its population were a direct result of divine anger at Israel's continued apostasy. The figure of Jeremiah became the subject of fascination in later history, as represented already in the Chronicler's history (2 Chr 35.25; 36.12,21–22) as well as in the books of Daniel (9.2) and in deuterocanonical traditions (2 Macc 2.1–7; 15.14–15).

GUIDE TO READING

The reader should take care to read each of the three cycles as an independent unit with its own chronological ordering. When beginning a new cycle, be prepared for a chronological displacement that carries the reader back in time. Read the relevant sections of the Deuteronomistic History, especially 2 Kings 21–25, as is appropriate for understanding the political backdrop to the oracles and narratives.

Rodney R. Hutton

1 The words of Jeremiah son of Hilkiah, of the priests who were in Anathoth in the land of Benjamin, ² to whom the word of the LORD came in the days of King Josiah son of Amon of Judah, in the thirteenth year of his reign. ³ It came also in the days of King Jehoiakim son of Josiah of Judah, and until the end of the eleventh year of King Zedekiah son of Josiah of Judah, until the captivity of Jerusalem in the fifth month.

⁴ Now the word of the LORD came to me saying,

⁵ "Before I formed you in the womb I knew you,
and before you were born I consecrated you;
I appointed you a prophet to the nations."
⁶ Then I said, "Ah, Lord GOD! Truly I do not know how to speak, for I am only a boy." ⁷ But the LORD said to me,

"Do not say, 'I am only a boy';
for you shall go to all to whom I send you,
and you shall speak whatever I command you.
⁸ Do not be afraid of them,
for I am with you to deliver you,
says the LORD."

⁹ Then the LORD put out his hand and touched my mouth; and the LORD said to me, "Now I have put my words in your mouth. ¹⁰ See, today I appoint you over nations and over kingdoms,

to pluck up and to pull down,
to destroy and to overthrow,
to build and to plant."

¹¹ The word of the LORD came to me, saying, "Jeremiah, what do you see?" And I said, "I see a branch of an almond tree."ᵃ ¹² Then the LORD said to me, "You have seen well, for I am watchingᵇ over my word to perform it." ¹³ The word of the LORD came to me a second time, saying, "What do you see?" And I said, "I see a boiling pot, tilted away from the north."

¹⁴ Then the LORD said to me: Out of the north disaster shall break out on all the inhabitants of the land. ¹⁵ For now I am calling all the tribes of the kingdoms of the north, says the LORD; and they shall come and all of them shall set their thrones at the

ᵃ Heb shaqed
ᵇ Heb shoqed

1.1–3: **Editor's superscription.** The superscription conforms to those of several of the prophetic books (Hos 1.1; Am 1.1; Mic 1.1; Zeph 1.1) and probably represents a stage in the gathering and editing of the books of the prophets as a whole. 1: *Priests . . . in Anathoth*, see the introduction. The *land of Benjamin* lay immediately north of Judah, and Anathoth was located about 3 mi (5 km) north of Jerusalem. 2: *Thirteenth year.* 627 BCE (see 25.3), taken by most to be the year when Jeremiah began his public ministry, one year after the reform movement of King Josiah of Judah began (2 Chr 34.3). 3: *Eleventh year of King Zedekiah*, 587 BCE. *In the fifth month* recalls the burning of the Temple and the razing of Jerusalem by the invading Babylonians (2 Kings 25.8–12; Zech 7.3–5).

1.4–19: **Jeremiah's call as a "prophet to the nations" and his initial visions. 1:4–10: The call.** The narrative of Jeremiah's call follows a typical pattern (see Ex 3–6; Judg 6.11–18; Isa 6) involving God's identification of a task and commission of the called one to be God's agent (v. 5), the excuses of the commissioned one (v. 6), God's promise to be with the commissioned one (vv. 7–8), and God's giving of a sign (vv. 9–10). 4: *Word of the LORD*, the prophets' primary area of responsibility was conveying the "word," often gained by visionary experience (see 18.18; Ezek 7.26). 5: *I formed you*, as a potter creates from clay (cf. Gen 2.7). *To the nations*, the call narrative introduces and presumes the entire book of Jeremiah, including the oracles against the nations. It portrays Jeremiah's ministry as a critical moment in world history (cf. Jer 25). 6: *A boy*, indicating apprentice or assistant status (see 2 Kings 4.12). Jeremiah protests his lack of experience. 9: *Touched my mouth*, the verb implying that this divine action involved an object, such as Isaiah's coal (Isa 6.7). Perhaps God's word was the object (15:16). 10: *To pluck up . . . to plant*, Jeremiah's twofold task of judgment and restoration, a common theme throughout the book. Compare 18.7–9; 24.6; 31.28.

1.11–19: **Two visions of pending judgment. 11:** *Almond tree*, a very early blooming tree, thus one that "wakes early and watches" for spring. See textual notes *a* and *b* for a play on these words in Heb. On God as "watching," see 31.28 and 44.27. 13–14: *Out of the north*, the mythological location of the mountain of the gods (Isa 14.13; Job 37.22) and of the ideal Zion (Ps 48.2); but also the direction from which Israel's mythical and historical enemies attacked (Isa 41.25; Zeph 2.13). The pot was *boiling* over as first Assyria and then Babylon exercised expansionist imperial policies against Judah and its neighbors. 15: *Set their thrones at the entrance of the gates*, at the place

entrance of the gates of Jerusalem, against all its surrounding walls and against all the cities of Judah. [16] And I will utter my judgments against them, for all their wickedness in forsaking me; they have made offerings to other gods, and worshiped the works of their own hands. [17] But you, gird up your loins; stand up and tell them everything that I command you. Do not break down before them, or I will break you before them. [18] And I for my part have made you today a fortified city, an iron pillar, and a bronze wall, against the whole land—against the kings of Judah, its princes, its priests, and the people of the land. [19] They will fight against you; but they shall not prevail against you, for I am with you, says the LORD, to deliver you.

2 The word of the LORD came to me, saying: [2] Go and proclaim in the hearing of Jerusalem, Thus says the LORD:

I remember the devotion of your youth,
    your love as a bride,
how you followed me in the wilderness,
    in a land not sown.
[3] Israel was holy to the LORD,
    the first fruits of his harvest.
All who ate of it were held guilty;
    disaster came upon them,
                    says the LORD.

[4] Hear the word of the LORD, O house of Jacob, and all the families of the house of Israel. [5] Thus says the LORD:

What wrong did your ancestors find in me
    that they went far from me,
and went after worthless things, and
        became worthless themselves?
[6] They did not say, "Where is the LORD
    who brought us up from the land of
        Egypt,
who led us in the wilderness,
    in a land of deserts and pits,
in a land of drought and deep darkness,
    in a land that no one passes through,
    where no one lives?"
[7] I brought you into a plentiful land
    to eat its fruits and its good things.
But when you entered you defiled my land,
    and made my heritage an abomination.
[8] The priests did not say, "Where is the
        LORD?"
Those who handle the law did not know
        me;
the rulers[a] transgressed against me;
    the prophets prophesied by Baal,
    and went after things that do not profit.

[9] Therefore once more I accuse you,
                        says the LORD,

---

[a] Heb *shepherds*

---

of judgment and justice; a sign of military conquest (39.3; 43.10). **16**: *Worshiped*, indicating bowing down in prostration. The *works of their own hands* are the images and idols of other gods fashioned by artisans (10.9). **17**: *Gird up your loins*, as if binding up a garment for hard travel on an assignment (2 Kings 4.29; 9.1) or strapping on battle gear (Job 38.3; Nah 2.1). **18**: *The whole land*, if the target is Judah. But Heb "'erets" also means "earth," and expresses the universal commission of Jeremiah against nations and kingdoms.

2.1–3.5: **Israel's apostasy.** Early oracles critical of Israel's fickle devotion to God and Baal. **1–3**: Recalls the wilderness period immediately after the Exodus in idealized terms as a period of fidelity to God (compare Hos 2.14–15). In a *land not sown* (v. 2) there was no temptation to worship the fertility gods of Canaan. **3**: *Israel was holy to the LORD*, recalling that some sacrifices were "most holy" and therefore reserved strictly for priestly consumption. Those who encroached upon them were *guilty* (Lev 5.15–16; 6.25–29), just as are the nations who have devoured Israel, God's own holy portion.

2.4–8: **Israel defiles the land.** **5**: *Worthless things*, or "vaporous puffs of wind" (Heb "hebel"), that which is mere "vanity" (Eccl 1.2). **6–7**: Israel is not only incapable of recalling its history, but is incapable of engaging in lament, of complaining "Where is the LORD?"! The loss of lament indicates the loss of relationship. **8**: *The priests did not say* reminds the priests that they were to lead the community in such complaint, and had failed to do so. If the community cannot complain to God, it cannot trust in God. *Those who handle the law*, that is, the priests, whose task it was to instruct the community with God's instruction or *law* (Heb "torah"). *Prophesied by Baal*, the Canaanite god, one of the common accusations against the prophets; cf. Hos 2.8–17. *Things that do not profit* (Heb "ya'al"), a play on the name Baal ("ba'al"), i.e., they worshiped Baal to no avail.

and I accuse your children's children.
¹⁰ Cross to the coasts of Cyprus and look,
  send to Kedar and examine with care;
  see if there has ever been such a thing.
¹¹ Has a nation changed its gods,
  even though they are no gods?
But my people have changed their glory
  for something that does not profit.
¹² Be appalled, O heavens, at this,
  be shocked, be utterly desolate,
          says the LORD,
¹³ for my people have committed two evils:
  they have forsaken me,
the fountain of living water,
  and dug out cisterns for themselves,
cracked cisterns
  that can hold no water.

¹⁴ Is Israel a slave? Is he a homeborn
    servant?
  Why then has he become plunder?
¹⁵ The lions have roared against him,
  they have roared loudly.
They have made his land a waste;
  his cities are in ruins, without
    inhabitant.
¹⁶ Moreover, the people of Memphis and
    Tahpanhes
  have broken the crown of your head.
¹⁷ Have you not brought this upon yourself
  by forsaking the LORD your God,

while he led you in the way?
¹⁸ What then do you gain by going to
    Egypt,
  to drink the waters of the Nile?
Or what do you gain by going to
    Assyria,
  to drink the waters of the Euphrates?
¹⁹ Your wickedness will punish you,
  and your apostasies will convict you.
Know and see that it is evil and bitter
  for you to forsake the LORD your God;
  the fear of me is not in you,
          says the Lord GOD of hosts.

²⁰ For long ago you broke your yoke
  and burst your bonds,
  and you said, "I will not serve!"
On every high hill
  and under every green tree
  you sprawled and played the whore.
²¹ Yet I planted you as a choice vine,
  from the purest stock.
How then did you turn degenerate
  and become a wild vine?
²² Though you wash yourself with lye
  and use much soap,
  the stain of your guilt is still before me,
          says the Lord GOD.
²³ How can you say, "I am not defiled,
  I have not gone after the Baals"?
Look at your way in the valley;

2.9–13: God's resulting legal accusation. 9: *I accuse you*, formal language for making a legal complaint.
10: From *the coasts of Cyprus* to *Kedar*, that is from the extremities of west to east. "Cyprus," better "Kittim"
(Heb "kittiyyim"; see Gen 10.4; Isa 23.1), a reference to the distant western lands in the Mediterranean (perhaps
Rome, as in Dan 11.30 or Greece, as in 1 Macc 1.1). On *Kedar* in northern Arabia, see 49.28n. **11:** As in v. 8, the
phrase *does not profit* indicates that the Canaanite god Baal is meant. That Israel acts against simple reason,
natural instinct, and plain common sense is a frequent theme in Jeremiah (see 8.7). **13:** *Cracked cisterns*, lit.
"broken," i.e., severely damaged.

  2.14–15: The consequences of Israel's apostasy. 14: The rhetorical questions beg a negative response. Of
course Israel is no slave. But that free status is dissonant with the present reality of subjugation. **15:** *The lions*,
that is, Israel's enemies.

  2.16–25: Israel's wild promiscuity. Israel is here addressed as a young woman. **16:** *Memphis* and *Tahpanhes*,
cities in Egypt (43.7; 44.1; 46.14,19). *Broken the crown of your head*, lit., "they have grazed the top of your head
bare," perhaps a reference to shaving a woman's head as a mark of humiliation. **18:** *Egypt . . . Assyria*, the temptation was to make alliances with a stronger neighbor, Egypt or Assyria, in order to protect against other enemies
(2 Kings 16.7; Isa 31.1). Such alliances could involve worshiping the gods of the major treaty power, resulting in
religious apostasy. **21:** God's *choice vine* from *purest stock* turned into something *wild*, lit. "foreign"; see Isa 5:2.
23: *The Baals*, local manifestations of the chief Canaanite god of fertility. The Heb word "ba'al" meant "master,
husband, owner," and Israel's God might also be thought of as Israel's "husband" or "baal" (3.14; 31.32; Hos 2.16),
thereby creating religious confusion. **23b–24:** The metaphor of animals *in heat* suggests the uncontrollable

know what you have done—
a restive young camel interlacing her
tracks,
²⁴ a wild ass at home in the wilderness,
in her heat sniffing the wind!
Who can restrain her lust?
None who seek her need weary
themselves;
in her month they will find her.
²⁵ Keep your feet from going unshod
and your throat from thirst.
But you said, "It is hopeless,
for I have loved strangers,
and after them I will go."

²⁶ As a thief is shamed when caught,
so the house of Israel shall be
shamed—
they, their kings, their officials,
their priests, and their prophets,
²⁷ who say to a tree, "You are my father,"
and to a stone, "You gave me birth."
For they have turned their backs to me,
and not their faces.
But in the time of their trouble they say,
"Come and save us!"
²⁸ But where are your gods
that you made for yourself?
Let them come, if they can save you,
in your time of trouble;
for you have as many gods
as you have towns, O Judah.

²⁹ Why do you complain against me?
You have all rebelled against me,
says the LORD.
³⁰ In vain I have struck down your
children;

they accepted no correction.
Your own sword devoured your
prophets
like a ravening lion.
³¹ And you, O generation, behold the word
of the LORD![a]
Have I been a wilderness to Israel,
or a land of thick darkness?
Why then do my people say, "We are free,
we will come to you no more"?
³² Can a girl forget her ornaments,
or a bride her attire?
Yet my people have forgotten me,
days without number.

³³ How well you direct your course
to seek lovers!
So that even to wicked women
you have taught your ways.
³⁴ Also on your skirts is found
the lifeblood of the innocent poor,
though you did not catch them breaking
in.
Yet in spite of all these things[a]
³⁵ you say, "I am innocent;
surely his anger has turned from me."
Now I am bringing you to judgment
for saying, "I have not sinned."
³⁶ How lightly you gad about,
changing your ways!
You shall be put to shame by Egypt
as you were put to shame by
Assyria.
³⁷ From there also you will come away
with your hands on your head;

---

[a] Meaning of Heb uncertain

---

nature of Israel's apostasy. **25:** As in v. 22, what is strange or foreign is the apostasy that defiles (v. 23). **2.26–28:** **Judah's confused apostasy. 26:** *A thief is shamed*, the use of "shame" (Heb "boshet") hints at Baal, since the word "shame" was often used in place of the name of Baal (see 2 Sam 3.8 textual note c). **27:** The *tree* or wood pole (Heb "'asherah") symbolized the goddess Asherah, and the standing *stone* symbolized the god Baal. But Israel even confuses its apostate iconography and cannot tell father from mother.

2.29–37: God's legal suit against Israel. 29: *Complain against*, formal language of legal complaint. **30:** *Devoured your prophets*, that Israel neglected the prophets is a refrain of the Deuteronomistic editor of Jeremiah (7.25; 25.4; 26.5; 29.19; 35.15; 44.4); on killing prophets, see 1 Kings 19.10; Neh 9.26. **31:** The rhetorical questions beg the answer "Of course not." *We are free*, or "We have wandered aimlessly," as though in a trackless wilderness or in the darkness of night. Israel cannot find its way to God. **32:** Continues the theme of vv. 10–11: Israel's behavior defies all logic, common sense and natural instinct (see also 8.4–5,7; 18.14–15). **33–37** are again addressed to the young woman. **34:** *You did not catch them breaking in*, if caught in the act of burglary, such violence directed against the thief might be excusable (Ex 22.2–3). **36:** Recalls the invasion of Judah and siege

for the LORD has rejected those in whom
  you trust,
  and you will not prosper through them.

3 If^a a man divorces his wife
  and she goes from him
and becomes another man's wife,
  will he return to her?
Would not such a land be greatly
  polluted?
You have played the whore with many
  lovers;
  and would you return to me?
  says the LORD.
² Look up to the bare heights,^b and see!
  Where have you not been lain with?
By the waysides you have sat waiting for
  lovers,
  like a nomad in the wilderness.
You have polluted the land
  with your whoring and
  wickedness.
³ Therefore the showers have been
  withheld,
  and the spring rain has not come;
yet you have the forehead of a whore,
  you refuse to be ashamed.
⁴ Have you not just now called to me,
  "My Father, you are the friend of my
  youth—
⁵ will he be angry forever,
  will he be indignant to the end?"

This is how you have spoken,
  but you have done all the evil that you
  could.

⁶ The LORD said to me in the days of King
Josiah: Have you seen what she did, that
faithless one, Israel, how she went up on
every high hill and under every green tree,
and played the whore there? ⁷ And I thought,
"After she has done all this she will return
to me"; but she did not return, and her false
sister Judah saw it. ⁸ She^c saw that for all the
adulteries of that faithless one, Israel, I had
sent her away with a decree of divorce; yet
her false sister Judah did not fear, but she
too went and played the whore. ⁹ Because
she took her whoredom so lightly, she polluted the land, committing adultery with
stone and tree. ¹⁰ Yet for all this her false
sister Judah did not return to me with her
whole heart, but only in pretense, says the
LORD.

¹¹ Then the LORD said to me: Faithless
Israel has shown herself less guilty than false
Judah. ¹² Go, and proclaim these words toward
the north, and say:
  Return, faithless Israel,
  says the LORD.

a   Q Ms Gk Syr: MT *Saying, If*
b   Or *the trails*
c   Q Ms Gk Mss Syr: MT *I*

of Jerusalem by the Assyrians in 701 BCE (2 Kings 18.13–19.28). **37:** *Your hands on your head*, a sign of deep mourning (2 Sam 13.19).

  3.1–5: No return is possible. 1: *Will he return?* The rhetorical question demands a negative answer; Deut 4.1–
4 prohibits second marriages to the same person. *Would you return to me?* Although the analogy would exclude
the possibility of repentance and reconciliation between people and God, later passages in the chapter envision such restoration of the covenant relationship. In both Hebrew and Greek this is a statement rather than
a question, suggesting inappropriate and bizarre behavior. **2:** *Lain with*, the MT contains alternate readings of
the verb. One is "ravished" (Heb "shagal"), which implies that Israel was a victim rather than complicit. Ancient
editors of the MT preferred to read "shakab" ("lain with") instead, pointing to Israel's complicity; cf. Zech 14.2
for the same distinction. *Like a nomad* (Heb "'arabi"): Greek suggests reading "like a raven" (= Heb "'oreb"); see
Isa 34.11; Zeph 2.14. **3:** Israel's behavior pollutes the environment and disrupts nature; see Hag 1.5–11. *Forehead*,
that is, stubbornness (cf. Isa 48.4). **4:** *The friend of my youth*, Heb "'allup" implies God's cozy intimacy.

  3.6–4.4: Call for faithless Israel and Judah to return. This section continues the theme of *return* (3.1).
3.6–13: Judah is worse than her sister Israel; cf. Ezek 16.45–52; 23.1–21. **6:** *Days of King Josiah*, 640–609 BCE.
High hill . . . green tree, high places were sites for illicit worship, and the wood pole/tree represented the
goddess Asherah (see 2.27n.). **8:** *Decree of divorce*, see Deut 24.1–4. **9:** *Stone and tree*, symbols of religious
apostasy; see 2.27n. **10:** *In pretense*, lit. "in the lie" (Heb "sheqer"), code language for the Canaanite god Baal.
12: *Toward the north*, the kingdom of Israel lay to the north of Judah, and had earlier been carried away by the
Assyrians into captivity by her own northern enemies. What follows is directed to the Northern Kingdom.

I will not look on you in anger,
    for I am merciful,
                says the LORD;
I will not be angry forever.
[13] Only acknowledge your guilt,
    that you have rebelled against the LORD
        your God,
and scattered your favors among strangers
    under every green tree,
    and have not obeyed my voice,
             says the LORD.
[14] Return, O faithless children,
             says the LORD,
    for I am your master;
I will take you, one from a city and two
    from a family,
    and I will bring you to Zion.

[15] I will give you shepherds after my own heart, who will feed you with knowledge and understanding. [16] And when you have multiplied and increased in the land, in those days, says the LORD, they shall no longer say, "The ark of the covenant of the LORD." It shall not come to mind, or be remembered, or missed; nor shall another one be made. [17] At that time Jerusalem shall be called the throne of the LORD, and all nations shall gather to it, to the presence of the LORD in Jerusalem, and they shall no longer stubbornly follow their own evil will. [18] In those days the house of Judah shall join the house of Israel, and together they shall come from the land of the north to the land that I gave your ancestors for a heritage.

[19] I thought
    how I would set you among my
        children,
and give you a pleasant land,
    the most beautiful heritage of all the
        nations.
And I thought you would call me, My
        Father,
    and would not turn from following me.
[20] Instead, as a faithless wife leaves her
        husband,
    so you have been faithless to me,
        O house of Israel,
                says the LORD.

[21] A voice on the bare heights[a] is heard,
    the plaintive weeping of Israel's
        children,
because they have perverted their way,
    they have forgotten the LORD their God:
[22] Return, O faithless children,
    I will heal your faithlessness.

[a] Or *the trails*

Merciful, also implying faithful and loyal. 13. *Strangers,* implying a dangerous and defiling foreignness. See 2.25n. 3.14–18: Israel's restoration. These words are now directed toward a masc. plural subject, a syntactical shift indicating that this oracle is independent of the previous one. 14: *I am your master* (Heb "ba'alti bakem"), the Hebrew word "ba'al" also means husband; see 2.23n. 15: *Shepherds,* that is, kings and leaders. The term *feed you* comes from the same Hebrew root (lit., "shepherd you"). 16: *Ark of the covenant,* Judah's central religious symbol had likely been removed in military attack and was no longer present in the Temple by Jeremiah's time. Later tradition ascribed to Jeremiah the securing of the final secret resting place for the Ark of the Covenant, where he hid it following the destruction of the Temple (2 Macc 2.4–5) on Mount Nebo, the same mountain near which Moses' secret burial site was located (Deut 34.1,6). On the removal of such important icons from religious memory, cf. the reference to the memory of the Exodus event (16.14; 23.7). 17: *Jerusalem . . . the throne,* as part of the divine throne, the ark was God's footstool (1 Chr 28.2; Ps 132.7–8). Now Jerusalem itself will become God's throne. 18: *Land of the north,* both Assyria and Babylon were symbolically located in the north; see 1.14n.

3.19–22a: Mixed oracles pleading for Israel to return. 19: Addressed to the young woman, whom God would honor by setting her among God's sons (NRSV "children") for an inheritance. Normally women did not inherit property, as illustrated by the case of the daughters of Zelophehad (Num 26.33; 27.1–7; 36.2–9; cf. also Job 42.15). 21: *Bare heights,* hot, dry, desolate, barren land, scene of Israel's misery (see 14.6).

3.22b–25: Israel's confession. 23. *A delusion* (Heb "sheqer"), as in 3.10 a play on code language for the Canaanite god Baal. *Orgies* is a strong translation; Heb "hamon" implies only the tumultuous noise of a crowd out of control. 24: *Shameful thing,* a reference to Baal; see 2.26n. *Devoured,* on Baal's voracious appetite see

"Here we come to you;
    for you are the LORD our God.
[23] Truly the hills are[a] a delusion,
    the orgies on the mountains.
Truly in the LORD our God
    is the salvation of Israel.
[24] "But from our youth the shameful thing
has devoured all for which our ancestors had
labored, their flocks and their herds, their
sons and their daughters. [25] Let us lie down
in our shame, and let our dishonor cover us;
for we have sinned against the LORD our God,
we and our ancestors, from our youth even to
this day; and we have not obeyed the voice of
the LORD our God."

4 If you return, O Israel,
                    says the LORD,
    if you return to me,
if you remove your abominations from my
        presence,
    and do not waver,
[2] and if you swear, "As the LORD lives!"
    in truth, in justice, and in
        uprightness,
then nations shall be blessed[b] by him,
    and by him they shall boast.
[3] For thus says the LORD to the people of
Judah and to the inhabitants of Jerusalem:
    Break up your fallow ground,
        and do not sow among thorns.
[4] Circumcise yourselves to the LORD,
    remove the foreskin of your hearts,
    O people of Judah and inhabitants of
        Jerusalem,

or else my wrath will go forth like fire,
    and burn with no one to quench it,
    because of the evil of your doings.

[5] Declare in Judah, and proclaim in Jerusalem, and say:
Blow the trumpet through the land;
    shout aloud[c] and say,
"Gather together, and let us go
    into the fortified cities!"
[6] Raise a standard toward Zion,
    flee for safety, do not delay,
for I am bringing evil from the north,
    and a great destruction.
[7] A lion has gone up from its thicket,
    a destroyer of nations has set out;
    he has gone out from his place
to make your land a waste;
    your cities will be ruins
    without inhabitant.
[8] Because of this put on sackcloth,
    lament and wail:
"The fierce anger of the LORD
    has not turned away from us."

[9] On that day, says the LORD, courage shall fail
the king and the officials; the priests shall be
appalled and the prophets astounded. [10] Then

---

[a] Gk Syr Vg: Heb *Truly from the hills is*
[b] Or *shall bless themselves*
[c] Or *shout, take your weapons*: Heb *shout, fill* (your hand)

51.33–44; cf. Bel 1.1–28. **25**: *Lie down in our shame.* As Israel "lay" with Baal (3.2), so now they will "lie" in their "shame" as the consequence mirrors the offense.

4.1–4: God's appeal for Israel's return, continuing the theme. 2: *As the LORD lives,* a call for sincere oath-taking in God's name in judicial cases. *Nations shall be blessed,* Israel's restoration would yield a blessing for the nations; cf. Gen 12.2–3; 18.18. **3**: The people are to live their lives as seed planted in freshly tilled soil; see Hos 10.12. **4**: *Circumcise . . . your hearts,* outward display must be matched by inward conversion; see Deut 10.16; 30.6.

4.5–6.26: The siege of Jerusalem by the enemy from the north. A lengthy section warning about the coming invasion and siege of Jerusalem.

4.5–10: The sentinels and leaders are commanded to signal the attack of the foe from the north (see 1.14n.). **5**: *The trumpet* was used for signaling, especially in battle (4.19; Judg 3.27; 6.34). But here the signal is for taking refuge inside the walled city. **6**: *A standard,* any visible marker, such as a pole or signal fire, that could be seen from a distance. The letters from Lachish, contemporary to this period, refer to the signal fire from Azekah as no longer visible, a signal that the end had come; see 34.7n. **7**: *A lion has gone up,* a reference to Nebuchadrez-zar II of Babylon (605–562 BCE). But it is a mixed metaphor, since God, too, can be described as a lion on the prowl (25.36–38; 49.19; 50.44), or as one watching the people as a predator watches its prey (1.12; 5.6; 44.27).

I said, "Ah, Lord GOD, how utterly you have deceived this people and Jerusalem, saying, 'It shall be well with you,' even while the sword is at the throat!"

11 At that time it will be said to this people and to Jerusalem: A hot wind comes from me out of the bare heights[a] in the desert toward my poor people, not to winnow or cleanse— 12 a wind too strong for that. Now it is I who speak in judgment against them.

13 Look! He comes up like clouds,
    his chariots like the
        whirlwind;
his horses are swifter than eagles—
    woe to us, for we are ruined!
14 O Jerusalem, wash your heart clean of
        wickedness
    so that you may be saved.
How long shall your evil schemes
    lodge within you?
15 For a voice declares from Dan
    and proclaims disaster from Mount
        Ephraim.
16 Tell the nations, "Here they are!"
    Proclaim against Jerusalem,
"Besiegers come from a distant land;
    they shout against the cities of
        Judah.
17 They have closed in around her like
        watchers of a field,
    because she has rebelled against me,
                    says the LORD.
18 Your ways and your doings
    have brought this upon you.

This is your doom; how bitter it is!
    It has reached your very heart."

19 My anguish, my anguish! I writhe in
        pain!
    Oh, the walls of my heart!
My heart is beating wildly;
    I cannot keep silent;
for I[b] hear the sound of the trumpet,
    the alarm of war.
20 Disaster overtakes disaster,
    the whole land is laid waste.
Suddenly my tents are destroyed,
    my curtains in a moment.
21 How long must I see the standard,
    and hear the sound of the trumpet?
22 "For my people are foolish,
    they do not know me;
they are stupid children,
    they have no understanding.
They are skilled in doing evil,
    but do not know how to do good."

23 I looked on the earth, and lo, it was
        waste and void;
    and to the heavens, and they had no
        light.
24 I looked on the mountains, and lo, they
        were quaking,
    and all the hills moved to and fro.
25 I looked, and lo, there was no one at all,
    and all the birds of the air had fled.

a Or the trails
b Another reading is for you, O my soul,

10. Jeremiah charges God with deceiving the people by convincing them that everything will be "peace" (Heb "shalom"). Normally attributed to the "lying" prophets (6.14; 8.11), this may reflect promises that God would be with the people (e.g., Deut 20.1; Isa 7.14). On the theme of God deceiving the prophets, see 1 Kings 22.18–23.

4.11–18: The siege is near. 11: From me is lacking in the Hebrew, though clearly God stands behind this invasion (v. 6). My poor people, lit. "the daughter of my people." There is no sympathy suggested. This wind is too strong to winnow, as it would blow both chaff and grain away. Cf. 51.1–2. 15: The enemy sweeps over Dan in the far north and through Ephraim in the center of Israel hurrying toward Jerusalem. 17: Like watchers, the term "besiegers" (v. 16) connotes those who "watch" or "guard" against anyone escaping from the city under siege; here a synonym is used of "watching" or "guarding" a field, perhaps indicating the ease of so doing.

4.19–28: The anguished voice of the prophet. Some scholars think that Jerusalem may be speaking in vv. 19–21, as in v. 31; cf. 6.24; 10.19–21. 19: For I hear, lit. "for you have heard, O my soul." The sound of the trumpet penetrates to the prophet's very core; see textual note b. 20: Tents . . . curtains, though often used of the sanctuary (see 10.20n.), here the terms likely refer to Israel as God's dwelling (see 49.29; Isa 54.2; Hab 3.7). 22: Skilled (lit. "wise") in doing evil, in fact they are fools, the opposite of wise. 23: Waste and void, echoing Gen 1.2, these verses envision the reduction of creation to primordial chaos. No light, even the first act of God's creation was undone. 25: No one, lit. "no "adam'," no first human being.

26 I looked, and lo, the fruitful land was a
  desert,
  and all its cities were laid in ruins
  before the LORD, before his fierce anger.
27 For thus says the LORD: The whole land
shall be a desolation; yet I will not make a full
end.
28 Because of this the earth shall mourn,
  and the heavens above grow black;
for I have spoken, I have purposed;
  I have not relented nor will I turn back.

29 At the noise of horseman and archer
  every town takes to flight;
they enter thickets; they climb among
  rocks;
  all the towns are forsaken,
  and no one lives in them.
30 And you, O desolate one,
what do you mean that you dress in crimson,
  that you deck yourself with ornaments
  of gold,
  that you enlarge your eyes with paint?
In vain you beautify yourself.
  Your lovers despise you;
  they seek your life.
31 For I heard a cry as of a woman in labor,
  anguish as of one bringing forth her
  first child,
the cry of daughter Zion gasping for
  breath,
  stretching out her hands,
"Woe is me! I am fainting before killers!"

5 Run to and fro through the streets of
  Jerusalem,
  look around and take note!
Search its squares and see
  if you can find one person
who acts justly
  and seeks truth—
so that I may pardon Jerusalem.ᵃ
2 Although they say, "As the LORD lives,"
  yet they swear falsely.

3 O LORD, do your eyes not look for
  truth?
You have struck them,
  but they felt no anguish;
you have consumed them,
  but they refused to take correction.
They have made their faces harder than
  rock;
  they have refused to turn back.

4 Then I said, "These are only the poor,
  they have no sense;
for they do not know the way of the LORD,
  the law of their God.
5 Let me go to the richᵇ
  and speak to them;
surely they know the way of the LORD,
  the law of their God."
But they all alike had broken the yoke,
  they had burst the bonds.

6 Therefore a lion from the forest shall kill
  them,
  a wolf from the desert shall destroy
  them.
A leopard is watching against their cities;
  everyone who goes out of them shall be
  torn in pieces—
because their transgressions are many,
  their apostasies are great.

7 How can I pardon you?
  Your children have forsaken me,
  and have sworn by those who are no
  gods.
When I fed them to the full,
  they committed adultery
  and trooped to the houses of
  prostitutes.
8 They were well-fed lusty stallions,
  each neighing for his neighbor's wife.

ᵃ Heb *it*
ᵇ Or *the great*

4.29–31: Israel the rejected whore. 30: *Crimson . . . gold,* signs of wealth (2 Sam 1.24). Bejeweled and fully made up, Israel hopes for a tryst but has already been rejected by her lovers; cf. Ezek 16.

5.1–9: No one is righteous. 1: In an extreme offer of vicarious merit, one righteous person would be enough to pardon the city; cf. Gen 18.23–33; Ezek 14.14,20. 2: *As the LORD lives,* see 4.2n. 4: *The poor,* implying helpless, not expected to know better. *Law,* lit. "justice" (so v. 1). 5: *The rich,* lit. "the great," the important people who ought to know by virtue of their social status. 6: Vicious predatory animals symbolize the coming enemy, but God too can be cast as such an animal; see 4.7n. 7: *Adultery . . . prostitutes,* used sym-

⁹ Shall I not punish them for these things?
　　　　says the LORD;
　and shall I not bring retribution
　　on a nation such as this?

¹⁰ Go up through her vine-rows and
　　　destroy,
　　but do not make a full end;
strip away her branches,
　for they are not the LORD's.
¹¹ For the house of Israel and the house of
　　Judah
　have been utterly faithless to me,
　　　　says the LORD.
¹² They have spoken falsely of the LORD,
　and have said, "He will do nothing.
No evil will come upon us,
　and we shall not see sword or famine."
¹³ The prophets are nothing but wind,
　for the word is not in them.
Thus shall it be done to them!

¹⁴ Therefore thus says the LORD, the God of
　　hosts:
Because theyª have spoken this word,
I am now making my words in your mouth
　a fire,
　and this people wood, and the fire shall
　　devour them.
¹⁵ I am going to bring upon you
　a nation from far away, O house of
　　　Israel,
　　　　says the LORD.
It is an enduring nation,
　it is an ancient nation,

a nation whose language you do not
　　know,
　nor can you understand what they
　　say.
¹⁶ Their quiver is like an open tomb;
　all of them are mighty warriors.
¹⁷ They shall eat up your harvest and your
　　food;
　they shall eat up your sons and your
　　daughters;
they shall eat up your flocks and your
　　herds;
　they shall eat up your vines and your
　　fig trees;
they shall destroy with the sword
　your fortified cities in which you
　　trust.

¹⁸ But even in those days, says the LORD, I
will not make a full end of you. ¹⁹ And when
your people say, "Why has the LORD our
God done all these things to us?" you shall
say to them, "As you have forsaken me and
served foreign gods in your land, so you
shall serve strangers in a land that is not
yours."

²⁰ Declare this in the house of Jacob,
　proclaim it in Judah:
²¹ Hear this, O foolish and senseless
　　people,
　who have eyes, but do not see,
　who have ears, but do not hear.

ª Heb *you*

bolically of religious apostasy, perhaps resulting from international contacts. **8:** *Neighing*, normally used only of humans shouting excitedly, it is used twice of horses (8.16; 50.11). God desires to pardon (v. 7), but cannot hold back punishment and must "avenge" divine honor (v. 9). **9:** A refrain in this section (see 5.29), repeated in 9.9.

5.10–19: Destruction comes in spite of Israel's deluded self-confidence. 10: *Vine-rows*, or perhaps rows of olive trees, where oil is pressed (see Job 24.11). *Do not make a full end*, there need to be witnesses left who can remember what happened (5.18–19; see also 4.27; 30.11; 46.28). **12:** *He will do nothing*, representing the false words of the prophets (v. 14). The Hebrew is ambiguous, perhaps "He is nothing" or "It will not happen." *Evil*, or "disaster," on God's inability to act either for good or ill, cf. Zeph 1.12. **13:** *Wind*, that is, "spirit," an ironic statement about the lack of inspiration of prophetic visions. For the prophet's responsibility for the "word," see 1.4n. **14:** The pronouns are confusing here. The syntax indicates that the people are the wood, and they will be set afire by Jeremiah's prophetic word, thereby consuming the ineffectual prophets of v. 13. **15:** This invading enemy is likely either Assyria (if this is an early oracle) or Babylon (if a later oracle). **17:** That enemies would devour the harvest is characteristic of curses; see Lev 26.16; Deut 28.25–37. **18:** God will not make a *full end* so that there might be some left who can ask what happened, and can witness to the disaster.

5.20–31: Israel's foolishness is evident in its lack of reverence for God and in its injustice toward the vulner-

²² Do you not fear me? says the Lord;
  Do you not tremble before me?
I placed the sand as a boundary for the
    sea,
  a perpetual barrier that it cannot pass;
though the waves toss, they cannot
    prevail,
  though they roar, they cannot pass
    over it.
²³ But this people has a stubborn and
    rebellious heart;
  they have turned aside and gone away.
²⁴ They do not say in their hearts,
  "Let us fear the Lord our God,
who gives the rain in its season,
  the autumn rain and the spring rain,
and keeps for us
  the weeks appointed for the harvest."
²⁵ Your iniquities have turned these away,
  and your sins have deprived you of
    good.
²⁶ For scoundrels are found among my
    people;
  they take over the goods of others.
Like fowlers they set a trap;[a]
  they catch human beings.
²⁷ Like a cage full of birds,
  their houses are full of treachery;
therefore they have become great and
    rich,
²⁸ they have grown fat and sleek.
They know no limits in deeds of
    wickedness;

they do not judge with justice
the cause of the orphan, to make it
    prosper,
  and they do not defend the rights of the
    needy.
²⁹ Shall I not punish them for these things?
                        says the Lord,
  and shall I not bring retribution
  on a nation such as this?

³⁰ An appalling and horrible thing
  has happened in the land:
³¹ the prophets prophesy falsely,
  and the priests rule as the prophets
    direct;[b]
my people love to have it so,
  but what will you do when the end
    comes?

6 Flee for safety, O children of Benjamin,
  from the midst of Jerusalem!
Blow the trumpet in Tekoa,
  and raise a signal on Beth-haccherem;
for evil looms out of the north,
  and great destruction.
² I have likened daughter Zion
  to the loveliest pasture.[c]
³ Shepherds with their flocks shall come
  against her.

---

a Meaning of Heb uncertain
b Or *rule by their own authority*
c Or *I will destroy daughter Zion, the loveliest pasture*

---

able. 21: Cf. Isa 6.9–10. 22: *Sand as a boundary for the sea*, like the waxing and waning of the tides of the ocean, God has set a limit for the primeval chaos surrounding creation, beyond which it cannot pass; see Gen 1.2–8; Job 38.8–11; Ps 104.9. 23: *Stubborn and rebellious* recalls the sort of perverse behavior by a child that has deadly consequences (Deut 21.18–21). Unlike such natural elements as the sea that honor their limits, Israel refuses that which is natural. 24: *The weeks appointed* refers to the seven-week period between the first cutting and the festival of weeks or Pentecost (Deut 16.9–10). 26: *They take over the goods of others*, or perhaps "They lurk like hunters crouching." Given what follows (v. 27), the image here is that of hunting birds and stuffing them into baskets. 28: As if trapping birds, the wicked trap *the orphan* and *the needy*, the most vulnerable members of society; cf. Isa 1.17; Am 2.6–7; Mic 3.1–3; Zech 7.10; Ex 22.21–24; Deut 24.17–18. 29: See 5.9n. 31: The prophets prophesy the lie (Heb "sheqer"), referring alternatively either to false confidence in God or else to devotion to the Canaanite god Baal, two aspects of the same offense. *The priests rule as the prophets direct*, lit. "the priests rule over their hands." Either the priests make decisions on the basis of false prophecy, or the priests dominate the prophets and censor their message (see 20.1–2; 29.26–27).

6.1–9: The attack surrounds Jerusalem. 1: The tribal territory of *Benjamin* was directly north of Jerusalem and *Tekoa*, hometown of the prophet Amos (Am 1.1), was ca. 11 mi (18km) to its south. Again the *trumpet* and *signal* (lit. "an uprising") warn of attack. The verb "blow (trumpet)" (Heb "tiq'u") plays on the name "Tekoa" ("teqoa'"); see 4.5–6n. *Beth-haccherem* ("vineyard house") is mentioned otherwise only in Neh 3.14, where it is a district in Judah. Some scholars identify it here as Ramat-rahel, ca. 3 mi (5 km) south of Jerusalem. 3: *Shepherds*,

They shall pitch their tents around her;
  they shall pasture, all in their places.
[4] "Prepare war against her;
  up, and let us attack at noon!"
"Woe to us, for the day declines,
  the shadows of evening lengthen!"
[5] "Up, and let us attack by night,
  and destroy her palaces!"
[6] For thus says the LORD of hosts:
Cut down her trees;
  cast up a siege ramp against Jerusalem.
This is the city that must be punished;[a]
  there is nothing but oppression within
    her.
[7] As a well keeps its water fresh,
  so she keeps fresh her wickedness;
violence and destruction are heard within
    her;
  sickness and wounds are ever before
    me.
[8] Take warning, O Jerusalem,
  or I shall turn from you in disgust,
and make you a desolation,
  an uninhabited land.

[9] Thus says the LORD of hosts:
Glean[b] thoroughly as a vine
  the remnant of Israel;
like a grape-gatherer, pass your hand again
  over its branches.

[10] To whom shall I speak and give warning,
  that they may hear?
See, their ears are closed,[c]
  they cannot listen.
The word of the LORD is to them an object
    of scorn;
  they take no pleasure in it.
[11] But I am full of the wrath of the LORD;
  I am weary of holding it in.

Pour it out on the children in the street,
  and on the gatherings of young men as
    well;
both husband and wife shall be taken,
  the old folk and the very aged.
[12] Their houses shall be turned over to
    others,
  their fields and wives together;
for I will stretch out my hand
  against the inhabitants of the land,
                                 says the LORD.

[13] For from the least to the greatest of
    them,
  everyone is greedy for unjust gain;
and from prophet to priest,
  everyone deals falsely.
[14] They have treated the wound of my
    people carelessly,
  saying, "Peace, peace,"
  when there is no peace.
[15] They acted shamefully, they committed
    abomination;
  yet they were not ashamed,
  they did not know how to blush.
Therefore they shall fall among those who
    fall;
  at the time that I punish them, they
    shall be overthrown,
                                 says the LORD.

[16] Thus says the LORD:
Stand at the crossroads, and look,
  and ask for the ancient paths,
where the good way lies; and walk in it,

[a] Or *the city of license*
[b] Cn: Heb *They shall glean*
[c] Heb *are uncircumcised*

enemy kings and their armies will surround Jerusalem. The verb used of "pitching" a tent is the same used of "blowing" a trumpet in v. 1. **4–5:** Alternating quotations of the enemy and the inhabitants of Jerusalem. *Prepare*, lit. "sanctify," since war involved blood and required a state of ritual purity (see 2 Sam 11.11; Jer 51.27; Joel 3.9). **6:** *Cut down her trees*, permitted for building siege ramps to storm defensive walls (see Deut 20.19–20). **8:** *Turn from you in disgust*, the verb used here (Heb "teqa'") again plays on the name Tekoa (see vv. 1n., 3n.) and indicates a dislocation of something, as in the dislocation of Jacob's hip (Gen 32.26). **9:** *Glean*, Israel will be stripped clean by its enemies. Gleaning was the practice of allowing the poor to come into a field to pick what remained after the regular harvest (Deut 24.21).

6.10–21: Israel refuses to heed the sentinel's warning. Vv. 12–15 are a near doublet of 8.10–12. **11:** The prophet's personal agony; see 20.9. *Taken*, that is, captured by the enemy. **14:** Prophetic promises of peace and well-

and find rest for your souls.
But they said, "We will not walk in it."
[17] Also I raised up sentinels for you:
"Give heed to the sound of the
trumpet!"
But they said, "We will not give heed."
[18] Therefore hear, O nations,
and know, O congregation, what will
happen to them.
[19] Hear, O earth; I am going to bring
disaster on this people,
the fruit of their schemes,
because they have not given heed to my
words;
and as for my teaching, they have
rejected it.
[20] Of what use to me is frankincense that
comes from Sheba,
or sweet cane from a distant land?
Your burnt offerings are not acceptable,
nor are your sacrifices pleasing to me.
[21] Therefore thus says the LORD:
See, I am laying before this people
stumbling blocks against which they
shall stumble;
parents and children together,
neighbor and friend shall perish.

[22] Thus says the LORD:
See, a people is coming from the land of
the north,
a great nation is stirring from the
farthest parts of the earth.
[23] They grasp the bow and the javelin,

they are cruel and have no mercy,
their sound is like the roaring sea;
they ride on horses,
equipped like a warrior for battle,
against you, O daughter Zion!
[24] "We have heard news of them,
our hands fall helpless;
anguish has taken hold of us,
pain as of a woman in labor.
[25] Do not go out into the field,
or walk on the road;
for the enemy has a sword,
terror is on every side."
[26] O my poor people, put on sackcloth,
and roll in ashes;
make mourning as for an only child,
most bitter lamentation:
for suddenly the destroyer
will come upon us.

[27] I have made you a tester and a refiner[a]
among my people
so that you may know and test their
ways.
[28] They are all stubbornly rebellious,
going about with slanders;
they are bronze and iron,
all of them act corruptly.
[29] The bellows blow fiercely,
the lead is consumed by the fire;

a   Or a fortress

being are delusional; cf. Ezek 13.10. **17:** Israel repeatedly refuses to heed the sentinel's warnings. On the prophet as a sentinel, cf. Ezek 3.17–21. **20:** *Sheba*, located in Arabia and valued for its spice trade (Isa 60.6; Ezek 27.22). All these items, including sweet cane, were offered to God in smoke (*burnt offerings*) as a pleasing odor in Israel's Temple worship (see Gen 8.20–21; Lev 1.9; Isa 43.24), but God rejects them if they are not accompanied by acts of justice and mercy (Am 5.21–24; 1 Sam 15.22).

6.22–26: Refusing the warning, the enemy comes and Israel is called to ritual mourning. 22: On the enemy from the north, see 1.14n. **23:** *Ride on horses*, that is, ride on horse-drawn chariots, which were the major battle-field war machines, rather than riding horseback. **24:** Now Israel hears the warning, but it is too late. *A woman in labor* is a common metaphor for being in agony and distress. See 4.31; 13.21; 22.23. **25:** *Terror is on every side*, a refrain in Jeremiah (20.3–4,10; 46.5; 49.29). **26:** *My poor people*, lit. "daughter of my people" (see 4.11). *Sackcloth . . . ashes*, ritual actions associated with mourning and entreaty for divine favor in crisis situations (see Jon 3.6; Isa 58.5; Dan 9.3).

6.27–30: Conclusion to the oracles from the time of King Josiah: Israel's final rejection. God appoints Jeremiah to refine Israel's metal (cf. Isa 48.10; Zech 13.9; Mal 3.2–4), but it is in vain. Jeremiah may be fortified with bronze and iron (1.18), but Israel has proved to be a match, as they too are bronze and iron (v. 28). Israel's dross cannot be removed by any process of refinement, no matter how hot the fire. The section concludes with final words of divine rejection, bringing this first section of the book to an ominous close.

in vain the refining goes on,
for the wicked are not removed.
³⁰ They are called "rejected silver,"
for the LORD has rejected them.

7 The word that came to Jeremiah from the LORD: ² Stand in the gate of the LORD's house, and proclaim there this word, and say, Hear the word of the LORD, all you people of Judah, you that enter these gates to worship the LORD. ³ Thus says the LORD of hosts, the God of Israel: Amend your ways and your doings, and let me dwell with youᵃ in this place. ⁴ Do not trust in these deceptive words: "This isᵇ the temple of the LORD, the temple of the LORD, the temple of the LORD."

⁵ For if you truly amend your ways and your doings, if you truly act justly one with another, ⁶ if you do not oppress the alien, the orphan, and the widow, or shed innocent blood in this place, and if you do not go after other gods to your own hurt, ⁷ then I will dwell with you in this place, in the land that I gave of old to your ancestors forever and ever.

⁸ Here you are, trusting in deceptive words to no avail. ⁹ Will you steal, murder, commit adultery, swear falsely, make offerings to Baal, and go after other gods that you have not known, ¹⁰ and then come and stand

before me in this house, which is called by my name, and say, "We are safe!"—only to go on doing all these abominations? ¹¹ Has this house, which is called by my name, become a den of robbers in your sight? You know, I too am watching, says the LORD. ¹² Go now to my place that was in Shiloh, where I made my name dwell at first, and see what I did to it for the wickedness of my people Israel. ¹³ And now, because you have done all these things, says the LORD, and when I spoke to you persistently, you did not listen, and when I called you, you did not answer, ¹⁴ therefore I will do to the house that is called by my name, in which you trust, and to the place that I gave to you and to your ancestors, just what I did to Shiloh. ¹⁵ And I will cast you out of my sight, just as I cast out all your kinsfolk, all the offspring of Ephraim.

¹⁶ As for you, do not pray for this people, do not raise a cry or prayer on their behalf, and do not intercede with me, for I will not hear you. ¹⁷ Do you not see what they are doing in the towns of Judah and in the streets of Jerusalem? ¹⁸ The children gather wood, the fathers kindle fire, and the women

ᵃ Or *and I will let you dwell*
ᵇ Heb *They are*

7.1–15: **The Temple sermon** opens the unit 7.1–10.25, which depicts the sickness, death, and funeral of Judah along with Judah's acceptance of its fate. The Temple sermon is generally associated with the events of ch 26 and Jeremiah's first arrest in 609 BCE, given the thematic connections of chs 7 and 26. 3: *Let me dwell*, this is not a request by God, but rather a promise expressing God's strong intentionality that God will indeed dwell with the people (or will indeed establish their dwelling, following both the MT and the Gk) under changed conditions. 4: The Temple was regarded as a place of sanctuary where one might seek refuge from reprisal (1 Kings 1.50; 2.28; see 17.1n.). The people believe that their mere presence in the Temple renders them safe (v. 10). Although liturgical tradition expressed God's protection of Jerusalem and the Temple (e.g., Pss 46; 48; 76; see also Isa 31.4; 37.35), it is deceptive (lit. a "lie," Heb "sheqer") to think that this necessarily assures God's protection. The threefold repetition implies that the phrase had become a cliché. 5–7: The requirements for true sincerity are consistent with the values expressed in Deuteronomy (5.7; 10.18–19; 24.17–22; 27.19) and in other prophets (Isa 10.2; 59.7; Hos 3.1). 9: Five of the Ten Commandments (Ex 20.1–17; Deut 5.6–21). 11: *Den of robbers*, they imagine the Temple to be a bandit cave or hideout. 12: *At first*, or "formerly." On Eli and the fate of Shiloh, destroyed during the early Philistine wars, see 1 Sam 4–6; Ps 78.60. The memory of Shiloh was important for Jeremiah's own family, descended from the priests of Shiloh through Abiathar, David's priest who was exiled to Anathoth by Solomon. 14: *Called by my name*, characteristic of Deuteronomic theology, which speaks of God choosing a place "to put his name there" (Deut 12.5; 14.23). 15: *Ephraim*, the tribe whose ancestor was the son of Joseph, and the most important within the northern tribal group, here as elsewhere symbolizing the entirety of the Northern Kingdom, which had been defeated and deported by the Assyrians more than a century earlier.

7.16–20: **Jeremiah prohibited from intercession**, a critical function of prophetic identity (Am 7.2,5); cf. 11.14; 14.11. 18: *Cakes for the queen of heaven*, a ritual custom honoring the goddess Astarte (Babylonian Ishtar), goddess of fecundity and fertility; see also 44.17–19 and cf. Judg 2.13; 10.6; 1 Sam 7.3–4; 2 Kings 23.13. Though the

knead dough, to make cakes for the queen of heaven; and they pour out drink offerings to other gods, to provoke me to anger. [19] Is it I whom they provoke? says the Lord. Is it not themselves, to their own hurt? [20] Therefore thus says the Lord God: My anger and my wrath shall be poured out on this place, on human beings and animals, on the trees of the field and the fruit of the ground; it will burn and not be quenched.

[21] Thus says the Lord of hosts, the God of Israel: Add your burnt offerings to your sacrifices, and eat the flesh. [22] For in the day that I brought your ancestors out of the land of Egypt, I did not speak to them or command them concerning burnt offerings and sacrifices. [23] But this command I gave them, "Obey my voice, and I will be your God, and you shall be my people; and walk only in the way that I command you, so that it may be well with you." [24] Yet they did not obey or incline their ear, but, in the stubbornness of their evil will, they walked in their own counsels, and looked backward rather than forward. [25] From the day that your ancestors came out of the land of Egypt until this day, I have persistently sent all my servants the prophets to them, day after day; [26] yet they did not listen to me, or pay attention, but they stiffened their necks. They did worse than their ancestors did.

[27] So you shall speak all these words to them, but they will not listen to you. You shall call to them, but they will not answer you. [28] You shall say to them: This is the nation that did not obey the voice of the Lord their God, and did not accept discipline; truth has perished; it is cut off from their lips.

[29] Cut off your hair and throw it away;
    raise a lamentation on the bare
        heights,[a]
for the Lord has rejected and forsaken
    the generation that provoked his wrath.

[30] For the people of Judah have done evil in my sight, says the Lord; they have set their abominations in the house that is called by my name, defiling it. [31] And they go on building the high place[b] of Topheth, which is in the valley of the son of Hinnom, to burn their sons and their daughters in the fire—which I did not command, nor did it come into my mind. [32] Therefore, the days are surely coming, says the Lord, when it will no more be called Topheth, or the valley of the son of Hinnom, but the valley of Slaughter: for they will bury in Topheth until there is no more room. [33] The corpses of this people will be food for the birds of the air, and for the animals of the earth; and no one will frighten

a   Or the trails
b   Gk Tg: Heb high places

worship of the queen of heaven was practiced chiefly by women (so 44.15,19), the texts here indicate that the entire family was actively involved; see also 44.17n. **19:** *To their own hurt*, or "to the shame (Heb "boshet") of their own face." The term "boshet" is code language for the Canaanite god Baal and for religious apostasy in general. See 2.26n.; 3.24.

7.21–26: Sacrifice and obedience. While part of the "sacrifice" was eaten by the one offering it, the "burnt offering" was offered up whole to God in smoke. The eating of both typifies the ritual abuses of Israel. **22:** *I did not speak . . . concerning . . . sacrifices*, the Exodus preceded the giving of the sacrificial laws at Sinai; see also Amos 5.25. The custom of sacrifice is but one illustration of the commitment one is to show toward God, and ritual actions are no substitute or replacement for moral integrity (Isa 1.11–17). **25:** *That God has persistently sent all my servants the prophets* is a principle of Deuteronomistic theology explicit in Jeremiah; see 25.4; 26.5; 29.19; 35.15; 44.4; 2 Kings 17.13,23; 21.10; 24.2.

7.27–8.3: Israel's death announced. Israel's lack of obedience leads to its death, consistent with the language of Deuteronomy (e.g., Deut 30.19). **27:** Like Isaiah (6.9–11), Jeremiah will preach to an audience unwilling or unable to hear. **29:** *Cut off your hair . . . raise a lamentation*, both were funeral rituals (see 16.6n.). **31:** *High place*, see 3.6n. *Topheth . . . in the valley of the son of Hinnom*, the valley skirting Jerusalem to the south and west was likely the site of many fire-pits for garbage, but also the site for sacrificing children in fire for divine favor. The custom was practiced even by Israel's kings (Deut 18.10; 2 Kings 16.3; 21.6) but was proscribed in the reform of King Josiah (2 Kings 23.10); see 19.2–5; 32.35. "Topheth" is also a "burning place" in Isa 30.33 (see textual note *b* there). The name Valley of Hinnom (Heb "ge' hinnom") lies behind the later name Gehenna, used for the netherworld as a fire-pit. **33:** *No one will frighten them away*, exposure of a dead corpse was an act of desecration and

them away. ³⁴ And I will bring to an end the sound of mirth and gladness, the voice of the bride and bridegroom in the cities of Judah and in the streets of Jerusalem; for the land shall become a waste.

8 At that time, says the LORD, the bones of the kings of Judah, the bones of its officials, the bones of the priests, the bones of the prophets, and the bones of the inhabitants of Jerusalem shall be brought out of their tombs; ² and they shall be spread before the sun and the moon and all the host of heaven, which they have loved and served, which they have followed, and which they have inquired of and worshiped; and they shall not be gathered or buried; they shall be like dung on the surface of the ground. ³ Death shall be preferred to life by all the remnant that remains of this evil family in all the places where I have driven them, says the LORD of hosts.

⁴ You shall say to them, Thus says the
  LORD:
When people fall, do they not get up
  again?
  If they go astray, do they not turn back?
⁵ Why then has this peopleª turned away
  in perpetual backsliding?
They have held fast to deceit,
  they have refused to return.
⁶ I have given heed and listened,
  but they do not speak honestly;
no one repents of wickedness,
  saying, "What have I done!"
All of them turn to their own course,
  like a horse plunging headlong into
    battle.
⁷ Even the stork in the heavens
  knows its times;
and the turtledove, swallow, and craneᵇ

observe the time of their coming;
but my people do not know
  the ordinance of the LORD.

⁸ How can you say, "We are wise,
  and the law of the LORD is with us,"
when, in fact, the false pen of the scribes
  has made it into a lie?
⁹ The wise shall be put to shame,
  they shall be dismayed and taken;
since they have rejected the word of the
  LORD,
  what wisdom is in them?
¹⁰ Therefore I will give their wives to others
  and their fields to conquerors,
because from the least to the greatest
  everyone is greedy for unjust gain;
from prophet to priest
  everyone deals falsely.
¹¹ They have treated the wound of my
    people carelessly,
  saying, "Peace, peace,"
  when there is no peace.
¹² They acted shamefully, they committed
    abomination;
  yet they were not at all ashamed,
  they did not know how to blush.
Therefore they shall fall among those who
    fall;
  at the time when I punish them, they
    shall be overthrown,
                            says the LORD.
¹³ When I wanted to gather them, says the
    LORD,
  there areᶜ no grapes on the vine,

ª One Ms Gk: MT *this people, Jerusalem,*
ᵇ Meaning of Heb uncertain
ᶜ Or *I will make an end of them, says the* LORD. *There
   are*

---

shaming. On the importance of keeping birds and animals away from a corpse, see 2 Sam 21.1–10. **34:** On this formulaic language see 16.9; 25.10; 33.11. **8.1–3:** On exhuming the remains as a way of shaming the deceased, see 16.4; 1 Kings 13.2; 2 Kings 23.14,16. Bones were also unclean, so spreading them upon sacred sites defiled the worship of the deities mentioned here. **2:** *All the host of heaven*, the stars, astral deities whose worship was forbidden (Deut 4.19; 17.3; 2 Kings 23.4–5; cf. 7.17–18).

8.4–9.26: Israel's wisdom is reduced to the funeral dirge. 8.4–12: Israel's false claim to wisdom. Though human behavior is conditioned by nature (v. 4) and though nature is infused with wisdom (8.7, birds migrate with seasons), Israel's claim to wisdom is a sham (8.8–9), both because of its moral failure (v. 10) and for promoting false optimism in a time of national crisis (v. 11). **8:** *False pen of the scribes*, normally it is the priest who is responsible for guarding and dispensing law or instruction (Heb "torah"). Perhaps what is meant here is the learned priest who also functions in such a literary capacity like Ezra the priest, who was also a scribe, a "scholar

nor figs on the fig tree;
even the leaves are withered,
and what I gave them has passed away
from them.ᵃ

¹⁴ Why do we sit still?
Gather together, let us go into the fortified
cities
and perish there;
for the LORD our God has doomed us to
perish,
and has given us poisoned water to
drink,
because we have sinned against the
LORD.
¹⁵ We look for peace, but find no good,
for a time of healing, but there is terror
instead.

¹⁶ The snorting of their horses is heard
from Dan;
at the sound of the neighing of their
stallions
the whole land quakes.
They come and devour the land and all
that fills it,
the city and those who live in it.
¹⁷ See, I am letting snakes loose among
you,
adders that cannot be charmed,
and they shall bite you,
says the LORD.

¹⁸ My joy is gone, grief is upon me,
my heart is sick.
¹⁹ Hark, the cry of my poor
people
from far and wide in the land:

"Is the LORD not in Zion?
Is her King not in her?"
("Why have they provoked me to anger
with their images,
with their foreign idols?")
²⁰ "The harvest is past, the summer is
ended,
and we are not saved."
²¹ For the hurt of my poor people I am
hurt,
I mourn, and dismay has taken hold
of me.

²² Is there no balm in Gilead?
Is there no physician there?
Why then has the health of my poor
people
not been restored?

9 ᵇ O that my head were a spring of
water,
and my eyes a fountain of tears,
so that I might weep day and night
for the slain of my poor people!
² ᶜ O that I had in the desert
a traveler's lodging place,
that I might leave my people
and go away from them!
For they are all adulterers,
a band of traitors.
³ They bend their tongues like bows;
they have grown strong in the land for
falsehood, and not for truth;

ᵃ Meaning of Heb uncertain
ᵇ Ch 8.23 in Heb
ᶜ Ch 9.1 in Heb

of the text" of the Torah (Ezra 7.11). **10–12:** Cf. the near doublet at 6.12–15. **13–14:** *Gather,* a term associated with "ingathering" of fruit at the fall harvest. There is no produce to be gathered, so the people seek to "gather themselves" for death. **16:** *Horses,* the horse was the chief animal of warfare (see 6.23n.), signaling that the enemy armies are pressing in from Dan, in the far north of the country; cf. 4.15. **17:** The *adder* represents those snakes known to be nonresponsive to being "charmed" by whispering; see Ps 58.4–5; Eccl 10.11.

8.18–9.3: Israel is sick unto death, and God grieves. 8.19: *My poor people,* lit. "daughter (of) my people." See 4.11; 6.26. Of course the *king* (God) is in *Zion,* and it is thus an offense that they have not removed the *images* and *idols* from God's presence. **20–21:** *The harvest is past,* see 8.13–14n. Death and mourning rituals are near at hand. **22:** *Balm in Gilead,* the region of Gilead, in the north of Israel's territory in Transjordan, was known for its medicinal herbs (46.11; Gen 37.25). The question begs a positive response, thereby setting up an intolerable incongruity between what ought to be and what is in fact the case. With plenty of medicine at hand, Jerusalem is dying. **9.1:** *Spring of water,* the people have drunk "poison water" (Heb "me-ro'sh," 8.14), but an entire "head of waters" (Heb "ro'shi mayim") cannot provide tears enough to mourn Israel's death. **3:** *Bend their tongues like*

for they proceed from evil to evil,
and they do not know me, says the LORD.

4 Beware of your neighbors,
and put no trust in any of your kin;[a]
for all your kin[b] are supplanters,
and every neighbor goes around like a
slanderer.
5 They all deceive their neighbors,
and no one speaks the truth;
they have taught their tongues to speak
lies;
they commit iniquity and are too weary
to repent.[c]
6 Oppression upon oppression, deceit[d]
upon deceit!
They refuse to know me, says the LORD.

7 Therefore thus says the LORD of hosts:
I will now refine and test them,
for what else can I do with my sinful
people?[e]
8 Their tongue is a deadly arrow;
it speaks deceit through the mouth.
They all speak friendly words to their
neighbors,
but inwardly are planning to lay an
ambush.
9 Shall I not punish them for these things?
says the LORD;
and shall I not bring retribution
on a nation such as this?

10 Take up[f] weeping and wailing for the
mountains,
and a lamentation for the pastures of
the wilderness,
because they are laid waste so that no one
passes through,

and the lowing of cattle is not heard;
both the birds of the air and the animals
have fled and are gone.
11 I will make Jerusalem a heap of ruins,
a lair of jackals;
and I will make the towns of Judah a
desolation,
without inhabitant.

12 Who is wise enough to understand this?
To whom has the mouth of the LORD spoken,
so that they may declare it? Why is the land
ruined and laid waste like a wilderness, so
that no one passes through? 13 And the LORD
says: Because they have forsaken my law that
I set before them, and have not obeyed my
voice, or walked in accordance with it, 14 but
have stubbornly followed their own hearts
and have gone after the Baals, as their ancestors taught them. 15 Therefore thus says the
LORD of hosts, the God of Israel: I am feeding
this people with wormwood, and giving them
poisonous water to drink. 16 I will scatter
them among nations that neither they nor
their ancestors have known; and I will send
the sword after them, until I have consumed
them.

17 Thus says the LORD of hosts:
Consider, and call for the mourning
women to come;

a Heb *in a brother*
b Heb *for every brother*
c Cn Compare Gk: Heb *they weary themselves with
iniquity. ⁶Your dwelling*
d Cn: Heb *Your dwelling in the midst of deceit*
e Or *my poor people*
f Gk Syr: Heb *I will take up*

bows. That is, they string (lit. "thread") their tongues so that their words can be shot like deadly arrows; cf. v. 8
where the tongue is now the arrow.

9.4–9: The LORD's warnings: *Supplanters* (Heb "'aqob ya'qob"), Israel is characterized by its name, Jacob
("ya'aqob"), and is full of oppression and deceit. On Jacob's twofold "supplanting" of his brother, see Gen 27.36;
cf. Gen 25.26 (textual note *d*); Hos 12.3. 4: *Slanderer* (Heb "rakil"), perhaps a play on the name of Jacob's wife
Rachel ("raḥel"). 7: *Refine and test them*, such efforts in purging Israel of its dross have already proven ineffective
(see 6.27–30n.). *Sinful people*, lit. "daughter (of) my people," as in 8.19. 9: See 5.9n.

9.10–26: Only the professional singers of the funeral dirge are truly wise. 10: *Lamentation* (Heb "qinah") is
the technical term for the funeral dirge. The displacement of domestic animals by wild animals is a conventional way of representing the destruction of a city or a land (Isa 13.20–22; 34.10–15). 12: The central question
is posed: "Who is wise enough?" 14: *Baals*, see 2.23n. 15: *Wormwood*, an extremely bitter and poisonous herbal
extract; cf. 23.15; Deut 29.17; Am 6.12. *Poisonous water*, cf. 8.14. Israel is experiencing death by poisoning. 17:

send for the skilled women to come;
[18] let them quickly raise a dirge over us,
so that our eyes may run down with
tears,
and our eyelids flow with water.
[19] For a sound of wailing is heard from
Zion:
"How we are ruined!
We are utterly shamed,
because we have left the land,
because they have cast down our
dwellings."

[20] Hear, O women, the word of the LORD,
and let your ears receive the word of his
mouth;
teach to your daughters a dirge,
and each to her neighbor a lament.
[21] "Death has come up into our
windows,
it has entered our palaces,
to cut off the children from the streets
and the young men from the squares."
[22] Speak! Thus says the LORD:
"Human corpses shall fall
like dung upon the open field,
like sheaves behind the reaper,
and no one shall gather them."

[23] Thus says the LORD: Do not let the
wise boast in their wisdom, do not let the
mighty boast in their might, do not let the
wealthy boast in their wealth; [24] but let
those who boast boast in this, that they
understand and know me, that I am the
LORD; I act with steadfast love, justice, and

righteousness in the earth, for in these
things I delight, says the LORD.
[25] The days are surely coming, says the
LORD, when I will attend to all those who are
circumcised only in the foreskin: [26] Egypt,
Judah, Edom, the Ammonites, Moab, and all
those with shaven temples who live in the
desert. For all these nations are uncircumcised, and all the house of Israel is uncircumcised in heart.

10 Hear the word that the LORD speaks to
you, O house of Israel. [2] Thus says the
LORD:
Do not learn the way of the nations,
or be dismayed at the signs of the
heavens;
for the nations are dismayed at them.
[3] For the customs of the peoples are false:
a tree from the forest is cut down,
and worked with an ax by the hands of
an artisan;
[4] people deck it with silver and gold;
they fasten it with hammer and nails
so that it cannot move.
[5] Their idols[a] are like scarecrows in a
cucumber field,
and they cannot speak;
they have to be carried,
for they cannot walk.
Do not be afraid of them,
for they cannot do evil,
nor is it in them to do good.

a   Heb *They*

Skilled women, lit. "the wise women." Only these professional dirge singers (cf. 2 Chr 35.25) are truly "wise,"
because they recognize death as a reality. **21:** Death sneaking in through the window echoes a theme from
Canaanite mythology regarding Baal's own palace. **22:** *No one shall gather them*, echoing the failure of the harvest (8.13–14). **25:** *Circumcised only in the foreskin*, other nations shared the custom of circumcision with Israel,
and shared Israel's guilt, in that physical circumcision is no substitute for circumcision of the heart; see 4.4n.
26: *Shaven temples*, lit. "cutting the corners," a practice of desert inhabitants (25.23; 49.32) but proscribed for
Israelites (Lev 19.27; 21.5).

10.1–18: Israel's judgment doxology. Custom dictated that persons condemned "give glory to God" as a
means of accepting any "bloodguilt" for a pending judgment upon them (13.16; Josh 7.19). **1–10:** A characteristic
satire of human-made idols, similar to Isa 44.9–20. **2:** *Dismayed at the signs of the heavens*, i.e., obsessed by
astrological phenomena, characteristic of Israel's neighbors. The gods were associated with stars and planets.
4: *Deck it*, that is "adorn it, beautify it" (cf. Isa 40.18–20; 41.6–7). *So that it cannot move*, or "so that it will not
teeter"; see Isa 28.7. **5:** *Like scarecrows in a cucumber field*, obscure reference, meaning they are either as stiff as
a post or totally lifeless, although made to look human (or divine); cf. Isa 1.8; Let Jer 1.70. *They have to be carried*, whereas God "carried" Israel, such idols have to be carried themselves (Isa 46.3–7). That such gods can do

[6] There is none like you, O Lord;
   you are great, and your name is great in
      might.
[7] Who would not fear you, O King of the
      nations?
   For that is your due;
among all the wise ones of the nations
   and in all their kingdoms
   there is no one like you.
[8] They are both stupid and foolish;
   the instruction given by idols
   is no better than wood![a]
[9] Beaten silver is brought from Tarshish,
   and gold from Uphaz.
They are the work of the artisan and of the
      hands of the goldsmith;
   their clothing is blue and purple;
   they are all the product of skilled
      workers.
[10] But the Lord is the true God;
   he is the living God and the everlasting
      King.
At his wrath the earth quakes,
   and the nations cannot endure his
      indignation.

[11] Thus shall you say to them: The gods
who did not make the heavens and the earth
shall perish from the earth and from under
the heavens.[b]

[12] It is he who made the earth by his power,
   who established the world by his
      wisdom,
   and by his understanding stretched out
      the heavens.
[13] When he utters his voice, there is a
      tumult of waters in the heavens,

and he makes the mist rise from the
      ends of the earth.
He makes lightnings for the rain,
   and he brings out the wind from his
      storehouses.
[14] Everyone is stupid and without
      knowledge;
   goldsmiths are all put to shame by their
      idols;
for their images are false,
   and there is no breath in them.
[15] They are worthless, a work of
      delusion;
   at the time of their punishment they
      shall perish.
[16] Not like these is the Lord,[c] the portion
      of Jacob,
   for he is the one who formed all things,
and Israel is the tribe of his inheritance;
   the Lord of hosts is his name.

[17] Gather up your bundle from the ground,
   O you who live under siege!
[18] For thus says the Lord:
I am going to sling out the inhabitants of
      the land
   at this time,
and I will bring distress on them,
   so that they shall feel it.

[19] Woe is me because of my hurt!
   My wound is severe.
But I said, "Truly this is my punishment,
   and I must bear it."

[a] Meaning of Heb uncertain
[b] This verse is in Aramaic
[c] Heb lacks the Lord

neither good nor harm is a complaint also used against God (Zeph 1.12). **6–10:** A hymn of praise, contrasting God with foreign idols. The incomparability of God is a common theme in such doxologies; see Ex 15.11; Deut 33.26; Ps 113.5. **8:** *Instruction . . . than wood,* perhaps a play on the concept that discipline was delivered by a rod of wood (Prov 13.24; 22.15). **9:** *Silver . . . from Tarshish,* most likely Tarsus in Turkey, or perhaps Tartessus in southern Spain; on Tarshish as a source of silver, see 1 Kings 10.22; Isa 60.9. *Uphaz,* unknown (Dan 10.5), perhaps an error for Ophir, a region in southern Arabia famous for gold (see 1 Kings 9.28). *Blue and purple,* the colors of royal clothing, indicating their pretentious claims in the face of God's kingship (v. 10). **11:** This verse is in Aramaic (see textual note b), indicating that it is a later gloss. **12–16:** Continues the doxology using traditional creation language (Isa 42.5; 44.24; Job 9.8; Zech 12.1). **12:** On creation as effected by divine *wisdom,* see Prov 8.22–31. **13:** An ancient mythological image was that of the creator god giving his *voice* in thunder, defeating the chaotic power of the primeval seas; see Ps 29.1–11. *Storehouses,* see Deut 28.12; Job 38.22; Pss 33.7; 135.7. **17–18:** Jerusalem is to *gather* together (cf. 8.13,14; 9.22) what little remains following the siege to be carried off into exile.

10.19–25: Israel accepts God's judgment. Following her doxology, Israel confesses her guilt and accepts

²⁰ My tent is destroyed,
  and all my cords are broken;
my children have gone from me,
  and they are no more;
there is no one to spread my tent again,
  and to set up my curtains.
²¹ For the shepherds are stupid,
  and do not inquire of the LORD;
therefore they have not prospered,
  and all their flock is scattered.

²² Hear, a noise! Listen, it is coming—
  a great commotion from the land of the
    north
to make the cities of Judah a desolation,
  a lair of jackals.

²³ I know, O LORD, that the way of human
    beings is not in their control,
  that mortals as they walk cannot direct
    their steps.
²⁴ Correct me, O LORD, but in just
    measure;
  not in your anger, or you will bring me
    to nothing.

²⁵ Pour out your wrath on the nations that
    do not know you,
  and on the peoples that do not call on
    your name;
for they have devoured Jacob;

they have devoured him and consumed
    him,
  and have laid waste his habitation.

11 The word that came to Jeremiah from the LORD: ² Hear the words of this covenant, and speak to the people of Judah and the inhabitants of Jerusalem. ³ You shall say to them, Thus says the LORD, the God of Israel: Cursed be anyone who does not heed the words of this covenant, ⁴ which I commanded your ancestors when I brought them out of the land of Egypt, from the iron-smelter, saying, Listen to my voice, and do all that I command you. So shall you be my people, and I will be your God, ⁵ that I may perform the oath that I swore to your ancestors, to give them a land flowing with milk and honey, as at this day. Then I answered, "So be it, LORD."

⁶ And the LORD said to me: Proclaim all these words in the cities of Judah, and in the streets of Jerusalem: Hear the words of this covenant and do them. ⁷ For I solemnly warned your ancestors when I brought them up out of the land of Egypt, warning them persistently, even to this day, saying, Obey my voice. ⁸ Yet they did not obey or incline their ear, but everyone walked in the stubbornness of an evil will. So I brought upon them all the words of this covenant, which I commanded them to do, but they did not.

divine punishment. **20–21:** *Tent . . . cords . . . curtains* are used metaphorically of Jerusalem and the Temple; see Ex 26.12; 35.18; 39.40. The invading Babylonians destroyed Judah's infrastructure in 586 BCE and carried the leaders (*shepherds*) and wealthy into captivity (52.1–30). **22:** As elsewhere, this invasion comes *from . . . the north* (1.13–15; 4.6; 6.22; 25.9). **23–25:** A prayer. The one who prays cites Prov 20.24 (v. 23) and Ps 79.6–7 (v. 25) to direct God's attention away from Judah and to neighboring nations instead. **24:** It was acceptable for Israel to plead for tempered justice (cf. 46.28; Ps 141.5). **25:** Biblical piety often allows the one experiencing divine judgment also to call for divine action against the enemies of God who "devour" God's portion; see 2.3; Ps 7.6,9.

11.1–17: The broken covenant. The disobedience of Israel's ancestors and their punishment has not prompted Israel to any greater faithfulness. They, like their ancestors, have also broken the covenant and are so cut off from divine favor that even intercession is of no assistance. Much of the language echoes the book of Deuteronomy (v. 3, Deut 27.26; v. 4, Deut 4.20; v. 5, *oath . . . ancestors*, Deut 7.8,12–13; *a land flowing with milk and honey*, Deut 6.3; 11.9; *as at this day*, Deut 6.24; 10.15). **1–5:** Recalls the curses and blessings that typically conclude a treaty or covenant agreement. **4:** *Your ancestors*, that is, those led by Moses from Egypt in the Exodus. In this tradition, the covenant was made with Moses at Sinai. **5:** *The oath that I swore to your ancestors*, here the reference is to the ancestors of those mentioned in v. 4—that is, to the generations of Abraham, Isaac, and Jacob. In this tradition, these ancestors did not receive a "covenant" but rather an "oath" or "promissory note." This promissory note was for the land of Canaan, flowing with milk and honey (see Ex 13.5; Deut 6.3; 11.9; 26.15). *So be it, LORD*, Jeremiah's response (Heb "'amen"), is the technical response accepting the consequences of a self-imprecation when swearing an oath; see Deut 27.15–26. **6–8:** Given the failure of their ancestors, the people are subject to the treaty curses. **7:** *Your ancestors*, that

⁹ And the LORD said to me: Conspiracy exists among the people of Judah and the inhabitants of Jerusalem. ¹⁰ They have turned back to the iniquities of their ancestors of old, who refused to heed my words; they have gone after other gods to serve them; the house of Israel and the house of Judah have broken the covenant that I made with their ancestors. ¹¹ Therefore, thus says the LORD, assuredly I am going to bring disaster upon them that they cannot escape; though they cry out to me, I will not listen to them. ¹² Then the cities of Judah and the inhabitants of Jerusalem will go and cry out to the gods to whom they make offerings, but they will never save them in the time of their trouble. ¹³ For your gods have become as many as your towns, O Judah; and as many as the streets of Jerusalem are the altars to shame you have set up, altars to make offerings to Baal.

¹⁴ As for you, do not pray for this people, or lift up a cry or prayer on their behalf, for I will not listen when they call to me in the time of their trouble. ¹⁵ What right has my beloved in my house, when she has done vile deeds? Can vows[a] and sacrificial flesh avert your doom? Can you then exult? ¹⁶ The LORD once called you, "A green olive tree, fair with goodly fruit"; but with the roar of a great tempest he will set fire to it, and its branches will be consumed. ¹⁷ The LORD of hosts, who planted you, has pronounced evil against you, because of the evil that the house of Israel and the house of Judah have done, provoking me to anger by making offerings to Baal.

¹⁸ It was the LORD who made it known to
me, and I knew;
    then you showed me their evil deeds.
¹⁹ But I was like a gentle lamb
    led to the slaughter.
And I did not know it was against me
    that they devised schemes, saying,
"Let us destroy the tree with its fruit,
    let us cut him off from the land of the
        living,
    so that his name will no longer be
        remembered!"
²⁰ But you, O LORD of hosts, who judge
    righteously,
    who try the heart and the mind,
let me see your retribution upon them,
    for to you I have committed my cause.

²¹ Therefore thus says the LORD concerning the people of Anathoth, who seek your life, and say, "You shall not prophesy in the name of the LORD, or you will die by our hand"— ²² therefore thus says the LORD of hosts: I am going to punish them; the young men shall die by the sword; their sons and their daughters shall die by famine; ²³ and not even a remnant shall be left of them. For I will bring disaster upon the people of Anathoth, the year of their punishment.

a Gk: Heb Can many

is, the generation of Moses. **8:** *All the words of this covenant.* The curse of v. 3, but more generally of Deut 28.15–44. **9–13:** Israel's present disobedience (going *after other gods*, v. 10) is a return to the ways of the ancestors, that is, to the generation of Moses. **9:** *Conspiracy*, used specifically of plots of rebellion against the king. See 2 Sam 15.12; 2 Kings 11.14. **13:** *Shame* (Heb "boshet") is a metaphor for the Canaanite god Baal (see 2.26n.; 3.24; 7.19). **14–17:** God's refusal to listen to Israel's cry (v. 11) has as its corollary God's refusal to allow Jeremiah to intercede on their behalf (see 7.16). **16:** *Green olive tree*, on the high status of this tree, see Judg 9.8–9; Hos 14.6; Ps 52.8.

11.18–12.17: Jeremiah's complaints and divine response. The first of Jeremiah's complaints, these words were shaped by the editor utilizing typical psalm language and attributed to Jeremiah in order to enhance the persona of the suffering prophet. See also 15.20–21; 17.14–18; 18.18–23; 20.7–13; 20.14–18. **11.18–23:** If Jeremiah cannot pray on behalf of the people (see v. 14), he will pray (lament) on his own behalf. **19:** *Lamb led to the slaughter,* cf. Isa 53.7. **20:** *Who try the heart and the mind*, the psalmist often appeals to God's testing as a basis for God to act for the sake of divine justice and mercy, convinced that God will find the heart free from sin and deceit. See Pss 17.3; 26.2. 139.23. **21:** *The people of Anathoth*, that is, from Jeremiah's own hometown, suggesting that Jeremiah was threatened with death if he continued to prophesy such things. On Anathoth, see 1.1n. and 7.12n. **22:** *Famine*, that is, a shortage of food prompted by the Babylonian siege; cf. 19.9 and 2 Kings 6.24–29.

12.1–17: The complaints of Jeremiah and God merge in their grief over Israel. Such accusation against God

12

You will be in the right, O LORD,
  when I lay charges against you;
  but let me put my case to you.
Why does the way of the guilty prosper?
  Why do all who are treacherous thrive?
[2] You plant them, and they take root;
  they grow and bring forth fruit;
you are near in their mouths
  yet far from their hearts.
[3] But you, O LORD, know me;
  You see me and test me—my heart is
    with you.
Pull them out like sheep for the slaughter,
  and set them apart for the day of
    slaughter.
[4] How long will the land mourn,
  and the grass of every field wither?
For the wickedness of those who live in it
  the animals and the birds are swept
    away,
  and because people said, "He is blind to
    our ways."[a]

[5] If you have raced with foot-runners and
    they have wearied you,
  how will you compete with horses?
And if in a safe land you fall down,
  how will you fare in the thickets of the
    Jordan?
[6] For even your kinsfolk and your own
    family,
  even they have dealt treacherously with
    you;
  they are in full cry after you;
do not believe them,

though they speak friendly words to
  you.
[7] I have forsaken my house,
  I have abandoned my heritage;
I have given the beloved of my heart
  into the hands of her enemies.
[8] My heritage has become to me
  like a lion in the forest;
she has lifted up her voice against me—
  therefore I hate her.
[9] Is the hyena greedy[b] for my heritage at
    my command?
  Are the birds of prey all around her?
Go, assemble all the wild animals;
  bring them to devour her.
[10] Many shepherds have destroyed my
    vineyard,
  they have trampled down my
    portion,
they have made my pleasant portion
  a desolate wilderness.
[11] They have made it a desolation;
  desolate, it mourns to me.
The whole land is made desolate,
  but no one lays it to heart.
[12] Upon all the bare heights[c] in the desert
    spoilers have come;
for the sword of the LORD devours
  from one end of the land to the other;
  no one shall be safe.

a Gk: Heb *to our future*
b Cn: Heb *Is the hyena, the bird of prey*
c Or *the trails*

and, at the same time, against one's enemies is characteristic of Israelite piety. Just as Jeremiah is alienated from his *own family* (v. 6), so God is alienated from God's own house (v. 7). 1: *Lay charges*, technical term for lodging a formal legal appeal. Like Job (Job 9.3; 23.1–17), Jeremiah wishes to sue God in court but knows that he cannot win. Conventional wisdom and the sentiments of Deuteronomic theology suggest that sin is punished and righteousness rewarded. Jeremiah frames his complaint in terms of general human suffering; cf. Hab 1.1–17. 3: *Know me . . . test me*, typical sentiments of the Psalms, where God's testing is invited to prove one's merit and righteousness (Pss 11.5; 17.3; 139.23–24). *Like sheep for the slaughter*, cf. 11.19.

12.5–6: God's response to Jeremiah. 5: *Foot-runners*, or more likely foot soldiers (Judg 20.2; 1 Sam 4.10; 15.4), as opposed to horse-drawn chariots. *Thickets of the Jordan*, the "pride" or lush river banks of the Jordan River was the abode of wild lions (49.19; Zech 11.3). 6: *Even your kinsfolk*, the people of Anathoth; see 11.21.

12.7–13: God's lament over Israel for abandoning her to her enemies. 8: *I hate her*, the term also has the technical sense in treaty contexts of becoming an enemy to another nation. God has become Israel's cove-nanted enemy. 9: The questions beg a negative answer, so the scavengers must be assembled to feed on the carcass of the victim. 10: *Many shepherds*, referring to Israel's kings; see 23.1–4. 11. *The whole land*, the Heb term "'erets" can mean "land" (of Israel) or "earth." The term here used of Israel introduces a cosmic element that is developed in what follows as all the nations are swept up in divine judgment.

[13] They have sown wheat and have reaped thorns,
   they have tired themselves out but profit nothing.
They shall be ashamed of their[a] harvests
   because of the fierce anger of the LORD.

[14] Thus says the LORD concerning all my evil neighbors who touch the heritage that I have given my people Israel to inherit: I am about to pluck them up from their land, and I will pluck up the house of Judah from among them. [15] And after I have plucked them up, I will again have compassion on them, and I will bring them again to their heritage and to their land, every one of them. [16] And then, if they will diligently learn the ways of my people, to swear by my name, "As the LORD lives," as they taught my people to swear by Baal, then they shall be built up in the midst of my people. [17] But if any nation will not listen, then I will completely uproot it and destroy it, says the LORD.

13 Thus said the LORD to me, "Go and buy yourself a linen loincloth, and put it on your loins, but do not dip it in water." [2] So I bought a loincloth according to the word of the LORD, and put it on my loins. [3] And the word of the LORD came to me a second time, saying, [4] "Take the loincloth that you bought and are wearing, and go now to the Euphrates,[b] and hide it there in a cleft of the rock." [5] So I went, and hid it by the Euphrates,[c] as the LORD commanded me. [6] And after many days the LORD said to me,

"Go now to the Euphrates,[b] and take from there the loincloth that I commanded you to hide there." [7] Then I went to the Euphrates,[b] and dug, and I took the loincloth from the place where I had hidden it. But now the loincloth was ruined; it was good for nothing.

[8] Then the word of the LORD came to me: [9] Thus says the LORD: Just so I will ruin the pride of Judah and the great pride of Jerusalem. [10] This evil people, who refuse to hear my words, who stubbornly follow their own will and have gone after other gods to serve them and worship them, shall be like this loincloth, which is good for nothing. [11] For as the loincloth clings to one's loins, so I made the whole house of Israel and the whole house of Judah cling to me, says the LORD, in order that they might be for me a people, a name, a praise, and a glory. But they would not listen.

[12] You shall speak to them this word: Thus says the LORD, the God of Israel: Every wine-jar should be filled with wine. And they will say to you, "Do you think we do not know that every wine-jar should be filled with wine?" [13] Then you shall say to them: Thus says the LORD: I am about to fill all the inhabitants of this land—the kings who sit on David's throne, the priests, the prophets, and all the inhabitants of Jerusalem—with drunkenness. [14] And I will dash them one against

---

a   Heb *your*
b   Or *to Parah*; Heb *perath*
c   Or *by Parah*; Heb *perath*

12.14–17: An addition to the divine lament, reshaping it to promise Judah's restoration in the midst of universal restoration. **14:** *Pluck them up,* a thematic term in Jeremiah, used of judgment (1.10). Here Judah's fate is placed in universal context as all the nations are uprooted, Judah among them. **15:** *Everyone of them* refers not simply to Judah but to all nations, who will live figuratively in Judah's midst (vv. 16–17). **16:** *Baal,* the Canaanite deity. **17:** *Uproot . . . destroy,* 1.10.

13.1–27: The sign of the loincloth. A series of oracles held together by word associations. The series is introduced with the symbolic story of Jeremiah's loincloth, representing God's intimacy with Israel and Israel's "clinging" to God (v. 11); it also represents the "ruined" nature of the relationship that was now "good for nothing" (v. 10). **1–11:** Sign-acts are a common feature of prophetic behavior (cf. chs 16; 18; 19; 32; Ezek 4.1–5.17). **4:** *Euphrates,* some doubt there were two trips to the Euphrates (Heb "perat"); instead they suggest that the town of Parah (textual note *b*), mentioned only in Josh 18.23, is meant. This sign is more likely a literary device. See also the prophetic sign associated with the Euphrates in 51.60–64. **9:** *Pride of Jerusalem,* majesty belongs to God, and national pride, whether that of Israel and Jerusalem (Hos 5.5; Am 6.8) or other nations (48.29; Isa 13.11,19; Ezek 16.49), is offensive to God. **12–14:** Taking up the term "ruin" from the earlier sign (v. 14, "destroy"), the image shifts to the nations being filled with wine, often a symbol of either drunkenness or even of poisoning

another, parents and children together, says the Lord. I will not pity or spare or have compassion when I destroy them.

¹⁵ Hear and give ear; do not be haughty,
 for the Lord has spoken.
¹⁶ Give glory to the Lord your God
 before he brings darkness,
and before your feet stumble
 on the mountains at twilight;
while you look for light,
 he turns it into gloom
 and makes it deep darkness.
¹⁷ But if you will not listen,
 my soul will weep in secret for your
 pride;
my eyes will weep bitterly and run down
 with tears,
 because the Lord's flock has been taken
 captive.

¹⁸ Say to the king and the queen mother:
 "Take a lowly seat,
for your beautiful crown
 has come down from your head."^a
¹⁹ The towns of the Negeb are shut up
 with no one to open them;
all Judah is taken into exile,
 wholly taken into exile.

²⁰ Lift up your eyes and see
 those who come from the north.
Where is the flock that was given you,
 your beautiful flock?
²¹ What will you say when they set as head
 over you
 those whom you have trained
 to be your allies?
Will not pangs take hold of you,
 like those of a woman in labor?

²² And if you say in your heart,
 "Why have these things come upon
 me?"
it is for the greatness of your iniquity
 that your skirts are lifted up,
 and you are violated.
²³ Can Ethiopians^b change their skin
 or leopards their spots?
Then also you can do good
 who are accustomed to do evil.
²⁴ I will scatter you^c like chaff
 driven by the wind from the desert.
²⁵ This is your lot,
 the portion I have measured out to you,
 says the Lord,
because you have forgotten me
 and trusted in lies.
²⁶ I myself will lift up your skirts over your
 face,
 and your shame will be seen.
²⁷ I have seen your abominations,
 your adulteries and neighings, your
 shameless prostitutions
 on the hills of the countryside.
Woe to you, O Jerusalem!
 How long will it be
 before you are made clean?

14 The word of the Lord that came to Jeremiah concerning the drought:
² Judah mourns
 and her gates languish;
they lie in gloom on the ground,
 and the cry of Jerusalem goes up.
³ Her nobles send their servants for water;
 they come to the cisterns,

---

a   Gk Syr Vg: Meaning of Heb uncertain
b   Or *Nubians*; Heb *Cushites*
c   Heb *them*

(25.15–16; 51.7; Ezek 23.33). **15–27:** Various oracles keyed to the terms "pride" (v. 17), "flock" (vv. 17,20), "head" (vv. 18,21), and "beauty" (vv. 18,20). **16:** *Give glory,* an invitation to provide a judgment doxology, as in 10.1–18. **18:** *The king,* either Jehoiakim, who reigned through most of the first Babylonian siege until 597 BCE, or his son Jehoiachin, who reigned briefly before Jerusalem finally fell. **19:** *Negeb,* the southernmost region of Judah. **20:** *From the north,* the invading Babylonian army; see 1.14n. **21:** The pains of childbirth symbolize agony and despair (Isa 13.8; Mic 4.9). **22,26:** Exposure and sexual violation was a form of punishment.; cf. Nah 3.5; Ezek 16.35–43. **23:** *Ethiopians,* the inhabitants of Cush, the land south of Egypt. In her present state, Jerusalem cannot change herself; cf. Hos 5.4. **27:** *Your . . . neighings,* the lust of horses was a strong symbol of sexual depravity symbolizing Israel's foreign dalliances and resulting religious apostasy (5.8; Ezek 23.20).

   14.1–15.21: Oracles concerning the drought. 14.1–10: In the face of critical drought (vv. 2–6), a lament and intercessory plea is voiced (vv. 7–9), only to be rejected by God (v. 10). **1:** *The drought,* the Heb term is general

they find no water,
  they return with their vessels empty.
They are ashamed and dismayed
  and cover their heads,
[4] because the ground is cracked.
  Because there has been no rain on the
    land
the farmers are dismayed;
  they cover their heads.
[5] Even the doe in the field forsakes her
    newborn fawn
  because there is no grass.
[6] The wild asses stand on the bare heights,[a]
  they pant for air like jackals;
their eyes fail
  because there is no herbage.

[7] Although our iniquities testify against us,
  act, O Lord, for your name's sake;
our apostasies indeed are many,
  and we have sinned against you.
[8] O hope of Israel,
  its savior in time of trouble,
why should you be like a stranger in the
    land,
  like a traveler turning aside for the
    night?
[9] Why should you be like someone
    confused,
  like a mighty warrior who cannot give
    help?
Yet you, O Lord, are in the midst of us,
  and we are called by your name;
  do not forsake us!

[10] Thus says the Lord concerning this
    people:
Truly they have loved to wander,
  they have not restrained their feet;

therefore the Lord does not accept them,
  now he will remember their iniquity
    and punish their sins.

[11] The Lord said to me: Do not pray for the welfare of this people. [12] Although they fast, I do not hear their cry, and although they offer burnt offering and grain offering, I do not accept them; but by the sword, by famine, and by pestilence I consume them. [13] Then I said: "Ah, Lord God! Here are the prophets saying to them, 'You shall not see the sword, nor shall you have famine, but I will give you true peace in this place.'" [14] And the Lord said to me: The prophets are prophesying lies in my name; I did not send them, nor did I command them or speak to them. They are prophesying to you a lying vision, worthless divination, and the deceit of their own minds. [15] Therefore thus says the Lord concerning the prophets who prophesy in my name though I did not send them, and who say, "Sword and famine shall not come on this land": By sword and famine those prophets shall be consumed. [16] And the people to whom they prophesy shall be thrown out into the streets of Jerusalem, victims of famine and sword. There shall be no one to bury them—themselves, their wives, their sons, and their daughters. For I will pour out their wickedness upon them.

[17] You shall say to them this word:
Let my eyes run down with tears night and
    day,
  and let them not cease,

[a] Or the trails

("the trouble," see Pss 9.9; 10.1), but the LXX uses a word that specifically refers to "drought." **3,4:** *Cover their heads* as a ritual sign of mourning (2 Sam 15.30; Esth 6.12). **7:** *For your name's sake,* Israelite theology understood that, in spite of one's sin, God might act simply for the sake of God's own reputation; cf. Num 14.13–16; Ezek 20.1–26; Pss 25.11; 79.9. **8:** *Stranger,* or "sojourner," a foreign resident and not a citizen with full rights and obligations, but nevertheless enjoying some social protections. **9:** *Called by your name,* indicates possession. The appeal here is to God's responsibility as "owner" of Israel. **10:** In spite of their appropriate and well-fashioned lament, God rejects their prayer using the technical language of worship. **11–16:** Immediately following this lament and rejection, Jeremiah is again instructed not to perform the prophetic task of intercession (cf. 7.16; 11.14; 14.11), and God restates the rejection, again using the technical language of worship. **14:** *They are prophesying,* using a form of the verb suggesting the ecstatic nature of prophetic utterance. *Lies,* a term used in Jeremiah to refer either to Baal worship or, as here, to the false confidence in God that "peace" (v. 13) is the order of the day (cf. 7.4). **17–18:** The theme of "sword and famine" from the previous verses shapes this lament. **17.** *Virgin*

for the virgin daughter—my people—is
    struck down with a crushing blow,
  with a very grievous wound.
[18] If I go out into the field,
  look—those killed by the sword!
And if I enter the city,
  look—those sick with[a] famine!
For both prophet and priest ply their trade
  throughout the land,
  and have no knowledge.

[19] Have you completely rejected Judah?
  Does your heart loathe Zion?
Why have you struck us down
  so that there is no healing for us?
We look for peace, but find no good;
  for a time of healing, but there is terror
    instead.
[20] We acknowledge our wickedness,
  O LORD,
  the iniquity of our ancestors,
  for we have sinned against you.
[21] Do not spurn us, for your name's sake;
  do not dishonor your glorious throne;
  remember and do not break your
    covenant with us.
[22] Can any idols of the nations bring rain?
  Or can the heavens give showers?
Is it not you, O LORD our God?
  We set our hope on you,
  for it is you who do all this.

15 Then the LORD said to me: Though
Moses and Samuel stood before me,
yet my heart would not turn toward this
people. Send them out of my sight, and let
them go! [2] And when they say to you, "Where
shall we go?" you shall say to them: Thus says
the LORD:
  Those destined for pestilence, to
    pestilence,
  and those destined for the sword, to the
    sword;
  those destined for famine, to famine,
  and those destined for captivity, to
    captivity.
[3] And I will appoint over them four kinds of
destroyers, says the LORD: the sword to kill,
the dogs to drag away, and the birds of the air
and the wild animals of the earth to devour
and destroy. [4] I will make them a horror to all
the kingdoms of the earth because of what
King Manasseh son of Hezekiah of Judah did
in Jerusalem.

[5] Who will have pity on you, O Jerusalem,
  or who will bemoan you?
Who will turn aside
  to ask about your welfare?
[6] You have rejected me, says the LORD,
  you are going backward;
so I have stretched out my hand against
    you and destroyed you—
  I am weary of relenting.
[7] I have winnowed them with a winnowing
    fork
  in the gates of the land;
I have bereaved them, I have destroyed my
    people;
  they did not turn from their ways.

a Heb *look—the sicknesses of*

daughter, the loss of a virgin daughter was particularly tragic. **18:** *Ply their trade*, the verb has the negative connotation that prophets and priests treat their responsibility for "word" and "instruction" as though they were merchandise for sale. **19–22:** Another lament by the people in which they seem to have a thoroughgoing change of heart. This outstanding example of confession of sin and of hope for divine mercy, as well stated as it is, is to no avail. **19:** Cf. Lam 5.22; Ps 74.1; 79.5. *Healing*, 3.22; 8.22. **20:** Cf. 3.25; Ps 79.8. **21:** *For your name's sake*, that is, for the sake of God's own reputation among the nations. See v. 7n.; Ps 79.10; 115.2. **22:** *Hope*, see v. 8. **15.1–4:** Moses and Samuel were honored as Israel's chief intercessors, repeatedly pleading for God's good favor in the face of the people's disobedience (Ex 32.11–14; Num 11.12; 21.7; 1 Sam 8.6). Israel's destruction cannot be mitigated. **2:** The usual triad is sword, famine, and pestilence; see Jer 14.12; 24.10; 27.8. But here the four terms are "death" (NRSV "pestilence"), "sword," "famine," and "captivity," each matched with one of the "four kinds of destroyers" (v. 3). **4:** *King Manasseh* (698/687–642 BCE) was blamed for singlehandedly assuring Judah's destruction, in spite of his son Josiah's reforming efforts (2 Kings 23.26–27).

15.5–9: God's lament over Jerusalem. 6: *Backward*, looking or going backward as a statement of going in the wrong direction in rebellion; cf. 7.24; Isa 50.5. *Relenting*, the term used of God "repenting of" or "regretting" a decision (Gen 6.6). The ability of God to "relent of punishment" was a standard aspect of Israel's faith (Jon 4.2;

⁸Their widows became more numerous
     than the sand of the seas;
I have brought against the mothers of
     youths
     a destroyer at noonday;
I have made anguish and terror
     fall upon her suddenly.
⁹She who bore seven has languished;
     she has swooned away;
her sun went down while it was yet day;
     she has been shamed and
          disgraced.
And the rest of them I will give to the
     sword
     before their enemies,
                              says the LORD.

¹⁰Woe is me, my mother, that you ever
bore me, a man of strife and contention to
the whole land! I have not lent, nor have I
borrowed, yet all of them curse me. ¹¹The
LORD said: Surely I have intervened in your
lifeᵃ for good, surely I have imposed enemies
on you in a time of trouble and in a time of
distress.ᵇ ¹²Can iron and bronze break iron
from the north?
¹³Your wealth and your treasures I will give
as plunder, without price, for all your sins,
throughout all your territory. ¹⁴I will make
you serve your enemies in a land that you
do not know, for in my anger a fire is kindled
that shall burn forever.
¹⁵O LORD, you know;
     remember me and visit me,

and bring down retribution for me on
     my persecutors.
In your forbearance do not take me away;
     know that on your account I suffer
          insult.
¹⁶Your words were found, and I ate them,
     and your words became to me a joy
     and the delight of my heart;
for I am called by your name,
     O LORD, God of hosts.
¹⁷I did not sit in the company of
     merrymakers,
     nor did I rejoice;
under the weight of your hand I sat alone,
     for you had filled me with indignation.
¹⁸Why is my pain unceasing,
     my wound incurable,
     refusing to be healed?
Truly, you are to me like a deceitful brook,
     like waters that fail.

¹⁹Therefore thus says the LORD:
If you turn back, I will take you back,
     and you shall stand before me.
If you utter what is precious, and not what
     is worthless,
     you shall serve as my mouth.
It is they who will turn to you,
     not you who will turn to them.
²⁰And I will make you to this people
     a fortified wall of bronze;

ᵃ   Heb *intervened with you*
ᵇ   Meaning of Heb uncertain

Joel 2.13). 7: *Bereaved them*, that is, made them childless. 9: Bearing seven children or sons was considered a sign
of blessing and good fortune (Gen 46.25; Ruth 4.15; 1 Sam 2.5; Job 42.13), just as the loss of seven was considered
absolute bereavement (2 Sam 21.5–14; 2 Macc 7.20).

15.10–21: Jeremiah's second complaint and God's response. See 11.18–12.17n. 10: Borrowing and lending represents Jeremiah's claim to overall and basic innocence. Israel had strict limits to borrowing and lending; see Ex
22.25; Deut 24.10–11; Neh 5.10–11; and cf. 1 Sam 12.3. 11: *The LORD said*, or perhaps, with LXX, Jeremiah continues,
"So be it LORD," with more claims of his innocence. See textual note *a*. 12: The question, though obscure, requires a negative response and must refer to the onslaught of the enemy *from the north* (see 1.14n.). Even Israel,
armored with bronze and iron (6.28), cannot withstand the enemy from the north. 13: This must represent God's
response. Israel is about to be plundered as punishment for its sins; cf. 17.3–4. 14: The notion of God's wrath
burning *forever* is not in the Hebrew. 15: *In your forbearance*, God's "slowness to anger" is normally prized (Ex
34.6; Num 14.18), but here it becomes a scandalous problem for the one hoping for speedy divine intervention
against the enemy. *On your account*, the psalmist can protest that he is suffering precisely because of devotion
to God; see Ps 69.7. 16: *Your words were found*, may refer either to 1.9 or to the finding of the book of the law in
the Temple (2 Kings 22.8); cf. Ezek 3.3. 17: *Merrymakers*, those who experience and celebrate the normal joys
of life. Jeremiah complains of being bereft of joy. 18: *Deceitful brook*, cf. Job 6.15–20. 19: *I will take you back*, or "I
shall bring you back." God's role might be more active than simply receiving Israel back. 20: *A fortified wall of*

they will fight against you,
    but they shall not prevail over you,
for I am with you
    to save you and deliver you,
            says the LORD.
²¹ I will deliver you out of the hand of the
    wicked,
    and redeem you from the grasp of the
        ruthless.

16 The word of the LORD came to me:
² You shall not take a wife, nor shall
you have sons or daughters in this place. ³ For
thus says the LORD concerning the sons and
daughters who are born in this place, and concerning the mothers who bear them and the
fathers who beget them in this land: ⁴ They
shall die of deadly diseases. They shall not
be lamented, nor shall they be buried; they
shall become like dung on the surface of the
ground. They shall perish by the sword and by
famine, and their dead bodies shall become
food for the birds of the air and for the wild
animals of the earth.

⁵ For thus says the LORD: Do not enter the
house of mourning, or go to lament, or bemoan them; for I have taken away my peace
from this people, says the LORD, my steadfast
love and mercy. ⁶ Both great and small shall
die in this land; they shall not be buried, and
no one shall lament for them; there shall be
no gashing, no shaving of the head for them.
⁷ No one shall break bread[a] for the mourner,
to offer comfort for the dead; nor shall anyone give them the cup of consolation to drink

for their fathers or their mothers. ⁸ You shall
not go into the house of feasting to sit with
them, to eat and drink. ⁹ For thus says the
LORD of hosts, the God of Israel: I am going
to banish from this place, in your days and
before your eyes, the voice of mirth and the
voice of gladness, the voice of the bridegroom
and the voice of the bride.

¹⁰ And when you tell this people all these
words, and they say to you, "Why has the
LORD pronounced all this great evil against
us? What is our iniquity? What is the sin
that we have committed against the LORD
our God?" ¹¹ then you shall say to them: It is
because your ancestors have forsaken me,
says the LORD, and have gone after other
gods and have served and worshiped them,
and have forsaken me and have not kept my
law; ¹² and because you have behaved worse
than your ancestors, for here you are, every
one of you, following your stubborn evil
will, refusing to listen to me. ¹³ Therefore
I will hurl you out of this land into a land
that neither you nor your ancestors have
known, and there you shall serve other
gods day and night, for I will show you no
favor.

¹⁴ Therefore, the days are surely coming,
says the LORD, when it shall no longer be said,
"As the LORD lives who brought the people
of Israel up out of the land of Egypt," ¹⁵ but
"As the LORD lives who brought the people of

---

[a] Two Mss Gk: MT *break for them*

---

bronze, God challenges Jeremiah to remain steadfast to his call and to the divine promise of being armored for
battle against his adversaries (1.18; 15.12) in the face of popular assault.

16.1–21: Further prohibitions for Jeremiah as sign-acts of coming judgment. Like the prohibition of intercession, now Jeremiah is prohibited from the normal patterns of family life and mourning rituals as signs of the
coming judgment. **1–4:** Jeremiah is prohibited from marrying and having children, taken by some scholars to
suggest a late date for his ministry, which could not then have begun until 609 BCE, when he was fairly young
(see Introduction). Most argue that this is a literary or symbolic device and downplay its biographical accuracy.
4: Common themes in Jeremiah relating to the desecration of corpses; cf. 7.33; 8.2; 9.21; 19.7; 22.18; 25.33. **5–13:**
Jeremiah is prohibited from performing mourning customs. The image of dead bodies conjures up the next image of the "house of mourning." **5:** *House of mourning* (Heb "bet marzeaḥ"), an uncommon word also found in
nonbiblical sources, likely referring to a banquet held in honor of the dead, thus involving feasting; see Am 6.7.
6: *Gashing* and *shaving of the head*, ritual actions of mourning; cf. 7.29; Lev 19.28; Deut 14.1; Hos 7.14. **8:** The house
of mourning, with its food rituals, is connected with the *house of feasting*, lit. "house of drinking" with emphasis
upon the consumption of wine. **9:** See 7.34n. **10–12:** Cf. Deut 4.25–28; 29.24–29. **12:** The people's sin is more
grievous even than that of their ancestors; cf. 11.6–10. **13:** The punishment will perfectly fit the crime: Israel will
be forced to worship other gods in the land of their exile. **14–15:** A brief interpolation from 23.7–8 promising
restoration. The Exodus will be forgotten in the face of God's new salvific event; cf. 3.16; 31.29; Isa 43.18. **16–18:**

Israel up out of the land of the north and out of all the lands where he had driven them." For I will bring them back to their own land that I gave to their ancestors.

[16] I am now sending for many fishermen, says the Lord, and they shall catch them; and afterward I will send for many hunters, and they shall hunt them from every mountain and every hill, and out of the clefts of the rocks. [17] For my eyes are on all their ways; they are not hidden from my presence, nor is their iniquity concealed from my sight. [18] And[a] I will doubly repay their iniquity and their sin, because they have polluted my land with the carcasses of their detestable idols, and have filled my inheritance with their abominations.

[19] O Lord, my strength and my stronghold,
    my refuge in the day of trouble,
to you shall the nations come
    from the ends of the earth and say:
Our ancestors have inherited nothing but
        lies,
    worthless things in which there is no
        profit.
[20] Can mortals make for themselves gods?
    Such are no gods!

[21] "Therefore I am surely going to teach them, this time I am going to teach them my

power and my might, and they shall know that my name is the Lord."

17 The sin of Judah is written with an iron pen; with a diamond point it is engraved on the tablet of their hearts, and on the horns of their altars, [2] while their children remember their altars and their sacred poles,[b] beside every green tree, and on the high hills, [3] on the mountains in the open country. Your wealth and all your treasures I will give for spoil as the price of your sin[c] throughout all your territory. [4] By your own act you shall lose the heritage that I gave you, and I will make you serve your enemies in a land that you do not know, for in my anger a fire is kindled[d] that shall burn forever.

[5] Thus says the Lord:
Cursed are those who trust in mere mortals
    and make mere flesh their strength,
    whose hearts turn away from the Lord.
[6] They shall be like a shrub in the desert,
    and shall not see when relief comes.

a   Gk: Heb *And first*
b   Heb *Asherim*
c   Cn: Heb *spoil your high places for sin*
d   Two Mss Theodotion: *you kindled*

Fishing and hunting as metaphors for divine judgment. **18:** *Doubly repay* as fullness of compensation; see Gen 43.15; Isa 40.2. Double punishment is warranted for the offense. Since dead carcasses pollute, as do things that are "detestable" (Lev 11.10–12), the dead carcasses of detestable things (*idols*) would be particularly defiling. **19–21:** A brief concluding hymn of praise and divine oath regarding the conversion of the nations. **19.** *Worthless things*, a term used of idols of false gods (Deut 22.31; Ps 31.6). *No profit*, an allusion to the Canaanite god Baal; see 2.8n. On the theme of the conversion of the nations, see Isa 2.2; 60.3; 66.18; Mic. 4.2; Zech 8.22; 14.16; Ps 86.9. **20:** See 10.5,8,14–15.

17.1–18: Various oracles gathered under the theme of the drought. Fragments brought together under the theme established in 14.1, these oracles present a collage of coming judgment. **1–4:** Israel's intransigence is likened to an engraver writing on rock; cf. Job 19.24. **1:** *Diamond point*, the term usually refers to sharp thorns, but can be used also of sharp hard stone, probably flint; cf. Ezek 3.9; Zech 7.12. *Tablet of their hearts*, combining the images of the Torah being written on the human heart (Deut 30.14) and on tablets of stone (Ex 24.12; 31.18). But now it is their sinfulness that is so engraved. The human heart represented the center of resolve and will. Its hardening was a common metaphor for human stubbornness. *Horns of their altars*, protrusions at each of the four corners of a cut-stone altar, symbolizing divine strength and functioning to hold in place the wood and animal parts. Sanctuary could be gained by seizing the horns; see 7.4n. **2:** *Sacred poles*, Heb "'asherim" (the "'asherah" represented the goddess Asherah), which were used even in the Temple itself (2 Kings 21.7; 23.4). *Green tree*, a symbol of high places, at which religious rituals were conducted in violation of the prohibitions in Deuteronomy; see 3.6,13; 1 Kings 14.23; 2 Kings 16.4. **3–4:** See 15.13. **4:** *A fire is kindled*, cf. 15.4, linking to the theme of drought. **5–8:** A curse and accompanying blessing, linked to the theme of drought in vv. 6 and 8. Cf. Ps 1 and the distinction between the righteous and the wicked, using similar imagery. **5:** *Flesh* symbolizes human

They shall live in the parched places of the
wilderness,
in an uninhabited salt land.

[7] Blessed are those who trust in the LORD,
whose trust is the LORD.
[8] They shall be like a tree planted by water,
sending out its roots by the stream.
It shall not fear when heat comes,
and its leaves shall stay green;
in the year of drought it is not anxious,
and it does not cease to bear fruit.

[9] The heart is devious above all else;
it is perverse—
who can understand it?
[10] I the LORD test the mind
and search the heart,
to give to all according to their ways,
according to the fruit of their doings.

[11] Like the partridge hatching what it did
not lay,
so are all who amass wealth unjustly;
in mid-life it will leave them,
and at their end they will prove to be
fools.

[12] O glorious throne, exalted from the
beginning,
shrine of our sanctuary!
[13] O hope of Israel! O LORD!
All who forsake you shall be put to shame;
those who turn away from you[a] shall be
recorded in the underworld,[b]
for they have forsaken the fountain of
living water, the LORD.

[14] Heal me, O LORD, and I shall be healed;
save me, and I shall be saved;
for you are my praise.
[15] See how they say to me,
"Where is the word of the LORD?
Let it come!"
[16] But I have not run away from being a
shepherd[c] in your service,
nor have I desired the fatal day.
You know what came from my lips;
it was before your face.
[17] Do not become a terror to me;
you are my refuge in the day of disaster;
[18] Let my persecutors be shamed,
but do not let me be shamed;
let them be dismayed,
but do not let me be dismayed;
bring on them the day of disaster;
destroy them with double destruction!

[19] Thus said the LORD to me: Go and stand
in the People's Gate, by which the kings of
Judah enter and by which they go out, and in
all the gates of Jerusalem, [20] and say to them:
Hear the word of the LORD, you kings of Judah, and all Judah, and all the inhabitants of
Jerusalem, who enter by these gates. [21] Thus
says the LORD: For the sake of your lives,
take care that you do not bear a burden on
the sabbath day or bring it in by the gates of
Jerusalem. [22] And do not carry a burden out of
your houses on the sabbath or do any work,
but keep the sabbath day holy, as I commanded your ancestors. [23] Yet they did not listen or

a   Heb *me*
b   Or *in the earth*
c   Meaning of Heb uncertain

weakness as opposed to divine strength. **9–10**: God tests the human heart. See Pss 11.5; 44.21. **9**: *Devious* (Heb
"'aqob"), a play on the name "Jacob" (Heb "ya'aqob"); see 9.4n. **10**: The question posed in v. 9 is immediately
answered: God tests the heart (*mind*) and examines the kidneys (*heart*). See 11.20. On the use of "kidneys" as
the seat of strong emotion and feeling, see Pss 7.9; 26.2; 73.21; Prov 23.16. **11**: A wisdom saying like those in the
book of Proverbs. **12–13**: A hymnic warning. **13**: *Hope of Israel* as a title for Israel's God, cf. 14.8. *Recorded in the
underworld*, lit. "written in the earth." The disobedient are doomed to die. The Heb word "'erets" means "earth,"
"land," or "country," (1.18; 12.11) but is also used for the netherworld (e.g., Pss 22.29; 44.26; 63.10). See Ps 69.28
for the concept of names being registered in a "book of life." *Fountain of living water*, cf. 2.13.

17.14–18: Jeremiah's third complaint (see 11.18–12.6n.). **15**: *Word of the LORD*, the prophetic oracle of judgment. They taunt Jeremiah regarding his oracles of coming disaster. **18**: *Double destruction*, see 16.18n. These
sentiments wishing for divine judgment upon one's adversaries are typical of pleas of intercession.

17.19–27: A command to honor the sabbath, concluding the section concerning the drought. The gates were
the control point for matters of sabbath keeping (Neh 13.15–19), so this word is to be delivered at all of the gates.

incline their ear; they stiffened their necks and would not hear or receive instruction.

[24] But if you listen to me, says the LORD, and bring in no burden by the gates of this city on the sabbath day, but keep the sabbath day holy and do no work on it, [25] then there shall enter by the gates of this city kings[a] who sit on the throne of David, riding in chariots and on horses, they and their officials, the people of Judah and the inhabitants of Jerusalem; and this city shall be inhabited forever. [26] And people shall come from the towns of Judah and the places around Jerusalem, from the land of Benjamin, from the Shephelah, from the hill country, and from the Negeb, bringing burnt offerings and sacrifices, grain offerings and frankincense, and bringing thank offerings to the house of the LORD. [27] But if you do not listen to me, to keep the sabbath day holy, and to carry in no burden through the gates of Jerusalem on the sabbath day, then I will kindle a fire in its gates; it shall devour the palaces of Jerusalem and shall not be quenched.

18 The word that came to Jeremiah from the LORD: [2] "Come, go down to the potter's house, and there I will let you hear my words." [3] So I went down to the potter's house, and there he was working at his wheel. [4] The vessel he was making of clay was spoiled in the potter's hand, and he reworked it into another vessel, as seemed good to him.

[5] Then the word of the LORD came to me: [6] Can I not do with you, O house of Israel, just as this potter has done? says the LORD. Just like the clay in the potter's hand, so are you in my hand, O house of Israel. [7] At one moment I may declare concerning a nation or a kingdom, that I will pluck up and break down and destroy it, [8] but if that nation, concerning which I have spoken, turns from its evil, I will change my mind about the disaster that I intended to bring on it. [9] And at another moment I may declare concerning a nation or a kingdom that I will build and plant it, [10] but if it does evil in my sight, not listening to my voice, then I will change my mind about the good that I had intended to do to it. [11] Now, therefore, say to the people of Judah and the inhabitants of Jerusalem: Thus says the LORD: Look, I am a potter shaping evil against you and devising a plan against you. Turn now, all of you from your evil way, and amend your ways and your doings.

[12] But they say, "It is no use! We will follow our own plans, and each of us will act according to the stubbornness of our evil will."

[13] Therefore thus says the LORD:
Ask among the nations:
  Who has heard the like of this?
The virgin Israel has done
  a most horrible thing.
[14] Does the snow of Lebanon leave
  the crags of Sirion?[b]

a Cn: Heb *kings and officials*
b Cn: Heb *of the field*

21: *Burden*, the term is also used for a divine "oracle"; cf. 23.33–40. **22:** *Keep the sabbath day holy*, Ex 20.8–11. **26:** *Benjamin . . . the Shephelah . . . the hill country . . . the Negeb*, the regions surrounding Jerusalem to the north, west, and south. **27:** *Kindle a fire*, cf. 15.14; 17.4, again tying this oracle into the theme of the drought.

18.1–23: The potter's house and pottery as signs of judgment. The beginning of a lengthy section (chs 18–20) focused on pottery and pottery-making as symbols of divine judgment. **1–17: A sign-act.** See 13.1–11n. At the potter's house, Jeremiah observes the potter at work as a sign of God's power to reshape Israel's future. **3:** *At his wheel*, lit. "upon the stones," referring to the stones used for turning pots. **8:** *I will change my mind about the disaster*, see 15.6n. Like the potter, God can rework the pot that is flawed. But the potter has control also to ruin his creation (v. 10); cf. Isa 45.9. The relationship between potter and clay is a metaphor of God's relationship to creation also in Isa 64.8; Sir 33.13. **10:** God can "repent" both of "disaster" and, as here, of "the good" that is planned. God can exercise total freedom to change the divine mind. **11:** The metaphor shifts from that of God's freedom to change course to that of God "plotting evil." That God "devises a plan" (or "plots a plot") against the people is taken up in the next verse. **12:** Although God may have a "plan," the people can only follow their own. The people express their fatalistic sense of doom, their inability to be "reworked." **14:** Israel acts contrary to the laws of nature by forgetting God, a common theme in the book; see 2.32n. *Lebanon*, the mountain range north of Israel that parallels the coast of the Mediterranean Sea. The name "Lebanon" is related to the word

Do the mountain[a] waters run dry,[b]
    the cold flowing streams?
[15] But my people have forgotten me,
    they burn offerings to a delusion;
they have stumbled[c] in their ways,
    in the ancient roads,
and have gone into bypaths,
    not the highway,
[16] making their land a horror,
    a thing to be hissed at forever.
All who pass by it are horrified
    and shake their heads.
[17] Like the wind from the east,
    I will scatter them before the
        enemy.
I will show them my back, not my face,
    in the day of their calamity.

[18] Then they said, "Come, let us make plots against Jeremiah—for instruction shall not perish from the priest, nor counsel from the wise, nor the word from the prophet. Come, let us bring charges against him,[d] and let us not heed any of his words."

[19] Give heed to me, O Lord,
    and listen to what my adversaries say!
[20] Is evil a recompense for good?
    Yet they have dug a pit for my life.
Remember how I stood before you
    to speak good for them,
    to turn away your wrath from them.

[21] Therefore give their children over to
        famine;
    hurl them out to the power of the
        sword,
let their wives become childless and
        widowed.
May their men meet death by
        pestilence,
    their youths be slain by the sword in
        battle.
[22] May a cry be heard from their houses,
    when you bring the marauder suddenly
        upon them!
For they have dug a pit to catch me,
    and laid snares for my feet.
[23] Yet you, O Lord, know
    all their plotting to kill me.
Do not forgive their iniquity,
    do not blot out their sin from your
        sight.
Let them be tripped up before you;
    deal with them while you are angry.

19 Thus said the Lord: Go and buy a potter's earthenware jug. Take with you[e] some of the elders of the people and some of

---

a Cn: Heb *foreign*
b Cn: Heb *Are ... plucked up?*
c Gk Syr Vg: Heb *they made them stumble*
d Heb *strike him with the tongue*
e Syr Tg Compare Gk: Heb lacks *take with you*

---

for "white," alluding to the snowy peaks. *Sirion* is a conjecture (see textual note *b*); if correct, it refers to Mount Hermon in Israel's far north (cf. Deut 3.9; Ps 29.6). *Mountain waters* is also a conjecture (see textual note *a*). **16:** Hissing and shaking the head are gestures of abhorrence and shaming. See 19.8; 1 Kings 9.8; Mic 6.16; 2 Chr 29.8;. **17:** *Show them my back*, lit "neck" or "back of the neck." This is a sign of stubbornness or neglect. Just as Israel can be "stiff-necked" (Ex 32.9), so can God; cf. 2.27; 7.26.

18.18–23: Jeremiah's fourth complaint, concerning his enemies (see 11.18–12.6n.). The sentiments are bitter, but not unusual for the piety of the Psalms. **18:** *Make plots*, this is a catchword in the section; cf. 18.8,11,12. *Priests, the wise,* and *prophets* were each associated with a primary form of divine revelation: *instruction* (Heb "torah"), *counsel,* and *word*; cf. Ezek 7.26. Jeremiah's adversaries claim these traditional forms of authority over Jeremiah's claim to an alternative word. **20:** A surprising claim, given prohibitions against Jeremiah interceding (7.16; 11.14). **23:** *While you are angry*, an appeal that God's mercy not be extended to the prophet's adversaries; see 15.15n.

19.1–20.18: The potter's flask and Jeremiah at Topheth. This section continues the theme of pottery as a symbol of divine judgment, concluding with Jeremiah's fifth complaint. No time reference is given, but by 605 BCE Jeremiah had been barred from the Temple (36.5), perhaps as a result of his confinement by the priest Pashhur, the chief officer of the Temple personnel (20.1–2). This section is the last of the oracles in the first cycle dated prior to the reign of Zedekiah.

19.1–20.6: Jeremiah at Topheth and its aftermath. On the rituals conducted at Topheth, see 7.31n. **2:** *Potsherd Gate*, nowhere else named. But since the Hinnom Valley was on the south of Jerusalem, this is likely the later

the senior priests, ² and go out to the valley of the son of Hinnom at the entry of the Potsherd Gate, and proclaim there the words that I tell you. ³ You shall say: Hear the word of the Lord, O kings of Judah and inhabitants of Jerusalem. Thus says the Lord of hosts, the God of Israel: I am going to bring such disaster upon this place that the ears of everyone who hears of it will tingle. ⁴ Because the people have forsaken me, and have profaned this place by making offerings in it to other gods whom neither they nor their ancestors nor the kings of Judah have known, and because they have filled this place with the blood of the innocent, ⁵ and gone on building the high places of Baal to burn their children in the fire as burnt offerings to Baal, which I did not command or decree, nor did it enter my mind; ⁶ therefore the days are surely coming, says the Lord, when this place shall no more be called Topheth, or the valley of the son of Hinnom, but the valley of Slaughter. ⁷ And in this place I will make void the plans of Judah and Jerusalem, and will make them fall by the sword before their enemies, and by the hand of those who seek their life. I will give their dead bodies for food to the birds of the air and to the wild animals of the earth. ⁸ And I will make this city a horror, a thing to be hissed at; everyone who passes by it will be horrified and will hiss because of all its disasters. ⁹ And I will make them eat the flesh of their sons and the flesh of their daughters, and all shall eat the flesh of their neighbors in the siege, and in the distress with which their enemies and those who seek their life afflict them.

¹⁰ Then you shall break the jug in the sight of those who go with you, ¹¹ and shall say to them: Thus says the Lord of hosts: So will I break this people and this city, as one breaks a potter's vessel, so that it can never

be mended. In Topheth they shall bury until there is no more room to bury. ¹² Thus will I do to this place, says the Lord, and to its inhabitants, making this city like Topheth. ¹³ And the houses of Jerusalem and the houses of the kings of Judah shall be defiled like the place of Topheth—all the houses upon whose roofs offerings have been made to the whole host of heaven, and libations have been poured out to other gods.

¹⁴ When Jeremiah came from Topheth, where the Lord had sent him to prophesy, he stood in the court of the Lord's house and said to all the people: ¹⁵ Thus says the Lord of hosts, the God of Israel: I am now bringing upon this city and upon all its towns all the disaster that I have pronounced against it, because they have stiffened their necks, refusing to hear my words.

20 Now the priest Pashhur son of Immer, who was chief officer in the house of the Lord, heard Jeremiah prophesying these things. ² Then Pashhur struck the prophet Jeremiah, and put him in the stocks that were in the upper Benjamin Gate of the house of the Lord. ³ The next morning when Pashhur released Jeremiah from the stocks, Jeremiah said to him, The Lord has named you not Pashhur but "Terror-all-around." ⁴ For thus says the Lord: I am making you a terror to yourself and to all your friends; and they shall fall by the sword of their enemies while you look on. And I will give all Judah into the hand of the king of Babylon; he shall carry them captive to Babylon, and shall kill them with the sword. ⁵ I will give all the wealth of this city, all its gains, all its prized belongings, and all the treasures of the kings of Judah into the hand of their enemies, who shall plunder them, and seize them, and carry them to Babylon. ⁶ And you, Pashhur, and all who live in your house, shall go into captivity, and to

Dung Gate (Neh 3.13–14), used to discard refuse (thus "Potsherd Gate"). **4:** *Blood of the innocent*, a reference to the practice of burning children to the Canaanite god Baal (or Molech) at this site in the Hinnom Valley; see 7.29n. **5:** *Baal*, but elsewhere Molech; see 32.35; 2 Kings 23.10. **7:** *Make void*, a verb (Heb "baqaq") related to the word for "jug" (Heb "baqbuq," vv. 1,10), thereby explaining the connection with the prophetic sign. **9:** The horrors of siege warfare; see 11.22n.; Deut 28.53–57. **10:** Jeremiah performs the sign-act, unleashing the curse he has spoken. **13:** *Host of heaven*, 7.18; 8.2n.; 2 Kings 21.3–5. **20.1:** *Chief officer*, the chief Temple administrator in charge of monitoring prophetic activity. Compare the role of Zephaniah in 29.26–28 and Amaziah in Am 7.10–13. Such an office was customary throughout the ancient Near East. **2:** *Stocks*, cf. 29.26 and 2 Chr 16.10, where they are similarly used to confine prophets. The Hebrew word suggests being subjected to a contorting position or

Babylon you shall go; there you shall die, and there you shall be buried, you and all your friends, to whom you have prophesied falsely.

7 O LORD, you have enticed me,
    and I was enticed;
you have overpowered me,
    and you have prevailed.
I have become a laughingstock all day long;
    everyone mocks me.
8 For whenever I speak, I must cry out,
    I must shout, "Violence and
        destruction!"
For the word of the LORD has become
        for me
    a reproach and derision all day long.
9 If I say, "I will not mention him,
    or speak any more in his name,"
then within me there is something like a
        burning fire
    shut up in my bones;
I am weary with holding it in,
    and I cannot.
10 For I hear many whispering:
    "Terror is all around!
Denounce him! Let us denounce him!"
    All my close friends
    are watching for me to stumble.
"Perhaps he can be enticed,
    and we can prevail against him,
    and take our revenge on him."
11 But the LORD is with me like a dread
        warrior;
    therefore my persecutors will stumble,
    and they will not prevail.

They will be greatly shamed,
    for they will not succeed.
Their eternal dishonor
    will never be forgotten.
12 O LORD of hosts, you test the righteous,
    you see the heart and the mind;
let me see your retribution upon them,
    for to you I have committed my cause.

13 Sing to the LORD;
    praise the LORD!
For he has delivered the life of the needy
    from the hands of evildoers.

14 Cursed be the day
    on which I was born!
The day when my mother bore me,
    let it not be blessed!
15 Cursed be the man
    who brought the news to my father,
        saying,
"A child is born to you, a son,"
    making him very glad.
16 Let that man be like the cities
    that the LORD overthrew without pity;
let him hear a cry in the morning
    and an alarm at noon,
17 because he did not kill me in the womb;
    so my mother would have been my
        grave,
    and her womb forever great.
18 Why did I come forth from the womb
    to see toil and sorrow,
    and spend my days in shame?

turned upside down. 3: *Terror-all-around*, see 17.17n. 6: *You have prophesied*, spoken of Pashhur the priest. Priests could function as prophets (so Jeremiah himself as well as Ezekiel), or perhaps it was because of his office (see v. 1) that he is attributed prophetic status.

20.7–18: **Jeremiah's final complaint** (see 11.18–12.6n.). Using strong language that has sexual overtones, Jeremiah complains of having been tricked or seduced by God. Jeremiah's own words are played upon by his enemies, who seek his ruin. A brief word of trust and praise (v. 11–13) gives way to a final self-imprecation as Jeremiah curses his own life. 7: *Enticed*, though the term can be used positively (Hos 2.14), it can also be used of seduction (Ex 22.16; Judg 14.15) and deception (2 Sam 3.25; Ps 78.36); see 1 Kings 22.20–21 for its use in a prophetic context. 10: *Terror is all around*, cf. v. 3; 6.25n. *Enticed . . . prevail*, key words in this section, cf. v. 7. 11: The expression of confidence is a common element in laments (e.g., Pss 6.8–10; 12.6–7). 12: Typical sentiments of complaint psalms in which the psalmist invites divine scrutiny and pleads for vengeance against adversaries. 13: A call to praise is typical of psalms of complaint, where deliverance is anticipated and a vow is made to lead the community in praise when deliverance is experienced (e.g., Pss 22.22–31; 31.19–24). 14–18: Raw words of bitterness concerning the human condition. Such sentiments regarding wished-for abortion or stillbirth are shocking, but not without parallels; see Job 3; Jon 4.3,8. 16: *The cities that the LORD overthrew*, Sodom and Gomorrah (Gen 19.21,25,29; Deut 29.23; Isa 13.19; Am 4.11). 17. *Forever great*, that is, "pregnant."

21 This is the word that came to Jeremiah from the LORD, when King Zedekiah sent to him Pashhur son of Malchiah and the priest Zephaniah son of Maaseiah, saying, [2] "Please inquire of the LORD on our behalf, for King Nebuchadrezzar of Babylon is making war against us; perhaps the LORD will perform a wonderful deed for us, as he has often done, and will make him withdraw from us."

[3] Then Jeremiah said to them: [4] Thus you shall say to Zedekiah: Thus says the LORD, the God of Israel: I am going to turn back the weapons of war that are in your hands and with which you are fighting against the king of Babylon and against the Chaldeans who are besieging you outside the walls; and I will bring them together into the center of this city. [5] I myself will fight against you with outstretched hand and mighty arm, in anger, in fury, and in great wrath. [6] And I will strike down the inhabitants of this city, both human beings and animals; they shall die of a great pestilence. [7] Afterward, says the LORD, I will give King Zedekiah of Judah, and his servants, and the people in this city—those who survive the pestilence, sword, and famine—into the hands of King Nebuchadrezzar of Babylon, into the hands of their enemies, into the hands of those who seek their lives. He shall strike them down with the edge of the sword; he shall not pity them, or spare them, or have compassion.

[8] And to this people you shall say: Thus says the LORD: See, I am setting before you the way of life and the way of death. [9] Those who stay in this city shall die by the sword, by famine, and by pestilence; but those who go out and surrender to the Chaldeans who are besieging you shall live and shall have their lives as a prize of war. [10] For I have set my face against this city for evil and not for good, says the LORD: it shall be given into the hands of the king of Babylon, and he shall burn it with fire.

[11] To the house of the king of Judah say: Hear the word of the LORD, [12] O house of David! Thus says the LORD:

Execute justice in the morning,
    and deliver from the hand of the
        oppressor
    anyone who has been robbed,
or else my wrath will go forth like fire,
    and burn, with no one to quench it,
    because of your evil doings.

[13] See, I am against you, O inhabitant of
    the valley,
    O rock of the plain,
                                    says the LORD;
you who say, "Who can come down
    against us,

21.1–24.10: Oracles from the reign of Zedekiah. The final phase of the first cycle of oracles. Zedekiah was the last of Judah's kings who reigned from the first deportation in 597 until the final fall of Jerusalem in 586 BCE. These oracles focus upon the royal house and establishment.

21.1–14: Oracles directed to Zedekiah, the people, and the royal house. In the face of the people's confidence, the LORD warns that he will fight against Judah (vv. 5–7), and Jerusalem and Zedekiah will fall to Nebuchadrezzar. Zedekiah repeatedly sent envoys to Jeremiah for divine guidance and information, always with similar results: Zedekiah should capitulate to the Babylonian armies; cf. 37.3–10; 38.1–3. The historical setting is apparently 588 BCE, after Zedekiah had committed himself to a rebellion against Babylon (see 52.3). **1:** *Pashhur son of Malchiah,* cf. 38.1. *Zephaniah son of Maaseiah,* the chief Temple officer who was apparently sympathetic toward Jeremiah (29.24–29). **2:** *Nebuchadrezzar,* the king of Babylon (605–562 BCE); his name is also written as "Nebuchadnezzar" (e.g., 27.6). **4:** *Chaldeans,* the inhabitants of the lower plain formed by the Tigris and Euphrates Rivers, a term that came to be used for Babylonians. **8:** *The way of life and the way of death,* Deuteronomic language (Deut 30.15,19). Ironically, Jeremiah offers the people the opportunity to choose, but their choices do not include the option of avoiding the Babylonian onslaught. The only possibility for life is surrender to the enemy besieging the city; Jerusalem, however, will be destroyed (38.17). **9:** *By the sword, by famine, and by pestilence,* a frequent triad in Jeremiah (14.12; 15.2; 18.21; 29.17–18). *A prize of war,* that is the "spoil" or "booty" that was divided among the soldiers after battle (Gen 49.27; Ex 15.9; Josh 22.8). **13:** Jerusalem was built on a narrow ridge and neighboring hill, protected on the west, south, and east, but it was vulnerable from the north. To refer to it as built in a "valley" and "plain" is derogatory language, as is the term "come *down* against," indicating its critical vulnerability in the current situation; one usually "went up" to Jerusalem. Compare the boast of the Jebusites in 2 Sam 5.6.

or who can enter our places of refuge?"
¹⁴ I will punish you according to the fruit of
your doings,

                says the LORD;
I will kindle a fire in its forest,
and it shall devour all that is around it.

22 Thus says the LORD: Go down to the
house of the king of Judah, and speak
there this word, ² and say: Hear the word
of the LORD, O King of Judah sitting on the
throne of David—you, and your servants,
and your people who enter these gates.
³ Thus says the LORD: Act with justice and
righteousness, and deliver from the hand of
the oppressor anyone who has been robbed.
And do no wrong or violence to the alien,
the orphan, and the widow, or shed in-
nocent blood in this place. ⁴ For if you will
indeed obey this word, then through the
gates of this house shall enter kings who sit
on the throne of David, riding in chariots
and on horses, they, and their servants, and
their people. ⁵ But if you will not heed these
words, I swear by myself, says the LORD, that
this house shall become a desolation. ⁶ For
thus says the LORD concerning the house of
the king of Judah:
You are like Gilead to me,
    like the summit of Lebanon;
but I swear that I will make you a
    desert,
an uninhabited city.^a

⁷ I will prepare destroyers against you,
    all with their weapons;
they shall cut down your choicest cedars
    and cast them into the fire.
⁸ And many nations will pass by this city,
and all of them will say one to another, "Why
has the LORD dealt in this way with that great
city?" ⁹ And they will answer, "Because they
abandoned the covenant of the LORD their
God, and worshiped other gods and served
them."

¹⁰ Do not weep for him who is dead,
    nor bemoan him;
weep rather for him who goes away,
    for he shall return no more
    to see his native land.
¹¹ For thus says the LORD concerning
Shallum son of King Josiah of Judah, who succeeded his father Josiah, and who went away
from this place: He shall return here no more,
¹² but in the place where they have carried
him captive he shall die, and he shall never
see this land again.

¹³ Woe to him who builds his house by
    unrighteousness,
and his upper rooms by injustice;
who makes his neighbors work for
    nothing,

a Cn: Heb *uninhabited cities*

22.1–9: Oracles directed to the king. Here the "house" refers to the palace; cf. 21.11–12, where it refers to the royal family and the dynasty. The king, as benefactor and symbol of justice, is instructed to perform the stand-ard duties of kingship to insure the continued existence of the Davidic dynasty. The criteria of justice recall Deuteronomy (Deut 16.11,14; 24.19–21); cf. Jer 7.5–7. **3:** The language repeats that of 21.12, tying these sections together thematically. **4:** Cf. 17.25. **6:** *Like Gilead*, well known for its rich cattle industry (Num 32.1; Song 4.1; 6.5) and trade in medicinal herbs (see 8.22n.; cf. 46.11). *Lebanon*, see 18.14n. **7:** *Prepare*, that is, "sanctify," indicating warfare; see 6.4n.; 51.27–28; Joel 4.9. **8–9:** A later comment (5.19; Deut 29.23–28; 1 Kings 9.8–9) referring to Jerusalem, not the palace.

22.10–30: A chronological survey of Israel's kings from Josiah to Zedekiah (see chart on p. 1058). **10–11:** *Him who is dead*, Josiah was killed at Megiddo in 609 BCE in a battle with Pharaoh Neco. Neco was leading the Egyptian army northward to come to the aid of the Assyrian army, which was under critical pressure from the Babylonians. Josiah's political program was governed by his revolt against Assyria, so he did not want Neco's campaign to relieve Assyria to succeed. *Him who goes away*, Josiah's son Jehoahaz (*Shallum*) reigned briefly but was taken captive by Pharaoh Neco II of Egypt (ruled 610–595 BCE), who placed his brother Jehoiakim (608–598 BCE) on the throne (2 Kings 23.31–34; 2 Chr 36:1–4; Ezek 19.4). **13–23:** An oracle against Jehoiakim, who is judged to be the antithesis of his father, Josiah (vv. 15–17). **13:** *Work for nothing*, the royal building projects were carried out by use of conscripted laborers, one of the realities of dynastic kingship as suggested by Samuel's warning (1 Sam 8.10–18). References to elaborate building projects completed by means of uncompensated

and does not give them their wages;
¹⁴ who says, "I will build myself a spacious
house
with large upper rooms,"
and who cuts out windows for it,
paneling it with cedar,
and painting it with vermilion.
¹⁵ Are you a king
because you compete in cedar?
Did not your father eat and drink
and do justice and
righteousness?
Then it was well with him.
¹⁶ He judged the cause of the poor and
needy;
then it was well.
Is not this to know me?
says the LORD.
¹⁷ But your eyes and heart
are only on your dishonest gain,
for shedding innocent blood,
and for practicing oppression and
violence.
¹⁸ Therefore thus says the LORD
concerning King Jehoiakim son of Josiah of
Judah:
They shall not lament for him, saying,
"Alas, my brother!" or "Alas, sister!"
They shall not lament for him, saying,
"Alas, lord!" or "Alas, his majesty!"
¹⁹ With the burial of a donkey he shall be
buried—
dragged off and thrown out beyond the
gates of Jerusalem.

²⁰ Go up to Lebanon, and cry out,
and lift up your voice in Bashan;
cry out from Abarim,
for all your lovers are crushed.

²¹ I spoke to you in your prosperity,
but you said, "I will not listen."
This has been your way from your youth,
for you have not obeyed my voice.
²² The wind shall shepherd all your
shepherds,
and your lovers shall go into captivity;
then you will be ashamed and dismayed
because of all your wickedness.
²³ O inhabitant of Lebanon,
nested among the cedars,
how you will groan[a] when pangs come
upon you,
pain as of a woman in labor!

²⁴ As I live, says the LORD, even if King
Coniah son of Jehoiakim of Judah were the
signet ring on my right hand, even from there
I would tear you off ²⁵ and give you into the
hands of those who seek your life, into the
hands of those of whom you are afraid, even
into the hands of King Nebuchadrezzar of
Babylon and into the hands of the Chaldeans.
²⁶ I will hurl you and the mother who bore
you into another country, where you were
not born, and there you shall die. ²⁷ But they
shall not return to the land to which they
long to return.

²⁸ Is this man Coniah a despised broken
pot,
a vessel no one wants?
Why are he and his offspring hurled out
and cast away in a land that they do not
know?
²⁹ O land, land, land,
hear the word of the LORD!
³⁰ Thus says the LORD:

---

a Gk Vg Syr: Heb *will be pitied*

labor suggest that Jehoiakim was perceived as imitating Solomon's grandeur and autocratic power (1 Kings
5.13–18). **14**: *Windows . . . cedar . . . vermilion*, signs of royal ostentation and arrogance. **15**: *Your father*, that is,
Josiah. **18**: The lack of professional mourners at one's funeral was a mark of shame and degradation; cf. 2 Kings
24.6, which suggests that nothing was unusual about Jehoiakim's death and burial. **20–23**: The addressee is
an individual feminine figure, presumably Jerusalem; cf. 2.20–25,33–37. **20**: From distant regions (*Lebanon,
Bashan* in northern Transjordan, *Abarim* east of the Dead Sea), lamentation will be made for Jerusalem, whose
lovers (military and political allies) have been defeated. **23**: *Inhabitant of Lebanon*, a figurative reference either
to Jerusalem or to King Jehoiakim. **24–30**: An oracle against Coniah (Jehoiachin), who reigned only briefly
before surrendering to the Babylonians in 597 BCE. **27**: Jehoiachin was maintained at the Babylonian court, and
continued to be the focus of hope for some Judeans and those in exile with him (compare the "good figs" of
24.4–7); see 2 Kings 25.27–30. **30**: *None of his offspring*, some evidence suggests that Sheshbazzar, "prince of
Judah" (Ezra 1.8), was the "Shenazzar" listed among the sons of Jehoiachin in 1 Chr 3.18, and was appointed by

Record this man as childless,
     a man who shall not succeed in his
          days;
     for none of his offspring shall succeed
          in sitting on the throne of David,
     and ruling again in Judah.

23 Woe to the shepherds who destroy and scatter the sheep of my pasture! says the LORD. [2] Therefore thus says the LORD, the God of Israel, concerning the shepherds who shepherd my people: It is you who have scattered my flock, and have driven them away, and you have not attended to them. So I will attend to you for your evil doings, says the LORD. [3] Then I myself will gather the remnant of my flock out of all the lands where I have driven them, and I will bring them back to their fold, and they shall be fruitful and multiply. [4] I will raise up shepherds over them who will shepherd them, and they shall not fear any longer, or be dismayed, nor shall any be missing, says the LORD.

[5] The days are surely coming, says the LORD, when I will raise up for David a righteous Branch, and he shall reign as king and deal wisely, and shall execute justice and righteousness in the land. [6] In his days Judah will be saved and Israel will live in safety. And this is the name by which he will be called: "The LORD is our righteousness."

[7] Therefore, the days are surely coming, says the LORD, when it shall no longer be said,

"As the LORD lives who brought the people of Israel up out of the land of Egypt," [8] but "As the LORD lives who brought out and led the offspring of the house of Israel out of the land of the north and out of all the lands where he[a] had driven them." Then they shall live in their own land.

[9] Concerning the prophets:
My heart is crushed within me,
     all my bones shake;
I have become like a drunkard,
     like one overcome by wine,
because of the LORD
     and because of his holy words.
[10] For the land is full of adulterers;
     because of the curse the land
          mourns,
     and the pastures of the wilderness are
          dried up.
Their course has been evil,
     and their might is not right.
[11] Both prophet and priest are ungodly;
     even in my house I have found their
          wickedness,
          says the LORD.
[12] Therefore their way shall be to them
     like slippery paths in the darkness,
     into which they shall be driven and fall;
for I will bring disaster upon them
     in the year of their punishment,
          says the LORD.

a Gk: Heb I

the Persians as governor of Judah (1 Esd 2.12).

23.1–8: Conclusion. The chronological survey of Judah's kings concludes with a general oracle against the "shepherds" (a common metaphor for kings; cf. 22.22; Ezek 34) and a veiled reference to Zedekiah (vv. 5–6). **2:** The shepherds have driven the flock away, but under divine purpose (vv. 3,8). *Not attended . . . attend to you*, an ambiguous term connoting both attentive care (Ex 3.16; 4.31) and especially scrutinizing punishment (Am 3.14; Zech 10.3). Both meanings are implied here. See also v. 4. **4:** *Be missing*, a third meaning of the term "attend." The basic meaning of the word is to "muster" or "count off." In counting and arranging in order some may be discovered to be missing. **5:** *Righteous Branch*, cf. 33.15; Isa 11.1; Zech 3.8; 6.12. The possession of wisdom and the execution of justice and righteousness were the hallmarks of the just king throughout the ancient Near East. **6:** This king's name is "yahweh-tsidqenu," "the LORD is our righteousness," a play on the name of Zedekiah ("tsidqi-yahu"), the last king of Judah (597–586 BCE) appointed to the throne by Nebuchadnezzar (2 Kings 24.17). The reversal of the two elements of the name suggests that he will be the antithesis of Zedekiah. Here the stress is upon the person of the future ruler; cf. 33.16, where the hope is placed not in the person of the king but in the city Jerusalem. **7–8:** See 16.14–15n. Future deliverance will surpass the past in significance, even the Exodus (cf. Isa 51.9–11; 52.11–12).

23.9–40: Oracles directed to the prophets as royal agents, who function alongside the priests in the Temple (v. 11) and who preach soothing words of well-being at a time of crisis. This oracle emphasizes words such as

¹³ In the prophets of Samaria
    I saw a disgusting thing:
they prophesied by Baal
    and led my people Israel astray.
¹⁴ But in the prophets of Jerusalem
    I have seen a more shocking thing:
they commit adultery and walk in lies;
    they strengthen the hands of evildoers,
    so that no one turns from wickedness;
all of them have become like Sodom to me,
    and its inhabitants like Gomorrah.
¹⁵ Therefore thus says the LORD of hosts
    concerning the prophets:
"I am going to make them eat wormwood,
    and give them poisoned water to drink;
for from the prophets of Jerusalem
    ungodliness has spread throughout the
    land."

¹⁶ Thus says the LORD of hosts: Do not
listen to the words of the prophets who
prophesy to you; they are deluding you. They
speak visions of their own minds, not from
the mouth of the LORD. ¹⁷ They keep saying
to those who despise the word of the LORD,
"It shall be well with you"; and to all who
stubbornly follow their own stubborn hearts,
they say, "No calamity shall come upon you."

¹⁸ For who has stood in the council of the
    LORD
    so as to see and to hear his word?
    Who has given heed to his word so as to
    proclaim it?
¹⁹ Look, the storm of the LORD!
    Wrath has gone forth,
a whirling tempest;
    it will burst upon the head of the
    wicked.

²⁰ The anger of the LORD will not turn back
    until he has executed and accomplished
    the intents of his mind.
In the latter days you will understand it
    clearly.

²¹ I did not send the prophets,
    yet they ran;
I did not speak to them,
    yet they prophesied.
²² But if they had stood in my council,
    then they would have proclaimed my
    words to my people,
and they would have turned them from
    their evil way,
    and from the evil of their doings.

²³ Am I a God near by, says the LORD, and
not a God far off? ²⁴ Who can hide in secret
places so that I cannot see them? says the
LORD. Do I not fill heaven and earth? says
the LORD. ²⁵ I have heard what the prophets
have said who prophesy lies in my name,
saying, "I have dreamed, I have dreamed!"
²⁶ How long? Will the hearts of the prophets
ever turn back—those who prophesy lies,
and who prophesy the deceit of their own
heart? ²⁷ They plan to make my people forget
my name by their dreams that they tell one
another, just as their ancestors forgot my
name for Baal. ²⁸ Let the prophet who has a
dream tell the dream, but let the one who has
my word speak my word faithfully. What has
straw in common with wheat? says the LORD.
²⁹ Is not my word like fire, says the LORD, and
like a hammer that breaks a rock in pieces?
³⁰ See, therefore, I am against the prophets,
says the LORD, who steal my words from one
another. ³¹ See, I am against the prophets, says

"driven" and "punishment" (v. 12; cf. vv. 2,3,4). **13:** *Samaria,* the capital of the Northern Kingdom of Israel. For *prophets* of the Canaanite God *Baal* there, see 1 Kings 18.20–24. **14:** Jerusalem outdoes Samaria with its offenses; cf. Ezek 16.46–55; 23.2–11. *Sodom . . . Gomorrah,* see 20.16n. **15:** *Wormwood,* see 9.15n. **18:** *Council of the LORD,* the abode of God was conceived of as a royal court with many divine beings present (1 Kings 22.19–23; Isa 6.1–7; Pss 82.1; 89.7). **19–20:** See 30.23–24. *Storm* imagery is frequently used to represent the coming of the LORD as a warrior. **21:** *They ran,* using the metaphor of a runner bringing a message (2 Sam 18.19–26; cf. Isa 52.7). **23:** *Am I a God near by?* a question supposing a negative response. God is not near by, but rather is far off, filling the heavens and seeing all things even in secret places; see 1 Kings 8.27. Jeremiah protests the assumptions of divine immanence and coziness. **28:** *Dream . . . word,* a contrast between common wishful thinking and powerful visionary experience producing God's fiery word. Num 12.6 and Joel 2.28, however, suggest that both dreams and visionary experiences were legitimate means of receiving oracles from God, so this is not likely a disparaging of the one for the sake of the other ("but" is not in the MT). The divine word surpasses any medium of its

the LORD, who use their own tongues and say, "Says the LORD." [32] See, I am against those who prophesy lying dreams, says the LORD, and who tell them, and who lead my people astray by their lies and their recklessness, when I did not send them or appoint them; so they do not profit this people at all, says the LORD.

[33] When this people, or a prophet, or a priest asks you, "What is the burden of the LORD?" you shall say to them, "You are the burden,[a] and I will cast you off, says the LORD." [34] And as for the prophet, priest, or the people who say, "The burden of the LORD," I will punish them and their households. [35] Thus shall you say to one another, among yourselves, "What has the LORD answered?" or "What has the LORD spoken?" [36] But "the burden of the LORD" you shall mention no more, for the burden is everyone's own word, and so you pervert the words of the living God, the LORD of hosts, our God. [37] Thus you shall ask the prophet, "What has the LORD answered you?" or "What has the LORD spoken?" [38] But if you say, "the burden of the LORD," thus says the LORD: Because you have said these words, "the burden of the LORD," when I sent to you, saying, You shall not say, "the burden of the LORD," [39] therefore, I will surely lift you up[b] and cast you away from my presence, you and the city that I gave to you and your ancestors. [40] And I will bring upon you everlasting disgrace and perpetual shame, which shall not be forgotten.

24 The LORD showed me two baskets of figs placed before the temple of the LORD. This was after King Nebuchadrez-zar of Babylon had taken into exile from Jerusalem King Jeconiah son of Jehoiakim of Judah, together with the officials of Judah, the artisans, and the smiths, and had brought them to Babylon. [2] One basket had very good figs, like first-ripe figs, but the other basket had very bad figs, so bad that they could not be eaten. [3] And the LORD said to me, "What do you see, Jeremiah?" I said, "Figs, the good figs very good, and the bad figs very bad, so bad that they cannot be eaten."

[4] Then the word of the LORD came to me: [5] Thus says the LORD, the God of Israel: Like these good figs, so I will regard as good the exiles from Judah, whom I have sent away from this place to the land of the Chaldeans. [6] I will set my eyes upon them for good, and I will bring them back to this land. I will build them up, and not tear them down; I will plant them, and not pluck them up. [7] I will give them a heart to know that I am the LORD; and they shall be my people and I will be their God, for they shall return to me with their whole heart.

[8] But thus says the LORD: Like the bad figs that are so bad they cannot be eaten, so will I treat King Zedekiah of Judah, his officials, the remnant of Jerusalem who remain in this land, and those who live in the land of Egypt. [9] I will make them a horror, an evil thing, to all the kingdoms of the earth—a disgrace, a byword, a taunt, and a curse in all the places where I shall drive them. [10] And I will send sword, famine, and pestilence upon them,

a   Gk Vg: Heb *What burden*
b   Heb Mss Gk Vg: MT *forget you*

conveyance, and is powerful (v. 29). **31**: *Says the LORD*, these prophets are not prophesying in the name of Baal (v. 27), but rather in the very name of God. They are, however, simply mimicking one another and plagiarizing each other's messages (v. 30). **33**: *Burden of the LORD*, a term also used for an "oracle" (see Nah 1.1; Zech 9.1; 12.1; Mal 1.1). A sarcastic play on words: the people seek an oracle from Jeremiah but they are declared to be a burden to God; cf. 17.21. **39**: *I will surely lift you up*, a further play on the term "burden," from the Heb verb "nasa'," which means "to carry or lift."

24.1–10: Conclusion to this group of oracles from the time of Zedekiah. The exiled Jeconiah (Jehoiachin) was held in high esteem by those exiled with him in Babylon and by the supporters of Jeremiah's program. Those left in Judah who supported Zedekiah were regarded as rotten and inedible figs; see further 22.27; 29.17; 2 Kings 24.10–17. In this perspective, the future hope lay with those in exile. This language was a polemical support for the community which eventually returned from exile and reestablished control in the postexilic reconstruction under Zerubbabel, Ezra, and Nehemiah. **5**: *Land of the Chaldeans*, Babylon (see 21.4n.). **6**: See 1.10. **8**: *In the land of Egypt*, many Judeans fled to Egypt, an ally of Judah's in its struggle against the Babylonians; cf. 42.13–14.

until they are utterly destroyed from the land that I gave to them and their ancestors.

25

The word that came to Jeremiah concerning all the people of Judah, in the fourth year of King Jehoiakim son of Josiah of Judah (that was the first year of King Nebuchadrezzar of Babylon), [2] which the prophet Jeremiah spoke to all the people of Judah and all the inhabitants of Jerusalem: [3] For twenty-three years, from the thirteenth year of King Josiah son of Amon of Judah, to this day, the word of the LORD has come to me, and I have spoken persistently to you, but you have not listened. [4] And though the LORD persistently sent you all his servants the prophets, you have neither listened nor inclined your ears to hear [5] when they said, "Turn now, every one of you, from your evil way and wicked doings, and you will remain upon the land that the LORD has given to you and your ancestors from of old and forever; [6] do not go after other gods to serve and worship them, and do not provoke me to anger with the work of your hands. Then I will do you no harm." [7] Yet you did not listen to me, says the LORD, and so you have provoked me to anger with the work of your hands to your own harm.

[8] Therefore thus says the LORD of hosts: Because you have not obeyed my words, [9] I am going to send for all the tribes of the north, says the LORD, even for King Nebuchadrezzar of Babylon, my servant, and I will bring them against this land and its inhabitants, and against all these nations around; I will utterly destroy them, and make them an object of horror and of hissing, and an everlasting disgrace.[a] [10] And I will banish from them the sound of mirth and the sound of gladness, the voice of the bridegroom and the voice of the bride, the sound of the millstones and the light of the lamp. [11] This whole land shall become a ruin and a waste, and these nations shall serve the king of Babylon seventy years. [12] Then after seventy years are completed, I will punish the king of Babylon and that nation, the land of the Chaldeans, for their iniquity, says the LORD, making the land an everlasting waste. [13] I will bring upon that land all the words that I have uttered against it, everything written in this book, which Jeremiah prophesied against all the nations. [14] For many nations and great kings shall make slaves of them also; and I will repay them according to their deeds and the work of their hands.

[15] For thus the LORD, the God of Israel, said to me: Take from my hand this cup of the wine of wrath, and make all the nations to whom I send you drink it. [16] They shall drink and stagger and go out of their minds because of the sword that I am sending among them.

[17] So I took the cup from the LORD's hand, and made all the nations to whom the LORD sent me drink it: [18] Jerusalem and the towns of Judah, its kings and officials, to make them a desolation and a waste, an object of hissing and of cursing, as they are today; [19] Pharaoh king of Egypt, his servants, his officials, and all his people; [20] all the mixed people;[b] all the kings of the land of Uz; all the kings of

---

a Gk Compare Syr: Heb *and everlasting desolations*
b Meaning of Heb uncertain

25.1–38: Judah among all the nations. The conclusion of the first cycle of oracles with its reference to the scroll of 605 BCE (see 36.1–32). With Nebuchadrezzar's victory over the Egyptians at Carchemish in 605, Judah's fate became a part of unfolding world events. Its destruction here is placed in cosmic perspective as God's wrath is directed against all the nations, and finally against Babylon itself. The LXX places the oracles against the nations (chs 46–51) here, following v. 13. **1:** *Fourth year,* 605 BCE. **3:** *Twenty-three years,* suggesting that Jeremiah's ministry began in 627 BCE. See 1.2 and the introduction. **4:** This role of the prophets is characteristic of Jeremiah; see 7.25n. **9:** *All the tribes of the north,* the direction of coming disaster; see 1.14. *All these nations around,* Judah's neighbors. **10:** See 7.34n. **11:** *Seventy years,* an expected lifetime; see Ps 90.10; Isa 23.15. No one alive will experience repatriation to their land. **13:** *This book,* that is, material in chs 1–25 or the scroll of 605 BCE. By placing the oracles against the nations at this point, however, the Septuagint takes "this book" to refer to chs 46–51. **15:** *Cup of the wine of wrath,* see 13.12–14n. **18:** *As they are today,* presumes an exilic perspective (after 586 BCE) rather than that of 605 BCE as indicated in 25.1. **19–25:** The nations are listed in their proximity to Judah from nearest to farthest. **20:** *Mixed people,* a term associated with desert dwellers in v. 24. *Uz* is in Edom, the

the land of the Philistines—Ashkelon, Gaza, Ekron, and the remnant of Ashdod; [21] Edom, Moab, and the Ammonites; [22] all the kings of Tyre, all the kings of Sidon, and the kings of the coastland across the sea; [23] Dedan, Tema, Buz, and all who have shaven temples; [24] all the kings of Arabia and all the kings of the mixed peoples[a] that live in the desert; [25] all the kings of Zimri, all the kings of Elam, and all the kings of Media; [26] all the kings of the north, far and near, one after another, and all the kingdoms of the world that are on the face of the earth. And after them the king of Sheshach[b] shall drink.

[27] Then you shall say to them, Thus says the LORD of hosts, the God of Israel: Drink, get drunk and vomit, fall and rise no more, because of the sword that I am sending among you.

[28] And if they refuse to accept the cup from your hand to drink, then you shall say to them: Thus says the LORD of hosts: You must drink! [29] See, I am beginning to bring disaster on the city that is called by my name, and how can you possibly avoid punishment? You shall not go unpunished, for I am summoning a sword against all the inhabitants of the earth, says the LORD of hosts.

[30] You, therefore, shall prophesy against them all these words, and say to them:
The LORD will roar from on high,
    and from his holy habitation utter his
        voice;
he will roar mightily against his fold,
    and shout, like those who tread grapes,
        against all the inhabitants of the earth.
[31] The clamor will resound to the ends of
        the earth,
    for the LORD has an indictment against
        the nations;

he is entering into judgment with all flesh,
    and the guilty he will put to the sword,
                says the LORD.

[32] Thus says the LORD of hosts:
See, disaster is spreading
    from nation to nation,
and a great tempest is stirring
    from the farthest parts of the earth!
[33] Those slain by the LORD on that day shall extend from one end of the earth to the other. They shall not be lamented, or gathered, or buried; they shall become dung on the surface of the ground.
[34] Wail, you shepherds, and cry out;
    roll in ashes, you lords of the flock,
for the days of your slaughter have come—
    and your dispersions,[a]
    and you shall fall like a choice vessel.
[35] Flight shall fail the shepherds,
    and there shall be no escape for the
        lords of the flock.
[36] Hark! the cry of the shepherds,
    and the wail of the lords of the flock!
For the LORD is despoiling their pasture,
        [37] and the peaceful folds are devastated,
    because of the fierce anger of the LORD.
[38] Like a lion he has left his covert;
    for their land has become a waste
because of the cruel sword,
    and because of his fierce anger.

26
At the beginning of the reign of King Jehoiakim son of Josiah of Judah, this word came from the LORD: [2] Thus says the LORD: Stand in the court of the LORD's house,

a   Meaning of Heb uncertain
b   *Sheshach* is a cryptogram for *Babel*, Babylon

home of Job (Job 1.1), though its precise location is unknown. **21:** *Edom, Moab, and the Ammonites*, nations in Transjordan, east of Israel and Judah. **23:** *Dedan, Tema, Buz*, cities in Arabia. *Shaven temples*, see 9.26n. **26:** *Sheshach*, code language for "Babel" (Babylon) derived by substituting the letters of the alphabet in reverse order, an encryption method called "atbash"; see also 51.1,41. **30:** Divine wrath is portrayed in conventional terms as a roaring lion (Am 1.2; Hos 11.10; Joel 3.16) or one treading out grapes like blood (Gen 49.11; Isa 63.1–3; Zech 9.15). **33:** Using common themes; cf. 16.4. **34:** *Roll in ashes*, characteristic mourning ritual; cf. 6.26. **38:** *He has left*, that is, God, the lion of Judah, has abandoned his abode.

26.1–29.32: Jeremiah in conflict. These narratives begin the second cycle of prophetic oracles, and detail several episodes where Jeremiah was in conflict with Temple and royal officials and other prophets. This cycle includes chs 26–35, and concludes with ch 36. It again spans the time from Jehoiakim's reign (609 BCE) down to the reign of Zedekiah and the final siege of Jerusalem (586 BCE). Some attribute this narrative material in chs

and speak to all the cities of Judah that come to worship in the house of the LORD; speak to them all the words that I command you; do not hold back a word. ³ It may be that they will listen, all of them, and will turn from their evil way, that I may change my mind about the disaster that I intend to bring on them because of their evil doings. ⁴ You shall say to them: Thus says the LORD: If you will not listen to me, to walk in my law that I have set before you, ⁵ and to heed the words of my servants the prophets whom I send to you urgently—though you have not heeded— ⁶ then I will make this house like Shiloh, and I will make this city a curse for all the nations of the earth.

⁷ The priests and the prophets and all the people heard Jeremiah speaking these words in the house of the LORD. ⁸ And when Jeremiah had finished speaking all that the LORD had commanded him to speak to all the people, then the priests and the prophets and all the people laid hold of him, saying, "You shall die! ⁹ Why have you prophesied in the name of the LORD, saying, 'This house shall be like Shiloh, and this city shall be desolate, without inhabitant'?" And all the people gathered around Jeremiah in the house of the LORD.

¹⁰ When the officials of Judah heard these things, they came up from the king's house to the house of the LORD and took their seat in the entry of the New Gate of the house of the LORD. ¹¹ Then the priests and the prophets said to the officials and to all the people,

"This man deserves the sentence of death because he has prophesied against this city, as you have heard with your own ears."

¹² Then Jeremiah spoke to all the officials and all the people, saying, "It is the LORD who sent me to prophesy against this house and this city all the words you have heard. ¹³ Now therefore amend your ways and your doings, and obey the voice of the LORD your God, and the LORD will change his mind about the disaster that he has pronounced against you. ¹⁴ But as for me, here I am in your hands. Do with me as seems good and right to you. ¹⁵ Only know for certain that if you put me to death, you will be bringing innocent blood upon yourselves and upon this city and its inhabitants, for in truth the LORD sent me to you to speak all these words in your ears."

¹⁶ Then the officials and all the people said to the priests and the prophets, "This man does not deserve the sentence of death, for he has spoken to us in the name of the LORD our God." ¹⁷ And some of the elders of the land arose and said to all the assembled people, ¹⁸ "Micah of Moresheth, who prophesied during the days of King Hezekiah of Judah, said to all the people of Judah: 'Thus says the LORD of hosts,

Zion shall be plowed as a field;
 Jerusalem shall become a heap of ruins,
 and the mountain of the house a
  wooded height.'

¹⁹ Did King Hezekiah of Judah and all Judah actually put him to death? Did he not fear the LORD and entreat the favor of the LORD,

26–29 to "Baruch's memoirs," but this is conjectural.

26.1–24: Jeremiah's Temple Sermon. Generally associated with ch 7 because of its location in the Temple and its reference to Shiloh (see 7.1,12–15). Attention is given here to the aftermath of the event and Jeremiah's near arrest and execution. **1:** *The beginning of the reign,* 609 BCE. **3:** *That I may change my mind,* see 18.8,10n., and the freedom God has to alter divine plans. **5:** See 7.25n. **6:** *Shiloh,* see 7.12n. **9:** To prophesy threats against the royal sanctuary was tantamount to treason. Compare Amos's reception at Bethel (Am 7.10–13). **10:** *Seat in the entry of the New Gate,* indicates that this is a formal judicial hearing, with justice being administered "in the gate" (Isa 29.21; Am 5.15). **12:** *It is the LORD who sent me,* as elsewhere in the ancient Near East, prophets were granted some degree of protection by virtue of the fact that they were constrained to bring their message by the gods (cf. v. 15). But such immunity had limits. **15:** *Innocent blood,* the killing of an innocent person was a horrific crime that had disastrous consequences, especially in the perspective of Deuteronomy (see Deut 19.10–13; 21.8–9; 27.25). **16–19:** The charge is mitigated for two reasons. First, they recognize the prophet's claim to immunity on the basis of being constrained by God to deliver a message (v. 16). Second, the precedent of Micah is invoked, with a rare quotation of an earlier book (Mic 3.12). Micah's prediction of disaster did not come to pass because, it is argued, he successfully prompted Hezekiah to plead for divine favor. There is no mention of this event in the historical books, where only Isaiah is mentioned in connection with Hezekiah and the Assyrian

and did not the LORD change his mind about the disaster that he had pronounced against them? But we are about to bring great disaster on ourselves!"

²⁰ There was another man prophesying in the name of the LORD, Uriah son of Shemaiah from Kiriath-jearim. He prophesied against this city and against this land in words exactly like those of Jeremiah. ²¹ And when King Jehoiakim, with all his warriors and all the officials, heard his words, the king sought to put him to death; but when Uriah heard of it, he was afraid and fled and escaped to Egypt. ²² Then King Jehoiakim sentª Elnathan son of Achbor and men with him to Egypt, ²³ and they took Uriah from Egypt and brought him to King Jehoiakim, who struck him down with the sword and threw his dead body into the burial place of the common people.

²⁴ But the hand of Ahikam son of Shaphan was with Jeremiah so that he was not given over into the hands of the people to be put to death.

27 In the beginning of the reign of King Zedekiahᵇ son of Josiah of Judah, this word came to Jeremiah from the LORD. ² Thus the LORD said to me: Make yourself a yoke of straps and bars, and put them on your neck. ³ Send wordᶜ to the king of Edom, the king of Moab, the king of the Ammonites, the king of Tyre, and the king of Sidon by the hand of the envoys who have come to Jerusalem to King Zedekiah of Judah. ⁴ Give them this charge for their masters: Thus says the LORD of hosts, the God of Israel: This is what you shall say to your masters: ⁵ It is I who by my great power and my outstretched arm have made the earth, with the people and animals that are on the earth, and I give it to whomever I please. ⁶ Now I have given all these lands into the hand of King Nebuchadnezzar of Babylon, my servant, and I have given him even the wild animals of the field to serve him. ⁷ All the nations shall serve him and his son and his grandson, until the time of his own land comes; then many nations and great kings shall make him their slave.

⁸ But if any nation or kingdom will not serve this king, Nebuchadnezzar of Babylon, and put its neck under the yoke of the king of Babylon, then I will punish that nation with

ª Heb adds *men to Egypt*
ᵇ Another reading is *Jehoiakim*
ᶜ Cn: Heb *send them*

crisis (2 Kings 18.13–20.19). **20–23:** The precedent of Uriah, however, indicated the danger facing Jeremiah. For exactly the same charge (v. 20) Uriah was hunted down by Jehoiakim and executed. **22:** *Elnathan,* see 36.12,25. **24:** *Ahikam son of Shaphan,* as Josiah's secretary, Shaphan had been instrumental in the reform movement of Josiah (2 Kings 22.3–13), of which Jeremiah was likely an enthusiastic supporter. This particular family, comprised of Shaphan's sons Ahikam and Gemariah and Ahikam's son Gedaliah, along with others, was one of Jeremiah's chief advocates within the royal ranks of the princes; see 36.11–19. That Ahikam had to rescue Jeremiah indicates that, in spite of the sentiments of the officials and people, Jeremiah was still in grave danger, as indicated by the precedent of Uriah.

27.1–28.17: Jeremiah's ox yoke and his confrontation with Hananiah. These conflict narratives are linked together syntactically and thematically. The date of Jeremiah's confrontation with Hananiah, according to 28.1, is August, 594 BCE (contrast 27.1, which has a scribal error, dating the event to the beginning of Jehoiakim's reign, under the influence of 26.1). In early 594 BCE a revolt in the Babylonian army prompted a conspiracy among the western states, including Judah, to revolt against Nebuchadrezzar. The meeting of these foreign emissaries in Jerusalem to consider the details for such a revolt is the occasion for the recorded prophetic sign in ch 27. Zedekiah did not join the conspiracy at this time, however, and Judah was spared the retaliatory strike by Babylon later that year.

27.1–11: Jeremiah's word to the foreign emissaries. 2: *A yoke of,* the phrase is lacking in the text. Jeremiah is simply told to make "straps" and "bars." But a yoke was comprised of straps and bars; see Lev 26.13; Ezek 34.27. **3:** *Send word,* the text ("Send them") suggests that it was the yoke itself that was sent via the emissaries. See textual note *c.* **6:** *Nebuchadnezzar,* this form of the name, used in chs 27–29, shows the influence of the Deuteronomistic editor. Elsewhere in Jeremiah the form is more correctly rendered as Nebuchadrezzar. *My servant,* a striking designation for a foreign ruler (cf. Isa 44.28–45.1). He is God's servant because he is the instrument of punishment against Judah and her neighbors. **7:** Cf. 25.11–14. **8–14:** Jeremiah offers a choice and limited hope:

the sword, with famine, and with pestilence, says the LORD, until I have completed its[a] destruction by his hand. [9] You, therefore, must not listen to your prophets, your diviners, your dreamers,[b] your soothsayers, or your sorcerers, who are saying to you, "You shall not serve the king of Babylon." [10] For they are prophesying a lie to you, with the result that you will be removed far from your land; I will drive you out, and you will perish. [11] But any nation that will bring its neck under the yoke of the king of Babylon and serve him, I will leave on its own land, says the LORD, to till it and live there.

[12] I spoke to King Zedekiah of Judah in the same way: Bring your necks under the yoke of the king of Babylon, and serve him and his people, and live. [13] Why should you and your people die by the sword, by famine, and by pestilence, as the LORD has spoken concerning any nation that will not serve the king of Babylon? [14] Do not listen to the words of the prophets who are telling you not to serve the king of Babylon, for they are prophesying a lie to you. [15] I have not sent them, says the LORD, but they are prophesying falsely in my name, with the result that I will drive you out and you will perish, you and the prophets who are prophesying to you.

[16] Then I spoke to the priests and to all this people, saying, Thus says the LORD: Do not listen to the words of your prophets who are prophesying to you, saying, "The vessels of the LORD's house will soon be brought back from Babylon," for they are prophesying a lie to you. [17] Do not listen to them; serve the king of Babylon and live. Why should this city become a desolation? [18] If indeed they are

prophets, and if the word of the LORD is with them, then let them intercede with the LORD of hosts, that the vessels left in the house of the LORD, in the house of the king of Judah, and in Jerusalem may not go to Babylon. [19] For thus says the LORD of hosts concerning the pillars, the sea, the stands, and the rest of the vessels that are left in this city, [20] which King Nebuchadnezzar of Babylon did not take away when he took into exile from Jerusalem to Babylon King Jeconiah son of Jehoiakim of Judah, and all the nobles of Judah and Jerusalem— [21] thus says the LORD of hosts, the God of Israel, concerning the vessels left in the house of the LORD, in the house of the king of Judah, and in Jerusalem: [22] They shall be carried to Babylon, and there they shall stay, until the day when I give attention to them, says the LORD. Then I will bring them up and restore them to this place.

28

In that same year, at the beginning of the reign of King Zedekiah of Judah, in the fifth month of the fourth year, the prophet Hananiah son of Azzur, from Gibeon, spoke to me in the house of the LORD, in the presence of the priests and all the people, saying, [2] "Thus says the LORD of hosts, the God of Israel: I have broken the yoke of the king of Babylon. [3] Within two years I will bring back to this place all the vessels of the LORD's house, which King Nebuchadnezzar of Babylon took away from this place and carried to Babylon. [4] I will also bring back to this place King Jeconiah son of Jehoiakim of Judah, and all the exiles from Judah who went

---

a   Heb *their*
b   Gk Syr Vg: Heb *dreams*

---

willing submission to vassalage or destruction. 9: *Diviners . . . dreamers . . . soothsayers . . . sorcerers*, though these intermediaries were banned by Deuteronomic tradition (Deut 18.10,14), the prophets inveigh against these customs, suggesting they were practiced also in Israel.

27.12–22: Jeremiah speaks similar words to Zedekiah and the people of Jerusalem. 16. *The vessels*, ritual paraphernalia used in the Temple; see 28.3; 2 Kings 24.13; Ezra 5.14–15. 19: *The pillars* Jachin and Boaz (1 Kings 7.15–22), the large basin known as the *sea* (1 Kings 7.23–26), and the *stands* and *vessels* (1 Kings 7.27–39) were furnishings of the Temple taken to Babylon in 586 BCE (2 Kings 25.13–17). The vessels, which were not broken up, were later returned by Cyrus in 538 BCE (Ezra 1.7–11).

28.1–17: Jeremiah's confrontation with the prophet Hananiah. Hananiah represented the message of "peace" being proclaimed by the "lying prophets," encouraging resistance to Babylon and false hopes of a quick end to the political crisis, a restoration not only of the Temple vessels but of King Jehoiachin to the throne. Jeremiah cites prophetic tradition in support of his message of disaster. The contest is resolved by the death of Hananiah two months later. 1: On the contradictory dates see 27.1–28.17n. 4: *Jeconiah*, Jehoiachin

to Babylon, says the LORD, for I will break the yoke of the king of Babylon."

⁵ Then the prophet Jeremiah spoke to the prophet Hananiah in the presence of the priests and all the people who were standing in the house of the LORD; ⁶ and the prophet Jeremiah said, "Amen! May the LORD do so; may the LORD fulfill the words that you have prophesied, and bring back to this place from Babylon the vessels of the house of the LORD, and all the exiles. ⁷ But listen now to this word that I speak in your hearing and in the hearing of all the people. ⁸ The prophets who preceded you and me from ancient times prophesied war, famine, and pestilence against many countries and great kingdoms. ⁹ As for the prophet who prophesies peace, when the word of that prophet comes true, then it will be known that the LORD has truly sent the prophet."

¹⁰ Then the prophet Hananiah took the yoke from the neck of the prophet Jeremiah, and broke it. ¹¹ And Hananiah spoke in the presence of all the people, saying, "Thus says the LORD: This is how I will break the yoke of King Nebuchadnezzar of Babylon from the neck of all the nations within two years." At this, the prophet Jeremiah went his way.

¹² Sometime after the prophet Hananiah had broken the yoke from the neck of the prophet Jeremiah, the word of the LORD came to Jeremiah: ¹³ Go, tell Hananiah, Thus says the LORD: You have broken wooden bars only to forge iron bars in place of them! ¹⁴ For thus says the LORD of hosts, the God of Israel:

I have put an iron yoke on the neck of all these nations so that they may serve King Nebuchadnezzar of Babylon, and they shall indeed serve him; I have even given him the wild animals. ¹⁵ And the prophet Jeremiah said to the prophet Hananiah, "Listen, Hananiah, the LORD has not sent you, and you made this people trust in a lie. ¹⁶ Therefore thus says the LORD: I am going to send you off the face of the earth. Within this year you will be dead, because you have spoken rebellion against the LORD."

¹⁷ In that same year, in the seventh month, the prophet Hananiah died.

29 These are the words of the letter that the prophet Jeremiah sent from Jerusalem to the remaining elders among the exiles, and to the priests, the prophets, and all the people, whom Nebuchadnezzar had taken into exile from Jerusalem to Babylon. ² This was after King Jeconiah, and the queen mother, the court officials, the leaders of Judah and Jerusalem, the artisans, and the smiths had departed from Jerusalem. ³ The letter was sent by the hand of Elasah son of Shaphan and Gemariah son of Hilkiah, whom King Zedekiah of Judah sent to Babylon to King Nebuchadnezzar of Babylon. It said: ⁴ Thus says the LORD of hosts, the God of Israel, to all the exiles whom I have sent into exile from Jerusalem to Babylon: ⁵ Build houses and live in them; plant gardens and eat what they produce. ⁶ Take wives and have sons and daughters; take wives for your sons, and give your daughters in marriage, that

---

(2 Kings 24.8–12). **5:** The first-person perspective of a Jeremiah memoir (27.2,12,16; 28.1) suddenly shifts to a third-person account. This illustrates the composite nature of this material. **6:** There is considerable debate as to whether Jeremiah is sincere in his wish or is speaking with bitter irony. Because the story, under Deuteronomistic editing, is committed to the theme of prophetic fulfillment (see v. 9), the reader cannot doubt Jeremiah's word. **8:** Commonly prophets issued oracles against foreign nations; see Am 1–2; Isa 13–24; Ezek 25–32. This is especially true of early forms of "war prophecy"; see Jer 46.1. **9:** On the criterion of prophetic fulfillment, see Deut 18.21–22. This Deuteronomistic perspective controls the narrative here, as indicated by 28.16–17. **16.** *Send you off,* a play on the fact that Hananiah has not been sent by God (v. 15).

29.1–32: Jeremiah in conflict with prophets among the exile community. Correspondence with leaders among the exiles in Babylon indicates their opposition to Jeremiah's message. Jeremiah's letter encouraging the exiles to prepare for a lengthy stay in captivity (vv. 4–14) is met with a letter of rebuke by Shemaiah (v. 25) instructing Zephaniah, the Temple overseer in Jerusalem, to clamp down on Jeremiah and control his oracles (vv. 25–28). This prompts another letter from Jeremiah to Shemaiah (v. 24) and a warning to all the exiles concerning Shemaiah's fate (vv. 31–32). **2:** *Jeconiah,* Jehoiachin (2 Kings 24.8–12). *The court officials,* or "eunuchs"; see 34.19n. **3:** *Elasah* (perhaps the brother of Ahikam; 26.24) and *Gemariah* (36.10), apparently supporters of Jeremiah's program and sensitive to Babylonian interests. *Hilkiah,* see 2 Kings 22–23. **5:** *Build . . . plant,* characteristic language

they may bear sons and daughters; multiply there, and do not decrease. [7] But seek the welfare of the city where I have sent you into exile, and pray to the LORD on its behalf, for in its welfare you will find your welfare. [8] For thus says the LORD of hosts, the God of Israel: Do not let the prophets and the diviners who are among you deceive you, and do not listen to the dreams that they dream,[a] [9] for it is a lie that they are prophesying to you in my name; I did not send them, says the LORD.

[10] For thus says the LORD: Only when Babylon's seventy years are completed will I visit you, and I will fulfill to you my promise and bring you back to this place. [11] For surely I know the plans I have for you, says the LORD, plans for your welfare and not for harm, to give you a future with hope. [12] Then when you call upon me and come and pray to me, I will hear you. [13] When you search for me, you will find me; if you seek me with all your heart, [14] I will let you find me, says the LORD, and I will restore your fortunes and gather you from all the nations and all the places where I have driven you, says the LORD, and I will bring you back to the place from which I sent you into exile.

[15] Because you have said, "The LORD has raised up prophets for us in Babylon,"— [16] Thus says the LORD concerning the king who sits on the throne of David, and concerning all the people who live in this city, your kinsfolk who did not go out with you into exile: [17] Thus says the LORD of hosts, I am going to let loose on them sword, famine, and pestilence, and I will make them like rotten figs that are so bad they cannot be eaten. [18] I will pursue them with the sword, with famine, and with pestilence, and will make them a horror to all the kingdoms of the earth, to be an object of cursing, and horror, and hissing, and a derision among all the nations where I have driven them, [19] because they did not heed my words, says the LORD, when I persis-

tently sent to you my servants the prophets, but they[b] would not listen, says the LORD. [20] But now, all you exiles whom I sent away from Jerusalem to Babylon, hear the word of the LORD: [21] Thus says the LORD of hosts, the God of Israel, concerning Ahab son of Kolaiah and Zedekiah son of Maaseiah, who are prophesying a lie to you in my name: I am going to deliver them into the hand of King Nebuchadrezzar of Babylon, and he shall kill them before your eyes. [22] And on account of them this curse shall be used by all the exiles from Judah in Babylon: "The LORD make you like Zedekiah and Ahab, whom the king of Babylon roasted in the fire," [23] because they have perpetrated outrage in Israel and have committed adultery with their neighbors' wives, and have spoken in my name lying words that I did not command them; I am the one who knows and bears witness, says the LORD.

[24] To Shemaiah of Nehelam you shall say: [25] Thus says the LORD of hosts, the God of Israel: In your own name you sent a letter to all the people who are in Jerusalem, and to the priest Zephaniah son of Maaseiah, and to all the priests, saying, [26] The LORD himself has made you priest instead of the priest Jehoiada, so that there may be officers in the house of the LORD to control any madman who plays the prophet, to put him in the stocks and the collar. [27] So now why have you not rebuked Jeremiah of Anathoth who plays the prophet for you? [28] For he has actually sent to us in Babylon, saying, "It will be a long time; build houses and live in them, and plant gardens and eat what they produce."

[29] The priest Zephaniah read this letter in the hearing of the prophet Jeremiah. [30] Then the word of the LORD came to Jeremiah: [31] Send to all the exiles, saying, Thus says

[a] Cn: Heb *your dreams that you cause to dream*
[b] Syr: Heb *you*

of Jeremiah's vision of restoration (Jer 1.10), which will first occur in Babylon itself. **7**: *Welfare*, that is "the peace" (Heb "shalom"). They are to pray for the peace not of Jerusalem (cf. Ps 122.6) but of Babylon. **10**: *Babylon's seventy years*, see 25.11n. **12–14**: See 23.3; 31.7–10. **16**: *This city*, that is, Jerusalem. **17**: *Rotten figs*, cf. 24.1–10. **19**: See 7.25n. **21**: *Ahab . . . Zedekiah*, two of the prophets among the exiled community referred to in v. 15. **22**: *Roasted in the fire*, cf. Dan 3.19–23. **26**: *Officers*, see 20.1n. *Madman*, indicating the ecstatic qualities of typical prophetic behavior. A fine line separated prophetic ecstasy and the behavior of the insane; see 1 Sam 10.10–13; 19.20–24. *Who plays the prophet*, that is, who engages in such ecstatic behavior. *Stocks and the collar*, cf. 20.2n.

the LORD concerning Shemaiah of Nehelam: Because Shemaiah has prophesied to you, though I did not send him, and has led you to trust in a lie, [32] therefore thus says the LORD: I am going to punish Shemaiah of Nehelam and his descendants; he shall not have anyone living among this people to see[a] the good that I am going to do to my people, says the LORD, for he has spoken rebellion against the LORD.

30 The word that came to Jeremiah from the LORD: [2] Thus says the LORD, the God of Israel: Write in a book all the words that I have spoken to you. [3] For the days are surely coming, says the LORD, when I will restore the fortunes of my people, Israel and Judah, says the LORD, and I will bring them back to the land that I gave to their ancestors and they shall take possession of it.

[4] These are the words that the LORD spoke concerning Israel and Judah:

[5] Thus says the LORD:
We have heard a cry of panic,
  of terror, and no peace.
[6] Ask now, and see,
  can a man bear a child?
Why then do I see every man
  with his hands on his loins like a
    woman in labor?
Why has every face turned pale?
[7] Alas! that day is so great
  there is none like it;
it is a time of distress for Jacob;
  yet he shall be rescued from it.
[8] On that day, says the LORD of hosts, I will break the yoke from off his[b] neck, and I will

burst his[b] bonds, and strangers shall no more make a servant of him. [9] But they shall serve the LORD their God and David their king, whom I will raise up for them.

[10] But as for you, have no fear, my servant
  Jacob, says the LORD,
  and do not be dismayed, O Israel;
for I am going to save you from far away,
  and your offspring from the land of
    their captivity.
Jacob shall return and have quiet and ease,
  and no one shall make him afraid.
[11] For I am with you, says the LORD, to save
  you;
I will make an end of all the nations
  among which I scattered you,
  but of you I will not make an end.
I will chastise you in just measure,
  and I will by no means leave you
    unpunished.

[12] For thus says the LORD:
Your hurt is incurable,
  your wound is grievous.
[13] There is no one to uphold your cause,
  no medicine for your wound,
  no healing for you.
[14] All your lovers have forgotten you;
  they care nothing for you;
for I have dealt you the blow of an enemy,
  the punishment of a merciless foe,

a Gk: Heb *and he shall not see*
b Cn: Heb *your*

30.1–31.40: The book of consolation, a cluster of oracles looking forward to God's restoration of Judah and Jerusalem, prompted by the reference to "the good" in 29.32. These oracles are said to be in a book or document (30.2,4) centering on the theme of "restoring the fortunes" of Israel/Judah. Since Israel (Ephraim) and Judah often appear as two separate political entities in this material, and because there is a frequent northern orientation (compare 30.4; 31.5,6,15), some of the oracles may be early, envisioning the desire of Josiah to re-unify Judah with the former territory of Israel. Jer 31.26 ("Thereupon I awoke") indicates that an original dream vision underlay some of this material, which has been reworked and expanded in its present form to address the hopes for the restoration of Judah following the Babylonian exile. 30.1–4: Introduction. The expressions "for the days are surely coming" and "restore the fortunes" sound the theme of this material. 3: *Fortunes*, or perhaps the spoils and persons lost in warfare, captivity or in crisis. 5–11: Using the imagery of breaking the yoke of captivity (v. 8), taken up from chs 27–28, God's salvation is promised. The language is akin to that of Second Isaiah, especially in vv. 10–11 (cf. Isa 35.4; 43.1). 6: The rhetorical question requires a negative response. The pain of pregnancy and labor in childbirth is a common metaphor for distress in the midst of crisis. See Jer 4.31; 6.24; 13.21. 11: *Not make an end*, see 4.27; 5.10,18. Israel will have to suffer the just consequence of its trans-gressions. 12–17: Shift to female subject. Lady Zion seems incurably wounded (cf. 14.17; 15.8,18) having suffered

because your guilt is great,
  because your sins are so numerous.
[15] Why do you cry out over your hurt?
  Your pain is incurable.
Because your guilt is great,
  because your sins are so numerous,
  I have done these things to you.
[16] Therefore all who devour you shall be
    devoured,
  and all your foes, every one of them,
    shall go into captivity;
those who plunder you shall be
    plundered,
  and all who prey on you I will make a
    prey.
[17] For I will restore health to you,
  and your wounds I will heal,
                    says the LORD,
because they have called you an
    outcast:
  "It is Zion; no one cares for her!"

[18] Thus says the LORD:
I am going to restore the fortunes of the
    tents of Jacob,
  and have compassion on his
    dwellings;
the city shall be rebuilt upon its mound,
  and the citadel set on its rightful site.
[19] Out of them shall come thanksgiving,
  and the sound of merrymakers.
I will make them many, and they shall not
    be few;
  I will make them honored, and they
    shall not be disdained.
[20] Their children shall be as of old,
  their congregation shall be established
    before me;
  and I will punish all who oppress them.
[21] Their prince shall be one of their own,
  their ruler shall come from their
    midst;

I will bring him near, and he shall
    approach me,
  for who would otherwise dare to
    approach me?
                    says the LORD.
[22] And you shall be my people,
  and I will be your God.

[23] Look, the storm of the LORD!
  Wrath has gone forth,
a whirling[a] tempest;
  it will burst upon the head of the
    wicked.
[24] The fierce anger of the LORD will not
    turn back
  until he has executed and accomplished
    the intents of his mind.
In the latter days you will understand this.

31 At that time, says the LORD, I will be
  the God of all the families of Israel, and
they shall be my people.

[2] Thus says the LORD:
The people who survived the sword
  found grace in the wilderness;
when Israel sought for rest,
  [3] the LORD appeared to him[b] from far
    away.[c]
I have loved you with an everlasting love;
  therefore I have continued my
    faithfulness to you.
[4] Again I will build you, and you shall be
    built,
  O virgin Israel!
Again you shall take[d] your
    tambourines,
  and go forth in the dance of the
    merrymakers.

a One Ms: Meaning of MT uncertain
b Gk: Heb *me*
c Or *to him long ago*
d Or *adorn yourself with*

God's punishment, but the time of healing and restoration is at hand. **14.** *Lovers*, that is, political allies. To be in alliance with a suzerain power, however, meant paying appropriate homage to its deities. This custom lay behind the connection of religious apostasy and the charge of committing adultery and fornication. **30.18–31.1:** Shift to male subject. The city and its ruler will be restored. **30.18:** *Its mound*, that is, its "tell." Cities were built on occupation mounds and, when destroyed, the mound was cleared, filled in, built higher and refortified. **21:** *Prince . . . ruler*, avoiding the term for "king," perhaps reflecting a more subdued expectation than that expressed in v. 9. **23–24** duplicates 23.19–20, and was likely a fragment appended to this section. **31.2–6:** Shift to female subject. "Virgin Israel" will dance and celebrate her vineyards. **2:** *Grace in the wilderness*, an Exodus theme (Ex 33.12–17) appropriated as a metaphor for return from exile (see Isa 40.3; 41.18–19; 43.19). **3:** *From far away*, see 23.23,

5 Again you shall plant vineyards
     on the mountains of Samaria;
the planters shall plant,
     and shall enjoy the fruit.
6 For there shall be a day when sentinels
     will call
in the hill country of Ephraim:
"Come, let us go up to Zion,
     to the LORD our God."

7 For thus says the LORD:
Sing aloud with gladness for Jacob,
     and raise shouts for the chief of the
          nations;
proclaim, give praise, and say,
     "Save, O LORD, your people,
     the remnant of Israel."
8 See, I am going to bring them from the
          land of the north,
and gather them from the farthest parts
          of the earth,
among them the blind and the lame,
     those with child and those in labor,
          together;
a great company, they shall return here.
9 With weeping they shall come,
     and with consolationsª I will lead them
          back,
I will let them walk by brooks of water,
     in a straight path in which they shall
          not stumble;
for I have become a father to Israel,
     and Ephraim is my firstborn.

10 Hear the word of the LORD, O nations,
     and declare it in the coastlands far
          away;
say, "He who scattered Israel will gather him,

and will keep him as a shepherd a
     flock."
11 For the LORD has ransomed Jacob,
     and has redeemed him from hands too
          strong for him.
12 They shall come and sing aloud on the
          height of Zion,
     and they shall be radiant over the
          goodness of the LORD,
over the grain, the wine, and the oil,
     and over the young of the flock and the
          herd;
their life shall become like a watered
          garden,
     and they shall never languish again.
13 Then shall the young women rejoice in
          the dance,
     and the young men and the old shall be
          merry.
I will turn their mourning into joy,
     I will comfort them, and give them
          gladness for sorrow.
14 I will give the priests their fill of fatness,
     and my people shall be satisfied with
          my bounty,
                              says the LORD.

15 Thus says the LORD:
A voice is heard in Ramah,
     lamentation and bitter weeping.
Rachel is weeping for her children;
     she refuses to be comforted for her
          children,
     because they are no more.
16 Thus says the LORD:
Keep your voice from weeping,

ª Gk Compare Vg Tg: Heb *supplications*

where God's nature is to be far away rather than close at hand. 31.7–9: Shift to male subject. The repatriation of the remnant of Israel. 7: *Save, O LORD*, a festival cry lying behind the term "Hosanna"; see Ps 118.25. 8. *Blind . . . lame*, those most pitiful and often discriminated against; cf. Lev 21.18; 2 Sam 5.8. 9: *Ephraim* was one of the Joseph tribes, the central power base of Israel (the north). Because of its significant political power base and its ancient associations with the Joseph traditions at Shechem, it was considered the *firstborn*; see Gen 48.8–20. 10–14: God's announcement to the nations. Using standard imagery, Israel's deliverance is declared. 10: Cf. 23.2–3. 12: *Grain . . . wine . . . oil*, images of agricultural bounty; see Deut 11.14; Hos 2.8; Joel 2.19,24. 13: Typical images of joy and celebration; cf. Ps 30.11; Isa 35.10. 14. *Fatness*, the fat of sacrifices was not to be eaten (Lev 3.17; 7.23–25), as it was reserved for God and was burned to ashes. This fatty ash residue was removed by the priests following sacrificial rites (Lev 6.3–4), and was a symbol of divine bounty (Ps 36.9). 15–20: *Rachel* comforted and her children restored. Rachel's sons were the ancestors of the Joseph tribes (Ephraim and Manasseh) and the tribe of Benjamin. Her death in childbirth was an occasion of mourning (see Gen 35.16–21). *Ramah* was in Benjaminite territory (Josh 18.21–25), and it was during Benjamin's birth that Rachel died. The Joseph tribes were

and your eyes from tears;
for there is a reward for your work,
    says the LORD:
they shall come back from the land of
    the enemy;
[17] there is hope for your future,
    says the LORD:
your children shall come back to their
    own country.

[18] Indeed I heard Ephraim pleading:
"You disciplined me, and I took the
    discipline;
  I was like a calf untrained.
Bring me back, let me come back,
  for you are the LORD my God.
[19] For after I had turned away I repented;
  and after I was discovered, I struck my
    thigh;
I was ashamed, and I was dismayed
  because I bore the disgrace of my
    youth."
[20] Is Ephraim my dear son?
  Is he the child I delight in?
As often as I speak against him,
  I still remember him.
Therefore I am deeply moved for him;
  I will surely have mercy on him,
    says the LORD.

[21] Set up road markers for yourself,
  make yourself signposts;
consider well the highway,
  the road by which you went.
Return, O virgin Israel,
  return to these your cities.

[22] How long will you waver,
  O faithless daughter?
For the LORD has created a new thing on
    the earth:
  a woman encompasses[a] a man.

[23] Thus says the LORD of hosts, the God of Israel: Once more they shall use these words in the land of Judah and in its towns when I restore their fortunes:
"The LORD bless you, O abode of
    righteousness,
  O holy hill!"
[24] And Judah and all its towns shall live there together, and the farmers and those who wander[b] with their flocks.
[25] I will satisfy the weary,
  and all who are faint I will
    replenish.
[26] Thereupon I awoke and looked, and my sleep was pleasant to me.
[27] The days are surely coming, says the LORD, when I will sow the house of Israel and the house of Judah with the seed of humans and the seed of animals. [28] And just as I have watched over them to pluck up and break down, to overthrow, destroy, and bring evil, so I will watch over them to build and to plant, says the LORD. [29] In those days they shall no longer say:

---

[a]   Meaning of Heb uncertain
[b]   Cn Compare Syr Vg Tg: Heb *and they shall wander*

taken captive by the Assyrians in 722 BCE, the occasion for Rachel's mourning. **18:** *Ephraim*, the more powerful of the Joseph tribes, and therefore representative of all Israel (the north); see 7.15. **19:** *Struck my thigh*, a sign of mourning and regret; see Ezek 21.12. **20:** Questions normally expecting a negative response. Though *Ephraim* does not act like a dear son or delightful child, nevertheless God cannot ultimately turn against him; cf. Hos 11.1–9. *Deeply moved*, strong language indicating the churning of one's intestines. **21–22:** The faithless daughter's return. **21:** *Road markers*, or more likely grave markers (see 2 Kings 23.17; Ezek 39.15). *Signposts*, term used in v. 15, so likely associated with the mourning at a grave. Israel is to recall its deadly path into exile. **22:** *A new thing*, cf. Isa 43.19. *A woman encompasses a man*, a cryptic phrase, perhaps playing on the term "faithless." The word translated "encompasses" is used of God's protective care in Deut 32.10. Normally women were under the protection of male members of their family. **23–26:** Conclusion to an earlier dream-vision sequence, a sign of the editing of this material.

    31.27–40: Three oracles looking forward to God's radically new future.

    31.27–30: God will build and plant the new Israel. 28: *Watched over . . . to build and to plant*, the central theme of the book; see 1.10,11–12. **29:** Cf. Ezek 18.1–4. Unlike Ezekiel, Jeremiah does not refute the saying but simply retires it from its traditional usage as a respected and honored truth about the nature of God; cf. Ex 20.5; 34.7.

"The parents have eaten sour grapes,
and the children's teeth are set on
edge."
³⁰ But all shall die for their own sins; the teeth of everyone who eats sour grapes shall be set on edge.

³¹ The days are surely coming, says the LORD, when I will make a new covenant with the house of Israel and the house of Judah. ³² It will not be like the covenant that I made with their ancestors when I took them by the hand to bring them out of the land of Egypt—a covenant that they broke, though I was their husband,ᵃ says the LORD. ³³ But this is the covenant that I will make with the house of Israel after those days, says the LORD: I will put my law within them, and I will write it on their hearts; and I will be their God, and they shall be my people. ³⁴ No longer shall they teach one another, or say to each other, "Know the LORD," for they shall all know me, from the least of them to the greatest, says the LORD; for I will forgive their iniquity, and remember their sin no more.

³⁵ Thus says the LORD,
who gives the sun for light by day
and the fixed order of the moon and the
stars for light by night,
who stirs up the sea so that its waves
roar—

the LORD of hosts is his name:
³⁶ If this fixed order were ever to cease
from my presence, says the LORD,
then also the offspring of Israel would
cease
to be a nation before me forever.

³⁷ Thus says the LORD:
If the heavens above can be measured,
and the foundations of the earth below
can be explored,
then I will reject all the offspring of Israel
because of all they have done,
says the LORD.

³⁸ The days are surely coming, says the LORD, when the city shall be rebuilt for the LORD from the tower of Hananel to the Corner Gate. ³⁹ And the measuring line shall go out farther, straight to the hill Gareb, and shall then turn to Goah. ⁴⁰ The whole valley of the dead bodies and the ashes, and all the fields as far as the Wadi Kidron, to the corner of the Horse Gate toward the east, shall be sacred to the LORD. It shall never again be uprooted or overthrown.

32 The word that came to Jeremiah from the LORD in the tenth year of King Zedekiah of Judah, which was the eighteenth

ᵃ Or *master*

This principle, however, was already coming under critique; see Deut 24.16; 2 Kings 14.6.

31.31–37: The renewed covenant. 32: *I was their husband*, using the term associated with the Canaanite god Baal; cf. Hos 2.16; Jer 3.14. God could function as "husband" or "master" (Heb "ba'al"), and this led to confusion between God and Baal. In functioning as "ba'al," it is God, not Baal, who gives Israel its "grain, wine and oil"; see Hos 2.8. **33–34:** Though the *law* (Heb "torah," which also means "teaching") was traditionally thought of as being "in the heart" (Deut 30.14), it would become so instinctual that "teaching" would become unnecessary, a radically new idea given the strong Deuteronomic concern for teaching (Deut 4.10; 5.1,31; 11.19; 31.12–13). **35–37:** Later additions using standard hymnic language. God's commitment is as sure as the cosmos is fixed and unfathomable; cf. 33.19–26.

31.38–40: Jerusalem rebuilt. A later oracle depicting the restoration of Jerusalem's walls around its perimeter. On these places, several of which are otherwise unknown, see Neh 3.1,28; 12.39; Zech 14.10; 2 Kings 14.13.

32.1–33.26: God's restoration of Israel. These chapters are thematically linked to the "Book of Consolation" (chs 30–31) and so are included here, even though they should follow ch 34 chronologically; they are dated to the very end of the reign of Zedekiah and of the Babylonian siege (588–586 BCE), during which Jeremiah was in confinement. Jer 32.1–44 centers on the theme that "fields shall be bought . . . and deeds shall be signed and sealed and witnessed" (v. 44), using Jeremiah's offer of redeeming family property in Anathoth as a sign. Jer 33.1–26 centers on the rebuilding of the city and the promise that the city will be given a new name, "the LORD is our righteousness" (v. 16).

32.1–25: Jeremiah purchases the family property. 1: *The tenth year . . . the eighteenth year*, 588 BCE. **3–5:** Jer-

year of Nebuchadrezzar. [2] At that time the army of the king of Babylon was besieging Jerusalem, and the prophet Jeremiah was confined in the court of the guard that was in the palace of the king of Judah, [3] where King Zedekiah of Judah had confined him. Zedekiah had said, "Why do you prophesy and say: Thus says the LORD: I am going to give this city into the hand of the king of Babylon, and he shall take it; [4] King Zedekiah of Judah shall not escape out of the hands of the Chaldeans, but shall surely be given into the hands of the king of Babylon, and shall speak with him face to face and see him eye to eye; [5] and he shall take Zedekiah to Babylon, and there he shall remain until I attend to him, says the LORD; though you fight against the Chaldeans, you shall not succeed?"

[6] Jeremiah said, The word of the LORD came to me: [7] Hanamel son of your uncle Shallum is going to come to you and say, "Buy my field that is at Anathoth, for the right of redemption by purchase is yours." [8] Then my cousin Hanamel came to me in the court of the guard, in accordance with the word of the LORD, and said to me, "Buy my field that is at Anathoth in the land of Benjamin, for the right of possession and redemption is yours; buy it for yourself." Then I knew that this was the word of the LORD.

[9] And I bought the field at Anathoth from my cousin Hanamel, and weighed out the money to him, seventeen shekels of silver. [10] I signed the deed, sealed it, got witnesses, and weighed the money on scales. [11] Then I took the sealed deed of purchase, containing the terms and conditions, and the open copy; [12] and I gave the deed of purchase to Baruch son of Neriah son of Mahseiah, in the presence of my cousin Hanamel, in the presence of the witnesses who signed the deed of purchase, and in the presence of all the Judeans who were sitting in the court of the guard. [13] In their presence I charged Baruch, saying, [14] Thus says the LORD of hosts, the God of Israel: Take these deeds, both this sealed deed of purchase and this open deed, and put them in an earthenware jar, in order that they may last for a long time. [15] For thus says the LORD of hosts, the God of Israel: Houses and fields and vineyards shall again be bought in this land.

[16] After I had given the deed of purchase to Baruch son of Neriah, I prayed to the LORD, saying: [17] Ah Lord GOD! It is you who made the heavens and the earth by your great power and by your outstretched arm! Nothing is too hard for you. [18] You show steadfast love to the thousandth generation,[a] but repay the guilt of parents into the laps of their children after them, O great and mighty God whose name is the LORD of hosts, [19] great in counsel and mighty in deed; whose eyes are open to all the ways of mortals, rewarding all according to their ways and according to the fruit of their doings. [20] You showed signs and wonders in the land of Egypt, and to this day in Israel and among all humankind, and have made yourself a name that continues to this very day. [21] You brought your people Israel out of the land of Egypt with signs and wonders, with a strong hand and outstretched arm, and with great terror; [22] and you gave them this land, which you swore to their ancestors to give them, a land flowing with milk and honey; [23] and they entered and took possession of it. But they did not obey your voice or follow your law; of all you commanded them to do, they did nothing. Therefore you have made all these disasters come upon them. [24] See, the siege ramps have been cast up against the city to take it, and the city,

[a] Or *to thousands*

emiah's arrest is narrated in 37.1–38.28. The prophetic oracle alluded to is 34.2–3. During a brief lifting of the siege (see 34.8–22) Jeremiah tried to leave the city, was accused of desertion, and was arrested (37.11–16). **4:** *Chaldeans*, i.e., Babylonians. **7:** *Right of redemption*, to keep property within the extended family, members who could do so were expected to "redeem" land that was in jeopardy of being forfeited or sold outside the family; see Lev 25.23–28. **9:** *Seventeen shekels*, ca. 7 oz (194 grams). At this time there was no coinage, and "money" was weighed. **11:** *Sealed deed . . . open copy*, contracts were sealed with a signet ring on a clay "bulla," but a copy or summary of the contents was left available on the outside of the scroll for reference and public scrutiny. Storage of such documents in clay jars was common practice. **12:** *Baruch, son of Neriah*, Jeremiah's scribe. See 36.4; 51.59. **17–18:** Standard hymnic language in creedal form; see Ex 20.5–6; 34.6–7. **20:** *Signs and wonders*, a refer-

faced with sword, famine, and pestilence, has been given into the hands of the Chaldeans who are fighting against it. What you spoke has happened, as you yourself can see. ²⁵ Yet you, O Lord GOD, have said to me, "Buy the field for money and get witnesses"—though the city has been given into the hands of the Chaldeans.

²⁶ The word of the LORD came to Jeremiah: ²⁷ See, I am the LORD, the God of all flesh; is anything too hard for me? ²⁸ Therefore, thus says the LORD: I am going to give this city into the hands of the Chaldeans and into the hand of King Nebuchadrezzar of Babylon, and he shall take it. ²⁹ The Chaldeans who are fighting against this city shall come, set it on fire, and burn it, with the houses on whose roofs offerings have been made to Baal and libations have been poured out to other gods, to provoke me to anger. ³⁰ For the people of Israel and the people of Judah have done nothing but evil in my sight from their youth; the people of Israel have done nothing but provoke me to anger by the work of their hands, says the LORD. ³¹ This city has aroused my anger and wrath, from the day it was built until this day, so that I will remove it from my sight ³² because of all the evil of the people of Israel and the people of Judah that they did to provoke me to anger—they, their kings and their officials, their priests and their prophets, the citizens of Judah and the inhabitants of Jerusalem. ³³ They have turned their backs to me, not their faces; though I have taught them persistently, they would not listen and accept correction. ³⁴ They set up their abominations in the house that bears my name, and defiled it. ³⁵ They built the high places of Baal in the valley of the son of Hinnom, to offer up their sons and daughters to Molech, though

I did not command them, nor did it enter my mind that they should do this abomination, causing Judah to sin.

³⁶ Now therefore thus says the LORD, the God of Israel, concerning this city of which you say, "It is being given into the hand of the king of Babylon by the sword, by famine, and by pestilence": ³⁷ See, I am going to gather them from all the lands to which I drove them in my anger and my wrath and in great indignation; I will bring them back to this place, and I will settle them in safety. ³⁸ They shall be my people, and I will be their God. ³⁹ I will give them one heart and one way, that they may fear me for all time, for their own good and the good of their children after them. ⁴⁰ I will make an everlasting covenant with them, never to draw back from doing good to them; and I will put the fear of me in their hearts, so that they may not turn from me. ⁴¹ I will rejoice in doing good to them, and I will plant them in this land in faithfulness, with all my heart and all my soul.

⁴² For thus says the LORD: Just as I have brought all this great disaster upon this people, so I will bring upon them all the good fortune that I now promise them. ⁴³ Fields shall be bought in this land of which you are saying, It is a desolation, without human beings or animals; it has been given into the hands of the Chaldeans. ⁴⁴ Fields shall be bought for money, and deeds shall be signed and sealed and witnessed, in the land of Benjamin, in the places around Jerusalem, and in the cities of Judah, of the hill country, of the Shephelah, and of the Negeb; for I will restore their fortunes, says the LORD.

33 The word of the LORD came to Jeremiah a second time, while he was still confined in the court of the guard: ² Thus

ence to the plagues tradition (cf. Ex 3.20; 4.21; Deut 34.11). **25:** After reviewing Israel's history of disobedience, Jeremiah is struck by the irony that, with the land about to be captured by the *Chaldeans* (the Babylonians) and all land-tenure about to be nullified, he is being asked to perform such a foolish transaction. **26–44:** In the face of Jeremiah's resistance, God restates the promise of restoration. A typically Deuteronomic sermon (vv. 26–35) is followed by words of promise. **29:** *Roofs* were commonly used for many purposes, including religious rituals both legitimate (Neh 8.16) and illegitimate (19.13; Zeph 1.5). **35:** On the rituals in the Hinnom Valley, see 7.31; 19.5–6. *Molech* is either the name of a foreign god (1 Kings 11.7) or an epithet for Baal, formed by combining the vowels of the word for "foolishness" (Heb "boshet") with the consonants of the word for "king" ("melek"). **36:** *Of which you say*, the pronoun here, as in v. 43, is plural, indicating that this is the popular sentiment at this critical time of the siege. **39–41:** As in 31.31–34, the saving action is here solely God's, who acts unilaterally in the face of Israel's own utter failure. **44:** *Benjamin . . . Negeb*, see 17.26n.

says the LORD who made the earth,[a] the LORD who formed it to establish it—the LORD is his name: [3] Call to me and I will answer you, and will tell you great and hidden things that you have not known. [4] For thus says the LORD, the God of Israel, concerning the houses of this city and the houses of the kings of Judah that were torn down to make a defense against the siege ramps and before the sword:[b] [5] The Chaldeans are coming in to fight[c] and to fill them with the dead bodies of those whom I shall strike down in my anger and my wrath, for I have hidden my face from this city because of all their wickedness. [6] I am going to bring it recovery and healing; I will heal them and reveal to them abundance[b] of prosperity and security. [7] I will restore the fortunes of Judah and the fortunes of Israel, and rebuild them as they were at first. [8] I will cleanse them from all the guilt of their sin against me, and I will forgive all the guilt of their sin and rebellion against me. [9] And this city[d] shall be to me a name of joy, a praise and a glory before all the nations of the earth who shall hear of all the good that I do for them; they shall fear and tremble because of all the good and all the prosperity I provide for it.

[10] Thus says the LORD: In this place of which you say, "It is a waste without human beings or animals," in the towns of Judah and the streets of Jerusalem that are desolate, without inhabitants, human or animal, there shall once more be heard [11] the voice of mirth and the voice of gladness, the voice of the bridegroom and the voice of the bride, the voices of those who sing, as they bring thank offerings to the house of the LORD:

"Give thanks to the LORD of hosts,
    for the LORD is good,
    for his steadfast love endures forever!"
For I will restore the fortunes of the land as at first, says the LORD.

[12] Thus says the LORD of hosts: In this place that is waste, without human beings or animals, and in all its towns there shall again be pasture for shepherds resting their flocks. [13] In the towns of the hill country, of the Shephelah, and of the Negeb, in the land of Benjamin, the places around Jerusalem, and in the towns of Judah, flocks shall again pass under the hands of the one who counts them, says the LORD.

[14] The days are surely coming, says the LORD, when I will fulfill the promise I made to the house of Israel and the house of Judah. [15] In those days and at that time I will cause a righteous Branch to spring up for David; and he shall execute justice and righteousness in the land. [16] In those days Judah will be saved and Jerusalem will live in safety. And this is the name by which it will be called: "The LORD is our righteousness."

[17] For thus says the LORD: David shall never lack a man to sit on the throne of the house of Israel, [18] and the levitical priests shall never lack a man in my presence to offer burnt offerings, to make grain offerings, and to make sacrifices for all time.

a   Gk: Heb *it*
b   Meaning of Heb uncertain
c   Cn: Heb *They are coming in to fight against the Chaldeans*
d   Heb *And it*

33.1–26: **Oracles of restoration,** connected to the previous oracles by their presumed location (Jeremiah in confinement). **4:** *Houses of this city,* introduces the theme of the restoration of Jerusalem's buildings. Now the city itself becomes the subject of visions of restoration; cf. v. 9. The desperation of the city is clear, as the buildings within it are dismantled to use as raw material to defend against the Babylonian siege ramps. **5:** *Chaldeans,* i.e., Babylonians. **7:** *At first,* or "formerly." **8–9:** God's favor will be lavished on Israel out of sheer divine mercy, with no preconditions, and the nations of the world will be astounded to see such beneficence. **10:** *Of which you say,* again the pronoun is plural, expressing popular pessimistic sentiment. **11:** Cf. 7.34; 16.9; 25.10. This thanksgiving uses standard psalmic language (Pss 106.1; 107.1; 136.1–26; Sir 51.12). **13:** *Shephelah . . . Negeb,* see 17.26n. **14–16:** Echoes 23.5–6, except that in v. 6 ("by which it will be called"), it is now the city of Jerusalem that is given the name rather than the anticipated Davidic ruler. **17–18:** The first of three appended oracles regarding Jerusalem's leadership, using late language reflecting 2 Chr 7.18. The term *levitical priests* is common to Deuteronomy but used only here in Jeremiah. **19–22:** Second appended oracle recalling the argument of 31.36–37. Again hopes are placed on both royal and levitical persons, characteristic of the postexilic hopes for both a Davidic and a

[19] The word of the LORD came to Jeremiah: [20] Thus says the LORD: If any of you could break my covenant with the day and my covenant with the night, so that day and night would not come at their appointed time, [21] only then could my covenant with my servant David be broken, so that he would not have a son to reign on his throne, and my covenant with my ministers the Levites. [22] Just as the host of heaven cannot be numbered and the sands of the sea cannot be measured, so I will increase the offspring of my servant David, and the Levites who minister to me.

[23] The word of the LORD came to Jeremiah: [24] Have you not observed how these people say, "The two families that the LORD chose have been rejected by him," and how they hold my people in such contempt that they no longer regard them as a nation? [25] Thus says the LORD: Only if I had not established my covenant with day and night and the ordinances of heaven and earth, [26] would I reject the offspring of Jacob and of my servant David and not choose any of his descendants as rulers over the offspring of Abraham, Isaac, and Jacob. For I will restore their fortunes, and will have mercy upon them.

34 The word that came to Jeremiah from the LORD, when King Nebuchadrezzar of Babylon and all his army and all the kingdoms of the earth and all the peoples under his dominion were fighting against Jerusalem and all its cities: [2] Thus says the LORD, the God of Israel: Go and speak to King Zedekiah of Judah and say to him: Thus says the LORD: I am going to give this city into the hand of the king of Babylon, and he shall burn it with fire. [3] And you yourself shall not escape from his hand, but shall surely be captured and handed over to him; you shall see the king of Babylon eye to eye and speak with him face to face; and you shall go to Babylon. [4] Yet hear the word of the LORD, O King Zedekiah of Judah! Thus says the LORD concerning you: You shall not die by the sword; [5] you shall die in peace. And as spices were burned[a] for your ancestors, the earlier kings who preceded you, so they shall burn spices[b] for you and lament for you, saying, "Alas, lord!" For I have spoken the word, says the LORD.

[6] Then the prophet Jeremiah spoke all these words to Zedekiah king of Judah, in Jerusalem, [7] when the army of the king of Babylon was fighting against Jerusalem and against all the cities of Judah that were left, Lachish and Azekah; for these were the only fortified cities of Judah that remained.

a Heb *as there was burning*
b Heb *shall burn*

priestly leader (compare Zech 4.11–14). **22:** Cf. Gen 22.17–18. **23–26:** Third appended oracle. Again celebrates the promise to the "two families," but now this is a reference to the entire land of Israel represented by Jacob (Israel) and David (Judah); cf. the cosmic argument of 31.36–37. **25:** *Covenant with day and night,* this radical language echoes the Priestly language explicit in Gen 9.8–16 that God's covenant is with "all flesh" and, indeed, with "the earth," that is, the cosmos. In this tradition, Gen 9 is understood as a recapitulation of creation itself (Gen 1).

34.1–7: Judgment against Zedekiah. This oracle, spoken during the Babylonian siege, recapitulates the speech that, according to 32.3–5, was the basis for Jeremiah's imprisonment. Though v. 5 sounds as though it is a threat against Zedekiah, it is rather a mitigation of divine judgment, promising Zedekiah a normal death and burial with full honor; contrast the fate of Jehoiakim in 22.18–19, for whom these normal rituals of burial would not be conducted. In fact, Zedekiah's fate was not this "peaceful," according to 52.9–11; 2 Kings 25.6–7. **7:** *Lachish* (21 mi [45 km] southwest of Jerusalem) *and Azekah* (11mi [18 km] north-northwest of Lachish) were two garrison cities defending Jerusalem on the southwest. Letters found at Lachish from this time indicate the drama of these final days, when at last even the signal fire from Azekah could no longer be seen and Lachish alone survived.

34.8–22: The aborted manumission of slaves. The context for this event is the period when the siege was briefly lifted because Egyptian forces under Pharaoh Hophra (Apries) arrived in Judah to attempt to break the siege of the Babylonian army. Babylonian forces temporarily withdrew from Jerusalem in order to face Hophra's army; see 37.5,11. The manumission was in accord with the principles of Ex 21.2 and Deut 15.12, as referenced in Jer 34.14. The manumission likely also served practical purposes, given scarcity of food resources and the need for male support troops. As soon as the siege was lifted, however, the people presumed that normality would

[8] The word that came to Jeremiah from the LORD, after King Zedekiah had made a covenant with all the people in Jerusalem to make a proclamation of liberty to them— [9] that all should set free their Hebrew slaves, male and female, so that no one should hold another Judean in slavery. [10] And they obeyed, all the officials and all the people who had entered into the covenant that all would set free their slaves, male or female, so that they would not be enslaved again; they obeyed and set them free. [11] But afterward they turned around and took back the male and female slaves they had set free, and brought them again into subjection as slaves. [12] The word of the LORD came to Jeremiah from the LORD: [13] Thus says the LORD, the God of Israel: I myself made a covenant with your ancestors when I brought them out of the land of Egypt, out of the house of slavery, saying, [14] "Every seventh year each of you must set free any Hebrews who have been sold to you and have served you six years; you must set them free from your service." But your ancestors did not listen to me or incline their ears to me. [15] You yourselves recently repented and did what was right in my sight by proclaiming liberty to one another, and you made a covenant before me in the house that is called by my name; [16] but then you turned around and profaned my name when each of you took back your male and female slaves, whom you had set free according to their desire, and you brought them again into subjection to be your slaves. [17] Therefore, thus says the

LORD: You have not obeyed me by granting a release to your neighbors and friends; I am going to grant a release to you, says the LORD—a release to the sword, to pestilence, and to famine. I will make you a horror to all the kingdoms of the earth. [18] And those who transgressed my covenant and did not keep the terms of the covenant that they made before me, I will make like[a] the calf when they cut it in two and passed between its parts: [19] the officials of Judah, the officials of Jerusalem, the eunuchs, the priests, and all the people of the land who passed between the parts of the calf [20] shall be handed over to their enemies and to those who seek their lives. Their corpses shall become food for the birds of the air and the wild animals of the earth. [21] And as for King Zedekiah of Judah and his officials, I will hand them over to their enemies and to those who seek their lives, to the army of the king of Babylon, which has withdrawn from you. [22] I am going to command, says the LORD, and will bring them back to this city; and they will fight against it, and take it, and burn it with fire. The towns of Judah I will make a desolation without inhabitant.

35 The word that came to Jeremiah from the LORD in the days of King Jehoiakim son of Josiah of Judah: [2] Go to the house of the Rechabites, and speak with them, and bring them to the house of the LORD, into one of

a   Cn: Heb lacks *like*

return and therefore the manumission was retracted. **17:** *A release to you,* using the term for the "amnesty" or "manumission," Jeremiah offers a play on words. **18:** *Like the calf when they cut it in two,* likely a reference to the fact that covenants were "cut" (Heb "karat," see v. 13) rather than "made," and were accompanied by ritual actions such as those suggested by Gen 15.9–18. **19:** *The eunuchs,* the Heb term "saris" is often used of court officials (1 Sam 8.15; 2 Kings 8.6; Jer 29.2; 52.25), indicating perhaps how highly in Judean court life such persons of ambiguous gender could ascend. Some scholars, however, suggest that the term has two distinct meanings ("official" and "eunuch"). There is no indication, however, that the "eunuch" was a social pariah. The common scholarly assumption that the laws of Lev 21.20; 22.24 and Deut 23.1 refer to eunuchs is far from certain. **22:** *Bring them back,* the siege will be resumed.

35.1–19: The sign of the Rechabites. The clan of the Rechabites traced their origins to Jonadab ben Rechab (v. 6), and rallied around the anti-agrarian policies indicated in vv. 8–10, perhaps as a fundamentalist reaction against cultural assimilation to the perceived values of the Canaanites. Jonadab was remembered as an ally of the conservative Yahwist Jehu (842–814 BCE) in his revolt against the syncretistic policies of the Omri dynasty in the Northern Kingdom of Israel (2 Kings 10.15,23). Their faithfulness to their extreme values was used by Jeremiah as a stark contrast with the faithlessness of the people of Jerusalem, who could not obey even divinely sanctioned norms. **1:** *King Jehoiakim* (608–598 BCE), a surprising regression in time, perhaps to prepare the

the chambers; then offer them wine to drink. [3] So I took Jaazaniah son of Jeremiah son of Habazziniah, and his brothers, and all his sons, and the whole house of the Rechabites. [4] I brought them to the house of the LORD into the chamber of the sons of Hanan son of Igdaliah, the man of God, which was near the chamber of the officials, above the chamber of Maaseiah son of Shallum, keeper of the threshold. [5] Then I set before the Rechabites pitchers full of wine, and cups; and I said to them, "Have some wine." [6] But they answered, "We will drink no wine, for our ancestor Jonadab son of Rechab commanded us, 'You shall never drink wine, neither you nor your children; [7] nor shall you ever build a house, or sow seed; nor shall you plant a vineyard, or even own one; but you shall live in tents all your days, that you may live many days in the land where you reside.' [8] We have obeyed the charge of our ancestor Jonadab son of Rechab in all that he commanded us, to drink no wine all our days, ourselves, our wives, our sons, or our daughters, [9] and not to build houses to live in. We have no vineyard or field or seed; [10] but we have lived in tents, and have obeyed and done all that our ancestor Jonadab commanded us. [11] But when King Nebuchadrezzar of Babylon came up against the land, we said, 'Come, and let us go to Jerusalem for fear of the army of the Chaldeans and the army of the Arameans.' That is why we are living in Jerusalem."

[12] Then the word of the LORD came to Jeremiah: [13] Thus says the LORD of hosts, the God of Israel: Go and say to the people of Judah and the inhabitants of Jerusalem, Can you not learn a lesson and obey my words?

says the LORD. [14] The command has been carried out that Jonadab son of Rechab gave to his descendants to drink no wine; and they drink none to this day, for they have obeyed their ancestor's command. But I myself have spoken to you persistently, and you have not obeyed me. [15] I have sent to you all my servants the prophets, sending them persistently, saying, "Turn now every one of you from your evil way, and amend your doings, and do not go after other gods to serve them, and then you shall live in the land that I gave to you and your ancestors." But you did not incline your ear or obey me. [16] The descendants of Jonadab son of Rechab have carried out the command that their ancestor gave them, but this people has not obeyed me. [17] Therefore, thus says the LORD, the God of hosts, the God of Israel: I am going to bring on Judah and on all the inhabitants of Jerusalem every disaster that I have pronounced against them; because I have spoken to them and they have not listened, I have called to them and they have not answered.

[18] But to the house of the Rechabites Jeremiah said: Thus says the LORD of hosts, the God of Israel: Because you have obeyed the command of your ancestor Jonadab, and kept all his precepts, and done all that he commanded you, [19] therefore thus says the LORD of hosts, the God of Israel: Jonadab son of Rechab shall not lack a descendant to stand before me for all time.

36 In the fourth year of King Jehoiakim son of Josiah of Judah, this word came to Jeremiah from the LORD: [2] Take a scroll and write on it all the words that I have spoken

reader for ch 36, also set during the reign of Jehoiakim. **4:** *Chamber*, prominent families had open rooms in the Temple complex where they gathered, shared sacrificial meals, and conducted other business (36.10; 2 Kings 23.11). *Keeper of the threshold*, on this important priestly function, see 2 Kings 12.9; 22.4; 23.4; 25.18. **11:** *When King Nebuchadrezzar . . . came up against the land*, must refer to the Babylonian (Chaldean) incursion into the Levant in 605–604 BCE, setting the stage for ch 36. *Arameans*, centered in Damascus (that is, Syria), who were often the historical enemies of Israel and perhaps always a problem for the nomadic clans of herdsmen in the eastern steppes. **15:** See 7.25n.

36.1–32: Commissioning and reading the scroll of 605 BCE. In a pivotal year, the Babylonians defeated the Egyptians in battle and asserted themselves as the dominant power over Judah, forcing the radical reshaping of Judean aspirations and allegiances, events introduced in 35.11. As in ch 25, so here the editor's use of the "scroll tradition" concludes a major section of the oracles (chs 26–35), the second such cycle. The oracles include the chief collection of Jeremiah's utterances from 627 down to 605 BCE (compare 25.3 and 36.2). At this time, Jeremiah was already under a temporary ban from the Temple quarters (36.5), so the story likely follows the event of his being arraigned and beaten by the Temple overseer Pashhur (20.1–6), a possible occa-

to you against Israel and Judah and all the nations, from the day I spoke to you, from the days of Josiah until today. [3] It may be that when the house of Judah hears of all the disasters that I intend to do to them, all of them may turn from their evil ways, so that I may forgive their iniquity and their sin.

[4] Then Jeremiah called Baruch son of Neriah, and Baruch wrote on a scroll at Jeremiah's dictation all the words of the LORD that he had spoken to him. [5] And Jeremiah ordered Baruch, saying, "I am prevented from entering the house of the LORD; [6] so you go yourself, and on a fast day in the hearing of the people in the LORD's house you shall read the words of the LORD from the scroll that you have written at my dictation. You shall read them also in the hearing of all the people of Judah who come up from their towns. [7] It may be that their plea will come before the LORD, and that all of them will turn from their evil ways, for great is the anger and wrath that the LORD has pronounced against this people." [8] And Baruch son of Neriah did all that the prophet Jeremiah ordered him about reading from the scroll the words of the LORD in the LORD's house.

[9] In the fifth year of King Jehoiakim son of Josiah of Judah, in the ninth month, all the people in Jerusalem and all the people who came from the towns of Judah to Jerusalem proclaimed a fast before the LORD. [10] Then, in the hearing of all the people, Baruch read the words of Jeremiah from the scroll, in the house of the LORD, in the chamber of Gemariah son of Shaphan the secretary, which was in the upper court, at the entry of the New Gate of the LORD's house.

[11] When Micaiah son of Gemariah son of Shaphan heard all the words of the LORD from the scroll, [12] he went down to the king's house, into the secretary's chamber; and all the officials were sitting there: Elishama the secretary, Delaiah son of Shemaiah, Elnathan son of Achbor, Gemariah son of Shaphan, Zedekiah son of Hananiah, and all the officials. [13] And Micaiah told them all the words that he had heard, when Baruch read the scroll in the hearing of the people. [14] Then all the officials sent Jehudi son of Nethaniah son of Shelemiah son of Cushi to say to Baruch, "Bring the scroll that you read in the hearing of the people, and come." So Baruch son of Neriah took the scroll in his hand and came to them. [15] And they said to him, "Sit down and read it to us." So Baruch read it to them. [16] When they heard all the words, they turned to one another in alarm, and said to Baruch, "We certainly must report all these words to the king." [17] Then they questioned Baruch, "Tell us now, how did you write all these words? Was it at his dictation?" [18] Baruch answered them, "He dictated all these words to me, and I wrote them with ink on the scroll." [19] Then the officials said to Baruch, "Go and hide, you and Jeremiah, and let no one know where you are."

[20] Leaving the scroll in the chamber of Elishama the secretary, they went to the court of the king; and they reported all the words to the king. [21] Then the king sent Jehudi to get the scroll, and he took it from the chamber of Elishama the secretary; and Jehudi read it to the king and all the officials who stood beside the king. [22] Now the king was sitting in his winter apartment (it was the ninth month), and there was a fire burning in the brazier before him. [23] As Jehudi read three or four columns, the

sion for the ban. As elsewhere, Jeremiah has the assistance of Baruch, who serves as his scribe (see 32.12–16; 51.59), and is supported by the family of Shaphan within the royal court and family (Gemariah and Micaiah), who send Baruch and Jeremiah into protective hiding (v. 19). Piece by piece Jehoiakim burned the scroll, likely as a means of mitigating the effects of the words of judgment, which would have been received as a type of "curse." Most scholars assume that the second scroll, produced to replace the first destroyed by Jehoiakim (vv. 27–32), contained the core of material now found in chs 1–24 (compare 36.29 with 7.20 and 21.6). 6: *On a fast day*, that is, on a day specially set aside for public mourning and divine intercession in the face of Judah's political crisis (v. 9). 12: *Elnathan son of Achbor*, perhaps the king's father-in-law (2 Kings 24.8) and head of the mission that brought the prophet Uriah back from Egypt for execution (Jer 26.22–23). 22: *Winter apartment*, or "harvest quarters." On the morality of the royal accumulation of such dwellings, see 22.13–17; Am 3.15. *Ninth month*, November-December.

king[a] would cut them off with a penknife and throw them into the fire in the brazier, until the entire scroll was consumed in the fire that was in the brazier. [24] Yet neither the king, nor any of his servants who heard all these words, was alarmed, nor did they tear their garments. [25] Even when Elnathan and Delaiah and Gemariah urged the king not to burn the scroll, he would not listen to them. [26] And the king commanded Jerahmeel the king's son and Seraiah son of Azriel and Shelemiah son of Abdeel to arrest the secretary Baruch and the prophet Jeremiah. But the LORD hid them.

[27] Now, after the king had burned the scroll with the words that Baruch wrote at Jeremiah's dictation, the word of the LORD came to Jeremiah: [28] Take another scroll and write on it all the former words that were in the first scroll, which King Jehoiakim of Judah has burned. [29] And concerning King Jehoiakim of Judah you shall say: Thus says the LORD, You have dared to burn this scroll, saying, Why have you written in it that the king of Babylon will certainly come and destroy this land, and will cut off from it human beings and animals? [30] Therefore thus says the LORD concerning King Jehoiakim of Judah: He shall have no one to sit upon the throne of David, and his dead body shall be cast out to the heat by day and the frost by night. [31] And I will punish him and his offspring and his servants for their iniquity; I will bring on them, and on the inhabitants of Jerusalem, and on the people of Judah, all the disasters with which I have threatened them—but they would not listen.

[32] Then Jeremiah took another scroll and gave it to the secretary Baruch son of Neriah, who wrote on it at Jeremiah's dictation all the words of the scroll that King Jehoiakim of Judah had burned in the fire; and many similar words were added to them.

37 Zedekiah son of Josiah, whom King Nebuchadrezzar of Babylon made king in the land of Judah, succeeded Coniah son of Jehoiakim. [2] But neither he nor his servants nor the people of the land listened to the words of the LORD that he spoke through the prophet Jeremiah.

[3] King Zedekiah sent Jehucal son of Shelemiah and the priest Zephaniah son of Maaseiah to the prophet Jeremiah saying, "Please pray for us to the LORD our God." [4] Now Jeremiah was still going in and out among the people, for he had not yet been put in prison. [5] Meanwhile, the army of Pharaoh had come out of Egypt; and when the Chaldeans who were besieging Jerusalem heard news of them, they withdrew from Jerusalem.

[6] Then the word of the LORD came to the prophet Jeremiah: [7] Thus says the LORD, God of Israel: This is what the two of you shall say to the king of Judah, who sent you to me to inquire of me: Pharaoh's army, which set out to help you, is going to return to its own land, to Egypt. [8] And the Chaldeans shall return and fight against this city; they shall take it and burn it with fire. [9] Thus says the LORD: Do not deceive yourselves, saying, "The Chaldeans will surely go away from us," for they will not go away. [10] Even if you defeated the whole army of Chaldeans who are fighting against you, and there remained of them only

a Heb *he*

37.1–38.28: The final arrest of Jeremiah. Two different accounts of what was likely one event have been juxtaposed, recounting the story of Jeremiah's final confinement just before the fall of Jerusalem in 586 BCE. The main story (37.1–21 and 38.14–28), concerning Jeremiah's desire to escape imprisonment in the house of the secretary Jonathan (37.15,20; 38.26), is embellished with the story of Jeremiah's rescue by the Ethiopian courtier, Ebed-melech (38.1–13). As this material begins the third cycle, it resets chronologically to a period prior to the events mentioned in chs 32–33. Jeremiah, not yet under arrest, is still prophesying publicly and openly (37.4; 38.1). During the brief lifting of the Babylonian siege (v. 5, see 34.8–22), Jeremiah attempted to leave Jerusalem to take care of some family business (vv. 11–12). He was arrested for desertion and his fate, which would have been severe at the hands of the officials, was softened by allowance of King Zedekiah. In both accounts, Jeremiah is threatened with harsh incarceration but is allowed to stay under royal protection in the court of the guard.

37.1–10: Jeremiah's response to Zedekiah's request for intercession. The context of the lifting of the siege provides the language for Jeremiah's oracle: the Babylonians (Chaldeans) will be right back, so take no comfort in the brief respite! 1: *Coniah*, Jehoiachin. 5: See 34.8–22n.

wounded men in their tents, they would rise up and burn this city with fire.

[11] Now when the Chaldean army had withdrawn from Jerusalem at the approach of Pharaoh's army, [12] Jeremiah set out from Jerusalem to go to the land of Benjamin to receive his share of property[a] among the people there. [13] When he reached the Benjamin Gate, a sentinel there named Irijah son of Shelemiah son of Hananiah arrested the prophet Jeremiah saying, "You are deserting to the Chaldeans." [14] And Jeremiah said, "That is a lie; I am not deserting to the Chaldeans." But Irijah would not listen to him, and arrested Jeremiah and brought him to the officials. [15] The officials were enraged at Jeremiah, and they beat him and imprisoned him in the house of the secretary Jonathan, for it had been made a prison. [16] Thus Jeremiah was put in the cistern house, in the cells, and remained there many days.

[17] Then King Zedekiah sent for him, and received him. The king questioned him secretly in his house, and said, "Is there any word from the LORD?" Jeremiah said, "There is!" Then he said, "You shall be handed over to the king of Babylon." [18] Jeremiah also said to King Zedekiah, "What wrong have I done to you or your servants or this people, that you have put me in prison? [19] Where are your prophets who prophesied to you, saying, 'The king of Babylon will not come against you and against this land'? [20] Now please hear me, my lord king: be good enough to listen to my plea, and do not send me back to the house of the secretary Jonathan to die there." [21] So King Zedekiah gave orders, and they committed Jeremiah to the court of the guard; and a loaf of bread was given him daily from the bakers' street, until all the bread of the city was gone. So Jeremiah remained in the court of the guard.

38 Now Shephatiah son of Mattan, Gedaliah son of Pashhur, Jucal son of Shelemiah, and Pashhur son of Malchiah heard the words that Jeremiah was saying to all the people, [2] Thus says the LORD, Those who stay in this city shall die by the sword, by famine, and by pestilence; but those who go out to the Chaldeans shall live; they shall have their lives as a prize of war, and live. [3] Thus says the LORD, This city shall surely be handed over to the army of the king of Babylon and be taken. [4] Then the officials said to the king, "This man ought to be put to death, because he is discouraging the soldiers who are left in this city, and all the people, by speaking such words to them. For this man is not seeking the welfare of this people, but their harm." [5] King Zedekiah said, "Here he is; he is in your hands; for the king is powerless against you." [6] So they took Jeremiah and threw him into the cistern of Malchiah, the king's son, which was in the court of the guard, letting Jeremiah down by ropes. Now there was no water in the cistern, but only mud, and Jeremiah sank in the mud.

[7] Ebed-melech the Ethiopian,[b] a eunuch in the king's house, heard that they had put Jeremiah into the cistern. The king happened to be sitting at the Benjamin Gate, [8] So Ebed-melech left the king's house and spoke

a   Meaning of Heb uncertain
b   Or *Nubian*; Heb *Cushite*

37.11–21: Jeremiah's incarceration in the Court of the Guard. 12: Jeremiah was from the Benjaminite town of Anathoth (1.1) and would later be invited to redeem some family property there (32.7–9). **16:** *Cistern house*, apparently a vaulted room formerly used as a cistern for water storage. Jeremiah believed that incarceration here would be deadly (v. 20), perhaps because while there he was under threat of some particularly hostile princes and did not enjoy any royal protection. **21:** *The court of the guard* was located in the royal palace itself, under direct supervision of the king (32.2).

38.1–13: An alternate account regarding Jeremiah and Ebed-melech. This story develops the theme of the conflict between Zedekiah and his pro-Egyptian advisers, who were particularly opposed to Jeremiah's message of capitulation to the Babylonians. The charge that Jeremiah was "discouraging the soldiers" is similar to a charge made in the Lachish letters against certain other royal princes (likely those associated with the Shaphan party) that they too were discouraging the troops. That the opposition of this party is lethal to Jeremiah's safety (v. 4) is brought out in this story. Here the cistern into which Jeremiah is thrown has a different name and is located in the court of the guard itself (v. 6). **1:** *Gedaliah son of Pashhur*, see 20.1; *Jucal* (Jehucal), see 37.3; *Pashhur*, see 21.1. **6:** The cistern was nearly dry, indicating a time shortly before Nebuchadrezzar's final assault, August

to the king, [9] "My lord king, these men have acted wickedly in all they did to the prophet Jeremiah by throwing him into the cistern to die there of hunger, for there is no bread left in the city." [10] Then the king commanded Ebed-melech the Ethiopian,[a] "Take three men with you from here, and pull the prophet Jeremiah up from the cistern before he dies." [11] So Ebed-melech took the men with him and went to the house of the king, to a wardrobe of[b] the storehouse, and took from there old rags and worn-out clothes, which he let down to Jeremiah in the cistern by ropes. [12] Then Ebed-melech the Ethiopian[a] said to Jeremiah, "Just put the rags and clothes between your armpits and the ropes." Jeremiah did so. [13] Then they drew Jeremiah up by the ropes and pulled him out of the cistern. And Jeremiah remained in the court of the guard.

[14] King Zedekiah sent for the prophet Jeremiah and received him at the third entrance of the temple of the LORD. The king said to Jeremiah, "I have something to ask you; do not hide anything from me." [15] Jeremiah said to Zedekiah, "If I tell you, you will put me to death, will you not? And if I give you advice, you will not listen to me." [16] So King Zedekiah swore an oath in secret to Jeremiah, "As the LORD lives, who gave us our lives, I will not put you to death or hand you over to these men who seek your life."

[17] Then Jeremiah said to Zedekiah, "Thus says the LORD, the God of hosts, the God of Israel, If you will only surrender to the officials of the king of Babylon, then your life shall be spared, and this city shall not be burned with fire, and you and your house shall live. [18] But if you do not surrender to the officials of the king of Babylon, then this city shall be handed over to the Chaldeans, and they shall burn it with fire, and you yourself shall not escape from their hand." [19] King Zedekiah said to Jeremiah, "I am afraid of the Judeans who have deserted to the Chaldeans, for I might be handed over to them and they would abuse me." [20] Jeremiah said, "That will not happen. Just obey the voice of the LORD in what I say to you, and it shall go well with you, and your life shall be spared. [21] But if you are determined not to surrender, this is what the LORD has shown me— [22] a vision of all the women remaining in the house of the king of Judah being led out to the officials of the king of Babylon and saying,

'Your trusted friends have seduced you
   and have overcome you;
Now that your feet are stuck in the mud,
   they desert you.'

[23] All your wives and your children shall be led out to the Chaldeans, and you yourself shall not escape from their hand, but shall be seized by the king of Babylon; and this city shall be burned with fire."

[24] Then Zedekiah said to Jeremiah, "Do not let anyone else know of this conversation, or you will die. [25] If the officials should hear that I have spoken with you, and they should come and say to you, 'Just tell us what you said to the king; do not conceal it from us, or we will put you to death. What did the king say to you?' [26] then you shall say to them, 'I was presenting my plea to the king not to send me back to the house of Jonathan to die there.'" [27] All the officials did come to Jeremiah and questioned him; and he answered them in the very words the king had commanded. So they stopped questioning him, for the conversation had not been overheard. [28] And Jeremiah remained in the court of the guard until the day that Jerusalem was taken.

---

[a] Or *Nubian*; Heb *Cushite*
[b] Cn: Heb *to under*

586 BCE (52.5–7). 7: *A eunuch in the king's house*, see 34.19n concerning the social position of such eunuchs. 9: *No bread left in the city*, an editorial comment, which does not suit the context but attempts to relate this alternate account sequentially to the main story line (see 37.21).

38.14–28: An alternate account of Jer 37.17–21. 17: *Surrender*, that is, "go out," abandon the city. 19. Zedekiah is afraid of reprisals against him by those who, already having surrendered, are aligned with King Jehoiachin in exile and who regard Zedekiah as an illegitimate heir to the throne; cf. the "good and bad figs" in ch 24. 22. *Your feet are stuck in the mud*, an image recalling Jeremiah's experience in v. 6 and possibly accounting for the linking of these variant traditions. 26. *House of Jonathan*, connecting this story to that of the main story line (Jer 37.20–21) rather than to the story line of 38.1–13.

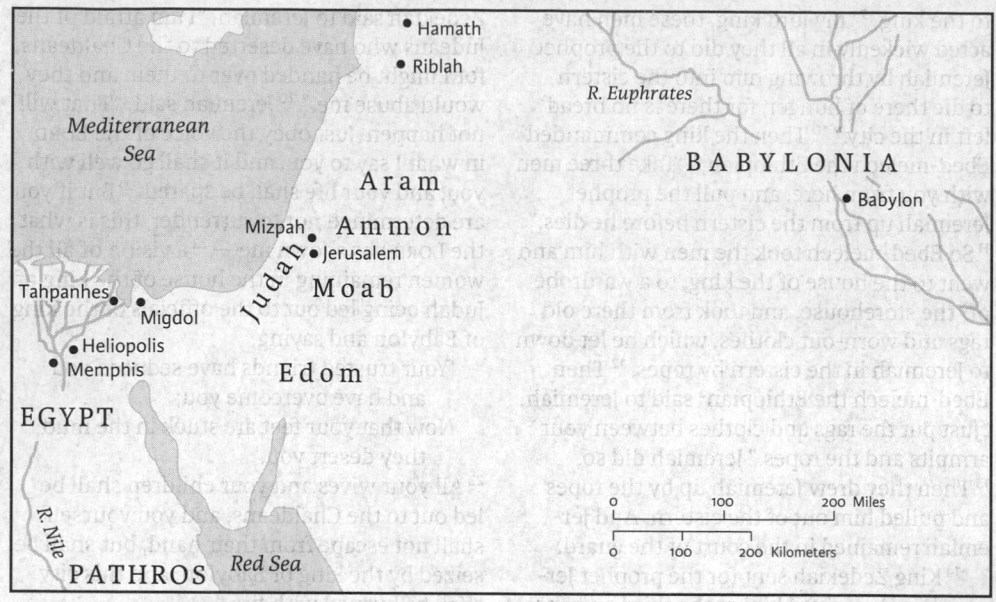

Chs 39, 52: Babylon and Judah in the early sixth century BCE.

39

In the ninth year of King Zedekiah of Judah, in the tenth month, King Nebuchadrezzar of Babylon and all his army came against Jerusalem and besieged it; ² in the eleventh year of Zedekiah, in the fourth month, on the ninth day of the month, a breach was made in the city. ³ When Jerusalem was taken,ᵃ all the officials of the king of Babylon came and sat in the middle gate: Nergal-sharezer, Samgar-nebo, Sarsechim the Rabsaris, Nergal-sharezer the Rabmag, with all the rest of the officials of the king of Babylon. ⁴ When King Zedekiah of Judah and all the soldiers saw them, they fled, going out of the city at night by way of the king's garden through the gate between the two walls; and they went toward the Arabah. ⁵ But the army of the Chaldeans pursued them, and overtook Zedekiah in the plains of Jericho; and when

they had taken him, they brought him up to King Nebuchadrezzar of Babylon, at Riblah, in the land of Hamath; and he passed sentence on him. ⁶ The king of Babylon slaughtered the sons of Zedekiah at Riblah before his eyes; also the king of Babylon slaughtered all the nobles of Judah. ⁷ He put out the eyes of Zedekiah, and bound him in fetters to take him to Babylon. ⁸ The Chaldeans burned the king's house and the houses of the people, and broke down the walls of Jerusalem. ⁹ Then Nebuzaradan the captain of the guard exiled to Babylon the rest of the people who were left in the city, those who had deserted to him, and the people who remained. ¹⁰ Nebuzaradan the captain of the guard left in the land of Judah some of the poor people who

ᵃ   This clause has been transposed from 38.28

39.1–18: The fall of Jerusalem. The Hebrew text indicates that ch 39 is a smooth continuation of ch 38 (see textual note *a* at 39.3), as does the reference to the court of the guard (Jer 39.14; see 38.28). The account here basically follows that of 52.4–16 and 2 Kings 25.1–22. **1–2:** *The ninth year . . . the eleventh year*, the siege of Jerusalem began in January 587 and lasted until July 586 BCE when the walls were breached. **3:** *Rabsaris* and *Rabmag* are titles of Babylonian officials. *Sat in the middle gate*, on the dispensing of justice in the gate as a sign of foreign conquest, see 1.15; 43.10. **4:** *Arabah*, the rift valley of the Jordan River and Dead Sea, which continues southward to the Gulf of Aqaba. **5:** *Riblah*, about 70 mi (110 km) north of Damascus, had earlier served as the Egyptian provincial capital (2 Kings 23.33), and was where the Babylonian governorship likewise was temporarily established. According to 52.6–13 and 2 Kings 25.3–9, there was a one-month lag between the breaching of the walls of Jerusalem and the sacking of the city. **9:** According to 52.29, the Babylonians deported a total

owned nothing, and gave them vineyards and fields at the same time.

[11] King Nebuchadrezzar of Babylon gave command concerning Jeremiah through Nebuzaradan, the captain of the guard, saying, [12] "Take him, look after him well and do him no harm, but deal with him as he may ask you." [13] So Nebuzaradan the captain of the guard, Nebushazban the Rabsaris, Nergalsharezer the Rabmag, and all the chief officers of the king of Babylon sent [14] and took Jeremiah from the court of the guard. They entrusted him to Gedaliah son of Ahikam son of Shaphan to be brought home. So he stayed with his own people.

[15] The word of the LORD came to Jeremiah while he was confined in the court of the guard: [16] Go and say to Ebed-melech the Ethiopian:[a] Thus says the LORD of hosts, the God of Israel: I am going to fulfill my words against this city for evil and not for good, and they shall be accomplished in your presence on that day. [17] But I will save you on that day, says the LORD, and you shall not be handed over to those whom you dread. [18] For I will surely save you, and you shall not fall by the sword; but you shall have your life as a prize

of war, because you have trusted in me, says the LORD.

40 The word that came to Jeremiah from the LORD after Nebuzaradan the captain of the guard had let him go from Ramah, when he took him bound in fetters along with all the captives of Jerusalem and Judah who were being exiled to Babylon. [2] The captain of the guard took Jeremiah and said to him, "The LORD your God threatened this place with this disaster; [3] and now the LORD has brought it about, and has done as he said, because all of you sinned against the LORD and did not obey his voice. Therefore this thing has come upon you. [4] Now look, I have just released you today from the fetters on your hands. If you wish to come with me to Babylon, come, and I will take good care of you; but if you do not wish to come with me to Babylon, you need not come. See, the whole land is before you; go wherever you think it good and right to go. [5] If you remain,[b] then return to Gedaliah son of Ahikam son of

---

a   Or *Nubian*; Heb *Cushite*
b   Syr: Meaning of Heb uncertain

---

of eight hundred thirty-two persons in this second deportation. **14:** Because Gedaliah was a member of the pro-Babylonian party, from the family of Shaphan, Nebuchadrezzar appointed him to serve as "governor" of the new Babylonian province (40.5). **15–18.** Words of deliverance for Ebed-melech and his family. See 38.7–13.

40.1–43.13: Political crisis results in the flight of Judeans to Egypt. Following the destruction of Jerusalem, the territorial governorship under Gedaliah was established in Mizpah, the venerable site associated with the ancient judgeship of Samuel (1 Sam 7.16), located between Jerusalem and Bethel. An attempted insurrection led by a member of the royal family, Ishmael son of Nethaniah (see 41.1), led to the assassination of Gedaliah and a debate by the Judeans who were left as to whether their future lay in staying in Judah or in flight to Egypt to avoid certain Babylonian repercussions. Against the advice of Jeremiah, the decision is made to flee to Egypt. **40.1–6:** With some slight changes in detail, 40.1–6 repeats the information from 39.11–14. Though the opening of the speech of the captain of the guard (vv. 2–4) is likely Deuteronomistic rhetoric, victorious kings in fact did claim the support of the deity of the conquered territory. So Cyrus of Media, after conquering Babylon, claimed to have been supported by Marduk, the god of Babylon. Compare 2 Kings 18.19–22, where the Assyrian official claims the support of Israel's God for the Assyrian invasion. **1:** *Ramah* (31.15n.) was a transit point for deportees. Jeremiah was allowed to choose exile or residence in Judah. Choosing the latter, he was placed in the custody of Gedaliah, the newly appointed governor of Judah with whose family Jeremiah had long been friendly (26.24; 36.10). Gedaliah's family figures prominently, not only in the life of Jeremiah but also at the Judean court and in relation to the Deuteronomic reform. Gedaliah's grandfather Shaphan delivered the newly discovered law scroll to King Josiah (2 Kings 22.3–13). Gedaliah's father, Ahikam, a member of the delegation sent to the prophetess Huldah (2 Kings 22.12–14), was Jeremiah's champion as well (26.24). Gedaliah's uncle Gemariah (36.24) and first cousin Micaiah (36.25) play similar, though unsuccessful, roles with regard to Jeremiah's scroll that was read to king Jehoiakim. Another of Gedaliah's uncles, Elasah, delivered Jeremiah's letter to the exiles (29.3). The close connection between this aristocratic family, the Deuteronomic movement, and the prose of the book of Jeremiah is intriguing.

Shaphan, whom the king of Babylon appointed governor of the towns of Judah, and stay with him among the people; or go wherever you think it right to go." So the captain of the guard gave him an allowance of food and a present, and let him go. [6] Then Jeremiah went to Gedaliah son of Ahikam at Mizpah, and stayed with him among the people who were left in the land.

[7] When all the leaders of the forces in the open country and their troops heard that the king of Babylon had appointed Gedaliah son of Ahikam governor in the land, and had committed to him men, women, and children, those of the poorest of the land who had not been taken into exile to Babylon, [8] they went to Gedaliah at Mizpah—Ishmael son of Nethaniah, Johanan son of Kareah, Seraiah son of Tanhumeth, the sons of Ephai the Netophathite, Jezaniah son of the Maacathite, they and their troops. [9] Gedaliah son of Ahikam son of Shaphan swore to them and their troops, saying, "Do not be afraid to serve the Chaldeans. Stay in the land and serve the king of Babylon, and it shall go well with you. [10] As for me, I am staying at Mizpah to represent you before the Chaldeans who come to us; but as for you, gather wine and summer fruits and oil, and store them in your vessels, and live in the towns that you have taken over." [11] Likewise, when all the Judeans who were in Moab and among the Ammonites and in Edom and in other lands heard that the king of Babylon had left a remnant in Judah and had appointed Gedaliah son of Ahikam son of Shaphan as governor over them, [12] then all the Judeans returned from all the places to which they had been scattered and came to the land of Judah, to Gedaliah at Mizpah; and they gathered wine and summer fruits in great abundance.

[13] Now Johanan son of Kareah and all the leaders of the forces in the open country came to Gedaliah at Mizpah [14] and said to him, "Are you at all aware that Baalis king of the Ammonites has sent Ishmael son of Nethaniah to take your life?" But Gedaliah son of Ahikam would not believe them. [15] Then Johanan son of Kareah spoke secretly to Gedaliah at Mizpah, "Please let me go and kill Ishmael son of Nethaniah, and no one else will know. Why should he take your life, so that all the Judeans who are gathered around you would be scattered, and the remnant of Judah would perish?" [16] But Gedaliah son of Ahikam said to Johanan son of Kareah, "Do not do such a thing, for you are telling a lie about Ishmael."

41 In the seventh month, Ishmael son of Nethaniah son of Elishama, of the royal family, one of the chief officers of the king, came with ten men to Gedaliah son of Ahikam, at Mizpah. As they ate bread together there at Mizpah, [2] Ishmael son of Nethaniah and the ten men with him got up and struck down Gedaliah son of Ahikam son of Shaphan with the sword and killed him, because the king of Babylon had appointed him governor in the land. [3] Ishmael also killed all the Judeans who were with Gedaliah at Mizpah, and the Chaldean soldiers who happened to be there.

[4] On the day after the murder of Gedaliah, before anyone knew of it, [5] eighty men arrived from Shechem and Shiloh and Samaria, with their beards shaved and their clothes torn, and their bodies gashed, bringing grain offerings and incense to present at the temple of the LORD. [6] And Ishmael son of Nethaniah came out from Mizpah to meet them, weeping as he came. As he met them, he said to them, "Come to Gedaliah son of Ahikam." [7] When they reached the middle of the city,

40.7–41.18: Gedaliah's governorship and his assassination. 40.7–12: Gedaliah assured his countrymen that he would represent them before the Babylonians (*Chaldeans*) and urged them to return to their fields and towns. When *they gathered wine and summer fruits in great abundance,* Gedaliah's assurance that life in the land could continue seemed confirmed. 14: The Ammonites, when not fighting Israel, were often their allies against larger imperial powers. Baalis of Ammon supported a nationalistic revolution in Judah led by Ishmael, a member of the royal family, but Gedaliah refused to heed the warnings for his own safety. 41.1: *As they ate bread,* ancient rules of hospitality and table fellowship bound host and guest to faithfulness toward one another. Ishmael's act was therefore particularly heinous. 3: *Chaldean,* Babylonian. 5: Eighty pilgrims from the north going to Jerusalem, likely to commemorate the day of atonement. Since animal sacrifice was suspended, they brought what might be appropriate for the occasion. To lure them to their deaths, Ishmael feigns their own ritual actions of

Ishmael son of Nethaniah and the men with him slaughtered them, and threw them[a] into a cistern. [8] But there were ten men among them who said to Ishmael, "Do not kill us, for we have stores of wheat, barley, oil, and honey hidden in the fields." So he refrained, and did not kill them along with their companions.

[9] Now the cistern into which Ishmael had thrown all the bodies of the men whom he had struck down was the large cistern[b] that King Asa had made for defense against King Baasha of Israel; Ishmael son of Nethaniah filled that cistern with those whom he had killed. [10] Then Ishmael took captive all the rest of the people who were in Mizpah, the king's daughters and all the people who were left at Mizpah, whom Nebuzaradan, the captain of the guard, had committed to Gedaliah son of Ahikam. Ishmael son of Nethaniah took them captive and set out to cross over to the Ammonites.

[11] But when Johanan son of Kareah and all the leaders of the forces with him heard of all the crimes that Ishmael son of Nethaniah had done, [12] they took all their men and went to fight against Ishmael son of Nethaniah. They came upon him at the great pool that is in Gibeon. [13] And when all the people who were with Ishmael saw Johanan son of Kareah and all the leaders of the forces with him, they were glad. [14] So all the people whom Ishmael had carried away captive from Mizpah turned around and came back, and went to Johanan son of Kareah. [15] But Ishmael son of Nethaniah escaped from Johanan with eight men, and went to the Ammonites. [16] Then Johanan son of Kareah and all the leaders of the forces with

him took all the rest of the people whom Ishmael son of Nethaniah had carried away captive[c] from Mizpah after he had slain Gedaliah son of Ahikam—soldiers, women, children, and eunuchs, whom Johanan brought back from Gibeon.[d] [17] And they set out, and stopped at Geruth Chimham near Bethlehem, intending to go to Egypt [18] because of the Chaldeans; for they were afraid of them, because Ishmael son of Nethaniah had killed Gedaliah son of Ahikam, whom the king of Babylon had made governor over the land.

42 Then all the commanders of the forces, and Johanan son of Kareah and Azariah[e] son of Hoshaiah, and all the people from the least to the greatest, approached [2] the prophet Jeremiah and said, "Be good enough to listen to our plea, and pray to the LORD your God for us—for all this remnant. For there are only a few of us left out of many, as your eyes can see. [3] Let the LORD your God show us where we should go and what we should do." [4] The prophet Jeremiah said to them, "Very well: I am going to pray to the LORD your God as you request, and whatever the LORD answers you I will tell you; I will keep nothing back from you." [5] They in their turn said to Jeremiah, "May the LORD be a true and faithful witness against us if we do

a   Syr: Heb lacks *and threw them*; compare verse 9
b   Gk: Heb *whom he had killed by the hand of Gedaliah*
c   Cn: Heb *whom he recovered from Ishmael son of Nethaniah*
d   Meaning of Heb uncertain
e   Gk: Heb *Jezaniah*

mourning. **9:** On the building projects of King Asa of Judah (908–867 BCE) in conjunction with his war against King Baasha of Israel (906–883 BCE), including those at Mizpah, see 1 Kings 15.16–22. **12.** *The great pool . . . in Gibeon,* the site of the battle between the forces of Joab and Abner (2 Sam 2.13). **17:** *Geruth Chimham,* perhaps meaning "fief of Chimham," referring to property given to Barzillai's son Chimham (see 2 Sam 19.37–40); precise location unknown.

42.1–22: The remnant under the leadership of Johanan son of Kareah asks Jeremiah for divine guidance regarding their plan to go to Egypt. That this takes place near Bethlehem (41.17) suggests that Jeremiah was not at his home in Mizpah but was with the group rescued by Johanan. At first the people seem to be open to whatever direction God provides (vv. 5–6). But as the conversation progresses, it is apparent that their earlier plan to go to Egypt was already set, and they were not open to divine direction. Even before hearing the people's response, Jeremiah presumes that they have disobeyed (v. 21). Much depends on the significance of the participle "saying" in v. 13 ("But if you continue to say . . .") and the use of the infinitive in v. 18 ("when you go . . ."). As in earlier times, Egypt was a place of refuge for those fleeing Judah for one reason or another; see 26.21; Gen 12.10; 46.6; 1 Kings 11.40. **1:** *Azariah,* MT reads "Jezaniah," but see textual note e and cf. 43.2.

not act according to everything that the Lord your God sends us through you. [6] Whether it is good or bad, we will obey the voice of the Lord our God to whom we are sending you, in order that it may go well with us when we obey the voice of the Lord our God."

[7] At the end of ten days the word of the Lord came to Jeremiah. [8] Then he summoned Johanan son of Kareah and all the commanders of the forces who were with him, and all the people from the least to the greatest, [9] and said to them, "Thus says the Lord, the God of Israel, to whom you sent me to present your plea before him: [10] If you will only remain in this land, then I will build you up and not pull you down; I will plant you, and not pluck you up; for I am sorry for the disaster that I have brought upon you. [11] Do not be afraid of the king of Babylon, as you have been; do not be afraid of him, says the Lord, for I am with you, to save you and to rescue you from his hand. [12] I will grant you mercy, and he will have mercy on you and restore you to your native soil. [13] But if you continue to say, 'We will not stay in this land,' thus disobeying the voice of the Lord your God [14] and saying, 'No, we will go to the land of Egypt, where we shall not see war, or hear the sound of the trumpet, or be hungry for bread, and there we will stay,' [15] then hear the word of the Lord, O remnant of Judah. Thus says the Lord of hosts, the God of Israel: If you are determined to enter Egypt and go to settle there, [16] then the sword that you fear shall overtake you there, in the land of Egypt; and the famine that you dread shall follow close after you into Egypt; and there you shall die. [17] All the people who have determined to go to Egypt to settle there shall die by the sword, by famine, and by pestilence; they shall have no remnant or survivor from the disaster that I am bringing upon them.

[18] "For thus says the Lord of hosts, the God of Israel: Just as my anger and my wrath were poured out on the inhabitants of Jerusalem, so my wrath will be poured out on you when you go to Egypt. You shall become an object of execration and horror, of cursing and ridicule. You shall see this place no more. [19] The Lord has said to you, O remnant of Judah, Do not go to Egypt. Be well aware that I have warned you today [20] that you have made a fatal mistake. For you yourselves sent me to the Lord your God, saying, 'Pray for us to the Lord our God, and whatever the Lord our God says, tell us and we will do it.' [21] So I have told you today, but you have not obeyed the voice of the Lord your God in anything that he sent me to tell you. [22] Be well aware, then, that you shall die by the sword, by famine, and by pestilence in the place where you desire to go and settle."

43

When Jeremiah finished speaking to all the people all these words of the Lord their God, with which the Lord their God had sent him to them, [2] Azariah son of Hoshaiah and Johanan son of Kareah and all the other insolent men said to Jeremiah, "You are telling a lie. The Lord our God did not send you to say, 'Do not go to Egypt to settle there'; [3] but Baruch son of Neriah is inciting you against us, to hand us over to the Chaldeans, in order that they may kill us or take us into exile in Babylon." [4] So Johanan son of Kareah and all the commanders of the forces and all the people did not obey the voice of the Lord, to stay in the land of Judah. [5] But Johanan son of Kareah and all the commanders of the forces took all the remnant of Judah who had returned to settle in the land of Judah from all the nations to which they had been driven— [6] the men, the women, the children, the princesses, and everyone whom Nebuzaradan the captain of the guard had left with Gedaliah son of Ahikam son of Shaphan; also the prophet Jeremiah and Baruch son of Neriah. [7] And they came into the land of Egypt, for they did not obey the voice of the Lord. And they arrived at Tahpanhes.

43.1–13: The flight to Tahpanhes and Jeremiah's oracle. The leaders dismiss Jeremiah's oracle as a "lie," suggesting that he is colluding with Baruch for their destruction. This insinuates a role for Baruch otherwise left unexplored in the book. The fears of Babylonian reprisal may not have been overdrawn, since 52.30 indicates that five years following the destruction of Jerusalem, there was a third deportation of Judeans, perhaps in response to political crises such as that of the assassination of Gedaliah. 6: Nebuzaradan, see 39.11–14; 40.1–6. 7: Tahpanhes was an Egyptian border fortress in the eastern Nile Delta; see 2.16. There were Judean refugee settlements in many areas of Egypt (see 44.1), especially at the military garrison of Elephantine in the upper Nile.

[8] Then the word of the Lord came to Jeremiah in Tahpanhes: [9] Take some large stones in your hands, and bury them in the clay pavement[a] that is at the entrance to Pharaoh's palace in Tahpanhes. Let the Judeans see you do it, [10] and say to them, Thus says the Lord of hosts, the God of Israel: I am going to send and take my servant King Nebuchadrezzar of Babylon, and he[b] will set his throne above these stones that I have buried, and he will spread his royal canopy over them. [11] He shall come and ravage the land of Egypt, giving

those who are destined for pestilence, to
pestilence,
and those who are destined for
captivity, to captivity,
and those who are destined for the
sword, to the sword.

[12] He[c] shall kindle a fire in the temples of the gods of Egypt; and he shall burn them and carry them away captive; and he shall pick clean the land of Egypt, as a shepherd picks his cloak clean of vermin; and he shall depart from there safely. [13] He shall break the obelisks of Heliopolis, which is in the land of Egypt; and the temples of the gods of Egypt he shall burn with fire.

44 The word that came to Jeremiah for all the Judeans living in the land of Egypt, at Migdol, at Tahpanhes, at Memphis, and in the land of Pathros, [2] Thus says the Lord of hosts, the God of Israel: You yourselves have seen all the disaster that I have brought on Jerusalem and on all the towns of Judah. Look at them; today they are a desolation, without an inhabitant in them, [3] because of the wickedness that they committed, provoking me to anger, in that they went to make offerings and serve other gods that they had not known, neither they, nor you, nor your ancestors. [4] Yet I persistently sent to you all my servants the prophets, saying, "I beg you not to do this abominable thing that I hate!" [5] But they did not listen or incline their ear, to turn from their wickedness and make no offerings to other gods. [6] So my wrath and my anger were poured out and kindled in the towns of Judah and in the streets of Jerusalem; and they became a waste and a desolation, as they still are today. [7] And now thus says the Lord God of hosts, the God of Israel: Why are you doing such great harm to

a   Meaning of Heb uncertain
b   Gk Syr: Heb *I*
c   Gk Syr Vg: Heb *I*

9–10: A prophetic sign-act indicating Babylonian control over Egypt. On setting up the royal throne at the gate, see 39.3. **12:** *Pick clean*, the Hebrew suggests a shepherd wrapping himself in a garment (see 1 Sam 28.14; Ps 109.19), but the LXX understood it to refer to removing lice. The verb can mean "to grasp tightly" (Isa 22.17). **13:** *Obelisks of Heliopolis*, the Hebrew reads "the stone pillars of Beth-shemesh," but Beth-shemesh means "house of the Sun." Heliopolis, or "city of the Sun," was the ancient center with a temple for the worship of the sun, as indicated by its name. It was located in the Nile Delta 6 mi (10 km) northeast of Cairo, and was also known as On (Gen 41.45,50; 46.20).

44.1–30: Dispute over disaster and divine purpose. A final oracle against the Jewish refugee communities in Egypt (cf. ch 43), in the context of a confrontation concerning why Judah has experienced the present crisis. In standard Deuteronomistic language, Jeremiah associates the disaster with the people's faithlessness toward God (vv. 2–10). He meets popular resistance from those who insist that the disaster has come precisely because they had discontinued their ancient syncretistic ritual practices, especially that of the adoration of and homage paid to the goddess known as the "queen of heaven," probably Astarte, variously known as Ishtar in Babylon and Ashtart in Canaan (vv. 15–19). The insinuation is that the reform movement of Josiah, with its restriction of worship to the Jerusalem Temple and its purging of the land of all syncretistic and foreign worship elements, was the cause of offense. Jeremiah's Deuteronomistic argument brackets that of the people, because it represents the fundamental theological principle of the book as prepared by its Deuteronomistic editors. **1:** Expands the focus far beyond the Jewish community in Tahpanhes (Jer 43.1–13). *Migdol*, like *Tahpanhes*, lay in the eastern Nile Delta and was associated with the Exodus (Ex 14.2). It was apparently the closest Egyptian garrison to Judah (Ezek 29.10). *Memphis* (or Noph), was the ancient imperial capital located at the head of the Nile Delta; see 2.16. *Pathros* was a designation for upper (i.e., southern) Egypt, and is listed alongside and parallel to Egypt in several lists (e.g., Isa 11.11); on the Jewish colony at Elephantine in upper Egypt, see 43.7n. **4:** See 7.25n.

yourselves, to cut off man and woman, child and infant, from the midst of Judah, leaving yourselves without a remnant? [8] Why do you provoke me to anger with the works of your hands, making offerings to other gods in the land of Egypt where you have come to settle? Will you be cut off and become an object of cursing and ridicule among all the nations of the earth? [9] Have you forgotten the crimes of your ancestors, of the kings of Judah, of their[a] wives, your own crimes and those of your wives, which they committed in the land of Judah and in the streets of Jerusalem? [10] They have shown no contrition or fear to this day, nor have they walked in my law and my statutes that I set before you and before your ancestors.

[11] Therefore thus says the LORD of hosts, the God of Israel: I am determined to bring disaster on you, to bring all Judah to an end. [12] I will take the remnant of Judah who are determined to come to the land of Egypt to settle, and they shall perish, everyone; in the land of Egypt they shall fall; by the sword and by famine they shall perish; from the least to the greatest, they shall die by the sword and by famine; and they shall become an object of execration and horror, of cursing and ridicule. [13] I will punish those who live in the land of Egypt, as I have punished Jerusalem, with the sword, with famine, and with pestilence, [14] so that none of the remnant of Judah who have come to settle in the land of Egypt shall escape or survive or return to the land of Judah. Although they long to go back to live there, they shall not go back, except some fugitives.

[15] Then all the men who were aware that their wives had been making offerings to other gods, and all the women who stood by, a great assembly, all the people who lived in Pathros in the land of Egypt, answered Jeremiah: [16] "As for the word that you have spoken to us in the name of the LORD, we are not going to listen to you. [17] Instead, we will do everything that we have vowed, make offerings to the queen of heaven and pour out libations to her, just as we and our ancestors, our kings and our officials, used to do in the towns of Judah and in the streets of Jerusalem. We used to have plenty of food, and prospered, and saw no misfortune. [18] But from the time we stopped making offerings to the queen of heaven and pouring out libations to her, we have lacked everything and have perished by the sword and by famine." [19] And the women said,[b] "Indeed we will go on making offerings to the queen of heaven and pouring out libations to her; do you think that we made cakes for her, marked with her image, and poured out libations to her without our husbands' being involved?"

[20] Then Jeremiah said to all the people, men and women, all the people who were giving him this answer: [21] "As for the offerings that you made in the towns of Judah and in the streets of Jerusalem, you and your ancestors, your kings and your officials, and the people of the land, did not the LORD remember them? Did it not come into his mind? [22] The LORD could no longer bear the sight of your evil doings, the abominations that you committed; therefore your land became a desolation and a waste and a curse, without inhabitant, as it is to this day. [23] It is because you burned offerings, and because you sinned against the LORD and did not obey the voice of the LORD or walk in his law and in his statutes and in his decrees, that this disaster has befallen you, as is still evident today."

[24] Jeremiah said to all the people and all the women, "Hear the word of the LORD, all you Judeans who are in the land of Egypt, [25] Thus says the LORD of hosts, the God of Israel: You and your wives have accomplished in deeds

---

a   Heb *his*
b   Compare Syr: Heb lacks *And the women said*

9: *Their wives*, the Hebrew "his wives" may have in mind the specific case of Solomon (1 Kings 11.1–13), whose wives led him to apostasy and the schism of the empire. **15**: It is strange that Jeremiah, who apparently settled as a hostage in Tahpanhes, is here addressed by Jews residing in upper Egypt. **17**: The worship of the *queen of heaven* was popular throughout the ancient world, including popular religious expression in Israel (compare the worship of Aphrodite and Venus). Her worship included the making of raisin cakes to her, expressive of prayers for fertility (v. 19). This goddess represented the evening-star phase of the planet Venus, while in Canaan her brother, Ashtar, represented the morning-star phase (see Isa 14.12–15, which refers to an ancient myth

what you declared in words, saying, 'We are determined to perform the vows that we have made, to make offerings to the queen of heaven and to pour out libations to her.' By all means, keep your vows and make your libations! ²⁶ Therefore hear the word of the LORD, all you Judeans who live in the land of Egypt: Lo, I swear by my great name, says the LORD, that my name shall no longer be pronounced on the lips of any of the people of Judah in all the land of Egypt, saying, 'As the Lord GOD lives.' ²⁷ I am going to watch over them for harm and not for good; all the people of Judah who are in the land of Egypt shall perish by the sword and by famine, until not one is left. ²⁸ And those who escape the sword shall return from the land of Egypt to the land of Judah, few in number; and all the remnant of Judah, who have come to the land of Egypt to settle, shall know whose words will stand, mine or theirs! ²⁹ This shall be the sign to you, says the LORD, that I am going to punish you in this place, in order that you may know that my words against you will surely be carried out: ³⁰ Thus says the LORD, I am going to give Pharaoh Hophra, king of Egypt, into the hands of his enemies, those who seek his life, just as I gave King Zedekiah of Judah into the hand of King Nebuchadrezzar of Babylon, his enemy who sought his life."

45 The word that the prophet Jeremiah spoke to Baruch son of Neriah, when he wrote these words in a scroll at the dictation of Jeremiah, in the fourth year of King Jehoiakim son of Josiah of Judah: ² Thus says the LORD, the God of Israel, to you, O Baruch: ³ You said, "Woe is me! The LORD has added sorrow to my pain; I am weary with my groaning, and I find no rest." ⁴ Thus you shall say to him, "Thus says the LORD: I am going to break down what I have built, and pluck up what I have planted—that is, the whole land. ⁵ And you, do you seek great things for yourself? Do not seek them; for I am going to bring disaster upon all flesh, says the LORD; but I will give you your life as a prize of war in every place to which you may go."

46 The word of the LORD that came to the prophet Jeremiah concerning the nations.

² Concerning Egypt, about the army of Pharaoh Neco, king of Egypt, which was by the river Euphrates at Carchemish and which King Nebuchadrezzar of Babylon defeated in the fourth year of King Jehoiakim son of Josiah of Judah:
³ Prepare buckler and shield,
    and advance for battle!
⁴ Harness the horses;
    mount the steeds!

associated with Ashtar, the "day star" who ushers in the light of morning); see also 7.18n. **27:** *Watch over them for harm*, it is deeply ironic that this last oracle addressed to the people echoes the language with which the book began (1.11–12), suggesting that, in spite of the hope of 31.28, the book tragically ends where it began for these Egyptian refugees. The promise resides with the exiles in Babylon. **30:** *Pharaoh Hophra* (Apries, ruled ca. 589–570 BCE) was assassinated by an enemy within the Egyptian court.

45.1–5: Words of promise to Baruch. This third and final cycle of oracles is concluded, as were the earlier two, by recollecting the scroll of 605 BCE (see 36.4–6,27–32). Using the central code language of the book, a final negative judgment is given: building yields to breaking down and planting yields to plucking up (see 1.10; etc.). But Baruch is reassured of his own survival. **5:** *Prize of war*, see 21.9; 38.2; 39.18.

46.1–51.64: Oracles against the nations. Prophetic books commonly have collections of such oracles directed against Israel's enemies (see Isa 13–23, Ezek 25–32, Am 1–2). These oracles may preserve one of the early functions of prophecy as "war prophecy": undermining the strength of the enemy with curses and psychologically fortifying the home troops for victory. The placement of these oracles is a major difference between the Hebrew and Greek traditions of the book of Jeremiah, with the latter (the Septuagint [LXX]) locating the oracles within the context of ch 25. The Hebrew and Greek traditions also differ in their ordering of the specific oracles. The Hebrew tradition begins with the oracle against Egypt, connecting with the geographical orientation of the previous chapters. The general sweep is then from west to east (or, using the language of the text, from "south" to "north") and concludes with the lengthy oracle against Babylon (chs 50–51), the major enemy in the book of Jeremiah.

46.2–28: Against Egypt, two oracles. The first oracle (vv. 3–12) is set in the context of Babylon's defeat of

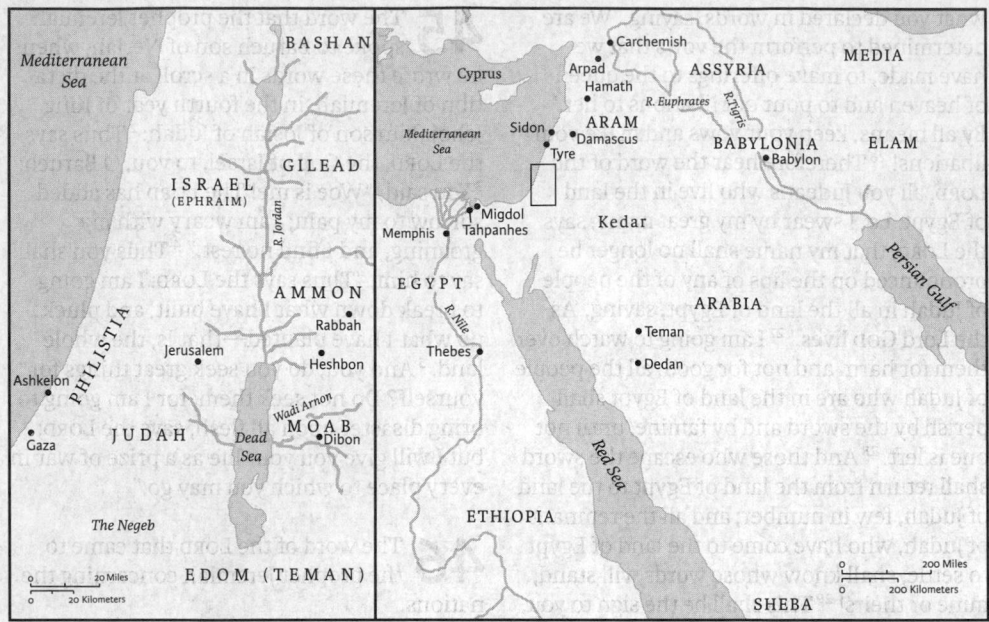

Chs 46–51: Places mentioned in the oracles against foreign nations.

Take your stations with your helmets,
  whet your lances,
  put on your coats of mail!
⁵ Why do I see them terrified?
  They have fallen back;
their warriors are beaten down,
  and have fled in haste.
They do not look back—
  terror is all around!

                says the LORD.

⁶ The swift cannot flee away,
  nor can the warrior escape;
in the north by the river Euphrates
  they have stumbled and fallen.

⁷ Who is this, rising like the Nile,
  like rivers whose waters surge?
⁸ Egypt rises like the Nile,
  like rivers whose waters surge.
It said, Let me rise, let me cover the
  earth,

let me destroy cities and their
  inhabitants.
⁹ Advance, O horses,
  and dash madly, O chariots!
Let the warriors go forth:
  Ethiopiaᵃ and Put who carry the shield,
  the Ludim, who drawᵇ the bow.
¹⁰ That day is the day of the Lord GOD of
  hosts,
a day of retribution,
  to gain vindication from his foes.
The sword shall devour and be sated,
  and drink its fill of their blood.
For the Lord GOD of hosts holds a sacrifice
  in the land of the north by the river
  Euphrates.

ᵃ Or *Nubia*; Heb *Cush*
ᵇ Cn: Heb *who grasp, who draw*

Egypt in 605 BCE at Carchemish on the Euphrates (vv. 6,10), solidifying Babylonian control over the Levant; cf. 36.1–32. The second oracle (vv. 13–28) is set in the context of the later invasion of Egypt by the Babylonian army (compare 43.9–13). **2:** *Pharaoh Neco* II ruled ca. 610–595 BCE. **3:** *Buckler . . . shield*, two different sizes of shields: the first smaller and the second covering the entire body. The unusual poetic meter of these verses mimics the sound of marching armies (compare Nah 2.1–9). **5:** *Terror is all around*, language celebrating the Egyptian defeat; see 6.25n.; 20.3,10; 49.29. **7–8:** Like the annual flooding of the Nile, Egypt's pretensions rose above manageable levels. **9:** *Ethiopia* (Heb "Cush"), *Put*, and *the Ludim* were all African nations known for their military prowess (see

¹¹ Go up to Gilead, and take balm,
  O virgin daughter Egypt!
In vain you have used many medicines;
  there is no healing for you.
¹² The nations have heard of your shame,
  and the earth is full of your cry;
for warrior has stumbled against warrior;
  both have fallen together.

¹³ The word that the Lord spoke to the prophet Jeremiah about the coming of King Nebuchadrezzar of Babylon to attack the land of Egypt:
¹⁴ Declare in Egypt, and proclaim in
    Migdol;
  proclaim in Memphis and Tahpanhes;
Say, "Take your stations and be ready,
  for the sword shall devour those around
    you."
¹⁵ Why has Apis fled?ᵃ
  Why did your bull not stand?
  —because the Lord thrust him down.
¹⁶ Your multitudeᵇ stumbled and fell,
  and one said to another,ᶜ
"Come, let us go back to our own people
  and to the land of our birth,
  because of the destroying sword."
¹⁷ Give Pharaoh, king of Egypt, the name
  "Braggart who missed his chance."

¹⁸ As I live, says the King,
  whose name is the Lord of hosts,
one is coming
  like Tabor among the mountains,
  and like Carmel by the sea.
¹⁹ Pack your bags for exile,
  sheltered daughter Egypt!
For Memphis shall become a waste,
  a ruin, without inhabitant.

²⁰ A beautiful heifer is Egypt—
  a gadfly from the north lights upon her.

²¹ Even her mercenaries in her midst
  are like fatted calves;
they too have turned and fled together,
  they did not stand;
for the day of their calamity has come
    upon them,
  the time of their punishment.

²² She makes a sound like a snake gliding
    away;
  for her enemies march in force,
and come against her with axes,
  like those who fell trees.
²³ They shall cut down her forest,
              says the Lord,
  though it is impenetrable,
because they are more numerous
  than locusts;
  they are without number.
²⁴ Daughter Egypt shall be put to shame;
  she shall be handed over to a people
    from the north.

²⁵ The Lord of hosts, the God of Israel, said: See, I am bringing punishment upon Amon of Thebes, and Pharaoh, and Egypt and her gods and her kings, upon Pharaoh and those who trust in him. ²⁶ I will hand them over to those who seek their life, to King Nebuchadrezzar of Babylon and his officers. Afterward Egypt shall be inhabited as in the days of old, says the Lord.

²⁷ But as for you, have no fear, my servant
    Jacob,
  and do not be dismayed, O Israel;
for I am going to save you from far
    away,

ᵃ Gk: Heb *Why was it swept away*
ᵇ Gk: Meaning of Heb uncertain
ᶜ Gk: Heb *and fell one to another and they said*

Gen 10.6,13; Ezek 27.10). **11:** *Gilead . . . balm,* see 8.22n. **14.** *Migdol . . . Memphis . . . Tahpanhes,* see 44.1n. **15:** *Why has Apis fled,* following the Greek text, underlying which is a different word division; MT reads "Why is it fallen?" Apis was a bull deity worshiped in Memphis and the subject of elaborate sacrificial and burial rituals. The flight of Apis represents the retreat of the imperial Egyptian armies. **18:** *Like Tabor,* a prominent mountain in the Galilee. *Like Carmel,* a prominent mountain point protecting the seaward (west) end of the Jezreel valley: **20:** *Gadfly from the north,* that is, Babylon. **21:** Egypt's troops have fled like their Apis bull (v. 15). **22:** The *snake gliding away* may recall the royal emblem on the Egyptian crown. **25:** *Amon of Thebes,* the major deity and religious center of upper Egypt. **26:** *Afterward Egypt shall be inhabited,* that the oracle concludes with a brief word of promise for the restoration of Egypt is strange, but consistent with 48.47; 49.6,39. **27–28:** A doublet of 30.10–11 in the exilic

and your offspring from the land of
their captivity.
Jacob shall return and have quiet and ease,
and no one shall make him afraid.
28 As for you, have no fear, my servant
Jacob,

says the LORD,
for I am with you.
I will make an end of all the nations
among which I have banished you,
but I will not make an end of you!
I will chastise you in just measure,
and I will by no means leave you
unpunished.

47

The word of the LORD that came to
the prophet Jeremiah concerning the
Philistines, before Pharaoh attacked Gaza:
2 Thus says the LORD:
See, waters are rising out of the north
and shall become an overflowing
torrent;
they shall overflow the land and all that
fills it,
the city and those who live in it.
People shall cry out,
and all the inhabitants of the land shall
wail.
3 At the noise of the stamping of the hoofs
of his stallions,
at the clatter of his chariots, at the
rumbling of their wheels,
parents do not turn back for children,
so feeble are their hands,
4 because of the day that is coming
to destroy all the Philistines,
to cut off from Tyre and Sidon
every helper that remains.
For the LORD is destroying the Philistines,

the remnant of the coastland of
Caphtor.
5 Baldness has come upon Gaza,
Ashkelon is silenced.
O remnant of their power!a
How long will you gash yourselves?
6 Ah, sword of the LORD!
How long until you are quiet?
Put yourself into your scabbard,
rest and be still!
7 How can itb be quiet,
when the LORD has given it an order?
Against Ashkelon and against the
seashore—
there he has appointed it.

48

Concerning Moab.

Thus says the LORD of hosts, the God of Israel:
Alas for Nebo, it is laid waste!
Kiriathaim is put to shame, it is taken;
the fortress is put to shame and broken
down;
2 the renown of Moab is no more.
In Heshbon they planned evil against her:
"Come, let us cut her off from being a
nation!"
You also, O Madmen, shall be brought to
silence;c
the sword shall pursue you.

3 Hark! a cry from Horonaim,
"Desolation and great destruction!"

a   Gk: Heb *their valley*
b   Gk Vg: Heb *you*
c   The place-name *Madmen* sounds like the Hebrew
    verb *to be silent*

language of Second Isaiah.

47.1–7: Against Philistia. This oracle alludes to the Babylonian destruction of the Philistine city of Ashkelon
in 694 BCE (see vv. 5, 7). **4:** *Tyre and Sidon* were part of Phoenicia rather than Philistia, and elsewhere are listed
separately from Philistia (25.20–22; Am 1.6–10; Ezek 25.15–28.26). The Philistines were associated with the ancestral land of Caphtor (Crete, Gen 10.14; Deut 2.23; Am 9.7), but Tyre, Sidon, and Philistia were connected in
tradition (Joel 3.4), all associated with incursions of Hellenic groups, and therefore are grouped together and
combined here. **5:** For similar signs of lamentation, cf. 16.6; 41.5. **6–7:** *Sword of the* LORD, 12.1; 25.31; Isa 34.6.

48.1–47: Against Moab. This lengthy oracle is comprised of a number of originally independent oracles,
several of which are found in other prophetic collections. **1:** Although *Nebo, Kiriathaim,* and other Moabite
cities were sometimes controlled by the Israelites (Mesha inscription; Num 32.37), they were traditionally part
of Moabite territory (Deut 32.49). **2:** *In Heshbon they planned evil,* a play on words, since "plot" or "plan" is Heb
"ḥashab." *Heshbon,* a northern Moabite city, is modern Hesban. **3–5:** On the place names *Horonaim* and the

⁴ "Moab is destroyed!"
  her little ones cry out.
⁵ For at the ascent of Luhith
  they go^a up weeping bitterly;
for at the descent of Horonaim
  they have heard the distressing cry of
    anguish.
⁶ Flee! Save yourselves!
  Be like a wild ass^b in the desert!

⁷ Surely, because you trusted in your
    strongholds^c and your treasures,
  you also shall be taken;
Chemosh shall go out into exile,
  with his priests and his attendants.
⁸ The destroyer shall come upon every
    town,
  and no town shall escape;
the valley shall perish,
  and the plain shall be destroyed,
  as the LORD has spoken.

⁹ Set aside salt for Moab,
  for she will surely fall;
her towns shall become a desolation,
  with no inhabitant in them.

¹⁰ Accursed is the one who is slack in doing
the work of the LORD; and accursed is the one
who keeps back the sword from bloodshed.

¹¹ Moab has been at ease from his youth,
  settled like wine^d on its dregs;
he has not been emptied from vessel to
    vessel,
  nor has he gone into exile;
therefore his flavor has remained
  and his aroma is unspoiled.
¹² Therefore, the time is surely coming,
says the LORD, when I shall send to him
decanters to decant him, and empty his
vessels, and break his^e jars in pieces. ¹³ Then
Moab shall be ashamed of Chemosh, as the

house of Israel was ashamed of Bethel, their
confidence.

¹⁴ How can you say, "We are heroes
  and mighty warriors"?
¹⁵ The destroyer of Moab and his towns has
    come up,
  and the choicest of his young men have
    gone down to slaughter,
  says the King, whose name is the LORD
    of hosts.
¹⁶ The calamity of Moab is near at hand
  and his doom approaches swiftly.
¹⁷ Mourn over him, all you his neighbors,
  and all who know his name;
say, "How the mighty scepter is broken,
  the glorious staff!"

¹⁸ Come down from glory,
  and sit on the parched ground,
  enthroned daughter Dibon!
For the destroyer of Moab has come up
    against you;
  he has destroyed your strongholds.
¹⁹ Stand by the road and watch,
  you inhabitant of Aroer!
Ask the man fleeing and the woman
    escaping;
  say, "What has happened?"
²⁰ Moab is put to shame, for it is broken
    down;
  wail and cry!
Tell it by the Arnon,
  that Moab is laid waste.

²¹ Judgment has come upon the tableland,
upon Holon, and Jahzah, and Mephaath,

---

a Cn: Heb *he goes*
b Gk Aquila: Heb *like Aroer*
c Gk: Heb *works*
d Heb lacks *like wine*
e Gk Aquila: Heb *their*

---

ascent of Luhith, see Isa 15.15. Their locations are unknown. **6**: *Like a wild ass* (Heb "'aro'er") *in the desert*, a reference to the Moabite town Aroer (17.6; Deut 2.36; 2 Kings 10.33). **7**: *Chemosh*, the national god of the Moabites; see Judg 11.24; 1 Kings 11.7. **9**: *Salt for Moab* refers to the ancient practice of "salting" a conquered territory to destroy its soil's fertility for generations to come; see Judges 9.45. But this is also a wordplay on the terms "salt" (Heb "tsits") and "fall" or "go out" (Heb "tetse'"). **10**: Probably an editorial comment. **11–12**: Uses language referring to Moab's well-known viticulture; see vv. 32–33. **13**: *Bethel* represented religious apostasy in prophetic critique (Hos 10.15; Am 3.14; 4.4; 5.5–6), because of the worship associated with the calf that Jeroboam installed there (1 Kings 12.26–31; 2 Kings 10.29). **18**: *Dibon*, a Moabite city located near Aroer north of the Wadi Arnon (v.

²² and Dibon, and Nebo, and Beth-diblathaim, ²³ and Kiriathaim, and Beth-gamul, and Beth-meon, ²⁴ and Kerioth, and Bozrah, and all the towns of the land of Moab, far and near. ²⁵ The horn of Moab is cut off, and his arm is broken, says the LORD.

²⁶ Make him drunk, because he magnified himself against the LORD; let Moab wallow in his vomit; he too shall become a laughingstock. ²⁷ Israel was a laughingstock for you, though he was not caught among thieves; but whenever you spoke of him you shook your head!

²⁸ Leave the towns, and live on the rock,
O inhabitants of Moab!
Be like the dove that nests
on the sides of the mouth of a gorge.
²⁹ We have heard of the pride of Moab—
he is very proud—
of his loftiness, his pride, and his
arrogance,
and the haughtiness of his heart.
³⁰ I myself know his insolence, says the
LORD;
his boasts are false,
his deeds are false.
³¹ Therefore I wail for Moab;
I cry out for all Moab;
for the people of Kir-heres I mourn.
³² More than for Jazer I weep for you,
O vine of Sibmah!
Your branches crossed over the sea,
reached as far as Jazer;ᵃ
upon your summer fruits and your vintage
the destroyer has fallen.
³³ Gladness and joy have been taken away
from the fruitful land of Moab;
I have stopped the wine from the wine
presses;
no one treads them with shouts of joy;
the shouting is not the shout of joy.

³⁴ Heshbon and Elealeh cry out;ᵇ as far as Jahaz they utter their voice, from Zoar to Horonaim and Eglath-shelishiyah. For even

the waters of Nimrim have become desolate. ³⁵ And I will bring to an end in Moab, says the LORD, those who offer sacrifice at a high place and make offerings to their gods. ³⁶ Therefore my heart moans for Moab like a flute, and my heart moans like a flute for the people of Kir-heres; for the riches they gained have perished.

³⁷ For every head is shaved and every beard cut off; on all the hands there are gashes, and on the loins sackcloth. ³⁸ On all the housetops of Moab and in the squares there is nothing but lamentation; for I have broken Moab like a vessel that no one wants, says the LORD. ³⁹ How it is broken! How they wail! How Moab has turned his back in shame! So Moab has become a derision and a horror to all his neighbors.

⁴⁰ For thus says the LORD:
Look, he shall swoop down like an eagle,
and spread his wings against Moab;
⁴¹ the townsᶜ shall be taken
and the strongholds seized.
The hearts of the warriors of Moab, on
that day,
shall be like the heart of a woman in
labor.
⁴² Moab shall be destroyed as a people,
because he magnified himself against
the LORD.
⁴³ Terror, pit, and trap
are before you, O inhabitants of Moab!
says the LORD.
⁴⁴ Everyone who flees from the terror
shall fall into the pit,
and everyone who climbs out of the pit
shall be caught in the trap.
For I will bring these thingsᵈ upon Moab
in the year of their punishment,
says the LORD.

ᵃ Two Mss and Isa 16.8: MT *the sea of Jazer*
ᵇ Cn: Heb *From the cry of Heshbon to Elealeh*
ᶜ Or *Kerioth*
ᵈ Gk Syr: Heb *bring upon it*

20). **19:** *Aroer*, see v. 6n. **31:** *Kir-heres*, otherwise known as Kir-hareseth (see Isa 16.7,11), is modern el-Kerak, the imposing and easily defended Moabite city 18 km (11 mi) east of the Dead Sea. **32:** *Vine of Sibmah*, see vv. 11–12n.; Isa 16.8,9. **34:** References several towns in Moab; see map on p. 1130. Cf. Isa 15.4–6; Num 32.3 **36:** *Moans . . . like a flute*, normally flutes are associated with joyful sounds (Isa 5.12; 30.29); cf. Isa 16.11. **37:** Characteristic rituals of mourning. *On all the hands*, or perhaps "between the hands," that is, marks made by slashing one's chest

⁴⁵ In the shadow of Heshbon
  fugitives stop exhausted;
for a fire has gone out from Heshbon,
  a flame from the house of Sihon;
it has destroyed the forehead of Moab,
  the scalp of the people of tumult.ᵃ
⁴⁶ Woe to you, O Moab!
  The people of Chemosh have perished,
for your sons have been taken captive,
  and your daughters into captivity.
⁴⁷ Yet I will restore the fortunes of Moab
  in the latter days, says the LORD.
Thus far is the judgment on Moab.

49

Concerning the Ammonites.

Thus says the LORD:
  Has Israel no sons?
  Has he no heir?
Why then has Milcom dispossessed Gad,
  and his people settled in its towns?
² Therefore, the time is surely coming,
  says the LORD,
when I will sound the battle alarm
  against Rabbah of the Ammonites;
it shall become a desolate mound,
  and its villages shall be burned with
    fire;
then Israel shall dispossess those who
  dispossessed him,
  says the LORD.

³ Wail, O Heshbon, for Ai is laid waste!
  Cry out, O daughtersᵇ of Rabbah!

Put on sackcloth,
  lament, and slash yourselves with
    whips!ᶜ
For Milcom shall go into exile,
  with his priests and his
    attendants.
⁴ Why do you boast in your strength?
  Your strength is ebbing,
O faithless daughter.
  You trusted in your treasures, saying,
  "Who will attack me?"
⁵ I am going to bring terror upon you,
  says the Lord GOD of hosts,
  from all your neighbors,
and you will be scattered, each
  headlong,
  with no one to gather the fugitives.
⁶ But afterward I will restore the fortunes
of the Ammonites, says the LORD.

⁷ Concerning Edom.

Thus says the LORD of hosts:
  Is there no longer wisdom in Teman?
  Has counsel perished from the
    prudent?
  Has their wisdom vanished?
⁸ Flee, turn back, get down low,
  inhabitants of Dedan!

ᵃ Or *of Shaon*
ᵇ Or *villages*
ᶜ Cn: Meaning of Heb uncertain

or back; see Zech 13.6. **45:** *Heshbon*, see v. 2n. *Sihon*, the legendary Amorite king of Heshbon; see the ancient ballad in Num 21.27–28. **47:** Moab's fortunes will be restored, as will those of Ammon (49.6) and Elam (49.39).

49.1–6: Against Ammon. The oracle against Ammon follows that of Moab, as the two are connected in tradition; see Gen 19.30–38; Deut 23.3. Both Moab and Ammon had recently been used by the Babylonians as proxies in the effort to subdue Judah (2 Kings 24.2). **1:** *Milcom . . . Gad*, as the east-Jordanian tribe of Reuben tried to establish itself in territory claimed by Moab, so the east-Jordanian tribe of Gad was in competition with the Ammonites, whose national god was Milcom (1 Kings 11.5,33) and who eventually became independent of Israel, thereby claiming their own territory (2 Kings 15.29). **3:** Reference to several major Ammonite towns, including Heshbon, the old Amorite city of Sihon (see 48.2n.; Num 21.21–24) and the capital, Rabbah (2 Sam 11.1), modern day Amman. *Ai* here probably does not refer to the ancient city of Ai near Bethel. The word is also the Heb term for "ruin," and may be used here in reference to Rabbah. **6:** *Restore the fortunes*, see 48.47n.

49.7–22: Against Edom. South of Ammon and Moab, Edom was the third east–Jordanian country that competed with Israel for territory and independence. Parts of this oracle are also found with variations in the book of Obadiah. **7–8:** *Teman*, perhaps in northern Arabia, was associated with Esau, the ancestor of Edom (Gen 36.1,8–11,15). Ancient traditions connected the God of Israel with Teman (Hab 3.3), and it was associated with ancient wisdom (Bar 3.22–23). As Edom's "brother," Israel recognized a strained kinship with the Edomites, but the relationship soured as Edom too was used as a proxy by Babylon (Ps 137.7–9). *Dedan*, a region in north-

For I will bring the calamity of Esau upon
him,
the time when I punish him.
⁹ If grape-gatherers came to you,
would they not leave gleanings?
If thieves came by night,
even they would pillage only what they
wanted.
¹⁰ But as for me, I have stripped Esau
bare,
I have uncovered his hiding places,
and he is not able to conceal himself.
His offspring are destroyed, his kinsfolk
and his neighbors; and he is no more.
¹¹ Leave your orphans, I will keep them
alive;
and let your widows trust in me.
¹² For thus says the LORD: If those who
do not deserve to drink the cup still have to
drink it, shall you be the one to go unpunished? You shall not go unpunished; you
must drink it. ¹³ For by myself I have sworn,
says the LORD, that Bozrah shall become an
object of horror and ridicule, a waste, and an
object of cursing; and all her towns shall be
perpetual wastes.
¹⁴ I have heard tidings from the LORD,
and a messenger has been sent among
the nations:
"Gather yourselves together and come
against her,
and rise up for battle!"
¹⁵ For I will make you least among the
nations,
despised by humankind.
¹⁶ The terror you inspire
and the pride of your heart have
deceived you,
you who live in the clefts of the rock,ᵃ
who hold the height of the hill.
Although you make your nest as high as
the eagle's,
from there I will bring you down,
says the LORD.

¹⁷ Edom shall become an object of horror;
everyone who passes by it will be horrified
and will hiss because of all its disasters. ¹⁸ As
when Sodom and Gomorrah and their neighbors were overthrown, says the LORD, no one
shall live there, nor shall anyone settle in it.
¹⁹ Like a lion coming up from the thickets of
the Jordan against a perennial pasture, I will
suddenly chase Edomᵇ away from it; and
I will appoint over it whomever I choose.ᶜ
For who is like me? Who can summon me?
Who is the shepherd who can stand before
me? ²⁰ Therefore hear the plan that the LORD
has made against Edom and the purposes
that he has formed against the inhabitants
of Teman: Surely the little ones of the flock
shall be dragged away; surely their fold shall
be appalled at their fate. ²¹ At the sound of
their fall the earth shall tremble; the sound
of their cry shall be heard at the Red Sea.ᵈ
²² Look, he shall mount up and swoop down
like an eagle, and spread his wings against
Bozrah, and the heart of the warriors of
Edom in that day shall be like the heart of a
woman in labor.

²³ Concerning Damascus.

Hamath and Arpad are confounded,
for they have heard bad news;
they melt in fear, they are troubled like the
seaᵉ
that cannot be quiet.
²⁴ Damascus has become feeble, she
turned to flee,
and panic seized her;
anguish and sorrows have taken hold of her,

ᵃ Or of Sela
ᵇ Heb him
ᶜ Or and I will single out the choicest of his rams:
Meaning of Heb uncertain
ᵈ Or Sea of Reeds
ᵉ Cn: Heb there is trouble in the sea

west Arabia associated with trade (Ezek 25.15–29). 13: *Bozrah*, modern Buseirah, a great fortress city in northern
Edom. 16: *Clefts of the rock*, Edom was known for its mountainous and hill-top dwellings such as at Sela ("rock");
see textual note *a*. 18: *Sodom and Gomorrah*, see 20.16n. A doublet of 50.40, but appropriately located here,
given Edomite associations with the southern Arabah. 19: *Lion . . . thickets of the Jordan*, see 12.5n. 21: *Red Sea*
or "Sea of Reeds" (see textual note *d*), here probably referring to the eastern arm of the Reed Sea, the Gulf of
Aqaba.
    49.23–27: Against Damascus, the capital of Aram, one of Israel's traditional enemies. **23:** On the connection

as of a woman in labor.
²⁵ How the famous city is forsaken,ᵃ
the joyful town!ᵇ
²⁶ Therefore her young men shall fall in her
squares,
and all her soldiers shall be destroyed in
that day,
says the LORD of hosts.
²⁷ And I will kindle a fire at the wall of
Damascus,
and it shall devour the strongholds of
Ben-hadad.

²⁸ Concerning Kedar and the kingdoms of
Hazor that King Nebuchadrezzar of Babylon
defeated.

Thus says the LORD:
Rise up, advance against Kedar!
Destroy the people of the east!
²⁹ Take their tents and their flocks,
their curtains and all their goods;
carry off their camels for yourselves,
and a cry shall go up: "Terror is all
around!"
³⁰ Flee, wander far away, hide in deep
places,
O inhabitants of Hazor!
says the LORD.
For King Nebuchadrezzar of Babylon
has made a plan against you
and formed a purpose against you.

³¹ Rise up, advance against a nation at ease,
that lives secure,
says the LORD,
that has no gates or bars,
that lives alone.
³² Their camels shall become booty,

their herds of cattle a spoil.
I will scatter to every wind
those who have shaven temples,
and I will bring calamity
against them from every side,
says the LORD.
³³ Hazor shall become a lair of jackals,
an everlasting waste;
no one shall live there,
nor shall anyone settle in it.

³⁴ The word of the LORD that came to the
prophet Jeremiah concerning Elam, at the
beginning of the reign of King Zedekiah of
Judah.
³⁵ Thus says the LORD of hosts: I am going
to break the bow of Elam, the mainstay of
their might; ³⁶ and I will bring upon Elam
the four winds from the four quarters of
heaven; and I will scatter them to all these
winds, and there shall be no nation to which
the exiles from Elam shall not come. ³⁷ I will
terrify Elam before their enemies, and before
those who seek their life; I will bring disaster
upon them, my fierce anger, says the LORD. I
will send the sword after them, until I have
consumed them; ³⁸ and I will set my throne
in Elam, and destroy their king and officials,
says the LORD.
³⁹ But in the latter days I will restore the
fortunes of Elam, says the LORD.

50 The word that the LORD spoke
concerning Babylon, concerning
the land of the Chaldeans, by the prophet
Jeremiah:

ᵃ Vg: Heb *is not forsaken*
ᵇ Syr Vg Tg: Heb *the town of my joy*

of the neighboring kingdoms of Arpad and Hamath, see 2 Kings 18.34; Isa 36.19; 10.9; 37.13. **27:** On this stylized
language, see Am 1.4,14. *Ben-hadad*, name of several of the kings of Aram-Damascus.

49.28–33: Against Kedar and Hazor. *Kedar* was a collective name for Ishmaelite nomadic tribes (Gen 25.13)
who lived in tents (Ps 120.5; Song 1.5) and grazed sheep and goats (Ezek 27.21). *Hazor* here must also refer
to desert nomadic wanderers. As such, they lived in unwalled villages (v. 31) and their economy was based
upon camel caravaneering (vv. 29,32). **28:** In midwinter 599–598 BCE Nebuchadrezzar led a successful campaign
against the Arab tribes in the eastern desert. **29:** *Terror is all around,* see 46.5n. **32:** *Shaven temples,* a mark of
eastern nomadic groups; see 9.26n.; 25.23.

49.34–39: Against Elam. The unusually long introduction to this oracle suggests that it was a later addition to the collection. One of the few dated oracles, it is placed in the context of the beginning of the reign
of Zedekiah following the first deportation (597 BCE). Elam, with its capital at Susa, lay to the east of Babylon.
The reference to the *bow of Elam* (v. 35) highlights its reputation (Isa 22.6). **36:** On the traditional division of the

² Declare among the nations and
   proclaim,
set up a banner and proclaim,
do not conceal it, say:
Babylon is taken,
   Bel is put to shame,
   Merodach is dismayed.
Her images are put to shame,
   her idols are dismayed.
³ For out of the north a nation has come up against her; it shall make her land a desolation, and no one shall live in it; both human beings and animals shall flee away.

⁴ In those days and in that time, says the LORD, the people of Israel shall come, they and the people of Judah together; they shall come weeping as they seek the LORD their God. ⁵ They shall ask the way to Zion, with faces turned toward it, and they shall come and join[a] themselves to the LORD by an everlasting covenant that will never be forgotten.

⁶ My people have been lost sheep; their shepherds have led them astray, turning them away on the mountains; from mountain to hill they have gone, they have forgotten their fold. ⁷ All who found them have devoured them, and their enemies have said, "We are not guilty, because they have sinned against

the LORD, the true pasture, the LORD, the hope of their ancestors."

⁸ Flee from Babylon, and go out of the land of the Chaldeans, and be like male goats leading the flock. ⁹ For I am going to stir up and bring against Babylon a company of great nations from the land of the north; and they shall array themselves against her; from there she shall be taken. Their arrows are like the arrows of a skilled warrior who does not return empty-handed. ¹⁰ Chaldea shall be plundered; all who plunder her shall be sated, says the LORD.

¹¹ Though you rejoice, though you exult,
   O plunderers of my heritage,
though you frisk about like a heifer on the
      grass,
   and neigh like stallions,
¹² your mother shall be utterly shamed,
   and she who bore you shall be
      disgraced.
Lo, she shall be the last of the nations,
   a wilderness, dry land, and a desert.
¹³ Because of the wrath of the LORD she
      shall not be inhabited,

---

a   Gk: Heb *toward it. Come! They shall join*

heavens into four quadrants, each with its wind, see Ezek 37.9; Zech 2.6; 6.5. **39:** On the restoration of Elam's fortunes, see 48.47; 49.6.

50.1–51.58: Against Babylon. The oracle against Babylon (Chaldea) appears last in the list, reflecting its historical importance and the cosmic aspects of Jeremiah's proclamation of judgment against the nations (25.11–14). This lengthy oracle, made up of numerous fragments, expresses both a harsh judgment upon Babylon and visions of restoration for Judah. Lacking is the sense expressed elsewhere that Babylon was an agent in God's purposeful design (see 27.6–11). Instead the oracle stresses the arrogance and defiance of Babylon, which will now face retribution from Israel's God.

50.1–3: Babylon's destruction is announced. 2: *Bel,* a title of Marduk, the chief deity of Babylon, related to the Canaanite title *ba'al,* "lord, master" (Isa 46.1); cf. Bel 1.1–22. *Merodach* refers to the chief patron deity of Babylon, Marduk, creator of the world in Babylonian mythology and founder of the city of Babylon. The name appears in the Bible only otherwise in the royal names Merodach-baladan (2 Kings 20.12=Isa 39.1) and Evil-merodach (52.31). **3:** Even Babylon, the enemy from the north, is subject to her own "enemies from the north" (1.14; 50.9,41–42). Babylon was conquered by Cyrus, head of a coalition of Medes and Persians, in 539 BCE, but the image here may be more literary and mythological than historical.

50.4–10: The restoration of Israel and Judah, envisioning the reestablishment of the united tribal alliance. **7:** Metaphor of lost sheep being devoured by predators, but compare with 2.3 and its ritual associations. **8:** Cf. Isa 48.20.

50.11–16: The LORD's vengeance against Babylon. 12: *Your mother,* that is, Babylon. Cities can often be spoken of as "mothers" to their inhabitants or surrounding villages.

but shall be an utter desolation;
everyone who passes by Babylon shall be
    appalled
and hiss because of all her wounds.
¹⁴ Take up your positions around Babylon,
all you that bend the bow;
shoot at her, spare no arrows,
for she has sinned against the LORD.
¹⁵ Raise a shout against her from all sides,
"She has surrendered;
her bulwarks have fallen,
her walls are thrown down."
For this is the vengeance of the LORD:
take vengeance on her,
do to her as she has done.
¹⁶ Cut off from Babylon the sower,
and the wielder of the sickle in time of
    harvest;
because of the destroying sword
all of them shall return to their own
    people,
and all of them shall flee to their own
    land.

¹⁷ Israel is a hunted sheep driven away by
lions. First the king of Assyria devoured it,
and now at the end King Nebuchadrezzar of
Babylon has gnawed its bones. ¹⁸ Therefore,
thus says the LORD of hosts, the God of Israel:
I am going to punish the king of Babylon and
his land, as I punished the king of Assyria. ¹⁹ I
will restore Israel to its pasture, and it shall
feed on Carmel and in Bashan, and on the
hills of Ephraim and in Gilead its hunger shall
be satisfied. ²⁰ In those days and at that time,
says the LORD, the iniquity of Israel shall be
sought, and there shall be none; and the sins
of Judah, and none shall be found; for I will
pardon the remnant that I have spared.

²¹ Go up to the land of Merathaim;ᵃ
go up against her,
and attack the inhabitants of Pekodᵇ
and utterly destroy the last of them,ᶜ
                says the LORD;

do all that I have commanded you.
²² The noise of battle is in the land,
and great destruction!
²³ How the hammer of the whole earth
is cut down and broken!
How Babylon has become
a horror among the nations!
²⁴ You set a snare for yourself and you were
    caught, O Babylon,
but you did not know it;
you were discovered and seized,
because you challenged the LORD.
²⁵ The LORD has opened his armory,
and brought out the weapons of his
    wrath,
for the Lord GOD of hosts has a task to do
in the land of the Chaldeans.
²⁶ Come against her from every quarter;
open her granaries;
pile her up like heaps of grain, and destroy
    her utterly;
let nothing be left of her.
²⁷ Kill all her bulls,
let them go down to the slaughter.
Alas for them, their day has come,
the time of their punishment!

²⁸ Listen! Fugitives and refugees from the
land of Babylon are coming to declare in Zion
the vengeance of the LORD our God, vengeance for his temple.

²⁹ Summon archers against Babylon, all
who bend the bow. Encamp all around her;
let no one escape. Repay her according to her
deeds; just as she has done, do to her—for
she has arrogantly defied the LORD, the Holy
One of Israel. ³⁰ Therefore her young men
shall fall in her squares, and all her soldiers
shall be destroyed on that day, says the LORD.

ᵃ Or of Double Rebellion
ᵇ Or of Punishment
ᶜ Tg: Heb destroy after them

50.17–20: Israel restored. 19: Carmel, a promontory in the western Jezreel Valley, and Bashan in Transjordan
were known for their fertility (Isa 33.9; Nah 1.4; Ezek 39.18).
50.21–32: The military assault on Babylon. 21: Merathaim, used only here, is perhaps a derisive term for
Babylon meaning "double rebellion," probably playing on the name of southern Babylon, "mat marrati," "land
of the lagoons." Pekod was a part of Babylonian territory or an allied territory; see Ezek 23.23. Also a play on
words, since Heb "paqad" commonly means to "attend to," as in punishing (vv. 18,27). 24: You set, Heb "I set."

31 I am against you, O arrogant one,
  says the Lord God of hosts;
for your day has come,
  the time when I will punish you.
32 The arrogant one shall stumble and fall,
  with no one to raise him up,
and I will kindle a fire in his cities,
  and it will devour everything around
    him.

33 Thus says the Lord of hosts: The people of Israel are oppressed, and so too are the people of Judah; all their captors have held them fast and refuse to let them go. 34 Their Redeemer is strong; the Lord of hosts is his name. He will surely plead their cause, that he may give rest to the earth, but unrest to the inhabitants of Babylon.

35 A sword against the Chaldeans, says the
    Lord,
  and against the inhabitants of Babylon,
  and against her officials and her sages!
36 A sword against the diviners,
  so that they may become fools!
A sword against her warriors,
  so that they may be destroyed!
37 A sword against her[a] horses and against
    her[a] chariots,
  and against all the foreign troops in her
    midst,
  so that they may become women!
A sword against all her treasures,
  that they may be plundered!
38 A drought[b] against her waters,
  that they may be dried up!
For it is a land of images,
  and they go mad over idols.

39 Therefore wild animals shall live with hyenas in Babylon,[c] and ostriches shall inhabit her; she shall never again be peopled, or inhabited for all generations. 40 As when God overthrew Sodom and Gomorrah and their neighbors, says the Lord, so no one shall live there, nor shall anyone settle in her.

41 Look, a people is coming from the north;
  a mighty nation and many kings
  are stirring from the farthest parts of
    the earth.
42 They wield bow and spear,
  they are cruel and have no mercy.
The sound of them is like the roaring sea;
  they ride upon horses,
set in array as a warrior for battle,
  against you, O daughter Babylon!

43 The king of Babylon heard news of them,
  and his hands fell helpless;
anguish seized him,
  pain like that of a woman in labor.

44 Like a lion coming up from the thickets of the Jordan against a perennial pasture, I will suddenly chase them away from her; and I will appoint over her whomever I choose.[d] For who is like me? Who can summon me? Who is the shepherd who can stand before me? 45 Therefore hear the plan that the Lord has made against Babylon, and the purposes that he has formed against the land of the Chaldeans: Surely the little ones of the flock shall be dragged away; surely their[e] fold shall be appalled at their fate. 46 At the sound of the capture of Babylon the earth shall tremble, and her cry shall be heard among the nations.

a Cn: Heb *his*
b Another reading is *A sword*
c Heb lacks *in Babylon*
d Or *and I will single out the choicest of her rams*: Meaning of Heb uncertain
e Syr Gk Tg Compare 49.20: Heb lacks *their*

50.33–34: Israel's redeemer will plead her cause. The terminology is of family redemption in a legal suit (cf. Isa 47.4).

50.35–40: Judgment against Babylon. Using a repeating phrase ("a sword [Heb "ḥereb"] against . . . "), changes images to "a drought [Heb "ḥoreb"] against" in v. 38. 36: *Diviners*, but Heb suggests a derogatory term for "those who prattle on about nothing." 37: *They may become women*, a common slander made against foreign soldiers. Compare 51.30; Isa 19.16; Nah 3.13. 40: *Sodom and Gomorrah*, see 20.16n.

50.41–43: The assault of the enemy from the north. See v. 3n.

50.44–46: The Lord is a lion. *Thickets of the Jordan*, see 12.5n. *Shepherd*, a metaphor for king.

51 Thus says the LORD:
I am going to stir up a destructive
wind[a]
against Babylon
and against the inhabitants of Leb-
qamai;[b]
[2] and I will send winnowers to Babylon,
and they shall winnow her.
They shall empty her land
when they come against her from every
side
on the day of trouble.
[3] Let not the archer bend his bow,
and let him not array himself in his coat
of mail.
Do not spare her young men;
utterly destroy her entire army.
[4] They shall fall down slain in the land of
the Chaldeans,
and wounded in her streets.
[5] Israel and Judah have not been forsaken
by their God, the LORD of hosts,
though their land is full of guilt
before the Holy One of Israel.

[6] Flee from the midst of Babylon,
save your lives, each of you!
Do not perish because of her guilt,
for this is the time of the LORD's
vengeance;
he is repaying her what is due.
[7] Babylon was a golden cup in the LORD's
hand,
making all the earth drunken;
the nations drank of her wine,
and so the nations went mad.
[8] Suddenly Babylon has fallen and is
shattered;
wail for her!
Bring balm for her wound;
perhaps she may be healed.

[9] We tried to heal Babylon,
but she could not be healed.
Forsake her, and let each of us go
to our own country;
for her judgment has reached up to heaven
and has been lifted up even to the skies.
[10] The LORD has brought forth our
vindication;
come, let us declare in Zion
the work of the LORD our God.

[11] Sharpen the arrows!
Fill the quivers!
The LORD has stirred up the spirit of the kings
of the Medes, because his purpose concerning Babylon is to destroy it, for that is the
vengeance of the LORD, vengeance for his
temple.
[12] Raise a standard against the walls of
Babylon;
make the watch strong;
post sentinels;
prepare the ambushes;
for the LORD has both planned and done
what he spoke concerning the
inhabitants of Babylon.
[13] You who live by mighty waters,
rich in treasures,
your end has come,
the thread of your life is cut.
[14] The LORD of hosts has sworn by himself:
Surely I will fill you with troops like a
swarm of locusts,
and they shall raise a shout of victory
over you.

a Or *stir up the spirit of a destroyer*
b *Leb-qamai* is a cryptogram for *Kasdim*, Chaldea

51.1–10: **A wind will blow against Babylon.** The image of winnowing is used ironically to depict a destructive wind that goes far beyond simply separating grain from chaff. 1: *Leb-qamai*, a cryptic 'atbash reading for
"Kasdim," meaning "Chaldea" or "Babylon"; see textual note *b*; cf. 25.26n.; 51.41. Also, the term *qamai* sounds
like the word for "standing grain" (Heb "qamah") which is being winnowed, so that *Leb-qamai* suggests "heart
of the standing grain." 7: On God's cup of wine, see 25.15–29. Here it is Babylon herself who is God's cup. The
nations drink and "go mad" (the same word as in 50.38).
51.11–14: **The Medes attack Babylon.** Cyrus was king of the empire of Media and Persia, and attacked Babylon in 539 BCE. 13: *Mighty waters*, Babylon was surrounded by the Euphrates and other water–ways as natural
defenses. 14: *Troops like a swarm of locusts*, cf. Joel 1.1–2.11 for the connection of a locust plague and the invasion
of enemy troops.

¹⁵ It is he who made the earth by his power,
 who established the world by his
  wisdom,
and by his understanding stretched out
 the heavens.
¹⁶ When he utters his voice there is a
  tumult of waters in the heavens,
and he makes the mist rise from the
  ends of the earth.
He makes lightnings for the rain,
 and he brings out the wind from his
  storehouses.
¹⁷ Everyone is stupid and without
  knowledge;
 goldsmiths are all put to shame by their
  idols;
for their images are false,
 and there is no breath in them.
¹⁸ They are worthless, a work of delusion;
 at the time of their punishment they
  shall perish.
¹⁹ Not like these is the LORD,ᵃ the portion
  of Jacob,
 for he is the one who formed all things,
and Israel is the tribe of his inheritance;
 the LORD of hosts is his name.

²⁰ You are my war club, my weapon of
  battle:
with you I smash nations;
 with you I destroy kingdoms;
²¹ with you I smash the horse and its rider;
 with you I smash the chariot and the
  charioteer;
²² with you I smash man and woman;
 with you I smash the old man and the
  boy;
with you I smash the young man and the
  girl;
²³ with you I smash shepherds and their
  flocks;

with you I smash farmers and their teams;
 with you I smash governors and
  deputies.

²⁴ I will repay Babylon and all the inhabitants of Chaldea before your very eyes for all the wrong that they have done in Zion, says the LORD.

²⁵ I am against you, O destroying
  mountain,
           says the LORD,
 that destroys the whole earth;
I will stretch out my hand against you,
 and roll you down from the crags,
 and make you a burned-out mountain.
²⁶ No stone shall be taken from you for a
  corner
 and no stone for a foundation,
but you shall be a perpetual waste,
 says the LORD.

²⁷ Raise a standard in the land,
 blow the trumpet among the nations;
prepare the nations for war against her,
 summon against her the kingdoms,
 Ararat, Minni, and Ashkenaz;
appoint a marshal against her,
 bring up horses like bristling locusts.
²⁸ Prepare the nations for war against her,
 the kings of the Medes, with their
  governors and deputies,
 and every land under their dominion.
²⁹ The land trembles and writhes,
 for the LORD's purposes against Babylon
  stand,
to make the land of Babylon a desolation,
 without inhabitant.

ᵃ Heb lacks *the LORD*

51.15–19: A hymn of praise to God. A doublet of 10.12–16 appended here to contrast the power of the God of Israel with the impotence of the idols of Babylon. **51.20–24: Refers back to the kings of the Medes** (v. 11) as God's weapon of war to be used against Babylon. The repeated term *I smash* (Heb "nipatsti") is related to the term for "war club" (Heb "mapets"), a common weapon in the ancient Near East. **51.25–33: Babylon is destroyed** and left desolate as Babylon's famous ziggurat (artificial temple mound) will be made an extinct burned-out volcano (v. 25). **26:** After cities were destroyed, their stone blocks were often reused in the rebuilding process. Even Babylon's ruins, however, will be unfit for future use. **27–33:** *Ararat*, ancient Urartu, modern Armenia, north of Lake Van. *Minni*, Manneans living south of Lake Urmia. *Ashkenaz*, the Scythians. See Gen 8.4; 10.3. All were defeated by the Medes in the early sixth century BCE. **27:** *Marshal*, a

³⁰ The warriors of Babylon have given up
fighting,
they remain in their strongholds;
their strength has failed,
they have become women;
her buildings are set on fire,
her bars are broken.
³¹ One runner runs to meet another,
and one messenger to meet another,
to tell the king of Babylon
that his city is taken from end to end:
³² the fords have been seized,
the marshes have been burned with
fire,
and the soldiers are in panic.
³³ For thus says the LORD of hosts, the God
of Israel:
Daughter Babylon is like a threshing floor
at the time when it is trodden;
yet a little while
and the time of her harvest will come.

³⁴ "King Nebuchadrezzar of Babylon has
devoured me,
he has crushed me;
he has made me an empty vessel,
he has swallowed me like a monster;
he has filled his belly with my delicacies,
he has spewed me out.
³⁵ May my torn flesh be avenged on
Babylon,"
the inhabitants of Zion shall say.
"May my blood be avenged on the
inhabitants of Chaldea,"
Jerusalem shall say.
³⁶ Therefore thus says the LORD:
I am going to defend your cause
and take vengeance for you.
I will dry up her sea

and make her fountain dry;
³⁷ and Babylon shall become a heap of
ruins,
a den of jackals,
an object of horror and of hissing,
without inhabitant.

³⁸ Like lions they shall roar together;
they shall growl like lions' whelps.
³⁹ When they are inflamed, I will set out
their drink
and make them drunk, until they
become merry
and then sleep a perpetual sleep
and never wake, says the LORD.
⁴⁰ I will bring them down like lambs to the
slaughter,
like rams and goats.

⁴¹ How Sheshach[a] is taken,
the pride of the whole earth seized!
How Babylon has become
an object of horror among the nations!
⁴² The sea has risen over Babylon;
she has been covered by its tumultuous
waves.
⁴³ Her cities have become an object of
horror,
a land of drought and a desert,
a land in which no one lives,
and through which no mortal passes.
⁴⁴ I will punish Bel in Babylon,
and make him disgorge what he has
swallowed.
The nations shall no longer stream to him;
the wall of Babylon has fallen.

---

[a] *Sheshach* is a cryptogram for *Babel*, Babylon

military official (Nah 3.17). **28:** *Prepare*, lit. "sanctify"; see 6.4n. **30:** *Become women*, see 50.37n.

51.34–44: God will seek vengeance against Babylon for devouring Judah. The theme of Babylon "devouring" Judah (v. 34) ushers in a theme pursued through this section. That Israel is "devoured" is a common theme (see 10.25; 30.16). But here the image is combined with the common mythological image of the sea-monster "swallowing" with a voracious appetite (v. 34; Ps 69.15; Prov 1.12), in turn combined with the polemic that Bel, the god of Babylon, has such a voracious appetite (v. 44), but will be forced by God to disgorge all he has devoured in conquest. See Jer 50.2 and the polemic in Bel 1.1–22, where Bel is characterized principally by his voracious appetite. **36:** *Dry up her sea*, that is, the mythological enemy, the sea-dragon with its all-consuming appetite, representing the power of destructive chaos. Marduk, the patron deity of Babylon, was the hero god who slew the dragon Tiamat, and who himself was depicted as a dragon on murals throughout Babylon. **41:** *Sheshach*, as in v. 1, cryptogram for Babel (*Babylon*); see 25.26n. **42:** See v. 36. **44:** *Bel*, see 50.2n. *Make him disgorge*, that is, "bring out," leading into what follows.

⁴⁵ Come out of her, my people!
  Save your lives, each of you,
  from the fierce anger of the LORD!
⁴⁶ Do not be fainthearted or fearful
  at the rumors heard in the land—
one year one rumor comes,
  the next year another,
rumors of violence in the land
  and of ruler against ruler.

⁴⁷ Assuredly, the days are coming
  when I will punish the images of
    Babylon;
her whole land shall be put to shame,
  and all her slain shall fall in her midst.
⁴⁸ Then the heavens and the earth,
  and all that is in them,
shall shout for joy over Babylon;
  for the destroyers shall come against
    them out of the north,
                              says the LORD.
⁴⁹ Babylon must fall for the slain of Israel,
  as the slain of all the earth have fallen
    because of Babylon.

⁵⁰ You survivors of the sword,
  go, do not linger!
Remember the LORD in a distant land,
  and let Jerusalem come into your mind:
⁵¹ We are put to shame, for we have heard
    insults;
  dishonor has covered our face,
for aliens have come
  into the holy places of the LORD's house.

⁵² Therefore the time is surely coming, says
    the LORD,
  when I will punish her idols,
and through all her land
  the wounded shall groan.
⁵³ Though Babylon should mount up to
    heaven,

and though she should fortify her
    strong height,
from me destroyers would come upon her,
  says the LORD.

⁵⁴ Listen!—a cry from Babylon!
  A great crashing from the land of the
    Chaldeans!
⁵⁵ For the LORD is laying Babylon waste,
  and stilling her loud clamor.
Their waves roar like mighty waters,
  the sound of their clamor resounds;
⁵⁶ for a destroyer has come against her,
  against Babylon;
her warriors are taken,
  their bows are broken;
for the LORD is a God of recompense,
  he will repay in full.
⁵⁷ I will make her officials and her sages
    drunk,
  also her governors, her deputies, and
    her warriors;
they shall sleep a perpetual sleep and
    never wake,
  says the King, whose name is the LORD
    of hosts.

⁵⁸ Thus says the LORD of hosts:
The broad wall of Babylon
  shall be leveled to the ground,
and her high gates
  shall be burned with fire.
The peoples exhaust themselves for
    nothing,
  and the nations weary themselves only
    for fire.ᵃ

⁵⁹ The word that the prophet Jeremiah
commanded Seraiah son of Neriah son of

ᵃ Gk Syr Compare Hab 2.13: Heb *and the nations for
fire, and they are weary*

51.45–49: Israel is urged to "come out" as that which is "disgorged" from Babylon. The figure of Babylon
continued for a long time to symbolize the power of God's great destructive enemy in biblical tradition; see
Rev 18.2–21.

51.50–58: Babylon's ultimate destruction. **50:** *Remember . . . distant land,* normally a difficult task; cf. Ps
137.4. **51:** *Aliens,* unlike "strangers" (sojourners), "aliens" are dangerous to the solidarity of the community and
threaten its integrity. Therefore "aliens" (Heb "zarim") are discriminated against in a way that goes far beyond
the favorable concern shown to sojourners. **53:** *Mount up to heaven,* that is, assert itself against God's authority;
cf. Isa 14.13.

51.59–64: The scroll thrown into the Euphrates. The oracles against Babylon ("all these words," v. 60) were,

Mahseiah, when he went with King Zedekiah of Judah to Babylon, in the fourth year of his reign. Seraiah was the quartermaster. [60] Jeremiah wrote in a[a] scroll all the disasters that would come on Babylon, all these words that are written concerning Babylon. [61] And Jeremiah said to Seraiah: "When you come to Babylon, see that you read all these words, [62] and say, 'O LORD, you yourself threatened to destroy this place so that neither human beings nor animals shall live in it, and it shall be desolate forever.' [63] When you finish reading this scroll, tie a stone to it, and throw it into the middle of the Euphrates, [64] and say, 'Thus shall Babylon sink, to rise no more, because of the disasters that I am bringing on her.'"[b]

Thus far are the words of Jeremiah.

52 Zedekiah was twenty-one years old when he began to reign; he reigned eleven years in Jerusalem. His mother's name was Hamutal daughter of Jeremiah of Libnah. [2] He did what was evil in the sight of the LORD, just as Jehoiakim had done. [3] Indeed, Jerusalem and Judah so angered the LORD that he expelled them from his presence.

Zedekiah rebelled against the king of Babylon. [4] And in the ninth year of his reign, in the tenth month, on the tenth day of the month, King Nebuchadrezzar of Babylon came with all his army against Jerusalem, and they laid siege to it; they built siegeworks against it all around. [5] So the city was besieged until the eleventh year of King Zedekiah. [6] On the ninth day of the fourth month the famine became so severe in the city that there was no food for the people of the land. [7] Then a breach was made in the city wall;[c] and all the soldiers fled and went out from the city by night by the way of the gate between the two walls, by the king's garden, though the Chaldeans were all around the city. They went in the direction of the Arabah. [8] But the army of the Chaldeans pursued the king, and overtook Zedekiah in the plains of Jericho; and all his army was scattered, deserting him. [9] Then they captured the king, and brought him up to the king of Babylon at Riblah in the land of Hamath, and he passed sentence on him. [10] The king of Babylon killed the sons of Zedekiah before his eyes, and also killed all the officers of Judah at Riblah. [11] He put out the eyes of Zedekiah, and bound him in fetters, and the king of Babylon took him to Babylon, and put him in prison until the day of his death.

[12] In the fifth month, on the tenth day of the month—which was the nineteenth year of King Nebuchadrezzar, king of Babylon—Nebuzaradan the captain of the bodyguard who served the king of Babylon, entered Jerusalem. [13] He burned the house of the LORD, the king's house, and all the houses of Jerusalem; every great house he burned down. [14] All the army of the Chaldeans, who were with the captain of the guard, broke down all the walls around Jerusalem. [15] Nebuzaradan the captain of the guard carried into exile

a Or *one*
b Gk: Heb *on her. And they shall weary themselves*
c Heb lacks *wall*

according to this account, sealed in a scroll and then taken to the Euphrates by courier and thrown in as a prophetic sign and curse that Babylon would so sink in divine disaster. This action is dated to 594 BCE, the year of the likely aborted revolt against Babylon; see 27.1–28.17n. The emissaries sent by Zedekiah to Babylon here may have been in response to a reaffirmation of treaty support by Zedekiah of his Babylonian overlords. **59:** *Seraiah . . . Neriah . . . Mahseiah,* apparently Seraiah was Baruch's brother; see 32.16. *Quartermaster,* or perhaps "chief of storage houses," an appropriate official to send to convince the king of Babylon that no revolt was planned. **64:** *Thus far are the words of Jeremiah,* an additional comment calling attention to the supplementary character of the appendix in ch 52.

52.1–34: The fall and looting of Jerusalem. Vv. 1–27 are nearly identical to 2 Kings 24.18–25.21. Vv. 28–30 provide statistics regarding the numbers of Judeans taken into exile during the three deportations, figures not recorded elsewhere. Vv. 31–34 are excerpted nearly verbatim from 2 Kings 25.27–30. This historical recitation from the Deuteronomistic History makes a fitting ending to the Deuteronomistically edited book of Jeremiah. **1:** *Zedekiah,* the last king of Judah, ruled ca. 597–586 BCE. **3:** A tragic theological conclusion consistent with the Deuteronomistic perspective; see 2 Kings 23.26–27. **4–11:** January 587 to August 586 BCE. On the attempted escape and capture of Zedekiah and his fate, cf. 39.1–10. **12–14:** *The fifth month* continued to be memorialized in

some of the poorest of the people and the rest of the people who were left in the city and the deserters who had defected to the king of Babylon, together with the rest of the artisans. [16] But Nebuzaradan the captain of the guard left some of the poorest people of the land to be vinedressers and tillers of the soil.

[17] The pillars of bronze that were in the house of the LORD, and the stands and the bronze sea that were in the house of the LORD, the Chaldeans broke in pieces, and carried all the bronze to Babylon. [18] They took away the pots, the shovels, the snuffers, the basins, the ladles, and all the vessels of bronze used in the temple service. [19] The captain of the guard took away the small bowls also, the firepans, the basins, the pots, the lampstands, the ladles, and the bowls for libation, both those of gold and those of silver. [20] As for the two pillars, the one sea, the twelve bronze bulls that were under the sea, and the stands,[a] which King Solomon had made for the house of the LORD, the bronze of all these vessels was beyond weighing. [21] As for the pillars, the height of the one pillar was eighteen cubits, its circumference was twelve cubits; it was hollow and its thickness was four fingers. [22] Upon it was a capital of bronze; the height of the capital was five cubits; latticework and pomegranates, all of bronze, encircled the top of the capital. And the second pillar had the same, with pomegranates. [23] There were ninety-six pomegranates on the sides; all the pomegranates encircling the latticework numbered one hundred.

[24] The captain of the guard took the chief priest Seraiah, the second priest Zephaniah, and the three guardians of the threshold;

[25] and from the city he took an officer who had been in command of the soldiers, and seven men of the king's council who were found in the city; the secretary of the commander of the army who mustered the people of the land; and sixty men of the people of the land who were found inside the city. [26] Then Nebuzaradan the captain of the guard took them, and brought them to the king of Babylon at Riblah. [27] And the king of Babylon struck them down, and put them to death at Riblah in the land of Hamath. So Judah went into exile out of its land.

[28] This is the number of the people whom Nebuchadrezzar took into exile: in the seventh year, three thousand twenty-three Judeans; [29] in the eighteenth year of Nebuchadrezzar he took into exile from Jerusalem eight hundred thirty-two persons; [30] in the twenty-third year of Nebuchadrezzar, Nebuzaradan the captain of the guard took into exile of the Judeans seven hundred forty-five persons; all the persons were four thousand six hundred.

[31] In the thirty-seventh year of the exile of King Jehoiachin of Judah, in the twelfth month, on the twenty-fifth day of the month, King Evil-merodach of Babylon, in the year he began to reign, showed favor to King Jehoiachin of Judah and brought him out of prison; [32] he spoke kindly to him, and gave him a seat above the seats of the other kings who were with him in Babylon. [33] So Jehoiachin put aside his prison clothes, and every day of his life he dined regularly at the king's table. [34] For his allowance, a regular daily allowance was given him by the king of Babylon, as long as he lived, up to the day of his death.

[a] Cn: Heb that were under the stands

commemoration of the destruction of the Temple; see Zech 7.3,5; 8.19. **17**: *Pillars of bronze*, see 1 Kings 7.15–16. On the *bronze sea* and Ahaz's reforms, see 1 Kings 7.23–26; 2 Kings 16.17. **22–23**: *Pomegranates* were a particularly important symbol used in Israel's ritual decorations, adorning both priestly wear and the Temple furnishings; see Ex 28.33; 39.24–25; 1 Kings 7.18–20,42. **24**: *Chief priest*, a relatively late title for the principal priest ("head" priest, or "first" priest), alongside his principal assistant, the "second" priest; compare with the term "high priest" (lit. "great" priest) in 2 Kings 12.10; 22.4,8; Hag 1.1. **30**: On the significance of the third deportation (581 BCE), see 43.1–13. **31**: *Evil-merodach* (562–560 BCE), Babylonian king whose name means "man of Marduk"; see 50.2n.

LAMENTATIONS

NAME, AUTHORSHIP, AND LOCATION IN CANON

The name Lamentations is a translation of the title of the book as it appears in the Septuagint, *Threnoi*. In the Hebrew Bible the book is titled *'Ekah*, literally "How," which is the first word of the initial verse, "How lonely sits the city."

In the Christian canon, Lamentations follows Jeremiah, who was traditionally thought to have been its author. While Jewish tradition also ascribes the book's authorship to Jeremiah, in the Hebrew Bible Lamentations is located in the Writings, among the Five Scrolls. It is read liturgically on the Ninth of Av, the day of public mourning in commemoration of the destruction of the First and Second Temples. (The First Temple was destroyed in 586 BCE by the Babylonians, and the Second Temple in 70 CE by the Romans.) In Christian tradition, readings from Lamentations are part of the Holy Week liturgies. The traditional ascription of authorship to Jeremiah derives from the impetus to ascribe all biblical books to inspired biblical authors as those books became authoritative or canonical. Jeremiah, a prophet who lived during the last days of the kingdom of Judah and prophesied its demise, was an obvious choice for Lamentations. According to 2 Chr 35.25, Jeremiah composed laments for the death of King Josiah. This suggests that already by the time of Chronicles, Jeremiah had a reputation as an author of laments.

DATE AND HISTORICAL CONTEXT

The five poems that comprise Lamentations, each with its distinctive tone and theme, were initially composed to lament the destruction of Jerusalem and the Temple by the Babylonians, which brought the independent country of Judah to an end (see 2 Kings 25.8–21). The sequence of the chapters is not chronological, and despite the vividness of their descriptions, the poems may not have been written by eyewitnesses to the events. The dating of the book is clearly after 586 BCE and before the end of the sixth century BCE, when the Temple was rebuilt, but the exact time, place, and reason for their composition is unknown. Perhaps the poems were used at the site of the ruined Temple to commemorate its loss.

GENRE

An ancient Near Eastern tradition of laments over the destruction of cities goes back to the Sumerian laments of the early second millennium BCE (e.g., "Lamentation over the Destruction of Ur," "Lamentation over the Destruction of Sumer and Ur," "Nippur Lament"). Despite the generic similarity, however, there is no direct line of influence from the Sumerian laments to the book of Lamentations. Moreover, the Sumerian laments were recited on the occasion of the rebuilding of a temple, so their "story" has a happy ending. Not so in the book of Lamentations, where hopes for the rebuilding of the Jerusalem Temple remain unrealized, and God, who is so movingly implored to end his people's suffering and exile and to restore them to their former condition, never responds. The poems in Lamentations resemble Pss 74 and 79, also written in the aftermath of Jerusalem's destruction (see also Ps 137), but the origin and development of the Jerusalem-laments in Israel remains unknown. The destruction of city and Temple was an unprecedented event in Judah; and perhaps a new genre arose to fill a new need.

STRUCTURE, INTERPRETATION, AND GUIDE TO READING

The book's first four poems (chs 1; 2; 3; 4) are alphabetic acrostics, a formal device found elsewhere in the Bible (e.g., Pss 111; 112; 145; Prov 31.10–31), in which each verse or stanza begins with successive letters of the Hebrew alphabet, twenty-two in all. Chapter 3 is a triple acrostic; all three verses of each stanza begin with the same letter. Chapter 5, although not an acrostic, also contains twenty-two verses. In Lamentations this formal device gives expression to the enormity or totality of the destruction (extending "from A to Z") and also attempts to give structure and closure to the incomprehensible events and unstructured pain that engulfed Judah and its inhabitants.

The language of the book is highly poetic and extraordinarily moving, so much so that at times we want to avert our eyes from the violence and suffering described. The experiences of warfare, siege, famine, and death are individualized—brave men reduced to begging, mothers unable to nourish their children. The national catastrophe is thus made real, as society disintegrates and people die or are deported. All of this is addressed to God, so that he may feel the suffering of his people and save them. The entire book may be thought of as an appeal for God's mercy. Yet God remains silent.

If the book fails to move God, it fulfills another function, that of public mourning which both relives and commemorates a catastrophe of incomprehensible proportion. Lamentations does not create a new theology. It assumes the theology of Deuteronomy, where sin leads to divine punishment and exile (see Deut 28). God is responsible for the disaster; the Babylonians are merely divine agents. So, God, whose power is not diminished despite the Temple's destruction, must be the one to end the Babylonian dominance and bring about the return from exile. Repentance, the antidote to sin, is mentioned but is not central (this is not penitential prayer); rather, the idea in Lamentations is that the punishment, even if deserved, outweighs the sin. The immediacy of the disproportionate punishment drowns out everything else.

As a short book, Lamentations can easily be read in one sitting. Each chapter is a window through which a poet attempts to render chaos into language in the formal structure of the acrostic.

Adele Berlin

1 How lonely sits the city
   that once was full of people!
How like a widow she has become,
   she that was great among the nations!
She that was a princess among the
      provinces
   has become a vassal.

[2] She weeps bitterly in the night,
   with tears on her cheeks;
among all her lovers
   she has no one to comfort her;
all her friends have dealt treacherously
      with her,
   they have become her enemies.

[3] Judah has gone into exile with suffering
   and hard servitude;
she lives now among the nations,
   and finds no resting place;
her pursuers have all overtaken her
   in the midst of her distress.

[4] The roads to Zion mourn,
   for no one comes to the festivals;

all her gates are desolate,
   her priests groan;
her young girls grieve,[a]
   and her lot is bitter.

[5] Her foes have become the masters,
   her enemies prosper,
because the LORD has made her suffer
   for the multitude of her
      transgressions;
her children have gone away,
   captives before the foe.

[6] From daughter Zion has departed
   all her majesty.
Her princes have become like stags
   that find no pasture;
they fled without strength
   before the pursuer.

[7] Jerusalem remembers,
   in the days of her affliction and
      wandering,

a   Meaning of Heb uncertain

1.1–22. Lament over the destroyed Jerusalem. The chapter has two sections, vv. 1–11, the lament of the narrator, and vv. 12–22, the lament of the city. Shame, mourning, and suffering are the main themes. The phrase "no one to comfort her/me" occurs four times (vv. 2,9,17,21; cf. vv. 7,16) and emphasizes unceasing mourning.

1.1–11: The poet laments Jerusalem. Jerusalem is personified as a woman, widowed, abandoned, and shamed. **1:** *How*, or "woe" is a common beginning of dirges (Isa 1.21; Jer 48.17; Lam 2.1; 4.1). **2:** *Lovers*, Judah's political allies who failed to support her. The term also hints that Jerusalem, by taking lovers, was unfaithful to God. **3:** *Suffering and hard servitude* is reminiscent of the Egyptian bondage (Ex 1.14; 2.23; 3.7,17; 4.31; 5.11; 6.6), to which the Babylonian exile is likened. **6:** *Daughter Zion*, or "Mistress Zion," a common epithet (e.g., 1.15; 2.1;

all the precious things
    that were hers in days of old.
When her people fell into the hand of the foe,
    and there was no one to help her,
the foe looked on mocking
    over her downfall.

[8] Jerusalem sinned grievously,
    so she has become a mockery;
all who honored her despise her,
    for they have seen her nakedness;
she herself groans,
    and turns her face away.

[9] Her uncleanness was in her skirts;
    she took no thought of her future;
her downfall was appalling,
    with none to comfort her.
"O LORD, look at my affliction,
    for the enemy has triumphed!"

[10] Enemies have stretched out their hands
    over all her precious things;
she has even seen the nations
    invade her sanctuary,
those whom you forbade
    to enter your congregation.

[11] All her people groan
    as they search for bread;
they trade their treasures for food
    to revive their strength.
Look, O LORD, and see
    how worthless I have become.

[12] Is it nothing to you,[a] all you who pass by?
    Look and see
if there is any sorrow like my sorrow,
    which was brought upon me,

which the LORD inflicted
    on the day of his fierce anger.

[13] From on high he sent fire;
    it went deep into my bones;
he spread a net for my feet;
    he turned me back;
he has left me stunned,
    faint all day long.

[14] My transgressions were bound[a] into a
    yoke;
    by his hand they were fastened
      together;
they weigh on my neck,
    sapping my strength;
the Lord handed me over
    to those whom I cannot withstand.

[15] The LORD has rejected
    all my warriors in the midst of me;
he proclaimed a time against me
    to crush my young men;
the Lord has trodden as in a wine press
    the virgin daughter Judah.

[16] For these things I weep;
    my eyes flow with tears;
for a comforter is far from me,
    one to revive my courage;
my children are desolate,
    for the enemy has prevailed.

[17] Zion stretches out her hands,
    but there is no one to comfort her;
the LORD has commanded against
    Jacob

a Meaning of Heb uncertain

4.22) conveying the sense of "dear little Zion." **8:** *Mockery,* or "banished." *Nakedness,* shame, especially sexual shame (cf. Isa 47.5; Jer 13.22; Ezek 16.37; Nah 3.5). **9:** *Uncleanness,* not from menstruation but from sexual impropriety. Jerusalem's sin was unfaithfulness to God, the taking of other "lovers." **10:** *Precious things,* the Temple treasures looted by the victors (cf. 2 Chr 36.10). The Babylonian invasion is conveyed in sexual terms, as a rape of Jerusalem by someone who had no rights of access to her. **11:** Jerusalem speaks in the final line, and continues speaking in vv. 12–16 and 18–22.

    1.12–22. Jerusalem's lament. 12: *Was brought,* the Heb word is much stronger and actually conveys violence (cf. 1 Sam 31.4; Jer 38.19; Judg 19.25). *Day . . . anger,* like "the day of the Lord," when God comes in judgment against Judah itself (e.g., Am 5.18). **15:** *Trodden as in a wine press,* crushed so the blood runs out (see Deut 32.14; Isa 63.1–2). *Virgin,* part of the epithet "daughter Zion" (see 1.6n.), Heb "betulah" means a girl of marriageable age. **17:** *Jacob,* a common term for Judah in postexilic literature. *Filthy thing,* a menstruant, who is ritually impure, not fit to come into contact with holy things and off-limits for sexual contact. Jerusalem's "lovers" (vv.

that his neighbors should become his
    foes;
Jerusalem has become
    a filthy thing among them.

[18] The Lord is in the right,
    for I have rebelled against his word;
but hear, all you peoples,
    and behold my suffering;
my young women and young men
    have gone into captivity.

[19] I called to my lovers
    but they deceived me;
my priests and elders
    perished in the city
while seeking food
    to revive their strength.

[20] See, O Lord, how distressed I am;
    my stomach churns,
my heart is wrung within me,
    because I have been very rebellious.
In the street the sword bereaves;
    in the house it is like death.

[21] They heard how I was groaning,
    with no one to comfort me.
All my enemies heard of my trouble;
    they are glad that you have done it.
Bring on the day you have announced,
    and let them be as I am.

[22] Let all their evil doing come before you;
    and deal with them

as you have dealt with me
    because of all my transgressions;
for my groans are many
    and my heart is faint.

2 How the Lord in his anger
    has humiliated[a] daughter Zion!
He has thrown down from heaven to earth
    the splendor of Israel;
he has not remembered his footstool
    in the day of his anger.

[2] The Lord has destroyed without mercy
    all the dwellings of Jacob;
in his wrath he has broken down
    the strongholds of daughter Judah;
he has brought down to the ground in
      dishonor
    the kingdom and its rulers.

[3] He has cut down in fierce anger
    all the might of Israel;
he has withdrawn his right hand from them
    in the face of the enemy;
he has burned like a flaming fire in Jacob,
    consuming all around.

[4] He has bent his bow like an enemy,
    with his right hand set like a foe;
he has killed all in whom we took pride
    in the tent of daughter Zion;
he has poured out his fury like fire.

a   Meaning of Heb uncertain

2,19) distance themselves from her. The narrator interrupts Jerusalem's speech, just as she did his (1.9c). **18:** An admission of sin, but the emphasis is on the suffering. **20:** *Stomach,* innards, the seat of emotions. *In the street,* better "outside," that is, outside the city walls where the fighting took place. Inside the besieged city the inhabitants were ravaged by famine and disease (see Ezek 7.15). **22:** Not simply vindictive revenge, this is a plea to restore the world order in which Israel is safe under God's protection and its enemies are banished. Chapters 3 and 4 end in a similar manner. The trope of the destruction of the enemy is common in psalms of lament.

    2.1–22: The Lord has become like an enemy. The tone changes from the despair of ch 1 to anger, with a concomitant shift from a focus on the victim to a focus on God, the perpetrator. Many verbs of strong military action portray God as a destroying enemy: e.g., "thrown down," "destroyed," "cut down," "burned," "bent his bow," "killed."

    2.1–10: God in his anger battles against Jerusalem, destroying the city and the country of Judah. **1:** *How,* see 1.1n. *Humiliated,* or "made loathsome." *The splendor of Israel,* the Temple, thought of as a link between heaven and earth. That link is now broken and formal ritual access to God is cut off. *Footstool,* i.e., the ark of the covenant or the Temple. God is envisioned as a king sitting in heaven with his feet touching the Temple (see Ps 132.7; Isa 60.13; Ezek 43.7; 1 Chr 28.2). **3:** *His right hand,* God's fighting arm and the symbol of his power and protection is intentionally withheld from Judah (Ex 15.6,12; Isa 41.10; Pss 48.10; 89.13; 98.1). **4:** *Tent,* an old-fashioned

⁵ The Lord has become like an enemy;
　he has destroyed Israel.
He has destroyed all its palaces,
　laid in ruins its strongholds,
and multiplied in daughter Judah
　mourning and lamentation.

⁶ He has broken down his booth like a
　　garden,
　he has destroyed his tabernacle;
the LORD has abolished in Zion
　festival and sabbath,
and in his fierce indignation has spurned
　king and priest.

⁷ The Lord has scorned his altar,
　disowned his sanctuary;
he has delivered into the hand of the
　　enemy
　the walls of her palaces;
a clamor was raised in the house of the
　　LORD
　as on a day of festival.

⁸ The LORD determined to lay in ruins
　the wall of daughter Zion;
he stretched the line;
　he did not withhold his hand from
　　destroying;
he caused rampart and wall to lament;
　they languish together.

⁹ Her gates have sunk into the ground;
　he has ruined and broken her bars;
her king and princes are among the
　　nations;
　guidance is no more,
and her prophets obtain
　no vision from the LORD.

¹⁰ The elders of daughter Zion
　sit on the ground in silence;
they have thrown dust on their heads
　and put on sackcloth;
the young girls of Jerusalem
　have bowed their heads to the ground.

¹¹ My eyes are spent with weeping;
　my stomach churns;
my bile is poured out on the ground
　because of the destruction of my
　　people,
because infants and babes faint
　in the streets of the city.

¹² They cry to their mothers,
　"Where is bread and wine?"
as they faint like the wounded
　in the streets of the city,
as their life is poured out
　on their mothers' bosom.

¹³ What can I say for you, to what compare
　you,
　O daughter Jerusalem?
To what can I liken you, that I may comfort
　you,
　O virgin daughter Zion?
For vast as the sea is your ruin;
　who can heal you?

¹⁴ Your prophets have seen for you
　false and deceptive visions;
they have not exposed your iniquity
　to restore your fortunes,
but have seen oracles for you
　that are false and misleading.

¹⁵ All who pass along the way
　clap their hands at you;

way of referring to the homes in Judah and to the Temple in Jerusalem (cf. 2 Sam 7.6). **6**: *His booth*, a temporary shelter (Job 27.18; Jon 4.5) and also the Temple (Pss 27.5; 76.3). *Like a garden*, the Temple was destroyed easily, as if it were a booth or hut in a garden. **7**: *Clamor*, the exultant crowing of the invading and plundering enemy has replaced the joyful sounds of the crowds coming to the Temple on festivals. **8–10**: We see the towers, walls, and gates disintegrate. The movement is from top to bottom, ending with the inhabitants sitting on the ground in mourning. **8**: *Stretched the line*, like an architect, God made a plan for unbuilding the city (cf. 2 Kings 21.13; Isa 34.11; Jer 31.39; Zech 1.16; Job 38.5). **9**: *Guidance*, Heb "torah."

2.11–19: The narrator's reaction. 11: The narrator's words echo those of Jerusalem in 1.20. *Streets*, broad places near the gates, squares. The babies are fainting and dying in public. **12**: *Where is bread and wine*, that is, the stored up food supplies, the staples. There is no food left anywhere. *Bread*, lit. "grain." *On their mother's bosom*, or, "lap." The mothers are holding their children where they should find comfort (Ruth 4.16) as they

they hiss and wag their heads
    at daughter Jerusalem;
"Is this the city that was called
    the perfection of beauty,
    the joy of all the earth?"

¹⁶ All your enemies
    open their mouths against you;
they hiss, they gnash their teeth,
    they cry: "We have devoured her!
Ah, this is the day we longed for;
    at last we have seen it!"

¹⁷ The LORD has done what he purposed,
    he has carried out his threat;
as he ordained long ago,
    he has demolished without pity;
he has made the enemy rejoice
        over you,
    and exalted the might of your foes.

¹⁸ Cry aloudᵃ to the Lord!
    O wall of daughter Zion!
Let tears stream down like a torrent
    day and night!
Give yourself no rest,
    your eyes no respite!

¹⁹ Arise, cry out in the night,
    at the beginning of the watches!
Pour out your heart like water
    before the presence of the Lord!
Lift your hands to him

for the lives of your children,
who faint for hunger
    at the head of every street.

²⁰ Look, O LORD, and consider!
    To whom have you done this?
Should women eat their offspring,
    the children they have borne?
Should priest and prophet be killed
    in the sanctuary of the Lord?

²¹ The young and the old are lying
    on the ground in the streets;
my young women and my young men
    have fallen by the sword;
in the day of your anger you have killed
        them,
    slaughtering without mercy.

²² You invited my enemies from all around
    as if for a day of festival;
and on the day of the anger of the LORD
    no one escaped or survived;
those whom I bore and reared
    my enemy has destroyed.

3 I am one who has seen affliction
    under the rod of God'sᵇ wrath;
² he has driven and brought me
    into darkness without any light;

ᵃ Cn: Heb *Their heart cried*
ᵇ Heb *his*

starve to death. **15:** *Clap . . . hiss . . . wag*, gestures of surprise and derision. The trope of the passer-by witnessing the shame of the victims and reacting with shock is common and provides an additional perspective to that of Zion and the narrator. *Perfection of beauty*, see Ezek 16.14; 27.3; Ps 50.2. *Joy of all the earth*, see Jer 51.41; Ps 48.2. **16:** The enemies mock and taunt the victims, taking credit for Judah's destruction, which v. 17 ascribes to God. The Babylonians never appear in the book (only Edom is named, in 4.21). **17:** *Ordained long ago*, the decree that if Judah sinned, the Temple would be destroyed and the people exiled from their land (1 Kings 9.6–9). **18:** *Wall*, the physical city should cry out to God on behalf of its people. **19:** *Watches*, the night was divided into three watches (see Ex 14.24; 1 Sam 11.11; Song 3.1–3; 5.7). Nighttime is when suffering seems hardest to bear and when many prayers are offered, with the expectation that God will respond in the morning (cf. Ps 30.5).

2.20–22: Jerusalem's address to God. **20:** *Eat their offspring*, cannibalism was a result of the famine during a siege (4.10; 2 Kings 6.28) and a punishment for violating the covenant (Deut 28.53–57); this is a common trope in describing a siege. It is the reversal of the norm, in which women feed their children. **21–22:** *Slaughtering*, as if preparing meat for food or sacrifice. The idea continues in the next verse, where God invites the enemies *as if for a day of festival* when they would participate in a sacrificial meal in the Temple. *Day of the anger of the LORD*, the time of punishment, like "the day of the LORD," when God will punish those who deserve it (cf. 1.12; 2.1).

3.1–66: The complaint of the one who has seen affliction. The longest and most complex poem of the book, arranged as a triple acrostic: each stanza has three short verses assigned to each successive letter of the alphabet. The logical subdivisions according to content do not correspond to the alphabetic structure,

³ against me alone he turns his hand,
   again and again, all day long.

⁴ He has made my flesh and my skin waste
   away,
   and broken my bones;
⁵ he has besieged and enveloped me
   with bitterness and tribulation;
⁶ he has made me sit in darkness
   like the dead of long ago.

⁷ He has walled me about so that I cannot
   escape;
   he has put heavy chains on me;
⁸ though I call and cry for help,
   he shuts out my prayer;
⁹ he has blocked my ways with hewn stones,
   he has made my paths crooked.

¹⁰ He is a bear lying in wait for me,
   a lion in hiding;
¹¹ he led me off my way and tore me to
   pieces;
   he has made me desolate;
¹² he bent his bow and set me
   as a mark for his arrow.

¹³ He shot into my vitals
   the arrows of his quiver;

¹⁴ I have become the laughingstock of all
   my people,
   the object of their taunt-songs all day
   long.
¹⁵ He has filled me with bitterness,
   he has sated me with wormwood.

¹⁶ He has made my teeth grind on
   gravel,
   and made me cower in ashes;
¹⁷ my soul is bereft of peace;
   I have forgotten what happiness is;
¹⁸ so I say, "Gone is my glory,
   and all that I had hoped for from the
   LORD."

¹⁹ The thought of my affliction and my
   homelessness
   is wormwood and gall!
²⁰ My soul continually thinks of it
   and is bowed down within me.
²¹ But this I call to mind,
   and therefore I have hope:

²² The steadfast love of the LORD never
   ceases,ᵃ
   his mercies never come to an end;

ᵃ Syr Tg: Heb LORD, we are not cut off

with the result that the reader is pulled along from one thought to the next and interrupted by a new stanza in mid-thought. The chapter uses the language of lament and of wisdom or theological reflection on God's punishment and mercy. The mood alternates between despair and hope. The identity of the male speaker has long been debated. Some think he was a historical individual (Jeremiah, Jehoiachin, or Zedekiah have been suggested), but it seems preferable to take him as a literary persona, the counterpart of the female city speaking in 1.12–22. He is a Job-like figure, using some phraseology similar to Job's (especially in vv. 25–39), crying out to God from his suffering, trying to make sense of the terrible event, and to provoke God's response. But unlike Job, this speaker is not successful, for God never answers him.

3.1–20: The lament of the male persona, who appears to be a survivor in exile, or perhaps the collective voice of the people. Verses 1–13 are constructed on the image of God as a bad shepherd who leads his flock into dark and dangerous places (exile), in stark contrast to the image of God as a good shepherd (as in Ps 23). 1: *I am one*, (lit. "I am the man"). Heb "geber" is clearly masculine although NRSV has stripped it of gender. *Rod of God's wrath*, the shepherd's rod, normally an instrument of protection, is here the rod with which God punishes, as in Isa 10.5, where Assyria is the rod of God's wrath. 2: *Driven and brought*, like a flock (cf. Isa 40.11; Ps 78.52–53). 6: *Darkness like the dead*, exile is often compared to darkness, prison, and death. In exile the Judeans were cut off from access to God's Temple, like a dead person. *The dead of long ago*, better, "like the eternally dead," those who have no hope of life. 8: *He shuts out my prayer*, see 3.44n. 10: *Bear . . . lion,* from being a bad shepherd God changes into the dangerous wild animals from whom the shepherd is supposed to protect his flock (cf. David in 1 Sam 17.34–37). 12–13: Instead of shooting at the wild animals, God shoots at the speaker. God is elsewhere a divine archer who shoots disaster from his bow; cf. Deut 32.23–24; Ps 38.2–3; Job 16.12–13. 15: *Bitterness . . . wormwood*, a common symbol of suffering, see 3.19; 4.21; Jer 9.14; Job 9.18. 17: *My soul*, my being or self.

3.21–24: Despair turns to hope in these transitional verses framed by *Therefore I have hope/Therefore I will*

²³ they are new every morning;
   great is your faithfulness.
²⁴ "The LORD is my portion," says my soul,
   "therefore I will hope in him."

²⁵ The LORD is good to those who wait for
   him,
   to the soul that seeks him.
²⁶ It is good that one should wait quietly
   for the salvation of the LORD.
²⁷ It is good for one to bear
   the yoke in youth,
²⁸ to sit alone in silence
   when the Lord has imposed it,
²⁹ to put one's mouth to the dust
   (there may yet be hope),
³⁰ to give one's cheek to the smiter,
   and be filled with insults.

³¹ For the Lord will not
   reject forever.
³² Although he causes grief, he will have
   compassion
   according to the abundance of his
   steadfast love;
³³ for he does not willingly afflict
   or grieve anyone.

³⁴ When all the prisoners of the land
   are crushed under foot,
³⁵ when human rights are perverted
   in the presence of the Most High,
³⁶ when one's case is subverted
   —does the Lord not see it?

³⁷ Who can command and have it done,
   if the Lord has not ordained it?
³⁸ Is it not from the mouth of the Most
   High
   that good and bad come?
³⁹ Why should any who draw breath
   complain
   about the punishment of their sins?

⁴⁰ Let us test and examine our ways,
   and return to the LORD.
⁴¹ Let us lift up our hearts as well as our
   hands
   to God in heaven.
⁴² We have transgressed and rebelled,
   and you have not forgiven.

⁴³ You have wrapped yourself with anger
   and pursued us,
   killing without pity;
⁴⁴ you have wrapped yourself with a cloud
   so that no prayer can pass through.
⁴⁵ You have made us filth and rubbish
   among the peoples.

⁴⁶ All our enemies
   have opened their mouths against us;
⁴⁷ panic and pitfall have come upon us,
   devastation and destruction.
⁴⁸ My eyes flow with rivers of tears
   because of the destruction of my
   people.

⁴⁹ My eyes will flow without ceasing,
   without respite,

hope in him. 22: *Steadfast love . . . mercies . . . faithfulness,* attributes of God representing covenant loyalty (Ex 34.6–7; see also 2 Sam 7.15; Ps 89.2–4).

   3.25–39: Drawing on wisdom thought, the poet finds reasons for hope in the face of suffering. **25–27:** *Good* begins each verse, applied to God and to human patience. Humans must wait for God's merciful help, and in the meantime accept the burden of their suffering (*bear the yoke*). **29:** *Put one's mouth to the dust,* accept God's discipline submissively (cf. Mic 7.17; Ps 72.9). **33:** *Willingly,* better "willfully" (lit. "from his heart"). God does not mete out punishment capriciously. **34–39:** Standard biblical theology: all is ordained by God, who is the source of both good and evil (cf. Job 2.10; Isa 45.7); punishment received is punishment deserved.

   3.40–47: Communal lament. The discourse shifts back to lament, although now in the first-person plural with direct address to God. At the beginning the tone is conciliatory, but then becomes accusatory. **40–41:** As if persuaded by 3.25–29, the speakers call for self-examination, repentance, and contrition. **41:** *Lift up our hearts as well as our hands,* a call for sincerity in repentance, not merely going through the motions of prayer. **42–44:** A devastating turning point: confession of sin does not bring forgiveness. **44:** *Wrapped yourself with a cloud,* the cloud through which God revealed himself at Sinai (Ex 19.16), and which protects the people from fatal direct contact with the divine, is here perceived as a barrier that God erected to prevent prayer from reaching him.

   3.48–66: Individual lament. The first-person singular "I" returns, emphasizing the personal dimension of

⁵⁰ until the Lord from heaven
    looks down and sees.
⁵¹ My eyes cause me grief
    at the fate of all the young women in
        my city.

⁵² Those who were my enemies without
        cause
    have hunted me like a bird;
⁵³ they flung me alive into a pit
    and hurled stones on me;
⁵⁴ water closed over my head;
    I said, "I am lost."

⁵⁵ I called on your name, O Lord,
    from the depths of the pit;
⁵⁶ you heard my plea, "Do not close your ear
    to my cry for help, but give me relief!"
⁵⁷ You came near when I called on you;
    you said, "Do not fear!"

⁵⁸ You have taken up my cause, O Lord,
    you have redeemed my life.
⁵⁹ You have seen the wrong done to me,
        O Lord;
    judge my cause.
⁶⁰ You have seen all their malice,
    all their plots against me.

⁶¹ You have heard their taunts, O Lord,
    all their plots against me.

⁶² The whispers and murmurs of my
        assailants
    are against me all day long.
⁶³ Whether they sit or rise—see,
    I am the object of their taunt-songs.

⁶⁴ Pay them back for their deeds, O Lord,
    according to the work of their hands!
⁶⁵ Give them anguish of heart;
    your curse be on them!
⁶⁶ Pursue them in anger and destroy
        them
    from under the Lord's heavens.

4 How the gold has grown dim,
    how the pure gold is changed!
The sacred stones lie scattered
    at the head of every street.

² The precious children of Zion,
    worth their weight in fine gold—
how they are reckoned as earthen pots,
    the work of a potter's hands!

³ Even the jackals offer the breast
    and nurse their young,
but my people has become cruel,
    like the ostriches in the wilderness.

⁴ The tongue of the infant sticks
    to the roof of its mouth for thirst;

the suffering. **53:** *Pit*, a cistern for holding water or for imprisoning people (cf. Jer 38.6), and also the grave or the netherworld (Sheol; cf. Isa 14.15; Pss 30.3; 88.4). **54:** *Water closed over my head*, the water in the cistern, but also a metaphor for desperation (see Jon 2.6–7; 2 Sam 22.5–6 = Ps 18.5–6). **56:** The verbs translated in the past tense here and in the following verses probably express a wish for the future. **58–60:** Legal language. The poet casts himself as a plaintiff in court where God will judge him innocent and the enemy guilty (cf. 3.34–36). **63:** *Whether they sit or rise*, whatever they do, at all times. **64–66:** A call for retribution; see 1.22. **66:** *From under the Lord's heavens*, there is no place in God's world for the wicked.

4.1–22: The community under siege in Jerusalem. The physical and social effects of starvation are graphically described. The progression is realistic: first the children and then the adults. Degradation and debasement is the main theme; those once well-off are now destitute, those once healthy are dying or dead. Much of the effect is achieved by the contrast in color, the "before" and the "after," as the rich palette of the colors of wealth and health (gold, scarlet, white, red, sapphire in vv. 1,2,5,7,8) is drained away to blackness. Heat is another dimension, the unrelenting heat of the summer siege, the dry and blackened skin (v. 8), the parched mouths (v. 4), God's burning anger setting fire to Zion (v. 11). There is no shade, no protection provided by God or the king (v. 20). Like chs 1 and 2, this chapter contains a single alphabetic acrostic and opens with the word *How* (see 1.1n).

4.1–10: The suffering of the siege. 1: *Sacred stones*, or gems, and gold, though appearing to be meant literally, are metaphors for the children (v. 2). **2:** *Earthen pots* were cheap and easily broken and discarded, while gold was an expensive and durable material. The children are likened to throw-away objects because no one can care for them. **3:** *Jackals*, considered despicable scavengers. *Ostriches*, thought to be cruel and neglectful parents (cf. Job 39.13–18). *My people has become cruel*, not willingly but from desperation; they are no longer able

the children beg for food,
　but no one gives them anything.

⁵ Those who feasted on delicacies
　perish in the streets;
those who were brought up in purple
　cling to ash heaps.

⁶ For the chastisement[a] of my people has
　been greater
　than the punishment[b] of Sodom,
which was overthrown in a moment,
　though no hand was laid on it.[c]

⁷ Her princes were purer than snow,
　whiter than milk;
their bodies were more ruddy than coral,
　their hair[c] like sapphire.[d]

⁸ Now their visage is blacker than soot;
　they are not recognized in the streets.
Their skin has shriveled on their bones;
　it has become as dry as wood.

⁹ Happier were those pierced by the sword
　than those pierced by hunger,
whose life drains away, deprived
　of the produce of the field.

¹⁰ The hands of compassionate women
　have boiled their own children;
they became their food
　in the destruction of my people.

¹¹ The LORD gave full vent to his wrath;
　he poured out his hot anger,
and kindled a fire in Zion
　that consumed its foundations.

¹² The kings of the earth did not believe,
　nor did any of the inhabitants of the
　world,
that foe or enemy could enter
　the gates of Jerusalem.

¹³ It was for the sins of her prophets
　and the iniquities of her priests,
who shed the blood of the righteous
　in the midst of her.

¹⁴ Blindly they wandered through the
　streets,
　so defiled with blood
that no one was able
　to touch their garments.

¹⁵ "Away! Unclean!" people shouted at
　them;
　"Away! Away! Do not touch!"
So they became fugitives and wanderers;
　it was said among the nations,
　"They shall stay here no longer."

¹⁶ The LORD himself has scattered them,
　he will regard them no more;
no honor was shown to the priests,
　no favor to the elders.

¹⁷ Our eyes failed, ever watching
　vainly for help;
we were watching eagerly
　for a nation that could not save.

a　Or *iniquity*
b　Or *sin*
c　Meaning of Heb uncertain
d　Or *lapis lazuli*

to care for their children. **4:** *The tongue . . . sticks to the roof of its mouth*, an expression meaning that no sound is uttered (Ezek 3.26; Ps 137.6; Job 29.10). The children are too weak even to cry. **6:** *Sodom*, whose punishment was legendary (Gen 19.24–25), was overthrown in an instant, whereas Jerusalem was made to suffer long agony. **7–8:** The colors associated with vigor have disappeared; now people are dried up. **10:** See 2.20n.

4.11–16: God's wrathful punishment. 12: The Judean belief in the inviolability of Zion, that God would never permit his city to be destroyed (see Pss 46.5; 48.3–8), is here attributed even to foreigners, a creative use of the "passers-by" trope (see 2.15n). **13–14:** *Prophets . . . priests*, those most associated with purity and vision are described as the most blind and defiled. **15:** *Away! Unclean!* The public warning that lepers must give so that no one will come in contact with them (Lev 13.45–46).

4.17–22: The voice of the community. As in 3.40–47, the speaker is "we," describing the final days of the siege and the fall of Jerusalem. **17:** *For a nation that could not save*, most likely Egypt, the major power opposed to Babylonia (see Jer 37.5–10; Isa 30.7). Contrary to what prophets like Jeremiah advised, Judah relied on help

18 They dogged our steps
    so that we could not walk in our streets;
our end drew near; our days were
        numbered;
    for our end had come.

19 Our pursuers were swifter
    than the eagles in the heavens;
they chased us on the mountains,
    they lay in wait for us in the wilderness.

20 The LORD's anointed, the breath of our
        life,
    was taken in their pits—
the one of whom we said, "Under his
        shadow
    we shall live among the nations."

21 Rejoice and be glad, O daughter Edom,
    you that live in the land of Uz;
but to you also the cup shall pass;
    you shall become drunk and strip
        yourself bare.

22 The punishment of your iniquity,
    O daughter Zion, is accomplished,
    he will keep you in exile no longer;

but your iniquity, O daughter Edom, he
        will punish,
    he will uncover your sins.

5 Remember, O LORD, what has befallen
        us;
    look, and see our disgrace!
2 Our inheritance has been turned over to
        strangers,
    our homes to aliens.
3 We have become orphans,
        fatherless;
    our mothers are like widows.
4 We must pay for the water we drink;
    the wood we get must be bought.
5 With a yoke[a] on our necks we are hard
        driven;
    we are weary, we are given no rest.
6 We have made a pact with[b] Egypt and
        Assyria,
    to get enough bread.
7 Our ancestors sinned; they are no
        more,
    and we bear their iniquities.

a Symmachus: Heb lacks *With a yoke*
b Heb *have given the hand to*

from another nation, not from God. **19:** Perhaps an allusion to the aftermath of the fall of Jerusalem, when Zedekiah and his soldiers fled the city and were pursued and captured by the Babylonian army (2 Kings 25.4–5). **20:** *The LORD's anointed, the breath of our life, . . . under his shadow,* royal epithets (1 Sam 24.7; 2 Sam 1.14,16; Pss 17.8; 91.1). The reference is most likely to Zedekiah, the last king of Judah, whose defeat signals the failure of the Davidic dynasty to protect the people. **21–22:** A curse on Edom, a neighbor of Judah who was a vassal to Babylonia. Edom is often singled out for negative comment in postexilic literature (Ezek 35; Ob 11; Ps 137.7). Edom is synonymous with Esau (Gen 36.1) and therefore the traditional enemy or rival of Jacob/Israel (=Judah). **21:** *Rejoice and be glad,* an ironic statement. *Daughter Edom,* an epithet parallel to "Daughter Zion." *Uz,* a region in southern Jordan or northwestern Arabia, often connected with Edom (Gen 36.28; Jer 25.20; Job 1.1; 1 Chr 1.42). *The cup,* of God's wrath (see 3.15; Jer 25.15–29; 49.12; 51.7; Hab 2.15–16), which will make Edom drunk. *Strip yourself bare,* expose your nakedness and be shamed as Jerusalem was (1.8–10). **22:** The most hopeful sentiment in the book (cf. Joel 4).

    5.1–22: A prayer of the survivors in Judah in the aftermath of the destruction. A call to God to notice the abject state of his people in Judah and to restore them to their previous condition. The chapter resembles communal laments and also penitential prayers of the Second Temple period. **1:** The plea to God to *remember* is framed by "Why have you forgotten" in v. 20. *Remember* means "to pay mind to" and "forget" means "to ignore." **2–3:** The breakdown of the institution of the family. **2:** *Our inheritance,* ancestral land was to be kept within the family. Here the reference may be to individual real estate or to the country as a whole. *Strangers,* those outside the family. *Aliens,* foreigners. **3:** *Fatherless,* an orphan is a person without a father. Widows and orphans are defenseless and required special protection (e.g., Isa 1.23; Ps 68.5). **4–5:** Harsh economic conditions; rampant inflation. *Water* and *wood* are basic necessities. **6:** *Egypt and Assyria,* traditional superpowers and enemy-invaders of Israel, are often found in parallelism even when, as in this period, Assyria was long gone (Isa 52.4; Zech 10.10–11). **7:** *Iniquities* also means "punishment." Earlier sinful generations did not suffer punishment like the current generation. Did the current generation also see itself as sinful and deserving of punishment, or do

⁸ Slaves rule over us;
  there is no one to deliver us from their
    hand.
⁹ We get our bread at the peril of our lives,
  because of the sword in the wilderness.
¹⁰ Our skin is black as an oven
  from the scorching heat of famine.
¹¹ Women are raped in Zion,
  virgins in the towns of Judah.
¹² Princes are hung up by their hands;
  no respect is shown to the elders.
¹³ Young men are compelled to grind,
  and boys stagger under loads of wood.
¹⁴ The old men have left the city gate,
  the young men their music.
¹⁵ The joy of our hearts has ceased;
  our dancing has been turned to mourning.
¹⁶ The crown has fallen from our head;

woe to us, for we have sinned!
¹⁷ Because of this our hearts are sick,
  because of these things our eyes have
    grown dim:
¹⁸ because of Mount Zion, which lies
    desolate;
  jackals prowl over it.

¹⁹ But you, O LORD, reign forever;
  your throne endures to all generations.
²⁰ Why have you forgotten us completely?
  Why have you forsaken us these many
    days?
²¹ Restore us to yourself, O LORD, that we
    may be restored;
  renew our days as of old—
²² unless you have utterly rejected us,
  and are angry with us beyond measure.

they think they are paying unfairly for the sins of their ancestors? The verse is ambiguous. **8:** *Slaves rule over us*, previously Judah was ruled by its own king but now it is governed by the lackeys of the Babylonian king (cf. 2 Kings 25.24). **9:** Food is scarce. *The sword in the wilderness*, a difficult phrase which may mean that scavenging in the countryside was dangerous because of marauders. Alternatively, it is a metaphor for the dehydration and starvation of the inhabitants of Judah, who suffer famine that resembles the famine of the siege (v. 10 and cf. 4.8). **11–14:** Social order has disintegrated; violence and indignity abound. Women are shamed sexually; leaders are shamed publicly; young and old are denied their proper calling and subjected to abusive labor. **12:** *Hung up*, impalement of corpses was a form of public shaming (Deut 21.22; Josh 10.26–27; 1 Sam 31.10). *By their hands*, probably meaning by the hands of the enemy (see v. 8), since victims were not generally hung by their hands. A better interpretation may be that this is not a form of execution or corpse display, but a form of torture and humiliation of the living, like putting a person in the stocks. **13:** *To grind*, a task normally done by women (Ex 11.5; Isa 47.2; Job 31.10) or slaves (Judg 16.21) and therefore demeaning if undertaken by a man. The Hebrew is "pull the millstone," which may refer to a large milling operation in which a donkey would normally pull the heavy millstone, making this line parallel in meaning to the next one. *Boys stagger under loads of wood*, humans are made to do the work of animals, beasts of burden. **14:** *City gate*, the location of business and legal transactions (Ruth 4.1; Job 29.7). **16:** *The crown*, the emblem of kingship, the Davidic dynasty. Or perhaps the crenellated walls of the city. *We have sinned*, an admission of guilt (cf. 3.42 and 5.7n). **18:** *Jackals*, or "foxes," proverbial inhabitants of ruined cities (see 4.3; Ezek 13.4; Isa 34.11–17; Zeph 2.13–15). **19:** A strong theological statement: Even though God's earthly throne, the Temple, lies in ruins, God continues to reign forever. **21:** A wish that the former relationship with God be reinstated. **22:** The book ends in tragic despair, with the suggestion that God's rejection of the people continues. *Unless* is difficult in the Hebrew; perhaps it is better translated "but instead," or even more literally, "for if," suggesting that the conclusion of the conditional clause has been withheld, thus perpetuating indefinitely the divine rejection with which the book ends.

EZEKIEL

NAME

The book is named for the prophet to whom it is attributed. His name, "Ezekiel," means "God strengthens." God's strengthening turns out to be imperative for Ezekiel, whose rebellious audience is characterized by ingrained defiance and stubbornness (see 2.5n. [rebellious house]; 3.8–9n. [hard]).

LOCATION IN CANON

Ezekiel is the last of the three major prophets, the others being Isaiah and Jeremiah. Their books are arranged in presumed chronological order: the first part of the book of Isaiah focuses on the prophet Isaiah's ministry in Jerusalem in the late eighth century BCE; the prophet Jeremiah was active in the late seventh and early sixth centuries; and Ezekiel's prophecies follow those of Jeremiah, his older contemporary. (In many English Bibles, following the order of the Septuagint [LXX], Lamentations comes between Jeremiah and Ezekiel.) According to the Talmud and in some manuscripts there was another order for the major prophets, in which Ezekiel's combined message of judgment and salvation appears between Jeremiah's predominant tone of sorrow and Isaiah's emphatic promises.

AUTHORSHIP

The only information we have about the prophet comes from the book itself. In this collection, God's divine prerogative overshadows and submerges the prophetic personality. Since Ezekiel is a literary character within his own prophecies, his shocking and mystifying actions must often be interpreted in a highly symbolic and theological manner, not necessarily as a window into the prophet's actual personality.

Some facts seem established. Ezekiel was a Judean exile in Babylonia, living in the deportee settlement of Tel-abib (see 3.15n.). His prophetic career stretched from 593 to at least 571 BCE. The prophet and his school— the followers who edited and preserved his prophecies—were members of a lineage of priests in Israel known as the Zadokites (see 1.1–3n.; 44.15–31n.).

At the time of Ezekiel's exile, the Zadokites controlled the Israelite high priesthood and held power at the Jerusalem Temple. They took a specific priestly theology with them into exile, preserved elsewhere in the Hebrew Bible as a source of the Pentateuch known as the "Holiness School." The priestly theology of the Holiness School thoroughly infuses the book of Ezekiel.

DATE OF COMPOSITION AND HISTORICAL CONTEXT

Ezekiel wrote his prophecies, and his followers edited, expanded, and preserved them, in the sixth century BCE in Babylonia, during the exile of the Judeans from their homeland. The exile thus forms the historical context of the book, and at several points, particularly in the allegory in 17.1–24, Ezekiel refers to the Babylonian subjugation of Judah.

The Babylonians under Nebuchadrezzar II (ruled 605–562 BCE) defeated the Egyptians in 605 at the battle of Carchemish. The Egyptians had allied with the great Assyrian empire, which the Babylonians destroyed between 614 and 609. Although these victories made Babylonia the leading political power in Syria-Palestine, including the territory of Judah, the Judeans, often acting in concert with other neighboring states, eventually rebelled. The Babylonians, in an escalating response to the continued efforts of the Judeans to throw them off, exiled the Judeans in two phases, spaced about a decade apart. They first besieged Jerusalem in 597 during the reign of King Jehoiakim, who died during the siege. When his successor, his son Jehoiachin, surrendered to the Babylonians, he, along with many of the Judean ruling class, was exiled to Babylon. The Babylonians installed a puppet king, Zedekiah; when he, too, attempted to rebel, they destroyed Jerusalem and the Temple in 586, and exiled much of the population, except the poorest, to Babylon.

Ezekiel was among the first group of exiles, taken to Babylonia in 597. Even so, he remained well informed about events in Judah, and his prophecies concern both the exiles and those who remained in Judah. He could address both communities as a single entity, since they were in frequent contact with each other, and both were passionately concerned about the fate of Jerusalem. Neither group accepted Ezekiel's indictment of their guilt or believed his prophecies about Jerusalem's coming destruction. After the destruction took place, the prophet's words turned to themes of renewed hope, regeneration, and blessing.

LITERARY HISTORY

The prophet and his followers composed the book in writing and preserved it for the specific purpose of instructing readers at a later time. The written composition and the careful preservation of Ezekiel contrast with much of the other prophetic literature in the Bible, which was spoken directly to a contemporaneous audience. Many of the words of prophets, such as Isaiah, were written down only a considerable time after they had been spoken; therefore they could be, and often were, modified to adapt them to situations that arose in later times. In Ezekiel, however, there are clear indications of an originally written composition and of an early intention to preserve the text. For instance, the thoroughgoing chronological notations show that Ezekiel and his followers took great care to demonstrate the timeliness and veracity of Ezekiel's oracles, and thereby their authority as prophecy. This care for the written text and its accurate transmission, as well as for the preservation of authoritative traditions such as the Holiness School material (see Interpretation section), mark a breakthrough in the development of written scripture in Israel, and therefore help us to understand the historical processes that created the biblical canon over the centuries.

STRUCTURE AND CONTENTS

The book of Ezekiel is complex, but fortunately its organization and outline are agreeably simple. Chapters 1–24 are set before the fall of Jerusalem and are largely prophecies of doom against the city and against Judah. An extended body of material on Ezekiel's call to prophesy begins this section in chs 1–3. Chapters 25–32 are prophecies against foreign nations, forming a bridge between Ezekiel's initial message of doom and his ultimate message of hope. The hope comes in the prophecies of restoration, chs 33–48, dating from the time after Jerusalem's fall. Clearly the capture and destruction of Jerusalem in 586 was the critical moment in Ezekiel's prophetic career. The prophecies of restoration include an apocalyptic passage (chs 38–39) and an extended blueprint for the restored Temple and land (chs 40–48).

INTERPRETATION

Ezekiel and his editors were Jerusalem priests at the center of Judean society, and as such were proponents of "Zion theology," the traditions that emphasized God's choice of Zion (Jerusalem), the holy city, as his home, and the protection that resulted from this choice (see 2 Sam 7.4–17; Pss 46; 132) both for the city and for the Davidic dynasty whose capital it was. The exile of the Judean elite and the destruction of Jerusalem directly challenged this theology, since they called into question God's promises to Zion of eternal protection. Ezekiel answered these challenges with cosmic, eschatological, and apocalyptic visions of a rebuilt Zion that will fulfill God's promises despite the fall of the earthly Jerusalem (see 1.22–25n.,26–28n.; 37.28n.; 38.12n.; 43.7n.; 48.35n.). In these visions particularly, Ezekiel anticipated much that was yet to come in the biblical writings, including later developments of apocalypticism (see especially Dan 7–12 and, in the New Testament, the book of Revelation).

The specific language and laws of the priests and the traditions of the Temple heavily influenced Ezekiel as a Zadokite. A significant body of these traditions, the "Holiness School" (HS) can be found in the Pentateuch. (Multiple references to the Pentateuch in this introduction and in the annotations that precede the notation [HS] are included in this body of material, except where noted.) The Holiness School material extends beyond the confines of Lev 17–26 (known as the "Holiness Code" or "Holiness Collection"), and includes other parts of the Pentateuch often identified as belonging to the Priestly source (P). The relationship between God and Israel assumed by the Holiness School is that of a vassal-covenant (see Lev 26.9,15,25), a type of agreement in which guarantees on one side are specifically linked to responsibilities on the other, with significant sanctions if the responsibilities of vassalage are not met. For Ezekiel this covenant form proved invaluable in interpreting the exile, since it allowed for the possibility that defilement, injustice, and covenant infidelity on Israel's part could lead to punishments, including exile, without annulling God's eternal promises to Israel (Lev 26.42).

In his allegory of the unfaithful wife (ch 16), the prophet rehearses the failed history of the Israelites' vassal-covenant with God. As in a marriage, with all its mutual obligations, God "pledged myself to you and entered into a covenant with you" (16.8). Because Jerusalem proves an adulterous wife, however, God determines to divorce her and expose her to be stoned (16.40; cf. Lev 20.10 [HS]). Jerusalem is doomed, because the people have "despised the oath, breaking the covenant" (16.59; cf. 17.19).

For the Holiness School, God's land is a delicately organized structure of holiness, subject to overthrow through the spread of uncleanness and bloodshed. It is like an uneasy stomach, ready to vomit out those who defile it (Lev 18.24–28). Ezekiel, in 36.16–19, insists that just such regurgitation has now happened. The land has fallen victim to defilement, and God's people have lost possession of it just as the Holiness School warned they would. Defiling any part of the land, God's holy territory, constitutes an assault of impurity on God's shrine (Lev 15.31; 19.30; 26.2; Num 5.3; 19.13; Ezek 8.6; 9.9). If the pollution of the sanctuary becomes willful and chronic, it will eventually force out God's glory (Num 35.34; Ezek 10.19; 11.22–23). Exposed to catastrophic judgment, the people become cut off (Ezek 37.11).

Despite Israel's lack of obedience to the covenant, Ezekiel prophesies a renewed covenantal relationship after the exile (16.60,62). God will guarantee this new vassal-covenant's success by transplanting new obedient hearts into the people (11.19–20; 16.60; 36.26–28; 37.23–27). Under God's new plan, the people will "follow my statutes and keep my ordinances and obey them. Then they shall be my people, and I will be their God" (11.20; cf. 36.27; Lev 26.3 [HS]).

The Holiness School stresses the unique sacredness of the people and land of Israel, in the midst of which dwells the glory of the LORD. This sacredness includes not only ritual and worship but also morality and social justice. The tangible dwelling of God's glory in the Temple at the center of Israel brings sanctity to all people and groups arrayed around it. It means the realization of Lev 20.26, where God proclaims: "You shall be holy to me; for I the LORD am holy, and I have separated you from the other peoples to be mine."

Since Israel is so intimately associated with God in this theology, the people must constantly grow in personal and collective holiness through their interaction with the divine presence (Ezek 11.12; 20.12; 37.28; Lev 11.44–45; 19.2; 20.7,26 [HS]). God's people, in Ezekiel's ideal world, emulate the holiness of God that sojourns in their midst (37.27; 43.9; cf. Ex 25.8; 29.45–46; 40.34; Lev 26.11; Num 5.3; 35.34 [HS]). From the midst of Israel, God radiates the divine holiness out to the entire land and to every sector of society (37.28; cf. Ex 31.13; Lev 21.15,23; 22.32 [HS]).

GUIDE TO READING

The prophecies in the book of Ezekiel are among the most fascinating and puzzling writings in the Bible. The prophet expresses his thought through a variety of literary forms, including symbolic action reports, visions, allegories, denunciations, and legal arguments. He sometimes uses bizarre or extreme imagery and elaborates it to an almost excessive point. He has inspired fear, awe, and wonder in readers because he attempts not merely to name but also to embody God's sovereignty, holiness, and mystery in words that come close to the limits of expression.

At first this variety, intricacy, and elaboration can seem confusing. It is easy to get lost in Ezekiel's images and forget his larger concerns; it is easy as well to pick out striking passages and ignore the context of the book as a whole. But Ezekiel makes a coherent effort to deal with profound and difficult issues, and readers should honor this effort by attending to the full sweep of the book in all its profundity. Ezekiel's book has been carefully put together and preserved for the instruction of later readers.

Ezekiel's character as a literary text makes it a complex book to read and interpret. Much of the other prophetic material of the Bible, as oral literature, generally uses less elaborate forms; Ezekiel, however, is made up of intricate, deliberately composed literary creations. Although some scholars have viewed such literary ornamentation and intricacy as indicating confused layers of literary growth, more recently scholars have argued for literary integrity in the texts, even when the final form has resulted from a process of transmission and editing. One of the characteristic features of the book is the frequent repetition of key words or phrases, such as "mortal" (literally, "son of man"), "for the sake of my holy name," and "so that you/they will know that I am the LORD." Important aspects of the theology of Ezekiel are reinforced by the repetition of these and other formulas.

The style of Ezekiel does not always render reality by direct representation. Instead, it probes behind or beyond observable things and events, using metaphors and mythic poetry to portray the underlying structure of existence or the transcendent realities beneath both plain sensory observation and historical records. The visions in Ezekiel show both inner and outer realities, going beyond or abolishing normal sensory and temporal bounds.

Because of these literary qualities, reading Ezekiel requires a sophisticated approach, in order to avoid mistaking some of the descriptions for historical events, observable behaviors, or factual reports. For example, some interpretations of Ezekiel's behavior take it as evidence of a disoriented or abnormal personality. But the descriptions of these acts—such as muteness (3.22–27), holding prolonged, agonizing postures (4.4–8), and a failure to mourn (24.15–27)—are not evidence of psychological illness but are instead literary images that have rich theological import. The book portrays Ezekiel engaging in bizarre and disturbing behavior in order to provoke recollection of preceding scripture and intense theological reflection. A profound reorientation in the relationship of God and Israel is imminent, the authors believe, and they ask their audience to detect radical implications for life and faith in the metaphorical and parabolic character of their descriptions.

Stephen L. Cook

1 In the thirtieth year, in the fourth month, on the fifth day of the month, as I was among the exiles by the river Chebar, the heavens were opened, and I saw visions of God. ² On the fifth day of the month (it was the fifth year of the exile of King Jehoiachin), ³ the word of the LORD came to the priest Ezekiel son of Buzi, in the land of the Chaldeans by the river Chebar; and the hand of the LORD was on him there.

⁴ As I looked, a stormy wind came out of the north: a great cloud with brightness around it and fire flashing forth continually, and in the middle of the fire, something like gleaming amber. ⁵ In the middle of it was something like four living creatures. This was their appearance: they were of human form. ⁶ Each had four faces, and each of them had four wings. ⁷ Their legs were straight, and the soles of their feet were like the sole of a calf's foot; and they sparkled like burnished bronze. ⁸ Under their wings on their four sides they had human hands. And the four had their faces and their wings thus: ⁹ their

1.1–3.27: The call of Ezekiel. 1.1–3: Superscription. Ezekiel was a Zadokite *priest* (v. 3; 4.5–6n.; 44.15–31n.), steeped in the theological traditions of Zion and of the Holiness School (see Introduction). Despite being a deportee, he never loses his priestly identity (cf. 43.12n.), although many priestly tasks would be impossible for him in exile away from Jerusalem. *The thirtieth year,* probably Ezekiel's own age. At the age for assuming his duties at the Jerusalem Temple (Num 4.3 [HS]), Ezekiel sought solitude outside his settlement (see 3.14–15) to reflect on what course his life might instead take in exile. *Fifth day* of the *fourth month . . . fifth year of the exile* would be July 31, 593 BCE. This would make Ezekiel fifty years old in 573 when he envisioned the ideal Temple at the end of his book (40.1n.), so his career fits the normal twenty-year span of a priest's active service (Num 4.3,23,30 [HS]). *Chebar,* a canal near Nippur, providing artificial irrigation from the Euphrates. It is mentioned also in fifth-century Babylonian documents. **3:** The name *Ezekiel* means "God strengthens." *Hand of the LORD* (3.14,22; 8.1; 33.22; 37.1; 40.1), a metaphor highlighting how God is about to seize the prophet, exercising control over his person, so that he will undergo the same types of divine compulsions and ecstatic trances experienced by Israel's early prophets, such as Elijah and Elisha (1 Kings 18.46; 2 Kings 3.15). The prophetic narratives of Ezekiel, like the prophetic legends of the books of Kings, depict stupendous, wondrous events in a manner intended to enliven readers' imaginations. *Chaldeans,* Babylonians.

1.4–28a: The throne-chariot vision. Cf. the imagery in 1 Kings 22.19–22; Isa 6.1–9. The first two-thirds of Ezekiel's vision of God describes the creatures and wheels below the platform supporting God's throne. In Ezekiel's theology of God's transcendence, God is clearly far removed from earthly perception. A graduated, spatial system of layered holiness with wheels, heavenly creatures, and a crystalline expanse separates the prophet from the divine presence. **4:** *Stormy wind . . . cloud . . .* and *fire* are phenomena often associated with the appearance of God (see Ps 18.8–12; Nah 1.3), as are "the sound of mighty waters" and "thunder" (v.24; see also 43.2; Ps 29.3). *Brightness . . . fire flashing forth continually,* as in the Holiness School, God's glory appears as a brilliant, fiery radiance (Ex 24.17; 40.38; Num 16.35, all HS). *Something like,* Ezekiel struggles to find words to express transcendent reality. **5–14:** The *living creatures* are later identified as cherubim (10.15,20), guardians of God's throne (see Ex 25.18–22; 1 Kings 6.23–28), namely winged, human-headed lions or bulls exhibiting the qualities of mobility, intelligence, and strength. Uncharacteristically, the creatures Ezekiel sees have four faces

wings touched one another; each of them moved straight ahead, without turning as they moved. [10] As for the appearance of their faces: the four had the face of a human being, the face of a lion on the right side, the face of an ox on the left side, and the face of an eagle; [11] such were their faces. Their wings were spread out above; each creature had two wings, each of which touched the wing of another, while two covered their bodies. [12] Each moved straight ahead; wherever the spirit would go, they went, without turning as they went. [13] In the middle of[a] the living creatures there was something that looked like burning coals of fire, like torches moving to and fro among the living creatures; the fire was bright, and lightning issued from the fire. [14] The living creatures darted to and fro, like a flash of lightning.

[15] As I looked at the living creatures, I saw a wheel on the earth beside the living creatures, one for each of the four of them.[b] [16] As for the appearance of the wheels and their construction: their appearance was like the gleaming of beryl; and the four had the same form, their construction being something like a wheel within a wheel. [17] When they moved, they moved in any of the four directions without veering as they moved. [18] Their rims were tall and awesome, for the rims of all four were full of eyes all around. [19] When the living creatures moved, the wheels moved beside them; and when the living creatures rose from the earth, the wheels rose. [20] Wherever the spirit would go, they went, and the wheels rose along with them; for the spirit of the living creatures was in the wheels.

[21] When they moved, the others moved; when they stopped, the others stopped; and when they rose from the earth, the wheels rose along with them; for the spirit of the living creatures was in the wheels.

[22] Over the heads of the living creatures there was something like a dome, shining like crystal,[c] spread out above their heads. [23] Under the dome their wings were stretched out straight, one toward another; and each of the creatures had two wings covering its body. [24] When they moved, I heard the sound of their wings like the sound of mighty waters, like the thunder of the Almighty,[d] a sound of tumult like the sound of an army; when they stopped, they let down their wings. [25] And there came a voice from above the dome over their heads; when they stopped, they let down their wings.

[26] And above the dome over their heads there was something like a throne, in appearance like sapphire;[e] and seated above the likeness of a throne was something that seemed like a human form. [27] Upward from what appeared like the loins I saw something like gleaming amber, something that looked like fire enclosed all around; and downward from what looked like the loins I saw something that looked like fire, and there was a splendor all around. [28] Like the bow in a cloud on a rainy day, such was the appearance of

a   Gk OL: Heb *And the appearance of*
b   Heb *of their faces*
c   Gk: Heb *like the awesome crystal*
d   Traditional rendering of Heb *Shaddai*
e   Or *lapis lazuli*

(v. 10). **13:** *Torches,* cf. Gen 15.17. **15–21:** *The four . . . wheels* (cf. the four faces of the creatures) to God's throne are a crucial element in Ezekiel's reconciling his central priestly belief that God had chosen and dwelled in Zion with the earthly Zion's coming destruction by the Babylonians (see Introduction). Its wheels mean that the real, cosmic Zion-throne has omnidirectional mobility and is not tied down to earthly Jerusalem. See also 1.26–28n. **18:** *Full of eyes,* symbolic of omniscience (10.12; Zech 4.2,5,10). **22–25:** *A dome,* referring to the cosmic firmament of Gen 1.6–8, which separates earth and heaven. Jerusalem and its Temple mount symbolize the cosmic mountain where heaven and earth intersect at the dome. **26–28:** Thus the LORD was still really enthroned atop the cosmos, even though Jerusalem, the symbol of God's cosmic dwelling (Pss 26.8; 63.2; 102.16), was to be destroyed by the Babylonians. **26:** *Seemed like a human form,* Ezekiel provides a rather humanlike image of God in keeping with the imagery of the Holiness School; the Mesopotamian god Ashur can also be depicted as a human figure with a glowing upper torso and a flaming lower body. Other biblical traditions, such as those in Isa 40–66 and in the Priestly Torah, would be aghast that Ezekiel would dare associate God with any sort of likeness or appearance (see Isa 40.18,25; 46.5). **28:** *Appearance of the likeness,* the qualified language again emphasizes God's transcendence and cosmic power (see 1.4n.). God's self is three levels removed from Ezekiel's

the splendor all around. This was the appearance of the likeness of the glory of the LORD.

When I saw it, I fell on my face, and I heard the voice of someone speaking.

2 He said to me: O mortal,[a] stand up on your feet, and I will speak with you. [2] And when he spoke to me, a spirit entered into me and set me on my feet; and I heard him speaking to me. [3] He said to me, Mortal, I am sending you to the people of Israel, to a nation[b] of rebels who have rebelled against me; they and their ancestors have transgressed against me to this very day. [4] The descendants are impudent and stubborn. I am sending you to them, and you shall say to them, "Thus says the Lord GOD." [5] Whether they hear or refuse to hear (for they are a rebellious house), they shall know that there has been a prophet among them. [6] And you, O mortal, do not be afraid of them, and do not be afraid of their words, though briers and thorns surround you and you live among scorpions; do not be afraid of their words, and do not be dismayed at their looks, for they are a rebellious house. [7] You shall speak my words to them, whether they hear or refuse to hear; for they are a rebellious house.

[8] But you, mortal, hear what I say to you; do not be rebellious like that rebellious house; open your mouth and eat what I give

you. [9] I looked, and a hand was stretched out to me, and a written scroll was in it. [10] He spread it before me; it had writing on the front and on the back, and written on it were words of lamentation and mourning and woe.

3 He said to me, O mortal, eat what is offered to you; eat this scroll, and go, speak to the house of Israel. [2] So I opened my mouth, and he gave me the scroll to eat. [3] He said to me, Mortal, eat this scroll that I give you and fill your stomach with it. Then I ate it; and in my mouth it was as sweet as honey.

[4] He said to me: Mortal, go to the house of Israel and speak my very words to them. [5] For you are not sent to a people of obscure speech and difficult language, but to the house of Israel— [6] not to many peoples of obscure speech and difficult language, whose words you cannot understand. Surely, if I sent you to them, they would listen to you. [7] But the house of Israel will not listen to you, for they are not willing to listen to me; because all the house of Israel have a hard forehead and a stubborn heart. [8] See, I have made your face hard against their faces, and

a   Or *son of man*; Heb *ben adam* (and so throughout the book when Ezekiel is addressed)

b   Syr: Heb *to nations*

description of God. *The glory of the LORD* is not God's self, but divine holiness made present, tangible, and accessible; see further 10.1–22n. It is Israel's divinely appointed role to receive this holiness, be transformed by it, and then reflect it back to God.

1.28b–3.27: Ezekiel's commissioning. The length of this section helps buttress Ezekiel's authority in the face of opposition and perhaps reflects his own resistance to God's commissioning. 1.28b–2.8a: Ezekiel is commissioned in a series of addresses. 1:28b: *Fell on my face*, a reaction of awe, and a gesture of submission to authority (also 3.23; 43.3). 2.1: *Mortal* (Heb "ben adam," see textual note *a*), a member of the category of "humanity." Ezekiel emphasizes that God and the divine realm tower above this category; the idiom occurs ninety-three times in the book. Yet in Ezekiel's Holiness School theology God brings the holy realm of the creator and the profane realm of creatures into permanent contact. 2: *Spirit* (see 3.12,14,24), a vigorous empowerment that Ezekiel experiences at receiving God's word. 3: *Transgressed*, violated the terms of the covenant with God of the Holiness School (Lev 26.9,15,25). In this type of covenant, there are punishments for disobedience: Israel can forfeit its status as God's people on God's land. 5: *Rebellious house*, a phrase unique to Ezekiel (2.5,6,8; 3.9,26,27; 12.2,3,9,25; 17.12; 24.3) that expresses one of his major themes: Judah's defiance and contempt for God's holiness (ch 20). The theme has roots in the Holiness School, which emphasizes the people's ingrained tendency toward stubbornness and irreverence (cf. Num 17.10). 6: *Briers and thorns . . . scorpions*, though Ezekiel is a priestly official, his message will be met with hostility.

2.8b–3.3: In keeping with the contemporary emergence of the concept of God's word as sacred text, Ezekiel is told to eat a *scroll* (cf. Jer 1.9; Zech 5.1–4). The scroll depicts the coming, fixed judgment of Judah; see 3.22–27n. 3.3: Jeremiah's metaphor (Jer 15.16) becomes concrete in Ezekiel. God's word is *sweet* (Ps 19.10), even when its contents involve pain. 3.4–9: Preparation for resistance. 5–6: *Obscure speech*, like the language of Judah's enemies, perceived as harsh and unintelligible (Isa 33.19; Jer 5.15). 8–9: *Hard*, or "strong"; compare the meaning

your forehead hard against their foreheads. ⁹ Like the hardest stone, harder than flint, I have made your forehead; do not fear them or be dismayed at their looks, for they are a rebellious house. ¹⁰ He said to me: Mortal, all my words that I shall speak to you receive in your heart and hear with your ears; ¹¹ then go to the exiles, to your people, and speak to them. Say to them, "Thus says the Lord GOD"; whether they hear or refuse to hear.

¹² Then the spirit lifted me up, and as the glory of the LORD rose[a] from its place, I heard behind me the sound of loud rumbling; ¹³ it was the sound of the wings of the living creatures brushing against one another, and the sound of the wheels beside them, that sounded like a loud rumbling. ¹⁴ The spirit lifted me up and bore me away; I went in bitterness in the heat of my spirit, the hand of the LORD being strong upon me. ¹⁵ I came to the exiles at Tel-abib, who lived by the river Chebar.[b] And I sat there among them, stunned, for seven days.

¹⁶ At the end of seven days, the word of the LORD came to me: ¹⁷ Mortal, I have made you a sentinel for the house of Israel; whenever you hear a word from my mouth, you shall give them warning from me. ¹⁸ If I say to the wicked, "You shall surely die," and you give them no warning, or speak to warn the wicked from their wicked way, in order to save their life, those wicked persons shall die for their iniquity; but their blood I will require at your hand. ¹⁹ But if you warn the wicked, and they do not turn from their wickedness, or from their wicked way, they shall die for their iniquity; but you will have saved your life. ²⁰ Again, if the righteous turn from their righteousness and commit iniquity, and I lay a stumbling block before them, they shall die; because you have not warned them, they shall die for their sin, and their righteous deeds that they have done shall not be remembered; but their blood I will require at your hand. ²¹ If, however, you warn the righteous not to sin, and they do not sin, they shall surely live, because they took warning; and you will have saved your life.

²² Then the hand of the LORD was upon me there; and he said to me, Rise up, go out into the valley, and there I will speak with you. ²³ So I rose up and went out into the valley; and the glory of the LORD stood there, like the glory that I had seen by the river Chebar; and I fell on my face. ²⁴ The spirit entered into me, and set me on my feet; and he spoke with me and said to me: Go, shut yourself inside your house. ²⁵ As for you, mortal, cords shall be placed on you, and you shall be bound with

ᵃ Cn: Heb *and blessed be the glory of the* LORD
ᵇ Two Mss Syr: Heb *Chebar, and to where they lived.* Another reading is *Chebar, and I sat where they sat*

of Ezekiel's name, "God strengthens" (1.3n.). **10–11:** A final charge.

3.12–15: Ezekiel returns to his people. 12: *Glory of the* LORD, see 10.1–22n. **14:** Ezekiel feels either God's anger at the people or his own distress over his difficult task. *The hand of the* LORD, see 1.3n. **15:** *Tel-abib,* ("mound of the deluge"), not modern Tel Aviv but a settlement of exiles near Nippur, not far from the Chebar canal. *Chebar,* 1.1–3n.

3.16–21: The sentinel. Prophets as sentries (Jer 6.17; Hab 2.1) provide early warnings of possible dangers (cf. 2 Kings 9.17). Ezekiel is assured that his personal responsibility is limited to delivering such warnings; the members of his audience are accountable for their responses (18.1–32; see also 33.1–9). **16:** *The word of the* LORD *came to me,* a form of expression occurring about fifty times in Ezekiel, which marks the beginnings of nearly all his main units of prophetic speech.

3.22–27: Ezekiel's speechlessness. *The hand of the* LORD *was upon me,* a phrase that in Ezekiel frequently introduces a vision; cf. 1.3n. *The valley,* a specific site near Tel-abib (see 37.1n.). It was probably a low-lying area, perhaps with a spring. Ezekiel's *speechless* state is best seen as one of the characteristic literary metaphors of the book, with a complex relationship to observable reality (Ezekiel is not literally speechless after this point; cf. 11.25). The metaphor's meaning is bound up with the growing significance of written, authoritative scripture in Ezekiel's time. In view of this development, Ezekiel must fall speechless, and let the scroll that he has swallowed (2.8b–3.3n.) have its fulfillment. The judgments of scripture (such as those of the book of Habakkuk) are now inevitable. The metaphor of speechlessness helps structure the book of Ezekiel. The judgments of the swallowed scroll play themselves out in the first half of Ezekiel, after which he regains his speech (24.25–27; 33.21–22).

them, so that you cannot go out among the people; ²⁶ and I will make your tongue cling to the roof of your mouth, so that you shall be speechless and unable to reprove them; for they are a rebellious house. ²⁷ But when I speak with you, I will open your mouth, and you shall say to them, "Thus says the Lord God"; let those who will hear, hear; and let those who refuse to hear, refuse; for they are a rebellious house.

4 And you, O mortal, take a brick and set it before you. On it portray a city, Jerusalem; ² and put siegeworks against it, and build a siege wall against it, and cast up a ramp against it; set camps also against it, and plant battering rams against it all around. ³ Then take an iron plate and place it as an iron wall between you and the city; set your face toward it, and let it be in a state of siege, and press the siege against it. This is a sign for the house of Israel.

⁴ Then lie on your left side, and place the punishment of the house of Israel upon it; you shall bear their punishment for the number of the days that you lie there. ⁵ For I assign to you a number of days, three hundred ninety days, equal to the number of the years of their punishment; and so you shall bear the punishment of the house of Israel. ⁶ When you have completed these, you shall lie down a second time, but on your right side, and bear the punishment of the house of Judah; forty days I assign you, one day for each year. ⁷ You shall set your face toward the siege of Jerusalem, and with your arm bared you shall prophesy against it. ⁸ See, I am putting cords on you so that you cannot turn from one side to the other until you have completed the days of your siege.

⁹ And you, take wheat and barley, beans and lentils, millet and spelt; put them into one vessel, and make bread for yourself. During the number of days that you lie on your side, three hundred ninety days, you shall eat it. ¹⁰ The food that you eat shall be twenty shekels a day by weight; at fixed times you shall eat it. ¹¹ And you shall drink water by measure, one-sixth of a hin; at fixed times you shall drink. ¹² You shall eat it as a barley-cake, baking it in their sight on human dung. ¹³ The LORD said, "Thus shall the people of Israel eat their bread, unclean, among the nations to which I will drive them." ¹⁴ Then I said, "Ah Lord God! I have never defiled

---

4.1–24,27: Prophecies of doom against Judah and Jerusalem. 4.1–5.17: Actions symbolizing Jerusalem's coming siege. Like Ezekiel's speechlessness, these actions appear to be literary metaphors rather than observable performances (e.g., see 4.4–8n.). In Ezekiel, reality is more complex than the merely observable. **4.1–3:** A *brick* (common in Babylonia) inscribed, before baking, with a drawing of Jerusalem. Archaeologists have unearthed several ancient clay bricks like this one, inscribed with city plans. *An iron plate,* a baking griddle, symbolizing the barrier between the city and God. **4–8:** More than simple, nonverbal dramatization, Ezekiel's symbolic actions contain complex layers of meaning. At one level the postures commanded of Ezekiel illustrate the coming siege of Jerusalem. At a deeper level, they also depict both God's pre-siege punishments of Israel in the land over the previous 390 years (v. 5; see Lev 26.14–32 [HS]) and God's post-siege punishment of Judah in exile over the course of forty years (v. 6; cf. Num 14.34 [HS]). **4–5:** *Punishment,* or "iniquity." Bearing the weight of Israel's iniquity was a normal function of Israelite priests such as Ezekiel (Num 18.1 [HS]). **5–6:** The figure of 390 years may be Ezekiel's retrospective tabulation of the years that Israel polluted the Temple with its iniquity, from the time of its dedication by Solomon until its imminent destruction. The second figure of forty years (roughly one generation) represents Judah's coming period of exile outside of the promised land. The figure echoes the period of wilderness wanderings in the book of Numbers (see Num 14.34 [HS]). As with the wanderings of Numbers, the exile in Babylonia may set the stage for a new beginning of God with Israel. **9–17:** Coarse bread and rationing symbolize the rigors of the coming siege of Jerusalem (cf. Jer 19.9; Lam 4.10). **9:** The necessity of mixing grains in odd combinations indicates scarcity of foodstuffs. **10–11:** *Twenty shekels,* approximately 8 oz. (228 gr). *One-sixth of a hin,* approximately .67 qt. (64 liters). On this extremely meager diet, Jerusalem's inhabitants would totter on the brink of starvation (vv. 16–17). **12–13:** Siege symbolism again blurs into exile symbolism here. *Human dung,* considered unclean (Deut 23.12–14), represents the defiling effects of exile to an unclean land. (Lands outside Israel were deemed *unclean,* since God's holy presence did not reside there to purify and sanctify the territory; cf. Josh 22.19; Hos 9.3; Amos 7.17. Zech 3.3–5 shows how those in the tradition of Ezekiel came to terms with the defilement of the exile after the return.) Ezekiel was allowed to substitute dried "cow's

myself; from my youth up until now I have never eaten what died of itself or was torn by animals, nor has carrion flesh come into my mouth." [15] Then he said to me, "See, I will let you have cow's dung instead of human dung, on which you may prepare your bread."

[16] Then he said to me, Mortal, I am going to break the staff of bread in Jerusalem; they shall eat bread by weight and with fearfulness; and they shall drink water by measure and in dismay. [17] Lacking bread and water, they will look at one another in dismay, and waste away under their punishment.

5 And you, O mortal, take a sharp sword; use it as a barber's razor and run it over your head and your beard; then take balances for weighing, and divide the hair. [2] One third of the hair you shall burn in the fire inside the city, when the days of the siege are completed; one third you shall take and strike with the sword all around the city;[a] and one third you shall scatter to the wind, and I will unsheathe the sword after them. [3] Then you shall take from these a small number, and bind them in the skirts of your robe. [4] From these, again, you shall take some, throw them into the fire and burn them up; from there a fire will come out against all the house of Israel.

[5] Thus says the Lord GOD: This is Jerusalem; I have set her in the center of the nations, with countries all around her. [6] But she has rebelled against my ordinances and my statutes, becoming more wicked than the nations and the countries all around her, rejecting my ordinances and not following my statutes. [7] Therefore thus says the Lord GOD: Because you are more turbulent than the nations that are all around you, and

have not followed my statutes or kept my ordinances, but have acted according to the ordinances of the nations that are all around you; [8] therefore thus says the Lord GOD: I, I myself, am coming against you; I will execute judgments among you in the sight of the nations. [9] And because of all your abominations, I will do to you what I have never yet done, and the like of which I will never do again. [10] Surely, parents shall eat their children in your midst, and children shall eat their parents; I will execute judgments on you, and any of you who survive I will scatter to every wind. [11] Therefore, as I live, says the Lord GOD, surely, because you have defiled my sanctuary with all your detestable things and with all your abominations—therefore I will cut you down;[b] my eye will not spare, and I will have no pity. [12] One third of you shall die of pestilence or be consumed by famine among you; one third shall fall by the sword around you; and one third I will scatter to every wind and will unsheathe the sword after them.

[13] My anger shall spend itself, and I will vent my fury on them and satisfy myself; and they shall know that I, the LORD, have spoken in my jealousy, when I spend my fury on them. [14] Moreover I will make you a desolation and an object of mocking among the nations around you, in the sight of all that pass by. [15] You shall be[c] a mockery and a taunt, a warning and a horror, to the nations around you, when I execute judgments on you in anger and fury, and with furious punishments—I, the LORD, have spoken— [16] when I

---

a Heb it
b Another reading is I will withdraw
c Gk Syr Vg Tg: Heb It shall be

---

dung" (v. 15), a common fuel in the Near East. **14:** Cf. Lev 17.10–16 (HS). **16:** In Ezekiel's antecedent text, Lev 26.26 (HS), God's breaking the *staff of bread* ("food supply") is a penalty for violating the Holiness School covenant. **5.1–17:** The *razor* symbolizes military defeat (Isa 7.20). The defeated people are then destroyed in three different ways. Even the surviving remnant undergoes further judgment. **3:** Objects could be carried in the folds of one's garments (Hag 2.12). **5:** *Center of the nations,* Jerusalem was viewed as the mythic center of the earth (see 38.12, "center [lit., navel] of the earth"; 43.13–17n.). **8:** Formulaic language for challenging someone to a duel. God is resolved to come against Jerusalem as an enemy. *Sight of the nations,* Ezekiel is concerned throughout the book that the nations, as well as Israel, understand God's holiness. Israel should have been an object lesson in holiness to other nations. **10:** Cannibalism was a curse for breaking the Holiness School covenant (Lev 26.29). **11:** If textual note *b* is the correct reading, this verse anticipates the departure of the LORD's glory from the Temple described in 10.1–22 and 11.22–25. **12:** *Pestilence . . . famine,* cf. the Holiness School covenant sanctions in Lev

loose against you[a] my deadly arrows of famine, arrows for destruction, which I will let loose to destroy you, and when I bring more and more famine upon you, and break your staff of bread. [17] I will send famine and wild animals against you, and they will rob you of your children; pestilence and bloodshed shall pass through you; and I will bring the sword upon you. I, the LORD, have spoken.

6 The word of the LORD came to me: [2] O mortal, set your face toward the mountains of Israel, and prophesy against them, [3] and say, You mountains of Israel, hear the word of the Lord GOD! Thus says the Lord GOD to the mountains and the hills, to the ravines and the valleys: I, I myself will bring a sword upon you, and I will destroy your high places. [4] Your altars shall become desolate, and your incense stands shall be broken; and I will throw down your slain in front of your idols. [5] I will lay the corpses of the people of Israel in front of their idols; and I will scatter your bones around your altars. [6] Wherever you live, your towns shall be waste and your high places ruined, so that your altars will be waste and ruined,[b] your idols broken and destroyed, your incense stands cut down, and your works wiped out. [7] The slain shall fall in your midst; then you shall know that I am the LORD.

[8] But I will spare some. Some of you shall escape the sword among the nations and be scattered through the countries. [9] Those of you who escape shall remember me among the nations where they are carried captive, how I was crushed by their wanton heart that turned away from me, and their wanton eyes that turned after their idols. Then they will be loathsome in their own sight for the evils that they have committed, for all their abominations. [10] And they shall know that I am the LORD; I did not threaten in vain to bring this disaster upon them.

[11] Thus says the Lord GOD: Clap your hands and stamp your foot, and say, Alas for all the vile abominations of the house of Israel! For they shall fall by the sword, by famine, and by pestilence. [12] Those far off shall die of pestilence; those nearby shall fall by the sword; and any who are left and are spared shall die of famine. Thus I will spend my fury upon them. [13] And you shall know that I am the LORD, when their slain lie among their idols around their altars, on every high hill, on all the mountain tops, under every green tree, and under every leafy oak, wherever they offered pleasing odor to all their idols. [14] I will stretch out my hand against them, and make the land

[a] Heb *them*

[b] Syr Vg Tg: Heb *and be made guilty*

26.25–26. **13:** *They shall know . . .* , 6.7n. **16:** *Staff of bread,* 4.16n. **17:** 14.21; Lev 26.22 (HS).

6.1–14: Two prophecies against Israel's idolatry. 1–10: *The mountains of Israel,* the central highland ridge of the promised land representing, in Ezekiel, the entire homeland territory (19.9; 33.38; 34.14; 35.12; 37.22; 38.8). Mountains symbolized the intersection of earth and heaven, so Israel's typography points to its unique status as God's holy land and the world's center (38.12; cf. Lev 26.11–12; Zech 2.12). Degrading this holy status, Israel's mountains are here associated with illegitimate worship (v. 9; cf. 18.6). **2:** *Set your face toward,* an idiom of Ezekiel (cf. 13.17; 20.46; 21.2; 25.2; 28.21; 29.2; 35.2; 38.2) calling for a hostile orientation based on God's angry disposition. **3:** *High places* were ritual installations or shrines. Their destruction was a curse for breaking the Holiness School covenant (Lev 26.30). **4:** *Idols* translates Ezekiel's characteristic term "gillulim," found in Lev 26.30 and thirty-nine times in Ezekiel, compared with eight times elsewhere in the Bible. The term is contemptuous, probably equating idols with sheep droppings. The people are devoted to vile futility. **6:** *Towns shall be waste,* Lev 26.31 (HS). **7:** *You shall know . . .* , one of over sixty similar closing declarations in Ezekiel (see vv. 10,13–14). Ezekiel shares an emphasis on recognition of the LORD with the Holiness School (e.g., Ex 6.7; 7.5; 10.2; 16.12; 31.13). He prophesies that God's judging and saving acts will prove God's sovereign identity and result in human recognition of God. The central purpose of God's work on earth is to evoke this recognition, which in the understanding of Ezekiel and the Holiness School means being drawn into direct experience of God's life. God is focused on making Israel holy, and nothing is more important than for Israel to align itself with this intention (see Ex 10.2; 16.32; Lev 23.43 [HS]). In general, the book of Ezekiel de-emphasizes the prophet's human experience, focusing instead on God's desire to reveal the mystery and "otherness" of God's own self. **9:** The people will finally despair of their state of alienation from God. **11–14:** A second prophecy of judgment, beginning with an expressive action (cf. 21.14n.) communicating divine distress and anger over the people's abominations. **11:**

desolate and waste, throughout all their settlements, from the wilderness to Riblah.[a] Then they shall know that I am the LORD.

7 The word of the LORD came to me: [2] You, O mortal, thus says the Lord GOD to the land of Israel:
An end! The end has come
    upon the four corners of the land.
[3] Now the end is upon you,
    I will let loose my anger upon you;
I will judge you according to your ways,
    I will punish you for all your
      abominations.
[4] My eye will not spare you, I will have no
    pity.
I will punish you for your ways,
    while your abominations are among you.
Then you shall know that I am the LORD.
[5] Thus says the Lord GOD:
Disaster after disaster! See, it comes.
    [6] An end has come, the end has come.
It has awakened against you; see, it comes!
[7] Your doom[b] has come to you,
    O inhabitant of the land.
The time has come, the day is near—
    of tumult, not of reveling on the
      mountains.
[8] Soon now I will pour out my wrath upon
    you;
I will spend my anger against you.
I will judge you according to your ways,
    and punish you for all your
      abominations.
[9] My eye will not spare; I will have no pity.
I will punish you according to your
    ways,
    while your abominations are among
      you.
Then you shall know that it is I the LORD who strike.

[10] See, the day! See, it comes!
    Your doom[b] has gone out.
The rod has blossomed, pride has
      budded.
[11] Violence has grown into a rod of
    wickedness.
None of them shall remain,
    not their abundance, not their
      wealth;
    no pre-eminence among them.[b]
[12] The time has come, the day draws near;
    let not the buyer rejoice, nor the seller
      mourn,
    for wrath is upon all their multitude.
[13] For the sellers shall not return to what has been sold as long as they remain alive. For the vision concerns all their multitude; it shall not be revoked. Because of their iniquity, they cannot maintain their lives.[b]
[14] They have blown the horn and made
    everything ready;
    but no one goes to battle,
    for my wrath is upon all their
      multitude.
[15] The sword is outside, pestilence and
    famine are inside;
    those in the field die by the sword;
    those in the city—famine and
      pestilence devour them.
[16] If any survivors escape,
    they shall be found on the mountains
    like doves of the valleys,
all of them moaning over their iniquity.
[17] All hands shall grow feeble,
    all knees turn to water.
[18] They shall put on sackcloth,
    horror shall cover them.
Shame shall be on all faces,

[a] Another reading is *Diblah*
[b] Meaning of Heb uncertain

Sword . . . famine . . . pestilence, Lev 26.25–26 (HS). **14:** *Stretch out my hand,* a repeated expression of Ezekiel denoting hard, crushing judgment (14.9,13; 16.27; 25.7; 35.3). *From the wilderness* of southern Judah *to Riblah* in central Syria was the maximum extent of Israelite territory.

7.1–27: Prophecies on the approaching end. 1–4: The theme, *the end,* is reminiscent of Am 8.2. **3:** Cf. Ps 78.49. **5–9:** *The day* (v. 7) of the end is "the day of the LORD," the time of God's appearance to defeat evil and establish justice (Am 5.18–20; Isa 2.11,12–17; Joel 1.15). The experience will be nothing short of cataclysmic, leaving nothing unchanged (Zeph 1.14–18). **9:** See v. 4. **10–27:** The end spells dissolution of normal life. **10:** *The rod,* the term both connotes "discipline" and evokes a similar Hebrew word meaning "injustice." **12:** The joys and sorrows of daily life and commerce (Prov 20.14) are rendered moot by the approach of Jerusalem's end. **14:** The trumpet calls to the defense, but the people are too enfeebled to respond. **18:** Wearing coarse *sackcloth* and shaving the

baldness on all their heads. [19] They shall fling their silver into the streets,

their gold shall be treated as unclean. Their silver and gold cannot save them on the day of the wrath of the Lord. They shall not satisfy their hunger or fill their stomachs with it. For it was the stumbling block of their iniquity. [20] From their[a] beautiful ornament, in which they took pride, they made their abominable images, their detestable things; therefore I will make of it an unclean thing to them.

[21] I will hand it over to strangers as booty,
to the wicked of the earth as plunder;
they shall profane it.
[22] I will avert my face from them,
so that they may profane my treasured[b] place;
the violent shall enter it,
they shall profane it.
[23] Make a chain![c]
For the land is full of bloody crimes;
the city is full of violence.
[24] I will bring the worst of the nations
to take possession of their houses.
I will put an end to the arrogance of the strong,
and their holy places shall be profaned.
[25] When anguish comes, they will seek peace,
but there shall be none.
[26] Disaster comes upon disaster,

rumor follows rumor;
they shall keep seeking a vision from the prophet;
instruction shall perish from the priest,
and counsel from the elders.
[27] The king shall mourn,
the prince shall be wrapped in despair,
and the hands of the people of the land shall tremble.
According to their way I will deal with them;
according to their own judgments I will judge them.
And they shall know that I am the Lord.

8 In the sixth year, in the sixth month, on the fifth day of the month, as I sat in my house, with the elders of Judah sitting before me, the hand of the Lord God fell upon me there. [2] I looked, and there was a figure that looked like a human being;[d] below what appeared to be its loins it was fire, and above the loins it was like the appearance of brightness, like gleaming amber. [3] It stretched out the form of a hand, and took me by a lock of my head; and the spirit lifted me up between earth and heaven, and brought me in visions of God to Jerusalem, to the entrance of the gateway of the inner court that faces north,

a Syr Symmachus: Heb *its*
b Or *secret*
c Meaning of Heb uncertain
d Gk: Heb *like fire*

head (*baldness*) were both intentional displays of mourning (cf. 27.31; Am 8.10; Isa 22.12). The disaster will also provoke involuntary reactions of *horror* and *shame*. **19:** Zeph 1.18. **20:** *Beautiful ornament,* perhaps the gold and silver of the Temple treasury, used to fashion idolatrous images (16.17; 2 Kings 21.7). **22:** *My treasured place,* the land of Israel, and particularly Jerusalem, containing God's Temple. **23a:** Perhaps a call to be chained together in a long train for exile (cf. Nah 3.10; Jer 40.1), but see textual note *c.* **23b:** Social ethics, as well as idolatry, concern Ezekiel and the Holiness School (12.19; 28.16; cf. Gen 6.11). **24:** Human *arrogance* has no place in the Zion theology used by Ezekiel (see Introduction), which stresses God's sovereignty (Lev 26.19 [HS]). **25–27:** The confusion and brutality of the invasion and siege.

8.1–11.25: The Temple visions. 8.1–18: The vision of idolatry (September 17, 592 BCE). In his vision of wickedness in Jerusalem's Temple, Ezekiel saw beyond the observable offenses of his time into the ingrained, polluted essence of the shrine. **1:** The *elders* in exile with the prophet (also his audience in 14.1; 20.1) were the traditional leaders, from premonarchic times, of Israel's family lines and kin groups. During the exile, they stepped in to fill the leadership vacuum among the deportees. *The hand of the Lord God* (see 1.3n.) grips Ezekiel suddenly, yanking him into a vision of a scene far removed, both spatially and temporally, from his setting in Babylonia. **2:** The *figure* is described in terms similar to those in 1.26–27. **3:** *By a lock of my head,* cf. Bel 36. The *gateway* to the Temple's inner court is also termed the *altar gate* (v. 5), as it led from the outer court to the great altar of sacrifice. The *image of jealousy* is probably the carved image of the goddess Asherah that King Manasseh set up in the Temple (2 Kings 21.7). Though removed by Ezekiel's time (2 Kings 23.6), it stood out starkly in the proph-

to the seat of the image of jealousy, which provokes to jealousy. [4] And the glory of the God of Israel was there, like the vision that I had seen in the valley.

[5] Then God[a] said to me, "O mortal, lift up your eyes now in the direction of the north." So I lifted up my eyes toward the north, and there, north of the altar gate, in the entrance, was this image of jealousy. [6] He said to me, "Mortal, do you see what they are doing, the great abominations that the house of Israel are committing here, to drive me far from my sanctuary? Yet you will see still greater abominations."

[7] And he brought me to the entrance of the court; I looked, and there was a hole in the wall. [8] Then he said to me, "Mortal, dig through the wall"; and when I dug through the wall, there was an entrance. [9] He said to me, "Go in, and see the vile abominations that they are committing here." [10] So I went in and looked; there, portrayed on the wall all around, were all kinds of creeping things, and loathsome animals, and all the idols of the house of Israel. [11] Before them stood seventy of the elders of the house of Israel, with Jaazaniah son of Shaphan standing among them. Each had his censer in his hand, and the fragrant cloud of incense was ascending. [12] Then he said to me, "Mortal, have you seen what the elders of the house of Israel are doing in the dark, each in his room of images?

For they say, 'The LORD does not see us, the LORD has forsaken the land.'" [13] He said also to me, "You will see still greater abominations that they are committing."

[14] Then he brought me to the entrance of the north gate of the house of the LORD; women were sitting there weeping for Tammuz. [15] Then he said to me, "Have you seen this, O mortal? You will see still greater abominations than these."

[16] And he brought me into the inner court of the house of the LORD; there, at the entrance of the temple of the LORD, between the porch and the altar, were about twenty-five men, with their backs to the temple of the LORD, and their faces toward the east, prostrating themselves to the sun toward the east. [17] Then he said to me, "Have you seen this, O mortal? Is it not bad enough that the house of Judah commits the abominations done here? Must they fill the land with violence, and provoke my anger still further? See, they are putting the branch to their nose! [18] Therefore I will act in wrath; my eye will not spare, nor will I have pity; and though they cry in my hearing with a loud voice, I will not listen to them."

9 Then he cried in my hearing with a loud voice, saying, "Draw near, you executioners of the city, each with his destroying weapon in his hand." [2] And six men came from

---

[a] Heb *he*

---

et's transhistorical perception. **4:** See 3.22–23. On *the glory of the God of Israel,* see 10.1–22n. **7–13:** The Temple stands infested by an ongoing rebellion against God's hierarchies of holiness that began in the wilderness period. The elders of Judah with censers inside the secret gatehouse chamber perform the very same improper act as that described in Num 16.2,17,35 (HS). Ezekiel views the scriptural story in Num 16 as prototypical, and it informs his assessment of the preexilic Temple's wickedness (see also 44.6–14n.). **10:** Cf. 23.14; Deut 4.17–18. **11:** The *elders* here are in the prophet's vision of Jerusalem, and are not the same as those in v. 1. The mention of *Jaazaniah* among the encroachers upon the holy precincts is particularly disturbing, given his family's record of faithfulness. His father *Shaphan* was active in King Josiah's reform movement (2 Kings 22), and his brother Ahikam and nephew Gedaliah assisted and protected Jeremiah (Jer 26.24; 39.14). **12:** The elders' idea that *the LORD has forsaken the land* becomes a self-fulfilling prophecy (see 11.22–23). **14–15:** *Tammuz,* a Mesopotamian god; the weeping was for his descent into the underworld. Transtemporal perception is again suggested here, since Ezekiel sees the weeping rite in the sixth month (v. 1) and not in the fourth month (June–July), when it was normally practiced. **16–18:** The climactic abomination seen by Ezekiel was sun worship. Its practice in Israel is evidenced by texts such as 2 Kings 23.5,11 and by an Israelite ritual stand found at Taanach that depicts the sun as a deity. **17:** The *branch* gesture may be an obscene expression. The Hebrew text originally referred to God's nose, but the scribes toned down the offensive image. **18:** The judgment is irrevocable (see 14.12–23n.).

9.1–11: The punishment of the guilty. 1–2: From the upper gate (Jer 20.2) come the *executioners* (divine functionaries sent to punish) and *a man clothed in linen,* who functions as the LORD's scribe, as did the Mesopotamian god Nabu among the seven Babylonian planetary deities. *Linen,* a bleached fabric signifying purity, was

the direction of the upper gate, which faces north, each with his weapon for slaughter in his hand; among them was a man clothed in linen, with a writing case at his side. They went in and stood beside the bronze altar.

³ Now the glory of the God of Israel had gone up from the cherub on which it rested to the threshold of the house. The LORD called to the man clothed in linen, who had the writing case at his side; ⁴ and said to him, "Go through the city, through Jerusalem, and put a mark on the foreheads of those who sigh and groan over all the abominations that are committed in it." ⁵ To the others he said in my hearing, "Pass through the city after him, and kill; your eye shall not spare, and you shall show no pity. ⁶ Cut down old men, young men and young women, little children and women, but touch no one who has the mark. And begin at my sanctuary." So they began with the elders who were in front of the house. ⁷ Then he said to them, "Defile the house, and fill the courts with the slain. Go!" So they went out and killed in the city. ⁸ While they were killing, and I was left alone, I fell prostrate on my face and cried out, "Ah Lord GOD! will you destroy all who remain of Israel as you pour out your wrath upon Jerusalem?" ⁹ He said to me, "The guilt of the house of Israel and Judah is exceedingly great; the land is full of bloodshed and the city full of perversity; for they say, 'The LORD has forsaken the land, and the LORD does not see.' ¹⁰ As for me, my eye will not spare, nor

will I have pity, but I will bring down their deeds upon their heads."

¹¹ Then the man clothed in linen, with the writing case at his side, brought back word, saying, "I have done as you commanded me."

10 Then I looked, and above the dome that was over the heads of the cherubim there appeared above them something like a sapphire,[a] in form resembling a throne. ² He said to the man clothed in linen, "Go within the wheelwork underneath the cherubim; fill your hands with burning coals from among the cherubim, and scatter them over the city." He went in as I looked on. ³ Now the cherubim were standing on the south side of the house when the man went in; and a cloud filled the inner court. ⁴ Then the glory of the LORD rose up from the cherub to the threshold of the house; the house was filled with the cloud, and the court was full of the brightness of the glory of the LORD. ⁵ The sound of the wings of the cherubim was heard as far as the outer court, like the voice of God Almighty[b] when he speaks.

⁶ When he commanded the man clothed in linen, "Take fire from within the wheelwork, from among the cherubim," he went in and stood beside a wheel. ⁷ And a cherub stretched out his hand from among the cherubim to the fire that was among the

---

a Or *lapis lazuli*
b Traditional rendering of Heb *El Shaddai*

---

worn by divine messengers (Dan 10.5) and also by priests (44.17; Lev 6.10 [HS]). **3:** On the departure of the *glory*, see 10.1–22n. *The cherub,* in the singular (also 10.4), is used of the inanimate pair of statues in the Temple that formed part of the divine throne. The actual living entities are referred to with the Heb plural, "cherubim." **4:** The *mark* was the Heb letter "taw," made like an X. **6:** The *elders* are those of 8.16. **7:** Ezekiel's Holiness School traditions stressed that corpses defile (Lev 21.1; Num 5.2–3; 9.6; 19.11,13 [HS]). **8:** *All who remain,* those remaining in Palestine after the initial deportation of 597 BCE.

10.1–22 and 11.22–25: The departure of the LORD's glory from the Temple is repeatedly described in each of three versions of Jerusalem's abandonment (9.3; 10.4; 11.22). *The glory of the LORD* is the revealed, objective presence of the majesty of God, manifesting God's holiness in fiery radiance (1.28n.; Lev 9.23; Num 20.6). The pattern of movement of the glory of the LORD helps structure the book of Ezekiel. The glory has been present in Jerusalem, even when the city's inhabitants felt forsaken by it (8.4,12b), but because of their wickedness it departs, first to the doorway of the Temple (also 9.3), and then to the east gate of the Temple's outer court (10.18–19). It then leaves the desecrated sanctuary. The departure continues in 11.22–25, where the glory heads east over the Mount of Olives toward Babylon. It was in Babylonia that Ezekiel first saw the glory of the LORD (1.28; 3.22–23; cf. 8.4; 11.16). Eventually, the prophet envisions it returning to the restored Temple (43.2–5; 44.4). **1:** *Cherubim,* see 1.5–14n. **2:** *Man clothed in linen,* see 9.1–2n. *Burning coals,* cf. Isa 31.9; Ps 18.10–13. **3–4:** The throne-chariot comes to collect the glory of the LORD from the cherub statues (see 9.3n.). The *cloud* filling the

cherubim, took some of it and put it into the hands of the man clothed in linen, who took it and went out. [8] The cherubim appeared to have the form of a human hand under their wings.

[9] I looked, and there were four wheels beside the cherubim, one beside each cherub; and the appearance of the wheels was like gleaming beryl. [10] And as for their appearance, the four looked alike, something like a wheel within a wheel. [11] When they moved, they moved in any of the four directions without veering as they moved; but in whatever direction the front wheel faced, the others followed without veering as they moved. [12] Their entire body, their rims, their spokes, their wings, and the wheels—the wheels of the four of them—were full of eyes all around. [13] As for the wheels, they were called in my hearing "the wheelwork." [14] Each one had four faces: the first face was that of the cherub, the second face was that of a human being, the third that of a lion, and the fourth that of an eagle.

[15] The cherubim rose up. These were the living creatures that I saw by the river Chebar. [16] When the cherubim moved, the wheels moved beside them; and when the cherubim lifted up their wings to rise up from the earth, the wheels at their side did not veer. [17] When they stopped, the others stopped, and when they rose up, the others rose up with them; for the spirit of the living creatures was in them.

[18] Then the glory of the LORD went out from the threshold of the house and stopped above the cherubim. [19] The cherubim lifted up their wings and rose up from the earth in my sight as they went out with the wheels beside them. They stopped at the entrance of the east gate of the house of the LORD; and the glory of the God of Israel was above them.

[20] These were the living creatures that I saw underneath the God of Israel by the river Chebar; and I knew that they were cherubim. [21] Each had four faces, each four wings, and underneath their wings something like human hands. [22] As for what their faces were like, they were the same faces whose appearance I had seen by the river Chebar. Each one moved straight ahead.

11 The spirit lifted me up and brought me to the east gate of the house of the LORD, which faces east. There, at the entrance of the gateway, were twenty-five men; among them I saw Jaazaniah son of Azzur, and Pelatiah son of Benaiah, officials of the people. [2] He said to me, "Mortal, these are the men who devise iniquity and who give wicked counsel in this city; [3] they say, 'The time is not near to build houses; this city is the pot, and we are the meat.' [4] Therefore prophesy against them; prophesy, O mortal."

[5] Then the spirit of the LORD fell upon me, and he said to me, "Say, Thus says the LORD: This is what you think, O house of Israel; I know the things that come into your mind. [6] You have killed many in this city, and have filled its streets with the slain. [7] Therefore thus says the Lord GOD: The slain whom you have placed within it are the meat, and this city is the pot; but you shall be taken out of it. [8] You have feared the sword; and I will bring the sword upon you, says the Lord GOD. [9] I will take you out of it and give you over to the hands of foreigners, and execute judgments

Temple recalls Ex 16.10; 40.34–35 (HS); it both conceals and reveals the divine presence. **12**: *Eyes all around*, see 1.18n. **14**: *That of the cherub,* the bull face of 1.10 (some ancient cherubim were bovine). **15**: *Chebar,* 1.1–3n.

11.1–25: Judgment and promise. 11.1–13: A disputation over the city. *Jaazaniah* and *Pelatiah* are otherwise unknown *officials of the people* (a postexilic title). *Wicked counsel* perhaps refers to the plot between Egypt and the pro-Egyptian counselors of King Zedekiah of Judah against the Babylonian king Nebuchadrezzar (Jer 27.1–3; 37.5,7,11). **3**: Having a false confidence in Zion's ironclad invulnerability (*the pot*), they assure the populace of the city's security. They put off domestic construction, perhaps because they have now appropriated the houses of the slain (v. 6) and of the deportees (v. 15). Alternatively, they are urging that all construction be concentrated on fortifying Jerusalem for their planned rebellion. *The pot,* an impenetrable metal cauldron or a sturdy crock where food was safely stored. Ezekiel returns to the symbol of the pot in 24.3–8. **5–13**: Ezekiel has formulated a far more sophisticated Zion theology than their rather denuded conception (see 1.15–21n.,26–28n.). Accusing the leaders of gross violence (7.23; ch 22), he tells them that a morally complacent trust in Zion will not protect them (cf. 24.1–14), but they will be judged at *the border of Israel* (v. 11; perhaps Riblah; see 6.14n.; 2 Kings

upon you. [10] You shall fall by the sword; I will judge you at the border of Israel. And you shall know that I am the LORD. [11] This city shall not be your pot, and you shall not be the meat inside it; I will judge you at the border of Israel. [12] Then you shall know that I am the LORD, whose statutes you have not followed, and whose ordinances you have not kept, but you have acted according to the ordinances of the nations that are around you."

[13] Now, while I was prophesying, Pelatiah son of Benaiah died. Then I fell down on my face, cried with a loud voice, and said, "Ah Lord GOD! will you make a full end of the remnant of Israel?"

[14] Then the word of the LORD came to me: [15] Mortal, your kinsfolk, your own kin, your fellow exiles,[a] the whole house of Israel, all of them, are those of whom the inhabitants of Jerusalem have said, "They have gone far from the LORD; to us this land is given for a possession." [16] Therefore say: Thus says the Lord GOD: Though I removed them far away among the nations, and though I scattered them among the countries, yet I have been a sanctuary to them for a little while[b] in the countries where they have gone. [17] Therefore say: Thus says the Lord GOD: I will gather you from the peoples, and assemble you out of the countries where you have been scattered, and I will give you the land of Israel. [18] When they come there, they will remove from it all its detestable things and all its abominations. [19] I will give them one[c] heart, and put a new spirit within them; I will remove the heart of stone from their flesh and give them a heart of flesh, [20] so that they may follow my statutes and keep my ordinances and obey them. Then they shall be my people, and I will be their God. [21] But as for those whose heart goes after their detestable things and their abominations,[d] I will bring their deeds upon their own heads, says the Lord GOD.

[22] Then the cherubim lifted up their wings, with the wheels beside them; and the glory of the God of Israel was above them. [23] And the glory of the LORD ascended from the middle of the city, and stopped on the mountain east of the city. [24] The spirit lifted me up and brought me in a vision by the spirit of God into Chaldea, to the exiles. Then the vision that I had seen left me. [25] And I told the exiles all the things that the LORD had shown me.

12 The word of the LORD came to me: [2] Mortal, you are living in the midst of a rebellious house, who have eyes to see but do not see, who have ears to hear but do not hear; [3] for they are a rebellious house.

a   Gk Syr: Heb *people of your kindred*
b   Or *to some extent*
c   Another reading is *a new*
d   Cn: Heb *And to the heart of their detestable things and their abominations their heart goes*

25.6,18–21). **13**: Pelatiah's death is a prediction within the prophetic vision, not an actual event. Ezekiel's desperate question at the end of this verse receives a reassuring negative answer in vv. 14–21, an authentically early (pre-586 BCE, see v. 15) oracle of promise in Ezekiel.

11.14–21: The future lies with the exiles. This passage disputes the claim of those who remained in the land that the exiles were bearing God's punishment, and that their property thus now belonged to those who remained. Ezekiel warns them that God is with his exiled people and will restore them. It is the exile group that constitutes the true Israel (cf. 20.41–42). **15**: *Your fellow exiles,* see textual note *a*; the rare Heb noun translated "kindred" denotes people who, according to the Holiness School, should be defended against the permanent alienation of their land (Lev 25.25–28). The Jerusalemites are violating Holiness School traditions (see 45.8–9n.). **16**: *A sanctuary,* the Hebrew indicates that the glory of the LORD is now tabernacling with the exiles in Babylonia rather than with those who remained behind (v. 23). **17–21**: Promise of restoration to the exiles. The prophecy is authentic to the prophet's message before the city's fall in 586 BCE, as shown by its concern with contemporaries inhabiting Jerusalem before its destruction (v. 21). **19**: New *heart,* see 36.26n. **20**: The new covenant, cf. 16.60; 36.27–28; 37.23,27. **24**: *Chaldea,* Babylonia.

11.22–25: Two reports conclude the Temple visions. **22–23**: See 10.1 **22n.** *The mountain east of the city* is the Mount of Olives.

12.1–20: Two symbolic actions. 12.1–16: First symbol, an exile's baggage. Ezekiel symbolizes the Jerusalemites' coming exile by collecting whatever goods exiles could carry (Jer 10.17; 46.19) and leaving the city. Features within this text later revealed themselves as stunningly applicable to events surrounding Zedekiah

Therefore, mortal, prepare for yourself an exile's baggage, and go into exile by day in their sight; you shall go like an exile from your place to another place in their sight. Perhaps they will understand, though they are a rebellious house. [4] You shall bring out your baggage by day in their sight, as baggage for exile; and you shall go out yourself at evening in their sight, as those do who go into exile. [5] Dig through the wall in their sight, and carry the baggage through it. [6] In their sight you shall lift the baggage on your shoulder, and carry it out in the dark; you shall cover your face, so that you may not see the land; for I have made you a sign for the house of Israel.

[7] I did just as I was commanded. I brought out my baggage by day, as baggage for exile, and in the evening I dug through the wall with my own hands; I brought it out in the dark, carrying it on my shoulder in their sight.

[8] In the morning the word of the LORD came to me: [9] Mortal, has not the house of Israel, the rebellious house, said to you, "What are you doing?" [10] Say to them, "Thus says the Lord GOD: This oracle concerns the prince in Jerusalem and all the house of Israel in it." [11] Say, "I am a sign for you: as I have done, so shall it be done to them; they shall go into exile, into captivity." [12] And the prince who is among them shall lift his baggage on his shoulder in the dark, and shall go out; he[a] shall dig through the wall and carry it through; he shall cover his face, so that he may not see the land with his eyes. [13] I will spread my net over him, and he shall be caught in my snare; and I will bring him to Babylon, the land of the Chaldeans, yet he shall not see it; and he shall die there. [14] I will scatter to every wind all who are around him, his helpers and all his troops; and I will unsheathe the sword behind them. [15] And they shall know that I am the LORD, when I disperse them among the nations and scatter them through the countries. [16] But I will let a few of them escape from the sword, from famine and pestilence, so that they may tell of all their abominations among the nations where they go; then they shall know that I am the LORD.

[17] The word of the LORD came to me: [18] Mortal, eat your bread with quaking, and drink your water with trembling and with fearfulness; [19] and say to the people of the land, Thus says the Lord GOD concerning the inhabitants of Jerusalem in the land of Israel: They shall eat their bread with fearfulness, and drink their water in dismay, because their land shall be stripped of all it contains, on account of the violence of all those who live in it. [20] The inhabited cities shall be laid waste, and the land shall become a desolation; and you shall know that I am the LORD.

[21] The word of the LORD came to me: [22] Mortal, what is this proverb of yours about the land of Israel, which says, "The days are prolonged, and every vision comes to nothing"? [23] Tell them therefore, "Thus says the Lord GOD: I will put an end to this proverb, and they shall use it no more as a proverb in Israel." But say to them, The days are near, and the fulfillment of every vision. [24] For there shall no longer be any false vision or flattering divination within the house of Israel. [25] But I the LORD will speak the word that I speak, and it will be fulfilled. It will no longer be delayed; but in your days, O rebellious house, I will speak the word and fulfill it, says the Lord GOD.

[a] Gk Syr: Heb *they*

(the *prince*, v. 12), who left Jerusalem by night at the city's fall. The oracle was then revised to bring out this applicability. It now specifies how Zedekiah was captured (17.20) and blinded (*may not see*, vv. 6,12; 2 Kings 25.4,7; Jer 39.1–10). 2: Cf. Isa 6.10. 3–4: *An exile's baggage*, deportees typically carried large sacks with supplies and personal items for the long trek into exile. Such sacks appear in several Assyrian reliefs, including a depiction of Judean captives from Lachish. 5: *Dig through the wall*, either the prophet switched roles and portrayed Jerusalem's besiegers breaching the city's walls (cf. Jer 39.2) or he depicts fugitives attempting to dig their way out of the city (through partially breached walls). 12: The Heb text may mean "they [the besiegers] will dig through the wall to bring [the prince] out through it" (see textual note *a*). 14: 5.2,12; 17.21; Lev 26.33 (HS). 15–16: 14.21–23.

12.17–20: **Second symbol, eating with trembling.** The people's emotional breakdown at the approaching invasion (cf. Ps 80.5) is prophesied.

12.21–28: **Disputations about prophecy.** Ezekiel condemns the people's skepticism about prophecies of

26 The word of the LORD came to me: 27 Mortal, the house of Israel is saying, "The vision that he sees is for many years ahead; he prophesies for distant times." 28 Therefore say to them, Thus says the Lord GOD: None of my words will be delayed any longer, but the word that I speak will be fulfilled, says the Lord GOD.

13 The word of the LORD came to me: 2 Mortal, prophesy against the prophets of Israel who are prophesying; say to those who prophesy out of their own imagination: "Hear the word of the LORD!" 3 Thus says the Lord GOD, Alas for the senseless prophets who follow their own spirit, and have seen nothing! 4 Your prophets have been like jackals among ruins, O Israel. 5 You have not gone up into the breaches, or repaired a wall for the house of Israel, so that it might stand in battle on the day of the LORD. 6 They have envisioned falsehood and lying divination; they say, "Says the LORD," when the LORD has not sent them, and yet they wait for the fulfillment of their word! 7 Have you not seen a false vision or uttered a lying divination, when you have said, "Says the LORD," even though I did not speak?

8 Therefore thus says the Lord GOD: Because you have uttered falsehood and en-visioned lies, I am against you, says the Lord GOD. 9 My hand will be against the prophets who see false visions and utter lying divina-tions; they shall not be in the council of my people, nor be enrolled in the register of the house of Israel, nor shall they enter the land of Israel; and you shall know that I am the Lord GOD. 10 Because, in truth, because they have misled my people, saying, "Peace," when there is no peace; and because, when the people build a wall, these prophets[a] smear whitewash on it. 11 Say to those who smear whitewash on it that it shall fall. There will be a deluge of rain,[b] great hailstones will fall, and a stormy wind will break out. 12 When the wall falls, will it not be said to you, "Where is the whitewash you smeared on it?" 13 There-fore thus says the Lord GOD: In my wrath I will make a stormy wind break out, and in my anger there shall be a deluge of rain, and hailstones in wrath to destroy it. 14 I will break down the wall that you have smeared with whitewash, and bring it to the ground, so that its foundation will be laid bare; when it falls, you shall perish within it; and you shall know that I am the LORD. 15 Thus I will spend my wrath upon the wall, and upon those who have smeared it with whitewash; and I will say to you, The wall is no more, nor those who smeared it— 16 the prophets of Israel who prophesied concerning Jerusalem and saw visions of peace for it, when there was no peace, says the Lord GOD.

17 As for you, mortal, set your face against the daughters of your people, who proph-esy out of their own imagination; prophesy against them 18 and say, Thus says the Lord GOD: Woe to the women who sew bands on all wrists, and make veils for the heads of persons of every height, in the hunt for hu-

---

a   Heb *they*
b   Heb *rain and you*

judgment (vv. 22,27; Jer 5.12; 17.15). **26–28**: Second disputation.

13.1–23: **Oracles against false prophecy. 1–16**: A major challenge for Ezekiel was opposing false prophets, particularly ones advocating nationalistic hope. Such prophets gave the people a false security that robbed them of their chance to find life amid the coming judgment. **4**: *Jackals among ruins* have no regard for their sur-roundings and actually contribute to their decay (Lam 5.18). **5**: True prophets would care enough about their people to go *up into the breaches* (like Moses, Ps 106.23), i.e., to risk their lives by arguing with God on the people's behalf (9.8; 11.13). *Day of the LORD*, see 7.5–9n. **10–16**: *Whitewash*, better "plaster." The false prophets' messages (Jer 23; 27–29), like mud-plaster that dissolves in a storm, were futile attempts to bolster the people, despite their ultimate defenselessness before God's inevitable coming judgment. *Peace . . . no peace*, cf. Jer 6.14; 8.11.

13.17–23: **Against sorceresses**. For a meager fee (v. 19), some exiles safeguarded the wicked and attacked their enemies through black magic. *Bands* and *veils* (perhaps "head clothes" or "necklaces" with amulets at-tached) were likely magical devices used in Babylonian witchcraft to attack and defend, respectively. Magic was prevalent in ancient Babylonia. **18**: The hunting may have involved snatching victims' souls from their bodies. The sorceresses entrap souls like hunters trapping prey, luring people to their deaths.

man lives! Will you hunt down lives among my people, and maintain your own lives? [19] You have profaned me among my people for handfuls of barley and for pieces of bread, putting to death persons who should not die and keeping alive persons who should not live, by your lies to my people, who listen to lies. [20] Therefore thus says the Lord God: I am against your bands with which you hunt lives;[a] I will tear them from your arms, and let the lives go free, the lives that you hunt down like birds. [21] I will tear off your veils, and save my people from your hands; they shall no longer be prey in your hands; and you shall know that I am the Lord. [22] Because you have disheartened the righteous falsely, although I have not disheartened them, and you have encouraged the wicked not to turn from their wicked way and save their lives; [23] therefore you shall no longer see false visions or practice divination; I will save my people from your hand. Then you will know that I am the Lord.

14 Certain elders of Israel came to me and sat down before me. [2] And the word of the Lord came to me: [3] Mortal, these men have taken their idols into their hearts, and placed their iniquity as a stumbling block before them; shall I let myself be consulted by them? [4] Therefore speak to them, and say to them, Thus says the Lord God: Any of those of the house of Israel who take their idols into their hearts and place their iniquity as a stumbling block before them, and yet come to the prophet—I the Lord will answer those who come with the multitude of their idols, [5] in order that I may take hold of the hearts of the house of Israel, all of whom are estranged from me through their idols.

[6] Therefore say to the house of Israel, Thus says the Lord God: Repent and turn away from your idols; and turn away your faces from all your abominations. [7] For any of those of the house of Israel, or of the aliens who reside in Israel, who separate themselves from me, taking their idols into their hearts and placing their iniquity as a stumbling block before them, and yet come to a prophet to inquire of me by him, I the Lord will answer them myself. [8] I will set my face against them; I will make them a sign and a byword and cut them off from the midst of my people; and you shall know that I am the Lord.

[9] If a prophet is deceived and speaks a word, I, the Lord, have deceived that prophet, and I will stretch out my hand against him, and will destroy him from the midst of my people Israel. [10] And they shall bear their punishment—the punishment of the inquirer and the punishment of the prophet shall be the same— [11] so that the house of Israel may no longer go astray from me, nor defile themselves any more with all their transgressions. Then they shall be my people, and I will be their God, says the Lord God.

[12] The word of the Lord came to me: [13] Mortal, when a land sins against me by acting faithlessly, and I stretch out my hand against it, and break its staff of bread and send famine upon it, and cut off from it human beings and animals, [14] even if Noah, Daniel,[b] and Job, these three, were in it, they would save only their own lives by their righteousness, says the Lord God. [15] If I send wild animals through the land to ravage it, so that it is made desolate, and no one may

---

a Gk Syr: Heb *lives for birds*
b Or, as otherwise read, *Danel*

14.1–11: A legal case involving consultation. Ezekiel uses the legal language of the Holiness School to indict sinful elders who try to consult God. Consultation is refused, since the words for the situation have already been inscribed as scripture (see 3.22–27n.). For now there will be no negotiation, only performance (12.28). **5:** *Idols,* not necessarily only false gods here, but any religious duplicity. **6:** *Repent,* cf. 18.21,30; 33.11. **7:** *Aliens,* see 47.21–23n. **9–11:** Deceived prophets will be punished similarly to those inquiring of them. For the Lord deceiving prophets, see 1 Kings 22.23.

14.12–23: The inevitability of God's judgment. Infamous Sodom might have been spared for a sufficient number of righteous people (Gen 18.22–33), but Jerusalem's impending punishment is inevitable (since it is already a matter of scriptural record, 2.8b–3.3n.). Under these circumstances, only righteous individuals themselves can be saved. **14:** Noah (Gen 6.9) and Job (Job 1.1) are renowned in the Bible for their righteousness. Ezekiel's references to Daniel (also 28.3) suggest the Canaanite Danel (see textual note *b*) of the Ugaritic texts (ca.

pass through because of the animals; [16] even if these three men were in it, as I live, says the Lord GOD, they would save neither sons nor daughters; they alone would be saved, but the land would be desolate. [17] Or if I bring a sword upon that land and say, "Let a sword pass through the land," and I cut off human beings and animals from it; [18] though these three men were in it, as I live, says the Lord GOD, they would save neither sons nor daughters, but they alone would be saved. [19] Or if I send a pestilence into that land, and pour out my wrath upon it with blood, to cut off humans and animals from it; [20] even if Noah, Daniel,[a] and Job were in it, as I live, says the Lord GOD, they would save neither son nor daughter; they would save only their own lives by their righteousness.

[21] For thus says the Lord GOD: How much more when I send upon Jerusalem my four deadly acts of judgment, sword, famine, wild animals, and pestilence, to cut off humans and animals from it! [22] Yet, survivors shall be left in it, sons and daughters who will be brought out; they will come out to you. When you see their ways and their deeds, you will be consoled for the evil that I have brought upon Jerusalem, for all that I have brought upon it. [23] They shall console you, when you see their ways and their deeds; and you shall know that it was not without cause that I did all that I have done in it, says the Lord GOD.

15 The word of the LORD came to me: [2] O mortal, how does the wood of the vine surpass all other wood—
the vine branch that is among the trees of the forest?

[3] Is wood taken from it to make anything? Does one take a peg from it on which to hang any object?
[4] It is put in the fire for fuel;
when the fire has consumed both ends of it
and the middle of it is charred,
is it useful for anything?
[5] When it was whole it was used for nothing;
how much less—when the fire has consumed it,
and it is charred—
can it ever be used for anything!

[6] Therefore thus says the Lord GOD: Like the wood of the vine among the trees of the forest, which I have given to the fire for fuel, so I will give up the inhabitants of Jerusalem. [7] I will set my face against them; although they escape from the fire, the fire shall still consume them; and you shall know that I am the LORD, when I set my face against them. [8] And I will make the land desolate, because they have acted faithlessly, says the Lord GOD.

16 The word of the LORD came to me: [2] Mortal, make known to Jerusalem her abominations, [3] and say, Thus says the Lord GOD to Jerusalem: Your origin and your birth were in the land of the Canaanites; your father was an Amorite, and your mother a Hittite. [4] As for your birth, on the day you were born your navel cord was not cut, nor were you washed with water to cleanse you, nor rubbed with salt, nor wrapped in cloths. [5] No eye pitied you, to do any of these things

a   Or, as otherwise read, *Danel*

1400 BCE), who is described as an ideally righteous ruler. **21:** On the four agents of divine judgment, see 5.17 (cf. 5.10n.; 33.27). The four scenarios in vv. 13–14,15–16,17–18, and 19–20 each highlighted one of the agents. **22–23:** *Console,* since their wicked behavior would prove the justice of God's judgment.

15.1–8: Analogy of the useless vine. The wood of the vine is good only when it is cultivated in a vineyard and produces; a wild vine of the forest is practically useless—its fruit may be poisonous (2 Kings 4.39–40), and it is unusable for woodworking. This metaphor for Jerusalem shows it has no worthiness on its own. **7:** *They escaped* from total destruction back in 597 BCE, when the Babylonians first attacked Jerusalem.

16.1–63: The allegory of the unfaithful wife. 1–8: Jerusalem, the foundling. 3: Jerusalem's historical ancestry here suggests a predisposition to apostasy. Ezekiel conveys a ruthless theological image of sin as deep rooted and ineradicable (cf. Gen 8.21; Ps 51.5). The *Canaanites, Amorites,* and *Hittites* were Israel's predecessors in the Promised Land (e.g., Ex 3.8,17; Josh 3.10), whom God commanded Israel to drive out. According to Ezekiel's Holiness School traditions, they were depraved peoples who defiled the land through their abominations (vv. 44–52; Lev 18.24–25). As Israel took root in the land, it did not fully drive out the inhabitants but often assimilated them, their practices, and their cities. The prophet is literally correct that Jerusalem was a Canaanite city, which

for you out of compassion for you; but you were thrown out in the open field, for you were abhorred on the day you were born.

⁶ I passed by you, and saw you flailing about in your blood. As you lay in your blood, I said to you, "Live! ⁷ and grow upᵃ like a plant of the field." You grew up and became tall and arrived at full womanhood;ᵇ your breasts were formed, and your hair had grown; yet you were naked and bare.

⁸ I passed by you again and looked on you; you were at the age for love. I spread the edge of my cloak over you, and covered your nakedness: I pledged myself to you and entered into a covenant with you, says the Lord GOD, and you became mine. ⁹ Then I bathed you with water and washed off the blood from you, and anointed you with oil. ¹⁰ I clothed you with embroidered cloth and with sandals of fine leather; I bound you in fine linen and covered you with rich fabric.ᶜ ¹¹ I adorned you with ornaments: I put bracelets on your arms, a chain on your neck, ¹² a ring on your nose, earrings in your ears, and a beautiful crown upon your head. ¹³ You were adorned with gold and silver, while your clothing was of fine linen, rich fabric,ᶜ and embroidered cloth. You had choice flour and honey and oil for food. You grew exceedingly beautiful, fit to be a queen. ¹⁴ Your fame spread among the nations on account of your beauty, for it was perfect because of my splendor that I had bestowed on you, says the Lord GOD.

¹⁵ But you trusted in your beauty, and played the whore because of your fame, and lavished your whorings on any passer-by.ᵈ ¹⁶ You took some of your garments, and made for yourself colorful shrines, and on them played the whore; nothing like this has ever been or ever shall be.ᶜ ¹⁷ You also took your beautiful jewels of my gold and my silver that I had given you, and made for yourself male images, and with them played the whore; ¹⁸ and you took your embroidered garments to cover them, and set my oil and my incense before them. ¹⁹ Also my bread that I gave you—I fed you with choice flour and oil and honey—you set it before them as a pleasing odor; and so it was, says the Lord GOD. ²⁰ You took your sons and your daughters, whom you had borne to me, and these you sacrificed to them to be devoured. As if your whorings were not enough! ²¹ You slaughtered my children and delivered them up as an offering to them. ²² And in all your abominations and your whorings you did not remember the days of your youth, when you were naked and bare, flailing about in your blood.

²³ After all your wickedness (woe, woe to you! says the Lord GOD), ²⁴ you built yourself a platform and made yourself a lofty place in every square; ²⁵ at the head of every

ᵃ Gk Syr: Heb *Live! I made you a myriad*
ᵇ Cn: Heb *ornament of ornaments*
ᶜ Meaning of Heb uncertain
ᵈ Heb adds *let it be his*

King David captured and assimilated (2 Sam 5.6–10). **4:** Rubbing the skin with salt may have been thought to make it firm; alternatively, the salt may have functioned as an antibacterial agent. Wrapping infants in swaddling *cloths* was a sign of care (Wis 7.4), which this infant was not given. **5–7:** By God's intervention, this abandoned and exposed infant grew into *full womanhood. Breasts* and pubic *hair* indicate sexual maturity. **8:** *Covering* a woman's *nakedness* with a garment is a euphemism for taking a wife and sharing in her sexuality (Ruth 3.9; Deut 22.30; 27.20). *I pledged myself*, see 20.5. The bilateral, mutually committed, and legally binding relationship of marriage constituted a *covenant* in the ancient world (Mal 2.14; Prov 2.17). Several biblical texts depict God's covenant with Israel as a marriage (Hos 1–3; Jer 2.2; 31.32; Isa 50.1; 54.5–6). In like manner, ancient Near Eastern vassal treaties spoke of the covenant relationship between sovereigns and their subjects in terms of love. **9–14:** **The beautiful bride. 9:** The *blood* may signify the breaking of the virginal bride's hymen (see Deut 22.13–21). Alternatively, due to the time compression of the allegory, the birth blood of v. 6 may still be in mind. **15–34: Sexual betrayal.** The image of Israel as a sexually unfaithful wife was first popularized by Hosea, for whom the image had both literal reference to sexualized worship (Hos 4.10–14) and metaphorical reference to religious apostasy in general (Hos 2.13). Ezekiel adopts the image as a metaphor from Hosea and Jeremiah (Jer 3.1–13), intensifies it to shocking extremes, and expands it into a quasi-biography of Israel's infidelity. This biography will climax in Jerusalem's destruction. **20–22:** Children were offered as human sacrifices (20.26,31; 23.37; 2 Kings 23.10; Jer 7.31; 32.35; Isa 57.5,9), against the prohibitions of the Holiness School (Lev 18.21; 20.2). **23–34:** The Zion

street you built your lofty place and prostituted your beauty, offering yourself to every passer-by, and multiplying your whoring. [26] You played the whore with the Egyptians, your lustful neighbors, multiplying your whoring, to provoke me to anger. [27] Therefore I stretched out my hand against you, reduced your rations, and gave you up to the will of your enemies, the daughters of the Philistines, who were ashamed of your lewd behavior. [28] You played the whore with the Assyrians, because you were insatiable; you played the whore with them, and still you were not satisfied. [29] You multiplied your whoring with Chaldea, the land of merchants; and even with this you were not satisfied.

[30] How sick is your heart, says the Lord God, that you did all these things, the deeds of a brazen whore; [31] building your platform at the head of every street, and making your lofty place in every square! Yet you were not like a whore, because you scorned payment. [32] Adulterous wife, who receives strangers instead of her husband! [33] Gifts are given to all whores; but you gave your gifts to all your lovers, bribing them to come to you from all around for your whorings. [34] So you were different from other women in your whorings: no one solicited you to play the whore; and you gave payment, while no payment was given to you; you were different.

[35] Therefore, O whore, hear the word of the Lord: [36] Thus says the Lord God, Because your lust was poured out and your nakedness uncovered in your whoring with your lovers, and because of all your abominable idols, and because of the blood of your children that you gave to them, [37] therefore, I will gather all your lovers, with whom you took pleasure, all those you loved and all those you hated; I will gather them against you from all around, and will uncover your nakedness to them, so that they may see all your nakedness. [38] I will judge you as women who commit adultery and shed blood are judged, and bring blood upon you in wrath and jealousy. [39] I will deliver you into their hands, and they shall throw down your platform and break down your lofty places; they shall strip you of your clothes and take your beautiful objects and leave you naked and bare. [40] They shall bring up a mob against you, and they shall stone you and cut you to pieces with their swords. [41] They shall burn your houses and execute judgments on you in the sight of many women; I will stop you from playing the whore, and you shall also make no more payments. [42] So I will satisfy my fury on you, and my jealousy shall turn away from you; I will be calm, and will be angry no longer. [43] Because you have not remembered the days of your youth, but have enraged me with all these things; therefore, I have returned your deeds upon your head, says the Lord God.

Have you not committed lewdness beyond all your abominations? [44] See, everyone who

theology (see Introduction), in which Ezekiel was steeped, advocated trust in God's exclusive sovereignty over geopolitics (cf. Isa 7.8–9). Given this divine prerogative, foreign alliances were a form of unfaithfulness. **26**: Israel's illicit relations with Egypt culminated for Ezekiel in the negotiations in the early sixth century BCE of King Zedekiah of Judah with Pharaoh Psammetichus II for assistance against Babylonia (17.7n.). *Lustful neighbors*, the Hebrew denotes their oversized genitals (cf. 23.20). **27**: A probable reference to the Assyrian king Sennacherib's transfer of Judean territory to the Philistine cities of Ashdod, Ekron, and Gaza in 701 BCE. Sennacherib's annals describe the event. *Who were ashamed*, even the foreign Philistines were embarrassed by Jerusalem's behavior. **28**: Judah willingly became an Assyrian vassal in 734 BCE (see 2 Kings 16.7–8), after which Assyria dominated the region until the rise of the Babylonians, who destroyed their empire between 614 and 609 BCE. Assyrian records mention that King Manasseh of Judah (698/687–642 BCE) was a loyal vassal. **29**: *Chaldea*, Babylonia. After the battle of Carchemish in 605 BCE, Babylonia became the leading political power in Syria-Palestine. Already in the eighth century BCE, King Hezekiah of Judah entertained a Babylonian embassy to the dismay of the prophet Isaiah, according to 2 Kings 20.12–19. Later, King Jehoiakim of Judah (608–598 BCE) became a vassal of Babylonia (2 Kings 24.1) as did King Zedekiah (597–586 BCE; 17.13–14; 2 Kings 24.20; 2 Chr 36.13). **30–34**: Instead of receiving income for her services, Jerusalem invited her lovers and paid them. **33**: *Gifts*, see 2 Kings 16.7–9; 18.14–16; 23.34–35; Jer 2.18 for examples of Judah's payment of tribute to foreign powers. **35–43**: **The threat of punishment.** Foreign nations (her lovers) will turn against her. God will divorce her and expose her to be stoned

uses proverbs will use this proverb about you, "Like mother, like daughter." [45] You are the daughter of your mother, who loathed her husband and her children; and you are the sister of your sisters, who loathed their husbands and their children. Your mother was a Hittite and your father an Amorite. [46] Your elder sister is Samaria, who lived with her daughters to the north of you; and your younger sister, who lived to the south of you, is Sodom with her daughters. [47] You not only followed their ways, and acted according to their abominations; within a very little time you were more corrupt than they in all your ways. [48] As I live, says the Lord GOD, your sister Sodom and her daughters have not done as you and your daughters have done. [49] This was the guilt of your sister Sodom: she and her daughters had pride, excess of food, and prosperous ease, but did not aid the poor and needy. [50] They were haughty, and did abominable things before me; therefore I removed them when I saw it. [51] Samaria has not committed half your sins; you have committed more abominations than they, and have made your sisters appear righteous by all the abominations that you have committed. [52] Bear your disgrace, you also, for you have brought about for your sisters a more favorable judgment; because of your sins in which you acted more abominably than they, they are more in the right than you. So be ashamed, you also, and bear your disgrace, for you have made your sisters appear righteous.

[53] I will restore their fortunes, the fortunes of Sodom and her daughters and the fortunes of Samaria and her daughters, and I will restore your own fortunes along with theirs, [54] in order that you may bear your disgrace and be ashamed of all that you have done, becoming a consolation to them. [55] As for your sisters, Sodom and her daughters shall return to their former state, Samaria and her daughters shall return to their former state, and you and your daughters shall return to your former state. [56] Was not your sister Sodom a byword in your mouth in the day of your pride, [57] before your wickedness was uncovered? Now you are a mockery to the daughters of Aram[a] and all her neighbors, and to the daughters of the Philistines, those all around who despise you. [58] You must bear the penalty of your lewdness and your abominations, says the LORD.

[59] Yes, thus says the Lord GOD: I will deal with you as you have done, you who have despised the oath, breaking the covenant; [60] yet I will remember my covenant with you in the days of your youth, and I will establish with you an everlasting covenant. [61] Then you will remember your ways, and be ashamed when I[b] take your sisters, both your elder and your younger, and give them to you as daughters, but not on account of my[c] covenant with you. [62] I will establish my covenant with you, and you shall know that I am the LORD, [63] in order that you may remember and be confounded, and never open your mouth again because of your shame, when I forgive you all that you have done, says the Lord GOD.

---

[a] Another reading is *Edom*
[b] Syr: Heb *you*
[c] Heb lacks *my*

(Lev 20.10). **44–58: Additional accusation.** This section elaborates the preceding theme, showing Jerusalem to be so much worse than *Samaria* (2 Kings 17) and *Sodom* (Gen 19), both of which were destroyed, that they *appear righteous* by comparison (Jer 3.11). **46:** *Elder sister,* better "bigger sister" (which makes more sense historically). Likewise, Sodom is a "smaller" sister, not necessarily a *younger* one (by Canaanite geopolitical standards, Sodom was an unimpressive city-state). **49:** Ezekiel does not represent Sodom's characteristic sin in sexual terms but primarily as social and moral injustice, especially toward the *poor and needy.* His perspective expands on Gen 18.20 and 19.13. Ezekiel's Holiness School traditions especially stressed social justice and care for the poor (Lev 19.9–15,33–35; 23.22; 25.13–17 [HS]). **53–58:** God will restore all three sisters, humiliating Jerusalem by putting it on the same footing as Samaria and Sodom. **57:** *Aram* should probably be read as "Edom" (see textual note *a*; cf. 36.5). **59–63: Jerusalem's restoration.** God will remember the covenant with the ancestors, as the Holiness School anticipated (Lev 26.43–45), as well as his marriage contract with Jerusalem (v. 8). **62:** *Will establish my covenant* (see also v. 60), a phrase characteristic of the Holiness School (e.g., Gen 17.7; Ex 6.4; Lev 26.9 [HS]).

17 The word of the LORD came to me: [2] O mortal, propound a riddle, and speak an allegory to the house of Israel. [3] Say: Thus says the Lord GOD:

A great eagle, with great wings and long pinions,
　rich in plumage of many colors,
　came to the Lebanon.
He took the top of the cedar,
　[4] broke off its topmost shoot;
he carried it to a land of trade,
　set it in a city of merchants.
[5] Then he took a seed from the land,
　placed it in fertile soil;
a plant[a] by abundant waters,
　he set it like a willow twig.
[6] It sprouted and became a vine
　spreading out, but low;
its branches turned toward him,
　its roots remained where it stood.
So it became a vine;
　it brought forth branches,
　put forth foliage.

[7] There was another great eagle,
　with great wings and much
　　plumage.
And see! This vine stretched out
　its roots toward him;
it shot out its branches toward him,
　so that he might water it.
From the bed where it was planted
　[8] it was transplanted
to good soil by abundant waters,
　so that it might produce branches
　and bear fruit
　and become a noble vine.
[9] Say: Thus says the Lord GOD:
Will it prosper?

Will he not pull up its roots,
　cause its fruit to rot[a] and wither,
　its fresh sprouting leaves to fade?
No strong arm or mighty army will be
　needed
　to pull it from its roots.
[10] When it is transplanted, will it thrive?
When the east wind strikes it,
　will it not utterly wither,
　wither on the bed where it grew?

[11] Then the word of the LORD came to me: [12] Say now to the rebellious house: Do you not know what these things mean? Tell them: The king of Babylon came to Jerusalem, took its king and its officials, and brought them back with him to Babylon. [13] He took one of the royal offspring and made a covenant with him, putting him under oath (he had taken away the chief men of the land), [14] so that the kingdom might be humble and not lift itself up, and that by keeping his covenant it might stand. [15] But he rebelled against him by sending ambassadors to Egypt, in order that they might give him horses and a large army. Will he succeed? Can one escape who does such things? Can he break the covenant and yet escape? [16] As I live, says the Lord GOD, surely in the place where the king resides who made him king, whose oath he despised, and whose covenant with him he broke—in Babylon he shall die. [17] Pharaoh with his mighty army and great company will not help him in war, when ramps are cast up and siege walls built to cut off many lives. [18] Because he despised the oath and broke the covenant, because he gave his hand and yet did all these things, he shall not escape. [19] Therefore thus says the

[a]　Meaning of Heb uncertain

17.1–24: The allegorical fable of the eagles. Verses 1–10 are the fable, and vv. 11–21 interpret it. **1–10: The fable. 3–4:** *Great eagle,* the Babylonian king Nebuchadrezzar; *Lebanon,* Jerusalem; *the top of the cedar,* house of David (Jer 22.23); *topmost shoot,* Jehoiachin, Judean king who was exiled to Babylon in 597 BCE (2 Kings 24.8–16); *land of trade,* Babylonia; *city of merchants,* Babylon; *seed from the land,* Zedekiah, the last king of Judah (597–586 BCE). **5:** *Placed it in fertile soil,* i.e., made him king in Judah (2 Kings 24.17). **6:** *Low,* submissive to King Nebuchadrezzar. *Branches turned toward him,* loyal in his vassalage. **7:** *Another great eagle,* Psammetichus II of Egypt (594–588 BCE), with whom Zedekiah negotiated for assistance against Babylonia (Jer 37.5). **9–10:** Zedekiah will be unable to resist Nebuchadrezzar (*he,* v. 9; *the east wind,* v. 10) for long, though the Babylonian siege of Jerusalem lasted nineteen months (2 Kings 25.1–4). **11–21: The interpretation. 13:** *Under oath,* 2 Chr 36.13. Nebuchadrezzar would have to punish Zedekiah for violating his oath of loyalty (see v. 7n.). **17:** The original text read, "and not with a mighty army shall he [Nebuchadrezzar] deal with him" (as in v. 9b). The verse was revised after the siege of Jerusalem to reflect historical detail, thus bringing out the prophecy's correlation with its fulfillment.

Lord God: As I live, I will surely return upon his head my oath that he despised, and my covenant that he broke. ²⁰ I will spread my net over him, and he shall be caught in my snare; I will bring him to Babylon and enter into judgment with him there for the treason he has committed against me. ²¹ All the pick[a] of his troops shall fall by the sword, and the survivors shall be scattered to every wind; and you shall know that I, the LORD, have spoken.

²² Thus says the Lord God:
I myself will take a sprig
    from the lofty top of a cedar;
    I will set it out.
I will break off a tender one
    from the topmost of its young twigs;
I myself will plant it
    on a high and lofty mountain.
²³ On the mountain height of Israel
    I will plant it,
in order that it may produce boughs and
        bear fruit,
    and become a noble cedar.
Under it every kind of bird will live;
    in the shade of its branches will nest
    winged creatures of every kind.
²⁴ All the trees of the field shall know
    that I am the LORD.

I bring low the high tree,
    I make high the low tree;
I dry up the green tree
    and make the dry tree flourish.
I the LORD have spoken;
    I will accomplish it.

18 The word of the LORD came to me: ² What do you mean by repeating this proverb concerning the land of Israel, "The parents have eaten sour grapes, and the children's teeth are set on edge"? ³ As I live, says the Lord God, this proverb shall no more be used by you in Israel. ⁴ Know that all lives are mine; the life of the parent as well as the life of the child is mine: it is only the person who sins that shall die.

⁵ If a man is righteous and does what is lawful and right— ⁶ if he does not eat upon the mountains or lift up his eyes to the idols of the house of Israel, does not defile his neighbor's wife or approach a woman during her menstrual period, ⁷ does not oppress anyone, but restores to the debtor his pledge, commits no robbery, gives his bread to the hungry and covers the naked with a garment, ⁸ does not take advance or accrued interest, withholds

a   Another reading is *fugitives*

19–21: Just as Nebuchadrezzar will not overlook Zedekiah's breaking his oath of loyalty, so also will God punish him for breaking the LORD's covenant with Israel (16.59). **22–24: The fable expanded,** an allegory about the restoration of the Davidic monarchy. As in v. 3, the *top of a cedar* is the house of David, but now God becomes the great eagle who is protecting and cultivating it. For the image of the coming king as a *twig* or branch, cf. Isa 11.1; Jer 23.5–6; 33.15; Zech 3.8; 6.12. Other passages in Ezekiel that speak of a new, ideal Davidic king include 29.21; 34.23–24; 37.24–25. *Lofty mountain,* Mount Zion (cf. Isa 2.2). *Noble cedar,* the archetypical "cosmic tree" in Near Eastern mythology. Planted at the center of the world, it connects heaven and earth and offers shelter to all peoples.

18.1–32: Being accountable. 1–4: The text does not necessarily deny the notion of corporate (communal) punishment or contradict the statement of Ex 20.5 that parents can pass on the consequences of sin to their children. In places such as 16.44 and 20.4,30 Ezekiel affirms that sins and their punishments may involve long-term consequences for individuals and for the corporate community. What Ezekiel is stressing is that the exiles cannot hide behind a defense of fatalism but must take responsibility for their present circumstances and their future. The prophet's audience is far from an innocent generation, and it is not appropriate for them to view their present fate as inexorably determined by past actions of their ancestors (cf. Jer 31.29–30, which quotes the same *proverb*). **4:** Ezekiel's stress on individual responsibility is not innovative but recalls Num 16:22–24 (HS; cf. Deut 24.16). God, who owns *all lives,* i.e., "the spirits of all flesh" (Num 16.22 [HS]), desires life for each human creature (cf. Ezek 18.23,32; 33:11), and those Israelites who separate themselves from all offenders against God's holiness will surely find salvation in the midst of God's judgment (Num 16.24 [HS]; cf. Deut 24.16). **5–9:** First, righteous generation. The list includes both ritual and ethical provisions; Ezekiel's theology shares with the Holiness School a concern with the entire range of sin from ceremonial to moral. **6:** *Eat upon the mountains,* idolatrous sacrifices at high places (6.1–14). *Lift up his eyes,* seek aid from (cf. 23.27; 33.25). *Defile his neighbor's wife,* Lev 18.20 (HS). *Menstrual period,* Lev 18.19 (HS). **7:** *Oppress anyone,* Lev 25.17 (HS). *Restores to the debtor his*

his hand from iniquity, executes true justice between contending parties, [9] follows my statutes, and is careful to observe my ordinances, acting faithfully—such a one is righteous; he shall surely live, says the Lord GOD.

[10] If he has a son who is violent, a shedder of blood, [11] who does any of these things (though his father[a] does none of them), who eats upon the mountains, defiles his neighbor's wife, [12] oppresses the poor and needy, commits robbery, does not restore the pledge, lifts up his eyes to the idols, commits abomination, [13] takes advance or accrued interest; shall he then live? He shall not. He has done all these abominable things; he shall surely die; his blood shall be upon himself.

[14] But if this man has a son who sees all the sins that his father has done, considers, and does not do likewise, [15] who does not eat upon the mountains or lift up his eyes to the idols of the house of Israel, does not defile his neighbor's wife, [16] does not wrong anyone, exacts no pledge, commits no robbery, but gives his bread to the hungry and covers the naked with a garment, [17] withholds his hand from iniquity,[b] takes no advance or accrued interest, observes my ordinances, and follows my statutes; he shall not die for his father's iniquity; he shall surely live. [18] As for his father, because he practiced extortion, robbed his brother, and did what is not good among his people, he dies for his iniquity.

[19] Yet you say, "Why should not the son suffer for the iniquity of the father?" When the son has done what is lawful and right, and has been careful to observe all my statutes, he shall surely live. [20] The person who sins shall die. A child shall not suffer for the iniquity of a parent, nor a parent suffer for the iniquity of a child; the righteousness of the righteous shall be his own, and the wickedness of the wicked shall be his own.

[21] But if the wicked turn away from all their sins that they have committed and keep all my statutes and do what is lawful and right, they shall surely live; they shall not die. [22] None of the transgressions that they have committed shall be remembered against them; for the righteousness that they have done they shall live. [23] Have I any pleasure in the death of the wicked, says the Lord GOD, and not rather that they should turn from their ways and live? [24] But when the righteous turn away from their righteousness and commit iniquity and do the same abominable things that the wicked do, shall they live? None of the righteous deeds that they have done shall be remembered; for the treachery of which they are guilty and the sin they have committed, they shall die.

[25] Yet you say, "The way of the Lord is unfair." Hear now, O house of Israel: Is my way unfair? Is it not your ways that are unfair? [26] When the righteous turn away from their righteousness and commit iniquity, they shall die for it; for the iniquity that they have committed they shall die. [27] Again, when the wicked turn away from the wickedness they have committed and do what is lawful and right, they shall save their life. [28] Because they considered and turned away from all the transgressions that they had committed, they shall surely live; they shall not die. [29] Yet the house of Israel says, "The way of the Lord is unfair." O house of Israel, are my ways unfair? Is it not your ways that are unfair?

[30] Therefore I will judge you, O house of Israel, all of you according to your ways, says the Lord GOD. Repent and turn from all your transgressions; otherwise iniquity will be your ruin.[c] [31] Cast away from you all

a   Heb *he*
b   Gk: Heb *the poor*
c   Or *so that they shall not be a stumbling block of iniquity to you*

pledge, returns any security on a loan once a debt is repaid. *Robbery,* Lev 19.13 (HS). **8:** *Interest,* Lev 25.36 (HS). *Executes true justice,* Lev 19.15 (HS); Zech 7.9. **10–13:** Second, wicked generation. A life opposite to that of the father is represented. **10:** *Shedder of blood,* 16.38; 22.3; 23.45; 33.25; Num 35.33–34 (HS). **14–18:** Third, righteous generation; another reversal. **19–20:** Summation: neither the righteousness nor the wickedness of a previous generation is transferable to the next; cf. Deut 24.16. **21–24:** Within an individual's life the same argument pertains. **23:** See v. 4n. **25–29:** To object is to misunderstand God's justice; cf. 33.17,20. **30–32:** The invitation to repentance is open (cf. 14.6; 33.11). The prophet's call that the people create for themselves a *new heart and a new spirit* is later replaced by an emphasis that God will have to take the initiative and perform this action (36.26n.; cf. 11.19; Jer 32.39). *Why will you die?* see 33.11n.

the transgressions that you have committed against me, and get yourselves a new heart and a new spirit! Why will you die, O house of Israel? ³² For I have no pleasure in the death of anyone, says the Lord GOD. Turn, then, and live.

19 As for you, raise up a lamentation for the princes of Israel, ² and say:

What a lioness was your mother
	among lions!
She lay down among young lions,
	rearing her cubs.
³ She raised up one of her cubs;
	he became a young lion,
and he learned to catch prey;
	he devoured humans.
⁴ The nations sounded an alarm against
	him;
	he was caught in their pit;
and they brought him with hooks
	to the land of Egypt.
⁵ When she saw that she was thwarted,
	that her hope was lost,
she took another of her cubs
	and made him a young lion.
⁶ He prowled among the lions;
	he became a young lion,
and he learned to catch prey;
	he devoured people.
⁷ And he ravaged their strongholds,ᵃ
	and laid waste their towns;
the land was appalled, and all in it,
	at the sound of his roaring.
⁸ The nations set upon him
	from the provinces all around;
they spread their net over him;
	he was caught in their pit.

⁹ With hooks they put him in a cage,
	and brought him to the king of
		Babylon;
	they brought him into custody,
so that his voice should be heard no more
	on the mountains of Israel.
¹⁰ Your mother was like a vine in a
		vineyardᵇ
	transplanted by the water,
fruitful and full of branches
	from abundant water.
¹¹ Its strongest stem became
	a ruler's scepter;ᶜ
it towered aloft
	among the thick boughs;
it stood out in its height
	with its mass of branches.
¹² But it was plucked up in fury,
	cast down to the ground;
the east wind dried it up;
	its fruit was stripped off,
its strong stem was withered;
	the fire consumed it.
¹³ Now it is transplanted into the
		wilderness,
	into a dry and thirsty land.
¹⁴ And fire has gone out from its stem,
	has consumed its branches and fruit,
so that there remains in it no strong stem,
	no scepter for ruling.

This is a lamentation, and it is used as a lamentation.

ᵃ Heb *his widows*
ᵇ Cn: Heb *in your blood*
ᶜ Heb *Its strongest stems became rulers' scepters*

19.1–14: Two funeral dirges. 1–9: First dirge. **1:** *Lamentation*, a parody of a dirge, condemning the exploitative and high-handed rule of Judah's last monarchs. *Princes*, monarchic rulers (cf. 12.10; 19.1; 34.24; 37.25; 44.1–3n.). **2:** The *lioness* is Judah (cf. Gen 49.9). **3–4:** The first cub is Jehoahaz, the king who was taken to Egypt in 609 BCE (2 Kings 23.30–34; Jer 22.10–12; 2 Chr 36.4). **5–9:** The identity of the second cub is less certain. It could be King Jehoiachin, who was exiled to Babylon in 597 BCE (Jer 22.24–30; 2 Kings 24.8–16), but is more likely King Zedekiah, likewise exiled to Babylon in 586 BCE (2 Kings 25.7; Jer 39.7). If the latter, the two cubs would have the same literal mother, Hamutal (2 Kings 23.31; 24.18; Jer 52.1). Alternatively, the second cub is Zedekiah's predecessor, King Jehoiakim, although the biblical references to his being brought *into custody* (v. 9) by Nebuchadrezzar and the Babylonians are of questionable historicity (2 Chr 36.6; Dan 1.1–2). Jehoiakim fits the description of the second cub in that *the land was appalled* (v. 7) during his reign (cf. 2 Kings 24.4; Jer 22.13–19).

19.10–14: Second dirge. 10: The *vine* is Judah, and its wild, towering growth signals arrogant pride. **11–13:** The *strongest stem* is King Zedekiah, who was dried up by *the east wind* (Nebuchadrezzar, 17.10) and *transplanted* (taken to Babylon). If the reading of textual note *c* is correct, however, two Judean kings, both Jehoiachin and Zedekiah, are in view.

20

In the seventh year, in the fifth month, on the tenth day of the month, certain elders of Israel came to consult the LORD, and sat down before me. ² And the word of the LORD came to me: ³ Mortal, speak to the elders of Israel, and say to them: Thus says the Lord GOD: Why are you coming? To consult me? As I live, says the Lord GOD, I will not be consulted by you. ⁴ Will you judge them, mortal, will you judge them? Then let them know the abominations of their ancestors, ⁵ and say to them: Thus says the Lord GOD: On the day when I chose Israel, I swore to the offspring of the house of Jacob—making myself known to them in the land of Egypt—I swore to them, saying, I am the LORD your God. ⁶ On that day I swore to them that I would bring them out of the land of Egypt into a land that I had searched out for them, a land flowing with milk and honey, the most glorious of all lands. ⁷ And I said to them, Cast away the detestable things your eyes feast on, every one of you, and do not defile yourselves with the idols of Egypt; I am the LORD your God. ⁸ But they rebelled against me and would not listen to me; not one of them cast away the detestable things their eyes feasted on, nor did they forsake the idols of Egypt.

Then I thought I would pour out my wrath upon them and spend my anger against them in the midst of the land of Egypt. ⁹ But I acted for the sake of my name, that it should not be profaned in the sight of the nations among whom they lived, in whose sight I made myself known to them in bringing them out of the land of Egypt. ¹⁰ So I led them out of the land of Egypt and brought them into the wilderness. ¹¹ I gave them my statutes and showed them my ordinances, by whose observance everyone shall live. ¹² Moreover I gave them my sabbaths, as a sign between me and them, so that they might know that I the LORD sanctify them. ¹³ But the house of Israel rebelled against me in the wilderness; they did not observe my statutes but rejected my ordinances, by whose observance everyone shall live; and my sabbaths they greatly profaned.

Then I thought I would pour out my wrath upon them in the wilderness, to make an end of them. ¹⁴ But I acted for the sake of my name, so that it should not be profaned in the sight of the nations, in whose sight I had brought them out. ¹⁵ Moreover I swore to them in the wilderness that I would not bring them into the land that I had given them, a land flowing with milk and honey, the most

---

20.1–44: Israel's pattern of rebellion. The passage is not intended as a chronological account but as a theological narrative about the people's ingrained waywardness, evident in a pattern of rebellion despite God's self-revelation (vv. 5–9,10–17,18–26). Israel has repeatedly failed to know the LORD, appreciate the LORD's holiness (vv. 12,20,26), and demonstrate this holiness before the world (vv. 9,14,22,39,41). The effect of Ezekiel's rhetoric is to drive home how this same rebellious pattern is inevitable for the present generation (vv. 30–32). **1–4:** Date: August 14, 591 BCE. All consultation of the LORD is prohibited (see v. 31n.; 3.22–27n.; 14.1–11n.). **5–9:** Rebellion in Egypt. **5:** *I am the LORD your God,* Ex 6.7 (HS). **6:** On God's oath to bring the people to the promised land, see Ex 6.8 (HS). *A land flowing with milk and honey,* v. 15; Lev 20.24 (HS; cf. Ex 3.8; Deut 6.3). *Most glorious of all lands,* in Ezekiel God is intensely, even patriotically devoted to the sacred land of Israel (Lev 25.23 [HS]; Ezek 7.22; 34.26; 35.10; 36.5). **7–8:** *I am the LORD your God,* Lev 19.4 (HS). Idolatrous worship in Egypt is mentioned explicitly in Josh 24.14. The Exodus narratives themselves lack information on Hebrew worship practices in Egypt, but Ex 32.1–6 suggests that the people had grown comfortable with worship of images and orgiastic rites. **9:** *For the sake of my name* (vv. 14,22,39,44; cf. 36.20–23; 39.7,25; 43.7–8), the motif in Ezekiel of God's intense concern with the honor of the divine name comes straight out of the Holiness School (see Lev 18.21; 19.12; 20.3; 21.6; 22.2,32 [HS]). The motif emphasizes the mystery of God's mercy (see 36.22–32n.) over against Israel's fossilized heart (cf. 2.4; 3.7; 20.33; 36.26). The people are not, and have not been, pleasing to God, so God must act in a manner set by God's character (God's "name") and by God's intention to infuse the world with divine holiness, not based on how humans make God feel. Only God's proactive grace has preserved Israel in the past and gives the people hope for the future. **10–17:** Rebellion in the wilderness. **11:** Lev 18.5 (HS). **12–13:** Ezekiel is influenced by the emphasis on the sabbath in the Holiness School (Ex 31.13; Lev 19.30; 26.2 [HS]). In this tradition, keeping the sabbath is a sign of the holiness and priestly service of all God's people. For a particular example of violation of the sabbath within the narratives of the Holiness School, see Ex 16.27–30. **13b–17:** Ex 32.9–14; Num 14.11–20;

glorious of all lands, [16] because they rejected my ordinances and did not observe my statutes, and profaned my sabbaths; for their heart went after their idols. [17] Nevertheless my eye spared them, and I did not destroy them or make an end of them in the wilderness.

[18] I said to their children in the wilderness, Do not follow the statutes of your parents, nor observe their ordinances, nor defile yourselves with their idols. [19] I the LORD am your God; follow my statutes, and be careful to observe my ordinances, [20] and hallow my sabbaths that they may be a sign between me and you, so that you may know that I the LORD am your God. [21] But the children rebelled against me; they did not follow my statutes, and were not careful to observe my ordinances, by whose observance everyone shall live; they profaned my sabbaths.

Then I thought I would pour out my wrath upon them and spend my anger against them in the wilderness. [22] But I withheld my hand, and acted for the sake of my name, so that it should not be profaned in the sight of the nations, in whose sight I had brought them out. [23] Moreover I swore to them in the wilderness that I would scatter them among the nations and disperse them through the countries, [24] because they had not executed my ordinances, but had rejected my statutes and profaned my sabbaths, and their eyes were set on their ancestors' idols. [25] Moreover I gave them statutes that were not good and ordinances by which they could not live. [26] I defiled them through their very gifts, in their offering up all their firstborn, in order that I might horrify them, so that they might know that I am the LORD.

[27] Therefore, mortal, speak to the house of Israel and say to them, Thus says the Lord GOD: In this again your ancestors blasphemed me, by dealing treacherously with me. [28] For when I had brought them into the land that I swore to give them, then wherever they saw any high hill or any leafy tree, there they offered their sacrifices and presented the provocation of their offering; there they sent up their pleasing odors, and there they poured out their drink offerings. [29] (I said to them, What is the high place to which you go? So it is called Bamah[a] to this day.) [30] Therefore say to the house of Israel, Thus says the Lord GOD: Will you defile yourselves after the manner of your ancestors and go astray after their detestable things? [31] When you offer your gifts and make your children pass through the fire, you defile yourselves with all your idols to this day. And shall I be consulted by you, O house of Israel? As I live, says the Lord GOD, I will not be consulted by you.

[32] What is in your mind shall never happen—the thought, "Let us be like the nations, like the tribes of the countries, and worship wood and stone."

[33] As I live, says the Lord GOD, surely with a mighty hand and an outstretched arm, and with wrath poured out, I will be king over you. [34] I will bring you out from the peoples and gather you out of the countries where you are scattered, with a mighty hand and an outstretched arm, and with wrath poured out; [35] and I will bring you into the wilderness of the peoples, and there I will enter into judgment with you face to face. [36] As I entered into judgment with your ancestors in the wilderness of the land of Egypt, so I will enter into judgment with you, says the Lord GOD. [37] I will make you pass under the staff,

[a] That is High Place

Deut 9.25–29. **18–26:** Rebellion of the next generation. **25–26:** The people may have been using the "law of the firstborn" (Ex 22.29; 34.19) to legitimate child sacrifice (16.20–22n.). The notion that God's law may be an occasion of punishment, unique in the Hebrew Bible, recurs in Rom 7.7–13. **27–32:** Application of the passage to Ezekiel's contemporaries. **29:** High place, 6.3n. The Heb word for "high place" ("bamah") is explained by the preceding words ("what" ["mah"] and "go" ["ba"]). **31:** On making children pass through the fire, see 16.20–22n.; 23.37; Deut 18.10; 2 Kings 16.3; 17.17; 21.6. The end of the verse echoes v. 3, forming an inclusio (envelope) around the passage. Judgment on the people's faithless state is fixed: Ezekiel can not intervene for them with God (see 3.22–27n.). **33–38:** A new Exodus and judgment in the wilderness. This is an oracle of promise, but with an angry tone dating prior to Jerusalem's destruction in 586 BCE. God will triumph with Israel, through force if necessary. (In accord with Zion theology, the election of God's people is ultimately irrevocable. See Introduction;

and will bring you within the bond of the covenant. ³⁸ I will purge out the rebels among you, and those who transgress against me; I will bring them out of the land where they reside as aliens, but they shall not enter the land of Israel. Then you shall know that I am the LORD.

³⁹ As for you, O house of Israel, thus says the Lord GOD: Go serve your idols, every one of you now and hereafter, if you will not listen to me; but my holy name you shall no more profane with your gifts and your idols.

⁴⁰ For on my holy mountain, the mountain height of Israel, says the Lord GOD, there all the house of Israel, all of them, shall serve me in the land; there I will accept them, and there I will require your contributions and the choicest of your gifts, with all your sacred things. ⁴¹ As a pleasing odor I will accept you, when I bring you out from the peoples, and gather you out of the countries where you have been scattered; and I will manifest my holiness among you in the sight of the nations. ⁴² You shall know that I am the LORD, when I bring you into the land of Israel, the country that I swore to give to your ancestors. ⁴³ There you shall remember your ways and all the deeds by which you have polluted yourselves; and you shall loathe yourselves for all the evils that you have committed. ⁴⁴ And you shall know that I am the LORD, when I deal with you for my name's sake, not according to your evil ways, or corrupt deeds, O house of Israel, says the Lord GOD.

⁴⁵ ᵃThe word of the LORD came to me: ⁴⁶ Mortal, set your face toward the south, preach against the south, and prophesy against the forest land in the Negeb; ⁴⁷ say to the forest of the Negeb, Hear the word of the LORD: Thus says the Lord GOD, I will kindle a fire in you, and it shall devour every green tree in you and every dry tree; the blazing flame shall not be quenched, and all faces from south to north shall be scorched by it. ⁴⁸ All flesh shall see that I the LORD have kindled it; it shall not be quenched. ⁴⁹ Then I said, "Ah Lord GOD! they are saying of me, 'Is he not a maker of allegories?'"

21 ᵇ The word of the LORD came to me: ² Mortal, set your face toward Jerusalem and preach against the sanctuaries; prophesy against the land of Israel ³ and say to the land of Israel, Thus says the LORD: I am coming against you, and will draw my sword out of its sheath, and will cut off from you both righteous and wicked. ⁴ Because I will cut off from you both righteous and wicked, therefore my sword shall go out of its sheath against all flesh from south to north; ⁵ and all flesh shall know that I the LORD have drawn my sword out of its sheath; it shall not be sheathed again. ⁶ Moan therefore, mortal; moan with breaking heart and bitter grief before their eyes. ⁷ And when they say to you, "Why do you moan?" you shall say, "Because of the news that has come. Every heart will melt and all hands will be feeble, every spirit will faint and all knees will turn to water. See, it comes and it will be fulfilled," says the Lord GOD.

⁸ And the word of the LORD came to me: ⁹ Mortal, prophesy and say: Thus says the Lord; Say:

A sword, a sword is sharpened,
    it is also polished;
¹⁰ it is sharpened for slaughter,
    honed to flash like lightning!
How can we make merry?
    You have despised the rod,
    and all discipline.ᶜ

ᵃ Ch 21.1 in Heb
ᵇ Ch 21.6 in Heb
ᶜ Meaning of Heb uncertain

Lev 26.42 [HS].) As in the wilderness (Num 14.26–35 [HS]), the unfaithful will be purged. 37: *Pass under the staff*, see Lev 27.32 (HS). **39–44: Final acceptance.** After the new Exodus, God will restore the people to Zion, and their sacrifices will again be acceptable. Deity, nation, and land will be united in covenant once and for all. **40:** Ezekiel's Zion theology (cf. 5.5n.; 28.14; 40:2; 43.12; Ob 16; Zech 8.3; Joel 3.17). *Mountain height of Israel,* 17.23; 34.14.

20.45–21.32: Sword prophecies (Lev 26.25,33 [HS]). **20.45–21.7: The sword against all flesh. 20.45–49:** *South* and *Negeb* both stand for Judah and Jerusalem, which lie south of their attackers. **49:** The people cannot take a claim of Jerusalem's vulnerability seriously (see 2.6n.; 3.7; 33.32). **21.1–5:** The preceding forest fire is interpreted as the sword of God. **6–7:** The message is reiterated through an expressive action.

21.8–17: Song of the sword. The sword is first polished (vv. 8–13), and then it will be engaged (vv. 14–17). **12:**

11 The sword[a] is given to be polished,
   to be grasped in the hand;
it is sharpened, the sword is polished,
   to be placed in the slayer's hand.
12 Cry and wail, O mortal,
   for it is against my people;
it is against all Israel's princes;
   they are thrown to the sword,
   together with my people.
   Ah! Strike the thigh!
13 For consider: What! If you despise the rod,
will it not happen?[b] says the Lord GOD.
14 And you, mortal, prophesy;
   strike hand to hand.
Let the sword fall twice, thrice;
   it is a sword for killing.
A sword for great slaughter—
   it surrounds them;
15 therefore hearts melt
   and many stumble.
At all their gates I have set
   the point[b] of the sword.
Ah! It is made for flashing,
   it is polished[c] for slaughter.
16 Attack to the right!
   Engage to the left!
   —wherever your edge is directed.
17 I too will strike hand to hand,
   I will satisfy my fury;
   I the LORD have spoken.
18 The word of the LORD came to me: 19 Mortal, mark out two roads for the sword of the king of Babylon to come; both of them shall issue from the same land. And make a signpost, make it for a fork in the road leading to a city; 20 mark out the road for the sword to come to Rabbah of the Ammonites or to Judah and to[d] Jerusalem the fortified. 21 For the king of Babylon stands at the parting of the way, at the fork in the two roads, to use divination; he shakes the arrows, he consults the teraphim,[e] he inspects the liver. 22 Into his right hand comes the lot for Jerusalem, to set battering rams, to call out for slaughter, for raising the battle cry, to set battering rams against the gates, to cast up ramps, to build siege towers. 23 But to them it will seem like a false divination; they have sworn solemn oaths; but he brings their guilt to remembrance, bringing about their capture.

24 Therefore thus says the Lord GOD: Because you have brought your guilt to remembrance, in that your transgressions are uncovered, so that in all your deeds your sins appear—because you have come to remembrance, you shall be taken in hand.[f]
25 As for you, vile, wicked prince of Israel,
   you whose day has come,
   the time of final punishment,
26 thus says the Lord GOD:
Remove the turban, take off the crown;
   things shall not remain as they are.
Exalt that which is low,
   abase that which is high.
27 A ruin, a ruin, a ruin—
   I will make it!
   (Such has never occurred.)
Until he comes whose right it is;
   to him I will give it.
28 As for you, mortal, prophesy, and say, Thus says the Lord GOD concerning the Ammonites, and concerning their reproach; say:

a Heb It
b Meaning of Heb uncertain
c Tg: Heb wrapped up
d Gk Syr: Heb Judah in
e Or the household gods
f Or be taken captive

Strike the thigh, a sign of mourning (Jer 31.19). 14: Strike hand to hand, in vexation (also v. 17; cf. 6.11).
   21.18–32: The sword of Nebuchadrezzar. 18–24: A symbolic act. 20: Rabbah (modern Amman, Jordan), capital of Ammon (25.5). 21: Perhaps from Riblah (see 2 Kings 25.6), Nebuchadrezzar uses divination to determine which rebel to attack first: belomancy (i.e., casting of arrows inscribed with names of projected victims); necromancy (teraphim were a traditional family's religious images, perhaps ancestor figurines [Gen 31.19; 1 Sam 19.13], sometimes expected to convey messages to the living [see Zech 10.2]); and hepatoscopy (making predictions based on the configurations and markings of animal livers). 22: The sword is about to fall—on Jerusalem! 23: The results of the divination seem false to the Jerusalemites, since they believe Jerusalem invulnerable (20.49n.). 25–27: The sword will strike Zedekiah, Judah's last king (Jer 21.7). To him, i.e., to Nebuchadrezzar. Ezekiel turns language drawn from Gen 49.10 upside down in order to destroy the false hopes of the Jerusalemites. 21.28–32: A poem addressing the Babylonian sword directly and telling it of its own eventual punishment. 28: A prose introduction alerts the Ammonites (see v. 20) that their glee over the sword's work (25.3,6) will be short-lived.

A sword, a sword! Drawn for slaughter,
    polished to consume,[a] to flash like
    lightning.
[29] Offering false visions for you,
    divining lies for you,
they place you over the necks
    of the vile, wicked ones—
those whose day has come,
    the time of final punishment.
[30] Return it to its sheath!
In the place where you were created,
    in the land of your origin,
    I will judge you.
[31] I will pour out my indignation upon you,
    with the fire of my wrath
    I will blow upon you.
I will deliver you into brutish hands,
    those skillful to destroy.
[32] You shall be fuel for the fire,
    your blood shall enter the earth;
you shall be remembered no more,
    for I the LORD have spoken.

22 The word of the LORD came to me: [2] You, mortal, will you judge, will you judge the bloody city? Then declare to it all its abominable deeds. [3] You shall say, Thus says the Lord GOD: A city! Shedding blood within itself; its time has come; making its idols, defiling itself. [4] You have become guilty by the blood that you have shed, and defiled by the idols that you have made; you have brought your day near, the appointed time of your years has come. Therefore I have made you a disgrace before the nations, and a mockery to all the countries. [5] Those who are near and those who are far from you will mock you, you infamous one, full of tumult.

[6] The princes of Israel in you, everyone according to his power, have been bent on shedding blood. [7] Father and mother are treated with contempt in you; the alien residing within you suffers extortion; the orphan and the widow are wronged in you. [8] You have

despised my holy things, and profaned my sabbaths. [9] In you are those who slander to shed blood, those in you who eat upon the mountains, who commit lewdness in your midst. [10] In you they uncover their fathers' nakedness; in you they violate women in their menstrual periods. [11] One commits abomination with his neighbor's wife; another lewdly defiles his daughter-in-law; another in you defiles his sister, his father's daughter. [12] In you, they take bribes to shed blood; you take both advance interest and accrued interest, and make gain of your neighbors by extortion; and you have forgotten me, says the Lord GOD.

[13] See, I strike my hands together at the dishonest gain you have made, and at the blood that has been shed within you. [14] Can your courage endure, or can your hands remain strong in the days when I shall deal with you? I the LORD have spoken, and I will do it. [15] I will scatter you among the nations and disperse you through the countries, and I will purge your filthiness out of you. [16] And I[b] shall be profaned through you in the sight of the nations; and you shall know that I am the LORD.

[17] The word of the LORD came to me: [18] Mortal, the house of Israel has become dross to me; all of them, silver,[c] bronze, tin, iron, and lead. In the smelter they have become dross. [19] Therefore thus says the Lord GOD: Because you have all become dross, I will gather you into the midst of Jerusalem. [20] As one gathers silver, bronze, iron, lead, and tin into a smelter, to blow the fire upon them in order to melt them; so I will gather you in my anger and in my wrath, and I will put you in and melt you. [21] I will gather you and blow upon

---

a   Cn: Heb *to contain*
b   Gk Syr Vg: Heb *you*
c   Transposed from the end of the verse; compare
    verse 20

29: Divination (v. 21) has directed the sword's use. **30–32:** Although Nebuchadrezzar served as God's agent, he himself, and Babylonia, will eventually face God's judgment.

22.1–31: Prophecies of smelting judgment. **22.1–16: A prophecy against Jerusalem, the bloody city.** The indictment of vv. 6–12 contains a catalogue of sins based on the regulations of the Holiness School (Lev 18–20). **13–16:** In scorn and anger (*strike my hands together*, 21.14,17) God will punish this bloody city (18.10n.; Num 35.33–34 [HS]).

22.17–22: Israel is dross. The judgment will be like a smelter in which base metals are removed.

you with the fire of my wrath, and you shall be melted within it. [22] As silver is melted in a smelter, so you shall be melted in it; and you shall know that I the LORD have poured out my wrath upon you.

[23] The word of the LORD came to me: [24] Mortal, say to it: You are a land that is not cleansed, not rained upon in the day of indignation. [25] Its princes[a] within it are like a roaring lion tearing the prey; they have devoured human lives; they have taken treasure and precious things; they have made many widows within it. [26] Its priests have done violence to my teaching and have profaned my holy things; they have made no distinction between the holy and the common, neither have they taught the difference between the unclean and the clean, and they have disregarded my sabbaths, so that I am profaned among them. [27] Its officials within it are like wolves tearing the prey, shedding blood, destroying lives to get dishonest gain. [28] Its prophets have smeared whitewash on their behalf, seeing false visions and divining lies for them, saying, "Thus says the Lord GOD," when the LORD has not spoken. [29] The people of the land have practiced extortion and committed robbery; they have oppressed the poor and needy, and have extorted from the alien without redress. [30] And I sought for anyone among them who would repair the wall and stand in the breach before me on behalf of the land, so that I would not destroy it; but I found no one. [31] Therefore I have poured out my indignation upon them; I have consumed them with the fire of my wrath; I have

returned their conduct upon their heads, says the LORD GOD.

23

The word of the LORD came to me: [2] Mortal, there were two women, the daughters of one mother; [3] they played the whore in Egypt; they played the whore in their youth; their breasts were caressed there, and their virgin bosoms were fondled. [4] Oholah was the name of the elder and Oholibah the name of her sister. They became mine, and they bore sons and daughters. As for their names, Oholah is Samaria, and Oholibah is Jerusalem.

[5] Oholah played the whore while she was mine; she lusted after her lovers the Assyrians, warriors[b] [6] clothed in blue, governors and commanders, all of them handsome young men, mounted horsemen. [7] She bestowed her favors upon them, the choicest men of Assyria all of them; and she defiled herself with all the idols of everyone for whom she lusted. [8] She did not give up her whorings that she had practiced since Egypt; for in her youth men had lain with her and fondled her virgin bosom and poured out their lust upon her. [9] Therefore I delivered her into the hands of her lovers, into the hands of the Assyrians, for whom she lusted. [10] These uncovered her nakedness; they seized her sons and her daughters; and they killed her with the sword. Judgment was executed upon her, and she became a byword among women.

[a] Gk: Heb *indignation.* [25]*A conspiracy of its prophets*
[b] Meaning of Heb uncertain

22.23–31: All classes are corrupt. This oracle seems to come after Jerusalem's fall in 586 BCE (see v. 31) and describes Judah's sinfulness in retrospect. All classes of Judean society were corrupt, and all must be punished; cf. Jer 8.8–10; Zeph 3.3–4. **26:** 42.20; 44.23; Lev 10.10–11 (HS). **28:** 13.10–16n. **30:** 13.5n.

23.1–49: The allegory of the sisters, Oholah and Oholibah (cf. ch 16). **1–4:** Introduction. **3:** *In Egypt,* thus Israel's apostasy was deep-rooted (20.5–9). **4:** The wordplay *Oholah,* "her [own] tent," (i.e., Samaria, which had been the northern kingdom of Israel), and *Oholibah,* "my tent [is] in her" (i.e., Jerusalem), may suggest that though the northern kingdom had shrines to Yahweh, God's real dwelling (tent) was in Jerusalem, thus emphasizing the enormity of Judah's apostasy. The two names are reminiscent of the Israelites' origins as tent-dwelling peoples (see Gen 36.2 for a similar type of name). Oholah/Samaria is a "bigger" sister, not necessarily an *elder* one (see 16.46n.). Ezekiel borrowed the image of the marrying of sisters from Jeremiah (Jer 3.6–11). **5–10:** Oholah. The northern kingdom is condemned for its alliances with Assyria (e.g., 2 Kings 15.19; 17.3). Like Jeremiah (4.30; same rare word for "*lovers*" as in Ezek 23.5,9), Ezekiel viewed foreign alliances as disloyalty to God. For Ezekiel, true realism was not political pragmatism but trust in God's geopolitical prerogative. **10:** The fall of Samaria to Assyria in 722 BCE. **11–21:** Indictment of Oholibah. Jerusalem, like Samaria, is condemned for its foreign alliances. Judah had allied itself with Assyria (2 Kings 16.7–9) and then with Babylon (17.13; 2 Kings 24.1,17;

[11] Her sister Oholibah saw this, yet she was more corrupt than she in her lusting and in her whorings, which were worse than those of her sister. [12] She lusted after the Assyrians, governors and commanders, warriors[a] clothed in full armor, mounted horsemen, all of them handsome young men. [13] And I saw that she was defiled; they both took the same way. [14] But she carried her whorings further; she saw male figures carved on the wall, images of the Chaldeans portrayed in vermilion, [15] with belts around their waists, with flowing turbans on their heads, all of them looking like officers—a picture of Babylonians whose native land was Chaldea. [16] When she saw them she lusted after them, and sent messengers to them in Chaldea. [17] And the Babylonians came to her into the bed of love, and they defiled her with their lust; and after she defiled herself with them, she turned from them in disgust. [18] When she carried on her whorings so openly and flaunted her nakedness, I turned in disgust from her, as I had turned from her sister. [19] Yet she increased her whorings, remembering the days of her youth, when she played the whore in the land of Egypt [20] and lusted after her paramours there, whose members were like those of donkeys, and whose emission was like that of stallions. [21] Thus you longed for the lewdness of your youth, when the Egyptians[b] fondled your bosom and caressed[c] your young breasts.

[22] Therefore, O Oholibah, thus says the Lord GOD: I will rouse against you your lovers from whom you turned in disgust, and I will bring them against you from every side: [23] the Babylonians and all the Chaldeans, Pekod and Shoa and Koa, and all the Assyrians with them, handsome young men, governors and commanders all of them, officers and warriors,[d] all of them riding on horses. [24] They shall come against you from the north[e] with chariots and wagons and a host of peoples; they shall set themselves against you on every side with buckler, shield, and helmet, and I will commit the judgment to them, and they shall judge you according to their ordinances. [25] I will direct my indignation against you, in order that they may deal with you in fury. They shall cut off your nose and your ears, and your survivors shall fall by the sword. They shall seize your sons and your daughters, and your survivors shall be devoured by fire. [26] They shall also strip you of your clothes and take away your fine jewels. [27] So I will put an end to your lewdness and your whoring brought from the land of Egypt; you shall not long for them, or remember Egypt any more. [28] For thus says the Lord GOD: I will deliver you into the hands of those whom you hate, into the hands of those from whom you turned in disgust; [29] and they shall deal with you in hatred, and take away all the fruit of your labor, and leave you naked and bare, and the nakedness of your whorings shall be exposed. Your lewdness and your whorings [30] have brought this upon you, because you played the whore with the nations, and polluted yourself with their idols. [31] You have gone the way of your sister; therefore I will give her cup into your hand. [32] Thus says the Lord GOD:

You shall drink your sister's cup,
    deep and wide;
you shall be scorned and derided,
    it holds so much.
[33] You shall be filled with drunkenness and
    sorrow.
A cup of horror and desolation
    is the cup of your sister Samaria;

---

[a] Meaning of Heb uncertain
[b] Two Mss: MT *from Egypt*
[c] Cn: Heb *for the sake of*
[d] Compare verses 6 and 12: Heb *officers and called ones*
[e] Gk: Meaning of Heb uncertain

---

cf. Isa 39.1–8). **17:** Judah swung to an anti-Babylonian policy (2 Kings 24.20; Jer 27.3). **19:** The passage moves to the contemporary event of Judah's alliance with Egypt (17.7,15). **20:** The reference is to oversized genitals and ejaculations; cf. 16.26n. Horses are proverbially oversexed (Jer 5.8). **22–35:** Announcements about Oholibah's punishment. **23:** Kindred allies of the *Babylonians* included *Pekod* (an important Aramean tribe in southeast Babylonia), *Shoa* and *Koa* (unknown tribes). The three names sound like Hebrew words for "punishment!" "war cry!" and "shriek!" and Ezekiel may have chosen the names to produce a striking wordplay. *Assyrian* troops were co-opted by their Babylonian conquerors. **32–34:** The poem of the cup of wrath (Jer 25.15–29; Hab 2.16; Ob 16)

³⁴ you shall drink it and drain it out,
and gnaw its sherds,
and tear out your breasts;
for I have spoken, says the Lord GOD. ³⁵ Therefore thus says the Lord GOD: Because you have forgotten me and cast me behind your back, therefore bear the consequences of your lewdness and whorings.

³⁶ The LORD said to me: Mortal, will you judge Oholah and Oholibah? Then declare to them their abominable deeds. ³⁷ For they have committed adultery, and blood is on their hands; with their idols they have committed adultery; and they have even offered up to them for food the children whom they had borne to me. ³⁸ Moreover this they have done to me: they have defiled my sanctuary on the same day and profaned my sabbaths. ³⁹ For when they had slaughtered their children for their idols, on the same day they came into my sanctuary to profane it. This is what they did in my house.

⁴⁰ They even sent for men to come from far away, to whom a messenger was sent, and they came. For them you bathed yourself, painted your eyes, and decked yourself with ornaments; ⁴¹ you sat on a stately couch, with a table spread before it on which you had placed my incense and my oil. ⁴² The sound of a raucous multitude was around her, with many of the rabble brought in drunken from the wilderness; and they put bracelets on the arms[a] of the women, and beautiful crowns upon their heads. ⁴³ Then I said, Ah, she is worn out with adulteries, but they carry on their sexual acts with her. ⁴⁴ For they have gone in to her, as one goes in to a whore. Thus they went in to Oholah and to Oholibah, wanton women. ⁴⁵ But righteous judges shall declare them guilty of adultery and of bloodshed; because they are adulteresses and blood is on their hands.

⁴⁶ For thus says the Lord GOD: Bring up an assembly against them, and make them an object of terror and of plunder. ⁴⁷ The assembly shall stone them and with their swords they shall cut them down; they shall kill their sons and their daughters, and burn up their houses. ⁴⁸ Thus will I put an end to lewdness in the land, so that all women may take warning and not commit lewdness as you have done. ⁴⁹ They shall repay you for your lewdness, and you shall bear the penalty for your sinful idolatry; and you shall know that I am the Lord GOD.

24 In the ninth year, in the tenth month, on the tenth day of the month, the word of the LORD came to me: ² Mortal, write down the name of this day, this very day. The king of Babylon has laid siege to Jerusalem this very day. ³ And utter an allegory to the rebellious house and say to them, Thus says the Lord GOD:
Set on the pot, set it on,
pour in water also;
⁴ put in it the pieces,
all the good pieces, the thigh and the
shoulder;
fill it with choice bones.
⁵ Take the choicest one of the flock,
pile the logs[b] under it;
boil its pieces,[c]
seethe[d] also its bones in it.

⁶ Therefore thus says the Lord GOD:
Woe to the bloody city,
the pot whose rust is in it,
whose rust has not gone out of it!

a Heb *hands*
b Compare verse 10: Heb *the bones*
c Two Mss: Heb *its boilings*
d Cn: Heb *its bones seethe*

links Jerusalem's fate with Samaria's. **36–49: The case against the sisters.** As adulterers are stoned (Lev 20.10), so the adultery (i.e., idolatry, child sacrifice, profanation of the sabbath, foreign alliances) of Samaria and Judah has been and will be punished—with death. **37:** 16.20–22n. **40:** Cf. vv. 16–17. **48:** Oholibah's fate becomes an object lesson (cf. v. 10; 26.16; 27.35; 30.9).

24:1–14: The allegory of the pot is a disputation with those still quoting nationalistic slogans about Jerusalem being as inviolable as a cauldron (11.3). Ezekiel turns the cauldron image on its head by depicting it as a dirty pot about to be cleaned by overheating (like a modern self-cleaning oven; vv. 5,9) until the bones inside are burned (v. 10). **1:** January 15, 588 BCE, the day that the Babylonian siege of Jerusalem began. **5:** Jerusalem will be *boiled* as its assailants heap siege equipment around it. **6–8:** Going beyond mere interpretation, these verses expand the image of the pot to provide reasons for Jerusalem's punishment. *Rust*, or, alternatively, "encrusted

Empty it piece by piece,
  making no choice at all.[a]
[7] For the blood she shed is inside it;
  she placed it on a bare rock;
she did not pour it out on the ground,
  to cover it with earth.
[8] To rouse my wrath, to take vengeance,
I have placed the blood she shed
  on a bare rock,
  so that it may not be covered.
[9] Therefore thus says the Lord God:
Woe to the bloody city!
  I will even make the pile great.
[10] Heap up the logs, kindle the fire;
  boil the meat well, mix in the spices,
  let the bones be burned.
[11] Stand it empty upon the coals,
  so that it may become hot, its copper
    glow,
  its filth melt in it, its rust be consumed.
[12] In vain I have wearied myself;[b]
  its thick rust does not depart.
  To the fire with its rust![c]
[13] Yet, when I cleansed you in your filthy
    lewdness,
  you did not become clean from your
    filth;
you shall not again be cleansed
  until I have satisfied my fury upon you.
[14] I the Lord have spoken; the time is coming,
I will act. I will not refrain, I will not spare, I
will not relent. According to your ways and
your doings I will judge you, says the Lord
God.
[15] The word of the Lord came to me:
[16] Mortal, with one blow I am about to take

away from you the delight of your eyes; yet
you shall not mourn or weep, nor shall your
tears run down. [17] Sigh, but not aloud; make
no mourning for the dead. Bind on your
turban, and put your sandals on your feet;
do not cover your upper lip or eat the bread
of mourners.[d] [18] So I spoke to the people in
the morning, and at evening my wife died.
And on the next morning I did as I was commanded.

[19] Then the people said to me, "Will you
not tell us what these things mean for us,
that you are acting this way?" [20] Then I said
to them: The word of the Lord came to me:
[21] Say to the house of Israel, Thus says the
Lord God: I will profane my sanctuary, the
pride of your power, the delight of your eyes,
and your heart's desire; and your sons and
your daughters whom you left behind shall
fall by the sword. [22] And you shall do as I have
done; you shall not cover your upper lip or
eat the bread of mourners.[d] [23] Your turbans
shall be on your heads and your sandals on
your feet; you shall not mourn or weep, but
you shall pine away in your iniquities and
groan to one another. [24] Thus Ezekiel shall be
a sign to you; you shall do just as he has done.
When this comes, then you shall know that I
am the Lord God.

[25] And you, mortal, on the day when I
take from them their stronghold, their joy

a Heb *piece, no lot has fallen on it*
b Cn: Meaning of Heb uncertain
c Meaning of Heb uncertain
d Vg Tg: Heb *of men*

gunk" (also vv. 11–12), represents injustice and bloodguilt (22.6–12).

  24.15–27: The sign of the death of Ezekiel's wife. Ezekiel's symbolic action shows the people that the loss
of the Temple and cherished persons at Jerusalem's fiery destruction in 586 BCE will bring profound recognition, reverent awe, and the submergence of ego. The people will mirror Aaron's silent mourning following the
release of holy fire in Lev 10.1–7, when God manifested the divine holiness and took two of Aaron's sons with
one blow. Ezek 24.17 uses the same Heb verb as Lev 10.3. **16–17:** The Lord commands the prophet to stifle all
expressions of grief and forgo all rituals of mourning, such as the unbinding of the hair, the removal of shoes,
the covering of the *upper lip*, and the eating of the *bread of mourners*. Ezekiel is again drawing from Lev 10.1–7,
where the Holiness School stresses that Aaron's silence at God's epiphany should properly include shunning
all participation in mourning and funerary rituals. Holiness and death are antithetical realities for the Holiness
School, and those in contact with God's holiness must avoid the realm of death, mourning, and burial (see
44.25n.). In acting out Aaron's avoidance of mourning, Ezekiel conveys to the people that the fall of Jerusalem
will be a major epiphany of divine holiness on earth. **22–24:** The people's deep, silent grief will signify a profound discernment of divine judgment (in contrast to their previous skepticism and enmity toward Ezekiel).
It will also entail recognition of God's otherness (v. 24), which will afford the exiles the gracious opportunity

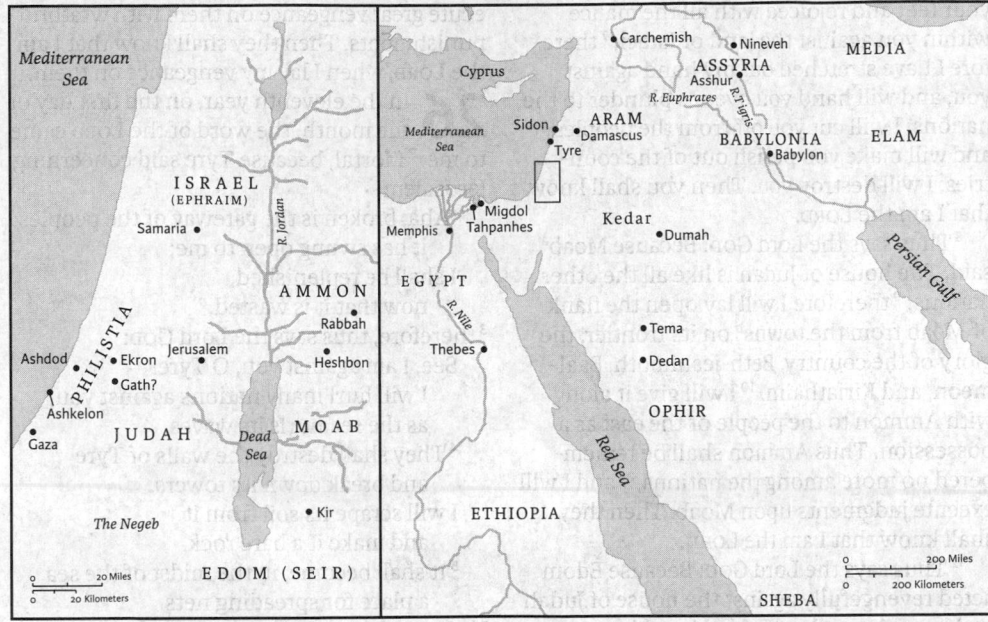

Chs 25–32: Places mentioned in the oracles against foreign nations.

and glory, the delight of their eyes and their heart's affection, and also[a] their sons and their daughters, ²⁶ on that day, one who has escaped will come to you to report to you the news. ²⁷ On that day your mouth shall be opened to the one who has escaped, and you shall speak and no longer be silent. So you shall be a sign to them; and they shall know that I am the LORD.

25 The word of the LORD came to me: ² Mortal, set your face toward the Ammonites and prophesy against them. ³ Say to the Ammonites, Hear the word of the Lord GOD: Thus says the Lord GOD, Because you

said, "Aha!" over my sanctuary when it was profaned, and over the land of Israel when it was made desolate, and over the house of Judah when it went into exile; ⁴ therefore I am handing you over to the people of the east for a possession. They shall set their encampments among you and pitch their tents in your midst; they shall eat your fruit, and they shall drink your milk. ⁵ I will make Rabbah a pasture for camels and Ammon a fold for flocks. Then you shall know that I am the LORD. ⁶ For thus says the Lord GOD: Because you have clapped your hands and stamped

---

a   Heb lacks *and also*

for self-transcendence. **25–27: The release from speechlessness predicted.** The prophet's muted response to the death of his wife has been a continuation of the divinely imposed bridling of his tongue in effect since his commissioning (3.22–27). When word of the fall of Jerusalem reaches Ezekiel (see 33.21–22), his tongue will be loosed (3.27), and he will proclaim a new message of restoration. At that time, Ezekiel's speechlessness will be transferred to and appropriated by the people (v. 23). That is, they will fully accept God's insistence from the start of the book on radically prioritizing the divine intention and its sure performance. They will drop a false reliance on *the pride of* their *power* (v. 21) and *their stronghold* (v. 25).

25.1–32.32: Oracles against the nations. This part of Ezekiel is an effective bridge between the book's message of doom and its message of hope. Here, doom for Israel's antagonists spells hope for Israel itself. Seven nations (Ammon, Moab, Edom, Philistia, Tyre, Sidon, and Egypt) will be punished before Israel is restored (36.5–7).

25.1–17: Oracles against Ammon, Moab, Edom, and Philistia. 1–7: Against Ammon (21.28; Am 1.13–15; Jer 49.1–6). Ammon, which had maliciously gloated over Judah's fall (Lam 2.15–16), is to be occupied by *the people of the east* (v. 4; cf. Isa 11.14), i.e., nomadic Arab tribes. **5:** *Rabbah* (modern Amman, Jordan) was the Ammonite

your feet and rejoiced with all the malice within you against the land of Israel, [7] therefore I have stretched out my hand against you, and will hand you over as plunder to the nations. I will cut you off from the peoples and will make you perish out of the countries; I will destroy you. Then you shall know that I am the LORD.

[8] Thus says the Lord GOD: Because Moab[a] said, The house of Judah is like all the other nations, [9] therefore I will lay open the flank of Moab from the towns[b] on its frontier, the glory of the country, Beth-jeshimoth, Baal-meon, and Kiriathaim. [10] I will give it along with Ammon to the people of the east as a possession. Thus Ammon shall be remembered no more among the nations, [11] and I will execute judgments upon Moab. Then they shall know that I am the LORD.

[12] Thus says the Lord GOD: Because Edom acted revengefully against the house of Judah and has grievously offended in taking vengeance upon them, [13] therefore thus says the Lord GOD, I will stretch out my hand against Edom, and cut off from it humans and animals, and I will make it desolate; from Teman even to Dedan they shall fall by the sword. [14] I will lay my vengeance upon Edom by the hand of my people Israel; and they shall act in Edom according to my anger and according to my wrath; and they shall know my vengeance, says the Lord GOD.

[15] Thus says the Lord GOD: Because with unending hostilities the Philistines acted in vengeance, and with malice of heart took revenge in destruction; [16] therefore thus says the Lord GOD, I will stretch out my hand against the Philistines, cut off the Cherethites, and destroy the rest of the seacoast. [17] I will ex-

ecute great vengeance on them with wrathful punishments. Then they shall know that I am the LORD, when I lay my vengeance on them.

26 In the eleventh year, on the first day of the month, the word of the LORD came to me: [2] Mortal, because Tyre said concerning Jerusalem,

"Aha, broken is the gateway of the peoples;
  it has swung open to me;
I shall be replenished,
  now that it is wasted,"
[3] therefore, thus says the Lord GOD:
  See, I am against you, O Tyre!
  I will hurl many nations against you,
    as the sea hurls its waves.
[4] They shall destroy the walls of Tyre
    and break down its towers.
  I will scrape its soil from it
    and make it a bare rock.
[5] It shall become, in the midst of the sea,
    a place for spreading nets.
I have spoken, says the Lord GOD.
  It shall become plunder for the nations,
    [6] and its daughter-towns in the country
    shall be killed by the sword.
Then they shall know that I am the LORD.

[7] For thus says the Lord GOD: I will bring against Tyre from the north King Nebuchadrezzar of Babylon, king of kings, together with horses, chariots, cavalry, and a great and powerful army.

[8] Your daughter-towns in the country
    he shall put to the sword.
He shall set up a siege wall against you,
    cast up a ramp against you,
    and raise a roof of shields against you.

---

[a] Gk Old Latin: Heb *Moab and Seir*
[b] Heb *towns from its towns*

capital. **8–11: Against Moab.** Cf. Jer 48. **8:** Cf. 20.32. **9:** God will lay bare Moab's high tableland (*flank*) through the destruction of the three northern fortified cities named. **12–14: Against Edom.** Cf. Jer 49.7–22; Ob; Ps 137.3. **12:** *Vengeance,* Ob 10–14; Ps 137.7. **13:** Destruction will stretch from *Teman* to *Dedan,* localities also associated with Edom in Jer 49.7–8. **15–17: Against Philistia.** Cf. Jer 47. *Cherethites,* probably Cretans (the Philistines originally came from the islands of the Aegean Sea; cf. 1 Sam 30.14; Am 9.7; Zeph 2.5; Jer 47.4).

26.1–28.19: Oracles against Tyre. 26.1–21: Tyre is to be destroyed by Nebuchadrezzar. 1–6: Tyre is judged for gloating over the fall of Jerusalem, a commercial rival, and for looking forward to taking over the city's trade. **1:** Both the (partially preserved) Hebrew and Septuagint texts date the passage several months before Jerusalem's fall, anticipating it as having occurred already (v. 2). **7–14:** Nebuchadrezzar will besiege the island city, which lay about a half-mile (1 km) offshore from the mainland city, after destroying the outlying settlements on the mainland (*daughter-towns,* v. 8). In fact, Nebuchadrezzar besieged the island of Tyre (after the mainland fell) for thirteen years. Tyre lost the war, but it was not destroyed or pillaged (as prophesied, v. 12). This state of affairs is

⁹ He shall direct the shock of his battering
    rams against your walls
and break down your towers with his
    axes.
¹⁰ His horses shall be so many
    that their dust shall cover you.
At the noise of cavalry, wheels, and
    chariots
    your very walls shall shake,
when he enters your gates
    like those entering a breached city.
¹¹ With the hoofs of his horses
    he shall trample all your streets.
He shall put your people to the sword,
    and your strong pillars shall fall to the
    ground.
¹² They will plunder your riches
    and loot your merchandise;
they shall break down your walls
    and destroy your fine houses.
Your stones and timber and soil
    they shall cast into the water.
¹³ I will silence the music of your songs;
    the sound of your lyres shall be heard
    no more.
¹⁴ I will make you a bare rock;
    you shall be a place for spreading nets.
You shall never again be rebuilt,
    for I the Lord have spoken,
    says the Lord God.

¹⁵ Thus says the Lord God to Tyre: Shall
not the coastlands shake at the sound of
your fall, when the wounded groan, when
slaughter goes on within you? ¹⁶ Then all the
princes of the sea shall step down from their
thrones; they shall remove their robes and
strip off their embroidered garments. They
shall clothe themselves with trembling, and
shall sit on the ground; they shall tremble
every moment, and be appalled at you. ¹⁷ And
they shall raise a lamentation over you, and
say to you:

How you have vanished[a] from the seas,
    O city renowned,
once mighty on the sea,
    you and your inhabitants,[b]
who imposed your[c] terror
    on all the mainland![d]
¹⁸ Now the coastlands tremble
    on the day of your fall;
the coastlands by the sea
    are dismayed at your passing.

¹⁹ For thus says the Lord God: When I make
you a city laid waste, like cities that are not
inhabited, when I bring up the deep over you,
and the great waters cover you, ²⁰ then I will
thrust you down with those who descend
into the Pit, to the people of long ago, and I
will make you live in the world below, among
primeval ruins, with those who go down to
the Pit, so that you will not be inhabited or
have a place[e] in the land of the living. ²¹ I will
bring you to a dreadful end, and you shall be
no more; though sought for, you will never be
found again, says the Lord God.

27 The word of the Lord came to me:
² Now you, mortal, raise a lamentation
over Tyre, ³ and say to Tyre, which sits at the
entrance to the sea, merchant of the peoples
on many coastlands, Thus says the Lord God:

O Tyre, you have said,
    "I am perfect in beauty."
⁴ Your borders are in the heart of the seas;
    your builders made perfect your beauty.
⁵ They made all your planks
    of fir trees from Senir;
they took a cedar from Lebanon
    to make a mast for you.

a   Gk OL Aquila: Heb *have vanished, O inhabited one,*
b   Heb *it and its inhabitants*
c   Heb *their*
d   Cn: Heb *its inhabitants*
e   Gk: Heb *I will give beauty*

addressed in 29.17–21. Tyre finally fell to Alexander the Great in 332 BCE. **11:** *Strong pillars* probably refer to standing stones that represented deities. **14:** Cf. vv. 4–5. **15–18:** Dirge of *the princes of the sea,* perhaps coastal cities in trade alliance with Tyre. **19–21:** The simile of the attack of the sea in v. 3 is here converted and heightened into mythic metaphor. The waters of the primordial *deep* (Gen 1.2) will cover the wasted city, which will *descend into the Pit* (Sheol, see 31.15–18; 32.17–32; Isa 14.15), the abode of the dead.

    27.1–36: Dirge over the ship Tyre. Ezekiel's use of metaphorical language here as elsewhere serves his need to push beyond the ordinarily observable and speak of ultimate realities. **1–25:** Tyre's glory. **2:** *Lamentation,* better, a funerary "dirge," in which present downfall is contrasted with past glory. **3:** *I am perfect in beauty* is supposed to be Jerusalem's epithet (16.14; Lam 2.15), not Tyre's. **5–9:** The text shifts directly into the ship metaphor.

[6] From oaks of Bashan
   they made your oars;
they made your deck of pines[a]
   from the coasts of Cyprus,
   inlaid with ivory.
[7] Of fine embroidered linen from Egypt
   was your sail,
   serving as your ensign;
blue and purple from the coasts of Elishah
   was your awning.
[8] The inhabitants of Sidon and Arvad
   were your rowers;
skilled men of Zemer[b] were within you,
   they were your pilots.
[9] The elders of Gebal and its artisans were
   within you,
   caulking your seams;
all the ships of the sea with their mariners
   were within you,
   to barter for your wares.
[10] Paras[c] and Lud and Put
   were in your army,
   your mighty warriors;
they hung shield and helmet in you;
   they gave you splendor.
[11] Men of Arvad and Helech[d]
   were on your walls all around;
   men of Gamad were at your towers.
They hung their quivers all around your
   walls;
   they made perfect your beauty.
[12] Tarshish did business with you out of
the abundance of your great wealth; silver,
iron, tin, and lead they exchanged for your
wares. [13] Javan, Tubal, and Meshech traded
with you; they exchanged human beings
and vessels of bronze for your merchandise. [14] Beth-togarmah exchanged for your
wares horses, war horses, and mules.
[15] The Rhodians[e] traded with you; many
coastlands were your own special markets; they brought you in payment ivory
tusks and ebony. [16] Edom[f] did business
with you because of your abundant goods;
they exchanged for your wares turquoise,
purple, embroidered work, fine linen, coral,
and rubies. [17] Judah and the land of Israel
traded with you; they exchanged for your
merchandise wheat from Minnith, millet,[g]
honey, oil, and balm. [18] Damascus traded
with you for your abundant goods—because of your great wealth of every kind—
wine of Helbon, and white wool. [19] Vedan
and Javan from Uzal[g] entered into trade for
your wares; wrought iron, cassia, and sweet
cane were bartered for your merchandise.
[20] Dedan traded with you in saddlecloths
for riding. [21] Arabia and all the princes of
Kedar were your favored dealers in lambs,
rams, and goats; in these they did business
with you. [22] The merchants of Sheba and

a   Or boxwood
b   Cn Compare Gen 10.18: Heb your skilled men,
    O Tyre
c   Or Persia
d   Or and your army
e   Gk: Heb The Dedanites
f   Another reading is Aram
g   Meaning of Heb uncertain

The good ship Tyre was constructed of the best materials. 5: *Senir* is Mount Hermon, located in southern Syria (Deut 3.9). 6: *Bashan* is east of the Sea of Galilee, known for its oak forests. 7: *Elishah* is probably Cyprus. 8–9: The ship's crew was from *Sidon, Arvad, Zemer* (textual note b), and *Gebal* (Byblos), Phoenician island and port cities. 10: The ship's warriors included those from Persia (textual note c), *Lud* (Lydia in western Asia Minor), and *Put* (Libya). 11: Literal reality (Tyre as a city) momentarily intrudes into Ezekiel's ship metaphor. *Arvad,* see v. 8. *Helech,* possibly Cilicia, in southeastern Asia Minor. The *men of Gamad* are perhaps the Cimmerians or Cappa-docians in eastern Asia Minor. 12–25: A (mostly prose) description of the gallant ship's cargo of rich wares from many nations. Tyre's commercial empire is described first in horizontal fashion from west to east (vv. 12–15): *Tar-shish,* perhaps Tartessus in southern Spain or Sardinia; *Javan,* Ionians, i.e., the Greeks of the Aegean; *Tubal* and *Meshech,* Assyrian "Tabal" and "Mushki," peoples settled in Asia Minor; *Beth-togarmah,* Assyrian "Tilgarimmu," in eastern Asia Minor (Armenia), east of the southernmost Halys River, east of Tubal. The description then moves vertically from south to northeast (vv. 16–19): *Edom; Judah* and *Israel; Minnith,* an Ammonite city (Judg 11.33); *Damascus; Helbon,* a famed wine center thirteen miles north of Damascus. The Arabian region is treated next (vv. 20–22): *Dedan,* in northwest Arabia; *Kedar,* a tribal group of northern Arabia; *Sheba* and *Raamah,* in southwest Arabia. Several Mesopotamian cities conclude the list (v. 23): *Haran,* in northwest Mesopotamia; *Canneh,* a town near Haran; *Eden,* the Aramaean state of Bit-Adini, south of Haran; *Asshur,* south of Nineveh;

Raamah traded with you; they exchanged
for your wares the best of all kinds of
spices, and all precious stones, and gold.
[23] Haran, Canneh, Eden, the merchants of
Sheba, Asshur, and Chilmad traded with
you. [24] These traded with you in choice garments, in clothes of blue and embroidered
work, and in carpets of colored material,
bound with cords and made secure; in
these they traded with you.[a] [25] The ships of
Tarshish traveled for you in your trade.

So you were filled and heavily laden
   in the heart of the seas.
[26] Your rowers have brought you
   into the high seas.
The east wind has wrecked you
   in the heart of the seas.
[27] Your riches, your wares, your
   merchandise,
   your mariners and your pilots,
your caulkers, your dealers in
   merchandise,
   and all your warriors within you,
with all the company
   that is with you,
sink into the heart of the seas
   on the day of your ruin.
[28] At the sound of the cry of your pilots
   the countryside shakes,
[29] and down from their ships
   come all that handle the oar.
The mariners and all the pilots of the sea
   stand on the shore
[30] and wail aloud over you,
   and cry bitterly.
They throw dust on their heads
   and wallow in ashes;
[31] they make themselves bald for you,
   and put on sackcloth,
and they weep over you in bitterness of soul,
   with bitter mourning.
[32] In their wailing they raise a lamentation
   for you,
   and lament over you:

"Who was ever destroyed[b] like Tyre
   in the midst of the sea?
[33] When your wares came from the seas,
   you satisfied many peoples;
with your abundant wealth and
   merchandise
   you enriched the kings of the earth.
[34] Now you are wrecked by the seas,
   in the depths of the waters;
your merchandise and all your crew
   have sunk with you.
[35] All the inhabitants of the coastlands
   are appalled at you;
and their kings are horribly afraid,
   their faces are convulsed.
[36] The merchants among the peoples hiss
   at you;
   you have come to a dreadful end
   and shall be no more forever."

28 The word of the LORD came to me:
[2] Mortal, say to the prince of Tyre,
Thus says the Lord GOD:
Because your heart is proud
   and you have said, "I am a god;
I sit in the seat of the gods,
   in the heart of the seas,"
yet you are but a mortal, and no god,
   though you compare your mind
   with the mind of a god.
[3] You are indeed wiser than Daniel;[c]
   no secret is hidden from you;
[4] by your wisdom and your
   understanding
   you have amassed wealth for yourself,
and have gathered gold and silver
   into your treasuries.
[5] By your great wisdom in trade
   you have increased your wealth,
   and your heart has become proud in
   your wealth.

a Cn: Heb *in your market*
b Tg Vg: Heb *like silence*
c Or, as otherwise read, *Danel*

Chilmad, unidentified. **25:** *Ships of Tarshish*, see 1 Kings 10.22; 22.48; Ps 48.7; Isa 23.1. **26–36:** With this section,
the dirge shifts from picturing Tyre's past glory to describing its sudden end. As in 19.12, the *east wind* (sirocco)
is an agent of destruction (cf. Ps 48.7). The sudden end of the great commercial city brings astonishment, fear,
and grief to seafarers, merchants, and inhabitants of the coastlands. **31:** 7.18n.
    28.1–10: Oracle against the leader of Tyre. 2: *Prince*, the Heb term means "leader" or "ruler" here. The leader,
who represents the whole people of Tyre, is judged for his pride (a universal offense, Prov 16.5). Hubris leads to
self-deification. Thus the prince of Tyre sat in *the seat of the gods* (cf. Isa 14.13–14). *Heart of the seas*, see 28.14n.

⁶ Therefore thus says the Lord God:
Because you compare your mind
  with the mind of a god,
⁷ therefore, I will bring strangers against
    you,
  the most terrible of the nations;
they shall draw their swords against the
    beauty of your wisdom
  and defile your splendor.
⁸ They shall thrust you down to the Pit,
  and you shall die a violent death
  in the heart of the seas.
⁹ Will you still say, "I am a god,"
  in the presence of those who kill you,
though you are but a mortal, and no god,
  in the hands of those who wound
    you?
¹⁰ You shall die the death of the
    uncircumcised
  by the hand of foreigners;
  for I have spoken, says the Lord God.
¹¹ Moreover the word of the Lord came to
me: ¹² Mortal, raise a lamentation over the
king of Tyre, and say to him, Thus says the
Lord God:

You were the signet of perfection,[a]
  full of wisdom and perfect in beauty.
¹³ You were in Eden, the garden of God;
  every precious stone was your
    covering,
carnelian, chrysolite, and moonstone,
  beryl, onyx, and jasper,
sapphire,[b] turquoise, and emerald;
  and worked in gold were your settings
    and your engravings.[a]
On the day that you were created
  they were prepared.
¹⁴ With an anointed cherub as guardian I
    placed you;[a]
  you were on the holy mountain of God;
  you walked among the stones of fire.
¹⁵ You were blameless in your ways
  from the day that you were created,
  until iniquity was found in you.
¹⁶ In the abundance of your trade
  you were filled with violence, and you
    sinned;

a Meaning of Heb uncertain
b Or *lapis lazuli*

3: In the Ugaritic tablets, *Danel* is the wise judge of widows and orphans (see 14.14n.). **6–10:** The leader will be slain by *the most terrible of the nations*, Babylonia (30.10–11), and come to an ignominious end (*the death of the uncircumcised*, v. 10) in *the Pit* (v. 8), that is, Sheol, where the unfortunate dead are cut off from life and community (32.30). Like the Israelites, the Phoenicians practiced circumcision, and would be shocked to experience a postmortem fate in the abysmal depths of the netherworld where unclean and vile souls were confined.

28.11–19: A dirge over the king of Tyre. The passage reworks 28.1–10 based on a mythic tale in which a celestial figure succumbed to ambition and met his downfall through hubris (cf. the Ugaritic myth of Athtar). Since this myth was familiar outside of Israel, it provided Ezekiel a basis for the judgment of a nation such as Tyre that was outside Israel's covenant. **12:** The judgment of the *king of Tyre* serves as a concrete instance of the downfall of an archetypal being, but the text (especially vv. 14 and 16) is ambiguous as to whether this being was *with* a cherub, or, more likely, was a great cherub himself (see v. 14n. and v. 16b n.). A cherub would fit Ezekiel's mythic tale well, since cherubim have an unstable, animalistic nature vulnerable to the lure of the cosmic center that they guard (cf. 28.2). Furthermore, in ancient Near Eastern myth, cherubim are nowhere companions to humans, as the NRSV translation would have it, but are interlocked with the divine presence itself (cf. 1.5–14n.). *Wisdom,* a characteristic trait of cherubim. Cf. the Ugaritic god Athtar, celebrated for knowledge and understanding, but unable successfully to occupy the throne at the cosmic center for which he longed. **13:** *Eden,* ancient images of cherubim often appear in association with highly stylized trees, which mark paradise, where God is present (cf. Gen 3.24; Ezek 31.9; 41.18). With the cherub's *covering* of precious stones, cf. the stones of the high priest's breastplate in Ex 28.17–20, which itself must have had a symbolic connection to Eden. **14:** The translation of the verse is contested (see textual note *a*). The Heb reads, "You were an anointed cherub." The outstretched, shielding wings of a cherub made it an effective *guardian* of the cosmic center. Tyre's ruler might initially have appreciated the comparison to a cherub. A magnificent, ninth-century Phoenician ivory depicts a human monarch in the guise of a semidivine cherub. The garden paradise of *Eden* (v. 13) sat atop the mythic cosmic mountain, *the holy mountain of God* that connects earth and heaven. Rivers flow from God's mountain to fill earth's lakes and oceans, making the mountain the "heart of the seas" (v. 2; cf. 47.1–12; Gen 2.10–14; Ps 46.4; Zech 14.8). *Stones of fire*, the stars of heaven, the astral coterie of the cherub. Arrayed in delicate balance

so I cast you as a profane thing from the
mountain of God,
and the guardian cherub drove you out
from among the stones of fire.
[17] Your heart was proud because of your
beauty;
you corrupted your wisdom for the sake
of your splendor.
I cast you to the ground;
I exposed you before kings,
to feast their eyes on you.
[18] By the multitude of your iniquities,
in the unrighteousness of your trade,
you profaned your sanctuaries.
So I brought out fire from within you;
it consumed you,
and I turned you to ashes on the earth
in the sight of all who saw you.
[19] All who know you among the peoples
are appalled at you;
you have come to a dreadful end
and shall be no more forever.
[20] The word of the LORD came to me:
[21] Mortal, set your face toward Sidon, and
prophesy against it, [22] and say, Thus says the
Lord GOD:
I am against you, O Sidon,
and I will gain glory in your midst.
They shall know that I am the LORD
when I execute judgments in it,
and manifest my holiness in it;
[23] for I will send pestilence into it,
and bloodshed into its streets;
and the dead shall fall in its midst,

by the sword that is against it on every
side.
And they shall know that I am the LORD.
[24] The house of Israel shall no longer find
a pricking brier or a piercing thorn among all
their neighbors who have treated them with
contempt. And they shall know that I am the
Lord GOD.
[25] Thus says the Lord GOD: When I gather
the house of Israel from the peoples among
whom they are scattered, and manifest my
holiness in them in the sight of the nations,
then they shall settle on their own soil that I
gave to my servant Jacob. [26] They shall live in
safety in it, and shall build houses and plant
vineyards. They shall live in safety, when I
execute judgments upon all their neighbors
who have treated them with contempt. And
they shall know that I am the LORD their God.

29 In the tenth year, in the tenth month,
on the twelfth day of the month, the
word of the LORD came to me: [2] Mortal, set
your face against Pharaoh king of Egypt, and
prophesy against him and against all Egypt;
[3] speak, and say, Thus says the Lord GOD:
I am against you,
Pharaoh king of Egypt,
the great dragon sprawling
in the midst of its channels,
saying, "My Nile is my own;
I made it for myself."
[4] I will put hooks in your jaws,
and make the fish of your channels
stick to your scales.

about the holy center of the universe, cherubim may covet the center's power. **16–19:** The dirge moves from the cherub's past glory to an account of his downfall through hubris. **16a:** The actual referent (Tyre's corrupt trade) intrudes into the allegorical figure (the primal cherub's sin) here. **16b:** The NRSV is following the Septuagint (cf. Gen 3.23–24). The Heb reads, "I drove you out, O guardian cherub." For demotions of supernatural figures, cf. Ps 82.6–7; Isa 14.12; Lk 10.18. **17–18:** The cherub arrogated to himself the "seat of the gods" (v. 2). Mimicking the hubris of this diabolical, celestial cherub, the earthly king of Tyre profaned his land. *To the ground,* in Ugaritic myth, Athtar's descent is also said to be to the "earth"/"underworld."

28.20–26: Oracle against Sidon, another Phoenician city, on the Mediterranean coast north of Tyre. **22:** A good example of Ezekiel's Priestly language (cf. Ex 14.17–18; Lev 10.3). **24–26:** Sidon's doom spells God's vindication. **24:** Cf. Num 33.55 (HS). **25–26:** Cf. 34.28; Lev 25.19.

29.1–32.32: Prophecies against Egypt. 29.1–16: Against Pharaoh (January 7, 587 BCE). **3:** In a prophecy with strong Egyptian flavoring, the pharaoh is depicted as a monstrous crocodile of the Nile, whom God will cast on the land as carrion. *Dragon,* the Heb term often refers to the mythical monster of watery chaos (see 32.2n.), but here, as in Ex 7.8–12, its basic denotation is the reptilian crocodile (a signature creature of Egypt). (The Heb term takes on more of its common mythological connotations in 32.1–16.) *Its channels,* the Nile delta and canals. *My own; I made it,* in Egyptian religion the pharaoh created and controlled the Nile. **4:** *Hooks,* cf. 38.4; Isa 37.29. *Fish of your channels,* the Egyptians and their mercenaries. **6b–9a:** *Staff of reed,* compare the Assyrian Rabshakeh's

I will draw you up from your channels,
    with all the fish of your channels
        sticking to your scales.
5 I will fling you into the wilderness,
    you and all the fish of your channels;
you shall fall in the open field,
    and not be gathered and buried.
To the animals of the earth and to the
        birds of the air
    I have given you as food.
6 Then all the inhabitants of Egypt shall
        know
    that I am the LORD
because you[a] were a staff of reed
    to the house of Israel;
7 when they grasped you with the hand,
        you broke,
    and tore all their shoulders;
and when they leaned on you, you broke,
    and made all their legs unsteady.[b]
8 Therefore, thus says the Lord GOD: I will
bring a sword upon you, and will cut off from
you human being and animal; 9 and the land
of Egypt shall be a desolation and a waste.
Then they shall know that I am the LORD.

Because you[c] said, "The Nile is mine, and
I made it," 10 therefore, I am against you, and
against your channels, and I will make the
land of Egypt an utter waste and desolation,
from Migdol to Syene, as far as the border
of Ethiopia.[d] 11 No human foot shall pass
through it, and no animal foot shall pass
through it; it shall be uninhabited forty years.
12 I will make the land of Egypt a desolation
among desolated countries; and her cities
shall be a desolation forty years among cities
that are laid waste. I will scatter the Egyptians
among the nations, and disperse them among
the countries.

13 Further, thus says the Lord GOD: At the
end of forty years I will gather the Egyptians
from the peoples among whom they were

scattered; 14 and I will restore the fortunes
of Egypt, and bring them back to the land of
Pathros, the land of their origin; and there
they shall be a lowly kingdom. 15 It shall be
the most lowly of the kingdoms, and never
again exalt itself above the nations; and
I will make them so small that they will
never again rule over the nations. 16 The
Egyptians[e] shall never again be the reliance
of the house of Israel; they will recall their
iniquity, when they turned to them for aid.
Then they shall know that I am the Lord
GOD.

17 In the twenty-seventh year, in the first
month, on the first day of the month, the
word of the LORD came to me: 18 Mortal, King
Nebuchadrezzar of Babylon made his army
labor hard against Tyre; every head was made
bald and every shoulder was rubbed bare;
yet neither he nor his army got anything
from Tyre to pay for the labor that he had
expended against it. 19 Therefore thus says the
Lord GOD: I will give the land of Egypt to King
Nebuchadrezzar of Babylon; and he shall
carry off its wealth and despoil it and plunder
it; and it shall be the wages for his army.
20 I have given him the land of Egypt as his
payment for which he labored, because they
worked for me, says the Lord GOD.

21 On that day I will cause a horn to sprout
up for the house of Israel, and I will open
your lips among them. Then they shall know
that I am the LORD.

30

The word of the LORD came to me:
2 Mortal, prophesy, and say, Thus says
the Lord GOD:

a   Gk Syr Vg: Heb *they*
b   Syr: Heb *stand*
c   Gk Syr Vg: Heb *he*
d   Or *Nubia*; Heb *Cush*
e   Heb *It*

similar belittlement of Egypt in 2 Kings 18.21; Isa 36.6. Pharaoh Hophra's attack against Nebuchadrezzar in the
spring of 588 had failed to relieve Jerusalem (Jer 37.5–10). **10:** *Migdol to Syene,* northern and southern Egyptian
localities, together signifying all Egypt. **11:** *Forty years,* 4.6; Num 14.33 (HS). **13–16:** The only promise of Egyptian
restoration in Ezekiel, though Egypt will be restored only as a *lowly kingdom.* **14:** *Pathros,* southern Egypt.

    29.17–21: Egypt as "wages" for Nebuchadrezzar, instead of Tyre. Ezekiel's latest dated oracle, April 26, 571
BCE. This unique passage amends the Tyre prophecies (26.12) in light of subsequent events. Nebuchadrezzar will
get sufficient plunder from Egypt to compensate for his lack of booty from the siege of Tyre. The preservation of
an earlier, embarrassingly unfulfilled prophecy (ch 26) in the book shows how quickly Ezekiel's prophecies took
on scriptural authority. **21:** *Horn* may refer to a reestablished Davidic monarch in Israel (Ps 132.17); cf. 17.22–24n.

Wail, "Alas for the day!"
³ For a day is near,
the day of the LORD is near;
it will be a day of clouds,
a time of doom[a] for the nations.
⁴ A sword shall come upon Egypt,
and anguish shall be in Ethiopia,[b]
when the slain fall in Egypt,
and its wealth is carried away,
and its foundations are torn down.
⁵ Ethiopia,[b] and Put, and Lud, and all Arabia,
and Libya,[c] and the people of the allied land[d]
shall fall with them by the sword.

⁶ Thus says the LORD:
Those who support Egypt shall fall,
and its proud might shall come down;
from Migdol to Syene
they shall fall within it by the sword,
says the Lord GOD.
⁷ They shall be desolated among other
desolated countries,
and their cities shall lie among cities
laid waste.
⁸ Then they shall know that I am the
LORD,
when I have set fire to Egypt,
and all who help it are broken.
⁹ On that day, messengers shall go out
from me in ships to terrify the unsuspecting
Ethiopians;[e] and anguish shall come upon
them on the day of Egypt's doom;[f] for it is
coming!

¹⁰ Thus says the Lord GOD:
I will put an end to the hordes of Egypt,
by the hand of King Nebuchadrezzar of
Babylon.
¹¹ He and his people with him, the most
terrible of the nations,
shall be brought in to destroy the land;

and they shall draw their swords against
Egypt,
and fill the land with the slain.
¹² I will dry up the channels,
and will sell the land into the hand of
evildoers;
I will bring desolation upon the land and
everything in it
by the hand of foreigners;
I the LORD have spoken.

¹³ Thus says the Lord GOD:
I will destroy the idols
and put an end to the images in
Memphis;
there shall no longer be a prince in the
land of Egypt;
so I will put fear in the land of Egypt.
¹⁴ I will make Pathros a desolation,
and will set fire to Zoan,
and will execute acts of judgment on
Thebes.
¹⁵ I will pour my wrath upon Pelusium,
the stronghold of Egypt,
and cut off the hordes of Thebes.
¹⁶ I will set fire to Egypt;
Pelusium shall be in great agony;
Thebes shall be breached,
and Memphis face adversaries by day.
¹⁷ The young men of On and of Pi-beseth
shall fall by the sword;
and the cities themselves[g] shall go into
captivity.

a   Heb lacks *of doom*
b   Or *Nubia*; Heb *Cush*
c   Compare Gk Syr Vg: Heb *Cub*
d   Meaning of Heb uncertain
e   Or *Nubians*; Heb *Cush*
f   Heb *the day of Egypt*
g   Heb *and they*

30.1–19: The doom of Egypt. 1–9: Since the time of the prophet Amos (Am 5.18–20), the "day of the LORD"
was God's judgment day on the Israelites (7.5–9n.; 13.5); later, as here, it became Israel's restoration day but
remained doomsday for the nations (38.18; 39.8). *Put, and Lud*, see 27.10n. **6–9:** Egypt's allies will collapse. *Migdol
to Syene*, see 29.10n. *Unsuspecting Ethiopians*, the enormity of Egypt's fall is emphasized by describing onlookers' reactions. **10–12:** Nebuchadrezzar is Egypt's destroyer. **12:** *Channels*, see 29.3n. **13–19:** All Egypt will be destroyed. *Images* are condemned in Holiness School texts, such as Lev 19.4; 26.1. *Memphis*, south of Cairo, was
the ancient capital of lower (northern) Egypt. *Pathros*, see 29.14n. *Zoan*, in the northeast delta region. *Thebes*,
capital of upper Egypt, is present-day Karnak and Luxor. *Pelusium*, east of Zoan, in the delta region. *On* is Heliopolis, slightly northeast of Memphis. *Pi-beseth*, Bubastis, in the eastern delta. *Tehaphnehes*, Tahpanhes, on
Egypt's northeastern frontier.

¹⁸ At Tehaphnehes the day shall be dark,
  when I break there the dominion of
    Egypt,
and its proud might shall come to an end;
  the city^a shall be covered by a cloud,
  and its daughter-towns shall go into
    captivity.
¹⁹ Thus I will execute acts of judgment on
    Egypt.
  Then they shall know that I am the
    Lord.

²⁰ In the eleventh year, in the first month, on the seventh day of the month, the word of the Lord came to me: ²¹ Mortal, I have broken the arm of Pharaoh king of Egypt; it has not been bound up for healing or wrapped with a bandage, so that it may become strong to wield the sword. ²² Therefore thus says the Lord God: I am against Pharaoh king of Egypt, and will break his arms, both the strong arm and the one that was broken; and I will make the sword fall from his hand. ²³ I will scatter the Egyptians among the nations, and disperse them throughout the lands. ²⁴ I will strengthen the arms of the king of Babylon, and put my sword in his hand; but I will break the arms of Pharaoh, and he will groan before him with the groans of one mortally wounded. ²⁵ I will strengthen the arms of the king of Babylon, but the arms of Pharaoh shall fall. And they shall know that I am the Lord, when I put my sword into the hand of the king of Babylon. He shall stretch it out against the land of Egypt, ²⁶ and I will scatter the Egyptians among the nations and disperse them throughout the countries. Then they shall know that I am the Lord.

31 In the eleventh year, in the third month, on the first day of the month, the word of the Lord came to me: ² Mor-

tal, say to Pharaoh king of Egypt and to his hordes:
  Whom are you like in your greatness?
    ³ Consider Assyria, a cedar of
      Lebanon,
  with fair branches and forest shade,
    and of great height,
    its top among the clouds.^b
⁴ The waters nourished it,
    the deep made it grow tall,
  making its rivers flow^c
    around the place it was planted,
  sending forth its streams
    to all the trees of the field.
⁵ So it towered high
    above all the trees of the field;
  its boughs grew large
    and its branches long,
    from abundant water in its shoots.
⁶ All the birds of the air
    made their nests in its boughs;
  under its branches all the animals of the field
    gave birth to their young;
  and in its shade
    all great nations lived.
⁷ It was beautiful in its greatness,
    in the length of its branches;
  for its roots went down
    to abundant water.
⁸ The cedars in the garden of God could
      not rival it,
    nor the fir trees equal its boughs;
  the plane trees were as nothing
    compared with its branches;
  no tree in the garden of God
    was like it in beauty.

a Heb *she*
b Gk: Heb *thick boughs*
c Gk: Heb *rivers going*

30.20–26: **Pharaoh disarmed.** April 29, 587 BCE. The body imagery of broken arms represents military defeat. Nebuchadrezzar had broken one arm of Hophra the year before (vv. 20–21; see 29.6b–9a n.). The next time, he will break both arms (vv. 22–26).

31.1–18: **The comparison between Assyria and Egypt.** Date, June 21, 587 BCE. Ezekiel uses the archetype of the "cosmic tree" (see 17.22–24n.) to emphasize that, as with Assyria, the cause for Egypt's fall will be pride (hubris). 3a: The fact of the downfall undergone by great Assyria, the superpower preceding Babylonia, supports the credibility of Ezekiel's judgments against Egypt. See Nah 3.8–10 for a similar comparison of Egypt and Assyria. Ezekiel's image of Assyria as a tree may have its source of inspiration in Isa 10.33–34. 3b–9: A dirge for the cosmic tree begins by describing its former glory. 4: *The deep* (Heb "tehom"), here, the world's subterranean sweet-waters (Gen 7.11), which nourished the tree so that it reached into the heavens and sheltered all life (cf. Dan 4). 7–9: The splendor of the great cedar was incomparable (v. 18), surpassing those *in the garden of*

⁹ I made it beautiful
  with its mass of branches,
the envy of all the trees of Eden
  that were in the garden of God.
¹⁰ Therefore thus says the Lord GOD: Because it[a] towered high and set its top among the clouds,[b] and its heart was proud of its height, ¹¹ I gave it into the hand of the prince of the nations; he has dealt with it as its wickedness deserves. I have cast it out. ¹² Foreigners from the most terrible of the nations have cut it down and left it. On the mountains and in all the valleys its branches have fallen, and its boughs lie broken in all the watercourses of the land; and all the peoples of the earth went away from its shade and left it.
¹³ On its fallen trunk settle
  all the birds of the air,
and among its boughs lodge
  all the wild animals.
¹⁴ All this is in order that no trees by the waters may grow to lofty height or set their tops among the clouds,[b] and that no trees that drink water may reach up to them in height.

For all of them are handed over to
    death,
  to the world below;
along with all mortals,
  with those who go down to the Pit.
¹⁵ Thus says the Lord GOD: On the day it went down to Sheol I closed the deep over it and covered it; I restrained its rivers, and its mighty waters were checked. I clothed Lebanon in gloom for it, and all the trees of the field fainted because of it. ¹⁶ I made the nations quake at the sound of its fall, when I cast it down to Sheol with those who go down to the Pit; and all the trees of Eden,

the choice and best of Lebanon, all that were well watered, were consoled in the world below. ¹⁷ They also went down to Sheol with it, to those killed by the sword, along with its allies,[c] those who lived in its shade among the nations.
¹⁸ Which among the trees of Eden was like you in glory and in greatness? Now you shall be brought down with the trees of Eden to the world below; you shall lie among the uncircumcised, with those who are killed by the sword. This is Pharaoh and all his horde, says the Lord GOD.

32 In the twelfth year, in the twelfth month, on the first day of the month, the word of the LORD came to me: ² Mortal, raise a lamentation over Pharaoh king of Egypt, and say to him:
You consider yourself a lion among the
    nations,
  but you are like a dragon in the
    seas;
you thrash about in your streams,
  trouble the water with your feet,
  and foul your[d] streams.
³ Thus says the Lord GOD:
  In an assembly of many peoples
  I will throw my net over you;
  and I[e] will haul you up in my
    dragnet.
⁴ I will throw you on the ground,
  on the open field I will fling you,

a Syr Vg: Heb *you*
b Gk: Heb *thick boughs*
c Heb *its arms*
d Heb *their*
e Gk Vg: Heb *they*

God (28.13). 10–18: The tree's two-phased disaster. God will have it cut down; the life it sheltered will be dispersed (vv. 10–14). Once felled, it will go down still farther (vv. 15–18), to the *Pit* (v. 14), i.e., to *Sheol*, the abode of the dead, where it will lie with those who died in untimely, violent, or dishonorable ways. 11: *Prince of the nations*, Nabopolassar (626–605 BCE), founder of the Neo-Babylonian Empire, who, in alliance with the Medes, destroyed the Assyrian Empire in a series of battles between 614 and 609 BCE. 18: *Uncircumcised*, see 28.6–10n., 32.17–32n.
    32.1–16: Dirge over Pharaoh. Date, March 3, 585 BCE. Although Pharaoh fancied himself *a lion* (v. 2; symbol of world-ranging power), Ezekiel declares he is better viewed as a sea-monster. 2: *Dragon*, a monstrous crocodile as in 29.3, but here with some of the fantastic proportions of the mythological chaos monster that the term signifies in Job 7.12; Ps 74.13; Isa 27.1; 51.9. In his hubris, Pharaoh aspires to rock the cosmos (*in the seas*, cf. Isa 27.1 and the watery chaos of Pss 46.3; 93.3). Verses 2,13–14 show, however, that in reality he can stir up only a little local trouble, muddying the water with his feet. 3–8: His punishment. Verses 6–8 recall the "day of the LORD" (see 30.1–9n.; Isa 13.10; Joel 2.2,30), in which God overcomes all opposing forces. They also echo the Exodus

and will cause all the birds of the air to
  settle on you,
and I will let the wild animals of the
  whole earth gorge themselves
  with you.
[5] I will strew your flesh on the mountains,
  and fill the valleys with your carcass.[a]
[6] I will drench the land with your flowing
  blood
up to the mountains,
  and the watercourses will be filled with
  you.
[7] When I blot you out, I will cover the
  heavens,
  and make their stars dark;
I will cover the sun with a cloud,
  and the moon shall not give its light.
[8] All the shining lights of the heavens
  I will darken above you,
  and put darkness on your land,
                    says the Lord God.
[9] I will trouble the hearts of many peoples,
  as I carry you captive[b] among the
  nations,
  into countries you have not known.
[10] I will make many peoples appalled at
  you;
  their kings shall shudder because of
  you.
When I brandish my sword before them,
  they shall tremble every moment
for their lives, each one of them,
  on the day of your downfall.
[11] For thus says the Lord God:
The sword of the king of Babylon shall
  come against you.
[12] I will cause your hordes to fall
  by the swords of mighty ones,
  all of them most terrible among the
  nations.
They shall bring to ruin the pride of
  Egypt,
  and all its hordes shall perish.

[13] I will destroy all its livestock
  from beside abundant waters;
and no human foot shall trouble them any
  more,
  nor shall the hoofs of cattle trouble
  them.
[14] Then I will make their waters clear,
  and cause their streams to run like oil,
                    says the Lord God.
[15] When I make the land of Egypt desolate
  and when the land is stripped of all that
  fills it,
when I strike down all who live in it,
  then they shall know that I am the
  Lord.
[16] This is a lamentation; it shall be chanted.
  The women of the nations shall chant
  it.
Over Egypt and all its hordes they shall
  chant it,
  says the Lord God.
[17] In the twelfth year, in the first month,[c]
on the fifteenth day of the month, the word
of the Lord came to me:
[18] Mortal, wail over the hordes of Egypt,
  and send them down,
with Egypt[d] and the daughters of majestic
  nations,
  to the world below,
  with those who go down to the Pit.
[19] "Whom do you surpass in beauty?
  Go down! Be laid to rest with the
  uncircumcised!"
[20] They shall fall among those who are killed
by the sword. Egypt[e] has been handed over to
the sword; carry away both it and its hordes.
[21] The mighty chiefs shall speak of them, with

a Symmachus Syr Vg: Heb *your height*
b Gk: Heb *bring your destruction*
c Gk: Heb lacks *in the first month*
d Heb *it*
e Heb *It*

plagues against Egypt: blood (Ex 7.17); darkness (Ex 10.21–23 [HS]). 9–10: The nations' reactions (cf. 26.16; 27.35).
11–15: The *sword* of God (v. 10; 30.4; Lev 26.25,33 [HS]) is concretely the Babylonians' sword (cf. 30.25). 14: Reversing v. 2, God restores the Nile's natural state (cf. Lev 26.34–35 [HS]).
  32.17–32: Egypt in the underworld. The Septuagint's date (textual note *c*) is April 27, 586 BCE. Like Tyre
(28.10), Egypt belongs in the section of the underworld ("the Pit," "Sheol") reserved for the uncircumcised
and those who are executed or who die violent or untimely deaths. They do not enjoy the status of the honored war-dead, who were properly buried (v. 27). The Egyptians apparently practiced circumcision, as did the
Edomites (v. 29) and the Sidonians (v. 30; cf. 28.10n.). Thus, their fate is to the disgrace of all three peoples.

their helpers, out of the midst of Sheol: "They have come down, they lie still, the uncircumcised, killed by the sword."

²² Assyria is there, and all its company, their graves all around it, all of them killed, fallen by the sword. ²³ Their graves are set in the uttermost parts of the Pit. Its company is all around its grave, all of them killed, fallen by the sword, who spread terror in the land of the living.

²⁴ Elam is there, and all its hordes around its grave; all of them killed, fallen by the sword, who went down uncircumcised into the world below, who spread terror in the land of the living. They bear their shame with those who go down to the Pit. ²⁵ They have made Elam[a] a bed among the slain with all its hordes, their graves all around it, all of them uncircumcised, killed by the sword; for terror of them was spread in the land of the living, and they bear their shame with those who go down to the Pit; they are placed among the slain.

²⁶ Meshech and Tubal are there, and all their multitude, their graves all around them, all of them uncircumcised, killed by the sword; for they spread terror in the land of the living. ²⁷ And they do not lie with the fallen warriors of long ago[b] who went down to Sheol with their weapons of war, whose swords were laid under their heads, and whose shields[c] are upon their bones; for the terror of the warriors was in the land of the living. ²⁸ So you shall be broken and lie among the uncircumcised, with those who are killed by the sword.

²⁹ Edom is there, its kings and all its princes, who for all their might are laid with those who are killed by the sword; they lie with the uncircumcised, with those who go down to the Pit.

³⁰ The princes of the north are there, all of them, and all the Sidonians, who have gone down in shame with the slain, for all the terror that they caused by their might; they lie uncircumcised with those who are killed by the sword, and bear their shame with those who go down to the Pit.

³¹ When Pharaoh sees them, he will be consoled for all his hordes—Pharaoh and all his army, killed by the sword, says the Lord GOD. ³² For he[d] spread terror in the land of the living; therefore he shall be laid to rest among the uncircumcised, with those who are slain by the sword—Pharaoh and all his multitude, says the Lord GOD.

33 The word of the LORD came to me: ² O Mortal, speak to your people and say to them, If I bring the sword upon a land, and the people of the land take one of their number as their sentinel; ³ and if the sentinel sees the sword coming upon the land and blows the trumpet and warns the people; ⁴ then if any who hear the sound of the trumpet do not take warning, and the sword comes and takes them away, their blood shall be upon their own heads. ⁵ They heard the sound of the trumpet and did not take warning; their blood shall be upon themselves. But if they had taken warning, they would have saved their lives. ⁶ But if the sentinel sees the sword coming and does not blow the trumpet, so that the people are not warned, and the sword comes and takes any of them, they are taken away in their iniquity, but their blood I will require at the sentinel's hand.

a Heb *it*
b Gk Old Latin: Heb *of the uncircumcised*
c Cn: Heb *iniquities*
d Cn: Heb *I*

22–30: A roster. In its dishonorable demise Egypt will join others who were objects of God's wrath (Isa 14.9–11), such as *Assyria* (31.3–17); *Elam* (defeated by Assyria, its western neighbor); *Meshech* and *Tubal* (see 27.12–25n.); *Edom* (25.12–14); *princes of the north* (unnamed rulers in Phoenicia and Syria); and *Sidon* (28.20–26). 23: *The uttermost parts of the Pit* constitute, in mythic poetry, a fate opposite to the goal of ascending to heaven (Isa 14.15).

33.1–39.29: Prophecies of Israel's restoration. 33.1–20: Clarification of Ezekiel's role. The social setting is given in v. 10. The exiles are now resigned to their condemnation and to Jerusalem's destruction, but this resignation has led to an unanticipated, paralyzing hopelessness. Ezekiel delivers two responses to their demoralized state: God desires people to live, and sin is forgivable. 1–9: God reminds Ezekiel of his commission as a *sentinel* (3.16–21). This metaphor had originally assuaged Ezekiel's personal reluctance about his calling. Here the prophet's role as sentinel is stressed again to explain how the intention behind Ezekiel's doom prophecy is not

⁷ So you, mortal, I have made a sentinel for the house of Israel; whenever you hear a word from my mouth, you shall give them warning from me. ⁸ If I say to the wicked, "O wicked ones, you shall surely die," and you do not speak to warn the wicked to turn from their ways, the wicked shall die in their iniquity, but their blood I will require at your hand. ⁹ But if you warn the wicked to turn from their ways, and they do not turn from their ways, the wicked shall die in their iniquity, but you will have saved your life.

¹⁰ Now you, mortal, say to the house of Israel, Thus you have said: "Our transgressions and our sins weigh upon us, and we waste away because of them; how then can we live?" ¹¹ Say to them, As I live, says the Lord God, I have no pleasure in the death of the wicked, but that the wicked turn from their ways and live; turn back, turn back from your evil ways; for why will you die, O house of Israel? ¹² And you, mortal, say to your people, The righteousness of the righteous shall not save them when they transgress; and as for the wickedness of the wicked, it shall not make them stumble when they turn from their wickedness; and the righteous shall not be able to live by their righteousnessᵃ when they sin. ¹³ Though I say to the righteous that they shall surely live, yet if they trust in their righteousness and commit iniquity, none of their righteous deeds shall be remembered; but in the iniquity that they have committed they shall die. ¹⁴ Again, though I say to the wicked, "You shall surely die," yet if they turn from their sin and do what is lawful and right— ¹⁵ if the wicked restore the pledge, give back what they have taken

by robbery, and walk in the statutes of life, committing no iniquity—they shall surely live, they shall not die. ¹⁶ None of the sins that they have committed shall be remembered against them; they have done what is lawful and right, they shall surely live.

¹⁷ Yet your people say, "The way of the Lord is not just," when it is their own way that is not just. ¹⁸ When the righteous turn from their righteousness, and commit iniquity, they shall die for it.ᵇ ¹⁹ And when the wicked turn from their wickedness, and do what is lawful and right, they shall live by it.ᵇ ²⁰ Yet you say, "The way of the Lord is not just." O house of Israel, I will judge all of you according to your ways!

²¹ In the twelfth year of our exile, in the tenth month, on the fifth day of the month, someone who had escaped from Jerusalem came to me and said, "The city has fallen." ²² Now the hand of the Lord had been upon me the evening before the fugitive came; but he had opened my mouth by the time the fugitive came to me in the morning; so my mouth was opened, and I was no longer unable to speak.

²³ The word of the Lord came to me: ²⁴ Mortal, the inhabitants of these waste places in the land of Israel keep saying, "Abraham was only one man, yet he got possession of the land; but we are many; the land is surely given us to possess." ²⁵ Therefore say to them, Thus says the Lord God: You eat flesh with the blood, and lift up your eyes to your idols, and shed blood; shall you then possess the land? ²⁶ You depend on your swords,

ᵃ Heb *by it*
ᵇ Heb *them*

death but life, to call the people to repentance. **10–20**: Repentance as the way to life. This oracle reemphasizes ch 18 and its stress on the moral autonomy of generations. Earlier this material had aimed to convict the exiles of their personal culpability. Here, Ezekiel's theme of taking responsibility is used to show that one's personal sinfulness is forgivable. **11**: Cf. 18.23n.; 18.31. God's impassioned plea is for all to find life, even the wicked.

33.21–22: Release from speechlessness. *Escaped from Jerusalem*, escaped death by exile to Babylonia. The exiles from Jerusalem arrived in Babylonia on January 19, 585 BCE, about half a year after Jerusalem's fall. (See Ezra 7.9 for a comparable travel time.) Ezekiel's concurrent release from the speechlessness of 3.26–27 was predicted at 24.27. The event is a watershed: the written judgment on Jerusalem of scripture, symbolized by the "written scroll" of 2.9–10, had been fulfilled, and now a new prophetic message of promise was possible.

33.23–33: Resistance in the homeland and in exile. 23–29: Disputation over possession of homeland property. Verse 24 reveals the social setting. The homelanders are repeating their earlier claim to the land (11.15; cf. Isa 51.2). Verses 25–26 indict them in terms echoing 18.1–20; 22.11; Lev 19.16,26 (HS). On the three punishments

you commit abominations, and each of you defiles his neighbor's wife; shall you then possess the land? [27] Say this to them, Thus says the Lord GOD: As I live, surely those who are in the waste places shall fall by the sword; and those who are in the open field I will give to the wild animals to be devoured; and those who are in strongholds and in caves shall die by pestilence. [28] I will make the land a desolation and a waste, and its proud might shall come to an end; and the mountains of Israel shall be so desolate that no one will pass through. [29] Then they shall know that I am the LORD, when I have made the land a desolation and a waste because of all their abominations that they have committed.

[30] As for you, mortal, your people who talk together about you by the walls, and at the doors of the houses, say to one another, each to a neighbor, "Come and hear what the word is that comes from the LORD." [31] They come to you as people come, and they sit before you as my people, and they hear your words, but they will not obey them. For flattery is on their lips, but their heart is set on their gain. [32] To them you are like a singer of love songs,[a] one who has a beautiful voice and plays well on an instrument; they hear what you say, but they will not do it. [33] When this comes— and come it will!—then they shall know that a prophet has been among them.

34 The word of the LORD came to me: [2] Mortal, prophesy against the shepherds of Israel: prophesy, and say to them— to the shepherds: Thus says the Lord GOD: Ah, you shepherds of Israel who have been feeding yourselves! Should not shepherds feed the sheep? [3] You eat the fat, you clothe yourselves with the wool, you slaughter the fatlings; but you do not feed the sheep. [4] You have not strengthened the weak, you have

not healed the sick, you have not bound up the injured, you have not brought back the strayed, you have not sought the lost, but with force and harshness you have ruled them. [5] So they were scattered, because there was no shepherd; and scattered, they became food for all the wild animals. [6] My sheep were scattered, they wandered over all the mountains and on every high hill; my sheep were scattered over all the face of the earth, with no one to search or seek for them.

[7] Therefore, you shepherds, hear the word of the LORD: [8] As I live, says the Lord GOD, because my sheep have become a prey, and my sheep have become food for all the wild animals, since there was no shepherd; and because my shepherds have not searched for my sheep, but the shepherds have fed themselves, and have not fed my sheep; [9] therefore, you shepherds, hear the word of the LORD: [10] Thus says the Lord GOD, I am against the shepherds; and I will demand my sheep at their hand, and put a stop to their feeding the sheep; no longer shall the shepherds feed themselves. I will rescue my sheep from their mouths, so that they may not be food for them.

[11] For thus says the Lord GOD: I myself will search for my sheep, and will seek them out. [12] As shepherds seek out their flocks when they are among their scattered sheep, so I will seek out my sheep. I will rescue them from all the places to which they have been scattered on a day of clouds and thick darkness. [13] I will bring them out from the peoples and gather them from the countries, and will bring them into their own land; and I will feed them on the mountains of Israel, by the watercourses, and in all the inhabited parts of the land. [14] I

a   Cn: Heb *like a love song*

in v. 27, cf. 5.17; 14.21. **30–33:** With the fulfillment of his prophecy of Jerusalem's destruction, Ezekiel's popularity grew among the exiles. Unfortunately, the response of many exiles to Ezekiel's words was shallow, lacking in personal commitment. **32:** *Love songs,* the Hebrew indicates that Ezekiel's words were just erotic entertainment to them; the same word is mistranslated "flattery" in v. 31.

34.1–31: The shepherds of Israel. 1–10: Israel's kings are symbolized by sheepherders, contracted by God to care for God's livestock, the people (*my sheep,* v. 6); the same metaphor is widely used in the ancient Near East. But they had abused their people and scattered them. The chapter combines priestly ("Holiness School," see below) and Jeremianic (Jer 10.21; 23.1–4) language. **5:** *Wild animals,* Judah's attackers, especially Babylonia. **7–10:** Punishment of the herders and rescue of the flock. **11–16: God is the good shepherd** (Isa 40.11; Jer 31.10) who will gather the entire dispersed flock. **12:** *Day of clouds and thick darkness,* the Day of the LORD, as in Joel 2.2 and

will feed them with good pasture, and the mountain heights of Israel shall be their pasture; there they shall lie down in good grazing land, and they shall feed on rich pasture on the mountains of Israel. [15] I myself will be the shepherd of my sheep, and I will make them lie down, says the Lord GOD. [16] I will seek the lost, and I will bring back the strayed, and I will bind up the injured, and I will strengthen the weak, but the fat and the strong I will destroy. I will feed them with justice.

[17] As for you, my flock, thus says the Lord GOD: I shall judge between sheep and sheep, between rams and goats: [18] Is it not enough for you to feed on the good pasture, but you must tread down with your feet the rest of your pasture? When you drink of clear water, must you foul the rest with your feet? [19] And must my sheep eat what you have trodden with your feet, and drink what you have fouled with your feet?

[20] Therefore, thus says the Lord GOD to them: I myself will judge between the fat sheep and the lean sheep. [21] Because you pushed with flank and shoulder, and butted at all the weak animals with your horns until you scattered them far and wide, [22] I will save my flock, and they shall no longer be ravaged; and I will judge between sheep and sheep.

[23] I will set up over them one shepherd, my servant David, and he shall feed them: he shall feed them and be their shepherd. [24] And I, the LORD, will be their God, and my servant David shall be prince among them; I, the LORD, have spoken.

[25] I will make with them a covenant of peace and banish wild animals from the land, so that they may live in the wild and sleep in the woods securely. [26] I will make them and the region around my hill a blessing; and I will send down the showers in their season; they shall be showers of blessing. [27] The trees of the field shall yield their fruit, and the earth shall yield its increase. They shall be secure on their soil; and they shall know that I am the LORD, when I break the bars of their yoke, and save them from the hands of those who enslaved them. [28] They shall no more be plunder for the nations, nor shall the animals of the land devour them; they shall live in safety, and no one shall make them afraid. [29] I will provide for them a splendid vegetation so that they shall no more be consumed with hunger in the land, and no longer suffer the insults of the nations. [30] They shall know that I, the LORD their God, am with them, and that they, the house of Israel, are my people, says the Lord GOD. [31] You are my sheep, the sheep of my pasture[a] and I am your God, says the Lord GOD.

35

The word of the LORD came to me: [2] Mortal, set your face against Mount Seir, and prophesy against it, [3] and say to it, Thus says the Lord GOD:

I am against you, Mount Seir;
    I stretch out my hand against you
        to make you a desolation and a waste.
[4] I lay your towns in ruins;
    you shall become a desolation,
        and you shall know that I am the LORD.
[5] Because you cherished an ancient enmity, and gave over the people of Israel to the power of the sword at the time of their calamity, at the time of their final punishment;

---

a   Gk OL: Heb *pasture, you are people*

Zeph 1.15 (see 30.1–9n.; 32.3–8n.) **16:** The focus shifts to God's care for needy individuals within the flock and to God's judgment of particular sheep (not just their shepherds). **17–31: A new order for Israel. 17–24:** Sheep, good and bad, are found in the flock; the bad must be separated out (20.38). **23–24:** God will install a Davidic ruler over the people (37.22–25; Jer 23.3–6; 30.9; Zech 6.12). *Prince,* see 44:1–3n. **25–31:** An announcement of future blessedness dependent on the Holiness School: God will *banish wild animals* (v. 25; see Lev 26.6 [HS]), bless the people from Mount Zion (*my hill,* v. 26), and break *the bars of their yoke* (v. 27; see Lev 26.13 [HS]). Thus, the people will *live in safety* (v. 28; see Lev 26.5–6 [HS]). **29:** *Insults,* see 36.15.

35.1–36.15: Oracle on behalf of the mountains of Israel. 35.1–15: Oracles against Edom. Edom has already been judged in Ezekiel's middle section (25.12–14). The present description of its grabbing of land belonging to Israel (v. 10; cf. 1 Esd 4.50) has been placed here as a foil for the restoration message of 35.1–36.15. Ezekiel's prophecies of restoration generally have as foils past wrongs, which they aim to reverse. **1–4:** First oracle. **2:** *Mount Seir* is the plateau in which Sela, the Edomite capital, was located. **5–9:** Second oracle. **5:** Cf. 25.12; Ob 10–14; Ps 137.7. *The ancient enmity* refers to the rivalry between Esau, the ancestor of the Edomites, and Jacob,

⁶ therefore, as I live, says the Lord GOD, I will prepare you for blood, and blood shall pursue you; since you did not hate bloodshed, bloodshed shall pursue you. ⁷ I will make Mount Seir a waste and a desolation; and I will cut off from it all who come and go. ⁸ I will fill its mountains with the slain; on your hills and in your valleys and in all your watercourses those killed with the sword shall fall. ⁹ I will make you a perpetual desolation, and your cities shall never be inhabited. Then you shall know that I am the LORD.

¹⁰ Because you said, "These two nations and these two countries shall be mine, and we will take possession of them,"—although the LORD was there— ¹¹ therefore, as I live, says the Lord GOD, I will deal with you according to the anger and envy that you showed because of your hatred against them; and I will make myself known among you,ᵃ when I judge you. ¹² You shall know that I, the LORD, have heard all the abusive speech that you uttered against the mountains of Israel, saying, "They are laid desolate, they are given us to devour." ¹³ And you magnified yourselves against me with your mouth, and multiplied your words against me; I heard it. ¹⁴ Thus says the Lord GOD: As the whole earth rejoices, I will make you desolate. ¹⁵ As you rejoiced over the inheritance of the house of Israel, because it was desolate, so I will deal with you; you shall be desolate, Mount Seir, and all Edom, all of it. Then they shall know that I am the LORD.

36 And you, mortal, prophesy to the mountains of Israel, and say: O mountains of Israel, hear the word of the LORD. ² Thus says the Lord GOD: Because

the enemy said of you, "Aha!" and, "The ancient heights have become our possession," ³ therefore prophesy, and say: Thus says the Lord GOD: Because they made you desolate indeed, and crushed you from all sides, so that you became the possession of the rest of the nations, and you became an object of gossip and slander among the people; ⁴ therefore, O mountains of Israel, hear the word of the Lord GOD: Thus says the Lord GOD to the mountains and the hills, the watercourses and the valleys, the desolate wastes and the deserted towns, which have become a source of plunder and an object of derision to the rest of the nations all around; ⁵ therefore thus says the Lord GOD: I am speaking in my hot jealousy against the rest of the nations, and against all Edom, who, with wholehearted joy and utter contempt, took my land as their possession, because of its pasture, to plunder it. ⁶ Therefore prophesy concerning the land of Israel, and say to the mountains and hills, to the watercourses and valleys, Thus says the Lord GOD: I am speaking in my jealous wrath, because you have suffered the insults of the nations; ⁷ therefore thus says the Lord GOD: I swear that the nations that are all around you shall themselves suffer insults.

⁸ But you, O mountains of Israel, shall shoot out your branches, and yield your fruit to my people Israel; for they shall soon come home. ⁹ See now, I am for you; I will turn to you, and you shall be tilled and sown; ¹⁰ and I will multiply your population, the whole house of Israel, all of it; the towns shall be

ᵃ Gk: Heb *them*

the ancestor of the Israelites; see Gen 25.21–34; 27, narratives informed by the history of the two peoples. **10–13:** Third oracle. **10:** *Two nations,* Israel and Judah. The LORD *was there* until the glory left (see 11.22–25n.); however, the glory will return (48.35). **14–15:** Fourth oracle. **15a:** As Edom rejoiced over Judah's fall (Ob 12), so the world will rejoice over Edom's fall. **36:1–12: Deliverance as "punishment."** *Mountains of Israel,* see 6.1–10n. The highlands, representing all Israel, are here promised deliverance and blessing as a sort of pseudo-punishment for being desolated and slandered. Though dispossessed by *Edom* (35.1–15) and surrounding nations (Neh 2.19), Israel will be restored to her heritage. This oracle reverses ch 6 (e.g., contrast v. 10 with 6.4–7). **5:** God's personal identification with the land of Israel is shown by the phrase *my land* (cf. Lev 25.23 [HS]). **8–12:** God's redemption goes beyond the people's repatriation and inner healing to include God's granting them a new fruitfulness within a physically transformed environment. See also vv. 33–38. **9:** Lev 26.9 (HS). **10:** *All of it,* including the northern kingdom (37.21–22). **11:** Lev 26.9 (HS). **12:** An editorial transition to vv. 13–15. **13–15: No more disgrace.** The land had been feared as a devouring land at least since the time that Israel first reconnoitered it (Num 13.32). In Ezekiel's new Exodus and settlement, there will be no place for such defamation.

inhabited and the waste places rebuilt; [11] and I will multiply human beings and animals upon you. They shall increase and be fruitful; and I will cause you to be inhabited as in your former times, and will do more good to you than ever before. Then you shall know that I am the LORD. [12] I will lead people upon you—my people Israel—and they shall possess you, and you shall be their inheritance. No longer shall you bereave them of children.

[13] Thus says the Lord GOD: Because they say to you, "You devour people, and you bereave your nation of children," [14] therefore you shall no longer devour people and no longer bereave your nation of children, says the Lord GOD; [15] and no longer will I let you hear the insults of the nations, no longer shall you bear the disgrace of the peoples; and no longer shall you cause your nation to stumble, says the Lord GOD.

[16] The word of the LORD came to me: [17] Mortal, when the house of Israel lived on their own soil, they defiled it with their ways and their deeds; their conduct in my sight was like the uncleanness of a woman in her menstrual period. [18] So I poured out my wrath upon them for the blood that they had shed upon the land, and for the idols with which they had defiled it. [19] I scattered them among the nations, and they were dispersed through the countries; in accordance with their conduct and their deeds I judged them. [20] But when they came to the nations, wherever they came, they profaned my holy name, in that it was said of them, "These are the people of the LORD, and yet they had to go out of his land." [21] But I had concern for my holy name, which the house of Israel had profaned among the nations to which they came.

[22] Therefore say to the house of Israel, Thus says the Lord GOD: It is not for your sake, O house of Israel, that I am about to act, but for the sake of my holy name, which you have profaned among the nations to which you came. [23] I will sanctify my great name, which has been profaned among the nations, and which you have profaned among them; and the nations shall know that I am the LORD, says the Lord GOD, when through you I display my holiness before their eyes. [24] I will take you from the nations, and gather you from all the countries, and bring you into your own land. [25] I will sprinkle clean water upon you, and you shall be clean from all your uncleannesses, and from all your idols I will cleanse you. [26] A new heart I will give you, and a new spirit I will put within you; and I will remove from your body the heart of stone and give you a heart of flesh. [27] I will put my spirit within you, and make you follow my statutes and be careful to observe my ordinances. [28] Then you shall live in the land that I gave to your ancestors; and you shall be my people, and I will be your God. [29] I will save you from all your unclean-

36.16–38: God's honor as the cause of the restoration. 16–21: Historical prologue. According to the Holiness School, when the homeland becomes defiled, it vomits out its inhabitants (Lev 18.25,28). This is what has happened to the exiled Israelites. 17: *Uncleanness*, see Lev 15.19–30 (Priestly tradition); 18.19 (HS). 20: *My holy name*, 20.9n. God's name was desecrated (cf. Lev 20.3; 22.2,32 [HS]) either because the exile made God look powerless to protect the Israelites (NRSV's interpretation; cf. Num 14.16) or because God's people from God's own land prove to be depraved (alternate sense of the Hebrew). 22–32: Verses 22 and 32 form an envelope around this section by their parallel assertions that the restoration is not something deserved. God's mercy is unmerited by the people and even precedes their repentance (see 20.9n). According to v. 31, the people show remorse only after their restoration to the land. This chapter thus moves beyond texts such as Lev 26.40–42; Jer 31.18–20, where repentance is the driving motivation behind restoration. 24: A reversal of v. 19. 25: God will *sprinkle* them (cf. Num 19.20 [HS]; Ps 51.7) with water, purifying them, inasmuch as human beings cannot make themselves clean. 26: Ezekiel's calls to repentance have failed (see 18.31n.). A radical, new creation (cf. 11.19; Ps 51.10) will be needed to break the people's bondage to the cycles of sin and retribution of Israel's past (ch 20). The concept of excising the people's old incorrigible *heart of stone* (cf. 2.4; 3.7–9; Zech 7.12) and engrafting a completely *new heart* goes beyond Jer 31.33 and Deut 30.1–6, and is in keeping with Ezekiel's focus on God's sovereignty in effecting salvation (20.33–34). 27: The infusion of God's spirit (cf. 37.14; 39.29; Ps 51.10–11; Joel 2.29; Zech 12.10) effects a fundamental regeneration of the people, so that obedience to the covenant (Lev 26.3

nesses, and I will summon the grain and make it abundant and lay no famine upon you. ³⁰ I will make the fruit of the tree and the produce of the field abundant, so that you may never again suffer the disgrace of famine among the nations. ³¹ Then you shall remember your evil ways, and your dealings that were not good; and you shall loathe yourselves for your iniquities and your abominable deeds. ³² It is not for your sake that I will act, says the Lord GOD; let that be known to you. Be ashamed and dismayed for your ways, O house of Israel.

³³ Thus says the Lord GOD: On the day that I cleanse you from all your iniquities, I will cause the towns to be inhabited, and the waste places shall be rebuilt. ³⁴ The land that was desolate shall be tilled, instead of being the desolation that it was in the sight of all who passed by. ³⁵ And they will say, "This land that was desolate has become like the garden of Eden; and the waste and desolate and ruined towns are now inhabited and fortified." ³⁶ Then the nations that are left all around you shall know that I, the LORD, have rebuilt the ruined places, and replanted that which was desolate; I, the LORD, have spoken, and I will do it.

³⁷ Thus says the Lord GOD: I will also let the house of Israel ask me to do this for them: to increase their population like a flock. ³⁸ Like the flock for sacrifices,ᵃ like the flock at Jerusalem during her appointed festivals, so shall the ruined towns be filled with flocks of people. Then they shall know that I am the LORD.

37 The hand of the LORD came upon me, and he brought me out by the spirit of the LORD and set me down in the middle of a valley; it was full of bones. ² He led me all around them; there were very many lying in the valley, and they were very dry. ³ He said to me, "Mortal, can these bones live?" I answered, "O Lord GOD, you know." ⁴ Then he said to me, "Prophesy to these bones, and say to them: O dry bones, hear the word of the LORD. ⁵ Thus says the Lord GOD to these bones: I will cause breathᵇ to enter you, and you shall live. ⁶ I will lay sinews on you, and will cause flesh to come upon you, and cover you with skin, and put breathᵇ in you, and you shall live; and you shall know that I am the LORD."

⁷ So I prophesied as I had been commanded; and as I prophesied, suddenly there was a noise, a rattling, and the bones came together, bone to its bone. ⁸ I looked, and there were sinews on them, and flesh had come upon them, and skin had covered them; but there was no breath in them. ⁹ Then he said to me, "Prophesy to the breath, prophesy, mortal, and say to the breath:ᶜ Thus says the Lord GOD: Come from the four winds, O breath,ᶜ and breathe upon these slain, that they may live." ¹⁰ I prophesied as he commanded me, and the breath came into them, and they lived, and stood on their feet, a vast multitude.

¹¹ Then he said to me, "Mortal, these bones are the whole house of Israel. They say, 'Our

ᵃ Heb *flock of holy things*

ᵇ Or *spirit*

ᶜ Or *wind* or *spirit*

[HS]) will come naturally from now on and the restoration will be permanent. **29–30**: Lev 26.4 (HS). **33–36**: The skeptical nations (v. 20) will recognize Israel's transformation to a paradise as God's act. **35**: *Garden of Eden*, Gen 2.4–14; cf. Ezek 47.1–12n.; Isa 51.3. God will now be at home in Israel just as in God's garden, Eden. **37–38**: Note the reversal of 14.3; 20.3,31. As Jerusalem always bustled with flocks at pilgrimage times, Israel will now teem with human interaction, mutuality, and spiritual energy (a blessing of the Holiness School covenant; Lev 26.9). Thus, the proliferation of the flock will signal its consecration (see textual note *a*).

37.1–14: Vision of the valley of dry bones. 1: *A valley*, in Heb, "the valley," suggesting that this is the same locale as in 3.22; 8.4. **3:** Ezekiel does not yet realize that this vision refers to the reestablishment of the exiles back in their homeland. Thus bodily resurrection was at least a theoretical possibility for Ezekiel (cf. 1 Kings 17.22; 2 Kings 4.35; 13.21). **4–8:** The first of two prophecies that are enfolded within the vision. As in Gen 2.7, life is generated here in two stages. **9–10:** Suspense builds, as a second prophesying is required in order to animate the bones. Hebrew "ruaḥ" can mean "spirit," "breath," or "wind"; thus there is a constant wordplay here. *Four winds* may refer to God's cosmic reach (1.17; Zech 6.5). *These slain*, the bones' identity is still unclear at this point, the assumption now being that Ezekiel is surveying an old battlefield. (The Hebrew word *multitude* in v. 10 com-

bones are dried up, and our hope is lost; we are cut off completely.' [12] Therefore prophesy, and say to them, Thus says the Lord GOD: I am going to open your graves, and bring you up from your graves, O my people; and I will bring you back to the land of Israel. [13] And you shall know that I am the LORD, when I open your graves, and bring you up from your graves, O my people. [14] I will put my spirit within you, and you shall live, and I will place you on your own soil; then you shall know that I, the LORD, have spoken and will act, says the LORD."

[15] The word of the LORD came to me: [16] Mortal, take a stick and write on it, "For Judah, and the Israelites associated with it"; then take another stick and write on it, "For Joseph (the stick of Ephraim) and all the house of Israel associated with it"; [17] and join them together into one stick, so that they may become one in your hand. [18] And when your people say to you, "Will you not show us what you mean by these?" [19] say to them, Thus says the Lord GOD: I am about to take the stick of Joseph (which is in the hand of Ephraim) and the tribes of Israel associated with it; and I will put the stick of Judah upon it,[a] and make them one stick, in order that they may be one in my hand. [20] When the sticks on which you write are in your hand before their eyes, [21] then say to them, Thus says the Lord GOD: I will take the people of Israel from the nations among which they have gone, and will gather them from every quarter, and bring them to their own land. [22] I will make them one nation in the land, on the mountains of Israel; and one king shall be king over them all. Never again shall they be two nations, and never again shall they be divided into two kingdoms. [23] They shall never again defile themselves with their idols and their detestable things, or with any of their transgressions. I will save them from all the apostasies into which they have fallen,[b] and will cleanse them. Then they shall be my people, and I will be their God.

[24] My servant David shall be king over them; and they shall all have one shepherd. They shall follow my ordinances and be careful to observe my statutes. [25] They shall live in the land that I gave to my servant Jacob, in which your ancestors lived; they and their children and their children's children shall live there forever; and my servant David shall be their prince forever. [26] I will make a covenant of peace with them; it shall be an everlasting covenant with them; and I will bless[c] them and multiply them, and will set my sanctuary among them forevermore. [27] My dwelling place shall be with them; and I will be their God, and they shall be my people. [28] Then the nations shall know that I the LORD sanctify Israel, when my sanctuary is among them forevermore.

38 The word of the LORD came to me: [2] Mortal, set your face toward Gog, of the land of Magog, the chief prince of

---

[a] Heb *I will put them upon it*

[b] Another reading is *from all the settlements in which they have sinned*

[c] Tg: Heb *give*

---

monly means "army.") **11–14:** The interpretation. Verse 11 finally reveals the actual life setting of the prophecy by citing words from a lament: The exiles' *bones are dried,* a metaphor for a downcast spirit (Prov 17.22; 15.30). The metaphor of resurrection is the antidote to such despair. *Cut off,* a metaphor for being within the power of death (Ps 88.5; Lam 3.54). In vv. 12–14, the passage shifts to a metaphor of disinterment as an antidote to this complaint.

37.15–28: The symbolic action of the two sticks (cf. Zech 11.7–14) envisions the reunification of the Southern ("Judah") and Northern ("Joseph/Ephraim/Israel") Kingdoms. Full restoration will then be realized (34.28; 36.10): law-abiding living (11.20) in the promised land (28.25) under the Davidic ruler (34.23–24) in a covenant of peace (34.25). At that time, God will permanently return to the central *sanctuary* (43.9). **22:** *Mountains of Israel,* 6.1–10n. **25:** *Prince,* monarchic ruler (cf. 12.10; 19.1; 34.24; 44.1–3n.). **27:** *Dwelling place,* in the theology of the Holiness School, God's glory properly dwells among God's people (cf. Ex 25.8; 29.45–46; 40.34; Lev 26.11; Num 5.3; 35.34 [HS]). **28:** As in the ideal of the Holiness School, God sanctifies Israel by radiating the divine holiness out to the entire land (cf. Ex 31.13; Lev 19.2; 21.15; 22.32[HS]).

38.1–39.29: The Gog of Magog oracles are early apocalyptic literature, describing the imminent attack on the promised land by an embodiment of evil from the north. After a cataclysmic, doomsday battle, God will

Meshech and Tubal. Prophesy against him ³and say: Thus says the Lord GOD: I am against you, O Gog, chief prince of Meshech and Tubal; ⁴I will turn you around and put hooks into your jaws, and I will lead you out with all your army, horses and horsemen, all of them clothed in full armor, a great company, all of them with shield and buckler, wielding swords. ⁵Persia, Ethiopia,ᵃ and Put are with them, all of them with buckler and helmet; ⁶Gomer and all its troops; Beth-togarmah from the remotest parts of the north with all its troops—many peoples are with you.

⁷Be ready and keep ready, you and all the companies that are assembled around you, and hold yourselves in reserve for them. ⁸After many days you shall be mustered; in the latter years you shall go against a land restored from war, a land where people were gathered from many nations on the mountains of Israel, which had long lain waste; its people were brought out from the nations and now are living in safety, all of them. ⁹You shall advance, coming on like a storm; you shall be like a cloud covering the land, you and all your troops, and many peoples with you.

¹⁰Thus says the Lord GOD: On that day thoughts will come into your mind, and you will devise an evil scheme. ¹¹You will say, "I will go up against the land of unwalled villages; I will fall upon the quiet people who

live in safety, all of them living without walls, and having no bars or gates"; ¹²to seize spoil and carry off plunder; to assail the waste places that are now inhabited, and the people who were gathered from the nations, who are acquiring cattle and goods, who live at the centerᵇ of the earth. ¹³Sheba and Dedan and the merchants of Tarshish and all its young warriorsᶜ will say to you, "Have you come to seize spoil? Have you assembled your horde to carry off plunder, to carry away silver and gold, to take away cattle and goods, to seize a great amount of booty?"

¹⁴Therefore, mortal, prophesy, and say to Gog: Thus says the Lord GOD: On that day when my people Israel are living securely, you will rouse yourselfᵈ ¹⁵and come from your place out of the remotest parts of the north, you and many peoples with you, all of them riding on horses, a great horde, a mighty army; ¹⁶you will come up against my people Israel, like a cloud covering the earth. In the latter days I will bring you against my land, so that the nations may know me, when through you, O Gog, I display my holiness before their eyes.

¹⁷Thus says the Lord GOD: Are you he of whom I spoke in former days by my ser-

ᵃ Or *Nubia*; Heb *Cush*
ᵇ Heb *navel*
ᶜ Heb *young lions*
ᵈ Gk: Heb *will you not know?*

be acknowledged by all nations as the undisputed victor (38.23; 39.21–29). At this point in the book, Ezekiel's prophecies of restoration, which aim to reverse preceding tragedies, have not yet reversed Israel's Babylonian destruction. The northern foe here is thus probably an end-time surrogate for Babylon, and for any super-power that has challenged the sovereignty of God. The followers of Ezekiel who recorded these apocalyptic oracles were central priests of their society, despite the claims of some scholars that all apocalyptic texts derive from peripheral groups. **38.1–9: Prophecy against Gog. 2:** *Gog*, a name perhaps derived from Gyges, a seventh-century BCE ruler of Lydia in Asia Minor. For Ezekiel's audience, the name would have conjured thoughts of mysterious and barbaric happenings in the far north. Gog is no symbol in this text but a mythic-realistic entity: tangibly real, but of mythological proportions. He is God's archetypal enemy, arising against God's people on doomsday. *Magog*, Gen 10.2. **3:** *Meshech and Tubal*, see 27.12–25n.; Gen 10.2. **5:** *Put*, Libya; Gen 10.5. **6:** *Gomer*, the Cimmerians in Asia Minor (Gen 10.2–3), far north of Israel. *Beth-togarmah*, see 27.12–25n. **10–13:** The per-spective shifts from God's external control (vv. 3–9) to Gog's interior motives. **12:** *Center*, see 5.5n. Ezekiel is affirming and re-envisioning Zion theology here. **13:** *Sheba, Dedan,* and *Tarshish* were all engaged in trade; see 27.12–25n. **14–16:** God's motive is God's glory. **17:** Transition. **18–23 (and 39.11–16): Expansion of the Gog ora-cles, radicalizing their apocalyptic and priestly fervor.** The radical magnitude of the apocalyptic threat is clear from the cosmic collapse (cf. Joel 2.10,30; Zech 14.4–5) and from the *seven months* (39.12) required to bury the enemy dead in the region east of the Dead Sea. In keeping with the Ezekiel group's status as priests, increasing priestly concern accompanies the increased apocalyptic feeling: This section draws heavily on Holiness School

vants the prophets of Israel, who in those days prophesied for years that I would bring you against them? [18] On that day, when Gog comes against the land of Israel, says the Lord GOD, my wrath shall be aroused. [19] For in my jealousy and in my blazing wrath I declare: On that day there shall be a great shaking in the land of Israel; [20] the fish of the sea, and the birds of the air, and the animals of the field, and all creeping things that creep on the ground, and all human beings that are on the face of the earth, shall quake at my presence, and the mountains shall be thrown down, and the cliffs shall fall, and every wall shall tumble to the ground. [21] I will summon the sword against Gog[a] in[b] all my mountains, says the Lord GOD; the swords of all will be against their comrades. [22] With pestilence and bloodshed I will enter into judgment with him; and I will pour down torrential rains and hailstones, fire and sulfur, upon him and his troops and the many peoples that are with him. [23] So I will display my greatness and my holiness and make myself known in the eyes of many nations. Then they shall know that I am the LORD.

39 And you, mortal, prophesy against Gog, and say: Thus says the Lord GOD: I am against you, O Gog, chief prince of Meshech and Tubal! [2] I will turn you around and drive you forward, and bring you up from the remotest parts of the north, and lead you against the mountains of Israel. [3] I will strike your bow from your left hand, and will make your arrows drop out of your right hand. [4] You shall fall on the mountains of Israel, you and all your troops and the peoples that are with you; I will give you to birds of prey of every kind and to the wild animals to be devoured. [5] You shall fall in the open field; for I have spoken, says the Lord GOD. [6] I will send fire on Magog and on those who live securely in the coastlands; and they shall know that I am the LORD.

[7] My holy name I will make known among my people Israel; and I will not let my holy name be profaned any more; and the nations shall know that I am the LORD, the Holy One in Israel. [8] It has come! It has happened, says the Lord GOD. This is the day of which I have spoken.

[9] Then those who live in the towns of Israel will go out and make fires of the weapons and burn them—bucklers and shields, bows and arrows, handpikes and spears—and they will make fires of them for seven years. [10] They will not need to take wood out of the field or cut down any trees in the forests, for they will make their fires of the weapons; they will despoil those who despoiled them, and plunder those who plundered them, says the Lord GOD.

[11] On that day I will give to Gog a place for burial in Israel, the Valley of the Travelers[c] east of the sea; it shall block the path of the travelers, for there Gog and all his horde will be buried; it shall be called the Valley of Hamon-gog.[d] [12] Seven months the house of Israel shall spend burying them, in order to cleanse the land. [13] All the people of the land shall bury them; and it will bring them honor on the day that I show my glory, says the Lord GOD. [14] They will set apart men to pass through the land regularly and bury any invaders[e] who remain on the face of the land, so as to cleanse it; for seven months they shall make their search. [15] As the searchers[e] pass through the land, anyone who sees a human bone shall set up a sign by it, until the buriers have buried it in the Valley of Hamon-gog.[d] [16] (A city Hamonah[f] is there also.) Thus they shall cleanse the land.

a Heb *him*
b Heb *to* or *for*
c Or *of the Abarim*
d That is, *the Horde of Gog*
e Heb *travelers*
f That is *The Horde*

traditions about the defiling effect of corpses (Lev 21.1; Num 5.2–3; 9.6; 19.11,13 [HS]). **18:** *That day,* i.e., the "day of the LORD"; see 30.1–9n.; 39.8. **39.1–10: The fall of Gog.** Gog will be defeated both in the field (vv. 1–5) and back at home (v. 6). God's holy name will then be established (vv. 7–8; cf. 20.9n.; 36.22). **9–10:** As in the biblical conquest narrative (Deut 7.2; 20.16–18; Josh 6.24), everything of the enemy's is burned as material devoted to the LORD alone. The huge quantities of war material (enough *wood* for fuel for *seven years*) identify this as an apocalyptic rather than a historical victory. **11–16:** See 38.18–23n. **11:** *Valley of the Travelers,* possibly in the Abarim range (Num 27.12; see textual note c) east of the Dead Sea. Alternatively, the *travelers* may be the departed,

[17] As for you, mortal, thus says the Lord GOD: Speak to the birds of every kind and to all the wild animals: Assemble and come, gather from all around to the sacrificial feast that I am preparing for you, a great sacrificial feast on the mountains of Israel, and you shall eat flesh and drink blood. [18] You shall eat the flesh of the mighty, and drink the blood of the princes of the earth—of rams, of lambs, and of goats, of bulls, all of them fatlings of Bashan. [19] You shall eat fat until you are filled, and drink blood until you are drunk, at the sacrificial feast that I am preparing for you. [20] And you shall be filled at my table with horses and charioteers,[a] with warriors and all kinds of soldiers, says the Lord GOD.

[21] I will display my glory among the nations; and all the nations shall see my judgment that I have executed, and my hand that I have laid on them. [22] The house of Israel shall know that I am the LORD their God, from that day forward. [23] And the nations shall know that the house of Israel went into captivity for their iniquity, because they dealt treacherously with me. So I hid my face from them and gave them into the hand of their adversaries, and they all fell by the sword. [24] I dealt with them according to their uncleanness and their transgressions, and hid my face from them.

[25] Therefore thus says the Lord GOD: Now I will restore the fortunes of Jacob, and have mercy on the whole house of Israel; and I will be jealous for my holy name. [26] They shall forget[b] their shame, and all the treachery they have practiced against me, when they live securely in their land with no one to make them afraid, [27] when I have brought them back from the peoples and gathered them from their enemies' lands, and through them have displayed my holiness in the sight of many nations. [28] Then they shall know that I am the LORD their God because I sent them into exile among the nations, and then gathered them into their own land. I will leave none of them behind; [29] and I will never again hide my face from them, when I pour out my spirit upon the house of Israel, says the Lord GOD.

40 In the twenty-fifth year of our exile, at the beginning of the year, on the tenth day of the month, in the fourteenth year after the city was struck down, on that very day, the hand of the LORD was upon me, and he brought me there. [2] He brought me, in visions of God, to the land of Israel, and set me down upon a very high mountain, on which was a structure like a city to the south. [3] When he brought me there, a man was there, whose appearance shone like bronze,

a Heb *chariots*
b Another reading is *They shall bear*

whose great numbers stop up passage to the underworld. **17–20:** Cf. 39.4b. An invitation to the animal world to attend an apocalyptic, sacrificial feast (cf. Isa 34.5–7; Zeph 1.7), perhaps a sacred, funerary banquet. **18:** Animal names were frequently used as titles of nobles. *Bashan,* in northern Transjordan, was noted for its cattle. **21–29: Secondary summary and concluding oracles. 25:** *Now I will restore,* a shift in focus to a stage before the end-times. The victory and restoration are linked here with the familiar language and narrative line of Ezekiel (5.8 [reversed]; 28.26; 34.28–30). *My holy name,* 20.9n. **29:** Cf. 36.27n.; 37.9,14; Ps 51.10–11; Zech 12.10; Joel 2.28–29.

40.1–48.35: Blueprint for the restored Temple and land. The blueprint that Ezekiel details here includes new ideal features that aim to prevent the wrongs of the past—those that led to the destruction of Solomon's Temple in 586 BCE—from ever happening again. New Temple fortifications and new land boundaries will demarcate the holiness of the land and people (e.g., 42.20n.) with the Temple functioning as an organizing center of this holiness (43.12). In accordance with the Holiness School, the plan provides for the settlements and entire people of Israel to be encompassed by the holiness of God, whose dwelling in their midst is now to be permanently safeguarded (43.7; 44.1–3; 48.35). This section of Ezekiel does not prophesy a literal future for the Temple; rather, it offers a Temple plan as an embodiment of the values of Ezekiel and his followers.

40.1–42.20: The new Temple. Ezekiel's Temple complex is modeled on that of Solomon (see 1 Kings 6 and 2 Chr 3), but with key modifications, such as immense gate-towers and graded zones of holiness, meant to secure the hierarchical world of the Holiness School. **40.1–27: The Temple area and gates: 1–5:** April 28, 573 BCE. On the twenty-fifth anniversary of his exile, Ezekiel is transported in a vision (cf. 8.2–3) to the Temple mountain

with a linen cord and a measuring reed in his hand; and he was standing in the gateway. [4] The man said to me, "Mortal, look closely and listen attentively, and set your mind upon all that I shall show you, for you were brought here in order that I might show it to you; declare all that you see to the house of Israel."

[5] Now there was a wall all around the outside of the temple area. The length of the measuring reed in the man's hand was six long cubits, each being a cubit and a handbreadth in length; so he measured the thickness of the wall, one reed; and the height, one reed. [6] Then he went into the gateway facing east, going up its steps, and measured the threshold of the gate, one reed deep.[a] There were [7] recesses, and each recess was one reed wide and one reed deep; and the space between the recesses, five cubits; and the threshold of the gate by the vestibule of the gate at the inner end was one reed deep. [8] Then he measured the inner vestibule of the gateway, one cubit. [9] Then he measured the vestibule of the gateway, eight cubits; and its pilasters, two cubits; and the vestibule of the gate was at the inner end. [10] There were three recesses on either side of the east gate; the three were of the same size; and the pilasters on either side were of the same size. [11] Then he measured the width of the opening of the gateway, ten cubits; and the width of the gateway, thirteen cubits. [12] There was a barrier before the recesses, one cubit on either side; and the recesses were six cubits on either side. [13] Then he measured the gate from the back[b] of the one recess to the back[b] of the other, a width of twenty-five cubits, from wall to wall.[c] [14] He measured[d] also the vestibule,

twenty cubits; and the gate next to the pilaster on every side of the court.[e] [15] From the front of the gate at the entrance to the end of the inner vestibule of the gate was fifty cubits. [16] The recesses and their pilasters had windows, with shutters[e] on the inside of the gateway all around, and the vestibules also had windows on the inside all around; and on the pilasters were palm trees.

[17] Then he brought me into the outer court; there were chambers there, and a pavement, all around the court; thirty chambers fronted on the pavement. [18] The pavement ran along the side of the gates, corresponding to the length of the gates; this was the lower pavement. [19] Then he measured the distance from the inner front of[f] the lower gate to the outer front of the inner court, one hundred cubits.[g]

[20] Then he measured the gate of the outer court that faced north—its depth and width. [21] Its recesses, three on either side, and its pilasters and its vestibule were of the same size as those of the first gate; its depth was fifty cubits, and its width twenty-five cubits. [22] Its windows, its vestibule, and its palm trees were of the same size as those of the gate that faced toward the east. Seven steps led up to it; and its vestibule was on the inside.[h] [23] Opposite the gate on the north, as on the east, was a gate to the inner court; he measured from gate to gate, one hundred cubits.

a Heb *deep, and one threshold, one reed deep*
b Gk: Heb *roof*
c Heb *opening facing opening*
d Heb *made*
e Meaning of Heb uncertain
f Compare Gk: Heb *from before*
g Heb adds *the east and the north*
h Gk: Heb *before them*

(*very high mountain*, 17.22; Isa 2.2). **3:** *Shone like bronze*, a radiant, supernatural figure (cf. 1.7). **5:** An outer wall surrounded the entire Temple area. The *long cubit* was 20.7 in (52.5 cm); the ordinary cubit was 17.5 in (44 cm). The *reed* was 10.3 ft (3.1 m) long. **6–16:** The outer court's east gate-tower was a massive, fortified complex consisting of a *threshold*, a long hallway with *recesses* (side rooms), a second threshold, and an *inner vestibule* room. Heavy *pilasters* (piers) with windows separated the recessed chambers, or guardrooms, inside the gate-tower (three on each side). This gate is treated further in 43.1–5; 44.1–3. The plan of the gate is similar to several excavated gateways, such as those at Megiddo, Hazor, and Gezer. **8:** *One cubit*, the Hebrew text is problematic here. **16:** *Palm trees*, see 28.13n.; cf. 1 Kings 6.29,35. **17–19:** The Temple area's outer courtyard. The thirty chambers around the court's periphery were probably for the use of the Levites and for people to meet and eat together (Jer 35.2; Neh 13.4–12). See also 46.21–24. **20–27:** The other two (northern and southern) gates of the outer courtyard were identical to the east gate-tower. That there were steps up to the gates (vv. 22,26) shows that the whole

²⁴ Then he led me toward the south, and there was a gate on the south; and he measured its pilasters and its vestibule; they had the same dimensions as the others. ²⁵ There were windows all around in it and in its vestibule, like the windows of the others; its depth was fifty cubits, and its width twenty-five cubits. ²⁶ There were seven steps leading up to it; its vestibule was on the inside.ᵃ It had palm trees on its pilasters, one on either side. ²⁷ There was a gate on the south of the inner court; and he measured from gate to gate toward the south, one hundred cubits.

²⁸ Then he brought me to the inner court by the south gate, and he measured the south gate; it was of the same dimensions as the others. ²⁹ Its recesses, its pilasters, and its vestibule were of the same size as the others; and there were windows all around in it and in its vestibule; its depth was fifty cubits, and its width twenty-five cubits. ³⁰ There were vestibules all around, twenty-five cubits deep and five cubits wide. ³¹ Its vestibule faced the outer court, and palm trees were on its pilasters, and its stairway had eight steps.

³² Then he brought me to the inner court on the east side, and he measured the gate; it was of the same size as the others. ³³ Its recesses, its pilasters, and its vestibule were of the same dimensions as the others; and there were windows all around in it and in its vestibule; its depth was fifty cubits, and its width twenty-five cubits. ³⁴ Its vestibule faced the outer court, and it had palm trees on its pilasters, on either side; and its stairway had eight steps.

³⁵ Then he brought me to the north gate, and he measured it; it had the same dimensions as the others. ³⁶ Its recesses, its pilas-

ters, and its vestibule were of the same size as the others;ᵇ and it had windows all around. Its depth was fifty cubits, and its width twenty-five cubits. ³⁷ Its vestibuleᶜ faced the outer court, and it had palm trees on its pilasters, on either side; and its stairway had eight steps.

³⁸ There was a chamber with its door in the vestibule of the gate,ᵈ where the burnt offering was to be washed. ³⁹ And in the vestibule of the gate were two tables on either side, on which the burnt offering and the sin offering and the guilt offering were to be slaughtered. ⁴⁰ On the outside of the vestibuleᵉ at the entrance of the north gate were two tables; and on the other side of the vestibule of the gate were two tables. ⁴¹ Four tables were on the inside, and four tables on the outside of the side of the gate, eight tables, on which the sacrifices were to be slaughtered. ⁴² There were also four tables of hewn stone for the burnt offering, a cubit and a half long, and one cubit and a half wide, and one cubit high, on which the instruments were to be laid with which the burnt offerings and the sacrifices were slaughtered. ⁴³ There were pegs, one handbreadth long, fastened all around the inside. And on the tables the flesh of the offering was to be laid.

⁴⁴ On the outside of the inner gateway there were chambers for the singers in the inner court, oneᶠ at the side of the north gate facing

a Gk: Heb *before them*
b One Ms: Compare verses 29 and 33: MT lacks *were of the same size as the others*
c Gk Vg Compare verses 26, 31, 34: Heb *pilasters*
d Cn: Heb *at the pilasters of the gates*
e Cn: Heb *to him who goes up*
f Heb lacks *one*

Temple platform was an elevated area. **28–46: The inner gate-towers.** Ezekiel is shown three gates (south, east, north) leading to the inner court corresponding to those leading to the outer court. Only priests could pass through these inner gates (42.14; 44.19; 46.3). **31:** *Eight steps,* the Temple was built on a succession of terraces, so that height demarcated gradations of holiness, just as did walled perimeters and gates (vv. 34,37). Holiness increased as one proceeded farther up and into the Temple. **38–43:** The vestibules of the inner gates contained facilities for the preparation of sacrifices. *Burnt, sin,* and *guilt* offerings, see Lev 1.1–7.38. **44–46:** Priests' chambers. On the north and south sides of the inner court were buildings for the use of the priests. These may be small cells (for priests on guard duty?), different from the chambers in 42.1–14. **44:** *The singers,* Levitical priests (cf. 1 Chr 9.33). *East gate,* read "south gate" with the Septuagint. **46b:** An editorial clarification that only Zadokite priests, such as Ezekiel and his group, may sacrifice at the altar (43.19; 44.15–31n.). **40.47–41.4:** The Temple

south, the other at the side of the east gate facing north. [45] He said to me, "This chamber that faces south is for the priests who have charge of the temple, [46] and the chamber that faces north is for the priests who have charge of the altar; these are the descendants of Zadok, who alone among the descendants of Levi may come near to the LORD to minister to him." [47] He measured the court, one hundred cubits deep, and one hundred cubits wide, a square; and the altar was in front of the temple.

[48] Then he brought me to the vestibule of the temple and measured the pilasters of the vestibule, five cubits on either side; and the width of the gate was fourteen cubits; and the sidewalls of the gate were three cubits[a] on either side. [49] The depth of the vestibule was twenty cubits, and the width twelve[b] cubits; ten steps led up[c] to it; and there were pillars beside the pilasters on either side.

41

Then he brought me to the nave, and measured the pilasters; on each side six cubits was the width of the pilasters.[d] [2] The width of the entrance was ten cubits; and the sidewalls of the entrance were five cubits on either side. He measured the length of the nave, forty cubits, and its width, twenty cubits. [3] Then he went into the inner room and measured the pilasters of the entrance, two cubits; and the width of the entrance, six cubits; and the sidewalls[e] of the entrance, seven cubits. [4] He measured the depth of the room, twenty cubits, and its width, twenty cubits, beyond the nave. And he said to me, This is the most holy place.

[5] Then he measured the wall of the temple, six cubits thick; and the width of the side chambers, four cubits, all around the temple. [6] The side chambers were in three stories, one over another, thirty in each story. There were offsets[f] all around the wall of the temple

to serve as supports for the side chambers, so that they should not be supported by the wall of the temple. [7] The passageway[g] of the side chambers widened from story to story; for the structure was supplied with a stairway all around the temple. For this reason the structure became wider from story to story. One ascended from the bottom story to the uppermost story by way of the middle one. [8] I saw also that the temple had a raised platform all around; the foundations of the side chambers measured a full reed of six long cubits. [9] The thickness of the outer wall of the side chambers was five cubits; and the free space between the side chambers of the temple [10] and the chambers of the court was a width of twenty cubits all around the temple on every side. [11] The side chambers opened onto the area left free, one door toward the north, and another door toward the south; and the width of the part that was left free was five cubits all around.

[12] The building that was facing the temple yard on the west side was seventy cubits wide; and the wall of the building was five cubits thick all around, and its depth ninety cubits.

[13] Then he measured the temple, one hundred cubits deep; and the yard and the building with its walls, one hundred cubits deep; [14] also the width of the east front of the temple and the yard, one hundred cubits.

[15] Then he measured the depth of the building facing the yard at the west, together

---

[a] Gk: Heb *and the width of the gate was three cubits*
[b] Gk: Heb *eleven*
[c] Gk: Heb *and by steps that went up*
[d] Compare Gk: Heb *tent*
[e] Gk: Heb *width*
[f] Gk Compare 1 Kings 6.6: Heb *they entered*
[g] Cn: Heb *it was surrounded*

---

proper. The successive entrances to the Temple's three rooms become more narrow, symbolizing increasing holiness (40.48; 41.2; 41.3). **40.49:** According to the Septuagint (textual note *c*), the Temple was *ten steps* (10 ft [3 m]; see 41.8) above the level of the inner court. (Again, steps indicate increasing holiness; cf. vv. 22,31.) In front of the vestibule were freestanding *pillars* (1 Kings 7.15–22). *The vestibule* (40.48–49) was 34 ft (10.5 m) x 20.5 ft (6.3 m). *The nave* (41.1–2), which Ezekiel could enter as a Zadokite priest, was 69 ft (21 m) x 34 ft (10.5 m). The adytum (*inner room* or *most holy place,* 41.3–4), which Ezekiel did not enter (Lev 16), was a square of 34 ft (10.5 m) per side (1 Kings 6.16; 7.50; 8.6; Ex 26.33–34). **41.5–15a: Annexes and surroundings.** The three tiers of thirty chambers per tier on the sides of the Temple (1 Kings 6.5–10) probably stored Temple treasures (cf. 44.30; 1 Kings 14.26; 2 Kings 14.14) and equipment for Temple services. **10:** *Chambers of the court,* 42.1–14.

with its galleries[a] on either side, one hundred cubits.

The nave of the temple and the inner room and the outer[b] vestibule [16] were paneled,[c] and, all around, all three had windows with recessed[d] frames. Facing the threshold the temple was paneled with wood all around, from the floor up to the windows (now the windows were covered), [17] to the space above the door, even to the inner room, and on the outside. And on all the walls all around in the inner room and the nave there was a pattern.[e] [18] It was formed of cherubim and palm trees, a palm tree between cherub and cherub. Each cherub had two faces: [19] a human face turned toward the palm tree on the one side, and the face of a young lion turned toward the palm tree on the other side. They were carved on the whole temple all around; [20] from the floor to the area above the door, cherubim and palm trees were carved on the wall.[f]

[21] The doorposts of the nave were square. In front of the holy place was something resembling [22] an altar of wood, three cubits high, two cubits long, and two cubits wide;[g] its corners, its base,[h] and its walls were of wood. He said to me, "This is the table that stands before the LORD." [23] The nave and the holy place had each a double door. [24] The doors had two leaves apiece, two swinging leaves for each door. [25] On the doors of the nave were carved cherubim and palm trees, such as were carved on the walls; and there was a canopy of wood in front of the vestibule outside. [26] And there were recessed windows and palm trees on either side, on the sidewalls of the vestibule.[i]

42 Then he led me out into the outer court, toward the north, and he brought me to the chambers that were opposite the temple yard and opposite the building on the north. [2] The length of the building that was on the north side[j] was[k] one hundred cubits, and the width fifty cubits. [3] Across the twenty cubits that belonged to the inner court, and facing the pavement that belonged to the outer court, the chambers rose[l] gallery[m] by gallery[m] in three stories. [4] In front of the chambers was a passage on the inner side, ten cubits wide and one hundred cubits deep,[n] and its[o] entrances were on the north. [5] Now the upper chambers were narrower, for the galleries[m] took more away from them than from the lower and middle chambers in the building. [6] For they were in three stories, and they had no pillars like the pillars of the outer[p] court; for this reason the upper chambers were set back from the ground more than the lower and the middle ones. [7] There was a wall outside parallel to the chambers, toward the outer court, opposite the chambers, fifty cubits long. [8] For the chambers on the outer court were fifty cubits long, while those opposite the temple were one hundred cubits long. [9] At the foot of these chambers ran a passage that one entered from the east in order to enter them from the outer court.

a Cn: Meaning of Heb uncertain
b Gk: Heb *of the court*
c Gk: Heb *the thresholds*
d Cn Compare Gk 1 Kings 6.4: Meaning of Heb uncertain
e Heb *measures*
f Cn Compare verse 25: Heb *and the wall*
g Gk: Heb lacks *two cubits wide*
h Gk: Heb *length*
i Cn: Heb *vestibule. And the side chambers of the temple and the canopies*
j Gk: Heb *door*
k Gk: Heb *before the length*
l Heb lacks *the chambers rose*
m Meaning of Heb uncertain
n Gk Syr: Heb *a way of one cubit*
o Heb *their*
p Gk: Heb lacks *outer*

12: A large auxiliary building stood west of the Temple; it may also have been intended for storage purposes. **15b–26: Wall decoration and interior furnishings. 16:** The windows were like those in the gates (40.16). **18–20:** The Temple aimed to model Eden, God's cosmic dwelling, where fantastic trees and cherubim are present (cf. 28.13n.; 1 Kings 6.29–30). **22:** The *table* in the nave was for the bread of the Presence, see Ex 25.23–30 (not HS); Lev 24.5–9 (HS).

42.1–14: The priests' chambers. Ezekiel first sees the north sacristy, which was behind (west of) the north gate-tower to the inner court. Similar chambers were on the Temple's south side (vv. 10–12). Perhaps the three stories of chambers were arranged terrace-fashion against the north and south walls retaining the inner court.

¹⁰ The width of the passage[a] was fixed by the wall of the court.

On the south[b] also, opposite the vacant area and opposite the building, there were chambers ¹¹ with a passage in front of them; they were similar to the chambers on the north, of the same length and width, with the same exits[c] and arrangements and doors. ¹² So the entrances of the chambers to the south were entered through the entrance at the head of the corresponding passage, from the east, along the matching wall.[d]

¹³ Then he said to me, "The north chambers and the south chambers opposite the vacant area are the holy chambers, where the priests who approach the LORD shall eat the most holy offerings; there they shall deposit the most holy offerings—the grain offering, the sin offering, and the guilt offering—for the place is holy. ¹⁴ When the priests enter the holy place, they shall not go out of it into the outer court without laying there the vestments in which they minister, for these are holy; they shall put on other garments before they go near to the area open to the people."

¹⁵ When he had finished measuring the interior of the temple area, he led me out by the gate that faces east, and measured the temple area all around. ¹⁶ He measured the east side with the measuring reed, five hundred cubits by the measuring reed. ¹⁷ Then he turned and measured[e] the north side, five hundred cubits by the measuring reed. ¹⁸ Then he turned and measured[e] the south side, five hundred cubits by the measuring reed. ¹⁹ Then he turned to the west side and measured, five hundred cubits by the measuring reed. ²⁰ He measured it on the four sides. It had a wall around it, five hundred cubits long and five hundred cubits

wide, to make a separation between the holy and the common.

43

Then he brought me to the gate, the gate facing east. ² And there, the glory of the God of Israel was coming from the east; the sound was like the sound of mighty waters; and the earth shone with his glory. ³ The[f] vision I saw was like the vision that I had seen when he came to destroy the city, and[g] like the vision that I had seen by the river Chebar; and I fell upon my face. ⁴ As the glory of the LORD entered the temple by the gate facing east, ⁵ the spirit lifted me up, and brought me into the inner court; and the glory of the LORD filled the temple.

⁶ While the man was standing beside me, I heard someone speaking to me out of the temple. ⁷ He said to me: Mortal, this is the place of my throne and the place for the soles of my feet, where I will reside among the people of Israel forever. The house of Israel shall no more defile my holy name, neither they nor their kings, by their whoring, and by the corpses of their kings at their death.[h] ⁸ When they placed their threshold by my threshold and their doorposts beside my doorposts, with only a wall between me and them, they were defiling my holy name by their abominations that they committed; therefore I have consumed them in my anger. ⁹ Now let them put away their idolatry and the corpses

---

a Heb lacks *of the passage*
b Gk: Heb *east*
c Heb *and all their exits*
d Meaning of Heb uncertain
e Gk: Heb *measuring reed all around. He measured*
f Gk: Heb *Like the vision*
g Syr: Heb *and the visions*
h Or *on their high places*

A second, smaller apartment building was opposite, on the outer-court side. **13**: On the sacrifices, see 40.38–39n.; 44.28–31; Lev 2.1–10; 7.7–10. **14**: See 44.19n. **15–20: The measuring completed.** The total Temple area was a square of 861 ft (262 m) per side. **20**: Marking boundaries of holiness, distinguishing between *the holy and the common,* was a central concern of Zadokites, such as Ezekiel (22.26; 44.23; Lev 10.10–11 [HS]).

43.1–12: Return of the glory of the LORD. As God on the throne-chariot had forsaken the Temple by the east gate (10.18–19; 11.22–23), so God's glory (see 10.1–22n.) returns through the same gate (40.6–16; 44.1–3) and dwells in the new Temple (Ex 40.34–38 [HS]; 1 Kings 8.10–11). **2**: *Sound of mighty waters,* see 1.4n. **3**: *Chebar,* 1.1–3n. *Fell upon my face,* 1.28n.; 3.23. **6–12**: God warns against any more defiling of the Temple. The text particularly attacks royal encroachment on the Temple, perhaps in constructing shrines to other deities in the Temple courtyard, and the practice of royal funerary offerings at the Temple (the Hebrew may refer not to *corpses* but to deification of deceased kings). **7**: Holiness School theology triumphs, as God's glory takes up permanent

of their kings far from me, and I will reside among them forever.

¹⁰ As for you, mortal, describe the temple to the house of Israel, and let them measure the pattern; and let them be ashamed of their iniquities. ¹¹ When they are ashamed of all that they have done, make known to them the plan of the temple, its arrangement, its exits and its entrances, and its whole form— all its ordinances and its entire plan and all its laws; and write it down in their sight, so that they may observe and follow the entire plan and all its ordinances. ¹² This is the law of the temple: the whole territory on the top of the mountain all around shall be most holy. This is the law of the temple.

¹³ These are the dimensions of the altar by cubits (the cubit being one cubit and a handbreadth): its base shall be one cubit high,ᵃ and one cubit wide, with a rim of one span around its edge. This shall be the height of the altar: ¹⁴ From the base on the ground to the lower ledge, two cubits, with a width of one cubit; and from the smaller ledge to the larger ledge, four cubits, with a width of one cubit; ¹⁵ and the altar hearth, four cubits; and from the altar hearth projecting upward, four horns. ¹⁶ The altar hearth shall be square, twelve cubits long by twelve wide. ¹⁷ The ledge also shall be square, fourteen cubits long by fourteen wide, with a rim around it half a cubit wide, and its surrounding base, one cubit. Its steps face east.

¹⁸ Then he said to me: Mortal, thus says the Lord GOD: These are the ordinances for the altar: On the day when it is erected for offer-ing burnt offerings upon it and for dashing blood against it, ¹⁹ you shall give to the levitical priests of the family of Zadok, who draw near to me to minister to me, says the Lord GOD, a bull for a sin offering. ²⁰ And you shall take some of its blood, and put it on the four horns of the altar, and on the four corners of the ledge, and upon the rim all around; thus you shall purify it and make atonement for it. ²¹ You shall also take the bull of the sin offering, and it shall be burnt in the appointed place belonging to the temple, outside the sacred area.

²² On the second day you shall offer a male goat without blemish for a sin offering; and the altar shall be purified, as it was purified with the bull. ²³ When you have finished purifying it, you shall offer a bull without blemish and a ram from the flock without blemish. ²⁴ You shall present them before the LORD, and the priests shall throw salt on them and offer them up as a burnt offering to the LORD. ²⁵ For seven days you shall provide daily a goat for a sin offering; also a bull and a ram from the flock, without blemish, shall be provided. ²⁶ Seven days shall they make atonement for the altar and cleanse it, and so consecrate it. ²⁷ When these days are over, then from the eighth day onward the priests shall offer upon the altar your burnt offerings and your offerings of well-being; and I will accept you, says the Lord GOD.

44 Then he brought me back to the outer gate of the sanctuary, which faces east; and it was shut. ² The LORD said to

---

ᵃ Gk: Heb lacks *high*

residence amid the Israelites (37.27n.; 37.28n.; 48.35n.). *My holy name,* 20.9n. **10–12:** Instructions and statement of purpose. The Temple plan of chs 40–42 provides for the holiness appropriate for God's eternal presence. **12:** *Law of the temple,* it was the priests, such as Ezekiel, who transmitted such law to people (44.23n.).

43.13–17: The altar of burnt offerings (40.47). The altar symbolizes a mythic cosmic center (cf. 5.5n.; 38.12n.), its shape resembling the Babylonian ziggurats meant to be cosmic centers and gateways to heaven (see Gen 11.4). *The base on the ground* (v. 14) is literally, "the bosom of the earth." The *altar hearth* (v. 15) in Hebrew is spelled like "the mountain of God." **13:** *Cubit,* see 40.5n. **15:** *Horns,* see 1 Kings 1.50n. **16:** *Hearth,* the altar's top layer, where sacrifices were burned. **17:** The height of the altar, over 17 ft (5.2 m), necessitated its having *steps* (contrast Ex 20.26). **43.18–27: The altar's consecration.** On the analogy of earlier consecratory rites (Ex 29.36–37 (not HS); 40.1–38 [HS]; Lev 8.14–15), the priests of Zadok (40.46n.; 44.15–31n.) are to dedicate the altar upon its completion. **21:** Lev 4.11–12; 8.16–17.

44.1–3: The outer east gate. This gate-tower (40.6–14) remains closed, symbolizing its consecration by God's entrance (43.4) and God's permanent presence inside the Temple (43.7). Thus shut, the gate-complex becomes a ceremonial room. As his sacral privilege, the *prince* was to enter it from the Temple's outer courtyard to eat his part of the sacrificial meal (43.27; Lev 7.15; 22.21). Ezekiel's preferred term for Israel's monarchic leader

me: This gate shall remain shut; it shall not be opened, and no one shall enter by it; for the LORD, the God of Israel, has entered by it; therefore it shall remain shut. ³ Only the prince, because he is a prince, may sit in it to eat food before the LORD; he shall enter by way of the vestibule of the gate, and shall go out by the same way.

⁴ Then he brought me by way of the north gate to the front of the temple; and I looked, and lo! the glory of the LORD filled the temple of the LORD; and I fell upon my face. ⁵ The LORD said to me: Mortal, mark well, look closely, and listen attentively to all that I shall tell you concerning all the ordinances of the temple of the LORD and all its laws; and mark well those who may be admitted to[a] the temple and all those who are to be excluded from the sanctuary. ⁶ Say to the rebellious house,[b] to the house of Israel, Thus says the Lord GOD: O house of Israel, let there be an end to all your abominations ⁷ in admitting foreigners, uncircumcised in heart and flesh, to be in my sanctuary, profaning my temple when you offer to me my food, the fat and the blood. You[c] have broken my covenant with all your abominations. ⁸ And you have not kept charge of my sacred offerings; but you have appointed foreigners[d] to act for you in keeping my charge in my sanctuary.

⁹ Thus says the Lord GOD: No foreigner, uncircumcised in heart and flesh, of all the foreigners who are among the people of Israel, shall enter my sanctuary. ¹⁰ But the Levites who went far from me, going astray from me after their idols when Israel went astray, shall bear their punishment. ¹¹ They shall be ministers in my sanctuary, having oversight at the gates of the temple, and serving in the temple; they shall slaughter the burnt offering and the sacrifice for the people, and they shall attend on them and serve them. ¹² Because they ministered to them before their idols and made the house of Israel stumble into iniquity, therefore I have sworn concerning them, says the Lord GOD, that they shall bear their punishment. ¹³ They shall not come near to me, to serve me as priest, nor come near any of my sacred offerings, the things that are most sacred; but they shall bear their shame, and the consequences of the abominations that they have committed. ¹⁴ Yet I will appoint them to keep charge of the temple, to do all its chores, all that is to be done in it.

¹⁵ But the levitical priests, the descendants of Zadok, who kept the charge of my sanctu-

a Cn: Heb *the entrance of*
b Gk: Heb lacks *house*
c Gk Syr Vg: Heb *They*
d Heb lacks *foreigners*

is *prince*. The term derives from Israel's tribal past, and Ezekiel uses it to uphold the kinship networks of the countryside and the landed patrimonies that supported them (see 45:8–9n.; 46:18n.). The Holiness School is concerned with organizing and stabilizing God's entire holy territory including the countryside, not just an isolated royal capital. In 34.24 and 37.25, the prince is a Davidic figure in the new era of restoration. Here in chs 40–48, the prince is less an ideal royal figure than a civil ruler with immediate, concrete tasks.

44.4–31: Temple ordinances. 4–5: A renewed commission. 6–16: Ezekiel's blueprint for the restored priesthood of Israel again redresses past wrongs. Under the influence of the Holiness School, Ezekiel finds these particular past wrongs encapsulated in Num 16–18, a text about the rebellion of Levites during Israel's wilderness wanderings. 7–8: The primary reference is to a prototypical narrative: the Levites' encroachment on priestly prerogatives in Num 16.40; 18.4,7. The Levites are *foreigners*, that is "outsiders," with respect to the priestly obligations of the sanctuary and the altar. 10–14: After their rebellion in the wilderness, the Levites were given circumscribed responsibilities. Here, the Levites are restored to these responsibilities in the new Temple, as the Holiness School had specified them (Num 18:3–4). 10: *When Israel went astray*, Num 16.2,22,41. *Bear their punishment*, Num 18.23. 11: The limitation of the slaughtering of sacrifices to the Levites, thus disenfranchising the general populace, is a new holiness stricture that goes beyond Lev 1.5,11. *Attend . . . and serve*, Num 16.9. 13: Num 18.3. 14: Num 18.4. 15–31: The Zadokite priesthood (see 40.46b n.; 43.19; 48.11). The Zadokites, one of at least three major priestly lineages in ancient Israel, had been the central priests at Jerusalem's preexilic Temple. Their origins trace back to Solomon's elevation of *Zadok*, the founder of the Zadokite lineage, to be chief priest after Abiathar's banishment (2 Sam 20.25; 1 Kings 1.7–8,41–45; 2.26–27). Ezekiel and his group were themselves Zadokite priests. 1 Chr 6.50–53 and 24.31 trace Zadok's ancestry back to Eleazar, Aaron's son. Here, vv. 15–16 refer

ary when the people of Israel went astray from me, shall come near to me to minister to me; and they shall attend me to offer me the fat and the blood, says the Lord God. [16] It is they who shall enter my sanctuary, it is they who shall approach my table, to minister to me, and they shall keep my charge. [17] When they enter the gates of the inner court, they shall wear linen vestments; they shall have nothing of wool on them, while they minister at the gates of the inner court, and within. [18] They shall have linen turbans on their heads, and linen undergarments on their loins; they shall not bind themselves with anything that causes sweat. [19] When they go out into the outer court to the people, they shall remove the vestments in which they have been ministering, and lay them in the holy chambers; and they shall put on other garments, so that they may not communicate holiness to the people with their vestments. [20] They shall not shave their heads or let their locks grow long; they shall only trim the hair of their heads. [21] No priest shall drink wine when he enters the inner court. [22] They shall not marry a widow, or a divorced woman, but only a virgin of the stock of the house of Israel, or a widow who is the widow of a priest. [23] They shall teach my people the difference between the holy and the common, and show them how to distinguish between the unclean and the clean. [24] In a controversy they shall act as judges, and they shall decide it according to my judgments. They shall keep my laws and my statutes regarding all my appointed festivals, and they shall keep my sabbaths holy. [25] They shall not defile themselves by going near to a dead person; for father or mother, however, and for son or daughter, and for brother or unmarried sister they may defile themselves. [26] After he has become clean, they shall count seven days for him. [27] On the day that he goes into the holy place, into the inner court, to minister in the holy place, he shall offer his sin offering, says the Lord God.

[28] This shall be their inheritance: I am their inheritance; and you shall give them no holding in Israel; I am their holding. [29] They shall eat the grain offering, the sin offering, and the guilt offering; and every devoted thing in Israel shall be theirs. [30] The first of all the first fruits of all kinds, and every offering of all kinds from all your offerings, shall belong to the priests; you shall also give to the priests the first of your dough, in order that a blessing may rest on your house. [31] The priests shall not eat of anything, whether bird or animal, that died of itself or was torn by animals.

45 When you allot the land as an inheritance, you shall set aside for the LORD a portion of the land as a holy district, twenty-five thousand cubits long and twenty[a] thousand cubits wide; it shall be holy throughout its entire extent. [2] Of this, a square plot of five hundred by five hundred cubits shall be for the sanctuary, with fifty cubits for an open space around it. [3] In the holy district you shall measure off a section twenty-five thousand cubits long and ten thousand wide, in which shall be the sanctu-

a Gk: Heb *ten*

to how Aaron and Eleazar had been faithful during the Levites' rebellion (Num 16.11,20–22,36–40,46–50). These priests were the ancestors of the Zadokites, and Ezekiel views the Zadokites as present "embryonically" in their actions. **15–16:** Num 18.7 (cf. Lev 16.14–15). **17–31: Priestly rules. 17:** *Linen vestments*, see 9.1–2n.; Ex 39.27–29 (HS). **19:** 42.14. *Communicate holiness*, cf. 46.20. Sanctity could sometimes be transmitted through direct contact with a sacred substance (see Lev 6.18,26–27). The goal here is to preserve gradations of sanctity. Failure in this regard was life-threatening (see Num 16.38 [HS]). **20:** The care of the hair, Lev 21.5 (HS). **21:** No *wine* before service, Lev 10.9 (HS). **22:** Proper marriage, Lev 21.7,13–15 (HS). **23:** Teaching of the people, Lev 10.10–11 (HS); 2 Chr 17.9; Hag 2.10–13. **24:** *Judges*, 1 Chr 23.4; 2 Chr 19.11. **25:** Defilement by a corpse, see 39.11–16n.; Lev 21.1–3 (HS). **28:** No *inheritance*, 45.1–5; 48.8–14; Num 18.20–24 (HS). **29–30:** Eating sacrifices and *first fruits*, Num 18.9–13 (HS); Lev 2.3; 6.16,26; 7.6–7. *Every devoted thing*, Num 18.14 (HS). **31:** Lev 7.24; 22.8 (HS).

45.1–9: The distribution of land (continued in 47.13–48.35) is idealized. A *holy district* is to contain a northern section for the Levites and a southern section for the sacrificing priests. The latter includes the square section for the Temple area (42.15–20) plus an enclosure space (not mentioned earlier). The property of Jerusalem south of the holy district (v. 6) makes with the holy district (v. 1) a square area of ca. 8 mi (13 km) per side. The prince

ary, the most holy place. ⁴ It shall be a holy portion of the land; it shall be for the priests, who minister in the sanctuary and approach the LORD to minister to him; and it shall be both a place for their houses and a holy place for the sanctuary. ⁵ Another section, twenty-five thousand cubits long and ten thousand cubits wide, shall be for the Levites who minister at the temple, as their holding for cities to live in.ᵃ

⁶ Alongside the portion set apart as the holy district you shall assign as a holding for the city an area five thousand cubits wide, and twenty-five thousand cubits long; it shall belong to the whole house of Israel.

⁷ And to the prince shall belong the land on both sides of the holy district and the holding of the city, alongside the holy district and the holding of the city, on the west and on the east, corresponding in length to one of the tribal portions, and extending from the western to the eastern boundary ⁸ of the land. It is to be his property in Israel. And my princes shall no longer oppress my people; but they shall let the house of Israel have the land according to their tribes.

⁹ Thus says the Lord GOD: Enough, O princes of Israel! Put away violence and oppression, and do what is just and right. Cease your evictions of my people, says the Lord GOD.

¹⁰ You shall have honest balances, an honest ephah, and an honest bath.ᵇ ¹¹ The ephah and the bath shall be of the same measure, the bath containing one-tenth of a homer, and the ephah one-tenth of a homer; the homer shall be the standard measure. ¹² The shekel shall be twenty gerahs. Twenty shekels, twenty-five shekels, and fifteen shekels shall make a mina for you.

¹³ This is the offering that you shall make: one-sixth of an ephah from each homer of wheat, and one-sixth of an ephah from each homer of barley, ¹⁴ and as the fixed portion of oil,ᶜ one-tenth of a bath from each cor (the cor,ᵈ like the homer, contains ten baths); ¹⁵ and one sheep from every flock of two hundred, from the pastures of Israel. This is the offering for grain offerings, burnt offerings, and offerings of well-being, to make atonement for them, says the Lord GOD. ¹⁶ All the people of the land shall join with the prince in Israel in making this offering. ¹⁷ But this shall be the obligation of the prince regarding the burnt offerings, grain offerings, and drink offerings, at the festivals, the new moons, and the sabbaths, all the appointed festivals of the house of Israel: he shall provide the sin offerings, grain offerings, the burnt offerings, and the offerings of well-being, to make atonement for the house of Israel.

¹⁸ Thus says the Lord GOD: In the first month, on the first day of the month, you shall take a young bull without blemish, and purify the sanctuary. ¹⁹ The priest shall take some of the blood of the sin offering and put it on the doorposts of the temple, the four corners of the ledge of the altar, and the posts of the gate of the inner court. ²⁰ You shall do the same on the seventh day of the month for anyone who has sinned through error or ignorance; so you shall make atonement for the temple.

²¹ In the first month, on the fourteenth day of the month, you shall celebrate the festival

---

ᵃ Gk: Heb as their holding, twenty chambers
ᵇ A Heb measure of volume
ᶜ Cn: Heb oil, the bath the oil
ᵈ Vg: Heb homer

(see 44.1–3n.) is to hold the strips of land to the west and east of this square area. **8–9**: In accordance with the ideals of the Holiness School (Lev 25.10,23–24,42), princes are denied the power to evict subjects from their family homesteads (cf. 11.15n.; 22.27; 46.18n.).

45.10-17: Weights and measures for offerings. For present-day equivalents of *ephah, bath, homer, shekel, gerah,* and *mina,* see Table of Weights and Measures. The Holiness School insisted on *honest* measures (see Lev 19.35–36). **13–17**: The people will bring gifts for the regular sacrifices to the prince, who, as their representative, will offer them to God. These offerings are additional to the donations given to the priests of 44.30.

45.18-25: Festival regulations. 18–20: A new annual ritual for purifying the Temple or a one-time, inaugural purification. **21–25**: Ezekiel's brief festival-calendar highlights the *passover* (Ex 12; Lev 23.4–8) and the festival of booths (the *festival* of the *seventh month* in v. 25; see Lev 23.33–36). It omits the festival of weeks (Pentecost;

of the passover, and for seven days unleavened bread shall be eaten. ²² On that day the prince shall provide for himself and all the people of the land a young bull for a sin offering. ²³ And during the seven days of the festival he shall provide as a burnt offering to the Lord seven young bulls and seven rams without blemish, on each of the seven days; and a male goat daily for a sin offering. ²⁴ He shall provide as a grain offering an ephah for each bull, an ephah for each ram, and a hin of oil to each ephah. ²⁵ In the seventh month, on the fifteenth day of the month and for the seven days of the festival, he shall make the same provision for sin offerings, burnt offerings, and grain offerings, and for the oil.

46 Thus says the Lord God: The gate of the inner court that faces east shall remain closed on the six working days; but on the sabbath day it shall be opened and on the day of the new moon it shall be opened. ² The prince shall enter by the vestibule of the gate from outside, and shall take his stand by the post of the gate. The priests shall offer his burnt offering and his offerings of well-being, and he shall bow down at the threshold of the gate. Then he shall go out, but the gate shall not be closed until evening. ³ The people of the land shall bow down at the entrance of that gate before the Lord on the sabbaths and on the new moons. ⁴ The burnt offering that the prince offers to the Lord on the sabbath day shall be six lambs without blemish and a ram without blemish; ⁵ and the grain offering with the ram shall be an ephah, and the grain offering with the lambs shall be as much as he wishes to give, together with a hin of oil to each ephah. ⁶ On the day of the new moon he shall offer a young bull without blemish, and six lambs and a ram, which shall be without blemish; ⁷ as a grain offering he shall provide an ephah with the bull and an ephah with the ram, and with the lambs as much as he wishes, together with a hin of oil to each ephah. ⁸ When the prince enters, he shall come in by the vestibule of the gate, and he shall go out by the same way.

⁹ When the people of the land come before the Lord at the appointed festivals, whoever enters by the north gate to worship shall go out by the south gate; and whoever enters by the south gate shall go out by the north gate: they shall not return by way of the gate by which they entered, but shall go out straight ahead. ¹⁰ When they come in, the prince shall come in with them; and when they go out, he shall go out.

¹¹ At the festivals and the appointed seasons the grain offering with a young bull shall be an ephah, and with a ram an ephah, and with the lambs as much as one wishes to give, together with a hin of oil to an ephah. ¹² When the prince provides a freewill offering, either a burnt offering or offerings of well-being as a freewill offering to the Lord, the gate facing east shall be opened for him; and he shall offer his burnt offering or his offerings of well-being as he does on the sabbath day. Then he shall go out, and after he has gone out the gate shall be closed.

¹³ He shall provide a lamb, a yearling, without blemish, for a burnt offering to the Lord daily; morning by morning he shall provide it. ¹⁴ And he shall provide a grain offering with it morning by morning regularly, one-sixth of an ephah, and one-third of a hin of oil to moisten the choice flour, as a grain offering to the Lord; this is the ordinance for all time. ¹⁵ Thus the lamb and the grain offering and the oil shall be provided, morning by morning, as a regular burnt offering.

¹⁶ Thus says the Lord God: If the prince makes a gift to any of his sons out of his

Lev 23.15–21). **24:** *Ephah* and *hin,* see Table of Weights and Measures.

46.1–15: Gate regulations and the prince's minor offerings. 1–7: Both weekly and monthly, the *prince* (see 44.1–3n.) shall bring offerings (vv. 4–7) into the inner east gate leading to the altar (40.32–34). Kings might have performed priestly functions in preexilic times (1 Kings 8.63; 2 Kings 16.12–13), but now they will stand by while the priests offer the sacrifices. For the *sabbath* sacrifices, see Num 28.9–10; on Ezekiel's emphasis on the sabbath here, see 20.12–13n. For the *new moon* (i.e., monthly) sacrifices, see Num 28.11–15. **8–10:** Exit procedures. The great festival crowds require regulations for controlled egress. **11–15:** Further rules. **11:** 45.24; 46.5,7. **12:** When the prince makes a *freewill offering* (Lev 22.18–23 [HS]), the inner east gate (v. 1) may be opened. **13–15:** The prince must also provide for daily sacrifices (Num 28.3–8; Ex 29.38–42 [HS]).

46.16–18: The prince's property. Crown property (45.7; 48.21–22) was to be inalienable from the royal line.

inheritance,[a] it shall belong to his sons, it is their holding by inheritance. [17] But if he makes a gift out of his inheritance to one of his servants, it shall be his to the year of liberty; then it shall revert to the prince; only his sons may keep a gift from his inheritance. [18] The prince shall not take any of the inheritance of the people, thrusting them out of their holding; he shall give his sons their inheritance out of his own holding, so that none of my people shall be dispossessed of their holding.

[19] Then he brought me through the entrance, which was at the side of the gate, to the north row of the holy chambers for the priests; and there I saw a place at the extreme western end of them. [20] He said to me, "This is the place where the priests shall boil the guilt offering and the sin offering, and where they shall bake the grain offering, in order not to bring them out into the outer court and so communicate holiness to the people."

[21] Then he brought me out to the outer court, and led me past the four corners of the court; and in each corner of the court there was a court— [22] in the four corners of the court were small[b] courts, forty cubits long and thirty wide; the four were of the same size. [23] On the inside, around each of the four courts[c] was a row of masonry, with hearths made at the bottom of the rows all around. [24] Then he said to me, "These are the kitchens where those who serve at the temple shall boil the sacrifices of the people."

47 Then he brought me back to the entrance of the temple; there, water was flowing from below the threshold of the temple toward the east (for the temple faced east); and the water was flowing down from below the south end of the threshold of the temple, south of the altar. [2] Then he brought

me out by way of the north gate, and led me around on the outside to the outer gate that faces toward the east;[d] and the water was coming out on the south side.

[3] Going on eastward with a cord in his hand, the man measured one thousand cubits, and then led me through the water; and it was ankle-deep. [4] Again he measured one thousand, and led me through the water; and it was knee-deep. Again he measured one thousand, and led me through the water; and it was up to the waist. [5] Again he measured one thousand, and it was a river that I could not cross, for the water had risen; it was deep enough to swim in, a river that could not be crossed. [6] He said to me, "Mortal, have you seen this?"

Then he led me back along the bank of the river. [7] As I came back, I saw on the bank of the river a great many trees on the one side and on the other. [8] He said to me, "This water flows toward the eastern region and goes down into the Arabah; and when it enters the sea, the sea of stagnant waters, the water will become fresh. [9] Wherever the river goes,[e] every living creature that swarms will live, and there will be very many fish, once these waters reach there. It will become fresh; and everything will live where the river goes. [10] People will stand fishing beside the sea[f] from En-gedi to En-eglaim; it will be a place for the spreading of nets; its fish will be of a great many kinds, like the fish of the Great Sea. [11] But its swamps and marshes will not

a Gk: Heb *it is his inheritance*
b Gk Syr Vg: Meaning of Heb uncertain
c Heb *the four of them*
d Meaning of Heb uncertain
e Gk Syr Vg Tg: Heb *the two rivers go*
f Heb *it*

When given to a nonrelative, it had to be returned on the *year of liberty* (jubilee year, Lev 25.8–17 [HS]). **18:** See 45.8–9n. Royal appropriation of others' ancestral lands (see 1 Kings 21.1–16; Isa 5.8; Mic 2.2) is strictly forbidden.

46.19–24: Sacrificial kitchens. 19–20: Behind (west of) the priest's chambers (42.1–14) were kitchens for preparing offerings (42.13) for priestly consumption. *Communicate holiness,* see 42.14; 44.19n. **21–24:** Kitchens, for the Levites to prepare the common-meal sacrifices of the general populace, were in all four corners of the outer court (40.17–19).

47.1–12: The sacred river. From the throne of God (the Temple; 43.7) issue the waters of life, making the land a new Paradise. This paradisiacal motif (see 28.14n.) is also found in Joel 3.18 and Zech 14.8 (both Zadokite apocalyptic texts that follow in the tradition of Ezekiel). **8:** *Arabah,* the Jordan valley, in which the Dead Sea (*the sea of stagnant waters*) is located. **10:** *En-gedi to En-eglaim,* two springs on the western side of the Dead Sea. *The*

become fresh; they are to be left for salt. ¹² On the banks, on both sides of the river, there will grow all kinds of trees for food. Their leaves will not wither nor their fruit fail, but they will bear fresh fruit every month, because the water for them flows from the sanctuary. Their fruit will be for food, and their leaves for healing."

¹³ Thus says the Lord GOD: These are the boundaries by which you shall divide the land for inheritance among the twelve tribes of Israel. Joseph shall have two portions. ¹⁴ You shall divide it equally; I swore to give it to your ancestors, and this land shall fall to you as your inheritance.

¹⁵ This shall be the boundary of the land: On the north side, from the Great Sea by way of Hethlon to Lebo-hamath, and on to Zedad,ᵃ ¹⁶ Berothah, Sibraim (which lies between the border of Damascus and the border of Hamath), as far as Hazer-hatticon, which is on the border of Hauran. ¹⁷ So the boundary shall run from the sea to Hazar-enon, which is north of the border of Damascus, with the border of Hamath to the north.ᵇ This shall be the north side.

¹⁸ On the east side, between Hauran and Damascus; along the Jordan between Gilead and the land of Israel; to the eastern sea and as far as Tamar.ᶜ This shall be the east side.

¹⁹ On the south side, it shall run from Tamar as far as the waters of Meribath-kadesh, from there along the Wadi of Egyptᵈ to the Great Sea. This shall be the south side.

²⁰ On the west side, the Great Sea shall be the boundary to a point opposite Lebo-hamath. This shall be the west side.

²¹ So you shall divide this land among you according to the tribes of Israel. ²² You

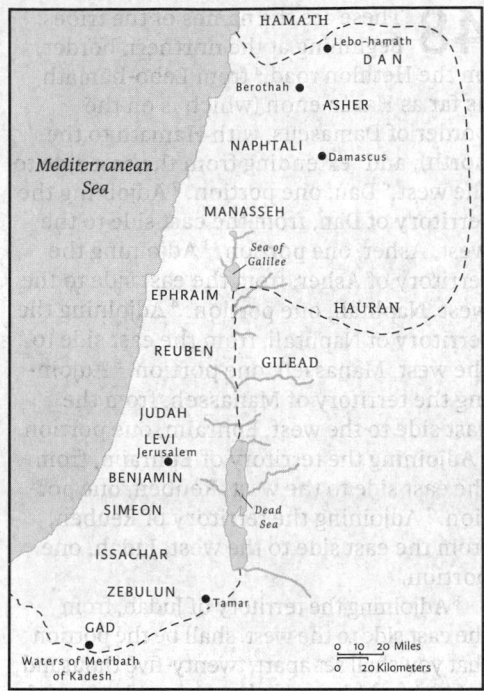

Chs 47–48: Tribal territories in the restored Israel.

shall allot it as an inheritance for yourselves and for the aliens who reside among you and have begotten children among you. They shall be to you as citizens of Israel; with you they shall be allotted an inheritance among the tribes of Israel. ²³ In whatever tribe aliens reside, there you shall assign them their inheritance, says the Lord GOD.

ᵃ Gk: Heb *Lebo-zedad,* ¹⁶*Hamath*
ᵇ Meaning of Heb uncertain
ᶜ Compare Syr: Heb *you shall measure*
ᵈ Heb lacks *of Egypt*

Great Sea, the Mediterranean. **11:** A source of salt would supply Temple rituals (43.24).

47.13–48.29: A new holy land. 47.13–23: Boundary and allotment instructions. Ezekiel's new Exodus and settlement (cf. 20.33–38n.; 36.8–12; 37.14) occasion a new allotment of the land. **14:** *I swore,* 20.6; 36.28. **15–20:** National boundaries. Several of the sites mentioned are unidentified. North border: roughly from the Mediterranean (*the Great Sea*) north of Tyre to Damascus (cf. Num 34.7–9). It is approximately the northern border of Solomon's territory (1 Kings 8.65). East border: along the Jordan to *Tamar,* a site south of the Dead Sea (*eastern sea*) (Num 34.10–12). Territory in the Transjordan is not included in the new land (contrast Num 34.13–15). South border: from Tamar along the southern Negeb through Kadesh-barnea (*Meribath-kadesh*) to *the Wadi of Egypt* (1 Kings 8.65n.) and the Mediterranean (Num 34.3–5). West border: the Mediterranean Sea (Num 34.6). **21–23:** Allotment. That resident *aliens* and native Israelites should be treated alike was a widespread principle in the Holiness School: Num 15.29; Lev 19.33–34; 24:22. Ezekiel radicalizes the principle to allow aliens to receive their own allotted portions of land.

48

These are the names of the tribes: Beginning at the northern border, on the Hethlon road,[a] from Lebo-hamath, as far as Hazar-enon (which is on the border of Damascus, with Hamath to the north), and[b] extending from the east side to the west,[c] Dan, one portion. [2] Adjoining the territory of Dan, from the east side to the west, Asher, one portion. [3] Adjoining the territory of Asher, from the east side to the west, Naphtali, one portion. [4] Adjoining the territory of Naphtali, from the east side to the west, Manasseh, one portion. [5] Adjoining the territory of Manasseh, from the east side to the west, Ephraim, one portion. [6] Adjoining the territory of Ephraim, from the east side to the west, Reuben, one portion. [7] Adjoining the territory of Reuben, from the east side to the west, Judah, one portion.

[8] Adjoining the territory of Judah, from the east side to the west, shall be the portion that you shall set apart, twenty-five thousand cubits in width, and in length equal to one of the tribal portions, from the east side to the west, with the sanctuary in the middle of it. [9] The portion that you shall set apart for the LORD shall be twenty-five thousand cubits in length, and twenty[d] thousand in width. [10] These shall be the allotments of the holy portion: the priests shall have an allotment measuring twenty-five thousand cubits on the northern side, ten thousand cubits in width on the western side, ten thousand in width on the eastern side, and twenty-five thousand in length on the southern side, with the sanctuary of the LORD in the middle of it. [11] This shall be for the consecrated priests, the descendants[e] of Zadok, who kept my charge, who did not go astray when the people of Israel went astray, as the Levites did. [12] It shall belong to them as a special portion from the holy portion of the land, a most holy place, adjoining the territory of the Levites. [13] Alongside the territory of the priests, the Levites shall have an allotment twenty-five thousand cubits in length and ten thousand in width. The whole length shall be twenty-five thousand cubits and the width twenty[f] thousand. [14] They shall not sell or exchange any of it; they shall not transfer this choice portion of the land, for it is holy to the LORD.

[15] The remainder, five thousand cubits in width and twenty-five thousand in length, shall be for ordinary use for the city, for dwellings and for open country. In the middle of it shall be the city; [16] and these shall be its dimensions: the north side four thousand five hundred cubits, the south side four thousand five hundred, the east side four thousand five hundred, and the west side four thousand five hundred. [17] The city shall have open land: on the north two hundred fifty cubits, on the south two hundred fifty, on the east two hundred fifty, on the west two hundred fifty. [18] The remainder of the length alongside the holy portion shall be ten thousand cubits to the east, and ten thousand to the west, and it shall be alongside the holy portion. Its produce shall be food for the workers of the city. [19] The workers of the city, from all the tribes of Israel, shall cultivate it. [20] The whole portion that you shall set apart shall be twenty-five thousand cubits square, that is, the holy portion together with the property of the city.

[21] What remains on both sides of the holy portion and of the property of the city shall belong to the prince. Extending from the twenty-five thousand cubits of the holy portion to the east border, and westward from the twenty-five thousand cubits to

a   Compare 47.15: Heb *by the side of the way*
b   Cn: Heb *and they shall be his*
c   Gk Compare verses 2–8: Heb *the east side the west*
d   Compare 45.1: Heb *ten*
e   One Ms Gk: Heb *of the descendants*
f   Gk: Heb *ten*

48.1–29: Tribal and holy-district allotments. All tribes receive equal allotments consisting of idealized strips of land. Ephraim and Manasseh ("Joseph," 47.13) receive a portion each, but Levi, the priestly tribe, is omitted, so that the tribal allotments number twelve in all. **1–7:** Seven tribes north of the central strip (vv. 8–22; 45.1–9). **1:** *Hethlon, Lebo-hamath,* sites on the land's northern border (47.15). **8–22:** The central strip. The description matches and expands 45.1–9. **11:** See 44.6–16n.; 44.15–31n. **15:** *Ordinary* ("common" as opposed to "holy") *use,* see 22.26; 42.20n.; 44.23; Lev 10.10 (HS). **16–17:** The area of Jerusalem, with the surrounding *open land,* was exactly one hundred times that of the Temple (42.20), i.e., a square of 1.6 mi (2.6 km) per side. **21–22:** The allot-

the west border, parallel to the tribal portions, it shall belong to the prince. The holy portion with the sanctuary of the temple in the middle of it, [22] and the property of the Levites and of the city, shall be in the middle of that which belongs to the prince. The portion of the prince shall lie between the territory of Judah and the territory of Benjamin.

[23] As for the rest of the tribes: from the east side to the west, Benjamin, one portion. [24] Adjoining the territory of Benjamin, from the east side to the west, Simeon, one portion. [25] Adjoining the territory of Simeon, from the east side to the west, Issachar, one portion. [26] Adjoining the territory of Issachar, from the east side to the west, Zebulun, one portion. [27] Adjoining the territory of Zebulun, from the east side to the west, Gad, one portion. [28] And adjoining the territory of Gad to the south, the boundary shall run from Tamar to the waters of Meribath-kadesh, from there along the Wadi of Egypt[a] to the Great Sea. [29] This is the land that you shall allot as an inheritance among the tribes of Israel, and these are their portions, says the Lord GOD.

[30] These shall be the exits of the city: On the north side, which is to be four thousand five hundred cubits by measure, [31] three gates, the gate of Reuben, the gate of Judah, and the gate of Levi, the gates of the city being named after the tribes of Israel. [32] On the east side, which is to be four thousand five hundred cubits, three gates, the gate of Joseph, the gate of Benjamin, and the gate of Dan. [33] On the south side, which is to be four thousand five hundred cubits by measure, three gates, the gate of Simeon, the gate of Issachar, and the gate of Zebulun. [34] On the west side, which is to be four thousand five hundred cubits, three gates,[b] the gate of Gad, the gate of Asher, and the gate of Naphtali. [35] The circumference of the city shall be eighteen thousand cubits. And the name of the city from that time on shall be, The LORD is There.

[a] Heb lacks *of Egypt*
[b] One Ms Gk Syr: MT *their gates three*

ment of the prince, as described in 45.7. **23–29:** Five tribes south of the central strip. **28:** See 47.19.

48.30–35: The new Jerusalem. Three gates on each of the city's four sides, each named after a tribe. **35:** The city's new name (cf. Isa 1.26; 60.14; 62.2; Zech 8.3) reflects how Holiness School theology has come into its own. The name *The LORD is There* (Heb "Yahweh-shammah") reverses 10.18–19.

DANIEL

NAME

The book of Daniel is named for its primary character, the exile from Judea who becomes a counselor and dream interpreter in the courts of the Babylonian, Median, and Persian kings (chs 1–6), and who himself is a recipient of mysterious revelations (chs 7–12).

The Daniel mentioned in Ezekiel (14.14,20; 28.3) is not the same character as the hero of the book of Daniel, but a figure of the remote past known also from Ugaritic texts of the fourteenth or thirteenth centuries BCE. In Ezekiel he is paired with Noah and Job: all three were non-Jews whose piety and wisdom were legendary. The hero of the book of Daniel is similar in knowledge and fidelity; he is, however, emphatically Jewish.

CONTENTS AND DATE OF COMPOSITION

The first six chapters are examples of the ancient Jewish short story, like Jonah, Esther, Tobit, and similar works. The purpose of such stories is to edify but also to entertain. More specifically, the stories in Daniel 1–6 are examples of "court tales," narratives that describe the dangers and triumphs experienced by Jewish heroes and heroines in the courts of foreign kings. Like Joseph in Gen 40–41, Daniel succeeds in service to the ruler through his ability to interpret dreams; like Mordecai in the book of Esther, he succeeds in such service despite challenges by rival politicians. Even though the court tales in Daniel are set in the time of the Babylonian exile and immediately following the fall of Babylon (in 539 BCE), they were most likely composed either in the late Persian (450–333 BCE) or early Hellenistic (333–170 BCE) periods, possibly in the eastern Diaspora. They reflect a time in which the imperial ruler is perceived as ignorant and dangerously unpredictable rather than malevolent, and a social context in which Jews can live at peace with their non-Jewish neighbors, although without complete security. The narratives also address a serious theological issue: How could Jews reconcile their belief in the sovereign power of God with the reality of Gentile imperial rule? In these stories the Gentile kings are shown as slowly recognizing that it is the "Most High" who is truly sovereign and that they rule only by divine permission.

The court tales in the first half of the book contrast with the apocalyptic materials in chs 7–12, which depict extreme hostility to foreign governments and feature lengthy periods of universal tribulation rather than temporary personal danger. In this second section, Daniel is not the interpreter of dream visions but the visionary himself, and he is now in need of an angel's interpretive skills. In a series of dreams, he learns of the history of the Near East from the Babylonian empire in the sixth century, through Persian rule, to the time of Alexander the Great in the late fourth century, and finally to the attacks against Jewish practice and belief as well as against the Jerusalem Temple by the Syrian-Greek ruler Antiochus IV Epiphanes (early second century BCE). The increasingly detailed descriptions of the period following the division of Alexander's empire to the rule of Antiochus suggest that the apocalyptic sections were composed between 167 and 164 BCE during the Maccabean revolt against the Hellenizing policies of Antiochus and his allies in Jerusalem's priestly circles (see 1 Macc 1). This dating makes the work the latest book in the Hebrew Bible. Its author may have been one of the "wise" who emphasized confidence in a divine plan to redeem Israel from idolatrous leaders, even in the face of martyrdom, and who rejected the armed resistance of the Maccabees (Dan 11.33–35); in the end, the author believed, God would punish the wicked and redeem the faithful (Dan 12.3). The visions are presented pseudonymously, that is, under the name of an ancient figure (in this case, Daniel, the sage of the sixth-fifth centuries BCE) who "foresees" what is to come, as in other apocalypses such as 2 Esdras, 2 Baruch, and the later Christian Apocalypse of Peter.

LANGUAGE AND CANONICAL STATUS

Daniel 2.4b–7.28 is written in Aramaic, the common language of the Near East during the Persian and early Hellenistic periods; chs 1.1–2.4a and chs 8–12 are in Hebrew, which had been eclipsed by Aramaic during this period, but which enjoyed a literary revival in the second century BCE. Complicating the history of the book of Daniel are additions to the story in some ancient Greek versions: Susanna, the Prayer of Azariah and the Song of the Three Jews, and Bel and the Dragon. These short works are considered Deuterocanonical by Catholic and Orthodox churches, that is, as having canonical status; Protestant churches regard them as part of the Apocrypha, and they have no canonical status in Judaism. (See the Introduction to the Apocryphal/Deuterocanonical books.)

Additional tales belonging to the cycle of stories about Daniel appear among the Dead Sea Scrolls. One text, the Prayer of Nabonidus (4QprNab), may represent an earlier version of Dan 4.

Jewish tradition places the book of Daniel among the Writings (Heb "Ketubim"), between the books of Esther and Ezra (see rabbinic discussion in *b. Meg.* 3a; *b. Sanh.* 94a). This decision may reflect the late date of composition of Daniel. Christian tradition locates the book among the Prophets, between the books of Ezekiel and Hosea.

INTERPRETATION

Despite the different genres and dates of composition, the book of Daniel does have a consistent theme: the sovereignty of God in history. By juxtaposing the wisdom of the Jewish courtiers in negotiating the difficulties of living under an often arbitrary and dangerous foreign rule with its visions of wars, persecutions, and, finally, salvation under God's sovereignty, the book of Daniel offers its readers both advice and consolation. The folktales speak to all peoples persecuted as religious and ethnic minorities. The apocalyptic materials, whose meanings would have been known to the author's own circle, have provided for more than two thousand years the occasion for speculation and, often, hope. Already 1 Macc 2.59–60 shows that Daniel and his three friends served as role models of resistance and deliverance. The apocalyptic materials, with their promise of divine salvation, also were often reinterpreted for later circumstances. For example, the apocalypse of 2 Esdras—a text originally written by a Jew but then edited and preserved by the Christian church—reinterprets the vision of Daniel 7 to express hope for the punishment of Rome and the redemption of Israel following the Roman destruction of Jerusalem in 70 CE. Early Christians saw in the figure of the "son of man" in Daniel 7 a reference to Jesus, and the synagogue saw in this same figure a reference to the covenant community of Israel.

Amy-Jill Levine

1 In the third year of the reign of King Jehoiakim of Judah, King Nebuchadnezzar of Babylon came to Jerusalem and besieged it. ² The Lord let King Jehoiakim of Judah fall into his power, as well as some of the vessels of the house of God. These he brought to the land of Shinar,ᵃ and placed the vessels in the treasury of his gods.

³ Then the king commanded his palace master Ashpenaz to bring some of the Israelites of the royal family and of the nobility, ⁴ young men without physical defect and handsome, versed in every branch of wisdom, endowed

ᵃ Gk Theodotion: Heb adds *to the house of his own gods*

1.1–21: The Babylonian exile. This first chapter introduces the young courtier Daniel, his companions in exile, and the difficulties they will face as Jews in the foreign court. **1:** *The third year of the reign of King Jehoiakim* is 606 BCE (see 2 Chr 36.5–7). *Nebuchadnezzar* reigned 605–562 BCE (see 2 Kings 24–25; 1 Chr 6; 2 Chr 36; Jer 27–29), and invaded Israel in 604, but did not attack Jerusalem until 597, when Jehoiakim's son Jehoiachin was king. The difficulties of the dating cannot be resolved; such chronological inaccuracy is typical of folktales (cf. Jdt 1.1). **2:** *Lord*, Israel's God, not the gods of Babylon, reigns over history. *Shinar*, an ancient term for Babylon (Gen 10.10; 14.1,9; Josh 7.21; Isa 11.11; Zech 5.11), is the site of the tower of Babel (Gen 11.2); both tower and Babylon fall through the sin of pride. *His gods*, Marduk, Babylon's national god, and Nabu, the king's personal deity; see Isa 46.1n. *Vessels*, noted in 2 Kings 24.13; 25.13–15; 2 Chr 36.7,10, foreshadow Belshazzar's feast (ch 5).

1.3–7: Courtiers in exile. 3: *Palace master* (lit. "chief of his eunuchs," although the term may have lost the literal meaning). Nobility from conquered kingdoms were typically brought into exile (see 2 Kings 24.14–16); educating their youth was thought to increase acceptance of foreign rule and minimize the likelihood of revolt. *Israelites*: lit. "children/sons of Israel." **4:** *Without physical defect* may suggest priests (Lev 21.17–23) as well as sacrificial animals (Lev 22.19–22), or may simply indicate attractive individuals (Absalom in 2 Sam 14.25; Song 4.7). *Versed in every branch of wisdom* also describes the heroes of the author's generation (11.33,35; 12.3). *Chaldeans* can refer either to the Babylonians in general (5.30; 9.1), or more specifically to magicians and astrologers (2.2–5,10; 4.7; 5.7,11). **5:** *Three years* are cited by Persian texts as the time required for gaining knowledge of reli-

with knowledge and insight, and competent to serve in the king's palace; they were to be taught the literature and language of the Chaldeans. [5] The king assigned them a daily portion of the royal rations of food and wine. They were to be educated for three years, so that at the end of that time they could be stationed in the king's court. [6] Among them were Daniel, Hananiah, Mishael, and Azariah, from the tribe of Judah. [7] The palace master gave them other names: Daniel he called Belteshazzar, Hananiah he called Shadrach, Mishael he called Meshach, and Azariah he called Abednego.

[8] But Daniel resolved that he would not defile himself with the royal rations of food and wine; so he asked the palace master to allow him not to defile himself. [9] Now God allowed Daniel to receive favor and compassion from the palace master. [10] The palace master said to Daniel, "I am afraid of my lord the king; he has appointed your food and your drink. If he should see you in poorer condition than the other young men of your own age, you would endanger my head with the king." [11] Then Daniel asked the guard whom the palace master had appointed over Daniel, Hananiah, Mishael, and Azariah: [12] "Please test your servants for ten days. Let us be given vegetables to eat and water to drink. [13] You can then compare our appearance with

the appearance of the young men who eat the royal rations, and deal with your servants according to what you observe." [14] So he agreed to this proposal and tested them for ten days. [15] At the end of ten days it was observed that they appeared better and fatter than all the young men who had been eating the royal rations. [16] So the guard continued to withdraw their royal rations and the wine they were to drink, and gave them vegetables. [17] To these four young men God gave knowledge and skill in every aspect of literature and wisdom; Daniel also had insight into all visions and dreams.

[18] At the end of the time that the king had set for them to be brought in, the palace master brought them into the presence of Nebuchadnezzar, [19] and the king spoke with them. And among them all, no one was found to compare with Daniel, Hananiah, Mishael, and Azariah; therefore they were stationed in the king's court. [20] In every matter of wisdom and understanding concerning which the king inquired of them, he found them ten times better than all the magicians and enchanters in his whole kingdom. [21] And Daniel continued there until the first year of King Cyrus.

2 In the second year of Nebuchadnezzar's reign, Nebuchadnezzar dreamed such dreams that his spirit was troubled and his

gious concerns. **6–7:** The original names are Jewish names, with "el" and "[y]ah" suffixes relating to Israel's God; all four occur in the book of Nehemiah (8.4; 10.2,6,23), although referring to different individuals. *Judah* is the tribe of Israel's monarchy. The new names refer to the Babylonian gods Bel (Marduk; see 1.2n; 2.26n.) and Nabu ("nego"). The meaning of the names Shadrach and Meshach is uncertain. Changing names was a well-known practice of kings (Gen 41.45; 2 Kings 24.17). Fidelity is marked when those whose names are changed preserve their ethnic and religious identity, such as Joseph and Daniel.

1.8–21: The first resistance. 8: *Defile himself* by eating the royal rations, which likely contained meat that had been sacrificed and wine that had been poured out as a libation to Babylon's gods. In the postexilic period, diet was a major indication of Jewish identity (Tob 1.10–11; 1 Macc 1.62–63; Jdt 12.1–4; 2 Macc 6–7; Esth 14.17); early followers of Jesus addressed the question of eating food offered to idols (Acts 15.29; 21.25; 1 Cor 8; Rev 2.14,20). **10:** *The palace master*, Ashpenaz (v. 3), is one of several sympathetic court functionaries in these tales (Gen 41.9–13; Esth 2.15; Achior of the book of Judith). **12:** *Test your servants* suggests trial by ordeal, a stock folktale motif. *Ten days*, see Rev 2.10. *Vegetables . . . and water*, not typically offered in sacrifice or libation, are in contrast to meat and wine. **17:** God grants the youths what Nebuchadnezzar had sought to teach them (v. 4). *Visions and dreams* associates Daniel with Joseph, another handsome youth carried into a foreign land (Gen 39–50), as well as with Mordecai in the Gk Additions to Esther. **20:** *Magicians* appear in the sagas of Joseph (Gen 41.8,24) and Moses and Aaron (Ex 7.11,22; 8.7,18–19; 9.11). *Enchanters* are priests who make incantations (2.2,10,27; 4.4; 5.7,11,15). **21:** *First year of King Cyrus,* 539 BCE (see 6.28, 10.1; 2 Chr 36.22–23; Ezra 1.1–2; 6.3; Isa 45; 1 Esdr 2.1–3).

2.1–13: Nebuchadnezzar's test. 1: *Second year* is 604 BCE. *Dreams* are a major motif in the book of Daniel; dreams, especially those of kings, were regarded as portents (Gen 15.12; 20.3; 28.11–15; 31.10–11,24; 37.5–10; 40.5; 41.1–32; Jdg 7.13–15; 1 Kings 3.5–15; Mt 1.20; 2.12,13,19,22; 27.19; Artemidorus's *Onirocritica*). *His spirit was troubled* also describes Pharaoh in Gen 41.8; Daniel in turn resembles Joseph in the foreign court. In Genesis 41

sleep left him. [2] So the king commanded that the magicians, the enchanters, the sorcerers, and the Chaldeans be summoned to tell the king his dreams. When they came in and stood before the king, [3] he said to them, "I have had such a dream that my spirit is troubled by the desire to understand it." [4] The Chaldeans said to the king (in Aramaic),[a] "O king, live forever! Tell your servants the dream, and we will reveal the interpretation." [5] The king answered the Chaldeans, "This is a public decree: if you do not tell me both the dream and its interpretation, you shall be torn limb from limb, and your houses shall be laid in ruins. [6] But if you do tell me the dream and its interpretation, you shall receive from me gifts and rewards and great honor. Therefore tell me the dream and its interpretation." [7] They answered a second time, "Let the king first tell his servants the dream, then we can give its interpretation." [8] The king answered, "I know with certainty that you are trying to gain time, because you see I have firmly decreed: [9] if you do not tell me the dream, there is but one verdict for you. You have agreed to speak lying and misleading words to me until things take a turn. Therefore, tell me the dream, and I shall know that you can give me its interpretation." [10] The Chaldeans answered the king, "There is no one on earth who can reveal what the king demands! In fact no king, however great and powerful, has ever asked such a thing of any magician or enchanter or Chaldean. [11] The thing that the king is asking is too difficult, and no one can reveal it to the king except the gods, whose dwelling is not with mortals."

[12] Because of this the king flew into a violent rage and commanded that all the wise men of Babylon be destroyed. [13] The decree was issued, and the wise men were about to be executed; and they looked for Daniel and his companions, to execute them. [14] Then Daniel responded with prudence and discretion to Arioch, the king's chief executioner, who had gone out to execute the wise men of Babylon; [15] he asked Arioch, the royal official, "Why is the decree of the king so urgent?" Arioch then explained the matter to Daniel. [16] So Daniel went in and requested that the king give him time and he would tell the king the interpretation.

[17] Then Daniel went to his home and informed his companions, Hananiah, Mishael, and Azariah, [18] and told them to seek mercy from the God of heaven concerning this mystery, so that Daniel and his companions with the rest of the wise men of Babylon might not perish. [19] Then the mystery was revealed

[a] The text from this point to the end of chapter 7 is in Aramaic

the reader is immediately told the content of the dream. Here, the content of the dream is withheld until Daniel's interpretation in vv. 31–45. **2:** *Magicians* and *Chaldeans*, see 1.4n.,20n.; they are not depicted favorably in biblical accounts. **4:** The greeting begins the Aramaic section; the book shifts back to Hebrew at 8.1. *Live forever*, a standard greeting to a ruler (3.9; 5.10; 6.6,21; 1 Kings 1.31; Neh 2.3). **5:** Nebuchadnezzar's insistence that the magicians *tell . . . the dream* as well as its interpretation tests their abilities; this hint of distrust anticipates his later celebration of Daniel's God. *Torn limb from limb* suggests the king's volatility (see also 3.29; 2 Macc 1.16). *Houses . . . laid in ruins*, cf. Ezra 6.11; Sir 21.18. **6:** *Gifts and rewards*, contrast Daniel's lack of interest in 5.17. **10–11:** The Chaldeans' admission, coupled with lack of prayer to their own gods, contrasts with Daniel's abilities and faith. **12–13:** Neither the magicians nor the executioners distinguish Daniel from the other *wise men*.

2.14–19: Daniel seeks divine aid. This section suggests that Daniel and his colleagues were not present at the earlier meeting with the king. **14:** Daniel's question indicates that at this point, he knows less than the magicians do. The name *Arioch* appears in Gen 14.1 and Jdt 1.6 to refer to a king from the distant east. Here, like Ashpenaz (1.10), he is a royal servant who willingly helps Daniel. **16:** Daniel's access to Nebuchadnezzar contrasts with v. 24, where he requires Arioch's intervention. This discrepancy, coupled with the reintroduction of Daniel's companions in v. 17, suggests that vv. 13–23 are an addition to the story. **17:** The companions were introduced in 1.6–7. **18:** *God of heaven* is a common phrase from the Persian and Hellenistic periods (vv. 19,37,44; 2 Chr 36.23; Ezra 1.2; 5.11–12; 6.9–10; 7.12,21,23; Neh 1.4–5; 2.4,20; Ps 136.26; Jon 1.9; Tob 7.12; 8.15; Jdt 5.8; 6.19; 11.17); its universalistic implications befit accounts set in exile. *Mystery* (2.19,27–30,47; 4.9; see also Rom 11.25; 16.25; 1 Cor 2.1; 15.51; Eph 1.9; 3.3–5,9; 5.32; 6.19), a term found frequently in the Dead Sea Scrolls, indicates a secret that can be learned through divine wisdom. *Rest of the wise men*, Daniel's intervention also saves the king's magicians; after Daniel's promotion (v. 48) they will turn on his colleagues (ch 3). **19:** Appropriately, Daniel

to Daniel in a vision of the night, and Daniel blessed the God of heaven. [20] Daniel said:

"Blessed be the name of God from age to age,
    for wisdom and power are his.
[21] He changes times and seasons,
    deposes kings and sets up kings;
he gives wisdom to the wise
    and knowledge to those who have understanding.
[22] He reveals deep and hidden things;
    he knows what is in the darkness,
    and light dwells with him.
[23] To you, O God of my ancestors,
    I give thanks and praise,
for you have given me wisdom and power,
    and have now revealed to me what we asked of you,
    for you have revealed to us what the king ordered."

[24] Therefore Daniel went to Arioch, whom the king had appointed to destroy the wise men of Babylon, and said to him, "Do not destroy the wise men of Babylon; bring me in before the king, and I will give the king the interpretation." [25] Then Arioch quickly brought Daniel before the king and said to him: "I have found among the exiles from Judah a man who can tell the king the interpretation." [26] The king said to Daniel, whose name was Belteshazzar, "Are you able to tell me the dream that I have seen and its interpretation?" [27] Daniel answered the king, "No wise men, enchanters, magicians, or diviners can show to the king the mystery that the king is asking, [28] but there is a God in heaven who reveals mysteries, and he has disclosed to King Nebuchadnezzar what will happen at the end of days. Your dream and the visions of your head as you lay in bed were these: [29] To you, O king, as you lay in bed, came thoughts of what would be hereafter, and the revealer of mysteries disclosed to you what is to be. [30] But as for me, this mystery has not been revealed to me because of any wisdom that I have more than any other living being, but in order that the interpretation may be known to the king and that you may understand the thoughts of your mind.

[31] "You were looking, O king, and lo! there was a great statue. This statue was huge, its brilliance extraordinary; it was standing before you, and its appearance was frightening. [32] The head of that statue was of fine gold, its chest and arms of silver, its middle and thighs of bronze, [33] its legs of iron, its feet partly of iron and partly of clay. [34] As you looked on, a

receives a *vision of the night*, i.e., a dream (1.17n; 2.1n; 7.2; Gen 46.2; Zech 1.8; see also Job 20.8; 33.15; Isa 29.7), that discloses the meaning of Nebuchadnezzar's dream. The author defers relating the content of the dream and so heightens suspense. Daniel's words of praise to God in the following verses hint at the content.

2.20–23: Daniel's doxology. This short psalm (see e.g., Pss 41.13; 106.48; 139.11–12) emphasizes the divine as the repository of wisdom (see also Prov 2.6; Isa 60.19–20; Hab 3.4; Job 12.13) and as one who controls the reigns of kings. Hymns and prayers are frequently inserted into postexilic narratives (Add Est, Jdt, Tob). **20:** *Blessed be the name of God* is a major theme in Jewish prayers (Job 1.21; Ps 113.2; Mt 6.9; the Kaddish). *Wisdom and power*, divine attributes that will be bestowed upon Daniel (v. 23). **21:** *Deposes kings*, Job 12.18–21; Lk 1.52. Here, ironically, Nebuchadnezzar is not deposed, although Belshazzar will be (ch.5). **22:** See Job 12.22–23. **23:** *God of . . . ancestors*, a traditional epithet (Ex 3.13,15–16; Deut 1.11,21; 4.1; 6.3; 12.1; 27.3; Josh 18.3; 2 Chr 13.12; 28.9; 29.5; Ezra 8.28; 10.11; Wis 9.1; Acts 7.32) here emphasizes Daniel's continuity with his community in exile. *Thanks and praise*, 2 Chr 31.2. *Revealed to us*: Daniel includes his colleagues in the revelation.

2.24–30: Daniel approaches the king. 24–25: See vv. 14–16. Arioch trusts Daniel's powers. **25:** Arioch locates Daniel not among the Babylonian magicians but among the Judean exiles (see 13n). **26:** *Belteshazzar*, see 1.7. The name in Babylonian would be *Balat-su-utsur*, "Protect his life" or *Balat-shar-utsur*, "Protect the life of the prince." **27:** Daniel agrees with the magicians (see 10–11), then distinguishes his power from human wisdom. **28:** *End of days* here means the distant future (10.14; see also Isa 2.2; Jer 23.20; 30.24; Ezek 38.16; Hos 3.5). **29–30:** The true *revealer of mysteries* is God (cf. Gen 41.16). Daniel gives God full glory, but the effect of the revelation is nonetheless that Daniel will be promoted.

2.31–35: Nebuchadnezzar's dream. 31: Giant figures are frequent in ancient Near Eastern dream records; there were also several famous giant statues. **32–33:** The metals are of decreasing worth; the descent from the golden age through silver, bronze, and iron periods appears in Greek (Hesiod, *Works and Days*), Roman (Ovid,

stone was cut out, not by human hands, and it struck the statue on its feet of iron and clay and broke them in pieces. [35] Then the iron, the clay, the bronze, the silver, and the gold, were all broken in pieces and became like the chaff of the summer threshing floors; and the wind carried them away, so that not a trace of them could be found. But the stone that struck the statue became a great mountain and filled the whole earth.

[36] "This was the dream; now we will tell the king its interpretation. [37] You, O king, the king of kings—to whom the God of heaven has given the kingdom, the power, the might, and the glory, [38] into whose hand he has given human beings, wherever they live, the wild animals of the field, and the birds of the air, and whom he has established as ruler over them all—you are the head of gold. [39] After you shall arise another kingdom inferior to yours, and yet a third kingdom of bronze, which shall rule over the whole earth. [40] And there shall be a fourth kingdom, strong as iron; just as iron crushes and smashes everything,[a] it shall crush and shatter all these. [41] As you saw the feet and toes partly of potter's clay and partly of iron, it shall be a divided kingdom; but some of the strength of iron shall be in it, as you saw the iron mixed with the clay. [42] As the toes of the feet were part iron and part clay, so the kingdom shall be partly strong and partly brittle. [43] As you saw the iron mixed with clay, so will they mix with one another in marriage,[b] but they will not hold together, just as iron does not mix with clay. [44] And in the days of those kings the God of heaven will set up a kingdom that shall never be destroyed, nor shall this kingdom be left to another people. It shall crush all these kingdoms and bring them to an end, and it shall stand forever; [45] just as you saw that a stone was cut from the mountain not by hands, and that it crushed the iron, the bronze, the clay, the silver, and the gold. The great God has informed the king what shall be hereafter. The dream is certain, and its interpretation trustworthy."

[46] Then King Nebuchadnezzar fell on his face, worshiped Daniel, and commanded that a grain offering and incense be offered to

---

a Gk Theodotion Syr Vg: Aram adds *and like iron that crushes*
b Aram *by human seed*

Metamorphoses) and Persian (*Bahman Yasht*) texts; see also 2 Esd 7.55–56. **33:** *Clay*, this substance cannot support the weightier metals. **34:** *A stone was cut out, not by human hands* indicates divine control of history. Idols are made with *human hands* (e.g., Deut 4.28; 2 Kings 19.18; 2 Chr 32.19; Pss 115.4; 135.15; Isa 17.19; Wis 13.10). **35:** *A great mountain* may suggest the permanence of the divine dwelling, Sinai, Zion, or the covenant community; see also v. 45.

2.36–45: **Daniel's first interpretation. 37–38:** Elaborating Nebuchadnezzar's powers, Daniel actually celebrates the rule of his God. For Nebuchadnezzar as a ruler designated by God, see Jer 25.9; 27.5–7. **37:** *King of kings* is used for Nebuchadnezzar in Ezek 26.7. For other references, see Ezra 7.12; 2 Mac 13.4; and the Christ, 1 Tim 6.15; Rev 17.14; 19.16. **38:** Interpreting the dream allegorically, Daniel equates Nebuchadnezzar, and by extension the neo-Babylonian empire with gold. **39–44:** The other kingdoms, although not named, are probably Media (silver), Persia (bronze), and Greece (iron and clay; the two elements probably represent the division of Alexander the Great's eastern empire into Ptolemaic and Seleucid kingdoms). This four-fold pattern of kingdoms appears also in *Sibylline Oracles* 4, Babylonian and Greek writings, and the Dead Sea Scrolls (4QPseudoDan). **41–42:** *A divided kingdom* is the division of Alexander the Great's empire: originally partitioned among four generals, for our author's history, the important part was the East: Judea was under (strong) Ptolemaic (Egyptian) control during 323–198 BCE, and then, until Maccabean rule in 163 BCE, under (brittle) Seleucid (Syrian–Greek) control. **43:** *In marriage* (lit. "by human seed"), intermarriage between Ptolemaic and Seleucid dynasties in 252 and again in 194/93 BCE (see also 11.6n.,17) did not prevent conflict. **44:** *A kingdom that shall never be destroyed* could refer to God's direct rule or to Israel. Cf. 7.27, where it is the people Israel ("the Holy Ones") who will possess the kingdom. **45:** *Cut from the mountain*, compare 2.35, where the stone became a mountain. The image of Israel as a *stone* occurs in Isa 51.1 (cf. 28.16); Ps 118.22 (cited in reference to Jesus in Mt 21.42; Mk 12.10; Lk 20.17; 1 Pet 2.7). See also Zech 12.13.

2.46–49: **Nebuchadnezzar's affirmation of Daniel's God, and Daniel's promotion. 46:** *Worshiped*, along with offerings of grain and incense, suggests that Nebuchadnezzar viewed Daniel as divine (see 3.5–7,10–12,14–

him. [47] The king said to Daniel, "Truly, your God is God of gods and Lord of kings and a revealer of mysteries, for you have been able to reveal this mystery!" [48] Then the king promoted Daniel, gave him many great gifts, and made him ruler over the whole province of Babylon and chief prefect over all the wise men of Babylon. [49] Daniel made a request of the king, and he appointed Shadrach, Meshach, and Abednego over the affairs of the province of Babylon. But Daniel remained at the king's court.

3 King Nebuchadnezzar made a golden statue whose height was sixty cubits and whose width was six cubits; he set it up on the plain of Dura in the province of Babylon. [2] Then King Nebuchadnezzar sent for the satraps, the prefects, and the governors, the counselors, the treasurers, the justices, the magistrates, and all the officials of the provinces, to assemble and come to the dedication of the statue that King Nebuchadnezzar had set up. [3] So the satraps, the prefects, and the governors, the counselors, the treasurers, the justices, the magistrates, and all the officials of the provinces, assembled for the dedication of the statue that King Nebuchadnezzar had set up. When they were standing before the statue that Nebuchadnezzar had set up, [4] the herald proclaimed aloud, "You are commanded, O peoples, nations, and languages, [5] that when you hear the sound of the horn, pipe, lyre, trigon, harp, drum, and entire musical ensemble, you are to fall down and worship the golden statue that King Nebuchadnezzar has set up. [6] Whoever does not fall down and worship shall immediately be thrown into a furnace of blazing fire." [7] Therefore, as soon as all the peoples heard the sound of the horn, pipe, lyre, trigon, harp, drum, and entire musical ensemble, all the peoples, nations, and languages fell down and worshiped the golden statue that King Nebuchadnezzar had set up.

[8] Accordingly, at this time certain Chaldeans came forward and denounced the Jews. [9] They said to King Nebuchadnezzar, "O king, live forever! [10] You, O king, have made a decree, that everyone who hears the sound of the horn, pipe, lyre, trigon, harp, drum, and entire musical ensemble, shall fall down and worship the golden statue, [11] and whoever does not fall down and worship shall be thrown into a furnace of blazing fire. [12] There are certain Jews whom you have appointed over the affairs of the province of Babylon: Shadrach, Meshach, and Abednego. These pay no heed to you, O king. They do not serve your gods and they do not worship the golden statue that you have set up." [13] Then Nebuchadnezzar in furious rage commanded that Shadrach, Meshach, and

15,18,28; Isa 44.15–19; 46.6; the term is typically used in reference to the worship of idols). **47:** *Your God*, Nebuchadnezzar respects Daniel's God, but he is not a convert. **48:** *Made him ruler* is reminiscent of Joseph (Gen 41.37–45; see also Esth 8.1–2). **49:** Daniel's concern for his colleagues anticipates 3.12.

3.1–7: The golden statue. 1: Even though ch 3 may originally have been an independent story (note Daniel's absence), Nebuchadnezzar's golden statue echoes the interpretation of the statue in the vision (2.38) that his kingship is the "head of gold." Ironically, first the king worships Daniel and praises Daniel's God (2.46); now he commands worship of an idol. The Greek historian Herodotus (fifth century BCE) mentions a golden statue of Zeus (Bel) in Babylon. Sixty cubits by 6 cubits (the Babylonians used a sexagesimal numerical system) is approximately 90 x 9 ft (30 x 3 m); ten times as high as wide, the statue was likely an obelisk or stele (if it could stand at all). The exaggerated dimensions suggest folktale style. *Dura* means "plain" or "fortress" and need not suggest a specific place. **2–3:** Repetition of officers, a folkloric motif, indicates the (almost) universal acceptance of Nebuchadnezzar's order. **5:** The list of instruments, reprised in vv. 7,10,15, echoes the hyperbole. Several of the terms are Greek loanwords. Jews faithful to their Torah could not obey the command. **6:** The *furnace* also functions as a symbol of testing and purifying (Ps 12.6; Prov 17.3; 27.21; Isa 48.10; Wis 3.6). The scenario anticipates the policies of Antiochus IV Epiphanes, one of the earliest instances of governmental persecution for refusing to worship the state's god.

3.8–15: The youths accused. 8: *Chaldeans*, see 1.4n.,2on. *Denounced* (lit., "ate the pieces of") indicates maliciousness and professional jealousy. In ch. 2, Daniel had saved their lives. **9:** *Live forever*: see 2.4n. **10:** The bynow humorous repetition decreases the threat of the story. **12:** *Appointed*, see 2.49. Ethnic prejudice surfaces again in Esth 3.8. *Shadrach, Meshach, and Abednego*, see 1.6–7n. **13–15:** Nebuchadnezzar's questioning repeats

Abednego be brought in; so they brought those men before the king. [14] Nebuchadnezzar said to them, "Is it true, O Shadrach, Meshach, and Abednego, that you do not serve my gods and you do not worship the golden statue that I have set up? [15] Now if you are ready when you hear the sound of the horn, pipe, lyre, trigon, harp, drum, and entire musical ensemble to fall down and worship the statue that I have made, well and good.[a] But if you do not worship, you shall immediately be thrown into a furnace of blazing fire, and who is the god that will deliver you out of my hands?"

[16] Shadrach, Meshach, and Abednego answered the king, "O Nebuchadnezzar, we have no need to present a defense to you in this matter. [17] If our God whom we serve is able to deliver us from the furnace of blazing fire and out of your hand, O king, let him deliver us.[b] [18] But if not, be it known to you, O king, that we will not serve your gods and we will not worship the golden statue that you have set up."

[19] Then Nebuchadnezzar was so filled with rage against Shadrach, Meshach, and Abednego that his face was distorted. He ordered the furnace heated up seven times more than was customary, [20] and ordered some of the strongest guards in his army to bind Shadrach, Meshach, and Abednego and to throw them into the furnace of blazing fire. [21] So the men were bound, still wearing their tunics,[c] their trousers,[c] their hats, and their other garments, and they were thrown into the furnace of blazing fire. [22] Because the king's command was urgent and the furnace was so overheated, the raging flames killed the men who lifted Shadrach, Meshach, and Abednego. [23] But the three men, Shadrach, Meshach, and Abednego, fell down, bound, into the furnace of blazing fire.

[24] Then King Nebuchadnezzar was astonished and rose up quickly. He said to his counselors, "Was it not three men that we threw bound into the fire?" They answered the king, "True, O king." [25] He replied, "But I see four men unbound, walking in the middle of the fire, and they are not hurt; and the fourth has the appearance of a god."[d] [26] Nebuchadnezzar then approached the door of the furnace of blazing fire and said, "Shadrach, Meshach, and Abednego, servants of the Most High God, come out! Come here!" So Shadrach, Meshach, and Abednego came out from the fire. [27] And the satraps, the prefects, the governors, and the king's counselors gathered together and saw that the fire had not had any power over the bodies of those men; the hair of their heads was not singed, their tunics[c] were not harmed, and not even the smell of fire came from them. [28] Nebuchadnezzar said, "Blessed be the God

---

a   Aram lacks *well and good*

b   Or *If our God whom we serve is able to deliver us, he will deliver us from the furnace of blazing fire and out of your hand, O king.*

c   Meaning of Aram word uncertain

d   Aram *a son of the gods*

---

the law, again. **15:** *Who is the god* may indicate that this story did not originally follow ch 2, where the king acknowledges the power of Daniel's God; given ch. 2, it shows that Nebuchadnezzar is at best capricious.

3.16–18: Resistance. 16: *Defense* (lit. "to answer, reply."). The refusal to respond continues the themes of Jewish resistance and divine power. **17–18:** Anticipating later martyrs, the youths assert their fidelity regardless of their fate.

3.19–27: The furnace. 19: Nebuchadnezzar's response continues to indicate volatility. **21:** Mention of clothing (the Aramaic has a rhythmic quality appropriate to folktales) foreshadows v. 27. **22:** The king's anger leads to his own soldiers' deaths. **23:** The Septuagint (LXX), Eastern Orthodox, and Roman Catholic Bibles insert here the Prayer of Azariah and the Song of the Three Jews; Protestant tradition places these texts in the Old Testament Apocrypha. **25:** The king is first to see the mysterious fourth figure. *Walking in the middle of the fire* without burning evokes the image of the burning bush (Ex 3.2). *Has the appearance of a god* (lit. "son of God") implies an angel or watcher (Gen 6.2,4; Job 1.6; 38.7; see also the "men" who aided Judas Maccabeus in 2 Macc 10.29–30, and Nebuchadnezzar's comment in 28). **26:** *Most High God*, Nebuchadnezzar answers the question he posed in v. 15. For this title, see also 4.2; 5.18,21; Ps 78.35,36; Jdt 13.18; Sir 7.9; 24.23; 41.8; Mk 5.7; Lk 8.28; Acts 16.17; Heb 7.1. **27:** The details enhance the miracle and evoke Isa 43.2.

3.28–30: Nebuchadnezzar's acknowledgment. 28: Ironically, Nebuchadnezzar celebrates that the youths

of Shadrach, Meshach, and Abednego, who has sent his angel and delivered his servants who trusted in him. They disobeyed the king's command and yielded up their bodies rather than serve and worship any god except their own God. ²⁹ Therefore I make a decree: Any people, nation, or language that utters blasphemy against the God of Shadrach, Meshach, and Abednego shall be torn limb from limb, and their houses laid in ruins; for there is no other god who is able to deliver in this way." ³⁰ Then the king promoted Shadrach, Meshach, and Abednego in the province of Babylon.

4 ᵃ King Nebuchadnezzar to all peoples, nations, and languages that live throughout the earth: May you have abundant prosperity! ² The signs and wonders that the Most High God has worked for me I am pleased to recount.

³ How great are his signs,
how mighty his wonders!
His kingdom is an everlasting kingdom,
and his sovereignty is from generation
to generation.

⁴ ᵇI, Nebuchadnezzar, was living at ease in my home and prospering in my palace. ⁵ I saw a dream that frightened me; my fantasies in bed and the visions of my head terrified me. ⁶ So I made a decree that all the wise men of Babylon should be brought before me, in order that they might tell me the interpretation of the dream. ⁷ Then the magicians, the enchanters,

the Chaldeans, and the diviners came in, and I told them the dream, but they could not tell me its interpretation. ⁸ At last Daniel came in before me—he who was named Belteshazzar after the name of my god, and who is endowed with a spirit of the holy godsᶜ—and I told him the dream: ⁹ "O Belteshazzar, chief of the magicians, I know that you are endowed with a spirit of the holy godsᶜ and that no mystery is too difficult for you. Hearᵈ the dream that I saw; tell me its interpretation.

¹⁰ ᵉUpon my bed this is what I saw;
there was a tree at the center of the
earth,
and its height was great.
¹¹ The tree grew great and strong,
its top reached to heaven,
and it was visible to the ends of the
whole earth.
¹² Its foliage was beautiful,
its fruit abundant,
and it provided food for all.
The animals of the field found shade
under it,
the birds of the air nested in its
branches,

a Ch 3.31 in Aram
b Ch 4.1 in Aram
c Or *a holy, divine spirit*
d Theodotion: Aram *The visions of*
e Theodotion Syr Compare Gk: Aram adds *The visions of my head*

disobeyed the king's command. His reaction, similar to those of 2.47; 4.37; and 6.26–27, is, in the context of the book, only temporarily good news. **29:** The historically improbable decree follows official form (see Ezra 6.6–12). **30:** The three, fidelity rewarded (or perhaps restored to their earlier status, see 2.49), now disappear from the story.

4.1–37: Nebuchadnezzar's praise of God, composed as a letter to the Babylonian empire. **1:** *Throughout the earth,* Nebuchadnezzar claims universal rule. **2:** *Most High God,* see 3.26n. **2–3:** *Signs and wonders,* popular description of God, e.g., 6.27; Ex 7.3; Deut 4.34; 6.22; 7.19; Neh 9.10; Ps 135.9; Jer 32.20–21; Heb 2.4. **3:** The traditional doxology recalls the king's earlier confession (2.47; 3.28–29). *Everlasting kingdom* (see 7.27; Ps 145.13) contrasts Nebuchadnezzar's Babylon; *his sovereignty,* a frequent term in chs 1–7, contrasts with Nebuchadnezzar's removal from this throne (see 4.33).

4.4–18: The king's vision. Much of this chapter is written as if Nebuchadnezzar is telling the story, although in vv. 19–33 it switches from first-person to third-person narration. **5–6:** The *dream* and the demand for *interpretation* recall ch 2. **7:** As in ch 2, the non-Jewish courtiers cannot solve mysteries. **7:** *Chaldeans,* see 1.4n., 20n. **8:** *Belteshazzar,* see 2.26n. Here Nebuchadnezzar interprets the name as containing the name of the god Bel (i.e., Marduk). This and the reference to the *holy gods* contrast with the letter's praise of the "Most High God" (v. 2). *Spirit of the holy gods,* see also vv. 9,18; 5:11,14,20. **9:** See 1.20; 2.4. *Mystery,* 1.18n. **10:** *A tree at the center of the earth* evokes cross-cultural myths of the center of the world and also symbolizes the king's self-image as the one who provides food and shelter (4.22; see also Ezek 17; 31; Mt 13.32; Mk 4.32; Lk 13.19). **11:** *Reached to*

and from it all living beings
were fed.

[13] "I continued looking, in the visions of my head as I lay in bed, and there was a holy watcher, coming down from heaven. [14] He cried aloud and said:
'Cut down the tree and chop off its branches,
strip off its foliage and scatter its fruit.
Let the animals flee from beneath it
and the birds from its branches.
[15] But leave its stump and roots in the ground,
with a band of iron and bronze,
in the tender grass of the field.
Let him be bathed with the dew of heaven,
and let his lot be with the animals of the field
in the grass of the earth.
[16] Let his mind be changed from that of a human,
and let the mind of an animal be given to him.
And let seven times pass over him.
[17] The sentence is rendered by decree of the watchers,
the decision is given by order of the holy ones,
in order that all who live may know
that the Most High is sovereign over the kingdom of mortals;
he gives it to whom he will
and sets over it the lowliest of human beings.'

[18] "This is the dream that I, King Nebuchadnezzar, saw. Now you, Belteshazzar, declare the interpretation, since all the wise men of my kingdom are unable to tell me the interpretation. You are able, however, for you are endowed with a spirit of the holy gods."[a]

[19] Then Daniel, who was called Belteshazzar, was severely distressed for a while. His thoughts terrified him. The king said, "Belteshazzar, do not let the dream or the interpretation terrify you." Belteshazzar answered, "My lord, may the dream be for those who hate you, and its interpretation for your enemies! [20] The tree that you saw, which grew great and strong, so that its top reached to heaven and was visible to the end of the whole earth, [21] whose foliage was beautiful and its fruit abundant, and which provided food for all, under which animals of the field lived, and in whose branches the birds of the air had nests— [22] it is you, O king! You have grown great and strong. Your greatness has increased and reaches to heaven, and your sovereignty to the ends of the earth. [23] And whereas the king saw a holy watcher coming down from heaven and saying, 'Cut down the tree and destroy it, but leave its stump and roots in the ground, with a band of iron and bronze, in the grass of the field; and let him be bathed with the dew of heaven, and let his lot be with the animals of the field, until seven times pass over him'— [24] this is the interpretation, O king, and it is a decree of the Most High that has come upon my lord the king: [25] You shall be driven away from human society, and your dwelling shall be with the wild animals. You shall be made to eat grass like oxen, you shall be bathed with the dew of heaven, and seven times shall pass over you, until you have learned that the Most High has sovereignty over the kingdom of mortals, and gives it to whom he will. [26] As it was commanded to leave the stump and roots of the tree, your kingdom shall be re-established for you from the time that you

[a] Or *a holy, divine spirit*

---

heaven suggests the tower of Babel (see 1.2n.). **13:** *Holy watcher* (4.17,23; also 3.25n; 8.13, *Jubilees*, and *1 Enoch*) indicates an angel. **14:** *Animals* and *birds* likely represent the peoples of the empire. **15:** With *let him* the symbolism changes from tree to beast (in Hebrew, there is no neuter pronoun). **16:** The king becomes insane. *Seven times* probably means seven years. **17:** *Watchers*, see v. 13n.

4.19–27: Daniel's second interpretation. 19: The story shifts to third-person narration. Whether Daniel is *distressed* because he is unsure of the interpretation, because he fears the king's repercussions upon hearing it, or because he has genuine concern for the king is not immediately clear. **20–22:** The repetition of the tree's greatness may indicate either sympathy or satire. **22:** For people symbolized by trees, see Jdg 9.8–15; Pss 1.3; 37.35; Jer 17.8. **23:** *Watcher*, see v. 13n. **24:** *Most High*, see 3.26n. **25:** *You have learned* contrasts with v. 17, where the watchers state that *all who live* will learn. **26:** *Heaven* as a circumlocution for God is common in the Deutero-

learn that Heaven is sovereign. [27] Therefore, O king, may my counsel be acceptable to you: atone for[a] your sins with righteousness, and your iniquities with mercy to the oppressed, so that your prosperity may be prolonged."

[28] All this came upon King Nebuchadnezzar. [29] At the end of twelve months he was walking on the roof of the royal palace of Babylon, [30] and the king said, "Is this not magnificent Babylon, which I have built as a royal capital by my mighty power and for my glorious majesty?" [31] While the words were still in the king's mouth, a voice came from heaven: "O King Nebuchadnezzar, to you it is declared: The kingdom has departed from you! [32] You shall be driven away from human society, and your dwelling shall be with the animals of the field. You shall be made to eat grass like oxen, and seven times shall pass over you, until you have learned that the Most High has sovereignty over the kingdom of mortals and gives it to whom he will." [33] Immediately the sentence was fulfilled against Nebuchadnezzar. He was driven away from human society, ate grass like oxen, and his body was bathed with the dew of heaven, until his hair grew as long as eagles' feathers and his nails became like birds' claws.

[34] When that period was over, I, Nebuchadnezzar, lifted my eyes to heaven, and my reason returned to me.

I blessed the Most High,
    and praised and honored the one who
        lives forever.

For his sovereignty is an everlasting
        sovereignty,
    and his kingdom endures from
        generation to generation.
[35] All the inhabitants of the earth are
        accounted as nothing,
    and he does what he wills with the host
        of heaven
    and the inhabitants of the earth.
There is no one who can stay his hand
    or say to him, "What are you doing?"
[36] At that time my reason returned to me; and my majesty and splendor were restored to me for the glory of my kingdom. My counselors and my lords sought me out, I was re-established over my kingdom, and still more greatness was added to me. [37] Now I, Nebuchadnezzar, praise and extol and honor the King of heaven,
    for all his works are truth,
        and his ways are justice;
    and he is able to bring low
        those who walk in pride.

5 King Belshazzar made a great festival for a thousand of his lords, and he was drinking wine in the presence of the thousand.

[2] Under the influence of the wine, Belshazzar commanded that they bring in the vessels of gold and silver that his father Nebuchadnezzar had taken out of the temple in Jerusa-

---

a Aram *break off*

canonical writings and the Gospel of Matthew. **27:** Correct behavior, mercy, and charity atone for sins against humanity. Daniel couches the interpretation in terms that allay the harshness of the sentence.

4.28–33: Nebuchadnezzar's punishment. 30: The king's prideful statements serve as catalyst for his fall (see also Ezek 31.10). **31:** The *voice . . . from heaven*, an increasingly common motif in the Second Temple period, can offer either good or distressing news (Mt 3.17; Mk 1.11; Lk 3.22; many instances in rabbinic texts). **32–33:** Although no sources indicate the banishment of Nebuchadnezzar, the later Babylonian king Nabonidus inexplicably left Babylon to spend several years at Tema in north Arabia; his son, Belshazzar (see ch 5) served as regent. The "Prayer of Nabonidus" in the Dead Sea Scrolls records the king's seven years of illness and his cure by a Jewish exorcist. **33:** Nebuchadnezzar's description may anticipate the humanlike beasts of Daniel's apocalyptic visions (chs 7–12).

4.34–37: Restoration. With the completion of the term of punishment and the restoration of the Nebuchadnezzar's sanity, the story resumes his first-person narration. Vv. 34–35 echo and expand upon the opening doxology (v. 3). See also 2.20–21; 6.26–27. This king's affirmation does not influence his "son," Belshazzar (5.2). **37:** *Bring low those who walk in pride* may be ironic, given Nebuchadnezzar's glorying in his restored status.

5.1–9: The handwriting on the wall. 1: *Belshazzar* was the son of Nabonidus, not of Nebuchadnezzar. He served as regent during Nabonidus's absence (see 4.32–33n.). The banquet is a standard motif in Second Temple literature (e.g., Esther). Lacking a statue of Israel's God to symbolize their conquest, the Babylonians took

lem, so that the king and his lords, his wives, and his concubines might drink from them. [3] So they brought in the vessels of gold and silver[a] that had been taken out of the temple, the house of God in Jerusalem, and the king and his lords, his wives, and his concubines drank from them. [4] They drank the wine and praised the gods of gold and silver, bronze, iron, wood, and stone.

[5] Immediately the fingers of a human hand appeared and began writing on the plaster of the wall of the royal palace, next to the lampstand. The king was watching the hand as it wrote. [6] Then the king's face turned pale, and his thoughts terrified him. His limbs gave way, and his knees knocked together. [7] The king cried aloud to bring in the enchanters, the Chaldeans, and the diviners; and the king said to the wise men of Babylon, "Whoever can read this writing and tell me its interpretation shall be clothed in purple, have a chain of gold around his neck, and rank third in the kingdom." [8] Then all the king's wise men came in, but they could not read the writing or tell the king the interpretation. [9] Then King Belshazzar became greatly terrified and his face turned pale, and his lords were perplexed.

[10] The queen, when she heard the discussion of the king and his lords, came into the banqueting hall. The queen said, "O king, live forever! Do not let your thoughts terrify you or your face grow pale. [11] There is a man in your kingdom who is endowed with a spirit of the holy gods.[b] In the days of your father he was found to have enlightenment, understanding, and wisdom like the wisdom of the gods. Your father, King Nebuchadnezzar, made him chief of the magicians, enchanters, Chaldeans, and diviners,[c] [12] because an excellent spirit, knowledge, and understanding to interpret dreams, explain riddles, and solve problems were found in this Daniel, whom the king named Belteshazzar. Now let Daniel be called, and he will give the interpretation."

[13] Then Daniel was brought in before the king. The king said to Daniel, "So you are Daniel, one of the exiles of Judah, whom my father the king brought from Judah? [14] I have heard of you that a spirit of the gods[d] is in you, and that enlightenment, understanding, and excellent wisdom are found in you. [15] Now the wise men, the enchanters, have been brought in before me to read this writing and tell me its interpretation, but they were not able to give the interpretation of the matter. [16] But I have heard that you can give interpretations and solve problems. Now if you are able to read the writing and tell me its interpretation, you shall be clothed in purple, have a chain of gold around your neck, and rank third in the kingdom."

[17] Then Daniel answered in the presence of the king, "Let your gifts be for yourself, or give your rewards to someone else! Nevertheless I will read the writing to the king and let him know the interpretation. [18] O king, the Most High God gave your father Nebuchadnezzar kingship, greatness, glory, and maj-

a   Theodotion Vg: Aram lacks *and silver*
b   Or *a holy, divine spirit*
c   Aram adds *the king your father*
d   Or *a divine spirit*

ritual vessels (1.2; Ezra 5.14; 6.5). **4:** The scene is one of sacrilegious debauchery; the Greek historians Herodotus and Xenophon describe such dissipation at the time of Babylon's fall. **5–6:** Although the writing is visible to all, only Belshazzar is alarmed; cf. 3.25. **7:** Like Nebuchadnezzar, Belshazzar summons Babylon's wise men; those familiar with the previous chapters can anticipate the magicians' failure and Daniel's success. *Rank third*: after the king and crown prince (see 2.48).

5.10–12: The queen's intervention. Like Ashpenaz (1.9) and Arioch (2.25), the queen—the only woman to speak in the book—recognizes Daniel's worth. The account may reflect knowledge of Nebuchadnezzar's wife who, according to Herodotus, had exceptional wisdom and political ability. She, as queen mother, knows of Daniel's abilities and rank, but Belshazzar does not (cf. Ex 1.8); Daniel, as representative of the Jews in exile, continually has to demonstrate the power of his God. **11:** *Holy gods*, the queen does not, however, recognize Daniel's theological claims. *Chaldeans*, see 1.4n., 2on. **12:** *Belteshazzar*, cf. 1.7; see 2.26n.

5.13–31: Deciphering the handwriting. 13: Reference to the *exiles* makes a fitting start to a chapter that concludes with the fall of Babylon (5.30). **14:** *Spirit of the gods* shows Belshazzar's lack of familiarity with Daniel's faith (see v. 11). **17:** Daniel disdains the offer, although later he appears to accept it (5.29). **18–21** recalls 4.30–37.

esty. ¹⁹ And because of the greatness that he gave him, all peoples, nations, and languages trembled and feared before him. He killed those he wanted to kill, kept alive those he wanted to keep alive, honored those he wanted to honor, and degraded those he wanted to degrade. ²⁰ But when his heart was lifted up and his spirit was hardened so that he acted proudly, he was deposed from his kingly throne, and his glory was stripped from him. ²¹ He was driven from human society, and his mind was made like that of an animal. His dwelling was with the wild asses, he was fed grass like oxen, and his body was bathed with the dew of heaven, until he learned that the Most High God has sovereignty over the kingdom of mortals, and sets over it whomever he will. ²² And you, Belshazzar his son, have not humbled your heart, even though you knew all this! ²³ You have exalted yourself against the Lord of heaven! The vessels of his temple have been brought in before you, and you and your lords, your wives and your concubines have been drinking wine from them. You have praised the gods of silver and gold, of bronze, iron, wood, and stone, which do not see or hear or know; but the God in whose power is your very breath, and to whom belong all your ways, you have not honored.

²⁴ "So from his presence the hand was sent and this writing was inscribed. ²⁵ And this is the writing that was inscribed: MENE, MENE, TEKEL, and PARSIN. ²⁶ This is the interpretation of the matter: MENE, God has numbered the days of[a] your kingdom and brought it to an end; ²⁷ TEKEL, you have been weighed on the scales and found wanting; ²⁸ PERES,[b] your

kingdom is divided and given to the Medes and Persians."

²⁹ Then Belshazzar gave the command, and Daniel was clothed in purple, a chain of gold was put around his neck, and a proclamation was made concerning him that he should rank third in the kingdom.

³⁰ That very night Belshazzar, the Chaldean king, was killed. ³¹[c] And Darius the Mede received the kingdom, being about sixty-two years old.

6 It pleased Darius to set over the kingdom one hundred twenty satraps, stationed throughout the whole kingdom, ² and over them three presidents, including Daniel; to these the satraps gave account, so that the king might suffer no loss. ³ Soon Daniel distinguished himself above all the other presidents and satraps because an excellent spirit was in him, and the king planned to appoint him over the whole kingdom. ⁴ So the presidents and the satraps tried to find grounds for complaint against Daniel in connection with the kingdom. But they could find no grounds for complaint or any corruption, because he was faithful, and no negligence or corruption could be found in him. ⁵ The men said, "We shall not find any ground for complaint against this Daniel unless we find it in connection with the law of his God."

⁶ So the presidents and satraps conspired and came to the king and said to him, "O King Darius, live forever! ⁷ All the presidents of

a   Aram lacks *the days of*
b   The singular of *Parsin*
c   Ch 6.1 in Aram

22: Belshazzar's memory is selective, as was Nebuchadnezzar's (ch 3). 25–28: The mysterious words are nouns that refer to various weights. Daniel will interpret them according to the related verbs. MENE (Heb "mina") is a large weight (ca. 20 oz [.5 kg]); the related verb means "to count" or "to number." TEKEL (Heb "shekel") is one-sixtieth of a mene; the related verb means "to weigh." PARSIN is the plural of "peres," which equals a half-shekel; the related verb means "to divide." The interpretation does not explain why the first word (*mene*) is repeated or why the last (*parsin*) is plural. The weights, which match the descending values of the metals in 2.32, symbolize Nebuchadnezzar's successors, from Belshazzar through the Medes and the Persians (see 2.39–44). 29: Belshazzar appears oblivious to the fateful prediction: did he think rewarding Daniel would forestall it? 31: No such person as *Darius the Mede* is known outside this biblical reference; later references in Jewish and Christian sources are dependent on Daniel's account. It was Cyrus the Persian who overthrew the Neo-Babylonian empire in 539 BCE. Darius I, not a Mede but a Persian, ruled 522–486 BCE; he facilitated the rebuilding of Jerusalem (Ezra 6).

6.1–9: **Persian plot against Daniel. 1:** *Darius*, see 5.31n. **2:** Like Joseph and Mordecai, Daniel advances in the foreign court; how Daniel impressed the Persian king is not recorded. **3:** Daniel distinguished himself apparently by political acumen, not supernatural powers. **5:** The first reference to Jewish *law* (Aram. "Dat", not "Torah")

the kingdom, the prefects and the satraps, the counselors and the governors are agreed that the king should establish an ordinance and enforce an interdict, that whoever prays to anyone, divine or human, for thirty days, except to you, O king, shall be thrown into a den of lions. [8] Now, O king, establish the interdict and sign the document, so that it cannot be changed, according to the law of the Medes and the Persians, which cannot be revoked." [9] Therefore King Darius signed the document and interdict.

[10] Although Daniel knew that the document had been signed, he continued to go to his house, which had windows in its upper room open toward Jerusalem, and to get down on his knees three times a day to pray to his God and praise him, just as he had done previously. [11] The conspirators came and found Daniel praying and seeking mercy before his God. [12] Then they approached the king and said concerning the interdict, "O king! Did you not sign an interdict, that anyone who prays to anyone, divine or human, within thirty days except to you, O king, shall be thrown into a den of lions?" The king answered, "The thing stands fast, according to the law of the Medes and Persians, which cannot be revoked." [13] Then they responded to the king, "Daniel, one of the exiles from Judah, pays no attention to you, O king, or to the interdict you have signed, but he is saying his prayers three times a day."

[14] When the king heard the charge, he was very much distressed. He was determined to save Daniel, and until the sun went down he made every effort to rescue him. [15] Then the conspirators came to the king and said to him, "Know, O king, that it is a law of the Medes and Persians that no interdict or ordinance that the king establishes can be changed."

[16] Then the king gave the command, and Daniel was brought and thrown into the den of lions. The king said to Daniel, "May your God, whom you faithfully serve, deliver you!" [17] A stone was brought and laid on the mouth of the den, and the king sealed it with his own signet and with the signet of his lords, so that nothing might be changed concerning Daniel. [18] Then the king went to his palace and spent the night fasting; no food was brought to him, and sleep fled from him.

[19] Then, at break of day, the king got up and hurried to the den of lions. [20] When he came near the den where Daniel was, he cried out anxiously to Daniel, "O Daniel, servant of the living God, has your God whom you faithfully serve been able to deliver you from the lions?" [21] Daniel then said to the king, "O king, live forever! [22] My God sent his angel and shut the lions' mouths so that they would not hurt me, because I was found blameless before him; and also before you, O king, I have done no wrong." [23] Then the king was exceedingly glad and commanded that Daniel be taken up out of the den. So Daniel was

in the book of Daniel. 7: The plot resembles that of ch 3. 8–9: The plot of the book of Esther (1.19; 8.8) also relies on the unalterable law of the Medes and the Persians; it is unlikely, despite occasional ancient testimony, that Median and Persian law functioned in this manner. Like Ahasuerus in Esther, Darius acts, without thinking, on his courtiers' advice. Historically, Persian rulers supported the various religious beliefs and practices of those under imperial rule.

6.10–17: Daniel's defiance. 10: Windows . . . open indicates either happenstance or Daniel's deliberate flouting of the edict (see Tob 2.8). Toward Jerusalem, the direction toward which Jews pray (1 Kings 8.35; 1 Esd 4.58). Three times a day for prayer was Jewish custom by early rabbinic (m. Ber. 4.5) and early Christian (Didache 8) times. 13: Exiles from Judah shows ethnic antagonism: the courtiers remind Darius that Daniel is not "one of them" (see 2.25; 5.13). 14: Sympathy for Darius may be compromised by his willingness to pronounce the edict that condemned Daniel (v. 9). 16: Darius prays for Daniel's safety, but does not himself acknowledge a worship of Daniel's God.

6.18–23: In the lions' den (cf. Bel 31–42). 18–19: Darius appears more agitated than Daniel. 18: Fasting is a cross-cultural practice often accompanying supplicatory prayer and repentance. Ironically, his not eating mirrors what he hopes the lions are doing. 20: The king continues to highlight Daniel's fidelity. 22: Sent his angel recalls the fourth man in the furnace (3.25). I have done no wrong, Daniel subtly faults the king for endangering an innocent person, even as he equates his blamelessness before God with his blamelessness before the king.

taken up out of the den, and no kind of harm was found on him, because he had trusted in his God. [24] The king gave a command, and those who had accused Daniel were brought and thrown into the den of lions—they, their children, and their wives. Before they reached the bottom of the den the lions overpowered them and broke all their bones in pieces.

[25] Then King Darius wrote to all peoples and nations of every language throughout the whole world: "May you have abundant prosperity! [26] I make a decree, that in all my royal dominion people should tremble and fear before the God of Daniel:

For he is the living God,
    enduring forever.
His kingdom shall never be destroyed,
    and his dominion has no end.
[27] He delivers and rescues,
    he works signs and wonders in heaven
        and on earth;
for he has saved Daniel
    from the power of the lions."

[28] So this Daniel prospered during the reign of Darius and the reign of Cyrus the Persian.

7 In the first year of King Belshazzar of Babylon, Daniel had a dream and visions of his head as he lay in bed. Then he wrote down the dream:[a] [2] I,[b] Daniel, saw in my vision by night the four winds of heaven stirring up the great sea, [3] and four great beasts came up out of the sea, different from one another. [4] The first was like a lion and had eagles' wings. Then, as I watched, its wings were plucked off, and it was lifted up from the ground and made to stand on two feet like a human being; and a human mind was given to it. [5] Another beast appeared, a second one, that looked like a bear. It was raised up on one side, had three tusks[c] in its mouth among its teeth and was told, "Arise, devour many bodies!" [6] After this, as I watched, another appeared, like a leopard. The beast had four wings of a bird on its back and four heads; and dominion was given to it. [7] After this I saw in the visions by night a fourth beast, terrifying and dreadful and exceedingly strong. It had great iron teeth and was devouring, breaking in pieces, and stamping what was left with its feet. It was different from all the beasts that preceded it, and it had ten horns. [8] I was considering the horns, when another horn appeared, a little one

a   Q Ms Theodotion: MT adds *the beginning of the words; he said*

b   Theodotion: Aram *Daniel answered and said, I*

c   Or *ribs*

6.24–28: Restitution. 24: *Children . . . wives* (see also Josh 7.24–26; Bel 21) indicate that family members suffer because of the misdeeds of the family leader. **25:** The letter and doxology resemble 4.1–3,34–37. **26:** The king, ironically, issues another law mandating a particular form of worship. **28:** Cyrus the Persian (ruled 590–530 BCE) promulgated the edict in 538 that permitted Judean exiles Babylon to return home (Ezra 1.1–4; 6.3–5; Isa 44.28; 45.1).

7.1–8: The first vision. Unlike Nebuchadnezzar's dreams and Belshazzar's visions, Daniel's apocalyptic revelations focus less on the dreamer's fate and more on international events. Also in contrast to the earlier scenes, Daniel is now himself in need of an interpreter. The history recorded in the visions suggests that they were composed sometime before 164 BCE, when Judas Maccabeus purified the Temple that Antiochus IV Epiphanes had profaned in 167. **1:** *The first year of King Belshazzar,* 553 BCE (Belshazzar served then as co-regent with Nabonidus). **2:** Daniel describes his dream in the first person. **3:** The *sea* is associated with chaos and beasts (e.g., Isa 27.1; Job 9.13); four beasts symbolize kingdoms, Babylon, Media, Persia, and Greece (2.31–45; 7.17; Pss 68.30; *1 Enoch,* and throughout the book of Revelation). **4:** *A lion,* the kingdom of Babylon. Hybrid creatures are a standard motif in late prophetic and early apocalyptic literature (see e.g., Ezek 1.5–7). The beast *like a human* reverses the image of Nebuchadnezzar (4.33). *Plucked* wings indicates both loss of power and transition to human form. *Human mind* may reflect Nebuchadnezzar's return to sanity in 4.34–35. **5:** The *bear* represents the Medes (cf. Jer 51.11 on the Medes attacking Babylon). **6:** The *leopard* is Persia. *Four heads* may anticipate the four Persian kings of 11.2. **7:** The *fourth beast* is the Greek kingdom, in particular the Seleucid kingdom founded by Seleucus I, one of Alexander the Great's generals, in Syria and Mesopotamia after Alexander's death in 323 BCE. *Different:* because of its non-Mesopotamian origins and more extensive geographical spread. *Stamping* may suggest the elephant, part of the Greek war effort (1 Macc 1.17; 3.34; 6.28–47). *Ten horns* is a round number representing the kings of the Seleucid empire from Seleucus I until the time of Antiochus IV Epiphanes. **8:** The

coming up among them; to make room for it, three of the earlier horns were plucked up by the roots. There were eyes like human eyes in this horn, and a mouth speaking arrogantly.

⁹ As I watched,
thrones were set in place,
    and an Ancient One[a] took his throne,
his clothing was white as snow,
    and the hair of his head like pure wool;
his throne was fiery flames,
    and its wheels were burning fire.
¹⁰ A stream of fire issued
    and flowed out from his presence.
A thousand thousands served him,
    and ten thousand times ten thousand
        stood attending him.
The court sat in judgment,
    and the books were opened.

¹¹ I watched then because of the noise of the arrogant words that the horn was speaking. And as I watched, the beast was put to death, and its body destroyed and given over to be burned with fire. ¹² As for the rest of the beasts, their dominion was taken away, but their lives were prolonged for a season and a time. ¹³ As I watched in the night visions,
I saw one like a human being[b]
    coming with the clouds of heaven.
And he came to the Ancient One[c]
    and was presented before him.
¹⁴ To him was given dominion

and glory and kingship,
    that all peoples, nations, and languages
        should serve him.
His dominion is an everlasting dominion
    that shall not pass away,
and his kingship is one
    that shall never be destroyed.

¹⁵ As for me, Daniel, my spirit was troubled within me,[d] and the visions of my head terrified me. ¹⁶ I approached one of the attendants to ask him the truth concerning all this. So he said that he would disclose to me the interpretation of the matter: ¹⁷ "As for these four great beasts, four kings shall arise out of the earth. ¹⁸ But the holy ones of the Most High shall receive the kingdom and possess the kingdom forever—forever and ever."

¹⁹ Then I desired to know the truth concerning the fourth beast, which was different from all the rest, exceedingly terrifying, with its teeth of iron and claws of bronze, and which devoured and broke in pieces, and stamped what was left with its feet; ²⁰ and concerning the ten horns that were on its head, and concerning the other horn, which came up and to make room for which three of them fell out—

a   Aram *an Ancient of Days*
b   Aram *one like a son of man*
c   Aram *the Ancient of Days*
d   Aram *troubled in its sheath*

little horn is Antiochus IV (8.9; 1 Macc 1.41–50), who attempted to outlaw Jewish practices. *Three of the earlier horns*, Antiochus IV was fourth in the line of succession, after his brother, Seleucus IV, and his brothers' sons, Antiochus and Demetrius. Seleucus was murdered by his prime minister, Heliodorus, and Demetrius was exiled to Rome. Antiochus IV was directly responsible only for the death of his nephew Antiochus, but the book of Daniel apparently holds him responsible for killing or displacing all three.

7.9–14: The heavenly throne room. See 1 Kings 22.19; Isa 6; Ezek 1.26–28; *1 Enoch* 14. 9: *Thrones*, although other parts of the Hebrew Bible and other Jewish apocalypses refer to only a single throne in heaven, the multiple thrones of the court setting in Daniel 7 are reflected in early Christian texts (see e.g., Mt 19.28; Rev 20.4). *Ancient One*, lit. "Ancient of Days," i.e., God. *White clothing*, Mt 28.3; Rev 3.5. *Fiery flames*, Ezek 1.4; *wheels*, Ezek 1.15–21; 10.2. 10: *The books* in which human deeds are recorded are commonly associated with the divine court (12.1n.; Isa 65.6; Mal 3.16; *1 Enoch* 90.20, Rev 20.12). 12: *Prolonged for a season and a time*, the empires are stripped of power, but they are not destroyed. 13: *One like a human being*, also translated "son of man," can be seen as the faithful community (a corporate symbol, for Daniel indicating faithful Jews), the angel Michael, Israel's guardian (10.13,21; see also Rev 12); Gabriel (see 9.21), Judas Maccabeus, Daniel himself. The term "son of man" can also mean "human being" (Ezek 2.1; Job 25.6), here in opposition to the animalistic nature of the previous kingdoms. In the Synoptic Gospels, the term is Jesus' preferred self-designation. 14: Cf. 4.3,34; 6.26.

7.15–28: The interpretation. 15: *Spirit was troubled* is a typical reaction to visions (2.1; 8.27; Gen 41.8); it is not clear whether Daniel has awakened or is still dreaming. 17: The *four kings* are the kingdoms of Babylon, Media, Persia, and Greece. 18: *The holy ones* are members of the heavenly court (e.g., Deut 33.2–3; Job 5.1; 15.15; Ps 89.5,7; Zech 14.5) as well as God's people (e.g., Ps 16.3; 34.9; Wis 3.9) The term may here specifically refer to

the horn that had eyes and a mouth that spoke arrogantly, and that seemed greater than the others. [21] As I looked, this horn made war with the holy ones and was prevailing over them, [22] until the Ancient One[a] came; then judgment was given for the holy ones of the Most High, and the time arrived when the holy ones gained possession of the kingdom.

[23] This is what he said: "As for the fourth beast,

there shall be a fourth kingdom on earth
    that shall be different from all the other
        kingdoms;
it shall devour the whole earth,
    and trample it down, and break it to
        pieces.
[24] As for the ten horns,
out of this kingdom ten kings shall arise,
    and another shall arise after them.
This one shall be different from the former
        ones,
    and shall put down three kings.
[25] He shall speak words against the Most
        High,
    shall wear out the holy ones of the Most
        High,
    and shall attempt to change the sacred
        seasons and the law;
and they shall be given into his power
    for a time, two times,[b] and half a time.
[26] Then the court shall sit in judgment,
    and his dominion shall be taken away,
    to be consumed and totally destroyed.
[27] The kingship and dominion
    and the greatness of the kingdoms
        under the whole heaven
    shall be given to the people of the holy
        ones of the Most High;

their kingdom shall be an everlasting
        kingdom,
    and all dominions shall serve and obey
        them."

[28] Here the account ends. As for me, Daniel, my thoughts greatly terrified me, and my face turned pale; but I kept the matter in my mind.

8 In the third year of the reign of King Belshazzar a vision appeared to me, Daniel, after the one that had appeared to me at first. [2] In the vision I was looking and saw myself in Susa the capital, in the province of Elam,[c] and I was by the river Ulai.[d] [3] I looked up and saw a ram standing beside the river.[e] It had two horns. Both horns were long, but one was longer than the other, and the longer one came up second. [4] I saw the ram charging westward and northward and southward. All beasts were powerless to withstand it, and no one could rescue from its power; it did as it pleased and became strong.

[5] As I was watching, a male goat appeared from the west, coming across the face of the whole earth without touching the ground. The goat had a horn[f] between its eyes. [6] It came toward the ram with the two horns that I had seen standing beside the river,[e] and it ran at it with savage force. [7] I saw it

a Aram *the Ancient of Days*
b Aram *a time, times*
c Gk Theodotion: MT Q Ms repeat *in the vision I was looking*
d Or *the Ulai Gate*
e Or *gate*
f Theodotion: Gk *one horn*; Heb *a horn of vision*

Jews persecuted by Antiochus. **22:** The prediction anticipates the reversal of fortune for the persecuted faithful, just as the folktales of chs 1–6 depict. **23–25:** The greater detail suggests a time closer to the author's own. The *fourth beast* and the *ten horns*, see 7.7–8n. **25:** *Words against the Most High*, Antiochus IV Epiphanes was the first Hellenistic king to use divine self-designations on coinage. *Sacred seasons and the law* are practices marking Jewish identity disrupted by Antiochus (1 Macc 1.45; 2 Macc 6.6). *A time, two times, and half a time* indicates three and a half years (see 4.36), approximately the time of Antiochus's persecution. Three and a half is also half of seven, the perfect number. **28:** *Kept the matter in my mind*, apocalyptic visions are often kept secret until an opportune time (2 Esd 14.45–46).

8.1–14: The second vision. With this chapter, the book of Daniel reverts from Aramaic to Hebrew. **1:** The earlier vision is that of ch 7. **2:** Susa, the royal city of Persia (Esth 1.2). *River Ulai*, a river near Susa; visionary experiences are occasionally associated with riverbank settings (Ezek 1.1). **3–4:** *Two horns* are Media and Persia (see v. 20). *The ram* may be connected to an astrological symbol. **5:** *The goat* may also be a zodiac sign; here it symbolizes Alexander the Great (see v. 21), whose empire originated *west* of Mesopotamia. *Across . . . the whole*

approaching the ram. It was enraged against it and struck the ram, breaking its two horns. The ram did not have power to withstand it; it threw the ram down to the ground and trampled upon it, and there was no one who could rescue the ram from its power. [8] Then the male goat grew exceedingly great; but at the height of its power, the great horn was broken, and in its place there came up four prominent horns toward the four winds of heaven.

[9] Out of one of them came another[a] horn, a little one, which grew exceedingly great toward the south, toward the east, and toward the beautiful land. [10] It grew as high as the host of heaven. It threw down to the earth some of the host and some of the stars, and trampled on them. [11] Even against the prince of the host it acted arrogantly; it took the regular burnt offering away from him and overthrew the place of his sanctuary. [12] Because of wickedness, the host was given over to it together with the regular burnt offering;[b] it cast truth to the ground, and kept prospering in what it did. [13] Then I heard a holy one speaking, and another holy one said to the one that spoke, "For how long is this vision concerning the regular burnt offering, the transgression that makes desolate, and the giving over of the sanctuary and host to be trampled?"[b] [14] And he answered him,[c]

"For two thousand three hundred evenings and mornings; then the sanctuary shall be restored to its rightful state."

[15] When I, Daniel, had seen the vision, I tried to understand it. Then someone appeared standing before me, having the appearance of a man, [16] and I heard a human voice by the Ulai, calling, "Gabriel, help this man understand the vision." [17] So he came near where I stood; and when he came, I became frightened and fell prostrate. But he said to me, "Understand, O mortal,[d] that the vision is for the time of the end."

[18] As he was speaking to me, I fell into a trance, face to the ground; then he touched me and set me on my feet. [19] He said, "Listen, and I will tell you what will take place later in the period of wrath; for it refers to the appointed time of the end. [20] As for the ram that you saw with the two horns, these are the kings of Media and Persia. [21] The male goat[e] is the king of Greece, and the great horn between its eyes is the first king. [22] As for the horn that was broken, in place of which four

a   Cn Compare 7.8: Heb *one*
b   Meaning of Heb uncertain
c   Gk Theodotion Syr Vg: Heb *me*
d   Heb *son of man*
e   Or *shaggy male goat*

earth suggests Alexander's swift eastern campaign. **8:** *Great horn was broken,* Alexander died in 323 BCE. *Four prominent horns* are Alexander's generals who divided his empire. **9:** The little horn is, again (see 7.8), Antiochus IV Epiphanes. *The beautiful land* is Israel or, more specifically, Jerusalem (11.16,41; Jer 3.19; Ezek 20.6,15). **10–11:** See Isa 14.12–16; Antiochus's outrages have cosmic import. *Host of heaven* can refer to stars or to heavenly beings or to both. Dan 12.3 connects the heavenly luminaries with God's faithful worshipers. Images of heavenly and human beings converge. For *threw down* some of the host, see Rev 12.4. **11:** *Prince of the host* is probably Michael, serving as God's representative; elsewhere *prince* designates angels (10.13,20–21). *Took the . . . offering away,* Antiochus and his supporters replaced the Temple's offerings (Ex 29.38–42; Num 28–29; Ezra 3.5; Neh 10.34; Ezek 46.1–5) with sacrifices to Zeus (1 Macc 1.45,59; 2 Macc 6.2). **12:** *Truth* or true religion is, for Daniel, worship of the God of Israel only. **13:** *Holy ones,* see 7.18n. *"How long"* is a major question of both penitential and apocalyptic literature (Ps 6.3; 79.5; 80.4; 90.13; Isa 6.11; Jer 12.4; Zech 1.12). *The transgression that makes desolate* is likely the structure erected on the altar of burnt offering in the Temple (1 Macc 1.54; 2 Macc 6.2); the Heb term ("pesha' shomem") is a play on the expression "Baal Shamem," or "lord of heaven," an epithet of Zeus.

8.15–27: Gabriel's interpretation. **15:** *Appearance of a man* indicates an angel; see 7.13n. **16:** *Ulai,* see v. 2n. *Gabriel,* whose name means "man of God" or "God is my hero/warrior," serves as a divine messenger (Lk 1.19,26). **17:** *Fell prostrate,* Daniel had not bowed to any Babylonian king or idol; the response is appropriate to an epiphany (10.9; Josh 5.14; Ezek 1.28; 3.23). *Mortal,* Heb "ben 'adam," or "son of man" (this is not the same term used in 7.13). *Time of the end* indicates the final judgment, restitution of the faithful, and punishment of the wicked (see Hab 2.3). **18:** *Trance* (lit. "deep sleep") is the same term used for Adam's (Gen 2.21) and Abraham's (Gen 15.12) sleep. Touch conveys heavenly concern (10.10,16,18; Isa 6.7; Jer 1.9). *Set me on my feet,* see Ezek 2.1–2.

others arose, four kingdoms shall arise from his[a] nation, but not with his power.

23 At the end of their rule,
  when the transgressions have reached
    their full measure,
a king of bold countenance shall arise,
  skilled in intrigue.
24 He shall grow strong in power,[b]
  shall cause fearful destruction,
  and shall succeed in what he does.
He shall destroy the powerful
  and the people of the holy ones.
25 By his cunning
  he shall make deceit prosper under his
    hand,
  and in his own mind he shall be great.
Without warning he shall destroy many
  and shall even rise up against the Prince
    of princes.
But he shall be broken, and not by human
  hands.

26 The vision of the evenings and the mornings that has been told is true. As for you, seal up the vision, for it refers to many days from now."

27 So I, Daniel, was overcome and lay sick for some days; then I arose and went about the king's business. But I was dismayed by the vision and did not understand it.

9 In the first year of Darius son of Ahasuerus, by birth a Mede, who became king over the realm of the Chaldeans— 2 in the first year of his reign, I, Daniel, perceived in the books the number of years that, according to the word of the LORD to the prophet Jeremiah, must be fulfilled for the devastation of Jerusalem, namely, seventy years.

3 Then I turned to the Lord God, to seek an answer by prayer and supplication with fasting and sackcloth and ashes. 4 I prayed to the LORD my God and made confession, saying,

"Ah, Lord, great and awesome God, keeping covenant and steadfast love with those who love you and keep your commandments, 5 we have sinned and done wrong, acted wickedly and rebelled, turning aside from your commandments and ordinances. 6 We have not listened to your servants the prophets, who spoke in your name to our kings, our princes, and our ancestors, and to all the people of the land.

7 "Righteousness is on your side, O Lord, but open shame, as at this day, falls on us, the people of Judah, the inhabitants of Jerusalem, and all Israel, those who are near and those who are far away, in all the lands to which you have driven them, because of the treachery that they have committed against you. 8 Open shame, O LORD, falls on us, our kings, our officials, and our ancestors, because we have sinned against you. 9 To the Lord our God belong mercy and forgiveness, for we have rebelled against him, 10 and have not obeyed the voice of the LORD our God by following his laws, which he set before us by his servants the prophets.

11 "All Israel has transgressed your law and turned aside, refusing to obey your voice. So

---

a Gk Theodotion Vg: Heb the
b Theodotion and one Gk Ms: Heb repeats (from 8.22) but not with his power

---

19: The period of wrath refers to the time of foreign domination. 23: On transgressions that must reach a certain number, see e.g., Gen 15.16; 2 Macc 6.14; 2 Esd 4.36–37. 25: Without warning may refer to the surprise attack against Jerusalem (1 Macc 1.29–30). Prince of princes, see v. 11n. Not by human hands, in contrast to the military resistance of the Maccabees, Daniel expects divine intervention (see 2.34). The circumstances of Antiochus IV's death are unclear. He died in Persia in late 164 BCE, either in the act of robbing a temple (so Polybius and 2 Macc 1.14–16) or of a sudden illness (so 1 Macc 6.1–17; 2 Macc 9.1–29). 26: See 7.28n.; Isa 29.11. 27: Cf. 7.28.

9.1–19: Daniel's prayer. 1: An attempt to resolve the chronological problem of 5.31 (see note) and ch 6. 2: Citing other scriptures is rare in the Hebrew Bible (cf. Jer 26.17–18; see also Tob 2.6n.); the reference is to Jer 25.11–12; 29.10–14. Devastation, Jerusalem was destroyed by the Babylonians in 586 BCE. 3: Fasting, sackcloth, and ashes are traditional indications of mourning and penance, including in perilous times (see 6.18n; 1 Kings 21.27; Isa 58.5; Ezra 8.21–23; Neh 9.1; Esth 4.1–4; 2 Macc 13.12; Jdt 4.9–11); fasting also serves as preparation for visionary experiences (Ex 34.28; 1 Kings 19.8). 4–19: The prayer is similar to other postexilic penitential prayers; cf. Ezra 9; Neh 9; Bar 1.15–3.8. Communal confession is typical of Jewish piety; even in cases where no sin is indicated, prayers begin with confession and repentance (see also 1 Kings 8.47; 2 Chr 6.37; Ps 106.6). 7: All Israel includes the ten tribes dispersed with the destruction of the northern kingdom of Israel by Assyria in 722 BCE. 10: Laws,

the curse and the oath written in the law of Moses, the servant of God, have been poured out upon us, because we have sinned against you. [12] He has confirmed his words, which he spoke against us and against our rulers, by bringing upon us a calamity so great that what has been done against Jerusalem has never before been done under the whole heaven. [13] Just as it is written in the law of Moses, all this calamity has come upon us. We did not entreat the favor of the LORD our God, turning from our iniquities and reflecting on his[a] fidelity. [14] So the LORD kept watch over this calamity until he brought it upon us. Indeed, the LORD our God is right in all that he has done; for we have disobeyed his voice.

[15] "And now, O Lord our God, who brought your people out of the land of Egypt with a mighty hand and made your name renowned even to this day—we have sinned, we have done wickedly. [16] O Lord, in view of all your righteous acts, let your anger and wrath, we pray, turn away from your city Jerusalem, your holy mountain; because of our sins and the iniquities of our ancestors, Jerusalem and your people have become a disgrace among all our neighbors. [17] Now therefore, O our God, listen to the prayer of your servant and to his supplication, and for your own sake, Lord,[b] let your face shine upon your desolated sanctuary. [18] Incline your ear, O my God, and hear. Open your eyes and look at our desolation and the city that bears your name. We do not present our supplication before you on the ground of our righteousness, but on the ground of your great mercies. [19] O Lord, hear; O Lord, forgive; O Lord, listen and act and do not delay! For your own sake, O my God, because your city and your people bear your name!"

[20] While I was speaking, and was praying and confessing my sin and the sin of my people Israel, and presenting my supplication before the LORD my God on behalf of the holy mountain of my God— [21] while I was speaking in prayer, the man Gabriel, whom I had seen before in a vision, came to me in swift flight at the time of the evening sacrifice. [22] He came[c] and said to me, "Daniel, I have now come out to give you wisdom and understanding. [23] At the beginning of your supplications a word went out, and I have come to declare it, for you are greatly beloved. So consider the word and understand the vision:

[24] "Seventy weeks are decreed for your people and your holy city: to finish the transgression, to put an end to sin, and to atone for iniquity, to bring in everlasting righteousness, to seal both vision and prophet, and to anoint a most holy place.[d] [25] Know therefore and understand: from the time that the word went out to restore and rebuild Jerusalem until the time of an anointed prince, there shall be seven weeks; and for sixty-two weeks it shall be built again with streets and moat, but in a troubled time. [26] After the sixty-two weeks, an anointed one shall be cut off and shall have nothing, and the troops of the prince who is to come shall destroy the city and the sanctuary. Its[e] end shall come with a flood, and to the end there shall be war. Desolations are decreed. [27] He shall make a strong

a Heb *your*
b Theodotion Vg Compare Syr: Heb *for the Lord's sake*
c Gk Syr: Heb *He made to understand*
d Or *thing* or *one*
e Or *His*

lit. "his Torahs." **11:** *Your law* (lit. "Your Torah" [singular]). *Curse* and *oath*, see Deut 28.15–45; Neh 10.30. **15:** The expressions echo Deuteronomy. **16:** Although in exile, Daniel's thoughts turn to Jerusalem. **17:** Reference to the *desolated sanctuary* would have particular meaning to those living during the time of Antiochus IV Epiphanes (see 8.13; 11.29–31). **19:** *Your city* is Jerusalem.

9.20–27: Gabriel's response. 21: See 8.16n. *Swift flight* indicates Gabriel's angelic nature. **24:** *Seventy weeks*, Jeremiah's seventy years (see v. 2n.) are interpreted to mean seventy weeks of years (70 x 7) or four hundred and ninety years (see Lev 25 on the jubilee, which may also be reflected in this interpretation). In Hebrew, the words for "weeks" and "seventy" have the same consonants, thus grounding Daniel's rereading of Jeremiah. The numbers are approximations. The *most holy place* is the Temple. **25:** The edict of Cyrus, sponsoring the restoration of *Jerusalem*, was promulgated in 538 BCE. The one *anointed* (Heb "mashiah" whence the English term "messiah") possibly Joshua the high priest or Zerubbabel, the descendant of King David (see Zech 4.14; also Ezra 2.2; 3.2; Hag 1.12–14). **26:** The deposed *anointed one* is the high priest Onias III (see 2 Macc 4.16), murdered in 171 BCE. *The*

covenant with many for one week, and for half of the week he shall make sacrifice and offering cease; and in their place[a] shall be an abomination that desolates, until the decreed end is poured out upon the desolator."

10 In the third year of King Cyrus of Persia a word was revealed to Daniel, who was named Belteshazzar. The word was true, and it concerned a great conflict. He understood the word, having received understanding in the vision.

[2] At that time I, Daniel, had been mourning for three weeks. [3] I had eaten no rich food, no meat or wine had entered my mouth, and I had not anointed myself at all, for the full three weeks. [4] On the twenty-fourth day of the first month, as I was standing on the bank of the great river (that is, the Tigris), [5] I looked up and saw a man clothed in linen, with a belt of gold from Uphaz around his waist. [6] His body was like beryl, his face like lightning, his eyes like flaming torches, his arms and legs like the gleam of burnished bronze, and the sound of his words like the roar of a multitude. [7] I, Daniel, alone saw the vision; the people who were with me did not see the vision, though a great trembling fell upon them, and they fled and hid themselves. [8] So I was left alone to see this great vision. My strength left me, and my complexion grew deathly pale, and I retained no strength. [9] Then I heard the sound of his words; and when I heard the sound of his words, I fell into a trance, face to the ground.

[10] But then a hand touched me and roused me to my hands and knees. [11] He said to me, "Daniel, greatly beloved, pay attention to the words that I am going to speak to you. Stand on your feet, for I have now been sent to you." So while he was speaking this word to me, I stood up trembling. [12] He said to me, "Do not fear, Daniel, for from the first day that you set your mind to gain understanding and to humble yourself before your God, your words have been heard, and I have come because of your words. [13] But the prince of the kingdom of Persia opposed me twenty-one days. So Michael, one of the chief princes, came to help me, and I left him there with the prince of the kingdom of Persia,[b] [14] and have come to help you understand what is to happen to your people at the end of days. For there is a further vision for those days."

[15] While he was speaking these words to me, I turned my face toward the ground and was speechless. [16] Then one in human form touched my lips, and I opened my mouth to speak, and said to the one who stood before me, "My lord, because of the vision such pains have come upon me that I retain no strength. [17] How can my lord's servant talk with my lord? For I am shaking,[c] no strength remains in me, and no breath is left in me."

[18] Again one in human form touched me and strengthened me. [19] He said, "Do not fear, greatly beloved, you are safe. Be strong and courageous!" When he spoke to me, I was

[a] Cn: Meaning of Heb uncertain
[b] Gk Theodotion: Heb *I was left there with the kings of Persia*
[c] Gk: Heb *from now*

prince is Antiochus IV Epiphanes. **27:** *Strong covenant*, Antiochus received support from Jason the high priest and various members of the Judean upper class (1 Macc 1.11). **27:** See 8.13n.

10.1–9: Daniel's visionary experience. The last three chapters of the book comprise a single vision. **1:** *Third year of King Cyrus* is 536 BCE. Reference to Daniel's Babylonian name (1.7; 2.24n.; 5.12) connects the apocalypse with the earlier tales. *Word*, accompanying the visual experience is auditory revelation. **3:** Daniel's regimen indicates mourning and repentance. **4:** The dating indicates that Daniel fasted during the feast of Passover (*first month* in this book's calendar is the spring month of Nisan). *On the bank*, see 8.2n. **5:** *Clothed in linen* suggests both the Temple priesthood (Ex 28) and angelic messengers (see Ezek 9.2–7). The "man" is probably Gabriel (cf. 9.21). *Uphaz*, perhaps Ophir in Arabia (see 1 Kings 9.28). **6:** The angel is described with elements that echo the divine glory in Ezek 1. **7:** *Alone saw the vision*, a similar experience occurs to Saul (Paul) according to Acts 9.7.

10.10–21: Gabriel's encouragement. 10: *Touched*, see 8.18n. **12:** *Do not fear* is standard exhortation for those receiving angelic revelation (also v. 19). **13:** War on earth is matched by war in heaven (a motif also found in the Dead Sea Scrolls and Rev 12); *Michael* is chief of the angelic princes (see Rev 12.7) and guardian of Israel (12.1). *Prince of the kingdom of Persia* is Persia's patron angel; cf. Deut 32.8; Sir 17.17. **16:** *Human form*, see 7.13n. Touching the *lips* recalls Isa 6.7; Jer 1.9. **17:** Reluctance is a frequent response by individuals called to prophetic tasks (see

strengthened and said, "Let my lord speak, for you have strengthened me." [20] Then he said, "Do you know why I have come to you? Now I must return to fight against the prince of Persia, and when I am through with him, the prince of Greece will come. [21] But I am to tell you what is inscribed in the book of truth. There is no one with me who contends against these princes except Michael, your prince. **11** [1] As for me, in the first year of Darius the Mede, I stood up to support and strengthen him.

[2] "Now I will announce the truth to you. Three more kings shall arise in Persia. The fourth shall be far richer than all of them, and when he has become strong through his riches, he shall stir up all against the kingdom of Greece. [3] Then a warrior king shall arise, who shall rule with great dominion and take action as he pleases. [4] And while still rising in power, his kingdom shall be broken and divided toward the four winds of heaven, but not to his posterity, nor according to the dominion with which he ruled; for his kingdom shall be uprooted and go to others besides these.

[5] "Then the king of the south shall grow strong, but one of his officers shall grow stronger than he and shall rule a realm greater than his own realm. [6] After some years they shall make an alliance, and the daughter of the king of the south shall come to the king of the north to ratify the agreement. But she shall not retain her power, and his offspring shall not endure. She shall be given up, she and her attendants and her child and the one who supported her.

"In those times [7] a branch from her roots shall rise up in his place. He shall come against the army and enter the fortress of the king of the north, and he shall take action against them and prevail. [8] Even their gods, with their idols and with their precious vessels of silver and gold, he shall carry off to Egypt as spoils of war. For some years he shall refrain from attacking the king of the north; [9] then the latter shall invade the realm of the king of the south, but will return to his own land.

[10] "His sons shall wage war and assemble a multitude of great forces, which shall advance like a flood and pass through, and again shall carry the war as far as his fortress. [11] Moved with rage, the king of the south shall go out and do battle against the king of the north, who shall muster a great multitude, which shall, however, be defeated by his enemy. [12] When the multitude has been carried off, his heart shall be exalted, and he shall overthrow tens of thousands, but he shall not prevail. [13] For the king of the north shall again raise a multitude, larger than the former, and after some years[a] he shall advance with a great army and abundant supplies.

[14] "In those times many shall rise against the king of the south. The lawless among

---

[a] Heb *and at the end of the times years*

Ex 3). **20:** *Prince of Greece* is another patron angel. **21:** *The book of truth*, see 7.10n.; perhaps different from the book of 12.1, describes the future; such determinism is typical of apocalyptic literature.

11.1–13: Succession of kings. 1. *Darius the Mede*, see 5.31n. **2:** see 7.6n.; there were however more than four kings of *Persia*; the numbers do not neatly match historical records. The fourth is likely Xerxes I (486–465 BCE). **3:** The *warrior king* is Alexander the Great. **4:** *Toward the four winds*, see 8.8n. **5:** *King of the south* is likely Ptolemy I Soter of Egypt (satrap, 323–305 BCE; king, 305–282); the *officer* is Seleucus I Nicanor (305–281), who established the Seleucid empire in Syria. **6:** *King of the north* is probably Antiochus II Theos of Syria (261–246), grandson of Seleucus, who married Berenice, the daughter of Ptolemy II Philadelphus, in 252 BCE. Berenice, her child, and her attendants were murdered. **7:** The *branch* is Berenice's brother, Ptolemy III Euergetes (246–221), who campaigned against the Seleucids. **8:** Ptolemy III captured many treasures from Egypt taken by the Persian king Cambyses in the fourth century and held in Babylon. **9:** The *latter* invader is Seleucus II Callinicus (246–225), whose invasion of Egypt in 242–240 BCE was unsuccessful. **10:** Callinicus's *sons* were Seleucus III Ceraunus (225–223) and Antiochus III the Great (223–187). **11:** Antiochus III campaigned against Ptolemy IV but was defeated by him at the battle of Raphia in 217. **13:** *King of the north* is Antiochus III, who waged successful campaigns during 212–205.

11.14–20: Campaigns of Antiochus III. The Ptolemies and Seleucids continued to fight until, in 198 BCE at the battle of Paneas, the Seleucids defeated the Egyptian forces and gained control of Judea. **14:** *Lawless* among

your own people shall lift themselves up in order to fulfill the vision, but they shall fail. [15] Then the king of the north shall come and throw up siegeworks, and take a well-fortified city. And the forces of the south shall not stand, not even his picked troops, for there shall be no strength to resist. [16] But he who comes against him shall take the actions he pleases, and no one shall withstand him. He shall take a position in the beautiful land, and all of it shall be in his power. [17] He shall set his mind to come with the strength of his whole kingdom, and he shall bring terms of peace[a] and perform them. In order to destroy the kingdom,[b] he shall give him a woman in marriage; but it shall not succeed or be to his advantage. [18] Afterward he shall turn to the coastlands, and shall capture many. But a commander shall put an end to his insolence; indeed,[c] he shall turn his insolence back upon him. [19] Then he shall turn back toward the fortresses of his own land, but he shall stumble and fall, and shall not be found.

[20] "Then shall arise in his place one who shall send an official for the glory of the kingdom; but within a few days he shall be broken, though not in anger or in battle. [21] In his place shall arise a contemptible person on whom royal majesty had not been conferred; he shall come in without warning and obtain the kingdom through intrigue. [22] Armies shall be utterly swept away and broken before him, and the prince of the covenant as well. [23] And after an alliance is made with him, he shall act deceitfully and become strong with a small party. [24] Without warning he shall come into the richest parts[d] of the province and do what none of his predecessors had ever done, lavishing plunder, spoil, and wealth on them. He shall devise plans against strongholds, but only for a time. [25] He shall stir up his power and determination against the king of the south with a great army, and the king of the south shall wage war with a much greater and stronger army. But he shall not succeed, for plots shall be devised against him [26] by those who eat of the royal rations. They shall break him, his army shall be swept away, and many shall fall slain. [27] The two kings, their minds bent on evil, shall sit at one table and exchange lies. But it shall not succeed, for there remains an end at the time appointed. [28] He shall return to his land with great wealth, but his heart shall be set against the holy covenant. He shall work his will, and return to his own land.

[29] "At the time appointed he shall return and come into the south, but this time it shall not be as it was before. [30] For ships of Kittim shall come against him, and he shall lose heart and withdraw. He shall be enraged and take action against the holy covenant. He shall turn back and pay heed to those

a   Gk: Heb kingdom, and upright ones with him
b   Heb it
c   Meaning of Heb uncertain
d   Or among the richest men

your own people may refer to the rivalry between the Tobiad family and the supporters of Onias III (see 9.26n.); both sought control of the Jerusalem Temple. 15–16: The well-fortified city is Sidon; its fall resulted in Antiochus III's personally taking possession of Judea, the beautiful land. 17: Terms of peace refers to the alliance formed when Antiochus III betrothed his daughter, Cleopatra I, to Ptolemy Epiphanes in 197 BCE. 18: Defeated by the Romans at Thermopylae in 191 and at Magnesia in 190, Antiochus III incurred massive tribute debt. 19: Antiochus III stumbled and fell at Elymais in 187, while attempting to plunder the temple of Bel in order to pay his debt to Rome. 20: The official is the tribute-collector, Heliodorus, sent by Seleucus IV Philopator (187–175 BCE) to plunder the Jerusalem Temple, but thwarted according to 2 Macc 3 by a divine apparition.

11.21–28: Antiochus IV. 21: The contemptible person is Antiochus IV Epiphanes (175–164 BCE). 22: The prince of the covenant is the high priest Onias III, deposed by Antiochus, who replaced him with Onias's assimilationist brother Jason (see 9.26n.). 23: The small party of Jews, those supporting Hellenization, receive rewards from the king's plundering. 25–28: Antiochus IV's successful first campaign against Egypt in 170 BCE. 26: Those who eat of the royal rations (cf. 1.5) are Eulaeus and Lenaeus, Ptolemaic courtiers whose plots against Antiochus IV prompted him to invade Egypt. 28: Against the holy covenant, either Antiochus's support in sponsoring anti-Jewish legislation or his attack on the Temple (1 Macc 1.20).

11.29–39: Attack against the Jews. 30: Kittim (Gen 10.4) here refers to Rome, which forced Antiochus to withdraw from Egypt in 168 BCE during his second campaign. That same year, Antiochus attacked Jerusalem

who forsake the holy covenant. [31] Forces sent by him shall occupy and profane the temple and fortress. They shall abolish the regular burnt offering and set up the abomination that makes desolate. [32] He shall seduce with intrigue those who violate the covenant; but the people who are loyal to their God shall stand firm and take action. [33] The wise among the people shall give understanding to many; for some days, however, they shall fall by sword and flame, and suffer captivity and plunder. [34] When they fall victim, they shall receive a little help, and many shall join them insincerely. [35] Some of the wise shall fall, so that they may be refined, purified, and cleansed,[a] until the time of the end, for there is still an interval until the time appointed.

[36] "The king shall act as he pleases. He shall exalt himself and consider himself greater than any god, and shall speak horrendous things against the God of gods. He shall prosper until the period of wrath is completed, for what is determined shall be done. [37] He shall pay no respect to the gods of his ancestors, or to the one beloved by women; he shall pay no respect to any other god, for he shall consider himself greater than all. [38] He shall honor the god of fortresses instead of these; a god whom his ancestors did not know he shall honor with gold and silver, with precious stones and costly gifts. [39] He shall deal with the strongest fortresses by the help of a foreign god. Those who acknowledge him he shall make more wealthy, and shall appoint them as rulers over many, and shall distribute the land for a price.

[40] "At the time of the end the king of the south shall attack him. But the king of the north shall rush upon him like a whirlwind, with chariots and horsemen, and with many ships. He shall advance against countries and pass through like a flood. [41] He shall come into the beautiful land, and tens of thousands shall fall victim, but Edom and Moab and the main part of the Ammonites shall escape from his power. [42] He shall stretch out his hand against the countries, and the land of Egypt shall not escape. [43] He shall become ruler of the treasures of gold and of silver, and all the riches of Egypt; and the Libyans and the Ethiopians[b] shall follow in his train. [44] But reports from the east and the north shall alarm him, and he shall go out with great fury to bring ruin and complete destruction to many. [45] He shall pitch his palatial tents between the sea and the beautiful holy mountain. Yet he shall come to his end, with no one to help him.

12 "At that time Michael, the great prince, the protector of your people, shall arise. There shall be a time of anguish, such as has never occurred since nations first came into existence. But at that time your people shall be delivered, everyone who is found written in the book. [2] Many of those who sleep in the dust of the earth[c] shall awake, some to everlasting life, and some to shame and everlasting contempt. [3] Those who are wise shall shine like the brightness

---

[a] Heb *made them white*
[b] Or *Nubians*; Heb *Cushites*
[c] Or *the land of dust*

(1 Macc 1.29–32). **31**: *Forces sent*, see 2 Macc 5.24. The *abomination* is an altar to Zeus Olympios set up in the Temple (see 8.13n.); this phrase reappears in early Christian literature (Mk 13.14). **32**: *People who are loyal* are those who resist the program of Hellenization, with its assimilationist and idolatrous practices. **33–34**: The visionary regards himself as one of the wise (Heb "maskilim"); they are distinguished from those of *little help*, probably the Maccabees, who rely on military force. On those who *fall by sword and flame*, cf. 1 Macc 1.63. **35**: Refining is a testing and purifying process (Ps 17.3; Jer 6.29; 9.6; Zech 13.9; Sir 2.5). **37**: *Beloved by women* is Tammuz (Adonis), a Mesopotamian god (Ezek 8.14). **38**: *God of fortresses* is Zeus Olympios; the fortress is likely the citadel in Jerusalem (the Akra) where occupation troops were stationed.

11.40–45: The end-time. 40: *The time of the end* moves into speculative material; no longer reporting what happened, the author envisions what will occur. **41–42**: *Edom, Moab*, and *Ammon* are ancient enemies of Israel, to its east and southeast. **45**: *The beautiful holy mountain* is Jerusalem; see 8.25n.

12.1–13: Michael's victory. 1: For the *book*, see 7.9–10n.; Ps 69.28; Isa 4.3; Mal 3.16–18; Rev 20.12,15; 21.27. Michael had been in battle with Persia and Greece (10.21–11.1). **2**: The first clear biblical reference to a resurrection, final judgment, and afterlife (see also 2 Macc 12.44–45 and cf. Ezek 37; Hos 6.2; Isa 26.19). *Many* may

of the sky,[a] and those who lead many to righteousness, like the stars forever and ever. [4] But you, Daniel, keep the words secret and the book sealed until the time of the end. Many shall be running back and forth, and evil[b] shall increase."

[5] Then I, Daniel, looked, and two others appeared, one standing on this bank of the stream and one on the other. [6] One of them said to the man clothed in linen, who was upstream, "How long shall it be until the end of these wonders?" [7] The man clothed in linen, who was upstream, raised his right hand and his left hand toward heaven. And I heard him swear by the one who lives forever that it would be for a time, two times, and half a time,[c] and that when the shattering of the power of the holy people comes to an end, all these things would be accomplished. [8] I heard but could not understand; so I said, "My lord, what shall be the outcome of these things?"

[9] He said, "Go your way, Daniel, for the words are to remain secret and sealed until the time of the end. [10] Many shall be purified, cleansed, and refined, but the wicked shall continue to act wickedly. None of the wicked shall understand, but those who are wise shall understand. [11] From the time that the regular burnt offering is taken away and the abomination that desolates is set up, there shall be one thousand two hundred ninety days. [12] Happy are those who persevere and attain the thousand three hundred thirty-five days. [13] But you, go your way,[d] and rest; you shall rise for your reward at the end of the days."

a   Or *dome*
b   Cn Compare Gk: Heb *knowledge*
c   Heb *a time, times, and a half*
d   Gk Theodotion: Heb adds *to the end*

suggest that not all will rise. 4: *The book sealed*, see 7.28n. 5–7: *The man clothed in linen* resembles a priest (see 10.5n.) and speaks like an angel. *Time, two times and half a time*, see 7.25n. 10: *Purified*, see 11.35n. 11–12: The numbers, likely added when the original timetable did not come to pass and different from the datings of 8.14, provide assurance that the end will come.

HOSEA

NAME, AUTHORSHIP, DATE OF COMPOSITION, AND HISTORICAL CONTEXT

The book of Hosea consists of a narrative about the prophet and sayings attributed to him. Hosea began his career in the final days of Jeroboam II (1.1), whose long reign (788–747 BCE) capped a century of political stability and economic prosperity in the Northern Kingdom of Israel under the dynasty found by Jehu in 842. Jeroboam died in 747, two years before Tiglath-pileser III came to power in Assyria (745) and initiated a program of imperial expansion. A prolonged national crisis ensued, which ended with the demise of the Northern Kingdom. Israel floundered under the Assyrian onslaught. Of the six kings who reigned in the next two decades, four were assassinated as the nation veered between appeasement, at the cost of heavy tribute, and rebellion, seeking futile alliances with Syria and Egypt (see 2 Kings 14.23–17.41). When Hosea's prophetic career ended is uncertain, though his oracles appear to allude to events right up to the Assyrian siege of Samaria in 722 (13.10–11,16).

After the destruction of Samaria, Hosea's words were preserved and transmitted in the Southern Kingdom of Judah. Some or all of the references to Judah may have been added in this era as Hosea's words were reinterpreted to address an analogous situation there (e.g., 1.7; 3.5; 11.12). It is also possible, however, that Hosea himself, though a northern prophet, addressed Judah as well.

As a prophet of the Northern Kingdom, Hosea presents a unique perspective among the prophets as an Israelite native, not a Judahite like his near contemporary Amos, who viewed the events from the south. The text gives little information about the prophet himself. Indeed, the only personal detail is the name of his father, Beeri (1.1). Chapters 1–3 narrate Hosea's marriage to the adulteress Gomer and the birth of their three children, Jezreel, Lo-ruhamah, and Lo-ammi, but it is debatable whether one can deduce actual biographical facts from this description of family life.

CANONICAL STATUS AND LOCATION IN CANON

The book of Hosea stands first in that part of the latter prophets called the Book of the Twelve, also known as the Minor Prophets because of their relative brevity in comparison with Isaiah, Jeremiah, and Ezekiel. Along with Amos, Hosea was the first of the "writing prophets," those prophets whose speeches were collected and edited as literary documents.

CONTENTS AND STRUCTURE

The book consists primarily of speeches critiquing the political, social, and, above all, religious life of the Northern Kingdom of Israel in the final days before its conquest and destruction by the Assyrians in 722. Hosea often refers to the Northern Kingdom under the titles of "Ephraim," its largest tribe, and "Samaria," its capital (see 4.17n.). Over the course of three decades (ca. 750–720 BCE), Hosea interpreted the unfolding disaster as a divine punishment—the Assyrians were merely God's tool—for violation of the exclusive demands of the LORD. With frequent allusions to Israelite historical traditions, Hosea portrayed Israel's entire history as a spiritual decline from an ideal time, its "youth" in the period of the Exodus from Egypt (2.15; 11.1).

During this national crisis, Hosea issued an unrelenting critique of existing political and religious institutions. Through dynastic kingship, political alliances with other nations, and, above all, illicit religious practices, Israel had violated the divine claim upon it for exclusive dependence upon and worship of the LORD. As divine punishment, Israel would be stripped of political and religious institutions too corrupt to be reformed and its land left desolate and barren. Israel would, in essence, find itself again in the wilderness. The severity of the prophetic critique is juxtaposed with language of divine longing and compassion (11.1–11; 13.4–7). In the short term, Hosea presented the annihilation of the Northern Kingdom as inevitable. Drawing, however, on a pattern discerned in Israel's sacred traditions, Hosea ultimately offered hope. In this new wilderness, as in the Sinai desert, Israel would recognize its dependence on the LORD and be restored to a harmonious state with God and with nature (2.14–23).

Hosea is best known for his metaphors, drawn from the natural world, agriculture, and, especially, kinship structures: Israel as the LORD's wife, Israel as the LORD's son. These familial metaphors are introduced in two narrative sections about the prophet's own life at the beginning of the book (1.2–2.1; 3.1–5). The prophet's personal life is presented as a paradigm of the relationship between the LORD and Israel.

Insofar as these chapters construct a biographical story for prophetic purposes, it can be said that Hosea deals with Gomer as the LORD deals with Israel. Gomer is "a wife of whoredom" (1.2), best understood as "a promiscuous woman." She bore three children, of whom Hosea was presumably not the father (2.4–5). After a period of marital separation, Hosea took her back (3.1–5). In a similar way, Israel, the LORD's unfaithful wife, will be separated from her husband and home but, just as Hosea bought back Gomer (3.2), the LORD will restore Israel. Hosea's image of Israel's sexual misconduct may be more than symbolic (e.g., 4.13–19; 9.1). Canaanite religious practice may have included sexual rites in imitation of the gods, who, presumably, generated terrestrial fertility through sexual intercourse.

The book has two major sections, which appear to be roughly chronological. Chapters 1–3 contain the material about Hosea's marriage and can be understood against the background of the last days of Jeroboam II, since 1.4 announces the demise of the Jehu dynasty of which Jeroboam was the final ruler. The second major section, chs 4–14, consists entirely of prophetic speeches that seem to allude to the chaotic days following the demise of the house of Jehu and the prolonged Assyria crisis. Boundaries between individual speech units in this second section are hard to discern. It seems to fall into two parts (chs 4–11; 12–14), rhetorically couched as legal indictments of Israel for breach of covenant (4.1; 12.2), and ending with images of restoration (11.1–11; 14.1–7).

Gregory Mobley

1 The word of the LORD that came to Hosea son of Beeri, in the days of Kings Uzziah, Jotham, Ahaz, and Hezekiah of Judah, and in the days of King Jeroboam son of Joash of Israel. ² When the LORD first spoke through Hosea, the LORD said to Hosea, "Go, take for yourself a wife of whoredom and have children of whoredom, for the land commits great whoredom by forsaking the LORD." ³ So he went and took Gomer daughter of Diblaim, and she conceived and bore him a son. ⁴ And the LORD said to him, "Name him Jezreel;ᵃ for in a little while I will punish the house of Jehu for the blood of Jezreel, and I will put an end to the kingdom of the house of Israel. ⁵ On that day I will break the bow of Israel in the valley of Jezreel."

⁶ She conceived again and bore a daughter. Then the LORD said to him, "Name her Loruhamah,ᵇ for I will no longer have pity on the house of Israel or forgive them. ⁷ But I will have pity on the house of Judah, and I will save them by the LORD their God; I will not

ᵃ That is *God sows*
ᵇ That is *Not pitied*

1.1: Superscription. *Word of the LORD,* the customary term for prophetic verbal revelation (Jer 18.18). For similar introductions to prophetic books, see Joel 1.1, Mic 1.1, Zeph 1.1, and Mal 1.1. *Hosea* (= Hoshea) is also the name for other persons in the Hebrew Bible (e.g., Num 13.8; 2 Kings 15.3; 1 Chr 27.20; Neh 10.23) and means "salvation" or "deliverance." *Days of Kings Uzziah . . . ,* these kings of Judah reigned in Jerusalem in the last half of the eighth century BCE (see 2 Kings 14.23–20.21). Uzziah was a contemporary of *Jeroboam* II, who ruled 788–747 in Samaria, the capital of the Northern Kingdom of Israel, and Ahaz was king in Judah when Samaria fell. Presumably Hosea prophesied late in Jeroboam's reign and after his death.

1.2–3.5: Hosea's family life as a symbolic vehicle for divine communication. The prophetic acts of Hosea, detailed in two sections (1.2–2.1; 3.1–5), exemplify God's relationship with Israel in allegorical fashion. Between the narrative sections, a prophetic speech (2.2–23) indicts Israel for unfaithfulness and offers hope for restoration after a period of punishment.

1.2–2.1: Hosea's marriage to Gomer, and the birth, naming, and renaming of their children as prophetic signs. The marital states of Jeremiah (Jer 16.1–2) and Ezekiel (Ezek 24) also took on prophetic significance; Isaiah gave children symbolic names (Isa 7.3,10,14; 8.1,3). **1.2:** *Wife of whoredom,* a promiscuous woman. *Children of whoredom,* children born of promiscuity. **4–8:** Birth of three children, each with symbolic names. **4:** *Jezreel* ("God sows"), the site where Jehu's bloody coup d'etat began (2 Kings 9–10). *House of Jehu,* the Israelite dynasty founded by Jehu in 842 BCE extended for a century, ending with Jeroboam II. **6:** *Lo-ruhamah,* "Not loved, not pitied"; cf. Ezek 16.4–5. **7:** This amendment to the doom promised in v. 6 is likely added by a later Judean editor.

save them by bow, or by sword, or by war, or by horses, or by horsemen."

[8] When she had weaned Lo-ruhamah, she conceived and bore a son. [9] Then the LORD said, "Name him Lo-ammi,[a] for you are not my people and I am not your God."[b]

[10][c] Yet the number of the people of Israel shall be like the sand of the sea, which can be neither measured nor numbered; and in the place where it was said to them, "You are not my people," it shall be said to them, "Children of the living God." [11] The people of Judah and the people of Israel shall be gathered together, and they shall appoint for themselves one head; and they shall take possession of[d] the land, for great shall be the day of Jezreel.

2 [e] Say to your brother,[f] Ammi,[g] and to your sister,[h] Ruhamah.[i]

[2] Plead with your mother, plead—
  for she is not my wife,
  and I am not her husband—
that she put away her whoring from her
    face,
  and her adultery from between her
    breasts,
[3] or I will strip her naked
  and expose her as in the day she was
    born,
and make her like a wilderness,
  and turn her into a parched land,
  and kill her with thirst.
[4] Upon her children also I will have no pity,
  because they are children of whoredom.
[5] For their mother has played the whore;

she who conceived them has acted
    shamefully.
For she said, "I will go after my lovers;
  they give me my bread and my water,
  my wool and my flax, my oil and my
    drink."
[6] Therefore I will hedge up her[j] way with
    thorns;
  and I will build a wall against her,
  so that she cannot find her paths.
[7] She shall pursue her lovers,
  but not overtake them;
and she shall seek them,
  but shall not find them.
Then she shall say, "I will go
  and return to my first husband,
  for it was better with me then than
    now."
[8] She did not know
  that it was I who gave her
  the grain, the wine, and the oil,
and who lavished upon her silver
  and gold that they used for Baal.

[a] That is *Not my people*
[b] Heb *I am not yours*
[c] Ch 2.1 in Heb
[d] Heb *rise up from*
[e] Ch 2.3 in Heb
[f] Gk: Heb *brothers*
[g] That is *My people*
[h] Gk Vg: Heb *sisters*
[i] That is *Pitied*
[j] Gk Syr: Heb *your*

8: *Weaned* the child, probably at age three (1 Sam 1.22; 2 Chr 31.16). **9**: *Lo-ammi,* "Not my people." *You are not my people,* God rejects the language of his covenant with Israel; see Ex 6.7; Deut 29.13. *I am not your God* can also be read, "I am not I Am" (see note *b*), as if God now withdraws the intimacy extended to Moses through revelation of the divine name (Ex 3.14). **1.10–2.1**: Jezreel's exaltation (1.11) and the renaming of Lo-ruhamah (2.1, *Ruhamah,* "Loved") and Lo-ammi (2.1, *Ammi,* "My people") signal restoration. **1.10**: For *the sand of the sea,* see the divine promise to Abraham (Gen 22.17) and Jacob (Gen 32.12); cf. Gen 15.5; 16.10; 1 Kings 3.8. *Children of the living God,* in contrast to "children of whoredom" (1.2). **11**: The prophet anticipates unification of the kingdoms of Israel and Judah, which had been separated since the tenth century BCE. *The day of Jezreel* will be one of triumph and glory; contrast 1.4–5.

2.2–23: A prophetic speech based on the preceding sign-acts. Israel wrongly attributed its agricultural fertility to Baal, a Canaanite god. For this infidelity, the Lord first initiates divorce against Israel, the promiscuous wife, then promises a rebetrothal. The metaphor of adulterous marriage and violent punishment should be interpreted with caution. It is a literary device to be viewed within its historical context, where a culture of honor and shame was used to control women's sexuality; it does not sanction domestic violence of any kind. **2**: *Plead with,* take legal action against. **3**: Ezekiel 16 expands this image. The covenant was first forged in the *wilderness* (Ex 19.1), though here "wilderness" is a symbol for barrenness and Israel's infidelity. **4**: *No pity,* a pun on Lo-ruhamah; see 1.6n. **5**: *My lovers,* foreign gods. *Wool and . . . flax,* pastoral and agricultural products, re-

⁹ Therefore I will take back
  my grain in its time,
  and my wine in its season;
and I will take away my wool and my flax,
  which were to cover her nakedness.
¹⁰ Now I will uncover her shame
  in the sight of her lovers,
  and no one shall rescue her out of my
    hand.
¹¹ I will put an end to all her mirth,
  her festivals, her new moons, her
    sabbaths,
  and all her appointed festivals.
¹² I will lay waste her vines and her fig trees,
  of which she said,
"These are my pay,
  which my lovers have given me."
I will make them a forest,
  and the wild animals shall devour them.
¹³ I will punish her for the festival days of
    the Baals,
  when she offered incense to them
and decked herself with her ring and
    jewelry,
  and went after her lovers,
  and forgot me, says the LORD.

¹⁴ Therefore, I will now allure her,
  and bring her into the wilderness,
  and speak tenderly to her.
¹⁵ From there I will give her her vineyards,
  and make the Valley of Achor a door of
    hope.

There she shall respond as in the days of
    her youth,
  as at the time when she came out of the
    land of Egypt.
¹⁶ On that day, says the LORD, you will call me,
"My husband," and no longer will you call
me, "My Baal."[a] ¹⁷ For I will remove the names
of the Baals from her mouth, and they shall
be mentioned by name no more. ¹⁸ I will make
for you[b] a covenant on that day with the wild
animals, the birds of the air, and the creeping
things of the ground; and I will abolish[c] the
bow, the sword, and war from the land; and I
will make you lie down in safety. ¹⁹ And I will
take you for my wife forever; I will take you
for my wife in righteousness and in justice,
in steadfast love, and in mercy. ²⁰ I will take
you for my wife in faithfulness; and you shall
know the LORD.
²¹ On that day I will answer, says the LORD,
  I will answer the heavens
  and they shall answer the earth;
²² and the earth shall answer the grain, the
    wine, and the oil,
  and they shall answer Jezreel;[d]
²³ and I will sow him[e] for myself in the
    land.

[a] That is, *"My master"*
[b] Heb *them*
[c] Heb *break*
[d] That is *God sows*
[e] Cn: Heb *her*

spectively, used for clothing. **6**: Sexual access will be prevented (see Song 8.9). **2.9–10**: *Nakedness*, a metaphor for Israel's unfaithfulness (see 1.3; Lam 1.8; Nah 3.5). **8**: The Lord, not Baal, is Israel's benefactor. **11**: The seasonal agricultural festivals (Ex 34.21–24) and the customary occasions for worship (Num 29.6; Ex 20.8) were now diluted by elements of the worship of Baal. **13**: *Baals*, manifestations of the god Baal at various shrines. *Offered incense*, incense itself was a lawful Israelite element of worship (Ex 30.7–8) but here, unlawfully, it is offered to other gods (cf. 1 Kings 22.44; Isa 65.3). *Decked herself*, cf. Isa 3.16–22. **14**: *Allure her*, courtship language. The *wilderness* signifies Israel's early years after the Exodus, remembered here, in terms of the marital metaphor, as a honeymoon (Jer 2.2). The wilderness can also be a place of judgment (Ezek 20.33–38). In both cases, the wilderness is a place for transformation. *Speak tenderly*, see Isa 40.2. **15**: *Achor*, a site just east of the Dead Sea where Israel got into "trouble" (the meaning of "Achor") soon after leaving the wilderness (Josh 7.22–26). **16**: *My Baal*, in secular usage, "ba'al" could also mean "husband." In this wordplay, Israel is to address the Lord as "husband" (Heb "'ish"), not as "husband" (Heb "ba'al"). **17**: *Baals*, see 2.13n. **18**: *Animals, birds . . ., creeping things*, the phrases recall Gen 1.27–31 and suggest a return to a state of blessing. See also Lev 26.6. **20**: *You shall know*, "knowledge" implies covenant faithfulness and, in terms of the marital metaphor employed, sexual intimacy. **21–23**: A conclusion to chs 1–2: The renaming of the children (see 1.4,6,9n.; 2.1n.) follows the rebetrothal of the Lord and Israel. **21–22**: Human faithfulness (or its lack) to the Lord has implications for the natural world. *Jezreel*, meaning "God sows," another symbol of restoration; see 1.4n.; 1.11n. Through a wordplay, the prophet indicates that the people will grow like plants upon their return to the land, that is, *they shall answer*, "God sows," *and I*

And I will have pity on Lo-ruhamah,[a]
and I will say to Lo-ammi,[b] "You are my
people";
and he shall say, "You are my God."

3 The LORD said to me again, "Go, love
a woman who has a lover and is an
adulteress, just as the LORD loves the people
of Israel, though they turn to other gods and
love raisin cakes." [2] So I bought her for fifteen
shekels of silver and a homer of barley and
a measure of wine.[c] [3] And I said to her, "You
must remain as mine for many days; you
shall not play the whore, you shall not have
intercourse with a man, nor I with you." [4] For
the Israelites shall remain many days without
king or prince, without sacrifice or pillar,
without ephod or teraphim. [5] Afterward the
Israelites shall return and seek the LORD their
God, and David their king; they shall come in
awe to the LORD and to his goodness in the
latter days.

4 Hear the word of the LORD, O people of
Israel;
for the LORD has an indictment against
the inhabitants of the land.
There is no faithfulness or loyalty,

and no knowledge of God in the land.
[2] Swearing, lying, and murder,
and stealing and adultery break out;
bloodshed follows bloodshed.
[3] Therefore the land mourns,
and all who live in it languish;
together with the wild animals
and the birds of the air,
even the fish of the sea are perishing.

[4] Yet let no one contend,
and let none accuse,
for with you is my contention, O priest.[d]
[5] You shall stumble by day;
the prophet also shall stumble with you
by night,
and I will destroy your mother.
[6] My people are destroyed for lack of
knowledge;
because you have rejected knowledge,
I reject you from being a priest to me.

a That is *Not pitied*
b That is *Not my people*
c Gk: Heb *a homer of barley and a lethech of barley*
d Cn: Meaning of Heb uncertain

will sow him for myself in the land. **23**: Cf. Ex 6.7; Lev 26.12.

3.1–5: The restoration of Hosea's marriage. In a like manner, the Lord's relationship to Israel will be restored. This section is in the first person while 1.2–2.1 was in the third. Gomer is not mentioned here by name. **1**: *Raisin cakes* were associated with illicit worship (Isa 16.7; Jer 7.18; 44.19). **2**: *Shekel,* ca. .4 oz (11.5 g); *homer,* about 230 l (6.5 bu). From whom Hosea *bought her* is not indicated. **3–4**: A transitional period is announced during which, on one level, the marital partners forgo relations, and on another, the covenant partners lack their customary mediators (king, prince) and religious mediations. *Pillar,* see 10.2n.; Gen 31.45. *Ephod,* Ex 28.6–14; 39.2–7; Judg 8.24–28; 1 Sam 2.18. *Teraphim,* Gen 31.19; probably ancestor statues. **5**: *David their king,* the only reference in Hosea to a specifically Judahite institution such as the Davidic dynasty, Jerusalem, or Zion; probably a later addition.

4.1–14.9: The prophetic speeches of Hosea indict Israel for unfaithfulness and announce the divine judgment, while offering hope of eventual restoration. The boundaries between individual speech units in the remainder of the book are unclear. This may in part reflect the style of the prophet and may in part be due to later editorial rearrangement.

4.1–12.1: The Lord has an indictment against Israel. 4.1: *Hear the word of the LORD,* an introduction in the prophetic style, which serves both the immediate speech and the remainder of the book. *Israel,* the primary referent here is the Northern Kingdom (also known as Ephraim) but, like all of Hosea's prophecies, after 722 the prophecy is transmitted in Judah; so the address is also to Israel in its broader sense as the people with whom God had made a covenant. *Indictment* is a legal term: On God's behalf, the prophet files suit against the people for breach of covenant. *Faithfulness, loyalty* (steadfast love), and *knowledge of God* are major theological terms in Hosea (2.19–20; 4.6; 5.4,7; 6.3,6; 10.12; 11.3–4,12b; 12.6). **2**: *Swearing . . .,* five of the Ten Commandments referred to (Ex 20.7,13–16; Deut 5.11,17–20). **3**: See 2.21n.

4.4–19: An indictment of corrupt religious practices. 4–8: The corruption issues from the priests. **4**: Legally, there are no grounds for a counterclaim against God. *Contend, contention,* the same legal terminology translated in 4.1 as "indictment." **5–6**: The phrases *destroy your mother* and *forget your children* build on the

And since you have forgotten the law of
    your God,
  I also will forget your children.

[7] The more they increased,
  the more they sinned against me;
  they changed[a] their glory into shame.
[8] They feed on the sin of my people;
  they are greedy for their iniquity.
[9] And it shall be like people, like priest;
  I will punish them for their ways,
  and repay them for their deeds.
[10] They shall eat, but not be satisfied;
  they shall play the whore, but not
    multiply;
because they have forsaken the LORD
  to devote themselves to [11] whoredom.

Wine and new wine
  take away the understanding.
[12] My people consult a piece of wood,
  and their divining rod gives them
    oracles.
For a spirit of whoredom has led them astray,
  and they have played the whore,
    forsaking their God.
[13] They sacrifice on the tops of the
    mountains,
  and make offerings upon the hills,
under oak, poplar, and terebinth,
  because their shade is good.

Therefore your daughters play the whore,
  and your daughters-in-law commit
    adultery.

[14] I will not punish your daughters when
  they play the whore,
  nor your daughters-in-law when they
    commit adultery;
for the men themselves go aside with
  whores,
  and sacrifice with temple prostitutes;
thus a people without understanding
  comes to ruin.

[15] Though you play the whore, O Israel,
  do not let Judah become guilty.
Do not enter into Gilgal,
  or go up to Beth-aven,
  and do not swear, "As the LORD lives."
[16] Like a stubborn heifer,
  Israel is stubborn;
can the LORD now feed them
  like a lamb in a broad pasture?

[17] Ephraim is joined to idols—
  let him alone.
[18] When their drinking is ended, they
  indulge in sexual orgies;
  they love lewdness more than their
    glory.[b]
[19] A wind has wrapped them[c] in its wings,
  and they shall be ashamed because of
    their altars.[d]

a Ancient Heb tradition: MT *I will change*
b Cn Compare Gk: Meaning of Heb uncertain
c Heb *her*
d Gk Syr: Heb *sacrifices*

foundation of 1.2–3.5. **7:** *The more . . . the more,* for a similar formulation, see 11.2. **8:** *They feed,* the priests depend on the sacrificial system for food. Since more sins require more sacrifices, Hosea accuses the priests of a debased relationship in their role in the process of atonement. **9–14:** The corruption, detailed here in terms of drunkenness, sexual activity, and divination, spreads from priests to the rest of society. **10:** Human fertility, also part of the divine blessing (Gen 1.28), is affected by human unfaithfulness. **11–12:** *Whoredom,* that is, improper worship and veneration of fertility deities. **12:** *Piece of wood, divining rod,* the exact referents are unknown. Trees or wooden symbols were associated with the worship of Asherah, a Canaanite goddess. **13:** A reference to high-place sanctuaries and their sacred groves (Deut 12.2). *Their shade,* note the contrast between this shade and that of 14.7. **14:** *Temple prostitutes,* lit. "sacred women," i.e., female ritual officials, a feature in Canaanite but not orthodox Israelite practice. *Without understanding,* see 2.20n. **15–19:** An admonishment to Judah: Do not let the contamination spread to you. **15:** *Gilgal, Beth-aven* (i.e., Bethel; Am 5.5), the northern shrines closest to Judah. *Beth-aven* (lit. "house of worthlessness") is a pejorative name for Bethel ("house of God"). **16:** *Stubborn heifer,* see 10.11. **17:** *Ephraim* was the name for the region surrounding Samaria. Though often used as a general term for the Northern Kingdom, its use here and Hosea's preference for it over Israel in the rest of the book could reflect a changed political situation. Israel gradually lost its territory in Transjordan, Galilee, and Jezreel in this period; in the end Ephraim was all that remained.

5

Hear this, O priests!
　Give heed, O house of Israel!
Listen, O house of the king!
　For the judgment pertains to you;
for you have been a snare at Mizpah,
　and a net spread upon Tabor,
[2] and a pit dug deep in Shittim;[a]
　but I will punish all of them.

[3] I know Ephraim,
　and Israel is not hidden from me;
for now, O Ephraim, you have played the
　whore;
　Israel is defiled.
[4] Their deeds do not permit them
　to return to their God.
For the spirit of whoredom is within them,
　and they do not know the LORD.

[5] Israel's pride testifies against him;
　Ephraim[b] stumbles in his guilt;
　Judah also stumbles with them.
[6] With their flocks and herds they shall go
　to seek the LORD,
but they will not find him;
　he has withdrawn from them.
[7] They have dealt faithlessly with the
　LORD;
　for they have borne illegitimate
　children.
Now the new moon shall devour them
　along with their fields.

[8] Blow the horn in Gibeah,
　the trumpet in Ramah.

Sound the alarm at Beth-aven;
　look behind you, Benjamin!
[9] Ephraim shall become a desolation
　in the day of punishment;
among the tribes of Israel
　I declare what is sure.
[10] The princes of Judah have
　become
　like those who remove the
　landmark;
on them I will pour out
　my wrath like water.
[11] Ephraim is oppressed, crushed in
　judgment,
　because he was determined to go after
　vanity.[c]
[12] Therefore I am like maggots to
　Ephraim,
　and like rottenness to the house of
　Judah.
[13] When Ephraim saw his sickness,
　and Judah his wound,
then Ephraim went to Assyria,
　and sent to the great king.[d]
But he is not able to cure you
　or heal your wound.
[14] For I will be like a lion to Ephraim,
　and like a young lion to the house of
　Judah.
I myself will tear and go away;

[a] Cn: Meaning of Heb uncertain
[b] Heb *Israel and Ephraim*
[c] Gk: Meaning of Heb uncertain
[d] Cn: Heb *to a king who will contend*

5.1–6.6: The people do not know the Lord. 5.1: *The judgment,* in a legal sense. *Mizpah,* a fortress city on the border between Judah and Israel (1 Kings 15.22), probably housed, like many border towns, a sanctuary. *Tabor,* a mountain in the north of Palestine, overlooking the Jezreel valley (Ps 89.12); probably the site of a sanctuary (Deut 33.18–19). 2: *Shittim,* a border town in Transjordan; the final encampment of the Israelites before they crossed the Jordan; also site of an infamy (Num 25.1–9). 3–4: Note the wordplay with "knowledge": The Lord *knows* (is aware of) *Ephraim* ('s deeds) but *they do not know* (demonstrate loyalty toward) the Lord. See 2.20n. *Spirit of whoredom,* see 4.11–12n. 5–7: Because of their disloyalty, the Lord will not be available to the people at festivals. 5: *Israel's pride,* also in 7.10. 6: *They shall go,* in pilgrimage festivals. 7: *New moon shall devour,* meaning obscure. 8–14: In the day of punishment the Lord will become the enemy of Israel (Am 9.2–4). This section may refer to the Syro-Ephraimite War (2 Kings 15.27–30) in 735, when Israel under Pekah formed a coalition with Syria to force Judah to join a rebellion against Assyria (see 2.11). 8: *Blow the horn,* the alarm signal used by sentinels. *Gibeah, Ramah,* Benjaminite towns just north of Jerusalem, situated on the path an invading army would take approaching from the south (Isa 10.28–32); *Beth-aven,* see 4.15n. This may refer to a Judahite counterattack after the Syro-Ephraimite initiative failed. 10–14: There is no defense against God. 10: *Remove the landmark,* a landmark is a boundary marker, defining the extent of property. See Deut 19.14; 27.17; Prov 22.28; 23.10. 13: *Went to Assyria,* Hoshea, the final king in Samaria (732–722 BCE), sought to appease Assyria in the wake of Pekah's

I will carry off, and no one shall rescue.
¹⁵ I will return again to my place
until they acknowledge their guilt and
seek my face.
In their distress they will beg my favor:

6
"Come, let us return to the LORD;
for it is he who has torn, and he will
heal us;
he has struck down, and he will bind
us up.
² After two days he will revive us;
on the third day he will raise us up,
that we may live before him.
³ Let us know, let us press on to know the
LORD;
his appearing is as sure as the dawn;
he will come to us like the showers,
like the spring rains that water the
earth."
⁴ What shall I do with you, O Ephraim?
What shall I do with you, O Judah?
Your love is like a morning cloud,
like the dew that goes away early.
⁵ Therefore I have hewn them by the
prophets,
I have killed them by the words of my
mouth,
and my^a judgment goes forth as the
light.
⁶ For I desire steadfast love and not
sacrifice,
the knowledge of God rather than burnt
offerings.

⁷ But at^b Adam they transgressed the
covenant;
there they dealt faithlessly with me.

⁸ Gilead is a city of evildoers,
tracked with blood.
⁹ As robbers lie in wait^c for someone,
so the priests are banded together;^d
they murder on the road to Shechem,
they commit a monstrous crime.
¹⁰ In the house of Israel I have seen a
horrible thing;
Ephraim's whoredom is there, Israel is
defiled.

¹¹ For you also, O Judah, a harvest is
appointed.

When I would restore the fortunes of my
people,

7
¹ when I would heal Israel,
the corruption of Ephraim is revealed,
and the wicked deeds of Samaria;
for they deal falsely,
the thief breaks in,
and the bandits raid outside.
² But they do not consider
that I remember all their wickedness.
Now their deeds surround them,
they are before my face.
³ By their wickedness they make the king
glad,
and the officials by their treachery.
⁴ They are all adulterers;

a Gk Syr: Heb *your*
b Cn: Heb *like*
c Cn: Meaning of Heb uncertain
d Syr: Heb *are a company*

failed rebellion (2 Kings 16.3). **14:** *Lion*, see Job 10.16; Lam 3.10.

5.15–6.6: God punishes not to annihilate but in order to inspire repentance. This section is in the form of a dialogue. **6.1:** God both punishes and *heals*; see Deut 32.39; Job 5.18. **6.2:** The punishment is temporary. *Two days . . . third day*, idiomatic expression for a brief period of time. **3:** *Spring rains*, the latter (March-April) rains (Deut 11.14). **4–6:** A summary of the entire speech. **4:** See the similar questions in 11.8. **6:** God desires covenant loyalty, a persistent theme of the prophets (Am 5.22–24; Mic 6.6–8). *Knowledge of God*, see 2.20n.

6.7–11a: An unholy gazetteer. 7: *At Adam*, a town in central Transjordan, close to where the Israelites crossed the Jordan (Josh 3.16). **8:** Men from *Gilead* participated in the assassination of King Pekahiah (2 Kings 15.25). **9:** *Shechem*, a major Ephraimite town, 12 km (7 mi) southeast of Samaria. Their *monstrous crime* is unspecified, though it may involve mistreatment of pilgrims, indecent religious acts, or brutal opposition to prophetic activity. **10:** *Ephraim's whoredom*, see 4.11–12n.; 4.17.

6.11b–7.7: A corrupt people and government. The author uses the metaphor of an oven to describe the heated activity of Israel's idolaters, the fervent celebration of the enthronement ritual, the hot anger of those who oppose the king, and the burning violence of assassination. **7.1:** The theme of healing again (5.13; 6.1). *Samaria,*

they are like a heated oven,
whose baker does not need to stir the fire,
from the kneading of the dough until it
is leavened.
5 On the day of our king the officials
became sick with the heat of wine;
he stretched out his hand with
mockers.
6 For they are kindled[a] like an oven, their
heart burns within them;
all night their anger smolders;
in the morning it blazes like a flaming
fire.
7 All of them are hot as an oven,
and they devour their rulers.
All their kings have fallen;
none of them calls upon me.

8 Ephraim mixes himself with the peoples;
Ephraim is a cake not turned.
9 Foreigners devour his strength,
but he does not know it;
gray hairs are sprinkled upon him,
but he does not know it.
10 Israel's pride testifies against[b] him;
yet they do not return to the LORD their
God,
or seek him, for all this.

11 Ephraim has become like a dove,
silly and without sense;
they call upon Egypt, they go to
Assyria.
12 As they go, I will cast my net over them;
I will bring them down like birds of the
air;
I will discipline them according to the
report made to their assembly.[c]

13 Woe to them, for they have strayed from
me!
Destruction to them, for they have
rebelled against me!
I would redeem them,
but they speak lies against me.

14 They do not cry to me from the heart,
but they wail upon their beds;
they gash themselves for grain and wine;
they rebel against me.
15 It was I who trained and strengthened
their arms,
yet they plot evil against me.
16 They turn to that which does not
profit;[d]
they have become like a defective bow;
their officials shall fall by the sword
because of the rage of their tongue.
So much for their babbling in the land of
Egypt.

8 Set the trumpet to your lips!
One like a vulture[c] is over the house of
the LORD,
because they have broken my covenant,
and transgressed my law.
2 Israel cries to me,
"My God, we—Israel—know you!"
3 Israel has spurned the good;
the enemy shall pursue him.

a   Gk Syr: Heb *brought near*
b   Or *humbles*
c   Meaning of Heb uncertain
d   Cn: Meaning of Heb uncertain

the capital of the Northern Kingdom. **4:** The time between the kneading of the dough and its fermentation is apparently when the oven was hottest. **5:** *Day of our king,* perhaps at an enthronement. **7:** *Devour their rulers,* four Israelite kings were assassinated between 747 and 732. **6:** An *oven* was typically a cylindrical earthenware structure with an opening at the top that permitted smoke or flames to escape (cf. Gen 15.17).

7.8–16: Mixing, religious and political, is bad. 8–10: Ephraim is a half-baked cake. **10:** Cf. 5.5. **11:** The *dove* was considered *silly* because it was overly familiar with humans and easily captured. *Egypt* and *Assyria* are the "foreigners" of v. 9. For the historical background, see 2 Kings 15.19–20; 17.3–4. **14:** The contrast is between acceptable forms of prayer, *crying to me from the heart,* and those which were unacceptable, such as *wailing upon their beds* (Isa 57.8) and self-mutilation (*they gash themselves*) (Deut 14.1; 1 Kings 18.28). **15:** Cf. 11.3–4. **16:** *Babbling,* i.e., negotiations conducted in the Egyptian language.

8.1–14: For the crime of assimilating foreign political models and religious practices, the punishment is foreign domination. 1–3: A military alarm signals the approach of an enemy, the Assyrians, the vehicle of divine judgment against Israel. This section is in the form of a dialogue. **1:** *Vulture,* or eagle, a symbol of the Assyrian

4 They made kings, but not through me;
　　they set up princes, but without my
　　　knowledge.
With their silver and gold they made idols
　　for their own destruction.
5 Your calf is rejected, O Samaria.
　　My anger burns against them.
How long will they be incapable of
　　　innocence?
6 For it is from Israel,
an artisan made it;
　it is not God.
The calf of Samaria
　　shall be broken to pieces.[a]

7 For they sow the wind,
　　and they shall reap the whirlwind.
The standing grain has no heads,
　　it shall yield no meal;
if it were to yield,
　　foreigners would devour it.
8 Israel is swallowed up;
　　now they are among the nations
　　as a useless vessel.
9 For they have gone up to Assyria,
　　a wild ass wandering alone;
　　Ephraim has bargained for lovers.
10 Though they bargain with the nations,
　　I will now gather them up.
They shall soon writhe
　　under the burden of kings and princes.

11 When Ephraim multiplied altars to
　　　expiate sin,
　　they became to him altars for sinning.
12 Though I write for him the multitude of
　　　my instructions,
　　they are regarded as a strange thing.
13 Though they offer choice sacrifices,[b]

though they eat flesh,
　　the LORD does not accept them.
Now he will remember their iniquity,
　　and punish their sins;
　　they shall return to Egypt.
14 Israel has forgotten his Maker,
　　and built palaces;
and Judah has multiplied fortified cities;
　　but I will send a fire upon his cities,
　　and it shall devour his strongholds.

9 Do not rejoice, O Israel!
　　Do not exult[c] as other nations do;
for you have played the whore, departing
　　　from your God.
　　You have loved a prostitute's pay
　　on all threshing floors.
2 Threshing floor and wine vat shall not
　　　feed them,
　　and the new wine shall fail them.
3 They shall not remain in the land of the
　　　LORD;
　　but Ephraim shall return to Egypt,
　　and in Assyria they shall eat unclean
　　　food.

4 They shall not pour drink offerings of
　　　wine to the LORD,
　　and their sacrifices shall not please him.
Such sacrifices shall be like mourners'
　　　bread;
　　all who eat of it shall be defiled;
for their bread shall be for their hunger
　　　only;

a Or *shall go up in flames*
b Cn: Meaning of Heb uncertain
c Gk: Heb *To exultation*

army (Jer 49.22). **2:** *Know*, see 2.20n. **4:** *They made kings . . . without my knowledge*, without endorsement from
the Lord by a prophet. **5–6:** There were calf images at the northern shrines of Dan and Bethel (1 Kings 12.28); the
singular *calf* here probably refers to that at Bethel (10.5), the shrine closest to the city of Samaria. *An artisan*, see
Isa 40.19–20. **7–10:** As punishment for political defection, Israel will be subjugated by foreigners. *Wind*, a reference to useless vanity (see Prov 11.29; Eccl 1.14,17), here implying Israel's idol worship, will become a destructive
whirlwind. See also 12.1. **9:** The phrase *a wild ass . . . Ephraim . . .* plays on the Heb words for wild ass ("pere'")
and Ephraim ("'eprayim"); cf. Jer 2.24. *Bargained for lovers*, had relations with Syria, Egypt, and Assyria. **11–14:** As
punishment for religious defection, Israel shall return to Egypt (cf. 9.3,6; 11.5; Deut 17.16). **12:** *My instructions*, my
"torahs," the legacy of Moses.

　9.1–6: Israel's festivals are condemned. 1: *Prostitute's pay*, Gen 38.17; Deut 23.17; Mic 1.7. *Threshing floors*,
harvest festivals were an occasion for communal worship; in this case, illicit worship. They were also the site of
sexual overtures (Deut 3). **3:** See 8.11–14n.; Am 7.17. **4:** *Drink offerings* were not, in themselves, forbidden; cf. Gen

it shall not come to the house of the
LORD.

5 What will you do on the day of appointed
festival,
and on the day of the festival of the
LORD?
6 For even if they escape destruction,
Egypt shall gather them,
Memphis shall bury them.
Nettles shall possess their precious things
of silver;[a]
thorns shall be in their tents.

7 The days of punishment have come,
the days of recompense have come;
Israel cries,[b]
"The prophet is a fool,
the man of the spirit is mad!"
Because of your great iniquity,
your hostility is great.
8 The prophet is a sentinel for my God over
Ephraim,
yet a fowler's snare is on all his ways,
and hostility in the house of his God.
9 They have deeply corrupted
themselves
as in the days of Gibeah;
he will remember their iniquity,
he will punish their sins.

10 Like grapes in the wilderness,
I found Israel.
Like the first fruit on the fig tree,
in its first season,
I saw your ancestors.
But they came to Baal-peor,
and consecrated themselves to a thing
of shame,
and became detestable like the thing
they loved.
11 Ephraim's glory shall fly away like a bird—
no birth, no pregnancy, no conception!
12 Even if they bring up children,
I will bereave them until no one is left.
Woe to them indeed
when I depart from them!
13 Once I saw Ephraim as a young palm
planted in a lovely meadow,[a]
but now Ephraim must lead out his
children for slaughter.
14 Give them, O LORD—
what will you give?
Give them a miscarrying womb
and dry breasts.

15 Every evil of theirs began at Gilgal;
there I came to hate them.
Because of the wickedness of their deeds

a   Meaning of Heb uncertain
b   Cn Compare Gk: Heb *shall know*

35.14. *Mourners' bread* was unclean because of association with the dead. 6: *Memphis* was the capital of Lower (northern) Egypt. *Tents* here probably refers to festival structures.

9.7–9: A response to the prophet's critics. 7: *Man of the spirit,* that is, the prophet (see Isa 11.2; 61.1; Ezek 2.2; Mic 3.8). 8: For the prophet as *sentinel* who sees at a distance and announces the divine approach, see Isa 21.6; Jer 6.17; Ezek 3.16–21; 33.6–8. *House of his God,* either the region as a whole or a former sanctuary where the prophet is no longer welcome (see 9.4). 9: *Gibeah,* the infamous episode there and its aftermath are detailed in Judg 19–21.

9.10–11.11: Before and after. This section consists of a series of four metaphors (Israel as grapes in the wilderness, a luxuriant vine, a heifer trained, a beloved child) used to characterize the people's former fidelity and health, and contrasted with their present corrupt state brought about by religious, social, and political misdeeds. As the first three metaphors unfold, the cumulative message appears to be that the covenant is irrevocably broken and Israel is to be abandoned (9.17; 10.10; 10.15). The fourth part, the culmination of the series and, for many, the culmination of the prophecies of Hosea, initially continues in this vein (11.1–7), but then dramatically shifts from an angry to a compassionate tone (11.8–11).

9.10–17: Israel, grapes in the wilderness found by God (v. 10), is now desiccated (v. 16). 10: *Baal-peor,* the site of an incident of grave disloyalty during the wilderness period (see Num 25.1–18). *First fruit,* a reference to Israel's divine election in the wilderness (see Deut 32.10; Jer 2.2–3). 15: *Gilgal,* a venerable Israelite shrine near Jericho (e.g., Josh 4.20; 10.43; 1 Sam 7.16); condemned here as the site of illicit worship (4.15; 12.11; Am 4.4; 5.5). Also, at Gilgal the Lord reluctantly acceded to the people's request for a king (1 Sam 10.14–11.25). *Thing of shame,* an epithet for Baal.

I will drive them out of my house.
I will love them no more;
    all their officials are rebels.

[16] Ephraim is stricken,
    their root is dried up,
    they shall bear no fruit.
Even though they give birth,
    I will kill the cherished offspring of
        their womb.
[17] Because they have not listened to him,
    my God will reject them;
    they shall become wanderers among
        the nations.

10

Israel is a luxuriant vine
    that yields its fruit.
The more his fruit increased
    the more altars he built;
as his country improved,
    he improved his pillars.
[2] Their heart is false;
    now they must bear their guilt.
The LORD[a] will break down their altars,
    and destroy their pillars.

[3] For now they will say:
"We have no king,
for we do not fear the LORD,
    and a king—what could he do for us?"
[4] They utter mere words;
    with empty oaths they make covenants;
so litigation springs up like poisonous weeds
    in the furrows of the field.
[5] The inhabitants of Samaria tremble
    for the calf[b] of Beth-aven.
Its people shall mourn for it,
    and its idolatrous priests shall wail[c]
        over it,
    over its glory that has departed from it.
[6] The thing itself shall be carried to Assyria
    as tribute to the great king.[d]
Ephraim shall be put to shame,

and Israel shall be ashamed of his
    idol.[e]

[7] Samaria's king shall perish
    like a chip on the face of the waters.
[8] The high places of Aven, the sin of Israel,
    shall be destroyed.
Thorn and thistle shall grow up
    on their altars.
They shall say to the mountains, Cover us,
    and to the hills, Fall on us.

[9] Since the days of Gibeah you have sinned,
    O Israel;
    there they have continued.
    Shall not war overtake them in Gibeah?
[10] I will come[f] against the wayward people
    to punish them;
    and nations shall be gathered against
        them
when they are punished[g] for their
    double iniquity.

[11] Ephraim was a trained heifer
    that loved to thresh,
    and I spared her fair neck;
but I will make Ephraim break the ground;
    Judah must plow;
    Jacob must harrow for himself.
[12] Sow for yourselves righteousness;
    reap steadfast love;
    break up your fallow ground;
for it is time to seek the LORD,
    that he may come and rain
    righteousness upon you.

a Heb *he*
b Gk Syr: Heb *calves*
c Cn: Heb *exult*
d Cn: Heb *to a king who will contend*
e Cn: Heb *counsel*
f Cn Compare Gk: Heb *In my desire*
g Gk: Heb *bound*

10.1–7: Israel, a luxuriant vine (v. 1), is now weedy (v. 4) and overrun with thorns (v. 8). **1–2:** In Canaan Israel increased in sin (here adopting illicit religious practices) as it increased in prosperity; cf. Deut 6.10–15. **2:** *Pillars*, standing stones, condemned in Ex 23.24; see 3.4. **4:** *Empty oaths*, Ex 20.7. **5:** *Calf*, 8.5n. *Beth-aven*, see 4.15n. **8:** *Aven*, 10.5n. *Mountains, Cover us . . .*, this phrase will be reused in New Testament depictions of divine judgment (Lk 23.30; Rev 6.16). **9:** *Gibeah*, 9.9n. **10:** God is a commander of the nations who will direct them against Israel. *Double iniquity*, Gibeah's former sin (see 9.9n.) and present guilt.

10.11–15: Heifer Israel now plows wickedness. **11:** *Trained heifer*, compare with 4.16. *Spared her . . . neck*, i.e., she was unyoked. **12:** *Break up your fallow ground*, Jer 4.3. *Rain* is a frequent prophetic symbol of divine restora-

¹³ You have plowed wickedness,
　you have reaped injustice,
　you have eaten the fruit of lies.
Because you have trusted in your power
　and in the multitude of your warriors,
¹⁴ therefore the tumult of war shall rise
　　against your people,
　and all your fortresses shall be destroyed,
as Shalman destroyed Beth-arbel on the
　　day of battle
　when mothers were dashed in pieces
　　with their children.
¹⁵ Thus it shall be done to you, O Bethel,
　because of your great wickedness.
At dawn the king of Israel
　shall be utterly cut off.

11 When Israel was a child, I loved him,
　and out of Egypt I called my son.
² The more I[a] called them,
　the more they went from me;[b]
they kept sacrificing to the Baals,
　and offering incense to idols.

³ Yet it was I who taught Ephraim to walk,
　I took them up in my[c] arms;
　but they did not know that I healed them.
⁴ I led them with cords of human kindness,
　with bands of love.
I was to them like those
　who lift infants to their cheeks.[d]
　I bent down to them and fed them.

⁵ They shall return to the land of Egypt,
　and Assyria shall be their king,
　because they have refused to return to me.
⁶ The sword rages in their cities,
　it consumes their oracle-priests,
　and devours because of their schemes.
⁷ My people are bent on turning away from
　　me.

To the Most High they call,
　but he does not raise them up at all.[e]

⁸ How can I give you up, Ephraim?
　How can I hand you over, O Israel?
How can I make you like Admah?
　How can I treat you like Zeboiim?
My heart recoils within me;
　my compassion grows warm and tender.
⁹ I will not execute my fierce anger;
　I will not again destroy Ephraim;
for I am God and no mortal,
　the Holy One in your midst,
　and I will not come in wrath.[e]

¹⁰ They shall go after the LORD,
　who roars like a lion;
when he roars,
　his children shall come trembling from
　　the west.
¹¹ They shall come trembling like birds
　　from Egypt,
　and like doves from the land of Assyria;
　and I will return them to their homes,
　　says the LORD.

¹² [f]Ephraim has surrounded me with lies,
　and the house of Israel with deceit;
but Judah still walks[g] with God,
　and is faithful to the Holy One.

a　Gk: Heb *they*
b　Gk: Heb *them*
c　Gk Syr Vg: Heb *his*
d　Or *who ease the yoke on their jaws*
e　Meaning of Heb uncertain
f　Ch 12.1 in Heb
g　Heb *roams* or *rules*

tion and blessing (Isa 44.3; 45.8; 55.10). **13:** Contrast Ps 20.7, 44.6, Isa 31.1. **14:** *Shalman . . . Beth-arbel,* the allusion is unknown, but perhaps refers to the Assyrian king Shalmaneser V (see 2 Kings 17.3) or the Moabite king Salamanu. **15:** *Bethel,* see 8.5–6n.

　11.1–11: Israel as God's wayward child. This speech employs the culminating, and most intimate, metaphor in the series: Israel as the Lord's child. It also ends this long section, which began in 4.1, on a hopeful note. Here, the divine mood shifts from anger to compassion. **1:** Cf. Ex 4.22. **2:** *Baals,* see 2.13n. **3:** Cf. 7.15. **5:** *Return to . . . Egypt,* 8.13; 9.3. **8–9:** At the pivotal point of this soliloquy, divine compassion overcomes divine anger. *Admah, Zeboiim,* cities destroyed along with Sodom and Gomorrah (Gen 19; Deut 29.23). **10:** In contrast with 5.14, this lion's *roar* is not aggressive but is a summons to its mate or cubs. **11:** *Doves,* contrast 7.11. These doves exhibit a homing instinct. *Egypt* and *Assyria,* contrast 9.3.

12
Ephraim herds the wind,
and pursues the east wind all day long;
they multiply falsehood and violence;
they make a treaty with Assyria,
and oil is carried to Egypt.

2 The LORD has an indictment against
Judah,
and will punish Jacob according to his
ways,
and repay him according to his
deeds.
3 In the womb he tried to supplant his
brother,
and in his manhood he strove with God.
4 He strove with the angel and prevailed,
he wept and sought his favor;
he met him at Bethel,
and there he spoke with him.[a]
5 The LORD the God of hosts,
the LORD is his name!
6 But as for you, return to your God,
hold fast to love and justice,
and wait continually for your God.

7 A trader, in whose hands are false balances,
he loves to oppress.
8 Ephraim has said, "Ah, I am rich,
I have gained wealth for myself;
in all of my gain
no offense has been found in me
that would be sin."[b]
9 I am the LORD your God
from the land of Egypt;
I will make you live in tents again,
as in the days of the appointed festival.

10 I spoke to the prophets;
it was I who multiplied visions,
and through the prophets I will bring
destruction.
11 In Gilead[c] there is iniquity,
they shall surely come to nothing.
In Gilgal they sacrifice bulls,
so their altars shall be like stone heaps
on the furrows of the field.
12 Jacob fled to the land of Aram,
there Israel served for a wife,
and for a wife he guarded sheep.[d]
13 By a prophet the LORD brought Israel up
from Egypt,
and by a prophet he was guarded.
14 Ephraim has given bitter offense,
so his Lord will bring his crimes down
on him
and pay him back for his insults.

13
When Ephraim spoke, there was
trembling;
he was exalted in Israel;
but he incurred guilt through Baal and
died.
2 And now they keep on sinning
and make a cast image for themselves,
idols of silver made according to their
understanding,
all of them the work of artisans.
"Sacrifice to these," they say.[e]

a Gk Syr: Heb *us*
b Meaning of Heb uncertain
c Compare Syr: Heb *Gilead*
d Heb lacks *sheep*
e Cn Compare Gk: Heb *To these they say sacrifices of people*

11.12–12.1: The futility of foreign alliances. 11.12: *But Judah still . . .*, perhaps a later addition. 12.1: Cf. 8.7. *Treaty with Assyria,* see 2 Kings 15.19–20; 17.3. *Oil . . . to Egypt,* Samaria was renowned for its olive oil, used here as a commodity of tribute to Egypt, which produced little.

12.2–14.9: Rebellion and restoration. Another major division in the book (like 4.1–12.1), which begins with the announcement of an indictment and ends with an oracle of hope.

12.2–13.16: A divine lawsuit against Israel, which mixes historical retrospection with contemporary critique. For a historical summary with a similar tone, see Ps 106. 12.2: *The LORD has an indictment,* cf. 4.1. 3: Gen 25.26; 32.22–30. 4–5: Gen 28.11–17; 35.5–8. 7: See Am 8.5. *Trader,* the Hebrew word can also mean "Canaanite," thus a doubly condemnatory pun. 8: As if prosperity were proof of virtue. 9: *I am the LORD your God,* see Ex 20.2; Deut 5.6; Ps 81.10; Isa 43.3. *Tents,* a customary feature of seasonal rites (Lev 23.34–43; Deut 16.13) and symbolic of the wilderness period, will be all that remains for Israel following the divine punishment. 11: *Gilead,* see 6.8n.; *Gilgal,* see 9.15n. 12–13: *Jacob . . . guarded sheep,* but Moses *guarded* the people of Israel; Gen 29.1–30. 13: *By a prophet,* the first reference is clearly to Moses; the second may be Moses as well, or Samuel (1 Sam 3.20) or Elijah (1 Kings 18.22). 13.1: An allusion to Ephraim's relative prosperity during much of the Divided Monarchy. 2:

People are kissing calves!
³ Therefore they shall be like the morning
mist
or like the dew that goes away early,
like chaff that swirls from the threshing
floor
or like smoke from a window.

⁴ Yet I have been the LORD your God
ever since the land of Egypt;
you know no God but me,
and besides me there is no savior.
⁵ It was I who fedᵃ you in the wilderness,
in the land of drought.
⁶ When I fedᵇ them, they were satisfied;
they were satisfied, and their heart was
proud;
therefore they forgot me.
⁷ So I will become like a lion to them,
like a leopard I will lurk beside the way.
⁸ I will fall upon them like a bear robbed of
her cubs,
and will tear open the covering of their
heart;
there I will devour them like a lion,
as a wild animal would mangle them.

⁹ I will destroy you, O Israel;
who can help you?ᶜ
¹⁰ Where now isᵈ your king, that he may
save you?
Where in all your cities are your rulers,
of whom you said,
"Give me a king and rulers"?
¹¹ I gave you a king in my anger,
and I took him away in my wrath.

¹² Ephraim's iniquity is bound up;
his sin is kept in store.
¹³ The pangs of childbirth come for him,
but he is an unwise son;

for at the proper time he does not present
himself
at the mouth of the womb.

¹⁴ Shall I ransom them from the power of
Sheol?
Shall I redeem them from Death?
O Death, where areᵉ your plagues?
O Sheol, where isᵉ your destruction?
Compassion is hidden from my eyes.

¹⁵ Although he may flourish among
rushes,ᶠ
the east wind shall come, a blast from
the LORD,
rising from the wilderness;
and his fountain shall dry up,
his spring shall be parched.
It shall strip his treasury
of every precious thing.
¹⁶ ᵍ Samaria shall bear her guilt,
because she has rebelled against her
God;
they shall fall by the sword,
their little ones shall be dashed in
pieces,
and their pregnant women ripped open.

14 Return, O Israel, to the LORD your God,
for you have stumbled because of your
iniquity.
² Take words with you

ᵃ Gk Syr: Heb *knew*
ᵇ Cn: Heb *according to their pasture*
ᶜ Gk Syr: Heb *for in me is your help*
ᵈ Gk Syr Vg: Heb *I will be*
ᵉ Gk Syr: Heb *I will be*
ᶠ Or *among brothers*
ᵍ Ch 14.1 in Heb

Kissing calves, see 8.5–6n.; 1 Kings 19.18. **3:** *Morning mist*, cf. 6.4. **4:** See 12.9n. **5:** Cf. 11.4. **8:** *A bear robbed of her cubs*, a popular image for ferocity (2 Sam 17.8; Prov 17.12). *Lion*, see 5.14; 11.10. **9–11:** This may refer to the deposing of Hoshea by the Assyrians in 723 (2 Kings 17.4). **10:** *King . . . may save*, read this in light of 13.4: The Lord alone is Israel's savior. *Give me a king*, Israel requested human leadership; see 1 Sam 8.6,19; 12.13,17. **11:** *I gave . . . a king in my anger*, cf. 1 Sam 12. **13:** The pain of divine judgment is designed not to kill but to induce new life, yet Israel, *unwise*, refuses to budge. **14:** *Sheol*, the abode of all dead, righteous and unrighteous. *Death* (Mot), the Canaanite deity of the underworld, is probably referred to here; cf. Job 18.13; Ps 49.14; Isa 28.15; Hab 2.5. *Sheol*, in this era, the abode of all dead, righteous and unrighteous. In this judgment speech, *compassion is hidden*, unlike 11.8. **15:** *Flourish among rushes*, alludes to political reliance on Egypt, which will be blown away by the "east wind," Assyria. *The east wind . . . a blast from the LORD*, contrasts the east wind, which was the vehicle of

and return to the Lord;
say to him,
   "Take away all guilt;
accept that which is good,
   and we will offer
   the fruit[a] of our lips.
³ Assyria shall not save us;
   we will not ride upon horses;
we will say no more, 'Our God,'
   to the work of our hands.
In you the orphan finds mercy."

⁴ I will heal their disloyalty;
   I will love them freely,
   for my anger has turned from them.
⁵ I will be like the dew to Israel;
   he shall blossom like the lily,
   he shall strike root like the forests of
      Lebanon.[b]
⁶ His shoots shall spread out;
   his beauty shall be like the olive tree,
   and his fragrance like that of Lebanon.
⁷ They shall again live beneath my[c]
      shadow,
   they shall flourish as a garden;[d]

they shall blossom like the vine,
   their fragrance shall be like the wine of
      Lebanon.

⁸ O Ephraim, what have I[e] to do with idols?
   It is I who answer and look after you.[f]
I am like an evergreen cypress;
   your faithfulness[g] comes from me.
⁹ Those who are wise understand these
      things;
   those who are discerning know
      them.
For the ways of the Lord are right,
   and the upright walk in them,
   but transgressors stumble in
      them.

a   Gk Syr: Heb *bulls*
b   Cn: Heb *like Lebanon*
c   Heb *his*
d   Cn: Heb *they shall grow grain*
e   Or *What more has Ephraim*
f   Heb *him*
g   Heb *your fruit*

the Lord's deliverance of Israel at the Reed Sea (Ex 14.21; 15.8). **16:** The ravages of conquering armies; cf. 10.14; 2 Kings 8.12; Ps 137.9; Am 1.13.

14.1–8: A final plea for repentance and a vision of restoration. 2–3: *Take words,* i.e., take these words: The prophet coaches Israel in repentance. **3:** *The work of our hands,* see 8.6. *Mercy* or "pity," the same root as in Lo-ruhamah/Ruhamah (1.6; 2.1). **5:** *Dew* is a life-sustaining necessity in the dry land of Israel (Ps 133.3); contrast the image in 6.4; 13.3. **6:** This *fragrance* is of the aromatic Lebanese cedar forest; in the next verse, of Lebanese scented wine. **7–8:** *My shadow,* more common is the poetic image of the "shade" under God's wings (Ps 17.8; 36.8); uniquely here, God's shade is that of a great tree. In contrast to the trees used in Canaanite worship (see 4.12n.), God's presence is everlasting, like the abundant foliage of an *evergreen*.

14.9: A postscript in the style of wisdom literature. For the first half of the verse, cf. Ps 107.43; Jer 9.12; for the second, Prov 10.29.

JOEL

NAME, AUTHORSHIP, AND DATE OF COMPOSITION

The book begins with a brief superscription stating that the word of the LORD came to Joel the son of Bethuel. No chronological formula is given to indicate the book's date, unlike the surrounding books of Hosea and Amos, which are both dated to the eighth century BCE. There is good reason to think that the book of Joel derives from a much later period, probably the Persian era (539–333 BCE), because (1) it refers to the Greeks (3.6); (2) it includes imagery attested elsewhere in late prophetic literature; (3) it alludes to other biblical texts, some of which were written in the late monarchic period (Obadiah) or the Persian period (Malachi); and (4) the name "Joel" is prominent in Persian-period biblical literature. Of the prophet himself nothing is known except his father's name.

LOCATION IN CANON

In the Masoretic Text (and in English translations that follow its order) Joel comes between two books attributed to much earlier prophets, Hosea and Amos. That may be due to two similar verses, Joel 3.16a and Am 1.2a. In the Septuagint (LXX), however, Joel is typically the fourth book of the Minor Prophets, after Hosea, Amos, and Micah.

STRUCTURE, CONTENTS, AND INTERPRETATION

The book of Joel describes a crisis in harrowing terms. The crisis and its resolution are reported in 1.1–2.27. Scholars, however, often attribute 2.28–3.21 to another author or authors. In this section, described as late prophetic or early apocalyptic literature, the world of ritual disappears and is replaced by the return of prophecy, cosmic symbolism, conflict with foreign nations, and images of fertility. These later verses also include more allusions to other biblical texts than 1.1–2.27.

The book offers multiple images of agricultural ruin and its impact on life in Judah. The prophet speaks of drought in the land (e.g., 1.10,12,17,20), and envisions a locust plague in the language of military attack. Locusts were known for their destructive potential to strip all vegetation from the countryside (see Ex 10.15) and are compared with military forces in other ancient Near Eastern literature.

Although the book's rhetoric of destruction is comparable to that found in other prophetic books, the poems or speeches are quite different. Rather than offering a critique of Israel's behavior, Joel summons the people to respond to the crisis by performing several rituals. Plural imperative verbs—fast, lament, wail, blow (the trumpet), put on sackcloth—are a hallmark of this summons.

The book has a distinctive theological position. Though Joel clearly thinks that God was the ultimate cause of the disaster (2.19), the prophet offers no reason for the deity's action. Hence, it is not clear that the crisis should be conceived as judgment for the people's prior misdeeds. Nonetheless, the book affirms that Israel's God is sovereign.

David L. Petersen

1

The word of the LORD that came to Joel
son of Pethuel:

² Hear this, O elders,
  give ear, all inhabitants of the land!
Has such a thing happened in your days,
  or in the days of your ancestors?
³ Tell your children of it,
  and let your children tell their
    children,
  and their children another generation.

⁴ What the cutting locust left,
  the swarming locust has eaten.
What the swarming locust left,
  the hopping locust has eaten,
and what the hopping locust left,
  the destroying locust has eaten.

⁵ Wake up, you drunkards, and weep;
  and wail, all you wine-drinkers,
over the sweet wine,
  for it is cut off from your mouth.
⁶ For a nation has invaded my land,
  powerful and innumerable;
its teeth are lions' teeth,
  and it has the fangs of a lioness.
⁷ It has laid waste my vines,
  and splintered my fig trees;

it has stripped off their bark and thrown
    it down;
  their branches have turned white.

⁸ Lament like a virgin dressed in
    sackcloth
  for the husband of her youth.
⁹ The grain offering and the drink offering
    are cut off
  from the house of the LORD.
The priests mourn,
  the ministers of the LORD.
¹⁰ The fields are devastated,
  the ground mourns;
for the grain is destroyed,
  the wine dries up,
  the oil fails.

¹¹ Be dismayed, you farmers,
  wail, you vinedressers,
over the wheat and the barley;
  for the crops of the field are ruined.
¹² The vine withers,
  the fig tree droops.
Pomegranate, palm, and apple—
  all the trees of the field are dried up;
surely, joy withers away
  among the people.

1.1: Superscription. Unlike Hos 1.1 and Am 1.1, there is no reference to a king during whose reign Joel prophesied. This may suggest a date when Israel was no longer a monarchy. **1.2–2.17: Crisis and call to action.** A series of staccato-like poems, some of which depict the crisis (e.g., 1.17–18), more of which call people to act (e.g., 1.14). **1.2–20:** Different groups are commanded to undertake various rituals of lament and petition to the LORD. **2–3:** The prophet strikes an intergenerational note, which involves both hearing and telling. *Elders*, probably village or regional officials (cf. Ezra 5.9; 6.8,14; 10.8,14), stand in parallel with the hyperbolic *all inhabitants of the land. Ancestors*, lit., "fathers." The rhetorical question, which has an obvious negative answer, does not reveal the nature of *such a thing.* **4:** Rather than different species, these nouns probably refer to the developmental stages of the *locust.* For Joel, the four forms represent four attacks on the vegetation (cf. Am 4.9). For other references to *locust* plagues see Ex 10.22; Pss 78.46; 105.34–35. **5–7:** *Drunkards* may be too negative a translation. In these speeches Joel does not regularly indict Israelites, so here he may simply be referring to those who enjoy wine. Joel 3.18 promises the return of *sweet wine.* The admonition to *wail* may involve ritual lament, not simply crying, as in Jer 4.8. **6–7:** The reference to *my land* (cf. 2.18; Lev 25.23) suggests that God is speaking. The poem offers the reason for the commands: *a nation* of vast numbers is ferocious; it is destroying Israel's *vines* (note the earlier reference to wine) and *fig trees*, both of which must grow for a long time before they bear fruit. **8–10:** *Virgin* may mean a young woman who is grief-stricken at the death of her husband. Again, the reason for the command follows the command itself, given to unidentified persons. Rituals at the temple—*grain offering, drink offering*—could not take place because *wine, grain,* and *oil* (cf. 2.19, which promises their return) were no longer available. **11–12:** Now farmers must lament the demise of eight different harvests, divided into *crops* and *trees.* **11:** *Vinedresser*, a person who prunes grape vines. **13–14:** *Priests* (cf. 1.9–11) are now commanded to lament and put on *sackcloth*, which was worn during mourning rites (e.g., Am 8.10) and other difficult times (e.g., Ps 35.13); see 2 Sam 12.16 for passing the night in

¹³ Put on sackcloth and lament, you priests;
  wail, you ministers of the altar.
Come, pass the night in sackcloth,
  you ministers of my God!
Grain offering and drink offering
  are withheld from the house of your God.

¹⁴ Sanctify a fast,
  call a solemn assembly.
Gather the elders
  and all the inhabitants of the land
to the house of the LORD your God,
  and cry out to the LORD.

¹⁵ Alas for the day!
For the day of the LORD is near,
  and as destruction from the Almighty[a]
    it comes.
¹⁶ Is not the food cut off
  before our eyes,
joy and gladness
  from the house of our God?

¹⁷ The seed shrivels under the clods,[b]
  the storehouses are desolate;
the granaries are ruined
  because the grain has failed.
¹⁸ How the animals groan!
  The herds of cattle wander about
because there is no pasture for them;
  even the flocks of sheep are dazed.[c]

¹⁹ To you, O LORD, I cry.
For fire has devoured
  the pastures of the wilderness,
and flames have burned
  all the trees of the field.
²⁰ Even the wild animals cry to you
  because the watercourses are dried up,

and fire has devoured
  the pastures of the wilderness.

2 Blow the trumpet in Zion;
  sound the alarm on my holy mountain!
Let all the inhabitants of the land tremble,
  for the day of the LORD is coming, it is
    near—
² a day of darkness and gloom,
  a day of clouds and thick darkness!
Like blackness spread upon the mountains
  a great and powerful army comes;
their like has never been from of old,
  nor will be again after them
    in ages to come.

³ Fire devours in front of them,
  and behind them a flame burns.
Before them the land is like the garden of
    Eden,
  but after them a desolate wilderness,
    and nothing escapes them.

⁴ They have the appearance of horses,
  and like war-horses they charge.
⁵ As with the rumbling of chariots,
  they leap on the tops of the mountains,
like the crackling of a flame of fire
  devouring the stubble,
like a powerful army
  drawn up for battle.

⁶ Before them peoples are in anguish,
  all faces grow pale.[b]

a Traditional rendering of Heb *Shaddai*
b Meaning of Heb uncertain
c Compare Gk Syr Vg: Meaning of Heb uncertain

a comparable ritual. *A fast* could be a public event (cf. Zech 7.3–5; 8.18–19; Ezra 8.21–23; Neh 1.4–11). For a different perspective on *a solemn assembly*, see Am 5.21; Isa 1.13. *Elders* and *all the inhabitants of the land* echo 1.2. **15–20:** These verses may be a single lament, spoken either by the prophet or the people (or their priests). *The day of the LORD* (see also 2.1,11,31; 3.14) symbolizes God's theophanic and judging presence (cf. Am 5.18; Ob 15; Zeph 1.7,14–15; Isa 13.6; Ezek 13.5). **16:** A rhetorical question, with an obvious response. **18:** Domestic animals also suffer. **20:** *Even the wild animals* completes the picture of all life—plant and animal—suffering through the attack, fire, and drought.

2.1–17: Though similar to ch 1, these poems focus more on describing the calamity than commanding a response. **1–2:** *The day of the LORD . . . is near* (see 1.15), even though catastrophe has already struck. *Darkness* is an anticipated feature of the *day* (see also Am 5.18; Zeph 1.15), highlighted in the advent of a *great and powerful army*. **3–4:** The prophet depicts the scene *before* the onslaught (2.3,6,10), *like the garden of Eden* (see Gen 2.8–9; 13.10; Isa 51.3), which contrasts with the description of the devastation afterward, *a desolate wilderness*. **5–7:**

⁷ Like warriors they charge,
    like soldiers they scale the wall.
Each keeps to its own course,
    they do not swerve from[a] their paths.
⁸ They do not jostle one another,
    each keeps to its own track;
they burst through the weapons
    and are not halted.
⁹ They leap upon the city,
    they run upon the walls;
they climb up into the houses,
    they enter through the windows like a
        thief.

¹⁰ The earth quakes before them,
    the heavens tremble.
The sun and the moon are darkened,
    and the stars withdraw their
        shining.
¹¹ The LORD utters his voice
    at the head of his army;
how vast is his host!
    Numberless are those who obey his
        command.
Truly the day of the LORD is great;
    terrible indeed—who can endure it?

¹² Yet even now, says the LORD,
    return to me with all your heart,
with fasting, with weeping, and with
        mourning;
    ¹³ rend your hearts and not your
        clothing.
Return to the LORD, your God,
    for he is gracious and merciful,
slow to anger, and abounding in steadfast
        love,
    and relents from punishing.

¹⁴ Who knows whether he will not turn
        and relent,
    and leave a blessing behind him,
a grain offering and a drink offering
    for the LORD, your God?

¹⁵ Blow the trumpet in Zion;
    sanctify a fast;
call a solemn assembly;
    ¹⁶ gather the people.
Sanctify the congregation;
    assemble the aged;
gather the children,
    even infants at the breast.
Let the bridegroom leave his room,
    and the bride her canopy.

¹⁷ Between the vestibule and the altar
    let the priests, the ministers of the
        LORD, weep.
Let them say, "Spare your people, O LORD,
    and do not make your heritage a
        mockery,
    a byword among the nations.
Why should it be said among the peoples,
    'Where is their God?'"

¹⁸ Then the LORD became jealous for his land,
    and had pity on his people.
¹⁹ In response to his people the LORD said:
I am sending you
    grain, wine, and oil,
    and you will be satisfied;
and I will no more make you
    a mockery among the nations.

a   Gk Syr Vg: Heb *they do not take a pledge along*

The similes *like a powerful army* and *like warriors* make it clear that locusts, not an army, are meant. **10–11:** *The earth quakes* is typical of a theophany (e.g., Ps 77.18), as is the darkening of astral objects (cf. Isa 13.10). God is the general of *his army*, which may describe the locusts and thus explains why the locusts are related to *the day of the LORD*. **12–13:** Language from ch 1 reappears, calling for a ritual response. The reference to *heart* reflects Deuteronomic idioms (Deut 10.16; 30.2). The characterization of the LORD in v. 13b appears elsewhere, though Joel omits mention of God's judgment (see, e.g., Ex 34.6–7; Num 14.18). **14:** *Who knows . . .* , cf. Jon 3.9. *The LORD* may leave an offering for himself. **15–16:** Cf. 1.14. **17:** *Vestibule* refers to the entry hall of the temple (see 1 Kings 6.3). The *altar* was in the temple courtyard. The priests, stationed between the altar and the vestibule, are to utter the prayer given to them by Joel. Cf. Ex 32.12; Deut 9.26–28 for similar logic.

2.18–27: The LORD responds. Since the deity responds, one may infer that the people, especially the priests, complied with Joel's commands, though the book does not report the people's actual response to Joel's admonitions. **18–19:** *Jealous*, better "zealous"; cf. Zech 1.14; Isa 9.7. God's first concern, even before the people, was *his land* (see 1.6–7n.). *Grain, wine, and oil* mentioned as absent in 1.10. The reference to *mockery among the nations*

²⁰ I will remove the northern army far from you,
  and drive it into a parched and desolate land,
its front into the eastern sea,
  and its rear into the western sea;
its stench and foul smell will rise up.
  Surely he has done great things!

²¹ Do not fear, O soil;
  be glad and rejoice,
  for the LORD has done great things!
²² Do not fear, you animals of the field,
  for the pastures of the wilderness are green;
the tree bears its fruit,
  the fig tree and vine give their full yield.

²³ O children of Zion, be glad
  and rejoice in the LORD your God;
for he has given the early rainᵃ for your vindication,
  he has poured down for you abundant rain,
  the early and the later rain, as before.
²⁴ The threshing floors shall be full of grain,
  the vats shall overflow with wine and oil.

²⁵ I will repay you for the years
  that the swarming locust has eaten,
the hopper, the destroyer, and the cutter,
  my great army, which I sent against you.

²⁶ You shall eat in plenty and be satisfied,
  and praise the name of the LORD your God,
  who has dealt wondrously with you.
And my people shall never again be put to shame.
²⁷ You shall know that I am in the midst of Israel,
  and that I, the LORD, am your God and there is no other.
And my people shall never again be put to shame.

²⁸ ᵇThen afterward
  I will pour out my spirit on all flesh;
your sons and your daughters shall prophesy,
  your old men shall dream dreams,
  and your young men shall see visions.
²⁹ Even on the male and female slaves,
  in those days, I will pour out my spirit.

³⁰ I will show portents in the heavens and on the earth, blood and fire and columns of smoke. ³¹ The sun shall be turned to darkness, and the moon to blood, before the great and terrible day of the LORD comes. ³² Then everyone who calls on the name of the LORD shall be saved; for in Mount Zion and in Jerusalem there shall be those who escape, as the LORD has said, and among the survivors shall be those whom the LORD calls.

ᵃ Meaning of Heb uncertain
ᵇ Ch 3.1 in Heb

suggests that God responded directly to the prayer in 2.17. **20:** *Northern army* is probably an allusion to the mythic enemy from the north (cf. Jer 1.13–15; 4.6; 6.1). *Eastern sea*, the Dead Sea; *western sea*, the Mediterranean. *Stench and foul smell* may reflect the plague traditions, cf. Ex 7.18; 8.14. **21:** The land is now personified as *soil.* **22:** The imagery represents a reversal of the earlier situation. *Animals of the field* will have pastureland (cf. 1.18), and *fig tree* and *vine* will bear fruit (cf. 1.12). **23:** *Abundant rain* replaces the earlier drought (1.20). *Children of Zion*, cf. Ps 149.2. Human life focuses on Jerusalem. *Early* rain, in late fall; *later rain*, in early spring. **25:** *Repay* often has legal connotations; cf. Ex 21.34. *Years* is much longer than the attack heretofore described. The four forms of locust appear here in a different order from that in 1.4. **26–27:** The promise of restoration is confirmed by allusion to the covenantal relationship with the only true God; cf. Isa 45.5; 45.17.

2.28–3.21. A future of well-being for Israel. Poetic and prose oracles focusing on Israel and their human enemies. God will again bring victory that will result in marvelous fertility. **2.28–29:** *Pour out my spirit* here implies enabling various forms of prophetic revelation (cf. Ezek 39.29). What had been limited to the house of David (Zech 12.10) or the prophets is now available to all Israel. Cf. Acts 2.16–21. **30–32:** These verses are probably poetic. *Portents* are cosmic events. On the sky darkening, cf. Isa 13.10; 34.4; Jer 4.23; Ezek 32.7–8; Am 8.9. In Joel 2.10, the locusts had darkened the sky; now God is the cause. *Calls on the name of the LORD*, i.e., worships the LORD. *Those who escape* and *survivors* probably refer to those not killed in an eschatological battle; cf. Zech 14.16,

3 ^a For then, in those days and at that time, when I restore the fortunes of Judah and Jerusalem, ² I will gather all the nations and bring them down to the valley of Jehoshaphat, and I will enter into judgment with them there, on account of my people and my heritage Israel, because they have scattered them among the nations. They have divided my land, ³ and cast lots for my people, and traded boys for prostitutes, and sold girls for wine, and drunk it down.

⁴ What are you to me, O Tyre and Sidon, and all the regions of Philistia? Are you paying me back for something? If you are paying me back, I will turn your deeds back upon your own heads swiftly and speedily. ⁵ For you have taken my silver and my gold, and have carried my rich treasures into your temples.^b ⁶ You have sold the people of Judah and Jerusalem to the Greeks, removing them far from their own border. ⁷ But now I will rouse them to leave the places to which you have sold them, and I will turn your deeds back upon your own heads. ⁸ I will sell your sons and your daughters into the hand of the people of Judah, and they will sell them to the Sabeans, to a nation far away; for the LORD has spoken.

⁹ Proclaim this among the nations:
Prepare war,^c
  stir up the warriors.
Let all the soldiers draw near,
  let them come up.
¹⁰ Beat your plowshares into swords,
and your pruning hooks into spears;
  let the weakling say, "I am a warrior."

¹¹ Come quickly,^d
  all you nations all around,
  gather yourselves there.
Bring down your warriors, O LORD.
¹² Let the nations rouse themselves,
  and come up to the valley of
      Jehoshaphat;
for there I will sit to judge
  all the neighboring nations.

¹³ Put in the sickle,
  for the harvest is ripe.
Go in, tread,
  for the wine press is full.
The vats overflow,
  for their wickedness is great.

¹⁴ Multitudes, multitudes,
  in the valley of decision!
For the day of the LORD is near
  in the valley of decision.
¹⁵ The sun and the moon are darkened,
  and the stars withdraw their shining.

¹⁶ The LORD roars from Zion,
  and utters his voice from Jerusalem,

^a Ch 4.1 in Heb
^b Or *palaces*
^c Heb *sanctify war*
^d Meaning of Heb uncertain

which includes non-Israelites. **3.1–3:** These verses are probably poetic. They depict an eschatological tradition that the LORD will judge *the nations*. **2:** *Valley of Jehoshaphat*, probably not the Kidron Valley in Jerusalem, but a symbolic place, a plain broad enough for *the nations* to be gathered and defeated, though cf. 2 Chr 20.20–26. **3:** On charges of enslavement, cf. Am 2.6; 8.6. On foreign nations that *cast lots,* see Ob 11; Nah 3.10.

3.4–21: Punishment of Tyre, Sidon, Philistia: In the tradition of oracles against foreign nations, coastal territories are indicted. Verses 4–8 may refer to events dating to the mid-fourth century BCE, a time when these regions could have worked in concert. Mercantile activity pervades these verses, which probably interrupt an original oracle 3.1–3,9–13 (16). **5:** According to 2 Kings 25.13–17, the Babylonians removed the gold from Jerusalem's Temple. **6:** On sale of children to Greece, cf. Ezek 27.13. **7–8:** Judah will requite the coastal regions by selling their children to the *Sabeans,* or the land of Sheba, in the southern Arabian peninsula. **9–13:** The oracle begun in vv. 1–3 resumes. Plural imperative verbs predominate in vv. 9–11, though speakers and audiences are ambiguous. The nations, or perhaps the divine council, are commanded to prepare for war. Verse 11b is directed to the LORD whereas in v. 12 the deity is speaking; v. 13 is addressed either to the divine council or to Israel. **12:** *Jehoshaphat* is a wordplay on *judge* (Heb "shaphat"). **13:** Images of fertility, as in ch 2, reappear. **14–21:** A series of poetic fragments (vv. 14–15,16,17,18,19–21) now ensues. **14–15:** The motif of darkening before the Day of the LORD appears echoes 2.30–31; cf. 2.1–2n. The motif of *valley* (see 3.2,12) may explain why this oracle appears here. **16a:** This part of the verse is identical with Am 1.2 and may explain why these two books are situated next

and the heavens and the earth
    shake.
But the Lord is a refuge for his people,
    a stronghold for the people of
        Israel.

[17] So you shall know that I, the Lord your
        God,
    dwell in Zion, my holy mountain.
And Jerusalem shall be holy,
    and strangers shall never again pass
        through it.

[18] In that day
the mountains shall drip sweet wine,
    the hills shall flow with milk,
and all the stream beds of Judah
    shall flow with water;

a fountain shall come forth from the house
    of the Lord
    and water the Wadi Shittim.

[19] Egypt shall become a desolation
    and Edom a desolate wilderness,
because of the violence done to the people
    of Judah,
    in whose land they have shed innocent
        blood.
[20] But Judah shall be inhabited forever,
    and Jerusalem to all generations.
[21] I will avenge their blood, and I will not
    clear the guilty,[a]
    for the Lord dwells in Zion.

a   Gk Syr: Heb *I will hold innocent their blood that I
have not held innocent*

to each other; see the Introduction. **17:** *You shall know*, cf. 2.27. **18:** The first part of this verse is almost identical
with the last part of Am 9:13. For such preternatural fertility, cf. Isa 65.17–25; Zech 14.6–11. On a *fountain* and
river flowing from the temple, see Ezek 47.1–12; Zech 14.8. *Wadi Shittim*, literally "Wadi of Acacias"; as with the
valley of Jehoshaphat (v. 12), the location is unknown. It may symbolize fertility. **19–21:** A final punitive oracle
against Egypt and Edom (cf. Ob; Ps 137; Mal 1.3–4; Sir 50.26), an unusual combination of an empire and a small
state. That the Lord dwells in or is located at Zion is an important motif near the end of the book (vv. 16,17,18,21).

AMOS

NAME, AUTHORSHIP, DATE OF COMPOSITION, AND HISTORICAL CONTEXT

The book of Amos is a compilation of sayings attributed to the prophet Amos, who was active in the first half of the eighth century BCE, during the long and peaceful reigns of Jeroboam II of Israel (788–747; Am 1.1) and Uzziah of Judah (785–733). In this period, Israel attained a height of territorial expansion and national prosperity never again reached. At the same time, this prosperity led to gross inequities between urban elites and the poor. Through manipulation of debt and credit, wealthy landowners amassed capital and estates at the expense of small farmers. The smallest debt served as the thin end of a wedge that lenders could use to separate farmers from their patrimonial farms and personal liberty.

Into this scene stepped Amos (of Tekoa, a small village in Judah), who was himself a farmer and herder, and was probably active during the decade 760–750 BCE. Amos denounced the society of the Northern Kingdom, Israel, in vivid language, bitterly describing the decadent opulence, immorality, and smug piety of elites who "trample the head of the poor into the dust of the earth" (2.7). Amos's program, in contrast, called for "justice" and "righteousness" (5.7,24; 6.12), terms that connote social equality and concern for the disadvantaged (Isa 5.7; Mic 6.8).

The narrative about Amos's encounter with Amaziah (7.1–7) and the superscription (1.1) yield the only portrait of the prophet. A native of the Southern Kingdom of Judah who raised livestock and tended fruit trees, Amos prophesied to and in the Northern Kingdom of Israel. At the royal sanctuary of Bethel (7.13), his bitter invective, voiced as divine word ("I hate, I despise your festivals," 5.21) no doubt scandalized pilgrims from Samaria, capital of the Northern Kingdom. His confrontation with Amaziah remains one of the unforgettable scenes in biblical prophecy. Expelled from Bethel and commanded not to prophesy there again, Amos perhaps returned to Judah where he, or like-minded scribes, wrote down the essence of his public preaching in substantially its present form.

Although the reigns of Jeroboam II and Uzziah were relatively peaceful and prosperous in Israel and Judah, the region experienced calamitous upheaval shortly thereafter when Tiglath-pileser III assumed the throne in Assyria (745–727). He began the period of Assyria's greatest expansion in the west, including conquering the smaller kingdoms of Syria-Palestine. His successors, Shalmaneser V (727–722) and Sargon II (722–705), invaded the Northern Kingdom and conquered Samaria in 722. Within a few decades of Amos's prophetic activity, the Northern Kingdom saw devastation and destruction which made his foreboding words all the more sobering.

CANONICAL STATUS AND LOCATION IN CANON

Amos's prophetic career was roughly contemporaneous with that of Hosea, though Amos probably preceded him. Chronologically, then, Amos inaugurated the era of classical prophecy. In some ancient manuscript traditions (the Septuagint [LXX], the ancient Greek translation of the Hebrew Bible), the book of Amos directly follows Hosea. The traditional arrangement of the Book of the Twelve in the Masoretic Text and in English translations, however, is based not solely on chronology but often on specific verbal similarities or catchwords that link the end of one book to the beginning of the next. Amos is linked to the preceding book of Joel by identical phrases (see Joel 3.16a and Am 1.2a) and to the following book of Obadiah by a similar subject (Edom in Am 9.12 and in Ob 1).

STRUCTURE, CONTENTS, AND GUIDE TO READING

The book of Amos has three major parts: chs 1–2 are presented as a single speech, an ethical tour of the region from the divine perspective, which climaxes in judgment on Israel itself; chs 3–6 are the least unified section, a collection of short prophetic sayings indicting Israel for sin and injustice; chs 7–9 contain the visions of Amos, as well as the Amaziah narrative (7.10–17) and a final speech of comfort (9.11–15) addressed not to Israel but to Judah. The best approach for readers is to follow the sequence of the book itself. The book contains a variety of material. Some of Amos's sayings are presented as messenger speeches ("thus says the LORD"), others as visions ("This is what the LORD showed me"), especially in chs 7–9. Amos, in a legal style of indictment followed by punishment ("therefore . . ."), announced judgments (e.g., 1.3–2.16), delivered funeral orations (e.g.,

5.1–2), and exhortations (e.g., 5.6). He rarely encouraged (but see 9.11–15 and the notes there). In addition to the above types of prophetic sayings, the book contains three fragments from a hymn (4.13; 5.8–9; 9.5–6) and one narrative about Amos's encounter with Amaziah, priest of the Northern Kingdom's royal sanctuary at Bethel (7.10–17).

INTERPRETATION

Against the background of Israelite tradition about "the Day of the LORD," occasions celebrated from the past and eagerly anticipated in the future when the LORD dramatically intervenes in human affairs, Amos announced that such a day was imminent. This time, however, the fortified palaces and temples of Israel would be leveled along with those of Israel's rival nations (1.3–2.3) when God executed the divine version of "justice and righteousness." Israel's covenant with God (3.2) did not absolve it from this ethical standard, which Amos, in so many words, universalized (9.7–8). Though Amos affirmed the special quality of God's relationship with Israel (9.8), he stressed that it entailed a special ethical responsibility (3.1). The agent of this divine punishment would be the Assyrian army (Isa 10.5–11). The frequent references to exile in Amos (e.g., 3.11; 6.7; 7.17) reflect a grim threat: the Assyrian imperial practice of deporting and transplanting conquered peoples.

Amos described himself as "a herdsman, and a dresser of sycamore trees" (7.14). The latter tree is not the same as a North American "sycamore" (*Platanus occidentalis*), but a type of wild fig tree (*Ficus sycomorus*). These wild figs were gathered by poor people. The small fruit of this tree was inferior to that from the domesticated fig tree (*Ficus carica*). By "dressing" or gashing the small fruit of this tree, Amos and his cohorts hastened their ripening. This single, vivid detail about Amos's background in 7.14 speaks volumes about the prophet's ethics and harsh tone. It explains his solidarity with the poor (2.6–7; 5.11; 8.4) who literally "scratched out" a living in rural Judah and Ephraim, desperate for any harvest, however sparse and bitter. As noted above, Amos rebuked far more often than he comforted. This arborist with his knife understood that pruning was required for revitalization and new growth. Amos lashed out at the elite's prosperity gained at the expense of the poor, upsetting their "baskets of summer fruit" (8.1–2).

The book of Amos begins and ends with references to an earthquake (1.1 and the images of shaking in 9.1–9). The exact year is unknown (760 has been proposed), but some archaeological evidence of a catastrophe exists. Did this earthquake, so severe that it was recalled centuries later (Zech 14.5), offer cosmic validation of Amos's preaching? One cannot know. Still, even today one can feel the aftershocks of Amos, the first in a brilliant succession of biblical prophets whose words, now preserved in written form, have left their indelible stamp on later thought about God and human history.

Gregory Mobley

1 The words of Amos, who was among the shepherds of Tekoa, which he saw concerning Israel in the days of King Uzziah of Judah and in the days of King Jeroboam son of Joash of Israel, two years[a] before the earthquake. [2] And he said:

The LORD roars from Zion,
  and utters his voice from
    Jerusalem;
the pastures of the shepherds wither,
  and the top of Carmel dries up.

[3] Thus says the LORD:
For three transgressions of Damascus,
  and for four, I will not revoke the
    punishment;[b]
because they have threshed Gilead
  with threshing sledges of iron.
[4] So I will send a fire on the house of
    Hazael,
  and it shall devour the strongholds of
    Ben-hadad.

[5] I will break the gate bars of Damascus,
  and cut off the inhabitants from the
    Valley of Aven,
and the one who holds the scepter from
    Beth-eden;
and the people of Aram shall go into
    exile to Kir,
              says the LORD.

[6] Thus says the LORD:
For three transgressions of Gaza,
  and for four, I will not revoke the
    punishment;[b]
because they carried into exile entire
    communities,
  to hand them over to Edom.
[7] So I will send a fire on the wall of
    Gaza,
  fire that shall devour its strongholds.

a Or *during two years*
b Heb *cause it to return*

1.1: Superscription. *Amos* means "one supported" (by the Lord). *Among the shepherds,* the word translated "shepherds" probably denotes a herder or owner of large flocks rather than a hired worker; the same word is translated "sheepbreeder" in 2 Kings 3.4, its only other occurrence. See also 7.14–15. *Tekoa* was a town in Judah, ca. 16 km (10 mi) south of Jerusalem. *He saw,* see Nah 1.1; visions were common among prophets from Judah (e.g., Isaiah and Ezekiel). *Uzziah* reigned over the Southern Kingdom 785–733 BCE. *Jeroboam* II reigned over the Northern Kingdom 788–747. The *earthquake,* mentioned again in Zech 14.5, cannot be precisely dated.

1.2–2.16: A speech against the nations. A common feature of Israelite prophecy was the indictment of foreign nations, which implied the Lord's universal sovereignty. In general, Amos indicts the neighboring peoples for ethical transgressions on the order of war crimes. The prophet condemns their actions not only against Israel and Judah, but against other neighboring peoples. Thus, the scope of God's concern spans the larger international community. Near the end of this section, when Amos addresses Judah and Israel, the ethical standard is more exacting. There is another way to look at the indictments directed toward these foreign nations. All the nations discussed were either subject to or allies of the Davidic and Solomonic monarchy, and therefore bound by treaties to which the Lord would have been a witness and now was acting as enforcer of the treaty curses. **1.2:** This introductory verse occurs in similar form in Joel 3.16 (cf. Jer 25.30). *The LORD roars,* Amos uses the image of God as lion again in 3.4,8. The sequence *from Jerusalem . . .* (to) *Carmel* traces the trajectory of the book as Amos, a southerner from the vicinity of Jerusalem, addresses the Northern Kingdom, whose northwest boundary was Mt. Carmel (see 9.3n.). **3,6,8, etc.:** *Thus says the LORD* and the conclusion *says the LORD* are standard formulas identifying prophetic oracles. The idiom *for three . . . and for four* indicates "more than enough" (Prov 30.18; Job 33.14).

1.3–5: Against Damascus (cf. Isa 17.1–3; Jer 49.23–27; Zech 9.1–4). *Damascus* was the capital of Syria (Aram). *They have threshed Gilead,* Gilead was Israelite territory in northern Transjordan, particularly vulnerable to Syrian aggression (2 Kings 10.32–33); threshing was often used to symbolize martial brutality (Isa 41.15; Mic 4.13). *Hazael* and *Ben-hadad* II were Syrian rulers (2 Kings 13.3). *The Valley of Aven* probably refers to the Beqa region between the Lebanon and Anti-Lebanon ranges. *Beth-eden,* known in Assyrian records as Bitidini, was a city-state on the Euphrates, between the Lebanon and Anti-Lebanon ranges. *Kir* is the place of Syrian origins (9.7) and exile (2 Kings 16.9); its precise location is unknown.

1.6–8: Against Philistia. Four cities of the Philistine pentapolis (1 Sam 6.17) on the southeast coast of the Mediterranean are condemned for their slave traffic with Edom (2 Chr 21.16–17; Joel 3.4–8; Zeph 2.4–7).

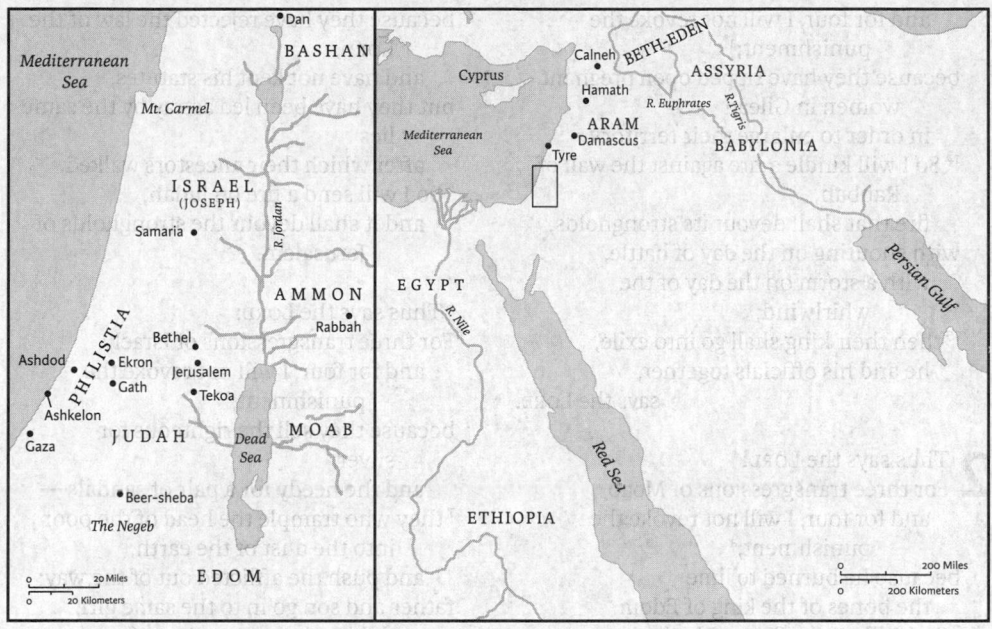

Chs 1–2: Places mentioned in the oracles against foreign nations.

8 I will cut off the inhabitants from Ashdod,
 and the one who holds the scepter from
  Ashkelon;
I will turn my hand against Ekron,
 and the remnant of the Philistines shall
  perish,
            says the Lord GOD.

9 Thus says the LORD:
For three transgressions of Tyre,
 and for four, I will not revoke the
  punishment;[a]
because they delivered entire communities
  over to Edom,
 and did not remember the covenant of
  kinship.
10 So I will send a fire on the wall of Tyre,
 fire that shall devour its strongholds.

11 Thus says the LORD:
For three transgressions of Edom,
 and for four, I will not revoke the
  punishment;[a]
because he pursued his brother with the
  sword
 and cast off all pity;
he maintained his anger perpetually,[b]
 and kept his wrath[c] forever.
12 So I will send a fire on Teman,
 and it shall devour the strongholds of
  Bozrah.

13 Thus says the LORD:
For three transgressions of the Ammonites,

a Heb *cause it to return*
b Syr Vg: Heb *and his anger tore perpetually*
c Gk Syr Vg: Heb *and his wrath kept*

1.9–10: Against Tyre (see Joel 3.4–8). Tyre was a Phoenician seaport north of Israel. *Covenant of kinship* (lit. "covenant of brothers"), cf. 1 Kings 5.12; 9.13.

1.11–12: Against Edom (Isa 34; Joel 3.19; Ezek 25.12). *Edom,* located south and east of the Dead Sea, was a perennial rival of neighboring Judah, especially in the exilic and postexilic era (Ps 137.7; Obadiah). The term *his brother,* i.e., Judah (Mal 1.2), draws on the ancient tradition of kinship between Jacob and Esau (Esau was "the father of Edom," Gen 36.43) and also connotes a treaty relationship (see vv. 9–10n.). *Teman,* a synonym for Edom. *Bozrah,* modern Buseirah, 40 km (25 mi) south of the Dead Sea.

1.13–15: Against Ammon (Zeph 2.8–11), which is condemned for atrocities against Israelites to its immediate north, in *Gilead. Rabbah,* the Ammonite capital (modern Amman).

and for four, I will not revoke the
    punishment;[a]
because they have ripped open pregnant
    women in Gilead
in order to enlarge their territory.
[14] So I will kindle a fire against the wall of
    Rabbah,
    fire that shall devour its strongholds,
with shouting on the day of battle,
    with a storm on the day of the
        whirlwind;
[15] then their king shall go into exile,
    he and his officials together,
                    says the LORD.

2 Thus says the LORD:
    For three transgressions of Moab,
        and for four, I will not revoke the
            punishment;[a]
because he burned to lime
    the bones of the king of Edom.
[2] So I will send a fire on Moab,
    and it shall devour the strongholds of
        Kerioth,
and Moab shall die amid uproar,
    amid shouting and the sound of the
        trumpet;
[3] I will cut off the ruler from its midst,
    and will kill all its officials with him,
                    says the LORD.

[4] Thus says the LORD:
    For three transgressions of Judah,
        and for four, I will not revoke the
            punishment;[a]

because they have rejected the law of the
    LORD,
    and have not kept his statutes,
but they have been led astray by the same
    lies
    after which their ancestors walked.
[5] So I will send a fire on Judah,
    and it shall devour the strongholds of
        Jerusalem.

[6] Thus says the LORD:
For three transgressions of Israel,
    and for four, I will not revoke the
        punishment;[a]
because they sell the righteous for
    silver,
    and the needy for a pair of sandals—
[7] they who trample the head of the poor
        into the dust of the earth,
    and push the afflicted out of the way;
father and son go in to the same girl,
    so that my holy name is profaned;
[8] they lay themselves down beside every
    altar
    on garments taken in pledge;
and in the house of their God they drink
    wine bought with fines they imposed.

[9] Yet I destroyed the Amorite before
    them,
    whose height was like the height of
        cedars,

---

[a] Heb *cause it to return*

2.1–3: Against Moab, Israel's neighbor and rival southeast of the Jordan (Isa 15.1–16.14). *Burned to lime,* for the practice of desecrating a corpse through disinterment and incineration, see 2 Kings 23.16–20; Isa 33.12. *Kerioth,* location uncertain; see Jer 48.24,41.

2.4–5: Against Judah. Because of similarities between its language and that of the Deuteronomistic Reform (e.g., 2 Kings 17.15) in the late seventh century, many scholars consider this oracle a later addition, but it is consistent with Amos's view that all nations stand accountable before God.

2.6–16: Against Israel. Amos's ethical tour finally reaches home, where it surely shocked its audience. Israel can refer both to the Northern Kingdom, as the counterpart of Judah (2.4), and to the entire people that God brought out of Egypt (see 2.10; 3.1). Using the same literary form, Amos shows that Israel stands under divine judgment too, for oppression of the poor and for immorality. **6:** *They sell the righteous . . . and the needy* into debt slavery. **7:** *Same girl* probably does not refer to ritual prostitutes but to young unmarried women who, like the "needy" and the *poor,* were being exploited. **8:** *Garments taken in pledge,* see the prohibitions in Ex 22.25; Deut 24.17. The exploitation of the poor is especially odious when commodities gained unjustly, the above *garments* and *wine,* were paraded before the deity at the *altar* of *the house of their God.* **9:** *The Amorite . . . whose height,* pre-Israelite inhabitants of Canaan such as the Amorites (see Ezek 16.3) were often depicted as gigantic (Num

and who was as strong as oaks;
I destroyed his fruit above,
and his roots beneath.
[10] Also I brought you up out of the land of
Egypt,
and led you forty years in the wilderness,
to possess the land of the Amorite.
[11] And I raised up some of your children to
be prophets
and some of your youths to be
nazirites.[a]
Is it not indeed so, O people of Israel?
says the LORD.

[12] But you made the nazirites[a] drink wine,
and commanded the prophets,
saying, "You shall not prophesy."

[13] So, I will press you down in your place,
just as a cart presses down
when it is full of sheaves.[b]
[14] Flight shall perish from the swift,
and the strong shall not retain their
strength,
nor shall the mighty save their lives;
[15] those who handle the bow shall not
stand,
and those who are swift of foot shall
not save themselves,
nor shall those who ride horses save
their lives;
[16] and those who are stout of heart among
the mighty
shall flee away naked in that day,
says the LORD.

3 Hear this word that the LORD has spoken
against you, O people of Israel, against
the whole family that I brought up out of the
land of Egypt:
[2] You only have I known
of all the families of the earth;
therefore I will punish you
for all your iniquities.

[3] Do two walk together
unless they have made an
appointment?
[4] Does a lion roar in the forest,
when it has no prey?
Does a young lion cry out from its den,
if it has caught nothing?
[5] Does a bird fall into a snare on the
earth,
when there is no trap for it?
Does a snare spring up from the ground,
when it has taken nothing?
[6] Is a trumpet blown in a city,
and the people are not afraid?
Does disaster befall a city,
unless the LORD has done it?
[7] Surely the Lord GOD does nothing,
without revealing his secret
to his servants the prophets.
[8] The lion has roared;
who will not fear?
The Lord GOD has spoken;
who can but prophesy?

a   That is, *those separated* or *those consecrated*
b   Meaning of Heb uncertain

13.32–33; Deut 1.28). **10:** Deut 1.19–21. In contrast to the preceding indictments, the prophet invokes God's history with Israel as grounds for impending punishment. **11–12:** *Nazirites,* consecrated individuals who undertook vows, including abstinence from wine; Num 6.2; Judg 13.5. **13:** The entire Israelite army is defenseless: archers, infantry, and cavalry. **16:** *Naked,* unarmed and exposed; cf. Isa 20.1–6.

3.1–6.14: Judgment speeches against Israel come in three sections, each with the same opening (3.1; 4.1; 5.1).

3.1–2: A chosen people are held to a higher standard. 2: *You only have I known,* knowledge here refers to a relationship through covenant. The phrase *all the families of the earth* recalls traditions about divine promises to Abram (Gen 12.3) and Moses (Ex 19.4–6; Deut 7.6).

3.3–8: A series of rhetorical questions, which permit only a single response, build to an inescapable conclusion in v. 8b: The call to prophecy, unsolicited, cannot be resisted (7.14–15). Furthermore, the self-evident truths of vv. 1–8a render the audience susceptible to a truth in 8b it would naturally resist: Amos speaks on behalf of the Lord. **4:** *A lion roar,* see 1.2. **6:** *Trumpet,* the shofar, the ram's horn. **7:** *His secret to his servants the prophets,* for positive and negative illustrations of this principle, see, respectively, Gen 18.17–19 and 2 Kings 4.27; cf. 2 Kings 4.13. Because the phrase "his servants the prophets" is Deuteronomistic (see 2 Kings 21.10), and because the verse is in a different form, some scholars consider it a later addition (see 2.3–4n.).

⁹ Proclaim to the strongholds in Ashdod,
  and to the strongholds in the land of
    Egypt,
and say, "Assemble yourselves on Mountª
    Samaria,
  and see what great tumults are within it,
  and what oppressions are in its
    midst."
¹⁰ They do not know how to do right, says
    the Lᴏʀᴅ,
  those who store up violence and
    robbery in their strongholds.
¹¹ Therefore thus says the Lord Gᴏᴅ:
An adversary shall surround the land,
  and strip you of your defense;
  and your strongholds shall be
    plundered.

¹² Thus says the Lᴏʀᴅ: As the shepherd
rescues from the mouth of the lion two legs,
or a piece of an ear, so shall the people of Israel who live in Samaria be rescued, with the
corner of a couch and partᵇ of a bed.

¹³ Hear, and testify against the house of
    Jacob,
  says the Lord Gᴏᴅ, the God of hosts:
¹⁴ On the day I punish Israel for its
    transgressions,
  I will punish the altars of Bethel,

and the horns of the altar shall be cut
    off
  and fall to the ground.
¹⁵ I will tear down the winter house as well
    as the summer house;
  and the houses of ivory shall perish,
  and the great housesᶜ shall come to an
    end,
                          says the Lᴏʀᴅ.

4 Hear this word, you cows of Bashan
  who are on Mount Samaria,
who oppress the poor, who crush the
    needy,
  who say to their husbands, "Bring
    something to drink!"
² The Lord Gᴏᴅ has sworn by his
    holiness:
  The time is surely coming upon you,
when they shall take you away with
    hooks,
  even the last of you with fishhooks.
³ Through breaches in the wall you shall
    leave,

ᵃ Gk Syr: Heb *the mountains of*
ᵇ Meaning of Heb uncertain
ᶜ Or *many houses*

3.9–15: Neighboring nations are invited to witness the Lord's complaint against the elites of Israelite society, who dwelt in *strongholds*, massive fortified palaces. **9:** *Ashdod*, a Philistine city on the Mediterranean coast;
see 1.6–8. **11:** God addresses Samaria directly and promises the coming of an *adversary*, though whether the
figure is a divine or human agent of God's judgment is difficult to say (cf. Isa 10.5; Jer 25.8; Lam 2.5). **12:** As Amos,
a pastoralist himself (7.14) knew, a *shepherd* was absolved of blame for loss of livestock if there were even small
remains, *legs, or a piece of an ear*, of a predator's attack. With sarcasm, Amos suggests that after the divine punishment, announced by the roar of a lion (1.2; 3.8), only scraps would remain from the palaces of Samaria. Thus,
Israel's remains do not signify the survival of a righteous remnant, but rather they justify God's judgment, just
as the remains of an animal's carcass vindicate the shepherd (Ex 22.13). **14:** *Bethel* was near the southern border
of the Northern Kingdom, ca. 18 km (11 mi) north of Jerusalem. For Bethel as a shrine, see 1 Kings 12.25–30; for
Amos and *Bethel*, see 4.4; 5.5–6; 7.10–13. *The horns of the altar,* the projections at the corners of an altar had
special significance; see Ex 21.14; 1 Kings 2.28–34. **15:** The Lord will raze the tokens of conspicuous Israelite
consumption: *the winter house, the summer house,* and the *houses* decorated with carved *ivory* inlay, such as the
royal palace in Samaria built by Ahab (1 Kings 22.39).

4.1–3: Israel's luxurious excesses. Wealthy and greedy women of Samaria would be punished along with
their husbands. **1:** *Cows of Bashan,* is not necessarily a derogatory remark against the prosperous women who
are identified with prized animal's from Bashan, a fertile region in the northern Transjordan renowned for its
cattle (Ps 22.12). However, the prophet suggests that the wealthy women make their husbands the instruments
of their oppressive greed. **2:** *Hooks . . . fishhooks,* the terms are obscure but perhaps refer to the practice of leading away prisoners with hooks through their noses, as depicted in ancient Near Eastern art (cf. Isa 37.29). **3:**
Straight ahead, with the city walls in ruins, the captives will be easily taken away.

each one straight ahead;
and you shall be flung out into
Harmon,[a]
      says the LORD.
4 Come to Bethel—and transgress;
to Gilgal—and multiply
transgression;
bring your sacrifices every morning,
your tithes every three days;
5 bring a thank offering of leavened bread,
and proclaim freewill offerings, publish
them;
for so you love to do, O people of
Israel!
      says the Lord GOD.

6 I gave you cleanness of teeth in all your
cities,
and lack of bread in all your places,
yet you did not return to me,
      says the LORD.

7 And I also withheld the rain from you
when there were still three months to
the harvest;
I would send rain on one city,
and send no rain on another city;
one field would be rained upon,
and the field on which it did not rain
withered;
8 so two or three towns wandered to one
town
to drink water, and were not satisfied;
yet you did not return to me,
      says the LORD.

9 I struck you with blight and mildew;
I laid waste[b] your gardens and your
vineyards;

the locust devoured your fig trees and
your olive trees;
yet you did not return to me,
      says the LORD.

10 I sent among you a pestilence after the
manner of Egypt;
I killed your young men with the sword;
I carried away your horses;[c]
and I made the stench of your camp go
up into your nostrils;
yet you did not return to me,
      says the LORD.

11 I overthrew some of you,
as when God overthrew Sodom and
Gomorrah,
and you were like a brand snatched
from the fire;
yet you did not return to me,
      says the LORD.

12 Therefore thus I will do to you,
O Israel;
because I will do this to you,
prepare to meet your God, O Israel!

13 For lo, the one who forms the
mountains, creates the wind,
reveals his thoughts to mortals,
makes the morning darkness,
and treads on the heights of the
earth—
the LORD, the God of hosts, is his name!

a Meaning of Heb uncertain
b Cn: Heb the multitude of
c Heb with the captivity of your horses

4.4–5: Israel's piety is satirized. 4: *Bethel*, see 3.14n. *Gilgal*, a venerable Israelite shrine near Jericho (e.g., Josh 4.20; 10.43; 1 Sam 7.16), condemned by Amos (5.5) and his contemporary Hosea (Hos 4.15; 9.15; 12.11). The ritual practices listed here are prescribed elsewhere; for the morning sacrifice, see Ex 29.29; *tithes,* see Lev 27.30–32; Deut 14.28–29; *thank offering of leavened bread,* see Lev 7.13; *freewill offerings,* see Num 15.3. Note the association of tithes with Bethel in Gen 28.22.

4.6–13: Israel has ignored the divine warnings issued through plagues. These plagues typify the curses a treaty partner brought on itself through disobedience. Israel's covenantal documents contained such curses (Lev 26.14–39; Deut 28.15–68). 6: *Cleanness of teeth,* i.e., famine. 10: *A pestilence after the manner of Egypt,* Ex 9.3–7,15. *The stench* of unburied corpses, as in Isa 34.3. 11: The verb *overthrew* here could refer to an earthquake, as it seems to in Gen 19.25,29, in which the destruction of *Sodom and Gomorrah* is described. 13: The first of three doxologies interspersed throughout Amos (5.8–9; 9.5–6). These hymn-like sections emphasize that the God Israel encounters in judgment is the creator.

5 Hear this word that I take up over you in lamentation, O house of Israel:
² Fallen, no more to rise,
is maiden Israel;
forsaken on her land,
with no one to raise her up.

³ For thus says the Lord GOD:
The city that marched out a thousand
shall have a hundred left,
and that which marched out a hundred
shall have ten left.ᵃ

⁴ For thus says the LORD to the house of
Israel:
Seek me and live;
⁵ but do not seek Bethel,
and do not enter into Gilgal
or cross over to Beer-sheba;
for Gilgal shall surely go into exile,
and Bethel shall come to nothing.

⁶ Seek the LORD and live,
or he will break out against the house of
Joseph like fire,
and it will devour Bethel, with no one to
quench it.
⁷ Ah, you that turn justice to wormwood,
and bring righteousness to the
ground!

⁸ The one who made the Pleiades and Orion,
and turns deep darkness into the
morning,
and darkens the day into night,

who calls for the waters of the sea,
and pours them out on the surface of
the earth,
the LORD is his name,
⁹ who makes destruction flash out against
the strong,
so that destruction comes upon the
fortress.

¹⁰ They hate the one who reproves in the
gate,
and they abhor the one who speaks the
truth.
¹¹ Therefore because you trample on the
poor
and take from them levies of grain,
you have built houses of hewn stone,
but you shall not live in them;
you have planted pleasant vineyards,
but you shall not drink their wine.
¹² For I know how many are your
transgressions,
and how great are your sins—
you who afflict the righteous, who take a
bribe,
and push aside the needy in the gate.
¹³ Therefore the prudent will keep silent in
such a time;
for it is an evil time.

ᵃ Heb adds *to the house of Israel*

5.1–3: Lament for Israel. Among the forms of prophetic speech was the lament; hearing one's own funeral speech delivered by a prophet must have had a sobering effect (cf. Jer 9.17–22).

5.4–7: A plea for repentance. Though the lament form was meant to convey a sense of inevitable judgment, there is yet time to *seek the LORD and live,* an exhortation to turn to God or abide by God's precepts (Ps 24.6; Prov 28.5; Isa 55.6). The prophet enjoins Israel to *seek* the Lord, not the sanctuaries of the Lord. **5:** For *Bethel* and *Gilgal,* see 3.14n.; 4.4n. *Beer-sheba,* though in the Negeb to the far south, was a shrine associated with Israel's ancestors (Gen 21.25–31; 26.23; 46.1–4) and would have attracted pilgrims from the north. **6:** *House of Joseph,* i.e., the Northern Kingdom. Its two main parts were Ephraim and Manasseh, named for the sons of Joseph (Gen 41.50–52; 48). **7:** The dried leaves of *wormwood* were aromatic and bitter; here, injustice leads to bitterness (see 6.12).

5.8–9: The second doxology (see 4.13n.). **8:** *Pleiades* and *Orion* also occur together in Job 9.9; 38.31. Though astral bodies could inspire illicit worship (e.g., 2 Kings 23.5), to the faithful they testified to God's power (e.g., Ps 8.3).

5.10–17: Amos condemns a corrupt legal system. 10–13: At the very site of legal proceedings, the city *gate,* the truth is rejected, the poor are plundered, and witnesses are bribed. See Prov 10.19. **11:** A futility curse, in which the connections between actions and their expected effects are broken; cf. Deut 28.30–31,38–46; Mic

¹⁴ Seek good and not evil,
 that you may live;
and so the Lord, the God of hosts, will be
 with you,
 just as you have said.
¹⁵ Hate evil and love good,
 and establish justice in the gate;
it may be that the Lord, the God of hosts,
 will be gracious to the remnant of
 Joseph.

¹⁶ Therefore thus says the Lord, the God of
 hosts, the Lord:
In all the squares there shall be wailing;
 and in all the streets they shall say,
 "Alas! alas!"
They shall call the farmers to mourning,
 and those skilled in lamentation, to
 wailing;
¹⁷ in all the vineyards there shall be
 wailing,
 for I will pass through the midst
 of you,
 says the Lord.

¹⁸ Alas for you who desire the day of the
 Lord!
Why do you want the day of the Lord?
It is darkness, not light;
 ¹⁹ as if someone fled from a lion,
 and was met by a bear;

or went into the house and rested a hand
 against the wall,
 and was bitten by a snake.
²⁰ Is not the day of the Lord darkness, not
 light,
 and gloom with no brightness in it?

²¹ I hate, I despise your festivals,
 and I take no delight in your solemn
 assemblies.
²² Even though you offer me your burnt
 offerings and grain offerings,
 I will not accept them;
and the offerings of well-being of your
 fatted animals
 I will not look upon.
²³ Take away from me the noise of your
 songs;
 I will not listen to the melody of your
 harps.
²⁴ But let justice roll down like waters,
 and righteousness like an ever-flowing
 stream.

²⁵ Did you bring to me sacrifices and offer-
ings the forty years in the wilderness, O house
of Israel? ²⁶ You shall take up Sakkuth your
king, and Kaiwan your star-god, your images,^a
which you made for yourselves; ²⁷ therefore I

---

a Heb *your images, your star-god*

6.14–15; Zeph 1.13. **12:** Cf. 2.6–7. **14–15:** Another plea for repentance; see vv. 4–7; *Joseph*, see 5.6n. **16–17:** Staying with the images of village life and returning to the motif of lament (5.1–3), Amos depicts the divine punishment for injustice. **16:** *Skilled in lamentation*, professional mourners; see Jer 9.17–21; Ezek 32.16; Eccl 12.5; 2 Chr 35.25.

5.18–6.14: A series of "woe" sayings (5.18–25; 6.1–3; 6.4–14) complete the section of judgment speeches.

5.18–20: The Day of the Lord, in which Israelites expected to be vindicated against their enemies, will be, as depicted already in 1.1–2.16, a day when Israel too receives its judgment. Amos's profound reinterpretation of this popular concept is among his most significant contributions. See also Isa 13.6,9; Jer 46.10; Joel 2.1–2; Mal 4.5.

5.21–27: The Lord delights not in abundance of festivals and sacrifices but in justice and righteousness. V. 24 expresses a central message of the prophets; see also Mic 6.6–8. **21–23:** The language is harsh. *Festivals* refers to the three pilgrimage feasts (Ex 23.14–17; 34.18,22–23; Deut 16.16), as does *solemn assemblies* (Lev 23.36; Deut 16.8). The sacrifices in v. 22 were prescribed; see, e.g., Lev 7.8–14. *Songs* is often used of hymns (see 8.3), such as the psalms (e.g., see title of Ps 120). For a similar view, see Isa 1.11–17. **24:** An *ever-flowing stream* is a riverbed that never fails, as opposed to a wadi, common in Israel's landscape, which had run-off water only in the rainy season. **25:** As in Jeremiah (2.2–3) and Hosea (2.14–20; 9.10), the period in the wilderness after the Exodus is recalled as an ideal. Like Jer 7.21–23, the rhetorical question presumes that sacrifice was not a compo-nent of Israel's religious system immediately after the Exodus. This is inconsistent with other biblical traditions (contrast Ex 20–Num 10). **26:** *Sakkuth* and *Kaiwan* (Saturn) designate known Assyrian deities. *Sakkuth* may be the same as the "Succoth" whose cult the Babylonians established in Samaria after its fall (2 Kings 17.30). **27:** *Damascus*, 1.3–5n.

will take you into exile beyond Damascus, says the LORD, whose name is the God of hosts.

6 Alas for those who are at ease in Zion,
and for those who feel secure on Mount
Samaria,
the notables of the first of the nations,
to whom the house of Israel resorts!
2 Cross over to Calneh, and see;
from there go to Hamath the great;
then go down to Gath of the Philistines.
Are you better[a] than these kingdoms?
Or is your[b] territory greater than their[c]
territory,
3 O you that put far away the evil day,
and bring near a reign of violence?

4 Alas for those who lie on beds of ivory,
and lounge on their couches,
and eat lambs from the flock,
and calves from the stall;
5 who sing idle songs to the sound of the
harp,
and like David improvise on
instruments of music;
6 who drink wine from bowls,
and anoint themselves with the finest
oils,
but are not grieved over the ruin of
Joseph!
7 Therefore they shall now be the first to go
into exile,
and the revelry of the loungers shall
pass away.

8 The Lord GOD has sworn by himself
(says the LORD, the God of hosts):

I abhor the pride of Jacob
and hate his strongholds;
and I will deliver up the city and all that
is in it.

9 If ten people remain in one house, they shall die. 10 And if a relative, one who burns the dead,[d] shall take up the body to bring it out of the house, and shall say to someone in the innermost parts of the house, "Is anyone else with you?" the answer will come, "No." Then the relative[e] shall say, "Hush! We must not mention the name of the LORD."

11 See, the LORD commands,
and the great house shall be shattered
to bits,
and the little house to pieces.
12 Do horses run on rocks?
Does one plow the sea with oxen?[f]
But you have turned justice into
poison
and the fruit of righteousness into
wormwood—
13 you who rejoice in Lo-debar,[g]
who say, "Have we not by our own
strength
taken Karnaim[h] for ourselves?"

a Or *Are they better*
b Heb *their*
c Heb *your*
d Or *who makes a burning for him*
e Heb *he*
f Or *Does one plow them with oxen*
g Or *in a thing of nothingness*
h Or *horns*

6.1–7: An indictment of conspicuous consumption. 1: Amos targets elite classes of the capitals of both the South (*Zion*, i.e., Jerusalem) and the North (*Mount Samaria*). **2:** Cf. Isa 10.9–11. *Calneh* and *Hamath* were prosperous cities of Syria, conquered by the Assyrians in 738 BCE; the allusion to *Gath*, the only Philistine city unmentioned in 1.6–8, could refer to its defeat at the hands of Syria (2 Kings 12.18) or Judah (2 Chr 26.6), or its conquest by the Assyrians in 711. **4:** *Beds of ivory*, see 3.15n. Over 500 ivory fragments have been excavated from the site of Samaria. **5:** *David*, 1 Sam 16.23; 1 Chr 23.5; Neh 12.36. **6–7:** Joseph, see 5.6n. The elites of Samaria, accustomed to the choicest products, will be the first chosen for deportation by the Assyrians. **7:** The *revelry* (Heb "marzeah") was a social and funerary ritual banquet of Canaanite origin; cf. Jer 16.5.

6.8–14: Judgment on Israel. *Jacob*, here referring to the Northern Kingdom. The house of Israel, both as a sociopolitical body and as representative of its palatial *strongholds*, is doomed. **10:** *Burns the dead* probably refers to practices employed to stop the spread of infection. In this extremity, the few survivors dare not *mention the name of the LORD*, out of fear of inviting their own destruction from a deity still intent on destruction. **12:** Israel's legal and moral machinations are a perversion bordering on the absurd. *Wormwood*, see 5.7n. **13:** *Lo-debar* and *Karnaim* are two cities east of the Jordan recovered for Israel by Jeroboam II (2 Kings 14.25). The

¹⁴ Indeed, I am raising up against you a
     nation,
     O house of Israel, says the LORD, the
         God of hosts,
and they shall oppress you from Lebo-
         hamath
     to the Wadi Arabah.

7 This is what the Lord GOD showed me:
     he was forming locusts at the time the
latter growth began to sprout (it was the latter
growth after the king's mowings). ² When they
had finished eating the grass of the land, I said,
"O Lord GOD, forgive, I beg you!
     How can Jacob stand?
     He is so small!"
³ The LORD relented concerning this;
     "It shall not be," said the LORD.

⁴ This is what the Lord GOD showed me:
the Lord GOD was calling for a shower of fire,ᵃ
and it devoured the great deep and was eating
up the land. ⁵ Then I said,
"O Lord GOD, cease, I beg you!
     How can Jacob stand?
     He is so small!"

⁶ The LORD relented concerning this;
     "This also shall not be," said the Lord
         GOD.

⁷ This is what he showed me: the Lord was
standing beside a wall built with a plumb
line, with a plumb line in his hand. ⁸ And the
LORD said to me, "Amos, what do you see?"
And I said, "A plumb line." Then the Lord
said,
"See, I am setting a plumb line
     in the midst of my people Israel;
     I will never again pass them by;
⁹ the high places of Isaac shall be made
         desolate,
     and the sanctuaries of Israel shall be
         laid waste,
     and I will rise against the house of
         Jeroboam with the sword."

¹⁰ Then Amaziah, the priest of Bethel, sent
to King Jeroboam of Israel, saying, "Amos
has conspired against you in the very center

ᵃ Or *for a judgment by fire*

verse puns on the names of the cities, which mean "No-thing" and "Horns [i.e., strength]," respectively. **14:** An
unnamed nation will be the instrument of God's judgement. *From Lebo-hamath to the Wadi Arabah,* the farthest
limits of Israelite territory (see 2 Kings 14.25), from the Orontes Valley in Lebanon to the north to the Rift Valley
in the southeast.

  7.1–9.15: The visions of Amos. The final section of the book consists of accounts and interpretations of
five visions (7.1–3; 7.4–6; 7.7–9; 8.1–3; 9.1–6), a biographical account about the prophet (7.10–17), and prophetic
oracles (8.4–14; 9.5–15).

  7.1–9: A series of three visions and attempted intercession. Amos acts as an intercessor on behalf of Israel
(see Gen 18.17; Ex 32.7–14). Yet prophetic intercession, while effective in the short term, will ultimately not deter
God from punishing sinful Israel.

  7.1–3: Judgment by locusts (cf. Joel 1.2–7). **1:** A locust plague at the time of *the latter growth* endangered the
spring planting, just sprouting, after the harvest of the winter grains. **2:** The prophet appeals to God's sense of
proportion: Israel (*Jacob*) is *so small* and, by implication, God is so big (cf. Job 7.20). **3:** *The LORD relented,* God's
mind changed concerning the punishment, although forgiveness is not offered, as Amos requested (see also
Ex 32.14; Joel 2.13; Jon 4.2).

  7.4–6: Judgment by fire. 4: *The great deep,* the cosmic waters under the earth and over the heavens (see Gen
1.2).

  7.7–9: Israel falls short. The *plumb line* (2 Kings 21.13–15), a device for determining the true vertical line of a
structure, reveals that Israel's religious and political institutions do not measure up and will be destroyed; here
the prophet offers no intercessory protest or plea. *High places* were open-air *sanctuaries.* Though acceptable in
earlier eras, Amos and Hosea (10.8) condemned them as places of illicit worship. *Isaac,* a rare designation for the
Northern Kingdom (see v. 16). *House of Jeroboam,* the royal dynasty of Jeroboam II (788–747 BCE).

  7.10–17: Amos and Amaziah. This piece, a narrative illustration of 2.12 in the form of a dramatic encounter between the royal priest and the prophet, the classic outsider, is placed at this point in the book perhaps
because its reference to *King Jeroboam* (v. 10) fits well next to the phrase "house of Jeroboam" (v. 9). Amaziah

of the house of Israel; the land is not able to bear all his words. [11] For thus Amos has said,

'Jeroboam shall die by the sword,
and Israel must go into exile
away from his land.'"

[12] And Amaziah said to Amos, "O seer, go, flee away to the land of Judah, earn your bread there, and prophesy there; [13] but never again prophesy at Bethel, for it is the king's sanctuary, and it is a temple of the kingdom."

[14] Then Amos answered Amaziah, "I am[a] no prophet, nor a prophet's son; but I am[a] a herdsman, and a dresser of sycamore trees, [15] and the LORD took me from following the flock, and the LORD said to me, 'Go, prophesy to my people Israel.'

[16] "Now therefore hear the word of the LORD.

You say, 'Do not prophesy against Israel,
and do not preach against the house of
Isaac.'

[17] Therefore thus says the LORD:

'Your wife shall become a prostitute in the city,
and your sons and your daughters shall fall by the sword,
and your land shall be parceled out by line;
you yourself shall die in an unclean land,

and Israel shall surely go into exile away from its land.'"

8 This is what the Lord GOD showed me—a basket of summer fruit.[b] [2] He said, "Amos, what do you see?" And I said, "A basket of summer fruit."[b] Then the LORD said to me, "The end[c] has come upon my people Israel;
I will never again pass them by.
[3] The songs of the temple[d] shall become wailings in that day,"
                              says the Lord GOD;
"the dead bodies shall be many,
cast out in every place. Be silent!"

[4] Hear this, you that trample on the needy,
and bring to ruin the poor of the land,
[5] saying, "When will the new moon be over so that we may sell grain;
and the sabbath,
so that we may offer wheat for sale?

a   Or *was*
b   Heb *qayits*
c   Heb *qets*
d   Or *palace*

was the official priest of the royal shrine at Bethel (see 3.14n.). **10:** Amos's prophecy equates to treason. **11:** *For thus Amos has said,* Amaziah does not attribute the prophet's words to God. The first utterance Amaziah cites (*Jeroboam shall die . . .*) is the rough but not exact equivalent of 7.9; the second phrase (*Israel must go . . .*) of 4.2–3; 5.5,26–27; 6.7; 9.4. **12:** *Earn your bread,* lit. "eat bread." **14:** Amos asserts that he is neither a professional prophet (1 Sam 9.6–10; Mic 3.5–8,11) nor a member of a prophetic guild (2 Kings 2.3; 1 Sam 10.5; 1 Kings 22.6). *Herdsman,* of large cattle (cf. 1.1n.); the word occurs only here in the Bible. *Dresser of sycamore trees,* the biblical sycamore was a type of fig tree whose fruit was gashed with knives to induce ripening. **15:** Cf. 2 Sam 7.8. **17:** A dreadful string of curses: May *your wife . . . become a prostitute;* may others acquire title to your land, i.e., *parcel it out* with a measuring *line. Israel shall surely go,* Amos closes his response to Amaziah by repeating the latter's words from v. 11.

8.1–9.15: Further visions and oracles. The final two chapters of Amos have a similar outline: Both begin with visions (8.1–3; 9.1–6), followed by oracles with many literary parallels (compare 8.8 with 9.5; 8.9 with 9.11; 8.11 with 9.13).

8.1–3: Fourth vision. A basket of ripe summer fruit symbolizes the immediacy of Israel's end. Note the pun in Hebrew between summer fruit, "qayits," and end, "qets." **2:** *I will never again pass them by,* God will no longer mitigate Israel's punishment, see 7.8. Contrast 5.17, where God's presence brings destruction. **3:** *Songs of the temple,* see 5.21–23n. *Wailings,* see 5.16. *Be silent,* see 6.10.

8.4–14: Judgment speeches against Israel akin to those in 3.1–6.14. **4–6:** Rapacious and fraudulent business practices victimize the poor. **5:** The merchants are impatient for the holy days to pass so they can resume their fraudulent business (Lev 19.35–36; Deut 25.13–16). *The new moon,* see Num 29.6. *Ephah small,* sell less than the apparent volume; an *ephah* was ca. 23 l (.66 bu). *Shekel great,* overcharge; a *shekel* weighed ca. 11.5 gr (.4 oz). *False*

We will make the ephah small and the
  shekel great,
 and practice deceit with false balances,
⁶ buying the poor for silver
 and the needy for a pair of sandals,
 and selling the sweepings of the wheat."

⁷ The Lᴏʀᴅ has sworn by the pride of Jacob:
Surely I will never forget any of their
  deeds.
⁸ Shall not the land tremble on this account,
 and everyone mourn who lives in it,
and all of it rise like the Nile,
  and be tossed about and sink again, like
    the Nile of Egypt?

⁹ On that day, says the Lord Gᴏᴅ,
 I will make the sun go down at noon,
 and darken the earth in broad daylight.
¹⁰ I will turn your feasts into mourning,
 and all your songs into lamentation;
I will bring sackcloth on all loins,
 and baldness on every head;
I will make it like the mourning for an only
    son,
 and the end of it like a bitter day.

¹¹ The time is surely coming, says the Lord
    Gᴏᴅ,
 when I will send a famine on the land;
not a famine of bread, or a thirst for water,
 but of hearing the words of the Lᴏʀᴅ.
¹² They shall wander from sea to sea,
 and from north to east;

they shall run to and fro, seeking the word
    of the Lᴏʀᴅ,
 but they shall not find it.

¹³ In that day the beautiful young women
  and the young men
 shall faint for thirst.
¹⁴ Those who swear by Ashimah of Samaria,
 and say, "As your god lives, O Dan,"
and, "As the way of Beer-sheba lives"—
 they shall fall, and never rise again.

9 I saw the Lᴏʀᴅ standing beside[a] the altar,
 and he said:
Strike the capitals until the thresholds
    shake,
 and shatter them on the heads of all the
    people;[b]
and those who are left I will kill with the
    sword;
 not one of them shall flee away,
 not one of them shall escape.

² Though they dig into Sheol,
 from there shall my hand take them;
though they climb up to heaven,
 from there I will bring them down.
³ Though they hide themselves on the top
    of Carmel,
 from there I will search out and take
    them;

ᵃ Or *on*
ᵇ Heb *all of them*

balances, scales rigged in the merchant's favor. **6**: *Buying the poor* probably refers to outright slavery, as opposed to *selling the righteous* (2.6) into debt slavery. *Sweepings of the wheat*, they sell the chaff as wheat. **7**: *Pride of Jacob*, may be an epithet for God (compare 1 Sam 15.29) or for Israel (see Ps 47.4). Here the term is ironic, for it is the sinful pride of Israel which prompts God's reproach (see 6.8; Jer 13.9; Hos 7.10). That God does not *forget* is often a comfort (see Deut 4.31; Ps 9.12; Isa 49.15), but here it brings judgment. **8**: *Like the Nile ... tossed about and sink*, the annual inundation of the Nile (9.5; Jer 46.7–8). **9–10**: A solar eclipse portends divine punishment and elicits mourning rituals. *Sackcloth* and *baldness* were customary expressions of mourning associated with national disaster (e.g., Isa 22.12). *An only son*, Jer 6.26; Zech 12.10. **11–12**: No longer will God's judgment come as a famine or drought (contrast 4.6), but rather as an absence of prophecy, thus extinguishing the intercessory role of prophets in times of turmoil. **14**: *Ashimah* (or "guilt") *of Samaria* could be a Syrian deity (2 Kings 17.30) or a disparaging reference ("the guilt") to the practice of treating the cosmic Lord merely as the patron of a local shrine, whether in the center of Israel (*Samaria*), the farthest north (*Dan*), or the farthest south (*Beer-sheba*).

9.1–6: Fifth vision. For other appearances of the Lord at shrines, see 1 Sam 3.1–18; Isa 6.1–13. **1**: Probably *the altar* at Bethel (3.14; 7.10) is intended. Capital, the top of a pillar. *Threshold*, the foundational slab of the door-posts. The entire structure, from ceiling to foundation, will *shake*; see Isa 6.4. **2**: *Sheol*, the place of the dead (Job 10.19–22; Isa 14.11,15), which, Amos asserts, is within God's purview (Ps 139.7–12), though many feared it was not (e.g., Ps 6.6; 88.3–5). **3**: Mount *Carmel*, which juts into the Mediterranean at the northwestern border of Israel,

and though they hide from my sight at the bottom of the sea,
there I will command the sea-serpent, and it shall bite them.
[4] And though they go into captivity in front of their enemies,
there I will command the sword, and it shall kill them;
and I will fix my eyes on them for harm and not for good.

[5] The Lord, GOD of hosts,
he who touches the earth and it melts, and all who live in it mourn,
and all of it rises like the Nile, and sinks again, like the Nile of Egypt;
[6] who builds his upper chambers in the heavens,
and founds his vault upon the earth;
who calls for the waters of the sea,
and pours them out upon the surface of the earth—
the LORD is his name.

[7] Are you not like the Ethiopians[a] to me, O people of Israel? says the LORD.
Did I not bring Israel up from the land of Egypt,
and the Philistines from Caphtor and the Arameans from Kir?
[8] The eyes of the Lord GOD are upon the sinful kingdom,
and I will destroy it from the face of the earth

—except that I will not utterly destroy the house of Jacob,
says the LORD.

[9] For lo, I will command,
and shake the house of Israel among all the nations
as one shakes with a sieve,
but no pebble shall fall to the ground.
[10] All the sinners of my people shall die by the sword,
who say, "Evil shall not overtake or meet us."

[11] On that day I will raise up
the booth of David that is fallen,
and repair its[b] breaches,
and raise up its[c] ruins,
and rebuild it as in the days of old;
[12] in order that they may possess the remnant of Edom
and all the nations who are called by my name,
says the LORD who does this.

[13] The time is surely coming, says the LORD,

a Or Nubians; Heb Cushites
b Gk: Heb their
c Gk: Heb his

reaches a summit of ca. 550 m (1,800 ft) above sea level and also boasts caves and forests for those who wish to hide. Sea-serpent, sea monsters, personifications of chaos, are at times cast as opponents of God (Ps 72.13); at other times, as here, as God's servants (Ps 104.25–26; Job 41). 5–6: The third hymn-like passage (4.13; 5.8–9). 5: See 8.8. 6: Upper chambers, Ps 104.3. The vault is another name for the celestial barrier thought to separate the earth from the cosmic waters (Gen 1.6–8; Prov 8.27).

9.7–10: Israel has no claim to special privilege. Amos refutes the idea that Israel's relationship with God implies its superiority. This oracle suggests, positively, that God has enacted other exoduses at other times and places and, negatively, that Israel stands in judgment alongside the nations; see 3.2. 7: Like the Ethiopians, even distant Nubia is within God's purview. Philistines from Caphtor (probably Crete) (Jer 47.4). Kir, see 1.5n. 8: House of Jacob, here referring to Judah. This exception to God's judgment is likely a later addition. 9: Sieve, used to separate grain from stones picked up on the threshing room floor.

9.11–15: An oracle of restoration. Prophetic collections often end on a similar, hopeful note; many, as above, refer to that day (Hos 14.1–7; Joel 3.18 21; Mic 7.11–20; Zeph 3.14–20; Hag 2.20; Zech 14.6,20; Mal 14.1–5). 11: Booth of David, elsewhere in Amos, the fate of the Davidic dynasty, depicted here as in ruins, had not been a concern. This verse, at least, sounds like it stems from a later time, after the dynasty had fallen. The phrase "booth of David" suggests a more fragile structure than the more frequent "house of David" (cf. 2 Sam 7.11; Isa 1.8). 12: Edom was a traditional rival of Judah, not Israel, so this is further evidence that part or all of this final

when the one who plows shall overtake
 the one who reaps,
 and the treader of grapes the one who
 sows the seed;
the mountains shall drip sweet wine,
 and all the hills shall flow with it.
[14] I will restore the fortunes of my people
 Israel,
 and they shall rebuild the ruined cities
 and inhabit them;

they shall plant vineyards and drink their
 wine,
 and they shall make gardens and eat
 their fruit.
[15] I will plant them upon their land,
 and they shall never again be plucked
 up
 out of the land that I have given them,
 says the LORD your God.

oracle was added after the fall of Samaria in 722, at a time when the book was reinterpreted for Judahites. **13:**
See Joel 3.18–21. *Shall overtake,* see Lev 26.5.

OBADIAH

NAME, AUTHORSHIP, AND CANONICAL STATUS

The name Obadiah, which means "servant of Yah[weh]," was a common one in ancient Israel. Other Obadiahs are mentioned in the books of Kings, Chronicles, Ezra, and Nehemiah. Because it has little information in its superscription, the name for the introductory labels of prophetic books, the book of Obadiah is functionally anonymous.

Obadiah is the shortest book in the Hebrew Bible, containing only verse numbers. It appears here, as in the Masoretic Text, between Amos and Jonah, although some ancient manuscripts place Obadiah between Joel and Jonah.

CONTENTS AND DATE OF COMPOSITION

Despite our lack of information about this particular Obadiah, his family background, or when he lived, most interpreters link the contents of the book to events in the sixth century BCE. Obadiah single-mindedly announces God's punishment on Edom, a nation east of Judah in Transjordan, for its mistreatment of Judah. The accusations leveled against Edom in vv. 10–14, that Edom stood aside while strangers attacked Jerusalem and even aided in the invasion of the city, are understood to refer to Edomite activity during the Babylonian destruction of Jerusalem in 586 BCE.

Other biblical books share Obadiah's anger against Edom. Anti-Edomite oracles appear in Isa 34.5–8; 63.1–4; Ezek 25.12–13; 35.5–6,15; 36.5; Joel 3.19; and Jer 49.7–22, the language of which closely parallels parts of Obadiah. Like Obadiah, Ps 137.7 calls for revenge against Edom. Obadiah is distinctive, however, in claiming that Edom's crimes are especially heinous because of the brotherhood between the nations: a brother should not do the things that Edom did to Judah. The tradition that Edom and Judah descend from the brothers Esau and Jacob is familiar to readers of Gen 25 and Mal 1.2–5, but only Obadiah uses the expectations of brotherhood to bolster criticism of Edom's behavior in the sixth century.

Archaeology has shown that the Babylonian armies left their mark not only on Judah but also on Edom; both countries suffered loss of population and stability. In the sixth and fifth centuries BCE, territorial boundaries between Judah and Edom, as well as ethnic boundaries between their populations, seem to have been fluid. This may be the situation reflected in the closing verses of Obadiah, which not only promise that Judah will reclaim the Negeb (disputed territory in southern Judah) but also envision the enlargement of Judah's borders in every direction. Hence, while many date Obadiah close to the traumatic events of 586, it instead may have been written in a later generation, as its author sought to establish Judah's land claims by recalling Edom's past crimes while appealing to the rhetoric of brotherhood.

Julia M. O'Brien

¹ The vision of Obadiah.

Thus says the Lord GOD concerning Edom:
We have heard a report from the LORD,
   and a messenger has been sent among
     the nations:
"Rise up! Let us rise against it for battle!"
² I will surely make you least among the
   nations;
   you shall be utterly despised.
³ Your proud heart has deceived you,
   you that live in the clefts of the rock,ᵃ
   whose dwelling is in the heights.
You say in your heart,
   "Who will bring me down to the ground?"
⁴ Though you soar aloft like the eagle,
   though your nest is set among the stars,
   from there I will bring you down,
              says the LORD.

⁵ If thieves came to you,
   if plunderers by night
   —how you have been destroyed!—
   would they not steal only what they
     wanted?
If grape-gatherers came to you,
   would they not leave gleanings?

⁶ How Esau has been pillaged,
   his treasures searched out!
⁷ All your allies have deceived you,
   they have driven you to the border;
your confederates have prevailed against you;
   those who ateᵇ your bread have set a
     trap for you—
there is no understanding of it.
⁸ On that day, says the LORD,
   I will destroy the wise out of Edom,
   and understanding out of Mount Esau.
⁹ Your warriors shall be shattered, O Teman,
   so that everyone from Mount Esau will
     be cut off.
¹⁰ For the slaughter and violence done to
     your brother Jacob,
   shame shall cover you,
   and you shall be cut off forever.
¹¹ On the day that you stood aside,
   on the day that strangers carried off his
     wealth,
and foreigners entered his gates
   and cast lots for Jerusalem,
   you too were like one of them.

ᵃ Or *clefts of Sela*
ᵇ Cn: Heb lacks *those who ate*

1a: Superscription. A distinctively prophetic term, *vision* also occurs in Isa 1.1 and Nah 1.1. It refers not to data simply registered by the eyes but rather to truth made known by God, as in Jer 23.16.

1b–4: Edom's pending destruction. These verses closely parallel Jer 49.12–16, although in Jeremiah feminine forms are used to describe Edom. The theme of reversal runs throughout the book: Edom's fortunes are about to change. **1b–2:** Both other nations and God are described as rising up against Edom. **3:** Prophetic books frequently condemn the *proud*, especially among the nations (Isa 10.12; 13.11,19; 16.6; Jer 48.29; Zeph 2.10; 9.6; Zech 10.11). **3–4:** *Clefts of the rock*, the same Heb word means "rock" and Sela, an Edomite city probably to be identified with Umm el-Biyara, a site on a mountain within the later city of Petra; cf. Ps 137.9. The mountainous terrain of Edom, however, will offer no protection.

5–7: Edom at the hand of the nations. These verses imply that Edom's former allies have already begun its devastation, as in Jer 49.9–10. **5:** A difficult verse, suggesting that Edom's loss is beyond that caused by simple thieves. *Leave gleanings*, see Deut 24.21. **6:** *Esau* is described as Judah's brother and the ancestor of the Edomites in Gen 25. **7:** Edom's former *allies* and *confederates* are not named.

8–9: Edom at the hand of God. God will complete Edom's devastation *on that day*, a common prophetic term for the Day of the LORD. Phrases are shared with Jer 49.7 and 22. **9:** *Teman* refers either to the northern region of Edom (as in Am 1.12) or to Edom as a whole.

10–14: Edom as treacherous brother. Edom's actions are especially treacherous because Esau/Edom was the brother of Jacob/Judah. *On the day* appears nine times in this unit, apparently referring to the traumatic day of Jerusalem's fall. The accusations against Edom increase—from *standing aside*, to *gloating*, to *boasting*, to *looting*, to physical acts against fleeing Judeans. Although the NRSV translates 12–14 as *you should not have*, the forms are Heb jussives: "may you not." While Ps 137.7 also blames Edomites for *rejoicing* in Jerusalem's destruction, 2 Kings 24.2 blames bands of Arameans, Moabites, and Ammonites for coming up against Jerusalem, with no mention of Edomites. Jeremiah 40.11 indicates that Judeans fleeing the Babylonians had escaped to Moab, Ammon, Edom and elsewhere. **11:** *Cast lots*, see Joel 3.3.

[12] But you should not have gloated[a] over[b]
  your brother
 on the day of his misfortune;
you should not have rejoiced over the
  people of Judah
 on the day of their ruin;
you should not have boasted
 on the day of distress.
[13] You should not have entered the gate of
  my people
 on the day of their calamity;
you should not have joined in the gloating
  over Judah's[c] disaster
 on the day of his calamity;
you should not have looted his goods
 on the day of his calamity.
[14] You should not have stood at the crossings
  to cut off his fugitives;
you should not have handed over his
  survivors
 on the day of distress.

[15] For the day of the LORD is near against all
  the nations.
As you have done, it shall be done to you;
 your deeds shall return on your own head.
[16] For as you have drunk on my holy
  mountain,
 all the nations around you shall drink;
they shall drink and gulp down,[d]
 and shall be as though they had never
  been.
[17] But on Mount Zion there shall be those
  that escape,
 and it shall be holy;

and the house of Jacob shall take possession
  of those who dispossessed them.
[18] The house of Jacob shall be a fire,
  the house of Joseph a flame,
  and the house of Esau stubble;
they shall burn them and consume them,
  and there shall be no survivor of the
   house of Esau;
       for the LORD has spoken.
[19] Those of the Negeb shall possess Mount
  Esau,
  and those of the Shephelah the land of
   the Philistines;
they shall possess the land of Ephraim and
   the land of Samaria,
  and Benjamin shall possess Gilead.
[20] The exiles of the Israelites who are in
  Halah[e]
  shall possess[f] Phoenicia as far as
   Zarephath;
and the exiles of Jerusalem who are in
  Sepharad
  shall possess the towns of the Negeb.
[21] Those who have been saved[g] shall go up
  to Mount Zion
  to rule Mount Esau;
  and the kingdom shall be the LORD's.

a   Heb *But do not gloat* (and similarly through verse 14)
b   Heb *on the day of*
c   Heb *his*
d   Meaning of Heb uncertain
e   Cn: Heb *in this army*
f   Cn: Meaning of Heb uncertain
g   Or *Saviors*

15–18: The Day of the LORD. Edom's fate will be shared by all hostile nations, as they suffer a reversal of fates on the *day* that God acts to (re-)establish justice. 16: As in other prophetic books, retribution is depicted as drinking a cup of wrath (Isa 51.17,22; Jer 25.17; Hab 2.16; Zech 12.2). 17–18: The reversal of fates will benefit Judah, whose devastation will turn to preeminence. 17: *Mount Zion*, a synonym for Jerusalem, is contrasted with *Mount Esau* in v. 8. 18: The *house of Jacob*, here southern Israel, i.e., Judah. The *house of Joseph* is Israel, the northern kingdom destroyed in 722 BCE. As in Mal 4.1, the day of the LORD will *burn* the unrighteous like *stubble*.

19–21: Reclamation and expansion of territory. 19: Those in the *Negeb*, an arid region in southern Judah, will expand eastward to take Edom. Those in the *Shephelah*, the western foothills of Judah, will seize territory from the neighboring *Philistines* and then advance northward, first into the tribal territory of *Ephraim* and then further northward to *Samaria*. The southern Judean tribe of *Benjamin* will expand eastward across the Jordan River to take the land of *Gilead*. 20: Survivors of both the Assyrian destruction of the Northern Kingdom in the eighth century BCE and the Babylonian destruction of the Southern Kingdom in the sixth century BCE will return to aid in Judah's territorial expansion. Those exiled to the Assyrian territory of *Halah* (2 Kings 17.6) will take *Zarephath* in Phoenicia, territory never previously possessed by Israel. Those exiled by the Babylonians will return from *Sepharad*, location unknown, and possess the *Negeb*, mentioned at the beginning of the unit. 21: The concluding verse justifies *Mount Zion's* control of *Mount Esau* (see 17n.), under the auspices of Judah's God.

JONAH

NAME AND LOCATION IN CANON

The book of Jonah, a story about a prophet and not a collection of his prophecies, is atypical of the prophetical books. It is the fifth of the Minor Prophets in the Hebrew Bible; the book's placement following Amos and Obadiah is likely topical: both Amos and Obadiah contain prophecies concerning foreign nations, and Jonah relates another prophecy concerning foreigners, the people of Nineveh. In the Septuagint (LXX), Jonah is the sixth book (between Obadiah and Nahum), the same order as in the list of the twelve minor prophets in 2 Esd 1.38–40.

Jonah son of Amittai is mentioned in 2 Kings 14 as a prophet who prophesied in the Northern Kingdom of Israel in the days of the King Jeroboam II in the mid-eighth century BCE: "[Jeroboam] restored the border of Israel from Lebo-hamath as far as the Sea of the Arabah, according to the word of the LORD, the God of Israel, which he spoke by his servant Jonah son of Amittai, the prophet, who was from Gath-hepher. For the LORD saw the distress of Israel was very bitter; there was no one left, bond or free, and no one to help Israel. But the LORD had not said that he would blot out the name of Israel from under heaven, so he saved them by the hand of Jeroboam son of Joash" (vv. 25–27). Jonah is not mentioned again. The author of our book seems to have chosen Jonah as his protagonist since attributing the events to a prophet mentioned in Israel's history grants authenticity, and because the event described in Kings deals with God's compassion and mercy, the central theme of the book of Jonah: In Kings the Northern Kingdom is spared, while in Jonah, the Assyrian Empire, its enemy, is forgiven.

STRUCTURE

The book is in two parts, each with three scenes:

Chs 1–2	God's first call to Jonah
1.1–3	Jonah's commission and attempt to flee
1.4–16	The moral: one cannot flee from God
2.1–11	Jonah, in the fish, prays and is saved
Chs 3–4	God's second call to Jonah
3.1–4	Jonah's mission and its completion
3.5–10	The repentance of Nineveh and God's forgiveness
4.1–11	Jonah's prayer-complaint, and the moral he learns from God

The two parts are symmetrical: the opening command assigning both missions is almost identical; the formulation of Jonah's flight and that of the fulfillment of the second mission open with the same words, "Jonah set out" (1.3; 3.3); both second scenes features foreigners who are depicted favorably in contrast with Jonah; similar phrasing is used when the ship captain and the king of Nineveh express their belief in God when they are in danger, though unsure their belief will save them (1.6; 3.6–9); Jonah prays to God in both final scenes: in 2.2 in order to save himself, and in 4.2–3 to express frustration over God's saving the people of Nineveh.

AUTHORSHIP AND DATE

The book of Jonah was written by an unknown author. Its language places it in the Second Temple period, its vocabulary and syntax corresponding with those of the Bible's later books, Aramaic sources, and rabbinic literature. The book was apparently written after the destruction of the Assyrian capital of Nineveh in 612 BCE, since it refers to that city in the past tense (3.3), and the king is not called the "King of Assyria" but the "King of Nineveh" (3.6), an inappropriate title. The book should be dated no later than the third century BCE.

A late date is also suggested by Jonah's broad and sophisticated use of earlier biblical texts. The evil of the Ninevites and their punishment is contrasted with that of the inhabitants of Sodom (1.2; 3.4; 4.5; cf. Gen 18.20; 19.24), while Jonah appears as Abraham's opposite. In the story of Sodom, Abraham pleads with God to save the city for the sake of the few righteous people without expecting the city's repentance (Gen 18.22–33). Jonah, in contrast, flees, refusing to warn the Ninevites lest they repent and be saved. Jonah is also depicted as the opposite of Abraham's nephew Lot, who warned his sons-in-law of imminent destruction until being taken from Sodom by angels; Jonah's proclamation, "Forty days more and Nineveh shall be overthrown!" (3.4) is recited unwillingly, and then he even leaves the city to watch events unfold with complete lack of interest (4.5). Jonah is also contrasted with Moses, who was willing to die if God did not forgive the Israelites after they made the golden calf (Ex 32). Jonah's actions are also patterned after those of Elijah, who fled from Jezebel and his mission and asked to die (1 Kings 19). Jonah 4.2 appears to quote God's attributes (Ex 34.6–7) as they are presented in Joel 2.13. Jeremiah's prophecies (Jer 26.3; 36.7) echo in the words of the king of Nineveh who, with Jonah behaving as an anti-prophet, himself assumes the role of prophet and rouses his people to repent (3.8).

INTERPRETATION AND GUIDE TO READING

Jonah is not a historical book in the sense of recalling events that actually occurred; its characters and setting provide the means for the writer to convey his message. Part of that message concerns the power of repentance. While not unimportant, however, repentance is not the book's central theme: were it so, the first three chapters would suffice, and Jonah's flight would be irrelevant. Instead, the book of Jonah revolves around the essence of prophecy. Jonah knows God's attributes, that he is "gracious and merciful, slow to anger, and abounding in steadfast love, and ready to relent from punishing" (4.2). He knows that God will relent from destroying Nineveh and he flees, certain that his prophecy of destruction will be proven false. Jonah represents the concept, expressed explicitly in Deut 18.21–22, that the single proof for a prophecy's truth is its realization. God seeks to teach Jonah values more lofty than a prophecy's realization or a prophet's reliability—the saving of God's creation when found worthy. The book therefore illustrates the position—voiced openly in Jer 28.9—that although a prophecy of peace must be fulfilled in order to prove that its deliverer is a true prophet, a prophecy of destruction is meant, from the outset, to educate and bring repentance. This holds true even for foreign nations: the prophecy of doom is a conditional prophecy that will come true only in the absence of repentance (Jer 18.7–8).

The book of Jonah is uncharacteristic, when compared to other writings in the prophetic tradition, in its use of humor or irony to make its point. Humorous qualities, such as exaggerated behavior (running away from God, 1.3); inappropriate actions (sleeping through a violent storm, 1.5); outlandish situations (offering a prayer of thanksgiving from inside a fish's belly, 2.1); ludicrous commands (animals must fast and wear sackcloth, 3.7–8); and emotions either contrary to expectation (anger at mercy, 4.1–2) or out of proportion (being angry enough to die because a plant has withered, 4.9) appear throughout the story. But all of these qualities serve to underline the book's themes.

The book has a role disproportionate to its size within religious tradition. Judaism, picking up on its theme of repentance, reads it liturgically on Yom Kippur, the Day of Atonement. It is cited several times in the New Testament, where Jonah prefigures Jesus who spent "three days and three nights . . . in the heart of the earth" (Mt 12.40).

Yair Zakovitch

1 Now the word of the LORD came to Jonah son of Amittai, saying, ² "Go at once to Nineveh, that great city, and cry out against it; for their wickedness has come up before me." ³ But Jonah set out to flee to Tarshish from the presence of the LORD. He went down to Joppa and found a ship going to Tarshish; so he paid his fare and went on board, to go with them to Tarshish, away from the presence of the LORD.

⁴ But the LORD hurled a great wind upon the sea, and such a mighty storm came upon the sea that the ship threatened to break up. ⁵ Then the mariners were afraid, and each cried to his god. They threw the cargo that was in the ship into the sea, to lighten it for them. Jonah, meanwhile, had gone down into the hold of the ship and had lain down, and was fast asleep. ⁶ The captain came and said to him, "What are you doing sound asleep? Get up, call on your god! Perhaps the god will spare us a thought so that we do not perish."

⁷ The sailors[a] said to one another, "Come, let us cast lots, so that we may know on whose account this calamity has come upon us." So they cast lots, and the lot fell on Jonah. ⁸ Then they said to him, "Tell us why this calamity has come upon us. What is your occupation? Where do you come from? What is your country? And of what people are you?" ⁹ "I am a Hebrew," he replied. "I worship the LORD, the God of heaven, who made the sea and the dry land." ¹⁰ Then the men were even more afraid, and said to him, "What is this that you have done!" For the men knew that he was fleeing from the presence of the LORD, because he had told them so.

¹¹ Then they said to him, "What shall we do to you, that the sea may quiet down for us?" For the sea was growing more and more tempestuous. ¹² He said to them, "Pick me up and throw me into the sea; then the sea will quiet down for you; for I know it is because of me that this great storm has come upon you." ¹³ Nevertheless the men rowed hard to bring the ship back to land, but they could not, for the sea grew more and more stormy against them. ¹⁴ Then they cried out to the LORD, "Please, O LORD, we pray, do not let us perish on account of this man's life. Do not make us guilty of innocent blood; for you, O LORD, have done as it pleased you." ¹⁵ So they picked Jonah up and threw him into the sea; and the sea ceased from its raging. ¹⁶ Then the men feared the LORD even more, and they offered a sacrifice to the LORD and made vows.

¹⁷ [b] But the LORD provided a large fish to swallow up Jonah; and Jonah was in

a Heb *They*
b Ch 2.1 in Heb

1–2: God's first call to Jonah. 1.1–3: Jonah's commission and attempt to flee. Neither what Jonah was commanded to say nor the reason for his flight is given. Jonah's name, which means "dove, the son of truth," may be symbolic. *Joppa*, modern Jaffa, is on the Mediterranean coast near Tel Aviv. *Tarshish* (Isa 23.1; Ezek 27.22,25) is probably Tarsus on the southeast coast of Turkey, or perhaps Tartessus in southwestern Spain, neither being in the direction of Nineveh. 4–16: The moral: one cannot flee from God. Jonah realizes the impossibility of flight—God, ruler of the seas, causes a great storm. The sailors, in their terror and awe, call to their gods for help, before turning to the practical matter of tossing the ship's cargo into the sea, whereas Jonah continues to flee, this time escaping into sleep. Ironically the prophet takes no part in the attempted rescue, and the ship's captain must rouse Jonah to call out to his God. 7: Using *lots*, a standard way of revealing the future in the ancient Near East, the sailors discover who is responsible; curious, they ask Jonah a series of questions. 9: Jonah's answer reveals another irony: although he knew that God *made the sea*, Jonah fled to the sea to escape him. Jonah identifies himself as a *Hebrew*, a term typically used when speaking to non-Hebrews. *The LORD, the God of heaven* is a title found only in Second Temple biblical texts. 12: Despite Jonah's words, the sailors' compassion spurs them to try to reach shore; only after the futility of their rowing becomes apparent do they pray to Jonah's God and throw him into the sea. 16: The section ends with the report of the sailors' awe ("feared"; cf. vv. 5,10) for the Lord; their *sacrifice* and *vows* show their belief in him. 17: Jonah in the fish's belly. *Provided*, the verb appears three more times in the story (4.6,7,8), always indicating a divine act that immediately affects Jonah's situation. *Three days and three nights*, with no deliverance in sight. Jonah had avoided turning to God on the ship, but now he has no other choice.

2.1–11: Jonah, in the fish, prays and is saved. The psalm (like those in 1 Sam 2.1–10 and Isa 38.9–10) was incorporated into the story at a secondary stage. It is a psalm of thanksgiving and not a prayer for salvation, and

the belly of the fish three days and three nights.

2 Then Jonah prayed to the LORD his God from the belly of the fish, ² saying,

"I called to the LORD out of my distress,
and he answered me;
out of the belly of Sheol I cried,
and you heard my voice.
³ You cast me into the deep,
into the heart of the seas,
and the flood surrounded me;
all your waves and your billows
passed over me.
⁴ Then I said, 'I am driven away
from your sight;
howª shall I look again
upon your holy temple?'
⁵ The waters closed in over me;
the deep surrounded me;
weeds were wrapped around my head
⁶ at the roots of the mountains.
I went down to the land
whose bars closed upon me forever;
yet you brought up my life from the Pit,
O LORD my God.
⁷ As my life was ebbing away,
I remembered the LORD;
and my prayer came to you,
into your holy temple.
⁸ Those who worship vain idols
forsake their true loyalty.
⁹ But I with the voice of thanksgiving
will sacrifice to you;

what I have vowed I will pay.
Deliverance belongs to the LORD!"
¹⁰ Then the LORD spoke to the fish, and it spewed Jonah out upon the dry land.

3 The word of the LORD came to Jonah a second time, saying, ² "Get up, go to Nineveh, that great city, and proclaim to it the message that I tell you." ³ So Jonah set out and went to Nineveh, according to the word of the LORD. Now Nineveh was an exceedingly large city, a three days' walk across. ⁴ Jonah began to go into the city, going a day's walk. And he cried out, "Forty days more, and Nineveh shall be overthrown!" ⁵ And the people of Nineveh believed God; they proclaimed a fast, and everyone, great and small, put on sackcloth.

⁶ When the news reached the king of Nineveh, he rose from his throne, removed his robe, covered himself with sackcloth, and sat in ashes. ⁷ Then he had a proclamation made in Nineveh: "By the decree of the king and his nobles: No human being or animal, no herd or flock, shall taste anything. They shall not feed, nor shall they drink water. ⁸ Human beings and animals shall be covered with sackcloth, and they shall cry mightily to God. All shall turn from their evil ways and from the violence that is in their hands. ⁹ Who knows? God may relent and change his mind;

ª Theodotion: Heb *surely*

---

does not correspond exactly to the context, although one can find associative connections with Jonah's situation. The image of the drowning poet reflects an ancient concept that the netherworld is found in the *deep*, at the *roots of the mountains*; its doors are bolted (v. 6) and none who enter will return. Despite the poet's being in *Sheol*, God, in his *holy temple*, nevertheless hears his prayer (v. 7). **2**: *Sheol*, the underworld, where all deceased go. **4**: The wish to visit the *temple*, God's home, is common in Psalms (e.g., 5.7). **9**: Cf. 1.16. **10**: God who made the sea and the dry land (1.9) returns Jonah from sea to the dry land. God speaks to the fish, not yet to Jonah directly. The term "spew" (literally, "vomit") mocks Jonah.

3–4: God's second call to Jonah. 3.1–10: Jonah's mission and its completion. This time Jonah obeys. Before we hear of Jonah entering Nineveh, the storyteller dwells on Nineveh's size, a significant detail in that all its inhabitants may perish. **3**: *A three days' walk across*, excavations have revealed a city three miles long and one and half miles wide; thus the description of its size is an exaggeration. Jonah's proclamation, after walking only a third of the way in, is cursory, even omitting the preliminary "Thus said the LORD." **4**: *Forty days* is frequently a symbolic period of time in the Bible (e.g., Gen 8.6; Ex 24.18). **5–10: The Ninevites repent and God forgives.** Despite Jonah's brevity, the Ninevites believe in God and perform customs of mourning and repentance (cf. 2 Sam 3.31; Job 2.12; Dan 9.3). Even the animals repent! Faced with the prophet's failure to fulfill his duties, the king functions as a prophet, calling out to his people to repent. **9**: Cf. 1.6. These two foreigners understand that supplications before God *may* awaken his mercy, a notion tightly linked with the lesson the author wishes to impart. The Ninevites' sincere repentance succeeds; God relents.

he may turn from his fierce anger, so that we do not perish."

¹⁰ When God saw what they did, how they turned from their evil ways, God changed his mind about the calamity that he had said he would bring upon them; and he did not do it.

4 But this was very displeasing to Jonah, and he became angry. ² He prayed to the LORD and said, "O LORD! Is not this what I said while I was still in my own country? That is why I fled to Tarshish at the beginning; for I knew that you are a gracious God and merciful, slow to anger, and abounding in steadfast love, and ready to relent from punishing. ³ And now, O LORD, please take my life from me, for it is better for me to die than to live." ⁴ And the LORD said, "Is it right for you to be angry?" ⁵ Then Jonah went out of the city and sat down east of the city, and made a booth for himself there. He sat under it in the shade, waiting to see what would become of the city.

⁶ The LORD God appointed a bush,ᵃ and made it come up over Jonah, to give shade over his head, to save him from his discomfort; so Jonah was very happy about the bush. ⁷ But when dawn came up the next day, God appointed a worm that attacked the bush, so that it withered. ⁸ When the sun rose, God prepared a sultry east wind, and the sun beat down on the head of Jonah so that he was faint and asked that he might die. He said, "It is better for me to die than to live."

⁹ But God said to Jonah, "Is it right for you to be angry about the bush?" And he said, "Yes, angry enough to die." ¹⁰ Then the LORD said, "You are concerned about the bush, for which you did not labor and which you did not grow; it came into being in a night and perished in a night. ¹¹ And should I not be concerned about Nineveh, that great city, in which there are more than a hundred and twenty thousand persons who do not know their right hand from their left, and also many animals?"

ᵃ Heb *qiqayon*, possibly *the castor bean plant*

4.1–11: Jonah's prayer-complaint, and the moral he learns from God. The foreigners fear the God of Israel, while Jonah, God's messenger, cannot accept God's actions and protests them. He is indignant that the Ninevites have been saved since his credibility is thereby questioned. **2–3:** Jonah's second prayer to God is ironic: previously he asked for mercy for himself (2.2), now he resents the mercy shown toward the Ninevites. The prayer is in two parts: in v. 2 he provides his reasoning, in v. 3 he makes his request. **2:** Jonah describes God's character with words taken from God's definition of his essence in Ex 34.6–7. Like other biblical texts (Pss 86.15; 103.8; 145.8; Neh 9.31; 2 Chr 30.9) that quote only the part about God's mercy (and not his severity—see Ex 34.7b), so also Jonah (cf. also Joel 2.13). Jonah objects to God's compassion, turning praise for God into condemnation. **3:** An ironic reversal of 1 Kings 19.4, where Elijah offers legitimate reasons to die. **5:** Such *booth*s were constructed to guard the crop during harvest time. **11:** The size of the city is again exaggerated. The book concludes with a question, suggesting that the reader must carefully ponder the nature of God.

MICAH

NAME, AUTHORSHIP, AND HISTORICAL CONTEXT

The book of Micah gives us little information about the prophet himself, for whom the book is named. According to 1.1, Micah prophesied in the days of Jotham, Ahaz, and Hezekiah, kings of Judah whose reigns spanned 759–687 BCE. Possible allusions to the fall of Samaria, the capital of the Northern Kingdom of Israel, in 722 (1.6), and to the campaign of Sennacherib, the Assyrian king, in 701 (1.10–16), place the prophet in the final quarter of the eighth century. As such he was a younger contemporary of Isaiah of Jerusalem. Like Hosea, Amos, and especially Isaiah, Micah lived in a tumultuous era, whose events are recounted in 2 Kings 16–19.

LOCATION IN CANON

The prophet Micah was among the earliest of the Minor Prophets. In the organization of the Book of the Twelve, Micah follows Jonah, an arrangement apparently based on chronology since, according to 2 Kings 14.25, Jonah also lived in the eighth century. Micah is connected to the book of Nahum, which follows, by catchword; compare the final section of Micah (7.18–19) with the initial unit of Nahum (1.1–3).

STRUCTURE AND CONTENTS

The book may be divided into three sections: chs 1–3; 4–5; 6–7. Some scholars think that chs 1–3 form the oldest core of the book; it is characterized by the judgmental tone for which Micah was most famous (Jer 26.18). Chs 1–3 consist mainly of oracles of judgment; chs 4–5 of oracles of hope. The final section, chs 6–7, begins with judgment and moves to hope. This alternation between judgment and hope may conform to some pattern in Micah's preaching or it may be an organizing device of later editors. The book of Micah may also have material from subsequent periods (e.g., 4.10 speaks of the Babylonian exile; 7.11 seems to reflect the postexilic period). Further evidence of editorial activity is the close correspondence between Micah 4.1–5 and Isaiah 2.2–5.

INTERPRETATION

Micah offered a theological interpretation of the dizzying events near the end of the eighth century: the fall of Samaria, the expansion of Jerusalem fueled by emigrants from the north, and the international situation made unstable by an aggressive superpower, Assyria. Micah, from a small town southwest of Jerusalem, Moresheth-gath, had a populist message. He expressed disdain for the corruptions and pretensions of Jerusalem and its leaders. He recalled the traditions of early Israel (3.9–10; 6.3–5), and condemned religious practice unaccompanied by ethical performance (6.6–8).

While Amos and Hosea condemned the high places, provincial shrines where the proper worship of the LORD was diluted by illicit elements, Micah called Jerusalem itself a high place (1.5) and announced its destruction (3.12), for which he was long remembered (see Jer 26.18). At the same time, Micah never lost faith in the future. The middle section of the book, chs 4–5, contains images of a restored and glorious Zion to which the nations make pilgrimage, and of an ideal king (5.2–5).

It is instructive to see how Micah's rural background shaped his populist vision of the ideal king, or "messiah." Isaiah, Micah's contemporary, used the birth of a royal child (Hezekiah, son of Ahaz, was probably intended) in the Judahite capital of Jerusalem as a symbol of hope (Isa 7.10–14). Micah affirmed the Davidic lineage of the ideal king by tracing his roots to Bethlehem (5.2), David's home village (1 Sam 17:12), but also reminded his audience that their greatest king once did and will again emerge from "one of the little clans of Judah" (5.2).

Gregory Mobley

1 The word of the LORD that came to Micah of Moresheth in the days of Kings Jotham, Ahaz, and Hezekiah of Judah, which he saw concerning Samaria and Jerusalem.

² Hear, you peoples, all of you;
    listen, O earth, and all that is in it;
and let the Lord GOD be a witness against
        you,
    the Lord from his holy temple.
³ For lo, the LORD is coming out of his
        place,
    and will come down and tread upon the
        high places of the earth.
⁴ Then the mountains will melt under him
    and the valleys will burst open,
like wax near the fire,
    like waters poured down a steep place.
⁵ All this is for the transgression of Jacob
    and for the sins of the house of Israel.
What is the transgression of Jacob?
    Is it not Samaria?
And what is the high place[a] of Judah?
    Is it not Jerusalem?
⁶ Therefore I will make Samaria a heap in
        the open country,
    a place for planting vineyards.
I will pour down her stones into the valley,
    and uncover her foundations.

⁷ All her images shall be beaten to pieces,
    all her wages shall be burned with fire,
    and all her idols I will lay waste;
for as the wages of a prostitute she
        gathered them,
    and as the wages of a prostitute they
        shall again be used.

⁸ For this I will lament and wail;
    I will go barefoot and naked;
I will make lamentation like the jackals,
    and mourning like the ostriches.
⁹ For her wound[b] is incurable.
    It has come to Judah;
it has reached to the gate of my people,
    to Jerusalem.

¹⁰ Tell it not in Gath,
    weep not at all;
in Beth-leaphrah
    roll yourselves in the dust.
¹¹ Pass on your way,
    inhabitants of Shaphir,
    in nakedness and shame;
the inhabitants of Zaanan
    do not come forth;

a Heb *what are the high places*
b Gk Syr Vg: Heb *wounds*

1.1: **Superscription.** Among the Minor Prophets, this superscription is closest in form to those for Hosea (1.1), Amos (1.1), and Zephaniah (1.1). *Micah* is a short form of the name Micaiah (1 Kings 22), which means, "Who is like Yahweh?" *Moresheth,* a small town in southwest Judah (cf. 1.14), probably Tell el-Judeidah, 37 km (23 mi) southwest of Jerusalem. *Which he saw,* Judean prophecy often had a visionary quality (e.g., Isa 1.1; Ezek 1.1.; Am 1.1; Ob 1; Nah 1.1; Hab 1.1). *Jotham* reigned from ca. 759 to 743 BCE; *Ahaz* from 743/735 to 727/715; *Hezekiah* from 727/715 to 698/687 (the data are inconsistent for the reigns of Ahaz and Hezekiah).

1.2–3.12: **Speeches condemning Judean society and its leaders.** This collection of speeches begins with an indictment of Samaria, capital of the Northern Kingdom, and ends with an indictment of Jerusalem, capital of the Southern Kingdom. This first major section of Micah is dominated by judgment speeches.

1.2–7: **The coming of the Lord.** In grand style, the Lord descends from heaven to punish Samaria. This oracle is to be dated before 722 BCE, when Samaria fell to the Assyrians. 2: Cf. Isa 1.2; Hab 2.20; and 1 Kings 22.28b. 3–4: Judg 5.4; Ps 68.8; 97.1–5; Isa 26.21. 5: *Jacob,* poetic synonym for Israel; cf. Gen 32.28. *High place* usually designates an open-air shrine, but seems to refer here to the Solomonic Temple. 7: This destruction of images is consistent with Deuteronomic law (Deut 7.25; 12.3). The phrase *wages of a prostitute* recalls the imagery of Hosea (Hos 2.2–13).

1.8–16: **A lament for Samaria, and Jerusalem too.** 8: *Barefoot . . . naked,* conventional mourning behavior (2 Sam 15.30; Ezek 24.17,23), employed for effect by Micah's contemporary Isaiah (Isa 20.2). *Jackals* and *ostriches,* associated with desolation because they frequented ruins and produced eerie howls or cries; see also Job 30.29; Isa 34.13.

1.10–16: These towns in southwestern Judah lay along the path of the Assyrian king Sennacherib's campaign in 701 (2 Kings 18–19; Isa 36–37), although the specific locations of several are unknown. There is a pun in virtually every verse of this section, lost in translation. For the flavor in Hebrew, consider v. 12: "the inhabitants of

Beth-ezel is wailing
  and shall remove its support from you.
¹² For the inhabitants of Maroth
    wait anxiously for good,
yet disaster has come down from the LORD
    to the gate of Jerusalem.
¹³ Harness the steeds to the chariots,
    inhabitants of Lachish;
it was the beginning of sin
    to daughter Zion,
for in you were found
    the transgressions of Israel.
¹⁴ Therefore you shall give parting gifts
    to Moresheth-gath;
the houses of Achzib shall be a deception
    to the kings of Israel.
¹⁵ I will again bring a conqueror upon you,
    inhabitants of Mareshah;
the glory of Israel
    shall come to Adullam.
¹⁶ Make yourselves bald and cut off your
      hair
    for your pampered children;
make yourselves as bald as the eagle,
    for they have gone from you into exile.

2 Alas for those who devise wickedness
    and evil deeds[a] on their beds!
When the morning dawns, they perform it,
    because it is in their power.
² They covet fields, and seize them;
    houses, and take them away;
they oppress householder and house,
    people and their inheritance.
³ Therefore thus says the LORD:
Now, I am devising against this family an
    evil
    from which you cannot remove your
      necks;

and you shall not walk haughtily,
    for it will be an evil time.
⁴ On that day they shall take up a taunt
      song against you,
    and wail with bitter lamentation,
and say, "We are utterly ruined;
    the LORD[b] alters the inheritance of my
      people;
how he removes it from me!
    Among our captors[c] he parcels out our
      fields."
⁵ Therefore you will have no one to cast the
    line by lot
    in the assembly of the LORD.

⁶ "Do not preach"—thus they preach—
    "one should not preach of such
      things;
    disgrace will not overtake us."
⁷ Should this be said, O house of Jacob?
    Is the LORD's patience exhausted?
    Are these his doings?
Do not my words do good
    to one who walks uprightly?
⁸ But you rise up against my people[d] as an
      enemy;
    you strip the robe from the peaceful,[e]
from those who pass by trustingly
    with no thought of war.
⁹ The women of my people you drive out
    from their pleasant houses;
from their young children you take away
    my glory forever.

a Cn: Heb *work evil*
b Heb *he*
c Cn: Heb *the rebellious*
d Cn: Heb *But yesterday my people rose*
e Cn: Heb *from before a garment*

Bitterness wait . . . for something sweet." **10**: *Gath,* one of the five Philistine cities on the coast; 2 Sam 1.20b. **13**: Sennacherib's siege of *Lachish,* an important city 45 km (28 mi) southwest of Jerusalem, is depicted in Assyrian records. **14**: *Moresheth-gath,* see 1.1n. **15**: *Mareshah,* later known as Marisa, is modern Tell Sandahanna, 5 km (3 mi) northeast of Lachish. **16**: *Make yourselves bald,* an extreme form of mourning behavior (e.g., Isa 15.2; Jer 7.29; 16.6; Am 8.10). *Pampered children* (better, "children of your delight") is not pejorative. It depicts the grief of parents bereft of exiled children. The *eagle,* more exactly, the griffon-vulture.

2.1–5: The Lord will punish the land barons. 1–2: Ps 36.4; Isa 5.8–12; 32.7. Micah condemns the injustice and inhumanity of creditors who, through manipulation of credit and courts, foreclose on family farms. **4**: *Taunt song,* cf. Num 21.27–30; Isa 23.15–16; Hab 2.6. **5**: *Cast the line by lot,* on a piece of land, thus acquiring title to it (Josh 18.6–10; Ps 16.6).

2.6–11: The prophet responds to criticism. Micah, like other prophets (Isa 30.10; Jer 5.31; Am 2.12), realizes his uncompromising message is not one his audience wants to hear.

¹⁰ Arise and go;
  for this is no place to rest,
because of uncleanness that destroys
  with a grievous destruction.^a
¹¹ If someone were to go about uttering
    empty falsehoods,
  saying, "I will preach to you of wine and
    strong drink,"
  such a one would be the preacher for
    this people!

¹² I will surely gather all of you, O Jacob,
  I will gather the survivors of Israel;
I will set them together
  like sheep in a fold,
like a flock in its pasture;
  it will resound with people.
¹³ The one who breaks out will go up before
    them;
  they will break through and pass the
    gate,
  going out by it.
Their king will pass on before them,
  the LORD at their head.

3 And I said:
Listen, you heads of Jacob
  and rulers of the house of Israel!
Should you not know justice?—
  ² you who hate the good and love the
    evil,
who tear the skin off my people,^b
  and the flesh off their bones;
³ who eat the flesh of my people,
  flay their skin off them,
break their bones in pieces,
  and chop them up like meat^c in a
    kettle,
  like flesh in a caldron.

⁴ Then they will cry to the LORD,
  but he will not answer them;
he will hide his face from them at that
    time,
  because they have acted wickedly.

⁵ Thus says the LORD concerning the
    prophets
  who lead my people astray,
who cry "Peace"
  when they have something to eat,
but declare war against those
  who put nothing into their mouths.
⁶ Therefore it shall be night to you, without
    vision,
  and darkness to you, without
    revelation.
The sun shall go down upon the prophets,
  and the day shall be black over them;
⁷ the seers shall be disgraced,
  and the diviners put to shame;
they shall all cover their lips,
  for there is no answer from God.
⁸ But as for me, I am filled with power,
  with the spirit of the LORD,
  and with justice and might,
to declare to Jacob his transgression
  and to Israel his sin.

⁹ Hear this, you rulers of the house of
    Jacob
  and chiefs of the house of Israel,
who abhor justice
  and pervert all equity,
¹⁰ who build Zion with blood
  and Jerusalem with wrong!

a Meaning of Heb uncertain
b Heb *from them*
c Gk: Heb *as*

2.12–13: **A shift to an oracle of encouragement.** Against the background of exile, whether in 722 or 587, this oracle counters despair with images of the Lord as shepherd (v. 12) and victorious king (v. 13). **13:** *The one who breaks out:* i.e., the Lord; see Ex 19.22; 2 Sam 5.20; 6.8.

3.1–4: **The Lord will punish the judicial leaders.** Corrupt judges are described as cannibals; Ezekiel also used this image (Ezek 11.5–12; 24.1–14). **1:** *Listen,* lit. "Hear," as in 1.1; 3.9; 6.1; 6.9b, a common introduction to Micah's oracles. **2:** For comparison, Isa 5.20; for contrast, Am 5.15. **4:** Futile *cry to the Lord* (i.e., prayer), cf. Isa 1.15.

3.5–8: **The Lord will punish the religious leaders.** Micah's rival prophets are crowd pleasers (see also 2.11), inspired on commission (v. 5); by contrast, see Micah's source of inspiration in v. 8. **6:** A time *without vision,* 1 Sam 3.1. **7:** *Seers,* see 1 Sam 9.9. *Cover their lips,* a sign of mourning (Lev 13.45; Ezek 24.17,22). **8:** *Filled . . . with the spirit,* Isa 11.2; 61.1–3; Ezek 2.2.

3.9–12: **Summary: Its leadership corrupt, Jerusalem is doomed.** The first section ends with Micah's bold

¹¹ Its rulers give judgment for a bribe,
  its priests teach for a price,
  its prophets give oracles for money;
yet they lean upon the LORD and say,
  "Surely the LORD is with us!
  No harm shall come upon us."
¹² Therefore because of you
  Zion shall be plowed as a field;
Jerusalem shall become a heap of ruins,
  and the mountain of the house a
    wooded height.

4 In days to come
  the mountain of the LORD's house
shall be established as the highest of the
    mountains,
  and shall be raised up above the hills.
Peoples shall stream to it,
  ² and many nations shall come and say:
"Come, let us go up to the mountain of the
    LORD,
  to the house of the God of Jacob;
that he may teach us his ways
  and that we may walk in his paths."
For out of Zion shall go forth instruction,
  and the word of the LORD from Jerusalem.
³ He shall judge between many peoples,
  and shall arbitrate between strong
    nations far away;
they shall beat their swords into
  plowshares,

and their spears into pruning hooks;
nation shall not lift up sword against
    nation,
  neither shall they learn war any
    more;
⁴ but they shall all sit under their own
    vines and under their own fig trees,
  and no one shall make them afraid;
  for the mouth of the LORD of hosts has
    spoken.

⁵ For all the peoples walk,
  each in the name of its god,
but we will walk in the name of the LORD
    our God
  forever and ever.

⁶ In that day, says the LORD,
  I will assemble the lame
and gather those who have been driven
    away,
  and those whom I have afflicted.
⁷ The lame I will make the remnant,
  and those who were cast off, a strong
    nation;
and the LORD will reign over them in
    Mount Zion
  now and forevermore.

⁸ And you, O tower of the flock,
  hill of daughter Zion,

assertion that Jerusalem and the Temple itself shall be destroyed because of the corruption of its leaders. **10:** *Who build Zion,* following the collapse of the northern state, Jerusalem expanded as it absorbed refugees; Hab 2.12. **11–12:** Prophecy is inseparable from context: Here, hopes in Zion's inviolability are dashed; contrast Ps 46, where they are confirmed. *Heap of ruins,* Jerusalem's fate shall be similar to that of Samaria (1.6). This parallel reveals a key strategy of the preexilic Judean prophets: The fall of Samaria served as an example to Judah. **12:** This prophecy was quoted at the trial of Jeremiah (Jer 26.18).

4.1–5.15: Speeches promising divine restoration and exaltation of the people Israel and the city Jerusalem. A series of poems depicts an ideal age ("that day") when God reigns, Israel triumphs, and the nations are judged. Some scholars date this section to the exilic or postexilic period (see 4.10n.). Alternately, possible allusions to the Babylonian exile (e.g., 4.6,10) could stem from editors who recast Micah's oracles for a later audience.

4.1–8: The ideal age is depicted in three poems, the first of which (vv. 1–4) is nearly identical to Isaiah 2.2–4. **1–2:** There is a universal pilgrimage to Mt. Zion, to which cosmic significance is ascribed here as *the mountain of the Lord's house.* **1:** *Highest of the mountains,* claims for Mt. Zion's height (Ps 48.3; Ezek 40.2) were symbolic, not topographic. **2:** *Instruction,* Heb "torah." **3–4:** A classic articulation of the Israelite prophetic ideal: peace and a social equality rooted in family ownership of land. **3:** *Swords into plowshares* (or "plowpoints," a stick with a small metal point), i.e., the transition from war to peace, as the militia man converts to farmer. For the opposite movement, see Joel 3.10. **4:** Zech 3.10; 1 Kings 4.25; 2 Kings 18.31 = Isa 36.16. **5:** Like its similarly worded parallel in Isa 2.5, this verse may have been read antiphonally, as an "Amen" to the visionary speech of 4.1–4 (= Isa 2.2–4). **6–7:** Cf. Zeph 3.19–20. **8:** *Tower of the flock,* an old epithet for Jerusalem (see "tower of Eder" in Gen

to you it shall come,
the former dominion shall come,
the sovereignty of daughter Jerusalem.

⁹ Now why do you cry aloud?
Is there no king in you?
Has your counselor perished,
that pangs have seized you like a
woman in labor?
¹⁰ Writhe and groan,ᵃ O daughter Zion,
like a woman in labor;
for now you shall go forth from the city
and camp in the open country;
you shall go to Babylon.
There you shall be rescued,
there the LORD will redeem you
from the hands of your enemies.

¹¹ Now many nations
are assembled against you,
saying, "Let her be profaned,
and let our eyes gaze upon Zion."
¹² But they do not know
the thoughts of the LORD;
they do not understand his plan,
that he has gathered them as sheaves to
the threshing floor.
¹³ Arise and thresh,
O daughter Zion,
for I will make your horn iron
and your hoofs bronze;
you shall beat in pieces many peoples,
and shallᵇ devote their gain to the LORD,
their wealth to the Lord of the whole
earth.

5 ᶜ Now you are walled around with a
wall;ᵈ
siege is laid against us;
with a rod they strike the ruler of Israel
upon the cheek.

² ᵉBut you, O Bethlehem of Ephrathah,
who are one of the little clans of Judah,
from you shall come forth for me
one who is to rule in Israel,
whose origin is from of old,
from ancient days.
³ Therefore he shall give them up until the
time
when she who is in labor has brought
forth;
then the rest of his kindred shall return
to the people of Israel.
⁴ And he shall stand and feed his flock in
the strength of the LORD,
in the majesty of the name of the LORD
his God.
And they shall live secure, for now he shall
be great
to the ends of the earth;
⁵ and he shall be the one of peace.

If the Assyrians come into our land
and tread upon our soil,ᶠ

ᵃ Meaning of Heb uncertain
ᵇ Gk Syr Tg: Heb *and I will*
ᶜ Ch 4.14 in Heb
ᵈ Cn Compare Gk: Meaning of Heb uncertain
ᵉ Ch 5.1 in Heb
ᶠ Gk: Heb *in our palaces*

35.21; "Eder" means "flock").

4.9–10: The Lord will rescue the exiles. This speech, which describes the exiles' march to Babylon and promises their redemption, addresses the situation of the sixth century, not the eighth. *Like a woman in labor,* Isa 13.8; 26.17; Jer 4.31.

4.11–12: Israel will crush its enemies. The Lord has planned a stunning reversal. At the very place outside Jerusalem where hostile nations assemble, the city gate (also the site of threshing floors), Israel shall trample them. **13:** For Israel as bovine, see Hos 10.11. *Devote their gain,* Deut 20.16; Josh 6.18–19.

5.1: *Strike . . . the cheek,* a gesture of insult; see 1 Kings 22.24; Job 16.10; Ps 3.7; Lam 3.30.

5.2–5a: A messianic poem. A new David shall arise, not from Jerusalem but from Bethlehem, David's place of birth, to rule in this ideal age. The New Testament interprets this poem as referring to the birth of Jesus (Mt 2.6; cf. Jn 7.40–43). **2:** *Bethlehem,* located 9 km (6 mi) south of Jerusalem; Gen 35.19; Ruth 4.11; 1 Sam 17.12. *Ephrathah,* the name of a Judahite clan and region; the latter includes the village of Bethlehem. The prophet Amos (9.11) also uses the phrase *of old* in reference to David. **3:** Isaiah of Jerusalem, a contemporary of Micah, also described the birth of an ideal king (7.14; 9.6).

5.5b–6: Assyria will be defeated. In the new age, Israel will not lack for leaders (contrast chs 2–3). **5:** *Seven . . .*

we will raise against them seven
  shepherds
  and eight installed as rulers.
⁶ They shall rule the land of Assyria with
    the sword,
  and the land of Nimrod with the drawn
    sword;ᵃ
theyᵇ shall rescue us from the Assyrians
  if they come into our land
  or tread within our border.

⁷ Then the remnant of Jacob,
  surrounded by many peoples,
shall be like dew from the Lord,
  like showers on the grass,
which do not depend upon people
  or wait for any mortal.
⁸ And among the nations the remnant of
    Jacob,
  surrounded by many peoples,
shall be like a lion among the animals of
    the forest,
  like a young lion among the flocks of
    sheep,
which, when it goes through, treads
    down
  and tears in pieces, with no one to
    deliver.
⁹ Your hand shall be lifted up over your
    adversaries,
  and all your enemies shall be cut off.

¹⁰ In that day, says the Lord,
  I will cut off your horses from among
    you
  and will destroy your chariots;

¹¹ and I will cut off the cities of your land
  and throw down all your strongholds;
¹² and I will cut off sorceries from your
    hand,
  and you shall have no more
    soothsayers;
¹³ and I will cut off your images
  and your pillars from among you,
and you shall bow down no more
  to the work of your hands;
¹⁴ and I will uproot your sacred polesᶜ from
    among you
  and destroy your towns.
¹⁵ And in anger and wrath I will execute
    vengeance
  on the nations that did not obey.

6 Hear what the Lord says:
  Rise, plead your case before the
    mountains,
  and let the hills hear your voice.
² Hear, you mountains, the controversy of
    the Lord,
  and you enduring foundations of the
    earth;
for the Lord has a controversy with his
    people,
  and he will contend with Israel.

³ "O my people, what have I done to you?
  In what have I wearied you? Answer
    me!

ᵃ Cn: Heb *in its entrances*
ᵇ Heb *he*
ᶜ Heb *Asherim*

---

eight, a sufficient number (see Am 1.3n). **6:** *Land of Nimrod,* Assyria; Gen 10.8–11 identifies Nimrod as a legendary warrior and king of Assyria.

5.7–9: Israel gains the upper hand. 7: *Dew,* the image is hostile; see 2 Sam 17.12.

5.10–15: But before reconstruction, demolition. The repetition of first-person verbs at the beginning of each line (*I will cut off,* four times; *I will uproot; I will execute vengeance*) sets the tone. **10:** *Cut off your horses . . . and . . . chariots,* Israel must rely on the Lord, not military force (Ps 20.17; 33.13–17; Zech 9.10). **11:** Jer 5.17; Hos 10.12–14. **12:** The precise forms these means of divination took are unknown; for the biblical prohibition, see Deut 18.10–11. **13–14:** *Pillars* and *sacred poles,* the equipment of Canaanite religion, banned for Israel (Ex 34.13). According to 2 Kings 18.4, King Hezekiah accomplished this.

6.1–7.20: A prophetic sampler moves from legal indictment of Israel's guilt to liturgical affirmation of God's mercy. The final section of Micah consists of four units, of different genres, which extend the themes of the first section (1.2–3.12).

6.1–8: A divine lawsuit. There are frequent shifts of speakers here, from the Lord (v. 1) to the prophet (v. 2) and back to the Lord (vv. 3–5), to a spokesperson for the community (vv. 6–7) and back to the prophet (v. 8), who delivers the punchline, the epitome of the entire Israelite prophetic tradition. **1–2:** The audience, in the style

⁴ For I brought you up from the land of
  Egypt,
 and redeemed you from the house of
  slavery;
and I sent before you Moses,
  Aaron, and Miriam.
⁵ O my people, remember now what King
  Balak of Moab devised,
 what Balaam son of Beor answered him,
and what happened from Shittim to Gilgal,
  that you may know the saving acts of
  the Lord."

⁶ "With what shall I come before the Lord,
  and bow myself before God on high?
Shall I come before him with burnt offerings,
  with calves a year old?
⁷ Will the Lord be pleased with thousands
  of rams,
 with ten thousands of rivers of oil?
Shall I give my firstborn for my
  transgression,
 the fruit of my body for the sin of my
  soul?"

⁸ He has told you, O mortal, what is good;
  and what does the Lord require of you
but to do justice, and to love kindness,
  and to walk humbly with your God?

⁹ The voice of the Lord cries to the city
  (it is sound wisdom to fear your name):
Hear, O tribe and assembly of the city!ᵃ
  ¹⁰ Can I forgetᵇ the treasures of
   wickedness in the house of the
   wicked,
  and the scant measure that is accursed?
¹¹ Can I tolerate wicked scales
  and a bag of dishonest weights?
¹² Yourᶜ wealthy are full of violence;
  yourᵈ inhabitants speak lies,
 with tongues of deceit in their mouths.

¹³ Therefore I have begunᵉ to strike you
  down,
 making you desolate because of your
  sins.
¹⁴ You shall eat, but not be satisfied,
  and there shall be a gnawing hunger
  within you;
you shall put away, but not save,
  and what you save, I will hand over to
  the sword.
¹⁵ You shall sow, but not reap;
  you shall tread olives, but not anoint
  yourselves with oil;
 you shall tread grapes, but not drink
  wine.
¹⁶ For you have kept the statutes of Omriᶠ
  and all the works of the house of Ahab,
 and you have followed their
  counsels.
Therefore I will make you a desolation,
  and yourᵍ inhabitants an object of
  hissing;
 so you shall bear the scorn of my
  people.

7 Woe is me! For I have become like one
  who,
 after the summer fruit has been gathered,
 after the vintage has been gleaned,
finds no cluster to eat;
  there is no first-ripe fig for which I
  hunger.

ᵃ Cn Compare Gk: Heb *tribe, and who has appointed
  it yet?*
ᵇ Cn: Meaning of Heb uncertain
ᶜ Heb *Whose*
ᵈ Heb *whose*
ᵉ Gk Syr Vg: Heb *have made sick*
ᶠ Gk Syr Vg Tg: Heb *the statutes of Omri are kept*
ᵍ Heb *its*

of ancient treaty witnesses, is the heavenly court. *Controversy,* lawsuit. **4:** Note the prominence of *Miriam* (Ex 15.20–21). **5:** *Balak, Balaam,* Num 22–24. **5:** *From Shittim* (Josh 3.1) *to Gilgal* (Josh 4.19) refers to the crossing of the Jordan. **6:** Cf. Pss 15.1; 24.3. **8:** In this single sentence the prophet sums up a century of brilliant prophecy; see Am 5.21–24; Hos 6.6; Isa 1.11–17. *Kindness,* "ḥesed," covenant loyalty.

6.9–16: Jerusalem, the corrupt city, is cursed. Jerusalem, as wicked as Samaria (see v. 16), must be destroyed. This speech can be read as a separate oracle or as the judicial sentence following the indictment in 6.1–8. **14–16:** For other "futility curses" in which actions fail to produce normal and expected results, see Deut 28.30–31,38–46. **16:** *Omri, Ahab,* of the Northern Kingdom in the ninth century BCE; see 1 Kings 16.25–34. *Object of hissing,* Zeph 2.15.

7.1–7: A lament for a desperate society. 1: *Gleaned,* Lev 19.9–10; 23.22; Deut 24.19–21; Ruth 2–3. The *first-ripe*

² The faithful have disappeared from the
land,
and there is no one left who is upright;
they all lie in wait for blood,
and they hunt each other with nets.
³ Their hands are skilled to do evil;
the official and the judge ask for a bribe,
and the powerful dictate what they desire;
thus they pervert justice.ᵃ
⁴ The best of them is like a brier,
the most upright of them a thorn hedge.
The day of theirᵇ sentinels, of theirᵇ
punishment, has come;
now their confusion is at hand.
⁵ Put no trust in a friend,
have no confidence in a loved one;
guard the doors of your mouth
from her who lies in your embrace;
⁶ for the son treats the father with contempt,
the daughter rises up against her
mother,
the daughter-in-law against her mother-
in-law;
your enemies are members of your own
household.
⁷ But as for me, I will look to the LORD,
I will wait for the God of my salvation;
my God will hear me.

⁸ Do not rejoice over me, O my enemy;
when I fall, I shall rise;
when I sit in darkness,
the LORD will be a light to me.
⁹ I must bear the indignation of the LORD,
because I have sinned against him,
until he takes my side
and executes judgment for me.
He will bring me out to the light;
I shall see his vindication.
¹⁰ Then my enemy will see,
and shame will cover her who said
to me,
"Where is the LORD your God?"

My eyes will see her downfall;ᶜ
now she will be trodden down
like the mire of the streets.

¹¹ A day for the building of your walls!
In that day the boundary shall be far
extended.
¹² In that day they will come to you
from Assyria toᵈ Egypt,
and from Egypt to the River,
from sea to sea and from mountain to
mountain.
¹³ But the earth will be desolate
because of its inhabitants,
for the fruit of their doings.

¹⁴ Shepherd your people with your staff,
the flock that belongs to you,
which lives alone in a forest
in the midst of a garden land;
let them feed in Bashan and Gilead
as in the days of old.
¹⁵ As in the days when you came out of the
land of Egypt,
show usᵉ marvelous things.
¹⁶ The nations shall see and be ashamed
of all their might;
they shall lay their hands on their mouths;
their ears shall be deaf;
¹⁷ they shall lick dust like a snake,
like the crawling things of the earth;
they shall come trembling out of their
fortresses;
they shall turn in dread to the LORD our
God,
and they shall stand in fear of you.

ᵃ Cn: Heb *they weave it*
ᵇ Heb *your*
ᶜ Heb lacks *downfall*
ᵈ One Ms: MT *Assyria and cities of*
ᵉ Cn: Heb *I will show him*

fig was the most delicious. **2:** Abraham (Gen 18.23–33), Jeremiah (Jer 5.1), and Ezekiel (Ezek 22.30) also searched for an honest man. **5:** Cf. Jer 9.4. **6:** Contrast Mal 4.6.

7.8–20: A final liturgy. This final unit contains shifts in content, if not speakers, and may have been designed for worship. It begins with lament (vv. 8–10), followed by an oracle of encouragement (vv. 11–13) and prayer (vv. 14–17), before closing with hopeful affirmation of God's great mercy. **8–10:** The prophet speaks as Israel. **9:** Jer 10.19. **10:** *Shame will cover her,* Ob 10. *Mire of the streets,* Isa 10.6. **11–13:** The references to the (re)*building of your walls* (Neh 2.17) and the restoration of former boundaries (Isa 54.2–3) suggest that this oracle was probably written in the early postexilic period. **12:** *The River,* the Euphrates. **14:** *Bashan* and *Gilead* in northern Transjordan

[18] Who is a God like you, pardoning
   iniquity
      and passing over the transgression
      of the remnant of your[a] possession?
He does not retain his anger forever,
   because he delights in showing
      clemency.
[19] He will again have compassion upon us;
   he will tread our iniquities under foot.

You will cast all our[b] sins
   into the depths of the sea.
[20] You will show faithfulness to Jacob
   and unswerving loyalty to Abraham,
as you have sworn to our ancestors
   from the days of old.

a   Heb *his*
b   Gk Syr Vg Tg: Heb *their*

were known for their fertility. **18–19:** Cf. Ex 34.6–7; Ps 103.8–10; contrast Nah 1.2–3. **18:** The sentence *Who is a God like you* is reminiscent of the prophet's name (1.1n.). **20:** Gen 12.1–3; 17.6–8.

NAHUM

NAME AND CANONICAL STATUS

The name Nahum derives from the Hebrew word for "comfort." It may be a shortened form of Nehemiah—"God has comforted."

The book is the seventh of the twelve Minor Prophets (see the Introduction to the Prophetic Books). In the books of Hosea, Amos, and Micah, those prophets devote much attention to explaining that Israel and Judah fell because of the people's sin. The next three books of the collection, begun by Nahum, explain God's sovereignty over the nations through which God carried out that punishment. Nahum insists that God will soon punish Nineveh, the capital of the Assyrian empire in the eighth century BCE. The Assyrians are infamous to the biblical writers for their destruction of the Northern Kingdom of Israel in 722 BCE, and even after Assyria passed from world dominance, it remained a symbol for brutal imperial control, as seen in works of the Hellenistic period such as the books of Judith and Tobit. Following Nahum, Habakkuk pointedly calls for God's action against the Babylonians, and Zephaniah joins oracles against Judah with oracles against the nations and offers a glimmer of hope for both.

DATE OF COMPOSITION

Nahum was written sometime after the fall of the Egyptian city of Thebes (mentioned in Nah 3.8) in 663 BCE. Because it looks forward to the fall of Nineveh, accomplished by a coalition of Babylonians and Medes in 612 BCE, the book is often dated to just before that major event. Recent interpretation of the prophetic books, however, suggests that they provide retrospective interpretations of Israel's history, so the book could date after 612 BCE. To readers aware that Nineveh had indeed fallen, Nahum would reveal not only God's powerful hand in international affairs but also the role of prophets in preparing each generation for events to come.

CONTENTS AND INTERPRETATION

A common genre within the prophetic books is the "oracle against the nations," which pronounces God's judgment on those other than Israel or Judah. While Isaiah, Jeremiah, Zephaniah, and others outline God's displeasure at multiple nations, Nahum focuses on only one: Assyria.

Throughout Nahum, God is cast as a mighty warrior whose armies violently defeat the foe. After an opening depiction of God as a cosmic power in ch 1, the book turns in chs 2 and 3 to vivid images of Nineveh in the midst of siege and defeat. The images of warfare are stark and disturbing: captive slave women beat their breasts (2.7), dead bodies fill Nineveh's streets (3.3), and Nineveh itself is portrayed as a woman who is sexually assaulted by God (3.5–7). The author shows no pity for Nineveh or its inhabitants, instead delighting in its overthrow and claiming that all nations do the same (3.19).

For this reason, many readers condemn the book and contrast it negatively with the book of Jonah, which insists that God cares about the Ninevites and which describes the Assyrians as repenting. The difference between the books, however, may be due less to different ancient assessments of the Assyrians than to the different messages the books proclaim. While Jonah demonstrates the depths of divine mercy by showing stereotypically evil Ninevites in the act of repentance, Nahum establishes the sovereignty of God over all tyrants by showing powerful Nineveh in defeat. The power of God is good news for Judah, as seen especially in Nah 1 where God's anger is presented as an act of care for Judah: God will serve as a stronghold to those who seek divine refuge (1.7), caring enough about their affliction to become angry on their behalf.

Reading Nahum raises issues that are disturbingly contemporary, such as justice, violence, revenge, and women as symbols of evil. Although the question that ends the book is rhetorical, perhaps Nahum leaves its readers with a more serious quandary: how can one appreciate Nahum's call for justice without embracing its celebration of violence?

Julia M. O'Brien

1

An oracle concerning Nineveh. The book of the vision of Nahum of Elkosh.

[2] A jealous and avenging God is the Lord,
    the Lord is avenging and wrathful;
the Lord takes vengeance on his adversaries
    and rages against his enemies.
[3] The Lord is slow to anger but great in
        power,
    and the Lord will by no means clear the
        guilty.

His way is in whirlwind and storm,
    and the clouds are the dust of his feet.
[4] He rebukes the sea and makes it dry,
    and he dries up all the rivers;
Bashan and Carmel wither,
    and the bloom of Lebanon fades.
[5] The mountains quake before him,
    and the hills melt;
the earth heaves before him,
    the world and all who live in it.

[6] Who can stand before his indignation?
    Who can endure the heat of his anger?
His wrath is poured out like fire,
    and by him the rocks are broken in
        pieces.

[7] The Lord is good,
    a stronghold in a day of trouble;
he protects those who take refuge in him,
    [8] even in a rushing flood.
He will make a full end of his adversaries,[a]
    and will pursue his enemies into
        darkness.
[9] Why do you plot against the Lord?
    He will make an end;
    no adversary will rise up twice.
[10] Like thorns they are entangled,
    like drunkards they are drunk;
    they are consumed like dry straw.
[11] From you one has gone out
    who plots evil against the Lord,
    one who counsels wickedness.

[12] Thus says the Lord,
"Though they are at full strength and
        many,[b]
    they will be cut off and pass away.
Though I have afflicted you,
    I will afflict you no more.
[13] And now I will break off his yoke from you
    and snap the bonds that bind you."

a Gk: Heb *of her place*
b Meaning of Heb uncertain

1.1: Superscription. Like other prophetic books, Nahum begins with a description of its contents. *Oracle* also begins prophetic collections in Isa 13; Hab 1; Zech 9; 12; and Mal 1. Although other prophetic books mention the writing of prophecy, Nahum is the only one explicitly called a *book*; the Hebrew term refers to anything that is written and may refer to a scroll. *Vision* in the Hebrew Bible refers almost exclusively to prophecy; seeing is linked with the reception of prophecy in the superscriptions of Amos, Micah, and Habakkuk. The location of *Elkosh* is unknown.

1.2–8: Establishing God's power. Before addressing the specific issue of Nineveh, the book seeks to establish God's power and might. These verses form a partial acrostic; that is, most lines in vv. 2–8 begin with successive letters of the first half of Hebrew alphabet. **2–3a:** First, God's attributes are named and God's character established: God is *jealous* for God's people and does not ignore wrongdoing. This version of Israel's familiar confession of faith (see Ex 34.6; Jon 4.2; Ps 86.15; etc.) highlights *vengeance*, the deity's willingness and power to right wrongs. **3b–5:** God's appearance on earth, the divine theophany, is as an angry, cosmic warrior (cf. 2 Sam 22.8–16 = Ps 18.7–15; Ps 29; Hab 3.3–12). **4:** The language may allude to ancient Near Eastern cosmologies, in which the deities "River" and "Sea" were defeated by a more powerful god (see also Hab 3; Ps 74.13). *Bashan* in northern Transjordan, *Carmel* on Israel's northern Mediterranean coast, and *Lebanon* are areas known for agricultural fertility; God is powerful enough to dry them up. **5:** God's appearance shakes *mountains* (Judg 5.5; Ps 18.7; Isa 64.1). **6–8:** As expressed in the first of several rhetorical questions in the book, no one who opposes this God can stand, while no one who seeks divine *refuge* will suffer. In biblical Hebrew as in English, *anger* is associated with *heat* (e.g., Ex 32.22; Judg 6.39; Jer 7.20; 17.4).

1.9–15: God's power turned against Nineveh. The shift in addressee to *you* marks a move from the general description of divine power to its specific application. The gender and identity of *you*, however, change in the course of the unit: the feminine *you* in 1.9–13 and 15 likely refers to Judah, and the masculine *you* in 1.14 likely is the king of Assyria. Many of the references in these verses, such as to the one *who plots evil* (v. 11), are unclear.

[14] The LORD has commanded concerning
 you:
  "Your name shall be perpetuated no
   longer;
from the house of your gods I will cut off
 the carved image and the cast image.
I will make your grave, for you are
 worthless."

[15] [a]Look! On the mountains the feet of one
 who brings good tidings,
  who proclaims peace!
Celebrate your festivals, O Judah,
 fulfill your vows,
for never again shall the wicked invade
 you;
  they are utterly cut off.

2 A shatterer[b] has come up against you.
 Guard the ramparts;
  watch the road;
gird your loins;
 collect all your strength.

[2] (For the LORD is restoring the majesty of
 Jacob,
  as well as the majesty of Israel,
though ravagers have ravaged them
 and ruined their branches.)

[3] The shields of his warriors are red;
 his soldiers are clothed in crimson.

The metal on the chariots flashes
 on the day when he musters them;
  the chargers[c] prance.
[4] The chariots race madly through the
 streets,
 they rush to and fro through the
  squares;
their appearance is like torches,
 they dart like lightning.
[5] He calls his officers;
 they stumble as they come
  forward;
they hasten to the wall,
 and the mantelet[d] is set up.
[6] The river gates are opened,
 the palace trembles.
[7] It is decreed[d] that the city[e] be
 exiled,
 its slave women led away,
moaning like doves
 and beating their breasts.
[8] Nineveh is like a pool
 whose waters[f] run away.

a Ch 2.1 in Heb
b Cn: Heb *scatterer*
c Cn Compare Gk Syr: Heb *cypresses*
d Meaning of Heb uncertain
e Heb *it*
f Cn Compare Gk: Heb *a pool, from the days that she has become, and they*

12: While acknowledging a role in Judah's oppression, God promises that its salvation has begun. **13:** *His yoke*, the political oppression of the king of Assyria, is about to break. **14:** Threats against the king of Assyria include loss of reputation, religious practice, and life itself. The king is *worthless* or, in Hebrew, a "trifling." **15:** A messenger brings the good news of the imminent death of the enemy to Judah, who can now celebrate its own religious traditions. *One who brings good tidings*, see 2 Sam 18.27,31; Isa 40.9; 41.27; 52.7. *Fulfill your vows*, presumably vows made to God during the oppression in hope of deliverance.

 2.1–13: The siege of Nineveh. A vivid description of the divine warrior's battle against the city of Nineveh. **1:** *You* is a feminine form, likely Nineveh. Here, as later in the book, the call for Nineveh to protect itself is sarcastic. *Shatterer*, "scatterer" in Hebrew (see translation note a), may be God, who leads warriors against Nineveh (vv. 3–6). A form of this word is used for the divine warrior's activity in Hab 3.14 and Isa 24.1. **2:** Parenthetical reminder that Nineveh's downfall avenges the devastation of the Northern Kingdom of *Israel* (722 BCE), whose ancestor is *Jacob*. **3–6:** Descriptive language and active verbs create arresting images of God's invading army. **5:** *He* likely is the king of Assyria, who tries in vain to defend the city by bolstering its walls. **6–8a:** The actual fall of the city is depicted with water imagery, conventional imagery found in other ancient Near Eastern documents and in Jer 51. **6:** *The river gates*, Nineveh was situated on the east bank of the Tigris River, whose tributary, the Khosr, flowed through the city, so it is possible that actual flooding occurred during the attack; see v. 8. **7:** The description of the mourning of the *slave women* adds poignancy to the scene; in Hebrew the sound of the words mimics mourning. **8b–10:** The NRSV has added quotation marks to highlight the writer's attempt to reproduce the shouts of the warriors. Incomplete sentences give a breathless feeling to the chaotic scene. **10a:** The first three words begin with the same letter in English, as the translators attempt to mirror the alliteration found in

"Halt! Halt!"—
but no one turns back.
⁹ "Plunder the silver,
plunder the gold!
There is no end of treasure!
An abundance of every precious thing!"

¹⁰ Devastation, desolation, and
destruction!
Hearts faint and knees tremble,
all loins quake,
all faces grow pale!
¹¹ What became of the lions' den,
the cave[a] of the young lions,
where the lion goes,
and the lion's cubs, with no one to
disturb them?
¹² The lion has torn enough for his
whelps
and strangled prey for his lionesses;
he has filled his caves with prey
and his dens with torn flesh.

¹³ See, I am against you, says the LORD
of hosts, and I will burn your[b] chariots in
smoke, and the sword shall devour your
young lions; I will cut off your prey from the
earth, and the voice of your messengers shall
be heard no more.

3 Ah! City of bloodshed,
utterly deceitful, full of booty—
no end to the plunder!

² The crack of whip and rumble of wheel,
galloping horse and bounding chariot!
³ Horsemen charging,
flashing sword and glittering spear,
piles of dead,
heaps of corpses,
dead bodies without end—
they stumble over the bodies!
⁴ Because of the countless debaucheries of
the prostitute,
gracefully alluring, mistress of sorcery,
who enslaves[c] nations through her
debaucheries,
and peoples through her sorcery,
⁵ I am against you,
says the LORD of hosts,
and will lift up your skirts over your
face;
and I will let nations look on your nakedness
and kingdoms on your shame.
⁶ I will throw filth at you
and treat you with contempt,
and make you a spectacle.
⁷ Then all who see you will shrink from
you and say,
"Nineveh is devastated; who will bemoan
her?"
Where shall I seek comforters for you?

a Cn: Heb pasture
b Heb her
c Heb sells

the Hebrew version of the phrase. **11–13:** The author begins a taunt of the Assyrian king by comparing him to a lion, an animal frequently associated with the Assyrian empire in its own art. Although the king (*lion*) has provided much wealth (*prey*) for his citizens (*his whelps*), God will cut off both. The *you* of v.13 is feminine, turning the taunt to Nineveh herself. The verse ties together previous parts of Nahum: the description of *chariots* in 2.4, the analogy of the den of the *lion* in 2.11–12, and the reference to a messenger in 1.15: while a messenger brought good news to Judah, now the *messengers* of the Assyrians are cut off.

3.1–19: Further taunts against feminine Nineveh and the Assyrian king. Nahum's personification of Nineveh as a woman, begun in the previous chapter, turns derogatory, as the city is envisioned as a prostitute who is taunted as well as assaulted. **1–3:** The absence of verbs creates a montage of horrific images of the city's destruction. **1:** *Ah* is an exclamation calling attention to woman Nineveh. *City of bloodshed,* similar language is used for Israel, Judah, and Jerusalem in Ezek 7.23; 9.9; and for Babylon in Hab 2.12. **4–7:** The punishment of the prostitute Nineveh begins. **4:** While the Hebrew term for *prostitute* can refer to one who receives money for sex acts, it also is used in the Bible to refer to promiscuity and unfaithfulness (Deut 22.21; 31.16; Ezek 23.3; Hos 4.13–14). Here the term may function as a slur against the city rather than a description of its activities. Nineveh's control over and appeal to other nations is attributed to *sorcery* and seduction. **5:** God will personally take action against Nineveh. The uncovering of *nakedness* is a matter of *shame* (Gen 9.22–23; Lev 18–20; Isa 47.3; Lam 1.8; Hab 2.15) and is often a prelude to sexual violation (Jer 13.22). **6:** Nineveh's nakedness will be made into a *spectacle,* as is the punished woman in Hos 2.10. **7:** The absence of *comforters* for Nineveh is ironic, given that "Nahum" derives from the word for "comfort." The image of Nineveh as a devastated woman finds a parallel in the depiction of Jerusalem in the book of Lamentations.

8 Are you better than Thebes[a]
    that sat by the Nile,
with water around her,
    her rampart a sea,
    water her wall?
9 Ethiopia[b] was her strength,
    Egypt too, and that without limit;
    Put and the Libyans were her[c] helpers.

10 Yet she became an exile,
    she went into captivity;
even her infants were dashed in pieces
    at the head of every street;
lots were cast for her nobles,
    all her dignitaries were bound in fetters.
11 You also will be drunken,
    you will go into hiding;[d]
you will seek
    a refuge from the enemy.
12 All your fortresses are like fig trees
    with first-ripe figs—
if shaken they fall
    into the mouth of the eater.
13 Look at your troops:
    they are women in your midst.
The gates of your land
    are wide open to your foes;
    fire has devoured the bars of your gates.

14 Draw water for the siege,
    strengthen your forts;
trample the clay,
    tread the mortar,
    take hold of the brick mold!

15 There the fire will devour you,
    the sword will cut you off.
    It will devour you like the locust.

Multiply yourselves like the locust,
    multiply like the grasshopper!
16 You increased your merchants
    more than the stars of the heavens.
    The locust sheds its skin and flies
        away.
17 Your guards are like grasshoppers,
    your scribes like swarms[d] of locusts
settling on the fences
    on a cold day—
when the sun rises, they fly away;
    no one knows where they have gone.

18 Your shepherds are asleep,
    O king of Assyria;
    your nobles slumber.
Your people are scattered on the
        mountains
    with no one to gather them.
19 There is no assuaging your hurt,
    your wound is mortal.
All who hear the news about you
    clap their hands over you.
For who has ever escaped
    your endless cruelty?

a   Heb *No-amon*
b   Or *Nubia*; Heb *Cush*
c   Gk: Heb *your*
d   Meaning of Heb uncertain

8–13: Nineveh is threatened with the same fate that befell Thebes, the most important city in southern Egypt, which was conquered by the Assyrians in 663 BCE. 8: The threat starts in the form of a rhetorical question, one of many in the book. 9–10: Thebes' sea defenses and her allies *Ethiopia*, *Put*, and the *Libyans* could not protect her. Just as she went into exile and her *infants were dashed in pieces* (see Isa 13.16; Ps 137.9), so Nineveh will suffer. 11: Military defeat is often described as stumbling as though drunken (Isa 51.22; Jer 25.16,27; 51.3). 13: Nineveh's *troops* are taunted as being as weak as *women*, language also used in Assyrian documents to describe defeated soldiers. *Gates* may be an allusion to female genitals (as also perhaps in Isa 3.26): Nineveh is open to violation. 14–17: The call for Nineveh to fortify itself for battle is sarcastic, as in 2.1: the city's fate is sealed. Locust imagery is used in several ways in these verses: Nineveh will be devoured as by *the locust* (v. 15a), even should its warriors multiply like *locusts* (v. 15b), and those charged with protecting the city are as undependable as *swarms of locusts* (v. 17). 16–17: *Merchants* may allude to Assyria's economic power in the ancient world. *Merchants*, *guards*, and *scribes*, each a part of a thriving society, all abandon Nineveh. 18–19: Shepherd imagery dominates the final taunt of the king of Assyria. Ironically, the one who was once called the "lion" (2.11–12) is here described as having incompetent *shepherds*, a common designation for leaders or *nobles* (Jer 3.15; 10.21; 25.35; Ezek 34.2–12). 19: All nations are described as celebrating the Assyrian king's defeat because of Nineveh's *endless cruelty*. A final rhetorical question ends this book, a feature shared with the book of Jonah, also concerned with Nineveh.

HABAKKUK

LOCATION IN CANON, AUTHORSHIP, AND LITERARY HISTORY

Habakkuk is the eighth of the twelve Minor Prophets (see Introduction to the Prophetic Books). Despite the book's first-person style, we know nothing about Habakkuk as a person. The superscription, the opening introductory title of a prophetic collection, only provides a label for the book. Unlike the complex superscriptions of Isaiah, Jeremiah, Amos, and Micah, the opening of Habakkuk does not give the prophet's family, location, or time period.

The prophet does appear as a character in later Jewish and Christian literature. In the Addition to Daniel known as Bel and the Dragon in the Apocrypha, Habakkuk is transported by an angel to feed Daniel in the lions' den (Bel 33–39). Other traditions locate him in the times of Manasseh or Jeremiah and Ezekiel, in the seventh and early sixth centuries BCE. A commentary on Habakkuk from Qumran, called a "pesher" for its style of applying the biblical text directly to events of the writer's own day, provides not only an early copy of the text itself but also a glimpse of how Habakkuk's words resonated with a later generation.

CONTENT AND LITERARY STYLE

Habakkuk complains about the violence of the Babylonians, called the Chaldeans in 1.6. Their empire came to power in the seventh century BCE after defeating the Assyrians. As described in 1 Kings 23–25, Babylonia soon dominated Judah's political life and in 586 BCE destroyed its independent existence as a state: Babylonian armies burned the Temple in Jerusalem and exiled many of the population.

Other prophetic collections such as Isa 14.3–23 and Jer 50–51 pronounce God's judgment on Babylon for its cruelty. While Habakkuk's anti-Babylonian rhetoric is similar, even sharing some vocabulary with Jeremiah, its literary style is different. The core of the book takes the form of alternating speeches of the prophet and God (1.2–17 and 2.1–20). In each case, the prophet voices the community's complaint in the first person, granting it immediacy and poignancy. God's ensuing speech does not directly answer the prophet but rather raises new issues for consideration. The book ends with the speech of the prophet, cast as a prayer for God to act as a warrior on behalf of the people. The divine warrior who was depicted as marching to right wrongs in Nah 1 is entreated here to return and save again.

DATE OF COMPOSITION

Because of its anti-Babylonian theme, the book is often dated to the late seventh century BCE, the height of Babylonian power. A key issue of interpretation, however, is whether the prophet's initial complaint in 1.2–4 concerns the Babylonians themselves or rather another enemy that will itself be conquered by the even more brutal Babylonians. Is God's rousing of the Babylonians in 1.5–11 offered as an answer to the prophet's complaint about someone else, or is it instead God's agreement about the nature of the Babylonians? The accusations in 1.4 of injustice and the perversion of the law could describe wrongdoing in a variety of contexts, including within Judah itself. These ambiguities, as well as the generic language of the book, rule out certainty in dating, yet the same features contribute to the book's ability to resonate in multiple times and places.

INTERPRETATION

A classic question in monotheistic traditions is why, if God is just and caring, do believers suffer? While the book of Job pointedly raises this question on behalf of an individual, the book of Habakkuk complains about the suffering of the community as a whole at the hand of tyrants. Nowhere does the book attempt to solve the problem of God's apparent injustice. Instead, it models the legitimacy of human protest as well as the power of trusting in God's power even when it is not apparent.

Julia M. O'Brien

1 The oracle that the prophet Habakkuk saw.

² O LORD, how long shall I cry for help,
  and you will not listen?
Or cry to you "Violence!"
  and you will not save?
³ Why do you make me see wrongdoing
  and look at trouble?
Destruction and violence are before me;
  strife and contention arise.
⁴ So the law becomes slack
  and justice never prevails.
The wicked surround the righteous—
  therefore judgment comes forth
    perverted.

⁵ Look at the nations, and see!
  Be astonished! Be astounded!
For a work is being done in your days
  that you would not believe if you were
    told.
⁶ For I am rousing the Chaldeans,
  that fierce and impetuous nation,
who march through the breadth of the earth
  to seize dwellings not their own.
⁷ Dread and fearsome are they;
  their justice and dignity proceed from
    themselves.

⁸ Their horses are swifter than
    leopards,
  more menacing than wolves at dusk;
  their horses charge.
Their horsemen come from far away;
  they fly like an eagle swift to
    devour.
⁹ They all come for violence,
  with faces pressing[a] forward;
  they gather captives like sand.
¹⁰ At kings they scoff,
  and of rulers they make sport.
They laugh at every fortress,
  and heap up earth to take it.
¹¹ Then they sweep by like the wind;
  they transgress and become guilty;
  their own might is their god!

¹² Are you not from of old,
  O LORD my God, my Holy One?
  You[b] shall not die.
O LORD, you have marked them for
    judgment;
  and you, O Rock, have established them
    for punishment.

---

a Meaning of Heb uncertain
b Ancient Heb tradition: MT *We*

1.1: Superscription. Like Nahum, which precedes it in the canon, the book of Habakkuk is called an *oracle*; Nahum is also called a vision, deriving from the same Hebrew verbal root as *saw* (cf. also Isa 1.1; Am 1.1). The book calls Habakkuk a *prophet* here and in 3.1. The superscription provides no family, geographical, or chronological information.

1.2–17: First interaction between the prophet and God. 2–4: The prophet speaks. While it is common for prophetic books to begin with the prophet speaking *for* God, Habakkuk pointedly begins with the prophet speaking *to* God, complaining about injustice. As in psalms of lament, *how long* introduces complaint and petition (Ps 6.3; 13.1; 35.17; 74.10; 79.5). Although he speaks in the first person, the prophet seems to speak for the community as a whole. The complaint that the *wicked surround the righteous* will be repeated in 1.13. **3:** Jer 20.8. **4:** *The law becomes slack*, this could refer to the reign of Jehoiakim (608–598 BCE), when the reforms of his father Josiah languished (2 Kings 23.35–37; cf. Jer 2.8). The *law* (Heb "torah") formed the basis of Josiah's reforms. **5–11: God speaks.** Rather than directly answering the prophet's questions, God addresses the community as a whole (*you* is plural), explaining that God is *rousing the Chaldeans* (the Neo-Babylonian empire, ca. 612–539 BCE); although they are fierce, they are being sent by God. The NRSV refers throughout this unit to *they*, but the Hebrew alternates between singular and plural references to the enemy. In response to the prophet's complaint of *violence* in 1.2, God explains that the Babylonians *come for violence*, and the complaint about the lack of *justice* in 1.4 is countered with the acknowledgment that the Babylonians make their own *justice*. God's words intensify rather than satisfy the prophet's claims. **12–17: The prophet speaks.** Having received no answer to his complaints, the prophet again appeals to God to save. **12–13:** As in numerous psalms, the prophet appeals to God's goodness and constancy as the basis for his request: why, if God is good, does God not act? **12:** *From of old*, Ps 74.12. As the note to the translation footnote explains, the Masoretic Text likely changed the original reading of *You* to *We* in order to avoid the possibility of suggesting that God could die. The metaphor of God as *Rock* appears frequently in the Bible (e.g., Deut 32.4; 2 Sam 23.3; Pss 18.2; 62.2,6–7; Isa 30.29). The claim that the

13 Your eyes are too pure to behold evil,
  and you cannot look on wrongdoing;
why do you look on the treacherous,
  and are silent when the wicked swallow
  those more righteous than they?
14 You have made people like the fish of the
  sea,
  like crawling things that have no ruler.

15 The enemy[a] brings all of them up with a
  hook;
  he drags them out with his net,
he gathers them in his seine;
  so he rejoices and exults.
16 Therefore he sacrifices to his net
  and makes offerings to his seine;
for by them his portion is lavish,
  and his food is rich.
17 Is he then to keep on emptying his net,
  and destroying nations without mercy?

2 I will stand at my watchpost,
  and station myself on the rampart;
I will keep watch to see what he will say
  to me,
  and what he[b] will answer concerning
  my complaint.
2 Then the LORD answered me and said:
Write the vision;
  make it plain on tablets,
  so that a runner may read it.
3 For there is still a vision for the appointed
  time;

it speaks of the end, and does not lie.
If it seems to tarry, wait for it;
  it will surely come, it will not delay.
4 Look at the proud!
  Their spirit is not right in them,
  but the righteous live by their faith.[c]
5 Moreover, wealth[d] is treacherous;
  the arrogant do not endure.
They open their throats wide as Sheol;
  like Death they never have enough.
They gather all nations for themselves,
  and collect all peoples as their own.

6 Shall not everyone taunt such people
and, with mocking riddles, say about them,
  "Alas for you who heap up what is not your
  own!"
  How long will you load yourselves with
  goods taken in pledge?
7 Will not your own creditors suddenly
  rise,
  and those who make you tremble wake
  up?
  Then you will be booty for them.
8 Because you have plundered many
  nations,
  all that survive of the peoples shall
  plunder you—

a Heb *He*
b Syr: Heb *I*
c Or *faithfulness*
d Other Heb Mss read *wine*

wicked oppress the *righteous* repeats the prophet's initial complaint in 1.4. **14–17:** *People*, Heb "'adam," the word used in Gen 1 to describe all humanity. There humanity was given dominion over the *fish of the sea* and *crawling things* (Gen 1.26,28); now the people have become *fish* in the *net* of the enemy. **16:** The enemy even treats his power, his *net*, as his god.

  2.1–20: Second interaction between the prophet and God. 1: The image of the prophet is that of a sentinel posted on the city walls, awaiting God's reply (cf. Isa 21.6–12; 62.7; Ezek 3.17; 33.7; Hos 9.8). **2:** God's reply will be a *vision*, from the same Hebrew word as "saw" in the book's superscription (1.1). It will be made plain to all, written largely enough that a *running* messenger can read it. **3–5:** All three verses constitute God's reply: the prophet is told to trust that an answer will come, despite its apparent *delay*. **4:** Although Rom 1.17; Gal 3.11; and Heb 10.38–39 draw heavily on this verse to prioritize *faith* over works, the Heb word is better understood as "faithfulness." Like the previous verse and 3.16, it stresses that the one who patiently awaits God's response will be rewarded. **5:** The *proud* of v. 4 are here linked with *wealth* and the *arrogant*. *Sheol*, the abode of the dead. In ancient Israelite and Canaanite literature death and the underworld are often depicted as an open mouth with an insatiable appetite; see Isa 5.14; Prov 30.15–16. **6–20: God's extended response, in five taunts.** Continuing the condemnation of pride and wealth are five taunts, each marked by *alas* (6b–8,9–11,12–14,15–17,18–19). The condemnation of rapaciousness, arrogance, and violence matches the description of Babylon in 1.6–11. **6–8:** The first taunt condemns the voracious appetite of the Babylonians. Common to prophetic literature is the affirmation that the evil will suffer the same pains they inflicted on others (Ob 15). **6b:** *Alas*, a term often used

because of human bloodshed, and
    violence to the earth,
        to cities and all who live in them.

9 "Alas for you who get evil gain for your
    house,
        setting your nest on high
        to be safe from the reach of harm!"
10 You have devised shame for your house
    by cutting off many peoples;
        you have forfeited your life.
11 The very stones will cry out from the
    wall,
        and the plaster[a] will respond from the
        woodwork.

12 "Alas for you who build a town by
    bloodshed,
        and found a city on iniquity!"
13 Is it not from the LORD of hosts
    that peoples labor only to feed the
        flames,
        and nations weary themselves for
        nothing?
14 But the earth will be filled
    with the knowledge of the glory of the
        LORD,
        as the waters cover the sea.

15 "Alas for you who make your neighbors
    drink,
        pouring out your wrath[b] until they are
        drunk,
            in order to gaze on their nakedness!"
16 You will be sated with contempt instead
    of glory.
        Drink, you yourself, and stagger!"[c]

The cup in the LORD's right hand
    will come around to you,
        and shame will come upon your glory!
17 For the violence done to Lebanon will
    overwhelm you;
        the destruction of the animals will
        terrify you—[d]
because of human bloodshed and violence
    to the earth,
        to cities and all who live in them.

18 What use is an idol
    once its maker has shaped it—
        a cast image, a teacher of lies?
For its maker trusts in what has been made,
    though the product is only an idol that
        cannot speak!
19 Alas for you who say to the wood, "Wake
    up!"
        to silent stone, "Rouse yourself!"
        Can it teach?
See, it is gold and silver plated,
    and there is no breath in it at all.

20 But the LORD is in his holy temple;
    let all the earth keep silence before him!

3 A prayer of the prophet Habakkuk ac-
    cording to Shigionoth.

2 O LORD, I have heard of your renown,
    and I stand in awe, O LORD, of your work.

a   Or *beam*
b   Or *poison*
c   Q Ms Gk: MT *be uncircumcised*
d   Gk Syr: Meaning of Heb uncertain

in funeral laments (1 Kings 13.30; Jer 22.18). **9–11**: Like Ob 3–4, the second taunt chastises the arrogance of the proud in setting their *nest* high; their very houses will rise up against them. **12–14**: The third taunt contrasts the aspirations of the peoples and the power of God. **14**: Isa 11.9. **15–17**: The fourth taunt insists that Babylon's fortunes will be reversed, using the imagery of drinking: she (Babylon) who made others *drink* of her *wrath* will herself drink God's cup of punishment (Jer 25.15–27; 51.7). Throughout the prophetic books, the punished suffer *shame* and *nakedness* (Jer 13.26; Ezek 7.18; Nah 3.5; Ob 10). **17**: Isa 14.8; 37.24 suggest that both Assyrian and Babylonian kings cut down the famous cedars of *Lebanon*; this verse suggests that the *animals* themselves will take revenge. *Bloodshed* and *violence* were mentioned earlier in 2.8. **18–20**: The fifth taunt differs from the others: *alas* does not begin the unit, and the theme of idolatry is introduced for the first time since 1.16. Isa 40.18–20; 44.9–20 also lampoon the making of an *idol*. **20**: Ps 11.4; Zeph 1.7; Zech 2.13.

3.1–19: The prayer of the prophet, in the form of a divine warrior hymn. The prophet, unsatisfied with God's previous responses, turns from complaint to petition. He invokes the biblical memory that God once marched as a divine warrior to vindicate the people (Nah 1; Ex 15; Deut 33; Isa 13) as the basis for his request that God march again to establish justice. **1**: The book's second superscription (see also 1.1) not only marks this chapter

In our own time revive it;
  in our own time make it known;
  in wrath may you remember mercy.
3 God came from Teman,
  the Holy One from Mount
    Paran.   Selah
His glory covered the heavens,
  and the earth was full of his
    praise.
4 The brightness was like the sun;
  rays came forth from his hand,
  where his power lay hidden.
5 Before him went pestilence,
  and plague followed close behind.
6 He stopped and shook the earth;
  he looked and made the nations
    tremble.
The eternal mountains were
    shattered;
  along his ancient pathways
  the everlasting hills sank low.
7 I saw the tents of Cushan under
    affliction;
  the tent-curtains of the land of Midian
    trembled.
8 Was your wrath against the rivers,a
    O Lord?
  Or your anger against the rivers,a
  or your rage against the sea,b
when you drove your horses,
  your chariots to victory?

9 You brandished your naked bow,
  satedc were the arrows at your
    command.d   Selah
You split the earth with rivers.
10 The mountains saw you, and writhed;
  a torrent of water swept by;
the deep gave forth its voice.
  The sune raised high its hands;
11 the moonf stood still in its exalted
    place,
  at the light of your arrows speeding by,
  at the gleam of your flashing spear.
12 In fury you trod the earth,
  in anger you trampled nations.
13 You came forth to save your people,
  to save your anointed.
You crushed the head of the wicked house,
  laying it bare from foundation
    to roof.d   Selah
14 You pierced with theirg own arrows the
    headh of his warriors,i

a Or *against River*
b Or *against Sea*
c Cn: Heb *oaths*
d Meaning of Heb uncertain
e Heb *It*
f Heb *sun, moon*
g Heb *his*
h Or *leader*
i Vg Compare Gk Syr: Meaning of Heb uncertain

as a *prayer* but also provides instruction for its musical performance. The singular form of *Shigionoth* appears in the superscription to Ps 7; its meaning is unknown. Other musical notations end vv. 3,9,13, and the book as a whole. They may indicate that, like the Psalms, Hab 3 originally was a musical composition, or perhaps that the chapter was written in the style of a musical composition. **2:** The prophet makes his opening petition for God to *revive* God's saving work in *our own time* and show *mercy*. **3–15:** A vision of the divine warrior. Although in Hebrew the verb tenses are ambiguous, the NRSV has rendered them in the past tense to underscore that the vision is a memory of how God acted in the past, particularly in delivering the Israelites from Egyptian bondage. **3:** As in Deut 33.2 and Judg 5.4, the divine warrior began his march from *Teman* (synonymous with Edom, as in Ob 9) and *Paran*, areas in Transjordan associated with God's dramatic deliverance of the Israelites from Egypt. **3:** *Selah*, here as in vv. 9 and 13, is a notation common to Psalms; its meaning is unclear, although it may indicate a musical pause. **4–11:** The description of God's dominance over *mountains*, *rivers*, etc., has strong mythical connotations and may allude to the cosmologies of other ancient Near Eastern cultures, in which *River* and *Sea* were deities defeated by a more powerful god (see translation notes *a* and *b*). Parallels are found in Pss 74.12–15; 89.9–10. The shaking of *mountains* is a common divine warrior motif (Judg 5.5; Ps 18.7; Isa 64.1). Throughout these verses, the warrior's scope is cosmic, as God brandishes *chariots, bow, arrows,* and *spear* while subduing all the earth. **5:** *Pestilence* and *plague* are pictured as divine attendants; cf. Ps 79.49. *Plague* (Heb "Resheph") is a well-attested deity in nonbiblical sources. **7:** Although the location of *Cushan* is unknown, it is here linked with *Midian*, another area connected with the Transjordanian wanderings of the Israelites. **10–11:** These and other verses are difficult to translate. *Mountains . . . writhed*, a common image in depictions of theophanies (divine appearances); cf. Pss 29.5–8; 114.3–7. **12:** As in Nah 1, God's *anger* is understood to be a positive force for action

who came like a whirlwind to scatter
us,[a]
gloating as if ready to devour the poor
who were in hiding.
[15] You trampled the sea with your horses,
churning the mighty waters.

[16] I hear, and I tremble within;
my lips quiver at the sound.
Rottenness enters into my bones,
and my steps tremble[b] beneath me.
I wait quietly for the day of calamity
to come upon the people who attack us.

[17] Though the fig tree does not blossom,
and no fruit is on the vines;

though the produce of the olive fails,
and the fields yield no food;
though the flock is cut off from the fold,
and there is no herd in the stalls,
[18] yet I will rejoice in the LORD;
I will exult in the God of my salvation.
[19] GOD, the Lord, is my strength;
he makes my feet like the feet of a deer,
and makes me tread upon the heights.[c]

To the leader: with stringed[d] instruments.

[a] Heb *me*
[b] Cn Compare Gk: Meaning of Heb uncertain
[c] Heb *my heights*
[d] Heb *my stringed*

against injustice. **15:** Further echoes of God's deliverance of the Israelites at the Red Sea (see Ex 15). **16–19a:** The prophet's response to the vision. **16:** After hearing a recital of the divine warrior's power, the prophet is awestruck, and is now able to trust that God will indeed act again. He has received the vision promised by God in 2.3 and can *wait quietly* (2.20; see also 2.4n.) for the *day of calamity* for his enemies. **17–19:** Although God's saving acts are not yet evident and the people and its land continue to suffer, the vision has allowed the prophet to trust in God's saving power. The book closes with a psalmlike affirmation that God is the prophet's *strength* (Ps 118.14) and makes his feet *like the feet of a deer* (Ps 18.33 = 2 Sam 22.34). **19:** The concluding instruction to the music *leader* to accompany the text with *stringed instruments* (see Pss 4; 6; 45; 54; 55; etc.) reinforces the psalmlike style of the chapter.

ZEPHANIAH

NAME, CANONICAL LOCATION, AND DATE OF COMPOSITION

Zephaniah is the ninth of the twelve Minor Prophets (see Introduction to Prophetic Literature). The book's superscription, its introductory title, provides more detailed information than do those of Nahum and Habakkuk, the two books that precede it in the canon.

After listing a four-generation genealogy, the superscription links the prophet (whose name means "the LORD has hidden" or "the LORD has stored up") with the reign of the Judean king Josiah. Second Kings 22–23 lauds Josiah as one of Judah's great religious reformers; before his death in 609 BCE, he removed foreign images from the Temple in Jerusalem, centralized worship practices, and established for Judah a degree of political independence from the Assyrian empire. Second Kings 16–23 also traces the close tie between worship practices and politics in this period. Submission to the Assyrians meant the inclusion of their religious statuary in the Temple (2 Kings 16.18), while resistance to Assyrian power both by Josiah and by his predecessor Hezekiah (see 1.1n.) was bolstered by the removal of such images. Resonating strongly with the narratives in 2 Kings, Zephaniah blames Judeans for mixing worship of the LORD with the worship of other deities (1.4–5) and accuses the royal court of dressing in foreign attire (1.8–9).

While the literary setting of the book in the seventh century BCE is obvious, the book may actually have been composed or at least substantially edited at a later date. The concluding promise of salvation for daughter Jerusalem (3.14–20), for example, reflects an exilic or postexilic perspective in its concern with the return of exiles to the city.

CONTENTS

Zephaniah is a typical prophetic book. It opens with a dramatic announcement of the Day of the LORD, prophetic language for a time in which God will act decisively to (re-)establish justice (Joel 1.15; 3.14; Am 5.18; Ob 15; Zech 12.4). It pairs oracles against foreign nations (cf. Isa 13–23; Jer 46–51; Ezek 25–32; Am 1.3–2.3) with oracles against Judah (cf. Isa 3; 5; Jer 1; 3; Am 2; Mic 2), accusing Judah of idolatry and injustice (cf. Isa 5.7; Jer 2.28; 11.13) and the nations of arrogance (cf. Isa 16.6; Jer 48.29; Zech 10.11). Zephaniah also ends with an announcement of salvation to daughter Jerusalem, similar to those found in other prophetic books (e.g., Mic 4; Zech 2; 9).

INTERPRETATION

The book's powerful language for divine judgment captivated the imagination of later interpreters. The *Dies Irae* ("day of wrath"), a thirteenth-century Christian hymn long included in the Mass for the Dead, derives from the Latin translation of the harrowing Day of the LORD imagery in ch 1. The *Apocalypse of Zephaniah*, a Jewish document usually dated between 100 BCE and 70 CE, describes the prophet's tour of hell as well as his brief visit to heaven. "Shoah," the Hebrew word for *ruin* in 1.15, is now a designation for the devastation of European Jewry known as the Holocaust.

Julia M. O'Brien

1 The word of the Lord that came to Zephaniah son of Cushi son of Gedaliah son of Amariah son of Hezekiah, in the days of King Josiah son of Amon of Judah.

2 I will utterly sweep away everything
  from the face of the earth, says the Lord.
3 I will sweep away humans and animals;
  I will sweep away the birds of the air
  and the fish of the sea.
I will make the wicked stumble.ᵃ
  I will cut off humanity
  from the face of the earth, says the
    Lord.
4 I will stretch out my hand against Judah,
  and against all the inhabitants of
    Jerusalem;
and I will cut off from this place every
    remnant of Baal
  and the name of the idolatrous priests;ᵇ
5 those who bow down on the roofs
  to the host of the heavens;
those who bow down and swear to the
    Lord,
  but also swear by Milcom;ᶜ
6 those who have turned back from
    following the Lord,
  who have not sought the Lord or
    inquired of him.

7 Be silent before the Lord God!
  For the day of the Lord is at hand;

the Lord has prepared a sacrifice,
  he has consecrated his guests.
8 And on the day of the Lord's sacrifice
I will punish the officials and the king's
    sons
  and all who dress themselves in foreign
    attire.
9 On that day I will punish
  all who leap over the threshold,
who fill their master's house
  with violence and fraud.

10 On that day, says the Lord,
  a cry will be heard from the Fish
    Gate,
a wail from the Second Quarter,
  a loud crash from the hills.
11 The inhabitants of the Mortar wail,
  for all the traders have perished;
  all who weigh out silver are cut off.
12 At that time I will search Jerusalem with
    lamps,
  and I will punish the people
who rest complacentlyᵈ on their dregs,
  those who say in their hearts,

ᵃ Cn: Heb *sea, and those who cause the wicked to stumble*
ᵇ Compare Gk: Heb *the idolatrous priests with the priests*
ᶜ Gk Mss Syr Vg: Heb *Malcam* (or, *their king*)
ᵈ Heb *who thicken*

1.1: Superscription. *Cushi* may be either a name or an ethnic designation, Ethiopian (see 2.12 and 3.10). *Gedaliah* and *Amariah* are otherwise unknown, although the names also appear in postexilic books. If *Hezekiah* is the eighth-century reformer King Hezekiah (727/715–698/687 BCE; 2 Kings 18), then Zephaniah would be a member of the royal family. The unusually long genealogy suggests this may have been the case. *Josiah* (640–609 BCE) was also a reformer (2 Kings 22–23), although his father *Amon* had sacrificed to carved images (2 Chr 33.22).

1.2–18: The Coming Day of the Lord. 2–3: Punishment is announced first against *everything from the face of the earth*. The language echoes that used in Gen 1 to describe creation and in Gen 6.7; 7.4; and 8.8 to describe God's punishment through the Flood. **4–5:** God's focus turns to Judah, whose inhabitants are charged with combining worship of the Lord with worship of other deities such as the Canaanite god *Baal,* the astral deities known as *the host of the heavens,* and the Ammonite god *Milcom.* These charges, as well as the term for *idolatrous priests,* fit well with the accounts of Manasseh's idolatry in 2 Kings 21 and Josiah's reforms in 2 Kings 23; see also Jer 19.13; 32.29. **7–18:** *The Day of the Lord* (Joel 1.15; 3.14; Am 5.18; Ob 15; Zech 12.4). **7–13:** First outlined are the implications of the Day for Judah. **7:** *Be silent,* cf. Hab 2.20. Judah is described as an animal *sacrificed* by God to serve *his guests.* **8–13:** A listing of Judah's crimes. **8–9:** The linkage between adoption of *foreign attire* with *leaping over the threshold,* likely a non-Judean religious custom (cf. 1 Sam 5.5), connects political assimilation with idolatry. **10–11:** *The Fish Gate* (Neh 3.3; 12.39), *the Second Quarter* (2 Kings 22.14), and *the Mortar* (unidentified) likely all refer to wealthy districts in Jerusalem, where *traders* work. **12–13:** Every one of the wealthy in these districts will be searched out and punished. Because they doubt God's oversight of the world (see also

"The LORD will not do good,
nor will he do harm."
[13] Their wealth shall be plundered,
and their houses laid waste.
Though they build houses,
they shall not inhabit them;
though they plant vineyards,
they shall not drink wine from them.

[14] The great day of the LORD is near,
near and hastening fast;
the sound of the day of the LORD is bitter,
the warrior cries aloud there.
[15] That day will be a day of wrath,
a day of distress and anguish,
a day of ruin and devastation,
a day of darkness and gloom,
a day of clouds and thick darkness,
[16] a day of trumpet blast and battle cry
against the fortified cities
and against the lofty battlements.

[17] I will bring such distress upon people
that they shall walk like the blind;
because they have sinned against the
LORD,
their blood shall be poured out like dust,
and their flesh like dung.
[18] Neither their silver nor their gold
will be able to save them
on the day of the LORD's wrath;
in the fire of his passion
the whole earth shall be consumed;
for a full, a terrible end
he will make of all the inhabitants of
the earth.

2 Gather together, gather,
O shameless nation,
[2] before you are driven away

like the drifting chaff,[a]
before there comes upon you
the fierce anger of the LORD,
before there comes upon you
the day of the LORD's wrath.
[3] Seek the LORD, all you humble of the land,
who do his commands;
seek righteousness, seek humility;
perhaps you may be hidden
on the day of the LORD's wrath.
[4] For Gaza shall be deserted,
and Ashkelon shall become a
desolation;
Ashdod's people shall be driven out at
noon,
and Ekron shall be uprooted.

[5] Ah, inhabitants of the seacoast,
you nation of the Cherethites!
The word of the LORD is against you,
O Canaan, land of the Philistines;
and I will destroy you until no
inhabitant is left.
[6] And you, O seacoast, shall be pastures,
meadows for shepherds
and folds for flocks.
[7] The seacoast shall become the possession
of the remnant of the house of Judah,
on which they shall pasture,
and in the houses of Ashkelon
they shall lie down at evening.
For the LORD their God will be mindful of
them
and restore their fortunes.

[8] I have heard the taunts of Moab
and the revilings of the Ammonites,

a   Cn Compare Gk Syr: Heb *before a decree is born;
like chaff a day has passed away*

Mal 2.17), their labor will not be successful (see Deut 28.30–31 and cf. Isa 65.21). **14–18:** The chapter ends as it began, with attention on *all the inhabitants of the earth*. As elsewhere in the prophets, the *Day* is one of divine wrath (Isa 13.9) from which *silver* and *gold* provide no protection (Ezek 7.19). **15:** Am 5.18–20.

2.1–3: Call to repentance. Although the Day of the LORD seems inevitable, Judah's repentance may yet stave off destruction. **1:** The *shameless nation* likely is Judah. **3:** As in Joel 2.14 and Jon 3.8–9, the prophet underscores that some could *perhaps* survive if they *seek righteousness* (Isa 51.1).

2.4–15: Judgment on the nations. The call for Judah to repent shifts to promises that Judah's enemies will be destroyed and that Judeans will possess their land. Throughout, the threats employ language common to ancient Near Eastern curses against those who break the terms of a treaty. **4:** *Gaza, Ashkelon, Ashdod,* and *Ekron* are four of the five major cities of the Philistines (Josh 13.3). Missing from the traditional list is Gath, destroyed by the Assyrians ca. 712 BCE. **5:** The *Cherethites* may be synonymous with "Philistines" (Ezek 25.16; 2 Sam 8.18),

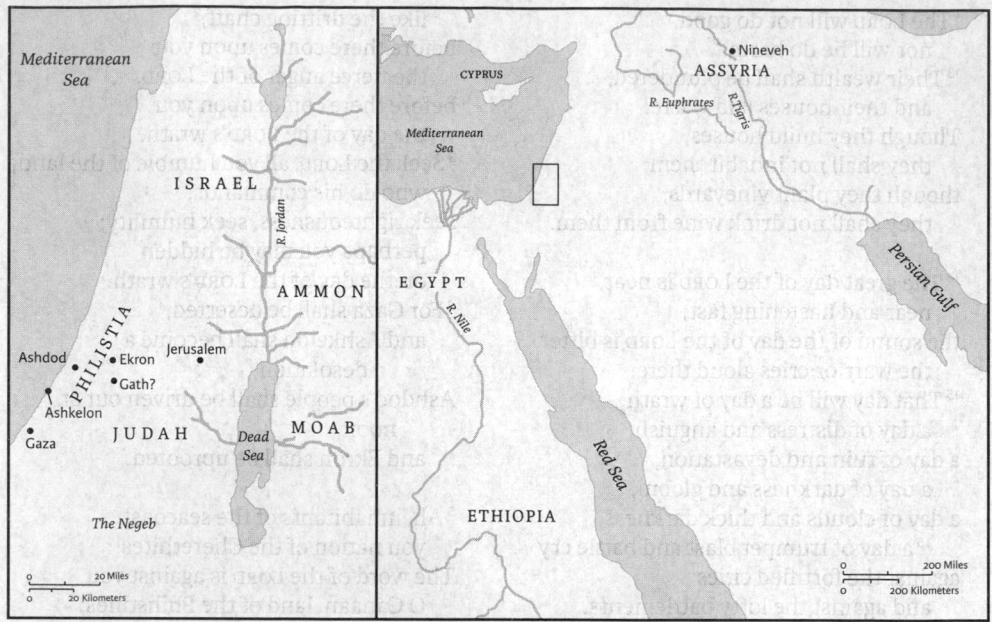

Ch 2.4–15: Places mentioned in the oracles against foreign nations.

how they have taunted my people
  and made boasts against their territory.
⁹ Therefore, as I live, says the LORD of
    hosts,
  the God of Israel,
Moab shall become like Sodom
  and the Ammonites like Gomorrah,
a land possessed by nettles and salt pits,
  and a waste forever.
The remnant of my people shall plunder
    them,
  and the survivors of my nation shall
    possess them.
¹⁰ This shall be their lot in return for their
    pride,
  because they scoffed and boasted
  against the people of the LORD of
    hosts.
¹¹ The LORD will be terrible against them;
  he will shrivel all the gods of the earth,

and to him shall bow down,
  each in its place,
  all the coasts and islands of the nations.

¹² You also, O Ethiopians,ᵃ
  shall be killed by my sword.

¹³ And he will stretch out his hand against
    the north,
  and destroy Assyria;
and he will make Nineveh a desolation,
  a dry waste like the desert.
¹⁴ Herds shall lie down in it,
  every wild animal;ᵇ
the desert owlᶜ and the screech owlᶜ
  shall lodge on its capitals;

ᵃ Or *Nubians*; Heb *Cushites*
ᵇ Tg Compare Gk: Heb *nation*
ᶜ Meaning of Heb uncertain

who ruled the area along the Mediterranean *seacoast*. In Hebrew, the cities are characterized as female. **8–11:** Threats against *Moab* and the *Ammonites*, two of Judah's eastern neighbors, are common in prophetic literature (Jer 48–49; Ezek 25; Am 1–2), as is the use of *Sodom* and *Gomorrah* to connote total annihilation (Gen 19; Isa 1.9; 13.19; Jer 23.14; 50.4). **9:** *Remnant* and *survivors* may reflect the situation of the Babylonian exile. **12:** The brief mention of the *Ethiopians* (Heb "Cush," see 1.1n.) seems out of place. **13–15:** *Assyria*, with its capital *Nineveh*, receives the greatest condemnation. While the translation of the animal vocabulary is difficult, the threat that a city become the *lair for wild animals* was common in the ancient world (Isa 13.19–22; 24.11–15), as was cursing by *hissing* and *shaking the fist* (Jer 19.8; 49.17; Lam 2.15).

the owl[a] shall hoot at the window,
  the raven[b] croak on the threshold;
  for its cedar work will be laid bare.
[15] Is this the exultant city
  that lived secure,
that said to itself,
  "I am, and there is no one else"?
What a desolation it has become,
  a lair for wild animals!
Everyone who passes by it
  hisses and shakes the fist.

3 Ah, soiled, defiled,
  oppressing city!
[2] It has listened to no voice;
  it has accepted no correction.
It has not trusted in the LORD;
  it has not drawn near to its God.

[3] The officials within it
  are roaring lions;
its judges are evening wolves
  that leave nothing until the morning.
[4] Its prophets are reckless,
  faithless persons;
its priests have profaned what is sacred,
  they have done violence to the law.
[5] The LORD within it is righteous;
  he does no wrong.
Every morning he renders his judgment,
  each dawn without fail;
but the unjust knows no shame.

[6] I have cut off nations;
  their battlements are in ruins;
I have laid waste their streets
  so that no one walks in them;
their cities have been made desolate,
  without people, without inhabitants.

[7] I said, "Surely the city[c] will fear me,
  it will accept correction;
it will not lose sight[d]
  of all that I have brought upon it."
But they were the more eager
  to make all their deeds corrupt.

[8] Therefore wait for me, says the LORD,
  for the day when I arise as a
    witness.
For my decision is to gather nations,
  to assemble kingdoms,
to pour out upon them my indignation,
  all the heat of my anger;
for in the fire of my passion
  all the earth shall be consumed.

[9] At that time I will change the speech of
    the peoples
  to a pure speech,
that all of them may call on the name of
    the LORD
  and serve him with one accord.
[10] From beyond the rivers of Ethiopia[e]
  my suppliants, my scattered ones,
  shall bring my offering.

[11] On that day you shall not be put to
    shame
  because of all the deeds by which you
    have rebelled against me;
for then I will remove from your midst
  your proudly exultant ones,

a   Cn: Heb *a voice*
b   Gk Vg: Heb *desolation*
c   Heb *it*
d   Gk Syr: Heb *its dwelling will not be cut off*
e   Or *Nubia*; Heb *Cush*

3.1–7: Judgment against Jerusalem. The *city* Jerusalem is no better than the nations previously judged. *Officials, judges, prophets,* and *priests* encompass the entire leadership of the city (Jer 6.13; 14.18). Their deceit contrasts the *righteousness* and just *judgments* of God. **6–7:** God's punishment of the *nations* should have served as a warning for Judah to fear God and repent (Am 4).

3.8–10: Judgment and salvation of the nations. 8: Language of the Day of the LORD, which dominated ch 1, returns; it is here described as a *day* of God's *decision* to act against the *nations* (Joel 3.14). The Hebrew Bible describes the emotion of anger as *heat* and *fire*. **9:** A more universal hope follows, in which all *peoples* will *call on* Judah's God (Isa 2; Mal 1.11; Ps 68.31). The punishment of those who built the Tower of Babel (Gen 11.9) is reversed. **10:** *Scattered ones,* Judeans who have been exiled to places such as *Ethiopia* (Heb "Cush"; see 1.1; 2.12), will join in this world-wide worship of God.

3.11–13: Salvation in Jerusalem. Focus returns to Jerusalem, for whom feminine Hebrew forms are used. **11:** At the time of salvation, God will remove the city's *shame* (3.19; Joel 2.26–27) and those who are proud (Isa

and you shall no longer be haughty
    in my holy mountain.
12 For I will leave in the midst of you
    a people humble and lowly.
They shall seek refuge in the name of the
    LORD—
13 the remnant of Israel;
they shall do no wrong
    and utter no lies,
nor shall a deceitful tongue
    be found in their mouths.
Then they will pasture and lie down,
    and no one shall make them afraid.

14 Sing aloud, O daughter Zion;
    shout, O Israel!
Rejoice and exult with all your heart,
    O daughter Jerusalem!
15 The LORD has taken away the judgments
    against you,
    he has turned away your enemies.
The king of Israel, the LORD, is in your midst;
    you shall fear disaster no more.
16 On that day it shall be said to Jerusalem:
Do not fear, O Zion;
    do not let your hands grow weak.

17 The LORD, your God, is in your midst,
    a warrior who gives victory;
he will rejoice over you with gladness,
    he will renew you[a] in his love;
he will exult over you with loud singing
    18 as on a day of festival.[b]
I will remove disaster from you,[c]
    so that you will not bear reproach
      for it.
19 I will deal with all your oppressors
    at that time.
And I will save the lame
    and gather the outcast,
and I will change their shame into praise
    and renown in all the earth.
20 At that time I will bring you home,
    at the time when I gather you;
for I will make you renowned and
    praised
    among all the peoples of the earth,
when I restore your fortunes
    before your eyes, says the LORD.

a Gk Syr: Heb *he will be silent*
b Gk Syr: Meaning of Heb uncertain
c Cn: Heb *I will remove from you; they were*

2.11,12,17), highly negative terms in prophetic books. *My holy mountain*, Mount Zion, site of the temple. **12–13:** As in 2.7,9, this verse envisions salvation not for all of Judah but only for a *remnant*. The *humble*, those urged in 2.3 to *seek righteousness*, will survive. Their peaceful state will be like that of guarded sheep.

    3.14–20: Salvation of daughter Jerusalem. The feminine characterization of *Jerusalem* expands to its depiction as a *daughter*, a designation of the city used throughout the prophets to underscore its vulnerability and utter dependency on God. The masculine characterization of God is essential to this unit as well: God is a virile *king* and *warrior* (cf. Ex 15.3) about to rescue daughter Zion (Zech 2.10–11; 9.9–10). **14:** *Zion*, *Israel*, and *Jerusalem* seem to be used interchangeably. **15–17:** The presence of God as strong *king* and *warrior* means that daughter Jerusalem does not need to *fear* or *grow weak*. **16:** Cf. Isa 41.10,13; 43.1,5. **17–18:** The Hebrew is obscure; see textual notes. **17:** God the *warrior* will *sing* and *rejoice*, just as Jerusalem was called to do in 3.14. **18–20:** *I will remove disaster from you*, contrasting with the beginning of the book, 1.2–3. The deep concern for the ingathering of exiles likely reflects postexilic sentiments, indicating either that these verses were later added to an Assyrian-period book or that the book itself was written in the postexilic period as a retrospective look at the time of King Josiah. The language is highly reminiscent of the promises made to Jerusalem in Zech 1–2, as well those made to daughter Zion in Mic 4.6–7, which also envisions the return of *the lame* and *the outcast* (the same Heb word is translated as "those who were cast off" in Mic 4.7).

HAGGAI

NAME, AUTHORSHIP, AND CANONICAL STATUS

The book offers no biographical information about Haggai, the prophet for whom the book is named. The name Haggai is related to the Hebrew word for festival (ḥag), perhaps indicating that he was born on a feast day. Some scholars have suggested that he had not been in exile. The book reports Haggai's prophetic activity during a brief period of less than four months. For Haggai as one of the twelve Minor Prophets, see the Introduction to the Prophetic Books (p. 961).

DATE AND HISTORICAL CONTEXT

The chronological formula with which the book begins (and which then reappears in 1.15b–2.1) is similar in style to those found in other books, e.g., 2 Kings 3.1; Hos 1.1; Am 1.1. The book of Haggai, however, records events after the destruction of the kingdom of Judah in 586 BCE and so has no native king to whom to refer (cf. Esth 3.7; Dan 7.1; 8.1; 9.1; 10.1; 11.1). Instead, Haggai is dated to the reign of a Persian ruler, Darius I. Although Cyrus, an earlier Persian king, had been remembered by one Israelite author as a "messiah" (Isa 45.1), Darius was the king during whose reign (522–486 BCE) the Temple in Jerusalem, which had to be rebuilt after the Neo-Babylonians destroyed it in 586 (see 2 Kings 26.8–21), was dedicated (515). This event inaugurates what biblical scholars refer to as the Second Temple period. Early in Darius's reign, several Persian colonies revolted, most notably Egypt, in response to which the empire launched both military and administrative campaigns to restore regional security. It was therefore in his interest to have a politically stable Syria-Palestine from which to move toward Egypt.

Because the book does not mention the completion of the Temple in 515 BCE, it was probably written before that event.

STRUCTURE, CONTENT, AND INTERPRETATION

Though many English translations construe the book as prose, substantial portions may be poetic, e.g., 1.4–9. The book presents a brief apologetic, historical narrative, focused on the rebuilding of the Temple, and in four dated oracles, on Haggai's role in persuading the community to complete that project. Haggai interpreted the plight of those in Yehud (the name given to the territory around Jerusalem by the Persians, formerly Judah) in light of the Temple, which was still in ruins. The book's final oracle broaches another issue, the royal prerogatives of Zerubbabel, heir to the Davidic throne. Haggai apparently addressed both the community's leaders—Joshua (high priest) and Zerubbabel (governor)—and the community directly.

GUIDE TO READING

Since this short book is arranged in chronological order, it can easily be read at one sitting, providing a contemporaneous perspective on the reconstruction of the Temple, as do chs 1–8 of the book of Zechariah that follows.

David L. Petersen

1 In the second year of King Darius, in the sixth month, on the first day of the month, the word of the LORD came by the prophet Haggai to Zerubbabel son of Shealtiel, governor of Judah, and to Joshua son of Jehozadak, the high priest: ² Thus says the LORD of hosts: These people say the time has not yet come to rebuild the LORD's house. ³ Then the word of the LORD came by the prophet Haggai, saying: ⁴ Is it a time for you yourselves to live in your paneled houses, while this house lies in ruins? ⁵ Now therefore thus says the LORD of hosts: Consider how you have fared. ⁶ You have sown much, and harvested little; you eat, but you never have enough; you drink, but you never have your fill; you clothe yourselves, but no one is warm; and you that earn wages earn wages to put them into a bag with holes.

⁷ Thus says the LORD of hosts: Consider how you have fared. ⁸ Go up to the hills and bring wood and build the house, so that I may take pleasure in it and be honored, says the LORD. ⁹ You have looked for much, and, lo, it came to little; and when you brought it home, I blew it away. Why? says the LORD of hosts. Because my house lies in ruins, while all of you hurry off to your own houses. ¹⁰ Therefore the heavens above you have withheld the dew, and the earth has withheld its produce. ¹¹ And I have called for a drought on the land and the hills, on the grain, the new wine, the oil, on what the soil produces, on human beings and animals, and on all their labors.

¹² Then Zerubbabel son of Shealtiel, and Joshua son of Jehozadak, the high priest, with all the remnant of the people, obeyed the voice of the LORD their God, and the words of the prophet Haggai, as the LORD their God had sent him; and the people feared the LORD. ¹³ Then Haggai, the messenger of the LORD, spoke to the people with the LORD's message, saying, I am with you, says the LORD. ¹⁴ And the LORD stirred up the spirit of Zerubbabel son of Shealtiel, governor of Judah, and the spirit of Joshua son of Jehozadak, the high priest, and the spirit of all the remnant of the people; and they came and worked on

1.1–11: Haggai indicts the people. 1: *The second year,* 520 BCE. *The sixth month,* Elul (August-September). *The first day of the month* was a time for special rituals; the date is ironic, since the place where such rituals took place is in ruins. *Zerubbabel* (1 Chr 3.19; Ezra 2.2; 3.2,8; 5.2; Neh 12.1; Zech 4.6–10), the grandson of Jehoiachin (2 Kings 24.8–17; 1 Chr 3.16–19), and thus a descendant of David. *Joshua,* Zech 3.1–10; 6.11 (= Jeshua in Ezra 2–5). Addressing the two together suggests that Yehud was led by both political and religious leaders. 2: For reasons unknown, the community has resisted rebuilding the Temple. 3–5: Even though Zerubbabel and Joshua had been addressed previously, Haggai appears to speak directly to the community. 4: Haggai charges the people not only with not building the Temple but also with living in lavish, i.e., *paneled,* houses. (Solomon's palace was paneled with cedar, 1 Kings 7.7.) The issue of *time* (vv. 2,4) is important. Haggai's rhetorical question receives no direct answer, but the answer is obviously "no." 5: *Consider,* literally, "set to your hearts," a phrase that will recur (1.7; 2.15,18). 6: Haggai analyzes the status quo, using imagery drawn from futility curses; cf. Deut 28.38; Hos 4.10. Such misfortune stands in marked contrast with the luxurious houses in which the people live. 7–11: A call to action. 7: *Consider,* see 1.5n. 8: Haggai's central admonition: build the Temple. 9–11: These verses are built around a wordplay: as long as the Temple is in *ruins* (Heb "hareb"), the people will suffer drought ("horeb"). 9: The prophet returns to the language of futility curses, though now explicitly identifying the LORD as the one who has caused such futility—*I blew it away.*

1.12–15a: The people respond. Unlike many earlier prophets, Haggai is successful in his admonitions. 12: *All the remnant of the people* suggests that Zerubbabel and Joshua had moved the people to obey. *Remnant* is ambiguous, perhaps referring to a group smaller than the preexilic population, or perhaps specifying those who had returned from exile. 13: Haggai is labeled *the messenger of the LORD,* a logical though unusual label for a prophet; cf. 2 Chr 35.15–16. The word *messenger* offers a wordplay on *message. I am with you* often occurs in oracles of salvation (e.g., Isa 41.10; 43.5). 14: A new perspective on the people's obedience (v. 12), which is due to the LORD's stirring up *the spirit* of both the leaders and the people. 15: *The sixth month,* Elul (August–September). The date seems out of place, since such dates elsewhere in the book occur at the beginning of an oracle. Three weeks have elapsed since Haggai initially addressed the governor and high priest.

1.15b–2.9: The Temple will be filled with splendor. Contrary to current experience, the LORD promises that this Temple will be even more glorious than the earlier one. 1.15b–2.1: *The twenty-fourth day of . . . the sixth*

the house of the Lord of hosts, their God, ¹⁵ on the twenty-fourth day of the month, in the sixth month. In the second year of King

2 Darius, ¹ in the seventh month, on the twenty-first day of the month, the word of the Lord came by the prophet Haggai, saying: ² Speak now to Zerubbabel son of Shealtiel, governor of Judah, and to Joshua son of Jehozadak, the high priest, and to the remnant of the people, and say, ³ Who is left among you that saw this house in its former glory? How does it look to you now? Is it not in your sight as nothing? ⁴ Yet now take courage, O Zerubbabel, says the Lord; take courage, O Joshua, son of Jehozadak, the high priest; take courage, all you people of the land, says the Lord; work, for I am with you, says the Lord of hosts, ⁵ according to the promise that I made you when you came out of Egypt. My spirit abides among you; do not fear. ⁶ For thus says the Lord of hosts: Once again, in a little while, I will shake the heavens and the earth and the sea and the dry land; ⁷ and I will shake all the nations, so that the treasure of all nations shall come, and I will fill this house with splendor, says the Lord of hosts. ⁸ The silver is mine, and the gold is mine, says the Lord of hosts. ⁹ The latter splendor of this house shall be greater than the former, says the Lord of hosts; and in this place I will give prosperity, says the Lord of hosts.

¹⁰ On the twenty-fourth day of the ninth month, in the second year of Darius, the word of the Lord came by the prophet Haggai, saying: ¹¹ Thus says the Lord of hosts: Ask the priests for a ruling: ¹² If one carries consecrated meat in the fold of one's garment, and with the fold touches bread, or stew, or wine, or oil, or any kind of food, does it become holy? The priests answered, "No." ¹³ Then Haggai said, "If one who is unclean by contact with a dead body touches any of these, does it become unclean?" The priests answered, "Yes, it becomes unclean." ¹⁴ Haggai then said, So is it with this people,

month, more than three weeks since construction began. *The seventh month*, Tishri (September–October). Haggai is commanded to address the community and its leaders. On this date, the community would have been celebrating the feast of booths (Lev 23.33–36,39–42). **2.3**: As was the case in v. 4, Haggai poses questions, the last two of which are rhetorical. The first question indicates that at least some of those present had seen the First Temple before it was destroyed in 586 BCE (cf. Ezra 3.12–13). They would have had to have been more than seventy years old to remember the First Temple. **4**: *Take courage*, cf. Zech 8.9,13,22–23, where the same Hebrew word occurs. In 1 Chr 28.10,20, David delivers a similar exhortation to Solomon, builder of the First Temple. *People of the land* probably refers to the same group known earlier as *the remnant of the people*, although some scholars have suggested that the former phrase refers to a rural population that did not go into exile. *I am with you*, see 1.13n. **5**: The Hebrew is difficult, reading literally, "The matter that I covenanted with you when you came out of Egypt." Haggai is clearly alluding to the Exodus and Sinai experiences, and claiming that God's covenant is still in force. The notion of God's *spirit* residing among the people is unusual. However, God could not be present as before, since the Temple had not yet been rebuilt.

2.6–9: An oracle announcing theophanic splendor. 6: God will now act on behalf of the Temple. *Once again, in a little while* is difficult in Hebrew, literally, "yet one, and it is only a little one." References to such shaking of the cosmos often occur in eschatological literature (e.g., v. 21; Isa 13.13; Joel 3.16; Heb 12.26). Here the very fabric of the universe quakes, not just mountains. This description of the universe—*heavens, earth, sea, dry land*—echoes that in Gen 1. **7**: *Splendor* refers to precious objects (see Hos 13.15; 2 Chr 32.27), which means that Haggai anticipates new ritual vessels will be provided for the Temple, the old ones having been plundered by the Neo-Babylonians (cf. 2 Kings 24.13). **8**: On silver and gold, cf. Zech 6.9–15, where they are products of fund-raising. **9**: *Prosperity*, Heb "shalom." The rebuilt Temple will engender well-being in Yehud, reversing the conditions described in 1.6,9.

2.10–14: The community is unclean. 10: December 18, 520 BCE, two months since the oracle promising splendor. *The word of the Lord* comes literally "to" Haggai, not "by" as was the case in 1.3 and 2.1; i.e., this is a private oracle. **11**: Literally, "Ask the priests for a torah." Priests were responsible for determining whether something or someone was holy or common, clean or unclean (Lev 10.10–11; Deut 33.10). Unlike the priests indicted in Ezek 22.26, those whom Haggai consults give proper responses. **12–13**: Two cases, one involving something holy, another involving something unclean, demonstrate the supremely contagious quality of the

and with this nation before me, says the LORD; and so with every work of their hands; and what they offer there is unclean. [15] But now, consider what will come to pass from this day on. Before a stone was placed upon a stone in the LORD's temple, [16] how did you fare?[a] When one came to a heap of twenty measures, there were but ten; when one came to the wine vat to draw fifty measures, there were but twenty. [17] I struck you and all the products of your toil with blight and mildew and hail; yet you did not return to me, says the LORD. [18] Consider from this day on, from the twenty-fourth day of the ninth month. Since the day that the foundation of the LORD's temple was laid, consider: [19] Is there any seed left in the barn? Do the vine, the fig tree, the pomegranate, and the olive tree still yield nothing? From this day on I will bless you.

[20] The word of the LORD came a second time to Haggai on the twenty-fourth day of the month: [21] Speak to Zerubbabel, governor of Judah, saying, I am about to shake the heavens and the earth, [22] and to overthrow the throne of kingdoms; I am about to destroy the strength of the kingdoms of the nations, and overthrow the chariots and their riders; and the horses and their riders shall fall, every one by the sword of a comrade. [23] On that day, says the LORD of hosts, I will take you, O Zerubbabel my servant, son of Shealtiel, says the LORD, and make you like a signet ring; for I have chosen you, says the LORD of hosts.

a   Gk: Heb *since they were*

latter. Corpse uncleanness is especially difficult to remove (Num 19). **14:** Haggai focuses on *what they offer there* as *unclean*. Sacrifices presented at the altar and the Temple, which was under construction, are unclean, presumably because the Temple itself has not yet been officially rededicated. The unclean Temple is analogous to a corpse in its ability to defile.

2.15–19: The Temple is rededicated. Since 2:20 refers to a second *word of the* LORD on the twenty-fourth day, 2.15–19 are part of the first word, which begins at 2.10. **15–17:** The repetition of *consider* in this oracle mirrors the twofold use in 1.5,7. Haggai appeals to past agricultural disaster, comparable to that depicted in 1.6,10–11. **18:** *This day* almost certainly refers to the day on which the Temple's foundation stone was relaid (cf. Zech 4.9; Ezra 3.10–11). Even though the Temple will not be completed and rededicated until 515 BCE, the Temple has now been purified. **19:** Haggai's questions (cf. the use of questions in 1.4; 2.3,16) affirms that seeds will be planted and that vines and trees will yield fruit. Prior agricultural disaster will give way to fertility. The final words are literally "I will bless," the implication being that the "shalom" foreseen in 2.9 will include both the people and the land.

2.20–23: Zerubbabel, my servant and signet ring. On that same *twenty-fourth day*, a second oracle focuses on Zerubbabel. **21:** The diction of "shaking" the nations resumes that in 2.6. **22:** God will destroy unnamed nations. The language is allusive, e.g., *chariots and their riders* echoes Jer 51.21, *overthrow* Gen 19.25, *sword of a comrade* Judg 7.22. **23:** *On that day*, a phrase routinely used to depict the eschatological "day of the LORD." *Son of Shealtiel* means that Zerubbabel stands in the Davidic line, the grandson of Jehoiachin, Judah's last reigning king. The diction of *choosing* (God "chose" David, Ps 78.70), *servant* (the Davidic king can be so labeled, 2 Sam 7.5), and *signet ring* (Jer 22.24) all suggest that Haggai thinks Zerubbabel will achieve royal status. Zerubbabel's fate, however, is unknown.

ZECHARIAH

NAME, AUTHORSHIP, AND CANONICAL STATUS

The name of the book derives from the prophet Zechariah, a contemporary of the prophet Haggai. Both prophesied in the early days of the restoration, when both returning exiles and those who had never left joined together to rebuild Judahite society. Although the book provides no biographical information, Zechariah is mentioned, along with Haggai, in Ezra 5.1 and 6.14. The book of Zechariah, however, is made up of diverse literature, deriving from different historical periods, and only the material in chs 1–8 pertains to the historical Zechariah. For Zechariah as one of the twelve Minor Prophets, see the Introduction to the Prophetic Books, p. 961.

DATE AND HISTORICAL CONTEXT

Chapters 1–8, often known as First Zechariah, include three chronological formulae (1.1,7; 7.1), which report that Zechariah was active between October and November in 520 BCE and December 7, 518 BCE. As with Haggai, Zechariah's work is dated early in the reign of the Persian emperor Darius I (522–486 BCE) and before the rededication of the Temple in 515. Though Haggai interacted with individuals also mentioned by Zechariah and both were active during 520 BCE, neither prophet refers to the other, although "the prophets" to whom Zechariah refers in 8.9 may include Haggai. Ezra 5.1 speaks of them as active together. Chapters 9–14, sometimes referred to as Deutero-Zechariah, stem from a later time, which is difficult to determine for at least two reasons. First, there are no explicit chronological formulas nor direct references to named individuals or recognizable historical events. Second, chs 9–14 are themselves heterogeneous. Zechariah 9:1 and 12:1 introduce two collections with comparable formulas: "The word of the LORD." The collections differ so much that it is unlikely they derive from the same time. Reference to Greece (9.13) may suggest that this section dates to the Hellenistic period, when Greece ruled Syria-Palestine. However, archaeology has shown that Greek imports were present in the Levant well before then.

STRUCTURE, CONTENTS, AND INTERPRETATION

In the month just before Haggai reported that the Temple foundation stone had been laid (Hag 2.10), Zechariah first speaks (Zech 1–8). Unlike Haggai, he is not overtly concerned with the rebuilding of the Temple, though he does refer to the Temple foundation stone ceremony (8.9). His message is broader, including both moral discourse and visionary rhetoric. As a result, Zech 1–8 is more literarily diverse than Haggai, including both oracles and vision reports. Haggai offers none of the latter. The oracles are themselves different. Some recapitulate rhetoric known from earlier prophets to whom he refers in general terms (1.5–6; 7.12); some encourage the people to return to the land (2.6–13); others offer ethical admonition (e.g., 7.8–10); still others announce a glorious future for Zion (8.1–7). Haggai's oracles sound similar to the one in 8.12.

The eight vision reports in chs 1–6 are truly distinctive. Other prophetic books include vision reports (e.g., Amos, Isaiah, Jeremiah, and Ezekiel) but none includes such a high proportion of them. In earlier visions, prophets apparently understood what they perceived. This changes with Zechariah. As prophet, he receives the visions, but he understands them only when they are interpreted by "the angel of the LORD" (e.g., Zech 1.9–10, literally "the LORD's messenger"). This situation will recur in later apocalyptic visions, e.g., Dan 7. Further, as was the case with Amos, the vision reports in Zech 1–6 constitute a carefully structured series. The first and last visions offer scenes populated by multicolored horses, whereas the central visions in chs 4 and 5 highlight the figures important to Yehud's polity, the high priest Joshua and the governor Zerubbabel. Zechariah's visions move beyond ordinary reality. They are filled with movement and color. Moreover, they span "the whole earth" (1.11). These visions explain the ways in which God is working providentially on behalf of the newly restored community.

The latter part of the book (Zech 9–14) has a less carefully worked-out structure. Two collections of prophetic sayings (chs 9–11 and 12–14) are introduced by the heading "An Oracle. The word of the LORD," as is the collection represented by Malachi, which follows. Chapters 9–11 are largely concerned with aspects of the victories of the LORD as Divine Warrior. The collection in chs 12–14 has a related focus on the imminent "day of the LORD" and is characterized by the repeated phrase "on that day."

GUIDE TO READING

The book of Zechariah is best read in conjunction with the books that precede and follow it: chs 1–8 in conjunction with Haggai, and chs 9–14 with Malachi. In terms of the development of apocalyptic literature in the Bible, Zechariah stands between Ezekiel (e.g., chs 38–39) and Daniel (chs 7–12).

David L. Petersen

1 In the eighth month, in the second year of Darius, the word of the LORD came to the prophet Zechariah son of Berechiah son of Iddo, saying: ² The LORD was very angry with your ancestors. ³ Therefore say to them, Thus says the LORD of hosts: Return to me, says the LORD of hosts, and I will return to you, says the LORD of hosts. ⁴ Do not be like your ancestors, to whom the former prophets proclaimed, "Thus says the LORD of hosts, Return from your evil ways and from your evil deeds." But they did not hear or heed me, says the LORD. ⁵ Your ancestors, where are they? And the prophets, do they live forever? ⁶ But my words and my statutes, which I commanded my servants the prophets, did they not overtake your ancestors? So they repented and said, "The LORD of hosts has dealt with us according to our ways and deeds, just as he planned to do."

⁷ On the twenty-fourth day of the eleventh month, the month of Shebat, in the second year of Darius, the word of the LORD came to the prophet Zechariah son of Berechiah son of Iddo; and Zechariah[a] said, ⁸ In the night I saw a man riding on a red horse! He was standing among the myrtle trees in the glen; and behind him were red, sorrel, and white horses. ⁹ Then I said, "What are these, my lord?" The angel who talked with me said to me, "I will show you what they are." ¹⁰ So the man who was standing among the myrtle trees answered, "They are those whom the LORD has sent to patrol the earth." ¹¹ Then they spoke to the angel of the LORD who was standing among the myrtle trees, "We have patrolled the earth, and lo, the whole earth remains at peace." ¹² Then the angel of the LORD said, "O LORD of hosts, how long will you withhold mercy from Jerusalem and the cities of Judah, with which you have been angry these seventy years?" ¹³ Then the LORD replied with gracious and comforting words to the angel who talked with me. ¹⁴ So the angel who talked with me said to me, Proclaim this message: Thus says the LORD of hosts; I am very jealous for Jerusalem and for Zion. ¹⁵ And I am extremely angry with the nations that are at ease; for while I was only a little angry, they made the disaster worse. ¹⁶ Therefore, thus says the LORD, I have returned to Jerusalem with compassion; my house shall be built in it, says the LORD of hosts, and the

a   Heb *and he*

1.1–8.23: Oracles and visions attributed to Zechariah ben Berechiah. This first major division of the book has three parts, each introduced by a date formula (1.1; 1.7; 7.1).

1.1–6: Prologue. 1: *The eighth month, in the second year,* Marheshvan (October-November), 520 BCE. *Darius* I, king of Persia, 522–486 BCE. A *Zechariah son of Iddo*, mentioned in Neh 12:16, belongs to a priestly lineage. *Zechariah* means "God remembered," which symbolizes God's remembering of the people, an important theme of the book. 2–6: An unusual oracle, which reflects on past prophetic admonitions and the *ancestors'* responses. *Return/repent* (Heb "shub," translated both ways) is the key word, appearing four times. For earlier prophetic calls to *return,* see, e.g., Joel 2.12; Jer 18.11; Ezek 33.11. 3: On mutual return, cf. Joel 2.12–14; Mal 3.7. 6: Though the *ancestors* did not initially *return,* they finally *repented,* which sets the stage for a glorious future.

1.7–17: The first vision: divine horsemen patrol the earth. 7: *The eleventh month . . . Shebat,* January-February; the year is 519 BCE. 8: *Glen,* or "cosmic deep"; cf. Mic 7.19. 9–12: A quiet scene in which horses graze, symbolizing peace over all the earth, elicits a protest by the angel. 10: *Patrol the earth,* cf. Job 1.7; 2.2. 12: *How long* regularly occurs in laments, e.g., Pss 6.4; 79.5. *Seventy years* also appears in Zech 7.4. The phrase is used in both biblical (e.g., Jer 25.11; Isa 23.15) and other ancient texts to refer to an unfortunate period of time. 13–17: The LORD expresses anger at the nations and promises that both Temple and cities will be rebuilt. 16: *The measuring line,* indicating new construction; (see 2.1–5; Jer 31.38–39; cf. Mic 2.4–5; Am 7.17).

measuring line shall be stretched out over Jerusalem. [17] Proclaim further: Thus says the LORD of hosts: My cities shall again overflow with prosperity; the LORD will again comfort Zion and again choose Jerusalem.

[18] [a]And I looked up and saw four horns. [19] I asked the angel who talked with me, "What are these?" And he answered me, "These are the horns that have scattered Judah, Israel, and Jerusalem." [20] Then the LORD showed me four blacksmiths. [21] And I asked, "What are they coming to do?" He answered, "These are the horns that scattered Judah, so that no head could be raised; but these have come to terrify them, to strike down the horns of the nations that lifted up their horns against the land of Judah to scatter its people."[b]

2 [c] I looked up and saw a man with a measuring line in his hand. [2] Then I asked, "Where are you going?" He answered me, "To measure Jerusalem, to see what is its width and what is its length." [3] Then the angel who talked with me came forward, and another angel came forward to meet him, [4] and said to him, "Run, say to that young man: Jerusalem shall be inhabited like villages without walls, because of the multitude of people and animals in it. [5] For I will be a wall of fire all around it, says the LORD, and I will be the glory within it."

[6] Up, up! Flee from the land of the north, says the LORD; for I have spread you abroad like the four winds of heaven, says the LORD. [7] Up! Escape to Zion, you that live with daughter Babylon. [8] For thus said the LORD of hosts (after his glory[d] sent me) regarding the nations that plundered you: Truly, one who touches you touches the apple of my eye.[e] [9] See now, I am going to raise[f] my hand against them, and they shall become plunder for their own slaves. Then you will know that the LORD of hosts has sent me. [10] Sing and rejoice, O daughter Zion! For lo, I will come and dwell in your midst, says the LORD. [11] Many nations shall join themselves to the LORD on that day, and shall be my people; and I will dwell in your midst. And you shall know that the LORD of hosts has sent me to you. [12] The LORD will inherit Judah as his portion in the holy land, and will again choose Jerusalem.

[a] Ch 2.1 in Heb
[b] Heb *it*
[c] Ch 2.5 in Heb
[d] Cn: Heb *after glory he*
[e] Heb *his eye*
[f] Or *wave*

1.18–21: The second vision: four horns and four smiths. 18: The *four horns* are ambiguous. They may refer to two pairs of animal horns, to horned helmets, or, most likely, to the four corners of a stone altar (cf. Ex 27.2; 38.2; Ezek 43.15). They are then interpreted as the totality of nations that destroyed Israel. 19: *Horns* elsewhere can symbolize nations (e.g., Deut 33.17 [the horns of a bull]; Jer 48.25; Dan 8.8). 20: *Blacksmiths*, the Hebrew word can refer to an artisan who works with wood, stone, or metal. 21: *These have come* probably refers to the artisans who will destroy *the horns of the nations*. Such artisans are elsewhere depicted as punitive agents (Ezek 21.31, "those skillful to destroy"). The world at peace in the first vision will now be disrupted.

2.1–5: The third vision: a surveyor measures Jerusalem. 1: A *measuring line*, see 1.16n. Such a line was used to determine divisions within a particular territory as in Ezek 40.3, a text that also foresees the rebuilding of Jerusalem and the Temple, using the categories of *width* and *length*. 2: Zechariah's questions presume that, in this vision, he understands what he sees. 4: Restoration focuses on *Jerusalem*, not the Temple, as was the case in Ezekiel. Here the absence of walls stands in stark contrast with the walls described in Ezek 40. Jerusalem's walls were eventually rebuilt (Neh 2.17–6.15). 5: *Wall of fire*, the Persian capital Pasargadae stood without walls and was surrounded by fire altars. God as *glory* will be located within the fiery circumference; cf. Ezek 43.2,4.

2.6–13: Admonitions and promises. 6–7: *Up, Up*, lit. "Woe, Woe," though here simply calling attention to what is being said; cf. Isa 1.24; Jer 27.6. *The land of the north*, the place where Israelites are in exile and from which they will return, so Jer 3.18; 16.15; 23.8; 31.8. *Daughter Babylon*, cf. Jer 50.42; 51.33; Ps 137.8. 8a: Literally, "after glory sent me to the nations." Cf. vv. 9,11, which also report that the LORD *sent me*. 8b: *Apple of my eye* refers to the pupil. 9: *My hand*, another bodily metaphor of the deity. Only when the nations are plundered will Israelites know that the LORD sent Zechariah. 10: *Sing and rejoice*, cf. Isa 12.6; Zeph 3.14–15. In all three texts, the command to sing accompanies the presence of the God *in your midst*. 11: On *join themselves to the LORD*, cf. 8.20–23; Isa 56.6–7. 12: *Holy land* does not occur elsewhere in the Hebrew Bible, but see Wis 12.3; 2 Macc 1.7.

[13] Be silent, all people, before the LORD; for he has roused himself from his holy dwelling.

3 Then he showed me the high priest Joshua standing before the angel of the LORD, and Satan[a] standing at his right hand to accuse him. [2] And the LORD said to Satan,[a] "The LORD rebuke you, O Satan![a] The LORD who has chosen Jerusalem rebuke you! Is not this man a brand plucked from the fire?" [3] Now Joshua was dressed with filthy clothes as he stood before the angel. [4] The angel said to those who were standing before him, "Take off his filthy clothes." And to him he said, "See, I have taken your guilt away from you, and I will clothe you with festal apparel." [5] And I said, "Let them put a clean turban on his head." So they put a clean turban on his head and clothed him with the apparel; and the angel of the LORD was standing by.

[6] Then the angel of the LORD assured Joshua, saying [7] "Thus says the LORD of hosts: If you will walk in my ways and keep my requirements, then you shall rule my house and have charge of my courts, and I will give you the right of access among those who are standing here. [8] Now listen, Joshua, high priest, you and your colleagues who sit before you! For they are an omen of things to come: I am going to bring my servant the Branch. [9] For on the stone that I have set before Joshua, on a single stone with seven facets, I will engrave its inscription, says the LORD of hosts, and I will remove the guilt of this land in a single day. [10] On that day, says the LORD of hosts, you shall invite each other to come under your vine and fig tree."

4 The angel who talked with me came again, and wakened me, as one is wakened from sleep. [2] He said to me, "What do you see?" And I said, "I see a lampstand all of gold, with a bowl on the top of it; there are seven lamps on it, with seven lips on each of the lamps that are on the top of it. [3] And by it there are two olive trees, one on the right of the bowl and the other on its left." [4] I said to the angel who talked with me, "What are these, my lord?" [5] Then the angel who talked with me answered me, "Do you not know what these are?" I said, "No, my lord." [6] He

a   Or *the Accuser*; Heb *the Adversary*

Zechariah emphasizes the sacred character of the land of Israel. **13:** *Be silent,* cf. Hab 2.20; Zeph 1.7. Sacrifices at the Temple were conducted in silence. *All people* is consistent with v. 11. *Holy dwelling* can refer to either the earthly temple (Ps 26.8) or the heavenly abode (Deut 26.15).

3.1–10: The fourth vision: Joshua and the satan. This vision differs from the prior three: Zechariah is shown something—he does not just see it; the usual question is missing; and no clarification is offered. **1:** The *angel of the LORD* is not an interpreter but a character in the vision, along with *Joshua,* the high priest (cf. Hag 1.1;2.2) and "the *satan,*" on whom see textual note *a.* This figure functions as the prosecuting attorney in the divine council; cf. Ps 109.6; 1 Chr 21.1 (only in this text does *Satan* appear as a name); Job 1–2. **2:** The accuser is rebuked, apparently for having charged Joshua improperly. **3:** The high priest is ritually unclean. **4:** *Festal apparel* (cf. Isa 3.22) symbolizes the cleansing of the high priest. **5:** *And I said* should read with LXX (Septuagint), "and he said." Zechariah is not an actor in the vision. *Turban,* the traditional headgear of the high priest, although not the same Hebrew word as in Lev 8.9. **6–7:** Admonitions of both general and specific sort; *keep my requirements* refers to priestly responsibilities (Num 3; Ezek 44). *Those standing here* belong to the divine council, to which Joshua is promised access. **8–10:** *The Branch,* (cf. Isa 11.1; Jer 23.5; 33.15) refers to a member of the royal family of David, probably Zerubbabel, the governor (Hag 1.1; 2.20–23). *Stone . . . with . . . facets,* probably the engraved gold plaque on the high priest's headdress (Ex 28.36–38); it signifies the ability of the high priest to remove guilt. **10:** *Under your vine and fig tree,* see 1 Kings 4.25; Mic 4.4.

4.1–14: The fifth vision: a lampstand and two olive trees. 1–6a: The angel roused Zechariah, whereupon he reported yet another vision. This vision builds on the previous one, since it alludes to Joshua. **2:** *Lampstand* (Heb "menorah") has a round *bowl* at the top with seven indentations for wicks; see Ex 25.31–40. Ceramic lampstands of this type have been discovered by archaeologists. **3:** *Olive trees* may be related to the olive oil that fueled the lamp. **6b–10a:** A distinct oracle. **6b–7:** An unnamed person is addressed as *O great mountain* and compared to Zerubbabel. The obvious candidate is the recently purified Joshua. Zerubbabel will achieve high status as the one who lays the foundation—*the top stone*—of the Temple. The ritual of temple rededication involved reus-

said to me, "This is the word of the LORD to Zerubbabel: Not by might, nor by power, but by my spirit, says the LORD of hosts. [7] What are you, O great mountain? Before Zerubbabel you shall become a plain; and he shall bring out the top stone amid shouts of 'Grace, grace to it!'"

[8] Moreover the word of the LORD came to me, saying, [9] "The hands of Zerubbabel have laid the foundation of this house; his hands shall also complete it. Then you will know that the LORD of hosts has sent me to you. [10] For whoever has despised the day of small things shall rejoice, and shall see the plummet in the hand of Zerubbabel.

"These seven are the eyes of the LORD, which range through the whole earth." [11] Then I said to him, "What are these two olive trees on the right and the left of the lampstand?" [12] And a second time I said to him, "What are these two branches of the olive trees, which pour out the oil[a] through the two golden pipes?" [13] He said to me, "Do you not know what these are?" I said, "No, my lord." [14] Then he said, "These are the two anointed ones who stand by the Lord of the whole earth."

5 Again I looked up and saw a flying scroll. [2] And he said to me, "What do you see?" I answered, "I see a flying scroll; its length is twenty cubits, and its width ten cubits." [3] Then he said to me, "This is the curse that goes out over the face of the whole land; for everyone who steals shall be cut off according to the writing on one side, and everyone who swears falsely[b] shall be cut off according to the writing on the other side. [4] I have sent it out, says the LORD of hosts, and it shall enter the house of the thief, and the house of anyone who swears falsely by my name; and it shall abide in that house and consume it, both timber and stones."

[5] Then the angel who talked with me came forward and said to me, "Look up and see what this is that is coming out." [6] I said, "What is it?" He said, "This is a basket[c] coming out." And he said, "This is their iniquity[d] in all the land." [7] Then a leaden cover was lifted, and there was a woman sitting in

[a] Cn: Heb *gold*
[b] The word *falsely* added from verse 4
[c] Heb *ephah*
[d] Gk Compare Syr: Heb *their eye*

ing a stone from the previous temple. **8–10a:** A second oracle, referring to the previous ritual, again highlights the role Zerubbabel will have in the reconstruction of the Temple. Kings were known as temple builders. **10a:** *The day of small things,* cf. Ezra 3.11. *Plummet* emphasizes Zerubbabel's role as builder. **10b–14:** The vision and its interpretation resume. **10b:** *Eyes of the LORD,* cf. 2 Chr 16.9, where the eyes represent divine benevolence. **11–14:** The *two olive trees* symbolize *the two anointed ones,* lit. "the two sons of the oil." The word "anoint" is not present in Hebrew, nor is the typical word for olive oil that is used in anointing. This *oil* was used both for food and for fueling such lamps. These two "sons" almost certainly refer to Joshua and Zerubbabel, who now stand in close relationship to the LORD, symbolized by the lamp. Zechariah envisions a government in which power is shared between the priest and the descendant of David.

5.1–4: The sixth vision: a flying scroll. 1–2: The scroll is apparently unrolled, rather like a flying carpet, and long, almost 30 ft (9 m). This scroll has a proportion of 2:1, more like a carpet than a document; the Qumran Isaiah scroll is about 24 ft (7.3 m) long and 11 in (30 cm) wide, a proportion of 24:1. **3:** *The curse* probably refers to the curses found in God's covenant with Israel (cf. Deut 29.11,13,18), curses that were written down on a scroll (cf. 2 Chr 34.24; Dan 9.11). *The whole land,* a phrase used through Zech 1–8 (1.11; 4.10b; 5.6; 6.5). *Steals. . . swears falsely* echoes, although does not quote exactly, the Decalogue (Ex 20.7,15,16). Scrolls were rarely written on both sides. **4:** Destruction of houses is a typical punishment (Hab 3.13b; Dan 2.5; 3.29; Ezra 6.11). Oddly, the perpetrators are not punished. The flying scroll symbolizes the administration of the LORD's covenant-based justice throughout the world.

5.5–11: The seventh vision: a woman in a basket. 5–6: This vision is so bizarre that, unlike the other visions, Zechariah cannot name or describe what he sees; only the angel can do so. **6:** *Basket,* Heb "ephah," which was a unit of measure, roughly two-thirds of a bushel (23 liters). Such an amount of grain or flour might have been held in a container made of textile, ceramic, or metal. *Iniquity,* see textual note d, the same word for evil that appeared in 3.4. The referent of *their* is unclear, though it may refer to Judeans, whose iniquity is being removed. **7–8:** An incongruous image, particularly since an "ephah" could not hold a human. This "ephah" was made of a

the basket!ª ⁸ And he said, "This is Wickedness." So he thrust her back into the basket,ª and pressed the leaden weight down on its mouth. ⁹ Then I looked up and saw two women coming forward. The wind was in their wings; they had wings like the wings of a stork, and they lifted up the basketª between earth and sky. ¹⁰ Then I said to the angel who talked with me, "Where are they taking the basket?"ª ¹¹ He said to me, "To the land of Shinar, to build a house for it; and when this is prepared, they will set the basketª down there on its base."

6 And again I looked up and saw four chariots coming out from between two mountains—mountains of bronze. ² The first chariot had red horses, the second chariot black horses, ³ the third chariot white horses, and the fourth chariot dappled grayᵇ horses. ⁴ Then I said to the angel who talked with me, "What are these, my lord?" ⁵ The angel answered me, "These are the four windsᶜ of heaven going out, after presenting themselves before the Lord of all the earth. ⁶ The chariot with the black horses goes toward the north country, the white ones go toward the west country,ᵈ and the dappled ones go toward the south

country." ⁷ When the steeds came out, they were impatient to get off and patrol the earth. And he said, "Go, patrol the earth." So they patrolled the earth. ⁸ Then he cried out to me, "Lo, those who go toward the north country have set my spirit at rest in the north country."

⁹ The word of the LORD came to me: ¹⁰ Collect silver and goldᵉ from the exiles—from Heldai, Tobijah, and Jedaiah—who have arrived from Babylon; and go the same day to the house of Josiah son of Zephaniah. ¹¹ Take the silver and gold and make a crown,ᶠ and set it on the head of the high priest Joshua son of Jehozadak; ¹² say to him: Thus says the LORD of hosts: Here is a man whose name is Branch: for he shall branch out in his place, and he shall build the temple of the LORD. ¹³ It is he that shall build the temple of the LORD; he shall bear royal honor, and shall sit upon his throne and rule. There

ª Heb *ephah*
ᵇ Compare Gk: Meaning of Heb uncertain
ᶜ Or *spirits*
ᵈ Cn: Heb *go after them*
ᵉ Cn Compare verse 11: Heb lacks *silver and gold*
ᶠ Gk Mss Syr Tg: Heb *crowns*

hard substance due to its lead lid. The entire image is thought to symbolize *Wickedness*. **9–11:** Gender continues to play a prominent role in this vision. *Two women* with wings, not cherubim, which were male. *Stork*, an unclean bird (Lev 11.19), and hence, in this simile, well suited to remove iniquity/wickedness. *The land of Shinar*, Babylon (Gen 10.10; 11.2; Dan 1.2; Josh 7.21). Isaiah 11.11 understands *Shinar* to be a place for exile and a place from which those exiled will return. Judeans are coming from Babylon; *Wickedness* is going to Babylon. *Build a house . . . its base*, the Babylonians, who will build a shrine for and permanently install *Wickedness*, will be polluted by the gesture that purifies Judah.

6.1–8: The eighth vision: four chariots. 1–3: A vision that like the first includes horses of many colors. The geographic setting is similar to that of the Mesopotamian sun god's appearance between two mountains. Here, chariots, rather than the sun, *come out* (a verb elsewhere used of the sun), with no explicit reference to charioteers. *Chariots* represent military might and dominion (cf. Hag 2.22), and could symbolize God's martial presence (Isa 66.15–16; Ps 68.17). **5–6:** That they go out in four directions (cf. Jer 49.36; Ezek 37.9; Dan 11.4) means that the LORD's military might will be present everywhere with the winds as the deity's agents; cf. Ps 104.4. *Four winds* are present in Zech 2.6. *Presented themselves*, cf. Job 1.6; 2.1. **7:** *Patrol*, see 1.7n. **8:** *The north country*, the land to which Judeans had been exiled; cf. 2.6. *My spirit*, the same Hebrew word as "wind" in v. 5. The Hebrew verb "go out" appears seven times in this vision report (vv. 1,5,6 [three times],7,8). The vision concludes with the deity having fulfilled the threats of the first and second visions (1.15, 21).

6.9–15: Wealth and coronation. Two oracles, one embedded in another, 6.9–11,14 and 6.12–13. **9–10:** *The exiles*, i.e., those who have returned from Mesopotamia. The three individuals are otherwise unknown. *Zephaniah*, father of *Josiah* may be the priest of 2 Kings 25.18, who was taken into exile. **11:** Literally "crowns," one of which was intended for *Joshua*. **12–13:** *Branch* in 3.8 and here refers to David's descendant Zerubbabel as is clear from his role as builder of the *Temple*. The oracle alludes to the diarchy envisioned in the fifth vision, though here the *Branch* appears to have a higher status than the priest. **14:** Hebrew reads "crowns." *Memorial in the temple* may

shall be a priest by his throne, with peaceful understanding between the two of them. [14] And the crown[a] shall be in the care of Heldai,[b] Tobijah, Jedaiah, and Josiah[c] son of Zephaniah, as a memorial in the temple of the LORD.

[15] Those who are far off shall come and help to build the temple of the LORD; and you shall know that the LORD of hosts has sent me to you. This will happen if you diligently obey the voice of the LORD your God.

7 In the fourth year of King Darius, the word of the LORD came to Zechariah on the fourth day of the ninth month, which is Chislev. [2] Now the people of Bethel had sent Sharezer and Regem-melech and their men, to entreat the favor of the LORD, [3] and to ask the priests of the house of the LORD of hosts and the prophets, "Should I mourn and practice abstinence in the fifth month, as I have done for so many years?" [4] Then the word of the LORD of hosts came to me: [5] Say to all the people of the land and the priests: When you fasted and lamented in the fifth month and in the seventh, for these seventy years, was it for me that you fasted? [6] And when you eat and when you drink, do you not eat and drink only for yourselves? [7] Were not these the words that the LORD proclaimed by the former prophets, when Jerusalem was inhabited and in prosperity, along with the towns around it, and when the Negeb and the Shephelah were inhabited?

[8] The word of the LORD came to Zechariah, saying: [9] Thus says the LORD of hosts: Render true judgments, show kindness and mercy to one another; [10] do not oppress the widow, the orphan, the alien, or the poor; and do not devise evil in your hearts against one another. [11] But they refused to listen, and turned a stubborn shoulder, and stopped their ears in order not to hear. [12] They made their hearts adamant in order not to hear the law and the words that the LORD of hosts had sent by his spirit through the former prophets. Therefore great wrath came from the LORD of hosts. [13] Just as, when I[d] called, they would not hear, so, when they called, I would not hear, says the LORD of hosts, [14] and I scattered them with a whirlwind among all the nations that they had not known. Thus the land they left was desolate, so that no one went to and fro, and a pleasant land was made desolate.

8 The word of the LORD of hosts came to me, saying: [2] Thus says the LORD of hosts: I am jealous for Zion with great jealousy, and I am jealous for her with great wrath. [3] Thus says the LORD: I will return to Zion, and will

a   Gk Syr: Heb *crowns*
b   Syr Compare verse 10: Heb *Helem*
c   Syr Compare verse 10: Heb *Hen*
d   Heb *he*

mean that the three donors are remembered for their gift at the Temple. **15:** A general comment about the help that those who return from exile would offer. *You shall know . . . sent me,* cf. 2.9.

7.1–8.23: Oracles. 7.1–7: A question answered by questions. **1:** December 7, 518 BCE., a date that introduces a miscellany of oracles. Two years after reporting visions (1.1), Zechariah now offers oracles. **2:** A delegation from *Bethel* travels the ca. 11 mi (17 km) south to Jerusalem for two reasons. *Entreat the favor of the LORD* means to seek help in a time of difficulty (so Ex 32.11; 1 Kings 13.6; 2 Kings 13.4; Jer 26.19; Ps 119.58). **3:** The question reflects a ritual commemorating the destruction of the Temple, which occurred *in the fifth month.* Gedeliah the governor was murdered in *the seventh* (2 Kings 25.8–9,25). It is possible to read the rest of the oracles in chs 7–8 as a response to this question. A definitive answer appears in 8.19. **4–6:** Zechariah addresses not only the delegation but also the priests whom they have come to consult. Zechariah again alludes to the words of *former prophets* (cf. 1.4,6) and poses three questions. In the first, he suggests that the rite has been *only for yourselves.* On inappropriate and appropriate fasting, see Isa 58.4b–5; Joel 2.12–13. Zechariah charges the people with both ineffectual fasting and feasting. **7:** *The Negeb and the Shephelah,* the southern and western regions of Judah.

7:8–14: Oracle and historical reprise. 9–10: Having referred to *former prophets* in v. 7, Zechariah now quotes what they said. For comparable admonitions and prohibitions, see Jer 7.5–6; 22.3; Mic 6.8. **11–12:** Language about *adamant hearts* was also used about Pharaoh (Ex 7.14). **13–14:** To *not hear* was reciprocal (cf. Ezek 8.18b; Jer 11.11b). The *whirlwind,* often a punitive agent, e.g., Jer 23.19).

8.1–23: Ten oracles of restoration (vv. 1–2; 3; 4–5; 6; 7–8; 9–13; 14–17; 18–19; 20–22; 23). **1–2:** Language of *jealousy* reprises 1.14; cf. Ezek 36.6b. **3:** This oracle echoes 1.14, with *dwell* referring to the Temple. *The faith-*

dwell in the midst of Jerusalem; Jerusalem shall be called the faithful city, and the mountain of the LORD of hosts shall be called the holy mountain. [4] Thus says the LORD of hosts: Old men and old women shall again sit in the streets of Jerusalem, each with staff in hand because of their great age. [5] And the streets of the city shall be full of boys and girls playing in its streets. [6] Thus says the LORD of hosts: Even though it seems impossible to the remnant of this people in these days, should it also seem impossible to me, says the LORD of hosts? [7] Thus says the LORD of hosts: I will save my people from the east country and from the west country; [8] and I will bring them to live in Jerusalem. They shall be my people and I will be their God, in faithfulness and in righteousness.

[9] Thus says the LORD of hosts: Let your hands be strong—you that have recently been hearing these words from the mouths of the prophets who were present when the foundation was laid for the rebuilding of the temple, the house of the LORD of hosts. [10] For before those days there were no wages for people or for animals, nor was there any safety from the foe for those who went out or came in, and I set them all against one another. [11] But now I will not deal with the remnant of this people as in the former days, says the LORD of hosts. [12] For there shall be a sowing of peace; the vine shall yield its fruit, the ground shall give its produce, and the skies shall give their dew; and I will cause the remnant of this people to possess all these things.

[13] Just as you have been a cursing among the nations, O house of Judah and house of Israel, so I will save you and you shall be a blessing. Do not be afraid, but let your hands be strong.

[14] For thus says the LORD of hosts: Just as I purposed to bring disaster upon you, when your ancestors provoked me to wrath, and I did not relent, says the LORD of hosts, [15] so again I have purposed in these days to do good to Jerusalem and to the house of Judah; do not be afraid. [16] These are the things that you shall do: Speak the truth to one another, render in your gates judgments that are true and make for peace, [17] do not devise evil in your hearts against one another, and love no false oath; for all these are things that I hate, says the LORD.

[18] The word of the LORD of hosts came to me, saying: [19] Thus says the LORD of hosts: The fast of the fourth month, and the fast of the fifth, and the fast of the seventh, and the fast of the tenth, shall be seasons of joy and gladness, and cheerful festivals for the house of Judah: therefore love truth and peace.

[20] Thus says the LORD of hosts: Peoples shall yet come, the inhabitants of many cities; [21] the inhabitants of one city shall go to another, saying, "Come, let us go to entreat the favor of the LORD, and to seek the LORD of hosts; I myself am going." [22] Many peoples and strong nations shall come to seek the LORD of hosts in Jerusalem, and to entreat the favor of the LORD. [23] Thus says the LORD of hosts: In those days ten men from nations of every language shall take hold of a Jew,

---

ful city, a new name for Jerusalem; cf. Isa 62.4; Jer 33.16; Ezek 48.35. On holy mountain, see Joel 3.17; Isa 52.1. 4–5: This oracle continues to portray prosperity in an urban setting, including multiple generations of both genders, on which see Jer 30.18–21. 6: This oracle highlights the key word "impossibility" (cf. Ps 139.4), just as v. 2 focused on "jealousy." 7–8: On saving from, see Jer 30.10–11; Isa 43.5–6. The covenantal relationship is reaffirmed (cf. Ex 6.7). 9–13: This oracle begins with an admonition, not just a promise. 9: An allusion to the ceremony reflected in 4.9; Hag 2.15,18. 10: A lamentable state portrayed similarly in Hag 1.6. 11–13: On remnant, see 8.6; Hag 1.12,14. Peace, Heb "shalom," which is described using fertility imagery, cf. Hag 1.10; Joel 3.18. Cursing/blessing draws on covenantal traditions, e.g., Deut 28. 14–17: The LORD promises a time of benevolence (do . . . good to Jerusalem); then turns to admonitions comparable to those in 7.9–10. Legal proceedings were conducted in city gates (Deut 21.19; Ruth 4.1). 18–19: This oracle responds to the question posed in 7.3. All prior rituals of fasting are to become occasions for feasting. The fourth month was when the Babylonians breached the walls of Jerusalem, and the tenth when they began their siege (2 Kings 25.1–4; Jer 39.2; 52.4–7). For the fifth and seventh months, see 7.3n. Again, a promise is juxtaposed with an admonition. 20–22: A pilgrimage of foreign nations to Jerusalem; cf. 14.16; Isa 2.2–4; 60.1–3; 66.18–21. 23: On the cloak, see Hag 2.12.

grasping his garment and saying, "Let us go with you, for we have heard that God is with you."

9 An Oracle.

The word of the LORD is against the land of Hadrach
  and will rest upon Damascus.
For to the LORD belongs the capital[a] of Aram,[b]
  as do all the tribes of Israel;
[2] Hamath also, which borders on it,
  Tyre and Sidon, though they are very wise.
[3] Tyre has built itself a rampart,
  and heaped up silver like dust,
  and gold like the dirt of the streets.
[4] But now, the Lord will strip it of its possessions
  and hurl its wealth into the sea,
  and it shall be devoured by fire.

[5] Ashkelon shall see it and be afraid;
  Gaza too, and shall writhe in anguish;
  Ekron also, because its hopes are withered.
The king shall perish from Gaza;
  Ashkelon shall be uninhabited;
[6] a mongrel people shall settle in Ashdod,
  and I will make an end of the pride of Philistia.

[7] I will take away its blood from its mouth,
  and its abominations from between its teeth;
it too shall be a remnant for our God;
  it shall be like a clan in Judah,
  and Ekron shall be like the Jebusites.
[8] Then I will encamp at my house as a guard,
  so that no one shall march to and fro;
no oppressor shall again overrun them,
  for now I have seen with my own eyes.

[9] Rejoice greatly, O daughter Zion!
  Shout aloud, O daughter Jerusalem!
Lo, your king comes to you;
  triumphant and victorious is he,
humble and riding on a donkey,
  on a colt, the foal of a donkey.
[10] He[c] will cut off the chariot from Ephraim
  and the war-horse from Jerusalem;
and the battle bow shall be cut off,
  and he shall command peace to the nations;
his dominion shall be from sea to sea,
  and from the River to the ends of the earth.

[11] As for you also, because of the blood of my covenant with you,

a Heb *eye*
b Cn: Heb *of Adam* (or *of humankind*)
c Gk: Heb I

9.1–11.17: The first "Oracle." "*An oracle. The word of the LORD*" also appears in Zech 12.1; and Mal 1.1., suggesting that three "oracles" have been appended to Zechariah 1–8. **9.1–8: An oracle of woe against foreign nations and of protection for the Temple.** The places named are all within Syria-Palestine. The initial sites are in the north; they subsequently move to the west and then south. **1:** *Hadrach*, Hatarikka in Neo-Assyrian texts, refers to a place in northern Syria. As is common in prophetic texts, the LORD controls land beyond the boundaries of Israel. **2:** *Tyre and Sidon*, Phoenician port cities, attested in earlier oracles against the nations (e.g., Isa 23; Ezek 26–28) and also important mercantile centers in the Persian period (Ezra 3.7; Neh 13.16). **4:** The LORD now acts as divine warrior. **5–6:** The sites are sometimes personified—*see, afraid, writhe*. Verses 5–6 highlight Philistine cities. **7–8:** God now speaks in the first person, promising to remove *abominations* (cf. Lev 7.21; 11.10–12) from Philistia's mouth, so that the Philistines will observe Jewish dietary laws (cf. Gen 9.4; Lev 11.2–47; Deut 14.3–21). *Jebusites*, pre-Israelite inhabitants of Jerusalem; see Josh 15.63; 2 Sam 5.6–9; 1 Chr 11.4–9. **8:** *Encamp*, an unusual word to depict God's presence at the Temple. It continues the military tone of the poem, with the LORD as *guard* (lit. "as a garrison").

9.9–17: God's sovereign rule. A series of poetic vignettes about God as king. **9–10:** The king welcomed. **9:** Personified Jerusalem is admonished to sing for joy; cf. Ps 32.11; 47.1. On *daughter Zion/Jerusalem*, see Lam 1.6; Zeph 3.14–15; Zech 2.13. *On a donkey, on a colt*, i.e., on one animal described in two parallel poetic lines; cf. Mt 21.2–7, which understands there are to be two animals. *The River* probably refers to the Euphrates. The demilitarized dominion described here is similar to Mic 4.3; Isa 2.4. **11–13:** Oracle advocating return and preparation for battle. **11:** *You* is feminine singular, referring still to *daughter Zion*. *Blood of my covenant* echoes Ex 24.8, the Sinai

I will set your prisoners free from the
waterless pit.
[12] Return to your stronghold, O prisoners
of hope;
today I declare that I will restore to you
double.
[13] For I have bent Judah as my bow;
I have made Ephraim its arrow.
I will arouse your sons, O Zion,
against your sons, O Greece,
and wield you like a warrior's sword.

[14] Then the LORD will appear over them,
and his arrow go forth like lightning;
the Lord GOD will sound the trumpet
and march forth in the whirlwinds of
the south.
[15] The LORD of hosts will protect them,
and they shall devour and tread down
the slingers;[a]
they shall drink their blood[b] like wine,
and be full like a bowl,
drenched like the corners of the altar.

[16] On that day the LORD their God will save
them
for they are the flock of his people;
for like the jewels of a crown
they shall shine on his land.
[17] For what goodness and beauty are his!
Grain shall make the young men
flourish,
and new wine the young women.

10
Ask rain from the LORD
in the season of the spring rain,
from the LORD who makes the storm
clouds,
who gives showers of rain to you,[c]
the vegetation in the field to everyone.

[2] For the teraphim[d] utter nonsense,
and the diviners see lies;
the dreamers tell false dreams,
and give empty consolation.
Therefore the people wander like sheep;
they suffer for lack of a shepherd.

[3] My anger is hot against the shepherds,
and I will punish the leaders;[e]
for the LORD of hosts cares for his flock,
the house of Judah,
and will make them like his proud war-
horse.
[4] Out of them shall come the cornerstone,
out of them the tent peg,
out of them the battle bow,
out of them every commander.
[5] Together they shall be like warriors in
battle,
trampling the foe in the mud of the
streets;
they shall fight, for the LORD is with
them,
and they shall put to shame the riders
on horses.

[6] I will strengthen the house of Judah,
and I will save the house of Joseph.
I will bring them back because I have
compassion on them,
and they shall be as though I had not
rejected them;
for I am the LORD their God and I will
answer them.

a   Cn: Heb *the slingstones*
b   Gk: Heb *shall drink*
c   Heb *them*
d   Or *household gods*
e   Or *male goats*

covenant. 13: Martial imagery returns, with *Judah* and *Ephraim*, the preexilic Southern and Northern Kingdoms, as weapons. *Greece*, along with Joel 3.6, is the earliest reference in the Bible to this enemy of the Persians. 14–15: Prophetic poem about the battle. 14: A military theophany. On a *march . . . of the south*, cf. Judg 5.4. 15: Typical of holy war, the divine warrior will fight and Israel will reap the benefits of victory, here described in graphic imagery, which also alludes to the Temple—*bowl* (Ex 27.3), *altar* (Ex 27.2). 16–17: The LORD as royal shepherd conveyed using the metaphor of a flock and a simile of jewelry. *Grain/new wine* symbolize fertility; cf. Hag 2.19.

10.1–12: The LORD, the militant shepherd. A poem that offers critique and solace. 1: God is affirmed as the source of fertility. 2: Three forms of divination are condemned. *Teraphim*, divinatory figurines often critiqued in the Bible (e.g., so Ezek 21.21). 3–5: God will turn *the house of Judah* into a military force. 3: *Shepherds*, i.e., rulers. *Leaders*, lit. "he-goats" (textual note *e*; Isa 14.9). 6: God speaks, reiterating the diction of *save* (9.16) and return (*bring back*; 9.12). Cf. Isa 54.8. The Northern Kingdom of Israel, *the house of Joseph* (called

[7] Then the people of Ephraim shall become
  like warriors,
  and their hearts shall be glad as with
  wine.
Their children shall see it and rejoice,
  their hearts shall exult in the LORD.

[8] I will signal for them and gather them in,
  for I have redeemed them,
  and they shall be as numerous as they
  were before.
[9] Though I scattered them among the
  nations,
  yet in far countries they shall remember
  me,
  and they shall rear their children and
  return.
[10] I will bring them home from the land of
  Egypt,
  and gather them from Assyria;
I will bring them to the land of Gilead and
  to Lebanon,
  until there is no room for them.
[11] They[a] shall pass through the sea of
  distress,
  and the waves of the sea shall be struck
  down,
  and all the depths of the Nile dried up.
The pride of Assyria shall be laid low,
  and the scepter of Egypt shall
  depart.
[12] I will make them strong in the LORD,
  and they shall walk in his name,
                                  says the LORD.

11 Open your doors, O Lebanon,
  so that fire may devour your cedars!
[2] Wail, O cypress, for the cedar has fallen,
  for the glorious trees are ruined!

Wail, oaks of Bashan,
  for the thick forest has been felled!
[3] Listen, the wail of the shepherds,
  for their glory is despoiled!
Listen, the roar of the lions,
  for the thickets of the Jordan are
  destroyed!

[4] Thus said the LORD my God: Be a shepherd of the flock doomed to slaughter.
[5] Those who buy them kill them and go
unpunished; and those who sell them say,
"Blessed be the LORD, for I have become rich";
and their own shepherds have no pity on
them. [6] For I will no longer have pity on the
inhabitants of the earth, says the LORD. I will
cause them, every one, to fall each into the
hand of a neighbor, and each into the hand of
the king; and they shall devastate the earth,
and I will deliver no one from their hand.
[7] So, on behalf of the sheep merchants, I
became the shepherd of the flock doomed
to slaughter. I took two staffs; one I named
Favor, the other I named Unity, and I tended
the sheep. [8] In one month I disposed of the
three shepherds, for I had become impatient
with them, and they also detested me. [9] So I
said, "I will not be your shepherd. What is to
die, let it die; what is to be destroyed, let it be
destroyed; and let those that are left devour
the flesh of one another!" [10] I took my staff
Favor and broke it, annulling the covenant
that I had made with all the peoples. [11] So
it was annulled on that day, and the sheep
merchants, who were watching me, knew
that it was the word of the LORD. [12] I then
said to them, "If it seems right to you, give

a Gk: Heb *He*

"Ephraim" in v. 7), will be saved along with Judah; cf. 9.13; Ezek 37.15–28. **7:** *Wine* making the *heart glad* symbolizes a good future; cf. Eccl 9.7; Ps 104.15. **8–12:** An oracle focusing on gathering and return from exile; cf.
Isa 43.1–7,14–21; Jer 23.3. **10–11:** On the flight to Egypt, see Jer 43. With part of Israel in Egypt, a new Exodus
can take place. **10:** *Gilead*, northern Transjordan. *Lebanon*, the mountainous region north of Israel, famous
for its forests (see 11.1).

11.1–3: Taunt against Israel's northern neighbors. In this ironic taunt, the region is personified and characterized by three trees, two of which are fabled—cedars of Lebanon (Ezek 31.3) and oaks of Bashan (Ezek 27.6),
which was in northern Transjordan. Shepherds and lions probably symbolize communal leaders. The destruction will affect foliage as far away as the Jordan Valley.

11.4–17: Shepherding a flock. Diverse oracles and reports, all using the metaphor of a shepherd for the community's leader; cf. 13.7–9. **4–6:** An unnamed person, perhaps the prophet Zechariah, is charged to lead the
community, which is doomed. **7–14:** The symbolic action is reported by the individual who wields and then

me my wages; but if not, keep them." So they weighed out as my wages thirty shekels of silver. [13] Then the LORD said to me, "Throw it into the treasury"[a]—this lordly price at which I was valued by them. So I took the thirty shekels of silver and threw them into the treasury[a] in the house of the LORD. [14] Then I broke my second staff Unity, annulling the family ties between Judah and Israel.

[15] Then the LORD said to me: Take once more the implements of a worthless shepherd. [16] For I am now raising up in the land a shepherd who does not care for the perishing, or seek the wandering,[b] or heal the maimed, or nourish the healthy,[c] but devours the flesh of the fat ones, tearing off even their hoofs.

[17] Oh, my worthless shepherd,
　　who deserts the flock!
May the sword strike his arm
　　and his right eye!
Let his arm be completely withered,
　　his right eye utterly blinded!

12　An Oracle.

The word of the LORD concerning Israel: Thus says the LORD, who stretched out the heavens and founded the earth and formed the human spirit within: [2] See, I am about to make Jerusalem a cup of reeling for all the surrounding peoples; it will be against Judah also in the siege against Jerusalem. [3] On that day I will make Jerusalem a heavy stone for all the peoples; all who lift it shall grievously hurt themselves. And all the nations of the earth shall come together against it. [4] On that day, says the LORD, I will strike every horse with panic, and its rider with madness. But on the house of Judah I will keep a watchful eye, when I strike every horse of the peoples with blindness. [5] Then the clans of Judah shall say to themselves, "The inhabitants of Jerusalem have strength through the LORD of hosts, their God."

[6] On that day I will make the clans of Judah like a blazing pot on a pile of wood, like a flaming torch among sheaves; and they shall devour to the right and to the left all the surrounding peoples, while Jerusalem shall again be inhabited in its place, in Jerusalem.

[7] And the LORD will give victory to the tents of Judah first, that the glory of the house of David and the glory of the inhabitants of Jerusalem may not be exalted over that of Judah. [8] On that day the LORD will shield the inhabitants of Jerusalem so that the feeblest among them on that day shall be like David, and the house of David shall be like God, like the angel of the LORD, at their head. [9] And on that day I will seek to destroy all the nations that come against Jerusalem.

[10] And I will pour out a spirit of compassion and supplication on the house of David and the inhabitants of Jerusalem, so that, when they look on the one[d] whom they have pierced, they shall mourn for him, as one mourns for an only child, and weep bitterly over him, as one weeps over a firstborn. [11] On that day the mourning in Jerusalem will be as great as the mourning for Hadad-rimmon

a　Syr: Heb *it to the potter*
b　Syr Compare Gk Vg: Heb *the youth*
c　Meaning of Heb uncertain
d　Heb *on me*

destroys two shepherd's staffs, symbolizing the end of a covenantal relationship. **12–13:** *Thirty shekels of silver:* Ex 21.32 stipulates this amount as restitution for a slave gored by an ox. Other ancient texts understand this to be a trifling amount of money; cf. Mt 26.15; 27.3–10. *Lordly price* is ironic. **15–16:** The deity commands a second symbolic action, again involving a shepherd's implements. **17:** Woe oracle against the community's leader.

12.1–14.21: The second "Oracle." See 9.1–11.17n. Divine oracles and prophetic sayings about the imminent day of the LORD, referred to as "that day." **12.1–9:** Through a *word . . . concerning Israel,* vv. 2–9 highlight the destruction of foreign nations, as did 9.1–8. The God who creates (v. 1; cf. Job 9.8; Isa 42.5; Jer 10,12) can also destroy. There will be conflict between Israel and the nations and even within Judah (v. 2). **2:** *Cup of reeling,* cf. Ps 75.8; Isa 51.17–23; Jer 25.15–18. **4:** *Madness* and *blindness,* curses in Deut 28.28–29. **7–8:** David's lineage continues to be a source of hope. **10–14:** The tone shifts to that of lamentation. **10:** *The one . . . pierced,* cf. 13.3. The referent is unclear but the Hebrew suggests it is the LORD; cf. Jn 19.37, which identifies it with Jesus. **11–14:** Lamentation over the one *pierced.* **11:** *Hadad-rimmon* is, according to 2 Chr 35.20–25, the site for mourning over Josiah's death. It is also the name of a Syrian storm god, also known as Baal, whose seasonal disappearance

in the plain of Megiddo. [12] The land shall mourn, each family by itself; the family of the house of David by itself, and their wives by themselves; the family of the house of Nathan by itself, and their wives by themselves; [13] the family of the house of Levi by itself, and their wives by themselves; the family of the Shimeites by itself, and their wives by themselves; [14] and all the families that are left, each by itself, and their wives by themselves.

13 On that day a fountain shall be opened for the house of David and the inhabitants of Jerusalem, to cleanse them from sin and impurity.

[2] On that day, says the LORD of hosts, I will cut off the names of the idols from the land, so that they shall be remembered no more; and also I will remove from the land the prophets and the unclean spirit. [3] And if any prophets appear again, their fathers and mothers who bore them will say to them, "You shall not live, for you speak lies in the name of the LORD"; and their fathers and their mothers who bore them shall pierce them through when they prophesy. [4] On that day the prophets will be ashamed, every one, of their visions when they prophesy; they will not put on a hairy mantle in order to deceive, [5] but each of them will say, "I am no prophet, I am a tiller of the soil; for the land has been my possession[a] since my youth." [6] And if anyone asks them, "What are these wounds on your chest?"[b] the answer will be "The wounds I received in the house of my friends."

[7] "Awake, O sword, against my shepherd, against the man who is my associate," says the LORD of hosts.
Strike the shepherd, that the sheep may be scattered;
I will turn my hand against the little ones.
[8] In the whole land, says the LORD, two-thirds shall be cut off and perish, and one-third shall be left alive.
[9] And I will put this third into the fire, refine them as one refines silver, and test them as gold is tested.
They will call on my name, and I will answer them.
I will say, "They are my people"; and they will say, "The LORD is our God."

14 See, a day is coming for the LORD, when the plunder taken from you will be divided in your midst. [2] For I will gather all the nations against Jerusalem to battle, and the city shall be taken and the houses looted and the women raped; half the city shall go into exile, but the rest of the people shall not be cut off from the city. [3] Then the LORD will go forth and fight against those nations as when he fights on a day of battle. [4] On that day his feet shall stand on the Mount of Olives, which lies before Jerusalem on the east; and the Mount of Olives shall be split in two from east to west by a very wide valley; so that one half of the Mount shall withdraw

a Cn: Heb *for humankind has caused me to possess*
b Heb *wounds between your hands*

was mourned in the agriculturally fertile area around Megiddo; see 2 Kings 5.18. **12–14:** *Their wives,* on women's lamentation, see 2 Chr 35.25; Jer 9.17,20. The lamentation will involve *the land* and *all the families,* not just the families named. The families are those of *the house of David* (1 Chr 14.14 reports that David bore Nathan) and *the house of Levi* (Shimei was a grandson of Levi, 1 Chr 6.16–17). **13.1:** Those who might have incurred corpse defilement during mourning will be cleansed by water from *a fountain.* On purification from such uncleanness, see Num 19. The *fountain* may be related to the motif of a river flowing from the Temple; cf. Zech 14.8; Ps 46.4 Ezek 47.1–12; Joel 3.18. **2–6:** Prophecy is viewed as negatively as idolatry, subject to punishment by death. Unlike the rebellious son, whom parents are to bring before the legal assembly (Deut 21.18–21), parents here can kill their prophetic offspring immediately. **4–6:** *Hairy mantle,* a garment, as in Gen 25.25, that symbolizes deception. *I am no prophet* quotes Am 7.14. Prophetic *wounds,* cf. 1 Kings 18.28.

13.7–9: A personified sword. A poem using imagery similar to 11.17. The fractional destruction is similar to that in Ezek 5.1–12. **8:** On imagery of refining, see Isa 1.25–26; Mal 3.2–4. **9:** *My people . . . our God* expresses the covenantal relationship (cf. Ex 6.7; Hos 2.23).

14.1–21: An eschatological depiction of the LORD's Day. 4: A theophany, in which the mountains are *split* (cf.

northward, and the other half southward. [5] And you shall flee by the valley of the LORD's mountain,[a] for the valley between the mountains shall reach to Azal;[b] and you shall flee as you fled from the earthquake in the days of King Uzziah of Judah. Then the LORD my God will come, and all the holy ones with him.

[6] On that day there shall not be[c] either cold or frost.[d] [7] And there shall be continuous day (it is known to the LORD), not day and not night, for at evening time there shall be light.

[8] On that day living waters shall flow out from Jerusalem, half of them to the eastern sea and half of them to the western sea; it shall continue in summer as in winter.

[9] And the LORD will become king over all the earth; on that day the LORD will be one and his name one.

[10] The whole land shall be turned into a plain from Geba to Rimmon south of Jerusalem. But Jerusalem shall remain aloft on its site from the Gate of Benjamin to the place of the former gate, to the Corner Gate, and from the Tower of Hananel to the king's wine presses. [11] And it shall be inhabited, for never again shall it be doomed to destruction; Jerusalem shall abide in security.

[12] This shall be the plague with which the LORD will strike all the peoples that wage war against Jerusalem: their flesh shall rot while they are still on their feet; their eyes shall rot in their sockets, and their tongues shall rot in their mouths. [13] On that day a great panic from the LORD shall fall on them, so that each will seize the hand of a neighbor, and the hand of the one will be raised against the hand of the other; [14] even Judah will fight at Jerusalem. And the wealth of all the surrounding nations shall be collected—gold, silver, and garments in great abundance. [15] And a plague like this plague shall fall on the horses, the mules, the camels, the donkeys, and whatever animals may be in those camps.

[16] Then all who survive of the nations that have come against Jerusalem shall go up year after year to worship the King, the LORD of hosts, and to keep the festival of booths.[e] [17] If any of the families of the earth do not go up to Jerusalem to worship the King, the LORD of hosts, there will be no rain upon them. [18] And if the family of Egypt do not go up and present themselves, then on them shall[f] come the plague that the LORD inflicts on the nations that do not go up to keep the festival of booths.[e] [19] Such shall be the punishment of Egypt and the punishment of all the nations that do not go up to keep the festival of booths.[e]

[20] On that day there shall be inscribed on the bells of the horses, "Holy to the LORD." And the cooking pots in the house of the LORD shall be as holy as[g] the bowls in front of the altar; [21] and every cooking pot in Jerusalem and Judah shall be sacred to the LORD of hosts, so that all who sacrifice may come and use them to boil the flesh of the sacrifice. And there shall no longer be traders[h] in the house of the LORD of hosts on that day.

a   Heb *my mountains*
b   Meaning of Heb uncertain
c   Cn: Heb *there shall not be light*
d   Compare Gk Syr Vg Tg: Meaning of Heb uncertain
e   Or *tabernacles*; Heb *succoth*
f   Gk Syr: Heb *shall not*
g   Heb *shall be like*
h   Or *Canaanites*

Mic 1.4; Hab 3.6). The new landscape allows Jerusalemites to flee from destruction. **5:** *Earthquake*, see Am 1.1n. *The holy ones*, members of the divine council; cf. Deut 33.2; Ps 89.5,7). **7:** The LORD's *day* will no longer be a day of darkness; cf. Am 5.18; Zeph 1.15. **8:** *Living waters*, see 13.1n. **9:** *The LORD* as monarch juxtaposed with an allusion to the "Shema" (Deut 6.4). **10–11:** Consistent with the Zion tradition (Ps 48.2; Isa 2.2; Mic 4.1), Jerusalem will be elevated and secure. The area *from Geba to Rimmon*, from (ca) 10 km (6mi) north-northeast to 60 km (37 mi) *south* of Jerusalem, represents the geographic limits of the old kingdom of Judah. **12–15:** The plague tradition (Ex 7–12; Pss 78; 105) is linked with holy war *panic* (cf. Deut 7.23; 1 Sam 5.9). **14:** Despoliation of the nations; cf. Isa 61.6; Hag 2.7). **16–19:** The tradition of a pilgrimage of nations (cf. 8.20–23; Isa 2.1–4; Mic 4.1–4) is related to *the festival of booths*, Sukkoth (Lev 23.33–36; Neh 8.13–18). Egypt is singled out for punishment, perhaps because of the allusion to plagues in vv.12,13. **20–21:** Imagery of radical holiness throughout Jerusalem, not just at the Temple. **20:** The book concludes as it began, with reference to horses. **21:** *Traders*, see textual note *h*, literally "Canaanites."

MALACHI

NAME, AUTHORSHIP, AND CANONICAL STATUS

Unlike the other compositions in the Book of the Twelve (the "Minor Prophets"), Malachi may not be named for a prophet. Malachi means literally "my messenger," and there is good reason not to construe the word in 1.1 as a proper name, especially since the name does not appear elsewhere in the Bible. The Septuagint (LXX) does not translate it as a name, and in fact the same word appears in Mal 3.1, where it is simply translated as "my messenger."

The book begins in similar fashion to Zech 9.1 and 12.1, suggesting that three collections (Zech 9–12; 12–14; and Malachi) were appended to Zech 1–8. An interest in creating a collection of twelve prophetic books may have resulted in the identification of Malachi as a separate book.

DATE OF COMPOSITION AND HISTORICAL CONTEXT

Scholars generally agree that the book of Malachi dates to the period after the rededication of the Temple in Jerusalem In 515 BCE. Reference to a governor (1.8), and not a king, clearly points to the postexilic era. The book may have been composed in Judah prior to the time that Ezra and Nehemiah were active, i.e., in the early decades of the fifth century BCE. Problems that Malachi addresses, such as tithing, are also attested in the book of Ezra-Nehemiah (Neh 13.5,12), suggesting that these three books date to roughly the same period. The book knows a number of earlier biblical traditions, particularly those in Deuteronomy and in ritual texts.

STRUCTURE, CONTENTS, AND INTERPRETATION

Malachi includes a distinctive form of literature, often characterized as a disputation. This genre has striking similarities to Greek diatribes. There are six such rhetorical units (1.2–5; 1.6.–2.9; 2.10–16; 2.17–3.5; 3.6–12; 3.13–4.3). In all of them, two parties—God and some group—engage in a stylized dialogue. All six units include questions, posed sometimes by the deity, other times by the people. Moreover, each disputation quotes the LORD's opponents. What the people say often seems outlandish, e.g., "All who do evil are good in the sight of the LORD, and he delights in them" (2.17) or "It is vain to serve God" (3.14).

The book addresses numerous topics: the permanence of the LORD's care for Israel, the need to venerate the LORD alone, the importance of tithing and justice, and hope for those who fear the LORD. Two topics are particularly prominent—the international scope of God's reign, and the ritual world of the Temple.

In the Hebrew Bible, Malachi ends the Book of the Twelve and the entire division of the canon called the Prophets. In Christian Bibles, it ends the Old Testament; its final words about Elijah as messenger are interpreted in the Gospels as referring to John the Baptist (Mt 14.10; Lk 1.17).

David L. Petersen

1 An oracle. The word of the LORD to Israel by Malachi.[a]

[2] I have loved you, says the LORD. But you say, "How have you loved us?" Is not Esau Jacob's brother? says the LORD. Yet I have loved Jacob [3] but I have hated Esau; I have made his hill country a desolation and his heritage a desert for jackals. [4] If Edom says, "We are shattered but we will rebuild the ruins," the LORD of hosts says: They may build, but I will tear down, until they are called the wicked country, the people with whom the LORD is angry forever. [5] Your own eyes shall see this, and you shall say, "Great is the LORD beyond the borders of Israel!"

[6] A son honors his father, and servants their master. If then I am a father, where is the honor due me? And if I am a master, where is the respect due me? says the LORD of hosts to you, O priests, who despise my name. You say, "How have we despised your name?" [7] By offering polluted food on my altar. And you say, "How have we polluted it?"[b] By thinking that the LORD's table may be despised. [8] When you offer blind animals in sacrifice, is that not wrong? And when you offer those that are lame or sick, is that not wrong? Try presenting that to your gover-

nor; will he be pleased with you or show you favor? says the LORD of hosts. [9] And now implore the favor of God, that he may be gracious to us. The fault is yours. Will he show favor to any of you? says the LORD of hosts. [10] Oh, that someone among you would shut the temple[c] doors, so that you would not kindle fire on my altar in vain! I have no pleasure in you, says the LORD of hosts, and I will not accept an offering from your hands. [11] For from the rising of the sun to its setting my name is great among the nations, and in every place incense is offered to my name, and a pure offering; for my name is great among the nations, says the LORD of hosts. [12] But you profane it when you say that the Lord's table is polluted, and the food for it[d] may be despised. [13] "What a weariness this is," you say, and you sniff at me,[e] says the LORD of hosts. You bring what has been taken by violence or is lame or sick, and this you bring as your offering! Shall I accept that from your hand? says the LORD. [14] Cursed be the cheat

a Or by my messenger
b Gk: Heb you
c Heb lacks temple
d Compare Syr Tg: Heb its fruit, its food
e Another reading is at it

1.1: Superscription. This verse begins in the same way as Zech 9.1 and Zech 12.1. Here the oracle (lit., "burden") is directed to Israel. Malachi, literally, "my messenger."

1.2–5: The God who loves and hates. God demonstrates love for Israel (Jacob) by hating Edom (Esau; see Gen 25.19–24; 36.1). Enmity toward Edom runs deep in the Hebrew Bible; see especially Obadiah (cf. Isa 34.5–17; Isa 63.1; Jer 49.7–22; Ezek 25.12–14; 35.1–15; Ps 137.7). Still, Israel's God was remembered as having given Edom its land (see Deut 2.4–5). **3:** Such destruction may be related to Nabonidus's campaign against Edom in 552 BCE. **5:** Great is the LORD, similar claims are made about God in Pss 35.27; 40.16; 70.4; 96.4, which emphasize the power of the divine king. The international significance of Israel's God is reiterated in 1.11,14.

1.6–2.9: Concerning priests and Levites. The longest of the disputations deals with the priesthood. **6:** The notion of honoring a parent is embedded in the Decalogue (Ex 20.12) and in proverbial literature (Prov 13.1; 19.26). To despise my name strikes at the heart of Israel's religious life since the Temple is "the place that the LORD your God will choose as a dwelling for his name" (Deut 12.11). **7:** Polluted food, an unusual phrase to describe unacceptable offerings. The word for "pollute" or "defile" is used in Ezra 2 of unacceptable priests (Ezra 2.62). **8:** Blind, lame, and sick animals were not acceptable as sacrifices (Deut 15.19–23; Lev 22.18–25). The prophet offers an ironic admonition, Try presenting that . . . **9:** And now implore the favor of God, an ironic call to worship placed in the mouths of the priests, which may echo the priestly blessing of Num 6.24–26. **10:** Doors, see textual note c. On the doors of the Temple, see 1 Kings 6.31; Ps 100.4; the Levites were doorkeepers at the Temple (Ezra 2.42; Neh 11.19). It is unclear whether altar refers to the altar of burnt offering or the incense altar. **11:** Using solar imagery (cf. 4.2), the prophet testifies to the vast territory in which the LORD is worshiped. Whether or not appropriate ritual is taking place at the Jerusalem Temple, the LORD's name is being venerated appropriately among the nations, including Jews in the Diaspora. **14:**

who has a male in the flock and vows to give it, and yet sacrifices to the Lord what is blemished; for I am a great King, says the LORD of hosts, and my name is reverenced among the nations.

2 And now, O priests, this command is for you. [2] If you will not listen, if you will not lay it to heart to give glory to my name, says the LORD of hosts, then I will send the curse on you and I will curse your blessings; indeed I have already cursed them,[a] because you do not lay it to heart. [3] I will rebuke your offspring, and spread dung on your faces, the dung of your offerings, and I will put you out of my presence.[b]

[4] Know, then, that I have sent this command to you, that my covenant with Levi may hold, says the LORD of hosts. [5] My covenant with him was a covenant of life and well-being, which I gave him; this called for reverence, and he revered me and stood in awe of my name. [6] True instruction was in his mouth, and no wrong was found on his lips. He walked with me in integrity and upright-

ness, and he turned many from iniquity. [7] For the lips of a priest should guard knowledge, and people should seek instruction from his mouth, for he is the messenger of the LORD of hosts. [8] But you have turned aside from the way; you have caused many to stumble by your instruction; you have corrupted the covenant of Levi, says the LORD of hosts, [9] and so I make you despised and abased before all the people, inasmuch as you have not kept my ways but have shown partiality in your instruction.

[10] Have we not all one father? Has not one God created us? Why then are we faithless to one another, profaning the covenant of our ancestors? [11] Judah has been faithless, and abomination has been committed in Israel and in Jerusalem; for Judah has profaned the sanctuary of the LORD, which he loves, and has married the daughter of a foreign god. [12] May the LORD cut off from the tents of Jacob

[a] Heb *it*

[b] Cn Compare Gk Syr: Heb *and he shall bear you to it*

Curse replaces the earlier style of questions (cf. the curses in Deut 27.15–16). On pledging something good to sacrifice and then replacing it with something inferior, see Lev 27.9–11. It appears that both worshiper and priest would suffer a curse. On the LORD as *great King*, see Pss 96.10; 97.1; 99.1. **2.1–3:** Admonition and threat to the priests. **1:** *This command* echoes language found in Deuteronomy (e.g. 27.1; 30.11). **2:** Veneration of the LORD's *name* is also at issue in Mal 1.6,11,14; 2.5; and the language of curse continues that of 1.14. *Your blessings* probably refers to the blessings that priests dispense (Num 6.23–27). **3:** *Offspring* implies the priestly lineage of Aaron, who were promised a covenant of peace (Num 25.12–13). *Dung*, either excrement or intestinal contents normally burned outside the Temple compound (Ex 29.14; Lev 4.11; 8.17; 16.27; Num 19.5). Smearing *dung* on the face of a priest would require the removal of that unclean priest from the Temple. **4–9:** The language of covenant and commandment continues, though now focusing on the Levites, whose status was below that of the priests who traced their ancestry back to Aaron. **4–5:** *Levi*, the third son of Jacob and ancestor of all priests (Gen 29.34). Jer 33.21 refers to a *covenant with Levi*; Deut 33.9 affirms the covenantal fidelity of the Levites. *Well-being* or "peace," (Heb "shalom"), is associated with the covenant with Phinehas in Num 25.12. **6:** *Instruction*, (Heb "torah"). Deut 33.10 characterizes Levites as responsible for teaching God's torah. To "walk" describes a proper covenantal relationship in Deuteronomy (10.12; 13.5). **7:** The language becomes prescriptive, though continuing to emphasize instruction. *Messenger of the LORD*, a phrase used of Haggai (Hag 1.13; see also Gen 19.1; 21.17). That Levi, personifying a group, would be so characterized underscores the high status priests receive here. **8:** *You* probably refers to the priests, indicted earlier in this disputation. The metaphor of walking (v. 6) continues here with turning *aside from the way*. **9:** The punishment is consistent with 2.2–3. Neh 13.19–20 may provide a context for understanding these charges. Nehemiah acted against those who had "defiled the priesthood, and the covenant of the priesthood and the Levites" (Neh 13.29).

2.10–16: Religious fidelity. Focus on covenant continues, but now between God and all Israel. Familial imagery is important. **10:** For a similar question, see Deut 32.6. On God as *one*, see Deut 6.4. *Covenant of our ancestors* (cf. Deut 4.3–31; 29.24–25; Jer 34.13–14, all referring to the Sinai covenant). **11:** *Abomination*, a religious sin. *The sanctuary of the LORD*, literally, "the holiness of Yahweh," which may refer to the Temple (Pss 63.2; 68.22). *Daughter of a foreign god* may refer to veneration of a goddess such as Asherah or, less likely, marriage to a

anyone who does this—any to witness[a] or answer, or to bring an offering to the LORD of hosts.

[13] And this you do as well: You cover the LORD's altar with tears, with weeping and groaning because he no longer regards the offering or accepts it with favor at your hand. [14] You ask, "Why does he not?" Because the LORD was a witness between you and the wife of your youth, to whom you have been faithless, though she is your companion and your wife by covenant. [15] Did not one God make her?[b] Both flesh and spirit are his.[c] And what does the one God[d] desire? Godly offspring. So look to yourselves, and do not let anyone be faithless to the wife of his youth. [16] For I hate[e] divorce, says the LORD, the God of Israel, and covering one's garment with violence, says the LORD of hosts. So take heed to yourselves and do not be faithless.

[17] You have wearied the LORD with your words. Yet you say, "How have we wearied him?" By saying, "All who do evil are good in the sight of the LORD, and he delights in them." Or by asking, "Where is the God of justice?"

3 See, I am sending my messenger to prepare the way before me, and the Lord whom you seek will suddenly come to his temple.

The messenger of the covenant in whom you delight—indeed, he is coming, says the LORD of hosts. [2] But who can endure the day of his coming, and who can stand when he appears? For he is like a refiner's fire and like fullers' soap; [3] he will sit as a refiner and purifier of silver, and he will purify the descendants of Levi and refine them like gold and silver, until they present offerings to the LORD in righteousness.[f] [4] Then the offering of Judah and Jerusalem will be pleasing to the LORD as in the days of old and as in former years.

[5] Then I will draw near to you for judgment; I will be swift to bear witness against the sorcerers, against the adulterers, against those who swear falsely, against those who oppress the hired workers in their wages, the widow and the orphan, against those who thrust aside the alien, and do not fear me, says the LORD of hosts.

[6] For I the LORD do not change; therefore you, O children of Jacob, have not perished.

a Cn Compare Gk: Heb *arouse*
b Or *Has he not made one?*
c Cn: Heb *and a remnant of spirit was his*
d Heb *he*
e Cn: Heb *he hates*
f Or *right offerings to the LORD*

non-Israelite woman, a major issue in the Persian period (see Ezra 9–10; Neh 13). **12:** The punishing curse. To *cut off* as a punishment, see Pss 12.3; 109.15. *Tents of Jacob,* see Jer 30.18. **13:** *Weeping* at the Temple may refer to foreign rituals similar to those described in Ezek 8.14. **14:** The identity of the characters is ambiguous. If *you* is Judah, then the *wife by covenant* would be the LORD. On marriage as a covenant, see also Ezek 16.8; Prov 2.17. **15:** Family symbolism continues with reference to *offspring.* **15b–16:** These verses, perhaps by another author, refer to human divorce; the issue is now marriage within the community, not idolatry as in vv. 10–14. Although Deut 24.1–4 permits *divorce,* it is likened to *violence* that the LORD hates.

2.17–3.5: Theodicy and theophany. The prospect of judgment brought by both a messenger and the LORD. **17:** The people are quoted three times. The second quotation ("Everyone who does evil . . .") reverses the usual biblical view about God and evildoers (cf. Deut 18.12; 25.16). *Where is the God of justice?* echoes language in psalms of lament, e.g., Pss 22.1; 89.49. **3.1–5:** These verses focus on an expected *messenger* and what he will do. **1:** *My messenger,* Heb. "mal'aki" (Eng. "Malachi"). This verse echoes Ex 23.20, "Behold, I send my messenger before you to guard your way" (cf. also Isa 40.3, "prepare the way of the LORD"). The messenger is apparently a forerunner of the Lord. *The messenger of the covenant* may be the same individual as *my messenger.* The epilogue in 4.5–6 identifies the messenger as the prophet Elijah. In the New Testament the messenger is identified as John the Baptist (Mt 11.10; Mk 1.2; Lk 1.17,76; 7.27). **2–3:** Metallurgy and the manufacture of textiles provide metaphors for purification. *Fullers' soap,* whitening and cleansing agent used in the processing of textiles. *The descendents of Levi* (see 2.4) become important again, though here as officiating priests, not teachers. **5:** All the infractions also appear in Deuteronomy, especially 24.14–17, which refers to the wage earner, sojourner, widow, and orphan (cf. also Zech 7.9–10).

3.6–12: Tithes, curses, and blessings. A disputation that addresses the responsibility of the entire community to bring tithes. **6:** *Children of Jacob* symbolize the unchanging commitment of the deity to Israel, as

7 Ever since the days of your ancestors you have turned aside from my statutes and have not kept them. Return to me, and I will return to you, says the LORD of hosts. But you say, "How shall we return?"

8 Will anyone rob God? Yet you are robbing me! But you say, "How are we robbing you?" In your tithes and offerings! 9 You are cursed with a curse, for you are robbing me—the whole nation of you! 10 Bring the full tithe into the storehouse, so that there may be food in my house, and thus put me to the test, says the LORD of hosts; see if I will not open the windows of heaven for you and pour down for you an overflowing blessing. 11 I will rebuke the locust[a] for you, so that it will not destroy the produce of your soil; and your vine in the field shall not be barren, says the LORD of hosts. 12 Then all nations will count you happy, for you will be a land of delight, says the LORD of hosts.

13 You have spoken harsh words against me, says the LORD. Yet you say, "How have we spoken against you?" 14 You have said, "It is vain to serve God. What do we profit by keeping his command or by going about as mourners before the LORD of hosts? 15 Now we count the arrogant happy; evildoers not only prosper, but when they put God to the test they escape."

16 Then those who revered the LORD spoke with one another. The LORD took note and listened, and a book of remembrance was written before him of those who revered the LORD and thought on his name. 17 They shall be mine, says the LORD of hosts, my special possession on the day when I act, and I will spare them as parents spare their children who serve them. 18 Then once more you shall see the difference between the righteous and the wicked, between one who serves God and one who does not serve him.

4 [b] See, the day is coming, burning like an oven, when all the arrogant and all evildoers will be stubble; the day that comes shall burn them up, says the LORD of hosts, so that it will leave them neither root nor branch. 2 But for you who revere my name the sun of righteousness shall rise, with healing in its wings. You shall go out leaping like calves from the stall. 3 And you shall tread down the wicked, for they will be ashes under the soles of your feet, on the day when I act, says the LORD of hosts.

4 Remember the teaching of my servant Moses, the statutes and ordinances that I commanded him at Horeb for all Israel.

a Heb devourer
b Ch 4.1-6 are Ch 3.19-24 in Heb

it has existed since the time of its ancient ancestor. 7: This verse picks up the theme of return found in Zech 1.2–6. 8–10: The deity responds to the people's question "How shall we return" (v. 7) by mandating proper tithes and offerings. 10: On the full tithe, see Lev 27.30,32. Num 18.21–32 allocates the tithe to the Levites (cf. Deut 14.22–29). The tithe was a matter of concern during the Persian period, see Neh 10.35,37–40 (cf. 12.44; 13.5). The people's testing of the LORD is attested elsewhere only in 3.15 and Ps 95.9, where it is an accusation. Here it is a challenge, and the LORD promises to pass the test and provide rain, which will create agricultural bounty. 11–12: Locust, literally, "devourer," which could refer to flies (Ps 78.45) or worms (Deut 28.39) as well as locusts (Joel 1.4). Deut 28.10–12 reflects a similar notion of rain, abundant harvest, and recognition by other peoples.
    3.13–4.3: Those who fear the LORD's name. This diatribe differs strikingly from the preceding ones by introducing a distinct group, "those who revered the LORD" (v. 16). 13: The LORD's charge could now refer to everything that the people have been quoted as saying throughout the book. 14–15: The people raise the issue of theodicy. Unlike those who venerate God, evildoers . . . prosper, even after they put God to the test (cf. 2.17; 3.10). The LORD offers no response to this charge; dialogue ceases. 16: On such God-fearers, see Pss 15.4; 22.23. Some psalms associate God-fearers with priestly houses; Ps 135.20 identifies them as the house of Levi, which has been prominent in Malachi. Book of remembrance (cf. Ps 139.16; Dan.10.21; Rev 13.8). In Ex 19.5, all Israel is God's special possession; here only a portion of Israel, the God-fearers, receives that honor. 17–18: God will spare those who serve him, who are righteous. Some will not be spared. The language of parents and children recurs in the book's final verse. 4.1: The day is the day of the LORD. Unlike the fire in 3.2–3, the oven will destroy, not purify. Cf. Isa 6.13 for the imagery of stubble consumed by fire. 2: Sun of righteousness alludes to the winged sun disk, which symbolized divine beneficence and protection in both Mesopotamia and Egypt.
    4.4–6: An epilogue, drawing on diverse biblical texts (Mal 1.6; Joel 2.31; 2 Kgs 2), that integrates the book of Malachi with individuals (Moses and Elijah) mentioned elsewhere in the Bible. 4: Teaching (Heb "torah") of

⁵ Lo, I will send you the prophet Elijah before the great and terrible day of the LORD comes. ⁶ He will turn the hearts of parents to their children and the hearts of children to their parents, so that I will not come and strike the land with a curse.ᵃ

ᵃ Or *a ban of utter destruction*

my servant Moses (cf. Josh 8.31; Neh 8.1). *Horeb* is an alternate name for Mount Sinai. 5–6: Elijah (see 3.1n.) can return because he never died (2 Kings 2.11). There was an expectation that a prophet or prophecy would return before the day of the Lord arrived (cf. Ezek 39.29; Joel 2.28; Sir 48.10). The book concludes with the imagery of familial reconciliation.

THE APOCRYPHA

The Apocryphal/ Deuterocanonical books of The Old Testament

New Revised Standard Version

INTRODUCTION TO THE APOCRYPHAL/ DEUTEROCANONICAL BOOKS

DEFINITIONS

The apocryphal/Deuterocanonical books are those works that were included in the Septuagint (the ancient Greek translation of the Hebrew Bible, referred to as LXX) or in the Old Latin and Vulgate translations, but are not included in the Hebrew text that forms both the canon for Judaism and the Protestant Old Testament. All of these works, whether they are individual books or additions to the Hebrew texts of Esther and Daniel, have been regarded as canonical by one or more Christian communities, but not by all. (The exception is 4 Macc, which appears only in an appendix to the Greek Bible.)

"Apocrypha" means "hidden things," but it is not clear why the term was chosen to describe these books. In antiquity "hidden books" sometimes referred to books that were restricted because they contained mysterious or esoteric teaching, too profound to be communicated to any except the initiated (see 2 Esd 14.45–46). Some early Christian writers used the term to describe works they considered to be spurious or heretical. But neither usage aptly describes the set of books that now goes by this name. The use of the term to refer to this group of books can be traced to the Christian scholar Jerome at the turn of the fifth century CE. It serves to distinguish them from books of the Christian Old Testament that are also found in the Jewish canon.

"Deuterocanonical," along with its coordinate term "protocanonical," is used in Roman Catholic tradition to describe the status of the two groups of books of the Old Testament. The "protocanon" consists of the books of the Hebrew Bible, concerning which there was no debate as to their canonical status. The "Deuterocanon" refers to those additional books whose canonical status was reaffirmed at a later date. This distinction, introduced by Sixtus of Sienna in 1566, acknowledges the differences between the two categories while making clear that Roman Catholics accept as fully canonical those books and parts of books that Protestants call the Apocrypha (except the Prayer of Manasseh, Psalm 151, 3 and 4 Maccabees, and 1 and 2 Esdras, which both groups regard as apocryphal). Thus, although the terms "Deuterocanonical" and "Apocryphal" can describe the same collections of writings, they clearly indicate the difference in status of the writings among different groups. In the NRSV translation, subheadings in the table of contents for these books, and in the text itself, explain the differing canonical status of various writings.

THE ROMAN CATHOLIC, ORTHODOX, AND PROTESTANT CANONS OF THE OLD TESTAMENT

Toward the end of the fourth century CE, Pope Damasus commissioned Jerome, the most learned Christian biblical scholar of his day, to prepare a standard Latin version of the scriptures (the translation that was to become known as the Latin Vulgate). In the Old Testament Jerome followed the Hebrew canon; though he also translated the apocryphal books, he called attention to their distinct status in prefaces. Subsequent copyists of the Latin Bible, however, did not always include Jerome's prefaces, and during the medieval period the Western Church generally regarded these books as scripture, without differentiation. After the Protestant reformers had denied the canonical status of these books, in 1546 the Council of Trent decreed that the canon of the Old Testament includes them (with the exceptions listed earlier). Subsequent editions of the Latin Vulgate text, officially approved by the Roman Catholic Church, placed these books within the Christian sequence of the Old Testament books. Thus Tobit and Judith come after Nehemiah; the Wisdom of Solomon and Ecclesiasticus (Sirach) come after the Song of Solomon; Baruch (with the Letter of Jeremiah as ch 6) comes after Lamentations; and 1 and 2 Maccabees conclude the books of the Old Testament. Esther is given in its longer (Greek) form rather than in the version based solely on the Hebrew text; the Prayer of Azariah and Song of the Three Jews appear as vv. 24–90 of ch 3 of Daniel, and the stories of Susanna and Bel and the Dragon as chs 13 and 14 of Daniel. An appendix after the New Testament contains the Prayer of Manasseh and 1 and 2 Esdras, without implying canonical status.

The Eastern Orthodox Churches recognize several other books as authoritative. Editions of the Old Testament approved by the Holy Synod of the Greek Orthodox Church contain, besides the Roman Catholic Deuterocanonical books, 1 Esdras, Psalm 151, the Prayer of Manasseh, and 3 Maccabees, while 4 Maccabees appears in an appendix. Slavonic Bibles approved by the Russian Orthodox Church contain, besides the Deuterocanonical books, 1 and 2 Esdras (called 2 and 3 Esdras), Psalm 151, and 3 Maccabees.

Protestant Bibles have followed the Hebrew canon, though in a different order. The disputed books, if they are included at all, have generally been placed in a separate section, usually bound between the Old and New Testaments, but occasionally placed after the close of the New Testament.

Here is a list of the Apocryphal/Deuterocanonical books in the order in which they are found in this Bible, showing which religious communities accept them as scripture:

	ROMAN CATHOLIC	GREEK ORTHODOX	SLAVONIC (RUSSIAN ORTHODOX)	LATIN VULGATE APPENDIX	GREEK APPENDIX	PROTESTANT/ ANGLICAN APOCRYPHA
Tobit	•	•	•			•
Judith	•	•	•			•
Additions to Esther	•	•	•			•
Wisdom of Solomon	•	•	•			•
Ecclesiasticus[1]	•	•	•			•
Baruch	•	•	•			•
Letter of Jeremiah (Baruch ch.6)	•	•	•			•
Additions to Daniel	•	•	•			•
1 Maccabees	•	•	•			•
2 Maccabees	•	•	•			•
1 Esdras[2]		•	•	•		•
Prayer of Manasseh		•	•	•		•
Psalm 151		•	•			
3 Maccabees		•	•			
2 Esdras[3]			•	•		•
4 Maccabees					•	

[1] Also called The Wisdom of Jesus, Son of Sirach, or simply Sirach.
[2] 2 Esdras in Slavonic; 3 Esdras in Appendix to Vulgate; In the Vulgate, Ezra-Nehemiah are 1 and 2 Esdras.
[3] 3 Esdras in Slavonic; 4 Esdras in Vulgate Appendix.

THE STATUS OF THE APOCRYPHAL/DEUTEROCANONICAL BOOKS IN CHRISTIANITY

During the first centuries of the Common Era, early Christian theologians (most of whom knew no Hebrew) quoted, in Greek, passages both from books in the Hebrew canon and from these additional works without making any distinction between them. Such citations were usually preceded by a word or phrase making it clear that the writer regarded the text being cited as canonical. During this time, only a few thinkers investigated the Jewish canon or distinguished between, for instance, the Hebrew text of Daniel and the addition of the story of Susanna in the Greek version.

By the fourth century, theologians in the Eastern (Greek) churches had begun to recognize a distinction between the books in the Hebrew canon and the rest, though they continued to cite all of them as scripture. During the following centuries the matter was debated and, consequently, practice varied in the East, but at the Synod of Jerusalem in 1672 (which expressed the Orthodox churches' reaction to the Protestant Reformation), Tobit, Judith, Ecclesiasticus (Sirach), Wisdom, Additions to Daniel, and 1 and 2 Maccabees were expressly designated as canonical.

In the Western (Latin) church, on the other hand, though there was some variety of opinion, in general theologians regarded these books as canonical. More than one local synodical council (e.g., Hippo, 393, and Carthage, 397 and 419) justified and authorized their use as scripture. The so-called *Decretum Gelasianum*, a Latin document probably dating to the sixth century, contains lists of the books to be read as scripture and of books to be avoided as apocryphal. The former list, which is not present in all the manuscripts, includes among the biblical books Tobit, Judith, Wisdom, Ecclesiasticus (Sirach), and 1 and 2 Maccabees.

Occasionally, however, theologians questioned the status of these books. Jerome, near the end of the fourth century, thought that books not in the Hebrew canon should be designated as apocryphal, and other thinkers, though always a minority, followed his view, at least theoretically. Toward the close of the fourteenth century John Wycliffe and his disciples produced the first English version of the Bible. This translation of the Latin Vulgate included all of the disputed books, with the exception of 2 Esdras. In the Prologue to the Old Testament, however, it makes a distinction between the books of the Hebrew canon, listed there, and the others which, the writer says, "shall be set among apocrypha, that is, without authority of belief." In the books of Esther and Daniel, the translators included a rendering of Jerome's notes calling the reader's attention to the additions.

At the time of the Reformation, Protestant thinkers came to the conclusion fairly early that they would need to determine which books were authoritative for the establishment of doctrine and which were not. For instance, disputes over the doctrine of purgatory and of the usefulness of prayers and masses for the dead involved the authority of 2 Maccabees, which contains what was held to be scriptural warrant for them (12.43–45). The first extensive Protestant discussion of the canon was Andreas Bodenstein's treatise *De Canonicis Scripturis Libellus* (1520). Bodenstein (or Carlstadt, after his place of birth) distinguished the books of the Hebrew Bible from the books of the Apocrypha, classifying the Apocrypha into two divisions. Concerning Wisdom, Ecclesiasticus (Sirach), Judith, Tobit, and 1 and 2 Maccabees, he says, "These are Apocrypha, that is, are outside the Hebrew canon; yet they are holy writings" (sect. 114). He continues:

> What they contain is not to be despised at once; still it is not right that Christians should relieve, much less slake, their thirst with them. . . . Before all things the best books must be read, that is, those that are canonical beyond all controversy; afterwards, if one has the time, it is allowed to peruse the controverted books, provided that you have the set purpose of comparing and collating the non-canonical books with those which are truly canonical (sect. 118).

The second group, 1 and 2 Esdras, Baruch, Prayer of Manasseh, and the Additions to Daniel, he declared without worth.

The first Bible in a modern vernacular language to segregate the apocryphal books from the others was the Dutch Bible published by Jacob van Liesveldt in 1526 at Antwerp. After Malachi there follows a section embodying the Apocrypha titled "The books which are not in the canon, that is to say, which one does not find among the Jews in the Hebrew."

The first edition of the Swiss-German Bible was published in six volumes (Zurich, 1527–29), the fifth of which contains the Apocrypha. The title page of this volume states, "These are the books which are not reckoned as biblical by the ancients, nor are found among the Hebrews." A one-volume edition of the Zurich Bible, which appeared in 1530, contains the apocryphal books grouped together after the New Testament. One Swiss reformer, Oecolampadius, declared in 1530: "We do not despise Judith, Tobit, Ecclesiasticus, Baruch, the last two books of Esdras, the three books of Maccabees, the Additions to Daniel; but we do not allow them divine authority with the others."

In reaction to Protestant criticism of the disputed books, in 1546 the Council of Trent gave what is regarded by Roman Catholics as the definitive declaration on the canon of the scriptures. After enumerating the books, which in the Old Testament include Tobit, Judith, Wisdom, Ecclesiasticus (Sirach), Baruch, and the two books of Maccabees, the decree pronounces an anathema upon anyone who "does not accept as sacred and canonical the aforesaid books in their entirety and with all their parts, as they have been accustomed to be read in the Catholic Church and as they are contained in the old Latin Vulgate Edition" (trans. H. J. Schroeder). The reference to "books in their entirety and with all their parts" is intended to cover the Letter of Jeremiah as ch 6 of Baruch, the Additions to Esther, and the chapters in Daniel including the Prayer of Azariah, the Song of the Three Jews, Susanna, and Bel and the Dragon. It is noteworthy, however, that the Prayer of Manasseh and 1 and 2 Esdras, although included in some manuscripts of the Latin Vulgate, were denied canonical status by the Council of Trent. In the official edition of the Vulgate, published in 1592, these three are printed as an appendix after the New Testament, "lest they should perish altogether."

In England, even though Protestants were unanimous in declaring that the apocryphal books were not to be used to establish any doctrine, differences arose as to the proper use and place of noncanonical books. A milder view prevailed in the Church of England, and the lectionary attached to the Book of Common Prayer, from 1549 on, has always contained prescribed lessons from the Apocrypha. In addition, portions of the Song of the Three Jews are used as a canticle, or song of praise, alongside selected Psalms in the service of Morning Prayer. In reply to those who urged the discontinuance of reading lessons from apocryphal books, as being inconsistent with the sufficiency of scripture, the bishops at the Savoy Conference, held in 1661, replied that the same objection could be raised against the preaching of sermons, and that it was much to be desired that all sermons should give as useful instruction as did the chapters selected from the Apocrypha.

The Puritans took a stricter view, and some Geneva Bibles, printed in 1599 mainly in the Low Countries, excluded the Apocrypha. The omission of the Apocrypha was presumably due to those responsible for binding the copies, since the titles of the apocryphal books occur in the table of contents. During subsequent centuries Bibles that lacked the books of the Apocrypha came to outnumber those that included them, and soon it became difficult to obtain ordinary editions of the King James Version containing the Apocrypha.

(For a more complete account of the formation of the various canons of scripture, see "The Canons of the Bible" on p 2185.)

THE HISTORICAL BACKGROUND TO THE APOCRYPHAL/DEUTEROCANONICAL BOOKS

With the destruction of Jerusalem and the Temple by the Babylonians under Nebuchadnezzar in 586 BCE, and the subsequent exile of many Judeans to Babylon, the history of Israel underwent a decisive break. Henceforth there would always be Jewish communities outside the land of Israel (the Diaspora), and even after the Persian king Cyrus allowed the exiles to return in 538 BCE, large communities flourished in Babylon and elsewhere.

For two centuries the Persians controlled the Near East. The rebuilt Temple became the institutional focus of the province of Judah. Although details are uncertain, this era probably saw important work on the editing of the Pentateuch and the prophetic writings, as well as the composition of other literature. The Persian period came to an end when Alexander the Great completed a series of conquests that put him in control of the former Persian empire, including Egypt. When Alexander died in 323, his empire was divided among his warring generals, and two of them—Seleucus, king of Syria, and Ptolemy, king of Egypt—and their successors fought over the territory of Judah, which fell first under Ptolemaic and then Seleucid dynastic control. Despite the political changes, however, the overall cultural influence remained: This was the era of the triumph of Hellenistic culture, including the use of the Greek language as the standard for the whole empire.

There had already been, in the Hebrew Bible, contention about such issues as intermarriage (Ezra 9.1–10.44; Neh 13.23–31). Now, with large numbers of Jews living outside the land as minorities within much larger and more dominant cultures, this issue and those of other religious observances came to be much more important. Stories of faithfully observant Jews among non-Jewish populations (Tobit, 3 Macc) were joined by expanded versions of books that strengthened this point (Greek Esther, the Prayer of Azariah, and Song of the Three Jews in ch 3 of Daniel).

Jews both in the Diaspora and in Judah appropriated many elements of Hellenistic culture, usually without incident. During the second century BCE, however, an attempt to establish Hellenistic educational and civic institutions in Jerusalem created a crisis when the persons involved bribed King Antiochus IV Epiphanes (175–164) to appoint Hellenizing high priests (Jason and Menelaus) and funds were taken from the Temple itself to pay the king. In response to the ensuing violence, Antiochus invaded Jerusalem in 169; in 167 he effectively outlawed the Jewish religion, making the teaching of the Torah a crime and establishing polytheistic worship in the Temple. This final provocation led to the ultimately successful Jewish revolt under the Hasmonean family, led by Mattathias and his five sons, one of whom, Judas, was known as Maccabeus, "the hammer." The revolt and the subsequent establishment of a Jewish government (which took more than twenty years to accomplish) are therefore referred to as Maccabean. This rule lasted for eighty years, until (because of constant power struggles among the various factions of Jews) the Romans were able to intervene and take direct control of the territory in 63 BCE.

The Apocryphal/Deuterocanonical books contain several different literary genres, including histories, historical fiction, wisdom, devotional writings, letters, and an apocalypse. Though several of the books combine more than one of these genres, most of the books can be classified as predominantly one type or another. Thus 1 Esdras, 1 Maccabees, and in a certain sense, 2 Maccabees are histories. First Esdras summarizes 2 Chr 35.1–36.23 and reproduces all of Ezra and Neh 7.38–8.12. Only 1 Esd 3.1–5.6 is a significant addition. First Maccabees recounts the history of the Seleucid persecutions and the rebellion and rise of the Maccabees. Second Maccabees, with its bombastic rhetoric and abundant use of invectives against the Seleucid tyrants and Hellenizing Jews, is an example of a popular Hellenistic genre, the "pathetic history," which uses highly charged language, exhortation, exaggeration, and other methods to stimulate the imaginations and emotions ("pathos") of readers. Third Maccabees is misleadingly named: It actually has nothing to do with the Maccabean period or the Seleucid dynasty, but deals with a period a half-century earlier and concerns the sufferings of the Jewish community in Egypt under the Ptolemaic rulers. It is a religious novel, written in Greek by an Alexandrian Jew sometime after 30 BCE. Using legendary elements, it tells three stories of conflict between Ptolemy IV (221–204) and the Jewish community in Egypt. The most dramatic section (5.1–6.21) describes Ptolemy's scheme to martyr the Jews: They were to be herded into an arena near Alexandria to be trampled under the feet of five hundred intoxicated elephants. The king's plan was finally foiled when angelic intervention terrorized those supervising the persecutions and also frightened the elephants into turning upon the Egyptian soldiers.

Fourth Maccabees is not a historical narrative but rather a Greek philosophical treatise addressed to Jews on the supremacy of reason over the passions of body and soul. In the form of a Stoic diatribe, or popular address, it uses narratives of exemplary behavior, and the conversations and arguments of characters in the narratives, to explore philosophical issues. The author begins with a theoretical exposition of his theme, which he then illustrates at length with examples of the martyrs drawn from 2 Maccabees, who preferred death to committing apostasy. The book was probably written by a Hellenistic Jew before 70 CE. In early Christianity the Maccabean martyrs were venerated as saints and eventually accorded a yearly festival in the ecclesiastical calendar (August 1).

Judith, Tobit, Susanna, and Bel and the Dragon are short historical fictions written to convey a moral point, as well as to entertain. Except for Judith, which is set in Judah, the rest are sometimes referred to as "Diaspora novels" since they are all set in the Jewish Diaspora of Mesopotamia. Yet they differ from one another in other respects. Like the canonical stories of Daniel 1–6, Bel and the Dragon is a court tale, in which the hero's relationship with the king and other members of the court provides the conflict of the plot. The motif of the lion's den, which occurs in Daniel 6, also occurs in the story of the dragon. In contrast to the earlier Daniel tales, however, Bel and the Dragon is preoccupied with the theme of the exposure of idols as false gods and their priests as fraudulent (see also the Letter of Jeremiah). Bel and the Dragon and Susanna are sometimes referred to as ancient examples of the detective story. Whereas Daniel functioned as an interpreter of dreams and visions in Daniel 1–6, in these stories Daniel uses cleverness and logical deduction to uncover deception.

Although Tobit, like Daniel, is presented as a court official of a Mesopotamian king, the story is concerned with personal and family affairs, not a rivalry at court. Thematically, Tobit may be compared with the prose story of Job, since it concerns the suffering of the righteous (both Tobit and his daughter-in-law Sarah). The book of Tobit is distinguished by the use of various folktale motifs (e.g., the motifs of the grateful dead, the angel in disguise, the dangerous bride, and the demon lover), and by its references to Ahikar, the hero of a non-Jewish folktale from Mesopotamia.

Judith might seem to bear comparison with 1 and 2 Maccabees, since it concerns a threat to the people from a foreign army. But whereas 1 and 2 Maccabees are histories, the fictional nature of Judith is evident from the story's flagrant historical inaccuracies, such as describing Nebuchadnezzar as king of Assyria and the invasion as taking place after the people's return from exile. A better comparison might be between Judith and Esther. Though set in Judah rather than the Diaspora, Judith, like Esther, tells how a courageous Jewish woman saves her people from enemies bent on destroying them.

Didactic literature is represented in the Apocrypha by the two treatises on wisdom: the Wisdom of Solomon, and the Wisdom of Jesus son of Sirach (also known as Ecclesiasticus). Sirach, which was originally composed in Hebrew ca. 180 BCE, shows particularly close connections with the style and content of the book of Proverbs in the Hebrew Bible, from which it is a natural development. The Wisdom of Solomon, by contrast, contains no proverbial material, such as characterizes the Hebrew wisdom tradition. It does, however, share with Proverbs and Sirach an interest in the figure of wisdom personified as a woman. What makes the Wisdom of Solomon distinctive is the strong influence of Greek literary styles and philosophical ideas. Thus, it comes from the Greek-speaking Diaspora, most probably from Alexandria in Egypt.

The Prayer of Manasseh is a hymnic lament of great feeling and literary skill. The Prayer of Azariah and the Song of the Three Jews are both modeled on psalms that are liturgical in form. In addition to the 150 psalms comprising the book of Psalms in the Hebrew Bible, during the Hellenistic and Roman periods such hymns were composed in Hebrew and in other languages; there are a number of such compositions in the Dead Sea Scrolls. Another, which celebrates the prowess of young David in slaying Goliath, is appended (as Ps 151) to the book of Psalms in Greek manuscripts.

The Hebrew Bible contains no books that are in the form of a letter, although letters or excerpts from letters occur at various places. There are decrees (Ezra 1.1–6), diplomatic correspondence (1 Kings 5.2–6), royal commands (2 Sam 11.14–15), even forgeries (1 Kings 21.8–10), but all are used to advance the narratives in which they occur, or explain incidents that follow, so it is unclear how representative they are. Twenty-one of the twenty-seven books of the New Testament are in the form of letters, but some (for instance, Hebrews) are more like sermons than letters. The Letter of Jeremiah, which dates from the Hellenistic period, may have provided later, Christian writers with an example of how this literary form could be used for religious purposes, combining theological content with a direct personal approach.

Finally, 2 Esdras, a book that purports to reveal the future, belongs to the genre of apocalypse, a word that literally means "an unveiling." Like the last six chapters of Daniel in the Hebrew Bible and the book of Revelation in the New Testament, which also are apocalypses, 2 Esdras uses metaphoric language, symbolic numbers, and angelic messengers who reveal hidden information.

Despite this diversity of genres, most of which parallel or are developed from similar ones in the Hebrew Bible, there is no correlative to classical prophecy. Even within the prophetic books of the Hebrew Bible, apocalyptic elements had already begun to supplant strict prophecy (for instance, Isa chs 24–27; Ezek chs 38–39; Joel ch 2; Zech chs 9–14). This absence perhaps supports the view of the late first-century CE historian Josephus (Ag. Ap. 1.8), that "the exact succession of the prophets" had been broken after the Persian period; a similar idea is found in later rabbinic literature. Sometimes there is a direct statement that "prophets ceased to appear" (1 Macc 9.27); at other times the writers express the hope that prophecy might one day return (1 Macc 4.46; 14.41). When a writer imitates prophetic style, as in the book of Baruch, he repeats with slight modifications the language of the older prophets. But the introductory phrase, "Thus says the Lord," which occurs so frequently in the prophetic literature of the Hebrew Bible, is absent from the Apocryphal/Deuterocanonical Books.

THE APOCRYPHAL/DEUTEROCANONICAL BOOKS WITHIN JUDAISM

All of the writings in the Apocryphal/Deuterocanonical books are Jewish in origin, but it is not clear that they were collected by any particular community of Jews. Some of them (for instance, Sirach) were quoted by rabbis, but for others no evidence exists that they were regarded as central to the Jewish community at any point. Some (Tobit, parts of Sirach, the Letter of Jeremiah, and Psalm 151) are among the Dead Sea Scrolls, and were therefore presumably of importance to the Essene community there, but whether or not they were considered canonical is not clear.

Nevertheless, influences from some of these works are apparent within Judaism. As mentioned above, rabbinic literature quotes and appropriates sayings from Sirach. The martyrdom of the woman and her seven sons (2 Macc 7.1–42; 4 Macc 8.3–18.24) is recounted in several places (Lam. Rab. 1.50; b. Git. 57b; Seder Eliyahu R. 29).

First and Second Maccabees (1 Macc 4.36–59; 2 Macc 10.1–8) provide the original accounts of the purification of the Temple in 164 BCE, which is commemorated in the festival of Hanukkah. The Talmudic legend (b. Shabb. 21b) that oil in the Temple, though only enough for one day nevertheless burned for eight—the supposed reason for the eight-day length of the observance—is not found in the books of Maccabees. Judith was, during the Middle Ages, associated with Hanukkah as well, on the grounds that both had to do with rallying an oppressed Jewish population to overthrow a threatening or occupying power.

Both Tobit and 2 Esdras influenced later Jewish literature and were popular during the Middle Ages. Baruch may have been read in synagogues at one time (see Bar 1.14), and Baruch himself, and therefore his writing, were regarded in some rabbinic writings as sharing Jeremiah's prophetic status (Sifre Num. 78; Seder Olam R. 20; b. B. Bat. 14b; Jer. Sot. 9.12). Susanna's story is recounted in the Babylonian Talmud (b. San. 93a).

The sense of a canon of scripture emerged only gradually in Judaism. During the time in which the Apocryphal/Deuterocanonical books were composed, the Torah (Pentateuch), the Prophets, and possibly the book of Psalms were considered authoritative. Many other writings, both those now in the Jewish canon and additional ones, were widely popular but did not have the status of scripture. A sense of a closed set of authoritative books emerged only in the first century CE, and even then there was some uncertainty about its extent. Josephus, however, says that "there are not with us myriads of books, discordant and discrepant, but only twenty-two, comprising the history of all time, which are justly accredited" (*Ag. Ap*.1.43).

Even if these additional writings were not considered scripture, they were often read and cited. Josephus himself makes use of 1 Esdras, 1 Maccabees, and the additions to Esther. Early rabbinic literature, however, makes no mention of any of these books except for Sirach, which is frequently quoted. The rabbis were, however, aware of the festival of Hanukkah, which is described in 1 and 2 Maccabees. During the Middle Ages, Jews became reacquainted with some of the Apocryphal/Deuterocanonical works from Christian sources and retranslated Tobit and Judith into Hebrew. The entire Apocrypha/Deuterocanon was translated into Hebrew in the early sixteenth century.

NEW TESTAMENT USES OF THE APOCRYPHAL/DEUTEROCANONICAL BOOKS

None of the books of the New Testament quotes directly from any Apocryphal book, in contrast to the frequent quotation of the thirty-nine books in the Hebrew Bible. Several New Testament writers, however, do allude to one or more apocryphal books. For example, what seem to be literary echoes from the Wisdom of Solomon are present in Paul's Letter to the Romans (compare Rom 1.20–29 with Wis 13.5,8; 14.24,27; and Rom 9.20–23 with Wis 12.12,20; 15.7) and in his correspondence with the Corinthians (compare 2 Cor 5.1,4 with Wis 9.15). The short Letter of James, a typical bit of "wisdom literature" in the New Testament, contains allusions not only to the book of Proverbs in the Hebrew Bible but to gnomic sayings in Sirach as well (compare Jas 1.19 with Sir 5.11; and Jas 1.13 with Sir 15.11–12).

THE FURTHER INFLUENCE OF THE APOCRYPHAL/DEUTEROCANONICAL BOOKS

The influence of the Apocrypha has been widespread, inspiring homilies, meditations, and liturgical forms, and providing subjects for poets, dramatists, composers, and artists. Some common expressions and proverbs have come from the Apocrypha. The sayings, "A good name endures forever" and "You can't touch pitch without being defiled," are derived from Sir 41.13 and 13.1. The affirmation in 1 Esd 4.41, "Great Is Truth, and mighty above all things" (King James Version), or its Latin form, *Magna est veritas et praevalet*, has been used as a motto or maxim in a wide variety of contexts.

The importance of these books extends to the information they supply concerning the development of Jewish life and thought just prior to the beginning of the Common Era. The stirring political fortunes of the Jews in the time of the Maccabees; the rise of what has been called normative Judaism, and the emergence of the sects of the Pharisees and the Sadducees; the lush growth of popular belief in the activities of angels and demons, and the use of magic to drive away malevolent influences; the first reflections on "original sin" and its relation to the "evil inclination" present in every person; the blossoming of apocalyptic hopes relating to the messiah, the resurrection of the body, and the vindication of the righteous—all these and many other topics are to be found in the Apocryphal/Deuterocanonical books.

(a) The books and parts of books from Tobit through 2 Maccabees are recognized as Deuterocanonical Scripture by the Roman Catholic, Greek, and Russian Orthodox Churches.

TOBIT

NAME AND CANONICAL STATUS

The book is named for its principal character, Tobit. The name is the Greek form of Hebrew *Tobi*, meaning "my good," possibly an abbreviation for *Tobiah*, "Yahweh is my good," or *Tobiel*, "God is my good." The book is not included in the Protestant or Jewish canons, but it is canonical in the Roman Catholic and Orthodox Churches. The Anglican Church and some other communions also recognize Tobit as Scripture for the purpose of edification but not for doctrine.

AUTHORSHIP, TEXT, AND DATE OF COMPOSITION

The author of the book is unknown. Although the original language was likely Aramaic, only fragments of that text have survived. The translation below is based on the Greek text of Codex Sinaiticus; other versions include two additional Greek recensions, the Old Latin, Jerome's Vulgate, a medieval Aramaic rendering, Coptic, Syriac, Ethiopic, and Armenian. Fragments in both Hebrew and Aramaic were found among the Dead Sea Scrolls. The book likely dates to sometime in the third or possibly early second century BCE; its place of composition remains unknown, with plausible suggestions including the eastern Diaspora, Egypt, and Israel.

CONTENTS AND STRUCTURE

After the Assyrian conquest of the Northern Kingdom of Israel in 722 BCE, Tobit, his wife Anna, and his son Tobias were exiled from their home in Galilee to Assyria. There Tobit, like Joseph (in Gen 39–50), Mordecai (in the book of Esther), and Daniel (in the book of Daniel), found himself in the service of a foreign ruler, as an officer in the court of the Assyrian king Shalmaneser. This pious Israelite too was tested: Shalmaneser's successor removed Tobit from his official position and then persecuted him for his insistence on burying the unattended corpses of his fellow Jews. One evening, following yet another burial, Tobit was blinded by a bird with unfortunate aim. Dependent on others, including his wife, for economic support, and following an argument with her in which she questioned the value of his piety, Tobit prayed for death. At the same time his relative Sarah was also praying for death. The demon Asmodeus, who was in love with her, had killed each of her seven successive grooms on their wedding nights. To resolve these improbable situations, the angel Raphael, in disguise as Tobias's traveling companion, escorts the young man first to Media to exorcise the demon and marry Sarah and then back to Nineveh to cure Tobit.

The complex plot is tied together by the parallel situations of Tobit and Sarah, prayers of praise and references to almsgiving, and frequent supernatural events. Its humorous aspects—from the angel in disguise to the attack of a magical fish—make the stories of Tobit and Sarah almost farcical and so prevent the book from becoming tragic or maudlin. Readers familiar with biblical literature will recognize familiar motifs and themes in the narrative: wisdom sayings; the antipathy between the matriarch Sarah and her slave Hagar (Gen 16; 21); the search for a bride for Isaac (Gen 24); the successes and trials of the Jew in the royal court; the problems of life in the Diaspora; Job's trials; the role of angels; the centrality of Jerusalem; the fulfillment of prophecy; and, especially, the importance of charity. The numerous personal prayers, similar to those found in the stories of Judith, Daniel (including the Additions), the Greek Additions to Esther, and elsewhere in postexilic Jewish literature, emphasize the universal authority and righteousness of God.

INTERPRETATION AND GUIDE TO READING

Combining ethical exhortation and prayers with broad humor, a rollicking plot, and vivid characters, the book of Tobit is both entertaining and edifying. It offers to a Diaspora community guidelines on how to preserve their identity, to historians indirect information about the postexilic period, and to theologians a view of a God who tests the faithful, responds to prayers, and redeems the covenant community.

The book of Tobit is also replete with information concerning family life, travel, burial and eating customs, gender roles, and medicine. These matters testify to the author's interest in providing guidance for life in Diaspora: Where Temple sacrifice is unavailable and the people are scattered, the story insists that Jews maintain their identity not only through piety and practice but also through strong bonds between parents and children, between husbands and wives, and with family members and fellow Jews. To preserve the community, Tobit insists that his son imitate Abraham, Isaac, and Jacob, who "took wives from among their kindred" (4.12–13).

The book also has connections to well-known folktale motifs, including the dangerous bride, the monster in the nuptial chamber, the supernatural being in disguise, the miraculous animal, and the grateful dead. Specifically mentioned are the characters of an Assyrian official Ahikar and his nephew, from a story well known in antiquity; there may also be hints of Homer's *Odyssey* and Sophocles's *Antigone*.

Amy-Jill Levine

1 This book tells the story of Tobit son of Tobiel son of Hananiel son of Aduel son of Gabael son of Raphael son of Raguel of the descendants[a] of Asiel, of the tribe of Naphtali, [2] who in the days of King Shalmaneser[b] of the Assyrians was taken into captivity from Thisbe, which is to the south of Kedesh Naphtali in Upper Galilee, above Asher toward the west, and north of Phogor.

[3] I, Tobit, walked in the ways of truth and righteousness all the days of my life. I performed many acts of charity for my kindred and my people who had gone with me in exile to Nineveh in the land of the Assyrians. [4] When I was in my own country, in the land of Israel, while I was still a young man, the whole tribe of my ancestor Naphtali deserted the house of David and Jerusalem. This city had been chosen from among all the tribes of Israel, where all the tribes of Israel should offer sacrifice and where the temple, the

dwelling of God, had been consecrated and established for all generations forever.

[5] All my kindred and our ancestral house of Naphtali sacrificed to the calf[c] that King Jeroboam of Israel had erected in Dan and on all the mountains of Galilee. [6] But I alone went often to Jerusalem for the festivals, as it is prescribed for all Israel by an everlasting decree. I would hurry off to Jerusalem with the first fruits of the crops and the firstlings of the flock, the tithes of the cattle, and the first shearings of the sheep. [7] I would give these to the priests, the sons of Aaron, at the altar; likewise the tenth of the grain, wine, olive oil, pomegranates, figs, and the rest of the fruits to the sons of Levi who ministered

[a] Other ancient authorities lack *of Raphael son of Raguel of the descendants*
[b] Gk *Enemessaros*
[c] Other ancient authorities read *heifer*

1.1–2: Exilic context. The superscription establishes Tobit's location and genealogy. 1: *Tobiel,* "God is my good"; *Hananiel,* "God has shown mercy"; the names of his family members have the suffix *el,* meaning "God." Genealogy becomes increasingly important in Second Temple Judaism (see Ezra 2; 8.1–20; Neh 7.5–73; 11.1–12.26; Jdt 8; Mt 1; Lk 3). 2: *Shalmaneser* V, ruled 727–722 BCE. Shalmaneser's predecessor, Tiglath-pileser III (ruled 745–727) deported the Naphtalites to Assyria (2 Kings 15.29); in 722 Sargon of Assyria, Shalmaneser's brother and successor, conquered Samaria, Israel's capital and resettled substantial portions of the population (2 Kings 17.1–6). *Kedesh,* in northern Galilee, defeated by Joshua (Josh 12.22; 19.37), was the home of Deborah's general Barak (Judg 4.6) and site of a Maccabean victory (1 Macc 11.63,73). *Asher* may be a Greek spelling of Hazor, ca. 6 mi (10 km) south-southeast of Kedesh. *Thisbe* and *Phogor* have not been identified.

1.3–9: Tobit's background. 3–4: Tobit, who speaks in the first person in 1.3–3.1, consistently emphasizes his own righteousness despite Israel's apostasy. Walking *in the ways of truth and righteousness* is a prominent motif of the Israelite wisdom tradition (see Prov 2.7–9; 4.11). 3: *Nineveh,* the capital of Assyria. 4: Tobit's life span, ranging from before 928 to after 722 BCE (but see 14.2), indicates the tale's fictional nature (the book of Judith similarly displays chronological fiction). *Naphtali* was one of the ten northern tribes that rebelled in 928 BCE against the dynasty founded by David (1 Kings 12.19–20); Tobit nevertheless consistently expresses concern for Jerusalem, the capital of the Southern Kingdom of Judah. 5: *Calf,* 1 Kings 12.28–29; *Dan* is northeast of Kedesh (see 1.2n.). 6: Participation in the pilgrimage *festivals* (Deut 12.11) of Booths (Sukkot), Passover (Pesach), and Weeks (Shavuot/Pentecost) entailed the giving of *first fruits* (Deut 26.1–11), *firstlings* (Ex 13.12), *tithes of the cattle* (Lev 27.32), and *first shearings of the sheep* (Deut 18.4). The extent of Tobit's pilgrimages and sacrificial activity emphasizes his faithfulness to the Torah, in contrast to his kin. 7–8: For tithing of produce, see Lev 27.30; Deut

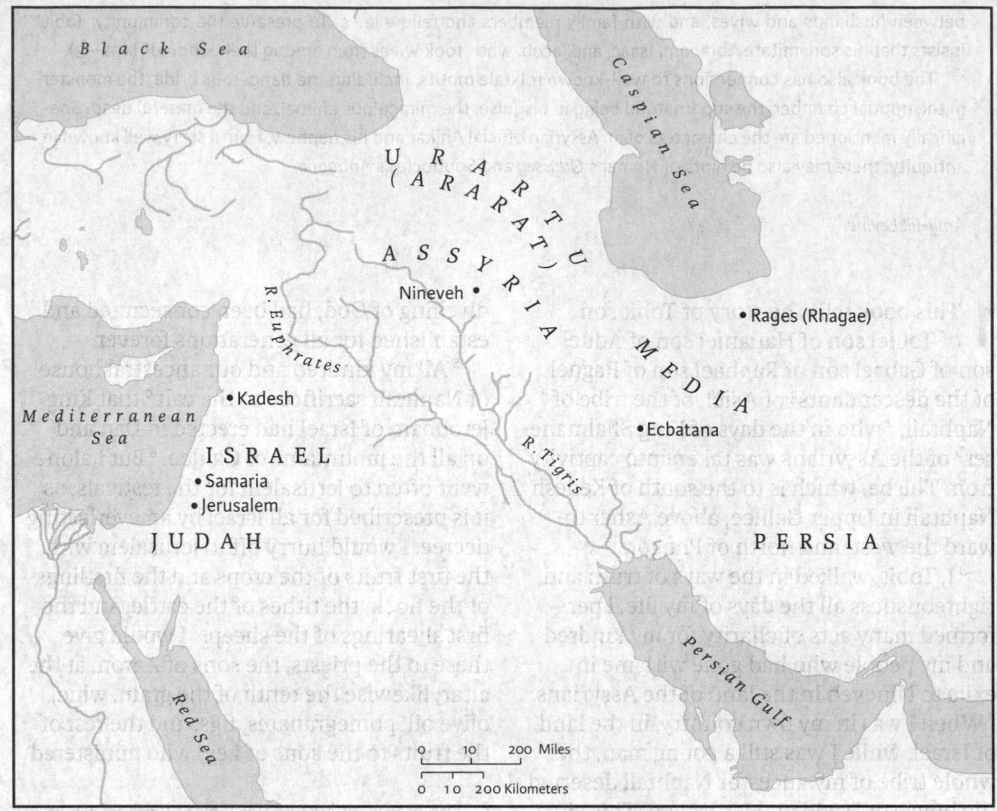

The geography of Tobit.

at Jerusalem. Also for six years I would save up a second tenth in money and go and distribute it in Jerusalem. ⁸ A third tenthᵃ I would give to the orphans and widows and to the converts who had attached themselves to Israel. I would bring it and give it to them in the third year, and we would eat it according to the ordinance decreed concerning it in the law of Moses and according to the instructions of Deborah, the mother of my father Tobiel,ᵇ for my father had died and left me an orphan. ⁹ When I became a man I married a woman,ᶜ a member of our own family, and by her I became the father of a son whom I named Tobias.

¹⁰ After I was carried away captive to Assyria and came as a captive to Nineveh, everyone of my kindred and my people ate the food of the Gentiles, ¹¹ but I kept myself from eating the food of the Gentiles. ¹² Because I was mindful of God with all my heart, ¹³ the Most High gave me favor and good

ᵃ *A third tenth* added from other ancient authorities
ᵇ Lat: Gk *Hananiel*
ᶜ Other ancient authorities add *Anna*

14.22. For the distribution of tithes to *Levites, orphans, and widows,* see Deut 14.27–29. **8:** *Deborah* indicates women's roles in religious education (see Prov 1.8; Sir 3.2); the name may have some connection to Kedesh and Naphtali (Judg 4–5; Tob 1.2n.). **9:** Endogamy, i.e., marriage within the kinship group, is a major theme (3.17; 4.12–13; 6.11–12; 7.10–11; cf. Gen 11.29; 24.3–4; 27.46–28.2; Deut 7.3–4; Ezra 9–10; Neh 10.28–30; but contrast the marriages of Ruth and Esther). Intermarriage became a particularly acute issue in the Diaspora.

1.10–22: Early captivity. The setting and Tobit's initial political success resemble that of Dan 1–6. Like Daniel and his companions (Dan 1.8–20), Esther (Add Esth 14.17), and Judith (Jdt 12.1–3), Tobit follows Jewish dietary laws (e.g., Lev 11.1–47; Deut 14.3–21). **13:** Tobit regards his political office as steward as a reward for righteous-

standing with Shalmaneser,[a] and I used to buy everything he needed. [14] Until his death I used to go into Media, and buy for him there. While in the country of Media I left bags of silver worth ten talents in trust with Gabael, the brother of Gabri. [15] But when Shalmaneser[a] died, and his son Sennacherib reigned in his place, the highways into Media became unsafe and I could no longer go there.

[16] In the days of Shalmaneser[a] I performed many acts of charity to my kindred, those of my tribe. [17] I would give my food to the hungry and my clothing to the naked; and if I saw the dead body of any of my people thrown out behind the wall of Nineveh, I would bury it. [18] I also buried any whom King Sennacherib put to death when he came fleeing from Judea in those days of judgment that the king of heaven executed upon him because of his blasphemies. For in his anger he put to death many Israelites; but I would secretly remove the bodies and bury them. So when Sennacherib looked for them he could not find them. [19] Then one of the Ninevites went and informed the king about me, that I was burying them; so I hid myself. But when I realized that the king knew about me and that I was being searched for to be put to death, I was afraid and ran away. [20] Then all my property was confiscated; nothing was left to me that was not taken into the royal treasury except my wife Anna and my son Tobias.

[21] But not forty[b] days passed before two of Sennacherib's[c] sons killed him, and they fled to the mountains of Ararat, and his son Esar-haddon[d] reigned after him. He appointed Ahikar, the son of my brother Hanael[e] over all the accounts of his kingdom, and he had authority over the entire administration. [22] Ahikar interceded for me, and I returned to Nineveh. Now Ahikar was chief cupbearer, keeper of the signet, and in charge of administration of the accounts under King Sennacherib of Assyria; so Esar-haddon[d] reappointed him. He was my nephew and so a close relative.

2 Then during the reign of Esar-haddon[d] I returned home, and my wife Anna and my son Tobias were restored to me. At our festival of Pentecost, which is the sacred festival of weeks, a good dinner was prepared for me and I reclined to eat. [2] When the table was set for me and an abundance of food placed before me, I said to my son Tobias, "Go, my child, and bring whatever poor person you may find of our people among the exiles in Nineveh, who is wholeheartedly mindful of God,[f] and he shall eat together with me. I will wait for you, until you come back." [3] So Tobias went to look for some poor person of our people. When he had returned he said, "Father!" And I replied, "Here I am, my child."

a   Gk *Enemessaros*
b   Other ancient authorities read either *forty-five* or *fifty*
c   Gk *his*
d   Gk *Sacherdonos*
e   Other authorities read *Hananael*
f   Lat: Gk *wholeheartedly mindful*

ness; later events temporarily question such justice. *Shalmaneser,* see 1.2n. **14:** *Media* (northern Iran) is east of Assyria; on Israelites exiled there, see 2 Kings 17.6. *Ten talents* is approximately 750 lb (350 kg). **15:** Sargon II (ruled 721–705 BCE), not Shalmaneser, was *Sennacherib*'s father (see 1.2n.,18–20n.). Similar historical inaccuracies mark the opening of the book of Judith. **16–17:** Tobit continues his earlier charitable works (1.3). Burying corpses is his principal sign of righteousness (1.18–20; 2.3–8; 4.3–4; 6.15; 14.10–133); their unburied presence indicates Assyria's brutality (Deut 28.26; 1 Kings 14.11; 21.24; Jer 7.33; Ezek 29.5), for even executed criminals deserved proper burial (Deut 21.22–23). *Nineveh,* see 1.3n. **18:** Sennacherib (ruled 705–681) succeeded his father Sargon II in 705 BCE. *Fleeing . . . in those days of judgment,* a reference to the defeat of Sennacherib by divine intervention; see 2 Kings 19.35–36. **19:** Like Sophocles's Antigone, Tobit is threatened with death for burying the executed; cf. 2 Sam 21.8–14. **20:** Like Daniel and his companions (Dan 3; 6), Tobit is persecuted for practicing Jewish piety. **21:** *Killed him,* see 2 Kings 19.37. *Esar-haddon* reigned 681–669 BCE. **21–22:** *Ahikar* is a well-known figure in Semitic stories; a copy of the Aramaic book of Ahikar, dating to the early fifth century BCE, was found among a cache of papyri from a Jewish colony in Elephantine in southern Egypt. Ahikar's relationship to Tobit, noted only in this book, enhances Tobit's status. Ahikar's own story is summarized in 14.10; cf. 2.10; 11.18.

2.1–10: Tobit's blindness. Tobit's charity toward others results in his being blinded. **1:** *Pentecost,* the spring harvest of Weeks, also known as Shavuot (Lev 23.15–21; Deut 16.9–12; 2 Chr 8.13). **2:** Tobit consistently demon-

Then he went on to say, "Look, father, one of our own people has been murdered and thrown into the market place, and now he lies there strangled." [4] Then I sprang up, left the dinner before even tasting it, and removed the body[a] from the square[b] and laid it[a] in one of the rooms until sunset when I might bury it.[a] [5] When I returned, I washed myself and ate my food in sorrow. [6] Then I remembered the prophecy of Amos, how he said against Bethel,[c]

> "Your festivals shall be turned into mourning,
>   and all your songs into lamentation."

And I wept.

[7] When the sun had set, I went and dug a grave and buried him. [8] And my neighbors laughed and said, "Is he still not afraid? He has already been hunted down to be put to death for doing this, and he ran away; yet here he is again burying the dead!" [9] That same night I washed myself and went into my courtyard and slept by the wall of the courtyard; and my face was uncovered because of the heat. [10] I did not know that there were sparrows on the wall; their fresh droppings fell into my eyes and produced white films. I went to physicians to be healed, but the more they treated me with ointments the more my vision was obscured by the white films, until I became completely blind. For four years I remained unable to see. All my kindred were sorry for me, and Ahikar took care of me for two years before he went to Elymais.

[11] At that time, also, my wife Anna earned money at women's work. [12] She used to send what she made to the owners and they would pay wages to her. One day, the seventh of Dystrus, when she cut off a piece she had woven and sent it to the owners, they paid her full wages and also gave her a young goat for a meal. [13] When she returned to me, the goat began to bleat. So I called her and said, "Where did you get this goat? It is surely not stolen, is it? Return it to the owners; for we have no right to eat anything stolen." [14] But she said to me, "It was given to me as a gift in addition to my wages." But I did not believe her, and told her to return it to the owners. I became flushed with anger against her over this. Then she replied to me, "Where are your acts of charity? Where are your righteous deeds? These things are known about you!"[d]

3 Then with much grief and anguish of heart I wept, and with groaning began to pray:

[2] "You are righteous, O Lord,
    and all your deeds are just;
all your ways are mercy and truth;
    you judge the world.[e]

---

a   Gk *him*
b   Other ancient authorities lack *from the square*
c   Other ancient authorities read *against Bethlehem*
d   Or *to you*; Gk *with you*
e   Other ancient authorities read *you render true and righteous judgment forever*

---

strates charity toward his people in exile (4.7–11,16). **5:** *Washed*, Num 19.11–13 commands washing as purification after contact with a corpse. **6:** *Amos* 8.10, one of the few scriptural citations in the book and another sign of composition in the Second Temple period. **9:** It is unclear why Tobit sleeps outside, especially since after moving the corpse he did return home to eat dinner (v. 5). If the concern is for ritual purity following contact with a corpse, see Num 19.11–22. A similar connection of dinner and gravedigging, but with humorous overtones, appears in 8.9–11. **10:** *Droppings*, Tobit is blinded in an ignominious and perhaps farcical manner. *Ahikar,* see 1.21–22n. *Elymais*, earlier Elam, a region in northwestern Persia.

2.11–14: The argument. Now dependent on others, Tobit becomes increasingly despondent. **11:** *Women's work* is weaving (cf. Prov 31.13,24); Tobit's earlier source of income, aside from investments, is unmentioned. **12:** At this verse and at 2.15–16, the Vulgate adds a comparison of Tobit to Job and thus an implied comparison of Anna to Job's wife. *Dystrus*, the fifth month in the Macedonian calendar (February/March), corresponding to the Jewish month of Shebat. The use of the Macedonian name is an indication of the Hellenistic date of Tobit. **13:** The outburst nuances Tobit's claims of righteousness and may also reflect his feeling of dishonor in being supported by a woman (Sir 25.22). **14:** Like Job's wife (Job 2.9), Anna questions the relationship between *righteous deeds* and a good life.

3.1–6: Tobit's prayer. The fight, coupled with Anna's observations about justice, not Tobit's blindness, causes him to seek death. Personal prayer is a major motif of this book (3.11–15; 8.4–8,15–17; 13.1–17) as well as

3 And now, O Lord, remember me
and look favorably upon me.
Do not punish me for my sins
and for my unwitting offenses
and those that my ancestors committed
before you.
They sinned against you,
4 and disobeyed your commandments.
So you gave us over to plunder, exile, and
death,
to become the talk, the byword, and an
object of reproach
among all the nations among whom
you have dispersed us.
5 And now your many judgments are true
in exacting penalty from me for my sins.
For we have not kept your commandments
and have not walked in accordance with
truth before you.
6 So now deal with me as you will;
command my spirit to be taken from
me,
so that I may be released from the face
of the earth and become dust.
For it is better for me to die than to live,
because I have had to listen to
undeserved insults,
and great is the sorrow within me.
Command, O Lord, that I be released from
this distress;
release me to go to the eternal home,
and do not, O Lord, turn your face away
from me.

For it is better for me to die
than to see so much distress in my life
and to listen to insults."

7 On the same day, at Ecbatana in Media,
it also happened that Sarah, the daughter of
Raguel, was reproached by one of her father's
maids. 8 For she had been married to seven
husbands, and the wicked demon Asmodeus
had killed each of them before they had
been with her as is customary for wives. So
the maid said to her, "You are the one who
kills[a] your husbands! See, you have already
been married to seven husbands and have
not borne the name of[b] a single one of them.
9 Why do you beat us? Because your husbands are dead? Go with them! May we never
see a son or daughter of yours!"
10 On that day she was grieved in spirit and
wept. When she had gone up to her father's
upper room, she intended to hang herself. But
she thought it over and said, "Never shall they
reproach my father, saying to him, 'You had
only one beloved daughter but she hanged
herself because of her distress.' And I shall
bring my father in his old age down in sorrow to Hades. It is better for me not to hang
myself, but to pray the Lord that I may die
and not listen to these reproaches anymore."

a Other ancient authorities read strangles
b Other ancient authorities read have had no benefit
   from

in Hellenistic Jewish literature in general (see Jdt 9; Esth 14.1–9; Song of Thr; Sus; 1 Macc 7.37–38). 3–4: Tobit
admits his own sin and the sin of his *ancestors* (see Ex 20.5–6). The theology, which posits that plunder, exile,
and death are occasioned by sin, is complicated by the plot, in which the righteous Tobit and Sarah suffer. Attribution of the exile to the people's sin is a common biblical idea. 6: *Command my spirit to be taken from me*,
Moses (Num 11.15), Elijah (1 Kings 19.4), and Jonah (Jon 4.8) similarly pray for release from suffering. Undeserved
insults were directed at Tobit by his neighbors (2.8); Tobit does not reflect upon his undeserved insult to Anna.
To *become dust* evokes Gen 3.19. The request for death is reminiscent of Job 3; cf. Jer 20.14–18. *The eternal home*
likely refers not to immortality of the soul or eternal life, but either to the grave (see Job 34.15; Ps 104.29) or to
Sheol, the realm of the dead (see Job 7.9–10; 14.10–13).

3.7–15: Sarah's plight and prayer. The scene shifts to Ecbatana in Media (modern Hamadan, in Iran), ca. 325
mi (525 km) east-southeast of Nineveh, and the narration shifts from first to third person as, *on the same day*,
Sarah's plight parallels that of Tobit. 7: *Reproached*, like Sarah of Gen 16.4–6, this Sarah also has no children and
abuses her tormentor. 8: The earliest literary mention of *Asmodeus*; his name derives from either the Persian
expression "aeshma Daeva" meaning "demon of wrath," or Heb "shamad," meaning "to destroy." 10: Sarah
intended to hang herself, but concern for her father prevents suicide. The Bible does not condemn those who
commit suicide (e.g. Saul [1 Sam 31.4–5], Ahithophel [2 Sam 17.23], Zimri [1 Kings 16.18], Razis [2 Macc 14.41–46]),
but suicide is implicitly forbidden in Gen 9.4–6 and Ex 20.13. *Hades*, for this text the Greek equivalent of Sheol,
the abode of the dead. Like Tobit, Sarah seeks to escape a woman's reproaches. 11: *Hands outstretched* is a com-

[11] At that same time, with hands outstretched toward the window, she prayed and said,

"Blessed are you, merciful God!
Blessed is your name forever;
let all your works praise you forever.
[12] And now, Lord,[a] I turn my face to you,
and raise my eyes toward you.
[13] Command that I be released from the earth
and not listen to such reproaches any
more.
[14] You know, O Master, that I am innocent
of any defilement with a man,
[15] and that I have not disgraced my name
or the name of my father in the land of
my exile.
I am my father's only child;
he has no other child to be his heir;
and he has no close relative or other
kindred
for whom I should keep myself as wife.
Already seven husbands of mine have died.
Why should I still live?
But if it is not pleasing to you, O Lord, to
take my life,
hear me in my disgrace."

[16] At that very moment, the prayers of both of them were heard in the glorious presence of God. [17] So Raphael was sent to heal both of them: Tobit, by removing the white films from his eyes, so that he might see God's light with his eyes; and Sarah, daughter of Raguel, by giving her in marriage to Tobias son of Tobit, and by setting her free from the wicked demon Asmodeus. For Tobias was entitled to have her before all others who had desired

to marry her. At the same time that Tobit returned from the courtyard into his house, Sarah daughter of Raguel came down from her upper room.

4 That same day Tobit remembered the money that he had left in trust with Gabael at Rages in Media, [2] and he said to himself, "Now I have asked for death. Why do I not call my son Tobias and explain to him about the money before I die?" [3] Then he called his son Tobias, and when he came to him he said, "My son, when I die,[b] give me a proper burial. Honor your mother and do not abandon her all the days of her life. Do whatever pleases her, and do not grieve her in anything. [4] Remember her, my son, because she faced many dangers for you while you were in her womb. And when she dies, bury her beside me in the same grave.

[5] "Revere the Lord all your days, my son, and refuse to sin or to transgress his commandments. Live uprightly all the days of your life, and do not walk in the ways of wrongdoing; [6] for those who act in accordance with truth will prosper in all their activities. To all those who practice righteousness[c] [7] give alms from your possessions,

a Other ancient authorities lack *Lord*
b Lat
c The text of codex Sinaiticus goes directly from verse 6 to verse 19, reading *To those who practice righteousness* [19] *the Lord will give good counsel.* In order to fill the lacuna verses 7 to 18 are derived from other ancient authorities

mon posture for prayer (Ezra 9.5; Dan 6.10). *Blessed are you* is the traditional opening of Jewish prayers (8.5,15; Jdt 13.17). **13–15:** Sarah more quickly than Tobit pleads for death, though, unlike Tobit, she adds only if death is *pleasing* to God; in contrast to Tobit, she does not confess sins but instead protests her innocence. **14–15:** Women's chastity and honor are also prominent themes in the books of Judith and Susanna. *A close relative* suggests levirate law (Deut 25.5–10); Sarah is not aware that another relative and thus a potential husband, Tobias, exists.

3.16–17: Divine response. The fates of the supplicants are intertwined by Raphael's dual mission. **16:** Seven angels stand *in the glorious presence of God* to express human prayers and fulfill God's replies (see 12.15n.). **17:** *Raphael's* name means "God has healed." *Entitled*, by being a near relation (6.12; see 3.14–15n.). The style shifts to third-person narration.

4.1–13: Tobit's advice on the family. Tobit offers a "testament" or "farewell discourse," a common literary genre in biblical texts (Gen 48–49 [Jacob]; the book of Deuteronomy [Moses]; Josh 22–24 [Joshua]; 1 Chr 28–29 [David]) as well as in Hellenistic writings (*1 Enoch* 81; *Testaments of the Twelve Patriarchs*), in which a father offers his children ethical advice and prophetic insight. Chapter 14 provides a second example. **1:** *Money*, see 1.14. *Rages* is just east of modern Teheran. **3:** *Burial*, Tobit asks for what he provided others (on this familial responsibility, see also Lk 9.59). *Honoring one's mother* is commanded in the Decalogue (Ex 20.12; Deut 5.16; see also Prov 23.22; Sir 3.12–15; 7.27–28). **6–7:** Tobit's circumstances (temporarily) conflict with the comments typical

and do not let your eye begrudge the gift when you make it. Do not turn your face away from anyone who is poor, and the face of God will not be turned away from you. [8] If you have many possessions, make your gift from them in proportion; if few, do not be afraid to give according to the little you have. [9] So you will be laying up a good treasure for yourself against the day of necessity. [10] For almsgiving delivers from death and keeps you from going into the Darkness. [11] Indeed, almsgiving, for all who practice it, is an excellent offering in the presence of the Most High.

[12] "Beware, my son, of every kind of fornication. First of all, marry a woman from among the descendants of your ancestors; do not marry a foreign woman, who is not of your father's tribe; for we are the descendants of the prophets. Remember, my son, that Noah, Abraham, Isaac, and Jacob, our ancestors of old, all took wives from among their kindred. They were blessed in their children, and their posterity will inherit the land. [13] So now, my son, love your kindred, and in your heart do not disdain your kindred, the sons and daughters of your people, by refusing to take a wife for yourself from among them. For in pride there is ruin and great confusion. And in idleness there is loss and dire poverty, because idleness is the mother of famine.

[14] "Do not keep over until the next day the wages of those who work for you, but pay them at once. If you serve God you will receive payment. Watch yourself, my son, in everything you do, and discipline yourself in all your conduct. [15] And what you hate, do not do to anyone. Do not drink wine to excess or let drunkenness go with you on your way. [16] Give some of your food to the hungry, and some of your clothing to the naked. Give all your surplus as alms, and do not let your eye begrudge your giving of alms. [17] Place your bread on the grave of the righteous, but give none to sinners. [18] Seek advice from every wise person and do not despise any useful counsel. [19] At all times bless the Lord God, and ask him that your ways may be made straight and that all your paths and plans may prosper. For none of the nations has understanding, but the Lord himself will give them good counsel; but if he chooses otherwise, he casts down to deepest Hades. So now, my child, remember these commandments, and do not let them be erased from your heart.

[20] "And now, my son, let me explain to you that I left ten talents of silver in trust with Gabael son of Gabrias, at Rages in Media. [21] Do not be afraid, my son, because we have become poor. You have great wealth if you fear God and flee from every sin and do what is good in the sight of the Lord your God."

of wisdom literature (e.g., Prov 10.27–30). **8:** Giving what one can is a prominent motif in Jewish-Hellenistic (*Testament of Issachar*), early Christian (Lk 21.1–4; 2 Cor 8.12), and rabbinic (*b. Git.* 7a) writing. **10:** *Delivers from death* probably suggests a long life, not an eternal one. *Darkness*, that is, the grave. **11:** *Almsgiving* is consistently emphasized (12.8–9; 14.10–11; see also Lev 23.22; Ps 112.9; Prov 14.21,31; Isa 58.6–8; Sir 3.30–31; 34.18–35.4). **12–13:** Consistent with the instructions of wisdom literature (Prov 5.20; 6.24), Tobit warns about the evils of sexual sin and foreign women. *Fornication* refers to any intercourse outside of marriage. On endogamy, see 1.9n. Genesis does not record the ancestry of Noah's wife, though *Jubilees* (4.33), an early Second Temple text, does. The reference to *pride* suggests Prov 16.18.

4.14–19: Popular wisdom. Following instructions on marriage, Tobit returns to the conventional advice begun in 4.5–10. **14:** *Do not keep over*, see Lev 19.13; Deut 24.15. **15:** The "golden rule" appears throughout ancient writing (*Ahikar*; Mt 7.12; Lk 6.31; *b. Shabb.* 31a). On *drunkenness*, see Prov 23.29–35; Sir 31.25–30; Tobit's point is not abstinence but avoiding excess. **16:** *Alms*, see v. 11n. **17:** *The grave of the righteous* may refer to food given to mourners (see Ps 106.28) or to meals offered to the dead. The *Tale of Ahikar* (see 1.21–22n.) mentions this latter forbidden (Deut 26:14) and decried (Sir 30.18) practice. **19:** *Ways . . . made straight*, see Prov 3.6; 11.5; Ps 5.8; Isa 45.13. The view that *none of the nations has understanding* (see Deut 32.28) comports with the condition of exile. *Hades*, see 3.10n.

4.20–5.3: Obtaining funds left in trust. Tobias is to obtain wealth from righteousness and, more directly, from his father's banked funds. The *fear of God* is a common theme in wisdom literature (see Prov 1.7; 10.27; 15.16; 22.4). **4.20:** *Ten talents*, see 1.14n. **5.1–2:** Tobias's positive response echoes Ex 19.8; Ruth 3.5. However, like Moses (Ex 3), he also questions his commission.

5 Then Tobias answered his father Tobit, "I will do everything that you have commanded me, father; [2] but how can I obtain the money[a] from him, since he does not know me and I do not know him? What evidence[b] am I to give him so that he will recognize and trust me, and give me the money? Also, I do not know the roads to Media, or how to get there." [3] Then Tobit answered his son Tobias, "He gave me his bond and I gave him my bond. I[c] divided his in two; we each took one part, and I put one with the money. And now twenty years have passed since I left this money in trust. So now, my son, find yourself a trustworthy man to go with you, and we will pay him wages until you return. But get back the money from Gabael."[d]

[4] So Tobias went out to look for a man to go with him to Media, someone who was acquainted with the way. He went out and found the angel Raphael standing in front of him; but he did not perceive that he was an angel of God. [5] Tobias[e] said to him, "Where do you come from, young man?" "From your kindred, the Israelites," he replied, "and I have come here to work." Then Tobias[f] said to him, "Do you know the way to go to Media?" [6] "Yes," he replied, "I have been there many times; I am acquainted with it and know all the roads. I have often traveled to Media, and would stay with our kinsman Gabael who lives in Rages of Media. It is a journey of two days from Ecbatana to Rages; for it lies in a mountainous area, while Ecbatana is in the middle of the plain." [7] Then Tobias said to him, "Wait for me, young man, until I go in and tell my father; for I do need you to travel with me, and I will pay you your wages." [8] He replied, "All right, I will wait; but do not take too long."

[9] So Tobias[f] went in to tell his father Tobit and said to him, "I have just found a man who is one of our own Israelite kindred!" He replied, "Call the man in, my son, so that I may learn about his family and to what tribe he belongs, and whether he is trustworthy enough to go with you."

[10] Then Tobias went out and called him, and said, "Young man, my father is calling for you." So he went in to him, and Tobit greeted him first. He replied, "Joyous greetings to you!" But Tobit retorted, "What joy is left for me any more? I am a man without eyesight; I cannot see the light of heaven, but I lie in darkness like the dead who no longer see the light. Although still alive, I am among the dead. I hear people but I cannot see them." But the young man[f] said, "Take courage; the time is near for God to heal you; take courage." Then Tobit said to him, "My son Tobias wishes to go to Media. Can you accompany him and guide him? I will pay your wages, brother." He answered, "I can go with him and I know all the roads, for I have often gone to Media and have crossed all its plains, and I am familiar with its mountains and all of its roads."

[11] Then Tobit[f] said to him, "Brother, of what family are you and from what tribe? Tell me, brother." [12] He replied, "Why do you need to know my tribe?" But Tobit[f] said, "I want to be sure, brother, whose son you are and what your name is." [13] He replied, "I am Azariah, the son of the great Hananiah, one of your

a Gk *it*
b Gk *sign*
c Other authorities read *He*
d Gk *from him*
e Gk *He*
f Gk *he*

5.4–17: **Raphael's disguise**. Disguised heavenly beings are a stock motif in folklore (as in *The Odyssey*, in which Athena accompanies Telemachus), and angelic appearances are frequent in biblical stories (e.g., Gen 18.1–15; Judg 13). That readers know more than Tobit and his family adds to the entertainment of the tale. **4**: *Standing in front of him*, the immediacy of the angel's appearance suggests the miraculous. *Raphael*, see 3.17n. **5**: *Young man*: Tobias better fits this description; the humor of mistaken identities continues. **6**: *Two days*: *Rages* is 185 mi (300 km) from *Ecbatana*; this journey would take far longer for anyone other than an angel. Ecbatana is not in *the middle of a plain*, but in the mountains; the story is as loose with geographical as with chronological and historical details (see 1.4n.; 1.15n.). **10**: Having prayed for death (3.6), Tobit perceives himself as among the dead. The reference to divine healing recalls Raphael's name (see 3.17n.). **11–12**: The angel appears to be reluctant to reveal his *family* and *tribe*. **13**: The pseudonyms point to Raphael's roles: *Azariah* is Hebrew for "God

relatives." [14] Then Tobit said to him, "Welcome! God save you, brother. Do not feel bitter toward me, brother, because I wanted to be sure about your ancestry. It turns out that you are a kinsman, and of good and noble lineage. For I knew Hananiah and Nathan,[a] the two sons of Shemeliah,[b] and they used to go with me to Jerusalem and worshiped with me there, and were not led astray. Your kindred are good people; you come of good stock. Hearty welcome!"

[15] Then he added, "I will pay you a drachma a day as wages, as well as expenses for yourself and my son. So go with my son, [16] and[c] I will add something to your wages." Raphael[d] answered, "I will go with him; so do not fear. We shall leave in good health and return to you in good health, because the way is safe." [17] So Tobit[e] said to him, "Blessings be upon you, brother."

Then he called his son and said to him, "Son, prepare supplies for the journey and set out with your brother. May God in heaven bring you safely there and return you in good health to me; and may his angel, my son, accompany you both for your safety."

Before he went out to start his journey, he kissed his father and mother. Tobit then said to him, "Have a safe journey."

[18] But his mother[f] began to weep, and said to Tobit, "Why is it that you have sent my child away? Is he not the staff of our hand as he goes in and out before us? [19] Do not heap money upon money, but let it be a ransom for our child. [20] For the life that is given to us by the Lord is enough for us."

[21] Tobit[d] said to her, "Do not worry; our child will leave in good health and return to us in good health. Your eyes will see him on the day when he returns to you in good health. Say no more! Do not fear for them, my sister. [22] For a good angel will accompany him; his journey will be successful, and he will come back in good health." [1] So she stopped weeping.

6

The young man went out and the angel went with him; [2] and the dog came out with him and went along with them. So they both journeyed along, and when the first night overtook them they camped by the Tigris river. [3] Then the young man went down to wash his feet in the Tigris river. Suddenly a large fish leaped up from the water and tried to swallow the young man's foot, and he cried out. [4] But the angel said to the young man, "Catch hold of the fish and hang on to it!" So the young man grasped the fish and drew it up on the land. [5] Then the angel said to him, "Cut open the fish and take out its gall, heart, and liver. Keep them with you, but throw away the intestines. For its gall, heart, and liver are useful as medicine." [6] So after cutting open

a   Other ancient authorities read *Jathan* or *Nathaniah*

b   Other ancient authorities read *Shemaiah*

c   Other ancient authorities add *when you return safely*

d   Gk *He*

e   Gk *he*

f   Other ancient authorities add *Anna*

has helped"; *Hananiah* means "God is merciful." **14:** Reference to the righteous sons of *Shemeliah* belies Tobit's claim (1.5–6) that he alone was faithful. **15:** Tobit's financial arrangements are generous. **17:** Tobit's prayer for angelic accompaniment (also 5.22) is already answered, adding an ironic note to the scene. Tobias's journey will resemble earlier quests for brides, although he does not yet know this (cf. Gen 24.40).

5.18–6.1a: Anna's lament. The couple alternate between practical observations and theological reflection (cf. 10.1–7). **18:** *My child,* Anna's maternal worry is palpable. *The staff of our hand,* a reliable person upon whom they can lean (see 2 Kings 18.21). **19:** *Ransom* suggests that Gabael should keep the funds as though they were ransom for Tobias. **21:** *My sister,* a term of affection for a lover or spouse (see Song 4.9,10). **22:** *A good angel* does accompany Tobias, although Tobit does not know this.

6.1b–9: Dangerous journey. Still disguised, Raphael will protect Tobias from dangerous fish and provide instruction for protection against lecherous demons. **2:** The *dog* (see also 11.4) adds an intimate touch and may suggest Odysseus's faithful pet (*Odyssey* 17.289–327). The *Tigris* is west of Nineveh; the geography remains fanciful. **3:** The unexpected *large fish* may be a parody of the Jonah story (Jon 1.7), in which a large fish swallows someone heading eventually toward Nineveh. **5:** Raphael's instructions are consistent with ancient medical texts that provide instructions for the use of fish organs. *Gall,* i.e., bile, is a bitter digestive juice recognized as

the fish the young man gathered together the gall, heart, and liver; then he roasted and ate some of the fish, and kept some to be salted.

The two continued on their way together until they were near Media.[a] [7] Then the young man questioned the angel and said to him, "Brother Azariah, what medicinal value is there in the fish's heart and liver, and in the gall?" [8] He replied, "As for the fish's heart and liver, you must burn them to make a smoke in the presence of a man or woman afflicted by a demon or evil spirit, and every affliction will flee away and never remain with that person any longer. [9] And as for the gall, anoint a person's eyes where white films have appeared on them; blow upon them, upon the white films, and the eyes[b] will be healed."

[10] When he entered Media and already was approaching Ecbatana,[c] [11] Raphael said to the young man, "Brother Tobias." "Here I am," he answered. Then Raphael[d] said to him, "We must stay this night in the home of Raguel. He is your relative, and he has a daughter named Sarah. [12] He has no male heir and no daughter except Sarah only, and you, as next of kin to her, have before all other men a hereditary claim on her. Also it is right for you to inherit her father's possessions. Moreover, the girl is sensible, brave, and very beautiful, and her father is a good man." [13] He continued, "You have every right to take her in marriage. So listen to me, brother; tonight I will speak to her father about the girl, so that we may take her to be your bride. When we return from Rages we will celebrate her marriage. For I know that Raguel can by no means keep her from you or promise her to another man without incurring the penalty

of death according to the decree of the book of Moses. Indeed he knows that you, rather than any other man, are entitled to marry his daughter. So now listen to me, brother, and tonight we shall speak concerning the girl and arrange her engagement to you. And when we return from Rages we will take her and bring her back with us to your house."

[14] Then Tobias said in answer to Raphael, "Brother Azariah, I have heard that she already has been married to seven husbands and that they died in the bridal chamber. On the night when they went in to her, they would die. I have heard people saying that it was a demon that killed them. [15] It does not harm her, but it kills anyone who desires to approach her. So now, since I am the only son my father has, I am afraid that I may die and bring my father's and mother's life down to their grave, grieving for me—and they have no other son to bury them."

[16] But Raphael[d] said to him, "Do you not remember your father's orders when he commanded you to take a wife from your father's house? Now listen to me, brother, and say no more about this demon. Take her. I know that this very night she will be given to you in marriage. [17] When you enter the bridal chamber, take some of the fish's liver and heart, and put them on the embers of the incense. An odor will be given off; [18] the demon will smell it and flee, and will never be seen near her any more. Now when you are

---

a Other ancient authorities read *Ecbatana*

b Gk *they*

c Other ancient authorities read *Rages*

d Gk *he*

---

having medicinal properties. **6:** No reference is made to the angel's eating (see Judg. 13.16). **8:** *To make a smoke*, or to fumigate, was a standard means for healing and exorcising demons. Explicit reference to a *woman* foreshadows Sarah's role.

6.10–18: Prenuptial instructions. Raphael now reveals the additional purpose of their journey; knowing Sarah's past luck with marriages, Tobias is understandably reluctant but quickly warms to the prospect of marrying her. **12:** *No male heir*, although Israelite inheritance laws were patrilineal, brotherless daughters could inherit if they married within the tribe (Num 27.1–11; 36.1–13). *Next of kin* refers to levirate law (3.14–15n.); by marrying Sarah, Tobias will obtain Raguel's estate. **13:** *Penalty of death*: no such law exists. **14–15:** Tobias's hesitancy—he mentions the death of Sarah's husbands four times in vv. 14–15—increases the tension; his fear is not primarily for his own life, but for the grief his death will cause his parents (see 3.10). **16:** Raphael eases Tobias's fear by repeating his concern for his parents, but changing his focus. **17:** On fumigating as an exorcism technique, see 6.8n. **18:** Raphael's advice, coupled with the announcement that the match was made in heaven and that Sarah is Tobias's relative, both calms the young man's fears and prompts his love.

about to go to bed with her, both of you must first stand up and pray, imploring the Lord of heaven that mercy and safety may be granted to you. Do not be afraid, for she was set apart for you before the world was made. You will save her, and she will go with you. I presume that you will have children by her, and they will be as brothers to you. Now say no more!" When Tobias heard the words of Raphael and learned that she was his kinswoman,[a] related through his father's lineage, he loved her very much, and his heart was drawn to her.

7 Now when they[b] entered Ecbatana, Tobias[c] said to him, "Brother Azariah, take me straight to our brother Raguel." So he took him to Raguel's house, where they found him sitting beside the courtyard door. They greeted him first, and he replied, "Joyous greetings, brothers; welcome and good health!" Then he brought them into his house. [2] He said to his wife Edna, "How much the young man resembles my kinsman Tobit!" [3] Then Edna questioned them, saying, "Where are you from, brothers?" They answered, "We belong to the descendants of Naphtali who are exiles in Nineveh." [4] She said to them, "Do you know our kinsman Tobit?" And they replied, "Yes, we know him." Then she asked them, "Is he[d] in good health?" [5] They replied, "He is alive and in good health." And Tobias added, "He is my father!" [6] At that Raguel jumped up and kissed him and wept. [7] He also spoke to him as follows, "Blessings on you, my child, son of a good and noble father![e] O most miserable of calamities that such an upright and beneficent man has become blind!" He then embraced his kinsman Tobias and wept. [8] His wife Edna also wept for him, and

their daughter Sarah likewise wept. [9] Then Raguel[c] slaughtered a ram from the flock and received them very warmly.

When they had bathed and washed themselves and had reclined to dine, Tobias said to Raphael, "Brother Azariah, ask Raguel to give me my kinswoman[a] Sarah." [10] But Raguel overheard it and said to the lad, "Eat and drink, and be merry tonight. For no one except you, brother, has the right to marry my daughter Sarah. Likewise I am not at liberty to give her to any other man than yourself, because you are my nearest relative. But let me explain to you the true situation more fully, my child. [11] I have given her to seven men of our kinsmen, and all died on the night when they went in to her. But now, my child, eat and drink, and the Lord will act on behalf of you both." But Tobias said, "I will neither eat nor drink anything until you settle the things that pertain to me." So Raguel said, "I will do so. She is given to you in accordance with the decree in the book of Moses, and it has been decreed from heaven that she be given to you. Take your kinswoman;[a] from now on you are her brother and she is your sister. She is given to you from today and forever. May the Lord of heaven, my child, guide and prosper you both this night and grant you mercy and peace." [12] Then Raguel summoned his daughter Sarah. When she came to him he took her by the hand and

a   Gk *sister*
b   Other ancient authorities read *he*
c   Gk *he*
d   Other ancient authorities add *alive and*
e   Other ancient authorities add *When he heard that Tobit had lost his sight, he was stricken with grief and wept. Then he said,*

7.1–16: Tobit and Sarah marry. *Raguel* and Edna's welcome repeats the themes of family connections. 1: *Raguel's* name is connected to Reuel, Moses' father-in-law (Ex 2.18; Num 10.29); the name is also shared with an archangel in *I Enoch* 20.4. *Ecbatana*, see 5.6n. 3: *Edna* asks the more pertinent questions; the scene echoes Gen 28.1–5. 5: Tobias does not mention his father's illness. 7: The source of Raguel's knowledge of Tobit's blindness is not cited. 9: *Bathed and washed* and *reclined to dine* indicate common customs of hospitality, cf. Gen 18.1–8; Lk 7.44–46. 10–11: The juxtaposition of death threats and joyous feasting is humorous; not every groom would appreciate Sarah's *true situation*. Raguel must follow the *decree in the book of Moses* regarding the rightful spouse for Sarah (see 3.14–15n.), but he is also concerned about the fate of her husbands. *I will neither eat nor drink*, Tobias begins to take charge of his fate. *Sister*, see 5.21n. 12–15: *The decree* is Num 36.8; Raguel repeats the idea (6.18) that Sarah is Tobias's divinely appointed wife. 12: *Raguel summoned his daughter* because neither she nor

gave her to Tobias,[a] saying, "Take her to be your wife in accordance with the law and decree written in the book of Moses. Take her and bring her safely to your father. And may the God of heaven prosper your journey with his peace." [13] Then he called her mother and told her to bring writing material; and he wrote out a copy of a marriage contract, to the effect that he gave her to him as wife according to the decree of the law of Moses. [14] Then they began to eat and drink.

[15] Raguel called his wife Edna and said to her, "Sister, get the other room ready, and take her there." [16] So she went and made the bed in the room as he had told her, and brought Sarah[b] there. She wept for her daughter.[b] Then, wiping away the tears,[c] she said to her, "Take courage, my daughter; the Lord of heaven grant you joy[d] in place of your sorrow. Take courage, my daughter." Then she went out.

8 When they had finished eating and drinking they wanted to retire; so they took the young man and brought him into the bedroom. [2] Then Tobias remembered the words of Raphael, and he took the fish's liver and heart out of the bag where he had them and put them on the embers of the incense. [3] The odor of the fish so repelled the demon that he fled to the remotest parts[e] of Egypt. But Raphael followed him, and at once bound him there hand and foot. [4] When the parents[f] had gone out and shut the door of the room, Tobias got out of bed and said to Sarah,[b] "Sister, get up,

and let us pray and implore our Lord that he grant us mercy and safety." [5] So she got up, and they began to pray and implore that they might be kept safe. Tobias[g] began by saying,

"Blessed are you, O God of our ancestors,
    and blessed is your name in all
        generations forever.
Let the heavens and the whole creation
    bless you forever.
[6] You made Adam, and for him you made
    his wife Eve
    as a helper and support.
    From the two of them the human race
        has sprung.
You said, 'It is not good that the man
        should be alone;
    let us make a helper for him like
        himself.'
[7] I now am taking this kinswoman of mine,
    not because of lust,
    but with sincerity.
Grant that she and I may find mercy
    and that we may grow old together."

[8] And they both said, "Amen, Amen." [9] Then they went to sleep for the night.

---

a   Gk *him*
b   Gk *her*
c   Other ancient authorities read *the tears of her daughter*
d   Other ancient authorities read *favor*
e   Or *fled through the air to the parts*
f   Gk *they*
g   Gk *He*

---

her mother participated in the original conversation about her fate; the match is arranged by the men. **13:** The Jewish marriage *contract* (Heb "ketubah") protects the wife's financial interests; this is the first recorded literary reference to this well-known practice; the earliest preserved example of a ketubah, dating to ca. 440 BCE, comes from the Jewish colony at Elephantine in Egypt. **16:** Edna's emotions encompass both fear and hope; she exhorts her daughter to courage, as Raphael had exhorted Tobias (6.18).

8.1–9a: Asmodeus is exorcised. Raphael's advice proves sound as the demon is exorcised, and the couple offers a prayer of thanksgiving. **2:** *The words of Raphael,* 6.8. **3:** *Repelled the demon,* see 6.8n. *Bound,* since binding restrains demons (see *1 Enoch* 10.4). **4–5:** The couple's praying contrasts with both Raguel's grave-digging (8.9–11) and the descriptions of ardent love-making found in non-Jewish Hellenistic romances. *Sister,* see 5.21n. **5–7:** Prayers are frequently attributed to characters in Second Temple Jewish literature (Jdt 9; Add Est 13; 14; Sus; Song of Three). **5:** *Blessed are you,* see 3.11n. *God of our ancestors,* see Ex 3.13; Deut 4.1. **6:** *Adam* and *Eve,* one of the earliest biblical references to these figures outside of Genesis. *You said,* introducing a quotation of Gen 2.18. **7:** *Not because of lust,* chastity is a popular theme in Jewish-Hellenistic literature; see also 3.14–15n. **8:** The text, discreetly, does not note when the marriage was consummated. *Amen, Amen* are Sarah's only words aside from her prayer (3.11–15).

8.9b–18: Raguel's fears are assuaged. **9–10:** Raguel's morbid planning contrasts with Tobias's piety; unlike

But Raguel arose and called his servants to him, and they went and dug a grave, [10] for he said, "It is possible that he will die and we will become an object of ridicule and derision." [11] When they had finished digging the grave, Raguel went into his house and called his wife, [12] saying, "Send one of the maids and have her go in to see if he is alive. But if he is dead, let us bury him without anyone knowing it." [13] So they sent the maid, lit a lamp, and opened the door; and she went in and found them sound asleep together. [14] Then the maid came out and informed them that he was alive and that nothing was wrong. [15] So they blessed the God of heaven, and Raguel[a] said,

"Blessed are you, O God, with every pure
      blessing;
let all your chosen ones bless you.[b]
Let them bless you forever.
[16] Blessed are you because you have made
      me glad.
It has not turned out as I expected,
but you have dealt with us according to
      your great mercy.
[17] Blessed are you because you had
      compassion
on two only children.
Be merciful to them, O Master, and keep
      them safe;
bring their lives to fulfillment
in happiness and mercy."

[18] Then he ordered his servants to fill in the grave before daybreak.

[19] After this he asked his wife to bake many loaves of bread; and he went out to the herd and brought two steers and four rams and ordered them to be slaughtered. So they began to make preparations. [20] Then he

called for Tobias and swore on oath to him in these words:[c] "You shall not leave here for fourteen days, but shall stay here eating and drinking with me; and you shall cheer up my daughter, who has been depressed. [21] Take at once half of what I own and return in safety to your father; the other half will be yours when my wife and I die. Take courage, my child. I am your father and Edna is your mother, and we belong to you as well as to your wife[d] now and forever. Take courage, my child."

9 Then Tobias called Raphael and said to him, [2] "Brother Azariah, take four servants and two camels with you and travel to Rages. Go to the home of Gabael, give him the bond, get the money, and then bring him with you to the wedding celebration. [4] For you know that my father must be counting the days, and if I delay even one day I will upset him very much. [3] You are witness to the oath Raguel has sworn, and I cannot violate his oath."[e] [5] So Raphael with the four servants and two camels went to Rages in Media and stayed with Gabael. Raphael[f] gave him the bond and informed him that Tobit's son Tobias had married and was inviting him to the wedding celebration. So Gabael[g] got up and counted out to him the money bags, with their seals intact; then they loaded

a Gk *they*
b Other ancient authorities lack this line
c Other ancient authorities read *Tobias and said to
   him*
d Gk *sister*
e In other ancient authorities verse 3 precedes verse 4
f Gk *He*
g Gk *he*

Tobit, Raguel prepares a grave *before* finding a corpse. **10:** *Ridicule and derision*, Raguel fears for his reputation, not his daughter's happiness or his son-in-law's life; Sarah had already become an object of derision (3.7–9). **12:** *Without anyone knowing* ignores Azariah/Raphael, the servants, and the concerns of Tobit and Anna. **15–17:** The prayer continues Raguel's wry perspective: he praises God for his own good fortune before mentioning the mercy extended to the couple.

    8.19–9.6: The wedding celebrated and tasks fulfilled. 8.20: *Fourteen days*, often seen as twice as long as a usual wedding celebration. *Depressed* either because of past deaths or the prospect of leaving her home. **21:** *Take courage* is what Edna advised Sarah (7.16), but under much different circumstances. The language of *father* and *mother* together with promises of inheritance suggests an adoption formula (see 10.12). **9.1:** Tobias now commands Raphael to obtain Tobit's money from Gabael; no longer the youth, he has become an adult. **4:** *I will upset him*, as demonstrated in 10.1–3. **5:** *Rages*, see 4.1n. **6:** Gabael's blessing indicates that the two families are regarded as one.

them on the camels.[a] [6] In the morning they both got up early and went to the wedding celebration. When they came into Raguel's house they found Tobias reclining at table. He sprang up and greeted Gabael,[b] who wept and blessed him with the words, "Good and noble son of a father good and noble, upright and generous! May the Lord grant the blessing of heaven to you and your wife, and to your wife's father and mother. Blessed be God, for I see in Tobias the very image of my cousin Tobit."

10 Now, day by day, Tobit kept counting how many days Tobias[c] would need for going and for returning. And when the days had passed and his son did not appear, [2] he said, "Is it possible that he has been detained? Or that Gabael has died, and there is no one to give him the money?" [3] And he began to worry. [4] His wife Anna said, "My child has perished and is no longer among the living." And she began to weep and mourn for her son, saying, [5] "Woe to me, my child, the light of my eyes, that I let you make the journey." [6] But Tobit kept saying to her, "Be quiet and stop worrying, my dear;[d] he is all right. Probably something unexpected has happened there. The man who went with him is trustworthy and is one of our own kin. Do not grieve for him, my dear;[d] he will soon be here." [7] She answered him, "Be quiet yourself! Stop trying to deceive me! My child has perished." She would rush out every day and watch the road her son had taken, and would heed no one.[e] When the sun had set she would go in and mourn and weep all night long, getting no sleep at all.

Now when the fourteen days of the wedding celebration had ended that Raguel had sworn to observe for his daughter, Tobias came to him and said, "Send me back, for I know that my father and mother do not believe that they will see me again. So I beg of you, father, to let me go so that I may return to my own father. I have already explained to you how I left him." [8] But Raguel said to Tobias, "Stay, my child, stay with me; I will send messengers to your father Tobit and they will inform him about you." [9] But he said, "No! I beg you to send me back to my father." [10] So Raguel promptly gave Tobias his wife Sarah, as well as half of all his property: male and female slaves, oxen and sheep, donkeys and camels, clothing, money, and household goods. [11] Then he saw them safely off; he embraced Tobias[b] and said, "Farewell, my child; have a safe journey. The Lord of heaven prosper you and your wife Sarah, and may I see children of yours before I die." [12] Then he kissed his daughter Sarah and said to her, "My daughter, honor your father-in-law and your mother-in-law,[f] since from now on they are as much your parents as those who gave you birth. Go in peace, daughter, and may I hear a good report about you as long as I live." Then he bade them farewell and let

a   Other ancient authorities lack *on the camels*

b   Gk *him*

c   Gk *he*

d   Gk *sister*

e   Other ancient authorities read *and she would eat nothing*

f   Other ancient authorities lack parts of *Then . . . mother-in-law*

10.1–7a: Anxiety at home. Tobit and Anna's concerns contrast with the celebration in Media. **1:** *And when the days had passed*, the two-week wedding celebrations, unknown to Tobit and Anna, extended the time of Tobias's absence long past what was required for the journey. **5:** *Light of my eyes*, perhaps a veiled reference to Tobit's blindness, recalls his words to Anna in 5.21. *I let you make the journey*, rather than again blaming Tobit (see 5.18), Anna suggests she had the power to prevent Tobias from leaving. **6:** In comforting Anna (cf. 5.21), Tobit masks his own fears. **7:** Unlike 5.21, here Anna does not heed Tobit's command to silence. Despite insisting that her *child has perished*, she continues to watch for him.

10.7b–13: Return to Nineveh. The couple's leave-taking is much less fraught with worry—and advice—than the parallel scene of 5.17–22. Tobias is mindful that his parents are likely worried (10.1–7a). **8:** Raguel desires his new son remain with him, but filial duty prompts Tobias to leave. **10:** Sarah's substantial dowry is part of the inheritance Tobias will receive (6.12). **12:** *Honor your father-in-law and your mother-in-law* extends the Decalogue's commandment (see 4.3n.). *Child and dear brother* intensifies the familial connection; more than just a marriage, the couple's relationship is the merging of two families. To *see children*, this prayer will be granted, as Raphael had remarked to Tobias (6.18). *Do nothing to grieve her*, the mother is vigilant for her daughter's happiness; the

them go. Then Edna said to Tobias, "My child and dear brother, the Lord of heaven bring you back safely, and may I live long enough to see children of you and of my daughter Sarah before I die. In the sight of the Lord I entrust my daughter to you; do nothing to grieve her all the days of your life. Go in peace, my child. From now on I am your mother and Sarah is your beloved wife.[a] May we all prosper together all the days of our lives." Then she kissed them both and saw them safely off. [13] Tobias parted from Raguel with happiness and joy, praising the Lord of heaven and earth, King over all, because he had made his journey a success. Finally, he blessed Raguel and his wife Edna, and said, "I have been commanded by the Lord to honor you all the days of my life."[b]

11 When they came near to Kaserin, which is opposite Nineveh, Raphael said, [2] "You are aware of how we left your father. [3] Let us run ahead of your wife and prepare the house while they are still on the way." [4] As they went on together Raphael[c] said to him, "Have the gall ready." And the dog[d] went along behind them.

[5] Meanwhile Anna sat looking intently down the road by which her son would come. [6] When she caught sight of him coming, she said to his father, "Look, your son is coming, and the man who went with him!"

[7] Raphael said to Tobias, before he had approached his father, "I knowthat his eyes will be opened. [8] Smear the gall of the fish on his eyes; the medicine will make the white films shrink and peel off from his eyes, and your father will regain his sight and see the light." [9] Then Anna ran up to her son and threw her arms around him, saying, "Now that I have seen you, my child, I am ready to die." And she wept. [10] Then Tobit got up and came

stumbling out through the courtyard door. Tobias went up to him, [11] with the gall of the fish in his hand, and holding him firmly, he blew into his eyes, saying, "Take courage, father." With this he applied the medicine on his eyes, [12] and it made them smart.[b] [13] Next, with both his hands he peeled off the white films from the corners of his eyes. Then Tobit[c] saw his son and[e] threw his arms around him, [14] and he wept and said to him, "I see you, my son, the light of my eyes!" Then he said,

"Blessed be God,
    and blessed be his great name,
    and blessed be all his holy angels.
May his holy name be blessed[f]
    throughout all the ages.
[15] Though he afflicted me,
    he has had mercy upon me.[g]
    Now I see my son Tobias!"

So Tobit went in rejoicing and praising God at the top of his voice. Tobias reported to his father that his journey had been successful, that he had brought the money, that he had married Raguel's daughter Sarah, and that she was, indeed, on her way there, very near to the gate of Nineveh.

[16] Then Tobit, rejoicing and praising God, went out to meet his daughter-in-law at the gate of Nineveh. When the people of Nineveh saw him coming, walking along in full vigor and with no one leading him, they were

a   Gk *sister*
b   Lat: Meaning of Gk uncertain
c   Gk *he*
d   Codex Sinaiticus reads *And the Lord*
e   Other ancient authorities lack *saw his son and*
f   Codex Sinaiticus reads *May his great name be upon us and blessed be all the angels*
g   Lat: Gk lacks this line

reader may recall the grief Tobit's insults brought Anna (2.11–14). **13:** Tobias confirms his bond with his in-laws; Sarah remains silent.

11.1–6: Tobias returns. 3: *Let us run ahead* may indicate Raphael's concern to avoid Sarah's company; unlike Asmodeus, he will not be tempted. **4:** *Gall,* see 6.5n. *The dog,* see 6.2n. **6:** Anna, ever watchful (see 10.7), brings the good news to Tobit.

11.7–18: Tobit is healed. 8: *Gall,* see 6.9. **11–13:** See Acts 9.18. **14:** *Light of my eyes,* fulfilling v. 8, has both metaphoric and literal implications (cf. 10.5). **14–15:** Tobit's doxology resembles those of Tobias (8.5–7) and Raguel (8.15–17); see also 8.5–7n. *Holy angels* is ironic, since Raphael has not revealed his identity. *Afflicted* (lit. "scourged") and *had mercy,* conventional terms for divine punishment and reconciliation upon the community's repentance, are applied to Israel in 13.2,5 (see 2 Macc 6.12–16). **16:** *Amazement* is the standard reaction

amazed. [17] Before them all, Tobit acknowledged that God had been merciful to him and had restored his sight. When Tobit met Sarah the wife of his son Tobias, he blessed her saying, "Come in, my daughter, and welcome. Blessed be your God who has brought you to us, my daughter. Blessed be your father and your mother, blessed be my son Tobias, and blessed be you, my daughter. Come in now to your home, and welcome, with blessing and joy. Come in, my daughter." So on that day there was rejoicing among all the Jews who were in Nineveh. [18] Ahikar and his nephew Nadab were also present to share Tobit's joy. With merriment they celebrated Tobias's wedding feast for seven days, and many gifts were given to him.[a]

12 When the wedding celebration was ended, Tobit called his son Tobias and said to him, "My child, see to paying the wages of the man who went with you, and give him a bonus as well." [2] He replied, "Father, how much shall I pay him? It would do no harm to give him half of the possessions brought back with me. [3] For he has led me back to you safely, he cured my wife, he brought the money back with me, and he healed you. How much extra shall I give him as a bonus?" [4] Tobit said, "He deserves, my child, to receive half of all that he brought back." [5] So Tobias[b] called him and said, "Take for your wages half of all that you brought back, and farewell."

[6] Then Raphael[b] called the two of them privately and said to them, "Bless God and acknowledge him in the presence of all the living for the good things he has done for

you. Bless and sing praise to his name. With fitting honor declare to all people the deeds[c] of God. Do not be slow to acknowledge him. [7] It is good to conceal the secret of a king, but to acknowledge and reveal the works of God, and with fitting honor to acknowledge him. Do good and evil will not overtake you. [8] Prayer with fasting[d] is good, but better than both is almsgiving with righteousness. A little with righteousness is better than wealth with wrongdoing.[e] It is better to give alms than to lay up gold. [9] For almsgiving saves from death and purges away every sin. Those who give alms will enjoy a full life, [10] but those who commit sin and do wrong are their own worst enemies.

[11] "I will now declare the whole truth to you and will conceal nothing from you. Already I have declared it to you when I said, 'It is good to conceal the secret of a king, but to reveal with due honor the works of God.' [12] So now when you and Sarah prayed, it was I who brought and read[f] the record of your prayer before the glory of the Lord, and likewise whenever you would bury the dead. [13] And that time when you did not hesitate to get up and leave your dinner to go and bury the dead, [14] I was sent to you to test you. And at the same time God sent me to heal you and

a Other ancient authorities lack parts of this sentence
b Gk *he*
c Gk *words*; other ancient authorities read *words of the deeds*
d Codex Sinaiticus *with sincerity*
e Lat
f Lat: Gk lacks *and read*

to a miraculous healing. **17:** *My daughter*, a repeated phrase, echoes the familial language of Raguel and Edna; Tobit greets the daughter-in-law for whom he had prayed (4.12–13). **18:** *Ahikar*, see 1.21–22n. *Nadab*, see 14.10n.

12.1–22: Raphael's revelations. Bringing the major plot lines to a conclusion, Raphael explains his role in testing Tobit and exhorts Tobit and his son to good deeds and piety. **2:** *How much shall I pay him?* The fee had been determined, but not the amount of the bonus (5.15–16). *Half of the possessions* is one-quarter of Raguel's estate plus half the loan. The generosity is consistent with Tobit's insistence on almsgiving. **6:** *Declare to all people* expresses a universalistic impulse (13.3–4,11; 14.6–7). **7:** *Secret of a king* anticipates Raphael's revelation in v. 11 and recalls Tobit's position at court (1.13–14); indeed, Tobit reveals no court secrets. *To acknowledge*, as Tobit had done in 11.17. **7b–10:** Proverbial sayings continue the emphasis on charitable deeds (4.6–11); for *fasting*, which becomes increasingly important in the postexilic period, see also 1 Macc 3.44–48; Esth 4.1–3,15; Mt 6.16–18; *almsgiving*, see 4.11n. **12–13:** The angelic task of conveying prayers and good deeds is mentioned in other Second Temple Jewish literature, such as 1 Enoch. **14:** *To test* indicates that Tobit's blindness and his subsequent trials resulted from God's active effort (Gen 22.1–22; Job 1–2); unmentioned is whether Sarah's trials were

Sarah your daughter-in-law. [15] I am Raphael, one of the seven angels who stand ready and enter before the glory of the Lord."

[16] The two of them were shaken; they fell face down, for they were afraid. [17] But he said to them, "Do not be afraid; peace be with you. Bless God forevermore. [18] As for me, when I was with you, I was not acting on my own will, but by the will of God. Bless him each and every day; sing his praises. [19] Although you were watching me, I really did not eat or drink anything—but what you saw was a vision. [20] So now get up from the ground,[a] and acknowledge God. See, I am ascending to him who sent me. Write down all these things that have happened to you." And he ascended. [21] Then they stood up, and could see him no more. [22] They kept blessing God and singing his praises, and they acknowledged God for these marvelous deeds of his, when an angel of God had appeared to them.

13

Then Tobit[b] said:
"Blessed be God who lives forever,
    because his kingdom[c] lasts throughout
        all ages.
[2] For he afflicts, and he shows mercy;
    he leads down to Hades in the lowest
        regions of the earth,
    and he brings up from the great abyss,[d]
    and there is nothing that can escape his
        hand.
[3] Acknowledge him before the nations,
        O children of Israel;
    for he has scattered you among them.
[4] He has shown you his greatness even
        there.

Exalt him in the presence of every living
        being,
    because he is our Lord and he is our
        God;
    he is our Father and he is God forever.
[5] He will afflict[e] you for your iniquities,
    but he will again show mercy on all of
        you.
He will gather you from all the nations
    among whom you have been scattered.
[6] If you turn to him with all your heart and
        with all your soul,
    to do what is true before him,
then he will turn to you
    and will no longer hide his face from
        you.
So now see what he has done for you;
    acknowledge him at the top of your voice.
Bless the Lord of righteousness,
    and exalt the King of the ages.[f]
In the land of my exile I acknowledge him,
    and show his power and majesty to a
        nation of sinners:
'Turn back, you sinners, and do what is
        right before him;
    perhaps he may look with favor upon
        you and show you mercy.'

[a] Other ancient authorities read *now bless the Lord on earth*
[b] Gk *he*
[c] Other ancient authorities read *forever, and his kingdom*
[d] Gk *from destruction*
[e] Other ancient authorities read *He afflicted*
[f] The lacuna in codex Sinaiticus, verses 6b to 10a, is filled in from other ancient authorities

also tests. 15: *Seven angels* (cf. Rev. 8.2) do not appear in earlier biblical material; Daniel mentions Gabriel (Dan 8.16; 9.21; cf. Lk 1.19,26) and Michael (Dan 10.13,21; 12.1; cf. Jude 9; Rev 12.7). *The glory of the Lord*, see 3.16. **16–17:** Fear and prostration are standard reactions to epiphanies (Dan 10.1–12), as is the response, *Do not be afraid*. **19:** *I really did not eat* reflects the traditional view that angels do not require food (Judg 13.16; see 6.6n.). **20:** Jesus' ascension in Acts 1.9 (cf. Jn 16.5) shares several motifs with this scene.

13.1–14.1: Tobit's hymn. The hymn expands upon 11.14–15; the vocabulary evokes Psalms 92–118, and the form may indicate liturgical models in use in the early Second Temple period. **2:** *Afflicts . . . and . . . shows mercy* (also v. 5), see 11.14–15n.; Tobit's (and Sarah's) trials encapsulate the difficulties of exile. Tobit repeats the Deuteronomic view that sin leads to punishment, and repentance to redemption (Deut 28–33; cf. Wis 12.22). Some interpreters see in *brings up from the great abyss* belief in resurrection; others associate the references with sickness and recovery, redemption from Sheol, or exile and return; see Deut 32.39; 1 Sam 2.6; Wis 16.13–15; 2 Macc 7.35. *Hades*, see 3.10n. **4:** *Our Father*, an address to God that becomes increasingly common in the postexilic period (e.g., Isa 63.16; 64.8; Sir 23.1,4; Wis 14.3; Mt 6.9). **5:** The in-gathering of the exiles, a popular theme in Second Temple Jewish literature, becomes in Jewish tradition a sign of the messianic age (14.7; Sir 36.13; Bar

7 As for me, I exalt my God,
   and my soul rejoices in the King of
      heaven.
8 Let all people speak of his majesty,
   and acknowledge him in Jerusalem.
9 O Jerusalem, the holy city,
   he afflicted[a] you for the deeds of your
      hands,[b]
   but will again have mercy on the
      children of the righteous.
10 Acknowledge the Lord, for he is good,[c]
   and bless the King of the ages,
   so that his tent[d] may be rebuilt in you
      in joy.
May he cheer all those within you who are
      captives,
   and love all those within you who are
      distressed,
   to all generations forever.
11 A bright light will shine to all the ends of
      the earth;
   many nations will come to you from far
      away,
the inhabitants of the remotest parts of
      the earth to your holy name,
   bearing gifts in their hands for the King
      of heaven.
Generation after generation will give
      joyful praise in you;
   the name of the chosen city will endure
      forever.
12 Cursed are all who speak a harsh word
      against you;
   cursed are all who conquer you
   and pull down your walls,
all who overthrow your towers
   and set your homes on fire.
But blessed forever will be all who
      revere you.[e]
13 Go, then, and rejoice over the children of
      the righteous,
   for they will be gathered together
   and will praise the Lord of the ages.

14 Happy are those who love you,
   and happy are those who rejoice in your
      prosperity.
Happy also are all people who grieve with
      you
   because of your afflictions;
for they will rejoice with you
   and witness all your glory forever.
15 My soul blesses[f] the Lord, the great King!
   16 For Jerusalem will be built[g] as his
      house for all ages.
How happy I will be if a remnant of my
      descendants should survive
   to see your glory and acknowledge the
      King of heaven.
The gates of Jerusalem will be built with
      sapphire and emerald,
   and all your walls with precious stones.
The towers of Jerusalem will be built with
      gold,
   and their battlements with pure gold.
The streets of Jerusalem will be paved
   with ruby and with stones of Ophir.
17 The gates of Jerusalem will sing hymns
      of joy,
   and all her houses will cry, 'Hallelujah!
Blessed be the God of Israel!'
   and the blessed will bless the holy name
      forever and ever."

14 So ended Tobit's words of praise.
² Tobit[h] died in peace when he was one
hundred twelve years old, and was buried with
great honor in Nineveh. He was sixty-two[i]

a Other ancient authorities read *will afflict*
b Other ancient authorities read *your children*
c Other ancient authorities read *Lord worthily*
d Or *tabernacle*
e Other ancient authorities read *who build you up*
f Or *O my soul, bless*
g Other ancient authorities add *for a city*
h Gk *He*
i Other ancient authorities read *fifty-eight*

4.21–5.9). *Afflict* and *show mercy*, see 11.14–15n. **6:** *Heart* and *soul* are to be inclined toward God (Deut 6.5). **8–17:** A celebration of *Jerusalem*, a focus with which the book began (1.4–10); now Tobit speaks of Jerusalem's glory rather than its destruction. **11:** *Many nations will come* is another sign of the messianic age (Isa 60.1–5; Zech 14.16). **12:** *Who conquer you* is anachronistic for Tobit's ostensible date; the reference shows knowledge of Nebuchadnezzar's attack on Jerusalem in 586 BCE. **14:** *Happy are . . . you* is a macarism or beatitude, cf. Mt 5.3–11; Lk 6.20–22. **16–17:** For similar views of Jerusalem's restoration, see Isa 54.11–14; Rev 21.9–27.

14.2–11a: Tobit's testament. Tobit's second testament (see 4.1–13n.) confirms his earlier insistence that piety will ultimately be rewarded. **2:** *Giving alms* and *blessing God* are the two major exhortations made throughout

years old when he lost his eyesight, and after regaining it he lived in prosperity, giving alms and continually blessing God and acknowledging God's majesty.

[3] When he was about to die, he called his son Tobias and the seven sons of Tobias[a] and gave this command: "My son, take your children [4] and hurry off to Media, for I believe the word of God that Nahum spoke about Nineveh, that all these things will take place and overtake Assyria and Nineveh. Indeed, everything that was spoken by the prophets of Israel, whom God sent, will occur. None of all their words will fail, but all will come true at their appointed times. So it will be safer in Media than in Assyria and Babylon. For I know and believe that whatever God has said will be fulfilled and will come true; not a single word of the prophecies will fail. All of our kindred, inhabitants of the land of Israel, will be scattered and taken as captives from the good land; and the whole land of Israel will be desolate, even Samaria and Jerusalem will be desolate. And the temple of God in it will be burned to the ground, and it will be desolate for a while.[b]

[5] "But God will again have mercy on them, and God will bring them back into the land of Israel; and they will rebuild the temple of God, but not like the first one until the period when the times of fulfillment shall come. After this they all will return from their exile and will rebuild Jerusalem in splendor; and in it the temple of God will be rebuilt, just as the prophets of Israel have said concerning it. [6] Then the nations in the whole world will all be converted and worship God in truth. They will all abandon their idols, which deceitfully have led them into their error; [7] and in righteousness they will praise the eternal God. All the Israelites who are saved in those days and are truly mindful of God will be gathered together; they will go to Jerusalem and live in safety forever in the land of Abraham, and it will be given over to them. Those who sincerely love God will rejoice, but those who commit sin and injustice will vanish from all the earth. [8,9] So now, my children, I command you, serve God faithfully and do what is pleasing in his sight. Your children are also to be commanded to do what is right and to give alms, and to be mindful of God and to bless his name at all times with sincerity and with all their strength. So now, my son, leave Nineveh; do not remain here. [10] On whatever day you bury your mother beside me, do not stay overnight within the confines of the city. For I see that there is much wickedness within it, and that much deceit is practiced within it, while the people are without shame. See, my son, what Nadab did to Ahikar who had reared him. Was he not, while still alive, brought down into the earth? For God repaid him to his face for this shameful treatment. Ahikar came out into the light, but Nadab went into the eternal darkness, because he tried to kill Ahikar. Because he gave alms, Ahikar[c] escaped the fatal trap that Nadab had set for him, but Nadab fell into it himself, and was destroyed. [11] So now, my children, see what almsgiving accomplishes, and what

a Lat: Gk lacks *and the seven sons of Tobias*
b Lat: Other ancient authorities read *of God will be in distress and will be burned for a while*
c Gk *he*; other ancient authorities read *Manasses*

the volume (see 3.1–6n.; 4.11n.). **3**: *Seven sons*: Edna's wish for grandchildren is granted (10.12; for the motif of seven sons, see Ruth 4.15; 2 Macc 7; 4 Macc 14.12). **4**: Unlike the first testament (ch 4), this one opens with predictions of the future; Tobit's comments are among the earliest claims that events are predetermined (see also Dan 10–12; Mk 13.7; Acts 1.7; Rev 1.1). The prophet *Nahum* predicted the destruction of *Assyria and Nineveh*; Babylon conquered Nineveh in 612 BCE (see v. 15; 13.12n.). **5–7**: With the restoration that began with the edict of Cyrus of Persia in 538 BCE, the hymn shifts to a vision of the splendid future of a renewed Jerusalem, glorified temple, return of the exiles (13.5n.), conversion of the Gentiles to the worship of the God of Israel, and elimination of sin. **10**: Recognizing that Anna will outlive him, Tobit insists his son provide for her in life and in death; reference to burial, now after a long life, contrasts positively with Tobit's interring of unburied corpses. *Nadab did to Ahikar*: see 1.21–22n. Nadab framed his uncle Ahikar, making it appear that he had committed treason against the king.

14.11b–15: Tobit and Anna die. Tobias is obedient to his father's command (v. 10) and fulfills his filial duty also by burying his in-laws. Of all the main characters, only Sarah's fate is left undeveloped in the final chapter.

injustice does—it brings death! But now my breath fails me."

Then they laid him on his bed, and he died; and he received an honorable funeral. [12] When Tobias's mother died, he buried her beside his father. Then he and his wife and children[a] returned to Media and settled in Ecbatana with Raguel his father-in-law. [13] He treated his parents-in-law[b] with great respect in their old age, and buried them in Ecbatana of Media. He inherited both the property of Raguel and that of his father Tobit. [14] He died highly respected at the age of one hundred seventeen[c] years. [15] Before he died he heard[d] of the destruction of Nineveh, and he saw its prisoners being led into Media, those whom King Cyaxares[e] of Media had taken captive. Tobias[f] praised God for all he had done to the people of Nineveh and Assyria; before he died he rejoiced over Nineveh, and he blessed the Lord God forever and ever. Amen.[g]

a Codex Sinaiticus lacks *and children*
b Gk *them*
c Other authorities read other numbers
d Codex Sinaiticus reads *saw and heard*
e Cn: Codex Sinaiticus *Ahikar*; other ancient authorities read *Nebuchadnezzar and Ahasuerus*
f Gk *He*
g Other ancient authorities lack *Amen*

13: *Ecbatana of Media*, see 3.7–15n. 15: Reference to the destruction of Nineveh (see v. 4n.) suggests that Tobit's other predictions (vv. 4–7) will also come to pass. *Cyaxares* was ruler of Media ca. 625–585 BCE. Appropriately, the book ends with praise to God.

JUDITH

NAME, DATE OF COMPOSITION, AND CANONICAL STATUS

The book of Judith, which is named for its spirited heroine, is an entertaining narrative that has engaged Jewish and Christian imaginations for centuries and in many different ways. In Jewish tradition Judith was a heroine who protected her people, while in Christian tradition Judith has represented various virtues, such as chastity slaying lust. It was probably composed in Hebrew near the end of the second century BCE in the aftermath of the Maccabean Revolt, which it appears to idealize. No Hebrew manuscript survives, probably because the book was not accorded canonical status in Judaism, but the book was preserved in the Christian tradition in Greek, Latin, and other translations. It is considered canonical in Roman Catholic and Eastern Orthodox churches, and as part of the Apocrypha by Protestants.

GENRE, STRUCTURE, AND INTERPRETATION

Although the book of Judith came to be considered historical, it was composed as a fictional novella, much like other Hebrew stories with a central female protagonist, such as Esther, Tobit, and Susanna, as well as the apocryphal story of *Joseph and Aseneth*, and many Greek novels. The book's fictional nature is evident from its blending of history and fiction, beginning in the very first verse, and is too prevalent thereafter to be considered as the result of mere historical mistakes. Thus, the great villain is "Nebuchadnezzar, who ruled over the Assyrians" (1.1), yet the historical Nebuchadnezzar was the famous king of the Babylonians. Other details are also patently unbelievable, such as fictional place names, the immense size of armies and fortifications, the dating of events, and the actions of the Assyrian general Holofernes. Like the books of Jonah and Job and the more contemporary novellas, Judith would not have been taken to be a factual account even at the time of its composition. With its blend of fiction and ancient history, it should also be read in light of historical events at the time it was written. The "Assyrian" Nebuchadnezzar may be a cipher or coded name for the Syrian Antiochus IV Epiphanes, who had also tried to enforce a foreign religion on Israel. The Maccabees, like Judith, showed strength of resolve and won their freedom. Judith later recounts that Israel had destroyed the cults of those on the land (8.18–20), and this also recalls contemporary history, because the successors of the Maccabees destroyed the Samaritan temple on Mount Gerizim.

The book of Judith entertains and instructs by combining irony and humor, bombast and fascinating detail, sexual suggestiveness and pious self-denial bordering on asceticism, outrageous reversals of the period's gender roles and conservative religious values, escapism, and celebration of military success. Moreover, the plot's careful structure and the commanding figure of Judith herself make this a compelling tale. The story has two parts or acts of approximately equal length. Chapters 1–7 describe the rise of the threat to Israel, led by the evil king Nebuchadnezzar of the Assyrians and his sycophantic general Holofernes. This first part concludes as Holofernes' world-wide campaign has converged at the mountain pass where Judith's village, Bethulia, is located. The second part, chs 8–16, introduces Judith and depicts her heroic actions to save her people. Each of the two parts has a clear chiastic pattern in which the order of events is reversed at a central moment in the narrative (*abcc'b'a'*).

Part I (1.1–7.23)
- A. Campaign against disobedient nations; the people surrender (1.1–2.13)
  - B. Israel is "greatly terrified" (2.14–3.10)
    - C. Joakim prepares for war (4.1–15)
      - D. Holofernes talks with Achior (5.1–6.9)
        - E. Achior is expelled by Assyrians (6.10–13)
        - E.' Achior is received in village of Bethulia (6.14–15)
      - D.' Achior talks with the people (6.16–21)
    - C.' Holofernes prepares for war (7.1–3)
  - B.' Israel is "greatly terrified" (7.4–5)
- A.' Campaign against Bethulia; the people want to surrender (7.6–32)

Part II (8.1–16.25)
- A. Introduction of Judith (8.1–8)
  - B. Judith plans to save Israel (8.9–10.8)
    - C. Judith and her maid leave Bethulia (10.9–10)
      - D. Judith beheads Holofernes (10.11–13.10a)
    - C.' Judith and her maid return to Bethulia (13.10b–11)
  - B.' Judith plans the destruction of Israel's enemy (13.12–16.20)
- A.' Conclusion about Judith (16.21–25)

Part I, although at times tedious in its description of the military developments, develops important themes by alternating battles with reflections and rousing action with rest. In contrast, the second half is devoted mainly to Judith's strength of character and the beheading scene, which is told quickly. Perhaps such terseness implies that the original audience would have known the story, but the artistry lies in describing not *what* will happen but *how* it will happen. Furthermore, that the scene is told quickly does not imply insignificance. On the contrary, its importance is evident in its position at the center of the story's second act. Other paired figures and expressions also contribute to the story's structure: Nebuchadnezzar and God each have a "general," Holofernes and Judith respectively, and each of them has a servant, Bagoas and Judith's maid.

The character of Judith is also larger than life, and she has won a place in Jewish and Christian lore, art, poetry, and drama. Her name, which means "Jewish woman," is the feminine form of *Yehudi* and suggests that she represents the heroic spirit of the Jewish people. Because of her unswerving religious devotion, she is able to step outside of her widow's role, dress and act in a sexually provocative manner, lie to the opposing general Holofernes, seduce him, and behead him, all without a moment of self-doubt. Yet the book does not undermine accepted social conventions, for in the end Judith returns to her life as an exemplary pious widow. Thus, like many comedies, the book of Judith allows for a release of social tensions, explores transgressions of everyday rules, and then reconstitutes society on acceptable lines.

The book constantly echoes biblical narratives, most notably the assassination of Sisera by Jael in Judg 4–5 and the revenge of Simeon and Levi on Shechem after the rape of Dinah in Gen 34. Judith's deliverance of her people from danger makes her like the judges of Israel. She echoes Moses, too, as when she responds to murmuring over water and the testing of God (8.9–27), and when her hand is likened to the hand of Moses (8.33; 13.14; cf. Ex 14.21). The story also recalls folk traditions about male heroes, but adds humor and irony by making the hero a pious widow who transgresses the social restrictions of her gender in order to save her people and defend her God. Although some modern interpreters have questioned Judith's morality, in the ancient world Judith was always remembered positively as a heroine of the faith.

Lawrence M. Wills

1 It was the twelfth year of the reign of Neb-uchadnezzar, who ruled over the Assyri-ans in the great city of Nineveh. In those days Arphaxad ruled over the Medes in Ecbatana. ² He built walls around Ecbatana with hewn stones three cubits thick and six cubits long; he made the walls seventy cubits high and fifty cubits wide. ³ At its gates he raised tow-ers one hundred cubits high and sixty cubits wide at the foundations. ⁴ He made its gates seventy cubits high and forty cubits wide to allow his armies to march out in force and his infantry to form their ranks. ⁵ Then King Nebuchadnezzar made war against King Arphaxad in the great plain that is on the borders of Ragau. ⁶ There rallied to him all the people of the hill country and all those who lived along the Euphrates, the Tigris, and the Hydaspes, and, on the plain, Arioch, king of the Elymeans. Thus, many nations joined the forces of the Chaldeans.ᵃ

⁷ Then Nebuchadnezzar, king of the As-syrians, sent messengers to all who lived in Persia and to all who lived in the west, those who lived in Cilicia and Damascus, Lebanon and Antilebanon, and all who lived along the seacoast, ⁸ and those among the nations of Carmel and Gilead, and Upper Galilee and the great plain of Esdraelon, ⁹ and all who were in Samaria and its towns, and beyond the Jordan as far as Jerusalem and Bethany and Chelous and Kadesh and the river of Egypt, and Tahpanhes and Raamses and the whole land of Goshen, ¹⁰ even beyond Tanis and Memphis, and all who lived in Egypt as far as the borders of Ethiopia. ¹¹ But all who lived in the whole region disregarded the summons of Nebuchadnezzar, king of the Assyrians, and refused to join him in the war; for they were not afraid of him, but regarded him as only one man.ᵇ So they sent back his messen-gers empty-handed and in disgrace.

¹² Then Nebuchadnezzar became very angry with this whole region, and swore by his throne and kingdom that he would take revenge on the whole territory of Cilicia and Damascus and Syria, that he would kill with his sword also all the inhabitants of the land of Moab, and the people of Ammon, and all Judea, and every one in Egypt, as far as the coasts of the two seas.

¹³ In the seventeenth year he led his forces against King Arphaxad and defeated him

ᵃ Syr: Gk Cheleoudites
ᵇ Or a man

1.1–7.32: Part I: A great empire rises up to attack Israel and other nations.

1.1–6: Nebuchadnezzar is introduced and declares war on Arphaxad, king of Media. 1: The dating of events in the reign of the great king is typical of histories, but although Nebuchadnezzar of Babylon had defeated the southern half of Israel (Judah) in 586 BCE (see 2 Kings 25.1–21) and the Assyrians had defeated the northern half of Israel in 722 BCE (see 2 Kings 17.5–6), the combination Nebuchadnezzar of the Assyrians is fictitious—yet it combines both bitter associations. There is also no known king of the Medes named Arphaxad. 2–4: The mas-sive fortifications of Arphaxad's capital Ecbatana, in northwestern Iran, are unrealistic: walls seventy cubits high and fifty cubits wide would measure 105 ft (32 m) by 75 ft (23 m). By beginning with the might and grandeur of Arphaxad, the threat of Nebuchadnezzar is made even more dramatic. 5–6: Although many of the place names in the book of Judith are well known, others are fictitious or unknown; together they give the impression that the entire world is involved. What seems repetitive to the modern reader serves to evoke the extent of the campaign. 6: Euphrates, Tigris, the principal rivers of Mesopotamia. Chaldeans is another name for Babylonians, reflecting the author's fictitious merging of the Assyrians and Babylonians for the purposes of the story.

1.7–11: Many nations rebuff Nebuchadnezzar's call to ally with him. Nebuchadnezzar's messengers move from east to west, through modern Iran, Syria, southern Turkey, Lebanon, Jordan, Palestine, Israel, and into Egypt. But all the nations reject his summons; he is nothing more than one man (v. 11). This judgment will be tested. 8: Esdraelon (older Jezreel), the great plain from Mount Carmel to the Jordan Valley. 9: Samaria and Je-rusalem are mentioned only in passing; at this point there is a world-wide focus, which will first narrow to the area of Syria-Palestine, then to Samaria and Judea, and finally to the tiny mountain village of Bethulia (4.6). (See map on p. 1394.)

1.12–16: Nebuchadnezzar vows to destroy the western nations and easily defeats Arphaxad without their aid. 12: Nebuchadnezzar swears to destroy the nations that figure so prominently in the Bible: Damascus, Syria, Moab, Ammon, Egypt; Judith and a small band of Jews will deliver all of the biblical lands. The two seas are pos-

in battle, overthrowing the whole army of Arphaxad and all his cavalry and all his chariots. ¹⁴ Thus he took possession of his towns and came to Ecbatana, captured its towers, plundered its markets, and turned its glory into disgrace. ¹⁵ He captured Arphaxad in the mountains of Ragau and struck him down with his spears, thus destroying him once and for all. ¹⁶ Then he returned to Nineveh, he and all his combined forces, a vast body of troops; and there he and his forces rested and feasted for one hundred twenty days.

2 In the eighteenth year, on the twenty-second day of the first month, there was talk in the palace of Nebuchadnezzar, king of the Assyrians, about carrying out his revenge on the whole region, just as he had said. ² He summoned all his ministers and all his nobles and set before them his secret plan and recounted fully, with his own lips, all the wickedness of the region.ᵃ ³ They decided that every one who had not obeyed his command should be destroyed.

⁴ When he had completed his plan, Nebuchadnezzar, king of the Assyrians, called Holofernes, the chief general of his army, second only to himself, and said to him, ⁵ "Thus says the Great King, the lord of the whole earth: Leave my presence and take with you men confident in their strength, one hundred twenty thousand foot soldiers and twelve thousand cavalry. ⁶ March out against all the land to the west, because they disobeyed my orders. ⁷ Tell them to prepare earth and water, for I am coming against them in my anger, and will cover the whole face of the earth with the feet of my troops, to whom I will hand them over to be plundered. ⁸ Their

wounded shall fill their ravines and gullies, and the swelling river shall be filled with their dead. ⁹ I will lead them away captive to the ends of the whole earth. ¹⁰ You shall go and seize all their territory for me in advance. They must yield themselves to you, and you shall hold them for me until the day of their punishment. ¹¹ But to those who resist show no mercy, but hand them over to slaughter and plunder throughout your whole region. ¹² For as I live, and by the power of my kingdom, what I have spoken I will accomplish by my own hand. ¹³ And you—take care not to transgress any of your lord's commands, but carry them out exactly as I have ordered you; do it without delay."

¹⁴ So Holofernes left the presence of his lord, and summoned all the commanders, generals, and officers of the Assyrian army. ¹⁵ He mustered the picked troops by divisions as his lord had ordered him to do, one hundred twenty thousand of them, together with twelve thousand archers on horseback, ¹⁶ and he organized them as a great army is marshaled for a campaign. ¹⁷ He took along a vast number of camels and donkeys and mules for transport, and innumerable sheep and oxen and goats for food; ¹⁸ also ample rations for everyone, and a huge amount of gold and silver from the royal palace.

¹⁹ Then he set out with his whole army, to go ahead of King Nebuchadnezzar and to cover the whole face of the earth to the west with their chariots and cavalry and picked foot soldiers. ²⁰ Along with them went a mixed crowd like a swarm of locusts, like the

---

ᵃ Meaning of Gk uncertain

---

sibly the Red Sea and the Mediterranean. **16:** The army *rested and feasted for one hundred twenty days*. This is the first of a series of well-placed pauses in the military history of the first half of the book (cf. 2.28; 3.10; 6.21; 7.32).

2.1–13: Nebuchadnezzar makes plans to destroy all the nations who opposed him. 1: *The eighteenth year*, 587 BCE, when the siege of Jerusalem began; see 2 Kings 25.1. **2:** Nebuchadnezzar summons *all his ministers* and threatens to destroy the whole region (cf. Dan 2.2–5; 3.2–9). **4:** *Holofernes* was the name of a general in the Persian army of Artaxerxes III Ochus, who invaded this same region in 350 and 343 BCE. His officer was named Bagoas, a name that will appear in 12:11. Real persons have likely been used as fictional opponents. **5:** *The lord of the whole earth*, Nebuchadnezzar and Holofernes will have delusions of grandeur and attribute terms to Nebuchadnezzar that should be reserved for God alone (cf. 3.8). **7:** It was Persian practice to demand *earth and water* from foreign states as a sign of submission (Herodotus, *Histories* 6.48).

2.14–3.10: Holofernes begins the campaign to destroy the disobedient nations.

2.15–20: The enormousness of the Assyrian army is emphasized, including animals, rations, gold and silver, even hangers-on—*a mixed crowd* (cf. Ex 12.38) *like a swarm of locusts* (cf. Judg 6.5; Joel 1.4–7), *like the dust of the*

dust[a] of the earth—a multitude that could not be counted.

²¹ They marched for three days from Nineveh to the plain of Bectileth, and camped opposite Bectileth near the mountain that is to the north of Upper Cilicia. ²² From there Holofernes[b] took his whole army, the infantry, cavalry, and chariots, and went up into the hill country. ²³ He ravaged Put and Lud, and plundered all the Rassisites and the Ishmaelites on the border of the desert, south of the country of the Chelleans. ²⁴ Then he followed[c] the Euphrates and passed through Mesopotamia and destroyed all the fortified towns along the brook Abron, as far as the sea. ²⁵ He also seized the territory of Cilicia, and killed everyone who resisted him. Then he came to the southern borders of Japheth, facing Arabia. ²⁶ He surrounded all the Midianites, and burned their tents and plundered their sheepfolds. ²⁷ Then he went down into the plain of Damascus during the wheat harvest, and burned all their fields and destroyed their flocks and herds and sacked their towns and ravaged their lands and put all their young men to the sword.

²⁸ So fear and dread of him fell upon all the people who lived along the seacoast, at Sidon and Tyre, and those who lived in Sur and Ocina and all who lived in Jamnia. Those who lived in Azotus and Ascalon feared him greatly.

3 They therefore sent messengers to him to sue for peace in these words: ² "We, the servants of Nebuchadnezzar, the Great King, lie prostrate before you. Do with us whatever you will. ³ See, our buildings and all our land and all our wheat fields and our flocks and herds and all our encampments[d] lie before you; do with them as you please. ⁴ Our towns and their inhabitants are also your slaves; come and deal with them as you see fit."

⁵ The men came to Holofernes and told him all this. ⁶ Then he went down to the seacoast with his army and stationed garrisons in the fortified towns and took picked men from them as auxiliaries. ⁷ These people and all in the countryside welcomed him with garlands and dances and tambourines. ⁸ Yet he demolished all their shrines[e] and cut down their sacred groves; for he had been commissioned to destroy all the gods of the land, so that all nations should worship Nebuchadnezzar alone, and that all their dialects and tribes should call upon him as a god.

⁹ Then he came toward Esdraelon, near Dothan, facing the great ridge of Judea; ¹⁰ he camped between Geba and Scythopolis, and remained for a whole month in order to collect all the supplies for his army.

4 When the Israelites living in Judea heard of everything that Holofernes, the general of Nebuchadnezzar, the king of the Assyrians, had done to the nations, and how he had plundered and destroyed all their temples, ² they were therefore greatly terrified at his approach; they were alarmed both for Jerusalem and for the temple of the Lord their God. ³ For they had only recently returned from exile, and all the people of Judea had

---

a   Gk *sand*
b   Gk *he*
c   Or *crossed*
d   Gk *all the sheepfolds of our tents*
e   Syr: Gk *borders*

---

earth. Such images depict the entire world at war. **21–27:** The campaign builds in intensity to include plundering, slaughter, and destruction, but the geography is confused. **21:** *Upper Cilicia*, in southeastern Asia Minor, is 400 mi (650 km) from Nineveh, a distance far too great to travel on foot in *three days*. **23:** *Put*, usually Libya; *Lud*, Lydia, in central Asia Minor; *Ishmaelites*, Arabs (Gen 16.11–12). **26:** *Midianites*, a group of people who lived in southern Transjordan, sometimes depicted as nomads (Gen 37.28; Judg 6.1–6).

2.28–3.10: The surrounding nations, who had caused trouble for Israel in the past, showed initial courage before Nebuchadnezzar (1.11), but now they succumb. **2.28:** *Sidon* and *Tyre* were two Phoenician cities on the Mediterranean coast north of Israel. *Jamnia, Azotus* (earlier Ashdod), and *Ascalon* (earlier Ashkelon), were on the Mediterranean coast of Palestine. **3.8:** *All nations, dialects, and tribes* (cf. Dan 3–4). **9:** *Dothan* was south of the plain of *Esdraelon* (see 1.8n.); *Scythopolis* (formerly Beth-shan) was at the plain's eastern end.

4.1–7: Israel, now standing alone, prepares for attack. The perspective now shifts to *the Israelites living in Judea* (v. 1), allowing an opportunity for a reflection on their history; however, it is telescoped: the Assyrians actually ruled before the Judeans *returned from exile* (v. 3). **3:** The consecration of the *sacred vessels, altar,* and

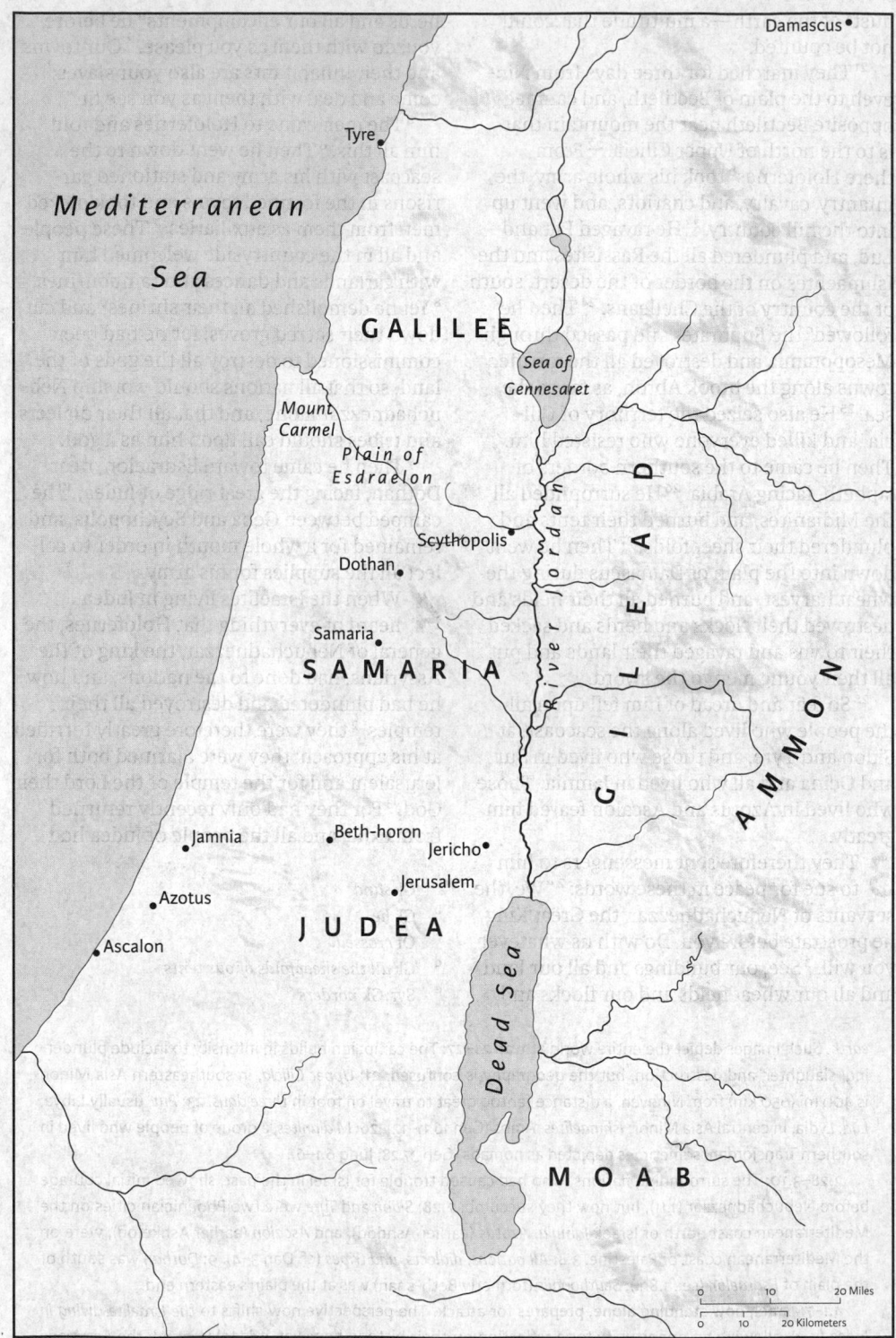

Damascus

Tyre

Mediterranean

Sea

GALILEE

Sea of
Gennesaret

Mount
Carmel

*Plain of
Esdraelon*

Scythopolis

Dothan

Samaria

S A M A R I A

River Jordan

G I L E A D

A M M O N

Jamnia

Beth-horon

Jericho

Jerusalem

Azotus

J U D E A

Dead Sea

Ascalon

M O A B

0   10   20 Miles

0   10   20 Kilometers

The geography of the book of Judith.

just now gathered together, and the sacred vessels and the altar and the temple had been consecrated after their profanation. ⁴ So they sent word to every district of Samaria, and to Kona, Beth-horon, Belmain, and Jericho, and to Choba and Aesora, and the valley of Salem. ⁵ They immediately seized all the high hilltops and fortified the villages on them and stored up food in preparation for war—since their fields had recently been harvested.

⁶ The high priest, Joakim, who was in Jerusalem at the time, wrote to the people of Bethulia and Betomesthaim, which faces Esdraelon opposite the plain near Dothan, ⁷ ordering them to seize the mountain passes, since by them Judea could be invaded; and it would be easy to stop any who tried to enter, for the approach was narrow, wide enough for only two at a time to pass.

⁸ So the Israelites did as they had been ordered by the high priest Joakim and the senate of the whole people of Israel, in session at Jerusalem. ⁹ And every man of Israel cried out to God with great fervor, and they humbled themselves with much fasting. ¹⁰ They and their wives and their children and their cattle and every resident alien and hired laborer and purchased slave—they all put sackcloth around their waists. ¹¹ And all the Israelite men, women, and children living at Jerusalem prostrated themselves before the temple and put ashes on their heads and spread out their sackcloth before the Lord.

¹² They even draped the altar with sackcloth and cried out in unison, praying fervently to the God of Israel not to allow their infants to be carried off and their wives to be taken as booty, and the towns they had inherited to be destroyed, and the sanctuary to be profaned and desecrated to the malicious joy of the Gentiles.

¹³ The Lord heard their prayers and had regard for their distress; for the people fasted many days throughout Judea and in Jerusalem before the sanctuary of the Lord Almighty. ¹⁴ The high priest Joakim and all the priests who stood before the Lord and ministered to the Lord, with sackcloth around their loins, offered the daily burnt offerings, the votive offerings, and freewill offerings of the people. ¹⁵ With ashes on their turbans, they cried out to the Lord with all their might to look with favor on the whole house of Israel.

5 It was reported to Holofernes, the general of the Assyrian army, that the people of Israel had prepared for war and had closed the mountain passes and fortified all the high hilltops and set up barricades in the plains. ² In great anger he called together all the princes of Moab and the commanders of Ammon and all the governors of the coastland, ³ and said to them, "Tell me, you Canaanites, what people is this that lives in the hill country? What towns do they inhabit? How large is their army, and in what does their power and strength consist? Who rules over them

temple ostensibly refers to the events in the late sixth century BCE after the exile (Ezra 6.13–22), but for the reader it would also evoke the more recent events after the victory of the Maccabees in 164 BCE (1 Macc 4:36–61; 2 Macc 10:1–8). Such telescoping distances the story from any specific historical event and so suggests that it concerns threats and responses in general. **4:** *Beth-horon,* 11 miles (18 km) northwest of Jerusalem. **6:** Judith's village, Bethulia ("virginity"), is named for the first time; if it is not a fictional place, its location is unknown. Although it is in Samaritan territory, Jerusalem and the Temple are always the focus.

4.8–15: Israel prays and fasts. The Israelites *humbled themselves with much fasting,* and *put sackcloth around their waists*—even the cattle! The humor is intentional (cf. Jon 3.8). The penitential theology found here became a staple of postexilic Judaism (cf. Ezra 9; Neh 9; Dan 9.4–19; Bar 1.1–3).**13:** *The Lord heard their prayers and had regard for their distress* (cf. Judg 3:9,15). Readers are assured that help is on the way, but in 7.23–31 this will be brought into question. Other novelistic texts of the period similarly predict happy endings despite building tension (Tob 3.16–17; Xenophon of Ephesus, *Ephesian Tale* 1.6). The question is not whether the protagonists will be saved, but how. **14:** For the various types of *offerings,* see Ex 29.38–41 and Lev 22.18–30.

5.1–21: Holofernes learns from Achior about Israelite identity. 1–4: Holofernes' campaign pauses for him to inquire concerning these Israelites who dare to oppose him. His military questions call forth a reflection on Jewish identity within a larger world: *In what does their power and strength consist? Who rules over them as king?* For the reader, God is king, which profoundly qualifies reverence for any earthly king. This scene introduces a recurring irony: the opponents perceive a worldly frame of reference, but Judith—and the audience—under-

as king and leads their army? [4] And why have they alone, of all who live in the west, refused to come out and meet me?"

[5] Then Achior, the leader of all the Ammonites, said to him, "May my lord please listen to a report from the mouth of your servant, and I will tell you the truth about this people that lives in the mountain district near you. No falsehood shall come from your servant's mouth. [6] These people are descended from the Chaldeans. [7] At one time they lived in Mesopotamia, because they did not wish to follow the gods of their ancestors who were in Chaldea. [8] Since they had abandoned the ways of their ancestors, and worshiped the God of heaven, the God they had come to know, their ancestors[a] drove them out from the presence of their gods. So they fled to Mesopotamia, and lived there for a long time. [9] Then their God commanded them to leave the place where they were living and go to the land of Canaan. There they settled, and grew very prosperous in gold and silver and very much livestock. [10] When a famine spread over the land of Canaan they went down to Egypt and lived there as long as they had food. There they became so great a multitude that their race could not be counted. [11] So the king of Egypt became hostile to them; he exploited them and forced them to make bricks. [12] They cried out to their God, and he afflicted the whole land of Egypt with incurable plagues. So the Egyptians drove them out of their sight. [13] Then God dried up the Red Sea before them, [14] and he led them by the way of Sinai and Kadesh-barnea. They drove out all the people of the desert, [15] and took up residence in the land of the Amorites, and by their might destroyed all the inhabitants of Heshbon; and crossing over the Jordan they took possession of all the hill country. [16] They drove out before them the Canaanites, the Perizzites, the Jebusites, the Shechemites, and all the Gergesites, and lived there a long time.

[17] "As long as they did not sin against their God they prospered, for the God who hates iniquity is with them. [18] But when they departed from the way he had prescribed for them, they were utterly defeated in many battles and were led away captive to a foreign land. The temple of their God was razed to the ground, and their towns were occupied by their enemies. [19] But now they have returned to their God, and have come back from the places where they were scattered, and have occupied Jerusalem, where their sanctuary is, and have settled in the hill country, because it was uninhabited.

[20] "So now, my master and lord, if there is any oversight in this people and they sin

a   Gk they

stand these discussions on a theological level. **5–21:** Achior's account of Israelite history is told from a Jewish, not an Ammonite, point of view and summarizes Israelite history from the time of Abraham until the return from exile. The character of the Ammonite Achior is probably inspired by the legendary Assyrian courtier Ahikar (cf. Tob 1.21–22; 14.10). He is similar to other righteous Gentiles (Josh 2–6; 2 Kings 5) and foreshadows Judith's role: he is heroic, in an almost prophetic way says many of the same things as she, and will attest to her achievements. **6–9:** The ancestral narratives from Gen 12–36. **6:** *Chaldeans,* Abraham came from Ur of the Chaldees (Gen 11.27–31), in southern Babylonia. It is characteristic of Greek and Roman ethnography to begin by noting the origins of a people. **7:** Early Jewish tradition explains that Abraham's family migrated from Chaldea because they wished to escape polytheism (*Jub.* 11.16–12.7; Josephus, *Ant.* 1.134–57). **10–13:** The descent into Egypt and the Exodus (Gen 37–Ex 18). **14:** *Sinai,* Ex 19–Num 10; *Kadesh-barnea,* Num 20.1. **15–16:** The conquests in Transjordan and Canaan (Num 20–Josh 11). **17–21:** Achior here states the Deuteronomic principle of God's conditional favor (Deut 28) that is prominent in the books of Joshua through Kings, later repeated by Judith (11. 9–15), and finally illustrated by the outcome of the story. **19:** The return from exile (Ezra 1–3).

5.22–6.21: Holofernes expels Achior, who is received in Bethulia. **6.2:** *Ephraim,* the northern part of Israel. Holofernes understands Achior's words as an attempt at prophecy and uses prophetic idioms to report Nebuchadnezzar's will (v. 4). He thus defines the conflict as a question of who is God. **6.5:** *You shall not see my face again,* highly ironic, since Achior will see Holofernes' face again—separated from the rest of his body (14.6)! Achior will not die in battle but will become a Jew (14.10). At least some of Holofernes' words will indeed come true, but not as he assumes. **20:** His banquet upon being received will be balanced by Judith's smaller banquet when she is received by Holofernes (12.1).

against their God and we find out their offense, then we can go up and defeat them. ²¹ But if they are not a guilty nation, then let my lord pass them by; for their Lord and God will defend them, and we shall become the laughingstock of the whole world."

²² When Achior had finished saying these things, all the people standing around the tent began to complain; Holofernes' officers and all the inhabitants of the seacoast and Moab insisted that he should be cut to pieces. ²³ They said, "We are not afraid of the Israelites; they are a people with no strength or power for making war. ²⁴ Therefore let us go ahead, Lord Holofernes, and your vast army will swallow them up."

6 When the disturbance made by the people outside the council had died down, Holofernes, the commander of the Assyrian army, said to Achior[a] in the presence of all the foreign contingents:

² "Who are you, Achior and you mercenaries of Ephraim, to prophesy among us as you have done today and tell us not to make war against the people of Israel because their God will defend them? What god is there except Nebuchadnezzar? He will send his forces and destroy them from the face of the earth. Their God will not save them; ³ we the king's[b] servants will destroy them as one man. They cannot resist the might of our cavalry. ⁴ We will overwhelm them;[c] their mountains will be drunk with their blood, and their fields will be full of their dead. Not even their footprints will survive our attack; they will utterly perish. So says King Nebuchadnezzar, lord of the whole earth. For he has spoken; none of his words shall be in vain.

⁵ "As for you, Achior, you Ammonite mercenary, you have said these words in a moment of perversity; you shall not see my face again from this day until I take revenge on this race that came out of Egypt. ⁶ Then at my return the sword of my army and the spear[d] of my servants shall pierce your sides, and you shall fall among their wounded. ⁷ Now my slaves are going to take you back into the hill country and put you in one of the towns beside the passes. ⁸ You will not die until you perish along with them. ⁹ If you really hope in your heart that they will not be taken, then do not look downcast! I have

spoken, and none of my words shall fail to come true."

¹⁰ Then Holofernes ordered his slaves, who waited on him in his tent, to seize Achior and take him away to Bethulia and hand him over to the Israelites. ¹¹ So the slaves took him and led him out of the camp into the plain, and from the plain they went up into the hill country and came to the springs below Bethulia. ¹² When the men of the town saw them,[e] they seized their weapons and ran out of the town to the top of the hill, and all the slingers kept them from coming up by throwing stones at them. ¹³ So having taken shelter below the hill, they bound Achior and left him lying at the foot of the hill, and returned to their master.

¹⁴ Then the Israelites came down from their town and found him; they untied him and brought him into Bethulia and placed him before the magistrates of their town, ¹⁵ who in those days were Uzziah son of Micah, of the tribe of Simeon, and Chabris son of Gothoniel, and Charmis son of Melchiel. ¹⁶ They called together all the elders of the town, and all their young men and women ran to the assembly. They set Achior in the midst of all their people, and Uzziah questioned him about what had happened. ¹⁷ He answered and told them what had taken place at the council of Holofernes, and all that he had said in the presence of the Assyrian leaders, and all that Holofernes had boasted he would do against the house of Israel. ¹⁸ Then the people fell down and worshiped God, and cried out:

¹⁹ "O Lord God of heaven, see their arrogance, and have pity on our people in their humiliation, and look kindly today on the faces of those who are consecrated to you."

²⁰ Then they reassured Achior, and praised him highly. ²¹ Uzziah took him from the assembly to his own house and gave a banquet for the elders; and all that night they called on the God of Israel for help.

---

a Other ancient authorities add *and to all the Moabites*

b Gk *his*

c Other ancient authorities add *with it*

d Lat Syr: Gk *people*

e Other ancient authorities add *on the top of the hill*

7 The next day Holofernes ordered his whole army, and all the allies who had joined him, to break camp and move against Bethulia, and to seize the passes up into the hill country and make war on the Israelites. [2] So all their warriors marched off that day; their fighting forces numbered one hundred seventy thousand infantry and twelve thousand cavalry, not counting the baggage and the foot soldiers handling it, a very great multitude. [3] They encamped in the valley near Bethulia, beside the spring, and they spread out in breadth over Dothan as far as Balbaim and in length from Bethulia to Cyamon, which faces Esdraelon.

[4] When the Israelites saw their vast numbers, they were greatly terrified and said to one another, "They will now strip clean the whole land; neither the high mountains nor the valleys nor the hills will bear their weight." [5] Yet they all seized their weapons, and when they had kindled fires on their towers, they remained on guard all that night.

[6] On the second day Holofernes led out all his cavalry in full view of the Israelites in Bethulia. [7] He reconnoitered the approaches to their town, and visited the springs that supplied their water; he seized them and set guards of soldiers over them, and then returned to his army.

[8] Then all the chieftains of the Edomites and all the leaders of the Moabites and the commanders of the coastland came to him and said, [9] "Listen to what we have to say, my lord, and your army will suffer no losses. [10] This people, the Israelites, do not rely on their spears but on the height of the mountains where they live, for it is not easy to reach the tops of their mountains. [11] Therefore, my lord, do not fight against them in regular formation, and not a man of your army will fall. [12] Remain in your camp, and keep all the men in your forces with you; let your servants take possession of the spring of water that flows from the foot of the mountain, [13] for this is where all the people of Bethulia get their water. So thirst will destroy them, and they will surrender their town. Meanwhile, we and our people will go up to the tops of the nearby mountains and camp there to keep watch to see that no one gets out of the town. [14] They and their wives and children will waste away with famine, and before the sword reaches them they will be strewn about in the streets where they live. [15] Thus you will pay them back with evil, because they rebelled and did not receive you peaceably."

[16] These words pleased Holofernes and all his attendants, and he gave orders to do as they had said. [17] So the army of the Ammonites moved forward, together with five thousand Assyrians, and they encamped in the valley and seized the water supply and the springs of the Israelites. [18] And the Edomites and Ammonites went up and encamped in the hill country opposite Dothan; and they sent some of their men toward the south and the east, toward Egrebeh, which is near Chusi beside the Wadi Mochmur. The rest of the Assyrian army encamped in the plain, and covered the whole face of the land. Their tents and supply trains spread out in great number, and they formed a vast multitude.

[19] The Israelites then cried out to the Lord their God, for their courage failed, because all their enemies had surrounded them, and there was no way of escape from them. [20] The whole Assyrian army, their infantry, chariots, and cavalry, surrounded them for thirty-four days, until all the water containers of every inhabitant of Bethulia were empty; [21] their cisterns were going dry, and on no day did they have enough water to drink, for their drinking water was rationed. [22] Their children were listless, and the women and young men fainted from thirst and were collapsing in the streets of the town and in the gateways; they no longer had any strength.

7.1–18: Holofernes advances on Bethulia and prepares for a siege. Again, the size of the army is emphasized, covering an entire valley (see 2.15–20n). They will *strip clean the whole land* like locusts. The action is drawn out and presented visually to give the full impression of the forces arrayed against Bethulia. 8: The historical enemies of Israel, *Edomites* and *Moabites*, recommend a siege, so that Bethulia will fall for lack of water.
7.19–32: Israelites in Bethulia begin to despair. The predictions of Holofernes' advisers appear to be coming true. Just as lack of water led to murmuring in Ex 17.1–7, so also here; Moses' role is paralleled by both Uzziah

23 Then all the people, the young men, the women, and the children, gathered around Uzziah and the rulers of the town and cried out with a loud voice, and said before all the elders, 24 "Let God judge between you and us! You have done us a great injury in not making peace with the Assyrians. 25 For now we have no one to help us; God has sold us into their hands, to be strewn before them in thirst and exhaustion. 26 Now summon them and surrender the whole town as booty to the army of Holofernes and to all his forces. 27 For it would be better for us to be captured by them.a We shall indeed become slaves, but our lives will be spared, and we shall not witness our little ones dying before our eyes, and our wives and children drawing their last breath. 28 We call to witness against you heaven and earth and our God, the Lord of our ancestors, who punishes us for our sins and the sins of our ancestors; do today the things that we have described!"

29 Then great and general lamentation arose throughout the assembly, and they cried out to the Lord God with a loud voice. 30 But Uzziah said to them, "Courage, my brothers and sisters!b Let us hold out for five days more; by that time the Lord our God will turn his mercy to us again, for he will not forsake us utterly. 31 But if these days pass by, and no help comes for us, I will do as you say."

32 Then he dismissed the people to their various posts, and they went up on the walls

and towers of their town. The women and children he sent home. In the town they were in great misery.

8 Now in those days Judith heard about these things: she was the daughter of Merari son of Ox son of Joseph son of Oziel son of Elkiah son of Ananias son of Gideon son of Raphain son of Ahitub son of Elijah son of Hilkiah son of Eliab son of Nathanael son of Salamiel son of Sarasadai son of Israel. 2 Her husband Manasseh, who belonged to her tribe and family, had died during the barley harvest. 3 For as he stood overseeing those who were binding sheaves in the field, he was overcome by the burning heat, and took to his bed and died in his town Bethulia. So they buried him with his ancestors in the field between Dothan and Balamon. 4 Judith remained as a widow for three years and four months 5 at home where she set up a tent for herself on the roof of her house. She put sackcloth around her waist and dressed in widow's clothing. 6 She fasted all the days of her widowhood, except the day before the sabbath and the sabbath itself, the day before the new moon and the day of the new moon, and the festivals and days of rejoicing of the house of Israel. 7 She was beautiful in appearance, and was very lovely to behold. Her husband Manasseh had left her gold and silver, men and women slaves, livestock, and fields; and she

a Other ancient authorities add *than to die of thirst*
b Gk *Courage, brothers*

and Judith. 28: *Our sins and the sins of our ancestors*, the Israelites blame themselves for their predicaments (cf. Judith's interpretation in 8.18,27). 30: Uzziah urges that they *hold out for five days more*. A similar story is told of the Greek city of Lindos, in which the citizens, besieged by the Persians, pray to Athena to send rain within five days. The goddess comes to their aid by bringing rain to them and drought to the Persians. Judith, however, will later have none of this; she will condemn the Bethulians for setting a deadline on God's help (see 8.11–17). 7.32: Calm descends on Bethulia, but it is the calm of despair. This makes an effective conclusion to the first half and a transition to the introduction of the person who will save Bethulia and thus Israel: Judith.

8.1–16.25: Part II: Judith rescues her people.

8.1–8: Judith is introduced. 1: Judith's name, in Greek "Ioudith," in Hebrew "Yehudit," is the feminine for Judean or Jew. Her name suggests that Bethulia and Jerusalem will be saved by the ideal Jewish woman, and it also echoes the name of one of the leaders of the Maccabean revolt, Judas Maccabeus. She is given the longest genealogy of any woman in the Bible, but it is likely fictitious. Many of the names are unknown, although it includes *Israel*, i.e., Jacob. 2–3: The death of her husband from sunstroke provides an unheroic contrast to Judith's actions. Other male characters will also be passive in contrast to her. 4–6: Judith's piety is exemplary, and her period of mourning is far greater than prescribed in Jewish law, suggesting a new mode of ascetic practice. In keeping with Jewish law, she does not fast on festive holidays. 7–8: Judith's beauty and wealth give her a larger-than-life quality, but her devotion to God is the source of her strength.

maintained this estate. [8] No one spoke ill of her, for she feared God with great devotion.

[9] When Judith heard the harsh words spoken by the people against the ruler, because they were faint for lack of water, and when she heard all that Uzziah said to them, and how he promised them under oath to surrender the town to the Assyrians after five days, [10] she sent her maid, who was in charge of all she possessed, to summon Uzziah and[a] Chabris and Charmis, the elders of her town. [11] They came to her, and she said to them:

"Listen to me, rulers of the people of Bethulia! What you have said to the people today is not right; you have even sworn and pronounced this oath between God and you, promising to surrender the town to our enemies unless the Lord turns and helps us within so many days. [12] Who are you to put God to the test today, and to set yourselves up in the place of[b] God in human affairs? [13] You are putting the Lord Almighty to the test, but you will never learn anything! [14] You cannot plumb the depths of the human heart or understand the workings of the human mind; how do you expect to search out God, who made all these things, and find out his mind or comprehend his thought? No, my brothers, do not anger the Lord our God. [15] For if he does not choose to help us within these five days, he has power to protect us within any time he pleases, or even to destroy us in the presence of our enemies. [16] Do not try to bind the purposes of the Lord our God; for God is not like a human being, to be threatened, or like a mere mortal, to be won over by pleading. [17] Therefore, while we wait for his deliverance, let us call upon him to help us, and he will hear our voice, if it pleases him.

[18] "For never in our generation, nor in these present days, has there been any tribe or family or people or town of ours that worships gods made with hands, as was done in days gone by. [19] That was why our ancestors were handed over to the sword and to pillage, and so they suffered a great catastrophe before our enemies. [20] But we know no other god but him, and so we hope that he will not disdain us or any of our nation. [21] For if we are captured, all Judea will be captured and our sanctuary will be plundered; and he will make us pay for its desecration with our blood. [22] The slaughter of our kindred and the captivity of the land and the desolation of our inheritance—all this he will bring on our heads among the Gentiles, wherever we serve as slaves; and we shall be an offense and a disgrace in the eyes of those who acquire us. [23] For our slavery will not bring us into favor, but the Lord our God will turn it to dishonor.

[24] "Therefore, my brothers, let us set an example for our kindred, for their lives depend upon us, and the sanctuary—both the temple and the altar—rests upon us. [25] In spite of everything let us give thanks to the Lord our God, who is putting us to the test as he did our ancestors. [26] Remember what he did with Abraham, and how he tested Isaac, and what happened to Jacob in Syrian Mesopotamia, while he was tending the sheep of Laban, his mother's brother. [27] For he has not tried us with fire, as he did them, to search their hearts, nor has he taken vengeance on us; but the Lord scourges those who are close to him in order to admonish them."

[28] Then Uzziah said to her, "All that you have said was spoken out of a true heart, and there is no one who can deny your words. [29] Today is not the first time your wisdom

---

a   Other ancient authorities lack *Uzziah and* (see verses 28 and 35)

b   Or *above*

8.9–27: Judith upbraids the town leaders. 10: Her unnamed *maid*, a slave, is responsible for her affairs. Slaves could wield the authority of their owners. **11:** That *they came to her* indicates Judith's important status in the community. **12:** Judith will insist that they pray to God (v.17), but they may not *put God to the test* by setting a date, a violation of Deut 6.16. **18–19:** A theme of this story is the Deuteronomic principle that if Jews sin, they will be defeated, but if they remain righteous, God will protect them (Deut 28). Judith's description of the present righteousness idealizes the period after the Maccabean Revolt when the Temple had been rededicated. **25–27:** Rather than testing God, it is God who tests Israel, as God tested *Abraham* (Gen 22), *Isaac*, and *Jacob* (Gen 29). Israelite history is echoed often in Judith.

8.28–36: Judith's powerful words win over Uzziah and the citizens. Just as Holofernes in the first half spends much of his time in war councils, Judith holds a war council with the Bethulians. **29:** The Bethulians have always

has been shown, but from the beginning of your life all the people have recognized your understanding, for your heart's disposition is right. ³⁰ But the people were so thirsty that they compelled us to do for them what we have promised, and made us take an oath that we cannot break. ³¹ Now since you are a God-fearing woman, pray for us, so that the Lord may send us rain to fill our cisterns. Then we will no longer feel faint from thirst."

³² Then Judith said to them, "Listen to me. I am about to do something that will go down through all generations of our descendants. ³³ Stand at the town gate tonight so that I may go out with my maid; and within the days after which you have promised to surrender the town to our enemies, the Lord will deliver Israel by my hand. ³⁴ Only, do not try to find out what I am doing; for I will not tell you until I have finished what I am about to do."

³⁵ Uzziah and the rulers said to her, "Go in peace, and may the Lord God go before you, to take vengeance on our enemies." ³⁶ So they returned from the tent and went to their posts.

9 Then Judith prostrated herself, put ashes on her head, and uncovered the sack-cloth she was wearing. At the very time when the evening incense was being offered in the house of God in Jerusalem, Judith cried out to the Lord with a loud voice, and said,

² "O Lord God of my ancestor Simeon, to whom you gave a sword to take revenge on those strangers who had torn off a virgin's clothing[a] to defile her, and exposed her thighs to put her to shame, and polluted her womb to disgrace her; for you said, 'It shall

not be done'—yet they did it; ³ so you gave up their rulers to be killed, and their bed, which was ashamed of the deceit they had practiced, was stained with blood, and you struck down slaves along with princes, and princes on their thrones. ⁴ You gave up their wives for booty and their daughters to captivity, and all their booty to be divided among your beloved children who burned with zeal for you and abhorred the pollution of their blood and called on you for help. O God, my God, hear me also, a widow.

⁵ "For you have done these things and those that went before and those that followed. You have designed the things that are now, and those that are to come. What you had in mind has happened; ⁶ the things you decided on presented themselves and said, 'Here we are!' For all your ways are prepared in advance, and your judgment is with fore-knowledge.

⁷ "Here now are the Assyrians, a greatly increased force, priding themselves in their horses and riders, boasting in the strength of their foot soldiers, and trusting in shield and spear, in bow and sling. They do not know that you are the Lord who crushes wars; the Lord is your name. ⁸ Break their strength by your might, and bring down their power in your anger; for they intend to defile your sanctuary, and to pollute the tabernacle where your glorious name resides, and to break off the horns[b] of your altar with the sword. ⁹ Look at their pride, and send your

a Cn: Gk *loosed her womb*
b Syr: Gk *horn*

respected Judith's wisdom; her traits are similar to personified Wisdom (Prov 8.6) and the capable wife (Prov 31.10–31). However, her wisdom will exceed the usual standards for wise women. **30**: Thirst had rendered the people weak, and the passive leaders, unlike Judith, had acquiesced. **32–34**: Judith keeps her plan secret, in contrast to Nebuchadnezzar who reveals his secret plan to his advisors (2.2), and places her confidence in God that it will succeed. It will be remembered by *all generations* (cf. 16.21–25).

9.1–14: Judith prepares through prayer. 1: *Ashes* and *sackcloth* are signs of mourning and affliction. Judith's prayer coincides with the offering of evening incense (Ex 30.8). **2–8**: She invokes the sins of the invaders and the revenge of *my ancestor Simeon* on Shechem for raping Dinah (Gen 34). Although Simeon's revenge is characterized as excessive and foolhardy in Gen 34.30; 49.5–7, here it is considered justified, as in *Jub.* 30. **8**: The *horns* of the altar were projections with symbolic importance; see Ex 27.2; 1 Kings 1.50; 2.28; Am 3.14. **9–10**: Judith prays that God strike down Holofernes by the hand of a *widow* and a *woman*, a reversal found also at Judg 4; 5; 9.53–54. Like Simeon, Judith will use *deceit*—not a last-minute expedient but the basis of her plan and her prayer all along. By contrast, a weaker male, Achior, insisted rightly that he would speak only truth (5.5). Although rejected in wisdom texts (Prov 6.16–19; Wis 1.8; Jas 3.5–12), deceit is celebrated in this story, and

wrath upon their heads. Give to me, a widow, the strong hand to do what I plan. [10] By the deceit of my lips strike down the slave with the prince and the prince with his servant; crush their arrogance by the hand of a woman.

[11] "For your strength does not depend on numbers, nor your might on the powerful. But you are the God of the lowly, helper of the oppressed, upholder of the weak, protector of the forsaken, savior of those without hope. [12] Please, please, God of my father, God of the heritage of Israel, Lord of heaven and earth, Creator of the waters, King of all your creation, hear my prayer! [13] Make my deceitful words bring wound and bruise on those who have planned cruel things against your covenant, and against your sacred house, and against Mount Zion, and against the house your children possess. [14] Let your whole nation and every tribe know and understand that you are God, the God of all power and might, and that there is no other who protects the people of Israel but you alone!"

10 When Judith[a] had stopped crying out to the God of Israel, and had ended all these words, [2] she rose from where she lay prostrate. She called her maid and went down into the house where she lived on sabbaths and on her festal days. [3] She removed the sackcloth she had been wearing, took off her widow's garments, bathed her body with water, and anointed herself with precious ointment. She combed her hair, put on a tiara, and dressed herself in the festive attire that she used to wear while her husband Manasseh was living. [4] She put sandals on her feet, and put on her anklets, bracelets, rings, earrings, and all her other jewelry. Thus she made herself very beautiful, to entice the eyes of all the men who might see her. [5] She gave her maid a skin of wine and a flask of oil, and filled a bag with roasted grain, dried fig cakes, and fine bread;[b] then she wrapped up all her dishes and gave them to her to carry.

[6] Then they went out to the town gate of Bethulia and found Uzziah standing there with the elders of the town, Chabris and Charmis. [7] When they saw her transformed in appearance and dressed differently, they were very greatly astounded at her beauty and said to her, [8] "May the God of our ancestors grant you favor and fulfill your plans, so that the people of Israel may glory and Jerusalem may be exalted." She bowed down to God.

[9] Then she said to them, "Order the gate of the town to be opened for me so that I may go out and accomplish the things you have just said to me." So they ordered the young men to open the gate for her, as she requested. [10] When they had done this, Judith went out, accompanied by her maid. The men of the town watched her until she had gone down the mountain and passed through the valley, where they lost sight of her.

[11] As the women[c] were going straight on through the valley, an Assyrian patrol met her [12] and took her into custody. They asked her, "To what people do you belong, and where are you coming from, and where are you going?" She replied, "I am a daughter of the Hebrews, but I am fleeing from them, for they are about

a Gk *she*
b Other ancient authorities add *and cheese*
c Gk *they*

elsewhere is often used by tricksters and those less powerful than their adversaries, such as Rebekah (Gen 27), Jacob (Gen 27), Rachel (Gen 31), Tamar (Gen 38), and Abraham (Gen 12; 20).

10.1–10: Judith puts her plan into motion. 1–4: Judith wore sackcloth while praying, but now dresses in beautiful clothes (cf. Add Esth 15). **3:** Given the lack of water in Bethulia, Judith's decision to bathe *her body with water* indicates the significance of her mission. **5:** Judith's provisions will allow her to keep the dietary laws while with the Assyrians (cf. Dan 1.8–16). Her maid will be a silent, efficient, loyal counterpart to Holofernes' talkative assistant, Bagoas. **6–10:** The ritualized departure slows the rhythm of the story here, and the visual detail is striking. Once Judith passes through the gate of the city, almost every word out of her mouth will be deceitful and every action sexually provocative or murderous.

10.11–23: Judith meets the guards and is taken to Holofernes. 13–16: Ironically and humorously, readers already see that her *true report* will be a lie. Nearly every line of dialogue that follows can be read ironically as well: *You have saved your life by hurrying down to see our lord* (v. 15) can be heard by the audience as referring to God. The obtuseness of the Assyrians, even about the meanings of their own words, is likely intended as

to be handed over to you to be devoured. ¹³ I am on my way to see Holofernes the commander of your army, to give him a true report; I will show him a way by which he can go and capture all the hill country without losing one of his men, captured or slain."

¹⁴ When the men heard her words, and observed her face—she was in their eyes marvelously beautiful—they said to her, ¹⁵ "You have saved your life by hurrying down to see our lord. Go at once to his tent; some of us will escort you and hand you over to him. ¹⁶ When you stand before him, have no fear in your heart, but tell him what you have just said, and he will treat you well."

¹⁷ They chose from their number a hundred men to accompany her and her maid, and they brought them to the tent of Holofernes. ¹⁸ There was great excitement in the whole camp, for her arrival was reported from tent to tent. They came and gathered around her as she stood outside the tent of Holofernes, waiting until they told him about her. ¹⁹ They marveled at her beauty and admired the Israelites, judging them by her. They said to one another, "Who can despise these people, who have women like this among them? It is not wise to leave one of their men alive, for if we let them go they will be able to beguile the whole world!"

²⁰ Then the guards of Holofernes and all his servants came out and led her into the tent. ²¹ Holofernes was resting on his bed under a canopy that was woven with purple and gold, emeralds and other precious stones. ²² When they told him of her, he came to the front of the tent, with silver lamps carried before him. ²³ When Judith came into the presence of Holofernes^a and his servants, they all marveled at the beauty of her face. She prostrated herself and did obeisance to him, but his slaves raised her up.

11 Then Holofernes said to her, "Take courage, woman, and do not be afraid in your heart, for I have never hurt anyone

who chose to serve Nebuchadnezzar, king of all the earth. ² Even now, if your people who live in the hill country had not slighted me, I would never have lifted my spear against them. They have brought this on themselves. ³ But now tell me why you have fled from them and have come over to us. In any event, you have come to safety. Take courage! You will live tonight and ever after. ⁴ No one will hurt you. Rather, all will treat you well, as they do the servants of my lord King Nebuchadnezzar."

⁵ Judith answered him, "Accept the words of your slave, and let your servant speak in your presence. I will say nothing false to my lord this night. ⁶ If you follow out the words of your servant, God will accomplish something through you, and my lord will not fail to achieve his purposes. ⁷ By the life of Nebuchadnezzar, king of the whole earth, and by the power of him who has sent you to direct every living being! Not only do human beings serve him because of you, but also the animals of the field and the cattle and the birds of the air will live, because of your power, under Nebuchadnezzar and all his house. ⁸ For we have heard of your wisdom and skill, and it is reported throughout the whole world that you alone are the best in the whole kingdom, the most informed and the most astounding in military strategy.

⁹ "Now as for Achior's speech in your council, we have heard his words, for the people of Bethulia spared him and he told them all he had said to you. ¹⁰ Therefore, lord and master, do not disregard what he said, but keep it in your mind, for it is true. Indeed our nation cannot be punished, nor can the sword prevail against them, unless they sin against their God.

¹¹ "But now, in order that my lord may not be defeated and his purpose frustrated, death

^a Gk *him*

---

humorous. **20–22:** Holofernes' tent is decorated with luxurious items like a harem chamber.
11.1–23: Judith's dialogue with Holofernes. **1:** Holofernes also speaks a mixture of truth and lies (see 3.2–8).
6: Judith's double meanings continue with the ambiguity in her statement: *My lord will not fail to achieve his purposes.* **7:** This grandiose view of Nebuchadnezzar is also played upon in Dan 2.37–38; 4.12 (cf. Jer 27.6; 28.14). Judith cleverly adapts the praise of Nebuchadnezzar to flatter Holofernes. **9–15:** That Holofernes would have believed any part of her story is preposterous, but this only makes the fictional world more enjoyable. **9:** *Achior's*

will fall upon them, for a sin has overtaken them by which they are about to provoke their God to anger when they do what is wrong. ¹² Since their food supply is exhausted and their water has almost given out, they have planned to kill their livestock and have determined to use all that God by his laws has forbidden them to eat. ¹³ They have decided to consume the first fruits of the grain and the tithes of the wine and oil, which they had consecrated and set aside for the priests who minister in the presence of our God in Jerusalem—things it is not lawful for any of the people even to touch with their hands. ¹⁴ Since even the people in Jerusalem have been doing this, they have sent messengers there in order to bring back permission from the council of the elders. ¹⁵ When the response reaches them and they act upon it, on that very day they will be handed over to you to be destroyed.

¹⁶ "So when I, your slave, learned all this, I fled from them. God has sent me to accomplish with you things that will astonish the whole world wherever people shall hear about them. ¹⁷ Your servant is indeed God-fearing and serves the God of heaven night and day. So, my lord, I will remain with you; but every night your servant will go out into the valley and pray to God. He will tell me when they have committed their sins. ¹⁸ Then I will come and tell you, so that you may go out with your whole army, and not one of them will be able to withstand you. ¹⁹ Then I will lead you through Judea, until you come to Jerusalem; there I will set your throne.ᵃ You will drive them like sheep that have no shepherd, and no dog will so much as growl at you. For this was told me to give me foreknowledge; it was announced to me, and I was sent to tell you."

²⁰ Her words pleased Holofernes and all his servants. They marveled at her wisdom and said, ²¹ "No other woman from one end of the earth to the other looks so beautiful or speaks so wisely!" ²² Then Holofernes said to her, "God has done well to send you ahead of the people, to strengthen our hands and bring destruction on those who have despised my lord. ²³ You are not only beautiful in appearance, but wise in speech. If you do as you have said, your God shall be my God, and you shall live in the palace of King Nebuchadnezzar and be renowned throughout the whole world."

12 Then he commanded them to bring her in where his silver dinnerware was kept, and ordered them to set a table for her with some of his own delicacies, and with some of his own wine to drink. ² But Judith said, "I cannot partake of them, or it will be an offense; but I will have enough with the things I brought with me." ³ Holofernes said to her, "If your supply runs out, where can we get you more of the same? For none of your people are here with us." ⁴ Judith replied, "As surely as you live, my lord, your servant will not use up the supplies I have with me before the Lord carries out by my hand what he has determined."

⁵ Then the servants of Holofernes brought her into the tent, and she slept until midnight. Toward the morning watch she got up ⁶ and sent this message to Holofernes: "Let my lord now give orders to allow your servant to go out and pray." ⁷ So Holofernes commanded his guards not to hinder her. She remained in the camp three days. She went out each night to the valley of Bethulia, and bathed at the spring in the camp.ᵇ ⁸ After bathing, she prayed the Lord God of Israel to direct her way for the triumph of hisᶜ people. ⁹ Then she returned purified and stayed in the tent until she ate her food toward evening.

ᵃ Or *chariot*
ᵇ Other ancient authorities lack *in the camp*
ᶜ Other ancient authorities read *her*

speech, see 5.5–21. **13**: *First fruits*, Ex 23.19; *tithes*, Lev 27.30. **17**: Even Judith's piety is deceitful; she establishes a prayer discipline that will allow her to escape unnoticed (13.3,10), just as her pouch for kosher food will also serve a different and macabre purpose. **22–23**: Holofernes unknowingly speaks the truth in double meanings: *bring destruction on those who have despised my lord; your God shall be my God*—in judgment!

12.1–9: Judith's daily schedule within Holofernes' camp. Judith imposes her schedule on Holofernes, which allows her to keep the dietary laws and to pray (cf. Dan 1.8–19). **8**: Her daily *bathing* may be a ritual bath; similar rituals were practiced at Qumran.

¹⁰ On the fourth day Holofernes held a banquet for his personal attendants only, and did not invite any of his officers. ¹¹ He said to Bagoas, the eunuch who had charge of his personal affairs, "Go and persuade the Hebrew woman who is in your care to join us and to eat and drink with us. ¹² For it would be a disgrace if we let such a woman go without having intercourse with her. If we do not seduce her, she will laugh at us."

¹³ So Bagoas left the presence of Holofernes, and approached her and said, "Let this pretty girl not hesitate to come to my lord to be honored in his presence, and to enjoy drinking wine with us, and to become today like one of the Assyrian women who serve in the palace of Nebuchadnezzar." ¹⁴ Judith replied, "Who am I to refuse my lord? Whatever pleases him I will do at once, and it will be a joy to me until the day of my death." ¹⁵ So she proceeded to dress herself in all her woman's finery. Her maid went ahead and spread for her on the ground before Holofernes the lambskins she had received from Bagoas for her daily use in reclining.

¹⁶ Then Judith came in and lay down. Holofernes' heart was ravished with her and his passion was aroused, for he had been waiting for an opportunity to seduce her from the day he first saw her. ¹⁷ So Holofernes said to her, "Have a drink and be merry with us!" ¹⁸ Judith said, "I will gladly drink, my lord, because today is the greatest day in my whole life." ¹⁹ Then she took what her maid had prepared and ate and drank before him. ²⁰ Holofernes was greatly pleased with her, and drank a great quantity of wine, much more than he had ever drunk in any one day since he was born.

13 When evening came, his slaves quickly withdrew. Bagoas closed the tent from outside and shut out the attendants from his master's presence. They went to bed, for they all were weary because the banquet had lasted so long. ² But Judith was left alone in the tent, with Holofernes stretched out on his bed, for he was dead drunk.

³ Now Judith had told her maid to stand outside the bedchamber and to wait for her to come out, as she did on the other days; for she said she would be going out for her prayers. She had said the same thing to Bagoas. ⁴ So everyone went out, and no one, either small or great, was left in the bedchamber. Then Judith, standing beside his bed, said in her heart, "O Lord God of all might, look in this hour on the work of my hands for the exaltation of Jerusalem. ⁵ Now indeed is the time to help your heritage and to carry out my design to destroy the enemies who have risen up against us."

⁶ She went up to the bedpost near Holofernes' head, and took down his sword that hung there. ⁷ She came close to his bed, took hold of the hair of his head, and said, "Give me strength today, O Lord God of Israel!" ⁸ Then she struck his neck twice with all her might, and cut off his head. ⁹ Next she rolled his body off the bed and pulled down the canopy from the posts. Soon afterward she went out and gave Holofernes' head to her maid, ¹⁰ who placed it in her food bag.

12.10–20: Holofernes invites Judith to a banquet. 11–13: *Bagoas,* see 2.4n. Both Holofernes and Bagoas reveal by their words that they are putty in Judith's hands, an ironic contrast with the power they think they have. In the Greek novels the beautiful heroine is often threatened with the prospect of being forced to marry a king or become a courtesan, but here Judith is fully in charge and can manipulate the suggestion. **15:** The lambskins may symbolically protect Judith from impurity (cf. Josephus, *Ant.* 3.270, *m. Sot.* 2:4). **16–20:** Holofernes thinks that he will seduce Judith, but it is *she* who seduces *him* into drinking *more than he had ever drunk* before. She seems as excited as Holofernes, but for an entirely different reason. Again, Judith speaks the truth that she intends to be misunderstood by Holofernes.

13.1–10a: Judith beheads Holofernes 1–3: Chs 1–12 have been building in tension for this moment. The story has been intentionally delayed before but proceeds quickly now, with the beheading scene told in seven verses. **6–10a:** Judith's actions and words also have biblical precedents, including David slaying Goliath (1 Sam 17.46) and Jael slaying Sisera (Judg 4–5). Holofernes' *canopy* and *head* are collected as trophies, which will be important later. The *food bag* is now seen to be part of her plan to kill Holofernes as well.

13.10b–20: Judith and her maid return to Bethulia. The daily prayers of Judith and her maid now make it

Then the two of them went out together, as they were accustomed to do for prayer. They passed through the camp, circled around the valley, and went up the mountain to Bethulia, and came to its gates. [11] From a distance Judith called out to the sentries at the gates, "Open, open the gate! God, our God, is with us, still showing his power in Israel and his strength against our enemies, as he has done today!"

[12] When the people of her town heard her voice, they hurried down to the town gate and summoned the elders of the town. [13] They all ran together, both small and great, for it seemed unbelievable that she had returned. They opened the gate and welcomed them. Then they lit a fire to give light, and gathered around them. [14] Then she said to them with a loud voice, "Praise God, O praise him! Praise God, who has not withdrawn his mercy from the house of Israel, but has destroyed our enemies by my hand this very night!"

[15] Then she pulled the head out of the bag and showed it to them, and said, "See here, the head of Holofernes, the commander of the Assyrian army, and here is the canopy beneath which he lay in his drunken stupor. The Lord has struck him down by the hand of a woman. [16] As the Lord lives, who has protected me in the way I went, I swear that it was my face that seduced him to his destruction, and that he committed no sin with me, to defile and shame me."

[17] All the people were greatly astonished. They bowed down and worshiped God, and said with one accord, "Blessed are you our God, who have this day humiliated the enemies of your people."

[18] Then Uzziah said to her, "O daughter, you are blessed by the Most High God above all other women on earth; and blessed be the Lord God, who created the heavens and the earth, who has guided you to cut off the head of the leader of our enemies. [19] Your praise[a] will never depart from the hearts of those who remember the power of God. [20] May God grant this to be a perpetual honor to you, and may he reward you with blessings, because you risked your own life when our nation was brought low, and you averted our ruin, walking in the straight path before our God." And all the people said, "Amen. Amen."

14 Then Judith said to them, "Listen to me, my friends. Take this head and hang it upon the parapet of your wall. [2] As soon as day breaks and the sun rises on the earth, each of you take up your weapons, and let every able-bodied man go out of the town; set a captain over them, as if you were going down to the plain against the Assyrian outpost; only do not go down. [3] Then they will seize their arms and go into the camp and rouse the officers of the Assyrian army. They will rush into the tent of Holofernes and will not find him. Then panic will come over them, and they will flee before you. [4] Then you and all who live within the borders of Israel will pursue them and cut them down in their tracks. [5] But before you do all this, bring Achior the Ammonite to me so that he may see and recognize the man who despised the house of Israel and sent him to us as if to his death."

[6] So they summoned Achior from the house of Uzziah. When he came and saw the head of Holofernes in the hand of one of the men in the assembly of the people, he fell down on his face in a faint. [7] When they raised him up he threw himself at Judith's feet, and did obeisance to her, and said, "Blessed are you in every tent of Judah! In every nation those who hear your name will be alarmed. [8] Now tell me what you have done during these days."

So Judith told him in the presence of the people all that she had done, from the day

---

[a] Other ancient authorities read *hope*

possible for them to arouse no suspicion as they escape (11.17; 12.7). **15:** *By the hand of a woman,* see 9.9–10n.

18–20: Judith's deed is met with a blessing similar to Deborah's blessing of Jael for killing the Canaanite general Sisera (Judg 5.24).

14.1–10: Judith plans for a military victory, and Achior converts. Judith again orders the Bethulians into action and demonstrates her control over the Assyrians. On exhibiting the enemy's *head,* cf. 1 Sam 17.54; 31.9–10; 2 Kings 10.7–8; Matt 14.8; 1 Macc 7.47; 2 Macc 15.35. The last two are significant because Judith's name may be a play on that of Judas Maccabeus, whose exhibition of the head of Nicanor also resulted in an annual celebra-

she left until the moment she began speaking to them. ⁹ When she had finished, the people raised a great shout and made a joyful noise in their town. ¹⁰ When Achior saw all that the God of Israel had done, he believed firmly in God. So he was circumcised, and joined the house of Israel, remaining so to this day.

¹¹ As soon as it was dawn they hung the head of Holofernes on the wall. Then they all took their weapons, and they went out in companies to the mountain passes. ¹² When the Assyrians saw them they sent word to their commanders, who then went to the generals and the captains and to all their other officers. ¹³ They came to Holofernes' tent and said to the steward in charge of all his personal affairs, "Wake up our lord, for the slaves have been so bold as to come down against us to give battle, to their utter destruction."

¹⁴ So Bagoas went in and knocked at the entry of the tent, for he supposed that he was sleeping with Judith. ¹⁵ But when no one answered, he opened it and went into the bedchamber and found him sprawled on the floor dead, with his head missing. ¹⁶ He cried out with a loud voice and wept and groaned and shouted, and tore his clothes. ¹⁷ Then he went to the tent where Judith had stayed, and when he did not find her, he rushed out to the people and shouted, ¹⁸ "The slaves have tricked us! One Hebrew woman has brought disgrace on the house of King Nebuchadnezzar. Look, Holofernes is lying on the ground, and his head is missing!"

¹⁹ When the leaders of the Assyrian army heard this, they tore their tunics and were greatly dismayed, and their loud cries and shouts rose up throughout the camp.

15 When the men in the tents heard it, they were amazed at what had happened. ² Overcome with fear and trembling, they did not wait for one another, but with one impulse all rushed out and fled by every path across the plain and through the hill country. ³ Those who had camped in the hills around Bethulia also took to flight. Then the Israelites, everyone that was a soldier, rushed out upon them. ⁴ Uzziah sent men to Beto-masthaim[a] and Choba and Kola, and to all the frontiers of Israel, to tell what had taken place and to urge all to rush out upon the enemy to destroy them. ⁵ When the Israelites heard it, with one accord they fell upon the enemy,[b] and cut them down as far as Choba. Those in Jerusalem and all the hill country also came, for they were told what had happened in the camp of the enemy. The men in Gilead and in Galilee outflanked them with great slaughter, even beyond Damascus and its borders. ⁶ The rest of the people of Bethulia fell upon the Assyrian camp and plundered it, acquiring great riches. ⁷ And the Israelites, when they returned from the slaughter, took possession of what remained. Even the villages and towns in the hill country and in the plain got a great amount of booty, since there was a vast quantity of it.

⁸ Then the high priest Joakim and the elders of the Israelites who lived in Jerusalem came to witness the good things that the Lord

[a] Other ancient authorities add *and Bebai*
[b] Gk *them*

tion. **6:** Cf. 6.5. It is ironic that Achior faints, since Judith was so resolute in taking the head. **10:** Like Judith, Achior recognizes that her heroism comes from God, and responds by converting. Although Deut 23.3 forbids the acceptance of Ammonites or Moabites to the tenth generation, in this romanticized narrative, he, like Ruth the Moabite, is permitted to join.

14.11–15.7: The Assyrians discover Holofernes' headless body and are put to flight. 14.11–14: Events occur just as Judith predicted (14.3), although the story is slowed somewhat so that the audience can relish the coming reversal. **18:** Honor and shame are now reversed; Judith has exhibited Holofernes' head, shaming him and his memory, and the status of weak and powerful is reversed: *Slaves* and *one Hebrew woman* prevail over and disgrace *the house of King Nebuchadnezzar*. **14.19–15.7:** Upon learning that Holofernes has lost his head, the Assyrians lose theirs as well: general chaos results, and they are easily vanquished by the outnumbered Israelites. Here the Assyrians experience the same *fear and trembling* that they caused other nations (cf. 2.3), including Israel (4.1–2). The depiction of victory and plundering is similar to 1 Macc 7.44–47 (cf. also Deut 20.10–18; Esth 9.1–19; Ps 48).

15.8–16.20: A series of celebrations. 15.8–10: The connection between Judith, Bethulia, and the Jerusalem

had done for Israel, and to see Judith and to wish her well. [9] When they met her, they all blessed her with one accord and said to her, "You are the glory of Jerusalem, you are the great boast of Israel, you are the great pride of our nation! [10] You have done all this with your own hand; you have done great good to Israel, and God is well pleased with it. May the Almighty Lord bless you forever!" And all the people said, "Amen."

[11] All the people plundered the camp for thirty days. They gave Judith the tent of Holofernes and all his silver dinnerware, his beds, his bowls, and all his furniture. She took them and loaded her mules and hitched up her carts and piled the things on them.

[12] All the women of Israel gathered to see her, and blessed her, and some of them performed a dance in her honor. She took ivy-wreathed wands in her hands and distributed them to the women who were with her; [13] and she and those who were with her crowned themselves with olive wreaths. She went before all the people in the dance, leading all the women, while all the men of Israel followed, bearing their arms and wearing garlands and singing hymns.

[14] Judith began this thanksgiving before

16 all Israel, and all the people loudly sang this song of praise. [1] And Judith said,

Begin a song to my God with tambourines,
      sing to my Lord with cymbals.
Raise to him a new psalm;[a]
      exalt him, and call upon his name.
[2] For the Lord is a God who crushes wars;
      he sets up his camp among his people;
      he delivered me from the hands of my
            pursuers.

[3] The Assyrian came down from the
            mountains of the north;
      he came with myriads of his warriors;
their numbers blocked up the wadis,
      and their cavalry covered the hills.
[4] He boasted that he would burn up my
            territory,
      and kill my young men with the sword,
and dash my infants to the ground,
      and seize my children as booty,
      and take my virgins as spoil.

[5] But the Lord Almighty has foiled them
      by the hand of a woman.[b]
[6] For their mighty one did not fall by the
            hands of the young men,
      nor did the sons of the Titans strike him
            down,
      nor did tall giants set upon him;
but Judith daughter of Merari
      with the beauty of her countenance
            undid him.

[7] For she put away her widow's clothing
      to exalt the oppressed in Israel.
She anointed her face with perfume;
      [8] she fastened her hair with a tiara
      and put on a linen gown to beguile
            him.
[9] Her sandal ravished his eyes,
      her beauty captivated his mind,
      and the sword severed his neck!
[10] The Persians trembled at her boldness,
      the Medes were daunted at her
            daring.

a   Other ancient authorities read *a psalm and praise*
b   Other ancient authorities add *he has confounded them*

Temple officials has often been emphasized in the story, and especially here in the co-celebration. **11:** A balanced and complete reversal of fortune can be seen here. Bethulia was under siege for thirty-four days (7.20) before Judith went to the Assyrian camp for four days, which the Israelites then plunder for thirty days. **12:** *The women . . . performed a dance in her honor,* women in Israel performed victory dances and songs (Ex 15.20–21; 1 Sam 18.6–7). *Ivy-wreathed wands* were Greek in origin, but 2 Macc 10.7 and 3 Macc 7.16 indicate that they had been adopted by Jews. **15.14–16.17:** Judith's victory song. This book, like Tobit, concludes with a long hymn of thanksgiving (cf. also Deut 32–33; Judg 5; 2 Sam 22; Jon 2; Prayer of Azariah, and the Song of the Three Jews). Especially close is Ex 15; Ex 15.3 (Greek) and Jdt 16.2 both read: *For the Lord is a God who crushes wars.* **16.1:** *Tambourines,* small hand-drums without the modern metal rattles, are known from ancient depictions (cf. Ps 150.4–5). *A new psalm* (cf. Ps 96.1; 98.1). **5:** *By the hand of a woman,* see 9.9–10n.; 13.15. **6:** *Titans* and *giants* are from Greek mythology, though here perhaps also referring to giants from Israelite tradition (Gen 6.4; Deut 3.11). **10:** The

[11] Then my oppressed people shouted;
    my weak people cried out,[a] and the
        enemy[b] trembled;
    they lifted up their voices, and the
        enemy[b] were turned back.
[12] Sons of slave-girls pierced them through
    and wounded them like the children of
        fugitives;
    they perished before the army of my Lord.

[13] I will sing to my God a new song:
O Lord, you are great and glorious,
    wonderful in strength, invincible.
[14] Let all your creatures serve you,
    for you spoke, and they were made.
You sent forth your spirit,[c] and it formed
        them;[d]
    there is none that can resist your voice.
[15] For the mountains shall be shaken to
        their foundations with the waters;
    before your glance the rocks shall melt
        like wax.
But to those who fear you
    you show mercy.
[16] For every sacrifice as a fragrant offering
        is a small thing,
    and the fat of all whole burnt offerings
        to you is a very little thing;
but whoever fears the Lord is great forever.

[17] Woe to the nations that rise up against
        my people!
    The Lord Almighty will take vengeance
        on them in the day of judgment;
he will send fire and worms into their
        flesh;
    they shall weep in pain forever.

[18] When they arrived at Jerusalem, they worshiped God. As soon as the people were purified, they offered their burnt offerings, their freewill offerings, and their gifts. [19] Judith also dedicated to God all the possessions of Holofernes, which the people had given her; and the canopy that she had taken for herself from his bedchamber she gave as a votive offering. [20] For three months the people continued feasting in Jerusalem before the sanctuary, and Judith remained with them.

[21] After this they all returned home to their own inheritances. Judith went to Bethulia, and remained on her estate. For the rest of her life she was honored throughout the whole country. [22] Many desired to marry her, but she gave herself to no man all the days of her life after her husband Manasseh died and was gathered to his people. [23] She became more and more famous, and grew old in her husband's house, reaching the age of one hundred five. She set her maid free. She died in Bethulia, and they buried her in the cave of her husband Manasseh; [24] and the house of Israel mourned her for seven days. Before she died she distributed her property to all those who were next of kin to her husband Manasseh, and to her own nearest kindred. [25] No one ever again spread terror among the Israelites during the lifetime of Judith, or for a long time after her death.

a   Other ancient authorities read *feared*
b   Gk *they*
c   Or *breath*
d   Other ancient authorities read *they were created*

Persians and *Medes* are surprising here; they have not figured in the narrative before. **13:** *A new song* (cf. 16.1n.; Ps 33; 149.1; Isa 42.10). **14:** Cf. Ps 104.30. **15:** Cf. Ps. 97.5. **19:** Offerings of military booty were common; David offered the sword of Goliath (1 Sam 21.9). Ironically, Judith does not offer Holofernes' sword but the inner canopy of his tent, which she penetrated to kill him. Even in death Holofernes is unmanned and shamed.

16.21–25: Conclusion. The hero or heroine in stories of many cultures does not generally reintegrate into society after saving the people, although Judith's status is unclear. She does not marry, gives away her wealth (cf. Num 27.11), and frees her slave, but does she reenter her hut (8.5)? At any rate, like the judges she brings peace and safety to the land for a period (Judg 3.11,30; 5.31).

ESTHER
(THE GREEK VERSION CONTAINING ADDITIONAL CHAPTERS)

NAME AND CANONICAL STATUS

The Greek version of Esther is a second- or first-century BCE translation for Greek-speaking Jews of the canonical Hebrew book of Esther (i.e., the one included in the "Hebrew Bible" portion of this edition). The earliest indication that the story was titled "Esther" after its Jewish heroine appears in connection with this Greek translation. The translator—very likely the Lysimachus of Jerusalem mentioned in 11.1—produced a systematic but relatively free translation of the Hebrew. Besides numerous small but often significant omissions and additions (see annotations that follow), the Greek version includes six extra sections with more than a hundred verses that have no counterparts in any Hebrew manuscript.

In the early centuries CE, as the rabbis worked out the official canon of Jewish scripture, they rejected the Greek translation of Esther, including its additional verses, along with all other non-Hebrew Jewish texts. By contrast the early Church adopted into its canon a number of Jewish writings in Greek, among them the "extra" verses in Greek Esther. Protestants follow the Jewish model and exclude the additional verses from their canon, while Roman Catholic and Orthodox Christians accept them. (Most editions of this Bible include these disputed Greek/Jewish texts in the Apocryphal/Deuterocanonical section.)

AUTHORSHIP, DATE, AND LITERARY HISTORY

The evidence from both Hebrew and Greek manuscripts suggests a complicated evolution of the Esther story that scholars have yet to disentangle fully. Originally, Additions A, C, D, and F were probably composed in either Hebrew or Aramaic, and if so may have already been part of the text from which the Greek translator worked. The florid rhetorical phraseology of B and E indicates that they must originally have been composed in Greek. It is impossible to say who authored either the Semitic or Greek Additions. Additions B and E may have been composed in a sophisticated Greek Jewish center, such as Alexandria, but a Palestinian provenance for the others is likely.

The additions were not composed at the same time. The latest possible date for B, C, D, and E is 93 CE when the historian Josephus paraphrased them in his *Jewish Antiquities*. The colophon's location (11.1) immediately after F suggests that A as well as F were part of the Semitic text at the time that Lysimachus made his Greek translation in the late second or first century BCE.

The additional sections are clearly intrusive and secondary, for they contradict the older Hebrew text at a number of points. What is clear, however, is that the Hellenistic author(s) of these extra portions of the story all followed the early Jewish tradition of biblical interpretation called *midrash* and felt called upon to resolve perceived narrative, theological, and moral ambiguities in Jewish scripture. Consequently, while the additions sometimes make the characters and events more vivid or dramatic, their main purpose is to transform the comparatively subtle and enigmatic Hebrew story of Esther into a more conventional tale of divine intervention and exemplary Jewish piety.

CONTENTS

The Greek Additions to the book of Esther comprise 105 verses. Their contents are as follows:
- Addition A: Mordecai's dream (11.2–12) and his discovery of a plot against the king (12.1–6)
- Addition B: The royal edict dictated by Haman, announcing a pogrom (a persecution to the death) against the Jews (13.1–7)
- Addition C: The prayers of Mordecai (13.8–18) and Esther (14.1–19)
- Addition D: Esther's appearance, unsummoned, before the king (15.4–19)
- Addition E: The royal edict dictated by Mordecai, counteracting the edict sent by Haman (16.1–24)
- Addition F: The interpretation of Mordecai's dream (10.4–13) and the colophon (an inscription at the end of a manuscript) to the Greek version (11.1)

Besides the Additions, the translators also made many minor changes as they interpreted the Hebrew text. These are mentioned in the annotations.

INTERPRETATION

Besides giving the story a more explicit religious character, the additions as they are arranged within the narrative create new emphases. A and F, which frame the story, graft onto it an apocalyptic perspective of cosmic struggle between good and evil. The juxtaposition of C's extensive praise of God with specific terms and phrases applied to Ahasuerus in D makes explicit the Greek version's intent throughout the story to contrast the capricious earthly king with God the faithful heavenly king. Similarly, the royal decrees in B and E highlight the theme of human commandments versus the divinely given Jewish law to which Esther also alludes when she prays in C.

There is no mention of God in the original Hebrew narrative, one important reason for the centuries of rabbinical debate over including Esther among the authoritative Jewish scriptures. By contrast, in the Greek Additions the terms "Lord" or "God" appear more than fifty times. Occasionally the Greek translation inserts references to God into verses that correspond to the original Hebrew text, as when Mordecai instructs Esther prior to her becoming queen that she should "fear God and keep his laws" (2.20) and then later urges her to "call upon the Lord" (4.8) before appearing unsummoned before the king. In 6.1 according to the Greek text, "That night the Lord took sleep from the king," whereas the Hebrew leaves the source of Ahasuerus's insomnia unspecified. Likewise in the Greek version, Haman's wife and his friends caution Haman that if Mordecai is Jewish, then "the living God is with him" (compare the Heb at 6.13).

The additions provide their authors with an opportunity to express their own particular theological views. Additions A and F introduce apocalyptic motifs to emphasize God's providential care for the people Israel in a universally hostile world. Addition C attests to the efficacy of prayer and expresses Queen Esther's abhorrence at being married to a Gentile, her loathing of all things worldly and courtly, and her strict observance of Jewish dietary laws—none of which are so much as hinted at in the Hebrew. Thanks largely to Addition D, the climax of the Greek version is reached when God miraculously changes to gentleness the king's "fierce anger" at Esther's unannounced entrance. This motif is lacking in the Hebrew. Taken together, the six additions deemphasize the establishment of Purim and express a deep distrust of Gentiles.

[For a full introduction to the book of Esther, see pp. 707–708 HB.]

Mary Joan Winn Leith

ADDITION A

11 ^a ² In the second year of the reign of Artaxerxes the Great, on the first day of Nisan, Mordecai son of Jair son of Shimei^b son of Kish, of the tribe of Benjamin, had a dream. ³ He was a Jew living in the city of Susa, a great man, serving in the court of the king. ⁴ He was one of the captives whom King Nebuchadnezzar of Babylon had brought from Jerusalem with King Jeconiah of Judea. And this was his dream: ⁵ Noises^c and confusion, thunders and earthquake, tumult on the earth! ⁶ Then two great dragons came forward, both ready to fight, and they roared terribly. ⁷ At their roaring every nation prepared for war, to fight against the righteous nation. ⁸ It was a day of darkness and gloom, of tribulation and distress, affliction and great tumult on the earth! ⁹ And the whole righteous nation was troubled; they feared the evils that threatened them,^d and were ready to perish. ¹⁰ Then they cried out to God; and at their outcry, as though from a tiny spring, there came a great river, with abun-

dant water; ¹¹ light came, and the sun rose, and the lowly were exalted and devoured those held in honor.

¹² Mordecai saw in this dream what God had determined to do, and after he awoke he had it on his mind, seeking all day to understand it in every detail.

12 Now Mordecai took his rest in the courtyard with Gabatha and Tharra, the two eunuchs of the king who kept watch in the courtyard. ² He overheard their conversation and inquired into their purposes, and learned that they were preparing to lay hands on King Artaxerxes; and he informed the king concerning them. ³ Then the king examined the two eunuchs, and after they had confessed it, they were led away to execution. ⁴ The king made a permanent record of these

---

^a Chapters 11.2—12.6 correspond to chapter A 1-17 in some translations.

^b Gk *Semeios*

^c Or *Voices*

^d Gk *their own evils*

Addidion A: 11.2—12: Mordecai's prophetic dream of impending danger to the Jews. 2: *Artaxerxes,* a mistranslation of the Heb "Ahasuerus," that is, Xerxes I (486–465 BCE); the *second year* would be 485. Month names in Esther are Babylonian; *Nisan,* March-April, is the first month of the new year. Thus, Mordecai's dream comes on New Year's Day. *Mordecai's* name derives from the name of the Babylonian god Marduk, whose creation of the world was reenacted every new year in Babylon. Mordecai's genealogy connecting him with King Saul (1 Sam 9.1; 2 Sam 16.5–18) is repeated in 2.5. **3:** *Jew* (Heb "yehudi"), originally meaning someone from the kingdom of Judah (2 Kings 16.6), is used here in its later sense of an adherent to Judaism. *Susa,* westernmost of the three capital cities of the Persian empire in northwestern Iran. In contrast to Heb Esther, Mordecai is already an important royal official. **4:** Mordecai would be well over one hundred years old by 485 BCE if he, along with Judah's last king *Jeconiah* (Jehoiachin), had been exiled by *Nebuchadnezzar* in 597 (2 Kings 24.8–16). As in other historical novellas, the author takes liberties with actual chronology. **5:** *Noises . . . tumult on the earth,* the language of cosmic chaos is typical of apocalyptic texts (see Isa 24.17–20; Dan 12.1,4). **6:** *Two great dragons,* Mordecai and Haman (see Addition F 10.7). God defeated the chaos dragon (a sea monster) at the time of creation (Pss 74.13; 89.10; Isa 27.1; 51.9–10; Job 26.12–13); imagery from this primordial battle is frequently used in apocalyptic literature (Dan 7; Rev 12.3; 13.2; 20.2). Two dragons (see 2 Esd 6.49–52), one good, one evil, are unusual and may reflect Persian influence. **7:** *Righteous nation,* the Jews (see Dan 7.27). Unlike the Heb, Gk Esther perceives the entire Gentile (non-Jewish) world as a danger to the Jews. **10:** *Cried out,* Ex 3.7; Jdt 4.9,12,15. *Tiny spring* and *great river* refer to Esther (10.6). **11:** *Light* and morning, symbolizing joy, salvation, and new life (Pss 30.5; 46.5; 112.4; Isa 33.2). *Lowly were exalted,* 1 Sam 2.4–9. One *held in honor* is Haman (12.6). **12:** *What God had determined to do,* in contrast to the Heb, all events in Gk Esther are foreordained by God, although Mordecai does not yet fully understand the dream's symbolism (10.4–9).

12.1–6: Mordecai saves the king's life. It is unclear whether this conspiracy is the same as the one in Esth 2.19–23 of the Heb text or an earlier intrigue. **5:** The king *rewarded* Mordecai immediately (in contrast to 6.1–3). **6:** The Gk text suggests (in contrast to the Heb) that Haman took part in the eunuchs' foiled plot and thus provides a motivation for Mordecai's and Haman's subsequent actions. *Bougean* (see also 3.1) is apparently an attempt to translate the Heb word "Agagite," which connects Haman to the Amalekite king, Agag, Saul's vanquished enemy (see 1 Sam 15.8). Mordecai and Haman share an ancestral enmity (Ex 17.8–16; Num 24.7).

things, and Mordecai wrote an account of them. [5] And the king ordered Mordecai to serve in the court, and rewarded him for these things. [6] But Haman son of Hammedatha, a Bougean, who was in great honor with the king, determined to injure Mordecai and his people because of the two eunuchs of the king.

END OF ADDITION A

1 It was after this that the following things happened in the days of Artaxerxes, the same Artaxerxes who ruled over one hundred twenty-seven provinces from India to Ethiopia.[a] [2] In those days, when King Artaxerxes was enthroned in the city of Susa, [3] in the third year of his reign, he gave a banquet for his Friends and other persons of various nations, the Persians and Median nobles, and the governors of the provinces. [4] After this, when he had displayed to them the riches of his kingdom and the splendor of his bountiful celebration during the course of one hundred eighty days, [5] at the end of the festivity[b] the king gave a drinking party for the people of various nations who lived in the city. This was held for six days in the courtyard of the royal palace, [6] which was adorned with curtains of fine linen and cotton, held by cords of purple linen attached to gold and silver blocks on pillars of marble and other stones. Gold and silver couches were placed on a mosaic floor of emerald, mother-of-pearl, and marble. There were coverings of gauze, embroidered in various colors, with roses arranged around them. [7] The cups were of gold and silver, and a miniature cup was displayed, made of ruby, worth thirty thousand talents. There was abundant sweet wine, such as the king himself drank. [8] The drinking was not according to a fixed rule; but the king wished to have it so, and he commanded his stewards to comply with his pleasure and with that of the guests.

[9] Meanwhile, Queen Vashti[c] gave a drinking party for the women in the palace where King Artaxerxes was.

[10] On the seventh day, when the king was in good humor, he told Haman, Bazan, Tharra, Boraze, Zatholtha, Abataza, and Tharaba, the seven eunuchs who served King Artaxerxes, [11] to escort the queen to him in order to proclaim her as queen and to place the diadem on her head, and to have her display her beauty to all the governors and the people of various nations, for she was indeed a beautiful woman. [12] But Queen Vashti[c] refused to obey him and would not come with the eunuchs. This offended the king and he became furious. [13] He said to his Friends, "This is how Vashti[c] has answered me.[d] Give therefore your ruling and judgment on this matter." [14] Arkesaeus, Sarsathaeus, and Malesear, then the governors of the Persians and Medes who were closest to the king—Arkesaeus, Sarsathaeus, and Malesear, who sat beside him in the chief seats—came to him [15] and told him what must be done

---

a Other ancient authorities lack *to Ethiopia*
b Gk *marriage feast*
c Gk *Astin*
d Gk *Astin has said thus and so*

1.1–9: Artaxerxes' banquet. 1: *Artaxerxes* see 11.2n. *Ethiopia* (Heb "Cush"), in the Bible this term refers to the territory of modern Sudan and Ethiopia. **3–4:** Greek writers mention fabulous feasts given by Persian kings; Ahasuerus's *banquet,* with its exaggerated length of *one hundred eighty days* (see Jdt 1.16), is the first of several that occur at key points in the story. *Friends,* a special class of courtiers. **5:** *Festivity,* or *marriage feast* (see textual note b), which would clarify the behavior of the king and Vashti (see 1.11). *Six days,* 1.10 (and Heb 1.5,10) says the party lasted seven days. **6–7:** The description, which emphasizes power and wealth, is more extravagant than in the Heb version. **8:** *According to a fixed rule,* ancient sources suggest that the king set the pace for drinking (Herodotus 1.33), and all guests drank when he drank. **9:** There are no ancient references to *Vashti,* whose name means "beloved"; Xerxes I's queen was Amestris (Herodotus 7.61). *Queen Vashti gave a drinking party for the women* emphasizes the separate gendered spheres of king and queen, a factor in Esther's later bravery.

1.10–22: Queen Vashti's downfall. 10: *Eunuchs* were castrated males who served in the Persian court. The list of their names lends the story an air of authenticity. **11:** *Proclaim her as queen,* in contrast to the Heb, Vashti is summoned for her official coronation as well as for display. **12:** The circumstances will be reversed when Esther approaches the king without having been summoned (4.11,16,15). **13–14:** Three *governors* rather than the seven

to Queen Vashti[a] for not obeying the order that the king had sent her by the eunuchs. [16] Then Muchaeus said to the king and the governors, "Queen Vashti[a] has insulted not only the king but also all the king's governors and officials" [17] (for he had reported to them what the queen had said and how she had defied the king). "And just as she defied King Artaxerxes, [18] so now the other ladies who are wives of the Persian and Median governors, on hearing what she has said to the king, will likewise dare to insult their husbands. [19] If therefore it pleases the king, let him issue a royal decree, inscribed in accordance with the laws of the Medes and Persians so that it may not be altered, that the queen may no longer come into his presence; but let the king give her royal rank to a woman better than she. [20] Let whatever law the king enacts be proclaimed in his kingdom, and thus all women will give honor to their husbands, rich and poor alike." [21] This speech pleased the king and the governors, and the king did as Muchaeus had recommended. [22] The king sent the decree into all his kingdom, to every province in its own language, so that in every house respect would be shown to every husband.

2 After these things, the king's anger abated, and he no longer was concerned about Vashti[a] or remembered what he had said and how he had condemned her. [2] Then the king's servants said, "Let beautiful and virtuous girls be sought out for the king. [3] The king shall appoint officers in all the provinces of his kingdom, and they shall select beautiful young virgins to be brought to the harem in Susa, the capital. Let them be entrusted to the king's eunuch who is in charge of the women, and let ointments and whatever else they need be given them. [4] And the woman who pleases the king shall be queen instead of Vashti."[a] This pleased the king, and he did so.

[5] Now there was a Jew in Susa the capital whose name was Mordecai son of Jair son of Shimei[b] son of Kish, of the tribe of Benjamin; [6] he had been taken captive from Jerusalem among those whom King Nebuchadnezzar of Babylon had captured. [7] And he had a foster child, the daughter of his father's brother, Aminadab, and her name was Esther. When her parents died, he brought her up to womanhood as his own. The girl was beautiful in appearance. [8] So, when the decree of the king was proclaimed, and many girls were gathered in Susa the capital in custody of Gai, Esther also was brought to Gai, who had custody of the women. [9] The girl pleased him

a Gk *Astin*
b Gk *Semeios*

---

officials named in the Heb. **16–18:** The fear of a feminine insurrection against patriarchal order lies just below the surface of many ancient myths and legends. Contrary to Muchaeus's dire imaginings, the real danger will come in the form of a conspiracy by palace bodyguards (2.21). **19:** There is no historical evidence that the *laws of the Medes and the Persians* (Esth 8.8; Dan 6.9,13) were unalterable. The phrase sets up a narrative tension between rigid legalism and the requirements of true justice. **20:** By issuing an absurdly unenforceable decree, the foolish king draws attention to his failure at ruling his own wife. **22:** The first of several decrees in the book (see 2.8; 3.12,13; 8.9–11; 9.20–22,29–32). Persian royal edicts were issued both in Aramaic, the official language of Persian diplomacy, and in the *languages* of subject peoples (see Ezra 6.3–5).

2.1–18: Esther becomes queen. 1–4: The king agrees to seek a new queen. 1: Here the search for a replacement occurs after the king forgets Vashti, while in the Heb the search begins because the king remembers Vashti's act. **2:** Consistent with its concern for moral rectitude, the Gk version adds that the winning *girl* (Heb "virgin") must be *virtuous* as well as *beautiful*. **3:** In patriarchal societies, a *virgin* bride ensures the paternity of children within the marriage (see Ex 22.16; Lev 21.13); here it may also be a convention of historical romance. Actual Persian law restricted kings to wives from certain noble Persian families.

2.5–7: Mordecai and Esther. 5–6: For a second time, the Gk introduces Mordecai (see 11.2–4n.). **7:** The name *Esther* derives from Ishtar, the Babylonian goddess of sexuality and war (the deities Marduk and Ishtar were cousins), or from the Persian word for "star," or both. The Gk fails to mention Esther's Heb name, Hadassah (see 2.7 in the Heb). *Aminadab*, in the Heb (2.15) Esther's father is Abihail. **8:** By beginning the book (11.2–12) with Mordecai's prophetic dream, the Gk version suggests that Esther arrives at court according to divine plan (see 10.4–6). Neither the Heb nor the Gk mentions Esther's feelings when she *was brought* to Susa. This is contra-

and won his favor, and he quickly provided her with ointments and her portion of food,[a] as well as seven maids chosen from the palace; he treated her and her maids with special favor in the harem. [10] Now Esther had not disclosed her people or country, for Mordecai had commanded her not to make it known. [11] And every day Mordecai walked in the courtyard of the harem, to see what would happen to Esther.

[12] Now the period after which a girl was to go to the king was twelve months. During this time the days of beautification are completed—six months while they are anointing themselves with oil of myrrh, and six months with spices and ointments for women. [13] Then she goes in to the king; she is handed to the person appointed, and goes with him from the harem to the king's palace. [14] In the evening she enters and in the morning she departs to the second harem, where Gai the king's eunuch is in charge of the women; and she does not go in to the king again unless she is summoned by name.

[15] When the time was fulfilled for Esther daughter of Aminadab, the brother of Mordecai's father, to go in to the king, she neglected none of the things that Gai, the eunuch in charge of the women, had commanded. Now Esther found favor in the eyes of all who saw her. [16] So Esther went in to King Artaxerxes in the twelfth month, which is Adar, in the seventh year of his reign. [17] And the king loved Esther and she found favor beyond all the other virgins, so he put on her the queen's

diadem. [18] Then the king gave a banquet lasting seven days for all his Friends and the officers to celebrate his marriage to Esther; and he granted a remission of taxes to those who were under his rule.

[19] Meanwhile Mordecai was serving in the courtyard. [20] Esther had not disclosed her country—such were the instructions of Mordecai; but she was to fear God and keep his laws, just as she had done when she was with him. So Esther did not change her mode of life.

[21] Now the king's eunuchs, who were chief bodyguards, were angry because of Mordecai's advancement, and they plotted to kill King Artaxerxes. [22] The matter became known to Mordecai, and he warned Esther, who in turn revealed the plot to the king. [23] He investigated the two eunuchs and hanged them. Then the king ordered a memorandum to be deposited in the royal library in praise of the goodwill shown by Mordecai.

3 After these events King Artaxerxes promoted Haman son of Hammedatha, a Bougean, advancing him and granting him precedence over all the king's[b] Friends. [2] So all who were at court used to do obeisance to Haman,[c] for so the king had commanded to be done. Mordecai, however, did not do obeisance. [3] Then the king's courtiers said to Mordecai, "Mordecai, why do you disobey the king's command?" [4] Day after day they spoke

---

a   Gk lacks *of food*
b   Gk *all his*
c   Gk *him*

---

dicted later in one of the Gk additions (14.15–18). **9:** In winning the *favor* of *Gai* (foreshadowing 2.15,17; 5.8; 7.3), Esther resembles Joseph in the house of Potiphar (Gen 39.2–6) and Daniel at the Babylonian court (Dan 1.9). **10:** Esther's silence about her Jewish identity (reiterated in v. 20) demonstrates her submissive nature even as it heightens narrative suspense.

2.12–18: Esther becomes queen. 14: The impossibility of seeing the king again unless *summoned by name* foreshadows Esther's dilemma in 4.11–16 and 15.1–6. **16:** *Adar*, February-March. The Heb gives a different month, Tebeth (December-January). *In the seventh year of his reign*, Ahasuerus has been testing queen candidates now for about four years. **18:** Another in the series of banquets (see 1.3n.) that will climax with the feast of Purim. *Remission of taxes*, the Gk correctly interprets the Hebrew term "holiday" in economic terms.

2.19–23: Mordecai and Esther save the king's life. This may be a second version of the plot in 12.1–6 or a different episode altogether. **20:** *Mode of life*, in contrast to the Heb, where Esther seems Jewish by ethnicity rather than religious observance. **21:** Unlike the Heb, the conspirators in the Gk are motivated by jealousy of Mordecai (see Dan 6.3–5). **23:** *Hanged*, impaled, not strangled with a rope, a foreshadowing of 5.14; 7.9–10; 9.13–14. *The royal library*, an official archive of royal decrees (cf. 10.2; 1 Kings 14.19,29; 2 Chr 25.26; 32.32).

3.1–13: Haman plots to annihilate the Jews. 1: *Bougean*, see 12.6n. **2:** The reasons for Mordecai's refusal to *do obeisance* are unclear but possibly explained in the Gk by Mordecai's prayer (13.14) or by the fact that Jews and

to him, but he would not listen to them. Then they informed Haman that Mordecai was resisting the king's command. Mordecai had told them that he was a Jew. [5] So when Haman learned that Mordecai was not doing obeisance to him, he became furiously angry, [6] and plotted to destroy all the Jews under Artaxerxes' rule.

[7] In the twelfth year of King Artaxerxes Haman[a] came to a decision by casting lots, taking the days and the months one by one, to fix on one day to destroy the whole race of Mordecai. The lot fell on the fourteenth[b] day of the month of Adar.

[8] Then Haman[a] said to King Artaxerxes, "There is a certain nation scattered among the other nations in all your kingdom; their laws are different from those of every other nation, and they do not keep the laws of the king. It is not expedient for the king to tolerate them. [9] If it pleases the king, let it be decreed that they are to be destroyed, and I will pay ten thousand talents of silver into the king's treasury." [10] So the king took off his signet ring and gave it to Haman to seal the decree[c] that was to be written against the Jews. [11] The king told Haman, "Keep the money, and do whatever you want with that nation."

[12] So on the thirteenth day of the first month the king's secretaries were summoned, and in accordance with Haman's instructions they wrote in the name of King Artaxerxes to the magistrates and the governors in every province from India to Ethiopia. There were one hundred twenty-seven provinces in all, and the governors were addressed each in his own language. [13] Instructions were sent by couriers throughout all the empire of Artaxerxes to destroy the Jewish people on a given day of the twelfth month, which is Adar, and to plunder their goods.

ADDITION B

13 [d] This is a copy of the letter: "The Great King, Artaxerxes, writes the following to the governors of the hundred twenty-seven provinces from India to Ethiopia and to the officials under them:

[2] "Having become ruler of many nations and master of the whole world (not elated with presumption of authority but always acting reasonably and with kindness), I have determined to settle the lives of my subjects in lasting tranquility and, in order to make my kingdom peaceable and open to travel throughout all its extent, to restore the peace desired by all people.

[3] "When I asked my counselors how this might be accomplished, Haman—who excels among us in sound judgment, and is distinguished for his unchanging goodwill and steadfast fidelity, and has attained the second place in the kingdom— [4] pointed out to us that among all the nations in the world there is scattered a certain hostile people, who have laws contrary to those of every nation and continually disregard the ordinances of kings, so that the unifying of the kingdom

---

a   Gk *he*

b   Other ancient witnesses read *thirteenth*; see 8.12

c   Gk lacks *the decree*

d   Chapter 13.1-7 corresponds to chapter B 1-7 in some translations.

Agagites were traditionally enemies; see 12.6n. **4:** *Day after day*, wording reminiscent of Joseph's resistance to the blandishments of Potiphar's wife (Gen 39.10). **7:** *The twelfth year*, Esther has been queen for five years. The Heb word for *lot*, "pur" (pl. "purim"), is borrowed from Babylonian. Haman resorts to this common form of divination (Herodotus 3.128) known also to the Israelites (1 Sam 14.42). *Adar*, February-March. Instead of the *fourteenth day*, 8.12 of the Gk and Heb rightly cite the thirteenth. **8:** Haman's manipulation of the pliable king (see 1.16–20) begins with the truth: the Jews were indeed *scattered* (Zech 7.14), and like other subject peoples in the Persian empire, their *laws* were different (Deut 4.5–6). He slides into falsehood in asserting that Jews *do not keep the laws of the king*. **9:** *Ten thousand talents of silver*, equal in value to hundreds of millions of US dollars. **10:** The king's *signet ring* gave Haman unlimited power to sign documents in the king's name (8.2,8; cf. Gen 41.41–42; 1 Kings 21.8–9). **12:** *In his own language*, see 1.22n. **13:** *Couriers*, the Persian empire's communication system was renowned (Herodotus 8.98). *A given day*, the thirteenth (see 8.12, Gk and Heb). *Adar*, February-March.

Addition B: **13.1–7:** The text of the king's letter authorizing the slaughter of the Jews. This addition to the Gk version of Esther was composed in Gk by the same author as 16.1–24 (Addition E). The brazen tone of the letter seems inconsistent with the king's general demeanor as depicted earlier in the story and reflects Haman's

that we honorably intend cannot be brought about. [5] We understand that this people, and it alone, stands constantly in opposition to every nation, perversely following a strange manner of life and laws, and is ill-disposed to our government, doing all the harm they can so that our kingdom may not attain stability.

[6] "Therefore we have decreed that those indicated to you in the letters written by Haman, who is in charge of affairs and is our second father, shall all—wives and children included—be utterly destroyed by the swords of their enemies, without pity or restraint, on the fourteenth day of the twelfth month, Adar, of this present year, [7] so that those who have long been hostile and remain so may in a single day go down in violence to Hades, and leave our government completely secure and untroubled hereafter."

END OF ADDITION B

3 [14] Copies of the document were posted in every province, and all the nations were ordered to be prepared for that day. [15] The matter was expedited also in Susa. And while the king and Haman caroused together, the city of Susa[a] was thrown into confusion.

4 When Mordecai learned of all that had been done, he tore his clothes, put on sackcloth, and sprinkled himself with ashes; then he rushed through the street of the city, shouting loudly: "An innocent nation is being destroyed!" [2] He got as far as the king's gate, and there he stopped, because no one was allowed to enter the courtyard clothed in sackcloth and ashes. [3] And in every province where the king's proclamation had been posted there was a loud cry of mourning and lamentation among the Jews, and they put on sackcloth and ashes. [4] When the queen's[b] maids and eunuchs came and told her, she was deeply troubled by what she heard had happened, and sent some

clothes to Mordecai to put on instead of sackcloth; but he would not consent. [5] Then Esther summoned Hachratheus, the eunuch who attended her, and ordered him to get accurate information for her from Mordecai.[c]

[7] So Mordecai told him what had happened and how Haman had promised to pay ten thousand talents into the royal treasury to bring about the destruction of the Jews. [8] He also gave him a copy of what had been posted in Susa for their destruction, to show to Esther; and he told him to charge her to go in to the king and plead for his favor in behalf of the people. "Remember," he said, "the days when you were an ordinary person, being brought up under my care—for Haman, who stands next to the king, has spoken against us and demands our death. Call upon the Lord; then speak to the king in our behalf, and save us from death."

[9] Hachratheus went in and told Esther all these things. [10] And she said to him, "Go to Mordecai and say, [11] 'All nations of the empire know that if any man or woman goes to the king inside the inner court without being called, there is no escape for that person. Only the one to whom the king stretches out the golden scepter is safe—and it is now thirty days since I was called to go to the king.'"

[12] When Hachratheus delivered her entire message to Mordecai, [13] Mordecai told him to go back and say to her, "Esther, do not say to yourself that you alone among all the Jews will escape alive. [14] For if you keep quiet at such a time as this, help and protection will come to the Jews from another quarter,

a   Gk *the city*
b   Gk *When her*
c   Other ancient witnesses add [6]*So Hachratheus went out to Mordecai in the street of the city opposite the city gate.*

voice. **6:** *Fourteenth* day, a correction of the Gk's "thirteenth" (see the Hebrew text 3.13; 8.12; 9.1; cf. Gk 16.20; 8.12). *Adar,* February-March. **7:** *Hades,* the underworld and abode of the dead (Heb "sheol").

3.14–15: Haman and the king celebrate the publication of the decree.

4.1–17: Mordecai persuades Esther to risk her life to save her people. **1:** *Sackcloth* and *ashes* and torn clothing were traditional signs of mourning and repentance (2 Sam 3.31; Job 42.6; Jon 3.5; Dan 9.3). **2:** No one rendered ritually unclean by mourning could *enter the courtyard.* **4:** Esther has obeyed Mordecai and kept her Jewish identity a secret; she is unaware of the edict. **11:** Like other biblical heroes called upon to save their people (Ex 3.11; 4.10; 10.28; Judg 6.15; Jer 1.6), Esther initially objects. *Since I was called to go to the king,* see 2.14. **14:** *From another quarter,* divine providence according to Gk 10.4–5; the phrase is ambiguous in Heb Esther. *Who*

but you and your father's family will perish. Yet, who knows whether it was not for such a time as this that you were made queen?" [15] Then Esther gave the messenger this answer to take back to Mordecai: [16] "Go and gather all the Jews who are in Susa and fast on my behalf; for three days and nights do not eat or drink, and my maids and I will also go without food. After that I will go to the king, contrary to the law, even if I must die." [17] So Mordecai went away and did what Esther had told him to do.

ADDITION C

13 [8] [a]Then Mordecai[b] prayed to the Lord, calling to remembrance all the works of the Lord.

[9] He said, "O Lord, Lord, you rule as King over all things, for the universe is in your power and there is no one who can oppose you when it is your will to save Israel, [10] for you have made heaven and earth and every wonderful thing under heaven. [11] You are Lord of all, and there is no one who can resist you, the Lord. [12] You know all things; you know, O Lord, that it was not in insolence or pride or for any love of glory that I did this, and refused to bow down to this proud Haman; [13] for I would have been willing to kiss the soles of his feet to save Israel! [14] But I did this so that I might not set human glory above the glory of God, and I will not bow down to anyone but you, who are my Lord; and I will not do these things in pride. [15] And now, O Lord God and King, God of Abraham, spare your people; for the eyes of our foes are upon us[c] to annihilate us, and they desire to destroy the inheritance that has been yours

from the beginning. [16] Do not neglect your portion, which you redeemed for yourself out of the land of Egypt. [17] Hear my prayer, and have mercy upon your inheritance; turn our mourning into feasting that we may live and sing praise to your name, O Lord; do not destroy the lips[d] of those who praise you."

[18] And all Israel cried out mightily, for their death was before their eyes.

14 Then Queen Esther, seized with deadly anxiety, fled to the Lord. [2] She took off her splendid apparel and put on the garments of distress and mourning, and instead of costly perfumes she covered her head with ashes and dung, and she utterly humbled her body; every part that she loved to adorn she covered with her tangled hair. [3] She prayed to the Lord God of Israel, and said: "O my Lord, you only are our king; help me, who am alone and have no helper but you, [4] for my danger is in my hand. [5] Ever since I was born I have heard in the tribe of my family that you, O Lord, took Israel out of all the nations, and our ancestors from among all their forebears, for an everlasting inheritance, and that you did for them all that you promised. [6] And now we have sinned before you, and you have handed us over to our enemies [7] because we glorified their gods. You are righteous, O Lord! [8] And now they are not satisfied that we are in bitter slavery, but they have covenanted with their idols [9] to abolish what your mouth has ordained, and to destroy

a   Chapters 13.8—15.16 correspond to chapters C 1-30 and D 1-16 in some translations.
b   Gk *he*
c   Gk *for they are eying us*
d   Gk *mouth*

---

knows? Often precedes an expression of hope for divine mercy (2 Sam 12.22; Joel 2.14; Jon 3.9). **16–17:** Resolving to act *contrary to the law* (see 4.11) on behalf of her people, Esther takes charge (anticipating 9.29). Communal or individual fasting was a rite of repentance believed to influence the deity (Lev 16.29–31; Judg 20.26; 2 Sam 12.16; 1 Kings 21.27; Jon 3.5,8; Ezra 8.21–23; Joel 1.14; 2.12,15; 1 Macc 3.47).

Addition C: 13.8–14.19: The prayers of Mordecai and Esther give the book an explicitly religious tone. Both contain themes common to national laments (Neh 9; Dan 9).

13.8–17: Mordecai's prayer and the people's response. 12–14: Mordecai justifies his refusal to bow down to Haman (3.2) on religious grounds (see Dan 3.12,16–18). **16:** Mordecai is confident in the god who liberated the Israelites, God's *portion* (Deut 32.9), from enslavement in *Egypt* (Ex 1–14).

14.1–19: Esther humbly petitions God. Her prayer (see especially Jdt 9) resembles Mordecai's in its sincere, if conventional, piety and concern for religious self-justification. **2:** Humble *garments*, filth, and disarray are appropriate to penitential prayer (2 Kings 19.1; Neh 1.4; Dan 9.3–4; Jdt 9.1). **8:** *Bitter slavery* interprets the exile and Diaspora in terms evocative of bondage in Egypt (Ex 1–14). **9:** *Your altar* and *your house* refer to the ruined

your inheritance, to stop the mouths of those who praise you and to quench your altar and the glory of your house, [10] to open the mouths of the nations for the praise of vain idols, and to magnify forever a mortal king.

[11] "O Lord, do not surrender your scepter to what has no being; and do not let them laugh at our downfall; but turn their plan against them, and make an example of him who began this against us. [12] Remember, O Lord; make yourself known in this time of our affliction, and give me courage, O King of the gods and Master of all dominion! [13] Put eloquent speech in my mouth before the lion, and turn his heart to hate the man who is fighting against us, so that there may be an end of him and those who agree with him. [14] But save us by your hand, and help me, who am alone and have no helper but you, O Lord. [15] You have knowledge of all things, and you know that I hate the splendor of the wicked and abhor the bed of the uncircumcised and of any alien. [16] You know my necessity—that I abhor the sign of my proud position, which is upon my head on days when I appear in public. I abhor it like a filthy rag, and I do not wear it on the days when I am at leisure. [17] And your servant has not eaten at Haman's table, and I have not honored the king's feast or drunk the wine of libations. [18] Your servant has had no joy since the day that I was brought here until now, except in you, O Lord God of Abraham. [19] O God, whose might is over all, hear the voice of the despairing, and save us from the hands of evildoers. And save me from my fear!"

END OF ADDITION C

15 On the third day, when she ended her prayer, she took off the garments in which she had worshiped, and arrayed herself in splendid attire. [2] Then, majestically adorned, after invoking the aid of the all-seeing God and Savior, she took two maids with her; [3] on one she leaned gently for support, [4] while the other followed, carrying her train. [5] She was radiant with perfect beauty, and she looked happy, as if beloved, but her heart was frozen with fear. [6] When she had gone through all the doors, she stood before the king. He was seated on his royal throne, clothed in the full array of his majesty, all covered with gold and precious stones. He was most terrifying.

[7] Lifting his face, flushed with splendor, he looked at her in fierce anger. The queen faltered, and turned pale and faint, and collapsed on the head of the maid who went in front of her. [8] Then God changed the spirit of the king to gentleness, and in alarm he sprang from his throne and took her in his arms until she came to herself. He comforted her with soothing words, and said to her, [9] "What is it, Esther? I am your husband.[a] Take courage; [10] You shall not die, for our law applies only to our subjects.[b] Come near."

[11] Then he raised the golden scepter and touched her neck with it; [12] he embraced her, and said, "Speak to me." [13] She said to him, "I saw you, my lord, like an angel of God, and my heart was shaken with fear at your glory.

[a] Gk *brother*
[b] Meaning of Gk uncertain

Temple in Jerusalem (2 Macc 14.33; 3 Macc 5.43), a subject ignored in the Heb. **13:** Despite her plea for *eloquent speech*, in 15.5 it is her beauty on which Esther initially relies. *Lion*, Artaxerxes (see Prov 19.12; 20.2). **15:** *Abhor the bed of the uncircumcised*, reflecting the Jewish prohibition of mixed marriage (Deut 7.3; Ezra 10.2; Neh 13.23–27). *Wicked, uncircumcised, alien*, non-Jews. Unlike the Heb text, Gk Esther takes a negative view of Gentiles. **16:** The *sign* upon Esther's *head* is the crown which she abhors as a *filthy* rag (lit. a rag soaked in menstrual blood; see Lev 15.19–24; Isa 64.6; contrast Deut 6.9). **17:** Esther observes the Jewish dietary laws (Lev 11; see Jdt 12.1–2).

Addition D: **15.1–16:** Esther approaches the king. This chapter expands 5.1–2 in the Heb text, heightening the suspense with added details and, consistent with the Gk version's theological perspective, crediting Esther's success to God's intervention. **1:** Esther's preparations call to mind an epic hero arming for battle (see *Iliad* 19.338–39; 360–91; 1 Sam 17.5–7,38–39; see Jdt 10.3; 12.15). **7–8:** This episode, absent in the Heb, portrays an Esther undone by feminine weakness and dependant upon God to succeed in her mission. *God changed the spirit of the king*, see 1 Sam 10.9. **9:** *Husband*, Gk "brother," a metaphorical expression of endearment found in Egyptian and Israelite love poetry (Song 4.9–10; 5.1–2). **13:** *Like an angel of God*, see 2 Sam 14.20. The phrase (not found in the Heb) implies wisdom and absence of evil intent. **15:** *Fainted*, see 15.7n.

¹⁴ For you are wonderful, my lord, and your countenance is full of grace." ¹⁵ And while she was speaking, she fainted and fell. ¹⁶ Then the king was agitated, and all his servants tried to comfort her.

END OF ADDITION D

5 ª ³ The king said to her, "What do you wish, Esther? What is your request? It shall be given you, even to half of my kingdom." ⁴ And Esther said, "Today is a special day for me. If it pleases the king, let him and Haman come to the dinner that I shall prepare today." ⁵ Then the king said, "Bring Haman quickly, so that we may do as Esther desires." So they both came to the dinner that Esther had spoken about. ⁶ While they were drinking wine, the king said to Esther, "What is it, Queen Esther? It shall be granted you." ⁷ She said, "My petition and request is: ⁸ if I have found favor in the sight of the king, let the king and Haman come to the dinner that I shall prepare them, and tomorrow I will do as I have done today."

⁹ So Haman went out from the king joyful and glad of heart. But when he saw Mordecai the Jew in the courtyard, he was filled with anger. ¹⁰ Nevertheless, he went home and summoned his friends and his wife Zosara. ¹¹ And he told them about his riches and the honor that the king had bestowed on him, and how he had advanced him to be the first in the kingdom. ¹² And Haman said, "The queen did not invite anyone to the dinner with the king except me; and I am invited again tomorrow. ¹³ But these things give me no pleasure as long as I see Mordecai the Jew in the courtyard." ¹⁴ His wife Zosara and his friends said to him, "Let a gallows be made, fifty cubits high, and

in the morning tell the king to have Mordecai hanged on it. Then, go merrily with the king to the dinner." This advice pleased Haman, and so the gallows was prepared.

6 That night the Lord took sleep from the king, so he gave orders to his secretary to bring the book of daily records, and to read to him. ² He found the words written about Mordecai, how he had told the king about the two royal eunuchs who were on guard and sought to lay hands on King Artaxerxes. ³ The king said, "What honor or dignity did we bestow on Mordecai?" The king's servants said, "You have not done anything for him." ⁴ While the king was inquiring about the goodwill shown by Mordecai, Haman was in the courtyard. The king asked, "Who is in the courtyard?" Now Haman had come to speak to the king about hanging Mordecai on the gallows that he had prepared. ⁵ The servants of the king answered, "Haman is standing in the courtyard." And the king said, "Summon him." ⁶ Then the king said to Haman, "What shall I do for the person whom I wish to honor?" And Haman said to himself, "Whom would the king wish to honor more than me?" ⁷ So he said to the king, "For a person whom the king wishes to honor, ⁸ let the king's servants bring out the fine linen robe that the king has worn, and the horse on which the king rides, ⁹ and let both be given to one of the king's honored Friends, and let him robe the person whom the king loves and mount him on the horse, and let it be proclaimed through the open square of the city, saying, 'Thus shall it be done to everyone

---

ª In Greek, Chapter D replaces verses 1 and 2 in Hebrew.

5.3–8: Esther invites the king and Haman to dinner. **3:** *Half of my kingdom* is customary folktale hyperbole. **4:** Esther frames her invitation in self-effacing terms. *Dinner*, see 1.3n. Food, reassuring and nurturing, is a frequent motif in stories of women confronting powerful men; Esther works indirectly to achieve her goal (Judg 5.25; Jdt 10.5; 12.1,17–20).

5.9–14: Haman's happiness is spoiled. **11–12:** Haman's boasting sets him up as an arrogant fool ripe for a fall, a theme also found in wisdom literature (Prov 11.28; 13.3; 16.5,18; 27.1; 29.20). **14:** *Zosara* is an exemplary son-bearing wife (9.7–10) whose husband heeds her loyal counsel. *Gallows* (also 9.13–14), see 2.23n. *Fifty cubits*, ca. 72 ft (22m), an exaggerated height. Only *the king* can order an execution.

6.1–13: Mordecai's triumph. **1:** *The Lord took sleep from the king*, unlike the Heb, the Gk ascribes the events of the Esther story to divine intention and intervention (11.1–12; 10.4–12; 4.14n.; 15.1–16). A sleepless king appears in numerous folktales (Dan 6.18; 1 Esd 3.3). **3:** Herodotus (8.85,90) notes that Persian kings kept records of courtiers' noble deeds. *You have not done anything for him*, in contrast to Mordecai's royal reward for reporting the earlier plot in Gk Addition A (see 12.5). **8:** A *robe* and a *horse* were gestures of favor (Gen 37.3; 41.42; 1 Sam

whom the king honors.'" [10] Then the king said to Haman, "You have made an excellent suggestion! Do just as you have said for Mordecai the Jew, who is on duty in the courtyard. And let nothing be omitted from what you have proposed." [11] So Haman got the robe and the horse; he put the robe on Mordecai and made him ride through the open square of the city, proclaiming, "Thus shall it be done to everyone whom the king wishes to honor." [12] Then Mordecai returned to the courtyard, and Haman hurried back to his house, mourning and with his head covered. [13] Haman told his wife Zosara and his friends what had befallen him. His friends and his wife said to him, "If Mordecai is of the Jewish people, and you have begun to be humiliated before him, you will surely fall. You will not be able to defend yourself, because the living God is with him."

[14] While they were still talking, the eunuchs arrived and hurriedly brought Haman to the banquet that Esther had prepared.

7 [1] So the king and Haman went in to drink with the queen. [2] And the second day, as they were drinking wine, the king said, "What is it, Queen Esther? What is your petition and what is your request? It shall be granted to you, even to half of my kingdom." [3] She answered and said, "If I have found favor with the king, let my life be granted me at my petition, and my people at my request. [4] For we have been sold, I and my people, to be destroyed, plundered, and made slaves—we and our children—male and female slaves. This has come to my knowledge. Our antagonist brings shame on[a] the king's court." [5] Then the king said, "Who is the person that would dare

to do this thing?" [6] Esther said, "Our enemy is this evil man Haman!" At this, Haman was terrified in the presence of the king and queen.

[7] The king rose from the banquet and went into the garden, and Haman began to beg for his life from the queen, for he saw that he was in serious trouble. [8] When the king returned from the garden, Haman had thrown himself on the couch, pleading with the queen. The king said, "Will he dare even assault my wife in my own house?" Haman, when he heard, turned away his face. [9] Then Bugathan, one of the eunuchs, said to the king, "Look, Haman has even prepared a gallows for Mordecai, who gave information of concern to the king; it is standing at Haman's house, a gallows fifty cubits high." So the king said, "Let Haman be hanged on that." [10] So Haman was hanged on the gallows he had prepared for Mordecai. With that the anger of the king abated.

8 On that very day King Artaxerxes granted to Esther all the property of the persecutor[b] Haman. Mordecai was summoned by the king, for Esther had told the king[c] that he was related to her. [2] The king took the ring that had been taken from Haman, and gave it to Mordecai; and Esther set Mordecai over everything that had been Haman's.

[3] Then she spoke once again to the king and, falling at his feet, she asked him to avert all the evil that Haman had planned against the Jews. [4] The king extended his golden scepter to Esther, and she rose and stood

a   Gk is not worthy of
b   Gk slanderer
c   Gk him

18.4; 1 Kings 1.33). **12:** Haman covered his head as a sign of grief (2 Sam 15.30; 19.4; Jer 14.4), foreshadowing his own demise, as his wife and friends recognize (v.13). **13:** Because the living God is with him (lacking in the Heb text), an example of Gentile wisdom, Zosara and Haman's friends make explicit the story's theme of divine retribution and Jewish triumph (11.1–12; 15.1–16; 6.1; 10.4–12; 4.14n.; see Josh 2.6–14; Jdt 5.20–21; 3 Macc 3.8–10,31).

6.14–7.10: Esther's second banquet and Haman's fall. **7.2:** Half of my kingdom, see 5.3n. **4:** Sold, probably an allusion to Haman's bribe in 3.11; (see 4.7; but note the metaphorical use of the verb in Deut 32.30; Judg 2.14; 3.8; 4.2,9; 10.7). Shame on the king's court, the king would be shamed if his queen were dishonored. **6:** Like Esther before the king in 15.5, now Haman is terrified in the presence of the king and queen. **8:** Assault my wife, Artaxerxes misinterprets Haman's gesture as a sexual assault on the queen, an unpardonable affront to both male and royal honor and, as such, a capital offense. **9–10:** Bugathan, Heb "Harbona." Gallows, see 2.23n., an ironic reversal of the death Haman intended for Mordecai.

8.1–12: The king shows favor to Esther, Mordecai, and the Jews. **1:** In 3.9, Haman offered the king money; now the king gives Haman's wealth to Esther. **2:** Haman's position as grand vizier (3.10) becomes Mordecai's with the transfer of the king's signet ring (see v. 8; 3.10n.), another ironic inversion of the two figures. **5:** That

before the king. ⁵ Esther said, "If it pleases you, and if I have found favor, let an order be sent rescinding the letters that Haman wrote and sent to destroy the Jews in your kingdom. ⁶ How can I look on the ruin of my people? How can I be safe if my ancestral nationᵃ is destroyed?" ⁷ The king said to Esther, "Now that Iᵇ have granted all of Haman's property to you and have hanged him on a tree because he acted against the Jews, what else do you request? ⁸ Write in my name what you think best and seal it with my ring; for whatever is written at the king's command and sealed with my ring cannot be contravened."

⁹ The secretaries were summoned on the twenty-third day of the first month, that is, Nisan, in the same year; and all that he commanded with respect to the Jews was given in writing to the administrators and governors of the provinces from India to Ethiopia, one hundred twenty-seven provinces, to each province in its own language. ¹⁰ The edict was writtenᶜ with the king's authority and sealed with his ring, and sent out by couriers. ¹¹ He ordered the Jews in every city to observe their own laws, to defend themselves, and to act as they wished against their opponents and enemies ¹² on a certain day, the thirteenth of the twelfth month, which is Adar, throughout all the kingdom of Artaxerxes.

ADDITION E

16 ᵈ The following is a copy of this letter: "The Great King, Artaxerxes, to the governors of the provinces from India to Ethiopia, one hundred twenty-seven provinces, and to those who are loyal to our government, greetings.

² "Many people, the more they are honored with the most generous kindness of their benefactors, the more proud do they become, ³ and not only seek to injure our subjects, but in their inability to stand prosperity, they even undertake to scheme against their own benefactors. ⁴ They not only take away thankfulness from others, but, carried away by the boasts of those who know nothing of goodness, they even assume that they will escape the evil-hating justice of God, who always sees everything. ⁵ And often many of those who are set in places of authority have been made in part responsible for the shedding of innocent blood, and have been involved in irremediable calamities, by the persuasion of friends who have been entrusted with the administration of public affairs, ⁶ when these persons by the false trickery of their evil natures beguile the sincere goodwill of their sovereigns.

⁷ "What has been wickedly accomplished through the pestilent behavior of those who exercise authority unworthily can be seen, not so much from the more ancient records that we hand on, as from investigation of matters close at hand.ᵉ ⁸ In the future we will take care to render our kingdom quiet and peaceable for all, ⁹ by changing our methods and always judging what comes before our eyes with more equitable consideration. ¹⁰ For Haman son of Hammedatha, a Macedonian

ᵃ Gk *country*
ᵇ Gk *If I*
ᶜ Gk *It was written*
ᵈ Chapter 16.1-24 corresponds to chapter E 1-24 in some translations.
ᵉ Gk *matters beside* (your) *feet*

Haman wrote, Esther diplomatically dissociates the king from the edict that condemned the Jews. **8:** The king's earlier edict *cannot be contravened* (1.19n.), but a new edict can neutralize the former's intent. **9:** *First month . . . Nisan* (March-April), Heb "third month . . . Sivan" (May-June). *In its own language*, see 1.22n. **11:** This explicit permission for the *Jews . . . to observe their own laws* (see 3.8n.; 13.4–5), which is a distinctly religious concern, is lacking in the Heb. **12:** The date of the intended extermination (3.7,13) becomes a day of triumph and relates to the Purim festival (see 9.21). *Adar*, February-March.

Addition E: 16.1–24: The king's second letter: Denunciation of Haman, praise of Mordecai and Esther, and direction to his subjects to help the Jews. Addition E to the Gk version of Esther provides a counterpoint to Addition C (13.1–17). Both were composed in Gk probably by the same author. The Gentile king refers in the most positive terms to the Jews and their God (Ex 9.27; 18.10–11; Num 22–24; 2 Kings 5.15; Dan 2.47; 3.29; 4.1–3,34–37; 6.26–27; Jdt 5.5–21). **2:** *Benefactors*, a reference to the king. **10:** Haman is actually a *Macedonian* scheming to overthrow Persian rule (v. 14; cf. 12.6), a plot twist not found in the Heb. This may be an allusion to the conquest of Persia by the Macedonian Alexander the Great in 333 BCE, an event already in the past when Addition E was composed.

(really an alien to the Persian blood, and quite devoid of our kindliness), having become our guest, [11] enjoyed so fully the goodwill that we have for every nation that he was called our father and was continually bowed down to by all as the person second to the royal throne. [12] But, unable to restrain his arrogance, he undertook to deprive us of our kingdom and our life,[a] [13] and with intricate craft and deceit asked for the destruction of Mordecai, our savior and perpetual benefactor, and of Esther, the blameless partner of our kingdom, together with their whole nation. [14] He thought that by these methods he would catch us undefended and would transfer the kingdom of the Persians to the Macedonians.

[15] "But we find that the Jews, who were consigned to annihilation by this thrice-accursed man, are not evildoers, but are governed by most righteous laws [16] and are children of the living God, most high, most mighty,[b] who has directed the kingdom both for us and for our ancestors in the most excellent order.

[17] "You will therefore do well not to put in execution the letters sent by Haman son of Hammedatha, [18] since he, the one who did these things, has been hanged at the gate of Susa with all his household—for God, who rules over all things, has speedily inflicted on him the punishment that he deserved.

[19] "Therefore post a copy of this letter publicly in every place, and permit the Jews to live under their own laws. [20] And give them reinforcements, so that on the thirteenth day of the twelfth month, Adar, on that very day, they may defend themselves against those who attack them at the time of oppression. [21] For God, who rules over all things, has made this day to be a joy for his chosen people instead of a day of destruction for them. [22] "Therefore you shall observe this with all good cheer as a notable day among your commemorative festivals, [23] so that both now

and hereafter it may represent deliverance for you[c] and the loyal Persians, but that it may be a reminder of destruction for those who plot against us.

[24] "Every city and country, without exception, that does not act accordingly shall be destroyed in wrath with spear and fire. It shall be made not only impassable for human beings, but also most hateful to wild animals and birds for all time.

END OF ADDITION E

8 [13] "Let copies of the decree be posted conspicuously in all the kingdom, and let all the Jews be ready on that day to fight against their enemies."

[14] So the messengers on horseback set out with all speed to perform what the king had commanded; and the decree was published also in Susa. [15] Mordecai went out dressed in the royal robe and wearing a gold crown and a turban of purple linen. The people in Susa rejoiced on seeing him. [16] And the Jews had light and gladness [17] in every city and province wherever the decree was published; wherever the proclamation was made, the Jews had joy and gladness, a banquet and a holiday. And many of the Gentiles were circumcised and became Jews out of fear of the Jews.

9 Now on the thirteenth day of the twelfth month, which is Adar, the decree written by the king arrived. [2] On that same day the enemies of the Jews perished; no one resisted, because they feared them. [3] The chief provincial governors, the princes, and the royal secretaries were paying honor to the Jews, because fear of Mordecai weighed upon them. [4] The king's decree required that Mordecai's name be held in honor throughout the

---

a Gk *our spirit*
b Gk *greatest*
c Other ancient authorities read *for us*

11: *Our father*, 13.6. *Second to the royal throne*, 13.3 (2 Chr 28.7; 1 Esd 3.7). **17:** *Letters sent by Haman*, see 8.8n. **18:** The Gk's reference to the death of Haman's family contradicts 7.9 and 9.7–10,13–14. **19:** *Their own laws* (absent in the Heb), see vv. 15–16; 8.11n. **21:** *Chosen people*, Deut 7.6; 1 Kings 3.8; 1 Chr 16.13; Ps 105.6; Isa 43.20 (see Esth 13.15–17). **22–23:** These verses, addressed to all the king's subjects, may hint at a non-Jewish origin for the Purim festival.

8.13–17: Dispatch of the king's decree. 14: See 3.13n. **17:** *Gentiles were circumcised and became Jews*, the Gk here interprets literally the ambiguous wording of the Heb.

9.1–19: The Jews triumph over their enemies. 2: *No one resisted*, contradicts the Heb ("no one could withstand them"), and vv. 11,16. **10:** The death of *the ten sons of Haman* agrees with the Heb but contradicts 16.18 (see

kingdom.[a] [6] Now in the city of Susa the Jews killed five hundred people, [7] including Pharsannestain, Delphon, Phasga, [8] Pharadatha, Barea, Sarbacha, [9] Marmasima, Aruphaeus, Arsaeus, Zabutheus, [10] the ten sons of Haman son of Hammedatha, the Bougean, the enemy of the Jews—and they indulged[b] themselves in plunder.

[11] That very day the number of those killed in Susa was reported to the king. [12] The king said to Esther, "In Susa, the capital, the Jews have destroyed five hundred people. What do you suppose they have done in the surrounding countryside? Whatever more you ask will be done for you." [13] And Esther said to the king, "Let the Jews be allowed to do the same tomorrow. Also, hang up the bodies of Haman's ten sons." [14] So he permitted this to be done, and handed over to the Jews of the city the bodies of Haman's sons to hang up. [15] The Jews who were in Susa gathered on the fourteenth and killed three hundred people, but took no plunder.

[16] Now the other Jews in the kingdom gathered to defend themselves, and got relief from their enemies. They destroyed fifteen thousand of them, but did not engage in plunder. [17] On the fourteenth day they rested and made that same day a day of rest, celebrating it with joy and gladness. [18] The Jews who were in Susa, the capital, came together also on the fourteenth, but did not rest. They celebrated the fifteenth with joy and gladness. [19] On this account then the Jews who are scattered around the country outside Susa keep the fourteenth of Adar as a joyful holiday, and send presents of food to one another, while those who live in the large cities keep the fifteenth day of Adar as their joyful holiday, also sending presents to one another.

[20] Mordecai recorded these things in a book, and sent it to the Jews in the kingdom of Artaxerxes both near and far, [21] telling them that they should keep the fourteenth and fifteenth days of Adar, [22] for on these days the Jews got relief from their enemies. The whole month (namely, Adar), in which their condition had been changed from sorrow into gladness and from a time of distress to a holiday, was to be celebrated as a time for feasting[c] and gladness and for sending presents of food to their friends and to the poor.

[23] So the Jews accepted what Mordecai had written to them [24]—how Haman son of Hammedatha, the Macedonian,[d] fought against them, how he made a decree and cast lots[e] to destroy them, [25] and how he went in to the king, telling him to hang Mordecai; but the wicked plot he had devised against the Jews came back upon himself, and he and his sons were hanged. [26] Therefore these days were called "Purim," because of the lots (for in their language this is the word that means "lots"). And so, because of what was written in this letter, and because of what they had experienced in this affair and what had befallen them, Mordecai established this festival,[f] [27] and the Jews took upon themselves, upon their descendants, and upon all who would join them, to observe it without fail.[g] These days of Purim should be a memorial and kept from generation to generation, in every city, family, and country. [28] These days of Purim were to be observed for all time, and the

[a] Meaning of Gk uncertain. Some ancient authorities add verse 5, *So the Jews struck down all their enemies with the sword, killing and destroying them, and they did as they pleased to those who hated them.*
[b] Other ancient authorities read *did not indulge*
[c] Gk *of weddings*
[d] Other ancient witnesses read *the Bougean*
[e] Gk *a lot*
[f] Gk *he established* (it)
[g] Meaning of Gk uncertain

note). *Indulged themselves in plunder* contradicted by both the Heb and Gk 9:15–16. **12–15:** Notice of the extra day for observing the king's edict is probably included to explain why the Jews of Susa celebrated Purim on the fifteenth of Adar and country Jews on the fourteenth (see 9.18–19). *Plunder*, see v.10n. **16:** *Destroyed fifteen thousand*, Heb "seventy-five thousand."

18–19: Differences in Purim dates are explained (see vv. 12–15n.). Jews today continue to observe Purim with feasting and *presents of food*.

9.20–32: The inauguration of the feast of Purim. The emphasis here upon the written word, a particular concern in postexilic Judaism, was probably intended to legitimate a festival not mentioned in the Torah (cf. the origin of Hanukkah: 1 Macc 4.56–59; 2 Macc 1.1–2.28; 10.1–8). **21:** See 9.12–15n. **22:** Purim commemorates not the day of the Jews' military triumph, but the day they obtained their *relief. Sorrow into gladness*, see Isa

commemoration of them was never to cease among their descendants.

[29] Then Queen Esther daughter of Aminadab along with Mordecai the Jew wrote down what they had done, and gave full authority to the letter about Purim.[a] [31] And Mordecai and Queen Esther established this decision on their own responsibility, pledging their own well-being to the plan.[b] [32] Esther established it by a decree forever, and it was written for a memorial.

10
The king levied a tax upon his kingdom both by land and sea. [2] And as for his power and bravery, and the wealth and glory of his kingdom, they were recorded in the annals of the kings of the Persians and the Medes. [3] Mordecai acted with authority on behalf of King Artaxerxes and was great in the kingdom, as well as honored by the Jews. His way of life was such as to make him beloved to his whole nation.

ADDITION F

[4][b] And Mordecai said, "These things have come from God; [5] for I remember the dream that I had concerning these matters, and none of them has failed to be fulfilled. [6] There was the little spring that became a river, and there was light and sun and abundant water—the river is Esther, whom the king married and made queen. [7] The two dragons are Haman and myself. [8] The nations are those that gathered to destroy the name of the Jews. [9] And my nation, this is Israel, who cried out to God and

was saved. The Lord has saved his people; the Lord has rescued us from all these evils; God has done great signs and wonders, wonders that have never happened among the nations. [10] For this purpose he made two lots, one for the people of God and one for all the nations, [11] and these two lots came to the hour and moment and day of decision before God and among all the nations. [12] And God remembered his people and vindicated his inheritance. [13] So they will observe these days in the month of Adar, on the fourteenth and fifteenth[c] of that month, with an assembly and joy and gladness before God, from generation to generation

11
forever among his people Israel." [1] In the fourth year of the reign of Ptolemy and Cleopatra, Dositheus, who said that he was a priest and a Levite,[d] and his son Ptolemy brought to Egypt[e] the preceding Letter about Purim, which they said was authentic and had been translated by Lysimachus son of Ptolemy, one of the residents of Jerusalem.

END OF ADDITION F

---

[a] Verse 30 in Heb is lacking in Gk: *Letters were sent to all the Jews, to the one hundred twenty-seven provinces of the kingdom of Ahasuerus, in words of peace and truth.*

[b] Chapter 10.4-13 and 11.1 correspond to chapter F 1-11 in some translations.

[c] Other ancient authorities lack *and fifteenth*

[d] Or *priest, and Levitas*

[e] Cn: Gk *brought in*

61.3; Jer 31.13. **24–26:** This plot summary, which does not mention Esther, differs slightly from the Heb version. The festival came to be called *"Purim"* for the lot, "pur" (pl. "purim"), which Haman cast (see 3.7n.). **32:** *Esther established it*, Queen Esther is the only woman in the Bible credited with establishing a religious observance.

10.1–3: The greatness of Artaxerxes and Mordecai. 1: This seemingly irrelevant comment may imply that the king prospered with Mordecai's assistance (see Gen 47.1–26). **2:** *Recorded in the annals*, a standard formula for historical reports in Kings and Chronicles (1 Kings 14.19,29; 2 Chr 25.26; 32.32).

Addition F: 10.4–13: Epilogue: Mordecai's dream explained. This addition rounds out the Gk version of Esther with an explanation of Mordecai's dream with which the book began (11.2–12n.). **4:** *These things have come from God*, the theme of Gk Esther (11.12; 4.14; 15.8; 6.1,13; 16.4; see Ps 118.23). **6:** *Light and sun*, 11.11n.; 8.16. **8:** *Name*, in ancient times, the essence of one's identity resided largely in one's name. **10:** *Two lots*, not mentioned in 11.2–12. This verse may represent an alternative derivation for Purim. It assumes a different context for the "lots" that give Purim its name (9.23; 3.7n.), understanding them as symbols of destiny (Dan 12.13; Isa 17.14; Jer 13.25). A similar concept appears in the Dead Sea Scrolls (1QS 2.2,5; 3.1–4.26). **13:** *So they will observe these days*, see 9.20–22.

11.1: The colophon to Gk Esther provides a probable date reference for the Gk translation. *Ptolemy and Cleopatra*, because three kings of Egypt named Ptolemy had wives named Cleopatra, the *fourth year* could be 114–113, 78–77, or 49–48 BCE. *Dositheus*, a common Hellenistic name (2 Macc 12.19,35; 3 Macc 1.3); presumably a copyist, he affirms the text's authenticity and his own religious authority. *Letter about Purim*, probably the entire book of Esther. *Lysimachus*, a Greek name (cf. 2 Macc 4.29), likely the translator of Heb Esther into Gk.

THE WISDOM OF SOLOMON

NAME AND CANONICAL STATUS

The title of the book in most manuscripts is "The Wisdom of Solomon." It is a Jewish writing, but it was preserved in Christian circles, like other Jewish writings in Greek. There is no evidence that the writing was accepted as canonical by any Jewish group, or even read by Jewish readers until many centuries after it had been written. The work seems to have been known to Clement of Rome and possibly Ignatius (late first-early second century CE). The Wisdom of Solomon was certainly used as Scripture by such early third-century writers as Tertullian, Clement of Alexandria, and Pseudo-Hippolytus. On the other hand, its canonicity was doubted by Origen, although he sometimes quotes it as if it were canonical. The book became a part of the Roman Catholic and Eastern Orthodox canons but is considered one of the Apocrypha by many Protestant groups.

AUTHORSHIP, DATE, AND HISTORICAL CONTEXT

Although the author claims to be King Solomon (with parts of ch 9 based on his prayer for wisdom in 1 Kings 3.6–9), this ascription has been recognized as a literary fiction since ancient times. Instead, the author is an anonymous Hellenistic Jew writing some time in the late first century BCE or early first century CE. The author most likely came from the Jewish community in Alexandria in Egypt or possibly from another major center in the Hellenistic world. In spite of seeming to appeal to Greek readers, the work is evidently aimed at an internal audience, probably the Jewish youth of Alexandria who might be tempted by the Hellenistic culture around them.

Some recent commentators view the book as originating in the historical context of the troubles experienced by the Alexandrian Jewish community in the period 38–41 CE, but the book gives no hint of a period of trauma or threat. Others have argued that the book is earlier, dating from the reign of the Roman emperor Augustus (27 BCE–14 CE). Nothing prevents the book from being this early. Typologically, The Wisdom of Solomon represents an earlier stage of development in the trajectory of biblical interpretation that reached its culmination in the Jewish philosopher Philo of Alexandria. A date about 20 BCE would fit the contents of the book.

GENRE, STRUCTURE, AND CONTENTS

The genre of the book has been analyzed in two distinct ways. One is as an "encomium," defined by Aristotle as a work praising someone or, in this case, something—the quality of wisdom. Much of the content of the book can be seen as part of an encomium if the structure is understood as follows:

Introduction	chs 1–6
Encomium proper	chs 6–9
Comparison	10.1–19.9
Epilogue and conclusion	19.10–22

Another suggestion is that The Wisdom of Solomon is an "exhortatory discourse." This is a much more specialized type of writing that was cultivated in philosophical schools and argued for and extolled a philosophical lifestyle. In addition to these two literary forms, The Wisdom of Solomon also has much in common with the "diatribe." The Hellenistic diatribe was a specific rhetorical form and should not be confused with the English term "diatribe"; it was essentially a type of moral discourse in the form of a speech or address, much favored by the philosophical street preachers among the Cynics and Stoics, though recent study has emphasized its home in an academic context. Its aim was to convince the hearers of a particular course of action, and it always had a moral theme.

Some scholars have argued that a concentric internal structure (or "chiastic" structure) with parallel elements can be found in various passages of The Wisdom of Solomon, indicating a deliberate arrangement of material. Some of these arrangements affect only individual passages of a few verses or so (for example, see chs 7–8). Others suggest an overall structure to the book. For example:

1–6	Book of Eschatology
7–10	Book of Wisdom
11–19	Book of History

Arguments about how to divide the book are often based on an inclusio, in which a section is delimited by having the same device (e.g., a word, a phrase, a sentence, a subject) at the beginning and the end. For example, the Book of Eschatology begins with an address to the rulers of the earth (ch 1) and ends with an address to the kings of the earth (ch 6), suggesting that chs 1–6 formed a complete unit in the mind of the author.

The Book of Eschatology (chs 1–6) contrasts the lives of the just and the wicked, dramatizing the eschatological destinies of the two groups. The next section, the Book of Wisdom (chs 7–10), celebrates the figure of divine Sophia (Wisdom). The author's persona as Solomon emerges most clearly here, as the king describes wisdom and his pursuit of her. The third section, the Book of History (chs 11–19), adopts the approach of historical comparison, presenting an elaborate system of contrasts based largely on Ex 7–14. A series of digressions in 11.17–15.19 explains why God's judgment manifested itself differently in dealing with the Egyptians and the Israelites. This adaptation of the Exodus story is meant to complement the arguments of the first two sections, providing biblical examples of the righteous and the unrighteous, and demonstrating how the power of divine wisdom operates in human history.

GUIDE TO READING

As a carefully crafted work, the book is best read in its entirety. For an understanding of its distinctive style and philosophical approach, comparing its summaries of biblical history in 10.1–11.14 with the corresponding passages in Genesis and Exodus will be fruitful.

Lester L. Grabbe

1 Love righteousness, you rulers of the
    earth,
think of the Lord in goodness
and seek him with sincerity of heart;
² because he is found by those who do not
    put him to the test,
and manifests himself to those who do not
    distrust him.
³ For perverse thoughts separate people
    from God,
and when his power is tested, it exposes
    the foolish;

⁴ because wisdom will not enter a deceitful
    soul,
or dwell in a body enslaved to sin.
⁵ For a holy and disciplined spirit will flee
    from deceit,
and will leave foolish thoughts behind,
and will be ashamed at the approach of
    unrighteousness.

⁶ For wisdom is a kindly spirit,
but will not free blasphemers from the
    guilt of their words;

1.1–6.21: The Book of Eschatology. Many scholars see this "book" as having a concentric structure, as follows:

   A. Address to judges: exhortation to justice (1.1–15)

     B. Speech of the wicked (1.16–2.24)

       C. Four paired contrasts of the just and the wicked (3.1–4.20)

     B.' Speech of the wicked (5.1–23)

   A.' Address to kings: exhortation to wisdom (6.1–21).

For those who analyze the book as an encomium (see Introduction), chs 1–6 function as the introduction ("exordium") whose theme is Wisdom's gift of immortality to the righteous. This section addresses "rulers of the earth" in what is mainly a discourse on righteousness and wickedness.

1.1–15: An exhortation to justice. The figure of Wisdom is introduced (v. 4) and seems to be equated with a *holy . . . spirit* (v. 5) or *the spirit of the Lord* (v. 7). Specific references to wisdom then disappear until ch 6. Much of the passage is framed negatively, focusing on those things that are the opposite of wisdom and God's spirit: *perverse thoughts* (v. 3), *sin* (v. 4), injustice (vv. 5,8), blasphemy (v. 6), *counsels of the ungodly* (v. 9), *lawless deeds* (v. 9), and so on. 1: The verse is reminiscent of Ps 2.2; other passages seem to presuppose this Psalm (see 2.10–20; 4.8,19; 6.1,21). The book begins with the literary device of the apostrophe, a direct address to the hearers or readers, though the actual audience is the Hellenistic Jewish community, not their Gentile rulers. This is one of the features of the diatribe that has influenced the rhetoric of Wisdom of Solomon; see also 2.10–20n. 5:

because God is witness of their inmost
feelings,
and a true observer of their hearts, and a
hearer of their tongues.
⁷ Because the spirit of the Lord has filled
the world,
and that which holds all things together
knows what is said,
⁸ therefore those who utter unrighteous
things will not escape notice,
and justice, when it punishes, will not pass
them by.
⁹ For inquiry will be made into the
counsels of the ungodly,
and a report of their words will come to
the Lord,
to convict them of their lawless deeds;
¹⁰ because a jealous ear hears all
things,
and the sound of grumbling does not go
unheard.
¹¹ Beware then of useless grumbling,
and keep your tongue from slander;
because no secret word is without
result,ᵃ
and a lying mouth destroys the soul.

¹² Do not invite death by the error of your
life,
or bring on destruction by the works of
your hands;
¹³ because God did not make death,
and he does not delight in the death of the
living.
¹⁴ For he created all things so that they
might exist;

the generative forcesᵇ of the world are
wholesome,
and there is no destructive poison in them,
and the dominionᶜ of Hades is not on
earth.
¹⁵ For righteousness is immortal.

¹⁶ But the ungodly by their words and
deeds summoned death;ᵈ
considering him a friend, they pined away
and made a covenant with him,
because they are fit to belong to his
company.

2 For they reasoned unsoundly, saying to
themselves,
"Short and sorrowful is our life,
and there is no remedy when a life comes
to its end,
and no one has been known to return from
Hades.
² For we were born by mere chance,
and hereafter we shall be as though we
had never been,
for the breath in our nostrils is smoke,
and reason is a spark kindled by the
beating of our hearts;
³ when it is extinguished, the body will
turn to ashes,
and the spirit will dissolve like empty air.
⁴ Our name will be forgotten in time,
and no one will remember our works;

ᵃ Or *will go unpunished*
ᵇ Or *the creatures*
ᶜ Or *palace*
ᵈ Gk *him*

Wisdom is a product of the *spirit* of God; cf. Isa 2.11. 6: *A kindly spirit*, literally "a philanthropic spirit," i.e., loving humanity (cf. 7.22–23; 12.19; 15.1). 7: See 12.1n. 11: *Tongue*, counsel on the vices of human speech is ubiquitous in wisdom literature (e.g., Prov 2.12; 4.24; 10.11,18–19,31–32; Sir 9.18; 20.24–26; 28.12–26). 12–15: These verses anticipate the discussion on immortality that follows in chs 2–6. 13: *Death* is eternal separation from God, the condition of the sinner. Here the author does not refer to the reality of physical death. 14: *Hades*, the abode of the dead in Greek tradition; comparable to Heb "Sheol." 15: Immortality is not an innate condition of the soul but God's gift to the righteous (see Philo, *On the Confusion of Tongues*, 149); see 2.23–24n.

1.16–2.24: The deluded reasoning of the ungodly. The passage's style resembles that of the Greco-Roman diatribe, which often included argumentative exchanges with a fictional adversary. Here the ungodly are made to explain their actions and motives *to themselves* (2.1–20). The writer then disproves the reasoning of the ungodly (vv. 21–24). The view expressed is Epicurean or a caricature of the Epicurean belief, which argued that everything was material, that life and the universe came about by accident, and that death was the end of the person. Epicureans were accused of being atheists and of promoting a sensual lifestyle. Some of this was broadly true, but in reality the Epicurean lifestyle was one of moderation, not excess. 1.16: For the *covenant* with *death* cf. Isa 28.15. 2.1–5: This view of death is reflected also in Job 7.9–10; 14.1–2; Eccl 2.14,16,24; 3.12,19; 6.12;

our life will pass away like the traces of a
cloud,
and be scattered like mist
that is chased by the rays of the sun
and overcome by its heat.
⁵ For our allotted time is the passing of a
shadow,
and there is no return from our death,
because it is sealed up and no one turns
back.

⁶ "Come, therefore, let us enjoy the good
things that exist,
and make use of the creation to the full as
in youth.
⁷ Let us take our fill of costly wine and
perfumes,
and let no flower of spring pass us by.
⁸ Let us crown ourselves with rosebuds
before they wither.
⁹ Let none of us fail to share in our revelry;
everywhere let us leave signs of
enjoyment,
because this is our portion, and this our lot.
¹⁰ Let us oppress the righteous poor man;
let us not spare the widow
or regard the gray hairs of the aged.
¹¹ But let our might be our law of right,
for what is weak proves itself to be useless.

¹² "Let us lie in wait for the righteous man,
because he is inconvenient to us and
opposes our actions;
he reproaches us for sins against the law,
and accuses us of sins against our training.
¹³ He professes to have knowledge of God,
and calls himself a childᵃ of the Lord.
¹⁴ He became to us a reproof of our
thoughts;

¹⁵ the very sight of him is a burden to us,
because his manner of life is unlike that of
others,
and his ways are strange.
¹⁶ We are considered by him as something
base,
and he avoids our ways as unclean;
he calls the last end of the righteous
happy,
and boasts that God is his father.
¹⁷ Let us see if his words are true,
and let us test what will happen at the end
of his life;
¹⁸ for if the righteous man is God's child, he
will help him,
and will deliver him from the hand of his
adversaries.
¹⁹ Let us test him with insult and torture,
so that we may find out how gentle he is,
and make trial of his forbearance.
²⁰ Let us condemn him to a shameful
death,
for, according to what he says, he will be
protected."

²¹ Thus they reasoned, but they were led
astray,
for their wickedness blinded them,
²² and they did not know the secret
purposes of God,
nor hoped for the wages of holiness,
nor discerned the prize for blameless
souls;
²³ for God created us for incorruption,
and made us in the image of his own
eternity,ᵇ

ᵃ Or servant
ᵇ Other ancient authorities read nature

9.2,7–9). 1: Hades, see 1.14n. 6–9: In the reasoning of the ungodly, the threat of death warrants sensuality (see Isa 22.13). In Eccl 9.7 enjoyment of pleasure is recommended as a proper response to life under the shadow of death. 10–20: The wicked are misled by an irrational antipathy for the righteous and the weak, persecuting those who call God their father. This passage draws on Isa 52.13–53.12: vv. 13 and 16 describe the righteous as child, Gk "pais," which can also be translated "servant" (as in LXX Isa 52.13); cf. also vv. 19–20 with Isa 53.7–9. Other parallels in following chapters include 3.2–3 and Isa 53.4; 3.6 and Isa 53.7–10; 4.19 and Isa 52.15; 5.2 and Isa 52.14; 5.3–4 and Isa 53.3,10; 5.6 and Isa 53.6. The passage also shows affinities with 1 Enoch 62–63, probably indicating that both 1 Enoch and Wis have drawn on Isa 52–53. 13: Knowledge of God, a gift of wisdom illuminating the path to immortality (6.22; 7.12,17; 8.4,9; 10.10; 15.2–3; 18.6). Conversely the wicked refuse to know God (2.22; 12.27; 13.1,9; 14.22; 15.11; 16.16). 22: For the idea of the afterlife as part of the secret purposes of God, see also 1 Cor 4.5; 15.51; 1 Enoch 103.2; and the Book of Mysteries in the Dead Sea Scrolls, 1Q27 1.3–4. 23–24: These verses explain further what has already been asserted in 1.13–14: Humanity was created for immortality. Through the

²⁴ but through the devil's envy death entered the world,
and those who belong to his company experience it.

3 But the souls of the righteous are in the hand of God,
and no torment will ever touch them.
² In the eyes of the foolish they seemed to have died,
and their departure was thought to be a disaster,
³ and their going from us to be their destruction;
but they are at peace.
⁴ For though in the sight of others they were punished,
their hope is full of immortality.
⁵ Having been disciplined a little, they will receive great good,
because God tested them and found them worthy of himself;
⁶ like gold in the furnace he tried them,
and like a sacrificial burnt offering he accepted them.
⁷ In the time of their visitation they will shine forth,
and will run like sparks through the stubble.
⁸ They will govern nations and rule over peoples,

and the Lord will reign over them forever.
⁹ Those who trust in him will understand truth,
and the faithful will abide with him in love,
because grace and mercy are upon his holy ones,
and he watches over his elect.ᵃ

¹⁰ But the ungodly will be punished as their reasoning deserves,
those who disregarded the righteousᵇ
and rebelled against the Lord;
¹¹ for those who despise wisdom and instruction are miserable.
Their hope is vain, their labors are unprofitable,
and their works are useless.
¹² Their wives are foolish, and their children evil;
¹³ their offspring are accursed.
For blessed is the barren woman who is undefiled,
who has not entered into a sinful union;
she will have fruit when God examines souls.

ᵃ Text of this line uncertain; omitted by some ancient authorities. Compare 4.15
ᵇ Or *what is right*

devil's envy death entered refers to Gen 3.1–24 (see 6.23; 2 Enoch 31.3–6). Consequently, immortality (*incorruption*) is no longer a natural condition but a reward from God, contrasted with the view of this time in the Greek world that the soul was naturally immortal (see 1.16–2.24n., however, for the Epicurean view).

3.1–4.20: Four pairs contrasting the just and the wicked. 3.1–11: The souls of the righteous will be rewarded, and the wicked, punished; 3.12–19: the offspring of the righteous and the wicked; 4.1–6: better the childlessness of the righteous than the fertility of the wicked; 4.7–20: better a short life and righteousness than long life and wickedness.

3.1–11: First contrast, on suffering and death. The suffering and even death of the righteous is only apparent (vv. 1–9; cf. 1 Enoch 102.4–103.4; 103.9–104.6), in contrast to the wicked (vv. 10–11; cf. 1 Enoch 103.5–8; 104.7–10) who are rightly punished. 1: Souls, the author repeatedly emphasizes the primacy of the soul in constituting human identity (1.4,11; 2.22; 3.13; 4.14; 7.27; 8.19; 9.15; 10.16; 15.8,11). 4: The emphasis on immortality rather than bodily resurrection reflects Greek influence (1.15; 2.23; 4.1; 6.18–19; 8.13, 17; 12.1; 15.3; 2 Esd 2.45; 7.13,96; 8.54; 4 Macc 9.22). 5–6: The value of divine discipline; cf. 11.8–10; 12.20–22; 16.3–6,11; 18.20; Deut 8.5; Job 5.17; Prov 3.11–12; Sir 2.1–5; 4.17; 18.13–14; 32.14; 2 Macc 6.12–16; 7.33. 7: Shine forth, the star-like appearance of the glorified righteous is frequently mentioned in apocalyptic literature (cf. Dan 12.3; 2 Esd 7.97; 1 Enoch 104.2). 9: Watches over his elect, see 4.15; Ps 1.6; 145.20; Sir 46.14; 2 Macc 7.6.

3.12–19: Second contrast, on offspring. Better is childlessness than children through adultery and unlawful union. Since children were considered a blessing in the ancient world (e.g., Ps 127.3–5; 128.3–4), the author shows how the apparent good fortune of the ungodly in having children is illusory. See also 3.16–19; 4.3–6; cf. Sir 16.1–4; 23.22–27. 41.5–9. In contrast, barrenness, which was often thought to indicate divine displeasure

14 Blessed also is the eunuch whose hands
  have done no lawless deed,
and who has not devised wicked things
  against the Lord;
for special favor will be shown him for his
  faithfulness,
and a place of great delight in the temple
  of the Lord.
15 For the fruit of good labors is
  renowned,
and the root of understanding does not
  fail.
16 But children of adulterers will not come
  to maturity,
and the offspring of an unlawful union will
  perish.
17 Even if they live long they will be held of
  no account,
and finally their old age will be without
  honor.
18 If they die young, they will have no
  hope
and no consolation on the day of
  judgment.
19 For the end of an unrighteous generation
  is grievous.

4 Better than this is childlessness with
  virtue,
for in the memory of virtue[a] is
  immortality,
because it is known both by God and by
  mortals.
2 When it is present, people imitate[b] it,
and they long for it when it has gone;
throughout all time it marches, crowned in
  triumph,
victor in the contest for prizes that are
  undefiled.

3 But the prolific brood of the ungodly will
  be of no use,
and none of their illegitimate seedlings
  will strike a deep root
or take a firm hold.
4 For even if they put forth boughs for a
  while,
standing insecurely they will be shaken by
  the wind,
and by the violence of the winds they will
  be uprooted.
5 The branches will be broken off before
  they come to maturity,
and their fruit will be useless,
not ripe enough to eat, and good for
  nothing.
6 For children born of unlawful unions
are witnesses of evil against their parents
  when God examines them.[c]
7 But the righteous, though they die early,
  will be at rest.
8 For old age is not honored for length of
  time,
or measured by number of years;
9 but understanding is gray hair for
  anyone,
and a blameless life is ripe old age.

10 There were some who pleased God and
  were loved by him,
and while living among sinners were taken
  up.
11 They were caught up so that evil might
  not change their understanding
or guile deceive their souls.

a Gk it
b Other ancient authorities read honor
c Gk at their examination

(Gen 30.23) if not sin (1 Enoch 98.5), may be the condition of the morally pure. **14:** Although Deut 23.1 excluded eunuchs from the cultic assembly, this author assures the virtuous eunuch a place in the temple of the Lord, referring perhaps to the heavenly temple; cf. Isa 56.4–5.

4.1–6: Third contrast, parallel to 3.13–19 on offspring. **1:** The memory of virtue, God's remembrance of the virtuous is their guarantee of eternal life (cf. 8.13; Ps 112.6; Prov 10.7; Sir 44.8–15; 2 Esd 12.47). Conversely, the memory of the wicked will perish (4.19; see 2.4; Eccl 9.5). **3–5:** Cf. Sir 23.22–27. For the imagery, cf. Job 15.32–34; Ps 1.4–5; Ezek 17.9; 31.10–14; Dan 4.14. **6:** Witnesses . . . against their parents, see 4.20.

4.7–20: Fourth contrast, parallel to 3.1–9, returning to the theme of suffering and death. A similar idea, that the righteous were taken away in order that they be removed from evil, is found in Isa 57.1–2. **7–9:** In contrast to the traditional association of old age with wisdom (Job 15.7–10), understanding, not length of time, is the true measure of righteousness (see 4.15; Philo, On Abraham 271). **10–11:** An allusion to Enoch who was taken up by God (Gen 5.24; cf. Sir 44.16). Gen Rab 25.1 also claims that the purpose of Enoch's removal was to

¹² For the fascination of wickedness
          obscures what is good,
and roving desire perverts the innocent
          mind.
¹³ Being perfected in a short time, they
          fulfilled long years;
¹⁴ for their souls were pleasing to the Lord,
therefore he took them quickly from the
          midst of wickedness.
¹⁵ Yet the peoples saw and did not
          understand,
or take such a thing to heart,
that God's grace and mercy are with his
          elect,
and that he watches over his holy ones.

¹⁶ The righteous who have died will
          condemn the ungodly who are living,
and youth that is quickly perfectedᵃ will
          condemn the prolonged old age of
          the unrighteous.
¹⁷ For they will see the end of the wise,
and will not understand what the Lord
          purposed for them,
and for what he kept them safe.
¹⁸ The unrighteousᵇ will see, and will have
          contempt for them,
but the Lord will laugh them to scorn.
After this they will become dishonored
          corpses,
and an outrage among the dead forever;
¹⁹ because he will dash them speechless to
          the ground,
and shake them from the foundations;
they will be left utterly dry and barren,
and they will suffer anguish,
and the memory of them will perish.

²⁰ They will come with dread when their
          sins are reckoned up,

and their lawless deeds will convict them
          to their face.

5 Then the righteous will stand with great
          confidence
in the presence of those who have
          oppressed them
and those who make light of their labors.
² When the unrighteousᶜ see them, they
          will be shaken with dreadful fear,
and they will be amazed at the unexpected
          salvation of the righteous.
³ They will speak to one another in
          repentance,
and in anguish of spirit they will groan,
          and say,
⁴ "These are persons whom we once held
          in derision
and made a byword of reproach—fools
          that we were!
We thought that their lives were
          madness
and that their end was without honor.
⁵ Why have they been numbered among
          the children of God?
And why is their lot among the saints?
⁶ So it was we who strayed from the way of
          truth,
and the light of righteousness did not
          shine on us,
and the sun did not rise upon us.
⁷ We took our fill of the paths of
          lawlessness and destruction,
and we journeyed through trackless
          deserts,
but the way of the Lord we have not
          known.

ᵃ Or *ended*
ᵇ Gk *They*
ᶜ Gk *they*

preserve his character. **12:** *Roving desire*, see 15.5–6; Eccl 6.9; 11.9; Sir 18.30–19.3. **14–15,17:** Premature death is interpreted not as a curse (cf. Ps 109.8–9) but as a sign of God's favor. These verses may be based on Isa 57.1–2. **17:** *They will see*, answering 2.17 (cf. 5.2). **18:** *The Lord will laugh*, cf. Ps 2.4; Prov 1.26. **18b–19:** These threats are familiar from prophetic announcements of judgment (Isa 13.6–16; 24.17–23; 66.24; Jer 15.7–9). **19:** *Memory*, see 4.1n.

5.1–23: Final judgment and the speech of the impious. In contrast to their arrogant speech of 2.1–20, *the unrighteous* now speak with remorse and self-condemnation (5.4–13). **1–8:** The reaction of *the unrighteous* to *the righteous* parallels the so-called servant song of Isa 52.13–53.12, which describes the astonishing restoration of Israel after terrible affliction. Cf. also *1 Enoch* 62–63. **4–13:** An imaginary monologue is placed in the mouths of the wicked, as in 2.1–20, a device common in diatribe. **5:** The righteous eventually become part of the heavenly host, a kind of astral immortality; cf. Dan. 12.2–3; *1 Enoch* 39.5; 104.2,6; 1QH 3.19–23; *2 Baruch* 51.5–13. **6–8:** Con-

⁸ What has our arrogance profited us?
And what good has our boasted wealth
    brought us?

⁹ "All those things have vanished like a
    shadow,
and like a rumor that passes by;
¹⁰ like a ship that sails through the billowy
    water,
and when it has passed no trace can be
    found,
no track of its keel in the waves;
¹¹ or as, when a bird flies through the air,
no evidence of its passage is found;
the light air, lashed by the beat of its
    pinions
and pierced by the force of its rushing
    flight,
is traversed by the movement of its wings,
and afterward no sign of its coming is
    found there;
¹² or as, when an arrow is shot at a target,
the air, thus divided, comes together at
    once,
so that no one knows its pathway.
¹³ So we also, as soon as we were born,
    ceased to be,
and we had no sign of virtue to show,
but were consumed in our wickedness."
¹⁴ Because the hope of the ungodly is like
    thistledown[a] carried by the wind,
and like a light frost[b] driven away by a
    storm;
it is dispersed like smoke before the wind,
and it passes like the remembrance of a
    guest who stays but a day.

¹⁵ But the righteous live forever,
and their reward is with the Lord;
the Most High takes care of them.
¹⁶ Therefore they will receive a glorious
    crown

and a beautiful diadem from the hand of
    the Lord,
because with his right hand he will cover
    them,
and with his arm he will shield them.
¹⁷ The Lord[c] will take his zeal as his whole
    armor,
and will arm all creation to repel[d] his
    enemies;
¹⁸ he will put on righteousness as a
    breastplate,
and wear impartial justice as a helmet;
¹⁹ he will take holiness as an invincible
    shield,
²⁰ and sharpen stern wrath for a sword,
and creation will join with him to fight
    against his frenzied foes.
²¹ Shafts of lightning will fly with true aim,
and will leap from the clouds to the target,
    as from a well-drawn bow,
²² and hailstones full of wrath will be
    hurled as from a catapult;
the water of the sea will rage against
    them,
and rivers will relentlessly overwhelm
    them;
²³ a mighty wind will rise against them,
and like a tempest it will winnow them
    away.
Lawlessness will lay waste the whole
    earth,
and evildoing will overturn the thrones of
    rulers.

6 Listen therefore, O kings, and
    understand;
learn, O judges of the ends of the earth.

a   Other ancient authorities read *dust*
b   Other ancient authorities read *spider's web*
c   Gk *He*
d   Or *punish*

fession of guilt by the wicked (cf. Isa 59.2–3,7–10). **6:** *The light . . . did not shine*, see 17.2–21. **9–14:** The ephemeral existence of *the ungodly*, cf. Ps. 1.4–5; Hos 13.3; 2 Esd 7.61; Jas 4.14. **10–11:** *A ship . . . a bird*, cf. Prov 30.18–19. **17–22:** **The armor of virtues** (see also 18.14–16; 19.13–17). The imagery of God putting on various attributes as divine armor derives from Isa 59.17; cf. Eph. 6.11–17. **16:** *Crown . . . diadem*, cf. Isa 62.3. **17:** *Will arm all creation*, see 5.20–23; 19.6; Sir 39.28–31. **21–22:** *Lightning . . . hailstones . . . water*, cf. 16.15–29.

6.1–21: An exhortation to wisdom. This section is parallel to 1.1–15, forming an inclusio that marks off 1.1–6.21 as a unit: just as the section began with an address to "the rulers of the earth" (1.1–15), it ends with an address to "the kings of the earth" (6.1–21). Some of the passage's themes are familiar from philosophical treatises on kingship (e.g., Plutarch, *To an Uneducated Ruler*), which generally stressed the need for rulers to be wise and

² Give ear, you that rule over multitudes,
and boast of many nations.
³ For your dominion was given you from
the Lord,
and your sovereignty from the Most High;
he will search out your works and inquire
into your plans.
⁴ Because as servants of his kingdom you
did not rule rightly,
or keep the law,
or walk according to the purpose of God,
⁵ he will come upon you terribly and
swiftly,
because severe judgment falls on those in
high places.
⁶ For the lowliest may be pardoned in
mercy,
but the mighty will be mightily tested.
⁷ For the Lord of all will not stand in awe of
anyone,
or show deference to greatness;
because he himself made both small and
great,
and he takes thought for all alike.
⁸ But a strict inquiry is in store for the
mighty.
⁹ To you then, O monarchs, my words are
directed,
so that you may learn wisdom and not
transgress.
¹⁰ For they will be made holy who observe
holy things in holiness,

and those who have been taught them will
find a defense.
¹¹ Therefore set your desire on my words;
long for them, and you will be instructed.

¹² Wisdom is radiant and unfading,
and she is easily discerned by those who
love her,
and is found by those who seek her.
¹³ She hastens to make herself known to
those who desire her.
¹⁴ One who rises early to seek her will have
no difficulty,
for she will be found sitting at the gate.
¹⁵ To fix one's thought on her is perfect
understanding,
and one who is vigilant on her account will
soon be free from care,
¹⁶ because she goes about seeking those
worthy of her,
and she graciously appears to them in
their paths,
and meets them in every thought.

¹⁷ The beginning of wisdomª is the most
sincere desire for instruction,
and concern for instruction is love of her,
¹⁸ and love of her is the keeping of her laws,
and giving heed to her laws is assurance of
immortality,

ª Gk *Her beginning*

benevolent (cf. 12.15–18n.). Kingship is also an important theme in Proverbs (e.g., 16.10–19; 20.26–28; 25.1–7; 29.4,12–14; 30.21–31), another book attributed to Solomon. **1–11:** Rulers of other nations are often condemned in the Bible and Jewish literature (e.g., Isa 14.3–21), yet this passage seems to assume that the ruler who heeds and gains wisdom will rule the world and gain many benefits. Thus, even Gentile rulers can gain favor in the eyes of God by living according to the law and God's will (6.4). *Law* (v. 4) here probably refers to universal law rather the specific Jewish Torah, though some Jewish writers of the time equated the two (*Ep. Aris.* 161,168–69; Philo, *Abraham*, especially 16,60–61,133–37). **1–2:** An apostrophe (see 1.1n.). **3:** Political authority is granted by God (cf. Prov 8.15–16; Jer 27.5–7; Dan 2.37–38; 4.17; Sir 10.4–5). **4–6:** For God's judgment against *the mighty*, cf. 1 Sam 2.3–5; Job 12.17–25; 34.24–30; Ps 2; Isa 2.11–17; Jer 25.15–29; Ezek 21.25–27; Sir 10.8–18. **7:** *Small and great*, cf. Job 34.19. **12:** *Wisdom* has been mentioned in passing at several points (1.4–6; 3.11; 6.9), but with this verse a discourse on the figure of personified Wisdom begins, continuing to the end of ch 10. The figure of Wisdom or Lady Wisdom occurs frequently in late Israelite and Jewish literature, especially Prov 1.20–33; 8; 9.1–6; Job 28.12–28; Sir 1.1–27; 4.11–19; 6.18–37; 14.20–15.10; 24; Bar 3.9–4.4. Later, Wisdom came to be equated with the Torah or elements of the Torah, rather than just intellectual or practical wisdom (e.g., Sir 24.23–29; Bar 4.1). **14:** *The gate*, the place in a city where legal and commercial transactions were carried out (Deut 22.15,24; Prov 22.22; Isa 29.21; Am 5.10–12,15); cf. Prov 1.20–21. **17–20:** The literary form called a "sorites" in Greek, defined as a set of statements that proceed step by step to a conclusion, with each statement picking up the last key word or phrase of the preceding one. The author of Wis clearly knows of the form and makes effective use of it. **18–19:** *Immortality*, see 3.4n.

[19] and immortality brings one near to God;
[20] so the desire for wisdom leads to a
   kingdom.

[21] Therefore if you delight in thrones and
   scepters, O monarchs over the peoples,
honor wisdom, so that you may reign
   forever.
[22] I will tell you what wisdom is and how
   she came to be,
and I will hide no secrets from you,
but I will trace her course from the
   beginning of creation,
and make knowledge of her clear,
and I will not pass by the truth;
[23] nor will I travel in the company of sickly
   envy,
for envy[a] does not associate with wisdom.
[24] The multitude of the wise is the
   salvation of the world,
and a sensible king is the stability of any
   people.
[25] Therefore be instructed by my words,
   and you will profit.

7 I also am mortal, like everyone else,
   a descendant of the first-formed child of
   earth;
and in the womb of a mother I was molded
   into flesh,
[2] within the period of ten months,
   compacted with blood,

from the seed of a man and the pleasure of
   marriage.
[3] And when I was born, I began to breathe
   the common air,
and fell upon the kindred earth;
my first sound was a cry, as is true of all.
[4] I was nursed with care in swaddling
   cloths.
[5] For no king has had a different beginning
   of existence;
[6] there is for all one entrance into life, and
   one way out.
[7] Therefore I prayed, and understanding
   was given me;
I called on God, and the spirit of wisdom
   came to me.
[8] I preferred her to scepters and thrones,
and I accounted wealth as nothing in
   comparison with her.
[9] Neither did I liken to her any priceless
   gem,
because all gold is but a little sand in her
   sight,
and silver will be accounted as clay before
   her.
[10] I loved her more than health and
   beauty,
and I chose to have her rather than
   light,
because her radiance never ceases.

---

[a] Gk *this*

6.22–10.21: The Book of Wisdom.

6.22–25: **Introduction:** the promise is made to reveal the mysteries of wisdom to the reader.

7.1–9.18: In this section the implied author speaks in the persona of Solomon, describing his life and quest for wisdom and the benefits wisdom is able to bestow. The pseudo-autobiographical narrative serves the dual function of gaining the empathy of the hearers and commending the quest for wisdom.

7.1–8.21: The first part of the autobiographical narrative consists of a speech by Solomon that has a concentric framework:

A. Birth of Solomon (7.1–6)
   B. Solomon asks for wisdom from God (7.7–12)
      C. Solomon given wealth and power (7.13–22a)
         D. Description of wisdom (7.22b–8.1)
      C.' Wisdom brings all good things (8.2–8)
   B.' Solomon becomes a great king through Wisdom (8.9–16)
A.' Wisdom available only through prayer (8.17–21).

7.1–6: By describing his birth *like everyone else*, "Solomon" shows his common humanity with the hearers. **2:** The conventional 40 weeks or 280 days of human gestation was usually interpreted as *ten months* in antiquity, because of the use of lunar rather than solar months. *Compacted with blood*, on conception as the coagulation of semen in the womb, cf. Job 10.10. **7–14:** Solomon prays for wisdom from God, as also in 1 Kings 3.4–14. God grants Solomon not only wisdom but also wealth and other benefits (cf. 1 Kings 3.10–14). **8–9:** Cf. Job 28.15–19;

¹¹ All good things came to me along with
her,
and in her hands uncounted wealth.
¹² I rejoiced in them all, because wisdom
leads them;
but I did not know that she was their
mother.
¹³ I learned without guile and I impart
without grudging;
I do not hide her wealth,
¹⁴ for it is an unfailing treasure for mortals;
those who get it obtain friendship with
God,
commended for the gifts that come from
instruction.

¹⁵ May God grant me to speak with
judgment,
and to have thoughts worthy of what I
have received;
for he is the guide even of wisdom
and the corrector of the wise.
¹⁶ For both we and our words are in his
hand,
as are all understanding and skill in crafts.
¹⁷ For it is he who gave me unerring
knowledge of what exists,
to know the structure of the world and the
activity of the elements;
¹⁸ the beginning and end and middle of
times,
the alternations of the solstices and the
changes of the seasons,
¹⁹ the cycles of the year and the
constellations of the stars,
²⁰ the natures of animals and the tempers
of wild animals,
the powers of spiritsᵃ and the thoughts of
human beings,

the varieties of plants and the virtues of
roots;
²¹ I learned both what is secret and what is
manifest,
²² for wisdom, the fashioner of all things,
taught me.

There is in her a spirit that is intelligent,
holy,
unique, manifold, subtle,
mobile, clear, unpolluted,
distinct, invulnerable, loving the good,
keen,
irresistible, ²³ beneficent, humane,
steadfast, sure, free from anxiety,
all-powerful, overseeing all,
and penetrating through all spirits
that are intelligent, pure, and altogether
subtle.
²⁴ For wisdom is more mobile than any
motion;
because of her pureness she pervades and
penetrates all things.
²⁵ For she is a breath of the power of God,
and a pure emanation of the glory of the
Almighty;
therefore nothing defiled gains entrance
into her.
²⁶ For she is a reflection of eternal light,
a spotless mirror of the working of God,
and an image of his goodness.
²⁷ Although she is but one, she can do all
things,
and while remaining in herself, she renews
all things;
in every generation she passes into holy
souls

ᵃ Or *winds*

Prov 2.4; 3.14–16. **14:** Abraham in particular was known for his *friendship with* God (2 Chr 20.7; Isa 41.8; Jas 2.23); see also 7.27; 8.18; Job 29.4; Ps 25.14; Jer 3.4. **15–22:** Divine wisdom is presented in scientific and philosophical terms; this sort of encyclopedic knowledge was a common interest of ancient wisdom literature; cf. 1 Kings 4.33.

7.22b–8.1: A description of wisdom, with two sets of lists. **7.22b–24:** The first list consists of 21 attributes (a multiple of 7 and 3, numbers signifying completeness and perfection). Most of the epithets have parallels in Greek philosophy (cf. Pseudo-Aristotle, *On the Cosmos* 400B–401B); a similar litany of attributes, glorifying the deity, is used in the *Apocalypse of Abraham* 17.8–15. **7.25–8.1:** The second list is made up of metaphors, a five-fold description of wisdom's relationship with God (breath, emanation, reflection, mirror, image). **25:** *Breath,* see 11.20; Sir 24.3. The description of wisdom as a *pure emanation* or effluence of God reflects the influence of philosophical concepts (e.g., Cicero, *The Nature of the Gods* 2.79; cf. Sir 1.9; 24.23–33). **26:** *Mirror,* cf. 2 Cor 3.18; Philo, *Quest. in Gen.* 1.57.

and makes them friends of God, and
  prophets;

28 for God loves nothing so much as the
  person who lives with wisdom.

29 She is more beautiful than the sun,
and excels every constellation of the stars.
Compared with the light she is found to be
  superior,

30 for it is succeeded by the night,
but against wisdom evil does not prevail.

8 She reaches mightily from one end of the
  earth to the other,
and she orders all things well.

2 I loved her and sought her from my youth;
I desired to take her for my bride,
and became enamored of her beauty.

3 She glorifies her noble birth by living
  with God,
and the Lord of all loves her.

4 For she is an initiate in the knowledge of
  God,
and an associate in his works.

5 If riches are a desirable possession in life,
what is richer than wisdom, the active
  cause of all things?

6 And if understanding is effective,
who more than she is fashioner of what
  exists?

7 And if anyone loves righteousness,
her labors are virtues;
for she teaches self-control and prudence,
justice and courage;
nothing in life is more profitable for
  mortals than these.

8 And if anyone longs for wide experience,
she knows the things of old, and infers the
  things to come;
she understands turns of speech and the
  solutions of riddles;
she has foreknowledge of signs and
  wonders
and of the outcome of seasons and times.

9 Therefore I determined to take her to live
  with me,

knowing that she would give me good
  counsel
and encouragement in cares and grief.

10 Because of her I shall have glory among
  the multitudes
and honor in the presence of the elders,
  though I am young.

11 I shall be found keen in judgment,
and in the sight of rulers I shall be
  admired.

12 When I am silent they will wait for me,
and when I speak they will give heed;
if I speak at greater length,
they will put their hands on their
  mouths.

13 Because of her I shall have immortality,
and leave an everlasting remembrance to
  those who come after me.

14 I shall govern peoples,
and nations will be subject to me;

15 dread monarchs will be afraid of me
  when they hear of me;
among the people I shall show myself
  capable, and courageous in war.

16 When I enter my house, I shall find rest
  with her;
for companionship with her has no
  bitterness,
and life with her has no pain, but gladness
  and joy.

17 When I considered these things inwardly,
and pondered in my heart
that in kinship with wisdom there is
  immortality,

18 and in friendship with her, pure delight,
and in the labors of her hands, unfailing
  wealth,
and in the experience of her company,
  understanding,
and renown in sharing her words,
I went about seeking how to get her for
  myself.

19 As a child I was naturally gifted,
and a good soul fell to my lot;

8.2–16: The extended metaphor of Solomon making Wisdom his bride. Erotic imagery in connection with Wisdom is found elsewhere, as in Prov. 9.1–6, which makes Wisdom a seductress. Even more erotically explicit is the Hebrew version of Sir 51.13–30, which circulated separately at Qumran as part of a Psalms scroll (11QPsa 21). 4–6: On wisdom's agency in creation, see Prov 8.22–31. 7: The four cardinal virtues of Greek thought: *self-control, prudence, justice,* and *courage.* Cf. 4 Macc 1.2–4. 8: *Turns of speech . . . riddles,* cf. Prov. 1.5–6. 10–12: Cf. Job 29.7–11,21–23; Sir 15.4–6. 13: *Everlasting remembrance,* see 4.1n. 15–16: *Rest,* see Sir 6.28.

8.17–21: Wisdom is available only as a gift from God. 17: *Immortality,* see 3.4n. 18: *Friendship,* see 7.8–9n.

20 or rather, being good, I entered an undefiled body.
21 But I perceived that I would not possess wisdom unless God gave her to me—
and it was a mark of insight to know whose gift she was—
so I appealed to the Lord and implored him,
and with my whole heart I said:

9 "O God of my ancestors and Lord of mercy,
who have made all things by your word,
2 and by your wisdom have formed humankind
to have dominion over the creatures you have made,
3 and rule the world in holiness and righteousness,
and pronounce judgment in uprightness of soul,
4 give me the wisdom that sits by your throne,
and do not reject me from among your servants.
5 For I am your servant[a] the son of your serving girl,
a man who is weak and short-lived,
with little understanding of judgment and laws;
6 for even one who is perfect among human beings
will be regarded as nothing without the wisdom that comes from you.
7 You have chosen me to be king of your people
and to be judge over your sons and daughters.
8 You have given command to build a temple on your holy mountain,
and an altar in the city of your habitation,
a copy of the holy tent that you prepared from the beginning.

9 With you is wisdom, she who knows your works
and was present when you made the world;
she understands what is pleasing in your sight
and what is right according to your commandments.
10 Send her forth from the holy heavens,
and from the throne of your glory send her,
that she may labor at my side,
and that I may learn what is pleasing to you.
11 For she knows and understands all things,
and she will guide me wisely in my actions
and guard me with her glory.
12 Then my works will be acceptable,
and I shall judge your people justly,
and shall be worthy of the throne[b] of my father.
13 For who can learn the counsel of God?
Or who can discern what the Lord wills?
14 For the reasoning of mortals is worthless,
and our designs are likely to fail;
15 for a perishable body weighs down the soul,
and this earthy tent burdens the thoughtful[c] mind.
16 We can hardly guess at what is on earth,
and what is at hand we find with labor;
but who has traced out what is in the heavens?
17 Who has learned your counsel,
unless you have given wisdom
and sent your holy spirit from on high?

a Gk *slave*
b Gk *thrones*
c Or *anxious*

19–20: The Platonic view of the soul as preexistent is reflected here, as in other Hellenistic Jewish writings (cf. Philo, *Giants* 6–14; *2 Enoch* 23.4–5). The author may be referring also to Hellenistic theories about the transmigration of souls, a belief attributed by Josephus to the Pharisees (*J.W.* 2.8.14).

9.1–18: Solomon's prayer (cf. 1 Kings 3.6–9; 2 Chr 1.8–10). Verses 1–5 parallel vv. 7–12: Address to God (vv. 1–3; 7–9); petition (vv. 4; 10a); motive (vv. 5; 10b–12). Verses 13–18 are a meditation on humanity's insignificance before God. 2: *Dominion*, see 10.2; Gen 1.26,28; Ps 8.6; Sir 17.2–4. 4: *Wisdom . . . sits by your throne*, see 9.10; 18.15; Prov 8.30; Sir 24.4; *1 Enoch* 84.3. 5: *Your servant*, see Pss 86.16; 116.16. 8: That the earthly temple on Mount Zion was only a *copy* of a heavenly archetype may be an interpretation of Ex 25.9,40; 26.30 (cf. Heb 8.2–5; Rev 11.19; *1 Enoch* 14.10–20). 9: Cf. Prov. 8.22–31. 12: *My father*, David. 13: Cf. Isa 40.12–14; Sir 1.2–6; Bar 3.29–31.15: That

18 And thus the paths of those on earth
were set right,
and people were taught what pleases you,
and were saved by wisdom."

10

Wisdom[a] protected the first-formed
father of the world, when he alone
had been created;
she delivered him from his transgression,
2 and gave him strength to rule all things.
3 But when an unrighteous man departed
from her in his anger,
he perished because in rage he killed his
brother.
4 When the earth was flooded because of
him, wisdom again saved it,
steering the righteous man by a paltry
piece of wood.

5 Wisdom[a] also, when the nations in
wicked agreement had been put to
confusion,
recognized the righteous man and
preserved him blameless before God,
and kept him strong in the face of his
compassion for his child.

6 Wisdom[a] rescued a righteous man when
the ungodly were perishing;
he escaped the fire that descended on the
Five Cities.[b]
7 Evidence of their wickedness still
remains:
a continually smoking wasteland,
plants bearing fruit that does not ripen,
and a pillar of salt standing as a
monument to an unbelieving soul.
8 For because they passed wisdom by,
they not only were hindered from
recognizing the good,

but also left for humankind a reminder of
their folly,
so that their failures could never go
unnoticed.

9 Wisdom rescued from troubles those
who served her.
10 When a righteous man fled from his
brother's wrath,
she guided him on straight paths;
she showed him the kingdom of God,
and gave him knowledge of holy
things;
she prospered him in his labors,
and increased the fruit of his toil.
11 When his oppressors were covetous,
she stood by him and made him rich.
12 She protected him from his
enemies,
and kept him safe from those who lay in
wait for him;
in his arduous contest she gave him the
victory,
so that he might learn that godliness is
more powerful than anything else.

13 When a righteous man was sold,
wisdom[c] did not desert him,
but delivered him from sin.
She descended with him into the
dungeon,
14 and when he was in prison she did not
leave him,
until she brought him the scepter of a
kingdom
and authority over his masters.

a Gk *She*
b Or *on Pentapolis*
c Gk *she*

---

the body *weighs down the soul* was a common philosophical belief (see Plato, *Phaedr* 81C). **18:** *Saved by wisdom,*
the attribution of a saving role to wisdom is one of the book's distinctive features; here as elsewhere activities
usually reserved for God are assigned to wisdom.

10.1–21: Biblical history illustrates wisdom's saving and punishing power. The author presents seven righteous heroes as evidence of wisdom's providential ordering of Israelite history, each contrasted with some
unrighteous villain. Personal names are avoided in favor of generic categories, but the descriptions make it
clear who they are. This chapter provides a transition to the third part of the book. **1–2:** The interpretation of
Adam is different in emphasis from the account in Gen 1.26–5.5. **2:** *Rule,* see 9.2n. **3:** Cain and Abel (Gen 4.1–16).
4: *Because of him,* Cain's crime is interpreted by the author as the cause of the Flood. *The righteous man,* Noah
(Gen 5.28–9.29). **5:** Abraham (Gen 11.26–25.10). *The nations,* referring to the Tower of Babel story (Gen 11.1–9).
Compassion for his child, cf. Gen 22.1–19. **6–8:** Lot (Gen 19.1–29). **9–12:** Jacob (Gen 27–33). **10:** *The kingdom of God,*

Those who accused him she showed to be
false,
and she gave him everlasting honor.

15 A holy people and blameless race
wisdom delivered from a nation of
oppressors.
16 She entered the soul of a servant of the
Lord,
and withstood dread kings with wonders
and signs.
17 She gave to holy people the reward of
their labors;
she guided them along a marvelous
way,
and became a shelter to them by day,
and a starry flame through the night.
18 She brought them over the Red Sea,
and led them through deep waters;
19 but she drowned their enemies,
and cast them up from the depth of the
sea.
20 Therefore the righteous plundered the
ungodly;
they sang hymns, O Lord, to your holy
name,
and praised with one accord your
defending hand;
21 for wisdom opened the mouths of those
who were mute,
and made the tongues of infants speak
clearly.

11 Wisdom[a] prospered their works by the
hand of a holy prophet.
2 They journeyed through an uninhabited
wilderness,
and pitched their tents in untrodden places.
3 They withstood their enemies and fought
off their foes.
4 When they were thirsty, they called upon
you,
and water was given them out of flinty rock,
and from hard stone a remedy for their
thirst.
5 For through the very things by which
their enemies were punished,
they themselves received benefit in their
need.
6 Instead of the fountain of an ever-flowing
river,
stirred up and defiled with blood
7 in rebuke for the decree to kill the infants,
you gave them abundant water
unexpectedly,
8 showing by their thirst at that time
how you punished their enemies.
9 For when they were tried, though they
were being disciplined in mercy,
they learned how the ungodly were
tormented when judged in wrath.
10 For you tested them as a parent[b] does in
warning,

a Gk She
b Gk a father

see Gen 28.12,17,22. **12:** *Arduous contest* (Gen 32.22–32; Hos 12.3–4). **13–14:** Joseph (Gen 37–50). **15–21:** Moses
(Ex 1–17).

11.1–19.22: The Book of History, a historical meditation contrasting God's dealings with the Israelites and
the Egyptians. The presentation of Moses in the preceding passage leads without a break into an elaborate
comparison consisting of seven historical contrasts, supplemented by a digression in 11.17–15.19. Although
based on the events of Ex 7–14, the author's interpretation is apologetic in nature, underscoring the Egyptians' culpability while omitting reference to any of Israel's failures. Three principles seem have been used in
constructing these historical contrasts: Israel would benefit from those things that were a punishment of the
Egyptians (11.5); the Egyptians' sins would themselves act as a punishment of them (11.16); Israel would also
suffer a mild form of the punishments, but this would be a means of understanding God's mercies (cf. 16.4).

11.1–14: First contrast: plague of the Nile versus water from the rock. The sin of the Egyptians was killing
the Israelite infants in the Nile (11.7); the punishment is that the Nile becomes undrinkable. The Israelite counterpart is the water brought forth from the rock in the desert (Ex 17.1–7; Num 20.1–13). **1–3:** Without making
specific references, the author establishes the historical setting for what follows, the Israelites' struggle in
the *wilderness*. **4,6–8:** See Ex 7.14–25; 17.1–7; Num 20.2–13. **5:** The principle behind all the contrasts: God uses
the same means for aiding Israel and punishing her *enemies* (see 11.13; 16.24; 18.8). **8–10:** The righteous must
also experience God's punishment, though not as a matter of condemnation but of compassionate testing and
discipline (see 3.5).

but you examined the ungodly[a] as a stern king does in condemnation.

[11] Whether absent or present, they were equally distressed,

[12] for a twofold grief possessed them,
and a groaning at the memory of what had occurred.

[13] For when they heard that through their own punishments
the righteous[b] had received benefit, they perceived it was the Lord's doing.

[14] For though they had mockingly rejected him who long before had been cast out and exposed,
at the end of the events they marveled at him,
when they felt thirst in a different way from the righteous.

[15] In return for their foolish and wicked thoughts,
which led them astray to worship irrational serpents and worthless animals,
you sent upon them a multitude of irrational creatures to punish them,

[16] so that they might learn that one is punished by the very things by which one sins.

[17] For your all-powerful hand,
which created the world out of formless matter,
did not lack the means to send upon them a multitude of bears, or bold lions,

[18] or newly-created unknown beasts full of rage,
or such as breathe out fiery breath,
or belch forth a thick pall of smoke,
or flash terrible sparks from their eyes;

[19] not only could the harm they did destroy people,[c]
but the mere sight of them could kill by fright.

[20] Even apart from these, people[b] could fall at a single breath
when pursued by justice
and scattered by the breath of your power.
But you have arranged all things by measure and number and weight.

[21] For it is always in your power to show great strength,
and who can withstand the might of your arm?

[22] Because the whole world before you is like a speck that tips the scales,
and like a drop of morning dew that falls on the ground.

[23] But you are merciful to all, for you can do all things,
and you overlook people's sins, so that they may repent.

[24] For you love all things that exist,
and detest none of the things that you have made,
for you would not have made anything if you had hated it.

[25] How would anything have endured if you had not willed it?
Or how would anything not called forth by you have been preserved?

[26] You spare all things, for they are yours, O Lord, you who love the living.

---

a   Gk *those*
b   Gk *they*
c   Gk *them*

11.15–16: Second contrast: the plague of small animals (see Ex 8.1–19; 9.1–7). Here the positive parallel with the Israelites is not developed; see further 16.1–4.

11.17–15.19: Two digressions that interrupt the interpretation of the Exodus, explaining how and why God judges the nations, contrasting the results of true worship (Jewish monotheism) and false worship (idolatry).

11.17–12.27: First digression. God's power and mercy, composed of two parallel sections and a conclusion: God punished the Egyptians by degrees so that they will have a chance to repent (11.17–12.2); God's punishment of the Canaanites was gradual, in spite of their heinous sins (12.3–18); God's punishment of Israel is very mild compared to that of their enemies (12.19–22).

11.17–12.2: God exercises power and mercy in judgment so as to free all creation from wickedness. **11.17:** *Formless matter*, a concept of Greek philosophy (see Plato, *Timaeus* 50D-E), here describing the chaos of Gen 1.2. **18–19:** Cf. Job 41.12–21. **21:** See 12.12n. **23:** *Merciful to all*, see 12.13,16,18; 15.1; Sir 16.11–14; 18.11–14; 2 Esd

12

For your immortal spirit is in all things.
² Therefore you correct little by little
those who trespass,
and you remind and warn them of the
things through which they sin,
so that they may be freed from wickedness
and put their trust in you, O Lord.

³ Those who lived long ago in your holy
land
⁴ you hated for their detestable practices,
their works of sorcery and unholy rites,
⁵ their merciless slaughterᵃ of children,
and their sacrificial feasting on human
flesh and blood.
These initiates from the midst of a
heathen cult,ᵇ
⁶ these parents who murder helpless
lives,
you willed to destroy by the hands of our
ancestors,
⁷ so that the land most precious of all to
you
might receive a worthy colony of the
servantsᶜ of God.
⁸ But even these you spared, since they
were but mortals,
and sent waspsᵈ as forerunners of your
army
to destroy them little by little,
⁹ though you were not unable to give
the ungodly into the hands of the
righteous in battle,
or to destroy them at one blow by dread
wild animals or your stern word.
¹⁰ But judging them little by little you gave
them an opportunity to repent,
though you were not unaware that their
originᵉ was evil
and their wickedness inborn,

and that their way of thinking would never
change.
¹¹ For they were an accursed race from the
beginning,
and it was not through fear of anyone that
you left them unpunished for their
sins.

¹² For who will say, "What have you done?"
or will resist your judgment?
Who will accuse you for the destruction of
nations that you made?
Or who will come before you to plead as an
advocate for the unrighteous?
¹³ For neither is there any god besides you,
whose care is for all people,ᶠ
to whom you should prove that you have
not judged unjustly;
¹⁴ nor can any king or monarch confront
you about those whom you have
punished.
¹⁵ You are righteous and you rule all things
righteously,
deeming it alien to your power
to condemn anyone who does not deserve
to be punished.
¹⁶ For your strength is the source of
righteousness,
and your sovereignty over all causes you to
spare all.
¹⁷ For you show your strength when people
doubt the completeness of your
power,

ᵃ Gk *slaughterers*
ᵇ Meaning of Gk uncertain
ᶜ Or *children*
ᵈ Or *hornets*
ᵉ Or *nature*
ᶠ Or *all things*

8.45. **12.1:** *Your . . . spirit is in all things*, see 1.7; 15.11; cf. Gen 6.3; Ps 104.30; Jdt 16.14. **2:** *You remind . . . them*, see 16.6,11n.

12.3–11: Divine judgment of the ancient Canaanites, a common theme of Jewish apologetic (see *Jub.*10.27–34; 22.20–22), gives an illustration for the preceding argument; although hating their *wickedness*, God showed forbearance in destroying them. **5:** Cf. Lev 20.2–5. **8:** *Wasps*, see Ex 23.28; Deut 7.20; Josh 24.12. **10:** *Little by little*, see 12.2,8; Ex 23.28–30. *Their origin was evil* (see textual note e), cf. Sir 33.10–15. **11:** *An accursed race*, see the curse placed on Canaan in Gen 9.25–27.

12.12–27: Divine righteousness and forbearance. God gives opportunity for *repentance* (v. 19; see also 11.23; 12.10) but condemns the obstinate. **12–14:** The affirmation of divine providence, making use of legal terminology. **12:** For similar rhetorical questions, see 9.13; 11.21; Job 9.12,19; Ps 76.7; Isa 40.13–14. **13:** *Any god besides you*, see Deut 32.39; cf. Ex 20.3. **15–18:** The portrayal of God's universal *power* and *forbearance* shares themes used

and you rebuke any insolence among
those who know it.[a]

[18] Although you are sovereign in strength,
you judge with mildness,
and with great forbearance you govern us;
for you have power to act whenever you
choose.

[19] Through such works you have taught
your people
that the righteous must be kind,
and you have filled your children with
good hope,
because you give repentance for sins.

[20] For if you punished with such great care
and indulgence[b]
the enemies of your servants[c] and those
deserving of death,
granting them time and opportunity to
give up their wickedness,

[21] with what strictness you have judged
your children,
to whose ancestors you gave oaths and
covenants full of good promises!

[22] So while chastening us you scourge our
enemies ten thousand times
more,
so that, when we judge, we may meditate
upon your goodness,
and when we are judged, we may expect
mercy.

[23] Therefore those who lived
unrighteously, in a life of folly,
you tormented through their own
abominations.

[24] For they went far astray on the paths of
error,
accepting as gods those animals that even
their enemies[d] despised;
they were deceived like foolish infants.

[25] Therefore, as though to children who
cannot reason,
you sent your judgment to mock them.

[26] But those who have not heeded the
warning of mild rebukes
will experience the deserved judgment of
God.

[27] For when in their suffering they became
incensed
at those creatures that they had thought
to be gods, being punished by means
of them,
they saw and recognized as the true God
the one whom they had before
refused to know.
Therefore the utmost condemnation came
upon them.

13 For all people who were ignorant of
God were foolish by nature;
and they were unable from the good
things that are seen to know the one
who exists,
nor did they recognize the artisan while
paying heed to his works;

[2] but they supposed that either fire or wind
or swift air,
or the circle of the stars, or turbulent
water,

---

a Meaning of Gk uncertain
b Other ancient authorities lack *and indulgence*;
   others read *and entreaty*
c Or *children*
d Gk *they*

---

to describe the ideal ruler in philosophical treatises on kingship (see 6.1–21n.). **17:** *You rebuke any insolence*,
see Ps 119.21; Isa 13.11; Jer 48.28–33; Sir 35.22–26; Bar 4.34; 3 Macc 2.3,21. **19–22:** Divine judgment is a model of
goodness and *mercy* for God's children. **20–21:** If repentance is available to the wicked, it is all the more available
to the heirs of God's *promises*. **23–27:** Condemnation of animal worshipers (see 11.15–16; 13.14; 15.18–19); divine
judgment forces them to recognize *the true God*. On their refusal *to know* God, see 2.13n. **25:** *To mock them*, cf.
Ex 10.2; Isa 66.4.

13.1–15.19: Second digression. False worship of nature, idols, and animals is castigated at length. The material is divided into two sections: a short section on worship of the natural world (13.1–9), and a much longer and
detailed section on idol worship (13.10–15.19).

13.1–9: Worship of the natural world. The natural philosophers are to be blamed, because they sought the
Creator but were unable to find him in spite of his works. **1:** *The one who exists* is used of the Supreme Being by
Platonists, whereas it is used by Jews (e.g., LXX Ex 3.14) to refer to the only God. Platonists considered the Su-
preme Being to be separate from the material creator. For Jews the Supreme Being is also the creator or *artisan*.

or the luminaries of heaven were the gods
    that rule the world.
³ If through delight in the beauty of these
        things people assumed them to be
        gods,
let them know how much better than
        these is their Lord,
for the author of beauty created them.
⁴ And if peopleª were amazed at their
        power and working,
let them perceive from them
how much more powerful is the one who
        formed them.
⁵ For from the greatness and beauty of
        created things
comes a corresponding perception of their
        Creator.
⁶ Yet these people are little to be blamed,
for perhaps they go astray
while seeking God and desiring to find
        him.
⁷ For while they live among his works, they
        keep searching,
and they trust in what they see, because
        the things that are seen are beautiful.
⁸ Yet again, not even they are to be
        excused;
⁹ for if they had the power to know so
        much

that they could investigate the world,
how did they fail to find sooner the Lord of
        these things?

¹⁰ But miserable, with their hopes set on
        dead things, are those
who give the name "gods" to the works of
        human hands,
gold and silver fashioned with skill,
and likenesses of animals,
or a useless stone, the work of an ancient
        hand.
¹¹ A skilled woodcutter may saw down a
        tree easy to handle
and skillfully strip off all its bark,
and then with pleasing workmanship
make a useful vessel that serves life's needs,
¹² and burn the cast-off pieces of his work
to prepare his food, and eat his fill.
¹³ But a cast-off piece from among them,
        useful for nothing,
a stick crooked and full of knots,
he takes and carves with care in his leisure,
and shapes it with skill gained in idleness;ᵇ
he forms it in the likeness of a human
        being,

ª   Gk *they*
ᵇ   Other ancient authorities read *with intelligent skill*

In Hellenistic literature, *ignorance* in this sort of context often implied impiety. **2:** The elements worshiped by those who do not know God. Associated with them are several philosophical terms; for example, the phrase *gods that rule the world* seems to refer to astral piety, the worship of the heavenly bodies (cf. 2 Kings 17.16; 23.4; Job 31.26–28; Cicero, *The Nature of the Gods* 2.15). **4:** Another technical philosophical expression, known from Aristotle (*Metaphysics*, 9.6.1–2 1048a), is *power and working*. **5:** The type of argumentation used here is Hellenistic, not biblical. It includes the common Hellenistic form of reasoning from analogy, and it argues that the beauty of the creation requires some overseer and source of beauty behind it. **6:** *Seeking God,* cf. Philo, *Abraham* 124–30; Acts 17.26–27. **9:** In Hellenistic speculation, the word translated *world* (Gk "aion") could mean both "world" and "age," but in Hellenistic speculation it was used of a mystical concept, the personification of a kind of world-soul, as in Plato's *Timaeus* 37D. The Stoics believed in an analogous cosmic "reason" or mind that governed all things.

13.10–15.19: Polemic against idolatry. The Jews came to regard idolatry as one of the most disgusting traits of paganism. Here it is stated that idolatry is "the beginning and cause and end of every evil" (14.27), leading to child murder, secret rites, pollution of marriages, adultery, bloodshed, murder, theft, deceit, sexual perversion, and debauchery. Jer 10.1–16 and Isa 44.9–20 engage in a similar polemic, describing at length the way in which a piece of wood could partly be burned for warmth and preparing food, and partly used to make a god for worship. This was a simplistic criticism, of course, since no pagans regarded themselves as worshiping a piece of wood, stone, or metal. The criticism is aimed at a Jewish audience, however, and the polemic may have been effective in this context. Yet similar comments about idols can be found in some Greco-Roman writers (Horace, *Satires* 1.8.1–7; Sophocles, according to a quotation in Clement of Alexandria, *Strom.* 5.14 113.1–2).

13.10–16: A sarcastic description of how idol "gods" are created from discarded wood (see 15.7–19). **13:** *In the*

14 or makes it like some worthless animal,
giving it a coat of red paint and coloring its
surface red
and covering every blemish in it with
paint;
15 then he makes a suitable niche for it,
and sets it in the wall, and fastens it there
with iron.
16 He takes thought for it, so that it may
not fall,
because he knows that it cannot help
itself,
for it is only an image and has need of
help.
17 When he prays about possessions and
his marriage and children,
he is not ashamed to address a lifeless
thing.
18 For health he appeals to a thing that is
weak;
for life he prays to a thing that is dead;
for aid he entreats a thing that is utterly
inexperienced;
for a prosperous journey, a thing that
cannot take a step;
19 for money-making and work and success
with his hands
he asks strength of a thing whose hands
have no strength.

14 Again, one preparing to sail and about
to voyage over raging waves
calls upon a piece of wood more fragile
than the ship that carries him.
2 For it was desire for gain that planned
that vessel,
and wisdom was the artisan who built it;
3 but it is your providence, O Father, that
steers its course,

because you have given it a path in the sea,
and a safe way through the waves,
4 showing that you can save from every
danger,
so that even a person who lacks skill may
put to sea.
5 It is your will that works of your wisdom
should not be without effect;
therefore people trust their lives even to
the smallest piece of wood,
and passing through the billows on a raft
they come safely to land.
6 For even in the beginning, when arrogant
giants were perishing,
the hope of the world took refuge on a raft,
and guided by your hand left to the world
the seed of a new generation.
7 For blessed is the wood by which
righteousness comes.

8 But the idol made with hands is accursed,
and so is the one who made it—
he for having made it, and the perishable
thing because it was named a god.
9 For equally hateful to God are the
ungodly and their ungodliness;
10 for what was done will be punished
together with the one who did it.
11 Therefore there will be a visitation also
upon the heathen idols,
because, though part of what God created,
they became an abomination,
snares for human souls
and a trap for the feet of the foolish.

12 For the idea of making idols was the
beginning of fornication,
and the invention of them was the
corruption of life;

likeness of a human being, cf. 14.19; Deut 4.16.

13.17–14.2: The ironically ineffective prayer of the idolater contrasts with that of Solomon in 9.1–18.

14.3–11: Safety and salvation come from God, not idols. 3: Providence, see 17.2,4; 4 Macc 9.24. O Father, cf. Isa 63.16; Tob 13.4; Sir 23.1; 3 Macc 6.3. 6–7: Arrogant giants, see Gen 6.1–4; cf. Sir 16.7; Bar 3.26–28; 3 Macc 2.4. A raft, Noah's ark (Gen 6.5–9.29). 8–11: The author's premise is that one takes on the status of what one worships; in this case both idols and idolaters are accursed by God. 11: Visitation, the occasion of God's judgment; see 3.7; Sir 16.18. Abomination, a common term for idolatry (see 12.23; 2 Chr 34.33; Ezra 9.1,11,14; Jer 2.7–8; Ezek 8.6–17; 18.12–13; Mal 2.11; 1 Macc 1.43–49).

14.12–31: Origins and repercussions of idolatry. The idea that the gods were originally human beings who have been elevated to divine status goes back to the Greek writer Euhemerus (ca. 300 BCE). He told a story about islands with a utopian society, in which the local gods (with Greek names) were originally kings who were promoted to divine status and worshiped by the people after their death (Diodorus Siculus 6.1). Although

13 for they did not exist from the beginning,
  nor will they last forever.
14 For through human vanity they entered
    the world,
  and therefore their speedy end has been
    planned.

15 For a father, consumed with grief at an
    untimely bereavement,
  made an image of his child, who had been
    suddenly taken from him;
  he now honored as a god what was once a
    dead human being,
  and handed on to his dependents secret
    rites and initiations.
16 Then the ungodly custom, grown strong
    with time, was kept as a law,
  and at the command of monarchs carved
    images were worshiped.
17 When people could not honor
    monarchs[a] in their presence, since
    they lived at a distance,
  they imagined their appearance far away,
  and made a visible image of the king
    whom they honored,
  so that by their zeal they might flatter the
    absent one as though present.

18 Then the ambition of the artisan
    impelled
  even those who did not know the king to
    intensify their worship.
19 For he, perhaps wishing to please his ruler,
  skillfully forced the likeness to take more
    beautiful form,
20 and the multitude, attracted by the
    charm of his work,
  now regarded as an object of worship the
    one whom shortly before they had
    honored as a human being.
21 And this became a hidden trap for
    humankind,
  because people, in bondage to misfortune
    or to royal authority,

bestowed on objects of stone or wood the
    name that ought not to be shared.

22 Then it was not enough for them to err
    about the knowledge of God,
  but though living in great strife due to
    ignorance,
  they call such great evils peace.
23 For whether they kill children in their
    initiations, or celebrate secret
    mysteries,
  or hold frenzied revels with strange
    customs,
24 they no longer keep either their lives or
    their marriages pure,
  but they either treacherously kill one
    another, or grieve one another by
    adultery,
25 and all is a raging riot of blood and
    murder, theft and deceit, corruption,
    faithlessness, tumult, perjury,
26 confusion over what is good,
    forgetfulness of favors,
  defiling of souls, sexual perversion,
  disorder in marriages, adultery, and
    debauchery.
27 For the worship of idols not to be
    named
  is the beginning and cause and end of
    every evil.
28 For their worshipers[b] either rave in
    exultation,
  or prophesy lies, or live unrighteously, or
    readily commit perjury;
29 for because they trust in lifeless idols
  they swear wicked oaths and expect to
    suffer no harm.
30 But just penalties will overtake them on
    two counts:
  because they thought wrongly about God
    in devoting themselves to idols,

a Gk *them*
b Gk *they*

the idea was not widespread among Greeks, the Jews latched on to it as an explanation for pagan worship, and it appears in several Jewish writings (e.g., Aristeas 135; Artapanus [Eusebius, *Praep. Ev.* 9.18,23,27; Clement of Alexandria, *Strom.* 1.23.154]; *Sib. Or.* 3.110–58). **12**: *Fornication*, the prophets sometimes spoke of idolatry metaphorically as sexual immorality (Jer 3.1–3; Ezek 16.28–41; Hos 2.2–15). **22–31.** The repercussions of idolatry include *strife, murder, adultery,* and *perjury*. **23**: Cf. 11.7; 12.4–5. **25**: Similar crimes are enumerated in Jer 7.9; Hos 4.2. **27**: Cf. 14.12. **29**: *They swear wicked oaths*, for the seriousness with which false oaths were regarded, see Hos 10.4; Sir 23.11; 41.19; 1 Macc 7.18; 1 Esd 1.48.

and because in deceit they swore
    unrighteously through contempt for
    holiness.
[31] For it is not the power of the things by
    which people swear,[a]
but the just penalty for those who sin,
that always pursues the transgression of
    the unrighteous.

15 But you, our God, are kind and true,
    patient, and ruling all things[b] in mercy.
[2] For even if we sin we are yours, knowing
    your power;
but we will not sin, because we know that
    you acknowledge us as yours.
[3] For to know you is complete
    righteousness,
and to know your power is the root of
    immortality.
[4] For neither has the evil intent of human
    art misled us,
nor the fruitless toil of painters,
a figure stained with varied colors,
[5] whose appearance arouses yearning in
    fools,
so that they desire[c] the lifeless form of a
    dead image.
[6] Lovers of evil things and fit for such
    objects of hope[d]
are those who either make or desire or
    worship them.

[7] A potter kneads the soft earth
and laboriously molds each vessel for our
    service,
fashioning out of the same clay
both the vessels that serve clean uses
and those for contrary uses, making all
    alike;
but which shall be the use of each of them
the worker in clay decides.
[8] With misspent toil, these workers form a
    futile god from the same clay—

these mortals who were made of earth a
    short time before
and after a little while go to the earth from
    which all mortals are taken,
when the time comes to return the souls
    that were borrowed.
[9] But the workers are not concerned that
    mortals are destined to die
or that their life is brief,
but they compete with workers in gold and
    silver,
and imitate workers in copper;
and they count it a glorious thing to mold
    counterfeit gods.
[10] Their heart is ashes, their hope is
    cheaper than dirt,
and their lives are of less worth than
    clay,
[11] because they failed to know the one who
    formed them
and inspired them with active souls
and breathed a living spirit into them.
[12] But they considered our existence an idle
    game,
and life a festival held for profit,
for they say one must get money however
    one can, even by base means.
[13] For these persons, more than all others,
    know that they sin
when they make from earthy matter fragile
    vessels and carved images.

[14] But most foolish, and more miserable
    than an infant,
are all the enemies who oppressed your
    people.
[15] For they thought that all their heathen
    idols were gods,

---

[a] Or *of the oaths people swear*
[b] Or *ruling the universe*
[c] Gk *and he desires*
[d] Gk *such hopes*

15.1–6: The benefits of true worship include *righteousness* and *immortality*. **1–3:** An apostrophe (direct address) to the deity. Allusion to Ex 34.6–9 makes it clear that the author associates authentic worship with the Sinai covenant. **5–6:** *Desire*, cf. 4.12; 6.11,13,17,20; 8.2; 13.6; 15.19.

15.7–19: The fabrication of idols (cf. 13.10–19). The image of clay and the potter occurs frequently (Isa 41.25; 45.9; 64.8; Jer 18.1–10), but it is usually about God as the potter and humans as clay. The image is turned here into the choice of the potter to turn the clay into base objects (e.g., a sewage pipe) or divine images, thus making the same point as at 13.11–19. **8:** That *souls* are *borrowed* was a philosophical conception (cf. 15.16). **12:** The image of life as a *game* or *festival* was common in ancient literature, e.g. Isa 22.12–13; Mt 11.16–17; Epictetus,

though these have neither the use of their
   eyes to see with,
nor nostrils with which to draw breath,
nor ears with which to hear,
nor fingers to feel with,
and their feet are of no use for walking.
[16] For a human being made them,
and one whose spirit is borrowed formed
   them;
for none can form gods that are like
   themselves.
[17] People are mortal, and what they make
   with lawless hands is dead;
for they are better than the objects they
   worship,
since[a] they have life, but the idols[b] never
   had.

[18] Moreover, they worship even the most
   hateful animals,
which are worse than all others when
   judged by their lack of intelligence;
[19] and even as animals they are not so
   beautiful in appearance that one
   would desire them,
but they have escaped both the praise of
   God and his blessing.

16 Therefore those people[c] were deservedly
   punished through such creatures,
and were tormented by a multitude of
   animals.
[2] Instead of this punishment you showed
   kindness to your people,
and you prepared quails to eat,
a delicacy to satisfy the desire of
   appetite;
[3] in order that those people, when they
   desired food,
might lose the least remnant of appetite[d]

because of the odious creatures sent to
   them,
while your people,[c] after suffering want a
   short time,
might partake of delicacies.
[4] For it was necessary that upon those
   oppressors inescapable want should
   come,
while to these others it was merely shown
   how their enemies were being
   tormented.

[5] For when the terrible rage of wild animals
   came upon your people[e]
and they were being destroyed by the bites
   of writhing serpents,
your wrath did not continue to the end;
[6] they were troubled for a little while as a
   warning,
and received a symbol of deliverance to
   remind them of your law's command.

[7] For the one who turned toward it was
   saved, not by the thing that was
   beheld,
but by you, the Savior of all.
[8] And by this also you convinced our
   enemies
that it is you who deliver from every
   evil.
[9] For they were killed by the bites of
   locusts and flies,

a   Other ancient authorities read *of which*
b   Gk *but they*
c   Gk *they*
d   Gk *loathed the necessary appetite*
e   Gk *them*

Discourses 2.14.23–29. **14:** *Most foolish* are the Egyptians who *oppressed* the Israelites. **18–19:** Egyptian animal worship was denounced by Romans as well as Jews, e.g., Juvenal, *Satire* 15.1–11; cf. Philo, *Decalogue* 76–80. **19:** *They have escaped . . . blessing*, referring perhaps to Gen 3.14–15 (cf. Wis 11.15; 1.5,10).

16.1–14: The contrasts, resumed (see 11.1–16). Each of the "elements" of classical antiquity (water, earth, air, and fire) is associated with one of the plagues in this section of the book; see 16.1–4; 16.5–14; 16.15–29; 17.1–18.4.

16.1–4: The second contrast, continued (see 11.15–16). The plague of frogs (cf. Ex 7.25–8.11) that came up from the Nile as punishment for the Egyptian attempt to kill the Israelite baby boys in the Nile is contrasted with the gift of God to the Israelites in the form of the quails from the sea to provide food in the wilderness (Ex 16.12–13; Num 11.31–34; Wis ignores the context in Num in which the demand for meat is actually criticized). This section also represents the element of water, with references to the river and the sea.

16.5–14: The third contrast: the plague of insects and the bronze serpent (Ex 8.20–32; 10.1–20; Num 21.4–9). Whereas the Egyptians were plagued by locusts and flies, the Israelites were saved from a plague of poisonous

and no healing was found for them,
because they deserved to be punished by
　　such things.
[10] But your children were not conquered
　　even by the fangs of venomous
　　serpents,
for your mercy came to their help and
　　healed them.
[11] To remind them of your oracles they
　　were bitten,
and then were quickly delivered,
so that they would not fall into deep
　　forgetfulness
and become unresponsive[a] to your
　　kindness.
[12] For neither herb nor poultice cured
　　them,
but it was your word, O Lord, that heals all
　　people.
[13] For you have power over life and death;
you lead mortals down to the gates of
　　Hades and back again.
[14] A person in wickedness kills another,
but cannot bring back the departed spirit,
or set free the imprisoned soul.

[15] To escape from your hand is impossible;
[16] for the ungodly, refusing to know you,
were flogged by the strength of your arm,
pursued by unusual rains and hail and
　　relentless storms,
and utterly consumed by fire.
[17] For—most incredible of all—in water,
　　which quenches all things,
the fire had still greater effect,
for the universe defends the righteous.
[18] At one time the flame was restrained,
so that it might not consume the creatures
　　sent against the ungodly,
but that seeing this they might know
that they were being pursued by the
　　judgment of God;
[19] and at another time even in the midst of
　　water it burned more intensely than
　　fire,
to destroy the crops of the unrighteous land.
[20] Instead of these things you gave your
　　people food of angels,
and without their toil you supplied them
　　from heaven with bread ready to eat,
providing every pleasure and suited to
　　every taste.
[21] For your sustenance manifested your
　　sweetness toward your children;
and the bread, ministering[b] to the desire of
　　the one who took it,
was changed to suit everyone's liking.
[22] Snow and ice withstood fire without
　　melting,
so that they might know that the crops of
　　their enemies
were being destroyed by the fire that
　　blazed in the hail
and flashed in the showers of rain;
[23] whereas the fire,[c] in order that the
　　righteous might be fed,
even forgot its native power.

[24] For creation, serving you who made it,
exerts itself to punish the unrighteous,
and in kindness relaxes on behalf of those
　　who trust in you.
[25] Therefore at that time also, changed into
　　all forms,
it served your all-nourishing bounty,
according to the desire of those who had
　　need,[d]
[26] so that your children, whom you loved,
　　O Lord, might learn

---

a　Meaning of Gk uncertain
b　Gk and it, ministering
c　Gk this
d　Or who made supplication

serpents through God's "word." **9:** Ex 8.16–32 and 10.12–20 do not speak of deaths from the lice/gnats/flies and locusts, but Josephus mentions them in connection with this plague (*Ant.* 2.14.3).

16.15–29: The fourth contrast: the plague of storms (cf. Ex 9.13–35). Because the Egyptians sinned by refusing to recognize God (16.16), their crops were destroyed by fire and hail. The Israelite counterpart of this plague is the rain of manna from heaven (Ex 16.11–35; Num. 11.6–9). **17:** *Water . . . fire*, referring to the hail and lightning of Ex 9.23–24. **18:** *So that it might not consume*, cf. 19.21. *The creatures*, the animals and insects of 16.1–14; apparently the author assumes that the plagues occurred at one time. **20:** *Food of angels*, cf. Ps 78.24–25. **21:** *Changed to suit everyone's liking*, a tradition also reflected in *Tosefta to Yoma* 75a and *Mekilta* on Ex 16.23. **24:** Since it was fashioned in accordance with wisdom, *creation* inherently assists providence, functioning as an instrument of

that it is not the production of crops that
feeds humankind
but that your word sustains those who
trust in you.
27 For what was not destroyed by fire
was melted when simply warmed by a
fleeting ray of the sun,
28 to make it known that one must rise
before the sun to give you thanks,
and must pray to you at the dawning of the
light;
29 for the hope of an ungrateful person will
melt like wintry frost,
and flow away like waste water.

17 Great are your judgments and hard to
describe;
therefore uninstructed souls have gone
astray.
2 For when lawless people supposed that
they held the holy nation in their
power,
they themselves lay as captives of
darkness and prisoners of long night,
shut in under their roofs, exiles from
eternal providence.
3 For thinking that in their secret sins they
were unobserved
behind a dark curtain of forgetfulness,
they were scattered, terribly[a] alarmed,
and appalled by specters.
4 For not even the inner chamber that held
them protected them from fear,
but terrifying sounds rang out around
them,
and dismal phantoms with gloomy faces
appeared.
5 And no power of fire was able to give light,
nor did the brilliant flames of the stars
avail to illumine that hateful night.

6 Nothing was shining through to them
except a dreadful, self-kindled fire,
and in terror they deemed the things that
they saw
to be worse than that unseen appearance.
7 The delusions of their magic art lay
humbled,
and their boasted wisdom was scornfully
rebuked.
8 For those who promised to drive off the
fears and disorders of a sick soul
were sick themselves with ridiculous
fear.
9 For even if nothing disturbing frightened
them,
yet, scared by the passing of wild animals
and the hissing of snakes
10 they perished in trembling fear,
refusing to look even at the air, though it
nowhere could be avoided.
11 For wickedness is a cowardly thing,
condemned by its own testimony;[b]
distressed by conscience, it has always
exaggerated[c] the difficulties.
12 For fear is nothing but a giving up of the
helps that come from reason;
13 and hope, defeated by this inward
weakness,
prefers ignorance of what causes the
torment.
14 But throughout the night, which was
really powerless
and which came upon them from the
recesses of powerless Hades,

a   Other ancient authorities read *unobserved,
they were darkened behind a dark curtain of
forgetfulness, terribly*
b   Meaning of Gk uncertain
c   Other ancient authorities read *anticipated*

both condemnation and blessing; see 8.4–6; 19.18–21 (cf. Josh 10.11–14; Judg 5.20–21). **28**: *Rise before the sun*, cf.
Ps 119.147; Sir 39.5. **29**: *Hope . . . will melt*, cf. 5.14; Job 14.19.
     17.1–18.4: The fifth contrast: the plague of darkness and the pillar of fire (Ex. 10.21–29; 13.21–22; 14.24–15).
Because the Egyptians sinned by taking the Israelites captive, they suffer by being taken captive by the darkness, which contrasts with the pillar of fire that goes with the Israelites day and night (18.3). This plague represents the element of air, since the darkness was caused by a strange atmosphere. **17.2–21**: The description of
the Egyptians' *terror* is reminiscent of the Greco-Roman genre of the "descent into Hades," of which Book 6 of
Virgil's *Aeneid* was a popular example. **3**: *A dark curtain of forgetfulness*, those who thought their sins were hidden are themselves concealed in darkness (cf. 16.11). **7**: See Ex 7.11,22; 8.7,18; 9.11. **11**: *Conscience*, a common topic
in moral literature (e.g., *T. Reuben* 4.3; Philo, *The Worse Attacks the Better* 22–26). **14**: *Powerless Hades*, see 1.14; cf.
Ps 88.10–12; Eccl 9.10; Isa 14.9–11. *Sleep*, the divine penalty includes nightmares (cf. 18.17–19; Job 7.14; Dan 4.5; Sir

they all slept the same sleep,
[15] and now were driven by monstrous specters,
and now were paralyzed by their souls' surrender;
for sudden and unexpected fear overwhelmed them.
[16] And whoever was there fell down,
and thus was kept shut up in a prison not made of iron;
[17] for whether they were farmers or shepherds
or workers who toiled in the wilderness,
they were seized, and endured the inescapable fate;
for with one chain of darkness they all were bound.
[18] Whether there came a whistling wind,
or a melodious sound of birds in wide-spreading branches,
or the rhythm of violently rushing water,
[19] or the harsh crash of rocks hurled down,
or the unseen running of leaping animals,
or the sound of the most savage roaring beasts,
or an echo thrown back from a hollow of the mountains,
it paralyzed them with terror.
[20] For the whole world was illumined with brilliant light,
and went about its work unhindered,
[21] while over those people alone heavy night was spread,
an image of the darkness that was destined to receive them;
but still heavier than darkness were they to themselves.

18 But for your holy ones there was very great light.
Their enemies[a] heard their voices but did not see their forms,
and counted them happy for not having suffered,

[2] and were thankful that your holy ones,[b]
though previously wronged, were doing them no injury;
and they begged their pardon for having been at variance with them.[b]
[3] Therefore you provided a flaming pillar of fire
as a guide for your people's[c] unknown journey,
and a harmless sun for their glorious wandering.
[4] For their enemies[d] deserved to be deprived of light and imprisoned in darkness,
those who had kept your children imprisoned,
through whom the imperishable light of the law was to be given to the world.

[5] When they had resolved to kill the infants of your holy ones,
and one child had been abandoned and rescued,
you in punishment took away a multitude of their children;
and you destroyed them all together by a mighty flood.
[6] That night was made known beforehand to our ancestors,
so that they might rejoice in sure knowledge of the oaths in which they trusted.
[7] The deliverance of the righteous and the destruction of their enemies
were expected by your people.
[8] For by the same means by which you punished our enemies
you called us to yourself and glorified us.
[9] For in secret the holy children of good people offered sacrifices,

a Gk *They*
b Meaning of Gk uncertain
c Gk *their*
d Gk *those persons*

40.5–7). **18–19:** They experience *terror* even at ordinary sounds (cf. 17.4; Lev 26.36–37; Job 15.20–21). **18.2:** This verse, the meaning of which is unclear, may be referring to Ex 12.31–33. **3:** See Ex 13.21–22; 14.24. **4:** *The law was to be given to the world,* cf. Isa 2.2–3; 42.6; 49.6; 2 Esd 7.20–24; 14.20–22.

18.5–25: The sixth contrast: the plague of the Egyptian firstborn and Israel's rescue (cf. Ex 11.1–12.32). The Egyptians sinned by killing the infants in the Nile. Their punishment is to have their firstborn die by the hand of the angel of death **5:** *One child,* Moses (Ex 1.15–2.10). **6–9:** A poetic description of the first Passover (Ex 12.1–28).

and with one accord agreed to the divine
    law,
so that the saints would share alike the
    same things,
both blessings and dangers;
and already they were singing the praises
    of the ancestors.[a]
[10] But the discordant cry of their enemies
    echoed back,
and their piteous lament for their children
    was spread abroad.
[11] The slave was punished with the same
    penalty as the master,
and the commoner suffered the same loss
    as the king;
[12] and they all together, by the one form[b]
    of death,
had corpses too many to count.
For the living were not sufficient even to
    bury them,
since in one instant their most valued
    children had been destroyed.
[13] For though they had disbelieved
    everything because of their magic arts,
yet, when their firstborn were destroyed,
    they acknowledged your people to be
    God's child.
[14] For while gentle silence enveloped all
    things,
and night in its swift course was now half
    gone,
[15] your all-powerful word leaped from
    heaven, from the royal throne,
into the midst of the land that was
    doomed,
a stern warrior
[16] carrying the sharp sword of your
    authentic command,
and stood and filled all things with death,
and touched heaven while standing on the
    earth.
[17] Then at once apparitions in dreadful
    dreams greatly troubled them,
and unexpected fears assailed them;
[18] and one here and another there, hurled
    down half dead,

made known why they were dying;
[19] for the dreams that disturbed them
    forewarned them of this,
so that they might not perish without
    knowing why they suffered.

[20] The experience of death touched also
    the righteous,
and a plague came upon the multitude in
    the desert,
but the wrath did not long continue.
[21] For a blameless man was quick to act as
    their champion;
he brought forward the shield of his
    ministry,
prayer and propitiation by incense;
he withstood the anger and put an end to
    the disaster,
showing that he was your servant.
[22] He conquered the wrath[c] not by strength
    of body,
not by force of arms,
but by his word he subdued the avenger,
appealing to the oaths and covenants
    given to our ancestors.
[23] For when the dead had already fallen on
    one another in heaps,
he intervened and held back the wrath,
and cut off its way to the living.
[24] For on his long robe the whole world
    was depicted,
and the glories of the ancestors were
    engraved on the four rows of
    stones,
and your majesty was on the diadem upon
    his head.
[25] To these the destroyer yielded, these he[d]
    feared;
for merely to test the wrath was enough.

a Other ancient authorities read *dangers, the
   ancestors already leading the songs of praise*
b Gk *name*
c Cn: Gk *multitude*
d Other ancient authorities read *they*

9: *Already they were singing*, cf. 2 Chr 30.21. 13: *God's child*, cf. 5.5; Ex 4.22–23; Jer 31.9; Hos 11.1. 15: *A stern warrior*,
cf. 5.17–20. 17–19: Cf. 17.14n. 20–25: *A blameless man*, Aaron makes atonement for the Israelites' rebellion against
God by burning *incense*, ending *a plague* that killed 14,700 people (Num 16.41–50). 22: *The avenger*, cf. Ps 99.8;
1 Thess 4.6. 24: See Ex 28.15–38. On the symbolism of the high priest's vestments, see Josephus, *Ant.* 3.7.7; Philo,
Moses 2.117–26 25: *The destroyer*, cf. 1 Cor 10:10.

19

But the ungodly were assailed to the end by pitiless anger,

for God[a] knew in advance even their future actions:

2 how, though they themselves had permitted[b] your people to depart

and hastily sent them out,

they would change their minds and pursue them.

3 For while they were still engaged in mourning,

and were lamenting at the graves of their dead,

they reached another foolish decision,

and pursued as fugitives those whom they had begged and compelled to leave.

4 For the fate they deserved drew them on to this end,

and made them forget what had happened,

in order that they might fill up the punishment that their torments still lacked,

5 and that your people might experience[c] an incredible journey,

but they themselves might meet a strange death.

6 For the whole creation in its nature was fashioned anew,

complying with your commands,

so that your children[d] might be kept unharmed.

7 The cloud was seen overshadowing the camp,

and dry land emerging where water had stood before,

an unhindered way out of the Red Sea,

and a grassy plain out of the raging waves,

8 where those protected by your hand passed through as one nation,

after gazing on marvelous wonders.

9 For they ranged like horses,

and leaped like lambs,

praising you, O Lord, who delivered them.

10 For they still recalled the events of their sojourn,

how instead of producing animals the earth brought forth gnats,

and instead of fish the river spewed out vast numbers of frogs.

11 Afterward they saw also a new kind[e] of birds,

when desire led them to ask for luxurious food;

12 for, to give them relief, quails came up from the sea.

13 The punishments did not come upon the sinners

without prior signs in the violence of thunder,

for they justly suffered because of their wicked acts;

for they practiced a more bitter hatred of strangers.

14 Others had refused to receive strangers when they came to them,

but these made slaves of guests who were their benefactors.

15 And not only so—but, while punishment of some sort will come upon the former

for having received strangers with hostility,

16 the latter, having first received them with festal celebrations,

afterward afflicted with terrible sufferings those who had already shared the same rights.

17 They were stricken also with loss of sight—

just as were those at the door of the righteous man—

when, surrounded by yawning darkness,

all of them tried to find the way through their own doors.

---

a Gk *he*
b Other ancient authorities read *had changed their minds to permit*
c Other ancient authorities read *accomplish*
d Or *servants*
e Or *production*

19.1–21: The seventh contrast: death and salvation at the Red Sea (Ex 14.1–31). **1:** *The ungodly,* the Egyptians. **4:** *Made them forget,* cf. 4.1; 17.3. *Fill up the punishment,* cf. Dan 8.23; 2 Macc 6.14. **6:** See 19.18–21. **7:** *Cloud,* Ex 13.21–22. **10:** Ex 8.1–19. **11–12:** See 16.1–4; cf. Num 11.31–32. **14:** *Others,* those of Sodom (Gen 19.1–11). *These,* the Egyptians. *Guests,* see Gen 45.16–20. *Benefactors,* referring to Joseph's service to Egypt. **17:** *Righteous man,* Lot;

18 For the elements changed[a] places with
  one another,
as on a harp the notes vary the nature of
  the rhythm,
while each note remains the same.[b]
This may be clearly inferred from the sight
  of what took place.
19 For land animals were transformed into
  water creatures,
and creatures that swim moved over to the
  land.
20 Fire even in water retained its normal
  power,
and water forgot its fire-quenching
  nature.

21 Flames, on the contrary, failed to
  consume
the flesh of perishable creatures that
  walked among them,
nor did they melt[c] the crystalline, quick-
  melting kind of heavenly food.

22 For in everything, O Lord, you have
  exalted and glorified your people,
and you have not neglected to help them
  at all times and in all places.

a   Gk *changing*
b   Meaning of Gk uncertain
c   Cn: Gk *nor could be melted*

cf. Gen 19.11; Ex 14.20. **18–21:** In the plagues and at the Red Sea nature *changed* its customary actions so as to
bring about God's purpose (16.24; 19.6). That the material elements could be transformed in various ways was
an assumption of ancient physics, e.g., Cicero, *The Nature of the Gods* 3.39.92.
  19.22: A final doxology or praise of God concludes the book.

18 For the elements changed places with
  one another,
  as on a harp the notes vary the nature of
  the rhythm,
  while each note remains the same.
  This may be clearly inferred from the sight
  of what took place.
19 For land animals were transformed into
  water creatures,
  and creatures that swim moved over to the
  land.
20 Fire even in water retained its normal
  power,
  and water forgot its fire-quenching
  nature.

21 Flames, on the contrary, failed to
  consume
  the flesh of perishable creatures that
  walked among them,
  nor did they melt the crystalline, quick-
  melting kind of heavenly food.

22 For in everything, O Lord, you have
  exalted and glorified your people,
  and you have not neglected to help them
  at all times and in all places.

a   *Bel and the*
   Dragon of Gk manuscripts
   Or *God represents the learned*

d Gen 1:20; Ex 7:19; 8:6 b In the plagues and at the Red Sea, nature changed its customary actions so as to bring about God's purpose (0-24:1992). That the material elements could be arranged in various ways without a disruption of created physics is a sign that the universe is governed by goodness.

ECCLESIASTICUS, OR THE WISDOM OF JESUS, SON OF SIRACH

NAME

In most Greek manuscripts the title given to this book is "The Wisdom of Jesus the Son of Sirach." Latin manuscripts refer to it as "The Book of Jesus the Son of Sirach." In the Latin tradition it is also known as "Ecclesiasticus," which means "church book" and was probably intended as a statement about the book's acceptance in the Christian canon of scripture. If the Hebrew original had a title, it was something like "The Wisdom of Yeshua the Son of Sira." Today some scholars refer to the book as "Sirach" and the original author as Ben Sira. Others use the title "Sirach" for the Greek version, "Ecclesiasticus" for the Latin text, and "Ben Sira" for the Hebrew original and/or its author.

CANONICAL STATUS

The book of Sirach was never part of the Hebrew canon of scripture, even though it was composed in Hebrew and was often quoted in Hebrew by later Jewish writers. It may have been considered too recent in its composition (early second century BCE) in comparison with the other canonical books. The Greek translation made by Ben Sira's grandson, however, was transmitted as part of the larger collection of Jewish writings in Greek known as the Septuagint (LXX). The Christian churches generally followed the wider Greek canon of scripture, and for fifteen centuries most Christians regarded Sirach as part of their Old Testament. When Martin Luther and other early Reformers sought to limit the Protestant Old Testament canon to the Jewish Hebrew canon, Sirach and other "deuterocanonical" books were relegated to the "Apocrypha" (see p. 1361). Roman Catholics and Orthodox Christians regard Sirach as canonical and place it among the other Old Testament books. Some Protestant Bibles today have revived the practice of the early Reformers and place it as part of the separate section between the Old and the New Testaments that is known as the Apocrypha.

AUTHOR AND HISTORICAL CONTEXT

Near the end of the Greek version of the book, the original author identifies himself as "Jesus son of Eleazar son of Sirach" (50.27). His Hebrew name would have been "Yeshua ben Eleazar ben Sira." He conducted a school ("a house of instruction," 51.23) for prospective scribes and sages, perhaps in association with the Jerusalem Temple complex. His book is a summary or compendium of his teachings, written down in Hebrew ca. 180 BCE. His grandson produced the Greek version in Egypt ca. 117 BCE.

If Ben Sira wrote his book ca. 180 BCE, he would have lived through the transition in control of Judea from the Ptolemies in Egypt to the Seleucids in Syria, and the political turmoil associated with that transition, which took place around 200 BCE. He may have died before the conflicts about the Jewish high priesthood beginning ca. 175 BCE, when the Seleucid ruler Antiochus IV Epiphanes and his Jewish collaborators attempted to eradicate the distinctive features of Jewish life (the Jerusalem Temple and the Torah) and sparked the Maccabean revolt (see Daniel and 1 and 2 Maccabees). Ben Sira was a traditional and conservative person by nature, and a strong supporter of the Temple and the Jewish high priesthood. Nevertheless, it is difficult to find clear references in his book to contemporary historical events (but perhaps 35.21–26 and 36.1–22 constitute exceptions) and figures (except for Simon the high priest in 50.1–24). For Ben Sira's autobiographical notices scattered throughout the book, see 24.30–34; 33.16–19; 34.9–13; 39.12–13; 50.27; and 51.13–30.

Ben Sira was a man of his place and time, that is, Palestine in the early second century BCE. His opinions on many social issues, especially on women and slaves, may strike modern readers as benighted, even outrageous. Ben Sira and his contemporaries perceived themselves as embedded in various groups (family, clan, village, city, etc.). They judged their own importance by what others thought of them, in what anthropologists call an honor-shame society. His social world was hierarchical, with everyone having a relatively fixed place and little opportunity for upward social mobility. People then considered wives to be naturally subordinate to their husbands, and children and slaves under the ultimate control of the male head of the household.

LITERARY HISTORY

The book of Sirach is best known through the grandson's Greek translation, which provides the basis for the present English version. As the Greek version became canonical for Christians, the Hebrew form became increasingly marginal for Jews. Large parts of the Hebrew text, however, have been found among the Dead Sea Scrolls (at Qumran and Masada) and in the Genizah (storehouse) of a medieval Jewish synagogue in Cairo. Nearly two-thirds of the Hebrew version has been retrieved in one form or another. Even in antiquity the Hebrew and Greek textual traditions developed short and long editions or recensions. The additional sayings in the longer recension appear in small type at the foot of the pages in this translation; this explains the "missing numbers" for verses throughout the main text of the book. Moreover, it appears that all the Greek manuscripts contained a textual displacement by which Sir 30.25–33.13a and 33.13b–36.16a changed places; this explains discrepancies in references between older and more recent translations and scholarly studies.

Sirach remains a valuable resource for understanding Judaism in the Second Temple period and the world in which Jesus and the early Christians lived. It was translated into various ancient languages and received much attention from patristic and medieval writers. It was treasured for its practical advice on many different topics and its emphasis on love of learning and the desire for God.

STRUCTURE AND CONTENTS

As with other ancient wisdom books, Sirach is an anthology or collection of short units on various topics. In many parts it is difficult to discover a logical progression of thought or to discern the principles of arrangement. However, a series of poems on seeking and finding wisdom (1.1–10; 4.11–19; 6.18–37; 14.20–15.10; 24.1–33; 38.24–39.11) seem to divide the book into something like chapters. The book reaches its climax with the praise of God's glory manifest in creation (42.15–43.33) and in the heroes of faith in ancient Israel's history (44.1–50.24).

In conveying his wisdom teachings, Ben Sira used a wide array of literary forms: analogies or comparisons (*meshalim*), maxims or proverbs, beatitudes and woes, numerical sayings, questions and answers, refrains and repetitions, "there is" sayings, "better than" sayings, prohibitions or admonitions ("Do not . . ."), instructions, prayers of petition, hymns, aretalogy (self-praise), autobiographical accounts, and biblical paraphrases. Many of these literary devices lend themselves to easy memorization, thus supplying Ben Sira's students and readers with a treasury of wisdom sayings by which to interpret the world around them and to conduct themselves wisely and righteously.

INTERPRETATION

Sirach is the largest wisdom book that we have from antiquity. It provides a window into life in ancient Israel at a pivotal point in Jewish history, illustrating how and what Jewish wisdom teachers taught, and offering wise teachings that have inspired and challenged readers for more than two millennia. Ben Sira gives his opinions on topics such as creation, death, fear of the Lord, friendship, happiness, and honor and shame. While conservative by nature, Ben Sira was an innovator in joining the wisdom traditions of the ancient Near East and the distinctive traditions of ancient Israel (cf. 24.23). The students at his school were expected to become equally adept at practical wisdom and biblical learning (39.1–5).

Ben Sira's students were mainly well-to-do young men preparing for careers as teachers and counselors in the public arena (39.6–11). He insisted that they view true wisdom as a gift from God and that they pray regularly for wisdom. He was an enthusiastic supporter of the Jerusalem Temple and high priesthood. As a teacher of young men, he issued warnings about the troubles that the wrong kinds of women might bring upon them. At several points, however, his caution borders on misogyny. With regard to human suffering, Ben Sira accepts the traditional understanding of theodicy, or divine justice, according to which wise and righteous persons prosper, while foolish and wicked persons suffer. He generally ignores the problem of innocent suffering raised by the book of Job, and at some points he may have been responding to the skepticism displayed by the book of Ecclesiastes. He takes a tentative stab at the problem of evil with his doctrine of the "pairs" (33.7–15), without proposing a full-fledged dualism. His poems about God's action in creation and in Israel's history urge his readers to seek and find the glory of God in all things (42.15–50.24). He viewed immortality mainly in terms of the good name or reputation that one leaves behind (38.16–23; 41.1–13).

GUIDE TO READING

One can read Sirach straight through from beginning to end, just as the book has come down to us. However, many find it difficult to read an anthology that way. Moreover, the various units in the book demand meditation, personal appropriation, and application. The reflections on wisdom and fear of the Lord in chapters 1 and 2 provide the theological framework for all that follows. The poem about wisdom personified and Ben Sira's identification of her with the covenant and the Torah in chapter 24 is the key to his integration of secular wisdom and biblical revelation. The other wisdom poems (4.11–19; 6.18–37; 14.20–15.10; 38.34–39.11) are also important for catching the flavor of Ben Sira's project. The description of Israel's heroes of faith as manifestations of God's glory in chapters 44–50 opens up fresh perspectives on the Bible as a whole. For the rest of the book, tracking specific themes through the various parts can be quite fruitful. For example, one might pursue several or all of the following ten topics: creation (16.24–17.24; 18.1–14; 33.7–15; 39.12–35; 42.15–43.33), death (11.26–28; 22.11–12; 38.16–23; 41.1–13), friendship (6.5–17; 9.10–16; 19.13–17; 22.19–26; 27.16–21; 36.23–37.15), happiness (25.1–11; 30.14–25; 40.1–30), honor and shame (4.20–6.4; 10.19–11.6; 41.14–42.8), money matters (3.30–4.10; 11.7–28; 13.1–14.19; 29.1–28; 31.1–11), sin (7.1–17; 15.11–20; 16.1–17.32; 18.30–19.3; 21.1–10; 22.27–23.27; 26.28–28.7), social justice (4.1–10; 34.21–27; 35.14–26), speech (5.9–15; 18.15–29; 19.4–17; 20.1–31; 23.7–15; 27.4–7; 27.11–15; 28.8–26), and women (9.1–9; 23.22–27; 25.13–26.27; 36.26–31; 42.9–14).

Daniel J. Harrington

THE PROLOGUE

Many great teachings have been given to us through the Law and the Prophets and the others[a] that followed them, and for these we should praise Israel for instruction and wisdom. Now, those who read the scriptures must not only themselves understand them, but must also as lovers of learning be able through the spoken and written word to help the outsiders. So my grandfather Jesus, who had devoted himself especially to the reading of the Law and the Prophets and the other books of our ancestors, and had acquired considerable proficiency in them, was himself also led to write something pertaining to instruction and wisdom, so that by becoming familiar also with his book[b] those who love learning might make even greater progress in living according to the law.

You are invited therefore to read it with goodwill and attention, and to be indulgent in cases where, despite our diligent labor in translating, we may seem to have rendered some phrases imperfectly. For what was originally expressed in Hebrew does not have exactly the same sense when translated into another language. Not only this book, but even the Law itself, the Prophecies, and the rest of the books differ not a little when read in the original.

When I came to Egypt in the thirty-eighth year of the reign of Euergetes and stayed for some time, I found opportunity for no little instruction.[c] It seemed highly necessary that

a   Or *other books*
b   Gk *with these things*
c   Other ancient authorities read *I found a copy affording no little instruction*

Prologue: Written in an elevated Greek style, the prologue to the Greek version of the book provides in three long sentences basic information about the original author and his purposes, the problems facing the translator, and the circumstances of the translation. It contains the earliest references to the threefold division of the Hebrew scriptures: *the Law and the Prophets and the other books* (cf. Lk 24.44). *Jesus* is the Greek form of the original author's Hebrew name, which was probably "Yeshua" or some other form of Joshua (50.27). In contrast to this translator, who admits that his book, as well as *the Law, the Prophecies, and the rest,* differ *not a little* from the *Hebrew* original, other early Jewish and Christian writers defended the accuracy of the Septuagint (LXX) in legends that have miraculous elements (Philo, *Life of Moses* 2.25–44). Ben Sira's grandson came to Egypt (most likely Alexandria) in *the thirty-eighth year* of the reign of Ptolemy VII Psychon *Euergetes* II, that is, in 132 BCE. He probably completed his work shortly after Ptolemy VII's death in 117 BCE. He intended his Greek translation especially for his fellow Jews *living abroad,* and in particular for the large Jewish community in Egypt. Thus he hoped that Diaspora Jews might profit from reading his grandfather's work in Greek just as Jews in Palestine had profited from the Hebrew original.

I should myself devote some diligence and labor to the translation of this book. During that time I have applied my skill day and night to complete and publish the book for those living abroad who wished to gain learning and are disposed to live according to the law.

1 All wisdom is from the Lord,
and with him it remains forever.
² The sand of the sea, the drops of rain,
and the days of eternity—who can
count them?
³ The height of heaven, the breadth of the
earth,
the abyss, and wisdomᵃ—who can
search them out?
⁴ Wisdom was created before all other things,
and prudent understanding from
eternity.ᵇ
⁶ The root of wisdom—to whom has it
been revealed?
Her subtleties—who knows them?ᶜ
⁸ There is but one who is wise, greatly to be
feared,
seated upon his throne—the Lord.
⁹ It is he who created her;
he saw her and took her measure;
he poured her out upon all his works,
¹⁰ upon all the living according to his gift;
he lavished her upon those who love him.ᵈ

¹¹ The fear of the Lord is glory and exultation,
and gladness and a crown of rejoicing.
¹² The fear of the Lord delights the heart,
and gives gladness and joy and long life.ᵉ
¹³ Those who fear the Lord will have a
happy end;
on the day of their death they will be
blessed.

¹⁴ To fear the Lord is the beginning of wisdom;
she is created with the faithful in the
womb.
¹⁵ She madeᶠ among human beings an
eternal foundation,
and among their descendants she will
abide faithfully.
¹⁶ To fear the Lord is fullness of wisdom;
she inebriates mortals with her fruits;
¹⁷ she fills theirᵍ whole house with
desirable goods,
and theirᵍ storehouses with her produce.
¹⁸ The fear of the Lord is the crown of
wisdom,
making peace and perfect health to
flourish.ʰ
¹⁹ She rained down knowledge and
discerning comprehension,
and she heightened the glory of those
who held her fast.

a Other ancient authorities read *the depth of the abyss*
b Other ancient authorities add as verse 5, *The source of wisdom is God's word in the highest heaven, and her ways are the eternal commandments.*
c Other ancient authorities add as verse 7, *The knowledge of wisdom—to whom was it manifested? And her abundant experience—who has understood it?*
d Other ancient authorities add *Love of the Lord is glorious wisdom; to those to whom he appears he apportions her, that they may see him.*
e Other ancient authorities add *The fear of the Lord is a gift from the Lord; also for love he makes firm paths.*
f Gk *made as a nest*
g Other ancient authorities read *her*
h Other ancient authorities add *Both are gifts of God for peace; glory opens out for those who love him. He saw her and took her measure.*

1.1-10: Wisdom's origin. Wisdom, described as a feminine figure, was created by God and is given to humans as a gift. **1:** *From the Lord,* created by and residing with God (Prov 8.22–23; Wis 7.25–26). **2-3:** The rhetorical questions (cf. 1.6) indicate that true wisdom is beyond mere human understanding (Job 38–39). **4:** *Created before all other things,* 24.3–7; Prov 8.22–26. **6-10:** God, the truly wise one, *created* wisdom and bestows *her* on those who *love him* (Job 28.23–27).

1.11–30: Wisdom and fear of the Lord. A programmatic statement of the proper response to God's gift of wisdom: *fear of the Lord*—the gratitude, respect, and conduct owed to God. **12:** *Long life,* v. 20; cf. Prov 3.16. In wisdom literature generally, the good are rewarded with a long, healthy, prosperous life. **13:** *Happy end,* immortality for Ben Sira consists primarily in the good name or reputation that one leaves behind (41.11–13). **14:** *The beginning of wisdom,* cf. Prov 1.7; 9.10; Ps 111.10. *In the womb,* a prophetic motif (49.7; Jer 1.5; Isa 44.2,24; 49.1,5; see also Ps 139.13). **15:** *Abide faithfully,* for wisdom's dwelling place, cf. 24.10–12; Prov 8.31; Wis 1.7. **20:** *Root,* wis-

²⁰ To fear the Lord is the root of wisdom,
and her branches are long life.^a

²² Unjust anger cannot be justified,
for anger tips the scale to one's ruin.
²³ Those who are patient stay calm until
the right moment,
and then cheerfulness comes back to
them.
²⁴ They hold back their words until the
right moment;
then the lips of many tell of their good
sense.

²⁵ In the treasuries of wisdom are wise
sayings,
but godliness is an abomination to a
sinner.
²⁶ If you desire wisdom, keep the
commandments,
and the Lord will lavish her upon you.
²⁷ For the fear of the Lord is wisdom and
discipline,
fidelity and humility are his delight.

²⁸ Do not disobey the fear of the Lord;
do not approach him with a divided
mind.
²⁹ Do not be a hypocrite before others,
and keep watch over your lips.
³⁰ Do not exalt yourself, or you may fall
and bring dishonor upon yourself.
The Lord will reveal your secrets
and overthrow you before the whole
congregation,
because you did not come in the fear of
the Lord,
and your heart was full of deceit.

2 My child, when you come to serve the Lord,
prepare yourself for testing.^b
² Set your heart right and be steadfast,
and do not be impetuous in time of
calamity.
³ Cling to him and do not depart,
so that your last days may be
prosperous.
⁴ Accept whatever befalls you,
and in times of humiliation be patient.
⁵ For gold is tested in the fire,
and those found acceptable, in the
furnace of humiliation.^c
⁶ Trust in him, and he will help you;
make your ways straight, and hope in
him.

⁷ You who fear the Lord, wait for his mercy;
do not stray, or else you may fall.
⁸ You who fear the Lord, trust in him,
and your reward will not be lost.
⁹ You who fear the Lord, hope for good
things,
for lasting joy and mercy.^d
¹⁰ Consider the generations of old and see:
has anyone trusted in the Lord and
been disappointed?
Or has anyone persevered in the fear of the
Lord^e and been forsaken?

^a Other ancient authorities add as verse 21, *The fear
of the Lord drives away sins; and where it abides, it
will turn away all anger.*
^b Or *trials*
^c Other ancient authorities add *in sickness and
poverty put your trust in him*
^d Other ancient authorities add *For his reward is an
everlasting gift with joy.*
^e Gk *of him*

dom is the tree that gives life (24.13–17; Prov 3.18; Gen 3.22). **22–24:** For the dangers of yielding to *unjust anger,*
cf. 27.30–28.11; Prov 12.16; 29.22. **25–27:** *The treasuries of wisdom* include proverbs and other sayings, while the
commandments are laws in the Torah (cf. 24.23). Sirach is the first wisdom book to relate Torah and wisdom in
this way; cf. Bar 4.1. **28:** *Divided mind,* 2.12. **29:** *Hypocrite,* 32.15; 33.2. **30:** Honor and *dishonor* are major themes in
Sirach (3.2–11; 4.21; 7.7; 10.19–11.6; 41.17–42.8).

2.1–18: Fear of the Lord. What it means to remain faithful to God and to the pursuit of wisdom. **1–6:** Those
who serve God must expect testing, remain patient, and accept suffering as a discipline. **1:** *My child,* literally
"my son," a common way for Ben Sira the teacher to address a pupil (3.17; 4.1; 6.8; 7.3; etc.; cf. Prov 1.8,10, etc.).
Testing reveals one's true character (4.17; 6.20–21; 44.20; Prov 3.11–12). **5.** *Tested in the fire,* cf. Prov 17.3; 27.21;
Wis 3.6. **7–9:** Those who *fear the Lord* must *wait, trust,* and *hope* during this life. Note another threefold repetition of *fear of the Lord* in 2.15–17. **10–11:** The three questions (cf. Pss 22.4–5; 37.25) expect negative responses,
though the case of Job renders dubious such easy answers. **11:** *The Lord is compassionate and merciful,* Ex 34.6–7;

Or has anyone called upon him and
    been neglected?
[11] For the Lord is compassionate and
    merciful;
    he forgives sins and saves in time of
    distress.

[12] Woe to timid hearts and to slack hands,
    and to the sinner who walks a double
    path!
[13] Woe to the fainthearted who have no trust!
    Therefore they will have no shelter.
[14] Woe to you who have lost your nerve!
    What will you do when the Lord's
    reckoning comes?

[15] Those who fear the Lord do not disobey
    his words,
    and those who love him keep his ways.
[16] Those who fear the Lord seek to please
    him,
    and those who love him are filled with
    his law.
[17] Those who fear the Lord prepare their
    hearts,
    and humble themselves before him.
[18] Let us fall into the hands of the Lord,
    but not into the hands of mortals;
for equal to his majesty is his mercy,
    and equal to his name are his works.[a]

3 Listen to me your father, O children;
    act accordingly, that you may be kept in
    safety.
[2] For the Lord honors a father above his
    children,
    and he confirms a mother's right over
    her children.

[3] Those who honor their father atone for
    sins,
    [4] and those who respect their mother
    are like those who lay up treasure.
[5] Those who honor their father will have
    joy in their own children,
    and when they pray they will be heard.
[6] Those who respect their father will have
    long life,
    and those who honor[b] their mother
    obey the Lord;
    [7] they will serve their parents as their
    masters.[c]
[8] Honor your father by word and deed,
    that his blessing may come upon you.
[9] For a father's blessing strengthens the
    houses of the children,
    but a mother's curse uproots their
    foundations.
[10] Do not glorify yourself by dishonoring
    your father,
    for your father's dishonor is no glory
    to you.
[11] The glory of one's father is one's own
    glory,
    and it is a disgrace for children not to
    respect their mother.

[12] My child, help your father in his old age,
    and do not grieve him as long as he lives;
[13] even if his mind fails, be patient with him;
    because you have all your faculties do
    not despise him.

a Syr: Gk lacks this line
b Heb: Other ancient authorities read *comfort*
c In other ancient authorities this line is preceded by
  Those who fear the Lord honor their father,

Pss 103.8–9; 145.8; Jon 4.2. For God as one who *forgives sins* and *saves*, cf. Pss 37.39–40; 103.3; 145.18–19. **12–14:** The three *woes* (41.8) are warnings or threats to the conflicted or *fainthearted*. *The Lord's reckoning* refers to the consequences during this life rather than to the last judgment. **15–17:** *Those who fear the Lord* observe God's commandments and approach God with proper reverence (cf. 2.7–9). **18:** *Fall into the hands of the Lord*, 2 Sam 24.14; 1 Chr 21.13. The *name* of the Lord here is "the merciful one"; see 2.11n.; 50.19.

3.1–16: Parents and children. Wisdom and fear of the Lord should extend to family relationships (Ex 20.12; Deut 5.16); those addressed (*O children*) are adults. **1–2:** The social order decreed by God places parents above their children. For the *father* as head of the family, see 7.23–26; 22.3–5; 26.1–27. Respect for the *mother* is also stressed here (cf. 3.16; Prov 1.8; 6.20; etc.). **3–7:** *Those who honor* their parents can expect spiritual and material benefits, including atonement for their sins (3.14) and a long life (Deut 5.16).

8–11: Honoring parents brings *honor* to the child, while *dishonoring* them brings shame (1.30; 4.21; 7.7; 10.19–11.6; 41.17–42.8). **12–16:** Caring for elderly parents will be rewarded by God and will provide atonement for sins (3.3), while dishonoring parents is the equivalent of blasphemy (3.1–2).

14 For kindness to a father will not be
forgotten,
and will be credited to you against your
sins;
15 in the day of your distress it will be
remembered in your favor;
like frost in fair weather, your sins will
melt away.
16 Whoever forsakes a father is like a
blasphemer,
and whoever angers a mother is cursed
by the Lord.

17 My child, perform your tasks with
humility;[a]
then you will be loved by those whom
God accepts.
18 The greater you are, the more you must
humble yourself;
so you will find favor in the sight of the
Lord.[b]
20 For great is the might of the Lord;
but by the humble he is glorified.
21 Neither seek what is too difficult for you,
nor investigate what is beyond your
power.
22 Reflect upon what you have been
commanded,
for what is hidden is not your concern.
23 Do not meddle in matters that are
beyond you,
for more than you can understand has
been shown you.
24 For their conceit has led many astray,
and wrong opinion has impaired their
judgment.

25 Without eyes there is no light;
without knowledge there is no
wisdom.[c]
26 A stubborn mind will fare badly at the
end,
and whoever loves danger will perish in it.

27 A stubborn mind will be burdened by
troubles,
and the sinner adds sin to sins.
28 When calamity befalls the proud, there
is no healing,
for an evil plant has taken root in him.
29 The mind of the intelligent appreciates
proverbs,
and an attentive ear is the desire of the
wise.

30 As water extinguishes a blazing fire,
so almsgiving atones for sin.
31 Those who repay favors give thought to
the future;
when they fall they will find support.

4 My child, do not cheat the poor of their
living,
and do not keep needy eyes waiting.
2 Do not grieve the hungry,
or anger one in need.
3 Do not add to the troubles of the desperate,
or delay giving to the needy.
4 Do not reject a suppliant in distress,
or turn your face away from the poor.
5 Do not avert your eye from the needy,
and give no one reason to curse you;
6 for if in bitterness of soul some should
curse you,
their Creator will hear their prayer.

7 Endear yourself to the congregation;
bow your head low to the great.
8 Give a hearing to the poor,
and return their greeting politely.
9 Rescue the oppressed from the oppressor;
and do not be hesitant in giving a verdict.

a   Heb: Gk *meekness*
b   Other ancient authorities add as verse 19, *Many are
lofty and renowned, but to the humble he reveals
his secrets.*
c   Heb: Other ancient authorities lack verse 25

3.17–29: **Humility before God.** Humility brings favor from God, while intellectual pride is to be avoided.
17–20: Humility (or meekness) glorifies God and wins favor from those *loved* by God (7.16–17; 10.28). **21–29:**
What is too difficult may refer to Greek philosophical and Jewish apocalyptic speculations. True wisdom is found
in *what you have been commanded* (in the Torah) and in *proverbs* (the teachings of the sages)—the two major
sources of wisdom in Ben Sira's school and his book.
    3.30–4.10: Almsgiving. The instructions assume that the sage will have sufficient wealth to act as a bene-
factor (cf. Job 29). **30:** *Atones for sin*, cf. 3.4,14. **4.1–5:** Ten things not to do when giving alms. The advice acknowledges and attempts to address the social and power differences that are present in acts of charity. **6:** *Curse*, cf.

¹⁰ Be a father to orphans,
　and be like a husband to their mother;
you will then be like a son of the Most
　　High,
　and he will love you more than does
　　your mother.

¹¹ Wisdom teachesᵃ her children
　and gives help to those who seek her.
¹² Whoever loves her loves life,
　and those who seek her from early
　　morning are filled with joy.
¹³ Whoever holds her fast inherits glory,
　and the Lord blesses the place sheᵇ
　　enters.
¹⁴ Those who serve her minister to the
　　Holy One;
　the Lord loves those who love her.
¹⁵ Those who obey her will judge the
　　nations,
　and all who listen to her will live secure.
¹⁶ If they remain faithful, they will inherit
　　her;
　their descendants will also obtain her.
¹⁷ For at first she will walk with them on
　　tortuous paths;
　she will bring fear and dread upon
　　them,
and will torment them by her discipline
　until she trusts them,ᶜ
and she will test them with her
　　ordinances.
¹⁸ Then she will come straight back to them
　　again and gladden them,
　and will reveal her secrets to them.
¹⁹ If they go astray she will forsake them,
　and hand them over to their ruin.

²⁰ Watch for the opportune time, and
　　beware of evil,
　and do not be ashamed to be yourself.

²¹ For there is a shame that leads to sin,
　and there is a shame that is glory and
　　favor.
²² Do not show partiality, to your own harm,
　or deference, to your downfall.
²³ Do not refrain from speaking at the
　　proper moment,ᵈ
　and do not hide your wisdom.ᵉ
²⁴ For wisdom becomes known through
　　speech,
　and education through the words of the
　　tongue.
²⁵ Never speak against the truth,
　but be ashamed of your ignorance.
²⁶ Do not be ashamed to confess your sins,
　and do not try to stop the current of a
　　river.
²⁷ Do not subject yourself to a fool,
　or show partiality to a ruler.
²⁸ Fight to the death for truth,
　and the Lord God will fight for you.

²⁹ Do not be reckless in your speech,
　or sluggish and remiss in your deeds.
³⁰ Do not be like a lion in your home,
　or suspicious of your servants.
³¹ Do not let your hand be stretched out to
　　receive
　and closed when it is time to give.

5 Do not rely on your wealth,
　or say, "I have enough."
² Do not follow your inclination and strength
　in pursuing the desires of your heart.

ᵃ Heb Syr: Gk *exalts*
ᵇ Or *he*
ᶜ Or *until they remain faithful in their heart*
ᵈ Heb: Gk *at a time of salvation*
ᵉ So some Gk Mss and Heb Syr Lat: Other Gk Mss
　lack *and do not hide your wisdom*

Deut 15.9. **10:** *Orphans*, cf. Ex 22.21–23; for God as father of orphans, see Ps 68.5.
　4.11–19. Wisdom's benefits. While the search for wisdom brings many benefits, it also involves testing and discipline. As often, wisdom is personified as a woman (cf. Prov 1.20–33; 8; Sir 24). **12:** Prov 8.35. **14:** Serving wisdom is the same as serving *the Holy One*. **15:** The expressions *judge the nations* and *live secure* probably refer to earthly existence rather than life after death. **17–19:** Wisdom as harsh disciplinarian but also giver of joy and security are key themes in Prov 1–9. **17:** *Discipline*, cf. 2.1. **18:** *Secrets*, 39.7; Dan 2.22.
　4.20–31: The need for self-restraint and truthfulness. 20–21: For proper and improper *shame*, see 41.17–42.8. **20–31:** The admonitions (*Do not . . .*) deal mainly with speech, especially truthfulness in speech, a frequent topic in wisdom literature (e.g., Prov 13.3; 25.11). **26:** *Stop the current of a river*, that is, trying to conceal one's sins from God is impossible. **30:** *Lion*, a frequent symbol of overpowering force (13.19; 21.2; 25.16; 27.10,28; 28.23; 47.3).

³ Do not say, "Who can have power over me?"
for the Lord will surely punish you.

⁴ Do not say, "I sinned, yet what has happened to me?"
for the Lord is slow to anger.
⁵ Do not be so confident of forgiveness[a]
that you add sin to sin.
⁶ Do not say, "His mercy is great,
he will forgive[b] the multitude of my sins,"
for both mercy and wrath are with him,
and his anger will rest on sinners.
⁷ Do not delay to turn back to the Lord,
and do not postpone it from day to day;
for suddenly the wrath of the Lord will come upon you,
and at the time of punishment you will perish.
⁸ Do not depend on dishonest wealth,
for it will not benefit you on the day of calamity.

⁹ Do not winnow in every wind,
or follow every path.[c]
¹⁰ Stand firm for what you know,
and let your speech be consistent.
¹¹ Be quick to hear,
but deliberate in answering.
¹² If you know what to say, answer your neighbor;
but if not, put your hand over your mouth.
¹³ Honor and dishonor come from speaking,
and the tongue of mortals may be their downfall.

¹⁴ Do not be called double-tongued[d]
and do not lay traps with your tongue;
for shame comes to the thief,
and severe condemnation to the double-tongued.
¹⁵ In great and small matters cause no harm,[e]

6

¹ and do not become an enemy instead of a friend;
for a bad name incurs shame and reproach;
so it is with the double-tongued sinner.

² Do not fall into the grip of passion,[f]
or you may be torn apart as by a bull.[g]
³ Your leaves will be devoured and your fruit destroyed,
and you will be left like a withered tree.
⁴ Evil passion destroys those who have it,
and makes them the laughingstock of their enemies.

⁵ Pleasant speech multiplies friends,
and a gracious tongue multiplies courtesies.

a   Heb: Gk *atonement*
b   Heb: Gk *he* (or *it*) *will atone for*
c   Gk adds *so it is with the double-tongued sinner* (see 6.1)
d   Heb: Gk *a slanderer*
e   Heb Syr: Gk *be ignorant*
f   Heb: Meaning of Gk uncertain
g   Meaning of Gk uncertain

5.1–8. Avoid presumption. Do not rely on wealth or presume on God's mercy as excuses for putting off repentance. **4:** *Slow to anger,* Ex 34.6. This ancient liturgical formula is frequently cited and adapted; cf. Num 14.18; Neh 9.17; Pss 86.15; 103.8; 145.8; Jon 4.2; etc. **6:** *Mercy and wrath,* although God is merciful, God's just demands cannot be ignored (16.11–12). **7:** *Wrath of the Lord,* Ex 32.10; Num 16.46; Deut 29.23; etc. The notion of sudden punishment, especially of the powerful, is a common motif in wisdom literature (10.10–11; Job 34.20–25; cf. Dan 5).

5.9–6.4: The need for truthfulness and self-restraint. Here speech is treated mainly in an honor-shame context (see 4.20–31).

10: For other treatments of *speech,* see 19.6–17; 20.16–20; 22.27–23.15; 28.12–26. **12:** *Hand over your mouth,* a gesture of humility and circumspection (Job 29.9; 40.4–5; Prov 30.32). **14:** *Double-tongued,* one who is duplicitous in speech or a slanderer (cf. 5.9 in Greek; 6.1). **6.2–4:** *Passion,* most likely sexual desire (18.30–19.3), though anger or envy is also possible. **6.3:** Cf. Ps 1.3.

⁶ Let those who are friendly with you be many,
  but let your advisers be one in a thousand.
⁷ When you gain friends, gain them through testing,
  and do not trust them hastily.
⁸ For there are friends who are such when it suits them,
  but they will not stand by you in time of trouble.
⁹ And there are friends who change into enemies,
  and tell of the quarrel to your disgrace.
¹⁰ And there are friends who sit at your table,
  but they will not stand by you in time of trouble.
¹¹ When you are prosperous, they become your second self,
  and lord it over your servants;
¹² but if you are brought low, they turn against you,
  and hide themselves from you.
¹³ Keep away from your enemies,
  and be on guard with your friends.

¹⁴ Faithful friends are a sturdy shelter:
  whoever finds one has found a treasure.
¹⁵ Faithful friends are beyond price;
  no amount can balance their worth.
¹⁶ Faithful friends are life-saving medicine;
  and those who fear the Lord will find them.
¹⁷ Those who fear the Lord direct their friendship aright,
  for as they are, so are their neighbors also.

¹⁸ My child, from your youth choose discipline,
  and when you have gray hair you will still find wisdom.
¹⁹ Come to her like one who plows and sows,
  and wait for her good harvest.
For when you cultivate her you will toil but little,
  and soon you will eat of her produce.
²⁰ She seems very harsh to the undisciplined;
  fools cannot remain with her.
²¹ She will be like a heavy stone to test them,
  and they will not delay in casting her aside.
²² For wisdom is like her name;
  she is not readily perceived by many.

²³ Listen, my child, and accept my judgment;
  do not reject my counsel.
²⁴ Put your feet into her fetters,
  and your neck into her collar.
²⁵ Bend your shoulders and carry her,
  and do not fret under her bonds.
²⁶ Come to her with all your soul,
  and keep her ways with all your might.
²⁷ Search out and seek, and she will become known to you;
  and when you get hold of her, do not let her go.
²⁸ For at last you will find the rest she gives,
  and she will be changed into joy for you.
²⁹ Then her fetters will become for you a strong defense,
  and her collar a glorious robe.

6.5–17: Friendship. While caution is necessary in making friends, a faithful friend is a treasure (cf. 9.10–16; 19.13–17; 22.19–26; 27.16–21; 37.1–6). Although the topic of friendship occasionally appears in earlier Israelite wisdom literature (Prov 17.17; 18.24; 27.6,10), it was a particularly prominent theme in Hellenistic writings. **6–7:** The difference between *those who are friendly* and true friends becomes clear only over time (*testing*). **8–13:** False *friends* can easily turn into enemies. **14–17:** *Faithful friends* are best sought and found among *those who fear the Lord*.

6.18–37: Discipline and the way to wisdom. Those who seek to become wise must accept the religious, intellectual, and moral formation (*discipline*) that produces wisdom and its rewards. **18–22:** Those who accept wisdom's *discipline* are like farmers who work hard and so enjoy abundant harvests, whereas discipline is *like a heavy stone* to those who refuse it. **18:** *My child,* each of the three segments begins with this address (vv.18,23,32); see 2.1n. **22:** *Wisdom is like her name,* probably a play on the Hebrew words "musar" (*discipline,* v. 18) and "sar" ("turn aside," i.e., become distant). **23–31:** The process of accepting wisdom's discipline is illustrated by images of the *yoke* and *rest* (51.26) and *glorious* royal apparel. **26:** *All your soul, and . . . all your might,* Deut

³⁰ Her yoke[a] is a golden ornament,
    and her bonds a purple cord.
³¹ You will wear her like a glorious robe,
    and put her on like a splendid crown.[b]

³² If you are willing, my child, you can be
    disciplined,
    and if you apply yourself you will
    become clever.
³³ If you love to listen you will gain
    knowledge,
    and if you pay attention you will
    become wise.
³⁴ Stand in the company of the elders.
    Who is wise? Attach yourself to such a
    one.
³⁵ Be ready to listen to every godly
    discourse,
    and let no wise proverbs escape you.
³⁶ If you see an intelligent person, rise
    early to visit him;
    let your foot wear out his doorstep.
³⁷ Reflect on the statutes of the Lord,
    and meditate at all times on his
    commandments.
It is he who will give insight to[c] your
    mind,
    and your desire for wisdom will be
    granted.

7 Do no evil, and evil will never overtake
    you.
² Stay away from wrong, and it will turn
    away from you.
³ Do[d] not sow in the furrows of injustice,
    and you will not reap a sevenfold
    crop.

⁴ Do not seek from the Lord high office,
    or the seat of honor from the king.
⁵ Do not assert your righteousness before
    the Lord,
    or display your wisdom before the king.

⁶ Do not seek to become a judge,
    or you may be unable to root out
    injustice;
you may be partial to the powerful,
    and so mar your integrity.
⁷ Commit no offense against the public,
    and do not disgrace yourself among the
    people.
⁸ Do not commit a sin twice;
    not even for one will you go
    unpunished.
⁹ Do not say, "He will consider the great
    number of my gifts,
    and when I make an offering to the
    Most High God, he will accept it."
¹⁰ Do not grow weary when you pray;
    do not neglect to give alms.
¹¹ Do not ridicule a person who is
    embittered in spirit,
    for there is One who humbles and
    exalts.
¹² Do not devise[e] a lie against your
    brother,
    or do the same to a friend.
¹³ Refuse to utter any lie,
    for it is a habit that results in no
    good.
¹⁴ Do not babble in the assembly of the
    elders,
    and do not repeat yourself when you
    pray.

¹⁵ Do not hate hard labor
    or farm work, which was created by the
    Most High.

a Heb: Gk *Upon her*
b Heb: Gk *crown of gladness*
c Heb: Gk *will confirm*
d Gk *My child, do*
e Heb: Gk *plow*

6.5. **30**: *Purple cord*; see Num 15.38–40. Although wisdom is often likened to an ornament (e.g., Prov 1.9; 3.22; 4.8–9), here the language evokes ritual garments like those of the high priest (50.11). **32–37**: The prospective sage should spend time in listening to the *elders*, attending to *godly discourse* and *wise proverbs*, and reflecting on and carrying out God's *commandments* (in the Torah).

   7.1–17: Evildoing and its consequences. Most of these instructions are presented as negative admonitions (*Do not . . .*; cf. Prov 3.1–4; 22.22–29). **1–3**: Avoiding *evil*, *wrong*, and *injustice* will protect one from their damaging consequences. **4–7**: Ambition for high offices and public prestige can be dangerous (Prov 25.6–7). **8–9**: For an earlier warning about presuming on God's mercy and patience, see 5.6–7. **10–14**: The unit begins and ends with

¹⁶ Do not enroll in the ranks of sinners;
  remember that retribution does not
    delay.
¹⁷ Humble yourself to the utmost,
  for the punishment of the ungodly is
    fire and worms.ᵃ

¹⁸ Do not exchange a friend for money,
  or a real brother for the gold of Ophir.
¹⁹ Do not dismissᵇ a wise and good wife,
  for her charm is worth more than gold.
²⁰ Do not abuse slaves who work
    faithfully,
  or hired laborers who devote
    themselves to their task.
²¹ Let your soul love intelligent slaves;ᶜ
  do not withhold from them their
    freedom.

²² Do you have cattle? Look after them;
  if they are profitable to you, keep them.
²³ Do you have children? Discipline them,
  and make them obedientᵈ from their
    youth.
²⁴ Do you have daughters? Be concerned
    for their chastity,ᵉ
  and do not show yourself too indulgent
    with them.
²⁵ Give a daughter in marriage, and you
    complete a great task;
  but give her to a sensible man.
²⁶ Do you have a wife who pleases you?ᶠ Do
    not divorce her;
  but do not trust yourself to one whom
    you detest.

²⁷ With all your heart honor your father,
  and do not forget the birth pangs of
    your mother.

²⁸ Remember that it was of your parentsᵍ
    you were born;
  how can you repay what they have
    given to you?

²⁹ With all your soul fear the Lord,
  and revere his priests.
³⁰ With all your might love your Maker,
  and do not neglect his ministers.
³¹ Fear the Lord and honor the priest,
  and give him his portion, as you have
    been commanded:
the first fruits, the guilt offering, the gift of
    the shoulders,
  the sacrifice of sanctification, and the
    first fruits of the holy things.

³² Stretch out your hand to the poor,
  so that your blessing may be complete.
³³ Give graciously to all the living;
  do not withhold kindness even from
    the dead.
³⁴ Do not avoid those who weep,
  but mourn with those who mourn.
³⁵ Do not hesitate to visit the sick,
  because for such deeds you will be
    loved.
³⁶ In all you do, remember the end of your
    life,
  and then you will never sin.

ᵃ Heb *for the expectation of mortals is worms*
ᵇ Heb: Gk *deprive yourself of*
ᶜ Heb *Love a wise slave as yourself*
ᵈ Gk *bend their necks*
ᵉ Gk *body*
ᶠ Heb Syr lack *who pleases you*
ᵍ Gk *them*

---

comments on prayer; the intervening material concerns faults connected with speech. **17**: *Fire and worms*, cf. Isa 66.24. The Hebrew has *worms* only.

7.18–36: Social relations. Directed to the male head of a household, these instructions pertain to his relationships with his *friend* or *brother*, *wife*, *slaves*, and *hired laborers*, *cattle*, *children*, *daughters*, *wife* again, *father* and *mother*, *priests*, the *poor*, the *dead*, and the *sick*. **18**: *Ophir* in southern Arabia or east Africa was famous for its *gold* (1 Kings 9.28; 10.11; Job 22.24; 28.16; Ps 45.9; Isa 13.12). **19**: *Dismiss a . . . wife*, Deut 24.1–4. **21**: *Freedom*, Ex 21.2; Lev 25.39–43; Deut 15.12–15. **24–25**: *Daughters*, cf. 22.3–6n.; 42.9–13. **27–28**: *Father . . . mother*, 3.1–16; cf. Ex 20.12; Deut 5.16.

31: *His portion*, Ex 29.27; Lev 7.31–34; Num 18.8–20; Deut 18.3. Earlier Israelite wisdom literature does not mention priests and seldom refers to ritual obligations; Prov 3.9 is a rare exception. **32**: *Poor*, Deut 14.28–29. **33**: *Dead*, cf. 38.16–18; Tob 1.17. **36**: *The end of your life* probably refers to one's good name at death (1.13; 28.6) rather than rewards in life after death.

8 Do not contend with the powerful,
    or you may fall into their hands.
² Do not quarrel with the rich,
    in case their resources outweigh yours;
for gold has ruined many,
    and has perverted the minds of kings.
³ Do not argue with the loud of mouth,
    and do not heap wood on their fire.

⁴ Do not make fun of one who is ill-bred,
    or your ancestors may be insulted.
⁵ Do not reproach one who is turning away
    from sin;
    remember that we all deserve
      punishment.
⁶ Do not disdain one who is old,
    for some of us are also growing old.
⁷ Do not rejoice over anyone's death;
    remember that we must all die.

⁸ Do not slight the discourse of the sages,
    but busy yourself with their maxims;
because from them you will learn
    discipline
    and how to serve princes.
⁹ Do not ignore the discourse of the
    aged,
    for they themselves learned from their
      parents;ᵃ
from them you learn how to understand
    and to give an answer when the need
      arises.

¹⁰ Do not kindle the coals of sinners,
    or you may be burned in their flaming
      fire.
¹¹ Do not let the insolent bring you to your
    feet,
    or they may lie in ambush against your
      words.

¹² Do not lend to one who is stronger than
    you;
    but if you do lend anything, count it as
      a loss.
¹³ Do not give surety beyond your means;
    but if you give surety, be prepared to
      pay.

¹⁴ Do not go to law against a judge,
    for the decision will favor him because
      of his standing.
¹⁵ Do not go traveling with the reckless,
    or they will be burdensome to you;
for they will act as they please,
    and through their folly you will perish
      with them.
¹⁶ Do not pick a fight with the quick-
      tempered,
    and do not journey with them through
      lonely country,
because bloodshed means nothing to
    them,
    and where no help is at hand, they will
      strike you down.
¹⁷ Do not consult with fools,
    for they cannot keep a secret.
¹⁸ In the presence of strangers do nothing
    that is to be kept secret,
    for you do not know what they will
      divulge.ᵇ
¹⁹ Do not reveal your thoughts to
    anyone,
    or you may drive away your
      happiness.ᶜ

ᵃ Or *ancestors*
ᵇ Or *it will bring forth*
ᶜ Heb: Gk *and let him not return a favor to you*

8.1–19: Caution in social relations. These negative admonitions (*Do not . . .*) are accompanied by reasons why certain persons and social situations should be avoided. The goal is to help one avoid public disgrace and shame. **1–2:** The *powerful* and *rich* as social categories are more prominent in Sirach than in earlier wisdom literature and may reflect the changing socio-economic realities of the Hellenistic world. **3:** The dangers of arguing with those who cannot control their speech is already a topic in ancient Egyptian wisdom literature (see, e.g., *Ptahhotep*). **5–7:** These motive clauses are more philosophical than the mainly pragmatic reasons given elsewhere in this instruction. **8–9:** *The discourse of the sages* and *of the aged* contain the wise learning of tradition, highly valued by the wisdom tradition (cf. Prov 4.1–4; Job 8.8–10). **10:** *Flaming fire,* 8.3; 28.8–12. **12–13:** Although Ben Sira was not opposed in principle to making loans and standing *surety* (29.1–7; cf. Prov 6.1–5; 11.15), he urges great caution. **17–19:** Avoiding self–revelation to *fools* and *strangers* is a prudent way to protect one's social standing. **18:** The Hebrew makes a play on words between "zar" (*stranger*) and "raz" (*secret*).

9 Do not be jealous of the wife of your bosom,
  or you will teach her an evil lesson to
    your own hurt.
[2] Do not give yourself to a woman
  and let her trample down your strength.
[3] Do not go near a loose woman,
  or you will fall into her snares.
[4] Do not dally with a singing girl,
  or you will be caught by her tricks.
[5] Do not look intently at a virgin,
  or you may stumble and incur penalties
    for her.
[6] Do not give yourself to prostitutes,
  or you may lose your inheritance.
[7] Do not look around in the streets of a city,
  or wander about in its deserted sections.
[8] Turn away your eyes from a shapely
    woman,
  and do not gaze at beauty belonging to
    another;
many have been seduced by a woman's
    beauty,
  and by it passion is kindled like a fire.
[9] Never dine with another man's wife,
  or revel with her at wine;
or your heart may turn aside to her,
  and in blood[a] you may be plunged into
    destruction.

[10] Do not abandon old friends,
  for new ones cannot equal them.
A new friend is like new wine;
  when it has aged, you can drink it with
    pleasure.

[11] Do not envy the success of sinners,
  for you do not know what their end will
    be like.

[12] Do not delight in what pleases the
    ungodly;
  remember that they will not be held
    guiltless all their lives.

[13] Keep far from those who have power to
    kill,
  and you will not be haunted by the fear
    of death.
But if you approach them, make no
    misstep,
  or they may rob you of your life.
Know that you are stepping among snares,
  and that you are walking on the city
    battlements.

[14] As much as you can, aim to know your
    neighbors,
  and consult with the wise.
[15] Let your conversation be with intelligent
    people,
  and let all your discussion be about the
    law of the Most High.
[16] Let the righteous be your dinner
    companions,
  and let your glory be in the fear of the
    Lord.

[17] A work is praised for the skill of the
    artisan;
  so a people's leader is proved wise by
    his words.
[18] The loud of mouth are feared in their
    city,
  and the one who is reckless in speech
    is hated.

---

a Heb: Gk *by your spirit*

9.1–9: Caution in relations with women. These admonitions concern the various types of women who can bring public disgrace and shame upon a sage. They continue the cautious tone of the preceding passage. **3–4:** *Loose,* literally "strange" woman (Heb. "zarah"); see Prov 2.16; 5.3,20; 7.5. The *singing girl* is apparently a prostitute (cf. Isa 23.15–16). **5:** The penalty for seducing a *virgin* involved financial payments to her father and marriage (Ex 22.16–17). **7:** *In the streets of a city,* cf. Prov 7.7–10. **9:** The penalty for adultery with *another man's wife* was death (Lev 20.10; Deut 22.22).

9.10–16: Caution in choosing and making friends. The best friends share the same spiritual values—*the law of the Most High* and *fear of the Lord.* See 6.5–17; 19.13–17; 22.19–26; 27.16–21; 37.1–6. **10:** As with *wine, old friends* are better than *new* ones.

11–13: *Sinners* and the *ungodly* pose a threat because they may entangle one in their own bad *end* (cf. Prov 1.10–19), but kings and rulers are dangerous because they themselves *have power to kill* (cf. Prov 16.14). **13:** *Battlements,* high on the city walls where one is exposed and easy to kill.

9.17–10.5: Wise rulers. The wise ruler is the good ruler (see Prov 25.4–5; 28.2–3,16; 29.4,12,14). **17–18:** Wise

10 A wise magistrate educates his people,
  and the rule of an intelligent person is
    well ordered.
² As the people's judge is, so are his
    officials;
  as the ruler of the city is, so are all its
    inhabitants.
³ An undisciplined king ruins his people,
  but a city becomes fit to live in through
    the understanding of its rulers.
⁴ The government of the earth is in the
    hand of the Lord,
  and over it he will raise up the right
    leader for the time.
⁵ Human success is in the hand of the Lord,
  and it is he who confers honor upon the
    lawgiver.ᵃ

⁶ Do not get angry with your neighbor for
    every injury,
  and do not resort to acts of insolence.
⁷ Arrogance is hateful to the Lord and to
    mortals,
  and injustice is outrageous to both.
⁸ Sovereignty passes from nation to nation
  on account of injustice and insolence
    and wealth.ᵇ
⁹ How can dust and ashes be proud?
  Even in life the human body decays.ᶜ
¹⁰ A long illness baffles the physician;ᵈ
  the king of today will die tomorrow.
¹¹ For when one is dead
  he inherits maggots and verminᵉ and
    worms.
¹² The beginning of human pride is to
    forsake the Lord;
  the heart has withdrawn from its
    Maker.
¹³ For the beginning of pride is sin,
  and the one who clings to it pours out
    abominations.

Therefore the Lord brings upon them
    unheard-of calamities,
  and destroys them completely.
¹⁴ The Lord overthrows the thrones of
    rulers,
  and enthrones the lowly in their place.
¹⁵ The Lord plucks up the roots of the
    nations,ᶠ
  and plants the humble in their place.
¹⁶ The Lord lays waste the lands of the
    nations,
  and destroys them to the foundations of
    the earth.
¹⁷ He removes some of them and destroys
    them,
  and erases the memory of them from
    the earth.
¹⁸ Pride was not created for human beings,
  or violent anger for those born of
    women.

¹⁹ Whose offspring are worthy of honor?
  Human offspring.
Whose offspring are worthy of honor?
  Those who fear the Lord.
Whose offspring are unworthy of honor?
  Human offspring.
Whose offspring are unworthy of honor?
  Those who break the commandments.
²⁰ Among family members their leader is
  worthy of honor,

a Heb: Gk *scribe*
b Other ancient authorities add here or after verse
   9a, *Nothing is more wicked than one who loves
   money, for such a person puts his own soul up for
   sale.*
c Heb: Meaning of Gk uncertain
d Heb Lat: Meaning of Gk uncertain
e Heb: Gk *wild animals*
f Other ancient authorities read *proud nations*

words are the tools of the good ruler. **10.1–3:** Rulers can have positive or negative effects on their city's *inhabitants* (Prov 28.3,16; 29.4,12). **4–5:** *The hand of the Lord,* Prov 8.15–16; Wis 6.1–3.

   10.6–18: Avoid arrogance and pride. Such behavior is hateful to not only to God but also to other people and has disastrous effects. Although arrogance is a traditional topic in wisdom literature, Sirach applies it specifically to rulers and nations, perhaps as a critique of the Ptolemaic and Seleucid kings of his day. **9–11:** Death is the great equalizer among humans (22.11–22; 38.16–23; 41.1–13), and the best remedy for pride. **9:** *Dust and ashes,* Gen 18.27; Job 30.19; 42.6. **12:** *To forsake the Lord* is the root of foolish *pride,* and pride is not what God intended for humankind (10.18). **14–17:** *Overthrows the thrones of rulers,* cf. 1 Sam 2.1–10; Lk 1.47–55.

   10.19–11.6: Honor and shame. True honor belongs not to the wealthy and powerful but rather to those who *fear the Lord* and keep God's *commandments* (cf. 4.20–6.4; 41.14–42.8; Prov 1.7; 9.10). **19:** *Human offspring,* giving

but those who fear the Lord are worthy
of honor in his eyes.ᵃ

22 The rich, and the eminent, and the
poor—
their glory is the fear of the Lord.

23 It is not right to despise one who is
intelligent but poor,
and it is not proper to honor one who
is sinful.

24 The prince and the judge and the ruler
are honored,
but none of them is greater than the
one who fears the Lord.

25 Free citizens will serve a wise servant,
and an intelligent person will not
complain.

26 Do not make a display of your wisdom
when you do your work,
and do not boast when you are in need.

27 Better is the worker who has goods in
plenty
than the boaster who lacks bread.

28 My child, honor yourself with humility,
and give yourself the esteem you
deserve.

29 Who will acquit those who condemnᵇ
themselves?
And who will honor those who
dishonor themselves?ᶜ

30 The poor are honored for their
knowledge,
while the rich are honored for their
wealth.

31 One who is honored in poverty, how
much more in wealth!
And one dishonored in wealth, how
much more in poverty!

11

The wisdom of the humble lifts their
heads high,
and seats them among the great.

2 Do not praise individuals for their good
looks,

or loathe anyone because of appearance
alone.

3 The bee is small among flying creatures,
but what it produces is the best of sweet
things.

4 Do not boast about wearing fine clothes,
and do not exalt yourself when you are
honored;
for the works of the Lord are wonderful,
and his works are concealed from
humankind.

5 Many kings have had to sit on the ground,
but one who was never thought of has
worn a crown.

6 Many rulers have been utterly disgraced,
and the honored have been handed
over to others.

7 Do not find fault before you investigate;
examine first, and then criticize.

8 Do not answer before you listen,
and do not interrupt when another is
speaking.

9 Do not argue about a matter that does not
concern you,
and do not sit with sinners when they
judge a case.

10 My child, do not busy yourself with
many matters;
if you multiply activities, you will not
be held blameless.
If you pursue, you will not overtake,
and by fleeing you will not escape.

11 There are those who work and struggle
and hurry,
but are so much the more in want.

12 There are others who are slow and need
help,

ᵃ Other ancient authorities add as verse 21, *The fear
of the Lord is the beginning of acceptance; obduracy
and pride are the beginning of rejection.*
ᵇ Heb: Gk *sin against*
ᶜ Heb Lat: Gk *their own life*

the same answer to opposite questions is a form of riddle, designed to provoke reflection. **26–27:** Boasting by
those in need brings only shame. **28:** *Humility* is appropriate to the wise (cf. 11.1). **11.3:** *The bee,* for other comparisons between animal and human behaviors, see Prov 6.6–8; 30.15–19,24–31.

11.7–9: Avoid hasty judgments. See 5.11–12.

11.10–28: True wealth. Since God is the real source of wealth, it is foolish to rely on earthly riches for security (cf. Prov 13.11; 20.21; 23.4–5; Eccl 5.10–12). **10–13:** Divine favor (*the eyes of the Lord*), and not human activity

who lack strength and abound in poverty;
but the eyes of the Lord look kindly upon
them;
he lifts them out of their lowly condition
[13] and raises up their heads
to the amazement of the many.

[14] Good things and bad, life and death,
poverty and wealth, come from the Lord.[a]
[17] The Lord's gift remains with the devout,
and his favor brings lasting success.
[18] One becomes rich through diligence and
self-denial,
and the reward allotted to him is this:
[19] when he says, "I have found rest,
and now I shall feast on my goods!"
he does not know how long it will be
until he leaves them to others and dies.

[20] Stand by your agreement and attend to it,
and grow old in your work.
[21] Do not wonder at the works of a sinner,
but trust in the Lord and keep at your
job;
for it is easy in the sight of the Lord
to make the poor rich suddenly, in an
instant.
[22] The blessing of the Lord is[b] the reward of
the pious,
and quickly God causes his blessing to
flourish.
[23] Do not say, "What do I need,
and what further benefit can be mine?"
[24] Do not say, "I have enough,
and what harm can come to me now?"
[25] In the day of prosperity, adversity is
forgotten,
and in the day of adversity, prosperity is
not remembered.
[26] For it is easy for the Lord on the day of
death
to reward individuals according to their
conduct.

[27] An hour's misery makes one forget past
delights,
and at the close of one's life one's deeds
are revealed.
[28] Call no one happy before his death;
by how he ends, a person becomes
known.[c]

[29] Do not invite everyone into your home,
for many are the tricks of the crafty.
[30] Like a decoy partridge in a cage, so is the
mind of the proud,
and like spies they observe your
weakness;[d]
[31] for they lie in wait, turning good into
evil,
and to worthy actions they attach blame.
[32] From a spark many coals are kindled,
and a sinner lies in wait to shed blood.
[33] Beware of scoundrels, for they devise evil,
and they may ruin your reputation
forever.
[34] Receive strangers into your home and
they will stir up trouble for you,
and will make you a stranger to your
own family.

12 If you do good, know to whom you do it,
and you will be thanked for your good
deeds.
[2] Do good to the devout, and you will be
repaid—

a   Other ancient authorities add as verses 15 and 16,
    [15]*Wisdom, understanding, and knowledge of the
    law come from the Lord; affection and the ways of
    good works come from him.* [16]*Error and darkness
    were created with sinners; evil grows old with those
    who take pride in malice.*
b   Heb: Gk *is in*
c   Heb: Gk *and through his children a person becomes
    known*
d   Heb: Gk *downfall*

alone, often brings success to some unlikely persons. **19:** A rich fool can be quickly deprived of material security
by death (cf. 11.26–28; Eccl 2.21; 4.8; 5.12–14). **26–28:** The *reward* most likely refers to the sage's good name
rather than to the last judgment and eternal rewards (22.11–22; 38.16–23; 41.1–13).

11.29–12.18: Caution in social relations. Even for those who approach them innocently and with good will,
social relations can be full of danger. **29–34:** *Scoundrels* and *strangers* can ruin one's reputation and turn a whole
household against its master. The Hebrew text makes a pun between "zar" (*stranger*) and "zahir" (*make you a
stranger*). **12.1–7:** Reserve almsgiving for the *devout, humble,* and *good* (cf. 18.15–18; 29.8–13). **8–18:** A warning
against potential enemies.

if not by them, certainly by the Most
High.
[3] No good comes to one who persists in evil
or to one who does not give alms.
[4] Give to the devout, but do not help the
sinner.
[5] Do good to the humble, but do not give
to the ungodly;
hold back their bread, and do not give it to
them,
for by means of it they might subdue you;
then you will receive twice as much evil
for all the good you have done to them.
[6] For the Most High also hates sinners
and will inflict punishment on the
ungodly.[a]
[7] Give to the one who is good, but do not
help the sinner.
[8] A friend is not known[b] in prosperity,
nor is an enemy hidden in adversity.
[9] One's enemies are friendly[c] when one
prospers,
but in adversity even one's friend
disappears.
[10] Never trust your enemy,
for like corrosion in copper, so is his
wickedness.
[11] Even if he humbles himself and walks
bowed down,
take care to be on your guard against
him.
Be to him like one who polishes a mirror,
to be sure it does not become
completely tarnished.
[12] Do not put him next to you,
or he may overthrow you and take your
place.
Do not let him sit at your right hand,
or else he may try to take your own seat,
and at last you will realize the truth of my
words,
and be stung by what I have said.

[13] Who pities a snake charmer when he is
bitten,
or all those who go near wild animals?
[14] So no one pities a person who associates
with a sinner

and becomes involved in the other's sins.
[15] He stands by you for a while,
but if you falter, he will not be there.
[16] An enemy speaks sweetly with his lips,
but in his heart he plans to throw you
into a pit;
an enemy may have tears in his eyes,
but if he finds an opportunity he will
never have enough of your blood.
[17] If evil comes upon you, you will find him
there ahead of you;
pretending to help, he will trip you up.
[18] Then he will shake his head, and clap his
hands,
and whisper much, and show his true
face.

13

Whoever touches pitch gets dirty,
and whoever associates with a proud
person becomes like him.
[2] Do not lift a weight too heavy for you,
or associate with one mightier and
richer than you.
How can the clay pot associate with the
iron kettle?
The pot will strike against it and be
smashed.
[3] A rich person does wrong, and even adds
insults;
a poor person suffers wrong, and must
add apologies.
[4] A rich person[d] will exploit you if you can
be of use to him,
but if you are in need he will abandon
you.
[5] If you own something, he will live with
you;
he will drain your resources without a
qualm.
[6] When he needs you he will deceive you,
and will smile at you and encourage
you;

a Other ancient authorities add *and he is keeping
them for the day of their punishment*
b Other ancient authorities read *punished*
c Heb: Gk *grieved*
d Gk *He*

13.1–23: **Rich and poor.** Associating with rich persons poses dangers to those dedicated to wisdom and
fear of the Lord. 1–7: The rich abuse and exploit the poor; they defile (like *pitch*) and destroy (like an *iron kettle*
striking a *clay pot*) poor persons. Although a prominent citizen, Sirach speaks from the perspective of the poor

he will speak to you kindly and say,
"What do you need?"
⁷ He will embarrass you with his delicacies,
until he has drained you two or three
times,
and finally he will laugh at you.
Should he see you afterwards, he will pass
you by
and shake his head at you.

⁸ Take care not to be led astray
and humiliated when you are enjoying
yourself.ᵃ
⁹ When an influential person invites you,
be reserved,
and he will invite you more insistently.
¹⁰ Do not be forward, or you may be rebuffed;
do not stand aloof, or you will be
forgotten.
¹¹ Do not try to treat him as an equal,
or trust his lengthy conversations;
for he will test you by prolonged talk,
and while he smiles he will be
examining you.
¹² Cruel are those who do not keep your
secrets;
they will not spare you harm or
imprisonment.
¹³ Be on your guard and very careful,
for you are walking about with your
own downfall.ᵇ

¹⁵ Every creature loves its like,
and every person the neighbor.
¹⁶ All living beings associate with their own
kind,
and people stick close to those like
themselves.
¹⁷ What does a wolf have in common with
a lamb?
No more has a sinner with the devout.
¹⁸ What peace is there between a hyena and
a dog?

And what peace between the rich and
the poor?
¹⁹ Wild asses in the wilderness are the prey
of lions;
likewise the poor are feeding grounds
for the rich.
²⁰ Humility is an abomination to the proud;
likewise the poor are an abomination to
the rich.
²¹ When the rich person totters, he is
supported by friends,
but when the humbleᶜ falls, he is
pushed away even by friends.
²² If the rich person slips, many come to
the rescue;
he speaks unseemly words, but they
justify him.
If the humble person slips, they even
criticize him;
he talks sense, but is not given a hearing.
²³ The rich person speaks and all are silent;
they extol to the clouds what he says.
The poor person speaks and they say,
"Who is this fellow?"
And should he stumble, they even push
him down.
²⁴ Riches are good if they are free from sin;
poverty is evil only in the opinion of the
ungodly.

²⁵ The heart changes the countenance,
either for good or for evil.ᵈ
²⁶ The sign of a happy heart is a cheerful face,

ᵃ Other ancient authorities read *in your folly*
ᵇ Other ancient authorities add as verse 14, *When
you hear these things in your sleep, wake up!
During all your life love the Lord, and call on him
for your salvation.*
ᶜ Other ancient authorities read *poor*
ᵈ Other ancient authorities add *and a glad heart
makes a cheerful countenance*

---

rather than from the perspective of the rich. **8–13:** In dealing with the rich and powerful, one must always be
on guard, since they can easily bring about one's *downfall*; see also 31.12–18. Similar cautious advice is found in
Egyptian wisdom literature (*Amenemope*, ch. 23), in Prov 23.1–3, and in later Jewish wisdom literature (*m. Abot*
2.3). **15–20:** The incompatibility between rich and poor is illustrated by comparisons taken from the animal
kingdom, which serve to naturalize the social antagonism. **17:** Cf. Isa 11.6. **21–23:** The *rich* customarily receive
better treatment than the *poor*.

13.24–14.2: Wealth and happiness. Happiness of *heart* (in biblical understanding where thinking and feeling
take place) is reflected in a *cheerful face* and in a clear conscience.

but to devise proverbs requires painful
    thinking.

14 Happy are those who do not blunder
    with their lips,
    and need not suffer remorse for sin.
2 Happy are those whose hearts do not
    condemn them,
    and who have not given up their hope.

3 Riches are inappropriate for a small-
    minded person;
    and of what use is wealth to a miser?
4 What he denies himself he collects for
    others;
    and others will live in luxury on his
    goods.
5 If one is mean to himself, to whom will
    he be generous?
    He will not enjoy his own riches.
6 No one is worse than one who is grudging
    to himself;
    this is the punishment for his
    meanness.
7 If ever he does good, it is by mistake;
    and in the end he reveals his meanness.
8 The miser is an evil person;
    he turns away and disregards people.
9 The eye of the greedy person is not
    satisfied with his share;
    greedy injustice withers the soul.
10 A miser begrudges bread,
    and it is lacking at his table.

11 My child, treat yourself well, according to
    your means,
    and present worthy offerings to the
    Lord.
12 Remember that death does not tarry,
    and the decree[a] of Hades has not been
    shown to you.
13 Do good to friends before you die,
    and reach out and give to them as much
    as you can.

14 Do not deprive yourself of a day's
    enjoyment;
    do not let your share of desired good
    pass by you.
15 Will you not leave the fruit of your labors
    to another,
    and what you acquired by toil to be
    divided by lot?
16 Give, and take, and indulge yourself,
    because in Hades one cannot look for
    luxury.
17 All living beings become old like a
    garment,
    for the decree[b] from of old is, "You must
    die!"
18 Like abundant leaves on a spreading
    tree
    that sheds some and puts forth others,
so are the generations of flesh and
    blood:
    one dies and another is born.
19 Every work decays and ceases to exist,
    and the one who made it will pass away
    with it.

20 Happy is the person who meditates on[c]
    wisdom
    and reasons intelligently,
21 who[d] reflects in his heart on her ways
    and ponders her secrets,
22 pursuing her like a hunter,
    and lying in wait on her paths;
23 who peers through her windows
    and listens at her doors;
24 who camps near her house
    and fastens his tent peg to her
    walls;

a Heb Syr: Gk *covenant*
b Heb: Gk *covenant*
c Other ancient authorities read *dies in*
d The structure adopted in verses 21–27 follows
    the Heb

14.3–10: **The miser.** While devoted to making money, the *miser* never really enjoys life and so leads a miserable existence, doing harm to himself and little good for others (cf. Prov 11.24–26).
    14.11–19: **Money and death.** Now is the time to use money to serve God, help others, and enjoy oneself. **12:**
Hades, the abode of the dead; Sheol in Hebrew. **14:** Cf. Eccl 8.15; 9.7. **17:** *Like a garment,* cf. Ps 102.26; Isa 50.9. *The
decree from of old,* see Gen 2.17; 3.3,19. **18–19:** Cf. Eccl 1.2–4; *Iliad* 6.146–49.
    14.20–27: **The search for wisdom.** One who seeks and finds wisdom may be declared *happy* (cf. Prov 3.13).
20: *Happy is* takes the form of a beatitude or makarism (cf. Ps 1.1; Prov 3.13; 8.34; etc.; Mt 5.3–11; Lk 6.20–23).
22–27: The search for wisdom is compared to going on a hunt, camping out by *her house,* and finding her as a

25 who pitches his tent near her,
and so occupies an excellent lodging
place;
26 who places his children under her
shelter,
and lodges under her boughs;
27 who is sheltered by her from the heat,
and dwells in the midst of her glory.

15 Whoever fears the Lord will do this,
and whoever holds to the law will
obtain wisdom.[a]
2 She will come to meet him like a mother,
and like a young bride she will welcome
him.
3 She will feed him with the bread of
learning,
and give him the water of wisdom to
drink.
4 He will lean on her and not fall,
and he will rely on her and not be put
to shame.
5 She will exalt him above his neighbors,
and will open his mouth in the midst of
the assembly.
6 He will find gladness and a crown of
rejoicing,
and will inherit an everlasting name.
7 The foolish will not obtain her,
and sinners will not see her.
8 She is far from arrogance,
and liars will never think of her.
9 Praise is unseemly on the lips of a sinner,
for it has not been sent from the Lord.

10 For in wisdom must praise be uttered,
and the Lord will make it prosper.

11 Do not say, "It was the Lord's doing that I
fell away";
for he does not do[b] what he hates.
12 Do not say, "It was he who led me astray";
for he has no need of the sinful.
13 The Lord hates all abominations;
such things are not loved by those who
fear him.
14 It was he who created humankind in the
beginning,
and he left them in the power of their
own free choice.
15 If you choose, you can keep the
commandments,
and to act faithfully is a matter of your
own choice.
16 He has placed before you fire and water;
stretch out your hand for whichever
you choose.
17 Before each person are life and death,
and whichever one chooses will be given.
18 For great is the wisdom of the Lord;
he is mighty in power and sees
everything;
19 his eyes are on those who fear him,
and he knows every human action.
20 He has not commanded anyone to be
wicked,

a Gk *her*
b Heb: Gk *you ought not to do*

shady tree. 23: *Peers through her windows,* cf. Song 2.9. 24: *Her house,* cf. the description of Ben Sira's school as the "house of instruction" in 51.23; see also Prov 8.32–35. 26: *Her boughs,* for wisdom as a tree, see 1.20; 24.13–17; Prov 3.18.

15.1–10: **The benefits of wisdom.** Wisdom is eager to be found and wants to lavish gifts on those who seek her out. 1: The three major theological themes of Sirach—*fear of Lord, the law,* and *wisdom*—come together in this verse (cf. 1.1–30; 6.32–37; 24.23). 2–6: Portrayed as a *mother* and as a *bride,* wisdom brings to those who seek her love, sustenance, security, success, and *an everlasting name* (immortality by remembrance). Cf. Prov 7.4; Wis 7.12; 8.2. 3: *Bread* and *water,* cf. 1.16; 24.19–21; Prov 9.1–5; Isa 55.1–2. 7–10: Wisdom has nothing to do with fools and sinners; only the wise can praise God properly.

15.11–20: **Human choice and sin.** Since God has given humans free will, they must take responsibility for their sins. 11–13: For texts that could suggest that God makes people sin, see Ex 11.10 and 2 Sam 24.1. 14–17: No attention is given here to Adam's sin (Gen 3.1–24) or the sins of "the sons of God" (Gen 6.1–4; but see Sir 16.7). Rather, the human person is regarded as free to choose between life and death (Deut 30.15–20) and so must be ready to accept the consequences. 14: *Free choice* (Heb "yetser") is a technical term, sometimes used in a good sense (Isa 26.3; 1 Chr 29.18), but usually to refer to an evil tendency or inclination toward sin (Gen 6.5; 8.21; cf. 2 Esd 4.30–31). In postbiblical times the doctrine arose of a good and an evil "yetser" that every person possesses (cf. 37.3). 18–20: God has no part in sin (cf. 15.11–13).

16 Do not desire a multitude of
worthless[a] children,
and do not rejoice in ungodly offspring.
[2] If they multiply, do not rejoice in them,
unless the fear of the Lord is in them.
[3] Do not trust in their survival,
or rely on their numbers;[b]
for one can be better than a thousand,
and to die childless is better than to
have ungodly children.
[4] For through one intelligent person a city
can be filled with people,
but through a clan of outlaws it
becomes desolate.

[5] Many such things my eye has seen,
and my ear has heard things more
striking than these.
[6] In an assembly of sinners a fire is kindled,
and in a disobedient nation wrath
blazes up.
[7] He did not forgive the ancient giants
who revolted in their might.
[8] He did not spare the neighbors of Lot,
whom he loathed on account of their
arrogance.
[9] He showed no pity on the doomed nation,
on those dispossessed because of their
sins;[c]
[10] or on the six hundred thousand foot
soldiers
who assembled in their stubbornness.[d]
[11] Even if there were only one stiff-necked
person,
it would be a wonder if he remained
unpunished.
For mercy and wrath are with the Lord;[e]
he is mighty to forgive—but he also
pours out wrath.

and he has not given anyone
permission to sin.

[12] Great as is his mercy, so also is his
chastisement;
he judges a person according to his or
her deeds.
[13] The sinner will not escape with plunder,
and the patience of the godly will not be
frustrated.
[14] He makes room for every act of mercy;
everyone receives in accordance with
his or her deeds.[f]

[17] Do not say, "I am hidden from the Lord,
and who from on high has me in
mind?
Among so many people I am unknown,
for what am I in a boundless creation?
[18] Lo, heaven and the highest heaven,
the abyss and the earth, tremble at his
visitation![g]
[19] The very mountains and the foundations
of the earth
quiver and quake when he looks upon
them.

a   Heb: Gk *unprofitable*
b   Other ancient authorities add *For you will groan in
untimely mourning, and will know of their sudden
end.*
c   Other ancient authorities add *All these things
he did to the hard-hearted nations, and by the
multitude of his holy ones he was not appeased.*
d   Other ancient authorities add *Chastising, showing
mercy, striking, healing, the Lord persisted in mercy
and discipline.*
e   Gk *him*
f   Other ancient authorities add *[15]The Lord hardened
Pharaoh so that he did not recognize him, in order
that his works might be known under heaven. [16]His
mercy is manifest to the whole of creation, and he
divided his light and darkness with a plumb line.*
g   Other ancient authorities add *The whole world past
and present is in his will.*

16.1–23: **Responsibility for sin.** God holds both individuals and groups responsible for their sins. 1–4: In
a society in which having many children was regarded as a sign of divine blessing (Prov 17.6; Ps 127.3–5), the
author counters that one good child *can be better than a thousand* bad ones. Cf. 40.15–16; 41.5–9. 5–10: God
has punished groups of sinners such as *the ancient giants* (Gen 6.1–4), *the neighbors of Lot* (Gen 18.16–19.29),
the doomed nation of Canaanites (Lev 18.3,24–25), and *the six hundred thousand foot soldiers* in the desert (Ex
12.37; Num 14.38). 11–14: God judges individuals according to their deeds (Ps 62.12; Ezek 18). 15–23: The speaker
quoted here claims that God is distant and has no concern for individuals and their moral responsibility (cf. Wis
2.1–20). The target may be Qoheleth/Ecclesiastes. The monologue is prefaced by an admonition (*Do not say*)
and is concluded with a judgment (16.23) that whoever says such things is a fool.

²⁰ But no human mind can grasp this,
    and who can comprehend his ways?
²¹ Like a tempest that no one can see,
    so most of his works are concealed.ᵃ
²² Who is to announce his acts of justice?
    Or who can await them? For his decreeᵇ
      is far off."ᶜ
²³ Such are the thoughts of one devoid of
    understanding;
    a senseless and misguided person
      thinks foolishly.

²⁴ Listen to me, my child, and acquire
    knowledge,
    and pay close attention to my words.
²⁵ I will impart discipline preciselyᵈ
    and declare knowledge accurately.

²⁶ When the Lord createdᵉ his works from
    the beginning,
    and, in making them, determined their
      boundaries,
²⁷ he arranged his works in an eternal order,
    and their dominionᶠ for all generations.
They neither hunger nor grow weary,
    and they do not abandon their tasks.
²⁸ They do not crowd one another,
    and they never disobey his word.
²⁹ Then the Lord looked upon the earth,
    and filled it with his good things.
³⁰ With all kinds of living beings he
    covered its surface,
    and into it they must return.

17 The Lord created human beings out of
    earth,
    and makes them return to it again.
² He gave them a fixed number of days,
    but granted them authority over
      everything on the earth.ᵍ
³ He endowed them with strength like his
    own,ʰ

and made them in his own image.
⁴ He put the fear of themⁱ in all living
    beings,
    and gave them dominion over beasts
      and birds.ʲ
⁶ Discretion and tongue and eyes,
    ears and a mind for thinking he gave
      them.
⁷ He filled them with knowledge and
    understanding,
    and showed them good and evil.
⁸ He put the fear of him intoᵏ their hearts
    to show them the majesty of his works.ˡ
¹⁰ And they will praise his holy name,
    ⁹ to proclaim the grandeur of his works.
¹¹ He bestowed knowledge upon them,
    and allotted to them the law of life.ᵐ
¹² He established with them an eternal
    covenant,
    and revealed to them his decrees.

ᵃ Meaning of Gk uncertain: Heb Syr *If I sin, no eye can see me, and if I am disloyal all in secret, who is to know?*
ᵇ Heb *the decree*: Gk *the covenant*
ᶜ Other ancient authorities add *and a scrutiny for all comes at the end*
ᵈ Gk *by weight*
ᵉ Heb: Gk *judged*
ᶠ Or *elements*
ᵍ Lat: Gk *it*
ʰ Lat: Gk *proper to them*
ⁱ Syr: Gk *him*
ʲ Other ancient authorities add as verse 5, *They obtained the use of the five faculties of the Lord; as sixth he distributed to them the gift of mind, and as seventh, reason, the interpreter of one's faculties.*
ᵏ Other ancient authorities read *He set his eye upon*
ˡ Other ancient authorities add *and he gave them to boast of his marvels forever*
ᵐ Other ancient authorities add *so that they may know that they who are alive now are mortal*

16.24–17.24: Creation and responsibility. God has put order into the world that can be discerned by reason and the law of Moses (the Torah), and God knows and judges the actions of every person. **16.26–17.4:** A paraphrase of Gen 1–3 and related texts, with an emphasis on the orderliness of creation. **26:** *Beginning,* Gen 1.1; Prov 8.22–23. *Their boundaries,* Job 38.10; Pss 104.9; 148.6. **27b–28:** Apparently referring to the heavenly bodies; see Ps 104.19; but cf. *1 En* 21. **29:** *Good things,* Gen 1.4,10,12, etc. **30:** *Must return,* 17.1; Gen 3.19. **17.1:** *Out of earth,* Gen 2.7 **2:** *Authority,* Gen 1.28. **3:** *His own image,* Gen 1.26. **4:** *Dominion,* Gen 1.28; 9.2. **6–10:** God has endowed humans with reason, and their proper response to God is *fear* and *praise* of the Lord. Thus there is no excuse for sin. **11–14:** The *law* (the Torah) is a further gift from God, and it enables humans to discern good from evil. **11:** *The law of life,* 45.5; Deut 30.15–20. **12–13:** When God made a *covenant* with the Israelites on Mount Sinai, they saw his *glorious majesty* (Ex 19).

¹³ Their eyes saw his glorious majesty,
   and their ears heard the glory of his voice.
¹⁴ He said to them, "Beware of all evil."
   And he gave commandment to each of
      them concerning the neighbor.
¹⁵ Their ways are always known to him;
   they will not be hid from his eyes.ᵃ
¹⁷ He appointed a ruler for every nation,
   but Israel is the Lord's own portion.ᵇ
¹⁹ All their works are as clear as the sun
      before him,
   and his eyes are ever upon their ways.
²⁰ Their iniquities are not hidden from him,
   and all their sins are before the Lord.ᶜ
²² One's almsgiving is like a signet ring
      with the Lord,ᵈ
   and he will keep a person's kindness
      like the apple of his eye.ᵉ
²³ Afterward he will rise up and repay them,
   and he will bring their recompense on
      their heads.
²⁴ Yet to those who repent he grants a return,
   and he encourages those who are losing
      hope.

²⁵ Turn back to the Lord and forsake your
      sins;
   pray in his presence and lessen your
      offense.
²⁶ Return to the Most High and turn away
      from iniquity,ᶠ
   and hate intensely what he abhors.
²⁷ Who will sing praises to the Most High
      in Hades
   in place of the living who give thanks?
²⁸ From the dead, as from one who does
      not exist, thanksgiving has ceased;
   those who are alive and well sing the
      Lord's praises.
²⁹ How great is the mercy of the Lord,
   and his forgiveness for those who
      return to him!
³⁰ For not everything is within human
      capability,

since human beings are not immortal.
³¹ What is brighter than the sun? Yet it can
      be eclipsed.
   So flesh and blood devise evil.
³² He marshals the host of the height of
      heaven;
   but all human beings are dust and ashes.

18 He who lives forever created the whole
      universe;
   ² the Lord alone is just.ᵍ
⁴ To none has he given power to proclaim
      his works;
   and who can search out his mighty deeds?
⁵ Who can measure his majestic power?
   And who can fully recount his mercies?
⁶ It is not possible to diminish or increase
      them,
   nor is it possible to fathom the wonders
      of the Lord.

ᵃ Other ancient authorities add ¹⁶*Their ways from
   youth tend toward evil, and they are unable to
   make for themselves hearts of flesh in place of their
   stony hearts.* ¹⁷*For in the division of the nations of
   the whole earth, he appointed*
ᵇ Other ancient authorities add as verse 18, *whom,
   being his firstborn, he brings up with discipline,
   and allotting to him the light of his love, he does not
   neglect him.*
ᶜ Other ancient authorities add as verse 21, *But the
   Lord, who is gracious and knows how they are
   formed, has neither left them nor abandoned them,
   but has spared them.*
ᵈ Gk *him*
ᵉ Other ancient authorities add *apportioning
   repentance to his sons and daughters*
ᶠ Other ancient authorities add *for he will lead you
   out of darkness to the light of health.*
ᵍ Other ancient authorities add *and there is no other
   beside him;* ³*he steers the world with the span of his
   hand, and all things obey his will; for he is king of
   all things by his power, separating among them the
   holy things from the profane.*

14: *Neighbor,* Ex 20.13–17; Lev 19.18; Deut 5.17–21. 15–23: Although God will judge each person with justice, almsgiving and repentance can delay or even temper God's judgment. 17: *The Lord's own portion,* Deut 32.8–9. 22: *Signet ring* (Jer 22.24; Hag 2.23) and *apple of his eye* (Deut 32.10; Ps 17.8; Prov 7.2) suggest a close personal relationship with God.

17.25–32: **A call to repent.** God's mercy makes repentance possible. 27: *Hades,* Heb "Sheol," the abode of the dead, where there is no praising God (Pss 6.5; 30.9; 88.10–12; 115.17–18; Isa 38.18; Bar 2.17). 31: *Eclipsed,* if the sun can fail by way of an eclipse, so mortal humans can also be expected to fail. 32: *Dust and ashes,* see 10.9n.

18.1–14: **God's majesty and mercy.** The all-powerful and just God shows mercy to weak and mortal humans.

7 When human beings have finished, they
   are just beginning,
   and when they stop, they are still
   perplexed.
8 What are human beings, and of what use
   are they?
   What is good in them, and what is evil?
9 The number of days in their life is great if
   they reach one hundred years.ᵃ
10 Like a drop of water from the sea and a
   grain of sand,
   so are a few years among the days of
   eternity.
11 That is why the Lord is patient with them
   and pours out his mercy upon them.
12 He sees and recognizes that their end is
   miserable;
   therefore he grants them forgiveness all
   the more.
13 The compassion of human beings is for
   their neighbors,
   but the compassion of the Lord is for
   every living thing.
He rebukes and trains and teaches them,
   and turns them back, as a shepherd his
   flock.
14 He has compassion on those who accept
   his discipline
   and who are eager for his precepts.

15 My child, do not mix reproach with your
   good deeds,
   or spoil your gift by harsh words.
16 Does not the dew give relief from the
   scorching heat?
   So a word is better than a gift.
17 Indeed, does not a word surpass a good gift?
   Both are to be found in a gracious person.
18 A fool is ungracious and abusive,
   and the gift of a grudging giver makes
   the eyes dim.

19 Before you speak, learn;
   and before you fall ill, take care of your
   health.
20 Before judgment comes, examine yourself;
   and at the time of scrutiny you will find
   forgiveness.
21 Before falling ill, humble yourself;
   and when you have sinned, repent.
22 Let nothing hinder you from paying a
   vow promptly,
   and do not wait until death to be
   released from it.
23 Before making a vow, prepare yourself;
   do not be like one who puts the Lord to
   the test.
24 Think of his wrath on the day of death,
   and of the moment of vengeance when
   he turns away his face.
25 In the time of plenty think of the time of
   hunger;
   in days of wealth think of poverty and
   need.
26 From morning to evening conditions
   change;
   all things move swiftly before the Lord.

27 One who is wise is cautious in
   everything;
   when sin is all around, one guards
   against wrongdoing.
28 Every intelligent person knows wisdom,
   and praises the one who finds her.
29 Those who are skilled in words become
   wise themselves,
   and pour forth apt proverbs.ᵇ

a   Other ancient authorities add *but the death of each
    one is beyond the calculation of all*
b   Other ancient authorities add *Better is confidence
    in the one Lord than clinging with a dead heart to a
    dead one.*

8: *What are human beings,* Ps 8.4. **9**: *The number of days,* Ps. 90.10. **13**: *As a shepherd his flock,* cf. Pss 23.1–4; 80.1; Isa 40.11; Ezek 34.11–16.

18.15–18: Words and gifts. Good gifts can be spoiled by bad words, whereas good words are better than material gifts and are the mark of a gracious person. For more texts on speech, see 18.19–29; 19.4–17; 20.1–8,18–31.

18.19–29: Reflection and action. Before, during, and after action there is need for planning and assessment. **22–23**: For similar advice see Prov 20.25; Eccl 5.4–5. *Test,* cf. Ex 17.2; Deut 6.16. **29**: *Apt proverbs* are intended as both interpretations of life experiences and guides to living wisely and correctly.

18.30–19.3: Self-control. Matters that need control are *base desires* such as greed and lust. Their negative effects include shame, poverty, debauchery (Prov 20.1; 31.3–5), and death.

SELF-CONTROL[a]

³⁰ Do not follow your base desires,
  but restrain your appetites.
³¹ If you allow your soul to take pleasure in
    base desire,
  it will make you the laughingstock of
      your enemies.
³² Do not revel in great luxury,
  or you may become impoverished by its
    expense.
³³ Do not become a beggar by feasting with
    borrowed money,
  when you have nothing in your purse.[b]

19 The one who does this[c] will not
  become rich;
  one who despises small things will fail
    little by little.
² Wine and women lead intelligent men
    astray,
  and the man who consorts with
    prostitutes is reckless.
³ Decay and worms will take possession of
    him,
  and the reckless person will be
    snatched away.

⁴ One who trusts others too quickly has a
    shallow mind,
  and one who sins does wrong to himself.
⁵ One who rejoices in wickedness[d] will be
    condemned,[e]
  ⁶ but one who hates gossip has less evil.
⁷ Never repeat a conversation,
  and you will lose nothing at all.
⁸ With friend or foe do not report it,
  and unless it would be a sin for you, do
    not reveal it;
⁹ for someone may have heard you and
    watched you,
  and in time will hate you.
¹⁰ Have you heard something? Let it die
    with you.
  Be brave, it will not make you burst!

¹¹ Having heard something, the fool suffers
    birth pangs
  like a woman in labor with a child.
¹² Like an arrow stuck in a person's thigh,
  so is gossip inside a fool.

¹³ Question a friend; perhaps he did not do it;
  or if he did, so that he may not do it again.
¹⁴ Question a neighbor; perhaps he did not
    say it;
  or if he said it, so that he may not repeat it.
¹⁵ Question a friend, for often it is slander;
  so do not believe everything you hear.
¹⁶ A person may make a slip without
    intending it.
  Who has not sinned with his tongue?
¹⁷ Question your neighbor before you
    threaten him;
  and let the law of the Most High take its
    course.[f]

²⁰ The whole of wisdom is fear of the Lord,
  and in all wisdom there is the
    fulfillment of the law.[g]

---

a   This heading is included in the Gk text.
b   Other ancient authorities add *for you will be
    plotting against your own life*
c   Heb: Gk *A worker who is a drunkard*
d   Other ancient authorities read *heart*
e   Other ancient authorities add *but one who
    withstands pleasures crowns his life.* ⁶*One who
    controls the tongue will live without strife,*
f   Other ancient authorities add *and do not be
    angry.* ¹⁸*The fear of the Lord is the beginning of
    acceptance, and wisdom obtains his love.* ¹⁹*The
    knowledge of the Lord's commandments is life-
    giving discipline; and those who do what is pleasing
    to him enjoy the fruit of the tree of immortality.*
g   Other ancient authorities add *and the knowledge of
    his omnipotence.* ²¹*When a slave says to his master,
    "I will not act as you wish," even if later he does it,
    he angers the one who supports him.*

19.4–17: The evils of gossip. Loose talk is destructive not only to its subject but also to its purveyors. **4–12:** A wise person should not accept slander or gossip too quickly and repeat it *unless it would be a sin* (19.8) to withhold it (cf. Lev 5.1). **13–17:** When a *friend* or *neighbor* is the subject of gossip, it is best to question that person directly. **17:** *The law of the Most High,* cf. Lev 19.17–18.

18–19: The verses included in the translators' note to 19.17 are generally regarded as a later addition to the text, since they refer explicitly to *immortality,* which is inconsistent with Sirach's statements elsewhere about the finality of death.

19.20–30: Wisdom and cleverness. Without *fear of the Lord* and fulfilling God's *law,* what may seem like

²² The knowledge of wickedness is not
  wisdom,
    nor is there prudence in the counsel of
      sinners.
²³ There is a cleverness that is detestable,
    and there is a fool who merely lacks
      wisdom.
²⁴ Better are the God-fearing who lack
    understanding
      than the highly intelligent who
        transgress the law.
²⁵ There is a cleverness that is exact but
    unjust,
      and there are people who abuse favors
        to gain a verdict.
²⁶ There is the villain bowed down in
    mourning,
  but inwardly he is full of deceit.
²⁷ He hides his face and pretends not to
    hear,
      but when no one notices, he will take
        advantage of you.
²⁸ Even if lack of strength keeps him from
    sinning,
      he will nevertheless do evil when he
        finds the opportunity.
²⁹ A person is known by his appearance,
    and a sensible person is known when
      first met, face to face.
³⁰ A person's attire and hearty laughter,
    and the way he walks, show what he is.

20 There is a rebuke that is untimely,
    and there is the person who is wise
      enough to keep silent.
² How much better it is to rebuke than to
    fume!
³ And the one who admits his fault will be
    kept from failure.
⁴ Like a eunuch lusting to violate a girl
    is the person who does right under
      compulsion.
⁵ Some people keep silent and are thought
    to be wise,

while others are detested for being
  talkative.
⁶ Some people keep silent because they
    have nothing to say,
      while others keep silent because they
        know when to speak.
⁷ The wise remain silent until the right
    moment,
      but a boasting fool misses the right
        moment.
⁸ Whoever talks too much is detested,
    and whoever pretends to authority is
      hated.ᵃ

⁹ There may be good fortune for a person
    in adversity,
      and a windfall may result in a loss.
¹⁰ There is the gift that profits you nothing,
    and the gift to be paid back double.
¹¹ There are losses for the sake of glory,
    and there are some who have raised
      their heads from humble
        circumstances.
¹² Some buy much for little,
    but pay for it seven times over.
¹³ The wise make themselves beloved by
    only few words,ᵇ
      but the courtesies of fools are wasted.
¹⁴ A fool's gift will profit you nothing,ᶜ
    for he looks for recompense sevenfold.ᵈ
¹⁵ He gives little and upbraids much;
    he opens his mouth like a town crier.
  Today he lends and tomorrow he asks it
    back;
      such a one is hateful to God and humans.ᵉ

ᵃ Other ancient authorities add *How good it is to
  show repentance when you are reproved, for so you
  will escape deliberate sin!*
ᵇ Heb: Gk *by words*
ᶜ Other ancient authorities add *so it is with the
  envious who give under compulsion*
ᵈ Syr: Gk *he has many eyes instead of one*
ᵉ Other ancient authorities lack *to God and humans*

wisdom may be only *detestable cleverness*. **20**: *Fear of the Lord*, cf. Prov 1.7; 9.10. **29**: A person's *appearance* may
be either deceiving or revealing.

20.1–31: Speech and related topics. These sayings concerning rebukes, silence, gifts and money, the fool,
inappropriate speech, shame, lies, and other matters are connected more by catchwords and topics than by logical progression or argument. The appeal throughout is to human experience and natural reasoning, not to fear
of the Lord or the commandments. **4**: *Like a eunuch*, a sinner cannot be forced to do *right* any more than a eunuch
can engage in sexual intercourse. **5–6**: *Keep silent*, Prov 17.27–28. **9–12**: Although wisdom literature attempted to

16 The fool says, "I have no friends,
    and I get no thanks for my good deeds.
    Those who eat my bread are evil-
        tongued."
17 How many will ridicule him, and how
    often![a]

18 A slip on the pavement is better than a
    slip of the tongue;
    the downfall of the wicked will occur
        just as speedily.
19 A coarse person is like an inappropriate
    story,
    continually on the lips of the ignorant.
20 A proverb from a fool's lips will be rejected,
    for he does not tell it at the proper time.

21 One may be prevented from sinning by
    poverty;
    so when he rests he feels no remorse.
22 One may lose his life through shame,
    or lose it because of human respect.[b]
23 Another out of shame makes promises
        to a friend,
    and so makes an enemy for nothing.

24 A lie is an ugly blot on a person;
    it is continually on the lips of the
        ignorant.
25 A thief is preferable to a habitual liar,
    but the lot of both is ruin.
26 A liar's way leads to disgrace,
    and his shame is ever with him.

PROVERBIAL SAYINGS[c]

27 The wise person advances himself by his
    words,
    and one who is sensible pleases the great.
28 Those who cultivate the soil heap up
    their harvest,
    and those who please the great atone
        for injustice.
29 Favors and gifts blind the eyes of the wise;
    like a muzzle on the mouth they stop
        reproofs.

30 Hidden wisdom and unseen treasure,
    of what value is either?
31 Better are those who hide their folly
    than those who hide their wisdom.[d]

21 Have you sinned, my child? Do so no
    more,
    but ask forgiveness for your past sins.
2 Flee from sin as from a snake;
    for if you approach sin, it will bite you.
Its teeth are lion's teeth,
    and can destroy human lives.
3 All lawlessness is like a two-edged sword;
    there is no healing for the wound it inflicts.

4 Panic and insolence will waste away riches;
    thus the house of the proud will be laid
        waste.[e]
5 The prayer of the poor goes from their
    lips to the ears of God,[f]
    and his judgment comes speedily.
6 Those who hate reproof walk in the
    sinner's steps,
    but those who fear the Lord repent in
        their heart.
7 The mighty in speech are widely known;
    when they slip, the sensible person
        knows it.

8 Whoever builds his house with other
    people's money
    is like one who gathers stones for his
        burial mound.[g]

a Other ancient authorities add *for he has not
    honestly received what he has, and what he does
    not have is unimportant to him*
b Other ancient authorities read *his foolish look*
c This heading is included in the Gk text.
d Other ancient authorities add 32*Unwearied
    endurance in seeking the Lord is better than a
    masterless charioteer of one's own life.*
e Other ancient authorities read *uprooted*
f Gk *his ears*
g Other ancient authorities read *for the winter*

discern clear cause-and-effect relationships, it also acknowledged the possibility of paradox and uncertainty; cf.
Prov 14.12; 16.25; Eccl 9.11–12. **24–26:** For the evil effects of a *lie*, see 7.13; 25.2; Prov 6.17; 12.22; Ps 5.6.
    21.1–10: The destructive effects of sin. Sin can destroy a person and lead to shame and death. **2–3:** Sin is
subtle and tempting like a *snake* (Gen 3.1–5), strong and destructive like a *lion's teeth* (27.10), and deadly like a
two-edged sword (Prov 5.4). **5:** The prayer of the poor, cf. 35.17–21. **9:** *Bundle of tow,* that is, combustible fibers.
Fire here refers to the sinner's destruction in this life rather than punishment after death. **10:** *Hades,* the abode

⁹ An assembly of the wicked is like a
  bundle of tow,
  and their end is a blazing fire.
¹⁰ The way of sinners is paved with smooth
  stones,
  but at its end is the pit of Hades.

¹¹ Whoever keeps the law controls his
  thoughts,
  and the fulfillment of the fear of the
  Lord is wisdom.
¹² The one who is not clever cannot be
  taught,
  but there is a cleverness that increases
  bitterness.
¹³ The knowledge of the wise will increase
  like a flood,
  and their counsel like a life-giving spring.
¹⁴ The mindᵃ of a fool is like a broken jar;
  it can hold no knowledge.

¹⁵ When an intelligent person hears a wise
  saying,
  he praises it and adds to it;
when a foolᵇ hears it, he laughs atᶜ it
  and throws it behind his back.
¹⁶ A fool's chatter is like a burden on a
  journey,
  but delight is found in the speech of the
  intelligent.
¹⁷ The utterance of a sensible person is
  sought in the assembly,
  and they ponder his words in their
  minds.

¹⁸ Like a house in ruins is wisdom to a fool,
  and to the ignorant, knowledge is talk
  that has no meaning.
¹⁹ To a senseless person education is fetters
  on his feet,
  and like manacles on his right hand.
²⁰ A fool raises his voice when he laughs,
  but the wiseᵈ smile quietly.

²¹ To the sensible person education is like a
  golden ornament,
  and like a bracelet on the right arm.

²² The foot of a fool rushes into a house,
  but an experienced person waits
  respectfully outside.
²³ A boor peers into the house from the
  door,
  but a cultivated person remains outside.
²⁴ It is ill-mannered for a person to listen
  at a door;
  the discreet would be grieved by the
  disgrace.

²⁵ The lips of babblers speak of what is not
  their concern,ᵉ
  but the words of the prudent are
  weighed in the balance.
²⁶ The mind of fools is in their mouth,
  but the mouth of the wise is inᶠ their
  mind.
²⁷ When an ungodly person curses an
  adversary,ᵍ
  he curses himself.
²⁸ A whisperer degrades himself
  and is hated in his neighborhood.

22 The idler is like a filthy stone,
    and every one hisses at his disgrace.
² The idler is like the filth of dunghills;
  anyone that picks it up will shake it off
  his hand.

ᵃ Syr Lat: Gk *entrails*
ᵇ Syr: Gk *reveler*
ᶜ Syr: Gk *dislikes*
ᵈ Syr Lat: Gk *clever*
ᵉ Other ancient authorities read *of strangers speak of these things*
ᶠ Other ancient authorities omit *in*
ᵍ Or *curses Satan*

of the dead (Heb "Sheol").

21.11–28: The sage and the fool. The opening saying gives the series of comparisons a specifically Jewish religious context by linking them to the *law, fear of the Lord,* and *wisdom*—the major themes of the book. Otherwise, the appeal is to common human experience and reason. The contrasts between the sage and the fool are especially evident with regard to speech (21.16–17,25–28), attitudes toward education (21.15,19,21), and behavior (21.22–24).

22.1–18: Dealing with fools. While the *idler* and the *fool* can be avoided, dealing with one's own foolish children is especially difficult. **1:** *Filthy stone,* a rock used for wiping oneself after a bowel movement. **3–6:** *Daughter,* sons were prized in Ben Sira's patriarchal society, whereas daughters were often regarded as a source of trouble for their

³ It is a disgrace to be the father of an
undisciplined son,
and the birth of a daughter is a loss.
⁴ A sensible daughter obtains a husband of
her own,
but one who acts shamefully is a grief
to her father.
⁵ An impudent daughter disgraces father
and husband,
and is despised by both.
⁶ Like music in time of mourning is ill-
timed conversation,
but a thrashing and discipline are at all
times wisdom.ᵃ

⁹ Whoever teaches a fool is like one who
glues potsherds together,
or who rouses a sleeper from deep
slumber.
¹⁰ Whoever tells a story to a fool tells it to a
drowsy man;
and at the end he will say, "What is it?"
¹¹ Weep for the dead, for he has left the
light behind;
and weep for the fool, for he has left
intelligence behind.
Weep less bitterly for the dead, for he is at
rest;
but the life of the fool is worse than death.
¹² Mourning for the dead lasts seven days,
but for the foolish or the ungodly it
lasts all the days of their lives.

¹³ Do not talk much with a senseless person
or visit an unintelligent person.ᵇ
Stay clear of him, or you may have trouble,
and be spattered when he shakes
himself off.
Avoid him and you will find rest,
and you will never be wearied by his
lack of sense.

¹⁴ What is heavier than lead?
And what is its name except "Fool"?
¹⁵ Sand, salt, and a piece of iron
are easier to bear than a stupid person.

¹⁶ A wooden beam firmly bonded into a
building
is not loosened by an earthquake;
so the mind firmly resolved after due
reflection
will not be afraid in a crisis.
¹⁷ A mind settled on an intelligent thought
is like stucco decoration that makes a
wall smooth.
¹⁸ Fencesᶜ set on a high place
will not stand firm against the wind;
so a timid mind with a fool's resolve
will not stand firm against any fear.

¹⁹ One who pricks the eye brings tears,
and one who pricks the heart makes
clear its feelings.
²⁰ One who throws a stone at birds scares
them away,
and one who reviles a friend destroys a
friendship.
²¹ Even if you draw your sword against a
friend,
do not despair, for there is a way back.
²² If you open your mouth against your
friend,
do not worry, for reconciliation is
possible.

ᵃ Other ancient authorities add ⁷Children who are
brought up in a good life, conceal the lowly birth of
their parents. ⁸Children who are disdainfully and
boorishly haughty stain the nobility of their kindred.
ᵇ Other ancient authorities add For being without
sense he will despise everything about you
ᶜ Other ancient authorities read Pebbles

fathers (cf. 7.24–25; 42.9–13). 6: *Thrashing*, corporal punishment was acceptable in this society (30.1–13; Prov 13.24; 23.13–14). 7–8: Translated in the marginal notes, these verses are probably not part of the original composition. 9: *Glues potsherds together*, reassembling a broken clay pot is futile and nearly impossible. 11–12: *The fool* is more deserving of pity and mourning than a dead person (cf. 38.16–23). 13: *Avoid him*, the best strategy for dealing with a fool. 14–15: The comparisons illustrate how burdensome a fool can be (cf. 21.16). Verse 14 has the structure of a riddle. 16–18: *A fool's resolve*, the comparisons contrast the strong resolve of the sage and the weak resolve of the fool.

22.19–26: **Preserving friendships.** Friendships are best preserved by keeping confidences and avoiding harsh words. A true friend remains faithful both in prosperity and in hard times (cf. 6.5–17; 9.10–16; 19.13–17; 27.16–21; 37.1–6). 19: *Eye*, just as the eye is sensitive to being hurt, so the heart (the place of thinking and feeling) suffers and expresses its own hurt *feelings*.

But as for reviling, arrogance, disclosure of
secrets, or a treacherous blow—
in these cases any friend will take to
flight.

23 Gain the trust of your neighbor in his
poverty,
so that you may rejoice with him in his
prosperity.
Stand by him in time of distress,
so that you may share with him in his
inheritance.[a]
24 The vapor and smoke of the furnace
precede the fire;
so insults precede bloodshed.
25 I am not ashamed to shelter a friend,
and I will not hide from him.
26 But if harm should come to me because
of him,
whoever hears of it will beware of him.

27 Who will set a guard over my mouth,
and an effective seal upon my lips,
so that I may not fall because of them,
and my tongue may not destroy me?

23 O Lord, Father and Master of my life,
do not abandon me to their designs,
and do not let me fall because of them!
2 Who will set whips over my thoughts,
and the discipline of wisdom over my
mind,
so as not to spare me in my errors,
and not overlook my[b] sins?
3 Otherwise my mistakes may be multiplied,
and my sins may abound,
and I may fall before my adversaries,
and my enemy may rejoice over me.[c]
4 O Lord, Father and God of my life,
do not give me haughty eyes,
5 and remove evil desire from me.
6 Let neither gluttony nor lust overcome me,
and do not give me over to shameless
passion.

DISCIPLINE OF THE TONGUE[d]

7 Listen, my children, to instruction
concerning the mouth;

the one who observes it will never be
caught.
8 Sinners are overtaken through their
lips;
by them the reviler and the arrogant are
tripped up.
9 Do not accustom your mouth to oaths,
nor habitually utter the name of the
Holy One;
10 for as a servant who is constantly under
scrutiny
will not lack bruises,
so also the person who always swears and
utters the Name
will never be cleansed[e] from sin.
11 The one who swears many oaths is full of
iniquity,
and the scourge will not leave his
house.
If he swears in error, his sin remains on
him,
and if he disregards it, he sins doubly;
if he swears a false oath, he will not be
justified,
for his house will be filled with
calamities.

12 There is a manner of speaking
comparable to death;[f]
may it never be found in the inheritance
of Jacob!
Such conduct will be far from the godly,
and they will not wallow in sins.
13 Do not accustom your mouth to coarse,
foul language,
for it involves sinful speech.

a Other ancient authorities add *For one should not
always despise restricted circumstances, or admire
a rich person who is stupid.*
b Gk *their*
c Other ancient authorities add *From them the hope
of your mercy is remote*
d This heading is included in the Gk text.
e Syr *be free*
f Other ancient authorities read *clothed about with
death*

22.27–23.6: Prayers for self-control. Two short units consisting of a question and a prayer ask for God's help
in the areas of speech and sexuality. **23.1,4:** *O Lord, Father,* cf. 51.10.

23.7–15: Sins of speech. Recognition of the need for self-control in matters of speech flows from the question and prayer in 22.27–23.1. **9:** *Oaths,* for avoiding rash or false oaths sworn in God's *name,* see Ex 20.7; Lev

14 Remember your father and mother
  when you sit among the great,
or you may forget yourself in their
    presence,
  and behave like a fool through bad habit;
then you will wish that you had never
    been born,
  and you will curse the day of your birth.
15 Those who are accustomed to using
    abusive language
  will never become disciplined as long as
    they live.

16 Two kinds of individuals multiply sins,
  and a third incurs wrath.
Hot passion that blazes like a fire
  will not be quenched until it burns
    itself out;
one who commits fornication with his
    near of kin
  will never cease until the fire burns
    him up.
17 To a fornicator all bread is sweet;
  he will never weary until he dies.
18 The one who sins against his marriage
    bed
  says to himself, "Who can see me?
Darkness surrounds me, the walls hide me,
  and no one sees me. Why should I
    worry?
  The Most High will not remember sins."
19 His fear is confined to human eyes
  and he does not realize that the eyes of
    the Lord
  are ten thousand times brighter than
    the sun;
they look upon every aspect of human
    behavior
  and see into hidden corners.
20 Before the universe was created, it was
    known to him,
  and so it is since its completion.

21 This man will be punished in the streets
    of the city,
  and where he least suspects it, he will
    be seized.

22 So it is with a woman who leaves her
    husband
  and presents him with an heir by
    another man.
23 For first of all, she has disobeyed the law
    of the Most High;
  second, she has committed an offense
    against her husband;
and third, through her fornication she has
    committed adultery
  and brought forth children by another
    man.
24 She herself will be brought before the
    assembly,
  and her punishment will extend to her
    children.
25 Her children will not take root,
  and her branches will not bear fruit.
26 She will leave behind an accursed
    memory
  and her disgrace will never be blotted
    out.
27 Those who survive her will recognize
    that nothing is better than the fear of
    the Lord,
  and nothing sweeter than to heed the
    commandments of the Lord.[a]

THE PRAISE OF WISDOM[b]

24 Wisdom praises herself,
  and tells of her glory in the midst of
    her people.

a Other ancient authorities add as verse 28, *It is a
great honor to follow God, and to be received by him
is long life.*
b This heading is included in the Gk text.

5.4; Deut 5.11. **12:** *Death,* the biblical penalty for blasphemy (Lev 24.16). *The inheritance of Jacob,* the Israelites. **14:**
Curse the day of your birth, see Job 3.3–5; Jer 20.14–18.

23.16–27: Sexual sins. This unit flows from the question and prayer in 23.2–6. **16–17:** *Two kinds . . . a third,*
the numerical proverb (cf. 25.1–2,7–11; 26.5–6,28; 50.25–26) condemns three kinds of sexual sins: *hot passion,*
incest, and *fornication.* **18–21:** How adulterers delude themselves. **21:** *Punished,* cf. Lev 20.10; Deut 22.22–27.
22–27: An adulteress who bears a child by another man offends both God and her husband (Ex 20.14; Deut.
5.18). **24:** *Before the assembly,* cf. Deut 22.22–24. **27:** The punishments visited upon those who commit adultery
highlight the importance of the *fear of the Lord* and God's *commandments.*

24.1–22: Wisdom praises herself. Wisdom is personified as a female figure (cf. Prov 8.22–36; Job 28; Bar

² In the assembly of the Most High she
  opens her mouth,
and in the presence of his hosts she
  tells of her glory:
³ "I came forth from the mouth of the Most
  High,
and covered the earth like a mist.
⁴ I dwelt in the highest heavens,
and my throne was in a pillar of cloud.
⁵ Alone I compassed the vault of heaven
and traversed the depths of the abyss.
⁶ Over waves of the sea, over all the earth,
and over every people and nation I have
  held sway.ᵃ
⁷ Among all these I sought a resting place;
in whose territory should I abide?

⁸ "Then the Creator of all things gave me a
  command,
and my Creator chose the place for my
  tent.
He said, 'Make your dwelling in Jacob,
and in Israel receive your inheritance.'
⁹ Before the ages, in the beginning, he
  created me,
and for all the ages I shall not cease to be.
¹⁰ In the holy tent I ministered before him,
and so I was established in Zion.
¹¹ Thus in the beloved city he gave me a
  resting place,
and in Jerusalem was my domain.
¹² I took root in an honored people,
in the portion of the Lord, his heritage.

¹³ "I grew tall like a cedar in Lebanon,
and like a cypress on the heights of
  Hermon.
¹⁴ I grew tall like a palm tree in En-gedi,ᵇ
and like rosebushes in Jericho;

like a fair olive tree in the field,
and like a plane tree beside waterᶜ I
  grew tall.
¹⁵ Like cassia and camel's thorn I gave forth
  perfume,
and like choice myrrh I spread my
  fragrance,
like galbanum, onycha, and stacte,
and like the odor of incense in the tent.
¹⁶ Like a terebinth I spread out my branches,
and my branches are glorious and
  graceful.
¹⁷ Like the vine I bud forth delights,
and my blossoms become glorious and
  abundant fruit.ᵈ

¹⁹ "Come to me, you who desire me,
and eat your fill of my fruits.
²⁰ For the memory of me is sweeter than
  honey,
and the possession of me sweeter than
  the honeycomb.
²¹ Those who eat of me will hunger for more,
and those who drink of me will thirst
  for more.
²² Whoever obeys me will not be put to
  shame,
and those who work with me will not
  sin."

ᵃ Other ancient authorities read *I have acquired a possession*
ᵇ Other ancient authorities read *on the beaches*
ᶜ Other ancient authorities omit *beside water*
ᵈ Other ancient authorities add as verse 18, *I am the mother of beautiful love, of fear, of knowledge, and of holy hope; being eternal, I am given to all my children, to those who are named by him.*

3.9–4.4) who dwells in the Jerusalem Temple. 1–2: *Her glory*, both the Hebrew (*hokhma*) and Greek (*sophia*) terms for *wisdom* are feminine in gender. The use of first-person singular language in praise of oneself (aretalogy) is characteristic of ancient texts associated with the Egyptian goddess Isis. *Her people*, i.e., Israel, and *the assembly of the Most High*, i.e., the divine council, cf. Ps 82.1,6–7. 3–7: Wisdom was created by God and has cosmic significance (Prov 8.22–31; Wis 1.7; 7.22–30). 4: *Pillar of cloud*, see Ex 13.21–22; 33.9–10. 7: *Resting place*, cf. Job 28.12–28; Wis 7.22–30; *1 Enoch* 42. 8–12: *Zion*, wisdom's dwelling place in Jacob (cf. Bar 3.36–37) is the Jerusalem Temple. 9: Cf. Prov 8.22–23. 10: *Holy tent*, i.e., the tabernacle; see Ex 25.8–9. 13–17: The comparisons stress wisdom's attractiveness and her life-giving power. 13: *Lebanon*, a high mountain range in modern Lebanon and Syria, famous in antiquity for its forests. *Hermon*, a high mountain on the border between modern Israel and Syria. 14: *En-gedi* and *Jericho* are oases in the Judean desert region, near the Dead Sea. 15: These items were ingredients for the *perfume* and *incense* used in the Jerusalem Temple; see Ex 30.22–38. 19–22: Wisdom's banquet provides delights and keeps one from sin (cf. 51.23–30; Prov 9.1–6).

²³ All this is the book of the covenant of
the Most High God,
the law that Moses commanded us
as an inheritance for the congregations
of Jacob.^a
²⁵ It overflows, like the Pishon, with wisdom,
and like the Tigris at the time of the
first fruits.
²⁶ It runs over, like the Euphrates, with
understanding,
and like the Jordan at harvest time.
²⁷ It pours forth instruction like the Nile,^b
like the Gihon at the time of vintage.
²⁸ The first man did not know wisdom^c
fully,
nor will the last one fathom her.
²⁹ For her thoughts are more abundant
than the sea,
and her counsel deeper than the great
abyss.

³⁰ As for me, I was like a canal from a river,
like a water channel into a garden.
³¹ I said, "I will water my garden
and drench my flower-beds."
And lo, my canal became a river,
and my river a sea.
³² I will again make instruction shine forth
like the dawn,
and I will make it clear from far away.
³³ I will again pour out teaching like
prophecy,
and leave it to all future generations.
³⁴ Observe that I have not labored for
myself alone,
but for all who seek wisdom.^c

25 I take pleasure in three things,
and they are beautiful in the sight of
God and of mortals:^d

agreement among brothers and sisters,
friendship among neighbors,
and a wife and a husband who live in
harmony.
² I hate three kinds of people,
and I loathe their manner of life:
a pauper who boasts, a rich person who lies,
and an old fool who commits adultery.

³ If you gathered nothing in your youth,
how can you find anything in your old
age?
⁴ How attractive is sound judgment in the
gray-haired,
and for the aged to possess good
counsel!
⁵ How attractive is wisdom in the aged,
and understanding and counsel in the
venerable!
⁶ Rich experience is the crown of the aged,
and their boast is the fear of the Lord.

⁷ I can think of nine whom I would call
blessed,
and a tenth my tongue proclaims:
a man who can rejoice in his children;
a man who lives to see the downfall of
his foes.
⁸ Happy the man who lives with a sensible
wife,

a   Other ancient authorities add as verse 24, *"Do not
cease to be strong in the Lord, cling to him so that
he may strengthen you; the Lord Almighty alone is
God, and besides him there is no savior."*
b   Syr: Gk *It makes instruction shine forth like light*
c   Gk *her*
d   Syr Lat: Gk *In three things I was beautiful and I
stood in beauty before the Lord and mortals.*

24.23–34: Ben Sira's commentary on the preceding poem about Wisdom. The identification of wisdom with the *covenant* and the *law* (24.23; Ex 24.7; Deut 33.4) combines the two great traditions taught at Ben Sira's school. **25–27:** Four of the rivers—Pishon, Tigris, Euphrates, and Gihon—appear in Gen 2.10–14. **28–29:** *The first man,* Adam did not know the Torah, the true wisdom, which was given first to Moses. **30–34:** As a wisdom teacher, Ben Sira regarded himself as a *canal* and a *water channel* for the wisdom conveyed in the Torah and the ancient Near Eastern wisdom tradition. See 33.16–19 and 51.13–30 for further autobiographical reflections on his role as a wisdom teacher.

25.1–11: Happiness. Two sets of numerical sayings (25.1–2,7–11) bracket an ideal picture of old age (25.3–6). **1–2:** The scenes of harmony stand in contrast with pictures of persons who act inappropriately. **3–6:** At their best the elderly manifest the value of *wisdom* and *fear of the Lord*. **7–11:** Ten beatitudes declare certain persons *happy* in the present. **8:** Plowing with an *ox and ass together* is forbidden by Deut 22.10. The reference here may

and the one who does not plow with ox
and ass together.ᵃ
Happy is the one who does not sin with
the tongue,
and the one who has not served an
inferior.
⁹ Happy is the one who finds a friend,ᵇ
and the one who speaks to attentive
listeners.
¹⁰ How great is the one who finds wisdom!
But none is superior to the one who
fears the Lord.
¹¹ Fear of the Lord surpasses everything;
to whom can we compare the one who
has it?ᶜ

¹³ Any wound, but not a wound of the
heart!
Any wickedness, but not the
wickedness of a woman!
¹⁴ Any suffering, but not suffering from
those who hate!
And any vengeance, but not the
vengeance of enemies!
¹⁵ There is no venomᵈ worse than a snake's
venom,ᵈ
and no anger worse than a woman'sᵉ
wrath.

¹⁶ I would rather live with a lion and a
dragon
than live with an evil woman.
¹⁷ A woman's wickedness changes her
appearance,
and darkens her face like that of a bear.
¹⁸ Her husband sitsᶠ among the neighbors,
and he cannot help sighingᵍ bitterly.
¹⁹ Any iniquity is small compared to a
woman's iniquity;
may a sinner's lot befall her!
²⁰ A sandy ascent for the feet of the aged—
such is a garrulous wife to a quiet
husband.

²¹ Do not be ensnared by a woman's beauty,
and do not desire a woman for her
possessions.ʰ
²² There is wrath and impudence and great
disgrace
when a wife supports her husband.
²³ Dejected mind, gloomy face,
and wounded heart come from an evil
wife.
Drooping hands and weak knees
come from the wife who does not make
her husband happy.
²⁴ From a woman sin had its beginning,
and because of her we all die.
²⁵ Allow no outlet to water,
and no boldness of speech to an evil wife.
²⁶ If she does not go as you direct,
separate her from yourself.

26 Happy is the husband of a good wife;
the number of his days will be doubled.
² A loyal wife brings joy to her husband,
and he will complete his years in peace.
³ A good wife is a great blessing;
she will be granted among the blessings
of the man who fears the Lord.
⁴ Whether rich or poor, his heart is
content,
and at all times his face is cheerful.

ᵃ Heb Syr: Gk lacks *and the one who does not plow
with ox and ass together*
ᵇ Lat Syr: Gk *good sense*
ᶜ Other ancient authorities add as verse 12, *The fear
of the Lord is the beginning of love for him, and
faith is the beginning of clinging to him.*
ᵈ Syr: Gk *head*
ᵉ Other ancient authorities read *an enemy's*
ᶠ Heb Syr: Gk *loses heart*
ᵍ Other ancient authorities read *and listening he
sighs*
ʰ Heb Syr: Other Gk authorities read *for her beauty*

be to polygamy with incompatible wives (cf. 26.6; 37.11).

25.13–26.18: Bad and good wives. Alternating sections describe a bad wife (25.13–26; 26.5–12) and a good
wife (26.1–4; 26.13–18). **25.13–26:** Advice for young male students about the bad effects of living with an evil
and angry woman. Sirach's very negative remarks about women are striking even in the context of a patriarchal
culture. **16:** Prov 21.19; 25.24; 27.15. **22:** *Disgrace,* for a husband to be dependent financially on his wife was regarded as a cause for shame. **24:** *From a woman sin had its beginning,* see Gen 3.6. Sirach's interpretation exceeds
Gen 3 in placing blame upon the woman (cf. 2 Cor 11.3; 1 Tim 2.14). **26:** *Separate,* only the husband could initiate
divorce proceedings (Deut 24.1–4). **26.1–4:** A *good wife* is a *great blessing* to her husband, and brings him a long

⁵ Of three things my heart is frightened,
  and of a fourth I am in great fear:ᵃ
Slander in the city, the gathering of
  a mob,
  and false accusation—all these are
    worse than death.
⁶ But it is heartache and sorrow when a
  wife is jealous of a rival,
  and a tongue-lashing makes it known
    to all.
⁷ A bad wife is a chafing yoke;
  taking hold of her is like grasping a
    scorpion.
⁸ A drunken wife arouses great anger;
  she cannot hide her shame.
⁹ The haughty stare betrays an unchaste
  wife;
  her eyelids give her away.

¹⁰ Keep strict watch over a headstrong
  daughter,
  or else, when she finds liberty, she will
    make use of it.
¹¹ Be on guard against her impudent eye,
  and do not be surprised if she sins
    against you.
¹² As a thirsty traveler opens his mouth
  and drinks from any water near him,
so she will sit in front of every tent peg
  and open her quiver to the arrow.

¹³ A wife's charm delights her husband,
  and her skill puts flesh on his bones.
¹⁴ A silent wife is a gift from the Lord,
  and nothing is so precious as her self-
    discipline.
¹⁵ A modest wife adds charm to charm,
  and no scales can weigh the value of her
    chastity.
¹⁶ Like the sun rising in the heights of the
  Lord,

so is the beauty of a good wife in her
    well-ordered home.
¹⁷ Like the shining lamp on the holy
  lampstand,
  so is a beautiful face on a stately figure.
¹⁸ Like golden pillars on silver bases,
  so are shapely legs and steadfast feet.

Other ancient authorities add verses 19-27:

¹⁹ *My child, keep sound the bloom of your*
  youth,
  and do not give your strength to
    strangers.
²⁰ *Seek a fertile field within the whole plain,*
  and sow it with your own seed, trusting
    in your fine stock.
²¹ *So your offspring will prosper,*
  and, having confidence in their good
    descent, will grow great.
²² *A prostitute is regarded as spittle,*
  and a married woman as a tower of
    death to her lovers.
²³ *A godless wife is given as a portion to a*
  lawless man,
  but a pious wife is given to the man who
    fears the Lord.
²⁴ *A shameless woman constantly acts*
  disgracefully,
  but a modest daughter will even be
    embarrassed before her husband.
²⁵ *A headstrong wife is regarded as a dog,*
  but one who has a sense of shame will
    fear the Lord.
²⁶ *A wife honoring her husband will seem*
  wise to all,
  but if she dishonors him in her pride she
    will be known to all as ungodly.
  Happy is the husband of a good wife;

ᵃ Syr: Meaning of Gk uncertain

life, joy, and peace (cf. Prov. 31.10–31). **26.5–12:** Warnings about a *jealous, bad, drunken,* and *unchaste wife* lead into advice about keeping strict control over a *headstrong daughter.* **5–6:** In numerical proverbs (see 23.16–17n) the last element is the climax. **6:** *Jealous of a rival,* probably referring to hostility among wives in a polygamous household. **12:** *Tent peg . . . quiver,* the language here about illicit sexual relations is very graphic. **26.13–18:** A good wife is praised for her virtues and physical beauty. **13:** *Her skill,* cf. Prov 31.10–31. **17–18:** Cf. Song 4.1–7.

27.19–27: More about women. While not in the Hebrew text, these verses appear in Greek and Syriac manuscripts and seem to have been part of Ben Sira's original work. **19–21:** The ideal for the young Jewish man is to marry a Jewish woman and raise up many children from her (Prov 5.7–23). **20:** An agricultural metaphor for reproduction. **22–27:** These further contrasts between bad and good wives (cf. 25.13–26.18) allow the positive ideal of the good Jewish wife to emerge more clearly.

*for the number of his years will be
doubled.*
27 *A loud-voiced and garrulous wife is like a
trumpet sounding the charge,
and every person like this lives in the
anarchy of war.*

---

28 At two things my heart is grieved,
and because of a third anger comes over
me:
a warrior in want through poverty,
intelligent men who are treated
contemptuously,
and a man who turns back from
righteousness to sin—
the Lord will prepare him for the sword!

29 A merchant can hardly keep from
wrongdoing,
nor is a tradesman innocent of sin.

27 Many have committed sin for gain,[a]
and those who seek to get rich will
avert their eyes.
2 As a stake is driven firmly into a fissure
between stones,
so sin is wedged in between selling and
buying.
3 If a person is not steadfast in the fear of
the Lord,
his house will be quickly overthrown.

4 When a sieve is shaken, the refuse
appears;
so do a person's faults when he speaks.
5 The kiln tests the potter's vessels;
so the test of a person is in his
conversation.
6 Its fruit discloses the cultivation of a tree;
so a person's speech discloses the
cultivation of his mind.
7 Do not praise anyone before he speaks,
for this is the way people are tested.

8 If you pursue justice, you will attain it
and wear it like a glorious robe.

9 Birds roost with their own kind,
so honesty comes home to those who
practice it.
10 A lion lies in wait for prey;
so does sin for evildoers.

11 The conversation of the godly is always
wise,
but the fool changes like the moon.
12 Among stupid people limit your time,
but among thoughtful people linger on.
13 The talk of fools is offensive,
and their laughter is wantonly sinful.
14 Their cursing and swearing make one's
hair stand on end,
and their quarrels make others stop
their ears.
15 The strife of the proud leads to
bloodshed,
and their abuse is grievous to hear.

16 Whoever betrays secrets destroys
confidence,
and will never find a congenial friend.
17 Love your friend and keep faith with
him;
but if you betray his secrets, do not
follow after him.
18 For as a person destroys his enemy,
so you have destroyed the friendship of
your neighbor.
19 And as you allow a bird to escape from
your hand,
so you have let your neighbor go, and
will not catch him again.
20 Do not go after him, for he is too far off,
and has escaped like a gazelle from a
snare.
21 For a wound may be bandaged,
and there is reconciliation after abuse,
but whoever has betrayed secrets is
without hope.

a Other ancient authorities read *a trifle*

26.28–27.29: Sin and speech. 26.28–27.7: How speech often reveals a person's character. 28: Another numerical proverb (see 23.16–17; 26.5–6). *Warrior*, the Greek translator may have mistaken *warrior* for the Hebrew word for "wealthy man." 27.2: *Sin is wedged*, business dealings often involve corruption (cf. Prov 11.1; 20.10,14). 4–7: Good speech is a paramount virtue in the wisdom tradition. A series of three comparisons from daily life disclose its diagnostic quality. 8–10: The contrasting effects of honesty and sin. 11–15: The contrast in the speech of the godly person and the fool. 16–21: Betraying confidences or *secrets* often brings friendships to an

²² Whoever winks the eye plots mischief,
  and those who know him will keep their
    distance.
²³ In your presence his mouth is all
    sweetness,
  and he admires your words;
but later he will twist his speech
  and with your own words he will trip
    you up.
²⁴ I have hated many things, but him above
    all;
  even the Lord hates him.
²⁵ Whoever throws a stone straight up
    throws it on his own head,
  and a treacherous blow opens up many
    wounds.
²⁶ Whoever digs a pit will fall into it,
  and whoever sets a snare will be caught
    in it.
²⁷ If a person does evil, it will roll back
    upon him,
  and he will not know where it came
    from.
²⁸ Mockery and abuse issue from the
    proud,
  but vengeance lies in wait for them like
    a lion.
²⁹ Those who rejoice in the fall of the godly
    will be caught in a snare,
  and pain will consume them before
    their death.

³⁰ Anger and wrath, these also are
    abominations,
  yet a sinner holds on to them.

28 The vengeful will face the Lord's
    vengeance,
  for he keeps a strict account of[a] their sins.
² Forgive your neighbor the wrong he has
    done,
  and then your sins will be pardoned
    when you pray.

³ Does anyone harbor anger against
    another,
  and expect healing from the Lord?
⁴ If one has no mercy toward another like
    himself,
  can he then seek pardon for his own sins?
⁵ If a mere mortal harbors wrath,
  who will make an atoning sacrifice for
    his sins?
⁶ Remember the end of your life, and set
    enmity aside;
  remember corruption and death, and be
    true to the commandments.
⁷ Remember the commandments, and do
    not be angry with your neighbor;
  remember the covenant of the Most
    High, and overlook faults.

⁸ Refrain from strife, and your sins will be
    fewer;
  for the hot-tempered kindle strife,
⁹ and the sinner disrupts friendships
  and sows discord among those who are
    at peace.
¹⁰ In proportion to the fuel, so will the fire
    burn,
  and in proportion to the obstinacy, so
    will strife increase;[b]
in proportion to a person's strength will be
    his anger,
  and in proportion to his wealth he will
    increase his wrath.
¹¹ A hasty quarrel kindles a fire,
  and a hasty dispute sheds blood.
¹² If you blow on a spark, it will glow;
  if you spit on it, it will be put out;
  yet both come out of your mouth.

---

a   Other ancient authorities read *for he firmly
    establishes*
b   Other ancient authorities read *burn*

---

end (Prov 20.19; 25.9). **21:** *Without hope,* of reconciliation (cf. 22.22). **22–24:** The hatefulness of the hypocrite.
25–29: How people destroy themselves with their own evil devices; cf. Prov 26.27; Eccl 10.8.
    27.30–28.7: Forgiveness of sins. Two very important attributes of God are justice and mercy. **27.30–28.1:**
Those who demand strict justice from others will have to face God's own strict justice (cf. Deut 32.35–36). **2–5:**
Those who seek God's mercy must be willing to show mercy to others (cf. Lev 19.18). **6–7:** Remembering *death,
the commandments,* and God's *covenant* can provide encouragement to forgive others. Death is frequently mentioned as a motivation for proper conduct in Sirach; see 7.36; 8.7; 14.12; 18.24; 38.20.
    28.8–26: Destructive speech. The mouth can be the instrument for all kinds of bad speech, and so it must
be carefully controlled. **8–12:** The mouth can either ignite or extinguish anger and *strife* (cf. Prov 26.20–21).

¹³ Curse the gossips and the double-
tongued,
for they destroy the peace of many.
¹⁴ Slander[a] has shaken many,
and scattered them from nation to
nation;
it has destroyed strong cities,
and overturned the houses of the
great.
¹⁵ Slander[a] has driven virtuous women
from their homes,
and deprived them of the fruit of their
toil.
¹⁶ Those who pay heed to slander[b] will not
find rest,
nor will they settle down in peace.
¹⁷ The blow of a whip raises a welt,
but a blow of the tongue crushes the
bones.
¹⁸ Many have fallen by the edge of the
sword,
but not as many as have fallen because
of the tongue.
¹⁹ Happy is the one who is protected from
it,
who has not been exposed to its
anger,
who has not borne its yoke,
and has not been bound with its
fetters.
²⁰ For its yoke is a yoke of iron,
and its fetters are fetters of bronze;
²¹ its death is an evil death,
and Hades is preferable to it.
²² It has no power over the godly;
they will not be burned in its flame.
²³ Those who forsake the Lord will fall into
its power;
it will burn among them and will not be
put out.
It will be sent out against them like a lion;
like a leopard it will mangle them.
²⁴ᵃ As you fence in your property with
thorns,

²⁵ᵇ so make a door and a bolt for your
mouth.
²⁴ᵇ As you lock up your silver and gold,
²⁵ᵃ so make balances and scales for your
words.
²⁶ Take care not to err with your tongue,[c]
and fall victim to one lying in wait.

29 The merciful lend to their neighbors;
by holding out a helping hand they
keep the commandments.
² Lend to your neighbor in his time of
need;
repay your neighbor when a loan falls
due.
³ Keep your promise and be honest with
him,
and on every occasion you will find
what you need.
⁴ Many regard a loan as a windfall,
and cause trouble to those who help
them.
⁵ One kisses another's hands until he gets
a loan,
and is deferential in speaking of his
neighbor's money;
but at the time for repayment he delays,
and pays back with empty promises,
and finds fault with the time.
⁶ If he can pay, his creditor[d] will hardly get
back half,
and will regard that as a windfall.
If he cannot pay, the borrower[d] has robbed
the other of his money,
and he has needlessly made him an
enemy;

a Gk *A third tongue*
b Gk *it*
c Gk *with it*
d Gk *he*

13–16: *Slander* can and does ruin lives (51.2–6). **17–23:** A series of comparisons illustrates the destructive effects of speech. **17:** *Bones,* cf. Prov 25.15. **21:** *Hades* (Heb "Sheol") is the abode of the dead. **24–26:** Various images highlight the need to guard against destructive speech. One's *words* should be guarded as carefully as one's prized possessions.

29.1–20: *Money matters.* **1–7:** *Lend*ing. While loans could be given to fellow Jews without charging interest (Ex 22.25; Lev 25.35–37; Deut 15.7–11; 23.19–20; 24.10–13; Neh 5.10–11), charging interest was allowed when one loaned to non-Jews (Deut 23.20–21). Ben Sira encourages a willingness to make loans, but warns that there is

he will repay him with curses and
reproaches,
and instead of glory will repay him with
dishonor.
⁷ Many refuse to lend, not because of
meanness,
but from fearᵃ of being defrauded
needlessly.

⁸ Nevertheless, be patient with someone in
humble circumstances,
and do not keep him waiting for your
alms.
⁹ Help the poor for the commandment's sake,
and in their need do not send them
away empty-handed.
¹⁰ Lose your silver for the sake of a brother
or a friend,
and do not let it rust under a stone and
be lost.
¹¹ Lay up your treasure according to the
commandments of the Most High,
and it will profit you more than gold.
¹² Store up almsgiving in your treasury,
and it will rescue you from every disaster;
¹³ better than a stout shield and a sturdy
spear,
it will fight for you against the enemy.

¹⁴ A good person will be surety for his
neighbor,
but the one who has lost all sense of
shame will fail him.
¹⁵ Do not forget the kindness of your
guarantor,
for he has given his life for you.
¹⁶ A sinner wastes the property of his
guarantor,
¹⁷ and the ungrateful person abandons
his rescuer.
¹⁸ Being surety has ruined many who were
prosperous,
and has tossed them about like waves of
the sea;

it has driven the influential into exile,
and they have wandered among foreign
nations.
¹⁹ The sinner comes to grief through surety;
his pursuit of gain involves him in
lawsuits.
²⁰ Assist your neighbor to the best of your
ability,
but be careful not to fall yourself.

²¹ The necessities of life are water, bread,
and clothing,
and also a house to assure privacy.
²² Better is the life of the poor under their
own crude roof
than sumptuous food in the house of
others.
²³ Be content with little or much,
and you will hear no reproach for being
a guest.ᵇ
²⁴ It is a miserable life to go from house to
house;
as a guest you should not open your
mouth;
²⁵ you will play the host and provide drink
without being thanked,
and besides this you will hear rude
words like these:
²⁶ "Come here, stranger, prepare the table;
let me eat what you have there."
²⁷ "Be off, stranger, for an honored guest
is here;
my brother has come for a visit, and I
need the guest-room."
²⁸ It is hard for a sensible person to bear
scolding about lodgingᶜ and the insults
of the moneylender.

a   Other ancient authorities read *many refuse to
lend, therefore, because of such meanness; they are
afraid*
b   Lat: Gk *reproach from your family*; other ancient
authorities lack this line
c   Or *scolding from the household*

no guarantee that one will be repaid and so one must always be cautious (cf. 8.12–13). **8–13:** Alms. Giving *alms* is
in accord with the Torah (Deut 15.7) and will contribute to one's spiritual treasury (cf. 3.30–4.10). **14–20:** *Surety.*
Ben Sira's encouragement to provide *surety* or collateral for another person contrasts with the advice given
repeatedly in Prov 6.1–5; 11.15; 17.18; 20.16; 22.2; 27.13.

    29.21–28: Not depending on others. While the Torah directs caring for indigent relatives (Lev 25.35), receiv-
ing such care can become demeaning and even shameful. **21:** *Necessities,* cf. the longer list in 39.26. **25:** *You will
play the host,* that is, you will be pressed into service in the household.

CONCERNING CHILDREN[a]

30 He who loves his son will whip him often,

so that he may rejoice at the way he turns out.

[2] He who disciplines his son will profit by him,

and will boast of him among acquaintances.

[3] He who teaches his son will make his enemies envious,

and will glory in him among his friends.

[4] When the father dies he will not seem to be dead,

for he has left behind him one like himself,

[5] whom in his life he looked upon with joy

and at death, without grief.

[6] He has left behind him an avenger against his enemies,

and one to repay the kindness of his friends.

[7] Whoever spoils his son will bind up his wounds,

and will suffer heartache at every cry.

[8] An unbroken horse turns out stubborn,

and an unchecked son turns out headstrong.

[9] Pamper a child, and he will terrorize you;

play with him, and he will grieve you.

[10] Do not laugh with him, or you will have sorrow with him,

and in the end you will gnash your teeth.

[11] Give him no freedom in his youth,

and do not ignore his errors.

[12] Bow down his neck in his youth,[b]

and beat his sides while he is young,

or else he will become stubborn and disobey you,

and you will have sorrow of soul from him.[c]

[13] Discipline your son and make his yoke heavy,[d]

so that you may not be offended by his shamelessness.

[14] Better off poor, healthy, and fit than rich and afflicted in body.

[15] Health and fitness are better than any gold,

and a robust body than countless riches.

[16] There is no wealth better than health of body,

and no gladness above joy of heart.

[17] Death is better than a life of misery,

and eternal sleep[e] than chronic sickness.

CONCERNING FOODS[f]

[18] Good things poured out upon a mouth that is closed

are like offerings of food placed upon a grave.

[19] Of what use to an idol is a sacrifice?

For it can neither eat nor smell.

So is the one punished by the Lord;

[20] he sees with his eyes and groans

as a eunuch groans when embracing a girl.[g]

[21] Do not give yourself over to sorrow,

and do not distress yourself deliberately.

---

a   This heading is included in the Gk text.
b   Other ancient authorities lack this line and the preceding line
c   Other ancient authorities lack this line
d   Heb: Gk *take pains with him*
e   Other ancient authorities lack *eternal sleep*
f   This heading is included in the Gk text; other ancient authorities place the heading before verse 16
g   Other ancient authorities add *So is the person who does right under compulsion*

30.1–13: Fathers and sons. A father's discipline of his son will benefit the son and add to the father's good reputation before others. **1–6:** Ben Sira's harsh views on raising children (cf. 22.6) were not unique (cf. Prov 13.24; 19.18; 22.15; 23.13–14; 29.15,17). **4:** The child is the image of the father (cf. Gen 5.3; Tob 9.6). **6:** *Avenger*, one who can vindicate his father's honor (cf. Ps 127.5). **7–13:** Lack of *discipline* will lead to shame and sorrow for both parent and child (Deut 21.18–21).

30.14–25: Happiness. Three elements that lead to happiness are good health, good food, and a good disposition. **17:** *Death is better*, cf. Job 3.11,13,17; Eccl 4.2–3; 6.3,10,13; Tob 3.6,10,13. **18–20:** *Food placed on a grave* (Tob

²² A joyful heart is life itself,
and rejoicing lengthens one's life span.
²³ Indulge yourself[a] and take comfort,
and remove sorrow far from you,
for sorrow has destroyed many,
and no advantage ever comes from it.
²⁴ Jealousy and anger shorten life,
and anxiety brings on premature old
age.
²⁵ Those who are cheerful and merry at
table
will benefit from their food.

31

Wakefulness over wealth wastes away
one's flesh,
and anxiety about it drives away
sleep.
² Wakeful anxiety prevents slumber,
and a severe illness carries off sleep.[b]
³ The rich person toils to amass a fortune,
and when he rests he fills himself with
his dainties.
⁴ The poor person toils to make a meager
living,
and if ever he rests he becomes needy.

⁵ One who loves gold will not be justified;
one who pursues money will be led
astray[c] by it.
⁶ Many have come to ruin because of gold,
and their destruction has met them face
to face.
⁷ It is a stumbling block to those who are
avid for it,
and every fool will be taken captive by
it.
⁸ Blessed is the rich person who is found
blameless,
and who does not go after gold.
⁹ Who is he, that we may praise him?
For he has done wonders among his
people.

¹⁰ Who has been tested by it and been
found perfect?
Let it be for him a ground for
boasting.
Who has had the power to transgress and
did not transgress,
and to do evil and did not do it?
¹¹ His prosperity will be established,[d]
and the assembly will proclaim his acts
of charity.

¹² Are you seated at the table of the great?[e]
Do not be greedy at it,
and do not say, "How much food there
is here!"
¹³ Remember that a greedy eye is a bad
thing.
What has been created more greedy
than the eye?
Therefore it sheds tears for any reason.
¹⁴ Do not reach out your hand for
everything you see,
and do not crowd your neighbor[f] at the
dish.
¹⁵ Judge your neighbor's feelings by your
own,
and in every matter be thoughtful.
¹⁶ Eat what is set before you like a well
brought-up person,[g]
and do not chew greedily, or you will
give offense.
¹⁷ Be the first to stop, as befits good
manners,

a   Other ancient authorities read *Beguile yourself*
b   Other ancient authorities read *sleep carries off a*
severe illness
c   Heb Syr: Gk *pursues destruction will be filled*
d   Other ancient authorities add *because of this*
e   Heb Syr: Gk *at a great table*
f   Gk *him*
g   Heb: Gk *like a human being*

4.17) is useless. An *idol* (Deut 4.28; Isa 44.9–20) and a *eunuch* (20.4) are unable to enjoy the pleasures of life. **23:**
Indulge yourself, cf. Eccl 2.10; 11.9–10.

   31.1–11: Riches and righteousness. Wealth does not guarantee happiness or righteousness (cf. Prov 30.8–9;
Eccl 5.10). **8–11:** The beatitude acknowledges that it is possible (by exception) for a rich person to be righteous
(cf. 13.24; Prov 28.20). **8:** *Gold,* the Hebrew text has *mammon* (cf. Mt 6.24; Lk 16.9,13).

   31.12–32.13: Table manners and moderation. In the upper-class milieu supposed here, cautious public behavior could help in establishing and maintaining one's good reputation. The topic of proper behavior at banquets was a frequent theme in ancient Egyptian wisdom literature, including *Ptahhotep* and *Amenemope.* **12–18:**
The goal behind observing good table manners (cf. Prov 23.1–3) is to avoid drawing undue and unwelcome

and do not be insatiable, or you will
give offense.
¹⁸ If you are seated among many persons,
do not help yourselfᵃ before they do.

¹⁹ How ample a little is for a well-
disciplined person!
He does not breathe heavily when in
bed.
²⁰ Healthy sleep depends on moderate
eating;
he rises early, and feels fit.
The distress of sleeplessness and of
nausea
and colic are with the glutton.
²¹ If you are overstuffed with food,
get up to vomit, and you will have relief.
²² Listen to me, my child, and do not
disregard me,
and in the end you will appreciate my
words.
In everything you do be moderate,ᵇ
and no sickness will overtake you.
²³ People bless the one who is liberal with
food,
and their testimony to his generosity is
trustworthy.
²⁴ The city complains of the one who is
stingy with food,
and their testimony to his stinginess is
accurate.

²⁵ Do not try to prove your strength by
wine-drinking,
for wine has destroyed many.
²⁶ As the furnace tests the work of the
smith,ᶜ
so wine tests hearts when the insolent
quarrel.
²⁷ Wine is very life to human beings
if taken in moderation.
What is life to one who is without wine?
It has been created to make people
happy.
²⁸ Wine drunk at the proper time and in
moderation
is rejoicing of heart and gladness of
soul.

²⁹ Wine drunk to excess leads to bitterness
of spirit,
to quarrels and stumbling.
³⁰ Drunkenness increases the anger of a
fool to his own hurt,
reducing his strength and adding
wounds.
³¹ Do not reprove your neighbor at a
banquet of wine,
and do not despise him in his
merrymaking;
speak no word of reproach to him,
and do not distress him by making
demands of him.

32 If they make you master of the feast,
do not exalt yourself;
be among them as one of their
number.
Take care of them first and then sit down;
² when you have fulfilled all your duties,
take your place,
so that you may be merry along with
them
and receive a wreath for your excellent
leadership.

³ Speak, you who are older, for it is your
right,
but with accurate knowledge, and do
not interrupt the music.
⁴ Where there is entertainment, do not
pour out talk;
do not display your cleverness at the
wrong time.
⁵ A ruby seal in a setting of gold
is a concert of music at a banquet of
wine.
⁶ A seal of emerald in a rich setting of gold
is the melody of music with good wine.

⁷ Speak, you who are young, if you are
obliged to,
but no more than twice, and only if
asked.

ᵃ Gk *reach out your hand*
ᵇ Heb Syr: Gk *industrious*
ᶜ Heb: Gk *tests the hardening of steel by dipping*

attention to oneself. **19–31:** The bad effects of drinking too much *wine* (cf. Prov 20.1; 23.29–35; 31.4–5) are contrasted with the good effects of the moderate use of wine (cf. Ps 104.15). **32.1–13:** Advice to various participants
at a banquet. **1:** *Master of the feast*, the one who cares for the needs of those who are eating (2 Macc 2.27). **3–10:**

8 Be brief; say much in few words;
  be as one who knows and can still hold
    his tongue.
9 Among the great do not act as their equal;
  and when another is speaking, do not
    babble.

10 Lightning travels ahead of the thunder,
  and approval goes before one who is
    modest.
11 Leave in good time and do not be the last;
  go home quickly and do not linger.
12 Amuse yourself there to your heart's
    content,
  but do not sin through proud speech.
13 But above all bless your Maker,
  who fills you with his good gifts.

14 The one who seeks God[a] will accept his
    discipline,
  and those who rise early to seek him[b]
    will find favor.
15 The one who seeks the law will be filled
    with it,
  but the hypocrite will stumble at it.
16 Those who fear the Lord will form true
    judgments,
  and they will kindle righteous deeds
    like a light.
17 The sinner will shun reproof,
  and will find a decision according to his
    liking.

18 A sensible person will not overlook a
    thoughtful suggestion;
  an insolent[c] and proud person will not
    be deterred by fear.[d]
19 Do nothing without deliberation,
  but when you have acted, do not regret
    it.
20 Do not go on a path full of hazards,
  and do not stumble at an obstacle
    twice.[e]

21 Do not be overconfident on a smooth[f]
    road,
22 and give good heed to your paths.[g]
23 Guard[h] yourself in every act,
  for this is the keeping of the
    commandments.

24 The one who keeps the law preserves
    himself,[i]
  and the one who trusts the Lord will
    not suffer loss.

33 No evil will befall the one who fears
    the Lord,
  but in trials such a one will be rescued
    again and again.
2 The wise will not hate the law,
  but the one who is hypocritical about it
    is like a boat in a storm.
3 The sensible person will trust in the law;
  for such a one the law is as dependable
    as a divine oracle.

4 Prepare what to say, and then you will be
    listened to;
  draw upon your training, and give your
    answer.
5 The heart of a fool is like a cart wheel,
  and his thoughts like a turning axle.
6 A mocking friend is like a stallion
  that neighs no matter who the rider is.

a Heb: Gk *who fears the Lord*
b Other ancient authorities lack *to seek him*
c Heb: Gk *alien*
d Meaning of Gk uncertain. Other ancient authorities
  add *and after acting, with him, without deliberation*
e Heb: Gk *stumble on stony ground*
f Or *an unexplored*
g Heb Syr: Gk *and beware of your children*
h Heb Syr: Gk *Trust*
i Heb: Gk *who believes the law heeds the
  commandments*

Directions to *older* persons and the *young.* **11–13:** Advice meant for all. **13:** *Bless your Maker,* by saying a prayer of
thanksgiving after the meal.

   32.14–33.6: The law, fear of the Lord, and wisdom. Ben Sira's ideal sage combines these three elements
(which are the book's central themes), and so differs sharply from fools and sinners. **14:** *Discipline,* a frequent
topic in the book; see 1.27; 4.17; 6.18,22; 21.19,21; 26.14; 42.5,8; 50.27). *Rise early,* for prayer (cf. 39.5). **15:** *The law,*
here and elsewhere in the passage the reference is to the law of Moses (the Torah). **17:** *Decision,* an interpretation of the Torah. **33.1:** Cf. Wis 10.1–21. **2:** Hebrew, "He who hates the law is not wise, and is tossed about like a
boat in a storm." **3:** *Divine oracle,* the Urim and Thummim (45.10; Ex 28.30; Num 27.21; 1 Sam 14.41–42).

⁷Why is one day more important than
    another,
  when all the daylight in the year is from
    the sun?
⁸By the Lord's wisdom they were
    distinguished,
  and he appointed the different seasons
    and festivals.
⁹Some days he exalted and hallowed,
  and some he made ordinary days.
¹⁰All human beings come from the ground,
  and humankindᵃ was created out of the
    dust.
¹¹In the fullness of his knowledge the Lord
    distinguished them
  and appointed their different ways.
¹²Some he blessed and exalted,
  and some he made holy and brought
    near to himself;
but some he cursed and brought low,
  and turned them out of their place.
¹³Like clay in the hand of the potter,
  to be molded as he pleases,
so all are in the hand of their Maker,
  to be given whatever he decides.

¹⁴Good is the opposite of evil,
  and life the opposite of death;
so the sinner is the opposite of the
    godly.
¹⁵Look at all the works of the Most High;
  they come in pairs, one the opposite of
    the other.

¹⁶Now I was the last to keep vigil;
  I was like a gleaner following the grape-
    pickers;

¹⁷by the blessing of the Lord I arrived first,
  and like a grape-picker I filled my wine
    press.
¹⁸Consider that I have not labored for
    myself alone,
  but for all who seek instruction.
¹⁹Hear me, you who are great among the
    people,
  and you leaders of the congregation,
    pay heed!

²⁰To son or wife, to brother or friend,
  do not give power over yourself, as long
    as you live;
and do not give your property to another,
  in case you change your mind and must
    ask for it.
²¹While you are still alive and have breath
    in you,
  do not let anyone take your place.
²²For it is better that your children should
    ask from you
  than that you should look to the hand
    of your children.
²³Excel in all that you do;
  bring no stain upon your honor.
²⁴At the time when you end the days of
    your life,
  in the hour of death, distribute your
    inheritance.

²⁵Fodder and a stick and burdens for a
    donkey;
  bread and discipline and work for a
    slave.

ᵃ Heb: Gk *Adam*

33.7–15: **The pairs.** God's plan for creation is based on opposites. Nevertheless, since the absolute sovereignty of God is assumed, this is not a full-scale dualism. Ben Sira may be influenced by Stoic philosophy. **7–9:**
Some days are holy days and others are *ordinary* (Gen 1.14; 2.3; Deut 16.1–15). **10–13:** A similar dualism occurs
among humans. Although all are made from *dust* (Gen 3.19), some are *blessed* and some are *cursed*; perhaps
referring to the different status of Israel (Gen 12.2–3; Ex 19.5) and the Canaanites (Gen 9.25–27; 12.6–7). **13:** *Clay*,
cf. Isa 29.16; 45.9; 64.8; Jer 18.1–12. **14–15:** The dualism of the pairs is modified, since the *Most High* remains
sovereign over all (Isa 45.7).
   33.16–19: **Ben Sira's vocation.** For other autobiographical notices, see 24.30–34; 34.9–13; 39.12–13; 50.27;
51.13–30. **16–17:** *A gleaner* collects the leftovers during the harvest. By study and hard work Ben Sira became a
grape-picker, that is, a wisdom teacher. **18–19:** *For all*, cf. 24.34.
   33.20–33: **Master of the household.** The advice given here is intended for an adult male with a family, financial resources, and slaves. **20–24:** Preserve your financial independence and do not distribute your property
until the hour of death. **25–33:** Human slavery was a socially and religiously sanctioned institution, and integral
to the economy, in Ben Sira's world (cf. 7.20–21). His harsh advice is tempered by recognizing the self-interest

26 Set your slave to work, and you will find
rest;
leave his hands idle, and he will seek
liberty.
27 Yoke and thong will bow the neck,
and for a wicked slave there are racks
and tortures.
28 Put him to work, in order that he may
not be idle,
29 for idleness teaches much evil.
30 Set him to work, as is fitting for him,
and if he does not obey, make his fetters
heavy.
Do not be overbearing toward anyone,
and do nothing unjust.

31 If you have but one slave, treat him like
yourself,
because you have bought him with
blood.
If you have but one slave, treat him like a
brother,
for you will need him as you need your
life.
32 If you ill-treat him, and he leaves you
and runs away,
33 which way will you go to seek him?

34 The senseless have vain and false
hopes,
and dreams give wings to fools.
2 As one who catches at a shadow and
pursues the wind,
so is anyone who believes in[a] dreams.
3 What is seen in dreams is but a
reflection,
the likeness of a face looking at itself.
4 From an unclean thing what can be
clean?
And from something false what can be
true?

5 Divinations and omens and dreams are
unreal,
and like a woman in labor, the mind has
fantasies.
6 Unless they are sent by intervention from
the Most High,
pay no attention to them.
7 For dreams have deceived many,
and those who put their hope in them
have perished.
8 Without such deceptions the law will be
fulfilled,
and wisdom is complete in the mouth
of the faithful.

9 An educated[b] person knows many
things,
and one with much experience knows
what he is talking about.
10 An inexperienced person knows few
things,
11 but he that has traveled acquires much
cleverness.
12 I have seen many things in my travels,
and I understand more than I can
express.
13 I have often been in danger of death,
but have escaped because of these
experiences.

14 The spirit of those who fear the Lord will
live,
15 for their hope is in him who saves
them.
16 Those who fear the Lord will not be
timid,
or play the coward, for he is their
hope.

a   Syr: Gk *pays heed to*
b   Other ancient authorities read *A traveled*

of someone who owns only *one slave* (33.31–33). **30:** *Do nothing unjust,* that is, act according to the biblical laws
pertaining to slaves (Ex 21.2–6,20–21,26–27; Lev 25.46; Deut 15.12–18). **32:** *Runs away,* Deut 23.15–16.

34.1–8: A critique of dreams. It is better to fulfill the law and to practice perfect wisdom than to rely on
dreams for wisdom and direction. Ben Sira may be criticizing the Jewish apocalyptic movement, which relied
extensively on dreams and visions for divine guidance (see the book of Daniel). **1:** *Dreams give wings to fools,* cf.
Deut 13.2–5; 18.9–14; Eccl 5.7; Jer 29.8. **2:** *Pursues the wind,* cf. Eccl 1.14; Hos 12.1. **3:** *Reflection,* dreams are often
merely mirrors of one's own concerns. **4:** *Unclean . . . clean,* cf. Job 14.4. **6:** *From the Most High,* an exception is
made for dreams that definitely come from God (as in Gen 37.5–10; Judg 7.13–15; Dan 2).

34.9–13: The value of experience through travel. See 39.4; 51.13.

34.14–20: Fear of the Lord. Blessings accompany *those who fear the Lord,* which is the proper human re-

¹⁷ Happy is the soul that fears the Lord!
  ¹⁸ To whom does he look? And who is
    his support?
¹⁹ The eyes of the Lord are on those who
    love him,
  a mighty shield and strong support,
a shelter from scorching wind and a shade
    from noonday sun,
  a guard against stumbling and a help
    against falling.
²⁰ He lifts up the soul and makes the eyes
    sparkle;
  he gives health and life and blessing.

²¹ If one sacrifices ill-gotten goods, the
    offering is blemished;^a
  ²² the gifts^b of the lawless are not
    acceptable.
²³ The Most High is not pleased with the
    offerings of the ungodly,
  nor for a multitude of sacrifices does he
    forgive sins.
²⁴ Like one who kills a son before his
    father's eyes
  is the person who offers a sacrifice from
    the property of the poor.
²⁵ The bread of the needy is the life of the
    poor;
  whoever deprives them of it is a
    murderer.
²⁶ To take away a neighbor's living is to
    commit murder;
  ²⁷ to deprive an employee of wages is to
    shed blood.

²⁸ When one builds and another tears
    down,
  what do they gain but hard work?

²⁹ When one prays and another curses,
  to whose voice will the Lord listen?
³⁰ If one washes after touching a corpse,
    and touches it again,
  what has been gained by washing?
³¹ So if one fasts for his sins,
  and goes again and does the same
    things,
who will listen to his prayer?
  And what has he gained by humbling
    himself?

35 The one who keeps the law makes
    many offerings;
  ² one who heeds the commandments
    makes an offering of well-being.
³ The one who returns a kindness offers
    choice flour,
  ⁴ and one who gives alms sacrifices a
    thank offering.
⁵ To keep from wickedness is pleasing to
    the Lord,
  and to forsake unrighteousness is an
    atonement.
⁶ Do not appear before the Lord empty-
    handed,
  ⁷ for all that you offer is in fulfillment of
    the commandment.
⁸ The offering of the righteous enriches the
    altar,
  and its pleasing odor rises before the
    Most High.
⁹ The sacrifice of the righteous is
    acceptable,
  and it will never be forgotten.

---

^a Other ancient authorities read *is made in mockery*
^b Other ancient authorities read *mockeries*

sponse to true wisdom (cf. 1.11–30; 2.1–18). **19:** *The eyes of the Lord,* cf. Ps 34.15. *Shelter,* cf. Pss 61.2–4; 91.1–4; 121.5–6; Isa 25.4.

34.21–31: True religion and social justice. Religious practices must be animated by and accomplished with a concern for social justice (cf. 1 Sam 15.22; Ps 51.16–19; Prov 15.8; 21.3; Hos 6.6; Amos 5.21–24). **21:** *Blemished,* cf. Lev 22.18–25. **26–27:** *Deprive an employee,* cf. Lev 19.13. **28:** *One builds and another tears down,* both the poor and the rich lose. **29:** *To whose voice,* cf. 4.5–6; 35.17–21. **30:** *Touching a corpse* makes a person ritually impure (Num 19.11). **31:** *Fasts for his sins,* most likely a reference to the Day of Atonement (Lev 23.27–32).

35.1–13: Good deeds and sacrifices. While Ben Sira was an enthusiastic supporter of the Jerusalem Temple and its priesthood (cf. 50.1–24), he also insisted that sacrifices be offered in the proper spirit and be accompanied by ethical obedience to the Torah (cf. Isa 1.11–18; Mic 6.6–8; Tob 1.6–8). **1–5:** Observing the *commandments,* performing kind actions, and avoiding sin are equivalent to offering sacrifices to God (cf. Ps 51.17; 1QS 8.1–4). **6–13:** But such observances are neither in opposition to the offering of material sacrifices nor substitutes for them. Here Ben Sira offers his endorsement of the sacrificial system carried out at the Jerusalem Temple.

¹⁰ Be generous when you worship the Lord,
    and do not stint the first fruits of your
      hands.
¹¹ With every gift show a cheerful face,
    and dedicate your tithe with gladness.
¹² Give to the Most High as he has given to
      you,
    and as generously as you can afford.
¹³ For the Lord is the one who repays,
    and he will repay you sevenfold.
¹⁴ Do not offer him a bribe, for he will not
      accept it;
    ¹⁵ and do not rely on a dishonest
        sacrifice;
for the Lord is the judge,
    and with him there is no partiality.
¹⁶ He will not show partiality to the poor;
    but he will listen to the prayer of one
      who is wronged.
¹⁷ He will not ignore the supplication of the
      orphan,
    or the widow when she pours out her
        complaint.
¹⁸ Do not the tears of the widow run down
      her cheek
    ¹⁹ as she cries out against the one who
        causes them to fall?
²⁰ The one whose service is pleasing to the
      Lord will be accepted,
    and his prayer will reach to the clouds.
²¹ The prayer of the humble pierces the
      clouds,
    and it will not rest until it reaches its
        goal;
it will not desist until the Most High
      responds
    ²² and does justice for the righteous, and
        executes judgment.
Indeed, the Lord will not delay,
    and like a warrior[a] will not be
        patient

until he crushes the loins of the
      unmerciful
    ²³ and repays vengeance on the nations;
until he destroys the multitude of the
      insolent,
    and breaks the scepters of the
        unrighteous;
²⁴ until he repays mortals according to
      their deeds,
    and the works of all according to their
        thoughts;
²⁵ until he judges the case of his people
    and makes them rejoice in his mercy.
²⁶ His mercy is as welcome in time of
      distress
    as clouds of rain in time of drought.

36 Have mercy upon us, O God[b] of all,
    ² and put all the nations in fear of you.
³ Lift up your hand against foreign nations
    and let them see your might.
⁴ As you have used us to show your
      holiness to them,
    so use them to show your glory to us.
⁵ Then they will know,[c] as we have known,
    that there is no God but you, O Lord.
⁶ Give new signs, and work other
      wonders;
    ⁷ make your hand and right arm
        glorious.
⁸ Rouse your anger and pour out your
      wrath;
    ⁹ destroy the adversary and wipe out the
        enemy.
¹⁰ Hasten the day, and remember the
      appointed time,[d]

a   Heb: Gk *and with them*
b   Heb: Gk *O Master, the God*
c   Heb: Gk *And let them know you*
d   Other ancient authorities read *remember your oath*

35.14–26: God's justice. As a just judge God will not be bribed by *dishonest sacrifice.* God will answer the prayers of those most in need. **15:** *No partiality,* cf. Deut 10.17; Job 34.19; Wis 6.7. **17:** *Orphan . . . widow,* God will defend the most vulnerable in society (cf. 4.9–10; Ps 68.5; Prov 23.10–11). **22–26:** This passage prepares for the prayer in 36.1–22. It may allude to political turmoil in Ben Sira's own time. **25:** *His people,* this suggests that the oppressors threatened here were foreign enemies of Israel, perhaps the Seleucids who had recently replaced the Ptolemies as rulers over the land of Israel.

36.1–22: Prayers for God's people. 1–12: A plea for deliverance from Israel's enemies, perhaps from the Seleucid rulers after 198 BCE (cf. Ps 44.1–8; 2 Macc 1.24–29). **1:** *God of all,* cf. 36.5,12; 50.22. **4:** As God manifested *holiness* in rescuing Israel from exile (Ezek 20.41; 28.25), so may God display *glory* by subduing its enemies now. **6–7:** *Signs . . . wonders . . . hand . . . right arm,* allusions to the Exodus from Egypt (Ex 11.9–10; 15.6; Deut 4.34; 7.19;

and let people recount your mighty
deeds.
[11] Let survivors be consumed in the fiery
wrath,
and may those who harm your people
meet destruction.
[12] Crush the heads of hostile rulers
who say, "There is no one but
ourselves."
[13] Gather all the tribes of Jacob,[a]
[16] and give them their inheritance, as at
the beginning.
[17] Have mercy, O Lord, on the people called
by your name,
on Israel, whom you have named[b] your
firstborn,
[18] Have pity on the city of your sanctuary,[c]
Jerusalem, the place of your dwelling.[d]
[19] Fill Zion with your majesty,[e]
and your temple[f] with your glory.
[20] Bear witness to those whom you created
in the beginning,
and fulfill the prophecies spoken in
your name.
[21] Reward those who wait for you
and let your prophets be found
trustworthy.
[22] Hear, O Lord, the prayer of your
servants, according to your goodwill
toward[g] your people,
and all who are on the earth will know
that you are the Lord, the God of the ages.

[23] The stomach will take any food,
yet one food is better than another.
[24] As the palate tastes the kinds of game,
so an intelligent mind detects false
words.
[25] A perverse mind will cause grief,
but a person with experience will pay
him back.
[26] A woman will accept any man as a
husband,

but one girl is preferable to another.
[27] A woman's beauty lights up a man's
face,
and there is nothing he desires more.
[28] If kindness and humility mark her
speech,
her husband is more fortunate than
other men.
[29] He who acquires a wife gets his best
possession,[h]
a helper fit for him and a pillar of
support.[i]
[30] Where there is no fence, the property
will be plundered;
and where there is no wife, a man
will become a fugitive and a
wanderer.[j]
[31] For who will trust a nimble robber
that skips from city to city?
So who will trust a man that has no nest,
but lodges wherever night overtakes
him?

37 Every friend says, "I too am a friend";
but some friends are friends only in
name.
[2] Is it not a sorrow like that for death itself
when a dear friend turns into an
enemy?

a   Owing to a dislocation in the Greek Mss of Sirach,
    the verse numbers 14 and 15 are not used in
    chapter 36, though no text is missing.
b   Other ancient authorities read *you have likened to*
c   Or *on your holy city*
d   Heb: Gk *your rest*
e   Heb Syr: Gk *the celebration of your wondrous deeds*
f   Heb Syr: Gk Lat *people*
g   Heb and two Gk witnesses: Lat and most Gk
    witnesses read *according to the blessing of Aaron for*
h   Heb: Gk *enters upon a possession*
i   Heb: Gk *rest*
j   Heb: Gk *wander about and sigh*

Neh 9.10). **10:** *The appointed time*, when Israel will be freed from its foreign oppressors. **13–22:** A prayer for the
ingathering of Israel and God's blessing on the Jerusalem Temple. **17:** *Called by your name*, see Deut 28.10; Jer
14.9. *Firstborn*, see Ex 4.22. **18:** *Your dwelling*, cf. Pss 26.8; 63.2; 102.16; 132.13–14.

 36.23–31: On choosing a wife. **23–25:** On discernment in general.

 26–31: On choosing a wife in particular (cf. 26.13–18). **26:** *Accept*, marriages were often arranged by the fathers (cf. 7.25). **29:** In a patriarchal family, the wife was regarded as the husband's *possession*. *A helper fit for him*,
see Gen 2.18. **30:** *A fugitive and a wanderer*, like Cain (Gen 4.12,14).

 37.1–15: On choosing a friend and a counselor. **1–7:** More warnings against false and fair-weather friends (cf.

³O inclination to evil, why were you
   formed
   to cover the land with deceit?
⁴Some companions rejoice in the
   happiness of a friend,
   but in time of trouble they are against
   him.
⁵Some companions help a friend for their
   stomachs' sake,
   yet in battle they will carry his shield.
⁶Do not forget a friend during the battle,ᵃ
   and do not be unmindful of him when
   you distribute your spoils.ᵇ

⁷All counselors praise the counsel they give,
   but some give counsel in their own
   interest.
⁸Be wary of a counselor,
   and learn first what is his interest,
   for he will take thought for himself.
He may cast the lot against you
   ⁹and tell you, "Your way is good,"
   and then stand aside to see what
   happens to you.
¹⁰Do not consult the one who regards you
   with suspicion;
   hide your intentions from those who
   are jealous of you.
¹¹Do not consult with a woman about her
   rival
   or with a coward about war,
with a merchant about business
   or with a buyer about selling,
with a miser about generosityᶜ
   or with the merciless about kindness,
with an idler about any work
   or with a seasonal laborer about
   completing his work,
with a lazy servant about a big task—
   pay no attention to any advice they give.
¹²But associate with a godly person
   whom you know to be a keeper of the
   commandments,
who is like-minded with yourself,
   and who will grieve with you if you fail.

¹³And heedᵈ the counsel of your own
   heart,
   for no one is more faithful to you than
   it is.
¹⁴For our own mind sometimes keeps us
   better informed
   than seven sentinels sitting high on a
   watchtower.
¹⁵But above all pray to the Most High
   that he may direct your way in truth.

¹⁶Discussion is the beginning of every
   work,
   and counsel precedes every
   undertaking.
¹⁷The mind is the root of all conduct;
   ¹⁸it sprouts four branches,ᵉ
good and evil, life and death;
   and it is the tongue that continually
   rules them.
¹⁹Some people may be clever enough to
   teach many,
   and yet be useless to themselves.
²⁰A skillful speaker may be hated;
   he will be destitute of all food,
²¹for the Lord has withheld the gift of
   charm,
   since he is lacking in all wisdom.
²²If a person is wise to his own
   advantage,
   the fruits of his good sense will be
   praiseworthy.ᶠ
²³A wise person instructs his own people,
   and the fruits of his good sense will
   endure.
²⁴A wise person will have praise heaped
   upon him,

ᵃ Heb: Gk *in your heart*
ᵇ Heb: Gk *him in your wealth*
ᶜ Heb: Gk *gratitude*
ᵈ Heb: Gk *establish*
ᵉ Heb: Gk *As a clue to changes of heart four kinds of
   destiny appear*
ᶠ Other ancient witnesses read *trustworthy*

6.5–17; 9.10–16; 19.13–17; 22.19–26; 27.16–21). **3:** *O inclination to evil,* the evil impulse (Heb *yetser*) is the origin of
sins and offenses against friendships (cf. 15.14n). **5:** *Carry his shield,* defend from attack (cf. Ps 35.2). **8–11:** By finding out a prospective counselor's own agenda, one can avoid relying on inappropriate counselors. **11:** *Her rival,*
perhaps another wife (26.6). **12–15:** The best sources of good counsel are *those who keep the commandments,*
one's own heart, and *the Most High.*

   37.16–26: Wisdom and action. 16–18: Wise action demands consultation, thought, and articulation. **19–26:**

and all who see him will call him happy.

²⁵ The days of a person's life are numbered,
 but the days of Israel are without
  number.

²⁶ One who is wise among his people will
 inherit honor,ᵃ
 and his name will live forever.

²⁷ My child, test yourself while you live;
 see what is bad for you and do not give
  in to it.

²⁸ For not everything is good for
 everyone,
 and no one enjoys everything.

²⁹ Do not be greedy for every delicacy,
 and do not eat without restraint;

³⁰ for overeating brings sickness,
 and gluttony leads to nausea.

³¹ Many have died of gluttony,
 but the one who guards against it
  prolongs his life.

38

Honor physicians for their services,
for the Lord created them;

² for their gift of healing comes from the
 Most High,
 and they are rewarded by the king.

³ The skill of physicians makes them
 distinguished,
 and in the presence of the great they are
  admired.

⁴ The Lord created medicines out of the
 earth,
 and the sensible will not despise them.

⁵ Was not water made sweet with a tree
 in order that itsᵇ power might be
  known?

⁶ And he gave skill to human beings
 that heᶜ might be glorified in his
  marvelous works.

⁷ By them the physicianᵈ heals and takes
 away pain;

⁸ the pharmacist makes a mixture from
 them.

God'sᵉ works will never be finished;
 and from him healthᶠ spreads over all
  the earth.

⁹ My child, when you are ill, do not delay,
 but pray to the Lord, and he will heal
  you.

¹⁰ Give up your faults and direct your
 hands rightly,
 and cleanse your heart from all sin.

¹¹ Offer a sweet-smelling sacrifice, and a
 memorial portion of choice flour,
 and pour oil on your offering, as much
  as you can afford.ᵍ

¹² Then give the physician his place, for the
 Lord created him;
 do not let him leave you, for you need
  him.

¹³ There may come a time when recovery
 lies in the hands of physicians,ʰ

¹⁴ for they too pray to the Lord
that he grant them success in
 diagnosisⁱ
 and in healing, for the sake of
  preserving life.

¹⁵ He who sins against his Maker,
 will be defiant toward the physician.ʲ

¹⁶ My child, let your tears fall for the
 dead,
 and as one in great pain begin the
  lament.

ᵃ Other ancient authorities read *confidence*
ᵇ Or *his*
ᶜ Or *they*
ᵈ Heb: Gk *he*
ᵉ Gk *His*
ᶠ Or *peace*
ᵍ Heb: Lat lacks *as much as you can afford*; Meaning
 of Gk uncertain
ʰ Gk *in their hands*
ⁱ Heb: Gk *rest*
ʲ Heb: Gk *may he fall into the hands of the physician*

There are *clever* persons who lack wisdom, while truly wise persons benefit themselves and their *people*. **25:** *The days of Israel are without number,* 2 Macc 14.15.

37.27–31: Moderation. Cf. 31.12–31. **28:** *Not everything is good for everyone,* Num 11.18–20.

38.1–15: Sickness and physicians. The wise person is respectful toward and cooperative with doctors, and regards medicines as gifts from God. **5:** *Water made sweet,* see Ex 15.23–25. **9–15:** The assumption is that illness is the effect of sin (Deut 28.21–22,27–28; Prov 3.7–8; Job 5.17–18), and so the sick must engage in prayer, repentance, and *sacrifice.*

Lay out the body with due ceremony,
and do not neglect the burial.
[17] Let your weeping be bitter and your
wailing fervent;
make your mourning worthy of the
departed,
for one day, or two, to avoid criticism;
then be comforted for your grief.
[18] For grief may result in death,
and a sorrowful heart saps one's
strength.
[19] When a person is taken away, sorrow is
over;
but the life of the poor weighs down the
heart.
[20] Do not give your heart to grief;
drive it away, and remember your own
end.
[21] Do not forget, there is no coming back;
you do the dead[a] no good, and you
injure yourself.
[22] Remember his[b] fate, for yours is like it;
yesterday it was his,[c] and today it is
yours.
[23] When the dead is at rest, let his
remembrance rest too,
and be comforted for him when his
spirit has departed.

[24] The wisdom of the scribe depends on
the opportunity of leisure;
only the one who has little business can
become wise.
[25] How can one become wise who handles
the plow,
and who glories in the shaft of a goad,
who drives oxen and is occupied with their
work,
and whose talk is about bulls?
[26] He sets his heart on plowing
furrows,
and he is careful about fodder for the
heifers.

[27] So it is with every artisan and master
artisan
who labors by night as well as by day;
those who cut the signets of seals,
each is diligent in making a great
variety;
they set their heart on painting a lifelike
image,
and they are careful to finish their
work.
[28] So it is with the smith, sitting by the
anvil,
intent on his iron-work;
the breath of the fire melts his flesh,
and he struggles with the heat of the
furnace;
the sound of the hammer deafens his
ears,[d]
and his eyes are on the pattern of the
object.
He sets his heart on finishing his
handiwork,
and he is careful to complete its
decoration.
[29] So it is with the potter sitting at his
work
and turning the wheel with his feet;
he is always deeply concerned over his
products,
and he produces them in quantity.
[30] He molds the clay with his arm
and makes it pliable with his feet;
he sets his heart to finish the glazing,
and he takes care in firing[e] the kiln.

[31] All these rely on their hands,
and all are skillful in their own work.

a   Gk *him*
b   Heb: Gk *my*
c   Heb: Gk *mine*
d   Cn: Gk *renews his ear*
e   Cn: Gk *cleaning*

38.16–23: Mourning. Grief over the death of a loved one (cf. 22.11–12; Tob 1.17–18; 4.3–4; 6.15; 12.12; 14.12–13) should be intense but circumscribed, lest the mourner suffer harm. **23:** *The dead is at rest,* while there is no explicit denial of life after death, there is no affirmation of it either.

38.24–34: Tradesmen and the scribe. Scribes trained at Ben Sira's school (51.23–28) learned not only to copy and produce legal documents but were also expected to become intellectuals, public figures, and leaders (cf. 39.1–11). **24:** *Leisure,* the scribe has time and circumstances to study, whereas farmers, artisans, smiths, and potters (38.25–30) are too occupied with working on their trades to do so. The contrast between the scribe and other occupations is also a topic in several Egyptian wisdom compositions, including the *Satire on the Trades*

³² Without them no city can be inhabited,
  and wherever they live, they will not go
    hungry.ᵃ
Yet they are not sought out for the council
  of the people,ᵇ
³³ nor do they attain eminence in the
    public assembly.
They do not sit in the judge's seat,
  nor do they understand the decisions of
    the courts;
they cannot expound discipline or
    judgment,
  and they are not found among the
    rulers.ᶜ
³⁴ But they maintain the fabric of the world,
  and their concern is forᵈ the exercise of
    their trade.

How different the one who devotes
    himself
  to the study of the law of the Most
    High!

39 He seeks out the wisdom of all the
    ancients,
  and is concerned with prophecies;
² he preserves the sayings of the famous
  and penetrates the subtleties of
    parables;
³ he seeks out the hidden meanings of
    proverbs
  and is at home with the obscurities of
    parables.
⁴ He serves among the great
  and appears before rulers;
he travels in foreign lands
  and learns what is good and evil in the
    human lot.
⁵ He sets his heart to rise early
  to seek the Lord who made him,
  and to petition the Most High;
he opens his mouth in prayer
  and asks pardon for his sins.

⁶ If the great Lord is willing,
  he will be filled with the spirit of
    understanding;
he will pour forth words of wisdom of his
    own
  and give thanks to the Lord in prayer.
⁷ The Lordᵉ will direct his counsel and
    knowledge,
  as he meditates on his mysteries.
⁸ He will show the wisdom of what he has
    learned,
  and will glory in the law of the Lord's
    covenant.
⁹ Many will praise his understanding;
  it will never be blotted out.
His memory will not disappear,
  and his name will live through all
    generations.
¹⁰ Nations will speak of his wisdom,
  and the congregation will proclaim his
    praise.
¹¹ If he lives long, he will leave a name
    greater than a thousand,
  and if he goes to rest, it is enoughᶠ for
    him.

¹² I have more on my mind to express;
  I am full like the full moon.
¹³ Listen to me, my faithful children, and
    blossom
  like a rose growing by a stream of water.
¹⁴ Send out fragrance like incense,
  and put forth blossoms like a lily.
Scatter the fragrance, and sing a hymn of
    praise;
  bless the Lord for all his works.

a Syr: Gk *and people can neither live nor walk there*
b Most ancient authorities lack this line
c Cn: Gk *among parables*
d Syr: Gk *prayer is in*
e Gk *He himself*
f Cn: Meaning of Gk uncertain

and the *Instruction of Kheti.* **32–33:** *Without them no city can be inhabited,* Ben Sira acknowledges the positive contributions of tradesmen to society. But they are not present in the *public assembly,* the *courts,* or *among the rulers.* **34:** *Law,* the Torah was an essential component in Ben Sira's curriculum (cf. Ezra 7.6,10).

39.1–11: Scribal education. The scribes dealt with the law, *wisdom,* and *prophecies* (see the Prologue for the threefold division of the Hebrew scriptures). **2–3:** Cf. Prov 1.5–6; 25.1. **4:** *Travels,* cf. 34.11; 51.13. **5:** *Prayer,* since God is the source of true wisdom (1.1–10), prayer must be part of the scribe's formation. **9:** *His memory* and *name will live,* cf. 37.26; 44.10–15. **11:** *Greater than a thousand,* cf. Job 9.3; 33.23; Eccl 7.28.

39.12–35: God's creation and evil. God can use everything, both *good* and *bad,* to carry out the divine pur-

¹⁵ Ascribe majesty to his name
  and give thanks to him with praise,
with songs on your lips, and with harps;
  this is what you shall say in
    thanksgiving:

¹⁶ "All the works of the Lord are very good,
  and whatever he commands will be
    done at the appointed time.
¹⁷ No one can say, 'What is this?' or 'Why is
    that?'—
  for at the appointed time all such
    questions will be answered.
At his word the waters stood in a heap,
  and the reservoirs of water at the word
    of his mouth.
¹⁸ When he commands, his every purpose
    is fulfilled,
  and none can limit his saving power.
¹⁹ The works of all are before him,
  and nothing can be hidden from his
    eyes.
²⁰ From the beginning to the end of time
  he can see everything,
  and nothing is too marvelous for him.
²¹ No one can say, 'What is this?' or 'Why is
    that?'—
  for everything has been created for its
    own purpose.

²² "His blessing covers the dry land like a
    river,
  and drenches it like a flood.
²³ But his wrath drives out the nations,
  as when he turned a watered land into
    salt.
²⁴ To the faithful his ways are straight,
  but full of pitfalls for the wicked.
²⁵ From the beginning good things were
    created for the good,
  but for sinners good things and bad.^a
²⁶ The basic necessities of human life
  are water and fire and iron and salt
and wheat flour and milk and honey,
  the blood of the grape and oil and
    clothing.

²⁷ All these are good for the godly,
  but for sinners they turn into evils.

²⁸ "There are winds created for
    vengeance,
  and in their anger they can dislodge
    mountains;^b
on the day of reckoning they will pour out
    their strength
  and calm the anger of their Maker.
²⁹ Fire and hail and famine and
    pestilence,
  all these have been created for
    vengeance;
³⁰ the fangs of wild animals and scorpions
    and vipers,
  and the sword that punishes the
    ungodly with destruction.
³¹ They take delight in doing his bidding,
  always ready for his service on earth;
  and when their time comes they never
    disobey his command."

³² So from the beginning I have been
    convinced of all this
  and have thought it out and left it in
    writing:
³³ All the works of the Lord are good,
  and he will supply every need in its
    time.
³⁴ No one can say, "This is not as good as
    that,"
  for everything proves good in its
    appointed time.
³⁵ So now sing praise with all your heart
    and voice,
  and bless the name of the Lord.

40 Hard work was created for everyone,
  and a heavy yoke is laid on the
    children of Adam,
from the day they come forth from their
    mother's womb

---

^a Heb Lat: Gk *sinners bad things*
^b Heb Syr: Gk *can scourge mightily*

pose. **16–31**: A hymn of praise (v. 14). **16**: *Very good*, cf. Gen 1.4,10,12,18,21,25,31. **17**: *The waters stood in a heap*, see Ex 15.8; Josh 3.16. *Water at the word of his mouth*, see Gen 1.9–10. **21**: *Created for its own purpose* may reflect the influence of Stoic philosophy. **23**: *Watered land into salt*, see Gen 19.24–26. **26**: *The basic necessities*, cf. 29.21. **28–30**: Things with bad effects punish the wicked. **33–34**: *Good*, cf. 39.16; 33.7–15.
  40.1–30: Miseries and joys. **1–11**: Fears and anxieties stem from the *heavy yoke* laid on *Adam's* descendants

until the day they return to[a] the mother of all the living.[b]
2 Perplexities and fear of heart are theirs,
and anxious thought of the day of their death.
3 From the one who sits on a splendid throne
to the one who grovels in dust and ashes,
4 from the one who wears purple and a crown
to the one who is clothed in burlap,
5 there is anger and envy and trouble and unrest,
and fear of death, and fury and strife.
And when one rests upon his bed,
his sleep at night confuses his mind.
6 He gets little or no rest;
he struggles in his sleep as he did by day.[c]
He is troubled by the visions of his mind
like one who has escaped from the battlefield.
7 At the moment he reaches safety he wakes up,
astonished that his fears were groundless.
8 To all creatures, human and animal,
but to sinners seven times more,
9 come death and bloodshed and strife and sword,
calamities and famine and ruin and plague.
10 All these were created for the wicked,
and on their account the flood came.
11 All that is of earth returns to earth,
and what is from above returns above.[d]
12 All bribery and injustice will be blotted out,
but good faith will last forever.
13 The wealth of the unjust will dry up like a river,
and crash like a loud clap of thunder in a storm.
14 As a generous person has cause to rejoice,
so lawbreakers will utterly fail.
15 The children of the ungodly put out few branches;
they are unhealthy roots on sheer rock.
16 The reeds by any water or river bank
are plucked up before any grass;
17 but kindness is like a garden of blessings,
and almsgiving endures forever.

18 Wealth and wages make life sweet,[e]
but better than either is finding a treasure.
19 Children and the building of a city establish one's name,
but better than either is the one who finds wisdom.
Cattle and orchards make one prosperous;[f]
but a blameless wife is accounted better than either.
20 Wine and music gladden the heart,
but the love of friends[g] is better than either.
21 The flute and the harp make sweet melody,
but a pleasant voice is better than either.
22 The eye desires grace and beauty,
but the green shoots of grain more than either.
23 A friend or companion is always welcome,
but a sensible wife[h] is better than either.
24 Kindred and helpers are for a time of trouble,
but almsgiving rescues better than either.

a Other Gk and Lat authorities read *are buried in*
b Heb: Gk *of all*
c Arm: Meaning of Gk uncertain
d Heb Syr: Gk Lat *from the waters returns to the sea*
e Heb: Gk *Life is sweet for the self-reliant worker*
f Heb Syr: Gk lacks *but better … prosperous*
g Heb: Gk *wisdom*
h Heb Compare Syr: Gk *wife with her husband*

(Gen 3.17–19). 1: *Mother's womb . . . mother,* cf. Job 1.21. 5–7: For restless *sleep* and bad dreams, see 34.1–8; Job 7.4; Eccl 2.23. 10: *Flood,* see Gen 6–8. 11: *Returns to earth,* cf. Gen 3.19. *What is from above,* cf. Eccl 12.7. 12–17: In the end righteousness will prevail. 15: Cf. Job 18.16. 18–27: The numerical sayings name two good things and

²⁵ Gold and silver make one stand firm,
    but good counsel is esteemed more
        than either.
²⁶ Riches and strength build up
        confidence,
    but the fear of the Lord is better than
        either.
There is no want in the fear of the Lord,
    and with it there is no need to seek for
        help.
²⁷ The fear of the Lord is like a garden of
        blessing,
    and covers a person better than any
        glory.

²⁸ My child, do not lead the life of a beggar;
    it is better to die than to beg.
²⁹ When one looks to the table of another,
    one's way of life cannot be considered
        a life.
One loses self-respect with another
        person's food,
    but one who is intelligent and well
        instructed guards against that.
³⁰ In the mouth of the shameless begging
        is sweet,
    but it kindles a fire inside him.

41 O death, how bitter is the thought of
        you
    to the one at peace among possessions,
who has nothing to worry about and is
        prosperous in everything,
    and still is vigorous enough to enjoy
        food!
² O death, how welcome is your sentence
    to one who is needy and failing in
        strength,
worn down by age and anxious about
        everything;
    to one who is contrary, and has lost all
        patience!
³ Do not fear death's decree for you;
    remember those who went before you
        and those who will come after.

⁴ This is the Lord's decree for all flesh;
    why then should you reject the will of
        the Most High?
Whether life lasts for ten years or a
        hundred or a thousand,
    there are no questions asked in Hades.

⁵ The children of sinners are abominable
        children,
    and they frequent the haunts of the
        ungodly.
⁶ The inheritance of the children of sinners
        will perish,
    and on their offspring will be a
        perpetual disgrace.
⁷ Children will blame an ungodly father,
    for they suffer disgrace because of him.
⁸ Woe to you, the ungodly,
    who have forsaken the law of the Most
        High God!
⁹ If you have children, calamity will be
        theirs;
    you will beget them only for groaning.
When you stumble, there is lasting joy;ᵃ
    and when you die, a curse is your lot.
¹⁰ Whatever comes from earth returns to
        earth;
    so the ungodly go from curse to
        destruction.

¹¹ The human body is a fleeting thing,
    but a virtuous name will never be
        blotted out.ᵇ
¹² Have regard for your name, since it will
        outlive you
    longer than a thousand hoards of gold.
¹³ The days of a good life are numbered,
    but a good name lasts forever.

¹⁴ My children, be true to your training and
        be at peace;

ᵃ Heb: Meaning of Gk uncertain
ᵇ Heb: Gk *People grieve over the death of the body,
    but the bad name of sinners will be blotted out*

assert that a third is even *better.* **26–27:** *Fear of the Lord* is best of all (cf. 1.11–30). **28–30:** The worst misery is to
be reduced to begging (29.24–28; 30.17).

41.1–13: Death and reputation. The most important mode of immortality for Ben Sira is through one's *name,*
the reputation that one leaves behind (cf. 14.11–19; 17.25–28; 38.16–23). **4:** *Decree for all,* cf. Gen 3.19. **Hades,** Heb
"Sheol," the abode of the dead (cf. Ps 88.10–11). **5:** *Abominable children,* merely having offspring does not guarantee immortality (Wis 3.12–13,16–18; 4.3–6). **11:** *Virtuous name,* cf. Prov 22.1; Eccl 7.1.

hidden wisdom and unseen treasure—
of what value is either?
[15] Better are those who hide their folly
than those who hide their wisdom.
[16] Therefore show respect for my words;
for it is not good to feel shame in every
circumstance,
nor is every kind of abashment to be
approved.[a]

[17] Be ashamed of sexual immorality, before
your father or mother;
and of a lie, before a prince or a ruler;
[18] of a crime, before a judge or magistrate;
and of a breach of the law, before the
congregation and the people;
of unjust dealing, before your partner or
your friend;
[19] and of theft, in the place where you
live.
Be ashamed of breaking an oath or
agreement,[b]
and of leaning on your elbow at meals;
of surliness in receiving or giving,
[20] and of silence, before those who greet
you;
of looking at a prostitute,
[21] and of rejecting the appeal of a
relative;
of taking away someone's portion or gift,
and of gazing at another man's wife;
[22] of meddling with his servant-girl—
and do not approach her bed;
of abusive words, before friends—
and do not be insulting after making a
gift.

42 Be ashamed of repeating what you
hear,
and of betraying secrets.
Then you will show proper shame,
and will find favor with everyone.

Of the following things do not be
ashamed,
and do not sin to save face:

[2] Do not be ashamed of the law of the Most
High and his covenant,
and of rendering judgment to acquit the
ungodly;
[3] of keeping accounts with a partner or
with traveling companions,
and of dividing the inheritance of
friends;
[4] of accuracy with scales and weights,
and of acquiring much or little;
[5] of profit from dealing with merchants,
and of frequent disciplining of
children,
and of drawing blood from the back of a
wicked slave.
[6] Where there is an untrustworthy wife, a
seal is a good thing;
and where there are many hands, lock
things up.
[7] When you make a deposit, be sure it is
counted and weighed,
and when you give or receive, put it all
in writing.
[8] Do not be ashamed to correct the stupid
or foolish
or the aged who are guilty of sexual
immorality.
Then you will show your sound training,
and will be approved by all.

[9] A daughter is a secret anxiety to her
father,
and worry over her robs him of sleep;
when she is young, for fear she may not
marry,
or if married, for fear she may be
disliked;
[10] while a virgin, for fear she may be
seduced
and become pregnant in her father's
house;

---

[a] Heb: Gk *and not everything is confidently esteemed
by everyone*
[b] Heb: Gk *before the truth of God and the covenant*

41.14–42.8: True and false shame. Cf. 4.20–6.4; 10.19–11.6. After an introduction (41.14–16), Ben Sira describes behaviors that properly bring shame (sexual misconduct, dishonesty, rudeness, 41.17–42.1a) and notes things of which one should not be ashamed (fidelity to the law, honesty, controlling one's household, giving reproof where needed, 42.1b–8). **42.2:** *The law of the Most High* leads the list of things not to be ashamed of.
42.9–14: A father's anxiety over his daughters. Cf. 7.24–25; 22.3–6. The major concern here is the father's good reputation (cf. 30.1–13). **9–10:** *Worry over her,* the father was responsible for arranging his daughter's

or having a husband, for fear she may go
astray,
or, though married, for fear she may be
barren.
¹¹ Keep strict watch over a headstrong
daughter,
or she may make you a laughingstock to
your enemies,
a byword in the city and the assembly of[a]
the people,
and put you to shame in public
gatherings.[b]
See that there is no lattice in her room,
no spot that overlooks the approaches
to the house.[c]
¹² Do not let her parade her beauty before
any man,
or spend her time among married
women;[a]
¹³ for from garments comes the moth,
and from a woman comes woman's
wickedness.
¹⁴ Better is the wickedness of a man than a
woman who does good;
it is woman who brings shame and
disgrace.

¹⁵ I will now call to mind the works of the
Lord,
and will declare what I have seen.
By the word of the Lord his works are
made;
and all his creatures do his will.[d]
¹⁶ The sun looks down on everything with
its light,
and the work of the Lord is full of his
glory.
¹⁷ The Lord has not empowered even his
holy ones
to recount all his marvelous works,
which the Lord the Almighty has
established

so that the universe may stand firm in
his glory.
¹⁸ He searches out the abyss and the
human heart;
he understands their innermost secrets.
For the Most High knows all that may be
known;
he sees from of old the things that are
to come.[e]
¹⁹ He discloses what has been and what is
to be,
and he reveals the traces of hidden things.
²⁰ No thought escapes him,
and nothing is hidden from him.
²¹ He has set in order the splendors of his
wisdom;
he is from all eternity one and the same.
Nothing can be added or taken away,
and he needs no one to be his
counselor.
²² How desirable are all his works,
and how sparkling they are to see![f]
²³ All these things live and remain forever;
each creature is preserved to meet a
particular need.[g]
²⁴ All things come in pairs, one opposite
the other,
and he has made nothing incomplete.
²⁵ Each supplements the virtues of the
other.
Who could ever tire of seeing his glory?

---

a   Heb: Meaning of Gk uncertain
b   Heb: Gk *to shame before the great multitude*
c   Heb: Gk lacks *See . . . house*
d   Syr Compare Heb: most Gk witnesses lack *and
    all . . . will*
e   Heb: Gk *he sees the sign(s) of the age*
f   Meaning of Gk uncertain
g   Heb: Gk *forever for every need, and all are obedient*

marriage, and a high premium was placed on her virginity and fertility (cf. Deut 22.13–29). **11–12:** *Headstrong
daughter,* a father who was unable to control the women of his household was subject to shame. Thus the
life of unmarried daughters was closely supervised. **13:** *From a woman comes woman's wickedness,* the woman
is Eve (cf. Gen 3.6; 1 Tim 3.14). **14:** *Better is the wickedness of a man,* the lowest point in Ben Sira's misogyny (cf.
25.13–26.27; 36.26–31).

42.15–43.33: God's glory made manifest in all creation. 15–25: The order and splendor of the whole cosmos
reflect God's omniscience and purpose. **15:** *By the word,* cf. Gen 1.1–31; Ps 33.6; Jdt 16.14; Wis 9.1. **17:** *Holy ones,*
that is, angels or members of the heavenly court. **19:** *What has been and what is to be,* cf. Isa 41.22–23; 44.7.
Reveals . . . hidden things, cf. Dan 2.22. **21:** *Counselor,* cf. Isa 40.13. **24:** *All things come in pairs,* cf. 33.7–15; 39.12–35;

43

The pride of the higher realms is the clear vault of the sky,
as glorious to behold as the sight of the heavens.
[2] The sun, when it appears, proclaims as it rises
what a marvelous instrument it is, the work of the Most High.
[3] At noon it parches the land,
and who can withstand its burning heat?
[4] A man tending[a] a furnace works in burning heat,
but three times as hot is the sun scorching the mountains;
it breathes out fiery vapors,
and its bright rays blind the eyes.
[5] Great is the Lord who made it;
at his orders it hurries on its course.

[6] It is the moon that marks the changing seasons,[b]
governing the times, their everlasting sign.
[7] From the moon comes the sign for festal days,
a light that wanes when it completes its course.
[8] The new moon, as its name suggests, renews itself;[c]
how marvelous it is in this change,
a beacon to the hosts on high,
shining in the vault of the heavens!
[9] The glory of the stars is the beauty of heaven,
a glittering array in the heights of the Lord.
[10] On the orders of the Holy One they stand in their appointed places;
they never relax in their watches.
[11] Look at the rainbow, and praise him who made it;
it is exceedingly beautiful in its brightness.
[12] It encircles the sky with its glorious arc;
the hands of the Most High have stretched it out.

[13] By his command he sends the driving snow
and speeds the lightnings of his judgment.
[14] Therefore the storehouses are opened,
and the clouds fly out like birds.
[15] In his majesty he gives the clouds their strength,
and the hailstones are broken in pieces.
[17a] The voice of his thunder rebukes the earth;
[16] when he appears, the mountains shake.
At his will the south wind blows;
[17b] so do the storm from the north and the whirlwind.
He scatters the snow like birds flying down,
and its descent is like locusts alighting.
[18] The eye is dazzled by the beauty of its whiteness,
and the mind is amazed as it falls.
[19] He pours frost over the earth like salt,
and icicles form like pointed thorns.
[20] The cold north wind blows,
and ice freezes on the water;
it settles on every pool of water,
and the water puts it on like a breastplate.
[21] He consumes the mountains and burns up the wilderness,
and withers the tender grass like fire.
[22] A mist quickly heals all things;
the falling dew gives refreshment from the heat.

[23] By his plan he stilled the deep
and planted islands in it.
[24] Those who sail the sea tell of its dangers,
and we marvel at what we hear.
[25] In it are strange and marvelous creatures,
all kinds of living things, and huge sea-monsters.

a Other ancient authorities read *blowing upon*
b Heb: Meaning of Gk uncertain
c Heb: Gk *The month is named after the moon*

40.8–10. 43.1–12: God's glory in the heavenly bodies (cf. Job 38.1–38; Ps 104). 7: *The sign for festal days,* this may suggest preference for a lunar rather than a solar calendar. 11: *Rainbow,* see Gen 9.12–17. 43.13–26: God's glory in storms (cf. Ps 29; Job 38–39). 16–17: The imagery is evocative of divine theophanies, cf. Ps 18.7–15. 23–25: Cf.

[26] Because of him each of his messengers
    succeeds,
  and by his word all things hold
    together.

[27] We could say more but could never say
    enough;
  let the final word be: "He is the all."
[28] Where can we find the strength to praise
    him?
  For he is greater than all his works.
[29] Awesome is the Lord and very great,
  and marvelous is his power.
[30] Glorify the Lord and exalt him as much
    as you can,
  for he surpasses even that.
When you exalt him, summon all your
    strength,
  and do not grow weary, for you cannot
    praise him enough.
[31] Who has seen him and can describe
    him?
  Or who can extol him as he is?
[32] Many things greater than these lie
    hidden,
  for I[a] have seen but few of his works.
[33] For the Lord has made all things,
  and to the godly he has given wisdom.

HYMN IN HONOR OF OUR ANCESTORS[b]

44 Let us now sing the praises of famous
    men,
  our ancestors in their generations.
[2] The Lord apportioned to them[c] great
    glory,
  his majesty from the beginning.
[3] There were those who ruled in their
    kingdoms,
  and made a name for themselves by
    their valor;
those who gave counsel because they were
    intelligent;
  those who spoke in prophetic oracles;

[4] those who led the people by their
    counsels
  and by their knowledge of the people's
    lore;
  they were wise in their words of
    instruction;
[5] those who composed musical tunes,
  or put verses in writing;
[6] rich men endowed with resources,
  living peacefully in their homes—
[7] all these were honored in their
    generations,
  and were the pride of their times.
[8] Some of them have left behind a
    name,
  so that others declare their praise.
[9] But of others there is no memory;
  they have perished as though they had
    never existed;
they have become as though they had
    never been born,
  they and their children after them.
[10] But these also were godly men,
  whose righteous deeds have not been
    forgotten;
[11] their wealth will remain with their
    descendants,
  and their inheritance with their
    children's children.[d]
[12] Their descendants stand by the
    covenants;
  their children also, for their sake.
[13] Their offspring will continue forever,
  and their glory will never be blotted
    out.
[14] Their bodies are buried in peace,
  but their name lives on generation after
    generation.

---

a Heb: Gk *we*
b This title is included in the Gk text.
c Heb: Gk *created*
d Heb Compare Lat Syr: Meaning of Gk uncertain

Pss 104.24–26; 107.23–24. **27–33:** God is *the all* in the sense that all creation reveals the presence of God as its creator and lord. The proper response from humans is praise and humility.

44.1–50.24: In praise of Israel's ancestors. Ben Sira celebrates the covenant with the patriarchs and Israel by recounting the great figures of Israel's history (44.1–49.16), culminating in the high priest Simon II (50.1–24).

44.1–15: God's glory made manifest in Israel. The great heroes in Israel's history are best understood as manifestations of God's glory (cf. 1 Macc 2.51–64). **1.** *Famous men*, the Hebrew and Syriac read *men of piety*. **3–8:** Twelve types of heroes are listed. **9–10:** Some good people have left no memorial, but they will not be *forgotten*. **14:** *Their name*, cf. 41.11–13.

15 The assembly declares[a] their wisdom,
    and the congregation proclaims their
        praise.

16 Enoch pleased the Lord and was taken
        up,
    an example of repentance to all
        generations.

17 Noah was found perfect and righteous;
    in the time of wrath he kept the race
        alive;[b]
therefore a remnant was left on the earth
    when the flood came.
18 Everlasting covenants were made with
        him
    that all flesh should never again be
        blotted out by a flood.

19 Abraham was the great father of a
        multitude of nations,
    and no one has been found like him in
        glory.
20 He kept the law of the Most High,
    and entered into a covenant with him;
he certified the covenant in his flesh,
    and when he was tested he proved
        faithful.
21 Therefore the Lord[c] assured him with an
        oath
    that the nations would be blessed
        through his offspring;
that he would make him as numerous as
    the dust of the earth,
and exalt his offspring like the stars,
and give them an inheritance from sea to
        sea
    and from the Euphrates[d] to the ends of
        the earth.
22 To Isaac also he gave the same assurance
    for the sake of his father Abraham.

The blessing of all people and the
        covenant
    23 he made to rest on the head of Jacob;
he acknowledged him with his blessings,
    and gave him his inheritance;
he divided his portions,
    and distributed them among twelve
        tribes.

From his descendants the Lord[c] brought
        forth a godly man,
    who found favor in the sight of all

45 1 and was beloved by God and people,
        Moses, whose memory is blessed.
2 He made him equal in glory to the holy
        ones,
    and made him great, to the terror of his
        enemies.
3 By his words he performed swift
        miracles;[e]
    the Lord[c] glorified him in the presence
        of kings.
He gave him commandments for his
        people,
    and revealed to him his glory.
4 For his faithfulness and meekness he
        consecrated him,
    choosing him out of all humankind.
5 He allowed him to hear his voice,
    and led him into the dark cloud,
and gave him the commandments face to
        face,
    the law of life and knowledge,

a Heb: Gk *Peoples declare*
b Heb: Gk *was taken in exchange*
c Gk *he*
d Syr: Heb Gk *River*
e Heb: Gk *caused signs to cease*

44.16–23: The patriarchs. 16: *Enoch* also ends the list (49.14). For his being *taken up*, see Gen 5.24. Why he is called an *example of repentance* is not clear. **17–18:** *Noah* was *perfect* (Gen 6.9) and *righteous* (Gen 7.1), and the vehicle for *everlasting covenants* (Gen 9.8–17). **19–21:** *Abraham*, the *great father* (Gen 17.4–5), *kept the law* before it was given to Moses on Sinai, entered into the *covenant* by circumcision (Gen 17), and *was tested* in the binding of Isaac (Gen 22.1–14). **21:** See Gen 12.3; 13.16; 15.5,18; 22.17–18. **22:** *Isaac*, Gen 17.19; 26.3–5. **23:** *Jacob*, Gen 27.27–29; 28.13–15; *his inheritance* is the promised land (Gen 28.4). The *twelve tribes* of Israel, descended from Jacob's sons; see Gen 49.

45.1–5: Moses as a miracle worker and teacher. 2: *Glory*, Ex 33.18–23. **3:** *Miracles*, specifically the signs and plagues in Egypt; Ex 7.1–11.10; 12.29–32. *Commandments*, the Decalogue (Ex 20.1–17; Deut 5.1–33); *glory* (Ex 33.18–23). **4:** *Meekness*, Num 12.3. **5:** *Dark cloud*, Ex 20.21; 24.18. *Face to face*, Num 12.8. *Teach*, Deut 4.1.

so that he might teach Jacob the covenant,
and Israel his decrees.

⁶ He exalted Aaron, a holy man like
Moses[a]
who was his brother, of the tribe of
Levi.
⁷ He made an everlasting covenant with
him,
and gave him the priesthood of the
people.
He blessed him with stateliness,
and put a glorious robe on him.
⁸ He clothed him in perfect splendor,
and strengthened him with the symbols
of authority,
the linen undergarments, the long robe,
and the ephod.
⁹ And he encircled him with
pomegranates,
with many golden bells all around,
to send forth a sound as he walked,
to make their ringing heard in the
temple
as a reminder to his people;
¹⁰ with the sacred vestment, of gold and
violet
and purple, the work of an
embroiderer;
with the oracle of judgment, Urim and
Thummim;
¹¹ with twisted crimson, the work of an
artisan;
with precious stones engraved like seals,
in a setting of gold, the work of a
jeweler,
to commemorate in engraved letters
each of the tribes of Israel;
¹² with a gold crown upon his turban,
inscribed like a seal with "Holiness,"
a distinction to be prized, the work of an
expert,
a delight to the eyes, richly adorned.
¹³ Before him such beautiful things did not
exist.
No outsider ever put them on,

but only his sons
and his descendants in perpetuity.
¹⁴ His sacrifices shall be wholly burned
twice every day continually.
¹⁵ Moses ordained him,
and anointed him with holy oil;
it was an everlasting covenant for him
and for his descendants as long as the
heavens endure,
to minister to the Lord[a] and serve as
priest
and bless his people in his name.
¹⁶ He chose him out of all the living
to offer sacrifice to the Lord,
incense and a pleasing odor as a memorial
portion,
to make atonement for the[b] people.
¹⁷ In his commandments he gave him
authority and statutes and[c]
judgments,
to teach Jacob the testimonies,
and to enlighten Israel with his law.
¹⁸ Outsiders conspired against him,
and envied him in the wilderness,
Dathan and Abiram and their followers
and the company of Korah, in wrath
and anger.
¹⁹ The Lord saw it and was not pleased,
and in the heat of his anger they were
destroyed;
he performed wonders against them
to consume them in flaming fire.
²⁰ He added glory to Aaron
and gave him a heritage;
he allotted to him the best of the first
fruits,
and prepared bread of first fruits in
abundance;
²¹ for they eat the sacrifices of the Lord,
which he gave to him and his
descendants.

a Gk *him*
b Other ancient authorities read *his* or *your*
c Heb: Gk *authority in covenants of*

45.6–26: Aaron and Phinehas. Attention to the priesthood prepares for the climactic description of Simon the high priest in 50.1–24. **6:** *His brother, of the tribe of Levi,* Ex 4.14. **7:** *Everlasting covenant* of priesthood, Ex 29.9; 40.15. **8–13:** *Perfect splendor,* see Ex 28–29 for the various priestly vestments. **10:** *Urim and Thummim,* see Ex 28.30; Num 27.21; 1 Sam 14.41–42. **14:** *Sacrifices,* Lev 6.8–15; Num 28.3–4. **15:** *Moses ordained . . . anointed,* Ex 28.41; Lev 8.1–30. *Bless his people,* see Num 6.22–27. **17:** *Teach,* Lev 10.11; Deut 33.10; Mal 2.7. **18–19:** *Dathan and Abiram*

22 But in the land of the people he has no
inheritance,
and he has no portion among the
people;
for the Lord[a] himself is his[b] portion and
inheritance.

23 Phinehas son of Eleazar ranks third in
glory
for being zealous in the fear of the
Lord,
and standing firm, when the people turned
away,
in the noble courage of his soul;
and he made atonement for Israel.
24 Therefore a covenant of friendship was
established with him,
that he should be leader of the
sanctuary and of his people,
that he and his descendants should
have
the dignity of the priesthood forever.
25 Just as a covenant was established with
David
son of Jesse of the tribe of Judah,
that the king's heritage passes only from
son to son,
so the heritage of Aaron is for his
descendants alone.

26 And now bless the Lord
who has crowned you with glory.[c]
May the Lord[a] grant you wisdom of
mind
to judge his people with justice,
so that their prosperity may not vanish,
and that their glory may endure
through all their generations.

46 Joshua son of Nun was mighty in war,
and was the successor of Moses in the
prophetic office.
He became, as his name implies,
a great savior of God's[d] elect,
to take vengeance on the enemies that
rose against them,

so that he might give Israel its
inheritance.
2 How glorious he was when he lifted his
hands
and brandished his sword against the
cities!
3 Who before him ever stood so firm?
For he waged the wars of the Lord.
4 Was it not through him that the sun
stood still
and one day became as long as two?
5 He called upon the Most High, the
Mighty One,
when enemies pressed him on every
side,
and the great Lord answered him
with hailstones of mighty power.
6 He overwhelmed that nation in
battle,
and on the slope he destroyed his
opponents,
so that the nations might know his
armament,
that he was fighting in the sight of the
Lord;
for he was a devoted follower of the
Mighty One.
7 And in the days of Moses he proved his
loyalty,
he and Caleb son of Jephunneh:
they opposed the congregation,[e]
restrained the people from sin,
and stilled their wicked grumbling.
8 And these two alone were spared
out of six hundred thousand
infantry,
to lead the people[f] into their inheritance,
the land flowing with milk and honey.

a Gk *he*
b Other ancient authorities read *your*
c Heb: Gk lacks *And . . . glory*
d Gk *his*
e Other ancient authorities read *the enemy*
f Gk *them*

. . . *Korah*, Num 16.1–35. **21:** *Eat the sacrifices*, Num 18.8–19. **22:** *No inheritance*, Num 18.20; Deut 12.12. **23–25:**
Phinehas, Num 25.10–13; Ps 106.30; 1 Macc 2.54. **26:** *You*, perhaps directed to Simon (50.1–24) and his successors.
    46.1–20: Joshua and Caleb, the judges, and Samuel. **1–10:** For Joshua's military exploits, see Josh 6–11. **1:**
Successor of Moses, Deut 34.9; Josh 1.1,5; 3.7. Joshua's *name* means "the Lord is salvation." **4:** *Sun stood still*, Josh
10.12–14. **5:** *Hailstones*, Josh 10.11. **7:** *Proved his loyalty*, Num 14.6–10. **8:** *Two alone*, Num 14.38; 26.65. *Six hundred*

⁹ The Lord gave Caleb strength,
  which remained with him in his old
    age,
so that he went up to the hill country,
  and his children obtained it for an
    inheritance,
¹⁰ so that all the Israelites might see
  how good it is to follow the Lord.

¹¹ The judges also, with their respective
    names,
  whose hearts did not fall into idolatry
and who did not turn away from the
    Lord—
  may their memory be blessed!
¹² May their bones send forth new life from
    where they lie,
  and may the names of those who have
    been honored
  live again in their children!

¹³ Samuel was beloved by his Lord;
  a prophet of the Lord, he established
    the kingdom
  and anointed rulers over his people.
¹⁴ By the law of the Lord he judged the
    congregation,
  and the Lord watched over Jacob.
¹⁵ By his faithfulness he was proved to be a
    prophet,
  and by his words he became known as a
    trustworthy seer.
¹⁶ He called upon the Lord, the Mighty
    One,
  when his enemies pressed him on every
    side,
  and he offered in sacrifice a suckling
    lamb.
¹⁷ Then the Lord thundered from
    heaven,
  and made his voice heard with a mighty
    sound;
¹⁸ he subdued the leaders of the enemy[a]
  and all the rulers of the Philistines.

¹⁹ Before the time of his eternal sleep,
  Samuel[b] bore witness before the Lord
    and his anointed:
"No property, not so much as a pair of
    shoes,
  have I taken from anyone!"
  And no one accused him.
²⁰ Even after he had fallen asleep, he
    prophesied
  and made known to the king his death,
and lifted up his voice from the ground
  in prophecy, to blot out the wickedness
    of the people.

47 After him Nathan rose up
  to prophesy in the days of David.
² As the fat is set apart from the offering of
    well-being,
  so David was set apart from the
    Israelites.
³ He played with lions as though they were
    young goats,
  and with bears as though they were
    lambs of the flock.
⁴ In his youth did he not kill a giant,
  and take away the people's disgrace,
when he whirled the stone in the sling
  and struck down the boasting
    Goliath?
⁵ For he called on the Lord, the Most
    High,
  and he gave strength to his right arm
to strike down a mighty warrior,
  and to exalt the power[c] of his people.
⁶ So they glorified him for the tens of
    thousands he conquered,
  and praised him for the blessings
    bestowed by the Lord,
  when the glorious diadem was given to
    him.

a Heb: Gk *leaders of the people of Tyre*
b Gk *he*
c Gk *horn*

thousand, Ex 12.37; Num 11.21. **9:** *Caleb's inheritance,* Josh 14.6–14. **11–12:** Only those *judges* who did not fall into idolatry (as Gideon did; Judg 8.22–35) are blessed. **12:** *Bones send forth new life,* 2 Kings 13.21. **13–20:** Samuel *anointed rulers* (1 Sam 10.1; 16.13) and served as a *judge* (1 Sam 7.3–17), *prophet* (1 Sam 3.19–20), and *priest* (1 Sam 7.9). **16–18:** 1 Sam 7.9–11. **19:** See 1 Sam 12.3. **20:** *Lifted up his voice from the ground,* 1 Sam 28.8–19.

  47.1–25: *Early kings.* **1:** *Nathan,* 2 Sam 7.2–3; 12.1; 1 Chr 17.1. **2–11:** *David* was chosen by God (1 Sam 16.1–12), was a great warrior, and initiated public worship in Jerusalem (1 Chr 16.4; 23.1–6,24–32). **2:** *The fat,* Lev 3.3–5. **3:** *Played with lions . . . and with bears,* 1 Sam 17.34–36. **4:** *Kill a giant,* Goliath (1 Sam 17.49–51). **6:** *Tens of thousands,*

⁷ For he wiped out his enemies on every
side,
and annihilated his adversaries the
Philistines;
he crushed their power[a] to our own
day.
⁸ In all that he did he gave thanks
to the Holy One, the Most High,
proclaiming his glory;
he sang praise with all his heart,
and he loved his Maker.
⁹ He placed singers before the altar,
to make sweet melody with their
voices.[b]
¹⁰ He gave beauty to the festivals,
and arranged their times throughout
the year,[c]
while they praised God's[d] holy name,
and the sanctuary resounded from
early morning.
¹¹ The Lord took away his sins,
and exalted his power[a] forever;
he gave him a covenant of kingship
and a glorious throne in Israel.

¹² After him a wise son rose up
who because of him lived in security:[e]
¹³ Solomon reigned in an age of peace,
because God made all his borders
tranquil,
so that he might build a house in his
name
and provide a sanctuary to stand
forever.
¹⁴ How wise you were when you were
young!
You overflowed like the Nile[f] with
understanding.
¹⁵ Your influence spread throughout the
earth,
and you filled it with proverbs having
deep meaning.
¹⁶ Your fame reached to far-off islands,
and you were loved for your peaceful
reign.
¹⁷ Your songs, proverbs, and parables,
and the answers you gave astounded
the nations.

¹⁸ In the name of the Lord God,
who is called the God of Israel,
you gathered gold like tin
and amassed silver like lead.
¹⁹ But you brought in women to lie at your
side,
and through your body you were
brought into subjection.
²⁰ You stained your honor,
and defiled your family line,
so that you brought wrath upon your
children,
and they were grieved[g] at your folly,
²¹ because the sovereignty was divided
and a rebel kingdom arose out of
Ephraim.
²² But the Lord will never give up his
mercy,
or cause any of his works to perish;
he will never blot out the descendants of
his chosen one,
or destroy the family line of him who
loved him.
So he gave a remnant to Jacob,
and to David a root from his own
family.

²³ Solomon rested with his ancestors,
and left behind him one of his sons,
broad in[h] folly and lacking in sense,
Rehoboam, whose policy drove the
people to revolt.
Then Jeroboam son of Nebat led Israel into
sin
and started Ephraim on its sinful
ways.

a Gk *horn*
b Other ancient authorities add *and daily they sing
his praises*
c Gk *to completion*
d Gk *his*
e Heb: Gk *in a broad place*
f Heb: Gk *a river*
g Other ancient authorities read *I was grieved*
h Heb (with a play on the name Rehoboam) Syr: Gk
the people's

1 Sam 18.7. **11:** *His sins,* 2 Sam 11–12. *Covenant of kingship,* 2 Sam 7.12–16; Ps 89.19–37. **12–22:** *Solomon* built the
Jerusalem Temple (1 Kings 5–8), became *wise* and wealthy (1 Kings 3.12–13; 4.21–34; 10.14–29) but succumbed
to lust and idolatry (1 Kings 11.1–11). **21:** When Solomon died, what had been one kingdom was *divided* into

²⁴ Their sins increased more and more,
  until they were exiled from their land.
²⁵ For they sought out every kind of
    wickedness,
  until vengeance came upon them.

48 Then Elijah arose, a prophet like fire,
  and his word burned like a torch.
² He brought a famine upon them,
  and by his zeal he made them few in
    number.
³ By the word of the Lord he shut up the
    heavens,
  and also three times brought down
    fire.
⁴ How glorious you were, Elijah, in your
    wondrous deeds!
  Whose glory is equal to yours?
⁵ You raised a corpse from death
  and from Hades, by the word of the
    Most High.
⁶ You sent kings down to destruction,
  and famous men, from their sickbeds.
⁷ You heard rebuke at Sinai
  and judgments of vengeance at Horeb.
⁸ You anointed kings to inflict
    retribution,
  and prophets to succeed you.ᵃ
⁹ You were taken up by a whirlwind of fire,
  in a chariot with horses of fire.
¹⁰ At the appointed time, it is written, you
    are destinedᵇ
  to calm the wrath of God before it
    breaks out in fury,
  to turn the hearts of parents to their
    children,
  and to restore the tribes of Jacob.
¹¹ Happy are those who saw you
  and were adornedᶜ with your love!
  For we also shall surely live.ᵈ

¹² When Elijah was enveloped in the
    whirlwind,
  Elisha was filled with his spirit.
He performed twice as many signs,
  and marvels with every utterance of his
    mouth.ᵉ
Never in his lifetime did he tremble before
    any ruler,
  nor could anyone intimidate him at all.
¹³ Nothing was too hard for him,
  and when he was dead, his body
    prophesied.
¹⁴ In his life he did wonders,
  and in death his deeds were marvelous.

¹⁵ Despite all this the people did not
    repent,
  nor did they forsake their sins,
until they were carried off as plunder from
    their land,
  and were scattered over all the earth.
The people were left very few in number,
  but with a ruler from the house of
    David.
¹⁶ Some of them did what was right,
  but others sinned more and more.

¹⁷ Hezekiah fortified his city,
  and brought water into its midst;
he tunneled the rock with iron tools,
  and built cisterns for the water.
¹⁸ In his days Sennacherib invaded the
    country;
  he sent his commanderᶠ and departed;

ᵃ Heb: Gk *him*
ᵇ Heb: Gk *are for reproofs*
ᶜ Other ancient authorities read *and have died*
ᵈ Text and meaning of Gk uncertain
ᵉ Heb: Gk lacks *He performed ... mouth*
ᶠ Other ancient authorities add *from Lachish*

two; 1 Kings 11.11–13,31–39; 12.15–20. **22:** *Root*, see Isa 11.10. **23–25:** *Rehoboam* and *Jeroboam*, 1 Kings 11.43–12.20; 12.28–30. **24:** *Exiled*, 2 Kings 17.6–8,18.

48.1–16: Elijah and Elisha. 1–11: How *Elijah* the *prophet* manifested God's glory. **3:** *Shut up the heavens*, 1 Kings 17.1. *Brought down fire*, 1 Kings 18.38; 2 Kings 1.10–12. **5:** *Raised a corpse*, 1 Kings 17.21–22. *Hades*, Heb "Sheol," the abode of the dead. **6:** *Sent kings*, 2 Kings 1.16. **7:** *Heard rebuke at Sinai*, 1 Kings 19.8. **8:** *Anointed kings*, 1 Kings 19.15–16. **9:** *Taken up*, 2 Kings 2.11. **10:** *It is written*, Mal 4.5–6. **12–14:** How the prophet *Elisha* manifested God's glory. **12:** *Filled with his spirit*, 2 Kings 2.9,13. **13:** *His body prophesied*, 2 Kings 13.20–21. **15–16:** The prophets could not overcome the people's sinfulness, which led to the defeat and exile of the northern kingdom of Israel in the eighth century BCE. **15:** *Were carried off*, 2 Kings 18.11–12.

48.17–49.16: Kings, prophets, and leaders of Judah. 17–22: The reign of King *Hezekiah*. **17:** *Water*, 2 Kings

he shook his fist against Zion,
    and made great boasts in his
        arrogance.
¹⁹ Then their hearts were shaken and their
    hands trembled,
    and they were in anguish, like women
        in labor.
²⁰ But they called upon the Lord who is
    merciful,
    spreading out their hands toward him.
The Holy One quickly heard them from
    heaven,
    and delivered them through Isaiah.
²¹ The Lord[a] struck down the camp of the
    Assyrians,
    and his angel wiped them out.
²² For Hezekiah did what was pleasing to
    the Lord,
    and he kept firmly to the ways of his
        ancestor David,
as he was commanded by the prophet
    Isaiah,
    who was great and trustworthy in his
        visions.
²³ In Isaiah's[b] days the sun went
    backward,
    and he prolonged the life of the king.
²⁴ By his dauntless spirit he saw the
    future,
    and comforted the mourners in Zion.
²⁵ He revealed what was to occur to the
    end of time,
    and the hidden things before they
        happened.

49 The name[c] of Josiah is like blended
    incense
    prepared by the skill of the perfumer;
his memory[d] is as sweet as honey to every
    mouth,
    and like music at a banquet of wine.
² He did what was right by reforming the
    people,
    and removing the wicked
        abominations.

³ He kept his heart fixed on the Lord;
    in lawless times he made godliness
        prevail.

⁴ Except for David and Hezekiah and
    Josiah,
    all of them were great sinners,
for they abandoned the law of the Most
    High;
    the kings of Judah came to an end.
⁵ They[e] gave their power to others,
    and their glory to a foreign nation,
⁶ who set fire to the chosen city of the
    sanctuary,
    and made its streets desolate,
    as Jeremiah had foretold.[f]
⁷ For they had mistreated him,
    who even in the womb had been
        consecrated a prophet,
to pluck up and ruin and destroy,
    and likewise to build and to plant.

⁸ It was Ezekiel who saw the vision of
    glory,
    which God[a] showed him above the
        chariot of the cherubim.
⁹ For God[g] also mentioned Job
    who held fast to all the ways of
        justice.[h]
¹⁰ May the bones of the Twelve Prophets
    send forth new life from where they lie,
for they comforted the people of Jacob
    and delivered them with confident
        hope.

a Gk *He*
b Gk *his*
c Heb: Gk *memory*
d Heb: Gk *it*
e Heb *He*
f Gk *by the hand of Jeremiah*
g Gk *he*
h Heb Compare Syr: Meaning of Gk uncertain

20.20. **18**: *Sennacherib*, the Assyrian king (705–681 BCE); 2 Kings 18.13,17; Isa 36.1. **20**: *Called upon the Lord*, 2 Kings 19.15–20. **21**: *The Lord struck down*, 2 Kings 19.35; Isa 37.36. **23–25**: The deeds of the prophet *Isaiah*. **23**: *Sun went backward*, 2 Kings 20.8–11; Isa 38.7–8. **24–25**: *He saw the future*, Isa 40.1–2; 42.9. **49.1–3**: The reign of King *Josiah*. **1**: *His memory*, 2 Kings 22.1–23.30. **6–7**: The prophet *Jeremiah*, 2 Chr 36.17–19; Jer 1.5–10; 38.2. **8**: The prophet *Ezekiel*, Ezek 1.3–15; 10.1–3; **9**: *Job*, Job 1–2; 42. **10**: *Twelve Prophets*, Hosea—Malachi, the so-called Minor Prophets, probably considered a single book by Ben Sira. **11–13**: Leaders after the exile: *Zerubbabel* (Ezra

¹¹ How shall we magnify Zerubbabel?
　He was like a signet ring on the right
　　hand,
¹² and so was Jeshua son of Jozadak;
in their days they built the house
　and raised a temple[a] holy to the Lord,
　　destined for everlasting glory.
¹³ The memory of Nehemiah also is lasting;
　he raised our fallen walls,
and set up gates and bars,
　and rebuilt our ruined houses.

¹⁴ Few have[b] ever been created on earth
　like Enoch,
　for he was taken up from the earth.
¹⁵ Nor was anyone ever born like Joseph;[c]
　even his bones were cared for.
¹⁶ Shem and Seth and Enosh were
　　honored,[d]
　but above every other created living
　　being was Adam.

50

The leader of his brothers and the
　pride of his people[e]
was the high priest, Simon son of Onias,
who in his life repaired the house,
　and in his time fortified the temple.
² He laid the foundations for the high
　　double walls,
　the high retaining walls for the temple
　　enclosure.
³ In his days a water cistern was dug,[f]
　a reservoir like the sea in
　　circumference.
⁴ He considered how to save his people
　　from ruin,
　and fortified the city against siege.
⁵ How glorious he was, surrounded by the
　　people,
　as he came out of the house of the
　　curtain.
⁶ Like the morning star among the clouds,
　like the full moon at the festal season;[f]
⁷ like the sun shining on the temple of the
　　Most High,

like the rainbow gleaming in splendid
　clouds;
⁸ like roses in the days of first fruits,
　like lilies by a spring of water,
　like a green shoot on Lebanon on a
　　summer day;
⁹ like fire and incense in the censer,
　like a vessel of hammered gold
　　studded with all kinds of precious
　　stones;
¹⁰ like an olive tree laden with fruit,
　and like a cypress towering in the
　　clouds.
¹¹ When he put on his glorious robe
　and clothed himself in perfect
　　splendor,
when he went up to the holy altar,
　he made the court of the sanctuary
　　glorious.
¹² When he received the portions from the
　　hands of the priests,
　as he stood by the hearth of the altar
with a garland of brothers around him,
　he was like a young cedar on
　　Lebanon
　surrounded by the trunks of palm
　　trees.
¹³ All the sons of Aaron in their splendor
　held the Lord's offering in their hands
　before the whole congregation of
　　Israel.
¹⁴ Finishing the service at the altars,[g]
　and arranging the offering to the Most
　　High, the Almighty,

a　Other ancient authorities read *people*
b　Heb Syr: Gk *No one has*
c　Heb Syr: Gk adds *the leader of his brothers, the
　support of the people*
d　Heb: Gk *Shem and Seth were honored by people*
e　Heb Syr: Gk lacks this line. Compare 49.15
f　Heb: Meaning of Gk uncertain
g　Other ancient authorities read *altar*

3.2; Hag 2.23), *Jeshua* (Ezra 3.2; Hag 1.12; 2.2; Zech 3.1); *Nehemiah* (Neh 7.1). **14–16:** Mentions of *Enoch* (44.16; Gen 5.18–24) and *Joseph* (Gen 39–50) as well as *Shem* (Gen 9.18), *Seth* (Gen 5.3) and *Enosh* (Gen 5.6–11) lead back to *Adam* (Gen 1.26–31).

　50.1–24: Simon the high priest. Simon II, son of Onias, was the high priest from 219 to 196 BCE (Josephus, *Ant.* 12.4.10). **1–4:** A summary of Simon's public works projects. **5–13:** For an earlier description of the high priest's vestments, cf. 45.6–13; cf. Ex 28.2–43; 39.1–31. **14–21:** A vivid description of the Temple ritual and sac-

¹⁵ he held out his hand for the cup
  and poured a drink offering of the blood
    of the grape;
he poured it out at the foot of the altar,
  a pleasing odor to the Most High, the
    king of all.
¹⁶ Then the sons of Aaron shouted;
  they blew their trumpets of hammered
    metal;
they sounded a mighty fanfare
  as a reminder before the Most High.
¹⁷ Then all the people together quickly
  fell to the ground on their faces
to worship their Lord,
  the Almighty, God Most High.

¹⁸ Then the singers praised him with their
    voices
  in sweet and full-toned melody.ᵃ
¹⁹ And the people of the Lord Most High
    offered
  their prayers before the Merciful One,
until the order of worship of the Lord was
    ended,
  and they completed his ritual.
²⁰ Then Simonᵇ came down and raised his
    hands
  over the whole congregation of
    Israelites,
to pronounce the blessing of the Lord with
    his lips,
  and to glory in his name;
²¹ and they bowed down in worship a
    second time,
  to receive the blessing from the Most
    High.

²² And now bless the God of all,
  who everywhere works great wonders,
who fosters our growth from birth,
  and deals with us according to his
    mercy.
²³ May he give usᶜ gladness of heart,

and may there be peace in ourᵈ days
  in Israel, as in the days of old.
²⁴ May he entrust to us his mercy,
  and may he deliver us in ourᵉ days!

²⁵ Two nations my soul detests,
  and the third is not even a people:
²⁶ Those who live in Seir,ᶠ and the
    Philistines,
  and the foolish people that live in
    Shechem.

²⁷ Instruction in understanding and
    knowledge
  I have written in this book,
Jesus son of Eleazar son of Sirachᵍ of
    Jerusalem,
  whose mind poured forth wisdom.
²⁸ Happy are those who concern
    themselves with these things,
  and those who lay them to heart will
    become wise.
²⁹ For if they put them into practice, they
    will be equal to anything,
  for the fearʰ of the Lord is their path.

PRAYER OF JESUS SON OF SIRACHⁱ

51 I give you thanks, O Lord and King,
  and praise you, O God my Savior.
I give thanks to your name,
  ² for you have been my protector and
    helper

ᵃ Other ancient authorities read *in sweet melody
  throughout the house*
ᵇ Gk *he*
ᶜ Other ancient authorities read *you*
ᵈ Other ancient authorities read *your*
ᵉ Other ancient authorities read *his*
ᶠ Heb Compare Lat: Gk *on the mountain of Samaria*
ᵍ Heb: Meaning of Gk uncertain
ʰ Heb: Other ancient authorities read *light*
ⁱ This title is included in the Gk text.

---

rifices, most likely for the Day of Atonement (Lev 16). **16:** *Trumpets,* Num 10.2; 31.6. **18:** *Singers,* 2 Chr 29.26–30. **20:** *The blessing,* Num 6.24–27. *His name,* only the high priest (and only once a year, on the Day of Atonement) could utter the ineffable name, YHWH. **22–24:** A concluding benediction.

50.25–26: A final numerical proverb. **26:** *Seir* (Edom) and the *Philistines* were historic enemies of the Israelites; here they refer to those who threatened them in Ben Sira's time, the Idumeans and the Greeks, along with the Samaritans, in *Shechem.*

50.27–29: Postscript. **27:** *Jesus,* the author's Hebrew name was probably Yeshua ben Eleazar ben Sira. **29:** *Fear of the Lord,* one of the book's major themes (1.11–30).

and have delivered me from destruction
  and from the trap laid by a slanderous
    tongue,
  from lips that fabricate lies.
In the face of my adversaries
  you have been my helper ³ and delivered
    me,
  in the greatness of your mercy and of
    your name,
from grinding teeth about to devour me,
  from the hand of those seeking my life,
  from the many troubles I endured,
⁴ from choking fire on every side,
  and from the midst of fire that I had not
    kindled,
⁵ from the deep belly of Hades,
  from an unclean tongue and lying
    words—
    ⁶ the slander of an unrighteous tongue
  to the king.
My soul drew near to death,
  and my life was on the brink of Hades
    below.
⁷ They surrounded me on every side,
  and there was no one to help me;
I looked for human assistance,
  and there was none.
⁸ Then I remembered your mercy,
    O Lord,
  and your kindnessᵃ from of old,
for you rescue those who wait for you
  and save them from the hand of their
    enemies.
⁹ And I sent up my prayer from the
    earth,
  and begged for rescue from death.
¹⁰ I cried out, "Lord, you are my Father;ᵇ
  do not forsake me in the days of
    trouble,
  when there is no help against the
    proud.
¹¹ I will praise your name continually,
  and will sing hymns of thanksgiving."
My prayer was heard,
  ¹² for you saved me from destruction
  and rescued me in time of trouble.
For this reason I thank you and praise you,
  and I bless the name of the Lord.

———————

Heb adds:

Give thanks to the LORD, for he is good,
  for his steadfast love endures forever;

Give thanks to the God of praises,
  for his steadfast love endures forever;

Give thanks to the guardian of Israel,
  for his steadfast love endures forever;

Give thanks to him who formed all things,
  for his steadfast love endures forever;

Give thanks to the redeemer of Israel,
  for his steadfast love endures forever;

Give thanks to him who gathers the
    dispersed of Israel,
  for his steadfast love endures forever;

Give thanks to him who rebuilt his city and
    his sanctuary,
  for his steadfast love endures forever;

Give thanks to him who makes a horn to
    sprout for the house of David,
  for his steadfast love endures forever;

Give thanks to him who has chosen the
    sons of Zadok to be priests,
  for his steadfast love endures forever;

Give thanks to the shield of Abraham,
  for his steadfast love endures forever;

Give thanks to the rock of Isaac,
  for his steadfast love endures forever;

Give thanks to the mighty one of Jacob,
  for his steadfast love endures forever;

Give thanks to him who has chosen Zion,
  for his steadfast love endures forever;

Give thanks to the King of the kings of kings,

ᵃ Other ancient authorities read *work*
ᵇ Heb: Gk *the Father of my lord*

51.1–30: Three appendixes. 1–12: A hymn in thanksgiving for deliverance. **5,6:** *Hades*, Heb "Sheol," the abode of the dead. **10:** *Father*, cf. 23.1,4. **12:** Following v. 12, the medieval Hebrew text includes a thanksgiving

for his steadfast love endures
forever;

He has raised up a horn for his people,
praise for all his loyal ones.

For the children of Israel, the people close
to him.
Praise the LORD!

---

¹³ While I was still young, before I went on
my travels,
I sought wisdom openly in my prayer.
¹⁴ Before the temple I asked for her,
and I will search for her until the end.

¹⁵ From the first blossom to the ripening
grape
my heart delighted in her;
my foot walked on the straight path;
from my youth I followed her steps.

¹⁶ I inclined my ear a little and received her,
and I found for myself much
instruction.
¹⁷ I made progress in her;
to him who gives wisdom I will give
glory.

¹⁸ For I resolved to live according to
wisdom,ᵃ
and I was zealous for the good,
and I shall never be disappointed.
¹⁹ My soul grappled with wisdom,ᵃ
and in my conduct I was strict;ᵇ

I spread out my hands to the heavens,
and lamented my ignorance of her.
²⁰ I directed my soul to her,
and in purity I found her.

With her I gained understanding from the
first;
therefore I will never be forsaken.

²¹ My heart was stirred to seek her;
therefore I have gained a prize
possession.
²² The Lord gave me my tongue as a reward,
and I will praise him with it.

²³ Draw near to me, you who are
uneducated,
and lodge in the house of instruction.
²⁴ Why do you say you are lacking in these
things,ᶜ
and why do you endure such great thirst?
²⁵ I opened my mouth and said,
Acquire wisdomᵈ for yourselves without
money.

²⁶ Put your neck under herᵉ yoke,
and let your souls receive instruction;
it is to be found close by.

²⁷ See with your own eyes that I have
labored but little
and found for myself much serenity.
²⁸ Hear but a little of my instruction,
and through me you will acquire silver
and gold.ᶠ

²⁹ May your soul rejoice in God'sᵍ mercy,
and may you never be ashamed to
praise him.
³⁰ Do your work in good time,
and in his own time Godʰ will give you
your reward.

ᵃ   Gk *her*
ᵇ   Meaning of Gk uncertain
ᶜ   Cn Compare Heb Syr: Meaning of Gk uncertain
ᵈ   Heb: Gk lacks *wisdom*
ᵉ   Heb: other ancient authorities read *the*
ᶠ   Syr Compare Heb: Gk *Get instruction with a large
sum of silver, and you will gain by it much gold.*
ᵍ   Gk *his*
ʰ   Gk *he*

hymn based on Ps 136. **13–30:** An autobiographical, acrostic poem on the search for wisdom. Another (some-what more erotic) version of this text appears in a Psalms scroll from Qumran (11QPsa). **13:** *Travels,* cf. 34.11; 39.4. **23:** *Draw near to me,* cf. 14.20–27; Prov 9.1–6. *House of instruction,* a wisdom school, presumably Ben Sira's own in Jerusalem. **26:** *Yoke,* cf. 6.23–31.

BARUCH

NAME AND AUTHORSHIP

The title of the book comes from its opening verse, which attributes the book to Baruch son of Neriah, the scribe of Jeremiah (cf. Jer 32.12; 36.4). This verse places Baruch in the Babylonian exile of the early sixth century BCE, but according to Jer 43.1–7, he and Jeremiah went to Egypt (not Babylon) in 582 BCE. This, along with historical errors in the introduction (1.1–14), suggests that the work was not actually written by Baruch. Following 1.1, later rabbinic tradition places Baruch in Babylon (*Mid. Rab. Song* 5.5; *b. Meg.* 16b; *Seder Olam R.* 26). The book is often referred to as 1 Baruch to distinguish it from several other books also attributed to Baruch, dating from the second century CE.

CANONICAL STATUS AND LOCATION IN CANON

In the Protestant tradition the book of Baruch is included in the Apocrypha; in the Roman Catholic and Eastern Orthodox churches it is one of the deuterocanonical books of the Old Testament. In Catholic Bibles the book is located between Lamentations and Ezekiel, with the Letter of Jeremiah (see p. 1537) appended as the final chapter of Baruch. In the Orthodox churches the book is between Lamentations and the Letter of Jeremiah. Baruch is not included in the Jewish canon of scripture.

DATE OF COMPOSITION AND HISTORICAL CONTEXT

Scholars often date the book of Baruch to the second or first centuries BCE. The book's themes of communal repentance, the gift of the Torah to Israel, and the glorification of Jerusalem through the return of the exiles may indicate a date during the national revival led by the Maccabees that began during the revolt against the Seleucid king Antiochus IV Epiphanes (175–164 BCE).

LITERARY HISTORY, STRUCTURE, AND CONTENTS

The existing text of Baruch is in Greek. On the basis of its literary style scholars think that the book was originally written in Hebrew and then translated into Greek, however, no Hebrew manuscript of Baruch is known. Ancient versions of Baruch in other languages, such as Latin and Syriac, are translations from the Greek.

The book has four major sections:

- A. Historical Introduction (1.1–14)
- B. Confession of Sin (1.15–3.8)
- C. Wisdom Poem (3.9–4.4)
- D. Poem of Consolation (4.5–5.9)

While themes such as confession of sin and exile are found throughout the work, these four sections differ significantly from one another in form and content (see, for example, 3.10n. and 4.10n.). Also, different names for God are used in the confession ("Lord"), in the Wisdom poem ("God"), and in the poem of consolation ("the Everlasting"). Thus the different sections may have been written separately and combined later. Much of the book is a pastiche of quotations and paraphrases of biblical texts (see the annotations). This type of composition, popular in the late Second Temple period, provided a means of interpreting canonical literature and creating new works.

INTERPRETATION

The Babylonian exile was not a living reality for the author of Baruch but a context for reflection on maintaining the vitality of the relationship between God and Israel. The book attributes the Babylonian exile to national sin (1.21–2.1). The curses of the covenant have now come upon the people (1.20; 2.2; compare 2.3 and Deut 28.53). The book offers a way to alleviate this difficult situation: confess your sins and turn to God. The people need to renew their dedication to God and the covenant. This is the core message of the prayer in 1.15–3.8. The poem in 3.9–4.4 encourages Israel to learn "where there is wisdom" (3.14)—God has found Wisdom, and he has given it to Israel in the form of the Torah (3.36–4.1a). Wisdom, as elsewhere in wisdom literature, is associated with life

(3.9; 4.1b; Prov 3.16). God, the book promises, will reward repentance by returning the exiles to Judah (4.36–5.9). The exile represents death and sin (2.17; 3.4,10–11); return to Zion symbolizes life and devotion to God.

Although the book of Baruch originated in the Jewish community, like other such works written in the Hellenistic and Roman eras, it fell out of use in rabbinic Judaism. Early Christian writers, however, frequently quoted the book as scripture. Baruch 3.36–37, which refers to Wisdom appearing on earth and living with humankind, was often cited because of its Christological interpretation (cf. Jn 1.14).

GUIDE TO READING

The opening verses of Baruch describe the book as having been read to the Jews exiled in Babylon; reading aloud was a common practice in antiquity. Modern readers can also appreciate the book's rhetorical appeal by listening to it rather than reading it silently. Even though the book consists of stylistically different sections, readers can experience its unity by noticing verses that reflect its main themes: sin and exile, repentance and the restoration of Zion. In antiquity Jewish education often involved memorizing large sections of scripture. Thus early readers would have recognized the many phrases adapted from biblical books, in particular Deuteronomy, Jeremiah, and Isaiah. The annotations will aid modern readers to identify and recognize these echoes of scripture.

Matthew Goff

1 These are the words of the book that Baruch son of Neriah son of Mahseiah son of Zedekiah son of Hasadiah son of Hilkiah wrote in Babylon, ² in the fifth year, on the seventh day of the month, at the time when the Chaldeans took Jerusalem and burned it with fire.

³ Baruch read the words of this book to Jeconiah son of Jehoiakim, king of Judah, and to all the people who came to hear the book, ⁴ and to the nobles and the princes, and to the elders, and to all the people, small and great, all who lived in Babylon by the river Sud. ⁵ Then they wept, and fasted, and prayed before the Lord; ⁶ they collected as much money as each could give, ⁷ and sent it to Jerusalem to the high priest[a] Jehoiakim son of Hilkiah son of Shallum, and to the priests, and to all the people who were present with

him in Jerusalem. ⁸ At the same time, on the tenth day of Sivan, Baruch[b] took the vessels of the house of the Lord, which had been carried away from the temple, to return them to the land of Judah—the silver vessels that Zedekiah son of Josiah, king of Judah, had made, ⁹ after King Nebuchadnezzar of Babylon had carried away from Jerusalem Jeconiah and the princes and the prisoners and the nobles and the people of the land, and brought them to Babylon.

¹⁰ They said: Here we send you money; so buy with the money burnt offerings and sin offerings and incense, and prepare a grain offering, and offer them on the altar of the Lord our God; ¹¹ and pray for the life of King

a   Gk *the priest*
b   Gk *he*

1.1–14: **Historical introduction. 1–2:** Authorship and date. **1:** *Baruch,* Jeremiah's scribe (Jer 36.4,15; 45.1). The genealogy here is more extensive than in Jer 32.12. **2:** *Fifth year,* after the destruction of Jerusalem in 586 BCE (2 Kings 25.8–12) by the Babylonians (*the Chaldeans*). **3–4:** Baruch reads his book to the other exiles (cf. Jer 36.10). **3:** *Jeconiah,* also called Jehoiachin. He was regarded by the exiles as king (2 Kings 24.15; 25.27–30; Jer 24.1; Ezek 1.2). **4:** *Sud,* the name is otherwise unknown. Perhaps a reference to the river Ahava (Ezra 8.15,21,31). **5–7:** The exiles react to Baruch's reading. **5:** In the book of Baruch the word *Lord* occurs only in 1.1–3.8. **6:** *They collected,* see Ezra 1.4,6. **7:** *The high priest Jehoiakim,* otherwise unknown. The Greek reads "the priest." The genealogy is derived from 1 Chr 6.13–15. **8:** *Sivan,* the third month of the Jewish calendar (May–June). This verse does not agree with Ezra 1.7–11, which states that Sheshbazzar returned the gold and *silver vessels* to Jerusalem after the edict of the Persian king Cyrus (538 BCE). *Zedekiah,* the king of Judah when Jerusalem fell (2 Kings 24.18–25.7). 2 Kings never claims that Zedekiah fashioned temple vessels. **9:** Jer 24.1; 2 Kings 24.10–16. **10–14:** Instruction that accompanies the scroll sent by exiles to the Jews who remained in Jerusalem. **10:** Jer 41.5 indicates that

Nebuchadnezzar of Babylon, and for the life of his son Belshazzar, so that their days on earth may be like the days of heaven. [12] The Lord will give us strength, and light to our eyes; we shall live under the protection[a] of King Nebuchadnezzar of Babylon, and under the protection of his son Belshazzar, and we shall serve them many days and find favor in their sight. [13] Pray also for us to the Lord our God, for we have sinned against the Lord our God, and to this day the anger of the Lord and his wrath have not turned away from us. [14] And you shall read aloud this scroll that we are sending you, to make your confession in the house of the Lord on the days of the festivals and at appointed seasons.

[15] And you shall say: The Lord our God is in the right, but there is open shame on us today, on the people of Judah, on the inhabitants of Jerusalem, [16] and on our kings, our rulers, our priests, our prophets, and our ancestors, [17] because we have sinned before the Lord. [18] We have disobeyed him, and have not heeded the voice of the Lord our God, to walk in the statutes of the Lord that he set before us. [19] From the time when the Lord brought our ancestors out of the land of Egypt until today, we have been disobedient to the Lord our God, and we have been negligent, in not heeding his voice. [20] So to this day there have clung to us the calamities and the curse that the Lord declared through his servant Moses at the time when he brought our ancestors out of the land of Egypt to give to us a land flowing with milk and honey. [21] We did not listen to the voice of the Lord our God in all the words of the prophets whom he sent to us, [22] but all of us followed the intent of our own wicked hearts by serving other gods and doing what is evil in the sight of the Lord our God.

2 So the Lord carried out the threat he spoke against us: against our judges who ruled Israel, and against our kings and our rulers and the people of Israel and Judah. [2] Under the whole heaven there has not been done the like of what he has done in Jerusalem, in accordance with the threats that were[b] written in the law of Moses. [3] Some of us ate the flesh of their sons and others the flesh of their daughters. [4] He made them subject to all the kingdoms around us, to be an object of scorn and a desolation among all the surrounding peoples, where the Lord has scattered them. [5] They were brought down and not raised up, because our nation[c] sinned against the Lord our God, in not heeding his voice.

[6] The Lord our God is in the right, but there is open shame on us and our ancestors this very day. [7] All those calamities with which the Lord threatened us have come upon us. [8] Yet we have not entreated the favor of the Lord by turning away, each of us, from the thoughts of our wicked hearts. [9] And the Lord has kept the calamities ready, and the Lord has brought them upon us, for the Lord is just in all the works that he has commanded us to do. [10] Yet we have not obeyed his voice, to walk in the statutes of the Lord that he set before us.

[11] And now, O Lord God of Israel, who brought your people out of the land of Egypt with a mighty hand and with signs and wonders and with great power and outstretched arm, and made yourself a name that continues to this day, [12] we have sinned, we have

a Gk *in the shadow*
b Gk *in accordance with what is*
c Gk *because we*

incense and *grain* offerings continued at the ruined temple; cf. Jer 17.26. **11:** Jer 29.7. Belshazzar was the son of Nabonidus. Dan 5 makes the same error.

1.15–3.8: Confession of sin. This prayer draws on numerous biblical texts, including Lev 26, Deut 28, and parts of Jeremiah. It also has many links with Dan 9.4–19. Bar 1.15–2.5 appears to be intended for the Jewish community in Palestine and 2.6–3.8 for Jews in exile; compare 1.15–16 and 2.13–14. **1.15–18:** The Jews in Judah confess their disobedience to God and his commandments (Dan 9.7–10). This refrain is similar to 2.6–10, which helps mark the division between the two sections of 1.15–3.8. **15:** *Open shame*, repeated in 2.6. See Dan 9.7–8; Ezra 9.7. **18:** 2.10; Dan 9.10. **1.19–2.5:** Israel's disobedience is given a historical context, from the Exodus to the Babylonian exile. **19:** 2 Kings 21.15; Jer 7.25. **20:** *Curse*, Lev 26; Deut 28; Jer 11.3–5. **21:** Jer 7.25–26; 26.4–5; Dan 9.5–6,10. **22:** 2.8. **2.1–2:** Dan 9.12–13. **3:** Lev 26.29; Deut 28.53; Jer 19.9; Lam 4.10. **4:** Cf. Jer 42.18. **5:** Deut 28.13. **6–10:** Confession of guilt. See 1.15–18; Dan 9.12–14. **11–26:** Supplication and confession. **11–14:** Dan 9.15–17. **11:**

been ungodly, we have done wrong, O Lord our God, against all your ordinances. [13] Let your anger turn away from us, for we are left, few in number, among the nations where you have scattered us. [14] Hear, O Lord, our prayer and our supplication, and for your own sake deliver us, and grant us favor in the sight of those who have carried us into exile; [15] so that all the earth may know that you are the Lord our God, for Israel and his descendants are called by your name.

[16] O Lord, look down from your holy dwelling, and consider us. Incline your ear, O Lord, and hear; [17] open your eyes, O Lord, and see, for the dead who are in Hades, whose spirit has been taken from their bodies, will not ascribe glory or justice to the Lord; [18] but the person who is deeply grieved, who walks bowed and feeble, with failing eyes and famished soul, will declare your glory and righteousness, O Lord.

[19] For it is not because of any righteous deeds of our ancestors or our kings that we bring before you our prayer for mercy, O Lord our God. [20] For you have sent your anger and your wrath upon us, as you declared by your servants the prophets, saying: [21] Thus says the Lord: Bend your shoulders and serve the king of Babylon, and you will remain in the land that I gave to your ancestors. [22] But if you will not obey the voice of the Lord and will not serve the king of Babylon, [23] I will make to cease from the towns of Judah and from the region around Jerusalem the voice of mirth and the voice of gladness, the voice of the bridegroom and the voice of the bride, and the whole land will be a desolation without inhabitants.

[24] But we did not obey your voice, to serve the king of Babylon; and you have carried out your threats, which you spoke by your servants the prophets, that the bones of our kings and the bones of our ancestors would be brought out of their resting place; [25] and indeed they have been thrown out to the heat of day and the frost of night. They perished in great misery, by famine and sword and pestilence. [26] And the house that is called by your name you have made as it is today, because of the wickedness of the house of Israel and the house of Judah.

[27] Yet you have dealt with us, O Lord our God, in all your kindness and in all your great compassion, [28] as you spoke by your servant Moses on the day when you commanded him to write your law in the presence of the people of Israel, saying, [29] "If you will not obey my voice, this very great multitude will surely turn into a small number among the nations, where I will scatter them. [30] For I know that they will not obey me, for they are a stiff-necked people. But in the land of their exile they will come to themselves [31] and know that I am the Lord their God. I will give them a heart that obeys and ears that hear; [32] they will praise me in the land of their exile, and will remember my name [33] and turn from their stubbornness and their wicked deeds; for they will remember the ways of their ancestors, who sinned before the Lord. [34] I will bring them again into the land that I swore to give to their ancestors, to Abraham, Isaac, and Jacob, and they will rule over it; and I will increase them, and they will not be diminished. [35] I will make an everlasting covenant with them to be their God and they shall be my people; and I will never again remove my people Israel from the land that I have given them."

3 O Lord Almighty, God of Israel, the soul in anguish and the wearied spirit cry out to you. [2] Hear, O Lord, and have mercy, for we have sinned before you. [3] For you are enthroned forever, and we are perishing

---

Ex 15.11–16; Jer 32.20–21. **12:** Cf. 1 Kings 8.47 and Ps 106.6. **13:** Deut 4.27; Jer 42.2. **15:** Cf. Deut 28.10; Jer 14.9. **16:** Deut 26.15; 1 Kings 8.39; Isa 63.15; Dan 9.18. **17:** Pss 6.5; 30.9; Isa 38.18; Sir 17.27–28. *Hades,* in Hebrew "Sheol," the underworld abode of the dead. **18:** Deut 28.65–66. **20:** Jer 36.7. **21:** Jer 27.11–12. **23:** Jer 7.34; 16.9; 33.10–11. **24:** Jer 8.1–2. **25:** Jer 36.30. **26:** Jer 7.14. **27–35:** Repentance and restoration illustrate God's compassion for Israel. The words attributed to Moses in vv. 29–34 have no verbatim match in the Hebrew Bible but resemble phrases from Deuteronomy and Jeremiah. **29:** Deut 28.58,62. **30:** 1 Kings 8.47. **31:** Jer 24.7. **34:** Lev 26.42–45; Deut 6.10; 30.1–5; Jer 32.37. **35:** Jer 24.6; 32.38–40. **3.1–8:** Appeal to God to hear the prayer of the exiles. **4:** The Greek word *dead* (see textual note *a*) may represent the confusion of two similar Hebrew terms, one which means "dead" and the other "men." Note, however, that elsewhere in the book exile is symbolically depicted as a form of death (2.17;

forever. ⁴ O Lord Almighty, God of Israel, hear now the prayer of the people[a] of Israel, the children of those who sinned before you, who did not heed the voice of the Lord their God, so that calamities have clung to us. ⁵ Do not remember the iniquities of our ancestors, but in this crisis remember your power and your name. ⁶ For you are the Lord our God, and it is you, O Lord, whom we will praise. ⁷ For you have put the fear of you in our hearts so that we would call upon your name; and we will praise you in our exile, for we have put away from our hearts all the iniquity of our ancestors who sinned against you. ⁸ See, we are today in our exile where you have scattered us, to be reproached and cursed and punished for all the iniquities of our ancestors, who forsook the Lord our God.

⁹ Hear the commandments of life, O Israel;
    give ear, and learn wisdom!
¹⁰ Why is it, O Israel, why is it that you are
        in the land of your enemies,
    that you are growing old in a foreign
        country,
    that you are defiled with the dead,
¹¹ that you are counted among those in
        Hades?
¹² You have forsaken the fountain of
        wisdom.
¹³ If you had walked in the way of God,
    you would be living in peace forever.
¹⁴ Learn where there is wisdom,
    where there is strength,
    where there is understanding,

so that you may at the same time discern
    where there is length of days, and life,
    where there is light for the eyes, and
        peace.

¹⁵ Who has found her place?
    And who has entered her storehouses?
¹⁶ Where are the rulers of the nations,
    and those who lorded it over the
        animals on earth;
¹⁷ those who made sport of the birds of the
        air,
    and who hoarded up silver and gold
    in which people trust,
        and there is no end to their getting;
¹⁸ those who schemed to get silver, and
        were anxious,
    but there is no trace of their works?
¹⁹ They have vanished and gone down to
        Hades,
    and others have arisen in their place.

²⁰ Later generations have seen the light of
        day,
    and have lived upon the earth;
    but they have not learned the way to
        knowledge,
    nor understood her paths,
    nor laid hold of her.
²¹ Their descendants have strayed far from
        her[b] way.
²² She has not been heard of in Canaan,
    or seen in Teman;

a   Gk *dead*
b   Other ancient authorities read *their*

3.10–11). 7: 1 Kings 8.47–48; Jer 32.40b. 8: 2.4. The exile is punishment for sins committed by earlier generations (2.33; 3.4–5; Ex 20.5; 34.7; Lam 5.7; cf. Jer 31.29–30; Ezek 18).

3.9–4.4: Wisdom poem. Wisdom, personified as a woman, is elusive but known to God, who gave her to Israel as the Torah. This section has many affinities with Sir 24 and Job 28. 3.9–14: Introduction to the poem, exhorting Israel to learn wisdom. 9: *The commandments of life*, Deut 30.15–20; Sir 45.5. 10: This verse connects the Wisdom poem of 3.9–4.4 to the confession of sin in 1.15–3.8. *Growing old*, the exile has continued for a long time (contrast 1.2). 11: Pss 28.1; 88.4. *Hades*, see 2.17n. 12: Prov 18.4; Jer 2.13; 2 Esd 14.47. 14: Prov 3.2,13–18; Job 12.13. 15–23: Gentile kings and nations do not possess wisdom. 15: Job 28.12,20. 16b–17a: Jer 27.6; Dan 2.37–38; Jdt 11.7. 17b–19: Those who searched for riches were unable to avoid death. The Torah, by contrast, is associated with life (4.1; cf. Prov 8.10–11,19). 22: *Canaan*, here probably a reference to the Phoenicians (cf. Gen 10.15), whose coastal cities Tyre and Sidon were associated with wisdom and mercantile skill (Isa 23.8; Ezek 28.3–5; Zech 9.2). *Teman*, in Edom, a region known for its wisdom (Jer 49.7; Ob 8–9; cf. Gen 36.9–11). 23: *The descendants of Hagar*, the Ishmaelites, who were Arabian tribal groups with a reputation for trade and commerce (Gen 25.12–15; 37.25). *Merran*, the word occurs nowhere else in the Bible. It may be a corruption of "Midian," an area well-known for its traders in the northern Hejaz region of Arabia, east of the Gulf of Aqaba

²³ the descendants of Hagar, who seek for
  understanding on the earth,
  the merchants of Merran and Teman,
  the story-tellers and the seekers for
    understanding,
have not learned the way to wisdom,
  or given thought to her paths.

²⁴ O Israel, how great is the house of God,
  how vast the territory that he possesses!
²⁵ It is great and has no bounds;
  it is high and immeasurable.
²⁶ The giants were born there, who were
    famous of old,
  great in stature, expert in war.
²⁷ God did not choose them,
  or give them the way to knowledge;
²⁸ so they perished because they had no
    wisdom,
  they perished through their folly.

²⁹ Who has gone up into heaven, and taken
    her,
  and brought her down from the clouds?
³⁰ Who has gone over the sea, and found
    her,
  and will buy her for pure gold?
³¹ No one knows the way to her,
  or is concerned about the path to her.
³² But the one who knows all things knows
    her,
  he found her by his understanding.
The one who prepared the earth for all time
  filled it with four-footed creatures;
³³ the one who sends forth the light, and
    it goes;
  he called it, and it obeyed him,
    trembling;

³⁴ the stars shone in their watches, and
    were glad;
  he called them, and they said, "Here we
    are!"
  They shone with gladness for him who
    made them.
³⁵ This is our God;
  no other can be compared to him.
³⁶ He found the whole way to knowledge,
  and gave her to his servant Jacob
  and to Israel, whom he loved.
³⁷ Afterward she appeared on earth
  and lived with humankind.

4 She is the book of the commandments
    of God,
  the law that endures forever.
All who hold her fast will live,
  and those who forsake her will die.
² Turn, O Jacob, and take her;
  walk toward the shining of her light.
³ Do not give your glory to another,
  or your advantages to an alien people.
⁴ Happy are we, O Israel,
  for we know what is pleasing to God.

⁵ Take courage, my people,
  who perpetuate Israel's name!
⁶ It was not for destruction
  that you were sold to the nations,
but you were handed over to your enemies
  because you angered God.
⁷ For you provoked the one who made you
  by sacrificing to demons and not to God.
⁸ You forgot the everlasting God, who
    brought you up,
  and you grieved Jerusalem, who reared
    you.

(Gen 25.2; 37.28; Isa 60.6). **24–28:** This section praises the magnitude of God's creation. **24:** *The house of God*, the context suggests that this refers to the created world rather than the Jerusalem temple. **26:** *The giants*, the legendary offspring of angels and women recounted in Gen 6.1–4; cf. *1 En.* 6–8; *Jub.* 5. **28:** Sir 16.7; Wis 14.6; 3 Macc 2.4. **29–37:** Only God has Wisdom, and he gives it to Israel. **29:** Deut 30.12–14; cf. Prov 30.4; Sir 24.4. **30:** Job 28.14–15. **32:** Job 28.23. God finds Wisdom (see v. 36), whereas in Ben Sira he creates Wisdom (Sir 24.3,9; cf. Prov 8:22). **33:** The trembling of *the light* denotes its fear and obedience before God (cf. Gen 1.3; Job 38.35). **34:** Job 38.7; Ps 148.3; Sir 43.10. **36:** Sir 24.8. **37:** Divine Wisdom appears on earth in Prov 8 and Sir 24.6–12 (cf. Wis 1.7; 9.10). Contrast *1 En.* 42. **4.1–4:** Identification of Wisdom as the Torah, which Israel should embrace. The personification of Wisdom as a woman is more prominent in Prov 8 and Sir 24 (cf. Wis 6–9). **1:** Prov 3.18; Sir 24.23 (cf. 6.37; 15.1). **4:** Deut 33.29.

4.5–5.9: Poem of consolation. 4.5–8: Introductory exhortation, stressing that God wished to punish, not destroy, Israel because of its sins. **5:** *Take courage*, a refrain of the poem (vv. 21,27,30; cf. Isa 40.1). **6:** Isa 50.1b; 52.3. **7:** Deut 32.16–17; Ps 106.37. **8:** Gen 21.33; Isa 40.28. **9b–16:** Jerusalem personified addresses neighboring

9 For she saw the wrath that came upon
    you from God,
  and she said:
Listen, you neighbors of Zion,
    God has brought great sorrow upon me;
10 for I have seen the exile of my sons and
    daughters,
  which the Everlasting brought upon
    them.
11 With joy I nurtured them,
  but I sent them away with weeping and
    sorrow.
12 Let no one rejoice over me, a widow
  and bereaved of many;
I was left desolate because of the sins of
    my children,
  because they turned away from the law
    of God.
13 They had no regard for his statutes;
  they did not walk in the ways of God's
    commandments,
  or tread the paths his righteousness
    showed them.
14 Let the neighbors of Zion come;
  remember the capture of my sons and
    daughters,
  which the Everlasting brought upon
    them.
15 For he brought a distant nation against
    them,
  a nation ruthless and of a strange
    language,
which had no respect for the aged
  and no pity for a child.
16 They led away the widow's beloved sons,
  and bereaved the lonely woman of her
    daughters.

17 But I, how can I help you?
18 For he who brought these calamities
    upon you
  will deliver you from the hand of your
    enemies.
19 Go, my children, go;
  for I have been left desolate.

20 I have taken off the robe of peace
  and put on sackcloth for my
    supplication;
  I will cry to the Everlasting all my days.

21 Take courage, my children, cry to God,
  and he will deliver you from the power
    and hand of the enemy.
22 For I have put my hope in the Everlasting
    to save you,
  and joy has come to me from the Holy
    One,
because of the mercy that will soon come
    to you
  from your everlasting savior.[a]
23 For I sent you out with sorrow and
    weeping,
  but God will give you back to me with
    joy and gladness forever.
24 For as the neighbors of Zion have now
    seen your capture,
  so they soon will see your salvation by
    God,
which will come to you with great glory
  and with the splendor of the
    Everlasting.
25 My children, endure with patience the
    wrath that has come upon you from
    God.
Your enemy has overtaken you,
  but you will soon see their destruction
  and will tread upon their necks.
26 My pampered children have traveled
    rough roads;
  they were taken away like a flock
    carried off by the enemy.

27 Take courage, my children, and cry to God,
  for you will be remembered by the one
    who brought this upon you.
28 For just as you were disposed to go
    astray from God,
  return with tenfold zeal to seek him.

a Or *from the Everlasting, your savior*

cities. **9:** Lam 1.12. **10:** *Everlasting*, a term for God characteristic of this poem that is not found in other sections
of the book of Baruch (vv. 14,20,22,24,35; 5.2). **12:** Isa 49.21; 54.4; Lam 1.1. **15:** Deut 28.49–50; Isa 33.19. **17–29:**
Jerusalem personified speaks to the exiles. **20:** Contrast Isa 52.1. *Robe of peace*, worn during a time of prosperity.
Sackcloth, worn in times of mourning and penitence (e.g., Isa 3.24; Jer 6.26; Lam 2.10). **22:** *The Holy One*, a name
for God that is prominent in Isaiah (e.g., 5.19; 12.6; 43.3; 47.4; 60.9) found also in 4.37; 5.5 but not elsewhere in
the book of Baruch. **23:** Ps 126.6; Isa 35.10; 51.11; Jer 31.12–13. **24:** Isa 60.1–3. **25:** Deut 33.29; Isa 51.23. *The wrath*

²⁹ For the one who brought these
   calamities upon you
will bring you everlasting joy with your
   salvation.

³⁰ Take courage, O Jerusalem,
   for the one who named you will
   comfort you.
³¹ Wretched will be those who mistreated
   you
   and who rejoiced at your fall.
³² Wretched will be the cities that your
   children served as slaves;
   wretched will be the city that received
   your offspring.
³³ For just as she rejoiced at your fall
   and was glad for your ruin,
   so she will be grieved at her own
   desolation.
³⁴ I will take away her pride in her great
   population,
   and her insolence will be turned to
   grief.
³⁵ For fire will come upon her from the
   Everlasting for many days,
   and for a long time she will be inhabited
   by demons.

³⁶ Look toward the east, O Jerusalem,
   and see the joy that is coming to you
   from God.
³⁷ Look, your children are coming, whom
   you sent away;
   they are coming, gathered from east
   and west,
at the word of the Holy One,
   rejoicing in the glory of God.

5 Take off the garment of your sorrow and
   affliction, O Jerusalem,
   and put on forever the beauty of the
   glory from God.
² Put on the robe of the righteousness that
   comes from God;
   put on your head the diadem of the
   glory of the Everlasting;
³ for God will show your splendor
   everywhere under heaven.
⁴ For God will give you evermore the name,
   "Righteous Peace, Godly Glory."

⁵ Arise, O Jerusalem, stand upon the
   height;
   look toward the east,
and see your children gathered from west
   and east
   at the word of the Holy One,
   rejoicing that God has remembered
   them.
⁶ For they went out from you on foot,
   led away by their enemies;
but God will bring them back to you,
   carried in glory, as on a royal throne.
⁷ For God has ordered that every high
   mountain and the everlasting hills be
   made low
   and the valleys filled up, to make level
   ground,
   so that Israel may walk safely in the
   glory of God.
⁸ The woods and every fragrant tree
   have shaded Israel at God's command.
⁹ For God will lead Israel with joy,
   in the light of his glory,
   with the mercy and righteousness that
   come from him.

has a short duration (cf. Isa 54.7–8). **4.30–5.9:** The narrator consoles Jerusalem with the prospect of the exiles'
return. **30–35:** Jerusalem is encouraged by the fall of her enemies, referring to Babylon and perhaps Edom (Ps
137.7–8; Isa 63.1–6; cf. Isa 13–14; 47; Jer 50–51). Contrast the attitude toward Babylon in 1.11–12. **30:** *The one who
named you*, see 5.4n. Cf. Isa 51.3. **35:** *Fire*, Jer 51.58; *demons*, Isa 13.21; 34.14. **4.36–5.4:** Jerusalem is exhorted to
watch the exiles return from the east. **36–37:** See 5.5n. **5.1–2:** 4.20; Isa 52.1; 61.3,10; *Pss. Sol.* 11.7. **4:** The renaming
of Jerusalem, which marks a change in status, is a theme in the prophetic books (Isa 1.26; 60.14; 62.2–4; Jer 33.16;
Ezek 48.35). *Righteous Peace*, Isa 32.17; 60.17. **5.5–9:** A second call for Jerusalem to watch God bring the exiles to
her. **5:** 4.36; Isa 40.9–11; 43.5; 49.18; 51.17; 60.4; *Pss. Sol.* 11.2–3. **6:** Isa 49.22; 66.20. **7:** Isa 40.4–5; 42.16; *Pss. Sol.*
11.4. **8:** *Pss. Sol.* 11.5–6. Cf. Isa 41.19.

THE LETTER OF JEREMIAH

NAME AND AUTHORSHIP

The work claims to be a copy of a letter written by the prophet Jeremiah for Judeans about to be exiled to Babylonia in 597 BCE. The Letter, however, never gives the impression that the siege of Jerusalem and the Babylonian exile are recent calamities. Moreover, it draws on the canonical book of Jeremiah and other biblical texts (see next sections). Thus the Letter was probably written much later and attributed to Jeremiah, inspired by the account in Jer 29 of Jeremiah's writing to the exilic community.

CANONICAL STATUS AND LOCATION IN CANON

The Letter is not part of the Jewish or Protestant canons. In the Roman Catholic and Orthodox traditions it is deuterocanonical. Major Greek Septuagint manuscripts, such as Vaticanus (fourth century CE) and Alexandrinus (fifth century CE), treat the Letter as a distinct work placed between Lamentations and Ezekiel. The Latin Vulgate, which is prominent in the Roman Catholic tradition, considers the text the sixth chapter of Baruch. The Letter appears in the NRSV as an independent book because it differs markedly from Baruch in terms of style and content; there is no strong evidence that it was originally part of Baruch (but see also note a).

DATE OF COMPOSITION AND HISTORICAL CONTEXT

Although the Letter purports to be sent to the Judeans about to be exiled to Babylonia in the early sixth century BCE, many scholars date the Letter to the Hellenistic period. The reference in v. 3 to an exile lasting seven generations (280 years) could, if taken literally, indicate that the text was written in 317 BCE. The "seven generations," however, should probably be read symbolically. 2 Macc 2.1–3 refers to the Letter, and a fragment of a Greek papyrus from Cave 7 of Qumran (7Q2) contains a portion of Let Jer 43–44; these factors indicate that the work was written before 100 BCE.

LITERARY HISTORY, STRUCTURE, AND CONTENTS

Although the oldest surviving manuscripts of the Letter are in Greek, there are indications that it was originally written in Hebrew or Aramaic and then translated into Greek (see 12n. and 72n.).

After a historical introduction (vv. 1–7), the body of the composition consists of ten warnings about idolatry. Each unit ends with a refrain that idols are not gods and that they should not be feared (vv. 16,23,29,40,44,52,56,65,69,72).

INTERPRETATION

The Letter of Jeremiah warns Jews to avoid pagan religion and asserts that idols are false gods that have no power. Since the veneration of idols was widespread, the text would have had relevance not only to Jewish exiles living in Babylon but to Jews living anywhere in the ancient world. The work is influenced by biblical condemnations of idolatry such as Deut 4.27–28; Isa 44.9–20; 46.5–7; Pss 115.3–8; 135.15–18; cf. Wis 13–15. The Letter also relies upon and expands Jer 10. Despite the identification of the composition as a letter, inspired by the prophet's epistle to the exiles in Jer 29, the work does not belong to the genre of ancient letters and is better classified as a homily or sermon.

GUIDE TO READING

The homiletical style of the Letter, with its vivid imagery, repeated refrains, reliance on formulaic biblical denunciations of idolatry, and sarcastic humor is intended to reinforce beliefs and values already held by its Jewish audience. The author shows no sympathy for actual pagan customs, and the Letter cannot be read as an accurate description of the way in which pagans understood their own religious practices.

Matthew Goff

6 ^a A copy of a letter that Jeremiah sent to those who were to be taken to Babylon as exiles by the king of the Babylonians, to give them the message that God had commanded him.

² Because of the sins that you have committed before God, you will be taken to Babylon as exiles by Nebuchadnezzar, king of the Babylonians. ³ Therefore when you have come to Babylon you will remain there for many years, for a long time, up to seven generations; after that I will bring you away from there in peace. ⁴ Now in Babylon you will see gods made of silver and gold and wood, which people carry on their shoulders, and which cause the heathen to fear. ⁵ So beware of becoming at all like the foreigners or of letting fear for these gods^b possess you ⁶ when you see the multitude before and behind them worshiping them. But say in your heart, "It is you, O Lord, whom we must worship." ⁷ For my angel is with you, and he is watching over your lives.

⁸ Their tongues are smoothed by the carpenter, and they themselves are overlaid with gold and silver; but they are false and cannot speak. ⁹ People^c take gold and make crowns for the heads of their gods, as they might for a girl who loves ornaments. ¹⁰ Sometimes the priests secretly take gold and silver from their gods and spend it on themselves, ¹¹ or even give some of it to the prostitutes on the terrace. They deck their gods^d out with garments like human beings—these gods of silver and gold and wood ¹² that cannot save themselves from rust and corrosion. When they have been dressed in purple robes, ¹³ their faces are wiped because of the dust from the temple, which is thick upon them. ¹⁴ One of them holds a scepter, like a district judge, but is unable to destroy anyone who offends it. ¹⁵ Another has a dagger in its right hand, and an ax, but cannot defend itself from war and robbers. ¹⁶ From this it is evident that they are not gods; so do not fear them.

¹⁷ For just as someone's dish is useless when it is broken, ¹⁸ so are their gods when they have been set up in the temples. Their eyes are full of the dust raised by the feet of those who enter. And just as the gates are shut on every side against anyone who has offended a king, as though under sentence of death, so the priests make their temples secure with doors and locks and bars, in order that they may not be plundered by robbers. ¹⁹ They light more lamps for them than they light for themselves, though their gods^e can see none of them. ²⁰ They are^f just like a beam of the temple, but their hearts, it is said, are eaten away when crawling creatures from the earth devour them and their robes. They do not notice ²¹ when their faces have been blackened by the smoke

^a The King James Version (like the Latin Vulgate) prints The Letter of Jeremiah as Chapter 6 of the Book of Baruch, and the chapter and verse numbers are here retained. In the Greek Septuagint, the Letter is separated from Baruch by the Book of Lamentations.
^b Gk *for them*
^c Gk *They*
^d Gk *them*
^e Gk *they*
^f Gk *It is*

6.1–7: Historical introduction. 1: The exile of 597 BCE (2 Kings 24.10–17). *Who were to be taken*, the work is composed for people about to be exiled. The letter in Jer 29 is written by the prophet to Jews already in exile. **3:** *Seven generations*, taken literally, the duration of the exile in Babylon. Contrast the different figures given in Jer 25.12; 29.10 (seventy years), Ezek 4.6 (forty years) and Dan 9.24 (seventy weeks of years). **4:** *Silver and gold*, overlaid on wood (v. 55; Jer 10.3–4; cf. Isa 40.19). *Which people carry on their shoulders*, this may refer to the procession that was part of the *Akitu*, the Babylonian New Year festival (see v. 26). **5:** Jer 10.2.

6.8–73: Warnings against idolatry. 8–16: First warning: the helplessness of idols. 8: *Carpenter*, Isa 40.20; 44.13; Jer. 10.3–4. *Cannot speak*, Pss 115.4–5; 135.15–16. **11:** *Prostitutes* may refer to women who earned money for vows through prostitution (cf. v. 43). **12:** *Purple robes*, a symbol of authority (cf. Jer 10.9). *Corrosion*, several Greek manuscripts give this word as either "food" or "meat." It is most likely a mistranslation of a Hebrew word for "moth." **15:** Vv. 48–49,57.

6.17–23: Second warning: the uselessness of idols. 17: V. 59; Jer 22.28; Hos 8.8. **18:** *Robbers*, see vv. 57–58n. **19:** Despite many lamps, the idols cannot see (Deut 4.28; Pss 115.5; 135.16; Isa 44.18). **20:** Being wooden, the idols are subject to decay and infestation. **22:** The earliest reference in Jewish literature to *cats*, first domesticated in Egypt.

of the temple. [22] Bats, swallows, and birds alight on their bodies and heads; and so do cats. [23] From this you will know that they are not gods; so do not fear them.

[24] As for the gold that they wear for beauty—it[a] will not shine unless someone wipes off the tarnish; for even when they were being cast, they did not feel it. [25] They are bought without regard to cost, but there is no breath in them. [26] Having no feet, they are carried on the shoulders of others, revealing to humankind their worthlessness. And those who serve them are put to shame [27] because, if any of these gods falls[b] to the ground, they themselves must pick it up. If anyone sets it upright, it cannot move itself; and if it is tipped over, it cannot straighten itself. Gifts are placed before them just as before the dead. [28] The priests sell the sacrifices that are offered to these gods[c] and use the money themselves. Likewise their wives preserve some of the meat[d] with salt, but give none to the poor or helpless. [29] Sacrifices to them may even be touched by women in their periods or at childbirth. Since you know by these things that they are not gods, do not fear them.

[30] For how can they be called gods? Women serve meals for gods of silver and gold and wood; [31] and in their temples the priests sit with their clothes torn, their heads and beards shaved, and their heads uncovered. [32] They howl and shout before their gods as some do at a funeral banquet. [33] The priests take some of the clothing of their gods[e] to clothe their wives and children. [34] Whether one does evil to them or good,

they will not be able to repay it. They cannot set up a king or depose one. [35] Likewise they are not able to give either wealth or money; if one makes a vow to them and does not keep it, they will not require it. [36] They cannot save anyone from death or rescue the weak from the strong. [37] They cannot restore sight to the blind; they cannot rescue one who is in distress. [38] They cannot take pity on a widow or do good to an orphan. [39] These things that are made of wood and overlaid with gold and silver are like stones from the mountain, and those who serve them will be put to shame. [40] Why then must anyone think that they are gods, or call them gods?

Besides, even the Chaldeans themselves dishonor them; for when they see someone who cannot speak, they bring Bel and pray that the mute may speak, as though Bel[f] were able to understand! [41] Yet they themselves cannot perceive this and abandon them, for they have no sense. [42] And the women, with cords around them, sit along the passage-ways, burning bran for incense. [43] When one of them is led off by one of the passers-by and is taken to bed by him, she derides the woman next to her, because she was not as attractive as herself and her cord was not broken. [44] Whatever is done for these idols[g] is

a Lat Syr: Gk *they*
b Gk *if they fall*
c Gk *to them*
d Gk *of them*
e Gk *some of their clothing*
f Gk *he*
g Gk *them*

6.24–29: Third warning: the lifelessness of idols. 25: *No breath*, Ps 135.17; Jer 10.14; 51.17; Hab 2.19. 26: V. 4; Isa 46.1, 7a; Jer 10.5. 27: Isa 46.7b; Jer 10.4 (cf. 1 Sam 5.3). *Gifts* for *the dead*, Ps 106.28; Tob 4.17; Sir 30.18–19. 29: Biblical purity regulations state that women during and shortly after menstruation and childbirth are not allowed to participate in worship (Lev 12.2–5; 15.19–24).

6.30–40a: Fourth warning: the powerlessness of idols. 30: Only men were priests in the Temple in Jerusalem; but see Ex 38.8; 1 Sam 2.22. 31–32: Ritual mourning, presumably for gods such as the Mesopotamian deity Tammuz, whose descent into the netherworld was annually observed with similar practices (Ezek 8.14; cf. Lev 21.5). *Funeral banquets*, Jer 16.5–9. 34b: V. 53; cf. Job 12.18; Dan 2.21. 35b: Deut 23.21. 36: Deut 32.39; 1 Sam 2.6. 37: Ps 146.8. 38: Deut 10.18; Ps 146.9. 39: Isa 44.11; Hab 2.19.

6.40b–44: Fifth warning: the folly of revering idols. 40b: *Chaldeans*, often a synonym for "Babylonians." The term can also refer to astrologers or diviners (e.g., Dan 2.2,4). *Bel* ("Lord"), a title for Marduk, the patron god of the city of Babylon (Isa 46.1; Jer 50.2; 51.44; Bel 1.3). 43: The Greek historian Herodotus (1.199) describes a similar practice among the Babylonians (cf. v. 11).

6.45–52: Sixth warning: idols are not divine but the work of human hands. 45: Isa 40.15; Jer 10.9; Pss 115.4;

false. Why then must anyone think that they are gods, or call them gods?

45 They are made by carpenters and goldsmiths; they can be nothing but what the artisans wish them to be. 46 Those who make them will certainly not live very long themselves; 47 how then can the things that are made by them be gods? They have left only lies and reproach for those who come after. 48 For when war or calamity comes upon them, the priests consult together as to where they can hide themselves and their gods.a 49 How then can one fail to see that these are not gods, for they cannot save themselves from war or calamity? 50 Since they are made of wood and overlaid with gold and silver, it will afterward be known that they are false. 51 It will be manifest to all the nations and kings that they are not gods but the work of human hands, and that there is no work of God in them. 52 Who then can fail to know that they are not gods?b

53 For they cannot set up a king over a country or give rain to people. 54 They cannot judge their own cause or deliver one who is wronged, for they have no power; 55 they are like crows between heaven and earth. When fire breaks out in a temple of wooden gods overlaid with gold or silver, their priests will flee and escape, but the godsc will be burned up like timbers. 56 Besides, they can offer no resistance to king or enemy. Why then must anyone admit or think that they are gods?

57 Gods made of wood and overlaid with silver and gold are unable to save themselves from thieves or robbers. 58 Anyone who can will strip them of their gold and silver and of the robes they wear, and go off with this booty, and they will not be able to help themselves. 59 So it is better to be a king who shows his courage, or a household utensil that serves its owner's need, than to be these false gods; better even the door of a house that protects its contents, than these false gods; better also a wooden pillar in a palace, than these false gods.

60 For sun and moon and stars are bright, and when sent to do a service, they are obedient. 61 So also the lightning, when it flashes, is widely seen; and the wind likewise blows in every land. 62 When God commands the clouds to go over the whole world, they carry out his command. 63 And the fire sent from above to consume mountains and woods does what it is ordered. But these idolsd are not to be compared with them in appearance or power. 64 Therefore one must not think that they are gods, nor call them gods, for they are not able either to decide a case or to do good to anyone. 65 Since you know then that they are not gods, do not fear them.

66 They can neither curse nor bless kings; 67 they cannot show signs in the heavens for the nations, or shine like the sun or give light like the moon. 68 The wild animals are better than they are, for they can flee to shelter and help themselves. 69 So we have no evidence whatever that they are gods; therefore do not fear them.

70 Like a scarecrow in a cucumber bed, which guards nothing, so are their gods of wood, overlaid with gold and silver. 71 In the

a Gk them
b Meaning of Gk uncertain
c Gk they
d Gk these things

135.15. 47: *Those who come after*, future generations. 50: *Afterward*, when the idols' overlay is stripped off (cf. vv. 10,58).

6.53–56: **Seventh warning: the impotence of idols.** 53: See v. 34b and note. *Give rain*, Deut 11.14; 28.12; Ps 147.8; Jer 14.22. 54: Vv. 36–37. 55: *Crows*, the sense is unclear; perhaps a mistranslation into Greek of the Hebrew word for "clouds."

6.57–65: **Eighth warning: the helplessness and uselessness of idols.** 57–58: The author mentions the plundering of idols several times (vv. 15,18,33; cf. 10). 59: V. 17. 60–63: God controls the natural world; the idols do not (cf. Sir 16.26–30; 1 En. 2–5). 61: Pss 97.4; 135.7. 64: V. 54; Ex 18.19; Isa 41.21.

6.66–69: **Ninth warning: idols cannot do what God can. Wild animals can do more than they can.** 66: V. 34; Jer 10.5; for the idiom see Gen 12.3; Num 22.6. 67: *Signs*, portents (cf. Jer 10.2; Joel 2.30).

6.70–73: **Tenth warning: idols are compared to a scarecrow, a thornbush, and a corpse.** 70: *Like a scarecrow in a cucumber bed*, the same comparison occurs in the Hebrew text of Jer 10.5 but not in its translation in the Greek Septuagint, suggesting that the Letter was originally written in Hebrew. 71: *Thornbush*, a common, use-

same way, their gods of wood, overlaid with gold and silver, are like a thornbush in a garden on which every bird perches; or like a corpse thrown out in the darkness. [72] From the purple and linen[a] that rot upon them you will know that they are not gods; and they will finally be consumed themselves, and be a reproach in the land. [73] Better, therefore, is someone upright who has no idols; such a person will be far above reproach.

[a] Cn: Gk *marble*, Syr *silk*

less shrub (cf. Judg 9.14–15). *A corpse thrown out*, the body is crudely discarded and not buried (cf. Isa 34.3; Jer 14.16; 22.19). **72:** The Greek word "marble" (see textual note *a*) is a mistranslation based on the confusion of two Hebrew homonyms (*shesh*), one of which means "alabaster" (or "marble") and the other "linen."

THE ADDITIONS TO DANIEL

CANONICAL STATUS AND LOCATION

The original book of Daniel is comprised of twelve chapters, six in Aramaic and six in Hebrew. The Greek translations of the book of Daniel, however, both in the Septuagint (LXX) version and in a version attributed to the second-century CE Jewish scholar Theodotion, include three Additions to the twelve original chapters: "The Prayer of Azariah and the Song of the Three Jews," "Susanna," and "Bel and the Dragon." The names given to these poetic compositions are descriptive titles provided by later editors and do not appear in the texts of the ancient manuscripts themselves.

The Additions to Daniel are considered canonical in Roman Catholic and Orthodox Christian traditions, whereas Protestants place them with the Apocrypha. They are not considered scriptural in Judaism.

The Prayer of Azariah and the Song of the Three Jews are found in all Greek versions between Dan 3.23 and 3.24. The Septuagint locates the other two Additions at the end of the book of Daniel, after 12.13; Theodotion's version places Susanna at the opening of the book of Daniel, and Bel and the Dragon at the conclusion of ch 6. The NRSV follows Theodotion's text but places the Additions with the other Apocryphal/Deuterocanonical texts rather than integrating them into the book of Daniel.

DATE AND HISTORICAL CONTEXT

Behind the Greek Additions may lie Hebrew or Aramaic originals, although no versions of the three stories have been found, even among the Dead Sea Scrolls. Like the folktales in Dan 1–6, the Additions may well have been written prior to the Maccabean revolt of the mid-second century BCE; the Prayer of Azariah (vs. 9) may reflect the crisis that led to the revolt. Scholars debate the place of composition: A Semitic (Hebrew or Aramaic) original would strengthen the argument for an origin in Israel or the eastern Diaspora; a Greek original would suggest Alexandria in Egypt, where there was a major Jewish community. The Additions likely circulated independently and only later, perhaps ca. 100 BCE when the book of Daniel was translated into Greek, were they added to it. The first independent citations of the Additions date from the church fathers of the second century CE.

Amy-Jill Levine

THE PRAYER OF AZARIAH AND THE SONG OF THE THREE JEWS

LOCATION

The Prayer of Azariah (vv. 1–22) and the Song of the Three Jews (vv. 28–68), along with a brief prose paragraph (vv. 23–27) concerning the fate of the three in Nebuchadnezzar's furnace, appear in ancient manuscripts between Dan 3.23 and 3.24. The Prayer and Song (with the exception of the end of the Song) may have had no original connection to the book of Daniel. They appear as numbers seven and eight of the fifteen "Odes" added to the book of Psalms in a few manuscripts of the Septuagint, a placement that complements the resemblance of these Additions to Ps 148 in terms of theme and to Ps 136 in terms of structure. The narrative context of Dan 3 gives their general emphasis on hope for deliverance, national repentance, and divine faithfulness a poignant focus as the three Jews face death in Babylonian exile.

DATE AND HISTORICAL CONTEXT

Whether the Prayer and Song were initially written in Hebrew or Aramaic or Greek remains debated, as does their place of composition. The Prayer contains references that correspond to the reign of the Seleucid king Antiochus IV (175–164 BCE), and so a second- (or perhaps first-) century BCE date of composition is possible.

CONTENTS AND INTERPRETATION

Prayers and hymns are a hallmark of Second Temple Jewish texts, and they are found in such works as Judith, Tobit, and Baruch, as well as in Dan 9 and among the scrolls discovered at Qumran (the Dead Sea Scrolls). The Additions to Daniel are especially comparable to the Additions to Esther—in both, prose narrative is supplemented with prayer and song that emphasize the piety of the main characters. The Prayer of Azariah resembles other postexilic works in its condemnation of the covenant community for its lack of fidelity to God, its emphasis on divine righteousness and mercy, and its appeal for deliverance (Ps 106; Ezra 9.6–15; Neh 1.5–11; Bar 1.15–3.8; and some Qumran texts). The Song of the Three Jews has allusions to numerous psalmic and prophetic passages in its exhortations to the heavens (vv. 36–41), nature (vv. 42–51), earth and its creatures (vv. 52–59), and humanity (vv. 60–68). Unlike the book of Daniel and the Prayer of Azariah, however, it does not suggest a period of persecution or a time when the Temple was either destroyed or profaned.

Amy-Jill Levine

¹They[a] walked around in the midst of the flames, singing hymns to God and blessing the Lord. ²Then Azariah stood still in the fire and prayed aloud:

³"Blessed are you, O Lord, God of our
  ancestors, and worthy of praise;
  and glorious is your name forever!
⁴For you are just in all you have done;
  all your works are true and your ways
    right,
  and all your judgments are true.
⁵You have executed true judgments in all
    you have brought upon us
  and upon Jerusalem, the holy city of our
    ancestors;
  by a true judgment you have brought all
    this upon us because of our
    sins.
⁶For we have sinned and broken your law
    in turning away from you;
  in all matters we have sinned
    grievously.
⁷We have not obeyed your
    commandments,
  we have not kept them or done what
    you have commanded us for our
    own good.
⁸So all that you have brought upon us,
  and all that you have done to us,
  you have done by a true judgment.

⁹You have handed us over to our enemies,
    lawless and hateful rebels,
  and to an unjust king, the most wicked
    in all the world.
¹⁰And now we cannot open our mouths;
  we, your servants who worship you,
    have become a shame and a
    reproach.
¹¹For your name's sake do not give us up
    forever,
  and do not annul your covenant.
¹²Do not withdraw your mercy from us,
  for the sake of Abraham your beloved
  and for the sake of your servant Isaac
  and Israel your holy one,
¹³to whom you promised
  to multiply their descendants like the
    stars of heaven
  and like the sand on the shore of the
    sea.
¹⁴For we, O Lord, have become fewer than
    any other nation,
  and are brought low this day in all the
    world because of our sins.
¹⁵In our day we have no ruler, or prophet,
    or leader,
  no burnt offering, or sacrifice, or
    oblation, or incense,

a That is, Hananiah, Mishael, and Azariah (Dan 2.17), the original names of Shadrach, Meshach, and Abednego (Dan 1.6-7)

1–22: The prayer of Azariah. 1: *They* refers to Daniel's three friends, Hananiah (named Shadrach), Mishael (Meshach), and Azariah (Abednego) in v. 66; Dan 1.6–7; 3.22–23. The Babylonian names given here in parentheses do not appear in these Additions; the use of the Hebrew names reinforces the friends' Jewish identity. 3: *Our ancestors*, see vv. 5,12,29; 1 Kings 8.53; Ezra 7.27; Dan 2.23; Tob 8.5. *Your name*, the praise of the divine name becomes increasingly common in Second Temple Jewish literature; cf. v. 30. 5: *True judgments*, v. 8; Neh 9.33; Lam 1.18; Tobit; and other texts attribute the Babylonian exile to the community's sin. 6–8: The confession of sin resembles Dan 9.5,15; Ezra 9.6; Neh 9.26. 9: The *unjust king* in the context of the book of Daniel is Nebuchadnezzar (Dan 3.19), but the vague reference makes the statement applicable to other tyrants, such as Antiochus IV Epiphanes (see 1 Macc 1 and notes to Dan 10–12); *rebels* may refer to Jews who supported Antiochus and the Hellenization of Jerusalem (1 Macc 1.11–15,41–60). 10: *Shame and a reproach*, see Dan 9.12. 11: *Covenant*, see Gen 15.18; 17.7–8. 12: *Abraham* is identified as beloved of God in Isa 41.8; 2 Chr 20.7; Jas 2.23, as well as the Qur'an (4.125). *Isaac* is called *servant* in Gen 24.14. *Israel*, i.e., Jacob (see Gen 32.28; 35.10). *Holy one* is more typically used for heavenly beings (Dan 4.10,20; 8.13). 13: On the *promise*, with references to the *stars* or the *sand*, see, e.g., Gen 15.5; 22.17; Ex 32.13; Jer 33.22. 15: *No ruler*, when read in the context of Dan 3, may refer to Nebuchadnezzar's blinding and exiling the Judean king (2 Kings 24.15); the lament is more generally expressed in Lam 2.9; Hos 3.4. No *prophet* is exaggerated for the Babylonian context, but it fits the early postexilic period (see Zech 13.3–6) and the time of Antiochus IV. *No burnt offering*, cessation of proper sacrifices occurred both when Nebuchadnezzar destroyed the Temple and when Antiochus IV profaned it. 16: Contrition and humility substitute for sacrifice (1 Sam 15.22; Pss 51.16–17; 141.2; Hos 6.6); the context of the prayer, the impending martyrdom of the

no place to make an offering before you
and to find mercy.
16 Yet with a contrite heart and a humble
spirit may we be accepted,
17 as though it were with burnt offerings
of rams and bulls,
or with tens of thousands of fat lambs;
such may our sacrifice be in your sight
today,
and may we unreservedly follow you,[a]
for no shame will come to those who
trust in you.
18 And now with all our heart we follow you;
we fear you and seek your presence.
19 Do not put us to shame,
but deal with us in your patience
and in your abundant mercy.
20 Deliver us in accordance with your
marvelous works,
and bring glory to your name, O Lord.
21 Let all who do harm to your servants be
put to shame;
let them be disgraced and deprived of
all power,
and let their strength be broken.
22 Let them know that you alone are the
Lord God,
glorious over the whole world."

23 Now the king's servants who threw them
in kept stoking the furnace with naphtha,
pitch, tow, and brushwood. 24 And the flames
poured out above the furnace forty-nine
cubits, 25 and spread out and burned those
Chaldeans who were caught near the furnace.
26 But the angel of the Lord came down

into the furnace to be with Azariah and his
companions, and drove the fiery flame out of
the furnace, 27 and made the inside of the furnace as though a moist wind were whistling
through it. The fire did not touch them at all
and caused them no pain or distress.
28 Then the three with one voice praised
and glorified and blessed God in the furnace:
29 "Blessed are you, O Lord, God of our
ancestors,
and to be praised and highly exalted
forever;
30 And blessed is your glorious, holy name,
and to be highly praised and highly
exalted forever.
31 Blessed are you in the temple of your
holy glory,
and to be extolled and highly glorified
forever.
32 Blessed are you who look into the depths
from your throne on the cherubim,
and to be praised and highly exalted
forever.
33 Blessed are you on the throne of your
kingdom,
and to be extolled and highly exalted
forever.
34 Blessed are you in the firmament of
heaven,
and to be sung and glorified forever.

35 "Bless the Lord, all you works of the Lord;
sing praise to him and highly exalt him
forever.

a   Meaning of Gk uncertain

three, makes the point acute. 21: *Put to shame*, in the context of the book of Daniel, anticipates Nebuchadnezzar's madness in Dan 4. See also Sir 36.9 on the hope for the enemy's demise.

23–27: **Protection in the furnace.** The plot follows Dan 3.22. 23: *Naphthah* is a type of petroleum (see
2 Macc 1.20–22,30–36). 24: *Forty-nine cubits* is 71 ft (22 m); the multiple of seven suggests Dan 3.19, in which
Nebuchadnezzar orders the furnace heated to seven times its usual temperature 25: *Burned those Chaldeans* is
noted in Dan 3:22; the king's agents die from the flames. 26: The protecting *angel* is an increasingly common
figure in Second Temple literature (Tobit; Sus 44–45 in the Old Greek version; *1 Enoch*); this verse makes the
angelic presence, implicit in the reference to a "fourth man" who appeared like a "son of the gods" in Dan 3.25,
explicit. 27: The verse is evoked in 3 Macc 6.6. *Moist* wind is dew; cf. Isa 26.19; Hos 14.5; Mic 5.7; etc., where dew
indicates God's salvation.

28–34: **Song of thanksgiving.** 29: The song begins with direct address to God. Verses 29–30 resemble Tob
8.5. 31: *Temple* may refer to the heavenly, not the Jerusalem, sanctuary, as in Ps 11.4; Hab 2.20. 32: *Cherubim* are
winged creatures who serve as the divine throne (Ex 25.18–20; 2 Sam 6.2; 22:11; Ps 18:10).

30–68: **The litany of praise.** 30: *Glorious, holy name*, Pss 29.2; 66.2; 79.9; etc. 31: *Temple of your . . . glory* may
indicate a heavenly temple, or the earthly one in a restored, purified state. 35: The song shifts to exhortations

36 Bless the Lord, you heavens;
  sing praise to him and highly exalt him
    forever.
37 Bless the Lord, you angels of the Lord;
  sing praise to him and highly exalt him
    forever.
38 Bless the Lord, all you waters above the
    heavens;
  sing praise to him and highly exalt him
    forever.
39 Bless the Lord, all you powers of the Lord;
  sing praise to him and highly exalt him
    forever.
40 Bless the Lord, sun and moon;
  sing praise to him and highly exalt him
    forever.
41 Bless the Lord, stars of heaven;
  sing praise to him and highly exalt him
    forever.

42 "Bless the Lord, all rain and dew;
  sing praise to him and highly exalt him
    forever.
43 Bless the Lord, all you winds;
  sing praise to him and highly exalt him
    forever.
44 Bless the Lord, fire and heat;
  sing praise to him and highly exalt him
    forever.
45 Bless the Lord, winter cold and summer
    heat;
  sing praise to him and highly exalt him
    forever.
46 Bless the Lord, dews and falling snow;
  sing praise to him and highly exalt him
    forever.
47 Bless the Lord, nights and days;
  sing praise to him and highly exalt him
    forever.
48 Bless the Lord, light and darkness;
  sing praise to him and highly exalt him
    forever.
49 Bless the Lord, ice and cold;
  sing praise to him and highly exalt him
    forever.
50 Bless the Lord, frosts and snows;
  sing praise to him and highly exalt him
    forever.

51 Bless the Lord, lightnings and clouds;
  sing praise to him and highly exalt him
    forever.

52 "Let the earth bless the Lord;
  let it sing praise to him and highly exalt
    him forever.
53 Bless the Lord, mountains and hills;
  sing praise to him and highly exalt him
    forever.
54 Bless the Lord, all that grows in the
    ground;
  sing praise to him and highly exalt him
    forever.
55 Bless the Lord, seas and rivers;
  sing praise to him and highly exalt him
    forever.
56 Bless the Lord, you springs;
  sing praise to him and highly exalt him
    forever.
57 Bless the Lord, you whales and all that
    swim in the waters;
  sing praise to him and highly exalt him
    forever.
58 Bless the Lord, all birds of the air;
  sing praise to him and highly exalt him
    forever.
59 Bless the Lord, all wild animals and
    cattle;
  sing praise to him and highly exalt him
    forever.

60 "Bless the Lord, all people on earth;
  sing praise to him and highly exalt him
    forever.
61 Bless the Lord, O Israel;
  sing praise to him and highly exalt him
    forever.
62 Bless the Lord, you priests of the Lord;
  sing praise to him and highly exalt him
    forever.
63 Bless the Lord, you servants of the Lord;
  sing praise to him and highly exalt him
    forever.
64 Bless the Lord, spirits and souls of the
    righteous;
  sing praise to him and highly exalt him
    forever.

to creation and thereby recalls the refrains of Pss 136 and 148. **38:** *Waters above,* see Gen 1.7; Ps 148.4. **39:** *Powers* suggests the heavenly host (see Ps 148.2–3). **57:** *Whales,* or sea monsters, suggest Leviathan (Isa 27.1; Ps 104.26; Job 41). **62:** *Priests* implies a Temple setting, but the song does not restrict its recitation to the Temple.

[65] Bless the Lord, you who are holy and
humble in heart;
sing praise to him and highly exalt him
forever.

[66] "Bless the Lord, Hananiah, Azariah, and
Mishael;
sing praise to him and highly exalt him
forever.
For he has rescued us from Hades and
saved us from the power[a] of death,
and delivered us from the midst of the
burning fiery furnace;

from the midst of the fire he has
delivered us.
[67] Give thanks to the Lord, for he is good,
for his mercy endures forever.
[68] All who worship the Lord, bless the God
of gods,
sing praise to him and give thanks to
him,
for his mercy endures forever."

[a] Gk *hand*

63: *Servants* could also refer to priests or other Temple functionaries, but the term is not limited to them. **66:** The friends are identified by their Hebrew names, as in Dan 1.6; 1 Macc 2.59. *Hananiah* means "the LORD is gracious"; *Azariah* is "the LORD has helped" (in the book of Tobit, the disguised angel Raphael assumes this name); and *Mishael* is "who is like God?" *Hades*, the abode of the dead. Their song strikes the same chord as numerous biblical comments on rescue from Sheol, e.g., 1 Sam 2.6; Pss 16.10; 30.3; 49.15; 86.13; Prov 23.14; Jon 2.2. **67:** *Give thanks . . . for his mercy endures forever*, see Ps 136; Sir 51; 1 Macc 4.24.

SUSANNA

NAME AND LOCATION

This addition to the book of Daniel is named for its heroine. Often called the first detective story, it appears in two different forms and locations in the early textual traditions. The Septuagint (and the Vulgate) locate it after Daniel 13; Theodotion, the version followed in this as well as most modern translations, locates the story at the beginning of the book of Daniel, since Sus 45 describes Daniel as a "young man." Perhaps composed as early as the Persian period (539–333 BCE), Susanna's tale was added to the cycle of tales about Daniel, probably ca. 100 BCE. The story may originally not have been about Daniel; the identification of the rescuing lad as Daniel would then be a secondary attribute of the story, added when the tale was attached to the other materials concerning Daniel, just as the Prayer of Azariah and the Song of the Three Jews may not have had an original connection to Dan 3. Susanna's setting in peaceful Babylon, in which the enemies are not wicked pagan kings but corrupt Jewish judges, contrasts with the threats emphasized in Dan 1–6.

CONTENT AND CANONICAL STATUS

Like Greek Esther, Judith, and Sarah of the book of Tobit, Susanna is beautiful and chaste, and, as in those books, prayer and piety are major motifs. Indeed, with the exception of the villainous elders, all the characters—including the narrator—mention God. First cited as having canonical status by the church father Irenaeus of Lyons in the late second century CE, Roman Catholic and Orthodox churches consider it canonical, while Protestants include it in the Apocrypha. Although the addition is not considered scriptural in Judaism, Susanna's story was also adapted by Samaritan and medieval Jewish writers.

Amy-Jill Levine

¹There was a man living in Babylon whose name was Joakim. ²He married the daughter of Hilkiah, named Susanna, a very beautiful woman and one who feared the Lord. ³Her parents were righteous, and had trained their daughter according to the law of Moses. ⁴Joakim was very rich, and had a fine garden adjoining his house; the Jews used to come to him because he was the most honored of them all.

⁵That year two elders from the people were appointed as judges. Concerning them the Lord had said: "Wickedness came forth from Babylon, from elders who were judges, who were supposed to govern the people." ⁶These men were frequently at Joakim's house, and all who had a case to be tried came to them there.

⁷When the people left at noon, Susanna would go into her husband's garden to walk. ⁸Every day the two elders used to see her, going in and walking about, and they began to lust for her. ⁹They suppressed their

1–4: Introduction. 1: Set in *Babylon*, the story is typically dated during the Babylonian exile (587–538 BCE) because of its connection to Daniel; however, an exact date is never specified. *Joakim* does not appear to be connected with others of the same name (2 Kings 24.15; Neh 12.10,12,26; Jdt 4.6; 15.8). **2:** *Susanna*, the name, which means "lily," appears in Lk 8.3, but not elsewhere in the Jewish or Christian canons. It is attested in late Babylonian sources. *Hilkiah* was a common name in priestly circles (2 Kings 22.4; Neh 12.7; Jer 1.1) and so perhaps suggests that Susanna's father was a priest. Beauty and piety are typically associated with heroines in the Deuterocanonical literature (Jdt 8:7–8; Tob 6:12; Est 2:7,20 [LXX]). **4:** The prosperity of some Jews in Babylon is attested by archaeological findings (see also Jer 29.5–7; 2 Esd 3:1b–2). *Joakim's* honor appears based on wealth. *Garden* (Gk "Paradeisos") recalls Eden (Gen 2–3).

5–14: The elders' plot. 5: The *year* is not identified. *Elders*, community leaders (Ruth 4.2–12; Ezek 8.1; 14.1; 20.1; Jer 29.1). The phrase *wickedness* (Gk "anomia," lit. "lawlessness") *came forth* is unattested in existing prophetic books, but see Jer 23.14–15; the church fathers Origin and Jerome associate the reference with Jer 29.20–23. The occasional suggestion that the Jewish community denied this story canonical status because it

consciences and turned away their eyes from looking to Heaven or remembering their duty to administer justice. [10] Both were overwhelmed with passion for her, but they did not tell each other of their distress, [11] for they were ashamed to disclose their lustful desire to seduce her. [12] Day after day they watched eagerly to see her.

[13] One day they said to each other, "Let us go home, for it is time for lunch." So they both left and parted from each other. [14] But turning back, they met again; and when each pressed the other for the reason, they confessed their lust. Then together they arranged for a time when they could find her alone.

[15] Once, while they were watching for an opportune day, she went in as before with only two maids, and wished to bathe in the garden, for it was a hot day. [16] No one was there except the two elders, who had hidden themselves and were watching her. [17] She said to her maids, "Bring me olive oil and ointments, and shut the garden doors so that I can bathe." [18] They did as she told them: they shut the doors of the garden and went out by the side doors to bring what they had been commanded; they did not see the elders, because they were hiding.

[19] When the maids had gone out, the two elders got up and ran to her. [20] They said, "Look, the garden doors are shut, and no one can see us. We are burning with desire for you; so give your consent, and lie with us. [21] If you refuse, we will testify against you that a young man was with you, and this was why you sent your maids away."

[22] Susanna groaned and said, "I am completely trapped. For if I do this, it will mean death for me; if I do not, I cannot escape your hands. [23] I choose not to do it; I will fall into your hands, rather than sin in the sight of the Lord."

[24] Then Susanna cried out with a loud voice, and the two elders shouted against her. [25] And one of them ran and opened the garden doors. [26] When the people in the house heard the shouting in the garden, they rushed in at the side door to see what had happened to her. [27] And when the elders told their story, the servants felt very much ashamed, for nothing like this had ever been said about Susanna.

[28] The next day, when the people gathered at the house of her husband Joakim, the two elders came, full of their wicked plot to have Susanna put to death. In the presence of the people they said, [29] "Send for Susanna daughter of Hilkiah, the wife of Joakim." [30] So they sent for her. And she came with her parents, her children, and all her relatives.

[31] Now Susanna was a woman of great refinement and beautiful in appearance. [32] As

criticized the elders is belied by the remarkable amount of self-critique the biblical text generates. **8:** *Lust*, in violation of Ex 20.17. **9:** *Turned away their eyes*, although they had no hesitance in looking at Susanna. *Heaven* is a circumlocution for God. **14:** *Pressed the other*, as if in cross-examination: their true testimony here will contrast with their false testimony regarding Susanna.

15–21: The attempted rape. 15: Contrary to most artistic depictions, Susanna never actually bathes. *In the garden*, the scene recollects depictions both of luxuriant beauty and physical love in the Song of Solomon, and of the garden of Eden (Gen 2–3) as a site of temptation. *Bathe* suggests both Bathsheba (2 Sam 11.2) and observations in Jewish-Hellenistic literature (*Jubilees* 22; *Testament of Reuben* 3) that Reuben sinned with his father's wife Bilhah after seeing her bathe; cf. Gen 35.22; 49.4. *Maids* frequently accompany heroines in the Deuterocanonical texts (Jdt, Tob, Add Esth). **17:** *Oil and ointments*, compare 2 Sam 12.20; Ruth 3.3; Jdt 10.3. *Shut the garden doors* attests to Susanna's modesty. **20:** *Give your consent*, Susanna's choice is adultery or death.

22–27: Susanna's response. 22: *Death*, because adultery was a capital crime (Lev 20.10; Deut 22.21–24; see also Jn 8:4–5). Susanna knows the "law of Moses" (v. 3). **23:** *Sin in the sight of the Lord* is the same concern voiced by Joseph in similar circumstances (Gen 39.9). **24:** Deut 22.24 legislates that a woman, facing rape, is to *cry out with a loud voice*; Susanna shows knowledge of and fidelity to the law. On crying out at times of oppression, see also Gen 21.16; Ex 2.23; 14.10; Deut 26.7; 1 Sam 4.13; 3 Macc 5.51; and elsewhere. **27:** That servants would be ashamed indicates the dishonor to the household. Although the elders (v. 11) and servants feel shame, Susanna is never described in this manner, despite being placed in a situation of public humiliation (vv. 31–32). *Nothing like this*, although she had an unblemished reputation, Susanna is presumed guilty.

28–41: Accusation. 30: Susanna is accompanied by all her family except Joakim. The Septuagint (LXX) notes she was veiled, the scoundrels ordered her to be unveiled, so that they might feast their eyes on her beauty. [33] Those who were with her and all who saw her were weeping.

[34] Then the two elders stood up before the people and laid their hands on her head. [35] Through her tears she looked up toward Heaven, for her heart trusted in the Lord. [36] The elders said, "While we were walking in the garden alone, this woman came in with two maids, shut the garden doors, and dismissed the maids. [37] Then a young man, who was hiding there, came to her and lay with her. [38] We were in a corner of the garden, and when we saw this wickedness we ran to them. [39] Although we saw them embracing, we could not hold the man, because he was stronger than we, and he opened the doors and got away. [40] We did, however, seize this woman and asked who the young man was, [41] but she would not tell us. These things we testify."

Because they were elders of the people and judges, the assembly believed them and condemned her to death.

[42] Then Susanna cried out with a loud voice, and said, "O eternal God, you know what is secret and are aware of all things before they come to be; [43] you know that

these men have given false evidence against me. And now I am to die, though I have done none of the wicked things that they have charged against me!"

[44] The Lord heard her cry. [45] Just as she was being led off to execution, God stirred up the holy spirit of a young lad named Daniel, [46] and he shouted with a loud voice, "I want no part in shedding this woman's blood!"

[47] All the people turned to him and asked, "What is this you are saying?" [48] Taking his stand among them he said, "Are you such fools, O Israelites, as to condemn a daughter of Israel without examination and without learning the facts? [49] Return to court, for these men have given false evidence against her."

[50] So all the people hurried back. And the rest of the[a] elders said to him, "Come, sit among us and inform us, for God has given you the standing of an elder." [51] Daniel said to them, "Separate them far from each other, and I will examine them."

[52] When they were separated from each other, he summoned one of them and said to him, "You old relic of wicked days, your sins have now come home, which you have

a   Gk lacks rest of the

---

that Susanna had four children. 31: *Refinement* and beauty are attributes of (Gk) Esther. 32: *Veiled* emphasizes her modesty; although the trial occurs in her home, the proceedings are public. The LXX describes Susanna as being uncovered (see Hos 2.3–10; Ezek 16.37–39). 34: *Laid their hands* indicates that the elders serve as witnesses (Lev 24.14; see Lev 8.14,18,22; Ex 29.10,15,19 for sacrificial imagery, and Lev 16.21–22 for the scapegoat ritual). The elders planned to lay their hands upon Susanna in order to rape her; now their gesture seeks to condemn her. Two witnesses are required (Num 35.30; Deut 17.6; 19.15). 41: *Condemned her* without cross-examination (Deut 19.15–21) or Susanna's own testimony; the "trial" is illegal according to both biblical and later rabbinic regulations.

42–43: **Susanna's prayer.** Like (Gk) Esther (14.3–19), Judith (9.2–14), and Sarah (Tob 2.10–15), as well as Azariah of the Additions to Daniel, Susanna offers personal prayer in a time of distress. 42: *Loud voice*, see v. 24. *Know what is secret* is a divine attribute stressed in Dan 2.22. 43: *Given false evidence*, Susanna's prayer locates God as the (true) judge and jury even as it again shows her knowledge of the law (Deut 19.15–21). *Now I am to die* leaves Susanna's request for justice implicit.

44–47: **Daniel responds.** 44: God responds to Susanna's prayer, not to the events that prompted it. 45: *Young lad* contrasts Daniel with the "elders"; the term indicates a youth of marriageable age (Tob 5.17) and subtly recalls the "young man" the elders claimed was with Susanna (37–39). *Holy spirit* is associated with both prophetic abilities and the possession of wisdom. The miraculous element in Susanna is not the work of an angel or a revelation of an undescribed dream, but the miracle of the inspired intellect. 46: *I want no part*, since the community is responsible for justice (Deut 22.20–21; Mt 27.24; Acts 24.26).

48–63: **Susanna's acquittal.** 48: *Examination*, or cross-examination, is required by Deut 19.15–20. *Daughter of Israel*, see also v. 57, which describes Susanna as a *daughter of Judah*. 50: Daniel's status appears miraculously granted. His youth contrasts with his *standing as an elder*. 50: *Rest of the elders* indicates that not all the leaders

committed in the past, ⁵³ pronouncing unjust judgments, condemning the innocent and acquitting the guilty, though the Lord said, 'You shall not put an innocent and righteous person to death.' ⁵⁴ Now then, if you really saw this woman, tell me this: Under what tree did you see them being intimate with each other?" He answered, "Under a mastic tree."^a ⁵⁵ And Daniel said, "Very well! This lie has cost you your head, for the angel of God has received the sentence from God and will immediately cut^a you in two."

⁵⁶ Then, putting him to one side, he ordered them to bring the other. And he said to him, "You offspring of Canaan and not of Judah, beauty has beguiled you and lust has perverted your heart. ⁵⁷ This is how you have been treating the daughters of Israel, and they were intimate with you through fear; but a daughter of Judah would not tolerate your wickedness. ⁵⁸ Now then, tell me: Under what tree did you catch them being intimate with each other?" He answered, "Under an evergreen oak."^b ⁵⁹ Daniel said to him, "Very

well! This lie has cost you also your head, for the angel of God is waiting with his sword to split^b you in two, so as to destroy you both."

⁶⁰ Then the whole assembly raised a great shout and blessed God, who saves those who hope in him. ⁶¹ And they took action against the two elders, because out of their own mouths Daniel had convicted them of bearing false witness; they did to them as they had wickedly planned to do to their neighbor. ⁶² Acting in accordance with the law of Moses, they put them to death. Thus innocent blood was spared that day.

⁶³ Hilkiah and his wife praised God for their daughter Susanna, and so did her husband Joakim and all her relatives, because she was found innocent of a shameful deed. ⁶⁴ And from that day onward Daniel had a great reputation among the people.

a   The Greek words for *mastic tree* and *cut* are similar, thus forming an ironic wordplay
b   The Greek words for *evergreen oak* and *split* are similar, thus forming an ironic wordplay

are wicked. 53: *Pronouncing unjust judgments*, Daniel accuses the first elder of a pattern of injustice. The citation evokes Ex 23.7. 54–55: *Mastic* (Gk "schinon") . . . *cut* (Gk "schisei"): "clove . . . cleave" provides an English approximation of the Greek pun. 55: *Angels* become increasingly common in Jewish Hellenistic literature (including Daniel; also Isa 37.36; Ezek 9). Here they serve as agents of punishment rather than of revelation. 56–57: The comment compares three nations. *Offspring of Canaan* suggests the sexual crimes attributed to the earlier inhabitants of the promised land (Lev 18.24–28); *daughters of Israel* refers to the Northern Kingdom, destroyed by Assyria in 722 BCE (2 Kings 17); *daughter of Judah*, Susanna is from the Southern Kingdom, whose exile in 586 BCE created the Babylonian Jewish community. 58–59: *Evergreen oak* (Gk "prinon") . . . *split* (Gk "kataprisei"): "yew" and "hew" provides an English approximation of the Greek pun. 59: *Sword* recalls Gen 3.24, as Susanna's garden suggests Eden (Gen 2–3). 62: *Law of Moses* is Deut 19.15–21.

64: Epilogue. If Susanna is placed at the opening of the book of Daniel, Daniel's *great reputation* is seen to increase in the subsequent stories.

BEL AND THE DRAGON

LOCATION AND NAME

These stories appear as ch 14 of the Greek version of the book of Daniel. In the Septuagint, as opposed to Theo-dotion's version, which is printed here, Daniel is identified as a priest and thus as a positive foil to the deceptive priests of the false gods. The title of the stories in the Septuagint is "From the prophecy of Habakkuk, the son of Joshua [Gk Jesus], of the tribe of Levi."

DATE, CONTENTS, AND INTERPRETATION

Perhaps composed as early as the Persian period (539–333 BCE), these two idol parodies (compare Isa 44) display the foolishness of pagan worship, divine protection of faithful Jews, and the cleverness of the court favorite, Daniel. In the first story, concerning Bel, Daniel demonstrates that the idol is not a god by proving that it does not eat the food set out for it each night; the second story reverses this scenario as Daniel proves that the drag-on is not divine by feeding it a noxious concoction that kills it. This second story recapitulates the account of Daniel in the lion's den (Dan 6.16–24) and adds to it Daniel's own miraculous feeding by the prophet Habakkuk. Food references culminate at the end, when Daniel's enemies are eaten by the lions into whose den Daniel had been thrown. Perhaps this second story is based on Jer 51.34,44, which is also set in Babylon, the filling of a belly with delicacies, and the punishment of Bel by having him "disgorge what he has swallowed."

Amy-Jill Levine

¹ When King Astyages was laid to rest with his ancestors, Cyrus the Persian succeeded to his kingdom. ² Daniel was a companion of the king, and was the most honored of all his Friends.

³ Now the Babylonians had an idol called Bel, and every day they provided for it twelve bushels of choice flour and forty sheep and six measures[a] of wine. ⁴ The king revered it and went every day to worship it. But Daniel worshiped his own God.

So the king said to him, "Why do you not worship Bel?" ⁵ He answered, "Because I do not revere idols made with hands, but the liv-ing God, who created heaven and earth and has dominion over all living creatures."

⁶ The king said to him, "Do you not think that Bel is a living god? Do you not see how much he eats and drinks every day?" ⁷ And Daniel laughed, and said, "Do not be deceived, O king, for this thing is only clay inside and bronze outside, and it never ate or drank anything."

⁸ Then the king was angry and called the priests of Bel[b] and said to them, "If you do not tell me who is eating these provisions, you shall die. ⁹ But if you prove that Bel is eating them, Daniel shall die, because he has spoken blasphemy against Bel." Daniel said to the king, "Let it be done as you have said."

a A little more than fifty gallons
b Gk *his priests*

1–2: Daniel in the Persian court. 1: *Astyages*, last king of Media (585–550 BCE), was defeated by his grandson, *Cyrus the Persian* (Dan 6.28). 2: *Companion of the king*, perhaps an official position (1 Macc 2.18), suggests a confidant. *Most honored*, see Dan 2.48.

3–7: The worship of Bel. 3: *Bel*, an epithet of Marduk, the god who headed the Babylonian pantheon (Jer 50.2). Ancient Babylonian sources confirm Bel's extensive diet. 4: *The king revered it*, although ancient sources indicate that in actual practice, the "leftovers" were sent to the king, and their consumption was considered to provide blessings. The king's support for the priests who were consuming the food is therefore ironic. 4: The question indicates the story's original independence from the book of Daniel, although in Dan 1–6 kings continually require reeducation about Daniel's faith and practices. 5: Daniel boldly confesses his own faith and criticizes that of the king. 7: *Laughed* (also in v. 19) indicates Daniel's familiarity with the king as well as his dis-dain for the worship of the idol; Bel is also ridiculed in Isa 46.1–2.

¹⁰ Now there were seventy priests of Bel, besides their wives and children. So the king went with Daniel into the temple of Bel. ¹¹ The priests of Bel said, "See, we are now going outside; you yourself, O king, set out the food and prepare the wine, and shut the door and seal it with your signet. ¹² When you return in the morning, if you do not find that Bel has eaten it all, we will die; otherwise Daniel will, who is telling lies about us." ¹³ They were unconcerned, for beneath the table they had made a hidden entrance, through which they used to go in regularly and consume the provisions. ¹⁴ After they had gone out, the king set out the food for Bel. Then Daniel ordered his servants to bring ashes, and they scattered them throughout the whole temple in the presence of the king alone. Then they went out, shut the door and sealed it with the king's signet, and departed. ¹⁵ During the night the priests came as usual, with their wives and children, and they ate and drank everything.

¹⁶ Early in the morning the king rose and came, and Daniel with him. ¹⁷ The king said, "Are the seals unbroken, Daniel?" He answered, "They are unbroken, O king." ¹⁸ As soon as the doors were opened, the king looked at the table, and shouted in a loud voice, "You are great, O Bel, and in you there is no deceit at all!"

¹⁹ But Daniel laughed and restrained the king from going in. "Look at the floor," he said, "and notice whose footprints these are." ²⁰ The king said, "I see the footprints of men and women and children." ²¹ Then the king was enraged, and he arrested the priests and their wives and children. They showed him the secret doors through which they used to enter to consume what was on the table. ²² Therefore the king put them to death, and gave Bel over to Daniel, who destroyed it and its temple.

²³ Now in that place[a] there was a great dragon, which the Babylonians revered. ²⁴ The king said to Daniel, "You cannot deny that this is a living god; so worship him." ²⁵ Daniel said, "I worship the Lord my God, for he is the living God. ²⁶ But give me permission, O king, and I will kill the dragon without sword or club." The king said, "I give you permission." ²⁷ Then Daniel took pitch, fat, and hair, and boiled them together and made cakes, which he fed to the dragon. The dragon ate them, and burst open. Then Daniel said, "See what you have been worshiping!"

²⁸ When the Babylonians heard about it, they were very indignant and conspired against the king, saying, "The king has become a Jew; he has destroyed Bel, and killed the dragon, and slaughtered the priests." ²⁹ Going to the king, they said, "Hand Daniel

---

a   Other ancient authorities lack *in that place*

8–22: Bel's trial. 8: The abruptness of *You shall die* (Dan 2.5; 3.6; 6.7) is conventional in folktales. 10: *Wives and children* contrasts Daniel's single status. 11: *Prepare the wine* by mixing it with water (2 Macc 15.39) or spices (Isa 5.22; Song 8.2). 14: *Ordered his servants*, unlike Dan chs 1–6, where Daniel relies on divine revelation and aid, here as well as in Susanna, he succeeds by his wits. The scene establishes what becomes a detective story convention, the "mystery of the locked room." 22: *Put them to death* echoes the punishment of the wicked elders (Sus 62; see Dan 2.12; 6.24); the corruption of the priests condemns also their wives and children. Bel's idol and *temple* were, according to the Greek historian Herodotus and other ancient sources, destroyed by the Persian king Xerxes in 479 BCE; Xerxes melted the temple's 20 ft (6 m) high statue of Bel into 800 lb (363 kg) of gold bullion. Daniel's action responds to Babylon's destruction of the Jerusalem Temple.

23–27: The destruction of the dragon. 23: *Great dragon*, dragons or snakes could symbolize the divine in ancient Near Eastern and Mediterranean cultures (see Num 2.8–9; 2 Kings 18.4), but there is no independent evidence of Babylonian snake worship. 24: *Living god* contrasts with the idol Bel, for the snake is clearly alive. 25: Daniel resists apostasy, a special concern for Jews in the Diaspora and during the persecution of Antiochus IV Epiphanes. 27: *Pitch, fat, and hair* would not necessarily be a noxious concoction; later versions of the story add details to increase the toxicity of the mixture. The snake eats and dies, unlike Bel who is proven false because he cannot eat; within the cycle of stories about Daniel, this detail offers subtle comparisons. Daniel and his friends prosper by restricting their diet (Dan 1); Belshazzar falls because of his blasphemous feasting (Dan 5).

28–42: Daniel in the lion pit. 28: *Become a Jew* anticipates v. 41, where the king affirms Daniel's God; he does not, however, convert. 29: The death threat repeats the punishment of Bel's priests and their families, but here

over to us, or else we will kill you and your household." [30] The king saw that they were pressing him hard, and under compulsion he handed Daniel over to them.

[31] They threw Daniel into the lions' den, and he was there for six days. [32] There were seven lions in the den, and every day they had been given two human bodies and two sheep; but now they were given nothing, so that they would devour Daniel.

[33] Now the prophet Habakkuk was in Judea; he had made a stew and had broken bread into a bowl, and was going into the field to take it to the reapers. [34] But the angel of the Lord said to Habakkuk, "Take the food that you have to Babylon, to Daniel, in the lions' den." [35] Habakkuk said, "Sir, I have never seen Babylon, and I know nothing about the den." [36] Then the angel of the Lord took him by the crown of his head and carried him by

his hair; with the speed of the wind[a] he set him down in Babylon, right over the den.

[37] Then Habakkuk shouted, "Daniel, Daniel! Take the food that God has sent you." [38] Daniel said, "You have remembered me, O God, and have not forsaken those who love you." [39] So Daniel got up and ate. And the angel of God immediately returned Habakkuk to his own place.

[40] On the seventh day the king came to mourn for Daniel. When he came to the den he looked in, and there sat Daniel! [41] The king shouted with a loud voice, "You are great, O Lord, the God of Daniel, and there is no other besides you!" [42] Then he pulled Daniel[b] out, and threw into the den those who had attempted his destruction, and they were instantly eaten before his eyes.

[a] Or by the power of his spirit
[b] Gk him

the king is threatened by his own people. **30:** The king's reluctance resembles that of Darius (Dan 6). **31:** *Lions' den,* see Dan 6.16–24, where Daniel spends one night, not six. Daniel destroyed Babylon's animal god; now the Babylonians anticipate that animals will destroy him. **32:** The description continues the author's interest in dietary matters, but it is only in this case that concerns for eating will be connected to the miraculous. **33:** *Habakkuk* prophesied ca. 612–597 BCE, well before the events recounted here. **34:** Angels appear in the book of Daniel as protectors (Dan 6.22) as well as apocalyptic revealers and interpreters (Dan 7–12). Along with the unlikely summoning of Habakkuk and his reluctance concerning this unexpected assignment, *the food* is part of the tale's humor: the lions, not Daniel, have the greater problem with hunger. **36:** *By his hair,* see Ezek 8.3. **41:** *You are great* replaces the king's praise of Bel in 18. **42:** References to food reach their conclusion as Daniel's accusers are consumed.

1 MACCABEES

NAME

The name "1 Maccabees" derives from the church fathers Hippolytus (ca. 170–236 CE), Origen (ca. 185–254 CE), and Jerome (ca. 342–420 CE), who notes that he found the first book of the Maccabees in Hebrew. The name "Maccabee," a nickname ("Hammer") given to Judas (1 Macc 3.4), was extended in Christian (but not Jewish) tradition to include his family. Origen said the book was titled *sarbethsabanaiel*, a Greek transliteration possibly suggesting an original Hebrew "The Book of the House of the Princes of Israel."

CANONICAL STATUS AND LOCATION

Jerome distinguished between Hebrew and Greek Jewish books, describing the latter as *apocrypha*, "hidden things." Perhaps because Jerome knew of a Hebrew version of 1 Maccabees, it was included in the Vulgate, the Latin Bible of the Western church. It is also one of the canonical scriptures of the Eastern Orthodox churches. The sixteenth-century Protestant reformers, unsympathetic toward non-Hebrew Jewish writings, placed it firmly among the Apocrypha, to be read for instruction in godly manners but not in Christian doctrine. The Roman Catholic church reaffirmed the canonical status of 1 Maccabees at the Council of Trent (1545–63). The book is not canonical in Jewish tradition, although it is an important religious text describing the origin of the festival of Hanukkah, the rededication of the Temple in 164 BCE. In Roman Catholic and Eastern Orthodox Bibles, 1 Maccabees is placed among the historical books, after the books of Tobit, Judith, and Esther. In Protestant Bibles it is included among the Apocrypha, usually after the Additions to Daniel.

AUTHORSHIP AND DATE

The author's identity is unknown. He was apparently an educated Jew, well versed in the Hebrew scriptures and the Temple liturgy, and with sufficient leisure and resources for authorship. He wrote in Hebrew but was able to use, translate, and incorporate Greek and Latin documents from Seleucid, Roman, and Spartan archives. His interests were political and historical rather than priestly; he firmly supported the Maccabean cause but was sufficiently scholarly and objective to avoid demonizing the Seleucid opposition (contrast 2 Maccabees).

The book covers Jewish history from the time of Alexander the Great to the high priesthood of John Hyrcanus (134–104 CE) and is thus usually dated to the later years of Hyrcanus's rule or soon after; the statements of 1 Macc 16.23–24, that his achievements were recorded in the chronicles of his high priesthood, and of 1 Macc 13.30, that the Maccabean family tomb built by Simon "remains to this day," suggest some passing of time. The book's positive attitude toward Rome makes it likely that it was written before the Roman general Pompey captured Jerusalem in 63 BCE.

LITERARY HISTORY

Sometime about the turn of the era, 1 Maccabees appeared in Greek translation; the late first-century BCE Jewish historian Josephus used this as a major source for his *Antiquities* (*Ant.* 12.242–13.212). Josephus perhaps found a copy in Jerusalem before the destruction of Jerusalem in 70 CE, or later in a Roman library. The fourth- and fifth-century manuscripts of Codex Sinaiticus and Codex Alexandrinus, and the eighth-century Codex Venetus preserve the Greek text; the presumed Hebrew original has been lost. The Old Latin translation, from the second or early third century CE, was later incorporated into the Vulgate tradition.

HISTORICAL CONTEXT

Judea had known a long period of relative peace and prosperity, first under Alexander the Great (332–323 BCE), then under the Ptolemies, the successors to Alexander's rule in Egypt. As a result of Alexander's rule, Hellenism (a mixture of Greek and Semitic cultures) had dominated all the countries of the eastern Mediterranean basin. By the second century BCE, however, when Judea came under the control of the Seleucids, the successors to Alexander's rule in Mesopotamia and Syria, Jews were divided over how to relate to Gentile culture. The upper classes in Jerusalem, the Hellenizers, had long adopted Greek ways, while the poorer people of the rural areas tended to cling to the customs of their ancestors. The book of 1 Maccabees consistently presents the Hellenizers as "renegades" or apostates (1 Macc 1.11–15), and their introduction of the Greek gymnasium and all that went with it (see 2 Macc 4.11–17) as the root of the following struggle.

In this situation of complex religious, economic, and political tensions, the actions of the Seleucid ruler Antiochus IV were a match in a tinderbox. In 169 BCE Antiochus IV invaded Egypt to reclaim Judea from Ptolemy IV Philometor. On Antiochus's return he pillaged the Jerusalem Temple (1 Macc 1.20–28) for purely financial reasons (he had at that point no political or religious quarrel with Judea). The following year, believing Judea to be in revolt (2 Macc 5.11), Antiochus attacked Jerusalem more viciously (1 Macc 1.29–40; cf. 2 Macc 5.11–14, Dan 11.29–31), and the subsequent attempt to suppress the Judeans by attacking the religious law (1 Macc 1.41–61), which apparently sustained the Jewish resistance, led to the war of independence and its horrors described in the following chapters of 1 Maccabees.

Into this crisis the author introduces the priestly family of Mattathias and his sons Judas, Jonathan, and Simon as the deliverers of Judea. Fearing that the policies of the Hellenizers would destroy Judaism, Judas Maccabeus and his men mounted a campaign of armed resistance against both enemies. Using a combination of guerrilla warfare and diplomacy, they succeeded in recovering and purifying the Temple after Antiochus had defiled it, fortifying Jerusalem and securing a measure of independence for Judea. By the end of the book three generations of Mattathias's family had fought for Judea's independence from the Seleucids and had established a ruling dynasty (called Hasmonean according to Josephus and other sources) that would remain in power until the Roman occupation in 63 BCE.

STRUCTURE AND CONTENTS

The book is clearly structured. Chapters 1 and 2 are introductory, giving the historical context and Mattathias's exhortation to his sons, and emphasizing the complementary roles of Simon and Judas (2.65–66). Chapters 3.1–9.22 describe the achievements of Judas, marked by an opening poetic eulogy of Judas (3.3–9) and a closure modeled on the regnal summaries in 1 and 2 Kings (9.22). Chapters 9.23–16.23 describe the activities of Jonathan, Simon, and Simon's son John, marked by the eulogy of Simon (14.4–15) and another regnal closure (16.23). Within this framework the author marshals his complex narrative. He presents the Maccabean relationships with the hostile Seleucids of Syria, the Ptolemies of Egypt, the cities of the Palestinian coast, and the tribes of Transjordan, and with two friendly Mediterranean powers, the Romans and the Spartans. The book condemns the "renegades" within Israel who would conform to the Greek way of life (1.11–15); Judas and Simon are presented as preserving the Jewish law and Temple against the enemies of their nation (14.29). The book ends with the firm establishment and solid achievements of the high priesthood of John Hyrcanus (16.23). For this author, it is through the Maccabean family alone that "deliverance was given to Israel" (5.62).

INTERPRETATION AND GUIDE TO READING

Historians value 1 Maccabees for its information on the second-century BCE Jewish-Hellenistic world. Jews and Christians alike have seen the Maccabees as champions against tyrants hostile to their faith aided by traitors within the fold. Some students of history, less sympathetic to the Jewish cause, have seen Antiochus as a cultivated Hellenistic monarch trying to unify his empire and control a disloyal subject on his borders. Others in modern times, less sympathetic to imperial causes, have interpreted the Maccabees as a rebel army struggling righteously on behalf of political minorities. Different circumstances make for different readings, as ever.

The reader will make sense of 1 Maccabees only by taking it as a coherent narrative from start to finish. Occasional dipping will yield only confusion. The author shapes his history clearly, quoting archival sources for information and adding short poems as theological commentary. Sympathetic reading will reveal, rewardingly, that the author was a man of scholarly ability, deep commitment to Israel, and trust in Israel's God.

John R. Bartlett

1 After Alexander son of Philip, the Macedonian, who came from the land of Kittim, had defeated[a] King Darius of the Persians and the Medes, he succeeded him as king. (He had previously become king of Greece.) [2] He fought many battles, conquered strongholds, and put to death the kings of the earth. [3] He advanced to the ends of the earth, and plundered many nations. When the earth became quiet before him, he was exalted, and his heart was lifted up. [4] He gathered a very strong army and ruled over countries, nations, and princes, and they became tributary to him.

[5] After this he fell sick and perceived that he was dying. [6] So he summoned his most honored officers, who had been brought up with him from youth, and divided his kingdom among them while he was still alive. [7] And after Alexander had reigned twelve years, he died.

[8] Then his officers began to rule, each in his own place. [9] They all put on crowns after his death, and so did their descendants after them for many years; and they caused many evils on the earth.

[10] From them came forth a sinful root, Antiochus Epiphanes, son of King Antiochus;

he had been a hostage in Rome. He began to reign in the one hundred thirty-seventh year of the kingdom of the Greeks.[b]

[11] In those days certain renegades came out from Israel and misled many, saying, "Let us go and make a covenant with the Gentiles around us, for since we separated from them many disasters have come upon us." [12] This proposal pleased them, [13] and some of the people eagerly went to the king, who authorized them to observe the ordinances of the Gentiles. [14] So they built a gymnasium in Jerusalem, according to Gentile custom, [15] and removed the marks of circumcision, and abandoned the holy covenant. They joined with the Gentiles and sold themselves to do evil.

[16] When Antiochus saw that his kingdom was established, he determined to become king of the land of Egypt, in order that he might reign over both kingdoms. [17] So he invaded Egypt with a strong force, with chariots and elephants and cavalry and with a large fleet. [18] He engaged King Ptolemy of

a Gk adds *and he defeated*
b 175 B.C.

1.1–10: Introduction. The author sketches the history of the Hellenistic world from Alexander the Great to Antiochus IV; cf. Dan 11.2–28. **1:** *Philip* II of Macedon (ruled 359–336 BCE) conquered the Greeks in 338 BCE; his son Alexander (336–323 BCE) marched from Greece (*the land of Kittim*) and defeated *Darius* III of Persia at Issus (333 BCE) and Gaugamela (331 BCE). Media (the land of *the Medes*) was south of the Caspian Sea. **2:** *Strongholds*, e.g., Tyre and Gaza. **3:** *To the ends of the earth*, i.e., present-day Afghanistan and India. *Exalted . . . his heart was lifted up* suggests deification as well as the biblical sin of pride (Isa 2.5–22; 2 Chr 26.16). **7:** Alexander *died* at Babylon, June 323 BCE. **8–9:** *Officers . . . descendants*, especially Seleucus I Nicator (305–281 BCE), who seized Babylonia and Syria, and Ptolemy I Soter (305–282 BCE), who took over Egypt and Palestine, and their successors in these regions. *Crowns* were of white cloth rather than precious metal. **10:** *Antiochus* IV (175–164 BCE), son of *Antiochus* III "the Great" (223–187 BCE), used the title "Theos Epiphanes" ("god manifest") on some of his later coins, but probably took such implied divinity less seriously than his Jewish subjects. *Hostage in Rome*, after the Roman defeat of Antiochus III at Magnesia (190 BCE); he escaped, succeeding his brother Seleucus IV in 175 BCE. *One hundred thirty-seventh year of* the Seleucid era, which began in either 312 BCE or 311 BCE.

1.11–15: Conflicts over Hellenization. 11: The author sees the *renegades* as Jewish apostates; 2 Macc 4.7–17 identifies the usurping high priest Jason as their leader. They hoped for the economic and political advantages of belonging to the wider Hellenistic world, rejecting the separation from the Gentiles required by the Law (cf. Deut 7.1–6) and demanded by Nehemiah (Neh 13.1–3,23–27). **14:** *Gymnasium*, the essential place of education and recreation for citizens of a Hellenistic city. This development did not break the Law, but according to Greek custom, athletes competed in the nude (2 Macc 4.14). *Removing the marks of circumcision* by surgery (epispasm) to make participants resemble Greek athletes was elsewhere seen as showing "irreverence to the divine laws" (2 Macc 4.17).

1.16–19: Antiochus IV and Egypt. See Dan 11.25–27. In 170 BCE Egypt, under Ptolemy VI Philometor (180–145 BCE), claimed Palestine under the terms of an earlier marriage settlement; Antiochus *invaded Egypt*, defeated Ptolemy (v. 18) at Mons Casius, and captured the fortress of Pelusium.

Egypt in battle, and Ptolemy turned and fled before him, and many were wounded and fell. ¹⁹ They captured the fortified cities in the land of Egypt, and he plundered the land of Egypt.

²⁰ After subduing Egypt, Antiochus returned in the one hundred forty-third year.^a He went up against Israel and came to Jerusalem with a strong force. ²¹ He arrogantly entered the sanctuary and took the golden altar, the lampstand for the light, and all its utensils. ²² He took also the table for the bread of the Presence, the cups for drink offerings, the bowls, the golden censers, the curtain, the crowns, and the gold decoration on the front of the temple; he stripped it all off. ²³ He took the silver and the gold, and the costly vessels; he took also the hidden treasures that he found. ²⁴ Taking them all, he went into his own land.

He shed much blood,
    and spoke with great arrogance.
²⁵ Israel mourned deeply in every
    community,
²⁶ rulers and elders groaned,
young women and young men became
    faint,
    the beauty of the women faded.

²⁷ Every bridegroom took up the lament;
    she who sat in the bridal chamber was
    mourning.
²⁸ Even the land trembled for its
    inhabitants,
    and all the house of Jacob was clothed
    with shame.

²⁹ Two years later the king sent to the cities of Judah a chief collector of tribute, and he came to Jerusalem with a large force. ³⁰ Deceitfully he spoke peaceable words to them, and they believed him; but he suddenly fell upon the city, dealt it a severe blow, and destroyed many people of Israel. ³¹ He plundered the city, burned it with fire, and tore down its houses and its surrounding walls. ³² They took captive the women and children, and seized the livestock. ³³ Then they fortified the city of David with a great strong wall and strong towers, and it became their citadel. ³⁴ They stationed there a sinful people, men who were renegades. These strengthened their position; ³⁵ they stored up arms and food, and collecting the spoils of Jerusalem they stored them there, and became a great menace,

---

^a 169 B.C.

1.20–28: Antiochus's first attack on Jerusalem. In autumn 169 BCE Antiochus, en route home from Egypt, pillaged the Jerusalem Temple (cf. the earlier attempt of Seleucus IV, 2 Macc 3). His motive was financial (see Dan 11.28); he had no political or religious quarrel with Judah. A Hellenistic king would not hesitate to enter a city temple; the Jewish author saw the entry of anyone but the high priest into the sanctuary as arrogance (v. 21; cf. Dan 7.8,25), requiring divine punishment. 21–23: Golden altar (of incense), Ex 30.1–10; lampstand, Ex 25.31–40; table, Ex 25.23–30; cf. 1 Kings 7.48–50. The bread of the Presence, see Lev 24.5–9; this symbolized the covenant between God and Israel, which 1 Macc sees as threatened by the current events. Crowns, diplomatic gifts stored in the Temple; see 13.37. Gold decoration, see 1 Kings 6.20–22. Hidden treasures, money deposited for safety by individuals; see 2 Macc 4.10–12. Later Judas restores these losses (4.49). 24b–28: Poetic comment (cf. the book of Lamentations) on the events described, as also in 1.36–40; 2.7–13. Blood, vv. 20–24 record no bloodshed, but see 2 Macc 5.11–14.

1.29–40: Capture and fortification of Jerusalem. 29: Two years later, probably 168 BCE, after Antiochus's second invasion of Egypt (2 Macc 5.1). Ejected from Egypt by Roman legions, learning that in Jerusalem his appointee the high priest Menelaus was under attack from his deposed predecessor Jason (2 Macc 5.5–10), and believing Judea was in revolt, Antiochus attacked Jerusalem viciously (2 Macc 5.11–14), later sending Apollonius with troops to enslave the citizens (2 Macc 5.24). Apollonius is probably the chief collector of tribute, this title perhaps mistranslates "captain of the Mysians" (mercenary troops from Asia; see 2 Macc 5.24). 30: The city . . . many people, the concern is political, to subjugate Jerusalem. 33: The city of David indicates historical identity rather than topography; the precise location of the citadel (Gk "akra") is debated; it overlooked and controlled the Temple (Josephus, Ant. 12.252,362), from the northwest or southeast corner, and was finally captured by Simon (13.49–50). 34: Renegades: see v. 11n. 36–40: Poetic lament, emphasizing the citadel's effect on the sanctuary. But Antiochus has not yet threatened Jewish religion.

³⁶for the citadelᵃ became an ambush
    against the sanctuary,
  an evil adversary of Israel at all times.
³⁷On every side of the sanctuary they shed
    innocent blood;
  they even defiled the sanctuary.
³⁸Because of them the residents of
    Jerusalem fled;
  she became a dwelling of strangers;
she became strange to her offspring,
  and her children forsook her.
³⁹Her sanctuary became desolate like a
    desert;
  her feasts were turned into mourning,
her sabbaths into a reproach,
  her honor into contempt.
⁴⁰Her dishonor now grew as great as her
    glory;
  her exaltation was turned into
    mourning.
⁴¹Then the king wrote to his whole kingdom that all should be one people, ⁴²and that
all should give up their particular customs.
⁴³All the Gentiles accepted the command of
the king. Many even from Israel gladly adopted
his religion; they sacrificed to idols and profaned the sabbath. ⁴⁴And the king sent letters
by messengers to Jerusalem and the towns
of Judah; he directed them to follow customs
strange to the land, ⁴⁵to forbid burnt offerings
and sacrifices and drink offerings in the sanctuary, to profane sabbaths and festivals, ⁴⁶to
defile the sanctuary and the priests, ⁴⁷to build
altars and sacred precincts and shrines for
idols, to sacrifice swine and other unclean animals, ⁴⁸and to leave their sons uncircumcised.
They were to make themselves abominable
by everything unclean and profane, ⁴⁹so that
they would forget the law and change all the

ordinances. ⁵⁰He added,ᵇ "And whoever does
not obey the command of the king shall die."
⁵¹In such words he wrote to his whole
kingdom. He appointed inspectors over all
the people and commanded the towns of Judah to offer sacrifice, town by town. ⁵²Many
of the people, everyone who forsook the law,
joined them, and they did evil in the land;
⁵³they drove Israel into hiding in every place
of refuge they had.
⁵⁴Now on the fifteenth day of Chislev,
in the one hundred forty-fifth year,ᶜ they
erected a desolating sacrilege on the altar of
burnt offering. They also built altars in the
surrounding towns of Judah, ⁵⁵and offered
incense at the doors of the houses and in
the streets. ⁵⁶The books of the law that they
found they tore to pieces and burned with
fire. ⁵⁷Anyone found possessing the book of
the covenant, or anyone who adhered to the
law, was condemned to death by decree of
the king. ⁵⁸They kept using violence against
Israel, against those who were found month
after month in the towns. ⁵⁹On the twenty-
fifth day of the month they offered sacrifice
on the altar that was on top of the altar of
burnt offering. ⁶⁰According to the decree,
they put to death the women who had their
children circumcised, ⁶¹and their families
and those who circumcised them; and they
hung the infants from their mothers' necks.
⁶²But many in Israel stood firm and were
resolved in their hearts not to eat unclean
food. ⁶³They chose to die rather than to be
defiled by food or to profane the holy cov-

ᵃ Gk it
ᵇ Gk lacks He added
ᶜ 167 B.C.

1.41–64: The decree of Antiochus and its consequences. 41–43: Antiochus did not attempt religious coer-
cion throughout his *whole kingdom*. His *letters* applied only to Jews in Jerusalem and Judea. 45–48: His prohibitions forced Jews to break the Law's fundamental commandments of *burnt offerings and sacrifices*, *sabbaths and
festivals*, rejection of idolatry, practice of circumcision, and the offering of proper sacrifice at Jerusalem only (Ex
20.4–6; Deut 12.2–28). 51: Thus *inspectors* required sacrifice outside Jerusalem in *the towns of Judah* (cf. v. 55).
2 Macc 6.7 adds that Jews had to offer pagan sacrifices monthly to celebrate the king's birthday, and to honor
the god Dionysus. 54: The date is December 168 or 167 BCE. *Desolating sacrilege* ("abomination of desolation";
cf. Dan 11.31; Mk 13.14) may pun on the Syrian "Ba'al Samen" ("Lord of Heaven"), identified as "Olympian Zeus"
in 2 Macc 6.2, or more likely indicate a pagan altar erected above the Jewish altar of burnt offering outside the
Temple (see v. 59). 56–57,60–61: The books of the Law, people owning copies, or keeping the Law, and those
practicing circumcision (cf. 2 Macc 6.10) were targeted. *Decree*, the instructions contained in the king's letters
(vv. 45–48 above). Antiochus's motives are debated; probably he wished to suppress rebellion by abolishing the

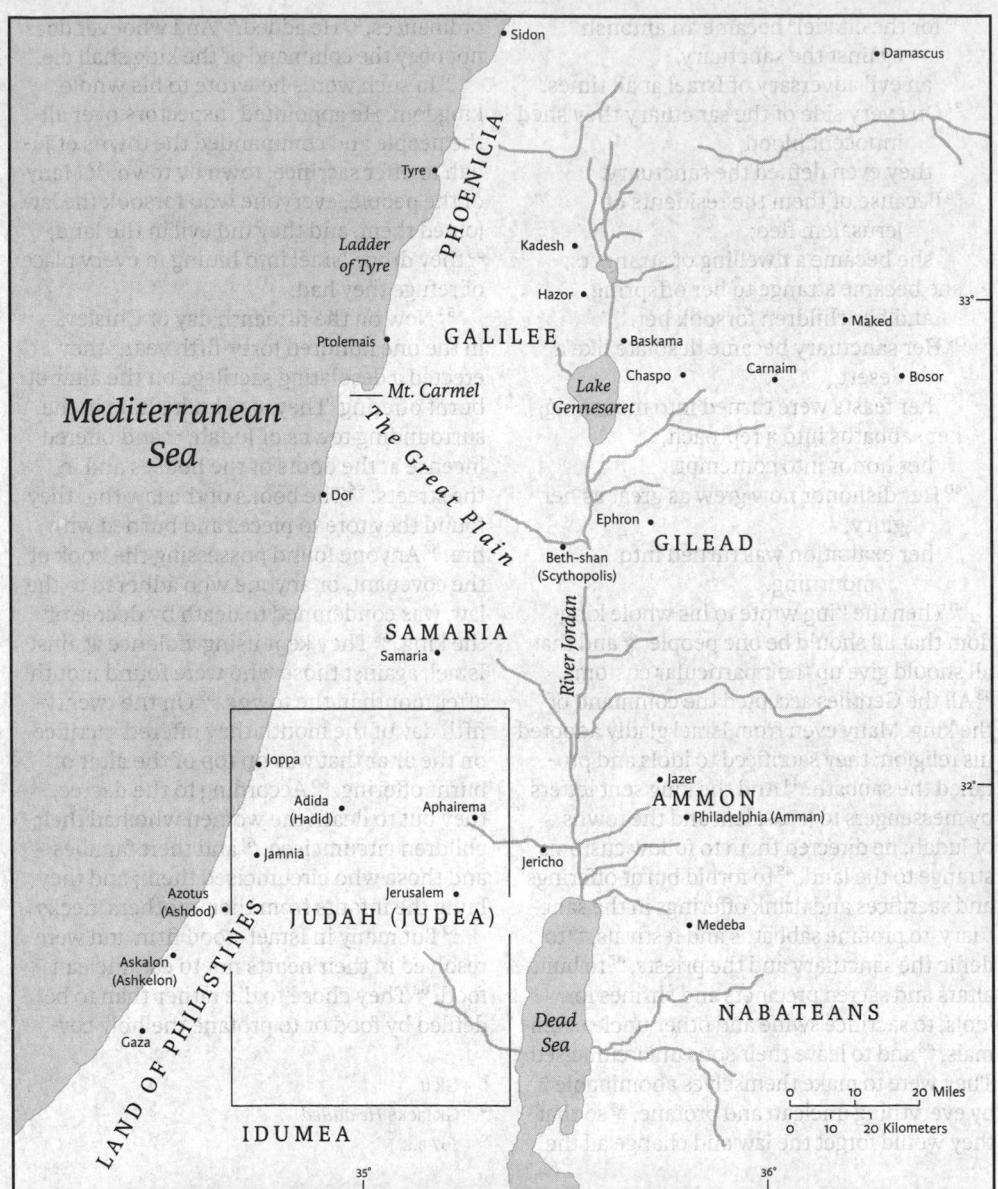

Chs 2–16: Campaigns of the Maccabees and Hasmoneans. See map on p. 1563 for sites in the Jerusalem vicinity.

enant; and they did die. [64] Very great wrath came upon Israel.

2 In those days Mattathias son of John son of Simeon, a priest of the family of Joarib, moved from Jerusalem and settled in Modein. [2] He had five sons, John surnamed Gaddi, [3] Simon called Thassi, [4] Judas called Maccabeus, [5] Eleazar called Avaran, and Jonathan called Apphus. [6] He saw the blasphemies being committed in Judah and Jerusalem, [7] and said,

"Alas! Why was I born to see this,
  the ruin of my people, the ruin of the
    holy city,
and to live there when it was given over to
    the enemy,
  the sanctuary given over to aliens?
[8] Her temple has become like a person
    without honor;[a]
[9] her glorious vessels have been carried
    into exile.
Her infants have been killed in her streets,
  her youths by the sword of the foe.
[10] What nation has not inherited her
    palaces[b]
  and has not seized her spoils?
[11] All her adornment has been taken away;
  no longer free, she has become a slave.
[12] And see, our holy place, our beauty,
    and our glory have been laid waste;
  the Gentiles have profaned them.
[13] Why should we live any longer?"

[14] Then Mattathias and his sons tore their clothes, put on sackcloth, and mourned greatly.

[15] The king's officers who were enforcing the apostasy came to the town of Modein to make them offer sacrifice. [16] Many from Israel came to them; and Mattathias and his sons were assembled. [17] Then the king's officers spoke to Mattathias as follows: "You are a leader, honored and great in this town, and supported by sons and brothers. [18] Now be the first to come and do what the king commands, as all the Gentiles and the people of Judah and those that are left in Jerusalem have done. Then you and your sons will be numbered among the Friends of the king, and you and your sons will be honored with silver and gold and many gifts."

[19] But Mattathias answered and said in a loud voice: "Even if all the nations that live under the rule of the king obey him, and have chosen to obey his commandments, every one of them abandoning the religion of their ancestors, [20] I and my sons and my brothers will continue to live by the covenant of our ancestors. [21] Far be it from us to desert the law and the ordinances. [22] We will not obey the king's words by turning aside from our religion to the right hand or to the left."

[23] When he had finished speaking these words, a Jew came forward in the sight of all to offer sacrifice on the altar in Modein, according to the king's command. [24] When Mattathias saw it, he burned with zeal and his heart was stirred. He gave vent to righteous anger; he ran and killed him on the altar. [25] At the same time he killed the king's officer who was forcing them to sacrifice, and he tore down the altar. [26] Thus he burned with zeal for the law, just as Phinehas did against Zimri son of Salu.

---

a   Meaning of Gk uncertain
b   Other ancient authorities read *has not had a part in her kingdom*

---

code that apparently sustained it. **64:** *Great wrath*, 1 Macc presents these events as God's punishment upon the sins of the renegades and their supporters.

2.1–14: Mattathias and his sons. 1: *Family of Joarib*, a senior priestly (not high priestly) family; 1 Chr 9.10; 24.7. *Modein* (cf. 13.25–30), a village near Lod, ca. 20 mi (32 km) northwest of Jerusalem. **2–5:** *Simon*, see chs 13–16; *Judas*, see 3.1–9.22. The nickname *Maccabeus* may mean "hammer" (see Introduction, 2 Macc). *Eleazar*, see 6.43. *Jonathan*, see 9.28–13.30. Jonathan and Simon became high priests. **7–13:** A poetic lament over Jerusalem personified as a captive woman, a comment on the events of 1.41–64; see Lam 1.

2.15–28: Confrontation at Modein. 15: *King's officers*, cf. "inspectors" (1.51). **18:** *What the king commands*, i.e., make local sacrifice away from Jerusalem, against the Jewish Law. *Friends of the king*, advisers at court appointed by the king. Jonathan was later enrolled among the king's "chief Friends" (10.65; cf. 10.20; 11.27) or "King's Kinsmen" (10.89). **22:** *Turning aside*, Mattathias rejects the invitation, quoting Deut 5.32. **23:** The Jew thus makes a direct challenge to Mattathias's leadership. **26:** Mattathias is directly compared with *Phinehas*, grandson of the high priest Aaron, who had killed an Israelite. The Israelite had compromised Israelite exclusivism by having

²⁷ Then Mattathias cried out in the town with a loud voice, saying: "Let every one who is zealous for the law and supports the covenant come out with me!" ²⁸ Then he and his sons fled to the hills and left all that they had in the town.

²⁹ At that time many who were seeking righteousness and justice went down to the wilderness to live there, ³⁰ they, their sons, their wives, and their livestock, because troubles pressed heavily upon them. ³¹ And it was reported to the king's officers, and to the troops in Jerusalem the city of David, that those who had rejected the king's command had gone down to the hiding places in the wilderness. ³² Many pursued them, and overtook them; they encamped opposite them and prepared for battle against them on the sabbath day. ³³ They said to them, "Enough of this! Come out and do what the king commands, and you will live." ³⁴ But they said, "We will not come out, nor will we do what the king commands and so profane the sabbath day." ³⁵ Then the enemy[a] quickly attacked them. ³⁶ But they did not answer them or hurl a stone at them or block up their hiding places, ³⁷ for they said, "Let us all die in our innocence; heaven and earth testify for us that you are killing us unjustly." ³⁸ So they attacked them on the sabbath, and they died, with their wives and children and livestock, to the number of a thousand persons.

³⁹ When Mattathias and his friends learned of it, they mourned for them deeply. ⁴⁰ And all said to their neighbors: "If we all do as our kindred have done and refuse to fight with the Gentiles for our lives and for our ordinances, they will quickly destroy us from the earth." ⁴¹ So they made this decision that day: "Let us fight against anyone who comes to attack us on the sabbath day; let us not all die as our kindred died in their hiding places."

⁴² Then there united with them a company of Hasideans, mighty warriors of Israel, all who offered themselves willingly for the law. ⁴³ And all who became fugitives to escape their troubles joined them and reinforced them. ⁴⁴ They organized an army, and struck down sinners in their anger and renegades in their wrath; the survivors fled to the Gentiles for safety. ⁴⁵ And Mattathias and his friends went around and tore down the altars; ⁴⁶ they forcibly circumcised all the uncircumcised boys that they found within the borders of Israel. ⁴⁷ They hunted down the arrogant, and the work prospered in their hands. ⁴⁸ They rescued the law out of the hands of the Gentiles and kings, and they never let the sinner gain the upper hand.

⁴⁹ Now the days drew near for Mattathias to die, and he said to his sons: "Arrogance and scorn have now become strong; it is a time of ruin and furious anger. ⁵⁰ Now, my children, show zeal for the law, and give your lives for the covenant of our ancestors.

⁵¹ "Remember the deeds of the ancestors, which they did in their generations; and you will receive great honor and an everlasting name. ⁵² Was not Abraham found faithful when tested, and it was reckoned to him as righteousness? ⁵³ Joseph in the time of his distress kept the commandment, and became lord of Egypt. ⁵⁴ Phinehas our ancestor, because he was deeply zealous, received the covenant of everlasting priesthood. ⁵⁵ Joshua, because he fulfilled the command, became a judge in Israel. ⁵⁶ Caleb, because he testified in the assembly, received an inheritance in

a Gk *they*

intercourse with a Midianite woman who worshiped Baal of Peor (Num 25.1–16). **28:** *Fled to the hills*, 2 Macc 5.27–6.2 dates this before Antiochus's religious persecution.

2.29–41: Passive resistance. 29: Mattathias's violence for Law and covenant (2.27) is contrasted favorably with the passive reaction of another group *seeking righteousness and justice*. **41:** Mattathias's followers decide that the necessity of self-preservation overrides even the command to keep the sabbath.

2:42–48: The Hasideans and Mattathias. The *Hasideans* (Heb "hasidim," "the pious," cf. Pss 79.2; 149.1) are another militaristic group, which *united* with Mattathias's *friends*; in 2 Macc 14.6 they are under Judas's leadership. 1 Macc 7.12 reports them as naively and fatally supporting a peace mission.

2:49–70: Mattathias's death-bed speech. Jacob (Gen 49), Moses (Deut 33), and Samuel (1 Sam 12) utter similar speeches; compare also the praises of famous men in Sir 44–50. **52:** *Abraham . . . faithful when tested*, Gen 22.1–18; *reckoned . . . as righteousness*, Gen 15.6. **53:** *Joseph*, Gen 39–50. **54:** *Phinehas*, see v. 26n. **55–56:** *Joshua*

the land. ⁵⁷ David, because he was merciful, inherited the throne of the kingdom forever. ⁵⁸ Elijah, because of great zeal for the law, was taken up into heaven. ⁵⁹ Hananiah, Azariah, and Mishael believed and were saved from the flame. ⁶⁰ Daniel, because of his innocence, was delivered from the mouth of the lions.

⁶¹ "And so observe, from generation to generation, that none of those who put their trust in him will lack strength. ⁶² Do not fear the words of sinners, for their splendor will turn into dung and worms. ⁶³ Today they will be exalted, but tomorrow they will not be found, because they will have returned to the dust, and their plans will have perished. ⁶⁴ My children, be courageous and grow strong in the law, for by it you will gain honor.

⁶⁵ "Here is your brother Simeon who, I know, is wise in counsel; always listen to him; he shall be your father. ⁶⁶ Judas Maccabeus has been a mighty warrior from his youth; he shall command the army for you and fight the battle against the peoples.ᵃ ⁶⁷ You shall rally around you all who observe the law, and avenge the wrong done to your people. ⁶⁸ Pay back the Gentiles in full, and obey the commands of the law."

⁶⁹ Then he blessed them, and was gathered to his ancestors. ⁷⁰ He died in the one hundred forty-sixth yearᵇ and was buried in the tomb of his ancestors at Modein. And all Israel mourned for him with great lamentation.

3 Then his son Judas, who was called Maccabeus, took command in his place. ² All his brothers and all who had joined his father helped him; they gladly fought for Israel.

³ He extended the glory of his people.
Like a giant he put on his breastplate;
he bound on his armor of war and waged battles,
protecting the camp by his sword.

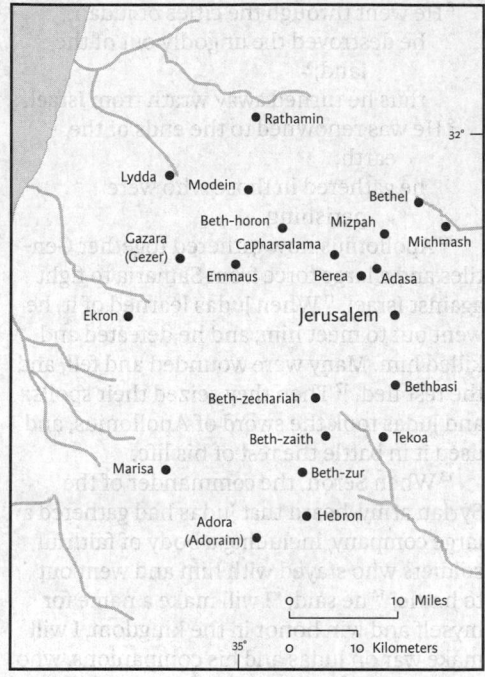

Chs 2–16: The Jerusalem vicinity.

⁴ He was like a lion in his deeds,
like a lion's cub roaring for prey.
⁵ He searched out and pursued those who broke the law;
he burned those who troubled his people.
⁶ Lawbreakers shrank back for fear of him;
all the evildoers were confounded;
and deliverance prospered by his hand.
⁷ He embittered many kings,
but he made Jacob glad by his deeds,
and his memory is blessed forever.

ᵃ Or *of the people*
ᵇ 166 B.C.

and *Caleb* appear together in Num 14.5–10 and Sir 46.1–10. **57:** *David . . . merciful,* perhaps "pious" or "loyal" is meant. *Throne . . . forever,* see 2 Sam 7.13,16. **58:** *Elijah . . . zeal for the law,* cf. 1 Kings 21.17–29; *into heaven,* 2 Kings 2.9–12. **59:** *Hananiah, Azariah, and Mishael,* see Dan 1.6–20. **60:** *Daniel . . . lions,* Dan 6.16–24. Mattathias commends these heroes especially for their loyalty to the Law and readiness to testify under trial. **65–66:** *Simeon* (Simon), *wise in counsel,* and *Judas, a mighty warrior,* thus 1 Macc presents them, but in reverse order. **70:** *Tomb,* described in 13.27–30.

3.1–9: Introducing Judas. The poem pictures Judas in terms of earlier heroes. **4:** *Like a lion,* cf. Judah (Gen 49.9). **5–8:** Judas attacks two groups, the *lawbreakers* (vv. 5,6) who accept Antiochus's decree, and foreign *kings* (v. 7), i.e., Antiochus IV and Demetrius. *Turned away wrath from Israel,* cf. Phinehas (Num 25.11); thus Judas cancels God's wrath (1.64).

[8] He went through the cities of Judah;
    he destroyed the ungodly out of the
      land;[a]
    thus he turned away wrath from Israel.
[9] He was renowned to the ends of the
      earth;
    he gathered in those who were
      perishing.

[10] Apollonius now gathered together Gentiles and a large force from Samaria to fight against Israel. [11] When Judas learned of it, he went out to meet him, and he defeated and killed him. Many were wounded and fell, and the rest fled. [12] Then they seized their spoils; and Judas took the sword of Apollonius, and used it in battle the rest of his life.

[13] When Seron, the commander of the Syrian army, heard that Judas had gathered a large company, including a body of faithful soldiers who stayed with him and went out to battle, [14] he said, "I will make a name for myself and win honor in the kingdom. I will make war on Judas and his companions, who scorn the king's command." [15] Once again a strong army of godless men went up with him to help him, to take vengeance on the Israelites.

[16] When he approached the ascent of Beth-horon, Judas went out to meet him with a small company. [17] But when they saw the army coming to meet them, they said to Judas, "How can we, few as we are, fight against so great and so strong a multitude? And we are faint, for we have eaten nothing today." [18] Judas replied, "It is easy for many to be hemmed in by few, for in the sight of Heaven there is no difference between saving by many or by few. [19] It is not on the size of the army that victory in battle depends, but strength comes from Heaven. [20] They come against us in great insolence and lawlessness to destroy us and our wives and our children, and to despoil us; [21] but we fight for our lives and our laws. [22] He himself will crush them before us; as for you, do not be afraid of them."

[23] When he finished speaking, he rushed suddenly against Seron and his army, and they were crushed before him. [24] They pursued them[b] down the descent of Beth-horon to the plain; eight hundred of them fell, and the rest fled into the land of the Philistines. [25] Then Judas and his brothers began to be feared, and terror fell on the Gentiles all around them. [26] His fame reached the king, and the Gentiles talked of the battles of Judas.

[27] When King Antiochus heard these reports, he was greatly angered; and he sent and gathered all the forces of his kingdom, a very strong army. [28] He opened his coffers and gave a year's pay to his forces, and ordered them to be ready for any need. [29] Then he saw that the money in the treasury was exhausted, and that the revenues from the country were small because of the dissension and disaster that he had caused in the land by abolishing the laws that had existed from the earliest days. [30] He feared that he might not have such funds as he had before for his expenses and for the gifts that he used to give more lavishly than preceding kings. [31] He was greatly perplexed in mind; then he determined to go to Persia and collect the revenues from those regions and raise a large fund.

a   Gk *it*
b   Other ancient authorities read *him*

3.10–26: Judas's campaigns against Apollonius and Seron. 10: *Apollonius*, possibly the Apollonius of 2 Macc 5.24, probably governor of Samaria (Josephus, *Ant.* 2.287). 1 Macc knows no details of this campaign. 12: *Sword of Apollonius*, cf. David's use of Goliath's sword (2 Sam 17.51). 13: *Seron . . . Syrian army*, in spite of the title, not a high-ranking officer, nor the main Syrian army, which in 166 BCE was on parade near Antioch. 16: *Ascent of Beth-horon*, a major pass ca. 12 mi (20 km) northwest of Jerusalem on the route from the coastal plain. The Seleucid general Bacchides later fortified it (9.50). Judas ambushed Seron here, as the Jews ambushed the Roman general Cestius in 65 CE (Josephus, *J.W.* 2.547). 18: *Heaven*, throughout 1 Macc, a pious substitution for the name of God; note "he himself" (v. 22). *Saving by many or by few*, an echo of 1 Sam 14.6. 24: *Philistines*, an anachronism illustrating the presentation of Judas as a latter-day David.

3.27–37: Antiochus's policy. 27: *Gathered all the forces* for a military review at Daphne near Antioch, 166 BCE. 29–30: Antiochus's shortage of cash was not caused, as the author likes to imagine, by *abolishing the* [Jewish] *laws* but by spending *lavishly* elsewhere. 31: Antiochus hoped to restore his finances by an expedition to *Persia*.

³² He left Lysias, a distinguished man of royal lineage, in charge of the king's affairs from the river Euphrates to the borders of Egypt. ³³ Lysias was also to take care of his son Antiochus until he returned. ³⁴ And he turned over to Lysias[a] half of his forces and the elephants, and gave him orders about all that he wanted done. As for the residents of Judea and Jerusalem, ³⁵ Lysias was to send a force against them to wipe out and destroy the strength of Israel and the remnant of Jerusalem; he was to banish the memory of them from the place, ³⁶ settle aliens in all their territory, and distribute their land by lot. ³⁷ Then the king took the remaining half of his forces and left Antioch his capital in the one hundred and forty-seventh year.[b] He crossed the Euphrates river and went through the upper provinces.

³⁸ Lysias chose Ptolemy son of Dorymenes, and Nicanor and Gorgias, able men among the Friends of the king, ³⁹ and sent with them forty thousand infantry and seven thousand cavalry to go into the land of Judah and destroy it, as the king had commanded. ⁴⁰ So they set out with their entire force, and when they arrived they encamped near Emmaus in the plain. ⁴¹ When the traders of the region heard what was said to them, they took silver and gold in immense amounts, and fetters,[c] and went to the camp to get the Israelites for slaves. And forces from Syria and the land of the Philistines joined with them.

⁴² Now Judas and his brothers saw that misfortunes had increased and that the forces were encamped in their territory. They also learned what the king had commanded to do to the people to cause their final destruction. ⁴³ But they said to one another, "Let us restore the ruins of our people, and fight for our people and the sanctuary." ⁴⁴ So the congregation assembled to be ready for battle, and to pray and ask for mercy and compassion.

⁴⁵ Jerusalem was uninhabited like a
    wilderness;
    not one of her children went in or out.
The sanctuary was trampled down,
    and aliens held the citadel;
    it was a lodging place for the Gentiles.
Joy was taken from Jacob;
    the flute and the harp ceased to play.

⁴⁶ Then they gathered together and went to Mizpah, opposite Jerusalem, because Israel formerly had a place of prayer in Mizpah. ⁴⁷ They fasted that day, put on sackcloth and sprinkled ashes on their heads, and tore their clothes. ⁴⁸ And they opened the book of the law to inquire into those matters about which the Gentiles consulted the likenesses of their gods. ⁴⁹ They also brought the vestments of the priesthood and the first fruits and the tithes, and they stirred up the nazirites[d] who had completed their days; ⁵⁰ and they cried aloud to Heaven, saying,

"What shall we do with these?
    Where shall we take them?
⁵¹ Your sanctuary is trampled down and
    profaned,
    and your priests mourn in humiliation.

---

a Gk *him*
b 165 B.C.
c Syr: Gk Mss, Vg *slaves*
d That is *those separated* or *those consecrated*

32: *Lysias . . . of royal lineage* was probably one of the King's "Kinsmen" (an honorary title; cf. 10.89) rather than a blood relative. 33: *His son Antiochus*, Antiochus V Eupator (ca. 164–162 BCE). 37: *Antioch*, modern Antakya in southern Turkey near the mouth of the Orontes River, founded by Seleucus I in 300 BCE. *Upper provinces*, Antiochus campaigned in Armenia, along the Persian Gulf, and in Elymais, probably in spring 165 BCE.

3.38–4.35: Judas's victory over Gorgias. 38: *Ptolemy son of Dorymenes*, probably the governor of Coelesyria and Phoenicia (2 Macc 8.8), and *Nicanor*, "son of Patroclus and one of the king's chief Friends" (2 Macc 8.9), play no further part in this campaign in 1 Macc; the enemy is led by *Gorgias*, another of the king's Friends (see 2.18) and governor of Idumea (2 Macc 12.32), but according to 2 Macc 8.10–29 by Nicanor (whose activities, however, seem to belong to Demetrius's reign; see 7.26–50). 40: *Emmaus* (not that of Lk 24.13), ca. 18 mi (28 km) west-northwest of Jerusalem, 8 mi (13 km) south of Modein. 41: *Slaves*, the sale of captured soldiers was usual in ancient warfare (see also 2 Macc 8.10–11). Some scholars think that *Syria* is an error for "Idumea" (cf. 4.29). *Philistines*, see v. 24n. 45–46: A poetic comment (cf. vv. 50–53). 46: *Mizpah*, 8 mi (13 km) north of Jerusalem, where Samuel gathered the Israelites against the Philistines (1 Sam 7.5–11). 48: A deliberate contrast: Jews consult *the book of the law*, Gentiles *their gods*. 49: *Nazirites* (cf. Num 6.1–21), perhaps a reminder of men like Samson (Judg

[52] Here the Gentiles are assembled against
  us to destroy us;
  you know what they plot against us.
[53] How will we be able to withstand them,
  if you do not help us?"
[54] Then they sounded the trumpets and gave a loud shout. [55] After this Judas appointed leaders of the people, in charge of thousands and hundreds and fifties and tens. [56] Those who were building houses, or were about to be married, or were planting a vineyard, or were fainthearted, he told to go home again, according to the law. [57] Then the army marched out and encamped to the south of Emmaus.

[58] And Judas said, "Arm yourselves and be courageous. Be ready early in the morning to fight with these Gentiles who have assembled against us to destroy us and our sanctuary. [59] It is better for us to die in battle than to see the misfortunes of our nation and of the sanctuary. [60] But as his will in heaven may be, so shall he do."

4 Now Gorgias took five thousand infantry and one thousand picked cavalry, and this division moved out by night [2] to fall upon the camp of the Jews and attack them suddenly. Men from the citadel were his guides. [3] But Judas heard of it, and he and his warriors moved out to attack the king's force in Emmaus [4] while the division was still absent from the camp. [5] When Gorgias entered the camp of Judas by night, he found no one there, so he looked for them in the hills, because he said, "These men are running away from us."

[6] At daybreak Judas appeared in the plain with three thousand men, but they did not have armor and swords such as they desired. [7] And they saw the camp of the Gentiles, strong and fortified, with cavalry all around it; and these men were trained in war. [8] But Judas said to those who were with him, "Do not fear their numbers or be afraid when they charge. [9] Remember how our ancestors were saved at the Red Sea, when Pharaoh with his forces pursued them. [10] And now, let us cry to Heaven, to see whether he will favor us and remember his covenant with our ancestors and crush this army before us today. [11] Then all the Gentiles will know that there is one who redeems and saves Israel."

[12] When the foreigners looked up and saw them coming against them, [13] they went out from their camp to battle. Then the men with Judas blew their trumpets [14] and engaged in battle. The Gentiles were crushed, and fled into the plain, [15] and all those in the rear fell by the sword. They pursued them to Gazara, and to the plains of Idumea, and to Azotus and Jamnia; and three thousand of them fell. [16] Then Judas and his force turned back from pursuing them, [17] and he said to the people, "Do not be greedy for plunder, for there is a battle before us; [18] Gorgias and his force are near us in the hills. But stand now against our enemies and fight them, and afterward seize the plunder boldly."

[19] Just as Judas was finishing this speech, a detachment appeared, coming out of the hills. [20] They saw that their army[a] had been put to flight, and that the Jews[a] were burning the camp, for the smoke that was seen showed what had happened. [21] When they perceived this, they were greatly frightened, and when they also saw the army of Judas drawn up in the plain for battle, [22] they all fled into the land of the Philistines. [23] Then Judas returned to plunder the camp, and they seized a great amount of gold and silver, and cloth dyed blue and sea purple, and great riches. [24] On their return they sang hymns

a   Gk they

13.7), Israel's champion against the Philistines. **55–56:** Judas *appointed leaders* (cf. Moses, Deut 1.15), sending *home* some groups (cf. Deut 20.5–8) and giving a pre-battle sermon (like Jehoshaphat; 2 Chr 20.15–17). **4.2:** *The citadel,* see 1.33n. **8:** *Do not fear their numbers,* the imbalance of Judas's 3,000 men opposing 35,000 infantry and 6,000 cavalry (see 3.39 and 4.1) is emphasized. 2 Macc 8.9,24 give different numbers. **9–11:** Judas appeals to Israel's victory at the Red Sea (Ex 14.21–31) and God's covenant with their *ancestors* Abraham, Isaac, and Jacob (Gen 17.1–8; 26.2–5; 35.9–15). **15:** *Gazara,* Gezer (1 Kings 9.15–17), and *Jamnia,* Jabneh (2 Chr 26.6), were both west of Emmaus, the site of the battle, and *Azotus,* Ashdod (1 Sam 5.5–6), was to the southwest. All were once Philistine cities. *Idumea* was south of Judah toward the Negeb. **23:** *Cloth dyed blue and sea purple,* luxury products of the Phoenician coast; see Ezek 27.7. **24:** Pss 118.1; 136.1.

and praises to Heaven—"For he is good, for his mercy endures forever." [25] Thus Israel had a great deliverance that day.

[26] Those of the foreigners who escaped went and reported to Lysias all that had happened. [27] When he heard it, he was perplexed and discouraged, for things had not happened to Israel as he had intended, nor had they turned out as the king had ordered. [28] But the next year he mustered sixty thousand picked infantry and five thousand cavalry to subdue them. [29] They came into Idumea and encamped at Beth-zur, and Judas met them with ten thousand men.

[30] When he saw that their army was strong, he prayed, saying, "Blessed are you, O Savior of Israel, who crushed the attack of the mighty warrior by the hand of your servant David, and gave the camp of the Philistines into the hands of Jonathan son of Saul, and of the man who carried his armor. [31] Hem in this army by the hand of your people Israel, and let them be ashamed of their troops and their cavalry. [32] Fill them with cowardice; melt the boldness of their strength; let them tremble in their destruction. [33] Strike them down with the sword of those who love you, and let all who know your name praise you with hymns."

[34] Then both sides attacked, and there fell of the army of Lysias five thousand men; they fell in action.[a] [35] When Lysias saw the rout of his troops and observed the boldness that inspired those of Judas, and how ready they were either to live or to die nobly, he withdrew to Antioch and enlisted mercenaries in order to invade Judea again with an even larger army.

[36] Then Judas and his brothers said, "See, our enemies are crushed; let us go up to cleanse the sanctuary and dedicate it." [37] So all the army assembled and went up to Mount Zion. [38] There they saw the sanctuary desolate, the altar profaned, and the gates burned. In the courts they saw bushes sprung up as in a thicket, or as on one of the mountains. They saw also the chambers of the priests in ruins. [39] Then they tore their clothes and mourned with great lamentation; they sprinkled themselves with ashes [40] and fell face down on the ground. And when the signal was given with the trumpets, they cried out to Heaven.

[41] Then Judas detailed men to fight against those in the citadel until he had cleansed the sanctuary. [42] He chose blameless priests devoted to the law, [43] and they cleansed the sanctuary and removed the defiled stones to an unclean place. [44] They deliberated what to do about the altar of burnt offering, which had been profaned. [45] And they thought it best to tear it down, so that it would not be a lasting shame to them that the Gentiles had defiled it. So they tore down the altar, [46] and stored the stones in a convenient place on the temple hill until a prophet should come to tell what to do with them. [47] Then they took unhewn[b] stones, as the law directs, and built a new altar like the former one. [48] They also rebuilt the sanctuary and the interior of the temple, and consecrated the courts. [49] They made new holy vessels, and brought the lampstand, the altar of incense, and the table into the temple. [50] Then they offered incense on the altar and lit the lamps on the lampstand, and these gave light in the tem-

a Or and some fell on the opposite side
b Gk whole

4.26–35: Judas defeats Lysias. 26: *Lysias*, see 3.32n. 28: *The next year*, i.e., year 148 (cf. 3.37), probably beginning in autumn 165 BCE. 1 Macc emphasizes the size of Lysias's army. 29: *Beth-zur*, 16 mi (25 km) south-southeast of Jerusalem; cf. 2 Macc 11.25. 30–33: Judas's prayer (cf. 4.8–11) recalls David's killing of Goliath (*the mighty warrior*; cf. 1 Sam 17.4–54) and Jonathan's success against the Philistines (1 Sam 14.1–15); 1 Macc again presents the struggle in biblical terms. 35: *To invade Judea again*, cf. 6.28–63. Some scholars suspect that these two campaigns are really one.

4.36–61: The cleansing of the Temple and dedication of the altar. 37: *Mount Zion*, an old name for the city of David (2 Sam 5.7) and the Temple site (Ps 2.6; Joel 2.1). 38: *Sanctuary desolate . . . altar profaned*, cf. 1.54,59. *Gates burned*, by Jason's men in 168 BCE, cf. 2 Macc 1.8; 5.5–6; 8.33. 41: Judas attacks the *citadel*, which controlled access to the Temple (see 1.33n.). 43: *Defiled stones*, i.e., those forming the "desolating sacrilege," 1.54n. 44: See 1.54,59. 46: *Stored the stones*, though defiled, they were still part of the original altar. *Prophet should come*, the author believed that prophecy had ceased (9.27) but awaited a future prophet to advise the people (14.41;

ple. [51] They placed the bread on the table and hung up the curtains. Thus they finished all the work they had undertaken.

[52] Early in the morning on the twenty-fifth day of the ninth month, which is the month of Chislev, in the one hundred forty-eighth year,[a] [53] they rose and offered sacrifice, as the law directs, on the new altar of burnt offering that they had built. [54] At the very season and on the very day that the Gentiles had profaned it, it was dedicated with songs and harps and lutes and cymbals. [55] All the people fell on their faces and worshiped and blessed Heaven, who had prospered them. [56] So they celebrated the dedication of the altar for eight days, and joyfully offered burnt offerings; they offered a sacrifice of well-being and a thanksgiving offering. [57] They decorated the front of the temple with golden crowns and small shields; they restored the gates and the chambers for the priests, and fitted them with doors. [58] There was very great joy among the people, and the disgrace brought by the Gentiles was removed.

[59] Then Judas and his brothers and all the assembly of Israel determined that every year at that season the days of dedication of the altar should be observed with joy and gladness for eight days, beginning with the twenty-fifth day of the month of Chislev.

[60] At that time they fortified Mount Zion with high walls and strong towers all around,

to keep the Gentiles from coming and trampling them down as they had done before. [61] Judas[b] stationed a garrison there to guard it; he also fortified Beth-zur to guard it, so that the people might have a stronghold that faced Idumea.

5 When the Gentiles all around heard that the altar had been rebuilt and the sanctuary dedicated as it was before, they became very angry, [2] and they determined to destroy the descendants of Jacob who lived among them. So they began to kill and destroy among the people. [3] But Judas made war on the descendants of Esau in Idumea, at Akrabattene, because they kept lying in wait for Israel. He dealt them a heavy blow and humbled them and despoiled them. [4] He also remembered the wickedness of the sons of Baean, who were a trap and a snare to the people and ambushed them on the highways. [5] They were shut up by him in their[c] towers; and he encamped against them, vowed their complete destruction, and burned with fire their towers and all who were in them. [6] Then he crossed over to attack the Ammonites, where he found a strong band and many people, with Timothy as their leader. [7] He engaged in many battles with them, and they

a   164 B.C.
b   Gk *He*
c   Gk *her*

cf. Deut 18.15; Mal 4.5; Jn 1.21). **47:** *As the law directs*, Ex 20.25; Deut 27.5–6. **49:** Cf. 1.21–23n. **51:** *Curtains*, see Ex 26.1–10,31–35. *Finished*, echoing the completion of Moses' work (Ex 40.33). **52:** *Chislev . . . the one hundred forty-eighth year*, i.e., December 165 BCE, exactly three years after the desecration (1.59); this dating places the Temple dedication, with 1 Macc, before Antiochus IV's death in 164 BCE. Some scholars, following 2 Macc 10.1–8, date the dedication soon after Antiochus's death in December 164 BCE. **56:** *Eight days*, as in Solomon's Temple dedication (1 Kings 8.66) and Hezekiah's purification (2 Chr 29.17). **57:** *Crowns*, cf. 1.22. **59:** *Assembly*, cf. 5.16; 14.19. Exactly who has authority to make this decision in 165 BCE is unclear. *Every year*, the letters of 2 Macc 1.1–9 and 1.10–2.18 instruct Egyptian Jews to keep this feast, associating it with lighting lamps (2 Macc 1.8) and holy fire (2 Macc 1.19–2.12). It is also called "the feast of Lights" (Josephus, *Ant.* 12.236) and "the festival of the Dedication" (Jn 10.22). **60–61:** *Mount Zion*, defending the Temple area against the citadel; *Beth-zur*, defending Jerusalem from the south (see 4.29n.).

5.1–68: Judas rescues Jews from neighboring peoples. The author inserts these undated events between chs 4 and 6 (2 Macc dates some of them later), constructing ch 5 carefully. Verses 1–8 show Judas attacking the sons of Esau and the Ammonites, balanced by 5.65–68 in which he attacks the sons of Esau again. In between, 5.9–64 show Simon rescuing Jews from Galilee (vv. 17,21–23), Judas rescuing Jews from Gilead (vv. 17,24–54), and Joseph and Azariah, left to guard Judea, being defeated (vv. 18–19,55–62). **3:** *Esau*, brother of Jacob, ancestor of Judah's enemy, Edom (see Gen 36). Judas defeats the Edomites as David did (2 Sam 8.13–14). *Idumea* (see 4.15n.). *Akrabattene*, located by Josephus (*J.W.* 2.235) in Samaria, by some scholars south of Judah (cf. Num 34.4). **4:** *Sons of Baean*, otherwise unknown. **6:** *Ammonites*, east of the Jordan; cf. Saul's victory (2 Sam 11). *Timothy*, cf.

were crushed before him; he struck them down. [8] He also took Jazer and its villages; then he returned to Judea.

[9] Now the Gentiles in Gilead gathered together against the Israelites who lived in their territory, and planned to destroy them. But they fled to the stronghold of Dathema, [10] and sent to Judas and his brothers a letter that said, "The Gentiles around us have gathered together to destroy us. [11] They are preparing to come and capture the stronghold to which we have fled, and Timothy is leading their forces. [12] Now then, come and rescue us from their hands, for many of us have fallen, [13] and all our kindred who were in the land of Tob have been killed; the enemy[a] have captured their wives and children and goods, and have destroyed about a thousand persons there."

[14] While the letter was still being read, other messengers, with their garments torn, came from Galilee and made a similar report; [15] they said that the people of Ptolemais and Tyre and Sidon, and all Galilee of the Gentiles,[b] had gathered together against them "to annihilate us." [16] When Judas and the people heard these messages, a great assembly was called to determine what they should do for their kindred who were in distress and were being attacked by enemies.[c] [17] Then Judas said to his brother Simon, "Choose your men and go and rescue your kindred in Galilee; Jonathan my brother and I will go to Gilead." [18] But he left Joseph, son of Zechariah, and Azariah, a leader of the people, with the rest of the forces, in Judea to guard it; [19] and he gave them this command, "Take charge of this people, but do not engage in battle with the Gentiles until we return." [20] Then three thousand men were assigned to Simon to go to Galilee, and eight thousand to Judas for Gilead.

[21] So Simon went to Galilee and fought many battles against the Gentiles, and the Gentiles were crushed before him. [22] He pursued them to the gate of Ptolemais; as many as three thousand of the Gentiles fell, and he despoiled them. [23] Then he took the Jews[d] of Galilee and Arbatta, with their wives and children, and all they possessed, and led them to Judea with great rejoicing.

[24] Judas Maccabeus and his brother Jonathan crossed the Jordan and made three days' journey into the wilderness. [25] They encountered the Nabateans, who met them peaceably and told them all that had happened to their kindred in Gilead: [26] "Many of them have been shut up in Bozrah and Bosor, in Alema and Chaspho, Maked and Carnaim"—all these towns were strong and large— [27] "and some have been shut up in the other towns of Gilead; the enemy[a] are getting ready to attack the strongholds tomorrow and capture and destroy all these people in a single day."

[28] Then Judas and his army quickly turned back by the wilderness road to Bozrah; and he took the town, and killed every male by the edge of the sword; then he seized all its spoils and burned it with fire. [29] He left the place at night, and they went all the way to the stronghold of Dathema.[e] [30] At dawn they looked out and saw a large company, which could not be counted, carrying ladders and engines of war to capture the stronghold, and attacking the Jews within.[f] [31] So Judas saw that the battle had begun and that the cry of the town went up to Heaven, with trumpets and loud shouts, [32] and he said to the men of his forces, "Fight today for your kindred!" [33] Then he came up behind them in three

a Gk they
b Gk aliens
c Gk them
d Gk those
e Gk lacks of Dathema. See verse 9
f Gk and they were attacking them

vv. 9,34,37,40 and 2 Macc 8.30–33. 8: Jazer, ca. 12 mi (20 km) northwest of Philadelphia (modern Amman); see Num 32.3. 9: Gilead, region north of Amman. Dathema, precise location uncertain. 13: Land of Tob, in southern Syria; see Judg 11.3. 15: Ptolemais, earlier Acco (Judg 1.31; modern Akko), renamed by Ptolemy II Philadelphus in 261 BCE, a Hellenistic port hostile to the Jews (see 2 Macc 6.8). 23: Arbatta, precise location uncertain. 25: Nabateans, people of northwest Arabia whose kings (e.g., Aretas, 2 Macc 5.8) ruled from Petra in southern Transjordan. 26: Bosrah, modern Bostra in southern Syria. The identifications of Bosor, Alema, Chaspho (perhaps the Caspin of 2 Macc 12.13–16), and Maked are debated. Carnaim (cf. 2 Macc 12.21) is Sheik Sad in southern Syria.

companies, who sounded their trumpets and cried aloud in prayer. [34] And when the army of Timothy realized that it was Maccabeus, they fled before him, and he dealt them a heavy blow. As many as eight thousand of them fell that day.

[35] Next he turned aside to Maapha,[a] and fought against it and took it; and he killed every male in it, plundered it, and burned it with fire. [36] From there he marched on and took Chaspho, Maked, and Bosor, and the other towns of Gilead.

[37] After these things Timothy gathered another army and encamped opposite Raphon, on the other side of the stream. [38] Judas sent men to spy out the camp, and they reported to him, "All the Gentiles around us have gathered to him; it is a very large force. [39] They also have hired Arabs to help them, and they are encamped across the stream, ready to come and fight against you." And Judas went to meet them.

[40] Now as Judas and his army drew near to the stream of water, Timothy said to the officers of his forces, "If he crosses over to us first, we will not be able to resist him, for he will surely defeat us. [41] But if he shows fear and camps on the other side of the river, we will cross over to him and defeat him."

[42] When Judas approached the stream of water, he stationed the officers[b] of the army at the stream and gave them this command, "Permit no one to encamp, but make them all enter the battle." [43] Then he crossed over against them first, and the whole army followed him. All the Gentiles were defeated before him, and they threw away their arms and fled into the sacred precincts at Carnaim. [44] But he took the town and burned the sacred precincts with fire, together with all who were in them. Thus Carnaim was conquered; they could stand before Judas no longer.

[45] Then Judas gathered together all the Israelites in Gilead, the small and the great, with their wives and children and goods, a very large company, to go to the land of Judah. [46] So they came to Ephron. This was a large and very strong town on the road, and they could not go around it to the right or to the left; they had to go through it. [47] But the people of the town shut them out and blocked up the gates with stones.

[48] Judas sent them this friendly message, "Let us pass through your land to get to our land. No one will do you harm; we will simply pass by on foot." But they refused to open to him. [49] Then Judas ordered proclamation to be made to the army that all should encamp where they were. [50] So the men of the forces encamped, and he fought against the town all that day and all the night, and the town was delivered into his hands. [51] He destroyed every male by the edge of the sword, and razed and plundered the town. Then he passed through the town over the bodies of the dead.

[52] Then they crossed the Jordan into the large plain before Beth-shan. [53] Judas kept rallying the laggards and encouraging the people all the way until he came to the land of Judah. [54] So they went up to Mount Zion with joy and gladness, and offered burnt offerings, because they had returned in safety; not one of them had fallen.

[55] Now while Judas and Jonathan were in Gilead and their[c] brother Simon was in Galilee before Ptolemais, [56] Joseph son of Zechariah, and Azariah, the commanders of the forces, heard of their brave deeds and of the heroic war they had fought. [57] So they said, "Let us also make a name for ourselves; let us go and make war on the Gentiles around us." [58] So they issued orders to the men of the forces that were with them and marched against Jamnia. [59] Gorgias and his men came out of the town to meet them

---

[a] Other ancient authorities read *Alema*

[b] Or *scribes*

[c] Gk *his*

33–34: Cf. Gideon's tactics in Judg 7.19–20. 35: *Maapha*, both text and site intended are uncertain. 37: *Raphon*, er-Rafeh, 9 mi (15 km) west of Carnaim. 43–44: *Sacred precincts*, of the goddess Atargatis, consort of the Syrian god Hadad; see 2 Macc 12.26. 46: *Ephron*, et-Taiyibeh, 12 mi (20 km) south-southeast of Lake Gennesaret (the Sea of Galilee); see 2 Macc 12.27. 48: Judas follows Moses' example, Num 21.21–24. 52: *Beth-shan*, in Hellenistic times Scythopolis (2 Macc 12.29–30), in the Jordan Valley ca. 16 mi (26 km) south-southwest of Lake Gennesaret (the Sea of Galilee). 56: *Joseph* and *Azariah* envy Judas's success; for the author, only members of Judas's family

in battle. [60] Then Joseph and Azariah were routed, and were pursued to the borders of Judea; as many as two thousand of the people of Israel fell that day. [61] Thus the people suffered a great rout because, thinking to do a brave deed, they did not listen to Judas and his brothers. [62] But they did not belong to the family of those men through whom deliverance was given to Israel.

[63] The man Judas and his brothers were greatly honored in all Israel and among all the Gentiles, wherever their name was heard. [64] People gathered to them and praised them.

[65] Then Judas and his brothers went out and fought the descendants of Esau in the land to the south. He struck Hebron and its villages and tore down its strongholds and burned its towers on all sides. [66] Then he marched off to go into the land of the Philistines, and passed through Marisa.[a] [67] On that day some priests, who wished to do a brave deed, fell in battle, for they went out to battle unwisely. [68] But Judas turned aside to Azotus in the land of the Philistines; he tore down their altars, and the carved images of their gods he burned with fire; he plundered the towns and returned to the land of Judah.

6 King Antiochus was going through the upper provinces when he heard that Elymais in Persia was a city famed for its wealth in silver and gold. [2] Its temple was very rich, containing golden shields, breastplates, and weapons left there by Alexander son of Philip, the Macedonian king who first reigned over the Greeks. [3] So he came and tried to take the city and plunder it, but he could not because his plan had become known to the citizens [4] and they withstood him in battle. So he fled and in great disappointment left there to return to Babylon.

[5] Then someone came to him in Persia and reported that the armies that had gone into the land of Judah had been routed; [6] that Lysias had gone first with a strong force, but had turned and fled before the Jews;[b] that the Jews[c] had grown strong from the arms, supplies, and abundant spoils that they had taken from the armies they had cut down; [7] that they had torn down the abomination that he had erected on the altar in Jerusalem; and that they had surrounded the sanctuary with high walls as before, and also Beth-zur, his town.

[8] When the king heard this news, he was astounded and badly shaken. He took to his bed and became sick from disappointment, because things had not turned out for him as he had planned. [9] He lay there for many days, because deep disappointment continually gripped him, and he realized that he was dying. [10] So he called all his Friends and said to them, "Sleep has departed from my eyes and I am downhearted with worry. [11] I said to myself, 'To what distress I have come! And into what a great flood I now am plunged! For I was kind and beloved in my power.' [12] But now I remember the wrong I did in Jerusalem. I seized all its vessels of silver and gold, and I sent to destroy the inhabitants of Judah without good reason. [13] I know that it is because of this that these misfortunes have come upon me; here I am, perishing of bitter disappointment in a strange land."

[14] Then he called for Philip, one of his Friends, and made him ruler over all his

---

a Other ancient authorities read *Samaria*
b Gk *them*
c Gk *they*

---

can claim to have saved Israel (v. 62). **58:** *Jamnia*, see 4.15. **65:** Hebron, where David ruled over Judah (1 Sam 5.5), now in Idumea; ca. 20 mi (31 km) south of Jerusalem. **66:** *Marisa*, 2 Macc 12.35, also in Idumea, ca. 12 mi (20 km) northwest of Hebron. **67:** The same point is made as in v. 62. **68:** *Azotus*, see 4.15. *Altars . . . images*, Judas, as at Carnaim (v. 44), destroys a pagan sanctuary, in accordance with Deuteronomy's command (Deut 7.5). Throughout the chapter 1 Macc presents Judas as a biblical hero.

6.1–17: Death of Antiochus IV and accession of Antiochus V. 1: *Upper provinces*, see 3.37n. *Elymais*, a region west of Persia, not a city. **2–3:** *Temple*, identified by 2 Macc 1.11–17 as the temple of the goddess Nanea (Gk Artemis), possibly located by 2 Macc 9.2 at Persepolis. **5–7:** *Reported*, these verses summarize 3.38–4.61, events from before Antiochus's death (see v. 16). **8–13:** The author's invention, suggesting (more charitably than 2 Macc 9) some remorse in Antiochus. **12:** See 1.20–23,30–31. **14–15:** Instead of Lysias, Antiochus appoints *Philip*, perhaps the "courtier" of 2 Macc 9.29 (cf. Manaen in Acts 13.1), as *ruler* and guardian of the child *Antiochus* V.

kingdom. [15] He gave him the crown and his robe and the signet, so that he might guide his son Antiochus and bring him up to be king. [16] Thus King Antiochus died there in the one hundred forty-ninth year.[a] [17] When Lysias learned that the king was dead, he set up Antiochus the king's[b] son to reign. Lysias[c] had brought him up from boyhood; he named him Eupator.

[18] Meanwhile the garrison in the citadel kept hemming Israel in around the sanctuary. They were trying in every way to harm them and strengthen the Gentiles. [19] Judas therefore resolved to destroy them, and assembled all the people to besiege them. [20] They gathered together and besieged the citadel[d] in the one hundred fiftieth year;[e] and he built siege towers and other engines of war. [21] But some of the garrison escaped from the siege and some of the ungodly Israelites joined them. [22] They went to the king and said, "How long will you fail to do justice and to avenge our kindred? [23] We were happy to serve your father, to live by what he said, and to follow his commands. [24] For this reason the sons of our people besieged the citadel[f] and became hostile to us; moreover, they have put to death as many of us as they have caught, and they have seized our inheritances. [25] It is not against us alone that they have stretched out their hands; they have also attacked all the lands on their borders. [26] And see, today they have encamped against the citadel in Jerusalem to take it; they have fortified both the sanctuary and Beth-zur; [27] unless you quickly prevent them, they will do still greater things, and you will not be able to stop them."

[28] The king was enraged when he heard this. He assembled all his Friends, the commanders of his forces and those in authority.[g] [29] Mercenary forces also came to him from other kingdoms and from islands of the seas. [30] The number of his forces was one hundred thousand foot soldiers, twenty thousand horsemen, and thirty-two elephants accustomed to war. [31] They came through Idumea and encamped against Beth-zur, and for many days they fought and built engines of war; but the Jews[h] sallied out and burned these with fire, and fought courageously.

[32] Then Judas marched away from the citadel and encamped at Beth-zechariah, opposite the camp of the king. [33] Early in the morning the king set out and took his army by a forced march along the road to Beth-zechariah, and his troops made ready for battle and sounded their trumpets. [34] They offered the elephants the juice of grapes and mulberries, to arouse them for battle. [35] They distributed the animals among the phalanxes; with each elephant they stationed a thousand men armed with coats of mail, and with brass helmets on their heads; and five hundred picked horsemen were assigned to each beast. [36] These took their position beforehand wherever the animal was; wherever it went, they went with it, and they never left it. [37] On the elephants[i] were wooden towers, strong and covered; they were fastened on each animal by special harness, and on each were four[j] armed men who fought from there,

a   163 B.C.
b   Gk *his*
c   Gk *He*
d   Gk *it*
e   162 B.C.
f   Meaning of Gk uncertain
g   Gk *those over the reins*
h   Gk *they*
i   Gk *them*
j   Cn: Some authorities read *thirty*; others *thirty-two*

Signet, the official seal, a symbol of authority together with the *crown* and the *robe*. **16:** *Died*, Antiochus's death is securely dated between 19/20 November and 18/19 December 164 BCE; *the one hundred forty-ninth year* began in spring or autumn 164 BCE. **17:** *Lysias* (see 3.32), in spite of Antiochus's wishes, remains regent for Antiochus V *Eupator*, "of a good father," and opposes Philip (see 6.55–56,63).

6.18–27: Judas attacks the citadel. 18: *Citadel*, see 1.33n. **20:** The *one hundred fiftieth year* began in spring or autumn 163 BCE; the event probably belongs to 163, not 162 BCE (cf. 2 Macc 13.1). *Siege towers* with other *engines* were commonly used in Hellenistic times; see 5.30; 6.51–52. **26:** *Fortified both the sanctuary and Beth-zur*, cf. 4.60–61.

6.28–63: Lysias's response. 31: *Beth-zur*, fortified by Judas (4.61). **32:** *Beth-zechariah*, ca. 7 mi (10 km) north of Beth-zur, between it and Jerusalem. Judas was blocking Lysias's approach to Jerusalem. **34:** The *elephants* are aroused by alcoholic *juice*; cf. 3 Macc 5.2. **35:** *Phalanxes*, infantry units in sixteen parallel columns sixteen ranks

and also its Indian driver. [38] The rest of the cavalry were stationed on either side, on the two flanks of the army, to harass the enemy while being themselves protected by the phalanxes. [39] When the sun shone on the shields of gold and brass, the hills were ablaze with them and gleamed like flaming torches.

[40] Now a part of the king's army was spread out on the high hills, and some troops were on the plain, and they advanced steadily and in good order. [41] All who heard the noise made by their multitude, by the marching of the multitude and the clanking of their arms, trembled, for the army was very large and strong. [42] But Judas and his army advanced to the battle, and six hundred of the king's army fell. [43] Now Eleazar, called Avaran, saw that one of the animals was equipped with royal armor. It was taller than all the others, and he supposed that the king was on it. [44] So he gave his life to save his people and to win for himself an everlasting name. [45] He courageously ran into the midst of the phalanx to reach it; he killed men right and left, and they parted before him on both sides. [46] He got under the elephant, stabbed it from beneath, and killed it; but it fell to the ground upon him and he died. [47] When the Jews[a] saw the royal might and the fierce attack of the forces, they turned away in flight.

[48] The soldiers of the king's army went up to Jerusalem against them, and the king encamped in Judea and at Mount Zion. [49] He made peace with the people of Bethzur, and they evacuated the town because they had no provisions there to withstand a siege, since it was a sabbatical year for the land. [50] So the king took Beth-zur and stationed a guard there to hold it. [51] Then he encamped before the sanctuary for many days. He set up siege towers, engines of war to throw fire and stones, machines to shoot arrows, and catapults. [52] The Jews[a] also made engines of war to match theirs, and fought for many days. [53] But they had no food in storage,[b] because it was the seventh

year; those who had found safety in Judea from the Gentiles had consumed the last of the stores. [54] Only a few men were left in the sanctuary; the rest scattered to their own homes, for the famine proved too much for them.

[55] Then Lysias heard that Philip, whom King Antiochus while still living had appointed to bring up his son Antiochus to be king, [56] had returned from Persia and Media with the forces that had gone with the king, and that he was trying to seize control of the government. [57] So he quickly gave orders to withdraw, and said to the king, to the commanders of the forces, and to the troops, "Daily we grow weaker, our food supply is scant, the place against which we are fighting is strong, and the affairs of the kingdom press urgently on us. [58] Now then let us come to terms with these people, and make peace with them and with all their nation. [59] Let us agree to let them live by their laws as they did before; for it was on account of their laws that we abolished that they became angry and did all these things."

[60] The speech pleased the king and the commanders, and he sent to the Jews[c] an offer of peace, and they accepted it. [61] So the king and the commanders gave them their oath. On these conditions the Jews[a] evacuated the stronghold. [62] But when the king entered Mount Zion and saw what a strong fortress the place was, he broke the oath he had sworn and gave orders to tear down the wall all around. [63] Then he set off in haste and returned to Antioch. He found Philip in control of the city, but he fought against him, and took the city by force.

7 In the one hundred fifty-first year[d] Demetrius son of Seleucus set out from Rome, sailed with a few men to a town by

[a] Gk *they*
[b] Other ancient authorities read *in the sanctuary*
[c] Gk *them*
[d] 161 B.C.

deep wielding long pikes. **43:** *Eleazar Avaran*, Judas's brother (2.5). **49–50:** *Beth-zur* had to be captured before the attack on Jerusalem. The *sabbatical year* (see Lev 25.2–7) began in autumn 164 BCE, with no harvesting in 163 BCE; cf. v. 53. **55:** *Philip*, see vv. 14–15. **57–59:** Threatened by Philip, isolated in Jerusalem, Lysias proposes *terms*, cancellation of the decree (1.51–60) for Jewish evacuation of Mount Zion (4.60). The letter of 2 Macc 11.22–27 probably reflects this situation. **62:** *Tear down the wall*, Lysias goes beyond the agreement.

the sea, and there began to reign. ² As he was entering the royal palace of his ancestors, the army seized Antiochus and Lysias to bring them to him. ³ But when this act became known to him, he said, "Do not let me see their faces!" ⁴ So the army killed them, and Demetrius took his seat on the throne of his kingdom.

⁵ Then there came to him all the renegade and godless men of Israel; they were led by Alcimus, who wanted to be high priest. ⁶ They brought to the king this accusation against the people: "Judas and his brothers have destroyed all your Friends, and have driven us out of our land. ⁷ Now then send a man whom you trust; let him go and see all the ruin that Judasᵃ has brought on us and on the land of the king, and let him punish them and all who help them."

⁸ So the king chose Bacchides, one of the king's Friends, governor of the province Beyond the River; he was a great man in the kingdom and was faithful to the king. ⁹ He sent him, and with him he sent the ungodly Alcimus, whom he made high priest; and he commanded him to take vengeance on the Israelites. ¹⁰ So they marched away and came with a large force into the land of Judah; and he sent messengers to Judas and his brothers with peaceable but treacherous words. ¹¹ But they paid no attention to their words, for they saw that they had come with a large force.

¹² Then a group of scribes appeared in a body before Alcimus and Bacchides to ask for just terms. ¹³ The Hasideans were first among the Israelites to seek peace from them, ¹⁴ for they said, "A priest of the line of Aaron has come with the army, and he will not harm us." ¹⁵ Alcimusᵇ spoke peaceable words to

them and swore this oath to them, "We will not seek to injure you or your friends." ¹⁶ So they trusted him; but he seized sixty of them and killed them in one day, in accordance with the word that was written,

¹⁷ "The flesh of your faithful ones and their blood
    they poured out all around Jerusalem,
    and there was no one to bury them."
¹⁸ Then the fear and dread of them fell on all the people, for they said, "There is no truth or justice in them, for they have violated the agreement and the oath that they swore."

¹⁹ Then Bacchides withdrew from Jerusalem and encamped in Beth-zaith. And he sent and seized many of the men who had deserted to him,ᶜ and some of the people, and killed them and threw them into a great pit. ²⁰ He placed Alcimus in charge of the country and left with him a force to help him; then Bacchides went back to the king.

²¹ Alcimus struggled to maintain his high priesthood, ²² and all who were troubling their people joined him. They gained control of the land of Judah and did great damage in Israel. ²³ And Judas saw all the wrongs that Alcimus and those with him had done among the Israelites; it was more than the Gentiles had done. ²⁴ So Judasᵃ went out into all the surrounding parts of Judea, taking vengeance on those who had deserted and preventing those in the cityᵈ from going out into the country. ²⁵ When Alcimus saw that Judas and those with

ᵃ Gk *he*
ᵇ Gk *He*
ᶜ Or *many of his men who had deserted*
ᵈ Gk *and they were prevented*

7.1–4: **Demetrius becomes king. 1:** *One hundred fifty-first year,* beginning in spring or autumn 162 BCE. *Demetrius* I Soter (162–150 BCE), son of Seleucus IV (Antiochus IV's brother), was held hostage in Rome (175–162 BCE). Helped by the historian Polybius, he escaped. *A few men,* Polybius says sixteen. *Town by the sea:* Tripolis (2 Macc 14.1), in northern Lebanon. **2:** *Palace,* at Antioch.

7.5–25: **Alcimus as high priest. 5:** *Renegades,* Hellenizing opponents of the Maccabees, cf. 1.11. *High priest,* Alcimus's predecessor Menelaus, of dubious priestly descent (2 Macc 3.4; 4.23), had bought his office (2 Macc 4.23). Alcimus, of a genuine high-priestly family (7.14; 2 Macc 14.7), was compromised in Maccabean eyes as Hellenizing (7.9; 2 Macc 14.3). **8:** *Beyond the River,* i.e., west of the Euphrates (cf. 3.32; Ezra 4.11). **12:** *Scribes,* i.e., scholars of the Law. **13:** *The Hasideans* (see 2.42n.) apparently joined the scribes and trusted Alcimus, but he mistrusted the Hasideans. **17:** Ps 79.2–3. **19:** *Beth-zaith,* location uncertain; either 15 mi (24 km) south or 9 mi (15 km) north of Jerusalem.

him had grown strong, and realized that he could not withstand them, he returned to the king and brought malicious charges against them. ²⁶ Then the king sent Nicanor, one of his honored princes, who hated and detested Israel, and he commanded him to destroy the people. ²⁷ So Nicanor came to Jerusalem with a large force, and treacherously sent to Judas and his brothers this peaceable message, ²⁸ "Let there be no fighting between you and me; I shall come with a few men to see you face to face in peace."

²⁹ So he came to Judas, and they greeted one another peaceably; but the enemy were preparing to kidnap Judas. ³⁰ It became known to Judas that Nicanorª had come to him with treacherous intent, and he was afraid of him and would not meet him again. ³¹ When Nicanor learned that his plan had been disclosed, he went out to meet Judas in battle near Caphar-salama. ³² About five hundred of the army of Nicanor fell, and the restᵇ fled into the city of David.

³³ After these events Nicanor went up to Mount Zion. Some of the priests from the sanctuary and some of the elders of the people came out to greet him peaceably and to show him the burnt offering that was being offered for the king. ³⁴ But he mocked them and derided them and defiled them and spoke arrogantly, ³⁵ and in anger he swore this oath, "Unless Judas and his army are delivered into my hands this time, then if I return safely I will burn up this house." And he went out in great anger. ³⁶ At this the priests went in and stood before the altar and the temple; they wept and said,

³⁷ "You chose this house to be called by
    your name,
  and to be for your people a house of
      prayer and supplication.

³⁸ Take vengeance on this man and on his
    army,
  and let them fall by the sword;
  remember their blasphemies,
    and let them live no longer."

³⁹ Now Nicanor went out from Jerusalem and encamped in Beth-horon, and the Syrian army joined him. ⁴⁰ Judas encamped in Adasa with three thousand men. Then Judas prayed and said, ⁴¹ "When the messengers from the king spoke blasphemy, your angel went out and struck down one hundred eighty-five thousand of the Assyrians.ᶜ ⁴² So also crush this army before us today; let the rest learn that Nicanorª has spoken wickedly against the sanctuary, and judge him according to this wickedness."

⁴³ So the armies met in battle on the thirteenth day of the month of Adar. The army of Nicanor was crushed, and he himself was the first to fall in the battle. ⁴⁴ When his army saw that Nicanor had fallen, they threw down their arms and fled. ⁴⁵ The Jewsᵇ pursued them a day's journey, from Adasa as far as Gazara, and as they followed they kept sounding the battle call on the trumpets. ⁴⁶ People came out of all the surrounding villages of Judea, and they outflanked the enemyᵈ and drove them back to their pursuers,ᵉ so that they all fell by the sword; not even one of them was left. ⁴⁷ Then the Jewsᵇ seized the spoils and the plunder; they cut off Nicanor's head and the right hand that he had so arrogantly stretched out, and brought them and displayed them just outside Jerusalem. ⁴⁸ The people rejoiced greatly and celebrated that day as a day of great gladness. ⁴⁹ They

a Gk *he*
b Gk *they*
c Gk *of them*
d Gk *them*
e Gk *these*

7.26–50: Judas and Nicanor. 26: *Nicanor*, possibly the Nicanor of 3.38 (in 2 Macc 14.12 an elephant commander and governor of Judea). 27,30: 1 Macc presents Nicanor as ever-treacherous, 2 Macc 14.18–25 as attempting friendly persuasion. 31: *Caphar-salama*, Khirbet Selma, ca. 7 mi (11 km) northwest of Jerusalem. 32: Nicanor lost men but remained in control; he demanded the surrender of Judas on pain of burning the Temple (v. 35, and replacing it with a temple to Dionysus, 2 Macc 14.33). 37: *Your name*, alluding to 1 Kings 8.29. 39: *Beth-horon*, see 3.16n. 40: *Adasa*, location uncertain, but somewhere between Beth-horon and Jerusalem. 41: Judas refers to 2 Kings 19.35. 43: *Adar*, i.e., March, probably 161 BCE. 45: The westward pursuit (cf. 1 Sam 14.31) to

decreed that this day should be celebrated each year on the thirteenth day of Adar. [50] So the land of Judah had rest for a few days.

8 Now Judas heard of the fame of the Romans, that they were very strong and were well-disposed toward all who made an alliance with them, that they pledged friendship to those who came to them, [2] and that they were very strong. He had been told of their wars and of the brave deeds that they were doing among the Gauls, how they had defeated them and forced them to pay tribute, [3] and what they had done in the land of Spain to get control of the silver and gold mines there, [4] and how they had gained control of the whole region by their planning and patience, even though the place was far distant from them. They also subdued the kings who came against them from the ends of the earth, until they crushed them and inflicted great disaster on them; the rest paid them tribute every year. [5] They had crushed in battle and conquered Philip, and King Perseus of the Macedonians,[a] and the others who rose up against them. [6] They also had defeated Antiochus the Great, king of Asia, who went to fight against them with one hundred twenty elephants and with cavalry and chariots and a very large army. He was crushed by them; [7] they took him alive and decreed that he and those who would reign after him should pay a heavy tribute and give hostages and surrender some of their best

provinces, [8] the countries of India, Media, and Lydia. These they took from him and gave to King Eumenes. [9] The Greeks planned to come and destroy them, [10] but this became known to them, and they sent a general against the Greeks[b] and attacked them. Many of them were wounded and fell, and the Romans[c] took captive their wives and children; they plundered them, conquered the land, tore down their strongholds, and enslaved them to this day. [11] The remaining kingdoms and islands, as many as ever opposed them, they destroyed and enslaved; [12] but with their friends and those who rely on them they have kept friendship. They have subdued kings far and near, and as many as have heard of their fame have feared them. [13] Those whom they wish to help and to make kings, they make kings, and those whom they wish they depose; and they have been greatly exalted. [14] Yet for all this not one of them has put on a crown or worn purple as a mark of pride, [15] but they have built for themselves a senate chamber, and every day three hundred twenty senators constantly deliberate concerning the people, to govern them well. [16] They trust one man each year to rule over them and to control all their land; they all heed the one man, and there is no envy or jealousy among them.

---

a   Or *Kittim*
b   Gk *them*
c   Gk *they*

Gazara (see 4.15n.), the complete annihilation, and the decapitation (cf. 1 Sam 17.54) recall famous past victories. **49:** *Celebrated each year*, but dropped from the calendar after 70 CE. 1 Macc sees this event as introducing a short period of peace; in 2 Macc 15.28–37 it marks the Jewish permanent repossession of Jerusalem.

  8.1–16: Eulogy of the Romans. 1 Macc lists Rome's achievements, presenting Rome as an ally against the Seleucids. Several of the details are inaccurate. **1:** *Friendship*, an official term indicating diplomatic relationship. **2:** Rome had conquered *Gauls* south of the Alps by 190 BCE. **3:** *Spain*, Roman exploitation began after Rome defeated Carthage (202 BCE). **4:** *Kings . . . of the earth*, identified in vv. 5–12. **5:** *Philip* V of Macedon was defeated at Cynoscephale in 197 BCE; his son *Perseus* was defeated at Pydna 168 BCE. **6:** The Seleucid *Antiochus* (III) *the Great* (223–187 BCE), who according to other sources had fifty-four, not *one hundred twenty elephants,* was *crushed* at Magnesia by Scipio Africanus (189 BCE). **7:** Antiochus remained free, but by the Treaty of Apamea (188 BCE) paid *tribute* of twelve thousand talents and gave *hostages* (including the future Antiochus IV). **8:** Rome transferred not *India* and *Media* but Asia Minor (including Lydia) to *King Eumenes* of Pergamum and to Rhodes. **9–10:** 1 Macc refers to the Achaean War of 146–145 BCE. *Strongholds*, particularly Corinth, mercilessly destroyed by L. Mummius. **11:** *Remaining kingdoms and islands*, including Carthage and Sicily. **14:** *Crown . . . purple,* the Roman republic banned kingship and its trappings, but magistrates wore togas with a purple hem. 1 Macc indirectly criticizes Jonathan (10.20,62,64) and Simon (14.43). **15:** The Roman *senate* numbered three hundred and did not meet daily. **16:** *One man each year*, i.e., a consul; in fact there were two.

¹⁷ So Judas chose Eupolemus son of John son of Accos, and Jason son of Eleazar, and sent them to Rome to establish friendship and alliance, ¹⁸ and to free themselves from the yoke; for they saw that the kingdom of the Greeks was enslaving Israel completely. ¹⁹ They went to Rome, a very long journey; and they entered the senate chamber and spoke as follows: ²⁰ "Judas, who is also called Maccabeus, and his brothers and the people of the Jews have sent us to you to establish alliance and peace with you, so that we may be enrolled as your allies and friends." ²¹ The proposal pleased them, ²² and this is a copy of the letter that they wrote in reply, on bronze tablets, and sent to Jerusalem to remain with them there as a memorial of peace and alliance:

²³ "May all go well with the Romans and with the nation of the Jews at sea and on land forever, and may sword and enemy be far from them. ²⁴ If war comes first to Rome or to any of their allies in all their dominion, ²⁵ the nation of the Jews shall act as their allies wholeheartedly, as the occasion may indicate to them. ²⁶ To the enemy that makes war they shall not give or supply grain, arms, money, or ships, just as Rome has decided; and they shall keep their obligations without receiving any return. ²⁷ In the same way, if war comes first to the nation of the Jews, the Romans shall willingly act as their allies, as the occasion may indicate to them. ²⁸ And to their enemies there shall not be given grain, arms, money, or ships, just as Rome has decided; and they shall keep these obligations and do so without deceit. ²⁹ Thus on these terms the Romans make a treaty with the Jewish people. ³⁰ If after these terms are in effect both parties shall determine to add or delete anything, they shall do so at their discretion, and any addition or deletion that they may make shall be valid.

³¹ "Concerning the wrongs that King Demetrius is doing to them, we have written to him as follows, 'Why have you made your yoke heavy on our friends and allies the Jews? ³² If now they appeal again for help against you, we will defend their rights and fight you on sea and on land.'"

9 When Demetrius heard that Nicanor and his army had fallen in battle, he sent Bacchides and Alcimus into the land of Judah a second time, and with them the right wing of the army. ² They went by the road that leads to Gilgal and encamped against Mesaloth in Arbela, and they took it and killed many people. ³ In the first month of the one hundred fifty-second year[a] they encamped against Jerusalem; ⁴ then they marched off and went to Berea with twenty thousand foot soldiers and two thousand cavalry.

⁵ Now Judas was encamped in Elasa, and with him were three thousand picked men. ⁶ When they saw the huge number of the enemy forces, they were greatly frightened, and many slipped away from the camp, until no more than eight hundred of them were left. ⁷ When Judas saw that his army had slipped away and the battle was imminent, he was crushed in spirit, for he had no time to assemble them. ⁸ He became faint, but he said to those who were left, "Let us get up and go against our enemies. We may have the strength to fight them." ⁹ But they tried to dissuade him, saying, "We do not have the strength. Let us rather save our own lives

a   160 B.C.

8.17–32: Alliance with Rome. 17: *Eupolemos,* grandson of *Accos,* of a priestly (Ezra 2.61) and diplomatic (2 Macc 4.11) family, may be the Jewish historian Eupolemus who wrote ca. 158 BCE. *Jason's* son Antipater also served on a mission to Rome (12.16; 14.22). These men had Greek names and presumably spoke Greek. 19: *Long journey,* over a month, probably in 161 BCE. 20: *Allies and friends,* Judas aims high; Judea was not even an independent state but subject to the Seleucid king. 22: *Bronze tablets,* cf. 14.27. 23–30: The format is standard, including mutual assistance in case of foreign aggression (vv. 24,27), prohibition of support for enemies (vv. 26,28), and provision for alterations (v. 30). 31–32: An appended letter from Rome to Demetrius, probably inauthentic.

9.1–22: The death of Judas. This resumes the narrative from 7.50. 1: *Bacchides and Alcimus,* see 7.19–20; *second time,* cf. 7.8–20. 2: The topography requires close examination. *Gilgal* was near Jericho. *Mesaloth* perhaps transliterates a Heb word for "trails" and *in Arbela* the Heb for "Mount Bethel." 3: The *one hundred fifty-second year* began in spring or autumn 161 BCE. 4: *Berea,* possibly el-Bireh near Ramallah 10 mi (16 km) north of Je-

now, and let us come back with our kindred and fight them; we are too few." [10] But Judas said, "Far be it from us to do such a thing as to flee from them. If our time has come, let us die bravely for our kindred, and leave no cause to question our honor."

[11] Then the army of Bacchides[a] marched out from the camp and took its stand for the encounter. The cavalry was divided into two companies, and the slingers and the archers went ahead of the army, as did all the chief warriors. [12] Bacchides was on the right wing. Flanked by the two companies, the phalanx advanced to the sound of the trumpets; and the men with Judas also blew their trumpets. [13] The earth was shaken by the noise of the armies, and the battle raged from morning until evening.

[14] Judas saw that Bacchides and the strength of his army were on the right; then all the stouthearted men went with him, [15] and they crushed the right wing, and he pursued them as far as Mount Azotus. [16] When those on the left wing saw that the right wing was crushed, they turned and followed close behind Judas and his men. [17] The battle became desperate, and many on both sides were wounded and fell. [18] Judas also fell, and the rest fled.

[19] Then Jonathan and Simon took their brother Judas and buried him in the tomb of their ancestors at Modein, [20] and wept for him. All Israel made great lamentation for him; they mourned many days and said,

[21] "How is the mighty fallen,
the savior of Israel!"

[22] Now the rest of the acts of Judas, and his wars and the brave deeds that he did, and his greatness, have not been recorded, but they were very many.

[23] After the death of Judas, the renegades emerged in all parts of Israel; all the wrongdoers reappeared. [24] In those days a very great famine occurred, and the country went over to their side. [25] Bacchides chose the godless and put them in charge of the country. [26] They made inquiry and searched for the friends of Judas, and brought them to Bacchides, who took vengeance on them and made sport of them. [27] So there was great distress in Israel, such as had not been since the time that prophets ceased to appear among them.

[28] Then all the friends of Judas assembled and said to Jonathan, [29] "Since the death of your brother Judas there has been no one like him to go against our enemies and Bacchides, and to deal with those of our nation who hate us. [30] Now therefore we have chosen you today to take his place as our ruler and leader, to fight our battle." [31] So Jonathan accepted the leadership at that time in place of his brother Judas.

[32] When Bacchides learned of this, he tried to kill him. [33] But Jonathan and his brother Simon and all who were with him heard of it, and they fled into the wilderness of Tekoa and camped by the water of the pool of Asphar. [34] Bacchides found this out on the sabbath day, and he with all his army crossed the Jordan.

[35] So Jonathan[b] sent his brother as leader of the multitude and begged the Nabateans, who were his friends, for permission to store with them the great amount of baggage that they had. [36] But the family of Jambri from Medeba came out and seized John and all that he had, and left with it.

[a] Gk lacks *of Bacchides*
[b] Gk *he*

rusalem. **5:** *Elasa*, .6 mi (1 km) from el-Bireh. **15:** *Mount Azotus*, perhaps a corruption of "to the slopes of the mountains." The whole campaign thus takes place in the central hill country north of Jerusalem. **19:** *Modein*, see 2.1n. **21:** *Mighty fallen*, quoting 2 Sam 1.19. **22:** 1 Macc imitates the formulae used in the books of Kings (cf. 1 Kings 11.41; 1 Macc 16.23).

9.23–31: Jonathan succeeds Judas. **23:** The author begins the second half of his history with the reappearance of the pro-Seleucid *renegades* (cf. 1.11,34), who assume control under Bacchides. **27:** For 1 Macc, this is the nadir of the post-prophetic age (cf. 4.46n.). **28:** *Jonathan*, apparently the youngest brother (2.5). **30:** *Ruler and leader*, cf. Judg 11.4–11.

9.32–53: Jonathan and Bacchides. The topography of this section, which intertwines the accounts of Bacchides's pursuit of Jonathan (vv. 32–34,43–49) and a Nabatean-Maccabean vendetta (vv. 35–42), is confusing. **33:** *Tekoa*, Amos's home (Am 1.1), 11 mi (18 km) south of Jerusalem. **34:** Topographically difficult here; probably

³⁷ After these things it was reported to Jonathan and his brother Simon, "The family of Jambri are celebrating a great wedding, and are conducting the bride, a daughter of one of the great nobles of Canaan, from Nadabath with a large escort." ³⁸ Remembering how their brother John had been killed, they went up and hid under cover of the mountain. ³⁹ They looked out and saw a tumultuous procession with a great amount of baggage; and the bridegroom came out with his friends and his brothers to meet them with tambourines and musicians and many weapons. ⁴⁰ Then they rushed on them from the ambush and began killing them. Many were wounded and fell, and the rest fled to the mountain; and the Jewsᵃ took all their goods. ⁴¹ So the wedding was turned into mourning and the voice of their musicians into a funeral dirge. ⁴² After they had fully avenged the blood of their brother, they returned to the marshes of the Jordan.

⁴³ When Bacchides heard of this, he came with a large force on the sabbath day to the banks of the Jordan. ⁴⁴ And Jonathan said to those with him, "Let us get up now and fight for our lives, for today things are not as they were before. ⁴⁵ For look! the battle is in front of us and behind us; the water of the Jordan is on this side and on that, with marsh and thicket; there is no place to turn. ⁴⁶ Cry out now to Heaven that you may be delivered from the hands of our enemies." ⁴⁷ So the battle began, and Jonathan stretched out his hand to strike Bacchides, but he eluded him and went to the rear. ⁴⁸ Then Jonathan and the men with him leaped into the Jordan and swam across to the other side, and the enemyᵃ did not cross the Jordan to attack them. ⁴⁹ And

about one thousand of Bacchides' men fell that day.

⁵⁰ Then Bacchidesᵇ returned to Jerusalem and built strong cities in Judea: the fortress in Jericho, and Emmaus, and Beth-horon, and Bethel, and Timnath, andᶜ Pharathon, and Tephon, with high walls and gates and bars. ⁵¹ And he placed garrisons in them to harass Israel. ⁵² He also fortified the town of Beth-zur, and Gazara, and the citadel, and in them he put troops and stores of food. ⁵³ And he took the sons of the leading men of the land as hostages and put them under guard in the citadel at Jerusalem.

⁵⁴ In the one hundred and fifty-third year,ᵈ in the second month, Alcimus gave orders to tear down the wall of the inner court of the sanctuary. He tore down the work of the prophets! ⁵⁵ But he only began to tear it down, for at that time Alcimus was stricken and his work was hindered; his mouth was stopped and he was paralyzed, so that he could no longer say a word or give commands concerning his house. ⁵⁶ And Alcimus died at that time in great agony. ⁵⁷ When Bacchides saw that Alcimus was dead, he returned to the king, and the land of Judah had rest for two years.

⁵⁸ Then all the lawless plotted and said, "See! Jonathan and his men are living in quiet and confidence. So now let us bring Bacchides back, and he will capture them all in one night." ⁵⁹ And they went and consulted with him. ⁶⁰ He started to come with a large force, and secretly sent letters to all his al-

ᵃ Gk *they*
ᵇ Gk *he*
ᶜ Some authorities omit *and*
ᵈ 159 B.C.

a gloss from v. 43. **35:** *Nabateans*, see 5.25n. **36:** *Family of Jambri*, a local tribe. *Medeba*, ca. 20 mi (32 km) south-southwest of Philadelphia (Amman). *John*, see 2.1. **37:** *Nadabath*, perhaps a corruption of Medeba. **43:** Bacchides comes from the west. **45:** Jonathan is on the marshy west bank, with the Jordan curving round him on each side. **48:** Jonathan retreats back across the Jordan. **50–52:** Bacchides ensures control of the eastern (*Jericho*), northern/northwestern (*Emmaus, Beth-horon, Bethel, Timnath, Pharathon, Tephon*), western (*Gazara*) and southern (*Beth-zur*) approaches to Jerusalem; see maps on pp. 1560, 1563. **53:** *Citadel*, see 1.33n.

  9.54–57: Death of Alcimus. 54: *The one hundred and fifty-third year* began in spring or autumn 160 BCE. *Wall*, probably that separating the outer, Gentile court from the inner courts reserved for Jews, perhaps with Hellenizing intentions. *Work of the prophets*: in what sense precisely is unclear. **57:** *Two years*, presumably ca. 159–158 BCE.

  9.58–73: The continuing struggle. 62: *Bethbasi*, perhaps Khirbet Beit Bassi, ca. 7 mi (11 km) south of Jerusa-

lies in Judea, telling them to seize Jonathan and his men; but they were unable to do it, because their plan became known. [61] And Jonathan's men[a] seized about fifty of the men of the country who were leaders in this treachery, and killed them.

[62] Then Jonathan with his men, and Simon, withdrew to Bethbasi in the wilderness; he rebuilt the parts of it that had been demolished, and they fortified it. [63] When Bacchides learned of this, he assembled all his forces, and sent orders to the men of Judea. [64] Then he came and encamped against Bethbasi; he fought against it for many days and made machines of war.

[65] But Jonathan left his brother Simon in the town, while he went out into the country; and he went with only a few men. [66] He struck down Odomera and his kindred and the people of Phasiron in their tents. [67] Then he[b] began to attack and went into battle with his forces; and Simon and his men sallied out from the town and set fire to the machines of war. [68] They fought with Bacchides, and he was crushed by them. They pressed him very hard, for his plan and his expedition had been in vain. [69] So he was very angry at the renegades who had counseled him to come into the country, and he killed many of them. Then he decided to go back to his own land.

[70] When Jonathan learned of this, he sent ambassadors to him to make peace with him and obtain release of the captives. [71] He agreed, and did as he said; and he swore to Jonathan[c] that he would not try to harm him as long as he lived. [72] He restored to him the captives whom he had taken previously from the land of Judah; then he turned and went back to his own land, and did not come again into their territory. [73] Thus the sword ceased from Israel.

Jonathan settled in Michmash and began to judge the people; and he destroyed the godless out of Israel.

10 In the one hundred sixtieth year[d] Alexander Epiphanes, son of Antiochus, landed and occupied Ptolemais. They welcomed him, and there he began to reign. [2] When King Demetrius heard of it, he assembled a very large army and marched out to meet him in battle. [3] Demetrius sent Jonathan a letter in peaceable words to honor him; [4] for he said to himself, "Let us act first to make peace with him[e] before he makes peace with Alexander against us, [5] for he will remember all the wrongs that we did to him and to his brothers and his nation." [6] So Demetrius[f] gave him authority to recruit troops, to equip them with arms, and to become his ally; and he commanded that the hostages in the citadel should be released to him.

[7] Then Jonathan came to Jerusalem and read the letter in the hearing of all the people and of those in the citadel. [8] They were greatly alarmed when they heard that the king had given him authority to recruit troops. [9] But those in the citadel released the hostages to Jonathan, and he returned them to their parents.

[10] And Jonathan took up residence in Jerusalem and began to rebuild and restore the city. [11] He directed those who were doing the work to build the walls and encircle Mount Zion with squared stones, for better fortification; and they did so.

---

a   Gk *they*
b   Other ancient authorities read *they*
c   Gk *him*
d   152 B.C.
e   Gk *them*
f   Gk *he*

---

lem. **65–66:** Simon *struck down Odomera and . . . the people of Phasiron* (as local supporters of Bacchides?), or by a slight change "summoned" them, in which case the Greek "they" (v. 67; see textual note *b*) makes sense. **68:** Bacchides, besieging Bethbasi, was *crushed* between attacks from both town and surrounding country. **70–73:** Peace is agreed upon, and captives are returned. *Michmash*, ca. 9 mi (14 km) north-northeast of Jerusalem; cf. 1 Sam 13.23. *Judge the people*, Jonathan appears as a biblical hero (cf. 1 Sam 7.6), but has no political or priestly office.

10.1–50: Alexander Epiphanes and Demetrius I compete for Jonathan's support. **1:** *The one hundred sixtieth year* probably began in spring or autumn 153, or possibly 152 BCE. *Alexander Epiphanes*, commonly called Balas, was an impostor who, helped by Eumenes of Pergamum (cf. 8.8), got Rome's support against Demetrius; he ruled until ca. 145. *Ptolemais*, see 5.15n. **6–8:** *Hostages . . . released* (cf. 9.53), an important concession. **10–11:**

¹² Then the foreigners who were in the strongholds that Bacchides had built fled; ¹³ all of them left their places and went back to their own lands. ¹⁴ Only in Beth-zur did some remain who had forsaken the law and the commandments, for it served as a place of refuge.

¹⁵ Now King Alexander heard of all the promises that Demetrius had sent to Jonathan, and he heard of the battles that Jonathanᵃ and his brothers had fought, of the brave deeds that they had done, and of the troubles that they had endured. ¹⁶ So he said, "Shall we find another such man? Come now, we will make him our friend and ally." ¹⁷ And he wrote a letter and sent it to him, in the following words:

¹⁸ "King Alexander to his brother Jonathan, greetings. ¹⁹ We have heard about you, that you are a mighty warrior and worthy to be our friend. ²⁰ And so we have appointed you today to be the high priest of your nation; you are to be called the king's Friend and you are to take our side and keep friendship with us." He also sent him a purple robe and a golden crown.

²¹ So Jonathan put on the sacred vestments in the seventh month of the one hundred sixtieth year,ᵇ at the festival of booths,ᶜ and he recruited troops and equipped them with arms in abundance. ²² When Demetrius heard of these things he was distressed and said, ²³ "What is this that we have done? Alexander has gotten ahead of us in forming a friendship with the Jews to strengthen himself. ²⁴ I

also will write them words of encouragement and promise them honor and gifts, so that I may have their help." ²⁵ So he sent a message to them in the following words:

"King Demetrius to the nation of the Jews, greetings. ²⁶ Since you have kept your agreement with us and have continued your friendship with us, and have not sided with our enemies, we have heard of it and rejoiced. ²⁷ Now continue still to keep faith with us, and we will repay you with good for what you do for us. ²⁸ We will grant you many immunities and give you gifts.

²⁹ "I now free you and exempt all the Jews from payment of tribute and salt tax and crown levies, ³⁰ and instead of collecting the third of the grain and the half of the fruit of the trees that I should receive, I release them from this day and henceforth. I will not collect them from the land of Judah or from the three districts added to it from Samaria and Galilee, from this day and for all time. ³¹ Jerusalem and its environs, its tithes and its revenues, shall be holy and free from tax. ³² I release also my control of the citadel in Jerusalem and give it to the high priest, so that he may station in it men of his own choice to guard it. ³³ And everyone of the Jews taken as a captive from the land of Judah into any part of my kingdom, I set free without payment; and let all officials cancel also the taxes on their livestock.

ᵃ Gk he
ᵇ 152 B.C.
ᶜ Or tabernacles

Jonathan restores the defenses built by Judas (4.60) and destroyed by Lysias (6.62). 12: *Strongholds*, cf. 9.50–53. 14: *Beth-zur*, cf. 6.50. 20: *We have appointed you . . . high priest*, Alexander had no right in Jewish law to do this. *King's Friend*, see 2.18n. *Purple robe*, appropriate both for a Friend and for the high priest (Ex 28.5). *Golden crown*, a gift: the high priest could wear a golden rosette and a "holy diadem" (Ex 28.36; 29.6) on the turban. 21: *Vestments*, Ex 28.1–39; 39.1–26. *The one hundred sixtieth year* here began in spring, as the references to *the seventh month* and the autumn *festival of booths* (Lev 23.33–43) require, possibly in 153 but probably in 152 BCE. 22–45: Demetrius offers new, remarkable concessions (vv. 29–45). Some major concessions reappear in Demetrius II's proposals (11.30–37: the exemption from *salt tax and crown levies* [v. 29; 11.35], from payments of *grain* and *fruit* [v. 30; 11.34]), and therefore were probably not part of Demetrius I's offer. Demetrius's astonishing offer of exemption from *tribute* (v. 29) is not granted until 13.39, as part of a peace agreement. Ceding *control of the citadel* (v. 32) (in fact never returned but captured by Simon, 13.50), the gift of *Ptolemais and its lands* (v. 39; cf. v. 1), the annual grant of *fifteen thousand shekels of silver* (v. 40), are also unlikely concessions at this stage. More realistically, Demetrius I may have conceded tax freedom and inviolability for *Jerusalem* (v. 31), *festivals* as *days of immunity and release* (v. 34), enrollment of Jews in the *king's forces* and administration with freedom to *live by their own laws* (vv. 36–37), the annexation to Judea of three Samarian districts (v. 38), various provisions for Temple finances and debtors taking sanctuary in the Temple (vv. 41–45), and the costs of *restoring the sanctuary* and

³⁴ "All the festivals and sabbaths and new moons and appointed days, and the three days before a festival and the three after a festival—let them all be days of immunity and release for all the Jews who are in my kingdom. ³⁵ No one shall have authority to exact anything from them or annoy any of them about any matter.

³⁶ "Let Jews be enrolled in the king's forces to the number of thirty thousand men, and let the maintenance be given them that is due to all the forces of the king. ³⁷ Let some of them be stationed in the great strongholds of the king, and let some of them be put in positions of trust in the kingdom. Let their officers and leaders be of their own number, and let them live by their own laws, just as the king has commanded in the land of Judah.

³⁸ "As for the three districts that have been added to Judea from the country of Samaria, let them be annexed to Judea so that they may be considered to be under one ruler and obey no other authority than the high priest. ³⁹ Ptolemais and the land adjoining it I have given as a gift to the sanctuary in Jerusalem, to meet the necessary expenses of the sanctuary. ⁴⁰ I also grant fifteen thousand shekels of silver yearly out of the king's revenues from appropriate places. ⁴¹ And all the additional funds that the government officials have not paid as they did in the first years,ᵃ they shall give from now on for the service of the temple.ᵇ ⁴² Moreover, the five thousand shekels of silver that my officialsᶜ have received every year from the income of the services of the temple, this too is canceled, because it belongs to the priests who minister there. ⁴³ And all who take refuge at the temple in Jerusalem, or in any of its precincts, because they owe money to the king or are in debt, let them be released and receive back all their property in my kingdom.

⁴⁴ "Let the cost of rebuilding and restoring the structures of the sanctuary be paid from the revenues of the king. ⁴⁵ And let the cost of rebuilding the walls of Jerusalem and fortifying it all around, and the cost of rebuilding the walls in Judea, also be paid from the revenues of the king."

⁴⁶ When Jonathan and the people heard these words, they did not believe or accept them, because they remembered the great wrongs that Demetriusᵈ had done in Israel and how much he had oppressed them. ⁴⁷ They favored Alexander, because he had been the first to speak peaceable words to them, and they remained his allies all his days.

⁴⁸ Now King Alexander assembled large forces and encamped opposite Demetrius. ⁴⁹ The two kings met in battle, and the army of Demetrius fled, and Alexanderᵉ pursued him and defeated them. ⁵⁰ He pressed the battle strongly until the sun set, and on that day Demetrius fell.

⁵¹ Then Alexander sent ambassadors to Ptolemy king of Egypt with the following message: ⁵² "Since I have returned to my kingdom and have taken my seat on the throne of my ancestors, and established my rule—for I crushed Demetrius and gained control of our country; ⁵³ I met him in battle, and he and his army were crushed by us, and we have taken our seat on the throne of his kingdom— ⁵⁴ now therefore let us establish friendship with one another; give me now your daughter as my wife, and I will become your son-in-law, and will make gifts to you and to her in keeping with your position."

⁵⁵ Ptolemy the king replied and said, "Happy was the day on which you returned to the land of your ancestors and took your seat on the throne of their kingdom. ⁵⁶ And now I will do for you as you wrote, but meet me at Ptolemais, so that we may see one another, and I will become your father-in-law, as you have said."

a Meaning of Gk uncertain
b Gk *house*
c Gk *they*
d Gk *he*
e Other ancient authorities read *Alexander fled, and Demetrius*

walls of Jerusalem and in Judea (vv. 44–45). **46:** *Great wrongs*, cf. chs 7–9. **47:** *First to speak*, in fact, Demetrius was (v. 3). The Greek perhaps means that Alexander provided the original opportunity for peace. **48–50:** This follows from v. 2. The battleground is unknown; see Josephus, *Ant.* 13.58–61. The date is probably summer 150 BCE.

10.51–66: Alexander, Ptolemy, and Jonathan. 51: *Ptolemy* VI Philometor (180–145 BCE), cf. 1.18. **54:** *Daughter*, Cleopatra Thea (v. 57). **55:** Ptolemy recognizes Alexander's legitimacy. **56:** *Ptolemais* (cf. v. 1), a symbol of Egyp-

⁵⁷ So Ptolemy set out from Egypt, he and his daughter Cleopatra, and came to Ptolemais in the one hundred sixty-second year.ᵃ ⁵⁸ King Alexander met him, and Ptolemyᵇ gave him his daughter Cleopatra in marriage, and celebrated her wedding at Ptolemais with great pomp, as kings do.

⁵⁹ Then King Alexander wrote to Jonathan to come and meet him. ⁶⁰ So he went with pomp to Ptolemais and met the two kings; he gave them and their Friends silver and gold and many gifts, and found favor with them. ⁶¹ A group of malcontents from Israel, renegades, gathered together against him to accuse him; but the king paid no attention to them. ⁶² The king gave orders to take off Jonathan's garments and to clothe him in purple, and they did so. ⁶³ The king also seated him at his side; and he said to his officers, "Go out with him into the middle of the city and proclaim that no one is to bring charges against him about any matter, and let no one annoy him for any reason." ⁶⁴ When his accusers saw the honor that was paid him, in accord with the proclamation, and saw him clothed in purple, they all fled. ⁶⁵ Thus the king honored him and enrolled him among his chiefᶜ Friends, and made him general and governor of the province. ⁶⁶ And Jonathan returned to Jerusalem in peace and gladness.

⁶⁷ In the one hundred sixty-fifth yearᵈ Demetrius son of Demetrius came from Crete to the land of his ancestors. ⁶⁸ When King Alexander heard of it, he was greatly distressed and returned to Antioch. ⁶⁹ And Demetrius appointed Apollonius the governor of Coelesyria, and he assembled a large force and encamped against Jamnia. Then he sent the following message to the high priest Jonathan:

⁷⁰ "You are the only one to rise up against us, and I have fallen into ridicule and disgrace because of you. Why do you assume authority against us in the hill country? ⁷¹ If you now have confidence in your forces, come down to the plain to meet us, and let us match strength with each other there, for I have with me the power of the cities. ⁷² Ask and learn who I am and who the others are that are helping us. People will tell you that you cannot stand before us, for your ancestors were twice put to flight in their own land. ⁷³ And now you will not be able to withstand my cavalry and such an army in the plain, where there is no stone or pebble, or place to flee."

⁷⁴ When Jonathan heard the words of Apollonius, his spirit was aroused. He chose ten thousand men and set out from Jerusalem, and his brother Simon met him to help him. ⁷⁵ He encamped before Joppa, but the people of the city closed its gates, for Apollonius had a garrison in Joppa. ⁷⁶ So they fought against it, and the people of the city became afraid and opened the gates, and Jonathan gained possession of Joppa.

⁷⁷ When Apollonius heard of it, he mustered three thousand cavalry and a large army, and went to Azotus as though he were going farther. At the same time he advanced into the plain, for he had a large troop of cavalry and put confidence in it. ⁷⁸ Jonathanᵇ pursued him to Azotus, and the armies engaged in battle. ⁷⁹ Now Apollonius had secretly left a thousand cavalry behind them. ⁸⁰ Jonathan learned that there was an ambush

ᵃ 150 B.C.
ᵇ Gk *he*
ᶜ Gk *first*
ᵈ 147 B.C.

tian presence on the coast. **57**: *The one hundred sixty-second year*, probably summer-autumn 150 BCE. **60**: *He*, i.e., Jonathan; *two kings*, Alexander and Ptolemy. **65**: *Chief Friends*, promotion, cf. v. 20. *General and governor*, i.e., military and civil head of the *province*, i.e., Judea. Jonathan is now a Seleucid official.

10.67–89: Jonathan defeats Apollonius. 67: *The one hundred sixty-fifth year* probably began in autumn 148 BCE; *Demetrius* II Nicator *came from Crete* to Cilicia in spring 147 BCE with Cretan mercenaries led by Lasthenes (cf. 11.32). **68**: *Returned to Antioch*, the Seleucid capital. **69**: *Apollonius*, known from Polybius (*Hist.* 31.11.19). *Coelesyria*, originally "hollow Syria" between the Lebanon and Anti-Lebanon ranges, then with wider reference. *Jamnia*, see 4.15n. Demetrius has to control Jonathan before attacking Alexander. **72**: *Twice put to flight*, perhaps referring to Judas's defeats, 6.47; 9.6–19. **73**: *No stone or pebble*, i.e., for ammunition. **74**: *Simon* (2.3) appears in action for the first time. **75**: *Joppa* (cf. 2 Macc 3–9), on the coast north of Jamnia, Azotus, and As-

behind him, for they surrounded his army and shot arrows at his men from early morning until late afternoon. [81] But his men stood fast, as Jonathan had commanded, and the enemy's[a] horses grew tired.

[82] Then Simon brought forward his force and engaged the phalanx in battle (for the cavalry was exhausted); they were overwhelmed by him and fled, [83] and the cavalry was dispersed in the plain. They fled to Azotus and entered Beth-dagon, the temple of their idol, for safety. [84] But Jonathan burned Azotus and the surrounding towns and plundered them; and the temple of Dagon, and those who had taken refuge in it, he burned with fire. [85] The number of those who fell by the sword, with those burned alive, came to eight thousand.

[86] Then Jonathan left there and encamped against Askalon, and the people of the city came out to meet him with great pomp.

[87] He and those with him then returned to Jerusalem with a large amount of booty. [88] When King Alexander heard of these things, he honored Jonathan still more; [89] and he sent to him a golden buckle, such as it is the custom to give to the King's Kinsmen. He also gave him Ekron and all its environs as his possession.

11 Then the king of Egypt gathered great forces, like the sand by the seashore, and many ships; and he tried to get possession of Alexander's kingdom by trickery and add it to his own kingdom. [2] He set out for Syria with peaceable words, and the people of the towns opened their gates to him and went to meet him, for King Alexander had commanded them to meet him, since he was Alexander's[b] father-in-law. [3] But when Ptole-

my entered the towns he stationed forces as a garrison in each town.

[4] When he[c] approached Azotus, they showed him the burnt-out temple of Dagon, and Azotus and its suburbs destroyed, and the corpses lying about, and the charred bodies of those whom Jonathan[d] had burned in the war, for they had piled them in heaps along his route. [5] They also told the king what Jonathan had done, to throw blame on him; but the king kept silent. [6] Jonathan met the king at Joppa with pomp, and they greeted one another and spent the night there. [7] And Jonathan went with the king as far as the river called Eleutherus; then he returned to Jerusalem.

[8] So King Ptolemy gained control of the coastal cities as far as Seleucia by the sea, and he kept devising wicked designs against Alexander. [9] He sent envoys to King Demetrius, saying, "Come, let us make a covenant with each other, and I will give you in marriage my daughter who was Alexander's wife, and you shall reign over your father's kingdom. [10] I now regret that I gave him my daughter, for he has tried to kill me." [11] He threw blame on Alexander[e] because he coveted his kingdom. [12] So he took his daughter away from him and gave her to Demetrius. He was estranged from Alexander, and their enmity became manifest.

[13] Then Ptolemy entered Antioch and put on the crown of Asia. Thus he put two crowns

a Gk *their*
b Gk *his*
c Other ancient authorities read *they*
d Gk *he*
e Gk *him*

calon; Jonathan thus separates Apollonius from Demetrius. **82:** Simon's forces complete the rout. **83–84:** *Azotus,* see 4.15n. *Beth-dagon,* lit. "the house of Dagon" (a West Semitic and later a Philistine god) at Azotus/Ashdod; see 1 Sam 5.1–5; cf. Judg 16.23. 1 Macc emphasizes Maccabean hostility to paganism. **86:** *Askalon,* earlier Ashkelon, about 10 mi (16 km) south of Azotus. **88–89:** *Buckle,* to fasten the cloak; cf. 11.58. *Kinsmen,* see 2.18. *Ekron,* Tel Miqne, a former Philistine city (Josh 14.3), important for olive oil production. Judea begins to extend her territory.

11.1–19: The end of Ptolemy VI and Alexander. 1: *By trickery,* Josephus (*Ant.* 13.106–8) claims that Ptolemy set out as Alexander's ally but changed his mind after Alexander plotted against his life. **4:** See 10.84. **5:** *The king kept silent,* needing Jonathan's support. **7:** *River called Eleutherus,* Nahr el-Kebir, north of Tripolis. **8:** *Seleucia,* Antioch's port at the mouth of the Orontes River, founded by Antiochus I. **9:** *Demetrius* II, see 10.67. *My daughter,* i.e., Cleopatra; see 10.57. **10:** *Tried to kill me,* a reference to the plot (v. 1). **12:** Ptolemy was supporting Demetrius to undermine *Alexander.* **13:** *Two crowns,* Antiochus IV had also wished (1.16) to "reign over both

on his head, the crown of Egypt and that of Asia. [14] Now King Alexander was in Cilicia at that time, because the people of that region were in revolt. [15] When Alexander heard of it, he came against him in battle. Ptolemy marched out and met him with a strong force, and put him to flight. [16] So Alexander fled into Arabia to find protection there, and King Ptolemy was triumphant. [17] Zabdiel the Arab cut off the head of Alexander and sent it to Ptolemy. [18] But King Ptolemy died three days later, and his troops in the strongholds were killed by the inhabitants of the strongholds. [19] So Demetrius became king in the one hundred sixty-seventh year.[a]

[20] In those days Jonathan assembled the Judeans to attack the citadel in Jerusalem, and he built many engines of war to use against it. [21] But certain renegades who hated their nation went to the king and reported to him that Jonathan was besieging the citadel. [22] When he heard this he was angry, and as soon as he heard it he set out and came to Ptolemais; and he wrote Jonathan not to continue the siege, but to meet him for a conference at Ptolemais as quickly as possible. [23] When Jonathan heard this, he gave orders to continue the siege. He chose some of the elders of Israel and some of the priests, and put himself in danger, [24] for he went to the king at Ptolemais, taking silver and gold and clothing and numerous other gifts. And

he won his favor. [25] Although certain renegades of his nation kept making complaints against him, [26] the king treated him as his predecessors had treated him; he exalted him in the presence of all his Friends. [27] He confirmed him in the high priesthood and in as many other honors as he had formerly had, and caused him to be reckoned among his chief[b] Friends. [28] Then Jonathan asked the king to free Judea and the three districts of Samaria[c] from tribute, and promised him three hundred talents. [29] The king consented, and wrote a letter to Jonathan about all these things; its contents were as follows:

[30] "King Demetrius to his brother Jonathan and to the nation of the Jews, greetings. [31] This copy of the letter that we wrote concerning you to our kinsman Lasthenes we have written to you also, so that you may know what it says. [32] 'King Demetrius to his father Lasthenes, greetings. [33] We have determined to do good to the nation of the Jews, who are our friends and fulfill their obligations to us, because of the goodwill they show toward us. [34] We have confirmed as their possession both the territory of Judea and the three districts of Aphairema and Lydda and Rathamin; the latter, with all

---

[a] 145 B.C.
[b] Gk *first*
[c] Cn: Gk *the three districts and Samaria*

---

kingdoms," the Ptolemaic and the Seleucid, but was prevented by Rome. **14:** *Cilicia*, on the southeast coast of Turkey. **15:** Strabo (*Geog.* 16.2.8) locates the *battle* on the river Oenoparus near Antioch. **16:** *Arabia*, the great desert east of Damascus and extending into southern Jordan; cf. Gal 1.17. **17:** *Zabdiel*; Diodorus 32.9,10 gives the name Diocles, blaming Alexander's death on two of his officers. **18:** Seriously wounded, *Ptolemy* died after surgery, having seen Alexander's severed head (Josephus, *Ant.* 13.118). *Strongholds*, cf. 11.3. **19:** *Demetrius* had arrived to claim his crown two years earlier (10.67), and took it in *the one hundred sixty-seventh year*, probably summer 145 BCE.

11.20–37: **Jonathan's agreement with Demetrius II. 20:** Jonathan's attack on the *citadel* shows that Demetrius's promise (10.32), if authentic, was not fulfilled. **23:** Jonathan negotiates from a position of strength. **26:** *Predecessors*, i.e., Demetrius I and Alexander. **27:** *High priesthood*, see 10.20n. *Other honors*, presumably his military and civil rule of Judea (10.65). *Chief Friends*, cf. Alexander's honors, 10.65. **28:** *To free . . . from tribute*, a major request; possession of the *three districts* (10.38) was confirmed, but *tribute* remission not granted (v. 34). *Three hundred talents*, in lieu of tribute; a talent weighed about 75 lb (34 kg). **32:** *Lasthenes*, not Demetrius's *father* but the general of his Cretan mercenaries. **34:** *Confirmed as their possession*, according to 10.38, specifically under the high priest's authority. *Aphairema* (Ephraim in Jn 11.54), *Lydda* (Lod, Ezra 2.2) and *Rathamin* (Arimathea in Lk 23.50) lie to the north and northwest of Judea; see maps on pp. 1560, 1563. *To all those who offer sacrifice in Jerusalem* (i.e., the priesthood), if taken with the preceding words, the revenues of the three districts benefit the priesthood (cf. 10.38); if with the following words (so NRSV), the priests are offered *release* from *taxes* on *crops* and *fruit, salt,* and *crown taxes* (v. 35; see 10.29–30). Demetrius is perhaps allowing that Jerusalem shall be "holy

the region bordering them, were added to Judea from Samaria. To all those who offer sacrifice in Jerusalem we have granted release from[a] the royal taxes that the king formerly received from them each year, from the crops of the land and the fruit of the trees. [35] And the other payments henceforth due to us of the tithes, and the taxes due to us, and the salt pits and the crown taxes due to us—from all these we shall grant them release. [36] And not one of these grants shall be canceled from this time on forever. [37] Now therefore take care to make a copy of this, and let it be given to Jonathan and put up in a conspicuous place on the holy mountain.'"

[38] When King Demetrius saw that the land was quiet before him and that there was no opposition to him, he dismissed all his troops, all of them to their own homes, except the foreign troops that he had recruited from the islands of the nations. So all the troops who had served under his predecessors hated him. [39] A certain Trypho had formerly been one of Alexander's supporters; he saw that all the troops were grumbling against Demetrius. So he went to Imalkue the Arab, who was bringing up Antiochus, the young son of Alexander, [40] and insistently urged him to hand Antiochus[b] over to him, to become king in place of his father. He also reported to Imalkue[b] what Demetrius had done and told of the hatred that the troops of Demetrius[c] had for him; and he stayed there many days.

[41] Now Jonathan sent to King Demetrius the request that he remove the troops of the citadel from Jerusalem, and the troops in the strongholds; for they kept fighting against Israel. [42] And Demetrius sent this message back to Jonathan: "Not only will I do these things for you and your nation, but I will confer great honor on you and your nation, if I find an opportunity. [43] Now then you will do well to send me men who will help me, for

all my troops have revolted." [44] So Jonathan sent three thousand stalwart men to him at Antioch, and when they came to the king, the king rejoiced at their arrival.

[45] Then the people of the city assembled within the city, to the number of a hundred and twenty thousand, and they wanted to kill the king. [46] But the king fled into the palace. Then the people of the city seized the main streets of the city and began to fight. [47] So the king called the Jews to his aid, and they all rallied around him and then spread out through the city; and they killed on that day about one hundred thousand. [48] They set fire to the city and seized a large amount of spoil on that day, and saved the king. [49] When the people of the city saw that the Jews had gained control of the city as they pleased, their courage failed and they cried out to the king with this entreaty: [50] "Grant us peace, and make the Jews stop fighting against us and our city." [51] And they threw down their arms and made peace. So the Jews gained glory in the sight of the king and of all the people in his kingdom, and they returned to Jerusalem with a large amount of spoil.

[52] So King Demetrius sat on the throne of his kingdom, and the land was quiet before him. [53] But he broke his word about all that he had promised; he became estranged from Jonathan and did not repay the favors that Jonathan[d] had done him, but treated him very harshly.

[54] After this Trypho returned, and with him the young boy Antiochus who began to reign and put on the crown. [55] All the troops that Demetrius had discharged gathered

a Or *Samaria, for all those who offer sacrifice in Jerusalem, in place of*
b Gk *him*
c Gk *his troops*
d Gk *he*

and tax-free" (cf. 10.31), the taxes going to support the official rituals. **37:** *Copy,* cf. 8.22; *holy mountain,* Mount Zion. Note that Demetrius rejects cancellation of tribute, and retains control of the citadel.

11.38–59: The appearance of Trypho. 39: *Trypho,* "self-indulgent," the nickname of Diodotus, former officer of Demetrius I and Alexander. *Imalkue,* possibly son of Zabdiel (11.17). *Antiochus,* born ca. 150 BCE. **41:** *Remove the troops,* presumably Jonathan had withdrawn his attack (11.20) under the agreement. *Strongholds,* Beth-zur and Gazara (see 9.52). **42–44:** Demetrius agrees, in return for military assistance. *Antioch,* ca. 300 mi (500 km) north of Jerusalem. **46–48:** Josephus (*Ant.* 13.135–41) describes the fighting. **53:** Demetrius reneges and, according to

around him; they fought against Demetrius,[a] and he fled and was routed. [56] Trypho captured the elephants[b] and gained control of Antioch. [57] Then the young Antiochus wrote to Jonathan, saying, "I confirm you in the high priesthood and set you over the four districts and make you one of the king's Friends." [58] He also sent him gold plates and a table service, and granted him the right to drink from gold cups and dress in purple and wear a gold buckle. [59] He appointed Jonathan's[c] brother Simon governor from the Ladder of Tyre to the borders of Egypt.

[60] Then Jonathan set out and traveled beyond the river and among the towns, and all the army of Syria gathered to him as allies. When he came to Askalon, the people of the city met him and paid him honor. [61] From there he went to Gaza, but the people of Gaza shut him out. So he besieged it and burned its suburbs with fire and plundered them. [62] Then the people of Gaza pleaded with Jonathan, and he made peace with them, and took the sons of their rulers as hostages and sent them to Jerusalem. And he passed through the country as far as Damascus.

[63] Then Jonathan heard that the officers of Demetrius had come to Kadesh in Galilee with a large army, intending to remove him from office. [64] He went to meet them, but left his brother Simon in the country. [65] Simon encamped before Beth-zur and fought against it for many days and hemmed it in. [66] Then they asked him to grant them terms of peace, and he did so. He removed them from there, took possession of the town, and set a garrison over it.

[67] Jonathan and his army encamped by the waters of Gennesaret. Early in the morning they marched to the plain of Hazor, [68] and there in the plain the army of the foreigners met him; they had set an ambush against him in the mountains, but they themselves met him face to face. [69] Then the men in ambush emerged from their places and joined battle. [70] All the men with Jonathan fled; not one of them was left except Mattathias son of Absalom and Judas son of Chalphi, commanders of the forces of the army. [71] Jonathan tore his clothes, put dust on his head, and prayed. [72] Then he turned back to the battle against the enemy[d] and routed them, and they fled. [73] When his men who were fleeing saw this, they returned to him and joined him in the pursuit as far as Kadesh, to their camp, and there they encamped. [74] As many as three thousand of the foreigners fell that day. And Jonathan returned to Jerusalem.

12 Now when Jonathan saw that the time was favorable for him, he chose men and sent them to Rome to confirm and renew the friendship with them. [2] He also sent letters to the same effect to the Spartans and to other places. [3] So they went to Rome and entered the senate chamber

a Gk him
b Gk animals
c Gk his
d Gk them

Josephus (*Ant.* 13.143), demands payment of back taxes. **54:** Trypho establishes *Antiochus* VI. **55:** *Discharged*, Gk "sent to the crows," suggesting contempt; this rebounded on Demetrius. **57:** The *four districts*, i.e., the three Samarian districts with Judea (11.34), or perhaps with Ekron (10.89). **58:** *Gold buckle*, cf. 10.89. **59:** Jonathan was already governor of Judea (10.65); *Simon* is now made Seleucid *governor* of the whole coastal region (with which he was familiar; see 10.74–85) from Ras en-Naqura, north of Ptolemais, to the Egyptian border (cf. Cendebaeus, 15.38).

11.60–74: Campaigns of Jonathan and Simon. 60: *Beyond the river*, the Greek means that Jonathan toured the province west of the Euphrates. *Askalon* (see 10.86n.) welcomed Jonathan; *Gaza* (ca. 12 mi [20 km] south of Askalon) opposed him, as it had Alexander the Great. **63:** *Kadesh in Galilee*, Tell Qades (Josh 12.22). **65–66:** *Bethzur*, cf. 9.52; 11.41. **67:** *The waters of Gennesaret*, the Sea of Galilee, to the north of which, in *the plain of Hazor*, Jonathan intended to counter Demetrius at Kadesh. **71:** Cf. Josh 7.6–9. **74:** This narrative continues in 12.24.

12.1–23: Alliances with Rome and Sparta. 1: *The time was favorable*, the date is between Antiochus VI's accession (145 BCE) and Jonathan's death (142 BCE; 13.23), after Rome's destruction of the Achaean League in Greece (see 8.9–10n.). *Renew*, see 8.17–32. **2:** The *Spartans* (v. 2), a militaristic people, the rival of Athens in Greece, whose constitution, founded by the lawgiver Lycurgus, may have seemed to the Jews comparable to the Law of Moses. **3–4:** The renewal is assumed; the Romans sent *letters* to *people in every place* (compare the list in 15.22–23) requesting *safe conduct* for the envoys' return; Josephus preserves a similar letter (*Ant.* 14.233). **5–18:**

and said, "The high priest Jonathan and the Jewish nation have sent us to renew the former friendship and alliance with them." [4] And the Romans[a] gave them letters to the people in every place, asking them to provide for the envoys[b] safe conduct to the land of Judah.

[5] This is a copy of the letter that Jonathan wrote to the Spartans: [6] "The high priest Jonathan, the senate of the nation, the priests, and the rest of the Jewish people to their brothers the Spartans, greetings. [7] Already in time past a letter was sent to the high priest Onias from Arius,[c] who was king among you, stating that you are our brothers, as the appended copy shows. [8] Onias welcomed the envoy with honor, and received the letter, which contained a clear declaration of alliance and friendship. [9] Therefore, though we have no need of these things, since we have as encouragement the holy books that are in our hands, [10] we have undertaken to send to renew our family ties and friendship with you, so that we may not become estranged from you, for considerable time has passed since you sent your letter to us. [11] We therefore remember you constantly on every occasion, both at our festivals and on other appropriate days, at the sacrifices that we offer and in our prayers, as it is right and proper to remember brothers. [12] And we rejoice in your glory. [13] But as for ourselves, many trials and many wars have encircled us; the kings around us have waged war against us. [14] We were unwilling to annoy you and our other allies and friends with these wars, [15] for we have the help that comes from Heaven for our aid, and so we were delivered from our enemies, and our enemies were humbled. [16] We therefore have chosen Numenius son of Antiochus and Antipater son of Jason, and have sent them to Rome to renew our former friendship and alliance with them. [17] We have commanded them to go also to you and greet you and deliver to you this letter from us concerning the renewal of our family ties. [18] And now please send us a reply to this."

[19] This is a copy of the letter that they sent to Onias: [20] "King Arius of the Spartans, to the high priest Onias, greetings. [21] It has been found in writing concerning the Spartans and the Jews that they are brothers and are of the family of Abraham. [22] And now that we have learned this, please write us concerning your welfare; [23] we on our part write to you that your livestock and your property belong to us, and ours belong to you. We therefore command that our envoys[a] report to you accordingly."

[24] Now Jonathan heard that the commanders of Demetrius had returned, with a larger force than before, to wage war against him. [25] So he marched away from Jerusalem and met them in the region of Hamath, for he gave them no opportunity to invade his own country. [26] He sent spies to their camp, and they returned and reported to him that the enemy[a] were being drawn up in formation to attack the Jews[b] by night. [27] So when the

a Gk *they*
b Gk *them*
c Vg Compare verse 20: Gk *Darius*

This *letter* is a fiction concocted by the author; behind it lies the letter of vv. 19–21. **6:** *Senate* (Gk "gerousia"), elsewhere "elders" (cf. 7.33); later the Sanhedrin. *Brothers,* see vv. 6,11,21. **7:** *High priest Onias, Arius,* either Onias I (323–300 BCE) and Arius I (309–265), though the contact is most unlikely at this date; or Onias III (so Josephus, *Ant.* 12.225) murdered in 174 BCE (2 Macc 4.34), though there was no contemporary king *Arius* of Sparta (the author perhaps used the only Spartan royal name known to him). *Appended copy,* vv. 19–21. **9:** *Holy books,* "the Law and the Prophets and the other books of our ancestors" (Sir *Prologue*). **11–12:** Surely insincere. **13–15:** If authentic, tactless, with no reference to Spartan political difficulties. **16:** *Numenius, Antipater,* cf. 8.17n.; 14.22. **17:** The sending of ambassadors to Rome *also to you* is equally undiplomatic. **19–21:** This letter is probably inauthentic, though perhaps deriving from a source also known to Josephus (*Ant.* 12.225–27). **21:** *Brothers, of the family of Abraham,* an idea unlikely from a Spartan king. **23:** *Livestock* and *property,* most unlikely between Sparta and Judea. Although these letters were fictional, however, the diplomatic contacts they presuppose were real; the Spartan "kinship" is noted in 2 Macc 5.9.

12.24–38: Jonathan's war with Demetrius, continued. This narrative continues from 11.74. **25:** Reference to Jerusalem here and in 11.74 suggests that Jonathan returned south for the winter. **25:** *Hamath,* on the Orontes

sun had set, Jonathan commanded his troops to be alert and to keep their arms at hand so as to be ready all night for battle, and he stationed outposts around the camp. ²⁸ When the enemy heard that Jonathan and his troops were prepared for battle, they were afraid and were terrified at heart; so they kindled fires in their camp and withdrew.ᵃ ²⁹ But Jonathan and his troops did not know it until morning, for they saw the fires burning. ³⁰ Then Jonathan pursued them, but he did not overtake them, for they had crossed the Eleutherus river. ³¹ So Jonathan turned aside against the Arabs who are called Zabadeans, and he crushed them and plundered them. ³² Then he broke camp and went to Damascus, and marched through all that region.

³³ Simon also went out and marched through the country as far as Askalon and the neighboring strongholds. He turned aside to Joppa and took it by surprise, ³⁴ for he had heard that they were ready to hand over the stronghold to those whom Demetrius had sent. And he stationed a garrison there to guard it.

³⁵ When Jonathan returned he convened the elders of the people and planned with them to build strongholds in Judea, ³⁶ to build the walls of Jerusalem still higher, and to erect a high barrier between the citadel and the city to separate it from the city, in order to isolate it so that its garrisonᵇ could neither buy nor sell. ³⁷ So they gathered together to rebuild the city; part of the wall on the valley to the east had fallen, and he repaired the section called Chaphenatha. ³⁸ Simon also built Adida in the Shephelah; he fortified it and installed gates with bolts.

³⁹ Then Trypho attempted to become king in Asia and put on the crown, and to raise his hand against King Antiochus. ⁴⁰ He feared that Jonathan might not permit him to do so, but might make war on him, so he kept seeking to seize and kill him, and he marched out and came to Beth-shan. ⁴¹ Jonathan went out to meet him with forty thousand picked warriors, and he came to Beth-shan. ⁴² When Trypho saw that he had come with a large army, he was afraid to raise his hand against him. ⁴³ So he received him with honor and commended him to all his Friends, and he gave him gifts and commanded his Friends and his troops to obey him as they would himself. ⁴⁴ Then he said to Jonathan, "Why have you put all these people to so much trouble when we are not at war? ⁴⁵ Dismiss them now to their homes and choose for yourself a few men to stay with you, and come with me to Ptolemais. I will hand it over to you as well as the other strongholds and the remaining troops and all the officials, and will turn around and go home. For that is why I am here."

⁴⁶ Jonathanᶜ trusted him and did as he said; he sent away the troops, and they returned to the land of Judah. ⁴⁷ He kept with himself three thousand men, two thousand of whom he left in Galilee, while one thousand accompanied him. ⁴⁸ But when Jonathan entered Ptolemais, the people of Ptolemais closed the gates and seized him, and they killed with the sword all who had entered with him.

⁴⁹ Then Trypho sent troops and cavalry into Galilee and the Great Plain to destroy all Jonathan's soldiers. ⁵⁰ But they realized that Jonathan had been seized and had perished

---

ᵃ Other ancient authorities omit *and withdrew*
ᵇ Gk *they*
ᶜ Gk *he*

River in northern Syria. **30:** *Crossed the Eleutherus river* (see 11.7n.), i.e., southwest toward the coast. **31:** *Zabadeans*, cf. Zabdiel (11.17), and modern Zebdani, north-northwest of *Damascus* (v. 32). **33–34:** Simon, in the south (11.64–65) surprises *Joppa* (previously taken by Jonathan, 10.76) and garrisons it. **35:** *Strongholds*, perhaps those built by Bacchides (9.50) and later deserted (10.12). **36:** *Still higher*, cf. 10.11. The *barrier* blockading the citadel and its garrison presaged its fall (13.49–52). **37:** *Valley to the east*, the Kidron. *Chaphenatha*, unidentified. **38:** *Adida*, Hadid (Ezra 2.33) near Lydda (11.34). *Shephelah*, foothills west of Judea.

12.39–53: Trypho captures Jonathan. 39: *King in Asia*, cf. 11.13. **40:** *Beth-shan* (see 5.52n.), at a strategic point in the Jordan Valley (5.52). **45:** *Ptolemais*, hostile to the Jews (5.15). Trypho repeats Demetrius's false promise (10.39). *Other strongholds*, apart from Beth-zur, Joppa, and Adida, already in Jewish hands. **48:** *Jonathan* is *seized*, but not yet killed (see 13.23). **49:** *Great Plain*, also called the Valley of Jezreel (Judg 6.33) and the plain of Es-

along with his men, and they encouraged one another and kept marching in close formation, ready for battle. [51] When their pursuers saw that they would fight for their lives, they turned back. [52] So they all reached the land of Judah safely, and they mourned for Jonathan and his companions and were in great fear; and all Israel mourned deeply. [53] All the nations around them tried to destroy them, for they said, "They have no leader or helper. Now therefore let us make war on them and blot out the memory of them from humankind."

13 Simon heard that Trypho had assembled a large army to invade the land of Judah and destroy it, [2] and he saw that the people were trembling with fear. So he went up to Jerusalem, and gathering the people together [3] he encouraged them, saying to them, "You yourselves know what great things my brothers and I and the house of my father have done for the laws and the sanctuary; you know also the wars and the difficulties that my brothers and I have seen. [4] By reason of this all my brothers have perished for the sake of Israel, and I alone am left. [5] And now, far be it from me to spare my life in any time of distress, for I am not better than my brothers. [6] But I will avenge my nation and the sanctuary and your wives and children, for all the nations have gathered together out of hatred to destroy us."

[7] The spirit of the people was rekindled when they heard these words, [8] and they answered in a loud voice, "You are our leader in place of Judas and your brother Jonathan. [9] Fight our battles, and all that you say to us we will do." [10] So he assembled all the warriors and hurried to complete the walls of Jerusalem, and he fortified it on every side. [11] He sent Jonathan son of Absalom to Joppa, and with him a considerable army; he drove out its occupants and remained there.

[12] Then Trypho left Ptolemais with a large army to invade the land of Judah, and Jonathan was with him under guard. [13] Simon encamped in Adida, facing the plain. [14] Trypho learned that Simon had risen up in place of his brother Jonathan, and that he was about to join battle with him, so he sent envoys to him and said, [15] "It is for the money that your brother Jonathan owed the royal treasury, in connection with the offices he held, that we are detaining him. [16] Send now one hundred talents of silver and two of his sons as hostages, so that when released he will not revolt against us, and we will release him."

[17] Simon knew that they were speaking deceitfully to him, but he sent to get the money and the sons, so that he would not arouse great hostility among the people, who might say, [18] "It was because Simon[a] did not send him the money and the sons, that Jonathan[b] perished." [19] So he sent the sons and the hundred talents, but Trypho[b] broke his word and did not release Jonathan.

[20] After this Trypho came to invade the country and destroy it, and he circled around by the way to Adora. But Simon and his army kept marching along opposite him to every place he went. [21] Now the men in the citadel kept sending envoys to Trypho urging him to come to them by way of the wilderness and to send them food. [22] So Trypho got all his cavalry

a Gk *I*
b Gk *he*

---

draelon (Jdt 1.8), extending from Mount Carmel to the Jordan Valley. **52–53**: *Mourned*, though Jonathan was not dead; *blot out the memory*, dramatic exaggeration (cf. 3.35).

13.1–11: Simon becomes leader. The date is somewhere between the accession of Demetrius II in 145 BCE (11.19) and the regaining of independence in 143 or 142 BCE (13.41). If Jonathan's campaigns (11.63–74; 12.24–32) belong to 144 BCE, Simon perhaps took over in 143 BCE. **4**: *Brothers . . . perished*, Eleazar (6.46), Judas (9.18), John (9.38); *I alone am left*, cf. 1 Kings 18.22. Jonathan, however, was still alive (cf. 13.23). **7–8**: These verses echo 2.67–68 and 9.28–31. In 2.67–68 Mattathias commissions his sons; in 9.28 the "friends of Judas" appointed Jonathan; now the people appoint Simon, an indication of political development. **10**: Simon urgently completes Jonathan's fortification of Jerusalem (12.35–37). **11**: *Jonathan son of Absalom*, perhaps brother of Mattathias (11.70). Simon strengthens his control of *Joppa* (cf. 12.33–34). The capture of this harbor was "to crown all his honor" (14.5).

13.12–30: Trypho invades Judea; the death of Jonathan. 13: *Adida*, see 12.38n. **16**: *Talents*, see 11.28n. **20**: *Ado-*

ready to go, but that night a very heavy snow fell, and he did not go because of the snow. He marched off and went into the land of Gilead. [23] When he approached Baskama, he killed Jonathan, and he was buried there. [24] Then Trypho turned and went back to his own land.

[25] Simon sent and took the bones of his brother Jonathan, and buried him in Modein, the city of his ancestors. [26] All Israel bewailed him with great lamentation, and mourned for him many days. [27] And Simon built a monument over the tomb of his father and his brothers; he made it high so that it might be seen, with polished stone at the front and back. [28] He also erected seven pyramids, opposite one another, for his father and mother and four brothers. [29] For the pyramids[a] he devised an elaborate setting, erecting about them great columns, and on the columns he put suits of armor for a permanent memorial, and beside the suits of armor he carved ships, so that they could be seen by all who sail the sea. [30] This is the tomb that he built in Modein; it remains to this day.

[31] Trypho dealt treacherously with the young King Antiochus; he killed him [32] and became king in his place, putting on the crown of Asia; and he brought great calamity on the land. [33] But Simon built up the strongholds of Judea and walled them all around, with high towers and great walls and gates and bolts, and he stored food in the strongholds. [34] Simon also chose emissaries and sent them to King Demetrius with a request to grant relief to the country, for all that Trypho did was to plunder. [35] King Demetrius sent him a favorable reply to this request, and wrote him a letter as follows, [36] "King Demetrius to Simon, the high priest and friend of kings, and to the elders and nation of the Jews, greetings. [37] We have received the gold crown and the palm branch that you[b] sent, and we are ready to make a general peace with you and to write to our officials to grant you release from tribute. [38] All the grants that we have made to you remain valid, and let the strongholds that you have built be your possession. [39] We pardon any errors and offenses committed to this day, and cancel the crown tax that you owe; and whatever other tax has been collected in Jerusalem shall be collected no longer. [40] And if any of you are qualified to be enrolled in our bodyguard,[c] let them be enrolled, and let there be peace between us."

[41] In the one hundred seventieth year[d] the yoke of the Gentiles was removed from Israel, [42] and the people began to write in their documents and contracts, "In the first year of Simon the great high priest and commander and leader of the Jews."

[43] In those days Simon[e] encamped against Gazara[f] and surrounded it with troops. He

a Gk For these
b The word you in verses 37-40 is plural
c Or court
d 142 B.C.
e Gk he
f Cn: Gk Gaza

ra (Adoraim, 2 Chr 11.9), a Hellenistic town in Idumea, southwest of Beth-zur, held by Simon. **22:** *Gilead*, east of the River Jordan. **23:** *Baskama*, unidentified, perhaps near the Sea of Galilee. **25–29:** *Modein*, see 2.1. Simon builds above the family tomb a typically Hellenistic victory *monument*, with *pyramids*, *columns*, *armor* (trophies), and *carved ships*; Simon (perhaps emulating Solomon; see 1 Kings 9.26–28; 10.11–12,22) was signaling Jewish marine ambitions for which the capture of Joppa was important.

13.31–53. Simon regains independence for Judea. 31–32: *Trypho . . . became king*, killing Antiochus, probably late 143, or 142 BCE. The last known coins of Antiochus VI are dated year 171, i.e., 142–141 BCE. *Crown of Asia*, cf. 12.39. **33:** *Strongholds*, Simon continues the policy of 11.66; 12.35,38. **34:** *Plunder*: the underlying Heb word ("ṭerepah") puns on Trypho. **36:** *High priest*, see 14.38,41. *Friend of kings*, an irregular and suspect phrase. *Elders*, see 7.33; 12.6n.,35. *Nation*, 11.30. **37:** *Gold crown, palm branch*, diplomatic gifts, tokens of allegiance (cf. 2 Macc 14.4). *General peace, release from tribute*, the latter, long sought (cf. 11.28) meant independence. **38:** *Strongholds*, Beth-zur, Adida, Joppa. **39:** *Crown tax, other tax*, ceded already (11.35). **40:** *Enrolled in our bodyguard*, cf. 10.36, which merely allowed enrollment in the king's forces. **41:** *Yoke of the Gentiles*, i.e., Seleucid rule. *The one hundred seventieth year*, reckoned from 312 or 311 BCE, began in spring 143 or 142 BCE; the date is therefore 142 or 141 BCE. **42:** *Documents and contracts*, unfortunately none survive. The titles *high priest* (14.27,38,41), *commander* (11.59), and *leader of the Jews* (perhaps the "ethnarch" of 14.47) were conferred by the Seleucids. **43:** *Gazara*, a correction

made a siege engine, brought it up to the city, and battered and captured one tower. ⁴⁴ The men in the siege engine leaped out into the city, and a great tumult arose in the city. ⁴⁵ The men in the city, with their wives and children, went up on the wall with their clothes torn, and they cried out with a loud voice, asking Simon to make peace with them; ⁴⁶ they said, "Do not treat us according to our wicked acts but according to your mercy." ⁴⁷ So Simon reached an agreement with them and stopped fighting against them. But he expelled them from the city and cleansed the houses in which the idols were located, and then entered it with hymns and praise. ⁴⁸ He removed all uncleanness from it, and settled in it those who observed the law. He also strengthened its fortifications and built in it a house for himself.

⁴⁹ Those who were in the citadel at Jerusalem were prevented from going in and out to buy and sell in the country. So they were very hungry, and many of them perished from famine. ⁵⁰ Then they cried to Simon to make peace with them, and he did so. But he expelled them from there and cleansed the citadel from its pollutions. ⁵¹ On the twenty-third day of the second month, in the one hundred seventy-first year,ᵃ the Jewsᵇ entered it with praise and palm branches, and with harps and cymbals and stringed instruments, and with hymns and songs, because a great enemy had been crushed and removed from Israel. ⁵² Simonᶜ decreed that every year they should celebrate this day with rejoicing. He strengthened the fortifications of the temple hill alongside the citadel, and he and his men lived there. ⁵³ Simon saw that his son John

had reached manhood, and so he made him commander of all the forces; and he lived at Gazara.

14 In the one hundred seventy-second yearᵈ King Demetrius assembled his forces and marched into Media to obtain help, so that he could make war against Trypho. ² When King Arsaces of Persia and Media heard that Demetrius had invaded his territory, he sent one of his generals to take him alive. ³ The generalᶜ went and defeated the army of Demetrius, and seized him and took him to Arsaces, who put him under guard.

⁴ The landᵉ had rest all the days of Simon.
  He sought the good of his nation;
his rule was pleasing to them,
    as was the honor shown him, all his
      days.
⁵ To crown all his honors he took Joppa for
    a harbor,
    and opened a way to the isles of the sea.
⁶ He extended the borders of his nation,
    and gained full control of the country.
⁷ He gathered a host of captives;
    he ruled over Gazara and Beth-zur and
      the citadel,
and he removed its uncleanness from it;
    and there was none to oppose him.
⁸ They tilled their land in peace;
    the ground gave its increase,
    and the trees of the plains their fruit.

ᵃ 141 B.C.
ᵇ Gk *they*
ᶜ Gk *He*
ᵈ 140 B.C.
ᵉ Other ancient authorities add *of Judah*

for Gk "Gaza" (11.61), which remained independent until 96 BCE. Gazara, garrisoned by Bacchides (9.52), was an important capture. **47:** *Idols*, cf. the treatment of Azotus (5.68). **48:** *House*, an inscription found in Gazara calls for fire to descend on Simon's palace. **49–50:** The *citadel* (cf. 12.36) is finally starved out and ritually cleansed. **51:** *Twenty-third day of the second month* (Iyyar), a major event, dated precisely in late May/early June 142 or 141 BCE, and celebrated annually (mentioned in *Megillat Taʻanith*, "Scroll of Fasting"). *Harps*, etc: cf. 4.54. **52:** *Fortifications of the temple hill*, cf. 12.36. **53:** *John*, see 16.1–24.

  14.1–3: Exile of Demetrius II. 1: The *one hundred and seventy-second year* began in autumn 141 BCE, and the campaign in spring 140 BCE. **2:** *Persia and Media*, formerly part of the Seleucid empire, were under Parthian control; *Arsaces* VI Mithradates I (171–138 BCE) occupied Seleucia on the Tigris. Demetrius attempted to recover Babylonia. **3:** Arsaces held Demetrius, but gave him his daughter as wife. Demetrius regained his throne and ruled 129–126 BCE.

  14.4–15: Poetic eulogy of Simon. Compare the ode in praise of Judas, 3.3–9. **4:** *Had rest*, cf. Judg 3.30; 5.31; etc. **5:** *Joppa*, 13.11. **6:** *Extended the borders*, Jonathan had added three districts (11.34); Simon settled Jews in

⁹ Old men sat in the streets;
  they all talked together of good things,
  and the youths put on splendid military
    attire.
¹⁰ He supplied the towns with food,
  and furnished them with the means of
    defense,
  until his renown spread to the ends of
    the earth.
¹¹ He established peace in the land,
  and Israel rejoiced with great joy.
¹² All the people sat under their own vines
    and fig trees,
  and there was none to make them
    afraid.
¹³ No one was left in the land to fight them,
  and the kings were crushed in those
    days.
¹⁴ He gave help to all the humble among his
    people;
  he sought out the law,
  and did away with all the renegades and
    outlaws.
¹⁵ He made the sanctuary glorious,
  and added to the vessels of the
    sanctuary.

¹⁶ It was heard in Rome, and as far away as Sparta, that Jonathan had died, and they were deeply grieved. ¹⁷ When they heard that his brother Simon had become high priest in his stead, and that he was ruling over the country and the towns in it, ¹⁸ they wrote to him on bronze tablets to renew with him the friendship and alliance that they had established with his brothers Judas and Jonathan.

¹⁹ And these were read before the assembly in Jerusalem.

²⁰ This is a copy of the letter that the Spartans sent:

"The rulers and the city of the Spartans to the high priest Simon and to the elders and the priests and the rest of the Jewish people, our brothers, greetings. ²¹ The envoys who were sent to our people have told us about your glory and honor, and we rejoiced at their coming. ²² We have recorded what they said in our public decrees, as follows, 'Numenius son of Antiochus and Antipater son of Jason, envoys of the Jews, have come to us to renew their friendship with us. ²³ It has pleased our people to receive these men with honor and to put a copy of their words in the public archives, so that the people of the Spartans may have a record of them. And they have sent a copy of this to the high priest Simon.'"

²⁴ After this Simon sent Numenius to Rome with a large gold shield weighing one thousand minas, to confirm the alliance with the Romans.ᵃ

²⁵ When the people heard these things they said, "How shall we thank Simon and his sons? ²⁶ For he and his brothers and the house of his father have stood firm; they have fought and repulsed Israel's enemies and established its freedom." ²⁷ So they made a record on bronze tablets and put it on pillars on Mount Zion.

ᵃ Gk *them*

Joppa and Gazara. **7:** The capture of *Gazara, Beth-zur,* and the *citadel* were major achievements. **8–15:** Simon's Judea is pictured in idyllic and scriptural terms from Lev 26.4; 1 Kings 4.25; Ezek 36.33–36; Mic 4.4; Zech 8.4; and elsewhere. **15:** *Made the sanctuary glorious,* no details are known.

14.16–24: Diplomacy with Rome and Sparta. These verses, interweaving contacts with Rome and Sparta, must be connected with 12.1–23 and 15.15–24, and present many problems. **16:** *As far away as Sparta,* an editorial link between two separate accounts. **18:** The Romans *wrote,* a most unlikely initiative. Probably they were responding to Simon's initiative described in v. 24. *Bronze tablets* suggest memorial plaques, not letters. *Renew . . . established with . . . Judas and Jonathan,* cf. 8.21; 12.1. **20–23:** This *letter* is clearly linked with that of 12.5–18 and seems equally inauthentic. **24:** *Numenius,* cf. 12.16; 14.22; 15.15. His travels are incomprehensible in their present sequence; this visit to Rome *to confirm the alliance* belongs before the Roman response of 14.8. *Gold shield . . . one thousand minas,* an enormous gift (weighing more than 1,100 lb [500 kg]) for a small nation.

14.25–49: Decree in honor of Simon. Such decrees were common in the Hellenistic world. They usually record the honorand's achievements in "whereas" clauses (cf. "since," v. 29), ending with the decree ("it seemed good to . . . "; cf. "have resolved," v. 41). **27:** *A record on bronze tablets,* cf. 8.21; 14.18. *Mount Zion,* 4.37; cf. Ps 2.6. *Copy,* vv. 27–45 seem partly quotation, partly reportage by 1 Macc. *The eighteenth day of Elul, in the one hundred seventy-second year,* a Jewish date, 13 September 141 or 140 BCE. Simon's *third year,* his first was year 170; cf. 13.41.

This is a copy of what they wrote: "On the eighteenth day of Elul, in the one hundred seventy-second year,[a] which is the third year of the great high priest Simon, 28 in Asaramel,[b] in the great assembly of the priests and the people and the rulers of the nation and the elders of the country, the following was proclaimed to us:

29 "Since wars often occurred in the country, Simon son of Mattathias, a priest of the sons[c] of Joarib, and his brothers, exposed themselves to danger and resisted the enemies of their nation, in order that their sanctuary and the law might be preserved; and they brought great glory to their nation. 30 Jonathan rallied the[d] nation, became their high priest, and was gathered to his people. 31 When their enemies decided to invade their country and lay hands on their sanctuary, 32 then Simon rose up and fought for his nation. He spent great sums of his own money; he armed the soldiers of his nation and paid them wages. 33 He fortified the towns of Judea, and Beth-zur on the borders of Judea, where formerly the arms of the enemy had been stored, and he placed there a garrison of Jews. 34 He also fortified Joppa, which is by the sea, and Gazara, which is on the borders of Azotus, where the enemy formerly lived. He settled Jews there, and provided in those towns[e] whatever was necessary for their restoration.

35 "The people saw Simon's faithfulness[f] and the glory that he had resolved to win for his nation, and they made him their leader and high priest, because he had done all these things and because of the justice and loyalty that he had maintained toward his nation. He sought in every way to exalt his people. 36 In his days things prospered in his hands, so that the Gentiles were put out of the[d] country, as were also those in the city of David in Jerusalem, who had built themselves a citadel from which they used to sally forth and defile the environs of the sanctuary, doing great damage to its purity. 37 He settled Jews in it and fortified it for the safety of the country and of the city, and built the walls of Jerusalem higher.

38 "In view of these things King Demetrius confirmed him in the high priesthood, 39 made him one of his Friends, and paid him high honors. 40 For he had heard that the Jews were addressed by the Romans as friends and allies and brothers, and that the Romans[g] had received the envoys of Simon with honor.

41 "The Jews and their priests have resolved that Simon should be their leader and high priest forever, until a trustworthy prophet should arise, 42 and that he should be governor over them and that he should take charge of the sanctuary and appoint officials over its tasks and over the country and the weapons and the strongholds, and that he should take charge of the sanctuary, 43 and that he should be obeyed by all, and that all contracts in the

a   140 B.C.
b   This word resembles the Hebrew words for the court of the people of God or the prince of the people of God
c   Meaning of Gk uncertain
d   Gk their
e   Gk them
f   Other ancient authorities read conduct
g   Gk they

28: *Asaramel,* a corruption (see textual note b), possibly of the title "prince of God's people." 30: *Became their high priest,* 10.20–21. This reference to Jonathan is intrusive in a decree honoring Simon. 31: *Enemies . . . invade their country,* i.e., Trypho, 13.1. 32: *His own money,* like other Hellenistic rulers, Simon paid for his army. 33–34: *Fortified . . . Judea* (12.38; 13.33), *Beth-zur* (11.65–66), *Joppa* (12.33–34), *Gazara* (13.43–48), near *Azotus* (14.34). 35: This verse, speaking of the people's actions, divides vv. 34 and 36, which belong together. 36: *Gentiles . . . put out,* from Beth-zur (11.66), Joppa (13.1), Gazara (13.47), *citadel* (13.50). 37: *Settled Jews in it and fortified it,* not mentioned in 13.50. *Built the walls of Jerusalem higher,* continuing Jonathan's work (12.36; 13.52). 38–39: 1 Macc reports *Demetrius* II's action, not explicitly stated in 13.36–37, and motivation, clearly not original to the decree. 40: The author similarly adds reference to Roman approval of Simon. 41–43: The actual decree making Simon *leader* (Gk "hegoumenos," 13.8,42), *high priest* ("archiereus," 13.36,42), and *governor* ("strategos"; cf. 13.42), with civil, religious and military powers. *High priest forever,* i.e., for life, or to create a priestly dynasty. *Until a trustworthy prophet should arise,* i.e., to approve this high priesthood or reveal another. 42: *Take charge of the sanctuary,* repeated later (v. 43) and additional here. 43: *All contracts,* cf. 13.42. *Purple and . . . gold* (buckle): the insignia

country should be written in his name, and that he should be clothed in purple and wear gold.

⁴⁴ "None of the people or priests shall be permitted to nullify any of these decisions or to oppose what he says, or to convene an assembly in the country without his permission, or to be clothed in purple or put on a gold buckle. ⁴⁵ Whoever acts contrary to these decisions or rejects any of them shall be liable to punishment."

⁴⁶ All the people agreed to grant Simon the right to act in accordance with these decisions. ⁴⁷ So Simon accepted and agreed to be high priest, to be commander and ethnarch of the Jews and priests, and to be protector of them all.ᵃ ⁴⁸ And they gave orders to inscribe this decree on bronze tablets, to put them up in a conspicuous place in the precincts of the sanctuary, ⁴⁹ and to deposit copies of them in the treasury, so that Simon and his sons might have them.

15 Antiochus, son of King Demetrius, sent a letter from the islands of the sea to Simon, the priest and ethnarch of the Jews, and to all the nation; ² its contents were as follows: "King Antiochus to Simon the high priest and ethnarch and to the nation of the Jews, greetings. ³ Whereas certain scoundrels have gained control of the kingdom of our ancestors, and I intend to lay claim to the kingdom so that I may restore it as it formerly was, and have recruited a host of mercenary troops and have equipped warships, ⁴ and intend to make a landing in the country so that I may proceed against those who have destroyed our country and those who have devastated many cities in my kingdom, ⁵ now therefore I confirm to you all the tax remis-

sions that the kings before me have granted you, and a release from all the other payments from which they have released you. ⁶ I permit you to mint your own coinage as money for your country, ⁷ and I grant freedom to Jerusalem and the sanctuary. All the weapons that you have prepared and the strongholds that you have built and now hold shall remain yours. ⁸ Every debt you owe to the royal treasury and any such future debts shall be canceled for you from henceforth and for all time. ⁹ When we gain control of our kingdom, we will bestow great honor on you and your nation and the temple, so that your glory will become manifest in all the earth."

¹⁰ In the one hundred seventy-fourth yearᵇ Antiochus set out and invaded the land of his ancestors. All the troops rallied to him, so that there were only a few with Trypho. ¹¹ Antiochus pursued him, and Tryphoᶜ came in his flight to Dor, which is by the sea; ¹² for he knew that troubles had converged on him, and his troops had deserted him. ¹³ So Antiochus encamped against Dor, and with him were one hundred twenty thousand warriors and eight thousand cavalry. ¹⁴ He surrounded the town, and the ships joined battle from the sea; he pressed the town hard from land and sea, and permitted no one to leave or enter it.

¹⁵ Then Numenius and his companions arrived from Rome, with letters to the kings and countries, in which the following was written: ¹⁶ "Lucius, consul of the Romans, to King Ptolemy, greetings. ¹⁷ The envoys of the Jews have come to us as our friends and allies

ᵃ Or *to preside over them all*
ᵇ 138 B.C.
ᶜ Gk *he*

of kings' Friends and high priests (cf. 10.20,89; 14.44). **44–45:** Safeguarding Simon's position. **47:** Simon *agreed* to be *high priest . . . commander* (Gk "strategos"), *and ethnarch*, an alternate Greek title for "leader of the people." **48:** *Bronze tablets*, cf. v. 27.

15.1–41: Antiochus VII, Trypho, and Simon. 1: With Antiochus VI dead and Demetrius II captive in Parthia, Demetrius's brother *Antiochus* VII Sidetes (named after his home town Side in Pamphylia) acceded in 139 or 138 BCE. *Islands of the sea*, probably Rhodes in the Aegean off the coast of Asia Minor. **2:** *Priest, ethnarch*, cf. 14.47. **5:** *Remissions*, cf. 10.25–45; 11.30–37; 13.38–39. **6:** *Coinage*, a new privilege (but soon withdrawn, v. 27), of minting copper (not silver or gold) coins. No coins of Simon are known. **7:** *Freedom to Jerusalem and the sanctuary* (cf. 10.31; 11.34) may have meant that Jerusalem was to be sacred, with right of asylum, rather than tax exempt. **9:** Antiochus clearly assumes that Judea, though with some independence, remains part of his empire. **10:** *Trypho*, cf. 12.39. *The one hundred and seventy-fourth year* began in autumn 139 BCE; Antiochus set out the following spring. **11:** *Dor*, an ancient port south of Mount Carmel. **15–24:** These verses interrupt the account of Antio-

to renew our ancient friendship and alliance. They had been sent by the high priest Simon and by the Jewish people [18] and have brought a gold shield weighing one thousand minas. [19] We therefore have decided to write to the kings and countries that they should not seek their harm or make war against them and their cities and their country, or make alliance with those who war against them. [20] And it has seemed good to us to accept the shield from them. [21] Therefore if any scoundrels have fled to you from their country, hand them over to the high priest Simon, so that he may punish them according to their law."

[22] The consul[a] wrote the same thing to King Demetrius and to Attalus and Ariarathes and Arsaces, [23] and to all the countries, and to Sampsames,[b] and to the Spartans, and to Delos, and to Myndos, and to Sicyon, and to Caria, and to Samos, and to Pamphylia, and to Lycia, and to Halicarnassus, and to Rhodes, and to Phaselis, and to Cos, and to Side, and to Aradus and Gortyna and Cnidus and Cyprus and Cyrene. [24] They also sent a copy of these things to the high priest Simon.

[25] King Antiochus besieged Dor for the second time, continually throwing his forces against it and making engines of war; and he shut Trypho up and kept him from going out or in. [26] And Simon sent to Antiochus[c] two thousand picked troops, to fight for him, and silver and gold and a large amount of military equipment. [27] But he refused to receive them, and broke all the agreements he formerly had made with Simon, and became estranged from

him. [28] He sent to him Athenobius, one of his Friends, to confer with him, saying, "You hold control of Joppa and Gazara and the citadel in Jerusalem; they are cities of my kingdom. [29] You have devastated their territory, you have done great damage in the land, and you have taken possession of many places in my kingdom. [30] Now then, hand over the cities that you have seized and the tribute money of the places that you have conquered outside the borders of Judea; [31] or else pay me five hundred talents of silver for the destruction that you have caused and five hundred talents more for the tribute money of the cities. Otherwise we will come and make war on you."

[32] So Athenobius, the king's Friend, came to Jerusalem, and when he saw the splendor of Simon, and the sideboard with its gold and silver plate, and his great magnificence, he was amazed. When he reported to him the king's message, [33] Simon said to him in reply: "We have neither taken foreign land nor seized foreign property, but only the inheritance of our ancestors, which at one time had been unjustly taken by our enemies. [34] Now that we have the opportunity, we are firmly holding the inheritance of our ancestors. [35] As for Joppa and Gazara, which you demand, they were causing great damage among the people and to our land; for them we will give you one hundred talents."

a Gk *He*
b The name is uncertain
c Gk *him*

chus's pursuit of Trypho and clearly belong with 14.24. **16:** *Lucius*, possibly Lucius Caecilius Metellus, *consul* in Rome 142 BCE, or Lucius Valerius Flaccus, praetor 134 BCE and consul 131 BCE, with whom Josephus (*Ant.* 145–148) associates an almost identical Jewish mission (though dating it to Hyrcanus II's time [63–40 BCE]). Josephus has perhaps confused consuls and dating. **18:** *Weighing one thousand minas* (see 14,24n.), according to Josephus (*Ant.* 14.147), "worth fifty thousand gold pieces." **22:** *Demetrius* II, cf. 11.19; 14.1; *Attalus* II (159–38) of Pergamum; *Ariarathes* V (162–131) of Cappadocia; *Arsaces*, cf. 14.2. **23:** A list of independent cities and states: *Sampsames*, possibly Samsun on the Black Sea. In Greece: the *Spartans* (see 12.2), and *Sicyon*, on the Gulf of Corinth. Aegean islands: *Delos*, a free port, notorious for its slave trade, with a Jewish population and synagogue; *Samos*; *Rhodes* (cf. Acts 21.1); *Cos* (cf. Acts 21.1). Crete: *Gortyna*. On the southwest coast of modern Turkey: *Caria* and *Lycia*, states; *Myndos*; *Halicarnassus*, birthplace of the Greek historian Herodotus; *Cnidus*. On the south coast of Turkey: *Pamphylia* (cf. Acts 13.13); *Phaselis*; *Side* (cf.15.1n.), later notorious for piracy. Phoenician coast: *Aradus*. Eastern Mediterranean: *Cyprus*. North Africa: *Cyrene* (cf. Mark 15.21). Ptolemy VIII of Egypt claimed these last two for his empire. **25:** *For the second time*, an inaccurate gloss probably caused by the intrusion of vv. 15–24 into this narrative. **26:** Simon sends military aid to Antiochus, thus accepting his political allegiance. **27:** *Agreements*, cf. vv. 5–9. **28:** *Joppa*, *Gazara*, and the *citadel* were Seleucid possessions before Simon took them, and Antiochus's claims (vv. 30–31) had some justification. **31:** *Or else* suggests that Antiochus was open to negotiation. *Talents*,

Athenobius[a] did not answer him a word, [36] but returned in wrath to the king and reported to him these words, and also the splendor of Simon and all that he had seen. And the king was very angry.

[37] Meanwhile Trypho embarked on a ship and escaped to Orthosia. [38] Then the king made Cendebeus commander-in-chief of the coastal country, and gave him troops of infantry and cavalry. [39] He commanded him to encamp against Judea, to build up Kedron and fortify its gates, and to make war on the people; but the king pursued Trypho. [40] So Cendebeus came to Jamnia and began to provoke the people and invade Judea and take the people captive and kill them. [41] He built up Kedron and stationed horsemen and troops there, so that they might go out and make raids along the highways of Judea, as the king had ordered him.

16 John went up from Gazara and reported to his father Simon what Cendebeus had done. [2] And Simon called in his two eldest sons Judas and John, and said to them: "My brothers and I and my father's house have fought the wars of Israel from our youth until this day, and things have prospered in our hands so that we have delivered Israel many times. [3] But now I have grown old, and you by Heaven's[b] mercy are mature in years. Take my place and my brother's, and go out and fight for our nation, and may the help that comes from Heaven be with you."

[4] So John[c] chose out of the country twenty thousand warriors and cavalry, and they marched against Cendebeus and camped for the night in Modein. [5] Early in the morning they started out and marched into the plain, where a large force of infantry and cavalry was coming to meet them; and a stream lay between them. [6] Then he and his army lined up against them. He saw that the soldiers were afraid to cross the stream, so he crossed over first; and when his troops saw him, they crossed over after him. [7] Then he divided the army and placed the cavalry in the center of the infantry, for the cavalry of the enemy were very numerous. [8] They sounded the trumpets, and Cendebeus and his army were put to flight; many of them fell wounded and the rest fled into the stronghold. [9] At that time Judas the brother of John was wounded, but John pursued them until Cendebeus[d] reached Kedron, which he had built. [10] They also fled into the towers that were in the fields of Azotus, and John[d] burned it with fire, and about two thousand of them fell. He then returned to Judea safely.

[11] Now Ptolemy son of Abubus had been appointed governor over the plain of Jericho; he had a large store of silver and gold, [12] for he was son-in-law of the high priest. [13] His heart was lifted up; he determined to get control of the country, and made treacherous plans against Simon and his sons, to do away with them. [14] Now Simon was visiting the towns of the country and attending to their needs, and he went down to Jericho with his sons Mattathias and Judas, in the one hundred seventy-seventh year,[e] in the eleventh month, which is the month of Shebat. [15] The son of Abubus received them treacherously

---

a   Gk *He*

b   Gk *his*

c   Other ancient authorities read *he*

d   Gk *he*

e   134 B.C.

---

see 11.28n. **32**: *Gold and silver plate*, the gifts of Trypho (11.58), provocatively displayed. **35**: Simon is prepared to negotiate over *Joppa* and *Gazara*. **37**: *Orthosia*, a Phoenician city north of Tripolis. **38**: *Commander-in-chief of the coastal country*, Simon was governor ("strategos") of the coast south of the Ladder of Tyre (cf. 11.59); Antiochus apparently replaces him with the higher ranking ("epistrategos") Cendebaeus. **39**: *Kedron*, cf. 16.9, near Jamnia, perhaps the village of Qatra. **40**: *Jamnia*, cf. 4.15n.; 10.69.

    16.1–10: **John defeats Cendebeus. 1**: *Gazara*, John's home, cf.13.53. **2–3**: Cf. Mattathias's speech, 2.49–68. **4**: *Modein*, see 2.1n. **8**: *Stronghold*, i.e., Kedron, cf. v. 9; 15.39. **10**: *Azotus*, burned by Jonathan (10.84). These verses give a confusing picture.

    16.11–22: The deaths of Simon and his sons Mattathias and Judas, and the accession of John Hyrcanus. 11–12: *Ptolemy son of Abubus*, Hellenized Semitic names. His wealth came from his governorship of the rich plain of Jericho (cf. Gen 13.10) and his father-in-law's income. **14**: Though retired (v. 3) Simon is still active. *Mattathias* and *Judas*, probably named after Simon's father and uncle. *Shebat*, the date, cast in Jewish form, is

in the little stronghold called Dok, which he had built; he gave them a great banquet, and hid men there. [16] When Simon and his sons were drunk, Ptolemy and his men rose up, took their weapons, rushed in against Simon in the banquet hall and killed him and his two sons, as well as some of his servants. [17] So he committed an act of great treachery and returned evil for good.

[18] Then Ptolemy wrote a report about these things and sent it to the king, asking him to send troops to aid him and to turn over to him the towns and the country. [19] He sent other troops to Gazara to do away with John; he sent letters to the captains asking them to come to him so that he might give them silver and gold and gifts; [20] and he sent other troops to take possession of Jerusalem and the temple hill. [21] But someone ran ahead and reported to John at Gazara that his father and brothers had perished, and that "he has sent men to kill you also." [22] When he heard this, he was greatly shocked; he seized the men who came to destroy him and killed them, for he had found out that they were seeking to destroy him.

[23] The rest of the acts of John and his wars and the brave deeds that he did, and the building of the walls that he completed, and his achievements, [24] are written in the annals of his high priesthood, from the time that he became high priest after his father.

January/February 135 or 134 BCE. **15:** *Dok*, the fortress on the Mount of Temptation above the spring 'Ain Duk, overlooking Jericho. **19:** *Gazara*, John's home (cf. v. 1), ca. 34 mi (55 km) west of Jericho. **20:** Ptolemy's plot failed, information reaching John before Ptolemy could take control. Ptolemy retreated to Dok, where John besieged him, and then fled to Philadelphia (Amman); Josephus, *Ant.* 13.230–235.

16.23–24: Epilogue. Compare the epilogue to Judas's career, 9.22. These verses imitate summaries familiar from 1–2 Kings, e.g., 2 Kings 14.28–29. **23:** John is presented as a worthy successor, with his *brave deeds* and *building of the walls* (probably walls destroyed by Antiochus VII, [Josephus, *Ant.* 13.247], who invaded Judea in 134 BCE, cf. his threat, 15.31). **24:** The author prefers not to describe John's career, referring the reader to *annals*: any existing were probably lost when the Romans destroyed the Temple (70 CE). John's *high priesthood* (134–104 BCE) appears to be in the past. 1 Macc was perhaps written during his high priesthood and completed shortly after it.

2 MACCABEES

The title Maccabees derives from Heb *maqqabi*, "hammer" (cf. Isa 44.12), the nickname given to Judas Maccabeus, the leader of the Jewish revolt that the story narrates. The original Greek title was "Book Recounting the Matters Pertaining to Maccabeus." The titles of the two main manuscripts of this work specifically refer to "the deeds of Judas Maccabeus" (terming it, respectively, an "epistle" or an "epitome" about those deeds). This title is especially appropriate for this work, in contrast to 1 Maccabees, which develops the history of several subsequent members of the Hasmonean dynasty after Judas.

CANONICAL STATUS

Second Maccabees is part of the Roman Catholic canon and Eastern Orthodox canons and the Protestant Apocrypha, but has no sacred status in Judaism. The text survived as part of the Septuagint (LXX), the Greek version of the Hebrew scriptures.

DATE, AUTHORSHIP, AND LITERARY HISTORY

In the introduction, the author tells us that the work is an abridgement of a longer work, now lost, written by Jason of Cyrene. Jason, otherwise unknown probably wrote in the mid-second century BCE, within a decade or so of the last events described in the work. The present abridgement was produced not long thereafter, around the same time as 1 Maccabees. Whereas 1 Maccabees was originally composed in Hebrew, 2 Maccabees was composed in Greek.

STRUCTURE AND CONTENTS

The body of the work (chs 4–15) deals with Judean history from King Antiochus IV Epiphanes' ascent to the Seleucid throne in 175 BCE to Judas Maccabeus's victory over the Seleucid general Nicanor in 161 BCE. It is prefaced (chs 1–2) by Palestinian letters urging the Jews of Egypt to celebrate the festival of Hanukkah, which commemorates Judas's purification and rededication of the Temple of Jerusalem in 164 BCE; by the abridger's introduction (2.19–32); and by a story (ch 3) about the way the Temple was miraculously preserved from desecration in the days of Antiochus's predecessor, an episode that in its present context serves as something of an idyllic prologue to the book's main story.

Chapter 4 begins that story with the introduction of Hellenized institutions into Jerusalem, which, according to the author, engendered sinful neglect of true Judaism. God, in response, "disregarded" (5.17) Jerusalem, i.e., suspended his providential care for it and thus allowed terrible things to happen, culminating in Antiochus's decrees against Judaism. These decrees then led to the noble martyrdom of those who refused to obey (chs 6–7).

Beginning in ch 8, however, God's anger changes to mercy (8.5; the pivotal verse of the book), and things go dramatically uphill: Judas Maccabeus wins battle after battle, Antiochus dies a terrible death (ch 9), Judas retakes Jerusalem and restores proper worship in the Temple (ch 10), and further victories bring about the repeal of Antiochus's decrees against Judaism (ch 11). More campaigns follow (chs 12–13) until the Seleucid army, commanded by Nicanor, is finally and decisively defeated. The book ends with the establishment of a holiday, "Nicanor's Day," to commemorate that event.

Accordingly, the main part of the book has two parts, in each of which, in the tradition of biblical dual causality, history and theology coincide. Chapters 4–7 present the problem: sin leads to persecution and Antiochus has the upper hand, while chs 8–15 present the solution: atonement makes for "reconciliation" (5.20; 7.33; 8.29) between the Jews and God, and Judas wins victory after victory until the circle is completed. The narrative opens in 3.1 with "the city" being once upon a time in ideal circumstances, and closes with the announcement in 15.37 that "the city" was restored to (other) ideal circumstances and so remained happily ever after.

INTERPRETATION

The book is a fascinating blend of Hellenism and Judaism. It was composed in the literary Greek of its day, comparable to that of the second-century BCE Greek historian Polybius, and has numerous allusions to Greek literature. For example, the author compares Antiochus's arrogance to that of the Persian king Xerxes (5.21; 9.8), portrays his heroes as complete Hellenistic gentlemen (4.37; 15.12,30), depicts his central martyr as a Jewish Socrates, and throughout the story, focuses upon Jerusalem as the Jews' *polis*, portraying Antiochus as a "barbarian" who tried to change the city's "constitution" and forbid Jews to "act as citizens" (6.1) according to Jewish law. But it is also a very Jewish book; its basic interpretative model is the Song of Moses (Deut 32), according to which God providentially cares for the Jews but hides his face when they sin, thus allowing foreigners to persecute them until the shedding of "his servants'" blood works atonement, so that God steps in, revenges himself upon their enemies, and restores his providential care for them. The author composes several substantial excurses (4.16–17; 5.17–20; 6.12–17), as well as various shorter remarks (e.g., 8.5; 9.13) to make sure readers understand his interpretation of events.

In addition to providing a parallel witness to the events reported in 1 Macc 1–7, this work (apart from the two introductory epistles) also bears witness to Judaism in the Hellenistic Diaspora. While those opening epistles have much in common with 1 Maccabees, the body of the book aligns more easily with such Diaspora works as 3 Maccabees, the Letter of Aristeas, and the works of Philo. This affinity is especially evident in the book's rosy picture of the Jews' usual relations with Gentiles (e.g. 4.35–36,49; contrast 1 Macc 5.1–2; 12.53), its assumption that Gentile rulers are usually benevolent (3.1–3; 5.16; contrast 1 Macc 1.9), its relative lack of interest in the Temple rituals (contrast 5.16 with the detail in 1 Macc 1.21–22 and note 2 Maccabees' emphasis upon God's residence in heaven in 3.39; 14.35), its high esteem for martyrs (see 6.11n.), and its insistence upon the priority of the people rather than the place (5.19; see also 5.6n).

Daniel R. Schwartz

---

1 The Jews in Jerusalem and those in the land of Judea,
To their Jewish kindred in Egypt,
Greetings and true peace.
² May God do good to you, and may he remember his covenant with Abraham and Isaac and Jacob, his faithful servants. ³ May he give you all a heart to worship him and to do his will with a strong heart and a willing spirit. ⁴ May he open your heart to his law and his commandments, and may he bring peace. ⁵ May he hear your prayers and be reconciled to you, and may he not forsake you in time of evil. ⁶ We are now praying for you here.
⁷ In the reign of Demetrius, in the one hundred sixty-ninth year,ᵃ we Jews wrote to you, in the critical distress that came upon us in those years after Jason and his company revolted from the holy land and the kingdom ⁸ and burned the gate and shed innocent blood. We prayed to the Lord and were heard, and we offered sacrifice and grain offering, and we lit the lamps and set out the loaves. ⁹ And now see that you keep the festival of booths in the month of Chislev, in the one hundred eighty-eighth year.ᵇ

ᵃ 143 B.C.
ᵇ 124 B.C.

1.1–9: Letter to the Jews in Egypt. This letter from Jerusalem invites the Jews of Egypt to observe the Hanukkah festival by referring to a previous letter written in the *one hundred sixty-ninth year* of the Seleucid era (v. 7), in the reign of Demetrius II, i.e., 143/142 BCE, which overlapped the first year of Hasmonean independence, according to 1 Macc 13.41. The letter portrays the Jews' troubles as having begun with Jason's revolt against the kingdom (v. 7), i.e., the kingdom of God; see ch 4. Thus, this epistle was written as something of a cover letter accompanying the body of the work, in an attempt to convince the Jews of Egypt to join in celebrating the Hasmoneans' victory. **2:** See Gen 15.18; 26.3; 35.12. **8:** *Lit the lamps and set out the loaves,* as mandated by Lev 24.1–9; see 10.3. **9:** *Festival of booths in the month of Chislev,* i.e., Hanukkah. The festival of booths (or tabernacles; Heb "Sukkoth") is celebrated in the autumn month of Tishri (September); Chislev (November/December) of 164 is when Judas retook the Temple, purified it, and rededicated it in a celebration reminiscent of that of the autumn festival (see 10.6–7). *In the one hundred eighty-eighth year,* if this date, ca. 124 BCE, is authentic, then this letter is quoting one of 143/142 BCE. But the date may be corrupt.

¹⁰ The people of Jerusalem and of Judea and the senate and Judas,

To Aristobulus, who is of the family of the anointed priests, teacher of King Ptolemy, and to the Jews in Egypt,

Greetings and good health.

¹¹ Having been saved by God out of grave dangers we thank him greatly for taking our side against the king,ᵃ ¹² for he drove out those who fought against the holy city. ¹³ When the leader reached Persia with a force that seemed irresistible, they were cut to pieces in the temple of Nanea by a deception employed by the priests of the goddessᵇ Nanea. ¹⁴ On the pretext of intending to marry her, Antiochus came to the place together with his Friends, to secure most of its treasures as a dowry. ¹⁵ When the priests of the temple of Nanea had set out the treasures and Antiochus had come with a few men inside the wall of the sacred precinct, they closed the temple as soon as he entered it. ¹⁶ Opening a secret door in the ceiling, they threw stones and struck down the leader and his men; they dismembered them and cut off their heads and threw them to the people outside. ¹⁷ Blessed in every way be our God, who has brought judgment on those who have behaved impiously.

¹⁸ Since on the twenty-fifth day of Chislev we shall celebrate the purification of the temple, we thought it necessary to notify you, in order that you also may celebrate the festival of booths and the festival of the fire given when Nehemiah, who built the temple and the altar, offered sacrifices.

¹⁹ For when our ancestors were being led captive to Persia, the pious priests of that time took some of the fire of the altar and secretly hid it in the hollow of a dry cistern, where they took such precautions that the place was unknown to anyone. ²⁰ But after many years had passed, when it pleased God, Nehemiah, having been commissioned by the king of Persia, sent the descendants of the priests who had hidden the fire to get it. And when they reported to us that they had not found fire but only a thick liquid, he ordered them to dip it out and bring it. ²¹ When the materials for the sacrifices were presented, Nehemiah ordered the priests to sprinkle the liquid on the wood and on the things laid upon it. ²² When this had been done and some time had passed,

ᵃ Cn: Gk *as those who array themselves against a king*

ᵇ Gk lacks *the goddess*

1.10–2.18: **Another letter to the Jews of Egypt.** This letter focuses on the history of the fire on the altar of the Temple of Jerusalem, working backward from Nehemiah through Jeremiah to Solomon. It claims that the fire that descended from heaven in the days of Solomon (2.10; 2 Chr 7.3) was hidden by pious priests at the time of the destruction of the First Temple (1.19). At the time of the restoration, it was found by Nehemiah, after a metamorphosis into a viscous and combustible liquid (1.20–36). He used some of it to rekindle the fire on the altar of the Second Temple, while the rest of it was preserved in rocks (1.31–32), from which Judas would eventually extract it when rededicating the Temple (10.3). So the restored Temple still had the original fire that descended from heaven. Thus, this letter constitutes an extended argument for the legitimacy of the Second Temple by connecting Nehemiah's restoration and Judas's rededication to Solomon's original dedication. **10:** *The senate,* lit. "council of elders." *Judas* Maccabeus; this letter is presented as if it were written in contemplation of the first Hanukkah or perhaps its first anniversary. *Aristobulus* was an Alexandrian Jewish philosopher and biblical exegete in the days of *Ptolemy* VI Philometor, king of Egypt, 180–145 BCE. By naming him merely "Ptolemy" the Judean authors show how little they care about that foreign king; contrast the use of "Philometor" in the body of the book (4.21; 9.29). **1.11–16: Antiochus Epiphanes' death in Persia.** For other versions of Antiochus's death during his eastern campaign, taken here to be part of God's rescue of the Jews, see ch 9 and 1 Macc 6.1–16. **14:** *His Friends,* courtiers of high rank; cf. 7.24; 14.11. This is not the only case of a fictive "sacred marriage" being used as a pretext to obtain money from a sanctuary. **18:** *The festival of booths,* cf. 1 Macc 10.21; 1 Kings 8.2; Neh 8.13–18.

1.19–36: **The latest link: the preservation of the fire.** This story assumes that Nehemiah rebuilt the Second Temple. In fact, he was active in the mid-fifth century BCE, several generations after the construction of the Second Temple. The mistake was common in Jewish tradition, which frequently remembered the Persian period as shorter than it really was. **19:** *Persia,* the exiles were actually led to Babylonia (cf. 2 Kings 24.14), which later became part of the Persian empire. **20:** *Nehemiah . . . commissioned,* Neh 2.7–8. **22:** *The sun . . . a great fire blazed*

and when the sun, which had been clouded over, shone out, a great fire blazed up, so that all marveled. [23] And while the sacrifice was being consumed, the priests offered prayer— the priests and everyone. Jonathan led, and the rest responded, as did Nehemiah. [24] The prayer was to this effect:

"O Lord, Lord God, Creator of all things, you are awe-inspiring and strong and just and merciful, you alone are king and are kind, [25] you alone are bountiful, you alone are just and almighty and eternal. You rescue Israel from every evil; you chose the ancestors and consecrated them. [26] Accept this sacrifice on behalf of all your people Israel and preserve your portion and make it holy. [27] Gather together our scattered people, set free those who are slaves among the Gentiles, look on those who are rejected and despised, and let the Gentiles know that you are our God. [28] Punish those who oppress and are insolent with pride. [29] Plant your people in your holy place, as Moses promised."

[30] Then the priests sang the hymns. [31] After the materials of the sacrifice had been consumed, Nehemiah ordered that the liquid that was left should be poured on large stones. [32] When this was done, a flame blazed up; but when the light from the altar shone back, it went out. [33] When this matter became known, and it was reported to the king of the Persians that, in the place where the exiled priests had hidden the fire, the liquid had appeared with which Nehemiah and his associates had burned the materials of the sacrifice, [34] the king investigated the matter, and enclosed the place and made it sacred. [35] And with those persons whom the king favored he exchanged many excellent gifts.

[36] Nehemiah and his associates called this "nephthar," which means purification, but by most people it is called naphtha.[a]

2 One finds in the records that the prophet Jeremiah ordered those who were being deported to take some of the fire, as has been mentioned, [2] and that the prophet, after giving them the law, instructed those who were being deported not to forget the commandments of the Lord, or to be led astray in their thoughts on seeing the gold and silver statues and their adornment. [3] And with other similar words he exhorted them that the law should not depart from their hearts.

[4] It was also in the same document that the prophet, having received an oracle, ordered that the tent and the ark should follow with him, and that he went out to the mountain where Moses had gone up and had seen the inheritance of God. [5] Jeremiah came and found a cave-dwelling, and he brought there the tent and the ark and the altar of incense; then he sealed up the entrance. [6] Some of those who followed him came up intending to mark the way, but could not find it. [7] When Jeremiah learned of it, he rebuked them and declared: "The place shall remain unknown until God gathers his people together again and shows his mercy. [8] Then the Lord will disclose these things, and the glory of the Lord and the cloud will appear, as they were shown in the case of Moses, and as Solomon asked that the place should be specially consecrated."

[9] It was also made clear that being possessed of wisdom Solomon[b] offered sacrifice

a Gk nephthai
b Gk he

up, with no human involvement, as in the days of Solomon (2.10; 2 Chr 7.3). The story also echoes one about Elijah in 1 Kings 18.33–38. 23: *Jonathan* is unknown, although it may refer to Mattaniah "who was the leader to begin the thanksgiving in prayer" (Neh 11.17) and whose name, like Jonathan, also means "God's gift" in Hebrew. 27: *Gather . . . set free those who are slaves among the Gentiles,* this Judean attitude contrasts diametrically with that of the Diaspora author of the body of the book. 29: *As Moses promised,* Ex 15.17; Deut 30.5. 34: The Persians considered fire holy and sometimes *enclosed* sites of *sacred* fire. 36: *"Nephthar," which means purification,* this etymology is obscure but Hanukkah is often seen as a purification; cf. 2.18; 10.3.

2.1–8: The penultimate link: Jeremiah. The tradition that Jeremiah saw to the hiding of various ritual objects at the time the First Temple was destroyed supplements the preceding one about what "pious priests" (1.19) did at the same time. For similar traditions, see *2 Baruch* 6. 2: *Instructed those who were being deported,* see Letter of Jeremiah. 4: *Mountain,* Nebo (Deut 32.49). *Inheritance of God* refers to the Holy Land in this Judean letter; elsewhere, notably in Deut 32.9, it often refers to the people (see 5.19n. and 6.16n.). 9–10: *Solomon,* 1 Kings 8.62–64;

for the dedication and completion of the temple. [10] Just as Moses prayed to the Lord, and fire came down from heaven and consumed the sacrifices, so also Solomon prayed, and the fire came down and consumed the whole burnt offerings. [11] And Moses said, "They were consumed because the sin offering had not been eaten." [12] Likewise Solomon also kept the eight days.

[13] The same things are reported in the records and in the memoirs of Nehemiah, and also that he founded a library and collected the books about the kings and prophets, and the writings of David, and letters of kings about votive offerings. [14] In the same way Judas also collected all the books that had been lost on account of the war that had come upon us, and they are in our possession. [15] So if you have need of them, send people to get them for you.

[16] Since, therefore, we are about to celebrate the purification, we write to you. Will you therefore please keep the days? [17] It is God who has saved all his people, and has returned the inheritance to all, and the kingship and the priesthood and the consecration, [18] as he promised through the law. We have hope in God that he will soon have mercy on us and will gather us from everywhere under heaven into his holy place, for he has rescued us from great evils and has purified the place.

[19] The story of Judas Maccabeus and his brothers, and the purification of the great temple, and the dedication of the altar, [20] and further the wars against Antiochus Epiphanes and his son Eupator, [21] and the appearances that came from heaven to those who fought bravely for Judaism, so that though few in number they seized the whole land and pursued the barbarian hordes, [22] and regained possession of the temple famous throughout the world, and liberated the city, and re-established the laws that were about to be abolished, while the Lord with great kindness became gracious to them— [23] all this, which has been set forth by Jason of Cyrene in five volumes, we shall attempt to condense into a single book. [24] For considering the flood of statistics involved and the difficulty there is for those who wish to enter upon the narratives of history because of the mass of material, [25] we have aimed to please those who wish to read, to make it easy for those who are inclined to memorize, and to profit all readers. [26] For us who have undertaken the toil of abbreviating, it is no light matter but calls for sweat and loss of sleep, [27] just as it is not easy for one who prepares a banquet and seeks the benefit of others. Nevertheless, to secure the gratitude of many we will gladly endure the uncomfortable toil, [28] leaving the responsibility for exact details to the compiler, while devoting our effort to arriving at the outlines of the condensation. [29] For as the master builder of a new house must be concerned with the whole construction, while the one who undertakes

---

2 Chr 7.1. **10**: *Moses prayed,* Lev 9.24. **11**: *"They were consumed . . ."* does not appear in the Bible, but may refer to the story in Lev 10.16–19. **12**: *The eight days* of dedicatory celebrations by Moses (Lev 8.33–9.1) and Solomon (2 Chr 7.9) are cited as precedents for Hanukkah (10.6). **13–14**: *Memoirs of Nehemiah . . . Judas also collected,* the biblical book of Nehemiah does not contain these references. Cf. Ezra 3.1–6; 1 Esd 5:46–50. It is important for the author, however, to underline these parallels between the putative founder of the Second Temple and its restorer, so that his claims are documented and thus should be believed by his addressees. Although there is no other evidence for the claim that Nehemiah *founded a library,* the reference to *kings and prophets, and the writings of David* sounds like a way of referring to the latter two parts of the Hebrew canon; compare the prologue to Sir and Lk 24.44. *Votive offerings,* such as those mentioned in 3.2 and 5.16. **17**: *All . . . to all,* including the Jews of Egypt. *Kingship and the priesthood,* a usual Jewish way of reading the promise of Ex 19.6.

2.19–32: The author's preface. 19–23. An involved sentence, in which the author shows his control of Greek from the outset. **21**: *Appearances* (Gk "epiphaneiai") . . . *from heaven* are given significant attention in the ensuing narrative at 3.24–26; 5.2–4; 10.29; 11.8; 12.22; etc. These true "epiphanies" are contrasted with the arrogant villain's byname, "Epiphanes." *Judaism,* the first known use of this term for the religion. *Barbarian hordes* as a term referring to the Greeks is a calculated reversal, which allows the author to mobilize the sympathies of Greek readers; so too 5.22; 13.9; 15.2. **23**: The five-volume work of *Jason of Cyrene,* of which 2 Macc is an abridgement, is no longer extant. *Cyrene,* in Libya. **29**: The author compares his work to that of a decorator, in

its painting and decoration has to consider only what is suitable for its adornment, such in my judgment is the case with us. [30] It is the duty of the original historian to occupy the ground, to discuss matters from every side, and to take trouble with details, [31] but the one who recasts the narrative should be allowed to strive for brevity of expression and to forego exhaustive treatment. [32] At this point therefore let us begin our narrative, without adding any more to what has already been said; for it would be foolish to lengthen the preface while cutting short the history itself.

3 While the holy city was inhabited in unbroken peace and the laws were strictly observed because of the piety of the high priest Onias and his hatred of wickedness, [2] it came about that the kings themselves honored the place and glorified the temple with the finest presents, [3] even to the extent that King Seleucus of Asia defrayed from his own revenues all the expenses connected with the service of the sacrifices.

[4] But a man named Simon, of the tribe of Benjamin, who had been made captain of the temple, had a disagreement with the high priest about the administration of the city market. [5] Since he could not prevail over Onias, he went to Apollonius of Tarsus,[a] who

at that time was governor of Coelesyria and Phoenicia, [6] and reported to him that the treasury in Jerusalem was full of untold sums of money, so that the amount of the funds could not be reckoned, and that they did not belong to the account of the sacrifices, but that it was possible for them to fall under the control of the king. [7] When Apollonius met the king, he told him of the money about which he had been informed. The king[b] chose Heliodorus, who was in charge of his affairs, and sent him with commands to effect the removal of the reported wealth. [8] Heliodorus at once set out on his journey, ostensibly to make a tour of inspection of the cities of Coelesyria and Phoenicia, but in fact to carry out the king's purpose.

[9] When he had arrived at Jerusalem and had been kindly welcomed by the high priest of[c] the city, he told about the disclosure that had been made and stated why he had come, and he inquired whether this really was the situation. [10] The high priest explained that there were some deposits belonging to widows and orphans, [11] and also some money of Hyrcanus son of Tobias, a man of very promi-

a   Gk *Apollonius son of Tharseas*
b   Gk *He*
c   Other ancient authorities read *and*

relation to Jason's original construction; for another analogy, see 15.39.

3.1–3: Prologue. Once upon a time everything was fine. **1:** *The holy city*, this opening bracket announces the book's topic; for the closing bracket, see 15.37. In the next two verses, the author quickly moves, using the inclusive term "place" (v. 2, compare 13.23), to the Temple. *Onias* III, son of Simeon II (whose praises are sung in Sir 50). He turned against Syria and collaborated with Egypt, while his cousins, the family of Tobias, to which Simon (v. 4) belonged, were pro-Syrian. For the notion that his piety guaranteed the stability of the city, compare Sir 10.2. *Hatred of wickedness*, a universal moral quality that also characterizes good Gentiles (4.36,49) and God himself (8.4). **3:** *King Seleucus* IV ruled 187–175 BCE. *Asia* was frequently used of the Seleucid kingdom.

3.4–40: Simon's plot against Onias. 4: *But* signals the beginning of the story; compare 12.2 and 14.26. *A man named Simon*, just as Greek kings are generally represented as benevolent and the villainous Antiochus is an exception, so too concerning Jewish villains, our author prefers lone wolves and bad apples, not parties; see 4.7 (contrast 1 Macc 1.13–14),40; 14.3 (contrast 1 Macc 7.5, also 1.11; 2.46). That is, the author in general portrays his world as good, with only occasional problems; contrast the world according to 1 Maccabees, which needed serious revision by the Hasmoneans. *Of the tribe of Benjamin*, since 4.23 identifies Menelaus as Simon's brother, many scholars prefer to read, with Latin witnesses, "of Bilgah" (a priestly clan, 1 Chr 24.14). **5:** *Tarsus*, capital of Cilicia in southern Asia Minor (Acts 21.39), then part of the Seleucid empire. *Coelesyria*, lit. "hollow Syria" (see 1 Macc 10.69n.), here used of Palestine. **6:** Simon apparently claimed that the royal budgets, earmarked for sacrifices (as in v. 3), were in fact being accumulated. **7:** *Heliodorus*, the prime minister of Seleucus IV, is known from inscriptions and historical sources. **11:** *Hyrcanus son of Tobias*, a well-known aristocratic Jewish family in Transjordan; see also 12.17. Hyrcanus was pro-Egyptian. He fled east of the Jordan after 198 BCE and built the fortress now known as Araq el-Emir. He committed suicide on the accession of Antiochus IV in 175. A *talent*

nent position, and that it totaled in all four hundred talents of silver and two hundred of gold. To such an extent the impious Simon had misrepresented the facts. [12] And he said that it was utterly impossible that wrong should be done to those people who had trusted in the holiness of the place and in the sanctity and inviolability of the temple that is honored throughout the whole world.

[13] But Heliodorus, because of the orders he had from the king, said that this money must in any case be confiscated for the king's treasury. [14] So he set a day and went in to direct the inspection of these funds.

There was no little distress throughout the whole city. [15] The priests prostrated themselves before the altar in their priestly vestments and called toward heaven upon him who had given the law about deposits, that he should keep them safe for those who had deposited them. [16] To see the appearance of the high priest was to be wounded at heart, for his face and the change in his color disclosed the anguish of his soul. [17] For terror and bodily trembling had come over the man, which plainly showed to those who looked at him the pain lodged in his heart. [18] People also hurried out of their houses in crowds to make a general supplication because the holy place was about to be brought into dishonor. [19] Women, girded with sackcloth under their breasts, thronged the streets. Some of the young women who were kept indoors ran together to the gates, and some to the walls, while others peered out of the windows. [20] And holding up their hands to heaven, they all made supplication. [21] There was something pitiable in the prostration of the whole populace and the anxiety of the high priest in his great anguish. [22] While they were calling upon the Almighty Lord that he would keep what had been entrusted safe and secure for those who had entrusted it, [23] Heliodorus went on with what had been decided. [24] But when he arrived at the treasury with his bodyguard, then and there the Sovereign of spirits and of all authority caused so great a manifestation that all who had been so bold as to accompany him were astounded by the power of God, and became faint with terror. [25] For there appeared to them a magnificently caparisoned horse, with a rider of frightening mien; it rushed furiously at Heliodorus and struck at him with its front hoofs. Its rider was seen to have armor and weapons of gold. [26] Two young men also appeared to him, remarkably strong, gloriously beautiful and splendidly dressed, who stood on either side of him and flogged him continuously, inflicting many blows on him. [27] When he suddenly fell to the ground and deep darkness came over him, his men took him up, put him on a stretcher, [28] and carried him away—this man who had just entered the aforesaid treasury with a great retinue and all his bodyguard but was now unable to help himself. They recognized clearly the sovereign power of God.

[29] While he lay prostrate, speechless because of the divine intervention and deprived of any hope of recovery, [30] they praised the Lord who had acted marvelously for his own place. And the temple, which a little while before was full of fear and disturbance, was filled with joy and gladness, now that the Almighty Lord had appeared.

[31] Some of Heliodorus's friends quickly begged Onias to call upon the Most High to grant life to one who was lying quite at his last breath. [32] So the high priest, fearing that the king might get the notion that some foul play had been perpetrated by the Jews with regard to Heliodorus, offered sacrifice for the man's recovery. [33] While the high priest was making an atonement, the same young men appeared again to Heliodorus dressed in the same clothing, and they stood and said, "Be very grateful to the high priest Onias, since for his sake the Lord has granted you your life. [34] And see that you, who have been

weighed ca. 75 lb (34 kg). 14–21: A purple passage, typical of Hellenistic "pathetic" historiography meant to make readers share in the emotions of the characters depicted by vivid rhetoric, as if they were being watched on stage. 15: *The law about deposits*, see Ex 22.7–13. 19: *Sackcloth* was a common sign of self-humiliation or mourning, used to support appeals for divine aid; compare 10.25 and Esth 4.1. *Young women who were kept indoors*, cf. Sir 42.9–12. 22–23: *They . . . Heliodorus*, the author often emphasizes the opposition of the two sides set for a showdown; cf. 10.28; 15.25–26. 26: *Two young men*, angelic figures, as in 10.30 and 3 Macc 6.18. 34:

flogged by heaven, report to all people the majestic power of God." Having said this they vanished.

[35] Then Heliodorus offered sacrifice to the Lord and made very great vows to the Savior of his life, and having bidden Onias farewell, he marched off with his forces to the king. [36] He bore testimony to all concerning the deeds of the supreme God, which he had seen with his own eyes. [37] When the king asked Heliodorus what sort of person would be suitable to send on another mission to Jerusalem, he replied, [38] "If you have any enemy or plotter against your government, send him there, for you will get him back thoroughly flogged, if he survives at all; for there is certainly some power of God about the place. [39] For he who has his dwelling in heaven watches over that place himself and brings it aid, and he strikes and destroys those who come to do it injury." [40] This was the outcome of the episode of Heliodorus and the protection of the treasury.

4 The previously mentioned Simon, who had informed about the money against[a] his own country, slandered Onias, saying that it was he who had incited Heliodorus and had been the real cause of the misfortune. [2] He dared to designate as a plotter against the government the man who was the benefactor of the city, the protector of his compatriots, and a zealot for the laws. [3] When his hatred progressed to such a degree that even

murders were committed by one of Simon's approved agents, [4] Onias recognized that the rivalry was serious and that Apollonius son of Menestheus,[b] and governor of Coelesyria and Phoenicia, was intensifying the malice of Simon. [5] So he appealed to the king, not accusing his compatriots but having in view the welfare, both public and private, of all the people. [6] For he saw that without the king's attention public affairs could not again reach a peaceful settlement, and that Simon would not stop his folly.

[7] When Seleucus died and Antiochus, who was called Epiphanes, succeeded to the kingdom, Jason the brother of Onias obtained the high priesthood by corruption, [8] promising the king at an interview[c] three hundred sixty talents of silver, and from another source of revenue eighty talents. [9] In addition to this he promised to pay one hundred fifty more if permission were given to establish by his authority a gymnasium and a body of youth for it, and to enroll the people of Jerusalem as citizens of Antioch. [10] When the king assented and Jason[d] came to office, he at once shifted his compatriots over to the Greek way of life.

[11] He set aside the existing royal concessions to the Jews, secured through John

a   Gk *and*
b   Vg Compare verse 21: Meaning of Gk uncertain
c   Or *by a petition*
d   Gk *he*

Flogged by heaven, in answer to prayers of vv. 15,20; note esp. v. 39. **36**: *He bore testimony*, as do others in this book who learned the same lesson (8.36; 9.17; 11.13). **39**: *Dwelling in heaven*, an important belief for Diaspora Jews; compare 5.19 and Acts 7.47–50.

4.1–6: Simon plots against Onias again. See 3.4n. The hostility resumes between the two rival Jewish families, contrasting in good Diaspora fashion the Jewish troublemaker Simon to the providential monarch. **4–5:** *Coelesyria,* see 3.5n.

4.7–17: Jason's reforms; "Antioch in Jerusalem." 7: *When Seleucus died,* 175 BCE. He was said to have been assassinated by Heliodorus (see 3.7). After the Roman defeat of Antiochus III at the battle of Magnesia (190 BCE) and Antiochus's capitulation to Rome in the subsequent Treaty of Apamea, one of his sons, *Antiochus* IV, was held hostage in Rome while another, *Seleucus* IV, reigned on the Syrian throne. With the death of *Seleucus, Antiochus* IV returned to Syria and ascended to the throne, being replaced in Rome by Demetrius I, Seleucus's young son; see 14.1n. **8:** *Talent,* see 3.11n. **9:** *Gymnasium,* a Greek school, the place not only of sport but also of political and cultural education, in short, the hallmark and bearer of Hellenism; cf. 1 Macc 1.14. *As citizens of Antioch,* that is, Jason received permission to establish a "polis," a Greek-style city-state in which citizenship status was essential to participation in political and economic life, called "Antioch in Jerusalem." **11:** *The existing royal concessions,* privileges recorded by Josephus granted by Antiochus III upon the establishment of Seleucid rule in Judea around 200 BCE, including the promise that Jewish law would be observed. The establishment of Antioch in Jerusalem is taken, by our pious author, to abrogate or undercut those privileges. *John the father of*

the father of Eupolemus, who went on the mission to establish friendship and alliance with the Romans; and he destroyed the lawful ways of living and introduced new customs contrary to the law. [12] He took delight in establishing a gymnasium right under the citadel, and he induced the noblest of the young men to wear the Greek hat. [13] There was such an extreme of Hellenization and increase in the adoption of foreign ways because of the surpassing wickedness of Jason, who was ungodly and no true[a] high priest, [14] that the priests were no longer intent upon their service at the altar. Despising the sanctuary and neglecting the sacrifices, they hurried to take part in the unlawful proceedings in the wrestling arena after the signal for the discus-throwing, [15] disdaining the honors prized by their ancestors and putting the highest value upon Greek forms of prestige. [16] For this reason heavy disaster overtook them, and those whose ways of living they admired and wished to imitate completely became their enemies and punished them. [17] It is no light thing to show irreverence to the divine laws—a fact that later events will make clear.

[18] When the quadrennial games were being held at Tyre and the king was present, [19] the vile Jason sent envoys, chosen as being Antiochian citizens from Jerusalem, to carry three hundred silver drachmas for the sacrifice to Hercules. Those who carried the money, however, thought best not to use it for sacrifice, because that was inappropriate, but to expend it for another purpose. [20] So this money was intended by the sender for the sacrifice to Hercules, but by the decision of its carriers it was applied to the construction of triremes.

[21] When Apollonius son of Menestheus was sent to Egypt for the coronation[b] of Philometor as king, Antiochus learned that Philometor[c] had become hostile to his government, and he took measures for his own security. Therefore upon arriving at Joppa he proceeded to Jerusalem. [22] He was welcomed magnificently by Jason and the city, and ushered in with a blaze of torches and with shouts. Then he marched his army into Phoenicia.

[23] After a period of three years Jason sent Menelaus, the brother of the previously mentioned Simon, to carry the money to the king and to complete the records of essential business. [24] But he, when presented to the king, extolled him with an air of authority, and secured the high priesthood for himself,

a Gk lacks true
b Meaning of Gk uncertain
c Gk he

Eupolemus is said, here, to have negotiated those privileges, just as his son, Eupolemus, was later to be a Jewish ambassador to Rome (1 Macc 8.17). The move from the father's Hebrew name to the son's Greek name illustrates the rise of Hellenism in contemporary Jerusalem, as does "Jason son of Eleazar," Eupolemus's partner (1 Macc 8.17). 12: The Greek hat was broad-rimmed; symbolic of the acceptance of Greek culture, it also allows our author to show off here with an impressive pun (Gk "hypotasson . . . hypo petason," "induced . . . the hat"). 16–17: An authorial excursus asserting that sin will not go unpunished.

4.18–22: Two pictures of life in Antioch in Jerusalem. The first story (vv. 18–20) shows that one may be a citizen of a "polis" and still avoid idolatry, and the second (vv. 21–22) shows the Jews were good subjects of the Seleucid king. 18: Tyre, a major city north of Palestine. Regular games had been held there since the late fourth century BCE. 19: Envoys were commonly sent by Greek cities to observe games and celebrations in others. A drachma was equivalent to a day's wages for a laborer. Hercules, the Greek name of the god Melkart of Tyre. 20: Triremes were standard Phoenician, Greek, and Roman war ships, with three benches of rowers on each side. 21–22: Apollonius, see v. 4. Coronation, or perhaps a coming-of-age ceremony. Ptolemy VI Philometor (ca. 180–145 BCE) became hostile to Syria, and claimed Palestine, which is why the Seleucid king travels east to secure his relationship with Jerusalem before proceeding to Phoenicia, the coastal plain. Jason and the city, as at 3.9, the high priest serves as something of a mayor; compare Sir 50.1–4.

4.23–50: Menelaus. The quality of the high priest now goes from bad to worse. If Jason, who supplanted Onias (4.7–8), was guilty of institutionalizing Hellenization in Jerusalem, Menelaus, who supplanted Jason (v. 26!), was a cruel (v. 25) and negligent (v. 27) governor who corruptly sought his own enrichment (v. 32) and did not shrink from murder (v. 34) and bribery (v. 45). He held onto his position, or tried to, until ca. 162 BCE

outbidding Jason by three hundred talents of silver. ²⁵ After receiving the king's orders he returned, possessing no qualification for the high priesthood, but having the hot temper of a cruel tyrant and the rage of a savage wild beast. ²⁶ So Jason, who after supplanting his own brother was supplanted by another man, was driven as a fugitive into the land of Ammon. ²⁷ Although Menelaus continued to hold the office, he did not pay regularly any of the money promised to the king. ²⁸ When Sostratus the captain of the citadel kept requesting payment—for the collection of the revenue was his responsibility—the two of them were summoned by the king on account of this issue. ²⁹ Menelaus left his own brother Lysimachus as deputy in the high priesthood, while Sostratus left Crates, the commander of the Cyprian troops.

³⁰ While such was the state of affairs, it happened that the people of Tarsus and of Mallus revolted because their cities had been given as a present to Antiochis, the king's concubine. ³¹ So the king went hurriedly to settle the trouble, leaving Andronicus, a man of high rank, to act as his deputy. ³² But Menelaus, thinking he had obtained a suitable opportunity, stole some of the gold vessels of the temple and gave them to Andronicus; other vessels, as it happened, he had sold to Tyre and the neighboring cities. ³³ When Onias became fully aware of these acts, he publicly exposed them, having first withdrawn to a place of sanctuary at Daphne near Antioch. ³⁴ Therefore Menelaus, taking Andronicus aside, urged him to kill Onias. Andronicus[a] came to Onias, and resorting to treachery, offered him sworn pledges and gave him his right hand; he persuaded him, though still suspicious, to come out from the place of sanctuary; then, with no regard for justice, he immediately put him out of the way.

³⁵ For this reason not only Jews, but many also of other nations, were grieved and displeased at the unjust murder of the man. ³⁶ When the king returned from the region of Cilicia, the Jews in the city[b] appealed to him with regard to the unreasonable murder of Onias, and the Greeks shared their hatred of the crime. ³⁷ Therefore Antiochus was grieved at heart and filled with pity, and wept because of the moderation and good conduct of the deceased. ³⁸ Inflamed with anger, he immediately stripped off the purple robe from Andronicus, tore off his clothes, and led him around the whole city to that very place where he had committed the outrage against Onias, and there he dispatched the bloodthirsty fellow. The Lord thus repaid him with the punishment he deserved.

³⁹ When many acts of sacrilege had been committed in the city by Lysimachus with the connivance of Menelaus, and when report of them had spread abroad, the populace gathered against Lysimachus, because many of the gold vessels had already been stolen. ⁴⁰ Since the crowds were becoming aroused and filled with anger, Lysimachus armed about three thousand men and launched an unjust attack, under the leadership of a certain Auranus, a man advanced in years and no less advanced in folly. ⁴¹ But when the Jews[c] became aware that Lysimachus was attacking them, some picked up stones, some blocks of wood, and others took handfuls of the ashes that were lying around, and threw them in wild confusion at Lysimachus and his men. ⁴² As a result, they wounded many of them, and killed some, and put all the rest to flight;

a   Gk *He*
b   Or *in each city*
c   Gk *they*

(see 13.3–8). **26**: *Land of Ammon*, east of the Jordan, near modern Amman. **30**: *Tarsus . . . Mallus* were cities in southeastern Asia Minor. Hellenistic kings often provided a wife or concubine with a regular income by giving her a city. Antiochus, being extravagant (see 1 Macc 3.30), was often in need of money. **31**: It is important for our author to claim that when injustice was done the king was absent, and that upon his return (v. 36) the king was enraged and meted out well-deserved punishment. **33**: *Sanctuary at Daphne*, of Apollo. Daphne is about 5 mi (8 km) from Antioch. Andronicus is thus shown to have violated the sanctity of a Greek temple in order to murder the Jewish high priest. **35–36**: *Not only Jews . . . other nations . . . Greeks*, the author insists on the basic unity of humanity and especially upon the Greeks' respect for Jews (see also v. 49 and 12.30–31); after all, Onias was a *man*. **37**: *Moderation and good conduct* were appropriate to a Hellenistic gentleman; cf. 15.12. **38**: *The Lord,*

the temple robber himself they killed close by the treasury. [43] Charges were brought against Menelaus about this incident. [44] When the king came to Tyre, three men sent by the senate presented the case before him. [45] But Menelaus, already as good as beaten, promised a substantial bribe to Ptolemy son of Dorymenes to win over the king. [46] Therefore Ptolemy, taking the king aside into a colonnade as if for refreshment, induced the king to change his mind. [47] Menelaus, the cause of all the trouble, he acquitted of the charges against him, while he sentenced to death those unfortunate men, who would have been freed uncondemned if they had pleaded even before Scythians. [48] And so those who had spoken for the city and the villages[a] and the holy vessels quickly suffered the unjust penalty. [49] Therefore even the Tyrians, showing their hatred of the crime, provided magnificently for their funeral. [50] But Menelaus, because of the greed of those in power, remained in office, growing in wickedness, having become the chief plotter against his compatriots.

5 About this time Antiochus made his second invasion of Egypt. [2] And it happened that, for almost forty days, there appeared over all the city golden-clad cavalry charging through the air, in companies fully armed with lances and drawn swords— [3] troops of cavalry drawn up, attacks and counterattacks made on this side and on that, brandishing of shields, massing of spears, hurling of missiles, the flash of golden trappings, and armor of all kinds. [4] Therefore everyone prayed that the apparition might prove to have been a good omen.

[5] When a false rumor arose that Antiochus was dead, Jason took no fewer than a thousand men and suddenly made an assault on the city. When the troops on the wall had been forced back and at last the city was being taken, Menelaus took refuge in the citadel. [6] But Jason kept relentlessly slaughtering his compatriots, not realizing that success at the cost of one's kindred is the greatest misfortune, but imagining that he was setting up trophies of victory over enemies and not over compatriots. [7] He did not, however, gain control of the government; in the end he got only disgrace from his conspiracy, and fled again into the country of the Ammonites. [8] Finally he met a miserable end. Accused[b] before Aretas the ruler of the Arabs, fleeing from city to city, pursued by everyone, hated as a rebel against the laws, and abhorred as the executioner of his country and his compatriots, he was cast ashore in Egypt. [9] There he who had driven many from their

a Other ancient authorities read *the people*
b Cn: Gk *Imprisoned*

---

an explicit statement of dual causality: Antiochus did the Lord's work. **39:** *The city,* Jerusalem. **42:** *Killed close by the treasury,* frequently the punishment fits the crime in 2 Maccabees, thus demonstrating God's equitable management of history; see also vv. 16,26,38. For Menelaus's own end, see 13.8. **45:** *Dorymenes* had fought for Ptolemy IV against Antiochus III; his son *Ptolemy* had been governor of Cyprus and had deserted to Antiochus IV (see 10.12–13). **47:** *Scythians,* a proverbially brutal people north of the Black Sea; see 7.4n. **48:** *The city and the villages and the holy vessels,* see textual note *a.* The reference first of all to the city, and only thereafter to the holy vessels, although the issue pertained to the latter, is typical for the orientation of this book; see 3.1n.

5.1–27: Antiochus IV desecrates the Temple. 1–4: Apparition over Jerusalem. **1:** *Antiochus made his second invasion of Egypt* in the spring of 168 BCE, the first having occurred in 170. The second was successful, although a Roman ultimatum forced him to withdraw (Dan 11.29–30). This humiliation may have created the "false rumor" of Antiochus's death (v. 5). **2–4:** *There appeared over all the city,* an apparition of a military nature. Because its meaning was ambiguous, all the Jerusalemites could do was pray that it be for the good; the rest of the chapter shows it was not. **5–10:** Jason attempts to take Jerusalem. Jason, who had been ousted by Menelaus and expelled from the city (4.26), now attempts a comeback. Because Jason had been forced out of the city (v. 7), although Menelaus had withdrawn to the *citadel* (the Temple mount, v. 5), there was probably a nationalist rebellion against Seleucid rule at the same time, as Antiochus inferred (v. 11). But our author prefers to ignore that; compare 3.4n. **6:** *Compatriots,* lit. "fellow citizens." *Trophies* commemorate victories over *enemies* (15.6), not *compatriots,* lit. "members of his people." In this sentence, the Diaspora author uses first a political (city-oriented) category and then two ethnic ones ("kindred," "members of his people"). **8:** *Aretas* I, king of Nabatean

own country into exile died in exile, having embarked to go to the Lacedaemonians in hope of finding protection because of their kinship. [10] He who had cast out many to lie unburied had no one to mourn for him; he had no funeral of any sort and no place in the tomb of his ancestors.

[11] When news of what had happened reached the king, he took it to mean that Judea was in revolt. So, raging inwardly, he left Egypt and took the city by storm. [12] He commanded his soldiers to cut down relentlessly everyone they met and to kill those who went into their houses. [13] Then there was massacre of young and old, destruction of boys, women, and children, and slaughter of young girls and infants. [14] Within the total of three days eighty thousand were destroyed, forty thousand in hand-to-hand fighting, and as many were sold into slavery as were killed.

[15] Not content with this, Antiochus[a] dared to enter the most holy temple in all the world, guided by Menelaus, who had become a traitor both to the laws and to his country. [16] He took the holy vessels with his polluted hands, and swept away with profane hands the votive offerings that other kings had made to enhance the glory and honor of the place. [17] Antiochus was elated in spirit, and did not perceive that the Lord was angered for a little while because of the sins of those who lived in the city, and that this was the reason he was disregarding the holy place. [18] But if it had not happened that they were involved in many sins, this man would have been flogged and turned back from his rash act as soon as he came forward, just as Heliodorus had been, whom King Seleucus sent to inspect the treasury. [19] But the Lord did not choose the nation for the sake of the holy place, but the place for the sake of the nation. [20] Therefore the place itself shared in the misfortunes that befell the nation and afterward participated in its benefits; and what was forsaken in the wrath of the Almighty was restored again in all its glory when the great Lord became reconciled.

[21] So Antiochus carried off eighteen hundred talents from the temple, and hurried away to Antioch, thinking in his arrogance that he could sail on the land and walk on the sea, because his mind was elated. [22] He left governors to oppress the people: at Jerusalem, Philip, by birth a Phrygian and in character more barbarous than the man who appointed him; [23] and at Gerizim, Andronicus; and besides these Menelaus, who lorded it over his compatriots worse than the others did. In his malice toward the Jewish citizens,[b] [24] Antiochus[a] sent Apollonius, the captain

a Gk *he*
b Or *worse than the others did in his malice toward the Jewish citizens*

Arabia, south and east of Palestine; his capital was at Petra. **9**: Rejected in Egypt, Jason fled to the *Lacedaemonians* in Sparta; other Jewish sources (e.g., 1 Macc 12.7,21) allege a kinship between the Jews and Spartans. **10**: *Unburied . . . no funeral*, a common theme in this book (9.15,28; 12.39; 13.7). **11–16**: Antiochus attacks Jerusalem thinking that all Judea, not just the villain Jason, was in revolt. He was *raging inwardly* because the Romans had forced him out of Egypt (the Roman envoy, Popillius Laenas, had threatened him with war if he attempted to annex Egypt; see 1 Macc 1.20); both his foreign and his domestic programs were collapsing. **12–13**: This account of murder of young and old, outside and inside, seems to allude to Deut 32.25. (On Deut 32 as the basic biblical subtext of this book, see the Introduction.) **15**: Even Jews were forbidden to enter *the most holy* parts of the *temple*. That the high priest Menelaus would guide Antiochus further indicts him as unfit (4.25). **16**: The relative lack of interest in ritual details (only "holy vessels"; contrast 1 Macc 1.21–23), and the need to underline that most Gentile kings are benevolent and respectful to Jews, are typically Diasporan.

5.17–20: Authorial excursus (cf. 4.16–17). The author explains that the Temple could suffer this profanation and robbery because it was secondary to the people; for a similar argument see Mk 2.27. **17**: *For a little while . . . disregarding* is the author's Greek way of rendering the biblical notion of God's hiding his face (Deut 32.20), something which he does at times "for a little while" (Isa 54.7–8) due to the Jews' sins. **18**: *Heliodorus*, see ch 3.

5.21–27: Further troubles. 21: *Thinking in his arrogance that he could sail on the land and walk on the sea* describes Antiochus according to the standard Greek topos of an arrogant oriental monarch. **22**: *Phrygia*, a region of western Asia Minor. **22–23**: *The people: at Jerusalem . . . at Gerizim*, the author considers Samaritans to be Jews, although they worshiped at a different temple. The author's evenhandedness reflects the situation of Diaspora

of the Mysians, with an army of twenty-two thousand, and commanded him to kill all the grown men and to sell the women and boys as slaves. ²⁵ When this man arrived in Jerusalem, he pretended to be peaceably disposed and waited until the holy sabbath day; then, finding the Jews not at work, he ordered his troops to parade under arms. ²⁶ He put to the sword all those who came out to see them, then rushed into the city with his armed warriors and killed great numbers of people.

²⁷ But Judas Maccabeus, with about nine others, got away to the wilderness, and kept himself and his companions alive in the mountains as wild animals do; they continued to live on what grew wild, so that they might not share in the defilement.

6 Not long after this, the king sent an Athenian[a] senator[b] to compel the Jews to forsake the laws of their ancestors and no longer to live by the laws of God; ² also to pollute the temple in Jerusalem and to call it the temple of Olympian Zeus, and to call the one in Gerizim the temple of Zeus-the-Friend-of-Strangers, as did the people who lived in that place.

³ Harsh and utterly grievous was the onslaught of evil. ⁴ For the temple was filled with debauchery and reveling by the Gentiles, who dallied with prostitutes and had intercourse with women within the sacred precincts, and besides brought in things

for sacrifice that were unfit. ⁵ The altar was covered with abominable offerings that were forbidden by the laws. ⁶ People could neither keep the sabbath, nor observe the festivals of their ancestors, nor so much as confess themselves to be Jews.

⁷ On the monthly celebration of the king's birthday, the Jews[c] were taken, under bitter constraint, to partake of the sacrifices; and when a festival of Dionysus was celebrated, they were compelled to wear wreaths of ivy and to walk in the procession in honor of Dionysus. ⁸ At the suggestion of the people of Ptolemais[d] a decree was issued to the neighboring Greek cities that they should adopt the same policy toward the Jews and make them partake of the sacrifices, ⁹ and should kill those who did not choose to change over to Greek customs. One could see, therefore, the misery that had come upon them. ¹⁰ For example, two women were brought in for having circumcised their children. They publicly paraded them around the city, with their babies hanging at their breasts, and then hurled them down headlong from the wall. ¹¹ Others who had assembled in the caves nearby, in order to observe the seventh day secretly, were betrayed to Philip and were

a   Other ancient authorities read *Antiochian*
b   Or *Geron an Athenian*
c   Gk *they*
d   Cn: Gk *suggestion of the Ptolemies* (or *of Ptolemy*)

Jews who worshiped at neither; cf. Jn 4.21. **24:** *Captain of the Mysians*, lit. "Mysarch," commander of mercenary troops from Mysia, a region of Asia Minor. **25:** *Parade under arms* recalls the apparition in vv. 1–3 and clarifies its meaning. **27:** *Judas Maccabeus*, the third son of Mattathias, of the Hasmonean family (1 Macc 2.1–28). Mention of him here provides a ray of hope throughout the next two chapters of suffering. He will reappear, with a much larger force, at the beginning of ch 8. *Live on what grew wild*, in observance of Jewish dietary laws that prohibited the consumption of unclean animals; cf. 11.31; 1 Macc 1.62–63; Dan 1.8.

    6.1–11: Decrees against Judaism. If Jason made Hellenization available in the social, political, and economic spheres, Antiochus now pollutes the Jews' Temple and attempts to force new rituals upon them which, however Semitic or syncretistic, were viewed by many Jews as Greek customs (v. 9), because a Greek king imposed them. **1:** *Athenian*, Antiochus's ties to Athens are well documented; compare 9.15. **2:** As at 5.22–23, the author has no problems about drawing a parallel between the Temple of Jerusalem and that of the Samaritans, which was considered illegitimate by some Jerusalemite Jews. **4:** *The temple* was polluted; see also 1 Macc 1.46–59 and Dan 11.31. **7:** Antiochus's *birthday* was celebrated on the twenty-fifth of each month (1 Macc 1.58–59). *Dionysus*, the Greek god of wine and harvest. **8:** *Ptolemais*, the Hellenistic city founded at Acco, north of Haifa. **10–11:** These first stories of martyrs are paralleled at 1 Macc 1.60–61 and 2.29–38. In contrast to 1 Maccabees, however, our "pathetic" work (see 3.14–21n.) refers (as at 3.19) to the mothers' breasts, not their necks; and as a Diaspora work it praises the martyrs in the caves who refused to fight on the sabbath, as opposed to 1 Macc 2, which uses them as foils for the Hasmoneans.

all burned together, because their piety kept them from defending themselves, in view of their regard for that most holy day.

[12] Now I urge those who read this book not to be depressed by such calamities, but to recognize that these punishments were designed not to destroy but to discipline our people. [13] In fact, it is a sign of great kindness not to let the impious alone for long, but to punish them immediately. [14] For in the case of the other nations the Lord waits patiently to punish them until they have reached the full measure of their sins; but he does not deal in this way with us, [15] in order that he may not take vengeance on us afterward when our sins have reached their height. [16] Therefore he never withdraws his mercy from us. Although he disciplines us with calamities, he does not forsake his own people. [17] Let what we have said serve as a reminder; we must go on briefly with the story.

[18] Eleazar, one of the scribes in high position, a man now advanced in age and of noble presence, was being forced to open his mouth to eat swine's flesh. [19] But he, welcoming death with honor rather than life with pollution, went up to the rack of his own accord, spitting out the flesh, [20] as all ought to go who have the courage to refuse things that it is not right to taste, even for the natural love of life.

[21] Those who were in charge of that unlawful sacrifice took the man aside because of their long acquaintance with him, and privately urged him to bring meat of his own providing, proper for him to use, and to pretend that he was eating the flesh of the sacrificial meal that had been commanded by the king, [22] so that by doing this he might be saved from death, and be treated kindly on account of his old friendship with them. [23] But making a high resolve, worthy of his years and the dignity

of his old age and the gray hairs that he had reached with distinction and his excellent life even from childhood, and moreover according to the holy God-given law, he declared himself quickly, telling them to send him to Hades.

[24] "Such pretense is not worthy of our time of life," he said, "for many of the young might suppose that Eleazar in his ninetieth year had gone over to an alien religion, [25] and through my pretense, for the sake of living a brief moment longer, they would be led astray because of me, while I defile and disgrace my old age. [26] Even if for the present I would avoid the punishment of mortals, yet whether I live or die I will not escape the hands of the Almighty. [27] Therefore, by bravely giving up my life now, I will show myself worthy of my old age [28] and leave to the young a noble example of how to die a good death willingly and nobly for the revered and holy laws."

When he had said this, he went[a] at once to the rack. [29] Those who a little before had acted toward him with goodwill now changed to ill will, because the words he had uttered were in their opinion sheer madness.[b] [30] When he was about to die under the blows, he groaned aloud and said: "It is clear to the Lord in his holy knowledge that, though I might have been saved from death, I am enduring terrible sufferings in my body under this beating, but in my soul I am glad to suffer these things because I fear him."

[31] So in this way he died, leaving in his death an example of nobility and a memorial of courage, not only to the young but to the great body of his nation.

a   Other ancient authorities read *was dragged*
b   Meaning of Gk uncertain

6.12–17: Authorial excursus (cf. 4.16–17; 5.17–20). The author explains to his readers that it is God's graciousness to his people that brings him to allow punishment for sins as they occur, thus enabling atonement and reconciliation. 12: *To discipline*, as in Deut 8.5. 14: *Full measure of their sins*, which would then bring upon them irrevocable punishment; Gen 15.16. 16: *He does not forsake his own people*, Ps 94.14.

6.18–31 Martyrdom of Eleazar. 18: *Scribes* were scholars of the Torah; cf. 1 Macc 7.12. 4 Macc 5.4 adds, on unknown authority but not improbably, that Eleazar was a priest. *Swine's flesh* is the best known of biblically prohibited meats (Lev 11.7–8). In this case the problem is compounded because the meat was sacrificed in a pagan rite (v. 21). 23: *Hades*, the Gk name of the underworld (Heb "Sheol"). 28: *Leave to the young a noble example*, Eleazar is presented as a Jewish Socrates; his speech resembles Socrates's final speech in Plato's *Apology*. 30: *Body . . . soul*, a distinction that reflects the influence of Greek anthropology on Jewish thought. *Fear*, revere. 31: *Not only to the young*, as he said in v. 28; the next chapter, however, focuses on the young.

7 It happened also that seven brothers and their mother were arrested and were being compelled by the king, under torture with whips and thongs, to partake of unlawful swine's flesh. ² One of them, acting as their spokesman, said, "What do you intend to ask and learn from us? For we are ready to die rather than transgress the laws of our ancestors."

³ The king fell into a rage, and gave orders to have pans and caldrons heated. ⁴ These were heated immediately, and he commanded that the tongue of their spokesman be cut out and that they scalp him and cut off his hands and feet, while the rest of the brothers and the mother looked on. ⁵ When he was utterly helpless, the king[a] ordered them to take him to the fire, still breathing, and to fry him in a pan. The smoke from the pan spread widely, but the brothers[b] and their mother encouraged one another to die nobly, saying, ⁶ "The Lord God is watching over us and in truth has compassion on us, as Moses declared in his song that bore witness against the people to their faces, when he said, 'And he will have compassion on his servants.'"[c]

⁷ After the first brother had died in this way, they brought forward the second for their sport. They tore off the skin of his head with the hair, and asked him, "Will you eat rather than have your body punished limb by limb?" ⁸ He replied in the language of his ancestors and said to them, "No." Therefore he in turn underwent tortures as the first brother had done. ⁹ And when he was at his last breath, he said, "You accursed wretch, you dismiss us from this present life, but the King of the universe will raise us up to an everlasting renewal of life, because we have died for his laws."

¹⁰ After him, the third was the victim of their sport. When it was demanded, he quickly put out his tongue and courageously stretched forth his hands, ¹¹ and said nobly, "I got these from Heaven, and because of his laws I disdain them, and from him I hope to get them back again." ¹² As a result the king himself and those with him were astonished at the young man's spirit, for he regarded his sufferings as nothing.

¹³ After he too had died, they maltreated and tortured the fourth in the same way. ¹⁴ When he was near death, he said, "One cannot but choose to die at the hands of mortals and to cherish the hope God gives of being raised again by him. But for you there will be no resurrection to life!"

¹⁵ Next they brought forward the fifth and maltreated him. ¹⁶ But he looked at the king,[d] and said, "Because you have authority among mortals, though you also are mortal, you do what you please. But do not think that God has forsaken our people. ¹⁷ Keep on, and see how his mighty power will torture you and your descendants!"

¹⁸ After him they brought forward the sixth. And when he was about to die, he said, "Do not deceive yourself in vain. For we are suffering these things on our own account, because of our sins against our own God. Therefore[e] astounding things have happened. ¹⁹ But do not think that you will go unpunished for having tried to fight against God!"

a Gk *he*
b Gk *they*
c Gk *slaves*
d Gk *at him*
e Lat: Other ancient authorities lack *Therefore*

7.1–42: Martyrdom of seven brothers and their mother. This story—which has a life of its own in Jewish literature, is the principal subject of 4 Maccabees, and may be inspired by Jer 15.9—may have been appropriated from an independent source, as is suggested by the king's presence and by the absence of political formulations so typical of this book. 1: *The king* is Antiochus IV (v. 24), although he returned to Syria in ch 5 and imposed the decrees through his agents. 2: *Ancestors*, lit. "fathers," who are thus made to compete with the king; compare "language of his ancestors" (i.e., Hebrew) in vv. 8,21,27. 4: *Scalp*, lit. "cut him around the Scythian way"; see 4.47n. 6: *As Moses declared*, Deut 32.36. On Deut 32, see Introduction. 9: *Raise us up*, resurrection is a recurrent theme in this chapter; see also 12.43–45 and 14.46. This belief's only clear attestation in the Hebrew Bible, Dan 12.1–3, seems to be a response to the same persecutions. 11: *Heaven*, a circumlocution for God; see v. 34. 18: *Because of our sins*, as in v. 32 and throughout this book; "our" is both specific (as in 12.40) and collective,

²⁰ The mother was especially admirable and worthy of honorable memory. Although she saw her seven sons perish within a single day, she bore it with good courage because of her hope in the Lord. ²¹ She encouraged each of them in the language of their ancestors. Filled with a noble spirit, she reinforced her woman's reasoning with a man's courage, and said to them, ²² "I do not know how you came into being in my womb. It was not I who gave you life and breath, nor I who set in order the elements within each of you. ²³ Therefore the Creator of the world, who shaped the beginning of humankind and devised the origin of all things, will in his mercy give life and breath back to you again, since you now forget yourselves for the sake of his laws."

²⁴ Antiochus felt that he was being treated with contempt, and he was suspicious of her reproachful tone. The youngest brother being still alive, Antiochusª not only appealed to him in words, but promised with oaths that he would make him rich and enviable if he would turn from the ways of his ancestors, and that he would take him for his Friend and entrust him with public affairs. ²⁵ Since the young man would not listen to him at all, the king called the mother to him and urged her to advise the youth to save himself. ²⁶ After much urging on his part, she undertook to persuade her son. ²⁷ But, leaning close to him, she spoke in their native language as follows, deriding the cruel tyrant: "My son, have pity on me. I carried you nine months in my womb, and nursed you for three years, and have reared you and brought you up to this point in your life, and have taken care of you.ᵇ ²⁸ I beg you, my child, to look at the heaven and the earth and see everything that is in them, and recognize that God did not make them out of things that existed.ᶜ And

in the same way the human race came into being. ²⁹ Do not fear this butcher, but prove worthy of your brothers. Accept death, so that in God's mercy I may get you back again along with your brothers."

³⁰ While she was still speaking, the young man said, "What are youᵈ waiting for? I will not obey the king's command, but I obey the command of the law that was given to our ancestors through Moses. ³¹ But you,ᵉ who have contrived all sorts of evil against the Hebrews, will certainly not escape the hands of God. ³² For we are suffering because of our own sins. ³³ And if our living Lord is angry for a little while, to rebuke and discipline us, he will again be reconciled with his own servants.ᶠ ³⁴ But you, unholy wretch, you most defiled of all mortals, do not be elated in vain and puffed up by uncertain hopes, when you raise your hand against the children of heaven. ³⁵ You have not yet escaped the judgment of the almighty, all-seeing God. ³⁶ For our brothers after enduring a brief suffering have drunkᵍ of ever-flowing life, under God's covenant; but you, by the judgment of God, will receive just punishment for your arrogance. ³⁷ I, like my brothers, give up body and life for the laws of our ancestors, appealing to God to show mercy soon to our nation and by trials and plagues to make you confess that he alone is God, ³⁸ and through me and my brothers to bring to an end the wrath of the Almighty that has justly fallen on our whole nation."

ª Gk *he*
ᵇ Or *have borne the burden of your education*
ᶜ Or *God made them out of things that did not exist*
ᵈ The Gk here for *you* is plural
ᵉ The Gk here for *you* is singular
ᶠ Gk *slaves*
ᵍ Cn: Gk *fallen*

as in the excurses (4.16–17; 5.18). *Astounding things have happened,* namely, your successes against the Jews. **22:** *It was not I who gave you life,* The mother's speech appears to combine references to Sir 1.1–3, which it refutes, with technical vocabulary from Greek philosophy (*set in order the elements*; Plato, *Theaetetus* 210e; Aristotle, *Metaphysics* 998a.23). The author argues that resurrection is a mystery analogous to the creation of the world, or of a human being. Just as God caused something to exist that had not existed previously (see v. 28), so God can resurrect a person who has ceased to exist. **24:** *His Friend,* see 1.14n. **28:** *Did not make them out of things that existed,* this verse was understood by Origen (185–254 CE) and subsequent Christian authors to be a statement of the doctrine that God created the universe out of nothing. **33:** *Angry for a little while,* see 5.17n. *Reconciled with his own servants,* alluding to Deut 32.36; see v. 6 above and 8.29. **34:** *Children of heaven,* the Jews; see v.11n. **38:** *Through me and my brothers to bring to an end the wrath,* their deaths are not in vain, but rather effective; con-

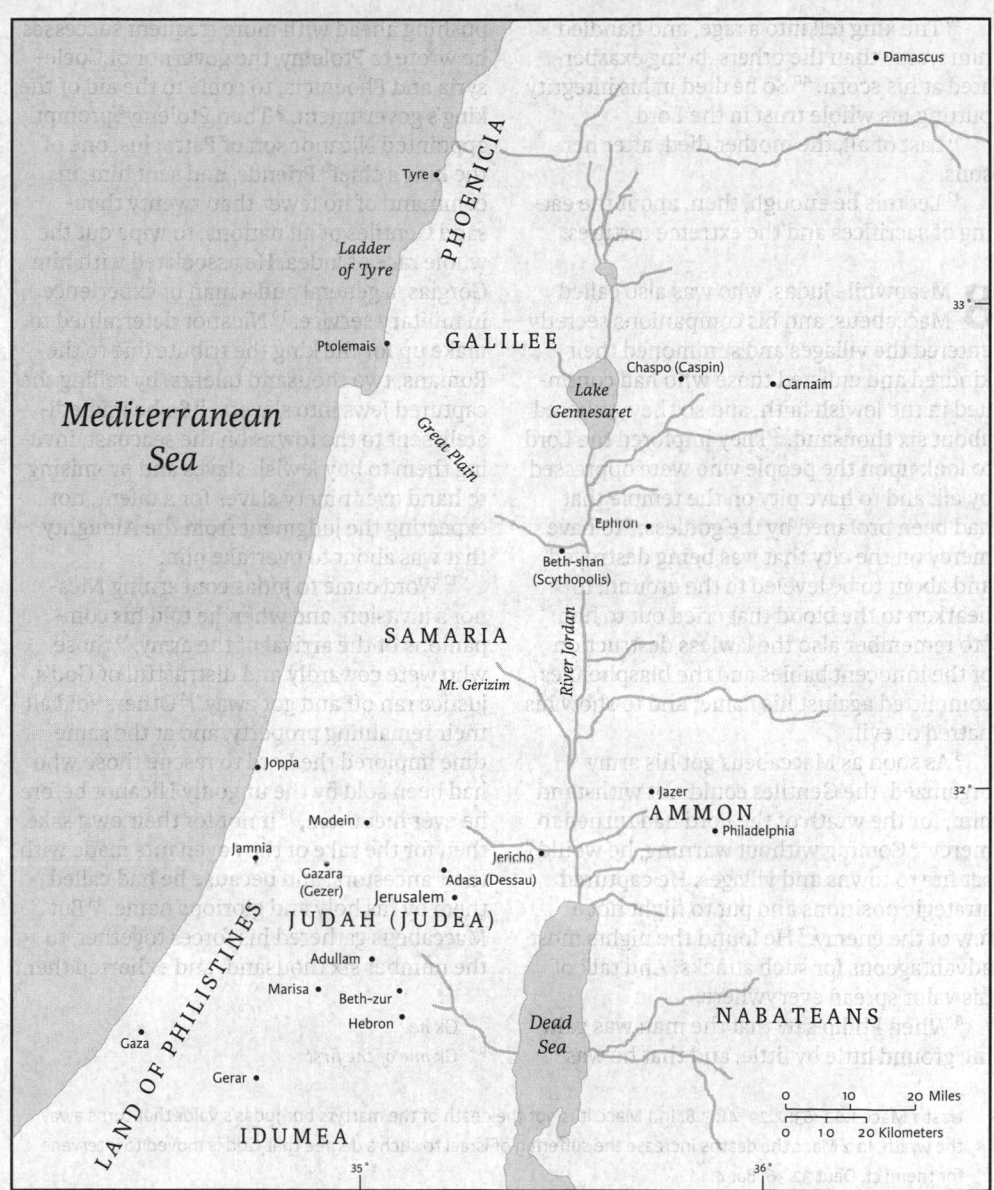

Places associated with the campaigns of the Maccabees in 2 Macc 8–15.

[39] The king fell into a rage, and handled him worse than the others, being exasperated at his scorn. [40] So he died in his integrity, putting his whole trust in the Lord.

[41] Last of all, the mother died, after her sons.

[42] Let this be enough, then, about the eating of sacrifices and the extreme tortures.

8 Meanwhile Judas, who was also called Maccabeus, and his companions secretly entered the villages and summoned their kindred and enlisted those who had continued in the Jewish faith, and so they gathered about six thousand. [2] They implored the Lord to look upon the people who were oppressed by all; and to have pity on the temple that had been profaned by the godless; [3] to have mercy on the city that was being destroyed and about to be leveled to the ground; to hearken to the blood that cried out to him; [4] to remember also the lawless destruction of the innocent babies and the blasphemies committed against his name; and to show his hatred of evil.

[5] As soon as Maccabeus got his army organized, the Gentiles could not withstand him, for the wrath of the Lord had turned to mercy. [6] Coming without warning, he would set fire to towns and villages. He captured strategic positions and put to flight not a few of the enemy. [7] He found the nights most advantageous for such attacks. And talk of his valor spread everywhere.

[8] When Philip saw that the man was gaining ground little by little, and that he was pushing ahead with more frequent successes, he wrote to Ptolemy, the governor of Coele-syria and Phoenicia, to come to the aid of the king's government. [9] Then Ptolemy[a] promptly appointed Nicanor son of Patroclus, one of the king's chief[b] Friends, and sent him, in command of no fewer than twenty thousand Gentiles of all nations, to wipe out the whole race of Judea. He associated with him Gorgias, a general and a man of experience in military service. [10] Nicanor determined to make up for the king the tribute due to the Romans, two thousand talents, by selling the captured Jews into slavery. [11] So he immediately sent to the towns on the seacoast, inviting them to buy Jewish slaves and promising to hand over ninety slaves for a talent, not expecting the judgment from the Almighty that was about to overtake him.

[12] Word came to Judas concerning Nicanor's invasion; and when he told his companions of the arrival of the army, [13] those who were cowardly and distrustful of God's justice ran off and got away. [14] Others sold all their remaining property, and at the same time implored the Lord to rescue those who had been sold by the ungodly Nicanor before he ever met them, [15] if not for their own sake, then for the sake of the covenants made with their ancestors, and because he had called them by his holy and glorious name. [16] But Maccabeus gathered his forces together, to the number six thousand, and exhorted them

---

a   Gk *he*
b   Gk *one of the first*

---

trast 1 Macc 1.62–63; 2.29–41; 3.8. In 1 Macc it is not the death of the martyrs but Judas's valor that turns away the wrath. In 2 Macc the deaths increase the suffering of Israel to such a degree that God is moved to intervene for them; cf. Deut 32.36; Bar 4.

8.1–7: Judas begins the revolt. See 1 Macc 3.1–41. **2–4:** The troops' prayer summarizes the events narrated by the book so far. **3:** *The blood that cried out to him,* cf. Gen 4.10. **4:** *Innocent babies,* 6.10; in context, this also refers, with some exaggeration, to the seven sons of ch 7. **7:** *The nights,* see 10:28; 12:6,9; 13:15; and especially 1 Macc 4:1–25.

8.8–36: First victory over Nicanor. See 1 Macc 3.38–4.25. **8:** *Philip,* see 5.22. *Ptolemy* (see 10.12–13, 1 Macc 3.38). **9:** *Nicanor son of Patroclus,* according to 1 Macc 3–4, *Gorgias* was the main figure in this campaign, but 2 Macc makes Nicanor the principal villain. Chs 14–15 narrate Judas's further clashes with him, and the book ends with the establishment of a festival commemorating his final defeat. **10:** *The tribute due to the Romans* imposed by the Treaty of Apamea (188 BCE; see 4.7n.); the Seleucids were in arrears. *Talent,* see 3.11n. **11:** *Ninety slaves for a talent* was half or less of the usual price. **13:** *Ran off,* 1 Macc 3.55–56 portrays this as part of a ceremony mandated by Deut 20.5–8, but 2 Macc uses the occasion to emphasize the courage of those who remained. **15:** *Covenants,* see 1.2n. *Because he had called them by his . . . name,* a standard argument in prayers asking God to

not to be frightened by the enemy and not to fear the great multitude of Gentiles who were wickedly coming against them, but to fight nobly, [17] keeping before their eyes the lawless outrage that the Gentiles[a] had committed against the holy place, and the torture of the derided city, and besides, the overthrow of their ancestral way of life. [18] "For they trust to arms and acts of daring," he said, "but we trust in the Almighty God, who is able with a single nod to strike down those who are coming against us, and even, if necessary, the whole world."

[19] Moreover, he told them of the occasions when help came to their ancestors; how, in the time of Sennacherib, when one hundred eighty-five thousand perished, [20] and the time of the battle against the Galatians that took place in Babylonia, when eight thousand Jews[b] fought along with four thousand Macedonians; yet when the Macedonians were hard pressed, the eight thousand, by the help that came to them from heaven, destroyed one hundred twenty thousand Galatians[c] and took a great amount of booty.

[21] With these words he filled them with courage and made them ready to die for their laws and their country; then he divided his army into four parts. [22] He appointed his brothers also, Simon and Joseph and Jonathan, each to command a division, putting fifteen hundred men under each. [23] Besides, he appointed Eleazar to read aloud[d] from the holy book, and gave the watchword, "The help of God"; then, leading the first division himself, he joined battle with Nicanor.

[24] With the Almighty as their ally, they killed more than nine thousand of the enemy, and wounded and disabled most of Nicanor's army, and forced them all to flee. [25] They captured the money of those who had come to buy them as slaves. After pursuing them for some distance, they were obliged to return because the hour was late. [26] It was the day before the sabbath, and for that reason they did not continue their pursuit. [27] When they had collected the arms of the enemy and stripped them of their spoils, they kept the sabbath, giving great praise and thanks to the Lord, who had preserved them for that day and allotted it to them as the beginning of mercy. [28] After the sabbath they gave some of the spoils to those who had been tortured and to the widows and orphans, and distributed the rest among themselves and their children. [29] When they had done this, they made common supplication and implored the merciful Lord to be wholly reconciled with his servants.[e]

[30] In encounters with the forces of Timothy and Bacchides they killed more than twenty thousand of them and got possession of some exceedingly high strongholds, and they divided a very large amount of plunder, giving to those who had been tortured and to the orphans and widows, and also to the aged, shares equal to their own. [31] They collected the arms of the enemy,[f] and carefully stored all of them in strategic places; the

a Gk *they*
b Gk lacks *Jews*
c Gk lacks *Galatians*
d Meaning of Gk uncertain
e Gk *slaves*
f Gk *their arms*

intervene: God's own reputation was at stake; cf. Ex 32.12; Deut 32.27; 1 Macc 4.33. 19: *Sennacherib*, king of Assyria; see Isa 37.36; 2 Kings 19.35; this miracle is also cited at 15.22 . 20: *Galatians*, a people of Asia Minor, known for their invasions westward in the third century BCE and for their service as mercenaries; the battle mentioned here is otherwise unknown. If "Jews" is omitted (see textual note b), Judas would be citing a case in which God helps worthy people regardless of their identity; see 4.35–36n. 21: *Four parts*, Judas commanded the first (v. 23). 22: *His brothers*, see 1 Macc 2.2–5. Although they scarcely figure in 2 Macc, *Simon* was high priest from 142 to 134 BCE (see 1 Macc 13–16), and *Jonathan* from 160 to 143 or 142 (see 1 Macc 9.23–12.53). *Joseph*, perhaps John is meant; see 1 Macc 2.2; 9.35–36. 23: *Eleazar*, another brother, was killed at Beth-zechariah (1 Macc 2.5; 6.43–46). 25: *Captured the money of those who had come to buy them*, the punishment fitting the crime, as often in this book (4.42n.). 26: *Day before the sabbath* required preparations; compare 12.38; Mk 15.42. 1 Macc 4.15–16 has no such religious explanation; rather, the Jews broke off the pursuit when it became too dangerous. 27–29: *Beginning of mercy . . . wholly reconciled with his servants*, completes the process predicted at 7.33. 30–33: This scene is located here, although out of place chronologically, to illustrate the pious practice of sharing spoils

rest of the spoils they carried to Jerusalem. [32] They killed the commander of Timothy's forces, a most wicked man, and one who had greatly troubled the Jews. [33] While they were celebrating the victory in the city of their ancestors, they burned those who had set fire to the sacred gates, Callisthenes and some others, who had fled into one little house; so these received the proper reward for their impiety.[a]

[34] The thrice-accursed Nicanor, who had brought the thousand merchants to buy the Jews, [35] having been humbled with the help of the Lord by opponents whom he regarded as of the least account, took off his splendid uniform and made his way alone like a runaway slave across the country until he reached Antioch, having succeeded chiefly in the destruction of his own army! [36] So he who had undertaken to secure tribute for the Romans by the capture of the people of Jerusalem proclaimed that the Jews had a Defender, and that therefore the Jews were invulnerable, because they followed the laws ordained by him.

9 About that time, as it happened, Antiochus had retreated in disorder from the region of Persia. [2] He had entered the city called Persepolis and attempted to rob the temples and control the city. Therefore the people rushed to the rescue with arms, and Antiochus and his army were defeated,[b] with the result that Antiochus was put to flight by the inhabitants and beat a shameful retreat. [3] While he was in Ecbatana, news came to him of what had happened to Nicanor and the forces of Timothy. [4] Transported with rage, he conceived the idea of turning upon the Jews the injury done by those who had put him to flight; so he ordered his charioteer to drive without stopping until he completed the journey. But the judgment of heaven rode with him! For in his arrogance he said, "When I get there I will make Jerusalem a cemetery of Jews."

[5] But the all-seeing Lord, the God of Israel, struck him with an incurable and invisible blow. As soon as he stopped speaking he was seized with a pain in his bowels, for which there was no relief, and with sharp internal tortures— [6] and that very justly, for he had tortured the bowels of others with many and strange inflictions. [7] Yet he did not in any way stop his insolence, but was even more filled with arrogance, breathing fire in his rage against the Jews, and giving orders to drive even faster. And so it came about that he fell out of his chariot as it was rushing along, and the fall was so hard as to torture every limb of his body. [8] Thus he who only a little while before had thought in his superhuman arrogance that he could command the waves of the sea, and had imagined that he could weigh the high mountains in a balance, was brought down to earth and carried in a litter, making the power of God manifest to all. [9] And so the ungodly man's body swarmed with worms, and while he was still living in anguish and pain, his flesh rotted away, and because of

---

[a] Meaning of Gk uncertain
[b] Gk *they were defeated*

---

with the needy (see Num 31.25–47; 1 Sam 30.21–25). **34:** *Thrice-accursed Nicanor*, as in 15.3. **35:** *Having succeeded chiefly in the destruction of his own army*, the author loves to gloat; compare e.g., v. 25; 3.28; 5.9–10; 9.8–10. **36:** *Proclaimed*, like Heliodorus (see 3.39n.), *that the Jews had a Defender*, i.e., God; compare 11.13.

9.1–12: Antiochus's retreat and illness. See 1 Macc 6.1–16. Antiochus IV Epiphanes began his eastern campaign in 165 BCE, leaving behind his young son Antiochus Eupator with a guardian, Lysias (1 Macc 3.31). 2 Macc simplifies matters by first mentioning that pair only after recounting Antiochus IV's demise; see 10.10–11. For another version of the king's defeat and death, see 1.11–17. **1:** *Antiochus* went to *Persia* to strengthen his authority there and to get funds. **2:** *Persepolis*, the capital of Persia, near modern Shiraz, founded by Darius I. **3:** Antiochus was on his way to Babylon (1 Macc 6.4) but apparently went north by way of Ecbatana (modern Hamadan). **4:** *But the judgment of heaven rode with him*, as elsewhere in this chapter, the author employs irony: Antiochus thinks he will punish the Jews but does not even know his own nemesis is riding along with him. **5:** *Incurable*, as in Isa 14.6. That chapter, on the fall of the king of Babylon, informs other parts of this chapter as well. **6:** *Tortured the bowels*, both by inflicting pain and by forcing Jews to eat forbidden foods (chs 6–7). **8:** *Command the waves of the sea*, 5.21. *Weigh the high mountains in a balance* is something only God can do (Isa 40.12).

the stench the whole army felt revulsion at his decay. [10] Because of his intolerable stench no one was able to carry the man who a little while before had thought that he could touch the stars of heaven. [11] Then it was that, broken in spirit, he began to lose much of his arrogance and to come to his senses under the scourge of God, for he was tortured with pain every moment. [12] And when he could not endure his own stench, he uttered these words, "It is right to be subject to God; mortals should not think that they are equal to God."[a]

[13] Then the abominable fellow made a vow to the Lord, who would no longer have mercy on him, stating [14] that the holy city, which he was hurrying to level to the ground and to make a cemetery, he was now declaring to be free; [15] and the Jews, whom he had not considered worth burying but had planned to throw out with their children for the wild animals and for the birds to eat, he would make, all of them, equal to citizens of Athens; [16] and the holy sanctuary, which he had formerly plundered, he would adorn with the finest offerings; and all the holy vessels he would give back, many times over; and the expenses incurred for the sacrifices he would provide from his own revenues; [17] and in addition to all this he also would become a Jew and would visit every inhabited place to proclaim the power of God. [18] But when his sufferings did not in any way abate, for the judgment of God had justly come upon him, he gave up all hope for himself and wrote to the Jews the following letter, in the form of a supplication. This was its content:

[19] "To his worthy Jewish citizens, Antiochus their king and general sends hearty greetings and good wishes for their health and prosperity. [20] If you and your children are well and your affairs are as you wish, I am glad. As my hope is in heaven, [21] I remember with affection your esteem and goodwill. On my way back from the region of Persia I suffered an annoying illness, and I have deemed it necessary to take thought for the general security of all. [22] I do not despair of my condition, for I have good hope of recovering from my illness, [23] but I observed that my father, on the occasions when he made expeditions into the upper country, appointed his successor, [24] so that, if anything unexpected happened or any unwelcome news came, the people throughout the realm would not be troubled, for they would know to whom the government was left. [25] Moreover, I understand how the princes along the borders and the neighbors of my kingdom keep watching for opportunities and waiting to see what will happen. So I have appointed my son Antiochus to be king, whom I have often entrusted and commended to most of you when I hurried off to the upper provinces; and I have written to him what is written here. [26] I therefore urge and beg you to remember the public

[a] Or *not think thoughts proper only to God*

9: *Worms*, a common motif in narratives about the death of tyrants, e.g., Jdt 16.17; Acts 12.23. *Stench*, from Joel 2.20, of "the northerner," who was easily identified as Antiochus Epiphanes (the "king of the north" of Dan 11). 10: *Touch the stars of heaven*, Isa 14.13.

9.13–27: Antiochus's vow and letter to the Jews. The author enjoys himself, concocting promises and self-humiliation by the desperate king. 14: *Free*, of taxes; perhaps also having asylum status. 15: *Not considered worth burying*, see 5.10n. 16: Cf. 3.3; 5.16. Antiochus's promises conform to his brother's practice (3.3). 17: *To proclaim the power of God*, as did Heliodorus (3.37–39) and Nicanor (8.36). 17–18: *Would visit . . . had justly come upon him*, the Greek verbs are identical, ironically underlining the contrast between Antiochus's confident promise and his inability to fulfill it. 19–27: The letter is no supplication (v. 18). Some scholars consider this to be an authentic letter, but one that was addressed only to Jews loyal to the king, bidding them to support his *son Antiochus* V (vv. 25–27); cf. the authentic letters in 11.16,22,27,34. If it is authentic, it does not fit the context. Alternatively, it may be an ironic composition by the author, designed to make Antiochus appear ridiculous. 19: *Citizens* means fellow-citizens (as in 5.6, "compatriots"), reflecting Antiochus's promise to become a Jew. By naming the addressees first Antiochus ascribes them greater importance, another example of the author's humor; contrast the authentic letters in ch 11. 23: *My father*, Antiochus III, who appointed Seleucus IV as his successor. *The upper country*, i.e., Babylonia and Persia, the inlands of Asia, as in 1 Macc 3.37; 6.1. 25: *What is written here*, lit. "What is written below," as if the letter had an appendix: more spoofing of official letters (such as 1 Macc 11.31; 12.7).

and private services rendered to you and to maintain your present goodwill, each of you, toward me and my son. [27] For I am sure that he will follow my policy and will treat you with moderation and kindness."

[28] So the murderer and blasphemer, having endured the more intense suffering, such as he had inflicted on others, came to the end of his life by a most pitiable fate, among the mountains in a strange land. [29] And Philip, one of his courtiers, took his body home; then, fearing the son of Antiochus, he withdrew to Ptolemy Philometor in Egypt.

10 Now Maccabeus and his followers, the Lord leading them on, recovered the temple and the city; [2] they tore down the altars that had been built in the public square by the foreigners, and also destroyed the sacred precincts. [3] They purified the sanctuary, and made another altar of sacrifice; then, striking fire out of flint, they offered sacrifices, after a lapse of two years, and they offered incense and lighted lamps and set out the bread of the Presence. [4] When they had done this, they fell prostrate and implored the Lord that they might never again fall into such misfortunes, but that, if they should ever sin, they might be disciplined by him with forbearance and not be handed over to blasphemous and barbarous nations. [5] It happened that on the same day on which the sanctuary had been profaned by the

foreigners, the purification of the sanctuary took place, that is, on the twenty-fifth day of the same month, which was Chislev. [6] They celebrated it for eight days with rejoicing, in the manner of the festival of booths, remembering how not long before, during the festival of booths, they had been wandering in the mountains and caves like wild animals. [7] Therefore, carrying ivy-wreathed wands and beautiful branches and also fronds of palm, they offered hymns of thanksgiving to him who had given success to the purifying of his own holy place. [8] They decreed by public edict, ratified by vote, that the whole nation of the Jews should observe these days every year.

[9] Such then was the end of Antiochus, who was called Epiphanes.

[10] Now we will tell what took place under Antiochus Eupator, who was the son of that ungodly man, and will give a brief summary of the principal calamities of the wars. [11] This man, when he succeeded to the kingdom, appointed one Lysias to have charge of the government and to be chief governor of Coelesyria and Phoenicia. [12] Ptolemy, who was called Macron, took the lead in showing justice to the Jews because of the wrong that had been done to them, and attempted to maintain peaceful relations with them. [13] As a result he was accused before Eupator by the king's Friends.

Cf. 11.17n. **26:** *Your present goodwill*, the way this contradicts the facts so blatantly again constitutes authorial humor.

9.28–29: Antiochus's death. *Philip* apparently tried to seize the Seleucid government (1 Macc 6.55–56) without success and so went over to their enemy, Ptolemy VI (see 4.21). As cuneiform evidence attests, Antiochus died late in 164 BCE, around the same time as the rededication of the Temple.

10.1–8: Rededication of the Temple (cf. 1 Macc 4.36–61). This passage, needed to support the invitation in the letters prefaced to the book, seems to have been inserted by the Judean authors of those letters. It interrupts the preceding account, which continues in 10.9, and in contrast to the book as a whole displays an interest in the Temple and an antipathy for Gentiles. **1:** *The temple and the city*, historical order reversed; contrast 3.1–3; 4.48; 15.17. **3:** *Striking fire out of flint*, lit. "igniting rocks and extracting fire from them"; see 1.10–2.18n. The *incense, lamps*, and *bread of the Presence*, prescribed by Ex 30.7–8; 25.30. **4:** *Disciplined*, see 6.12n. **5–6:** *Chislev . . . festival of booths*, (December 164 BCE); see 1.9,18. The Hanukkah festival, celebrated *for eight days* like Solomon's dedication of the first Temple (1 Kings 8.65–66) and Hezekiah's reconsecration (2 Chr 29.17), commemorates this event. See also 1 Macc 4.52–59. *In the mountains and caves like wild animals*, see 5.27. **7:** *Ivy-wreathed wands*, contrast 6.7. *Fronds of palm*, cf. 1 Macc 13.51; Jn 12.13.

10.9–13: Antiochus V Eupator ascends to throne. See 9.1–12n. *Antiochus V*, son of Antiochus IV Epiphanes, ruled 164–162 BCE, when he was murdered by order of Demetrius I at the age of eleven. **10:** *Eupator, who was the son of that ungodly man* is ironic, since "Eupator" means "who has a good father." **11:** *Lysias*, see 1 Macc 3.32–33. **12:** *Ptolemy Macron*, see 4.45. We know no more about his fair policy toward the Jews. **13:** *Philometor*, see 1.10n.

He heard himself called a traitor at every turn, because he had abandoned Cyprus, which Philometor had entrusted to him, and had gone over to Antiochus Epiphanes. Unable to command the respect due his office,[a] he took poison and ended his life.

[14] When Gorgias became governor of the region, he maintained a force of mercenaries, and at every turn kept attacking the Jews. [15] Besides this, the Idumeans, who had control of important strongholds, were harassing the Jews; they received those who were banished from Jerusalem, and endeavored to keep up the war. [16] But Maccabeus and his forces, after making solemn supplication and imploring God to fight on their side, rushed to the strongholds of the Idumeans. [17] Attacking them vigorously, they gained possession of the places, and beat off all who fought upon the wall, and slaughtered those whom they encountered, killing no fewer than twenty thousand.

[18] When at least nine thousand took refuge in two very strong towers well equipped to withstand a siege, [19] Maccabeus left Simon and Joseph, and also Zacchaeus and his troops, a force sufficient to besiege them; and he himself set off for places where he was more urgently needed. [20] But those with Simon, who were money-hungry, were bribed by some of those who were in the towers, and on receiving seventy thousand drachmas let some of them slip away. [21] When word of what had happened came to Maccabeus, he gathered the leaders of the people, and accused these men of having sold their kindred for money by setting their enemies free to fight against them. [22] Then he killed these men who had turned traitor, and immediately captured the two towers. [23] Having

success at arms in everything he undertook, he destroyed more than twenty thousand in the two strongholds.

[24] Now Timothy, who had been defeated by the Jews before, gathered a tremendous force of mercenaries and collected the cavalry from Asia in no small number. He came on, intending to take Judea by storm. [25] As he drew near, Maccabeus and his men sprinkled dust on their heads and girded their loins with sackcloth, in supplication to God. [26] Falling upon the steps before the altar, they implored him to be gracious to them and to be an enemy to their enemies and an adversary to their adversaries, as the law declares. [27] And rising from their prayer they took up their arms and advanced a considerable distance from the city; and when they came near the enemy they halted. [28] Just as dawn was breaking, the two armies joined battle, the one having as pledge of success and victory not only their valor but also their reliance on the Lord, while the other made rage their leader in the fight.

[29] When the battle became fierce, there appeared to the enemy from heaven five resplendent men on horses with golden bridles, and they were leading the Jews. [30] Two of them took Maccabeus between them, and shielding him with their own armor and weapons, they kept him from being wounded. They showered arrows and thunderbolts on the enemy, so that, confused and blinded, they were thrown into disorder and cut to pieces. [31] Twenty thousand five hundred were slaughtered, besides six hundred cavalry.

[32] Timothy himself fled to a stronghold called Gazara, especially well garrisoned,

[a] Cn: Meaning of Gk uncertain

In claiming that Seleucid courtiers condemned Ptolemy Macron for moving his loyalty to the Seleucids, our author is condemning them, as usual; cf. 14.11.

10.14–23: Fighting the Idumeans. Cf. 1 Macc 5.3–5. 14: The region, of Idumea (southern Palestine) according to 12.32, which explains the link to the next verse. 15: Those who were banished from Jerusalem, apparently by Judas when he retook the city. 17: Twenty thousand, a favorite number (see also v. 23; 8.9,30). 20: Drachma, see 4.19n.

10.24–38: Fighting Timothy. 24: Timothy, who had been defeated by the Jews before, this might be a secondary gloss (see 8.30–33n.). To take Judea, but according to 1 Macc 5.6–8,11 this warfare was in Transjordan; see v. 32n. 25: Sprinkled dust, or possibly "ashes," as in Esth 4.1; cf. 14.15 and Josh 7.6. 26: The steps before the altar, compare Joel 2.17 and see 9.9n. As the law declares, at Ex 23.22. The very next verse there promises that God's angel will go before the Jews; see below, v. 29. 28: The one . . . the other, cf. 3.22–23n. 29: Horses with golden bridles, as at 3.25. 32:

where Chaereas was commander. [33] Then Maccabeus and his men were glad, and they besieged the fort for four days. [34] The men within, relying on the strength of the place, kept blaspheming terribly and uttering wicked words. [35] But at dawn of the fifth day, twenty young men in the army of Maccabeus, fired with anger because of the blasphemies, bravely stormed the wall and with savage fury cut down everyone they met. [36] Others who came up in the same way wheeled around against the defenders and set fire to the towers; they kindled fires and burned the blasphemers alive. Others broke open the gates and let in the rest of the force, and they occupied the city. [37] They killed Timothy, who was hiding in a cistern, and his brother Chaereas, and Apollophanes. [38] When they had accomplished these things, with hymns and thanksgivings they blessed the Lord who shows great kindness to Israel and gives them the victory.

11

Very soon after this, Lysias, the king's guardian and kinsman, who was in charge of the government, being vexed at what had happened, [2] gathered about eighty thousand infantry and all his cavalry and came against the Jews. He intended to make the city a home for Greeks, [3] and to levy tribute on the temple as he did on the sacred places of the other nations, and to put up the high priesthood for sale every year. [4] He took no account whatever of the power of God, but was elated with his ten thousands of infantry, and his thousands of cavalry, and his eighty

elephants. [5] Invading Judea, he approached Beth-zur, which was a fortified place about five stadia[a] from Jerusalem, and pressed it hard.

[6] When Maccabeus and his men got word that Lysias[b] was besieging the strongholds, they and all the people, with lamentations and tears, prayed the Lord to send a good angel to save Israel. [7] Maccabeus himself was the first to take up arms, and he urged the others to risk their lives with him to aid their kindred. Then they eagerly rushed off together. [8] And there, while they were still near Jerusalem, a horseman appeared at their head, clothed in white and brandishing weapons of gold. [9] And together they all praised the merciful God, and were strengthened in heart, ready to assail not only humans but the wildest animals or walls of iron. [10] They advanced in battle order, having their heavenly ally, for the Lord had mercy on them. [11] They hurled themselves like lions against the enemy, and laid low eleven thousand of them and sixteen hundred cavalry, and forced all the rest to flee. [12] Most of them got away stripped and wounded, and Lysias himself escaped by disgraceful flight.

[13] As he was not without intelligence, he pondered over the defeat that had befallen him, and realized that the Hebrews were invincible because the mighty God fought

a   Meaning of Gk uncertain
b   Gk *he*

Gazara (Gezer) was conquered by the Hasmoneans only decades later (1 Macc 13.43–48); here we should probably read (as in 1 Macc 5.8) "Jazer," a town in Transjordan, west of Amman. *Chaereas*, Timothy's brother, according to v. 37. **37**: *Timothy, who was hiding in a cistern*. A *cistern* was a large pit with plaster walls that stored water. The author often denies his enemies honorable death in battle; compare 8.34–35; 9.1–2; 11.12; 12.35.

11.1–15: Beth-zur campaign. Compare 1 Macc 4.26–35 and 6.31. Beth-zur was a fortress 16 mi (25 km) southsoutheast of Jerusalem. **1**: *Lysias*, see 9.1–12n. *Kinsman*, honorific usage, as at 1 Macc 11.31; compare v. 22, "brother." **2**: *He intended*, lit. "thinking"; see v. 4n. **3**: *High priesthood for sale every year*, which would demean it greatly, for traditionally, until Jason (4.7; cf. 4.24), it had been held for life and passed from father to son. **4**: *He took no account whatever*, lit. "not thinking more," responding to the verb in v. 2: i.e., Lysias depended upon his own thoughts, and did not give more consideration to the power of God. He will learn: see v. 13. *Elephants*, often used to force openings in opposing ranks of soldiers (cf. 1 Macc 1.17; 3.34; 6.34–35. **5**: *Five stadia*, lit. "five schoinoi"; a "schoinos" was a Persian measure popular in Egypt, equivalent to ca. thirty stadia (see 12.10–28n.), so the distance here is approximately 18 mi (29 km), which is close to the actual distance of 16 mi (26 km). **6**: *A good angel*, as at 15.23; see 10.26n. **12**: *Lysias himself escaped by disgraceful flight*, see 10.37n. **13–15**: According to 1 Macc 4.35 no peace was made, but Lysias returned to Antioch for reinforcements. He may have heard of Antiochus's death and hastened home to take control. **13**: *God fought on their side*, as at 8.36.

on their side. So he sent to them [14] and persuaded them to settle everything on just terms, promising that he would persuade the king, constraining him to be their friend.[a] [15] Maccabeus, having regard for the common good, agreed to all that Lysias urged. For the king granted every request in behalf of the Jews which Maccabeus delivered to Lysias in writing.

[16] The letter written to the Jews by Lysias was to this effect:

"Lysias to the people of the Jews, greetings. [17] John and Absalom, who were sent by you, have delivered your signed communication and have asked about the matters indicated in it. [18] I have informed the king of everything that needed to be brought before him, and he has agreed to what was possible. [19] If you will maintain your goodwill toward the government, I will endeavor in the future to help promote your welfare. [20] And concerning such matters and their details, I have ordered these men and my representatives to confer with you. [21] Farewell. The one hundred forty-eighth year,[b] Dioscorinthius twenty-fourth."

[22] The king's letter ran thus:

"King Antiochus to his brother Lysias, greetings. [23] Now that our father has gone on to the gods, we desire that the subjects of the kingdom be undisturbed in caring for their own affairs. [24] We have heard that the Jews do not consent to our father's change to Greek customs, but prefer their own way of living and ask that their own customs be allowed them. [25] Accordingly, since we choose that this nation also should be free from disturbance, our decision is that their temple be restored to them and that they shall live according to the customs of their ancestors. [26] You will do well, therefore, to send word to them and give them pledges of friendship, so that they may know our policy and be of good cheer and go on happily in the conduct of their own affairs."

[27] To the nation the king's letter was as follows:

"King Antiochus to the senate of the Jews and to the other Jews, greetings. [28] If you are well, it is as we desire. We also are in good health. [29] Menelaus has informed us that you wish to return home and look after your own affairs. [30] Therefore those who go home by the thirtieth of Xanthicus will have our pledge of friendship and full permission [31] for the Jews to enjoy their own food and laws, just as formerly, and none of them shall be molested in any way for what may have been done in ignorance. [32] And I have also sent Menelaus to encourage you.

a Meaning of Gk uncertain
b 164 B.C.

11.16–38: Four official letters. These are usually assumed to be authentic, but their location here, after the death of Antiochus IV (ch 9) and ascent of Eupator to the throne (ch 10), is problematic. True, the second letter is definitely by Antiochus Eupator, who refers to his father's death in v. 23. But the other three bear dates in 164 BCE, when Antiochus IV Epiphanes was still alive and ruling, although campaigning in the east; see 9.28–29n. The author's mistaken assumption that all four letters are from the period after that king's death caused problems in the narrative; see 12.1n., 12.10n., and 13.23n.

11.16–21: Lysias's letter to the Jews. 17: John, perhaps Judas's brother (1 Macc 2.2); for Absalom, see 1 Macc 11.70; 13.11. Your signed communication, read "your communication attached below"; the reference is to the document mentioned in v. 15, which was unfortunately not preserved. **18:** And he has agreed, read "and I have agreed" (see vv. 35–36); Lysias distinguishes between decisions he is authorized to take and others that require the king's attention. **19:** Maintain your goodwill, Lysias diplomatically ignores the warfare. **21:** The one hundred forty-eighth year of the Seleucid era ran from autumn 165 to autumn 164; the name of the month is corrupt. The date is before Judas rededicated the Temple.

11.22–26: The king's letter to Lysias. 24: We have heard that the Jews do not consent, more diplomatic understatement. **25:** Temple be restored . . . live according to the customs of their ancestors, Antiochus rescinds his father's decrees against Judaism (ch 6), ignoring the fact that the Temple was already in Jewish hands.

11.27–33: The king's letter to the Jews. 29: Menelaus as late as spring 164 BCE was attempting to mediate between Antiochus and the Jews. **30:** Thirtieth of Xanthicus, equivalent to Heb Nisan (March/April). **31:** Their own food and laws, the special emphasis upon food corresponds to that focus of the decrees (chs 6–7; 1 Macc 1.62–63). **33:** Xanthicus fifteenth, the amnesty's deadline was only two weeks later (v. 30), which is unlikely. Given

[33] Farewell. The one hundred forty-eighth year,[a] Xanthicus fifteenth."

[34] The Romans also sent them a letter, which read thus:

"Quintus Memmius and Titus Manius, envoys of the Romans, to the people of the Jews, greetings. [35] With regard to what Lysias the kinsman of the king has granted you, we also give consent. [36] But as to the matters that he decided are to be referred to the king, as soon as you have considered them, send some one promptly so that we may make proposals appropriate for you. For we are on our way to Antioch. [37] Therefore make haste and send messengers so that we may have your judgment. [38] Farewell. The one hundred forty-eighth year,[a] Xanthicus fifteenth."

12 When this agreement had been reached, Lysias returned to the king, and the Jews went about their farming.

[2] But some of the governors in various places, Timothy and Apollonius son of Gennaeus, as well as Hieronymus and Demophon, and in addition to these Nicanor the governor of Cyprus, would not let them live quietly and in peace. [3] And the people of Joppa did so ungodly a deed as this: they invited the Jews who lived among them to embark, with their wives and children, on boats that they had provided, as though there were no ill will to the Jews;[b] [4] and this was done by public vote of the city. When they accepted, because they wished to live peaceably and suspected nothing, the people of Joppa[c] took them out to sea and drowned them, at least two hundred. [5] When Judas heard of the cruelty visited on his compatriots, he gave orders to his men [6] and, calling upon God, the righteous judge, attacked the murderers of his kindred. He set fire to the harbor by night, burned the boats, and massacred those who had taken refuge there. [7] Then, because the city's gates were closed, he withdrew, intending to come again and root out the whole community of Joppa. [8] But learning that the people in Jamnia meant in the same way to wipe out the Jews who were living among them, [9] he attacked the Jamnites by night and set fire to the harbor and the fleet, so that the glow of the light was seen in Jerusalem, thirty miles[d] distant.

[10] When they had gone more than a mile[e] from there, on their march against Timothy, at least five thousand Arabs with five

a   164 B.C.
b   Gk *to them*
c   Gk *they*
d   Gk *two hundred forty stadia*
e   Gk *nine stadia*

the identity of the date in v. 38, which too is suspicious, it is likely that this date is corrupt.

11.34–38: Letter of the Romans to the Jews. 34: *The Romans* in this period were periodically sending embassies to the East. Judas apparently asked them to use their influence with the Seleucids, just as a few years later he would establish a mutual defense pact with them (1 Macc 8). **35–36:** *What Lysias . . . has granted . . . referred to the king,* see v. 18n.

12.1–9: Clashes in coastal towns. 1: *This agreement,* lit. "these covenants." But the documents in ch 11 are not covenants; they are one–sided decisions. Chapter 13, in contrast, does end with "covenants" (13.25, same term in Greek). Given the author's difficulties coordinating ch 13 with earlier material (see 13.1–26n.), perhaps it originally preceded ch 12. *The Jews went about their farming,* a pastoral image of returning "to their own affairs" (11.23,26,29). **2:** *Timothy,* 8.30–33; 10.24–37. *Governor of Cyprus,* read "Cypriarch," i.e., commander of mercenaries from Cyprus (cf. 5.24n.). **3:** *Joppa,* Jaffa, next to modern Tel Aviv; a major port on the Mediterranean, later conquered by the Hasmoneans (1 Macc 12.33–34). **8:** *Jamnia,* ca. 14 mi (22 km) south of Joppa; compare v. 40 and 1 Macc 5.58.

12.10–28: Fighting in Transjordan. This section parallels much of 1 Macc 5, which contains a fuller account. The order is confused here, for "one mile" (v. 10, lit. "nine stadia"; a stadion was ca. 625 ft [190 m]) would not take Judas's forces from the Mediterranean coast to Transjordan; "ninety–five miles" (v. 17) could. Perhaps the two stories have been erroneously exchanged. **10:** *Timothy,* some confusion is present here too, as he had been killed at 10.37; see 11.16–38n. **10–11:** *Arabs . . . nomads,* the author often varies his terminology; compare "no light matter . . . not easy" in 2.26–27 and "festival of weeks . . . Pentecost" in 12.31–32. 1 Macc 5.25 identifies these Arabs as Nabateans and claims they were peaceable from the outset; 2 Macc first allows Judas another heroic

hundred cavalry attacked them. ¹¹ After a hard fight, Judas and his companions, with God's help, were victorious. The defeated nomads begged Judas to grant them pledges of friendship, promising to give him livestock and to help his peopleª in all other ways. ¹² Judas, realizing that they might indeed be useful in many ways, agreed to make peace with them; and after receiving his pledges they went back to their tents.

¹³ He also attacked a certain town that was strongly fortified with earthworksᵇ and walls, and inhabited by all sorts of Gentiles. Its name was Caspin. ¹⁴ Those who were within, relying on the strength of the walls and on their supply of provisions, behaved most insolently toward Judas and his men, railing at them and even blaspheming and saying unholy things. ¹⁵ But Judas and his men, calling upon the great Sovereign of the world, who without battering rams or engines of war overthrew Jericho in the days of Joshua, rushed furiously upon the walls. ¹⁶ They took the town by the will of God, and slaughtered untold numbers, so that the adjoining lake, a quarter of a mileᶜ wide, appeared to be running over with blood.

¹⁷ When they had gone ninety-five milesᵈ from there, they came to Charax, to the Jews who are called Toubiani. ¹⁸ They did not find Timothy in that region, for he had by then left there without accomplishing anything, though in one place he had left a very strong garrison. ¹⁹ Dositheus and Sosipater, who were captains under Maccabeus, marched out and destroyed those whom Timothy had left in the stronghold, more than ten thousand men. ²⁰ But Maccabeus arranged his army in divisions, set menª in command of the divisions, and hurried after Timothy, who had with him one hundred twenty thousand infantry and two thousand five hundred cavalry. ²¹ When Timothy learned of

the approach of Judas, he sent off the women and the children and also the baggage to a place called Carnaim; for that place was hard to besiege and difficult of access because of the narrowness of all the approaches. ²² But when Judas's first division appeared, terror and fear came over the enemy at the manifestation to them of him who sees all things. In their flight they rushed headlong in every direction, so that often they were injured by their own men and pierced by the points of their own swords. ²³ Judas pressed the pursuit with the utmost vigor, putting the sinners to the sword, and destroyed as many as thirty thousand.

²⁴ Timothy himself fell into the hands of Dositheus and Sosipater and their men. With great guile he begged them to let him go in safety, because he held the parents of most of them, and the brothers of some, to whom no consideration would be shown. ²⁵ And when with many words he had confirmed his solemn promise to restore them unharmed, they let him go, for the sake of saving their kindred.

²⁶ Then Judasᵉ marched against Carnaim and the temple of Atargatis, and slaughtered twenty-five thousand people. ²⁷ After the rout and destruction of these, he marched also against Ephron, a fortified town where Lysias lived with multitudes of people of all nationalities.ᵇ Stalwart young men took their stand before the walls and made a vigorous defense; and great stores of war engines and missiles were there. ²⁸ But the Jewsᶠ called upon the Sovereign who with power shatters

ª Gk *them*
ᵇ Meaning of Gk uncertain
ᶜ Gk *two stadia*
ᵈ Gk *seven hundred fifty stadia*
ᵉ Gk *he*
ᶠ Gk *they*

victory before they make peace. **13:** *All sorts of Gentiles* is pejorative, as in v. 27. *Caspin,* ca. 10 mi (16 km) east of Lake Gennesaret (the Sea of Galilee). **15:** *Overthrew Jericho,* Josh 6.1–21. **16:** *Adjoining lake,* perhaps a swamp. **17:** *Charax,* "fortified camp"; location unknown. *Toubiani,* Jews associated with the Tobiad family (3.11n.); cf. 1 Macc 5.13. **21:** *Women . . . children . . . baggage,* lit. "women, children, and other baggage," reflecting patriarchal values. *Carnaim,* farther east in Transjordan (1 Macc 5.26–27). **22:** *Manifestation,* epiphany; see 2.21n. *Injured by their own men,* a literary convention in battle scenes. **26:** *Carnaim,* see v. 21n. *Atargatis* was a Syrian goddess, corresponding to the Canaanite Ashtoreth; cf. "Ashteroth-karnaim" in Gen 14.5. **27:** *Ephron,* ca. 8 mi (13 km) east of the Jordan River, opposite Scythopolis (v. 29; 1 Macc 5.46–51). *War engines,* large catapults.

the might of his enemies, and they got the town into their hands, and killed as many as twenty-five thousand of those who were in it.

²⁹ Setting out from there, they hastened to Scythopolis, which is seventy-five miles[a] from Jerusalem. ³⁰ But when the Jews who lived there bore witness to the goodwill that the people of Scythopolis had shown them and their kind treatment of them in times of misfortune, ³¹ they thanked them and exhorted them to be well disposed to their race in the future also. Then they went up to Jerusalem, as the festival of weeks was close at hand.

³² After the festival called Pentecost, they hurried against Gorgias, the governor of Idumea, ³³ who came out with three thousand infantry and four hundred cavalry. ³⁴ When they joined battle, it happened that a few of the Jews fell. ³⁵ But a certain Dositheus, one of Bacenor's men, who was on horseback and was a strong man, caught hold of Gorgias, and grasping his cloak was dragging him off by main strength, wishing to take the accursed man alive, when one of the Thracian cavalry bore down on him and cut off his arm; so Gorgias escaped and reached Marisa.

³⁶ As Esdris and his men had been fighting for a long time and were weary, Judas called upon the Lord to show himself their ally and leader in the battle. ³⁷ In the language of their ancestors he raised the battle cry, with hymns; then he charged against Gorgias's troops when they were not expecting it, and put them to flight.

³⁸ Then Judas assembled his army and went to the city of Adullam. As the seventh day was coming on, they purified themselves according to the custom, and kept the sabbath there.

³⁹ On the next day, as had now become necessary, Judas and his men went to take up the bodies of the fallen and to bring them back to lie with their kindred in the sepulchres of their ancestors. ⁴⁰ Then under the tunic of each one of the dead they found sacred tokens of the idols of Jamnia, which the law forbids the Jews to wear. And it became clear to all that this was the reason these men had fallen. ⁴¹ So they all blessed the ways of the Lord, the righteous judge, who reveals the things that are hidden; ⁴² and they turned to supplication, praying that the sin that had been committed might be wholly blotted out. The noble Judas exhorted the people to keep themselves free from sin, for they had seen with their own eyes what had happened as the result of the sin of those who had fallen. ⁴³ He also took up a collection, man by man, to the amount of two thousand drachmas of silver, and sent it to Jerusalem to provide for a sin offering. In doing this he acted very well and honorably, taking account of the resurrection. ⁴⁴ For if he were not expecting that those who had fallen would rise again, it would have been superfluous and foolish to pray for the dead. ⁴⁵ But if he was looking to the splendid reward that is laid up for those who fall asleep in godliness, it was a holy and pious thought. Therefore he made atonement for the dead, so that they might be delivered from their sin.

13 In the one hundred forty-ninth year[b] word came to Judas and his men that Antiochus Eupator was coming with a great

---

[a] Gk *six hundred stadia*

[b] 163 B.C.

12.29–31: Return to Jerusalem. 29: *Scythopolis* (Hellenistic Beth-shan), a major city west of the Jordan River, ca. 16 mi (26 km) south of the Sea of Galilee (Judg 1.27; 1 Kings 4.12). **31:** *Went up,* the usual verb for pilgrimage to Jerusalem; e.g. 1 Sam 1.3; Acts 21.15. **31–32:** *Festival of weeks . . . Pentecost,* this holiday comes seven weeks ("Pentecost" = fifty [days]) after Passover (Lev 23.15–16; Acts 2.1). **35:** *Thracians* were well-known mercenaries in the Hellenistic period. *Marisa* was a major Idumean town, 20 mi (32 km) southwest of Jerusalem. **37:** *Language of their ancestors,* i.e., Hebrew. **38:** *Adullam,* ca. 10 mi (16 km) southeast of Marisa. **40:** Although only "a few" Jews had died (v. 34), it is important for the author that it is sin, not the chances of war, that caused their death. *Sacred tokens of the idols of Jamnia,* probably taken as booty. *Which the law forbids,* see Num 33.52; Deut 7.25–26. **43–45:** The author expounds upon Judas's care for the dead as evidence of his belief that their lives did not end with death; see 7.9n. **45:** *Fall asleep,* a common metaphor for death.

13.1–26: A new invasion. This chapter, which makes no allusion to ch 11, reports yet another campaign by Lysias and Antiochus Eupator that focuses on Beth-zur (vv. 18–22). This is problematic, both because no at-

army against Judea, [2] and with him Lysias, his guardian, who had charge of the government. Each of them had a Greek force of one hundred ten thousand infantry, five thousand three hundred cavalry, twenty-two elephants, and three hundred chariots armed with scythes.

[3] Menelaus also joined them and with utter hypocrisy urged Antiochus on, not for the sake of his country's welfare, but because he thought that he would be established in office. [4] But the King of kings aroused the anger of Antiochus against the scoundrel; and when Lysias informed him that this man was to blame for all the trouble, he ordered them to take him to Beroea and to put him to death by the method that is customary in that place. [5] For there is a tower there, fifty cubits high, full of ashes, and it has a rim running around it that on all sides inclines precipitously into the ashes. [6] There they all push to destruction anyone guilty of sacrilege or notorious for other crimes. [7] By such a fate it came about that Menelaus the lawbreaker died, without even burial in the earth. [8] And this was eminently just; because he had committed many sins against the altar whose fire and ashes were holy, he met his death in ashes.

[9] The king with barbarous arrogance was coming to show the Jews things far worse than those that had been done[a] in his father's time. [10] But when Judas heard of this, he ordered the people to call upon the Lord day and night, now if ever to help those who were on the point of being deprived of the law and their country and the holy temple, [11] and not to let the people who had just begun to revive fall into the hands of the blasphemous Gentiles. [12] When they had all joined in the same petition and had implored the merciful Lord with weeping and fasting and lying prostrate for three days without ceasing, Judas exhorted them and ordered them to stand ready.

[13] After consulting privately with the elders, he determined to march out and decide the matter by the help of God before the king's army could enter Judea and get possession of the city. [14] So, committing the decision to the Creator of the world and exhorting his troops to fight bravely to the death for the laws, temple, city, country, and commonwealth, he pitched his camp near Modein. [15] He gave his troops the watchword, "God's victory," and with a picked force of the bravest young men, he attacked the king's pavilion at night and killed as many as two thousand men in the camp. He stabbed[b] the leading elephant and its rider. [16] In the end they filled the camp with terror and confusion and withdrew in triumph. [17] This happened, just as day was dawning, because the Lord's help protected him.

[18] The king, having had a taste of the daring of the Jews, tried strategy in attacking their positions. [19] He advanced against Beth-

a Or *the worst of the things that had been done*
b Meaning of Gk uncertain

tempt is made to coordinate this narrative with that of ch 11, and because according to the parallel narrative in 1 Maccabees this second campaign began around Beth-zur (1 Macc 6.31) but quickly moved north to Beth-zechariah (1 Macc 6.32–47), which is not mentioned here. Similarly, Philip's role is puzzling; see 13.23n. It appears that the author was confused. **3–8:** Death of Menelaus. This interruptive interlude takes care of a loose end. **3:** *Menelaus,* see 4.23–50n. **4:** *King of kings,* a typical Persian epithet. Here it refers to God. *Beroea,* Aleppo in northern Syria. **5:** *Fifty cubits high,* cf. Esth 7.9; a cubit was ca. 18 in (45 cm). This method was Persian; we are not told here whether the ashes were hot, so that Menelaus died by burning, or cold, and so by suffocating. **7:** *Without even burial,* see 5.10n. **8:** The apparent artificiality of this explanation of poetic justice shows how important the notion is for 2 Macc; see 4.42n. **9:** To explain why the invasion continued although the real troublemaker had been recognized and executed, the author can only claim that the king's attitude toward the Jews changed for the worse; no reason is given. **11:** *Just begun to revive,* so relapse would be all the worse; cf. 14.36. **12:** *Fasting . . . for three days,* as in Esth 4.16. **14:** *Modein,* ca. 20 mi (32 km) northwest of Jerusalem, the hometown of the Hasmoneans (1 Macc 2.1). **15:** *Watchword,* as in 8.23. *Leading elephant and its rider,* cf. 1 Macc 6.43–46, where Eleazar dies after heroically killing the lead elephant. **16:** According to 1 Macc 6.47, the Jews fled. **19:** *Beth-zur,*

zur, a strong fortress of the Jews, was turned back, attacked again,[a] and was defeated. [20] Judas sent in to the garrison whatever was necessary. [21] But Rhodocus, a man from the ranks of the Jews, gave secret information to the enemy; he was sought for, caught, and put in prison. [22] The king negotiated a second time with the people in Beth-zur, gave pledges, received theirs, withdrew, attacked Judas and his men, was defeated; [23] he got word that Philip, who had been left in charge of the government, had revolted in Antioch; he was dismayed, called in the Jews, yielded and swore to observe all their rights, settled with them and offered sacrifice, honored the sanctuary and showed generosity to the holy place. [24] He received Maccabeus, left Hegemonides as governor from Ptolemais to Gerar, [25] and went to Ptolemais. The people of Ptolemais were indignant over the treaty; in fact they were so angry that they wanted to annul its terms.[b] [26] Lysias took the public platform, made the best possible defense, convinced them, appeased them, gained their goodwill, and set out for Antioch. This is how the king's attack and withdrawal turned out.

14 Three years later, word came to Judas and his men that Demetrius son of Seleucus had sailed into the harbor of Tripolis with a strong army and a fleet, [2] and had taken possession of the country, having made away with Antiochus and his guardian Lysias.

[3] Now a certain Alcimus, who had formerly been high priest but had willfully defiled himself in the times of separation,[c] realized that there was no way for him to be safe or to have access again to the holy altar, [4] and went to King Demetrius in about the one hundred fifty-first year,[d] presenting to him a crown of gold and a palm, and besides these some of the customary olive branches from the temple. During that day he kept quiet. [5] But he found an opportunity that furthered his mad purpose when he was invited by Demetrius to a meeting of the council and was asked about the attitude and intentions of the Jews. He answered:

[6] "Those of the Jews who are called Hasideans, whose leader is Judas Maccabeus, are keeping up war and stirring up sedition, and will not let the kingdom attain tranquility. [7] Therefore I have laid aside my ancestral glory—I mean the high priesthood—and have

---

a Or *faltered*
b Meaning of Gk uncertain
c Other ancient authorities read *of mixing*
d 161 B.C.

see 11.1–15n. **23:** *Philip, who had been left in charge of the government, had revolted,* this comment is confusing, since 9.29 reported that Philip had fled to Egypt out of fear of Eupator; see 11.16–38n. **24:** *Received Maccabeus,* formally taking leave of him, as at 3.35. *Hegemonides,* like Heliodorus (3.7) and Ptolemy Macron (10:12), this Seleucid official is known from inscriptions. *From Ptolemais to Gerar,* the Palestinian coastal region from Acco down to below Gaza; for this administrative district, see also 1 Macc 11.59 and 15.38. **25:** *The treaty,* see 12.1n.

14.1–25: Alcimus and Nicanor. Enter a new villain, Alcimus, said to have formerly been high priest, which is possible if Antiochus V appointed him after the death of Menelaus. He incites the new Seleucid king against Judas, and a royal expedition is sent out, commanded by Nicanor, who is taken by the author, perhaps mistakenly, to be identical with the "thrice-accursed" (8.34; 15.3) villain of ch 8. According to 1 Macc 7.12–25 the first campaign incited by Alcimus was commanded by Bacchides; 2 Macc assigns it to Nicanor in light of its general focus upon him, culminating in his defeat in ch 15 and the festival established to celebrate it (15.36); cf. 8.9n. **1:** *Three years later,* about 162 or 161 BCE. *Demetrius I, son of Seleucus* IV (reigned 162–150), had been sent to Rome to replace Antiochus IV Epiphanes as a hostage. When Seleucus IV died in 175 BCE, Demetrius was still a child, and Antiochus assumed the throne (see 4.7n.). After the death of Antiochus IV, Demetrius viewed his cousin Antiochus V Eupator as a usurper (see 4.7n.). Demetrius escaped from Rome in the late summer of 162 BCE and quickly established himself upon the Seleucid throne. *Tripolis,* in northern Lebanon. **2:** See 1 Macc 7.3–4. **3:** *A certain Alcimus,* alone; compare 1 Macc 7.5, where he leads a delegation; see 3.4n. *Times of separation* refers to the days of Antiochus's decrees. **4:** *Crown of gold and a palm,* customary gifts to kings; compare 1 Macc 13.37. **6–11:** Alcimus's speech is meant to be understood as self-serving. His concern for the commonweal is a parody serving to contrast him with Onias (4.1–6) **6:** *Hasideans,* meaning "pious ones"; see also 1 Macc 7.13 where they are a party separate from the Maccabees, and Judas is not their leader. In 1 Macc their pious peace-seeking is represented as naïve, and many of them are killed, making them, in 1 Macc 1.62–63 and 2.29–38, foils for the

now come here, [8] first because I am genuinely concerned for the interests of the king, and second because I have regard also for my compatriots. For through the folly of those whom I have mentioned our whole nation is now in no small misfortune. [9] Since you are acquainted, O king, with the details of this matter, may it please you to take thought for our country and our hard-pressed nation with the gracious kindness that you show to all. [10] For as long as Judas lives, it is impossible for the government to find peace."
[11] When he had said this, the rest of the king's Friends,[a] who were hostile to Judas, quickly inflamed Demetrius still more. [12] He immediately chose Nicanor, who had been in command of the elephants, appointed him governor of Judea, and sent him off [13] with orders to kill Judas and scatter his troops, and to install Alcimus as high priest of the great[b] temple. [14] And the Gentiles throughout Judea, who had fled before[c] Judas, flocked to join Nicanor, thinking that the misfortunes and calamities of the Jews would mean prosperity for themselves.

[15] When the Jews[d] heard of Nicanor's coming and the gathering of the Gentiles, they sprinkled dust on their heads and prayed to him who established his own people forever and always upholds his own heritage by manifesting himself. [16] At the command of the leader, they[e] set out from there immediately and engaged them in battle at a village called Dessau.[c] [17] Simon, the brother of Judas, had encountered Nicanor, but had been temporarily[f] checked because of the sudden consternation created by the enemy.

[18] Nevertheless Nicanor, hearing of the valor of Judas and his troops and their courage in battle for their country, shrank from deciding the issue by bloodshed. [19] Therefore he sent Posidonius, Theodotus, and Mattathias to give and receive pledges of friendship. [20] When the terms had been fully considered,

and the leader had informed the people, and it had appeared that they were of one mind, they agreed to the covenant. [21] The leaders[d] set a day on which to meet by themselves. A chariot came forward from each army; seats of honor were set in place; [22] Judas posted armed men in readiness at key places to prevent sudden treachery on the part of the enemy; so they duly held the consultation.

[23] Nicanor stayed on in Jerusalem and did nothing out of the way, but dismissed the flocks of people that had gathered. [24] And he kept Judas always in his presence; he was warmly attached to the man. [25] He urged him to marry and have children; so Judas[e] married, settled down, and shared the common life.

[26] But when Alcimus noticed their goodwill for one another, he took the covenant that had been made and went to Demetrius. He told him that Nicanor was disloyal to the government, since he had appointed that conspirator against the kingdom, Judas, to be his successor. [27] The king became excited and, provoked by the false accusations of that depraved man, wrote to Nicanor, stating that he was displeased with the covenant and commanding him to send Maccabeus to Antioch as a prisoner without delay.

[28] When this message came to Nicanor, he was troubled and grieved that he had to annul their agreement when the man had done no wrong. [29] Since it was not possible to oppose the king, he watched for an opportunity to accomplish this by a stratagem. [30] But Maccabeus, noticing that Nicanor was more aus-

a   Gk of the Friends
b   Gk greatest
c   Meaning of Gk uncertain
d   Gk they
e   Gk he
f   Other ancient authorities read slowly

smarter, more violent, Hasmoneans. Cf. 15.27n. **11:** *Friends,* see 1.14n. **14:** Cf. 8.11. **15:** *Dust,* see 10.25n. **16:** *Dessau,* precise location uncertain. **17:** As at 10.20, Simon is something of a foil for Judas, although not condemned. **18:** *Country,* lit. "fatherland"; see 7.2n. **23–25:** Idyllic relations between Nicanor and Judas. The author again portrays mutual respect between Jew and Gentile, as long as troublemakers do not interfere; see 4.35–36n.

14.26–15.36: Alcimus and Nicanor, continued. As elsewhere (3.4; 12.2), the idyll is destroyed, and so the story resumes, with a heavy "But." Alcimus again misrepresents the good relations between Nicanor and Judas to Demetrius, and the king responds by renewing his orders to Nicanor to assert royal rule and arrest Judas.

tere in his dealings with him and was meeting him more rudely than had been his custom, concluded that this austerity did not spring from the best motives. So he gathered not a few of his men, and went into hiding from Nicanor. ³¹ When the latter became aware that he had been cleverly outwitted by the man, he went to the great[a] and holy temple while the priests were offering the customary sacrifices, and commanded them to hand the man over. ³² When they declared on oath that they did not know where the man was whom he wanted, ³³ he stretched out his right hand toward the sanctuary, and swore this oath: "If you do not hand Judas over to me as a prisoner, I will level this shrine of God to the ground and tear down the altar, and build here a splendid temple to Dionysus."

³⁴ Having said this, he went away. Then the priests stretched out their hands toward heaven and called upon the constant Defender of our nation, in these words: ³⁵ "O Lord of all, though you have need of nothing, you were pleased that there should be a temple for your habitation among us; ³⁶ so now, O holy One, Lord of all holiness, keep undefiled forever this house that has been so recently purified."

³⁷ A certain Razis, one of the elders of Jerusalem, was denounced to Nicanor as a man who loved his compatriots and was very well thought of and for his goodwill was called father of the Jews. ³⁸ In former times, when there was no mingling with the Gentiles, he had been accused of Judaism, and he had most zealously risked body and life for Judaism. ³⁹ Nicanor, wishing to exhibit the enmity that he had for the Jews, sent more than five hundred soldiers to arrest him; ⁴⁰ for he thought that by arresting[b] him he would do them an injury. ⁴¹ When the troops were about to capture the tower and were forcing the door of the courtyard, they ordered that fire be brought and the doors burned. Being surrounded, Razis[c] fell upon his own sword, ⁴² preferring to die nobly rather than to fall into the hands of sinners and suffer outrages unworthy of his noble birth. ⁴³ But in the heat of the struggle he did not hit exactly, and the crowd was now rushing in through the doors. He courageously ran up on the wall, and bravely threw himself down into the crowd. ⁴⁴ But as they quickly drew back, a space opened and he fell in the middle of the empty space. ⁴⁵ Still alive and aflame with anger, he rose, and though his blood gushed forth and his wounds were severe he ran through the crowd; and standing upon a steep rock, ⁴⁶ with his blood now completely drained from him, he tore out his entrails, took them in both hands and hurled them at the crowd, calling upon the Lord of life and spirit to give them back to him again. This was the manner of his death.

15 When Nicanor heard that Judas and his troops were in the region of Samaria, he made plans to attack them with complete safety on the day of rest. ² When the Jews who were compelled to follow him said, "Do not destroy so savagely and barbarously, but show respect for the day that he who sees all things has honored and hallowed above other

---

a Gk *greatest*
b Meaning of Gk uncertain
c Gk *he*

Nicanor has no choice but to obey, and so the way is paved for a new clash. **28–33:** Cf. 1 Macc 7.30–38. **30:** Cf. Gen 31.2. **33:** *Stretched out his right hand*, usually a gesture of prayer (3.20; 15.12), but here it is a threat, apparently modeled on Isa 10.32, where it is ascribed to an Assyrian king leading an army against Jerusalem. The threatening gesture is answered first in the next verse and then, conclusively, at 15.32. **34:** *Toward heaven*, to protect the Temple, as in 3.39. **35:** In contrast to the parallel in 1 Macc 7.36–38, the Diaspora theology of 2 Macc emphasizes that God resides in heaven, not in what the Bible calls "the house of God." **36:** *Been so recently purified*, see 10.1–8; 13.11.

14.37–46: Martyrdom of Razis. This account of martyrdom functions similarly to those in chs 6–7. It is the premise of the victory over Nicanor depicted in the next chapter. **37:** *Father of the Jews*, honorifically; compare 11.1n. **38:** *Risked body and life for Judaism*, the reference to *Judaism* shows that Razis fought, in his way, for the same cause as did Judas and his men in theirs (2.21; 8.1). **42:** *Die nobly*, like Eleazar (6.28). **43–44:** *Courageously . . . bravely*: the Diaspora author emphasizes that martyrs share the same qualities as heroic soldiers. **46:** See 7.9n.

15.1–36: Death of Nicanor. 1: *Attack . . . on the day of rest*, cf. 5.25; 8.26. **3:** *Thrice-accursed* Nicanor, as 8.34.

days," [3] the thrice-accursed wretch asked if there were a sovereign in heaven who had commanded the keeping of the sabbath day. [4] When they declared, "It is the living Lord himself, the Sovereign in heaven, who ordered us to observe the seventh day," [5] he replied, "But I am a sovereign also, on earth, and I command you to take up arms and finish the king's business." Nevertheless, he did not succeed in carrying out his abominable design.

[6] This Nicanor in his utter boastfulness and arrogance had determined to erect a public monument of victory over Judas and his forces. [7] But Maccabeus did not cease to trust with all confidence that he would get help from the Lord. [8] He exhorted his troops not to fear the attack of the Gentiles, but to keep in mind the former times when help had come to them from heaven, and so to look for the victory that the Almighty would give them. [9] Encouraging them from the law and the prophets, and reminding them also of the struggles they had won, he made them the more eager. [10] When he had aroused their courage, he issued his orders, at the same time pointing out the perfidy of the Gentiles and their violation of oaths. [11] He armed each of them not so much with confidence in shields and spears as with the inspiration of brave words, and he cheered them all by relating a dream, a sort of vision,[a] which was worthy of belief.

[12] What he saw was this: Onias, who had been high priest, a noble and good man, of modest bearing and gentle manner, one who spoke fittingly and had been trained from childhood in all that belongs to excellence, was praying with outstretched hands for the whole body of the Jews. [13] Then in the same fashion another appeared, distinguished by his gray hair and dignity, and of marvelous majesty and authority. [14] And Onias spoke, saying, "This is a man who loves the family of Israel and prays much for the people and the holy city—Jeremiah, the prophet of God."

[15] Jeremiah stretched out his right hand and gave to Judas a golden sword, and as he gave it he addressed him thus: [16] "Take this holy sword, a gift from God, with which you will strike down your adversaries."

[17] Encouraged by the words of Judas, so noble and so effective in arousing valor and awaking courage in the souls of the young, they determined not to carry on a campaign[b] but to attack bravely, and to decide the matter by fighting hand to hand with all courage, because the city and the sanctuary and the temple were in danger. [18] Their concern for wives and children, and also for brothers and sisters[c] and relatives, lay upon them less heavily; their greatest and first fear was for the consecrated sanctuary. [19] And those who had to remain in the city were in no little distress, being anxious over the encounter in the open country.

[20] When all were now looking forward to the coming issue, and the enemy was already close at hand with their army drawn up for battle, the elephants[d] strategically stationed and the cavalry deployed on the flanks, [21] Maccabeus, observing the masses that were in front of him and the varied supply of arms and the savagery of the elephants, stretched out his hands toward heaven and called upon the Lord who works wonders; for he knew that it is not by arms, but as the Lord[e] decides, that he gains the victory for those who deserve it. [22] He called upon him in these words: "O Lord, you sent your angel in the time of King Hezekiah of Judea, and he killed fully one hundred eighty-five thousand in the camp of Sennacherib. [23] So now, O Sovereign of the heavens, send a good angel to spread terror and trembling before us. [24] By the

---

[a] Meaning of Gk uncertain
[b] Or *to remain in camp*
[c] Gk *for brothers*
[d] Gk *animals*
[e] Gk *he*

4–5: *Sovereign in heaven . . . sovereign also, on earth*, see 3.22–23n. 8–9: Cf. v. 22 and 8.19. 9: *The law and the prophets*, the Torah (Pentateuch) and the prophetic books were now regarded as scripture (see Prologue to Sirach). 10: *Violation of oaths*, 11.27–32; 14.18–29. 12–16: Judas receives the support of both priest (Onias) and prophet (Jeremiah) to defend the Jews on the Sabbath; compare the treatment of the sabbath question in 1 Macc 2.39–41. 12: On *Onias's* qualities, see 4.37n. *Was praying*, as a priest invoking God's blessing upon a congregation; see Lev 9.22 and Sir 50.20. 20: *Elephants . . . cavalry*, compare 1 Macc 6.34–38. 22: See 8.19n. 23: *Good angel*, as at

might of your arm may these blasphemers who come against your holy people be struck down." With these words he ended his prayer.

25 Nicanor and his troops advanced with trumpets and battle songs, 26 but Judas and his troops met the enemy in battle with invocations to God and prayers. 27 So, fighting with their hands and praying to God in their hearts, they laid low at least thirty-five thousand, and were greatly gladdened by God's manifestation.

28 When the action was over and they were returning with joy, they recognized Nicanor, lying dead, in full armor. 29 Then there was shouting and tumult, and they blessed the Sovereign Lord in the language of their ancestors. 30 Then the man who was ever in body and soul the defender of his people, the man who maintained his youthful goodwill toward his compatriots, ordered them to cut off Nicanor's head and arm and carry them to Jerusalem. 31 When he arrived there and had called his compatriots together and stationed the priests before the altar, he sent for those who were in the citadel. 32 He showed them the vile Nicanor's head and that profane man's arm, which had been boastfully stretched out against the holy house of the Almighty. 33 He cut out the tongue of the ungodly Nicanor and said that he would feed it piecemeal to the birds and would hang up these rewards of his folly opposite the sanctuary. 34 And they all, looking to heaven, blessed the Lord who had manifested himself, saying, "Blessed is he who has kept his own place undefiled!" 35 Judas[a] hung Nicanor's head from the citadel, a clear and conspicuous sign to everyone of the help of the Lord. 36 And they all decree by public vote never to let this day go unobserved, but to celebrate the thirteenth day of the twelfth month—which is called Adar in the Aramaic language—the day before Mordecai's day.

37 This, then, is how matters turned out with Nicanor, and from that time the city has been in the possession of the Hebrews. So I will here end my story. 38 If it is well told and to the point, that is what I myself desired; if it is poorly done and mediocre, that was the best I could do. 39 For just as it is harmful to drink wine alone, or, again, to drink water alone, while wine mixed with water is sweet and delicious and enhances one's enjoyment, so also the style of the story delights the ears of those who read the work. And here will be the end.

a Gk He

11.6. 24: *Might of your arm,* Ex 15.16. 27: *Fighting with their hands and praying,* Ps 149.6. 29: *Shouting and tumult,* words that usually bespeak fear; see 3.30; 10.30; 11.25; 12.37; 13.16. Indeed, some fear is expected among those who witness divine intervention, even on their behalf; compare Ex 14.30–31; Ps 52.6; Mk 4.41; Lk 1.65. *Language of their ancestors,* i.e., Hebrew; Palestinian Jews spoke Aramaic, but formal prayer, using the language of scripture, was typically in Hebrew. 30–36: Disposition of Nicanor's corpse; cf. 1 Macc 7.47–49. 31: *The citadel,* the garrison north of the Temple was still held by the Syrians (1 Macc 1.33; 6.18), but the Jews had built another fort (1 Macc 4.60). 32: See 14.33. 34: *Who has kept his own place undefiled,* answering, verbatim, the prayer of 14.36. 35: 1 Sam 31.9; Jdt 14.1; 1 Macc 7.47. 36: *Decreed by public vote,* as at 10.8. Compare 1 Macc 7.48–49. *Adar,* February/March. *Aramaic,* the contemporary vernacular, as opposed to Hebrew, "the language of their ancestors" (12.37; 15.29; cf. 7.8,21,27). *Mordecai's day,* the festival of Purim, celebrated on the fourteenth day of Adar (Esth 9.21). There is evidence for the celebration of Nicanor's Day even centuries later.

15.37–39: Conclusion. 37: *So I will here end,* by using the first person the author reintroduces himself and thus announces the conclusion of his work, clearly explaining that it is the restoration of Jerusalem that ends his story, thus closing the circle that began with the idyllic Jerusalem of 3.1–3. The fact that the city was under Seleucid rule in ch 3 and now it was *in the possession of the Hebrews* does not interest the Diaspora author. For the history of Jerusalem, and the revolt, from this point on, see 1 Macc 8ff. 39: *Harmful to drink wine alone,* in the Greco-Roman world it was usual to drink wine mixed with water; only barbarians, famously the Scythians (see 4.47n.), drank it undiluted. As at 2.29, the author emphasizes that his job was only to beautify Jason of Cyrene's work, making it more palatable and enjoyable.

(b) The books from 1 Esdras through 3 Maccabees are recognized as Deuterocanonical Scripture by the Greek and the Russian Orthodox Churches. They are not so recognized by the Roman Catholic Chruch, but 1 Esdras and the Prayer of Manasseh (together with 2 Esdras) are placed in an appendix to the Latin Vulgate Bible.

1 ESDRAS

NAME AND CANONICAL STATUS

First Esdras (the Greek form of Ezra) is one of several books bearing the name of Ezra. It is included in the canon by Greek and Russian Orthodox churches. Known in the early Greek mss as Esdras Apocrypha or 1 Esdras; the book is called 3 Esdras in the Latin Vulgate Bible, where it was often placed in an appendix after the New Testament.

DATE OF COMPOSITION AND LITERARY HISTORY

The book has been preserved in Greek and reflects Hellenistic values and vocabulary. Although the latest events it narrates are from the mid-fifth century, it probably dates in its current form to the second century BCE. It is unclear whether the book is a translation of an earlier Hebrew or Aramaic version (possibly as ancient as Ezra-Nehemiah) or a late adaptation of 2 Chronicles and Ezra-Nehemiah composed originally in Greek. The work in Greek was used by the late first-century CE historian Josephus for his account of the return from the exile.

   With one significant exception, the book repeats, with minor (yet often significant) variations, sections from the books of 2 Chronicles and Ezra-Nehemiah. First Esdras begins with King Josiah's Passover celebration in Jerusalem in 622 BCE, reproducing the substance of 2 Chr 35.1–36.21. It continues directly with all of the canonical book of Ezra (with a few changes), which describes the return to Judea beginning in 538 BCE, followed by Nehemiah 8, which describes events that ostensibly (in 1 Esdras) transpired in 458–457 BCE in which Ezra participated. The only material unique to 1 Esdras is the story of the three young bodyguards in the court of King Darius (3.1–5.6).

STRUCTURE AND CONTENTS

Although the book largely overlaps other biblical books, its compositional pattern offers a distinct perspective on the history it recounts. It traces a trajectory between Josiah's Passover (1.1–24) and an unnamed holy day in the time of Ezra (9.49–55 || Neh 8:1–13). The destruction of Jerusalem, exile, and rebuilding that it narrates are framed by celebrations, which imply complete restoration and a return to the "good old days." It thereby depicts a more positive historical development than the longer report in Ezra-Nehemiah, which begins and concludes with challenges rather than festivities. The main divisions of the book are:

1.1–24	An ideal state of affairs: Josiah's Passover celebration (=2 Chr 35.1–27)
1.25–58	Decline and destruction (=2 Chr 36.1–21)
2.1–9.55 [except 3.1-5.6]	Stages of return and restoration (=Ezra 1–10 and Neh 8):
2.1–30	Initial preparations for a return and rebuilding (||Ezra 1 and 4.7–24)
3.1–5.6	The three bodyguards and the commissioning of Zerubbabel
5.7–7.15	Zerubbabel leads the rebuilding of the altar and the temple (||Ezra 2:1–4:6 and 5.1–6.22)
8.1–9.55	Ezra leads the reforms and introduces the law (||Ezra 7–9; Neh 8.1–13a)

INTERPRETATION AND GUIDE TO READING

The book begins and concludes with a ceremony in Jerusalem in front of the Temple—highlighting the unquestioned centrality of the Temple. The troubled time between the ceremonies—namely, the destruction of the Temple and Jerusalem, and the exile to Babylon—is treated as a brief period, followed immediately by a gradual but effective restoration of the altar, the Temple, and the community. Whereas the book of Ezra-Nehemiah contrasts the preexilic period with that of the return from exile, 1 Esdras, like Chronicles, underscores continuities between them. First Esdras also contrasts with the accounts in Ezra-Nehemiah in glorifying leaders, especially King David's descendant Zerubbabel, whose role it expands significantly. In particular, the lengthy story (unique to 1 Esdras) of the three bodyguards in Darius's court focuses on Zerubbabel's achievements. This story portrays

Zerubbabel as the wise hero who wins Darius's support for the reconstruction of the Temple and successfully accomplishes his goal. Ezra the priest also rises to a higher level than in Ezra-Nehemiah, explicitly called a chief priest (but see Ezra 7.5n.). Ezra's prominence is further increased by the absence of collaboration with Nehemiah (who is portrayed in Nehemiah 1–13 as a governor responsible for rebuilding Jerusalem's walls). In First Esdras, Ezra is the dominant figure in the final stages of the restoration and the climax of the entire story (8.1–9.55).

Tamara Cohn Eskenazi

1 Josiah kept the passover to his Lord in Jerusalem; he killed the passover lamb on the fourteenth day of the first month, ² having placed the priests according to their divisions, arrayed in their vestments, in the temple of the Lord. ³ He told the Levites, the temple servants of Israel, that they should sanctify themselves to the Lord and put the holy ark of the Lord in the house that King Solomon, son of David, had built; ⁴ and he said, "You need no longer carry it on your shoulders. Now worship the Lord your God and serve his people Israel; prepare yourselves by your families and kindred, ⁵ in accordance with the directions of King David of Israel and the magnificence of his son Solomon. Stand in order in the temple according to the groupings of the ancestral houses of you Levites, who minister before your kindred the people of Israel, ⁶ and kill the passover lamb and prepare the sacrifices for your kindred, and keep the passover according to the commandment of the Lord that was given to Moses."

⁷ To the people who were present Josiah gave thirty thousand lambs and kids, and three thousand calves; these were given from the king's possessions, as he promised, to the people and the priests and Levites. ⁸ Hilkiah, Zechariah, and Jehiel,ᵃ the chief officers of the temple, gave to the priests for the passover two thousand six hundred sheep and three hundred calves. ⁹ And Jeconiah and Shemaiah and his brother Nethanel, and Hashabiah and Ochiel and Joram, captains over thousands, gave the Levites for the passover five thousand sheep and seven hundred calves.

¹⁰ This is what took place. The priests and the Levites, having the unleavened bread, stood in proper order according to kindred ¹¹ and the grouping of the ancestral houses, before the people, to make the offering to the Lord as it is written in the book of Moses; this they did in the morning. ¹² They roasted the passover lamb with fire, as required; and they boiled the sacrifices in bronze pots and caldrons, with a pleasing odor, ¹³ and carried them to all the people. Afterward they prepared the passover for themselves and for their kindred the priests, the sons of Aaron, ¹⁴ because the priests were offering the fat until nightfall; so the Levites prepared it for themselves and for their kindred the priests, the sons of Aaron. ¹⁵ The temple singers, the sons of Asaph, were in their place according to the arrangement made by David, and also Asaph, Zechariah, and Eddinus, who represented the king. ¹⁶ The gatekeepers were at each gate; no one needed to interrupt his

ᵃ Gk *Esyelus*

1.1–24: An ideal state of affairs: Josiah's Passover celebration (2 Chr 35.1–19). This event constitutes a high point just prior to the destruction of Jerusalem and its Temple. According to 2 Kings 23.21–23 and 2 Chr 34.14–33, the Passover celebration of 622 BCE was the culmination of the religious reforms of Josiah, king of Judah (640–609 BCE). First Esdras does not include an account of the reforms. The author of 1 Esdras is interested in the continuity between the First and Second Temples, and thus shapes its narrative as a movement from one high point (Passover celebration under Josiah) to another, at the time of Ezra (1 Esdras 9), with the destruction and exile but a brief interlude (1 Esdras 1.25–58), followed directly by return and restoration. **3**: *The Levites* were religious functionaries; the priests (v.2) were a subgroup of Levites who, according to tradition, were descended from Aaron, the first priest (see Ex 28.1) with unique responsibilities for the sanctuary. For rules concerning Levites, see 1 Chr 3.1–5.1. **5**: For an understanding of David's role, see 1 Chr 23; 28.13,21; 2 Chr 8.14. **6**: For Passover rules, see Ex 12.1–13; Deut 16.1–8. **7–9**: The list of offerings differs slightly from that in 2 Chr 35.7–9.

daily duties, for their kindred the Levites prepared the passover for them.

[17] So the things that had to do with the sacrifices to the Lord were accomplished that day: the passover was kept [18] and the sacrifices were offered on the altar of the Lord, according to the command of King Josiah. [19] And the people of Israel who were present at that time kept the passover and the festival of unleavened bread seven days. [20] No passover like it had been kept in Israel since the times of the prophet Samuel; [21] none of the kings of Israel had kept such a passover as was kept by Josiah and the priests and Levites and the people of Judah and all of Israel who were living in Jerusalem. [22] In the eighteenth year of the reign of Josiah this passover was kept.

[23] And the deeds of Josiah were upright in the sight of the Lord, for his heart was full of godliness. [24] In ancient times the events of his reign have been recorded—concerning those who sinned and acted wickedly toward the Lord beyond any other people or kingdom, and how they grieved the Lord[a] deeply, so that the words of the Lord fell upon Israel.

[25] After all these acts of Josiah, it happened that Pharaoh, king of Egypt, went to make war at Carchemish on the Euphrates, and Josiah went out against him. [26] And the king of Egypt sent word to him saying, "What have we to do with each other, O king of Judea? [27] I was not sent against you by the Lord God, for my war is at the Euphrates. And now the Lord is with me! The Lord is with me, urging me on! Stand aside, and do not oppose the Lord."

[28] Josiah, however, did not turn back to his chariot, but tried to fight with him, and did not heed the words of the prophet Jeremiah from the mouth of the Lord. [29] He joined battle with him in the plain of Megiddo, and the commanders came down against King Josiah. [30] The king said to his servants, "Take me away from the battle, for I am very weak." And immediately his servants took him out of the line of battle. [31] He got into his second chariot; and after he was brought back to Jerusalem he died, and was buried in the tomb of his ancestors.

[32] In all Judea they mourned for Josiah. The prophet Jeremiah lamented for Josiah, and the principal men, with the women,[b] have made lamentation for him to this day; it was ordained that this should always be done throughout the whole nation of Israel. [33] These things are written in the book of the histories of the kings of Judea; and every one of the acts of Josiah, and his splendor, and his understanding of the law of the Lord, and the things that he had done before, and these that are now told, are recorded in the book of the kings of Israel and Judah.

[34] The men of the nation took Jeconiah[c] son of Josiah, who was twenty-three years old, and made him king in succession to his father Josiah. [35] He reigned three months in Judah and Jerusalem. Then the king of Egypt deposed him from reigning in Jerusalem, [36] and fined the nation one hundred talents of silver and one talent of gold. [37] The king of Egypt made his brother Jehoiakim king of Judea and Jerusalem. [38] Jehoiakim put the nobles in prison, and seized his brother Zarius and brought him back from Egypt.

a   Gk *him*
b   Or *their wives*
c   2 Kings 23.30; 2 Chr 36.1 *Jehoahaz*

12: See 2 Chr 35.13n. **20:** Cf. 2 Kings 23.22. **22:** *The eighteenth year,* 622 BCE. **23–24:** The evaluation of Josiah in 1 Esdras elaborates on Chronicles.

1.25–58: Decline and destruction. 25-33: Josiah's death and the beginning of decline in 1 Esdras largely follow the account in 2 Chr 35.20–27, omitting the report that Josiah disguised himself, and that he was struck by an arrow. **28:** The author of 1 Esdras probably found the Chronicler's account difficult because it depicts the Pharaoh as a prophet, and revised it to suggest that Josiah's death resulted from ignoring the warning of Jeremiah, though no passage in the book of Jeremiah explicitly relates to the battle in which Josiah died. **33:** Josiah is the last good king in the books of Kings and Chronicles, and his death in 609 BCE marks the end of an era.

1.34–49: The last kings of Judah (2 Chr 36.1–14). The good king Josiah is followed by evil kings. **34:** *Jeconiah* as successor to Josiah does not appear in 2 Chr or 2 Kings, and is probably an error for Jehoahaz (ruled briefly in 609 BCE; see 2 Kings 23.30–31; 2 Chr 36.1–2). Jeconiah is an alternate form of the name of Jehoiachin (see v. 43); see Jer 28.4; cf. Jer 22.24. *Men of the nation,* this corresponds to "the people of the land" of 2 Chr 36.1; in preexilic times these were probably landowners who often came to the support of reforming kings or who themselves

³⁹ Jehoiakim was twenty-five years old when he began to reign in Judea and Jerusalem; he did what was evil in the sight of the Lord. ⁴⁰ King Nebuchadnezzar of Babylon came up against him; he bound him with a chain of bronze and took him away to Babylon. ⁴¹ Nebuchadnezzar also took some holy vessels of the Lord, and carried them away, and stored them in his temple in Babylon. ⁴² But the things that are reported about Jehoiakim,ᵃ and his uncleanness and impiety, are written in the annals of the kings.

⁴³ His son Jehoiachinᵇ became king in his place; when he was made king he was eighteen years old, ⁴⁴ and he reigned three months and ten days in Jerusalem. He did what was evil in the sight of the Lord. ⁴⁵ A year later Nebuchadnezzar sent and removed him to Babylon, with the holy vessels of the Lord, ⁴⁶ and made Zedekiah king of Judea and Jerusalem.

Zedekiah was twenty-one years old, and he reigned eleven years. ⁴⁷ He also did what was evil in the sight of the Lord, and did not heed the words that were spoken by the prophet Jeremiah from the mouth of the Lord. ⁴⁸ Although King Nebuchadnezzar had made him swear by the name of the Lord, he broke his oath and rebelled; he stiffened his neck and hardened his heart and transgressed the laws of the Lord, the God of Israel. ⁴⁹ Even the leaders of the people and of the priests committed many acts of sacrilege and lawlessness beyond all the unclean deeds of all the nations, and polluted the temple of the Lord in Jerusalem—the temple that God had made holy. ⁵⁰ The God of their ancestors sent his messenger to call them back, because he would have spared them and his dwelling place. ⁵¹ But they mocked his messengers, and whenever the Lord spoke, they scoffed at his prophets, ⁵² until in his anger against his people because of their ungodly acts he gave command to bring against them the kings of the Chaldeans. ⁵³ These killed their young men with the sword around their holy temple, and did not spare young man or young woman,ᶜ old man or child, for he gave them all into their hands. ⁵⁴ They took all the holy vessels of the Lord, great and small, the treasure chests of the Lord, and the royal stores, and carried them away to Babylon. ⁵⁵ They burned the house of the Lord, broke down the walls of Jerusalem, burned their towers with fire, ⁵⁶ and utterly destroyed all its glorious things. The survivors he led away to Babylon with the sword, ⁵⁷ and they were servants to him and to his sons until the Persians began to reign, in fulfillment of the word of the Lord by the mouth of Jeremiah, ⁵⁸ saying, "Until the land has enjoyed its sabbaths, it shall keep sabbath all the time of its desolation until the completion of seventy years."

2 In the first year of Cyrus as king of the Persians, so that the word of the Lord by the mouth of Jeremiah might be accomplished— ² the Lord stirred up the spirit of

ᵃ Gk *him*
ᵇ Gk *Jehoiakim*
ᶜ Gk *virgin*

instituted reforms (2 Kings 12.18,20; 21.24; 23.30). **36:** A talent weighed about 75 lb (34 kg). **38:** The author recasts 2 Chr 36.4, in which Neco of Egypt removed Jehoahaz from the throne and installed Josiah's elder son Eliakim as king, changing his name to Jehoiakim. Jehoahaz was taken to Egypt, where presumably he died (Jer 22.10–12). In 1 Esdras, Jehoiakim brings up his brother Zarius from Egypt; the name Zarius may be a corruption of Jehoahaz or of Zedekiah, both of whom were brothers of Jehoiakim (2 Kings 24.17; 2 Chr 36.4,10). **39:** According to 2 Chr 36.5, Jehoiakim reigned eleven years (608–598). **43:** 1 Esdras (in contrast to 2 Chr and 2 Kings) gives the name Jehoiakim rather than Jehoiachin to this king's son and successor; but the king's age at the beginning of his reign is more credible (eighteen years; not eight, as in 2 Chr 36.9; cf. 2 Kings 24.8); he ruled in 597. **46:** *Zedekiah*, the last king of Judah, ruled 597–586.

1.50–58: Jerusalem falls to the Babylonians (2 Chr 36.15–21). **52: Chaldeans,** a late biblical name for the Babylonians. **58:** To keep sabbath means here that the land is to lie untended, as in the seventh or sabbatical years, until the exiles return (Jer 25.11–12; 29.10; cf. Lev 25.1–7; 26.27–39,43). Like Chronicles, 1 Esdras stresses the temporary nature of exile, in contrast to 2 Kings 25 and Jer 52, which present it as a tragedy with only a glimmer of hope.

2.1–9.55: Stages of return and restoration. Except for the new material in 3.1–5.6, from here on 1 Esdras

King Cyrus of the Persians, and he made a proclamation throughout all his kingdom and also put it in writing:

³ "Thus says Cyrus king of the Persians: The Lord of Israel, the Lord Most High, has made me king of the world, ⁴ and he has commanded me to build him a house at Jerusalem, which is in Judea. ⁵ If any of you, therefore, are of his people, may your Lord be with you; go up to Jerusalem, which is in Judea, and build the house of the Lord of Israel—he is the Lord who dwells in Jerusalem— ⁶ and let each of you, wherever you may live, be helped by the people of your place with gold and silver, ⁷ with gifts and with horses and cattle, besides the other things added as votive offerings for the temple of the Lord that is in Jerusalem."

⁸ Then arose the heads of families of the tribes of Judah and Benjamin, and the priests and the Levites, and all whose spirit the Lord had stirred to go up to build the house in Jerusalem for the Lord; ⁹ their neighbors helped them with everything, with silver and gold,

with horses and cattle, and with a very great number of votive offerings from many whose hearts were stirred.

¹⁰ King Cyrus also brought out the holy vessels of the Lord that Nebuchadnezzar had carried away from Jerusalem and stored in his temple of idols. ¹¹ When King Cyrus of the Persians brought these out, he gave them to Mithridates, his treasurer, ¹² and by him they were given to Sheshbazzar,ᵃ the governor of Judea. ¹³ The number of these was: one thousand gold cups, one thousand silver cups, twenty-nine silver censers, thirty gold bowls, two thousand four hundred ten silver bowls, and one thousand other vessels. ¹⁴ All the vessels were handed over, gold and silver, five thousand four hundred sixty-nine, ¹⁵ and they were carried back by Sheshbazzar with the returning exiles from Babylon to Jerusalem.

¹⁶ In the time of King Artaxerxes of the Persians, Bishlam, Mithridates, Tabeel, Rehum,

ᵃ Gk *Sanabassaros*

follows Ezra 1–10 and Neh 8, reshaping the material through artful composition that shifts the emphases from the community to exceptional leaders, mostly Zerubbabel the governor and Ezra the priest and scribe. Some changes in sequence highlight these emphases (see 2.16–30).

2.1–15: Cyrus, king of Persia permits the exiles to return (Ezra 1.1–11). The text is almost identical with the end of 2 Chr and the beginning of Ezra, which are also nearly identical. 1: *First year of Cyrus,* 538 BCE; the year after he conquered Babylon. 3–7: The substance of the decree is consistent with Persian religious and political policy; ancient inscriptions depict Cyrus as the restorer of several temples. *Jeremiah* lived through the destruction of Judah and repeatedly promised a restoration; see, e.g., Jer 29.10. 8–9: These verses sum up the enthusiastic response by the people to the decree, a response that leads to the reconstruction described in 5.47–7.15. 8: *Judah and Benjamin,* these tribes had constituted the Southern Kingdom of Judah. They now represent the sole remnant of the twelve tribes of ancient Israel. According to 2 Kings 17, the other tribes were deported, and their land was repopulated by foreigners. 10–15: The return of the sacred vessels symbolizes continuity with the destroyed Temple, whose looting is described in 1.54. The inventory of the sacred vessels is smoother in 1 Esdras than in Ezra. 12: *Sheshbazzar,* a Jewish leader and the first governor of the province of Yehud (Judea) appointed by the Persians. He may have been a descendant of David.

2.16–30: Opposition to the rebuilding of the Temple and the city walls (Ezra 4.7–24). This account in Ezra 4 represents a later stage in the process of return and reconstruction, describing opposition to rebuilding the walls of Jerusalem in the time of Artaxerxes I (465–424 BCE), after the Temple had been founded (Ezra 3). Its location in the Ezra narrative is out of chronological order and seeks to explain why Zerubbabel and Joshua were unable to finish rebuilding the Temple. Here it serves to explain why nothing was accomplished until the hero Zerubbabel took charge. The sequence is still out of chronological order because it presents Artaxerxes (who ruled after Darius I) as preceding Darius. The fact that the Persian Empire had several kings with the same names may have facilitated this error. As in Ezra 4, adversaries led by Samarians (from the former Northern Kingdom of Israel) allege seditious activities by the returnees and successfully halt the rebuilding of Jerusalem. Historical records show that Cyrus was followed by Cambyses (530–522) and after him by Darius I (522–486). Josephus (*Ant.* 11.2.1–3), who typically follows 1 Esdras, substitutes Cambyses for Artaxerxes, thus providing the correct sequence of Persian kings. 16–20: The opponents' letter claims that rebuilding the Temple and city

Beltethmus, the scribe Shimshai, and the rest of their associates, living in Samaria and other places, wrote him the following letter, against those who were living in Judea and Jerusalem:

17 "To King Artaxerxes our lord, your servants the recorder Rehum and the scribe Shimshai and the other members of their council, and the judges in Coelesyria and Phoenicia: 18 Let it now be known to our lord the king that the Jews who came up from you to us have gone to Jerusalem and are building that rebellious and wicked city, repairing its market places and walls and laying the foundations for a temple. 19 Now if this city is built and the walls finished, they will not only refuse to pay tribute but will even resist kings. 20 Since the building of the temple is now going on, we think it best not to neglect such a matter, 21 but to speak to our lord the king, in order that, if it seems good to you, search may be made in the records of your ancestors. 22 You will find in the annals what has been written about them, and will learn that this city was rebellious, troubling both kings and other cities, 23 and that the Jews were rebels and kept setting up blockades in it from of old. That is why this city was laid waste. 24 Therefore we now make known to you, O lord and king, that if this city is built

and its walls finished, you will no longer have access to Coelesyria and Phoenicia."

25 Then the king, in reply to the recorder Rehum, Beltethmus, the scribe Shimshai, and the others associated with them and living in Samaria and Syria and Phoenicia, wrote as follows:

26 "I have read the letter that you sent me. So I ordered search to be made, and it has been found that this city from of old has fought against kings, 27 that the people in it were given to rebellion and war, and that mighty and cruel kings ruled in Jerusalem and exacted tribute from Coelesyria and Phoenicia. 28 Therefore I have now issued orders to prevent these people from building the city and to take care that nothing more be done 29 and that such wicked proceedings go no further to the annoyance of kings."

30 Then, when the letter from King Artaxerxes was read, Rehum and the scribe Shimshai and their associates went quickly to Jerusalem, with cavalry and a large number of armed troops, and began to hinder the builders. And the building of the temple in Jerusalem stopped until the second year of the reign of King Darius of the Persians.

3 Now King Darius gave a great banquet for all that were under him, all that were born in his house, and all the nobles of Media

walls will lead to rebellion. **16:** The name *Beltethmus* is an awkward Greek transliteration of the Aramaic title ("be'el te'em") of the office ("royal deputy") held by Rehum. **17:** *Rehum,* designated "the royal deputy" in Ezra 4.8; the title is supported by Josephus. The persons named are officials of the region called "Beyond the River" (Ezra 4.10), which included the lands of (Coele-) Syria, Phoenicia, Samaria, and Judah. **20:** The account differs from that in Ezra 4.14, which contains no reference to the rebuilding of the Temple at this point. However, Ezra 4.24 states that work on the Temple stopped. This revision and reworking of material is consistent with the focus of 1 Esdras on the Temple. **21:** *Records of your ancestors,* the Assyrians and Babylonians kept careful records, and the Persians inherited and enlarged their bureaucracy. Here, as in ch 8, written records play a crucial role in establishing authority. **24:** Revolt in Jerusalem will endanger Persian rule throughout the western region of the empire. **25–30:** The king's investigation confirms the danger inherent in the rebuilding of the city, and he issues an order to stop it. **29:** Ezra 4.21 includes "until I make a decree," setting the stage for a reversal at a later date. **30:** *Until the second year of . . . Darius,* King Darius I (522–486), the ruler in the subsequent narrative, is identified also in Haggai and Zechariah as the Persian king during whose reign the Temple was rebuilt. 1 Esdras (like Ezra 1–6) does not allow for the prospect that work on the Temple stopped because of Judean inertia (as Haggai and Zechariah indicate) but rather attributes the neglect to external opposition.

3.1–7.15: Zerubbabel leads the return and restoration. In 1 Esdras, Samarian opponents successfully stop rebuilding before any restoration takes place (in contrast to Ezra 3–6, where Zerubbabel and Joshua lead in laying the Temple's foundation before being stopped). This arrangement of the narrative magnifies the accomplishments of Zerubbabel, making him responsible for the very first successful return. Here, then, Zerubbabel wins King Darius's favor and as a result receives permission to go and restore the Temple.

3.1–5.6: The three young bodyguards in the court of Darius. This lively story, unique to 1 Esdras, describes

and Persia, [2] and all the satraps and generals and governors that were under him in the hundred twenty-seven satrapies from India to Ethiopia. [3] They ate and drank, and when they were satisfied they went away, and King Darius went to his bedroom; he went to sleep, but woke up again.

[4] Then the three young men of the body-guard, who kept guard over the person of the king, said to one another, [5] "Let each of us state what one thing is strongest; and to the one whose statement seems wisest, King Darius will give rich gifts and great honors of victory. [6] He shall be clothed in purple, and drink from gold cups, and sleep on a gold bed,[a] and have a chariot with gold bridles, and a turban of fine linen, and a necklace around his neck; [7] and because of his wisdom he shall sit next to Darius and shall be called Kinsman of Darius."

[8] Then each wrote his own statement, and they sealed them and put them under the pillow of King Darius, [9] and said, "When the king wakes, they will give him the writing; and to the one whose statement the king and the three nobles of Persia judge to be wisest the victory shall be given according to what is written." [10] The first wrote, "Wine is strongest." [11] The second wrote, "The king is strong-est." [12] The third wrote, "Women are strong-est, but above all things truth is victor."[b]

[13] When the king awoke, they took the writing and gave it to him, and he read it. [14] Then he sent and summoned all the nobles of Persia and Media and the satraps and generals and governors and prefects, [15] and he took his seat in the council chamber, and the writing was read in their presence. [16] He said, "Call the young men, and they shall explain their statements." So they were summoned, and came in. [17] They said to them, "Explain to us what you have written."

Then the first, who had spoken of the strength of wine, began and said: [18] "Gentle-men, how is wine the strongest? It leads astray the minds of all who drink it. [19] It makes equal the mind of the king and the orphan, of the slave and the free, of the poor and the rich. [20] It turns every thought to feasting and mirth, and forgets all sorrow and debt. [21] It makes all hearts feel rich, forgets kings and satraps, and makes everyone talk in millions.[c] [22] When people drink they forget to be friendly with friends and kindred, and

a   Gk on gold
b   Or but truth is victor over all things
c   Gk talents

how Zerubbabel found favor in King Darius's eyes. It magnifies the role of Zerubbabel, the last Davidic heir to have political power, making him the first great hero of the restoration. In Ezra-Nehemiah, Zerubbabel is no more prominent than his co-worker, Jeshua the priest. Although Zerubbabel the governor is a key figure in Haggai and Zechariah, along with the high priest Joshua (Jeshua in Ezra-Nehemiah and 1 Esdras), no other text suggests direct contact between him and the king. The story probably originated as a secular tale praising the relative strength of kings, wine, and women, to which praise of truth was added (4.33–41); it has close parallels in Greek literature. The author of 1 Esdras adopted the story, identified the third, wisest youth with Zerubbabel (4.13), and added a sequel to the tale, relating how Darius rewarded Zerubbabel by supporting the rebuilding of Jerusalem and its Temple (4.42–5.6). Josephus, who includes this story (Ant. 11.3.2–9), has a slightly different version of it.

3.1–17a: The three royal bodyguards plan a contest. The royal banquet scene is a favorite Hellenistic motif, though this case is unusual in that the bodyguards, not the king, choose the entertainment. 1–3: Although the location is not explicitly mentioned, the Persian capital Susa may be implied (cf. Esth 1.2–3). Media, one of the two main original kingdoms of the Persian Empire, in northern Iran. 2: Satraps, high officials in the Persian government, usually provincial governors. There were only about twenty provinces (satrapies) during Darius's reign (522–486 BCE); this number was later increased, and the total one hundred twenty-seven became conven-tional in later Jewish literature (Esth 1.1; Josephus, Ant. 11.3.2). 4–12: The three bodyguards decide of their own initiative to entertain the king, thereby bringing riches and honor to one of them. In Josephus (Ant. 11.3.2), the king proposes the contest. 13–17a: The entire court is assembled to hear the three men defend their respective answers; the scene accurately depicts court practices in the ancient world.

3.17b–24: The first guard praises the strength of wine. As the great equalizer of society, wine takes away the capacity for discernment and remembrance, overpowering king and commoner alike.

before long they draw their swords. [23] And when they recover from the wine, they do not remember what they have done. [24] Gentlemen, is not wine the strongest, since it forces people to do these things?" When he had said this, he stopped speaking.

4 Then the second, who had spoken of the strength of the king, began to speak: [2] "Gentlemen, are not men strongest, who rule over land and sea and all that is in them? [3] But the king is stronger; he is their lord and master, and whatever he says to them they obey. [4] If he tells them to make war on one another, they do it; and if he sends them out against the enemy, they go, and conquer mountains, walls, and towers. [5] They kill and are killed, and do not disobey the king's command; if they win the victory, they bring everything to the king—whatever spoil they take and everything else. [6] Likewise those who do not serve in the army or make war but till the soil; whenever they sow and reap, they bring some to the king; and they compel one another to pay taxes to the king. [7] And yet he is only one man! If he tells them to kill, they kill; if he tells them to release, they release; [8] if he tells them to attack, they attack; if he tells them to lay waste, they lay waste; if he tells them to build, they build; [9] if he tells them to cut down, they cut down; if he tells them to plant, they plant. [10] All his people and his armies obey him. Furthermore, he reclines, he eats and drinks and sleeps, [11] but they keep watch around him, and no one may go away to attend to his own affairs, nor do they disobey him. [12] Gentlemen, why is not the king the strongest, since he is to be obeyed in this fashion?" And he stopped speaking.

[13] Then the third, who had spoken of women and truth (and this was Zerubbabel), began to speak: [14] "Gentlemen, is not the king great, and are not men many, and is not wine strong? Who is it, then, that rules them, or has the mastery over them? Is it not women? [15] Women gave birth to the king and to every people that rules over sea and land. [16] From women they came; and women brought up the very men who plant the vineyards from which comes wine. [17] Women make men's clothes; they bring men glory; men cannot exist without women. [18] If men gather gold and silver or any other beautiful thing, and then see a woman lovely in appearance and beauty, [19] they let all those things go, and gape at her, and with open mouths stare at her, and all prefer her to gold or silver or any other beautiful thing. [20] A man leaves his own father, who brought him up, and his own country, and clings to his wife. [21] With his wife he ends his days, with no thought of his father or his mother or his country. [22] Therefore you must realize that women rule over you!

"Do you not labor and toil, and bring everything and give it to women? [23] A man takes his sword, and goes out to travel and rob and steal and to sail the sea and rivers; [24] he faces lions, and he walks in darkness, and when he steals and robs and plunders, he brings it back to the woman he loves. [25] A man loves his wife more than his father or his mother. [26] Many men have lost their minds because of women, and have become slaves because of them. [27] Many have perished, or stumbled, or sinned because of women. [28] And now do you not believe me?

"Is not the king great in his power? Do not all lands fear to touch him? [29] Yet I have seen him with Apame, the king's concubine, the daughter of the illustrious Bartacus; she would sit at the king's right hand [30] and take the crown from the king's head and put it on her own, and slap the king with her left hand. [31] At this the king would gaze at her with mouth agape. If she smiles at him, he laughs; if she loses her temper with him, he flatters

4.1–12: The second guard praises the strength of kings. The unchecked power of ancient kings is accurately portrayed here, but this passage should not be viewed as a polemic against kingship.

4.13–32: The third guard praises the strength of women as well as wisdom. He first depicts women as those who give birth to kings, who receive from men the treasures won in warfare through heroic deeds, who can humiliate their masters, including kings, and yet are sought after and fawned upon even by those whom they humiliate. 13: *The third . . . (and this was Zerubbabel),* according to 1 Chr 3.19, Zerubbabel is a descendant of David. His name is added here as the traditional tale is incorporated into 1 Esdras (see 3.1–5.6n.). 20: *Clings to his wife,* see Gen 2.24. 29: *Apame, the king's concubine,* is not mentioned in other ancient sources.

her, so that she may be reconciled to him. [32] Gentlemen, why are not women strong, since they do such things?"

[33] Then the king and the nobles looked at one another; and he began to speak about truth: [34] "Gentlemen, are not women strong? The earth is vast, and heaven is high, and the sun is swift in its course, for it makes the circuit of the heavens and returns to its place in one day. [35] Is not the one who does these things great? But truth is great, and stronger than all things. [36] The whole earth calls upon truth, and heaven blesses it. All God's works[a] quake and tremble, and with him there is nothing unrighteous. [37] Wine is unrighteous, the king is unrighteous, women are unrighteous, all human beings are unrighteous, all their works are unrighteous, and all such things. There is no truth in them and in their unrighteousness they will perish. [38] But truth endures and is strong forever, and lives and prevails forever and ever. [39] With it there is no partiality or preference, but it does what is righteous instead of anything that is unrighteous or wicked. Everyone approves its deeds, [40] and there is nothing unrighteous in its judgment. To it belongs the strength and the kingship and the power and the majesty of all the ages. Blessed be the God of truth!" [41] When he stopped speaking, all the people shouted and said, "Great is truth, and strongest of all!"

[42] Then the king said to him, "Ask what you wish, even beyond what is written, and we will give it to you, for you have been found to be the wisest. You shall sit next to me, and be called my Kinsman." [43] Then he said to the king, "Remember the vow that you made on the day when you became king, to build Jerusalem, [44] and to send back all the vessels that were taken from Jerusalem, which Cyrus set apart when he began[b] to destroy Babylon, and vowed to send them back there. [45] You also vowed to build the temple, which the Edomites burned when Judea was laid waste by the Chaldeans. [46] And now, O lord the king, this is what I ask and request of you, and this befits your greatness. I pray therefore that you fulfill the vow whose fulfillment you vowed to the King of heaven with your own lips."

[47] Then King Darius got up and kissed him, and wrote letters for him to all the treasurers and governors and generals and satraps, that they should give safe conduct to him and to all who were going up with him to build Jerusalem. [48] And he wrote letters to all the governors in Coelesyria and Phoenicia and to those in Lebanon, to bring cedar timber from Lebanon to Jerusalem, and to help him build the city. [49] He wrote in behalf of all the Jews who were going up from his kingdom to Judea, in the interest of their freedom, that no officer or satrap or governor or treasurer should forcibly enter their doors; [50] that all the country that they would occupy should be theirs without tribute; that the Idumeans should give up the villages of the Jews that they held; [51] that twenty talents a year should

a Gk All the works
b Cn: Gk vowed

4.33–41: Zerubbabel adds praise of truth. This addition to the original story was probably made prior to the story's adaptation to the Jewish author's purpose. Truth is portrayed in imagery familiar in Greek literature, although the Jewish adapter of the story may have modified the original to conform to the meaning of the Hebrew word for truth, which conveys firmness and reliability. **40:** A clever maneuver by a Jewish adapter of the story to suggest that truth is virtually equivalent to the will of God. **41:** The Latin Vulgate translation of the people's response, "Magna est veritas et praevalet," became a famous proverb.

4.42–57: Zerubbabel's reward. At Zerubbabel's request, Darius agrees to authorize Zerubbabel to return to Jerusalem and rebuild the Temple, with generous support from the Persian treasury. **43:** This improbable vow of Darius to rebuild Jerusalem and its Temple upon his accession to kingship is not otherwise attested and is likely the creation of the author. **45:** *Edomites,* this group is not mentioned in 1.55 as having burned the Temple, but see Ob 11–14 and Ps 137.7. **48–57:** Darius magnificently supports the program outlined by Zerubbabel. The extravagant royal support depicted here is improbable. A more plausible version is found in the decree Darius issues later after receiving a report about building activities (Ezra 6.1–13; 1 Esd 6.23–34). **50:** *Idumeans,* a later designation of the Edomites. The demand that they give back their villages to the returning exiles implies that Edomites encroached upon Judean land during the exile.

be given for the building of the temple until it was completed, [52] and an additional ten talents a year for burnt offerings to be offered on the altar every day, in accordance with the commandment to make seventeen offerings; [53] and that all who came from Babylonia to build the city should have their freedom, they and their children and all the priests who came. [54] He wrote also concerning their support and the priests' vestments in which[a] they were to minister. [55] He wrote that the support for the Levites should be provided until the day when the temple would be finished and Jerusalem built. [56] He wrote that land and wages should be provided for all who guarded the city. [57] And he sent back from Babylon all the vessels that Cyrus had set apart; everything that Cyrus had ordered to be done, he also commanded to be done and to be sent to Jerusalem.

[58] When the young man went out, he lifted up his face to heaven toward Jerusalem, and praised the King of heaven, saying, [59] "From you comes the victory; from you comes wisdom, and yours is the glory. I am your servant. [60] Blessed are you, who have given me wisdom; I give you thanks, O Lord of our ancestors."

[61] So he took the letters, and went to Babylon and told this to all his kindred. [62] And they praised the God of their ancestors, because he had given them release and permission [63] to go up and build Jerusalem and the temple that is called by his name; and they feasted, with music and rejoicing, for seven days.

5 After this the heads of ancestral houses were chosen to go up, according to their tribes, with their wives and sons and daughters, and their male and female servants, and their livestock. [2] And Darius sent with them a

thousand cavalry to take them back to Jerusalem in safety, with the music of drums and flutes; [3] all their kindred were making merry. And he made them go up with them.

[4] These are the names of the men who went up, according to their ancestral houses in the tribes, over their groups: [5] the priests, the descendants of Phinehas son of Aaron; Jeshua son of Jozadak son of Seraiah and Joakim son of Zerubbabel son of Shealtiel, of the house of David, of the lineage of Phares, of the tribe of Judah, [6] who spoke wise words before King Darius of the Persians, in the second year of his reign, in the month of Nisan, the first month.

[7] These are the Judeans who came up out of their sojourn in exile, whom King Nebuchadnezzar of Babylon had carried away to Babylon [8] and who returned to Jerusalem and the rest of Judea, each to his own town. They came with Zerubbabel and Jeshua, Nehemiah, Seraiah, Resaiah, Eneneus, Mordecai, Beelsarus, Aspharasus, Reeliah, Rehum, and Baanah, their leaders.

[9] The number of those of the nation and their leaders: the descendants of Parosh, two thousand one hundred seventy-two. The descendants of Shephatiah, four hundred seventy-two. [10] The descendants of Arah, seven hundred fifty-six. [11] The descendants of Pahath-moab, of the descendants of Jeshua and Joab, two thousand eight hundred twelve. [12] The descendants of Elam, one thousand two hundred fifty-four. The descendants of Zattu, nine hundred forty-five. The descendants of Chorbe, seven hundred five. The descendants of Bani, six hundred forty-eight. [13] The descendants of Bebai, six hundred twenty-three. The descendants of

---

a Gk *in what priestly vestments*

4.58–60: Zerubbabel's prayer. The language of this prayer resembles a prayer of Daniel (Dan 2.20–23) and may be dependent upon it.

4.61–5.6: Preparations for the return to Judah. Zerubbabel journeys (perhaps from Susa) to Babylon and there recruits leaders from the priestly and royal families for the returning exiles (5.4–6). The genealogies of the leaders are hopelessly confused. The material unique to 1 Esdras concludes here, with the rest of the book paralleling Ezra 2–10 and Neh 8.

5.7–46: A list of the returning exiles (Ezra 2.1–70 and Neh 7.6–73a). The list in 1 Esdras differs somewhat from that in Ezra 2 and Nehemiah 7, both in the names and numbers listed. The totals, however, are identical, and the numbers of the priests and Levites are almost identical in the three lists, an indication that priestly and levitical genealogies were more carefully preserved than others. 6: *Nisan,* March-April. 9–23: Lay Israelites are

Azgad, one thousand three hundred twenty-two. [14] The descendants of Adonikam, six hundred sixty-seven. The descendants of Bigvai, two thousand sixty-six. The descendants of Adin, four hundred fifty-four. [15] The descendants of Ater, namely of Hezekiah, ninety-two. The descendants of Kilan and Azetas, sixty-seven. The descendants of Azaru, four hundred thirty-two. [16] The descendants of Annias, one hundred one. The descendants of Arom. The descendants of Bezai, three hundred twenty-three. The descendants of Arsiphurith, one hundred twelve. [17] The descendants of Baiterus, three thousand five. The descendants of Bethlomon, one hundred twenty-three. [18] Those from Netophah, fifty-five. Those from Anathoth, one hundred fifty-eight. Those from Bethasmoth, forty-two. [19] Those from Kiriatharim, twenty-five. Those from Chephirah and Beeroth, seven hundred forty-three.

[20] The Chadiasans and Ammidians, four hundred twenty-two. Those from Kirama and Geba, six hundred twenty-one. [21] Those from Macalon, one hundred twenty-two. Those from Betolio, fifty-two. The descendants of Niphish, one hundred fifty-six. [22] The descendants of the other Calamolalus and Ono, seven hundred twenty-five. The descendants of Jerechus, three hundred forty-five. [23] The descendants of Senaah, three thousand three hundred thirty.

[24] The priests: the descendants of Jedaiah son of Jeshua, of the descendants of Anasib, nine hundred seventy-two. The descendants of Immer, one thousand and fifty-two. [25] The descendants of Pashhur, one thousand two hundred forty-seven. The descendants of Charme, one thousand seventeen.

[26] The Levites: the descendants of Jeshua and Kadmiel and Bannas and Sudias, seventy-four. [27] The temple singers: the descendants of Asaph, one hundred twenty-eight. [28] The gatekeepers: the descendants of Shallum, the descendants of Ater, the descendants of Talmon, the descendants of Akkub, the descendants of Hatita, the descendants of Shobai, in all one hundred thirty-nine.

[29] The temple servants: the descendants of Esau, the descendants of Hasupha, the descendants of Tabbaoth, the descendants of Keros, the descendants of Sua, the descendants of Padon, the descendants of Lebanah, the descendants of Hagabah, [30] the descendants of Akkub, the descendants of Uthai, the descendants of Ketab, the descendants of Hagab, the descendants of Subai, the descendants of Hana, the descendants of Cathua, the descendants of Geddur, [31] the descendants of Jairus, the descendants of Daisan, the descendants of Noeba, the descendants of Chezib, the descendants of Gazera, the descendants of Uzza, the descendants of Phinoe, the descendants of Hasrah, the descendants of Basthai, the descendants of Asnah, the descendants of Maani, the descendants of Nephisim, the descendants of Acuph,[a] the descendants of Hakupha, the descendants of Asur, the descendants of Pharakim, the descendants of Bazluth, [32] the descendants of Mehida, the descendants of Cutha, the descendants of Charea, the descendants of Barkos, the descendants of Serar, the descendants of Temah, the descendants of Neziah, the descendants of Hatipha.

[33] The descendants of Solomon's servants: the descendants of Assaphioth, the descendants of Peruda, the descendants of Jaalah, the descendants of Lozon, the descendants of Isdael, the descendants of Shephatiah, [34] the descendants of Agia, the descendants of Pochereth-hazzebaim, the descendants of Sarothie, the descendants of Masiah, the descendants of Gas, the descendants of Addus, the descendants of Subas, the descendants of Apherra, the descendants of Barodis, the descendants of Shaphat, the descendants of Allon.

[35] All the temple servants and the descendants of Solomon's servants were three hundred seventy-two.

[36] The following are those who came up from Tel-melah and Tel-harsha, under the leadership of Cherub, Addan, and Immer,

---

[a] Other ancient authorities read *Acub* or *Acum*

listed by family ancestral names (vv. 9–17, 21b–23) and towns of origin (vv. 18–21a). **24-25:** *Priests* include four families claiming descent from Aaron (cf. 1 Chr 24). **26–27:** *Levites* are listed according to their Temple functions in the postexilic period. **29–35:** Other Temple personnel and miscellaneous groups. **36–37:** The inability of some

37 though they could not prove by their ancestral houses or lineage that they belonged to Israel: the descendants of Delaiah son of Tobiah, and the descendants of Nekoda, six hundred fifty-two.

38 Of the priests the following had assumed the priesthood but were not found registered: the descendants of Habaiah, the descendants of Hakkoz, and the descendants of Jaddus who had married Agia, one of the daughters of Barzillai, and was called by his name. 39 When a search was made in the register and the genealogy of these men was not found, they were excluded from serving as priests. 40 And Nehemiah and Attharias[a] told them not to share in the holy things until a high priest should appear wearing Urim and Thummim.[b]

41 All those of Israel, twelve or more years of age, besides male and female servants, were forty-two thousand three hundred sixty; 42 their male and female servants were seven thousand three hundred thirty-seven; there were two hundred forty-five musicians and singers. 43 There were four hundred thirty-five camels, and seven thousand thirty-six horses, two hundred forty-five mules, and five thousand five hundred twenty-five donkeys.

44 Some of the heads of families, when they came to the temple of God that is in Jerusalem, vowed that, to the best of their ability, they would erect the house on its site, 45 and that they would give to the sacred treasury for the work a thousand minas of gold, five thousand minas of silver, and one hundred priests' vestments.

46 The priests, the Levites, and some of the people[c] settled in Jerusalem and its vicinity; and the temple singers, the gatekeepers, and all Israel in their towns.

47 When the seventh month came, and the Israelites were all in their own homes,

a   Or the governor
b   Gk Manifestation and Truth
c   Or those who were of the people

returnees to prove their Israelite ancestry is recorded, but without mention of any repercussions. 38–40: Proof of legitimate priestly genealogies is needed for any who may serve in the Temple in order to preserve the holiness of the Temple and protect the community from danger. Priests whose credentials are in question cannot serve until a mechanism for verification becomes available. 38: Barzillai, see 2 Sam 17.27; 19.31. The adoption of the father-in-law's name suggests that Barzillai did not have a male heir. 40: The name Nehemiah, not found in the parallel in Ezra-Nehemiah, is added here to compensate for the fact that 1 Esdras omits the story of Nehemiah (who, according to Neh 5.14 and 8.9 was the governor at the time of Ezra) in order to focus on Zerubbabel as governor and Ezra as high priest. Attharias, in Neh 8:9 a similar word, understood as the title "governor," describes Nehemiah. Urim and Thummim are the sacred lots used by the priests to receive oracular decisions (Ex 28.30; Lev 8.8; Deut 33.8; 1 Sam 14.41). This type of divine communication was a means of verification in the absence of other sources. 41: The total of 42,360 returnees exceeds the sum total of the several groups listed but is identical with that in Ezra 2.66 and Neh 7.64. This larger number may include women and older children. Twelve or more years, this detail, which marks a boy's entry into formal standing in the community, is unique to 1 Esdras (see Luke 2:42 for a later allusion to this life stage). 45: The precise monetary value of this contribution to the Temple (for which different amounts are given in Ezra 2.69) is uncertain because the value of the mina fluctuated. Nevertheless, the passage suggests that the community invested a great deal in restoring its Temple. The priests' vestments are specialized garments for official service.

5.47–73: Work on the Temple commences and is interrupted (Ezra 3.1–4.5; cf. Josephus, Ant. 11.4.1–3). Ezra 3–6 places the building of the Temple in both the reign of Cyrus (539–530 BCE) and that of Darius (522–486), merging several returns of exiles in a chronologically confusing fashion. First Esdras offers a more coherent and historically credible sequence, with Sheshbazzar beginning the work under Cyrus, and Zerubbabel working only under Darius. The likely sequence of events is that Sheshbazzar returned to Yehud shortly after 538, restored the sacrificial altar, reestablished public worship and perhaps even attempted to start building the Temple by laying its foundation, but with little success. The work on the Temple only resumed around 520 with Zerubbabel and Jeshua (during King Darius's reign). The prophets Haggai and Zechariah encouraged the community to complete the Temple, and the Temple was finally dedicated in 515.

5.47–55: Building the altar and resumption of sacrifices. The restoration of the altar and a functioning

they gathered with a single purpose in the square before the first gate toward the east. ⁴⁸ Then Jeshua son of Jozadak, with his fellow priests, and Zerubbabel son of Shealtiel, with his kinsmen, took their places and prepared the altar of the God of Israel, ⁴⁹ to offer burnt offerings upon it, in accordance with the directions in the book of Moses the man of God. ⁵⁰ And some joined them from the other peoples of the land. And they erected the altar in its place, for all the peoples of the land were hostile to them and were stronger than they; and they offered sacrifices at the proper times and burnt offerings to the Lord morning and evening. ⁵¹ They kept the festival of booths, as it is commanded in the law, and offered the proper sacrifices every day, ⁵² and thereafter the regular offerings and sacrifices on sabbaths and at new moons and at all the consecrated feasts. ⁵³ And all who had made any vow to God began to offer sacrifices to God, from the new moon of the seventh month, though the temple of God was not yet built. ⁵⁴ They gave money to the masons and the carpenters, and food and drink ⁵⁵ and carts[a] to the Sidonians and the Tyrians, to bring cedar logs from Lebanon and convey them in rafts to the harbor of Joppa, according to the decree that they had in writing from King Cyrus of the Persians.

⁵⁶ In the second year after their coming to the temple of God in Jerusalem, in the second month, Zerubbabel son of Shealtiel and Jeshua son of Jozadak made a beginning, together with their kindred and the levitical priests and all who had come back to Jerusalem from exile; ⁵⁷ and they laid the foundation of the temple of God on the new moon of the second month in the second year after they came to Judea and Jerusalem. ⁵⁸ They appointed the Levites who were twenty or more years of age to have charge of the work of the Lord. And Jeshua arose, and his sons and kindred and his brother Kadmiel and the sons of Jeshua Emadabun and the sons of Joda son of Iliadun, with their sons and kindred, all the Levites, pressing forward the work on the house of God with a single purpose.

So the builders built the temple of the Lord. ⁵⁹ And the priests stood arrayed in their vestments, with musical instruments and trumpets, and the Levites, the sons of Asaph, with cymbals, ⁶⁰ praising the Lord and blessing him, according to the directions of King David of Israel; ⁶¹ they sang hymns, giving thanks to the Lord, "For his goodness and his glory are forever upon all Israel." ⁶² And all the people sounded trumpets and shouted with a great shout, praising the Lord for the erection of the house of the Lord. ⁶³ Some of the levitical priests and heads of ancestral houses, old men who had seen the former house, came to the building of this one with outcries and loud weeping, ⁶⁴ while many

---

[a] Meaning of Gk uncertain

---

priesthood indicates the resumption of sacrificial worship, a central means of religious expression in the ancient world. Here 1 Esdras credits Zerubbabel and Jeshua (v. 48) with the successful rebuilding, beginning with the altar itself, now during the reign of Darius. Ezra 3 places this event earlier, still at the time of Cyrus. **47:** *The seventh month,* Tishri (September–October). **49:** *The book of Moses,* the Torah. Conformity to God's teachings embodied in the Torah plays a major role in accounts of the restoration period. **50:** Although the returnees elsewhere oppose marriages with peoples of the land, they do allow persons to join the community under certain conditions that are not specified in this text. This phrase does not appear in the parallel in Ezra 3, but the idea appears in Ezra 6.21. **51:** *The festival of booths* is celebrated in autumn, beginning on the fifteenth day of the seventh month (Lev 23.34). **52:** *New moons,* see Num 29.6. **55:** Sidon and Tyre helped build Solomon's Temple (1 Kings 5–7).

5.56–65: The Temple's foundation is laid (Ezra 3.8–13). **56:** Ezra 3 implies the second year of Cyrus, but 1 Esdras implies the second year of Darius (520 BCE), a date which more closely conforms to material in Haggai and Zechariah. **59–62:** Celebration of temple-foundings is a common ancient Near Eastern practice. **61:** The quoted words paraphrase a frequently occurring refrain in late Psalms (e.g., 106.1; 107.1; 118.1, 136.1). **63:** *The former house,* Solomon's Temple, destroyed in 586. *Loud weeping,* the founding of the Temple is an emotionally charged event. It is unclear whether the tears of the old result from sorrow about what had been lost (since the new Temple is presumably smaller than the one they remember) or from joy at seeing the beginning of restoration and the fulfillment of earlier hopes.

came with trumpets and a joyful noise, [65] so that the people could not hear the trumpets because of the weeping of the people.

For the multitude sounded the trumpets loudly, so that the sound was heard far away; [66] and when the enemies of the tribe of Judah and Benjamin heard it, they came to find out what the sound of the trumpets meant. [67] They learned that those who had returned from exile were building the temple for the Lord God of Israel. [68] So they approached Zerubbabel and Jeshua and the heads of the ancestral houses and said to them, "We will build with you. [69] For we obey your Lord just as you do and we have been sacrificing to him ever since the days of King Esar-haddon[a] of the Assyrians, who brought us here." [70] But Zerubbabel and Jeshua and the heads of the ancestral houses in Israel said to them, "You have nothing to do with us in building the house for the Lord our God, [71] for we alone will build it for the Lord of Israel, as Cyrus, the king of the Persians, has commanded us." [72] But the peoples of the land pressed hard[b] upon those in Judea, cut off their supplies, and hindered their building; [73] and by plots and demagoguery and uprisings they prevented the completion of the building as long as King Cyrus lived. They were kept from building for two years, until the reign of Darius.

6 Now in the second year of the reign of Darius, the prophets Haggai and Zechariah son of Iddo prophesied to the Jews who were in Judea and Jerusalem; they prophesied to them in the name of the Lord God of Israel. [2] Then Zerubbabel son of Shealtiel and Jeshua son of Jozadak began to build the house of the Lord that is in Jerusalem, with the help of the prophets of the Lord who were with them.

[3] At the same time Sisinnes the governor of Syria and Phoenicia and Sathrabuzanes and their associates came to them and said, [4] "By whose order are you building this house and this roof and finishing all the other things? And who are the builders that are finishing these things?" [5] Yet the elders of the Jews were dealt with kindly, for the providence of the Lord was over the captives; [6] they were not prevented from building until word could be sent to Darius concerning them and a report made.

[7] A copy of the letter that Sisinnes the governor of Syria and Phoenicia, and Sathrabuzanes, and their associates the local rulers in Syria and Phoenicia, wrote and sent to Darius:

[8] "To King Darius, greetings. Let it be fully known to our lord the king that, when we went to the country of Judea and entered the city of Jerusalem, we found the elders of the Jews, who had been in exile, [9] building in the city of Jerusalem a great new house for the Lord, of hewn stone, with costly timber laid in the walls. [10] These operations are going on rapidly, and the work is prospering in their hands and being completed with all splendor and care. [11] Then we asked these elders, 'At whose command are you build-

a Gk *Asbasareth*
b Meaning of Gk uncertain

5.66–73: **Enemies interrupt the work of the returned exiles** (Ezra 4.1–5). The returnees refuse to rebuild the Temple with outsiders who by their own admission did not belong to the Israelite community. 2 Kings 17 describes the resettling of non-Israelites in the territory of Samaria after its destruction by Assyria in 722 BCE. **69:** Instead of *Esar-haddon,* the Assyrian king who ruled 681–669 BCE, Josephus (*Ant.* 11.4.3) has Shalmaneser (727–722) as in 2 Kings 17.3; 18.9. **73:** This verse smoothes over the more problematic sequence in Ezra 3–6 (which inserts material from the reign of later kings, Xerxes and Artaxerxes, at this point; see Ezra 4.6–24).

6.1–34: **Temple work resumes** (Ezra 5.1–6.12). The prophets Haggai and Zechariah encourage the resumption of work on the Temple and succeed in gaining support for Zerubbabel and Jeshua (Joshua; cf. Hag 1.1–4; 2.1–4; Zech 4.9; 6.15). Although investigated by the governor of the entire Persian province Beyond the River (west of Babylon and encompassing Judah as well as Lebanon and Syria), the Judeans nonetheless are able to work with no interruption. **3:** *Sisinnes the governor of Syria and Phoenicia* is Tattenai in Ezra 5.3, and governor of the province Beyond the River, namely the Persian province west of Babylon, including Judah; *Phoenicia* corresponds to modern Lebanon. *Sathrabuzanes* is Shethar-bozenai in Ezra 5.3.

6.7–22: **The governor's report and request.** In this letter, the provincial governor seeks to find out whether King Darius will confirm and authorize the permission to build the Temple first granted by Cyrus. The report is

ing this house and laying the foundations of this structure?' [12] In order that we might inform you in writing who the leaders are, we questioned them and asked them for a list of the names of those who are at their head. [13] They answered us, 'We are the servants of the Lord who created the heaven and the earth. [14] The house was built many years ago by a king of Israel who was great and strong, and it was finished. [15] But when our ancestors sinned against the Lord of Israel who is in heaven, and provoked him, he gave them over into the hands of King Nebuchadnezzar of Babylon, king of the Chaldeans; [16] and they pulled down the house, and burned it, and carried the people away captive to Babylon. [17] But in the first year that Cyrus reigned over the country of Babylonia, King Cyrus wrote that this house should be rebuilt. [18] And the holy vessels of gold and of silver, which Nebuchadnezzar had taken out of the house in Jerusalem and stored in his own temple, these King Cyrus took out again from the temple in Babylon, and they were delivered to Zerubbabel and Sheshbazzar[a] the governor [19] with the command that he should take all these vessels back and put them in the temple at Jerusalem, and that this temple of the Lord should be rebuilt on its site. [20] Then this Sheshbazzar, after coming here, laid the foundations of the house of the Lord that is in Jerusalem. Although it has been in process of construction from that time until now, it has not yet reached completion.' [21] Now therefore, O king, if it seems wise to do so, let search be made in the royal archives of our lord[b] the king that are in Babylon; [22] if it is found that the building of the house of the Lord in Jerusalem was done with the consent of King Cyrus, and if it is approved by our lord the king, let him send us directions concerning these things."

[23] Then Darius commanded that search be made in the royal archives that were deposited in Babylon. And in Ecbatana, the fortress that is in the country of Media, a scroll[c] was found in which this was recorded: [24] "In the first year of the reign of King Cyrus, he ordered the building of the house of the Lord in Jerusalem, where they sacrifice with perpetual fire; [25] its height to be sixty cubits and its width sixty cubits, with three courses of hewn stone and one course of new native timber; the cost to be paid from the treasury of King Cyrus; [26] and that the holy vessels of the house of the Lord, both of gold and of silver, which Nebuchadnezzar took out of the house in Jerusalem and carried away to Babylon, should be restored to the house in Jerusalem, to be placed where they had been."

[27] So Darius[d] commanded Sisinnes the governor of Syria and Phoenicia, and Sathrabuzanes, and their associates, and those who were appointed as local rulers in Syria and Phoenicia, to keep away from the place, and to permit Zerubbabel, the servant of the Lord and governor of Judea, and the elders of the Jews to build this house of the Lord on its site. [28] "And I command that it be built completely, and that full effort be made to help those who have returned from the exile of Judea, until the house of the Lord is finished; [29] and that out of the tribute of Coelesyria and Phoenicia a portion be scrupulously given to these men, that is, to Zerubbabel the governor, for sacrifices to the Lord, for bulls and rams and lambs, [30] and likewise wheat and salt and wine and oil, regularly every

---

a   Gk *Sanabassarus*
b   Other ancient authorities read *of Cyrus*
c   Other authorities read *passage*
d   Gk *he*

---

neutral in tone. **14:** *A king of Israel,* namely Solomon (1 Kings 6). **15:** *Chaldeans,* the Babylonians; see 1.52n. **18:** *Zerubbabel,* who is more prominent in 1 Esdras than in Ezra 3–6, is added here and in vv. 27, 29; only *Sheshbazzar* is mentioned in Ezra 5.14 and in Josephus (*Ant.* 11.4.4).

6.23–34: Darius's authorization of rebuilding and generous support for the Temple. The king's investigation recovers a copy of Cyrus's memorandum, which King Darius then confirms, thus adding his support to the Judeans' rebuilding efforts. In following the account in Ezra 5–6, 1 Esdras ignores the earlier report (1 Esd 5.42–57) in which Darius authorizes the bodyguard Zerubbabel to build the Temple; this reflects the complicated history of composition of 1 Esdras. **23:** *Ecbatana* was the summer residence of Persian kings, now Hamadan in Iran. **24–26:** The discovered copy of Cyrus's authorization confirms the claims of the Judean builders. See

year, without quibbling, for daily use as the priests in Jerusalem may indicate, [31] in order that libations may be made to the Most High God for the king and his children, and prayers be offered for their lives."

[32] He commanded that if anyone should transgress or nullify any of the things herein written,[a] a beam should be taken out of the house of the perpetrator, who then should be impaled upon it, and all property forfeited to the king.

[33] "Therefore may the Lord, whose name is there called upon, destroy every king and nation that shall stretch out their hands to hinder or damage that house of the Lord in Jerusalem.

[34] "I, King Darius, have decreed that it be done with all diligence as here prescribed."

7 Then Sisinnes the governor of Coelesyria and Phoenicia, and Sathrabuzanes, and their associates, following the orders of King Darius, [2] supervised the holy work with very great care, assisting the elders of the Jews and the chief officers of the temple. [3] The holy work prospered, while the prophets Haggai and Zechariah prophesied; [4] and they completed it by the command of the Lord God of Israel. So with the consent of Cyrus and Darius and Artaxerxes, kings of the Persians, [5] the holy house was finished by the twenty-third day of the month of Adar, in the sixth year of King Darius. [6] And the people of Israel, the priests, the Levites, and the rest of those who returned from exile who joined them, did according to what was written in the book

of Moses. [7] They offered at the dedication of the temple of the Lord one hundred bulls, two hundred rams, four hundred lambs, [8] and twelve male goats for the sin of all Israel, according to the number of the twelve leaders of the tribes of Israel; [9] and the priests and the Levites stood arrayed in their vestments, according to kindred, for the services of the Lord God of Israel in accordance with the book of Moses; and the gatekeepers were at each gate.

[10] The people of Israel who came from exile kept the passover on the fourteenth day of the first month, after the priests and the Levites were purified together. [11] Not all of the returned captives were purified, but the Levites were all purified together,[b] [12] and they sacrificed the passover lamb for all the returned captives and for their kindred the priests and for themselves. [13] The people of Israel who had returned from exile ate it, all those who had separated themselves from the abominations of the peoples of the land and sought the Lord. [14] They also kept the festival of unleavened bread seven days, rejoicing before the Lord, [15] because he had changed the will of the king of the Assyrians concerning them, to strengthen their hands for the service of the Lord God of Israel.

8 After these things, when Artaxerxes, the king of the Persians, was reigning, Ezra came, the son of Seraiah, son of Aza-

---

[a] Other authorities read *stated above* or *added in writing*

[b] Meaning of Gk uncertain

Ezra 6.3–5n. **25:** A cubit is about 18 in (45 cm). **27–34:** Darius's own support exceeds that of Cyrus. **32:** Ezra 6.11 prescribes further that the houses of violators of the decree be made a dunghill.

7.1–9: The Temple is completed (Ezra 6.13–18). At last, the builders are able to complete work on the Temple in 516 BCE and celebrate their success. **4:** *Artaxerxes* I (465–424 BCE) appears here anachronistically (see 8.1–9.36). This reference to him is taken from Ezra 6.14, where it functions ideologically, linking all the stages of the return. The verse is more problematic in 1 Esdras because, unlike Ezra-Nehemiah (see Neh 1–6), this book does not depict any Temple-building activities under Artaxerxes; Josephus omits the name. **5:** February-March, 516 BCE. **7–8:** Compare the account of the dedication of the first Temple (1 Kings 8.8,63). **9:** Compare Ezra 6.18.

7.10–15: The Passover celebration (Ezra 6.19–22). The celebration marks the restoration of Jewish life, resuming life and practices that were first disrupted with Josiah's death in ch 1. **11:** *Not all . . . were purified,* this comment is not in Ezra 6, but is perhaps borrowed from 2 Chr 30.18. **13:** Contrary to Ezra 6.21, the account here suggests that only the returned exiles participated in the Passover. But see 5.50. **15:** *The king of the Assyrians,* an anachronistic reference to the Persian king, alluding to the earliest exile by Assyria, which is now reversed. Josephus (*Ant.* 11.4.8) refers to the Persian king.

8.1–9.55: Final return and restoration under Ezra (Ezra 7.1–10.44; Neh 7.73–8.12). Ezra, who like Zerubbabel is a key figure in 1 Esdras, is first introduced here. 1 Esdras closely parallels Ezra-Nehemiah on the matters they

riah, son of Hilkiah, son of Shallum, [2] son of Zadok, son of Ahitub, son of Amariah, son of Uzzi, son of Bukki, son of Abishua, son of Phineas, son of Eleazar, son of Aaron the high[a] priest. [3] This Ezra came up from Babylon as a scribe skilled in the law of Moses, which was given by the God of Israel; [4] and the king showed him honor, for he found favor before the king[b] in all his requests. [5] There came up with him to Jerusalem some of the people of Israel and some of the priests and Levites and temple singers and gatekeepers and temple servants, [6] in the seventh year of the reign of Artaxerxes, in the fifth month (this was the king's seventh year); for they left Babylon on the new moon of the first month and arrived in Jerusalem on the new moon of the fifth month, by the prosperous journey that the Lord gave them.[c] [7] For Ezra possessed great knowledge, so that he omitted nothing from the law of the Lord or the commandments, but taught all Israel all the ordinances and judgments.

[8] The following is a copy of the written commission from King Artaxerxes that was delivered to Ezra the priest and reader of the law of the Lord:

[9] "King Artaxerxes to Ezra the priest and reader of the law of the Lord, greeting. [10] In accordance with my gracious decision, I have given orders that those of the Jewish nation and of the priests and Levites and others in our realm, those who freely choose to do so, may go with you to Jerusalem. [11] Let as many as are so disposed, therefore, leave with you, just as I and the seven Friends who are my counselors have decided, [12] in order to look into matters in Judea and Jerusalem, in accordance with what is in the law of the Lord, [13] and to carry to Jerusalem the gifts for the Lord of Israel that I and my Friends have vowed, and to collect for the Lord in Jerusalem all the gold and silver that may be found in the country of Babylonia, [14] together with what is given by the nation for the temple of their Lord that is in Jerusalem, both gold and silver for bulls and rams and lambs and what goes with them, [15] so as to offer sacrifices on the altar of their Lord that is in Jerusalem. [16] Whatever you and your kindred are minded to do with the gold and silver, perform it in accordance with the will of your God; [17] deliver the holy vessels of the Lord that are given you for the use of the temple of your God that is in Jerusalem. [18] And whatever else occurs to

---

a Gk *the first*
b Gk *him*
c Other authorities add *for him* or *upon him*

both discuss, although its author ignores the work of Nehemiah (Neh 1–7), as Sirach ignores the work of Ezra (Sir 49.13). Given the interest of the author of 1 Esdras in the Temple and its personnel, it is not surprising that Ezra the priest, rather than Nehemiah the governor, is highlighted. For the author of 1 Esdras, the restoration was accomplished by a descendant of King David—Zerubbabel—and by the priest Ezra. Both 1 Esdras and Ezra 7 set the mission of Ezra at the time of King Artaxerxes of Persia, most likely Artaxerxes I (465–424 BCE), although some scholars have suggested that it was at the time of the later king, Artaxerxes II (404–358 BCE).

8.1–7: Ezra's credentials and mission (Ezra 7.1–10). 1–2: The genealogy is briefer than that in Ezra 7.1–5 but establishes the impeccable credentials of Ezra as belonging to the most important priestly line. 3: *Scribe*, a highly educated person, often in an important advisory position to kings. 6: *The seventh year . . . of Artaxerxes* was 458 BCE if Artaxerxes I is meant. *The fifth month*, Ab (July-August). *The new moon of the first month*, i.e., Nisan (March-April), two weeks before Passover. The dates may be symbolic, reflecting the Exodus from Egypt in the first month (Ex 12.2; Num 33.3) and the destruction of the Temple in the fifth (2 Kings 25.8). However, five months would be a reasonable time for a journey from Babylon to Jerusalem. 7: A paraphrase of Ezra 7.10 defining Ezra's qualifications as scribe and teacher. *Law of the Lord,* the book of Torah ("the law of Moses," v. 3), some early version of the Pentateuch. *Law,* Gk "nomos," an equivalent term for Hebrew "torah," a term that can refer to a specific work as well as to authoritative, normative teachings.

8.8–24: The letter of Artaxerxes authorizing Ezra (Ezra 7.12–26). Ezra is authorized to lead a return to Judah, bring extensive gifts for the Temple, and teach the law of Ezra's God, namely the distinctive Jewish tradition that now has the backing of the king. 11: *The seven Friends* or counselors of the king (see Ezra 7.14) are referred to in Esth 1.14 and Herodotus, *Histories* 3.84. 13–17: The royal privileges include financial support for the Temple by the king himself, voluntary contributions from Babylonian Jews for the Temple, and a free hand to use the sur-

you as necessary for the temple of your God, you may provide out of the royal treasury. [19] "I, King Artaxerxes, have commanded the treasurers of Syria and Phoenicia that whatever Ezra the priest and reader of the law of the Most High God sends for, they shall take care to give him, [20] up to a hundred talents of silver, and likewise up to a hundred cors of wheat, a hundred baths of wine, and salt in abundance. [21] Let all things prescribed in the law of God be scrupulously fulfilled for the Most High God, so that wrath may not come upon the kingdom of the king and his sons. [22] You are also informed that no tribute or any other tax is to be laid on any of the priests or Levites or temple singers or gatekeepers or temple servants or persons employed in this temple, and that no one has authority to impose any tax on them.

[23] "And you, Ezra, according to the wisdom of God, appoint judges and justices to judge all those who know the law of your God, throughout all Syria and Phoenicia; and you shall teach it to those who do not know it. [24] All who transgress the law of your God or the law of the kingdom shall be strictly punished, whether by death or some other punishment, either fine or imprisonment."

[25] Then Ezra the scribe said,[a] "Blessed be the Lord alone, who put this into the heart of the king, to glorify his house that is in Jerusalem, [26] and who honored me in the sight of the king and his counselors and all his Friends and nobles. [27] I was encouraged by the help of the Lord my God, and I gathered men from Israel to go up with me."

[28] These are the leaders, according to their ancestral houses and their groups, who went up with me from Babylon, in the reign of King Artaxerxes: [29] Of the descendants of Phineas, Gershom. Of the descendants of Ithamar, Gamael. Of the descendants of David, Hattush son of Shecaniah. [30] Of the descendants of Parosh, Zechariah, and with him a hundred fifty men enrolled. [31] Of the descendants of Pahath-moab, Eliehoenai son of Zerahiah, and with him two hundred men. [32] Of the descendants of Zattu, Shecaniah son of Jahaziel, and with him three hundred men. Of the descendants of Adin, Obed son of Jonathan, and with him two hundred fifty men. [33] Of the descendants of Elam, Jeshaiah son of Gotholiah, and with him seventy men. [34] Of the descendants of Shephatiah, Zeraiah son of Michael, and with him seventy men. [35] Of the descendants of Joab, Obadiah son of Jehiel, and with him two hundred twelve men. [36] Of the descendants of Bani, Shelomith son of Josiphiah, and with him a hundred sixty men. [37] Of the descendants of Bebai, Zechariah son of Bebai, and with him twenty-eight men. [38] Of the descendants of Azgad, Johanan son of Hakkatan, and with him a hundred ten men. [39] Of the descendants of Adonikam, the last ones, their names being Eliphelet, Jeuel, and Shemaiah, and with them seventy men. [40] Of the descendants of Bigvai, Uthai son of Istalcurus, and with him seventy men.

[41] I assembled them at the river called Theras, and we encamped there three days,

a   Other ancient authorities lack *Then Ezra the scribe said*

plus. **18:** Artaxerxes virtually gives Ezra a blank check, showing great trust in Ezra. **19–22:** Artaxerxes assures a generous year's supply of provisions for the Temple. **19:** Additional support is to come from local officials. **20:** A *talent* was 75 lb (34 kg); a *cor* 6.5 bu (230 L); and a *bath* about 6 gal (23 L). **22:** Temple personnel are exempt from all taxes. **23–24:** Ezra is given authority to appoint judges throughout the entire province in order to maintain Jewish law. **24:** *The law of your God or the law of the kingdom,* the imperial authorization of the specific Jewish Law is important in that it grants the Jewish community the ability to preserve its distinctive religious heritage. The king's letter presents royal law and Jewish law as equally binding.

8.25–60: Ezra's report: leading the exiles to Jerusalem (Ezra 7.27–8.30). In a first-person account (sometimes called "the Ezra memoir"), Ezra describes his response to the royal letter, his prayer of thanks, and preparations for the journey to Jerusalem. **25–27:** Ezra's first words are a prayer of thanksgiving. **28–40:** Having thanked God, Ezra lists the names of exiles who went to Jerusalem with him. The list differs only slightly from the parallel in Ezra, although the numbers are higher, with a total of about 1,700 males. **29:** *Hattush,* several persons with this name appear in the Hebrew Bible but here and in the parallel in Ezra 8.2 only this Hattush is identified as a descendant of David.

8.41–60: Communal preparations (Ezra 8.15–30) include surveying the company, fasting, and commis-

and I inspected them. ⁴² When I found there none of the descendants of the priests or of the Levites, ⁴³ I sent word to Eliezar, Iduel, Maasmas, ⁴⁴ Elnathan, Shemaiah, Jarib, Nathan, Elnathan, Zechariah, and Meshullam, who were leaders and men of understanding; ⁴⁵ I told them to go to Iddo, who was the leading man at the place of the treasury, ⁴⁶ and ordered them to tell Iddo and his kindred and the treasurers at that place to send us men to serve as priests in the house of our Lord. ⁴⁷ And by the mighty hand of our Lord they brought us competent men of the descendants of Mahli son of Levi, son of Israel, namely Sherebiahᵃ with his descendants and kinsmen, eighteen; ⁴⁸ also Hashabiah and Annunus and his brother Jeshaiah, of the descendants of Hananiah, and their descendants, twenty men; ⁴⁹ and of the temple servants, whom David and the leaders had given for the service of the Levites, two hundred twenty temple servants; the list of all their names was reported.

⁵⁰ There I proclaimed a fast for the young men before our Lord, to seek from him a prosperous journey for ourselves and for our children and the livestock that were with us. ⁵¹ For I was ashamed to ask the king for foot soldiers and cavalry and an escort to keep us safe from our adversaries; ⁵² for we had said to the king, "The power of our Lord will be with those who seek him, and will support them in every way." ⁵³ And again we prayed to our Lord about these things, and we found him very merciful.

⁵⁴ Then I set apart twelve of the leaders of the priests, Sherebiah and Hashabiah, and ten of their kinsmen with them; ⁵⁵ and I weighed out to them the silver and the gold and the holy vessels of the house of our Lord, which the king himself and his counselors and the nobles and all Israel had given. ⁵⁶ I weighed and gave to them six hundred fifty talents of silver, and silver vessels worth a hundred talents, and a hundred talents of gold, ⁵⁷ and twenty golden bowls, and twelve bronze vessels of fine bronze that glittered like gold. ⁵⁸ And I said to them, "You are holy to the Lord, and the vessels are holy, and the silver and the gold are vowed to the Lord, the Lord of our ancestors. ⁵⁹ Be watchful and on guard until you deliver them to the leaders of the priests and the Levites, and to the heads of the ancestral houses of Israel, in Jerusalem, in the chambers of the house of our Lord." ⁶⁰ So the priests and the Levites who took the silver and the gold and the vessels that had been in Jerusalem carried them to the temple of the Lord.

⁶¹ We left the river Theras on the twelfth day of the first month; and we arrived in Jerusalem by the mighty hand of our Lord, which was upon us; he delivered us from every enemy on the way, and so we came to Jerusalem. ⁶² When we had been there three days, the silver and the gold were weighed and delivered in the house of our Lord to the priest Meremoth son of Uriah; ⁶³ with him was Eleazar son of Phinehas, and with them were Jozabad son of Jeshua and Moeth son of Binnui,ᵇ the Levites. ⁶⁴ The whole was counted and weighed, and the weight of everything was recorded at that very time. ⁶⁵ And those

---

ᵃ Gk Asbebias
ᵇ Gk Sabannus

sioning cult personnel as conveyers of vessels for the Temple. 41: The river . . . Theras is probably a tributary of the Euphrates. 42–49: Because neither priests nor Levites were among the group first assembled by Ezra, special measures had to be taken to secure the required number of both (Ezra 8 mentions only missing Levites). 45: The treasury, Ezra 8.17 mentions a place name, Casiphia, of unknown location. The treasure may be derived from interpretation of Casiphia, a word related to silver (Heb "kesep"). 50: Fasting prior to an important undertaking was common, especially in the postexilic period (2 Chr 20.3; Esth 4.16). 56: Talents weighed about 34 kg (75 lb) each. 58: Holy objects could be entrusted only to those who were holy themselves.

8.61–67: Arrival in Jerusalem (Ezra 8.31–36). Upon arriving, Ezra ensured that the treasures were turned over to the Jerusalem Temple personnel. This is followed by sacrifices to God and delivering the king's orders to the provincial officers, who are given no choice but to respect Ezra's mission. 61: Twelfth day of the first month (Nisan [March-April]), two days before the Passover commemorating the Exodus. A new Exodus may be implicit; however, for reasons of weather, spring was the season for expeditions (see 2 Sam 11.1).

who had returned from exile offered sacrifices to the Lord, the God of Israel, twelve bulls for all Israel, ninety-six rams, [66] seventy-two lambs, and as a thank offering twelve male goats—all as a sacrifice to the Lord. [67] They delivered the king's orders to the royal stewards and to the governors of Coelesyria and Phoenicia; and these officials[a] honored the people and the temple of the Lord.

[68] After these things had been done, the leaders came to me and said, [69] "The people of Israel and the rulers and the priests and the Levites have not put away from themselves the alien peoples of the land and their pollutions, the Canaanites, the Hittites, the Perizzites, the Jebusites, the Moabites, the Egyptians, and the Edomites. [70] For they and their descendants have married the daughters of these people,[b] and the holy race has been mixed with the alien peoples of the land; and from the beginning of this matter the leaders and the nobles have been sharing in this iniquity."

[71] As soon as I heard these things I tore my garments and my holy mantle, and pulled out hair from my head and beard, and sat down in anxiety and grief. [72] And all who were ever moved at[c] the word of the Lord of Israel gathered around me, as I mourned over this iniquity, and I sat grief-stricken until the evening sacrifice. [73] Then I rose from my fast, with my garments and my holy mantle torn, and kneeling down and stretching out my hands to the Lord [74] I said,

"O Lord, I am ashamed and confused before your face. [75] For our sins have risen higher than our heads, and our mistakes have mounted up to heaven [76] from the times of our ancestors, and we are in great sin to this day. [77] Because of our sins and the sins of our ancestors, we with our kindred and our kings and our priests were given over to the kings of the earth, to the sword and exile and plundering, in shame until this day. [78] And now in some measure mercy has come to us from you, O Lord, to leave to us a root and a name in your holy place, [79] and to uncover a light for us in the house of the Lord our God, and to give us food in the time of our servitude. [80] Even in our bondage we were not forsaken by our Lord, but he brought us into favor with the kings of the Persians, so that they have given us food [81] and glorified the temple of our Lord, and raised Zion from desolation, to give us a stronghold in Judea and Jerusalem.

[82] "And now, O Lord, what shall we say, when we have these things? For we have transgressed your commandments, which you gave by your servants the prophets, saying, [83] 'The land that you are entering to take possession of is a land polluted with the pollution of the aliens of the land, and they have filled it with their uncleanness. [84] Therefore do not give your daughters in marriage to their de-

a   Gk *they*
b   Gk *their daughters*
c   Or *zealous for*

8.68–9.36: The crisis of mixed marriages in Judah (Ezra 9.1–10.44). Ezra records that he was told about marriages of Judeans and "alien people of the land," which he viewed as violation of God's commandments. It appears that Ezra and his supporters considered the ethnic and religious cohesiveness of the returned exiles to be in danger when living as a minority in the land, among more numerous ethnicities and groups. This best explains the harsh, separatist measures that Ezra and his supporters take to protect communal boundaries. 1 Esdras follows the parallel in Ezra 9–10 with but a few, albeit important, differences.

8.68–70: The nature of the crisis (Ezra 9.1–2). Some members of the community, including leaders, have married women from the residents of the land, who are described as "alien." The parallel in Ezra 9.1–2 charges that the objectionable people's practices were like the ancient Canaanites, Moabites, and other groups mentioned in Deuteronomy as proscribed (see Deut 7.1–5 and 23.4–7). 1 Esdras gives the impression that the peoples of the land are in fact these earlier proscribed groups. **70:** *Holy*, that is dedicated to God. *Race*, lit. "seed" (offspring).

8.71–90: Ezra's response to the crisis: mourning and prayer (Ezra 9.3–15). Ezra interprets for the community the significance of mixed marriages, noting that they may again cause an exile. **71:** *Holy*, Ezra 9.3 does not ascribe holiness to Ezra's mantle; the addition in 1 Esdras stresses Ezra's significant position as high priest (see note on 9.39). **82–85:** The prophetic books contain no such statement; the author may have in mind such passages as Lev 18.24–30 and Deut 7.3–4, attributed to Moses as a prophet.

scendants, and do not take their daughters for your descendants; [85] do not seek ever to have peace with them, so that you may be strong and eat the good things of the land and leave it for an inheritance to your children forever.' [86] And all that has happened to us has come about because of our evil deeds and our great sins. For you, O Lord, lifted the burden of our sins [87] and gave us such a root as this; but we turned back again to transgress your law by mixing with the uncleanness of the peoples of the land. [88] Were you not angry enough with us to destroy us without leaving a root or seed or name? [89] O Lord of Israel, you are faithful; for we are left as a root to this day. [90] See, we are now before you in our iniquities; for we can no longer stand in your presence because of these things."

[91] While Ezra was praying and making his confession, weeping and lying on the ground before the temple, there gathered around him a very great crowd of men and women and youths from Jerusalem; for there was great weeping among the multitude. [92] Then Shecaniah son of Jehiel, one of the men of Israel, called out, and said to Ezra, "We have sinned against the Lord, and have married foreign women from the peoples of the land; but even now there is hope for Israel. [93] Let us take an oath to the Lord about this, that we will put away all our foreign wives, with their children, [94] as seems good to you and to all who obey the law of the Lord. [95] Rise up[a] and take action, for it is your task, and we are with you to take strong measures."
[96] Then Ezra rose up and made the leaders of the priests and Levites of all Israel swear that they would do this. And they swore to it.

9 Then Ezra set out and went from the court of the temple to the chamber of Jehohanan son of Eliashib, [2] and spent the night there; and he did not eat bread or drink water, for he was mourning over the great iniquities of the multitude. [3] And a proclamation was made throughout Judea and Jerusalem to all who had returned from exile that they should assemble at Jerusalem, [4] and that if any did not meet there within two or three days, in accordance with the decision of the ruling elders, their livestock would be seized for sacrifice and the men themselves[b] expelled from the multitude of those who had returned from the captivity.

[5] Then the men of the tribe of Judah and Benjamin assembled at Jerusalem within three days; this was the ninth month, on the twentieth day of the month. [6] All the multitude sat in the open square before the temple, shivering because of the bad weather that prevailed. [7] Then Ezra stood up and said to them, "You have broken the law and married foreign women, and so have increased the sin of Israel. [8] Now then make confession and give glory to the Lord the God of our ancestors, [9] and do his will; separate yourselves from the peoples of the land and from your foreign wives."

[10] Then all the multitude shouted and said with a loud voice, "We will do as you have said. [11] But the multitude is great and it is winter, and we are not able to stand in the open air. This is not a work we can do in one day or two, for we have sinned too much in these things. [12] So let the leaders of the multitude stay, and let all those in our settlements who have foreign wives come at the time appointed, [13] with the elders and judges of each place,

[a] Other ancient authorities read *as seems good to you." And all who obeyed the law of the Lord rose and said to Ezra,* [95]*"Rise up*
[b] Gk *he himself*

8.91–9.36: The people repent and dismiss their foreign wives (Ezra 10.1–44). As in Ezra 10, the account switches from a first-person report ("the Ezra Memoirs") to a third-person report about Ezra's reforms. **8.91–96:** A proposal to remove foreign wives is made. **93:** The children of such marriages are to be sent away as well, thereby not being separated from their mothers. **9.1–17:** Ezra leads the communal process toward dismissing foreign wives. **1:** *The chamber,* an office within the Temple complex that as a priest, Ezra may use. **4:** The ruling elders issue orders for the entire community to assemble; Ezra exercises religious, not political, authority in the land. **7:** *The law,* an allusion to Deut 7.3. **8:** *To give glory to the Lord* is to acknowledge themselves to be in the wrong (cf. Josh 7.19). **5–6:** Cold weather and heavy rains are typical of the *ninth month*, Chislev (November–December). **11–13:** Because of the severe winter weather and the complexity of the task, it is agreed that the separation should be handled by a committee, with the help of leaders from various districts. The multitude

until we are freed from the wrath of the Lord over this matter."

¹⁴ Jonathan son of Asahel and Jahzeiah son of Tikvah[a] undertook the matter on these terms, and Meshullam and Levi and Shabbethai served with them as judges. ¹⁵ And those who had returned from exile acted in accordance with all this.

¹⁶ Ezra the priest chose for himself the leading men of their ancestral houses, all of them by name; and on the new moon of the tenth month they began their sessions to investigate the matter. ¹⁷ And the cases of the men who had foreign wives were brought to an end by the new moon of the first month.

¹⁸ Of the priests, those who were brought in and found to have foreign wives were: ¹⁹ of the descendants of Jeshua son of Jozadak and his kindred, Maaseiah, Eliezar, Jarib, and Jodan. ²⁰ They pledged themselves to put away their wives, and to offer rams in expiation of their error. ²¹ Of the descendants of Immer: Hanani and Zebadiah and Maaseiah and Shemaiah and Jehiel and Azariah. ²² Of the descendants of Pashhur: Elioenai, Maaseiah, Ishmael, and Nathanael, and Gedaliah, and Salthas.

²³ And of the Levites: Jozabad and Shimei and Kelaiah, who was Kelita, and Pethahiah and Judah and Jonah. ²⁴ Of the temple singers: Eliashib and Zaccur.[b] ²⁵ Of the gatekeepers: Shallum and Telem.[c]

²⁶ Of Israel: of the descendants of Parosh: Ramiah, Izziah, Malchijah, Mijamin, and Eleazar, and Asibias, and Benaiah. ²⁷ Of the descendants of Elam: Mattaniah and Zechariah, Jezrielus and Abdi, and Jeremoth and Elijah. ²⁸ Of the descendants of Zamoth: Eliadas, Eliashib, Othoniah, Jeremoth, and Zabad and Zerdaiah. ²⁹ Of the descendants of Bebai: Jehohanan and Hananiah and Zabbai and Emathis. ³⁰ Of the descendants of Mani: Olamus, Mamuchus, Adaiah, Jashub, and Sheal and Jeremoth. ³¹ Of the descendants of Addi: Naathus and Moossias, Laccunus and Naidus, and Bescaspasmys and Sesthel, and Belnuus and Manasseas. ³² Of the descendants of Annan, Elionas and Asaias and Melchias and Sabbaias and Simon Chosamaeus. ³³ Of the descendants of Hashum: Mattenai and Mattattah and Zabad and Eliphelet and Manasseh and Shimei. ³⁴ Of the descendants of Bani: Jeremai, Momdius, Maerus, Joel, Mamdai and Bedeiah and Vaniah, Carabasion and Eliashib and Mamitanemus, Eliasis, Binnui, Elialis, Shimei, Shelemiah, Nethaniah. Of the descendants of Ezora: Shashai, Azarel, Azael, Samatus, Zambris, Joseph. ³⁵ Of the descendants of Nooma: Mazitias, Zabad, Iddo, Joel, Benaiah. ³⁶ All these had married foreign women, and they put them away together with their children.

³⁷ The priests and the Levites and the Israelites settled in Jerusalem and in the

a Gk *Thocanos*
b Gk *Bacchurus*
c Gk *Tolbanes*

is dismissed. **16–17:** Investigating the cases of intermarriage takes three months, from the first of the tenth month, Tebet (December–January) to the first of the first month, Nisan (March–April). **18–36:** Ezra 10.18–44. The list of those who put away foreign wives, which includes priests, Levites, and the laity, may have been preserved in the Temple archives. **20:** The priests, whose violation of genealogical purity endangers the sanctity of the Temple, are required to make a guilt offering in expiation of the sin. **36:** *They put them away,* only 1 Esdras specifies that the women and children were expelled. The parallel in Ezra 10.44 does not; verses 18–44 only indicate that priests put away their wives. Many translators, however, append 1 Esd 9.36 to Ezra 10.44.

9.37–55: The restoration is complete with Ezra's public reading of the law (Neh 7.73–8.12). First Esdras concludes with a grand celebration, reminiscent of the Passover celebration with which the book began (see ch 1), thereby rendering the destruction and exile as a temporary crisis that has been fully overcome by the end of the book; 1 Esdras departs markedly from Ezra-Nehemiah at this juncture. In Ezra-Nehemiah the reading of the Torah (NRSV "law"; see 8.7n.) follows the rebuilding of Jerusalem's walls under Nehemiah's leadership (Neh 1–6). For the author of 1 Esdras, the only important leaders are David's descendant Zerubbabel and Ezra the priest, who together restore (rather than transform) Israel's institutions and communal life. The celebrative, public reading of the book constitutes the completion of the restoration. Thus the ceremony recalls Sinai as the receiving of God's teachings by the entire people, transforming them into "the people of the Book." **37:** *The new moon* or first day of the seventh month, Tishri (September–October), was a day of holy convocation (Lev 23.23–

country. On the new moon of the seventh month, when the people of Israel were in their settlements, [38] the whole multitude gathered with one accord in the open square before the east gate of the temple; [39] they told Ezra the chief priest and reader to bring the law of Moses that had been given by the Lord God of Israel. [40] So Ezra the chief priest brought the law, for all the multitude, men and women, and all the priests to hear the law, on the new moon of the seventh month. [41] He read aloud in the open square before the gate of the temple from early morning until midday, in the presence of both men and women; and all the multitude gave attention to the law. [42] Ezra the priest and reader of the law stood on the wooden platform that had been prepared; [43] and beside him stood Mattathiah, Shema, Ananias, Azariah, Uriah, Hezekiah, and Baalsamus on his right, [44] and on his left Pedaiah, Mishael, Malchijah, Lothasubus, Nabariah, and Zechariah. [45] Then Ezra took up the book of the law in the sight of the multitude, for he had the place of honor in the presence of all. [46] When he opened the law, they all stood erect. And Ezra blessed the Lord God Most High, the God of hosts, the Almighty, [47] and the multitude answered, "Amen." They lifted up their hands, and fell to the ground and worshiped the Lord. [48] Jeshua and Anniuth and Sherebiah, Jadinus, Akkub, Shabbethai, Hodiah, Maiannas and Kelita, Azariah and Jozabad, Hanan, Pelaiah, the Levites, taught the law of the Lord,[a] at the same time explaining what was read.

[49] Then Attharates[b] said to Ezra the chief priest and reader, and to the Levites who were teaching the multitude, and to all, [50] "This day is holy to the Lord"—now they were all weeping as they heard the law— [51] "so go your way, eat the fat and drink the sweet, and send portions to those who have none; [52] for the day is holy to the Lord; and do not be sorrowful, for the Lord will exalt you." [53] The Levites commanded all the people, saying, "This day is holy; do not be sorrowful." [54] Then they all went their way, to eat and drink and enjoy themselves, and to give portions to those who had none, and to make great rejoicing; [55] because they were inspired by the words which they had been taught. And they came together.[c]

a Other ancient authorities add *and read the law of the Lord to the multitude*

b Or *the governor*

c The Greek text ends abruptly: compare Neh 8.13

24; Num 29.1). The date for the ceremony is September 444 (or perhaps 443). **38:** *The east gate of the temple,* Neh 8 does not mention the Temple and includes no other priests except Ezra in this ceremony of reading. **39:** *They told Ezra,* the people, not Ezra, initiate the ceremony. Ezra is not identified elsewhere as *the chief priest. The law of Moses,* i.e., the Torah. From the people's reaction and other details in Ezra-Nehemiah, scholars conclude that some form of today's Pentateuch, especially Deuteronomy, is being used. **40–41:** Both men and women participate in this ceremony of hearing and receiving the Torah (see Deut 31.12). **42:** The *platform* erected for Ezra probably continued the tradition whereby kings would appear before the people to reaffirm the covenant law on the festal occasion (cf. 2 Chr 20.5; 23.13; 29.4). It also served a practical need: to make the book of the Torah visible and audible to all. **43:** *Beside him stood . . .* Ezra's assistants include laity, as well as Levites, who are elsewhere connected to the study of the law. Their participation expresses broadened access to the authoritative teachings, a move away from exclusive control by priests (see Jer 18.18). **48:** The *Levites* explained the law to the people or possibly translated it into Aramaic for those who may not have been familiar with Hebrew.

9.49–55: The concluding celebration. 49: *Attharates* (see also 5.40) is a corruption of "tirshatha" (governor) in Neh 8.9. The author of 1 Esdras does not intend to indicate that Nehemiah, the named governor in Neh 8.9, was a participant in the festivity. **50–55:** The people are to rejoice even though the words of the law cause them to recognize their sin, because the law is associated with joy. **55:** *They came together,* some consider the ending abrupt, with the continuation in the parallel in Neh 8 (a second gathering and the feast of booths in Neh 8.13–18) a more fitting conclusion. Nevertheless, coming together as a community around the law and celebrating in the Temple in Jerusalem constitute an appropriate ending for a book that began with a celebration under Josiah in the same location.

THE PRAYER OF MANASSEH

NAME AND DATE

Manasseh, the idolatrous seventh-century BCE king of Judah, uttered a prayer, according to 2 Chr 33, while lying in shackles as a captive of Babylon. The Chronicler suggests that he had before him a text containing the king's actual words; the Prayer of Manasseh purports to be that very source. In reality, this composition was most likely written around the turn of the Common Era, perhaps even in Greek rather than in Hebrew.

CANONICAL STATUS AND LOCATION

Evidence for the Prayer of Manasseh is first found in a Syriac translation of a third-century CE Greek work, the *Didascalia Apostolorum*, and in the fourth-century Greek work *The Apostolic Constitutions*. It is appended to the Psalter in a few manuscripts of the Septuagint, and though beloved by many Christian communities, became canonical only in the Eastern Orthodox churches.

STRUCTURE, CONTENTS, AND INTERPRETATION

This prayer for forgiveness follows a typical structure: praise of God (vv. 1–8), lament (vv. 9–10), petition (vv. 11–13), and vow of additional praise (vv. 14–15). Like other late biblical prayers (Ezra 9.1–15; Neh 1.4–11; 9.6–37; Dan 9.4–19; Bar 1.15–3.8), it dwells on sin in order to emphasize the extent of the need for divine intervention. Such sin must be removed for the petitioner to be released from suffering. The way the prayer uses an emergent doctrine of repentance is novel. With his power, God has "made heaven and earth with all their order" (v. 2), and, in his mercy, he has "appointed repentance for sinners" (v. 7). Manasseh praises God for his creation of the world and thereby gains an opportunity to remind him that he also "created" repentance at that time. He establishes the basis, as a penitent, on which he can expect, even demand, to have his petition favorably received.

The distinctive theology of repentance found in the prayer may be profitably compared to a variety of late Hebrew and Greek texts. Nehemiah 1.8–9 and Bar 3.5–7 allude to a divine promise based on the book of Deuteronomy to redeem those who turn away from sin, but the focus of these texts is on the nation, not individuals. With its interest in the individual sinner, the Prayer of Manasseh resembles rabbinic texts with their interpretation of Deuteronomy's promise as applying to individuals and their view that repentance was established at the time of creation. The notion that repentance is a grant ("promised," v. 7; "appointed," vv. 8–9) probably comes from Greek military terminology; amnesty is granted to those who repent of their rebellion. The sense of repentance as having an established existence is also found in such Greek texts as the pagan *Tabula of Cebes*, the Hellenistic Jewish *Joseph and Aseneth* and the Christian *Shepherd of Hermas*.

David Lambert

¹O Lord Almighty,
God of our ancestors,
of Abraham and Isaac and Jacob
and of their righteous offspring;
²you who made heaven and earth
with all their order;
³who shackled the sea by your word of
command,
who confined the deep

and sealed it with your terrible and
glorious name;
⁴at whom all things shudder,
and tremble before your power,
⁵for your glorious splendor cannot be
borne,
and the wrath of your threat to sinners is
unendurable;
⁶yet immeasurable and unsearchable

1–8: Praise of the creator. 1: *God of our ancestors*, Ex 3.15–16; Dan 2.23; cf. Acts 3.13. *Their righteous offspring*, an unusual phrase, which may indicate that the prayer was meant to be uttered by a convert. 3: The restraining of the sea by the creator is a common poetic theme of the Bible (Pss 29.10; 104.7–9; 148.5–6; Job 38.8–11). 5: God's power, exemplified by creation and his mastery over the deep, naturally leads to the utter destruction of

is your promised mercy,

[7] for you are the Lord Most High,
of great compassion, long-suffering, and
     very merciful,
and you relent at human suffering.
O Lord, according to your great goodness
you have promised repentance and
     forgiveness
to those who have sinned against you,
and in the multitude of your mercies
you have appointed repentance for
     sinners,
so that they may be saved.[a]

[8] Therefore you, O Lord, God of the
     righteous,
have not appointed repentance for the
     righteous,
for Abraham and Isaac and Jacob, who did
     not sin against you,
but you have appointed repentance for me,
     who am a sinner.

[9] For the sins I have committed are more in
     number than the sand of the sea;
my transgressions are multiplied, O Lord,
     they are multiplied!
I am not worthy to look up and see the
     height of heaven
because of the multitude of my iniquities.

[10] I am weighted down with many an iron
     fetter,
so that I am rejected[b] because of my sins,
and I have no relief;

for I have provoked your wrath
and have done what is evil in your sight,
setting up abominations and multiplying
     offenses.

[11] And now I bend the knee of my heart,
imploring you for your kindness.

[12] I have sinned, O Lord, I have sinned,
and I acknowledge my transgressions.

[13] I earnestly implore you,
forgive me, O Lord, forgive me!
Do not destroy me with my transgressions!
Do not be angry with me forever or store
     up evil for me;
do not condemn me to the depths of the
     earth.
For you, O Lord, are the God of those who
     repent,

[14] and in me you will manifest your
     goodness;
for, unworthy as I am, you will save me
     according to your great mercy,

[15] and I will praise you continually all the
     days of my life.
For all the host of heaven sings your
     praise,
and yours is the glory forever. Amen.

---

a Other ancient authorities lack *O Lord, according . . .
be saved*

b Other ancient authorities read *so that I cannot lift
up my head*

sinners. **6–7:** His power is tempered by equally boundless mercy. In late biblical texts (e.g. 2 Chr 30.9), the "turn away from sin" enables divine mercy to operate. In the Prayer, God's establishment of repentance as a perennial opportunity is itself an expression of his mercy. **7:** Cf. Ex 34.6–7; the Greek is very close to the LXX translation of Joel 2.13 and Jon 4.21.

    9–10: Lament. A presentation of the central problem: the petitioner's sin has ruined him. **10:** *An iron fetter*, cf. 2 Chr 33.11. *I . . . have done what is evil in your sight*, Ps 51.4 (LXX 50.6).

    11–13: Petition. 11: *And now*, the dramatic climax. *I bend the knee*, usually an act of supplication. *Of my heart* probably serves as an indication of the supplicant's inner sincerity. That Manasseh is bound in fetters (v. 10), makes "bending the knee of the heart" ironically the only method of prostration available.

    14–15: Vow of praise. Reminder of how heeding the petitioner's request will benefit God. Such a vow is often found at the end of laments in the Psalms (e.g., 22.22–31; 80.18). **15:** *Host of heaven*, the multitude of angelic beings (Job 38.7; Neh 9.6; cf. Lk 2.13).

PSALM 151

CANONICAL STATUS, ANCIENT VERSIONS, AND DATE OF COMPOSITION

Although Psalm 151 does not appear in the Masoretic Text, it is the final psalm in the book of Psalms in the Greek Septuagint (LXX). One manuscript of the Septuagint contains a postscript to Psalm 151 that reads "the 151 Psalms of David," thus attributing the entire collection to King David. Other Septuagint manuscripts, however, contain a superscription to the psalm that indicates it is "outside the number" (of 150 psalms). A more expansive version of Psalm 151 was discovered among the Dead Sea Scrolls toward the end of the long psalms scroll from Cave 11 (11QPsa). This version comprises two distinct psalms, referred to as Psalm 151A (roughly LXX Ps 151) and 151B (fragmentary), each with its own superscription. The psalm also appears in somewhat expanded form as the first of five additional psalms in the Syriac translation. Psalm 151 is part of the canon of Orthodox churches and is included in the Apocrypha.

Psalm 151 was likely composed no later than the third century BCE when the exact content and ordering of the book of Psalms was not yet fixed. Such fluidity in form and content suggests that the psalms were used, memorized, and transmitted orally.

CONTENTS

In contrast to the final psalms of the canonical Psalter (146–150), which all offer praise to the LORD, Psalm 151 focuses on David, making explicit reference to incidents from David's life as described in 1 Samuel 16–17.

Verses 1 and 4b–5 of the psalm form a unit (with framed references to "brothers," "father's sheep") before the transition in vv. 6–7 to David's conflict with Goliath.

Judith H. Newman

This psalm is ascribed to David as his own composition (though it is outside the number[a]), after he had fought in single combat with Goliath.

¹I was small among my brothers,
    and the youngest in my father's house;
I tended my father's sheep.

²My hands made a harp;
    my fingers fashioned a lyre.

³And who will tell my Lord?
    The Lord himself; it is he who hears.[b]

⁴It was he who sent his messenger[c]
    and took me from my father's sheep,
    and anointed me with his
        anointing oil.

⁵My brothers were handsome and tall,
    but the Lord was not pleased with them.

⁶I went out to meet the Philistine,[d]
    and he cursed me by his idols.

⁷But I drew his own sword;
    I beheaded him, and took away disgrace
        from the people of Israel.

a Other ancient authorities add *of the one hundred fifty* (psalms)

b Other ancient authorities add *everything*; others add *me*; others read *who will hear me*

c Or *angel*

d Or *foreigner*

1: *The youngest,* cf. 1 Sam 16.11; 17.14. **2:** David's ability to play the *lyre* allowed him to soothe Saul's "evil spirit" (1 Sam 16.14–23; 18.10). Such musical ability was closely associated with the gift of poetry in antiquity and likely contributed to David's reputation as the author of the psalms. **4:** *His messenger,* specified in 11QPsa as the prophet Samuel; see 1 Sam 16.1–13. **6–7:** The focus of the psalm shifts to David's feat of slaying "the Philistine" Goliath (1 Sam 17). *Idols,* see 1 Sam 17.43. On Israel's subjugation by Goliath as a "disgrace" see Sir 47.4.

3 MACCABEES

NAME AND CANONICAL STATUS

The title of the book known as 3 Maccabees is a misnomer, for it is not a historical account of the Maccabees but a fictional story about Egyptian Jews under Ptolemy IV Philopator (221–204 BCE), half a century before the Maccabean period. The book is preserved in the Greek Septuagint (LXX) and the Syriac Peshitta, as well as in most manuscripts of the Armenian Bible. It is not, however, included in the Latin Vulgate. This may explain why it was not included in the canon of the Roman Catholic Church or in the traditional Protestant Apocrypha. It is included in the canon of the Eastern Orthodox churches.

CONTENTS

Third Maccabees begins with a brief account of how Ptolemy was saved from assassination at the battle of Raphia by the intervention of a Jew (1.1–5). This brief story of Jewish loyalty provides a foil against which the king's hostility to the Jews must be seen. The second episode (1.6–2.24) tells of the king's unsuccessful attempt to enter the holy of holies in the Jerusalem Temple. The desecration is averted by divine intervention in response to the prayer of the high priest Simon. The third episode, which takes up most of the book, describes the persecution of the Jews in Egypt. Upon his return there, the king determines to take vengeance upon the Jews for his humiliation in Jerusalem. He radically alters their legal status and attempts to force them to worship the Greek god Dionysus, promising to those who comply full citizenship in Alexandria (2.25–33). The vast majority of Jews resist, and with great cruelty they are herded together to be registered, tortured, and put to death. Again divine intervention averts disaster; after forty days the writing materials have been exhausted, and the registration cannot be completed (3.1–4.21). Finally, the king decrees that drugged elephants be turned upon the Jews, who have been detained in the city's arena. Twice this is providentially delayed, and the third miracle occurs in answer to the prayer of the aged priest Eleazar, paralleling the prayer of the high priest in the second episode. The elephants turn on the king's forces, and he repents, allowing the Jews to return to their homes (5.1–6.21). The book ends with a royal letter decreeing protection for the Jews, who punish those of their number who had apostatized, and rejoice at the providential deliverance (ch 7).

DATE AND HISTORICAL CONTEXT

The work was originally written in Greek by an unknown Egyptian Jew. The date of composition is disputed. Some scholars argue that the language of the book and its familiarity with the terminology of the Ptolemaic court argue for a date about 100 BCE. Others hold that the threatened change in the status of the Jews, and the promise of Alexandrian citizenship to those who abandoned their religion, reflect the situation of the Alexandrian Jews after Rome conquered Egypt in 30 BCE. Non-Jews were subjected to a new tax, called the "laographia" (the word used in connection with the change of status in 3 Macc 2.28). Citizenship normally required the worship of other gods, and so was unacceptable to most Jews, but some Jews who abandoned their religion rose to prominence in Roman service (most notably Tiberius Julius Alexander, nephew of the philosopher Philo). The book is not a historical account, although it does depict some earlier historical events, such as the battle of Raphia, known from other sources.

Although the book is written in a bombastic style, it provides a colorful drama of danger and deliverance. It also conveys a strict message of the need for solidarity in the Jewish community.

GUIDE TO READING

Third Maccabees belongs to a narrative genre that was especially popular among Jews who lived in the Diaspora, outside the land of Israel. Other examples are found in the book of Esther and in Daniel 2–6. These stories tell of some great danger that threatens the Jewish community, which is then averted, either through heroic action (Esther) or, more typically, through divine intervention. Such stories provided both entertainment and edification, allowing the Jewish readers to confront their fears of destruction and then allaying those fears by the happy ending.

John J. Collins

1 When Philopator learned from those who returned that the regions that he had controlled had been seized by Antiochus, he gave orders to all his forces, both infantry and cavalry, took with him his sister Arsinoë, and marched out to the region near Raphia, where the army of Antiochus was encamped. ² But a certain Theodotus, determined to carry out the plot he had devised, took with him the best of the Ptolemaic arms that had been previously issued to him,ᵃ and crossed over by night to the tent of Ptolemy, intending single-handed to kill him and thereby end the war. ³ But Dositheus, known as the son of Drimylus, a Jew by birth who later changed his religion and apostatized from the ancestral traditions, had led the king away and arranged that a certain insignificant man should sleep in the tent; and so it turned out that this man incurred the vengeance meant for the king.ᵇ ⁴ When a bitter fight resulted, and matters were turning out rather in favor of Antiochus, Arsinoë went to the troops with wailing and tears, her locks all disheveled, and exhorted them to defend themselves and their children and wives bravely, promising to give them each two minas of gold if they won the battle. ⁵ And so it came about that the enemy was routed in the action, and many captives also were taken. ⁶ Now that he had foiled the plot, Ptolemyᶜ decided to visit the neighboring cities and encourage them. ⁷ By doing this, and by endowing their sacred enclosures with gifts, he strengthened the morale of his subjects.

⁸ Since the Jews had sent some of their council and elders to greet him, to bring him gifts of welcome, and to congratulate him on what had happened, he was all the more eager to visit them as soon as possible. ⁹ After he had arrived in Jerusalem, he offered sacrifice to the supreme Godᵈ and made thank offerings and did what was fitting for the holy place.ᵉ Then, upon entering the place and being impressed by its excellence and its beauty, ¹⁰ he marveled at the good order of the temple, and conceived a desire to enter the sanctuary. ¹¹ When they said that this was not permitted, because not even members of their own nation were allowed to enter,

---

ᵃ Or *the best of the Ptolemaic soldiers previously put under his command*
ᵇ Gk *that one*
ᶜ Gk *he*
ᵈ Gk *the greatest God*
ᵉ Gk *the place*

1.1–7: The battle of Raphia (217 BCE). The abruptness with which the book opens and the use of the Greek conjunctive particle "de" may indicate that the introduction to 3 Maccabees has not survived (see also 2.25n.). Alternatively, the account of the battle may have been excerpted from a historical source. It resembles the account given by the second-century BCE historian Polybius (book 5), who also reports a plot to kill the king, but not the role of Dositheus in foiling it. **1**: Ptolemy IV [Philopator] was king of Egypt 221–204. *From those who returned,* fugitives who had escaped. *Antiochus* III, later called the Great, was king of Syria 223–187. *Raphia,* a city of Palestine, three miles from Gaza and not far from the Egyptian frontier. *Arsinoë,* Ptolemy's sister, who became his wife, was later put to death at the instigation of her husband. **2**: *Theodotus* had been chief commander of the Egyptian forces in Syria, but subsequently became disaffected and deserted to Antiochus III (Polybius, 5.40). **3**: *Dositheus* is mentioned in Hibeh papyrus 90 as priest of Alexander in 222 BCE, a very exalted position, and he is also mentioned in earlier papyri as a Ptolemaic administrator. The papyri, however, do not identify him as Jewish. *A certain insignificant* man, Polybius identifies the man as Andreas, the king's physician. **4**: *Two minas,* ca. 2.5 lb (1.1 kg). **5**: According to Polybius (5.86.5–6), Antiochus lost nearly 10,000 infantry, 300 cavalry, and 4,000 prisoners; Ptolemy lost 1,500 infantry and 700 cavalry.

1.8–15: Ptolemy attempts to enter the sanctuary at Jerusalem. 9: Reference to *the supreme God,* Greek "megistos theos," occurs frequently in 3 Maccabees (1.9,16; 3.11; 4.16; 5.25; 7.22) as well as in 2 Maccabees (3.36). The God of the Jews was often known as The Most High God in antiquity. It was customary for kings to show respect to local deities. According to Josephus (*Ant.* 11.336), Alexander the Great had offered sacrifice in the Jerusalem Temple. *The holy place,* an alternative term for "the Temple" in 3 Maccabees and other Jewish literature. **10**: No attempt by a Ptolemy to enter the holy of holies is otherwise known. The Roman general Pompey did enter it in 63 BCE, but the closest parallel to 3 Maccabees on this point is found in the story of Heliodorus in 2 Macc 3, although the details of the stories are different (Heliodorus was attempting to seize the Temple treasure). **11**: *High priest . . . once a year,* Lev 16.2,34.

not even all of the priests, but only the high priest who was pre-eminent over all—and he only once a year—the king was by no means persuaded. [12] Even after the law had been read to him, he did not cease to maintain that he ought to enter, saying, "Even if those men are deprived of this honor, I ought not to be." [13] And he inquired why, when he entered every other temple,[a] no one there had stopped him. [14] And someone answered thoughtlessly that it was wrong to take that as a portent.[b] [15] "But since this has happened," the king[c] said, "why should not I at least enter, whether they wish it or not?"

[16] Then the priests in all their vestments prostrated themselves and entreated the supreme God[d] to aid in the present situation and to avert the violence of this evil design, and they filled the temple with cries and tears; [17] those who remained behind in the city were agitated and hurried out, supposing that something mysterious was occurring. [18] Young women who had been secluded in their chambers rushed out with their mothers, sprinkled their hair with dust,[e] and filled the streets with groans and lamentations. [19] Those women who had recently been arrayed for marriage abandoned the bridal chambers[f] prepared for wedded union, and, neglecting proper modesty, in a disorderly rush flocked together in the city. [20] Mothers and nurses abandoned even newborn children here and there, some in houses and some in the streets, and without a backward look they crowded together at the most high temple. [21] Various were the supplications of those gathered there because of what the king was profanely plotting. [22] In addition, the bolder of the citizens would not tolerate the completion of his plans or the fulfillment of his intended purpose.

[23] They shouted to their compatriots to take arms and die courageously for the ancestral law, and created a considerable disturbance in the holy place;[g] and being barely restrained by the old men and the elders,[h] they resorted to the same posture of supplication as the others. [24] Meanwhile the crowd, as before, was engaged in prayer, [25] while the elders near the king tried in various ways to change his arrogant mind from the plan that he had conceived. [26] But he, in his arrogance, took heed of nothing, and began now to approach, determined to bring the aforesaid plan to a conclusion. [27] When those who were around him observed this, they turned, together with our people, to call upon him who has all power to defend them in the present trouble and not to overlook this unlawful and haughty deed. [28] The continuous, vehement, and concerted cry of the crowds[i] resulted in an immense uproar; [29] for it seemed that not only the people but also the walls and the whole earth around echoed, because indeed all at that time[j] preferred death to the profanation of the place.

2 Then the high priest Simon, facing the sanctuary, bending his knees and extending his hands with calm dignity, prayed as

---

a   Or *entered the temple precincts*
b   Or *to boast of this*
c   Gk *he*
d   Gk *the greatest God*
e   Other ancient authorities add *and ashes*
f   Or *the canopies*
g   Gk *the place*
h   Other ancient authorities read *priests*
i   Other ancient authorities read *vehement cry of the assembled crowds*
j   Other ancient authorities lack *at that time*

1.16–29: Jewish reaction to Ptolemy's determination to enter the sanctuary. Compare the reaction to the attempt of Heliodorus in 2 Macc 3.14–21, and also the historical episodes when Pontius Pilate introduced the sacrilegious Roman standards into Jerusalem (Josephus, *War* 1.169–74; *Ant.* 18.55–59) and when Caligula attempted to have his statue installed in the Temple (*War* 2.184–203; *Ant.* 18.269–72). 18: *Young women* were not permitted to appear in public before marriage; cf. 2 Macc 3.19. 19: For other references to bridal chambers see Joel 2.16; 2 Esd 16.33–34; Bar 2.23. 23: *Die courageously for the ancestral law,* 1 Macc 2.40; 3.21; 13.3–4; 2 Macc 8.21. It is noteworthy that the militants are restrained by the elders here, in contrast to the Maccabean rebellion and to the later Jewish revolt against Rome.

2.1–20: The prayer of Simon, the high priest. Simon II, son of Onias II and called "the Just," was high priest about 219–196 BCE (see Sir 50.1n.). The prayer is in a classic Jewish form that, like Eleazar's prayer in 6.1–15, follows the pattern of Ps 105 and 106 in confessing the sins of the people but calling on God to deliver them as he follows:[a] [2] "Lord, Lord, king of the heavens, and sovereign of all creation, holy among the holy ones, the only ruler, almighty, give attention to us who are suffering grievously from an impious and profane man, puffed up in his audacity and power. [3] For you, the creator of all things and the governor of all, are a just Ruler, and you judge those who have done anything in insolence and arrogance. [4] You destroyed those who in the past committed injustice, among whom were even giants who trusted in their strength and boldness, whom you destroyed by bringing on them a boundless flood. [5] You consumed with fire and sulfur the people of Sodom who acted arrogantly, who were notorious for their vices;[b] and you made them an example to those who should come afterward. [6] You made known your mighty power by inflicting many and varied punishments on the audacious Pharaoh who had enslaved your holy people Israel. [7] And when he pursued them with chariots and a mass of troops, you overwhelmed him in the depths of the sea, but carried through safely those who had put their confidence in you, the Ruler over the whole creation. [8] And when they had seen works of your hands, they praised you, the Almighty. [9] You, O King, when you had created the boundless and immeasurable earth, chose this city and sanctified this place for your name, though you have no need of anything; and when you had glorified it by your magnificent manifestation,[c] you made it a firm foundation for the glory of your great and honored name. [10] And because you love the house of Israel, you promised that if we should have reverses and tribulation should overtake us, you would listen to our petition when we come to this place and pray.

[11] And indeed you are faithful and true. [12] And because oftentimes when our fathers were oppressed you helped them in their humiliation, and rescued them from great evils, [13] see now, O holy King, that because of our many and great sins we are crushed with suffering, subjected to our enemies, and overtaken by helplessness. [14] In our downfall this audacious and profane man undertakes to violate the holy place on earth dedicated to your glorious name. [15] For your dwelling is the heaven of heavens, unapproachable by human beings. [16] But because you graciously bestowed your glory on your people Israel, you sanctified this place. [17] Do not punish us for the defilement committed by these men, or call us to account for this profanation, otherwise the transgressors will boast in their wrath and exult in the arrogance of their tongue, saying, [18] 'We have trampled down the house of the sanctuary as the houses of the abominations are trampled down.' [19] Wipe away our sins and disperse our errors, and reveal your mercy at this hour. [20] Speedily let your mercies overtake us, and put praises in the mouth of those who are downcast and broken in spirit, and give us peace."

[21] Thereupon God, who oversees all things, the first Father of all, holy among the holy ones, having heard the lawful supplication, scourged him who had exalted himself in insolence and audacity. [22] He shook him on this side and that as a reed is shaken by the wind, so that he lay helpless on the ground and, besides being paralyzed in his limbs, was unable even to speak, since

---

[a] Other ancient authorities lack verse 1
[b] Other ancient authorities read *secret in their vices*
[c] Or *epiphany*

---

did in the past. **2:** *Holy among the holy ones,* Isa 57.15 LXX. The *holy ones* are members of the divine council (see Deut 33.2; Ps 89.5), in this period understood as angels. **3:** Ex 18.11; Ps 31.23. **4:** *Giants,* the race of heroes whose origins are described in Gen 6.1–4, also mentioned in Wis 14.6; Sir 16.7; Bar 3.26; 1 Enoch 7.2; 15.8. **5:** *Sodom,* Gen 19.24; Deut 29.23; Wis 10.7. *An example,* cf. 2 Pet 2.6. **6:** Exodus 5–12. *Your holy people Israel,* Ex 19.6; Wis 10.15. **7:** *Overwhelmed him,* Exodus 14. **8:** *They praised,* Ex 15.1–21; Wis 19.8–9. **9:** *This city,* Jerusalem. *Place,* see 1.9n. *No need of anything,* 2 Macc 14.35–36. **10:** *Promised . . . you would listen,* Deut 30.1–6; 1 Kings 8.33–34,48–50. **12:** *Our fathers . . . you . . . rescued,* 1 Sam 12.10–11; Pss 22.4–5; 106.43; Neh 9.28. **13:** *Because of our many and great sins,* even though the Jewish community has done nothing wrong in this instance, such confession of sin was a standard element in prayers of this type. **14:** *Glorious name,* Jdt 9.8. **15:** *The heaven of heavens,* 1 Kings 8.27; Isa 66.1. **18:** *Trampled down,* Isa 63.18; Dan 8.13; 1 Macc 3.45. **19:** *Wipe away our sins,* Ps 51.2,9. **20:** *Mercies,* Ps 79.8,13. **2.21–24: The punishment of Ptolemy. 21:** *Holy ones,* v. 2n. **22:** *Paralyzed,* compare the punishment of Heli-

he was smitten[a] by a righteous judgment. ²³ Then both friends and bodyguards, seeing the severe punishment that had overtaken him, and fearing that he would lose his life, quickly dragged him out, panic-stricken in their exceedingly great fear. ²⁴ After a while he recovered, and though he had been punished, he by no means repented, but went away uttering bitter threats.

²⁵ When he arrived in Egypt, he increased in his deeds of malice, abetted by the previously mentioned drinking companions and comrades, who were strangers to everything just. ²⁶ He was not content with his uncounted licentious deeds, but even continued with such audacity that he framed evil reports in the various localities; and many of his friends, intently observing the king's purpose, themselves also followed his will. ²⁷ He proposed to inflict public disgrace on the Jewish community,[b] and he set up a stone[c] on the tower in the courtyard with this inscription: ²⁸ "None of those who do not sacrifice shall enter their sanctuaries, and all Jews shall be subjected to a registration involving poll tax and to the status of slaves. Those who object to this are to be taken by force and put to death; ²⁹ those who are registered are also to be branded on their bodies by fire with the ivy-leaf symbol of Dionysus, and they shall also be reduced to their former

limited status." ³⁰ In order that he might not appear to be an enemy of all, he inscribed below: "But if any of them prefer to join those who have been initiated into the mysteries, they shall have equal citizenship with the Alexandrians."

³¹ Now some, however, with an obvious abhorrence of the price to be exacted for maintaining the religion of their city,[d] readily gave themselves up, since they expected to enhance their reputation by their future association with the king. ³² But the majority acted firmly with a courageous spirit and did not abandon their religion; and by paying money in exchange for life they confidently attempted to save themselves from the registration. ³³ They remained resolutely hopeful of obtaining help, and they abhorred those who separated themselves from them, considering them to be enemies of the Jewish nation,[b] and depriving them of companionship and mutual help.

3 When the impious king comprehended this situation, he became so infuriated that not only was he enraged against those Jews who lived in Alexandria, but was still

---

a   Other ancient authorities read *pierced*
b   Gk *the nation*
c   Gk *stele*
d   Meaning of Gk uncertain

---

odorus (2 Macc 3.24–30) and of Antiochus (2 Macc 9.5–6). **23:** *Friends,* the higher officers and courtiers of the king (4 Macc 8.5n.). *Lose his life,* cf. 2 Macc 3.31. **24:** *By no means repented,* compare Antiochus Epiphanes in 2 Macc 9.7 (Antiochus is subsequently forced to repent).

2.25–33: Hostile measures against the Jews of Egypt. 25: These *companions* have not, in fact, been *previously mentioned* in the present text of 3 Maccabees; this is additional evidence that the opening section has been lost (see 1.1–7n.). **26:** *Friends,* see v. 23n. **28:** The Jews are forbidden to *enter their sanctuaries,* that is, their synagogues. Synagogue worship was disrupted during a pogrom in Alexandria in 38 CE. *Registration,* for which the Greek term, "laographia," literally means census, is often used in connection with taxation. It is especially associated with the *poll tax* imposed by the Romans in 24 BCE. This is the only tax that is known to have entailed a reduction of the status of the Jews, since it classified them with the Egyptians, not with the Greeks. **29:** Ptolemy Philopator was in fact a devotee of the Greek god Dionysus. Branding was associated with the worship of Dionysus, and the king himself may have been branded. Judaism was sometimes thought by Gentile observers to be a form of the worship of Dionysus (see especially Plutarch, *Table Talk* 4.6.1–2). According to 2 Macc 6.7, Antiochus Epiphanes tried to make the people of Jerusalem observe the festival of Dionysus. Branding was also used to identify slaves in case they ran away. 3 Maccabees seems to confuse the two kinds of branding. *Their former limited status,* perhaps referring to the status of Jewish captives before they were released by Ptolemy II (see *Letter of Aristeas* 22). **32:** *Paying money,* as bribes. **33:** *Enemies of the Jewish nation,* renegade Jews are viewed with even greater opprobrium than the Gentile persecutors.

3.1–10: The Jews and their neighbors. 1: The distinction between Jews in *Alexandria* and those in the *countryside* is made also in 4.11–12. The emphasis on Jews from the countryside is odd and may reflect a historical

more bitterly hostile toward those in the countryside; and he ordered that all should promptly be gathered into one place, and put to death by the most cruel means. [2] While these matters were being arranged, a hostile rumor was circulated against the Jewish nation by some who conspired to do them ill, a pretext being given by a report that they hindered others[a] from the observance of their customs. [3] The Jews, however, continued to maintain goodwill and unswerving loyalty toward the dynasty; [4] but because they worshiped God and conducted themselves by his law, they kept their separateness with respect to foods. For this reason they appeared hateful to some; [5] but since they adorned their style of life with the good deeds of upright people, they were established in good repute with everyone. [6] Nevertheless those of other races paid no heed to their good service to their nation, which was common talk among all; [7] instead they gossiped about the differences in worship and foods, alleging that these people were loyal neither to the king nor to his authorities, but were hostile and greatly opposed to his government. So they attached no ordinary reproach to them.

[8] The Greeks in the city, though wronged in no way, when they saw an unexpected tumult around these people and the crowds that suddenly were forming, were not strong enough to help them, for they lived under tyranny. They did try to console them, being grieved at the situation, and expected that matters would change; [9] for such a great community ought not be left to its fate when it had committed no offense. [10] And already some of their neighbors and friends and business associates had taken some of them aside privately and were pledging to protect them and to exert more earnest efforts for their assistance.

[11] Then the king, boastful of his present good fortune, and not considering the might of the supreme God,[b] but assuming that he would persevere constantly in his same purpose, wrote this letter against them:

[12] "King Ptolemy Philopator to his generals and soldiers in Egypt and all its districts, greetings and good health:

[13] "I myself and our government are faring well. [14] When our expedition took place in Asia, as you yourselves know, it was brought to conclusion, according to plan, by the gods' deliberate alliance with us in battle, [15] and we considered that we should not rule the nations inhabiting Coelesyria and Phoenicia by the power of the spear, but should cherish them with clemency and great benevolence, gladly treating them well. [16] And when we had granted very great revenues to the temples in the cities, we came on to Jerusalem also, and went up to honor the temple of those wicked people, who never cease from their folly. [17] They accepted our presence by word, but insincerely by deed, because when we proposed to enter their inner temple and honor it with magnificent and most beautiful offerings, [18] they were carried away by their traditional arrogance, and excluded us from entering; but they were spared the exercise of

---

[a] Gk *them*

[b] Gk *the greatest God*

---

attempt by Ptolemy to take a census of the Jews in rural areas. **2**: The *rumor* maliciously represents the Jews as hostile to the best interests of the state (cf. Esth 3.8), whereas the author insists on their loyalty. Some scholars think 3 Maccabees was written by a Jew from the countryside. His Greek is less sophisticated than that of Alexandrian Jews, such as Philo. **4**: *Separateness with respect to foods* was one of the barriers between Jew and Gentile, cf. 1 Macc 1.62–63; 2 Macc 11.30–31. Many Hellenistic Jewish writings avoid the subject. For a defense of the observance of Jewish dietary rules, by explaining them allegorically, see the *Letter of Aristeas,* 128–66. **5**: Deut 4.5–6. **7**: For similar charges see Esth 3.8; Add Esth 13.4–5. **8**: *The Greeks,* the elite, cultivated class, in distinction from *those of other races* (v. 6). The Alexandrian Greeks were bitter enemies of the Jews in the Roman period, but the author portrays a relationship of support and respect between the two groups, even though the king and his friends were obviously Greek.

3.11–30: Ptolemy orders the arrest of all Jews in his kingdom. 11: The king is *boastful,* and therefore guilty of "hubris," the sin that leads to disaster in Greek tragedy. *Assuming that he would persevere,* an anticipatory reference to the calamity that came upon him by which he forgot his own previous commands (5.27–28). **15**: *Coelesyria,* western Syria. *Phoenicia,* modern Lebanon. *Benevolence,* Greek "philanthropia" (see vv. 18,20), was

our power because of the benevolence that we have toward all. [19] By maintaining their manifest ill-will toward us, they become the only people among all nations who hold their heads high in defiance of kings and their own benefactors, and are unwilling to regard any action as sincere.

[20] "But we, when we arrived in Egypt victorious, accommodated ourselves to their folly and did as was proper, since we treat all nations with benevolence. [21] Among other things, we made known to all our amnesty toward their compatriots here, both because of their alliance with us and the myriad affairs liberally entrusted to them from the beginning; and we ventured to make a change, by deciding both to deem them worthy of Alexandrian citizenship and to make them participants in our regular religious rites.[a] [22] But in their innate malice they took this in a contrary spirit, and disdained what is good. Since they incline constantly to evil, [23] they not only spurn the priceless citizenship, but also both by speech and by silence they abominate those few among them who are sincerely disposed toward us; in every situation, in accordance with their infamous way of life, they secretly suspect that we may soon alter our policy. [24] Therefore, fully convinced by these indications that they are ill-disposed toward us in every way, we have taken precautions so that, if a sudden disorder later arises against us, we shall not have these impious people behind our backs as traitors and barbarous enemies. [25] Therefore we have given orders that, as soon as this letter arrives, you are to send to us those who live among you, together with their wives and children, with insulting and harsh treatment, and bound securely with iron fetters, to suffer the sure and shameful death

that befits enemies. [26] For when all of these have been punished, we are sure that for the remaining time the government will be established for ourselves in good order and in the best state. [27] But those who shelter any of the Jews, whether old people or children or even infants, will be tortured to death with the most hateful torments, together with their families. [28] Any who are willing to give information will receive the property of those who incur the punishment, and also two thousand drachmas from the royal treasury, and will be awarded their freedom.[b] [29] Every place detected sheltering a Jew is to be made unapproachable and burned with fire, and shall become useless for all time to any mortal creature." [30] The letter was written in the above form.

4 In every place, then, where this decree arrived, a feast at public expense was arranged for the Gentiles with shouts and gladness, for the inveterate enmity that had long ago been in their minds was now made evident and outspoken. [2] But among the Jews there was incessant mourning, lamentation, and tearful cries; everywhere their hearts were burning, and they groaned because of the unexpected destruction that had suddenly been decreed for them. [3] What district or city, or what habitable place at all, or what streets were not filled with mourning and wailing for them? [4] For with such a harsh and ruthless spirit were they being sent off, all together, by the generals in the several cities, that at the sight of their unusual punishments, even some of their enemies, perceiving the common object of pity before their eyes, reflected

---

[a] Other ancient authorities read *partners of our regular priests*

[b] Gk *crowned with freedom*

---

regarded as a major political virtue during the Hellenistic period. **21:** For the confidence placed in Jews, see 6.25 and Josephus, *Ag. Ap.* 2.49, who says that Ptolemy VI Philometor gave two Jewish generals, Onias and Dositheus, command of his whole army. Jews were often employed in Egypt as mercenaries. *Alexandrian citizenship* normally entailed participation in Greek religious ceremonies. Alexandrian Greeks, such as the first-century CE scholar Apion, complained that the Jews wanted the privileges of citizenship but were unwilling to fulfill the religious obligations that it usually entailed. **24:** *Behind our backs*, cf. Ex 1.10. **28:** *Awarded their freedom*, another rendering is "crowned at the Eleutheria" (a festival of Dionysus; see 2.29n.). **29:** *Useless for all time*, cf. Add Esth 16.24.

4.1–21: The Jews brought to Alexandria and imprisoned. 1: *Enmity* on the part of native-born Egyptians for the Jews is assumed in 3 Maccabees; contrast the depiction of the Greeks in 3.8. **2:** *Mourning, lamentation, and*

on the uncertainty of life and shed tears at the most miserable expulsion of these people. [5] For a multitude of gray-headed old men, sluggish and bent with age, was being led away, forced to march at a swift pace by the violence with which they were driven in such a shameful manner. [6] And young women who had just entered the bridal chamber[a] to share married life exchanged joy for wailing, their myrrh-perfumed hair sprinkled with ashes, and were carried away unveiled, all together raising a lament instead of a wedding song, as they were torn by the harsh treatment of the heathen.[b] [7] In bonds and in public view they were violently dragged along as far as the place of embarkation. [8] Their husbands, in the prime of youth, their necks encircled with ropes instead of garlands, spent the remaining days of their marriage festival in lamentations instead of good cheer and youthful revelry, seeing death immediately before them.[c] [9] They were brought on board like wild animals, driven under the constraint of iron bonds; some were fastened by the neck to the benches of the boats, others had their feet secured by unbreakable fetters, [10] and in addition they were confined under a solid deck, so that, with their eyes in total darkness, they would undergo treatment befitting traitors during the whole voyage.

[11] When these people had been brought to the place called Schedia, and the voyage was concluded as the king had decreed, he commanded that they should be enclosed in the hippodrome that had been built with a monstrous perimeter wall in front of the city, and that was well suited to make them an obvious spectacle to all coming back into the city and to those from the city[d] going out into the country, so that they could neither communicate with the king's forces nor in any way claim to be inside the circuit of the city.[e] [12] And when this had happened, the king, hearing that the Jews' compatriots

from the city frequently went out in secret to lament bitterly the ignoble misfortune of their kindred, [13] ordered in his rage that these people be dealt with in precisely the same fashion as the others, not omitting any detail of their punishment. [14] The entire race was to be registered individually, not for the hard labor that has been briefly mentioned before, but to be tortured with the outrages that he had ordered, and at the end to be destroyed in the space of a single day. [15] The registration of these people was therefore conducted with bitter haste and zealous intensity from the rising of the sun until its setting, coming to an end after forty days but still uncompleted.

[16] The king was greatly and continually filled with joy, organizing feasts in honor of all his idols, with a mind alienated from truth and with a profane mouth, praising speechless things that are not able even to communicate or to come to one's help, and uttering improper words against the supreme God.[f] [17] But after the previously mentioned interval of time the scribes declared to the king that they were no longer able to take the census of the Jews because of their immense number, [18] though most of them were still in the country, some still residing in their homes, and some at the place;[g] the task was impossible for all the generals in Egypt. [19] After he had threatened them severely, charging that they had been bribed to contrive a means of escape, he was clearly convinced about the matter [20] when they said and proved that

a Or *the canopy*
b Other ancient authorities read *as though torn by heathen whelps*
c Gk *seeing Hades already lying at their feet*
d Gk *those of them*
e Or *claim protection of the walls*; meaning of Gk uncertain
f Gk *the greatest God*
g Other ancient authorities read *on the way*

tearful cries, cf. Esth 4.3. **11:** *Schedia*, a promontory about three miles from Alexandria. *The hippodrome* (arena) was situated at the east or Canobic gate of Alexandria; according to Strabo (17.1.10,16) a canal joined Schedia and the Canobic gate. *Inside . . . the city*, implies that Jews living in Alexandria (see v. 12, *compatriots from the city*) had been thus far unmolested (but cf. 3.1). **14:** *Mentioned before*, see 2.28. The registration for poll tax and slave status is transformed into an instrument for the execution of *the entire race* of Jews. **16:** *Speechless things*, see Ps 115.3–7; Jer 10.5; Hab 2.18; Bar 6.7. *Supreme God*, see 1.9n. **17:** *Their immense number*, an obvious hyperbole. **19:** *Bribed*, see 2.32.

both the paper[a] and the pens they used for writing had already given out. [21] But this was an act of the invincible providence of him who was aiding the Jews from heaven.

5 Then the king, completely inflexible, was filled with overpowering anger and wrath; so he summoned Hermon, keeper of the elephants, [2] and ordered him on the following day to drug all the elephants—five hundred in number—with large handfuls of frankincense and plenty of unmixed wine, and to drive them in, maddened by the lavish abundance of drink, so that the Jews might meet their doom. [3] When he had given these orders he returned to his feasting, together with those of his Friends and of the army who were especially hostile toward the Jews. [4] And Hermon, keeper of the elephants, proceeded faithfully to carry out the orders. [5] The servants in charge of the Jews[b] went out in the evening and bound the hands of the wretched people and arranged for their continued custody through the night, convinced that the whole nation would experience its final destruction. [6] For to the Gentiles it appeared that the Jews were left without any aid, [7] because in their bonds they were forcibly confined on every side. But with tears and a voice hard to silence they all called upon the Almighty Lord and Ruler of all power, their merciful God and Father, praying [8] that he avert with vengeance the evil plot against them and in a glorious manifestation rescue them from the fate now prepared for them. [9] So their entreaty ascended fervently to heaven.

[10] Hermon, however, when he had drugged the pitiless elephants until they had been filled with a great abundance of wine and satiated with frankincense, presented himself at the courtyard early in the morning to report to the king about these preparations. [11] But the Lord[c] sent upon the king a portion of sleep, that beneficence that from the beginning, night and day, is bestowed by him who grants it to whomever he wishes. [12] And by the action of the Lord he was overcome by so pleasant and deep a sleep[d] that he quite failed in his lawless purpose and was completely frustrated in his inflexible plan. [13] Then the Jews, since they had escaped the appointed hour, praised their holy God and again implored him who is easily reconciled to show the might of his all-powerful hand to the arrogant Gentiles.

[14] But now, since it was nearly the middle of the tenth hour, the person who was in charge of the invitations, seeing that the guests were assembled, approached the king and nudged him. [15] And when he had with difficulty roused him, he pointed out that the hour of the banquet was already slipping by, and he gave him an account of the situation. [16] The king, after considering this, returned to his drinking, and ordered those present for the banquet to recline opposite him. [17] When this was done he urged them to give themselves over to revelry and to make the present[e] portion of the banquet joyful by celebrating all the more. [18] After the party had been going on for some time, the king summoned Hermon and with sharp threats demanded to know why the Jews had been allowed to remain alive through the present day. [19] But when he, with the corroboration of the king's[f] Friends, pointed out that while it was still night he had carried out completely the order given him, [20] the king,[c] possessed by a savagery

a Or *paper factory*
b Gk *them*
c Gk *he*
d Other ancient authorities add *from evening until the ninth hour*
e Other ancient authorities read *delayed* (Gk *untimely*)
f Gk *his*

5.1–51: Ptolemy orders the execution of the Jews, but is thwarted. A variant of this story is told in Josephus, *Ag. Ap.* 2.53–55, but there the Ptolemy is Ptolemy VIII Euergetes II Physcon (144–117 BCE). 1: *Hermon*, the name of the keeper of the elephants, recalls the figure of Haman in Esther. 2: *Elephants—five hundred* is an exaggeration; according to Polybius, Ptolemy had seventy-three elephants at the battle of Raphia. After Alexander the Great encountered them in India, war-*elephants* were often a component of Hellenistic armies; see 1 Macc 1.17. Similar stimulation of war-elephants is reported in 1 Macc 6.34. 3: *Returned to his feasting*, 4.16. 7: *Father*, see Isa 63.16; Mal 2.10; Tob 13.4; Wis 11.10. 11: The divine gift of *sleep* is extolled by Roman poets (e.g., Seneca, *Hercules Furens* 1065–78; Statius, *Silvae* 5.4); see Ps 127.2. 14: *Middle of the tenth hour*, 3:30 pm. 19: *Friends*, see 2.23n. 20: *Phalaris*,

worse than that of Phalaris, said that the Jews[a] were benefited by today's sleep, "but," he added, "tomorrow without delay prepare the elephants in the same way for the destruction of the lawless Jews!" [21] When the king had spoken, all those present readily and joyfully with one accord gave their approval, and all went to their own homes. [22] But they did not so much employ the duration of the night in sleep as in devising all sorts of insults for those they thought to be doomed.

[23] Then, as soon as the cock had crowed in the early morning, Hermon, having equipped[b] the animals, began to move them along in the great colonnade. [24] The crowds of the city had been assembled for this most pitiful spectacle and they were eagerly waiting for daybreak. [25] But the Jews, at their last gasp—since the time had run out—stretched their hands toward heaven and with most tearful supplication and mournful dirges implored the supreme God[c] to help them again at once. [26] The rays of the sun were not yet shed abroad, and while the king was receiving his Friends, Hermon arrived and invited him to come out, indicating that what the king desired was ready for action. [27] But he, on receiving the report and being struck by the unusual invitation to come out—since he had been completely overcome by incomprehension—inquired what the matter was for which this had been so zealously completed for him. [28] This was the act of God who rules over all things, for he had implanted in the king's mind a forgetfulness of the things he had previously devised. [29] Then Hermon and all the king's Friends[d] pointed out that the animals and the armed forces were ready, "O king, according to your eager purpose."[e] [30] But at these words he was filled with an overpowering wrath, because by the providence of God his whole mind had been deranged concerning these matters; and with a threatening look he said, [31] "If your parents or children were present, I would have prepared them to be a rich feast for the savage animals instead of the Jews, who give me no ground for complaint and have exhibited to an extraordinary degree a full and firm loyalty to

my ancestors. [32] In fact you would have been deprived of life instead of these, if it were not for an affection arising from our nurture in common and your usefulness." [33] So Hermon suffered an unexpected and dangerous threat, and his eyes wavered and his face fell. [34] The king's Friends one by one sullenly slipped away and dismissed[f] the assembled people to their own occupations. [35] Then the Jews, on hearing what the king had said, praised the manifest Lord God, King of kings, since this also was his aid that they had received.

[36] The king, however, reconvened the party in the same manner and urged the guests to return to their celebrating. [37] After summoning Hermon he said in a threatening tone, "How many times, you poor wretch, must I give you orders about these things? [38] Equip[g] the elephants now once more for the destruction of the Jews tomorrow!" [39] But the officials who were at table with him, wondering at his instability of mind, remonstrated as follows: [40] "O king, how long will you put us to the test, as though we are idiots, ordering now for a third time that they be destroyed, and again revoking your decree in the matter?[h] [41] As a result the city is in a tumult because of its expectation; it is crowded with masses of people, and also in constant danger of being plundered."

[42] At this the king, a Phalaris in everything and filled with madness, took no account of the changes of mind that had come about within him for the protection of the Jews, and he firmly swore an irrevocable oath that he would send them to death[i] without

---

a Gk *they*
b Or *armed*
c Gk *the greatest God*
d Gk *all the Friends*
e Other ancient authorities read *pointed to the beasts and the armed forces, saying, "They are ready, O king, according to your eager purpose."*
f Other ancient authorities read *he dismissed*
g Or *Arm*
h Other ancient authorities read *when the matter is in hand*
i Gk *Hades*

---

tyrant of Agrigentum in Sicily (ca. 570–554 BCE) whose cruelty was proverbial (Polybius 12.25). **28:** *The act of God,* cf. Prov 21.1. **29:** An addition in several Greek manuscripts indicates that though Ptolemy was moved by compassion and determined to release the Jews, Hermon influenced him to proceed with his plans to destroy

delay, mangled by the knees and feet of the animals, [43] and would also march against Judea and rapidly level it to the ground with fire and spear, and by burning to the ground the temple inaccessible to him[a] would quickly render it forever empty of those who offered sacrifices there. [44] Then the Friends and officers departed with great joy, and they confidently posted the armed forces at the places in the city most favorable for keeping guard.

[45] Now when the animals had been brought virtually to a state of madness, so to speak, by the very fragrant draughts of wine mixed with frankincense and had been equipped with frightful devices, the elephant keeper [46] entered at about dawn into the courtyard—the city now being filled with countless masses of people crowding their way into the hippodrome—and urged the king on to the matter at hand. [47] So he, when he had filled his impious mind with a deep rage, rushed out in full force along with the animals, wishing to witness, with invulnerable heart and with his own eyes, the grievous and pitiful destruction of the aforementioned people.

[48] When the Jews saw the dust raised by the elephants going out at the gate and by the following armed forces, as well as by the trampling of the crowd, and heard the loud and tumultuous noise, [49] they thought that this was their last moment of life, the end of their most miserable suspense, and giving way to lamentation and groans they kissed each other, embracing relatives and falling into one another's arms[b]—parents and children, mothers and daughters, and others with babies at their breasts who were drawing their last milk.

[50] Not only this, but when they considered the help that they had received before from heaven, they prostrated themselves with one accord on the ground, removing the babies from their breasts, [51] and cried out in a very loud voice, imploring the Ruler over every power to manifest himself and be merciful to them, as they stood now at the gates of death.[c]

6 Then a certain Eleazar, famous among the priests of the country, who had attained a ripe old age and throughout his life had been adorned with every virtue, directed the elders around him to stop calling upon the holy God, and he prayed as follows: [2] "King of great power, Almighty God Most High, governing all creation with mercy, [3] look upon the descendants of Abraham, O Father, upon the children of the sainted Jacob, a people of your consecrated portion who are perishing as foreigners in a foreign land. [4] Pharaoh with his abundance of chariots, the former ruler of this Egypt, exalted with lawless insolence and boastful tongue, you destroyed together with his arrogant army by drowning them in the sea, manifesting the light of your mercy on the nation of Israel. [5] Sennacherib exulting in his countless forces, oppressive king of the Assyrians, who had already gained control of the whole world by the spear and was lifted up against your holy city, speaking grievous words with boasting and insolence, you, O Lord, broke in pieces, showing your power to many nations. [6] The three companions in Babylon who had

a Gk us
b Gk falling upon their necks
c Gk Hades

them. **42**: *Phalaris*, see v. 20n. **45**: The *frightful devices* were probably scythes, knives, and other military equipment attached to different parts of the bodies of the elephants. **49**: *Embracing*, but according to 6.27 they are still bound. **50–51**: The author continues to build up his thesis that God was the only resort for the captives, and that their hope would not be frustrated. **51**: *Gates of death*, Pss 9.13; 107.18.

6.1–15: The prayer of Eleazar. Like Simon's prayer in 2.1–20, it is plainly Jewish in form and style, containing doxology, thanksgiving for God's earlier interventions in Israel's history, and petition for a new miracle. The emphasis is on the exclusiveness and separate standing of Israel before God (v. 3). Eleazar expects God's intervention, not on account of Israel's virtues or merits, but because of divine mercy. Unlike many Jewish prayers from this period, however, there is little confession of sin (but see v. 10). **1**: *Eleazar*, the name of one of Aaron's sons (Ex 6.23), of a martyr in 2 Macc 6 and 4 Macc 5–6, and of a high priest in the *Letter of Aristeas*. Priests were always numerous in the Jewish community. There was a Jewish temple at Leontopolis in Egypt, erected by an exiled high priest (Onias IV) in the second century BCE, in defiance of Deuteronomistic law (Deut 12). **4**: *Pharaoh*, Ex 14.28. **5**: *Sennacherib*, 2 Kings 18.13; 19.35–37. **6**: *Three companions in Babylon*, Dan 3.22,27; Song of Thr 22–27.

voluntarily surrendered their lives to the flames so as not to serve vain things, you rescued unharmed, even to a hair, moistening the fiery furnace with dew and turning the flame against all their enemies. [7] Daniel, who through envious slanders was thrown down into the ground to lions as food for wild animals, you brought up to the light unharmed. [8] And Jonah, wasting away in the belly of a huge, sea-born monster, you, Father, watched over and restored[a] unharmed to all his family. [9] And now, you who hate insolence, all-merciful and protector of all, reveal yourself quickly to those of the nation of Israel[b]—who are being outrageously treated by the abominable and lawless Gentiles.

[10] "Even if our lives have become entangled in impieties in our exile, rescue us from the hand of the enemy, and destroy us, Lord, by whatever fate you choose. [11] Let not the vain-minded praise their vanities[c] at the destruction of your beloved people, saying, 'Not even their god has rescued them.' [12] But you, O Eternal One, who have all might and all power, watch over us now and have mercy on us who by the senseless insolence of the lawless are being deprived of life in the manner of traitors. [13] And let the Gentiles cower today in fear of your invincible might, O honored One, who have power to save the nation of Jacob. [14] The whole throng of infants and their parents entreat you with tears. [15] Let it be shown to all the Gentiles that you are with us, O Lord, and have not turned your face from us; but just as you have said, 'Not even when they were in the land of their enemies did I neglect them,' so accomplish it, O Lord."

[16] Just as Eleazar was ending his prayer, the king arrived at the hippodrome with the animals and all the arrogance of his forces. [17] And when the Jews observed this they raised great cries to heaven so that even the nearby valleys resounded with them and brought an uncontrollable terror upon the army. [18] Then the most glorious, almighty, and true God revealed his holy face and opened the heavenly gates, from which two glorious angels of fearful aspect descended, visible to all but the Jews. [19] They opposed the forces of the enemy and filled them with confusion and terror, binding them with immovable shackles. [20] Even the king began to shudder bodily, and he forgot his sullen insolence. [21] The animals turned back upon the armed forces following them and began trampling and destroying them.

[22] Then the king's anger was turned to pity and tears because of the things that he had devised beforehand. [23] For when he heard the shouting and saw them all fallen headlong to destruction, he wept and angrily threatened his Friends, saying, [24] "You are committing treason and surpassing tyrants in cruelty; and even me, your benefactor, you are now attempting to deprive of dominion and life by secretly devising acts of no advantage to the kingdom. [25] Who has driven from their homes those who faithfully kept our country's fortresses, and foolishly gathered every one of them here? [26] Who is it that has so lawlessly encompassed with outrageous treatment those who from the beginning differed from[d] all nations in their goodwill toward us and often have accepted willingly the worst of human dangers? [27] Loose and untie their unjust bonds! Send them back to their homes in peace, begging pardon for your former actions![e] [28] Release the children of the almighty and living God of heaven, who from the time of our ancestors until now has granted an unimpeded and notable sta-

---

a   Other ancient authorities read *rescued and restored*; others, *mercifully restored*
b   Other ancient authorities read *to the saints of Israel*
c   Or *bless their vain gods*
d   Or *excelled above*
e   Other ancient authorities read *revoking your former commands*

7: *Daniel,* Dan 6.22. 8: *Jonah,* Jon 2.10. 11: Ps 115.2. 13: *Let the Gentiles cower,* the prayer overlooks the exception made for the Greeks in 3.8. 15: *As you have said,* Lev 26.44.

6.16–29: The Jews are delivered, and the king now favors them. 18: *Most glorious,* Greek "megalodoxos," compare *1 Enoch* 14.20 and *Testament of Levi* 3.4, where God is called "the Great Glory." *Angels of fearful aspect,* for similar terror-inspiring apparitions, see 2 Macc 3.25–29; 10.29. 21: *The animals turned* upon the king's own *forces,* a detail found also in Josephus's account (*Ag. Ap.* 2.5). For the principle, see Pss 7.15–16; 9.15–16; 35.8; 57.6. 25: *Faithfully,* see 3.21n.; contrast the king's language in 3.24. 28: *Children of . . . God,* Wis 18.13.

bility to our government." [29] These then were the things he said; and the Jews, immediately released, praised their holy God and Savior, since they now had escaped death.

[30] Then the king, when he had returned to the city, summoned the official in charge of the revenues and ordered him to provide to the Jews both wines and everything else needed for a festival of seven days, deciding that they should celebrate their rescue with all joyfulness in that same place in which they had expected to meet their destruction. [31] Accordingly those disgracefully treated and near to death,[a] or rather, who stood at its gates, arranged for a banquet of deliverance instead of a bitter and lamentable death, and full of joy they apportioned to celebrants the place that had been prepared for their destruction and burial. [32] They stopped their chanting of dirges and took up the song of their ancestors, praising God, their Savior and worker of wonders.[b] Putting an end to all mourning and wailing, they formed choruses[c] as a sign of peaceful joy. [33] Likewise also the king, after convening a great banquet to celebrate these events, gave thanks to heaven unceasingly and lavishly for the unexpected rescue that he[d] had experienced. [34] Those who had previously believed that the Jews would be destroyed and become food for birds, and had joyfully registered them, groaned as they themselves were overcome by disgrace, and their fire-breathing boldness was ignominiously[e] quenched.

[35] The Jews, as we have said before, arranged the aforementioned choral group[f] and passed the time in feasting to the accompaniment of joyous thanksgiving and psalms. [36] And when they had ordained a public rite for these things in their whole community and for their descendants, they instituted the observance of the aforesaid

days as a festival, not for drinking and gluttony, but because of the deliverance that had come to them through God. [37] Then they petitioned the king, asking for dismissal to their homes. [38] So their registration was carried out from the twenty-fifth of Pachon to the fourth of Epeiph,[g] for forty days; and their destruction was set for the fifth to the seventh of Epeiph,[h] the three days [39] on which the Lord of all most gloriously revealed his mercy and rescued them all together and unharmed. [40] Then they feasted, being provided with everything by the king, until the fourteenth day,[i] on which also they made the petition for their dismissal. [41] The king granted their request at once and wrote the following letter for them to the generals in the cities, magnanimously expressing his concern:

7 "King Ptolemy Philopator to the generals in Egypt and all in authority in his government, greetings and good health:

[2] "We ourselves and our children are faring well, the great God guiding our affairs according to our desire. [3] Certain of our friends, frequently urging us with malicious intent, persuaded us to gather together the Jews of the kingdom in a body and to punish them

---

a   Gk *Hades*
b   Other ancient authorities read *praising Israel and the wonder-working God*; or *praising Israel's Savior, the wonder-working God*
c   Or *dances*
d   Other ancient authorities read *they*
e   Other ancient authorities read *completely*
f   Or *dance*
g   July 7—August 15
h   August 16—18
i   August 25

6.30–41: The Jews celebrate their deliverance. 32: *The song of their ancestors,* perhaps Ps 136, which often was used earlier as a hymn of thanksgiving (1 Chr 16.41; 2 Chr 5.13; 7.3; Ezra 3.11). **34:** *Food for birds,* Gen 40.19; Deut 28.26; Ezek 39.4; 2 Macc 9.15. **36:** The institution of Jewish festivals is a common feature in this period (Esth 9.20–23; 1 Macc 4.59; 7.49; 13.51–52).

7.1–9: Ptolemy's letter on behalf of the Jews. Compare the letters of Ahasuerus (Esth 8; Add Esth 16.1–24), of Nebuchadnezzar (Dan 4), and of Antiochus Epiphanes (2 Macc 9.19–27). **2:** *Children,* Philopator had only one legitimate son, born in 210 BCE, who reigned later as Ptolemy V Epiphanes (204–180). Either the author had no knowledge of Philopator's family life, or the king is using a general term for the members of his court. **3:** The

with barbarous penalties as traitors; [4] for they declared that our government would never be firmly established until this was accomplished, because of the ill-will that these people had toward all nations. [5] They also led them out with harsh treatment as slaves, or rather as traitors, and, girding themselves with a cruelty more savage than that of Scythian custom, they tried without any inquiry or examination to put them to death. [6] But we very severely threatened them for these acts, and in accordance with the clemency that we have toward all people we barely spared their lives. Since we have come to realize that the God of heaven surely defends the Jews, always taking their part as a father does for his children, [7] and since we have taken into account the friendly and firm goodwill that they had toward us and our ancestors, we justly have acquitted them of every charge of whatever kind. [8] We also have ordered all people to return to their own homes, with no one in any place[a] doing them harm at all or reproaching them for the irrational things that have happened. [9] For you should know that if we devise any evil against them or cause them any grief at all, we always shall have not a mortal but the Ruler over every power, the Most High God, in everything and inescapably as an antagonist to avenge such acts. Farewell."

[10] On receiving this letter the Jews[b] did not immediately hurry to make their departure, but they requested of the king that at their own hands those of the Jewish nation who had willfully transgressed against the holy God and the law of God should receive the punishment they deserved. [11] They declared that those who for the belly's sake had transgressed the divine commandments would never be favorably disposed toward the king's government. [12] The king[c]

then, admitting and approving the truth of what they said, granted them a general license so that freely, and without royal authority or supervision, they might destroy those everywhere in his kingdom who had transgressed the law of God. [13] When they had applauded him in fitting manner, their priests and the whole multitude shouted the Hallelujah and joyfully departed. [14] And so on their way they punished and put to a public and shameful death any whom they met of their compatriots who had become defiled. [15] In that day they put to death more than three hundred men; and they kept the day as a joyful festival, since they had destroyed the profaners. [16] But those who had held fast to God even to death and had received the full enjoyment of deliverance began their departure from the city, crowned with all sorts of very fragrant flowers, joyfully and loudly giving thanks to the one God of their ancestors, the eternal Savior[d] of Israel, in words of praise and all kinds of melodious songs.

[17] When they had arrived at Ptolemais, called "rose-bearing" because of a characteristic of the place, the fleet waited for them, in accordance with the common desire, for seven days. [18] There they celebrated their deliverance,[e] for the king had generously provided all things to them for their journey until all of them arrived at their own houses. [19] And when they had all landed in peace with appropriate thanksgiving, there too in

a   Other ancient authorities read way
b   Gk they
c   Gk He
d   Other ancient authorities read the holy Savior; others, the holy one
e   Gk they made a cup of deliverance

king seeks to exonerate himself, blaming others (see 6.24). 4: Ill-will, 3.2,7. 5: Scythian custom, see 2 Macc 4.47n.; 4 Macc 10.7n. The Scythians were known for barbarism. 6: Threatened them, that is, the enemies of the Jews. Father, 5.7n.; Ps 103.13. 8: In any place through which the Jews might pass on their return.

7.10–23: The Jews punish the renegades and return home. 10: They requested of the king, in the Hellenistic and Roman periods the Jews were often obliged to seek permission from their foreign rulers to carry out their own laws pertaining to capital punishment (Deut 13.6–18; Esth 8.8–11). 13: Hallelujah, see Ps 105n.; Tob 13.18. 17: This Ptolemais was probably not the city of this name near Thebes in Upper Egypt, but "Ptolemais at the harbor" in the Arsinoite nome (province), about twelve miles from present-day Cairo. Rose-bearing is not elsewhere applied to Ptolemais. 22–23: The book closes with a benediction to the supreme God; cf. 4 Macc 18.24.

like manner they decided to observe these days as a joyous festival during the time of their stay. [20] Then, after inscribing them as holy on a pillar and dedicating a place of prayer at the site of the festival, they departed unharmed, free, and overjoyed, since at the king's command they had all of them been brought safely by land and sea and river to their own homes. [21] They also possessed greater prestige among their enemies, being held in honor and awe; and they were not subject at all to confiscation of their belongings by anyone. [22] Besides, they all recovered all of their property, in accordance with the registration, so that those who held any of it restored it to them with extreme fear.[a] So the supreme God perfectly performed great deeds for their deliverance. [23] Blessed be the Deliverer of Israel through all times! Amen.

[a] Other ancient authorities read *with a very large supplement*

2 ESDRAS

NAME

The book known as 2 Esdras is actually a composite work made up of three separate writings: 5 Ezra (chs 1–2), 4 Ezra (chs 3–14), and 6 Ezra (chs 15–16). "Esdras" is the Greek form of the name "Ezra.".

CANONICAL STATUS

2 Esdras is considered "apocryphal"—that is, noncanonical but instructive—in both the Roman Catholic and Protestant traditions. Since the Council of Trent (1546), it has been placed, together with 1 Esdras and the Prayer of Manasseh, in an appendix to the Latin Vulgate Bible. 2 Esdras is not included in the Septuagint or in any Jewish canon.

AUTHORSHIP

Traditionally, 2 Esdras has been considered a writing of the biblical figure Ezra. For modern scholars, however, "Ezra" is a pseudonym, and all three components of 2 Esdras are thought to be of unknown authorship. It should be noted that 6 Ezra, as it stands, is anonymous.

DATE AND HISTORICAL CONTEXT

Fourth Ezra, the longest and most complex of the three parts of 2 Esdras, is also the earliest. Written in Hebrew by an anonymous Jew in Israel near the end of the first century CE, it sets forth its author's anguished reflections on the destruction of Jerusalem and its Temple by the Romans in 70 CE. Sometime in the second century CE, 4 Ezra was translated into Greek and, subsequently, into many other languages. Although both the original Hebrew text and the Greek translation were lost over time, the book is known in no less than eight versions: Latin, Syriac, Ethiopic, Georgian, Armenian, two independent Arabic versions, and a fragmentary Coptic version. This large number of translations attests to the book's immense popularity in the many Christian churches of the early Middle Ages.

Fifth Ezra, a Christian writing of the second or third century CE, is also attributed to Ezra. It was composed in either Greek or Latin; its place of composition is uncertain.

Sixth Ezra is a Christian composition of the third century, probably from Asia Minor. Although 6 Ezra survives in full only in Latin, a fourth-century Greek parchment fragment of 15.57–59 found at Oxyrhynchus, Egypt, indicates that the book was composed in Greek.

Some time before 400 CE, a Latin form of 6 Ezra was appended to the end of 4 Ezra. In turn, a Latin form of 5 Ezra was later added to the end of that composite, probably before 450. Then, prior to 800, 5 Ezra was moved to the beginning of the collection, resulting in the form of the book known today.

STRUCTURE AND CONTENTS

The author of 4 Ezra adopts the pseudonym "Ezra," whom he presents as living after the destruction of the First Temple by the Babylonians in 586 BCE, and the author also refers to Rome by the pseudonym "Babylon." Thus he writes on two levels, comparing his own situation with that of his biblical hero. The book's central concern is the issue of theodicy: How could a just God allow such misfortunes to happen to God's chosen people?

The author of 4 Ezra is a deeply reflective and highly imaginative thinker, who with skill and sophistication presents divergent theological viewpoints in different parts of the book. In the first three of the book's seven "visions," Ezra, the book's spirited and loquacious hero, persuasively argues a profoundly humanistic viewpoint that stresses the ideals of God's mercy, justice, and care for humanity, especially Israel. Ezra is rebuffed time and again, however, by an angel, who emphasizes the limitations of human reasoning.

In the fourth vision, the book's central and pivotal section, Ezra experiences a profound psychological shift from his previous attitude to a state of unquestioning acceptance of God's will. As a sign of this transition he receives a mystical vision of the heavenly Jerusalem. Equipped with his newly acquired state of mind, Ezra in the last section of the book receives two further mystical visions (the fifth and sixth), both indicating that the true solution to the problem of God's justice is an apocalyptic one: The suffering righteous will receive their reward at the end of the world. Finally, in the climactic seventh vision, the inspired Ezra is granted permission by God to rewrite the scriptures that had been burned by the "Babylonians," but with one variation: In addition to the traditional books of the Hebrew canon, he writes seventy secret books meant for the "wise" among his people. Fourth Ezra's author thus displays his penchant for mystical, esoteric, and apocalyptic modes of thinking, and his conviction that these hold the answers to the ethical and theological dilemmas of Israel, and indeed of all humankind.

Fifth Ezra reflects the growing tension between Christian and Jewish communities. It indicts the people of Israel for their sins and "predicts" the coming of a new people (the Christians) who will inherit the promises originally made to Israel. One is best advised to read the book as a pseudonymous effort by an anonymous Christian author to place a "prophecy" of the coming of Christianity in the mouth of a respected Jewish figure of the fifth century BCE. The "prophecy" is made more convincing by the fact that the author strives to be historically authentic, never referring to "Christianity" explicitly and never mentioning Jesus by name.

In 6 Ezra, an anonymous prophet predicts terrible catastrophes that will afflict the whole earth as a result of human iniquity and warns God's "elect" to abstain from sin if they wish to escape the calamities. The book reflects a situation in which its Christian community was experiencing persecution and strives to convince its audience to stand firm. The author seeks to make sense of the severe persecution threatening the Christian community, and, as in the case of 4 Ezra, 6 Ezra's eschatology is presented as a solution to a situation of extreme social and religious challenge.

INTERPRETATION

Because of its position on the margins of the canon, 2 Esdras has not received a great deal of interpretive attention. Traditional exegetes have generally interpreted 2 Esdras as a genuine prophecy of future events by the biblical figure Ezra. Modern scholars, however, tend to regard it as prophecy formulated after the fact, or as inspired by historical exigencies of the periods in which the book's components were written.

Theodore A. Bergren

COMPRISING WHAT IS SOMETIMES CALLED 5 EZRA (CHAPTERS 1–2), 4 EZRA (CHAPTERS 3–14), AND 6 EZRA (CHAPTERS 15–16)

1 The book[a] of the prophet Ezra son of Seraiah, son of Azariah, son of Hilkiah, son of Shallum, son of Zadok, son of Ahitub, ² son of Ahijah, son of Phinehas, son of Eli, son of Amariah, son of Azariah, son of Meraimoth, son of Arna, son of Uzzi, son of Borith, son of Abishua, son of Phinehas, son of Eleazar, ³ son of Aaron, of the tribe of Levi, who was a captive in the country of the Medes in the reign of Artaxerxes, king of the Persians.[b]

⁴ The word of the Lord came to me, saying, ⁵ "Go, declare to my people their evil deeds, and to their children the iniquities that they

have committed against me, so that they may tell[c] their children's children ⁶ that the sins of their parents have increased in them, for they have forgotten me and have offered sacrifices to strange gods. ⁷ Was it not I who brought them out of the land of Egypt, out of the house of bondage? But they have angered me and despised my counsels. ⁸ Now you,

a   Other ancient authorities read *The second book*
b   Other ancient authorities, which place chapters 1 and 2 after 16.78, lack verses 1-3 and begin the chapter: *The word of the Lord that came to Ezra son of Chusi in the days of King Nebuchadnezzar, saying, "Go,*
c   Other ancient authorities read *nourish*

Chapters 1–2 comprise a separate literary composition also known as 5 Ezra (see Introduction).

1.1–3: **Ascription.** Ezra is given a high-priestly genealogy similar to Ezra 7.1–5 and 1 Esd 8.1–2, but with several differences (cf. 1 Sam 14.3). 1: *Prophet* is unusual; Ezra is usually called "priest" or "scribe" (Ezra 7.6,11; see 2 Esd 12.42n.). 3: Probably *Artaxerxes* I (465–424 BCE).

1.4–2.9: **A prophetic indictment against Israel. 1.4–23: Prophetic historical recital of God's benefits during the Exodus** (cf. Pss 78; 106; Neh 9). 4: *The word of the Lord came . . .*, a typical expression in narratives about prophets. 5: Isa 58.1; Ezek 23.36; Joel 1.3. 6: *Strange gods,* cf. Deut 32.16. 7: *Was it not I . . . ?*, the Exodus was God's

pull out the hair of your head and hurl[a] all evils upon them, for they have not obeyed my law—they are a rebellious people. ⁹ How long shall I endure them, on whom I have bestowed such great benefits? ¹⁰ For their sake I have overthrown many kings; I struck down Pharaoh with his servants and all his army. ¹¹ I destroyed all nations before them, and scattered in the east the peoples of two provinces,[b] Tyre and Sidon; I killed all their enemies.

¹² "But speak to them and say, Thus says the Lord: ¹³ Surely it was I who brought you through the sea, and made safe highways for you where there was no road; I gave you Moses as leader and Aaron as priest; ¹⁴ I provided light for you from a pillar of fire, and did great wonders among you. Yet you have forgotten me, says the Lord.

¹⁵ "Thus says the Lord Almighty:[c] The quails were a sign to you; I gave you camps for your protection, and in them you complained. ¹⁶ You have not exulted in my name at the destruction of your enemies, but to this day you still complain.[d] ¹⁷ Where are the benefits that I bestowed on you? When you were hungry and thirsty in the wilderness, did you not cry out to me, ¹⁸ saying, 'Why have you led us into this wilderness to kill us? It would have been better for us to serve the Egyptians than to die in this wilderness.' ¹⁹ I pitied your groanings and gave you manna for food; you ate the bread of angels. ²⁰ When you were thirsty, did I not split the rock so that waters flowed in abundance? Because of the heat I clothed you with the leaves of trees.[e] ²¹ I divided fertile lands among you; I drove out the Canaanites, the Perizzites, and the Philistines[f] before you. What more can I do

for you? says the Lord. ²² Thus says the Lord Almighty:[c] When you were in the wilderness, at the bitter stream, thirsty and blaspheming my name, ²³ I did not send fire on you for your blasphemies, but threw a tree into the water and made the stream sweet.

²⁴ "What shall I do to you, O Jacob? You, Judah, would not obey me. I will turn to other nations and will give them my name, so that they may keep my statutes. ²⁵ Because you have forsaken me, I also will forsake you. When you beg mercy of me, I will show you no mercy. ²⁶ When you call to me, I will not listen to you; for you have defiled your hands with blood, and your feet are swift to commit murder. ²⁷ It is not as though you had forsaken me; you have forsaken yourselves, says the Lord.

²⁸ "Thus says the Lord Almighty: Have I not entreated you as a father entreats his sons or a mother her daughters or a nurse her children, ²⁹ so that you should be my people and I should be your God, and that you should be my children and I should be your father? ³⁰ I gathered you as a hen gath-

a   Other ancient authorities read *and shake out*
b   Other ancient authorities read *Did I not destroy the city of Bethsaida because of you, and to the south burn two cities…?*
c   Other ancient authorities lack *Almighty*
d   Other ancient authorities read verse 16, *Your pursuer with his army I sank in the sea, but still the people complain also concerning their own destruction.*
e   Other ancient authorities read *I made for you trees with leaves*
f   Other ancient authorities read *Perizzites and their children*

paradigmatic mighty act for Israel. **8:** Ezra is to *pull out* his *hair* as a prophetic sign signaling his disgust with the people (see Ezra 9.3; Neh 13.25; Jer 6.19). *Rebellious people*, see Deut 28.50; Isa 30.9. **9:** *How long shall I endure them … ?* Frequent rhetorical questions like this highlight God's exasperation (see Num 14.27). **10:** Ex 14.28; Pss 135.9–11; 136.17. **11:** The scattering of the peoples of *Tyre and Sidon* is not recorded in other Exodus traditions. **13:** Ex 14.21–22,29; Num 33.1; Pss 77.20; 78.13. **14:** Ex 13.21. *You have forgotten me*, God indicts the people. **15:** Ex 16.13; Num 11.1,31–34; Deut 1.27; Ps 105.40; Wis 15.2–3. **17–18:** Num 14.3; Ps 77.11. **19:** *The bread of angels*, manna; Ps 78.24–25; Ex 16.13–16; Num 11.4–9; Wis 16.20. **20:** *Split the rock*, Num 20.11; Wis 11.4. *I clothed you with the leaves*, this is not mentioned in other Exodus traditions; protection from the heat is sometimes attributed to the pillar of cloud (Ex 13.21). **22–23:** Ex 15.22–25; Sir 38.5.

1.24–34: Pronouncement of judgment against Israel. 24: Isa 43.22. *I will turn to other nations*, the pivotal point of 5 Ezra, in which God decisively rejects the former nation (see Mt 21.43). See also Ex 32.10; Num 14.12. **25:** Jer 13.14. **26:** Prov 1.28; Isa 1.15; 59.3,7; Jer 7.16. **29:** Lev 26.12; Jer 7.23 24.7; 2 Cor 6.16–18; Heb 8.10. **30–33:** Compare

ers her chicks under her wings. But now, what shall I do to you? I will cast you out from my presence. [31] When you offer oblations to me, I will turn my face from you; for I have rejected your[a] festal days, and new moons, and circumcisions of the flesh.[b] [32] I sent you my servants the prophets, but you have taken and killed them and torn their bodies[c] in pieces; I will require their blood of you, says the Lord.[d]

[33] "Thus says the Lord Almighty: Your house is desolate; I will drive you out as the wind drives straw; [34] and your sons will have no children, because with you[e] they have neglected my commandment and have done what is evil in my sight. [35] I will give your houses to a people that will come, who without having heard me will believe. Those to whom I have shown no signs will do what I have commanded. [36] They have seen no prophets, yet will recall their former state.[f] [37] I call to witness the gratitude of the people that is to come, whose children rejoice with gladness;[g] though they do not see me with bodily eyes, yet with the spirit they will believe the things I have said.

[38] "And now, father,[h] look with pride and see the people coming from the east; [39] to them I will give as leaders Abraham, Isaac, and Jacob, and Hosea and Amos and Micah and Joel and Obadiah and Jonah [40] and Nahum and Habakkuk, Zephaniah, Haggai, Zechariah and Malachi, who is also called the messenger of the Lord.[i]

2 "Thus says the Lord: I brought this people out of bondage, and I gave them commandments through my servants the prophets; but they would not listen to them, and made my counsels void. [2] The mother who bore them[j] says to them, 'Go, my children, be-

cause I am a widow and forsaken. [3] I brought you up with gladness; but with mourning and sorrow I have lost you, because you have sinned before the Lord God and have done what is evil in my sight.[k] [4] But now what can I do for you? For I am a widow and forsaken. Go, my children, and ask for mercy from the Lord.' [5] Now I call upon you, father, as a witness in addition to the mother of the

a Other ancient authorities read *I have not commanded for you*

b Other ancient authorities lack *of the flesh*

c Other ancient authorities read *the bodies of the apostles*

d Other ancient authorities add *Thus says the Lord Almighty: Recently you also laid hands on me, crying out before the judge's seat for him to deliver me to you. You took me as a sinner, not as a father who freed you from slavery, and you delivered me to death by hanging me on the tree; these are the things you have done. Therefore, says the Lord, let my Father and his angels return and judge between you and me; if I have not kept the commandment of the Father, if I have not nourished you, if I have not done the things my Father commanded, I will contend in judgment with you, says the Lord.*

e Other ancient authorities lack *with you*

f Other ancient authorities read *their iniquities*

g Other ancient authorities read *The apostles bear witness to the coming people with joy*

h Other ancient authorities read *brother*

i Other ancient authorities read *and Jacob, Elijah and Enoch, Zechariah and Hosea, Amos, Joel, Micah, Obadiah, Zephaniah, [40]Nahum, Jonah, Mattia (or Mattathias), Habakkuk, and twelve angels with flowers*

j Other ancient authorities read *They begat for themselves a mother who*

k Other ancient authorities read *in his sight*

Mt 23.30–38. This is the closest New Testament parallel in 5 Ezra, and it suggests Christian authorship. See also Lk 11.49–51; 13.34–35. **31:** Isa 1.11–15. The rejection of circumcision also reveals the Christian identity of the author. **32:** Jer 7.25; 25.4. **33:** Job 21.18; Ps 1.4; Jer 13.24.

1.35–40: Description and vision of the coming people. Emphasis is placed on the untutored goodness of the *people that will come.* **35:** *A people that will come,* that is, the Gentile Christians. *Signs,* cf. Num 14.11. **36-37:** Heb 2.3–4; 1 Pet 1.8–12. *With bodily eyes,* Jn 20.29. **38:** God addresses Ezra as *father,* a term of respect. The people coming *from the east* suggests a return from exile (see Bar 4.36–37; 5.5). **39–40:** The three patriarchs, and the twelve minor prophets arranged in the order of the Septuagint (see Mt 8.11–12; Lk 13.28–29).

2.1–9: Further pronouncement of judgment. The "mother" of the old people is consigned to destruction. **1:** Jer 7.25–26; Ezra 9.10–11; Dan 9.10. **2:** *The mother who bore them,* Jerusalem (Isa 49.21; 54.1). **2–4:** This section, like 1.38, draws on the last chapters of the book of Baruch (Bar 4.8–23). **5:** This time it is God who is invoked as

children, because they would not keep my covenant, [6] so that you may bring confusion on them and bring their mother to ruin, so that they may have no offspring. [7] Let them be scattered among the nations; let their names be blotted out from the earth, because they have despised my covenant.

[8] "Woe to you, Assyria, who conceal the unrighteous within you! O wicked nation, remember what I did to Sodom and Gomorrah, [9] whose land lies in lumps of pitch and heaps of ashes.[a] That is what I will do to those who have not listened to me, says the Lord Almighty."

[10] Thus says the Lord to Ezra: "Tell my people that I will give them the kingdom of Jerusalem, which I was going to give to Israel. [11] Moreover, I will take back to myself their glory, and will give to these others the everlasting habitations, which I had prepared for Israel.[b] [12] The tree of life shall give them fragrant perfume, and they shall neither toil nor become weary. [13] Go[c] and you will receive; pray that your days may be few, that they may be shortened. The kingdom is already prepared for you; be on the watch! [14] Call, O call heaven and earth to witness: I set aside evil and created good; for I am the Living One, says the Lord.

[15] "Mother, embrace your children; bring them up with gladness, as does a dove; strengthen their feet, because I have chosen you, says the Lord. [16] And I will raise up the dead from their places, and bring them out from their tombs, because I recognize my name

in them. [17] Do not fear, mother of children, for I have chosen you, says the Lord. [18] I will send you help, my servants Isaiah and Jeremiah. According to their counsel I have consecrated and prepared for you twelve trees loaded with various fruits, [19] and the same number of springs flowing with milk and honey, and seven mighty mountains on which roses and lilies grow; by these I will fill your children with joy.

[20] "Guard the rights of the widow, secure justice for the ward, give to the needy, defend the orphan, clothe the naked, [21] care for the injured and the weak, do not ridicule the lame, protect the maimed, and let the blind have a vision of my splendor. [22] Protect the old and the young within your walls. [23] When you find any who are dead, commit them to the grave and mark it,[d] and I will give you the first place in my resurrection. [24] Pause and be quiet, my people, because your rest will come.

[25] "Good nurse, nourish your children; strengthen their feet. [26] Not one of the servants[e] whom I have given you will perish, for I will require them from among your number. [27] Do not be anxious, for when the day of tribulation and anguish comes, others

[a] Other ancient authorities read *Gomorrah, whose land descends to hell*
[b] Lat *for those*
[c] Other ancient authorities read *Seek*
[d] Or *seal it*; or *mark them and commit them to the grave*
[e] Or *slaves*

father, in conjunction with Jerusalem as *mother* (cf. 1.38). 6: *Bring their mother to ruin*, a reference to the fall of Jerusalem in 70 or 135 CE (cf. Mt 22.1–14). 7: *Let them be scattered*, as punishment, see Lev 26.33; Deut 4.27; Ps 44.11; Jer 9.16. The endurance of *names* is a form of immortality (see Sir 41:11–13). 8–9: Woe against Assyria. The exact significance of this reference is uncertain; some scholars view *Assyria* as a reference to Rome. Here Assyria is cursed for concealing the Jews (cf. Zeph 2.13-3.5). *Sodom and Gomorrah*, Gen 19.

2.10–41: Prophetic exhortation of the new people. 10–14: Blessing and instruction; listing of eschatological delights. 10: *My people*, the newly chosen Christians. See Mt 21.43. 11: *Everlasting habitations*, dwelling places in the world to come; see Lk 16.9; Jn 14.2–3; 2 Cor 5.1,4; Rev 21.3. 12: *Tree of life*, Gen 2.9; 3.17–19,22; Rev 2.7; 22.2,14; 1 Enoch 24.4–25.7. 13: Mt 7.7–8; 13.20,33–37; 14.34–38; 24.22; 25.34; Mk 13.37; Jn 16.24. 14: *Heaven and earth*, Deut 4.26; Isa 1.2. *Living One*, Rev 1.18.

2.15–32: Exhortation of the mother. In distinction to 2.2–6, it is now the church, not Jerusalem, that is addressed as *mother*. 15: *Dove*, Song 2.13–14. *Chosen*, Isa 44.1–2; 49.7; 16: Resurrection is promised; see Isa 26.19; Ezek 37.12; Rev 3.12; 14.1; 22.4. 18–19: 1 Enoch 24–25; 31–32; 48; Hermas *Sim.* 9. 18: *Twelve trees*, Rev 22.2. 19: *Springs . . . mountains*, 1 Enoch 18.6; 24.2–3; 32.1; 48.1. 20–23: A recital of the traditional "works of mercy" of the church (see Isa 58.6–10; Tob 1.17–19; Mt 25.35–45; Hermas *Mand.* 8.10). 22: *The old and the young*, Joel 2.16. 23: Concern for proper burial, cf. Ezek 39.15; Sir 38.16. 24: *Rest*, an eschatological reward; cf. Dan 12.13; Heb 3.18–19.

shall weep and be sorrowful, but you shall rejoice and have abundance. [28] The nations shall envy you, but they shall not be able to do anything against you, says the Lord. [29] My power will protect[a] you, so that your children may not see hell.[b]

[30] "Rejoice, O mother, with your children, because I will deliver you, says the Lord. [31] Remember your children that sleep, because I will bring them out of the hiding places of the earth, and will show mercy to them; for I am merciful, says the Lord Almighty. [32] Embrace your children until I come, and proclaim mercy to them; because my springs run over, and my grace will not fail."

[33] I, Ezra, received a command from the Lord on Mount Horeb to go to Israel. When I came to them they rejected me and refused the Lord's commandment. [34] Therefore I say to you, O nations that hear and understand, "Wait for your shepherd; he will give you everlasting rest, because he who will come at the end of the age is close at hand. [35] Be ready for the rewards of the kingdom, because perpetual light will shine on you forevermore. [36] Flee from the shadow of this age, receive the joy of your glory; I publicly call on my savior to witness.[c] [37] Receive what the Lord has entrusted to you and be joyful, giving thanks to him who has called you to the celestial kingdoms. [38] Rise, stand erect and see the number of those who have been sealed at the feast of the Lord. [39] Those who have departed from the shadow of this age have received glorious garments from the Lord. [40] Take again your full number, O Zion, and close the list of your people who are clothed in white,

who have fulfilled the law of the Lord. [41] The number of your children, whom you desired, is now complete; implore the Lord's authority that your people, who have been called from the beginning, may be made holy."

[42] I, Ezra, saw on Mount Zion a great multitude that I could not number, and they all were praising the Lord with songs. [43] In their midst was a young man of great stature, taller than any of the others, and on the head of each of them he placed a crown, but he was more exalted than they. And I was held spellbound. [44] Then I asked an angel, "Who are these, my lord?" [45] He answered and said to me, "These are they who have put off mortal clothing and have put on the immortal, and have confessed the name of God. Now they are being crowned, and receive palms." [46] Then I said to the angel, "Who is that young man who is placing crowns on them and putting palms in their hands?" [47] He answered and said to me, "He is the Son of God, whom they confessed in the world." So I began to praise those who had stood valiantly for the name of the Lord.[d] [48] Then the angel said to me, "Go, tell my people how great and how many are the wonders of the Lord God that you have seen."

3 In the thirtieth year after the destruction of the city, I was in Babylon—I, Salathiel, who am also called Ezra. I was troubled as I

a   Lat *hands will cover*
b   Lat *Gehenna*
c   Other ancient authorities read *I testify that my savior has been commissioned by the Lord*
d   Other ancient authorities read *to praise and glorify the Lord*

25: *Nurse*, the church; cf. 2.15; Num 11.12. **26:** Jn 17.12; 18.9. **27–32:** The author emphasizes eschatology and resurrection. **31:** *Sleep*, i.e., death; Dan 12.2. *Hiding places*, cf. 1 Enoch 22. **32:** See 2.15n.

2.33–41: Description of the glorified state to be enjoyed by God's newly chosen people. **33:** *On Mount Horeb*, depicting Ezra as a second Moses; see 14.1–4,30,37–38; Ex 3.1. *Rejected me*, Acts 13.46. **34:** *Nations*, Gentiles; *Shepherd*, Christ; cf. 1 Pet 5.4. **35:** *Light will shine*, cf. Isa 9.2; 60.19–20; Rev 21.23–25; 22.5. **38:** *Sealed*, Rev 7.4. **39:** *Glorious garments*, 1 Enoch 62.15–16. See also Bar 5.1–3; Rev 3.4–5. **40:** *Full number*, see 4.36–37; Rev 6.11; *Clothed in white*, Rev 3.4; 6.11; 7.14; 1 Enoch 71.1. **41:** 1 Enoch 47.4.

2.42–48: Ezra's vision of a great multitude (cf. Rev 7.9–17). **42:** *Mount Zion*, contrasted here with the *Mount Horeb* of 2.33. *Great multitude*, 13.5,12,35; Rev 7.9; 14.1; 2 Bar 40; 1 Enoch 39.12–40.1. *Songs*, Rev 14.1–5; 15.2–4. **43:** *Young man*, a messianic figure, here referring to Jesus. See 13.5,35; Rev 14.1; *Gospel of Peter* 40; Hermas *Sim.* 9.6.1. *Crown*, 2 Tim 4.8; 1 Pet 5.4; Rev 2.10; 3.11. *Spellbound*, 13.11; Rev 17.6–7. **44–47:** Rev 7.13–14. **45:** *Put off mortal clothing*, 1 Cor 15.53–54; 2 Cor 5.2–4. *Palms*, Rev 7.9. **47:** *Son of God*, here a Christian designation, can also be Jewish (see 7.28–29; 13.32,37,52). *Confessed in the world*, signifying Christian martyrs.

lay on my bed, and my thoughts welled up in my heart, [2] because I saw the desolation of Zion and the wealth of those who lived in Babylon. [3] My spirit was greatly agitated, and I began to speak anxious words to the Most High, and said, [4] "O sovereign Lord, did you not speak at the beginning when you planted[a] the earth—and that without help—and commanded the dust[b] [5] and it gave you Adam, a lifeless body? Yet he was the creation of your hands, and you breathed into him the breath of life, and he was made alive in your presence. [6] And you led him into the garden that your right hand had planted before the earth appeared. [7] And you laid upon him one commandment of yours; but he transgressed it, and immediately you appointed death for him and for his descendants. From him there sprang nations and tribes, peoples and clans without number. [8] And every nation walked after its own will; they did ungodly things in your sight and rejected your commands, and you did not hinder them. [9] But again, in its time you brought the flood upon the inhabitants of the world and destroyed them. [10] And the same fate befell all of them: just as death came upon Adam, so the flood upon them. [11] But you left one of them, Noah with his household, and all the righteous who have descended from him.

[12] "When those who lived on earth began to multiply, they produced children and peoples and many nations, and again they began to be more ungodly than were their ancestors. [13] And when they were committing iniquity in your sight, you chose for yourself one of them, whose name was Abraham; [14] you loved him, and to him alone you revealed the end of the times, secretly by night. [15] You made an everlasting covenant with him, and promised him that you would never forsake his descendants; and you gave him Isaac, and to Isaac you gave Jacob and Esau. [16] You set apart Jacob for yourself, but Esau you rejected; and Jacob became a great multitude. [17] And when you led his descendants out of Egypt, you brought them to Mount Sinai. [18] You bent down the heavens and shook[c] the earth, and moved the world, and caused the depths to tremble, and troubled the times. [19] Your glory passed through the four gates of fire and earthquake and wind and ice, to give

---

a   Other ancient authorities read *formed*
b   Syr Ethiop: Lat *people* or *world*
c   Syr Ethiop Arab 1 Georg: Lat *set fast*

Chapters 3–14 comprise a separate literary composition also known as 4 Ezra (see Introduction).

3.1–5.20: The first vision. 3.1–3: Introduction. 1: *The thirtieth year after the destruction* of Jerusalem by Nebuchadnezzar in 586 BCE (2 Kings 25.1–21) would be 556. The date specified may imply that the author was writing about 100 CE (i.e., thirty years after the fall of Jerusalem in 70 CE). The historical Ezra lived almost a century after the claimed setting of the book. *Babylon*, the historical Ezra was born in Babylon, then led a group of exiled Jews returning to Jerusalem about 458 BCE; see Ezra 7.7n. *Salathiel* is the Greek form of "Shealtiel" (Ezra 3.2; 5.2; Neh 12.1), appropriately meaning in Hebrew, "I asked God." The identification of Salathiel with Ezra has never been adequately explained. *On my bed*, cf. Dan 7.1. **2:** *Zion*, Jerusalem. **3:** *My spirit was greatly agitated*, the author immediately signals Ezra's emotional sensitivity.

3.4–36: Addressing God, the author raises perplexing questions. What is the origin of sin with its consequent misery? How can Israel's continuing affliction be reconciled with God's justice? Each of the first four visions opens with a long, reflective prayer of Ezra addressed to God (see 5.23–30; 6.38–59; 9.29–37). Here Ezra presents a historical review of God's interactions with humanity and with Israel. **4–5:** The creation of *Adam*, based on Gen 2.7, draws on the concept of creation by divine speech in Gen 1. **6–8:** Adam's disobedience (see Gen 2.16–17; 3.1–13) gives rise to sin and death for all humans. **7:** The words *immediately you appointed death* imply that Adam was not originally intended to be mortal (see Gen 3.22; cf. Wis 1.13–14; 2.23–24). *Death for him and his descendants*, see also 3.21,26; 4.30; 7.116–118. Similar ideas are expressed by Paul in Rom 5.12–21; 1 Cor 15.21–22. **8:** Gen 6.12. **9–11:** *The flood* (Gen 6.11–8.22). **12–15:** The choice of and covenant with Abraham (Gen 12.1; 17.5). **14:** *The end of the times* is not the topic of Gen 15. See, however, *The Apocalypse of Abraham*, roughly contemporary with chs 3–14. *By night*, Gen 15.5,12,17. **15–16:** *Jacob and Esau*, Gen 25.19–26. **17–19:** The Exodus and the giving of the law. **18:** Compare Ex 19.16–18; Ps 68.7–8. **19:** *Four gates*, according to certain early Jewish cosmological models, meteorological phenomena passed from heaven to earth through *gates* in the heavenly firmament, here enumerated as *four*. See *1 Enoch* 36.1,76; cf. Ps 78.23; 1 Kings 19.11–12. Here God's

the law to the descendants of Jacob, and your commandment to the posterity of Israel.

20 "Yet you did not take away their evil heart from them, so that your law might produce fruit in them. 21 For the first Adam, burdened with an evil heart, transgressed and was overcome, as were also all who were descended from him. 22 Thus the disease became permanent; the law was in the hearts of the people along with the evil root; but what was good departed, and the evil remained. 23 So the times passed and the years were completed, and you raised up for yourself a servant, named David. 24 You commanded him to build a city for your name, and there to offer you oblations from what is yours. 25 This was done for many years; but the inhabitants of the city transgressed, 26 in everything doing just as Adam and all his descendants had done, for they also had the evil heart. 27 So you handed over your city to your enemies.

28 "Then I said in my heart, Are the deeds of those who inhabit Babylon any better? Is that why it has gained dominion over Zion? 29 For when I came here I saw ungodly deeds without number, and my soul has seen many sinners during these thirty years.[a] And my heart failed me, 30 because I have seen how you endure those who sin, and have spared those who act wickedly, and have destroyed your people, and protected your enemies, 31 and have not shown to anyone how your way may be comprehended.[b] Are the deeds

of Babylon better than those of Zion? 32 Or has another nation known you besides Israel? Or what tribes have so believed the covenants as these tribes of Jacob? 33 Yet their reward has not appeared and their labor has borne no fruit. For I have traveled widely among the nations and have seen that they abound in wealth, though they are unmindful of your commandments. 34 Now therefore weigh in a balance our iniquities and those of the inhabitants of the world; and it will be found which way the turn of the scale will incline. 35 When have the inhabitants of the earth not sinned in your sight? Or what nation has kept your commandments so well? 36 You may indeed find individuals who have kept your commandments, but nations you will not find."

4 Then the angel that had been sent to me, whose name was Uriel, answered 2 and said to me, "Your understanding has utterly failed regarding this world, and do you think you can comprehend the way of the Most High?" 3 Then I said, "Yes, my lord." And he replied to me, "I have been sent to show you three ways, and to put before you three problems. 4 If you can solve one of them for me, then I will show you the way you desire to see, and will teach you why the heart is evil."

5 I said, "Speak, my lord."

---

a Ethiop Arab 1 Arm: Lat Syr *in this thirtieth year*
b Syr; compare Ethiop: Lat *how this way should be forsaken*

---

glory descends through these *gates* to *give the law* on Mount Sinai. **20–27:** The tendency to sin is universal and permanent. **20:** *You did not take away*, here, as in 3.8 (*you did not hinder them*), Ezra implies that God bears some responsibility for human sinfulness. *Evil heart*, possibly, in the Hebrew (now lost), the evil "yetser," an inclination or tendency to sin (Gen 6.5; 2 Esd 4.30–31). The "yetser" can also be an inclination to good (Isa 26.3; 1 Chr 29.18). *Fruit*, see 8.6. **22:** Contrast 9.34–37. *Evil root*, cf. 8.53. **23–27:** *David*, see 1 Sam 16.1–13; 2 Sam 7.1–17; Ps 89.19–29. The *city* is Jerusalem. **27:** *Handed over your city*, the Babylonian conquest of Jerusalem in 586 BCE (2 Kings 25.1–21). **28–36:** Ezra questions whether the deeds of Babylon are any better than those of Israel. **28:** *Babylon*, here, as regularly in the book, stands for Rome (compare Rev 14.8). **30–31:** Here the author expresses the essence of the problem: God permits evildoers to continue in their wickedness, does not spare the suffering people of God, and does not let anyone understand why this should be so. **33–36:** Ezra claims that God's judgment regarding the present world order has been faulty. **34:** *Scale*, see Job 31.6; Dan 5.27; 1 Enoch 4.1; 61.8. **36:** *Individuals* among the Gentiles.

4.1–25: Dialogic dispute between Ezra and the angel Uriel. The message is that God's ways are beyond human understanding. **1–12:** Three riddles illustrate the limitations of human knowledge. **1:** *Angel*, representing the viewpoint of God. The name *Uriel* in Hebrew means "God is my fire" (or "my light"). According to 1 Enoch 20.2, Uriel is a watcher over both the world and Tartaros, the lowest part of hell (cf. 2 Pet 2.4, textual note *e*). **5:** The angel's method of instructing Ezra regularly employs analogies drawn from nature;

And he said to me, "Go, weigh for me the weight of fire, or measure for me a blast[a] of wind, or call back for me the day that is past."
[6] I answered and said, "Who of those that have been born can do that, that you should ask me about such things?"
[7] And he said to me, "If I had asked you, 'How many dwellings are in the heart of the sea, or how many streams are at the source of the deep, or how many streams are above the firmament, or which are the exits of Hades, or which are the entrances[b] of paradise?'
[8] perhaps you would have said to me, 'I never went down into the deep, nor as yet into Hades, neither did I ever ascend into heaven.'
[9] But now I have asked you only about fire and wind and the day—things that you have experienced and from which you cannot be separated, and you have given me no answer about them." [10] He said to me, "You cannot understand the things with which you have grown up; [11] how then can your mind comprehend the way of the Most High? And how can one who is already worn out[c] by the corrupt world understand incorruption?"[d] When I heard this, I fell on my face[e] [12] and said to him, "It would have been better for us not to be here than to come here and live in ungodliness, and to suffer and not understand why."
[13] He answered me and said, "I went into a forest of trees of the plain, and they made a plan [14] and said, 'Come, let us go and make war against the sea, so that it may recede before us and so that we may make for ourselves more forests.' [15] In like manner the waves of the sea also made a plan and said, 'Come, let us go up and subdue the forest of the plain so that there also we may gain more territory for ourselves.' [16] But the plan of the forest was in vain, for the fire came and consumed it; [17] likewise also the plan of the waves of the sea was in vain,[f] for the sand stood firm and

blocked it. [18] If now you were a judge between them, which would you undertake to justify, and which to condemn?"
[19] I answered and said, "Each made a foolish plan, for the land has been assigned to the forest, and the locale of the sea a place to carry its waves."
[20] He answered me and said, "You have judged rightly, but why have you not judged so in your own case? [21] For as the land has been assigned to the forest and the sea to its waves, so also those who inhabit the earth can understand only what is on the earth, and he who is[g] above the heavens can understand what is above the height of the heavens."
[22] Then I answered and said, "I implore you, my lord, why[h] have I been endowed with the power of understanding? [23] For I did not wish to inquire about the ways above, but about those things that we daily experience: why Israel has been given over to the Gentiles in disgrace; why the people whom you loved has been given over to godless tribes, and the law of our ancestors has been brought to destruction and the written covenants no longer exist. [24] We pass from the world like locusts, and our life is like a mist,[i] and we are not worthy to obtain mercy. [25] But what will he do for his[j] name that is invoked over us? It is about these things that I have asked."

a Syr Ethiop Arab 1 Arab 2 Georg *a measure*
b Syr Compare Ethiop Arab 2 Arm: Lat lacks *of Hades, or which are the entrances*
c Meaning of Lat uncertain
d Syr Ethiop *the way of the incorruptible?*
e Syr Ethiop Arab 1: Meaning of Lat uncertain
f Lat lacks *was in vain*
g Or *those who are*
h Syr Ethiop Arm: Meaning of Lat uncertain
i Syr Ethiop Arab Georg: Lat *a trembling*
j Ethiop adds *holy*

see 4.13–21,28–32,40–42,48–50; 5.36–37,46–55. **7:** *How many dwellings . . . ?* In many apocalypses, these types of questions are in fact issues of proper concern. **8:** See Deut 30.11–13. *Hades,* the underworld. **10–11:** See Job 38–41; Jn 3.12. **12:** For the seer, to live without understanding of life's meaning is intolerable. **13–21:** Parable of the conflict between the forest and the sea. **18–19:** As a skillful teacher, the angel leads Ezra to answer his own question; see also 5.36–40, 46–47; 7.52–58. **21:** Isa 55.8–9. **22–25:** Ezra protests that he is inquiring only about the meaning of earthly, historical happenings, not about cosmic events. **24:** Ps 109.23; Wis 2.4.

4.26–52: Dialogic prediction regarding the future. 26–32: The angel's concern shifts to the end of the present, evil age and the distinction between this age and the next. This section marks the beginning of the

²⁶ He answered me and said, "If you are alive, you will see, and if you live long,ᵃ you will often marvel, because the age is hurrying swiftly to its end. ²⁷ It will not be able to bring the things that have been promised to the righteous in their appointed times, because this age is full of sadness and infirmities. ²⁸ For the evil about whichᵇ you ask me has been sown, but the harvest of it has not yet come. ²⁹ If therefore that which has been sown is not reaped, and if the place where the evil has been sown does not pass away, the field where the good has been sown will not come. ³⁰ For a grain of evil seed was sown in Adam's heart from the beginning, and how much ungodliness it has produced until now—and will produce until the time of threshing comes! ³¹ Consider now for yourself how much fruit of ungodliness a grain of evil seed has produced. ³² When heads of grain without number are sown, how great a threshing floor they will fill!"

³³ Then I answered and said, "How long?ᵇ When will these things be? Why are our years few and evil?" ³⁴ He answered me and said, "Do not be in a greater hurry than the Most High. You, indeed, are in a hurry for yourself,ᶜ but the Highest is in a hurry on behalf of many. ³⁵ Did not the souls of the righteous in their chambers ask about these matters, saying, 'How long are we to remain here?ᵈ And when will the harvest of our reward come?' ³⁶ And the archangel Jeremiel answered and said, 'When the number of those like yourselves is completed;ᵉ for he has weighed the age in the balance, ³⁷ and measured the times by measure, and numbered the times by number; and he will not move or arouse them until that measure is fulfilled.'"

³⁸ Then I answered and said, "But, O sovereign Lord, all of us also are full of ungodliness. ³⁹ It is perhaps on account of us that the time of threshing is delayed for the righteous—on account of the sins of those who inhabit the earth."

⁴⁰ He answered me and said, "Go and ask a pregnant woman whether, when her nine months have been completed, her womb can keep the fetus within her any longer."

⁴¹ And I said, "No, lord, it cannot."

He said to me, "In Hades the chambers of the souls are like the womb. ⁴² For just as a woman who is in labor makes haste to escape the pangs of birth, so also do these places hasten to give back those things that were committed to them from the beginning. ⁴³ Then the things that you desire to see will be disclosed to you."

⁴⁴ I answered and said, "If I have found favor in your sight, and if it is possible, and if I am worthy, ⁴⁵ show me this also: whether more time is to come than has passed, or whether for us the greater part has gone by. ⁴⁶ For I know what has gone by, but I do not know what is to come."

⁴⁷ And he said to me, "Stand at my right side, and I will show you the interpretation of a parable."

⁴⁸ So I stood and looked, and lo, a flaming furnace passed by before me, and when the

---

a Syr: Lat *live*
b Syr Ethiop: Meaning of Lat uncertain
c Syr Ethiop Arab Arm: Meaning of Lat uncertain
d Syr Ethiop Arab 2 Georg: Lat *How long do I hope thus?*
e Syr Ethiop Arab 2: Lat *number of seeds is completed for you*

---

angel's esoteric eschatological teaching, the main focus of 4 Ezra. **28–32:** *Harvest*, the time of judgment. Cf. Mt 3.12; 13.24–30. **29:** Cf. the fourth vision, 9.26–10.59. **30:** The *grain of evil seed*, or evil "yetser" (see 3.20n.) *sown in Adam's heart*, introduced in 3.7–27, must ripen and be harvested before the coming, righteous age can appear. **33–52:** Ezra's questions concerning the time of the end. **33:** *How long?*, the question is a prophetic and apocalyptic commonplace; see 4.35; 6.59; Isa 6.11; Dan 8.13; 12.6; Zech 1.12; Rev 6.10. Ezra's concerns, like the angel's, also move to the end of the age. **34:** An exhortation to patience in the face of coming judgment. **35–37:** This passage is similar to Rev 6.9–11. **35:** *Souls of the righteous in their chambers*, according to Jewish thought of the time, the souls of the righteous dead are placed in "chambers," or "treasuries," to await the last judgment (see 2.31; 4.41; 7.32,80,95,101; 1 Enoch 22; 2 Apoc. Bar. 21.23). **36:** *Archangel Jeremiel*, see 1 Enoch 20.8, Apoc. Zeph. 6.11–17; 2 Bar. 53–74. In 1 Enoch 20.8 the angel, called Remiel, is "in charge of those who rise." *When the number . . . is completed*, cf. 2.40–41; Rev 6.11. **36–37:** *Weighed . . . measured . . . numbered*, God has determined the times and periods of history (see Sir 36.10). **40–43:** The analogy of *a woman who is in labor* explains the inevitability of the end (cf. 5.46–55; 16.38–39; 1 Thess 5.3). **41:** *Hades*, the underworld. *Chambers*, see v. 35n. **44–50:** The seer

flame had gone by I looked, and lo, the smoke remained. ⁴⁹ And after this a cloud full of water passed before me and poured down a heavy and violent rain, and when the violent rainstorm had passed, drops still remained in the cloud.ª

⁵⁰ He said to me, "Consider it for yourself; for just as the rain is more than the drops, and the fire is greater than the smoke, so the quantity that passed was far greater; but drops and smoke remained."

⁵¹ Then I prayed and said, "Do you think that I shall live until those days? Or who will be alive in those days?"

⁵² He answered me and said, "Concerning the signs about which you ask me, I can tell you in part; but I was not sent to tell you concerning your life, for I do not know.

5 "Now concerning the signs: lo, the days are coming when those who inhabit the earth shall be seized with great terror,ᵇ and the way of truth shall be hidden, and the land shall be barren of faith. ² Unrighteousness shall be increased beyond what you yourself see, and beyond what you heard of formerly. ³ And the land that you now see ruling shall be a trackless waste, and people shall see it desolate. ⁴ But if the Most High grants that you live, you shall see it thrown into confusion after the third period;ᶜ

and the sun shall suddenly begin to shine at night,
and the moon during the day.
⁵ Blood shall drip from wood,
and the stone shall utter its voice;
the peoples shall be troubled,
and the stars shall fall.ᵈ
⁶ And one shall reign whom those who inhabit the earth do not expect, and the birds shall fly

away together; ⁷ and the Dead Seaᵉ shall cast up fish; and one whom the many do not know shall make his voice heard by night, and all shall hear his voice.ᶠ ⁸ There shall be chaos also in many places, fire shall often break out, the wild animals shall roam beyond their haunts, and menstruous women shall bring forth monsters. ⁹ Salt waters shall be found in the sweet, and all friends shall conquer one another; then shall reason hide itself, and wisdom shall withdraw into its chamber, ¹⁰ and it shall be sought by many but shall not be found, and unrighteousness and unrestraint shall increase on earth. ¹¹ One country shall ask its neighbor, 'Has righteousness, or anyone who does right, passed through you?' And it will answer, 'No.' ¹² At that time people shall hope but not obtain; they shall labor, but their ways shall not prosper. ¹³ These are the signs that I am permitted to tell you, and if you pray again, and weep as you do now, and fast for seven days, you shall hear yet greater things than these."

¹⁴ Then I woke up, and my body shuddered violently, and my soul was so troubled that it fainted. ¹⁵ But the angel who had come and talked with me held me and strengthened me and set me on my feet.

ª Lat *in it*
ᵇ Syr Ethiop: Meaning of Lat uncertain
ᶜ Literally *after the third*; Ethiop *after three months*; Arm *after the third vision*; Georg *after the third day*
ᵈ Ethiop Compare Syr and Arab: Meaning of Lat uncertain
ᵉ Lat *Sea of Sodom*
ᶠ Cn: Lat *fish; and it shall make its voice heard by night, which the many have not known, but all shall hear its voice.*

---

asks what proportion of time remains; he is told by a parable that the end is near (see 5.50–55; 14.10–12). **48:** *Flaming furnace . . . smoke*, see also Gen 15.17; Zech 12.6.

5.1–13: Direct prediction of the future by the angel, who uses classical apocalyptic "signs" to describe the end of this age (cf. the "synoptic apocalypse" in Mt 24.4–31; Mk 13.5–27; Lk 21.8–28). Each of the first three visions contains similar lists of apocalyptic signs (see 6.11–29; 7.26–44; 8.63–9.13). **2:** Mt 24.12. **3:** Rome will be destroyed. **4–9:** The natural order, mirroring the moral order, will be confused and overturned (cf. Joel 2.10; Mt 24.3–35; Mk 13.3–31; Lk 21.7–28). **4:** The reference to *the third period* is cryptic (cf. 14.10–12). **5:** *The stone shall utter its voice*, Hab 2.11; Lk 19.40. **7:** Cf. Ezek 47.8–10. **8a:** Syriac, "There shall be chasms also in many places" (cf. Zech 14.4). **8:** *Menstruous women*, cf. 6.21; Mt 24.19; Mk 13.17. **9–11:** *Wisdom*, personified as in the wisdom literature, *shall withdraw*, another classic apocalyptic theme (cf. Isa 59.14–15; 2 *Apoc. Bar.* 48.36). **13:** For the author, fasting, prayer, and mourning prepared one to receive a divine revelation; he refers to four such preparatory periods of seven days (5.20; 6.35; 9.23–25; 12.51).

5.14–20: Transition to the second vision. 14: *Then I woke up*, from the dream vision. *My soul . . . fainted*, cf.

[16] Now on the second night Phaltiel, a chief of the people, came to me and said, "Where have you been? And why is your face sad? [17] Or do you not know that Israel has been entrusted to you in the land of their exile? [18] Rise therefore and eat some bread, and do not forsake us, like a shepherd who leaves the flock in the power of savage wolves."

[19] Then I said to him, "Go away from me and do not come near me for seven days; then you may come to me."

He heard what I said and left me. [20] So I fasted seven days, mourning and weeping, as the angel Uriel had commanded me.

[21] After seven days the thoughts of my heart were very grievous to me again. [22] Then my soul recovered the spirit of understanding, and I began once more to speak words in the presence of the Most High. [23] I said, "O sovereign Lord, from every forest of the earth and from all its trees you have chosen one vine, [24] and from all the lands of the world you have chosen for yourself one region,[a] and from all the flowers of the world you have chosen for yourself one lily, [25] and from all the depths of the sea you have filled for yourself one river, and from all the cities that have been built you have consecrated Zion for yourself, [26] and from all the birds that have been created you have named for yourself one dove, and from all the flocks that have been made you have provided for yourself one sheep, [27] and from all the multitude of peoples you have gotten for yourself one people; and to this people, whom you have loved, you have given the law that is approved by all. [28] And now, O Lord, why have you handed the one over to the many, and dishonored[b] the one root beyond the others, and scattered your only one among the many? [29] And those who opposed your promises have trampled on those who believed your covenants. [30] If you really hate your people, they should be punished at your own hands."

[31] When I had spoken these words, the angel who had come to me on a previous night was sent to me. [32] He said to me, "Listen to me, and I will instruct you; pay attention to me, and I will tell you more."

[33] Then I said, "Speak, my lord." And he said to me, "Are you greatly disturbed in mind over Israel? Or do you love him more than his Maker does?"

[34] I said, "No, my lord, but because of my grief I have spoken; for every hour I suffer agonies of heart, while I strive to understand the way of the Most High and to search out some part of his judgment."

[35] He said to me, "You cannot." And I said, "Why not, my lord? Why then was I born? Or why did not my mother's womb become my grave, so that I would not see the travail of Jacob and the exhaustion of the people of Israel?"

[36] He said to me, "Count up for me those who have not yet come, and gather for me the scattered raindrops, and make the withered flowers bloom again for me; [37] open for me the closed chambers, and bring out for me the winds shut up in them, or show me the picture of a voice; and then I will explain to you the travail that you ask to understand."[c]

---

a   Ethiop: Lat *pit*
b   Syr Ethiop Arab: Lat *prepared*
c   Lat *see*

Dan 7.28; 8.27; 10.9–10,17b–19. **16–19:** *Phaltiel, a chief of the people,* named only here, tries unsuccessfully to dissuade Ezra from his solitary visionary quest. See also 12.40–51.

5.21–6.34: The second vision. 5.21–22: Introduction; cf. 3.1–3.

5.23–30: Addressing God, the seer reiterates his complaints of divine injustice in dealing with Israel. 23–28: In this series of comparisons, most of the *chosen* elements are biblical figures representing Israel: the *vine* (v. 23), Ps 80.8–15; Jer 2.21; the *lily* (v. 24), Song 2.2 (interpreted allegorically); Hos 14.5; the *river* (v. 25), Isa 8.6; the city of *Zion* (v. 25), Ps 132.13; the *dove* (v. 26), Ps 74.19; the *sheep* (v. 26), Ps 79.13; Isa 53.7; the *root* (v. 28), *1 Enoch* 93.8. The author has a penchant for compiling similar, long lists of synonymous or analogous elements (see 5.36–37; 6.1–5; 8.52–54; 10.21–23). **27:** The claim that God has *loved* Israel (see Deut 7.8) is contrasted with the idea of *hate* in v. 30. **30:** Ezra wishes that punishment would come directly from God, not human agents; see also 2 Sam 24.14; Sir 2.18.

5.31–40: Dialogic dispute with the angel. The issue of contention is the same as in the first vision. **31:** *The angel who had come to me,* see 4.1n. **33:** The angel answers Ezra's concern for God's *love* for Israel. **35:** Job 3.11;

[38] I said, "O sovereign Lord, who is able to know these things except him whose dwelling is not with mortals? [39] As for me, I am without wisdom, and how can I speak concerning the things that you have asked me?"

[40] He said to me, "Just as you cannot do one of the things that were mentioned, so you cannot discover my judgment, or the goal of the love that I have promised to my people."

[41] I said, "Yet, O Lord, you have charge of those who are alive at the end, but what will those do who lived before me, or we, ourselves, or those who come after us?"

[42] He said to me, "I shall liken my judgment to a circle;[a] just as for those who are last there is no slowness, so for those who are first there is no haste."

[43] Then I answered and said, "Could you not have created at one time those who have been and those who are and those who will be, so that you might show your judgment the sooner?"

[44] He replied to me and said, "The creation cannot move faster than the Creator, nor can the world hold at one time those who have been created in it."

[45] I said, "How have you said to your servant that you[b] will certainly give life at one time to your creation? If therefore all creatures will live at one time[c] and the creation will sustain them, it might even now be able to support all of them present at one time."

[46] He said to me, "Ask a woman's womb, and say to it, 'If you bear ten[d] children, why one after another?' Request it therefore to produce ten at one time."

[47] I said, "Of course it cannot, but only each in its own time."

[48] He said to me, "Even so I have given the womb of the earth to those who from time to time are sown in it. [49] For as an infant does not bring forth, and a woman who has become old does not bring forth any longer, so I have made the same rule for the world that I created."

[50] Then I inquired and said, "Since you have now given me the opportunity, let me speak before you. Is our mother, of whom you have told me, still young? Or is she now approaching old age?"

[51] He replied to me, "Ask a woman who bears children, and she will tell you. [52] Say to her, 'Why are those whom you have borne recently not like those whom you bore before, but smaller in stature?' [53] And she herself will answer you, 'Those born in the strength of youth are different from those born during the time of old age, when the womb is failing.' [54] Therefore you also should consider that you and your contemporaries are smaller in stature than those who were before you, [55] and those who come after you will be smaller than you, as born of a creation that already is aging and passing the strength of youth."

[56] I said, "I implore you, O Lord, if I have found favor in your sight, show your servant through whom you will visit your creation."

6 He said to me, "At the beginning of the circle of the earth, before[e] the portals of the world were in place, and before the

---

a   Or *crown*
b   Syr Ethiop Arab 1: Meaning of Lat uncertain
c   Lat lacks *If … one time*
d   Syr Ethiop Arab 2 Arm: Meaning of Lat uncertain
e   Meaning of Lat uncertain: Compare Syr *The beginning by the hand of humankind, but the end by my own hands. For as before the land of the world existed there, and before*; Ethiop: *At first by the Son of Man, and afterwards I myself. For before the earth and the lands were created, and before*

10.18–19; Jer 20.17. **36–40:** As in the first vision (4.5), the angel poses unanswerable riddles from nature. **40:** *My … I*, the angel speaks in God's name.

   5.41–6.10: Dialogic prediction concerning the future. 5.41–49: Ezra's concern is for fair treatment of all at the judgment. **41:** *You have charge*, Ezra immediately resumes his questioning about the details of the end. The problem of the faithful who die before the end time was also an issue in early Christianity (1 Thess 4.13–15). **45:** *How have you said … ?* Ezra points out an apparent contradiction in the logic: *All … will live at one time*, namely at the resurrection. **48:** *The womb of the earth*, see Job 1.21. **50–55:** As in the first vision (4.44–46), Ezra asks about the timing of the end. **54:** Ezra's generation being *smaller in stature* shows that the end is near. Various traditions refer to an ancient race of giants (Gen 6.4; Num 13.33; Deut 3.11; *1 Enoch* 6–11). **5.56–6.6:** To Ezra's question concerning an eschatological agent, the angel responds that God alone will act. **6.1:** *Portals of the*

assembled winds blew, [2] and before the rumblings of thunder sounded, and before the flashes of lightning shone, and before the foundations of paradise were laid, [3] and before the beautiful flowers were seen, and before the powers of movements[a] were established, and before the innumerable hosts of angels were gathered together, [4] and before the heights of the air were lifted up, and before the measures of the firmaments were named, and before the footstool of Zion was established, [5] and before the present years were reckoned and before the imaginations of those who now sin were estranged, and before those who stored up treasures of faith were sealed— [6] then I planned these things, and they were made through me alone and not through another; just as the end shall come through me alone and not through another."

[7] I answered and said, "What will be the dividing of the times? Or when will be the end of the first age and the beginning of the age that follows?"

[8] He said to me, "From Abraham to Isaac,[b] because from him were born Jacob and Esau, for Jacob's hand held Esau's heel from the beginning. [9] Now Esau is the end of this age, and Jacob is the beginning of the age that follows. [10] The beginning of a person is the hand, and the end of a person is the heel;[c] seek for nothing else, Ezra, between the heel and the hand, Ezra!"

[11] I answered and said, "O sovereign Lord, if I have found favor in your sight, [12] show your servant the last of your signs of which you showed me a part on a previous night."

[13] He answered and said to me, "Rise to your feet and you will hear a full, resounding voice. [14] And if the place where you are standing is greatly shaken [15] while the voice is speaking, do not be terrified; because the word concerns the end, and the foundations of the earth will understand [16] that the speech concerns them. They will tremble and be shaken, for they know that their end must be changed."

[17] When I heard this, I got to my feet and listened; a voice was speaking, and its sound was like the sound of mighty[d] waters. [18] It said, "The days are coming when I draw near to visit the inhabitants of the earth, [19] and when I require from the doers of iniquity the penalty of their iniquity, and when the humiliation of Zion is complete. [20] When the seal is placed upon the age that is about to pass away, then I will show these signs: the books shall be opened before the face of the firmament, and all shall see my judgment[e] together. [21] Children a year old shall speak with their voices, and pregnant women shall give birth to premature children at three and four months, and these shall live and leap about. [22] Sown places shall suddenly appear unsown, and full storehouses shall suddenly be found to be empty; [23] the trumpet shall sound aloud, and when all hear it, they shall suddenly be terrified. [24] At that time friends shall make war on friends like enemies, the earth and those who inhabit it shall be terrified, and the springs of the fountains shall stand still, so that for three hours they shall not flow.

[25] "It shall be that whoever remains after all that I have foretold to you shall be saved

---

a Or *earthquakes*
b Other ancient authorities read *to Abraham*
c Syr: Meaning of Lat uncertain
d Lat *many*
e Syr: Lat lacks *my judgment*

---

world, here, as elsewhere, the author shows a fascination with natural phenomena and their origins (vv. 1–5). **4**: *Footstool*, see Pss 99.5; 132.7. **7–10**: The division of the ages. In allegorical language the seer is told that the present corrupt age (symbolized by *Esau*) will be followed immediately, without a break, by the glorious age to come (symbolized by *Jacob*). **8**: *Heel*, see Gen 25.26.

    6.11–29: Direct prediction of the future, this time in response to Ezra's query (6.11–12). As in 5.1–13, the author uses classical apocalyptic signs. **14–16**: God's appearance causes the very foundations of the earth to shake; see Joel 3.16. **17**: *A voice . . . like the sound of mighty waters* signifies direct address by God. The image is developed from the vision of Ezekiel (Ezek 1.24–25). Compare Rev 1.15; 14.2; 19.6. **18**: *Visit*, bring judgment. **20**: *The books shall be opened*, the heavenly books in which are written the deeds of humankind (Dan 7.10; 12.1; Mal 3.16; cf. Ex 32.32; Ps 69.28). The motif is also common in Christian writings roughly contemporary with chs 3–14 (Lk 10.20; Heb 12.23; Rev 20.12). **23**: *The trumpet shall sound*, a common eschatological motif (1 Cor 15.52; 1 Thess

and shall see my salvation and the end of my world. ²⁶ And they shall see those who were taken up, who from their birth have not tasted death; and the heart of the earth's[a] inhabitants shall be changed and converted to a different spirit. ²⁷ For evil shall be blotted out, and deceit shall be quenched; ²⁸ faithfulness shall flourish, and corruption shall be overcome, and the truth, which has been so long without fruit, shall be revealed."

²⁹ While he spoke to me, little by little the place where I was standing began to rock to and fro.[b] ³⁰ And he said to me, "I have come to show you these things this night.[c] ³¹ If therefore you will pray again and fast again for seven days, I will again declare to you greater things than these,[d] ³² because your voice has surely been heard by the Most High; for the Mighty One has seen your uprightness and has also observed the purity that you have maintained from your youth. ³³ Therefore he sent me to show you all these things, and to say to you: 'Believe and do not be afraid! ³⁴ Do not be quick to think vain thoughts concerning the former times; then you will not act hastily in the last times.'"

³⁵ Now after this I wept again and fasted seven days in the same way as before, in order to complete the three weeks that had been prescribed for me. ³⁶ Then on the eighth night my heart was troubled within me again, and I began to speak in the presence of the Most High. ³⁷ My spirit was greatly aroused, and my soul was in distress.

³⁸ I said, "O Lord, you spoke at the beginning of creation, and said on the first day, 'Let heaven and earth be made,' and your word accomplished the work. ³⁹ Then the spirit was blowing, and darkness and silence embraced everything; the sound of human voices was not yet there.[e] ⁴⁰ Then you commanded a ray of light to be brought out from your storechambers, so that your works could be seen.

⁴¹ "Again, on the second day, you created the spirit of the firmament, and commanded it to divide and separate the waters, so that one part might move upward and the other part remain beneath.

⁴² "On the third day you commanded the waters to be gathered together in a seventh part of the earth; six parts you dried up and kept so that some of them might be planted and cultivated and be of service before you. ⁴³ For your word went forth, and at once the work was done. ⁴⁴ Immediately fruit came forth in endless abundance and of varied appeal to the taste, and flowers of inimitable color, and odors of inexpressible fragrance. These were made on the third day.

⁴⁵ "On the fourth day you commanded the brightness of the sun, the light of the moon, and the arrangement of the stars to come into being; ⁴⁶ and you commanded them to serve humankind, about to be formed.

⁴⁷ "On the fifth day you commanded the seventh part, where the water had been gathered together, to bring forth living creatures, birds, and fishes; and so it was done. ⁴⁸ The dumb and lifeless water produced living creatures, as it was commanded, so that therefore the nations might declare your wondrous works.

[a] Syr Compare Ethiop Arab 1 Arm: Lat lacks *earth's*
[b] Syr Ethiop Compare Arab Arm: Meaning of Lat uncertain
[c] Syr Compare Ethiop: Meaning of Lat uncertain
[d] Syr Ethiop Arab 1 Arm: Lat adds *by day*
[e] Syr Ethiop: Lat *was not yet from you*

4.16). **25:** *See my salvation*, see 7.27; 9.8; 13.48,50; Ps 98.3; Isa 52.10; Lk 2.30. **26:** *Those who were taken up*, such as Enoch (Gen 5.24; Sir 44.16) and Elijah (2 Kings 2.11–12); cf. 8.19; 14.9. **26–28:** The transition from evil to truth.

6.30–34: The conclusion of the vision (compare 5.14–20). **34:** The seer is cautioned against being presumptuous.

6.35–9.25: The third vision. 6.35–7.44: The first section of the third vision. **6.35–37: Introduction** (cf. 3.1–3 and 5.21–22). **35:** *I . . . fasted seven days*, see 5.13n. *The three weeks* (cf. Dan 10.2–3), so far only two fasts of seven days have been mentioned (here and at 5.20). The author may be referring to this as Ezra's third vision.

6.38–59: Addressing God, the seer recounts God's work in six days of creation. If the world was created for Israel (v. 55), why has the nation not possessed its inheritance? This is similar in theme and content to the addresses in 3.4–36 and 5.23–30. **38–54:** A summary of creation, roughly following Gen 1. **42:** *A seventh part . . . six parts*, although there is no exact parallel to this division in Genesis or other literature, explorers like Christopher

⁴⁹ "Then you kept in existence two living creatures;ᵃ the one you called Behemothᵇ and the name of the other Leviathan. ⁵⁰ And you separated one from the other, for the seventh part where the water had been gathered together could not hold them both. ⁵¹ And you gave Behemothᵇ one of the parts that had been dried up on the third day, to live in it, where there are a thousand mountains; ⁵² but to Leviathan you gave the seventh part, the watery part; and you have kept them to be eaten by whom you wish, and when you wish.

⁵³ "On the sixth day you commanded the earth to bring forth before you cattle, wild animals, and creeping things; ⁵⁴ and over these you placed Adam, as ruler over all the works that you had made; and from him we have all come, the people whom you have chosen.

⁵⁵ "All this I have spoken before you, O Lord, because you have said that it was for us that you created this world.ᶜ ⁵⁶ As for the other nations that have descended from Adam, you have said that they are nothing, and that they are like spittle, and you have compared their abundance to a drop from a bucket. ⁵⁷ And now, O Lord, these nations, which are reputed to be as nothing, domineer over us and devour us. ⁵⁸ But we your people, whom you have called your firstborn, only begotten, zealous for you,ᵈ and most dear, have been given into their hands. ⁵⁹ If the world has indeed been created for us, why do we not possess our world as an inheritance? How long will this be so?"

7 When I had finished speaking these words, the angel who had been sent to me on the former nights was sent to me again. ² He said to me, "Rise, Ezra, and listen to the words that I have come to speak to you." ³ I said, "Speak, my lord." And he said to me, "There is a sea set in a wide expanse so that it is deep and vast, ⁴ but it has an entrance set in a narrow place, so that it is like a river. ⁵ If there are those who wish to reach the sea, to look at it or to navigate it, how can they come to the broad part unless they pass through the narrow part? ⁶ Another example: There is a city built and set on a plain, and it is full of all good things; ⁷ but the entrance to it is narrow and set in a precipitous place, so that there is fire on the right hand and deep water on the left. ⁸ There is only one path lying between them, that is, between the fire and the water, so that only one person can walk on the path. ⁹ If now the city is given to someone as an inheritance, how will the heir receive the inheritance unless by passing through the appointed danger?"

¹⁰ I said, "That is right, lord." He said to me, "So also is Israel's portion. ¹¹ For I made the world for their sake, and when Adam transgressed my statutes, what had been made was judged. ¹² And so the entrances of this world were made narrow and sorrowful and toilsome; they are few and evil, full of dangers and involved in great hardships. ¹³ But the entrances of the greater world are broad and safe, and yield the fruit of immortality. ¹⁴ Therefore unless the living pass through the difficult and futile experiences, they can never receive those things that have been reserved for them. ¹⁵ Now therefore why are you disturbed, seeing that you are to perish? Why are you moved, seeing that you are mortal? ¹⁶ Why have you not considered in your mind what is to come, rather than what is now present?"

ᵃ Syr Ethiop: Lat *two souls*

ᵇ Other Lat authorities read *Enoch*

ᶜ Syr Ethiop Arab 2: Lat *the firstborn world* Compare Arab 1 *first world*

ᵈ Meaning of Lat uncertain

Columbus took this verse as an indicator of the world's layout. **49–52:** The land creature *Behemoth* and the sea creature *Leviathan* are two primeval monsters frequently found in Israelite mythology (see Job 7.12; 26.12–13; Pss 74.12–15; 89.10–11; Isa 30.7; 51.9–10). Their eschatological function is to serve as food for the elect (*2 Apoc. Bar.* 29.4; *1 Enoch* 60.7–10). **55:** *For us* (Israel) *that you created this world*, a notion developed from such passages as Ex 4.22; Deut 10.15; 14.2. See 7.11. **56:** *A drop from a bucket*, Isa 40.15 (note especially the Septuagint version).

7.1–25: Dispute between Ezra and the angel. It is necessary first to undergo the trials of this world before one can receive the rewards of the next. **1:** *The former nights*, 4.1; 5.31. **3–9:** The angel tells two parables, of a sea and a city, to illustrate his point. **3:** *Sea*, the world to come. **4:** *Narrow place*, see also Mt 7.13–14; Lk 13.24. **11:** By implication, the *world* was created entirely good for Israel's *sake, and when Adam transgressed*, that inheritance

¹⁷ Then I answered and said, "O sovereign Lord, you have ordained in your law that the righteous shall inherit these things, but that the ungodly shall perish. ¹⁸ The righteous, therefore, can endure difficult circumstances while hoping for easier ones; but those who have done wickedly have suffered the difficult circumstances and will never see the easier ones."

¹⁹ He said to me, "You are not a better judge than the Lord,[a] or wiser than the Most High! ²⁰ Let many perish who are now living, rather than that the law of God that is set before them be disregarded! ²¹ For the Lord[b] strictly commanded those who came into the world, when they came, what they should do to live, and what they should observe to avoid punishment. ²² Nevertheless they were not obedient, and spoke against him;

they devised for themselves vain thoughts,
²³ and proposed to themselves wicked frauds;
they even declared that the Most High does not exist,
and they ignored his ways.
²⁴ They scorned his law,
and denied his covenants;
they have been unfaithful to his statutes,
and have not performed his works.
²⁵ That is the reason, Ezra, that empty things are for the empty, and full things are for the full.

²⁶ "For indeed the time will come, when the signs that I have foretold to you will come to pass, that the city that now is not seen shall appear,[c] and the land that now is hidden shall be disclosed. ²⁷ Everyone who has been delivered from the evils that I have foretold shall see my wonders. ²⁸ For my son the Messiah[d] shall be revealed with those who are with him, and those who remain shall rejoice four hundred years. ²⁹ After those years my son the Messiah shall die, and all who draw human breath.[e] ³⁰ Then the world shall be turned back to primeval silence for seven days, as it was at the first beginnings, so that no one shall be left. ³¹ After seven days the world that is not yet awake shall be roused, and that which is corruptible shall perish. ³² The earth shall give up those who are asleep in it, and the dust those who rest there in silence; and the chambers shall give up the souls that have been committed to them. ³³ The Most High shall be revealed on the seat of judgment, and compassion shall pass away, and patience shall be withdrawn.[f] ³⁴ Only judgment shall remain, truth shall stand, and faithfulness shall grow strong. ³⁵ Recompense shall follow, and the reward shall be manifested; righteous deeds shall awake, and unrighteous deeds shall not sleep.[g] ³⁶ The pit[h] of torment shall appear,

a   Other ancient authorities read God; Ethiop Georg the only One
b   Other ancient authorities read God
c   Arm: Lat Syr that the bride shall appear, even the city appearing
d   Syr Arab 1: Ethiop my Messiah; Arab 2 the Messiah; Arm the Messiah of God; Lat my son Jesus
e   Arm all who have continued in faith and in patience
f   Lat shall gather together
g   The passage from verse 36 to verse 105, formerly missing, has been restored to the text
h   Syr Ethiop: Lat place

was despoiled (see 3.7,21). **12–13:** This world . . . evil is contrasted with the greater world to come. **17:** Cf. Deut 8.1; Ps 37.9. **17–18:** The seer exhibits a heartfelt, characteristic concern for the ungodly but is told that their punishment is deserved (vv. 19–25). **21:** Commanded, Deut 30:15–19.

7.26–44: Direct prediction of the future by the angel, again using classical apocalyptic signs (cf. 5.1–13; 6.11–29). In this section the focus is on God's judgment (cf. Mt 25.31–46). **26:** The city, the heavenly Jerusalem; see 10.25–54. **28:** My son the Messiah, a term used often in this book (see 13.32,37,52; 14.9). The precise connection between this term and Christian notions of Jesus "the Messiah" as "son of God" is uncertain, and in any event is indirect. Those who are with him, 13.52; 14.9. **29:** My son the Messiah shall die, this idea is unparalleled in Jewish sources. **30:** Primeval silence, as before creation. See 6.39. **32:** Dan 12.2. Chambers, see 4.35n. Resurrection precedes the day of judgment. **33–34:** On the day of judgment, only judgment shall remain; mercy is put aside (see 7.104–5). **36–105:** These verses are lacking from the standard editions of the Latin Vulgate, and from the King James Version. They are present in the Syriac, Ethiopic, Arabic, and Armenian versions, and in seven Latin manuscripts. The section was probably deliberately cut out of an ancestor of most surviving Latin manuscripts for dogmatic reasons, because the passage contains an emphatic denial of the value of prayers for the dead (v. 105). **36–38:** There exist only two possible destinations for those who are judged: a place of reward and a place

and opposite it shall be the place of rest; and the furnace of hell[a] shall be disclosed, and opposite it the paradise of delight. [37]Then the Most High will say to the nations that have been raised from the dead, 'Look now, and understand whom you have denied, whom you have not served, whose commandments you have despised. [38]Look on this side and on that; here are delight and rest, and there are fire and torments.' Thus he will[b] speak to them on the day of judgment— [39]a day that has no sun or moon or stars, [40]or cloud or thunder or lightning, or wind or water or air, or darkness or evening or morning, [41]or summer or spring or heat or winter[c] or frost or cold, or hail or rain or dew, [42]or noon or night, or dawn or shining or brightness or light, but only the splendor of the glory of the Most High, by which all shall see what has been destined. [43]It will last as though for a week of years. [44]This is my judgment and its prescribed order; and to you alone I have shown these things."

[45] I answered and said, "O sovereign Lord, I said then and[d] I say now: Blessed are those who are alive and keep your commandments! [46]But what of those for whom I prayed? For who among the living is there that has not sinned, or who is there among mortals that has not transgressed your covenant? [47]And now I see that the world to come will bring delight to few, but torments to many. [48]For an evil heart has grown up in us, which has alienated us from God,[e] and has brought us into corruption and the ways of death, and has shown us the paths of perdition and removed us far from life—and that not merely for a few but for almost all who have been created."

[49] He answered me and said, "Listen to me, Ezra,[f] and I will instruct you, and will admonish you once more. [50]For this reason the Most High has made not one world but two. [51]Inasmuch as you have said that the righteous are not many but few, while the ungodly abound, hear the explanation for this.

[52] "If you have just a few precious stones, will you add to them lead and clay?"[g] [53]I said, "Lord, how could that be?" [54]And he said to me, "Not only that, but ask the earth and she will tell you; defer to her, and she will declare it to you. [55]Say to her, 'You produce gold and silver and bronze, and also iron and lead and clay; [56]but silver is more abundant than gold, and bronze than silver, and iron than bronze, and lead than iron, and clay than lead.' [57]Judge therefore which things are precious and desirable, those that are abundant or those that are rare?"

[58] I said, "O sovereign Lord, what is plentiful is of less worth, for what is more rare is more precious."

[59] He answered me and said, "Consider within yourself[h] what you have thought, for the person who has what is hard to get rejoices more than the person who has what is plentiful. [60]So also will be the judgment[i] that I have promised; for I will rejoice over the few who shall be saved, because it is they who have made my glory to prevail now, and through them my name has now been honored. [61]I will not grieve over the great number of those who perish; for it is they who are now like a mist, and are similar to a flame and

a Lat Syr Ethiop *Gehenna*
b Syr Ethiop Arab 1: Lat *you shall*
c Or *storm*
d Syr: Lat *And I answered, "I said then, O Lord, and*
e Cn: Lat Syr Ethiop *from these*
f Syr Arab 1 Georg: Lat Ethiop lack *Ezra*
g Arab 1: Meaning of Lat Syr Ethiop uncertain
h Syr Ethiop Arab 1: Meaning of Lat uncertain
i Syr Arab 1: Lat *creation*

of punishment. See also 7.79–99. **36:** *Pit*, Isa 38.17–18; Rev 9.2. **39–43:** A description of the day of judgment; cf. Gen 8.22; Zech 14.6–7. **42:** Isa 60.19–20; Rev 21.23. **42:** *The glory of the Most High* is the revelation of God's appearance, see 3.19; 7.60,112,122. **43:** *A week of years*, seven years; cf. Dan 9.24,26.

7.45–8.3: The second section of the third vision. **45–74:** Dispute between Ezra and the angel. God rejoices over the few who will be saved and does not lament the many wicked who perish. **45–48:** Ezra again bemoans the fate of sinners. **46:** Cf. 1 Kings 8.46; Prov 20.9. **48:** *An evil heart*, see 3.20n. *The ways of death* affect nearly all; see 3.7–11. **52–57:** *Precious*, that is, the righteous, as opposed to common metals and substances; see the

smoke—they are set on fire and burn hotly, and are extinguished."

⁶² I replied and said, "O earth, what have you brought forth, if the mind is made out of the dust like the other created things? ⁶³ For it would have been better if the dust itself had not been born, so that the mind might not have been made from it. ⁶⁴ But now the mind grows with us, and therefore we are tormented, because we perish and we know it. ⁶⁵ Let the human race lament, but let the wild animals of the field be glad; let all who have been born lament, but let the cattle and the flocks rejoice. ⁶⁶ It is much better with them than with us; for they do not look for a judgment, and they do not know of any torment or salvation promised to them after death. ⁶⁷ What does it profit us that we shall be preserved alive but cruelly tormented? ⁶⁸ For all who have been born are entangled inᵃ iniquities, and are full of sins and burdened with transgressions. ⁶⁹ And if after death we were not to come into judgment, perhaps it would have been better for us."

⁷⁰ He answered me and said, "When the Most High made the world and Adam and all who have come from him, he first prepared the judgment and the things that pertain to the judgment. ⁷¹ But now, understand from your own words—for you have said that the mind grows with us. 72 For this reason, therefore, those who live on earth shall be tormented, because though they had understanding, they committed iniquity; and though they received the commandments, they did not keep them; and though they obtained the law, they dealt unfaithfully with what they received. ⁷³ What, then, will they have to say in the judgment, or how will they answer in the last times? ⁷⁴ How long the Most High has been patient with those who

inhabit the world!—and not for their sake, but because of the times that he has foreordained."

⁷⁵ I answered and said, "If I have found favor in your sight, O Lord, show this also to your servant: whether after death, as soon as everyone of us yields up the soul, we shall be kept in rest until those times come when you will renew the creation, or whether we shall be tormented at once?"

⁷⁶ He answered me and said, "I will show you that also, but do not include yourself with those who have shown scorn, or number yourself among those who are tormented. ⁷⁷ For you have a treasure of works stored up with the Most High, but it will not be shown to you until the last times. ⁷⁸ Now concerning death, the teaching is: When the decisive decree has gone out from the Most High that a person shall die, as the spirit leaves the body to return again to him who gave it, first of all it adores the glory of the Most High. ⁷⁹ If it is one of those who have shown scorn and have not kept the way of the Most High, who have despised his law and hated those who fear God— ⁸⁰ such spirits shall not enter into habitations, but shall immediately wander about in torments, always grieving and sad, in seven ways. ⁸¹ The first way, because they have scorned the law of the Most High. ⁸² The second way, because they cannot now make a good repentance so that they may live. ⁸³ The third way, they shall see the reward laid up for those who have trusted the covenants of the Most High. ⁸⁴ The fourth way, they shall consider the torment laid up for themselves in the last days. ⁸⁵ The fifth way, they shall see how the habitations of the others are guarded by angels in profound quiet. ⁸⁶ The sixth way, they shall see how some of them will cross

ᵃ Syr *defiled with*

similar arguments in 8.1–3. *62–69*: Ezra's heated lament (*better if . . . had not been born*) is typical of his reactions to the angel's arguments (see 4.12; 5.35). *64–68*: The *human race*, aware of their sins and their fate, are worse off than the blissfully ignorant *wild animals*. Knowledge has adverse effects; cf. Gen 3.7. *72*: Humans who are sinful deserve their fate.

7.75–101: Dialogic prediction of the future. The state of souls after death and before the judgment. *76–77*: *Do not include yourself*, the angel repeatedly asserts that Ezra is specially favored by God (see 6.32–33; 7.44; 8.19,47–54; 13.53–56; 14.9). *77*: *A treasure of works*, 8.33,36. Cf. Mt 6.20; Mk 10.21; Lk 12.33. *79–99*: The fates of two different types of souls, good and evil, are laid out in parallel fashion. *80–87*: Seven kinds of torment for the wicked; cf. Lk 16.19–31. *80*: *Habitations*, elsewhere called "chambers," see 4.35n. *85*: *Guarded by angels*, see v.

over[a] into torments. [87] The seventh way, which is worse[b] than all the ways that have been mentioned, because they shall utterly waste away in confusion and be consumed with shame,[c] and shall wither with fear at seeing the glory of the Most High in whose presence they sinned while they were alive, and in whose presence they are to be judged in the last times.

[88] "Now this is the order of those who have kept the ways of the Most High, when they shall be separated from their mortal body.[d] [89] During the time that they lived in it,[c] they laboriously served the Most High, and withstood danger every hour so that they might keep the law of the Lawgiver perfectly. [90] Therefore this is the teaching concerning them: [91] First of all, they shall see with great joy the glory of him who receives them, for they shall have rest in seven orders. [92] The first order, because they have striven with great effort to overcome the evil thought that was formed with them, so that it might not lead them astray from life into death. [93] The second order, because they see the perplexity in which the souls of the ungodly wander and the punishment that awaits them. [94] The third order, they see the witness that he who formed them bears concerning them, that throughout their life they kept the law with which they were entrusted. [95] The fourth order, they understand the rest that they now enjoy, being gathered into their chambers and guarded by angels in profound quiet, and the glory waiting for them in the last days. [96] The fifth order, they rejoice that they have now escaped what is corruptible and shall inherit what is to come; and besides they see the straits and toil[e] from which they have been delivered, and the spacious liberty that they are to receive and enjoy in immortality. [97] The sixth order, when it is shown them how their face is to shine like the sun, and how they are to be made like the light of the stars, being incor-

ruptible from then on. [98] The seventh order, which is greater than all that have been mentioned, because they shall rejoice with boldness, and shall be confident without confusion, and shall be glad without fear, for they press forward to see the face of him whom they served in life and from whom they are to receive their reward when glorified. [99] This is the order of the souls of the righteous, as henceforth is announced;[f] and the previously mentioned are the ways of torment that those who would not give heed shall suffer hereafter."

[100] Then I answered and said, "Will time therefore be given to the souls, after they have been separated from the bodies, to see what you have described to me?"

[101] He said to me, "They shall have freedom for seven days, so that during these seven days they may see the things of which you have been told, and afterwards they shall be gathered in their habitations."

[102] I answered and said, "If I have found favor in your sight, show further to me, your servant, whether on the day of judgment the righteous will be able to intercede for the ungodly or to entreat the Most High for them— [103] fathers for sons or sons for parents, brothers for brothers, relatives for their kindred, or friends for those who are most dear."

[104] He answered me and said, "Since you have found favor in my sight, I will show you this also. The day of judgment is decisive[g] and displays to all the seal of truth. Just as now a father does not send his son, or a son his father, or a master his servant, or a friend his dearest friend, to be ill[a] or sleep or eat or

---

[a] Cn: Meaning of Lat uncertain
[b] Lat Syr Ethiop *greater*
[c] Syr Ethiop: Meaning of Lat uncertain
[d] Lat *the corruptible vessel*
[e] Syr Ethiop: Lat *fullness*
[f] Syr: Meaning of Lat uncertain
[g] Lat *bold*

95; 1 Enoch 100.5. **87:** *Glory*, see 6.14–16; 7.42n. **88–99:** Seven kinds of joyous rest for the righteous. Compare the teaching regarding death in Dan 12.2–3; Wis 3–5. **92:** *The evil thought*, the evil "yetser" (see 3.20n.). **95:** *Chambers*, see 4.35n. **97:** *Sun . . . stars*, v. 125; Dan 12.3; Mt 13.43; 2 Bar. 51. **98:** *To see the face* of God (Ex 33.20; 1 Jn 3.2; Rev 22.4). *Reward*, cf. Rev 22.12. **99–101:** *The souls of the righteous* are gathered in their *habitations* (see 4.35n.), while the souls of the unjust wander aimlessly.

7.102–115: Dispute between Ezra and the angel, mainly concerning the idea that there will be no interces-

be healed in his place, [105] so no one shall ever pray for another on that day, neither shall anyone lay a burden on another;[b] for then all shall bear their own righteousness and unrighteousness."

[36] [106] I answered and said, "How then do we find that first Abraham prayed for the people of Sodom, and Moses for our ancestors who sinned in the desert, [37] [107] and Joshua after him for Israel in the days of Achan, [38] [108] and Samuel in the days of Saul,[c] and David for the plague, and Solomon for those at the dedication, [39] [109] and Elijah for those who received the rain, and for the one who was dead, that he might live, [40] [110] and Hezekiah for the people in the days of Sennacherib, and many others prayed for many? [41] [111] So if now, when corruption has increased and unrighteousness has multiplied, the righteous have prayed for the ungodly, why will it not be so then as well?"

[42] [112] He answered me and said, "This present world is not the end; the full glory does not[d] remain in it;[e] therefore those who were strong prayed for the weak. [43] [113] But the day of judgment will be the end of this age and the beginning[f] of the immortal age to come, in which corruption has passed away, [44] [114] sinful indulgence has come to an end, unbelief has been cut off, and righteousness has increased and truth has appeared. [45] [115] Therefore no one will then be able to have mercy on someone who has been condemned in the judgment, or to harm[g] someone who is victorious."

[46] [116] I answered and said, "This is my first and last comment: it would have been better if the earth had not produced Adam, or else, when it had produced him, had restrained him from sinning. [47] [117] For what good is it to all that they live in sorrow now and expect punishment after death? [48] [118] O Adam, what have you done? For though it was you who sinned, the fall was not yours alone, but ours also who are your descendants. [49] [119] For what good is it to us, if an immortal time has been promised to us, but we have done deeds that bring death? [50] [120] And what good is it that an everlasting hope has been promised to us, but we have miserably failed? [51] [121] Or that safe and healthful habitations have been reserved for us, but we have lived wickedly? [52] [122] Or that the glory of the Most High will defend those who have led a pure life, but we have walked in the most wicked ways? [53] [123] Or that a paradise shall be revealed, whose fruit remains unspoiled and in which are abundance and healing, but we shall not enter it [54] [124] because we have lived in perverse ways?[h] [55] [125] Or that the faces of those who practiced self-control shall shine more than the stars, but our faces shall be blacker than darkness? [56] [126] For while we lived and committed iniquity we did not consider what we should suffer after death."

[57] [127] He answered and said, "This is the significance of the contest that all who are born on earth shall wage: [58] [128] if they are defeated they shall suffer what you have said, but if they are victorious they shall receive what I have said.[i] [59] [129] For this is the way of which Moses, while he was alive, spoke to the peo-

a Syr Ethiop Arm: Lat *to understand*
b Syr Ethiop: Lat lacks *on that … another*
c Syr Ethiop Arab 1: Lat Arab 2 Arm lack *in the days of Saul*
d Lat lacks *not*
e Or *the glory does not continuously abide in it*
f Syr Ethiop: Lat lacks *the beginning*
g Syr Ethiop: Lat *overwhelm*
h Cn: Lat Syr *places*
i Syr Ethiop Arab 1: Lat *what I say*

sion for the evil on the day of judgment (cf. Deut 24.16; Jer 31.30; Ezek 18.1–32). *104: Decisive*, 7.33–34. *106:* At v. 106 we come to the continuation of ch 7 as preserved in the standard editions of the Latin Vulgate (see. vv. *36–105*n.); NRSV resumes the Latin numbering here, designating verses *106–140* as *36–70*, but with the numbers *106–140* in italics added as well. *106: Abraham*, Gen 18.23; *Moses*, Ex 32.11. *107: Joshua*, Josh 7.6–7. *108: Samuel*, 1 Sam 7.9; 12.23. *David*, 2 Sam 24.17. *Solomon*, 1 Kings 8.22–23,30. *109: Elijah*, 1 Kings 18.42,45; 17.20–21. *110: Hezekiah*, 2 Kings 19.15–19. *112–115:* The angel again contrasts the present and future ages. *7.116–8.3:* Further dispute between Ezra and the angel, returning to the issue of the seeming unfairness of the human condition. *7.116–126:* Ezra again laments the fate of humans (cf. 4.12,22–24; 5.35; 7.62–69). *116: My first … comment*, 3.5–7. See also Job 3. *118:* 3.7–10; 4.30–31. *123: Fruit*, cf. Ezek 47.12; Rev 22.2. *125: Shine more than the stars*, see 7.97n. *Darkness*, *1 Enoch* 62.10. *127–131:* The idea of life as a *contest*, in which one can be *defeated* or *victorious*. *129: Moses*, Deut 30.19. *130: Prophets*, 2 Chr 36.15–16; cf. Mt 5.17; 23.31–37. *132–140:* As the angel had quoted scripture

ple, saying, 'Choose life for yourself, so that you may live!'[60] [130]But they did not believe him or the prophets after him, or even myself who have spoken to them. [61][131]Therefore there shall not be[a] grief at their destruction, so much as joy over those to whom salvation is assured."

[62,132]I answered and said, "I know, O Lord, that the Most High is now called merciful, because he has mercy on those who have not yet come into the world; [63,133]and gracious, because he is gracious to those who turn in repentance to his law; [64,134]and patient, because he shows patience toward those who have sinned, since they are his own creatures; [65][135]and bountiful, because he would rather give than take away;[b] [66][136]and abundant in compassion, because he makes his compassions abound more and more to those now living and to those who are gone and to those yet to come—[67][137]for if he did not make them abound, the world with those who inhabit it would not have life—[68][138]and he is called the giver, because if he did not give out of his goodness so that those who have committed iniquities might be relieved of them, not one ten-thousandth of humankind could have life; [69][139]and the judge, because if he did not pardon those who were created by his word and blot out the multitude of their sins,[c] [70][140]there would probably be left only very few of the innumerable multitude."

8 He answered me and said, "The Most High made this world for the sake of many, but the world to come for the sake of only a few. [2]But I tell you a parable, Ezra. Just as, when you ask the earth, it will tell you that it provides a large amount of clay from which earthenware is made, but only a little dust from which gold comes, so is the course of the present world. [3]Many have been created, but only a few shall be saved."

[4]I answered and said, "Then drink your fill of understanding,[d] O my soul, and drink wisdom, O my heart. [5]For not of your own will did you come into the world,[e] and against your will you depart, for you have been given only a short time to live. [6]O Lord above us, grant to your servant that we may pray before you, and give us a seed for our heart and cultivation of our understanding so that fruit may be produced, by which every mortal who bears the likeness[f] of a human being may be able to live. [7]For you alone exist, and we are a work of your hands, as you have declared. [8]And because you give life to the body that is now fashioned in the womb, and furnish it with members, what you have created is preserved amid fire and water, and for nine months the womb[g] endures your creature that has been created in it. [9]But that which keeps and that which is kept shall both be kept by your keeping.[e] And when the womb gives up again what has been created in it, [10]you have commanded that from the members themselves (that is, from the breasts) milk, the fruit of the breasts, should be supplied, [11]so that what has been fashioned may be nourished for a time; and afterwards you will still guide it in your mercy. [12]You have nurtured it in your righteousness, and instructed it in your law, and reproved it in your wisdom. [13]You put it to death as your creation, and make it live as your work. [14]If then you will suddenly and quickly[h] destroy what with so great labor was fashioned by your command, to what purpose was it made? [15]And now I will speak

---

a   Syr: Lat *there was not*
b   Or *he is ready to give according to requests*
c   Lat *contempts*
d   Syr: Lat *Then release understanding*
e   Syr: Meaning of Lat uncertain
f   Syr: Lat *place*
g   Lat *what you have formed*
h   Syr: Lat *will with a light command*

(Deut 30.19), the seer responds with a rabbinic-like exegesis, or "midrash," of Ex 34.6–7. He pleads that God *is now called merciful . . . and gracious . . . and patient. 138: Life*, eternal life. 8.1–3: The angel repeats the arguments and parable used in 7.52–61. 3: Cf. Mt 22.14.

8.4–9.25: The third section of the third vision. 8.4–19a: Monologue of Ezra: Why should God wonderfully fashion and sustain all humankind, only to destroy a great majority? 6: Ezra seeks *a seed . . . so that fruit may be produced* that will counteract the effect of the *evil seed . . . sown in Adam's heart* (4.30). 7: *You alone* exist, a confession of God's sovereignty, see Deut 4.35; 6.4; Isa 44.6; 45.11; 60.21. 8–14: The enigma of God's creative activity

out: About all humankind you know best; but I will speak about your people, for whom I am grieved, [16] and about your inheritance, for whom I lament, and about Israel, for whom I am sad, and about the seed of Jacob, for whom I am troubled. [17] Therefore I will pray before you for myself and for them, for I see the failings of us who inhabit the earth; [18] and now also[a] I have heard of the swiftness of the judgment that is to come. [19] Therefore hear my voice and understand my words, and I will speak before you."

The beginning of the words of Ezra's prayer,[b] before he was taken up. He said: [20] "O Lord, you who inhabit eternity,[c] whose eyes are exalted[d] and whose upper chambers are in the air, [21] whose throne is beyond measure and whose glory is beyond comprehension, before whom the hosts of angels stand trembling [22] and at whose command they are changed to wind and fire,[e] whose word is sure and whose utterances are certain, whose command is strong and whose ordinance is terrible, [23] whose look dries up the depths and whose indignation makes the mountains melt away, and whose truth is established[f] forever— [24] hear, O Lord, the prayer of your servant, and give ear to the petition of your creature; attend to my words. [25] For as long as I live I will speak, and as long as I have understanding I will answer. [26] O do not look on the sins of your people, but on those who serve you in truth. [27] Do not take note of the endeavors of those who act wickedly, but of the endeavors of those who have kept your covenants amid afflictions. [28] Do not think of those who have

lived wickedly in your sight, but remember those who have willingly acknowledged that you are to be feared. [29] Do not will the destruction of those who have the ways of cattle, but regard those who have gloriously taught your law.[g] [30] Do not be angry with those who are deemed worse than wild animals, but love those who have always put their trust in your glory. [31] For we and our ancestors have passed our lives in ways that bring death;[h] but it is because of us sinners that you are called merciful. [32] For if you have desired to have pity on us, who have no works of righteousness, then you will be called merciful. [33] For the righteous, who have many works laid up with you, shall receive their reward in consequence of their own deeds. [34] But what are mortals, that you are angry with them; or what is a corruptible race, that you are so bitter against it? [35] For in truth there is no one among those who have been born who has not acted wickedly; among those who have existed[i] there is no one who has not done wrong. [36] For in this, O Lord, your righteousness and goodness will

a   Syr: Lat *but*
b   Syr Ethiop; Lat *beginning of Ezra's words*
c   Or *you who abide forever*
d   Another Lat text reads *whose are the highest heavens*
e   Syr: Lat *they whose service takes the form of wind and fire*
f   Arab 2: Other authorities read *truth bears witness*
g   Syr *have received the brightness of your law*
h   Syr Ethiop: Meaning of Lat uncertain
i   Syr: Meaning of Lat uncertain

and providential care followed by destruction recalls Job 10.8–13. **15–16:** The seer leaves the fate of *humankind* in God's hands, and speaks particularly about Israel, God's *inheritance* (Ps 28.9). **17:** *I will pray,* in 8.19b–36.

8.19b–36: Ezra's prayer, a beautiful and liturgically structured piece (invocation to God, whose attributes are recalled, vv. 20–23; petitions, interspersed with confession and intercessions, vv. 24–35; concluding ascription of praise, v. 36). This prayer also occurs separately, with the title "Confessio Esdrae," in the section of canticles and hymns contained in many manuscripts of the Latin Vulgate Bible. This circumstance probably accounts for the presence (in v. 19b) of a superscription in the third person. **19b:** The words *before he was taken up* point to the belief that Ezra, like Enoch and Elijah, was taken up to heaven without dying (see 6.26n.). **20:** *Upper chambers,* see Ps 104.3; Amos 9.6. **21:** *Hosts of angels* are a traditional element in the description of the heavenly throne room; see 1 Kings 22.19; Isa 6.2–3; Dan 7.9–10; Rev 5.11–12; 7.11–12. **22:** *Wind and fire,* Ps 104.4; Heb 1.7. **23:** *Dries up,* Isa 50.2; 51.10. *Mountains melt,* Mic 1.4; Sir 16.18–19. **26–36:** A strikingly developed series of rhetorical contrasts between sinners and the righteous introduces an appeal to the mercy of God, the quality highlighted in the influential liturgical formula found in Ex 34.6–7. See also 7.132–140n. **33–36:** Ezra is concerned not for those who have *many works laid up* with God (see 7.77), but for those who have *no store of good works* (v. 36). **34:** Cf. Ps 8.4.

be declared, when you are merciful to those who have no store of good works."

37 He answered me and said, "Some things you have spoken rightly, and it will turn out according to your words. 38 For indeed I will not concern myself about the fashioning of those who have sinned, or about their death, their judgment, or their destruction; 39 but I will rejoice over the creation of the righteous, over their pilgrimage also, and their salvation, and their receiving their reward. 40 As I have spoken, therefore, so it shall be.

41 "For just as the farmer sows many seeds in the ground and plants a multitude of seedlings, and yet not all that have been sown will come up[a] in due season, and not all that were planted will take root; so also those who have been sown in the world will not all be saved."

42 I answered and said, "If I have found favor in your sight, let me speak. 43 If the farmer's seed does not come up, because it has not received your rain in due season, or if it has been ruined by too much rain, it perishes.[b] 44 But people, who have been formed by your hands and are called your own image because they are made like you, and for whose sake you have formed all things—have you also made them like the farmer's seed? 45 Surely not, O Lord[c] above! But spare your people and have mercy on your inheritance, for you have mercy on your own creation."

46 He answered me and said, "Things that are present are for those who live now, and things that are future are for those who will live hereafter. 47 For you come far short of being able to love my creation more than I love it. But you have often compared yourself[d] to the unrighteous. Never do so! 48 But even in this respect you will be praiseworthy before the Most High, 49 because you have humbled yourself, as is becoming for you, and have not considered yourself to be among the righteous. You will

receive the greatest glory, 50 for many miseries will affect those who inhabit the world in the last times, because they have walked in great pride. 51 But think of your own case, and inquire concerning the glory of those who are like yourself, 52 because it is for you that paradise is opened, the tree of life is planted, the age to come is prepared, plenty is provided, a city is built, rest is appointed,[e] goodness is established and wisdom perfected beforehand. 53 The root of evil[f] is sealed up from you, illness is banished from you, and death[g] is hidden; Hades has fled and corruption has been forgotten;[h] 54 sorrows have passed away, and in the end the treasure of immortality is made manifest. 55 Therefore do not ask any more questions about the great number of those who perish. 56 For when they had opportunity to choose, they despised the Most High, and were contemptuous of his law, and abandoned his ways. 57 Moreover, they have even trampled on his righteous ones, 58 and said in their hearts that there is no God—though they knew well that they must die. 59 For just as the things that I have predicted await[i] you, so the thirst and torment that are prepared await them. For the Most High did not intend that anyone should be destroyed; 60 but those who were created have themselves defiled the name of him who made them, and have been ungrateful to him

a   Syr Ethiop *will live*; Lat *will be saved*
b   Cn: Compare Syr Arab 1 Arm Georg 2: Meaning of Lat uncertain
c   Ethiop Arab Compare Syr: Lat lacks *O Lord*
d   Syr Ethiop: Lat *brought yourself near*
e   Syr Ethiop: Lat *allowed*
f   Lat lacks *of evil*
g   Syr Ethiop Arm: Lat lacks *death*
h   Syr: Lat *Hades and corruption have fled into oblivion*; or *corruption has fled into Hades to be forgotten*
i   Syr: Lat *will receive*

8.37–62a: Dispute between Ezra and the angel. 37–40: God's reply to Ezra's prayer is characteristic (see 7.60–61; 7.127–131). As after 7.132–140, Ezra's plea for mercy goes unacknowledged. In stating that God will *not concern* himself with sinners but will *rejoice over . . . the righteous*, the angel playfully admits that Ezra has ironically *spoken rightly* about *some things*, namely, in Ezra's plea (vv. 26–36) that God ignore the wicked and pay attention only to the righteous. **41–45:** To God's analogy of *seeds* (cf. Mt 13.3–9), Ezra protests that surely humans are more valuable than plants. **46–62a:** The final divine reply: The seer is assured that his lot is with the blessed and is advised to think no more about sinners, who deserve their doom because they have *despised the Most High* (v. 56). **46:** 7.14–18,25. **47:** See 5.33; 7.76–77n. **48–54:** The angel praises Ezra's character and offers a list of delights awaiting *those who are like* him (see 14.9). **52:** *Paradise*, 7.123; *tree of life*, Gen 2.9; Rev 2.7; 22.2. *City*, the

who prepared life for them now. [61] Therefore my judgment is now drawing near; [62] I have not shown this to all people, but only to you and a few like you."

Then I answered and said, [63] "O Lord, you have already shown me a great number of the signs that you will do in the last times, but you have not shown me when you will do them."

9 He answered me and said, "Measure carefully in your mind, and when you see that some of the predicted signs have occurred, [2] then you will know that it is the very time when the Most High is about to visit the world that he has made. [3] So when there shall appear in the world earthquakes, tumult of peoples, intrigues of nations, wavering of leaders, confusion of princes, [4] then you will know that it was of these that the Most High spoke from the days that were of old, from the beginning. [5] For just as with everything that has occurred in the world, the beginning is evident,[a] and the end manifest; [6] so also are the times of the Most High: the beginnings are manifest in wonders and mighty works, and the end in penalties[b] and in signs.

[7] "It shall be that all who will be saved and will be able to escape on account of their works, or on account of the faith by which they have believed, [8] will survive the dangers that have been predicted, and will see my salvation in my land and within my borders, which I have sanctified for myself from the beginning. [9] Then those who have now abused my ways shall be amazed, and those who have rejected them with contempt shall live in torments. [10] For as many as did not acknowledge me in their lifetime, though they received my benefits, [11] and as many as scorned my law while they still had freedom, and did not understand but despised it[c] while an opportunity of repentance was still open to them, [12] these must in torment acknowledge it[c] after death. [13] Therefore, do not continue to be curious about how the ungodly will be punished; but inquire how the righteous will be saved, those to whom the age belongs and for whose sake the age was made."[d]

[14] I answered and said, [15] "I said before, and I say now, and will say it again: there are more who perish than those who will be saved, [16] as a wave is greater than a drop of water."

[17] He answered me and said, "As is the field, so is the seed; and as are the flowers, so are the colors; and as is the work, so is the product; and as is the farmer, so is the threshing floor. [18] For there was a time in this age when I was preparing for those who now exist, before the world was made for them to live in, and no one opposed me then, for no one existed; [19] but now those who have been created in this world, which is supplied both with an unfailing table and an inexhaustible pasture,[e] have become corrupt in their ways. [20] So I considered my world, and saw that it was lost. I saw that my earth was in peril because of the devices of those who[f] had come into it. [21] And I saw and spared some[g] with great difficulty, and saved for myself one grape out of a cluster, and one plant out of a great forest.[h] [22] So let the multitude perish that has been born in vain, but let my grape

---

a Syr: Ethiop *is in the word*; Meaning of Lat uncertain
b Syr: Lat Ethiop *in effects*
c Or *me*
d Syr: Lat *saved, and whose is the age and for whose sake the age was made and when*
e Cn: Lat *law*
f Cn: Lat *devices that*
g Lat *them*
h Syr Ethiop Arab 1: Lat *tribe*

---

heavenly Jerusalem; see 7.26; 10.27,44,54. **53:** *Hades*, the realm of the dead. **58:** Cf. Pss 14.1; 53.1. **59:** *Torment*, 7.80–87. **61:** *Drawing near*, see 4.50; 5.55. **62:** *Only to you*, see 7.44. *A few like you*, see 8.51; 14.9,46.

8.62b–9.22: Direct prediction of the future by the angel, now in response to Ezra's request, and again using the key word *signs* (v. 63) (cf. 5.1–13; 6.11–29; 7.26–44). **8.63:** *When*, see 4.33; Mk 13.4. **9.1–4:** The author uses classical apocalyptic signs (see Mk 13.7–8,29). **7:** *Able to escape*, cf. 13.23; Mk 13.14–16. The author counts both *works* and *faith* as valid criteria for salvation. **8:** *See my salvation*, cf. Mk 13.13. *Within my borders*, 12.34; 13.48. **9:** *Torments*, 7.79–87. **11:** *Scorned . . . despised*, 7.22–24,37,72,79–81; 8.56–60. **13:** 8.38–39,55. *For whose sake*, 6.59; 7.11. **14–22:** The final explanation of why so few are saved: The many *have become corrupt in their ways*. Cf. Gen 6.5, where the corruption of humankind provokes the flood, which kills all but Noah and his family. **22:** *Let the multitude perish*, God disclaims responsibility for the fates of the mass of humanity.

and my plant be saved, because with much labor I have perfected them.

23 "Now, if you will let seven days more pass—do not, however, fast during them, 24 but go into a field of flowers where no house has been built, and eat only of the flowers of the field, and taste no meat and drink no wine, but eat only flowers— 25 and pray to the Most High continually, then I will come and talk with you."

26 So I went, as he directed me, into the field that is called Ardat;[a] there I sat among the flowers and ate of the plants of the field, and the nourishment they afforded satisfied me. 27 After seven days, while I lay on the grass, my heart was troubled again as it was before. 28 Then my mouth was opened, and I began to speak before the Most High, and said, 29 "O Lord, you showed yourself among us, to our ancestors in the wilderness when they came out from Egypt and when they came into the untrodden and unfruitful wilderness; 30 and you said, 'Hear me, O Israel, and give heed to my words, O descendants of Jacob. 31 For I sow my law in you, and it shall bring forth fruit in you, and you shall be glorified through it forever.' 32 But though our ancestors received the law, they did not keep it and did not observe the[b] statutes; yet the fruit of the law did not perish—for it could not, because it was yours. 33 Yet those who received it perished, because they did not keep what had been sown in them. 34 Now this is the general rule that, when the ground has received seed, or the sea a ship, or any dish food or drink, and when it comes about that what was sown or what was launched or what was put in is destroyed, 35 they are destroyed, but the things that held them remain; yet with us it has not been so. 36 For we who have received the law and sinned will perish, as well as our hearts that received it; 37 the law, however, does not perish but survives in its glory."

38 When I said these things in my heart, I looked around,[c] and on my right I saw a woman; she was mourning and weeping with a loud voice, and was deeply grieved at heart; her clothes were torn, and there were ashes on her head. 39 Then I dismissed the thoughts with which I had been engaged, and turned to her 40 and said to her, "Why are you weeping, and why are you grieved at heart?"

41 She said to me, "Let me alone, my lord, so that I may weep for myself and continue to mourn, for I am greatly embittered in spirit and deeply distressed."

42 I said to her, "What has happened to you? Tell me."

43 And she said to me, "Your servant was barren and had no child, though I lived with my husband for thirty years. 44 Every hour and every day during those thirty years I prayed to the Most High, night and day. 45 And after thirty years God heard your servant, and looked upon my low estate, and considered my distress, and gave me a son. I rejoiced greatly over him, I and my husband

---

a   Syr Ethiop *Arpad*; Arm *Ardab*

b   Lat *my*

c   Syr Arab Arm: Lat *I looked about me with my eyes*

9.23–25: Conclusion and injunctions. Ezra's prescribed diet of *flowers* recalls Dan 1.8–16 (cf. 2 Macc 5.27). **24:** *Where no house has been built*, see 10.51–54.

9.26–10.59: The fourth vision. 9.26–28: Introduction. 26: *Ardat*, an unknown location. **27:** *As it was before*, before each of the first three visions.

9.29–37: Ezra's address. Instead of challenging God, as he had done in the first three visions, Ezra praises the *law*, which *survives in its glory* despite the perishing of humankind, its vessel. **29:** An allusion to the theophany at Mount Sinai, Ex 19.9; 24.10; Deut 4.12. **30–37:** Unlike the normal case, where the container outlasts what is placed in it, with humankind it is just the opposite: We perish, while God's law, implanted within us, survives intact. **30:** *Hear me, O Israel*, Deut 6.4. **31:** See 3.20.

9.38–10.4: The first part of the vision. Ezra converses with a disconsolate woman. The sudden departure from the pattern of the first three visions, wherein the angel had appeared, signals a shift in tone. **9.38:** *Clothes were torn, ashes*, signs of mourning; Josh 7.6; Job 2.12–13. **39:** *I dismissed the thoughts*, for the first time in the book, Ezra turns his attention from his own concerns to those of another (see also 10.5). **40:** Now it is the woman who is *weeping* and *grieved*, as Ezra had been during the first three visions. **45:** *After thirty years*, see 3.1. Like Sarah (Gen 18.11–14), Hannah (1 Sam 1.20), and Elizabeth (Lk 1.24), the woman conceives a child in her old

and all my neighbors;[a] and we gave great glory to the Mighty One. [46] And I brought him up with much care. [47] So when he grew up and I came to take a wife for him, I set a day for the marriage feast.

10 "But it happened that when my son entered his wedding chamber, he fell down and died. [2] So all of us put out our lamps, and all my neighbors[a] attempted to console me; I remained quiet until the evening of the second day. [3] But when all of them had stopped consoling me, encouraging me to be quiet, I got up in the night and fled, and I came to this field, as you see. [4] And now I intend not to return to the town, but to stay here; I will neither eat nor drink, but will mourn and fast continually until I die."

[5] Then I broke off the reflections with which I was still engaged, and answered her in anger and said, [6] "You most foolish of women, do you not see our mourning, and what has happened to us? [7] For Zion, the mother of us all, is in deep grief and great distress. [8] It is most appropriate to mourn now, because we are all mourning, and to be sorrowful, because we are all sorrowing; you are sorrowing for one son, but we, the whole world, for our mother.[b] [9] Now ask the earth, and she will tell you that it is she who ought to mourn over so many who have come into being upon her. [10] From the beginning all have been born of her, and others will come; and, lo, almost all go[c] to perdition, and a multitude of them will come to doom. [11] Who then ought to mourn the more, she who lost so great a multitude, or you who are griev-

ing for one alone? [12] But if you say to me, 'My lamentation is not like the earth's, for I have lost the fruit of my womb, which I brought forth in pain and bore in sorrow; [13] but it is with the earth according to the way of the earth—the multitude that is now in it goes as it came'; [14] then I say to you, 'Just as you brought forth in sorrow, so the earth also has from the beginning given her fruit, that is, humankind, to him who made her.' [15] Now, therefore, keep your sorrow to yourself, and bear bravely the troubles that have come upon you. [16] For if you acknowledge the decree of God to be just, you will receive your son back in due time, and will be praised among women. [17] Therefore go into the town to your husband."

[18] She said to me, "I will not do so; I will not go into the city, but I will die here."

[19] So I spoke again to her, and said, [20] "Do not do that, but let yourself be persuaded—for how many are the adversities of Zion?—and be consoled because of the sorrow of Jerusalem. [21] For you see how our sanctuary has been laid waste, our altar thrown down, our temple destroyed; [22] our harp has been laid low, our song has been silenced, and our rejoicing has been ended; the light of our lampstand has been put out, the ark of our covenant has been plundered, our holy things have been polluted, and the name by which we are called has been almost profaned; our

a   Literally *all my citizens*
b   Compare Syr: Meaning of Lat uncertain
c   Literally *walk*

age. **10.1:** Cf. Tob 7.11; 8.10. **4:** *Mourn and fast*, as Ezra had done previously.

10.5–24: The second part of the vision. Ezra tries to convince the woman of the relative insignificance of her own sorrows in relation to the broader concerns of *the whole world* (v. 8), just as the angel had done with Ezra in the earlier visions. **5:** *Broke off the reflections*, as before (*dismissed the thoughts*, 9.39), Ezra is forced to leave aside his prior concerns. **5–6:** *In anger . . . you most foolish*, Ezra's highly emotional disposition, evident in the first three visions, continues here, but is redirected. **7:** *Zion, the mother of us all*, Isa 50.1; Jer 50.12; Bar 4.8–5.9; Gal 4.26. For *Zion* in *deep grief*, see Lam 1.12–22. **9–10:** Ezra's arguments recall those of the angel in the first three visions. **9:** *Ask the earth*, who is also the mother of all humankind (v. 10). Thus, the figure of the mother functions on three levels: Ezra's interlocutor, Zion (Jerusalem), and the whole earth. **10:** This is the perspective Ezra refused to accept in the third vision. **16:** *If you acknowledge*, as the angel had earlier encouraged Ezra to do. *You will receive your son back in due time*, perhaps in the resurrection; Heb 11.35; 2 Macc 7.23,29. **18:** *I will not*, the woman's stubbornness recalls Ezra's earlier attitude. **21–23:** Ezra sadly recalls the desolation of Jerusalem (cf. Lam 1.10; 2.7; 1 Macc 1.36–40; 2.7–13); ultimately, this refers to the destruction of the city in 70 CE. **22:** *Harp* symbolizes the service of praise. The extinction of the perpetually burning lamp marked the cessation of Temple services. *Our holy things* are enumerated in 1 Macc 4.49–51. *The name* "Israel" was bestowed by God (Gen 32.28).

children[a] have suffered abuse, our priests have been burned to death, our Levites have gone into exile, our virgins have been defiled, and our wives have been ravished; our righteous men[b] have been carried off, our little ones have been cast out, our young men have been enslaved and our strong men made powerless. [23] And, worst of all, the seal of Zion has been deprived of its glory, and given over into the hands of those that hate us. [24] Therefore shake off your great sadness and lay aside your many sorrows, so that the Mighty One may be merciful to you again, and the Most High may give you rest, a respite from your troubles."

[25] While I was talking to her, her face suddenly began to shine exceedingly; her countenance flashed like lightning, so that I was too frightened to approach her, and my heart was terrified. While[c] I was wondering what this meant, [26] she suddenly uttered a loud and fearful cry, so that the earth shook at the sound. [27] When I looked up, the woman was no longer visible to me, but a city was being built,[d] and a place of huge foundations showed itself. I was afraid, and cried with a loud voice and said, [28] "Where is the angel Uriel, who came to me at first? For it was he who brought me into this overpowering bewilderment; my end has become corruption, and my prayer a reproach."

[29] While I was speaking these words, the angel who had come to me at first came to me, and when he saw me [30] lying there like a corpse, deprived of my understanding, he grasped my right hand and strengthened me and set me on my feet, and said to me, [31] "What is the matter with you? And why are you troubled? And why are your understanding and the thoughts of your mind troubled?"

[32] I said, "It was because you abandoned me. I did as you directed, and went out into the field, and lo, what I have seen and can still see, I am unable to explain."

[33] He said to me, "Stand up like a man, and I will instruct you."

[34] I said, "Speak, my lord; only do not forsake me, so that I may not die before my time.[e] [35] For I have seen what I did not know, and I hear[f] what I do not understand [36]—or is my mind deceived, and my soul dreaming? [37] Now therefore I beg you to give your servant an explanation of this bewildering vision."

[38] He answered me and said, "Listen to me, and I will teach you, and tell you about the things that you fear; for the Most High has revealed many secrets to you. [39] He has seen your righteous conduct, and that you have sorrowed continually for your people and mourned greatly over Zion. [40] This therefore is the meaning of the vision. [41] The woman who appeared to you a little while ago, whom you saw mourning and whom you began to console [42] (you do not now see the form of a woman, but there appeared to you a city being built)[g] [43] and who

a   Ethiop *free men*
b   Syr *our seers*
c   Syr Ethiop Arab 1: Lat lacks *I was too … terrified. While*
d   Lat: Syr Ethiop Arab 1 Arab 2 Arm *but there was an established city*
e   Syr Ethiop Arab: Lat *die to no purpose*
f   Other ancient authorities read *have heard*
g   Lat: Syr Ethiop Arab 1 Arab 2 Arm *an established city*

23: *The seal … has been deprived of its glory*, i.e., the city is under enemy control. 24: In Ezra's final words to the woman, he has fully become a consoler to her, just as the angel earlier had been to him.

10.25–27a: A vision of the transformed Jerusalem. 25: *Suddenly began to shine*, the figure of the woman had only been a foil for the inner transformation of Ezra, who is now worthy to receive the vision. 27: *A city was being built*, Zech 2.1–5; Rev 21.9–21. Jerusalem, whose destruction was movingly described in vv. 21–23, is being transformed or rebuilt in a way open only to visionary experience.

10.27b–37: The appearance of the angel. 28: *At first*, 4.1. Although the angel (Uriel; 4.1) has had no part in this vision, it is he upon whom Ezra immediately calls for guidance. 30: *Like a corpse*, cf. Dan 8.18; 10.9; Rev 1.17. 32: *And can still see*, the vision is still before the seer's eyes. The seer is *unable to explain* the vision, much as he had earlier been unable to come to terms with the angel's more rational explanations. 33: Cf. Job 38.3; 40.7; see 5.15; 6.13,17; 7.2. 34–37: Cf. 12.3b–9; 13.13b–15. 34: *Do not forsake me*, Ezra's plea is ironic. See 5.18 and 12.41, where Ezra's compatriots beg him not to "forsake" them.

10.38–54: Interpretation of the vision. 38–39: See 7.76–77n. 44: *Zion*, the transformed Jerusalem. 45: *Three*

told you about the misfortune of her son—this is the interpretation: [44] The woman whom you saw is Zion, which you now behold as a city being built.[a] [45] And as for her telling you that she was barren for thirty years, the reason is that there were three thousand[b] years in the world before any offering was offered in it.[c] [46] And after three thousand[d] years Solomon built the city, and offered offerings; then it was that the barren woman bore a son. [47] And as for her telling you that she brought him up with much care, that was the period of residence in Jerusalem. [48] And as for her saying to you, 'My son died as he entered his wedding chamber,' and that misfortune had overtaken her,[e] this was the destruction that befell Jerusalem. [49] So you saw her likeness, how she mourned for her son, and you began to console her for what had happened.[f] [50] For now the Most High, seeing that you are sincerely grieved and profoundly distressed for her, has shown you the brilliance of her glory, and the loveliness of her beauty. [51] Therefore I told you to remain in the field where no house had been built, [52] for I knew that the Most High would reveal these things to you. [53] Therefore I told you to go into the field where there was no foundation of any building, [54] because no work of human construction could endure in a place where the city of the Most High was to be revealed.

[55] "Therefore do not be afraid, and do not let your heart be terrified; but go in and see the splendor or[g] the vastness of the building, as far as it is possible for your eyes to see it, [56] and afterward you will hear as much as your ears can hear. [57] For you are more blessed than many, and you have been called to be with[h] the Most High as few have been.

[58] But tomorrow night you shall remain here, [59] and the Most High will show you in those dream visions what the Most High will do to those who inhabit the earth in the last days."

So I slept that night and the following one, as he had told me.

11 On the second night I had a dream: I saw rising from the sea an eagle that had twelve feathered wings and three heads. [2] I saw it spread its wings over[i] the whole earth, and all the winds of heaven blew upon it, and the clouds were gathered around it.[j] [3] I saw that out of its wings there grew opposing wings; but they became little, puny wings. [4] But its heads were at rest; the middle head was larger than the other heads, but it too was at rest with them. [5] Then I saw that the eagle flew with its wings, and it reigned over the earth and over those who inhabit it. [6] And I saw how all things under heaven were subjected to it, and no one spoke against it—not a single creature that was on the earth. [7] Then I saw the eagle rise upon its talons, and it uttered a cry to its wings, saying, [8] "Do not all watch at the same time; let each sleep in its

a Cn: Lat *an established city*
b Most Lat Mss read *three*
c Cn: Lat Syr Arab Arm *her*
d Syr Ethiop Arab Arm: Lat *three*
e Or *him*
f Most Lat Mss and Arab 1 add *These were the things to be opened to you*
g Other ancient authorities read *and*
h Or *been named by*
i Arab 2 Arm: Lat Syr Ethiop *in*
j Syr: Compare Ethiop Arab: Lat lacks *the clouds* and *around it*

thousand years, the time between the creation of the world and construction of the Temple. **46:** *A son*, the historical Jerusalem. *Solomon*, although David established Jerusalem as an Israelite city, Solomon built the Temple (1 Kings 5–6). **48:** *The destruction*, see 10.21–23 and note. In its context, this passage refers to the destruction of Jerusalem in 586 BCE. **49:** *Zion*, in the universal sense, *mourned for* the destruction of her physical manifestation, the earthly city. **49–50:** Ezra's vision is a direct reward for his sincere consolation of the mourning woman (see 10.41).

10.55–59: Conclusion and injunctions. 55–56: *Go in and see*, the city is conceived as still present to Ezra (see vv. 32,42,44). **59:** The remainder of the book will consist of *dream visions* rather than argumentation.

11.1–12.51: The fifth vision (the eagle vision). 11.1–12.3a: Description of the vision. 11.1: The interpretation of the fifth vision that is set forth in the notes to 11.1–12.3a anticipates that given in the text of 2 Esdras itself in 12.10–36. *From the sea*, Dan 7.3; Rev 13.1. *An eagle*, symbol of the Roman Empire, used on the standards of Roman legions **2:** *Spread its wings*, asserted its dominion. *The winds*, 13.2; Dan 7.2. At the time of 4 Ezra's composition, the Romans ruled almost the *whole* inhabited *earth*. **3:** *Opposing wings*, symbolizing usurpers who revolted

own place, and watch in its turn; [9] but let the heads be reserved for the last."

[10] I looked again and saw that the voice did not come from its heads, but from the middle of its body. [11] I counted its rival wings, and there were eight of them. [12] As I watched, one wing on the right side rose up, and it reigned over all the earth. [13] And after a time its reign came to an end, and it disappeared, so that even its place was no longer visible. Then the next wing rose up and reigned, and it continued to reign a long time. [14] While it was reigning its end came also, so that it disappeared like the first. [15] And a voice sounded, saying to it, [16] "Listen to me, you who have ruled the earth all this time; I announce this to you before you disappear. [17] After you no one shall rule as long as you have ruled, not even half as long."

[18] Then the third wing raised itself up, and held the rule as the earlier ones had done, and it also disappeared. [19] And so it went with all the wings; they wielded power one after another and then were never seen again. [20] I kept looking, and in due time the wings that followed[a] also rose up on the right[b] side, in order to rule. There were some of them that ruled, yet disappeared suddenly; [21] and others of them rose up, but did not hold the rule.

[22] And after this I looked and saw that the twelve wings and the two little wings had disappeared, [23] and nothing remained on the eagle's body except the three heads that were at rest and six little wings.

[24] As I kept looking I saw that two little wings separated from the six and remained under the head that was on the right side; but four remained in their place. [25] Then I saw that these little wings[c] planned to set themselves up and hold the rule. [26] As I kept looking, one was set up, but suddenly disappeared; [27] a second also, and this disappeared more quickly than the first. [28] While I continued to look the two that remained were planning between themselves to reign together; [29] and while they were planning, one of the heads that were at rest (the one that was in the middle) suddenly awoke; it was greater than the other two heads. [30] And I saw how it allied the two heads with itself, [31] and how the head turned with those that were with it and devoured the two little wings[c] that were planning to reign. [32] Moreover this head gained control of the whole earth, and with much oppression dominated its inhabitants; it had greater power over the world than all the wings that had gone before.

[33] After this I looked again and saw the head in the middle suddenly disappear, just as the wings had done. [34] But the two heads remained, which also in like manner ruled over the earth and its inhabitants. [35] And while I looked, I saw the head on the right side devour the one on the left.

[36] Then I heard a voice saying to me, "Look in front of you and consider what you see." [37] When I looked, I saw what seemed to be a lion roused from the forest, roaring; and I heard how it uttered a human voice to the eagle, and spoke, saying, [38] "Listen and I will speak to you. The Most High says to you, [39] 'Are you not the one that remains of the four beasts that I had made to reign in my world, so that the end of my times might come through them? [40] You, the fourth that has come, have conquered all the beasts that have gone before; and you have held sway over the world with great terror, and over all the earth with grievous oppression; and for so long you have lived on the earth with deceit.[d] [41] You have judged the earth, but not with truth, [42] for you have oppressed the meek and injured the peaceable; you have hated those who tell the truth, and have loved liars; you have destroyed the homes of those who brought forth fruit, and have laid low the walls of those who did you no harm.

a   Syr Arab 2 *the little wings*
b   Some Ethiop Mss read *left*
c   Syr: Lat *underwings*
d   Syr Arab Arm: Lat Ethiop *The fourth came, however, and conquered ... and held sway ... and for so long lived*

against the Roman emperors. *But they became little*, they were subdued. **11:** *Rival wings*, the "opposing wings" of v. 3. **13:** *Its reign came to an end*, the ruler symbolized by the wing perished. **35:** At this point, only the *head on the right* and the two little wings under it remain. **37:** The *lion* is a symbol of the messiah; cf. Rev 5.5. **39:** *Four beasts*, Dan 7. In Daniel, however, the fourth beast is not an eagle but a horned monster. **40:** *With grievous oppression*, at this time in history, after the Romans had destroyed Jerusalem and its Temple, they were considered evil op-

43 Your insolence has come up before the Most High, and your pride to the Mighty One. **44** The Most High has looked at his times; now they have ended, and his ages have reached completion. **45** Therefore you, eagle, will surely disappear, you and your terrifying wings, your most evil little wings, your malicious heads, your most evil talons, and your whole worthless body, **46** so that the whole earth, freed from your violence, may be refreshed and relieved, and may hope for the judgment and mercy of him who made it.'"

12 While the lion was saying these words to the eagle, I looked **2** and saw that the remaining head had disappeared. The two wings that had gone over to it rose up and[a] set themselves up to reign, and their reign was brief and full of tumult. **3** When I looked again, they were already vanishing. The whole body of the eagle was burned, and the earth was exceedingly terrified.

Then I woke up in great perplexity of mind and great fear, and I said to my spirit, **4** "You have brought this upon me, because you search out the ways of the Most High. **5** I am still weary in mind and very weak in my spirit, and not even a little strength is left in me, because of the great fear with which I have been terrified tonight. **6** Therefore I will now entreat the Most High that he may strengthen me to the end."

7 Then I said, "O sovereign Lord, if I have found favor in your sight, and if I have been accounted righteous before you beyond many others, and if my prayer has indeed come up before your face, **8** strengthen me and show me, your servant, the interpretation and meaning of this terrifying vision so that you may fully comfort my soul. **9** For you have judged me worthy to be shown the end of the times and the last events of the times."

10 He said to me, "This is the interpretation of this vision that you have seen: **11** The eagle that you saw coming up from the sea is the fourth kingdom that appeared in a vision to your brother Daniel. **12** But it was not explained to him as I now explain to you or have explained it. **13** The days are coming when a kingdom shall rise on earth, and it shall be more terrifying than all the kingdoms that have been before it. **14** And twelve kings shall reign in it, one after another. **15** But the second that is to reign shall hold sway for a longer time than any other one of the twelve. **16** This is the interpretation of the twelve wings that you saw.

17 "As for your hearing a voice that spoke, coming not from the eagle's[b] heads but from the midst of its body, this is the interpretation: **18** In the midst of[c] the time of that kingdom great struggles shall arise, and it shall be in danger of falling; nevertheless it shall not fall then, but shall regain its former power.[d] **19** As for your seeing eight little wings[e] clinging to its wings, this is the interpretation: **20** Eight kings shall arise in it, whose times shall be short and their years swift; **21** two of them shall perish when the middle of its time draws near; and four shall be kept for the time when its end approaches, but two shall be kept until the end.

22 "As for your seeing three heads at rest, this is the interpretation: **23** In its last days the Most High will raise up three kings,[f] and

a Ethiop: Lat lacks *rose up and*
b Lat *his*
c Syr Arm: Lat *After*
d Ethiop Arab 1 Arm: Lat Syr *its beginning*
e Syr: Lat *underwings*
f Syr Ethiop Arab Arm: Lat *kingdoms*

pressors by the Jews. **44**: God's judgment of the fourth beast is a sign that the *ages have reached completion* (see 11.39). **12.3a**: This is the beginning of the end times.

12.3b–9: The seer's response. Ezra, terrified, seeks an explanation of the vision (cf. 10.27–37; 13.13b–20).

12.10–36: The interpretation. 11: *The fourth kingdom* in Daniel's vision (Dan 7.7) symbolized the Greek or Macedonian Empire; here, however, it is reinterpreted (cf. v. 12) to refer to the Roman Empire (see 11.1n.; 11.39n.). **13**: *The days are coming*, since the seer is represented as prophesying during the exile, the rise of the Roman Empire is depicted as a future event. **14**: *Kings*, the Roman emperors. **15**: *The second* king is Augustus (ruled 27 BCE–14 CE); cf. 11.17. **18**: There is nothing in the vision that corresponds to what is said in this verse. The author may refer to *the time of . . . great struggles* for power that followed the death of Nero in 68 CE. **19**: *Little wings*, 11.3,11. **20–21**: These apparently represent imperial usurpers or pretenders; they cannot be identified precisely.

they[a] shall renew many things in it, and shall rule the earth [24] and its inhabitants more oppressively than all who were before them. Therefore they are called the heads of the eagle, [25] because it is they who shall sum up his wickedness and perform his last actions. [26] As for your seeing that the large head disappeared, one of the kings[b] shall die in his bed, but in agonies. [27] But as for the two who remained, the sword shall devour them. [28] For the sword of one shall devour him who was with him; but he also shall fall by the sword in the last days.

[29] "As for your seeing two little wings[c] passing over to[d] the head which was on the right side, [30] this is the interpretation: It is these whom the Most High has kept for the eagle's[e] end; this was the reign which was brief and full of tumult, as you have seen.

[31] "And as for the lion whom you saw rousing up out of the forest and roaring and speaking to the eagle and reproving him for his unrighteousness, and as for all his words that you have heard, [32] this is the Messiah[f] whom the Most High has kept until the end of days, who will arise from the offspring of David, and will come and speak[g] with them. He will denounce them for their ungodliness and for their wickedness, and will display before them their contemptuous dealings. [33] For first he will bring them alive before his judgment seat, and when he has reproved them, then he will destroy them. [34] But in mercy he will set free the remnant of my people, those who have been saved throughout my borders, and he will make them joyful until the end comes, the day of judgment, of which I spoke to you at the beginning. [35] This is the dream that you saw, and this is its interpretation. [36] And you alone were worthy to learn this secret of the

Most High. [37] Therefore write all these things that you have seen in a book, put it[h] in a hidden place; [38] and you shall teach them to the wise among your people, whose hearts you know are able to comprehend and keep these secrets. [39] But as for you, wait here seven days more, so that you may be shown whatever it pleases the Most High to show you." Then he left me.

[40] When all the people heard that the seven days were past and I had not returned to the city, they all gathered together, from the least to the greatest, and came to me and spoke to me, saying, [41] "How have we offended you, and what harm have we done you, that you have forsaken us and sit in this place? [42] For of all the prophets you alone are left to us, like a cluster of grapes from the vintage, and like a lamp in a dark place, and like a haven for a ship saved from a storm. [43] Are not the disasters that have befallen us enough? [44] Therefore if you forsake us, how much better it would have been for us if we also had been consumed in the burning of Zion. [45] For we are no better than those who died there." And they wept with a loud voice.

Then I answered them and said, [46] "Take courage, O Israel; and do not be sorrowful, O house of Jacob; [47] for the Most High has you in remembrance, and the Mighty One has not forgotten you in your struggle. [48] As for me, I have neither forsaken you nor withdrawn

---

a   Syr Ethiop Arm: Lat *he*
b   Lat *them*
c   Arab 1: Lat *underwings*
d   Syr Ethiop: Lat lacks *to*
e   Lat *his*
f   Literally *anointed one*
g   Syr: Lat lacks *of days… and speak*
h   Ethiop Arab 1 Arab 2 Arm: Lat Syr *them*

22: *Three heads*, the Flavian emperors (Vespasian, 69–79 CE; Titus, 79–81; and Domitian, 81–96). **23–25:** 11.30–32. **26:** The *large head*, Vespasian. Vespasian did *die in his bed*, perhaps a rarity for Roman emperors, but the attendant *agonies* are otherwise unattested. **30:** *As you have seen*, vv. 2–3. **32:** *Messiah*, 7.28–29n.; *1 Enoch* 62.7. **33-34:** See *2 Bar.* 40. **33:** Here, unlike earlier in the book (6.6; 7.28–44), the Messiah functions as eschatological judge. **34:** *Throughout my borders*, 9.8; 13.48. *He will make them joyful*, 7.28. This verse envisions a second *day of judgment* after that described in v. 33.

12.37–39: Conclusion and injunctions. 37–38: The angel's command to *write* a secret *book* for the *wise* anticipates 14.23–26,37–48 (cf. Isa 8.16; Dan 12.3–4; Rev 1.11; 22.10).

12.40–51: The seer comforts those who were grieved because of his absence (cf. 5.16–19). **40:** *The seven days*, 9.23,27. **42:** Only here and in 1.1 in biblical and apocryphal literature is Ezra called a prophet. *Cluster of grapes*, see 9.21. **44–45:** The people's lament recalls Ezra's earlier words (4.12; 5.35; 7.63). **46–47:** Ezra's reply in

from you; but I have come to this place to pray on account of the desolation of Zion, and to seek mercy on account of the humiliation of our[a] sanctuary. [49] Now go to your homes, every one of you, and after these days I will come to you." [50] So the people went into the city, as I told them to do. [51] But I sat in the field seven days, as the angel[b] had commanded me; and I ate only of the flowers of the field, and my food was of plants during those days.

13 After seven days I dreamed a dream in the night. [2] And lo, a wind arose from the sea and stirred up[c] all its waves. [3] As I kept looking the wind made something like the figure of a man come up out of the heart of the sea. And I saw[d] that this man flew[e] with the clouds of heaven; and wherever he turned his face to look, everything under his gaze trembled, [4] and whenever his voice issued from his mouth, all who heard his voice melted as wax melts[f] when it feels the fire.

[5] After this I looked and saw that an innumerable multitude of people were gathered together from the four winds of heaven to make war against the man who came up out of the sea. [6] And I looked and saw that he carved out for himself a great mountain, and flew up on to it. [7] And I tried to see the region or place from which the mountain was carved, but I could not.

[8] After this I looked and saw that all who had gathered together against him, to wage war with him, were filled with fear, and yet they dared to fight. [9] When he saw the onrush of the approaching multitude, he neither lifted his hand nor held a spear or any weapon of war; [10] but I saw only how he sent forth from his mouth something like a stream of fire, and from his lips a flaming breath, and from his tongue he shot forth a storm of sparks.[g] [11] All these were mingled together, the stream of fire and the flaming breath and the great storm, and fell on the onrushing multitude that was prepared to fight, and burned up all of them, so that suddenly nothing was seen of the innumerable multitude but only the dust of ashes and the smell of smoke. When I saw it, I was amazed.

[12] After this I saw the same man come down from the mountain and call to himself another multitude that was peaceable. [13] Then many people[h] came to him, some of whom were joyful and some sorrowful; some of them were bound, and some were bringing others as offerings.

Then I woke up in great terror, and prayed to the Most High, and said, [14] "From the beginning you have shown your servant these wonders, and have deemed me worthy to have my prayer heard by you; [15] now show me the interpretation of this dream also. [16] For as I consider it in my mind, alas for those who will be left in those days! And still more, alas for those who are not left! [17] For those who are not left will be sad [18] because they understand the things that are reserved for the last days, but cannot attain them. [19] But alas for those also who are left, and for that very reason! For they shall see great dangers and much distress, as these dreams show. [20] Yet it is better[i] to come into these things,[j] though

a Syr Ethiop: Lat *your*
b Literally *he*
c Other ancient authorities read *I saw a wind arise from the sea and stir up*
d Syr: Lat lacks *the wind … I saw*
e Syr Ethiop Arab Arm: Lat *grew strong*
f Syr: Lat *burned as the earth rests*
g Meaning of Lat uncertain
h Lat Syr Arab 2 literally *the faces of many people*
i Ethiop Compare Arab 2: Lat *easier*
j Syr: Lat *this*

turn recalls the earlier encouragement of the angel. **51**: 9.24–26. Ezra's vegetarian diet is clearly linked to the onset of his dream visions.

13.1–58: The sixth vision (the man from the sea). **1–13a: Description of the vision. 2**: *A wind . . . from the sea*, 11.1–2; Dan 7.2. **3**: *Something like the figure of a man*, a messianic figure (cf. Dan 7.13), later in the vision called God's *Son* (13.32; Ezek 1.26). *Flew with the clouds*, Isa 19.1; Dan 7.13; Mk 13.26; Rev 1.7. **4**: *As wax melts*, Mic 1.4; Jdt 16.15. **5**: *Innumerable multitude*, see 13.33–34n. *Four winds of heaven*, Dan 7.2. **6**: *Carved out*, Dan 2.45. **10**: Cf. Isa 11.4; 2 Thess 2.8. **11**: *Burned up*, 12.3; cf. Rev 20.9. **12**: See *2 Bar.* 40.2. **13a**: *Some . . . were bound*, Jews who came from captivity. *Others as offerings*, cf. Isa 66.20.

13.13b–20a: The seer prays that God will interpret the vision to him. See *7.116–126n.*; 10.34–37n. **14**: *My prayer*, 9.25–37. **20**: Contrast 4.12.

incurring peril, than to pass from the world like a cloud, and not to see what will happen in the last days."

He answered me and said, [21] "I will tell you the interpretation of the vision, and I will also explain to you the things that you have mentioned. [22] As for what you said about those who survive, and concerning those who do not survive,[a] this is the interpretation: [23] The one who brings the peril at that time will protect those who fall into peril, who have works and faith toward the Almighty. [24] Understand therefore that those who are left are more blessed than those who have died.

[25] "This is the interpretation of the vision: As for your seeing a man come up from the heart of the sea, [26] this is he whom the Most High has been keeping for many ages, who will himself deliver his creation; and he will direct those who are left. [27] And as for your seeing wind and fire and a storm coming out of his mouth, [28] and as for his not holding a spear or weapon of war, yet destroying the onrushing multitude that came to conquer him, this is the interpretation: [29] The days are coming when the Most High will deliver those who are on the earth. [30] And bewilderment of mind shall come over those who inhabit the earth. [31] They shall plan to make war against one another, city against city, place against place, people against people, and kingdom against kingdom. [32] When these things take place and the signs occur that I showed you before, then my Son will be revealed, whom you saw as a man coming up from the sea.[b]

[33] "Then, when all the nations hear his voice, all the nations shall leave their own lands and the warfare that they have against one another; [34] and an innumerable multitude shall be gathered together, as you saw, wishing to come and conquer him. [35] But he shall stand on the top of Mount Zion. [36] And Zion shall come and be made manifest to all people, prepared and built, as you saw the mountain carved out without hands. [37] Then he, my Son, will reprove the assembled nations for their ungodliness (this was symbolized by the storm), [38] and will reproach them to their face with their evil thoughts and the torments with which they are to be tortured (which were symbolized by the flames), and will destroy them without effort by means of the law[c] (which was symbolized by the fire).

[39] "And as for your seeing him gather to himself another multitude that was peaceable, [40] these are the nine[d] tribes that were taken away from their own land into exile in the days of King Hoshea, whom Shalmaneser, king of the Assyrians, made captives; he took them across the river, and they were taken into another land. [41] But they formed this plan for themselves, that they would leave the multitude of the nations and go to a more distant region, where no human beings had ever lived, [42] so that there at least they might keep their statutes that they had not kept in their own land. [43] And they went in by the narrow passages of the Euphrates river. [44] For at that time the Most High performed signs for them, and stopped the channels of the river until they had crossed over. [45] Through that region there was a long way to go, a journey of a year and a half; and that country is called Arzareth.[e]

[46] "Then they lived there until the last times; and now, when they are about to come again, [47] the Most High will stop[f] the channels of the river again, so that they may be able to cross over. Therefore you saw the multitude

---

[a] Syr Arab 1: Lat lacks *and . . . not survive*
[b] Syr and most Lat Mss lack *from the sea*
[c] Syr: Lat *effort and the law*
[d] Other Lat Mss *ten*; Syr Ethiop Arab 1 Arm *nine and a half*
[e] That is *Another Land*
[f] Syr: Lat *stops*

13.20b–55: The interpretation. 21: *Things . . . mentioned*, in vv. 16–20. 23: *The one who brings the peril*, the Messiah; vv. 3–13a. *Works and faith*, see 9.7n. 24: Contrast 5.41–42. 26: *He whom the Most High has been keeping for many ages*, the Messiah, v. 52; 12.32. 31: Cf. Isa 19.2; Mt 24.7. 32: Cf. 6.20; 7.26–28; 9.1–2; Mk 13.29. 33–34: Cf. Rev 16.14–16; 19.19; 20.7–9. 35: Cf. Heb 12.22–24; Rev 14.1; 2 Bar. 40. 36: *Zion shall come and be made manifest*, 7.26; 10.25–54; Rev 21.2,9–14. *Without hands*, Dan 2.34,45. 37–38: *Reprove . . . reproach . . . destroy*, as in 11.37–46; 12.31–33. 40: 2 Kings 17.1–6. *The nine tribes*, the northern kingdom of Israel (usually "ten tribes"; see textual note d). *The river*, the Euphrates. 44: *Stopped . . . the river*, cf. Josh 3.14–16. 45: *Arzareth*, Heb for "Another Land" (cf.

gathered together in peace. [48] But those who are left of your people, who are found within my holy borders, shall be saved.[a] [49] Therefore when he destroys the multitude of the nations that are gathered together, he will defend the people who remain. [50] And then he will show them very many wonders."

[51] I said, "O sovereign Lord, explain this to me: Why did I see the man coming up from the heart of the sea?"

[52] He said to me, "Just as no one can explore or know what is in the depths of the sea, so no one on earth can see my Son or those who are with him, except in the time of his day.[b] [53] This is the interpretation of the dream that you saw. And you alone have been enlightened about this, [54] because you have forsaken your own ways and have applied yourself to mine, and have searched out my law; [55] for you have devoted your life to wisdom, and called understanding your mother. [56] Therefore I have shown you these things; for there is a reward laid up with the Most High. For it will be that after three more days I will tell you other things, and explain weighty and wondrous matters to you."

[57] Then I got up and walked in the field, giving great glory and praise to the Most High for the wonders that he does[c] from time to time, [58] and because he governs the times and whatever things come to pass in their seasons. And I stayed there three days.

14 On the third day, while I was sitting under an oak, suddenly a voice came out of a bush opposite me and said, "Ezra, Ezra!" [2] And I answered, "Here I am, Lord," and I rose to my feet. [3] Then he said to me, "I revealed myself in a bush and spoke to Moses when my people were in bondage in Egypt; [4] and I sent him and led[d] my people out of Egypt; and I led

him up on Mount Sinai, where I kept him with me many days. [5] I told him many wondrous things, and showed him the secrets of the times and declared to him[e] the end of the times. Then I commanded him, saying, [6] 'These words you shall publish openly, and these you shall keep secret.' [7] And now I say to you: [8] Lay up in your heart the signs that I have shown you, the dreams that you have seen, and the interpretations that you have heard; [9] for you shall be taken up from among humankind, and henceforth you shall live with my Son and with those who are like you, until the times are ended. [10] The age has lost its youth, and the times begin to grow old. [11] For the age is divided into twelve parts, and nine[f] of its parts have already passed, [12] as well as half of the tenth part; so two of its parts remain, besides half of the tenth part.[g] [13] Now therefore, set your house in order, and reprove your people; comfort the lowly among them, and instruct those that are wise.[h] And now renounce the life that is corruptible, [14] and put away from you mortal thoughts; cast away from you the burdens of humankind, and divest yourself now of your weak nature; [15] lay to one side the thoughts that are most grievous to you, and hurry to escape from these times. [16] For evils worse than those that you have now seen

a Syr: Lat lacks *shall be saved*
b Syr: Ethiop *except when his time and his day have come.* Lat lacks *his*
c Lat *did*
d Syr Arab 1 Arab 2 *he led*
e Syr Ethiop Arab Arm: Lat lacks *declared to him*
f Cn: Lat Ethiop *ten*
g Syr lacks verses 11, 12: Ethiop *For the world is divided into ten parts, and has come to the tenth, and half of the tenth remains. Now…*
h Lat lacks *and…wise*

Deut 29.28). **47:** *Will stop … the river*, cf. Isa 11.15–16. **48:** *Within my … borders*, presumably the borders of Israel (cf. 9.8; 12.34). This answers the seer's previous questions about the fate of Israel. **52:** *Those who are with him*, perhaps "those who were taken up," 6.26. Cf. 8.51; 14.9. **53–55:** See 7.76–77n.

13.56–58: Conclusion and injunctions. Ezra's giving *great glory and praise* to God shows the change in attitude that he has experienced since his earlier petulance.

14.1–48: The seventh vision (the legend of Ezra and the holy scriptures). **1–18: God speaks to Ezra. 1–2:** *A bush … "Here I am,"* cf. Ex 3.4. **2:** *I rose*, in contrast to previous occasions, when Ezra was asked to rise (6.13; 7.2; 10.33). **3:** This chapter explicitly draws a parallel between Ezra and *Moses*. **4:** Cf. Ex 34.28. **5–6:** The biblical Moses was never instructed to *keep* some teachings *secret*. Further, see 12.37–38; 14.26,45–47. **5:** *Secrets … the end of the times*, see 3.14n. **9:** *You shall be taken up*, see 6.26n. *My Son*, the Messiah (7.28–29; 13.32,37,52). *Those who are like you*, 8.51; cf. 13.52. **10:** 4.44–50n.; 5.50–55. **11:** See *2 Bar.* 53–70 for a similar division of world history into

happen shall take place hereafter. [17] For the weaker the world becomes through old age, the more shall evils be increased upon its inhabitants. [18] Truth shall go farther away, and falsehood shall come near. For the eagle[a] that you saw in the vision is already hurrying to come."

[19] Then I answered and said, "Let me speak[b] in your presence, Lord. [20] For I will go, as you have commanded me, and I will reprove the people who are now living; but who will warn those who will be born hereafter? For the world lies in darkness, and its inhabitants are without light. [21] For your law has been burned, and so no one knows the things which have been done or will be done by you. [22] If then I have found favor with you, send the holy spirit into me, and I will write everything that has happened in the world from the beginning, the things that were written in your law, so that people may be able to find the path, and that those who want to live in the last days may do so."

[23] He answered me and said, "Go and gather the people, and tell them not to seek you for forty days. [24] But prepare for yourself many writing tablets, and take with you Sarea, Dabria, Selemia, Ethanus, and Asiel—these five, who are trained to write rapidly; [25] and you shall come here, and I will light in your heart the lamp of understanding, which shall not be put out until what you are about to write is finished. [26] And when you have finished, some things you shall make public, and some you shall deliver in secret to the wise; tomorrow at this hour you shall begin to write."

[27] Then I went as he commanded me, and I gathered all the people together, and said, [28] "Hear these words, O Israel. [29] At first our ancestors lived as aliens in Egypt,

and they were liberated from there [30] and received the law of life, which they did not keep, which you also have transgressed after them. [31] Then land was given to you for a possession in the land of Zion; but you and your ancestors committed iniquity and did not keep the ways that the Most High commanded you. [32] And since he is a righteous judge, in due time he took from you what he had given. [33] And now you are here, and your people[c] are farther in the interior.[d] [34] If you, then, will rule over your minds and discipline your hearts, you shall be kept alive, and after death you shall obtain mercy. [35] For after death the judgment will come, when we shall live again; and then the names of the righteous shall become manifest, and the deeds of the ungodly shall be disclosed. [36] But let no one come to me now, and let no one seek me for forty days."

[37] So I took the five men, as he commanded me, and we proceeded to the field, and remained there. [38] And on the next day a voice called me, saying, "Ezra, open your mouth and drink what I give you to drink." [39] So I opened my mouth, and a full cup was offered to me; it was full of something like water, but its color was like fire. [40] I took it and drank; and when I had drunk it, my heart poured forth understanding, and wisdom increased in my breast, for my spirit retained its memory, [41] and my mouth was opened and was no longer closed. [42] Moreover, the Most High gave understanding to the five men, and

---

a   Syr Ethiop Arab Arm: Meaning of Lat uncertain
b   Most Lat Mss lack *Let me speak*
c   Lat *brothers*
d   Syr Ethiop Arm: Lat *are among you*

---

twelve parts. 16–18: Mk 13.7–8. 18: 5.9–11. *The eagle*, chs 11–12.

14.19–26: Ezra's prayer for inspiration to restore the holy scriptures is granted. 20: *Who will warn?*, Ezra's characteristic concern for his fellow Jews finally bears fruit in his desire to rewrite the scriptures. *Without light*, without the light of God's law (cf. Ps 19.8b). 21: According to one tradition, the *law* had *been burned* by the Babylonians when they destroyed Jerusalem in 586 BCE (4.23). 22: *The holy spirit* will guide Ezra in rewriting the law. 23: *Forty days*, cf. Ex 24.18; 34.28; Deut 9.9,18. 26: *Some things . . . make public*, namely, the rewritten books of the Jewish scriptures. *Some . . . deliver in secret*, namely, some extracanonical books (see 12.37–38; 14.5–6,45–47).

14.27–36: Ezra reproves the people (14.13,20), reminding them of the reasons for their state of exile. 28: See 9.30; Deut 6.4. 33: *Farther*, apparently referring to the ten northern tribes (13.39–45).

14.37–48: The revelation of scriptures. 37: *The five men*, v. 24. *The field*, the same one in which Ezra has received the fourth through the seventh visions (see 9.24). 39: *A full cup* of inspiration, containing the fire of the spirit (v. 22). 42: *Using characters that they did not know*, in a new script for Hebrew, the Aramaic square

by turns they wrote what was dictated, using characters that they did not know.[a] They sat forty days; they wrote during the daytime, and ate their bread at night. [43] But as for me, I spoke in the daytime and was not silent at night. [44] So during the forty days, ninety-four[b] books were written. [45] And when the forty days were ended, the Most High spoke to me, saying, "Make public the twenty-four[c] books that you wrote first, and let the worthy and the unworthy read them; [46] but keep the seventy that were written last, in order to give them to the wise among your people. [47] For in them is the spring of understanding, the fountain of wisdom, and the river of knowledge." [48] And I did so.[d]

15 [e] Speak in the ears of my people the words of the prophecy that I will put in your mouth, says the Lord, [2] and cause them to be written on paper; for they are trustworthy and true. [3] Do not fear the plots against you, and do not be troubled by the unbelief of those who oppose you. [4] For all unbelievers shall die in their unbelief.[f]

[5] Beware, says the Lord, I am bringing evils upon the world, the sword and famine, death and destruction, [6] because iniquity has spread throughout every land, and their harmful doings have reached their limit. [7] Therefore, says the Lord, [8] I will be silent no longer concerning their ungodly acts that they impiously commit, neither will I tolerate their wicked practices. Innocent and righteous blood cries out to me, and the souls of the righteous cry out continually. [9] I will surely avenge them,

says the Lord, and will receive to myself all the innocent blood from among them. [10] See, my people are being led like a flock to the slaughter; I will not allow them to live any longer in the land of Egypt, [11] but I will bring them out with a mighty hand and with an uplifted arm, and will strike Egypt with plagues, as before, and will destroy all its land.

[12] Let Egypt mourn, and its foundations, because of the plague of chastisement and castigation that the Lord will bring upon it. [13] Let the farmers that till the ground mourn, because their seed shall fail to grow[g] and their trees shall be ruined by blight and hail and by a terrible tempest. [14] Alas for the world and for those who live in it! [15] For the sword and misery draw near them, and nation shall rise up to fight against nation, with swords in their

[a] Syr Compare Ethiop Arab 2 Arm: Meaning of Lat uncertain

[b] Syr Ethiop Arab 1 Arm: Meaning of Lat uncertain

[c] Syr Arab 1: Lat lacks *twenty-four*

[d] Syr adds *in the seventh year of the sixth week, five thousand years and three months and twelve days after creation. At that time Ezra was caught up, and taken to the place of those who are like him, after he had written all these things. And he was called the scribe of the knowledge of the Most High for ever and ever.* Ethiop Arab 1 Arm have a similar ending

[e] Chapters 15 and 16 (except 15.57-59, which has been found in Greek) are extant only in Lat

[f] Other ancient authorities add *and all who believe shall be saved by their faith*

[g] Lat lacks *to grow*

characters. **45:** *Twenty-four books* is one traditional reckoning of the Hebrew canon: the five books of the Law (Gen, Ex, Lev, Num, Deut), eight books of the Prophets (the former prophets: Josh; Judg; 1 and 2 Sam [as one book]; 1 and 2 Kings [as one book]; the latter prophets: Isa; Jer; Ezek; and the Twelve [as one book]), and eleven books of the Writings (Ps; Prov; Job; Song; Ruth; Lam; Eccl; Esth; Dan; Ezra-Neh [as one book]; 1 and 2 Chr [as one book]). **46:** *The seventy* are esoteric, apocryphal books (see 12.37–38; 14.26). **48:** The original version of 4 Ezra probably ended with an account of Ezra's being taken up into heaven and functioning as a heavenly scribe (see textual note *d;* cf. 8.19bn.; 14.9). This ending was apparently dropped from the Latin version to make way for the prophecies of chs 15–16 when they were added at a later time.

Chapters 15–16 comprise a separate literary composition also known as 6 Ezra (see Introduction).

15.1–4: The commissioning of the prophet, who in this context is not named. See Jer 1.7–9; 26.2; Hab 2.2. **2:** Cf. Rev 21.5,22b. **3:** Cf. Jer 18.20–23.

15.5–16.34: Prediction of worldwide catastrophes. 15.5–27: God will destroy the world because of human sinfulness. **8:** *Innocent and righteous blood cries out,* cf. Gen 4.10; Rev 6.9–10. **9:** Cf. Deut 32.43. **10–11:** *Egypt* and the *plagues* are probably symbols for the author's own situation of crisis. Cf. Ps 44.22; Isa 53.7. See also Deut 4.34; 26.8; Jer 51.40. **13:** Joel 1.11. **14:** The destruction will be universal. **15–17:** Cf. 2 Chr 15.5–6. **15:** *Nation . . .*

hands. [16] For there shall be unrest among people; growing strong against one another, they shall in their might have no respect for their king or the chief of their leaders. [17] For a person will desire to go into a city, and shall not be able to do so. [18] Because of their pride the cities shall be in confusion, the houses shall be destroyed, and people shall be afraid. [19] People shall have no pity for their neighbors, but shall make an assault upon[a] their houses with the sword, and plunder their goods, because of hunger for bread and because of great tribulation.

[20] See how I am calling together all the kings of the earth to turn to me, says God, from the rising sun and from the south, from the east and from Lebanon; to turn and repay what they have given them. [21] Just as they have done to my elect until this day, so I will do, and will repay into their bosom. Thus says the Lord God: [22] My right hand will not spare the sinners, and my sword will not cease from those who shed innocent blood on earth. [23] And a fire went forth from his wrath, and consumed the foundations of the earth and the sinners, like burnt straw. [24] Alas for those who sin and do not observe my commandments, says the Lord;[b] [25] I will not spare them. Depart, you faithless children! Do not pollute my sanctuary. [26] For God[c] knows all who sin against him; therefore he will hand them over to death and slaughter. [27] Already calamities have come upon the whole earth, and you shall remain in them; God[c] will not deliver you, because you have sinned against him.

[28] What a terrifying sight, appearing from the east! [29] The nations of the dragons of Arabia shall come out with many chariots, and from the day that they set out, their hissing shall spread over the earth, so that all who hear them will fear and tremble. [30] Also the Carmonians, raging in wrath, shall go forth like wild boars[d] from the forest, and with great power they shall come and engage them in battle, and with their tusks they shall devastate a portion of the land of the Assyrians with their teeth. [31] And then the dragons,[e] remembering their origin, shall become still stronger; and if they combine in great power and turn to pursue them, [32] then these shall be disorganized and silenced by their power, and shall turn and flee.[f] [33] And from the land of the Assyrians an enemy in ambush shall attack them and destroy one of them, and fear and trembling shall come upon their army, and indecision upon their kings.

[34] See the clouds from the east, and from the north to the south! Their appearance is exceedingly threatening, full of wrath and storm. [35] They shall clash against one another and shall pour out a heavy tempest on the earth, and their own tempest;[g] and there shall be blood from the sword as high as a horse's belly [36] and a man's thigh and a camel's hock. [37] And there shall be fear and great trembling on the earth; those who see that wrath shall be horror-stricken, and they shall be seized with trembling. [38] After that, heavy storm clouds shall be stirred up from the south, and from the north, and another part from the west. [39] But the winds from the east shall prevail over the cloud that was[h] raised in wrath, and shall dispel it; and the tempest[g] that was to cause destruction by the east wind shall be driven violently toward the south and west. [40] Great and mighty

---

a Cn: Lat *shall empty*
b Other ancient authorities read *God*
c Other ancient authorities read *the Lord*
d Other ancient authorities lack *like wild boars*
e Cn: Lat *dragon*
f Other ancient authorities read *turn their face to the north*
g Meaning of Lat uncertain
h Literally *that he*

---

against nation, cf. Mk 13.8. **18:** Cf. Lk 21.26. *Confusion* and social unrest is the result of pride; cf. Gen 11.7–8. **20:** Ps 72.11. **21:** Isa 65.6. **22–27:** Woes against *sinners.* **23:** Cf. Jer 4.4.

15.28–33: A vision of warfare in the east. This section may reflect conflicts between Odenathus of Palmyra (*dragons of Arabia*) and Shapur I of Persia (*Carmonians*) that took place on the eastern borders of the Roman Empire between 261 and 267 CE. **30:** *The Carmonians,* from Carmania (Kerman in modern Iran), a southern province of the Parthian Empire.

15.34–63: A vision of destructive storm clouds. The exact historical referents of this section, if any, are un-

clouds, full of wrath and tempest, shall rise and destroy all the earth and its inhabitants, and shall pour out upon every high and lofty place[a] a terrible tempest, [41] fire and hail and flying swords and floods of water, so that all the fields and all the streams shall be filled with the abundance of those waters. [42] They shall destroy cities and walls, mountains and hills, trees of the forests, and grass of the meadows, and their grain. [43] They shall go on steadily to Babylon and blot it out. [44] They shall come to it and surround it; they shall pour out on it the tempest[b] and all its fury;[c] then the dust and smoke shall reach the sky, and all who are around it shall mourn for it. [45] And those who survive shall serve those who have destroyed it.

[46] And you, Asia, who share in the splendor of Babylon and the glory of her person— [47] woe to you, miserable wretch! For you have made yourself like her; you have decked out your daughters for prostitution to please and glory in your lovers, who have always lusted after you. [48] You have imitated that hateful one in all her deeds and devices.[d] Therefore God[e] says, [49] I will send evils upon you: widowhood, poverty, famine, sword, and pestilence, bringing ruin to your houses, bringing destruction and death. [50] And the glory of your strength shall wither like a flower when the heat shall rise that is sent upon you. [51] You shall be weakened like a wretched woman who is beaten and wounded, so that you cannot receive your mighty lovers. [52] Would I have dealt with you so violently, says the Lord, [53] if you had not killed my chosen people continually, exulting and clapping your hands and talking about their death when you were drunk?

[54] Beautify your face! [55] The reward of a prostitute is in your lap; therefore you shall receive your recompense. [56] As you will do to my chosen people, says the Lord, so God will do to you, and will hand you over to adversi-

ties. [57] Your children shall die of hunger, and you shall fall by the sword; your cities shall be wiped out, and all your people who are in the open country shall fall by the sword. [58] Those who are in the mountains and highlands[f] shall perish of hunger, and they shall eat their own flesh in hunger for bread and drink their own blood in thirst for water. [59] Unhappy above all others, you shall come and suffer fresh miseries. [60] As they pass by they shall crush the hateful[g] city, and shall destroy a part of your land and abolish a portion of your glory, when they return from devastated Babylon. [61] You shall be broken down by them like stubble,[h] and they shall be like fire to you. [62] They shall devour you and your cities, your land and your mountains; they shall burn with fire all your forests and your fruitful trees. [63] They shall carry your children away captive, plunder your wealth, and mar the glory of your countenance.

16

Woe to you, Babylon and Asia! Woe to you, Egypt and Syria! [2] Bind on sackcloth and cloth of goats' hair,[i] and wail for your children, and lament for them; for your destruction is at hand. [3] The sword has been sent upon you, and who is there to turn it back? [4] A fire has been sent upon you, and who is there to quench it? [5] Calamities have been sent upon you, and who is there to drive

---

a   Or *eminent person*
b   Meaning of Lat uncertain
c   Other ancient authorities add *until they destroy it to its foundations*
d   Other ancient authorities read *devices, and you have followed after that one about to gratify her magnates and leaders so that you may be made proud and be pleased by her fornications*
e   Other ancient authorities read *the Lord*
f   Gk: Lat omits *and highlands*
g   Another reading is *idle* or *unprofitable*
h   Other ancient authorities read *like dry straw*
i   Other ancient authorities lack *cloth of goats' hair*

---

clear. 35: *As high as . . .* , cf. Rev 14.20. 43: *Babylon*, Rome. 43–44: Cf. Rev 18.9–10,15; 19.3. 46–63: Polemic against *Asia*, imitator of the corrupt *splendor of Babylon* (Rome). *Asia*, here and in 16.1, probably designates the whole of Asia Minor. 47–48: Cf. Ezek 16.33; Rev 14.8; 17.2–5; 18.3. 49: Cf. Rev 18.7–8. 50: Cf. Rev 17.16. 51: Cf. Jer 3.1; etc.; Rev 18.9–10. 52–53: Cf. Rev 17.6; 18.24. 56: Cf. Rev 19.2. 57–59: This section survives in Greek in a parchment fragment from Oxyrhynchus, Egypt. 57: Cf. Jer 18.21. 60: Cf. Rev 18.21. *The hateful city*, Babylon/Rome. 63: Cf. Rev 18.14.

16.1–17: The inevitability of God's judgment (cf. Am 3.3–8). 1–2: A reprise of ch 15. 2: *Sackcloth and cloth of*

them away? [6] Can one drive off a hungry lion in the forest, or quench a fire in the stubble once it has started to burn?[a] [7] Can one turn back an arrow shot by a strong archer? [8] The Lord God sends calamities, and who will drive them away? [9] Fire will go forth from his wrath, and who is there to quench it? [10] He will flash lightning, and who will not be afraid? He will thunder, and who will not be terrified? [11] The Lord will threaten, and who will not be utterly shattered at his presence? [12] The earth and its foundations quake, the sea is churned up from the depths, and its waves and the fish with them shall be troubled at the presence of the Lord and the glory of his power. [13] For his right hand that bends the bow is strong, and his arrows that he shoots are sharp and when they are shot to the ends of the world will not miss once. [14] Calamities are sent forth and shall not return until they come over the earth. [15] The fire is kindled, and shall not be put out until it consumes the foundations of the earth. [16] Just as an arrow shot by a mighty archer does not return, so the calamities that are sent upon the earth shall not return. [17] Alas for me! Alas for me! Who will deliver me in those days?

[18] The beginning of sorrows, when there shall be much lamentation; the beginning of famine, when many shall perish; the beginning of wars, when the powers shall be terrified; the beginning of calamities, when all shall tremble. What shall they do, when the calamities come? [19] Famine and plague, tribulation and anguish are sent as scourges for the correction of humankind. [20] Yet for all this they will not turn from their iniquities, or ever be mindful of the scourges. [21] Indeed, provisions will be so cheap upon earth that people will imagine that peace is assured for them, and then calamities shall spring up on the earth—the sword, famine, and great confusion. [22] For many of those who live on the earth shall perish by famine; and those who survive the famine shall die by the sword. [23] And the dead shall be thrown out like dung, and there shall be no one to console

them; for the earth shall be left desolate, and its cities shall be demolished. [24] No one shall be left to cultivate the earth or to sow it. [25] The trees shall bear fruit, but who will gather it? [26] The grapes shall ripen, but who will tread them? For in all places there shall be great solitude; [27] a person will long to see another human being, or even to hear a human voice. [28] For ten shall be left out of a city; and two, out of the field, those who have hidden themselves in thick groves and clefts in the rocks. [29] Just as in an olive orchard three or four olives may be left on every tree, [30] or just as, when a vineyard is gathered, some clusters may be left[b] by those who search carefully through the vineyard, [31] so in those days three or four shall be left by those who search their houses with the sword. [32] The earth shall be left desolate, and its fields shall be plowed up,[c] and its roads and all its paths shall bring forth thorns, because no sheep will go along them. [33] Virgins shall mourn because they have no bridegrooms; women shall mourn because they have no husbands; their daughters shall mourn, because they have no help. [34] Their bridegrooms shall be killed in war, and their husbands shall perish of famine.

[35] Listen now to these things, and understand them, you who are servants of the Lord. [36] This is the word of the Lord; receive it and do not disbelieve what the Lord says.[d] [37] The calamities draw near, and are not delayed. [38] Just as a pregnant woman, in the ninth month when the time of her delivery draws near, has great pains around her womb for two or three hours beforehand, but when the child comes forth from the womb, there will not be a moment's delay, [39] so the calamities will not

a   Other ancient authorities read *fire when dry straw has been set on fire*
b   Other ancient authorities read *a cluster may remain exposed*
c   Other ancient authorities read *be for briers*
d   Cn: Lat *do not believe the gods of whom the Lord speaks*

goats' hair, signs of mourning. **9:** Cf. Jer 4.4. **12–13:** 6.14–16n.; 2 Sam 22.8,16; Pss 7.3; 18.7,14–15; Isa 51.15; Sir 16.19. **14:** Cf. Jer 30.23–24. **15:** Cf. Deut 32.22; 2 Pet 3.10. **17:** A plaintive, personal interlude by the prophet.

16.18–34: Prediction of desolation on the earth. 19: Calamity is for the *correction of humankind*, see Amos 4.6–12. **20:** Cf. Hag 2.17; Rev 9.20–21. **23:** Cf. Jer 9.22. **28:** Cf. Am 5.3. **29–31:** Cf. Isa 17.6. **30:** *Clusters*, see 9.21; 12.42. **32:** Cf. Isa 7.23–25. **33:** Cf. Isa 33.8. **34:** Cf. Joel 1.8.

16.35–78: Exhortation of God's people. 35–52: Advice and instruction. **38–39:** 4.40–42; cf. 1 Thess 5.3. **40–**

delay in coming upon the earth, and the world will groan, and pains will seize it on every side.

⁴⁰ Hear my words, O my people; prepare for battle, and in the midst of the calamities be like strangers on the earth. ⁴¹ Let the one who sells be like one who will flee; let the one who buys be like one who will lose; ⁴² let the one who does business be like one who will not make a profit; and let the one who builds a house be like one who will not live in it; ⁴³ let the one who sows be like one who will not reap; so also the one who prunes the vines, like one who will not gather the grapes; ⁴⁴ those who marry, like those who will have no children; and those who do not marry, like those who are widowed. ⁴⁵ Because of this, those who labor, labor in vain; ⁴⁶ for strangers shall gather their fruits, and plunder their goods, overthrow their houses, and take their children captive; for in captivity and famine they will produce their children.ᵃ ⁴⁷ Those who conduct business, do so only to have it plundered; the more they adorn their cities, their houses and possessions, and their persons, ⁴⁸ the more angry I will be with them for their sins, says the Lord. ⁴⁹ Just as a respectable and virtuous woman abhors a prostitute, ⁵⁰ so righteousness shall abhor iniquity, when she decks herself out, and shall accuse her to her face when he comes who will defend the one who searches out every sin on earth.

⁵¹ Therefore do not be like her or her works. ⁵² For in a very short time iniquity will be removed from the earth, and righteousness will reign over us. ⁵³ Sinners must not say that they have not sinned;ᵇ for Godᶜ will burn coals of fire on the head of everyone who says, "I have not sinned before God and his glory." ⁵⁴ The Lordᵈ certainly knows everything that people do; he knows their imaginations and their thoughts and their hearts. ⁵⁵ He said, "Let the earth be made," and it was made, and "Let the heaven be made," and it was made. ⁵⁶ At his word the stars were fixed in their places, and he knows the number of the stars. ⁵⁷ He searches the abyss and its treasures; he has measured the sea and its contents; ⁵⁸ he has confined the sea in the midst of the waters;ᵉ and by his word he has suspended the earth over the water. ⁵⁹ He has spread out the heaven like a dome and made it secure upon the waters; ⁶⁰ he has put springs of water in the desert, and pools on the tops of the mountains, so as to send rivers from the heights to water the earth. ⁶¹ He formed human beings and put a heart in the midst of each body, and gave each person breath and life and understanding ⁶² and the spiritᶠ of Almighty God,ᵍ who surely made all things and searches out hidden things in hidden places. ⁶³ He knows your imaginations and what you think in your hearts! Woe to those who sin and want to hide their sins! ⁶⁴ The Lord will strictly examine all their works, and will make a public spectacle of all of you. ⁶⁵ You shall be put to shame when your sins come out before others, and your own iniquities shall stand as your accusers on that day. ⁶⁶ What will you do? Or how will you hide your sins before the Lord and his glory? ⁶⁷ Indeed, Godʰ is the judge; fear him! Cease from your sins, and forget your iniquities, never to commit them again; so Godʰ will lead you forth and deliver you from all tribulation.

⁶⁸ The burning wrath of a great multitude is kindled over you; they shall drag some of you away and force you to eat what was sacri-

---

a Other ancient authorities read *therefore those who are married may know that they will produce children for captivity and famine*
b Other ancient authorities add *or the unjust done injustice*
c Lat *for he*
d Other ancient authorities read *Lord God*
e Other ancient authorities read *confined the world between the waters and the waters*
f Or *breath*
g Other ancient authorities read *of the Lord Almighty*
h Other ancient authorities read *the Lord*

47: Every form of worldly activity is useless. See Deut 28.30–33,38–42; 1 Cor 7.29–31. 46: Cf. Lev 26.16; Deut 28.33.

16.53–67: The impossibility of hiding sins from God. 53: Cf. Prov 25.22. 54: Cf. Ps 33.15; Sir 15.18–19; 39.19. 55–62: This recital of God's acts of creation underscores God's omniscience; cf. Job 38; Sir 43. 55: See Gen 1.6,9. 56: Cf. Ps 147.4. 58–59: Cf. Ps 136.6; Prov 8.29; Isa 44.24. 59: Cf. Isa 40.22; Ps 104.2. 60: Cf. Ps 107.35; Isa 41.18. 61-62: Cf. Job 32.8; 33.4. 62: Cf. Rev 2.23.

16.68–73: Prediction of persecutions. These descriptions have close parallels with third- and early fourth-

ficed to idols. [69] And those who consent to eat shall be held in derision and contempt, and shall be trampled under foot. [70] For in many places[a] and in neighboring cities there shall be a great uprising against those who fear the Lord. [71] They shall[b] be like maniacs, sparing no one, but plundering and destroying those who continue to fear the Lord.[c] [72] For they shall destroy and plunder their goods, and drive them out of house and home. [73] Then the tested quality of my elect shall be manifest, like gold that is tested by fire.

[74] Listen, my elect ones, says the Lord; the days of tribulation are at hand, but I will deliver you from them. [75] Do not fear or doubt, for God[d] is your guide. [76] You who keep my commandments and precepts, says the Lord God, must not let your sins weigh you down, or your iniquities prevail over you. [77] Woe to those who are choked by their sins and overwhelmed by their iniquities! They are like a field choked with underbrush and its path[e] overwhelmed with thorns, so that no one can pass through. [78] It is shut off and given up to be consumed by fire.

---

a   Meaning of Lat uncertain
b   Other ancient authorities read *For people, because of their misfortunes, shall*
c   Other ancient authorities read *fear God*
d   Other ancient authorities read *the Lord*
e   Other ancient authorities read *seed*

---

century Roman persecutions of Christians. **68:** Eating food *sacrificed to idols* was forbidden for many Jewish and early Christian groups. See Ex 34.15; Acts 15.20,29; 1 Cor 8.1–13; 10.14–22; Rev 2.14,20; 4 Macc 5.2. **73:** Cf. Zech 13.9; 1 Pet 1.7. **74:** Cf. Dan 12.1.

16.74–78: Concluding instructions to the elect. 77–78: Cf. 2 Sam 23.6–7; Heb 6.8. **77:** Cf. Prov 5.22.

(d) The following book appears in an appendix to the Greek Bible.

4 MACCABEES

NAME

This book is linked with 1 and 2 Maccabees on the basis of its focus on the events also related in them, the conflict between Jewish factions that eventually precipitated the persecution by the Seleucid king Antiochus IV Epiphanes (reigned 175–164 BCE) and the Jewish revolt led by Judas Maccabeus. In 4 Maccabees, however, the family of Judas Maccabeus and its exploits are never mentioned. The focus is rather on the torture and death of the martyrs (see 2 Macc 7). The work was also known as *On the Supremacy of Reason* in the early church (Eusebius, *Hist. eccl.* 3.10.6; Jerome, *De vir. ill.* 13).

CANONICAL STATUS

No modern religious community regards the work as strictly canonical, although it is included in two important copies of the Bible from the fourth and fifth century Christian Church.

AUTHORSHIP

The anonymous author is a Torah-observant Jew who exhibits a greater mastery of Greek language, philosophy, literature, and rhetoric than any canonical author. The church fathers Eusebius and Jerome both attributed the work to Josephus, the first-century CE Jewish historian, though it does not suit his style, greater historical accuracy, and more indulgent attitude toward assimilation.

DATE AND HISTORICAL CONTEXT

Plausible arguments have been made for a date of composition anywhere between 20 and 130 CE, with a date later in that range more likely. Many earlier scholars thought that 4 Maccabees was written in Alexandria in Egypt, the generally assumed place of origin for Hellenistic Jewish literature. But the interest in these martyrs in Antioch (in northern Syria), and the fact that the literary epitaph in 17.9–10 reflects the wording of actual Jewish epitaphs in Cilicia (in southeast Turkey), point to an origin in the northeast Mediterranean basin. The author does not write in response to any known crisis affecting the Jewish community, but instead addresses the everyday challenge of maintaining pride in, and commitment to, the Jewish way of life in an often hostile environment.

LITERARY HISTORY

4 Maccabees is a thoroughly original composition rather than the product of editing various sources. The author has read 2 Macc 3–7, but completely recasts the story in keeping with his own interests and goals. The work appears to have been written, in Greek, for oral delivery on a particular occasion (1.10; 3.20), perhaps during a celebration of Hanukkah, which celebrates the reconsecration of the Temple in 164 BCE, or a festival connected with the giving of the Torah (e.g., the Feast of Weeks).

STRUCTURE AND CONTENTS

The author presents the work as a philosophical demonstration of the popular maxim that reason is able to master the passions, with the added dimension that Torah observance provides the most effective training to achieve this goal. The work has two main parts: a more deductive development of the thesis (1.13–3.18), and a narrative demonstration of the thesis focused on the historical example of nine martyrs (3.19–17.6). The combination of logical argumentation and extended examples is found in other Greek and Roman ethical works. The author prepares the hearers for this two-part structure (1.1,7–8,12), and the two parts of the work are thoroughly integrated, as its outline shows:

INTERPRETATION

Fourth Maccabees is one of several texts from the Second Temple period interpreting the Jewish law and way of life in terms of Greco-Roman philosophy. Rather than using an allegorical approach, as did Philo of Alexandria, this author casts the Torah as a training program in the right exercise of reason and the cultivation of the cardinal virtues of justice, courage, self-control, and wisdom. It belongs thus to a larger literary movement promoting the Jewish way of life in close dialogue with the Greek cultural milieu.

As with other Jewish writings composed in Greek, it was not influential in the rabbinic Judaism that emerged in the wake of the disastrous revolts against Rome (66–70 and 132–35 CE). While early Christian authors recognized its philosophical dimensions, 4 Maccabees exercised its most enduring influence in the development of Christian martyrology during the second through fourth centuries.

GUIDE TO READING

The author gives several cues concerning how the work is to be read. He uses the language of "demonstration" (1.1; 3.19), suggesting that it can be read as an essay marshaling evidence for an ethical thesis: reason can rise above the passions and choose the path of virtue. He uses the language of praise or eulogy (1.10), suggesting that it can also be read as a celebration of the achievement of particular individuals, whose virtue is therefore to be imitated by all who strive for a praiseworthy remembrance. His exhortations to the audience (1.1, 18.1) and his interest in demonstrating that the Jewish law provides the surest path to ethical virtue add a third dimension, that of the "protreptic speech" that promotes a particular philosophy or way of life as worth following. Finally, the work can be read as resistance literature, both within the frame of the story of the martyrdoms and from the vantage point of an author who has mastered the dominant culture's tools as resources for promoting a minority culture's way of life.

David A. deSilva

1 The subject that I am about to discuss is most philosophical, that is, whether devout reason is sovereign over the emotions. So it is right for me to advise you to pay earnest attention to philosophy. [2] For the subject is essential to everyone who is seeking knowledge, and in addition it includes the praise of the highest virtue—I mean, of course, rational judgment. [3] If, then, it is evident that reason rules over those emotions that hinder self-control, namely, gluttony and lust, [4] it is also clear that it masters the emotions that hinder one from justice, such as malice, and those that stand in the way of courage, namely anger, fear, and pain. [5] Some might perhaps ask, "If reason rules the emotions, why is it not sovereign over forgetfulness and ignorance?" Their attempt at argument is ridiculous![a] [6] For reason does not rule its own emotions, but those that are opposed to justice, courage, and self-control;[b] and it is not for the purpose of destroying them, but so that one may not give way to them.

[7] I could prove to you from many and various examples that reason[c] is dominant over the emotions, [8] but I can demonstrate it best from the noble bravery of those who died for the sake of virtue, Eleazar and the seven brothers and their mother. [9] All of these, by despising sufferings that bring death, demonstrated that reason controls the emotions. [10] On this anniversary[d] it is fitting for me to praise for their virtues those who, with their mother, died for the sake of nobility and goodness, but I would also call them blessed for the honor in which they are held. [11] All people, even their torturers, marveled at their courage and endurance, and they became the cause of the downfall of tyranny over their nation. By their endurance they conquered the tyrant, and thus their native land was purified through them. [12] I shall shortly have an opportunity to speak of this; but, as my custom is, I shall begin by stating my main principle, and then I shall turn to their story, giving glory to the all-wise God.

[13] Our inquiry, accordingly, is whether reason is sovereign over the emotions. [14] We shall decide just what reason is and what emotion is, how many kinds of emotions there are, and whether reason rules over all these.

---

a   Or *They are attempting to make my argument ridiculous!*

b   Other ancient authorities add *and rational judgment*

c   Other ancient authorities read *devout reason*

d   Gk *At this time*

1.1–12: Introduction. 1: *Reason . . . emotions*, the Greek word translated "emotions" includes desires and drives, emotional responses, and physical sensations. Greco-Roman philosophical writers regularly promoted mastery of these experiences, or self-mastery, as the path to lead a consistently virtuous life. *Devout reason*, the mind shaped by training in and obedience to the Jewish Torah (2.21–23; 5.19–26; 18.1–2). The author will claim for Judaism the status of a *philosophy* (as do the first-century CE Jewish writers Josephus and Philo), and argue for its superiority for achieving the Greek ideal of virtue. **3–4:** These topics are covered sequentially in 1.30–2.6a, 2.6b–3.18, and 5.1–17.6. **4:** *Anger* is more properly an obstacle to justice, not to courage, and is so treated in 2.6b,16–20. **5–6a:** The first-century CE Roman writer Cicero (*Fin.* 5.1.3.36), as well as Philo (*Migr.* 206), made similar distinctions between voluntary and involuntary defects or passions, holding the individual morally responsible only for the former. **6b:** The author, aware of this larger debate, aligns himself with philosophers promoting mastery and moderation of the emotions, drives, and sensations rather than with hardline Stoics who sought to eliminate such experiences; see also 3.2–18. **7:** *Examples* function here, as in Greek rhetoric generally, as a form of inductive proof. The extreme case of the martyrs will prove the general rule. **8:** See 2 Macc 6.18–7.42. **10:** Those who are most committed to the Jewish law thus achieve *nobility and goodness*, the highest Greek ideal. **11:** The author avoids all mention of the Maccabean revolutionaries throughout the speech and locates the cause for Judea's liberation squarely in the martyrs' effective, nonviolent resistance to imperialism.

1.13–3.18: Development of the thesis. 1.13–30a: Definitions of terms. 13: The author is not, strictly speaking, concerned with *whether*, but rather what enables reason to achieve such mastery. **16–17:** The author shares this definition of *wisdom* with Greco-Roman philosophers but reveals his particular allegiance to the Jewish "philosophy" by naming the Torah, *the law*, as the path to this *wisdom* (Sir 1:26; 19:20; Wis 6:17–20). *Education* (Gk "paideia") was what distinguished the civilized Greeks from the barbarians; the author claims for Torah-

¹⁵ Now reason is the mind that with sound logic prefers the life of wisdom. ¹⁶ Wisdom, next, is the knowledge of divine and human matters and the causes of these. ¹⁷ This, in turn, is education in the law, by which we learn divine matters reverently and human affairs to our advantage. ¹⁸ Now the kinds of wisdom are rational judgment, justice, courage, and self-control. ¹⁹ Rational judgment is supreme over all of these, since by means of it reason rules over the emotions. ²⁰ The two most comprehensive types[a] of the emotions are pleasure and pain; and each of these is by nature concerned with both body and soul. ²¹ The emotions of both pleasure and pain have many consequences. ²² Thus desire precedes pleasure and delight follows it. ²³ Fear precedes pain and sorrow comes after. ²⁴ Anger, as a person will see by reflecting on this experience, is an emotion embracing pleasure and pain. ²⁵ In pleasure there exists even a malevolent tendency, which is the most complex of all the emotions. ²⁶ In the soul it is boastfulness, covetousness, thirst for honor, rivalry, and malice; ²⁷ in the body, indiscriminate eating, gluttony, and solitary gormandizing.

²⁸ Just as pleasure and pain are two plants growing from the body and the soul, so there are many offshoots of these plants,[b] ²⁹ each of which the master cultivator, reason, weeds and prunes and ties up and waters and thoroughly irrigates, and so tames the jungle of habits and emotions. ³⁰ For reason is the guide of the virtues, but over the emotions it is sovereign.

Observe now, first of all, that rational judgment is sovereign over the emotions by virtue of the restraining power of self-control. ³¹ Self-control, then, is dominance over the desires. ³² Some desires are mental, others are physical, and reason obviously rules over both. ³³ Otherwise, how is it that when we are attracted to forbidden foods we abstain from the pleasure to be had from them? Is it not because reason is able to rule over appetites? I for one think so. ³⁴ Therefore when we crave seafood and fowl and animals and all sorts of foods that are forbidden to us by the law, we abstain because of domination by reason. ³⁵ For the emotions of the appetites are restrained, checked by the temperate mind, and all the impulses of the body are bridled by reason.

2 And why is it amazing that the desires of the mind for the enjoyment of beauty are rendered powerless? ² It is for this reason, certainly, that the temperate Joseph is praised, because by mental effort[c] he overcame sexual desire. ³ For when he was young and in his prime for intercourse, by his reason he nullified the frenzy[d] of the passions. ⁴ Not only is reason proved to rule over the frenzied urge of sexual desire, but also over every desire.[e] ⁵ Thus the law says, "You shall not covet your neighbor's wife or

---

a Or *sources*
b Other ancient authorities read *these emotions*
c Other ancient authorities add *in reasoning*
d Or *gadfly*
e Or *all covetousness*

---

observance the status and fruits of such education. **18–19:** The four cardinal virtues of Platonic and Stoic ethics. The elevation of *rational judgment* as supreme emerges from the focus on the contest between reason and the emotions. **20:** The author follows Aristotle's twofold classification of the emotions based on *pleasure* and *pain* (*Rh.* 2.1–11) rather than the fourfold Stoic classification of desire, pain, pleasure, and fear; but see 1.22–23. **24:** The definition of anger as a mixture of pleasure and pain is particularly Aristotelian (*Rh.* 2.2.1–2). **28–29:** The author employs common agricultural analogies for the cultivation of the soul. *Habits*, predispositions particularly associated with the stages of life like youth, adulthood, and old age. The author treats the mastery of these challenges specifically in 2.3; 7.13–14.

1.30b–3.18: Evidence from the scriptures. 1.33–34: The author offers the ability of Jews to observe the dietary restrictions of the Torah (here, Lev 11.4–23,41–42; Deut 14.4–21) as proof of the power of self-control over desire. The commandments, however, also provide the training necessary to develop self-control (2.6b–9; 5.22–26). This represents a significant defense against Gentile ridicule of the Torah's restrictions as barbaric or superstitious (Josephus, *Ag. Ap.* 2.137; Tacitus, *Hist.* 5.4.3; Juvenal, *Sat.* 14.98–99; Plutarch, *Mor.* 169C). **2.2:** *Joseph* (Gen 39.7–12) is a model of temperance also in *T. Jos.* 2.7–10.4. **3:** *Young*, see 1.29n. **5:** Ex 20.17; Deut 5.21. **6a:** Contrast Paul's claim that the commandment awakens sin, rather than proves that sin can be mastered (Rom 7.7–24). **6b:** *Justice* involves giving to each person his or her due, which includes giving

anything that is your neighbor's." [6] In fact, since the law has told us not to covet, I could prove to you all the more that reason is able to control desires.

Just so it is with the emotions that hinder one from justice. [7] Otherwise how could it be that someone who is habitually a solitary gormandizer, a glutton, or even a drunkard can learn a better way, unless reason is clearly lord of the emotions? [8] Thus, as soon as one adopts a way of life in accordance with the law, even though a lover of money, one is forced to act contrary to natural ways and to lend without interest to the needy and to cancel the debt when the seventh year arrives. [9] If one is greedy, one is ruled by the law through reason so that one neither gleans the harvest nor gathers the last grapes from the vineyard.

In all other matters we can recognize that reason rules the emotions. [10] For the law prevails even over affection for parents, so that virtue is not abandoned for their sakes. [11] It is superior to love for one's wife, so that one rebukes her when she breaks the law. [12] It takes precedence over love for children, so that one punishes them for misdeeds. [13] It is sovereign over the relationship of friends, so that one rebukes friends when they act wickedly. [14] Do not consider it paradoxical when reason, through the law, can prevail even over

enmity. The fruit trees of the enemy are not cut down, but one preserves the property of enemies from marauders and helps raise up what has fallen.[a]

[15] It is evident that reason rules even[b] the more violent emotions: lust for power, vainglory, boasting, arrogance, and malice. [16] For the temperate mind repels all these malicious emotions, just as it repels anger—for it is sovereign over even this. [17] When Moses was angry with Dathan and Abiram, he did nothing against them in anger, but controlled his anger by reason. [18] For, as I have said, the temperate mind is able to get the better of the emotions, to correct some, and to render others powerless. [19] Why else did Jacob, our most wise father, censure the households of Simeon and Levi for their irrational slaughter of the entire tribe of the Shechemites, saying, "Cursed be their anger"? [20] For if reason could not control anger, he would not have spoken thus. [21] Now when God fashioned human beings, he planted in them emotions and inclinations, [22] but at the same time he enthroned the mind among the senses as a sacred governor over them all. [23] To the mind he gave the law; and one who lives subject to this will rule a kingdom that is temperate, just, good, and courageous.

a   Or *the beasts that have fallen*
b   Other ancient authorities read *through*

God God's due by honoring God's right thus to regulate human relationships. **8–9:** *Lend without interest*, Ex 22:25; Deut 23:19–20; *the seventh year*, Deut 15:1–2,9; *neither gleans*, so as to leave something for the poor, Ex 23:10–11; Lev 19:9–10. Specific commandments of the Torah provide ways to remedy specific vices. **10–13:** Commitment to virtue must outweigh even positive emotions like love for one's family and friends (cf. Deut 13.6–11). The author will return to this topic at length (13.19–14.1; 14.13–20; 15.4–23). **12:** See Prov 13.24; 19.18; 23.13–14; 29.15,17. **14:** Ex 23.4–5; Deut 20.19–20,24. Far from being a law that promotes hatred of foreigners (a frequent criticism; Diod. Sic. 34/35.1.1–4; Tacitus, *Hist.* 5.5; Josephus, *Ag. Ap.* 2.121), the Torah teaches kindness and humaneness toward one's enemies. **17:** When challenged by Dathan and Abiram, Moses acted justly by submitting the matter to God's adjudication (Num 16.1–35). **19–20:** Jacob's deathbed censure of Simeon and Levi (Gen 49:7) for their refusal to reconcile with the inhabitants of Shechem after the seduction of their sister Dinah (see Gen 34:1–31) indicates that reason should be expected to master anger. Other Jewish authors praise Simeon and Levi for this act, suggesting that Jacob was at fault (Jdt 8.2–4; *T. Levi* 5–6). **21–23:** The author regards inclinations and emotions to be part of God's design of the human being, and therefore aligns with the schools that seek to master rather than eliminate them. Diligent observance of the Torah promises the enjoyment of the "kingship" familiar from Stoic discourse, the exercise of perfect rule over the passions and enjoyment of the fruits of virtuous self-governance. **2.24–3.2:** See 1.5–6a n. **3.2–5:** See 1.6b n. **6–18:** The story of David's thirst (2 Sam 23.13–17; 1 Chr 11.15–19) provides a proof from example of the position taken in 3.2. David regards the water as *blood* (v. 15) because the soldiers risked their lives. Although he still experiences thirst at the close (hence does not eliminate his craving), David does not allow it to lead him

[24] How is it then, one might say, that if reason is master of the emotions, it does not control forgetfulness and ignorance?

3 [1] But this argument is entirely ridiculous; for it is evident that reason rules not over its own emotions, but over those of the body. [2] No one of us[a] can eradicate that kind of desire, but reason can provide a way for us not to be enslaved by desire. [3] No one of us can eradicate anger from the mind, but reason can help to deal with anger. [4] No one of us can eradicate malice, but reason can fight at our side so that we are not overcome by malice. [5] For reason does not uproot the emotions but is their antagonist.

[6] Now this can be explained more clearly by the story of King David's thirst. [7] David had been attacking the Philistines all day long, and together with the soldiers of his nation had killed many of them. [8] Then when evening fell, he[b] came, sweating and quite exhausted, to the royal tent, around which the whole army of our ancestors had encamped. [9] Now all the rest were at supper, [10] but the king was extremely thirsty, and though springs were plentiful there, he could not satisfy his thirst from them. [11] But a certain irrational desire for the water in the enemy's territory tormented and inflamed him, undid and consumed him. [12] When his guards complained bitterly because of the king's craving, two staunch young soldiers, respecting[c] the king's desire, armed themselves fully, and taking a pitcher climbed over the enemy's ramparts. [13] Eluding the sentinels at the gates, they went searching throughout the enemy camp [14] and found the spring, and from it boldly brought the king a drink. [15] But David,[d] though he was burning with thirst, considered it an altogether fearful danger to his soul to drink what was regarded as equivalent to blood. [16] Therefore, opposing reason to desire, he poured out the drink as an offering to God. [17] For the temperate mind can conquer the drives of the emotions and quench the flames of frenzied desires; [18] it can overthrow bodily agonies even when they are extreme, and by nobility of reason spurn all domination by the emotions.

[19] The present occasion now invites us to a narrative demonstration of temperate reason.

[20] At a time when our ancestors were enjoying profound peace because of their observance of the law and were prospering, so that even Seleucus Nicanor, king of Asia, had both appropriated money to them for the temple service and recognized their commonwealth— [21] just at that time certain persons attempted a revolution against the public harmony and caused many and various disasters.

4 Now there was a certain Simon, a political opponent of the noble and good man, Onias, who then held the high priesthood for life. When despite all manner of slander he was unable to injure Onias in the eyes of the nation, he fled the country with the purpose of betraying it. [2] So he came to Apollonius, governor of Syria, Phoenicia, and Cilicia, and said, [3] "I have come here because I am loyal to the king's government, to report that in the Jerusalem treasuries there are deposited tens of thousands in private funds, which are not the property of the temple but belong to

a Gk *you*
b Other ancient authorities read *he hurried and*
c Or *embarrassed because of*
d Gk *he*

into an act of pride (hence he masters his craving). The author modifies the story to underscore the severity of David's thirst and the irrational element of his desire for water beyond his reach (3.10 has no parallel in the biblical narratives).

3.19–17.24: Narrative demonstration of the thesis. **3.19–4.26:** Historical background. A highly condensed version of 2 Macc 3:1–6:11. **3.19:** The martyrdoms provide the primary proof from historical example for the author's thesis, a connection made explicit in 6.31–35; 13.1–5; 16.1–2. **20–21:** *Seleucus Nicanor*, Seleucus IV Philopator (king of Syria, 187–175 BCE), not Seleucus I Nicator (305–281). Jerusalem is portrayed as the ideal Greek city-state, exhibiting *peace*, lawful *observance*, and *public harmony* through observing its native way of life; ironically, the Hellenization of the city will destroy this ideal. **4.1:** *Simon*, see 2 Macc 3.4; 4.1–6. *Onias* III was the legitimate high priest (son of the Simon celebrated in Sir 50.1–21). **3:** *Private funds* were deposited in temples for safekeeping. **5:** In 2 Macc 3.7–8 Heliodorus, not Apollonius, is put in command. **7:** Burdensome tribute imposed by Rome led the Seleucid kings to raid several temple treasur-

King Seleucus." [4] When Apollonius learned the details of these things, he praised Simon for his service to the king and went up to Seleucus to inform him of the rich treasure. [5] On receiving authority to deal with this matter, he proceeded quickly to our country accompanied by the accursed Simon and a very strong military force. [6] He said that he had come with the king's authority to seize the private funds in the treasury. [7] The people indignantly protested his words, considering it outrageous that those who had committed deposits to the sacred treasury should be deprived of them, and did all that they could to prevent it. [8] But, uttering threats, Apollonius went on to the temple. [9] While the priests together with women and children were imploring God in the temple to shield the holy place that was being treated so contemptuously, [10] and while Apollonius was going up with his armed forces to seize the money, angels on horseback with lightning flashing from their weapons appeared from heaven, instilling in them great fear and trembling. [11] Then Apollonius fell down half dead in the temple area that was open to all, stretched out his hands toward heaven, and with tears begged the Hebrews to pray for him and propitiate the wrath of the heavenly army. [12] For he said that he had committed a sin deserving of death, and that if he were spared he would praise the blessedness of the holy place before all people. [13] Moved by these

words, the high priest Onias, although otherwise he had scruples about doing so, prayed for him so that King Seleucus would not suppose that Apollonius had been overcome by human treachery and not by divine justice. [14] So Apollonius,[a] having been saved beyond all expectations, went away to report to the king what had happened to him.

[15] When King Seleucus died, his son Antiochus Epiphanes succeeded to the throne, an arrogant and terrible man, [16] who removed Onias from the priesthood and appointed Onias's[b] brother Jason as high priest. [17] Jason[c] agreed that if the office were conferred on him he would pay the king three thousand six hundred sixty talents annually. [18] So the king appointed him high priest and ruler of the nation. [19] Jason[c] changed the nation's way of life and altered its form of government in complete violation of the law, [20] so that not only was a gymnasium constructed at the very citadel[d] of our native land, but also the temple service was abolished. [21] The divine justice was angered by these acts and caused Antiochus himself to make war on them. [22] For when he was warring against Ptolemy in Egypt, he heard that a rumor of his death had spread and that the people of Jerusalem

a   Gk *he*
b   Gk *his*
c   Gk *He*
d   Or *high place*

ies (see 1 Macc 6.9–13; 2 Macc 1.11–17; 9.1–2,13–16), despite the taboos against sacrilege. 9–12: As long as the people adhere to the Torah, they enjoy God's patronage and protection from their enemies (compare 3 Macc 1.8–2.24). 13: Perhaps better, "Moved by these words, although in other respects concerned so that King Seleucus would not suppose that Apollonius had been overcome . . . , the high priest Onias prayed for him." Onias is not scrupulous about offering prayers for Apollonius. 15: *Antiochus* IV *Epiphanes* (reigned 175–164 BCE) was in fact the son of Antiochus III (the Great) and the brother of *Seleucus* IV. 16–17: *Jason*, Onias's younger brother and an avid reformer. The (exaggerated) sum he offers as a bribe signals the breadth of his support among Jerusalem's elite. 19–20: Like many cities following Alexander the Great's conquests in the late fourth century BCE, Jerusalem's plan is now altered to conform to the pattern of the Greek city. *Gymnasium*, a center for Greek education and enculturation as well as athletic contests. According to 2 Macc 4.10–15, *the temple service* was not abolished under Jason, only neglected. 21: God uses the Gentile king Antiochus IV to punish the people who turned from the covenant (see Deut 28.49–50), as for example he had used Nebuchadnezzar in 586 BCE. The author affirms Deuteronomy's theology of history, encouraging the hearers to follow the Torah as the means to advance the peace and prosperity of the Jewish community. 22–23: *Ptolemy* VI Philometor (180–145 BCE). 2 Macc 5.5–12 cites rumors of an insurrection in Jerusalem as the reason for Antiochus's response. This author, by contrast, portrays Antiochus's persecution of the Jews as an irrational, heated response to their joy at the rumor of his death; cf. 8.2; 9.10–11.

had rejoiced greatly. He speedily marched against them, [23] and after he had plundered them he issued a decree that if any of them were found observing the ancestral law they should die. [24] When, by means of his decrees, he had not been able in any way to put an end to the people's observance of the law, but saw that all his threats and punishments were being disregarded [25] —even to the extent that women, because they had circumcised their sons, were thrown headlong from heights along with their infants, though they had known beforehand that they would suffer this— [26] when, I say, his decrees were despised by the people, he himself tried through torture to compel everyone in the nation to eat defiling foods and to renounce Judaism.

5 The tyrant Antiochus, sitting in state with his counselors on a certain high place, and with his armed soldiers standing around him, [2] ordered the guards to seize each and every Hebrew and to compel them to eat pork and food sacrificed to idols. [3] If any were not willing to eat defiling food, they were to be broken on the wheel and killed. [4] When many persons had been rounded up, one man, Eleazar by name, leader of the flock, was brought[a] before the king. He was a man of priestly family, learned in the law, advanced in age, and known to many in the tyrant's court because of his philosophy.[b]

[5] When Antiochus saw him he said, [6] "Before I begin to torture you, old man, I would advise you to save yourself by eating pork, [7] for I respect your age and your gray hairs. Although you have had them for so long a time, it does not seem to me that you are a philosopher when you observe the religion of the Jews. [8] When nature has granted it to us, why should you abhor eating the very excellent meat of this animal? [9] It is senseless not to enjoy delicious things that are not shameful, and wrong to spurn the gifts of nature. [10] It seems to me that you will do something even more senseless if, by holding a vain opinion concerning the truth, you continue to despise me to your own hurt. [11] Will you not awaken from your foolish philosophy, dispel your futile reasonings, adopt a mind appropriate to your years, philosophize according to the truth of what is beneficial, [12] and have compassion on your old age by honoring my humane advice? [13] For consider this: if there is some power watching over this religion of yours, it will excuse you from any transgression that arises out of compulsion."

[14] When the tyrant urged him in this fashion to eat meat unlawfully, Eleazar asked to have a word. [15] When he had received permission to speak, he began to address the people as follows: [16] "We, O Antiochus, who have been persuaded to govern our lives by the divine law, think that there is no compulsion more powerful than our obedience to the law. [17] Therefore we consider that we should not transgress it in any respect. [18] Even if, as you suppose, our law were not truly divine and we had wrongly held it to be divine, not even so would it be right for us to invalidate our reputation for piety. [19] Therefore do not suppose that it would be a petty sin if we were to eat defiling food; [20] to transgress the law in

---

[a] Or was the first of the flock to be brought

[b] Other ancient authorities read his advanced age

5.1–6.30: The example of Eleazar. 5.1–4: Antiochus is presented throughout the book as a stereotypical *tyrant*, inventing cruel torments, displaying arrogance, and suppressing time-honored, local laws. The scene of the tyrant confronting the sage is familiar in Greco-Roman philosophical texts, except that here an aged Jewish priest is cast in the role of the sage. 5–38: The "speech duel" between Antiochus and Eleazar gives the author an opportunity to state and refute the dominant culture's case against Judaism. 7–8: Philosophers claimed that the universal law of *nature* trumped the imperfect, particularistic laws of any one people. The prohibition of pork (see Lev 11.7; Deut 14.8) was frequently targeted for ridicule as a barbaric peculiarity that flew in the face of nature. 9: Antiochus critiques the avoidance of pork as unjust, as it shows ingratitude toward *the gifts of nature*, and a sign of ignorance concerning what is truly permissible and what is truly shameful. 13: Transgression of a law under compulsion was excusable according to Greek philosophers. 15: Eleazar addresses not only the tyrant, but also the audience, which includes the other Jewish captives. He seeks as much to encourage the latter as to answer the former. 19–21: Like the Stoics, Eleazar considers all sins to be *of equal seriousness* since all show

matters either small or great is of equal seriousness, [21] for in either case the law is equally despised. [22] You scoff at our philosophy as though living by it were irrational, [23] but it teaches us self-control, so that we master all pleasures and desires, and it also trains us in courage, so that we endure any suffering willingly; [24] it instructs us in justice, so that in all our dealings we act impartially,[a] and it teaches us piety, so that with proper reverence we worship the only living God.

[25] "Therefore we do not eat defiling food; for since we believe that the law was established by God, we know that in the nature of things the Creator of the world in giving us the law has shown sympathy toward us. [26] He has permitted us to eat what will be most suitable for our lives,[b] but he has forbidden us to eat meats that would be contrary to this. [27] It would be tyrannical for you to compel us not only to transgress the law, but also to eat in such a way that you may deride us for eating defiling foods, which are most hateful to us. [28] But you shall have no such occasion to laugh at me, [29] nor will I transgress the sacred oaths of my ancestors concerning the keeping of the law, [30] not even if you gouge out my eyes and burn my entrails. [31] I am not so old and cowardly as not to be young in reason on behalf of piety. [32] Therefore get your torture wheels ready and fan the fire more vehemently! [33] I do not so pity my old age as to break the ancestral law by my own act. [34] I will not play false to you, O law that trained me, nor will I renounce you, beloved self-control. [35] I will not put you to shame, philosophical reason, nor will I reject you, honored priesthood and knowledge of the law. [36] You, O king,[c] shall not defile the honorable mouth of my old age, nor my long life lived lawfully. [37] My ancestors will receive me as pure, as one who does not fear your violence even to death. [38] You may tyrannize the ungodly, but you shall not dominate my religious principles, either by words or through deeds."

6 When Eleazar in this manner had made eloquent response to the exhortations of the tyrant, the guards who were standing by dragged him violently to the instruments of torture. [2] First they stripped the old man, though he remained adorned with the gracefulness of his piety. [3] After they had tied his arms on each side they flogged him, [4] while a herald who faced him cried out, "Obey the king's commands!" [5] But the courageous and noble man, like a true Eleazar, was unmoved, as though being tortured in a dream; [6] yet while the old man's eyes were raised to heaven, his flesh was being torn by scourges, his blood flowing, and his sides were being cut to pieces. [7] Although he fell to the ground because his body could not endure the agonies, he kept his reason upright and unswerving. [8] One of the cruel guards rushed at him and began to kick him in the side to make him get up again after he fell. [9] But he bore the pains and scorned the punishment and endured the tortures. [10] Like a noble athlete the old man, while being beaten, was victorious over his torturers; [11] in fact, with his face bathed in sweat, and gasping heavily for breath, he amazed even his torturers by his courageous spirit.

a   Or *so that we hold in balance all our habitual inclinations*
b   Or *souls*
c   Gk lacks *O king*

equal affront to God, whether or not an outsider like Antiochus considers the particular issue weighty. **22–24:** Eleazar counters Antiochus's challenge to Judaism's status as a worthy philosophy (5.7,11) with the functional proof that obedience to the Torah nurtures the cardinal virtues prized by Platonic and Stoic philosophers (*piety* replaces "rational judgment" here; see 1.18). **25–26:** *In the nature of things*, lit., "according to nature." Stoics sought to live in accordance with the divine order inherent in creation. Eleazar counters Antiochus's criticism that the Torah contradicts nature (5.8–9) by affirming the Torah's origin in the mind of the *Creator* of nature, thus providing an even more reliable guide to virtue. **29:** *Sacred oaths*, Ex 24.3,7; Josh 24.18,21,24. **38:** Eleazar exhibits the freedom of the sage prized by Stoic philosophy. **6.2:** Eleazar's honor was not diminished by the degrading treatment he received. **5:** *Like a true Eleazar*, "Eleazar" means "God has helped," hence, "like someone truly helped by God." **7:** Keeping *reason upright* is the goal of the sage, even as it is for Eleazar. **10:** The victim becomes the victor by being able to endure, without capitulation, more than the torturers can inflict. Comparing Eleazar to *a noble athlete* reflects widespread philosophical usage of athletic imagery to transform passive

[12] At that point, partly out of pity for his old age, [13] partly out of sympathy from their acquaintance with him, partly out of admiration for his endurance, some of the king's retinue came to him and said, [14] "Eleazar, why are you so irrationally destroying yourself through these evil things? [15] We will set before you some cooked meat; save yourself by pretending to eat pork."

[16] But Eleazar, as though more bitterly tormented by this counsel, cried out: [17] "Never may we, the children of Abraham,[a] think so basely that out of cowardice we feign a role unbecoming to us! [18] For it would be irrational if having lived in accordance with truth up to old age and having maintained in accordance with law the reputation of such a life, we should now change our course [19] and ourselves become a pattern of impiety to the young by setting them an example in the eating of defiling food. [20] It would be shameful if we should survive for a little while and during that time be a laughingstock to all for our cowardice, [21] and be despised by the tyrant as unmanly by not contending even to death for our divine law. [22] Therefore, O children of Abraham, die nobly for your religion! [23] And you, guards of the tyrant, why do you delay?"

[24] When they saw that he was so courageous in the face of the afflictions, and that he had not been changed by their compassion, the guards brought him to the fire. [25] There they burned him with maliciously contrived instruments, threw him down, and poured stinking liquids into his nostrils. [26] When he was now burned to his very bones and about to expire, he lifted up his eyes to God and said, [27] "You know, O God, that though I might have saved myself, I am dying in burning torments for the sake of the law. [28] Be merciful to your people, and let our punishment suffice for them. [29] Make my blood their purification, and take my life in exchange for theirs." [30] After he said this, the holy man died nobly in his tortures; even in the tortures of death he resisted, by virtue of reason, for the sake of the law.

[31] Admittedly, then, devout reason is sovereign over the emotions. [32] For if the emotions had prevailed over reason, we would have testified to their domination. [33] But now that reason has conquered the emotions, we properly attribute to it the power to govern. [34] It is right for us to acknowledge the dominance of reason when it masters even external agonies. It would be ridiculous to deny it.[b] [35] I have proved not only that reason has mastered agonies, but also that it masters pleasures and in no respect yields to them.

7 For like a most skillful pilot, the reason of our father Eleazar steered the ship of religion over the sea of the emotions, [2] and though buffeted by the stormings of the tyrant and overwhelmed by the mighty waves of tortures, [3] in no way did he turn the rudder of religion until he sailed into the haven of immortal victory. [4] No city besieged with many ingenious war machines has ever held out as did that most holy man. Although his sacred life was consumed by tortures and racks, he conquered the besiegers with the shield of his devout reason. [5] For in setting his mind firm like a jutting cliff, our father Eleazar broke the maddening waves of the emotions. [6] O priest, worthy of the priesthood, you neither defiled your sacred teeth

a   Or *O children of Abraham*
b   Syr: Meaning of Gk uncertain

endurance into active resistance. This imagery recurs in 9.23; 11.20; 12.11,14; 13.13,15; 16.16; 17.11–16. **12–23**: See 2 Macc 6.21–22. Eleazar's rejection of the ruse recalls Socrates' rejection of the escape planned by his friends. Neither consented to purchasing a few more years of life at the cost of preserving the virtue of that life unblemished (5.36; 6.18–21; Plato, *Cri.* 52A–54C). Eleazar cannot maintain his private integrity without also preserving his public witness and example. **28–29**: The author combines the belief that a display of covenant obedience would bring an end to God's wrath upon the disobedient nation (Deut 30.1–5) with the sacrificial practice of using a victim's blood to atone for a life (Lev 17.11) to interpret the significance of the martyrdoms (cf. 17.21–22). This is an instructive parallel development to early Christian reflection on the death of Jesus as an act of atonement for the unrighteous. Greek drama also frequently features voluntary deaths as sacrifices that allow others to live or a nation to survive.

6.31–7.23: Reflection on Eleazar's example. 6.31–35: See 3.19n. **7.1–5**: The author uses a series of images familiar from popular ethical philosophy to praise Eleazar's achievement of mastery over emotions and sensa-

nor profaned your stomach, which had room only for reverence and purity, by eating defiling foods. [7] O man in harmony with the law and philosopher of divine life! [8] Such should be those who are administrators of the law, shielding it with their own blood and noble sweat in sufferings even to death. [9] You, father, strengthened our loyalty to the law through your glorious endurance, and you did not abandon the holiness that you praised, but by your deeds you made your words of divine[a] philosophy credible. [10] O aged man, more powerful than tortures; O elder, fiercer than fire; O supreme king over the passions, Eleazar! [11] For just as our father Aaron, armed with the censer, ran through the multitude of the people and conquered the fiery[b] angel, [12] so the descendant of Aaron, Eleazar, though being consumed by the fire, remained unmoved in his reason. [13] Most amazing, indeed, though he was an old man, his body no longer tense and firm,[c] his muscles flabby, his sinews feeble, he became young again [14] in spirit through reason; and by reason like that of Isaac he rendered the many-headed rack ineffective. [15] O man of blessed age and of venerable gray hair and of law-abiding life, whom the faithful seal of death has perfected!

[16] If, therefore, because of piety an aged man despised tortures even to death, most certainly devout reason is governor of the emotions. [17] Some perhaps might say, "Not all have full command of their emotions, because not all have prudent reason." [18] But as many as attend to religion with a whole heart, these alone are able to control the passions of the flesh, [19] since they believe that they, like our patriarchs Abraham and Isaac and Jacob, do not die to God, but live to God. [20] No contradiction therefore arises when some persons appear to be dominated by their emotions because of the weakness of their reason. [21] What person who lives as a philosopher by the whole rule of philosophy, and trusts in God, [22] and knows that it is blessed to endure any suffering for the sake of virtue, would not be able to overcome the emotions through godliness? [23] For only the wise and courageous are masters of their emotions.

8 For this is why even the very young, by following a philosophy in accordance with devout reason, have prevailed over the most painful instruments of torture. [2] For when the tyrant was conspicuously defeated in his first attempt, being unable to compel an aged man to eat defiling foods, then in violent rage he commanded that others of the Hebrew captives be brought, and that any who ate defiling food would be freed after eating, but if any were to refuse, they would be tortured even more cruelly.

[3] When the tyrant had given these orders, seven brothers—handsome, modest, noble, and accomplished in every way—were brought before him along with their aged mother. [4] When the tyrant saw them, grouped about their mother as though a chorus, he was pleased with them. And struck by

---

[a] Other ancient authorities lack *divine*
[b] Other ancient authorities lack *fiery*
[c] Gk *the tautness of the body already loosed*

---

tions. **6**: Far from devaluing his body, Eleazar honors it in his choice of endurance over capitulation. **9**: Consistency in word and speech is the test of the value of one's *philosophy*, or way of life. **11–12**: *Aaron*, see Num 16.41–50; Wis 18.20–25. Both priests courageously took a stand in a place of great danger for the sake of the nation in order to perform an act of expiation. **14**: *Isaac*, see Gen 22.1–19. **15**: *The faithful seal of death . . . perfected*, because Eleazar preserved his honor and virtue intact to the end, and they are now unassailable forever. **18**: *Religion*, specifically Judaism, is here affirmed as essential to achieving the ethical goal of the Greco-Roman philosophers. **19**: Freedom from the fear of death is essential if one is to be free to make the sacrifices that virtue sometimes demands.

8.1–12.19: The example of the seven brothers. 8.2: *Conspicuously defeated*, Antiochus is aware that the martyrs' effective resistance unto death publicly shames him. *In violent rage*, Antiochus fails to master his own emotions, giving them instead the upper hand. The Greco-Syrian king falls short of the Greek ideal so fully embodied by the non-Greek martyrs (see 9.10–11), and is indeed unfit to rule others (Plato, *Gorg.* 491D; Dio Chrys., *Or.* 62.1). **3–5**: Embodying the Greek ideal of male beauty and skill, the brothers do not lack the potential for success in the Greek world. **4**: *Chorus*, an image from the Greek stage, often speaking in unison and represent-

their appearance and nobility, he smiled at them, and summoned them nearer and said, [5] "Young men, with favorable feelings I admire each and every one of you, and greatly respect the beauty and the number of such brothers. Not only do I advise you not to display the same madness as that of the old man who has just been tortured, but I also exhort you to yield to me and enjoy my friendship. [6] Just as I am able to punish those who disobey my orders, so I can be a benefactor to those who obey me. [7] Trust me, then, and you will have positions of authority in my government if you will renounce the ancestral tradition of your national life. [8] Enjoy your youth by adopting the Greek way of life and by changing your manner of living. [9] But if by disobedience you rouse my anger, you will compel me to destroy each and every one of you with dreadful punishments through tortures. [10] Therefore take pity on yourselves. Even I, your enemy, have compassion for your youth and handsome appearance. [11] Will you not consider this, that if you disobey, nothing remains for you but to die on the rack?"

[12] When he had said these things, he ordered the instruments of torture to be brought forward so as to persuade them out of fear to eat the defiling food. [13] When the guards had placed before them wheels and joint-dislocators, rack and hooks[a] and catapults[b] and caldrons, braziers and thumbscrews and iron claws and wedges and bellows, the tyrant resumed speaking: [14] "Be afraid, young fellows; whatever justice you revere will be merciful to you when you transgress under compulsion."

[15] But when they had heard the inducements and saw the dreadful devices, not only were they not afraid, but they also opposed the tyrant with their own philosophy, and by their right reasoning nullified his tyranny. [16] Let us consider, on the other hand, what arguments might have been used if some

of them had been cowardly and unmanly. Would they not have been the following? [17] "O wretches that we are and so senseless! Since the king has summoned and exhorted us to accept kind treatment if we obey him, [18] why do we take pleasure in vain resolves and venture upon a disobedience that brings death? [19] O men and brothers, should we not fear the instruments of torture and consider the threats of torments, and give up this vain opinion and this arrogance that threatens to destroy us? [20] Let us take pity on our youth and have compassion on our mother's age; [21] and let us seriously consider that if we disobey we are dead! [22] Also, divine justice will excuse us for fearing the king when we are under compulsion. [23] Why do we banish ourselves from this most pleasant life and deprive ourselves of this delightful world? [24] Let us not struggle against compulsion[c] or take hollow pride in being put to the rack. [25] Not even the law itself would arbitrarily put us to death for fearing the instruments of torture. [26] Why does such contentiousness excite us and such a fatal stubbornness please us, when we can live in peace if we obey the king?"

[27] But the youths, though about to be tortured, neither said any of these things nor even seriously considered them. [28] For they were contemptuous of the emotions and sovereign over agonies, [29] so that as soon as the tyrant had ceased counseling them to eat defiling food, all with one voice together, as from one mind, said:

9 "Why do you delay, O tyrant? For we are ready to die rather than transgress our ancestral commandments; [2] we are obviously putting our forebears to shame unless we should practice ready obedience to the

[a] Meaning of Gk uncertain
[b] Here and elsewhere in 4 Macc an instrument of torture
[c] Or *fate*

ing a single role. The image underscores their harmonious agreement (see 8.29–9.9; 13.8–18; 17.23). **5:** *Friendship* here indicates personal patronage and the promise of holding offices in the king's government (see 8.7). **9:** *You will compel me*, the king is less free than his victims, who cannot be compelled by his most coercive tortures. **14:** See 5.13n. **16–26:** The author creates a hypothetical response to throw the brothers' actual resolve into sharper relief. While it may seem reasonable enough, it is also laced with expressions of cowardice found elsewhere (e.g., Aristotle, *Virt.* 6.5–6; Sophocles, *Ant.* 58–68). If members of the audience have similarly rationalized the loosening of adherence to the Torah's commandments, the effect will be to shame and challenge them. **29:**

law and to Moses[a] our counselor. [3] Tyrant and counselor of lawlessness, in your hatred for us do not pity us more than we pity ourselves.[b] [4] For we consider this pity of yours, which insures our safety through transgression of the law, to be more grievous than death itself. [5] You are trying to terrify us by threatening us with death by torture, as though a short time ago you learned nothing from Eleazar. [6] And if the aged men of the Hebrews because of their religion lived piously[c] while enduring torture, it would be even more fitting that we young men should die despising your coercive tortures, which our aged instructor also overcame. [7] Therefore, tyrant, put us to the test; and if you take our lives because of our religion, do not suppose that you can injure us by torturing us. [8] For we, through this severe suffering and endurance, shall have the prize of virtue and shall be with God, on whose account we suffer; [9] but you, because of your bloodthirstiness toward us, will deservedly undergo from the divine justice eternal torment by fire."

[10] When they had said these things, the tyrant was not only indignant, as at those who are disobedient, but also infuriated, as at those who are ungrateful. [11] Then at his command the guards brought forward the eldest, and having torn off his tunic, they bound his hands and arms with thongs on each side. [12] When they had worn themselves out beating him with scourges, without accomplishing anything, they placed him upon the wheel. [13] When the noble youth was stretched out around this, his limbs were dislocated, [14] and with every member disjointed he denounced the tyrant, saying, [15] "Most abominable tyrant, enemy of heavenly justice, savage of mind, you are mangling me in this manner, not because I am a murderer, or as one who acts impiously, but because I protect the divine law." [16] And when the guards said, "Agree to eat so that you may be released from the tortures," [17] he replied, "You abominable lackeys, your wheel is not so powerful as to strangle my reason. Cut my limbs, burn my flesh, and twist my joints; [18] through all these tortures I will convince you that children of the Hebrews alone are invincible where virtue is concerned." [19] While he was saying these things, they spread fire under him, and while fanning the flames[b] they tightened the wheel further. [20] The wheel was completely smeared with blood, and the heap of coals was being quenched by the drippings of gore, and pieces of flesh were falling off the axles of the machine. [21] Although the ligaments joining his bones were already severed, the courageous youth, worthy of Abraham, did not groan, [22] but as though transformed by fire into immortality, he nobly endured the rackings. [23] "Imitate me, brothers," he said. "Do not leave your post in my struggle[d] or renounce our courageous family ties. [24] Fight the sacred and noble battle for religion. Thereby the just Providence of our ancestors may become merciful to our nation and take vengeance on the accursed tyrant." [25] When he had said this, the saintly youth broke the thread of life.

[26] While all were marveling at his courageous spirit, the guards brought in the next eldest, and after fitting themselves with iron gauntlets having sharp hooks, they bound

a   Other ancient authorities read *knowledge*
b   Meaning of Gk uncertain
c   Other ancient authorities read *died*
d   Other ancient authorities read *post forever*

With one voice, see 8.4n. **9.6:** *More fitting*, because the young were deemed stronger and more courageous than the elderly. **7:** The ideal sage acknowledges no injury from outside, but fears only self-inflicted injury to his or her moral determination. **8–9:** Expectation of reward or punishment after death underlies the martyrs' commitment to the Law throughout the work. **10–11:** See 8.2n. **12:** See 6.10n. **15:** The first brother refuses to accept the deviant status that the tortures are meant to inscribe on him: he is in the right, and the imperial power is acting unjustly. **17–18:** The sage refuses to allow physical maltreatment to give an enemy leverage against his or her will, thus remaining *invincible* (also 11.21,27). The claim that *children of the Hebrews alone* achieve the Greek philosophical ideal encourages the audience to prize their own distinctive heritage in the context of Greek cultural imperialism (see 7.18–19). **21:** *Did not groan*, a familiar topic of fortitude (e.g., Plutarch, *Mor.* 234A, 498E). **23–24:** Military imagery transforms the endurance of degrading torture into the battle line against the enemy that must be held at all costs, hence an opportunity to display courage. **25:** *Thread of life*, an image from Greek

him to the torture machine and catapult. [27] Before torturing him, they inquired if he were willing to eat, and they heard his noble decision.[a] [28] These leopard-like beasts tore out his sinews with the iron hands, flayed all his flesh up to his chin, and tore away his scalp. But he steadfastly endured this agony and said, [29] "How sweet is any kind of death for the religion of our ancestors!" [30] To the tyrant he said, "Do you not think, you most savage tyrant, that you are being tortured more than I, as you see the arrogant design of your tyranny being defeated by our endurance for the sake of religion? [31] I lighten my pain by the joys that come from virtue, [32] but you suffer torture by the threats that come from impiety. You will not escape, you most abominable tyrant, the judgments of the divine wrath."

10 When he too had endured a glorious death, the third was led in, and many repeatedly urged him to save himself by tasting the meat. [2] But he shouted, "Do you not know that the same father begot me as well as those who died, and the same mother bore me, and that I was brought up on the same teachings? [3] I do not renounce the noble kinship that binds me to my brothers."[b] [5] Enraged by the man's boldness, they disjointed his hands and feet with their instruments, dismembering him by prying his limbs from their sockets, [6] and breaking his fingers and arms and legs and elbows. [7] Since they were not able in any way to break his spirit,[c] they abandoned the instruments[d] and scalped him with their fingernails in a Scythian fashion. [8] They immediately brought him to the wheel, and while his vertebrae were being dislocated by this, he saw his own flesh torn all around and drops of blood flowing from his entrails. [9] When he was about to die, he said, [10] "We, most abominable tyrant, are suffering be-

cause of our godly training and virtue, [11] but you, because of your impiety and bloodthirstiness, will undergo unceasing torments."

[12] When he too had died in a manner worthy of his brothers, they dragged in the fourth, saying, [13] "As for you, do not give way to the same insanity as your brothers, but obey the king and save yourself." [14] But he said to them, "You do not have a fire hot enough to make me play the coward. [15] No—by the blessed death of my brothers, by the eternal destruction of the tyrant, and by the everlasting life of the pious, I will not renounce our noble family ties. [16] Contrive tortures, tyrant, so that you may learn from them that I am a brother to those who have just now been tortured." [17] When he heard this, the bloodthirsty, murderous, and utterly abominable Antiochus gave orders to cut out his tongue. [18] But he said, "Even if you remove my organ of speech, God hears also those who are mute. [19] See, here is my tongue; cut it off, for in spite of this you will not make our reason speechless. [20] Gladly, for the sake of God, we let our bodily members be mutilated. [21] God will visit you swiftly, for you are cutting out a tongue that has been melodious with divine hymns."

11 When he too died, after being cruelly tortured, the fifth leaped up, saying, [2] "I will not refuse, tyrant, to be tortured for the sake of virtue. [3] I have come of my own accord, so that by murdering me you will incur punishment from the heavenly justice for even

a Other ancient authorities read *having heard his noble decision, they tore him to shreds*
b Other ancient authorities add verse 4, *So if you have any instrument of torture, apply it to my body; for you cannot touch my soul, even if you wish."*
c Gk *to strangle him*
d Other ancient authorities read *they tore off his skin*

mythology. **28:** The representatives of Greek civilization become more and more like barbarians and *beasts* as the speech progresses. **29:** Compare Horace, *Odes* 3.2.13: "Sweet and fitting it is to die for one's country." **31–32:** Plato taught that virtue brought its own sweetness, and vice its own punishment (*Gorg.* 470E–471A; 507B; also Plutarch, *Mor.* 498C–E). **10.5:** *Boldness* was an ideal of Greek democracy, especially important as a means of critique where democracy was threatened or replaced by tyranny or monarchy. *Enraged*, Antiochus's lackeys share in the king's failure to master their own passions (8.2; 9.10–11). **7:** The representatives of Greek culture show themselves to be the true barbarians; the Scythians, in the vicinity of the Black Sea, had a reputation for cruelty (2 Macc 4.47; 3 Macc 7.5). **15:** The fourth brother rejects the torturers' assessment of his brothers' conduct as "madness" (Gk "manian," 10.13), asserting instead that they died a *blessed* (Gk "makarion") death because they maintained their integrity to the end. **11.1, 3:** *Of my own accord*, by seizing what little initiative is available, the

more crimes. [4] Hater of virtue, hater of human-kind, for what act of ours are you destroying us in this way? [5] Is it because[a] we revere the Creator of all things and live according to his virtuous law? [6] But these deeds deserve honors, not tortures."[b] [9] While he was saying these things, the guards bound him and dragged him to the catapult; [10] they tied him to it on his knees, and fitting iron clamps on them, they twisted his back[c] around the wedge on the wheel,[d] so that he was completely curled back like a scorpion, and all his members were disjointed. [11] In this condition, gasping for breath and in anguish of body, [12] he said, "Tyrant, they are splendid favors that you grant us against your will, because through these noble sufferings you give us an opportunity to show our endurance for the law."

[13] When he too had died, the sixth, a mere boy, was led in. When the tyrant inquired whether he was willing to eat and be released, he said, [14] "I am younger in age than my brothers, but I am their equal in mind. [15] Since to this end we were born and bred, we ought likewise to die for the same principles. [16] So if you intend to torture me for not eating defiling foods, go on torturing!" [17] When he had said this, they led him to the wheel. [18] He was carefully stretched tight upon it, his back was broken, and he was roasted[e] from underneath. [19] To his back they applied sharp spits that had been heated in the fire, and pierced his ribs so that his entrails were burned through. [20] While being tortured he said, "O contest befitting holiness, in which so many of us brothers have been summoned to an arena of sufferings for religion, and in which we have not been defeated! [21] For religious knowledge, O tyrant, is invincible. [22] I also, equipped with nobility, will die with my brothers, [23] and I my-

self will bring a great avenger upon you, you inventor of tortures and enemy of those who are truly devout. [24] We six boys have paralyzed your tyranny. [25] Since you have not been able to persuade us to change our mind or to force us to eat defiling foods, is not this your downfall? [26] Your fire is cold to us, and the catapults painless, and your violence powerless. [27] For it is not the guards of the tyrant but those of the divine law that are set over us; therefore, unconquered, we hold fast to reason."

12 When he too, thrown into the caldron, had died a blessed death, the seventh and youngest of all came forward. [2] Even though the tyrant had been vehemently reproached by the brothers, he felt strong compassion for this child when he saw that he was already in fetters. He summoned him to come nearer and tried to persuade him, saying, [3] "You see the result of your brothers' stupidity, for they died in torments because of their disobedience. [4] You too, if you do not obey, will be miserably tortured and die before your time, [5] but if you yield to persuasion you will be my friend and a leader in the government of the kingdom." [6] When he had thus appealed to him, he sent for the boy's mother to show compassion on her who had been bereaved of so many sons and to influence her to persuade the surviving son to obey and save himself.

---

[a] Other ancient authorities read *Or does it seem evil to you that*

[b] Other authorities add verses 7 and 8, [7]*If you but understood human feelings and had hope of salvation from God—* [8]*but, as it is, you are a stranger to God and persecute those who serve him."*

[c] Gk *loins*

[d] Meaning of Gk uncertain

[e] Other ancient authorities add *by fire*

fifth brother comes forward as a contender rather than a victim. **4:** The charge of hatred of humanity, frequently leveled against the Jews by those who held the Jewish law to be xenophobic (see 2.14n.), is turned back upon those who would persecute the Jews on account of their different religion and way of life. **6:** See 9.15n. **12:** The ideal sage engages hardships as a means of demonstrating commitment to virtue. These are the only *favors* the pious Jews will accept from Antiochus (contrast 8.6–7). **20:** *Contest . . . arena*, see 6.10n. *Not been defeated*, since their wills could not be corrupted. **24–25:** Antiochus has failed in his primary goal of forcing assimilation. **26:** *Fire is cold*, in the sense of powerless or ineffective to subvert the Judeans' will. The martyrs have not, however, extinguished the awareness of pain, as a Stoic might strive to do (11.11; 14.9–10). **12.2:** *Vehemently reproached*, better, "frightfully abused." With skillful irony, the author suggests that Antiochus is the one who has been beaten down here. **6:** Although the author presents Antiochus as acting out of *compassion* here, persuading the last brother to surrender would also effectively cancel his previous seven defeats. **7:** The use of the *Hebrew*

[7] But when his mother had exhorted him in the Hebrew language, as we shall tell a little later, [8] he said, "Let me loose, let me speak to the king and to all his friends that are with him." [9] Extremely pleased by the boy's declaration, they freed him at once. [10] Running to the nearest of the braziers, [11] he said, "You profane tyrant, most impious of all the wicked, since you have received good things and also your kingdom from God, were you not ashamed to murder his servants and torture on the wheel those who practice religion? [12] Because of this, justice has laid up for you intense and eternal fire and tortures, and these throughout all time[a] will never let you go. [13] As a man, were you not ashamed, you most savage beast, to cut out the tongues of men who have feelings like yours and are made of the same elements as you, and to maltreat and torture them in this way? [14] Surely they by dying nobly fulfilled their service to God, but you will wail bitterly for having killed without cause the contestants for virtue." [15] Then because he too was about to die, he said, [16] "I do not desert the excellent example[b] of my brothers, [17] and I call on the God of our ancestors to be merciful to our nation;[c] [18] but on you he will take vengeance both in this present life and when you are dead." [19] After he had uttered these imprecations, he flung himself into the braziers and so ended his life.[d]

13 Since, then, the seven brothers despised sufferings even unto death, everyone must concede that devout reason is sovereign over the emotions. [2] For if they had been slaves to their emotions and had eaten defiling food, we would say that they had been conquered by these emotions. [3] But in fact it was not so. Instead, by reason, which is praised before God, they prevailed over their emotions. [4] The supremacy of the mind over these cannot be overlooked, for the brothers[e] mastered both emotions and pains. [5] How then can one fail to confess the sovereignty of right reason over emotion in those who were not turned back by fiery agonies? [6] For just as towers jutting out over harbors hold back the threatening waves and make it calm for those who sail into the inner basin, [7] so the seven-towered right reason of the youths, by fortifying the harbor of religion, conquered the tempest of the emotions. [8] For they constituted a holy chorus of religion and encouraged one another, saying, [9] "Brothers, let us die like brothers for the sake of the law; let us imitate the three youths in Assyria who despised the same ordeal of the furnace. [10] Let us not be cowardly in the demonstration of our piety." [11] While one said, "Courage, brother," another said, "Bear up nobly," [12] and another reminded them, "Remember whence you came, and the father by whose hand Isaac would have submitted to being slain for the sake of religion." [13] Each of them and all of them together looking at one another, cheerful and undaunted, said, "Let us with all our hearts consecrate

---

a Gk throughout the whole age
b Other ancient authorities read the witness
c Other ancient authorities read my race
d Gk and so gave up; other ancient authorities read gave up his spirit or his soul
e Gk they

---

language here both hides the meaning of her speech from the king and is an act of resistance to Greek imperialism. When the speech is actually recounted a little later, however, the mother speaks to all her sons during Eleazar's ordeal (16.15–25). **11, 13:** The last brother charges Antiochus with injustice against the God who gave him his authority (cf. Dan 4:25), since he has used that power to harm God's loyal clients rather than benefit them and serve God's cause. He also condemns Antiochus for violating the universal bond of humanity that unites all people by brutally torturing fellow human beings. The charges that Jews do not give the gods their due and violate the universal bond of humanity are thus again turned back upon the dominant culture. **19:** The youngest brother seizes what little control he can by committing suicide; see 17.1n. Contrast 2 Macc 7.39–40.

13.1–14.10: Reflection on the seven brothers' example. 13.1–5: See 3.19n. **8:** The brothers' harmony in their collective commitment to the Torah helps each individually to remain steadfast. Such harmony (see 8.4n.) was considered a valuable civic virtue, since it enhanced social reinforcement of the group's norms. **9:** Dan 3 (esp. 3.17–18). The three youths, together with Daniel himself (Dan 6), were prototypes of resistance against a tyrant's coercive threats and laws for the sake of maintaining their piety; see also 16.21; 18.12–13. **12:** Gen 22.1–19. The mother will also be compared to Abraham, with whom she shared a willingness to put obedience to God's command above the life of her children (14.20; 15.28). **13:** The brothers regard obedience to God to the point of death

ourselves to God, who gave us our lives,[a] and let us use our bodies as a bulwark for the law. [14] Let us not fear him who thinks he is killing us, [15] for great is the struggle of the soul and the danger of eternal torment lying before those who transgress the commandment of God. [16] Therefore let us put on the full armor of self-control, which is divine reason. [17] For if we so die,[b] Abraham and Isaac and Jacob will welcome us, and all the fathers will praise us." [18] Those who were left behind said to each of the brothers who were being dragged away, "Do not put us to shame, brother, or betray the brothers who have died before us."

[19] You are not ignorant of the affection of family ties, which the divine and all-wise Providence has bequeathed through the fathers to their descendants and which was implanted in the mother's womb. [20] There each of the brothers spent the same length of time and was shaped during the same period of time; and growing from the same blood and through the same life, they were brought to the light of day. [21] When they were born after an equal time of gestation, they drank milk from the same fountains. From such embraces brotherly-loving souls are nourished; [22] and they grow stronger from this common nurture and daily companionship, and from both general education and our discipline in the law of God.

[23] Therefore, when sympathy and brotherly affection had been so established, the brothers were the more sympathetic to one another. [24] Since they had been educated by the same law and trained in the same virtues and brought up in right living, they loved one another all the more. [25] A common zeal for nobility strengthened their goodwill toward

one another, and their concord, [26] because they could make their brotherly love more fervent with the aid of their religion. [27] But although nature and companionship and virtuous habits had augmented the affection of family ties, those who were left endured for the sake of religion, while watching their brothers being maltreated and tortured to death.

14 Furthermore, they encouraged them to face the torture, so that they not only despised their agonies, but also mastered the emotions of brotherly love.

[2] O reason,[c] more royal than kings and freer than the free! [3] O sacred and harmonious concord of the seven brothers on behalf of religion! [4] None of the seven youths proved coward or shrank from death, [5] but all of them, as though running the course toward immortality, hastened to death by torture. [6] Just as the hands and feet are moved in harmony with the guidance of the mind, so those holy youths, as though moved by an immortal spirit of devotion, agreed to go to death for its sake. [7] O most holy seven, brothers in harmony! For just as the seven days of creation move in choral dance around religion, [8] so these youths, forming a chorus, encircled the sevenfold fear of tortures and dissolved it. [9] Even now, we ourselves shudder as we hear of the suffering of these young men; they not only saw what was happening, not only heard the direct word of threat, but also bore the sufferings patiently, and in agonies of fire at that. [10] What could

a Or *souls*

b Other ancient authorities read *suffer*

c Or *O minds*

a fitting return of gratitude for the gift of life itself; see also 16.18–19. **14:** *Who thinks he is killing,* see 9.7n.; cf. Mt 10.28. **19–26:** Almost every detail in the author's discussion of the love between siblings has a counterpart in Greco-Roman philosophical discussions of this topic, another indication of how immersed the author was in Greek culture and learning while remaining fully committed to the Jewish way of life. **13.27–14.1:** Because of their training in the Torah, the brothers are able to strengthen rather than weaken each other's resolve, enabling one another to walk in line with virtue, thus fulfilling the Aristotelian ideal of friendship. **14.2:** The sage cannot be compelled to sacrifice virtue, bowing to any external pressure, and so remains *free* and exercises *royal* self-governance. **7:** *Seven* was mystically associated with the harmony of God's creation and created order (Philo, *Opif.* 90–128). **8:** *Chorus,* see 8.4n. and 13.8n. **9:** The author has justifiable confidence in his power of vivid description to make his audience squirm. He has used this rhetorical technique in order to heighten the audience's appreciation of the sensations the martyrs withstood, so as to embolden them to remain steadfast in their commitment to the Jewish way of life in the face of far less daunting difficulties.

be more excruciatingly painful than this? For the power of fire is intense and swift, and it consumed their bodies quickly.

[11] Do not consider it amazing that reason had full command over these men in their tortures, since the mind of woman despised even more diverse agonies, [12] for the mother of the seven young men bore up under the rackings of each one of her children.

[13] Observe how complex is a mother's love for her children, which draws everything toward an emotion felt in her inmost parts. [14] Even unreasoning animals, as well as human beings, have a sympathy and parental love for their offspring. [15] For example, among birds, the ones that are tame protect their young by building on the housetops, [16] and the others, by building at the tops of mountains and the depths of chasms, in holes of trees, and on tree-tops, hatch the nestlings and ward off the intruder. [17] If they are not able to keep the intruder[a] away, they do what they can to help their young by flying in circles around them in the anguish of love, warning them with their own calls. [18] And why is it necessary to demonstrate sympathy for children by the example of unreasoning animals, [19] since even bees at the time for making honeycombs defend themselves against intruders and, as though with an iron dart, sting those who approach their hive and defend it even to the death? [20] But sympathy for her children did not sway the mother of the young men; she was of the same mind as Abraham.

15 O reason of the children, tyrant over the emotions! O religion, more desirable to the mother than her children! [2] Two courses were open to this mother, that of religion, and that of preserving her seven sons for a time, as the tyrant had promised. [3] She loved religion more, the religion that preserves them for eternal life according to God's promise.[b]

[4] In what manner might I express the emotions of parents who love their children? We impress upon the character of a small child a wondrous likeness both of mind and of form. Especially is this true of mothers, who because of their birth pangs have a deeper sympathy toward their offspring than do the fathers. [5] Considering that mothers are the weaker sex and give birth to many, they are more devoted to their children.[c] [6] The mother of the seven boys, more than any other mother, loved her children. In seven pregnancies she had implanted in herself tender love toward them, [7] and because of the many pains she suffered with each of them she had sympathy for them; [8] yet because of the fear of God she disdained the temporary safety of her children. [9] Not only so, but also because of the nobility of her sons and their ready obedience to the law, she felt a greater tenderness toward them. [10] For they were righteous and self-controlled and brave and magnanimous, and loved their brothers and their mother, so that they obeyed her even to death in keeping the ordinances.

[11] Nevertheless, though so many factors influenced the mother to suffer with them out of love for her children, in the case of none of them were the various tortures strong enough to pervert her reason. [12] But each child separately and all of them together the mother urged on to death for religion's sake. [13] O sacred nature and affection of parental love, yearning of parents toward offspring, nurture and indomitable suffering by mothers! [14] This mother, who saw them tortured and burned one by one, because of religion

a   Gk *it*
b   Gk *according to God*
c   Or *For to the degree that mothers are weaker and the more children they bear, the more they are devoted to their children.*

14.11–17.6: The example of the mother and reflection. The climactic example of the Torah's ability to empower the mind for mastery of the emotions is the mother of the seven brothers. **14.11:** *Since the mind of woman*, perhaps more accurately, "since even the mind of a woman." Women were generally held to be more prone to yield to the emotions and sensations than men (Aristotle, *Pol.* 1.13; Philo, *Leg. all.* 2.44–50), with the result that a female's mastery of such overwhelming experiences proves the efficacy of the Torah as a philosophical way of life beyond contradiction. **13–20:** The author's description of love for offspring once again shares many details with Greco-Roman writings on the topic; see 13.19–26n. **20:** See 13.12n. **15.1:** *O reason . . . O religion . . .!* The author makes extensive use of "apostrophe" (direct address to some ideal or person not physically present) throughout his oration in order to heighten its emotionally evocative power. **2–3:** *For a time . . . for eternal*

did not change her attitude. [15] She watched the flesh of her children being consumed by fire, their toes and fingers scattered[a] on the ground, and the flesh of the head to the chin exposed like masks.

[16] O mother, tried now by more bitter pains than even the birth pangs you suffered for them! [17] O woman, who alone gave birth to such complete devotion! [18] When the firstborn breathed his last, it did not turn you aside, nor when the second in torments looked at you piteously nor when the third expired; [19] nor did you weep when you looked at the eyes of each one in his tortures gazing boldly at the same agonies, and saw in their nostrils the signs of the approach of death. [20] When you saw the flesh of children burned upon the flesh of other children, severed hands upon hands, scalped heads upon heads, and corpses fallen on other corpses, and when you saw the place filled with many spectators of the torturings, you did not shed tears. [21] Neither the melodies of sirens nor the songs of swans attract the attention of their hearers as did the voices of the children in torture calling to their mother. [22] How great and how many torments the mother then suffered as her sons were tortured on the wheel and with the hot irons! [23] But devout reason, giving her heart a man's courage in the very midst of her emotions, strengthened her to disregard, for the time, her parental love.

[24] Although she witnessed the destruction of seven children and the ingenious and various rackings, this noble mother disregarded all these[b] because of faith in God. [25] For as in the council chamber of her own soul she saw mighty advocates—nature, family, parental love, and the rackings of her children— [26] this

mother held two ballots, one bearing death and the other deliverance for her children. [27] She did not approve the deliverance that would preserve the seven sons for a short time, [28] but as the daughter of God-fearing Abraham she remembered his fortitude.

[29] O mother of the nation, vindicator of the law and champion of religion, who carried away the prize of the contest in your heart! [30] O more noble than males in steadfastness, and more courageous than men in endurance! [31] Just as Noah's ark, carrying the world in the universal flood, stoutly endured the waves, [32] so you, O guardian of the law, overwhelmed from every side by the flood of your emotions and the violent winds, the torture of your sons, endured nobly and withstood the wintry storms that assail religion.

16 If, then, a woman, advanced in years and mother of seven sons, endured seeing her children tortured to death, it must be admitted that devout reason is sovereign over the emotions. [2] Thus I have demonstrated not only that men have ruled over the emotions, but also that a woman has despised the fiercest tortures. [3] The lions surrounding Daniel were not so savage, nor was the raging fiery furnace of Mishael so intensely hot, as was her innate parental love, inflamed as she saw her seven sons tortured in such varied ways. [4] But the mother quenched so many and such great emotions by devout reason.

[5] Consider this also: If this woman, though a mother, had been fainthearted, she would

---

[a] Or *quivering*

[b] Other ancient authorities read *having bidden them farewell, surrendered them*

---

life, see 9.8–9n. **4–7:** See 14.11n.; 14.13–20n. **8:** See 9.8–9n. **16–17:** *O mother . . . O woman,* see 15.1n. **18–22:** The author provides a concentrated summary of the brothers' sufferings to sharpen the audience's impression of the assaults that tortured the mother, pressing upon her to cry out and beg her sons to save themselves (see 12.6; 16.12). **19:** *Gazing boldly,* literally, "gazing bull-like," a classical Greek expression (Aristophanes, *Ran.* 804; Plato, *Phaed.* 1176). **21:** *The melodies of sirens* were so irresistible they lured sailors to their death (Homer, *Od.* 12.44–52), and *swans* (which do not sing) were believed to sing a beautiful song just before they died. **26:** *Two ballots,* a judicial image, one for acquittal, one for condemnation. **28:** See 13.12n. **30:** *More courageous than men,* an especially poignant pun in Greek where "courageous" ("andreia") is derived from the noun for "male human being" ("aner, andros"), like English "manly." See also 15.23; 16.14. Plutarch celebrates the stories of women who exemplified courage greater than or equal to men ("On the Bravery of Women," *Mor.* 242E–263C), with whose stories the mother's story shares several traits. **31–32:** See 7.1–3n. Philo gives a similar interpretation of Noah's ark (*Quaest. in Gen.* 2.18). **16.1–4:** See 3.19n. **2:** *Not only that men . . . but also that a woman,* see 14.11n. **3:**

have mourned over them and perhaps spoken as follows: [6] "O how wretched am I and many times unhappy! After bearing seven children, I am now the mother of none! [7] O seven childbirths all in vain, seven profitless pregnancies, fruitless nurturings and wretched nursings! [8] In vain, my sons, I endured many birth pangs for you, and the more grievous anxieties of your upbringing. [9] Alas for my children, some unmarried, others married and without offspring.[a] I shall not see your children or have the happiness of being called grandmother. [10] Alas, I who had so many and beautiful children am a widow and alone, with many sorrows.[b] [11] And when I die, I shall have none of my sons to bury me."

[12] Yet that holy and God-fearing mother did not wail with such a lament for any of them, nor did she dissuade any of them from dying, nor did she grieve as they were dying. [13] On the contrary, as though having a mind like adamant and giving rebirth for immortality to the whole number of her sons, she implored them and urged them on to death for the sake of religion. [14] O mother, soldier of God in the cause of religion, elder and woman! By steadfastness you have conquered even a tyrant, and in word and deed you have proved more powerful than a man. [15] For when you and your sons were arrested together, you stood and watched Eleazar being tortured, and said to your sons in the Hebrew language, [16] "My sons, noble is the contest to which you are called to bear witness for the nation. Fight zealously for our ancestral law. [17] For it would be shameful if, while an aged man endures such agonies for the sake of religion, you young men were to be terrified by

tortures. [18] Remember that it is through God that you have had a share in the world and have enjoyed life, [19] and therefore you ought to endure any suffering for the sake of God. [20] For his sake also our father Abraham was zealous to sacrifice his son Isaac, the ancestor of our nation; and when Isaac saw his father's hand wielding a knife[c] and descending upon him, he did not cower. [21] Daniel the righteous was thrown to the lions, and Hananiah, Azariah, and Mishael were hurled into the fiery furnace and endured it for the sake of God. [22] You too must have the same faith in God and not be grieved. [23] It is unreasonable for people who have religious knowledge not to withstand pain."

[24] By these words the mother of the seven encouraged and persuaded each of her sons to die rather than violate God's commandment. [25] They knew also that those who die for the sake of God live to God, as do Abraham and Isaac and Jacob and all the patriarchs.

17 Some of the guards said that when she also was about to be seized and put to death she threw herself into the flames so that no one might touch her body.

[2] O mother, who with your seven sons nullified the violence of the tyrant, frustrated his evil designs, and showed the courage of your faith! [3] Nobly set like a roof on the pillars of your sons, you held firm and unswerving against the earthquake of the tortures. [4] Take courage, therefore, O holy-minded mother,

a   Gk *without benefit*
b   Or *much to be pitied*
c   Gk *sword*

Daniel, Dan 6.1–24. *Mishael*, also called Meshach, Dan 1.7; 3.1–30. **5–11**: As for the brothers (8.16–26), the author provides a speech reflective of the mind-set that the mother refused to adopt. Almost every element in the hypothetical lament composed for the mother reflects the laments of bereaved mothers in the tragedies of Euripides (see especially *Tro.* 380–82, 473–88, 503–505, 758–60). Having raised many children only to lose them in a single struggle, the mother is worthy of comparison with Queen Hecuba of Troy. **12–13**: The author stresses, however, that despite similar loss she did not grieve like Hecuba, since she considered the faithful deaths of her sons the best course for them and for her. Her pregnancies were not profitless (v. 7) since she gave *rebirth for immortality* to all her sons. *Dissuade*, see 12.6–7. *Adamant,* here a hard metal or diamond. **15**: *Hebrew*, see 12.7n. **16**: *Noble . . . contest*, see 6.10n. The martyrs *bear witness* in this public arena to the value of the Jewish way of life and the nation's character. *Fight zealously*, again turning the passive experience of victimization into active resistance. **18–19**: See 13.12–13n. **20**: *Abraham . . . Isaac*, Gen 22.1–19. **21**: *Daniel . . . Mishael*, see 13.9n.; 16.3n. **22**: *Have the same faith*, or "show the same loyalty toward God." **25**: See 7.19n.; 9.8–9n. **17.1**: The mother commits suicide rather than allow herself to be inappropriately handled by other men. Suicide under such circumstances

maintaining firm an enduring hope in God. [5] The moon in heaven, with the stars, does not stand so august as you, who, after lighting the way of your star-like seven sons to piety, stand in honor before God and are firmly set in heaven with them. [6] For your children were true descendants of father Abraham.[a]

[7] If it were possible for us to paint the history of your religion as an artist might, would not those who first beheld it have shuddered as they saw the mother of the seven children enduring their varied tortures to death for the sake of religion? [8] Indeed it would be proper to inscribe on their tomb these words as a reminder to the people of our nation:[b] [9] "Here lie buried an aged priest and an aged woman and seven sons, because of the violence of the tyrant who wished to destroy the way of life of the Hebrews. [10] They vindicated their nation, looking to God and enduring torture even to death."

[11] Truly the contest in which they were engaged was divine, [12] for on that day virtue gave the awards and tested them for their endurance. The prize was immortality in endless life. [13] Eleazar was the first contestant, the mother of the seven sons entered the competition, and the brothers contended. [14] The tyrant was the antagonist, and the world and the human race were the spectators. [15] Reverence for God was victor and gave the crown to its own athletes. [16] Who did not admire the athletes of the divine[c] legislation? Who were not amazed? [17] The tyrant himself and all his council marveled at their[d] endurance, [18] because

of which they now stand before the divine throne and live the life of eternal blessedness. [19] For Moses says, "All who are consecrated are under your hands." [20] These, then, who have been consecrated for the sake of God,[e] are honored, not only with this honor, but also by the fact that because of them our enemies did not rule over our nation, [21] the tyrant was punished, and the homeland purified—they having become, as it were, a ransom for the sin of our nation. [22] And through the blood of those devout ones and their death as an atoning sacrifice, divine Providence preserved Israel that previously had been mistreated.

[23] For the tyrant Antiochus, when he saw the courage of their virtue and their endurance under the tortures, proclaimed them to his soldiers as an example for their own endurance, [24] and this made them brave and courageous for infantry battle and siege, and he ravaged and conquered all his enemies.

18 O Israelite children, offspring of the seed of Abraham, obey this law and exercise piety in every way, [2] knowing that devout reason is master of all emotions, not only of sufferings from within, but also of those from without.

[a] Gk For your childbearing was from Abraham the father; other ancient authorities read For… Abraham the servant
[b] Or as a memorial to the heroes of our people
[c] Other ancient authorities read true
[d] Other ancient authorities add virtue and
[e] Other ancient authorities lack for the sake of God

(see also 12.19) was considered noble (1 Sam 31.1–6; 2 Macc 14.41–46; Josephus, J.W. 7.324–34, 377; Plutarch, Mor. 253D-E). 5: The hearers are invited to imagine the martyrs enjoying their eternal reward, confirming their hope.
17.7–18.24: Epilogue. 17.7–18.5: Summary of the martyrs' accomplishments and exhortation. 17.7: Jurists were known to bring a painting of the crime into a courtroom to sway a jury's emotions (Quintilian, Inst. 6.1.32), although the author does not regard this as possible here, whether because of scruples about images (Ex 20.4) or good taste. Religion, better "piety." 8–10: Literary epitaphs often appear in Greek speeches about the dead. 11–16: See 6.10n. 20–22: The martyrs' deaths are ennobled further by stressing the benefit they brought to their nation (see also 1.11; 18.4). 19: Deut 33.3. 21–22: Atoning sacrifice translates the Greek "hilasterion" (perhaps better "propitiation"), a term also used in Rom 3.25 to interpret the significance of a violent death in obedience to God's covenant. See 6.28–29n. 23–24: The idea of becoming an example that even one's enemies would recognize and admire appears elsewhere; while historically improbable in this case, it is nevertheless rhetorically effective. Ravaged and conquered, a rhetorical flourish meant to underscore the power of the martyrs' example of courage. In fact, Antiochus suffered crushing defeat in the East shortly after leaving Jerusalem (see 1 Macc 6.1–4; 2 Macc 9.1), as 18.5 implies. 18.1–2: The philosophical demonstration (18.2) ultimately serves a protreptic goal, namely promoting continued or intensified commitment to the Jewish way of life, particular the commandments of the Torah. An exhortation to imitate the virtuous conduct of the fallen is common in eulogistic speeches.

[3] Therefore those who gave over their bodies in suffering for the sake of religion were not only admired by mortals, but also were deemed worthy to share in a divine inheritance. [4] Because of them the nation gained peace, and by reviving observance of the law in the homeland they ravaged the enemy. [5] The tyrant Antiochus was both punished on earth and is being chastised after his death. Since in no way whatever was he able to compel the Israelites to become pagans and to abandon their ancestral customs, he left Jerusalem and marched against the Persians.

[6] The mother of seven sons expressed also these principles to her children: [7] "I was a pure virgin and did not go outside my father's house; but I guarded the rib from which woman was made.[a] [8] No seducer corrupted me on a desert plain, nor did the destroyer, the deceitful serpent, defile the purity of my virginity. [9] In the time of my maturity I remained with my husband, and when these sons had grown up their father died. A happy man was he, who lived out his life with good children, and did not have the grief of bereavement. [10] While he was still with you, he taught you the law and the prophets. [11] He read to you about Abel slain by Cain, and Isaac who was offered as a burnt offering, and about Joseph in prison. [12] He told you of the zeal of Phinehas, and he taught you about Hananiah, Azariah, and Mishael in the fire.

[13] He praised Daniel in the den of the lions and blessed him. [14] He reminded you of the scripture of Isaiah, which says, 'Even though you go through the fire, the flame shall not consume you.' [15] He sang to you songs of the psalmist David, who said, 'Many are the afflictions of the righteous.' [16] He recounted to you Solomon's proverb, 'There is a tree of life for those who do his will.' [17] He confirmed the query of Ezekiel, 'Shall these dry bones live?' [18] For he did not forget to teach you the song that Moses taught, which says, [19] 'I kill and I make alive: this is your life and the length of your days.'"

[20] O bitter was that day—and yet not bitter—when that bitter tyrant of the Greeks quenched fire with fire in his cruel caldrons, and in his burning rage brought those seven sons of the daughter of Abraham to the catapult and back again to more[b] tortures, [21] pierced the pupils of their eyes and cut out their tongues, and put them to death with various tortures. [22] For these crimes divine justice pursued and will pursue the accursed tyrant. [23] But the sons of Abraham with their victorious mother are gathered together into the chorus of the fathers, and have received pure and immortal[c] souls from God, [24] to whom be glory forever and ever. Amen.

[a] Gk the rib that was built
[b] Other ancient authorities read to all his
[c] Other ancient authorities read victorious

18.6–19: The mother's testimony to feminine virtue and additional exhortation. This second speech of the mother is possibly a later addition, but nevertheless one well crafted to suit the larger text. **7–9a:** Though celebrated mainly for her courage, the mother here reflects on her careful preservation throughout her life of her modesty and chastity, quintessential female virtues in the ancient world. **7:** Rib, Gen 2.22. **8:** Desert plain, Deut 22.25–27. Serpent, Gen 3.13; cf. 2 Cor 11.2–3. **10:** The father laudably fulfilled the obligations to teach his children (Deut 4.9; 6.7; 11.19) the scriptures (the law and the prophets). **11:** As Abel was attacked by Cain (Gen 4.8), so the ungodly continue to assault the pious. Isaac, Gen 22.1–19. Joseph endured prison rather than transgress virtue (Gen 39.1–23). **12a:** Phinehas exemplified zeal for the Torah and watchfulness against assimilation (Num 25.1–9; Sir 45.23–24; 1 Macc 2.26, 54). **12b:** Hananiah . . . Daniel, see 13.9n. **14–19:** The quotations from scripture encourage perseverance in hardship for the sake of covenant loyalty. **14:** Isa 43.2. The firm conviction in an afterlife allows the promise to remain true in an ultimate sense. **15:** Ps 34.19. The context may be important and assumed, as the constant refrain of this psalm speaks of God's deliverance of the righteous from every trial (Ps 34.4, 6, 7, 17, 19). **16:** Prov 3.18, slightly altered. **17:** Ezek 37.2–3, as appropriate a question in Ezekiel's valley as in the courtyard where the tortures occurred. Even those who were "burned to the very bones" (6.26) will not fail to enjoy God's reward. **18:** Song, Deut 31.30–32.44. **19:** Deut 32.39; 30.20. The word order is crucial and climactic: God will make alive those righteous whom he has permitted to be killed. Length of your days is now transferred to eternity.

18.20–24: Conclusion. 18.20: Speaking of a tyrant of the Greeks is a bitterly ironic criticism of the imperialism of Alexander the Great and his successors, since the Greeks prized themselves on perfecting democracy. **22–24:** The fates after death of martyrs and tyrant, foundational to the martyrs' resistance, are here confirmed in the author's closing sentences. Now the chorus (see 8.4n.) is in heaven.

THE NEW TESTAMENT

The new covenant
commonly called
The New Testament of our
Lord and Savior Jesus Christ

New Revised Standard Version

INTRODUCTION TO THE GOSPELS

THE LITERARY GENRE OF THE GOSPELS

The English word "gospel" originally meant "good news," and it is an exact translation of the Gk word *euangelion* (from which the English word "evangelist" is derived). The opening of Mark's Gospel, "The beginning of the good news [or "gospel"] of Jesus Christ, the Son of God" (1.1), uses the word "gospel" for the message about salvation through Jesus. In the New Testament the word "gospel" (Gk *euangelion*) refers either to the act of preaching (1 Thess 1.5, NRSV: "our message of the gospel") or its content (Acts 15.7, NRSV: "message of the good news"; 20.24, NRSV: "good news"). Outside the New Testament and other early Christian writings, the term is used for happy announcements, such as a military victory, the birth of a son, or a wedding. An inscription from 9 BCE uses the noun (in the plural) to refer to the past event of the birth of the Roman emperor Augustus: "the birthday of the god was for the world the beginning of 'joyful messages' which have gone forth because of him." The idea that an emperor's birth, coming of age, and ascent to the throne was "good news" for the world would have come to mind when Christian missionaries came preaching "good news." Not until the mid-second century CE was the word for "gospel" used of a literary genre (Justin Martyr, *Dialogue with Trypho* 10.2; Irenaeus, *Adv. Haer.* 50.26.6).

The use of the word "gospel" in Mark's introduction presumably led to its being adopted as the designation for written accounts of the ministry, teaching, death, and resurrection of Jesus. Short formulas in Paul's letters show that the "good news" of early preaching focused on the death, resurrection, and exaltation of Jesus (1 Thess 1.9–10; Rom 1.2–4; 1 Cor 15.3–5). Mark expanded this to include Jesus' own preaching of the kingdom of God (Mk 1.14–15). So far as we know, Mark was the first to create a distinctive literary form by combining early Christian preaching about Jesus with a narrative account of Jesus' life and ministry. Writings that some scholars date earlier than Mark are collections of sayings with little or no narrative framework.

By presenting a narrative about Jesus as the basis of Christian preaching (see Lk 1.1–4), the Gospel writers (the "evangelists") assume that the life of Jesus provides evidence to support Christian beliefs about him. By providing an account of Jesus from the time of his emergence on the public stage through his trial and death, Mark presents a "life" (Gk *bios*) of his subject. The ancient *bios* should not be confused with a modern biography, which explicates the subject's origins, family, cultural influences, and character development, and tends to emphasize uniqueness and individuality. Ancient writers often characterized persons as types, and the narratives of their lives reflected a view that individuals had fixed characters from birth rather than personalities that developed through life.

Still, scholars disagree over the extent to which the Gospels follow conventions of ancient biography. Because the story of Jesus concerns a figure with a crucial place in the history of God's relationship with Israel, it is closer to Jewish accounts of Moses or a prophet like Elijah than to typical Greek and Roman biographies of rulers or philosophers (e.g., Xenophon, *Agesilaus*; Isocrates, *Evagoras*; Tacitus, *Agricola*; Lucian, *Demonax*), which had a wider scope, including an account of the preliminary education of the subject of the biography. Greco-Roman biographies were addressed to a social and literary elite, which may explain why the Gospels, addressed to a much broader audience, do not match them very closely. Philo's *Life of Moses* adopts a Hellenistic-style laudatory biography for a Jewish subject. Echoes of the life of Moses as related in the book of Exodus and other Jewish sources appear in Matthew's version of the birth and infancy of Jesus (Mt 1–2).

Since the genre "biography" emerged from Greek historical writing, the question of whether the Gospels belong to this genre often involves a prior judgment concerning their historical plausibility. Scholars who reject biography as a description of the Gospels often overemphasize the ideological or legendary elements found in the narratives. They prefer to read the Gospels as etiological legends that explain the emergence of a new religion or as ideological representations of the Christology of particular early Christian communities. Such writings do not intend to provide historical information about their subject. Rather, they operate like myths and symbols to support Christian beliefs and practices.

Second-century CE authors, on the other hand, both adherents of Christianity like Justin Martyr and opponents like Celsus, presumed that the evangelists intended to provide information. Justin Martyr's designation of the Gospels as "memoirs" (Gk *hypomnemata*; *1 Apology* 1.67.3) suggests something less than a full literary biography, something more like a gathering of notes about the subject and his teaching. This perception may have been enhanced by the fact that early Christians disseminated their writings using a codex (similar to a bound book) rather than a scroll. Though some modern readers think of the codex as a technological advance over the scroll, the ancients did not. Serious literary works were copied onto scrolls. Notes, preliminary drafts, and all sorts of records were kept in codices. Thus their physical appearance would suggest to an ancient reader that the Gospels were more educational handbooks than examples of high literary art. Papias's comment that Mark is "not in order" (Eusebius, *Hist. eccl.* 3.39.5) shows that even some Christian readers considered it an unfinished composition. Papias also noted that Matthew was a more polished work (Eusebius, *Hist. eccl.* 3.39.16). Luke's prologue states that he intends to correct the deficiencies in earlier accounts (1.1–4). Such comments indicate that Mark's earliest readers treated the Gospel as a rough life of Jesus. A "biography" of this type naturally invited expansions in content and revisions of style like those that Matthew and Luke subsequently undertook.

THE SOURCES OF THE GOSPELS

A historical genre does not necessarily guarantee historical accuracy or reliability, and neither the evangelists nor their first readers engaged in historical analysis. Their aim was to confirm Christian faith (Lk 1.4; Jn 20.31). Scholars generally agree that the Gospels were written forty to sixty years after the death of Jesus. They thus do not present eyewitness or contemporary accounts of Jesus' life and teaching. Even the language has changed. Though Greek had become the common language used between groups whose primary languages were different in the eastern Roman Empire, and inscriptions and fragments of Greek translations of the Hebrew Bible show that Greek was used even among Jews within Judea, Jesus, his disciples, and the crowds would have spoken Aramaic, a Semitic language closely related to Hebrew, which it had replaced as the principal spoken language of Palestine. Despite scholarly efforts to detect an underlying Aramaic original for Mark or Matthew, it is probable that all the evangelists wrote in the common ("koine") Greek of their day. Further, the vast majority of Hebrew Bible citations in the New Testament are taken from the Greek translation of the Hebrew Bible (the Septuagint).

Large sections of Matthew, Mark, and Luke repeat stories about and sayings of Jesus in nearly identical words. Hence these three Gospels are referred to as the "Synoptic" Gospels (from Gk *synoptikos*, "viewed together"). On a linguistic level, both Luke and Matthew improve on Mark's style, smoothing out inelegant expressions and repetitions. Luke eliminates Mark's characteristic use of parataxis (one short phrase following another without indicating how they are related) by employing balancing particles and subordinate clauses. Matthew follows Mark's outline, though the insertion of considerable sections of discourse material may obscure that relationship for the casual reader. Luke knows most of Mark but has no parallels to Mk 6.45–8.26; whether Luke chose to omit this section or had a different version of Mark remains unclear. Detailed analysis of the traditions shared by Matthew, Mark, and Luke provides strong support for the view that Mark was the earliest Gospel. But, given its rough, draftlike composition, both Matthew and Luke revised it extensively.

Further study of additional material shared by Matthew and Luke shows a number of close verbal parallels in passages such as the temptation of Jesus (Mt 4.2–11; Lk 4.2–13), the Beatitudes (Lk 6.20–23; Mt 5.3,6,4,11–12), the parable of the lost sheep (Lk 15.4–7; Mt 18.12–14), and the Lord's Prayer (Lk 11.2–4; Mt 6.9–13). These parallels include various types of sayings, controversy stories, and parables. Scholars have hypothesized that a collection of such material must have been circulating in the early churches, and they have designated it with the symbol "Q," from the German *Quelle* ("source"). In 1945, a library of religious treatises in Coptic was discovered near Nag Hammadi in Egypt. They included just such a "sayings book," the *Gospel of Thomas*. Subsequently, sayings from a variant tradition of this Gospel in Greek were identified among Greek papyri. The *Gospel of Thomas* is not "Q": Some of its sayings and parables appear to have been taken from the Synoptic Gospels rather than from earlier oral tradition. But its discovery provides evidence that such sayings collections existed.

Scholars presume that the Gospel writers may have had other such notebook-like collections of material such as parables and miracle stories. Presumably additional items, such as genealogies, hymnic prayers, and legends in the infancy narratives of Matthew and Luke, were not created by the evangelists but come from earlier tradition. Similarly, some of the material found only in Matthew or in Luke is not likely to be the author's creation. The following diagram shows the understanding of a majority of scholars about the sources and literary relationships of the Synoptic Gospels.

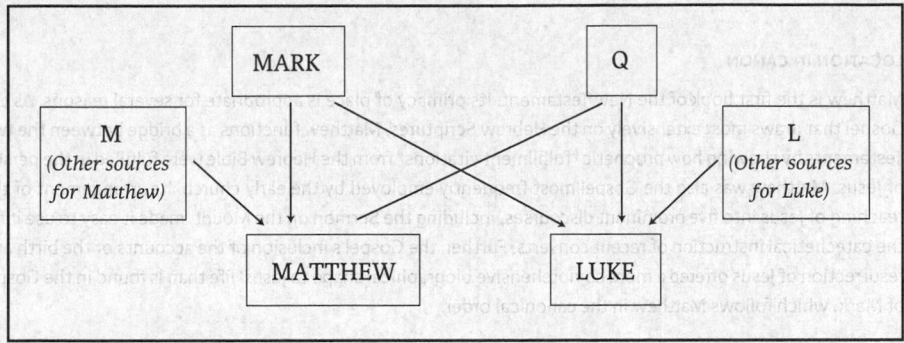

Four Source Hypothesis. In composing their Gospels, both Matthew and Luke independently used two earlier sources: the gospel of Mark, and "Q," the collection of sayings of Jesus. Each also used other sources specific to each of them

There may also have been an earlier narrative of the passion and death of Jesus; some scholars think that most of Mark's narrative came from such a source, while others maintain that there is no evidence for such an account. The origin of the story of Jesus' passion is unclear, and some details may have been based on biblical descriptions of the suffering righteous one.

While the Synoptic Gospels have a close relationship based on their literary connections, the Fourth Gospel, the Gospel of John, presents a much greater puzzle. Its chronology of Jesus' ministry is quite different from that of the Synoptics, as are many narrative details. Jesus spends three years preaching, during which he journeys between Galilee and Jerusalem; in the Synoptic Gospels he visits Jerusalem only once, at the end of a ministry that apparently lasted less than a year. The episode denouncing the sellers in the Temple, which enrages the religious authorities and leads to his death in the Synoptics, occurs near the beginning of the three-year ministry in John (Jn 2.13–22). John claims that Jesus' popularity with Jerusalem crowds after he dramatically restored Lazarus to life awakened political fears for the safety of the nation (Jn 11.45–57; 12.9–11). John's account of the passion also differs markedly: There is no agony. Conscious of his unity with the Father and the cross as his exaltation and return to preexistent glory, Jesus controls all the events; he engages Pilate, the Roman governor, in an ironic discussion of kingship; and John has a disciple-witness, a resident of Jerusalem, who does not flee with the others. Is this unnamed "disciple whom Jesus loved" (Jn 21.7,20; cf. 19.26; 20.2) a symbolic creation of the Evangelist? Some scholars think so; others suggest that he was a historical individual, the source of much of the Fourth Gospel's unique tradition and theology, as the text alleges (19.35; 21.24). What led the author of the Gospel of John to compose such a unique variant on an outline of Jesus' life that still has a recognizable similarity to Mark (and in some instances to Luke)? Some scholars use the parallels as indications of a shorter sketch of Jesus' life known to both authors. Others think that the Gospel of Mark, and perhaps also Luke, were already circulating in the Evangelist's area. He assumed that readers knew some other account of Jesus' life and teaching, and formulated a different version of who Jesus is and what he taught based on the insight that Jesus of Nazareth was not just a miracle-worker, a prophet, or a charismatic Jewish teacher, but the incarnate Son of God. That claim constitutes the flash point between Jesus and the Jewish authorities throughout the narrative.

The Evangelists did more than compile a notebook of traditions about Jesus. Rather, each shaped the narrative to emphasize particular features of Jesus and his teaching. Readers may approach every Gospel in a similar way, asking what are the special characteristics of Jesus and of his followers in each Evangelist's presentation of Jesus and of those who follow Jesus.

THE GOSPEL ACCORDING TO MATTHEW

LOCATION IN CANON

Matthew is the first book of the New Testament. Its primacy of place is appropriate for several reasons. As the Gospel that draws most extensively on the Hebrew Scriptures, Matthew functions as a bridge between the two Testaments by showing how prophetic "fulfillment citations" from the Hebrew Bible were fulfilled in the person of Jesus. Matthew was also the Gospel most frequently employed by the early church. Its arrangement of the teaching of Jesus into five prominent discourses, including the Sermon on the Mount, made it easy to use it for the catechetical instruction of recent converts. Further, the Gospel's inclusion of the accounts of the birth and resurrection of Jesus offered a more comprehensive biographical shape to Jesus' life than is found in the Gospel of Mark, which follows Matthew in the canonical order.

AUTHORSHIP, DATE, AND PLACE OF COMPOSITION

Some scholars have seen the Gospel's replacement of Mark's tax-collector Levi (Mk 2.13–17) with Matthew (9.9–13) as a sort of authorial signature. Yet, the fact that the Evangelist was so reliant upon Mark and a collection of Jesus' sayings ("Q") seems to point to a later, unknown author. The Gospel's time of writing is likewise unknown. As it appears to be familiar with events of the first Jewish Revolt (66–70 CE; see 22.7), Matthew must have been composed sometime afterward. Since, however, Christian writers show a broad familiarity with the Gospel from an early period, it cannot date from much beyond the final decade of the first century. Scholars usually settle on the 80s CE as a likely decade for the Gospel's composition.

Evidence for the Gospel's place of composition is also largely conjectural. The author's familiarity with Judaism and his acquaintance with the geography of Palestine are two of the chief considerations. Thus, large cities proximate to Palestine with a substantial Jewish presence are the most plausible locales. Syrian Antioch, the third largest city in the Roman Empire, has the added distinction of being associated with Matthew in church tradition. Nevertheless, other sites continue to be proposed, such as Caesarea Maritima or Sepphoris, a Greco-Roman city located near Nazareth. Certainty is hardly possible.

LITERARY FORM

A proper reading of the Gospel requires being attuned to its literary form. For instance, it is important to remember that the division into chapters and verses is a relatively recent modification (1551 CE) and occasionally overlooks natural divisions in the Gospel. Temporarily disregarding chapter and verse numbers will bring out the literary contours of the text and allow one to approximate the experience of the Gospel's first readers.

Without doubt, the most distinctive of these literary contours are the Gospel's five discourses. More of Matthew is devoted to Jesus' teaching than any other Gospel (estimates are Matthew 43 percent; Mark 20 percent; Luke 37 percent; and John 34 percent).

The Evangelist has assembled five discourses comprising different aspects of Jesus' teaching, probably a deliberate parallel to the five books of the Torah/Pentateuch. Each of these discourses ends with the phrase, "when Jesus had finished saying these things . . ." The first, the Sermon on the Mount (chs 5–7), is justly famous as an encapsulation of the "entry requirements of the kingdom," while a number of "parables of the kingdom" can be found in ch 13's "parable discourse." Taken together, the discourses afford an overview of the progress of the kingdom: it begins with teaching about the kingdom (chs 5–7), moves to the preaching of the kingdom (ch 10), its mysteries (ch 13), its application to the church (ch 18), and finally, its implications for the last days and final judgment (chs 24–25).

That the last discourse contains parables of judgment is characteristic of Matthew as a whole; in fact, each of his discourses ends with references to judgment. His view of the world is highly polarized. One either walks according to Jesus' "way of righteousness" and produces spiritual fruit, or one does not. For Matthew, the consequences of this decision are momentous: the coming judgment will be swift, unexpected, and inexorable.

Another of the Gospel's literary contours is the way in which it approximates the ancient Greek literary form of the *bios* ("life"). The *bios* differs from modern biography in its concern to provide episodes that reveal the underlying character of its subject. Rather than display the psychological development of Jesus, Matthew depicts him as the humble and compassionate Messiah over the entirety of his Gospel. Jesus acts throughout the Gospel as the exemplar for every Christian.

INTERPRETATION

Matthew's utility for the Christian church is no coincidence. The issues of his own church and community were of pressing importance to the Evangelist; Matthew's is the only Gospel to use the word "church" expressly (Gk *ekklesia*, 16.18; 18.17) and to include issues of church authority and discipline (ch 18). Matthew's Gospel gives vivid insights into the concerns of his own church. The evangelist has telescoped the experiences of Christians in his day with the story of Jesus so that Jesus' words and actions apply to both the time of Jesus and that of Matthew a half century later.

This procedure explains some of the Gospel's apparent anomalies. One of the most striking is the narrative's conflicted portrayal of Jewish piety and religious leaders. Its high regard for the Jewish Torah (5.17–20; 23.1–3) is noteworthy, as is the extensive use of prophecies from the Hebrew Bible, and its occasional disdain for non-Jews (5.47; 6.7,32; 16.17). These features suggest a positive assessment of Judaism. On the other hand, the Gospel displays a strident and unrelenting condemnation of the Jewish leadership—the chief priests, elders, Sadducees, Pharisees, and scribes. These groups are indiscriminately paired with each other in a manner inconsistent with the historical distinctions between these groups in Jesus' day. The Gospel's treatment of the Pharisees, routinely condemned as hypocrites (e.g., 23.5–7), in particular, has led many scholars to suggest that their portrayal reflects later tensions between Matthew's church and emergent Rabbinic Judaism. In other words, the conflict between Jesus and the Pharisees reflects tensions that emerged fifty years after Jesus' death.

The crucifixion narrative also displays this telescoping of perspective. Responsibility for Jesus' passion is shifted from Pontius Pilate and the Romans to the Jewish people and their leadership (27.20–25). The horrific pronouncement "His blood be on us and on our children!" (27.25) is Matthew's way of attributing the destruction of Jerusalem and the Temple in 70 CE to Israel's rejection of Jesus. The vehemence with which the evangelist expresses such sentiments was likely intended to shock both Jewish Christians and their Jewish neighbors into reconsidering the claims made by the Gospel, and discounting rival claims being advanced by the leadership of emergent Rabbinic Judaism, such as the Jewish explanation for the resurrection of Jesus (Matt 27.52–66; 28.11–15).

While such deliberately shocking rhetoric was characteristic of debates between groups in the first century CE, its long-term consequences have been disastrous. Subsequent non-Jewish Christians interpreted the Gospel as a warrant to exact retribution from Jews for the death of Jesus and persecution of his first followers. A proper reading of the Gospel, therefore, requires being attuned to the polemical context in which it was written, and recognizing that the conflict between emerging Rabbinic Judaism and the smaller Jewish Christian minority ceased being relevant nearly two millennia ago.

What remains unchanged about the Gospel of Matthew, however, is its place as one of the richest and most fascinating documents within the Christian Bible—one that will reward long and detailed study with treasures both new and old (13.52).

J. R. C. Cousland

1

An account of the genealogy[a] of Jesus the Messiah,[b] the son of David, the son of Abraham.

[2] Abraham was the father of Isaac, and Isaac the father of Jacob, and Jacob the father of Judah and his brothers, [3] and Judah the father of Perez and Zerah by Tamar, and Perez the father of Hezron, and Hezron the father of Aram, [4] and Aram the father of Aminadab, and Aminadab the father of Nahshon, and Nahshon the father of Salmon, [5] and Salmon the father of Boaz by Rahab, and Boaz the father of Obed by Ruth, and Obed the father of Jesse, [6] and Jesse the father of King David.

And David was the father of Solomon by the wife of Uriah, [7] and Solomon the father of Rehoboam, and Rehoboam the father of Abijah, and Abijah the father of Asaph,[c] [8] and Asaph[c] the father of Jehoshaphat, and Jehoshaphat the father of Joram, and Joram the father of Uzziah, [9] and Uzziah the father of Jotham, and Jotham the father of Ahaz, and Ahaz the father of Hezekiah, [10] and Hezekiah the father of Manasseh, and Manasseh the father of Amos,[d] and Amos[d] the father of Josiah, [11] and Josiah the father of Jechoniah and his brothers, at the time of the deportation to Babylon.

[12] And after the deportation to Babylon: Jechoniah was the father of Salathiel, and Salathiel the father of Zerubbabel, [13] and Zerubbabel the father of Abiud, and Abiud

the father of Eliakim, and Eliakim the father of Azor, [14] and Azor the father of Zadok, and Zadok the father of Achim, and Achim the father of Eliud, [15] and Eliud the father of Eleazar, and Eleazar the father of Matthan, and Matthan the father of Jacob, [16] and Jacob the father of Joseph the husband of Mary, of whom Jesus was born, who is called the Messiah.[e]

[17] So all the generations from Abraham to David are fourteen generations; and from David to the deportation to Babylon, fourteen generations; and from the deportation to Babylon to the Messiah,[e] fourteen generations.

[18] Now the birth of Jesus the Messiah[b] took place in this way. When his mother Mary had been engaged to Joseph, but before they lived together, she was found to be with child from the Holy Spirit. [19] Her husband Joseph, being a righteous man and unwilling to expose her to public disgrace, planned to dismiss her quietly. [20] But just when he had resolved to do this, an angel of the Lord appeared to him in a dream and said, "Joseph, son of David, do not be afraid to take Mary as your wife, for

a Or birth
b Or Jesus Christ
c Other ancient authorities read Asa
d Other ancient authorities read Amon
e Or the Christ

1.1–17: Jesus' genealogy (Lk 3.23–38). 1: Jesus, "Jeshua" (Heb "Yeshua'") is a later, abbreviated, form of the name "Joshua," meaning "The Lord (YHWH) is help (or salvation)." Messiah, Gk "Christos," "Anointed One." Those anointed by God—typically kings or priests—were set apart by God for a specific purpose (1 Sam 10.1). The designation son indicates Jesus' familial descent. That he is both the son of David, the king, and son of Abraham, the patriarch, demonstrates that Jesus is a scion of the royal family of David, and a true Israelite. 2–17: The genealogy continues the "descent" motif by furnishing a stylized ancestral tree consisting of roughly three groups of fourteen: from Abraham to David, from David to the deportation to Babylon in 586 BCE (2 Kings 24.8–16), and from the deportation to Jesus. The numerical value of David's name in Hebrew is fourteen, which may account for this arrangement. While this genealogy is not complete (cf. 1 Chr 3.11–12), it establishes that David and Abraham were Jesus' forebears. Genealogies are common in the Hebrew Bible (e.g., 1 Chr 1–9) and were a matter of pride and importance for demonstrating one's status as true Israelites (Neh 7.61–4). Jesus' genealogy is unusual, however, not simply because it includes women, but also because it features non-Israelite (i.e., Gentile) women, some of questionable repute: Tamar (v. 3; Gen 38), Rahab (v. 5; Josh 2.1–21; 6.22–25), Ruth (v. 5; Ruth 2–4), and Bathsheba, the wife of Uriah (v. 6; 2 Sam 11–12). Their inclusion may prefigure Mary's own marital dilemma (vv. 18–19), and the coming mission to the Gentiles (28.18–20).

1.18–25: The conception and birth of Jesus Christ (Lk 2.1–7). Chapter 1 stresses that Jesus was of the line of David, but then indicates that Mary was a virgin and Joseph was not his father. This apparent difficulty is resolved by Joseph's formal adoption of Jesus, which legally situates Jesus within Joseph's line. 20: Dreams are

the child conceived in her is from the Holy Spirit. [21] She will bear a son, and you are to name him Jesus, for he will save his people from their sins." [22] All this took place to fulfill what had been spoken by the Lord through the prophet:

[23] "Look, the virgin shall conceive and bear a son,
and they shall name him Emmanuel,"

which means, "God is with us." [24] When Joseph awoke from sleep, he did as the angel of the Lord commanded him; he took her as his wife, [25] but had no marital relations with her until she had borne a son;[a] and he named him Jesus.

2 In the time of King Herod, after Jesus was born in Bethlehem of Judea, wise men[b] from the East came to Jerusalem, [2] asking, "Where is the child who has been born king of the Jews? For we observed his star at its rising,[c] and have come to pay him homage." [3] When King Herod heard this, he was frightened, and all Jerusalem with him; [4] and calling together all the chief priests and scribes of the people, he inquired of them where the Messiah[d] was to be born. [5] They told him, "In Bethlehem of Judea; for so it has been written by the prophet:

[6] 'And you, Bethlehem, in the land of Judah,
are by no means least among the rulers of Judah;

for from you shall come a ruler
who is to shepherd[e] my people Israel.'"

[7] Then Herod secretly called for the wise men[b] and learned from them the exact time when the star had appeared. [8] Then he sent them to Bethlehem, saying, "Go and search diligently for the child; and when you have found him, bring me word so that I may also go and pay him homage." [9] When they had heard the king, they set out; and there, ahead of them, went the star that they had seen at its rising,[c] until it stopped over the place where the child was. [10] When they saw that the star had stopped,[f] they were overwhelmed with joy. [11] On entering the house, they saw the child with Mary his mother; and they knelt down and paid him homage. Then, opening their treasure chests, they offered him gifts of gold, frankincense, and myrrh. [12] And having been warned in a dream not to return to Herod, they left for their own country by another road.

[13] Now after they had left, an angel of the Lord appeared to Joseph in a dream and said, "Get up, take the child and his mother, and flee to Egypt, and remain there until I

a Other ancient authorities read *her firstborn son*
b Or *astrologers*; Gk *magi*
c Or *in the East*
d Or *the Christ*
e Or *rule*
f Gk *saw the star*

a common means of revelation in Matthew (2.12,13,19–20,22; 27.19). **21**: The angel's reference to Jesus "saving his people" probably alludes to Jesus' name (see v. 1n.). **23**: The first of Matthew's fulfillment citations (Isa 7.14), showing how Jesus' life conforms to prophecies of the Hebrew Bible.

2.1–12: The visit of the wise men. 1: *King Herod* is Herod the Great (ruled 37–4 BCE), who was confirmed as the client king of Judea by the emperor Augustus (31 BCE–14 CE). Herod was only partly Jewish and was notorious for reacting savagely to potential rivals, particularly Jewish rivals. *Bethlehem* was David's hometown and where he was anointed king of Israel (1 Sam 16.1–13). The *wise men* or Magi were a class of Parthian (Persian) priests, renowned as astrologers. **2:** As Gentiles, the Magi do not ask for the king of Israel, but for the *king of the Jews* (27.11,37). The *star* has been variously explained as a supernova, a comet, or a notable conjunction of the planets, but its meaning is probably symbolic; see Num 24.17. **4:** The *chief priests* would have included the current high priest and a larger priestly college, based in Jerusalem. The *scribes* were lawyers, teachers, and interpreters of the Torah (Sir 39.1–11). **5–6:** Mic 5.1,3; cf. 2 Sam 5.2. **11:** *Frankincense* and *myrrh* were costly, resinous gums derived from trees and shrubs (Isa 60.6; Song 3.6). Because of their aromatic qualities they were often employed in religious rituals. The mention of three gifts is probably the origin of the postbiblical tradition that there were three wise men.

2.13–23: The escape to Egypt and return. 15: A fulfillment citation from Hos 11.1, where *son* refers to the people of Israel (Ex 4.22). The citation calls to mind Israel's sojourn in Egypt and God's mighty deliverance of Israel

tell you; for Herod is about to search for the child, to destroy him." [14] Then Joseph[a] got up, took the child and his mother by night, and went to Egypt, [15] and remained there until the death of Herod. This was to fulfill what had been spoken by the Lord through the prophet, "Out of Egypt I have called my son."

[16] When Herod saw that he had been tricked by the wise men,[b] he was infuriated, and he sent and killed all the children in and around Bethlehem who were two years old or under, according to the time that he had learned from the wise men.[b] [17] Then was fulfilled what had been spoken through the prophet Jeremiah:

[18] "A voice was heard in Ramah,
     wailing and loud lamentation,
Rachel weeping for her children;
     she refused to be consoled, because
          they are no more."

[19] When Herod died, an angel of the Lord suddenly appeared in a dream to Joseph in Egypt and said, [20] "Get up, take the child and his mother, and go to the land of Israel, for those who were seeking the child's life are dead." [21] Then Joseph[a] got up, took the child and his mother, and went to the land of Israel. [22] But when he heard that Archelaus was ruling over Judea in place of his father Herod, he was afraid to go there. And after

being warned in a dream, he went away to the district of Galilee. [23] There he made his home in a town called Nazareth, so that what had been spoken through the prophets might be fulfilled, "He will be called a Nazorean."

3 In those days John the Baptist appeared in the wilderness of Judea, proclaiming, [2] "Repent, for the kingdom of heaven has come near."[c] [3] This is the one of whom the prophet Isaiah spoke when he said,

"The voice of one crying out in the
     wilderness:
'Prepare the way of the Lord,
     make his paths straight.'"

[4] Now John wore clothing of camel's hair with a leather belt around his waist, and his food was locusts and wild honey. [5] Then the people of Jerusalem and all Judea were going out to him, and all the region along the Jordan, [6] and they were baptized by him in the river Jordan, confessing their sins.

[7] But when he saw many Pharisees and Sadducees coming for baptism, he said to them, "You brood of vipers! Who warned you to flee from the wrath to come? [8] Bear

a   Gk *he*
b   Or *astrologers*; Gk *magi*
c   Or *is at hand*

through Moses. **16:** Herod's action recalls the command of the king of Egypt in Ex 1.16. **18:** A fulfillment citation from Jer 31.15. The tomb of *Rachel*, the wife of Jacob, the father of the twelve "tribes" of Israel, was near Bethlehem (Gen 35.16–20). **20:** Cf. Ex 4.19. **22:** Upon Herod's death in 4 BCE, his kingdom was divided among his sons *Archelaus* (4 BCE–6 CE), ethnarch (prince) over Judea, Samaria, and Idumea; Herod Antipas (4 BCE–39 CE), tetrarch (minor prince) over Galilee and Perea; and Philip (4 BCE–33/34 CE), tetrarch of smaller territories northeast of the Sea of Galilee. **23:** *Nazareth* in Jesus' day was not so much a "city" (NRSV *town*) as a village. *Nazorean*, this fulfillment citation does not explicitly correspond to any passage in the Hebrew Bible, though it echoes passages such as Isa 11.12 and Judg 13.5.

3.1–12: The preaching of John the Baptist (Mk 1.1–8; Lk 3.1–9,15–17; Jn 1.19–28; Josephus, *Ant.* 18.116–19). **1:** *In those days*, a general reference to the time when Jesus began his public ministry. *John the Baptist*, the prophetic forerunner of Jesus. In Matthew, although John is subordinate to Jesus, their ministries display strong parallels (compare 3.2 with 4.17). *Wilderness of Judea*, the barren eastern slopes of the Judean mountains that face the Dead Sea and lower Jordan valley. **2:** *Kingdom of heaven* is Matthew's circumlocution for kingdom of God, one that avoids mentioning the name of God directly (though the phrase "kingdom of God" remains unchanged at 6.33; 12.28; 21.31,43). The kingdom of heaven (or God) refers to the absolute rule of God over human affairs. Its establishment marks the onset of the new age and God's ultimate dominion. **3:** A fulfillment citation from Isa 40.3 (Mk 1.2–3; cf. CD 10.16; 16.15). John acts as a herald announcing the coming of the king. **4:** John's manner of dress recalled the prophet Elijah (2 Kings 1.8) while his *food* was that of an ascetic; *locusts* are one of the few types of insects not regarded as unclean (Lev 11.20–23). In Matthew, John is more closely identified with Elijah than in the other Gospels (17.11–13). **7:** The Pharisees and Sadducees were two of the most important groups of

fruit worthy of repentance. ⁹ Do not presume to say to yourselves, 'We have Abraham as our ancestor'; for I tell you, God is able from these stones to raise up children to Abraham. ¹⁰ Even now the ax is lying at the root of the trees; every tree therefore that does not bear good fruit is cut down and thrown into the fire.

¹¹ "I baptize you with[a] water for repentance, but one who is more powerful than I is coming after me; I am not worthy to carry his sandals. He will baptize you with[a] the Holy Spirit and fire. ¹² His winnowing fork is in his hand, and he will clear his threshing floor and will gather his wheat into the granary; but the chaff he will burn with unquenchable fire."

¹³ Then Jesus came from Galilee to John at the Jordan, to be baptized by him. ¹⁴ John would have prevented him, saying, "I need to be baptized by you, and do you come to me?" ¹⁵ But Jesus answered him, "Let it be so now; for it is proper for us in this way to fulfill all righteousness." Then he consented. ¹⁶ And when Jesus had been baptized, just as he came up from the water, suddenly the heavens were opened to him and he saw the Spirit of God descending like a dove and alighting on him. ¹⁷ And a voice from heaven said, "This is my Son, the Beloved,[b] with whom I am well pleased."

4 Then Jesus was led up by the Spirit into the wilderness to be tempted by the devil. ² He fasted forty days and forty nights,

and afterwards he was famished. ³ The tempter came and said to him, "If you are the Son of God, command these stones to become loaves of bread." ⁴ But he answered, "It is written,

'One does not live by bread alone,
    but by every word that comes from the
        mouth of God.'"

⁵ Then the devil took him to the holy city and placed him on the pinnacle of the temple, ⁶ saying to him, "If you are the Son of God, throw yourself down; for it is written,

'He will command his angels concerning
        you,'
    and 'On their hands they will bear you
        up,
so that you will not dash your foot against
    a stone.'"

⁷ Jesus said to him, "Again it is written, 'Do not put the Lord your God to the test.'"

⁸ Again, the devil took him to a very high mountain and showed him all the kingdoms of the world and their splendor; ⁹ and he said to him, "All these I will give you, if you will fall down and worship me." ¹⁰ Jesus said to him, "Away with you, Satan! for it is written,

'Worship the Lord your God,
    and serve only him.'"

a Or *in*
b Or *my beloved Son*

the Second Temple period, though little can be said with certainty about membership in either. The *Pharisees* appear to have been a reform movement in Judaism, advocating stringent observance of the Law and their own "oral Torah." The *Sadducees* may have been the aristocratic descendants of Zadok the priest (2 Sam 8.17), who considered the written, but not the "oral Torah" binding on Israel. In contrast to the Pharisees (Acts 23.6–10), they did not believe in resurrection (22.22–23). **8:** *Repentance*, the beginning of a new relationship with God. **12:** A *winnowing fork* was a forked shovel that was used to toss the threshed grain into the wind, separating the kernels of *wheat* from the husks and straw, the *chaff*, which was blown away.

3.13–17: The baptism of Jesus (Mk 1.9–11; Lk 3.21–22; Jn 1.31–34). **15:** *Righteousness* is a central theme in Matthew, and means acting in accordance with the will of God. It furnishes the justification for the greater (Jesus) being baptized by the lesser (the Baptist; 11.11). **16:** *Spirit*, 28.19; Gen 1.2; Isa 61.1. **17:** *My beloved Son* (see textual note b), 17.5; Ps 2.7; Isa 42.1.

4.1–11: The temptation of Jesus (Mk 1.12–13; Lk 4.1–13). **1:** *The devil*, a transcendent evil being, also described in this chapter as the tempter (v. 3) and Satan ("the enemy"; v. 10). **2:** The *forty days* recall the testing of Israel in the wilderness (Ex 34.28), and Elijah's forty-day journey into the Sinai wilderness (1 Kings 19.8). **3:** *Son of God*, the most comprehensive christological designation for Jesus in Matthew (3.17; 16.16; 17.5; 27.54; 28.19). **4:** Deut 8.3. **5:** *Holy city*, Jerusalem; cf. 27.53; *pinnacle*, possibly the southeast corner of the Temple's terrace where there was a steep drop to the Kidron Valley below. **6:** Ps 91.11–12. **7:** Deut 6.16. **8:** Mountains figure prominently in Matthew as places of revelation (5.1; 14.23; 15.29; 17.1; 24.3; 28.16). **10:** Deut 6.13. All of Jesus' responses to Satan are

[11] Then the devil left him, and suddenly angels came and waited on him.

[12] Now when Jesus[a] heard that John had been arrested, he withdrew to Galilee. [13] He left Nazareth and made his home in Capernaum by the sea, in the territory of Zebulun and Naphtali, [14] so that what had been spoken through the prophet Isaiah might be fulfilled:
[15] "Land of Zebulun, land of Naphtali,
 on the road by the sea, across the
 Jordan, Galilee of the Gentiles—
[16] the people who sat in darkness
 have seen a great light,
and for those who sat in the region and
 shadow of death
 light has dawned."
[17] From that time Jesus began to proclaim, "Repent, for the kingdom of heaven has come near."[b]

[18] As he walked by the Sea of Galilee, he saw two brothers, Simon, who is called Peter, and Andrew his brother, casting a net into the sea—for they were fishermen. [19] And he said to them, "Follow me, and I will make you fish for people." [20] Immediately they left their nets and followed him. [21] As he went from there, he saw two other brothers, James son of Zebedee and his brother John, in the boat with their father Zebedee, mending their nets, and he called them. [22] Immediately they left the boat and their father, and followed him.

[23] Jesus[c] went throughout Galilee, teaching in their synagogues and proclaiming the good news[d] of the kingdom and curing every disease and every sickness among the people. [24] So his fame spread throughout all Syria, and they brought to him all the sick, those who were afflicted with various diseases and pains, demoniacs, epileptics, and paralytics, and he cured them. [25] And great crowds followed him from Galilee, the Decapolis, Jerusalem, Judea, and from beyond the Jordan.

5 When Jesus[a] saw the crowds, he went up the mountain; and after he sat down, his disciples came to him. [2] Then he began to speak, and taught them, saying:
[3] "Blessed are the poor in spirit, for theirs is the kingdom of heaven.
[4] "Blessed are those who mourn, for they will be comforted.

a Gk he
b Or is at hand
c Gk He
d Gk gospel

citations from Deuteronomy. **11:** The *angels* feed Jesus as they had once fed Elijah (1 Kings 19.5–8).

4.12–25: The beginning of the Galilean ministry (Mk 1.14–20; Lk 4.14–15; 5.1–11; 6.17–19). **12:** *Galilee* was a region in northern Israel, one of the chief areas of Jesus' activity. It was separated from Judea (and Jerusalem) by Samaria. **13:** *Capernaum*, a village on the northwest shore of the Sea of Galilee. Fishing was an important and lucrative economic activity in the region. **15–16:** Fulfillment citation of Isa 9.1–2. The name "Galilee" is derived from the Hebrew phrase "circle *of the Gentiles*" (Isa 8.23). After the fall of the Northern Kingdom of Israel to Assyria (722 BCE), much of the area had been repopulated by Gentiles, although by Jesus' day it was predominantly Jewish. **17:** Some scholars argue that the phrase *from that time* marks the beginning of the second of three major divisions in the Gospel; cf. 16.21. **18:** *Sea of Galilee*, not a sea but a fresh-water lake, also known as Gennesaret (Lk 5.1) and the Lake of Tiberias (Jn 21.1). **24:** *Syria* is mentioned in no other Gospel; many scholars think that its capital, Antioch-on-the-Orontes, was the location of Matthew's church. *Demoniacs,* those thought to be possessed by demons. **25:** The *crowds* generally represent the Jewish people as distinguished from their leaders. *Decapolis*: A league of some ten cities with all but Scythopolis (earlier Beth-shan) situated east of the Jordan River. Their populations were largely Gentile, though they also contained substantial Jewish minorities.

5.1–7.29: The first discourse: The Sermon on the Mount. Matthew postpones his account of the Galilean ministry in order to introduce Jesus' teaching in the Sermon on the Mount, the first and longest of Jesus' five discourses in Matthew (compare the much briefer "Sermon on the Plain" in Lk 6.20–49). Its prominence within Matthew testifies to its importance for understanding Jesus and the requirements for "entering the kingdom." Whether the Sermon advocates an idealized or a realizable ethic continues to be debated. **1:** *Mountain*, recalling the figure of Moses giving the law to Israel (Ex 19–24). Just as the Law of Moses had five books, the Gospel of Matthew contains five discourses of Jesus. *He sat down*, the posture normally assumed by Jewish teachers.

⁵ "Blessed are the meek, for they will inherit the earth.

⁶ "Blessed are those who hunger and thirst for righteousness, for they will be filled.

⁷ "Blessed are the merciful, for they will receive mercy.

⁸ "Blessed are the pure in heart, for they will see God.

⁹ "Blessed are the peacemakers, for they will be called children of God.

¹⁰ "Blessed are those who are persecuted for righteousness' sake, for theirs is the kingdom of heaven.

¹¹ "Blessed are you when people revile you and persecute you and utter all kinds of evil against you falsely[a] on my account. ¹² Rejoice and be glad, for your reward is great in heaven, for in the same way they persecuted the prophets who were before you.

¹³ "You are the salt of the earth; but if salt has lost its taste, how can its saltiness be restored? It is no longer good for anything, but is thrown out and trampled under foot.

¹⁴ "You are the light of the world. A city built on a hill cannot be hid. ¹⁵ No one after lighting a lamp puts it under the bushel basket, but on the lampstand, and it gives light to all in the house. ¹⁶ In the same way, let your light shine before others, so that they may see your good works and give glory to your Father in heaven.

¹⁷ "Do not think that I have come to abolish the law or the prophets; I have come not to abolish but to fulfill. ¹⁸ For truly I tell you, until heaven and earth pass away, not one letter,[b] not one stroke of a letter, will pass from the law until all is accomplished. ¹⁹ Therefore, whoever breaks[c] one of the least of these commandments, and teaches others to do the same, will be called least in the kingdom of heaven; but whoever does them and teaches them will be called great in the kingdom of heaven. ²⁰ For I tell you, unless your righteousness exceeds that of the scribes and Pharisees, you will never enter the kingdom of heaven.

²¹ "You have heard that it was said to those of ancient times, 'You shall not murder'; and 'whoever murders shall be liable to judgment.' ²² But I say to you that if you are angry with a brother or sister,[d] you will be liable to judgment; and if you insult[e] a brother or sister,[f] you will be liable to the council; and if you say, 'You fool,' you will be liable to the hell[g]

a   Other ancient authorities lack *falsely*
b   Gk *one iota*
c   Or *annuls*
d   Gk *a brother*; other ancient authorities add *without cause*
e   Gk *say Raca to* (an obscure term of abuse)
f   Gk *a brother*
g   Gk *Gehenna*

Disciples, for Jesus' named disciples, see 9.9–13; 10.2. **5.3–12: The Beatitudes** (Lk 6.20–23). Luke has only four beatitudes to Matthew's nine, and his four have a more this-worldly focus. **3:** The term "Beatitudes" is derived from the Latin word "beatus," meaning "blessed" or "favored by God." Matthew's beatitudes emphasize that God's blessings will be bestowed on believers in the new age (Isa 61.2). *The poor in spirit*, Lk 6.20 has "the poor." **4.** *Mourn*, perhaps for one's sins. **5:** *Meek*, Ps 37.11. **8:** *Pure in heart*, Pss 24.4; 73.1. **12:** *Persecuted the prophets*, Matthew assumes that all true prophets were persecuted (1 Kings 19.10; Neh 9.26), John the Baptist and Jesus among them.

5.13–16: Salt and light (Mk 9.50; Lk 14.34–35). **13:** *Lost its taste*, genuine salt can leach away from impure salt, leaving only a tasteless residue. **16:** *Father* is one of Jesus' favorite expressions for God in Matthew.

5.17–20: Teaching about the law. The rest of ch 5 deals with issues relating to the Torah. **17:** *Prophets*, the second of the three divisions of the Hebrew Bible. **18:** The phrase *truly* ("amen") *I tell you* in Jesus' mouth frequently involves pronouncements pertaining to the end time. *Until . . . all*: both temporal clauses refer to the end of the present age and the onset of the eschatological age. The verse suggests that the Torah remained in force among Jewish Christians in Matthew's church.

5.21–48: The outworking of the law (Lk 6.27–36; cf. Lev 19.18; *m. Abot* 1.12). The phrase "you have heard that it was said" occurs six times in ch 5, each followed by a reference to one of the commandments in the Hebrew Bible. In three of these "antitheses," Jesus' purpose is not to abrogate the Law, but to express the deeper significance of God's commandments. **21:** Ex 20.13; Deut 5.17. **22:** *I say to you* occurs twelve other times in the Sermon, and emphasizes Jesus' unprecedented authority to determine God's will (7.29; 28.18). *Council*, the Sanhedrin;

of fire. ²³ So when you are offering your gift at the altar, if you remember that your brother or sister[a] has something against you, ²⁴ leave your gift there before the altar and go; first be reconciled to your brother or sister,[a] and then come and offer your gift. ²⁵ Come to terms quickly with your accuser while you are on the way to court[b] with him, or your accuser may hand you over to the judge, and the judge to the guard, and you will be thrown into prison. ²⁶ Truly I tell you, you will never get out until you have paid the last penny.

²⁷ "You have heard that it was said, 'You shall not commit adultery.' ²⁸ But I say to you that everyone who looks at a woman with lust has already committed adultery with her in his heart. ²⁹ If your right eye causes you to sin, tear it out and throw it away; it is better for you to lose one of your members than for your whole body to be thrown into hell.[c] ³⁰ And if your right hand causes you to sin, cut it off and throw it away; it is better for you to lose one of your members than for your whole body to go into hell.[c]

³¹ "It was also said, 'Whoever divorces his wife, let him give her a certificate of divorce.' ³² But I say to you that anyone who divorces his wife, except on the ground of unchastity, causes her to commit adultery; and whoever marries a divorced woman commits adultery.

³³ "Again, you have heard that it was said to those of ancient times, 'You shall not swear falsely, but carry out the vows you have made to the Lord.' ³⁴ But I say to you, Do not swear at all, either by heaven, for it is the throne of God, ³⁵ or by the earth, for it is his footstool,

or by Jerusalem, for it is the city of the great King. ³⁶ And do not swear by your head, for you cannot make one hair white or black. ³⁷ Let your word be 'Yes, Yes' or 'No, No'; anything more than this comes from the evil one.[d]

³⁸ "You have heard that it was said, 'An eye for an eye and a tooth for a tooth.' ³⁹ But I say to you, Do not resist an evil-doer. But if anyone strikes you on the right cheek, turn the other also; ⁴⁰ and if anyone wants to sue you and take your coat, give your cloak as well; ⁴¹ and if anyone forces you to go one mile, go also the second mile. ⁴² Give to everyone who begs from you, and do not refuse anyone who wants to borrow from you.

⁴³ "You have heard that it was said, 'You shall love your neighbor and hate your enemy.' ⁴⁴ But I say to you, Love your enemies and pray for those who persecute you, ⁴⁵ so that you may be children of your Father in heaven; for he makes his sun rise on the evil and on the good, and sends rain on the righteous and on the unrighteous. ⁴⁶ For if you love those who love you, what reward do you have? Do not even the tax collectors do the same? ⁴⁷ And if you greet only your brothers and sisters,[e] what more are you doing than others? Do not even the Gentiles do the same? ⁴⁸ Be perfect, therefore, as your heavenly Father is perfect.

a Gk *your brother*
b Gk lacks *to court*
c Gk *Gehenna*
d Or *evil*
e Gk *your brothers*

see 26.59n. **24:** *Gift,* true worship of God requires full reconciliation with one's neighbors. **25:** Imprisonment for debt was a Gentile, not a Jewish, practice. **27:** For the remaining three antitheses, Jesus proposes a different ethic for his followers. *Adultery,* cf. Ex. 20.14; Deut 5.18; cf. 5.32; 15.19; 19.9. Jesus not only condemns adultery but even entertaining thoughts that would lead to adultery. **31:** *Divorce,* Deut 24.1–4; cf. 19.7–9. Jesus indicates that the only justification for divorcing one's wife is sexual infidelity; otherwise the divorce is invalid, and any future marriages adulterous. **33:** Lev 19.12; Num 30.2; Deut 23.21. **34–36:** *Heaven, earth,* and *Jerusalem* are all circumlocutions for "God;" they, along with one's *head,* are in God's keeping and, therefore, not under humans' dominion. **35:** Isa 66.1; Ps 48.2. **38:** Jesus qualifies the law of retaliation, the "lex talionis" ("an eye for an eye . . .," Ex 21.23–24; Lev 24.19–20; Deut 19.21), by advocating the return of good for evil. **40:** Cf. Ex 22.26–27; Deut 24.12–13. **43:** *Love your neighbor* quotes Lev 19.18, but *hate your enemy* is not found in the Hebrew Bible. **44:** *Those who persecute you,* Matthew's version (cf. Lk 6.27–28) may refer to actual persecution experienced by his church, demonstrating the radical nature of the commandment (cf. 10.17). **46:** *Tax collectors* though Jewish, were popularly regarded as unclean, Roman collaborators. **47:** *Gentiles* occasionally have a negative connotation in the Gospel

6 "Beware of practicing your piety before others in order to be seen by them; for then you have no reward from your Father in heaven.

² "So whenever you give alms, do not sound a trumpet before you, as the hypocrites do in the synagogues and in the streets, so that they may be praised by others. Truly I tell you, they have received their reward. ³ But when you give alms, do not let your left hand know what your right hand is doing, ⁴ so that your alms may be done in secret; and your Father who sees in secret will reward you.ᵃ

⁵ "And whenever you pray, do not be like the hypocrites; for they love to stand and pray in the synagogues and at the street corners, so that they may be seen by others. Truly I tell you, they have received their reward. ⁶ But whenever you pray, go into your room and shut the door and pray to your Father who is in secret; and your Father who sees in secret will reward you.ᵃ

⁷ "When you are praying, do not heap up empty phrases as the Gentiles do; for they think that they will be heard because of their many words. ⁸ Do not be like them, for your Father knows what you need before you ask him.

⁹ "Pray then in this way:
Our Father in heaven,
    hallowed be your name.
¹⁰ Your kingdom come.
    Your will be done,
        on earth as it is in heaven.
¹¹ Give us this day our daily bread.ᵇ

¹² And forgive us our debts,
    as we also have forgiven our debtors.
¹³ And do not bring us to the time of trial,ᶜ
    but rescue us from the evil one.ᵈ

¹⁴ For if you forgive others their trespasses, your heavenly Father will also forgive you; ¹⁵ but if you do not forgive others, neither will your Father forgive your trespasses.

¹⁶ "And whenever you fast, do not look dismal, like the hypocrites, for they disfigure their faces so as to show others that they are fasting. Truly I tell you, they have received their reward. ¹⁷ But when you fast, put oil on your head and wash your face, ¹⁸ so that your fasting may be seen not by others but by your Father who is in secret; and your Father who sees in secret will reward you.ᵃ

¹⁹ "Do not store up for yourselves treasures on earth, where moth and rustᵉ consume and where thieves break in and steal; ²⁰ but store up for yourselves treasures in heaven, where neither moth nor rustᵉ consumes and where thieves do not break in and steal. ²¹ For where your treasure is, there your heart will be also.

²² "The eye is the lamp of the body. So, if your eye is healthy, your whole body will be

ᵃ Other ancient authorities add *openly*
ᵇ Or *our bread for tomorrow*
ᶜ Or *us into temptation*
ᵈ Or *from evil*. Other ancient authorities add, in some form, *For the kingdom and the power and the glory are yours forever. Amen.*
ᵉ Gk *eating*

(5.47; 6.7,32; 15.26; 16.17). **48:** The word *perfect* occurs only here and at 19.21 in the Gospels. This understanding of "perfection" is closely linked with the love commandment (19.19).

6.1–18: Almsgiving, prayer, and fasting. 1: This segment opens with a general principle, followed by three particular applications. True piety or righteousness, which is inconspicuous, is contrasted with false piety, which is motivated by ostentation. **2:** Giving *alms* involved not only the donation of money but also the performance of other merciful and charitable actions. Sounding a *trumpet* is probably metaphorical (as in "blow your own horn"). *Hypocrites* originally signified "actors." Here the word takes on some of that sense; elsewhere in Matthew it is used more pejoratively, particularly of the Pharisees and scribes, in the sense of "frauds," not the outstanding examples of piety people thought them to be. **5:** Performance of the daily Jewish prayers in the morning, at noon, and in the evening (Lk 11.2–4). *Stand*, standing with the face directed toward Jerusalem was the typical Jewish posture for prayer (1 Kings 8.35–48; Mk 11.25; Lk 18.13). **9:** *Pray*, Matthew's version of the Lord's Prayer is considerably longer than Luke's (11.2–4). The final doxology (see textual note *d*) appears to have been added later under the influence of 1 Chr 29.1–13. **17:** *Oil on your head*, anointing and washing oneself were a feature of day-to-day hygiene and not necessarily a sign of festivity.

6.19–34: Life and livelihood (Lk 12.22–34; 11.34–36). This section illustrates how to live in the world, without

full of light; [23] but if your eye is unhealthy, your whole body will be full of darkness. If then the light in you is darkness, how great is the darkness!

[24] "No one can serve two masters; for a slave will either hate the one and love the other, or be devoted to the one and despise the other. You cannot serve God and wealth.[a]

[25] "Therefore I tell you, do not worry about your life, what you will eat or what you will drink,[b] or about your body, what you will wear. Is not life more than food, and the body more than clothing? [26] Look at the birds of the air; they neither sow nor reap nor gather into barns, and yet your heavenly Father feeds them. Are you not of more value than they? [27] And can any of you by worrying add a single hour to your span of life?[c] [28] And why do you worry about clothing? Consider the lilies of the field, how they grow; they neither toil nor spin, [29] yet I tell you, even Solomon in all his glory was not clothed like one of these. [30] But if God so clothes the grass of the field, which is alive today and tomorrow is thrown into the oven, will he not much more clothe you—you of little faith? [31] Therefore do not worry, saying, 'What will we eat?' or 'What will we drink?' or 'What will we wear?' [32] For it is the Gentiles who strive for all these things; and indeed your heavenly Father knows that you need all these things. [33] But strive first for the kingdom of God[d] and his[e] righteousness, and all these things will be given to you as well.

[34] "So do not worry about tomorrow, for tomorrow will bring worries of its own. Today's trouble is enough for today.

7 "Do not judge, so that you may not be judged. [2] For with the judgment you make you will be judged, and the measure you give will be the measure you get. [3] Why do you see the speck in your neighbor's[f] eye, but do not notice the log in your own eye? [4] Or how can you say to your neighbor,[g] 'Let me take the speck out of your eye,' while the log is in your own eye? [5] You hypocrite, first take the log out of your own eye, and then you will see clearly to take the speck out of your neighbor's[f] eye.

[6] "Do not give what is holy to dogs; and do not throw your pearls before swine, or they will trample them under foot and turn and maul you.

[7] "Ask, and it will be given you; search, and you will find; knock, and the door will be opened for you. [8] For everyone who asks receives, and everyone who searches finds, and for everyone who knocks, the door will be opened. [9] Is there anyone among you who, if your child asks for bread, will give a stone? [10] Or if the child asks for a fish, will give a snake? [11] If you then, who are evil, know how to give good gifts to your children, how much more will your Father in heaven give good things to those who ask him!

[12] "In everything do to others as you would have them do to you; for this is the law and the prophets.

[13] "Enter through the narrow gate; for the gate is wide and the road is easy[h] that leads to destruction, and there are many who take it. [14] For the gate is narrow and the road is hard that leads to life, and there are few who find it.

[a] Gk *mammon*
[b] Other ancient authorities lack *or what you will drink*
[c] Or *add one cubit to your height*
[d] Other ancient authorities lack *of God*
[e] Or *its*
[f] Gk *brother's*
[g] Gk *brother*
[h] Other ancient authorities read *for the road is wide and easy*

being subject to it. **22–23:** A sincere *eye is healthy* and has no hidden agenda, while an "unhealthy" or insincere eye was thought to occlude the entry of *light*. **26–30:** These verses demonstrate a "less to greater" ("a fortiori") argument, where one establishes a greater premise from a lesser one (cf. 12.9–11). **29:** *Solomon*, 1 Kings 10; 2 Chr 1. **30:** *Thrown into the oven*, grass was used to fire baking ovens. **32:** 5.47n.

7.1–6: Judging others (Lk 6.37–38,41–42). **1:** *Be judged*, by God. **6:** *Holy*, meat from the sacrifice or possibly the deeper truths of the Gospel; *dogs* were considered scavengers and *swine* were unclean animals.

7.7–23: The way of righteousness (Lk 11.9–13; 6.43–44; 13.24–27). The following sayings from Q embody Matthew's ethic of righteousness. **12:** The "Golden Rule" epitomizing Jesus' ethical teaching. A similar principle is attributed to the Pharisee Hillel (*b. Shabb* 31a; cf. Tob 4.15). **13:** *Narrow gate*, a metaphor for entering

¹⁵ "Beware of false prophets, who come to you in sheep's clothing but inwardly are ravenous wolves. ¹⁶ You will know them by their fruits. Are grapes gathered from thorns, or figs from thistles? ¹⁷ In the same way, every good tree bears good fruit, but the bad tree bears bad fruit. ¹⁸ A good tree cannot bear bad fruit, nor can a bad tree bear good fruit. ¹⁹ Every tree that does not bear good fruit is cut down and thrown into the fire. ²⁰ Thus you will know them by their fruits.

²¹ "Not everyone who says to me, 'Lord, Lord,' will enter the kingdom of heaven, but only the one who does the will of my Father in heaven. ²² On that day many will say to me, 'Lord, Lord, did we not prophesy in your name, and cast out demons in your name, and do many deeds of power in your name?' ²³ Then I will declare to them, 'I never knew you; go away from me, you evildoers.'

²⁴ "Everyone then who hears these words of mine and acts on them will be like a wise man who built his house on rock. ²⁵ The rain fell, the floods came, and the winds blew and beat on that house, but it did not fall, because it had been founded on rock. ²⁶ And everyone who hears these words of mine and does not act on them will be like a foolish man who built his house on sand. ²⁷ The rain fell, and the floods came, and the winds blew and beat against that house, and it fell—and great was its fall!"

²⁸ Now when Jesus had finished saying these things, the crowds were astounded at his teaching, ²⁹ for he taught them as one having authority, and not as their scribes.

8 When Jesus[a] had come down from the mountain, great crowds followed him; ² and there was a leper[b] who came to him and knelt before him, saying, "Lord, if you choose, you can make me clean." ³ He stretched out his hand and touched him, saying, "I do choose. Be made clean!" Immediately his leprosy[b] was cleansed. ⁴ Then Jesus said to him, "See that you say nothing to anyone; but go, show yourself to the priest, and offer the gift that Moses commanded, as a testimony to them."

⁵ When he entered Capernaum, a centurion came to him, appealing to him ⁶ and saying, "Lord, my servant is lying at home paralyzed, in terrible distress." ⁷ And he said to him, "I will come and cure him." ⁸ The cen-

a   Gk *he*
b   The terms *leper* and *leprosy* can refer to several diseases

the kingdom of God. **15:** *False prophets*, possibly itinerant Christian prophets 7.22; 23.34; *Did.* 11.7–12. **16:** *Fruits*, repentance and righteous behavior. **22:** *That day*, the day of judgment. *In your name*, "on behalf of" or "with the authority of." **23:** *Evildoers*, Ps 6.8.

7.24–29: The two foundations (Lk 6.47–49). **24:** *These words of mine*, obedience to Jesus' words, as to the will of God (7.21), is the only way to achieve righteousness and enter the kingdom. In the Sermon, Jesus has provided his hearers with a solid foundation of *rock* (16.18). **28:** The *crowds*, not mentioned at the beginning of the discourse, appear as the audience beyond the inner circle of disciples. Their presence suggests that Jesus' words are directed not only to the disciples but to all followers of Jesus. **29:** *Scribes*, 2.4n. All five of Matthew's discourses close with a reference to judgment.

8.1–9.38: The deeds of the Messiah. Matthew follows his epitome of Jesus' teaching with a collection of Jesus' miracles: the Messiah of word is succeeded by the Messiah of deed. While Matthew conforms to the order of Mark in a general way, he has made considerable use of Q and his own traditions (two of which are doublets; see 9.27–31 and 9.32–34). To create the Messiah of deed sequence Matthew has introduced five miracle stories so that chs 8–9 form a composite of ten miracle accounts interleaved with two discipleship narratives (8.18–22; 9.9–17).

8.1–4: The cleansing of a leper (Mk 1.40–45; Lk 5.12–16). Matthew emphasizes Jesus' divine calm by eliminating Mark's reference to Jesus' emotions (1.41,43). **2:** *Make me clean*, the skin condition of lepers rendered them ceremonially unclean (Lev 13.1–59; Num 5.1–4). **3:** *Leprosy* was a serious skin disease, including what we describe as leprosy (Hansen's disease), as well as many other disorders such as psoriasis, lupus, ringworm, and favus. **4:** *The gift that Moses commanded*, offerings for the cleansing of a leper (Lev. 14.10–32). This leper heeds Jesus' command to tell no one (contrast Mk 1.40–5).

8.5–17: Many healings (Lk 7.1–10; Jn 4.43–54; Mk 1.29–34; Lk 4.38–41). **5:** *Centurion*, a Roman officer com-

turion answered, "Lord, I am not worthy to have you come under my roof; but only speak the word, and my servant will be healed. [9] For I also am a man under authority, with soldiers under me; and I say to one, 'Go,' and he goes, and to another, 'Come,' and he comes, and to my slave, 'Do this,' and the slave does it." [10] When Jesus heard him, he was amazed and said to those who followed him, "Truly I tell you, in no one[a] in Israel have I found such faith. [11] I tell you, many will come from east and west and will eat with Abraham and Isaac and Jacob in the kingdom of heaven, [12] while the heirs of the kingdom will be thrown into the outer darkness, where there will be weeping and gnashing of teeth." [13] And to the centurion Jesus said, "Go; let it be done for you according to your faith." And the servant was healed in that hour.

[14] When Jesus entered Peter's house, he saw his mother-in-law lying in bed with a fever; [15] he touched her hand, and the fever left her, and she got up and began to serve him. [16] That evening they brought to him many who were possessed with demons; and he cast out the spirits with a word, and cured all who were sick. [17] This was to fulfill what had been spoken through the prophet Isaiah, "He took our infirmities and bore our diseases."

[18] Now when Jesus saw great crowds around him, he gave orders to go over to the other side. [19] A scribe then approached and said, "Teacher, I will follow you wherever you go." [20] And Jesus said to him, "Foxes have holes, and birds of the air have nests; but the Son of Man has nowhere to lay his head." [21] Another of his disciples said to him, "Lord, first let me go and bury my father." [22] But Jesus said to him, "Follow me, and let the dead bury their own dead."

[23] And when he got into the boat, his disciples followed him. [24] A windstorm arose on the sea, so great that the boat was being swamped by the waves; but he was asleep. [25] And they went and woke him up, saying, "Lord, save us! We are perishing!" [26] And he said to them, "Why are you afraid, you of little faith?" Then he got up and rebuked the winds and the sea; and there was a dead calm. [27] They were amazed, saying, "What sort of man is this, that even the winds and the sea obey him?"

[28] When he came to the other side, to the country of the Gadarenes,[b] two demoniacs coming out of the tombs met him. They were so fierce that no one could pass that way. [29] Suddenly they shouted, "What have you to do with us, Son of God? Have you come here to torment us before the time?" [30] Now a large herd of swine was feeding at some distance from them. [31] The demons begged him, "If you cast us out, send us into the herd of swine." [32] And he said to them, "Go!" So they came out and entered the swine; and

[a] Other ancient authorities read *Truly I tell you, not even*

[b] Other ancient authorities read *Gergesenes*; others, *Gerasenes*

manding about a hundred men. **6:** *Servant,* or "child." **8:** *I am not worthy,* contact with Gentiles could make Jews ceremonially unclean (Acts 10.28; *m. Avoda Zara*) **10:** *Faith,* in Matthew the two figures commended by Jesus for their faith are Gentiles (cf. 15.28). **11:** *Eat . . . in the kingdom,* the messianic banquet (22.1–10; Isa 25.6). **12:** *1 Enoch* 10.4–6; 62.11. *Gnashing of teeth,* an indication of sharp pain or vexation. This phrase, which occurs six times in Matthew, expresses the dire consequences of exclusion from the kingdom (13.42,50; 22.13; 24.51; 25.30; cf. Lk 12.47; 13.28). **17:** A fulfillment citation of Isaiah 53.4. Matthew's form of the citation emphasizes physical rather than spiritual healing.

8.18–22: Would-be followers of Jesus (Lk 9.57–62). **18:** *Other side,* the eastern shore of the Sea of Galilee. **20:** *Son of Man,* an enigmatic self-designation used by Jesus that has at least three senses in Matthew: Jesus as a human being; Jesus as a figure who must suffer and die; Jesus as divine judge at the end of days (cf. Dan 7.13–14). The first sense is in view here. **21:** *Bury my father,* although the burial of kinsmen was among the most pressing of sacred duties for Jews (Tob 1.18–19), it is entirely eclipsed by the call to follow Jesus.

8.23–34: The calming of a storm and the healing of two demoniacs (Mk 4.35–5.20; Lk 8.22–39). **26:** This nature miracle is Jesus' only nonhealing miracle in the first half of the Gospel. **28:** *Gadarenes,* Matthew situates the healing in Gadara, instead of Gerasa (Mk 5.1), which was located ca. 35 mi (56 km) from the sea. Gadara's territory was far closer to the Sea of Galilee. **29:** *Before the time,* the day of judgment. **30:** *Swine* suggest a Gentile region (7.6n.).

suddenly, the whole herd rushed down the steep bank into the sea and perished in the water. ³³ The swineherds ran off, and on going into the town, they told the whole story about what had happened to the demoniacs. ³⁴ Then the whole town came out to meet Jesus; and when they saw him, they begged

9 him to leave their neighborhood. ¹ And after getting into a boat he crossed the sea and came to his own town.

² And just then some people were carrying a paralyzed man lying on a bed. When Jesus saw their faith, he said to the paralytic, "Take heart, son; your sins are forgiven." ³ Then some of the scribes said to themselves, "This man is blaspheming." ⁴ But Jesus, perceiving their thoughts, said, "Why do you think evil in your hearts? ⁵ For which is easier, to say, 'Your sins are forgiven,' or to say, 'Stand up and walk'? ⁶ But so that you may know that the Son of Man has authority on earth to forgive sins"—he then said to the paralytic— "Stand up, take your bed and go to your home." ⁷ And he stood up and went to his home. ⁸ When the crowds saw it, they were filled with awe, and they glorified God, who had given such authority to human beings.

⁹ As Jesus was walking along, he saw a man called Matthew sitting at the tax booth; and he said to him, "Follow me." And he got up and followed him.

¹⁰ And as he sat at dinner[a] in the house, many tax collectors and sinners came and were sitting[b] with him and his disciples. ¹¹ When the Pharisees saw this, they said to his disciples, "Why does your teacher eat with tax collectors and sinners?" ¹² But when he heard this, he said, "Those who are well have no need of a physician, but those who are sick. ¹³ Go and learn what this means, 'I desire mercy, not sacrifice.' For I have come to call not the righteous but sinners."

¹⁴ Then the disciples of John came to him, saying, "Why do we and the Pharisees fast often,[c] but your disciples do not fast?" ¹⁵ And Jesus said to them, "The wedding guests cannot mourn as long as the bridegroom is with them, can they? The days will come when the bridegroom is taken away from them, and then they will fast. ¹⁶ No one sews a piece of unshrunk cloth on an old cloak, for the patch pulls away from the cloak, and a worse tear is made. ¹⁷ Neither is new wine put into old wineskins; otherwise, the skins burst, and the wine is spilled, and the skins are destroyed; but new wine is put into fresh wineskins, and so both are preserved."

¹⁸ While he was saying these things to them, suddenly a leader of the synagogue[d] came in and knelt before him, saying, "My daughter has just died; but come and lay your hand on her, and she will live." ¹⁹ And Jesus got up and followed him, with his disciples. ²⁰ Then suddenly a woman who had been suffering from hemorrhages for twelve years came up behind him and touched the fringe of his cloak, ²¹ for she said to herself, "If I only touch his cloak, I will be made well." ²² Jesus turned, and seeing her he said, "Take heart, daughter; your faith has made you well." And instantly the woman was made well. ²³ When Jesus came to the leader's house and saw the flute players and the crowd making a commotion, ²⁴ he said, "Go away; for the girl is not dead but sleeping." And they laughed at him. ²⁵ But when the crowd had been put outside, he went in and took her by the hand, and the girl got up. ²⁶ And the report of this spread throughout that district.

a Gk *reclined*
b Gk *were reclining*
c Other ancient authorities lack *often*
d Gk lacks *of the synagogue*

9.1–17: The ministry in Capernaum (Mk 2.1–22; Lk 5.17–39). **1:** *His own town*, Capernaum. **3:** *Blaspheming*, they accuse Jesus of dishonoring God's name because he claims that he, like God, can forgive sins. **8:** *To human beings*, Jesus' own authority to forgive has been bequeathed to Matthew's church. **9:** The change of Levi's name (Mk 2.14) has led some scholars to consider "Matthew" to be the evangelist's own signature; see also 5.46n. **13:** Jesus cites Hos. 6.6 here and again at 12.7. **15:** *Bridegroom*, Jesus' association with the coming of the kingdom makes him a festal figure like a bridegroom (cf. 22.1–14).
9.18–34: Four healings (Mk 5.21–43; Lk 8.40–56). **21:** *Touch his cloak*, if the hemorrhage was menstrual, the woman was ritually impure and would have made Jesus impure by touching him. **23:** *Flute players* were a feature of funeral rites. **27–31:** This healing narrative is a doublet of 20.29–34. The evangelist frequently doubles

²⁷ As Jesus went on from there, two blind men followed him, crying loudly, "Have mercy on us, Son of David!" ²⁸ When he entered the house, the blind men came to him; and Jesus said to them, "Do you believe that I am able to do this?" They said to him, "Yes, Lord." ²⁹ Then he touched their eyes and said, "According to your faith let it be done to you." ³⁰ And their eyes were opened. Then Jesus sternly ordered them, "See that no one knows of this." ³¹ But they went away and spread the news about him throughout that district.

³² After they had gone away, a demoniac who was mute was brought to him. ³³ And when the demon had been cast out, the one who had been mute spoke; and the crowds were amazed and said, "Never has anything like this been seen in Israel." ³⁴ But the Pharisees said, "By the ruler of the demons he casts out the demons."ᵃ

³⁵ Then Jesus went about all the cities and villages, teaching in their synagogues, and proclaiming the good news of the kingdom, and curing every disease and every sickness. ³⁶ When he saw the crowds, he had compassion for them, because they were harassed and helpless, like sheep without a shepherd. ³⁷ Then he said to his disciples, "The harvest is plentiful, but the laborers are few; ³⁸ therefore ask the Lord of the harvest to send out laborers into his harvest."

10 Then Jesusᵇ summoned his twelve disciples and gave them authority over unclean spirits, to cast them out, and to cure every disease and every sickness. ² These are the names of the twelve apostles: first, Simon, also known as Peter, and his brother Andrew; James son of Zebedee, and his brother John; ³ Philip and Bartholomew; Thomas and Matthew the tax collector; James son of Alphaeus, and Thaddaeus;ᶜ ⁴ Simon the Cananaean, and Judas Iscariot, the one who betrayed him.

⁵ These twelve Jesus sent out with the following instructions: "Go nowhere among the Gentiles, and enter no town of the Samaritans, ⁶ but go rather to the lost sheep of the house of Israel. ⁷ As you go, proclaim the good news, 'The kingdom of heaven has come near.'ᵈ ⁸ Cure the sick, raise the dead, cleanse the lepers,ᵉ cast out demons. You received without payment; give without payment. ⁹ Take no gold, or silver, or copper in your belts, ¹⁰ no bag for your journey, or two tunics, or sandals, or a staff; for laborers deserve their food. ¹¹ What-

---

a   Other ancient authorities lack this verse
b   Gk *he*
c   Other ancient authorities read *Lebbaeus*, or *Lebbaeus called Thaddaeus*
d   Or *is at hand*
e   The terms *leper* and *leprosy* can refer to several diseases

---

the number of figures in his sources (8.28–34; 9.27–31), possibly in keeping with the Jewish legal tradition of furnishing double witnesses to testify to the truth of something (Deut 19.15). **27**: The sick and marginalized often address Jesus as *Son of David* (1.1) in order to be healed. In the other Gospels the title does not have such therapeutic associations. **32–34**: A doublet of 12.22–24. **34**: *Ruler of the demons*: cf. 12.24–32.

9.35–38: The compassion of Jesus. 35: *Their synagogues* may indicate that Jewish Christians in Matthew's day were no longer participants in Jewish synagogues. In Jesus' day, synagogue buildings were well established as places of worship. **36**: Jesus' compassion for the leaderless people of Israel is a defining feature of Matthew's Jesus; cf. Num 27.17; Ezek 34.5. **37**: Normally a symbol for the final judgment, the *harvest* appears here as a metaphor for Jesus' mission, and forms a fitting introduction to the mission discourse.

10.1–11.1: The second (mission) discourse. This discourse appears to reflect both the time of Jesus and that of the early church. While Jesus delimits the disciples' mission to the people of Israel (10.5–6), the discourse goes on to speak of a later phase where the disciples were dragged before governors and provided testimony to the Gentiles (10.18).

10.1–15: The commissioning of the twelve (Mk 3.13–19; Lk 6.12–16; Mk 6.7–13; Lk 9.1–6). The miraculous acts performed by Jesus now become a feature of the disciples' own ministry. **2**: *Twelve apostles*, this is the first time Matthew explicitly names the twelve; their number reflects the twelve tribes of Israel (19.28). **3**: Matthew has added *tax collector*. **4**: *Iscariot* may mean "from Kerioth," a town in southern Judea. **5**: *Gentiles*, only Matthew has Jesus delimit his own and his disciples' ministry to *Israel*. *Samaritans* were the inhabitants of Samaria, a region that had been part of the Northern Kingdom of Israel until its defeat by the Assyrians in 722 BCE. Those Jews who were not deported were thought to have intermarried with Gentiles, and their descendants, the Samari-

ever town or village you enter, find out who in it is worthy, and stay there until you leave. [12] As you enter the house, greet it. [13] If the house is worthy, let your peace come upon it; but if it is not worthy, let your peace return to you. [14] If anyone will not welcome you or listen to your words, shake off the dust from your feet as you leave that house or town. [15] Truly I tell you, it will be more tolerable for the land of Sodom and Gomorrah on the day of judgment than for that town.

[16] "See, I am sending you out like sheep into the midst of wolves; so be wise as serpents and innocent as doves. [17] Beware of them, for they will hand you over to councils and flog you in their synagogues; [18] and you will be dragged before governors and kings because of me, as a testimony to them and the Gentiles. [19] When they hand you over, do not worry about how you are to speak or what you are to say; for what you are to say will be given to you at that time; [20] for it is not you who speak, but the Spirit of your Father speaking through you. [21] Brother will betray brother to death, and a father his child, and children will rise against parents and have them put to death; [22] and you will be hated by all because of my name. But the one who endures to the end will be saved. [23] When they persecute you in one town, flee to the next; for truly I tell you, you will not have gone through all the towns of Israel before the Son of Man comes.

[24] "A disciple is not above the teacher, nor a slave above the master; [25] it is enough for the disciple to be like the teacher, and the slave like the master. If they have called the master of the house Beelzebul, how much more will they malign those of his household!

[26] "So have no fear of them; for nothing is covered up that will not be uncovered, and nothing secret that will not become known. [27] What I say to you in the dark, tell in the light; and what you hear whispered, proclaim from the housetops. [28] Do not fear those who kill the body but cannot kill the soul; rather fear him who can destroy both soul and body in hell.[a] [29] Are not two sparrows sold for a penny? Yet not one of them will fall to the ground apart from your Father. [30] And even the hairs of your head are all counted. [31] So do not be afraid; you are of more value than many sparrows.

[32] "Everyone therefore who acknowledges me before others, I also will acknowledge before my Father in heaven; [33] but whoever denies me before others, I also will deny before my Father in heaven.

[34] "Do not think that I have come to bring peace to the earth; I have not come to bring peace, but a sword.

[35] For I have come to set a man against his
　　father,
and a daughter against her mother,
and a daughter-in-law against her mother-
　　in-law;
[36] and one's foes will be members of one's
　　own household.

[37] Whoever loves father or mother more than me is not worthy of me; and whoever loves son or daughter more than me is not worthy of me; [38] and whoever does not take up the cross and follow me is not worthy of me. [39] Those who find their life will lose it, and those who lose their life for my sake will find it.

[40] "Whoever welcomes you welcomes me, and whoever welcomes me welcomes the one who sent me. [41] Whoever welcomes a

[a] Gk Gehenna

---

tans, were reviled by Jews (see Jn 4.9). **6:** *Lost sheep of the house of Israel,* see 9.36n. **15:** *Sodom and Gomorrah,* Gen 18.16–19.39.

10.16–25: Coming persecutions (Mk 13.9–13; Lk 21.12–17). **17:** *Their synagogues,* see 9.35n. **18:** *Governors,* Roman officials, including prefects and procurators. *Gentiles,* an anticipation of the post-resurrection mission (28.19). **23:** *Son of Man,* most scholars interpret this difficult verse as a reference to Jesus' return (the Second Coming or Parousia). **25:** *They,* the Pharisees (9.34; 12.24). *Beelzebul,* a ruler of demons often identified with Satan; originally the name for the Canaanite deity Baal-zebul, "Baal (or "Lord") the Prince" (2 Kings 1.2–6). See 9.34; 12.24.

10.26–11.1: The consequences of mission (Lk 12.2–9; 12.51–53; 14.26–27; Mk 9.41). **26:** *Them,* the scribes and Pharisees. **29:** *Sparrows,* the least expensive of edible birds. **34–39:** The affliction and pain that must come prior to the messianic age of peace. **38:** *Cross,* a Roman punishment reserved for slaves and rebels. The condemned

prophet in the name of a prophet will receive a prophet's reward; and whoever welcomes a righteous person in the name of a righteous person will receive the reward of the righteous; [42] and whoever gives even a cup of cold water to one of these little ones in the name of a disciple—truly I tell you, none of these will lose their reward."

11 Now when Jesus had finished instructing his twelve disciples, he went on from there to teach and proclaim his message in their cities.

[2] When John heard in prison what the Messiah[a] was doing, he sent word by his[b] disciples [3] and said to him, "Are you the one who is to come, or are we to wait for another?" [4] Jesus answered them, "Go and tell John what you hear and see: [5] the blind receive their sight, the lame walk, the lepers[c] are cleansed, the deaf hear, the dead are raised, and the poor have good news brought to them. [6] And blessed is anyone who takes no offense at me."

[7] As they went away, Jesus began to speak to the crowds about John: "What did you go out into the wilderness to look at? A reed shaken by the wind? [8] What then did you go out to see? Someone[d] dressed in soft robes? Look, those who wear soft robes are in royal palaces. [9] What then did you go out to see? A prophet?[e] Yes, I tell you, and more than a prophet. [10] This is the one about whom it is written,

'See, I am sending my messenger ahead of you,
   who will prepare your way before you.'

[11] Truly I tell you, among those born of women no one has arisen greater than John the Baptist; yet the least in the kingdom of heaven is greater than he. [12] From the days of John the Baptist until now the kingdom of heaven has suffered violence,[f] and the violent take it by force. [13] For all the prophets and the law prophesied until John came; [14] and if you are willing to accept it, he is Elijah who is to come. [15] Let anyone with ears[g] listen!

[16] "But to what will I compare this generation? It is like children sitting in the marketplaces and calling to one another,

[17] 'We played the flute for you, and you did not dance;
   we wailed, and you did not mourn.'

[18] For John came neither eating nor drinking, and they say, 'He has a demon'; [19] the Son of Man came eating and drinking, and they say, 'Look, a glutton and a drunkard, a friend of tax collectors and sinners!' Yet wisdom is vindicated by her deeds."[h]

[20] Then he began to reproach the cities in which most of his deeds of power had been done, because they did not repent. [21] "Woe

a   Or *the Christ*
b   Other ancient authorities read *two of his*
c   The terms *leper* and *leprosy* can refer to several diseases
d   Or *Why then did you go out? To see someone*
e   Other ancient authorities read *Why then did you go out? To see a prophet?*
f   Or *has been coming violently*
g   Other ancient authorities add *to hear*
h   Other ancient authorities read *children*

were forced to carry their cross to the place of execution (27.32). **41:** *In the name of a prophet*, i.e., because he is a prophet. **42:** *Little ones*, those disciples occupying a humble or lowly position (18.6).

11.2–19: The messengers from John the Baptist (Lk 7.18–35). **2:** *Prison*, Herod's stronghold Machaerus, 5 mi (8 km) east of the Dead Sea (see 14.1–12). **3:** *The one who is to come*, the Messiah. **5:** *The blind . . . to them*, the deeds predicted of the Messiah (Isa 35.5–6; 61.1). **5:** *Lepers*: 8.3n. **11:** *The least*: The least are greater through having witnessed the kingdom's arrival in Jesus and through having been given the opportunity to act on that knowledge (5.19; 18.4). **12:** As had happened with many true prophets, violence would soon be visited on John and Jesus. **14:** John is the *Elijah* to come before the day of the Lord: he ushers in the kingdom (Mal 3.1; cf. 17.12–13). **15:** 13.9. **16:** *This generation*, the entire generation of Israel contemporaneous with Jesus. **19:** *Son of Man*, 8.20n. *Wisdom*, Jesus, like John, embodies wisdom, and is justified by his actions (11.4–5).

11.20–24: Woes to unrepentant cities (Lk 10.13–15). **21:** A woe oracle against Galilean towns for failing to respond to Jesus. *Chorazin* has been identified with Kerazeh, a town situated close to Capernaum. After Jerusalem and Capernaum, *Bethsaida* is the place most commonly associated with Jesus' ministry in the Gospels (Mk 8.22–6). *Sackcloth*, a rough fabric worn as a symbol of mourning and repentance. **21–23:** *Tyre* and *Sidon*, on the Mediterranean coast north of Israel, were often linked in prophetic oracles (Isa 23; Jer 25.22; 27.3–7; 47.4; Ezek

to you, Chorazin! Woe to you, Bethsaida! For if the deeds of power done in you had been done in Tyre and Sidon, they would have repented long ago in sackcloth and ashes. ²² But I tell you, on the day of judgment it will be more tolerable for Tyre and Sidon than for you. ²³ And you, Capernaum,

will you be exalted to heaven?

No, you will be brought down to Hades. For if the deeds of power done in you had been done in Sodom, it would have remained until this day. ²⁴ But I tell you that on the day of judgment it will be more tolerable for the land of Sodom than for you."

²⁵ At that time Jesus said, "I thank^a you, Father, Lord of heaven and earth, because you have hidden these things from the wise and the intelligent and have revealed them to infants; ²⁶ yes, Father, for such was your gracious will.^b ²⁷ All things have been handed over to me by my Father; and no one knows the Son except the Father, and no one knows the Father except the Son and anyone to whom the Son chooses to reveal him.

²⁸ "Come to me, all you that are weary and are carrying heavy burdens, and I will give you rest. ²⁹ Take my yoke upon you, and learn from me; for I am gentle and humble in heart, and you will find rest for your souls. ³⁰ For my yoke is easy, and my burden is light."

12 At that time Jesus went through the grainfields on the sabbath; his disciples were hungry, and they began to pluck heads of grain and to eat. ² When the Pharisees saw it, they said to him, "Look, your disciples are doing what is not lawful to do on the sabbath." ³ He said to them, "Have you not read what David did when he and his companions were hungry? ⁴ He entered the house of God and ate the bread of the Presence, which it was not lawful for him or his companions to eat, but only for the priests. ⁵ Or have you not read in the law that on the sabbath the priests in the temple break the sabbath and yet are guiltless? ⁶ I tell you, something greater than the temple is here. ⁷ But if you had known what this means, 'I desire mercy and not sacrifice,' you would not have condemned the guiltless. ⁸ For the Son of Man is lord of the sabbath."

⁹ He left that place and entered their synagogue; ¹⁰ a man was there with a withered hand, and they asked him, "Is it lawful to cure on the sabbath?" so that they might accuse him. ¹¹ He said to them, "Suppose one of you has only one sheep and it falls into a pit on the sabbath; will you not lay hold of it and lift it out? ¹² How much more valuable is a human being than a sheep! So it is lawful to do good on the sabbath." ¹³ Then he said to the man, "Stretch out your hand." He stretched it out, and it was restored, as sound as the other. ¹⁴ But the Pharisees went out and conspired against him, how to destroy him.

¹⁵ When Jesus became aware of this, he departed. Many crowds^c followed him, and he cured all of them, ¹⁶ and he ordered them not to make him known. ¹⁷ This was to fulfill what had been spoken through the prophet Isaiah:

¹⁸ "Here is my servant, whom I have
     chosen,

---

^a Or *praise*

^b Or *for so it was well-pleasing in your sight*

^c Other ancient authorities lack *crowds*

28.11–23; Joel 3.4–8), while *Sodom* was a stock example of an evil and unrepentant city (see 10.15n.).

11.25–30: Come to me and rest (Lk 11.21–22). **28:** *Heavy burdens*, 23.4. *Rest*, a defining feature of the new age (*1 Enoch* 63.6). **29:** *Yoke*, either Jesus' way of life or his teaching of the Torah's requirements. Jesus may be addressing his disciples here, but it is more likely the crowds of Israel (v. 7).

12.1–8: Plucking grain on the sabbath (Mk 2.23–28; Lk 6.1–5). **1:** *Grainfields*, wheat or barley. *Sabbath*, Ex 20.8–11; 34.21. Plucking grain was considered to be "work." **3:** *David*, 1 Sam 21.1–6. **4:** Priests were permitted to eat the *bread of the Presence* once it had been replaced with freshly consecrated loaves (Ex 25.30; Lev 24.5–9). **7:** A second citation (see 9.13) of Hos 6.6. For God, acts of mercy outweigh ritual observances. **8:** *Lord of the sabbath*, Jesus' authority exceeds even that of divinely established institutions.

12.9–21: The healing Messiah (Mk 3.1–6; Lk 6.6–11). **10:** Healing would be permitted if the afflicted person was unlikely to survive the sabbath. See also 6.26–30n. **11:** *One sheep*, most authorities permitted the rescue of animals on the sabbath (cf. *m. Shabb* 18.3; for a ruling against doing so, see CD 11.13–14). **15–21:** Isa 42.1–4, the longest fulfillment citation in Matthew. Here the servanthood of Jesus is strongly emphasized.

my beloved, with whom my soul is well pleased.

I will put my Spirit upon him,
and he will proclaim justice to the Gentiles.

[19] He will not wrangle or cry aloud,
nor will anyone hear his voice in the streets.

[20] He will not break a bruised reed
or quench a smoldering wick
until he brings justice to victory.

[21] And in his name the Gentiles will hope."

[22] Then they brought to him a demoniac who was blind and mute; and he cured him, so that the one who had been mute could speak and see. [23] All the crowds were amazed and said, "Can this be the Son of David?" [24] But when the Pharisees heard it, they said, "It is only by Beelzebul, the ruler of the demons, that this fellow casts out the demons." [25] He knew what they were thinking and said to them, "Every kingdom divided against itself is laid waste, and no city or house divided against itself will stand. [26] If Satan casts out Satan, he is divided against himself; how then will his kingdom stand? [27] If I cast out demons by Beelzebul, by whom do your own exorcists[a] cast them out? Therefore they will be your judges. [28] But if it is by the Spirit of God that I cast out demons, then the kingdom of God has come to you. [29] Or how can one enter a strong man's house and plunder his property, without first tying up the strong man? Then indeed the house can be plundered. [30] Whoever is not with me is against me, and whoever does not gather with me scatters. [31] Therefore I tell you, people will be forgiven for every sin and blasphemy, but blasphemy against the Spirit will not be forgiven. [32] Whoever speaks a word against the Son of Man will be forgiven, but whoever speaks against the Holy Spirit will not be forgiven, either in this age or in the age to come.

[33] "Either make the tree good, and its fruit good; or make the tree bad, and its fruit bad; for the tree is known by its fruit. [34] You brood of vipers! How can you speak good things, when you are evil? For out of the abundance of the heart the mouth speaks. [35] The good person brings good things out of a good treasure, and the evil person brings evil things out of an evil treasure. [36] I tell you, on the day of judgment you will have to give an account for every careless word you utter; [37] for by your words you will be justified, and by your words you will be condemned."

[38] Then some of the scribes and Pharisees said to him, "Teacher, we wish to see a sign from you." [39] But he answered them, "An evil and adulterous generation asks for a sign, but no sign will be given to it except the sign of the prophet Jonah. [40] For just as Jonah was three days and three nights in the belly of the sea monster, so for three days and three nights the Son of Man will be in the heart of the earth. [41] The people of Nineveh will rise up at the judgment with this generation and condemn it, because they repented at the proclamation of Jonah, and see, something greater than Jonah is here! [42] The queen of the South will rise up at the judgment with this generation and condemn it, because she came from the ends of the earth to listen to the wisdom of Solomon, and see, something greater than Solomon is here!

[43] "When the unclean spirit has gone out of a person, it wanders through waterless regions looking for a resting place, but it finds none. [44] Then it says, 'I will return to my house from which I came.' When it comes, it finds it empty, swept, and put in order.

---

[a] Gk sons

12.22–37: Jesus and Beelzebul (Mk 3.20–30; Lk 11.14–23; 12.10; 6.43–45). 22–24: A doublet of 9.32–34. 23: The title *Son of David* is synonymous with the Messiah of Israel (1.1; 9.27n.; Ezek 34; *Pss. Sol.* 17). The crowds merely broach the question of Jesus' identity, but their question is framed in such a way as to expect a negative answer: "This isn't . . . , is it?" 24: *Beelzebul*, 10.25n. 31: *Blasphemy*, impious denigration. 33: 7.17. 34: 3.7. 37: Jas 3.1–12.

12.38–45: The demand for a sign (Mk 8.11–12; Lk 11.29–32; 11.24–26). 38: 16.1n. 39: *Adulterous*, unfaithful to God. *Sign of the prophet Jonah*, Jesus' resurrection after three days and nights. 41: *Nineveh*, capital of the Assyrian empire, proverbial for its size and power. It was the subject of numerous prophetic oracles (Jon; Nah; Zeph 2.13; Tob 14). 42: *Queen of the South*, the queen of Sheba (1 Kings 10.1–13; 2 Chr 9.1–12). 43: *Waterless regions*, demons

[45] Then it goes and brings along seven other spirits more evil than itself, and they enter and live there; and the last state of that person is worse than the first. So will it be also with this evil generation."

[46] While he was still speaking to the crowds, his mother and his brothers were standing outside, wanting to speak to him. [47] Someone told him, "Look, your mother and your brothers are standing outside, wanting to speak to you."[a] [48] But to the one who had told him this, Jesus[b] replied, "Who is my mother, and who are my brothers?" [49] And pointing to his disciples, he said, "Here are my mother and my brothers! [50] For whoever does the will of my Father in heaven is my brother and sister and mother."

13 That same day Jesus went out of the house and sat beside the sea. [2] Such great crowds gathered around him that he got into a boat and sat there, while the whole crowd stood on the beach. [3] And he told them many things in parables, saying: "Listen! A sower went out to sow. [4] And as he sowed, some seeds fell on the path, and the birds came and ate them up. [5] Other seeds fell on rocky ground, where they did not have much soil, and they sprang up quickly, since they had no depth of soil. [6] But when the sun rose, they were scorched; and since they had no root, they withered away. [7] Other seeds fell among thorns, and the thorns grew up and choked them. [8] Other seeds fell on good soil and brought forth grain, some a hundredfold, some sixty, some thirty. [9] Let anyone with ears[c] listen!"

[10] Then the disciples came and asked him, "Why do you speak to them in parables?" [11] He answered, "To you it has been given to know the secrets[d] of the kingdom of heaven, but to them it has not been given. [12] For to those who have, more will be given, and they will have an abundance; but from those who have nothing, even what they have will be taken away. [13] The reason I speak to them in parables is that 'seeing they do not perceive, and hearing they do not listen, nor do they understand.' [14] With them indeed is fulfilled the prophecy of Isaiah that says:

'You will indeed listen, but never understand,
  and you will indeed look, but never perceive.
[15] For this people's heart has grown dull,
  and their ears are hard of hearing,
    and they have shut their eyes;
      so that they might not look with their eyes,
  and listen with their ears,
    and understand with their heart and turn—
      and I would heal them.'

[16] But blessed are your eyes, for they see, and your ears, for they hear. [17] Truly I tell you, many prophets and righteous people longed

---

a   Other ancient authorities lack verse 47
b   Gk *he*
c   Other ancient authorities add *to hear*
d   Or *mysteries*

---

were thought to reside in deserts (4.1; Tob 8.3). **45**: *Seven* often symbolizes "completeness," here suggesting complete possession. *This evil generation*, 11.16n.

12.46–50: The mother and brothers of Jesus (Mk 3.31–35; Lk 8.19–21). Obedience to God the Father is not only the most fundamental of familial obligations (8.21n.), it is also the ultimate basis of kinship.

13.1–53: The third discourse (the parable discourse). The word "parable" is derived from Gk "parabolē," "a placing beside," where a literary figure or story illumines something "placed beside" it—here, the nature of the kingdom of heaven: "It is the same with the kingdom of heaven as when . . ." In ch 13, only the parable of the sower is not introduced as a "kingdom" parable (but see v. 19). Four of the parables in this chapter and one of the interpretations (vv. 36–43) are unique to Matthew. The theme of growth in the first four parables emphasizes the inexorable expansion of the kingdom.

13.1–23: The parable of the sower and its interpretation (Mk 4.1–20; Lk 8.4–15). **1**: *Sea*, of Galilee. *Sat*, 5.1n. **2**: *Crowds*, 4.25n. **8**: These yields are exceptional, but not impossible. **11**: *Secrets*, the mysteries of the end of days (Dan 2.28). **13**: Where Mk 4.12 suggests that the purpose of Jesus' parabolic speech is to promote incomprehension, Matthew indicates that Jesus speaks in parables as a consequence of incomprehension by Jesus' audience. **14–15**: Isa 6.9–10. **16**: The disciples are *blessed* because, unlike "this people" (v. 15), they comprehend Jesus and

to see what you see, but did not see it, and to hear what you hear, but did not hear it.

¹⁸ "Hear then the parable of the sower. ¹⁹ When anyone hears the word of the kingdom and does not understand it, the evil one comes and snatches away what is sown in the heart; this is what was sown on the path. ²⁰ As for what was sown on rocky ground, this is the one who hears the word and immediately receives it with joy; ²¹ yet such a person has no root, but endures only for a while, and when trouble or persecution arises on account of the word, that person immediately falls away.^a ²² As for what was sown among thorns, this is the one who hears the word, but the cares of the world and the lure of wealth choke the word, and it yields nothing. ²³ But as for what was sown on good soil, this is the one who hears the word and understands it, who indeed bears fruit and yields, in one case a hundredfold, in another sixty, and in another thirty."

²⁴ He put before them another parable: "The kingdom of heaven may be compared to someone who sowed good seed in his field; ²⁵ but while everybody was asleep, an enemy came and sowed weeds among the wheat, and then went away. ²⁶ So when the plants came up and bore grain, then the weeds appeared as well. ²⁷ And the slaves of the householder came and said to him, 'Master, did you not sow good seed in your field? Where, then, did these weeds come from?' ²⁸ He answered, 'An enemy has done this.' The slaves said to him, 'Then do you want us to go and gather them?' ²⁹ But he replied, 'No; for in gathering the weeds you would uproot the wheat along with them. ³⁰ Let both of them grow together until the harvest; and at harvest time I will tell the reapers, Collect the weeds first and

bind them in bundles to be burned, but gather the wheat into my barn.'"

³¹ He put before them another parable: "The kingdom of heaven is like a mustard seed that someone took and sowed in his field; ³² it is the smallest of all the seeds, but when it has grown it is the greatest of shrubs and becomes a tree, so that the birds of the air come and make nests in its branches."

³³ He told them another parable: "The kingdom of heaven is like yeast that a woman took and mixed in with^b three measures of flour until all of it was leavened."

³⁴ Jesus told the crowds all these things in parables; without a parable he told them nothing. ³⁵ This was to fulfill what had been spoken through the prophet:^c

"I will open my mouth to speak in
    parables;
I will proclaim what has been hidden
    from the foundation of the
    world."^d

³⁶ Then he left the crowds and went into the house. And his disciples approached him, saying, "Explain to us the parable of the weeds of the field." ³⁷ He answered, "The one who sows the good seed is the Son of Man; ³⁸ the field is the world, and the good seed are the children of the kingdom; the weeds are the children of the evil one, ³⁹ and the enemy who sowed them is the devil; the harvest is the end of the age, and the reapers are angels. ⁴⁰ Just as the weeds are collected and burned up with fire, so will it be at the end of the age. ⁴¹ The Son of Man will send his angels, and

---

^a Gk *stumbles*
^b Gk *hid in*
^c Other ancient authorities read *the prophet Isaiah*
^d Other ancient authorities lack *of the world*

---

his message. **18–23:** In the Gospels only a few of Jesus' parables are provided with interpretations. **19:** *Does not understand it*, a characteristic Matthean addition.

13.24–33: Three parables of growth (Mk 4.30–32; Lk 13.18–21). **25:** *Weeds*, perhaps darnel, a weed resembling wheat. **31:** *Mustard seed*, the precise species cannot be determined, though mustard seed was popularly regarded as the smallest of seeds planted by farmers. **32:** *Tree*, actually a shrub growing to a height of ca. 10 ft (3 m). *Birds*, Ezek 17.23; Dan 4.10–12. **33:** *Yeast*, not yeast but leaven, a remnant of fermented dough used as a "starter" for raising a new batch of dough. *Three measures*, ca. 2/3 bu (21 L).

13.34–35: The use of parables (Mk 4.33–34). A fulfillment citation (Ps 78.2) attributed to Asaph the seer (2 Chr 29.30). In this half of the discourse Jesus' teaching is reserved for the disciples.

13.36–43: The parable of the weeds explained. 36: *House*, 13.1. **38:** *Children of the kingdom*, those worthy of the kingdom. **41:** *Out of his kingdom*, some scholars have identified the kingdom with the church, but in view

they will collect out of his kingdom all causes of sin and all evildoers, [42] and they will throw them into the furnace of fire, where there will be weeping and gnashing of teeth. [43] Then the righteous will shine like the sun in the kingdom of their Father. Let anyone with ears[a] listen!

[44] "The kingdom of heaven is like treasure hidden in a field, which someone found and hid; then in his joy he goes and sells all that he has and buys that field.

[45] "Again, the kingdom of heaven is like a merchant in search of fine pearls; [46] on finding one pearl of great value, he went and sold all that he had and bought it.

[47] "Again, the kingdom of heaven is like a net that was thrown into the sea and caught fish of every kind; [48] when it was full, they drew it ashore, sat down, and put the good into baskets but threw out the bad. [49] So it will be at the end of the age. The angels will come out and separate the evil from the righteous [50] and throw them into the furnace of fire, where there will be weeping and gnashing of teeth.

[51] "Have you understood all this?" They answered, "Yes." [52] And he said to them, "Therefore every scribe who has been trained for the kingdom of heaven is like the master of a household who brings out of his treasure what is new and what is old." [53] When Jesus had finished these parables, he left that place.

[54] He came to his hometown and began to teach the people[b] in their synagogue, so that they were astounded and said, "Where did this man get this wisdom and these deeds

of power? [55] Is not this the carpenter's son? Is not his mother called Mary? And are not his brothers James and Joseph and Simon and Judas? [56] And are not all his sisters with us? Where then did this man get all this?" [57] And they took offense at him. But Jesus said to them, "Prophets are not without honor except in their own country and in their own house." [58] And he did not do many deeds of power there, because of their unbelief.

14 At that time Herod the ruler[c] heard reports about Jesus; [2] and he said to his servants, "This is John the Baptist; he has been raised from the dead, and for this reason these powers are at work in him." [3] For Herod had arrested John, bound him, and put him in prison on account of Herodias, his brother Philip's wife,[d] [4] because John had been telling him, "It is not lawful for you to have her." [5] Though Herod[e] wanted to put him to death, he feared the crowd, because they regarded him as a prophet. [6] But when Herod's birthday came, the daughter of Herodias danced before the company, and she pleased Herod [7] so much that he promised on oath to grant her whatever she might ask. [8] Prompted by her mother, she said, "Give me the head of John the Baptist here on a platter." [9] The king was grieved, yet out of regard for his oaths and for the guests, he

a Other ancient authorities add *to hear*
b Gk *them*
c Gk *tetrarch*
d Other ancient authorities read *his brother's wife*
e Gk *he*

of v. 38 it is better understood as the world. *Causes of sin,* 16.23; 18.7. *Evildoers,* 7.23. **42:** 8.12n. **43:** *Shine like the sun,* Dan 12.3.

13.44–53: Four more parables. 44: *Field,* in the absence of banks, valuables were often buried for safekeeping (25.25). **47:** *Net,* a seine net. **51:** The final parable in the chapter. *Understood,* in contrast to Jesus' disciples in Mk 4.13,33–34, here the disciples confirm their understanding of Jesus' teaching. **52:** *Scribe,* perhaps a self-portrait of the Gospel's author, or an indication of early Christian scribes (23.34). *His treasure,* the storeroom from which he draws his understanding of Jesus' ministry (the *new*) and of the Jewish Scriptures (the *old*).

13.54–58: The rejection of Jesus at Nazareth (Mk 6.1–6; Lk 4.16–30). **54:** *His hometown,* Nazareth. **55:** *Carpenter's son* contrasts with "carpenter" (Mk 6.3). The word translated here as "carpenter" can also mean "builder" or "stonemason." What Mk 6.5 describes as an inability to perform mighty deeds becomes, in Matthew, an unwillingness to do so in the face of the Nazarenes' disbelief (13.58). *His brothers,* Mk 6.3; Jude 1.

14.1–12: The death of John the Baptist (Mk 6.14–29; Lk 9.7–9). **1:** *Herod,* Matthew uses the correct designation "Herod the Tetrarch" (see textual note *c*) for Herod Antipas (2.22n.) in contrast to the "King Herod" of Mk 6.14. **4:** Lev 18.16; 20.21. **6:** *Daughter of Herodias,* Josephus identifies her as Salome (*Ant.* 18.136; for Josephus's account of John's death, see *Ant.* 18.116–19). Compare Esth 2.9.

commanded it to be given; [10] he sent and had John beheaded in the prison. [11] The head was brought on a platter and given to the girl, who brought it to her mother. [12] His disciples came and took the body and buried it; then they went and told Jesus.

[13] Now when Jesus heard this, he withdrew from there in a boat to a deserted place by himself. But when the crowds heard it, they followed him on foot from the towns. [14] When he went ashore, he saw a great crowd; and he had compassion for them and cured their sick. [15] When it was evening, the disciples came to him and said, "This is a deserted place, and the hour is now late; send the crowds away so that they may go into the villages and buy food for themselves." [16] Jesus said to them, "They need not go away; you give them something to eat." [17] They replied, "We have nothing here but five loaves and two fish." [18] And he said, "Bring them here to me." [19] Then he ordered the crowds to sit down on the grass. Taking the five loaves and the two fish, he looked up to heaven, and blessed and broke the loaves, and gave them to the disciples, and the disciples gave them to the crowds. [20] And all ate and were filled; and they took up what was left over of the broken pieces, twelve baskets full. [21] And those who ate were about five thousand men, besides women and children.

[22] Immediately he made the disciples get into the boat and go on ahead to the other side, while he dismissed the crowds. [23] And after he had dismissed the crowds, he went up the mountain by himself to pray. When evening came, he was there alone, [24] but by this time the boat, battered by the waves, was far from the land,[a] for the wind was against them. [25] And early in the morning he came walking toward them on the sea. [26] But when the disciples saw him walking on the sea, they were terrified, saying, "It is a ghost!" And they cried out in fear. [27] But immediately Jesus spoke to them and said, "Take heart, it is I; do not be afraid."

[28] Peter answered him, "Lord, if it is you, command me to come to you on the water." [29] He said, "Come." So Peter got out of the boat, started walking on the water, and came toward Jesus. [30] But when he noticed the strong wind,[b] he became frightened, and beginning to sink, he cried out, "Lord, save me!" [31] Jesus immediately reached out his hand and caught him, saying to him, "You of little faith, why did you doubt?" [32] When they got into the boat, the wind ceased. [33] And those in the boat worshiped him, saying, "Truly you are the Son of God."

[34] When they had crossed over, they came to land at Gennesaret. [35] After the people of that place recognized him, they sent word throughout the region and brought all who were sick to him, [36] and begged him that they might touch even the fringe of his cloak; and all who touched it were healed.

15 Then Pharisees and scribes came to Jesus from Jerusalem and said, [2] "Why do your disciples break the tradition of the elders? For they do not wash their hands before they eat." [3] He answered them, "And why do you break the commandment of God for the sake of your tradition? [4] For God said,[c] 'Honor your father and your mother,' and, 'Whoever speaks evil of father or mother must surely die.' [5] But you say that whoever tells father or mother, 'Whatever support you might have had from me is given to God,'[d]

---

a   Other ancient authorities read *was out on the sea*
b   Other ancient authorities read *the wind*
c   Other ancient authorities read *commanded, saying*
d   Or *is an offering*

14.13–36: The feeding of the five thousand and the walking on the water (Mk 6.30–56; Lk 9.10–17; Jn 6.1–21). These are the only miracles found in all four Gospels. There is a doublet for the feeding in 15.32–38; cf. also 1 Kings 17.8–16; 2 Kings 4.42–44. **19:** *Looked . . . blessed . . . broke . . . gave . . .* , the language suggests a liturgical action; cf. 26.26. **21:** Matthew increases the magnitude of the miracle by adding *besides women and children*. **22:** The *other side* of the Sea of Galilee. **25:** *Early in the morning*, lit., "in the fourth watch of the night," i.e., between 3 and 6 AM. **27:** *It is I*, lit., "I am," a reference to the divine name (Ex 3.14). **28:** Peter's walking on the water is unique to Matthew and brings out both the role of Peter as the representative of the disciples, and his—and their— need for faith. **34:** *Gennesaret*, either a narrow plain on the west side of the Sea, or a town on that plain; 4.18n.

15.1–20: The tradition of the elders (Mk 7.1–23). **2:** *Tradition of the elders*, Pharisaic oral law designed to elucidate and protect the law of Moses (3.8n.). *Wash*, eat food in a state of ritual purity. **3:** Hand-washing was a

then that person need not honor the father.[a] [6] So, for the sake of your tradition, you make void the word[b] of God. [7] You hypocrites! Isaiah prophesied rightly about you when he said:

[8] 'This people honors me with their lips,
  but their hearts are far from me;
[9] in vain do they worship me,
  teaching human precepts as doctrines.'"

[10] Then he called the crowd to him and said to them, "Listen and understand: [11] it is not what goes into the mouth that defiles a person, but it is what comes out of the mouth that defiles." [12] Then the disciples approached and said to him, "Do you know that the Pharisees took offense when they heard what you said?" [13] He answered, "Every plant that my heavenly Father has not planted will be uprooted. [14] Let them alone; they are blind guides of the blind.[c] And if one blind person guides another, both will fall into a pit." [15] But Peter said to him, "Explain this parable to us." [16] Then he said, "Are you also still without understanding? [17] Do you not see that whatever goes into the mouth enters the stomach, and goes out into the sewer? [18] But what comes out of the mouth proceeds from the heart, and this is what defiles. [19] For out of the heart come evil intentions, murder, adultery, fornication, theft, false witness, slander. [20] These are what defile a person, but to eat with unwashed hands does not defile."

[21] Jesus left that place and went away to the district of Tyre and Sidon. [22] Just then a Canaanite woman from that region came out and started shouting, "Have mercy on me, Lord, Son of David; my daughter is tormented by a demon." [23] But he did not answer her at all. And his disciples came and urged him, saying, "Send her away, for she keeps shouting after us." [24] He answered, "I was sent only to the lost sheep of the house of Israel." [25] But she came and knelt before him, saying, "Lord, help me." [26] He answered, "It is not fair to take the children's food and throw it to the dogs." [27] She said, "Yes, Lord, yet even the dogs eat the crumbs that fall from their masters' table." [28] Then Jesus answered her, "Woman, great is your faith! Let it be done for you as you wish." And her daughter was healed instantly.

[29] After Jesus had left that place, he passed along the Sea of Galilee, and he went up the mountain, where he sat down. [30] Great crowds came to him, bringing with them the lame, the maimed, the blind, the mute, and many others. They put them at his feet, and he cured them, [31] so that the crowd was amazed when they saw the mute speaking, the maimed whole, the lame walking, and the blind seeing. And they praised the God of Israel.

[32] Then Jesus called his disciples to him and said, "I have compassion for the crowd, because they have been with me now for three days and have nothing to eat; and I do not want to send them away hungry, for they might faint on the way." [33] The disciples said to him, "Where are we to get enough bread in the desert to feed so great a crowd?" [34] Jesus asked them, "How many loaves have you?" They said, "Seven, and a few small fish." [35] Then ordering the crowd to sit down on the ground, [36] he took the seven loaves and the fish; and after giving thanks he broke them and gave them to the disciples, and the disciples gave them to the crowds. [37] And all

a Other ancient authorities add *or the mother*
b Other ancient authorities read *law*; others, *commandment*
c Other ancient authorities lack *of the blind*

Pharisaic *tradition*, not stipulated by the Torah. **4**: *God said*, Ex 20.12; 21.17; Lev 20.9; Deut 5.16. **7–9**: Isa 29.13. **11**: *Defiles*, renders one ritually unclean. **14**: *Blind guides*, 23.16,24. **15**: Significantly, Matthew stops short of Mark's conclusion, "Thus he declared all foods clean" (Mk 7.19).

15.21–28: The Canaanite woman's faith (Mk 7.24–30). **21**: *District*, perhaps the largely Jewish enclave in Syria bordering on northwest Galilee. **22**: *Canaanite* replaces Mark's more accurate, political designation "Syrophoenician." The archaic term "Canaanite" may be designed to recall Israel's traditional enemies (Deut 7.1). *Son of David*, see 9.27n. **24**: The limited mission to Israel enjoined on the disciples at 10.5–6 also applies to Jesus' own ministry. **27**: *Dogs*, "little dogs" or household pets as metaphors for Gentiles. **28**: Like the Roman centurion (8.5–10), the Gentile woman is praised for exemplary *faith*.

15.29–39: The feeding and healing of many people (Mk 8.1–10). There is a doublet to the feeding in 14.13–23.

of them ate and were filled; and they took up the broken pieces left over, seven baskets full. [38] Those who had eaten were four thousand men, besides women and children. [39] After sending away the crowds, he got into the boat and went to the region of Magadan.[a]

16 The Pharisees and Sadducees came, and to test Jesus[b] they asked him to show them a sign from heaven. [2] He answered them, "When it is evening, you say, 'It will be fair weather, for the sky is red.' [3] And in the morning, 'It will be stormy today, for the sky is red and threatening.' You know how to interpret the appearance of the sky, but you cannot interpret the signs of the times.[c] [4] An evil and adulterous generation asks for a sign, but no sign will be given to it except the sign of Jonah." Then he left them and went away.

[5] When the disciples reached the other side, they had forgotten to bring any bread. [6] Jesus said to them, "Watch out, and beware of the yeast of the Pharisees and Sadducees." [7] They said to one another, "It is because we have brought no bread." [8] And becoming aware of it, Jesus said, "You of little faith, why are you talking about having no bread? [9] Do you still not perceive? Do you not remember the five loaves for the five thousand, and how many baskets you gathered? [10] Or the seven loaves for the four thousand, and how many baskets you gathered? [11] How could you fail

to perceive that I was not speaking about bread? Beware of the yeast of the Pharisees and Sadducees!" [12] Then they understood that he had not told them to beware of the yeast of bread, but of the teaching of the Pharisees and Sadducees.

[13] Now when Jesus came into the district of Caesarea Philippi, he asked his disciples, "Who do people say that the Son of Man is?" [14] And they said, "Some say John the Baptist, but others Elijah, and still others Jeremiah or one of the prophets." [15] He said to them, "But who do you say that I am?" [16] Simon Peter answered, "You are the Messiah,[d] the Son of the living God." [17] And Jesus answered him, "Blessed are you, Simon son of Jonah! For flesh and blood has not revealed this to you, but my Father in heaven. [18] And I tell you, you are Peter,[e] and on this rock[f] I will build my church, and the gates of Hades will not prevail against it. [19] I will give you the keys of the kingdom of heaven, and whatever you bind on earth will be bound

a   Other ancient authorities read *Magdala* or *Magdalan*
b   Gk *him*
c   Other ancient authorities lack [2]*When it is . . . of the times*
d   Or *the Christ*
e   Gk *Petros*
f   Gk *petra*

30: 9.35–36n. **38:** The four thousand may be Gentiles but are more likely Israelites. **39:** *Magadan* (see textual note *a*) replaces Mark's "district of Dalmanutha" (Mk 8.10); both locales are unknown.

16.1–12: The Pharisees and Sadducees (Mk 8.11–21; Lk 12.54–56). **1:** 3.7n. *Sign*, probably a cosmic event. **4:** *Sign of Jonah*, see 12.38–41. **6:** Here *yeast* (leaven) is a metaphor for teaching, but teaching that has the capacity to corrupt everything with which it comes into contact. At 13.33 the metaphor is used positively. **8:** 14.28n. **9:** 14.13–21. **10:** 15.32–39.

16.13–20: Peter's confession about Jesus (Mk 8.27–30; Lk 9.18–21). **13:** *Caesarea Philippi*, a city 25 mi (40 km) north of the Sea of Galilee, formerly Baneas and renamed by Philip in honor of Augustus. It is to be distinguished from Caesarea Maritima, the Hellenistic city redesigned and expanded by Herod the Great on the Mediterranean coast that served as the headquarters of the Roman governor (Acts 8.40; 21.8,16). *Son of Man*, 8.20n. **14:** *Jeremiah*, Matthew's inclusion of Jeremiah among the prophets emphasizes the parallels between Jesus and Jeremiah (also mentioned in Mt 2.17; 27.9). **16:** *Son of the living God* is found only in Matthew's version of Peter's confession (cf. 26.63; Ps 42.2). The title has strong messianic overtones (4Q174.10–14). **17:** *Son of Jonah*, either a variant of "son of John" (Jn 1.42) or an indication that Peter has a prophetic gift like Jonah's. *Flesh and blood*, humans. **18:** This promise to Peter is found only in Matthew. *Peter . . . rock*, Jesus' nickname for Simon (Gk "petros") means "stone" or "rock." The same pun works with its Aramaic equivalent, Kephas (1 Cor 1.12; 15.5; Gal 1.18). *Church*, the only occurrences of the word "church" ("ekklesia") in the Gospels are here and at 18.17. *Hades* is the Greek term for both the god of the dead and his realm, the latter roughly equivalent to Heb Sheol, the shadowy domain of all the dead. The *gates of Hades* may mean the "powers of death." **19:** *Keys*, a symbolic ascription of power (see Isa 22.22), bequeathing Peter the authority to oversee admission to the church (cf. 18.18).

in heaven, and whatever you loose on earth will be loosed in heaven." [20] Then he sternly ordered the disciples not to tell anyone that he was[a] the Messiah.[b]

[21] From that time on, Jesus began to show his disciples that he must go to Jerusalem and undergo great suffering at the hands of the elders and chief priests and scribes, and be killed, and on the third day be raised. [22] And Peter took him aside and began to rebuke him, saying, "God forbid it, Lord! This must never happen to you." [23] But he turned and said to Peter, "Get behind me, Satan! You are a stumbling block to me; for you are setting your mind not on divine things but on human things."

[24] Then Jesus told his disciples, "If any want to become my followers, let them deny themselves and take up their cross and follow me. [25] For those who want to save their life will lose it, and those who lose their life for my sake will find it. [26] For what will it profit them if they gain the whole world but forfeit their life? Or what will they give in return for their life?

[27] "For the Son of Man is to come with his angels in the glory of his Father, and then he will repay everyone for what has been done. [28] Truly I tell you, there are some standing here who will not taste death before they see the Son of Man coming in his kingdom."

17 Six days later, Jesus took with him Peter and James and his brother John and led them up a high mountain, by themselves. [2] And he was transfigured before them, and his face shone like the sun, and his clothes became dazzling white. [3] Suddenly there appeared to them Moses and Elijah, talking with him. [4] Then Peter said to Jesus, "Lord, it is good for us to be here; if you wish, I[c] will make three dwellings[d] here, one for you, one for Moses, and one for Elijah." [5] While he was still speaking, suddenly a bright cloud overshadowed them, and from the cloud a voice said, "This is my Son, the Beloved;[e] with him I am well pleased; listen to him!" [6] When the disciples heard this, they fell to the ground and were overcome by fear. [7] But Jesus came and touched them, saying, "Get up and do not be afraid." [8] And when they looked up, they saw no one except Jesus himself alone.

[9] As they were coming down the mountain, Jesus ordered them, "Tell no one about the vision until after the Son of Man has been raised from the dead." [10] And the disciples asked him, "Why, then, do the scribes say that Elijah must come first?" [11] He replied, "Elijah is indeed coming and will restore all things; [12] but I tell you that Elijah has already come, and they did not recognize him, but they did to him whatever they pleased. So also the Son of Man is about to suffer at their hands." [13] Then the disciples understood that he was speaking to them about John the Baptist.

[14] When they came to the crowd, a man came to him, knelt before him, [15] and said, "Lord, have mercy on my son, for he is an epileptic and he suffers terribly; he often falls into the fire and often into the water. [16] And I brought him to your disciples, but they could not cure him." [17] Jesus answered, "You faithless and perverse generation, how much longer must I be with you? How much longer must

a   Other ancient authorities add *Jesus*
b   Or *the Christ*
c   Other ancient authorities read *we*
d   Or *tents*
e   Or *my beloved Son*

16.21–28: Jesus foretells his death and resurrection (Mk 8.31–9.1; Lk 9.22–27). 21: The phrase *from that time on* may be a marker signaling the last third of the Gospel (4.17n.). The first of three passion predictions (17.22–23; 20.17–19; cf. 26.1–2). 23: *Stumbling block* or obstacle. 24: 10.38n. 28: *Some standing here*, possibly a reference to Jesus' transfiguration (17.1–13).

17.1–13: The transfiguration of Jesus (Mk 9.2–13; Lk 9.28–36). 1: *High mountain*, traditionally identified with Mount Tabor or, because of its proximity to Caesarea Philippi, with Mount Hermon. The setting is reminiscent of God's revelation to Moses, and later Elijah, on Sinai (Horeb) (Ex 34.1–9; 1 Kings 19.1–18). 3: *Moses and Elijah* symbolize, respectively, the Law and the prophets, the first two divisions of the Hebrew Bible. 5: *My Son*, 3.17n. 10: *Elijah must come first*, according to the traditional interpretation of Mal 4.5, Elijah would come "before the day of the Lord." 12: *Elijah has already come* in the person of John the Baptist.

17.14–21: The healing of a boy with a demon (Mk 9.14–29; Lk 9.37–43). 17: *Faithless and perverse generation*,

I put up with you? Bring him here to me." [18] And Jesus rebuked the demon,[a] and it[b] came out of him, and the boy was cured instantly. [19] Then the disciples came to Jesus privately and said, "Why could we not cast it out?" [20] He said to them, "Because of your little faith. For truly I tell you, if you have faith the size of a[c] mustard seed, you will say to this mountain, 'Move from here to there,' and it will move; and nothing will be impossible for you."[d]

[22] As they were gathering[e] in Galilee, Jesus said to them, "The Son of Man is going to be betrayed into human hands, [23] and they will kill him, and on the third day he will be raised." And they were greatly distressed.

[24] When they reached Capernaum, the collectors of the temple tax[f] came to Peter and said, "Does your teacher not pay the temple tax?"[f] [25] He said, "Yes, he does." And when he came home, Jesus spoke of it first, asking, "What do you think, Simon? From whom do kings of the earth take toll or tribute? From their children or from others?" [26] When Peter[g] said, "From others," Jesus said to him, "Then the children are free. [27] However, so that we do not give offense to them, go to the sea and cast a hook; take the first fish that comes up; and when you open its mouth, you will find a coin;[h] take that and give it to them for you and me."

18 At that time the disciples came to Jesus and asked, "Who is the greatest in the kingdom of heaven?" [2] He called a child,

whom he put among them, [3] and said, "Truly I tell you, unless you change and become like children, you will never enter the kingdom of heaven. [4] Whoever becomes humble like this child is the greatest in the kingdom of heaven. [5] Whoever welcomes one such child in my name welcomes me.

[6] "If any of you put a stumbling block before one of these little ones who believe in me, it would be better for you if a great millstone were fastened around your neck and you were drowned in the depth of the sea. [7] Woe to the world because of stumbling blocks! Occasions for stumbling are bound to come, but woe to the one by whom the stumbling block comes!

[8] "If your hand or your foot causes you to stumble, cut it off and throw it away; it is better for you to enter life maimed or lame than to have two hands or two feet and to be thrown into the eternal fire. [9] And if your eye causes you to stumble, tear it out and throw it away; it is better for you to enter life with one

a Gk *it* or *him*
b Gk *the demon*
c Gk *faith as a grain of*
d Other ancient authorities add verse 21, *But this kind does not come out except by prayer and fasting*
e Other ancient authorities read *living*
f Gk *didrachma*
g Gk *he*
h Gk *stater*; the stater was worth two didrachmas

Jesus' disciples; cf. Deut 32.5,20. **20:** *Little faith* is the main problem besetting Jesus' disciples in Matthew. *Mustard seed*, 13.31n.

17.22–23: Jesus' second prediction of his death and resurrection (Mk 9.30–32; Lk 9.43–45). **22:** *Were gathering*, in order to visit Jerusalem for Passover. **23:** Whereas in Mk 9.32 the disciples are perplexed, Matthew's disciples are *greatly distressed*.

17.24–27: Payment of the temple tax. **24:** *Temple tax*, lit., "the didrachma." This "double drachma" was equivalent to half a shekel, an amount enjoined on all Israel (Ex 30.11–16). Used in Jesus' day for sacrifices and the upkeep of the Temple, the tax (the "fiscus judaicus") continued to be levied by Rome after the Temple's destruction in 70 CE, as a penalty for the Jewish people's revolt. **26:** *The children are free*, just as a king's children are tax-exempt, so too are God's children, i.e., Jesus and his brothers and sisters (12.50). **27:** *Give offense*, offend the devout people who collect the tax.

18.1–35: The fourth discourse, on community or church. This discourse focuses on community interrelations and church discipline—specifically the need for the church to care for their disadvantaged and forgive one another.

18.1–9: The greatest in the kingdom and temptations to sin (Mk 9.33–37; 42–48; Lk 9.46–48; 17.1–2). **3–6:** *Children* and *little ones*, humble Christian disciples. **6:** *Great millstone*, a stone harnessed to a donkey to grind grain. *Sea*, millstones were sometimes used as anchors (cf. Rev 18.21). **9:** *Hell*, lit., "Gehenna," the valley of Ben Hinnom to the immediate south of Jerusalem, formerly a place of child sacrifice (Jer 7.31), used in Jesus' day as

eye than to have two eyes and to be thrown into the hell[a] of fire.

10 "Take care that you do not despise one of these little ones; for, I tell you, in heaven their angels continually see the face of my Father in heaven.[b] 12 What do you think? If a shepherd has a hundred sheep, and one of them has gone astray, does he not leave the ninety-nine on the mountains and go in search of the one that went astray? 13 And if he finds it, truly I tell you, he rejoices over it more than over the ninety-nine that never went astray. 14 So it is not the will of your[c] Father in heaven that one of these little ones should be lost.

15 "If another member of the church[d] sins against you,[e] go and point out the fault when the two of you are alone. If the member listens to you, you have regained that one.[f] 16 But if you are not listened to, take one or two others along with you, so that every word may be confirmed by the evidence of two or three witnesses. 17 If the member refuses to listen to them, tell it to the church; and if the offender refuses to listen even to the church, let such a one be to you as a Gentile and a tax collector. 18 Truly I tell you, whatever you bind on earth will be bound in heaven, and whatever you loose on earth will be loosed in heaven. 19 Again, truly I tell you, if two of you agree on earth about anything you ask, it will be done for you by my Father in heaven. 20 For where two or three are gathered in my name, I am there among them."

21 Then Peter came and said to him, "Lord, if another member of the church[g] sins against me, how often should I forgive? As many as seven times?" 22 Jesus said to him, "Not seven times, but, I tell you, seventy-seven[h] times.

23 "For this reason the kingdom of heaven may be compared to a king who wished to settle accounts with his slaves. 24 When he began the reckoning, one who owed him ten thousand talents[i] was brought to him; 25 and, as he could not pay, his lord ordered him to be sold, together with his wife and children and all his possessions, and payment to be made. 26 So the slave fell on his knees before him, saying, 'Have patience with me, and I will pay you everything.' 27 And out of pity for him, the lord of that slave released him and forgave him the debt. 28 But that same slave, as he went out, came upon one of his fellow slaves who owed him a hundred denarii;[j] and seizing him by the throat, he said, 'Pay what you owe.' 29 Then his fellow slave fell down and pleaded with him, 'Have patience with me, and I will pay you.' 30 But he refused; then he went and threw him into prison until he would pay the debt. 31 When his fellow slaves saw what had happened, they were greatly distressed, and they went and reported to their lord all that had taken place. 32 Then his lord summoned him and said to him, 'You wicked slave! I forgave you all that debt because you pleaded with me. 33 Should you not have had mercy

a   Gk Gehenna
b   Other ancient authorities add verse 11, For the Son of Man came to save the lost
c   Other ancient authorities read my
d   Gk If your brother
e   Other ancient authorities lack against you
f   Gk the brother
g   Gk if my brother
h   Or seventy times seven
i   A talent was worth more than fifteen years' wages of a laborer
j   The denarius was the usual day's wage for a laborer

a garbage dump and incinerator.

18.10–20: Lost sheep and sinning brothers (Lk 15.3–7; 17.3). **10:** *Their angels*, both individuals and nations were thought to have guardian angels (Dan 10.20–21; Acts 12.15). *Face of my Father*, receive God's special attention. **12:** Luke's parable varies considerably; in Matthew the emphasis is not on the shepherd's joy at finding the lost sheep, but on his responsibility not to lose a straying sheep. **15:** *Alone*, to avoid publicly shaming the church member. *Witnesses*, 9.27–31n. **17:** *Gentile . . . tax collector*, 5.46,47n. **18:** 16.16. This authority is extended to the church as a whole.

18.21–35: The parable of the unforgiving servant. 21–22: *Seven*, 12.45n.; cf. Gen 4.24. **23:** *A king*, God. **24:** *Ten thousand talents*, a vast sum amounting to more than the entire tribute paid by Galilee to Rome over a fifteen-year period. A talent was equivalent to six thousand denarii (a denarius was a day-laborer's wage). **25:** *Ordered him to be sold*, slaves, their families and possessions were chattel. **28:** *A hundred denarii*, roughly three month's

on your fellow slave, as I had mercy on you?' [34] And in anger his lord handed him over to be tortured until he would pay his entire debt. [35] So my heavenly Father will also do to every one of you, if you do not forgive your brother or sister[a] from your heart."

19

When Jesus had finished saying these things, he left Galilee and went to the region of Judea beyond the Jordan. [2] Large crowds followed him, and he cured them there.

[3] Some Pharisees came to him, and to test him they asked, "Is it lawful for a man to divorce his wife for any cause?" [4] He answered, "Have you not read that the one who made them at the beginning 'made them male and female,' [5] and said, 'For this reason a man shall leave his father and mother and be joined to his wife, and the two shall become one flesh'? [6] So they are no longer two, but one flesh. Therefore what God has joined together, let no one separate." [7] They said to him, "Why then did Moses command us to give a certificate of dismissal and to divorce her?" [8] He said to them, "It was because you were so hard-hearted that Moses allowed you to divorce your wives, but from the beginning it was not so. [9] And I say to you, whoever divorces his wife, except for unchastity, and marries another commits adultery."[b]

[10] His disciples said to him, "If such is the case of a man with his wife, it is better not to marry." [11] But he said to them, "Not everyone can accept this teaching, but only those to whom it is given. [12] For there are eunuchs who have been so from birth, and there are eunuchs who have been made eunuchs by others, and there are eunuchs who have made themselves eunuchs for the sake of the kingdom of heaven. Let anyone accept this who can."

[13] Then little children were being brought to him in order that he might lay his hands on them and pray. The disciples spoke sternly to those who brought them; [14] but Jesus said, "Let the little children come to me, and do not stop them; for it is to such as these that the kingdom of heaven belongs." [15] And he laid his hands on them and went on his way.

[16] Then someone came to him and said, "Teacher, what good deed must I do to have eternal life?" [17] And he said to him, "Why do you ask me about what is good? There is only one who is good. If you wish to enter into life, keep the commandments." [18] He said to him, "Which ones?" And Jesus said, "You shall not murder; You shall not commit adultery; You shall not steal; You shall not bear false witness; [19] Honor your father and mother; also, You shall love your neighbor as yourself." [20] The young man said to him, "I have kept all these;[c] what do I still lack?" [21] Jesus said to him, "If you wish to be perfect, go, sell your possessions, and give the money[d] to the poor, and you will have treasure in heaven; then come, follow me." [22] When the young man heard this word, he went away grieving, for he had many possessions.

[23] Then Jesus said to his disciples, "Truly I tell you, it will be hard for a rich person to enter the kingdom of heaven. [24] Again I tell

a   Gk *brother*
b   Other ancient authorities read *except on the ground of unchastity, causes her to commit adultery*; others add at the end of the verse *and he who marries a divorced woman commits adultery*
c   Other ancient authorities add *from my youth*
d   Gk lacks *the money*

wages. **30**: 5.25n. **34**: *Tortured*, to ascertain the location of the slave's money or to coerce money from his family.

    19.1–20.34: Jesus moves from Galilee to Judea. In Matthew, this transition marks Jesus' first (and final) trip to Judea.

    19.1–12: Teaching about divorce (Mk 10.1–12). **1**: *Beyond the Jordan*, the Transjordan or Perea, regions on the east side of the Jordan river. Galileans traveling to Jerusalem for Passover would often cross over the Jordan to bypass Samaria (Lk 9.51–56). **2**: *Large crowds*, 4.25n. **3**: The Pharisaic schools of Hillel and Shammai both permitted divorce but differed over the appropriate grounds. **4–5**: Gen 1.27; 2.24. **7**: *Moses*, Deut 24.1–4. **9**: *Except for unchastity*, this exception clause has been added by Matthew. **12**: *Made themselves eunuchs*, hyperbole for the voluntary practice of celibacy; a eunuch is a castrated male.

    19.13–30: Little children and the rich young man (Mk 10.13–31; Lk 18.15–30). **13–15**: Cf. 18.1–5. **17**: *Only one*, God; Mk 10.18. To *enter into life* means both "to enter the kingdom" and "to gain eternal life" (vv. 16,23,24). **19**: Ex 20.12–16; Deut 5.16–20; Matthew adds the love commandment from Lev 19.18 (cf. 22.39). **21**: *Perfect*, 5.48. **22**:

you, it is easier for a camel to go through the eye of a needle than for someone who is rich to enter the kingdom of God." ²⁵ When the disciples heard this, they were greatly astounded and said, "Then who can be saved?" ²⁶ But Jesus looked at them and said, "For mortals it is impossible, but for God all things are possible."

²⁷ Then Peter said in reply, "Look, we have left everything and followed you. What then will we have?" ²⁸ Jesus said to them, "Truly I tell you, at the renewal of all things, when the Son of Man is seated on the throne of his glory, you who have followed me will also sit on twelve thrones, judging the twelve tribes of Israel. ²⁹ And everyone who has left houses or brothers or sisters or father or mother or children or fields, for my name's sake, will receive a hundredfold,ᵃ and will inherit eternal life. ³⁰ But many who are first will be last, and the last will be first.

20 "For the kingdom of heaven is like a landowner who went out early in the morning to hire laborers for his vineyard. ² After agreeing with the laborers for the usual daily wage,ᵇ he sent them into his vineyard. ³ When he went out about nine o'clock, he saw others standing idle in the marketplace; ⁴ and he said to them, 'You also go into the vineyard, and I will pay you whatever is right.' So they went. ⁵ When he went out again about noon and about three o'clock, he did the same. ⁶ And about five o'clock he went out and found others standing around; and he said to them, 'Why are you standing here idle all day?' ⁷ They said to him, 'Because no one has hired us.' He said to them, 'You also go into the vineyard.' ⁸ When evening came, the owner of the vineyard said to his manager, 'Call the laborers and give them their pay, beginning with the last and then going to the first.' ⁹ When those hired about five o'clock came, each of them received the usual daily wage.ᵇ ¹⁰ Now when the first came, they thought they would receive more; but each of them also received the usual daily wage.ᵇ ¹¹ And when they received it, they grumbled against the landowner, ¹² saying, 'These last worked only one hour, and you have made them equal to us who have borne the burden of the day and the scorching heat.' ¹³ But he replied to one of them, 'Friend, I am doing you no wrong; did you not agree with me for the usual daily wage?ᵇ ¹⁴ Take what belongs to you and go; I choose to give to this last the same as I give to you. ¹⁵ Am I not allowed to do what I choose with what belongs to me? Or are you envious because I am generous?'ᶜ ¹⁶ So the last will be first, and the first will be last."ᵈ

¹⁷ While Jesus was going up to Jerusalem, he took the twelve disciples aside by themselves, and said to them on the way, ¹⁸ "See, we are going up to Jerusalem, and the Son of Man will be handed over to the chief priests and scribes, and they will condemn him to death; ¹⁹ then they will hand him over to the Gentiles to be mocked and flogged and crucified; and on the third day he will be raised."

²⁰ Then the mother of the sons of Zebedee came to him with her sons, and kneeling before him, she asked a favor of him. ²¹ And he said to her, "What do you want?" She said to him, "Declare that these two sons of mine will sit, one at your right hand and one at your left, in your kingdom." ²² But Jesus answered, "You do not know what you are asking. Are you able to drink the cup that I

ᵃ Other ancient authorities read *manifold*
ᵇ Gk *a denarius*
ᶜ Gk *is your eye evil because I am good?*
ᵈ Other ancient authorities add *for many are called but few are chosen*

Young, only found in Matthew. **24:** *Camel*, the largest animal in the region (23.24). **28:** *Renewal*, the new age on earth, featuring a general resurrection. *Thrones*, Dan 7.9–14. **30:** 20.16.

20.1–16: The workers in the vineyard. 2: 18.28n. **15:** *Envious*, lit., "Is your eye evil?" (cf. 6.22–23n.). **16:** See 19.30.

20.17–19: A third time Jesus foretells his death and resurrection (Mk 10.32–34; Lk 18.31–34). **17–19:** Cf. 16.21–28; 17.22–23. This prediction explicitly indicts the Gentiles in Jesus' death.

20.20–28: The request of James and John (Mk 10.35–45). In contrast to Mark, the request here originates with their mother. **21:** *Right . . . left*, indicates those figures who, flanking a monarch, would rank as second and

am about to drink?"[a] They said to him, "We are able." [23] He said to them, "You will indeed drink my cup, but to sit at my right hand and at my left, this is not mine to grant, but it is for those for whom it has been prepared by my Father."

[24] When the ten heard it, they were angry with the two brothers. [25] But Jesus called them to him and said, "You know that the rulers of the Gentiles lord it over them, and their great ones are tyrants over them. [26] It will not be so among you; but whoever wishes to be great among you must be your servant, [27] and whoever wishes to be first among you must be your slave; [28] just as the Son of Man came not to be served but to serve, and to give his life a ransom for many."

[29] As they were leaving Jericho, a large crowd followed him. [30] There were two blind men sitting by the roadside. When they heard that Jesus was passing by, they shouted, "Lord,[b] have mercy on us, Son of David!" [31] The crowd sternly ordered them to be quiet; but they shouted even more loudly, "Have mercy on us, Lord, Son of David!" [32] Jesus stood still and called them, saying, "What do you want me to do for you?" [33] They said to him, "Lord, let our eyes be opened." [34] Moved with compassion, Jesus touched their eyes. Immediately they regained their sight and followed him.

21 When they had come near Jerusalem and had reached Bethphage, at the Mount of Olives, Jesus sent two disciples,

[2] saying to them, "Go into the village ahead of you, and immediately you will find a donkey tied, and a colt with her; untie them and bring them to me. [3] If anyone says anything to you, just say this, 'The Lord needs them.' And he will send them immediately.[c]" [4] This took place to fulfill what had been spoken through the prophet, saying,

[5] "Tell the daughter of Zion,
Look, your king is coming to you,
    humble, and mounted on a donkey,
        and on a colt, the foal of a donkey."
[6] The disciples went and did as Jesus had directed them; [7] they brought the donkey and the colt, and put their cloaks on them, and he sat on them. [8] A very large crowd[d] spread their cloaks on the road, and others cut branches from the trees and spread them on the road. [9] The crowds that went ahead of him and that followed were shouting,

"Hosanna to the Son of David!
    Blessed is the one who comes in the name of the Lord!
Hosanna in the highest heaven!"
[10] When he entered Jerusalem, the whole city was in turmoil, asking, "Who is this?" [11] The crowds were saying, "This is the prophet Jesus from Nazareth in Galilee."

a   Other ancient authorities add *or to be baptized with the baptism that I am baptized with?*
b   Other ancient authorities lack *Lord*
c   Or *'The Lord needs them and will send them back immediately.'*
d   Or *Most of the crowd*

third in authority. **23:** *My cup*, Acts 12.2 mentions James' martyrdom; according to postbiblical tradition, his brother John was also martyred. **28:** *Ransom*, the price paid to liberate a slave.

20.29–34: The healing of two blind men (Mk 10.46–52; Lk 18.35–43); a doublet of 9.27–31. **29:** *Jericho*, city and oasis 15 mi (24 km) east of Jerusalem and 8 mi (13 km) north of the Dead Sea. **30:** *Two blind men*, in Mk 10.46 the single blind man is identified as Bartimaeus, son of Timaeus. **31:** *Son of David*, see 9.27n.

21.1–11: The triumphal entry into Jerusalem (Mk 11.1–11; Lk 19.28–38; Jn 12:12–19). **1:** *Bethphage* ("House of Figs"), a village on the Mount of Olives ca. 1 mi (1.6 km) east of the Jerusalem Temple. **2:** *Village*, perhaps Bethany (see v. 17; Mk 11.1). *Donkey*, instead of a warhorse connoting a military leader (*Pss. Sol.* 17), Jesus rides a donkey symbolizing peace (Zech 9.9–10). **4–5:** A composite fulfillment citation of Isa 62.11 and Zech 9.9. *Daughter of Zion*, Jerusalem and its residents. **7:** *Colt*, while Zechariah refers to only one donkey, expressed by poetic parallelism, Matthew's fulfillment citation interprets the expression as two: a donkey and its foal. **8:** *Cloaks*, an act of royal homage; 2 Kings 9.13. **9:** The cry *Hosanna* (lit., in Heb "Help" or "Save, I pray") had become by Jesus' day an exclamation of praise. *Blessed*, a citation of Ps 118.26, which was used as a traditional greeting for pilgrims arriving in Jerusalem for the great festivals. **11:** *Prophet*, 21.46. Not a reference to the prophet resembling Moses (Deut 18.18).

21.12–27: The Temple and the fig tree (Mk 11.12–24; 27–33; Lk 19.45–48; 20.1–8). **12:** In Jn 2.13–22 this episode

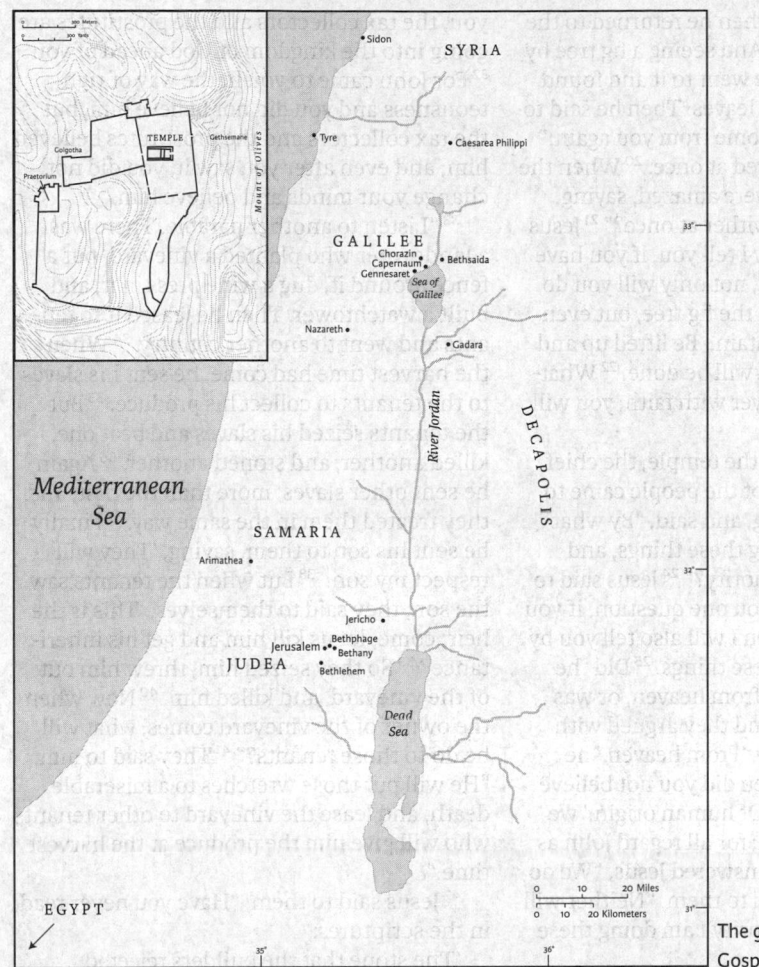

The geography of the Gospel of Matthew.

---

¹² Then Jesus entered the temple[a] and drove out all who were selling and buying in the temple, and he overturned the tables of the money changers and the seats of those who sold doves. ¹³ He said to them, "It is written,

'My house shall be called a house of prayer';
    but you are making it a den of robbers."

¹⁴ The blind and the lame came to him in the temple, and he cured them. ¹⁵ But when the chief priests and the scribes saw the amazing things that he did, and heard[b] the children crying out in the temple, "Hosanna to the Son of David," they became angry ¹⁶ and said to him, "Do you hear what these are saying?" Jesus said to them, "Yes; have you never read,

'Out of the mouths of infants and nursing babies
    you have prepared praise for yourself'?"

¹⁷ He left them, went out of the city to Bethany, and spent the night there.

a Other ancient authorities add *of God*
b Gk lacks *heard*

is situated early in Jesus' ministry, in Mk 11.11–19 on the day after Jesus' arrival in Jerusalem. *Selling and buying*, animals for sacrifice. *Money changers*, Roman money had to be changed into Tyrian shekels, the only currency acceptable for use within the Temple. *Doves*, offerings typical of the poor (Lev 5.7–10). Business transactions took place in the large outer Court of the Gentiles; it was here that Jesus' "cleansing" took place. **13:** *Written*, Isa 56.7; Jer 7.11. **14:** Jesus' cleansing culminates in the healing of the *blind and the lame*, who were normally excluded

[18] In the morning, when he returned to the city, he was hungry. [19] And seeing a fig tree by the side of the road, he went to it and found nothing at all on it but leaves. Then he said to it, "May no fruit ever come from you again!" And the fig tree withered at once. [20] When the disciples saw it, they were amazed, saying, "How did the fig tree wither at once?" [21] Jesus answered them, "Truly I tell you, if you have faith and do not doubt, not only will you do what has been done to the fig tree, but even if you say to this mountain, 'Be lifted up and thrown into the sea,' it will be done. [22] Whatever you ask for in prayer with faith, you will receive."

[23] When he entered the temple, the chief priests and the elders of the people came to him as he was teaching, and said, "By what authority are you doing these things, and who gave you this authority?" [24] Jesus said to them, "I will also ask you one question; if you tell me the answer, then I will also tell you by what authority I do these things. [25] Did the baptism of John come from heaven, or was it of human origin?" And they argued with one another, "If we say, 'From heaven,' he will say to us, 'Why then did you not believe him?' [26] But if we say, 'Of human origin,' we are afraid of the crowd; for all regard John as a prophet." [27] So they answered Jesus, "We do not know." And he said to them, "Neither will I tell you by what authority I am doing these things.

[28] "What do you think? A man had two sons; he went to the first and said, 'Son, go and work in the vineyard today.' [29] He answered, 'I will not'; but later he changed his mind and went. [30] The father[a] went to the second and said the same; and he answered, 'I go, sir'; but he did not go. [31] Which of the two did the will of his father?" They said, "The first." Jesus said to them, "Truly I tell you, the tax collectors and the prostitutes are going into the kingdom of God ahead of you. [32] For John came to you in the way of righteousness and you did not believe him, but the tax collectors and the prostitutes believed him; and even after you saw it, you did not change your minds and believe him.

[33] "Listen to another parable. There was a landowner who planted a vineyard, put a fence around it, dug a wine press in it, and built a watchtower. Then he leased it to tenants and went to another country. [34] When the harvest time had come, he sent his slaves to the tenants to collect his produce. [35] But the tenants seized his slaves and beat one, killed another, and stoned another. [36] Again he sent other slaves, more than the first; and they treated them in the same way. [37] Finally he sent his son to them, saying, 'They will respect my son.' [38] But when the tenants saw the son, they said to themselves, 'This is the heir; come, let us kill him and get his inheritance.' [39] So they seized him, threw him out of the vineyard, and killed him. [40] Now when the owner of the vineyard comes, what will he do to those tenants?" [41] They said to him, "He will put those wretches to a miserable death, and lease the vineyard to other tenants who will give him the produce at the harvest time."

[42] Jesus said to them, "Have you never read in the scriptures:

'The stone that the builders rejected
        has become the cornerstone;[b]
    this was the Lord's doing,
        and it is amazing in our eyes'?

[43] Therefore I tell you, the kingdom of God will be taken away from you and given to a people that produces the fruits of the

a   Gk *He*
b   Or *keystone*

from the Temple (Lev 21.16–23). **16:** Ps 8.2. **19:** *Fig tree*, "it was not the season for figs" (Mk 11.13) is omitted. As fig trees often symbolized Jerusalem or the Temple, Jesus' action is best understood as a prophecy of judgment (23.37–24.2). **23:** *Authority*, 7.29; 9.6–8. **25:** *From heaven*, from God.

  21.28–22.14: Three parables (Mk 12.1–12; Lk 20.9–19; Lk 14.15–24). **21.28–32:** The first of three consecutive parables condemning the Jewish religious leadership. **31:** *The tax collectors and the prostitutes*, the people who were presumed to have the lowest morals (5.46n.). **33–37:** The second parable is an allegory based on Isa 5.1–7, outlining the history of God and Israel. The *vineyard* is a metaphor for Israel, with God as the *landowner*, the Jewish leadership as the *tenants*, the prophets as the *slaves*, and Jesus as the *son*. **42:** Ps 118.22–23; *cornerstone*, the keystone of an arch. **43:** *A people that produces the fruits*, a reference to the Christian church and its practice

kingdom.[a] [44] The one who falls on this stone will be broken to pieces; and it will crush anyone on whom it falls."[b]

[45] When the chief priests and the Pharisees heard his parables, they realized that he was speaking about them. [46] They wanted to arrest him, but they feared the crowds, because they regarded him as a prophet.

22 Once more Jesus spoke to them in parables, saying: [2] "The kingdom of heaven may be compared to a king who gave a wedding banquet for his son. [3] He sent his slaves to call those who had been invited to the wedding banquet, but they would not come. [4] Again he sent other slaves, saying, 'Tell those who have been invited: Look, I have prepared my dinner, my oxen and my fat calves have been slaughtered, and everything is ready; come to the wedding banquet.' [5] But they made light of it and went away, one to his farm, another to his business, [6] while the rest seized his slaves, mistreated them, and killed them. [7] The king was enraged. He sent his troops, destroyed those murderers, and burned their city. [8] Then he said to his slaves, 'The wedding is ready, but those invited were not worthy. [9] Go therefore into the main streets, and invite everyone you find to the wedding banquet.' [10] Those slaves went out into the streets and gathered all whom they found, both good and bad; so the wedding hall was filled with guests.

[11] "But when the king came in to see the guests, he noticed a man there who was not wearing a wedding robe, [12] and he said to him, 'Friend, how did you get in here without a wedding robe?' And he was speechless. [13] Then the king said to the attendants, 'Bind him hand and foot, and throw him into the outer darkness, where there will be weeping and gnashing of teeth.' [14] For many are called, but few are chosen."

[15] Then the Pharisees went and plotted to entrap him in what he said. [16] So they sent their disciples to him, along with the Herodians, saying, "Teacher, we know that you are sincere, and teach the way of God in accordance with truth, and show deference to no one; for you do not regard people with partiality. [17] Tell us, then, what you think. Is it lawful to pay taxes to the emperor, or not?" [18] But Jesus, aware of their malice, said, "Why are you putting me to the test, you hypocrites? [19] Show me the coin used for the tax." And they brought him a denarius. [20] Then he said to them, "Whose head is this, and whose title?" [21] They answered, "The emperor's." Then he said to them, "Give therefore to the emperor the things that are the emperor's, and to God the things that are God's." [22] When they heard this, they were amazed; and they left him and went away.

[23] The same day some Sadducees came to him, saying there is no resurrection;[c] and they asked him a question, saying, [24] "Teacher, Moses said, 'If a man dies childless, his brother shall marry the widow, and raise up children for his brother.' [25] Now there were seven brothers among us; the first married, and died childless, leaving the widow to his brother. [26] The second did the same, so also the third, down to the seventh. [27] Last of all, the woman herself died. [28] In the resurrection, then, whose wife of the seven will she be? For all of them had married her."

[29] Jesus answered them, "You are wrong, because you know neither the scriptures nor the power of God. [30] For in the resurrection

a   Gk *the fruits of it*
b   Other ancient authorities lack verse 44
c   Other ancient authorities read *who say that there is no resurrection*

of righteousness. **44:** If this verse is Matthean (see textual note *b*), it refers to the dire consequences of misunderstanding who Jesus is. **46:** *Prophet,* v. 11. **22.1–14:** The third parable. **7:** *Burned their city*, an allusion to the destruction of Jerusalem in 70 CE. **11–14:** These four verses are a Matthean addition to the parable. **11:** A *wedding robe* may suggest the righteous deeds necessary for believers to enter the kingdom (see Mt 7.21–23). **13:** 8.12n.

22.15–46: Attempts to ensnare Jesus (Mk 12.13–37; Lk 20.20–44; 10.25–28). The preceding three parables are followed by three trick questions meant to entrap Jesus in his own words. **16:** *Herodians*, possibly supporters of Herod Antipas and his family. **17:** *Taxes*, on agricultural yield and personal property amounting to about a denarius a year. *Emperor*, Tiberius Caesar (14–37 CE). **18:** *Hypocrites*, 6.2n. **20:** A typical silver denarius of Tiberias' day would have his portrait on the obverse and the Latin inscription "Tiberius Caesar Augustus, Son of the Divine Augustus" on the reverse. **23:** *Sadducees*, 3.7n. **24:** *Moses said*, Deut 25.5; cf. Gen 38.7–11. **30:** *Marry,*

they neither marry nor are given in marriage, but are like angels[a] in heaven. [31] And as for the resurrection of the dead, have you not read what was said to you by God, [32] 'I am the God of Abraham, the God of Isaac, and the God of Jacob'? He is God not of the dead, but of the living." [33] And when the crowd heard it, they were astounded at his teaching.

[34] When the Pharisees heard that he had silenced the Sadducees, they gathered together, [35] and one of them, a lawyer, asked him a question to test him. [36] "Teacher, which commandment in the law is the greatest?" [37] He said to him, " 'You shall love the Lord your God with all your heart, and with all your soul, and with all your mind.' [38] This is the greatest and first commandment. [39] And a second is like it: 'You shall love your neighbor as yourself.' [40] On these two commandments hang all the law and the prophets."

[41] Now while the Pharisees were gathered together, Jesus asked them this question: [42] "What do you think of the Messiah?[b] Whose son is he?" They said to him, "The son of David." [43] He said to them, "How is it then that David by the Spirit[c] calls him Lord, saying,

[44] 'The Lord said to my Lord,
"Sit at my right hand,
    until I put your enemies under your feet"'?

[45] If David thus calls him Lord, how can he be his son?" [46] No one was able to give him an answer, nor from that day did anyone dare to ask him any more questions.

23 Then Jesus said to the crowds and to his disciples, [2] "The scribes and the Pharisees sit on Moses' seat; [3] therefore, do whatever they teach you and follow it; but do not do as they do, for they do not practice what they teach. [4] They tie up heavy burdens, hard to bear,[d] and lay them on the shoulders of others; but they themselves are unwilling to lift a finger to move them. [5] They do all their deeds to be seen by others; for they make their phylacteries broad and their fringes long. [6] They love to have the place of honor at banquets and the best seats in the synagogues, [7] and to be greeted with respect in the marketplaces, and to have people call them rabbi. [8] But you are not to be called rabbi, for you have one teacher, and you are all students.[e] [9] And call no one your father on earth, for you have one Father—the one in heaven. [10] Nor are you to be called instructors, for you have one instructor, the Messiah.[f] [11] The greatest among you will be your servant. [12] All who exalt themselves will be humbled, and all who humble themselves will be exalted.

[13] "But woe to you, scribes and Pharisees, hypocrites! For you lock people out of the

---

a   Other ancient authorities add *of God*
b   Or *Christ*
c   Gk *in spirit*
d   Other ancient authorities lack *hard to bear*
e   Gk *brothers*
f   Or *the Christ*

---

in the coming age men no longer marry and women are no longer given in marriage. *Like angels*, since angels are eternal, they do not need to reproduce; the same holds true for the resurrected dead. **32:** Ex 3.6. Otherwise God would have said, "I *was* the God of Abraham." **34–40:** For Matthew, the love commandment is preeminent; all other commandments are subsidiary and to be interpreted and performed out of love for God and one's neighbor. **37:** Deut 6.5. **39:** 19.19; Lev 19.18. **44–45:** Jesus replies with a query of his own. In Ps 110.1 David (reputed author of the Psalms) describes the *Lord* (God) as speaking to *my Lord* (the Messiah). How can David's Lord be his son, since it is invariably sons who call their fathers "my lord"?

23.1–39: The denunciation of the scribes and Pharisees (Mk 12.38–40; Lk 11.37–52; 13.34–35; 20.45–47). This chapter contains the harshest and most sustained criticism of the scribes and Pharisees in the Gospels. Some scholars regard ch 23 as part of Matthew's fifth discourse (chs 24–25), but Matthew shifts the latter to a new setting (see 24.1). **2:** *Moses' seat*, a stone seat for synagogue leaders or a receptacle for the Torah scroll. **3:** *Do whatever they teach you*, a surprising directive from Matthew's Jesus. It may mean, "Follow their guidelines if you must, but by no means follow their example." **4:** *Heavy burdens*, contrast 11.30. **5:** *Phylacteries*, small cases, often made of leather, containing scriptural passages such as Deut 6.4–9. They were strapped to the left arm and forehead during prayer (Deut 6.8). *Fringes*, tassels ("tsitsit") attached to the corners of an outer garment or prayer shawl (Num 15.38). **6:** *Place of honor*, normally, the place nearest the host. **7:** *Rabbi*, a designation of respect; lit., "my great one" or "my teacher." **9:** *Father*, do not use "father" as an honorific title. **13:** *Woe*, lit., "Alas!"

kingdom of heaven. For you do not go in yourselves, and when others are going in, you stop them.[a] [15] Woe to you, scribes and Pharisees, hypocrites! For you cross sea and land to make a single convert, and you make the new convert twice as much a child of hell[b] as yourselves.

[16] "Woe to you, blind guides, who say, 'Whoever swears by the sanctuary is bound by nothing, but whoever swears by the gold of the sanctuary is bound by the oath.' [17] You blind fools! For which is greater, the gold or the sanctuary that has made the gold sacred? [18] And you say, 'Whoever swears by the altar is bound by nothing, but whoever swears by the gift that is on the altar is bound by the oath.' [19] How blind you are! For which is greater, the gift or the altar that makes the gift sacred? [20] So whoever swears by the altar, swears by it and by everything on it; [21] and whoever swears by the sanctuary, swears by it and by the one who dwells in it; [22] and whoever swears by heaven, swears by the throne of God and by the one who is seated upon it.

[23] "Woe to you, scribes and Pharisees, hypocrites! For you tithe mint, dill, and cummin, and have neglected the weightier matters of the law: justice and mercy and faith. It is these you ought to have practiced without neglecting the others. [24] You blind guides! You strain out a gnat but swallow a camel!

[25] "Woe to you, scribes and Pharisees, hypocrites! For you clean the outside of the cup and of the plate, but inside they are full of greed and self-indulgence. [26] You blind Pharisee! First clean the inside of the cup,[c] so that the outside also may become clean.

[27] "Woe to you, scribes and Pharisees, hypocrites! For you are like whitewashed tombs, which on the outside look beautiful, but inside they are full of the bones of the dead and of all kinds of filth. [28] So you also on the outside look righteous to others, but inside you are full of hypocrisy and lawlessness.

[29] "Woe to you, scribes and Pharisees, hypocrites! For you build the tombs of the prophets and decorate the graves of the righteous, [30] and you say, 'If we had lived in the days of our ancestors, we would not have taken part with them in shedding the blood of the prophets.' [31] Thus you testify against yourselves that you are descendants of those who murdered the prophets. [32] Fill up, then, the measure of your ancestors. [33] You snakes, you brood of vipers! How can you escape being sentenced to hell?[b] [34] Therefore I send you prophets, sages, and scribes, some of whom you will kill and crucify, and some you will flog in your synagogues and pursue from town to town, [35] so that upon you may come all the righteous blood shed on earth, from the blood of righteous Abel to the blood of Zechariah son of Barachiah, whom you murdered between the sanctuary and the altar. [36] Truly I tell you, all this will come upon this generation.

[37] "Jerusalem, Jerusalem, the city that kills the prophets and stones those who are sent to it! How often have I desired to gather your children together as a hen gathers her brood under her wings, and you were not willing! [38] See, your house is left to you, desolate.[d] [39] For I tell you, you will not see me again until you say, 'Blessed is the one who comes in the name of the Lord.'"

---

a   Other authorities add here (or after verse 12) verse 14, *Woe to you, scribes and Pharisees, hypocrites! For you devour widows' houses and for the sake of appearance you make long prayers; therefore you will receive the greater condemnation*
b   Gk *Gehenna*
c   Other ancient authorities add *and of the plate*
d   Other ancient authorities lack *desolate*

The seven woes given here contrast with the beatitudes at 5.3–12. **15:** *Hypocrites,* 6.2n. *You cross sea and land,* "you do everything possible." *New convert,* a proselyte, or Gentile convert to Judaism. **16:** *Gold of the sanctuary,* perhaps the Temple treasury, which was also used as a bank. **25:** *Cup . . . plate* may symbolize the Pharisees themselves. **27:** Tombs were *whitewashed* during festivals to prevent pilgrims from touching them and polluting themselves by contact with the dead. **34:** *Prophets . . . scribes,* Christian missionaries. *Synagogues,* see 9.35n. **35:** *Abel,* Gen 4.8–11. The allusion to *Zechariah, son of Barachiah* likely conflates Zechariah the martyr (son of Jehoiada, 2 Chr 24.20–22) with Zechariah the prophet (son of Berechiah, Zech 1.1). **38:** *Your house,* Jerusalem. **39:** Ps 118.26; cf. Mt 21.9.

24.1–51: The fifth (apocalyptic) discourse. As with the mission discourse (ch 10), it is not clear whether

24

As Jesus came out of the temple and was going away, his disciples came to point out to him the buildings of the temple. ² Then he asked them, "You see all these, do you not? Truly I tell you, not one stone will be left here upon another; all will be thrown down."

³ When he was sitting on the Mount of Olives, the disciples came to him privately, saying, "Tell us, when will this be, and what will be the sign of your coming and of the end of the age?" ⁴ Jesus answered them, "Beware that no one leads you astray. ⁵ For many will come in my name, saying, 'I am the Messiah!'ᵃ and they will lead many astray. ⁶ And you will hear of wars and rumors of wars; see that you are not alarmed; for this must take place, but the end is not yet. ⁷ For nation will rise against nation, and kingdom against kingdom, and there will be faminesᵇ and earthquakes in various places: ⁸ all this is but the beginning of the birth pangs.

⁹ "Then they will hand you over to be tortured and will put you to death, and you will be hated by all nations because of my name. ¹⁰ Then many will fall away,ᶜ and they will betray one another and hate one another. ¹¹ And many false prophets will arise and lead many astray. ¹² And because of the increase of lawlessness, the love of many will grow cold. ¹³ But the one who endures to the end will be saved. ¹⁴ And this good newsᵈ of the kingdom will be proclaimed throughout the world, as a testimony to all the nations; and then the end will come.

¹⁵ "So when you see the desolating sacrilege standing in the holy place, as was spoken of by the prophet Daniel (let the reader understand), ¹⁶ then those in Judea must flee to the mountains; ¹⁷ the one on the housetop must not go down to take what is in the house; ¹⁸ the one in the field must not turn back to get a coat. ¹⁹ Woe to those who are pregnant and to those who are nursing infants in those days! ²⁰ Pray that your flight may not be in winter or on a sabbath. ²¹ For at that time there will be great suffering, such as has not been from the beginning of the world until now, no, and never will be. ²² And if those days had not been cut short, no one would be saved; but for the sake of the elect those days will be cut short. ²³ Then if anyone says to you, 'Look! Here is the Messiah!'ᵃ or 'There he is!'—do not believe it. ²⁴ For false messiahsᵉ and false prophets will appear and produce great signs and omens, to lead astray, if possible, even the elect. ²⁵ Take note, I have told you beforehand. ²⁶ So, if they say to you, 'Look! He is in the wilderness,' do not go out. If they say, 'Look! He is in the inner rooms,' do not believe it. ²⁷ For as the lightning comes from the east and flashes as far as the west, so will be the coming of the Son of Man. ²⁸ Wherever the corpse is, there the vultures will gather.

ᵃ Or the Christ
ᵇ Other ancient authorities add and pestilences
ᶜ Or stumble
ᵈ Or gospel
ᵉ Or christs

these prophetic words speak of events that are imminent or had already occurred when the Gospel was written; probably they combine both perspectives. Matthew regards some of the tribulations as consequent upon the destruction of Jerusalem in 70 CE and others as the prelude to the Second Coming.

24.1–14: The Temple's destruction and the beginning of woes (Mk 13.1–13; Lk 21.5–19). 2: Buildings of the temple, the Jerusalem Temple was one of the most magnificent sanctuaries of the ancient world. The reconstruction begun by Herod the Great spanned eighty years (20 BCE–63 CE) and came to include separate courtyards for Gentiles, Jewish women, Jewish males, and priests. 3: Mount of Olives, a low mountain facing the east side of the Temple from across the Kidron Valley. Jesus and his disciples may have camped here during the crowded Passover festival. Zech 14.1–10 indicates that the Messiah would appear here. 8: Birth pangs, a metaphor for the onset of the end-time woes. 14: See 28.19–20.

24.15–28: The great tribulation (Mk 13.14–23; Lk 21.20–24). 15: Desolating sacrilege standing in the holy place, the image of Zeus Olympios erected in the Temple by Antiochus Epiphanes in 167 BCE (Dan 9.27; 11.31; 12.11; 1 Macc 1.54; 6.7). The phrase may also refer to Gaius Caligula's attempt in 40 CE to install an image of himself in the Jerusalem Temple. The reader, either an editorial aside (as it is translated above) or Jesus' reference to the readers of Daniel. 16: Mountains had caves where one might hide. 19: Lk.23.28–31. 20: Winter or on a sabbath, times when travel was difficult or prohibited.

²⁹ "Immediately after the suffering of those days

the sun will be darkened,
and the moon will not give its light;
the stars will fall from heaven,
and the powers of heaven will be shaken.

³⁰ Then the sign of the Son of Man will appear in heaven, and then all the tribes of the earth will mourn, and they will see 'the Son of Man coming on the clouds of heaven' with power and great glory. ³¹ And he will send out his angels with a loud trumpet call, and they will gather his elect from the four winds, from one end of heaven to the other.

³² "From the fig tree learn its lesson: as soon as its branch becomes tender and puts forth its leaves, you know that summer is near. ³³ So also, when you see all these things, you know that he^a is near, at the very gates. ³⁴ Truly I tell you, this generation will not pass away until all these things have taken place. ³⁵ Heaven and earth will pass away, but my words will not pass away.

³⁶ "But about that day and hour no one knows, neither the angels of heaven, nor the Son,^b but only the Father. ³⁷ For as the days of Noah were, so will be the coming of the Son of Man. ³⁸ For as in those days before the flood they were eating and drinking, marrying and giving in marriage, until the day Noah entered the ark, ³⁹ and they knew nothing until the flood came and swept them all away, so too will be the coming of the Son of Man. ⁴⁰ Then two will be in the field; one will be taken and one will be left. ⁴¹ Two women will be grinding meal together; one will be taken and one will be left. ⁴² Keep awake therefore, for you do not know on what day^c your Lord is coming. ⁴³ But understand this: if the owner of the house had known in what part of the night the thief was coming, he would have stayed awake and would not have let his house be broken into. ⁴⁴ Therefore you also must be ready, for the Son of Man is coming at an unexpected hour.

⁴⁵ "Who then is the faithful and wise slave, whom his master has put in charge of his household, to give the other slaves^d their allowance of food at the proper time? ⁴⁶ Blessed is that slave whom his master will find at work when he arrives. ⁴⁷ Truly I tell you, he will put that one in charge of all his possessions. ⁴⁸ But if that wicked slave says to himself, 'My master is delayed,' ⁴⁹ and he begins to beat his fellow slaves, and eats and drinks with drunkards, ⁵⁰ the master of that slave will come on a day when he does not expect him and at an hour that he does not know. ⁵¹ He will cut him in pieces^e and put him with the hypocrites, where there will be weeping and gnashing of teeth.

25

"Then the kingdom of heaven will be like this. Ten bridesmaids^f took their lamps and went to meet the bridegroom.^g ² Five of them were foolish, and five were wise. ³ When the foolish took their lamps, they took no oil with them; ⁴ but the wise took flasks of oil with their lamps. ⁵ As the bridegroom was delayed, all of them became drowsy and slept. ⁶ But at midnight there was a shout, 'Look! Here is the bridegroom! Come out to meet him.' ⁷ Then all those bridesmaids^f got up and trimmed their lamps. ⁸ The foolish said to the wise, 'Give us some of your oil, for our lamps are going out.' ⁹ But the wise replied, 'No! there will not be enough for you and for us; you had better go to the dealers and buy some for yourselves.' ¹⁰ And while they went to buy it, the bridegroom came, and those who were ready went with him into the wedding banquet; and the door was shut.

---

a   Or *it*
b   Other ancient authorities lack *nor the Son*
c   Other ancient authorities read *at what hour*
d   Gk *to give them*
e   Or *cut him off*
f   Gk *virgins*
g   Other ancient authorities add *and the bride*

24.29–51: The coming of the Son of Man (Mk 13.24–37; Lk 21.25–33: Lk 17.26–30, 34–36; Lk 12.41–48). **29:** Isa 13.1; 34.4. **30:** The Son of Man is himself the *sign*; see Dan 7.13. **31:** *Trumpet*, see Isa 27.13; Zech 9.14; 1 Thess 4.16. **35:** Cf. 5.18. **38:** *Noah*, Gen 7.7. **51:** *Cut him in pieces*, perhaps a figurative expression for "cut off from the community" (1QS 2.16–17).

25.1–30: Two parables of the end-times (Lk 19.11–27). **1:** *Lamps*, torches made from rags wrapped around the end of a pole and soaked in olive oil. *Bridegroom*, 9.15n. **2:** *Foolish . . . wise*, 7.24–27. **7:** *Trimmed their lamps*, cut

[11] Later the other bridesmaids[a] came also, saying, 'Lord, lord, open to us.' [12] But he replied, 'Truly I tell you, I do not know you.' [13] Keep awake therefore, for you know neither the day nor the hour.[b]

[14] "For it is as if a man, going on a journey, summoned his slaves and entrusted his property to them; [15] to one he gave five talents,[c] to another two, to another one, to each according to his ability. Then he went away. [16] The one who had received the five talents went off at once and traded with them, and made five more talents. [17] In the same way, the one who had the two talents made two more talents. [18] But the one who had received the one talent went off and dug a hole in the ground and hid his master's money. [19] After a long time the master of those slaves came and settled accounts with them. [20] Then the one who had received the five talents came forward, bringing five more talents, saying, 'Master, you handed over to me five talents; see, I have made five more talents.' [21] His master said to him, 'Well done, good and trustworthy slave; you have been trustworthy in a few things, I will put you in charge of many things; enter into the joy of your master.' [22] And the one with the two talents also came forward, saying, 'Master, you handed over to me two talents; see, I have made two more talents.' [23] His master said to him, 'Well done, good and trustworthy slave; you have been trustworthy in a few things, I will put you in charge of many things; enter into the joy of your master.' [24] Then the one who had received the one talent also came forward, saying, 'Master, I knew that you were a harsh man, reaping where you did not sow, and gathering where you did not scatter seed; [25] so I was afraid, and I went and hid your talent in the ground. Here you have what is yours.' [26] But his master replied, 'You wicked and lazy slave! You knew, did you, that I reap where I did not sow, and gather where I did not scatter? [27] Then you ought to have invested my money with the bankers, and on my return I would have received what was my own with interest. [28] So take the talent from him, and give it to the one with the ten talents. [29] For to all those who have, more will be given, and they will have an abundance; but from those who have nothing, even what they have will be taken away. [30] As for this worthless slave, throw him into the outer darkness, where there will be weeping and gnashing of teeth.'

[31] "When the Son of Man comes in his glory, and all the angels with him, then he will sit on the throne of his glory. [32] All the nations will be gathered before him, and he will separate people one from another as a shepherd separates the sheep from the goats, [33] and he will put the sheep at his right hand and the goats at the left. [34] Then the king will say to those at his right hand, 'Come, you that are blessed by my Father, inherit the kingdom prepared for you from the foundation of the world; [35] for I was hungry and you gave me food, I was thirsty and you gave me something to drink, I was a stranger and you welcomed me, [36] I was naked and you gave me clothing, I was sick and you took care of me, I was in prison and you visited me.' [37] Then the righteous will answer him, 'Lord, when was it that we saw you hungry and gave you food, or thirsty and gave you something to drink? [38] And when was it that we saw you a stranger and welcomed you, or naked and gave you clothing? [39] And when was it that we saw you sick or in prison and visited you?' [40] And the

a Gk *virgins*
b Other ancient authorities add *in which the Son of Man is coming*
c A talent was worth more than fifteen years' wages of a laborer

away the charred cloth wicks and added more oil. **13**: 24.42. **14**: *Slaves*, in Jesus' day, it was not unusual to entrust slaves with large amounts of money and responsibility. **15**: *Talents*, 18.24n. This parable furnishes the basis for the English word "talent." **18**: 13.44n. **19**: The delay of the parousia (Jesus' return). **23**: *Joy of your master*, possibly the messianic banquet (8.11n.). **29**: Cf. 13.12.

25.31–46: The judgment of the nations. 31: *The Son of Man*, 8.2On. **32**: 24.9; 28.19; Isa 66.18; Joel 3.2. **33**: *Right*, the auspicious side, while *left* was the bad or unlucky side. The distinction between sheep and goats may reside in the fabrics the two produce: goats produce dark hair, which was used to make ill-omened sackcloth (11.21n.), while white wool was a sign of prosperity.

king will answer them, 'Truly I tell you, just as you did it to one of the least of these who are members of my family,[a] you did it to me.' [41] Then he will say to those at his left hand, 'You that are accursed, depart from me into the eternal fire prepared for the devil and his angels; [42] for I was hungry and you gave me no food, I was thirsty and you gave me nothing to drink, [43] I was a stranger and you did not welcome me, naked and you did not give me clothing, sick and in prison and you did not visit me.' [44] Then they also will answer, 'Lord, when was it that we saw you hungry or thirsty or a stranger or naked or sick or in prison, and did not take care of you?' [45] Then he will answer them, 'Truly I tell you, just as you did not do it to one of the least of these, you did not do it to me.' [46] And these will go away into eternal punishment, but the righteous into eternal life."

26

When Jesus had finished saying all these things, he said to his disciples, [2] "You know that after two days the Passover is coming, and the Son of Man will be handed over to be crucified."

[3] Then the chief priests and the elders of the people gathered in the palace of the high priest, who was called Caiaphas, [4] and they conspired to arrest Jesus by stealth and kill him. [5] But they said, "Not during the festival, or there may be a riot among the people."

[6] Now while Jesus was at Bethany in the house of Simon the leper,[b] [7] a woman came to him with an alabaster jar of very costly ointment, and she poured it on his head as he sat at the table. [8] But when the disciples saw it, they were angry and said, "Why this waste? [9] For this ointment could have been sold for a large sum, and the money given to the poor." [10] But Jesus, aware of this, said to them,

"Why do you trouble the woman? She has performed a good service for me. [11] For you always have the poor with you, but you will not always have me. [12] By pouring this ointment on my body she has prepared me for burial. [13] Truly I tell you, wherever this good news[c] is proclaimed in the whole world, what she has done will be told in remembrance of her."

[14] Then one of the twelve, who was called Judas Iscariot, went to the chief priests [15] and said, "What will you give me if I betray him to you?" They paid him thirty pieces of silver. [16] And from that moment he began to look for an opportunity to betray him.

[17] On the first day of Unleavened Bread the disciples came to Jesus, saying, "Where do you want us to make the preparations for you to eat the Passover?" [18] He said, "Go into the city to a certain man, and say to him, 'The Teacher says, My time is near; I will keep the Passover at your house with my disciples.'" [19] So the disciples did as Jesus had directed them, and they prepared the Passover meal.

[20] When it was evening, he took his place with the twelve;[d] [21] and while they were eating, he said, "Truly I tell you, one of you will betray me." [22] And they became greatly distressed and began to say to him one after another, "Surely not I, Lord?" [23] He answered, "The one who has dipped his hand into the bowl with me will betray me. [24] The Son of Man goes as it is written of him, but woe to that one by whom the Son of Man is betrayed! It would have been better for that one not to have been born." [25] Judas, who

a Gk *these my brothers*
b The terms *leper* and *leprosy* can refer to several diseases
c Or *gospel*
d Other ancient authorities add *disciples*

26.1–16: **Preliminaries to the Passover** (Mk 14.3–11; Lk 22.3–6; Jn 12.1–8). **1:** The conclusion of Jesus' final discourse. **2:** *Passover*, the annual Jewish festival celebrating Israel's exodus from Egypt (Ex 12.1–20). **3:** *Caiaphas*, high priest ca.18–36 CE, was the son-in-law of the high priest Annas (6–15 CE; 26.57). **5:** *Riots* were always a possibility during the major festivals. **6:** *Bethany*, a village on the Mount of Olives just east of Jerusalem. **7:** *Alabaster jar*, a small vial or bottle called an alabastron. **14:** *Judas Iscariot*, 10.4n. *Thirty pieces of silver*, tetradrachmas worth about one hundred and twenty denarii, a third of a year's wages; cf. Zech 11.12.

26.17–35: **The Passover and Lord's Supper** (Mk 14.12–31; Lk 22.7–23,31–34 Jn 13.21–30, 36–38; cf. 1 Cor 11.23–25). **17:** *First day*, the fourteenth of Nisan (March-April), sometimes described as "the preparation of the Passover." It marks the beginning of the week-long festival. **25:** *Rabbi*, a title for Jesus that is typically used by non-disciples in Matthew (23.7n.); Judas is the only disciple to use the title in Matthew. *You have said so* means

betrayed him, said, "Surely not I, Rabbi?" He replied, "You have said so."

²⁶ While they were eating, Jesus took a loaf of bread, and after blessing it he broke it, gave it to the disciples, and said, "Take, eat; this is my body." ²⁷ Then he took a cup, and after giving thanks he gave it to them, saying, "Drink from it, all of you; ²⁸ for this is my blood of theᵃ covenant, which is poured out for many for the forgiveness of sins. ²⁹ I tell you, I will never again drink of this fruit of the vine until that day when I drink it new with you in my Father's kingdom."

³⁰ When they had sung the hymn, they went out to the Mount of Olives.

³¹ Then Jesus said to them, "You will all become deserters because of me this night; for it is written,

'I will strike the shepherd,
    and the sheep of the flock will be
        scattered.'

³² But after I am raised up, I will go ahead of you to Galilee." ³³ Peter said to him, "Though all become deserters because of you, I will never desert you." ³⁴ Jesus said to him, "Truly I tell you, this very night, before the cock crows, you will deny me three times." ³⁵ Peter said to him, "Even though I must die with you, I will not deny you." And so said all the disciples.

³⁶ Then Jesus went with them to a place called Gethsemane; and he said to his disciples, "Sit here while I go over there and pray." ³⁷ He took with him Peter and the two sons of Zebedee, and began to be grieved and agitated. ³⁸ Then he said to them, "I am deeply grieved, even to death; remain here, and stay awake with me." ³⁹ And going a little farther, he threw himself on the ground and prayed, "My Father, if it is possible, let this cup pass from me; yet not what I want but what you want." ⁴⁰ Then he came to the disciples and found them sleeping; and he said to Peter, "So, could you not stay awake with me one hour? ⁴¹ Stay awake and pray that you may not come into the time of trial;ᵇ the spirit indeed is willing, but the flesh is weak." ⁴² Again he went away for the second time and prayed, "My Father, if this cannot pass unless I drink it, your will be done." ⁴³ Again he came and found them sleeping, for their eyes were heavy. ⁴⁴ So leaving them again, he went away and prayed for the third time, saying the same words. ⁴⁵ Then he came to the disciples and said to them, "Are you still sleeping and taking your rest? See, the hour is at hand, and the Son of Man is betrayed into the hands of sinners. ⁴⁶ Get up, let us be going. See, my betrayer is at hand."

⁴⁷ While he was still speaking, Judas, one of the twelve, arrived; with him was a large crowd with swords and clubs, from the chief priests and the elders of the people. ⁴⁸ Now the betrayer had given them a sign, saying, "The one I will kiss is the man; arrest him." ⁴⁹ At once he came up to Jesus and said, "Greetings, Rabbi!" and kissed him. ⁵⁰ Jesus said to him, "Friend, do what you are here to do." Then they came and laid hands on Jesus and arrested him. ⁵¹ Suddenly, one of those with Jesus put his hand on his sword, drew it, and struck the slave of the high priest, cutting off his ear. ⁵² Then Jesus said to him, "Put your sword back into its place; for all who take the sword will perish by the sword. ⁵³ Do you think that I cannot appeal to my Father, and he will at once send me more than twelve legions of angels? ⁵⁴ But how then would the scriptures be fulfilled, which say it must happen in this way?" ⁵⁵ At that hour Jesus said to the crowds, "Have you come out with swords and clubs to arrest me as though I were a bandit? Day after day I sat in the temple teaching, and you did not arrest me. ⁵⁶ But all

---

ᵃ   Other ancient authorities add *new*
ᵇ   Or *into temptation*

"Yes." **26**: Cf. 14.19; 15.36. **28**: *Blood of the covenant*, Ex 24.8. **30**: *The hymn*, the second half of the Hallel Psalms (113–18). **31**: *I will strike . . .*, Zech 13.7. **32**: See 28.7,10,16–20.

26.36–56: The arrest in Gethsemane (Mk 14.32–50; Lk 22.39–53; Jn 18.3–12). **36**: *Gethsemane*, the name means "garden of oil," so the site was likely an olive grove on the Mount of Olives (Lk 22.39) with olive presses nearby. **37**: *Sons of Zebedee*, James and John (4.21; 17.1; 20.20–23n.). **38**: Cf. Ps 42.6; Jon 4.9. **39**: *Cup*, see 20.22. **49**: *Rabbi*, see 26.25n. **53**: In the Roman army a *legion* was about five thousand soldiers. **56**: *Scriptures*, not individual passages, but the Jewish scriptures as a whole.

this has taken place, so that the scriptures of the prophets may be fulfilled." Then all the disciples deserted him and fled.

⁵⁷ Those who had arrested Jesus took him to Caiaphas the high priest, in whose house the scribes and the elders had gathered. ⁵⁸ But Peter was following him at a distance, as far as the courtyard of the high priest; and going inside, he sat with the guards in order to see how this would end. ⁵⁹ Now the chief priests and the whole council were looking for false testimony against Jesus so that they might put him to death, ⁶⁰ but they found none, though many false witnesses came forward. At last two came forward ⁶¹ and said, "This fellow said, 'I am able to destroy the temple of God and to build it in three days.'" ⁶² The high priest stood up and said, "Have you no answer? What is it that they testify against you?" ⁶³ But Jesus was silent. Then the high priest said to him, "I put you under oath before the living God, tell us if you are the Messiah,ᵃ the Son of God." ⁶⁴ Jesus said to him, "You have said so. But I tell you,

From now on you will see the Son of Man
    seated at the right hand of Power
    and coming on the clouds of heaven."

⁶⁵ Then the high priest tore his clothes and said, "He has blasphemed! Why do we still need witnesses? You have now heard his blasphemy. ⁶⁶ What is your verdict?" They answered, "He deserves death." ⁶⁷ Then they spat in his face and struck him; and some slapped him, ⁶⁸ saying, "Prophesy to us, you Messiah!ᵃ Who is it that struck you?"

⁶⁹ Now Peter was sitting outside in the courtyard. A servant-girl came to him and said, "You also were with Jesus the Galilean." ⁷⁰ But he denied it before all of them, saying, "I do not know what you are talking about." ⁷¹ When he went out to the porch, another servant-girl saw him, and she said to the bystanders, "This man was with Jesus of Nazareth."ᵇ ⁷² Again he denied it with an oath, "I do not know the man." ⁷³ After a little while the bystanders came up and said to Peter, "Certainly you are also one of them, for your accent betrays you." ⁷⁴ Then he began to curse, and he swore an oath, "I do not know the man!" At that moment the cock crowed. ⁷⁵ Then Peter remembered what Jesus had said: "Before the cock crows, you will deny me three times." And he went out and wept bitterly.

27 When morning came, all the chief priests and the elders of the people conferred together against Jesus in order to bring about his death. ² They bound him, led him away, and handed him over to Pilate the governor.

³ When Judas, his betrayer, saw that Jesusᶜ was condemned, he repented and brought back the thirty pieces of silver to the chief priests and the elders. ⁴ He said, "I have sinned by betraying innocentᵈ blood." But they said, "What is that to us? See to it yourself." ⁵ Throwing down the pieces of silver in the temple, he departed; and he went and hanged himself. ⁶ But the chief priests, taking the pieces of silver, said, "It is not lawful to put them into the treasury, since they are blood money." ⁷ After conferring together, they used them to buy the potter's field as a place to bury foreigners. ⁸ For this reason that field has been called the Field of Blood to this day. ⁹ Then was fulfilled what had been spoken through the prophet Jeremiah,ᵉ "And they tookᶠ the thirty pieces of silver, the price of the one on whom a price had been set,ᵍ on whom some of the people of

ᵃ Or Christ
ᵇ Gk the Nazorean
ᶜ Gk he
ᵈ Other ancient authorities read righteous
ᵉ Other ancient authorities read Zechariah or Isaiah
ᶠ Or I took
ᵍ Or the price of the precious One

26.57–27.2: Jesus before the council and Pilate (Mk 14.53–15.1; Lk 22.54–23.2; Jn 18.13–27). **26.59:** *Whole council*, the Sanhedrin, the highest council of the Jews, possessing judicial authority in noncapital cases. **61:** Cf. 24.2. **63:** *Messiah, the Son of God*, 16.16n. **64:** *You have said so:* Jesus' response confirms the high priest's identification (25.25n.; 27.11). *Son of Man*, 8.20n. Cf. Ps 110.1; Dan 7.13. **75:** 26.34. **27.2:** *Pilate the governor*, Roman administrator of Judea, 26–36 CE.

27.3–10: The death of Judas. Compare Acts 1.18–20. **9–10:** A fulfillment citation from Zech 11.12–13, with echoes of Jer 32.6–9.

Israel had set a price, [10] and they gave[a] them for the potter's field, as the Lord commanded me."

[11] Now Jesus stood before the governor; and the governor asked him, "Are you the King of the Jews?" Jesus said, "You say so." [12] But when he was accused by the chief priests and elders, he did not answer. [13] Then Pilate said to him, "Do you not hear how many accusations they make against you?" [14] But he gave him no answer, not even to a single charge, so that the governor was greatly amazed.

[15] Now at the festival the governor was accustomed to release a prisoner for the crowd, anyone whom they wanted. [16] At that time they had a notorious prisoner, called Jesus[b] Barabbas. [17] So after they had gathered, Pilate said to them, "Whom do you want me to release for you, Jesus[b] Barabbas or Jesus who is called the Messiah?"[c] [18] For he realized that it was out of jealousy that they had handed him over. [19] While he was sitting on the judgment seat, his wife sent word to him, "Have nothing to do with that innocent man, for today I have suffered a great deal because of a dream about him." [20] Now the chief priests and the elders persuaded the crowds to ask for Barabbas and to have Jesus killed. [21] The governor again said to them, "Which of the two do you want me to release for you?" And they said, "Barabbas." [22] Pilate said to them, "Then what should I do with Jesus who is called the Messiah?"[c] All of them said, "Let him be crucified!" [23] Then he asked, "Why, what evil has he done?" But they shouted all the more, "Let him be crucified!"

[24] So when Pilate saw that he could do nothing, but rather that a riot was beginning, he took some water and washed his hands before the crowd, saying, "I am innocent of this man's blood;[d] see to it yourselves." [25] Then the people as a whole answered, "His blood be on us and on our children!" [26] So he released Barabbas for them; and after flogging Jesus, he handed him over to be crucified.

[27] Then the soldiers of the governor took Jesus into the governor's headquarters,[e] and they gathered the whole cohort around him. [28] They stripped him and put a scarlet robe on him, [29] and after twisting some thorns into a crown, they put it on his head. They put a reed in his right hand and knelt before him and mocked him, saying, "Hail, King of the Jews!" [30] They spat on him, and took the reed and struck him on the head. [31] After mocking him, they stripped him of the robe and put his own clothes on him. Then they led him away to crucify him.

[32] As they went out, they came upon a man from Cyrene named Simon; they compelled this man to carry his cross. [33] And when they came to a place called Golgotha (which means Place of a Skull), [34] they offered him wine to drink, mixed with gall; but when he tasted it, he would not drink it. [35] And when they had crucified him, they divided his clothes among themselves by casting lots;[f] [36] then they sat down there and kept watch over him. [37] Over his head they put the charge against him, which read, "This is Jesus, the King of the Jews."

[38] Then two bandits were crucified with him, one on his right and one on his left.

---

[a] Other ancient authorities read *I gave*
[b] Other ancient authorities lack *Jesus*
[c] Or *the Christ*
[d] Other ancient authorities read *this righteous blood*, or *this righteous man's blood*
[e] Gk *the praetorium*
[f] Other ancient authorities add *in order that what had been spoken through the prophet might be fulfilled, "They divided my clothes among themselves, and for my clothing they cast lots."*

27.11–31: Jesus on trial before Pilate (Mk 15.2–20; Lk 23.3–5,13–25; Jn 18.33–19.16). **11:** 26.64n. **16:** *Barabbas*, ("son of the Father") was a common name in Israel. **19:** *Judgment seat*, a raised, paved area outside Pilate's residence. *Dream*, this episode is unique to Matthew. **24:** *Washed his hands*, Deut 21.6; Ps 73.13. **25:** *Children*, an indication that the next generation would experience the destruction of Jerusalem in 70 CE. **27:** *The governor's headquarters* (see textual note e), Pilate's residence (Jn 19.13). *Whole cohort*, ca. 600–1,000 men.

27.32–56: The crucifixion and death of Jesus (Mk 15.21–41; Lk 23.26–49; Jn 19.17–30). **32:** *Simon*, Mk 15.21. **34:** *Gall*, a bitter, poisonous plant (see Ps 69.21). **35:** See Ps 22.18. **37:** *King of the Jews*, the official charge against

[39] Those who passed by derided[a] him, shaking their heads [40] and saying, "You who would destroy the temple and build it in three days, save yourself! If you are the Son of God, come down from the cross." [41] In the same way the chief priests also, along with the scribes and elders, were mocking him, saying, [42] "He saved others; he cannot save himself.[b] He is the King of Israel; let him come down from the cross now, and we will believe in him. [43] He trusts in God; let God deliver him now, if he wants to; for he said, 'I am God's Son.'" [44] The bandits who were crucified with him also taunted him in the same way.

[45] From noon on, darkness came over the whole land[c] until three in the afternoon. [46] And about three o'clock Jesus cried with a loud voice, "Eli, Eli, lema sabachthani?" that is, "My God, my God, why have you forsaken me?" [47] When some of the bystanders heard it, they said, "This man is calling for Elijah." [48] At once one of them ran and got a sponge, filled it with sour wine, put it on a stick, and gave it to him to drink. [49] But the others said, "Wait, let us see whether Elijah will come to save him."[d] [50] Then Jesus cried again with a loud voice and breathed his last.[e] [51] At that moment the curtain of the temple was torn in two, from top to bottom. The earth shook, and the rocks were split. [52] The tombs also were opened, and many bodies of the saints who had fallen asleep were raised. [53] After his resurrection they came out of the tombs and entered the holy city and appeared to many. [54] Now when the centurion and those with him, who were keeping watch over Jesus, saw the earthquake and what took place, they were terrified and said, "Truly this man was God's Son!"[f]

[55] Many women were also there, looking on from a distance; they had followed Jesus from Galilee and had provided for him. [56] Among them were Mary Magdalene, and Mary the mother of James and Joseph, and the mother of the sons of Zebedee.

[57] When it was evening, there came a rich man from Arimathea, named Joseph, who was also a disciple of Jesus. [58] He went to Pilate and asked for the body of Jesus; then Pilate ordered it to be given to him. [59] So Joseph took the body and wrapped it in a clean linen cloth [60] and laid it in his own new tomb, which he had hewn in the rock. He then rolled a great stone to the door of the tomb and went away. [61] Mary Magdalene and the other Mary were there, sitting opposite the tomb.

[62] The next day, that is, after the day of Preparation, the chief priests and the Pharisees gathered before Pilate [63] and said, "Sir, we remember what that impostor said while he was still alive, 'After three days I will rise again.' [64] Therefore command the tomb to be made secure until the third day; otherwise his disciples may go and steal him away, and tell the people, 'He has been raised from the dead,' and the last deception would be worse than the first." [65] Pilate said to them, "You have a guard[g] of soldiers; go, make it as secure as you can."[h] [66] So they went with the guard and made the tomb secure by sealing the stone.

[a] Or blasphemed
[b] Or is he unable to save himself?
[c] Or earth
[d] Other ancient authorities add And another took a spear and pierced his side, and out came water and blood
[e] Or gave up his spirit
[f] Or a son of God
[g] Or Take a guard
[h] Gk you know how

Jesus was inscribed on a tablet. The charge suggests that he was considered a political threat (2.2). **46:** Eli . . . , an Aramaic translation of Ps 22.1. The invocation to God ("Eli," "my God") sounds similar to the name Elijah ("The Lord is my God"). **47:** Elijah was popularly regarded as a helper to those in need. **51:** The curtain of the temple, a large tapestry that hung in front of the Holy of Holies, the innermost room of the Temple. The earth shook, 28.2. **53:** The holy city, Jerusalem. **54:** God's Son, the first acclamation of Jesus as Son of God by a Gentile. **56:** Mary Magdalene, 27.61; 28.1; Mk 16.9; Lk 8.2. Magdala was a fishing town on the west coast of the Sea of Galilee, northwest of Tiberias. Sons of Zebedee, see 26.37n.

27.57–66: The burial of Jesus and the guard at the tomb. (Mk 15.42–47; Lk 23.50–56; Jn 19.38–42). **61:** Other Mary, the mother of James and Joseph (27.56; 28.1). **62:** After the day of Preparation, the sabbath (Saturday). Friday was the day of Preparation. The Pharisees, last mentioned at 23.29, were not involved in Jesus' crucifixion. **65:** Guard of soldiers, Roman soldiers, not the Temple police.

28

After the sabbath, as the first day of the week was dawning, Mary Magdalene and the other Mary went to see the tomb. [2] And suddenly there was a great earthquake; for an angel of the Lord, descending from heaven, came and rolled back the stone and sat on it. [3] His appearance was like lightning, and his clothing white as snow. [4] For fear of him the guards shook and became like dead men. [5] But the angel said to the women, "Do not be afraid; I know that you are looking for Jesus who was crucified. [6] He is not here; for he has been raised, as he said. Come, see the place where he[a] lay. [7] Then go quickly and tell his disciples, 'He has been raised from the dead,[b] and indeed he is going ahead of you to Galilee; there you will see him.' This is my message for you." [8] So they left the tomb quickly with fear and great joy, and ran to tell his disciples. [9] Suddenly Jesus met them and said, "Greetings!" And they came to him, took hold of his feet, and worshiped him. [10] Then Jesus said to them, "Do not be afraid; go and tell my brothers to go to Galilee; there they will see me."

[11] While they were going, some of the guard went into the city and told the chief priests everything that had happened. [12] After the priests[c] had assembled with the elders, they devised a plan to give a large sum of money to the soldiers, [13] telling them, "You must say, 'His disciples came by night and stole him away while we were asleep.' [14] If this comes to the governor's ears, we will satisfy him and keep you out of trouble." [15] So they took the money and did as they were directed. And this story is still told among the Jews to this day.

[16] Now the eleven disciples went to Galilee, to the mountain to which Jesus had directed them. [17] When they saw him, they worshiped him; but some doubted. [18] And Jesus came and said to them, "All authority in heaven and on earth has been given to me. [19] Go therefore and make disciples of all nations, baptizing them in the name of the Father and of the Son and of the Holy Spirit, [20] and teaching them to obey everything that I have commanded you. And remember, I am with you always, to the end of the age."[d]

a Other ancient authorities read *the Lord*
b Other ancient authorities lack *from the dead*
c Gk *they*
d Other ancient authorities add *Amen*

28.1–15: The resurrection of Jesus and the guards' report (Mk 16.1–8; Lk 24.1–12; Jn 20.1–10). **1:** *First day of the week,* Sunday. *The other Mary,* 27.61n. **2:** 27.51. **7:** *Galilee,* 26.32; Mk 16.7; contrast Acts 1.4; Jn 20.19. **9:** Here, as in the other Gospels, Jesus' women disciples are the first to witness the risen Jesus. **10:** *My brothers,* Jesus identifies his disciples as "brothers," indicating his ongoing love for them despite their lapses. **14:** *Governor's ears,* an investigation before Pilate. **15:** Not *among the Jews* but "among Jews," i.e., among Jews who had not accepted the Christian message.

28.16–20: The commissioning of the disciples (Mk 16.14–18; Lk 24.36–49; Jn 20.19–23; Acts 1.6–8). **17:** *Some doubted,* doubt still characterizes some of the disciples in Matthew. **18:** *All authority,* 7.29n.; 9.6. **19:** *All nations,* all people, including the Jews. *I am with you,* 18.20; cf. 1.23.

THE GOSPEL ACCORDING TO MARK

AUTHORSHIP AND DATE

Although the Gospel is anonymous, an ancient tradition ascribes it to John Mark (mentioned in Acts 12.12; 15.37), who is supposed to have composed it at Rome as a summary of Peter's preaching (see 1 Pet 5.13). Modern scholars find little first-century CE evidence to support this tradition. Mark is the shortest of the four canonical Gospels and is generally thought to be the earliest and to have been used as a source for both Matthew and Luke. The vague references to the destruction of Jerusalem in Mark 13 (contrast Mt 22.7; Lk 19.43) could be clues that the Gospel was composed just prior to the Jewish revolt that began in 66 CE and the Roman reconquest and destruction of Jerusalem and the Temple in 70 CE.

STYLE AND CONTENT

The language of the Gospel is that of popular spoken Greek. Its style features rapid sequences of brief and vivid concrete episodes linked simply by "and" or "and immediately," frequently omitted in translation for less awkward reading in English. The narrative often shifts from the past tense into the present tense, enlivening the action. The content of the Gospel consists mostly of stories about Jesus' actions and disputes with scribes and Pharisees, including some of Jesus' sayings, with two speeches (one mostly of parables) interrupting the rapid flow of episodes. Mark appears to have drawn upon a rich variety of oral traditions of Jesus' actions and teachings, including chains of miracle stories, sets of parables, and stories of controversies with the Pharisees. Some scholars think that the Gospel may have been a text that was still performed orally by Christian storytellers. The overall narrative weaves sequences of episodes together into a complex plot with several interrelated themes and conflicts. In the earliest manuscripts, Mark ends abruptly at 16.8. This (apparently original) open ending invites the reader to continue the story of Jesus and the kingdom. In some later manuscripts Mark's story was "completed" with resurrection appearances of amalgamated elements from the other canonical Gospels, to make it conform to their common pattern.

STRUCTURE

The Gospel story unfolds in an escalating series of steps. After Jesus' baptism by John, he proclaims the kingdom of God and manifests its miraculous power in rural Galilee as the renewal of Israel, over against the Jerusalem priestly establishment and its representatives, the scribes and Pharisees (chs 1–3). In the first long speech of the Gospel, Jesus then teaches the mysterious plan of the kingdom in parables to large audiences and especially to his disciples (4.1–34). Jesus continues his program of the renewal of Israel in a sustained program of sea crossings, exorcisms, healings, and wilderness feedings reminiscent of the activities of Moses and Elijah (the great prophets of the past who, respectively, founded and renewed Israel), along with continuing disputes with the scribes and Pharisees (4.35–8.21). In the next step of the story, one framed by healings of blind men that highlight the disciples' misunderstanding, Jesus repeatedly makes clear that, besides being a new prophet equal in significance to Moses and Elijah in his restoration of covenantal Israel, it is necessary that he carry out the agenda of a martyr-messiah of Israel who must be condemned by the rulers, be killed, and rise again (8.22–10.52). After his dramatic messianic entry into Jerusalem and his provocative prophetic condemnation of the Temple, Jesus confronts the Jerusalem priestly establishment and its representatives (chs 11–12). In a second major speech, Jesus warns the disciples about fanatical misinterpretation of the coming political struggles (ch 13). In the final section of the Gospel, following Jesus' last meal with the disciples and his betrayal and arrest by the rulers' posse, he is accused of treason, blasphemy, and insurrection, condemned, and turned over to Pilate, the Roman governor, who orders him executed by crucifixion (chs 14–15). The Gospel then ends abruptly with the story of the empty tomb and the women's fear (16.1–8).

INTERPRETATION

Modern readers often hear the Gospel as a story of Christian discipleship, but it is much more than that. Mark is a story of multiple conflicts, exciting to read and with a compelling message. In the dominant conflict that builds to a climax throughout the Gospel, Jesus' challenge to the Jewish religious leaders and their Roman imperial overlords escalates from his preaching and practice of the kingdom of God in the village gatherings of Galilee to his dramatic demonstration against the Temple and confrontation with the rulers in Jerusalem. That results in his torturous death by crucifixion at the hands of the Romans as an insurrectionary. In Jesus' exorcisms, moreover, God is winning the struggle with Satan and the demonic "unclean spirits" (1.27; 5.10–12) that have taken possession of the people like an occupying Roman legion. Surprisingly, a conflict between Jesus and the very disciples he designates as representative of the renewed people of Israel also develops in the course of the story. Although Jesus teaches them the mystery of the kingdom, they persistently fail to understand what he is teaching and doing, and at the end they betray, deny, and desert him. By contrast with the misunderstanding and faithless disciples, women, who play an increasingly prominent role in Mark's story, serve as models of faithfulness.

The Gospel of Mark presents Jesus' preaching and manifestation of the kingdom of God as a decisive new development in the history of Israel, not as the beginning of a new religion. Indeed, in this story religion is inseparable from the social, political, economic, even the physiological aspects of life. Throughout the Gospel, Jesus is portrayed in terms of popular Israelite memories of the great prophets, especially Moses, who had led Israel's Exodus from subjection to alien rule in Egypt; Elijah, who had led the renewal of Israel in resistance to oppressive monarchs; and Jeremiah, who had proclaimed God's judgment on the Temple and the rulers based there. At the beginning, in the middle, and toward the end, Mark also presents Jesus as a specially designated son of God, or king. Jesus, however, turns out to be a messiah (anointed one) who is a martyr, in contrast to the disciples' expectations that Jesus would be invested with political power in Jerusalem. And Jesus' role as both prophet and martyr-messiah is pointedly distinguished from the expectations of the Jewish elite, such as the scribes (see esp. 9.11–13; 12.35–37).

GUIDE TO READING

Because the Gospel presents a sustained narrative of escalating conflicts, it should be read as a whole so its components are understood in their connection with the overall story—a story that did not end at the tomb, as the prophecy of a new encounter between Jesus and his disciples reminds the audience (14.27–28; 16.7).

Richard A. Horsley

1 The beginning of the good news[a] of Jesus Christ, the Son of God.[b] ² As it is written in the prophet Isaiah,[c]
"See, I am sending my messenger ahead
  of you,[d]
who will prepare your way;
³ the voice of one crying out in the
  wilderness:
'Prepare the way of the Lord,
make his paths straight,'"

⁴ John the baptizer appeared[e] in the wilderness, proclaiming a baptism of repentance for the forgiveness of sins. ⁵ And people from the whole Judean countryside and all

a   Or *gospel*
b   Other ancient authorities lack *the Son of God*
c   Other ancient authorities read *in the prophets*
d   Gk *before your face*
e   Other ancient authorities read *John was baptizing*

1.1–13: **Preparing the way of the Lord. 1:** In the context of the Roman Empire, *the good news* (gospel) *of Jesus Christ,* i.e., Jesus the "anointed" king of Israel, a people subject to Rome, would have been understood over against the "gospel" of Caesar as the "Savior" who brought peace to the world. *Son of God* is missing in the earliest manuscripts. **1.2–8: John's baptism of repentance** (Mt 3.1–12; Lk 3.1–20; Jn 1.6–15,19–28) preparing the *way* as the new Exodus and covenant renewal. **2–3:** See Ex 23.20; Mal 3.1 (cf. Mt 11.10; Lk 7.27); Isa 40.3. That this is not all a quotation from Isaiah suggests that it is rooted in a popular (non-scribal) oral conflation of "prophecies." It is not clear whether *my messenger ahead of you* refers to John sent ahead of Jesus, or Jesus sent ahead of the addressees. *"Prepare the way of the Lord"* proclaims a new Exodus, as in Isa 40. The *wilderness,* also suggestive of a new Exodus, was a place where other popular prophets and movements often originated (e.g., Acts 5.36; cf. Josephus, *Ant.* 20.5.1). **4–5:** Acts 13.24. *Baptism of repentance for the forgiveness of sins,* John proclaims and performs a ritual of entrance into God's renewed covenant with Israel in which those ready to change their ways are baptized as forgiven for having broken the covenantal laws. **5:** *The whole Judean countryside and all the people of Jerusalem,* i.e., all the people of Israel, from the capital city as well as from the villages, were baptized. **6:** John's garb evokes an image of the prophet Elijah, as in 2 Kings 1.8; cf. 9.11–13. Jesus is also taken to be Elijah in 6.15; 8.28; 15.35–36. **7–8:** John also proclaims *one . . . more powerful* who will bring the enabling divine power of the *Holy Spirit.*

the people of Jerusalem were going out to him, and were baptized by him in the river Jordan, confessing their sins. ⁶ Now John was clothed with camel's hair, with a leather belt around his waist, and he ate locusts and wild honey. ⁷ He proclaimed, "The one who is more powerful than I is coming after me; I am not worthy to stoop down and untie the thong of his sandals. ⁸ I have baptized you withᵃ water; but he will baptize you withᵃ the Holy Spirit."

⁹ In those days Jesus came from Nazareth of Galilee and was baptized by John in the Jordan. ¹⁰ And just as he was coming up out of the water, he saw the heavens torn apart and the Spirit descending like a dove on him. ¹¹ And a voice came from heaven, "You are my Son, the Beloved;ᵇ with you I am well pleased."

¹² And the Spirit immediately drove him out into the wilderness. ¹³ He was in the wilderness forty days, tempted by Satan; and he was with the wild beasts; and the angels waited on him.

¹⁴ Now after John was arrested, Jesus came to Galilee, proclaiming the good newsᶜ of God,ᵈ ¹⁵ and saying, "The time is fulfilled, and the kingdom of God has come near;ᵉ repent, and believe in the good news."ᶜ

¹⁶ As Jesus passed along the Sea of Galilee, he saw Simon and his brother Andrew casting a net into the sea—for they were fishermen. ¹⁷ And Jesus said to them, "Follow me and I will make you fish for people." ¹⁸ And immediately they left their nets and followed him. ¹⁹ As he went a little farther, he saw James son of Zebedee and his brother John, who were in their boat mending the nets. ²⁰ Immediately he called them; and they left their father Zebedee in the boat with the hired men, and followed him.

²¹ They went to Capernaum; and when the sabbath came, he entered the synagogue and taught. ²² They were astounded at his teaching, for he taught them as one having authority, and not as the scribes. ²³ Just then there was in their synagogue a man with an

a   Or *in*
b   Or *my beloved Son*
c   Or *gospel*
d   Other ancient authorities read *of the kingdom*
e   Or *is at hand*

1.9–11: Jesus' baptism (Mt 3.13–17; Lk 3.21–22; Jn 1.29–34). Jesus himself is baptized into the renewal movement that began before him. *From Nazareth of Galilee,* a small village about 25 km (16 mi) west of the Sea of Galilee in the district now governed by "King" Herod Antipas (see 6.14), son of Herod the Great. 10–11: *The heavens torn apart,* as the divine *Spirit* breaks through empowering Jesus as the anointed king of Israel. A traditional designation for the king was "son of God," as in 2 Sam 7.14; Pss 2.7; 89.26 (cf. Lk 9.35). *Beloved,* cf. Isa 42.1.

1.12–13: Jesus' testing (cf. the particular "temptations" added in Mt 4.1–11; Lk 4.1–13). Jesus undergoes a forty-day time of trial and testing in the wilderness for a prophet, such as Elijah in 1 Kings 19.8; cf. Ex 24.18. The battle against Satan (see 3.23–27) is already engaged.

1.14–3.35: Proclaiming and manifesting the kingdom of God as the renewal of Israel, over against the Jerusalem priestly rulers.

1.14–15: Jesus' opening proclamation of the kingdom of God (Mt 4.12–17; Lk 4.14–15). 14: *John was arrested* (see 6.17) indicates the ominous situation as Jesus begins his mission centered in Galilee, a remote area of a country subjected to Rome. 15: A summary of Jesus' program and of the Gospel according to Mark. At the right time, in fulfillment of long-standing yearnings and hopes, God is finally acting to reestablish his beneficent will for the people. *Repent,* return to God's way, in response to the good news of God's action.

1.16–20: Call of disciples (Mt 4.18–22; Lk 5.1–11; Jn 1.35–42). *Sea of Galilee* or the Lake of Gennesaret is a large lake in a deep basin mostly surrounded by high hills. *Simon,* also called Peter (3.16).

1.21–28: Exorcism and teaching with authority (Mt 7.28–29; Lk 4.33–37). 21–22: *Capernaum,* a village at the north of the Lake, is the base of Jesus' activity in Galilee and the surrounding areas. *The synagogue* is the village assembly, here gathering on the sabbath (when Jesus performs the ensuing exorcism); at this time village assemblies apparently did not yet construct public buildings in which to gather. *His teaching* is inclusive of his healings and exorcisms, as the rest of this story indicates. *Authority,* the Greek word also means "power." *Scribes,* the literate elite of scholars-lawyers who represented the Jerusalem priestly rulers. 23: *A man with an*

unclean spirit, [24] and he cried out, "What have you to do with us, Jesus of Nazareth? Have you come to destroy us? I know who you are, the Holy One of God." [25] But Jesus rebuked him, saying, "Be silent, and come out of him!" [26] And the unclean spirit, convulsing him and crying with a loud voice, came out of him. [27] They were all amazed, and they kept on asking one another, "What is this? A new teaching—with authority! He[a] commands even the unclean spirits, and they obey him." [28] At once his fame began to spread throughout the surrounding region of Galilee.

[29] As soon as they[b] left the synagogue, they entered the house of Simon and Andrew, with James and John. [30] Now Simon's mother-in-law was in bed with a fever, and they told him about her at once. [31] He came and took her by the hand and lifted her up. Then the fever left her, and she began to serve them.

[32] That evening, at sunset, they brought to him all who were sick or possessed with demons. [33] And the whole city was gathered around the door. [34] And he cured many who were sick with various diseases, and cast out many demons; and he would not permit the demons to speak, because they knew him.

[35] In the morning, while it was still very dark, he got up and went out to a deserted place, and there he prayed. [36] And Simon and his companions hunted for him. [37] When they found him, they said to him, "Everyone is searching for you." [38] He answered, "Let us go on to the neighboring towns, so that I may proclaim the message there also; for that is what I came out to do." [39] And he went throughout Galilee, proclaiming the message in their synagogues and casting out demons.

[40] A leper[c] came to him begging him, and kneeling[d] he said to him, "If you choose, you can make me clean." [41] Moved with pity,[e] Jesus[f] stretched out his hand and touched him, and said to him, "I do choose. Be made

a Or *A new teaching! With authority he*
b Other ancient authorities read *he*
c The terms *leper* and *leprosy* can refer to several diseases
d Other ancient authorities lack *kneeling*
e Other ancient authorities read *anger*
f Gk *he*

---

unclean spirit, possessed by an alien force or demon. **24:** In Mark the unclean spirits immediately recognize who Jesus is, as again in 1.34; 3.11; 5.7. *Holy One of God,* a prophet possessed of divine power, as Elisha, 2 Kings 4.9. **25–26:** The exorcism involves a violent struggle. In Pss 6.9; 68.31; 78.6; 80.16; Zech 3.2 and the War Scroll from Qumran (1QM14.9–11), the Heb equivalent of the Gk term here translated "rebuke" referred to God defeating foreign conquerors or even Satan. Jesus is defeating the alien demonic forces in battle. **27:** With v. 22 these exclamations frame Jesus' exorcism: In contrast to the scribal "authorities," Jesus teaches and acts with authority and power over the unclean spirits for the benefit of the people. In Jesus' struggle against the superhuman demonic spirits his political conflict with the rulers and their scribal representatives is also engaged. **28:** From his very first exorcism, Jesus' fame spreads rapidly throughout the region; see also 1.45; 3.7–8.

1.29–34: Healings and exorcisms (Mt 8.14–17; Lk 4.38–41). **30–31:** The first of several key healings of women in Mark; see 5.21–43. **32–34:** A Markan summary, cf. 1.39; 3.7–8. **33:** Mark often uses *city* with reference to a village. **34:** *Not permit the demons to speak,* Jesus commands the demons, who know who he is, not to make him known (see 3.12) and sometimes asks people who witness healings not to tell anyone (e.g., 1.44; 5.43; 7.36). Nevertheless, his fame spreads rapidly and widely (e.g., 1.37; 1.45; 3.7–8; 7.36). The readers of Mark, of course, like the demons, know who he is from the beginning (1.1).

1.35–39: Summary of Jesus' activity (Mt 4.23–25; Lk 4.42–44). A Markan summary of Jesus' program of proclaiming the kingdom of God and exorcism of demons throughout the villages of Galilee. **39:** *In their synagogues,* the Greek word means "assemblies." Jesus' proclamations, exorcisms, and healings take place largely in the village assemblies (see vv. 21–22n.).

1.40–45: Healing a leper (Mt 8.2–4; Lk 5.12–16). *Leper,* a person suffering from skin lesions of any sort, and interpreted in priestly sources (see Lev 13–14) as a channel of "unclean" contamination for individuals and society. **40–42:** The leper dares Jesus to declare him *clean,* and Jesus responds to the challenge, In defiance of the elaborate and costly procedures prescribed in biblical law. **41:** *Moved with pity,* some manuscripts have "with anger" (see textual note *e*), which is the more difficult, hence the preferred reading; Jesus is angry at the institutionalized procedures and prescribed offerings in the Temple necessary for the "leper" to be declared free of

clean!" [42] Immediately the leprosy[a] left him, and he was made clean. [43] After sternly warning him he sent him away at once, [44] saying to him, "See that you say nothing to anyone; but go, show yourself to the priest, and offer for your cleansing what Moses commanded, as a testimony to them." [45] But he went out and began to proclaim it freely, and to spread the word, so that Jesus[b] could no longer go into a town openly, but stayed out in the country; and people came to him from every quarter.

2 When he returned to Capernaum after some days, it was reported that he was at home. [2] So many gathered around that there was no longer room for them, not even in front of the door; and he was speaking the word to them. [3] Then some people[c] came, bringing to him a paralyzed man, carried by four of them. [4] And when they could not bring him to Jesus because of the crowd, they removed the roof above him; and after having dug through it, they let down the mat on which the paralytic lay. [5] When Jesus saw their faith, he said to the paralytic, "Son, your sins are forgiven." [6] Now some of the scribes were sitting there, questioning in their hearts, [7] "Why does this fellow speak in this way? It is blasphemy! Who can forgive sins but God alone?" [8] At once Jesus perceived in his spirit that they were discussing these

questions among themselves; and he said to them, "Why do you raise such questions in your hearts? [9] Which is easier, to say to the paralytic, 'Your sins are forgiven,' or to say, 'Stand up and take your mat and walk'? [10] But so that you may know that the Son of Man has authority on earth to forgive sins"—he said to the paralytic— [11] "I say to you, stand up, take your mat and go to your home." [12] And he stood up, and immediately took the mat and went out before all of them; so that they were all amazed and glorified God, saying, "We have never seen anything like this!"

[13] Jesus[d] went out again beside the sea; the whole crowd gathered around him, and he taught them. [14] As he was walking along, he saw Levi son of Alphaeus sitting at the tax booth, and he said to him, "Follow me." And he got up and followed him.

[15] And as he sat at dinner[e] in Levi's[f] house, many tax collectors and sinners were also sit-

---

a   The terms *leper* and *leprosy* can refer to several diseases
b   Gk *he*
c   Gk *they*
d   Gk *He*
e   Gk *reclined*
f   Gk *his*

---

the stigma (*clean*). 44: Since Jesus has already made the man clean, his instructions must be intended either as a demonstrative *testimony* or "witness" against the priest and the costly offerings required by their code (Lev 14.10–32) or as a facetious remark (the now-clean man does pointedly disobey the instructions).

2.1–12: Healing paralysis and forgiveness of sins (Mt 9.1–8; Lk 5.17–26). This controversy story, which is also a healing story, begins a series of controversies in which the scribes (see 1.21–22n.) and Pharisees attack or question Jesus, whose sharp response is decisive. The scribes were the literate expert interpreters and guardians of the official law codes, the Pharisees a particular party or faction within the wider class of scribes. Both were based in the Jerusalem Temple (3.22; 7.1) and worked for and represented the priestly rulers in dealings with the people. 4: Houses often had a flat roof consisting of mud plaster over a wood framework. 5–11: Jesus equates the declaration "*Your sins are forgiven*" with "*Stand up . . . and walk*." The man's paralysis is believed to be due to his own sin (or that of his parents; see Ex 34.7; Jn 9.2). The scribes, the authorities who socially reinforced such self-blame for illness and misfortune, accuse Jesus of *blasphemy*, a capital offense (Lev 24.16), since forgiveness can be done by *God alone* through the established procedures in the Temple, according to these his official interpreters. The accusation prefigures that by the high priest at his trial (Mk 14.64). Again Jesus asserts his own prophetic authority and power over against the scribes, as in 1.22–27. *Son of Man* means either "human being" or refers to Jesus as an exalted figure representative of a finally restored Israel (derived from Dan 7.13), or both.

2.13–17: Eating with sinners (Mt 9.9–13; Lk 5.27–32). **14**: *Levi*, identified as "Matthew" in Mt 9.9, is a customs officer at Capernaum, a border village, presumably working under an officer of Herod Antipas. **15–16**: *Eating with sinners and tax collectors* (or rather "toll collectors") would have entailed contact with impure people and social outcasts, according to *the scribes of the Pharisees*.

ting[a] with Jesus and his disciples—for there were many who followed him. [16] When the scribes of[b] the Pharisees saw that he was eating with sinners and tax collectors, they said to his disciples, "Why does he eat[c] with tax collectors and sinners?" [17] When Jesus heard this, he said to them, "Those who are well have no need of a physician, but those who are sick; I have come to call not the righteous but sinners."

[18] Now John's disciples and the Pharisees were fasting; and people[d] came and said to him, "Why do John's disciples and the disciples of the Pharisees fast, but your disciples do not fast?" [19] Jesus said to them, "The wedding guests cannot fast while the bridegroom is with them, can they? As long as they have the bridegroom with them, they cannot fast. [20] The days will come when the bridegroom is taken away from them, and then they will fast on that day.

[21] "No one sews a piece of unshrunk cloth on an old cloak; otherwise, the patch pulls away from it, the new from the old, and a worse tear is made. [22] And no one puts new wine into old wineskins; otherwise, the wine will burst the skins, and the wine is lost, and so are the skins; but one puts new wine into fresh wineskins."[e]

[23] One sabbath he was going through the grainfields; and as they made their way his disciples began to pluck heads of grain. [24] The Pharisees said to him, "Look, why are they doing what is not lawful on the sabbath?" [25] And he said to them, "Have you never read what David did when he and his companions were hungry and in need of food? [26] He entered the house of God, when Abiathar was high priest, and ate the bread of the Presence, which it is not lawful for any but the priests to eat, and he gave some to his companions." [27] Then he said to them, "The sabbath was made for humankind, and not humankind for the sabbath; [28] so the Son of Man is lord even of the sabbath."

3 Again he entered the synagogue, and a man was there who had a withered hand. [2] They watched him to see whether he would cure him on the sabbath, so that they might accuse him. [3] And he said to the man who had the withered hand, "Come forward." [4] Then he said to them, "Is it lawful to do good or to do harm on the sabbath, to save life or to kill?" But they were silent. [5] He looked around at them with anger; he was grieved at their hardness of heart and said to the man, "Stretch out your hand." He stretched it out, and his hand was restored. [6] The Pharisees went out and immediately conspired with the Herodians against him, how to destroy him.

a Gk *reclining*
b Other ancient authorities read *and*
c Other ancient authorities add *and drink*
d Gk *they*
e Other ancient authorities lack *but one puts new wine into fresh wineskins*

2.18–22: Fasting (Mt 9.14–17; Lk 5.33–39). **19:** A wedding feast, one of the principal times of celebration and feasting among peasants, was a traditional symbol of the future time of fulfillment, a time of justice and plenty; cf. Isa 62.5; Lk 17.22. **20:** *The bridegroom . . . taken away*, after the crucifixion when Jesus, understood as the bridegroom, is gone. **21–22:** With Jesus' preaching and manifestation of the kingdom something new has come, calling for suspension of old forms such as fasting.

2.23–28: The sabbath and hunger (Mt 12.1–8; Lk 6.1–5). **23–24:** The disciples' action may have violated the Pharisees' restrictions against travel as well as harvesting on the sabbath, meant to implement the fourth commandment (Ex 20.8–10). **25–26:** Jesus' reply summarizes a story about David commandeering food for his soldiers that appears in 1 Sam 21.1–6, in which Ahimelech, Abiathar's father, is the priest (cf. 2 Sam 15.35). The point of the story: David's men were *hungry*, a detail not found in 1 Sam 21. **27:** Ex 23.12; Deut 5.14–15. **28:** *Son of Man*, even more clearly than in 2.10, could mean either "human being," in parallelism with "humankind" in v. 27, or the future Jesus as an exalted figure representing a renewed Israel.

3.1–6: Healing on the sabbath (Mt 12.9–14; Lk 6.6–11). **1:** *Synagogue*, see 1.21–22n. **2–4:** Having already performed an exorcism on the sabbath (1.22–27), Jesus now pointedly performs a healing on the sabbath in the presence of the Pharisees, who remain silent. **5:** Juxtaposition of Jesus' anger and grief at the Pharisees' program and his compassion in curing the man's withered hand. **6:** In response to this and Jesus' previous actions, the Pharisees conspire with the *Herodians*, representatives of Herod Antipas, the ruler of Galilee, *to destroy him*.

3.7–12: Summary of Jesus' activity (Mt 4.24–25; 12.15–21; Lk 6.17–19; 4.41). A summary of Jesus' program and

⁷ Jesus departed with his disciples to the sea, and a great multitude from Galilee followed him; ⁸ hearing all that he was doing, they came to him in great numbers from Judea, Jerusalem, Idumea, beyond the Jordan, and the region around Tyre and Sidon. ⁹ He told his disciples to have a boat ready for him because of the crowd, so that they would not crush him; ¹⁰ for he had cured many, so that all who had diseases pressed upon him to touch him. ¹¹ Whenever the unclean spirits saw him, they fell down before him and shouted, "You are the Son of God!" ¹² But he sternly ordered them not to make him known.

¹³ He went up the mountain and called to him those whom he wanted, and they came to him. ¹⁴ And he appointed twelve, whom he also named apostles,ᵃ to be with him, and to be sent out to proclaim the message, ¹⁵ and to have authority to cast out demons. ¹⁶ So he appointed the twelve:ᵇ Simon (to whom he gave the name Peter); ¹⁷ James son of Zebedee and John the brother of James (to whom he gave the name Boanerges, that is, Sons of Thunder); ¹⁸ and Andrew, and Philip, and Bartholomew, and Matthew, and Thomas, and James son of Alphaeus, and Thaddaeus, and Simon the Cananaean, ¹⁹ and Judas Iscariot, who betrayed him.

Then he went home; ²⁰ and the crowd came together again, so that they could not even eat. ²¹ When his family heard it, they went out to restrain him, for people were saying, "He has gone out of his mind." ²² And the scribes who came down from Jerusalem said, "He has Beelzebul, and by the ruler of the demons he casts out demons." ²³ And he called them to him, and spoke to them in parables, "How can Satan cast out Satan? ²⁴ If a kingdom is divided against itself, that kingdom cannot stand. ²⁵ And if a house is divided against itself, that house will not be able to stand. ²⁶ And if Satan has risen up against himself and is divided, he cannot stand, but his end has come. ²⁷ But no one can enter a strong man's house and plunder his property without first tying up the strong man; then indeed the house can be plundered.

²⁸ "Truly I tell you, people will be forgiven for their sins and whatever blasphemies they utter; ²⁹ but whoever blasphemes against the Holy Spirit can never have forgiveness, but is guilty of an eternal sin"— ³⁰ for they had said, "He has an unclean spirit."

ᵃ Other ancient authorities lack *whom he also named apostles*

ᵇ Other ancient authorities lack *So he appointed the twelve*

the burgeoning response it evokes. **8:** Peoples of Israelite heritage from all these areas flock to Jesus, indicating that a renewal of all Israel is happening. *The region around* indicates that they are mainly from rural villages. See map on p. 1800.

3.13–19a: Appointing the twelve (Mt 10.1–4; Lk 6.12–16). **13–14:** *Up the mountain . . . appointed twelve,* suggests a new Sinai, on which Jesus is constituting a renewed Israel symbolized by the twelve. **14–15:** The twelve are invested with the same proclamation (of the kingdom) and authority and power to exorcize demons as Jesus, an extension of his program.

3.19b–35: Defeat of Satan, and the new community (Mt 12.22–27; Lk 11.14–23; 12.10; 16.43–45). In a repeated narrative technique, Mark "sandwiches" one story into another. **21:** To those who knew Jesus before he assumed the role of prophet or are concerned lest he be seized by the authorities, he appears to be *out of his mind* (cf. 6.1–3). **22–27:** Both Jesus and the scribes (see 1.21–22n.) think that current personal and social-political life is caught in the struggle for dominion between God and Satan. **22:** The threatened scribes attribute Jesus' power to demonic possession: He is a witch! *Beelzebul,* possibly "Lord of the (divine) house" (cf. Mt 10.25), or "Baal, the prince," originally a title of the Canaanite storm and fertility god (2 Kings 1.2), later demonized into the chief power of evil. **23:** *In parables,* in extended metaphors or analogies; cf. 4.2,33. **24–26:** A kingdom was thought of as a household on a large scale, and both kingdom and household were metaphors for God's and Satan's power or control. Jesus argues both that the scribes' charge is absurd and that even assuming they are right, Satan's rule is at an end. **27:** By analogy, in his exorcism of demons Jesus (the "more powerful one," 1.7) has broken into Satan's house, tied up "the strong man," and "plundered his property." This further implies that God's is now the only kingdom left, by which Jesus is acting. **28–30:** From Mark's viewpoint, attacks on Jesus during his mission can be forgiven, but not attacks against the *Holy Spirit* acting in his movement. **31–35:** Not necessarily an attack on his family (but see v. 21), but rather an indication that within the Jesus-movement and its communi-

31 Then his mother and his brothers came; and standing outside, they sent to him and called him. 32 A crowd was sitting around him; and they said to him, "Your mother and your brothers and sisters[a] are outside, asking for you." 33 And he replied, "Who are my mother and my brothers?" 34 And looking at those who sat around him, he said, "Here are my mother and my brothers! 35 Whoever does the will of God is my brother and sister and mother."

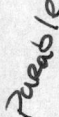

4 Again he began to teach beside the sea. Such a very large crowd gathered around him that he got into a boat on the sea and sat there, while the whole crowd was beside the sea on the land. 2 He began to teach them many things in parables, and in his teaching he said to them: 3 "Listen! A sower went out to sow. 4 And as he sowed, some seed fell on the path, and the birds came and ate it up. 5 Other seed fell on rocky ground, where it did not have much soil, and it sprang up quickly, since it had no depth of soil. 6 And when the sun rose, it was scorched; and since it had no root, it withered away. 7 Other seed fell among thorns, and the thorns grew up and choked it, and it yielded no grain. 8 Other seed fell into good soil and brought forth grain, growing up and increasing and yielding thirty and sixty and a hundredfold." 9 And he said, "Let anyone with ears to hear listen!"

10 When he was alone, those who were around him along with the twelve asked him about the parables. 11 And he said to them, "To you has been given the secret[b] of the kingdom of God, but for those outside, everything comes in parables; 12 in order that

'they may indeed look, but not perceive,
  and may indeed listen, but not understand;
so that they may not turn again and be forgiven.'"

13 And he said to them, "Do you not understand this parable? Then how will you understand all the parables? 14 The sower sows the word. 15 These are the ones on the path where the word is sown: when they hear, Satan immediately comes and takes away the word that is sown in them. 16 And these are the ones sown on rocky ground: when they hear the word, they immediately receive it with joy. 17 But they have no root, and endure only for a while; then, when trouble or persecution arises on account of the word, immediately they fall away.[c] 18 And others are those sown among the thorns: these are the ones who hear the word, 19 but the cares of the world, and the lure of wealth, and the desire for other things come in and choke the word, and it yields nothing. 20 And these are the ones sown on the good soil: they hear the word and accept it and bear fruit, thirty and sixty and a hundredfold."

21 He said to them, "Is a lamp brought in to be put under the bushel basket, or under the bed, and not on the lampstand? 22 For there is nothing hidden, except to be disclosed; nor is anything secret, except to come to light. 23 Let anyone with ears to hear listen!" 24 And he said to them, "Pay attention to what you hear; the measure you give will be the measure you

a Other ancient authorities lack *and sisters*
b Or *mystery*
c Or *stumble*

ties, those who do *the will of God* are Jesus' and each others' *brother and sister and mother.*

4.1–34: Teaching the mystery of the kingdom of God in parables (Mt 13; Lk 8.4–18; 13.18–21). **2:** *In parables,* in extended metaphors or analogies. **3–8:** Parable of the sower and the seeds. Despite all the obstacles, there is an amazing and unprecedented bumper crop (normal good yield was 7 to 1). **10:** The rest of the teaching is directed to the twelve (3.16–19) and other members of the movement. **11–12:** *The secret of the kingdom of God,* to them is disclosed the "mystery" or hidden plan of God (cf. Dan 2.28) for the fulfillment of history in the kingdom of God now being proclaimed and manifested. Since outsiders do not understand this "mystery" or "plan," the parables are opaque to them, just as Isaiah's contemporaries did not understand his prophecies (Isa 6.9–10). **13–20:** Explains the parable of the sower allegorically, with each principal symbol of the analogy standing for some aspect of the listeners' experiences of the effects of Jesus' preaching of the kingdom—and corresponding to later episodes in Mark. **15:** The struggle with Satan continues, as it also will in Peter's misunderstanding in 8.29–33. **16–17:** Cf. 9.42–48; 13.19,24; 14.27,29. **18–19:** *The lure of wealth,* cf. 10.17–22,25. **21–23:** These sayings repeat and reinforce the message of 4.3–10,20; the kingdom, *hidden* now, will *come to light.* **24–25:** These sayings make most sense as a warning not to accept any cynical "realistic" advice that the established power-relations

get, and still more will be given you. [25] For to those who have, more will be given; and from those who have nothing, even what they have will be taken away."

[26] He also said, "The kingdom of God is as if someone would scatter seed on the ground, [27] and would sleep and rise night and day, and the seed would sprout and grow, he does not know how. [28] The earth produces of itself, first the stalk, then the head, then the full grain in the head. [29] But when the grain is ripe, at once he goes in with his sickle, because the harvest has come."

[30] He also said, "With what can we compare the kingdom of God, or what parable will we use for it? [31] It is like a mustard seed, which, when sown upon the ground, is the smallest of all the seeds on earth; [32] yet when it is sown it grows up and becomes the greatest of all shrubs, and puts forth large branches, so that the birds of the air can make nests in its shade."

[33] With many such parables he spoke the word to them, as they were able to hear it; [34] he did not speak to them except in parables, but he explained everything in private to his disciples.

[35] On that day, when evening had come, he said to them, "Let us go across to the other side." [36] And leaving the crowd behind, they took him with them in the boat, just as he was. Other boats were with him. [37] A great windstorm arose, and the waves beat into the boat, so that the boat was already being swamped.

[38] But he was in the stern, asleep on the cushion; and they woke him up and said to him, "Teacher, do you not care that we are perishing?" [39] He woke up and rebuked the wind, and said to the sea, "Peace! Be still!" Then the wind ceased, and there was a dead calm. [40] He said to them, "Why are you afraid? Have you still no faith?" [41] And they were filled with great awe and said to one another, "Who then is this, that even the wind and the sea obey him?"

5 They came to the other side of the sea, to the country of the Gerasenes.[a] [2] And when he had stepped out of the boat, immediately a man out of the tombs with an unclean spirit met him. [3] He lived among the tombs; and no one could restrain him any more, even with a chain; [4] for he had often been restrained with shackles and chains, but the chains he wrenched apart, and the shackles he broke in pieces; and no one had the strength to subdue him. [5] Night and day among the tombs and on the mountains he was always howling and bruising himself with stones. [6] When he saw Jesus from a distance, he ran and bowed down before him; [7] and he shouted at the top of his voice, "What have you to do with me, Jesus, Son of the Most High God? I adjure you by God, do not torment me." [8] For he had said to him, "Come out of the man, you unclean spirit!" [9] Then Jesus[b] asked him, "What is your

---

a Other ancient authorities read *Gergesenes*; others, *Gadarenes*

b Gk *he*

---

will inevitably continue. **26–29:** The kingdom of God will surely come to full fruition, just as the seed inevitably sprouts, grows, and produces a harvest (cf. Joel 3.13). **30–32:** The climax of the process by which the kingdom of God is growing is like the tiniest seed producing a large bush that provides homes for the birds. Note the modest metaphor, in contrast with the imperial metaphor of the cedar tree in Ezek 17; 31; Dan 4.

4.35–8.21: Continuing the prophetic renewal of Israel (and other peoples) despite opposition and the disciples' misunderstanding. This section is organized around two sequences of Moses- and Elijah-like sea crossings, exorcisms, healings, and wilderness feedings.

4.35–41: First sea crossing (Mt 8.18,23–27; Lk 8.22–25; cf. Mk 6.45–52). Emphasis falls on the disciples' lack of faith and their *great awe . . . "that even the wind and the sea obey him."* Control of the sea is a divine characteristic (e.g., Job 26.12; 38.8–11; see Ps 89.9; cf. Ps 89.25).

5.1–20: Exorcism of the demon whose name is "Legion" (Mt 8.28–34; Lk 8.26–39). This is the most embellished such episode in Mark. **1:** The territory of the city of Gerasa (modern Jerash) was in central Transjordan; its population was largely non-Jewish. Mt 8.28 situates this event in Gadara, southeast of the Sea of Galilee, a setting that better fits the narrative. **2–5:** The man's possession by the alien force generated such violence that his community had not been able to restrain him, even with chains. **7:** *Most High God* is not an Israelite but a Hellenistic name, found mainly in Luke-Acts. **9:** Once the unclean spirit is cast out, it is possible to find

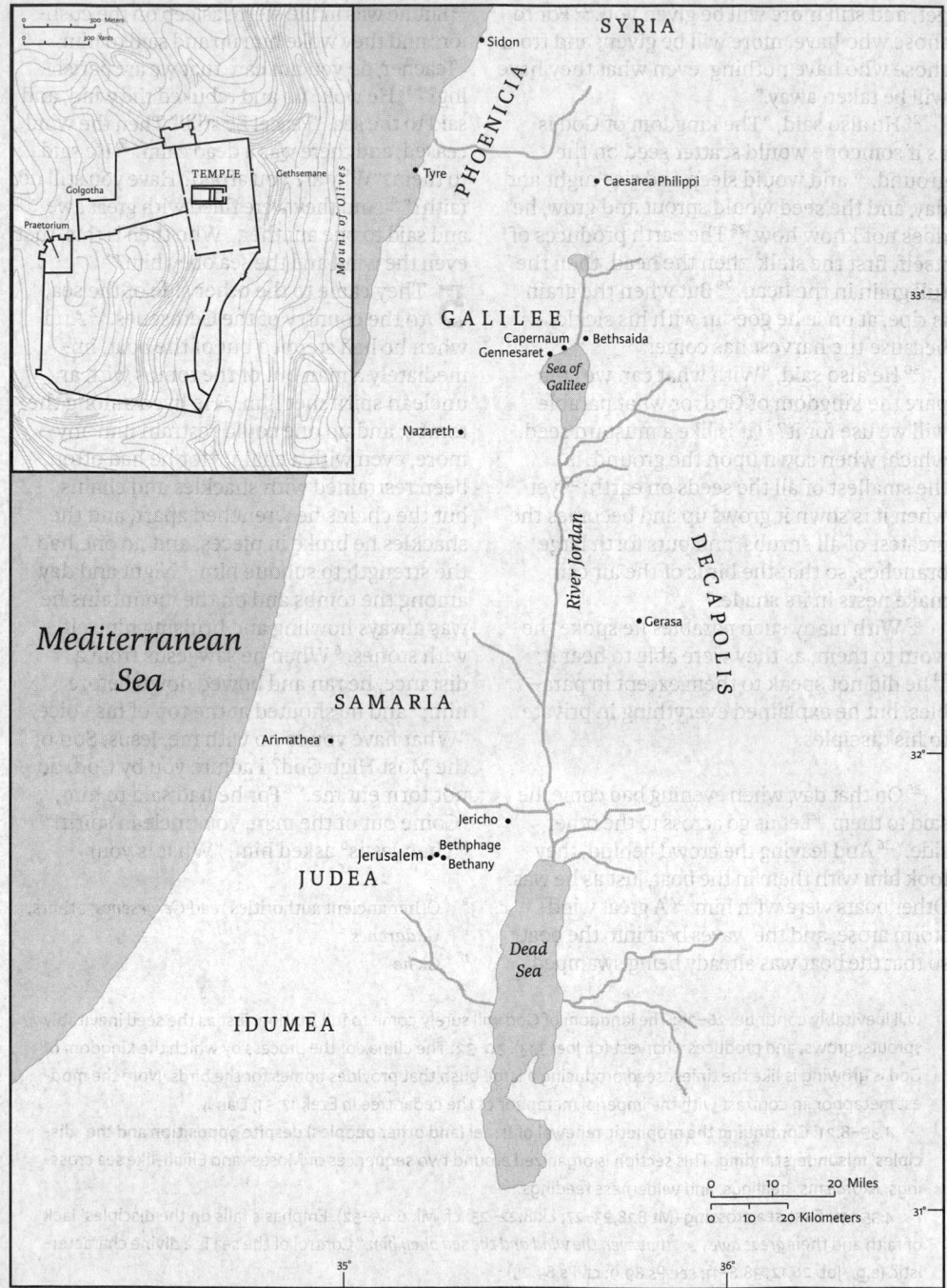

The geography of the Gospel of Mark.

name?" He replied, "My name is Legion; for we are many." [10] He begged him earnestly not to send them out of the country. [11] Now there on the hillside a great herd of swine was feeding; [12] and the unclean spirits[a] begged him, "Send us into the swine; let us enter them." [13] So he gave them permission. And the unclean spirits came out and entered the swine; and the herd, numbering about two thousand, rushed down the steep bank into the sea, and were drowned in the sea.

[14] The swineherds ran off and told it in the city and in the country. Then people came to see what it was that had happened. [15] They came to Jesus and saw the demoniac sitting there, clothed and in his right mind, the very man who had had the legion; and they were afraid. [16] Those who had seen what had happened to the demoniac and to the swine reported it. [17] Then they began to beg Jesus[b] to leave their neighborhood. [18] As he was getting into the boat, the man who had been possessed by demons begged him that he might be with him. [19] But Jesus[c] refused, and said to him, "Go home to your friends, and tell them how much the Lord has done for you, and what mercy he has shown you." [20] And he went away and began to proclaim in the Decapolis how much Jesus had done for him; and everyone was amazed.

[21] When Jesus had crossed again in the boat[d] to the other side, a great crowd gathered around him; and he was by the sea. [22] Then one of the leaders of the synagogue named Jairus came and, when he saw him,

fell at his feet [23] and begged him repeatedly, "My little daughter is at the point of death. Come and lay your hands on her, so that she may be made well, and live." [24] So he went with him.

And a large crowd followed him and pressed in on him. [25] Now there was a woman who had been suffering from hemorrhages for twelve years. [26] She had endured much under many physicians, and had spent all that she had; and she was no better, but rather grew worse. [27] She had heard about Jesus, and came up behind him in the crowd and touched his cloak, [28] for she said, "If I but touch his clothes, I will be made well." [29] Immediately her hemorrhage stopped; and she felt in her body that she was healed of her disease. [30] Immediately aware that power had gone forth from him, Jesus turned about in the crowd and said, "Who touched my clothes?" [31] And his disciples said to him, "You see the crowd pressing in on you; how can you say, 'Who touched me?'" [32] He looked all around to see who had done it. [33] But the woman, knowing what had happened to her, came in fear and trembling, fell down before him, and told him the whole truth. [34] He said to her, "Daughter, your faith has made you well; go in peace, and be healed of your disease."

a Gk *they*
b Gk *him*
c Gk *he*
d Other ancient authorities lack *in the boat*

out its identity. A *legion* was a division (usually consisting of about five or six thousand troops) of the Roman military, who had conquered and, in effect, still occupied the country. **11–13:** Having entered the herd of pigs (which Jews were not permitted to eat, Lev 11.7; Deut 14.8), the Roman "legion" of unclean spirits, in a military image, charged into the sea and were destroyed, alluding to the destruction of Pharaoh's army in Israel's Exodus deliverance (Ex 15.4). Cf. the image of the (Temple-) mount "thrown into the sea," 11.23. **14–17:** The people were apprehensive that Jesus had disrupted their delicately balanced adjustment to the alien possession. **20:** The liberated man carried the good news about Jesus' actions into the wider *Decapolis*, the district of "ten cities" in the Jordan valley and in Transjordan. They were Hellenistic in character, with a largely non-Israelite population.

5.21–43: Healings of Jairus's daughter and the hemorrhaging woman (Mt 9.18–26; Lk 8.40–56). Again (see 3.19b–25) Mark has "sandwiched" one story into another. The healings of both the woman who had been hemorrhaging for twelve years and the almost dead twelve-year-old woman are also symbolic of Jesus' renewal of Israel. **22:** *Leaders of the synagogue,* i.e., of the village assembly. **25–26:** The woman is poverty-stricken from the worsening hemorrhaging that no physicians could stop. According to the official Jerusalem purity code (Lev 15.25–30), she would have been "unclean." It is doubtful that this code affected village life. The story itself does not mention ritual purity. **27–33:** The initiative and action are entirely hers, Jesus being the passive conduit through which the healing power goes forth. **34:** Her confidence that she would be healed is a paradigm of trust

35 While he was still speaking, some people came from the leader's house to say, "Your daughter is dead. Why trouble the teacher any further?" 36 But overhearing[a] what they said, Jesus said to the leader of the synagogue, "Do not fear, only believe." 37 He allowed no one to follow him except Peter, James, and John, the brother of James. 38 When they came to the house of the leader of the synagogue, he saw a commotion, people weeping and wailing loudly. 39 When he had entered, he said to them, "Why do you make a commotion and weep? The child is not dead but sleeping." 40 And they laughed at him. Then he put them all outside, and took the child's father and mother and those who were with him, and went in where the child was. 41 He took her by the hand and said to her, "Talitha cum," which means, "Little girl, get up!" 42 And immediately the girl got up and began to walk about (she was twelve years of age). At this they were overcome with amazement. 43 He strictly ordered them that no one should know this, and told them to give her something to eat.

6 He left that place and came to his hometown, and his disciples followed him. 2 On the sabbath he began to teach in the synagogue, and many who heard him were astounded. They said, "Where did this man get all this? What is this wisdom that has been given to him? What deeds of power are being done by his hands! 3 Is not this the carpenter, the son of Mary[b] and brother of James and Joses and Judas and Simon, and are not his sisters here with us?" And they took offense[c] at him. 4 Then Jesus said to them, "Prophets are not without honor, except in their hometown, and among their own kin, and in their own house." 5 And he could do no deed of power there, except that he laid his hands on a few sick people and cured them. 6 And he was amazed at their unbelief.

Then he went about among the villages teaching. 7 He called the twelve and began to send them out two by two, and gave them authority over the unclean spirits. 8 He ordered them to take nothing for their journey except a staff; no bread, no bag, no money in their belts; 9 but to wear sandals and not to put on two tunics. 10 He said to them, "Wherever you enter a house, stay there until you leave the place. 11 If any place will not welcome you and they refuse to hear you, as you leave, shake off the dust that is on your feet as a testimony against them." 12 So they went out and proclaimed that all should repent. 13 They cast out many demons, and anointed with oil many who were sick and cured them.

14 King Herod heard of it, for Jesus'[d] name had become known. Some were[e] saying, "John the baptizer has been raised from the dead; and for this reason these powers are at work in him." 15 But others said, "It is Elijah." And others said, "It is a prophet, like one of the prophets of old." 16 But when Herod heard of it, he said, "John, whom I beheaded, has been raised."

a Or *ignoring*; other ancient authorities read *hearing*
b Other ancient authorities read *son of the carpenter and of Mary*
c Or *stumbled*
d Gk *his*
e Other ancient authorities read *He was*

(*faith*) in the renewal that is happening through Jesus. 41: The phrase *talitha cum* is Aramaic; cf. 7.34; 14.36; 15.34. 42: The young woman, at twelve approaching marriage, appears to be dead, yet Jesus restores her to life and, presumably, the ability to reproduce new life in and of Israel.

6.1–6a: Rejection in his hometown (Mt. 13.53–58; Lk 4.16–30). Those who knew Jesus from his early years, before he was called into service as a prophet mediating extraordinary powers, cannot respond in faith as others can; cf. 3.21. 5: The powers that work through such a prophet are dependent on people's positive response with faith.

6.6b–13: Commissioning the twelve (Mt 10.1,9–11,14; Lk 9.1–6; cf. Lk 10.2–16). Jesus commissions the twelve, appointed as symbolic heads of the renewed Israel in 3.13–19, to expand his mission of proclamation, exorcism, and healing. They work in villages, staying in sympathetic households, building the renewal movement.

6.14–29: Herod's execution of John (Mt 14.1–12; Lk 9.7–9). 14–16: *Herod*, Antipas, son of Herod the Great, technically appointed tetrarch, but popularly known as "King," ruled Galilee and part of Transjordan 4 BCE–39 CE. Clearly people were responding to and identifying Jesus out of their cultivation of popular tradition as "Elijah" or "one of the prophets." Herod, however, is anxiously superstitious because he had beheaded John.

¹⁷ For Herod himself had sent men who arrested John, bound him, and put him in prison on account of Herodias, his brother Philip's wife, because Herod[a] had married her. ¹⁸ For John had been telling Herod, "It is not lawful for you to have your brother's wife." ¹⁹ And Herodias had a grudge against him, and wanted to kill him. But she could not, ²⁰ for Herod feared John, knowing that he was a righteous and holy man, and he protected him. When he heard him, he was greatly perplexed;[b] and yet he liked to listen to him. ²¹ But an opportunity came when Herod on his birthday gave a banquet for his courtiers and officers and for the leaders of Galilee. ²² When his daughter Herodias[c] came in and danced, she pleased Herod and his guests; and the king said to the girl, "Ask me for whatever you wish, and I will give it." ²³ And he solemnly swore to her, "Whatever you ask me, I will give you, even half of my kingdom." ²⁴ She went out and said to her mother, "What should I ask for?" She replied, "The head of John the baptizer." ²⁵ Immediately she rushed back to the king and requested, "I want you to give me at once the head of John the Baptist on a platter." ²⁶ The king was deeply grieved; yet out of regard for his oaths and for the guests, he did not want to refuse her. ²⁷ Immediately the king sent a soldier of the guard with orders to bring John's[d] head. He went and beheaded him in the prison, ²⁸ brought his head on a platter, and gave it to the girl. Then the girl gave it to her mother. ²⁹ When his disciples heard about it, they came and took his body, and laid it in a tomb.

³⁰ The apostles gathered around Jesus, and told him all that they had done and taught. ³¹ He said to them, "Come away to a deserted place all by yourselves and rest a while." For many were coming and going, and they had no leisure even to eat. ³² And they went away in the boat to a deserted place by themselves. ³³ Now many saw them going and recognized them, and they hurried there on foot from all the towns and arrived ahead of them. ³⁴ As he went ashore, he saw a great crowd; and he had compassion for them, because they were like sheep without a shepherd; and he began to teach them many things. ³⁵ When it grew late, his disciples came to him and said, "This is a deserted place, and the hour is now very late; ³⁶ send them away so that they may go into the surrounding country and villages and buy something for themselves to eat." ³⁷ But he answered them, "You give them something to eat." They said to him, "Are we to go and buy two hundred denarii[e] worth of bread, and give it to them to eat?" ³⁸ And he said to them, "How many loaves have you? Go and

a   Gk *he*

b   Other ancient authorities read *he did many things*

c   Other ancient authorities read *the daughter of Herodias herself*

d   Gk *his*

e   The denarius was the usual day's wage for a laborer

17–29: A popular tale of the decadent life at Herod's court and of the gruesome beheading of John that sounds an ominous note for Jesus' prophetic renewal of Israel over against the king appointed by Rome. 17–18: Royal marriages were instruments of international politics. John's prophecy against Herod Antipas's marriage to his brother's wife, which was illegal (Lev 18.16; 20.21) and which alienated the Nabatean king Aretas IV, father of his first wife, was politically incendiary (see Josephus, *J.W.* 2.182; *Ant.* 18.240–44). 19–20: Herod's and Herodias's respective feelings about John are reminiscent of Ahab's and Jezebel's stances toward Elijah in 1 Kings 18–19,21. 21: *Leaders,* better "the first ones," i.e., high-ranking officials at court. 22: *His daughter,* called Salome by Josephus (*Ant.* 18.5.136). 29: John also had disciples, and perhaps headed a prophetic movement parallel to that of Jesus.

    6.30–44: Wilderness feeding of five thousand (Mt 14.13–21; Lk 9.10–17; Jn 6.1–13; cf. Mk 8.1–10). First of two wilderness feedings reminiscent of God's feeding early Israel in the wilderness through Moses (Ex 16; Num 11). 30–33: In need of a temporary retreat from the rigors of their mission, Jesus and his apostles withdraw, but hordes of people clamor to them even in the wilderness. 34: *Sheep without a shepherd,* a frequent image for a people without a prophet or king to lead them (see Num 27.17; 1 Kings 22.17; Ezek 34.8; Zech 10.2). Coming right after Herod's execution of John, it also alludes to the prophetic tradition of political criticism of predatory and exploitative kings who become rich by "fleecing" rather than caring for their people (see Ezek 34.2–5; Zech 11.4–17). 35–37: The disciples' suggestion and protest both represent a misunderstanding of Jesus' program. That the villagers could no longer feed themselves from their own produce and had to become laborers to earn

see." When they had found out, they said, "Five, and two fish." [39] Then he ordered them to get all the people to sit down in groups on the green grass. [40] So they sat down in groups of hundreds and of fifties. [41] Taking the five loaves and the two fish, he looked up to heaven, and blessed and broke the loaves, and gave them to his disciples to set before the people; and he divided the two fish among them all. [42] And all ate and were filled; [43] and they took up twelve baskets full of broken pieces and of the fish. [44] Those who had eaten the loaves numbered five thousand men.

[45] Immediately he made his disciples get into the boat and go on ahead to the other side, to Bethsaida, while he dismissed the crowd. [46] After saying farewell to them, he went up on the mountain to pray.

[47] When evening came, the boat was out on the sea, and he was alone on the land. [48] When he saw that they were straining at the oars against an adverse wind, he came towards them early in the morning, walking on the sea. He intended to pass them by. [49] But when they saw him walking on the sea, they thought it was a ghost and cried out; [50] for they all saw him and were terrified. But immediately he spoke to them and said, "Take heart, it is I; do not be afraid." [51] Then he got into the boat with them and the wind ceased. And they were utterly astounded, [52] for they did not understand about the loaves, but their hearts were hardened.

[53] When they had crossed over, they came to land at Gennesaret and moored the boat. [54] When they got out of the boat, people at once recognized him, [55] and rushed about that whole region and began to bring the sick on mats to wherever they heard he was. [56] And wherever he went, into villages or cities or farms, they laid the sick in the marketplaces, and begged him that they might touch even the fringe of his cloak; and all who touched it were healed.

7 Now when the Pharisees and some of the scribes who had come from Jerusalem gathered around him, [2] they noticed that some of his disciples were eating with defiled hands, that is, without washing them. [3] (For the Pharisees, and all the Jews, do not eat unless they thoroughly wash their hands,[a] thus observing the tradition of the elders; [4] and they do not eat anything from the market unless they wash it;[b] and there are also many other traditions that they observe, the washing of cups, pots, and bronze kettles.[c]) [5] So the Pharisees and the scribes asked him, "Why do your disciples not live[d] according to the tradition of the elders, but eat with defiled hands?" [6] He said to them, "Isaiah

a   Meaning of Gk uncertain
b   Other ancient authorities read *and when they come from the marketplace, they do not eat unless they purify themselves*
c   Other ancient authorities add *and beds*
d   Gk *walk*

money to buy food is just the problem! **38–44:** One of the dreams of peasants, who are always economically marginal and therefore hungry, is a future good time when food is plentiful (cf. Lk 6.20–21). Both the multiplication of the food and the twelve baskets left over suggest that this story is reminiscent of Elijah-Elisha stories of feeding in times of famine (e.g., 2 Kings 4.42–44) and of their restoration of Israel symbolized in its twelve tribes. **39–40:** Groups of hundreds and fifties are an allusion to Moses' organization of Israel following the Exodus (Ex 18.21–25). **41:** Christian readers usually find eucharistic overtones in Jesus' blessing and breaking of the loaves (cf. 14.22).

6.45–52: Second sea crossing (Mt 14.22–33; Jn 6.15–21; cf. Mk 4.35–41). **45:** *Bethsaida*, a village at the north of the Sea of Galilee, transformed into a small "city" by Herod Philip. **47–52:** Again the disciples are terrified, not only at the wind but also at the apparition. **50:** Mark compares Jesus to God, using the phrase "I am" (Gk "ego eimi," NRSV: "It is I"; cf. Ex 3.14). **51–52:** Yet the disciples not only lack faith, as in 4.40, but *their hearts were hardened*, as had occurred with enemies of God in earlier times (e.g., Ex 7.3,14; Deut 2.30; Josh 11.20; 1 Sam 6.6).

6.53–56: A summary passage highlighting the widening response to Jesus. Mt 14.34–36. **56:** *His cloak . . . were healed*, cf. 5.25–34.

7.1–23: Traditions of the elders vs. the commandment of God (Mt 15.1–20). **1–5:** As representatives of the Jerusalem Temple, the political-economic as well as religious capital of Judea, the Pharisees and scribes cultivated oral *tradition of the elders* supplementary to the law of Moses, in this story focused on purity codes for processing and eating food. **3–4:** The parenthetical explanation claims that "all the Judeans/NRSV "all the

prophesied rightly about you hypocrites, as it is written,

'This people honors me with their lips,
  but their hearts are far from me;
[7] in vain do they worship me,
  teaching human precepts as doctrines.'
[8] You abandon the commandment of God and hold to human tradition."

[9] Then he said to them, "You have a fine way of rejecting the commandment of God in order to keep your tradition! [10] For Moses said, 'Honor your father and your mother'; and, 'Whoever speaks evil of father or mother must surely die.' [11] But you say that if anyone tells father or mother, 'Whatever support you might have had from me is Corban' (that is, an offering to God[a])— [12] then you no longer permit doing anything for a father or mother, [13] thus making void the word of God through your tradition that you have handed on. And you do many things like this."

[14] Then he called the crowd again and said to them, "Listen to me, all of you, and understand: [15] there is nothing outside a person that by going in can defile, but the things that come out are what defile."[b]

[17] When he had left the crowd and entered the house, his disciples asked him about the parable. [18] He said to them, "Then do you also fail to understand? Do you not see that whatever goes into a person from outside cannot defile, [19] since it enters, not the heart but the stomach, and goes out into the sewer?" (Thus he declared all foods clean.) [20] And he said,

"It is what comes out of a person that defiles. [21] For it is from within, from the human heart, that evil intentions come: fornication, theft, murder, [22] adultery, avarice, wickedness, deceit, licentiousness, envy, slander, pride, folly. [23] All these evil things come from within, and they defile a person."

[24] From there he set out and went away to the region of Tyre.[c] He entered a house and did not want anyone to know he was there. Yet he could not escape notice, [25] but a woman whose little daughter had an unclean spirit immediately heard about him, and she came and bowed down at his feet. [26] Now the woman was a Gentile, of Syrophoenician origin. She begged him to cast the demon out of her daughter. [27] He said to her, "Let the children be fed first, for it is not fair to take the children's food and throw it to the dogs." [28] But she answered him, "Sir,[d] even the dogs under the table eat the children's crumbs." [29] Then he said to her, "For saying that, you may go—the demon has left your daughter." [30] So she went home, found the child lying on the bed, and the demon gone.

[31] Then he returned from the region of Tyre, and went by way of Sidon towards the Sea of Galilee, in the region of the Decapo-

---

a   Gk lacks to God
b   Other ancient authorities add verse 16, "Let anyone with ears to hear listen"
c   Other ancient authorities add and Sidon
d   Or Lord; other ancient authorities prefix Yes

Jews"), not just the Pharisees, observed their hand-washing regulations. **6–8:** In reply, quoting Isa 29.13 (LXX), Jesus claims that the Pharisees in effect replace the basic covenantal *commandment of God* with their merely *human tradition.* **9–13:** Jesus focuses the dispute in concrete terms on the *commandment of God* concerning *Honor your father and your mother* (cf. Ex 20.12; 21.17), which includes economic support in their declining years. He claims that the Pharisees make it void with their *tradition* of *Corban,* encouraging people to dedicate the produce of their land to the Jerusalem Temple—thus siphoning off produce that otherwise could have been used to support parents. *Corban* is an Aramaic word meaning "offering dedicated (to God)." **14–19a:** Addresses purity codes with a touch of earthy humor regarding eating and resultant bodily functions. **17:** *Parable* here has the sense of "riddle." **19b:** Perhaps a later addition to the text. **20–23:** Shifts the focus from bodily functions to the inner motivations of "defiling," socially destructive behavior.

7.24–30: The Syrophoenician woman (Mt 15.21–28). **24–26:** In *the region of Tyre,* not in the city itself, a "Greek" woman intrudes with her plea on behalf of her possessed daughter. **27–28:** To Jesus' insistence that the manifestation of the kingdom (*food*) is primarily for Israelites (*children*), she gives a reply that wins the debate. **29–30:** The representative figure of the peoples surrounding Israel insists on receiving the benefits of the kingdom, and her insistence produces precisely that.

7.31–37: Healing the deaf (Mt 15.29–31). Healing the deaf-mute, which is symbolic of a more general restoration of hearing and speech, confirms that the kingdom of God and the movement of renewal has extended to

lis. ³² They brought to him a deaf man who had an impediment in his speech; and they begged him to lay his hand on him. ³³ He took him aside in private, away from the crowd, and put his fingers into his ears, and he spat and touched his tongue. ³⁴ Then looking up to heaven, he sighed and said to him, "Ephphatha," that is, "Be opened." ³⁵ And immediately his ears were opened, his tongue was released, and he spoke plainly. ³⁶ Then Jesusᵃ ordered them to tell no one; but the more he ordered them, the more zealously they proclaimed it. ³⁷ They were astounded beyond measure, saying, "He has done everything well; he even makes the deaf to hear and the mute to speak."

8 In those days when there was again a great crowd without anything to eat, he called his disciples and said to them, ² "I have compassion for the crowd, because they have been with me now for three days and have nothing to eat. ³ If I send them away hungry to their homes, they will faint on the way—and some of them have come from a great distance." ⁴ His disciples replied, "How can one feed these people with bread here in the desert?" ⁵ He asked them, "How many loaves do you have?" They said, "Seven." ⁶ Then he ordered the crowd to sit down on the ground; and he took the seven loaves, and after giving thanks he broke them and gave them to his disciples to distribute; and they distributed them to the crowd. ⁷ They had also a few small fish; and after blessing them, he ordered that these too should be distributed. ⁸ They ate and were filled; and they took up the broken pieces left over, seven baskets

full. ⁹ Now there were about four thousand people. And he sent them away. ¹⁰ And immediately he got into the boat with his disciples and went to the district of Dalmanutha.ᵇ

¹¹ The Pharisees came and began to argue with him, asking him for a sign from heaven, to test him. ¹² And he sighed deeply in his spirit and said, "Why does this generation ask for a sign? Truly I tell you, no sign will be given to this generation." ¹³ And he left them, and getting into the boat again, he went across to the other side.

¹⁴ Now the disciplesᶜ had forgotten to bring any bread; and they had only one loaf with them in the boat. ¹⁵ And he cautioned them, saying, "Watch out—beware of the yeast of the Pharisees and the yeast of Herod."ᵈ ¹⁶ They said to one another, "It is because we have no bread." ¹⁷ And becoming aware of it, Jesus said to them, "Why are you talking about having no bread? Do you still not perceive or understand? Are your hearts hardened? ¹⁸ Do you have eyes, and fail to see? Do you have ears, and fail to hear? And do you not remember? ¹⁹ When I broke the five loaves for the five thousand, how many baskets full of broken pieces did you collect?" They said to him, "Twelve." ²⁰ "And the seven for the four thousand, how many baskets full of broken pieces did you collect?" And they said to him, "Seven." ²¹ Then he said to them, "Do you not yet understand?"

ᵃ Gk *he*
ᵇ Other ancient authorities read *Mageda* or *Magdala*
ᶜ Gk *they*
ᵈ Other ancient authorities read *the Herodians*

the peoples round about Israel. **34:** The word *ephphatha* is Aramaic; see 5.41n.

8.1–9: Wilderness feeding of four thousand (Mt 15.32–38; cf. Mk 6.30–44). As he had fed the earlier crowd in the wilderness, implicitly composed of Israelites, now Jesus also feeds the surrounding peoples in the wilderness. *Seven* is symbolic of the surrounding peoples, as twelve was of Israel (6.43). The two wilderness feedings echo the two accounts of the giving of food to the Israelites in the wilderness (Ex 16; Num 11).

8.10–12: No sign will be given (Mt 16.1–4; 12.28–39; Lk 11.29; 11.16; 12.54–56). This passage would make better sense if v. 10 were in one paragraph with vv. 11–12, and v. 13 were joined to the following paragraph (vv. 14–21). Blind to the sequences of Moses- and Elijah-like actions Jesus has just taken, the Pharisees again press Jesus, asking *for a sign from heaven, to test him*, which they do again in 10.2 and 12.15. **10:** *Dalmanutha*, the parallel in Mt 15.39 reads "Magadan" (see note there).

8.13–21: The disciples misunderstand (Mt 16.4–12; Lk 12.1). In a bridge to the next section, the disciples simply do not understand what is happening, either the scheming of the religious and political authorities seeking to destroy Jesus (cf. 3.6) or the renewal movement underway among the surrounding peoples as well as among Israelite villages. **17–18:** 4.9–12; 6.52. **19:** 6.41–44. **20:** 8.5–8.

22 They came to Bethsaida. Some people[a] brought a blind man to him and begged him to touch him. 23 He took the blind man by the hand and led him out of the village; and when he had put saliva on his eyes and laid his hands on him, he asked him, "Can you see anything?" 24 And the man[b] looked up and said, "I can see people, but they look like trees, walking." 25 Then Jesus[b] laid his hands on his eyes again; and he looked intently and his sight was restored, and he saw everything clearly. 26 Then he sent him away to his home, saying, "Do not even go into the village."[c]

27 Jesus went on with his disciples to the villages of Caesarea Philippi; and on the way he asked his disciples, "Who do people say that I am?" 28 And they answered him, "John the Baptist; and others, Elijah; and still others, one of the prophets." 29 He asked them, "But who do you say that I am?" Peter answered him, "You are the Messiah."[d] 30 And he sternly ordered them not to tell anyone about him.

31 Then he began to teach them that the Son of Man must undergo great suffering, and be rejected by the elders, the chief priests, and the scribes, and be killed, and after three days rise again. 32 He said all this quite openly. And Peter took him aside and began to rebuke him. 33 But turning and looking at his disciples, he rebuked Peter and said, "Get behind me, Satan! For you are setting your mind not on divine things but on human things."

34 He called the crowd with his disciples, and said to them, "If any want to become my followers, let them deny themselves and take up their cross and follow me. 35 For those who want to save their life will lose it, and those who lose their life for my sake, and for the sake of the gospel,[e] will save it. 36 For what will it profit them to gain the whole world and forfeit their life? 37 Indeed, what can they give in return for their life? 38 Those who are ashamed of me and of my words[f] in this adulterous and sinful generation, of them the Son of Man will also be ashamed

a   Gk They
b   Gk he
c   Other ancient authorities add or tell anyone in the village
d   Or the Christ
e   Other ancient authorities read lose their life for the sake of the gospel
f   Other ancient authorities read and of mine

8.22–10.52: Jesus confirms and continues his prophetic role in the renewal of Israel while announcing his agenda as martyr-messiah to the misunderstanding disciples.

8.22–26: Healing of a blind man (Jn 9.1–7). This restoration of a blind man's sight and that of Bartimaeus in 10.46–52 frame this part of Mark in which the disciples are "blind" to what is said and done.

8.27–33: Jesus' first announcement and Peter's misunderstanding (Mt 16.13–23; Lk 9.18–22). **27:** The villages of Caesarea Philippi, villages subject to Herod Philip in the northernmost area of (formerly) Israelite territory. **28:** Again, not surprisingly given his program, Jesus is popularly understood as Elijah, one of the prophets, or even John. **29–30:** There is very little evidence for expectations of "the messiah," which was hardly standardized at the time. The role and title the Messiah would fit Jesus' subsequent actions (e.g., in 11.2–10) and statements about him, but not his previous actions in Mark. **31:** The translation softens a key Greek term: "it is necessary that . . . ," i.e., in God's plan, given the historical situation. The Son of Man, meaning "human being" or the future figure representing a restored Israel, or both (see 2.10n.), is clearly Jesus' self-reference. This is the first of three clear announcements that "it is necessary" that he be condemned by the rulers, be killed, and rise again (see 9.31–32; 10.32–34). **32–33:** Following Peter's rebuke (presumably about having to be killed), Jesus in turn rebukes Peter in startling terms, contrasting the purpose or will of God for human beings with the purposes those human beings would have for themselves. Jesus will be a martyr-messiah.

8.34–9.1: The cost of following Jesus (Mt 16.24–28; Lk 9.23–27; cf. Mt 10.28–33; Lk 12.4–9). Pointedly telling the crowd to join the disciples, Jesus warns that, like himself, his followers must also be prepared to suffer martyrdom for the gospel, the cause of the kingdom. **34:** Take up their cross, the Romans used crucifixion as a gruesome means of terrorizing subject peoples by hanging rebels and agitators from crosses for several days until they suffocated to death. They required condemned provincials to carry the crossbeam on which they were to be hung. **38:** How the followers stand toward Jesus and his gospel when facing trial will determine how the Son of Man will stand toward them when, in God's final condemnation of the oppressive empire,

9 when he comes in the glory of his Father with the holy angels." [1] And he said to them, "Truly I tell you, there are some standing here who will not taste death until they see that the kingdom of God has come with[a] power."

[2] Six days later, Jesus took with him Peter and James and John, and led them up a high mountain apart, by themselves. And he was transfigured before them, [3] and his clothes became dazzling white, such as no one[b] on earth could bleach them. [4] And there appeared to them Elijah with Moses, who were talking with Jesus. [5] Then Peter said to Jesus, "Rabbi, it is good for us to be here; let us make three dwellings,[c] one for you, one for Moses, and one for Elijah." [6] He did not know what to say, for they were terrified. [7] Then a cloud overshadowed them, and from the cloud there came a voice, "This is my Son, the Beloved;[d] listen to him!" [8] Suddenly when they looked around, they saw no one with them any more, but only Jesus.

[9] As they were coming down the mountain, he ordered them to tell no one about what they had seen, until after the Son of Man had risen from the dead. [10] So they kept the matter to themselves, questioning what this rising from the dead could mean. [11] Then they asked him, "Why do the scribes say that Elijah must come first?" [12] He said to them, "Elijah is indeed coming first to restore all things. How then is it written about the Son of Man, that

he is to go through many sufferings and be treated with contempt? [13] But I tell you that Elijah has come, and they did to him whatever they pleased, as it is written about him."

[14] When they came to the disciples, they saw a great crowd around them, and some scribes arguing with them. [15] When the whole crowd saw him, they were immediately overcome with awe, and they ran forward to greet him. [16] He asked them, "What are you arguing about with them?" [17] Someone from the crowd answered him, "Teacher, I brought you my son; he has a spirit that makes him unable to speak; [18] and whenever it seizes him, it dashes him down; and he foams and grinds his teeth and becomes rigid; and I asked your disciples to cast it out, but they could not do so." [19] He answered them, "You faithless generation, how much longer must I be among you? How much longer must I put up with you? Bring him to me." [20] And they brought the boy[e] to him. When the spirit saw him, immediately it convulsed the boy,[e] and he fell on the ground and rolled about, foaming at the mouth. [21] Jesus[f] asked the father, "How long has this been happening to him?"

a Or *in*
b Gk *no fuller*
c Or *tents*
d Or *my beloved Son*
e Gk *him*
f Gk *He*

he comes in judgment as well as restoration of the people (cf. Mk 13.26–27; 14.62; Dan 7.13–14). **9.1:** *The kingdom of God* will *come with power* already during their lifetime.

9.2–8: Transfiguration of Jesus (Mt 17.1–8; Lk 9.28–36). **2–4:** The mountain setting is reminiscent of Moses and the elders of Israel on Sinai (Ex 24). *Transfigured . . . dazzling white*, in the disciples' visionary experience, Jesus appears as a vindicated martyr (see Dan 11.36; Rev 3.5,18; 4.4; 6.9–11; 7.9,13–14), linked to what he had just told the disciples in 8.31. With him are Elijah and Moses, the prophetic restorer and founder of Israel, respectively, whose great actions of deliverance Jesus' actions, just performed in 4.35–8.26, resemble. **5–6:** Peter, mystified and *terrified*, addresses Jesus not as "messiah," but as *Rabbi*, as he does again in 11.21 when he is again mystified, and as Judas does in his betrayal, 14.45. **7:** Now Peter, James, and John hear the same voice that Jesus heard at his baptism in 1.11.

9.9–13: Correction of scribal teaching about Elijah (Mt 17.9–13). **9–11:** The disciples, still not understanding the necessity of his martyrdom, remain oriented toward the teachings of the Jerusalem scribes, as in Sir 48.10 (cf. Mal 4.4–5). **12–13:** First pointing to the obvious contradiction between the official scribal teaching and what he has just told them, mockingly couching it in scribal terms as scriptural, "it is written," he asserts that in fact Elijah has already come in John, and he was ignominiously killed.

9.14–29: Healing of epileptic child (Mt 17.14–21; Lk 9.37–42). Since Matthew and Luke have no parallels to vv. 15–16,21–27 of this unusually elaborate story in Mark, the text may have been much shorter originally.

And he said, "From childhood. [22] It has often cast him into the fire and into the water, to destroy him; but if you are able to do anything, have pity on us and help us." [23] Jesus said to him, "If you are able!—All things can be done for the one who believes." [24] Immediately the father of the child cried out,[a] "I believe; help my unbelief!" [25] When Jesus saw that a crowd came running together, he rebuked the unclean spirit, saying to it, "You spirit that keeps this boy from speaking and hearing, I command you, come out of him, and never enter him again!" [26] After crying out and convulsing him terribly, it came out, and the boy was like a corpse, so that most of them said, "He is dead." [27] But Jesus took him by the hand and lifted him up, and he was able to stand. [28] When he had entered the house, his disciples asked him privately, "Why could we not cast it out?" [29] He said to them, "This kind can come out only through prayer."[b]

[30] They went on from there and passed through Galilee. He did not want anyone to know it; [31] for he was teaching his disciples, saying to them, "The Son of Man is to be betrayed into human hands, and they will kill him, and three days after being killed, he will rise again." [32] But they did not understand what he was saying and were afraid to ask him.

[33] Then they came to Capernaum; and when he was in the house he asked them, "What were you arguing about on the way?" [34] But they were silent, for on the way they had argued with one another who was the greatest. [35] He sat down, called the twelve, and said to them, "Whoever wants to be first must be last of all and servant of all." [36] Then he took a little child and put it among them; and taking it in his arms, he said to them, [37] "Whoever welcomes one such child in my name welcomes me, and whoever welcomes me welcomes not me but the one who sent me."

[38] John said to him, "Teacher, we saw someone[c] casting out demons in your name, and we tried to stop him, because he was not following us." [39] But Jesus said, "Do not stop him; for no one who does a deed of power in my name will be able soon afterward to speak evil of me. [40] Whoever is not against us is for us. [41] For truly I tell you, whoever gives you a cup of water to drink because you bear the name of Christ will by no means lose the reward.

[42] "If any of you put a stumbling block before one of these little ones who believe in me,[d] it would be better for you if a great millstone were hung around your neck and you were thrown into the sea. [43] If your hand causes you to stumble, cut it off; it is better for you to enter life maimed than to have two hands and to go to hell,[e] to the unquenchable fire.[f] [45] And if your foot causes you to stumble, cut it off; it is better for you to enter life lame than to have two feet and to be thrown into hell.[e,f] [47] And if your eye causes you to stumble, tear it out; it is better for you to enter the kingdom of God with one eye than

a   Other ancient authorities add *with tears*
b   Other ancient authorities add *and fasting*
c   Other ancient authorities add *who does not follow us*
d   Other ancient authorities lack *in me*
e   Gk *Gehenna*
f   Verses 44 and 46 (which are identical with verse 48) are lacking in the best ancient authorities

9.30–37: Second announcement and misunderstanding (Mt 17.22–23; 18.1–5; Lk 9.43–48). Despite his teaching, again (see 8.31n.), that the Son of Man would be killed and rise again, the disciples still do not understand, as illustrated in their blithe discussion of *who was the greatest*. **36–37:** A *child* was the lowest-status person in a household.

9.38–41: Unknown exorcist (Lk 9.49–50). An allusion to the story in Num 11.27–29. The movement is not to be defensive or controlling.

9.42–50: Warning on discipline (Mt 18.6–9; 5.29–30; 5.13; Lk 17.1–2; 14.34–35). A series of warnings on male sexual discipline, judging from references in rabbinic literature, beginning with sexual abuse of children. **43:** *Hand* probably refers to prohibition of masturbation (See *Mishnah Niddah* 2.1). *Hell*, lit., "Gehenna," the valley of the son of Hinnom (2 Kings 23.10; Jer 7.31), symbolizing the place of eternal punishment by fire. **45:** *Foot* is a standard euphemism in Heb for the male genitals (Isa 6.2; 7.20), and there is probably double-entendre here.

to have two eyes and to be thrown into hell,[a] [48] where their worm never dies, and the fire is never quenched.

[49] "For everyone will be salted with fire.[b] [50] Salt is good; but if salt has lost its saltiness, how can you season it?[c] Have salt in yourselves, and be at peace with one another."

10 He left that place and went to the region of Judea and[d] beyond the Jordan. And crowds again gathered around him; and, as was his custom, he again taught them.

[2] Some Pharisees came, and to test him they asked, "Is it lawful for a man to divorce his wife?" [3] He answered them, "What did Moses command you?" [4] They said, "Moses allowed a man to write a certificate of dismissal and to divorce her." [5] But Jesus said to them, "Because of your hardness of heart he wrote this commandment for you. [6] But from the beginning of creation, 'God made them male and female.' [7] 'For this reason a man shall leave his father and mother and be joined to his wife,[e] [8] and the two shall become one flesh.' So they are no longer two, but one flesh. [9] Therefore what God has joined together, let no one separate."

[10] Then in the house the disciples asked him again about this matter. [11] He said to them, "Whoever divorces his wife and marries another commits adultery against her; [12] and if she divorces her husband and marries another, she commits adultery."

[13] People were bringing little children to him in order that he might touch them; and the disciples spoke sternly to them. [14] But when Jesus saw this, he was indignant and said to them, "Let the little children come to me; do not stop them; for it is to such as these that the kingdom of God belongs. [15] Truly I tell you, whoever does not receive the kingdom of God as a little child will never enter it." [16] And he took them up in his arms, laid his hands on them, and blessed them.

[17] As he was setting out on a journey, a man ran up and knelt before him, and asked him, "Good Teacher, what must I do to inherit eternal life?" [18] Jesus said to him, "Why do you call me good? No one is good but God alone. [19] You know the commandments: 'You shall not murder; You shall not commit adultery; You shall not steal; You shall not bear false witness; You shall not defraud; Honor your father and mother.'" [20] He said to him, "Teacher, I have kept all these since my youth." [21] Jesus, looking at him, loved him and said, "You lack one thing; go, sell what you own, and give the money[f] to the poor, and you will have treasure in heaven; then come, follow me." [22] When he heard this, he was shocked and went away grieving, for he had many possessions.

a Gk *Gehenna*
b Other ancient authorities either add or substitute *and every sacrifice will be salted with salt*
c Or *how can you restore its saltiness?*
d Other ancient authorities lack *and*
e Other ancient authorities lack *and be joined to his wife*
f Gk lacks *the money*

47: *Eye* here refers to lustful gazes. 48: See Isa 66.24.

10.1–16: Marriage and children in the kingdom (Mt 19.1–15; Lk 18.15–17). 1: Jesus moves into Israelite territory beyond Galilee, now concentrating on teaching. 2–12: The first step in a series of covenantal instructions and exhortations focuses on (the commandment against) adultery (Ex 20.12; Deut 5.18), i.e., on marriage and divorce. 3–4: See Deut 24.1–4; Jer 3.8. 5–9: To the Pharisees' focus on divorce as a male prerogative, Jesus insists upon the equality of marriage intended in the creation stories, Gen 1.27; 2.24. 10–12: Cf. Mt 5.31–32. The juxtaposition of vv. 2–9 and vv. 11–12 indicates that Jesus' restrictive interpretation of the commandment against adultery, allowing divorce but prohibiting remarriage, was grounded in creation. Jesus' formulation with both the man and the woman as active agents stands in contrast to the ancient assumption that adultery was an offense against the husband. 13–16: Not an idealization of childhood. Against the disciples' restriction of access to Jesus and his movement, Jesus uses children, who occupied the lowest status in society, as a symbol for how one should receive the kingdom.

10.17–31: Egalitarian economic relations in the kingdom (Mt 19.16–30; Lk 18.18–30). An exhortation for egalitarian covenantal economic relations. 17: The man's address is flattering and his question unusual for Mark, in which the common people have more concrete concerns. 19: Recitation of covenantal commandments, Ex 20.12–16, adding *defraud*. 21–22: Jesus' test exposes the man as adamantly attached to his wealth, which (from the covenantal viewpoint) he might have gained by defrauding peasants by charging interest on loans, etc.,

²³ Then Jesus looked around and said to his disciples, "How hard it will be for those who have wealth to enter the kingdom of God!" ²⁴ And the disciples were perplexed at these words. But Jesus said to them again, "Children, how hard it is[a] to enter the kingdom of God! ²⁵ It is easier for a camel to go through the eye of a needle than for someone who is rich to enter the kingdom of God." ²⁶ They were greatly astounded and said to one another,[b] "Then who can be saved?" ²⁷ Jesus looked at them and said, "For mortals it is impossible, but not for God; for God all things are possible."

²⁸ Peter began to say to him, "Look, we have left everything and followed you." ²⁹ Jesus said, "Truly I tell you, there is no one who has left house or brothers or sisters or mother or father or children or fields, for my sake and for the sake of the good news,[c] ³⁰ who will not receive a hundredfold now in this age—houses, brothers and sisters, mothers and children, and fields, with persecutions—and in the age to come eternal life. ³¹ But many who are first will be last, and the last will be first."

³² They were on the road, going up to Jerusalem, and Jesus was walking ahead of them; they were amazed, and those who followed were afraid. He took the twelve aside again and began to tell them what was to happen to him, ³³ saying, "See, we are going up to Jerusalem, and the Son of Man will be handed over to the chief priests and the scribes, and they will condemn him to death; then they will hand him over to the Gentiles; ³⁴ they will mock him, and spit upon him, and flog him, and kill him; and after three days he will rise again."

³⁵ James and John, the sons of Zebedee, came forward to him and said to him, "Teacher, we want you to do for us whatever we ask of you." ³⁶ And he said to them, "What is it you want me to do for you?" ³⁷ And they said to him, "Grant us to sit, one at your right hand and one at your left, in your glory." ³⁸ But Jesus said to them, "You do not know what you are asking. Are you able to drink the cup that I drink, or be baptized with the baptism that I am baptized with?" ³⁹ They replied, "We are able." Then Jesus said to them, "The cup that I drink you will drink; and with the baptism with which I am baptized, you will be baptized; ⁴⁰ but to sit at my right hand or at my left is not mine to grant, but it is for those for whom it has been prepared."

⁴¹ When the ten heard this, they began to be angry with James and John. ⁴² So Jesus

---

a   Other ancient authorities add *for those who trust in riches*

b   Other ancient authorities read *to him*

c   Or *gospel*

---

thus also violating the commandment against stealing. **23–25:** Jesus consolidates the point just illustrated with a little proverbial peasant humor: It is impossible for a rich person to enter the kingdom of God. **26–27:** Jesus' reply to the disciples' incomprehension, although precisely how it connects with the previous discussion is unclear. **28–31:** To Peter's anxious plea, Jesus' reply is serious about the concrete restoration (houses, fields, families) but teasingly facetious as well. The obvious exaggeration about the degree is canceled out by the *persecutions,* and the promise of *eternal life in the age to come* is a throw-away line mocking the rich man's concern (v. 17).

10.32–45: Egalitarian social-political relations in the kingdom and the third announcement and misunderstanding (Mt 20.17–28; Lk 18.31–34, 22.24–27). Mark uses Jesus' third explanation to the disciples that the Son of Man will be condemned, killed, and rise again (see 8.31n.), combined with the disciples' stubborn misunderstanding, as a foil for exhortation on egalitarian social-political relations in the movement and its communities. **32–34:** The tone becomes ominous as they head toward Jerusalem and the climax of Jesus' escalating conflict with the rulers there, as explicitly dramatized in the details added to this third announcement of his destiny there. **35–37:** James and John's request indicates that they have completely misunderstood Jesus' mission and movement as well as refused to hear what Jesus has repeatedly told them. **38–40:** They claim they are prepared to follow the path of Jesus into martyrdom for the cause, which he promises will happen. But he rejects their request as presumptuous. On the metaphor of *cup,* see 14.24,36; Isa 51.17; Lam 4.21. **41–45:** The request for positions of power and privilege results in conflict among the disciples. But in contrast to the imperial practices of the nations, there will be no rulers in Jesus' movement or communities. Rather, would-be leaders must take

called them and said to them, "You know that among the Gentiles those whom they recognize as their rulers lord it over them, and their great ones are tyrants over them. [43] But it is not so among you; but whoever wishes to become great among you must be your servant, [44] and whoever wishes to be first among you must be slave of all. [45] For the Son of Man came not to be served but to serve, and to give his life a ransom for many."

[46] They came to Jericho. As he and his disciples and a large crowd were leaving Jericho, Bartimaeus son of Timaeus, a blind beggar, was sitting by the roadside. [47] When he heard that it was Jesus of Nazareth, he began to shout out and say, "Jesus, Son of David, have mercy on me!" [48] Many sternly ordered him to be quiet, but he cried out even more loudly, "Son of David, have mercy on me!" [49] Jesus stood still and said, "Call him here." And they called the blind man, saying to him, "Take heart; get up, he is calling you." [50] So throwing off his cloak, he sprang up and came to Jesus. [51] Then Jesus said to him, "What do you want me to do for you?" The blind man said to him, "My teacher,[a] let me see again." [52] Jesus said to him, "Go; your faith has made you well." Immediately he regained his sight and followed him on the way.

11 When they were approaching Jerusalem, at Bethphage and Bethany, near the Mount of Olives, he sent two of his disciples [2] and said to them, "Go into the village ahead of you, and immediately as you enter it, you will find tied there a colt that has never been ridden; untie it and bring it. [3] If anyone says to you, 'Why are you doing this?' just say this, 'The Lord needs it and will send it back here immediately.'" [4] They went away and found a colt tied near a door, outside in the street. As they were untying it, [5] some of the bystanders said to them, "What are you doing, untying the colt?" [6] They told them what Jesus had said; and they allowed them to take it. [7] Then they brought the colt to Jesus and threw their cloaks on it; and he sat on it. [8] Many people spread their cloaks on the road, and others spread leafy branches that they had cut in the fields. [9] Then those who went ahead and those who followed were shouting,

"Hosanna!
　Blessed is the one who comes in the
　　name of the Lord!
[10] Blessed is the coming kingdom of our
　　ancestor David!
Hosanna in the highest heaven!"

---

[a] Aramaic *Rabbouni*

the role of servants, following the paradigm of the Son of Man, Jesus, whose martyrdom will be a ransom (paid for redemption from slavery or indebtedness; see God's "ransom" or "redemption" of Israel from subjection to Egypt, Ex. 6.6; 15.13; Isa 43.1–7) of many.

10.46–52: Healing of the blind Bartimaeus (Mt 20.29–34; Lk 18.35–43). The second healing of a blind man (see 8.22–26) that frames and completes this section focuses partly on the blindness of the disciples. 46: *Jericho* is in the Jordan Valley ca. 21 km (13 mi) east-northeast of Jerusalem; a secondary road connected the two cities (see 11.1; Lk 10.30). *Bartimaeus* means *son of Timaeus* in Aramaic. 47–48: Though blind, Bartimaeus nevertheless sees or knows that Jesus is the *Son of David*. In some circles a "son of David" was expected to restore the fortunes of Israel as king (2 Sam 5.1–5). In Mk 12.35–37 Jesus himself explains that the messiah is not the "son of David." 52: After his sight is restored, he pointedly *followed* Jesus *on the way*, in striking contrast to the disciples, who remained blind to what was happening.

11.1–13.2: Confronting the rulers and ruling institutions in Jerusalem.

11.1–11: A messianic demonstration (Mt 21.1–9; Lk 19.28–38; Jn 12.12–15). As Jesus and his followers enter into the capital city, they stage a "messianic" demonstration, in fulfillment of the prophecy of Zech 9.9–10 of a peasant king riding on a donkey (cf. 1 Kings 1.38), not in an imperial war-chariot. 1: *Bethphage and Bethany*, villages just east of Jerusalem. 8: *Spread their cloaks on the road*, before the messiah, the "anointed" king, just as was done when Elisha anointed Jehu to lead the rebellion against the oppressive dynasty founded by Omri (2 Kings 9.1–13). The *leafy branches* appear to have a similar significance; cf. the "palm branches" waved in victorious celebration (with hymns, etc.) of the newly established independence of Jerusalem and Judea in 1 Macc 13.51. 9: The throng shouts a psalm of thanksgiving (Ps 118.25–26) for victory over Israel's enemies, one that was sung at the Passover festival. *Hosanna* means "Save us!" 10: Added to the psalm, linking the festal demonstration with

¹¹ Then he entered Jerusalem and went into the temple; and when he had looked around at everything, as it was already late, he went out to Bethany with the twelve.

¹² On the following day, when they came from Bethany, he was hungry. ¹³ Seeing in the distance a fig tree in leaf, he went to see whether perhaps he would find anything on it. When he came to it, he found nothing but leaves, for it was not the season for figs. ¹⁴ He said to it, "May no one ever eat fruit from you again." And his disciples heard it.

¹⁵ Then they came to Jerusalem. And he entered the temple and began to drive out those who were selling and those who were buying in the temple, and he overturned the tables of the money changers and the seats of those who sold doves; ¹⁶ and he would not allow anyone to carry anything through the temple. ¹⁷ He was teaching and saying, "Is it not written,

'My house shall be called a house of prayer
    for all the nations'?
But you have made it a den of
    robbers."

¹⁸ And when the chief priests and the scribes heard it, they kept looking for a way to kill him; for they were afraid of him, because the whole crowd was spellbound by his teaching. ¹⁹ And when evening came, Jesus and his disciples[a] went out of the city.

²⁰ In the morning as they passed by, they saw the fig tree withered away to its roots. ²¹ Then Peter remembered and said to him, "Rabbi, look! The fig tree that you cursed has withered." ²² Jesus answered them, "Have[b] faith in God. ²³ Truly I tell you, if you say to this mountain, 'Be taken up and thrown into the sea,' and if you do not doubt in your heart, but believe that what you say will come to pass, it will be done for you. ²⁴ So I tell you, whatever you ask for in prayer, believe that you have received[c] it, and it will be yours.

²⁵ "Whenever you stand praying, forgive, if you have anything against anyone; so that

a   Gk *they*: other ancient authorities read *he*
b   Other ancient authorities read *"If you have*
c   Other ancient authorities read *are receiving*

the hope of Israel's future restoration and independence led by the anointed "son of David," as in Bartimaeus's repeated cry in 10.48–49 that just preceded the demonstration. **11:** On *the temple*, see 11.12–25n. *Looked around*, after the messianic demonstration in seeming anticipation of the restoration of Israel, Jesus enters Jerusalem, but only to reconnoiter before launching his aggressive face-off with the rulers the next day.

11.12–25 [26]: Prophetic demonstration against the Temple (Mt 21.12–13,18–22; Lk 19.45–48). Mark again sandwiches one story into another (cf. 3.19b–35; 5.21–43), framing the prophetic demonstration against the Temple with the cursing of the fig tree (which is bearing no fruit), a figure for God's judgment in Israelite tradition (e.g., Isa 34.4; Jer 5.17). The *temple* in Jerusalem was the political-economic center of power as well as the sanctuary where the priests offered sacrifices to God. Supported by the tithes and offerings of the people, it had been rebuilt. In 20 BCE Herod the Great had mounted a massive rebuilding of the Temple into a vast complex of colonnades and shops as well as a center of Jewish pilgrimage and one of the wonders of the Roman imperial world. **15–16:** Jesus took forcible action against the sellers and buyers in the large Court of the Gentiles, the principal open public space in Jerusalem, where anyone—including non-Israelites—could go. Commerce, including moneychanging, was necessary in connection with sacrifices and offerings in the semi-monetarized Temple economy. **17:** Quoting Isa 56.7, and Jeremiah's prophecy against the first Temple (Jer 7.11), Jesus interprets his action as a prophetic demonstration of God's condemnation of the Temple. *Den of robbers* is better translated "bandits' stronghold," conveying more the original sense in Jeremiah that the rulers plunder the people like bandits and then seek refuge in the Temple. **18–19:** In response to Jesus' prophetic demonstration, the Jerusalem rulers intensify the long-standing scheme to kill him, known since 3.6. In preindustrial cities, rulers had to worry at festival times about touching off mob action by taking repressive measures against agitators, as indicated in 14.1–2. But Jesus and his disciples strategically withdraw from the city at evening. **20–24:** This astounding statement about the mount of the Temple upon which Jesus has just demonstrated God's condemnation says, in effect, to trust God to do what has been prophesied. **25–[26]:** Early manuscripts omit v. 26, as does the NRSV translation. If original to Mark, it establishes mutual forgiveness (as in the Lord's Prayer, Lk 11.2–4) as the focus of prayer, now that the Temple, the official site for prayer and for obtaining divine forgiveness (see Lev 6.7), stands under God's condemnation.

your Father in heaven may also forgive you your trespasses."[a]

²⁷ Again they came to Jerusalem. As he was walking in the temple, the chief priests, the scribes, and the elders came to him ²⁸ and said, "By what authority are you doing these things? Who gave you this authority to do them?" ²⁹ Jesus said to them, "I will ask you one question; answer me, and I will tell you by what authority I do these things. ³⁰ Did the baptism of John come from heaven, or was it of human origin? Answer me." ³¹ They argued with one another, "If we say, 'From heaven,' he will say, 'Why then did you not believe him?' ³² But shall we say, 'Of human origin'?"—they were afraid of the crowd, for all regarded John as truly a prophet. ³³ So they answered Jesus, "We do not know." And Jesus said to them, "Neither will I tell you by what authority I am doing these things."

12 Then he began to speak to them in parables. "A man planted a vineyard, put a fence around it, dug a pit for the wine press, and built a watchtower; then he leased it to tenants and went to another country. ² When the season came, he sent a slave to the tenants to collect from them his share of the produce of the vineyard. ³ But they seized him, and beat him, and sent him away empty-handed. ⁴ And

again he sent another slave to them; this one they beat over the head and insulted. ⁵ Then he sent another, and that one they killed. And so it was with many others; some they beat, and others they killed. ⁶ He had still one other, a beloved son. Finally he sent him to them, saying, 'They will respect my son.' ⁷ But those tenants said to one another, 'This is the heir; come, let us kill him, and the inheritance will be ours.' ⁸ So they seized him, killed him, and threw him out of the vineyard. ⁹ What then will the owner of the vineyard do? He will come and destroy the tenants and give the vineyard to others. ¹⁰ Have you not read this scripture:

'The stone that the builders rejected
  has become the cornerstone;[b]
¹¹ this was the Lord's doing,
  and it is amazing in our eyes'?"

¹² When they realized that he had told this parable against them, they wanted to arrest him, but they feared the crowd. So they left him and went away.

¹³ Then they sent to him some Pharisees and some Herodians to trap him in what

---

[a] Other ancient authorities add verse 26, *"But if you do not forgive, neither will your Father in heaven forgive your trespasses."*

[b] Or *keystone*

11.27–33: Jesus' authority (Mt 21.23–27; Lk 20.1–8; cf. Jn 2.18–22). The first in a series of sharp charges and countercharges in the escalating conflict between Jesus and the Roman-backed Jewish priestly rulers and their representatives. **27–28:** *The chief priests, the scribes, and the elders,* authorized presumably by God as well as imperial Rome, challenge Jesus on the *authority* by which he acts and speaks, referring to the confrontation regarding "authority and power" with which the whole gospel story began in 1.22–28. **29–30:** In his counter question Jesus cleverly entraps them and exposes their lack of authority among the people, while avoiding any statement that might seem to justify his seizure by them.

12.1–12: Parable of the vineyard (Mt 21.33–46; Lk 20.9–19). Building on the traditional image of Israel as the vineyard of God in Isa 5.1–7, Jesus tells a parable that invites listeners to see the chief priests, who were themselves absentee landlords of estates with tenant labor, as tenants of God's vineyard. It also resonated with the resentment of indebted peasants who feared nothing more than becoming such share-cropping tenants on their own ancestral land and would have reveled at such role-reversal. In Mark the parable virtually passes over into allegory, with the landlord's "slaves" being analogous to the prophets God sent to "tenants" to demand the fruit of justice, and the *beloved son* clearly being Jesus himself, as in 1.11 and 9.7, and the rejected *stone* becoming the *cornerstone* (citing Ps 118.22–23) of the new political-religious order that will replace the Temple establishment.

12.13–17: Paying taxes to the emperor (Mt 22.15–22; Lk 20.20–26). As in 3.6, the representatives of both the Jerusalem priestly establishment and Herod Antipas's regime conspire to entrap Jesus into giving some pretext to arrest and kill him. **14:** They preface the entrapping question with heavy, insincere flattery. *Is it lawful to pay taxes to the emperor?* A genuine dilemma. In the strict adherence to the covenantal law (commandment) of Moses, supposedly advocated by the Pharisees themselves, it was not lawful because God was their exclusive sovereign. Yet the Romans treated nonpayment of tribute as rebellion. Some decades earlier the teacher Judas and

he said. ¹⁴ And they came and said to him, "Teacher, we know that you are sincere, and show deference to no one; for you do not regard people with partiality, but teach the way of God in accordance with truth. Is it lawful to pay taxes to the emperor, or not? ¹⁵ Should we pay them, or should we not?" But knowing their hypocrisy, he said to them, "Why are you putting me to the test? Bring me a denarius and let me see it." ¹⁶ And they brought one. Then he said to them, "Whose head is this, and whose title?" They answered, "The emperor's." ¹⁷ Jesus said to them, "Give to the emperor the things that are the emperor's, and to God the things that are God's." And they were utterly amazed at him.

¹⁸ Some Sadducees, who say there is no resurrection, came to him and asked him a question, saying, ¹⁹ "Teacher, Moses wrote for us that if a man's brother dies, leaving a wife but no child, the manᵃ shall marry the widow and raise up children for his brother. ²⁰ There were seven brothers; the first married and, when he died, left no children; ²¹ and the second married the widowᵇ and died, leaving no children; and the third likewise; ²² none of the seven left children. Last of all the woman herself died. ²³ In the resurrectionᶜ whose wife will she be? For the seven had married her."

²⁴ Jesus said to them, "Is not this the reason you are wrong, that you know neither the scriptures nor the power of God? ²⁵ For when they rise from the dead, they neither marry nor are given in marriage, but are like angels in heaven. ²⁶ And as for the dead being raised, have you not read in the book of Moses, in the story about the bush, how God said to him, 'I am the God of Abraham, the God of Isaac, and the God of Jacob'? ²⁷ He is God not of the dead, but of the living; you are quite wrong."

²⁸ One of the scribes came near and heard them disputing with one another, and seeing that he answered them well, he asked him, "Which commandment is the first of all?" ²⁹ Jesus answered, "The first is, 'Hear, O Israel: the Lord our God, the Lord is one; ³⁰ you shall love the Lord your God with all your heart, and with all your soul, and with all your mind, and with all your strength.' ³¹ The second is this, 'You shall love your neighbor as yourself.' There is no other commandment greater than these." ³² Then the scribe said to him, "You are right, Teacher; you have truly said that 'he is one, and besides him there is no other'; ³³ and 'to love him with all the heart, and with all the understanding, and with all the strength,' and 'to love one's neighbor as oneself,'—this is much more important than all whole burnt offerings and sacrifices." ³⁴ When Jesus saw that he answered wisely, he said to him, "You are not

ᵃ Gk *his brother*
ᵇ Gk *her*
ᶜ Other ancient authorities add *when they rise*

the Pharisee Saddok had led a movement to refuse payment of the tribute, appealing to the same covenantal commandment, that God was their true and sole ruler (Acts 5.37; Josephus, *Ant.* 18.4–23). **16:** Turning the trick question back upon the questioners, Jesus exposes their own collaboration with the Romans by asking them to show him a coin—literally forcing their hand. **17:** Jesus ingeniously gives an ambiguous answer that does not literally advocate nonpayment of tribute to the emperor, but could be understood that way by those committed to the first commandment of the covenantal law of Moses: *the things that are the emperor's,* i.e., nothing; *the things that are God's,* i.e., everything.

12.18–27: Dispute with the Sadducees (Mt 22.23–33; Lk 20.27–40). **18–23:** The Sadducees, the aristocratic priestly party of property, power, and privilege, denied that there could be a future resurrection of the dead. While their question took the form of academic casuistry, their focus on levirate marriage (Deut 25.5) hinted at their real agenda: the protection of property rights and power through patriarchal marriage that perpetuated the male lineage. **24–25:** Life after resurrection will not involve marriage. **26–27:** God's words to Moses (Ex 3.6) speak of Abraham, Isaac, and Jacob in the present tense, i.e., as *living* not *dead.*

12.28–34: Love your neighbor (Mt 22.34–40; Lk 10.25–28). The polemic softens, but the argument sets up the sharp condemnation of the scribes in 12.38–44. **29–31:** Jesus satisfies the scribe by immediately reciting Deut 6.4, but he quickly insists that love of God means love of neighbor by reciting Lev 19.18 as well, which climaxes a series of prohibitions against exploiting and oppressing the poor (cf. Lev 19.9–17; Lk 6.27–36; Mt 5.38–48). **32–33:** The scribe admits that love of God and love of neighbor are more important than the elaborate

far from the kingdom of God." After that no one dared to ask him any question.

[35] While Jesus was teaching in the temple, he said, "How can the scribes say that the Messiah[a] is the son of David? [36] David himself, by the Holy Spirit, declared,

'The Lord said to my Lord,
   "Sit at my right hand,
      until I put your enemies under your
         feet."'

[37] David himself calls him Lord; so how can he be his son?" And the large crowd was listening to him with delight.

[38] As he taught, he said, "Beware of the scribes, who like to walk around in long robes, and to be greeted with respect in the marketplaces, [39] and to have the best seats in the synagogues and places of honor at banquets! [40] They devour widows' houses and for the sake of appearance say long prayers. They will receive the greater condemnation."

[41] He sat down opposite the treasury, and watched the crowd putting money into the treasury. Many rich people put in large sums. [42] A poor widow came and put in two small copper coins, which are worth a penny. [43] Then he called his disciples and said to

them, "Truly I tell you, this poor widow has put in more than all those who are contributing to the treasury. [44] For all of them have contributed out of their abundance; but she out of her poverty has put in everything she had, all she had to live on."

13 As he came out of the temple, one of his disciples said to him, "Look, Teacher, what large stones and what large buildings!" [2] Then Jesus asked him, "Do you see these great buildings? Not one stone will be left here upon another; all will be thrown down."

[3] When he was sitting on the Mount of Olives opposite the temple, Peter, James, John, and Andrew asked him privately, [4] "Tell us, when will this be, and what will be the sign that all these things are about to be accomplished?" [5] Then Jesus began to say to them, "Beware that no one leads you astray. [6] Many will come in my name and say, 'I am he!'[b] and they will lead many astray. [7] When you hear of wars and rumors of wars, do not

a   Or *the Christ*
b   Gk *I am*

sacrifices at the Temple, from which he draws his living. **34:** The scribe does not "resign" his position, and Jesus does not invite him into the movement. Jesus has outmaneuvered all segments of the Temple establishment in the series of attacks and counterattacks from 11.27.

12.35–37: How can the messiah be David's son? (Mt 22.41–46; Lk 20.41–44). This passage constitutes a rejection of any triumphalist restoration of the Davidic state (which Bartimaeus and the shouts of the crowd may have suggested; see 10.47–48n.; 11.10), reciting one of the imperial Davidic psalms (Ps 110.1) in the refutation.

12.38–44: Beware of the scribes (Mt 23.1,6; Lk 20.45–47; 21.1–4; 11.43; 14.7–11). **38–40:** Condemnation of the scribes, moving from their craving for honor to a concrete example of their exploitation of the poor. *Widows' houses* refers to all their inheritance and resources. **41–44:** Illustrates how the scribes "devour widow's houses": by inducing them to give their meager resources to the Temple. For this "they will receive the greater condemnation" (v. 40), confirmed by the immediately ensuing prophecy of the destruction of the Temple which they serve (13.1–2).

13.1–2: Destruction of Jerusalem and the Temple (Mt 24.1–3; Lk 21.5–7). This section of the Gospel, which began with Jesus' prophetic demonstration against the Temple (11.15–17), ends with his prophecy of its destruction—also implicating those whose base of power it constituted.

13.3–37: Exhortation not to be distracted from the movement by distressing events (Mt 24.3–36; Lk 21.7–36). Jesus' second speech uses prophetic and apocalyptic motifs in order to caution against an apocalyptic interpretation of historical crises of resistance, repression, and reconquest under Roman imperial rule, but to remain disciplined and vigilant in the struggle, despite persecution. The Israelite prophetic and Judean revelatory traditions are framed, balanced, and interpreted by the exhortation in vv. 5–6,9–13, and 28–37, particularly by the carefully positioned and repeated "beware/ be alert" in vv. 5,9,23,33. Judging from v. 14, these paragraphs must be written from a viewpoint outside both Jerusalem and Judea. **3:** Addressed through Peter and other disciples to the whole movement. **4:** Despite this apparent link with the destruction of the Temple just prophesied in v. 2, nothing in the rest of ch 13 implies that the events prophesied have anything to do with Jerusalem. **6:** *I*

be alarmed; this must take place, but the end is still to come. [8] For nation will rise against nation, and kingdom against kingdom; there will be earthquakes in various places; there will be famines. This is but the beginning of the birth pangs.

[9] "As for yourselves, beware; for they will hand you over to councils; and you will be beaten in synagogues; and you will stand before governors and kings because of me, as a testimony to them. [10] And the good news[a] must first be proclaimed to all nations. [11] When they bring you to trial and hand you over, do not worry beforehand about what you are to say; but say whatever is given you at that time, for it is not you who speak, but the Holy Spirit. [12] Brother will betray brother to death, and a father his child, and children will rise against parents and have them put to death; [13] and you will be hated by all because of my name. But the one who endures to the end will be saved.

[14] "But when you see the desolating sacrilege set up where it ought not to be (let the reader understand), then those in Judea must flee to the mountains; [15] the one on the housetop must not go down or enter the house to take anything away; [16] the one in the field must not turn back to get a coat. [17] Woe to those who are pregnant and to those who are nursing infants in those days! [18] Pray that it may not be in winter. [19] For in those days there will be suffering, such as has not been from the beginning of the creation that God created until now, no, and never will be.

[20] And if the Lord had not cut short those days, no one would be saved; but for the sake of the elect, whom he chose, he has cut short those days. [21] And if anyone says to you at that time, 'Look! Here is the Messiah!'[b] or 'Look! There he is!'—do not believe it. [22] False messiahs[c] and false prophets will appear and produce signs and omens, to lead astray, if possible, the elect. [23] But be alert; I have already told you everything.

[24] "But in those days, after that suffering,
the sun will be darkened,
    and the moon will not give its light,
[25] and the stars will be falling from heaven,
    and the powers in the heavens will be
        shaken.
[26] Then they will see 'the Son of Man coming in clouds' with great power and glory. [27] Then he will send out the angels, and gather his elect from the four winds, from the ends of the earth to the ends of heaven.

[28] "From the fig tree learn its lesson: as soon as its branch becomes tender and puts forth its leaves, you know that summer is near. [29] So also, when you see these things taking place, you know that he[d] is near, at the very gates. [30] Truly I tell you, this generation will not pass away until all these things have taken place. [31] Heaven and earth will pass away, but my words will not pass away.

a   Gk *gospel*
b   Or *the Christ*
c   Or *christs*
d   Or *it*

am he, lit., "I am"; see 6.50n. **7–8:** Stereotypical phrases from Israelite prophetic and Judean revelatory literature. *Rumors of wars* may refer to the intense resistance to the order of Emperor Gaius Caligula (37–41 CE) to install his bust in the Temple. *Famines* may refer to the disastrous effects of the severe drought in the late 40s. **9–13:** Cf. Lk 12.2–12,51–53; Mk 8.34–38. Far from being distracted by wars and famines, the movement should expect repressions, but not worry, expect to be hated by all, but endure. **14a:** A shift from the past to the present and future, from the readers' standpoint. *The desolating sacrilege,* cf. Dan 9.27; 11.31; 12.11. In contrast to Mt 24.15, nothing in Mark's vague phrase or the literary context points to Jerusalem or the Temple, let alone its destruction. **14b–20:** Anticipation of events in Judea and Galilee, where political conflict escalated during the 50s and 60s, based on long experience of how the Romans reacted to actual or perceived resistance with severe repressive measures and "scorched earth" reconquest of the people. **21–22:** Other prophets and messiahs were already familiar features in Judea in particular, and more appeared around the mid-first century. **24–25:** Traditional prophetic portrayal of God's coming in judgment, drawn from Isa 13.10; 34.4; Ezek 32.7–8; Joel 2.10,31; 3.15. **26–27:** In contrast to Dan 7.13, where the "human-like one" symbolizes the elect generally, *the Son of Man* here presides over the gathering of the elect (cf. Zech 2.6; Deut 30.4). **28–31:** Reassurance that the resolution of the historical crisis is near, as symbolized by the impending coming of the Son of Man, and that Jesus' words are utterly credible. **28:** Reverses the image of the fig tree from 11.12–14, now symbolizing new blessing for the people. **30:** Cf. 9.1. **31:** Cf.

[32] "But about that day or hour no one knows, neither the angels in heaven, nor the Son, but only the Father. [33] Beware, keep alert;[a] for you do not know when the time will come. [34] It is like a man going on a journey, when he leaves home and puts his slaves in charge, each with his work, and commands the doorkeeper to be on the watch. [35] Therefore, keep awake—for you do not know when the master of the house will come, in the evening, or at midnight, or at cockcrow, or at dawn, [36] or else he may find you asleep when he comes suddenly. [37] And what I say to you I say to all: Keep awake."

14 It was two days before the Passover and the festival of Unleavened Bread. The chief priests and the scribes were looking for a way to arrest Jesus[b] by stealth and kill him; [2] for they said, "Not during the festival, or there may be a riot among the people."

[3] While he was at Bethany in the house of Simon the leper,[c] as he sat at the table, a woman came with an alabaster jar of very costly ointment of nard, and she broke open the jar and poured the ointment on his head. [4] But some were there who said to one another in anger, "Why was the ointment wasted in this way? [5] For this ointment could have been sold for more than three hundred denarii,[d] and the money given to the poor." And they scolded her. [6] But Jesus said, "Let her alone; why do you trouble her? She has performed a good service for me. [7] For you always have the poor with you, and you can show kindness to them whenever you wish;

but you will not always have me. [8] She has done what she could; she has anointed my body beforehand for its burial. [9] Truly I tell you, wherever the good news[e] is proclaimed in the whole world, what she has done will be told in remembrance of her."

[10] Then Judas Iscariot, who was one of the twelve, went to the chief priests in order to betray him to them. [11] When they heard it, they were greatly pleased, and promised to give him money. So he began to look for an opportunity to betray him.

[12] On the first day of Unleavened Bread, when the Passover lamb is sacrificed, his disciples said to him, "Where do you want us to go and make the preparations for you to eat the Passover?" [13] So he sent two of his disciples, saying to them, "Go into the city, and a man carrying a jar of water will meet you; follow him, [14] and wherever he enters, say to the owner of the house, 'The Teacher asks, Where is my guest room where I may eat the Passover with my disciples?' [15] He will show you a large room upstairs, furnished and ready. Make preparations for us there." [16] So the disciples set out and went to the city, and found everything as he had told them; and they prepared the Passover meal.

a   Other ancient authorities add *and pray*
b   Gk *him*
c   The terms *leper* and *leprosy* can refer to several diseases
d   The denarius was the usual day's wage for a laborer
e   Or *gospel*

Isa 51.6; 40.8. **32–37:** Since no one knows precisely when the crisis will be resolved, they must simply maintain discipline and *Keep awake*.

14.1–15.47: Jesus' death as martyr-messiah (Mt 26.1–27.66; Lk 22.1–23.56; Jn 18.1–19.42). **1–2:** *Passover and the festival of Unleavened Bread,* in March/April, celebrated Israel's deliverance from foreign rule in ancient Egypt. Repressive actions by rulers repeatedly touched off massive protest demonstrations at Passover. The concern of the Jerusalem rulers and their representatives to kill Jesus, signaled in 3.6 and indicated again in 11.18 and 12.12, finally focuses on a specific plot.

14.3–8: Anointing for burial (Mt 26.6–13; Jn 12.1–8). As a prophet had poured oil on the head of (anointed, made a messiah of) David and other popular kings leading Israel, so *a woman . . . poured ointment on* Jesus' head, but to prepare his body for burial. In reply to strenuous objections, Jesus recognizes what she has done as part of the gospel itself. **3:** *Nard* was imported from the Himalayan mountains.

14.10–11: Anticipation of betrayal (Mt 26.14–16; Lk 22.3–6). It is from within the twelve, representatives of the renewed Israel, that the betrayal comes.

14.12–25: The Last Supper (Mt 26.17–29; Lk 22.7–20). **12–16:** Just as the chief priests and scribes had resorted to covert means "to arrest Jesus by stealth" (14.1), so Jesus and his disciples are now operating covertly, "underground," as indicated by Jesus' instructions for discreet movement inside the city and the carefully planned

¹⁷ When it was evening, he came with the twelve. ¹⁸ And when they had taken their places and were eating, Jesus said, "Truly I tell you, one of you will betray me, one who is eating with me." ¹⁹ They began to be distressed and to say to him one after another, "Surely, not I?" ²⁰ He said to them, "It is one of the twelve, one who is dipping bread[a] into the bowl[b] with me. ²¹ For the Son of Man goes as it is written of him, but woe to that one by whom the Son of Man is betrayed! It would have been better for that one not to have been born."

²² While they were eating, he took a loaf of bread, and after blessing it he broke it, gave it to them, and said, "Take; this is my body." ²³ Then he took a cup, and after giving thanks he gave it to them, and all of them drank from it. ²⁴ He said to them, "This is my blood of the[c] covenant, which is poured out for many. ²⁵ Truly I tell you, I will never again drink of the fruit of the vine until that day when I drink it new in the kingdom of God."

²⁶ When they had sung the hymn, they went out to the Mount of Olives. ²⁷ And Jesus said to them, "You will all become deserters; for it is written,

'I will strike the shepherd,
and the sheep will be scattered.'

²⁸ But after I am raised up, I will go before you to Galilee." ²⁹ Peter said to him, "Even though all become deserters, I will not." ³⁰ Jesus said to him, "Truly I tell you, this day, this very night, before the cock crows twice, you will deny me three times." ³¹ But he said vehemently, "Even though I must die with you, I will not deny you." And all of them said the same.

³² They went to a place called Gethsemane; and he said to his disciples, "Sit here while I pray." ³³ He took with him Peter and James and John, and began to be distressed and agitated. ³⁴ And he said to them, "I am deeply grieved, even to death; remain here, and keep awake." ³⁵ And going a little farther, he threw himself on the ground and prayed that, if it were possible, the hour might pass from him. ³⁶ He said, "Abba,[d] Father, for you all things are possible; remove this cup from me; yet, not what I want, but what you want." ³⁷ He came and found them sleeping; and he said to Peter, "Simon, are you asleep? Could you not keep awake one hour? ³⁸ Keep awake and pray that you may not come into the time of trial;[e] the spirit indeed is willing, but the flesh is weak." ³⁹ And again he went away and prayed, saying the same words. ⁴⁰ And once more he came and found them sleeping, for their eyes were very heavy; and they did not know what to say to him. ⁴¹ He came a third time and said to them, "Are you still sleeping and taking your rest? Enough! The hour has

---

a   Gk lacks *bread*
b   Other ancient authorities read *same bowl*
c   Other ancient authorities add *new*
d   Aramaic for *Father*
e   Or *into temptation*

---

signal of a *man carrying a jar of water* (a task that a woman would usually have performed). **18:** Cf. Ps 41.9. **20:** *Dipping bread into the bowl with me,* the common meal was the most intimate form of fellowship. **22–25:** Mt 26.26–29; Lk 22.15–20; 1 Cor 11.23–26. Jesus' words at the Last Supper became the words of institution of the regularly celebrated Lord's Supper. **22:** *My body,* without "for you" as in 1 Cor 11.24, clearly a collective symbol of the community. **24:** *My blood of the covenant,* thus renewing the covenant between God and the people, alluding to the covenant ceremony on Sinai (Ex 24.4–8). *For many,* see Isa 53.12. **25:** The Supper is eaten in anticipation of celebrating it *new in the kingdom of God,* whereas in 1 Cor 11.25–26 it is eaten also in memory.

14.26–52: Agony and betrayal in Gethsemane (Mt 26.30–56; Lk 22.31–53). Jesus' prediction of the disciples' desertion and their actual desertion frames his agonized prayer over his impending martyrdom and his enemies' surreptitious seizure of him. **26:** The Passover ended with the singing of Pss 115–118. **27:** Zech 13.7; Jn 16.32. See 6.34n. **28:** Although the disciples are all about to desert, the movement will continue as Jesus will go back to Galilee after his martyr's death; see 16.7. **29–31:** Cf. 8.34; 14.66–72; Jn 13.36–38; 18.15–18,25–27. **32:** *Gethsemane,* meaning "garden of oil," was an olive orchard or "garden" (Jn 18.1) on the slope of the Mount of Olives just east of Jerusalem. **33–35:** *Distressed and agitated . . . deeply grieved, even to death . . . threw himself on the ground.* The language and action are very strong, v. 34 echoing Pss 42.5,11; 43.5. **36:** *Abba,* Aramaic for "father" (see 5.41n.). *This cup,* refers to both vv. 23–24 and 10.39, implicating the disciples, especially James and John. **37–41:** The disciples are utterly incapable of doing what Jesus had emphasized in teaching about future crises; see 13.35–37.

come; the Son of Man is betrayed into the hands of sinners. [42] Get up, let us be going. See, my betrayer is at hand."

[43] Immediately, while he was still speaking, Judas, one of the twelve, arrived; and with him there was a crowd with swords and clubs, from the chief priests, the scribes, and the elders. [44] Now the betrayer had given them a sign, saying, "The one I will kiss is the man; arrest him and lead him away under guard." [45] So when he came, he went up to him at once and said, "Rabbi!" and kissed him. [46] Then they laid hands on him and arrested him. [47] But one of those who stood near drew his sword and struck the slave of the high priest, cutting off his ear. [48] Then Jesus said to them, "Have you come out with swords and clubs to arrest me as though I were a bandit? [49] Day after day I was with you in the temple teaching, and you did not arrest me. But let the scriptures be fulfilled." [50] All of them deserted him and fled.

[51] A certain young man was following him, wearing nothing but a linen cloth. They caught hold of him, [52] but he left the linen cloth and ran off naked.

[53] They took Jesus to the high priest; and all the chief priests, the elders, and the scribes were assembled. [54] Peter had followed him at a distance, right into the courtyard of the high priest; and he was sitting with the guards, warming himself at the fire. [55] Now the chief priests and the whole council were looking for testimony against Jesus to put him to death; but they found none. [56] For many gave false testimony against him, and their testimony did not agree. [57] Some stood up and gave false testimony against him, saying, [58] "We heard him say, 'I will destroy this temple that is made with hands, and in three days I will build another, not made with hands.'" [59] But even on this point their testimony did not agree. [60] Then the high priest stood up before them and asked Jesus, "Have you no answer? What is it that they testify against you?" [61] But he was silent and did not answer. Again the high priest asked him, "Are you the Messiah,[a] the Son of the Blessed One?" [62] Jesus said, "I am; and

'you will see the Son of Man
seated at the right hand of the Power,'
and 'coming with the clouds of heaven.'"

[63] Then the high priest tore his clothes and said, "Why do we still need witnesses? [64] You have heard his blasphemy! What is your

a   Or *the Christ*

43–50: Emphasis is on the excessive force used by the Jerusalem rulers in their covert action to capture Jesus, as if Jesus were a violent bandit-chieftain. Jesus mocks their reluctance simply to seize him when he had been teaching in the Temple courtyard, which betrays their lack of "authority" and their political impotence with the people. **45:** *Rabbi,* see 9.5–6n. **47:** In contrast to Mt 26.52–53, Lk 22.51, and Jn 18.10–11, Jesus in Mark does not rebuke the spontaneous violent response by *one of those who stood near* (not necessarily a disciple, although identified as Peter in Jn 18.10). **49:** *Let the scriptures be fulfilled,* Jesus' arrest, trial, and death in particular proceed "as written" in the scripture (vv. 21,27; etc.); *fulfilled,* only here and 1.15, marks a highly significant point in the overall gospel story. **51–52:** *Young man . . . naked,* presumably symbolic in the narrative, of the disciples now standing exposed as unfaithful deserters and of Jesus as defenseless before the rulers. The "young man" appears once more in the narrative in 16.5–7.

14.53–72: Jesus condemned by chief priests and council and Peter's denial (Mt 26.57–75; Lk 22.54–71). Jesus is condemned twice, first by the ruling chief priest and council, then by the Roman governor. While the accounts are integral parts of the Gospel, not historical transcripts, they have historical plausibility against the background of Roman imperial rule in Judea. **53:** Convening the council at night would have been highly unusual, but by this point due process was hardly a concern of the Jerusalem rulers. **55–59:** Although Jesus had been speaking and acting in public (see v. 49), the council had no witnesses with credible testimony to justify his execution. The *false testimony* appears to be a confusing parody of Jesus' prophetic condemnation of the Temple and his renewal of Israel (the "house of God" "not made with hands"?) in opposition to the Temple (the "house of God" "made with hands"?). **61–62:** *The Messiah,* it is unclear whether this is a charge. *"I am"* would be an uncharacteristic answer for Jesus (but see 6.50n.). It stands in sharp contrast with his answer to Pilate in 15.2: "You say so," and both Mt 26.64 and Lk 22.70 have "You say (that I am)," which suggests that Mk 14.62 also originally read "You say so" or "Am I?" But in immediately confessing *the Son of Man . . . coming with the clouds of heaven* (quoting Dan 7.13 and Ps 110.1), Jesus gives the high priest all he needs for condemnation. **63–64:**

decision?" All of them condemned him as deserving death. [65] Some began to spit on him, to blindfold him, and to strike him, saying to him, "Prophesy!" The guards also took him over and beat him.

[66] While Peter was below in the courtyard, one of the servant-girls of the high priest came by. [67] When she saw Peter warming himself, she stared at him and said, "You also were with Jesus, the man from Nazareth." [68] But he denied it, saying, "I do not know or understand what you are talking about." And he went out into the forecourt.[a] Then the cock crowed.[b] [69] And the servant-girl, on seeing him, began again to say to the bystanders, "This man is one of them." [70] But again he denied it. Then after a little while the bystanders again said to Peter, "Certainly you are one of them; for you are a Galilean." [71] But he began to curse, and he swore an oath, "I do not know this man you are talking about." [72] At that moment the cock crowed for the second time. Then Peter remembered that Jesus had said to him, "Before the cock crows twice, you will deny me three times." And he broke down and wept.

15 As soon as it was morning, the chief priests held a consultation with the elders and scribes and the whole council.

They bound Jesus, led him away, and handed him over to Pilate. [2] Pilate asked him, "Are you the King of the Jews?" He answered him, "You say so." [3] Then the chief priests accused him of many things. [4] Pilate asked him again, "Have you no answer? See how many charges they bring against you." [5] But Jesus made no further reply, so that Pilate was amazed.

[6] Now at the festival he used to release a prisoner for them, anyone for whom they asked. [7] Now a man called Barabbas was in prison with the rebels who had committed murder during the insurrection. [8] So the crowd came and began to ask Pilate to do for them according to his custom. [9] Then he answered them, "Do you want me to release for you the King of the Jews?" [10] For he realized that it was out of jealousy that the chief priests had handed him over. [11] But the chief priests stirred up the crowd to have him release Barabbas for them instead. [12] Pilate spoke to them again, "Then what do you wish me to do[c] with the

a Or *gateway*

b Other ancient authorities lack *Then the cock crowed*

c Other ancient authorities read *what should I do*

Blasphemy would presumably refer to the confession of being the Son of Man, rather than his threat against the Temple. For the prescribed punishment, see Lev 24.16. See also 2.7. **66–72:** Cf. v. 54. Peter's denial of Jesus is juxtaposed to and simultaneous with Jesus' confession and condemnation. Even the servants of the high priest share the prejudice against and contempt of Galileans such as Jesus, "the man from Nazareth," and Peter. **71:** Peter's third denial is very strong language. *I do not know this man* had double meaning: As indicated repeatedly throughout the Gospel, Peter indeed does not understand who Jesus is and what he is doing. **72:** See v. 30.

15.1–15: Jesus condemned by Pilate (Mt 27.1–2,11–26; Lk 23.1–5,18–25; Jn 18.28–40; 19.4–16). The second trial, before the Roman governor Pilate (26–37 CE). **1:** This further *consultation* suggests that the specific charge(s) against Jesus were still not clear, and that this continued in the hearing before Pilate (v. 3). **2:** It is the Roman governor who defines the charge as one of indigenous kingship in potential insurrection against the Roman order. The formulation of the question is that of outsiders to Israel, who viewed Galileans and others subject to Herodian rulers as "Judeans." It is surely significant also that the title *King of the Jews* (i.e., Judeans) occurs only in speech by Pilate or the Roman soldiers and the inscription on the cross presumably placed there by Pilate's order, in vv. 2,9,12,18,26, in contrast with "the Messiah, the King of Israel," used by the chief priests and scribes in v. 32. Thus Jesus' answer: "That is what *you* say." **4–5:** As in 14.60–61, Jesus is just "above it all," or is deliberately refusing to cooperate in his own interrogation. **6–15:** There is no evidence outside the New Testament of such a custom by Roman governors of Judea generally. Mark does not in any way suggest that "the Jews" demanded Jesus' death. The crowd is stirred up by the chief priests. Infamous in sources outside the New Testament for his tough stance, provocations, and violence as Roman governor, Pilate is portrayed here as an experienced imperial official who understands both that Jesus is politically more dangerous to the Roman order than an anti-imperial assassin and how to mollify the crowd while manipulating them into a choice. On crucifixion as the intensely cruel Roman form of torture and execution for provincial rebels, see 8.34n. Beating was standard treatment of political prisoners, whether they were to be executed or not.

man you call[a] the King of the Jews?" [13] They shouted back, "Crucify him!" [14] Pilate asked them, "Why, what evil has he done?" But they shouted all the more, "Crucify him!" [15] So Pilate, wishing to satisfy the crowd, released Barabbas for them; and after flogging Jesus, he handed him over to be crucified.

[16] Then the soldiers led him into the courtyard of the palace (that is, the governor's headquarters[b]); and they called together the whole cohort. [17] And they clothed him in a purple cloak; and after twisting some thorns into a crown, they put it on him. [18] And they began saluting him, "Hail, King of the Jews!" [19] They struck his head with a reed, spat upon him, and knelt down in homage to him. [20] After mocking him, they stripped him of the purple cloak and put his own clothes on him. Then they led him out to crucify him.

[21] They compelled a passer-by, who was coming in from the country, to carry his cross; it was Simon of Cyrene, the father of Alexander and Rufus. [22] Then they brought Jesus[c] to the place called Golgotha (which means the place of a skull). [23] And they offered him wine mixed with myrrh; but he did not take it. [24] And they crucified him, and divided his clothes among them, casting lots to decide what each should take.

[25] It was nine o'clock in the morning when they crucified him. [26] The inscription of the charge against him read, "The King of the Jews." [27] And with him they crucified two bandits, one on his right and one on his left.[d] [29] Those who passed by derided[e] him, shaking their heads and saying, "Aha! You who would destroy the temple and build it in three days, [30] save yourself, and come down from the cross!" [31] In the same way the chief priests, along with the scribes, were also mocking him among themselves and saying, "He saved others; he cannot save himself. [32] Let the Messiah,[f] the King of Israel, come down from the cross now, so that we may see and believe." Those who were crucified with him also taunted him.

[33] When it was noon, darkness came over the whole land[g] until three in the afternoon. [34] At three o'clock Jesus cried out with a loud voice, "Eloi, Eloi, lema sabachthani?" which

a   Other ancient authorities lack *the man you call*
b   Gk *the praetorium*
c   Gk *him*
d   Other ancient authorities add verse 28, *And the scripture was fulfilled that says, "And he was counted among the lawless."*
e   Or *blasphemed*
f   Or *the Christ*
g   Or *earth*

15.16–38: The crucifixion (Mt 27.27–48; Lk 23.18–43). 16–20: Along with the *purple cloak* symbolizing royalty, the mockery, by the whole cohort, of Jesus as "King of the Judeans," includes several allusions to worship of the Roman emperor whom Jesus has the audacity to challenge: The crown of thorns suggests the laurel wreath crowning the emperor's head, the hailing suggests the acclamation of the emperor, and kneeling in homage suggests the prostration to the emperor. The mutual hostility between Mark's Jesus and the imperial army is unmistakably intense. 16: A *cohort* consisted of about five hundred soldiers. 21: *Simon of Cyrene,* a peasant *coming in from the country,* had perhaps moved back to Judea from the Diaspora Jewish community in Cyrene, west of Egypt; his sons apparently later joined the movement. This Simon in effect replaces Peter, whose original name was Simon, and who had just proven incapable of "taking up his cross" by denying Jesus instead of himself (8.34; 14.66–72). Perhaps they "compel" Simon to carry the cross because Jesus is already too weak from repeated beatings, 14.65; 15.15,19. Once hung on the cross he died more quickly than expected (vv. 44–45). 23: Jesus declines the offer of a sedative to mitigate the pain. 24: *Casting lots,* see Ps 22.18; the first of three allusions to this psalm. 26: The inscription indicates the crime: As "King of the Judeans" Jesus threatened to bring about a rebellion against the law and order of the empire, which was maintained by such gruesome, terrorizing violence against subject peoples. 27: *Two bandits,* perhaps actually ancient "Robin Hoods"; but the Romans used the term contemptuously to demean rebels against Roman rule. *On his right . . . on his left,* cf. 10.37–40; not James and John, but the two "bandits" undergo the baptism of death with Jesus. 29–30: *Shaking their heads,* cf. Ps 22.7–8. The mocking passers-by would appear to be hostile, using the same terms as the false witnesses in 14.56–58. 31: *He saved others; he cannot save himself,* double meaning: cf. 8.34; 10.45. 33–38: Mt 27.45–53; Lk 23.44–48. 33: *Darkness came over the whole land,* crisis in the natural order indicating God coming in judgment (cf. Joel 2.2; Am 5.18–20; Zeph 1.15). 34: *"Eloi, Eloi,"* Jesus crying out in abandonment in the words of Ps 22.1 in

means, "My God, my God, why have you for-saken me?"[a] [35] When some of the bystanders heard it, they said, "Listen, he is calling for Elijah." [36] And someone ran, filled a sponge with sour wine, put it on a stick, and gave it to him to drink, saying, "Wait, let us see whether Elijah will come to take him down." [37] Then Jesus gave a loud cry and breathed his last. [38] And the curtain of the temple was torn in two, from top to bottom. [39] Now when the centurion, who stood facing him, saw that in this way he[b] breathed his last, he said, "Truly this man was God's Son!"[c]

[40] There were also women looking on from a distance; among them were Mary Magdalene, and Mary the mother of James the younger and of Joses, and Salome. [41] These used to follow him and provided for him when he was in Galilee; and there were many other women who had come up with him to Jerusalem.

[42] When evening had come, and since it was the day of Preparation, that is, the day before the sabbath, [43] Joseph of Arimathea, a respected member of the council, who was also himself waiting expectantly for the king-dom of God, went boldly to Pilate and asked for the body of Jesus. [44] Then Pilate wondered if he were already dead; and summoning the centurion, he asked him whether he had been dead for some time. [45] When he learned from the centurion that he was dead, he granted the body to Joseph. [46] Then Joseph[d] bought a linen cloth, and taking down the body,[e] wrapped it in the linen cloth, and laid it in a tomb that had been hewn out of the rock. He then rolled a stone against the door of the tomb. [47] Mary Magdalene and Mary the mother of Joses saw where the body[e] was laid.

16 When the sabbath was over, Mary Magdalene, and Mary the mother of James, and Salome bought spices, so that they might go and anoint him. [2] And very early on the first day of the week, when the sun had risen, they went to the tomb. [3] They had been saying to one another, "Who will roll away the stone for us from the entrance to the tomb?" [4] When they looked up, they saw that the stone, which was very large, had already been rolled back. [5] As they entered

a Other ancient authorities read *made me a reproach*
b Other ancient authorities add *cried out and*
c Or *a son of God*
d Gk *he*
e Gk *it*

Aramaic (see 5.41n.). **35–36:** Voyeurs, misinterpreting the word "Eloi," suggest that he is calling for Elijah, and want to revive him, prolonging the ordeal, to see if Elijah comes. **37–38:** As Jesus dies, the curtain of the Temple (see Ex 26.33), separating but also protecting the people from the presence of God, is torn in two, in judgment on the Temple's mediation of the Holy but also opening access to God for the people; see also 1.10.

15.39–47: Jesus' burial (Mt 27.54–61; Lk 23.49–56). Three interrelated responses to Jesus' death: by a mili-tary representative of the Roman rulers, by a representative of the Jerusalem religious establishment, and by loyal women followers. **39:** Just as Jesus' other opponents earlier in the Gospel know who he is, so the Roman centurion (the equivalent of a company commander) presiding at his crucifixion recognizes that he was truly "a son of God." While neither a confession of faith (the centurion continues his duties in 15.44–45) nor the final resolution of the "messianic secret," contrary to previous interpretations, Mark ironically has the officer who presides at Jesus' execution recognize his true identity. He also confirms to Pilate that Jesus is dead in 15.44–45. **40–41:** As the disciples, commissioned as the leaders of the movement, consistently misunderstood, women were healed by Jesus as symbolic of the renewal of Israel. Now, after the disciples had betrayed, denied, and abandoned Jesus, some of the many women who had followed him and provided for him stood by him, at a distance, throughout the ordeal. Neither of the two women named here has been mentioned earlier. Both will witness the burial site (v. 47) and the empty tomb (16.1). **42–46:** *Joseph of Arimathea*, a *member of the council* that had condemned Jesus (see 14.64), but like the scribe in 12.28–34, interested in the kingdom of God, asked for the body. Apparently eager to dispose of it *before the sabbath*, he *wrapped it*, and secured it in a rock tomb sealed with a heavy stone (cf. 16.3n), without even a gesture of proper burial rites. **47:** Although the disciples, having completely disappeared, make no effort to afford Jesus proper burial (contrast John's disciples in 6.22), the two Marys witness *where the body was laid*.

16.1–8: The empty tomb, the call back to Galilee, and *they were afraid* (Mt 28.1–8a; Lk 24.1–11). **1:** The women go finally to perform proper rites of burial. **3:** The disk-shaped stone rolled in a groove to close the tomb's entry. **5:** The

the tomb, they saw a young man, dressed in a white robe, sitting on the right side; and they were alarmed. [6] But he said to them, "Do not be alarmed; you are looking for Jesus of Nazareth, who was crucified. He has been raised; he is not here. Look, there is the place they laid him. [7] But go, tell his disciples and Peter that he is going ahead of you to Galilee; there you will see him, just as he told you." [8] So they went out and fled from the tomb, for terror and amazement had seized them; and they said nothing to anyone, for they were afraid.[a]

THE SHORTER ENDING OF MARK

⟦And all that had been commanded them they told briefly to those around Peter. And afterward Jesus himself sent out through them, from east to west, the sacred and imperishable proclamation of eternal salvation.[b]⟧

THE LONGER ENDING OF MARK

[9] ⟦Now after he rose early on the first day of the week, he appeared first to Mary Magdalene, from whom he had cast out seven demons. [10] She went out and told those who had been with him, while they were mourning and weeping. [11] But when they heard that he was alive and had been seen by her, they would not believe it.

[12] After this he appeared in another form to two of them, as they were walking into the country. [13] And they went back and told the rest, but they did not believe them.

[14] Later he appeared to the eleven themselves as they were sitting at the table; and he upbraided them for their lack of faith and stubbornness, because they had not believed those who saw him after he had risen.[c] [15] And he said to them, "Go into all the world and proclaim the good news[d] to the whole creation. [16] The one who believes and is baptized will be saved; but the one who does not believe will be condemned. [17] And these signs will accompany those who believe: by using my name they will cast out demons; they will speak in new tongues; [18] they will pick up snakes in their hands,[e] and if they drink any deadly thing, it will not hurt them; they will lay their hands on the sick, and they will recover."

a   Some of the most ancient authorities bring the book to a close at the end of verse 8. One authority concludes the book with the shorter ending; others include the shorter ending and then continue with verses 9-20. In most authorities verses 9-20 follow immediately after verse 8, though in some of these authorities the passage is marked as being doubtful.

b   Other ancient authorities add *Amen*

c   Other ancient authorities add, in whole or in part, *And they excused themselves, saying, "This age of lawlessness and unbelief is under Satan, who does not allow the truth and power of God to prevail over the unclean things of the spirits. Therefore reveal your righteousness now"—thus they spoke to Christ. And Christ replied to them, "The term of years of Satan's power has been fulfilled, but other terrible things draw near. And for those who have sinned I was handed over to death, that they may return to the truth and sin no more, that they may inherit the spiritual and imperishable glory of righteousness that is in heaven."*

d   Or *gospel*

e   Other ancient authorities lack *in their hands*

young man (cf. 14.51–52) is *dressed in a white robe*, as a martyr vindicated by God would be dressed (cf. Dan 11.35; Rev 7.9,13), reminiscent of Jesus' garments becoming "dazzling white" in the transfiguration, 9.3. **6:** The "young man" tells the women *He has been raised;* there was apparently no resurrection appearance in the original text of Mark that ended at 16.8. **7:** The risen Jesus is *going ahead . . . to Galilee* (cf. 14.28), where they *will see him,* in the same way as Jesus twice before said people would "see the Son of Man coming with the clouds of heaven," i.e., the standard symbol of the renewed Israel. Jesus is vindicated and his movement is to continue. Mark's Gospel is open-ended and must be completed by the hearers and readers of the Gospel. **8:** The narrative ends with the women terrified. Obviously, however, they eventually told the tale, or Mark's Gospel could not have been written.

16.9–20: Two attempts to provide a more satisfactory ending to the Gospel of Mark. **The shorter ending.** Although present in some manuscripts, this ending is clearly different from the rest of Mark in style and understanding of Jesus. It was evidently not added before the fourth century CE. **The longer ending.** Possibly written in the early second century and appended to the Gospel later in the second century. These sentences borrow

¹⁹ So then the Lord Jesus, after he had spoken to them, was taken up into heaven and sat down at the right hand of God. ²⁰ And they went out and proclaimed the good news everywhere, while the Lord worked with them and confirmed the message by the signs that accompanied it.ᵃ⟧

ᵃ Other ancient authorities add *Amen*

some motifs from the other Gospels and contain several unusual apocryphal elements. **9–10:** Mary is alone in Jn 20.1–2,11–19. *Seven demons,* Lk 8.2. **11:** Lk 24.11,22–25; Jn 20.19–29. **12–13:** Lk 24.12–35. **13:** Cf. Lk 24.34. **14–18:** Mt 28.19; Lk 24.47. **16:** Acts 2.37–42; 10.47–48; Rom 10.9. **17–18:** Exorcisms, Acts 8.6–7; 16.18; 19.11–20; *new tongues,* Acts 2.4–11n.; 10.46; 19.6; and possibly 1 Cor 12.10,28; 14.2–33; snakes and drinking poison lack New Testament parallels. **19–20:** Jesus' exaltation, Phil 2.9–11; Heb 1.3; *taken up,* Acts 1.2,11,22; *right hand of God,* Ps 110.1; Acts 7.55; Heb 1.3.

THE GOSPEL ACCORDING TO LUKE

NAME AND AUTHORSHIP

The Third Gospel, traditionally called the Gospel according to Luke, is a unique literary and theological contribution to the story of Jesus Christ. The oldest traditions of the Christian church identify Luke, a physician who was a traveling companion and co-worker with Paul (Philem 1.24; Col 4.14), as the author of the Gospel and its sequel, the Acts of the Apostles. At times the tradition further identifies Luke as a Syrian from Antioch, but practically nothing else is remembered of the writer of the Third Gospel. The earliest of these traditions about the author are from the late second century, and scholarly analysis of the Gospel and Acts raises critical questions about the accuracy of the attribution of the writings to the Luke who was Paul's associate. The strongest argument in favor of identifying Luke the physician as the author of the Gospel and Acts is the relative obscurity of this figure in early Christianity. Yet, even defenders of the traditional identity of Luke recognize difficulties with that connection. Though Luke's familiarity with Judaism is extensive, he seems to have more book-knowledge than practical experience of its particular rituals and beliefs. Similarly, when Luke provides details about Palestinian locations and practices, they exhibit a tendency toward setting the story in an urban environment rather than the predominantly nonurban village culture that Jesus would have known. Above all, Luke never mentions in Acts that Paul wrote letters nor does he use theological themes from the letters attributed to the apostle.

SOURCES

Luke's Gospel is dependent on other earlier writings, especially the Gospel according to Mark. That Luke knew and used still other materials, both oral and written, in composing this Gospel is certain, if not demonstrable. In fact, Luke shares a body of material (probably in written form) with the author of the Gospel according to Matthew that accounts for approximately one-fifth of the overall Gospel story. Scholars designate this common material as "Q" (German "Quelle," "source"). Whether Luke had additional written sources for episodes and teaching found only in his Gospel—such as the account of Jesus' birth, childhood, certain parables, and some materials peculiar to Luke's account of Jesus' passion and resurrection—is debated, though possible. Luke's concern with sources—with acknowledging and using them profitably—is clear from his prologue to the Gospel (1.1–4). (See Introduction to the Gospels, p. 1743.)

DATE AND PLACE OF COMPOSITION

The time and place of the writing of this Gospel are uncertain. Tradition identifies Luke's account with both Antioch and Rome (where Acts comes to its end), but no firm tradition specifies a precise time and place of composition. Any major urban center in the Greek-speaking areas of the Roman empire would be a suitable location for such a document to be written and read. As for its date, all one can say with certainty is that Luke wrote this account after Mark composed his Gospel. The typical suggestion that Luke wrote around 85 CE is plausible, though the Gospel could have been completed five to fifteen years earlier or even five to ten years later.

STYLE, CONTENTS, AND STRUCTURE

In telling this story, Luke demonstrates an ability to write in different literary styles. The initial four verses of the book are a single Greek sentence that forms a highly stylized introductory statement typical of ancient historical writings. The language is formal and refined in a fashion familiar to well-educated citizens of the Roman empire in the first century CE. After this distinctive preface, however, the narrative shifts into a style of Greek reminiscent of the Septuagint (the ancient Greek translation of the Hebrew Bible). (In the annotations, places where Luke's quotations from the scriptures follow the Septuagint rather than the Hebrew are marked with the standard abbreviation for the Septuagint, LXX.) This Semitic-influenced form of Greek permeates the stories about the birth and childhood of Jesus. The Septuagint-like style lightens into a more normal (and more typically secular) form of first-century Greek (called "koine") in the narrative that comprises the remainder of the Gospel. As situations shift in the story, the language used varies appropriately to suit the locale and characters in the narrative. Luke's appreciation of stylistic variation in narrative communication is apparent from his skilled employment of this technique. Indeed, it seems that the Gospel communicates the universal significance of its story of God's salvation in and through Jesus Christ in the variety of styles that Luke uses to tell the story. Readers from different religious, ethnic, and social backgrounds would find one level or another of the overall account familiar and, thereby, a point of identity and entry into the story of Jesus Christ.

In broad strokes, Luke tells the same basic story that one reads in the other canonical Gospels: Jesus appears, ministers in Galilee, and moves to Judea and Jerusalem where he encounters deadly hostility that leads to his suffering, death, and resurrection. Yet, Luke's story of Jesus has logic and content that distinguish it among the four Gospels. The advent of Jesus among pious Jews, who observed ancestral traditions, highlights the continuity of Jesus' story with the history of Israel and presents it as the fulfillment of his people's hopes. In Luke's remembrance of Jesus, one finds an emphasis on God's compassion as Jesus reaches out to live and work among the marginal members of his society. Women, the less-than-pious, tax collectors, the poor, the sick, the oppressed, and even noble Pharisees are present and interact with Jesus more prominently in this account than in any other. As stated in Acts, "Jesus of Nazareth . . . went about doing good . . . for God was with him" (Acts 10.38). Both the coming of Jesus and his ministry of compassion are the direct results of God's anointing Jesus with the power of the Holy Spirit. Such an outpouring of the Spirit was neither unprecedented nor singular, however. The same Spirit of God that was active in the history of Israel is clearly present in the infancy stories concerning John the Baptist and Jesus with which the Gospel begins, and later reappears in Acts as the church spreads the message of salvation to all the peoples of the known world.

Luke has structured the narrative in a deliberate and logical way. A prologue (1.1–4) prepares readers for the significance of the story that follows. The infancy and childhood of Jesus is told in a series of scenes that alternate with an account of the origins of John the Baptist so that readers understand the role of both these figures in God's bringing salvation to all humanity, though Jesus is clearly presented as superior to the Baptist in this arrangement (1.5–2.52). As an adult Jesus prepares for his ministry through an encounter with John (then, readers learn Jesus' genealogy), and he undergoes temptations by the devil (3.1–4.13); Jesus ministers in Galilee, provoking controversy, calling disciples, preaching, working miracles, teaching, commissioning the initial ministry of his followers, and dealing compassionately with the masses of people (4.14–9.50). Jesus and his followers journey to Jerusalem and he ministers along the way (9.51–19.27). Jesus enters Jerusalem, working in the Temple area and teaching about the future (19.28–21.38). Jesus directs the Last Supper, suffers, dies, and is buried (22.1–23.56), and Jesus' empty tomb is found before he appears to the disciples and then ascends to heaven (24.1–53).

INTERPRETATION

The carefully crafted beginning of Luke's narrative contains anticipations of the story that follows and declarations that highlight the significance of the whole story. The narrative unfolds smoothly. Initial incidents are told in such a way that they anticipate later developments in the narrative. Readers who become actively involved with Luke's account will find hints and signals that provoke questions and expectations that are answered after one has read the whole story. In general, wondering about the nature of salvation, the character of the kingdom of God, the reality of repentance, and the person and work of Jesus as the Lord—God's messiah, son, and savior—will lead readers to ask about the deeper significance of the story that Luke is telling. Luke's primary concern is to inform the reader who Jesus of Nazareth was—and now, who he is as the suffering, crucified savior and the risen, exalted Lord. Furthermore, in the wake of Luke's purposeful presentation of the person and work of Jesus Christ, there is another dimension of the story that preserves and communicates Jesus' teaching about what it means to be his follower. Discipleship is a secondary theme that is closely related to the primary theme of Jesus' identity and significance. Discipleship, however, is sometimes a difficult dimension of the story for contemporary readers to grasp, for discipleship is a way of life as a member of the repentant and saved people of God. For Luke, one is not a disciple alone, but one finds profound personal significance in becoming one of the people of God who live as citizens of God's kingdom in a manner consistent with God's intentions for the life of all humanity as brought and taught, shown and known in Jesus Christ.

Luke's elegantly crafted account of Jesus' life and teaching shows him to be "the Lord," God's son who is the universal savior of humanity. Jesus inaugurates a mission to all humankind as the kingdom of God draws near to the ordinary lives of people in Jesus' person and work. Luke's version of Jesus' story presents Jesus' coming among humanity—in birth, life, ministry, suffering, death, and resurrection—as the fulfillment of God's promises of salvation, which brings peace and well-being in a definitive way. This saving event inaugurated the final stage of God's dealings with humanity in anticipation of the "Last Day," "the Day of the Lord." Jesus himself and, in turn, his disciples call people to true repentance, which means a new relationship to God and to other human beings in a manner of life that embodies God's will for human existence.

Marion L. Soards

1 Since many have undertaken to set down an orderly account of the events that have been fulfilled among us, [2] just as they were handed on to us by those who from the beginning were eyewitnesses and servants of the word, [3] I too decided, after investigating everything carefully from the very first,[a] to write an orderly account for you, most excellent Theophilus, [4] so that you may know the truth concerning the things about which you have been instructed.

[5] In the days of King Herod of Judea, there was a priest named Zechariah, who belonged to the priestly order of Abijah. His wife was a descendant of Aaron, and her name was Elizabeth. [6] Both of them were righteous before God, living blamelessly according to all the commandments and regulations of the Lord. [7] But they had no children, because Elizabeth was barren, and both were getting on in years.

[8] Once when he was serving as priest before God and his section was on duty, [9] he was chosen by lot, according to the custom of the priesthood, to enter the sanctuary of the Lord and offer incense. [10] Now at the time of the incense offering, the whole assembly of the people was praying outside. [11] Then there appeared to him an angel of the Lord, standing at the right side of the altar of incense. [12] When Zechariah saw him, he was terrified; and fear overwhelmed him. [13] But the angel said to him, "Do not be afraid, Zechariah, for your prayer has been heard. Your wife Elizabeth will bear you a son, and you will name him John. [14] You will have joy and gladness, and many will rejoice at his birth, [15] for he will be great in the sight of the Lord. He must never drink wine or strong drink; even before his birth he will be filled with the Holy

a Or *for a long time*

1.1–4: The prologue (Mt 1.1; Mk 1.1). See Acts 1.1–2. Jn 20.30–31; 21.25 show similar awareness of sources used by the Gospel writers. This literary prologue resembles the openings of many classical or Hellenistic Greek works, particularly histories. Accordingly, Luke refers to previous early Christian writings, acknowledges sources, and explains the need or purpose of his own work. 3: *Theophilus* means "friend of God" and may address a person of prominent social standing, since Theophilus is designated "most excellent," terminology typically applied to persons of high official or socioeconomic status. If Theophilus is a specific prominent person, then, he is likely to be the patron of the author of the Gospel, one who would use his influence to have the Gospel copied and distributed. While the address may be to a specific person, the symbolic sense of the name may designate any ideal Christian, as it has been understood since the earliest interpretations of Luke's Gospel.
1.5–2.52: The infancy and childhood of Jesus.
1.5–25: The annunciation of the birth of John the Baptist. 5: *In the days of King Herod of Judea* refers broadly to 37–4 BCE. The specific time in view in this story is probably 7–6 BCE (see Mt 2.1,15). *The priestly order of Abijah* was the eighth of twenty-four divisions of priests (1 Chr 24.10) who served twice annually, for one week at a time, in the Jerusalem Temple. These priests were Levites who served God both in behalf of and in the place of the firstborn males of all the tribes of Israel (Num 3.11–13). As *a descendant of Aaron,* Israel's first priest, Elizabeth was also from a priestly family. 5–7: The mention of Elizabeth, the righteousness of the couple, their childlessness, and their advanced age all anticipate the appearance of the angel and are not directly related to Zechariah's Temple service. The description also echoes images and lines from the Hebrew Bible (Gen 15.3; 16.1; 25.2; 29.31; Judg 13.2–3; 1 Sam 1.2; Ex 30.6–8). 9: The privilege of offering the incense was normally granted only once in a lifetime. 13: The name *John* (Heb "J[eh]ohanan") means "The Lord has shown favor." 15: Num 6.1–4; Judg

Spirit. [16] He will turn many of the people of Israel to the Lord their God. [17] With the spirit and power of Elijah he will go before him, to turn the hearts of parents to their children, and the disobedient to the wisdom of the righteous, to make ready a people prepared for the Lord." [18] Zechariah said to the angel, "How will I know that this is so? For I am an old man, and my wife is getting on in years." [19] The angel replied, "I am Gabriel. I stand in the presence of God, and I have been sent to speak to you and to bring you this good news. [20] But now, because you did not believe my words, which will be fulfilled in their time, you will become mute, unable to speak, until the day these things occur."

[21] Meanwhile the people were waiting for Zechariah, and wondered at his delay in the sanctuary. [22] When he did come out, he could not speak to them, and they realized that he had seen a vision in the sanctuary. He kept motioning to them and remained unable to speak. [23] When his time of service was ended, he went to his home.

[24] After those days his wife Elizabeth conceived, and for five months she remained in seclusion. She said, [25] "This is what the Lord has done for me when he looked favorably on me and took away the disgrace I have endured among my people."

[26] In the sixth month the angel Gabriel was sent by God to a town in Galilee called Nazareth, [27] to a virgin engaged to a man whose name was Joseph, of the house of David. The virgin's name was Mary. [28] And he came to her and said, "Greetings, favored one! The Lord is with you."[a] [29] But she was much perplexed by his words and pondered what sort

of greeting this might be. [30] The angel said to her, "Do not be afraid, Mary, for you have found favor with God. [31] And now, you will conceive in your womb and bear a son, and you will name him Jesus. [32] He will be great, and will be called the Son of the Most High, and the Lord God will give to him the throne of his ancestor David. [33] He will reign over the house of Jacob forever, and of his kingdom there will be no end." [34] Mary said to the angel, "How can this be, since I am a virgin?"[b] [35] The angel said to her, "The Holy Spirit will come upon you, and the power of the Most High will overshadow you; therefore the child to be born[c] will be holy; he will be called Son of God. [36] And now, your relative Elizabeth in her old age has also conceived a son; and this is the sixth month for her who was said to be barren. [37] For nothing will be impossible with God." [38] Then Mary said, "Here am I, the servant of the Lord; let it be with me according to your word." Then the angel departed from her.

[39] In those days Mary set out and went with haste to a Judean town in the hill country, [40] where she entered the house of Zechariah and greeted Elizabeth. [41] When Elizabeth heard Mary's greeting, the child leaped in her womb. And Elizabeth was filled with the Holy Spirit [42] and exclaimed with a loud cry, "Blessed are you among women, and blessed is the fruit of your womb. [43] And why has this happened to me, that the mother of my Lord

[a] Other ancient authorities add *Blessed are you among women*
[b] Gk *I do not know a man*
[c] Other ancient authorities add *of you*

13.4–5; 1 Sam 1.11 LXX. **17:** *He will go before him,* that is, he will be the forerunner of the messiah (Mal 4.5–6; Mt 11.14); on *Elijah,* see 1 Kings 17–19; 21. **19:** *Gabriel* is one of two angels named in the Hebrew Bible (Dan 8.16; 9.21). **25:** Among Jews sterility was regarded as a sign of divine disfavor and therefore a *disgrace* (see Gen 16.2; 25.21; 30.23; 1 Sam 1.1–18; Lev 20.20–21; Ps 128.3; Jer 22.30).

1.26–38: The annunciation of Jesus' birth. 26: *In the sixth month,* after the conception of John. *Nazareth,* a small village (cf. Jn 1.46) in southern Galilee. **27:** There is a clear emphasis on Mary's status as a *virgin,* a term used twice in this verse; see 1.34. *Mary,* Gk "Mariam," from Heb "Miryam." **31:** *Jesus,* the Greek form of the Hebrew name Joshua, meaning "The Lord has saved" (see Mt 1.21). **32:** *The Son of the Most High* implies both divinity (see Sir 4.10) and royal authority (see 2 Sam 7.13–16; cf. Lk 2.35,76; 6.35; 8.28; Acts 7.48; 16.17). **32–33:** Jesus will fulfil the expectation that David's heir will reign eternally; see 2 Sam 7.12–17. **36:** *Elizabeth . . . conceived,* the angel offers Mary some corroboration, on which she acts (v. 39).

1.39–56: Mary and Elizabeth. 41: Elizabeth's being *filled with the Holy Spirit* may also acknowledge the presence and the power of the Holy Spirit at work in relation to the unborn John *in her womb.* **43:** Prior to his birth

comes to me? [44] For as soon as I heard the sound of your greeting, the child in my womb leaped for joy. [45] And blessed is she who believed that there would be[a] a fulfillment of what was spoken to her by the Lord."

[46] And Mary[b] said,

"My soul magnifies the Lord,
[47] and my spirit rejoices in God my
    Savior,
[48] for he has looked with favor on the
    lowliness of his servant.
  Surely, from now on all generations will
    call me blessed;
[49] for the Mighty One has done great things
    for me,
  and holy is his name.
[50] His mercy is for those who fear him
  from generation to generation.
[51] He has shown strength with his arm;
  he has scattered the proud in the
    thoughts of their hearts.
[52] He has brought down the powerful from
    their thrones,
  and lifted up the lowly;
[53] he has filled the hungry with good
    things,
  and sent the rich away empty.
[54] He has helped his servant Israel,
  in remembrance of his mercy,
[55] according to the promise he made to our
    ancestors,
  to Abraham and to his descendants
    forever."

[56] And Mary remained with her about three months and then returned to her home.

[57] Now the time came for Elizabeth to give birth, and she bore a son. [58] Her neighbors and relatives heard that the Lord had shown his great mercy to her, and they rejoiced with her. [59] On the eighth day they came to circumcise the child, and they were going to name him Zechariah after his father. [60] But his mother said, "No; he is to be called John." [61] They said to her, "None of your relatives has this name." [62] Then they began motioning to his father to find out what name he wanted to give him. [63] He asked for a writing tablet and wrote, "His name is John." And all of them were amazed. [64] Immediately his mouth was opened and his tongue freed, and he began to speak, praising God. [65] Fear came over all their neighbors, and all these things were talked about throughout the entire hill country of Judea. [66] All who heard them pondered them and said, "What then will this child become?" For, indeed, the hand of the Lord was with him.

[67] Then his father Zechariah was filled with the Holy Spirit and spoke this prophecy:

[68] "Blessed be the Lord God of Israel,
  for he has looked favorably on his
    people and redeemed them.
[69] He has raised up a mighty savior[c] for us
  in the house of his servant David,
[70] as he spoke through the mouth of his
  holy prophets from of old,
[71] that we would be saved from our
    enemies and from the hand of all
    who hate us.
[72] Thus he has shown the mercy promised
    to our ancestors,
  and has remembered his holy covenant,
[73] the oath that he swore to our ancestor
    Abraham,
  to grant us [74] that we, being rescued
    from the hands of our enemies,
  might serve him without fear, [75] in holiness
    and righteousness
  before him all our days.

---

[a] Or believed, for there will be
[b] Other ancient authorities read Elizabeth
[c] Gk a horn of salvation

Jesus is designated Lord. **44:** *Joy* indicates the positive nature of the relationship of John the Baptist and Jesus. **46–55:** These verses form the first of four "canticles" or "hymns" in the infancy narrative of Luke. This "song" is the "Magnificat" (so called from its first word in the Latin or Vulgate translation); compare the prayer of Hannah in 1 Sam 2.1–10, a passage to which these verses relate. **55:** Gen 17.7; 18.18; 22.17; Mic 7.20.

1.57–80: The birth and naming of John. 58: Here, *the Lord* refers to God. **59:** Lev 12.3; Gen 17.12; Lk 2.21. **65:** *Fear* (rendered "awe" in 5.26) designates humble, reverent recognition of the limits of human understanding and power before God (2.9; 7.16; Acts 2.43,46–47; 5.5,11; 19.17). **66:** The question anticipates the appearance of the adult John, 3.1–18. **67–79:** The second hymn, called the "Benedictus." **69:** *A mighty savior,* lit., "a horn of salvation," uses a biblical metaphor ("horn") for power (Pss 18.3; 75.5–6; 89.18; 112.9; 148.14) and here refers to

76 And you, child, will be called the prophet
of the Most High;
for you will go before the Lord to
prepare his ways,
77 to give knowledge of salvation to his
people
by the forgiveness of their sins.
78 By the tender mercy of our God,
the dawn from on high will break upon[a]
us,
79 to give light to those who sit in darkness
and in the shadow of death,
to guide our feet into the way of peace."
80 The child grew and became strong in
spirit, and he was in the wilderness until the
day he appeared publicly to Israel.

2 In those days a decree went out from Emperor Augustus that all the world should
be registered. 2 This was the first registration
and was taken while Quirinius was governor of Syria. 3 All went to their own towns
to be registered. 4 Joseph also went from the
town of Nazareth in Galilee to Judea, to the
city of David called Bethlehem, because he
was descended from the house and family of David. 5 He went to be registered with
Mary, to whom he was engaged and who was
expecting a child. 6 While they were there,
the time came for her to deliver her child.
7 And she gave birth to her firstborn son and
wrapped him in bands of cloth, and laid him
in a manger, because there was no place for
them in the inn.

8 In that region there were shepherds living
in the fields, keeping watch over their flock
by night. 9 Then an angel of the Lord stood
before them, and the glory of the Lord shone
around them, and they were terrified. 10 But
the angel said to them, "Do not be afraid; for
see—I am bringing you good news of great
joy for all the people: 11 to you is born this
day in the city of David a Savior, who is the
Messiah,[b] the Lord. 12 This will be a sign for
you: you will find a child wrapped in bands of
cloth and lying in a manger." 13 And suddenly
there was with the angel a multitude of the
heavenly host,[c] praising God and saying,

14 "Glory to God in the highest heaven,
and on earth peace among those whom
he favors!"[d]

15 When the angels had left them and
gone into heaven, the shepherds said to one
another, "Let us go now to Bethlehem and
see this thing that has taken place, which the
Lord has made known to us." 16 So they went
with haste and found Mary and Joseph, and
the child lying in the manger. 17 When they
saw this, they made known what had been
told them about this child; 18 and all who
heard it were amazed at what the shepherds
told them. 19 But Mary treasured all these

a Other ancient authorities read *has broken upon*
b Or *the Christ*
c Gk *army*
d Other ancient authorities read *peace, goodwill
among people*

one who will bring salvation; see Pss 92.10–11; 132.17–18. **76:** See 3.4. **80:** Compare 1.80 with 2.52. These words
cover a period of approximately thirty years (see 3.23). *In the wilderness,* see 3.4.

2.1–7: The birth of Jesus (Mt 1.18–25). **1:** General censuses of Roman citizens are known from 28 BCE, 8 BCE,
and 14 CE; but outside the New Testament this enrollment under Caesar *Augustus* is not attested. Caesar *Augustus* reigned 27 BCE–14 CE. His rule marked a time of peace, the "pax Augusta", which caused the populace to
hail him as lord and savior of the world. **2:** *Quirinius* was at this time legate or commissioner of *Augustus* in a war
against a rebellious tribe, the Homonadenses. As such he was a military governor of Syria, while civil administration was in the hands of Varus. It is possible that *Quirinius* was affiliated with Syria as a governmental authority on two different occasions, 6–4 BCE and 6–9 CE. *City of David called Bethlehem,* see 1 Sam 1–13. **7:** *Firstborn
son* indicates nothing about Mary's subsequent childbearing; the word is more a technical term in reference to
the child upon which God laid full claim (Num 3.11–13). *Bands of cloth* were normally used to bundle and provide
warmth and comfort for infants. *Manger,* a feeding trough for animals.

2.8–20: Annunciation to shepherds and their visit (cf. Mt 2.1–12). **8:** That the shepherds were *living in the
fields* indicates nothing about the season of Jesus' birth. **11:** Jesus is identified by three primary titles of Christian
belief, *Savior, Messiah,* and *Lord* (see Mt 1.21; 16.16; Jn 4.42; Acts 2.36; 5.31; Phil 2.11). The designation of the newborn Jesus as Lord is striking (see 1.43), for that word in Greek ("kyrios") is the precise term used consistently
throughout the LXX to translate the tetragrammaton, God's holy and personal name (Heb "YHWH"). **14:** The

words and pondered them in her heart. [20] The shepherds returned, glorifying and praising God for all they had heard and seen, as it had been told them.

[21] After eight days had passed, it was time to circumcise the child; and he was called Jesus, the name given by the angel before he was conceived in the womb.

[22] When the time came for their purification according to the law of Moses, they brought him up to Jerusalem to present him to the Lord [23] (as it is written in the law of the Lord, "Every firstborn male shall be designated as holy to the Lord"), [24] and they offered a sacrifice according to what is stated in the law of the Lord, "a pair of turtledoves or two young pigeons."

[25] Now there was a man in Jerusalem whose name was Simeon;[a] this man was righteous and devout, looking forward to the consolation of Israel, and the Holy Spirit rested on him. [26] It had been revealed to him by the Holy Spirit that he would not see death before he had seen the Lord's Messiah.[b] [27] Guided by the Spirit, Simeon[c] came into the temple; and when the parents brought in the child Jesus, to do for him what was customary under the law, [28] Simeon[d] took him in his arms and praised God, saying,

[29] "Master, now you are dismissing your
   servant[e] in peace,
   according to your word;
[30] for my eyes have seen your salvation,
   [31] which you have prepared in the
      presence of all peoples,
[32] a light for revelation to the Gentiles
   and for glory to your people Israel."

[33] And the child's father and mother were amazed at what was being said about him. [34] Then Simeon[a] blessed them and said to his mother Mary, "This child is destined for the falling and the rising of many in Israel, and to be a sign that will be opposed [35] so that the inner thoughts of many will be revealed— and a sword will pierce your own soul too."

[36] There was also a prophet, Anna[f] the daughter of Phanuel, of the tribe of Asher. She was of a great age, having lived with her husband seven years after her marriage, [37] then as a widow to the age of eighty-four. She never left the temple but worshiped there with fasting and prayer night and day. [38] At that moment she came, and began to praise God and to speak about the child[g] to all who were looking for the redemption of Jerusalem.

[39] When they had finished everything required by the law of the Lord, they returned to Galilee, to their own town of Nazareth. [40] The child grew and became strong, filled with wisdom; and the favor of God was upon him.

[41] Now every year his parents went to Jerusalem for the festival of the Passover. [42] And when he was twelve years old, they went up as usual for the festival. [43] When the festival was ended and they started to return, the boy Jesus stayed behind in Jerusalem, but his parents did not know it. [44] Assuming that he was in the group of travelers, they went a day's journey. Then they started to look for him among their

a Gk Symeon
b Or the Lord's Christ
c Gk In the Spirit, he
d Gk he
e Gk slave
f Gk Hanna
g Gk him

third hymn. 19: See 1.66; 2.51.

2.21–38: Jesus' circumcision and presentation. 21: See 1.59. 22–23: Ex 13.2,12,15; Lev 5.11; 12.8. The phrase *their purification* is ambiguous and likely refers to the parents, though there was no rite of purification for the father (or the newborn). Luke's interest in this ritual is to recognize the occasion of the parents' taking Jesus to the Temple. 25–38: *Simeon* and *Anna*, not otherwise known, acclaim Jesus as savior and redeemer. 29–32: The fourth hymn, whose opening words in Latin are "Nunc dimittis." 30–31: See 3.6. 32: See Isa 49.6; 46.13. 32: See Acts 2.21; 10.28,34–35; 22.21. 33: Luke calls Joseph the *father* of Jesus (notwithstanding 1.34–35) since he was Mary's husband and Jesus' legal father (cf. Mt 13.55; Lk 2.48; 3.23).

2.39–40: Jesus' childhood in Nazareth (Mt 2.22–23).

2.41–52: Young Jesus in the Temple. This story of Jesus' boyhood is unique to Luke among the canonical Gospels, though later legendary writings also show interest in this otherwise unknown period of Jesus' life.

relatives and friends. [45] When they did not find him, they returned to Jerusalem to search for him. [46] After three days they found him in the temple, sitting among the teachers, listening to them and asking them questions. [47] And all who heard him were amazed at his understanding and his answers. [48] When his parents[a] saw him they were astonished; and his mother said to him, "Child, why have you treated us like this? Look, your father and I have been searching for you in great anxiety." [49] He said to them, "Why were you searching for me? Did you not know that I must be in my Father's house?"[b] [50] But they did not understand what he said to them. [51] Then he went down with them and came to Nazareth, and was obedient to them. His mother treasured all these things in her heart.

[52] And Jesus increased in wisdom and in years,[c] and in divine and human favor.

3 In the fifteenth year of the reign of Emperor Tiberius, when Pontius Pilate was governor of Judea, and Herod was ruler[d] of Galilee, and his brother Philip ruler[d] of the region of Ituraea and Trachonitis, and Lysanias ruler[d] of Abilene, [2] during the high priesthood of Annas and Caiaphas, the word of God came to John son of Zechariah in the wilderness. [3] He went into all the region around the Jordan, proclaiming a baptism of repentance for the forgiveness of sins, [4] as it is written in the book of the words of the prophet Isaiah,

"The voice of one crying out in the
    wilderness:
'Prepare the way of the Lord,
    make his paths straight.
[5] Every valley shall be filled,
    and every mountain and hill shall be
        made low,
and the crooked shall be made straight,
    and the rough ways made smooth;
[6] and all flesh shall see the salvation of
        God.'"

[7] John said to the crowds that came out to be baptized by him, "You brood of vipers! Who warned you to flee from the wrath to come? [8] Bear fruits worthy of repentance. Do not begin to say to yourselves, 'We have Abraham as our ancestor'; for I tell you, God is able from these stones to raise up children to Abraham. [9] Even now the ax is lying at the root of the trees; every tree therefore that does not bear good fruit is cut down and thrown into the fire."

a Gk *they*
b Or *be about my Father's interests?*
c Or *in stature*
d Gk *tetrarch*

41: Ex 23.15; Deut 16.1–8. 49: *My Father's house* recognizes the special relationship between Jesus and God and contrasts with Mary's reference to Joseph as "your father" (v. 48). 51: See 2.19. 52: 1 Sam 2.26; Lk 1.80; 2.40.

3.1–4.13: Jesus' preparation for ministry (Mt 3.1–4.11; Mk 1.2–13).

3.1–6: The appearance of John the Baptist (Mt 3.1–6; Mk 1.2–6). 1: *Tiberius* Caesar succeeded Augustus in 14 CE and ruled until 37. Thus, depending on the manner of reckoning years, sometime between 26 and 29 CE is indicated. *Pontius Pilate,* a Roman governor, held authority in *Judea,* Samaria, and Idumea 26–36 CE; see 23.1, etc. The remainder of the kingdom of Herod the Great had been divided between his sons *Herod* Antipas who ruled Galilee and Perea (23.6–7) and Philip (see map on p. 1800). Initially another son, Herod Archelaus, had ruled Judea as ethnarch from 4 BCE, but he was deposed and banished for incompetence and replaced by a Roman official in 6 CE (see Mt 2.22). Lysanias was a Roman tetrarch of Abilenem ca. 25–30 CE. 2: *Annas* was high priest 6–15 CE when the Romans deposed him. He was followed by relatives; initially by his son, Eleazar; then by his son-in-law *Caiaphas* (18–36 CE), and thereafter by four more sons. Because Jewish custom was for the high priest to serve for life, even when out of office, Annas's influence and authority continued to be recognized by the population. 3: A summary statement of the shape and substance of John's ministry. Proclamation led to baptism, *a baptism of repentance,* a symbolic act of cleansing to indicate realignment with the will of God in forgiveness of the one baptized. 4–6: Isa 40.3–5. 6: *All flesh* refers to all humanity and emphasizes that God's salvation was universal in character; see 2.30–32; Acts 2.21.

3.7–9: John's call to repentance (Mt 3.7–10). 8: The assertion to have *Abraham as . . . ancestor* was a claim to privileged standing with God through natural birth (see Jn 8.33,39; Rom 2.28–29). 9: *Fire,* a symbol of judgment, often eschatological judgment (see 3.16; 16.24).

¹⁰ And the crowds asked him, "What then should we do?" ¹¹ In reply he said to them, "Whoever has two coats must share with anyone who has none; and whoever has food must do likewise." ¹² Even tax collectors came to be baptized, and they asked him, "Teacher, what should we do?" ¹³ He said to them, "Collect no more than the amount prescribed for you." ¹⁴ Soldiers also asked him, "And we, what should we do?" He said to them, "Do not extort money from anyone by threats or false accusation, and be satisfied with your wages."

¹⁵ As the people were filled with expectation, and all were questioning in their hearts concerning John, whether he might be the Messiah,ᵃ ¹⁶ John answered all of them by saying, "I baptize you with water; but one who is more powerful than I is coming; I am not worthy to untie the thong of his sandals. He will baptize you withᵇ the Holy Spirit and fire. ¹⁷ His winnowing fork is in his hand, to clear his threshing floor and to gather the wheat into his granary; but the chaff he will burn with unquenchable fire."

¹⁸ So, with many other exhortations, he proclaimed the good news to the people. ¹⁹ But Herod the ruler,ᶜ who had been rebuked by him because of Herodias, his brother's wife, and because of all the evil things that Herod had done, ²⁰ added to them all by shutting up John in prison.

²¹ Now when all the people were baptized, and when Jesus also had been baptized and was praying, the heaven was opened, ²² and the Holy Spirit descended upon him in bod-

ily form like a dove. And a voice came from heaven, "You are my Son, the Beloved;ᵈ with you I am well pleased."ᵉ

²³ Jesus was about thirty years old when he began his work. He was the son (as was thought) of Joseph son of Heli, ²⁴ son of Matthat, son of Levi, son of Melchi, son of Jannai, son of Joseph, ²⁵ son of Mattathias, son of Amos, son of Nahum, son of Esli, son of Naggai, ²⁶ son of Maath, son of Mattathias, son of Semein, son of Josech, son of Joda, ²⁷ son of Joanan, son of Rhesa, son of Zerubbabel, son of Shealtiel,ᶠ son of Neri, ²⁸ son of Melchi, son of Addi, son of Cosam, son of Elmadam, son of Er, ²⁹ son of Joshua, son of Eliezer, son of Jorim, son of Matthat, son of Levi, ³⁰ son of Simeon, son of Judah, son of Joseph, son of Jonam, son of Eliakim, ³¹ son of Melea, son of Menna, son of Mattatha, son of Nathan, son of David, ³² son of Jesse, son of Obed, son of Boaz, son of Sala,ᵍ son of Nahshon, ³³ son of Amminadab, son of Admin, son of Arni,ʰ son of Hezron, son of Perez, son of Judah, ³⁴ son of Jacob, son of Isaac,

a   Or the Christ
b   Or in
c   Gk tetrarch
d   Or my beloved Son
e   Other ancient authorities read You are my Son, today I have begotten you
f   Gk Salathiel
g   Other ancient authorities read Salmon
h   Other ancient authorities read Amminadab, son of Aram; others vary widely

3.10–14: John's directions to the crowd. 11: Two coats, lit., "two tunics," usually worn as undergarments. Sharing possessions is a theme of Luke and Acts; see 4.18; 6.30; 10.7,25–37; Acts 2.42–47; 4.32–37.

3.15–18: John's heralding of the messiah (Mt 3.11–12; Mk 1.7–8). 16: He will baptize you with the Holy Spirit and fire, a promise or prophecy fulfilled at Pentecost (Acts 2.1–4). 17: Winnowing fork, a tool used in threshing grain. 18: John's judgmental message about the coming of the Messiah is, nevertheless, characterized as good news: 4.17–21.

3.19–20: John's imprisonment by Herod. Herod Antipas had divorced the daughter of the Nabatean king in order to marry his niece, Herodias, who had been married to Antipas's brother, Herod Philip. In Luke, John's imprisonment is placed before the baptism of Jesus; cf. Mt 14.3–4; Mk 6.17–18.

3.21–22: The baptism of Jesus (Mt 3.13–17; Mk 1.9–11). 21: Prayer is a regular activity of Jesus and a prominent theme in Luke's portrait (5.16; 6.12; 9.18,28; 11.1; 22.32,41–46). 22: See Ps 2.7; Isa 42.1. The voice from heaven speaks again at the Transfiguration (9.35).

3.23–38: The genealogy of Jesus (Mt 1.1–17). Luke traces the lineage of Jesus back to Adam, the first human (Gen 5.1); linking Jesus' line with God's original creation shows Jesus' common humanity and establishes his credentials as the universal savior. 23–38: The genealogy traced through the line of Joseph includes the paragons David and Abraham as well as other notable figures. 23–27: The persons named from Heli to Zerubbabel are otherwise unknown. For the rest of the genealogy cf. Gen 5.3–32; 11.10–26; Ruth 4.18–22; 1 Chr 1.1–4,24–28; 2.1–15.

son of Abraham, son of Terah, son of Nahor, [35] son of Serug, son of Reu, son of Peleg, son of Eber, son of Shelah, [36] son of Cainan, son of Arphaxad, son of Shem, son of Noah, son of Lamech, [37] son of Methuselah, son of Enoch, son of Jared, son of Mahalaleel, son of Cainan, [38] son of Enos, son of Seth, son of Adam, son of God.

4 Jesus, full of the Holy Spirit, returned from the Jordan and was led by the Spirit in the wilderness, [2] where for forty days he was tempted by the devil. He ate nothing at all during those days, and when they were over, he was famished. [3] The devil said to him, "If you are the Son of God, command this stone to become a loaf of bread." [4] Jesus answered him, "It is written, 'One does not live by bread alone.'"

[5] Then the devil[a] led him up and showed him in an instant all the kingdoms of the world. [6] And the devil[a] said to him, "To you I will give their glory and all this authority; for it has been given over to me, and I give it to anyone I please. [7] If you, then, will worship me, it will all be yours." [8] Jesus answered him, "It is written,

'Worship the Lord your God,
    and serve only him.'"

[9] Then the devil[a] took him to Jerusalem, and placed him on the pinnacle of the temple, saying to him, "If you are the Son of God, throw yourself down from here, [10] for it is written,

'He will command his angels concerning
        you,
    to protect you,'

[11] and

'On their hands they will bear you up,
    so that you will not dash your foot
        against a stone.'"

[12] Jesus answered him, "It is said, 'Do not put the Lord your God to the test.'" [13] When the devil had finished every test, he departed from him until an opportune time.

[14] Then Jesus, filled with the power of the Spirit, returned to Galilee, and a report about him spread through all the surrounding country. [15] He began to teach in their synagogues and was praised by everyone.

[16] When he came to Nazareth, where he had been brought up, he went to the synagogue on the sabbath day, as was his custom. He stood up to read, [17] and the scroll of the prophet Isaiah was given to him. He unrolled the scroll and found the place where it was written:

[18] "The Spirit of the Lord is upon me,
    because he has anointed me
        to bring good news to the poor.
He has sent me to proclaim release to the
        captives
    and recovery of sight to the blind,
        to let the oppressed go free,
[19] to proclaim the year of the Lord's
        favor."

[20] And he rolled up the scroll, gave it back to the attendant, and sat down. The eyes of all in the synagogue were fixed on him. [21] Then he began to say to them, "Today this scripture has been fulfilled in your hearing." [22] All

---

[a] Gk *he*

4.1–13: The temptation of Jesus (Mt 4.1–11; Mk 1.12–13). Note the emphasis on the (Holy) Spirit. The order of the temptations differs from Matthew's, but the particular tests are the same. 2: The mention of *forty days* in relation to the stay in the "wilderness" recalls Israel's forty years of wandering in the wilderness after the Exodus (Deut 8.2; see also Deut 9.9; 1 Kings 19.8). 4: Deut 8.3. 8: Deut 6.13; 10.20. 10–11: Ps 91.11–12. 12: Deut 6.16. 13: *Until an opportune time*, see 22.3,28,53.

4.14–9.50: Jesus' ministry in Galilee (Mt 4.12–18.35; Mk 1.14–9.50).

4.14–15: The beginning of the Galilean ministry (Mt 4.12–17; Mk 1.14–15). 14: Luke mentions Jesus' fame repeatedly, see v. 37; 5.15; 7.17. 15: Synagogues, local places of Jewish worship and instruction; see 4.44.

4.16–30: Jesus in Nazareth (Mt 13.53–58; Mk 6.1–6). Luke has transposed this incident to make it a frontispiece at the outset of Jesus' ministry. The parallel account in Mark 6.1–6 follows earlier appearances and work in Galilee; statements in Luke's version of this incident seem out of sequence because Jesus has not yet engaged in the specific ministry to which he refers in this speech (v. 23). The details given here of synagogue worship are the earliest accounts of them. 17: *The scroll of . . . Isaiah was given to* Jesus by the attendant of the synagogue (v. 20). Scrolls were kept in a special place in the synagogue and were given to readers by the attendant. 18–19: Isa

spoke well of him and were amazed at the gracious words that came from his mouth. They said, "Is not this Joseph's son?" [23] He said to them, "Doubtless you will quote to me this proverb, 'Doctor, cure yourself!' And you will say, 'Do here also in your hometown the things that we have heard you did at Capernaum.'" [24] And he said, "Truly I tell you, no prophet is accepted in the prophet's hometown. [25] But the truth is, there were many widows in Israel in the time of Elijah, when the heaven was shut up three years and six months, and there was a severe famine over all the land; [26] yet Elijah was sent to none of them except to a widow at Zarephath in Sidon. [27] There were also many lepers[a] in Israel in the time of the prophet Elisha, and none of them was cleansed except Naaman the Syrian." [28] When they heard this, all in the synagogue were filled with rage. [29] They got up, drove him out of the town, and led him to the brow of the hill on which their town was built, so that they might hurl him off the cliff. [30] But he passed through the midst of them and went on his way.

[31] He went down to Capernaum, a city in Galilee, and was teaching them on the sabbath. [32] They were astounded at his teaching, because he spoke with authority. [33] In the synagogue there was a man who had the spirit of an unclean demon, and he cried out with a loud voice, [34] "Let us alone! What have you to do with us, Jesus of Nazareth? Have you come to destroy us? I know who you are, the Holy One of God." [35] But Jesus rebuked him, saying, "Be silent, and come out of him!" When the demon had thrown him down before them, he came out of him without having done him any harm. [36] They were all amazed and kept saying to one another, "What kind of utterance is this? For with authority and power he commands the unclean spirits, and out they come!" [37] And a report about him began to reach every place in the region.

[38] After leaving the synagogue he entered Simon's house. Now Simon's mother-in-law was suffering from a high fever, and they asked him about her. [39] Then he stood over her and rebuked the fever, and it left her. Immediately she got up and began to serve them.

[40] As the sun was setting, all those who had any who were sick with various kinds of diseases brought them to him; and he laid his hands on each of them and cured them. [41] Demons also came out of many, shouting, "You are the Son of God!" But he rebuked them and would not allow them to speak, because they knew that he was the Messiah.[b]

[42] At daybreak he departed and went into a deserted place. And the crowds were looking

---

a   The terms *leper* and *leprosy* can refer to several diseases
b   Or *the Christ*

61.1; 58.6; 61.2. **22:** The initial reaction to Jesus was strikingly positive. **24–27:** Traditions of the prophets (1 Kings 17.8–16; 2 Kings 5.1–14) illustrate that foreigners sometimes experienced God's aid when Israel did not. **28:** The hostile reaction comes in response to Jesus' references to Gentiles (vv. 24–27), not to his apparent messianic claims (v. 21).

4.31–37: Jesus in the synagogue at Capernaum (Mt 4.13; 7.28–29; Mk 1.21–28). Demons were thought of as nonmaterial existences of a personal kind, hostile to human welfare and rebellious against God. The Gospels reflect widespread dread of demons and a general sense of helplessness before demonic activity. Jesus is portrayed here and elsewhere (11.20–22) as one who can deliver persons from demonic oppression and from Satan himself (see 13.16). **31:** This incident is the first of five sabbath healings or exorcisms by Jesus (4.31,38; 6.6; 13.10; 14.1). **32:** Jesus produced astonishment; 2.48; 9.43. **34–36:** The *demon* recognized Jesus' true identity, whereas the people were simply amazed; see 4.41.

4.38–39: The healing of Simon Peter's mother-in-law (Mt 8.14–15; Mk 1.29–31). While not stated explicitly, this incident is another "sabbath healing" (see 4.31n.). Simon Peter is more fully introduced in 5.1–11; 6.13–14. **38–39:** *Simon* a Greek personal name meaning "flat-nosed," is used in the New Testament as an alternative for the Hebrew name "Simeon," which means "hearing."

4.40–41: Healings and exorcisms at sunset (Mt 8.16–17; Mk 1.32–34). With the sabbath ending at sundown, people began to present their problems and maladies to Jesus for attention and healing.

4.42–44: Departure and further preaching in Galilee (Mt 4.23; Mk 1.35–39). **44:** This is the only express men-

for him; and when they reached him, they wanted to prevent him from leaving them. [43] But he said to them, "I must proclaim the good news of the kingdom of God to the other cities also; for I was sent for this purpose." [44] So he continued proclaiming the message in the synagogues of Judea.[a]

5 Once while Jesus[b] was standing beside the lake of Gennesaret, and the crowd was pressing in on him to hear the word of God, [2] he saw two boats there at the shore of the lake; the fishermen had gone out of them and were washing their nets. [3] He got into one of the boats, the one belonging to Simon, and asked him to put out a little way from the shore. Then he sat down and taught the crowds from the boat. [4] When he had finished speaking, he said to Simon, "Put out into the deep water and let down your nets for a catch." [5] Simon answered, "Master, we have worked all night long but have caught nothing. Yet if you say so, I will let down the nets." [6] When they had done this, they caught so many fish that their nets were beginning to break. [7] So they signaled their partners in the other boat to come and help them. And they came and filled both boats, so that they began to sink. [8] But when Simon Peter saw it, he fell down at Jesus' knees, saying, "Go away from me, Lord, for I am a sinful man!" [9] For he and all who were with him were amazed at the catch of fish that they had taken; [10] and so also were James and John, sons of Zebedee, who were partners with Simon. Then Jesus said to Simon, "Do not be afraid; from now on you will be catching people." [11] When they had brought their boats to shore, they left everything and followed him.

[12] Once, when he was in one of the cities, there was a man covered with leprosy.[c] When he saw Jesus, he bowed with his face to the ground and begged him, "Lord, if you choose, you can make me clean." [13] Then Jesus[b] stretched out his hand, touched him, and said, "I do choose. Be made clean." Immediately the leprosy[c] left him. [14] And he ordered him to tell no one. "Go," he said, "and show yourself to the priest, and, as Moses commanded, make an offering for your cleansing, for a testimony to them." [15] But now more than ever the word about Jesus[d] spread abroad; many crowds would gather to hear him and to be cured of their diseases. [16] But he would withdraw to deserted places and pray.

[17] One day, while he was teaching, Pharisees and teachers of the law were sitting near by (they had come from every village of Galilee and Judea and from Jerusalem); and the power of the Lord was with him to heal.[e] [18] Just then some men came, carrying a paralyzed man on a bed. They were trying to bring him in and lay him before Jesus;[d] [19] but finding no way to bring him in because of the crowd, they went up on the roof and let him down with his bed

a   Other ancient authorities read *Galilee*
b   Gk *he*
c   The terms *leper* and *leprosy* can refer to several diseases
d   Gk *him*
e   Other ancient authorities read *was present to heal them*

tion outside the Fourth Gospel of Jesus' early Judean ministry (but compare the implication of Mt 23.37 and Lk 13.34). Here, however, Luke may simply employ *Judea* to refer to the broader Palestinian region as the land of the Jews.

5.1–11: The great catch of fish (Mt 13.1–3a; 4.18–22; Mk 4.1–2; 1.16–20). 1: *Lake of Gennesaret,* Sea of Galilee.

5.12–16: The healing of a leper (Mt 8.1–4; Mk 1.40–45). 12–16: The biblical descriptions of *leprosy* make clear that the term was a generic reference to skin ailments from psoriasis to true leprosy, as well as mold, mildew, and fungus. 14: Lev 13.2–3; 14.2–32. Jesus' touching this man countered the common religious assumption that such contact rendered a person unclean. The healing demonstrates the power of God in Jesus overcoming that which was deemed unclean.

5.17–26: Healing and forgiveness of sins (Mt 9.1–8; Mk 2.1–12). 17: The *Pharisees* were lay persons who were part of a religious movement (a sectarian group within Judaism) that was devoted to strict and faithful observance of the law of Moses. The concern of the Pharisees was with both the written form of the law and the interpretation of the law offered and preserved in oral tradition. *The law* is the law of Moses or the Torah. 19: *Through the tiles* is Luke's adjustment of Mark's story to present a tiled roof rather than the mud-plaster roof in which

through the tiles into the middle of the crowd[a] in front of Jesus. [20] When he saw their faith, he said, "Friend,[b] your sins are forgiven you." [21] Then the scribes and the Pharisees began to question, "Who is this who is speaking blasphemies? Who can forgive sins but God alone?" [22] When Jesus perceived their questionings, he answered them, "Why do you raise such questions in your hearts? [23] Which is easier, to say, 'Your sins are forgiven you,' or to say, 'Stand up and walk'? [24] But so that you may know that the Son of Man has authority on earth to forgive sins"—he said to the one who was paralyzed—"I say to you, stand up and take your bed and go to your home." [25] Immediately he stood up before them, took what he had been lying on, and went to his home, glorifying God. [26] Amazement seized all of them, and they glorified God and were filled with awe, saying, "We have seen strange things today."

[27] After this he went out and saw a tax collector named Levi, sitting at the tax booth; and he said to him, "Follow me." [28] And he got up, left everything, and followed him.

[29] Then Levi gave a great banquet for him in his house; and there was a large crowd of tax collectors and others sitting at the table[c] with them. [30] The Pharisees and their scribes were complaining to his disciples, saying, "Why do you eat and drink with tax collectors and sinners?" [31] Jesus answered, "Those who are well have no need of a physician, but those who are sick; [32] I have come to call not the righteous but sinners to repentance."

[33] Then they said to him, "John's disciples, like the disciples of the Pharisees, frequently fast and pray, but your disciples eat and drink." [34] Jesus said to them, "You cannot make wedding guests fast while the bridegroom is with them, can you? [35] The days will come when the bridegroom will be taken away from them, and then they will fast in those days." [36] He also told them a parable: "No one tears a piece from a new garment and sews it on an old garment; otherwise the new will be torn, and the piece from the new will not match the old. [37] And no one puts new wine into old wineskins; otherwise the new wine will burst the skins and will be spilled, and the skins will be destroyed. [38] But new wine must be put into fresh wineskins. [39] And no one after drinking old wine desires new wine, but says, 'The old is good.'"[d]

6 One sabbath[e] while Jesus[f] was going through the grainfields, his disciples plucked some heads of grain, rubbed them in their hands, and ate them. [2] But some of the Pharisees said, "Why are you doing what is not lawful[g] on the sabbath?" [3] Jesus answered,

a   Gk *into the midst*
b   Gk *Man*
c   Gk *reclining*
d   Other ancient authorities read *better*; others lack verse 39
e   Other ancient authorities read *On the second first sabbath*
f   Gk *he*
g   Other ancient authorities add *to do*

Mark's account says the people "dug" a hole through which to lower the paralytic. **20:** The connection here between forgiveness of sins and healing reflects an ancient belief that sickness resulted from sin (see Ex 34.7; Jn 9.2). **21:** *Scribes,* the group called "teachers of the law" at 5.17, were Jewish specialists in the law of Moses. Luke also refers to these persons as "lawyers," e.g., 7.30. **21:** "Blasphemy" was a capital offense; see Lev 24.14–16. **24:** *Son of Man,* Jesus' self-designation here and in other Gospel accounts is an ambiguous title that can be understood either to refer to Jesus as a human being among humans (e.g., Ps 8.4; Ezek 2.1) or to identify Jesus with the apocalyptic figure of Dan 7.13–14, who was often understood to be the coming messiah and deputy of God.

5.27–32: The call of Levi (Mt 9.9–13; Mk 2.13–17). **27:** Tax collectors worked directly or indirectly for the Roman overlords and were generally despised by the Jewish population. *Levi* is identified by some as Matthew (6.15; cf. Mt 10.3).

5.33–39: Debate about fasting (Mt 9.14–17; Mk 2.18–22). **34–35:** Jesus' words refer to him as the *bridegroom* and to days *when the bridegroom will be taken away from them* as the time after his death and resurrection. **36:** *Parable,* memorable word-pictures or stories that captured and communicated in sometimes cryptic form the essence of Jesus' message concerning God and God's kingdom. **39:** Found only in Luke, this saying is difficult to interpret. It may be ironic, indicating that contentment with *the old* prevents openness to the *new*.

6.1–11: Eating and healing on the sabbath (Mt 12.1–14; Mk 2.23–3.6). **2:** Harvesting violated the sabbath

"Have you not read what David did when he and his companions were hungry? [4] He entered the house of God and took and ate the bread of the Presence, which it is not lawful for any but the priests to eat, and gave some to his companions?" [5] Then he said to them, "The Son of Man is lord of the sabbath."

[6] On another sabbath he entered the synagogue and taught, and there was a man there whose right hand was withered. [7] The scribes and the Pharisees watched him to see whether he would cure on the sabbath, so that they might find an accusation against him. [8] Even though he knew what they were thinking, he said to the man who had the withered hand, "Come and stand here." He got up and stood there. [9] Then Jesus said to them, "I ask you, is it lawful to do good or to do harm on the sabbath, to save life or to destroy it?" [10] After looking around at all of them, he said to him, "Stretch out your hand." He did so, and his hand was restored. [11] But they were filled with fury and discussed with one another what they might do to Jesus.

[12] Now during those days he went out to the mountain to pray; and he spent the night in prayer to God. [13] And when day came, he called his disciples and chose twelve of them, whom he also named apostles: [14] Simon, whom he named Peter, and his brother Andrew, and James, and John, and Philip, and Bartholomew, [15] and Matthew, and Thomas, and James son of Alphaeus, and Simon, who was called the Zealot, [16] and Judas son of James, and Judas Iscariot, who became a traitor.

[17] He came down with them and stood on a level place, with a great crowd of his disciples and a great multitude of people from all Judea, Jerusalem, and the coast of Tyre and Sidon. [18] They had come to hear him and to be healed of their diseases; and those who were troubled with unclean spirits were cured. [19] And all in the crowd were trying to touch him, for power came out from him and healed all of them.

[20] Then he looked up at his disciples and said:

"Blessed are you who are poor,
    for yours is the kingdom of God.
[21] "Blessed are you who are hungry now,
    for you will be filled.
"Blessed are you who weep now,
    for you will laugh.
[22] "Blessed are you when people hate you, and when they exclude you, revile you, and defame you[a] on account of the Son of Man. [23] Rejoice in that day and leap for joy, for surely your reward is great in heaven; for that is what their ancestors did to the prophets.
[24] "But woe to you who are rich,
    for you have received your consolation.

---

[a] Gk cast out your name as evil

rest (Ex 34.21). **3–4:** Luke's version of this story does not name the priest as in Mk 2.23–26. **3:** 1 Sam 21.1–6. **4:** Lev 24.5–9. **5:** See 5.24n. **6:** See 4.31n. **11:** The Gk word "anioa" translated "fury" more exactly means "lack of understanding."

6.12–16: Jesus' selection of the twelve (Mt 10.1–4; Mk 3.13–19a). Other lists of the twelve occur at Mt 10.2–4; Mk 3.16–19; Acts 1.13; while there is variation, Peter is always named first and Judas Iscariot is always named last. **13:** "The twelve" (8.1; Acts 6.2; etc.) are a recognized and remembered group in early Christianity, and Luke designates the *twelve* to be *apostles* in such a way that the two titles are strictly equated. "Apostle" (from the Gk verb "apostellein," "to send") occurs in the New Testament to designate a Christian who was commissioned to preach the gospel, essentially as a missionary. **14:** The "name" *Peter* is a nickname, meaning "rock." **15:** Zealots were a distinct faction of revolutionaries in the Jewish war with Rome of 66–70 CE, but whether this designation indicates that this *Simon* was zealous in a political fashion is debatable since it is unlikely that a Zealot party existed during Jesus' life. **16:** *Iscariot* is a peculiar term that probably means "the man from Kerioth" (see Josh 15.25); if so, then this Judas was the only Judean among the twelve.

6.17–49: The Sermon on the Plain (Mt 5–7).

6.17–19: The occasion of the preaching (Mt 4.24–5.2; Mk 3.7–13a). **18:** *Unclean spirits* designates "spirits" that are contrary to God. "Clean" and "unclean" were religious terms, not strictly descriptions of sanitary conditions, and can be understood as categories of "holiness" or "sanctity." **19:** Luke emphasizes both that the throngs pressed on Jesus and that Jesus was a source of miraculous power.

6.20–23: The beatitudes (Mt 5.3–12). The focus is on economic and social conditions, not spiritual states.

²⁵ "Woe to you who are full now,
   for you will be hungry.
"Woe to you who are laughing now,
   for you will mourn and weep.

²⁶ "Woe to you when all speak well of you, for that is what their ancestors did to the false prophets.

²⁷ "But I say to you that listen, Love your enemies, do good to those who hate you, ²⁸ bless those who curse you, pray for those who abuse you. ²⁹ If anyone strikes you on the cheek, offer the other also; and from anyone who takes away your coat do not withhold even your shirt. ³⁰ Give to everyone who begs from you; and if anyone takes away your goods, do not ask for them again. ³¹ Do to others as you would have them do to you.

³² "If you love those who love you, what credit is that to you? For even sinners love those who love them. ³³ If you do good to those who do good to you, what credit is that to you? For even sinners do the same. ³⁴ If you lend to those from whom you hope to receive, what credit is that to you? Even sinners lend to sinners, to receive as much again. ³⁵ But love your enemies, do good, and lend, expecting nothing in return.ᵃ Your reward will be great, and you will be children of the Most High; for he is kind to the ungrateful and the wicked. ³⁶ Be merciful, just as your Father is merciful.

³⁷ "Do not judge, and you will not be judged; do not condemn, and you will not be condemned. Forgive, and you will be forgiven; ³⁸ give, and it will be given to you. A good measure, pressed down, shaken together, running over, will be put into your lap; for the measure you give will be the measure you get back."

³⁹ He also told them a parable: "Can a blind person guide a blind person? Will not both fall into a pit? ⁴⁰ A disciple is not above the teacher, but everyone who is fully qualified will be like the teacher. ⁴¹ Why do you see the speck in your neighbor'sᵇ eye, but do not notice the log in your own eye? ⁴² Or how can you say to your neighbor,ᶜ 'Friend,ᶜ let me take out the speck in your eye,' when you yourself do not see the log in your own eye? You hypocrite, first take the log out of your own eye, and then you will see clearly to take the speck out of your neighbor'sᵇ eye.

⁴³ "No good tree bears bad fruit, nor again does a bad tree bear good fruit; ⁴⁴ for each tree is known by its own fruit. Figs are not gathered from thorns, nor are grapes picked from a bramble bush. ⁴⁵ The good person out of the good treasure of the heart produces good, and the evil person out of evil treasure produces evil; for it is out of the abundance of the heart that the mouth speaks.

⁴⁶ "Why do you call me 'Lord, Lord,' and do not do what I tell you? ⁴⁷ I will show you what someone is like who comes to me, hears my words, and acts on them. ⁴⁸ That one is like a man building a house, who dug deeply and laid the foundation on rock; when a flood arose, the river burst against that house but could not shake it, because it had been well built.ᵈ ⁴⁹ But the one who hears and does not act is like a man who built a house on the

ᵃ Other ancient authorities read *despairing of no one*
ᵇ Gk *brother's*
ᶜ Gk *brother*
ᵈ Other ancient authorities read *founded upon the rock*

6.24–26: The woes. These verses provide a point-by-point antithesis to the previous statements of blessing in vv. 20–23. Again, actual circumstances are the point of Jesus' statements. In Jesus' declarations of blessings and woes, the earthly status of those addressed will be reversed in the divinely determined future.

6.27–36: The love of enemies (Mt 5.38–48; 7.12). Jesus demands love and forbids spite or retaliation. **28:** In Luke, Jesus gives an example of this on the cross in 23.34, if that verse is authentic. **31:** Luke's version of the "Golden Rule," see Mt 7.12. **34–35:** For Israelite laws concerning loans, see Ex 22.25; Lev 25.36–37; Deut 23.19–20. **36:** Cf. Mt 5.48; God's own actions and character provide the standard.

6.37–42: On judging others (Mt 7.1–5; 12.36–37; 15.14; Mk 4.24–25). **41–42:** The form of this teaching is hyperbole.

6.43–45: The sources of good and evil (Mt 7.15–20; 12.33–35). Cf. Jas 3.11–12. **45:** *Heart,* for the ancients the heart was the body's mental and spiritual center.

6.46–49: The wise and the foolish builders (Mt 7.21–27). Cf. Jas 1.22–25.

ground without a foundation. When the river burst against it, immediately it fell, and great was the ruin of that house."

7 After Jesus[a] had finished all his sayings in the hearing of the people, he entered Capernaum. [2] A centurion there had a slave whom he valued highly, and who was ill and close to death. [3] When he heard about Jesus, he sent some Jewish elders to him, asking him to come and heal his slave. [4] When they came to Jesus, they appealed to him earnestly, saying, "He is worthy of having you do this for him, [5] for he loves our people, and it is he who built our synagogue for us." [6] And Jesus went with them, but when he was not far from the house, the centurion sent friends to say to him, "Lord, do not trouble yourself, for I am not worthy to have you come under my roof; [7] therefore I did not presume to come to you. But only speak the word, and let my servant be healed. [8] For I also am a man set under authority, with soldiers under me; and I say to one, 'Go,' and he goes, and to another, 'Come,' and he comes, and to my slave, 'Do this,' and the slave does it." [9] When Jesus heard this he was amazed at him, and turning to the crowd that followed him, he said, "I tell you, not even in Israel have I found such faith." [10] When those who had been sent returned to the house, they found the slave in good health.

[11] Soon afterwards[b] he went to a town called Nain, and his disciples and a large crowd went with him. [12] As he approached the gate of the town, a man who had died was being carried out. He was his mother's only son, and she was a widow; and with her was a large crowd from the town. [13] When the Lord saw her, he had compassion for her and said to her, "Do not weep." [14] Then he came forward and touched the bier, and the bearers stood still. And he said, "Young man, I say to you, rise!" [15] The dead man sat up and began to speak, and Jesus[a] gave him to his mother. [16] Fear seized all of them; and they glorified God, saying, "A great prophet has risen among us!" and "God has looked favorably on his people!" [17] This word about him spread throughout Judea and all the surrounding country.

[18] The disciples of John reported all these things to him. So John summoned two of his disciples [19] and sent them to the Lord to ask, "Are you the one who is to come, or are we to wait for another?" [20] When the men had come to him, they said, "John the Baptist has sent us to you to ask, 'Are you the one who is to come, or are we to wait for another?'" [21] Jesus[c] had just then cured many people of diseases, plagues, and evil spirits, and had given sight to many who were blind. [22] And he answered them, "Go and tell John what you have seen and heard: the blind receive their sight, the lame walk, the lepers[d] are cleansed, the deaf hear, the dead are raised, the poor have good news brought to them. [23] And blessed is anyone who takes no offense at me."

[a] Gk *he*

[b] Other ancient authorities read *Next day*

[c] Gk *He*

[d] The terms *leper* and *leprosy* can refer to several diseases

7.1–10: The centurion's slave (Mt 8.5–13). This story parallels the account of Peter's conversion of the Gentile centurion Cornelius, who was also generous to the Jews; see Acts 10.2,34–35. **2:** *Centurion,* an officer in charge of a company of 100 soldiers. Clearly a Gentile, this particular centurion was either an employee of Herod Antipas, a member of the Roman police force, or an official attached to the customs service. **3:** *Elders,* leaders in the Jewish community. **6:** According to Acts 10.28, the house of a Gentile was considered unclean, and entering such a home defiled a Jew (see also *m. Oholot* 18.7). **9:** Though Luke lacks the climactic utterance of Mt 8.13, his intent is the same: The faith of a Gentile is acceptable to Jesus (4.27; 5.32).

7.11–17: The widow's son at Nain. Cf. 1 Kings 17.17–24; 2 Kings 4.32–37; see Lk 4.25–26. **11:** *Nain,* about 37 km (23 mi) southwest of Capernaum. **12:** Cemeteries were usually located outside a city or town. This description of the widow implies that she is utterly destitute with the death of her son. **16:** Apparently the similarity of Jesus' action to that of Elijah in raising the only son of a widow of Zarephath (1 Kings 17) elicits the reaction of the crowd. **17:** See 4.42–44n.

7.18–35: Jesus and John the Baptist (Mt 11.2–19). **18:** *John* the Baptist was at this time in prison (see 2.9) at Machaerus, east of the Dead Sea. **19:** *Lord,* Luke's own title for Jesus. *The one who is to come,* the messiah.

[24] When John's messengers had gone, Jesus[a] began to speak to the crowds about John:[b] "What did you go out into the wilderness to look at? A reed shaken by the wind? [25] What then did you go out to see? Someone[c] dressed in soft robes? Look, those who put on fine clothing and live in luxury are in royal palaces. [26] What then did you go out to see? A prophet? Yes, I tell you, and more than a prophet. [27] This is the one about whom it is written,

'See, I am sending my messenger ahead of you,

who will prepare your way before you.'

[28] I tell you, among those born of women no one is greater than John; yet the least in the kingdom of God is greater than he." [29] (And all the people who heard this, including the tax collectors, acknowledged the justice of God,[d] because they had been baptized with John's baptism. [30] But by refusing to be baptized by him, the Pharisees and the lawyers rejected God's purpose for themselves.)

[31] "To what then will I compare the people of this generation, and what are they like? [32] They are like children sitting in the marketplace and calling to one another,

'We played the flute for you, and you did not dance;

we wailed, and you did not weep.'

[33] For John the Baptist has come eating no bread and drinking no wine, and you say, 'He has a demon'; [34] the Son of Man has come eating and drinking, and you say, 'Look, a glutton and a drunkard, a friend of tax collectors and sinners!' [35] Nevertheless, wisdom is vindicated by all her children."

[36] One of the Pharisees asked Jesus[b] to eat with him, and he went into the Phari-see's house and took his place at the table. [37] And a woman in the city, who was a sinner, having learned that he was eating in the Pharisee's house, brought an alabaster jar of ointment. [38] She stood behind him at his feet, weeping, and began to bathe his feet with her tears and to dry them with her hair. Then she continued kissing his feet and anointing them with the ointment. [39] Now when the Pharisee who had invited him saw it, he said to himself, "If this man were a prophet, he would have known who and what kind of woman this is who is touching him—that she is a sinner." [40] Jesus spoke up and said to him, "Simon, I have something to say to you." "Teacher," he replied, "speak." [41] "A certain creditor had two debtors; one owed five hundred denarii,[e] and the other fifty. [42] When they could not pay, he canceled the debts for both of them. Now which of them will love him more?" [43] Simon answered, "I suppose the one for whom he canceled the greater debt." And Jesus[a] said to him, "You have judged rightly." [44] Then turning toward the woman, he said to Simon, "Do you see this woman? I entered your house; you gave me no water for my feet, but she has bathed my feet with her tears and dried them with her hair. [45] You gave me no kiss, but from the time I came in she has not stopped kissing my feet. [46] You did not anoint my head with oil, but she has anointed my feet with oint-

a   Gk he
b   Gk him
c   Or Why then did you go out? To see someone
d   Or praised God
e   The denarius was the usual day's wage for a laborer

22: This verse contains phrases from Isa 29.18; 42.18; 26.19; see also Isa 35.5–6; 61.1; Lk 4.18–19. 24–30: Jesus' statements concerning John indicate the nature of the relationship between them. John is Jesus' precursor, the messenger mentioned in Mal 3.1 and identified in Mal 3.23 as Elijah. John, then, is an Elijah-like figure, not Elijah reincarnated. 27: Ex 23.20; Mal 3.1. 28: A pivotal point arises with the ministries of John and Jesus. 30: *The Pharisees and the lawyers* are specific, not simply all, members of their classes. 33: *Demon* possession is offered as the explanation of unconventional behavior or attitudes that were deemed unacceptable or inappropriate. 35: The personification of "Wisdom" is a way to speak of God and God's purposes; thus, Wisdom's *children* are those who do God's will.

7.36–50: Simon the Pharisee, Jesus, and the woman with the ointment (Mt 26.6–13; Mk 14.3–9; Jn 12.1–8). 37: Houses seem to have been open to intrusion of this kind (cf. Mk 1.33; 2.2). The story seems to presuppose a previous encounter between Jesus and the woman, a story not told in this Gospel. 38: Jesus reclined at the banquet table, stretching out his feet on a couch. The motivation for the woman's anointing Jesus' feet rather than

ment. [47] Therefore, I tell you, her sins, which were many, have been forgiven; hence she has shown great love. But the one to whom little is forgiven, loves little." [48] Then he said to her, "Your sins are forgiven." [49] But those who were at the table with him began to say among themselves, "Who is this who even forgives sins?" [50] And he said to the woman, "Your faith has saved you; go in peace."

[8] Soon afterwards he went on through cities and villages, proclaiming and bringing the good news of the kingdom of God. The twelve were with him, [2] as well as some women who had been cured of evil spirits and infirmities: Mary, called Magdalene, from whom seven demons had gone out, [3] and Joanna, the wife of Herod's steward Chuza, and Susanna, and many others, who provided for them[a] out of their resources.

[4] When a great crowd gathered and people from town after town came to him, he said in a parable: [5] "A sower went out to sow his seed; and as he sowed, some fell on the path and was trampled on, and the birds of the air ate it up. [6] Some fell on the rock; and as it grew up, it withered for lack of moisture. [7] Some fell among thorns, and the thorns grew with it and choked it. [8] Some fell into good soil, and when it grew, it produced a hundredfold." As he said this, he called out, "Let anyone with ears to hear listen!"

[9] Then his disciples asked him what this parable meant. [10] He said, "To you it has been given to know the secrets[b] of the kingdom of God; but to others I speak[c] in parables, so that

'looking they may not perceive,
and listening they may not understand.'

[11] "Now the parable is this: The seed is the word of God. [12] The ones on the path are those who have heard; then the devil comes and takes away the word from their hearts, so that they may not believe and be saved. [13] The ones on the rock are those who, when they hear the word, receive it with joy. But these have no root; they believe only for a while and in a time of testing fall away. [14] As for what fell among the thorns, these are the ones who hear; but as they go on their way, they are choked by the cares and riches and pleasures of life, and their fruit does not mature. [15] But as for that in the good soil, these are the ones who, when they hear the word, hold it fast in an honest and good heart, and bear fruit with patient endurance.

[16] "No one after lighting a lamp hides it under a jar, or puts it under a bed, but puts it

a   Other ancient authorities read *him*
b   Or *mysteries*
c   Gk lacks *I speak*

his head, which was the normal action, is uncertain. 47: *Hence she has shown great love,* her great love proving that her many sins had been forgiven. Cf. v. 48; 5.20. 50: Cf. 8.48; 17.19; 18.42. The story combines the ideas of faith, salvation, forgiveness, and peace.

8.1–3: Jesus' tour and the ministering women. These verses recall the itinerant character of Jesus' preaching, teaching, and healing. His entourage included the unusual combination of male and female followers. Given ancient Palestinian attitudes toward women, this association of these Galilean women with Jesus' ministry is remarkable, as is the mixture of the sexes among the followers. Many of those persons mentioned here later follow Jesus to Jerusalem and witness his arrest, crucifixion, death, burial, empty tomb, and resurrection appearances. See 23.49. 2: *Mary, called Magdalene,* apparently came from Magdala on the western coast of the Sea of Galilee. There is no evidence to identify her with the woman in 7.36–50. 3: Herod's *steward* was probably a domestic administrator. *Others,* i.e., other women.

8.4–8: Parable of the sower (Mt 13.1–9; Mk 4.1–9). 4–8: The parable invites allegorization, which follows in 8.11–15.

8.9–10: Jesus' explanation of parables (Mt 13.10–17; Mk 4.1–10). 10: Paraphrase of Isa 6.9–10. See Mk 4.11; Mt 13.11; Jer 5.21; Ezek 12.2. The meaning of the statement is enigmatic and implies that parables deliberately created obscurity while actually revealing a message.

8.11–15: Interpretation of the parable of the sower (Mt 13.18–23; Mk 4.13–20). 15: The words *honest and good,* here spoken of the heart (cf. Mk 7.21–23), echo the classical Greek description of the true gentleman. *Heart,* see 6.45n.

8.16–18: On obedient listening (Mt 5.15; 10.26; 13.12; Mk 4.21–25).

on a lampstand, so that those who enter may see the light. [17] For nothing is hidden that will not be disclosed, nor is anything secret that will not become known and come to light. [18] Then pay attention to how you listen; for to those who have, more will be given; and from those who do not have, even what they seem to have will be taken away."

[19] Then his mother and his brothers came to him, but they could not reach him because of the crowd. [20] And he was told, "Your mother and your brothers are standing outside, wanting to see you." [21] But he said to them, "My mother and my brothers are those who hear the word of God and do it."

[22] One day he got into a boat with his disciples, and he said to them, "Let us go across to the other side of the lake." So they put out, [23] and while they were sailing he fell asleep. A windstorm swept down on the lake, and the boat was filling with water, and they were in danger. [24] They went to him and woke him up, shouting, "Master, Master, we are perishing!" And he woke up and rebuked the wind and the raging waves; they ceased, and there was a calm. [25] He said to them, "Where is your faith?" They were afraid and amazed, and said to one another, "Who then is this, that he commands even the winds and the water, and they obey him?"

[26] Then they arrived at the country of the Gerasenes,[a] which is opposite Galilee. [27] As he stepped out on land, a man of the city who had demons met him. For a long time he had worn[b] no clothes, and he did not live in a house but in the tombs. [28] When he saw Jesus, he fell down before him and shouted at the top of his voice, "What have you to do with me, Jesus, Son of the Most High God? I beg you, do not torment me"— [29] for Jesus[c] had commanded the unclean spirit to come out of the man. (For many times it had seized him; he was kept under guard and bound with chains and shackles, but he would break the bonds and be driven by the demon into the wilds.) [30] Jesus then asked him, "What is your name?" He said, "Legion"; for many demons had entered him. [31] They begged him not to order them to go back into the abyss.

[32] Now there on the hillside a large herd of swine was feeding; and the demons[d] begged Jesus[e] to let them enter these. So he gave them permission. [33] Then the demons came

a Other ancient authorities read *Gadarenes*; others, *Gergesenes*

b Other ancient authorities read *a man of the city who had had demons for a long time met him. He wore*

c Gk *he*

d Gk *they*

e Gk *him*

8.19–21: Jesus' true relatives (Mt 12.46–50; Mk 3.31–35). **19:** *Brothers,* four names are given in Mk 6.3, and there is also a mention of sisters. A variety of explanations come from the early church, usually arguing that they were sons of Joseph by a previous marriage, or that they were cousins, or that they were the natural children of Joseph and Mary. **21:** Luke seems to soften Mark's version of Jesus' reply, not reporting items such as Mk 3.20–21,33, so that the natural family of Jesus is not rejected as Jesus highlights the importance of obedience to God as the essential criterion for intimacy and mutual concern among Jesus' followers.

8.22–25: Winds and water obey (Mt 8.23–27; Mk 4.35–41). Power over the elements is a divine capacity often celebrated in the Psalms and other texts (see Ps 107.28–30).

8.26–39: The Gerasene demoniac (Mt 8.28–34; Mk 5.1–20). **26:** *Gerasenes,* the territory of the city of Gerasa (modern Jerash) was in central Transjordan; its population was largely non-Jewish. Mt 8.28 situates this event in Gadara, southeast of the Sea of Galilee, a setting that fits the narrative somewhat better. **28:** The demon-possessed man recognized Jesus' true identity. **30:** The inquiry after the name of the demon-possessed man probably reflects the ancient idea that knowledge of the name of a supernatural power gave one an advantage over it (see, e.g., Gen 32.29). *Legion,* the technical term for a division of the Roman army, usually consisting of about five thousand troops; thus the name suggests a horde of demons (see 11.24–26). **31:** *Abyss,* a place of confinement for demonic forces which, though hostile to God, are ultimately under his control (Rev 9.1–11; 11.7; 17.8; 20.1–3). The words attribute a judicial authority to Jesus (as do Mt 7.21–23; 11.20–24). **32:** *Swine,* Jews were prohibited from eating pork (Lev 11.7; Deut 14.8), but the pigs were raised for the large Gentile population that lived in sections of Palestine. Contrast Jesus' instructions to "declare how much God has done for you" with the man's action of "proclaiming throughout the city how much Jesus has done for him."

out of the man and entered the swine, and the herd rushed down the steep bank into the lake and was drowned.

[34] When the swineherds saw what had happened, they ran off and told it in the city and in the country. [35] Then people came out to see what had happened, and when they came to Jesus, they found the man from whom the demons had gone sitting at the feet of Jesus, clothed and in his right mind. And they were afraid. [36] Those who had seen it told them how the one who had been possessed by demons had been healed. [37] Then all the people of the surrounding country of the Gerasenes[a] asked Jesus[b] to leave them; for they were seized with great fear. So he got into the boat and returned. [38] The man from whom the demons had gone begged that he might be with him; but Jesus[c] sent him away, saying, [39] "Return to your home, and declare how much God has done for you." So he went away, proclaiming throughout the city how much Jesus had done for him.

[40] Now when Jesus returned, the crowd welcomed him, for they were all waiting for him. [41] Just then there came a man named Jairus, a leader of the synagogue. He fell at Jesus' feet and begged him to come to his house, [42] for he had an only daughter, about twelve years old, who was dying.

As he went, the crowds pressed in on him. [43] Now there was a woman who had been suffering from hemorrhages for twelve years; and though she had spent all she had on physicians,[d] no one could cure her. [44] She came up behind him and touched the fringe of his clothes, and immediately her hemorrhage stopped. [45] Then Jesus asked, "Who touched me?" When all denied it, Peter[e] said, "Master, the crowds surround you and press in on you." [46] But Jesus said, "Someone touched me; for I noticed that power had gone out from me." [47] When the woman saw that she could not remain hidden, she came

trembling; and falling down before him, she declared in the presence of all the people why she had touched him, and how she had been immediately healed. [48] He said to her, "Daughter, your faith has made you well; go in peace."

[49] While he was still speaking, someone came from the leader's house to say, "Your daughter is dead; do not trouble the teacher any longer." [50] When Jesus heard this, he replied, "Do not fear. Only believe, and she will be saved." [51] When he came to the house, he did not allow anyone to enter with him, except Peter, John, and James, and the child's father and mother. [52] They were all weeping and wailing for her; but he said, "Do not weep; for she is not dead but sleeping." [53] And they laughed at him, knowing that she was dead. [54] But he took her by the hand and called out, "Child, get up!" [55] Her spirit returned, and she got up at once. Then he directed them to give her something to eat. [56] Her parents were astounded; but he ordered them to tell no one what had happened.

9

Then Jesus[c] called the twelve together and gave them power and authority over all demons and to cure diseases, [2] and he sent them out to proclaim the kingdom of God and to heal. [3] He said to them, "Take nothing for your journey, no staff, nor bag, nor bread, nor money—not even an extra tunic. [4] Whatever house you enter, stay there, and leave from there. [5] Wherever they do not welcome you, as you are leaving that town shake

a Other ancient authorities read *Gadarenes*; others, *Gergesenes*

b Gk *him*

c Gk *he*

d Other ancient authorities lack *and though she had spent all she had on physicians*

e Other ancient authorities add *and those who were with him*

8.40–56: Jairus's daughter and the hemorrhaging woman (Mt 9.18–26; Mk 5.21–43). **41:** *Leader of the synagogue,* one who held responsibility for overseeing and arranging the worship and life of the congregation. **42:** Parallel elements in the two stories incorporate them into a larger whole—e.g., *daughter,* 8.42 and 48; *twelve years,* 8.42 and 43. **43:** Cf. Lev 15.25–30. Since the exact nature of this issue of blood is not specified, precise diagnoses are speculative. Cf. 7.50. **55:** Cf. 1 Kings 17.22.

9.1–6: Commissioning the twelve (Mt 10.1–14; Mk 6.6b–13). The sharing of power by Jesus with the disciples indicates their continuation and extension of his ministry as seen in the preceding stories. **3–4:** These instructions contrast with the practices of Cynic philosophers. **3:** The command to *take nothing for [the] journey* forces

the dust off your feet as a testimony against them." [6] They departed and went through the villages, bringing the good news and curing diseases everywhere.

[7] Now Herod the ruler[a] heard about all that had taken place, and he was perplexed, because it was said by some that John had been raised from the dead, [8] by some that Elijah had appeared, and by others that one of the ancient prophets had arisen. [9] Herod said, "John I beheaded; but who is this about whom I hear such things?" And he tried to see him.

[10] On their return the apostles told Jesus[b] all they had done. He took them with him and withdrew privately to a city called Bethsaida. [11] When the crowds found out about it, they followed him; and he welcomed them, and spoke to them about the kingdom of God, and healed those who needed to be cured.

[12] The day was drawing to a close, and the twelve came to him and said, "Send the crowd away, so that they may go into the surrounding villages and countryside, to lodge and get provisions; for we are here in a deserted place." [13] But he said to them, "You give them something to eat." They said, "We have no more than five loaves and two fish— unless we are to go and buy food for all these people." [14] For there were about five thousand men. And he said to his disciples, "Make them sit down in groups of about fifty each." [15] They did so and made them all sit down. [16] And taking the five loaves and the two fish, he looked up to heaven, and blessed and broke them, and gave them to the disciples to set before the crowd. [17] And all ate and were filled. What was left over was gathered up, twelve baskets of broken pieces.

[18] Once when Jesus[c] was praying alone, with only the disciples near him, he asked them, "Who do the crowds say that I am?" [19] They answered, "John the Baptist; but others, Elijah; and still others, that one of the ancient prophets has arisen." [20] He said to them, "But who do you say that I am?" Peter answered, "The Messiah[d] of God."

[21] He sternly ordered and commanded them not to tell anyone, [22] saying, "The Son of Man must undergo great suffering, and be rejected by the elders, chief priests, and scribes, and be killed, and on the third day be raised."

[23] Then he said to them all, "If any want to become my followers, let them deny themselves and take up their cross daily and follow me. [24] For those who want to save

a   Gk *tetrarch*
b   Gk *him*
c   Gk *he*
d   Or *The Christ*

the twelve to rely completely on God for their ministry. 5: The act of shaking off dust was a graphic demonstration of renunciation of further responsibility for those who did not welcome the twelve; cf. 10.10–12.

9.7–9: Herod's curiosity about Jesus (Mt 14.1–2; Mk 6.14–16). *Herod* Antipas, son of Herod the Great; see 3.1n. Cf. 9.18–19. 9: *John I beheaded*, see Mk 6.17–29.

9.10–11: The apostles' return and the crowds' following Jesus (Mt 14.12–14; Mk 6.30–34). 10: *Bethsaida*, located just north of the Sea of Galilee.

9.12–17: Feeding of the five thousand (Mt 14.15–21; Mk 6.35–44; Jn 6.5–14). The one story from the account of Jesus' ministry that occurs in all four canonical Gospels. 14: *Five thousand men*, not counting any women and children. 16: The language of this sentence anticipates the account of the Last Supper in 22.17–20.

9.18–20: Peter's confession (Mt 16.13–19; Mk 8.27–29). 19: The answers to Jesus' question illustrate the variety of expectations (some messianic) among Jews of Jesus' day. *The Messiah of God,* translates Gk "ho christos tou theou," lit., "God's anointed one," a title that typically named a royal Davidic leader who would reconstitute the former political glory of Israel for the people and the nation.

9.21–22: Jesus' command to silence and first prediction of his death (Mt 16.20–21; Mk 8.30–31). Jesus' forceful direction to silence probably reflects his attempt to prevent misunderstandings of his "messianic" work. In turn, Luke's version of this first prediction does not include the attempt of Peter to redirect Jesus' thinking and commitments, so that Peter's previous confession (9.20) maintains more force in this version of the story than in Mark's account, in which Jesus sharply rebukes him (Mk 8.32–33).

9.23–27: The requirements of discipleship (Mt 16.24–28; Mk 8.34–9.1). *Take up their cross daily and follow me,* the Greek is not cast in the plural (*any . . . their*) but in the singular (lit., "anyone . . . his"), so that the challenge

their life will lose it, and those who lose their life for my sake will save it. [25] What does it profit them if they gain the whole world, but lose or forfeit themselves? [26] Those who are ashamed of me and of my words, of them the Son of Man will be ashamed when he comes in his glory and the glory of the Father and of the holy angels. [27] But truly I tell you, there are some standing here who will not taste death before they see the kingdom of God."

[28] Now about eight days after these sayings Jesus[a] took with him Peter and John and James, and went up on the mountain to pray. [29] And while he was praying, the appearance of his face changed, and his clothes became dazzling white. [30] Suddenly they saw two men, Moses and Elijah, talking to him. [31] They appeared in glory and were speaking of his departure, which he was about to accomplish at Jerusalem. [32] Now Peter and his companions were weighed down with sleep; but since they had stayed awake,[b] they saw his glory and the two men who stood with him. [33] Just as they were leaving him, Peter said to Jesus, "Master, it is good for us to be here; let us make three dwellings,[c] one for you, one for Moses, and one for Elijah"—not knowing what he said. [34] While he was saying this, a cloud came and overshadowed them; and they were terrified as they entered the cloud. [35] Then from the cloud came a voice that said, "This is my Son, my Chosen;[d] listen to him!" [36] When the voice had spoken, Jesus

was found alone. And they kept silent and in those days told no one any of the things they had seen.

[37] On the next day, when they had come down from the mountain, a great crowd met him. [38] Just then a man from the crowd shouted, "Teacher, I beg you to look at my son; he is my only child. [39] Suddenly a spirit seizes him, and all at once he[e] shrieks. It convulses him until he foams at the mouth; it mauls him and will scarcely leave him. [40] I begged your disciples to cast it out, but they could not." [41] Jesus answered, "You faithless and perverse generation, how much longer must I be with you and bear with you? Bring your son here." [42] While he was coming, the demon dashed him to the ground in convulsions. But Jesus rebuked the unclean spirit, healed the boy, and gave him back to his father. [43] And all were astounded at the greatness of God.

While everyone was amazed at all that he was doing, he said to his disciples, [44] "Let these words sink into your ears: The Son of Man is going to be betrayed into human hands." [45] But they did not understand this saying; its meaning was concealed from

a Gk *he*
b Or *but when they were fully awake*
c Or *tents*
d Other ancient authorities read *my Beloved*
e Or *it*

is intensely personal. The temporal qualifier *daily* makes clear the ongoing character of discipleship. **26:** Jesus' words anticipate a final day of divine judgment. **27:** Jesus' enigmatic statement invites various interpretations; one is that it refers to the time after the resurrection.

9.28–36: The Transfiguration (Mt 17.1–9; Mk 9.2–10). This account recalls an intense religious experience, the exact nature of which is uncertain. The aura of unnatural brilliance is associated with mystical experiences elsewhere (Ex 34.29–35; Acts 9.3). **28:** *About eight days,* may merely indicate the passage of a week, but in the early church "the eighth day" became a designation for both the Lord's day and the day of Jesus' resurrection, the first day of a new creation. **30:** *Moses and Elijah,* two paragons of the faith of Israel: Moses was the lawgiver and Elijah the great prophet. **31:** *Departure,* lit., "exodus," probably referring to Jesus' death, resurrection, and ascension. **32:** The sleepy condition of the disciples may indicate that this event transpired at night (cf. 22.45). **33:** Peter's suggestion concerning *three dwellings* demonstrates his desire to preserve the experience. **34:** The association of God with a cloud in reminiscent of Israel's exodus experience of God, see Ex 13.17–22. **35:** The *voice* is clearly that of God (see 3.22), and the command, *listen to him,* focuses the attention and obedience of the disciples on Jesus above all others.

9.37–43a: Jesus heals an afflicted boy (Mt 17.14–21; Mk 9.14–29). The description of the boy's malady leads some scholars to conclude that the boy had epilepsy, but any diagnosis is speculative.

9.43b–45: A second prediction (Cf. 9.22; 18.31–33. **44:** 9.22; 18.31–34; 17.25. **45:** The comment is based on the view that (a) the messiah's death was not part of the disciples' Jewish faith, and

them, so that they could not perceive it. And they were afraid to ask him about this saying.

[46] An argument arose among them as to which one of them was the greatest. [47] But Jesus, aware of their inner thoughts, took a little child and put it by his side, [48] and said to them, "Whoever welcomes this child in my name welcomes me, and whoever welcomes me welcomes the one who sent me; for the least among all of you is the greatest."

[49] John answered, "Master, we saw someone casting out demons in your name, and we tried to stop him, because he does not follow with us." [50] But Jesus said to him, "Do not stop him; for whoever is not against you is for you."

[51] When the days drew near for him to be taken up, he set his face to go to Jerusalem. [52] And he sent messengers ahead of him. On their way they entered a village of the Samaritans to make ready for him; [53] but they did not receive him, because his face was set toward Jerusalem. [54] When his disciples James and John saw it, they said, "Lord, do you want us to command fire to come down from heaven and consume them?"[a] [55] But he turned and rebuked them. [56] Then[b] they went on to another village.

[57] As they were going along the road, someone said to him, "I will follow you wherever you go." [58] And Jesus said to him, "Foxes have holes, and birds of the air have nests; but the Son of Man has nowhere to lay his head." [59] To another he said, "Follow me." But he said, "Lord, first let me go and bury my father." [60] But Jesus[c] said to him, "Let the dead bury their own dead; but as for you, go and proclaim the kingdom of God." [61] Another said, "I will follow you, Lord; but let me first say farewell to those at my home." [62] Jesus said to him, "No one who puts a hand to the plow and looks back is fit for the kingdom of God."

10 After this the Lord appointed seventy[d] others and sent them on ahead of him in pairs to every town and place where he himself intended to go. [2] He said to them, "The harvest is plentiful, but the laborers

a   Other ancient authorities add *as Elijah did*
b   Other ancient authorities read *rebuked them, and said, "You do not know what spirit you are of,* [56]*for the Son of Man has not come to destroy the lives of human beings but to save them." Then*
c   Gk *he*
d   Other ancient authorities read *seventy-two*

(b) spiritual truth must be revealed (see 24.16).

9.46–48: **True greatness** (Mt 18.1–5; Mk 9.33–37). An acted parable rejecting self-centered ambition. **47:** The reception of the *little child* requires generosity without expectation of gain.

9.49–50: **The unknown exorcist** (Mk 9.38–41). This incident records Jesus' repudiation of intolerance, though contrast the statement in 11.23, which indicates the necessity of aligning actions and concerns with Jesus' values and work.

9.51–19.27: **Jesus' journey to Jerusalem with his followers** (Mt 19.1–20.34; Mk 10.1–52). This section, most of which is found only in Luke, reports the ministry of Jesus in Samaria and Judea.

9.51: **Jesus' resolve to go to Jerusalem** (Mt 19.1–2; Mk 10.1). *To be taken up,* explicitly refers to the ascension, but probably also designates Jesus' suffering, death, and resurrection that led to his departure into heaven. *He set his face to go to Jerusalem,* states Jesus' resolve using a Semitic idiom (see Isa 50.7).

9.52–56: **Samaritans' rejection of Jesus. 52–53:** The Samaritans did not help pilgrims going to keep a feast at what they regarded as the wrong sanctuary (cf. Jn 4.20). **52:** *Samaritan* is a geographical designation used also to name an inhabitant of Samaria, which was originally the capital of the former Northern Kingdom of Israel that fell to the Assyrians in 722 BCE. *Samaritan* became a term for persons living between Judea and Galilee who came to be regarded as a distinct ethnic and religious group. Tensions existed between Samaritans and Jews after the return of the Jews from exile in Babylon (538 BCE) and remained, as this story recognizes, in Jesus' day. **54:** Incorporates wordings parallel to 2 Kings 1.10–12. Elijah had called down fire from heaven on hostile troops (see 2 Kings 1.9–16). See 9.3–5 for Jesus' instructions for dealing with rejection.

9.57–62: **The demands of following Jesus** (Mt 8.18–22). **59:** From the statement that follows (v. 60), the man's father was almost certainly not yet dead; rather, the man used this responsibility to procrastinate complete commitment to discipleship. **60:** *Let the dead bury their own dead,* suggests that the spiritually dead should be left to bury the physically dead. **61:** See 1 Kings 19.20.

10.1–12: **The mission of the seventy** (Mt 9.37–38; 10.7–16). **1:** 9.1–5,51–52; Mk 6.7–11. **4:** *Greet no one,* which

are few; therefore ask the Lord of the harvest to send out laborers into his harvest. ³ Go on your way. See, I am sending you out like lambs into the midst of wolves. ⁴ Carry no purse, no bag, no sandals; and greet no one on the road. ⁵ Whatever house you enter, first say, 'Peace to this house!' ⁶ And if anyone is there who shares in peace, your peace will rest on that person; but if not, it will return to you. ⁷ Remain in the same house, eating and drinking whatever they provide, for the laborer deserves to be paid. Do not move about from house to house. ⁸ Whenever you enter a town and its people welcome you, eat what is set before you; ⁹ cure the sick who are there, and say to them, 'The kingdom of God has come near to you.'ᵃ ¹⁰ But whenever you enter a town and they do not welcome you, go out into its streets and say, ¹¹ 'Even the dust of your town that clings to our feet, we wipe off in protest against you. Yet know this: the kingdom of God has come near.'ᵇ ¹² I tell you, on that day it will be more tolerable for Sodom than for that town.

¹³ "Woe to you, Chorazin! Woe to you, Bethsaida! For if the deeds of power done in you had been done in Tyre and Sidon, they would have repented long ago, sitting in sackcloth and ashes. ¹⁴ But at the judgment it will be more tolerable for Tyre and Sidon than for you. ¹⁵ And you, Capernaum,

will you be exalted to heaven?

No, you will be brought down to Hades.

¹⁶ "Whoever listens to you listens to me, and whoever rejects you rejects me, and whoever rejects me rejects the one who sent me."

¹⁷ The seventyᶜ returned with joy, saying, "Lord, in your name even the demons submit to us!" ¹⁸ He said to them, "I watched Satan fall from heaven like a flash of lightning. ¹⁹ See, I have given you authority to tread on snakes and scorpions, and over all the power of the enemy; and nothing will hurt you. ²⁰ Nevertheless, do not rejoice at this, that the spirits submit to you, but rejoice that your names are written in heaven."

²¹ At that same hour Jesusᵈ rejoiced in the Holy Spiritᵉ and said, "I thankᶠ you, Father, Lord of heaven and earth, because you have hidden these things from the wise and the intelligent and have revealed them to infants; yes, Father, for such was your gracious will.ᵍ ²² All things have been handed over to me by my Father; and no one knows who the Son is except the Father, or who the Father is except the Son and anyone to whom the Son chooses to reveal him."

²³ Then turning to the disciples, Jesusᵈ said to them privately, "Blessed are the eyes that see what you see! ²⁴ For I tell you that many prophets and kings desired to see what you see, but did not see it, and to hear what you hear, but did not hear it."

ᵃ Or is at hand for you
ᵇ Or is at hand
ᶜ Other ancient authorities read seventy-two
ᵈ Gk he
ᵉ Other authorities read in the spirit
ᶠ Or praise
ᵍ Or for so it was well-pleasing in your sight

---

might cause delay, underscoring the urgency of the mission. **9–11:** The emphasis here on the kingdom of God distinguishes these instructions from those given at 9.3–5. **5:** 1 Sam 25.6. **7:** Deut 24.15. **10–11:** Cf. 9.5n. **12:** Gen 19.24–28.

10.13–15: Woes to unrepentant cities (Mt 11.20–24). **13:** Chorazin, a town 3 km (2 mi) north of Capernaum. Tyre and Sidon were Gentile cities on the Mediterranean coast north of Galilee. Sackcloth and ashes recalls the repentance of Nineveh in Jon 3. **15:** The words echo Isa 14.13–15 (see v. 18). Hades, equivalent to Heb "Sheol," the abode of the dead.

10.16: Jesus' interpretation of the mission (Mt 10.40).

10.17–20: Return of the seventy (Mt 11.25–27). **17:** Even the demons submit to us, unlike the twelve (9.1), the seventy had not been promised this power. **18:** I watched Satan fall from heaven, alluding to the victory of the seventy over the demons; cf. Isa 14.15; Jn 12.31; Rev 12.7–12. **20:** Jesus did not regard exorcism in itself as a sign of God's kingdom (11.19). Written in heaven, Dan 12.1; Ps 69.28; Ex 32.32.

10.21–22: Jesus' thanksgiving to God (Mt 11.25–27). **21:** In the Holy Spirit, in communion with God. **22:** Cf. Jn 3.35; 10.14–15; 13.1; 17.25.

10.23–24: Jesus' blessing of the disciples (Mt 13.16–17).

²⁵ Just then a lawyer stood up to test Jesus.ª "Teacher," he said, "what must I do to inherit eternal life?" ²⁶ He said to him, "What is written in the law? What do you read there?" ²⁷ He answered, "You shall love the Lord your God with all your heart, and with all your soul, and with all your strength, and with all your mind; and your neighbor as yourself." ²⁸ And he said to him, "You have given the right answer; do this, and you will live."

²⁹ But wanting to justify himself, he asked Jesus, "And who is my neighbor?" ³⁰ Jesus replied, "A man was going down from Jerusalem to Jericho, and fell into the hands of robbers, who stripped him, beat him, and went away, leaving him half dead. ³¹ Now by chance a priest was going down that road; and when he saw him, he passed by on the other side. ³² So likewise a Levite, when he came to the place and saw him, passed by on the other side. ³³ But a Samaritan while traveling came near him; and when he saw him, he was moved with pity. ³⁴ He went to him and bandaged his wounds, having poured oil and wine on them. Then he put him on his own animal, brought him to an inn, and took care of him. ³⁵ The next day he took out two denarii,ᵇ gave them to the innkeeper, and said, 'Take care of him; and when I come back, I will repay you whatever more you spend.' ³⁶ Which of these three, do you think, was a neighbor to the man who fell into the hands of the robbers?" ³⁷ He said, "The one who showed him mercy." Jesus said to him, "Go and do likewise."

³⁸ Now as they went on their way, he entered a certain village, where a woman named Martha welcomed him into her home.

³⁹ She had a sister named Mary, who sat at the Lord's feet and listened to what he was saying. ⁴⁰ But Martha was distracted by her many tasks; so she came to him and asked, "Lord, do you not care that my sister has left me to do all the work by myself? Tell her then to help me." ⁴¹ But the Lord answered her, "Martha, Martha, you are worried and distracted by many things; ⁴² there is need of only one thing.ᶜ Mary has chosen the better part, which will not be taken away from her."

11 He was praying in a certain place, and after he had finished, one of his disciples said to him, "Lord, teach us to pray, as John taught his disciples." ² He said to them, "When you pray, say:

> Father,ᵈ hallowed be your name.
> Your kingdom come.ᵉ
> ³ Give us each day our daily bread.ᶠ
> ⁴ And forgive us our sins,
> for we ourselves forgive everyone indebted to us.
> And do not bring us to the time of trial."ᵍ

a Gk *him*
b The denarius was the usual day's wage for a laborer
c Other ancient authorities read *few things are necessary, or only one*
d Other ancient authorities read *Our Father in heaven*
e A few ancient authorities read *Your Holy Spirit come upon us and cleanse us.* Other ancient authorities add *Your will be done, on earth as in heaven*
f Or *our bread for tomorrow*
g Or *us into temptation.* Other ancient authorities add *but rescue us from the evil one* (or *from evil*)

10.25–28: A lawyer's question (Mt 22.34–40; Mk 12.28–34; cf. Lk 18.9–14). **25:** *Lawyer,* an expert in the law of Moses, probably synonymous with "scribe" and likely affiliated with or belonging to the party of the Pharisees. **27:** Deut 6.5; Lev 19.18. **27:** Josh 22.5.

10.29–37: Parable of the Good Samaritan. 29: *Justify himself* means to show himself to be righteous, acceptable to God. **30:** *Down from Jerusalem to Jericho,* about 18 mi (30 km) with a drop in elevation from about 2,500 ft (760 m) above sea level to about 820 ft (250 m) below sea level. The road between the cities was notoriously dangerous. **31–33:** The *priest* represented the highest religious leadership among the Jews; the *Levite* (v. 32) belonged to minor clergy below the priest. In contrast, it was a *Samaritan* (see 9.52n.), a foreigner not expected to show sympathy to Jews, who was moved with pity. **34:** The *oil* served as a salve (see Isa 1.6) and the *wine* as an antiseptic. **35:** *Two denarii* would provide approximately two months of lodging in an ancient inn.

10.38–42: Martha and Mary. This enigmatic account affirms the importance of listening to Jesus and at the same time the account shows Jesus' openness to and acceptance of women among his followers. According to Jn 11.1, Martha and Mary were the sisters of Lazarus and lived in Bethany, just east of Jerusalem.

11.1–4: The Lord's Prayer. This model prayer appears in a more elaborate form in Mt 6.9–13. In both Matthew and Luke there is an eschatological cast to the petitions, yet the concerns specified are related to daily life.

⁵ And he said to them, "Suppose one of you has a friend, and you go to him at midnight and say to him, 'Friend, lend me three loaves of bread; ⁶ for a friend of mine has arrived, and I have nothing to set before him.' ⁷ And he answers from within, 'Do not bother me; the door has already been locked, and my children are with me in bed; I cannot get up and give you anything.' ⁸ I tell you, even though he will not get up and give him anything because he is his friend, at least because of his persistence he will get up and give him whatever he needs.

⁹ "So I say to you, Ask, and it will be given you; search, and you will find; knock, and the door will be opened for you. ¹⁰ For everyone who asks receives, and everyone who searches finds, and for everyone who knocks, the door will be opened. ¹¹ Is there anyone among you who, if your child asks for[a] a fish, will give a snake instead of a fish? ¹² Or if the child asks for an egg, will give a scorpion? ¹³ If you then, who are evil, know how to give good gifts to your children, how much more will the heavenly Father give the Holy Spirit[b] to those who ask him!"

¹⁴ Now he was casting out a demon that was mute; when the demon had gone out, the one who had been mute spoke, and the crowds were amazed. ¹⁵ But some of them said, "He casts out demons by Beelzebul, the ruler of the demons." ¹⁶ Others, to test him, kept demanding from him a sign from heaven. ¹⁷ But he knew what they were thinking and said to them, "Every kingdom divided against itself becomes a desert, and house falls on house. ¹⁸ If Satan also is divided against himself, how will his kingdom stand? —for you say that I cast out the demons by Beelzebul. ¹⁹ Now if I cast out the demons by Beelzebul, by whom do your exorcists[c] cast them out? Therefore they will be your judges. ²⁰ But if it is by the finger of God that I cast out the demons, then the kingdom of God has come to you. ²¹ When a strong man, fully armed, guards his castle, his property is safe. ²² But when one stronger than he attacks him and overpowers him, he takes away his armor in which he trusted and divides his plunder. ²³ Whoever is not with me is against me, and whoever does not gather with me scatters.

²⁴ "When the unclean spirit has gone out of a person, it wanders through waterless regions looking for a resting place, but not finding any, it says, 'I will return to my house from which I came.' ²⁵ When it comes, it finds it swept and put in order. ²⁶ Then it goes and brings seven other spirits more evil than itself, and they enter and live there; and the last state of that person is worse than the first."

²⁷ While he was saying this, a woman in the crowd raised her voice and said to him, "Blessed is the womb that bore you and the breasts that nursed you!" ²⁸ But he said, "Blessed rather are those who hear the word of God and obey it!"

²⁹ When the crowds were increasing, he began to say, "This generation is an evil

a   Other ancient authorities add *bread, will give a stone; or if your child asks for*

b   Other ancient authorities read *the Father give the Holy Spirit from heaven*

c   Gk *sons*

11.5–8: Teaching about persistence (Mt 7.7–11). Cf. Lk 18.1–5. **5–8:** Following the Lord's Prayer, this parable in Luke relates to persistence in prayer.

11.9–13: A parabolic admonition and assurance concerning prayer (Mt 7.7–11). **9–13:** The promise of *the Holy Spirit* focuses the substance of petitions in prayers in a pointed fashion.

11.14–23: The Beelzebul controversy (Mt 12.22–30; Mk 3.22–27). **15:** *Beelzebul, the ruler of the demons*, Satan (see v. 18); Beelzebul was originally a title of the Canaanite storm and fertility god Baal (see 2 Kings 1.2). **16:** The request for a sign comes almost immediately after Jesus restores the power of speech to one afflicted with muteness. **20:** Ex 8.19. *Finger* stands for God's power. *The kingdom of God has come to you* indicates Jesus' interpretation of the meaning of his ministry. **21–22:** Jesus seems to cast himself in this parable as the *one stronger than he*. **23:** Cf. 9.50. This statement registers the uncompromising demands of Jesus' call to discipleship, and in relation to the preceding parable the saying declares that in the struggle between Jesus and Beelzebul neutrality is not an option.

11.24–26: The return of unclean spirits (Mt 12.43–45).

11.27–28: True blessedness. Cf. 8.21.

11.29–32: The sign of Jonah (Mt 12.38–42; Mk 8.11–12). **29:** *The sign of Jonah* was given through Jonah's preach-

generation; it asks for a sign, but no sign will be given to it except the sign of Jonah. [30] For just as Jonah became a sign to the people of Nineveh, so the Son of Man will be to this generation. [31] The queen of the South will rise at the judgment with the people of this generation and condemn them, because she came from the ends of the earth to listen to the wisdom of Solomon, and see, something greater than Solomon is here! [32] The people of Nineveh will rise up at the judgment with this generation and condemn it, because they repented at the proclamation of Jonah, and see, something greater than Jonah is here!

[33] "No one after lighting a lamp puts it in a cellar,[a] but on the lampstand so that those who enter may see the light. [34] Your eye is the lamp of your body. If your eye is healthy, your whole body is full of light; but if it is not healthy, your body is full of darkness. [35] Therefore consider whether the light in you is not darkness. [36] If then your whole body is full of light, with no part of it in darkness, it will be as full of light as when a lamp gives you light with its rays."

[37] While he was speaking, a Pharisee invited him to dine with him; so he went in and took his place at the table. [38] The Pharisee was amazed to see that he did not first wash before dinner. [39] Then the Lord said to him, "Now you Pharisees clean the outside of the cup and of the dish, but inside you are full of greed and wickedness. [40] You fools! Did not the one who made the outside make the inside also? [41] So give for alms those things that are within; and see, everything will be clean for you.

[42] "But woe to you Pharisees! For you tithe mint and rue and herbs of all kinds, and neglect justice and the love of God; it is these you ought to have practiced, without neglecting the others. [43] Woe to you Pharisees! For you love to have the seat of honor in the synagogues and to be greeted with respect in the marketplaces. [44] Woe to you! For you are like unmarked graves, and people walk over them without realizing it."

[45] One of the lawyers answered him, "Teacher, when you say these things, you insult us too." [46] And he said, "Woe also to you lawyers! For you load people with burdens hard to bear, and you yourselves do not lift a finger to ease them. [47] Woe to you! For you build the tombs of the prophets whom your ancestors killed. [48] So you are witnesses and approve of the deeds of your ancestors; for they killed them, and you build their tombs. [49] Therefore also the Wisdom of God said, 'I will send them prophets and apostles, some of whom they will kill and persecute,' [50] so that this generation may be charged with the blood of all the prophets shed since the foundation of the world, [51] from the blood of Abel to the blood of Zechariah, who perished between the altar and the sanctuary. Yes, I tell you, it will be charged against this generation. [52] Woe to you lawyers! For you have taken away the key of knowledge; you did not enter yourselves, and you hindered those who were entering."

[53] When he went outside, the scribes and the Pharisees began to be very hostile toward him and to cross-examine him about many things, [54] lying in wait for him, to catch him in something he might say.

---

[a] Other ancient authorities add *or under the bushel basket*

ing to the Ninevites; here, Jesus is not referring to his resurrection. **30:** Jon 3.4. **31:** 1 Kings 10.1–10; 2 Chr 9.1–9.

11.33: Light and sight (Mt 5.15; Mk 4.21). Cf. 8.16.

11.34–36: The healthy eye (Mt 6.22–23). **34–36:** One theory of vision held that the eye produced fire or light, which made sight possible.

11.37–54: Sayings against Pharisees and lawyers (Mt 15.1–9; Mk 7.1–9; Mt 23.1–36, in different order). **37:** 7.36; 14.1. **38:** *Wash before dinner,* ceremonial washing (lit., "baptize before dinner"; cf. Mk 7.1–5). **39–41:** Mt 23.25–26. Jesus turns back the Pharisees' criticism that the outside is unwashed by insisting that the inner life is equal in importance to the outer (v. 40), indeed, that it exercises a cleansing or corrupting power over the outer (v. 41; Mk 7.23). **41:** *Alms,* charitable gifts for the poor. **42:** *Tithe,* see Deut 14.22–29. *Mint and rue* were common herbs of little value. **44:** Graves were carefully marked and even whitewashed (Mt 23.27) to prevent defilement through unintentional contact with the dead. **49:** *The Wisdom of God said,* introduces an apparent quotation, but from neither the Hebrew Bible nor the nonbiblical writings of Judaism. **49:** Cf. Jer 7.25–26. **51:** *Abel* is the first person murdered in the Bible (Gen 4.8), and *Zechariah* seems to be the person murdered in 2 Chr 24.20–22. **54:**

12 Meanwhile, when the crowd gathered by the thousands, so that they trampled on one another, he began to speak first to his disciples, "Beware of the yeast of the Pharisees, that is, their hypocrisy. [2] Nothing is covered up that will not be uncovered, and nothing secret that will not become known. [3] Therefore whatever you have said in the dark will be heard in the light, and what you have whispered behind closed doors will be proclaimed from the housetops.

[4] "I tell you, my friends, do not fear those who kill the body, and after that can do nothing more. [5] But I will warn you whom to fear: fear him who, after he has killed, has authority[a] to cast into hell.[b] Yes, I tell you, fear him! [6] Are not five sparrows sold for two pennies? Yet not one of them is forgotten in God's sight. [7] But even the hairs of your head are all counted. Do not be afraid; you are of more value than many sparrows.

[8] "And I tell you, everyone who acknowledges me before others, the Son of Man also will acknowledge before the angels of God; [9] but whoever denies me before others will be denied before the angels of God. [10] And everyone who speaks a word against the Son of Man will be forgiven; but whoever blasphemes against the Holy Spirit will not be forgiven. [11] When they bring you before the synagogues, the rulers, and the authorities, do not worry about how[c] you are to defend yourselves or what you are to say; [12] for the Holy Spirit will teach you at that very hour what you ought to say."

[13] Someone in the crowd said to him, "Teacher, tell my brother to divide the family inheritance with me." [14] But he said to him, "Friend, who set me to be a judge or arbitrator over you?" [15] And he said to them, "Take care! Be on your guard against all kinds of greed; for one's life does not consist in the abundance of possessions." [16] Then he told them a parable: "The land of a rich man produced abundantly. [17] And he thought to himself, 'What should I do, for I have no place to store my crops?' [18] Then he said, 'I will do this: I will pull down my barns and build larger ones, and there I will store all my grain and my goods. [19] And I will say to my soul, Soul, you have ample goods laid up for many years; relax, eat, drink, be merry.' [20] But God said to him, 'You fool! This very night your life is being demanded of you. And the things you have prepared, whose will they be?' [21] So it is with those who store up treasures for themselves but are not rich toward God."

[22] He said to his disciples, "Therefore I tell you, do not worry about your life, what you will eat, or about your body, what you

---

a   Or *power*
b   Gk *Gehenna*
c   Other ancient authorities add *or what*

Cf. 6.11; 19.47–48; 20.19–20; 22.2.

12.1: The yeast of the Pharisees (Mt 16.5–6; Mk 8.14–15). **1:** Leaven/yeast was often a symbol of corruption for ancient Jews; cf. 1 Cor 5.6–8.

12.2–9: Calls to fearless confession (Mt 10.26–33). **5:** *Him who . . . has authority to cast into hell,* God alone. *Hell* is "Gehenna," not Hades as in 10.5; Gehenna was a deep ravine to the south of Jerusalem. Human sacrifices were allegedly made there during the Judean monarchy (2 Kings 23.10), and it came to symbolize the place of eternal punishment. **6:** The *penny* ("assarion") was one-sixteenth of a denarius (see 12.59n.). **8–9:** Cf. 9.26; Mk 8.38.

12.10: Blaspheming the Holy Spirit (Mt 12.31–32; Mk 3.28–30). Blasphemy *against the Holy Spirit* is attributing the genuine work of the Spirit to the forces of evil rather than to God.

12.11–12: Aid from the Holy Spirit (Mt 10.19–20; Mk 13.11).

12.13–15: Warning against greed. 13: According to Deut 21.17 the oldest son received double the younger's share. Jesus shows no interest in ensuring equitable division and subsequently warns against greed and material self-satisfaction.

12.16–21: Parable of the rich fool. 19: *Relax, eat, drink, be merry,* see Eccl 8.15. The maxim is reminiscent of similar declarations in Tob 7.10; *1 Enoch* 97.8–9; Euripides; Meander. **20:** Cf. Jer 17.11; Lk 12.33–34. The declaration by God in Greek is difficult, reading literally, "Fool! In this night your soul they demand from you." The subject "they" may be a circumlocution for God, but more likely it is "the things" that now own the man and that claim his life.

will wear. [23] For life is more than food, and the body more than clothing. [24] Consider the ravens: they neither sow nor reap, they have neither storehouse nor barn, and yet God feeds them. Of how much more value are you than the birds! [25] And can any of you by worrying add a single hour to your span of life?[a] [26] If then you are not able to do so small a thing as that, why do you worry about the rest? [27] Consider the lilies, how they grow: they neither toil nor spin;[b] yet I tell you, even Solomon in all his glory was not clothed like one of these. [28] But if God so clothes the grass of the field, which is alive today and tomorrow is thrown into the oven, how much more will he clothe you—you of little faith! [29] And do not keep striving for what you are to eat and what you are to drink, and do not keep worrying. [30] For it is the nations of the world that strive after all these things, and your Father knows that you need them. [31] Instead, strive for his[c] kingdom, and these things will be given to you as well.

[32] "Do not be afraid, little flock, for it is your Father's good pleasure to give you the kingdom. [33] Sell your possessions, and give alms. Make purses for yourselves that do not wear out, an unfailing treasure in heaven, where no thief comes near and no moth destroys. [34] For where your treasure is, there your heart will be also.

[35] "Be dressed for action and have your lamps lit; [36] be like those who are waiting for their master to return from the wedding banquet, so that they may open the door for him as soon as he comes and knocks. [37] Blessed are those slaves whom the master finds alert when he comes; truly I tell you, he will fasten his belt and have them sit down to eat, and he will come and serve them. [38] If he comes during the middle of the night, or near dawn, and finds them so, blessed are those slaves.

[39] "But know this: if the owner of the house had known at what hour the thief was coming, he[d] would not have let his house be broken into. [40] You also must be ready, for the Son of Man is coming at an unexpected hour."

[41] Peter said, "Lord, are you telling this parable for us or for everyone?" [42] And the Lord said, "Who then is the faithful and prudent manager whom his master will put in charge of his slaves, to give them their allowance of food at the proper time? [43] Blessed is that slave whom his master will find at work when he arrives. [44] Truly I tell you, he will put that one in charge of all his possessions. [45] But if that slave says to himself, 'My master is delayed in coming,' and if he begins to beat the other slaves, men and women, and to eat and drink and get drunk, [46] the master of that slave will come on a day when he does not expect him and at an hour that he does not know, and will cut him in pieces,[e] and put him with the unfaithful. [47] That slave who knew what his master wanted, but did not prepare himself or do what was wanted, will receive a severe beating. [48] But the one who did not know and did what deserved a beating will receive a light beating. From everyone to whom much has been given, much will be required; and from the one to whom much has been entrusted, even more will be demanded.

[49] "I came to bring fire to the earth, and how I wish it were already kindled! [50] I have a baptism with which to be baptized, and what stress I am under until it is completed! [51] Do

a   Or *add a cubit to your stature*
b   Other ancient authorities read *Consider the lilies; they neither spin nor weave*
c   Other ancient authorities read *God's*
d   Other ancient authorities add *would have watched and*
e   Or *cut him off*

12.22–32: Anxiety concerning life (Mt 6.25–34). **24:** *Ravens*, members of the crow family, act as scavengers and are listed among the unclean birds in the Hebrew Bible (Lev 11.15; Deut 14.14; cf. Job 38.41). **27:** See 1 Kings 10. **32:** *Flock* refers to the messiah's people (Ezek 34.23).

12.33–34: Treasure in heaven (Mt 6.19–21). Compare Mk 10.21; Lk 18.22; Acts 2.45; 4.32–35.

12.35–48: Sayings on watchfulness and faithfulness (Mt 24.42–51). **35:** *Dressed for action,* lit., "your loins girded"; see Ex 12.11. **37:** The language suggests the messianic banquet (13.29; 14.15; 22.16), to which a marriage feast served as an analogy. For the action of this master in serving the servants, see 17.7–8; cf. Jn 13.3–16; Lk 22.27. **40:** Cf. Mk 13.35; 1 Thess 5.2. **48:** 8.18; 19.26.

12.49–53: The controversial character of Jesus' mission (Mt 10.34–36). **49:** *Fire,* a symbol of judgment (Mt

you think that I have come to bring peace to the earth? No, I tell you, but rather division! ⁵² From now on five in one household will be divided, three against two and two against three; ⁵³ they will be divided:

father against son
    and son against father,
mother against daughter
    and daughter against mother,
mother-in-law against her daughter-in-law
    and daughter-in-law against mother-in-law."

⁵⁴ He also said to the crowds, "When you see a cloud rising in the west, you immediately say, 'It is going to rain'; and so it happens. ⁵⁵ And when you see the south wind blowing, you say, 'There will be scorching heat'; and it happens. ⁵⁶ You hypocrites! You know how to interpret the appearance of earth and sky, but why do you not know how to interpret the present time?

⁵⁷ "And why do you not judge for yourselves what is right? ⁵⁸ Thus, when you go with your accuser before a magistrate, on the way make an effort to settle the case,ᵃ or you may be dragged before the judge, and the judge hand you over to the officer, and the officer throw you in prison. ⁵⁹ I tell you, you will never get out until you have paid the very last penny."

13 At that very time there were some present who told him about the Galileans whose blood Pilate had mingled with their sacrifices. ² He asked them, "Do you think that because these Galileans suffered in this way they were worse sinners than all other Galileans? ³ No, I tell you; but unless you repent, you will all perish as they did.

⁴ Or those eighteen who were killed when the tower of Siloam fell on them—do you think that they were worse offenders than all the others living in Jerusalem? ⁵ No, I tell you; but unless you repent, you will all perish just as they did."

⁶ Then he told this parable: "A man had a fig tree planted in his vineyard; and he came looking for fruit on it and found none. ⁷ So he said to the gardener, 'See here! For three years I have come looking for fruit on this fig tree, and still I find none. Cut it down! Why should it be wasting the soil?' ⁸ He replied, 'Sir, let it alone for one more year, until I dig around it and put manure on it. ⁹ If it bears fruit next year, well and good; but if not, you can cut it down.'"

¹⁰ Now he was teaching in one of the synagogues on the sabbath. ¹¹ And just then there appeared a woman with a spirit that had crippled her for eighteen years. She was bent over and was quite unable to stand up straight. ¹² When Jesus saw her, he called her over and said, "Woman, you are set free from your ailment." ¹³ When he laid his hands on her, immediately she stood up straight and began praising God. ¹⁴ But the leader of the synagogue, indignant because Jesus had cured on the sabbath, kept saying to the crowd, "There are six days on which work ought to be done; come on those days and be cured, and not on the sabbath day." ¹⁵ But the Lord answered him and said, "You hypocrites! Does not each of you on the sabbath untie his ox or his donkey from the manger, and lead it away to give it water? ¹⁶ And ought not this woman,

ᵃ   Gk *settle with him*

3.11; 7.19; Mk 9.48; Lk 3.16). **50**: *Baptism,* Jesus' death. **53**: Incorporates phrases from Mic 7.6.

12.54–56: Interpreting the times (Mt 16.2–3). Winds from the west blew off the Mediterranean, those from the south off the desert. Jesus says there are signs of crisis that human beings neglect.

12.57–59: Settling with an accuser (Mt 5.25–26). **59**: *Penny,* Greek "lepton," the smallest Greek coin in circulation. There were two lepta to a quadrans ("penny" in Mt 5.26; Mk 12.42), eight to an assarion ("penny" in Lk 12.6), and one hundred twenty-eight to a denarius, the daily wage in Mt 20.2.

13.1–9: Parable of the unfruitful fig tree (compare Mt 21.18–19; Mk 11.12–14). **1**: The Galileans had been slain by the order of Pilate (see 3.1n.) while sacrificing in the Temple at Jerusalem. This incident is otherwise unattested. **2**: The reports carried with them questions of a deeper meaning. According to common Jewish belief, painful experiences were signs of God's judgments (see 5.20n.). Jesus issues a call to repentance so that catastrophe would not overtake his hearers. **4**: *Siloam,* in the southeast corner of Jerusalem, where the pool of Siloam (Isa 8.6; Neh 3.15; Jn 9.7) was located. **7**: See 3.9.

13.10–17: Healing of a crippled woman on the sabbath. A similar sabbath healing follows in 14.1–6; see

a daughter of Abraham whom Satan bound for eighteen long years, be set free from this bondage on the sabbath day?" [17] When he said this, all his opponents were put to shame; and the entire crowd was rejoicing at all the wonderful things that he was doing.

[18] He said therefore, "What is the kingdom of God like? And to what should I compare it? [19] It is like a mustard seed that someone took and sowed in the garden; it grew and became a tree, and the birds of the air made nests in its branches."

[20] And again he said, "To what should I compare the kingdom of God? [21] It is like yeast that a woman took and mixed in with[a] three measures of flour until all of it was leavened."

[22] Jesus[b] went through one town and village after another, teaching as he made his way to Jerusalem. [23] Someone asked him, "Lord, will only a few be saved?" He said to them, [24] "Strive to enter through the narrow door; for many, I tell you, will try to enter and will not be able. [25] When once the owner of the house has got up and shut the door, and you begin to stand outside and to knock at the door, saying, 'Lord, open to us,' then in reply he will say to you, 'I do not know where you come from.' [26] Then you will begin to say, 'We ate and drank with you, and you taught in our streets.' [27] But he will say, 'I do not know where you come from; go away from me, all you evildoers!' [28] There will be weeping and gnashing of teeth when you see Abraham and Isaac and Jacob

and all the prophets in the kingdom of God, and you yourselves thrown out. [29] Then people will come from east and west, from north and south, and will eat in the kingdom of God. [30] Indeed, some are last who will be first, and some are first who will be last."

[31] At that very hour some Pharisees came and said to him, "Get away from here, for Herod wants to kill you." [32] He said to them, "Go and tell that fox for me,[c] 'Listen, I am casting out demons and performing cures today and tomorrow, and on the third day I finish my work. [33] Yet today, tomorrow, and the next day I must be on my way, because it is impossible for a prophet to be killed outside of Jerusalem.' [34] Jerusalem, Jerusalem, the city that kills the prophets and stones those who are sent to it! How often have I desired to gather your children together as a hen gathers her brood under her wings, and you were not willing! [35] See, your house is left to you. And I tell you, you will not see me until the time comes when[d] you say, 'Blessed is the one who comes in the name of the Lord.'"

14 On one occasion when Jesus[e] was going to the house of a leader of the Pharisees to eat a meal on the sabbath,

a Gk *hid in*
b Gk *He*
c Gk lacks *for me*
d Other ancient authorities lack *the time comes when*
e Gk *he*

4.31n.; cf. 8.43–48. **14:** Ex 20.9–10. Lev 23.3; Deut 5.13–14. **16:** Jesus relates the physical disorder of the woman to the work of Satan (cf. 11.14). Such afflictions conflict with God's purpose of salvation in his covenant with Abraham and are the concern of Jesus' ministry (4.18).

13.18–19: Parable of the mustard seed (Mt 13.31–32; Mk 4.30–32). **19:** The last phrase of this verse reflects the wording of Ps 104.12; Dan 4.12,21.

13.20–21: Parable of the yeast (Mt 13.33). This parable, like the preceding one (vv. 18–19), contrasts the future grandeur of the kingdom with the seemingly small start that was occurring in the ministry of Jesus. **21:** *Three measures,* ca. 63 dry quarts (69 liters).

13.22–30: The necessity of discipline for salvation (Mt 7.13–14,22–23; 8.11–12; 19.30; Mk 10.31). **27:** The wording of this verse bears similarities to Ps 6.8. **29:** Ps 107.3.

13.31–33: Report and reply concerning Herod. **31:** Some Pharisees who appear to be well intentioned toward Jesus are noteworthy and show that not all Pharisees were negatively disposed toward Jesus. *Here,* Herod's domain of Galilee and Perea (see 3.1n.). **32:** *Fox,* an unflattering metaphor. Jesus denies that Herod's intended opposition can hinder his ministry, which has not reached its goal. **33:** *It is impossible . . . ,* bitter irony that leads to the ensuing laments (see 13.34–35; 19.41–42).

13.34–35: Jesus' lament over Jerusalem (Mt 23.37–39). **35:** See Jer 22.5. The quotation is from Ps 118.26; see Lk 19.37–38.

14.1–6: Healing of a man with dropsy on the sabbath. This healing story forms the second part of a balanced

they were watching him closely. ² Just then, in front of him, there was a man who had dropsy. ³ And Jesus asked the lawyers and Pharisees, "Is it lawful to cure people on the sabbath, or not?" ⁴ But they were silent. So Jesus[a] took him and healed him, and sent him away. ⁵ Then he said to them, "If one of you has a child[b] or an ox that has fallen into a well, will you not immediately pull it out on a sabbath day?" ⁶ And they could not reply to this.

⁷ When he noticed how the guests chose the places of honor, he told them a parable. ⁸ "When you are invited by someone to a wedding banquet, do not sit down at the place of honor, in case someone more distinguished than you has been invited by your host; ⁹ and the host who invited both of you may come and say to you, 'Give this person your place,' and then in disgrace you would start to take the lowest place. ¹⁰ But when you are invited, go and sit down at the lowest place, so that when your host comes, he may say to you, 'Friend, move up higher'; then you will be honored in the presence of all who sit at the table with you. ¹¹ For all who exalt themselves will be humbled, and those who humble themselves will be exalted."

¹² He said also to the one who had invited him, "When you give a luncheon or a dinner, do not invite your friends or your brothers or your relatives or rich neighbors, in case they may invite you in return, and you would be repaid. ¹³ But when you give a banquet, invite the poor, the crippled, the lame, and the blind. ¹⁴ And you will be blessed, because they cannot repay you, for you will be repaid at the resurrection of the righteous."

¹⁵ One of the dinner guests, on hearing this, said to him, "Blessed is anyone who will eat bread in the kingdom of God!" ¹⁶ Then Jesus[a] said to him, "Someone gave a great dinner and invited many. ¹⁷ At the time for the dinner he sent his slave to say to those who had been invited, 'Come; for everything is ready now.' ¹⁸ But they all alike began to make excuses. The first said to him, 'I have bought a piece of land, and I must go out and see it; please accept my regrets.' ¹⁹ Another said, 'I have bought five yoke of oxen, and I am going to try them out; please accept my regrets.' ²⁰ Another said, 'I have just been married, and therefore I cannot come.' ²¹ So the slave returned and reported this to his master. Then the owner of the house became angry and said to his slave, 'Go out at once into the streets and lanes of the town and bring in the poor, the crippled, the blind, and the lame.' ²² And the slave said, 'Sir, what you ordered has been done, and there is still room.' ²³ Then the master said to the slave, 'Go out into the roads and lanes, and compel people to come in, so that my house may be filled. ²⁴ For I tell you,[c] none of those who were invited will taste my dinner.'"

²⁵ Now large crowds were traveling with him; and he turned and said to them, ²⁶ "Whoever comes to me and does not hate father and mother, wife and children, brothers and sisters, yes, and even life itself, cannot be my disciple. ²⁷ Whoever does not carry the cross and follow me cannot be my disciple. ²⁸ For which of you, intending to

---

a   Gk *he*

b   Other ancient authorities read *a donkey*

c   The Greek word for *you* here is plural

---

pair with the foregoing account of Jesus' healing the crippled woman (13.1–16), exhibiting Luke's concern to show the inclusive nature of Jesus' ministry. **2:** *Dropsy*, swelling from abnormal fluid retention. **5:** The variant reading, "a donkey" instead of "a child" (see note b) was a scribal alteration to make this verse conform to the wording of 13.15. Cf. Ex 23.5; Deut 22.4.

14.7–14: Parable on humility. 8: Prov 25.6–7. **11:** See 13.30; 18.14; Mt 18.4; 23.12.

14.15–24: Parable of the great dinner (Mt 22.1–14). **18–20:** Cf. Deut 20.5–8. **24:** *You* is plural here, whereas the master in the parable was speaking to only one servant ("you" singular). Thus, Jesus seems to have completed the parabolic form in v. 23 and, now, he speaks to the guests directly in this verse (v. 24) as a reply to the statement by the guest in v. 15. *My dinner* suggests the messianic banquet (see 12.37n.).

14.25–33: The costs of discipleship (Mt 10.37–38). A series of sayings declaring the necessity of the disciples' total devotion to following Jesus. **26:** Jn 12.25. *Hate* is vivid language; the parallel passage in Mt 10.37 is

build a tower, does not first sit down and estimate the cost, to see whether he has enough to complete it? ²⁹ Otherwise, when he has laid a foundation and is not able to finish, all who see it will begin to ridicule him, ³⁰ saying, 'This fellow began to build and was not able to finish.' ³¹ Or what king, going out to wage war against another king, will not sit down first and consider whether he is able with ten thousand to oppose the one who comes against him with twenty thousand? ³² If he cannot, then, while the other is still far away, he sends a delegation and asks for the terms of peace. ³³ So therefore, none of you can become my disciple if you do not give up all your possessions.

³⁴ "Salt is good; but if salt has lost its taste, how can its saltiness be restored?^a ³⁵ It is fit neither for the soil nor for the manure pile; they throw it away. Let anyone with ears to hear listen!"

15

Now all the tax collectors and sinners were coming near to listen to him. ² And the Pharisees and the scribes were grumbling and saying, "This fellow welcomes sinners and eats with them."

³ So he told them this parable: ⁴ "Which one of you, having a hundred sheep and losing one of them, does not leave the ninety-nine in the wilderness and go after the one that is lost until he finds it? ⁵ When he has found it, he lays it on his shoulders and rejoices. ⁶ And when he comes home, he calls together his friends and neighbors, saying to them, 'Rejoice with me, for I have found my sheep that was lost.' ⁷ Just so, I tell you, there will be more joy in heaven over one sinner who repents than over ninety-nine righteous persons who need no repentance.

⁸ "Or what woman having ten silver coins,^b if she loses one of them, does not light a lamp, sweep the house, and search carefully until she finds it? ⁹ When she has found it, she calls together her friends and neighbors, saying, 'Rejoice with me, for I have found the coin that I had lost.' ¹⁰ Just so, I tell you, there is joy in the presence of the angels of God over one sinner who repents."

¹¹ Then Jesus^c said, "There was a man who had two sons. ¹² The younger of them said to his father, 'Father, give me the share of the property that will belong to me.' So he divided his property between them. ¹³ A few days later the younger son gathered all he had and traveled to a distant country, and there he squandered his property in dissolute living. ¹⁴ When he had spent everything, a severe famine took place throughout that country, and he began to be in need. ¹⁵ So he went and hired himself out to one of the citizens of that country, who sent him to his fields to feed the pigs. ¹⁶ He would gladly have filled himself with^d the pods that the pigs were eating; and no one gave him anything. ¹⁷ But when he came to himself he said, 'How many of my father's hired hands have bread enough and to spare, but here I am dying of hunger! ¹⁸ I will get up and go to my father, and I will say to him, "Father, I have sinned against heaven and before you; ¹⁹ I am no longer worthy to be called your son; treat me like one of your

^a Or *how can it be used for seasoning?*
^b Gk *drachmas*, each worth about a day's wage for a laborer
^c Gk *he*
^d Other ancient authorities read *filled his stomach with*

softer. **27:** See Mk 8.34. **31–32:** Possibly alludes to some contemporary event. **33:** The stark severity of this statement suggests that it is to be understood as hyperbole. See 12.33; 18.22.

14.34–35: Saying about salt (Mt 5.13; Mk 9.49–50). This saying warns against lackadaisical discipleship. Ancient salt was not pure sodium chloride, so the other material in the salt could go bad and cause the salt to be no good.

15.1–7: Parable of the lost sheep (Mt 18.12–14). God is frequently called the shepherd, both of Israel (e.g., Pss 78.52; 80.1; 100.3) and of the individual (Ps 23); for the image of lost sheep, see Ps 119.176; Jer 50.6; Ezek 34.15–16. **6–7:** The mention of joy anticipates the declarations of joy in the following two parables, which share the theme of lost and found.

15.8–10: Parable of the lost coin. The woman sweeping and seeking the coin is freely cast in the parable to depict the activity of God. **8:** The coins are Greek drachmas; see note *b.*

15.11–32: Parable of the lost prodigal son. 12: On inheritance, see Deut 21.17. See 12.13n. **15:** *Pigs,* see 8.32n.

hired hands.'" [20] So he set off and went to his father. But while he was still far off, his father saw him and was filled with compassion; he ran and put his arms around him and kissed him. [21] Then the son said to him, 'Father, I have sinned against heaven and before you; I am no longer worthy to be called your son.'[a] [22] But the father said to his slaves, 'Quickly, bring out a robe—the best one—and put it on him; put a ring on his finger and sandals on his feet. [23] And get the fatted calf and kill it, and let us eat and celebrate; [24] for this son of mine was dead and is alive again; he was lost and is found!' And they began to celebrate.

[25] "Now his elder son was in the field; and when he came and approached the house, he heard music and dancing. [26] He called one of the slaves and asked what was going on. [27] He replied, 'Your brother has come, and your father has killed the fatted calf, because he has got him back safe and sound.' [28] Then he became angry and refused to go in. His father came out and began to plead with him. [29] But he answered his father, 'Listen! For all these years I have been working like a slave for you, and I have never disobeyed your command; yet you have never given me even a young goat so that I might celebrate with my friends. [30] But when this son of yours came back, who has devoured your property with prostitutes, you killed the fatted calf for him!' [31] Then the father[b] said to him, 'Son, you are always with me, and all that is mine is yours. [32] But we had to celebrate and rejoice, because this brother of yours was dead and has come to life; he was lost and has been found.'"

16 Then Jesus[b] said to the disciples, "There was a rich man who had a manager, and charges were brought to him that this man was squandering his property. [2] So he summoned him and said to him, 'What is this that I hear about you? Give me an accounting of your management, because you cannot be my manager any longer.' [3] Then the manager said to himself, 'What will I do, now that my master is taking the position away from me? I am not strong enough to dig, and I am ashamed to beg. [4] I have decided what to do so that, when I am dismissed as manager, people may welcome me into their homes.' [5] So, summoning his master's debtors one by one, he asked the first, 'How much do you owe my master?' [6] He answered, 'A hundred jugs of olive oil.' He said to him, 'Take your bill, sit down quickly, and make it fifty.' [7] Then he asked another, 'And how much do you owe?' He replied, 'A hundred containers of wheat.' He said to him, 'Take your bill and make it eighty.' [8] And his master commended the dishonest manager because he had acted shrewdly; for the children of this age are more shrewd in dealing with their own generation than are the children of light. [9] And I tell you, make friends for yourselves

a   Other ancient authorities add *Treat me like one of your hired servants*

b   Gk *he*

22–24: His place as son is freely restored, though his inheritance is gone. The parable illustrates God's grace toward those who rebel and return. 22: *Robe*, a festal garment (not worn while working); *ring*, symbol of authority; *sandals*, slaves would have been barefooted. Cf. Gen 41.42; Zech 3.4. 23: *Fatted calf*, a luxury; see 1 Sam 28.24; Am 6.4. 25–32: Rivalry between brothers is a common biblical theme (see Gen 4.2–8; 25.27–34; 27.1–36; 37.1–4). Note the elder son's pique ("this son of yours," v. 30). 31: See v. 12n.

16.1–9: Parable of the dishonest manager. The culmination of this enigmatic story appears to be v. 8, and Jesus' exposition follows in v. 9. The meaning of the story for those hearing Jesus' teaching is that the dishonest manager was prudent in using the things of this life to ensure the future, so believers should do the same. More generally, however, the probable sense of the story itself is that the steward was dishonest in his squandering his master's estate. When confronted, he does not necessarily engage in dishonest behavior (in fact he is praised for his actions), but he calls in the debtors and reduces their bills by eliminating his own commission. Thus, he shrewdly uses material goods to win gratitude from his master's debtors. 8: *His master*, lit., "the lord"; perhaps indicating a reference by Luke to Jesus ("the Lord") rather than being the words of Jesus' conclusion to the parable. *Children of light*, those who are spiritually enlightened; this phrase appears in Jn 12.36; Eph 5.8; 1 Thess 5.5, as well as in the Dead Sea Scrolls where it is contrasted with the phrase "children of darkness." 9: *Wealth*, lit., "mammon," is the Greek transliteration of a Semitic word probably meaning "that in which one trusts."

by means of dishonest wealth[a] so that when it is gone, they may welcome you into the eternal homes.[b]

[10] "Whoever is faithful in a very little is faithful also in much; and whoever is dishonest in a very little is dishonest also in much. [11] If then you have not been faithful with the dishonest wealth,[a] who will entrust to you the true riches? [12] And if you have not been faithful with what belongs to another, who will give you what is your own? [13] No slave can serve two masters; for a slave will either hate the one and love the other, or be devoted to the one and despise the other. You cannot serve God and wealth."[a]

[14] The Pharisees, who were lovers of money, heard all this, and they ridiculed him. [15] So he said to them, "You are those who justify yourselves in the sight of others; but God knows your hearts; for what is prized by human beings is an abomination in the sight of God.

[16] "The law and the prophets were in effect until John came; since then the good news of the kingdom of God is proclaimed, and everyone tries to enter it by force.[c] [17] But it is easier for heaven and earth to pass away, than for one stroke of a letter in the law to be dropped.

[18] "Anyone who divorces his wife and marries another commits adultery, and whoever marries a woman divorced from her husband commits adultery.

[19] "There was a rich man who was dressed in purple and fine linen and who feasted sumptuously every day. [20] And at his gate lay a poor man named Lazarus, covered with sores, [21] who longed to satisfy his hunger with what fell from the rich man's table; even the dogs would come and lick his sores. [22] The poor man died and was carried away by the angels to be with Abraham.[d] The rich man also died and was buried. [23] In Hades, where he was being tormented, he looked up and saw Abraham far away with Lazarus by his side.[e] [24] He called out, 'Father Abraham, have mercy on me, and send Lazarus to dip the tip of his finger in water and cool my tongue; for I am in agony in these flames.' [25] But Abraham said, 'Child, remember that during your lifetime you received your good things, and Lazarus in like manner evil things; but now he is comforted here, and you are in agony. [26] Besides all this, between you and us a great chasm has been fixed, so that those who might want to pass from here to you cannot do so, and no one can cross from there to us.' [27] He said, 'Then, father, I beg you to send him to my father's house— [28] for I have five brothers—that he may warn them, so that they will not also come into this place of torment.' [29] Abraham replied, 'They have Moses and the prophets; they should listen to them.' [30] He said, 'No, father Abraham; but

[a] Gk mammon
[b] Gk tents
[c] Or everyone is strongly urged to enter it
[d] Gk to Abraham's bosom
[e] Gk in his bosom

16.10–18: A series of sayings. 10–12: Sayings on faithfulness. The sayings take the form of "from lesser to greater." 11,13: Wealth, see v. 9n. 13: The impossibility of serving two masters (Mt 6.24; cf. Deut 6.13). 14–15: Strong criticism of the Pharisees. 16–17: Sayings concerning the law (Mt 11.12–13; 5.18; cf. Lk 21.33). 16: Here, John the Baptist is presented as the figure through whom the fulfillment of God's promises began to appear. The law and the prophets, the first two parts of what became the three divisions of the Hebrew Bible, the Torah or "law" of Moses, and the prophets (the books of Joshua through 2 Kings and Isaiah through Malachi; see the Prologue to Sirach; 2 Macc 15.9; Lk 16.29; 24.27,44). 18: Saying concerning divorce (Mt 19.9; Mk 10.11–12). This statement may condemn the simultaneous actions of divorce and marrying another; in other words, a divorce that occurred to facilitate remarriage. Herod Antipas had done exactly that; see 3.19–20n.

16.19–31: Parable of the rich man and Lazarus. A clear emphasis of this parable (vv. 27–31) is that the Hebrew Bible speaks an urgent and sufficient call to repentance (v. 17). As a whole the story seems to illustrate vv. 10–15. 19: The rich man, though unnamed, is commonly called "Dives," which is Latin for "rich man." Purple was an expensive cloth dyed with the liquid obtained from a species of shellfish. 20: The person named here is not to be identified with the Lazarus of Jn 11.1–44; 12.1,9. 21–22: The moral character of Lazarus is passed over to illustrate the fatal deficiency in the life of the indifferent rich man and the impossibility of altering his condemnation. 22: With Abraham, traditional terminology for a blessed condition in the afterlife; see 13.28–29. 23: Hades, 10.15n.

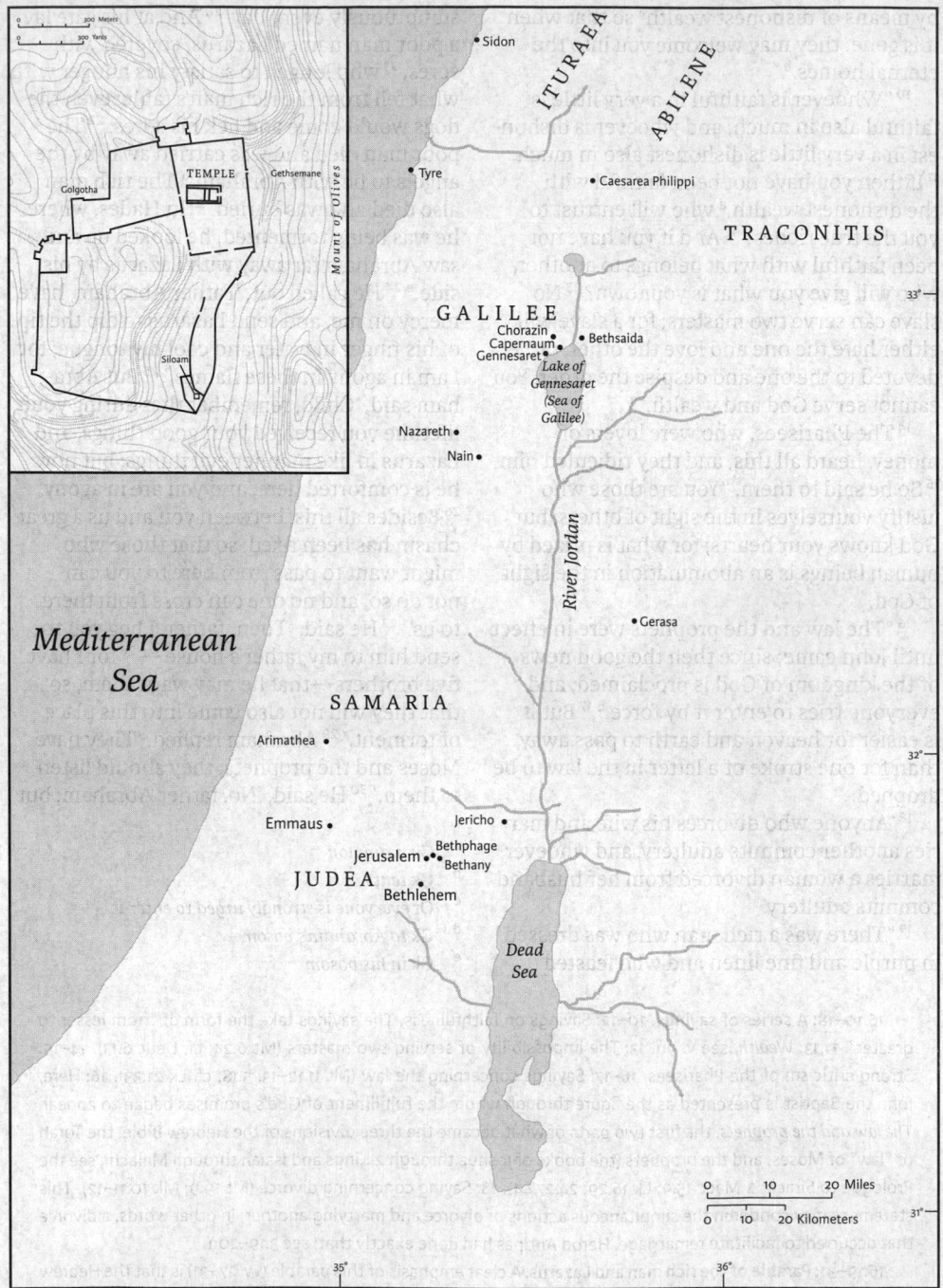

The geography of the Gospel of Luke.

if someone goes to them from the dead, they will repent.' ³¹ He said to him, 'If they do not listen to Moses and the prophets, neither will they be convinced even if someone rises from the dead.'"

17 Jesusᵃ said to his disciples, "Occasions for stumbling are bound to come, but woe to anyone by whom they come! ² It would be better for you if a millstone were hung around your neck and you were thrown into the sea than for you to cause one of these little ones to stumble. ³ Be on your guard! If another discipleᵇ sins, you must rebuke the offender, and if there is repentance, you must forgive. ⁴ And if the same person sins against you seven times a day, and turns back to you seven times and says, 'I repent,' you must forgive."

⁵ The apostles said to the Lord, "Increase our faith!" ⁶ The Lord replied, "If you had faith the size of aᶜ mustard seed, you could say to this mulberry tree, 'Be uprooted and planted in the sea,' and it would obey you.

⁷ "Who among you would say to your slave who has just come in from plowing or tending sheep in the field, 'Come here at once and take your place at the table'? ⁸ Would you not rather say to him, 'Prepare supper for me, put on your apron and serve me while I eat and drink; later you may eat and drink'? ⁹ Do you thank the slave for doing what was commanded? ¹⁰ So you also, when you have done all that you were ordered to do, say, 'We are worthless slaves; we have done only what we ought to have done!'"

¹¹ On the way to Jerusalem Jesusᵈ was going through the region between Samaria and Galilee. ¹² As he entered a village, ten lepersᵉ approached him. Keeping their distance, ¹³ they called out, saying, "Jesus, Master, have mercy on us!" ¹⁴ When he saw them, he said to them, "Go and show yourselves to the priests." And as they went, they were made clean. ¹⁵ Then one of them, when he saw that he was healed, turned back, praising God with a loud voice. ¹⁶ He prostrated himself at Jesus'ᶠ feet and thanked him. And he was a Samaritan. ¹⁷ Then Jesus asked, "Were not ten made clean? But the other nine, where are they? ¹⁸ Was none of them found to return and give praise to God except this foreigner?" ¹⁹ Then he said to him, "Get up and go on your way; your faith has made you well."

²⁰ Once Jesusᵈ was asked by the Pharisees when the kingdom of God was coming, and he answered, "The kingdom of God is not coming with things that can be observed; ²¹ nor will they say, 'Look, here it is!' or 'There it is!' For, in fact, the kingdom of God is amongᵍ you."

ᵃ Gk *He*
ᵇ Gk *your brother*
ᶜ Gk *faith as a grain of*
ᵈ Gk *he*
ᵉ The terms *leper* and *leprosy* can refer to several diseases
ᶠ Gk *his*
ᵍ Or *within*

29: *Moses and the prophets*, see v. 16n. 31: *Rises from the dead*, a clear reference to Jesus' resurrection (see 9.22) and the ensuing refusal of some to believe it.

17.1–3a: The peril of causing temptation (Mt 18.6–7; Mk 9.42). 2: *Millstone*, stone (used in pairs) to grind grain; it was typically made of basalt and ca. 12–18 in (30–40 cm) in diameter and 2–4 in (5–10 cm) thick. *Little ones*, disciples.

17.3b–4: Sayings concerning forgiveness (Mt 18.15,21–22).

17.5–6: Saying concerning faith (Mt 17.19–21; Mk 9.28–29). 6: *The size of a mustard seed*, see Mk 4.31.

17.7–10: The obligation to obedience. For the apostles, obedience to God is a duty to be fulfilled and not an occasion for reward; yet, cf. 12.35–38.

17.11–19: The cleansing of ten lepers. (See 5.12–16n.) 12: Lev 13.45–46. 14: *Priests*, Lev 13.2–3; 14.2–32. 16: *Samaritan*, see 9.52n. 17: *The other nine* were, presumably, Jews. 18: The Gk word translated *foreigner* more literally means "another race," 7.9n. 19: 7.50; 8.48; 18.42. *Made you well*, lit., "saved you."

17.20–21: The coming of the kingdom of God. 20: 19.11; 21.7; Acts 1.6. 21: The questioners had in mind a kingdom bringing material and political benefits. Jesus shifted the emphasis from future expectation to the observable presence of the kingdom in his ministry; see 11.20.

17.22–37: The day of the Son of Man (Mt 24.17–18,23,26–28,37–41; Mk 13.14–16,19–23). Mt 24 has similar

22 Then he said to the disciples, "The days are coming when you will long to see one of the days of the Son of Man, and you will not see it. 23 They will say to you, 'Look there!' or 'Look here!' Do not go, do not set off in pursuit. 24 For as the lightning flashes and lights up the sky from one side to the other, so will the Son of Man be in his day.ᵃ 25 But first he must endure much suffering and be rejected by this generation. 26 Just as it was in the days of Noah, so too it will be in the days of the Son of Man. 27 They were eating and drinking, and marrying and being given in marriage, until the day Noah entered the ark, and the flood came and destroyed all of them. 28 Likewise, just as it was in the days of Lot: they were eating and drinking, buying and selling, planting and building, 29 but on the day that Lot left Sodom, it rained fire and sulfur from heaven and destroyed all of them 30 —it will be like that on the day that the Son of Man is revealed. 31 On that day, anyone on the housetop who has belongings in the house must not come down to take them away; and likewise anyone in the field must not turn back. 32 Remember Lot's wife. 33 Those who try to make their life secure will lose it, but those who lose their life will keep it. 34 I tell you, on that night there will be two in one bed; one will be taken and the other left. 35 There will be two women grinding meal together; one will be taken and the other left."ᵇ 37 Then they asked him, "Where, Lord?" He said to them, "Where the corpse is, there the vultures will gather."

18 Then Jesusᶜ told them a parable about their need to pray always and not to lose heart. 2 He said, "In a certain city there was a judge who neither feared God nor had respect for people. 3 In that city there was a widow who kept coming to him and saying, 'Grant me justice against my opponent.' 4 For a while he refused; but later he said to himself, 'Though I have no fear of God and no respect for anyone, 5 yet because this widow keeps bothering me, I will grant her justice, so that she may not wear me out by continually coming.'"ᵈ 6 And the Lord said, "Listen to what the unjust judge says. 7 And will not God grant justice to his chosen ones who cry to him day and night? Will he delay long in helping them? 8 I tell you, he will quickly grant justice to them. And yet, when the Son of Man comes, will he find faith on earth?"

9 He also told this parable to some who trusted in themselves that they were righteous and regarded others with contempt: 10 "Two men went up to the temple to pray, one a Pharisee and the other a tax collector. 11 The Pharisee, standing by himself, was praying thus, 'God, I thank you that I am not like other people: thieves, rogues, adulterers, or even like this tax collector. 12 I fast twice a week; I give a tenth of all my income.' 13 But the tax collector, standing far off, would not even look up to heaven, but was beating his breast and saying, 'God, be merciful to me, a sinner!' 14 I tell you, this man went down to

---

ᵃ Other ancient authorities lack *in his day*
ᵇ Other ancient authorities add verse 36, *"Two will be in the field; one will be taken and the other left."*
ᶜ Gk *he*
ᵈ Or *so that she may not finally come and slap me in the face*

---

teachings in a different order and setting. **24:** The coming will be sudden and discernible to all. **25:** 9.22. An allusion to Jesus' suffering and death. **26–36:** The emphasis is on the unexpected nature of events. **26–27:** Gen 6.5–8; 7.6–24. **28–30:** Gen 18.16–19.28. **31:** *On the housetop,* a flat-top roof reached by an exterior staircase. **32:** Gen 19.26. **33:** 9.24. **[36]:** This verse is a scribal addition to Luke to incorporate a saying from Mt 24.20. **37:** Mt 24.28. The questioners wish to know *where* the messiah and his people will be located. Instead of answering them directly, Jesus warns: As surely as vultures find the carcass, so surely will divine judgment come; therefore always be ready!

18.1–8: Parable of the unjust judge and the persistent widow. **1:** The aim is carefully stated (cf. 11.5–8), perhaps because the details are incongruous (as in 16.1–9). **3:** Cf. Deut 27.19. **8:** *Comes,* from heaven, in judgment (see Dan 7.13–14). This verse links the parable with 17.20–37.

18.9–14: Parable of the Pharisee and the tax collector. **9:** *Righteous,* that is, acceptable to God because of their strict observance of the law. **10:** Tax collector, see 5.27n. **11:** *Standing by himself, was praying thus,* more literally, "standing to himself these things prayed," a suggestively ambiguous statement. **12:** *Twice a week,* Mondays and Thursdays; such a practice was apparently voluntary rather than prescribed. **13:** *Beating his breast,* a sign of contrition. **14:** *Justified* means "right with God" or "accepted by God." All who exalt

his home justified rather than the other; for all who exalt themselves will be humbled, but all who humble themselves will be exalted."

¹⁵ People were bringing even infants to him that he might touch them; and when the disciples saw it, they sternly ordered them not to do it. ¹⁶ But Jesus called for them and said, "Let the little children come to me, and do not stop them; for it is to such as these that the kingdom of God belongs. ¹⁷ Truly I tell you, whoever does not receive the kingdom of God as a little child will never enter it."

¹⁸ A certain ruler asked him, "Good Teacher, what must I do to inherit eternal life?" ¹⁹ Jesus said to him, "Why do you call me good? No one is good but God alone. ²⁰ You know the commandments: 'You shall not commit adultery; You shall not murder; You shall not steal; You shall not bear false witness; Honor your father and mother.'" ²¹ He replied, "I have kept all these since my youth." ²² When Jesus heard this, he said to him, "There is still one thing lacking. Sell all that you own and distribute the money[a] to the poor, and you will have treasure in heaven; then come, follow me." ²³ But when he heard this, he became sad; for he was very rich. ²⁴ Jesus looked at him and said, "How hard it is for those who have wealth to enter the kingdom of God! ²⁵ Indeed, it is easier for a camel to go through the eye of a needle than for someone who is rich to enter the kingdom of God." ²⁶ Those who heard it said, "Then who can be saved?" ²⁷ He replied, "What is impossible for mortals is possible for God."

²⁸ Then Peter said, "Look, we have left our homes and followed you." ²⁹ And he said to them, "Truly I tell you, there is no one who has left house or wife or brothers or parents or children, for the sake of the kingdom of God, ³⁰ who will not get back very much more in this age, and in the age to come eternal life."

³¹ Then he took the twelve aside and said to them, "See, we are going up to Jerusalem, and everything that is written about the Son of Man by the prophets will be accomplished. ³² For he will be handed over to the Gentiles; and he will be mocked and insulted and spat upon. ³³ After they have flogged him, they will kill him, and on the third day he will rise again." ³⁴ But they understood nothing about all these things; in fact, what he said was hidden from them, and they did not grasp what was said.

³⁵ As he approached Jericho, a blind man was sitting by the roadside begging. ³⁶ When he heard a crowd going by, he asked what was happening. ³⁷ They told him, "Jesus of Nazareth[b] is passing by." ³⁸ Then he shouted, "Jesus, Son of David, have mercy on me!" ³⁹ Those who were in front sternly ordered him to be quiet; but he shouted even more loudly, "Son of David, have mercy on me!" ⁴⁰ Jesus stood still and ordered the man to be brought to him; and when he came near, he

---

a Gk lacks the money
b Gk the Nazorean

themselves . . . , see 14.11n.

18.15–17: Jesus and the little children (Mt 19.13–15; Mk 10.13–16). Located between the preceding parable and the subsequent incident with the rich ruler, this brief story with its sayings contrasts humility with self-righteousness and self-satisfaction.

18.18–30: The rich ruler, wealth, and salvation (Mt 19.16–30; Mk 10.17–31). **18:** 10.25. **20:** The order of the commandments, varying from the Hebrew Bible, follows the ancient Greek translation, the Septuagint (LXX); see Ex 20.12–16; Deut 5.16–20. **22:** *Treasure in heaven,* see 12.33–34. See 14.33n. **23:** The story does not tell what the rich ruler ultimately did in relation to Jesus' statement at 18.22. **26:** To be *saved* refers to the same spiritual experience as to *inherit eternal life* (v. 18), and to *enter the kingdom of God* (v. 25). **27:** Gen 18.14; Job 42.2; Jer 32.17; Lk 1.37. **28:** 5.1–11. **30:** *In this age, and in the age to come,* traditional apocalyptic language contrasting the present evil age and the age of God's kingdom or reign.

18.31–34: Jesus' third prediction of his death (Mt 20.17–19; Mk 10.32–34). Cf. 9.22,44–45; 17.25. The details of this prediction form an outline of the events in chs 22–24. **31:** *Everything that is written . . . by the prophets,* an allusion to passages such as Ps 22; Isa 53; Zech 13.7.

18.35–43: Healing of a blind man (Mt 20.29–34; Mk 10.46–52). **38:** *Son of David,* a phrase identifying Jesus with the messianic expectations associated with the dynasty founded by David, probably indicating political

asked him, 41 "What do you want me to do for you?" He said, "Lord, let me see again." 42 Jesus said to him, "Receive your sight; your faith has saved you." 43 Immediately he regained his sight and followed him, glorifying God; and all the people, when they saw it, praised God.

19 He entered Jericho and was passing through it. 2 A man was there named Zacchaeus; he was a chief tax collector and was rich. 3 He was trying to see who Jesus was, but on account of the crowd he could not, because he was short in stature. 4 So he ran ahead and climbed a sycamore tree to see him, because he was going to pass that way. 5 When Jesus came to the place, he looked up and said to him, "Zacchaeus, hurry and come down; for I must stay at your house today." 6 So he hurried down and was happy to welcome him. 7 All who saw it began to grumble and said, "He has gone to be the guest of one who is a sinner." 8 Zacchaeus stood there and said to the Lord, "Look, half of my possessions, Lord, I will give to the poor; and if I have defrauded anyone of anything, I will pay back four times as much." 9 Then Jesus said to him, "Today salvation has come to this house, because he too is a son of Abraham. 10 For the Son of Man came to seek out and to save the lost."

11 As they were listening to this, he went on to tell a parable, because he was near Jerusalem, and because they supposed that the kingdom of God was to appear immediately. 12 So he said, "A nobleman went to a distant country to get royal power for himself and then return. 13 He summoned ten of his slaves, and gave them ten pounds,ª and said to them, 'Do business with these until I come back.' 14 But the citizens of his country hated him and sent a delegation after him, saying, 'We do not want this man to rule over us.' 15 When he returned, having received royal power, he ordered these slaves, to whom he had given the money, to be summoned so that he might find out what they had gained by trading. 16 The first came forward and said, 'Lord, your pound has made ten more pounds.' 17 He said to him, 'Well done, good slave! Because you have been trustworthy in a very small thing, take charge of ten cities.' 18 Then the second came, saying, 'Lord, your pound has made five pounds.' 19 He said to him, 'And you, rule over five cities.' 20 Then the other came, saying, 'Lord, here is your pound. I wrapped it up in a piece of cloth, 21 for I was afraid of you, because you are a harsh man; you take what you did not deposit, and reap what you did not sow.' 22 He said to him, 'I will judge you by your own words, you wicked slave! You knew, did you, that I was a harsh man, taking what I did not deposit and reaping what I did not sow? 23 Why then did you not put my money into the bank? Then when I returned, I could have collected it with interest.' 24 He said to the bystanders, 'Take the pound from him and give it to the one who has ten pounds.' 25 (And they said to him, 'Lord, he has ten pounds!') 26 'I tell you, to all those who have, more will be given; but from those who have nothing, even what they have will be taken away. 27 But as for these enemies of mine who did not want me to be king over them—bring them here and slaughter them in my presence.'"

ª The mina, rendered here by *pound*, was about three months' wages for a laborer

and nationalistic aspirations. **42:** See 17.19n.

19.1–10: Zacchaeus's salvation. Although he is rich, Zacchaeus's response to Jesus is a striking contrast to that of the rich man in 18.18–23. **1:** Because of its location *Jericho* was an important customs center. **2:** As *chief tax collector* Zacchaeus had contracted with the Roman overlords for the right to collect revenues (lit., "tolls") in the district. His neighbors despised him for sharing in the Roman domination (v. 7). **7:** 5.29–30; 15.1–2. **8:** *I will give,* henceforth, a vow amounting to repentance. *Four times as much,* cf. Ex 22.1; Lev 6.5; Num 5.6–7. **9:** *Salvation,* or the kingdom of God, *has come* in Jesus' presence and message and evinces itself in Zacchaeus's transformation. **10:** A summary of Jesus' ministry in the entire Gospel; see ch 15.

19.11–27: Parable of the ten pounds (Mt 25.14–30; Mk 13.34). The parable may allude to the journey of Archelaus to Rome in 4 BCE to assure his succession to his father Herod's throne; his mission was opposed by a delegation of leaders from Judea (Josephus *Ant.* 17.9.4; 17.10). **11:** 9.51; 13.22; 17.11; 18.31. **13:** *Ten pounds,* lit., "ten minas," golden coins, each of which equaled a hundred drachmas (see 15.8n.). **17:** 16.10. **26:** See 8.18.

²⁸ After he had said this, he went on ahead, going up to Jerusalem.

²⁹ When he had come near Bethphage and Bethany, at the place called the Mount of Olives, he sent two of the disciples, ³⁰ saying, "Go into the village ahead of you, and as you enter it you will find tied there a colt that has never been ridden. Untie it and bring it here. ³¹ If anyone asks you, 'Why are you untying it?' just say this, 'The Lord needs it.'" ³² So those who were sent departed and found it as he had told them. ³³ As they were untying the colt, its owners asked them, "Why are you untying the colt?" ³⁴ They said, "The Lord needs it." ³⁵ Then they brought it to Jesus; and after throwing their cloaks on the colt, they set Jesus on it. ³⁶ As he rode along, people kept spreading their cloaks on the road. ³⁷ As he was now approaching the path down from the Mount of Olives, the whole multitude of the disciples began to praise God joyfully with a loud voice for all the deeds of power that they had seen, ³⁸ saying,

"Blessed is the king
    who comes in the name of the Lord!
Peace in heaven,
    and glory in the highest heaven!"

³⁹ Some of the Pharisees in the crowd said to him, "Teacher, order your disciples to stop." ⁴⁰ He answered, "I tell you, if these were silent, the stones would shout out."

⁴¹ As he came near and saw the city, he wept over it, ⁴² saying, "If you, even you, had only recognized on this day the things that make for peace! But now they are hidden from your eyes. ⁴³ Indeed, the days will come upon you, when your enemies will set up ramparts around you and surround you, and hem you in on every side. ⁴⁴ They will crush you to the ground, you and your children within you, and they will not leave within you one stone upon another; because you did not recognize the time of your visitation from God."ᵃ

⁴⁵ Then he entered the temple and began to drive out those who were selling things there; ⁴⁶ and he said, "It is written,

'My house shall be a house of prayer';
    but you have made it a den of robbers."

⁴⁷ Every day he was teaching in the temple. The chief priests, the scribes, and the leaders of the people kept looking for a way to kill him; ⁴⁸ but they did not find anything they could do, for all the people were spellbound by what they heard.

20 One day, as he was teaching the people in the temple and telling the good news, the chief priests and the scribes came with the elders ² and said to him, "Tell us, by what authority are you doing these things? Who is it who gave you this authority?" ³ He answered them, "I will also ask you a question, and you tell me: ⁴ Did the baptism of John come from heaven, or was it of human

---

ᵃ Gk lacks *from God*

19.28–21.38: Jesus' ministry in Jerusalem (Mt 21.1–24.36; Mk 11.1–13.37).

19.28–40: The entry into Jerusalem (Mt 21.1–9; Mk 11.1–10; Jn 12.12–18). **29:** *Bethphage and Bethany*, villages just east of Jerusalem. **30:** Zech. 9.9. **31:** While the situation in the story shows that it is "Jesus" who needs the colt, the saying could be understood to mean "God needs it." **32:** 22.13. **36:** Cf. 2 Kings 9.13. **37:** The road crossed a ridge into the Kidron valley. **38:** Incorporates a phrase from Ps 118.26; see Zech 9.9; Lk 13.35. This scene depicts a royal entry, naming Jesus as *king*, a title that will be used in the charges against Jesus before Pilate in 23.2. Portions of this verse echo the words of the angels at 2.14. **39–40:** Hab 2.11.

19.41–44: Weeping over Jerusalem. See 13.33–34; cf. 23.27–31. These verses may reflect historical knowledge of the actual destruction of Jerusalem in 70 CE. **42–44:** The "you" here is a singular form, indicating that Jesus spoke to "Jerusalem." **43:** 21.20–24; 21.6; Isa 29.3; Jer 6.6; Ezek 4.2. *Your enemies*, the Roman army. *Ramparts*, palisade that would keep out all supplies of food. **44:** Ps 137.9; Hos 10.14; 13.16. *Children*, the inhabitants of Jerusalem.

19.45–46: Cleansing of the Temple (Mt 21.12–13; Mk 11.15–17; Jn 2.13–17). In this display of authority in the Temple, Jesus dramatically acts out Mal 3.1–2. **45:** *Selling* the prescribed offerings, as in 2.24; Lev 1.14. **46:** Isa 56.7; Jer 7.11.

19.47–48: The religious leaders' hostility toward Jesus (Mk 11.18–19). **47:** *The chief priests, the scribes, and the leaders of the people* were Jesus' adversaries once he reached Jerusalem.

20.1–8: Questioning Jesus' authority (Mt 21.23–27; Mk 11.27–33; Jn 2.18–22). **4:** *The baptism of John,* 3.3–21.

origin?" ⁵ They discussed it with one another, saying, "If we say, 'From heaven,' he will say, 'Why did you not believe him?' ⁶ But if we say, 'Of human origin,' all the people will stone us; for they are convinced that John was a prophet." ⁷ So they answered that they did not know where it came from. ⁸ Then Jesus said to them, "Neither will I tell you by what authority I am doing these things."

⁹ He began to tell the people this parable: "A man planted a vineyard, and leased it to tenants, and went to another country for a long time. ¹⁰ When the season came, he sent a slave to the tenants in order that they might give him his share of the produce of the vineyard; but the tenants beat him and sent him away empty-handed. ¹¹ Next he sent another slave; that one also they beat and insulted and sent away empty-handed. ¹² And he sent still a third; this one also they wounded and threw out. ¹³ Then the owner of the vineyard said, 'What shall I do? I will send my beloved son; perhaps they will re-spect him.' ¹⁴ But when the tenants saw him, they discussed it among themselves and said, 'This is the heir; let us kill him so that the inheritance may be ours.' ¹⁵ So they threw him out of the vineyard and killed him. What then will the owner of the vineyard do to them? ¹⁶ He will come and destroy those ten-ants and give the vineyard to others." When they heard this, they said, "Heaven forbid!" ¹⁷ But he looked at them and said, "What then does this text mean:

'The stone that the builders rejected
    has become the cornerstone'?ᵃ

¹⁸ Everyone who falls on that stone will be broken to pieces; and it will crush anyone on whom it falls." ¹⁹ When the scribes and chief priests realized that he had told this parable against them, they wanted to lay hands on him at that very hour, but they feared the people.

²⁰ So they watched him and sent spies who pretended to be honest, in order to trap him by what he said, so as to hand him over to the jurisdiction and authority of the governor. ²¹ So they asked him, "Teacher, we know that you are right in what you say and teach, and you show deference to no one, but teach the way of God in accordance with truth. ²² Is it lawful for us to pay taxes to the emperor, or not?" ²³ But he perceived their craftiness and said to them, ²⁴ "Show me a denarius. Whose head and whose title does it bear?" They said, "The emperor's." ²⁵ He said to them, "Then give to the emperor the things that are the emperor's, and to God the things that are God's." ²⁶ And they were not able in the presence of the people to trap him by what he said; and being amazed by his answer, they became silent.

²⁷ Some Sadducees, those who say there is no resurrection, came to him ²⁸ and asked him a question, "Teacher, Moses wrote for us that if a man's brother dies, leaving a wife but no children, the manᵇ shall marry the widow and raise up children for his brother. ²⁹ Now there were seven brothers; the first married, and died childless; ³⁰ then the second ³¹ and the third married her, and so in the same way all seven died childless. ³² Finally the woman also died. ³³ In the resurrection, therefore,

ᵃ Or keystone
ᵇ Gk his brother

20.9–19: Parable of the vineyard and tenants (Mt 21.33–46; Mk 12.1–12). 9: Isa 5.1–7. 13: The use of beloved (see 3.22) identifies the son with Jesus. 15: The murder of the son outside the vineyard may reflect Jesus' cruci-fixion outside the city of Jerusalem; see Jn 19.17; Heb 13.12; cf. Acts 7.52–53. 17: Ps 118.22; see Isa 28.16; Acts 4.11. 18: Isa 8.14–15. 19: Lk 19.47.

20.20–26: Paying taxes to the emperor (Mt 22.15–22; Mk 12.13–17). 20: Honest translates a Greek word that normally means "correct according to the law," i.e., "righteous." It is used here in the same sense of false pre-tense that it has in Mt 23.28. 22–25: A falsified version of this incident lies behind the charge against Jesus before Pilate in 23.2. 24: Denarius, a coin that had the head of the emperor on one side. Strict, pious Jews did not use these Roman coins, but specially minted Jewish coinage.

20.27–40: Question concerning resurrection (Mt 22.23–33; Mk 12.18–27). 27: Sadducees were the elite class of landed Jerusalem gentry who operated the Temple and wielded power from that religious base of operations; cf. Acts 4.1–2; 23.6–10. 27: Sadducees recognized only the Pentateuch (first five books of the Hebrew Bible) as authoritative, so they denied resurrection because they insisted that it was not taught there. 28: The question

whose wife will the woman be? For the seven had married her."

34 Jesus said to them, "Those who belong to this age marry and are given in marriage; 35 but those who are considered worthy of a place in that age and in the resurrection from the dead neither marry nor are given in marriage. 36 Indeed they cannot die anymore, because they are like angels and are children of God, being children of the resurrection. 37 And the fact that the dead are raised Moses himself showed, in the story about the bush, where he speaks of the Lord as the God of Abraham, the God of Isaac, and the God of Jacob. 38 Now he is God not of the dead, but of the living; for to him all of them are alive." 39 Then some of the scribes answered, "Teacher, you have spoken well." 40 For they no longer dared to ask him another question.

41 Then he said to them, "How can they say that the Messiah[a] is David's son? 42 For David himself says in the book of Psalms,

'The Lord said to my Lord,
"Sit at my right hand,
43 until I make your enemies your
footstool."'

44 David thus calls him Lord; so how can he be his son?"

45 In the hearing of all the people he said to the[b] disciples, 46 "Beware of the scribes, who like to walk around in long robes, and love to be greeted with respect in the marketplaces, and to have the best seats in the synagogues and places of honor at banquets. 47 They devour widows' houses and for the sake of appearance say long prayers. They will receive the greater condemnation."

21 He looked up and saw rich people putting their gifts into the treasury; 2 he also saw a poor widow put in two small copper coins. 3 He said, "Truly I tell you, this poor widow has put in more than all of them; 4 for all of them have contributed out of their abundance, but she out of her poverty has put in all she had to live on."

5 When some were speaking about the temple, how it was adorned with beautiful stones and gifts dedicated to God, he said, 6 "As for these things that you see, the days will come when not one stone will be left upon another; all will be thrown down."

7 They asked him, "Teacher, when will this be, and what will be the sign that this is about to take place?" 8 And he said, "Beware that you are not led astray; for many will come in my name and say, 'I am he!'[c] and, 'The time is near!'[d] Do not go after them. 9 "When you hear of wars and insurrections, do not be terrified; for these things must take place first, but the end will not follow immediately." 10 Then he said to them,

a Or the Christ
b Other ancient authorities read his
c Gk I am
d Or at hand

reflects the practice of levirate marriage in Deut 25.5–10; see Gen 38.8. **34–36:** Human relations in marriage do not exist in the same way beyond death. Jesus distinguishes two ages and kinds of existence. Mortals are part of this age by their physical birth, and of the age to come by resurrection. **37:** Ex 3.6. Jesus cites the words of Moses from the Pentateuch to refute the Sadducees' argument. **39:** Note the praise of Jesus by the scribes, affirmation that shows that all scribes were not simply aligned against Jesus.

20.41–44: A question about David's son (Mt 22.41–46; Mk 12.35–37a). **42–43:** Ps 110.1. No solution is given for the riddle that Jesus offered. **44:** King David was traditionally viewed as the author of most of the Psalms. The question is: How can the messiah be David's descendant if David calls him Lord? Ps 110 was frequently referred to in early Christian writings; see Acts 2.34–35; 1 Cor 15.25; Heb 1.5.

20.45–47: Warning concerning the scribes (Mt 23.1–36; Mk 12.37b–40). **46:** 11.43.

21.1–4: The widow's offering (Mk 12.41–44). **1:** The treasury refers here to a container (shaped like an inverted trumpet for protection against theft) to receive offerings; there were thirteen of these receptacles in "the court of the women" of the Temple; in Jn 8.20 the term refers to a room in the Temple. **2:** The copper coin (Gk "lepton") was of little monetary value (see 12.59n.) but of great cost to this giver.

21.5–6: Foretelling the destruction of the Temple (Mt 24.1–2; Mk 13.1–2). Jesus' teachings in these and the following verses are related to the material in Mk 13, but Luke's version of that eschatological discourse has distinctive elements and perspectives. **6:** See 19.44n.

21.7–11: Sayings about end-time signs (Mt 24.3–8; Mk 13.3–8). **7:** 17.20; Acts 1.6. **10:** 2 Chr 15.6; Isa 19.2.

"Nation will rise against nation, and kingdom against kingdom; [11] there will be great earthquakes, and in various places famines and plagues; and there will be dreadful portents and great signs from heaven.

[12] "But before all this occurs, they will arrest you and persecute you; they will hand you over to synagogues and prisons, and you will be brought before kings and governors because of my name. [13] This will give you an opportunity to testify. [14] So make up your minds not to prepare your defense in advance; [15] for I will give you words[a] and a wisdom that none of your opponents will be able to withstand or contradict. [16] You will be betrayed even by parents and brothers, by relatives and friends; and they will put some of you to death. [17] You will be hated by all because of my name. [18] But not a hair of your head will perish. [19] By your endurance you will gain your souls.

[20] "When you see Jerusalem surrounded by armies, then know that its desolation has come near.[b] [21] Then those in Judea must flee to the mountains, and those inside the city must leave it, and those out in the country must not enter it; [22] for these are days of vengeance, as a fulfillment of all that is written. [23] Woe to those who are pregnant and to those who are nursing infants in those days! For there will be great distress on the earth and wrath against this people; [24] they will fall by the edge of the sword and be taken away as captives among all nations; and Jerusalem will be trampled on by the Gentiles, until the times of the Gentiles are fulfilled.

[25] "There will be signs in the sun, the moon, and the stars, and on the earth distress among nations confused by the roaring of the sea and the waves. [26] People will faint from fear and foreboding of what is coming upon the world, for the powers of the heavens will be shaken. [27] Then they will see 'the Son of Man coming in a cloud' with power and great glory. [28] Now when these things begin to take place, stand up and raise your heads, because your redemption is drawing near."

[29] Then he told them a parable: "Look at the fig tree and all the trees; [30] as soon as they sprout leaves you can see for yourselves and know that summer is already near. [31] So also, when you see these things taking place, you know that the kingdom of God is near. [32] Truly I tell you, this generation will not pass away until all things have taken place. [33] Heaven and earth will pass away, but my words will not pass away.

[34] "Be on guard so that your hearts are not weighed down with dissipation and drunkenness and the worries of this life, and that day does not catch you unexpectedly, [35] like a trap. For it will come upon all who live on the face of the whole earth. [36] Be alert at all times, praying that you may have the strength to escape all these things that will take place, and to stand before the Son of Man."

[37] Every day he was teaching in the temple, and at night he would go out and spend the night on the Mount of Olives, as it was called.

[a] Gk a mouth
[b] Or is at hand

21.12–19: **Foretelling the persecution of the disciples** (Mt 24.9–14; Mk 13.9–13). **14–15:** 12.11–12. These themes developed in the narrative of Acts. **18:** 12.7; Acts 27.34; 1 Sam 14.45.

21.20–24: **The desolation of Jerusalem** (Mt 24.15–22; Mk 13.14–20. See 19.41–44n.). **20–22:** 19.41–44; 23.28–31; 17.31. **20:** *Armies*, the Roman forces. **22:** Cf. Isa 63.4; Jer 5.29; Hos 9.7. **24:** Isa 63.18; Dan 8.13. *The times of the Gentiles* may mean the divinely imposed limit on Roman dominance, or the extension of salvation to all people (20.16).

21.25–28: **The coming of the Son of Man** (Mt 24.29–31; Mk 13.24–27). **25–27:** These verses reflect language and elements of thought from Joel 3.3–4; Isa 24.19 (LXX); Pss 65.8; 46.4; 89.10; Wis 5.22; Jon 1.15. **25:** Isa 13.10; Joel 2.10; Zeph 1.15. **26:** Incorporates wording parallel to Isa 34.4. *The powers of the heavens* are likely the celestial bodies mentioned in v. 25. **27:** Incorporates wording parallel to Dan 7.13–14.

21.29–33: **The lesson of the fig tree** (Mt 24.32–36; Mk 13.28–32). **32:** Cf. 9.27. **33:** 16.17.

21.34–36: **Admonition to alertness** (cf. Mt 24.43–51; 25.13; Mk 13.33–37). **34–36:** 12.35–48. **34:** 8.14; 12.22; 1 Thess 5.6–7. **36:** 2 Cor 5.10.

21.37–38: **Summary concerning Jesus' ministry in Jerusalem. 38:** The story of the woman caught in adultery (Jn 8.1–11) appears after this verse in some ancient manuscripts; see Jn 8.11, note *c*.

[38] And all the people would get up early in the morning to listen to him in the temple.

22 Now the festival of Unleavened Bread, which is called the Passover, was near. [2] The chief priests and the scribes were looking for a way to put Jesus[a] to death, for they were afraid of the people.

[3] Then Satan entered into Judas called Iscariot, who was one of the twelve; [4] he went away and conferred with the chief priests and officers of the temple police about how he might betray him to them. [5] They were greatly pleased and agreed to give him money. [6] So he consented and began to look for an opportunity to betray him to them when no crowd was present.

[7] Then came the day of Unleavened Bread, on which the Passover lamb had to be sacrificed. [8] So Jesus[b] sent Peter and John, saying, "Go and prepare the Passover meal for us that we may eat it." [9] They asked him, "Where do you want us to make preparations for it?" [10] "Listen," he said to them, "when you have entered the city, a man carrying a jar of water will meet you; follow him into the house he enters [11] and say to the owner of the house, 'The teacher asks you, "Where is the guest room, where I may eat the Passover with my disciples?"' [12] He will show you a large room upstairs, already furnished. Make preparations for us there." [13] So they went and found everything as he had told them; and they prepared the Passover meal.

[14] When the hour came, he took his place at the table, and the apostles with him. [15] He said to them, "I have eagerly desired to eat this Passover with you before I suffer; [16] for I tell you, I will not eat it[c] until it is fulfilled in the kingdom of God." [17] Then he took a cup, and after giving thanks he said, "Take this and divide it among yourselves; [18] for I tell you that from now on I will not drink of the fruit of the vine until the kingdom of God comes." [19] Then he took a loaf of bread, and when he had given thanks, he broke it and gave it to them, saying, "This is my body, which is given for you. Do this in remembrance of me." [20] And he did the same with the cup after supper, saying, "This cup that is poured out for you is the new covenant in my blood.[d] [21] But see, the one who betrays me is with me, and his hand is on the table. [22] For the Son of Man is going as it has been

a   Gk *him*
b   Gk *he*
c   Other ancient authorities read *never eat it again*
d   Other ancient authorities lack, in whole or in part, verses 19b-20 (*which is given … in my blood*)

22.1–23.56: The Last Supper and Jesus' trials, death, and burial (Mt 26.1–27.61; Mk 14.1–15.47; Jn 13.1–19.42).

22.1–6: The deadly conspiracy against Jesus. 1–2: Mt 26.2–5; Mk 14.1–2; Jn 11.47–53. The word "called" is a concession to the Gentile readers for whom Luke wrote. **3–6:** Mt 26.14–16; Mk 14.10–11; Jn 13.2. **3:** The entry of *Satan* into *Judas* (see 6.16n.) reintroduces the theme from 4.13. Cf. Jn 13.2. **4:** *Chief priests . . .* , see 19.47n. **5:** Judas's motive for betrayal is made explicit here.

22.7–13: Preparations for the Passover (Mt 26.17–19; Mk 14.12–16; Jn 13.1). **7:** Ex 12.18–20; Deut 16.5–8. **10:** The plans appear to rest on some prior arrangement; a man carrying a jar of water would be doing woman's work and would be easily noticeable. **11:** The identity of the householder is unknown. **12:** The *large room upstairs* was on the second floor, probably served by an outside staircase; such rooms were regularly available and rented to pilgrims to Jerusalem.

22.14–20: The Last Supper (Mt 26.26–29; Mk 14.22–25; cf. Jn 6.51–58). **14:** *The hour,* of the meal, after sundown. **15:** 12.49–50. **16:** Jesus thinks of the meal as pointing forward to the meal celebrating the fulfilling of God's kingdom (12.37n.; 13.28–29; 14.15; 22.28–30). **17:** Some Jewish meals included prayers over the cup of wine, and several such prayers might be offered during the meal (see v. 20). Luke's order of events may be related to this practice, or to a variation among early Christians in the way they remembered and observed the "Lord's supper." Luke's inclusion of a cup before the bread, as well as the usual cup after the bread, is unique. Jesus transformed a Jewish devotional meal into a continuing expression of association with himself in death and victory. **19:** 1 Cor 11.23–26. **21:** Ps 41.9; Jn 13.21–30.

22.21–23: The foretelling of the betrayal (Mt 26.21–25; Mk 14.18–21; Jn 13.21–30). **22:** Jesus (*the Son of Man*) moves toward a destiny determined by God and even Judas's actions are a part of a process beyond human control, although Judas is still responsible for his betrayal.

determined, but woe to that one by whom he is betrayed!" [23] Then they began to ask one another which one of them it could be who would do this.

[24] A dispute also arose among them as to which one of them was to be regarded as the greatest. [25] But he said to them, "The kings of the Gentiles lord it over them; and those in authority over them are called benefactors. [26] But not so with you; rather the greatest among you must become like the youngest, and the leader like one who serves. [27] For who is greater, the one who is at the table or the one who serves? Is it not the one at the table? But I am among you as one who serves.

[28] "You are those who have stood by me in my trials; [29] and I confer on you, just as my Father has conferred on me, a kingdom, [30] so that you may eat and drink at my table in my kingdom, and you will sit on thrones judging the twelve tribes of Israel.

[31] "Simon, Simon, listen! Satan has demanded[a] to sift all of you like wheat, [32] but I have prayed for you that your own faith may not fail; and you, when once you have turned back, strengthen your brothers." [33] And he said to him, "Lord, I am ready to go with you to prison and to death!" [34] Jesus[b] said, "I tell you, Peter, the cock will not crow this day, until you have denied three times that you know me."

[35] He said to them, "When I sent you out without a purse, bag, or sandals, did you lack anything?" They said, "No, not a thing." [36] He said to them, "But now, the one who has a purse must take it, and likewise a bag. And the one who has no sword must sell his cloak and buy one. [37] For I tell you, this scripture must be fulfilled in me, 'And he was counted among the lawless'; and indeed what is written about me is being fulfilled." [38] They said, "Lord, look, here are two swords." He replied, "It is enough."

[39] He came out and went, as was his custom, to the Mount of Olives; and the disciples followed him. [40] When he reached the place, he said to them, "Pray that you may not come into the time of trial."[c] [41] Then he withdrew from them about a stone's throw, knelt down, and prayed, [42] "Father, if you are willing, remove this cup from me; yet, not my will but yours be done." [43] Then an angel from heaven appeared to him and gave him strength. [44] In his anguish he prayed more earnestly, and his sweat became like great drops of blood falling down on the ground.[d] [45] When he got up from prayer, he came to the disciples and found them sleeping because of grief, [46] and he said to them, "Why are you sleeping? Get up and pray that you may not come into the time of trial."[c]

[47] While he was still speaking, suddenly a crowd came, and the one called Judas, one of the twelve, was leading them. He approached Jesus to kiss him; [48] but Jesus said to him, "Judas, is it with a kiss that you are betraying the Son of Man?" [49] When those who were around him saw what was coming, they asked, "Lord, should we strike with the sword?" [50] Then one of them struck the slave of the high priest and cut off his right ear.

a   Or has obtained permission
b   Gk He
c   Or into temptation
d   Other ancient authorities lack verses 43 and 44

22.24–30: True discipleship (Mt 20.24–28; Mk 10.41–45). These verses and those of the two sections that follow (21.31–34,35–38) form a brief farewell discourse delivered by Jesus to his disciples. 24: Jn 13.3–16. 25: Benefactors, a title bestowed on Hellenistic kings. 27: See 12.37n.

22.31–34: The foretelling of Peter's denial (Mt 26.30–35; Mk 14.26–31; Jn 13.36–38). 31: Job 1.6–12; . 32: You in this verse is singular (contrast v. 31). 34: See vv. 54–62.

22.35–38: Sayings about the coming crisis. 35: See 10.4; cf. 9.3. 36: An example of Jesus' fondness for striking metaphors, but the disciples take it literally (v. 38). 37: Isa 53.12. 38: An ironic rebuke.

22.39–46: Jesus' prayer on the Mount of Olives (Mt 26.36–46; Mk 14.32–42; Jn 18.1–2). 40: See 11.4. 42: Cup, metaphor for that which is allotted by God, whether blessing (Pss 16.5; 116.13) or judgment (Isa 51.17; Lam 4.21). Here it refers to Jesus' suffering and death. 43–44: Important early manuscripts lack these verses, but they were known to Christian writers of the second century CE and reflect tradition concerning the suffering of Jesus. Whether they were a part of the original text is debatable.

22.47–53: The betrayal and arrest of Jesus (Mt 26.47–56; Mk 14.43–52; Jn 18.2–12). 52: Isa 53.12. Only in Luke

⁵¹ But Jesus said, "No more of this!" And he touched his ear and healed him. ⁵² Then Jesus said to the chief priests, the officers of the temple police, and the elders who had come for him, "Have you come out with swords and clubs as if I were a bandit? ⁵³ When I was with you day after day in the temple, you did not lay hands on me. But this is your hour, and the power of darkness!"

⁵⁴ Then they seized him and led him away, bringing him into the high priest's house. But Peter was following at a distance. ⁵⁵ When they had kindled a fire in the middle of the courtyard and sat down together, Peter sat among them. ⁵⁶ Then a servant-girl, seeing him in the firelight, stared at him and said, "This man also was with him." ⁵⁷ But he denied it, saying, "Woman, I do not know him." ⁵⁸ A little later someone else, on seeing him, said, "You also are one of them." But Peter said, "Man, I am not!" ⁵⁹ Then about an hour later still another kept insisting, "Surely this man also was with him; for he is a Galilean." ⁶⁰ But Peter said, "Man, I do not know what you are talking about!" At that moment, while he was still speaking, the cock crowed. ⁶¹ The Lord turned and looked at Peter. Then Peter remembered the word of the Lord, how he had said to him, "Before the cock crows today, you will deny me three times." ⁶² And he went out and wept bitterly.

⁶³ Now the men who were holding Jesus began to mock him and beat him; ⁶⁴ they also blindfolded him and kept asking him, "Prophesy! Who is it that struck you?" ⁶⁵ They kept heaping many other insults on him.

⁶⁶ When day came, the assembly of the elders of the people, both chief priests and scribes, gathered together, and they brought him to their council. ⁶⁷ They said, "If you are the Messiah,ᵃ tell us." He replied, "If I tell you, you will not believe; ⁶⁸ and if I question you, you will not answer. ⁶⁹ But from now on the Son of Man will be seated at the right hand of the power of God." ⁷⁰ All of them asked, "Are you, then, the Son of God?" He said to them, "You say that I am." ⁷¹ Then they said, "What further testimony do we need? We have heard it ourselves from his own lips!"

23 Then the assembly rose as a body and brought Jesusᵇ before Pilate. ² They began to accuse him, saying, "We found this man perverting our nation, forbidding us to pay taxes to the emperor, and saying that he himself is the Messiah, a king."ᶜ ³ Then Pilate asked him, "Are you the king of the Jews?" He answered, "You say so." ⁴ Then Pilate said to the chief priests and the crowds, "I find no basis for an accusation against this man." ⁵ But they were insistent and said, "He stirs up the people by teaching throughout all Judea, from Galilee where he began even to this place."

⁶ When Pilate heard this, he asked whether the man was a Galilean. ⁷ And when he learned that he was under Herod's jurisdiction, he sent him off to Herod, who was himself in Jerusalem at that time. ⁸ When Herod saw Jesus,

ᵃ Or the Christ
ᵇ Gk him
ᶜ Or is an anointed king

are the chief priests themselves present. **53:** Jesus' words recognize the moment as a time of supreme evil, see 4.13; 22.3.

22.54–62: Peter's denials (Mt 26.69–75; Mk 14.66–72; Jn 18.25–27). **54–55:** Jn 18.12–16. **56–62:** Jn 18.16–18,25–27. **61:** 22.34. Jesus' turning to face Peter is a detail found only in Luke .

22.63–65: The mockery of Jesus (Mt 26.67–68; 27.27–31a; Mk 14.65; 15.16–20a). See Jn 18.22–24. This scene in Luke's account is located differently in the sequence of the narrative from the parallels in the other Gospels.

22.66–71: Jesus before the council (Mt 27.1; 26.59–65; Mk 15.1; 14.55–63; Jn 18.13–14,19–23). **66:** Council, Gk "synedrion," Sanhedrin. **67:** The demand put to Jesus, If you are the Messiah, tell us, becomes an element of the charges against Jesus before Pilate in 23.2. **69:** See Ps 110.1; Dan 7.13. **71:** From what follows in 23.1–2, it seems here that Jesus' adversaries (the authorities at the assembly) conclude that he is guilty of sedition.

23.1–5: Jesus before Pilate (Mt 27.1–14; Mk 15.1–5; Jn 18.28–38). **1:** Pilate, see 3.1n. **2:** Cf. 19.38; 20.25; see Acts 24.5. The charge is phrased to sound like treason. **3:** Jesus' answer, translated from the Gk as "You say so," more literally is the ambiguous statement, "You yourself say." **4:** 23.14,22,41; Jn 19.4,6; Acts 13.28. Pilate refused to take religious ideas in a political sense. Here, and later, Pilate sought to free Jesus but then yielded to pressures.

23.6–12: Jesus before Herod. Only Luke reports this episode. Herod Antipas was a son of Herod the Great

he was very glad, for he had been wanting to see him for a long time, because he had heard about him and was hoping to see him perform some sign. [9] He questioned him at some length, but Jesus[a] gave him no answer. [10] The chief priests and the scribes stood by, vehemently accusing him. [11] Even Herod with his soldiers treated him with contempt and mocked him; then he put an elegant robe on him, and sent him back to Pilate. [12] That same day Herod and Pilate became friends with each other; before this they had been enemies.

[13] Pilate then called together the chief priests, the leaders, and the people, [14] and said to them, "You brought me this man as one who was perverting the people; and here I have examined him in your presence and have not found this man guilty of any of your charges against him. [15] Neither has Herod, for he sent him back to us. Indeed, he has done nothing to deserve death. [16] I will therefore have him flogged and release him."[b]

[18] Then they all shouted out together, "Away with this fellow! Release Barabbas for us!" [19] (This was a man who had been put in prison for an insurrection that had taken place in the city, and for murder.) [20] Pilate, wanting to release Jesus, addressed them again; [21] but they kept shouting, "Crucify, crucify him!" [22] A third time he said to them, "Why, what evil has he done? I have found in him no ground for the sentence of death; I will therefore have him flogged and then release him." [23] But they kept urgently demanding with loud shouts that he should be crucified; and their voices prevailed.

[24] So Pilate gave his verdict that their demand should be granted. [25] He released the man they asked for, the one who had been put in prison for insurrection and murder, and he handed Jesus over as they wished.

[26] As they led him away, they seized a man, Simon of Cyrene, who was coming from the country, and they laid the cross on him, and made him carry it behind Jesus. [27] A great number of the people followed him, and among them were women who were beating their breasts and wailing for him. [28] But Jesus turned to them and said, "Daughters of Jerusalem, do not weep for me, but weep for yourselves and for your children. [29] For the days are surely coming when they will say, 'Blessed are the barren, and the wombs that never bore, and the breasts that never nursed.' [30] Then they will begin to say to the mountains, 'Fall on us'; and to the hills, 'Cover us.' [31] For if they do this when the wood is green, what will happen when it is dry?"

[32] Two others also, who were criminals, were led away to be put to death with him. [33] When they came to the place that is called The Skull, they crucified Jesus[c] there with the criminals, one on his right and one on his left. [34] Then Jesus said, "Father, forgive them; for they do not know what they are

a   Gk he
b   Here, or after verse 19, other ancient authorities add verse 17, *Now he was obliged to release someone for them at the festival*
c   Gk him

(see 3.1n.). Herod [Antipas] had arrested (3.19–20) and beheaded (9.9) John the Baptist. **8:** 9.9; Acts 4.27–28. **9:** Jesus' silence, noted in Mt 27.12 and Mk 15.5, occurs in Luke's account as Jesus stands before Herod Antipas, a scene unique to Luke. **11:** Jn 19.2–3.

23.13–16 [17]: Pilate's declaration of Jesus' innocence. 14: Vv. 4,22,41. **16:** Jn 19.12–14. **[17]:** An addition to Luke's account from Mk 15.6; see note there.

23.18–25: The sentencing of Jesus to death (Mt 27.15–26; Mk 15.6–15; Jn 18.39–40; 19.16; see Acts 3.13–14). **18:** The Barabbas incident is recounted in further detail in Mt 27.15–23; Mk 15.6–14; Jn 18.39–40.

23.26–31: On the way to the cross (Mt 27.31b–32; Mk 15.20b–21; Jn 19.17a). **26:** *Cyrene*, in Libya. *The cross*, i.e., the horizontal cross-beam. **27:** Here *beating their breasts* seems to indicate more mourning than repentance (cf. 18.3; 23.48). **28–32:** 21.23–24; 19.41–44. **30:** Incorporates wording parallel to Hos 10.8. **31:** Cf. Prov 11.31. This proverb may mean either that if the innocent Jesus meets such a fate, then a worse fate awaits the guilty Jerusalem, or that if such takes place with Jesus present and active, what will happen when he is no longer present? Cf. 1 Pet 4.17–18.

23.32: Two criminals with Jesus. The Gk word for *criminal* gives no indication of the nature of the crime(s) committed by these two who were crucified with Jesus.

23.33–38: The scene of the crucifixion (Mt 27.33–43; Mk 15.22–32a; Jn 19.17b–27). **33:** *The Skull*, its Aramaic

doing." [a] And they cast lots to divide his clothing. [35] And the people stood by, watching; but the leaders scoffed at him, saying, "He saved others; let him save himself if he is the Messiah[b] of God, his chosen one!" [36] The soldiers also mocked him, coming up and offering him sour wine, [37] and saying, "If you are the King of the Jews, save yourself!" [38] There was also an inscription over him,[c] "This is the King of the Jews."

[39] One of the criminals who were hanged there kept deriding[d] him and saying, "Are you not the Messiah?[b] Save yourself and us!" [40] But the other rebuked him, saying, "Do you not fear God, since you are under the same sentence of condemnation? [41] And we indeed have been condemned justly, for we are getting what we deserve for our deeds, but this man has done nothing wrong." [42] Then he said, "Jesus, remember me when you come into[e] your kingdom." [43] He replied, "Truly I tell you, today you will be with me in Paradise."

[44] It was now about noon, and darkness came over the whole land[f] until three in the afternoon, [45] while the sun's light failed;[g] and the curtain of the temple was torn in two. [46] Then Jesus, crying with a loud voice, said, "Father, into your hands I commend my spirit." Having said this, he breathed his last. [47] When the centurion saw what had taken place, he praised God and said, "Certainly this man was innocent."[h] [48] And when all

the crowds who had gathered there for this spectacle saw what had taken place, they returned home, beating their breasts. [49] But all his acquaintances, including the women who had followed him from Galilee, stood at a distance, watching these things.

[50] Now there was a good and righteous man named Joseph, who, though a member of the council, [51] had not agreed to their plan and action. He came from the Jewish town of Arimathea, and he was waiting expectantly for the kingdom of God. [52] This man went to Pilate and asked for the body of Jesus. [53] Then he took it down, wrapped it in a linen cloth, and laid it in a rock-hewn tomb where no one had ever been laid. [54] It was the day of Preparation, and the sabbath was beginning.[i] [55] The women who had come with him from Galilee followed, and they saw the tomb and

a Other ancient authorities lack the sentence *Then Jesus … what they are doing*
b Or *the Christ*
c Other ancient authorities add *written in Greek and Latin and Hebrew* (that is, *Aramaic*)
d Or *blaspheming*
e Other ancient authorities read *in*
f Or *earth*
g Or *the sun was eclipsed.* Other ancient authorities read *the sun was darkened*
h Or *righteous*
i Gk *was dawning*

name, Golgotha, is found in the other Gospels. **34:** See textual note *a*; cf. Acts 7.60. The final phrase alludes to Ps 22.18. **36:** Ps 69.21.

23.39–43: The exchange between Jesus and the two criminals (Mt 27.44; Mk 15.32b). **41:** Vv. 4,14,22. **42:** The criminal's appeal may be based on the charge against Jesus (vv. 2,3,38); he thinks in terms of 21.27–28. Jesus promises him more than he asked, intimating that God's kingly power is a present reality, not merely future. **43:** *Paradise*, originally a term for the garden of Eden (Gen 2.8–10), was a contemporary term for the lodging place of the righteous dead prior to the resurrection; cf. 16.22.

23.44–48: The death of Jesus (Mt 27.45–54; Mk 15.33–39; Jn 19.28–30). **45:** Ex 26.31–35. *The sun's light failed*, the translation is uncertain; see Am 8.9; Joel 2.31. **46:** Jesus' words quote Ps 31.6. **47:** In the context of Luke's Gospel, the centurion (see 7.2n.) declares Jesus to be "righteous" rather than merely *innocent*. **48:** The cause of this popular agitation is not clear (Zech 12.10), though compare 18.13–14 for a possible meaning of the crowd's reaction.

23.49: Jesus' acquaintances at the crucifixion (Mt 27.55–56; Mk 15.40–41; Jn 19.25–27). See 23.55; cf. 8.1–3; 24.10; Ps 38.11. **49:** Luke often uses *all* to indicate a large number of persons, not actually "all"; cf. 3.21.

23.50–54: The burial of Jesus (Mt 27.57–60; Mk 15.42–46; Jn 19.38–42). **50:** *The council,* 22.66n. **54:** *The sabbath* began at sundown. Luke, perhaps having Gentile readers in mind, indicates the urgency of the burial in Jewish custom.

23.55–56: Women at the burial (Mt 27.61; Mk 15.47–16.1). **55:** Cf. 24.10. **56:** Ex 12.16; 20.10. *Spices and ointments* were applied to the corpse; see Mk 16.1; Jn 19.40.

how his body was laid. [56] Then they returned, and prepared spices and ointments.

On the sabbath they rested according to the commandment.

24 But on the first day of the week, at early dawn, they came to the tomb, taking the spices that they had prepared. [2] They found the stone rolled away from the tomb, [3] but when they went in, they did not find the body.[a] [4] While they were perplexed about this, suddenly two men in dazzling clothes stood beside them. [5] The women[b] were terrified and bowed their faces to the ground, but the men[c] said to them, "Why do you look for the living among the dead? He is not here, but has risen.[d] [6] Remember how he told you, while he was still in Galilee, [7] that the Son of Man must be handed over to sinners, and be crucified, and on the third day rise again." [8] Then they remembered his words, [9] and returning from the tomb, they told all this to the eleven and to all the rest. [10] Now it was Mary Magdalene, Joanna, Mary the mother of James, and the other women with them who told this to the apostles. [11] But these words seemed to them an idle tale, and they did not believe them. [12] But Peter got up and ran to the tomb; stooping and looking in, he saw the linen cloths by themselves; then he went home, amazed at what had happened.[e]

[13] Now on that same day two of them were going to a village called Emmaus, about seven miles[f] from Jerusalem, [14] and talking with each other about all these things that had happened. [15] While they were talking and discussing, Jesus himself came near and went with them, [16] but their eyes were kept from recognizing him. [17] And he said to them, "What are you discussing with each other while you walk along?" They stood still, looking sad.[g] [18] Then one of them, whose name was Cleopas, answered him, "Are you the only stranger in Jerusalem who does not know the things that have taken place there in these days?" [19] He asked them, "What things?" They replied, "The things about Jesus of Nazareth,[h] who was a prophet mighty in deed and word before God and all the people, [20] and how our chief priests and leaders handed him over to be condemned to death and crucified him. [21] But we had hoped that he was the one to redeem Israel.[i] Yes, and besides all this, it is now the third day since these things took place. [22] Moreover, some women of our group astounded us. They were at the tomb early this morning, [23] and when they did not find his body there, they came back and told us that they had indeed seen a vision of angels who said that he was alive. [24] Some of those who were with us went to the tomb and found it just as the women had said; but they did not see him." [25] Then he said to them, "Oh, how foolish you are, and how slow of heart to believe all that the prophets have declared! [26] Was it not necessary that the Messiah[j] should suffer these things and then enter into his glory?" [27] Then beginning with Moses and

a Other ancient authorities add *of the Lord Jesus*
b Gk *They*
c Gk *but they*
d Other ancient authorities lack *He is not here, but has risen*
e Other ancient authorities lack verse 12
f Gk *sixty stadia;* other ancient authorities read *a hundred sixty stadia*
g Other ancient authorities read *walk along, looking sad?"*
h Other ancient authorities read *Jesus the Nazorean*
i Or *to set Israel free*
j Or *the Christ*

24.1–53: **The empty tomb and the resurrection** (Mt 28.1–10,16–20; Mk 16.1–8; Jn 20–21).

24.1–12: **The women at the tomb** (Mt 28.1–8; Mk 16.1–8; Jn 20.1–13). **4:** The *two men* wear clothing that identifies them as angels, not ordinary humans (see v. 23), as do their sudden appearance and supernatural knowledge (vv. 5–7). **6:** 9.22; 13.32–33. *You* here suggests that Jesus' disciples as a group often included others in addition to those of the inner circle. **10:** 8.1–3; Jn 19.25; 20.2. **12:** This verse, though appearing in many ancient manuscripts, may be an addition to the original text of Luke based on Jn 20.3–10.

24.13–35: **The Emmaus incident. 13:** *Seven miles,* lit., "sixty stadia"; a stade was approximately 180 m (600 ft). The exact location of Emmaus is uncertain. **16:** The inability of these persons to recognize Jesus is typical of initial reactions to Jesus in resurrection stories (cf. 24.37). **19:** 7.16; 13.33; Acts 3.22; 10.38. **26:** *Necessary* because of God's divine plan (see 7.30; Acts 2.23; 13.36; 20.27). **27:** *Moses,* the traditional author of the first five books of the Bible. *The prophets,* a major section of the Jewish scriptures more extensive in scope than the prophetic works

all the prophets, he interpreted to them the things about himself in all the scriptures.

²⁸ As they came near the village to which they were going, he walked ahead as if he were going on. ²⁹ But they urged him strongly, saying, "Stay with us, because it is almost evening and the day is now nearly over." So he went in to stay with them. ³⁰ When he was at the table with them, he took bread, blessed and broke it, and gave it to them. ³¹ Then their eyes were opened, and they recognized him; and he vanished from their sight. ³² They said to each other, "Were not our hearts burning within usᵃ while he was talking to us on the road, while he was opening the scriptures to us?" ³³ That same hour they got up and returned to Jerusalem; and they found the eleven and their companions gathered together. ³⁴ They were saying, "The Lord has risen indeed, and he has appeared to Simon!" ³⁵ Then they told what had happened on the road, and how he had been made known to them in the breaking of the bread.

³⁶ While they were talking about this, Jesus himself stood among them and said to them, "Peace be with you."ᵇ ³⁷ They were startled and terrified, and thought that they were seeing a ghost. ³⁸ He said to them, "Why are you frightened, and why do doubts arise in your hearts? ³⁹ Look at my hands and my feet; see that it is I myself. Touch me and see; for a ghost does not have flesh and bones as you see that I have." ⁴⁰ And when he had said this, he showed them his hands and his feet.ᶜ ⁴¹ While in their joy they were disbelieving and still wondering, he said to them, "Have you anything here to eat?"

⁴² They gave him a piece of broiled fish, ⁴³ and he took it and ate in their presence.

⁴⁴ Then he said to them, "These are my words that I spoke to you while I was still with you—that everything written about me in the law of Moses, the prophets, and the psalms must be fulfilled." ⁴⁵ Then he opened their minds to understand the scriptures, ⁴⁶ and he said to them, "Thus it is written, that the Messiahᵈ is to suffer and to rise from the dead on the third day, ⁴⁷ and that repentance and forgiveness of sins is to be proclaimed in his name to all nations, beginning from Jerusalem. ⁴⁸ You are witnessesᵉ of these things. ⁴⁹ And see, I am sending upon you what my Father promised; so stay here in the city until you have been clothed with power from on high."

⁵⁰ Then he led them out as far as Bethany, and, lifting up his hands, he blessed them. ⁵¹ While he was blessing them, he withdrew from them and was carried up into heaven.ᶠ ⁵² And they worshiped him, andᵍ returned to Jerusalem with great joy; ⁵³ and they were continually in the temple blessing God.ʰ

ᵃ Other ancient authorities lack *within us*
ᵇ Other ancient authorities lack *and said to them, "Peace be with you."*
ᶜ Other ancient authorities lack verse 40
ᵈ Or *the Christ*
ᵉ Or *nations. Beginning from Jerusalem ⁴⁸you are witnesses*
ᶠ Other ancient authorities lack *and was carried up into heaven*
ᵍ Other ancient authorities lack *worshiped him, and*
ʰ Other ancient authorities add *Amen*

of the Hebrew Bible (see 16.16n.; 24.44; Acts 28.23). **30:** *Took, blessed,* and *broke,* echo the actions of Jesus at the Last Supper (22.19) and the multiplication of the loaves (9.16). **34:** 1 Cor 15.5. Peter's experience is not described. **35:** *Breaking of the bread,* see Acts 2.42; 20.7; 1 Cor 10.16.

24.36–43: Jesus' appearance to his disciples (Jn 20.19–23). See 1 Cor 15.5. The experience of Jesus, affirmed in v. 36, is tentatively interpreted in v. 37 as an encounter with the dead, but this explanation is rejected in v. 39. **39–40:** Cf. Jn 20.25,27. **42:** *Broiled fish,* cf. Jn 21.9–13.

24.44–53: Jesus' final words and withdrawal into heaven (cf. elements of the longer ending of Mark: Mk 16.15,19). **44:** Vv. 26–27; Acts 28.23. The Psalms formed the opening and the longest part of the third division of the Hebrew Bible; see 16.16n. **45:** 24.32. **46:** Hos 6.2; cf. 1 Cor 15.3–4. **47:** Acts 1.4–8; 5.31; 10.43; 13.38; 26.18. **48:** Acts 1.8. **49:** *Power from on high,* the words allude to the energy of the Spirit of God referred to in Joel 2.28–32 (cf. Acts 2.1–21). The new age has begun, but its power is not yet fully realized. **50:** *Bethany,* see 19.29n. **51:** Acts 1.9–11. **52–53:** Acts 1.12–14; 2.46–47.

THE GOSPEL ACCORDING TO JOHN

NAME, AUTHORSHIP, AND DATE

The Fourth Gospel is named for John, the son of Zebedee, one of the Twelve (see Mk 1.19; 3.17; etc.), traditionally thought to be its author and identified as the "beloved disciple" repeatedly mentioned in the Gospel. Modern scholars think it was more likely written by a disciple of John. It may have been the "beloved disciple," who is never called John in the Gospel, or someone to whom he dictated it (see Jn 21.24n.). Most scholars date the Gospel to about 90 CE, although some have proposed an earlier date for it, or for an earlier version of it.

RELATIONSHIP TO THE SYNOPTIC GOSPELS

The author of the Fourth Gospel was apparently familiar with the earlier Synoptic Gospels or with traditions they contain. It includes sayings of Jesus that resemble some in the Synoptics, and such narratives as Jesus and the money changers in the Temple, Jesus multiplying bread and fish, and Jesus walking on water are found in all four Gospels. Moreover, the narrative structure of the Fourth Gospel in general follows that of the earlier Gospels: the preaching of John the Baptist; preaching and healing by Jesus in Galilee and Judea; journey to Jerusalem to celebrate the Passover; arrest, trial, death, burial, and resurrection there; and appearances of Jesus after the resurrection both in Judea and in Galilee.

Within this general framework, however, John is very different in many details and in content. For example, the scene in the Temple, which the Synoptic Gospels place in the week before Jesus' death, appears in John near the beginning of Jesus' ministry (2.13–23). In the Synoptics, the adult Jesus journeys to Jerusalem only once, implying that his ministry lasted less than a year, whereas in John, Jesus makes several journeys to Jerusalem, including three Passovers (2.13; 6.4; 11.55), meaning that his ministry lasted several years. Although there is a Last Supper in John, it is not a Passover meal as in the Synoptic Gospels. Rather, in John the first day of Passover is the day of Jesus' death, when he is symbolically identified as the Passover lamb (see 19.36; cf. 1.29,36), and thus the account of the Last Supper does not include the institution of the Eucharist.

Most significant are the differences in content. John has a very high Christology: Jesus is repeatedly identi-fied and identifies himself as divine. Many of Jesus' speeches in the Gospel reflect this perspective, and they have few parallels in the Synoptic tradition.

HISTORICAL CONTEXT

The Gospel of John thus seems to represent a relatively late stage in the development of earliest Christian beliefs. Its views have much in common with the other Johannine literature, the Letters of John and the book of Revelation. Although it is no longer thought likely that these works have a single author, they do seem to be the product of a "Johannine school," which ancient tradition perhaps correctly locates at Ephesus in western Asia Minor at a time when persecution by Roman authorities was becoming more frequent, and conflicts between Gentile Christians and Jewish Christians as well as between Christians in general and Jews were becoming more intense.

STYLE, STRUCTURE, AND INTERPRETATION

The audience of John consists of Greek speakers, for many Hebrew words are translated into Greek. The "be-loved disciple" is considered the "witness" to the story, presumably written in Ephesus. The author (composer and writer), who differs from the "witness," displays sophisticated literary and rhetorical abilities. He knows the encomium that praises a person because of origins (geography and generation), education and training, virtuous actions, and noble death. Here we find two encomiums, one praiseworthy and one condemnatory, both arguing from the same topics. Opponents know that Jesus comes from Nazareth of Galilee, an insignifi-cant place; his father is the peasant Joseph; he never studied; as for his actions, he deceives and violates the Law; and he died a death befitting a sinner. But insiders know that his geography is heaven, God's world; his generation, son of a heavenly Father; his education, God's instruction on what to say and do; his actions virtu-ous (obedience, courage, and justice); and his death noble. Antitheses like these occur regularly as crowds voice contrasting judgments about Jesus, either sinner or saint.

The Gospel argues through the rhetorical figure "comparison" the superiority of Jesus to Israel's patriarchs: he is "greater than" Jacob (4.12), Abraham (8.52), and Moses (1.17; 3.13–14; 5.45–47). When Jesus says that "I am . . . (something)," he is claiming superiority over some element of Israelite tradition and ritual as well as of nature. "I am . . . bread . . . from heaven" (6.41; not mere manna); "light of the world" (8.12; not mere sunlight); "gate" (10.9; no other broker provides access to God); "noble shepherd" (see 10.11n.; not thieves or bandits); "resurrection and . . . life" (11.25; apart from me, death), and "vine" (15.1). Jesus speaks eight statements, each of which begin with a demand "Unless . . ."; these require something be done, either to join the group (3.3,5; 12.24; 13.8) or remain in it (8.24; 15.4). They all demand behavior surpassing Israel's transformative and confirmatory rituals.

The following division is suggested by the Gospel itself: the prologue (1.1–18); the book of Jesus' signs that he is the revelation of the Father (1.19–12.50); the book of Jesus' glory as it is revealed to those who accept him through his crucifixion, resurrection, and ascension (13.1–20.31); the epilogue, which contains additional accounts of Jesus' postresurrection appearances and comments on the future of Peter and the "beloved disciple" (21.1–25).

The author knows traditional literary forms, such as the shape of a miracle narrative. Commonly noted are (1) the severity of the disease; (2) cure by command or use of spit and mud; (3) proof of the cure; and (4) honor awarded the healer. This form illuminates the structure of many of the "signs," especially 5.1–10; 9.1–11 and 11.38–44. The genre of the "farewell address," known from both Jewish and Greek literature, structures the discourse in John 14–17. It typically contains (1) notice of death or departure (13.33; 14.2–3,28); (2) review of the person's life (14.32; 17.4–8,18,26); (3) relationships to be maintained (14.3–17; 15.1–17); (4) knowledge and revelations given (14.4–11,20–26; 15.25–26); (5) predictions of forthcoming events (14.29; 15.18–25; 16.1–4,29–22); (6) exhortation to virtue ("believe," 14.10–11; "love," 14.21–24; 15.12–17; "abide," 15.1–10); (7) successor named (14.25–26; 16.7–15); and (8) legacy ("greater works," 14.12–14; "name of God" bestowed, 17.6,11–12,26; knowledge, 17.3–8).

Other patterns appear. Four times people request Jesus to act; he refuses, but shortly thereafter acts positively (2.3–7; 4.47–50; 7.3–10; 11.3–7). Only Jesus knows his "hour," and all actions are of his own choosing, a display of his honor and of control. Conflict, which pervades this Gospel, is expressed in forensic trials, which consist of: person charged; witnesses pro and con; judge; sentence and verdict. All trials occur in Jerusalem (chs 5; 7–11; 18–19) where the elite accuse Jesus of violating the sabbath (5.17; 7.21; 9.16) and blasphemy (5.18; 10.33). Witnesses testify both favorably and critically. The judges, who claim to judge according to the law, judge instead according to appearances (7.24; 8.15). Despite their guilty verdict, they cannot execute sentence, and in time they themselves will be judged.

Jesus reveals and conceals. As revealer, he is the Word of God who speaks God's words. But he also conceals in that only insiders hear and know his revelation (e.g., 10.27). Outsiders like Nicodemus barely know the workings of the world of matter and flesh below (see 3.12). In one of the notable patterns here, Jesus uses words with double meanings. Nicodemus must be born "again," he thinks, but Jesus meant "from above." The Samaritan woman discusses "water" with Jesus but never realizes that Jesus is not speaking of well water (4.7–15); nor do the disciples understand Jesus' "food" (4.31–34). Some interpret "I am going . . ." as departure or suicide (7.35; 8.22), not as glorious return to the Father. Jesus hides himself (8.59; 12.36), dissembles with his brothers (7.1–11), speaks in parables (10.1–18) and figures of speech (16.25,29–30). A strategy of mystery and concealment occurs frequently in the pattern of statement, misunderstanding, and clarification. Jesus speaks, but all misunderstand; to insiders he clarifies, but to outsiders, he proves them incapable of understanding (e.g., 3.3–5; 6.51–58; 14.4–6,7–11). Readers appreciate the irony of situations and statements, such as claims by enemies and outsiders to "know" (7.27; 9.29) or the prophecy of Caiaphas (11.48–50).

The Gospel discredits the religious authorities, whom it calls "the Jews," by portraying them as mercenary and uncaring shepherds (10.12–13), as haughty and condescending to the people (7.15,49; 9.34), as being more concerned with worldly honor than divine favor (12.43), and as maliciously plotting to kill Jesus (11.53). Although its scathing portrayal of "the Jews" has opened John to charges of anti-Semitism, a careful reading reveals "the Jews" to be a class designation, not a religious or ethnic grouping; rather than denoting adherents to Judaism in general, the term primarily refers to the hereditary Temple religious authorities. The Gospel further acknowledges their influential status by including among "the Jews" those who have accepted the worldview and class interests of the hereditary religious authorities as their own. This larger group includes the Pharisees (1.19,24) and even the "crowd" of laypersons whose worth the religious authorities dismissed (7.49; cf. 6.22,41). Thus the rejection and persecution of Jesus by "the Jews" is shown to be not only the result of his words and deeds, but a result of the fact that his healings, pronouncements, and person lack the pedigree and imprimatur of the governing religious elite (7.15,48–49; cf. 9.34).

The Gospel of John celebrates Jesus, albeit differently from the other Gospels. Indeed, Jesus is acclaimed Messiah, Son of God, king of Israel, prophet, and Son of Man. But the author understands Jesus in more elevated terms. For example, in the prologue we learn at once that Jesus is a heavenly figure existing with God before the world was created. Thus he is uncreated in the past and brokers God's creative power. Jesus comes from God, is not merely sent by him, and entered this world, becoming flesh. Jesus, moreover, returns to that heavenly world when God glorifies him, God thus vindicating all that he said and did. This descent-ascent motif permeates the narrative, from beginning (1.1–18; 3.13) to end (13.1–3; 20.18).

It is false to claim that Jesus "makes himself" anything, for God makes him equal to himself, especially in terms of creative power (1.1–3; all healings) and eschatological power (5.19–29; 10.17–18; 11.38–44). God gives Jesus his own name, which he in turn gives to the disciples: the name "I AM" in 8.58 (see also 4.26n.; cf. Ex 3.14; Isa 43.10; 46.4) expresses uncreated existence in the past and imperishability in the future. All of Jesus' qualities and endowments serve to make him a superior broker or mediator between God who is patron and the disciples who are clients. Disciples pray always in Jesus' name; God's word and power comes to the world through Jesus. In fact, no one can know or see God except through Jesus. Jesus is the ideal broker because he belongs equally to the patron's world and that of the clients.

GUIDE TO READING

The Gospel is best read straight through, but readers may wish to attend to significant aspects such as the signs, the "I am" sayings, and other characteristics noted in this introduction. The Gospel itself claims that its narrative should be viewed in service to a larger goal: "that . . . you [the reader] may have life" (20.31).

Jerome H. Neyrey

1 In the beginning was the Word, and the Word was with God, and the Word was God. [2] He was in the beginning with God. [3] All things came into being through him, and without him not one thing came into being. What has come into being [4] in him was life,[a] and the life was the light of all people. [5] The light shines in the darkness, and the darkness did not overcome it.

[6] There was a man sent from God, whose name was John. [7] He came as a witness to testify to the light, so that all might believe through him. [8] He himself was not the light, but he came to testify to the light. [9] The true light, which enlightens everyone, was coming into the world.[b]

[10] He was in the world, and the world came into being through him; yet the world did not know him. [11] He came to what was his own,[c] and his own people did not accept him. [12] But

a Or *[3]through him. And without him not one thing came into being that has come into being. [4]In him was life*

b Or *He was the true light that enlightens everyone coming into the world*

c Or *to his own home*

1.1–18: Prologue. The Gospel begins with a prologue containing important topics to be developed. Jesus is eternal (uncreated and imperishable); the Word who speaks God's words; the light of the world; the one who faces rejection and acceptance; is compared with Israel's patriarchs; and mediates God's blessings (creation, grace, and truth). Here also is the plot of the story: Jesus begins with God in heaven, sojourns on earth, and returns there (3.13; 6.62; 13.1–3), which appears in the repeated discussion of where Jesus comes from and where he is going. **3:** Jesus as mediator or broker: *through him* all things were made, and through him come grace and truth (v. 17); later the disciples will address God in his name, that is, through him (14.13–14; 16.26). **5:** The world is hostile to the light and "hates" him (7.7; 15.18–19); this is developed in vv. 10–11, and dramatized in the trials in chs 18–19. **6–8:** In contrast to those rejecting the light, John (the Baptist) acknowledges it, even brokering Jesus to Israel. John's subordination to Jesus is found in 1.15,29–34; 3.27–30. **9:** Jesus, *true light* of the *world* (see 8.12). *True* means "authentic, unique"; cf. "true bread" (6.32); "true vine" (15.1). Disciples walk in light (10.9–10) but many prefer darkness (3.19–20; 12.25–26). **10–11:** *The world did not know him* (i.e., acknowledge him; see 4.44; 7.1–7); nor did *his own* (blood relatives and Israel) become disciples. The Word is in a hostile place. **12–13:** But he meets with acceptance and gives believers kinship with him and God. This depends not on birth, circumcision,

to all who received him, who believed in his name, he gave power to become children of God, [13] who were born, not of blood or of the will of the flesh or of the will of man, but of God.

[14] And the Word became flesh and lived among us, and we have seen his glory, the glory as of a father's only son,[a] full of grace and truth. [15] (John testified to him and cried out, "This was he of whom I said, 'He who comes after me ranks ahead of me because he was before me.'") [16] From his fullness we have all received, grace upon grace. [17] The law indeed was given through Moses; grace and truth came through Jesus Christ. [18] No one has ever seen God. It is God the only Son,[b] who is close to the Father's heart,[c] who has made him known.

[19] This is the testimony given by John when the Jews sent priests and Levites from Jerusalem to ask him, "Who are you?" [20] He confessed and did not deny it, but confessed, "I am not the Messiah."[d] [21] And they asked him, "What then? Are you Elijah?" He said, "I am not." "Are you the prophet?" He answered, "No." [22] Then they said to him, "Who are you? Let us have an answer for those who sent us. What do you say about yourself?" [23] He said,
"I am the voice of one crying out in the
    wilderness,

'Make straight the way of the Lord,'"
as the prophet Isaiah said.

[24] Now they had been sent from the Pharisees. [25] They asked him, "Why then are you baptizing if you are neither the Messiah,[d] nor Elijah, nor the prophet?" [26] John answered them, "I baptize with water. Among you stands one whom you do not know, [27] the one who is coming after me; I am not worthy to untie the thong of his sandal." [28] This took place in Bethany across the Jordan where John was baptizing.

[29] The next day he saw Jesus coming toward him and declared, "Here is the Lamb of God who takes away the sin of the world! [30] This is he of whom I said, 'After me comes a man who ranks ahead of me because he was before me.' [31] I myself did not know him; but I came baptizing with water for this reason, that he might be revealed to Israel." [32] And John testified, "I saw the Spirit descending from heaven like a dove, and it remained on him. [33] I myself did not know him, but the one who sent me to baptize with water said to me, 'He on whom you see the Spirit descend and remain is the one who baptizes with the Holy

a   Or *the Father's only Son*
b   Other ancient authorities read *It is an only Son,
    God,* or *It is the only Son*
c   Gk *bosom*
d   Or *the Christ*

or adoption, but on acceptance of Jesus and honoring his name. **14:** Along with Heb 2.11,14,17, this is the clearest statement of Jesus' humanity; he not only "came into the world" (1.10) but suffered thirst, weariness, and death. *Lived among us,* lit., "tented among us," just as the *"glory* of the LORD" took up residence in the tent of meeting (Ex 40.34). **15:** John repeats the statement about Jesus' eternity in 1.1–2. Temporally Jesus follows John but existed before John, from the beginning: John's testimony is quoted by anticipation from v. 30. **16–17:** Moses gave the *law,* the Torah; the comparison of Jesus and Moses inaugurates a pattern, which argues that Jesus was "greater" than Moses (see also 3.14; 5.45–46), Jacob (4.12), and Abraham (8.53).

    1.19–34: John's testimony to hostile outsiders and receptive insiders. On John the Baptist, cf. Mt 3.1–17; Mk 1.1–11; Lk 3.1–22. In the Gospel of John, John the Baptist does not actually baptize Jesus. **19–23:** Two groups question John, first priests and Levites, then Pharisees. They do not seek information but attempt to discredit him, with questions acting as weapons. He replies that he is not the *Messiah,* nor *Elijah* the prophet (despite Mt 11.14; Mk 9.11–12; cf. Mal 4.5), nor another prophet (cf. Deut 18.15), but rather the one described in Isa 40.3. **19:** *The Jews,* here, as often in this Gospel, referring to religious authorities in Jerusalem. **24–25:** Pharisees continue the attack, demanding to know why he baptizes. John deflects the attack by talking about the one whom he heralds. **26:** They *do not know* (cf. v. 10) this honorable person in their midst. **28:** *Bethany across the Jordan,* an unknown location, but different from the Bethany in 11.18. **29–30:** John also testifies about Jesus to receptive people as *Lamb of God,* a reference to the Passover lamb (Ex 12), as 19.36 makes explicit; cf. Rev 6.6–14. John admits that he *did not know* him (1.31,33), but God revealed his son to John (cf. Gal 1.15) that he might testify. **30:** cf. v. 15. **32:** The spirit *remained* on Jesus, a word repeatedly used in this Gospel and in 1 and 2 John that signals belonging and attachment; not a transitory Spirit, it remains upon Jesus. As in the Synoptic Gospels (see Mk

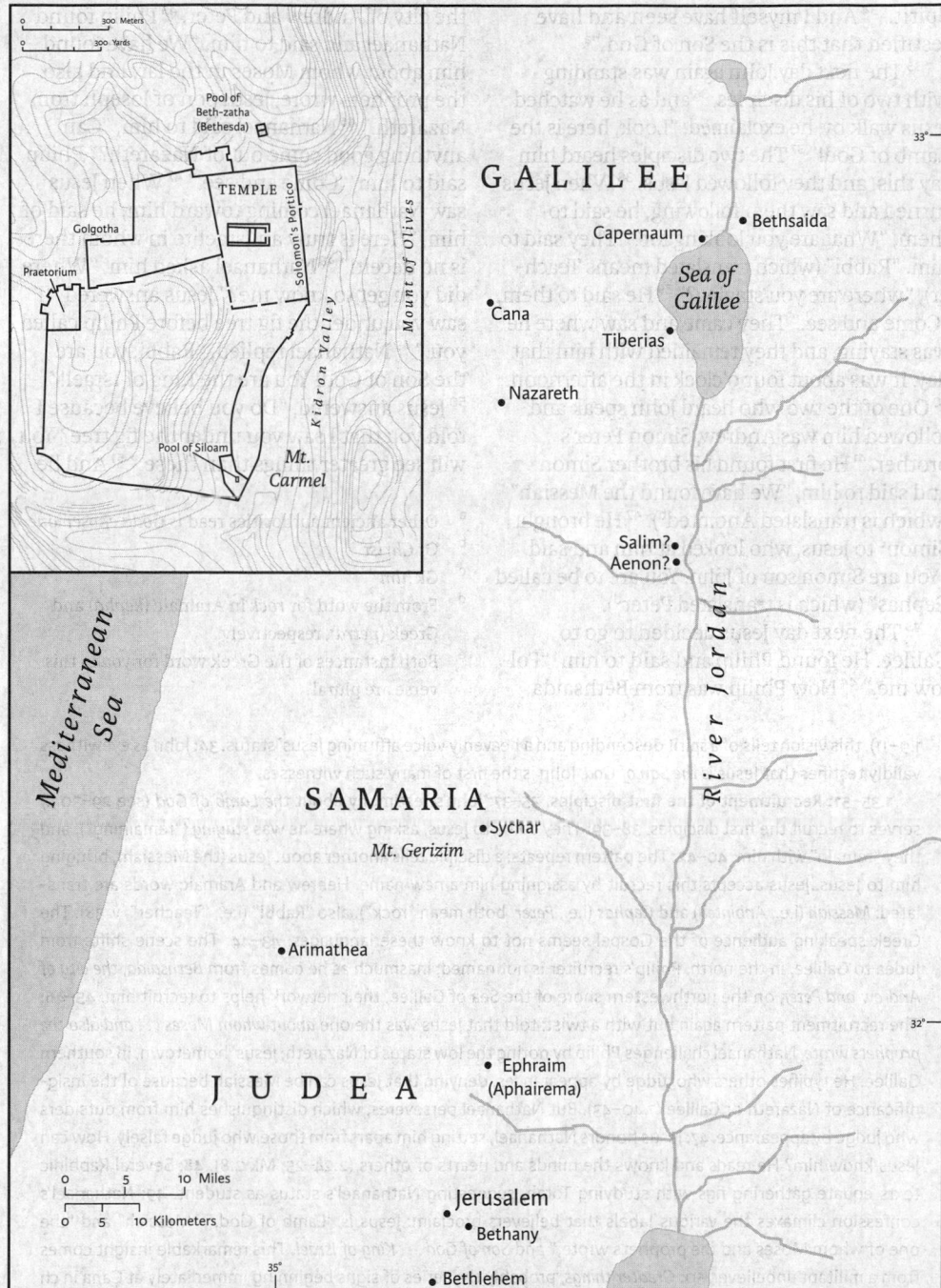

The geography of the Gospel of John.

Labels within the map:

Inset map:
- Pool of Beth-zatha (Bethesda)
- TEMPLE
- Golgotha
- Solomon's Portico
- Praetorium
- Pool of Siloam
- Kidron Valley
- Mount of Olives
- Mt. Carmel
- 0 300 Meters
- 0 300 Yards

Main map:
- GALILEE
- Capernaum
- Bethsaida
- Sea of Galilee
- Cana
- Tiberias
- Nazareth
- Salim?
- Aenon?
- River Jordan
- Mediterranean Sea
- SAMARIA
- Sychar
- Mt. Gerizim
- Arimathea
- Ephraim (Aphairema)
- JUDEA
- Jerusalem
- Bethany
- Bethlehem
- 0 5 10 Miles
- 0 5 10 Kilometers
- 33°
- 32°
- 35°

Spirit.' [34] And I myself have seen and have testified that this is the Son of God."[a]

[35] The next day John again was standing with two of his disciples, [36] and as he watched Jesus walk by, he exclaimed, "Look, here is the Lamb of God!" [37] The two disciples heard him say this, and they followed Jesus. [38] When Jesus turned and saw them following, he said to them, "What are you looking for?" They said to him, "Rabbi" (which translated means Teacher), "where are you staying?" [39] He said to them, "Come and see." They came and saw where he was staying, and they remained with him that day. It was about four o'clock in the afternoon. [40] One of the two who heard John speak and followed him was Andrew, Simon Peter's brother. [41] He first found his brother Simon and said to him, "We have found the Messiah" (which is translated Anointed[b]). [42] He brought Simon[c] to Jesus, who looked at him and said, "You are Simon son of John. You are to be called Cephas" (which is translated Peter[d]).

[43] The next day Jesus decided to go to Galilee. He found Philip and said to him, "Follow me." [44] Now Philip was from Bethsaida, the city of Andrew and Peter. [45] Philip found Nathanael and said to him, "We have found him about whom Moses in the law and also the prophets wrote, Jesus son of Joseph from Nazareth." [46] Nathanael said to him, "Can anything good come out of Nazareth?" Philip said to him, "Come and see." [47] When Jesus saw Nathanael coming toward him, he said of him, "Here is truly an Israelite in whom there is no deceit!" [48] Nathanael asked him, "Where did you get to know me?" Jesus answered, "I saw you under the fig tree before Philip called you." [49] Nathanael replied, "Rabbi, you are the Son of God! You are the King of Israel!" [50] Jesus answered, "Do you believe because I told you that I saw you under the fig tree? You will see greater things than these." [51] And he

---

a   Other ancient authorities read *is God's chosen one*
b   Or *Christ*
c   Gk *him*
d   From the word for *rock* in Aramaic (*kepha*) and Greek (*petra*), respectively
e   Both instances of the Greek word for *you* in this verse are plural

---

1.9–11), this vision tells of a spirit descending and a heavenly voice affirming Jesus' status. **34:** John as eyewitness validly testifies that Jesus is *the Son of God.* John is the first of many such witnesses.

1.35–51: Recruitment of the first disciples. 35–37: John's testimony about *the Lamb of God* (see 29–30n.) serves to recruit the first disciples. **38–39:** They come to Jesus, asking where he was *staying* ("remaining"), and they "remain" with him. **40–42:** The pattern repeats: a disciple tells another about Jesus (the Messiah), bringing him to Jesus. Jesus accepts this recruit by assigning him a new name. Hebrew and Aramaic words are translated: *Messiah* (i.e., *Anointed*) and *Cephas* (i.e., *Peter*, both mean "rock"), also "Rabbi" (i.e., "Teacher"; v. 38). The Greek-speaking audience of the Gospel seems not to know these languages. **43–44:** The scene shifts from Judea to Galilee, in the north. Philip's recruiter is not named; inasmuch as he comes from *Bethsaida, the city of Andrew and Peter,* on the northwestern shore of the Sea of Galilee, their network helps to recruit him. **45–46:** The recruitment pattern again but with a twist: told that Jesus was the one *about whom Moses . . . and also the prophets wrote,* Nathanael challenges Philip by noting the low status of Nazareth, Jesus' hometown, in southern Galilee. He typifies others who judge by appearances, denying that Jesus can be Messiah because of the insignificance of Nazareth or Galilee (7.40–43). But Nathanael perseveres, which distinguishes him from outsiders who judge by appearance. **47:** Jesus honors Nathanael, setting him apart from those who judge falsely. How can Jesus know him? He reads and knows the minds and hearts of others (2.24–25; Mk 2.8). **48:** Several Rabbinic texts equate gathering figs with studying Torah, suggesting Nathanael's status as student. **49:** Nathanael's confession climaxes the various labels that believers proclaim: Jesus is "Lamb of God," "Messiah" and "the one of whom Moses and the prophets wrote," and *Son of God . . . King of Israel.* This remarkable insight comes from a militant unbeliever. **50:** *Greater things,* probably the series of signs beginning immediately at Cana in ch 2. **51:** Jesus promises a theophany to all of them: they will see the *Son of Man* (cf. 3.13–15n.; Dan 7.13), who first descends from heaven's center, then re-ascends to it, with angels streaming toward him from all directions (cf. Gen 28.12). This vision is realized when he ascends "to my God and your God" (20.18), thus returning to the glory he had before the world was made (17.5).

2.1–12: The first sign. 1: *On the third day,* not necessarily actual, but symbolic time: John's testimony = day one, recruitment = day two, and signs = day three. *Wedding,* a family affair for Jesus and his mother, presum-

said to him, "Very truly, I tell you,[e] you will see heaven opened and the angels of God ascending and descending upon the Son of Man."

2 On the third day there was a wedding in Cana of Galilee, and the mother of Jesus was there. [2] Jesus and his disciples had also been invited to the wedding. [3] When the wine gave out, the mother of Jesus said to him, "They have no wine." [4] And Jesus said to her, "Woman, what concern is that to you and to me? My hour has not yet come." [5] His mother said to the servants, "Do whatever he tells you." [6] Now standing there were six stone water jars for the Jewish rites of purification, each holding twenty or thirty gallons. [7] Jesus said to them, "Fill the jars with water." And they filled them up to the brim. [8] He said to them, "Now draw some out, and take it to the chief steward." So they took it. [9] When the steward tasted the water that had become wine, and did not know where it came from (though the servants who had drawn the water knew), the steward called the bridegroom [10] and said to him, "Everyone serves the good wine first, and then the inferior wine after the guests have become drunk. But you have kept the good wine until now." [11] Jesus did this, the first of his signs, in Cana of Galilee, and revealed his glory; and his disciples believed in him.

[12] After this he went down to Capernaum with his mother, his brothers, and his disciples; and they remained there a few days.

[13] The Passover of the Jews was near, and Jesus went up to Jerusalem. [14] In the temple he found people selling cattle, sheep, and doves, and the money changers seated at their tables. [15] Making a whip of cords, he drove all of them out of the temple, both the sheep and the cattle. He also poured out the coins of the money changers and overturned their tables. [16] He told those who were selling the doves, "Take these things out of here! Stop making my Father's house a marketplace!" [17] His disciples remembered that it was written, "Zeal for your house will consume me." [18] The Jews then said to him, "What sign can you show us for doing this?" [19] Jesus answered them, "Destroy this temple, and in three days I will raise it up." [20] The Jews then said, "This temple has been under construction for forty-six years, and will you raise it up in three days?" [21] But he was speaking of the temple of his body. [22] After he was raised from the dead, his disciples remembered that he had said this;

ably kinfolk of the couple married. The family's honor is on display, taxing its resources. *Cana*, a town in central Galilee, about 8 mi (14 km) north of Nazareth. **3–4**: A request is made, denied, then responded to; this pattern repeats later (4.47–50; 7.3–10; 11.3–7). *The mother*, never named in the Gospel, challenges Jesus by her request to do something he does not wish to do. *Woman* intentionally downplays her claim to blood ties (1.11–13). **4**: *My hour*, cf. 7.30; 8.20; 12.23; 13.1; 17.1. **6–8**: Jesus acts because he chooses to. Wine is needed, so he provides a superabundance of good wine. *Twenty or thirty gallons*, just as bread is multiplied superabundantly (6.1–14), so too is wine (see 10.10). **8–9**: The steward *did not know* where the wine came from, but provides proof of the miracles (cf. 9.18–21; 11.43–44; Mk 2.10–12). **11**: The *first . . . sign* of seven (4.47–50; 5.1–9; 6.1–14; 6.15–21; 9.1–12; 11.17–44). *Signs* are credentials, which the apostles acknowledge: Jesus could not do them unless God were with him (cf. 9.32–33). **12**: *Capernaum*, a town on the northwestern shore of the Sea of Galilee. On Jesus' *brothers*, see 7.3,10; 20.17; 21.23; Mk 6.3.

2.13–25: Jesus and the Temple. In the Synoptic Gospels, this episode occurs at the end of Jesus' ministry (Mt 21.12–17; Mk 11.15–19; Lk 19.45–46); here it is toward the beginning. **13–16**: *Passover*, in this Gospel, Jesus celebrates three Passovers. Here Jesus replaces the Jerusalem Temple, not with another building but with his body; later Jesus is bread, not manna (6.41), and Jesus' body, not the lamb, is sacrifice (13.1). **14**: The Temple alone supplied unblemished sacrificial animals; the half-shekel of Tyre, required for entry, was procured from the *money changers*. **15–17**: Jesus halts sacrificial worship and renders the Temple as non-sacred space. **16**: He attacks the sellers for profaning it by making it a market. **17**: Remembering the event, also interpreting it by means of Ps 69.9: *zeal for your house* is virtuous, despite the attacks by his critics; it *will consume me*, that is, occasion Jesus' death. **18**: *What sign*, this challenge seeks to discredit Jesus. **19**: *Destroy . . . temple . . . three days*, similar to the testimony in Mk 14.58; but Jesus himself speaks here. **20**: Another pattern: Jesus speaks, listeners misunderstand, so Jesus speaks again either in clarification or to demonstrate the listeners' obtuseness. Jesus says *temple . . . three days*; outsiders misunderstand, thinking that he means the Temple whose construction began under Herod the Great in the late first century BCE. **21–22**: Not an earthly *temple* (cf. 4.21) but his risen

and they believed the scripture and the word that Jesus had spoken.

23 When he was in Jerusalem during the Passover festival, many believed in his name because they saw the signs that he was doing. 24 But Jesus on his part would not entrust himself to them, because he knew all people 25 and needed no one to testify about anyone; for he himself knew what was in everyone.

3 Now there was a Pharisee named Nicodemus, a leader of the Jews. 2 He came to Jesus[a] by night and said to him, "Rabbi, we know that you are a teacher who has come from God; for no one can do these signs that you do apart from the presence of God." 3 Jesus answered him, "Very truly, I tell you, no one can see the kingdom of God without being born from above."[b] 4 Nicodemus said to him, "How can anyone be born after having grown old? Can one enter a second time into the mother's womb and be born?" 5 Jesus answered, "Very truly, I tell you, no one can enter the kingdom of God without being born of water and Spirit. 6 What is born of the flesh is flesh, and what is born of the Spirit is spirit.[c] 7 Do not be astonished that I said to you, 'You[d] must be born from above.'[e] 8 The wind[c] blows where it chooses, and you hear the sound of it, but you do not know where it comes from or where it goes. So it is with everyone who is born of the Spirit." 9 Nicodemus said to him, "How can these things be?" 10 Jesus answered

him, "Are you a teacher of Israel, and yet you do not understand these things?

11 "Very truly, I tell you, we speak of what we know and testify to what we have seen; yet you[f] do not receive our testimony. 12 If I have told you about earthly things and you do not believe, how can you believe if I tell you about heavenly things? 13 No one has ascended into heaven except the one who descended from heaven, the Son of Man.[g] 14 And just as Moses lifted up the serpent in the wilderness, so must the Son of Man be lifted up, 15 that whoever believes in him may have eternal life.[h]

16 "For God so loved the world that he gave his only Son, so that everyone who believes in him may not perish but may have eternal life.

17 "Indeed, God did not send the Son into the world to condemn the world, but in order that the world might be saved through him.

a   Gk *him*
b   Or *born anew*
c   The same Greek word means both *wind* and *spirit*
d   The Greek word for *you* here is plural
e   Or *anew*
f   The Greek word for *you* here and in verse 12 is plural
g   Other ancient authorities add *who is in heaven*
h   Some interpreters hold that the quotation concludes with verse 15

body, which replaces all temples. After his vindication, believers remember and understand Jesus' remark. **23:** This Gospel contains many people with ambiguous loyalties (3.1–12; 7.1–10; 8.31–45). Hypocrisy and cowardice abound (see 9.22), making it hard to distinguish insiders from outsiders, true from false. **24–25:** Jesus knows all (18.4), especially human hearts; prophets could read hearts and not be fooled by hypocrisy.

    3.1–21: Nicodemus listens but does not hear. 1–2: A high-ranking Pharisee comes in darkness to Jesus. *Teacher . . . come from God* reveals little when compared with what insiders had said (1.34,36,41,49). **3–5:** A pattern repeated (see 2.20n.): Jesus speaks, Nicodemus misunderstands a double-meaning word: he thinks Jesus means "again" (see textual note *b*), whereas Jesus meant *from above.* Nicodemus ridicules Jesus' word, thinking about birth as the impossible return to the womb. **5:** *No one can . . . without* introduces absolute claims by Jesus. *Born of water and Spirit* introduces the double–meaning word *Spirit,* which could be "heavenly agent" or "wind" (v. 8). Scholars disagree about whether there is a reference to baptism here. **6:** A typical Johannine dichotomy dividing the world in two: Nicodemus is *flesh,* knowing earthy things. **8:** Nicodemus cannot understand even where the wind comes from or where it goes. **9:** He claimed knowledge (3.2), but is now reduced to questioning, proof that he is flesh. **10:** Nicodemus's remark about Jesus ("a teacher . . . from God," v. 3), is now sarcastically turned back on him. **11–12:** In contrast, "we" speak true testimony about what we *know* and have *seen,* which he cannot *receive.* Even as "flesh," he still cannot understand earthly things, like wind; he is incapable of comprehending *heavenly* things. **13–15:** *The Son of Man* first mentioned in 1.51 was ambiguous; but *Son of Man* refers to the heavenly figure who first descended then re-ascended, confirming his heavenly origin. *Serpent,* see Num 21.9. **16:** God's own plan, who as a benevolent patron, sent his agent Jesus out of love. **17–18:** *Not . . .*

[18] Those who believe in him are not condemned; but those who do not believe are condemned already, because they have not believed in the name of the only Son of God. [19] And this is the judgment, that the light has come into the world, and people loved darkness rather than light because their deeds were evil. [20] For all who do evil hate the light and do not come to the light, so that their deeds may not be exposed. [21] But those who do what is true come to the light, so that it may be clearly seen that their deeds have been done in God."[a]

[22] After this Jesus and his disciples went into the Judean countryside, and he spent some time there with them and baptized. [23] John also was baptizing at Aenon near Salim because water was abundant there; and people kept coming and were being baptized [24]—John, of course, had not yet been thrown into prison. [25] Now a discussion about purification arose between John's disciples and a Jew.[b] [26] They came to John and said to him, "Rabbi, the one who was with you across the Jordan, to whom you testified, here he is baptizing, and all are going to him." [27] John answered, "No one can receive anything except what has been given from heaven. [28] You yourselves are my witnesses that I said, 'I am not the Messiah,[c] but I have been sent ahead of him.' [29] He who has the bride is the bridegroom. The friend of the bridegroom, who stands and hears him, rejoices greatly at the bridegroom's voice. For this reason my joy has been fulfilled. [30] He must increase, but I must decrease."[d]

[31] The one who comes from above is above all; the one who is of the earth belongs to the earth and speaks about earthly things. The one who comes from heaven is above all. [32] He testifies to what he has seen and heard, yet no one accepts his testimony. [33] Whoever has accepted his testimony has certified[e] this, that God is true. [34] He whom God has sent speaks the words of God, for he gives the Spirit without measure. [35] The Father loves the Son and has placed all things in his hands. [36] Whoever believes in the Son has eternal life; whoever disobeys the Son will not see life, but must endure God's wrath.

4 Now when Jesus[f] learned that the Pharisees had heard, "Jesus is making and baptizing more disciples than John" [2]—although it was not Jesus himself but his disciples who baptized—[3] he left Judea and started back to Galilee. [4] But he had to go through Samaria. [5] So he came to a Samaritan city called Sychar, near the plot of ground that Jacob had given to his son Joseph. [6] Jacob's well was

---

a   Some interpreters hold that the quotation concludes with verse 15
b   Other ancient authorities read *the Jews*
c   Or *the Christ*
d   Some interpreters hold that the quotation continues through verse 36
e   Gk *set a seal to*
f   Other ancient authorities read *the Lord*

---

condemn . . . but . . . be saved, confirms God's benevolence. **19–21:** God gave grace, but some prefer darkness (3.1; 13.30), where they cannot be seen. But believers come into the light to receive God's saving *judgment*.

   3.22–30: John's testimony again (cf. 1.15,29–36). **22–23:** With two groups of baptizers—Jesus and his disciples, and John and his disciples—competition is inevitable; see further 4.1–2. The locations of *Aenon* and *Salim* are uncertain. **24:** See Mk 6.14–29. **27:** All Jesus has and does is because he is God's agent. **28:** John happily holds second place, as his herald. **29:** *Friend,* the best man or groomsman is not a rival of the *bridegroom*; cf. Mk 2.18–20. **30:** Jesus' *increase* does not shame John, because John's *decrease* is voluntary, thus honorable.

   3.31–36: Concluding summary. 31: Nicodemus misunderstood the double-meaning word as "again" (3.3), which here describes Jesus who *comes from above* (3.13,31). As "flesh" contrasts with "spirit" (3.6) and "earthly" with "heavenly" knowledge (3.12), so the speaker *from above* is contrasted with the one *of the earth* speaking earthly things. **32:** Cf. 1.10–11. **34:** *Spirit* in 3.5–8 meant "wind," but now is it God's gift *without measure*.

   4.1–42: Success in Samaria. 1–2: The Pharisees' concern over Jesus' baptizing balances the controversy with John's disciples (3.22–26). **3:** Chs 3 and 4 are antithetical: from Judea and unbelief to Samaria and acceptance, from night to noon, from water for birth to water of life, from Israelite male to Samaritan female. **4:** *Samaria,* between Judea and Galilee (v. 3), was inhabited by the Samaritans, who worshiped the Lord God and used the Torah. But Jews did not consider Samaritan observances to be authentic; see further v. 9. **5–6:** *Jacob's well,*

there, and Jesus, tired out by his journey, was sitting by the well. It was about noon.

[7] A Samaritan woman came to draw water, and Jesus said to her, "Give me a drink." [8] (His disciples had gone to the city to buy food.) [9] The Samaritan woman said to him, "How is it that you, a Jew, ask a drink of me, a woman of Samaria?" (Jews do not share things in common with Samaritans.)[a] [10] Jesus answered her, "If you knew the gift of God, and who it is that is saying to you, 'Give me a drink,' you would have asked him, and he would have given you living water." [11] The woman said to him, "Sir, you have no bucket, and the well is deep. Where do you get that living water? [12] Are you greater than our ancestor Jacob, who gave us the well, and with his sons and his flocks drank from it?" [13] Jesus said to her, "Everyone who drinks of this water will be thirsty again, [14] but those who drink of the water that I will give them will never be thirsty. The water that I will give will become in them a spring of water gushing up to eternal life." [15] The woman said to him, "Sir, give me this water, so that I may never be thirsty or have to keep coming here to draw water."

[16] Jesus said to her, "Go, call your husband, and come back." [17] The woman answered him, "I have no husband." Jesus said to her, "You are right in saying, 'I have no husband'; [18] for you have had five husbands, and the one you have now is not your husband. What you have said is true!" [19] The woman said to him, "Sir, I see that you are a prophet. [20] Our ancestors worshiped on this mountain, but you[b] say that the place where people must worship is in Jerusalem." [21] Jesus said to her,

"Woman, believe me, the hour is coming when you will worship the Father neither on this mountain nor in Jerusalem. [22] You worship what you do not know; we worship what we know, for salvation is from the Jews. [23] But the hour is coming, and is now here, when the true worshipers will worship the Father in spirit and truth, for the Father seeks such as these to worship him. [24] God is spirit, and those who worship him must worship in spirit and truth." [25] The woman said to him, "I know that Messiah is coming" (who is called Christ). "When he comes, he will proclaim all things to us." [26] Jesus said to her, "I am he,[c] the one who is speaking to you."

[27] Just then his disciples came. They were astonished that he was speaking with a woman, but no one said, "What do you want?" or, "Why are you speaking with her?" [28] Then the woman left her water jar and went back to the city. She said to the people, [29] "Come and see a man who told me everything I have ever done! He cannot be the Messiah,[d] can he?" [30] They left the city and were on their way to him.

[31] Meanwhile the disciples were urging him, "Rabbi, eat something." [32] But he said to them, "I have food to eat that you do not know about." [33] So the disciples said to one another, "Surely no one has brought him something to eat?" [34] Jesus said to them, "My food is to do the will of him who sent me and to complete his

a   Other ancient authorities lack this sentence

b   The Greek word for *you* here and in verses 21 and 22 is plural

c   Gk *I am*

d   Or *the Christ*

traditionally located near ancient Shechem, where Jacob acquired land (Gen 33.18–20; Josh 24.32). **7–12:** Jesus speaks (*give me a drink*), which the Samaritan woman understands but never fulfills. Jesus speaks again, but she misunderstands *living water* as flowing water (as opposed to the still water of a well), rather than what Jesus means. If she had understood, gender roles would reverse: the female would ask the male to serve her. **12:** She challenges Jesus by comparing this peasant Jew to the patriarch Jacob. **16–18:** Jesus speaks, and now she dissembles. Jesus, knowing the truth, praises her for her clever evasion, but exposes what she hides: no husband, but five previous ones and now a paramour. **19–20:** She mocks Jesus' prophetic knowledge, testing him to solve an unsolvable problem: where to worship, the holy mountain of the Samaritans, Mount Gerizim, or Jerusalem. **21–24:** The prophet Jesus desacralizes both sites; worship will be apart from fixed temple space. **26:** Jesus' self-revelation makes him greater than previously acknowledged. *I am he*, lit., "I am," (cf. Ex 3.14; Isa 41.4; 43.10; 46.4; see also Jn 6.20; 8.24,28,58; 13.19; 18.5. **27:** Male talking to female in public is irregular. **28–30:** The woman does not go home to call her husband (v. 16), but invites all to *come and see* (cf. 1.46). *Everything I have ever done* can only be her sexual history (4.16–18). She does not acknowledge Jesus as Messiah, but only suggests he might be. **31–34:** Vv. 8–15 dealt with drink; vv. 31–38 emphasize food. Jesus says "*I have food,*" which

work. ³⁵ Do you not say, 'Four months more, then comes the harvest'? But I tell you, look around you, and see how the fields are ripe for harvesting. ³⁶ The reaper is already receiving[a] wages and is gathering fruit for eternal life, so that sower and reaper may rejoice together. ³⁷ For here the saying holds true, 'One sows and another reaps.' ³⁸ I sent you to reap that for which you did not labor. Others have labored, and you have entered into their labor."

³⁹ Many Samaritans from that city believed in him because of the woman's testimony, "He told me everything I have ever done." ⁴⁰ So when the Samaritans came to him, they asked him to stay with them; and he stayed there two days. ⁴¹ And many more believed because of his word. ⁴² They said to the woman, "It is no longer because of what you said that we believe, for we have heard for ourselves, and we know that this is truly the Savior of the world."

⁴³ When the two days were over, he went from that place to Galilee ⁴⁴ (for Jesus himself had testified that a prophet has no honor in the prophet's own country). ⁴⁵ When he came to Galilee, the Galileans welcomed him, since they had seen all that he had done in Jerusalem at the festival; for they too had gone to the festival.

⁴⁶ Then he came again to Cana in Galilee where he had changed the water into wine. Now there was a royal official whose son lay ill in Capernaum. ⁴⁷ When he heard that Jesus had come from Judea to Galilee, he went and begged him to come down and heal his son, for he was at the point of death. ⁴⁸ Then Jesus said to him, "Unless you[b] see signs and wonders you will not believe." ⁴⁹ The official said to him, "Sir, come down before my little boy dies." ⁵⁰ Jesus said to him, "Go; your son will live." The man believed the word that Jesus spoke to him and started on his way. ⁵¹ As he was going down, his slaves met him and told him that his child was alive. ⁵² So he asked them the hour when he began to recover, and they said to him, "Yesterday at one in the afternoon the fever left him." ⁵³ The father realized that this was the hour when Jesus had said to him, "Your son will live." So he himself believed, along with his whole household. ⁵⁴ Now this was the second sign that Jesus did after coming from Judea to Galilee.

5 After this there was a festival of the Jews, and Jesus went up to Jerusalem.

² Now in Jerusalem by the Sheep Gate there is a pool, called in Hebrew[c] Beth-zatha,[d] which has five porticoes. ³ In these lay many invalids—blind, lame, and paralyzed.[e] ⁵ One

---

a   Or ³⁵ . . . the fields are already ripe for harvesting. ³⁶ The reaper is receiving
b   Both instances of the Greek word for you in this verse are plural
c   That is, Aramaic
d   Other ancient authorities read Bethesda, others Bethsaida
e   Other ancient authorities add, wholly or in part, waiting for the stirring of the water; ⁴ for an angel of the Lord went down at certain seasons into the pool, and stirred up the water; whoever stepped in first after the stirring of the water was made well from whatever disease that person had.

---

they misunderstand; Jesus explains: obeying God is food for him (cf. Deut 8.3; Mt 4.4). **35–36:** Jesus expands the metaphor by including harvest of grain, which is recruitment of disciples; cf. Mt 9.37–38. **37–38:** Normally sowers and reapers are the same people; unlike the proverb in Mic 6.15 (see also Deut 6.10–11), here, although they are distinguished, it is done is a positive light. Jesus' command should neutralize any competition. **39–42:** Samaritans first believed for a curious reason: Jesus revealed the woman's personal history. Eventually they believe because of Jesus' own words; the result is a climactic acknowledgment: he is *Savior of the world*, which dismisses earlier ethnic points of conflict.

4.43–54: Progress of the prophet (cf. Mt 8.5–15; Lk 7.1–10). **43–46:** *Cana* (see 2.1n.) and *Galilee* symbolize places favorable to Jesus, not just actual locations. Just as the Galileans saw Jesus' signs earlier, now an official seeks a sign. **46–47:** High-ranking people normally sent messages by an intermediary, but this one comes himself. **48–49:** The earlier pattern of request, refusal, then positive action (2.3–4) recurs. **50–54:** The boy lived and the father *believed*, as Jesus had said to him; in fact his *whole household* believed. *Second sign*, after Cana and the wine (2.1–11), before the feeding (ch 6).

5.1–18: The sign that failed. 1: Jesus attended this unnamed feast as well as Passover (see 2.13–16n.), Booths (7.2), and Dedication (10.22). **2–3:** *Jerusalem*, where Jesus is repeatedly rejected. Water links this episode with 3.5 and 4.7; and *pool* links it with 9.7. See map on p. 1862. **5–9:** Typical miracles have these elements: the severity

man was there who had been ill for thirty-eight years. ⁶ When Jesus saw him lying there and knew that he had been there a long time, he said to him, "Do you want to be made well?" ⁷ The sick man answered him, "Sir, I have no one to put me into the pool when the water is stirred up; and while I am making my way, someone else steps down ahead of me." ⁸ Jesus said to him, "Stand up, take your mat and walk." ⁹ At once the man was made well, and he took up his mat and began to walk.

Now that day was a sabbath. ¹⁰ So the Jews said to the man who had been cured, "It is the sabbath; it is not lawful for you to carry your mat." ¹¹ But he answered them, "The man who made me well said to me, 'Take up your mat and walk.'" ¹² They asked him, "Who is the man who said to you, 'Take it up and walk'?" ¹³ Now the man who had been healed did not know who it was, for Jesus had disappeared inᵃ the crowd that was there. ¹⁴ Later Jesus found him in the temple and said to him, "See, you have been made well! Do not sin any more, so that nothing worse happens to you." ¹⁵ The man went away and told the Jews that it was Jesus who had made him well. ¹⁶ Therefore the Jews started persecuting Jesus, because he was doing such things on the sabbath. ¹⁷ But Jesus answered them, "My Father is still working, and I also am working." ¹⁸ For this reason the Jews were seeking all the more to kill him, because he was not only breaking the sabbath, but was also calling God his own Father, thereby making himself equal to God.

¹⁹ Jesus said to them, "Very truly, I tell you, the Son can do nothing on his own, but only what he sees the Father doing; for whatever the Fatherᵇ does, the Son does likewise. ²⁰ The Father loves the Son and shows him all that he himself is doing; and he will show him greater works than these, so that you will be astonished. ²¹ Indeed, just as the Father raises the dead and gives them life, so also the Son gives life to whomever he wishes. ²² The Father judges no one but has given all judgment to the Son, ²³ so that all may honor the Son just as they honor the Father. Anyone who does not honor the Son does not honor the Father who sent him. ²⁴ Very truly, I tell you, anyone who hears my word and believes him who sent me has eternal life, and does not come under judgment, but has passed from death to life.

²⁵ "Very truly, I tell you, the hour is coming, and is now here, when the dead will hear the voice of the Son of God, and those who hear will live. ²⁶ For just as the Father has life in himself, so he has granted the Son also to have life in himself; ²⁷ and he has given him authority to execute judgment, because he is the Son of Man. ²⁸ Do not be astonished at this; for the hour is coming when all who are in their graves will hear his voice ²⁹ and will come out—those who have done good, to the resurrection of life, and those who have done evil, to the resurrection of condemnation.

ᵃ Or had left because of
ᵇ Gk that one

of the disease (*ill for thirty-eight years*); cure, either by the use of spittle and clay (as in 9.5) or by a command (*stand up*); proof of healing (*he . . . began to walk*); and grant of honor to the healer, absent here. Healing on the *sabbath* (5.10; 7.23 and 9.14) persuades many that Jesus is sinner—a judgment by appearances. **7:** *The water is stirred up*, explained by an addition in some manuscripts (see textual note on v. 3). **10–18:** Jesus' first trial begins; the man healed is charged with sabbath violation; he shifts the blame to his healer, whom he *did not know*. This witness brings no glory to the healer, but shame. After meeting Jesus again, he testified who the healer was. Punishment follows crime: they *persecuted* Jesus for *breaking the sabbath*. A defense is offered: if God works on the sabbath, Jesus' working cannot be sinful. The charge is elevated to blasphemy, whose punishment was death (see 10.30–32n.).

5.19–47: Two trials and two defenses. 19–29: The two charges (sabbath violation and blasphemous claims) require different defenses. The first defense denies that Jesus makes himself anything; rather, God honors him: because "the Father loves the Son," Jesus is not vaingloriously claiming anything. But he is truly "equal to God" (v. 18) because God gave him God's two comprehensive powers: lifegiver (cf. 1.1–3) and judge. **21:** God's power over death is exercised by Jesus. **22:** God twice invested Jesus with judgment (5.22,27). **23:** God demands that the respect owed him be given to Jesus. **25,28–29:** Jesus has power over the dead, to call them from tombs, raise them, and reward or punish them. This will be proved in Jesus' own case (10.17–18) and in that of Lazarus

30 "I can do nothing on my own. As I hear, I judge; and my judgment is just, because I seek to do not my own will but the will of him who sent me. 31 "If I testify about myself, my testimony is not true. 32 There is another who testifies on my behalf, and I know that his testimony to me is true. 33 You sent messengers to John, and he testified to the truth. 34 Not that I accept such human testimony, but I say these things so that you may be saved. 35 He was a burning and shining lamp, and you were willing to rejoice for a while in his light. 36 But I have a testimony greater than John's. The works that the Father has given me to complete, the very works that I am doing, testify on my behalf that the Father has sent me. 37 And the Father who sent me has himself testified on my behalf. You have never heard his voice or seen his form, 38 and you do not have his word abiding in you, because you do not believe him whom he has sent.

39 "You search the scriptures because you think that in them you have eternal life; and it is they that testify on my behalf. 40 Yet you refuse to come to me to have life. 41 I do not accept glory from human beings. 42 But I know that you do not have the love of God ina you. 43 I have come in my Father's name, and you do not accept me; if another comes in his own name, you will accept him. 44 How can you believe when you accept glory from one another and do not seek the glory that comes from the one who alone is God? 45 Do not think that I will accuse you before the Father; your accuser is Moses, on whom you have set your hope. 46 If you believed Moses, you would believe me, for he wrote about me. 47 But if you do not believe what he wrote, how will you believe what I say?"

6 After this Jesus went to the other side of the Sea of Galilee, also called the Sea of Tiberias.b 2 A large crowd kept following him, because they saw the signs that he was doing for the sick. 3 Jesus went up the mountain and sat down there with his disciples. 4 Now the Passover, the festival of the Jews, was near. 5 When he looked up and saw a large crowd coming toward him, Jesus said to Philip, "Where are we to buy bread for these people to eat?" 6 He said this to test him, for he himself knew what he was going to do. 7 Philip answered him, "Six months' wagesc would not buy enough bread for each of them to get a little." 8 One of his disciples, Andrew, Simon Peter's brother, said to him, 9 "There is a boy here who has five barley loaves and two fish. But what are they among so many people?" 10 Jesus said, "Make the people sit down." Now there was a great deal of grass in the place; so theyd sat down, about five thousand in all. 11 Then Jesus took the loaves, and when he had given thanks, he distributed them to those who were seated; so also the fish, as much as they wanted. 12 When they were satisfied, he told his disciples, "Gather up the fragments left over, so that nothing may be lost." 13 So they gathered them up, and from the fragments of the five barley loaves, left by those who had eaten, they filled twelve baskets. 14 When the people saw the sign that he had

a Or among
b Gk of Galilee of Tiberias
c Gk Two hundred denarii; the denarius was the usual day's wage for a laborer
d Gk the men

(11.43–44). 27: Son of Man, see 1.51n., 3.13–15n. 30–35: The defense against sabbath violation consists of calling witnesses to testify that Jesus is a saint, not a sinner. John the Baptist is acceptable to this court which valued him as a burning and shining lamp (see 1.29,34; 3.28–30). 36: Jesus' second witness—his works—proves God's favor (9.33). 37–38: God is also Jesus' witness. Although the Israelites never saw God at Sinai (see Deut 4.15), Jesus was face-to-face with God; he alone has seen God (contrast Ex 34.17–23). 39: Scripture witnesses to Jesus because "Moses . . . wrote about me" (v. 46; cf. 1.45). 40–44: The trial turns upside down: accusers are accused, the one judged becomes the judge. Jesus charges his accusers with a deadly crime: You do not have the love of God in you. Their accuser is Moses, once their defender (Ex 32.11–14; Num 14.13–19). The death sentence they would bring upon Jesus (v. 18) will be turned on them: they will never enjoy "eternal life" (vv. 24,39).

6.1–21: Fourth sign: multiplication of bread. Cf. Mt 14.13–21; Mk 6.32–44; Lk 9.10–17. 1: The other side, the eastern shore. 5–6: Jesus tests Philip by asking him how the crowd is to be fed; the Synoptic Gospels make Jesus' humanitarian motive explicit.

done, they began to say, "This is indeed the prophet who is to come into the world."

¹⁵ When Jesus realized that they were about to come and take him by force to make him king, he withdrew again to the mountain by himself.

¹⁶ When evening came, his disciples went down to the sea, ¹⁷ got into a boat, and started across the sea to Capernaum. It was now dark, and Jesus had not yet come to them. ¹⁸ The sea became rough because a strong wind was blowing. ¹⁹ When they had rowed about three or four miles,ᵃ they saw Jesus walking on the sea and coming near the boat, and they were terrified. ²⁰ But he said to them, "It is I;ᵇ do not be afraid." ²¹ Then they wanted to take him into the boat, and immediately the boat reached the land toward which they were going.

²² The next day the crowd that had stayed on the other side of the sea saw that there had been only one boat there. They also saw that Jesus had not got into the boat with his disciples, but that his disciples had gone away alone. ²³ Then some boats from Tiberias came near the place where they had eaten the bread after the Lord had given thanks.ᶜ ²⁴ So when the crowd saw that neither Jesus nor his disciples were there, they themselves got into the boats and went to Capernaum looking for Jesus.

²⁵ When they found him on the other side of the sea, they said to him, "Rabbi, when did you come here?" ²⁶ Jesus answered them, "Very truly, I tell you, you are looking for me, not because you saw signs, but because you ate your fill of the loaves. ²⁷ Do not work for the food that perishes, but for the food that endures for eternal life, which the Son of Man will give you. For it is on him that God the Father has set his seal." ²⁸ Then they said to him, "What must we do to perform the works of God?" ²⁹ Jesus answered them, "This is the work of God, that

you believe in him whom he has sent." ³⁰ So they said to him, "What sign are you going to give us then, so that we may see it and believe you? What work are you performing? ³¹ Our ancestors ate the manna in the wilderness; as it is written, 'He gave them bread from heaven to eat.'" ³² Then Jesus said to them, "Very truly, I tell you, it was not Moses who gave you the bread from heaven, but it is my Father who gives you the true bread from heaven. ³³ For the bread of God is that whichᵈ comes down from heaven and gives life to the world." ³⁴ They said to him, "Sir, give us this bread always."

³⁵ Jesus said to them, "I am the bread of life. Whoever comes to me will never be hungry, and whoever believes in me will never be thirsty. ³⁶ But I said to you that you have seen me and yet do not believe. ³⁷ Everything that the Father gives me will come to me, and anyone who comes to me I will never drive away; ³⁸ for I have come down from heaven, not to do my own will, but the will of him who sent me. ³⁹ And this is the will of him who sent me, that I should lose nothing of all that he has given me, but raise it up on the last day. ⁴⁰ This is indeed the will of my Father, that all who see the Son and believe in him may have eternal life; and I will raise them up on the last day."

⁴¹ Then the Jews began to complain about him because he said, "I am the bread that came down from heaven." ⁴² They were saying, "Is not this Jesus, the son of Joseph, whose father and mother we know? How can he now say, 'I have come down from heaven'?" ⁴³ Jesus answered them, "Do not complain among yourselves. ⁴⁴ No one can come to me

ᵃ Gk *about twenty-five or thirty stadia*
ᵇ Gk *I am*
ᶜ Other ancient authorities lack *after the Lord had given thanks*
ᵈ Or *he who*

6.16–21: Jesus walks on the sea. Cf. Mt 14.22–27; Mk 6.45–52. Jesus' mysterious presence anticipates his going away but coming back (see 14.3,28). 20: *It is I*, lit., "I am"; see 4.26n.

6.22–59: Bread from heaven. *The crowd* are not true insiders because they challenge Jesus with hostile questions. Jesus responds by accusing them of hypocrisy and demands acknowledgment as God's agent, declaring that he is the *bread from heaven* (v. 31). 24: *Capernaum*, see 2.12n. 27: *Son of Man*, see 3.13–15n. 31–32: They challenge Jesus with a scripture (see Ex 16.4–5 and Ps 78.24), and he reinterprets each word in it as a reference to himself. 34: As in 4.15, the questioners misunderstand. 35–40: Jesus explains: *I am the bread of life . . . come down from heaven.* 41: They complained, like the Israelites in the wilderness before and after the manna was given (Ex 16.2; Num 11.1). 42: Reference to Jesus' earthly parents should refute his claim to have *come*

unless drawn by the Father who sent me; and I will raise that person up on the last day. ⁴⁵ It is written in the prophets, 'And they shall all be taught by God.' Everyone who has heard and learned from the Father comes to me. ⁴⁶ Not that anyone has seen the Father except the one who is from God; he has seen the Father. ⁴⁷ Very truly, I tell you, whoever believes has eternal life. ⁴⁸ I am the bread of life. ⁴⁹ Your ancestors ate the manna in the wilderness, and they died. ⁵⁰ This is the bread that comes down from heaven, so that one may eat of it and not die. ⁵¹ I am the living bread that came down from heaven. Whoever eats of this bread will live forever; and the bread that I will give for the life of the world is my flesh."

⁵² The Jews then disputed among themselves, saying, "How can this man give us his flesh to eat?" ⁵³ So Jesus said to them, "Very truly, I tell you, unless you eat the flesh of the Son of Man and drink his blood, you have no life in you. ⁵⁴ Those who eat my flesh and drink my blood have eternal life, and I will raise them up on the last day; ⁵⁵ for my flesh is true food and my blood is true drink. ⁵⁶ Those who eat my flesh and drink my blood abide in me, and I in them. ⁵⁷ Just as the living Father sent me, and I live because of the Father, so whoever eats me will live because of me. ⁵⁸ This is the bread that came down from heaven, not like that which your ancestors ate, and they died. But the one who eats this bread will live forever." ⁵⁹ He said these things while he was teaching in the synagogue at Capernaum.

⁶⁰ When many of his disciples heard it, they said, "This teaching is difficult; who can accept it?" ⁶¹ But Jesus, being aware that his disciples were complaining about it, said to them, "Does this offend you? ⁶² Then what if you were to see the Son of Man ascending to where he was before? ⁶³ It is the spirit that gives life; the flesh is useless. The words that I have spoken to you are spirit and life. ⁶⁴ But among you there are some who do not believe." For Jesus knew from the first who were the ones that did not believe, and who was the one that would betray him. ⁶⁵ And he said, "For this reason I have told you that no one can come to me unless it is granted by the Father."

⁶⁶ Because of this many of his disciples turned back and no longer went about with him. ⁶⁷ So Jesus asked the twelve, "Do you also wish to go away?" ⁶⁸ Simon Peter answered him, "Lord, to whom can we go? You have the words of eternal life. ⁶⁹ We have come to believe and know that you are the Holy One of God."ᵃ ⁷⁰ Jesus answered them, "Did I not choose you, the twelve? Yet one of you is a devil." ⁷¹ He was speaking of Judas son of Simon Iscariot,ᵇ for he, though one of the twelve, was going to betray him.

7 After this Jesus went about in Galilee. He did not wishᶜ to go about in Judea because the Jews were looking for an

---

a Other ancient authorities read *the Christ, the Son of the living God*

b Other ancient authorities read *Judas Iscariot son of Simon*; others, *Judas son of Simon from Karyot* (Kerioth)

c Other ancient authorities read *was not at liberty*

---

down from heaven, a literal understanding. **45:** Isa 54.13. **49–50:** The contrast between Moses' manna and Jesus' true bread looks to results: one dies after eating manna but has eternal life from Jesus' bread. **51–59:** Another instance of statement (v. 51), misunderstanding (v. 52), and restatement (vv. 53–58). In these verses, the author (who does not include an account of the institution of the Lord's Supper) presents teachings with unmistakable eucharistic overtones. So far only bread was discussed, now *blood*. Consumption of blood was taboo to Israel: in the blood was life (Deut 12.23), but life belongs to God alone (Gen 9.4). Ordinarily taking Jesus literally is folly, but here Jesus intends to be both literal and outrageous. **59:** *In the synagogue at Capernaum*, cf. Mk 1.21; Lk 4.31.

6.60–71: Separating wheat from chaff. 60–65: Even some disciples reject Jesus' bread; they too complained (see v. 41n.). **61–62:** If they reject his claim to descend from heaven, his return there will be impossible to accept. **64–65:** Jesus knew from the start both the unbelieving crowds and who would betray him. Knowing all things, he commands the scene. **66–69:** A typical Johannine schism: some leave; others remain, but even they are challenged. **67:** *The twelve*, Jesus' inner circle, mentioned only here and in 20.24 in this Gospel. Peter's confession resembles that at Caesarea Philippi (Mk 8.28–29), substituting *Holy One of God* for "Messiah." **70–71:** Jesus' knowledge of the betrayer (v. 64) indicates that he voluntarily accepts death; see 13.11,21–30.

7.1–10: Blood relationships don't count. 1: *The Jews*, see 1.19n. **2:** *Booths* (also called "Tabernacles"), a seven-

opportunity to kill him. [2] Now the Jewish festival of Booths[a] was near. [3] So his brothers said to him, "Leave here and go to Judea so that your disciples also may see the works you are doing; [4] for no one who wants[b] to be widely known acts in secret. If you do these things, show yourself to the world." [5] (For not even his brothers believed in him.) [6] Jesus said to them, "My time has not yet come, but your time is always here. [7] The world cannot hate you, but it hates me because I testify against it that its works are evil. [8] Go to the festival yourselves. I am not[c] going to this festival, for my time has not yet fully come." [9] After saying this, he remained in Galilee.

[10] But after his brothers had gone to the festival, then he also went, not publicly but as it were[d] in secret. [11] The Jews were looking for him at the festival and saying, "Where is he?" [12] And there was considerable complaining about him among the crowds. While some were saying, "He is a good man," others were saying, "No, he is deceiving the crowd." [13] Yet no one would speak openly about him for fear of the Jews.

[14] About the middle of the festival Jesus went up into the temple and began to teach. [15] The Jews were astonished at it, saying, "How does this man have such learning,[e] when he has never been taught?" [16] Then Jesus answered them, "My teaching is not mine but his who sent me. [17] Anyone who resolves to do the will of God will know whether the teaching is from God or whether I am speaking on my own. [18] Those who speak on their own seek their own glory; but the one who seeks the glory of him who sent him is true, and there is nothing false in him.

[19] "Did not Moses give you the law? Yet none of you keeps the law. Why are you looking for an opportunity to kill me?" [20] The crowd answered, "You have a demon! Who is trying to kill you?" [21] Jesus answered them, "I performed one work, and all of you are astonished. [22] Moses gave you circumcision (it is, of course, not from Moses, but from the patriarchs), and you circumcise a man on the sabbath. [23] If a man receives circumcision on the sabbath in order that the law of Moses may not be broken, are you angry with me because I healed a man's whole body on the sabbath? [24] Do not judge by appearances, but judge with right judgment."

[25] Now some of the people of Jerusalem were saying, "Is not this the man whom they are trying to kill? [26] And here he is, speaking openly, but they say nothing to him! Can it be that the authorities really know that this is the Messiah?[f] [27] Yet we know where this man is from; but when the Messiah[f] comes, no one will know where he is from." [28] Then Jesus cried out as he was teaching in the temple, "You know me, and you know where I am from. I have not come on my own. But the one who sent me is true, and you do not know him. [29] I know him, because I am from him, and he sent me." [30] Then they tried to arrest him, but no one laid hands on him, because his hour had not yet come. [31] Yet many in the crowd believed in him and were saying, "When the Messiah[f] comes, will he do more signs than this man has done?"[g]

a Or *Tabernacles*
b Other ancient authorities read *wants it*
c Other ancient authorities add *yet*
d Other ancient authorities lack *as it were*
e Or *this man know his letters*
f Or *the Christ*
g Other ancient authorities read *is doing*

day harvest feast in the fall during which petitions for rains and sunlight were expressed in daily water libations and nightly lighting of menorahs. **3–5:** *Brothers* (see 2.12n.), here opposed to Jesus (cf. 1.12). **6,8:** *My time,* cf. "my hour" in 2.4; 7.30; 8.20; 13.1. **8–10:** Jesus regularly controls his fate with a strategy of secrecy.

7.11–52: Second trial in Jerusalem. 11–13: Another schism: some accuse Jesus of deception, but others praise him (cf. 7.40–44,45–52; 10.19–21). *Fear of the Jews* muzzles possible disciples (9.22; 12.42; 19.38–39). **14–17:** Can Jesus teach if not schooled? His Father taught him (5.20); and godly people recognize this (9.29–30). **18:** Telling false from true speakers: Those who *seek their own glory* are false (5.44); but *the one who seeks the glory of him who sent him* is true (8.50). **25–27:** Testimony against Jesus: "*We know*" where he comes from (see 1.45–46; 6.42), but no one knows where the Messiah comes from. **28–29:** Jesus' challenge, "*You do not know him*," because you know according to the flesh. But "*I know him, because I am from him.*" **30–31:** A negative schism again (*they*

³² The Pharisees heard the crowd muttering such things about him, and the chief priests and Pharisees sent temple police to arrest him. ³³ Jesus then said, "I will be with you a little while longer, and then I am going to him who sent me. ³⁴ You will search for me, but you will not find me; and where I am, you cannot come." ³⁵ The Jews said to one another, "Where does this man intend to go that we will not find him? Does he intend to go to the Dispersion among the Greeks and teach the Greeks? ³⁶ What does he mean by saying, 'You will search for me and you will not find me' and 'Where I am, you cannot come'?"

³⁷ On the last day of the festival, the great day, while Jesus was standing there, he cried out, "Let anyone who is thirsty come to me, ³⁸ and let the one who believes in me drink. As^a the scripture has said, 'Out of the believer's heart^b shall flow rivers of living water.'" ³⁹ Now he said this about the Spirit, which believers in him were to receive; for as yet there was no Spirit,^c because Jesus was not yet glorified.

⁴⁰ When they heard these words, some in the crowd said, "This is really the prophet." ⁴¹ Others said, "This is the Messiah."^d But some asked, "Surely the Messiah^d does not come from Galilee, does he? ⁴² Has not the scripture said that the Messiah^d is descended from David and comes from Bethlehem, the village where David lived?" ⁴³ So there was a division in the crowd because of him. ⁴⁴ Some of them wanted to arrest him, but no one laid hands on him.

⁴⁵ Then the temple police went back to the chief priests and Pharisees, who asked them, "Why did you not arrest him?" ⁴⁶ The police answered, "Never has anyone spoken like this!" ⁴⁷ Then the Pharisees replied, "Surely you have not been deceived too, have you? ⁴⁸ Has any one of the authorities or of the Pharisees believed in him? ⁴⁹ But this crowd, which does not know the law—they are accursed." ⁵⁰ Nicodemus, who had gone to Jesus^e before, and who was one of them, asked, ⁵¹ "Our law does not judge people without first giving them a hearing to find out what they are doing, does it?" ⁵² They replied, "Surely you are not also from Galilee, are you? Search and you will see that no prophet is to arise from Galilee."

8 ⟦ ⁵³ Then each of them went home, ¹ while Jesus went to the Mount of Olives. ² Early in the morning he came again to the temple. All the people came to him and he sat down and began to teach them. ³ The scribes and the Pharisees brought a woman who had been caught in adultery; and making her stand before all of them, ⁴ they said to him, "Teacher, this woman was caught in the very act of committing adultery. ⁵ Now in the law Moses commanded us to stone such women. Now what do you say?" ⁶ They said this to test him, so that they might have some charge to

a Or *come to me and drink.* ³⁸*The one who believes in me, as*
b Gk *out of his belly*
c Other ancient authorities read *for as yet the Spirit* (others, *Holy Spirit*) *had not been given*
d Or *the Christ*
e Gk *him*

tried to arrest him), followed by a positive judgment: Will the Messiah do more signs than Jesus? **32–36:** Debate about where Jesus is going. They think he may be going to Jews in *the Dispersion among the Greeks*, but his actual destination—*to him who sent me*—is known only by insiders. *You will search for me* means "seek to kill me," but *"Where I am, you cannot come."* **37–39:** The water ritual of the feast of Tabernacles (see 7.2n.) transformed: Jesus replaces with his water the festal libations; cf. the blood and water from his *heart* at his death (19.34). Jesus is *glorified* only at death when he hands over the Spirit (19:30). **38:** *Scripture has said,* no biblical passage contains these exact words; for the general sense, see Prov 18.4; Isa 44.3; 58.11. **40–43:** Some accept Jesus' testimony, but others reject it, judging according to appearances: the Messiah cannot come from Galilee but must come from Bethlehem; see 1.45–46n. **44:** Jesus tried in absentia: they accuse him, find testimony against him, seek to kill him, but cannot carry out the sentence. **45–48:** Soldiers sent to arrest Jesus return acclaiming him, proof that Jesus is a deceiver. **49:** Who is fit to judge? Not the accursed *crowd, which does not know the law*; the *Pharisees* claim to, but they too violate the law. **50–51:** Nicodemus says nothing positive about Jesus but only defends the law. **52:** Another judgment according to appearances.

8.1–11: Jesus and the adulteress. 1: This story is absent in major manuscripts. **3–6:** Opponents *test* Jesus, cit-

bring against him. Jesus bent down and wrote with his finger on the ground. [7] When they kept on questioning him, he straightened up and said to them, "Let anyone among you who is without sin be the first to throw a stone at her." [8] And once again he bent down and wrote on the ground.[a] [9] When they heard it, they went away, one by one, beginning with the elders; and Jesus was left alone with the woman standing before him. [10] Jesus straightened up and said to her, "Woman, where are they? Has no one condemned you?" [11] She said, "No one, sir."[b] And Jesus said, "Neither do I condemn you. Go your way, and from now on do not sin again."]][c]

[12] Again Jesus spoke to them, saying, "I am the light of the world. Whoever follows me will never walk in darkness but will have the light of life." [13] Then the Pharisees said to him, "You are testifying on your own behalf; your testimony is not valid." [14] Jesus answered, "Even if I testify on my own behalf, my testimony is valid because I know where I have come from and where I am going, but you do not know where I come from or where I am going. [15] You judge by human standards;[d] I judge no one. [16] Yet even if I do judge, my judgment is valid; for it is not I alone who judge, but I and the Father[e] who sent me. [17] In your law it is written that the testimony of two witnesses is valid. [18] I testify on my own behalf, and the Father who sent me testifies on my behalf." [19] Then they said to him, "Where is your Father?" Jesus answered, "You know neither me nor my Father. If you knew me, you would know my Father also." [20] He spoke these words while he was teaching

in the treasury of the temple, but no one arrested him, because his hour had not yet come.

[21] Again he said to them, "I am going away, and you will search for me, but you will die in your sin. Where I am going, you cannot come." [22] Then the Jews said, "Is he going to kill himself? Is that what he means by saying, 'Where I am going, you cannot come'?" [23] He said to them, "You are from below, I am from above; you are of this world, I am not of this world. [24] I told you that you would die in your sins, for you will die in your sins unless you believe that I am he."[f] [25] They said to him, "Who are you?" Jesus said to them, "Why do I speak to you at all?[g] [26] I have much to say about you and much to condemn; but the one who sent me is true, and I declare to the world what I have heard from him." [27] They did not understand that he was speaking to them about the Father. [28] So Jesus said, "When you have lifted up the Son of Man, then you will realize that I am he,[f] and that I do nothing on my own, but I speak these things as the Father instructed me. [29] And the one who sent me is with me; he has not left me alone, for I always do what is pleasing to

a Other ancient authorities add *the sins of each of them*

b Or *Lord*

c The most ancient authorities lack 7.53—8.11; other authorities add the passage here or after 7.36 or after 21.25 or after Luke 21.38, with variations of text; some mark the passage as doubtful.

d Gk *according to the flesh*

e Other ancient authorities read *he*

f Gk *I am*

g Or *What I have told you from the beginning*

ing the law (Deut 22.23–24) and its punishment. **7:** Jesus' challenge is answered: only the sinless may stone her. **9:** Sinful opponents put to shame. **10–11:** Unlike his challengers, Jesus does not condemn her.

8.12–20: The feast of Tabernacles, continued. 12: Jesus claims to replace the rain (7.37–38) and sunlight (8.12) for which Israel prayed. **13–14:** The trial is resumed: Jesus' testimony is declared invalid; but because Jesus knows his origin and destination, i.e., his authorization, it is *valid*. **15–16:** They judge by appearances (7.24). Jesus does not but does judge because God stands with him (5.22,27). **17–18:** Two valid witnesses (see Deut 19.15): Jesus and the Father who sent him. **19:** *Know* means to acknowledge or honor. **20:** Jesus in public space (cf. 18.20).

8.21–30: Jesus judges. 21–25: Jesus' topic statement contains four points: *Going away* may imply suicide; *search for me*, "attempt to kill"; *die in your sins*, sentence for failing to keep my law (see 4.26n.;7.19,25; 8.58–59); *you cannot come*, because they belong to irreconcilable worlds (see 3.5–8). **28:** *Lifted up*, either lifting Jesus on the cross or his glorious return to heaven. *I am he*, lit., "I am," the name of God in Ex 3.14; here, a being who is both eternal in the past and imperishable in the future.

him." ³⁰ As he was saying these things, many believed in him.

³¹ Then Jesus said to the Jews who had believed in him, "If you continue in my word, you are truly my disciples; ³² and you will know the truth, and the truth will make you free." ³³ They answered him, "We are descendants of Abraham and have never been slaves to anyone. What do you mean by saying, 'You will be made free'?"

³⁴ Jesus answered them, "Very truly, I tell you, everyone who commits sin is a slave to sin. ³⁵ The slave does not have a permanent place in the household; the son has a place there forever. ³⁶ So if the Son makes you free, you will be free indeed. ³⁷ I know that you are descendants of Abraham; yet you look for an opportunity to kill me, because there is no place in you for my word. ³⁸ I declare what I have seen in the Father's presence; as for you, you should do what you have heard from the Father."ᵃ

³⁹ They answered him, "Abraham is our father." Jesus said to them, "If you were Abraham's children, you would be doingᵇ what Abraham did, ⁴⁰ but now you are trying to kill me, a man who has told you the truth that I heard from God. This is not what Abraham did. ⁴¹ You are indeed doing what your father does." They said to him, "We are not illegitimate children; we have one father, God himself." ⁴² Jesus said to them, "If God were your Father, you would love me, for I came from God and now I am here. I did not come on my own, but he sent me. ⁴³ Why do you not understand what I say? It is because you cannot accept my word. ⁴⁴ You are from your father the devil, and you choose to do your father's desires. He was a murderer from the beginning and does not stand in the truth, because there is no truth in him. When he lies, he speaks according to his own nature, for he is a liar and the father of lies. ⁴⁵ But because I tell the truth, you do not believe me. ⁴⁶ Which of you convicts me of sin? If I tell the truth, why do you not believe me? ⁴⁷ Whoever is from God hears the words of God. The reason you do not hear them is that you are not from God."

⁴⁸ The Jews answered him, "Are we not right in saying that you are a Samaritan and have a demon?" ⁴⁹ Jesus answered, "I do not have a demon; but I honor my Father, and you dishonor me. ⁵⁰ Yet I do not seek my own glory; there is one who seeks it and he is the judge. ⁵¹ Very truly, I tell you, whoever keeps my word will never see death." ⁵² The Jews said to him, "Now we know that you have a demon. Abraham died, and so did the prophets; yet you say, 'Whoever keeps my word will never taste death.' ⁵³ Are you greater than our father Abraham, who died? The prophets also died. Who do you claim to be?" ⁵⁴ Jesus answered, "If I glorify myself, my glory is nothing. It is my Father who glorifies me, he of whom you say, 'He is our God,' ⁵⁵ though you do not know him. But I know him; if I would say that I do not know him, I would be a liar like you. But I do know him and I keep his word. ⁵⁶ Your ancestor Abraham rejoiced that he would see my day; he saw it and was glad." ⁵⁷ Then the Jews said to him, "You are not yet fifty years old, and have you seen Abraham?"ᶜ ⁵⁸ Jesus

ᵃ Other ancient authorities read *you do what you have heard from your father*
ᵇ Other ancient authorities read *If you are Abraham's children, then do*
ᶜ Other ancient authorities read *has Abraham seen you?*

8.31–59: Exposing lies. 31–32: As judge, Jesus examines their testimony according to his criterion for true discipleship. **31:** *Believed in him,* it is unclear whether this is genuine or a deception. **33:** Abraham had two sons, Ishmael (slave) and Isaac (free); their claim that Isaac was their father is proven false. **34–36:** Slaves of sin (Ishmael) do not remain in the house, but free sons (Isaac) do (Gen 21.9–14). **37:** They are children of Ishmael, sinners trying to kill Jesus. The criterion "continue in my word" (v. 31) is verified: *There is no place in you for my word.* **38–42:** Abraham did not try to kill heavenly messengers at Mamre (Gen 18.1–9). Masking their illegitimacy, they lie, claiming God as father. But if he were, they would do what their Father does, love Jesus. **43:** The criterion repeated. **44:** Their paternity is revealed: the *devil,* a *murderer,* and a *liar,* like them. **48:** *Samaritan,* not one of us; see 4.4n. *Have a demon,* not of God. **49–50:** Denial of demon charge because Jesus honors God and God honors him. **51–52:** Jesus says *"never see death,"* which they misunderstand as *"never taste death."* **54–55:** God makes Jesus who he is, but they do not know God; Jesus does not lie, for he knows God and keeps his word. **56–58:** Jesus is "greater" than Abraham (v. 53) because Abraham came into being and died but Jesus as divine (*I am*; see

said to them, "Very truly, I tell you, before Abraham was, I am." [59] So they picked up stones to throw at him, but Jesus hid himself and went out of the temple.

9 As he walked along, he saw a man blind from birth. [2] His disciples asked him, "Rabbi, who sinned, this man or his parents, that he was born blind?" [3] Jesus answered, "Neither this man nor his parents sinned; he was born blind so that God's works might be revealed in him. [4] We[a] must work the works of him who sent me[b] while it is day; night is coming when no one can work. [5] As long as I am in the world, I am the light of the world." [6] When he had said this, he spat on the ground and made mud with the saliva and spread the mud on the man's eyes, [7] saying to him, "Go, wash in the pool of Siloam" (which means Sent). Then he went and washed and came back able to see. [8] The neighbors and those who had seen him before as a beggar began to ask, "Is this not the man who used to sit and beg?" [9] Some were saying, "It is he." Others were saying, "No, but it is someone like him." He kept saying, "I am the man." [10] But they kept asking him, "Then how were your eyes opened?" [11] He answered, "The man called Jesus made mud, spread it on my eyes, and said to me, 'Go to Siloam and wash.' Then I went and washed and received my sight." [12] They said to him, "Where is he?" He said, "I do not know."

[13] They brought to the Pharisees the man who had formerly been blind. [14] Now it was a sabbath day when Jesus made the mud and opened his eyes. [15] Then the Pharisees also began to ask him how he had received his sight. He said to them, "He put mud on my eyes. Then I washed, and now I see." [16] Some of the Pharisees said, "This man is not from God, for he does not observe the sabbath." But others said, "How can a man who is a sin-

ner perform such signs?" And they were divided. [17] So they said again to the blind man, "What do you say about him? It was your eyes he opened." He said, "He is a prophet."

[18] The Jews did not believe that he had been blind and had received his sight until they called the parents of the man who had received his sight [19] and asked them, "Is this your son, who you say was born blind? How then does he now see?" [20] His parents answered, "We know that this is our son, and that he was born blind; [21] but we do not know how it is that now he sees, nor do we know who opened his eyes. Ask him; he is of age. He will speak for himself." [22] His parents said this because they were afraid of the Jews; for the Jews had already agreed that anyone who confessed Jesus[c] to be the Messiah[d] would be put out of the synagogue. [23] Therefore his parents said, "He is of age; ask him."

[24] So for the second time they called the man who had been blind, and they said to him, "Give glory to God! We know that this man is a sinner." [25] He answered, "I do not know whether he is a sinner. One thing I do know, that though I was blind, now I see." [26] They said to him, "What did he do to you? How did he open your eyes?" [27] He answered them, "I have told you already, and you would not listen. Why do you want to hear it again? Do you also want to become his disciples?" [28] Then they reviled him, saying, "You are his disciple, but we are disciples of Moses. [29] We know that God has spoken to Moses, but as for this man, we do not know where he comes from." [30] The man answered, "Here is an astonishing thing! You do not know where he comes from, and

---

a Other ancient authorities read *I*
b Other ancient authorities read *us*
c Gk *him*
d Or *the Christ*

8.28.) is uncreated and imperishable. **59:** Trying to stone Jesus, they prove their guilt.

9.1–41: A sign, trial, and testimony. 1–12: The healing. **1–3:** Human explanations for blindness are rejected; now it reveals God's works. **4–5:** *Day* includes sunlight and *light* of the world (8.12). **6–7:** As a cure Jesus uses *saliva* and *mud* (cf. Mk 8.23), then commands washing. *Pool*, cf. 5.1–9. *Siloam*, an ancient pool in Jerusalem (see 2 Kings 20.20).

9.13–34: Jesus tried in absentia. 13–17: The man whose sight had been restored repeats the facts and interprets them: Jesus is a *prophet* (see 6.14). **18–23:** To prove whether he was born blind, his parents testify affirmatively that their son was born blind, but they refuse to speak about the healer and the cure because they fear reprisals for witnessing to Jesus (see 12.42–43). **24–27:** Jesus is now on trial. The healed man mocks their demand to repeat the facts of the case, already narrated twice: Will hearing it again make them *disciples*? **30–33:**

yet he opened my eyes. [31] We know that God does not listen to sinners, but he does listen to one who worships him and obeys his will. [32] Never since the world began has it been heard that anyone opened the eyes of a person born blind. [33] If this man were not from God, he could do nothing." [34] They answered him, "You were born entirely in sins, and are you trying to teach us?" And they drove him out.

[35] Jesus heard that they had driven him out, and when he found him, he said, "Do you believe in the Son of Man?"[a] [36] He answered, "And who is he, sir?[b] Tell me, so that I may believe in him." [37] Jesus said to him, "You have seen him, and the one speaking with you is he." [38] He said, "Lord,[b] I believe." And he worshiped him. [39] Jesus said, "I came into this world for judgment so that those who do not see may see, and those who do see may become blind." [40] Some of the Pharisees near him heard this and said to him, "Surely we are not blind, are we?" [41] Jesus said to them, "If you were blind, you would not have sin. But now that you say, 'We see,' your sin remains.

10
"Very truly, I tell you, anyone who does not enter the sheepfold by the gate but climbs in by another way is a thief and a bandit. [2] The one who enters by the gate is the shepherd of the sheep. [3] The gatekeeper opens the gate for him, and the sheep hear his voice. He calls his own sheep by name and leads them out. [4] When he has brought out all his own, he goes ahead of them, and the sheep follow him because they know his voice. [5] They will not follow a stranger, but they will run from him because they do not know the voice of strangers." [6] Jesus used this

figure of speech with them, but they did not understand what he was saying to them.

[7] So again Jesus said to them, "Very truly, I tell you, I am the gate for the sheep. [8] All who came before me are thieves and bandits; but the sheep did not listen to them. [9] I am the gate. Whoever enters by me will be saved, and will come in and go out and find pasture. [10] The thief comes only to steal and kill and destroy. I came that they may have life, and have it abundantly.

[11] "I am the good shepherd. The good shepherd lays down his life for the sheep. [12] The hired hand, who is not the shepherd and does not own the sheep, sees the wolf coming and leaves the sheep and runs away—and the wolf snatches them and scatters them. [13] The hired hand runs away because a hired hand does not care for the sheep. [14] I am the good shepherd. I know my own and my own know me, [15] just as the Father knows me and I know the Father. And I lay down my life for the sheep. [16] I have other sheep that do not belong to this fold. I must bring them also, and they will listen to my voice. So there will be one flock, one shepherd. [17] For this reason the Father loves me, because I lay down my life in order to take it up again. [18] No one takes[c] it from me, but I lay it down of my own accord. I have power to lay it down, and I have power to take it up again. I have received this command from my Father."

[19] Again the Jews were divided because of these words. [20] Many of them were saying,

---

a   Other ancient authorities read the Son of God
b   Sir and Lord translate the same Greek word
c   Other ancient authorities read has taken

Their judgment is judged: if Jesus were not from God, he could do nothing. **34:** The disciples attributed blindness to sin (9.2); now the court judges the man to be a sinner. His fate is that which his parents feared: expulsion from the synagogue.

9.35–41: Final verdicts. Jesus vindicates the man by leading him into greater *believing*. He knows that *the Son of Man* is Jesus; his knowledge becomes belief. Ironically, Jesus makes the blind see and the sighted blind (see 12.40). Physical blindness is morally neutral, not so false claims to sight.

10.1–21: Authentic shepherding (cf. Ezek 34.11–16; Pss 23; 78.52; 95.7; Isa 40.10–11). **6:** Jesus' parables and words are generally misunderstood (Mk 4.33–34; 16.25,29). **7–9:** *I am the gate*, Jesus' exclusive claim to be broker of salvation and pasturage. **11:** *Good*, better "noble," a word applied to the death of a soldier or hero when voluntarily accepted, which benefitted the city, when experienced virtuously, when the hero died unconquered, and which was awarded posthumous honors. **12–13:** Hirelings lack virtue, justice, and courage. **14–15:** The noble shepherd manifests justice: his death benefits the sheep and is performed virtuously. **16:** Recruiting envisioned (4.35–38; 17.20–21). **17–18:** Noble death: voluntary, virtuous, and unconquered in death (cf. 5.26), a power that

"He has a demon and is out of his mind. Why listen to him?" [21] Others were saying, "These are not the words of one who has a demon. Can a demon open the eyes of the blind?"

[22] At that time the festival of the Dedication took place in Jerusalem. It was winter, [23] and Jesus was walking in the temple, in the portico of Solomon. [24] So the Jews gathered around him and said to him, "How long will you keep us in suspense? If you are the Messiah,[a] tell us plainly." [25] Jesus answered, "I have told you, and you do not believe. The works that I do in my Father's name testify to me; [26] but you do not believe, because you do not belong to my sheep. [27] My sheep hear my voice. I know them, and they follow me. [28] I give them eternal life, and they will never perish. No one will snatch them out of my hand. [29] What my Father has given me is greater than all else, and no one can snatch it out of the Father's hand.[b] [30] The Father and I are one."

[31] The Jews took up stones again to stone him. [32] Jesus replied, "I have shown you many good works from the Father. For which of these are you going to stone me?" [33] The Jews answered, "It is not for a good work that we are going to stone you, but for blasphemy, because you, though only a human being, are making yourself God." [34] Jesus answered, "Is it not written in your law,[c] 'I said, you are gods'? [35] If those to whom the word of God came were called 'gods'—and the scripture cannot be annulled— [36] can you say that the one whom the Father has sanctified and sent into the world is blaspheming because

I said, 'I am God's Son'? [37] If I am not doing the works of my Father, then do not believe me. [38] But if I do them, even though you do not believe me, believe the works, so that you may know and understand[d] that the Father is in me and I am in the Father." [39] Then they tried to arrest him again, but he escaped from their hands.

[40] He went away again across the Jordan to the place where John had been baptizing earlier, and he remained there. [41] Many came to him, and they were saying, "John performed no sign, but everything that John said about this man was true." [42] And many believed in him there.

11 Now a certain man was ill, Lazarus of Bethany, the village of Mary and her sister Martha. [2] Mary was the one who anointed the Lord with perfume and wiped his feet with her hair; her brother Lazarus was ill. [3] So the sisters sent a message to Jesus,[e] "Lord, he whom you love is ill." [4] But when Jesus heard it, he said, "This illness does not lead to death; rather it is for God's glory, so that the Son of God may be glorified through it." [5] Accordingly, though Jesus loved Martha and her sister and Lazarus, [6] after

a   Or the Christ
b   Other ancient authorities read My Father who has given them to me is greater than all, and no one can snatch them out of the Father's hand
c   Other ancient authorities read in the law
d   Other ancient authorities lack and understand; others read and believe
e   Gk him

belongs exclusively to God. **19–21:** Cf. 7.20; 8.48; 9.16; 10.20.

10.22–42: Trial in the Temple. This episode resembles the trial before the Sanhedrin in the Synoptic Gospels, especially the question, "Are you the Messiah?" (Mt 26.62–64). **22–24:** *Dedication* (Hanukkah; see 1 Macc 4.36–59), the fourth holy day that Jesus attended in Jerusalem. **25–27:** Because they act in bad faith and do not judge his works properly, they cannot be his disciples. In contrast, true *sheep* hear his *voice*, he acknowledges them, and they *follow* him. **28–29:** *Eternal life*, the promise made in v. 10 is abundant life. Death cannot snatch them from the hands of Jesus or the Father: both have power over death (5.21–29). **30–32:** Jesus' signs and works are evidence of his agency from God, as the healed blind man had said earlier (8.30–33). Stoning was the penalty for blasphemy (Lev 24.16). **33–36:** Jesus defends himself against the charge that he is making himself God by quoting Ps 82.6, which is interpreted as declaring some mortals to be "gods," that is, immortals. All the more is Jesus holy, because God *sanctified and sent* him. **37–38:** Jesus' works attest to his relationship with the Father. **40–42:** Signs do not persuade the Jerusalemites, but the signs work where John testified to Jesus (1.29–34).

11.1–45: The raising of Lazarus. 1–16: Jesus delays. 1–2: Introducing beloved disciples: Lazarus, Mary, Martha. *Bethany*, see v. 18. *Anointed*, see 12.3. **3–6:** Hearing of Lazarus's illness, Jesus reacts predictably (2.4; 4.48; 7.8–9); he will not act until his time is ripe, *for God's glory* and that of the *Son of God* (cf. 9.3). The delay allows

having heard that Lazarus[a] was ill, he stayed two days longer in the place where he was.

[7] Then after this he said to the disciples, "Let us go to Judea again." [8] The disciples said to him, "Rabbi, the Jews were just now trying to stone you, and are you going there again?" [9] Jesus answered, "Are there not twelve hours of daylight? Those who walk during the day do not stumble, because they see the light of this world. [10] But those who walk at night stumble, because the light is not in them." [11] After saying this, he told them, "Our friend Lazarus has fallen asleep, but I am going there to awaken him." [12] The disciples said to him, "Lord, if he has fallen asleep, he will be all right." [13] Jesus, however, had been speaking about his death, but they thought that he was referring merely to sleep. [14] Then Jesus told them plainly, "Lazarus is dead. [15] For your sake I am glad I was not there, so that you may believe. But let us go to him." [16] Thomas, who was called the Twin,[b] said to his fellow disciples, "Let us also go, that we may die with him."

[17] When Jesus arrived, he found that Lazarus[a] had already been in the tomb four days. [18] Now Bethany was near Jerusalem, some two miles[c] away, [19] and many of the Jews had come to Martha and Mary to console them about their brother. [20] When Martha heard that Jesus was coming, she went and met him, while Mary stayed at home. [21] Martha said to Jesus, "Lord, if you had been here, my brother would not have died. [22] But even now I know that God will give you whatever you ask of him." [23] Jesus said to her, "Your brother will rise again." [24] Martha said to him, "I know that he will rise again in the resurrection on the last day." [25] Jesus said to her, "I am the resurrection and the life.[d] Those who believe in me, even though they die, will live, [26] and everyone who lives and believes in me will never die. Do you believe this?" [27] She said to him, "Yes, Lord, I believe that you are the Messiah,[e] the Son of God, the one coming into the world."

[28] When she had said this, she went back and called her sister Mary, and told her privately, "The Teacher is here and is calling for you." [29] And when she heard it, she got up quickly and went to him. [30] Now Jesus had not yet come to the village, but was still at the place where Martha had met him. [31] The Jews who were with her in the house, consoling her, saw Mary get up quickly and go out. They followed her because they thought that she was going to the tomb to weep there. [32] When Mary came where Jesus was and saw him, she knelt at his feet and said to him, "Lord, if you had been here, my brother would not have died." [33] When Jesus saw her weeping, and the Jews who came with her also weeping, he was greatly disturbed in spirit and deeply moved. [34] He said, "Where have you laid him?" They said to him, "Lord, come and see." [35] Jesus began to weep. [36] So the Jews said, "See how he loved him!" [37] But some of them said, "Could not he who opened the eyes of the blind man have kept this man from dying?"

[38] Then Jesus, again greatly disturbed, came to the tomb. It was a cave, and a stone

a   Gk *he*
b   Gk *Didymus*
c   Gk *fifteen stadia*
d   Other ancient authorities lack *and the life*
e   Or *the Christ*

the severity of the illness to increase. **7–8:** Love characterizes Bethany, hate characterizes Judea. Ironically, raising Lazarus will cause Jesus' death (vv. 45–52). **9–10:** Cf. 9.4–5. **11–15:** Lazarus's sleep is misunderstood as restorative sleep, but Jesus means that he is dead. Sleep is a frequent euphemism for death; see Ps 13.3; Acts 7.60, textual note *a*; 1 Cor 15.6, textual note *b*; 1 Thess 4.13, textual note *b*. **15:** The severity of the disease enhances honor of the healer: cf. 5.5; 9.1.

11.17–37: The lament of the sisters. 17–19: Jerusalemites console the sisters and criticize Jesus. **20–23:** Reproach and implicit petition are followed by the statement that "*Your brother will rise,*" which Martha misunderstands. **24–26:** Misunderstanding is clarified. **27:** Martha still misunderstands: her belief in Jesus as *the Messiah, the Son of God* does not include belief that he is "the resurrection and the life" (v. 25). **28–30:** Private conversations between men and women are unusual (cf. 4.6–25; 20.16–18). **33–35:** First Mary weeps, then the Jews, then Jesus.

11.38–44: Calling forth the dead. Raising Lazarus, the final, greatest sign, proves Jesus' earlier claim in 5.25–29 but is also the catalyst for his death. **38a:** *Greatly disturbed*, one of few emotions ascribed to Jesus; cf.

was lying against it. [39] Jesus said, "Take away the stone." Martha, the sister of the dead man, said to him, "Lord, already there is a stench because he has been dead four days." [40] Jesus said to her, "Did I not tell you that if you believed, you would see the glory of God?" [41] So they took away the stone. And Jesus looked upward and said, "Father, I thank you for having heard me. [42] I knew that you always hear me, but I have said this for the sake of the crowd standing here, so that they may believe that you sent me." [43] When he had said this, he cried with a loud voice, "Lazarus, come out!" [44] The dead man came out, his hands and feet bound with strips of cloth, and his face wrapped in a cloth. Jesus said to them, "Unbind him, and let him go."

[45] Many of the Jews therefore, who had come with Mary and had seen what Jesus did, believed in him. [46] But some of them went to the Pharisees and told them what he had done. [47] So the chief priests and the Pharisees called a meeting of the council, and said, "What are we to do? This man is performing many signs. [48] If we let him go on like this, everyone will believe in him, and the Romans will come and destroy both our holy place[a] and our nation." [49] But one of them, Caiaphas, who was high priest that year, said to them, "You know nothing at all! [50] You do not understand that it is better for you to have one man die for the people than to have the whole nation destroyed." [51] He did not say this on his own, but being high priest that year he prophesied that Jesus was about to die for the nation, [52] and not for the nation only, but to gather into one the dispersed children of God. [53] So from that day on they planned to put him to death.

[54] Jesus therefore no longer walked about openly among the Jews, but went from there to a town called Ephraim in the region near the wilderness; and he remained there with the disciples.

[55] Now the Passover of the Jews was near, and many went up from the country to Jerusalem before the Passover to purify themselves. [56] They were looking for Jesus and were asking one another as they stood in the temple, "What do you think? Surely he will not come to the festival, will he?" [57] Now the chief priests and the Pharisees had given orders that anyone who knew where Jesus[b] was should let them know, so that they might arrest him.

12 Six days before the Passover Jesus came to Bethany, the home of Lazarus, whom he had raised from the dead. [2] There they gave a dinner for him. Martha served, and Lazarus was one of those at the table with him. [3] Mary took a pound of costly perfume made of pure nard, anointed Jesus' feet, and wiped them[c] with her hair. The house was filled with the fragrance of the perfume. [4] But Judas Iscariot, one of his disciples (the one who was about to betray him), said, [5] "Why was this perfume not sold for three hundred denarii[d] and the money given to the poor?" [6] (He said this not because he cared about the poor, but because he was a thief; he kept the common purse and used to steal what was put into it.) [7] Jesus said, "Leave her alone. She bought it[e] so that she might keep it for the day of my burial. [8] You always have the

---

a   Or *our temple*; Greek *our place*

b   Gk *he*

c   Gk *his feet*

d   Three hundred denarii would be nearly a year's wages for a laborer

e   Gk lacks *She bought it*

"weary" (4.6), "troubled" about his own death (12.27; 13.21). **38b–39:** The cave tomb was closed by a round stone rolled in front (Lk 24.2).

11.45–57: The plot to kill Jesus intensifies. 47–48: John did not envy Jesus' success (3.25–30), but this court, threatened by his success, envies him: his honor and fame mean their disgrace. **49–52:** Ironically Caiaphas (who was high priest 18–36 CE) repeats the virtue of the "noble shepherd" (see 10.11n.): one who dies for others. While Caiaphas was promoting Jesus' destruction, he states that Jesus' death will benefit the people. The audience knows the secret: Jesus' enemy, this unwitting prophet; death sentence, death to benefit the people; saving the nation by killing Jesus, Jesus saves it by voluntary death. **53:** Another trial in absentia (7.50–52). **54:** *Ephraim*, also Aphairema, ca. 12 mi (20 km) north of Jerusalem. **55–57:** Another division among the people: folk from the country look for Jesus, while Pharisees' spies are seeking to arrest Jesus.

12.1–11: Jesus returns to Bethany, the home of beloved disciples. 5: Costly perfume: *three hundred denarii*

poor with you, but you do not always have me."

⁹ When the great crowd of the Jews learned that he was there, they came not only because of Jesus but also to see Lazarus, whom he had raised from the dead. ¹⁰ So the chief priests planned to put Lazarus to death as well, ¹¹ since it was on account of him that many of the Jews were deserting and were believing in Jesus.

¹² The next day the great crowd that had come to the festival heard that Jesus was coming to Jerusalem. ¹³ So they took branches of palm trees and went out to meet him, shouting,

"Hosanna!
Blessed is the one who comes in the name
      of the Lord—
   the King of Israel!"

¹⁴ Jesus found a young donkey and sat on it; as it is written:

¹⁵ "Do not be afraid, daughter of Zion.
Look, your king is coming,
   sitting on a donkey's colt!"

¹⁶ His disciples did not understand these things at first; but when Jesus was glorified, then they remembered that these things had been written of him and had been done to him. ¹⁷ So the crowd that had been with him when he called Lazarus out of the tomb and raised him from the dead continued to testify.ᵃ ¹⁸ It was also because they heard that he had performed this sign that the crowd went to meet him. ¹⁹ The Pharisees then said to one another, "You see, you can do nothing. Look, the world has gone after him!"

²⁰ Now among those who went up to worship at the festival were some Greeks. ²¹ They came to Philip, who was from Bethsaida in Galilee, and said to him, "Sir, we wish to see Jesus." ²² Philip went and told Andrew; then Andrew and Philip went and told Jesus. ²³ Jesus answered them, "The hour has come for the Son of Man to be glorified. ²⁴ Very truly, I tell you, unless a grain of wheat falls into the earth and dies, it remains just a single grain; but if it dies, it bears much fruit. ²⁵ Those who love their life lose it, and those who hate their life in this world will keep it for eternal life. ²⁶ Whoever serves me must follow me, and where I am, there will my servant be also. Whoever serves me, the Father will honor.

²⁷ "Now my soul is troubled. And what should I say—'Father, save me from this hour'? No, it is for this reason that I have come to this hour. ²⁸ Father, glorify your name." Then a voice came from heaven, "I have glorified it, and I will glorify it again." ²⁹ The crowd standing there heard it and said that it was thunder. Others said, "An angel has spoken to him." ³⁰ Jesus answered, "This voice has come for your sake, not for mine. ³¹ Now is the judgment of this world; now the ruler of this world will be driven out. ³² And I, when I am lifted up from the earth, will draw all peopleᵇ to myself." ³³ He said this to indicate the kind of death he was to die. ³⁴ The crowd answered him, "We have heard from the law that the Messiahᶜ remains forever. How can you say that the Son of Man must be lifted up? Who is this Son of Man?" ³⁵ Jesus

ᵃ Other ancient authorities read *with him began to testify that he had called . . . from the dead*
ᵇ Other ancient authorities read *all things*
ᶜ Or *the Christ*

was the equivalent of a year's wages. **7:** The anointing, a gesture of hospitality, also anticipates Jesus' burial. **9:** As in 6.26–29, people fixate on Jesus' signs rather than on him. **10–11:** Lazarus also threatened with death, but this time for Jesus' sake.

12.12–36: Confusion in Jerusalem. 12–15: Cf. Mt 21.1–9; Mk 11.1–10; Lk 19.28–38. The people quote Ps 118.26; Jesus' entry is interpreted as a fulfillment of Zeph 3.16; Zech 9.9. **16:** These events, typically, are opaque until Jesus is glorified. **17–19:** Again Lazarus draws crowds, provoking hostile reactions from the religious authorities (11.47–52; 12.9–11). **20:** *Some Greeks*, visitors for Passover, most likely Greek-speaking Jews. **21–22:** Compare 1.43–44. **23:** *Hour. . . to be glorified*, Jesus' death; cf. 2.4, challenging these volunteers with difficult discipleship. **24:** *Unless*, an uncompromising demand for disciples (3.3; 8.24; 13.8). The metaphor of seeds dying in order to grow and live explains Jesus' death and return to God. **25:** For this paradoxical saying, cf. Mt 10.39; Mk 8.3; Lk 9.24; 14.26. **26:** True *followers* serve Jesus and share his relationship with God, who honors them. **27–28:** This resembles Jesus' prayers in Mk 14.34–36. Here, however, the prayer is answered. **29:** Again the crowd is divided. **31:** *Ruler of this world*, Satan; see also 14.30n.; 16.11. **32:** *Lifted up*, referring both to the shame of death by crucifixion

said to them, "The light is with you for a little longer. Walk while you have the light, so that the darkness may not overtake you. If you walk in the darkness, you do not know where you are going. 36 While you have the light, believe in the light, so that you may become children of light."

After Jesus had said this, he departed and hid from them. 37 Although he had performed so many signs in their presence, they did not believe in him. 38 This was to fulfill the word spoken by the prophet Isaiah:

"Lord, who has believed our message,
    and to whom has the arm of the Lord
        been revealed?"

39 And so they could not believe, because Isaiah also said,

40 "He has blinded their eyes
    and hardened their heart,
so that they might not look with their eyes,
    and understand with their heart and
        turn—
    and I would heal them."

41 Isaiah said this because[a] he saw his glory and spoke about him. 42 Nevertheless many, even of the authorities, believed in him. But because of the Pharisees they did not confess it, for fear that they would be put out of the synagogue; 43 for they loved human glory more than the glory that comes from God.

44 Then Jesus cried aloud: "Whoever believes in me believes not in me but in him who sent me. 45 And whoever sees me sees him who sent me. 46 I have come as light into the world, so that everyone who believes in me should not remain in the darkness. 47 I do not judge anyone who hears my words and does not keep them, for I came not to judge the world, but to save the world. 48 The one who rejects me and does not receive my word has a judge;

on the last day the word that I have spoken will serve as judge, 49 for I have not spoken on my own, but the Father who sent me has himself given me a commandment about what to say and what to speak. 50 And I know that his commandment is eternal life. What I speak, therefore, I speak just as the Father has told me."

13 Now before the festival of the Passover, Jesus knew that his hour had come to depart from this world and go to the Father. Having loved his own who were in the world, he loved them to the end. 2 The devil had already put it into the heart of Judas son of Simon Iscariot to betray him. And during supper 3 Jesus, knowing that the Father had given all things into his hands, and that he had come from God and was going to God, 4 got up from the table,[b] took off his outer robe, and tied a towel around himself. 5 Then he poured water into a basin and began to wash the disciples' feet and to wipe them with the towel that was tied around him. 6 He came to Simon Peter, who said to him, "Lord, are you going to wash my feet?" 7 Jesus answered, "You do not know now what I am doing, but later you will understand." 8 Peter said to him, "You will never wash my feet." Jesus answered, "Unless I wash you, you have no share with me." 9 Simon Peter said to him, "Lord, not my feet only but also my hands and my head!" 10 Jesus said to him, "One who has bathed does not need to wash, except for the feet,[c] but is entirely clean. And you[d] are clean, though not all of you." 11 For he knew

a Other ancient witnesses read when
b Gk from supper
c Other ancient authorities lack except for the feet
d The Greek word for you here is plural

12.37–50: Judgment time. 37: Signs fail to create acceptance of Jesus (6.26–29; 11.45–52). 38–40: Isaiah prophesied failure: a rejected message (Isa 53.1), and blind eyes (Isa 6.10). 41: Saw his glory, the eternal Jesus appeared to the prophet Isaiah, as he had to Abraham (cf. 8.56; Isa 6.1–6). 42–43: Fear of expulsion paralyzed even those who believed, like the parents of the blind man (9.22). 44–45: The only issue for judgment is whether Jesus is God's agent. 47: Repeats 3.16–17; yet Jesus indeed judges in 8.15–16,31–59.

13.1–20: Foot washing. 1–3: Whereas 1.1–18 stressed Jesus' coming into the world, 13.1–3 focuses on his departure from this world. 1: In John the Passover begins on Friday (see 19.14); contrast Mk.14.12–16; Lk 22.15. 4–5: Dressed as a servant, Jesus washes their feet, a reversal of roles. 6–11: Simon Peter challenges Jesus, who demands compliance: Unless, the familiar demand (3.3; 6.53; 12.24). By requesting a total bath, Simon misunderstands Jesus, who states that only this washing is necessary. 11: All disciples are clean except the traitor,

who was to betray him; for this reason he said, "Not all of you are clean."

¹² After he had washed their feet, had put on his robe, and had returned to the table, he said to them, "Do you know what I have done to you? ¹³ You call me Teacher and Lord—and you are right, for that is what I am. ¹⁴ So if I, your Lord and Teacher, have washed your feet, you also ought to wash one another's feet. ¹⁵ For I have set you an example, that you also should do as I have done to you. ¹⁶ Very truly, I tell you, servants[a] are not greater than their master, nor are messengers greater than the one who sent them. ¹⁷ If you know these things, you are blessed if you do them. ¹⁸ I am not speaking of all of you; I know whom I have chosen. But it is to fulfill the scripture, 'The one who ate my bread[b] has lifted his heel against me.' ¹⁹ I tell you this now, before it occurs, so that when it does occur, you may believe that I am he.[c] ²⁰ Very truly, I tell you, whoever receives one whom I send receives me; and whoever receives me receives him who sent me."

²¹ After saying this Jesus was troubled in spirit, and declared, "Very truly, I tell you, one of you will betray me." ²² The disciples looked at one another, uncertain of whom he was speaking. ²³ One of his disciples—the one whom Jesus loved—was reclining next to him; ²⁴ Simon Peter therefore motioned to him to ask Jesus of whom he was speaking. ²⁵ So while reclining next to Jesus, he asked him, "Lord, who is it?" ²⁶ Jesus answered, "It is the one to whom I give this piece of bread when I have dipped it in the dish."[d] So when he had dipped the piece of bread, he gave it to Judas

son of Simon Iscariot.[e] ²⁷ After he received the piece of bread,[f] Satan entered into him. Jesus said to him, "Do quickly what you are going to do." ²⁸ Now no one at the table knew why he said this to him. ²⁹ Some thought that, because Judas had the common purse, Jesus was telling him, "Buy what we need for the festival"; or, that he should give something to the poor. ³⁰ So, after receiving the piece of bread, he immediately went out. And it was night.

³¹ When he had gone out, Jesus said, "Now the Son of Man has been glorified, and God has been glorified in him. ³² If God has been glorified in him,[g] God will also glorify him in himself and will glorify him at once. ³³ Little children, I am with you only a little longer. You will look for me; and as I said to the Jews so now I say to you, 'Where I am going, you cannot come.' ³⁴ I give you a new commandment, that you love one another. Just as I have loved you, you also should love one another. ³⁵ By this everyone will know that you are my disciples, if you have love for one another."

³⁶ Simon Peter said to him, "Lord, where are you going?" Jesus answered, "Where I am

a Gk *slaves*
b Other ancient authorities read *ate bread with me*
c Gk *I am*
d Gk *dipped it*
e Other ancient authorities read *Judas Iscariot son of Simon*; others, *Judas son of Simon from Karyot* (Kerioth)
f Gk *After the piece of bread*
g Other ancient authorities lack *If God has been glorified in him*

already possessed by the devil (v. 2). **12–14:** Dressed again as *Teacher* and *Lord,* Jesus explains the foot washing as example of a master serving his servants (cf. Mt 10.24; Lk 6.40). **15–16:** Foot washing in 13.4–11 is a one-time status transformation of the disciples, but in 13.12–16, a ceremony exemplifying and confirming that the greater serves the lesser. The master serves, so too the disciples. **17:** First beatitude: acting upon wisdom (cf. 20.29n.).

13.18–19: Judas exposed. The traitor identified in 13.11 is now exposed. **18:** Ps 41.9; see v. 26. **19:** *I am he,* see 8.28,58. **20:** Receiving the agent means acknowledging the sender. **23:** *The one whom Jesus loved,* see 19.26; 20.2; 21.7; 21.20; he is the apparent narrator (21.24). **26–27:** An unusual gesture, because individuals dipped in a common bowl. **29:** Cf. 12.6. **30:** *Night,* a terrible time: when Nicodemus comes (3.2), when no one can work (9.4), what people love (3.19), hence the time for evil.

13.31–38: Tender words. 31–32: To outsiders his death is shame; to insiders, the occasion when God honors the one who honors him. Death is not Jesus' punishment but his voluntary obedience to God. **33:** Restatement of 7.33–34, to be explained in 14.1–3. *Little children,* cf. 1 Jn 2.1,12,28; etc. **34–35:** First statement of the love commandment (15.12–17). *Love,* faithfulness and loyalty, not material support (1 Jn 3.17). **36–38:** Despite Jesus' remark in 13.33, Simon challenges Jesus with a question and a claim: *"I will lay down my life for you"* (cf. 10.11,15,17). But shame, not honor awaits Simon in his triple denial of Jesus (18.15–27).

going, you cannot follow me now; but you will follow afterward." [37] Peter said to him, "Lord, why can I not follow you now? I will lay down my life for you." [38] Jesus answered, "Will you lay down your life for me? Very truly, I tell you, before the cock crows, you will have denied me three times.

14 "Do not let your hearts be troubled. Believe[a] in God, believe also in me. [2] In my Father's house there are many dwelling places. If it were not so, would I have told you that I go to prepare a place for you?[b] [3] And if I go and prepare a place for you, I will come again and will take you to myself, so that where I am, there you may be also. [4] And you know the way to the place where I am going."[c] [5] Thomas said to him, "Lord, we do not know where you are going. How can we know the way?" [6] Jesus said to him, "I am the way, and the truth, and the life. No one comes to the Father except through me. [7] If you know me, you will know[d] my Father also. From now on you do know him and have seen him."

[8] Philip said to him, "Lord, show us the Father, and we will be satisfied." [9] Jesus said to him, "Have I been with you all this time, Philip, and you still do not know me? Whoever has seen me has seen the Father. How can you say, 'Show us the Father'? [10] Do you not believe that I am in the Father and the Father is in me? The words that I say to you I do not speak on my own; but the Father who dwells in me does his works. [11] Believe me that I am in the Father and the Father is in me; but if you

do not, then believe me because of the works themselves. [12] Very truly, I tell you, the one who believes in me will also do the works that I do and, in fact, will do greater works than these, because I am going to the Father. [13] I will do whatever you ask in my name, so that the Father may be glorified in the Son. [14] If in my name you ask me[e] for anything, I will do it.

[15] "If you love me, you will keep[f] my commandments. [16] And I will ask the Father, and he will give you another Advocate,[g] to be with you forever. [17] This is the Spirit of truth, whom the world cannot receive, because it neither sees him nor knows him. You know him, because he abides with you, and he will be in[h] you.

[18] "I will not leave you orphaned; I am coming to you. [19] In a little while the world will no longer see me, but you will see me; because I live, you also will live. [20] On that day you will know that I am in my Father, and you in me, and I in you. [21] They who have my command-

a Or *You believe*
b Or *If it were not so, I would have told you; for I go to prepare a place for you*
c Other ancient authorities read *Where I am going you know, and the way you know*
d Other ancient authorities read *If you had known me, you would have known*
e Other ancient authorities lack *me*
f Other ancient authorities read *me, keep*
g Or *Helper*
h Or *among*

14.1–14: The household of God. 1: Predictions of future crises should evoke loyalty in the disciples (14.27; 16.1–4,33). **2:** *House*, not a building but household relationships; *preparing a place* means mediating a relationship between God and disciples. **3:** Jesus never brings them to a *place* (17.15); *"Where I am,"* not a location, but relationship of mutual loyalty. **4–6:** *You know the way* is misunderstood by Thomas who claims that they do not know either *place* or *way*. Jesus clarifies: *"I am the way, and the truth and the life"*; he is God's unique, authentic broker (cf. 5.21,26; 6.44). **7:** If they *know* Jesus, they *know* the Father, which illustrates relationships. **8–9:** Knowing includes seeing, but not face to face (1.18). To see Jesus is to see God; to be in relationship with Jesus is to be such with God. **10–11:** Like "house" (v. 2n.) *in* is not spatial but relational. To the two parts of the relationship (the Father and Jesus; Jesus and the disciples) a third is added: the Father and disciple, because Jesus is broker, related to God and representing God's interests, just as he is related to the disciples and loyal to their interests. Thus the Father and the disciples are in relationship because Jesus is broker to both. **12:** Relationship with Jesus gives access to God's power to match and surpass Jesus' works. **13–14:** Petitionary prayer (*ask*) grounded in relationship (*in my name*); cf. Mt 21.22.

14.15–24: Knowing, loving, abiding. 15–17: Loving Jesus brings an *Advocate* (or "Paraclete") who *abides* in those who *know him*. This Advocate brokers the relationship of Jesus and disciples. **18:** *Orphans*, those lacking home and household relationships, are in crisis. **19:** Confirmation of relationship with Jesus: he will return when raised and they will see and live. **20:** Again, relationships are expressed by *in*, with Jesus as perfect mediator:

ments and keep them are those who love me; and those who love me will be loved by my Father, and I will love them and reveal myself to them." [22] Judas (not Iscariot) said to him, "Lord, how is it that you will reveal yourself to us, and not to the world?" [23] Jesus answered him, "Those who love me will keep my word, and my Father will love them, and we will come to them and make our home with them. [24] Whoever does not love me does not keep my words; and the word that you hear is not mine, but is from the Father who sent me.

[25] "I have said these things to you while I am still with you. [26] But the Advocate,[a] the Holy Spirit, whom the Father will send in my name, will teach you everything, and remind you of all that I have said to you. [27] Peace I leave with you; my peace I give to you. I do not give to you as the world gives. Do not let your hearts be troubled, and do not let them be afraid. [28] You heard me say to you, 'I am going away, and I am coming to you.' If you loved me, you would rejoice that I am going to the Father, because the Father is greater than I. [29] And now I have told you this before it occurs, so that when it does occur, you may believe. [30] I will no longer talk much with you, for the ruler of this world is coming. He has no power over me; [31] but I do as the Father has commanded me, so that the world may know that I love the Father. Rise, let us be on our way.

15 "I am the true vine, and my Father is the vinegrower. [2] He removes every branch in me that bears no fruit. Every branch that bears fruit he prunes[b] to make it bear more fruit. [3] You have already been cleansed[b] by the word that I have spoken to you. [4] Abide in me as I abide in you. Just as the branch cannot bear fruit by itself unless it abides in the vine, neither can you unless you abide in me. [5] I am the vine, you are the branches. Those who abide in me and I in them bear much fruit, because apart from me you can do nothing. [6] Whoever does not abide in me is thrown away like a branch and withers; such branches are gathered, thrown into the fire, and burned. [7] If you abide in me, and my words abide in you, ask for whatever you wish, and it will be done for you. [8] My Father is glorified by this, that you bear much fruit and become[c] my disciples. [9] As the Father has loved me, so I have loved you; abide in my love. [10] If you keep my commandments, you will abide in my love, just as I have kept my Father's commandments and abide in his love. [11] I have said these things to you so that my joy may be in you, and that your joy may be complete.

[12] "This is my commandment, that you love one another as I have loved you. [13] No one has greater love than this, to lay down one's life for one's friends. [14] You are my friends if you do what I command you. [15] I do not call you servants[d] any longer, because the servant[e]

[a] Or *Helper*
[b] The same Greek root refers to pruning and cleansing
[c] Or *be*
[d] Gk *slaves*
[e] Gk *slave*

Jesus is *in* the Father and *in* them, and they are *in* him. **21**: The same relationships are expressed through *love*. **22**: *Judas* (see Lk 6.16; Acts 1.13) asks: is revelation only for insiders? **23–24**: Jesus replies indirectly: Only insiders *love* him and *keep* his *word*. Only to insiders will Jesus and his Father come and make a *home*, which again is not a place but a relationship. Outsiders do *not love* Jesus or *keep* his *words*.

14.25–31: Comings and goings. 25–26: Now Jesus speaks, but the Advocate/Holy Spirit will speak later. The Advocate functions to link past and future, *remind*ing them of Jesus' words and *teach*ing all things. The Spirit, then, is Jesus' broker. **28**: *Going away*, both Jesus' death and return to God. **29**: Forewarned about the crisis to come means forearmed. **30**: *Ruler of this world*, either the father of lies and murder (8.44; 12.31), or the Roman emperor and his legions in Palestine; see also 16.11.

15.1–25: Exhortations: abide and love. 1–11: The first exhortation. *Abide* occurs nine times and is the focus of the exhortation. As in 14.1–3, it is not spatial but relational, referring to loyalty and faithfulness. On the image of the vine and God as the vinegrower, cf. Isa 5.1–7; Jer 2.21; Ezek 19.10–14; Mk 12.1–12 par. **3**: The disciples are already *cleansed* (13.10); see also textual note *b*. **5–9**: Argument from advantage: those abiding profit, those not abiding perish. **6**: Cf. Mt 3.10; 7.19. **10**: Keeping produces a durable relationship of loving: the disciples *abide* in Jesus' love who *abides in* God's love. **12–17**: The second exhortation: *Love*. **14**: *Friends* expresses the polite relationship of clients and patron. Pilate is a "friend" of Caesar, his patron, not an intimate (19.12). **15**: Not *ser-*

does not know what the master is doing; but I have called you friends, because I have made known to you everything that I have heard from my Father. [16] You did not choose me but I chose you. And I appointed you to go and bear fruit, fruit that will last, so that the Father will give you whatever you ask him in my name. [17] I am giving you these commands so that you may love one another.

[18] "If the world hates you, be aware that it hated me before it hated you. [19] If you belonged to the world,[a] the world would love you as its own. Because you do not belong to the world, but I have chosen you out of the world—therefore the world hates you. [20] Remember the word that I said to you, 'Servants[b] are not greater than their master.' If they persecuted me, they will persecute you; if they kept my word, they will keep yours also. [21] But they will do all these things to you on account of my name, because they do not know him who sent me. [22] If I had not come and spoken to them, they would not have sin; but now they have no excuse for their sin. [23] Whoever hates me hates my Father also. [24] If I had not done among them the works that no one else did, they would not have sin. But now they have seen and hated both me and my Father. [25] It was to fulfill the word that is written in their law, 'They hated me without a cause.'

[26] "When the Advocate[c] comes, whom I will send to you from the Father, the Spirit of truth who comes from the Father, he will testify on my behalf. [27] You also are to testify because you have been with me from the beginning.

16

"I have said these things to you to keep you from stumbling. [2] They will put you out of the synagogues. Indeed, an hour is coming when those who kill you will think that by doing so they are offering worship to God. [3] And they will do this because they have not known the Father or me. [4] But I have said these things to you so that when their hour comes you may remember that I told you about them.

"I did not say these things to you from the beginning, because I was with you. [5] But now I am going to him who sent me; yet none of you asks me, 'Where are you going?' [6] But because I have said these things to you, sorrow has filled your hearts. [7] Nevertheless I tell you the truth: it is to your advantage that I go away, for if I do not go away, the Advocate[c] will not come to you; but if I go, I will send him to you. [8] And when he comes, he will prove the world wrong about[d] sin and righteousness and judgment: [9] about sin, because they do not believe in me; [10] about righteousness, because I am going to the Father and you will see me no longer; [11] about judgment, because the ruler of this world has been condemned.

[12] "I still have many things to say to you, but you cannot bear them now. [13] When the Spirit of truth comes, he will guide you into all the truth; for he will not speak on his own, but will speak whatever he hears, and he will declare to you the things that are to come.

---

[a] Gk *were of the world*
[b] Gk *Slaves*
[c] Or *Helper*
[d] Or *convict the world of*

---

vants, but not peers: see 13.13. **16:** A return to the vine imagery of the first exhortation. **17:** *Love one another,* the second exhortation ends as it began (15.12). **18–25:** Exhortation on hatred, balancing the preceding exhortation on love. Hatred is proof that disciples belong to Jesus and not the world. **20:** See 13.16. The disciples are both "friends" because Jesus brokers wisdom (see v. 14n.), and also *servants* because they are followers of the master (see 13.13). **22–24:** When Jesus is *hated,* God who sent him is also *hated.* **25:** Pss 35.19; 69.4.

15.26–27: Testifying. 26: The role of the *Advocate* (see 14.16n.) is not just forensic but also that of a mediator or broker. *I will send,* cf. "The Father will send" (14.26). **26:** As in 8.13–14, there are two witnesses: here the Spirit and the disciples, both confirming Jesus' role as unique broker.

16.1–15: What Jesus now has to say. 1–4a: Predictions defuse crises to come. **4b–7:** Announcement of departure, which causes consternation. Yet his departure is an advantage, because he will send the *Advocate* (see 14.16n.), partly replacement and partly broker. **8:** Like Jesus, the Advocate plays many roles, especially that of forensic witness. **11:** *Ruler of this world,* see 12.31n. **12–15:** The Advocate will clarify to the disciples both things said and not said. As Jesus' agent and broker, he looks back to Jesus' past remarks and looks to what is forthcoming.

¹⁴ He will glorify me, because he will take what is mine and declare it to you. ¹⁵ All that the Father has is mine. For this reason I said that he will take what is mine and declare it to you.

¹⁶ "A little while, and you will no longer see me, and again a little while, and you will see me." ¹⁷ Then some of his disciples said to one another, "What does he mean by saying to us, 'A little while, and you will no longer see me, and again a little while, and you will see me'; and 'Because I am going to the Father'?" ¹⁸ They said, "What does he mean by this 'a little while'? We do not know what he is talking about." ¹⁹ Jesus knew that they wanted to ask him, so he said to them, "Are you discussing among yourselves what I meant when I said, 'A little while, and you will no longer see me, and again a little while, and you will see me'? ²⁰ Very truly, I tell you, you will weep and mourn, but the world will rejoice; you will have pain, but your pain will turn into joy. ²¹ When a woman is in labor, she has pain, because her hour has come. But when her child is born, she no longer remembers the anguish because of the joy of having brought a human being into the world. ²² So you have pain now; but I will see you again, and your hearts will rejoice, and no one will take your joy from you. ²³ On that day you will ask nothing of me.ᵃ Very truly, I tell you, if you ask anything of the Father in my name, he will give it to you.ᵇ ²⁴ Until now you have not asked for anything in my name. Ask and you will receive, so that your joy may be complete.

²⁵ "I have said these things to you in figures of speech. The hour is coming when I will no longer speak to you in figures, but will tell you plainly of the Father. ²⁶ On that day you will ask in my name. I do not say to you that I will ask the Father on your behalf; ²⁷ for the Father himself loves you, because you have loved me and have believed that I came from God.ᶜ ²⁸ I came from the Father and have come into the world; again, I am leaving the world and am going to the Father."

²⁹ His disciples said, "Yes, now you are speaking plainly, not in any figure of speech! ³⁰ Now we know that you know all things, and do not need to have anyone question you; by this we believe that you came from God." ³¹ Jesus answered them, "Do you now believe? ³² The hour is coming, indeed it has come, when you will be scattered, each one to his home, and you will leave me alone. Yet I am not alone because the Father is with me. ³³ I have said this to you, so that in me you may have peace. In the world you face persecution. But take courage; I have conquered the world!"

17 After Jesus had spoken these words, he looked up to heaven and said, "Father, the hour has come; glorify your Son so that the Son may glorify you, ² since you have given him authority over all people,ᵈ to give eternal life to all whom you have given him. ³ And this is eternal life, that they may know you, the only true God, and Jesus Christ whom you have sent. ⁴ I glorified you on earth by finishing the work that you gave me to do. ⁵ So now, Father, glorify me in your own presence with the glory that I had in your presence before the world existed.

ᵃ Or *will ask me no question*
ᵇ Other ancient authorities read *Father, he will give it to you in my name*
ᶜ Other ancient authorities read *the Father*
ᵈ Gk *flesh*

16.16–24: "A little while." 20: Jesus does not yet explain what he meant but focuses attention on the disciples and their distress. 21–22: The labor pains of childbirth and the joy of a birth parallel the disciples' experience. 23–24: Instruction for petitionary prayer, as in 14.13–14; cf. Mt 21.22. 25–33: Full explanation. 26: Petitionary prayer with direct access to God, not through broker. 27: Secure relationships: the Father *loves you* because you love and believe me. 28: As ideal broker, Jesus belongs both to God's world and the disciples'. He came from the Father into the world and now returns to the Father (1.1–18; 3.13; 13.1–3). 32: Like sheep *scattered* they will leave Jesus *alone*, yet he is not truly *alone* because of his relationship with God. 33: A crisis foretold to strengthen them.

17.1–26: Jesus praying. For previous prayers of Jesus, see 11.41–42; 12.27–28. 1: Mutual glorifying indicates ideal relationship; cf. 8.50,54; 16.14. 3: *Eternal life*, a two-part confession: to *know you, the only true God* (monotheism) and to acknowledge Jesus Christ as agent (broker). 5: The relationship demands that God in turn glorify

6 "I have made your name known to those whom you gave me from the world. They were yours, and you gave them to me, and they have kept your word. 7 Now they know that everything you have given me is from you; 8 for the words that you gave to me I have given to them, and they have received them and know in truth that I came from you; and they have believed that you sent me. 9 I am asking on their behalf; I am not asking on behalf of the world, but on behalf of those whom you gave me, because they are yours. 10 All mine are yours, and yours are mine; and I have been glorified in them. 11 And now I am no longer in the world, but they are in the world, and I am coming to you. Holy Father, protect them in your name that you have given me, so that they may be one, as we are one. 12 While I was with them, I protected them in your name that[a] you have given me. I guarded them, and not one of them was lost except the one destined to be lost,[b] so that the scripture might be fulfilled. 13 But now I am coming to you, and I speak these things in the world so that they may have my joy made complete in themselves.[c] 14 I have given them your word, and the world has hated them because they do not belong to the world, just as I do not belong to the world. 15 I am not asking you to take them out of the world, but I ask you to protect them from the evil one.[d] 16 They do not belong to the world, just as I do not belong to the world. 17 Sanctify them in the truth; your word is truth. 18 As you have sent me into the world, so I have sent them into the world. 19 And for their sakes I sanctify myself, so that they also may be sanctified in truth.

20 "I ask not only on behalf of these, but also on behalf of those who will believe in me through their word, 21 that they may all be one. As you, Father, are in me and I am in you, may they also be in us,[e] so that the world may believe that you have sent me. 22 The glory that you have given me I have given them, so that they may be one, as we are one, 23 I in them and you in me, that they may become completely one, so that the world may know that you have sent me and have loved them even as you have loved me. 24 Father, I desire that those also, whom you have given me, may be with me where I am, to see my glory, which you have given me because you loved me before the foundation of the world.

25 "Righteous Father, the world does not know you, but I know you; and these know that you have sent me. 26 I made your name known to them, and I will make it known, so that the love with which you have loved me may be in them, and I in them."

18 After Jesus had spoken these words, he went out with his disciples across the Kidron valley to a place where there was a garden, which he and his disciples en-

a Other ancient authorities read *protected in your name those whom*
b Gk *except the son of destruction*
c Or *among themselves*
d Or *from evil*
e Other ancient authorities read *be one in us*

Jesus in heaven, not with earned honor but restoration of Jesus' eternal glory (1.1–2). **6:** Besides petition and praise, Jesus prays a self-focused prayer: Jesus tells God of his honorable behavior, the accomplishment of what he was sent to do. *Name,* not God or "Lord," but "I AM," the name revealed to Moses (Ex 3.14); see 8.28,58. **7–8:** Words given by God to Jesus are given to them, acknowledging him as broker. **9:** Jesus brokers only the needs of insiders. **10:** Sender and agent equally share *all,* establishing Jesus as the ideal broker. **11:** Reason for petition: your broker is in transit to you; petition: You protect them, i.e., keep them loyal. **12:** Again (see. v. 6) a self-focused prayer. **13:** An implied petition: the broker, who is in transit, desires them to have *my joy* in abundance (16.20–22). **14:** As in Jesus' case, the world hates them, for, like him, they do not belong below (7.7; 8.23). **15–17:** Further petitions. **18:** Cf. 20.21. **19:** *Sanctify* means total dedication to God; Jesus *sanctifies* himself so that the disciples might be totally loyal. **20–21:** Petition: Jesus intercedes for them and those recruited by them (v. 18). *One,* unified, in the same proper relationship as Jesus and the Father. *In me . . . in you . . . in us, . . .* recalling the household language of 14.2. **24:** Petition: not contradicting v. 15, but suggesting a relationship with the heavenly Jesus. *See my glory* explains the promise in 1.51. **25–26:** *Know* means "acknowledge"; the world *does not know* God because it rejects God's broker; Jesus knows God as his agent; disciples *know* God because they acknowledge Jesus as agent. That knowledge cements perfect relationships in *love.*

tered. [2] Now Judas, who betrayed him, also knew the place, because Jesus often met there with his disciples. [3] So Judas brought a detachment of soldiers together with police from the chief priests and the Pharisees, and they came there with lanterns and torches and weapons. [4] Then Jesus, knowing all that was to happen to him, came forward and asked them, "Whom are you looking for?" [5] They answered, "Jesus of Nazareth."[a] Jesus replied, "I am he."[b] Judas, who betrayed him, was standing with them. [6] When Jesus[c] said to them, "I am he,"[b] they stepped back and fell to the ground. [7] Again he asked them, "Whom are you looking for?" And they said, "Jesus of Nazareth."[a] [8] Jesus answered, "I told you that I am he.[b] So if you are looking for me, let these men go." [9] This was to fulfill the word that he had spoken, "I did not lose a single one of those whom you gave me." [10] Then Simon Peter, who had a sword, drew it, struck the high priest's slave, and cut off his right ear. The slave's name was Malchus. [11] Jesus said to Peter, "Put your sword back into its sheath. Am I not to drink the cup that the Father has given me?"

[12] So the soldiers, their officer, and the Jewish police arrested Jesus and bound him. [13] First they took him to Annas, who was the father-in-law of Caiaphas, the high priest that year. [14] Caiaphas was the one who had advised the Jews that it was better to have one person die for the people.

[15] Simon Peter and another disciple followed Jesus. Since that disciple was known to the high priest, he went with Jesus into the courtyard of the high priest, [16] but Peter was standing outside at the gate. So the other disciple, who was known to the high priest, went out, spoke to the woman who guarded the gate, and brought Peter in. [17] The woman said to Peter, "You are not also one of this man's disciples, are you?" He said, "I am not." [18] Now the slaves and the police had made a charcoal fire because it was cold, and they were standing around it and warming themselves. Peter also was standing with them and warming himself.

[19] Then the high priest questioned Jesus about his disciples and about his teaching. [20] Jesus answered, "I have spoken openly to the world; I have always taught in synagogues and in the temple, where all the Jews come together. I have said nothing in secret. [21] Why do you ask me? Ask those who heard what I said to them; they know what I said." [22] When he had said this, one of the police standing nearby struck Jesus on the face, saying, "Is that how you answer the high priest?" [23] Jesus answered, "If I have spoken wrongly, testify to the wrong. But if I have spoken rightly, why do you strike me?" [24] Then Annas sent him bound to Caiaphas the high priest.

[25] Now Simon Peter was standing and warming himself. They asked him, "You are not also one of his disciples, are you?" He

[a] Gk *the Nazorean*
[b] Gk *I am*
[c] Gk *he*

18.1–19.42: **The arrest, trials, death, and burial of Jesus** (cf. Mt 26.30–27.61; Mk 14.26–15.47; Lk 22.39–23.56).

18.1–11: **Jesus surrenders.** 1–2: *Across the Kidron valley,* east of the city, to the Mount of Olives. *Garden,* an olive orchard frequented by Jesus, called Gethsemane in Mk 14.32; Mt 26.36; cf. Lk 21.37; 22.39. 4: Jesus controls events 6: When Jesus reveals himself as "I AM" (see 4.26n.), his questioners fall to the ground, as at a theophany. 8–9: The "noble shepherd" (see 10.11n.) rescues all his sheep, except for Judas (17.12); none are snatched (10.28; cf. 6.39). 10: Peter defends Jesus as an earthly king; cf. 18.36. *Simon Peter . . . Malchus,* both identified by name only in this Gospel. 11: *Cup,* a metaphor for what God allots; see Ps 16.5; Isa 51.17; Lam 4.21. Jesus shows his nobility by voluntarily and virtuously accepting his fate.

18.12–27: **In the high priests' palaces.** 12–14: Earlier Caiaphas ironically described Jesus' death as noble (11.50–52) because it benefits others. *Annas* was Caiphas's father-in-law and predecessor as high priest.15–16: The beloved disciple acts as a shepherd (see 10.1–3): he talks to the gatekeeper and leads Peter in. Their relationship will be reversed in 21.15–18. 17–18: Peter cancels all relationship to Jesus, not merely denying knowledge about him, but like the parents of the blind man (9.22) and certain Pharisees (12.42) by cowardly hiding allegiance to Jesus. 19–21: Public figure in public places, thus honorable (7.26; 10.22–23; Matt 26.55). 25–27: *The cock crowed,* see 13.38.

denied it and said, "I am not." ²⁶ One of the slaves of the high priest, a relative of the man whose ear Peter had cut off, asked, "Did I not see you in the garden with him?" ²⁷ Again Peter denied it, and at that moment the cock crowed.

²⁸ Then they took Jesus from Caiaphas to Pilate's headquarters.^a It was early in the morning. They themselves did not enter the headquarters,^a so as to avoid ritual defilement and to be able to eat the Passover. ²⁹ So Pilate went out to them and said, "What accusation do you bring against this man?" ³⁰ They answered, "If this man were not a criminal, we would not have handed him over to you." ³¹ Pilate said to them, "Take him yourselves and judge him according to your law." The Jews replied, "We are not permitted to put anyone to death." ³² (This was to fulfill what Jesus had said when he indicated the kind of death he was to die.)

³³ Then Pilate entered the headquarters^a again, summoned Jesus, and asked him, "Are you the King of the Jews?" ³⁴ Jesus answered, "Do you ask this on your own, or did others tell you about me?" ³⁵ Pilate replied, "I am not a Jew, am I? Your own nation and the chief priests have handed you over to me. What have you done?" ³⁶ Jesus answered, "My kingdom is not from this world. If my kingdom were from this world, my followers would be fighting to keep me from being handed over to the Jews. But as it is, my kingdom is not from here." ³⁷ Pilate asked him, "So you are a king?" Jesus answered, "You say that I am a king. For this I was born, and for this I came into the world, to testify to the truth. Everyone who belongs to the truth listens to my voice." ³⁸ Pilate asked him, "What is truth?"

After he had said this, he went out to the Jews again and told them, "I find no case against him. ³⁹ But you have a custom that I release someone for you at the Passover. Do you want me to release for you the King of the Jews?" ⁴⁰ They shouted in reply, "Not this man, but Barabbas!" Now Barabbas was a bandit.

19 Then Pilate took Jesus and had him flogged. ² And the soldiers wove a crown of thorns and put it on his head, and they dressed him in a purple robe. ³ They kept coming up to him, saying, "Hail, King of the Jews!" and striking him on the face. ⁴ Pilate went out again and said to them, "Look, I am bringing him out to you to let you know that I find no case against him." ⁵ So Jesus came out, wearing the crown of thorns and the purple robe. Pilate said to them, "Here is the man!" ⁶ When the chief priests and the police saw him, they shouted, "Crucify him! Crucify him!" Pilate said to them, "Take him yourselves and crucify him; I find no case against him." ⁷ The Jews answered him, "We have a law, and according to that law he ought to die because he has claimed to be the Son of God."

⁸ Now when Pilate heard this, he was more afraid than ever. ⁹ He entered his headquarters^a again and asked Jesus, "Where are you from?" But Jesus gave him no answer. ¹⁰ Pilate therefore said to him, "Do you refuse to speak to me? Do you not know that I have power to release you, and power to crucify you?" ¹¹ Jesus answered him, "You would have no

^a Gk *the praetorium*

18.28–40: In Roman hands. 28: *Pilate's headquarters,* the Praetorium (see textual note *a* and map on p. 1883) was located on the west side of Jerusalem. It was the official residence of Pontius Pilate, the Roman governor of Judea (ca. 26–37 CE). Ironically, killing Jesus is permitted, but ritual impunity must be avoided. 31: Moreover, the religious authorities are powerless. 36: Jesus' kingdom is otherworldly, and no threat to Rome or Judea (see 18.10–11). 37–38a: Pilate's question receives an honest response, but Jesus now challenges with a focus on *truth*. 38b: Pilate's declaration of Jesus' innocence should end the trial. 39–40: Jesus, king of the Jews, again rejected by his own in favor of a *bandit* (or revolutionary insurrectionist). The custom of a releasing a prisoner at Passover is attested only in the New Testament.

19.1–16: Jesus' second trial before Pilate. 1: *Flogging,* judicial warning (Lk 23.22); Paul often received such (2 Cor 11.23–25). 2–3: A mock coronation: crown of thorns; royal purple robe; acclamation. 4–5: Pilate again declares Jesus innocent, taunting the powerless crowd. 7: The penalty for blasphemy was death (see 10.39–32n.). 8–9: Jesus' true origin is known only by insiders (13.1–3; 16.28). *No answer,* silence generally signals defeat; here

power over me unless it had been given you from above; therefore the one who handed me over to you is guilty of a greater sin." [12] From then on Pilate tried to release him, but the Jews cried out, "If you release this man, you are no friend of the emperor. Everyone who claims to be a king sets himself against the emperor."

[13] When Pilate heard these words, he brought Jesus outside and sat[a] on the judge's bench at a place called The Stone Pavement, or in Hebrew[b] Gabbatha. [14] Now it was the day of Preparation for the Passover; and it was about noon. He said to the Jews, "Here is your King!" [15] They cried out, "Away with him! Away with him! Crucify him!" Pilate asked them, "Shall I crucify your King?" The chief priests answered, "We have no king but the emperor." [16] Then he handed him over to them to be crucified.

So they took Jesus; [17] and carrying the cross by himself, he went out to what is called The Place of the Skull, which in Hebrew[b] is called Golgotha. [18] There they crucified him, and with him two others, one on either side, with Jesus between them. [19] Pilate also had an inscription written and put on the cross. It read, "Jesus of Nazareth,[c] the King of the Jews." [20] Many of the Jews read this inscription, because the place where Jesus was crucified was near the city; and it was written in Hebrew,[b] in Latin, and in Greek. [21] Then the chief priests of the Jews said to Pilate, "Do not write, 'The King of the Jews,' but, 'This man said, I am King of the Jews.'" [22] Pilate answered, "What I have

written I have written." [23] When the soldiers had crucified Jesus, they took his clothes and divided them into four parts, one for each soldier. They also took his tunic; now the tunic was seamless, woven in one piece from the top. [24] So they said to one another, "Let us not tear it, but cast lots for it to see who will get it." This was to fulfill what the scripture says,

"They divided my clothes among
       themselves,
    and for my clothing they cast lots."

[25] And that is what the soldiers did.

Meanwhile, standing near the cross of Jesus were his mother, and his mother's sister, Mary the wife of Clopas, and Mary Magdalene. [26] When Jesus saw his mother and the disciple whom he loved standing beside her, he said to his mother, "Woman, here is your son." [27] Then he said to the disciple, "Here is your mother." And from that hour the disciple took her into his own home.

[28] After this, when Jesus knew that all was now finished, he said (in order to fulfill the scripture), "I am thirsty." [29] A jar full of sour wine was standing there. So they put a sponge full of the wine on a branch of hyssop and held it to his mouth. [30] When Jesus had received the wine, he said, "It is finished." Then he bowed his head and gave up his spirit.

[a] Or seated him

[b] That is, Aramaic

[c] Gk the Nazorean

---

it challenges Pilate. **10–11:** Pilate's power comes from God, not from Caesar. *Greater sin*, rejection by his own surpasses Pilate's injustice. **12:** Pilate cannot release Caesar's rival and be his client (friend). **13:** *Gabbatha,* occurring only here, probably means "the elevated (place)" in Aramaic (see textual note *b*); it was probably near the Praetorium (see 18.28n.) **14–15:** *Noon* on the *day of Preparation*: time when Passover lambs were slaughtered. *We have no king but the emperor,* an example of the "greater sin" (v. 11), rejection of God and of Jesus.

19.17–30: The crucifixion: killing the king. 17: *Golgotha*, in the northwest section of the city; see map on p. 1883. *Hebrew*, see textual note *b*. **18:** *Crucified*, like "flogged" (v. 1), focuses not just on pain but on shame. **19:** The sign states Jesus' "crime," but ironically it is true. **20:** Three languages suggests openness to all (cf. "savior of the world," 4.42). **23–24:** *Clothes*, spoils for executioners, whose refusal to cut the tunic necessitates casting lots, fulfilling Ps 22.18. **25:** *His mother,* unnamed as in 2.4, as also is her sister, who is not mentioned elsewhere in the New Testament. *Mary . . . of Clopas,* perhaps to be identified with the mother of James and Joses (Mk 15.40; etc.). **26–27:** Jesus provides his mother with a new son to protect her. *The disciple whom he loved,* see 13.23n. **28:** *Thirsty*, fulfilling Ps 69.21. **29:** *Hyssop*, a wild shrub whose branches were used for sprinkling liquids in religious rituals. **30:** *Finished*, either life ended or mission accomplished (17.4). *Gave up his Spirit*, a double meaning: "spirit" can mean "breath," but the phrase is also indicative of a Pentecostal event (see 7.39; Acts 2.4).

³¹ Since it was the day of Preparation, the Jews did not want the bodies left on the cross during the sabbath, especially because that sabbath was a day of great solemnity. So they asked Pilate to have the legs of the crucified men broken and the bodies removed. ³² Then the soldiers came and broke the legs of the first and of the other who had been crucified with him. ³³ But when they came to Jesus and saw that he was already dead, they did not break his legs. ³⁴ Instead, one of the soldiers pierced his side with a spear, and at once blood and water came out. ³⁵ (He who saw this has testified so that you also may believe. His testimony is true, and he knowsᵃ that he tells the truth.) ³⁶ These things occurred so that the scripture might be fulfilled, "None of his bones shall be broken." ³⁷ And again another passage of scripture says, "They will look on the one whom they have pierced."

³⁸ After these things, Joseph of Arimathea, who was a disciple of Jesus, though a secret one because of his fear of the Jews, asked Pilate to let him take away the body of Jesus. Pilate gave him permission; so he came and removed his body. ³⁹ Nicodemus, who had at first come to Jesus by night, also came, bringing a mixture of myrrh and aloes, weighing about a hundred pounds. ⁴⁰ They took the body of Jesus and wrapped it with the spices in linen cloths, according to the burial custom of the Jews. ⁴¹ Now there was a garden in the place where he was crucified, and in the garden there was a new tomb in which no one had ever been laid. ⁴² And so, because it was the Jewish day of Preparation, and the tomb was nearby, they laid Jesus there.

20 Early on the first day of the week, while it was still dark, Mary Magdalene came to the tomb and saw that the stone had been removed from the tomb. ² So she ran and went to Simon Peter and the other disciple, the one whom Jesus loved, and said to them, "They have taken the Lord out of the tomb, and we do not know where they have laid him." ³ Then Peter and the other disciple set out and went toward the tomb. ⁴ The two were running together, but the other disciple outran Peter and reached the tomb first. ⁵ He bent down to look in and saw the linen wrappings lying there, but he did not go in. ⁶ Then Simon Peter came, following him, and went into the tomb. He saw the linen wrappings lying there, ⁷ and the cloth that had been on Jesus' head, not lying with the linen wrappings but rolled up in a place by itself. ⁸ Then the other disciple, who reached the tomb first, also went in, and he saw and believed; ⁹ for as yet they did not understand the scripture, that he must rise from the dead. ¹⁰ Then the disciples returned to their homes.

¹¹ But Mary stood weeping outside the tomb. As she wept, she bent over to lookᵇ into the tomb; ¹² and she saw two angels in white, sitting where the body of Jesus had been lying, one at the head and the other at the feet. ¹³ They said to her, "Woman, why are you weeping?" She said to them, "They have taken away my Lord, and I do not know where they have laid him." ¹⁴ When she had said this, she turned around and saw Jesus standing there, but she did not

ᵃ Or *there is one who knows*
ᵇ Gk lacks *to look*

19.31–42: Final affairs. 31: *Legs . . . broken*: to forestall asphyxiation, the crucified pulled up with their arms and pushed up with their legs. With legs broken, the arms cramp quickly, bringing death. 34: Either senseless mutilation or fluids suggesting benefits: baptism (*water*) and Eucharist (*blood*; 6.53–56; 1 Jn 5.6–8). 35: The witness is not the actual writer, but guarantor of the narrative. 36–37: *Scriptures . . . fulfilled*, a claim that God providentially controls Jesus' death. 36: Ex 12.46, referring to the Passover lamb; see 1.29–30n. Cf. Ps 34.20. 37: Zech 12.10. 38: *Joseph of Arimathea*'s fear of censure (cf. 9.22; 12.42) is balanced by his public attempt to bury Jesus. 39: *Nicodemus* (3.2), brings excessive spices. 40–42: An honorable burial: a new tomb, burial clothes, excessive spices, all according to Judean burial customs.

20.1–18: The resurrection (cf. Mt 28; Mk 16; Lk 24). 1: *The first day of the week*, Sunday. 2–5: *The one whom Jesus loved* (see 13.23n.) arrives first; not entering indicates respect for Peter; contrast 13.23–25. 6–7: Peter arrives, inventories the tomb's contents, and leaves knowing nothing. 8: *The other disciple* sees all Peter saw, but *believed*. 9: *As yet they did not understand the scripture*: see 2.17 (Ps 69.9); 3.14 (Num 21.9); 19.24 (Ps 22.18); etc.

know that it was Jesus. [15] Jesus said to her, "Woman, why are you weeping? Whom are you looking for?" Supposing him to be the gardener, she said to him, "Sir, if you have carried him away, tell me where you have laid him, and I will take him away." [16] Jesus said to her, "Mary!" She turned and said to him in Hebrew,[a] "Rabbouni!" (which means Teacher). [17] Jesus said to her, "Do not hold on to me, because I have not yet ascended to the Father. But go to my brothers and say to them, 'I am ascending to my Father and your Father, to my God and your God.'" [18] Mary Magdalene went and announced to the disciples, "I have seen the Lord"; and she told them that he had said these things to her.

[19] When it was evening on that day, the first day of the week, and the doors of the house where the disciples had met were locked for fear of the Jews, Jesus came and stood among them and said, "Peace be with you." [20] After he said this, he showed them his hands and his side. Then the disciples rejoiced when they saw the Lord. [21] Jesus said to them again, "Peace be with you. As the Father has sent me, so I send you." [22] When he had said this, he breathed on them and said to them, "Receive the Holy Spirit. [23] If you forgive the sins of any, they are forgiven

them; if you retain the sins of any, they are retained."

[24] But Thomas (who was called the Twin[b]), one of the twelve, was not with them when Jesus came. [25] So the other disciples told him, "We have seen the Lord." But he said to them, "Unless I see the mark of the nails in his hands, and put my finger in the mark of the nails and my hand in his side, I will not believe."

[26] A week later his disciples were again in the house, and Thomas was with them. Although the doors were shut, Jesus came and stood among them and said, "Peace be with you." [27] Then he said to Thomas, "Put your finger here and see my hands. Reach out your hand and put it in my side. Do not doubt but believe." [28] Thomas answered him, "My Lord and my God!" [29] Jesus said to him, "Have you believed because you have seen me? Blessed are those who have not seen and yet have come to believe."

[30] Now Jesus did many other signs in the presence of his disciples, which are not written in this book. [31] But these are written so that you may come to believe[c] that Jesus

[a] That is, *Aramaic*

[b] Gk *Didymus*

[c] Other ancient authorities read *may continue to believe*

11–13: The angels tell Mary nothing, unlike Mt 28.5–7. She repeats her lines (see v. 2). 14: She *saw*, but *did not know.* 15: More confusion and ambiguity. 16: Jesus rarely addresses people by name in this Gospel; exceptions are Lazarus (11.43), Simon, son of John (21.15), now Mary. She addresses Jesus by his role, *Rabbouni* (a variant of "rabbi"), *Teacher* (1.38; 3.2; 11.28; 13.13). 17a: Only members of his inner circle touch Jesus: Mary (12.3–4); the beloved disciple (13.23); Thomas (20.25,27); Jesus rarely touches others (but see 9.6; 13.5). 17b: The Gospel's greatest revelation, communicated only to Mary: As Jesus lays down his life, he takes it back (10.17); he travels by his own power. She in turn is sent only to insiders, but her role is of limited duration.

20.19–29: Commissioning. 19–21: *Peace be with you,* a traditional Jewish greeting (e.g., Tob 12.17) is repeated twice, erasing their cowardice (16.32; 18.25–27). *Showed them his hands and his side,* proving he is no ghost (see Lk 24.38–39,41–42). 21: Typically the risen Jesus commissions disciples to roles of service (Mt 28.16–28; Lk 24.48; Jn 21.15–18). *As the Father has sent . . . I send,"* identical to 17.18, this sending will endure, unlike Mary's. 22: *Breathed,* cf. Gen 2.7. *Receive the Holy Spirit,* resurrection, "ascension" (v. 17) and "Pentecost" (v. 22) all occur on one day; thus Jesus confirms his brokerage. 24–25: Thomas, absent from the group, refused the apostles' "gospel" about Jesus. 26: The setting is the same as in v. 19, but Thomas is in attendance. 27: *"See . . . reach out your hand,"* gentler treatment than with those demanding signs (2.18; 4.48; 6.2,26). Unlike these previous requests, Jesus gives in to Thomas completely. 28: Thomas surrenders and honors Jesus as *Lord* and *God.* This recalls 1.1–3 and 5.19–29. 29: John's second beatitude (see 13.17). In the Synoptic Gospels, the beatitudes honor people suffering for Jesus (Lk 6.22–24); this honors insiders who believe the gospel.

20.30–31: First conclusion to the Gospel. In the Gospel, seven signs have been narrated out of a collection of many. These signs are credentials and proof of Jesus' relationship with God. Thus believing, one has access to eternal *life* by having Jesus as broker, *in his name.*

is the Messiah,[a] the Son of God, and that through believing you may have life in his name.

21 After these things Jesus showed himself again to the disciples by the Sea of Tiberias; and he showed himself in this way. [2] Gathered there together were Simon Peter, Thomas called the Twin,[b] Nathanael of Cana in Galilee, the sons of Zebedee, and two others of his disciples. [3] Simon Peter said to them, "I am going fishing." They said to him, "We will go with you." They went out and got into the boat, but that night they caught nothing.

[4] Just after daybreak, Jesus stood on the beach; but the disciples did not know that it was Jesus. [5] Jesus said to them, "Children, you have no fish, have you?" They answered him, "No." [6] He said to them, "Cast the net to the right side of the boat, and you will find some." So they cast it, and now they were not able to haul it in because there were so many fish. [7] That disciple whom Jesus loved said to Peter, "It is the Lord!" When Simon Peter heard that it was the Lord, he put on some clothes, for he was naked, and jumped into the sea. [8] But the other disciples came in the boat, dragging the net full of fish, for they were not far from the land, only about a hundred yards[c] off.

[9] When they had gone ashore, they saw a charcoal fire there, with fish on it, and bread. [10] Jesus said to them, "Bring some of the fish that you have just caught." [11] So Simon Peter went aboard and hauled the net ashore, full of large fish, a hundred fifty-three of them; and though there were so many, the net was not torn. [12] Jesus said to them, "Come and have breakfast." Now none of the disciples dared to ask him, "Who are you?" because they knew it was the Lord. [13] Jesus came and took the bread and gave it to them, and did the same with the fish. [14] This was now the third time that Jesus appeared to the disciples after he was raised from the dead.

[15] When they had finished breakfast, Jesus said to Simon Peter, "Simon son of John, do you love me more than these?" He said to him, "Yes, Lord; you know that I love you." Jesus said to him, "Feed my lambs." [16] A second time he said to him, "Simon son of John, do you love me?" He said to him, "Yes, Lord; you know that I love you." Jesus said to him, "Tend my sheep." [17] He said to him the third time, "Simon son of John, do you love me?" Peter felt hurt because he said to him the third time, "Do you love me?" And he said to him, "Lord, you know everything; you know that I love you." Jesus said to him, "Feed my sheep. [18] Very truly, I tell you, when you were younger, you used to fasten your own belt and to go wherever you wished. But when you grow old, you will stretch out your hands, and someone else will fasten a belt around you and take you where you do not wish to go." [19] (He said this to indicate the kind of death by

a   Or *the Christ*

b   Gk *Didymus*

c   Gk *two hundred cubits*

21.1–19: **Simon Peter: fisherman, table servant, and shepherd. 1:** *By the Sea of Tiberias,* in Galilee (see 6.1). **2:** Typical boats held six comfortably; here, seven: Simon Peter, Thomas, Nathanael (see 1.45–51), the sons of Zebedee (James and John), and two others. **3:** *Simon Peter,* returns to his occupation as a fisherman (Lk 5.1–10). **6:** Abundance is typical of Jesus' benefactions: wine (2.6–7), bread (6.5–13), life (10.10), now fish. **7:** Only the *disciple whom Jesus loved* (see 13.23n.) recognizes Jesus (20.8), upon whom Simon Peter totally depends for knowledge (13.25; 18.15–16). Neither nakedness nor working clothes are suitable for the presence of the Lord. **9–10:** *Fire, fish,* and *bread* provided by Jesus the host. *Fish* and *bread* have eucharistic overtones (see 6.11). **11:** *A hundred fifty-three,* either gematria (a numerical code) for Simon's name or just a very large number. **12–13:** Jesus' service continues the foot washing (13.13–15). **15:** Presumably they speak publicly before the others. *Love* suggests exceptional loyalty; if Peter's triple denial (18.17,25–27) meant rejection of all relationship with Jesus, now his assertion of *love* means the opposite. *Feed my lambs,* Jesus authorizes Peter to be the new shepherd. **17:** *Third time,* paralleling the triple denial. Peter now acknowledges Jesus and professes complete loyalty. **18:** Peter, as "noble" shepherd (see 10.11n.), will die in service of Jesus (10.11,15); his boast in 13.37 ironically will come true. **19:** Peter's death will *glorify* God, as did Jesus' (13.31–32; 17.1). Although now a shepherd, he is still Jesus' sheep: *Follow me.*

which he would glorify God.) After this he said to him, "Follow me."

²⁰ Peter turned and saw the disciple whom Jesus loved following them; he was the one who had reclined next to Jesus at the supper and had said, "Lord, who is it that is going to betray you?" ²¹ When Peter saw him, he said to Jesus, "Lord, what about him?" ²² Jesus said to him, "If it is my will that he remain until I come, what is that to you? Follow me!" ²³ So the rumor spread in the community[a] that this disciple would not die. Yet Jesus did not say to him that he would not die, but, "If it is my will that he remain until I come, what is that to you?"[b]

²⁴ This is the disciple who is testifying to these things and has written them, and we know that his testimony is true. ²⁵ But there are also many other things that Jesus did; if every one of them were written down, I suppose that the world itself could not contain the books that would be written.

a Gk *among the brothers*
b Other ancient authorities lack *what is that to you*

21.20–25: Rivalry, continued. 20: The disciple's high status comes from his touching Jesus, learning his secrets, courageously standing with him at the cross, and recognizing him (see 13.24n.). **22:** Simon's question challenges Jesus about the status of the disciple. His response resembles 2.3–4; it is none of your business. **23:** Jesus' statement is typically misunderstood. They construe *remain* as *he would not die* (see 5.24; 8.51–52; 1 Cor 15.50–52), but Jesus clarifies.

21.24–25: Second conclusion to the Gospel. *The disciple who is testifying,* most likely the beloved disciple (13.25–26; 19.35; 21.7), as opposed to the one who *has written,* just as Pilate caused the title on the cross to be written by another (19.19). *Other things,* cf. 20.30.

THE ACTS OF THE APOSTLES

NAME

The anonymous author of the third Gospel and its sequel, the Acts of the Apostles, supplied no titles for these works. By the end of the second century CE this author was thought to be Luke, and his second volume was referred to as "Acts" in the sense of the "activities" or "deeds" of the apostles. As a descriptive title, however, Acts of the Apostles is a misnomer, since Peter is the only one of the twelve apostles whose deeds and speeches are recounted in detail. Paul, the subject of the second half of the book, refers to himself as "apostle" in his letters but is not presented as such by Luke. Nevertheless, the title does capture a key concept of the book, namely, that the twelve apostles collectively guaranteed the early church's continuity with Jesus. In Luke's view they did so because they had been witnesses to everything that happened during Jesus' ministry, and especially to his resurrection (Acts 1.21–22; 10.39–41).

CANONICAL STATUS

Acts is the fifth book of the New Testament, immediately following the four Gospels. Although modern interpreters now understand Luke-Acts as a unified literary work in two parts, in the canonical arrangement the Gospel of John comes between these two books. Moreover, Luke's two works never appear in sequence in any ancient manuscript. In its canonical position, Acts connects the four Gospels to the collection of letters that follow, and its narrative focus, first on Peter and then on Paul, whether by accident or design allows it to function as an appropriate transition from the accounts about Jesus to the writings of the apostles.

AUTHORSHIP

Although Acts nowhere identifies its author, by the end of the second century it was possible to argue that Luke was the obvious candidate, and it has become conventional to refer to the author with this traditional name. This identification was based on the occurrence of Luke's name in Philemon 24 and in two other letters attributed to Paul (Col 4.14; 2 Tim 4.11), and also on passages in Acts in which the author presents himself as a traveling companion of Paul. Irenaeus (ca. 180 CE) pointed to these "we" passages (Acts 16.10–17; 20.5–15; 21.1–18; 27.1–28.16), in which the text shifts from third-person to first-person plural narration, as proof that Luke had been Paul's inseparable collaborator (Irenaeus, *Adv. Haer.* 3.14.1). Many modern scholars, however, challenge the assumption that the "we" passages demonstrate personal familiarity with Paul. In fact, one consequence of Luke's larger narrative goals is that his presentation of Paul is inconsistent with biographical and theological details in Paul's own letters. For example, Luke's denial of the formal status of "apostle" to Paul in Acts is almost unimaginable for an actual companion of Paul. In his letters Paul repeatedly claims to be one divinely called to be an apostle (e.g., Rom 1.1; 1 Cor 1.1; Gal 1.1). Luke's reluctance to use this term for Paul is connected to his view that only the Twelve, who had been present with Jesus throughout his public activity (Acts 1.21–22), were apostles. This disqualifies Paul, even if there is an echo of this contested status within Acts itself (14.4,14).

Although there is reason to doubt the identification of Luke as a companion of Paul, it cannot be denied that Luke admired Paul and viewed his missionary career as decisive for the establishment of Christianity in Asia Minor and Greece. Indeed, Luke's portrayal suggests that Paul's fame and influence extended from Jerusalem to Rome. Luke was probably someone from the Pauline mission area who, a generation or so after Paul, addressed issues facing Christians who found themselves in circumstances different from those addressed by Paul himself. Precisely where Luke carried out this task is uncertain. Ancient tradition placed him in Antioch, but his obvious respect for Paul and the Pauline tradition might indicate that he was connected with any of the cities of the Pauline mission around the Aegean Sea.

DATE

According to its opening words, Acts was written sometime after Luke's Gospel, which scholarly consensus currently dates to 85–95 CE (though some arguments have been advanced for an early second-century date). The considerations on the relation between Luke and Paul just reviewed support this late first-century date. Discrepancies between the undisputed Pauline letters and the narrative about Paul in Acts have long been recognized, and a temporal gap between the two does much to clarify the situation. During the period in which Luke was writing, Paul's image was undergoing revision (as is shown in the Pastoral Epistles; see 1 and 2 Tim; Titus, p. 2084). For example, Luke does not hesitate to portray Paul as subject to Jewish law; this depiction is consistent with Luke's emphasis on the continuity of the history of Israel and of the church. Moreover, according to Luke it was not Paul's theological arguments but the conversion of Cornelius through Peter, ratified by the apostolic council (Acts 10.1–11.18), that established that Gentile Christians were not required to observe the law of Moses in its entirety. Such contradictions arise because Acts preserves an image of Paul from a period some decades after his death. Thus Paul's role in Acts is dictated not primarily by biographical details but rather by the needs of Luke's theology as well as the circumstances of his readers.

LITERARY HISTORY

Luke gives no information about the sources upon which the narrative presented in Acts is based. He appears to have relied on a mixture of traditional information uncovered by his own investigation (see Lk 1.3) and his imagination about how the founding events unfolded in Jerusalem and reverberated throughout the Mediterranean world. Like many Greek historians, whom Luke imitates in part, Luke supplemented his narrative with speeches appropriate to significant occasions. These speeches, which amount to nearly one-third of the total text, are Luke's own literary creations, inserted into the narrative to instruct and please the reader. They also serve to demonstrate the unity of the earliest Christian preaching, even as they present Luke's own interpretation of the "events" (Lk 1.1) surrounding the emergence of the church. Scholars have attempted to identify traditional material and sources behind Luke's account, but no consensus has emerged from these efforts. To the extent that Luke did use preexisting sources and traditions, his rewriting of them leaves few clues about what they were. While scholars previously have made much of Luke's apparent lack of use of Paul's letters, some now believe that Luke in fact was familiar with at least some of them. It may be that Luke used Paul's letters in a way most appropriate to his narrative genre: not by explicitly citing them but more generally as an aid in fashioning his picture of Paul and the early church.

STRUCTURE AND CONTENTS

The book of Acts tells a dramatic story of the birth and expansion of the church from the time of the ascension of Jesus until the arrival of Paul in Rome. The plot line of Acts begins with Jesus' ascent to heaven. The narrative first portrays the life and dynamic growth of the primitive community in Jerusalem, energized by the Spirit and led by Peter and the apostles up through the martyrdom of Stephen (chs 1–7). The persecution initiated with Stephen's death resulted in mission activity outside Jerusalem highlighted by approaches to non-Jews by Philip (ch 8). After narrating the conversion of Saul (ch 9), Luke presents Peter as the individual through whom God established the inclusion of the Gentiles (10.1–11.18). Next, the early missionary tour of Barnabas and Saul/Paul on behalf of Antioch is narrated (11.19–14.28), along with a story about Peter's miraculous escape from death (ch 12). The center of the book recounts the apostolic council's vindication of the efforts to free the Gentile mission from the requirements of Jewish ritual law (ch 15). Then Paul's further missionary travels are depicted (15.36–21.26) in Philippi, Thessalonica, Athens, Corinth, Ephesus, Miletus, Caesarea, and Jerusalem. Finally, the book recounts Paul's arrest, imprisonment, and trials in Jerusalem and Caesarea, and his transfer to Rome (21.27–28.31), closing with the uplifting image of Paul, while under house arrest, preaching and teaching without hindrance in the capital city of the empire.

INTERPRETATION

Written from the perspective of the late first or perhaps early second century CE, Acts alone among the documents of the earliest Christian period offers a narrative sequel to the accounts of Jesus' words and deeds found in the Gospels. Its author, identified by tradition as Luke, had already produced the Gospel (Acts 1.1–2). His purpose in writing again was more than a matter of antiquarian interest, although Acts can be compared with Hellenistic historical monographs. The account was intended to give Christians of his day an unshakable confidence in their future through an instructive survey of their past. In carrying out that overarching purpose, Acts addresses social and theological problems brought about by the church's relationship to its Jewish heritage and its Greco-Roman cultural and political environment. Luke sought to clarify both how the church was faithful to the God of the Jewish scriptures and how Christianity was not incompatible with civic order and morality in the cities of the Roman Empire. Luke devotes half of the narrative to Paul, constructing for Christians of the era after Paul an image of this important figure consistent with the stance taken on Jewish and Roman concerns in the book. Beginning with Irenaeus and especially with Eusebius (d. ca. 339 CE), readers drew on Acts more strictly as a historical account or for information useful for solving later theological problems, no longer observing how in Acts Luke addressed the situation of the original audience. Moreover, such later uses were aided and abetted by the canonical arrangement of Luke's works, which gave no indication that his two books were to be read as a single work in two parts. Thus, for most ancient readers and their modern successors, Acts has been viewed not as a supplement to Luke's Gospel in particular but to the Gospels in general.

GUIDE TO READING

For Luke, who was likely a Gentile Christian (though a minority of scholars contend that he was a Diaspora Jew), that God's promises in scripture had been made to the ancient people of God required the church to stand in continuity with Israel. But since most Jews did not accept Jesus as the Messiah, and since the increasingly Gentile Christian community ceased to observe Jewish ritual, this historical continuity had been called into question. Luke responds to this threat by depicting the earliest Christians as faithful Jews in Jerusalem until persecution pushed them out. Then, by means of multiple elaborations of the Cornelius episode (10.1–48; 11.1–18; 15.7–9) and of the story of Paul's conversion (9.1–19; 22.4–16; 26.9–18), he stresses that the entrance of Gentiles into the church is nothing less than an act of God, and so by definition in continuity with Israel's history. It is significant that Luke's ideal Gentile convert is one who continues to practice Jewish piety (10.2), and that Gentile Christians are urged to adhere to conduct that would permit association with Jews (15.20). Luke's portrayal of Paul's visits to synagogues and his Jewish lifestyle serve to reinforce this maintaining of continuity with Jewish roots.

Apart from any value Acts has as a work of history, it is an important example of early Christian theology. Luke develops the idea of the church as a historical entity with its own distinctive era. Moreover, the earliest church, by being confined to Jerusalem, was set apart from the church of Luke's day. The ideal and unrepeatable structures of the early community resulted from the presence of the apostles and eyewitnesses. Luke's concern to highlight the continuity between Israel and the church is expressed by the continued observance of Jewish practices in the early period, implicitly in contrast to Luke's later situation. The gap between Luke's generation and the earlier time is bridged by the endorsement of the Gentile mission in the deliberations of the apostolic council and the promulgation of the apostolic decree (15.20,29; 21.25). The latter pronouncement may have been of practical value for Luke's community by creating the conditions necessary to allow table fellowship between Jewish and Gentile Christians. Luke's portrayal of Christianity's close ties to Judaism and thus as possessing a venerable heritage (24.14) also bolsters his appeal to Roman officials not to concern themselves with internal religious disputes (25.19,20). Acts portrays influential Romans expressing interest in Christianity (13.12; 19.31), or at least concluding that it posed no threat to the state (18.15; 19.37; 23.29; 25.25; 26.32). In this way Luke demonstrates the nonsubversive nature of the church, possibly in an effort to convince citizen elites of his own day that their membership in the Christian community was not incompatible with their status as Roman citizens. Luke's argument is designed for internal consumption; it was neither intended to persuade non-Christians nor would it have been likely to do so.

Key among the factors promoting continuity within the church itself throughout the narrative are the descriptions of the church's proclamation and teaching about Jesus and the constant presence of the Spirit as the prime mover at the crucial junctures of early Christian history (e.g., 8.29; 10.19; 16.6–7). Yet in Acts it is God who occupies the dominant place. Jesus is described as a man whom God legitimated by mighty works, wonders, and signs (2.22). The view of Jesus' death as atoning occurs only once in an expression taken over from earlier tradition (20.28). The focal point of salvation is the resurrection, which is viewed as the turning point of history. The combination of all of these forces allows Luke to portray the successful expansion of the early Christian mission throughout the Roman Empire under the direction of the Spirit according to the purpose of God.

Christopher R. Matthews

1 In the first book, Theophilus, I wrote about all that Jesus did and taught from the beginning ² until the day when he was taken up to heaven, after giving instructions through the Holy Spirit to the apostles whom he had chosen. ³ After his suffering he presented himself alive to them by many convincing proofs, appearing to them during forty days and speaking about the kingdom of God. ⁴ While staying^a with them, he ordered them not to leave Jerusalem, but to wait there for the promise of the Father. "This," he said, "is what you have heard from me; ⁵ for John baptized with water, but you will be baptized with^b the Holy Spirit not many days from now."

⁶ So when they had come together, they asked him, "Lord, is this the time when you will restore the kingdom to Israel?" ⁷ He replied, "It is not for you to know the times or periods that the Father has set by his own authority. ⁸ But you will receive power when the Holy Spirit has come upon you; and you will be my witnesses in Jerusalem, in all Judea and Samaria, and to the ends of the earth." ⁹ When he had said this, as they were watch-ing, he was lifted up, and a cloud took him out of their sight. ¹⁰ While he was going and they were gazing up toward heaven, suddenly two men in white robes stood by them. ¹¹ They said, "Men of Galilee, why do you stand looking up toward heaven? This Jesus, who has been taken up from you into heaven, will come in the same way as you saw him go into heaven."

¹² Then they returned to Jerusalem from the mount called Olivet, which is near Jerusalem, a sabbath day's journey away. ¹³ When they had entered the city, they went to the room upstairs where they were staying, Peter, and John, and James, and Andrew, Philip and Thomas, Bartholomew and Matthew, James son of Alphaeus, and Simon the Zealot, and Judas son of^c James. ¹⁴ All these were constantly devoting themselves to prayer, together with certain women, including Mary the mother of Jesus, as well as his brothers.

a Or *eating*
b Or *by*
c Or *the brother of*

1.1–14: Introduction and summary. The author (hereafter, "Luke") summarizes information from *the first book*, the Gospel of Luke. **1:** *Theophilus*, "dear to God"; perhaps a patron sponsoring publication of the two books (note the respectful address "most excellent" in Lk 1.3), or symbolic for any ideal reader. An opening dedication and reference to previous work is a common pattern in ancient literature. **3:** Examples of the *many convincing proofs* are given in Lk 24.13–53. *Appearing to them during forty days*, note that Lk 24.50–53 seems to place the ascension on Easter; *forty*, a symbolic number in the Bible frequently used for important transitions (e.g., Gen 7.12; Ex 24.18; Num 14.23), and here parallels the beginning of Jesus' ministry (Lk 4.2). *Kingdom of God* stands for the Christian proclamation (8.12; 19.8; 20.25) and indicates continuity with the teaching of Jesus (Lk 4.43; 8.1; 9.2,11). **4:** The Gk word translated *staying* means "to eat at the same table with" (see note *a*) and likely refers to Lk 24.30,31,35,41–43. *Promise of the Father*, that is, the Spirit; see Lk 11.13; 24.49. The promise is fulfilled in Acts 2.1–4 (see 2.33). *Jerusalem*, Luke locates all of the significant founding events in this holy city; the other Gospels report resurrection appearances in Galilee. **5:** *John* the Baptist, Lk 3.1–20. The *Holy Spirit* is one of the major characters of Acts. **6–11:** The ascension, cf. Lk 24.44–51. **6:** The apostles suppose that Jesus intends to *restore the kingdom to Israel* (Lk 22.28–30) and reestablish the dominion once enjoyed by David (Lk 1.32). **7:** The nationalistic tenor of the question is deflected. **8:** The theme of the apostles as *witnesses* (Lk 24.48) recurs often (1.22; 2.32; 3.15; 5.32; 10.39,41; 13.31). *Jerusalem . . . Judea . . . Samaria . . . the ends of the earth*, the progress of the mission is given in geographical terms (8.38n.). **9:** Elsewhere in the New Testament the ascension is found only at Lk 24.51 (cf. Mk 16.19). **10:** *Two men in white robes*, angels (24.4; Jn 20.12); in Lk 9.30 the two men are Moses and Elijah. There are other parallels between Luke's Transfiguration account (Lk 9.28–36) and the ascension scene. **11:** *Will come in the same way*, note the cloud in v. 9; Lk 21.27; cf. Mk 14.62; Dan 7.13. **12:** *Olivet*, the Mount of Olives is just east of Jerusalem. *A sabbath day's journey*, about 3,000 ft. (1,000 m.), the distance it was permissible for an observant Jew to walk on the sabbath (*Tr. Eruvin*) without breaking the command not to leave one's "place" on the sabbath (Ex 6.29). **13:** The same list as in Lk 6.14–16, but in a different order (and without Judas Iscariot). **14:** Jesus' family is incorporated into the church. *Brothers*, see Mt 13.55; Mk 6.3; James later appears as the leader of the Jerusalem church (12.17; 15.13; 21.18).

¹⁵ In those days Peter stood up among the believers[a] (together the crowd numbered about one hundred twenty persons) and said, ¹⁶ "Friends,[b] the scripture had to be fulfilled, which the Holy Spirit through David foretold concerning Judas, who became a guide for those who arrested Jesus— ¹⁷ for he was numbered among us and was allotted his share in this ministry." ¹⁸ (Now this man acquired a field with the reward of his wickedness; and falling headlong,[c] he burst open in the middle and all his bowels gushed out. ¹⁹ This became known to all the residents of Jerusalem, so that the field was called in their language Hakeldama, that is, Field of Blood.) ²⁰ "For it is written in the book of Psalms,

'Let his homestead become desolate,
    and let there be no one to live in it';
and
'Let another take his position of overseer.'
²¹ So one of the men who have accompanied us during all the time that the Lord Jesus went in and out among us, ²² beginning from the baptism of John until the day when he was taken up from us—one of these must become a witness with us to his resurrection." ²³ So they proposed two, Joseph called Barsabbas, who was also known as Justus, and Matthias. ²⁴ Then they prayed and said, "Lord, you know everyone's heart. Show us which one of these two you have chosen ²⁵ to take the place[d] in this ministry and apostleship from which Judas turned aside to go to his own place." ²⁶ And they cast lots for them, and the lot fell on Matthias; and he was added to the eleven apostles.

2 When the day of Pentecost had come, they were all together in one place. ² And suddenly from heaven there came a sound like the rush of a violent wind, and it filled the entire house where they were sitting. ³ Divided tongues, as of fire, appeared among them, and a tongue rested on each of them. ⁴ All of them were filled with the Holy Spirit and began to speak in other languages, as the Spirit gave them ability.

⁵ Now there were devout Jews from every nation under heaven living in Jerusalem. ⁶ And at this sound the crowd gathered and was bewildered, because each one heard them speaking in the native language of each. ⁷ Amazed and astonished, they asked, "Are not all these who are speaking Galileans? ⁸ And how is it that we hear, each of us, in our own

[a] Gk *brothers*
[b] Gk *Men, brothers*
[c] Or *swelling up*
[d] Other ancient authorities read *the share*

1.15–26: **The restoration of the twelve.** The selection of Matthias restores the number of apostles to twelve, corresponding to the twelve tribes of Israel. **16:** *Through David,* in the Psalms quoted in v. 20; King David was traditionally viewed as the author of the Psalms. *Judas,* see Lk 22.3–6,47–48. **17:** *Us,* the apostles. **18:** Compare the gruesome death of Herod Agrippa in 12.23. According to Mt 27.5, Judas hanged himself. **19:** *Their language,* Aramaic, a language closely related to Hebrew; the information is clearly for Luke's Gk readers, not Peter's Aramaic-speaking audience. **20:** Scripture foresaw the situation (Ps 69.25) and dictates a course of action (Ps 109.8). In Acts, citations from the Hebrew Bible are based on the Gk version, the Septuagint. **21:** The requirements stipulated here explain why Paul does not qualify as an apostle in Acts. **22:** *The baptism of John* (Lk 3.1–21) marks the beginning of Jesus' ministry (10.37). To *become a witness . . . to* Jesus' *resurrection* in Acts means to become one of the twelve apostles, who function in a special sense as witnesses (v. 8; 2.32). **23:** Nothing else is known about Joseph and Matthias. **24:** *Know . . . heart,* see Lk 9.47; Acts 15.8. **26:** *Cast lots,* allowing the "Lord" (v. 24; Jesus, or perhaps God) to choose. Lots were widely used in the ancient world for religious and social decisions and are often mentioned in the Hebrew Bible (e.g., Lev 16.8; 1 Sam 10.20–21; 1 Chr 25.8).

2.1–41: **The day of Pentecost.** The Feast of Weeks or Pentecost (Lev 23.15–21), the spring barley harvest, falls fifty days after Passover. In Jewish tradition the law was given on this day. **1–13:** The coming of the Holy Spirit. **2:** *Rush of a violent wind,* perhaps an allusion to Gen 1.2 ("while a mighty wind swept over the face of the waters" [alternate version]), though this and other features here are typical of theophanies—manifestations of God (Ex 19.16–19; 1 Kings 19.11; Isa 66.15). **3:** John the Baptist had predicted a baptism "with the Holy Spirit and fire" (Lk 3.16; Mt 3.11; cf. Mk 1.8; Jn 1.33). **4:** This baptism (1.5) or filling with the Spirit is clearly foundational for Acts but is not referred to elsewhere in the New Testament (but cf. Jn 20.22). **5:** *Devout Jews from every nation,* emphasizing the universal character of the Pentecost event. **6:** The *other languages* (v. 4) are foreign languages, not the "tongues" of 1 Cor 14.1–33. Perhaps the author thinks of a reversal of the confusion of languages at the tower

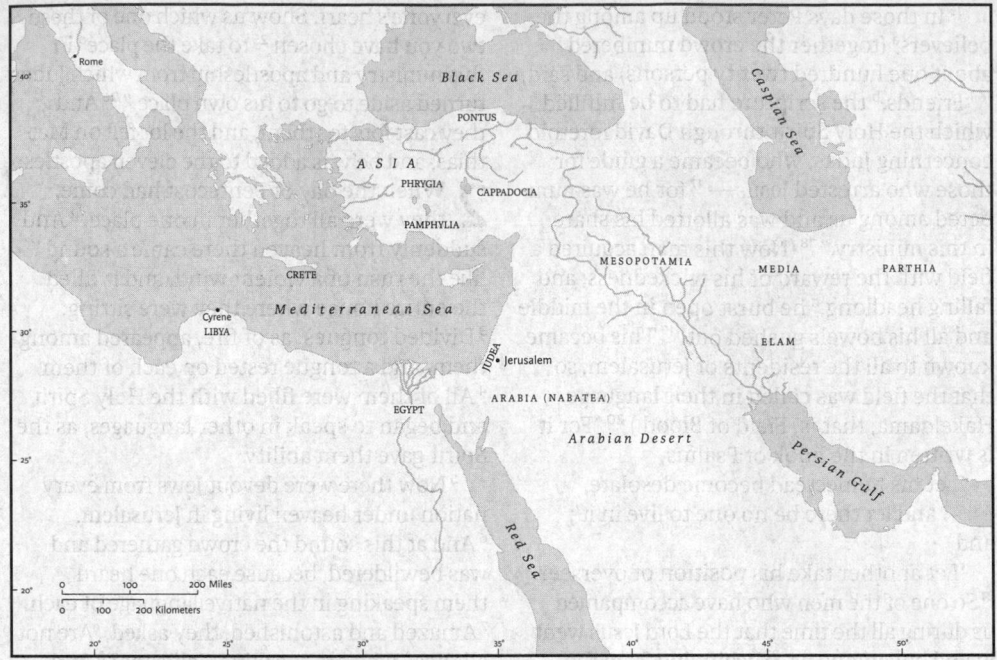

2.9–11: The native lands of Pentecost pilgrims.

native language? ⁹ Parthians, Medes, Elamites, and residents of Mesopotamia, Judea and Cappadocia, Pontus and Asia, ¹⁰ Phrygia and Pamphylia, Egypt and the parts of Libya belonging to Cyrene, and visitors from Rome, both Jews and proselytes, ¹¹ Cretans and Arabs—in our own languages we hear them speaking about God's deeds of power." ¹² All were amazed and perplexed, saying to one another, "What does this mean?" ¹³ But others sneered and said, "They are filled with new wine."

¹⁴ But Peter, standing with the eleven, raised his voice and addressed them, "Men of Judea and all who live in Jerusalem, let this be known to you, and listen to what I say. ¹⁵ Indeed, these are not drunk, as you suppose, for it is only nine o'clock in the morning. ¹⁶ No, this is what was spoken through the prophet Joel:

¹⁷ 'In the last days it will be, God declares,
that I will pour out my Spirit upon all
  flesh,
and your sons and your daughters shall
  prophesy,
and your young men shall see visions,
  and your old men shall dream dreams.
¹⁸ Even upon my slaves, both men and
  women,
in those days I will pour out my Spirit;
  and they shall prophesy.
¹⁹ And I will show portents in the heaven
  above
and signs on the earth below,
  blood, and fire, and smoky mist.
²⁰ The sun shall be turned to darkness
  and the moon to blood,
before the coming of the Lord's great
  and glorious day.

of Babel (Gen 11.1–9). **9–11:** The list of countries and races, generally moving from east to west, suggests universal participation in the Pentecost event. **10:** *Proselytes,* full converts to Judaism. **13:** *Filled with new wine,* i.e., drunk (v. 15). **14–36:** Peter's sermon. Like other Hellenistic historians Luke provides characters with speeches appropriate to their circumstances. These may use traditional material but also convey Luke's viewpoint. The speeches use the same biblical style in which Luke has written the early chapters of Acts. **14:** *Peter* remains the spokesman for the apostles (1.15); individualized actions by the others are not portrayed in Acts. **16:** The event is interpreted as a fulfillment of scripture. **17:** *In the last days* is added to the beginning of the quotation

²¹ Then everyone who calls on the name of the Lord shall be saved.'

²² "You that are Israelites,ᵃ listen to what I have to say: Jesus of Nazareth,ᵇ a man attested to you by God with deeds of power, wonders, and signs that God did through him among you, as you yourselves know— ²³ this man, handed over to you according to the definite plan and foreknowledge of God, you crucified and killed by the hands of those outside the law. ²⁴ But God raised him up, having freed him from death,ᶜ because it was impossible for him to be held in its power. ²⁵ For David says concerning him,

'I saw the Lord always before me,
    for he is at my right hand so that I will
        not be shaken;
²⁶ therefore my heart was glad, and my
    tongue rejoiced;
    moreover my flesh will live in hope.
²⁷ For you will not abandon my soul to
    Hades,
    or let your Holy One experience
        corruption.
²⁸ You have made known to me the ways
    of life;
    you will make me full of gladness with
        your presence.'

²⁹ "Fellow Israelites,ᵈ I may say to you confidently of our ancestor David that he both died and was buried, and his tomb is with us to this day. ³⁰ Since he was a prophet, he knew that God had sworn with an oath to him that he would put one of his descendants on his throne. ³¹ Foreseeing this, Davidᵉ spoke of the resurrection of the Messiah,ᶠ saying,

'He was not abandoned to Hades,
    nor did his flesh experience corruption.'

³² This Jesus God raised up, and of that all of us are witnesses. ³³ Being therefore exalted atᵍ the right hand of God, and having received from the Father the promise of the Holy Spirit, he has poured out this that you both see and hear. ³⁴ For David did not ascend into the heavens, but he himself says,

'The Lord said to my Lord,
    "Sit at my right hand,
³⁵ until I make your enemies your
    footstool."'

³⁶ Therefore let the entire house of Israel know with certainty that God has made him both Lord and Messiah,ʰ this Jesus whom you crucified."

³⁷ Now when they heard this, they were cut to the heart and said to Peter and to the other apostles, "Brothers,ᵈ what should we do?" ³⁸ Peter said to them, "Repent, and be baptized every one of you in the name of Jesus Christ so that your sins may be forgiven; and you will receive the gift of the Holy Spirit. ³⁹ For the promise is for you, for your children, and for all who are far away, everyone whom the Lord our God calls to him." ⁴⁰ And he testified with many other arguments and exhorted them, saying, "Save yourselves from this corrupt generation." ⁴¹ So those who welcomed his message were baptized,

ᵃ Gk *Men, Israelites*
ᵇ Gk *the Nazorean*
ᶜ Gk *the pains of death*
ᵈ Gk *Men, brothers*
ᵉ Gk *he*
ᶠ Or *the Christ*
ᵍ Or *by*
ʰ Or *Christ*

of Joel 2.28–32. **22:** *A man,* Luke does not think of the incarnation of a divine being. *Deeds of power, wonders, and signs,* biblical language (e.g., Deut 4.34; 6.22; 26.8) used often in Acts. **23:** The crucifixion of Jesus by Jews and Gentiles was part of a *plan,* see Lk 22.22; 24.26; Acts 4.27–28. **25:** Ps 16.8–11. *David,* see 1.16n. **29:** *His tomb,* see, e.g., Josephus, *Ant.* 7.392–394. **30:** 2 Sam 7.12–13; Ps 132.11. **31:** *The Messiah* is assumed to come from the line of *David* (cf. Rom 1.3). **32:** *Witnesses,* see 1.22n. **33:** *Exalted,* a reference to the ascension. *The promise,* see 1.4n. **34–35:** Ps 110.1, like Ps 16.8–11 (vv. 25,31), here also refers not to *David* but to Jesus. It was widely used in early Christian thought about Jesus (Mk 12.36; 1 Cor 15.25; Heb 1.13). **36:** *Made him both Lord and Messiah,* apparently at the resurrection. This "adoptionist" christology appears to conflict with Luke's account of Jesus' baptism (Lk 3.21–22); see 10.38n. Such tensions in Acts may indicate the use of sources with contrasting viewpoints. **37–41:** The call to repentance. **37:** Lk 3.10. **38:** Here the gift of the *Spirit* follows baptism, but there is variety elsewhere (8.16; 10.44; 18.26; 19.5–6). **39:** Isa 57.19; Joel 2.32. *All who are far away,* the universal nature of the church is clear from the beginning (cf. Lk 2.32). **41:** *Three thousand persons were added,* illustrating the phenomenal success of Peter's speech.

and that day about three thousand persons were added. [42] They devoted themselves to the apostles' teaching and fellowship, to the breaking of bread and the prayers.

[43] Awe came upon everyone, because many wonders and signs were being done by the apostles. [44] All who believed were together and had all things in common; [45] they would sell their possessions and goods and distribute the proceeds[a] to all, as any had need. [46] Day by day, as they spent much time together in the temple, they broke bread at home[b] and ate their food with glad and generous[c] hearts, [47] praising God and having the goodwill of all the people. And day by day the Lord added to their number those who were being saved.

3 One day Peter and John were going up to the temple at the hour of prayer, at three o'clock in the afternoon. [2] And a man lame from birth was being carried in. People would lay him daily at the gate of the temple called the Beautiful Gate so that he could ask for alms from those entering the temple. [3] When he saw Peter and John about to go into the temple, he asked them for alms. [4] Peter looked intently at him, as did John, and said, "Look at us." [5] And he fixed his attention on them, expecting to receive something from them. [6] But Peter said, "I have no silver or gold, but what I have I give you; in the name of Jesus Christ of Nazareth,[d] stand up and walk." [7] And he took him by the right hand and raised him up; and immediately his feet and ankles were made strong. [8] Jumping up, he stood and began to walk, and he entered the temple with them, walking and leaping and praising God. [9] All the people saw him walking and praising God, [10] and they recognized him as the one who used to sit and ask for alms at the Beautiful Gate of the temple; and they were filled with wonder and amazement at what had happened to him.

[11] While he clung to Peter and John, all the people ran together to them in the portico called Solomon's Portico, utterly astonished. [12] When Peter saw it, he addressed the people, "You Israelites,[e] why do you wonder at this, or why do you stare at us, as though by our own power or piety we had made him walk? [13] The God of Abraham, the God of Isaac, and the God of Jacob, the God of our ancestors has glorified his servant[f] Jesus, whom you handed over and rejected in the presence of Pilate, though he had decided to release him.

---

a Gk *them*
b Or *from house to house*
c Or *sincere*
d Gk *the Nazorean*
e Gk *Men, Israelites*
f Or *child*

2.42–47: Life in the first Christian community. (The terms "Christian" and "Christianity" are used here for convenience, but strictly speaking are inaccurate for the time portrayed in the narrative; see 9.2n.; 11.25–26n.) **42:** *The breaking of bread* (v. 46) describes both a common Christian meal (e.g., 20.7,11) and the Lord's Supper (27.33–38; cf. 1 Cor 11.17–34). **43–47:** Luke portrays life in the early Jerusalem community as a golden age. **43:** By performing *wonders and signs* the apostles fulfill Joel's prophecy (2.19) and imitate Jesus (2.22). **44–45:** The ideal use of possessions and money illustrates the proper response to the preaching of Jesus on this subject in the Gospel (see Lk 6.20; 12.13–21,33–34; 14.12–24,33). For community of goods in the Dead Sea scrolls, see 1QS 1.11–12; cf. Josephus, *J.W.* 2.122 on the Essenes. **46:** Members of the growing Christian group are simultaneously devout Jews who remain close to *the temple*.

3.1–10: Peter's healing miracle in the Temple. An illustration of the apostles' "wonders and signs" (2.43). **1:** The apostles center their activity in *the temple* (see 2.46) and so imitate Jesus' practice in Jerusalem (note the distinctive portrayal in Lk 20–21). *John* appears here and elsewhere with *Peter* but with no individualized role. *Three o'clock in the afternoon*, when sacrifice was offered with prayer (Ex 29.39; Lev 6.20; Josephus, *Ant.* 14.65). **2:** *The Beautiful Gate*, perhaps the Nicanor Gate of Corinthian bronze on the east side of the Temple; see Josephus, *J.W.* 5.201. **6:** *The name* is a key concept in Acts (v. 16; 2.21,38), as 4.7–12 will underline (see also 4.17,18,30; 10.43; 19.13).

3.11–26: Peter's explanation. In a second sermon Peter links Jesus with the patriarchs and Moses. **11:** *Solomon's Portico*, a colonnade located by Josephus (*J.W.* 5.185; *Ant.* 20.221) on the east side of the Temple. **13:** The word *servant* recalls Isa 52.13 and the suffering servant of the Lord (4.27; 8.30–35). *Pilate*, Pontius Pilate, the Roman governor of Judea, who sentenced Jesus to death (Lk 3.1; 23.24). Roman responsibility for the death of

¹⁴ But you rejected the Holy and Righteous One and asked to have a murderer given to you, ¹⁵ and you killed the Author of life, whom God raised from the dead. To this we are witnesses. ¹⁶ And by faith in his name, his name itself has made this man strong, whom you see and know; and the faith that is through Jesus[a] has given him this perfect health in the presence of all of you.

¹⁷ "And now, friends,[b] I know that you acted in ignorance, as did also your rulers. ¹⁸ In this way God fulfilled what he had foretold through all the prophets, that his Messiah[c] would suffer. ¹⁹ Repent therefore, and turn to God so that your sins may be wiped out, ²⁰ so that times of refreshing may come from the presence of the Lord, and that he may send the Messiah[d] appointed for you, that is, Jesus, ²¹ who must remain in heaven until the time of universal restoration that God announced long ago through his holy prophets. ²² Moses said, 'The Lord your God will raise up for you from your own people[b] a prophet like me. You must listen to whatever he tells you. ²³ And it will be that everyone who does not listen to that prophet will be utterly rooted out of the people.' ²⁴ And all the prophets, as many as have spoken, from Samuel and those after him, also predicted these days. ²⁵ You are the descendants of the prophets and of the covenant that God gave to your ancestors, saying to Abraham, 'And in your descendants all the families of the earth shall be blessed.' ²⁶ When God raised up his servant,[e] he sent him first to you, to

bless you by turning each of you from your wicked ways."

4 While Peter and John[f] were speaking to the people, the priests, the captain of the temple, and the Sadducees came to them, ² much annoyed because they were teaching the people and proclaiming that in Jesus there is the resurrection of the dead. ³ So they arrested them and put them in custody until the next day, for it was already evening. ⁴ But many of those who heard the word believed; and they numbered about five thousand.

⁵ The next day their rulers, elders, and scribes assembled in Jerusalem, ⁶ with Annas the high priest, Caiaphas, John,[g] and Alexander, and all who were of the high-priestly family. ⁷ When they had made the prisoners[h] stand in their midst, they inquired, "By what power or by what name did you do this?" ⁸ Then Peter, filled with the Holy Spirit, said to them, "Rulers of the people and elders, ⁹ if we are questioned today because of a good deed done to someone who was sick and are asked how this man has been healed, ¹⁰ let it be known to all of you, and to all the people of Israel, that this man is standing before you

a   Gk *him*
b   Gk *brothers*
c   Or *his Christ*
d   Or *the Christ*
e   Or *child*
f   Gk *While they*
g   Other ancient authorities read *Jonathan*
h   Gk *them*

Jesus is downplayed here as in Lk 23.4,14–16,20–25; contrast Acts 4.27. **14:** *A murderer,* Barabbas (Lk 23.18–19). **15:** *Author,* the word can mean "pioneer" or "founder" (of a new city); in 5.31 it is "leader" (cf. Heb 2.10; 12.2). The testimony of the *witnesses* is again emphasized (1.22n.). **16:** *Name,* see v. 6n. **17:** *You acted in ignorance,* mitigating the guilt emphasized in vv. 13–15 (see 4.10). Compare 14.16 and 17.30. **18:** The necessity that the *Messiah would suffer* was *foretold,* see Lk 24.25–27,46; Acts 17.2–3; 26.22–23. Recall the "plan" of 2.23. **19:** Lk 3.3. **22:** 7.37. Jesus is successor of Moses (Deut 18.15) as well as David. **23:** Deut 18.19; Lev 23.29. **24:** *These days,* i.e., the last days (2.17). **25:** Gen 12.3; 18.18; 22.18. **26:** *First to you,* implying the later mission to the Gentiles.

   4.1–22: Arrest and release of Peter and John. The first of many incidents in which the apostles defend the faith before the authorities. **1–2:** *Captain of the temple,* the officer in charge of the Temple police. *Sadducees,* a circle composed of priestly and lay nobility who according to Luke denied the *resurrection of the dead* (23.6–8). **3:** It was not legal to hold a judicial inquiry at night. **4:** *Five thousand,* the rapid growth of the community of believers continues (see 2.41). This is a recurrent theme in Acts, typically in the face of opposition. **5–6:** Perhaps the *rulers* are priests; with the *elders* and *scribes* they made up the Sanhedrin, or council (v. 15), of which *the high priest* was head. *Annas* held this office from 6–14 CE; *Caiaphas* was his son-in-law (Jn 18.13) and became high priest in 18 CE (Lk 3.2); *John* may be Jonathan, the son of Annas who succeeded Caiaphas in 37 CE. **8–12:** A condensed version of the speeches in chs 2, 3, 10, and 13. The scene in v. 8 represents the fulfillment of Jesus'

in good health by the name of Jesus Christ of Nazareth,[a] whom you crucified, whom God raised from the dead. [11] This Jesus[b] is

'the stone that was rejected by you, the builders;

it has become the cornerstone.'[c]

[12] There is salvation in no one else, for there is no other name under heaven given among mortals by which we must be saved."

[13] Now when they saw the boldness of Peter and John and realized that they were uneducated and ordinary men, they were amazed and recognized them as companions of Jesus. [14] When they saw the man who had been cured standing beside them, they had nothing to say in opposition. [15] So they ordered them to leave the council while they discussed the matter with one another. [16] They said, "What will we do with them? For it is obvious to all who live in Jerusalem that a notable sign has been done through them; we cannot deny it. [17] But to keep it from spreading further among the people, let us warn them to speak no more to anyone in this name." [18] So they called them and ordered them not to speak or teach at all in the name of Jesus. [19] But Peter and John answered them, "Whether it is right in God's sight to listen to you rather than to God, you must judge; [20] for we cannot keep from speaking about what we have seen and heard." [21] After threatening them again, they let them go, finding no way to punish them because of the people, for all of them praised God for what had happened. [22] For the man on whom this sign of healing had been performed was more than forty years old.

[23] After they were released, they went to their friends[d] and reported what the chief priests and the elders had said to them.

[24] When they heard it, they raised their voices together to God and said, "Sovereign Lord, who made the heaven and the earth, the sea, and everything in them, [25] it is you who said by the Holy Spirit through our ancestor David, your servant:[e]

'Why did the Gentiles rage,
and the peoples imagine vain things?
[26] The kings of the earth took their stand,
and the rulers have gathered together
against the Lord and against his
Messiah.'[f]

[27] For in this city, in fact, both Herod and Pontius Pilate, with the Gentiles and the peoples of Israel, gathered together against your holy servant[e] Jesus, whom you anointed, [28] to do whatever your hand and your plan had predestined to take place. [29] And now, Lord, look at their threats, and grant to your servants[g] to speak your word with all boldness, [30] while you stretch out your hand to heal, and signs and wonders are performed through the name of your holy servant[e] Jesus." [31] When they had prayed, the place in which they were gathered together was shaken; and they were all filled with the Holy Spirit and spoke the word of God with boldness.

[32] Now the whole group of those who believed were of one heart and soul, and no one claimed private ownership of any possessions, but everything they owned was held in common. [33] With great power the apostles

---

a   Gk *the Nazorean*
b   Gk *This*
c   Or *keystone*
d   Gk *their own*
e   Or *child*
f   Or *his Christ*
g   Gk *slaves*

---

promise in Lk 12.12; compare the prediction of Lk 21.15. **11:** Ps 118.22 was popular in Christian arguments (Mt 21.42; Mk 12.10; Lk 20.17; 1 Pet 2.7). **12:** *No other name* underlines the answer (v. 10) to the question posed (v. 7) about the name; see 3.6,16; 4.17–18,30. **13:** *Boldness,* this word and its cognates are used often in Acts and connote frank and courageous speech (e.g., 13.46; 18.26). *Uneducated and ordinary men,* lacking legal training. **19:** The reply here and in 5.29 is reminiscent of Socrates' famous words (Plato, *Apology* 29d).

4.23–31: Prayer of the community. 24: Ps 146.6. **25–26:** Ps 2.1–2. **27:** *Servant,* see 3.13n.; the same term is used of David in v. 25. *Herod,* Herod Antipas, Lk 3.1n.; 23.12. *Pontius Pilate,* see 3.13n. **28:** See 2.23n.; 3.18. **29:** *Look at their threats,* a prayer to be shielded from harm. **31:** *The place . . . was shaken,* meaning that the prayer was heard (cf. 16.25–26).

4.32–5.11: The sharing of goods. 4.32–35: The ideal handling of possessions in the early Jerusalem commu-

gave their testimony to the resurrection of the Lord Jesus, and great grace was upon them all. [34] There was not a needy person among them, for as many as owned lands or houses sold them and brought the proceeds of what was sold. [35] They laid it at the apostles' feet, and it was distributed to each as any had need. [36] There was a Levite, a native of Cyprus, Joseph, to whom the apostles gave the name Barnabas (which means "son of encouragement"). [37] He sold a field that belonged to him, then brought the money, and laid it at the apostles' feet.

5 But a man named Ananias, with the consent of his wife Sapphira, sold a piece of property; [2] with his wife's knowledge, he kept back some of the proceeds, and brought only a part and laid it at the apostles' feet. [3] "Ananias," Peter asked, "why has Satan filled your heart to lie to the Holy Spirit and to keep back part of the proceeds of the land? [4] While it remained unsold, did it not remain your own? And after it was sold, were not the proceeds at your disposal? How is it that you have contrived this deed in your heart? You did not lie to us[a] but to God!" [5] Now when Ananias heard these words, he fell down and died. And great fear seized all who heard of it. [6] The young men came and wrapped up his body,[b] then carried him out and buried him.

[7] After an interval of about three hours his wife came in, not knowing what had happened. [8] Peter said to her, "Tell me whether you and your husband sold the land for such and such a price." And she said, "Yes, that was the price." [9] Then Peter said to her, "How is it that you have agreed together to put the Spirit of the Lord to the test? Look, the feet of those who have buried your husband are at the door, and they will carry you out." [10] Immediately she fell down at his feet and died. When the young men came in they found her dead, so they carried her out and buried her beside her husband. [11] And great fear seized the whole church and all who heard of these things.

[12] Now many signs and wonders were done among the people through the apostles. And they were all together in Solomon's Portico. [13] None of the rest dared to join them, but the people held them in high esteem. [14] Yet more than ever believers were added to the Lord, great numbers of both men and women, [15] so that they even carried out the sick into the streets, and laid them on cots and mats, in order that Peter's shadow might fall on some of them as he came by. [16] A great number of people would also gather from the towns around Jerusalem, bringing the sick and those tormented by unclean spirits, and they were all cured.

[17] Then the high priest took action; he and all who were with him (that is, the sect of the Sadducees), being filled with jealousy, [18] arrested the apostles and put them in the public prison. [19] But during the night an angel of the Lord opened the prison doors, brought them out, and said, [20] "Go, stand in the temple and tell the people the whole message about this life." [21] When they heard this, they entered the temple at daybreak and went on with their teaching.

When the high priest and those with him arrived, they called together the council and

a Gk *to men*
b Meaning of Gk uncertain

nity (see 2.44–45n.). **36–37:** *Levite,* a member of the priestly tribe of Levi. *Barnabas,* who later appears as Paul's missionary companion in 13.1–14.28 (cf. 1 Cor 9.6), embodies the response of the ideal believer. **5.1–11:** The negative example of *Ananias* and *Sapphira.* Compare the story of Achan in Josh 7. **3:** *Satan,* Lk 22.3. The apostles, or perhaps the church, represent *the Holy Spirit;* cf. 9.4; 15.28. **4:** The property was at Ananias's *disposal* (although this contradicts 4.32,34) until he pretended to dedicate all his goods. **11:** *Church,* used here for the first time, designates the entire congregation of believers, which is still restricted to Jerusalem. Elsewhere it means either local communities in Jerusalem (8.1,3; 11.22; 12.5; 15.4,22; 18.22), Antioch (11.26; 13.1; 14.27; 15.3), Ephesus (20.17), and other places (14.23; 15.41; 16.5), or, occasionally, the universal body of all believers (20.28).

5.12–16: Signs and wonders. **12:** *Solomon's Portico,* see 3.11n. **13:** *None of the rest,* i.e., nonbelievers; the Christians now stand out as a clearly defined group. **16:** Compare Mk 1.32–34.

5.17–42: Second arrest of the apostles. The motif of obeying God rather than human beings is played out again before the council (cf. ch 4). **19:** *An angel . . . opened the prison doors,* see 12.6–11; cf. 16.25–26. **21:** *Body of*

the whole body of the elders of Israel, and sent to the prison to have them brought. [22] But when the temple police went there, they did not find them in the prison; so they returned and reported, [23] "We found the prison securely locked and the guards standing at the doors, but when we opened them, we found no one inside." [24] Now when the captain of the temple and the chief priests heard these words, they were perplexed about them, wondering what might be going on. [25] Then someone arrived and announced, "Look, the men whom you put in prison are standing in the temple and teaching the people!" [26] Then the captain went with the temple police and brought them, but without violence, for they were afraid of being stoned by the people.

[27] When they had brought them, they had them stand before the council. The high priest questioned them, [28] saying, "We gave you strict orders not to teach in this name,[a] yet here you have filled Jerusalem with your teaching and you are determined to bring this man's blood on us." [29] But Peter and the apostles answered, "We must obey God rather than any human authority.[b] [30] The God of our ancestors raised up Jesus, whom you had killed by hanging him on a tree. [31] God exalted him at his right hand as Leader and Savior that he might give repentance to Israel and forgiveness of sins. [32] And we are witnesses to these things, and so is the Holy Spirit whom God has given to those who obey him."

[33] When they heard this, they were enraged and wanted to kill them. [34] But a Pharisee in the council named Gamaliel, a teacher of the law, respected by all the people, stood up and ordered the men to be put outside for a short time. [35] Then he said to them, "Fellow Israelites,[c] consider carefully what you pro-

pose to do to these men. [36] For some time ago Theudas rose up, claiming to be somebody, and a number of men, about four hundred, joined him; but he was killed, and all who followed him were dispersed and disappeared. [37] After him Judas the Galilean rose up at the time of the census and got people to follow him; he also perished, and all who followed him were scattered. [38] So in the present case, I tell you, keep away from these men and let them alone; because if this plan or this undertaking is of human origin, it will fail; [39] but if it is of God, you will not be able to overthrow them—in that case you may even be found fighting against God!"

They were convinced by him, [40] and when they had called in the apostles, they had them flogged. Then they ordered them not to speak in the name of Jesus, and let them go. [41] As they left the council, they rejoiced that they were considered worthy to suffer dishonor for the sake of the name. [42] And every day in the temple and at home[d] they did not cease to teach and proclaim Jesus as the Messiah.[e]

6 Now during those days, when the disciples were increasing in number, the Hellenists complained against the Hebrews because their widows were being neglected in the daily distribution of food. [2] And the twelve called together the whole community of the disciples and said, "It is not right that we should neglect the word of God in order

---

a   Other ancient authorities read *Did we not give you strict orders not to teach in this name?*

b   Gk *than men*

c   Gk *Men, Israelites*

d   Or *from house to house*

e   Or *the Christ*

---

the elders, another word for *council* or Sanhedrin. **29:** See 4.19n. **30:** The reference to the *tree* (cross; 10.39; 13.29) recalls Deut 21.22–23, but it is not developed; cf. Gal 3.13. **31:** A concise summary of the theology of Acts. *Leader,* the same Gk word is translated "Author" in 3.15. *Savior,* a term widely used in the Hellenistic world (e.g., 11.19n.). **34:** *A Pharisee* (see 15.5n.), the famous Rabban *Gamaliel,* the Elder, later identified as Paul's teacher (22.3). **36–37:** The historical order of the figures referred to is reversed. *Theudas,* according to Josephus (*Ant.* 20.97–98), raised his revolt (ca. 44–46 CE) some years after Gamaliel's speech. *Judas the Galilean,* a revolutionary leader who in 6 or 7 CE opposed the imposition of new taxes following *the census* of Quirinius (Lk 2.2). **40:** *Had them flogged,* to reinforce the warning.

6.1–7: Choice of the seven. The seven are identified as the first deacons by later tradition but hold no ecclesiastical office here. **1:** *The Hellenists,* Greek-speaking Jewish Christians; the *Hebrews,* Aramaic-speaking Jewish

to wait on tables.[a] [3] Therefore, friends,[b] select from among yourselves seven men of good standing, full of the Spirit and of wisdom, whom we may appoint to this task, [4] while we, for our part, will devote ourselves to prayer and to serving the word." [5] What they said pleased the whole community, and they chose Stephen, a man full of faith and the Holy Spirit, together with Philip, Prochorus, Nicanor, Timon, Parmenas, and Nicolaus, a proselyte of Antioch. [6] They had these men stand before the apostles, who prayed and laid their hands on them.

[7] The word of God continued to spread; the number of the disciples increased greatly in Jerusalem, and a great many of the priests became obedient to the faith.

[8] Stephen, full of grace and power, did great wonders and signs among the people. [9] Then some of those who belonged to the synagogue of the Freedmen (as it was called), Cyrenians, Alexandrians, and others of those from Cilicia and Asia, stood up and argued with Stephen. [10] But they could not withstand the wisdom and the Spirit[c] with which he spoke. [11] Then they secretly instigated some men to say, "We have heard him speak blasphemous words against Moses and God." [12] They stirred up the people as well as the elders and the scribes; then they suddenly confronted him, seized him, and brought him before the council. [13] They set up false witnesses who said, "This man never stops saying things against this holy place and the law; [14] for we have heard him say that this Jesus of Nazareth[d] will

destroy this place and will change the customs that Moses handed on to us." [15] And all who sat in the council looked intently at him, and they saw that his face was like the face of an angel.

7 Then the high priest asked him, "Are these things so?" [2] And Stephen replied: "Brothers[e] and fathers, listen to me. The God of glory appeared to our ancestor Abraham when he was in Mesopotamia, before he lived in Haran, [3] and said to him, 'Leave your country and your relatives and go to the land that I will show you.' [4] Then he left the country of the Chaldeans and settled in Haran. After his father died, God had him move from there to this country in which you are now living. [5] He did not give him any of it as a heritage, not even a foot's length, but promised to give it to him as his possession and to his descendants after him, even though he had no child. [6] And God spoke in these terms, that his descendants would be resident aliens in a country belonging to others, who would enslave them and mistreat them during four hundred years. [7] 'But I will judge the nation that they serve,' said God, 'and after that they shall come out and worship me in this place.' [8] Then he gave him the covenant of circumcision. And so Abraham[f] became the father of

a   Or *keep accounts*
b   Gk *brothers*
c   Or *spirit*
d   Gk *the Nazorean*
e   Gk *Men, brothers*
f   Gk *he*

Christians. **2:** *The twelve* is used to designate the apostles only here in Acts. *To wait on tables,* i.e., to feed the hungry. **5:** *Stephen, Philip,* and the other names are Greek. *Proselyte,* a Gentile convert to Judaism, implying that the others were born Jews. **6:** *Laid . . . hands,* a ritual of consecration and appointment; see Num 8.10; 27.23; 1 Tim 4.14; 2 Tim 1.6 (13.3). **7:** Not all *priests* are hostile. Acts throughout reports the partial success of the Christian movement among Jews (21.20n.; 28.24).

6.8–8.1a: Preaching and martyrdom of Stephen. Elements of Stephen's trial and death reflect the passion of Jesus. **6.8:** Stephen does *wonders and signs* like the apostles (2.43; 4.30; 5.12). **9:** Diaspora Jews *argued with Stephen. Freedmen,* former slaves, either Jews or proselytes; an inscription found in Jerusalem possibly refers to this *synagogue. Cyrenians,* from Cyrene in northern Africa (see 11.20n.). *Cilicia,* the southeastern portion of Asia Minor where Paul was from (21.39; 22.3; 23.34). *Asia,* the Roman province of that name in western Asia Minor. **10:** A fulfillment of Jesus' prediction in Lk 21.15. **13:** *False witnesses,* cf. Mk 14.55–57. **14:** *Jesus . . . will destroy this place,* Mk 14.58; Lk 21.6; Jn 2.19. The *change* in *customs* reported by Mk 7.15,19 is not recorded in Lk. These charges had not been made in the earlier examinations of the apostles. **7.2–50:** Stephen's speech contains some thirty citations from the Greek version of the Hebrew Bible (the Septuagint), which was the Bible of the early Christians. Accordingly, Stephen makes reference to *Abraham* (v. 2), *Joseph* (v. 9), *Moses* (v. 20), and others (cf. 13.16–24; Heb 11.4–40). **3:** Gen 12.1; according to Gen 11.31 Abraham was already in Haran (against v. 2). **5:** Gen 12.7; 13.15;

Isaac and circumcised him on the eighth day; and Isaac became the father of Jacob, and Jacob of the twelve patriarchs.

9 "The patriarchs, jealous of Joseph, sold him into Egypt; but God was with him, 10 and rescued him from all his afflictions, and enabled him to win favor and to show wisdom when he stood before Pharaoh, king of Egypt, who appointed him ruler over Egypt and over all his household. 11 Now there came a famine throughout Egypt and Canaan, and great suffering, and our ancestors could find no food. 12 But when Jacob heard that there was grain in Egypt, he sent our ancestors there on their first visit. 13 On the second visit Joseph made himself known to his brothers, and Joseph's family became known to Pharaoh. 14 Then Joseph sent and invited his father Jacob and all his relatives to come to him, seventy-five in all; 15 so Jacob went down to Egypt. He himself died there as well as our ancestors, 16 and their bodies[a] were brought back to Shechem and laid in the tomb that Abraham had bought for a sum of silver from the sons of Hamor in Shechem.

17 "But as the time drew near for the fulfillment of the promise that God had made to Abraham, our people in Egypt increased and multiplied 18 until another king who had not known Joseph ruled over Egypt. 19 He dealt craftily with our race and forced our ancestors to abandon their infants so that they would die. 20 At this time Moses was born, and he was beautiful before God. For three months he was brought up in his father's house; 21 and when he was abandoned, Pharaoh's daughter adopted him and brought him up as her own son. 22 So Moses was instructed in all the wisdom of the Egyptians and was powerful in his words and deeds.

23 "When he was forty years old, it came into his heart to visit his relatives, the Israelites.[b] 24 When he saw one of them being wronged, he defended the oppressed man and avenged him by striking down the Egyp-

tian. 25 He supposed that his kinsfolk would understand that God through him was rescuing them, but they did not understand. 26 The next day he came to some of them as they were quarreling and tried to reconcile them, saying, 'Men, you are brothers; why do you wrong each other?' 27 But the man who was wronging his neighbor pushed Moses[c] aside, saying, 'Who made you a ruler and a judge over us? 28 Do you want to kill me as you killed the Egyptian yesterday?' 29 When he heard this, Moses fled and became a resident alien in the land of Midian. There he became the father of two sons.

30 "Now when forty years had passed, an angel appeared to him in the wilderness of Mount Sinai, in the flame of a burning bush. 31 When Moses saw it, he was amazed at the sight; and as he approached to look, there came the voice of the Lord: 32 'I am the God of your ancestors, the God of Abraham, Isaac, and Jacob.' Moses began to tremble and did not dare to look. 33 Then the Lord said to him, 'Take off the sandals from your feet, for the place where you are standing is holy ground. 34 I have surely seen the mistreatment of my people who are in Egypt and have heard their groaning, and I have come down to rescue them. Come now, I will send you to Egypt.'

35 "It was this Moses whom they rejected when they said, 'Who made you a ruler and a judge?' and whom God now sent as both ruler and liberator through the angel who appeared to him in the bush. 36 He led them out, having performed wonders and signs in Egypt, at the Red Sea, and in the wilderness for forty years. 37 This is the Moses who said to the Israelites, 'God will raise up a prophet for you from your own people[d] as he raised me up.' 38 He is the one who was in the

a Gk they
b Gk his brothers, the sons of Israel
c Gk him
d Gk your brothers

17.8; 48.4. 6–7: Four hundred years, see Gen 15.13–14; cf. Ex 12.40. 8: Gen 17.10–13. 9: Gen 37. 10–16: Gen 39–50. 14: Seventy-five, according to the Septuagint of Gen 46.27; Ex 1.5. 16: Shechem, but according to Gen 50.13 Jacob was buried at Hebron. Abraham, but according to Gen 33.19 and Josh 24.32 it was Jacob who bought the tomb at Shechem. 17–19: Ex 1–2. 20–22: Ex 2.1–10. 20: The importance of Moses is stressed by the amount of space devoted to him in the following verses. 23–29: Ex 2.11–22. 29: Midian, northwestern Arabia, on the east coast of the Gulf of Aqaba (Eilat). 30–34: Ex 3.1–10. 30: In Ex 3.1 the mountain is Horeb, not Sinai. 35: Ex 2.14. 37: A

congregation in the wilderness with the angel who spoke to him at Mount Sinai, and with our ancestors; and he received living oracles to give to us. ³⁹ Our ancestors were unwilling to obey him; instead, they pushed him aside, and in their hearts they turned back to Egypt, ⁴⁰ saying to Aaron, 'Make gods for us who will lead the way for us; as for this Moses who led us out from the land of Egypt, we do not know what has happened to him.' ⁴¹ At that time they made a calf, offered a sacrifice to the idol, and reveled in the works of their hands. ⁴² But God turned away from them and handed them over to worship the host of heaven, as it is written in the book of the prophets:

'Did you offer to me slain victims and sacrifices
     forty years in the wilderness, O house
          of Israel?
⁴³ No; you took along the tent of Moloch,
     and the star of your god Rephan,
          the images that you made to
               worship;
so I will remove you beyond Babylon.'

⁴⁴ "Our ancestors had the tent of testimony in the wilderness, as God[a] directed when he spoke to Moses, ordering him to make it according to the pattern he had seen. ⁴⁵ Our ancestors in turn brought it in with Joshua when they dispossessed the nations that God drove out before our ancestors. And it was there until the time of David, ⁴⁶ who found favor with God and asked that he might find a dwelling place for the house of Jacob.[b] ⁴⁷ But it was Solomon who built a house for him. ⁴⁸ Yet the Most High does not dwell in houses made with human hands;[c] as the prophet says,

⁴⁹ 'Heaven is my throne,
     and the earth is my footstool.
What kind of house will you build for me,
     says the Lord,
          or what is the place of my rest?
⁵⁰ Did not my hand make all these
          things?'

⁵¹ "You stiff-necked people, uncircumcised in heart and ears, you are forever opposing the Holy Spirit, just as your ancestors used to do. ⁵² Which of the prophets did your ancestors not persecute? They killed those who foretold the coming of the Righteous One, and now you have become his betrayers and murderers. ⁵³ You are the ones that received the law as ordained by angels, and yet you have not kept it."

⁵⁴ When they heard these things, they became enraged and ground their teeth at Stephen.[d] ⁵⁵ But filled with the Holy Spirit, he gazed into heaven and saw the glory of God and Jesus standing at the right hand of God. ⁵⁶ "Look," he said, "I see the heavens opened and the Son of Man standing at the right hand of God!" ⁵⁷ But they covered their ears, and with a loud shout all rushed together against him. ⁵⁸ Then they dragged him out of the city and began to stone him; and the witnesses laid their coats at the feet of a young man named Saul. ⁵⁹ While they were stoning Stephen, he prayed, "Lord Jesus, receive my spirit." ⁶⁰ Then he knelt down and cried out in a loud voice, "Lord,

a Gk *he*
b Other ancient authorities read *for the God of Jacob*
c Gk *with hands*
d Gk *him*

prophet, Deut 18.15; see 3.22. **38:** In the Hebrew Bible God, not an *angel,* speaks to Moses and gives him the law (*living oracles*); cf. v. 53. **40:** Ex 32.1. **42–43:** Am 5.25–27 is quoted to support the charge of idolatry raised in vv. 40–42. The *book of the* (twelve minor) *prophets* (Hosea through Malachi) was thought of as a unit. **42:** *The host of heaven,* the stars (2 Kings 17.16), which are associated with various supernatural beings. **43:** *Moloch,* a deity to whom children were offered as sacrifices (Jer 32.35). *Rephan,* an astral deity (Saturn). **44:** *The tent of testimony,* the tabernacle (Ex 27.21), is brought forward in the following verses as preferable to the Temple; compare the "true tent" of Heb 8.1–5. **45:** Josh 3.7–4.18. **46:** Ps 132.5; cf. 2 Sam 7.1–2. **47:** 1 Kings 6. **48:** Since *made with human hands* is language associated with idolatry in the Hebrew Bible (see Ps 115.4; Isa 2.8), its application to the Temple would be offensive to a Jewish audience. Cf. 17.24–25. **49–50:** Isa 66.1–2. **51:** *Stiff-necked people, uncircumcised in heart and ears,* see Ex 33.3,5; Lev 26.41; Jer 9.26; cf. Rom 2.29. **52:** The question is hyperbolic but recalls Lk 11.47–48. **53:** *The law,* being *ordained by angels* (cf. v. 38) is considered valid (Heb 2.2); but Paul used this Jewish tradition to argue that the law is secondary (Gal 3.19). **54–58a:** Here Stephen is described as the victim of a lynching. **55–56:** Lk 22.69. *Son of Man* in the Gospels often denotes Jesus as the glorified heavenly judge;

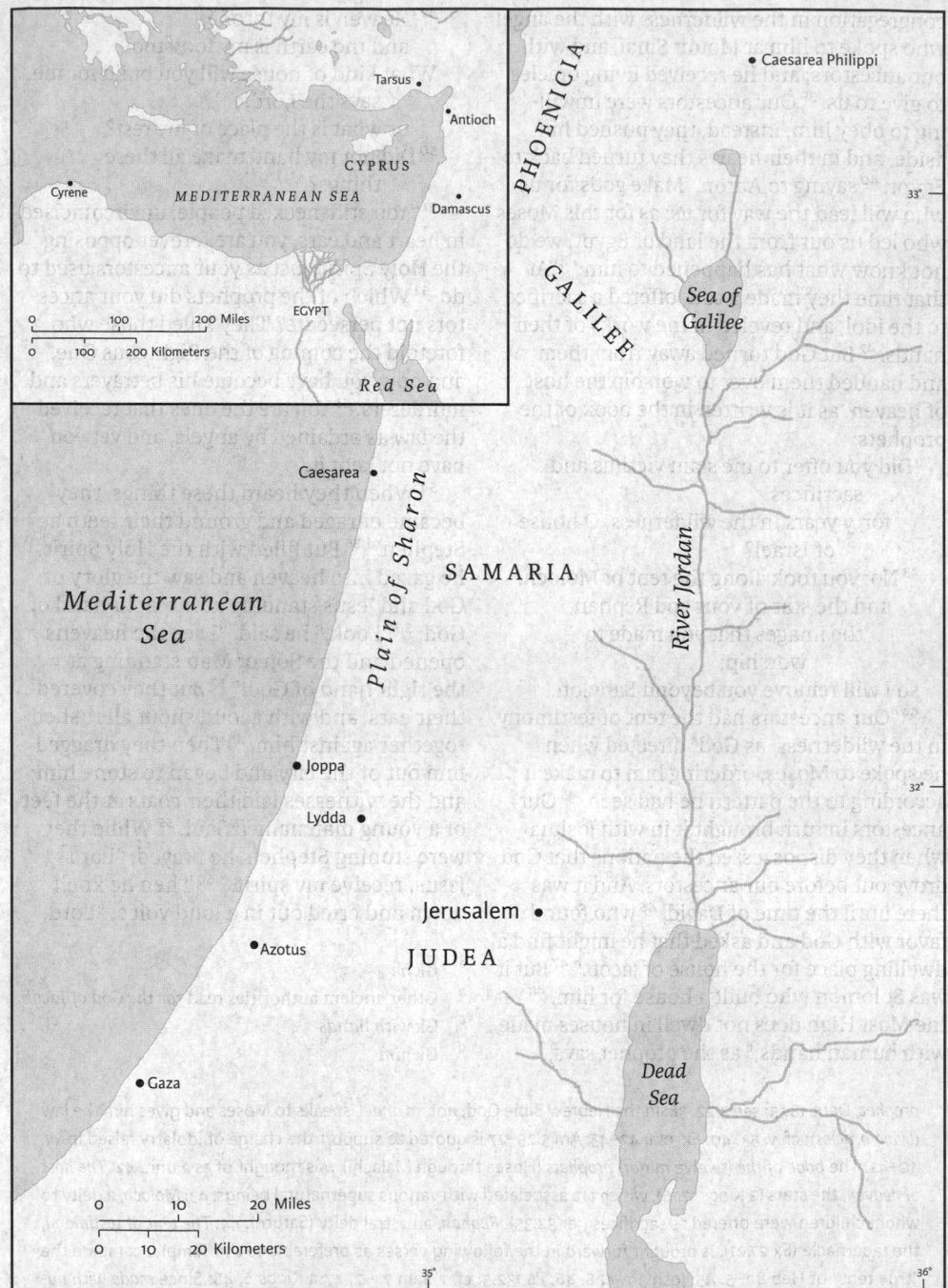

Chs 8–11: Sites of early Christian missionary activities.

do not hold this sin against them." When he had said this, he died.[a] 1 And Saul approved of their killing him.

8 That day a severe persecution began against the church in Jerusalem, and all except the apostles were scattered throughout the countryside of Judea and Samaria. 2 Devout men buried Stephen and made loud lamentation over him. 3 But Saul was ravaging the church by entering house after house; dragging off both men and women, he committed them to prison.

4 Now those who were scattered went from place to place, proclaiming the word. 5 Philip went down to the city[b] of Samaria and proclaimed the Messiah[c] to them. 6 The crowds with one accord listened eagerly to what was said by Philip, hearing and seeing the signs that he did, 7 for unclean spirits, crying with loud shrieks, came out of many who were possessed; and many others who were paralyzed or lame were cured. 8 So there was great joy in that city.

9 Now a certain man named Simon had previously practiced magic in the city and amazed the people of Samaria, saying that he was someone great. 10 All of them, from the least to the greatest, listened to him eagerly, saying, "This man is the power of God that is called Great." 11 And they listened eagerly to him because for a long time he had amazed them with his magic. 12 But when they believed Philip, who was proclaiming the good news about the kingdom of God and the name of Jesus Christ, they were baptized, both men and women. 13 Even Simon himself believed. After being baptized, he stayed constantly with Philip and was amazed when he saw the signs and great miracles that took place.

14 Now when the apostles at Jerusalem heard that Samaria had accepted the word of God, they sent Peter and John to them. 15 The two went down and prayed for them that they might receive the Holy Spirit 16 (for as yet the Spirit had not come[d] upon any of them; they had only been baptized in the name of the Lord Jesus). 17 Then Peter and John[e] laid their hands on them, and they received the Holy Spirit. 18 Now when Simon saw that the Spirit was given through the laying on of the apostles' hands, he offered them money, 19 saying, "Give me also this power so that anyone on whom I lay my hands may receive the Holy Spirit." 20 But Peter said to him, "May your silver perish with you, because you thought you could obtain God's gift with money! 21 You have no part or share in this, for your heart is not right before God. 22 Repent therefore of this wickedness of yours, and pray to the Lord that, if possible, the intent of your heart may be forgiven you. 23 For I see that you are in the gall of bitterness and the chains of wickedness." 24 Simon answered, "Pray for me

a   Gk *fell asleep*
b   Other ancient authorities read *a city*
c   Or *the Christ*
d   Gk *fallen*
e   Gk *they*

elsewhere in the New Testament the term is found only here and in Rev 1.13; 14.14. **58b–8.1:** The presence of *witnesses*, who were legally required to cast the first stones at the offender (Deut 17.7), suggests not a lynching but a judicial execution. **58b:** *Saul*, Luke's dramatic introduction of Paul. His presence may have been suggested by 1 Cor 15.9 and Gal 1.13 but is not confirmed by these references. **59:** Lk 23.46. **60:** See Lk 23.34n.

8.1b–40: Spread of the gospel to Samaria and beyond. Christianity now reaches non-Jewish regions. **1:** *Except the apostles*, although unrealistic, it is important for Luke that the apostles remain in *Jerusalem*. *Samaria*, between Galilee to the north and Judea to the south, was inhabited by remnants of the northern tribes who worshiped the Lord God and used the Pentateuch. Jews despised them (2 Kings 17.24–41; cf. Mt 10.5). **3:** *Saul was ravaging the church*, 9.1–2; cf. Gal 1.13. **4:** Ironically, severe persecution leads to *proclaiming the word* in new places. **5:** *Philip*, one of the seven mentioned in 6.5, is now active as an evangelist (21.8). All second-century references to this individual consider him to be one of the twelve apostles, but according to the idealized account of Acts the apostles remain in Jerusalem during this period. **9:** Acts displays great interest in distinguishing between *magic* and Christian signs (see 13.6–12; 19.13–20). **12:** Philip breaks religious barriers and fulfills the expectations about Samaritans generated by Luke's Gospel (Lk 10.30–37; 17.11–19) and the promise of 1.8. **14:** *Jerusalem* is represented as coordinating the ever-growing church (see 11.1,22). **16–17:** *Spirit had not come*, see 2.38. *Laid . . . hands*, see 6.6n. **18–24:** The medieval term "simony" (buying church offices) is derived from

to the Lord, that nothing of what you[a] have said may happen to me."

25 Now after Peter and John[b] had testified and spoken the word of the Lord, they returned to Jerusalem, proclaiming the good news to many villages of the Samaritans.

26 Then an angel of the Lord said to Philip, "Get up and go toward the south[c] to the road that goes down from Jerusalem to Gaza." (This is a wilderness road.) 27 So he got up and went. Now there was an Ethiopian eunuch, a court official of the Candace, queen of the Ethiopians, in charge of her entire treasury. He had come to Jerusalem to worship 28 and was returning home; seated in his chariot, he was reading the prophet Isaiah. 29 Then the Spirit said to Philip, "Go over to this chariot and join it." 30 So Philip ran up to it and heard him reading the prophet Isaiah. He asked, "Do you understand what you are reading?" 31 He replied, "How can I, unless someone guides me?" And he invited Philip to get in and sit beside him. 32 Now the passage of the scripture that he was reading was this:

"Like a sheep he was led to the slaughter,
    and like a lamb silent before its shearer,
        so he does not open his mouth.
33 In his humiliation justice was denied him.
    Who can describe his generation?
        For his life is taken away from the
            earth."

34 The eunuch asked Philip, "About whom, may I ask you, does the prophet say this, about himself or about someone else?" 35 Then Philip began to speak, and starting with this scripture, he proclaimed to him the good news about Jesus. 36 As they were going along the road, they came to some water; and the eunuch said, "Look, here is water! What is to prevent me from being baptized?"[d] 38 He commanded the chariot to stop, and both of them, Philip and the eunuch, went down into the water, and Philip[e] baptized him. 39 When they came up out of the water, the Spirit of the Lord snatched Philip away; the eunuch saw him no more, and went on his way rejoicing. 40 But Philip found himself at Azotus, and as he was passing through the region, he proclaimed the good news to all the towns until he came to Caesarea.

9 Meanwhile Saul, still breathing threats and murder against the disciples of the Lord, went to the high priest 2 and asked him for letters to the synagogues at Damascus, so that if he found any who belonged to the Way, men or women, he might bring them bound to Jerusalem. 3 Now as he was going along and approaching Damascus, suddenly a light from heaven flashed around him. 4 He fell to the ground and heard a voice saying to him, "Saul, Saul, why

a   The Greek word for *you* and the verb *pray* are plural
b   Gk *after they*
c   Or *go at noon*
d   Other ancient authorities add all or most of verse 37, *And Philip said, "If you believe with all your heart, you may." And he replied, "I believe that Jesus Christ is the Son of God."*
e   Gk *he*

this account. **27:** *An Ethiopian*, see Ps 68.31; Zeph 3.10. *The Candace* was the title of the *queen of the Ethiopians*. Although *he had come to Jerusalem to worship*, a *eunuch* could not have become a proselyte (Deut 23.1). The passage may envisage fulfillment of Isa 56.3–5. **28:** *He was reading* aloud to himself (as was customary in antiquity); hence Philip *heard him* (v. 30). **32–33:** Isa 53.7–8; see Acts 3.13n. **35:** Cf. Lk 24.27. **38:** As in the case of the Samaritans, the baptism of an Ethiopian eunuch breaks social and ritual barriers (v. 12n.). Since in the ancient Mediterranean world Ethiopia was often considered to be located at the "ends of the earth" (e.g., Homer, *Od.* 1.22–23; Herodotus 3.25), this conversion fulfills the prediction of 1.8. **39:** *The Spirit of the Lord snatched Philip away*, cf. 1 Kings 18.12; 2 Kings 2.16. **40:** *Philip*'s evangelizing journey proceeds along the Mediterranean coast from Gaza (v. 26) through *Azotus* (ancient Ashdod, ca. 23 mi [37 km] north-northeast of Gaza) to *Caesarea* (ca. 55 mi [90 km] farther north). Caesarea was an important seaport and the headquarters of the Roman governor; see 10.1; 21.8.

9.1–19a: The conversion and call of Saul of Tarsus. Slightly different versions are found in 22.4–16; 26.9–18; Paul's own account is in Gal 1.13–17; see 1 Cor 15.8. Key narratives in Acts are stressed by repetition. **1–2:** Acts connects Paul with Jerusalem (7.58; 9.13,26), although Paul claimed he was unknown by sight in Judea (Gal 1.22–23). **2:** *The Way* stands for Christianity (18.25; 19.9,23; 22.4; 24.14,22), but its origin is uncertain. The closest parallels can be found in the Dead Sea Scrolls; cf. Isa 40.3. **3–9:** The passage incorporates various features of theophanies (e.g., 2 Macc 3; Acts 2.2n.) and stories of the call of prophets (e.g., Isa 6.1–13). **4–5:** In persecuting

do you persecute me?" [5] He asked, "Who are you, Lord?" The reply came, "I am Jesus, whom you are persecuting. [6] But get up and enter the city, and you will be told what you are to do." [7] The men who were traveling with him stood speechless because they heard the voice but saw no one. [8] Saul got up from the ground, and though his eyes were open, he could see nothing; so they led him by the hand and brought him into Damascus. [9] For three days he was without sight, and neither ate nor drank.

[10] Now there was a disciple in Damascus named Ananias. The Lord said to him in a vision, "Ananias." He answered, "Here I am, Lord." [11] The Lord said to him, "Get up and go to the street called Straight, and at the house of Judas look for a man of Tarsus named Saul. At this moment he is praying, [12] and he has seen in a vision[a] a man named Ananias come in and lay his hands on him so that he might regain his sight." [13] But Ananias answered, "Lord, I have heard from many about this man, how much evil he has done to your saints in Jerusalem; [14] and here he has authority from the chief priests to bind all who invoke your name." [15] But the Lord said to him, "Go, for he is an instrument whom I have chosen to bring my name before Gentiles and kings and before the people of Israel; [16] I myself will show him how much he must suffer for the sake of my name." [17] So Ananias went and entered the house. He laid his hands on Saul[b] and said, "Brother Saul, the Lord Jesus, who appeared to you on your way here, has sent me so that you may regain your sight and be filled with the Holy Spirit." [18] And immediately something like scales fell from his eyes, and his sight was restored. Then he got up and was baptized, [19] and after taking some food, he regained his strength.

For several days he was with the disciples in Damascus, [20] and immediately he began to proclaim Jesus in the synagogues, saying, "He is the Son of God." [21] All who heard him were amazed and said, "Is not this the man who made havoc in Jerusalem among those who invoked this name? And has he not come here for the purpose of bringing them bound before the chief priests?" [22] Saul became increasingly more powerful and confounded the Jews who lived in Damascus by proving that Jesus[c] was the Messiah.[d]

[23] After some time had passed, the Jews plotted to kill him, [24] but their plot became known to Saul. They were watching the gates day and night so that they might kill him; [25] but his disciples took him by night and let him down through an opening in the wall,[e] lowering him in a basket.

[26] When he had come to Jerusalem, he attempted to join the disciples; and they were all afraid of him, for they did not believe that he was a disciple. [27] But Barnabas took him, brought him to the apostles, and described for them how on the road he had seen the Lord, who had spoken to him, and how in Damascus he had spoken boldly in the name of Jesus. [28] So he went in and out among them in Jerusalem, speaking boldly in the name of the Lord. [29] He spoke and argued with the

[a] Other ancient authorities lack *in a vision*
[b] Gk *him*
[c] Gk *that this*
[d] Or *the Christ*
[e] Gk *through the wall*

the disciples, he persecuted *Jesus* (cf. Mt 25.40). **10:** *Ananias*, evidently one of the leaders of the believers at *Damascus* (see 22.12). Acts does not record how or when Christians first arrived in Damascus. **11:** *The street called Straight*, commonly identified as Darbel-Mostakim, an east-to-west street in the Old City of Damascus. *Tarsus*, see v. 30n. **13:** *Saints*, holy ones, i.e., Christians as sanctified by their faith (see 26.18). **15:** Saul, like the prophets, was chosen for a special purpose (Jer 1.5; Gal 1.15). **17:** *Laid his hands*, see 6.6n.

9.19b–31: Saul's preaching in Damascus and first visit to Jerusalem. 20: *Immediately he began to proclaim Jesus in the synagogues,* this will be the consistent pattern followed by Paul in Acts; according to Paul himself, he went immediately to Arabia (Gal 1.17). *Son of God* occurs only here in Acts; cf. Gal 1.15–16. **24–25:** In 2 Cor 11.32–33 Paul flees the governor of Damascus appointed by Aretas IV, king of the Nabateans. **26:** See vv. 1–2n. In Gal 1.18 Paul states that his first visit to Jerusalem was three years after his conversion. Luke associates Paul with Jerusalem from the beginning. **27–28:** *Barnabas* (see 4.36–37) intercedes with the *apostles* on Paul's behalf. Paul himself (Gal 1.18–19) claimed only to have seen Peter and James, the Lord's brother (not considered an apostle in Acts). **29:** Paul, from the Diaspora himself, contends with the *Hellenists,* namely, Stephen's Greek-speaking,

Hellenists; but they were attempting to kill him. [30] When the believers[a] learned of it, they brought him down to Caesarea and sent him off to Tarsus.

[31] Meanwhile the church throughout Judea, Galilee, and Samaria had peace and was built up. Living in the fear of the Lord and in the comfort of the Holy Spirit, it increased in numbers.

[32] Now as Peter went here and there among all the believers,[b] he came down also to the saints living in Lydda. [33] There he found a man named Aeneas, who had been bedridden for eight years, for he was paralyzed. [34] Peter said to him, "Aeneas, Jesus Christ heals you; get up and make your bed!" And immediately he got up. [35] And all the residents of Lydda and Sharon saw him and turned to the Lord.

[36] Now in Joppa there was a disciple whose name was Tabitha, which in Greek is Dorcas.[c] She was devoted to good works and acts of charity. [37] At that time she became ill and died. When they had washed her, they laid her in a room upstairs. [38] Since Lydda was near Joppa, the disciples, who heard that Peter was there, sent two men to him with the request, "Please come to us without delay." [39] So Peter got up and went with them; and when he arrived, they took him to the room upstairs. All the widows stood beside him,

weeping and showing tunics and other clothing that Dorcas had made while she was with them. [40] Peter put all of them outside, and then he knelt down and prayed. He turned to the body and said, "Tabitha, get up." Then she opened her eyes, and seeing Peter, she sat up. [41] He gave her his hand and helped her up. Then calling the saints and widows, he showed her to be alive. [42] This became known throughout Joppa, and many believed in the Lord. [43] Meanwhile he stayed in Joppa for some time with a certain Simon, a tanner.

10

In Caesarea there was a man named Cornelius, a centurion of the Italian Cohort, as it was called. [2] He was a devout man who feared God with all his household; he gave alms generously to the people and prayed constantly to God. [3] One afternoon at about three o'clock he had a vision in which he clearly saw an angel of God coming in and saying to him, "Cornelius." [4] He stared at him in terror and said, "What is it, Lord?" He answered, "Your prayers and your alms have ascended as a memorial before God. [5] Now send men to Joppa for a certain Simon who is called Peter; [6] he is lodging with Simon, a tanner, whose

a Gk *brothers*
b Gk *all of them*
c The name Tabitha in Aramaic and the name Dorcas in Greek mean *a gazelle*

Jewish opponents (6.9–14). **30:** *Tarsus,* Paul's home city according to 21.39 (see 11.25; cf. Gal 1.21), was in Cilicia on the southern coast of Asia Minor. **31:** The familiar note of growth. The persecution of 8.1 has apparently passed. Here *church* moves beyond its usual meaning of a local community (see 5.11n.) to believers spread over a larger geographical area.

9.32–43: Peter in Lydda and Joppa. 32: *Lydda,* northwest of Jerusalem between Azotus and Caesarea (see 8.40n.), about 11 mi (17 km) southeast of Joppa (v. 36). There are already *believers* in both places, perhaps the result of Philip's activity (8.40). **34:** Lk 5.24–25. **35:** *Sharon,* the coastal plain between Joppa and Caesarea. **36–42:** Cf. Lk 8.41–42,49–56 (Mk 5.22–24,35–43); 2 Kings 4.33. **36:** *Joppa,* modern Jaffa, on the coast in the Plain of Sharon, ca. 30 mi (50 km) south of Caesarea. **39:** *Widows,* see 6.1; 1 Tim 5.3–16. **43:** Peter's lodging with *a tanner,* who would be ritually unclean, may suggest preparation for his encounter with Cornelius.

10.1–48: The conversion of Cornelius. This key narrative in which the inclusion of Gentiles is directed by God is essentially repeated in 11.1–18 and referred to in significant terms at 15.7–9. Luke ascribes to Peter the honor of converting the first Gentile; but recall the Ethiopian (8.26–39) and see 11.19–21. **1:** *Caesarea,* see 8.40n. *A centurion,* an officer in the Roman army. Luke may want to show that Roman citizenship was compatible with Christianity (13.7n.; 16.37–38n.; 18.14–15n.; 22.25–29n.; 23.27–30n.; 25.8n.). On "friendly" centurions, see 27.3,43. **2:** Cornelius was *devout* and *feared God,* i.e., worshiped him (see v. 22); although he had not adopted the Jewish religion (i.e., undergone circumcision), he practiced the characteristic acts of Jewish piety: almsgiving and prayer. The similar profile of the centurion in Lk 7.1–10 shows that Luke is particularly interested in Gentiles who practice Jewish piety (v. 35). **3:** *About three o'clock,* the time of afternoon prayer (3.1). Angels often appear in Acts in service of the divine will. **7:** *A devout soldier,* suggests that those with Cornelius shared his piety (see

house is by the seaside." [7] When the angel who spoke to him had left, he called two of his slaves and a devout soldier from the ranks of those who served him, [8] and after telling them everything, he sent them to Joppa.

[9] About noon the next day, as they were on their journey and approaching the city, Peter went up on the roof to pray. [10] He became hungry and wanted something to eat; and while it was being prepared, he fell into a trance. [11] He saw the heaven opened and something like a large sheet coming down, being lowered to the ground by its four corners. [12] In it were all kinds of four-footed creatures and reptiles and birds of the air. [13] Then he heard a voice saying, "Get up, Peter; kill and eat." [14] But Peter said, "By no means, Lord; for I have never eaten anything that is profane or unclean." [15] The voice said to him again, a second time, "What God has made clean, you must not call profane." [16] This happened three times, and the thing was suddenly taken up to heaven.

[17] Now while Peter was greatly puzzled about what to make of the vision that he had seen, suddenly the men sent by Cornelius appeared. They were asking for Simon's house and were standing by the gate. [18] They called out to ask whether Simon, who was called Peter, was staying there. [19] While Peter was still thinking about the vision, the Spirit said to him, "Look, three[a] men are searching for you. [20] Now get up, go down, and go with them without hesitation; for I have sent them." [21] So Peter went down to the men and said, "I am the one you are looking for; what is the reason for your coming?" [22] They answered, "Cornelius, a centurion, an upright and God-fearing man, who is well spoken of by the whole Jewish nation, was directed by a holy angel to send for you to come to his house and to hear what you have to say." [23] So Peter[b] invited them in and gave them lodging.

The next day he got up and went with them, and some of the believers[c] from Joppa accompanied him. [24] The following day they came to Caesarea. Cornelius was expecting them and had called together his relatives and close friends. [25] On Peter's arrival Cornelius met him, and falling at his feet, worshiped him. [26] But Peter made him get up, saying, "Stand up; I am only a mortal." [27] And as he talked with him, he went in and found that many had assembled; [28] and he said to them, "You yourselves know that it is unlawful for a Jew to associate with or to visit a Gentile; but God has shown me that I should not call anyone profane or unclean. [29] So when I was sent for, I came without objection. Now may I ask why you sent for me?"

[30] Cornelius replied, "Four days ago at this very hour, at three o'clock, I was praying in my house when suddenly a man in dazzling clothes stood before me. [31] He said, 'Cornelius, your prayer has been heard and your alms have been remembered before God. [32] Send therefore to Joppa and ask for Simon, who is called Peter; he is staying in the home of Simon, a tanner, by the sea.' [33] Therefore I sent for you immediately, and you have been kind enough to come. So now all of us are here in the presence of God to listen to all that the Lord has commanded you to say."

[34] Then Peter began to speak to them: "I truly understand that God shows no partiality, [35] but in every nation anyone who fears him and does what is right is acceptable to him. [36] You know the message he sent to the people of Israel, preaching peace by Jesus Christ—he is Lord of all. [37] That message spread throughout Judea, beginning in Gali-

---

a   One ancient authority reads *two*; others lack the word
b   Gk *he*
c   Gk *brothers*

16.15n.,33). **9:** *Noon,* the usual Roman time for luncheon. **14:** *Profane,* only some animals might be eaten (Lev 11). **15:** In Mk 7.14–19 Jesus declared all foods clean, but this statement is not included in Luke's Gospel and Peter seems unaware of it. Some conditions regarding food will still apply at 15.20,29. **16:** *Three times,* for emphasis and warning. **19–20:** The *Spirit*'s message obliquely refers to Cornelius's vision and is reminiscent of the coordinated visions of Ananias and Paul in ch 9. **23:** *Invited them in,* Peter is prepared to associate with Gentiles. **28:** *You yourselves know,* the audience is aware that association with Gentiles can be a cause of defilement for Jews (the centurion in Lk 7.6–7 seems to be sensitive to this). *But God has shown me,* Peter now understands the vision about food (vv. 11–17) to refer allegorically to people—i.e., defilement is no longer an issue. **30:** See v. 3n. **34:** *No partiality,* lit., "God is no respecter of persons"; cf. Rom 2.10–11. **36–43:** A synopsis of Luke's Gospel. **36:**

lee after the baptism that John announced: [38] how God anointed Jesus of Nazareth with the Holy Spirit and with power; how he went about doing good and healing all who were oppressed by the devil, for God was with him. [39] We are witnesses to all that he did both in Judea and in Jerusalem. They put him to death by hanging him on a tree; [40] but God raised him on the third day and allowed him to appear, [41] not to all the people but to us who were chosen by God as witnesses, and who ate and drank with him after he rose from the dead. [42] He commanded us to preach to the people and to testify that he is the one ordained by God as judge of the living and the dead. [43] All the prophets testify about him that everyone who believes in him receives forgiveness of sins through his name."

[44] While Peter was still speaking, the Holy Spirit fell upon all who heard the word. [45] The circumcised believers who had come with Peter were astounded that the gift of the Holy Spirit had been poured out even on the Gentiles, [46] for they heard them speaking in tongues and extolling God. Then Peter said, [47] "Can anyone withhold the water for baptizing these people who have received the Holy Spirit just as we have?" [48] So he ordered them to be baptized in the name of Jesus Christ. Then they invited him to stay for several days.

11 Now the apostles and the believers[a] who were in Judea heard that the Gentiles had also accepted the word of God. [2] So when Peter went up to Jerusalem, the circumcised believers[b] criticized him, [3] saying, "Why did you go to uncircumcised men and eat with them?" [4] Then Peter began to explain it to them, step by step, saying, [5] "I was in the city of Joppa praying, and in a trance I saw a vision. There was something like a large sheet coming down from heaven, being lowered by its four corners; and it came close to me. [6] As I looked at it closely I saw four-footed animals, beasts of prey, reptiles, and birds of the air. [7] I also heard a voice saying to me, 'Get up, Peter; kill and eat.' [8] But I replied, 'By no means, Lord; for nothing profane or unclean has ever entered my mouth.' [9] But a second time the voice answered from heaven, 'What God has made clean, you must not call profane.' [10] This happened three times; then everything was pulled up again to heaven. [11] At that very moment three men, sent to me from Caesarea, arrived at the house where we were. [12] The Spirit told me to go with them and not to make a distinction between them and us.[c] These six brothers also accompanied me, and we entered the man's house. [13] He told us how he had seen the angel standing in his house and saying, 'Send to Joppa and bring Simon, who is called Peter; [14] he will give you a message by which you and your entire household will be saved.' [15] And as I began to speak, the Holy Spirit fell upon them just as it had upon us at the beginning. [16] And I remembered the word of the Lord, how he had said, 'John baptized with water, but you will be baptized with the Holy Spirit.' [17] If then God gave them the same gift that he

a Gk *brothers*

b Gk lacks *believers*

c Or *not to hesitate*

Lord of all, both Jews and Gentiles. **38**: *God anointed Jesus,* seems to refer to the baptism at Lk 3.22 (see also Lk 4.14); but note Lk 2.11; Acts 2.36n.; 3.20. **39**: *We are witnesses,* also v. 41, see 1.8n.; 1.21–22; *tree,* 5.30n. **41**: Jesus was seen only by those *chosen* (Lk 24.48; Acts 1.8,22). *Ate and drank with him,* 1.4n.; Lk 24.30–31,41–43. **42**: *Judge,* 17.31. **43**: *All the prophets,* Lk 24.25–27,44–47; *forgiveness of sins,* Lk 24.47; Acts 2.38; 13.26,39; *through his name,* 3.6. **44–48**: The *circumcised believers* knew by the *speaking in tongues* (2.4–11) that *the Holy Spirit* fell upon *the Gentiles* before baptism (see 2.38n.).

11.1–18: Peter's defense. The Jerusalem church requires an explanation for the baptism of Gentiles. **1**: News of the new development reaches Jerusalem, cf. 8.14; 11.22. **2**: Up to this point all believers were *circumcised* (see note *b*; at 10.45 the text says "circumcised believers," but the meaning is the same, as v. 18 makes clear). **3**: The question is framed in terms of association with Gentiles, not their entry into the church; cf. Gal 2.12. **4–17**: *Peter* answers by retelling 10.1–48 in abbreviated fashion. **12**: *Not to make a distinction,* clarifies "go . . . without hesitation" in 10.20. *Six,* replaces "some" in 10.23. **14**: Unlike 10.33, here it is made clear that Cornelius is expecting a *message* of salvation (4.12). **15**: See 2.1–4. **16**: See 1.5n. **17–18**: The "Gentile Pentecost" (v. 15; 10.47; 15.8) was an act of *God.* Although the issue of Gentile inclusion seems to be decisively settled, controversy

gave us when we believed in the Lord Jesus Christ, who was I that I could hinder God?" [18] When they heard this, they were silenced. And they praised God, saying, "Then God has given even to the Gentiles the repentance that leads to life."

[19] Now those who were scattered because of the persecution that took place over Stephen traveled as far as Phoenicia, Cyprus, and Antioch, and they spoke the word to no one except Jews. [20] But among them were some men of Cyprus and Cyrene who, on coming to Antioch, spoke to the Hellenists[a] also, proclaiming the Lord Jesus. [21] The hand of the Lord was with them, and a great number became believers and turned to the Lord. [22] News of this came to the ears of the church in Jerusalem, and they sent Barnabas to Antioch. [23] When he came and saw the grace of God, he rejoiced, and he exhorted them all to remain faithful to the Lord with steadfast devotion; [24] for he was a good man, full of the Holy Spirit and of faith. And a great many people were brought to the Lord. [25] Then Barnabas went to Tarsus to look for Saul, [26] and when he had found

him, he brought him to Antioch. So it was that for an entire year they met with[b] the church and taught a great many people, and it was in Antioch that the disciples were first called "Christians."

[27] At that time prophets came down from Jerusalem to Antioch. [28] One of them named Agabus stood up and predicted by the Spirit that there would be a severe famine over all the world; and this took place during the reign of Claudius. [29] The disciples determined that according to their ability, each would send relief to the believers[c] living in Judea; [30] this they did, sending it to the elders by Barnabas and Saul.

12 About that time King Herod laid violent hands upon some who belonged to the church. [2] He had James, the brother of John, killed with the sword. [3] After he saw that it pleased the Jews, he proceeded to arrest Peter also. (This was during the festival of Unleavened Bread.) [4] When he had seized

a Other ancient authorities read *Greeks*

b Or *were guests of*

c Gk *brothers*

will resurface in ch 15.

11.19–26: Mission to the Greeks in Antioch. The narrative now rejoins the mission initiated by the *persecution* following Stephen's death (8.1,4). **19:** *Antioch* on the Orontes River, capital of the Roman province of Syria, which included Galilee and Judea, and according to Josephus (*J.W.* 3.29), the third largest city (after Rome and Alexandria) in the Roman Empire. Antioch was a popular city name in Syria and Asia Minor, reflecting the rule of Antiochus I (whose epithet was "savior"), son of Seleucus I, one of the successors of Alexander the Great. **20:** *Cyrene,* a great North African city (2.10; 6.9; 13.1; Lk 23.26), had a large Jewish colony. *Hellenists* (unlike 6.1 and 9.29) here apparently refers to non-Jewish, Greek-speaking residents of *Antioch.* **22–24:** *Barnabas* came from Cyprus (4.36), and there were Cypriots in Antioch (v. 20). He investigates and expresses approval over the latest developments on behalf of *Jerusalem* (cf. 8.14–17; 11.1–18). Compare his description (v. 24) with that of Stephen (6.5). **25–26:** *Saul* was in *Tarsus* (9.30), cf. Gal 1.21. An extended collaboration with Barnabas is initiated (see Gal 2.1,9,13; 1 Cor 9.6). *Christians,* a Latin word meaning "partisans of Christ," perhaps at first a term of reproach. It occurs elsewhere in the New Testament only at 26.28 and 1 Pet 4.16. It appears to be a term gaining currency in Luke's day that has been retrojected into the time portrayed by the narrative.

11.27–30: Antioch aids Jerusalem. 27: *Prophets* (13.1; 15.32) were numerous in the early church and in Acts characterize the last days (2.17–18). Here they predict the future (see 21.10). According to 1 Cor 14.3–4,31 they teach and build up the church. **28:** *Agabus,* 21.10–11. The *famine* probably occurred in 47 CE; it was not worldwide (see Josephus, *Ant.* 20.51–53,101). The Roman emperor *Claudius* ruled 41–54 CE. **29:** The *relief* operation resembles the arrangements for Paul's collection (20.4n.; 1 Cor 16.2; 2 Cor 9.7); the days of selling all (2.44–45; 4.32–35) are gone. **30:** *Elders,* as Christian leaders are first mentioned here ("old men" in 2.17 translates the same Greek word); their emergence may reflect synagogue practice. According to Gal 2.1–10, Paul's second visit to Jerusalem coincided with the discussion narrated in Acts 15.1–29.

12.1–19: Persecution touches the apostles. 1: *Herod* Agrippa I, grandson of Herod the Great, nephew of Herod Antipas (4.27; 13.1; the Herod of Luke's Gospel), was made king of Judea by Claudius in 41 CE. **2:** An apostle, *James* the son of Zebedee, is martyred. No replacement is made (cf. 1.15–26). **3:** *Peter,* like Jesus, is arrested at

him, he put him in prison and handed him over to four squads of soldiers to guard him, intending to bring him out to the people after the Passover. [5] While Peter was kept in prison, the church prayed fervently to God for him.

[6] The very night before Herod was going to bring him out, Peter, bound with two chains, was sleeping between two soldiers, while guards in front of the door were keeping watch over the prison. [7] Suddenly an angel of the Lord appeared and a light shone in the cell. He tapped Peter on the side and woke him, saying, "Get up quickly." And the chains fell off his wrists. [8] The angel said to him, "Fasten your belt and put on your sandals." He did so. Then he said to him, "Wrap your cloak around you and follow me." [9] Peter[a] went out and followed him; he did not realize that what was happening with the angel's help was real; he thought he was seeing a vision. [10] After they had passed the first and the second guard, they came before the iron gate leading into the city. It opened for them of its own accord, and they went outside and walked along a lane, when suddenly the angel left him. [11] Then Peter came to himself and said, "Now I am sure that the Lord has sent his angel and rescued me from the hands of Herod and from all that the Jewish people were expecting."

[12] As soon as he realized this, he went to the house of Mary, the mother of John whose other name was Mark, where many had gathered and were praying. [13] When he knocked at the outer gate, a maid named Rhoda came to answer. [14] On recognizing Peter's voice, she was so overjoyed that, instead of opening the gate, she ran in and announced that Peter was standing at the gate. [15] They said to her, "You are out of your mind!" But she insisted that it was so. They said, "It is his angel." [16] Meanwhile Peter continued knocking; and when they opened the gate, they saw him and were amazed. [17] He motioned to them with his hand to be silent, and described for them how the Lord had brought him out of the prison. And he added, "Tell this to James and to the believers."[b] Then he left and went to another place.

[18] When morning came, there was no small commotion among the soldiers over what had become of Peter. [19] When Herod had searched for him and could not find him, he examined the guards and ordered them to be put to death. Then he went down from Judea to Caesarea and stayed there.

[20] Now Herod[c] was angry with the people of Tyre and Sidon. So they came to him in a body; and after winning over Blastus, the king's chamberlain, they asked for a reconciliation, because their country depended on the king's country for food. [21] On an appointed day Herod put on his royal robes, took his seat on the platform, and delivered a public address to them. [22] The people kept shouting, "The voice of a god, and not of a mortal!" [23] And immediately, because he had not given the glory to God, an angel of the Lord struck

[a] Gk *He*
[b] Gk *brothers*
[c] Gk *he*

Passover season (v. 4), *the festival of Unleavened Bread* (v. 3). **4:** *Four squads of soldiers*, emphasizes the impossibility of escape (similarly v. 6). **6–11:** Cf. 5.17–23; 16.23–28. Miraculous escapes were a staple of ancient literature. **6:** *Bring him out*, for execution. **12:** *John . . . Mark* is connected with Peter elsewhere (1 Pet 5.13), and tradition credited him with authoring the second Gospel as Peter's interpreter (Eusebius, *Hist. eccl.* 3.39.15; 5.8.3). In 12.25–13.13 he travels with Paul and Barnabas. According to Col 4.10 he was Barnabas's cousin (see also Philem 24; 2 Tim 4.11). **13:** *Outer gate*, a significant house is suggested. **15:** A person's guardian *angel* (Mt 18.10) was thought to resemble the person protected. **17:** *James*, the brother of Jesus next in age (1.14n.), soon emerges as the leader of the Jerusalem church (15.13; see Gal 1.19; 2.12). Peter goes to *another place*, appearing one last time at the Jerusalem council (15.7–11).

12.20–23: Death of Herod Agrippa. Josephus (*Ant.* 19.343–353) gives a somewhat similar account in which, after flatterers address Herod as a god, he is stricken by a fatal disease and dies after five days of pain—but he acknowledges the false title and accepts his fate. **23:** Herod's death in 44 CE occurred before the probable date of the famine mentioned at 11.28 — Acts does not necessarily present all events in correct chronological order. *Died*, the Gk word here is used elsewhere in the New Testament only to describe the deaths of Ananias and Sapphira (5.5,10).

him down, and he was eaten by worms and died.

²⁴ But the word of God continued to advance and gain adherents. ²⁵ Then after completing their mission Barnabas and Saul returned toᵃ Jerusalem and brought with them John, whose other name was Mark.

13 Now in the church at Antioch there were prophets and teachers: Barnabas, Simeon who was called Niger, Lucius of Cyrene, Manaen a member of the court of Herod the ruler,ᵇ and Saul. ² While they were worshiping the Lord and fasting, the Holy Spirit said, "Set apart for me Barnabas and Saul for the work to which I have called them." ³ Then after fasting and praying they laid their hands on them and sent them off.

⁴ So, being sent out by the Holy Spirit, they went down to Seleucia; and from there they sailed to Cyprus. ⁵ When they arrived at Salamis, they proclaimed the word of God in the synagogues of the Jews. And they had John also to assist them. ⁶ When they had gone through the whole island as far as Paphos, they met a certain magician, a Jewish false prophet, named Bar-Jesus. ⁷ He was with the proconsul, Sergius Paulus, an intelligent man, who summoned Barnabas and Saul and wanted to hear the word of God. ⁸ But

the magician Elymas (for that is the translation of his name) opposed them and tried to turn the proconsul away from the faith. ⁹ But Saul, also known as Paul, filled with the Holy Spirit, looked intently at him ¹⁰ and said, "You son of the devil, you enemy of all righteousness, full of all deceit and villainy, will you not stop making crooked the straight paths of the Lord? ¹¹ And now listen—the hand of the Lord is against you, and you will be blind for a while, unable to see the sun." Immediately mist and darkness came over him, and he went about groping for someone to lead him by the hand. ¹² When the proconsul saw what had happened, he believed, for he was astonished at the teaching about the Lord.

¹³ Then Paul and his companions set sail from Paphos and came to Perga in Pamphylia. John, however, left them and returned to Jerusalem; ¹⁴ but they went on from Perga and came to Antioch in Pisidia. And on the sabbath day they went into the synagogue and sat down. ¹⁵ After the reading of the law and the prophets, the officials of the synagogue sent them a message, saying, "Brothers, if you have any word of exhortation for the people, give it." ¹⁶ So Paul stood up and with a gesture began to speak:

ᵃ Other ancient authorities read *from*
ᵇ Gk *tetrarch*

12.24–13.3: **Commission at Antioch.** 12.24: The attack on the church's leaders fails to stem growth. 25: *Barnabas and Saul returned* from *Jerusalem* to Antioch (see note *a*) after the relief visit (11.29–30). 13.1: *Prophets and teachers* were important leaders in the early church (see 11.27n.; 1 Cor 12.28; Eph 4.11). *Manaen,* Gk form of Heb Menahem. *Herod the ruler,* Herod Antipas (4.27; Lk 3.19; 8.3; 9.7,9; 13.31; 23.7–15), not Herod Agrippa (12.1n.). 2: As is usual in Acts *the Holy Spirit* initiates new developments. *Set apart,* cf. Rom 1.1; Gal 1.15. 3: *Laid . . . hands,* see 6.6n.

13.4–12: **Cyprus.** 4: *Seleucia* Pieria, Antioch's seaport, about 12 mi (20 km) west at the mouth of the Orontes River. 5: *Salamis,* important port and former capital city at the eastern end of Cyprus. *Synagogues,* there was a large Jewish population on Cyprus. According to Acts, Paul regularly begins mission work in a new place in the local synagogue (13.14; 14.1; 17.1,10,17; 18.4,19; 19.8; see 9.20n.; cf. Rom 1.16). *John,* see 12.12n. According to 11.19, missionaries had previously reached the island. 6: *Paphos,* capital of Cyprus, located in the extreme west. *Magician,* see 8.9n. *Bar-Jesus,* "son of Jesus [or Joshua]." 7: The island was a senatorial province ruled by a *proconsul. Sergius Paulus,* another Roman official favorable to Christianity (see 10.1n.). 8: *Elymas* does not mean "Bar-Jesus." 9: *Saul* was his Jewish name, used up to this point to stress his origin; *Paul* was his Roman name, the one he was generally known by, and is used from now on in Acts as missionary activity aims at both Jews and Gentiles. 10–11: Compare Peter's rebuke of Simon (8.20–24).

13.13–52: **Journey to Antioch of Pisidia and Iconium.** The focus now clearly shifts to Paul as his first work in inner Asia Minor is depicted. 13: *Perga* is inland 8 mi (13 km) from Attalia (14.25), main seaport of *Pamphylia,* a small province south of the Taurus mountains, between Cilicia and Lycia. *John . . . left,* v. 5; see 15.38. 14: Strictly, *Antioch* near *Pisidia,* a Roman city and colony (see 11.19n.). *Synagogue,* v. 5n. 15: One lesson each from *the law and the prophets* was customary. 16: *Gesture,* an orator's move. *Others who fear God,* here and v. 26 probably equivalent to "devout converts" to Judaism in v. 43 (where "convert" is the Gk word for proselyte; see 6.5n.).

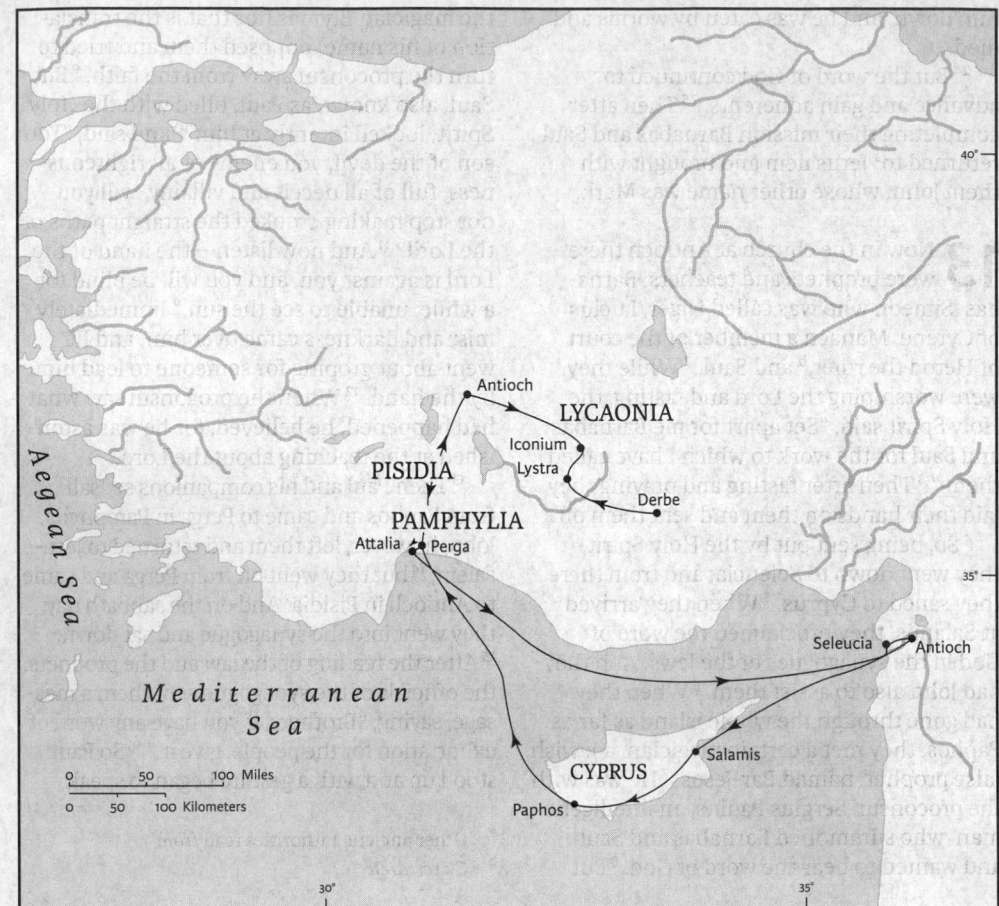

Chs 13–14: First missionary journey of Paul.

"You Israelites,[a] and others who fear God, listen. [17] The God of this people Israel chose our ancestors and made the people great during their stay in the land of Egypt, and with uplifted arm he led them out of it. [18] For about forty years he put up with[b] them in the wilderness. [19] After he had destroyed seven nations in the land of Canaan, he gave them their land as an inheritance [20] for about four hundred fifty years. After that he gave them judges until the time of the prophet Samuel. [21] Then they asked for a king; and God gave them Saul son of Kish, a man of the tribe of Benjamin, who reigned for forty years. [22] When he had removed him, he made David their king. In his testimony about him he said, 'I have found David, son of Jesse, to be a man after my heart, who will carry out all my wishes.' [23] Of this man's posterity God has brought to Israel a Savior, Jesus, as he promised; [24] before his coming John had already proclaimed a baptism of repentance to all the people of Israel. [25] And as John was finishing

a Gk *Men*, Israelites

b Other ancient authorities read *cared for*

17–25: The survey of biblical history emphasizes the theme of fulfillment in the latter part of the speech (vv. 23,27,29,32,33). **18:** Context requires the reading *he put up with them in the wilderness* with Deut 1.31 (note *b*). **19:** *Seven nations*, Deut 7.1; Josh 3.10; 24.11. **20:** *Four hundred fifty years* from the entrance into Canaan to the building of the Temple may be an approximation. *Samuel*, 1 Sam 4.1. **21:** 1 Sam 8.5; 9.15–17. **22:** Ps 89.20; 1 Sam 13.14. **23:** *Posterity*, see Lk 3.31. *Savior*, see 5.31n. The promise is found in 2 Sam 7.12. **24:** Lk 3.3. **25:** The Baptist's emphatic

his work, he said, 'What do you suppose that I am? I am not he. No, but one is coming after me; I am not worthy to untie the thong of the sandals[a] on his feet.'

²⁶ "My brothers, you descendants of Abraham's family, and others who fear God, to us[b] the message of this salvation has been sent. ²⁷ Because the residents of Jerusalem and their leaders did not recognize him or understand the words of the prophets that are read every sabbath, they fulfilled those words by condemning him. ²⁸ Even though they found no cause for a sentence of death, they asked Pilate to have him killed. ²⁹ When they had carried out everything that was written about him, they took him down from the tree and laid him in a tomb. ³⁰ But God raised him from the dead; ³¹ and for many days he appeared to those who came up with him from Galilee to Jerusalem, and they are now his witnesses to the people. ³² And we bring you the good news that what God promised to our ancestors ³³ he has fulfilled for us, their children, by raising Jesus; as also it is written in the second psalm,

'You are my Son;
    today I have begotten you.'

³⁴ As to his raising him from the dead, no more to return to corruption, he has spoken in this way,

'I will give you the holy promises made to
    David.'

³⁵ Therefore he has also said in another psalm,

'You will not let your Holy One experience
    corruption.'

³⁶ For David, after he had served the purpose of God in his own generation, died,[c] was laid beside his ancestors, and experienced corruption; ³⁷ but he whom God raised up experienced no corruption. ³⁸ Let it be known to you therefore, my brothers, that through this man forgiveness of sins is proclaimed to you; ³⁹ by this Jesus[d] everyone who believes is set free from all those sins[e] from which you could not be freed by the law of Moses. ⁴⁰ Beware, therefore, that what the prophets said does not happen to you:

⁴¹ 'Look, you scoffers!
    Be amazed and perish,
for in your days I am doing a work,
    a work that you will never believe, even
        if someone tells you.'"

⁴² As Paul and Barnabas[f] were going out, the people urged them to speak about these things again the next sabbath. ⁴³ When the meeting of the synagogue broke up, many Jews and devout converts to Judaism followed Paul and Barnabas, who spoke to them and urged them to continue in the grace of God.

⁴⁴ The next sabbath almost the whole city gathered to hear the word of the Lord.[g] ⁴⁵ But when the Jews saw the crowds, they were filled with jealousy; and blaspheming, they contradicted what was spoken by Paul. ⁴⁶ Then both Paul and Barnabas spoke out boldly, saying, "It was necessary that the word of God should be spoken first to you. Since you reject it and judge yourselves to be unworthy of eternal life, we are now turning to the Gentiles. ⁴⁷ For so the Lord has commanded us, saying,

'I have set you to be a light for the Gentiles,
    so that you may bring salvation to the
        ends of the earth.'"

⁴⁸ When the Gentiles heard this, they were glad and praised the word of the Lord; and as

a   Gk untie the sandals
b   Other ancient authorities read you
c   Gk fell asleep
d   Gk this
e   Gk all
f   Gk they
g   Other ancient authorities read God

denial here (cf. Lk 3.16; Mk 1.7; Mt 3.11; Jn 1.20) may be aimed at those who continued to be his disciples (18.25; 19.3). **26:** *Salvation,* 4.12; in vv. 38–39 it is forgiveness of sins (2.38; 10.43; Lk 24.47). **26–41:** For argument and style compare Peter's speeches in 2.14–36; 3.12–26; 10.34–43. **27:** *Did not recognize . . . or understand,* see 3.17. **28:** *No cause,* Lk 23.4,14–15,22,47. *Pilate,* 3.13n. **29:** *Tree,* 5.30n. **30:** The resurrection is the heart of the gospel in Acts (3.15; 4.10; 10.40. 13.37). **31:** *Witnesses,* 1.8n. **33:** Ps 2.7. *Raising Jesus,* here in the sense of bringing him on the scene (in contrast to v. 34; cf. 3.22,26). **34:** Isa 55.3. **35:** Ps 16.10 (see Acts 2.27). **38:** *Forgiveness of sins,* v. 26n. **39:** *Set free,* Greek "justified"; the only reference to justification by faith in Acts fittingly appears on Paul's lips even if the sense is not fully that found in Paul's letters. **41:** Hab 1.5. **43:** *Devout converts to Judaism,* see v. 16n. **46:** The same dramatic announcement of turning to the *Gentiles* occurs in 18.5–6; 28.25–28. *Spoke out boldly,* 14.3; 18.26;

many as had been destined for eternal life became believers. [49] Thus the word of the Lord spread throughout the region. [50] But the Jews incited the devout women of high standing and the leading men of the city, and stirred up persecution against Paul and Barnabas, and drove them out of their region. [51] So they shook the dust off their feet in protest against them, and went to Iconium. [52] And the disciples were filled with joy and with the Holy Spirit.

14 The same thing occurred in Iconium, where Paul and Barnabas[a] went into the Jewish synagogue and spoke in such a way that a great number of both Jews and Greeks became believers. [2] But the unbelieving Jews stirred up the Gentiles and poisoned their minds against the brothers. [3] So they remained for a long time, speaking boldly for the Lord, who testified to the word of his grace by granting signs and wonders to be done through them. [4] But the residents of the city were divided; some sided with the Jews, and some with the apostles. [5] And when an attempt was made by both Gentiles and Jews, with their rulers, to mistreat them and to stone them, [6] the apostles[a] learned of it and fled to Lystra and Derbe, cities of Lycaonia, and to the surrounding country; [7] and there they continued proclaiming the good news.

[8] In Lystra there was a man sitting who could not use his feet and had never walked, for he had been crippled from birth. [9] He listened to Paul as he was speaking. And Paul, looking at him intently and seeing that he had faith to be healed, [10] said in a loud voice, "Stand upright on your feet." And the man[b] sprang up and began to walk. [11] When the crowds saw what Paul had done, they shouted in the Lycaonian language, "The gods have come down to us in human form!" [12] Barnabas they called Zeus, and Paul they called Hermes, because he was the chief speaker. [13] The priest of Zeus, whose temple was just outside the city,[c] brought oxen and garlands to the gates; he and the crowds wanted to offer sacrifice. [14] When the apostles Barnabas and Paul heard of it, they tore their clothes and rushed out into the crowd, shouting, [15] "Friends,[d] why are you doing this? We are mortals just like you, and we bring you good news, that you should turn from these worthless things to the living God, who made the heaven and the earth and the sea and all that is in them. [16] In past generations he allowed all the nations to follow their own ways; [17] yet he has not left himself without a witness in doing good— giving you rains from heaven and fruitful seasons, and filling you with food and your hearts with joy." [18] Even with these words, they scarcely restrained the crowds from offering sacrifice to them.

[19] But Jews came there from Antioch and Iconium and won over the crowds. Then they stoned Paul and dragged him out of the city,

a Gk *they*
b Gk *he*
c Or *The priest of Zeus-Outside-the-City*
d Gk *Men*

19.8; 26.26; see 4.13n. **47:** Isa 49.6; cf. Lk 2.32. **49:** A typical summary that makes it clear that Acts claims only to be a partial report of the spread of Christianity; cf. 9.10n. **50:** The scene depicted here (see 2 Tim 3.11) is repeated in subsequent accounts (see 14.2,19; 17.5,13). **51:** *They shook the dust off* (18.6) to show that their responsibility ended (Lk 9.5; 10.11; Mt 10.14). *Iconium,* modern Konya, ca. 75 mi (120 km) southeast of Antioch.

14.1–28: Ministry in the Iconium region and return to Antioch. 1: In spite of the announcement of 13.46, *Paul and Barnabas* again start at the *Jewish synagogue.* **2:** 13.50n. **4:** The Gk word *apostles* is used of Paul and Barnabas in Acts only here and in v. 14. Since the term otherwise is limited to the twelve, here the meaning may be "apostles (i.e., emissaries) of the church of Antioch," the church that sent them (13.2–3). **6:** *Lystra,* according to 16.1 the home of Timothy, was a Roman colony 24 mi (40 km) south-southwest of Iconium. *Derbe,* another town in Lycaonia 60 mi (96 km) southeast of Lystra. **7:** In Acts persecution always leads to new opportunities. **8–18:** Cf. 3.1–8. In this and other episodes in Acts Paul replicates the experiences of Peter. **11–12:** According to a myth of this region, the gods *Zeus* and *Hermes* visited Baucis and Philemon *in human form* and rewarded their hospitality (Ovid, *Metamorphoses,* 8.618–724). Paul, *the chief speaker,* was hailed as the messenger of the gods, not the chief god. **14:** *Apostles,* see 14.4n. *Tore their clothes,* a sign of horror and dismay at what they looked upon as blasphemy (cf. Mk 14.63). **15–17:** Cf. 17.22–31; 1 Thess 1.9–10. Paul (v. 15), like Peter (10.26), rejects worship of

supposing that he was dead. [20] But when the disciples surrounded him, he got up and went into the city. The next day he went on with Barnabas to Derbe.

[21] After they had proclaimed the good news to that city and had made many disciples, they returned to Lystra, then on to Iconium and Antioch. [22] There they strengthened the souls of the disciples and encouraged them to continue in the faith, saying, "It is through many persecutions that we must enter the kingdom of God." [23] And after they had appointed elders for them in each church, with prayer and fasting they entrusted them to the Lord in whom they had come to believe.

[24] Then they passed through Pisidia and came to Pamphylia. [25] When they had spoken the word in Perga, they went down to Attalia. [26] From there they sailed back to Antioch, where they had been commended to the grace of God for the work[a] that they had completed. [27] When they arrived, they called the church together and related all that God had done with them, and how he had opened a door of faith for the Gentiles. [28] And they stayed there with the disciples for some time.

15 Then certain individuals came down from Judea and were teaching the brothers, "Unless you are circumcised according to the custom of Moses, you cannot be saved." [2] And after Paul and Barnabas had no small dissension and debate with them, Paul and Barnabas and some of the others were appointed to go up to Jerusalem to discuss this question with the apostles and the elders. [3] So they were sent on their way by the church, and as they passed through both Phoenicia and Samaria, they reported the conversion of the Gentiles, and brought great joy to all the believers.[b] [4] When they came to Jerusalem, they were welcomed by the church and the apostles and the elders, and they reported all that God had done with them. [5] But some believers who belonged to the sect of the Pharisees stood up and said, "It is necessary for them to be circumcised and ordered to keep the law of Moses."

[6] The apostles and the elders met together to consider this matter. [7] After there had been much debate, Peter stood up and said to them, "My brothers,[c] you know that in the early days God made a choice among you, that I should be the one through whom the Gentiles would hear the message of the good news and become believers. [8] And God, who knows the human heart, testified to them by giving them the Holy Spirit, just as he did to us; [9] and in cleansing their hearts by faith he has made no distinction between them and us. [10] Now therefore why are you putting God to the test by placing on the neck of the disciples a yoke that neither our ancestors nor we have been able to bear? [11] On the contrary, we believe that we will be saved through the grace of the Lord Jesus, just as they will."

[12] The whole assembly kept silence, and listened to Barnabas and Paul as they told of all the

a   Or *committed in the grace of God to the work*
b   Gk *brothers*
c   Gk *Men, brothers*

himself. **19:** 13.50n. Paul tells of receiving a stoning in 2 Cor 11.25; see 2 Tim 3.11. **20:** Perhaps a miraculous recovery. **23:** In Acts, Paul's churches are ruled by *elders* (cf. 20.17). Their presence may reflect conditions in Luke's day read back into the earlier period (see 15.2n.). The word is not used in Paul's own letters (but see 1 Tim 4.14; 5.17; Titus 1.5). See 11.30n. **25:** *Attalia*, the seaport of Perga (13.13n.). **26:** *Antioch*, their starting point for the *work* (13.2) now *completed.*

15.1–35: Jerusalem affirms the admission of Gentiles. 1: *Certain individuals*, cf. v. 5, Pharisees; Gal 2.4, "false believers." *Unless you are circumcised* and "keep the law" (v. 5), reopens issues seemingly settled with the approval of the "circumcised believers" (11.2n.,18) in 11.1–18. If the right of Gentile admission to the church was confirmed in ch 11, the present discussion may raise the issue of the conditions that might nevertheless apply. **2:** *Were appointed,* in Gal 2.2 Paul says he went "by revelation" (Gal 2.2). *Elders* (11.30n.; 14.23n.) now appear with the *apostles* (vv. 4,6,22,23; 16.4n.) as leaders of the Jerusalem church under James (vv. 13,19). Peter is the only apostle named; the others function as a corporate symbol as they have throughout. **5:** In Acts *Pharisees* are portrayed as *believers* (26.5) or tolerant of Christianity (5.34), often in sharp contrast to Sadducees (4.1–2; 5.17; 23.6–9). **7–9:** Peter's second summary (see 11.1–18) of the events narrated in 10.1–48. *I should be the one,* contrast Gal 2.7–8. **10:** The *yoke* is that of the law (Lk 11.46); Paul's view (Rom 7.12; Phil 3.6) is different. **11:** Peter's words echo Paul's language (Rom 3.24). **12:** 14.27; 15.4. The contentious debate reported in Gal 2 is passed

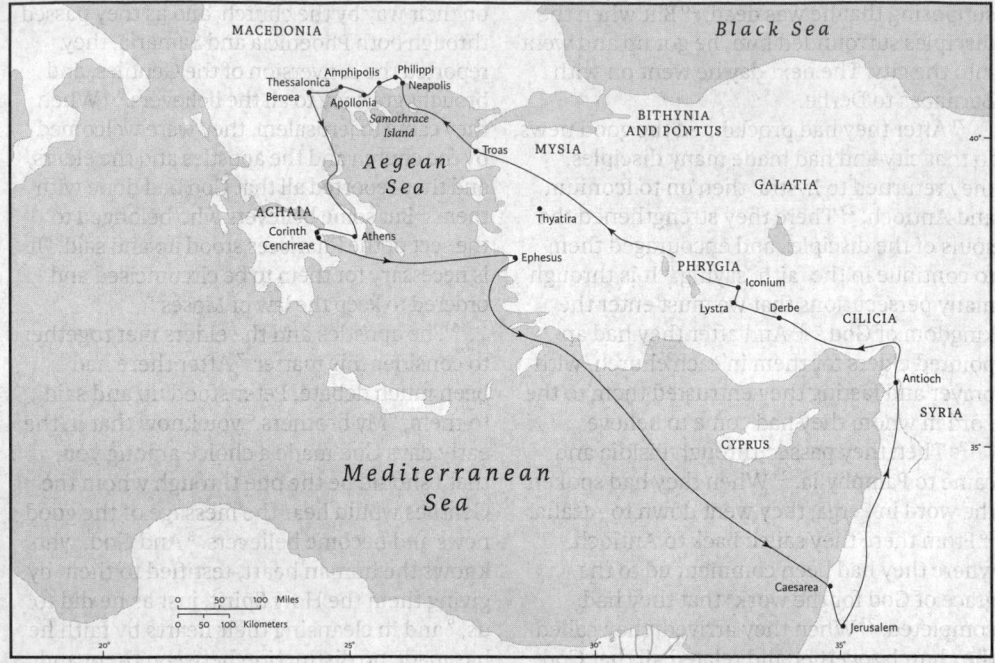

Chs 15–18: Second missionary journey of Paul.

signs and wonders that God had done through them among the Gentiles. [13] After they finished speaking, James replied, "My brothers,[a] listen to me. [14] Simeon has related how God first looked favorably on the Gentiles, to take from among them a people for his name. [15] This agrees with the words of the prophets, as it is written,

[16] 'After this I will return,
and I will rebuild the dwelling of David, which has fallen;
    from its ruins I will rebuild it,
        and I will set it up,
[17] so that all other peoples may seek the
    Lord—
even all the Gentiles over whom my
    name has been called.

Thus says the Lord, who has been
    making these things [18] known
        from long ago.'[b]
[19] Therefore I have reached the decision that we should not trouble those Gentiles who are turning to God, [20] but we should write to them to abstain only from things polluted by idols and from fornication and from whatever has been strangled[c] and from blood. [21] For in every city, for generations past,

---

a   Gk *Men, brothers*
b   Other ancient authorities read *things. [18]Known to God from of old are all his works.'*
c   Other ancient authorities lack *and from whatever has been strangled*

---

over in silence in Acts. **13:** *James,* see 12.17n. **14:** *Simeon,* the Semitic form of Peter's given name, emphasizing connections with Judaism even as the church is becoming a mixed group (v. 19) of Jews and Gentiles (see 14.1; 17.4,11–12; 18.4,8; 19.10). **16–18:** Am 9.11–12; Jer 12.15; Isa 45.21. **20:** *Things polluted by idols,* i.e., food sacrificed to them—prohibiting by extension idolatry itself (note Paul's more liberal stance in 1 Cor 10.27–29). *Whatever has been strangled,* i.e., meat not ritually butchered, which may mean the same thing as *blood* (omitted by some manuscripts), although the latter could mean murder. Suggested backgrounds for the items included in the "apostolic decree" include the so-called Noachian precepts (regulations to be observed by all peoples; see Gen 9.4–6) and the regulations for Gentiles living among Jews in Lev 17–18. The list may have a more practical function (avoid non-kosher food and *fornication*) or stipulate matters beyond compromise (idolatry, murder, and incest). **21:** *Moses,* selections from the Torah (the first five books of the Bible), traditionally thought to have been

Moses has had those who proclaim him, for he has been read aloud every sabbath in the synagogues."

22 Then the apostles and the elders, with the consent of the whole church, decided to choose men from among their members[a] and to send them to Antioch with Paul and Barnabas. They sent Judas called Barsabbas, and Silas, leaders among the brothers, 23 with the following letter: "The brothers, both the apostles and the elders, to the believers[b] of Gentile origin in Antioch and Syria and Cilicia, greetings. 24 Since we have heard that certain persons who have gone out from us, though with no instructions from us, have said things to disturb you and have unsettled your minds,[c] 25 we have decided unanimously to choose representatives[d] and send them to you, along with our beloved Barnabas and Paul, 26 who have risked their lives for the sake of our Lord Jesus Christ. 27 We have therefore sent Judas and Silas, who themselves will tell you the same things by word of mouth. 28 For it has seemed good to the Holy Spirit and to us to impose on you no further burden than these essentials: 29 that you abstain from what has been sacrificed to idols and from blood and from what is strangled[e] and from fornication. If you keep yourselves from these, you will do well. Farewell."

30 So they were sent off and went down to Antioch. When they gathered the congregation together, they delivered the letter. 31 When its members[f] read it, they rejoiced at the exhortation. 32 Judas and Silas, who were

themselves prophets, said much to encourage and strengthen the believers.[b] 33 After they had been there for some time, they were sent off in peace by the believers[b] to those who had sent them.[g] 35 But Paul and Barnabas remained in Antioch, and there, with many others, they taught and proclaimed the word of the Lord.

36 After some days Paul said to Barnabas, "Come, let us return and visit the believers[b] in every city where we proclaimed the word of the Lord and see how they are doing." 37 Barnabas wanted to take with them John called Mark. 38 But Paul decided not to take with them one who had deserted them in Pamphylia and had not accompanied them in the work. 39 The disagreement became so sharp that they parted company; Barnabas took Mark with him and sailed away to Cyprus. 40 But Paul chose Silas and set out, the believers[b] commending him to the grace of the Lord. 41 He went through Syria and Cilicia, strengthening the churches.

a   Gk *from among them*
b   Gk *brothers*
c   Other ancient authorities add *saying, 'You must be circumcised and keep the law,'*
d   Gk *men*
e   Other ancient authorities lack *and from what is strangled*
f   Gk *When they*
g   Other ancient authorities add verse 34, *But it seemed good to Silas to remain there*

written by Moses, *read aloud* in weekly Jewish services. The necessity of the decree (v. 20) is explained in terms of the pervasiveness of Jewish practices, which continued to be observed by Jewish Christians (cf. 21.20–25). **22:** *Silas* may be the Silvanus of 2 Cor 1.19; 1 Thess 1.1; 2 Thess 1.1. He becomes a missionary companion of Paul at 15.40. **28:** *To the Holy Spirit and to us*, see 5.3n. *No further burden than these essentials*, cf. Gal 2.10. **32:** *Prophets*, 13.1n. **35:** 11.26; 14.28.

15.36–16.5: Paul revisits the churches of the previous mission. 15.37–38: *John called Mark . . . had deserted*, see 12.12n.; 13.13. **39:** Compare the *disagreement* here over John *Mark* with the report in Gal 2.11–13 that Barnabas disagreed with Paul over the legitimacy of Jews and Gentiles eating together. According to Acts, this problem had already been dealt with in 10.1–11.18, although the apostolic decree (15.20,29) may have been intended to make such meals acceptable for Jewish Christians. Barnabas and Mark revisit *Cyprus* (13.4–12), which had been omitted on the return journey to Antioch described in 14.24–26. **40:** *Paul* now sets out as an "independent" missionary, accompanied by *Silas* (v. 22). Paul's ties with Antioch may have been strained at this point (see Gal 2.11–14). **16.1:** *Derbe and . . . Lystra*, 14.6n. *Timothy* (17.14–15; 18.5; 19.22; 20.4) was a more important companion of Paul than the picture in Acts suggests (see Rom 16.21; 1 Cor 16.10; 2 Cor 1.1,19; Phil 1.1; 1 Thess 1.1); he is referred to as Paul's "child in the Lord" at 1 Cor 4.17. The pseudonymous letters 1 and 2 Timothy are ostensibly addressed

16

Paul[a] went on also to Derbe and to Lystra, where there was a disciple named Timothy, the son of a Jewish woman who was a believer; but his father was a Greek. [2] He was well spoken of by the believers[b] in Lystra and Iconium. [3] Paul wanted Timothy to accompany him; and he took him and had him circumcised because of the Jews who were in those places, for they all knew that his father was a Greek. [4] As they went from town to town, they delivered to them for observance the decisions that had been reached by the apostles and elders who were in Jerusalem. [5] So the churches were strengthened in the faith and increased in numbers daily.

[6] They went through the region of Phrygia and Galatia, having been forbidden by the Holy Spirit to speak the word in Asia. [7] When they had come opposite Mysia, they attempted to go into Bithynia, but the Spirit of Jesus did not allow them; [8] so, passing by Mysia, they went down to Troas. [9] During the night Paul had a vision: there stood a man of Macedonia pleading with him and saying, "Come over to Macedonia and help us." [10] When he had seen the vision, we immediately tried to cross over to Macedonia, being convinced that God had called us to proclaim the good news to them.

[11] We set sail from Troas and took a straight course to Samothrace, the following day to Neapolis, [12] and from there to Philippi, which is a leading city of the district[c] of Macedonia and a Roman colony. We remained in this city for some days. [13] On the sabbath day we went outside the gate by the river, where we supposed there was a place of prayer; and we sat down and spoke to the women who had gathered there. [14] A certain woman named Lydia, a worshiper of God, was listening to us; she was from the city of Thyatira and a dealer in purple cloth. The Lord opened her heart to listen eagerly to what was said by Paul. [15] When she and her household were baptized, she urged us, saying, "If you have judged me to be faithful to the Lord, come and stay at my home." And she prevailed upon us.

a Gk He
b Gk brothers
c Other authorities read a city of the first district

to him. Timothy's mother (see 2 Tim 1.5) is said to be Jewish, while his father was a Greek. 3: That Paul . . . had him circumcised seems unimaginable in view of passages such as 1 Cor 7.18 and Gal 5.2. Paul stresses in Gal 2.3 that Titus "was not compelled to be circumcised, though he was a Greek." Timothy's case might be different because his mother was Jewish (v. 1), yet the principle of matrilineal descent (the ethnicity of the child is determined by the mother) does not appear to have been in effect at this time. Luke may have allowed his theme of Paul's faithfulness to the law in all respects (21.23–24; 22.3) to color the narrative here and refute the charge raised in 21.21 in advance. 4: The decisions, the apostolic decree of 15.20. The apostles are mentioned here for the last time—their era is now over.

16.6–10: Directed by the Spirit through Asia Minor to Troas. Journey through the interior to the Aegean Sea. 6: The region is probably the country northwest of Iconium where both Phrygians and Galatians lived. Asia, the Roman province of that name in western Asia Minor (6.9). 7: Opposite Mysia, a northwestern part of the province of Asia; Bithynia was to its east. Spirit of Jesus, equivalent to the Holy Spirit in v. 6. 8: Troas, on the western coast of Mysia. 9: Macedonia, a Roman province in Europe including the cities of Philippi, Thessalonica, and Beroea. 10: The "we" passages (16.10–17; 20.5–15; 21.1–18; 27.1–28.16; see Introduction) begin here and bring additional vividness to the story.

16.11–40: Paul and Silas in Philippi. 11: Samothrace, an island in the northern Aegean, midway between Troas and Neapolis, the seaport of Philippi. 12: Philippi was a leading city, but not the capital, of Macedonia. It was populated by discharged soldiers who received grants of land and enjoyed the special civic rights that pertained to a Roman colony (freedom from taxation, Roman legal procedures). 13: The Gk word normally rendered "prayer" in the New Testament can also mean a place of prayer, as here, which may or may not imply a building (synagogue). By the river, some evidence suggests that Diaspora synagogues were frequently located near water. As usual in Acts, Paul seeks out the Jewish community in a new place. 14: Worshiper of God, the same word is used to describe proselytes in 13.43 but is applied to "women of high standing" in 13.50 in contradistinction to Jews. The term might simply describe Lydia as pious or suggest that she is a Jewish sympathizer. Thyatira (Rev 2.18–29), a city of Lydia, a country in western Asia Minor, was a center for the dyeing industry. 15: She and her household were baptized, dependents followed the head of the household in religious matters (v. 31; 10.2; 1 Cor

[16] One day, as we were going to the place of prayer, we met a slave-girl who had a spirit of divination and brought her owners a great deal of money by fortune-telling. [17] While she followed Paul and us, she would cry out, "These men are slaves of the Most High God, who proclaim to you[a] a way of salvation." [18] She kept doing this for many days. But Paul, very much annoyed, turned and said to the spirit, "I order you in the name of Jesus Christ to come out of her." And it came out that very hour.

[19] But when her owners saw that their hope of making money was gone, they seized Paul and Silas and dragged them into the marketplace before the authorities. [20] When they had brought them before the magistrates, they said, "These men are disturbing our city; they are Jews [21] and are advocating customs that are not lawful for us as Romans to adopt or observe." [22] The crowd joined in attacking them, and the magistrates had them stripped of their clothing and ordered them to be beaten with rods. [23] After they had given them a severe flogging, they threw them into prison and ordered the jailer to keep them securely. [24] Following these instructions, he put them in the innermost cell and fastened their feet in the stocks.

[25] About midnight Paul and Silas were praying and singing hymns to God, and the prisoners were listening to them. [26] Suddenly there was an earthquake, so violent that the foundations of the prison were shaken; and immediately all the doors were opened and everyone's chains were unfastened. [27] When the jailer woke up and saw the prison doors wide open, he drew his sword and was about to kill himself, since he supposed that the prisoners had escaped. [28] But Paul shouted in a loud voice, "Do not harm yourself, for we are all here." [29] The jailer[b] called for lights, and rushing in, he fell down trembling before Paul and Silas. [30] Then he brought them outside and said, "Sirs, what must I do to be saved?" [31] They answered, "Believe on the Lord Jesus, and you will be saved, you and your household." [32] They spoke the word of the Lord[c] to him and to all who were in his house. [33] At the same hour of the night he took them and washed their wounds; then he and his entire family were baptized without delay. [34] He brought them up into the house and set food before them; and he and his entire household rejoiced that he had become a believer in God.

[35] When morning came, the magistrates sent the police, saying, "Let those men go." [36] And the jailer reported the message to Paul, saying, "The magistrates sent word to let you go; therefore come out now and go in peace." [37] But Paul replied, "They have beaten us in public, uncondemned, men who are Roman citizens, and have thrown us into prison; and now are they going to discharge us in secret? Certainly not! Let them come and take us out themselves." [38] The police reported these words to the magistrates, and they were afraid when they heard that they were Roman citizens; [39] so they came and apologized to them. And they took them out and asked them to leave the city. [40] After leaving the prison they went to Lydia's home; and when

---

a   Other ancient authorities read to us
b   Gk He
c   Other ancient authorities read word of God

1.16). **17:** In Lk 8.28 the Gerasene demoniac identifies Jesus as Son of *the Most High God*. The epithet is common for God in the Psalms of the Septuagint. The "we" passage (v. 10n.) stops here and resumes at 20.5. **19:** Acts frowns on *making money* by magical or supernatural means (see 8.18–24; 19.25n.). **20:** *Magistrates*, Gk "generals"; here probably not a military but a civic term (apparently to be distinguished from the "authorities," v. 19). **21:** It was *not lawful* for Jews to make converts of *Romans*. **22–23:** Cf. 2 Cor 11.23–25 ("imprisonments . . . floggings . . . beaten with rods"). **24:** The familiar motif of escape-proof security (5.19–20; 12.6). **26:** *An earthquake*, here a supernatural event (see 4.31). *Doors* open and bonds are loosened for Dionysus in Euripides' *Bacchae* 447–448; see also Ovid, *Metamorphoses* 15.669–671. See 12.6–11n. **27:** *Drew his sword*, a Roman jailer whose prisoner escaped was liable to forfeit his life (cf. 12.19; 27.42). **30:** The question is elicited by the supernatural circumstances. **33:** The entire household is *baptized* (v. 15). **35:** *Police*, lictors, officials who enforced the decisions of a magistrate. **37–38:** With dramatic flair the reader suddenly learns that both *Paul* and *Silas* are *Roman citizens* protected by law against scourging (22.25; contrast 2 Cor 11.23–25). This surprising increase in Paul's credentials strongly endorses the theme of the compatibility of Christianity with Roman life (see 10.1n.; 13.7n.).

they had seen and encouraged the brothers and sisters[a] there, they departed.

17 After Paul and Silas[b] had passed through Amphipolis and Apollonia, they came to Thessalonica, where there was a synagogue of the Jews. [2] And Paul went in, as was his custom, and on three sabbath days argued with them from the scriptures, [3] explaining and proving that it was necessary for the Messiah[c] to suffer and to rise from the dead, and saying, "This is the Messiah,[c] Jesus whom I am proclaiming to you." [4] Some of them were persuaded and joined Paul and Silas, as did a great many of the devout Greeks and not a few of the leading women. [5] But the Jews became jealous, and with the help of some ruffians in the marketplaces they formed a mob and set the city in an uproar. While they were searching for Paul and Silas to bring them out to the assembly, they attacked Jason's house. [6] When they could not find them, they dragged Jason and some believers[a] before the city authorities,[d] shouting, "These people who have been turning the world upside down have come here also, [7] and Jason has entertained them as guests. They are all acting contrary to the decrees of the emperor, saying that there is another king named Jesus." [8] The people and the city officials were disturbed when they heard this, [9] and after they had taken bail from Jason and the others, they let them go.

[10] That very night the believers[a] sent Paul and Silas off to Beroea; and when they arrived, they went to the Jewish synagogue.

[11] These Jews were more receptive than those in Thessalonica, for they welcomed the message very eagerly and examined the scriptures every day to see whether these things were so. [12] Many of them therefore believed, including not a few Greek women and men of high standing. [13] But when the Jews of Thessalonica learned that the word of God had been proclaimed by Paul in Beroea as well, they came there too, to stir up and incite the crowds. [14] Then the believers[a] immediately sent Paul away to the coast, but Silas and Timothy remained behind. [15] Those who conducted Paul brought him as far as Athens; and after receiving instructions to have Silas and Timothy join him as soon as possible, they left him.

[16] While Paul was waiting for them in Athens, he was deeply distressed to see that the city was full of idols. [17] So he argued in the synagogue with the Jews and the devout persons, and also in the marketplace[e] every day with those who happened to be there. [18] Also some Epicurean and Stoic philosophers debated with him. Some said, "What does this babbler want to say?" Others said, "He seems to be a proclaimer of foreign divinities." (This was because he was telling the good news about Jesus and the resurrection.) [19] So they took him and brought

a Gk *brothers*
b Gk *they*
c Or *the Christ*
d Gk *politarchs*
e Or *civic center*; Gk *agora*

17.1–15: From Thessalonica to Athens. Paul founds churches in Thessalonica and Beroea. **1:** *Amphipolis and Apollonia* were on the Via Egnatia between Philippi and *Thessalonica* (modern Saloniki), capital of the second district of Macedonia. **2:** *His custom,* the pattern of starting a new mission in a synagogue (vv. 1,10,17) is explicitly stated (see 13.5n.; 14.1n.). **3:** See 3.18n. **4:** *Devout Greeks,* see 16.14n. *Leading women,* v. 12; contrast 13.50. **5:** *Jealous,* 13.45. On the typical nature of the scene, see 13.50n.; cf. 1 Thess 2.14–16. **6–7:** *City authorities,* i.e., politarchs, a Macedonian title for non-Roman magistrates. Serious charges of activities that threaten Roman order are made; cf. Lk 23.2. **9:** *Had taken bail from Jason,* had made him financially and legally responsible for future good behavior. **10:** *Beroea,* a city of Macedonia, 36 mi (58 km) west-southwest of Thessalonica. **11–12:** *Jews* and Gentiles believe (15.14n.). *Greek women and men of high standing,* Christianity is attracting people with status (16.37–38n.). **14:** *To the coast,* where he would take a ship to Athens (v. 15).

17.16–34: Paul at Athens. The apostle is portrayed as the first Christian philosopher, using Stoic and Jewish arguments. **16:** *Waiting . . . in Athens,* cf. 1 Thess 3.1–2. *Full of idols,* v. 22; cf. 1 Thess 1.9. **18:** *Epicurean and Stoic philosophers,* recognizable tenets from both groups are incorporated into Paul's speech in vv. 22–31. *Babbler,* a term of disparagement; the Gk word is literally used in reference to birds to mean "picking up seeds," of persons "one who makes a living by picking up scraps" (here implied: "of learning"). *Jesus and* Anastasis (the Gk word for

him to the Areopagus and asked him, "May we know what this new teaching is that you are presenting? [20] It sounds rather strange to us, so we would like to know what it means." [21] Now all the Athenians and the foreigners living there would spend their time in nothing but telling or hearing something new.

[22] Then Paul stood in front of the Areopagus and said, "Athenians, I see how extremely religious you are in every way. [23] For as I went through the city and looked carefully at the objects of your worship, I found among them an altar with the inscription, 'To an unknown god.' What therefore you worship as unknown, this I proclaim to you. [24] The God who made the world and everything in it, he who is Lord of heaven and earth, does not live in shrines made by human hands, [25] nor is he served by human hands, as though he needed anything, since he himself gives to all mortals life and breath and all things. [26] From one ancestor[a] he made all nations to inhabit the whole earth, and he allotted the times of their existence and the boundaries of the places where they would live, [27] so that they would search for God[b] and perhaps grope for him and find him—though indeed he is not far from each one of us. [28] For 'In him we live

and move and have our being'; as even some of your own poets have said,

'For we too are his offspring.'
[29] Since we are God's offspring, we ought not to think that the deity is like gold, or silver, or stone, an image formed by the art and imagination of mortals. [30] While God has overlooked the times of human ignorance, now he commands all people everywhere to repent, [31] because he has fixed a day on which he will have the world judged in righteousness by a man whom he has appointed, and of this he has given assurance to all by raising him from the dead."

[32] When they heard of the resurrection of the dead, some scoffed; but others said, "We will hear you again about this." [33] At that point Paul left them. [34] But some of them joined him and became believers, including Dionysius the Areopagite and a woman named Damaris, and others with them.

18 After this Paul[c] left Athens and went to Corinth. [2] There he found a Jew named Aquila, a native of Pontus, who had recently

a Gk *From one*; other ancient authorities read *From one blood*
b Other ancient authorities read *the Lord*
c Gk *he*

resurrection) are mistaken for two *foreign divinities*. **19**: *Took him,* could either imply arrest or friendly escort, and *Areopagus* could refer either to arraignment before the Council of the Areopagus (essentially the chief Roman court in Athens) or the Areopagus hill west of the Acropolis. The request *"May we know . . . ?"* suggests a more relaxed setting for discussion, though allusions to Socrates before the Areopagus court are surely intended (see v. 34). **21**: The curiosity of *the Athenians* was proverbial. **22–31**: Contrast the approach to Gentiles attributed to Paul in this speech with Rom 1.18–31. **22**: *Extremely religious,* can be taken in a good or bad sense. It connects to "idols" in v. 16 and leads to v. 23. **23**: *To an unknown god,* such an inscription has not been found in Athens to date; the plural form is attested. The scene intends to illustrate the anxiety of the "extremely religious" (v. 22) lest the honor due to any deity be inadvertently omitted and gives Paul an opening to *proclaim* the Christian message. **24–25**: *God* as the creator (14.15) is an idea common to Jews (Gen 1.1) and Greeks (e.g., Plato, *Timaeus*). *Shrines made by human hands,* 7.48n. **26**: *From one ancestor,* Adam. **27**: God created "all nations" (v. 26) to *search for God* (cf. 14.17). That God was near to all people was a Stoic belief. **28**: Although the first quotation is sometimes attributed to Epimenides, its language is probably to be associated with Posidonius (based on Plato); the second quotation is from Aratus (*Phaenomena* 5), a Greek poet of Cilicia educated as a Stoic. In Paul's usage the original pantheistic sense of both "quotations" is reinterpreted. **30**: *Ignorance,* cf. 14.16. **31**: That the *world* will be *judged* (10.42) . . . *by a man,* i.e., Jesus (2.22,36), *appointed* by God has been guaranteed by the resurrection. **32**: *Some scoffed,* Greek thought made no provision for resurrection of the body (e.g., Aeschylus, *Eumenides,* 647–648; cf. 1 Cor 15.12,35), *but others* were intrigued. **34**: The conversion of *Dionysius,* a member of the Areopagus court, contributes to the theme of rulers attracted to Christianity. The note about *Damaris* conforms to a pattern found in both the Gospel (e.g., Lk 15.3–10) and Acts (e.g., 5.1–11) of juxtaposing characters of both genders.

18.1–17: Paul in Corinth. See 1 Cor 1–4 for Paul's own account. **1**: *Corinth,* the old city was famous but was razed in 146 BCE by the Romans. It was refounded as a colony in 44 BCE by Julius Caesar, became the capital of the

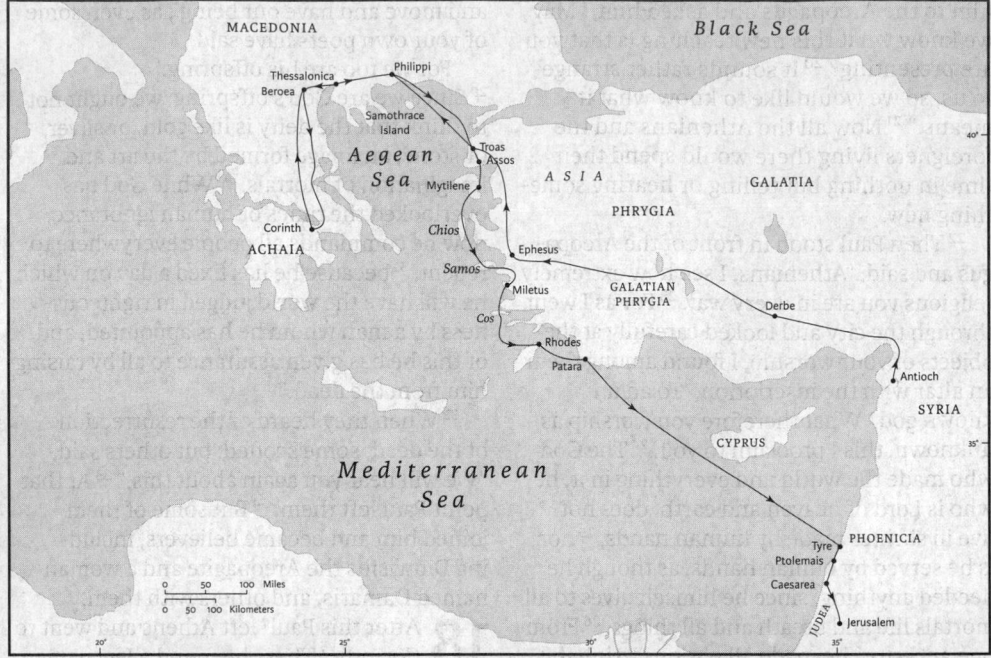

Chs 18–21: Third missionary journey of Paul.

come from Italy with his wife Priscilla, because Claudius had ordered all Jews to leave Rome. Paul[a] went to see them, [3] and, because he was of the same trade, he stayed with them, and they worked together—by trade they were tentmakers. [4] Every sabbath he would argue in the synagogue and would try to convince Jews and Greeks.

[5] When Silas and Timothy arrived from Macedonia, Paul was occupied with proclaiming the word,[b] testifying to the Jews that the Messiah[c] was Jesus. [6] When they opposed and reviled him, in protest he shook the dust from his clothes[d] and said to them, "Your blood be on your own heads! I am innocent. From now on I will go to the Gentiles." [7] Then

he left the synagogue[e] and went to the house of a man named Titius[f] Justus, a worshiper of God; his house was next door to the synagogue. [8] Crispus, the official of the synagogue, became a believer in the Lord, together with all his household; and many of the Corinthians who heard Paul became believers and were baptized. [9] One night the Lord said to Paul in a vision, "Do not be afraid, but speak

a   Gk *He*
b   Gk *with the word*
c   Or *the Christ*
d   Gk *reviled him, he shook out his clothes*
e   Gk *left there*
f   Other ancient authorities read *Titus*

senatorial province of Achaia in 27 BCE, and quickly emerged as an important commercial center owing to its location on the isthmus linking the Peloponnesus to mainland Greece with neighboring seaports to the east and west. **2:** *Pontus,* a Roman province of Asia Minor on the Black Sea. An edict issued by the emperor *Claudius* (see Suetonius, *Claudius* 25) expelling the *Jews* from *Rome* can probably be dated to 49 CE; this verse suggests that the trouble was connected with Jewish Christians. *Aquila* and *Priscilla* (or Prisca) worked with Paul, according to Rom 16.3–5. The fact that a church met in their house (Rom 16.5; 1 Cor 16.19) suggests that they were wealthy. In the epistles (including 2 Tim 4.19) their names appear in reverse order. **3:** *Same trade . . . tentmakers,* see 20.34. *He stayed with them,* possibly "lodged with them." **4:** *Synagogue,* 13.5n.; *Jews and Greeks,* 15.14n. **6:** 13.46n.,51n. *Your blood . . . ,* 2 Sam 1.16; Mt 27.25. **7:** *Worshiper of God,* 16.14n. **8:** *Crispus,* his baptism by Paul is mentioned as an exceptional case in 1 Cor 1.14. The conversion of the *official of the synagogue* (i.e., president; see 13.15) and his

and do not be silent; [10] for I am with you, and no one will lay a hand on you to harm you, for there are many in this city who are my people." [11] He stayed there a year and six months, teaching the word of God among them.

[12] But when Gallio was proconsul of Achaia, the Jews made a united attack on Paul and brought him before the tribunal. [13] They said, "This man is persuading people to worship God in ways that are contrary to the law." [14] Just as Paul was about to speak, Gallio said to the Jews, "If it were a matter of crime or serious villainy, I would be justified in accepting the complaint of you Jews; [15] but since it is a matter of questions about words and names and your own law, see to it yourselves; I do not wish to be a judge of these matters." [16] And he dismissed them from the tribunal. [17] Then all of them[a] seized Sosthenes, the official of the synagogue, and beat him in front of the tribunal. But Gallio paid no attention to any of these things.

[18] After staying there for a considerable time, Paul said farewell to the believers[b] and sailed for Syria, accompanied by Priscilla and Aquila. At Cenchreae he had his hair cut, for he was under a vow. [19] When they reached Ephesus, he left them there, but first he himself went into the synagogue and had a discussion with the Jews. [20] When they asked him to stay longer, he declined; [21] but on taking leave of them, he said, "I[c] will return to you, if God wills." Then he set sail from Ephesus.

[22] When he had landed at Caesarea, he went up to Jerusalem[d] and greeted the church, and then went down to Antioch. [23] After spending some time there he departed and went from place to place through the region of Galatia[e] and Phrygia, strengthening all the disciples.

[24] Now there came to Ephesus a Jew named Apollos, a native of Alexandria. He was an eloquent man, well-versed in the scriptures. [25] He had been instructed in the Way of the Lord; and he spoke with burning enthusiasm and taught accurately the things concerning Jesus, though he knew only the baptism of John. [26] He began to speak boldly in the synagogue; but when Priscilla and Aquila heard him, they took him aside and explained the Way of God to him more accurately. [27] And when he wished to cross over to Achaia, the believers[b] encouraged him and wrote to the disciples to welcome him. On his arrival he greatly helped those who through grace had become believers, [28] for he powerfully refuted the Jews in public, showing by the scriptures that the Messiah[f] is Jesus.

a   Other ancient authorities read *all the Greeks*
b   Gk *brothers*
c   Other ancient authorities read *I must at all costs keep the approaching festival in Jerusalem, but I*
d   Gk *went up*
e   Gk *the Galatian region*
f   Or *the Christ*

household (16.15n.) illustrates the continued success of Paul's mission among Jews (in spite of v. 6) in addition to Gentiles (*many of the Corinthians . . . became believers*). **12:** L. Junius *Gallio,* older brother of the philosopher Seneca, *proconsul of Achaia* about 52 CE. The dating of Gallio's proconsulship is crucial for the chronological reconstruction of Paul's career. **13:** *The law,* could mean the Jewish law (as Gallio takes it in v. 15) or Roman law, i.e., charges of sedition similar to the complaints raised in 16.21 and 17.7 (the latter would make more sense to present before a proconsul). **14–15:** *Gallio* again voices one of the subthemes of the book: Christianity is not a cause of concern for Rome. Roman representatives tend to be either outwardly favorable (e.g., Cornelius, Sergius Paulus) or at worst indifferent to Christianity, suggesting that it need not be viewed as incompatible with Rome (see 10.1n.). **17:** *Sosthenes* may be the one mentioned in 1 Cor 1.1, but the name is common.

18.18–23: End of the second missionary journey and beginning of the third. Paul returns to Antioch and goes back to Asia Minor. **18:** Paul *had his hair cut* as a temporary nazirite *vow* (21.23–24; Num 6.1–21), but the rule was to cut the hair off at the end of the vow. *Cenchreae,* the eastern port of Corinth (Rom 16.1). **19:** *Ephesus,* on the Aegean coast, was the capital of the Roman province of Asia. **22:** *Caesarea,* see 8.40n. *Jerusalem* still appears as the mother church. *Antioch,* see 11.19n. **23:** *The region of Galatia and Phrygia,* see 16.6n.

18.24–28: Apollos in Ephesus. 25: *The Way,* see 9.2n. Although he *taught accurately,* he had not received Christian baptism (13.25n.). **26:** *Speak boldly,* 13.46n. It is not disclosed in what sense things were *explained . . . more accurately.* **27–28:** For his activity in Corinth, see 1 Cor 1.12; 3.1–9,21–23.

19 While Apollos was in Corinth, Paul passed through the interior regions and came to Ephesus, where he found some disciples. [2] He said to them, "Did you receive the Holy Spirit when you became believers?" They replied, "No, we have not even heard that there is a Holy Spirit." [3] Then he said, "Into what then were you baptized?" They answered, "Into John's baptism." [4] Paul said, "John baptized with the baptism of repentance, telling the people to believe in the one who was to come after him, that is, in Jesus." [5] On hearing this, they were baptized in the name of the Lord Jesus. [6] When Paul had laid his hands on them, the Holy Spirit came upon them, and they spoke in tongues and prophesied— [7] altogether there were about twelve of them.

[8] He entered the synagogue and for three months spoke out boldly, and argued persuasively about the kingdom of God. [9] When some stubbornly refused to believe and spoke evil of the Way before the congregation, he left them, taking the disciples with him, and argued daily in the lecture hall of Tyrannus.[a] [10] This continued for two years, so that all the residents of Asia, both Jews and Greeks, heard the word of the Lord.

[11] God did extraordinary miracles through Paul, [12] so that when the handkerchiefs or aprons that had touched his skin were brought to the sick, their diseases left them, and the evil spirits came out of them. [13] Then some itinerant Jewish exorcists tried to use the name of the Lord Jesus over those who had evil spirits, saying, "I adjure you by the Jesus whom Paul proclaims." [14] Seven sons of a Jewish high priest named Sceva were doing this. [15] But the evil spirit said to them in reply, "Jesus I know, and Paul I know; but who are you?" [16] Then the man with the evil spirit leaped on them, mastered them all, and so overpowered them that they fled out of the house naked and wounded. [17] When this became known to all residents of Ephesus, both Jews and Greeks, everyone was awestruck; and the name of the Lord Jesus was praised. [18] Also many of those who became believers confessed and disclosed their practices. [19] A number of those who practiced magic collected their books and burned them publicly; when the value of these books[b] was calculated, it was found to come to fifty thousand silver coins. [20] So the word of the Lord grew mightily and prevailed.

[21] Now after these things had been accomplished, Paul resolved in the Spirit to go through Macedonia and Achaia, and then to go on to Jerusalem. He said, "After I have gone there, I must also see Rome." [22] So he sent two of his helpers, Timothy and Erastus, to Macedonia, while he himself stayed for some time longer in Asia.

[23] About that time no little disturbance broke out concerning the Way. [24] A man named Demetrius, a silversmith who made

---

a Other ancient authorities read *of a certain Tyrannus, from eleven o'clock in the morning to four in the afternoon*

b Gk *them*

19.1–41: Paul's long ministry in Ephesus. Paul wrote 1 and 2 Corinthians during the period of more than two years (v. 10; cf. 20.31) portrayed here. **1:** *The interior regions* of Asia Minor (18.23). *Disciples* elsewhere in Acts means Christians. **2:** All who read the Jewish scriptures would know of *a Holy Spirit* (Ps 51.11; Isa 63.10,11). The reference may be to outward signs of the Spirit's presence (v. 6; 10.44–48n.). **3:** *John's baptism,* 13.25n. **5–6:** See 6.6n.; 8.17. **8:** *Synagogue,* 13.5n. *Kingdom of God,* 1.3n. **9:** *The Way,* v. 23; see 9.2n. *Tyrannus,* perhaps a local philosopher; the name appears in inscriptions in Ephesus. The hours mentioned in note *a* suggest the building was available to Paul during siesta time. **10:** During Paul's stay of *two years . . . all the residents of Asia* heard the word (note the churches of Rev 2–3). The mixed character of the audience (*Jews and Greeks*) continues to be noted (15.14n.). **12:** Compare 5.15; on parallels between Peter and Paul, see 14.8–18n. **13:** For *Jewish exorcists,* see Lk 11.19. For use of the *name* outside the circle of Jesus, see Mk 9.38–39. **14:** *Sceva,* a high priest by this name is not known. **15–16:** The story makes it clear that the name (v. 17; 3.6n.) does not belong to the realm of magic. On a number of occasions Acts attempts to distinguish Christian miracle working from the activities of religious charlatans and profiteers (8.18–24; 13.6–12; 16.16–19). **19:** Ephesus was such a noted center of *magic* that magical books were often called "Ephesian Scripts." **21:** *Must . . . see Rome,* 23.11; 27.24; cf. Rom 1.13–15; 15.22–29. **22:** A city treasurer named *Erastus* is mentioned at Rom 16.23; the city of his office is not named, but Romans was likely written in Corinth; the name also appears at 2 Tim 4.20 ("Erastus remained in Corinth"). A Corinthian

silver shrines of Artemis, brought no little business to the artisans. ²⁵ These he gathered together, with the workers of the same trade, and said, "Men, you know that we get our wealth from this business. ²⁶ You also see and hear that not only in Ephesus but in almost the whole of Asia this Paul has persuaded and drawn away a considerable number of people by saying that gods made with hands are not gods. ²⁷ And there is danger not only that this trade of ours may come into disrepute but also that the temple of the great goddess Artemis will be scorned, and she will be deprived of her majesty that brought all Asia and the world to worship her."

²⁸ When they heard this, they were enraged and shouted, "Great is Artemis of the Ephesians!" ²⁹ The city was filled with the confusion; and people[a] rushed together to the theater, dragging with them Gaius and Aristarchus, Macedonians who were Paul's travel companions. ³⁰ Paul wished to go into the crowd, but the disciples would not let him; ³¹ even some officials of the province of Asia,[b] who were friendly to him, sent him a message urging him not to venture into the theater. ³² Meanwhile, some were shouting one thing, some another; for the assembly was in confusion, and most of them did not know why they had come together. ³³ Some of the crowd gave instructions to Alexander, whom the Jews had pushed forward. And Alexander motioned for silence and tried to make a defense before the people. ³⁴ But when they recognized that he was a Jew, for about two hours all of them shouted in unison, "Great is Artemis of the Ephesians!"

³⁵ But when the town clerk had quieted the crowd, he said, "Citizens of Ephesus, who is there that does not know that the city of the Ephesians is the temple keeper of the great Artemis and of the statue that fell from heaven?[c] ³⁶ Since these things cannot be denied, you ought to be quiet and do nothing rash. ³⁷ You have brought these men here who are neither temple robbers nor blasphemers of our[d] goddess. ³⁸ If therefore Demetrius and the artisans with him have a complaint against anyone, the courts are open, and there are proconsuls; let them bring charges there against one another. ³⁹ If there is anything further[e] you want to know, it must be settled in the regular assembly. ⁴⁰ For we are in danger of being charged with rioting today, since there is no cause that we can give to justify this commotion." ⁴¹ When he had said this, he dismissed the assembly.

20 After the uproar had ceased, Paul sent for the disciples; and after encouraging them and saying farewell, he left for Macedonia. ² When he had gone through those regions and had given the believers[f] much encouragement, he came to Greece, ³ where he stayed for three months. He was about to set sail for Syria when a plot was made against him by the Jews, and so he decided to return through Macedonia. ⁴ He

a Gk *they*
b Gk *some of the Asiarchs*
c Meaning of Gk uncertain
d Other ancient authorities read *your*
e Other ancient authorities read *about other matters*
f Gk *given them*

inscription mentions a Roman official (an aedile) by this name. **24:** *Shrines,* apparently miniature temples for use in religious ceremonies or as souvenirs or amulets. *Artemis,* chief divinity of Ephesus; her temple was one of the seven wonders of the ancient world. **25:** *Wealth,* the story joins others in which gain by religious means is criticized (see vv. 15–16n.). **29:** The *theater* has been excavated and could seat at least 24,000. **31:** *Asiarchs* (in note b) held office in a league of the cities of Asia and promoted the worship of the emperor. They were *friendly to* Paul and so portray again the favorable disposition of high officials toward Christianity. Such acceptance by high-status individuals suggested to Christian readers that social respectability was not beyond their grasp (16.37–38n.). **35:** *Temple keeper,* a designation assumed by Asiatic cities that had built a temple in honor of their patron god or the emperor. *The statue that fell from heaven,* apparently a meteorite. **36–40:** An argument that Christians were entitled to due process and that the actions taken thus far were unwarranted is put into the mouth of the town clerk.

20.1–6: The last visit to Greece. 2: *Through those regions,* revisiting the churches of Philippi, Thessalonica, and Beroea (see 19.21). **3:** *Three months,* at Corinth (see 2 Cor 12.14; 13.1; the problems evident in 2 Corinthians are not mentioned). *A plot . . . by the Jews,* 9.24; 20.19; 23.12. **4:** Paul's companions seem to be local representa-

was accompanied by Sopater son of Pyrrhus from Beroea, by Aristarchus and Secundus from Thessalonica, by Gaius from Derbe, and by Timothy, as well as by Tychicus and Trophimus from Asia. [5] They went ahead and were waiting for us in Troas; [6] but we sailed from Philippi after the days of Unleavened Bread, and in five days we joined them in Troas, where we stayed for seven days.

[7] On the first day of the week, when we met to break bread, Paul was holding a discussion with them; since he intended to leave the next day, he continued speaking until midnight. [8] There were many lamps in the room upstairs where we were meeting. [9] A young man named Eutychus, who was sitting in the window, began to sink off into a deep sleep while Paul talked still longer. Overcome by sleep, he fell to the ground three floors below and was picked up dead. [10] But Paul went down, and bending over him took him in his arms, and said, "Do not be alarmed, for his life is in him." [11] Then Paul went upstairs, and after he had broken bread and eaten, he continued to converse with them until dawn; then he left. [12] Meanwhile they had taken the boy away alive and were not a little comforted.

[13] We went ahead to the ship and set sail for Assos, intending to take Paul on board there; for he had made this arrangement, intending to go by land himself. [14] When he met us in Assos, we took him on board and went to Mitylene. [15] We sailed from there, and on the following day we arrived opposite Chios. The next day we touched at Samos, and[a] the

day after that we came to Miletus. [16] For Paul had decided to sail past Ephesus, so that he might not have to spend time in Asia; he was eager to be in Jerusalem, if possible, on the day of Pentecost.

[17] From Miletus he sent a message to Ephesus, asking the elders of the church to meet him. [18] When they came to him, he said to them:

"You yourselves know how I lived among you the entire time from the first day that I set foot in Asia, [19] serving the Lord with all humility and with tears, enduring the trials that came to me through the plots of the Jews. [20] I did not shrink from doing anything helpful, proclaiming the message to you and teaching you publicly and from house to house, [21] as I testified to both Jews and Greeks about repentance toward God and faith toward our Lord Jesus. [22] And now, as a captive to the Spirit,[b] I am on my way to Jerusalem, not knowing what will happen to me there, [23] except that the Holy Spirit testifies to me in every city that imprisonment and persecutions are waiting for me. [24] But I do not count my life of any value to myself, if only I may finish my course and the ministry that I received from the Lord Jesus, to testify to the good news of God's grace.

[25] "And now I know that none of you, among whom I have gone about proclaim-

a Other ancient authorities add *after remaining at Trogyllium*

b Or *And now, bound in the spirit*

tives of churches that have contributed to the collection for Jerusalem organized by Paul (see 11.29n.) who are traveling with him to deliver it (Rom 15.25–29; 1 Cor 16.3–4). Apart from 24.17 there is no hint of this major project of Paul's in Acts. *Sopater,* perhaps the Sosipater of Rom 16.21. *Aristarchus,* 19.29; 27.2 (Col 4.10; Philem 24). A *Gaius* from Macedonia is mentioned in 19.29, but Derbe is in the same region as *Timothy's* home (Lystra, see 16.1). *Tychicus,* Eph 6.21; Col 4.7; 2 Tim 4.12; Titus 3.12. *Trophimus,* 2 Tim 4.20. 5: The "we" passages (16.10n.) resume here at Philippi, the city where the previous passage ended (16.17). 6: *Days of Unleavened Bread,* 12.3n.

20.7–38: The raising of Eutychus and the speech to the Ephesian elders. 7: *The first day of the week,* Sunday. *Break bread,* see 2.42n.; 27.36–37. 9: *Eutychus,* a not uncommon name meaning "fortunate." *Three floors,* a tenement-style building is pictured. 10: An understated miraculous resurrection (cf. 14.19–20). 13: *Assos,* a port town on the coast, southwest of Troas, opposite the northern end of the island of Lesbos. 14: *Mitylene,* capital city of Lesbos. 15: *Chios,* an island south of Lesbos. *Samos,* an island southwest of Chios. *Miletus,* an important port on the western coast of Asia Minor at the mouth of the Meander River. The "we" passages resume again at 21.1. 16: *Sail past Ephesus,* while on route from Chios to Samos. *Pentecost,* see 2.1–41n. 17: *Elders,* 14.23n. 18–35: Paul's "farewell" address, the only speech in Acts explicitly addressed to Christians. It reviews Paul's accomplishments as depicted in Acts and looks forward to paint a picture of the church in Luke's day. 21: Paul's mission has been consistently portrayed as directed to both *Jews and Greeks.* 24–25: *Finish my course . . . testify,* a premonition of

ing the kingdom, will ever see my face again. [26] Therefore I declare to you this day that I am not responsible for the blood of any of you, [27] for I did not shrink from declaring to you the whole purpose of God. [28] Keep watch over yourselves and over all the flock, of which the Holy Spirit has made you overseers, to shepherd the church of God[a] that he obtained with the blood of his own Son.[b] [29] I know that after I have gone, savage wolves will come in among you, not sparing the flock. [30] Some even from your own group will come distorting the truth in order to entice the disciples to follow them. [31] Therefore be alert, remembering that for three years I did not cease night or day to warn everyone with tears. [32] And now I commend you to God and to the message of his grace, a message that is able to build you up and to give you the inheritance among all who are sanctified. [33] I coveted no one's silver or gold or clothing. [34] You know for yourselves that I worked with my own hands to support myself and my companions. [35] In all this I have given you an example that by such work we must support the weak, remembering the words of the Lord Jesus, for he himself said, 'It is more blessed to give than to receive.'"

[36] When he had finished speaking, he knelt down with them all and prayed. [37] There was much weeping among them all; they embraced Paul and kissed him, [38] grieving especially because of what he had said, that they would not see him again. Then they brought him to the ship.

21 When we had parted from them and set sail, we came by a straight course to Cos, and the next day to Rhodes, and from

there to Patara.[c] [2] When we found a ship bound for Phoenicia, we went on board and set sail. [3] We came in sight of Cyprus; and leaving it on our left, we sailed to Syria and landed at Tyre, because the ship was to unload its cargo there. [4] We looked up the disciples and stayed there for seven days. Through the Spirit they told Paul not to go on to Jerusalem. [5] When our days there were ended, we left and proceeded on our journey; and all of them, with wives and children, escorted us outside the city. There we knelt down on the beach and prayed [6] and said farewell to one another. Then we went on board the ship, and they returned home.

[7] When we had finished[d] the voyage from Tyre, we arrived at Ptolemais; and we greeted the believers[e] and stayed with them for one day. [8] The next day we left and came to Caesarea; and we went into the house of Philip the evangelist, one of the seven, and stayed with him. [9] He had four unmarried daughters[f] who had the gift of prophecy. [10] While we were staying there for several days, a prophet named Agabus came down from Judea. [11] He came to us and took Paul's belt, bound his own feet and hands with it, and said, "Thus says the Holy Spirit, 'This is the way the Jews in Jerusalem will bind the man who owns this belt and will hand him over to the Gentiles.'" [12] When we heard this, we and

a   Other ancient authorities read *of the Lord*
b   Or *with his own blood*; Gk *with the blood of his Own*
c   Other ancient authorities add *and Myra*
d   Or *continued*
e   Gk *brothers*
f   Gk *four daughters, virgins,*

martyrdom (2 Tim 4.6). **27**: *Purpose of God*, cf. 2.23; 4.28; 5.38–39; 13.36. **28**: *Overseers* (Gk "episkopoi"), used to designate officials in secular institutions; here it indicates those described as elders in v. 17. *Shepherd*, an image for leadership both in the Hebrew Bible (Jer 3.15; 23.1–4; Ezek 34.1–24) and in nonbiblical writings that also appears in the New Testament (Jn 21.15–17; Eph 4.11, "pastors"). In 1 Pet 5.1–4 elders are exhorted to "tend the flock of God." *With his own blood* (note b), understanding Jesus as a representative of God. *Church* has universal overtones; see 5.11n. Elsewhere in Luke-Acts, emphasis is placed on the resurrection, not the redemptive death of Christ. **29–30**: Mt 7.15; Mk 13.22; the Pastoral Epistles. **34**: 18.3; 1 Cor 9.1–18. **35**: A saying of *Jesus* not found in the Gospels.

21.1–16: Journey to Jerusalem. 1: The "we" passages (16.10n.) resume. *Cos*, an island off the southwestern coast of Asia Minor. **4:** V. 12; 20.23. **7:** *Ptolemais*, a port town in Phoenicia (modern Akko, near Haifa), 22 mi (35 km) south of Tyre. **8:** *Philip the evangelist* (8.5n.) had arrived in *Caesarea* (8.40n.) some time before. *One of the seven*, see 6.1–7. **9:** Philip's *daughters* became important figures in the church traditions of Hierapolis and Ephesus. **10–11:** *Agabus* (11.28), like Hebrew prophets (1 Kings 11.29–32; Isa 20.2–6), performs

the people there urged him not to go up to Jerusalem. [13] Then Paul answered, "What are you doing, weeping and breaking my heart? For I am ready not only to be bound but even to die in Jerusalem for the name of the Lord Jesus." [14] Since he would not be persuaded, we remained silent except to say, "The Lord's will be done."

[15] After these days we got ready and started to go up to Jerusalem. [16] Some of the disciples from Caesarea also came along and brought us to the house of Mnason of Cyprus, an early disciple, with whom we were to stay.

[17] When we arrived in Jerusalem, the brothers welcomed us warmly. [18] The next day Paul went with us to visit James; and all the elders were present. [19] After greeting them, he related one by one the things that God had done among the Gentiles through his ministry. [20] When they heard it, they praised God. Then they said to him, "You see, brother, how many thousands of believers there are among the Jews, and they are all zealous for the law. [21] They have been told about you that you teach all the Jews living among the Gentiles to forsake Moses, and that you tell them not to circumcise their children or observe the customs. [22] What then is to be done? They will certainly hear that you have come. [23] So do what we tell you. We have four men who are under a vow. [24] Join these men, go through the rite of purification with them, and pay for the shaving of their heads. Thus all will know that there is nothing in what they have been told about you, but that you yourself observe and guard the law. [25] But as for the Gentiles who have become believers, we have sent a letter with our judgment that they should abstain from what has been sacrificed to idols and from blood and from what is strangled[a] and from fornication." [26] Then Paul took the men, and the next day, having purified himself, he entered the temple with them, making public the completion of the days of purification when the sacrifice would be made for each of them.

[27] When the seven days were almost completed, the Jews from Asia, who had seen him in the temple, stirred up the whole crowd. They seized him, [28] shouting, "Fellow Israelites, help! This is the man who is teaching everyone everywhere against our people, our law, and this place; more than that, he has actually brought Greeks into the temple and has defiled this holy place." [29] For they had previously seen Trophimus the Ephesian with him in the city, and they supposed that Paul had brought him into the temple. [30] Then all the city was aroused, and the people rushed together. They seized Paul and dragged him out of the temple, and immediately the doors were shut. [31] While they were trying to kill him, word came to the tribune of the cohort that all Jerusalem was in an uproar. [32] Immediately he took soldiers and centurions and ran down to them. When they saw the tribune and the soldiers, they stopped beating Paul. [33] Then the tribune came, arrested him, and ordered him to be

---

a   Other ancient authorities lack *and from what is strangled*

---

a symbolic act. The prediction is not strictly fulfilled in the chapters that follow. **12**: V. 4. **14**: Paul appears as a heroic figure, cf. Lk 22.42. **16**: *An early disciple,* note Christianity in connection with *Cyprus* at 4.36; 11.19–20; 13.4–12.

21.17–26: Paul's observance of Jewish tradition. 17–20: The *Jerusalem* church accepts Paul and his accomplishments as complementary to their own in a harmonious portrait of unity (cf. Gal 2). **18**: *James,* see 12.17n.; *the elders,* 11.30n. The "we" passage stops here. **20**: *Thousands of believers,* Acts represents the success of Christianity among *Jews* as phenomenal (cf. 6.7). *Zealous for the law,* see 11.2n.; 15.1n., 15.5n.; cf. Gal 2. **21**: *Moses,* see 15.21n. The charge has been anticipated (16.3n.). The informants are not identified (see v. 28). **23–24**: Paul can demonstrate his faithfulness to the law by undergoing *purification* for uncleanness with some others and paying the expenses upon their release from a nazirite *vow* (18.18n.). **25**: He is told of the decree (15.20, 29) as though he had not heard of it (see 16.4).

21.27–40: Uproar in the Temple and arrest of Paul. Seized after a disturbance in the Temple, Paul begins his defense. **28**: It was a capital offense for non-Jews to pass beyond the Court of the Gentiles; an inscription stating this has been discovered (cf. Josephus, *J.W.* 5.193–194; 6.125–126). **29**: *Trophimus,* 20.4; 2 Tim 4.20. **31**: A military *tribune* commanded a *cohort* (a detachment of 1,000 men); this would have been stationed in the cita-

bound with two chains; he inquired who he was and what he had done. [34] Some in the crowd shouted one thing, some another; and as he could not learn the facts because of the uproar, he ordered him to be brought into the barracks. [35] When Paul[a] came to the steps, the violence of the mob was so great that he had to be carried by the soldiers. [36] The crowd that followed kept shouting, "Away with him!"

[37] Just as Paul was about to be brought into the barracks, he said to the tribune, "May I say something to you?" The tribune[b] replied, "Do you know Greek? [38] Then you are not the Egyptian who recently stirred up a revolt and led the four thousand assassins out into the wilderness?" [39] Paul replied, "I am a Jew, from Tarsus in Cilicia, a citizen of an important city; I beg you, let me speak to the people." [40] When he had given him permission, Paul stood on the steps and motioned to the people for silence; and when there was a great hush, he addressed them in the Hebrew[c] language, saying:

22 "Brothers and fathers, listen to the defense that I now make before you."

[2] When they heard him addressing them in Hebrew,[c] they became even more quiet. Then he said:

[3] "I am a Jew, born in Tarsus in Cilicia, but brought up in this city at the feet of Gamaliel, educated strictly according to our ancestral law, being zealous for God, just as all of you are today. [4] I persecuted this Way up to the point of death by binding both men and women and putting them in prison, [5] as the high priest and the whole council of elders can testify about me. From them I also received letters to the brothers in Damascus, and I went there in order to bind those who

were there and to bring them back to Jerusalem for punishment.

[6] "While I was on my way and approaching Damascus, about noon a great light from heaven suddenly shone about me. [7] I fell to the ground and heard a voice saying to me, 'Saul, Saul, why are you persecuting me?' [8] I answered, 'Who are you, Lord?' Then he said to me, 'I am Jesus of Nazareth[d] whom you are persecuting.' [9] Now those who were with me saw the light but did not hear the voice of the one who was speaking to me. [10] I asked, 'What am I to do, Lord?' The Lord said to me, 'Get up and go to Damascus; there you will be told everything that has been assigned to you to do.' [11] Since I could not see because of the brightness of that light, those who were with me took my hand and led me to Damascus.

[12] "A certain Ananias, who was a devout man according to the law and well spoken of by all the Jews living there, [13] came to me; and standing beside me, he said, 'Brother Saul, regain your sight!' In that very hour I regained my sight and saw him. [14] Then he said, 'The God of our ancestors has chosen you to know his will, to see the Righteous One and to hear his own voice; [15] for you will be his witness to all the world of what you have seen and heard. [16] And now why do you delay? Get up, be baptized, and have your sins washed away, calling on his name.'

[17] "After I had returned to Jerusalem and while I was praying in the temple, I fell into a trance [18] and saw Jesus[e] saying to me, 'Hurry

a   Gk *he*
b   Gk *He*
c   That is, *Aramaic*
d   Gk *the Nazorean*
e   Gk *him*

---

del Antonia, which had access to the Temple courtyard (see Josephus, *J.W.* 5.244). **33:** Paul's case came into the hands of Roman, not Jewish, authorities. **36:** *Away with him,* 22.22; cf. Lk 23.18. **38:** The question in Greek may be: "Are you not the Egyptian?" Concerning *the Egyptian,* a pseudo-messiah who, with thousands of followers, had planned to take Jerusalem from the Romans, see Josephus, *J.W.* 2.261–263 (which puts the number at about 30,000); *Ant.* 20.169–172. **39:** *Paul* gives assurances that he is not the Egyptian. *Tarsus,* 9.30n.

22.1–29: Defense in the Temple and Roman custody. 1: *Defense* is the principal theme of the next chapters (24.10; 25.8,16; 26.1–2). It has a clear function at the level of the narrative and also allows Luke to endorse Paul for readers who may have had questions about him. **3:** *Brought up,* educated. *Gamaliel,* see 5.34n. *Zealous,* 21.20; in Gal 1.14 as a self-description of Paul. **4–21:** Cf. 9.1–18; 26.9–18. **9:** In 9.7 the companions heard the voice but saw no one. **14–15:** What Ananias says here is roughly parallel to what the Lord tells him in 9.15. **17–21:** The report of the vision is not given in the other conversion accounts. Paul's commission to the Gentiles is signifi-

and get out of Jerusalem quickly, because they will not accept your testimony about me.' [19] And I said, 'Lord, they themselves know that in every synagogue I imprisoned and beat those who believed in you. [20] And while the blood of your witness Stephen was shed, I myself was standing by, approving and keeping the coats of those who killed him.' [21] Then he said to me, 'Go, for I will send you far away to the Gentiles.'"

[22] Up to this point they listened to him, but then they shouted, "Away with such a fellow from the earth! For he should not be allowed to live." [23] And while they were shouting, throwing off their cloaks, and tossing dust into the air, [24] the tribune directed that he was to be brought into the barracks, and ordered him to be examined by flogging, to find out the reason for this outcry against him. [25] But when they had tied him up with thongs,[a] Paul said to the centurion who was standing by, "Is it legal for you to flog a Roman citizen who is uncondemned?" [26] When the centurion heard that, he went to the tribune and said to him, "What are you about to do? This man is a Roman citizen." [27] The tribune came and asked Paul,[b] "Tell me, are you a Roman citizen?" And he said, "Yes." [28] The tribune answered, "It cost me a large sum of money to get my citizenship." Paul said, "But I was born a citizen." [29] Immediately those who were about to examine him drew back from him; and the tribune also was afraid, for he realized that Paul was a Roman citizen and that he had bound him.

[30] Since he wanted to find out what Paul[c] was being accused of by the Jews, the next day he released him and ordered the chief priests and the entire council to meet. He brought Paul down and had him stand before them.

23 While Paul was looking intently at the council he said, "Brothers,[d] up to this day I have lived my life with a clear conscience before God." [2] Then the high priest Ananias ordered those standing near him to strike him on the mouth. [3] At this Paul said to him, "God will strike you, you whitewashed wall! Are you sitting there to judge me according to the law, and yet in violation of the law you order me to be struck?" [4] Those standing nearby said, "Do you dare to insult God's high priest?" [5] And Paul said, "I did not realize, brothers, that he was high priest; for it is written, 'You shall not speak evil of a leader of your people.'"

[6] When Paul noticed that some were Sadducees and others were Pharisees, he called out in the council, "Brothers, I am a Pharisee, a son of Pharisees. I am on trial concerning the hope of the resurrection[e] of the dead." [7] When he said this, a dissension began between the Pharisees and the Sadducees, and the assembly was divided. [8] (The Sadducees say that there is no resurrection, or angel, or spirit; but the Pharisees acknowledge all three.) [9] Then a great clamor arose, and certain scribes of the Pharisees' group stood up and contended, "We find nothing wrong with this man. What if a spirit or an angel has spoken to him?" [10] When the dissension became violent, the tribune, fearing that they would tear Paul to pieces, ordered the soldiers to go down, take him by force, and bring him into the barracks.

[a] Or *up for the lashes*
[b] Gk *him*
[c] Gk *he*
[d] Gk *Men, brothers*
[e] Gk *concerning hope and resurrection*

cantly located in the *temple*. **20**: See 7.58. **24**: *Examined by flogging* to determine the truth of the matter (2 Cor 11.23). **25–29**: That Paul is *a Roman citizen* is disclosed at the last moment; see 16.37–38n. In the early part of the emperor Claudius's reign *citizenship* was often purchased for *a large sum*. The scene increases Paul's status for readers of Acts and reinforces the theme of the compatibility of Christianity and Roman life; there is nothing in Paul's letters to indicate that he was a Roman citizen.

22.30–23.11: Paul before the Sanhedrin. The tribune brings him before it to get evidence, not to try him. **22.30**: The tribune calls for an advisory meeting of the *council;* see 5.21n. **23.2**: *Ananias, high priest* in the reigns of Claudius and Nero, was murdered by rebels about 66 CE. **3**: *Whitewashed wall*, cf. Ezek 13.10–15; Mt 23.27. **5**: Ex 22.28. It is strange that Paul does not recognize the *high priest*. **6**: *Paul* as a *Pharisee* (26.5; Phil 3.5) realizes he can exploit a difference of opinion between *Sadducees* and *Pharisees* over the *resurrection* (see Josephus, *J.W.* 2.163–165). **8**: *Sadducees* denied a *resurrection* (Mk 12.18). **9**: The *Pharisees* side with Paul (see 15.5n.). **10**: Paul is

[11] That night the Lord stood near him and said, "Keep up your courage! For just as you have testified for me in Jerusalem, so you must bear witness also in Rome."

[12] In the morning the Jews joined in a conspiracy and bound themselves by an oath neither to eat nor drink until they had killed Paul. [13] There were more than forty who joined in this conspiracy. [14] They went to the chief priests and elders and said, "We have strictly bound ourselves by an oath to taste no food until we have killed Paul. [15] Now then, you and the council must notify the tribune to bring him down to you, on the pretext that you want to make a more thorough examination of his case. And we are ready to do away with him before he arrives."

[16] Now the son of Paul's sister heard about the ambush; so he went and gained entrance to the barracks and told Paul. [17] Paul called one of the centurions and said, "Take this young man to the tribune, for he has something to report to him." [18] So he took him, brought him to the tribune, and said, "The prisoner Paul called me and asked me to bring this young man to you; he has something to tell you." [19] The tribune took him by the hand, drew him aside privately, and asked, "What is it that you have to report to me?" [20] He answered, "The Jews have agreed to ask you to bring Paul down to the council tomorrow, as though they were going to inquire more thoroughly into his case. [21] But do not be persuaded by them, for more than forty of their men are lying in ambush for him. They have bound themselves by an oath neither to eat nor drink until they kill him. They are ready now and are waiting for your consent."

[22] So the tribune dismissed the young man, ordering him, "Tell no one that you have informed me of this."

[23] Then he summoned two of the centurions and said, "Get ready to leave by nine o'clock tonight for Caesarea with two hundred soldiers, seventy horsemen, and two hundred spearmen. [24] Also provide mounts for Paul to ride, and take him safely to Felix the governor." [25] He wrote a letter to this effect:

[26] "Claudius Lysias to his Excellency the governor Felix, greetings. [27] This man was seized by the Jews and was about to be killed by them, but when I had learned that he was a Roman citizen, I came with the guard and rescued him. [28] Since I wanted to know the charge for which they accused him, I had him brought to their council. [29] I found that he was accused concerning questions of their law, but was charged with nothing deserving death or imprisonment. [30] When I was informed that there would be a plot against the man, I sent him to you at once, ordering his accusers also to state before you what they have against him.[a]"

[31] So the soldiers, according to their instructions, took Paul and brought him during the night to Antipatris. [32] The next day they let the horsemen go on with him, while they returned to the barracks. [33] When they came to Caesarea and delivered the letter to the governor, they presented Paul also before him. [34] On reading the letter, he asked what province he belonged to, and when he learned that he was from Cilicia, [35] he said, "I will give you a hearing when your accus-

---

a   Other ancient authorities add *Farewell*

rescued from mob violence for a second time by an agent of Rome (21.33–36). **11**: A vision (cf. 18.9–10) provides assurance that martyrdom will not occur in Jerusalem (21.13).

23.12–35: A plot to kill Paul results in his transfer to Caesarea, the seat of the Roman governor. **12**: *Conspiracy*, 9.24; 20.19. **16**: There is no other extant information about Paul's family. The notion of Paul's education in Jerusalem (22.3) could suggest that other family members were there. **17–22**: The prisoner Paul's remarkable access to the commanders shows some favoritism. **23**: *Caesarea*, 8.40n. The number of *soldiers* emphasizes the danger faced. The Gk word translated *spearmen* is obscure. **24**: Antonius *Felix*, procurator of Judea (ca. 52–56 CE), brother of Pallas, a favorite freedman of the emperor Claudius. **26**: *His Excellency*, the same word used in addressing Theophilus (Lk 1.3). **27–30**: The letter summarizes the preceding events and perhaps casts the tribune in a better light. As was the case with Jesus (Lk 23.4,14–16,20–25), Romans find no serious charges (v. 29; cf. 18.14–16). **31**: *Antipatris*, a city in the Plain of Sharon on the main road to Caesarea. **35**: *Herod's headquarters*, a palace built by Herod the Great and occupied by the Roman governors in Palestine.

ers arrive." Then he ordered that he be kept under guard in Herod's headquarters.[a]

24 Five days later the high priest Ananias came down with some elders and an attorney, a certain Tertullus, and they reported their case against Paul to the governor. [2] When Paul[b] had been summoned, Tertullus began to accuse him, saying:

"Your Excellency,[c] because of you we have long enjoyed peace, and reforms have been made for this people because of your foresight. [3] We welcome this in every way and everywhere with utmost gratitude. [4] But, to detain you no further, I beg you to hear us briefly with your customary graciousness. [5] We have, in fact, found this man a pestilent fellow, an agitator among all the Jews throughout the world, and a ringleader of the sect of the Nazarenes.[d] [6] He even tried to profane the temple, and so we seized him.[e] [8] By examining him yourself you will be able to learn from him concerning everything of which we accuse him."

[9] The Jews also joined in the charge by asserting that all this was true.

[10] When the governor motioned to him to speak, Paul replied:

"I cheerfully make my defense, knowing that for many years you have been a judge over this nation. [11] As you can find out, it is not more than twelve days since I went up to worship in Jerusalem. [12] They did not find me disputing with anyone in the temple or stirring up a crowd either in the synagogues or throughout the city. [13] Neither can they prove to you the charge that they now bring against me. [14] But this I admit to you, that according to the Way, which they call a sect, I worship the God of our ancestors, believing everything laid down according to the law or written in the prophets. [15] I have a hope in God—a hope

that they themselves also accept—that there will be a resurrection of both[f] the righteous and the unrighteous. [16] Therefore I do my best always to have a clear conscience toward God and all people. [17] Now after some years I came to bring alms to my nation and to offer sacrifices. [18] While I was doing this, they found me in the temple, completing the rite of purification, without any crowd or disturbance. [19] But there were some Jews from Asia—they ought to be here before you to make an accusation, if they have anything against me. [20] Or let these men here tell what crime they had found when I stood before the council, [21] unless it was this one sentence that I called out while standing before them, 'It is about the resurrection of the dead that I am on trial before you today.'"

[22] But Felix, who was rather well informed about the Way, adjourned the hearing with the comment, "When Lysias the tribune comes down, I will decide your case." [23] Then he ordered the centurion to keep him in custody, but to let him have some liberty and not to prevent any of his friends from taking care of his needs.

[24] Some days later when Felix came with his wife Drusilla, who was Jewish, he sent for Paul and heard him speak concerning faith in Christ Jesus. [25] And as he discussed justice, self-control, and the coming judgment, Felix

a Gk *praetorium*
b Gk *he*
c Gk lacks *Your Excellency*
d Gk *Nazoreans*
e Other ancient authorities add *and we would have judged him according to our law.* [7] *But the chief captain Lysias came and with great violence took him out of our hands,* [8] *commanding his accusers to come before you.*
f Other ancient authorities read *of the dead, both of*

24.1–27: Paul before Felix. The apostle denies the charges, and the governor postpones the case. **2–4:** *Tertullus* begins the prosecution with the customary method of opening a speech with praise that is intended to attract the attention and good will of the one being addressed. **5:** *Agitator,* a charge of political sedition (see 16.21; 17.7; 18.13) would be taken seriously by a Roman court. *Sect,* or party, is used in a bad sense here and at 24.14; 28.22; it is used of the Sadducees at 5.17. *Nazarenes,* the term otherwise used in the singular to identify Jesus (2.22; 3.6; 4.10; 6.14; 22.8) is here used in the plural to describe Christians for Christians. **6:** *Profane the temple,* 21.28. **10:** See 22.1n. **14:** *The Way* (see 9.2n.) is compatible with the ancestral religion. **15:** *Resurrection,* here general belief in resurrection as common ground (also v. 21). **16:** *Clear conscience,* 20.20,27,33; 23.1. **17:** *To bring alms,* may connect to 21.23–26 but is reminiscent of Paul's plan in Rom 15.25–29 to deliver the collection (see 11.29n.; 20.4n.). **23:** *Custody,* perhaps protective custody. **24:** *Drusilla* was the sister of Herod Agrippa II and Bernice (25.13); she had left her husband Azizus, king of Emesa, to marry Felix. **25–26:** Cf. Mk 6.20. *Felix embod-*

became frightened and said, "Go away for the present; when I have an opportunity, I will send for you." [26] At the same time he hoped that money would be given him by Paul, and for that reason he used to send for him very often and converse with him.

[27] After two years had passed, Felix was succeeded by Porcius Festus; and since he wanted to grant the Jews a favor, Felix left Paul in prison.

25 Three days after Festus had arrived in the province, he went up from Caesarea to Jerusalem [2] where the chief priests and the leaders of the Jews gave him a report against Paul. They appealed to him [3] and requested, as a favor to them against Paul,[a] to have him transferred to Jerusalem. They were, in fact, planning an ambush to kill him along the way. [4] Festus replied that Paul was being kept at Caesarea, and that he himself intended to go there shortly. [5] "So," he said, "let those of you who have the authority come down with me, and if there is anything wrong about the man, let them accuse him."

[6] After he had stayed among them not more than eight or ten days, he went down to Caesarea; the next day he took his seat on the tribunal and ordered Paul to be brought. [7] When he arrived, the Jews who had gone down from Jerusalem surrounded him, bringing many serious charges against him, which they could not prove. [8] Paul said in his defense, "I have in no way committed an offense against the law of the Jews, or against the temple, or against the emperor." [9] But Festus, wishing to do the Jews a favor, asked Paul, "Do you wish to go up to Jerusalem and be tried there before me on these charges?" [10] Paul said, "I am appealing to the emperor's

tribunal; this is where I should be tried. I have done no wrong to the Jews, as you very well know. [11] Now if I am in the wrong and have committed something for which I deserve to die, I am not trying to escape death; but if there is nothing to their charges against me, no one can turn me over to them. I appeal to the emperor." [12] Then Festus, after he had conferred with his council, replied, "You have appealed to the emperor; to the emperor you will go."

[13] After several days had passed, King Agrippa and Bernice arrived at Caesarea to welcome Festus. [14] Since they were staying there several days, Festus laid Paul's case before the king, saying, "There is a man here who was left in prison by Felix. [15] When I was in Jerusalem, the chief priests and the elders of the Jews informed me about him and asked for a sentence against him. [16] I told them that it was not the custom of the Romans to hand over anyone before the accused had met the accusers face to face and had been given an opportunity to make a defense against the charge. [17] So when they met here, I lost no time, but on the next day took my seat on the tribunal and ordered the man to be brought. [18] When the accusers stood up, they did not charge him with any of the crimes[b] that I was expecting. [19] Instead they had certain points of disagreement with him about their own religion and about a certain Jesus, who had died, but whom Paul asserted to be alive. [20] Since I was at a loss how to investigate these questions, I asked whether he wished to go to Jerusalem and be tried there on these

a Gk *him*

b Other ancient authorities read *with anything*

---

ies both positive and negative features, but ultimately his corruption means that Paul remains in prison. **27:** *After two years had passed,* either from Felix's appointment or Paul's arrest. *Porcius Festus,* appointed procurator of Judea by the emperor Nero in 60 CE.

25.1–12: Appeal to the emperor. Paul insists on a Roman trial, and Festus consents to send him to Rome. **3:** See 23.12. **8:** Paul maintains that he is both a good Jew and a good Roman citizen. **9:** *Favor,* 24.27. **10:** Paul fears being turned over to a Jewish court; therefore he insists on *the emperor's tribunal,* i.e., trial according to Roman law. **11–12:** Paul's *appeal* to the *emperor* becomes the mechanism that takes him to Rome (19.21; 23.11). Details of the law of appeals are unclear.

25.13–26.32: Paul's defense before Agrippa. Paul's speech is intended to present a model defense of Christianity and allows for the pronouncement of a symbolic Roman acquittal. **25.13:** *King Agrippa,* Herod Agrippa II (ruled 53–ca. 93 CE), sided with the Romans in the First Jewish Revolt. He and his sister *Bernice* were children of Herod Agrippa I (12.1n.). **16:** Roman judicial process is put in a good light. **18–20:** The *accusers* do not bring a

charges.[a] [21] But when Paul had appealed to be kept in custody for the decision of his Imperial Majesty, I ordered him to be held until I could send him to the emperor." [22] Agrippa said to Festus, "I would like to hear the man myself." "Tomorrow," he said, "you will hear him."

[23] So on the next day Agrippa and Bernice came with great pomp, and they entered the audience hall with the military tribunes and the prominent men of the city. Then Festus gave the order and Paul was brought in. [24] And Festus said, "King Agrippa and all here present with us, you see this man about whom the whole Jewish community petitioned me, both in Jerusalem and here, shouting that he ought not to live any longer. [25] But I found that he had done nothing deserving death; and when he appealed to his Imperial Majesty, I decided to send him. [26] But I have nothing definite to write to our sovereign about him. Therefore I have brought him before all of you, and especially before you, King Agrippa, so that, after we have examined him, I may have something to write— [27] for it seems to me unreasonable to send a prisoner without indicating the charges against him."

26 Agrippa said to Paul, "You have permission to speak for yourself." Then Paul stretched out his hand and began to defend himself:

[2] "I consider myself fortunate that it is before you, King Agrippa, I am to make my defense today against all the accusations of the Jews, [3] because you are especially familiar with all the customs and controversies of the Jews; therefore I beg of you to listen to me patiently.

[4] "All the Jews know my way of life from my youth, a life spent from the beginning among my own people and in Jerusalem. [5] They have known for a long time, if they are willing to testify, that I have belonged to the strictest sect of our religion and lived as a Pharisee. [6] And now I stand here on trial on account of my hope in the promise made by God to our ancestors, [7] a promise that our twelve tribes hope to attain, as they earnestly worship day and night. It is for this hope, your Excellency,[b] that I am accused by Jews! [8] Why is it thought incredible by any of you that God raises the dead?

[9] "Indeed, I myself was convinced that I ought to do many things against the name of Jesus of Nazareth.[c] [10] And that is what I did in Jerusalem; with authority received from the chief priests, I not only locked up many of the saints in prison, but I also cast my vote against them when they were being condemned to death. [11] By punishing them often in all the synagogues I tried to force them to blaspheme; and since I was so furiously enraged at them, I pursued them even to foreign cities.

[12] "With this in mind, I was traveling to Damascus with the authority and commission of the chief priests, [13] when at midday along the road, your Excellency,[b] I saw a light from heaven, brighter than the sun, shining around me and my companions. [14] When we had all fallen to the ground, I heard a voice saying to me in the Hebrew[d] language, 'Saul, Saul, why are you persecuting me? It hurts you to kick against the goads.' [15] I asked, 'Who are you, Lord?' The Lord answered, 'I am Jesus whom you are persecuting. [16] But get up and stand on your feet; for I have appeared

a   Gk *on them*
b   Gk *O king*
c   Gk *the Nazorean*
d   That is, *Aramaic*

charge of sedition (24.5). Cf. 18.13–16; but in this case Festus does not dismiss the charges. **25**: *Nothing deserving death* is the repeated verdict of the Roman authorities handling Paul's case (26.31; cf. Lk 23.4,15,22). *His Imperial Majesty,* lit., "Augustus," one of the imperial titles. **26.1**: The scene set for Paul's speech fulfills 9.15 and Lk 21.12–15. Compare Jesus' appearance before Herod Antipas (Lk 23.6–12). **2**: *Defense,* 22.1n. **3**: The narrative assumes that Agrippa was a practicing Jew. **4**: *Among my own people,* stresses Paul's thoroughly Jewish upbringing (22.3n.; Phil 3.5). **8**: *You,* i.e., the Jewish people. **9–20**: A third account of Paul's conversion (9.1–8; 22.4–16). **10**: *In Jerusalem,* according to 9.1–2 Paul's authorization concerned Damascus. *Saints,* see 9.13n. **14**: Here *all fall to the ground* and the *voice* speaks *Hebrew,* quoting a common Greek proverb about the futility of resisting the divine will (cf. 9.4; 22.7); a goad is a pointed stick used to prod an ox or other animals. **16**: Only in

to you for this purpose, to appoint you to serve and testify to the things in which you have seen me[a] and to those in which I will appear to you. [17] I will rescue you from your people and from the Gentiles—to whom I am sending you [18] to open their eyes so that they may turn from darkness to light and from the power of Satan to God, so that they may receive forgiveness of sins and a place among those who are sanctified by faith in me.'

[19] "After that, King Agrippa, I was not disobedient to the heavenly vision, [20] but declared first to those in Damascus, then in Jerusalem and throughout the countryside of Judea, and also to the Gentiles, that they should repent and turn to God and do deeds consistent with repentance. [21] For this reason the Jews seized me in the temple and tried to kill me. [22] To this day I have had help from God, and so I stand here, testifying to both small and great, saying nothing but what the prophets and Moses said would take place: [23] that the Messiah[b] must suffer, and that, by being the first to rise from the dead, he would proclaim light both to our people and to the Gentiles."

[24] While he was making this defense, Festus exclaimed, "You are out of your mind, Paul! Too much learning is driving you insane!" [25] But Paul said, "I am not out of my mind, most excellent Festus, but I am speaking the sober truth. [26] Indeed the king knows about these things, and to him I speak freely; for I am certain that none of these things has escaped his notice, for this was not done in a corner. [27] King Agrippa, do you believe the prophets? I know that you believe." [28] Agrippa said to Paul, "Are you so quickly persuading me to become a Christian?"[c] [29] Paul replied,

"Whether quickly or not, I pray to God that not only you but also all who are listening to me today might become such as I am—except for these chains."

[30] Then the king got up, and with him the governor and Bernice and those who had been seated with them; [31] and as they were leaving, they said to one another, "This man is doing nothing to deserve death or imprisonment." [32] Agrippa said to Festus, "This man could have been set free if he had not appealed to the emperor."

27 When it was decided that we were to sail for Italy, they transferred Paul and some other prisoners to a centurion of the Augustan Cohort, named Julius. [2] Embarking on a ship of Adramyttium that was about to set sail to the ports along the coast of Asia, we put to sea, accompanied by Aristarchus, a Macedonian from Thessalonica. [3] The next day we put in at Sidon; and Julius treated Paul kindly, and allowed him to go to his friends to be cared for. [4] Putting out to sea from there, we sailed under the lee of Cyprus, because the winds were against us. [5] After we had sailed across the sea that is off Cilicia and Pamphylia, we came to Myra in Lycia. [6] There the centurion found an Alexandrian ship bound for Italy and put us on board. [7] We sailed slowly for a number of days and arrived with difficulty off Cnidus, and as the wind was against us, we sailed under the lee of Crete off Salmone. [8] Sailing past it

a Other ancient authorities read *the things that you have seen*

b Or *the Christ*

c Or *Quickly you will persuade me to play the Christian*

this account does Paul's commission on the road come directly from Jesus (cf. Gal 1.1); there is no mention of Ananias or Paul's blindness. **20**: Paul's mission is universal, directed to both Jews and Greeks. **21**: *For this reason*, i.e., inclusion of the Gentiles. **22–23**: *The prophets and Moses . . . the Messiah must suffer*, 3.18n.; 10.43; 15.21n.; Lk 24.25–27,44–47. **27**: See v. 3. **28**: *Christian*, see 11.25–26n. **31**: *Nothing to deserve death or imprisonment*, a further "acquittal" (25.25n.). **32**: See 25.11–12n.

27.1–44: Shipwreck. A dangerous winter voyage ends in shipwreck. **1**: The "we" passages (16.10n.) resume here. *The Augustan Cohort*, a unit of this name was stationed in Syria in the first century. **2**: *Adramyttium*, a seaport south of Troas (16.8). *Aristarchus*, 19.29; 20.4. *Thessalonica*, 17.1n. **3**: *Sidon*, a Phoenician seaport, north of Tyre. *Julius treated Paul kindly*, compare the centurions of Lk 7.1–10; 23.47; and Cornelius (10.1–2n.). *Friends*, i.e., Christians. **4**: *Under the lee of Cyprus*, apparently north of the island. **5–6**: *Myra* on the southern coast of Asia Minor was a regular stage in the route of Egyptian grain ships bound for Italy (see v. 38). **7**: *Cnidus*, on the mainland northwest of Rhodes. *Under the lee of Crete*, to its south for shelter from the *wind*; *Salmone* is at the northeast tip of the island. **8**: *Fair Havens*, a bay on the southern coast of Crete. *Lasea*, a city somewhat inland

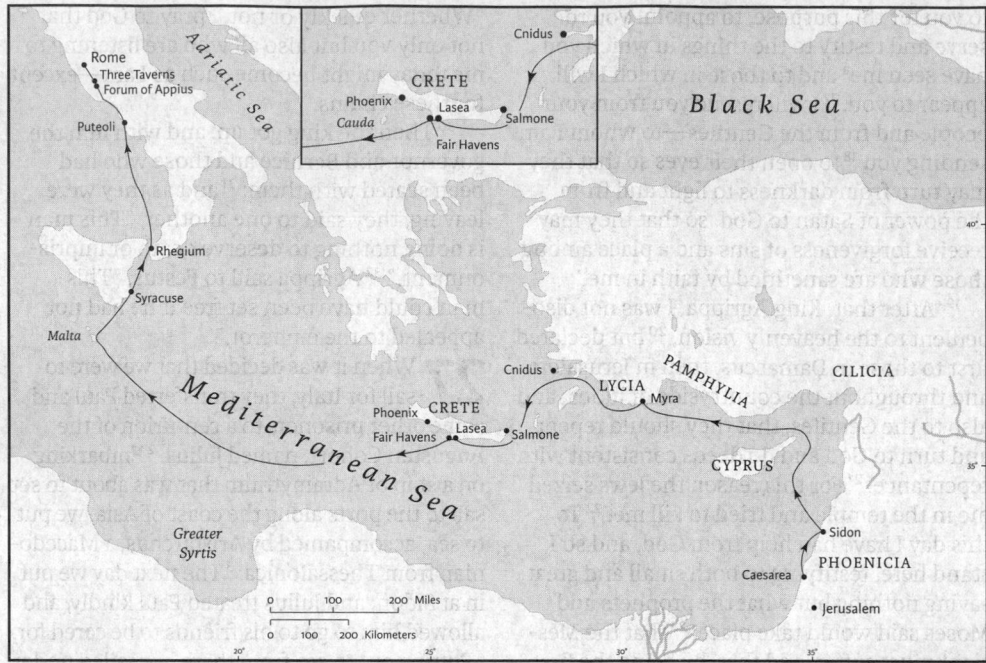

Chs 27–28: Paul's journey to Rome.

with difficulty, we came to a place called Fair Havens, near the city of Lasea.

⁹ Since much time had been lost and sailing was now dangerous, because even the Fast had already gone by, Paul advised them, ¹⁰ saying, "Sirs, I can see that the voyage will be with danger and much heavy loss, not only of the cargo and the ship, but also of our lives." ¹¹ But the centurion paid more attention to the pilot and to the owner of the ship than to what Paul said. ¹² Since the harbor was not suitable for spending the winter, the majority was in favor of putting to sea from there, on the chance that somehow they could reach Phoenix, where they could spend the winter. It was a harbor of Crete, facing southwest and northwest.

¹³ When a moderate south wind began to blow, they thought they could achieve their purpose; so they weighed anchor and began to sail past Crete, close to the shore. ¹⁴ But soon a violent wind, called the northeaster,

rushed down from Crete.ᵃ ¹⁵ Since the ship was caught and could not be turned head-on into the wind, we gave way to it and were driven. ¹⁶ By running under the lee of a small island called Caudaᵇ we were scarcely able to get the ship's boat under control. ¹⁷ After hoisting it up they took measuresᶜ to undergird the ship; then, fearing that they would run on the Syrtis, they lowered the sea anchor and so were driven. ¹⁸ We were being pounded by the storm so violently that on the next day they began to throw the cargo overboard, ¹⁹ and on the third day with their own hands they threw the ship's tackle overboard. ²⁰ When neither sun nor stars appeared for many days, and no small tempest raged, all hope of our being saved was at last abandoned.

ᵃ Gk it
ᵇ Other ancient authorities read *Clauda*
ᶜ Gk *helps*

and east of Fair Havens. 9: *Sailing was . . . dangerous* after September and ceased from mid-November until mid-March. *The Fast*, the Day of Atonement, in September or October. 16: *Cauda*, south of Crete. *The ship's boat* (see vv. 30–32) was in tow. 17: The *measures* undertaken by the crew are not clear. *The Syrtis*, a dangerous shoal west of Cyrene on the north coast of Africa. *Sea anchor*, a conjecture for the Gk word meaning "vessel" or "implement," i.e., a device to slow the ship. 18: Jon 1.5 and numerous Greek and Roman parallels (e.g., Josephus, *J.W.*

[21] Since they had been without food for a long time, Paul then stood up among them and said, "Men, you should have listened to me and not have set sail from Crete and thereby avoided this damage and loss. [22] I urge you now to keep up your courage, for there will be no loss of life among you, but only of the ship. [23] For last night there stood by me an angel of the God to whom I belong and whom I worship, [24] and he said, 'Do not be afraid, Paul; you must stand before the emperor; and indeed, God has granted safety to all those who are sailing with you.' [25] So keep up your courage, men, for I have faith in God that it will be exactly as I have been told. [26] But we will have to run aground on some island."

[27] When the fourteenth night had come, as we were drifting across the sea of Adria, about midnight the sailors suspected that they were nearing land. [28] So they took soundings and found twenty fathoms; a little farther on they took soundings again and found fifteen fathoms. [29] Fearing that we might run on the rocks, they let down four anchors from the stern and prayed for day to come. [30] But when the sailors tried to escape from the ship and had lowered the boat into the sea, on the pretext of putting out anchors from the bow, [31] Paul said to the centurion and the soldiers, "Unless these men stay in the ship, you cannot be saved." [32] Then the soldiers cut away the ropes of the boat and set it adrift.

[33] Just before daybreak, Paul urged all of them to take some food, saying, "Today is the fourteenth day that you have been in suspense and remaining without food, having eaten nothing. [34] Therefore I urge you to take some food, for it will help you survive; for none of you will lose a hair from your heads." [35] After he had said this, he took bread; and giving thanks to God in the presence of all, he broke it and began to eat. [36] Then all of them were encouraged and took food for themselves. [37] (We were in all two hundred seventy-six[a] persons in the ship.) [38] After they had satisfied their hunger, they lightened the ship by throwing the wheat into the sea.

[39] In the morning they did not recognize the land, but they noticed a bay with a beach, on which they planned to run the ship ashore, if they could. [40] So they cast off the anchors and left them in the sea. At the same time they loosened the ropes that tied the steering-oars; then hoisting the foresail to the wind, they made for the beach. [41] But striking a reef,[b] they ran the ship aground; the bow stuck and remained immovable, but the stern was being broken up by the force of the waves. [42] The soldiers' plan was to kill the prisoners, so that none might swim away and escape; [43] but the centurion, wishing to save Paul, kept them from carrying out their plan. He ordered those who could swim to jump overboard first and make for the land, [44] and the rest to follow, some on planks and others on pieces of the ship. And so it was that all were brought safely to land.

28 After we had reached safety, we then learned that the island was called Malta. [2] The natives showed us unusual kindness. Since it had begun to rain and was cold, they kindled a fire and welcomed all of us around it. [3] Paul had gathered a bundle of brushwood and was putting it on the fire, when a viper, driven out by the heat, fastened itself on his hand. [4] When the natives saw the creature hanging from his hand, they said to one another, "This man must be a murderer; though he has escaped from the sea, justice has not allowed him to live." [5] He, however, shook off the creature into the fire and suffered no harm. [6] They were expecting him to swell up

a Other ancient authorities read *seventy-six*; others, *about seventy-six*

b Gk *place of two seas*

1.280). **22:** Cf. v. 10. **24:** 23.11; 25.11–12. **27:** The *sea of Adria* then included the central Mediterranean. **30:** *Escape* of the crew is a popular motif found in Greco-Roman novels. **35–36:** *He took bread,* gave *thanks,* and *broke it,* cf. Lk 22.19; 24.30,35 (see 2.42n.). The meal in which all partake has clear eucharistic overtones. **37:** *Two hundred seventy-six* people on board is quite possible. **41:** *A reef,* Gk "a place of two seas." **42:** The *soldiers* were responsible for the *prisoners*(see 12.19; 16.27). **43:** The "good" *centurion* intervenes (see v. 3n.; 10.1n.).

28.1–10: Paul on Malta. Unharmed though bitten by a viper, Paul heals the father of Publius. **1:** *Malta,* a significant island south of Sicily controlled by the Romans. **2:** *Natives* (lit., "barbarians"), used of non-Greek

or drop dead, but after they had waited a long time and saw that nothing unusual had happened to him, they changed their minds and began to say that he was a god.

⁷ Now in the neighborhood of that place were lands belonging to the leading man of the island, named Publius, who received us and entertained us hospitably for three days. ⁸ It so happened that the father of Publius lay sick in bed with fever and dysentery. Paul visited him and cured him by praying and putting his hands on him. ⁹ After this happened, the rest of the people on the island who had diseases also came and were cured. ¹⁰ They bestowed many honors on us, and when we were about to sail, they put on board all the provisions we needed.

¹¹ Three months later we set sail on a ship that had wintered at the island, an Alexandrian ship with the Twin Brothers as its figurehead. ¹² We put in at Syracuse and stayed there for three days; ¹³ then we weighed anchor and came to Rhegium. After one day there a south wind sprang up, and on the second day we came to Puteoli. ¹⁴ There we found believersᵃ and were invited to stay with them for seven days. And so we came to Rome. ¹⁵ The believersᵃ from there, when they heard of us, came as far as the Forum of Appius and Three Taverns to meet us. On seeing them, Paul thanked God and took courage.

¹⁶ When we came into Rome, Paul was allowed to live by himself, with the soldier who was guarding him.

¹⁷ Three days later he called together the local leaders of the Jews. When they had assembled, he said to them, "Brothers, though I had done nothing against our people or the customs of our ancestors, yet I was arrested in Jerusalem and handed over to the Romans. ¹⁸ When they had examined me, the Romansᵇ wanted to release me, because there was no reason for the death penalty in my case. ¹⁹ But when the Jews objected, I was compelled to appeal to the emperor—even though I had no charge to bring against my nation. ²⁰ For this reason therefore I have asked to see you and speak with you,ᶜ since it is for the sake of the hope of Israel that I am bound with this chain." ²¹ They replied, "We have received no letters from Judea about you, and none of the brothers coming here has reported or spoken anything evil about you. ²² But we would like to hear from you what you think, for with regard to this sect we know that everywhere it is spoken against."

²³ After they had set a day to meet with him, they came to him at his lodgings in great numbers. From morning until evening he explained the matter to them, testifying to the kingdom of God and trying to convince them about Jesus both from the law of Moses and from the prophets. ²⁴ Some were convinced by what he had said, while others refused to believe. ²⁵ So they disagreed with each other; and as they were leaving, Paul made one further statement: "The Holy Spirit was right in saying to your ancestors through the prophet Isaiah,

²⁶ 'Go to this people and say,
You will indeed listen, but never understand,
and you will indeed look, but never perceive.

ᵃ Gk brothers
ᵇ Gk they
ᶜ Or I have asked you to see me and speak with me

speakers. 4: *Justice*, here a deity. 5: Lk 10.19; Mk 16.18 (Ps 91.13). 7: *Leading man*, a local official on Malta. 8–9: Lk 4.38–40.

28.11–16: The journey to Rome. Paul goes by sea to Syracuse, Rhegium, and Puteoli, then by land to the capital. 11: *Three months* (see 27.9n.) would be too soon to have set sail but is just an approximation. *The Twin Brothers*, the Dioscuri, Castor and Pollux, patron deities of sailors. 12: *Syracuse*, capital city of the island of Sicily. 13: *Rhegium*, port city on the Italian coast opposite Sicily. *Puteoli*, modern Pozzuoli, on the north side of the Bay of Naples. 14: *Believers*, there are already Christians at Rome (see 18.2n.). 15: The *Forum of Appius* was 40 mi (65 km) from Rome, and the *Three Taverns* 30 mi (50 km), both on the Via Appia. 16: The "we" passages (16.10n.) end here. *By himself*, apparently in private quarters.

28.17–28: Paul and the Jews of Rome. 17: Even as a captive Paul sticks to the pattern of speaking to Jews first (9.20n.; 13.5n.; 17.2n.). 20: The *hope of Israel* is now bound up with Christianity. 23: *Kingdom of God*, 1.3n.; *the prophets*, 26.22–23n. 24: The reception is mixed as it has been all along (17.11–12n.). 26–27: Isa 6.9–10 is used

27 For this people's heart has grown dull,
   and their ears are hard of hearing,
      and they have shut their eyes;
         so that they might not look with
            their eyes,
      and listen with their ears,
   and understand with their heart and turn—
      and I would heal them.'
28 Let it be known to you then that this salvation of God has been sent to the Gentiles; they will listen."[a]

30 He lived there two whole years at his own expense[b] and welcomed all who came to him, 31 proclaiming the kingdom of God and teaching about the Lord Jesus Christ with all boldness and without hindrance.

[a] Other ancient authorities add verse 29, *And when he had said these words, the Jews departed, arguing vigorously among themselves*

[b] Or *in his own hired dwelling*

elsewhere to explain Jewish rejection of the gospel (see Mt 13.14–15; Jn 12.40; cf. Rom 9–11). **28:** The "turn to the *Gentiles*" of 13.46; 18.6 is repeated. It is no more a final rejection than the previous instances were but may indicate the social reality of Luke's day.

   28.30–31: Conclusion. Though under house arrest (v. 16) Paul preached *without hindrance* for *two whole years.*

INTRODUCTION TO THE LETTERS/EPISTLES IN THE NEW TESTAMENT

CLASSIFICATION AND AUTHORSHIP OF THE NEW TESTAMENT LETTERS

Letters, or epistles, are the earliest documents in the New Testament and its most common literary form: Some scholars date 1 Thessalonians before 50 CE, about twenty years before Mark, the earliest of the Gospels, and there are twenty-one separate letters in the New Testament. Thirteen are from Paul or his missionary associates: Romans, 1 and 2 Corinthians, Ephesians, Philippians, Colossians, Galatians, 1 and 2 Thessalonians, 1 and 2 Timothy, Titus, and Philemon. When the book of Hebrews was attributed to Paul, the number of Pauline letters in ancient manuscripts and lists came to fourteen. Another seven letters, which appear to be pseudonymously attributed to other apostles, round out the group: 1 and 2 Peter; 1, 2, and 3 John; James; and Jude. The Greek word *epistole* ("letter") originally referred to an oral communication sent by messenger (Herodotus, *Histories* 4.10.1). Even in the New Testament period, the letter-carrier might be entrusted with crucial information about a letter's content that was conveyed to its recipients orally. Paul often includes missionary associates in the greeting of his letters (1 Cor 1.1; 2 Cor 1.1; Phil 1.1; Col 1.1; 1 Thess 1.1; Philem 1). He omits them in Galatians, where he has no future plans to visit the region, and in Romans, addressed to a church he did not found. Ephesians lacks a specific destination in the best manuscripts and may be an exhortation sent to several churches in Asia Minor by a later disciple of Paul.

Several other Pauline epistles also differ in language and theological emphasis from the major Pauline letters. The Pastoral Epistles (1 and 2 Timothy and Titus; see p. 2084), addressed to his key assistants, treat them as youthful leaders of local churches. The Pastoral Epistles look to a future in which Christians are established in the larger society. While both 1 and 2 Thessalonians have as their principal theme the return of the Lord Jesus in the end time, the second letter seeks to moderate expectations that the last days are at hand. This change in eschatological perspective, as well as its warning against pseudo-Pauline writings, has led some scholars to conclude that 2 Thessalonians was written by a later disciple of Paul as well. Since Paul had a number of close associates in his missionary activities, it would not be surprising if they used a familiar medium, the apostolic letter, to continue dealing with concrete issues in the churches of the Pauline mission. Although many of the letters unquestionably by Paul are considerably longer than ordinary private letters, they address concrete situations in the churches.

Ephesians, however, lacks not only an address but also references to specific individuals or problems. Among the non-Pauline letters, Hebrews and James also appear to be tractates or general exhortations, rather than letters to specific communities. Jude addresses a sharp apocalyptic warning to Christians in general. First John speaks to concrete problems in its church circles, but lacks the form of a letter; 2 and 3 John are both personal letters, though addressed to different problems. First Peter uses the letter form as exhortation for suffering Christians in Asia Minor. Finally, 2 Peter appears to be the latest epistle in the New Testament. It contains a possible allusion to the Gospel account of the transfiguration of Jesus (1.16–18; see Mk 9.2–8) and refers to Christians who misinterpret Paul's letters (3.15–16). Like 2 Timothy, 2 Peter is presented as the last testament of an apostle. It affirms the unity of apostolic teaching concerning the "day of the Lord" (3.1–14) against some who used Paul's authority to deny that God would end the world.

WRITING AND SENDING LETTERS IN THE GRECO-ROMAN WORLD

Letters from Greco-Roman antiquity include imperial decrees addressed to subjects in a particular area, such as that by the Roman emperor Claudius to "the city of Alexandria" in Egypt in 41 CE concerning Jewish agitation for citizen rights; collections of philosophical letters by prominent figures like Cicero, Pliny, and Seneca; and hundreds of papyri from Egypt documenting the concerns of ordinary people. Royal diplomatic correspondence has its own formalities of language, which are echoed in the so-called letters that the heavenly Christ addresses to the angels of the churches in Revelation 2–3. Philosophical letters often use a highly formal rhetoric, which indicates that such letters were intended to be preserved for posterity. They are typically longer than private letters, which are generally described as "documentary" to distinguish them from such literary creations. Authors often retained copies of and revised literary correspondence before committing it to copying for posterity. Documentary letters existed only for one or more immediate purposes, such as dealing with problems at home, urging an absent husband or son to return, reporting on a military posting, pleading for legal redress, engaging in commerce, describing one's circumstances to family or friends, and recommending the bearer of the letter to its recipient.

The existence of so many letters from private individuals does not necessarily imply a high rate of literacy among craftsmen, traders, or women. A letter could be dictated to a scribe who would be charged with the actual writing. Even those who could write often preferred to employ the services of a scribe (Rom 16.22; Gal 6.11). The letter-carrier or another party might read the letter at its destination and, depending upon the carrier's relationship to the sender, might also interpret the content of the letter. Some documentary letters in Egypt suggest that after the letter had been read in Greek, it would have been translated into the local dialect so that the women in the sender's audience could understand it.

The formal parts of an ancient letter—to be distinguished from other rhetorical patterns authors of literary epistles might use—are straightforward. The opening or superscription identifies sender(s) and recipient(s) and concludes with a greeting or salutation. Epithets, information about geographical locations, and terms of endearment often expand on individuals named. Paul regularly shifts to a Semitic form of salutation, "grace and peace," expanded with reference to God and Christ Jesus (2 Cor 1.2). When his apostolic authority is an issue between himself and the recipients, that note may be attached as a self-designation (2 Cor 1.1; Rom 1.1–5, a community for which Paul is not a founding apostle). In ancient letters, the opening is often followed by a formal statement of the sender's wish for the health of the recipients. Such formulas may also be used to close the letter. Another common formula expresses the sender's prayer to the gods or thanksgiving on behalf of the recipients. In the Pauline letter type, this conventional way of opening a letter usually develops into a much longer thanksgiving or blessing section. That section often previews items from the body of the letter that follows.

After the opening formalities, the body of the letter states the actual business or request that is the reason for the letter. The sender may either give information about his own future travel plans or request it about others. Paul usually has such travel reports near the end of the body of the letter. Various formulas can be used to conclude the letter. Often greetings are given from or to others not mentioned in the body of the letter.

Once the letter was written, the sender had to find a person to deliver the letter to its recipient. Often the presence of someone who was on the way to the desired location provided an opportunity for writing. There was no guaranteed overnight delivery in antiquity! Even letters entrusted to friends for delivery had an uncertain fate. Under the best of circumstances a response was weeks or months away. The sender would ordinarily retain a copy, and some scholars have suggested that the first collection of Paul's letters was due to the apostle's own editing of his copies of Romans, 1 and 2 Corinthians, and Galatians. This hypothesis accounts for the start of the process of collecting and editing Pauline letters, but lacking any specific manuscript evidence, it remains speculative.

THE LETTER OF PAUL TO THE ROMANS

NAME AND AUTHORSHIP

This letter is named for its recipients, the community of believers in Christ in the city of Rome. Although, because of its length, it is the first of the letters of Paul in the New Testament, Romans was probably the latest of Paul's undisputed letters to be written (see "Letters/Epistles in the New Testament," pp. 1973–74).

DATE OF COMPOSITION AND HISTORICAL CONTEXT

The letter was occasioned in part by circumstances in Rome during the reign of the emperor Nero (54–68 CE). Among those to whom Paul sends greetings in ch 16 are Prisca and Aquila, known from Acts 18.2 as among the Jews expelled from Rome by the emperor Claudius around 49 CE. Their presence in Rome at the time Paul writes may reflect Nero's suspension of that edict (Suetonius, *Life of Claudius* 25.3). The recent return of Jews to the imperial capital, including Jewish believers in Christ like Prisca and Aquila, who had been driven out and probably lost property and community ties during their exile, may have aroused tensions within house groups (see 16.5n.) in which non-Judean ("Gentile") believers had become predominant.

Paul's appeal to Gentiles among the Roman faithful not to "boast" over Jews (11.13–36) comes at the end of chs 9–11, the climax of the letter. Paul's argument responds to an incipient anti-Judaism, which was already established among Roman aristocrats and was beginning to emerge among Gentile believers as well. Given the horrors of an anti-Jewish pogrom in Alexandria in Egypt (38–41 CE), and even more recent market tax riots that had turned deadly in Puteoli, a city south of Rome, Paul was concerned to prevent in Rome the sort of civic disturbance in which the city's minority Jewish population would be especially vulnerable. This danger may explain the notorious exhortation to "be subject to the governing authorities" (13.1–7n.). Similarly, Paul's admonitions regarding the "weak in faith," concerned with the observance of diet and special days (14.1–15.13), address tensions between Jews who retained their observance of the law and Gentile believers in Christ who did not.

CONTENTS AND STRUCTURE

The letter to the Romans contains the longest and most complex sustained argument in any of Paul's letters even though it is addressed to believers in Christ whom he has never met (1.13). For these reasons the letter, especially chs 1–8, has often been read as Paul's theological last will and testament, a reflection on and a summary of the gospel of salvation in Christ. It was also intended to persuade the faithful in Rome to support Paul's intended mission to Spain (15.23–24).

Paul had more in view than creating a base for future missionary endeavors. He meant to proclaim to the faithful in Rome the gospel, "the power of God for salvation" (1.15–16; 15.18–19), and by so doing strengthen and encourage them (1.11–12). Romans is, like Paul's other letters, an instrument of moral instruction and exhortation (see 15.14–15).

A dogmatically oriented reading of Romans has traditionally identified a "thesis" in 1.16–17, which is developed in proofs that all humanity has sinned (1.18–3.20) and that God nevertheless justifies human beings through faith, bringing freedom from sin, law, and death (3.21–8.39). On this reading, chs 9–11 have seemed somewhat tangential, as Paul defends his gospel from implications that in it God's covenant with Israel is nullified. Chapters 12–15 are read as stereotyped exhortations with little bearing on the Roman situation (Paul's declaration of confidence in 15.14 being taken at face value), followed by standard greetings in Rom 16.

A different outline follows if we take seriously the indications that chs 9–11 are the climax of the letter. Elements that ordinarily mark the beginning of a letter body appear first at 9.1: the disclosure formula, intensified by an oath, and an expression of deep pathos. The burden of argument in 9–11 is to warn the Gentile audience not to boast against an apparently vanquished Israel. But if these chapters are the letter's climax, all that comes before can be seen as a long *insinuatio*—the "indirect approach" recommended when a speaker's topic is controversial or unpopular (as we may imagine the status of Judeans under Roman rule had become, after recent events in Alexandria, Judea, and Rome itself). Readers may get a sense of the intended rhetorical effect if they first read 8.18–39—a familiar and much-treasured assurance of the love of God—then follow it immediately with 9.1–4, noticing how the testimony of the Spirit, the status of "children of God," and the theme of separation from God play a role in both passages.

The "theme" of the letter is universal accountability to God's justice, developed first in 1.18–2.16, then augmented rhetorically as Paul calls on a fellow Jew to agree that no one is free from God's judgment (2.17–3.31). Abraham's faithfulness makes him the ancestor of all the faithful, not Jews only (ch 4); salvation in Christ means more than exoneration, it means freedom from the power of sin (chs 5–6), and only on that basis is it freedom from law (ch 7). The exultant description of empowered life in the Spirit as children of God (ch 8) provides a rhetorical foil for the appeal on behalf of Israel, to whom that status first belongs (9.4–5). In this light, the hortatory chs 12–15 are directed to shape a life of respectful mutuality between Jews and Gentiles in Rome.

INTERPRETATION AND GUIDE TO READING

The theme of God's "righteousness" (1.17) or "justice" (as the same Gk word is translated in 3.5) resonates throughout the letter. At stake is God's faithfulness in the face of human faithlessness, as the rhetorical questions that punctuate the letter show (2.3–4,21–23; 3.3,5,7,9,27,29; 4.1; 6.1–3,15–16; 7.7,13; 9.14,19,30; 11.1,11). God's justice is manifest in the uncompromising judgment of all impiety and wickedness, and also in unwavering loyalty to the covenant with Israel. Paul wants the faithful of Rome to respect God's integrity in the salvation offered them through the faithful obedience of Jesus (5.6,18–19; see 3.22,26n.).

Paul is Christ's apostle, obligated to "bring about the obedience of faith among all the Gentiles" (or "nations"), among whom he includes his Roman audience (1.1–6). He declares the gospel of God's salvation to all who believe, Jews and Greeks alike, but "to the Jew first" (1.16). The priority of the Jews in God's plan of salvation is an important theme in the letter (3.1–2; 9.1–4). Paul's mission to Gentiles should provoke his fellow Jews to jealousy (11.13–14), perhaps by convincing them that the last days prophesied by Isaiah were at hand (see 15.12). At last, Paul declares, "all Israel will be saved" (11.26), and all the nations will join Israel in the worship of the one true God (15.7–13).

As he writes, the apostle is about to present to the "saints" in Jerusalem both monetary aid from churches in his mission field (15.25–27) and an embassy of Gentile converts (1 Cor 16.3–4; on the catastrophe of this Jerusalem mission, see Acts 21.27–30). Although the Roman believers have not had the opportunity to contribute to this collection, Paul asks for their prayers (15.30–32). He also invites his readers to participate in the "offering of the Gentiles" (15.15–16) by exhorting them to holy living, which he describes as their sacrificial offering to God (12.1–3; 15.7–9).

The theological convictions expressed in the Letter to the Romans resemble those in letters to congregations Paul himself had founded. Those who have been baptized into Christ must no longer let sin have dominion over them (6.1–14). They are no longer to live as the unbelieving world does (1.18–32), but to give "spiritual worship" to God through sobriety of thought and bodily purity (12.1–3). Just so Paul had reminded the Corinthians, Galatians, and Thessalonians that they must no longer live as "the Gentiles who do not know God," having been sanctified by Christ (1 Cor 6.9–11; Gal 5.22–24; 1 Thess 4.1–5).

Universal accountability before God, Paul's theme in the early chapters of the letter, is more specifically applied in chs 12–15. Rather than being a treatise on salvation in Christ, Romans is a sustained appeal for holy living, directed to Gentiles tempted to look down on their beleaguered Jewish neighbors, within the community of believers in Christ and without. The apostle's call to realize in common life the justice of God which believers celebrate is the letter's enduring legacy.

Neil Elliott

1

Paul, a servant[a] of Jesus Christ, called to be an apostle, set apart for the gospel of God, [2] which he promised beforehand through his prophets in the holy scriptures, [3] the gospel concerning his Son, who was descended from David according to the flesh [4] and was declared to be Son of God with power according to the spirit[b] of holiness by resurrection from the dead, Jesus Christ our Lord, [5] through whom we have received grace and apostleship to bring about the obedience of faith among all the Gentiles for the sake of his name, [6] including yourselves who are called to belong to Jesus Christ,

[7] To all God's beloved in Rome, who are called to be saints:

Grace to you and peace from God our Father and the Lord Jesus Christ.

[8] First, I thank my God through Jesus Christ for all of you, because your faith is proclaimed throughout the world. [9] For God, whom I serve with my spirit by announcing the gospel[c] of his Son, is my witness that without ceasing I remember you always in my prayers, [10] asking that by God's will I may somehow at last succeed in coming to you. [11] For I am longing to see you so that I may share with you some spiritual gift to strengthen you— [12] or rather so that we may be mutually encouraged by each other's faith, both yours and mine. [13] I want you to know, brothers and sisters,[d] that I have often intended to come to you (but thus far have been prevented), in order that I may reap some harvest among you as I have among the rest of the Gentiles. [14] I am a debtor both to Greeks and to barbarians, both to the wise and to the foolish [15]—hence my eagerness to proclaim the gospel to you also who are in Rome.

[16] For I am not ashamed of the gospel; it is the power of God for salvation to everyone who has faith, to the Jew first and also to the Greek. [17] For in it the righteousness of God is

a   Gk *slave*
b   Or *Spirit*
c   Gk *my spirit in the gospel*
d   Gk *brothers*

1.1–7: Salutation. Ancient letters began with the names of sender and recipient and a short greeting (see Acts 23.26). Paul's expansion of this form reflects the liturgical context in which his letter would be read. **1:** *A servant . . . called . . . set apart,* the characteristic marks of Israel's prophets (Jer 1.5; Am 7.14), *Apostle,* lit., one "sent forth," i.e., by God (Isa 6.8; Jer 1.7; Ezek 2.3–4). **3:** *Gospel,* see 1.16n. *Descended from David,* messiah in David's royal lineage; cf. the genealogies in Mt 1.1–17; Lk 3.23–28. **4:** *The spirit of holiness,* God's Spirit (see 8.2n.). The corresponding Heb phrase is translated "holy spirit" in Ps 51.11; Isa 63.10–11 (cf. 1QS 4.21; 8.16; 9.3; 1QH 7.6–7; 9.32). **5–6:** Despite the presence of Jews among his audience (see 16.3,7,11), Paul addresses his hearers as Gentiles (1.13–15). **7:** *Saints,* lit., "holy ones."

1.8–17: Thanksgiving. Ancient letters continued with an expression of thanksgiving. Paul's thanksgivings signal important themes in a letter. He describes his obligation to *proclaim the gospel* to the Romans as priestly service (v. 9; see 15.16,25), grounded in the revelation of God's righteousness (vv. 16–17). **10–13:** *By God's will . . . prevented,* apostolic obligations have delayed Paul's visiting the Romans (15.18–22). **11–13:** *Share . . . reap some harvest,* Paul seeks an active response from the Romans (15.14n.). *Strengthen . . . encouraged,* see 1 Thess 3.2. Polite circumspection dominates here and at 15.14–15. **14:** *To Greeks and . . . barbarians,* Paul describes the world as Roman orators saw it, divided into more or less civilized peoples (cf. 1.16n.). **15:** *To you also,* the Romans stand within Paul's mission as apostle to the Gentiles (15.14–19). **16–17:** Often taken as the thesis or theme of the letter, these verses explain Paul's eagerness to *proclaim the gospel* (v. 15) to the Romans. **16:** *I am not ashamed,* a confession of faith (cf. 4 Macc 5.34–38; 6.20; 9.2). Paul's "boast" in God's power is a recurrent theme in the letter (5.1–4,11; 15.17; cf. 1 Thess 1.5; 1 Cor 2.4). *The gospel,* "euangelion," in nonbiblical Greek, celebrated the triumph of a ruler; Paul announces God's triumph. Salvation is the result of the life-giving and right-making *power of God* (see 4.17; 5.11,12–21; 6.1–14; 8.1–4,10–11,21–25; 11.15,23; 15.18–19). *To the Jew first,* 2.9–10; 3.1–2; 9.4. *And also to the Greek,* Paul now describes the world from a Jewish point of view (cf. 1.14). **17:** *The righteousness of God,* or "justice" (as at 3.5). God's character as righteous, which is being *revealed* as God brings human beings into right relationship (see 3.21–26), is a sign of the last days (see 13.11–12). God's vindication before the nations is in view (Ps 98.2; Isa 51.5). *Through faith,* i.e., God's faithfulness (as at 3.3). *For faith,* God's faithfulness elicits human trust. *The one who . . . by faith,* Hab 2.4. Like other Jews, Paul may have read the verse as a messianic prophecy: The Righteous One, the messiah (Acts 3.14; 7.52;

revealed through faith for faith; as it is written, "The one who is righteous will live by faith."[a]

[18] For the wrath of God is revealed from heaven against all ungodliness and wickedness of those who by their wickedness suppress the truth. [19] For what can be known about God is plain to them, because God has shown it to them. [20] Ever since the creation of the world his eternal power and divine nature, invisible though they are, have been understood and seen through the things he has made. So they are without excuse; [21] for though they knew God, they did not honor him as God or give thanks to him, but they became futile in their thinking, and their senseless minds were darkened. [22] Claiming to be wise, they became fools; [23] and they exchanged the glory of the immortal God for images resembling a mortal human being or birds or four-footed animals or reptiles.

[24] Therefore God gave them up in the lusts of their hearts to impurity, to the degrading of their bodies among themselves, [25] because they exchanged the truth about God for a lie and worshiped and served the creature rather than the Creator, who is blessed forever! Amen. [26] For this reason God gave them up to degrading passions. Their women exchanged natural intercourse for unnatural, [27] and in the same way also the men, giving up natural intercourse with women, were consumed with passion for one another. Men committed shameless acts with men and received in their own persons the due penalty for their error.

[28] And since they did not see fit to acknowledge God, God gave them up to a debased mind and to things that should not be done. [29] They were filled with every kind of wickedness, evil, covetousness, malice. Full of envy, murder, strife, deceit, craftiness, they are gossips, [30] slanderers, God-haters,[b] insolent, haughty, boastful, inventors of evil, rebellious toward parents, [31] foolish, faithless, heartless, ruthless. [32] They know God's decree, that those who practice such things deserve to die—yet they not only do them but even applaud others who practice them.

2 Therefore you have no excuse, whoever you are, when you judge others; for in passing judgment on another you condemn yourself, because you, the judge, are doing the very same things. [2] You say,[c] "We know

a   Or *The one who is righteous through faith will live*
b   Or *God-hated*
c   Gk lacks *You say*

22.14), will live on the basis of faithfulness (see 3.22n.).

1.18–32: An indictment of human wickedness and injustice. Paul argues in 1.18–3.20 that God's justice allows no impunity for any who willfully do wrong. **18:** *The wrath of God,* 2.5; 4.9. God's righteousness (1.17) requires that God no longer pass over sins with forbearance (see 3.25). *Wickedness,* lit., "injustice." **19–23:** Idolatry is an attempt to deny awareness of God, thus evading accountability for one's actions. Its opposite is the "spiritual worship" offered by renewed minds (12.1–2). **20:** *Without excuse,* 2.1; 3.19; compare Wis 13.1–9. **23:** *Images,* idolatry was condemned by the Torah (Ex 20.4–6) and ridiculed by the prophets (Isa 40.18–20; 42.17; 45.16,20; Jer 10.1–16). Like other Jews, Paul attributes the wickedness characteristic of the Greco-Roman world to idolatry. A more irenic tone is attributed to Paul in Acts 17.22–23. **24–27:** *Impurity,* disordered thinking and behavior, to be left behind in baptism (6.6–14; 12.1). **24–25:** *God gave them up,* in a spiral of depravity, injustice leads mortals to suppress their awareness of truth and turn from God (vv. 18–23); God abandons them to increasing wickedness (vv. 24–32). *The Creator, who is blessed forever,* spontaneous praise to God (6.17; 7.25; 9.5; 11.33–36; 16.25–27). **26–27:** *Degrading passions,* while Torah forbids a male lying "with a male as with a woman" (Lev 18.22), Paul's Jewish contemporaries criticized a range of sexual behaviors common in the Greco-Roman world. Although widely read today as a reference to homosexuality, the language of *unnatural* intercourse was more often used in Paul's day to denote not the orientation of sexual desire but its immoderate indulgence, which was believed to weaken the body (*the due penalty*). **28–31:** The spiraling descent into wickedness reaches its nadir in these vices, presented here in a list as elsewhere in the New Testament (e.g., Gal 5.19–21; 1 Tim 1.9–10; 1 Pet 4.3) and in Greek and Roman literature. *Full of envy, murder, strife,* the notorious perversity and brutality of emperors like Gaius (Caligula), or Nero, Paul's contemporary, come readily to mind. **32:** *They know God's decree,* they cannot plead ignorance as an excuse (see 1.20).

2.1–16: All are accountable before God for their works. 1: Paul attacks as hypocritical the presumption that

that God's judgment on those who do such things is in accordance with truth." [3] Do you imagine, whoever you are, that when you judge those who do such things and yet do them yourself, you will escape the judgment of God? [4] Or do you despise the riches of his kindness and forbearance and patience? Do you not realize that God's kindness is meant to lead you to repentance? [5] But by your hard and impenitent heart you are storing up wrath for yourself on the day of wrath, when God's righteous judgment will be revealed. [6] For he will repay according to each one's deeds: [7] to those who by patiently doing good seek for glory and honor and immortality, he will give eternal life; [8] while for those who are self-seeking and who obey not the truth but wickedness, there will be wrath and fury. [9] There will be anguish and distress for everyone who does evil, the Jew first and also the Greek, [10] but glory and honor and peace for everyone who does good, the Jew first and also the Greek. [11] For God shows no partiality.

[12] All who have sinned apart from the law will also perish apart from the law, and all who have sinned under the law will be judged by the law. [13] For it is not the hearers of the law who are righteous in God's sight, but the doers of the law who will be justified. [14] When Gentiles, who do not possess the law, do instinctively what the law requires, these, though not having the law, are a law to themselves. [15] They show that what the law requires is written on their hearts, to which their own conscience also bears witness; and their conflicting thoughts will accuse or perhaps excuse them [16] on the day when, according to my gospel, God, through Jesus Christ, will judge the secret thoughts of all.

[17] But if you call yourself a Jew and rely on the law and boast of your relation to God [18] and know his will and determine what is best because you are instructed in the law, [19] and if you are sure that you are a guide to the blind, a light to those who are in darkness, [20] a corrector of the foolish, a teacher of children, having in the law the embodiment of knowledge and truth, [21] you, then, that teach others, will you not teach yourself? While you preach against stealing, do you steal? [22] You that forbid adultery, do you commit adultery? You that abhor idols, do you rob temples? [23] You that boast in the law, do you dishonor God by breaking the law? [24] For,

God will have mercy on some by exempting them from punishment (2.4). **2:** *You say*, these words, lacking in Gk, have been added to express one interpretation of this passage as a "trap" for "the Jew," who judges those indicted in 1.18–32. Jews are not clearly addressed before 2.17. Here, any are condemned who *know that God's judgment . . . is in accordance with truth*, yet do *the very same things* they condemn in others (2.1,3). **4:** *Do you despise . . . kindness*, the question is rhetorical. Paul warns the baptized not to presume God's grace in 6.1,15. **5:** *Day of wrath*, the time of divine judgment (see Isa 2.12n.; 13.9,13; Lam 2.1; 1 Thess 1.10; etc.), understood in early Christian thought to be imminent and universal (e.g., 13.12; 2 Pet 3.10). God's punishment of sin coheres with God's righteousness (see 1.17–18). **6–11:** Judgment according to one's works: see 2 Cor 11.15; in Jas 2.14–26 the Gk word "erga," translated *deeds* here, is "works." **9–10:** The Jew is first in salvation (1.16; 3.1–2), therefore also in responsibility. *Anguish and distress*, eschatological woe (2 Cor 4.8). **11:** *No partiality*, Deut 10.17; 2 Chr 19.7. No discrimination compromises God's justice. **12:** *Apart from the law*, or "in a lawless manner"; *under the law*, or "while living within the law." The translation given here implies a distinction between Gentiles and Jews. Paul's larger point is that all shall be judged by the same standard: doing what the law requires (v. 15). **13:** *Hearers* and *doers*, Mt 7.21; Jas 1.22–25. *Doers of the law . . . will be justified*, see 3.20n. **14–15:** Ancient Judaism acknowledged righteous Gentiles who did "by nature" *what the law requires*, lit., "the work of the law." For Paul, those who walk according to the Spirit fulfill the law's "just requirement" (8.4). **15:** *Their own conscience also bears witness*, thus they acknowledge the validity of God's law. A similar argument appears in 7.14–22.

2.17–29: Does being a Jew relieve one from accountability to God? Paul makes his point through imaginary conversation with a Jew (the diatribe style). **17:** Although vv. 17–24 have often been read as an "indictment" of the Jew, Paul considers Israel's privileges real (see 3.1–9; 9.1–4). *Boast*, Paul warns repeatedly against groundless boasting before God (see 2.23; 3.27; 4.5; 5.1–3,11; 11.17–20). **21–23:** *Will you not teach yourself?* Paul interrogates an imaginary witness, whose testimony leads to the conclusions in vv. 25–29. Israel's covenantal privileges do not lessen accountability before God. **22:** *Do you rob temples?* While the Torah forbade idolatry, Jews in Paul's day were careful not to dishonor shrines to other gods (Philo, *De Conf. Ling.* 163; Josephus, *Ap.* 269; *Ant.* 4.207).

as it is written, "The name of God is blasphemed among the Gentiles because of you."

²⁵ Circumcision indeed is of value if you obey the law; but if you break the law, your circumcision has become uncircumcision. ²⁶ So, if those who are uncircumcised keep the requirements of the law, will not their uncircumcision be regarded as circumcision? ²⁷ Then those who are physically uncircumcised but keep the law will condemn you that have the written code and circumcision but break the law. ²⁸ For a person is not a Jew who is one outwardly, nor is true circumcision something external and physical. ²⁹ Rather, a person is a Jew who is one inwardly, and real circumcision is a matter of the heart—it is spiritual and not literal. Such a person receives praise not from others but from God.

3 Then what advantage has the Jew? Or what is the value of circumcision? ² Much, in every way. For in the first place the Jewsᵃ were entrusted with the oracles of God. ³ What if some were unfaithful? Will their faithlessness nullify the faithfulness of God? ⁴ By no means! Although everyone is a liar, let God be proved true, as it is written,

"So that you may be justified in your
        words,
    and prevail in your judging."ᵇ

⁵ But if our injustice serves to confirm the justice of God, what should we say? That God is unjust to inflict wrath on us? (I speak in a human way.) ⁶ By no means! For then how could God judge the world? ⁷ But if through my falsehood God's truthfulness abounds to his glory, why am I still being condemned as a sinner? ⁸ And why not say (as some people slander us by saying that we say), "Let us do evil so that good may come"? Their condemnation is deserved!

⁹ What then? Are we any better off?ᶜ No, not at all; for we have already charged that all, both Jews and Greeks, are under the power of sin, ¹⁰ as it is written:

"There is no one who is righteous, not
        even one;
    ¹¹ there is no one who has
        understanding,
    there is no one who seeks God.
¹² All have turned aside, together they have
        become worthless;
    there is no one who shows kindness,
        there is not even one."
¹³ "Their throats are opened graves;
    they use their tongues to deceive."
"The venom of vipers is under their lips."
    ¹⁴ "Their mouths are full of cursing and
        bitterness."
¹⁵ "Their feet are swift to shed blood;
    ¹⁶ ruin and misery are in their paths,
    ¹⁷ and the way of peace they have not
        known."
    ¹⁸ "There is no fear of God before their
        eyes."
¹⁹ Now we know that whatever the law says, it speaks to those who are under the law,

ᵃ Gk *they*
ᵇ Gk *when you are being judged*
ᶜ Or *at any disadvantage?*

23: *Do you dishonor God,* some translations render this sentence as a statement, but it is a question in the earliest punctuated Gk manuscript. **24:** Isa 52.5; cf. Ezek 36.20. **25–29:** These verses expand the principle that "all who have sinned under the law will be judged by the law" (v. 12). **26:** *The requirements of the law,* see v. 14; 8.1–4n. **29:** *Real circumcision . . . the heart,* Deut 10.16; 30.6,8; Jer 4.4; 9.26; Ezek 44.9.

3.1–9: God's integrity in the covenant with Israel. 1: Paul continues to question an imaginary dialogue partner, who agrees that the *advantage* of being a Jew is real (see 9.1–4), but does not provide immunity from God's just judgment. **3:** The faithlessness of some Jews—often read as a lack of faith in Christ, but possibly meaning their disobedience—does not alter God's *faithfulness* to the covenant. **4:** Pss 116.11; 51.4. **5:** *The justice of God* (see 1.17n.) requires the judgment of injustice. **8:** *As some people slander us,* it is not clear who is slandering whom. Jews like Philo protested being "slandered" (*Flaccus* 21–23) by hostile stereotypes. In 6.1,15 Paul uses similar language to refute a possible misunderstanding of God's grace in Christ. **9:** *Are we any better off?* This translation echoes v. 2, yet reaches a different conclusion. The Gk may also be translated "Do we have a defense?"

3.10–20: The universality of God's judgment. These quotations from the Hebrew Bible insist that no one may claim to satisfy God's standards. **10–12:** Pss 14.1–2; 53.1–2. **13:** Pss 5.9; 140.3. **14:** Ps 10.7. **15–17:** Prov 1.16; Isa 59.7–8. **18:** Ps 36.1. **19:** The law holds everyone accountable before God, not only Jews (cf. 2.13). The previous

so that every mouth may be silenced, and the whole world may be held accountable to God. [20] For "no human being will be justified in his sight" by deeds prescribed by the law, for through the law comes the knowledge of sin.

[21] But now, apart from law, the righteousness of God has been disclosed, and is attested by the law and the prophets, [22] the righteousness of God through faith in Jesus Christ[a] for all who believe. For there is no distinction, [23] since all have sinned and fall short of the glory of God; [24] they are now justified by his grace as a gift, through the redemption that is in Christ Jesus, [25] whom God put forward as a sacrifice of atonement[b] by his blood, effective through faith. He did this to show his righteousness, because in his divine forbearance he had passed over the sins previously committed; [26] it was to prove at the present time that he himself is righteous and that he justifies the one who has faith in Jesus.[c]

[27] Then what becomes of boasting? It is excluded. By what law? By that of works? No, but by the law of faith. [28] For we hold that a person is justified by faith apart from works prescribed by the law. [29] Or is God the God of Jews only? Is he not the God of Gentiles also? Yes, of Gentiles also, [30] since God is one; and he will justify the circumcised on the ground of faith and the uncircumcised through that same faith. [31] Do we then overthrow the law by this faith? By no means! On the contrary, we uphold the law.

4 What then are we to say was gained by[d] Abraham, our ancestor according to the flesh? [2] For if Abraham was justified by works, he has something to boast about, but not before God. [3] For what does the scripture say? "Abraham believed God, and it was reckoned to him as righteousness." [4] Now to one who works, wages are not reckoned as a gift but as something due. [5] But to one who without works trusts him who justi-

a Or *through the faith of Jesus Christ*
b Or *a place of atonement*
c Or *who has the faith of Jesus*
d Other ancient authorities read *say about*

scriptures emphasize sins of false speech (cf. 1.18). **20:** Ps 143.2. The lack of human righteousness is a theme throughout the Psalms and other Jewish writings (e.g., *1 Enoch* 81.5; 1QH 8.20; 17.14–15). *By deeds prescribed by the law,* lit., "works of the law," is Paul's addition to the Psalm text (see 3.28n.; Dan 9.18; 1QH 15.17). The "doers of the law" who "will be justified" (2.13) are not those who merely possess the law, but those who by God's Spirit fulfill its "just requirement" (8.4), by "doing," lit., working, "good" (2.7,10).

3.21–31: The revelation of God's justice. 21–22: *Apart from the law,* where no one might lay hold of the law as a defense from God's judgment. *Disclosed,* see 1.17n. The *righteousness of God* involves God's action in Christ to "justify" (make right) those who trust in God (see 6.1–23). **22:** The alternate translation in note *a, the faith of Jesus Christ,* is increasingly preferred. It conforms this phrase to identically structured phrases in 3.3 ("the faithfulness of God") and 4.12,16 ("the faith of . . . Abraham") and reflects the importance for Paul of Jesus' faithful obedience (5.19; Phil 2.8). **25–26:** Paul emphasizes God's integrity and justice, now "revealed" (1.17), not in putting up with sin but in dealing with it decisively through the *faith of Jesus* (see textual note *c*). *Sacrifice of atonement,* cf. 4 Macc 17.22. The translation in textual note *b* (see Ex 25.17–22) is less likely. *Divine forbearance,* God has patiently withheld wrath, not to indulge sin but to lead sinners to repentance (2.4; see Wis 11.23). **27:** *Boasting* is *excluded* by *the law of faith,* i.e., by the law rightly understood as eliciting trust in God's saving power (see 2.17n.; 4.5; 11.18n.; Deut 9.4–6; Dan 9.18). **28:** *We hold,* Paul's language resembles that of Dead Sea Scroll fragments listing "works of the law" that will be "reckoned as righteousness" for those who perform them (4Q397, 398). Paul's point is that one is *justified by faith,* meaning either one's faithful obedience to God (see 1.5,16), God's faithfulness (as in 3.3), or Jesus' faithfulness (see 3.22n.,26n.). **29–31:** *God is one* (see Deut 6.4), judging Jew and Gentile alike on the basis of *faith,* i.e., faithful obedience (2.13–16), which will indeed *uphold the law* (7.7,12–16).

4.1–25: Abraham as ancestor. 1: *Abraham . . . the flesh,* this translation implies Paul refers only to Jews. The Gk may also be translated "What shall we say: Have we found Abraham to be our ancestor according to the flesh?" which leads to the negative answer in 4.11–12,16 (cf. 9.6–9). Thus Abraham is ancestor of the faithful, Gentiles as well as Jews. **2–5:** Paul finds in Gen 15.6 proof that righteousness was *reckoned* to Abraham as a *gift,* not as *wages* paid as *something due* (6.23). God is free from any obligation to mortals (see 4.16). **5:** God *justifies*

fies the ungodly, such faith is reckoned as righteousness. [6] So also David speaks of the blessedness of those to whom God reckons righteousness apart from works:

[7] "Blessed are those whose iniquities are forgiven,
  and whose sins are covered;
[8] blessed is the one against whom the Lord will not reckon sin."

[9] Is this blessedness, then, pronounced only on the circumcised, or also on the uncircumcised? We say, "Faith was reckoned to Abraham as righteousness." [10] How then was it reckoned to him? Was it before or after he had been circumcised? It was not after, but before he was circumcised. [11] He received the sign of circumcision as a seal of the righteousness that he had by faith while he was still uncircumcised. The purpose was to make him the ancestor of all who believe without being circumcised and who thus have righteousness reckoned to them, [12] and likewise the ancestor of the circumcised who are not only circumcised but who also follow the example of the faith that our ancestor Abraham had before he was circumcised.

[13] For the promise that he would inherit the world did not come to Abraham or to his descendants through the law but through the righteousness of faith. [14] If it is the adherents of the law who are to be the heirs, faith is null and the promise is void. [15] For the law brings wrath; but where there is no law, neither is there violation.

[16] For this reason it depends on faith, in order that the promise may rest on grace and be guaranteed to all his descendants, not only to the adherents of the law but also to those who share the faith of Abraham (for he is the father of all of us, [17] as it is written, "I have made you the father of many nations")—in the presence of the God in whom he believed, who gives life to the dead and calls into existence the things that do not exist. [18] Hoping against hope, he believed that he would become "the father of many nations," according to what was said, "So numerous shall your descendants be." [19] He did not weaken in faith when he considered his own body, which was already[a] as good as dead (for he was about a hundred years old), or when he considered the barrenness of Sarah's womb. [20] No distrust made him waver concerning the promise of God, but he grew strong in his faith as he gave glory to God, [21] being fully convinced that God was able to do what he had promised. [22] Therefore his faith[b] "was reckoned to him as righteousness." [23] Now the words, "it was reckoned to him," were written not for

a Other ancient authorities lack *already*
b Gk *Therefore it*

the ungodly, Paul shares his contemporaries' view that God had called Abraham out of idolatry (see Gen 12.1–4; 13.4; 17.9–14,23–27). Abraham's faithful response stands in contrast with the "ungodliness" of the Greco-Roman world (1.18) and provides the prototype for God's justification of the ungodly through Christ's death (5.6). **6–8:** Paul quotes Ps 32.1–2 (LXX) to introduce the theme of *blessedness* (Gen 12.2–3; Gal 3.8). **9–12:** Abraham was justified (Gen 15.6) *before he was circumcised* (Gen 17.24), on account of his *faith*; therefore he could be ancestor of both circumcised (Gen 12.2; 15.13–14) and uncircumcised (Gen 17.5; see v. 17). **12:** *The faith that . . . Abraham had*, his faithful response to God (vv. 5,17). **13–15:** God's promise comes through *the righteousness of faith*, or "faithful righteousness," like that of Abraham (vv. 16,20), not through the law. **14:** *The adherents of the law*, compare "hearers of the law" in 2.13. *Faith is null and the promise is void*, if God's blessing included only those who had already performed the law they possessed (3.3–4; 9.6–9). **15:** *The law brings wrath*, Paul may have in mind the solemn curses pronounced on the disobedient in Lev 26 and Deut 28. *But where there is no law . . . violation*, Abraham did not stand under the law when he responded to God in faith.

  4.16–25: Inclusion in the heritage of Abraham's faith. 16: *Not only . . . but also*, Jews and Gentiles alike inherit God's promise as they *share the faith of Abraham*. **17:** Gen 17.5. Abraham's faith in God's promise despite his own "dead" body (v. 19) is an example for all those who trust God *who raised Jesus . . . from the dead* (v. 24). God's power to *call into existence the things that do not exist* is a key theme in the letter (v. 24; 6.4–5,9–11; 8.11; 9.25–26; 11.5). Contrast Abraham's faith with those who refuse to acknowledge God through creation (1.20–22). **18:** Gen 15.5. *Hoping against hope*, see 8.24–25. **19:** See Gen 17.17. **20–21:** God's ability *to do what he had promised* is at stake throughout Romans, especially regarding Israel (3.3–4; 9.6). *Gave glory to God*, again Abraham is contrasted with the ungodly of 1.21–24; see 15.9–12. **22–23:** Gen 15.6.

his sake alone, ²⁴ but for ours also. It will be reckoned to us who believe in him who raised Jesus our Lord from the dead, ²⁵ who was handed over to death for our trespasses and was raised for our justification.

5 Therefore, since we are justified by faith, we[a] have peace with God through our Lord Jesus Christ, ² through whom we have obtained access[b] to this grace in which we stand; and we[c] boast in our hope of sharing the glory of God. ³ And not only that, but we[c] also boast in our sufferings, knowing that suffering produces endurance, ⁴ and endurance produces character, and character produces hope, ⁵ and hope does not disappoint us, because God's love has been poured into our hearts through the Holy Spirit that has been given to us.

⁶ For while we were still weak, at the right time Christ died for the ungodly. ⁷ Indeed, rarely will anyone die for a righteous person—though perhaps for a good person someone might actually dare to die. ⁸ But God proves his love for us in that while we still were sinners Christ died for us. ⁹ Much more surely then, now that we have been justified by his blood, will we be saved through him from the wrath of God.[d] ¹⁰ For if while we were enemies, we were reconciled to God through the death of his Son, much more surely, having been reconciled, will we be saved by his life. ¹¹ But more than that, we even boast in God through our Lord Jesus Christ, through whom we have now received reconciliation.

¹² Therefore, just as sin came into the world through one man, and death came through sin, and so death spread to all because all have sinned— ¹³ sin was indeed in the world before the law, but sin is not reckoned when there is no law. ¹⁴ Yet death exercised dominion from Adam to Moses, even over those whose sins were not like the transgression of Adam, who is a type of the one who was to come.

¹⁵ But the free gift is not like the trespass. For if the many died through the one man's trespass, much more surely have the grace of God and the free gift in the grace of the one man, Jesus Christ, abounded for the many. ¹⁶ And the free gift is not like the effect of the one man's sin. For the judgment following one trespass brought condemnation, but the free gift following many trespasses brings justification. ¹⁷ If, because of the one man's trespass, death exercised dominion through

a   Other ancient authorities read *let us*
b   Other ancient authorities add *by faith*
c   Or *let us*
d   Gk *the wrath*

5.1–21: The nature of justification in Christ. In light of the preceding argument, Paul declares that those justified in Christ may *boast* (vv. 2–3,11), not merely of being forgiven their sins (see vv. 8–10), but *much more surely*, of being saved from *wrath* (v. 9) and the *dominion* of *death* (vv. 14–17). This chapter prepares for the call to righteous living in ch 6. 1: Being *justified by faith* (see 3.28n.) means entering God's life-giving and right-making *dominion* (v. 21), as ch 6 will make clear. Justification *by faith* may mean by the faith of Jesus, i.e., his obedience to God as shown in his death (v. 19). Thus Paul can speak of being justified *through Jesus Christ* (vv. 11,21), by Jesus' *blood* (v. 9), i.e., through his *death* (v. 10), or by his *obedience* (v. 19). 2–5: *Hope* in the coming *glory of God*, see 8.16–25. 2: *We boast* (or "let us boast," see v. 11), not in our own works (3.27; 4.2) but in God's power. 3: *Sufferings*, see 8.18,35–36. 5: *The Holy Spirit*, see 1.4n.; 8.2n. On the work of *the Spirit*, see 8.2–17,23–27. 6: *While we were still weak*, God's grace preceded any human act that might constitute a claim to righteousness before God (see 3.27; 4.2; 9.11–12,16; regarding the Gentiles, 9.30). 9–11: Paul stresses that God's saving purpose is *much more* than a reprieve from the punishment due for sins (vv. 15,17). 9–10: *Justified by his blood . . . reconciled . . . through the death of his Son*, see v. 1n.

5.12–21: Adam and Christ. Christ's saving work surpasses even the effects of Adam's disobedience. (A different comparison of Christ and Adam is made in 1 Cor 15.21–23,45–49.) 12–14: The catastrophe in Adam's transgression (Gen 3) is greater than the punishments reckoned for individual transgressions. It also introduced the *dominion* of sin (see v. 21; 6.6,12,14), and *much more*, allowed for *death* to invade creation (Gen 3.19,22–24). 14: *To Moses*, until the law was given to Moses; see v. 20. *The one who was to come*, the messiah. 15–21: Salvation much more than forgiveness. 15–16: Despite an apparent similarity between their effects on *the many*, Christ's obedience accomplished *much more* than to reverse the effects of Adam's sin. 17–18: Christ's *act of righteousness* (see

that one, much more surely will those who receive the abundance of grace and the free gift of righteousness exercise dominion in life through the one man, Jesus Christ.

[18] Therefore just as one man's trespass led to condemnation for all, so one man's act of righteousness leads to justification and life for all. [19] For just as by the one man's disobedience the many were made sinners, so by the one man's obedience the many will be made righteous. [20] But law came in, with the result that the trespass multiplied; but where sin increased, grace abounded all the more, [21] so that, just as sin exercised dominion in death, so grace might also exercise dominion through justification[a] leading to eternal life through Jesus Christ our Lord.

6 What then are we to say? Should we continue in sin in order that grace may abound? [2] By no means! How can we who died to sin go on living in it? [3] Do you not know that all of us who have been baptized into Christ Jesus were baptized into his death? [4] Therefore we have been buried with him by baptism into death, so that, just as Christ was raised from the dead by the glory of the Father, so we too might walk in newness of life.

[5] For if we have been united with him in a death like his, we will certainly be united with him in a resurrection like his. [6] We know that our old self was crucified with him so that the body of sin might be destroyed, and we might no longer be enslaved to sin. [7] For whoever has died is freed from sin. [8] But if we have died with Christ, we believe that we will also live with him. [9] We know that Christ, being raised from the dead, will never die again; death no longer has dominion over him. [10] The death he died, he died to sin, once for all; but the life he lives, he lives to God. [11] So you also must consider yourselves dead to sin and alive to God in Christ Jesus.

[12] Therefore, do not let sin exercise dominion in your mortal bodies, to make you obey their passions. [13] No longer present your members to sin as instruments[b] of wickedness, but present yourselves to God as those who have been brought from death to life, and present your members to God as instruments[b] of righteousness. [14] For sin will have no dominion over you, since you are not under law but under grace.

[15] What then? Should we sin because we are not under law but under grace? By no means! [16] Do you not know that if you present yourselves to anyone as obedient slaves, you are slaves of the one whom you obey, either of sin, which leads to death, or of obedience, which leads to righteousness? [17] But thanks be to God that you, having once been slaves of sin, have become obedient from the heart to the form of teaching to which you were entrusted, [18] and that you,

a Or *righteousness*

b Or *weapons*

8.1–4n.) brought the dominion of *life* (6.13–14,23–24). **20:** The giving of the law is a minor episode, serving only to document sin's dominion through the increase of trespasses (7.7–11). The law could not bring that dominion to an end; God's powerful grace could (8.1–4; CD A 3.1–12).

6.1–23: Life in Christ requires obedience. 1: Compare other leading questions in 4.1; 6.15,21; 7.7,13. *Should we continue in sin,* (see v. 2; 3.8n.) only if grace were simply a matter of being relieved of the punishment for trespasses. But it is "much more" (5.12–21). **2–6:** Baptism is a dying with Christ (v. 6; 7.6; Gal 2.19) to the power of sin, assuring that *we will also live with him* (v. 8). Contrast Eph 2.5–6; Col 2.12–13, where the baptized are said already to be *raised* with Christ. **7–11:** *Whoever has died,* whether Christ, through his own death (v. 10), or those who have been baptized into his death (v. 14); see 7.1–6. **9–10:** The lethal collusion of sin and death is evident (see 5.12–14,21). The Gk word translated *has dominion* is related to the word translated "lord" (see vv. 16–17n.); in 5.21 a different word is used. **12–13:** *Instruments of wickedness . . . of righteousness,* lit., "weapons of injustice . . . of justice." Through martial imagery Paul calls the baptized not to surrender themselves as sin's prisoners of war. **14–15:** If grace provided immunity from the law's verdict, then we might well "continue in sin" (see v. 1). **16–20:** An analogy from slavery. Since war captives were often enslaved, these verses may continue the imagery of vv. 13–14. **16–17:** *Slaves . . . obedient,* human existence is inevitably some form of obedience. Note that Paul refrains here from describing God as "Lord," lit., "master." **17:** *Obedient from the heart,* not in slavish obedience but with

having been set free from sin, have become slaves of righteousness. [19] I am speaking in human terms because of your natural limitations.[a] For just as you once presented your members as slaves to impurity and to greater and greater iniquity, so now present your members as slaves to righteousness for sanctification.

[20] When you were slaves of sin, you were free in regard to righteousness. [21] So what advantage did you then get from the things of which you now are ashamed? The end of those things is death. [22] But now that you have been freed from sin and enslaved to God, the advantage you get is sanctification. The end is eternal life. [23] For the wages of sin is death, but the free gift of God is eternal life in Christ Jesus our Lord.

7 Do you not know, brothers and sisters[b]—for I am speaking to those who know the law—that the law is binding on a person only during that person's lifetime? [2] Thus a married woman is bound by the law to her husband as long as he lives; but if her husband dies, she is discharged from the law concerning the husband. [3] Accordingly, she will be called an adulteress if she lives with another man while her husband is alive. But if her husband dies, she is free from that law, and if she marries another man, she is not an adulteress.

[4] In the same way, my friends,[b] you have died to the law through the body of Christ, so that you may belong to another, to him who has been raised from the dead in order that we may bear fruit for God. [5] While we were living in the flesh, our sinful passions, aroused by the law, were at work in our members to bear fruit for death. [6] But now we are discharged from the law, dead to that which held us captive, so that we are slaves not under the old written code but in the new life of the Spirit.

[7] What then should we say? That the law is sin? By no means! Yet, if it had not been for the law, I would not have known sin. I would not have known what it is to covet if the law had not said, "You shall not covet." [8] But sin, seizing an opportunity in the commandment, produced in me all kinds of covetousness. Apart from the law sin lies dead. [9] I was once alive apart from the law, but when the commandment came, sin revived [10] and I died, and the very commandment that promised life proved to be death to me. [11] For sin, seizing an opportunity in the commandment, deceived me and through it killed me. [12] So the law is holy, and the commandment is holy and just and good.

[13] Did what is good, then, bring death to me? By no means! It was sin, working death in me through what is good, in order that sin might be shown to be sin, and through the commandment might become sinful beyond measure.

a   Gk *the weakness of your flesh*
b   Gk *brothers*

genuine intention (12.1–2). **18–20:** "Not under law" (v. 15) does not imply freedom from moral obligation. **21:** *The things of which you now are ashamed,* 1.24–32.

7.1–25: A defense of the law. Paul relies on an analogy from marriage law. One is "free from the law" (v. 3) only when free from the circumstances to which the law rightly applies; here, free from the dominion of sin (6.6–11). Just as marriage law remains valid, so the Torah remains *holy* (v. 12), *spiritual* (v. 14), and *good* (v. 16). **1:** *Those who know the law,* i.e., marriage law. Paul may not be presuming specific knowledge of the Torah. **4:** The one who is in Christ has *died to the law,* and is thus "discharged" from it (v. 6). **5:** *Sinful passions, aroused by the law,* 5.20; 7.7–11. **6:** *That which held us captive,* the law, which bound us in our relationship to sin (6.15–23).

7.7–13: Sin's poisonous interaction with the law. 7: Leading questions (see v. 13) express Paul's concern to exonerate the law. *I would not have known sin,* Paul is not speaking autobiographically (v. 9; Phil 3.6); some have suggested he refers to Adam (v. 10). More likely he presents a "speech in character," reflecting a typical human experience of the law. Although the law (here, Ex 20.17; Deut 5.21) aggravates the dominion of sin in one's members, the law itself remains valid. **8:** *Covetousness,* or "desire," was regarded by Paul's contemporaries as the root of all evil (see Jas 1.15; 4 Macc 2.4–6; Philo, *De spec. leg.* 4.84–94), even the source of Adam's sin (Philo, *Leg. all.* 3.115). *Sin lies dead,* cf. 5.13–14. **10:** *Promised life,* possibly an allusion to Lev 18.5, or to Deut 30.6–20; Paul juxtaposes those passages in 10.5–7 (cf. Gal 3.21). **11:** *Sin . . . deceived me,* Gen 3.13. **13:** *That sin might be shown to be sin,* 5.13.

[14] For we know that the law is spiritual; but I am of the flesh, sold into slavery under sin.[a] [15] I do not understand my own actions. For I do not do what I want, but I do the very thing I hate. [16] Now if I do what I do not want, I agree that the law is good. [17] But in fact it is no longer I that do it, but sin that dwells within me. [18] For I know that nothing good dwells within me, that is, in my flesh. I can will what is right, but I cannot do it. [19] For I do not do the good I want, but the evil I do not want is what I do. [20] Now if I do what I do not want, it is no longer I that do it, but sin that dwells within me.

[21] So I find it to be a law that when I want to do what is good, evil lies close at hand. [22] For I delight in the law of God in my inmost self, [23] but I see in my members another law at war with the law of my mind, making me captive to the law of sin that dwells in my members. [24] Wretched man that I am! Who will rescue me from this body of death? [25] Thanks be to God through Jesus Christ our Lord!

So then, with my mind I am a slave to the law of God, but with my flesh I am a slave to the law of sin.

8 There is therefore now no condemnation for those who are in Christ Jesus. [2] For the law of the Spirit[b] of life in Christ Jesus has set you[c] free from the law of sin and of death. [3] For God has done what the law, weakened by the flesh, could not do: by sending his own Son in the likeness of sinful flesh, and to deal with sin,[d] he condemned sin in the flesh, [4] so that the just requirement of the law might be fulfilled in us, who walk not according to the flesh but according to the Spirit.[b] [5] For those who live according to the flesh set their minds on the things of the flesh, but those who live according to the Spirit[b] set their minds on the things of the Spirit.[b] [6] To set the mind on the flesh is death, but to set the mind on the Spirit[b] is life and peace. [7] For this reason the mind that is set on the flesh is hostile to God; it does not submit to God's law—indeed it cannot, [8] and those who are in the flesh cannot please God.

[9] But you are not in the flesh; you are in the Spirit,[b] since the Spirit of God dwells in you. Anyone who does not have the Spirit of Christ does not belong to him. [10] But if Christ is in you, though the body is dead because of sin,

a Gk *sold under sin*

b Or *spirit*

c Here the Greek word *you* is singular number; other ancient authorities read *me* or *us*

d Or *and as a sin offering*

7.14–25: Even the disobedient acknowledge the rightness of the law's verdict. 14: *The flesh*, where *sin . . . dwells* (vv. 17–20); the Dead Sea Scrolls similarly speak of the "dominion" of sin in the flesh (e.g., 1QH 4.25), or of the "evil impulse" that prevents the fulfillment of God's law, until God intervenes (1QH 13.6). 15–16: *I do not do what I want,* this is not Paul's view of existence in Christ (see 12.1–2), but an illustration of the point made in 2.15: The law declares God's valid judgment on all human conduct. 18: *I cannot do it,* 8.4,7–8. 25: The "I" is hypothetical; Paul has already declared that those baptized into Christ are "no longer . . . enslaved to sin" (6.6).

8.1–39: Life in the Spirit. A turning point in the letter, summing up Paul's previous argument (*therefore,* v. 1) and serving as a foil for the dramatic appeal that follows. 1–4: The inclination of human *flesh* (see 5.20n.) prevented earlier generations from fulfilling the *just requirement of the law* (2.14–15,26). The law is thus *weakened by the flesh* (v. 3). Now that Christ has satisfied that *just requirement* through his own "act of righteousness" (5.18, translating the same Gk word), those who are *in Christ* or *in the Spirit* (v. 9) likewise fulfill the law's *requirement,* in that they *walk . . . according to the Spirit* (v. 4). 2: *The law of the Spirit of life* and *of death,* Paul speaks not of two different laws, but of God's law experienced under two opposing dominions, of sin and of righteousness (6.12–14; 7.6). *The Spirit of life,* capitalized to refer to the "Spirit of God" (vv. 9,11,14; "the Spirit that is from God," 1 Cor 2.14). Paul can use the word "spirit" indefinitely (e.g., "a spirit of slavery . . . a spirit of adoption," v. 15), or personally (vv. 26–27; 1 Cor 2.10–14). The latter meaning is conventionally capitalized in Christian usage, i.e., *the Holy Spirit* (5.5; 9.1; 1 Thess 4.8). 3: *God has done what the law . . . could not do,* Jews in Paul's day regarded Israel's subjection to unjust powers as realizing God's curses on the disobedient (9.31; 10.3). Paul sees Israel's destiny as bound up with Christ's obedience (9.4–5). 5–17: Life in the Spirit and life in the flesh are contrasted. Paul thinks not of a sharp dualism of "spirit" or "mind" over body, but of different dispositions of the mind (vv. 5–7) corresponding to different ways of comporting one's body (6.12–19; 12.1–2). 7: *Hostile to God,* 5.10. *Does not submit to God's law,* that is, to the law's "just requirement," which remains the standard of righteous living (v. 4; 2.14–15).

the Spirit[a] is life because of righteousness. [11] If the Spirit of him who raised Jesus from the dead dwells in you, he who raised Christ[b] from the dead will give life to your mortal bodies also through[c] his Spirit that dwells in you.

[12] So then, brothers and sisters,[d] we are debtors, not to the flesh, to live according to the flesh— [13] for if you live according to the flesh, you will die; but if by the Spirit you put to death the deeds of the body, you will live. [14] For all who are led by the Spirit of God are children of God. [15] For you did not receive a spirit of slavery to fall back into fear, but you have received a spirit of adoption. When we cry, "Abba![e] Father!" [16] it is that very Spirit bearing witness[f] with our spirit that we are children of God, [17] and if children, then heirs, heirs of God and joint heirs with Christ—if, in fact, we suffer with him so that we may also be glorified with him.

[18] I consider that the sufferings of this present time are not worth comparing with the glory about to be revealed to us. [19] For the creation waits with eager longing for the revealing of the children of God; [20] for the creation was subjected to futility, not of its own will but by the will of the one who subjected it, in hope [21] that the creation itself will be set free from its bondage to decay and will obtain the freedom of the glory of the children of God. [22] We know that the whole creation has been groaning in labor pains until now; [23] and not only the creation, but we ourselves, who have the first fruits of the Spirit, groan inwardly while we wait for adoption, the redemption of our bodies. [24] For in[g] hope we were saved. Now hope that is seen is not hope. For who hopes[h] for what is seen? [25] But if we hope for what we do not see, we wait for it with patience.

[26] Likewise the Spirit helps us in our weakness; for we do not know how to pray as we ought, but that very Spirit intercedes[i] with sighs too deep for words. [27] And God,[j] who searches the heart, knows what is the mind of the Spirit, because the Spirit[k] intercedes for the saints according to the will of God.[l]

[28] We know that all things work together for good[m] for those who love God, who are

a Or *spirit*
b Other ancient authorities read *the Christ* or *Christ Jesus* or *Jesus Christ*
c Other ancient authorities read *on account of*
d Gk *brothers*
e Aramaic for *Father*
f Or [15]*a spirit of adoption, by which we cry, "Abba! Father!"* [16]*The Spirit itself bears witness*
g Or *by*
h Other ancient authorities read *awaits*
i Other ancient authorities add *for us*
j Gk *the one*
k Gk *he* or *it*
l Gk *according to God*
m Other ancient authorities read *God makes all things work together for good*, or *in all things God works for good*

9–10: Paul shifts from speaking of being "in Christ" (v. 1) or *in the Spirit* to having the Spirit or Christ dwell within oneself (6.22; 7.4). 11: *He who raised Christ*, 4.17,24; 11.15. 13: *Deeds of the body*, here Paul uses "body" interchangeably with *flesh*. See 6.6–8. 15–17: *Adoption* by the Spirit: Those who live according to the Spirit (or by "faith," i.e., faithfulness, 4.12,16) are the *heirs* of the promises given to Abraham, even if not his descendants according to the flesh (4.1,11–14; Gal 4.5–7). 15: *Abba*, an Aramaic word which Jesus may have used in his own prayer (Mk 14.36), was retained in prayer by early Christians (Gal 4.6). 17: *If . . . we suffer*, the tension between suffering and hope in the glory to come (5.3–5) is characteristic of life during "this present time" (v. 18; 12.12; 1 Cor 4.8–13).

8.18–39: Suffering, and hope in God's promise. God's purposes toward his children are much greater than the circumstances of *this present time* would indicate. This theme is crucial in chs 9–11. 19–22: Paul shares an apocalyptic viewpoint that the present age is evil (see Gal 1.4), having been *subjected* by God to malevolent spiritual forces (v. 20; 1 Cor 15.20–28; Phil 3.21). 21: Creation itself will participate in the liberation of the *children of God*. 22: *Groaning in labor pains*, a frequent apocalyptic metaphor (2 Esd 4.42; 10.5–14; Mt 24.8; Mk 13.8). 23: The inner testimony of the Spirit (vv. 16,26–27) is experienced as intense yearning and hope (5.1–5). *Adoption*, lit., "sonship," see 9.4n. 26–27: If we "groan inwardly" (v. 23), it is because of the Spirit at work in our prayers, interceding *for the saints*. This dramatic language is resumed in 9.1–3. 28–30: The alternative translations in the footnote represent the reading in the earliest manuscript. Paul means, not that all circumstances of this life are good for us (the lament in 8.36 is genuine), but that amid *all* these *things* God's purpose prevails. *Those . . . who are called*, preeminently Israel (9.4; 11.2); also all those who are "the children of the promise," including Gentiles

called according to his purpose. ²⁹ For those whom he foreknew he also predestined to be conformed to the image of his Son, in order that he might be the firstborn within a large family.ᵃ ³⁰ And those whom he predestined he also called; and those whom he called he also justified; and those whom he justified he also glorified.

³¹ What then are we to say about these things? If God is for us, who is against us? ³² He who did not withhold his own Son, but gave him up for all of us, will he not with him also give us everything else? ³³ Who will bring any charge against God's elect? It is God who justifies. ³⁴ Who is to condemn? It is Christ Jesus, who died, yes, who was raised, who is at the right hand of God, who indeed intercedes for us.ᵇ ³⁵ Who will separate us from the love of Christ? Will hardship, or distress, or persecution, or famine, or nakedness, or peril, or sword? ³⁶ As it is written,

"For your sake we are being killed all day
    long;
we are accounted as sheep to be
    slaughtered."

³⁷ No, in all these things we are more than conquerors through him who loved us. ³⁸ For I am convinced that neither death, nor life,

nor angels, nor rulers, nor things present, nor things to come, nor powers, ³⁹ nor height, nor depth, nor anything else in all creation, will be able to separate us from the love of God in Christ Jesus our Lord.

9 I am speaking the truth in Christ—I am not lying; my conscience confirms it by the Holy Spirit— ² I have great sorrow and unceasing anguish in my heart. ³ For I could wish that I myself were accursed and cut off from Christ for the sake of my own people,ᶜ my kindred according to the flesh. ⁴ They are Israelites, and to them belong the adoption, the glory, the covenants, the giving of the law, the worship, and the promises; ⁵ to them belong the patriarchs, and from them, according to the flesh, comes the Messiah,ᵈ who is over all, God blessed forever.ᵉ Amen.

⁶ It is not as though the word of God had failed. For not all Israelites truly belong to

ᵃ Gk *among many brothers*
ᵇ Or *Is it Christ Jesus … for us?*
ᶜ Gk *my brothers*
ᵈ Or *the Christ*
ᵉ Or *Messiah, who is God over all, blessed forever*; or
   Messiah. May he who is God over all be blessed forever

(9.8,23–26). *Conformed to the image of his Son,* Phil 3.21; 2 Cor 4.4. Christ the *firstborn,* 1 Cor 15.20; Col 1.18. **31–39:** Previous assurances of God's love (5.1–11) are reaffirmed; despite all present adversities, God's purpose will prevail. **34:** The heavenly Christ *intercedes for us,* as in vv. 26–27 the Spirit intercedes for the saints. **35–36:** *Hardship . . . or sword,* very real afflictions, as Israel's experience testifies; Ps 44.22 is quoted.

Chapters 9–11: The certainty of God's purposes toward Israel. The preceding argument reaches its climax in these extraordinary chapters, which combine earnest emotional appeal (9.1–5; 10.1–2), exegetical argument (9.6–13,25–29,33; 10.5–13,15–21; 11.2–4,8–10), the stylized dialogue of the diatribe (9.14,19–21,30–32; 10.14,18; 11.1,4,7,11; see 2.17-29n.), and the stark pronouncement style of the prophets (11.25–27). The dramatic contrast in tone between chs 8 and 9, and the continuity of theme across chs 8–11, confirm Paul's overarching purpose. Despite present appearances, God has not abandoned promises made to Israel (9.6; 11.1,11–12,29). The same power that raised Jesus Christ from the dead (10.6–9) can restore Israel as well (11.15,23).

9.1–5: Paul's anguish for Israel is deeply personal—he speaks of his *own people* (v. 3)—yet also grounded in God's *promises* (v. 4). **1:** A solemn oath, confirmed by the Spirit (8.16,23,26–27). **2–3:** Paul's willingness to be *cut off from Christ* for the sake of Israel is especially poignant after the assurance in 8.39. **4:** *To them belong the adoption,* lit., "sonship." The same Gk word appeared in 8.15,23. Paul's point is not that the people of Israel are more "naturally" God's children (vv. 6–9; 4.11–12), but that their "sonship" (see Ex 4.22–23; Hos 11.1) is prior to that of the Gentiles called in Christ (11.17–24). *The glory,* Ex 16.10; 24.16–17. *The covenants,* plural because several are recorded in scripture (Gen 15.8; 17.2,7,9; Ex 2.24; 24.8). *Giving of the law,* Israel's privilege (2.17–20). *The worship,* Israel's covenant obligation (Ex 3.12; 4.23; 40.16–33; 1 Kings 8.54–66). *The promises,* of the land (see Gen 15.7; Ex 6.8), or more broadly "the world" (4.13). **5:** *The patriarchs,* Abraham, Isaac, and Jacob, see Ex 2.24. *According to the flesh,* see 1.3; 15.8–9. *Messiah . . . God blessed forever,* whether Christ is called God here depends on the punctuation inserted (see textual note e). Similar Gk phrases are translated as spontaneous praise to God in 1.25; 11.36; 16.25–27.

Israel, [7] and not all of Abraham's children are his true descendants; but "It is through Isaac that descendants shall be named for you." [8] This means that it is not the children of the flesh who are the children of God, but the children of the promise are counted as descendants. [9] For this is what the promise said, "About this time I will return and Sarah shall have a son." [10] Nor is that all; something similar happened to Rebecca when she had conceived children by one husband, our ancestor Isaac. [11] Even before they had been born or had done anything good or bad (so that God's purpose of election might continue, [12] not by works but by his call) she was told, "The elder shall serve the younger." [13] As it is written,

"I have loved Jacob,
　　but I have hated Esau."

[14] What then are we to say? Is there injustice on God's part? By no means! [15] For he says to Moses,

"I will have mercy on whom I have mercy,
　　and I will have compassion on whom I
　　　　have compassion."

[16] So it depends not on human will or exertion, but on God who shows mercy. [17] For the scripture says to Pharaoh, "I have raised you up for the very purpose of showing my power in you, so that my name may be proclaimed in all the earth." [18] So then he has mercy on whomever he chooses, and he hardens the heart of whomever he chooses.

[19] You will say to me then, "Why then does he still find fault? For who can resist his will?" [20] But who indeed are you, a human being, to argue with God? Will what is molded say to the one who molds it, "Why have you made me like this?" [21] Has the potter no right over the clay, to make out of the same lump one object for special use and another for ordinary use? [22] What if God, desiring to show his wrath and to make known his power, has endured with much patience the objects of wrath that are made for destruction; [23] and what if he has done so in order to make known the riches of his glory for the objects of mercy, which he has prepared beforehand for glory— [24] including us whom he has called, not from the Jews only but also from the Gentiles? [25] As indeed he says in Hosea,

"Those who were not my people I will call
　　'my people,'
and her who was not beloved I will call
　　'beloved.'"
[26] "And in the very place where it was said
　　to them, 'You are not my people,'
there they shall be called children of
　　the living God."

[27] And Isaiah cries out concerning Israel, "Though the number of the children of Israel were like the sand of the sea, only a remnant of them will be saved; [28] for the Lord will

---

9.6–29: God's unwavering purpose. Paul's concern to vindicate God's *purpose of election* (v. 11) runs throughout these verses, as rhetorical questions in vv. 14,19–24 and 30–32 show. 6: The theme of all that follows is that *the word of God* has not *failed. Not all Israelites . . . Israel,* or "these who are Israel are not all who are descended from Israel." Paul's point is not to restrict the number of those who are "truly Israel," but to insist, as did other Jews, that being "Abraham's children" (v. 7) was never a matter either of accomplishment or of physical descent (v. 8). Because the promise came to Abraham through faith (4.13), his "true descendants" are "children of the promise." 7: Though Abraham had other sons (Gen 25.2,12,19), only Isaac was his heir (Gen 21.12). 9: God's promise was given to Sarah (Gen 18.10), not Hagar; Gal 4.21–31. 10–12: God chose Jacob, not Esau (Gen 25.21,23), without regard to any human accomplishment (v. 16). 13: Mal 1.2–3. 14–29: If election is not the result of human *will or exertion* (v. 16), is God unjust? Paul rejects this conclusion, not by appealing to moral principle, but by affirming God's sovereignty. 15: Ex 33.19. 17–18: *Hardens the heart,* see Ex 4.21; Deut 2.30; Josh 11.20. God hardened Pharaoh (Ex 9.16) in order to show God's power (see 11.7–12). 19–21: Paul drives his point home in diatribe style, using biblical metaphors; see Isa 29.16; 45.9; Jer 18.6; Wis 15.7. 22–24: *Objects of wrath,* sinners toward whom God has paradoxically shown *much patience,* as in 2.4–5; 3.25–26. *Objects of mercy . . . glory,* not Israel alone (see 9.4; 11.31) but those who are *called . . . from the Gentiles* as well. Paul insists that present circumstances do not reveal God's final purposes. Mortals may not presume God's judgment on others, to vindicate or to condemn (see 8.1; 11.30–32; 14.3–4,10–13). 25–26: The prophet Hosea spoke of the redemption of Israel (Hos 2.23; 1.10). Paul applies the passage to those God has called, *Jews* and *Gentiles* alike (v. 24). 27–29: God's preservation of *a remnant* in Israel (Isa 10.22; 1.9) shows God's faithfulness (see 11.1–6). The word *only* does not appear in Gk. Paul's point is not that the circle of the elect is contracting, but that God has preserved a remnant out of faith-

execute his sentence on the earth quickly and decisively."ᵃ ²⁹ And as Isaiah predicted,

"If the Lord of hosts had not left survivorsᵇ
    to us,
  we would have fared like Sodom
    and been made like Gomorrah."

³⁰ What then are we to say? Gentiles, who did not strive for righteousness, have attained it, that is, righteousness through faith; ³¹ but Israel, who did strive for the righteousness that is based on the law, did not succeed in fulfilling that law. ³² Why not? Because they did not strive for it on the basis of faith, but as if it were based on works. They have stumbled over the stumbling stone, ³³ as it is written,

"See, I am laying in Zion a stone that will
    make people stumble, a rock that will
    make them fall,
  and whoever believes in himᶜ will not
    be put to shame."

10 Brothers and sisters,ᵈ my heart's desire and prayer to God for them is that they may be saved. ² I can testify that they have a zeal for God, but it is not enlightened. ³ For, being ignorant of the righteousness that comes from God, and seeking to establish their own, they have not submitted to God's righteousness. ⁴ For Christ is the end of the law so that there may be righteousness for everyone who believes.

⁵ Moses writes concerning the righteousness that comes from the law, that "the per-

son who does these things will live by them." ⁶ But the righteousness that comes from faith says, "Do not say in your heart, 'Who will ascend into heaven?'" (that is, to bring Christ down) ⁷ "or 'Who will descend into the abyss?'" (that is, to bring Christ up from the dead). ⁸ But what does it say?

"The word is near you,
  on your lips and in your heart"

(that is, the word of faith that we proclaim); ⁹ becauseᵉ if you confess with your lips that Jesus is Lord and believe in your heart that God raised him from the dead, you will be saved. ¹⁰ For one believes with the heart and so is justified, and one confesses with the mouth and so is saved. ¹¹ The scripture says, "No one who believes in him will be put to shame." ¹² For there is no distinction between Jew and Greek; the same Lord is Lord of all and is generous to all who call on him. ¹³ For, "Everyone who calls on the name of the Lord shall be saved."

¹⁴ But how are they to call on one in whom they have not believed? And how are they

---

ᵃ Other ancient authorities read *for he will finish his work and cut it short in righteousness, because the Lord will make the sentence shortened on the earth*
ᵇ Or *descendants*; Gk *seed*
ᶜ Or *trusts in it*
ᵈ Gk *Brothers*
ᵉ Or *namely, that*

---

fulness to his promise.

9.30–11.12: What went wrong? Paul addresses the surprising circumstances of Israel and the Gentiles. **9.30–33:** A fixed footrace. The Gk "diokein" ("strive for") can mean "chase after" as in a race. The Gentiles' success and Israel's failure to reach the goal or finish line have nothing to do with effort. Israel *stumbled over the stumbling stone,* tripped up, as it were, by God (v. 33; 11.7–8). **32:** Israel approached the law on the basis of *works* (3.20n.,27). Paul does not elaborate, since he considers the ultimate responsibility for Israel's "hardening" lies with God (11.25–26). He does not speak here (or in 10.3) of the desire to obey the law, but perhaps of what he perceives as Israel's failure in his own day to achieve recognition or public vindication through the keeping of the law, a concern among Jewish apologetic writers. **33:** Isa 8.14–15; 28.16. Other early Christians interpreted these verses in relation to Christ (Mt 21.42; 1 Pet 2.6–8). For Paul, the *stone* laid *in Zion* may be the law itself. **10.1–3:** See 9.1–5. **3:** In Paul's view, Israel failed to submit *to God's righteousness* because they were *ignorant* of the vindication God would bring about through the "faith of Jesus Christ" (see 3.22n.). **4:** *The end of the law* almost certainly means its goal, not its termination (3.31; 7.12,16,22; 9.30–32). **5–13:** Using a common Jewish technique, Paul interprets one passage of scripture (Lev 18.5) in light of others (Deut 30.11–14; cf. Ps 107.26). **5–7:** *The righteousness . . . from the law* and *from faith* are not opposed, since there is only "God's righteousness" (10.3). The promise of life to *the person who does these things* (Lev 18.5) requires not human effort to produce the messiah, but faith in the messiah whom God has sent. Such is Paul's Christological reading of Deut 30.11–14. **9–13:** Salvation through "faith" (1.15–17). **11:** Isa 28.16. **12:** *No distinction,* see 3.22,29. **13:** Joel 2.32. Early Christians often applied to Jesus certain biblical references to the *Lord,* references, which in their original context, refer to God. **14–21:** God's faithfulness

to believe in one of whom they have never heard? And how are they to hear without someone to proclaim him? [15] And how are they to proclaim him unless they are sent? As it is written, "How beautiful are the feet of those who bring good news!" [16] But not all have obeyed the good news;[a] for Isaiah says, "Lord, who has believed our message?" [17] So faith comes from what is heard, and what is heard comes through the word of Christ.[b]

[18] But I ask, have they not heard? Indeed they have; for

"Their voice has gone out to all the earth,
    and their words to the ends of the world."

[19] Again I ask, did Israel not understand? First Moses says,

"I will make you jealous of those who are
        not a nation;
    with a foolish nation I will make you
        angry."

[20] Then Isaiah is so bold as to say,

"I have been found by those who did not
        seek me;
    I have shown myself to those who did
        not ask for me."

[21] But of Israel he says, "All day long I have held out my hands to a disobedient and contrary people."

11

I ask, then, has God rejected his people? By no means! I myself am an Israelite, a descendant of Abraham, a member of the tribe of Benjamin. [2] God has not rejected his people whom he foreknew. Do you not know what the scripture says of Elijah, how he pleads with God against Israel? [3] "Lord, they have killed your prophets, they have demolished your altars; I alone am left, and they are seeking my life." [4] But what is the divine reply

to him? "I have kept for myself seven thousand who have not bowed the knee to Baal." [5] So too at the present time there is a remnant, chosen by grace. [6] But if it is by grace, it is no longer on the basis of works, otherwise grace would no longer be grace.[c]

[7] What then? Israel failed to obtain what it was seeking. The elect obtained it, but the rest were hardened, [8] as it is written,

"God gave them a sluggish spirit,
    eyes that would not see
    and ears that would not hear,
    down to this very day."

[9] And David says,

"Let their table become a snare and a trap,
    a stumbling block and a retribution for
        them;
[10] let their eyes be darkened so that they
        cannot see,
    and keep their backs forever bent."

[11] So I ask, have they stumbled so as to fall? By no means! But through their stumbling[d] salvation has come to the Gentiles, so as to make Israel[e] jealous. [12] Now if their stumbling[d] means riches for the world, and if their defeat means riches for Gentiles, how much more will their full inclusion mean!

[13] Now I am speaking to you Gentiles. Inasmuch then as I am an apostle to the Gentiles,

a Or *gospel*
b Or *about Christ*; other ancient authorities read *of God*
c Other ancient authorities add *But if it is by works, it is no longer on the basis of grace, otherwise work would no longer be work*
d Gk *transgression*
e Gk *them*

to Israel continues as *good news* is preached to them. **15:** Isa 52.17. **16:** Isa 53.1. *But not all have obeyed,* the disobedience of some in Israel does not alter God's faithfulness (see 3.3). *Good news,* the same word is elsewhere translated "gospel"; see 1.16n. **18:** Ps 19.4. **19:** Deut 32.21. Israel's disobedience does not indicate God's failure; to the contrary, God's purpose is to make Israel jealous. **20–21:** See 11.11–12. The Gentiles are the "foolish nation" (Deut 32.21), *those who did not seek me* (Isa 65.1–2). *All day long,* Paul emphasizes God's persistent faithfulness to a disobedient Israel.

11.1–12: God has preserved a remnant. 1: Paul himself is evidence that God has not *rejected his people.* **2–5:** The *divine reply* to the prophet Elijah was a rebuke for presuming he *alone* was left (1 Kings 19.10,18). Similarly, the *remnant* in Paul's day does not exhaust God's gracious purpose (see vv. 12,15,25–27). **7–12:** Astonishingly, Paul concludes Israel *failed* (9.31–10.4) because they *were hardened* by God (9.18). **8:** Isa 29.10; Deut 29.4; cf. Isa 6.10. **9–10:** Ps 69.22–23. **11–12:** Previous rhetorical questions concerned God's righteousness or faithfulness (3.3,29; 9.14,19); now Paul asks about God's faithfulness to the covenant with Israel. The obedience of the Gentiles will *make Israel jealous* (see 10.19–20). *Their full inclusion,* see vv. 15,26.

I glorify my ministry [14] in order to make my own people[a] jealous, and thus save some of them. [15] For if their rejection is the reconciliation of the world, what will their acceptance be but life from the dead! [16] If the part of the dough offered as first fruits is holy, then the whole batch is holy; and if the root is holy, then the branches also are holy.

[17] But if some of the branches were broken off, and you, a wild olive shoot, were grafted in their place to share the rich root[b] of the olive tree, [18] do not boast over the branches. If you do boast, remember that it is not you that support the root, but the root that supports you. [19] You will say, "Branches were broken off so that I might be grafted in." [20] That is true. They were broken off because of their unbelief, but you stand only through faith. So do not become proud, but stand in awe. [21] For if God did not spare the natural branches, perhaps he will not spare you.[c] [22] Note then the kindness and the severity of God: severity toward those who have fallen, but God's kindness toward you, provided you continue in his kindness; otherwise you also will be cut off. [23] And even those of Israel,[d] if they do not persist in unbelief, will be grafted in, for God has the power to graft them in again. [24] For if you have been cut from what is by nature a wild olive tree and grafted, contrary to nature, into a cultivated olive tree,

how much more will these natural branches be grafted back into their own olive tree.

[25] So that you may not claim to be wiser than you are, brothers and sisters,[e] I want you to understand this mystery: a hardening has come upon part of Israel, until the full number of the Gentiles has come in. [26] And so all Israel will be saved; as it is written,

"Out of Zion will come the Deliverer;
    he will banish ungodliness from Jacob."
[27] "And this is my covenant with them,
    when I take away their sins."

[28] As regards the gospel they are enemies of God[f] for your sake; but as regards election they are beloved, for the sake of their ancestors; [29] for the gifts and the calling of God are irrevocable. [30] Just as you were once disobedient to God but have now received mercy because of their disobedience, [31] so they have now been disobedient in order that, by the mercy shown to you, they too may now[g]

a   Gk *my flesh*
b   Other ancient authorities read *the richness*
c   Other ancient authorities read *neither will he spare you*
d   Gk lacks *of Israel*
e   Gk *brothers*
f   Gk lacks *of God*
g   Other ancient authorities lack *now*

11.13–36: A warning to the Gentile faithful in Rome. The climax of chs 9–11, these verses reveal the heart of the letter's purpose. Paul is obliged as apostle to the Gentiles to address the believers in Rome (see 1.1–13), and to pronounce the solemn warning that follows (see 15.14–16). **13:** *I glorify my ministry,* 15.18–21. **14:** *To make my own people jealous,* possibly by eliciting their acceptance of the Christ (see 10.14–21), though Paul does not say this explicitly. **15:** *Life from the dead,* see v. 23. **16:** The remnant preserved by God (see 9.27–29; 11.1–5), like a portion of *dough* offered in worship (Num 15.18–21) or the *root* of a tree (Jer 11.16–17), guarantees God's continuing care for the whole of Israel.

11.17–24: The metaphor of the olive tree. The tree, root and branches, is Israel (Jer 11.16; Hos 14.6); the *wild olive shoot* (v. 17) represents the Gentiles who believe in Christ. **17–18:** *Broken off,* the passive voice here and in vv. 19–20 reflects divine action (see v. 21). The grafting, "contrary to nature" (v. 24), of a *wild olive shoot* gives life to the shoot, but does not benefit the root. *Do not boast,* the tone of warning earlier (2.17n.) reaches its target here. **19–21:** Paul concedes the perception among Gentile believers that *branches were broken off,* but warns against pride (see 12.3). **22:** *The kindness . . . severity,* God's kindness is meant to lead to repentance and obedience (see 2.4–10). **24:** Grafting branches from a *wild olive tree . . . into a cultivated olive tree* is more difficult than restoring *natural branches* that have been broken off.

11.25–36: The hardening of Israel. A warning against arrogance on the part of Gentile believers in Christ, the heart of the letter (see 2.1–4; 3.27; 12.3). **25:** *I want you to understand,* such solemn disclosures indicate Paul's concerns in his letters (1 Cor 10.1–6; 12.1; 2 Cor 1.8; 1 Thess 4.13). *This mystery,* a truth revealed by God (Dan 2.18–30,47; 1 Cor 2.7; 13.2; 14.2). *A hardening,* vv. 7–8; 9.18. This hardening is temporary, until *the full number of the Gentiles,* those destined to trust in God, *has come in.* **26:** Isa 59.20–21; 27.9. *All Israel,* in view already in 11.16,23. *Saved,* delivered from *ungodliness* and forgiven their sins. **28–32:** God's mysterious course of action fulfills the

receive mercy. [32] For God has imprisoned all in disobedience so that he may be merciful to all.

[33] O the depth of the riches and wisdom and knowledge of God! How unsearchable are his judgments and how inscrutable his ways! [34] "For who has known the mind of the Lord?
Or who has been his counselor?"
[35] "Or who has given a gift to him,
to receive a gift in return?"
[36] For from him and through him and to him are all things. To him be the glory forever. Amen.

12 I appeal to you therefore, brothers and sisters,[a] by the mercies of God, to present your bodies as a living sacrifice, holy and acceptable to God, which is your spiritual[b] worship. [2] Do not be conformed to this world,[c] but be transformed by the renewing of your minds, so that you may discern what is the will of God—what is good and acceptable and perfect.[d]

[3] For by the grace given to me I say to everyone among you not to think of yourself more highly than you ought to think, but to think with sober judgment, each according to the measure of faith that God has assigned. [4] For as in one body we have many members, and not all the members have the same function, [5] so we, who are many, are one body in Christ, and individually we are members one of another. [6] We have gifts that differ according to the grace given to us: prophecy, in proportion to faith; [7] ministry, in ministering; the teacher, in teaching; [8] the exhorter, in exhortation; the giver, in generosity; the leader, in diligence; the compassionate, in cheerfulness.

[9] Let love be genuine; hate what is evil, hold fast to what is good; [10] love one another with mutual affection; outdo one another in showing honor. [11] Do not lag in zeal, be ardent in spirit, serve the Lord.[e] [12] Rejoice in hope, be patient in suffering, persevere in prayer. [13] Contribute to the needs of the saints; extend hospitality to strangers.

[14] Bless those who persecute you; bless and do not curse them. [15] Rejoice with those who rejoice, weep with those who weep. [16] Live in harmony with one another; do not be haughty, but associate with the lowly;[f] do not claim to be wiser than you are. [17] Do not repay anyone evil for evil, but take thought for what is noble in the sight of all. [18] If it is possible, so far as it depends on you, live peaceably with all. [19] Beloved, never avenge yourselves, but leave room for the wrath of God;[g] for it is written, "Ven-

a   Gk *brothers*
b   Or *reasonable*
c   Gk *age*
d   Or *what is the good and acceptable and perfect will of God*
e   Other ancient authorities read *serve the opportune time*
f   Or *give yourselves to humble tasks*
g   Gk *the wrath*

election of Israel (3.2; 9.6; 11.1) and precludes the possibility of human boasting (v. 32; 3.9–30). **34:** Isa 40.13. **35:** Job 35.7; 41.11. **36:** A blessing, as at 1.25; 9.5; 16.25–27.

12.1–15.13: Exhortation to holy living. On the basis of the argument in previous chapters, Paul now exhorts the faithful of Rome to right conduct. **12.1:** Holy living is *spiritual worship* (15.15–16), the opposite of "ungodliness" (1.21–28), made possible through baptism (6.12–23). Paul makes his *appeal* (the Gk phrase marks exhortations in his letters: 1 Cor 1.10; 2 Cor 10.1; 1 Thess 4.1; Philem 9) on the basis of *the mercies of God* (11.22–23,30–32) and the "grace given" to him as apostle (v. 3; 1.5; 15.15). **2:** The faithful are to live no longer as belonging to *this world* (Gal 1.4; Phil 2.15; 1 Cor 7.29–31). The *renewing of . . . minds*, possible because of baptism (6.4), enables discerning *the will of God* (see Phil 1.9; 3.8–9). **3–8: A warning against arrogance. 3:** *I say*, direct speech echoes 11.1,11,13. *Not to think . . . more highly*, similar Gk phrases are translated "do not become proud" in 11.20, and "do not be haughty" in v. 16. **4–8:** *Gifts* are given to nourish the community as *one body in Christ;* 1 Cor 12.4–31 has a similar list.

12.9–21: Goodwill within the community and without. 9–10: *Love*, 13.8–10; 1 Cor 13. **12:** *Hope* and patience in *suffering*, see 5.3–5; 8.18–39. **13:** *Hospitality* was a crucial virtue in the early churches (see 16.1–2; Heb 13.2; 3 Jn 5–8). **14:** Here and in vv. 17,21, Paul may allude to sayings of Jesus (Mt 5.44). **16:** See v. 3n. *The lowly*, almost certainly people (despite the alternative in textual note *f*), as in Lk 1.52; Jas 1.9; the same word is translated "humble" in Mt 11.29; Jas 4.6; 1 Pet 5.5, and "oppressed" throughout the Hebrew Bible. **17:** Mt 5.44. **19:** Deut

geance is mine, I will repay, says the Lord." ²⁰ No, "if your enemies are hungry, feed them; if they are thirsty, give them something to drink; for by doing this you will heap burning coals on their heads." ²¹ Do not be overcome by evil, but overcome evil with good.

13 Let every person be subject to the governing authorities; for there is no authority except from God, and those authorities that exist have been instituted by God. ² Therefore whoever resists authority resists what God has appointed, and those who resist will incur judgment. ³ For rulers are not a terror to good conduct, but to bad. Do you wish to have no fear of the authority? Then do what is good, and you will receive its approval; ⁴ for it is God's servant for your good. But if you do what is wrong, you should be afraid, for the authorityᵃ does not bear the sword in vain! It is the servant of God to execute wrath on the wrongdoer. ⁵ Therefore one must be subject, not only because of wrath but also because of conscience. ⁶ For the same reason you also pay taxes, for the authorities are God's servants, busy with this very thing. ⁷ Pay to all what is due them—taxes to whom taxes are due, revenue to whom revenue is due, respect to whom respect is due, honor to whom honor is due.

⁸ Owe no one anything, except to love one another; for the one who loves another has fulfilled the law. ⁹ The commandments, "You shall not commit adultery; You shall not murder; You shall not steal; You shall not covet"; and any other commandment, are summed up in this word, "Love your neighbor as yourself." ¹⁰ Love does no wrong to a neighbor; therefore, love is the fulfilling of the law.

¹¹ Besides this, you know what time it is, how it is now the moment for you to wake from sleep. For salvation is nearer to us now than when we became believers; ¹² the night is far gone, the day is near. Let us then lay aside the works of darkness and put on the armor of light; ¹³ let us live honorably as in the day, not in reveling and drunkenness, not in debauchery and licentiousness, not in quarreling and jealousy. ¹⁴ Instead, put on the Lord Jesus Christ, and make no provision for the flesh, to gratify its desires.

14 Welcome those who are weak in faith,ᵇ but not for the purpose of quarreling over opinions. ² Some believe in eating

ᵃ   Gk *it*
ᵇ   Or *conviction*

32.35. *Wrath*, see 2.5n. **20**: To *heap burning coals* . . . makes enemies feel ashamed and perhaps remorseful (Prov 25.21–22). **21**: Mt 5.39.

   13.1–7: Subjection to governing authorities. Sometimes read as Paul's "theology of the state," these verses stand in tension with his view elsewhere of the "rulers of this age" (1 Cor 2.6–8; 15.24–26; 1 Thess 5.3–11), and with his own willingness to suffer punishment from civil authorities (2 Cor 11.23,25–27). This teaching appears conventional (Wis 6.1–3; 1 Pet 2.13–17; 3.13), and there are other attitudes to civil authorities in the New Testament (Acts 5.29; Rev 13.2,5,11–18). These verses may have had a very specific application (see the Introduction). **1**: Empires rise and fall by the will of God (Isa 10.5–6; Jer 27.4–8,11; Dan 3.28–32). *Instituted*, lit., "put in their place"; the Gk word is related to the word translated *be subject*. **2**: Do not *resist* authority; contrast 12.2. *Resists what God has appointed*, 8.7; 9.19. **3–4**: The proper role of civil authorities; Paul was aware they could act otherwise. *God's servant*, a title applied to the Babylonian king Nebuchadrezzar (Jer 27.6), as well as to many leaders of Israel. The authority may punish; the individual Christian may not (12.19–21). *The sword*, a symbol of power over life and death (see 8.35). Paul's remark is in some tension with claims, current at the time, that the emperor Nero did not need the sword to rule. *Wrath*, elsewhere usually "the wrath of God" (1.18; 2.5; 5.9). **5–6**: Proper civil behavior is motivated both by fear of "wrath" (but see v. 3) and *conscience*. **6–7**: *Taxes*, the Roman tribute (as in Mt 22.21; Mk 12.17; Lk 20.25), from which Roman citizens were exempt. *Revenue*, commercial taxes. *Respect*, lit., "fear"; the same word is translated "terror" in v. 3. The one *to whom respect*, or fear, *is due* may be God alone (1 Pet 2.17).

   13.8–14: Other exhortations. 8–10: *Love* fulfills *the law*, 2.14; 8.4; 12.9; Mt 22.39–40; Mk 12.31; Gal 5.14; Jas 2.8; 1 Jn 4.11. **9**: Ex 20.13–17; Deut 5.17–21; Lev 19.18. **11–14**: Imminent *salvation*, i.e., the return of Christ, makes it urgent to *wake* to holy and honorable living (1 Thess 5.1–11; Eph 5.8–18). **14**: *Put on the Lord Jesus*, an early metaphor based in the practice of receiving a new garment after baptism (Gal 3.27).

   14.1–15.13: Exhortations regarding those considered "weak." The observance of special days (14.5–6) and a

anything, while the weak eat only vegetables. ³ Those who eat must not despise those who abstain, and those who abstain must not pass judgment on those who eat; for God has welcomed them. ⁴ Who are you to pass judgment on servants of another? It is before their own lord that they stand or fall. And they will be upheld, for the Lordᵃ is able to make them stand.

⁵ Some judge one day to be better than another, while others judge all days to be alike. Let all be fully convinced in their own minds. ⁶ Those who observe the day, observe it in honor of the Lord. Also those who eat, eat in honor of the Lord, since they give thanks to God; while those who abstain, abstain in honor of the Lord and give thanks to God.

⁷ We do not live to ourselves, and we do not die to ourselves. ⁸ If we live, we live to the Lord, and if we die, we die to the Lord; so then, whether we live or whether we die, we are the Lord's. ⁹ For to this end Christ died and lived again, so that he might be Lord of both the dead and the living.

¹⁰ Why do you pass judgment on your brother or sister?ᵇ Or you, why do you despise your brother or sister?ᵇ For we will all stand before the judgment seat of God.ᶜ ¹¹ For it is written,

"As I live, says the Lord, every knee shall
     bow to me,
   and every tongue shall give praise toᵈ
        God."
¹² So then, each of us will be accountable to God.ᵉ

¹³ Let us therefore no longer pass judgment on one another, but resolve instead never to put a stumbling block or hindrance in the way of another.ᶠ ¹⁴ I know and am persuaded in the Lord Jesus that nothing is unclean in itself; but it is unclean for anyone who thinks it unclean. ¹⁵ If your brother or sisterᵇ is being injured by what you eat, you are no longer walking in love. Do not let what you eat cause the ruin of one for whom Christ died. ¹⁶ So do not let your good be spoken of as evil. ¹⁷ For the kingdom of God is not food and drink but righteousness and peace and joy in the Holy Spirit. ¹⁸ The one who thus serves Christ is acceptable to God and has human approval. ¹⁹ Let us then pursue what makes for peace and for mutual upbuilding. ²⁰ Do not, for the sake of food, destroy the work of God. Everything is indeed clean, but it is wrong for you to make others fall by what you eat; ²¹ it is good not to eat meat or drink wine or do anything that makes your brother or sisterᵇ stumble.ᵍ ²² The faith that you have, have as your own conviction before God. Blessed are those who have no reason to condemn themselves because of what they approve. ²³ But those who have doubts are condemned if they eat, because they do not act from faith;ʰ

ᵃ Other ancient authorities read for God
ᵇ Gk brother
ᶜ Other ancient authorities read of Christ
ᵈ Or confess
ᵉ Other ancient authorities lack to God
ᶠ Gk of a brother
ᵍ Other ancient authorities add or be upset or be weakened
ʰ Or conviction

kosher diet (vv. 2,14n.) are marks of Jewish observance. They were also objects of ridicule among some Roman satirists, being seen as superstition on the part of the weak. Paul warns against such disparaging judgments (v. 3). **14.1–12: Tolerance for others' observance. 1–2:** Those who eat only vegetables are most likely keeping kosher by avoiding "unclean" meat (v. 14), or meat "sacrificed to idols" (Acts 15.29; 1 Cor 8.1; Dan 1.3–16; Esth 3.28; 14.17; Jdt 12.1–2). Paul calls them weak in faith, not because they adhere to the Torah (see vv. 4,6; 7.12), but perhaps because they are scandalized by Gentile believers who eat nonkosher food (vv. 13,15,20), or because the circumstances of Jews in Rome had been so clearly reduced in the eyes of their neighbors in the wake of the edict of Claudius (see Introduction). **4:** The Lord is able, 11.23. **5–9:** Jews and Gentiles can, each in their own way, live in honor of the Lord. **11:** Isa 45.23. **13–23: Freedom is not license to give offense. 13:** Stumbling block . . . hindrance, 9.32–33; 1 Cor 8.9. **14:** Nothing is unclean in itself, lit., "common," as opposed to "clean" (v. 20; 1 Macc 1.47,62; Mk 7.19; Acts 10.14; 11.8). For the observant, however, nonkosher food is unclean. **17:** The kingdom of God, a rare phrase in Paul's letters (1 Cor 4.20; 6.9–10). **19:** Peace . . . mutual upbuilding, 1 Cor 14.3–5,12,26. **20–23:** Faith does not allow one to violate the conscience of others, e.g., by encouraging them to act against their

for whatever does not proceed from faith[a] is sin.[b]

15 We who are strong ought to put up with the failings of the weak, and not to please ourselves. [2] Each of us must please our neighbor for the good purpose of building up the neighbor. [3] For Christ did not please himself; but, as it is written, "The insults of those who insult you have fallen on me." [4] For whatever was written in former days was written for our instruction, so that by steadfastness and by the encouragement of the scriptures we might have hope. [5] May the God of steadfastness and encouragement grant you to live in harmony with one another, in accordance with Christ Jesus, [6] so that together you may with one voice glorify the God and Father of our Lord Jesus Christ.

[7] Welcome one another, therefore, just as Christ has welcomed you, for the glory of God. [8] For I tell you that Christ has become a servant of the circumcised on behalf of the truth of God in order that he might confirm the promises given to the patriarchs, [9] and in order that the Gentiles might glorify God for his mercy. As it is written,

"Therefore I will confess[c] you among the Gentiles,
    and sing praises to your name";
[10] and again he says,
"Rejoice, O Gentiles, with his people";
[11] and again,
"Praise the Lord, all you Gentiles,
    and let all the peoples praise him";
[12] and again Isaiah says,
"The root of Jesse shall come,
    the one who rises to rule the Gentiles;
in him the Gentiles shall hope."

[13] May the God of hope fill you with all joy and peace in believing, so that you may abound in hope by the power of the Holy Spirit.

[14] I myself feel confident about you, my brothers and sisters,[d] that you yourselves are full of goodness, filled with all knowledge, and able to instruct one another. [15] Nevertheless on some points I have written to you rather boldly by way of reminder, because of the grace given me by God [16] to be a minister of Christ Jesus to the Gentiles in the priestly service of the gospel of God, so that the offering of the Gentiles may be acceptable, sanctified by the Holy Spirit. [17] In Christ Jesus, then, I have reason to boast of my work for God. [18] For I will not venture to speak of anything except what Christ has accomplished[e] through me to win obedience from the Gentiles, by word and deed, [19] by the power of signs and wonders, by the power of the Spirit of God,[f] so that from Jerusalem and as far around as Illyricum I have fully proclaimed the good news[g] of Christ. [20] Thus I make it my ambition to proclaim the good news,[g] not where Christ has already been named, so that

a   Or *conviction*
b   Other authorities, some ancient, add here 16.25–27
c   Or *thank*
d   Gk *brothers*
e   Gk *speak of those things that Christ has not accomplished*
f   Other ancient authorities read *of the Spirit* or *of the Holy Spirit*
g   Or *gospel*

conscience. **15.1–13: Christ's example. 1:** *We who are strong,* lit., "powerful," a term that could connote status in Roman society. Paul does not speak of the strong "in faith" (in contrast to the *weak in faith* in 14.1). *Put up with the failings of the weak,* lit., "sustain the powerless in their weaknesses" (see Gal 6.2). **2–3:** Ps 69.9 is read in terms of Christ's humbling himself (Phil 2.5–8; 2 Cor 8.9). **4:** See 4.23–25; 1 Cor 9.10. **5–6:** The goal of Paul's exhortation is that Gentiles and Jews should *with one voice glorify . . . God.* **8:** Christ came to *confirm the promises* given to Israel (9.3–5). **9:** Ps 18.49. **10:** Deut 32.43. **11:** Ps 117.1. **12:** Isa 11.10. (The Gk word for *Gentiles* in vv. 9–12 is translated "nations" in the biblical passages that Paul quotes.)

15.14–32: The letter's argument brought to a close. 14–16: Despite confidence in the Romans (1.8,11,12), Paul has written *boldly,* compelled by the *grace given* him (1.5). **16:** *Minister . . . priestly service,* Paul will present a holy *offering* to God, i.e., the Gentile believers themselves (1.9; 12.2). Paul may have in mind Isaiah's prophecies of the "wealth of the nations" being brought to Israel (Isa. 60.4–7, 11; see 66.20); his language also echoes imperial language about the "gifts of the peoples" being brought before Caesar. **17–32: The broader context of Paul's apostolate.** As at the letter's beginning (1.1–15), Paul links his letter to the Romans with his *work for God.* **19:** *Signs and wonders,* 1 Cor 12.10; 2 Cor 12.12; Gal 3.5. *Illyricum,* a Roman province on the east coast of the Adriatic

I do not build on someone else's foundation, ²¹ but as it is written,

"Those who have never been told of him shall see,
and those who have never heard of him shall understand."

²² This is the reason that I have so often been hindered from coming to you. ²³ But now, with no further place for me in these regions, I desire, as I have for many years, to come to you ²⁴ when I go to Spain. For I do hope to see you on my journey and to be sent on by you, once I have enjoyed your company for a little while. ²⁵ At present, however, I am going to Jerusalem in a ministry to the saints; ²⁶ for Macedonia and Achaia have been pleased to share their resources with the poor among the saints at Jerusalem. ²⁷ They were pleased to do this, and indeed they owe it to them; for if the Gentiles have come to share in their spiritual blessings, they ought also to be of service to them in material things. ²⁸ So, when I have completed this, and have delivered to them what has been collected,ᵃ I will set out by way of you to Spain; ²⁹ and I know that when I come to you, I will come in the fullness of the blessingᵇ of Christ.

³⁰ I appeal to you, brothers and sisters,ᶜ by our Lord Jesus Christ and by the love of the Spirit, to join me in earnest prayer to God on my behalf, ³¹ that I may be rescued from the unbelievers in Judea, and that my ministryᵈ to Jerusalem may be acceptable to the saints,

³² so that by God's will I may come to you with joy and be refreshed in your company. ³³ The God of peace be with all of you.ᵉ Amen.

16 I commend to you our sister Phoebe, a deaconᶠ of the church at Cenchreae, ² so that you may welcome her in the Lord as is fitting for the saints, and help her in whatever she may require from you, for she has been a benefactor of many and of myself as well.

³ Greet Prisca and Aquila, who work with me in Christ Jesus, ⁴ and who risked their necks for my life, to whom not only I give thanks, but also all the churches of the Gentiles. ⁵ Greet also the church in their house. Greet my beloved Epaenetus, who was the first convertᵍ in Asia for Christ. ⁶ Greet Mary, who has worked very hard among you. ⁷ Greet Andronicus and Junia,ʰ my relativesⁱ who were in prison with me; they are prominent among the apostles, and they were in Christ before I was. ⁸ Greet Ampliatus, my beloved in the Lord.

---

a Gk *have sealed to them this fruit*

b Other ancient authorities add *of the gospel*

c Gk *brothers*

d Other ancient authorities read *my bringing of a gift*

e One ancient authority adds 16.25-27 here

f Or *minister*

g Gk *first fruits*

h Or *Junias*; other ancient authorities read *Julia*

i Or *compatriots*

Sea, mentioned only here in the New Testament. *Good news,* see 1.16n. **21:** Isa 52.15. **22–29:** Travel plans and further requests. **23:** *No further place,* Paul sees himself as a herald more than a pastor. **24:** Paul says nothing now of wishing to "proclaim the gospel" to the Romans (1.10–15); perhaps this letter has done that. **25–29:** The *ministry to the saints,* the collection mentioned in 1 Cor 16.1–4; 2 Cor 8–9; Gal 2.10. **26:** *Macedonia and Achaia,* Roman provinces in Greece. **30–33: Apprehensions regarding Jerusalem.** The Roman faithful may participate in the "offering of the Gentiles" (v. 16) through their own holiness (12.2) and their *earnest prayer* for Paul. The *unbelievers in Judea,* perhaps Jews who have not believed in Jesus (see 9.1–5; 10.1–2,14) who are the ultimate targets of his work (11.13–14). On the fate of this *ministry to Jerusalem,* see Acts 21.7–28.31.

16.1–23: A recommendation and greetings. Some early manuscripts do not include 16.1–24; these verses nevertheless appear to be an authentic part of the letter (see also vv. 25–27n.). **1–2:** Paul commends *Phoebe,* an officer of a church in *Cenchreae* near Corinth (Acts 18.18), to the hospitality and support of the Roman believers, thus honoring his obligations to her as his *benefactor.* On the early Christian office of *deacon,* see Phil 1.1; 1 Tim 3.8,12; Titus 1.9. **3–16:** A list of greetings shows Paul's personal connections with the Roman community. Most of the individuals named are mentioned only here; a number are Hebrew names. **3–4:** *Prisca and Aquila,* identified in Acts 18.2 as exiles from Rome, now returned (1 Cor 16.19; 2 Tim 4.19). **5:** Congregations of believers in Christ first met in private homes, or in common areas in the upper floors of apartment buildings. **7:** *Junia,* a woman; many manuscripts read "Junias," an otherwise unattested male Latin name; our earliest manuscript reads "Julia." *Relatives,* fellow Jews (vv. 11,21; 9.3). *The apostles,* Paul uses the term to mean more than the twelve (see 1 Cor

[9] Greet Urbanus, our co-worker in Christ, and my beloved Stachys. [10] Greet Apelles, who is approved in Christ. Greet those who belong to the family of Aristobulus. [11] Greet my relative[a] Herodion. Greet those in the Lord who belong to the family of Narcissus. [12] Greet those workers in the Lord, Tryphaena and Tryphosa. Greet the beloved Persis, who has worked hard in the Lord. [13] Greet Rufus, chosen in the Lord; and greet his mother—a mother to me also. [14] Greet Asyncritus, Phlegon, Hermes, Patrobas, Hermas, and the brothers and sisters[b] who are with them. [15] Greet Philologus, Julia, Nereus and his sister, and Olympas, and all the saints who are with them. [16] Greet one another with a holy kiss. All the churches of Christ greet you.

[17] I urge you, brothers and sisters,[b] to keep an eye on those who cause dissensions and offenses, in opposition to the teaching that you have learned; avoid them. [18] For such people do not serve our Lord Christ, but their own appetites,[c] and by smooth talk and flattery they deceive the hearts of the simpleminded. [19] For while your obedience is known to all, so that I rejoice over you, I want you to be wise in what is good and guileless in what is evil. [20] The God of peace will shortly crush Satan under your feet. The grace of our Lord Jesus Christ be with you.[d]

[21] Timothy, my co-worker, greets you; so do Lucius and Jason and Sosipater, my relatives.[e]

[22] I Tertius, the writer of this letter, greet you in the Lord.[f]

[23] Gaius, who is host to me and to the whole church, greets you. Erastus, the city treasurer, and our brother Quartus, greet you.[g]

[25] Now to God[h] who is able to strengthen you according to my gospel and the proclamation of Jesus Christ, according to the revelation of the mystery that was kept secret for long ages [26] but is now disclosed, and through the prophetic writings is made known to all the Gentiles, according to the command of the eternal God, to bring about the obedience of faith— [27] to the only wise God, through Jesus Christ, to whom[i] be the glory forever! Amen.[j]

a Or *compatriot*
b Gk *brothers*
c Gk *their own belly*
d Other ancient authorities lack this sentence
e Or *compatriots*
f Or *I Tertius, writing this letter in the Lord, greet you*
g Other ancient authorities add verse 24, *The grace of our Lord Jesus Christ be with all of you. Amen.*
h Gk *the one*
i Other ancient authorities lack *to whom*. The verse then reads, *to the only wise God be the glory through Jesus Christ forever. Amen.*
j Other ancient authorities lack 16.25-27 or include it after 14.23 or 15.33; others put verse 24 after verse 27

15.5,7; Phil 2.25). **13:** *A mother to me also,* an expression of affection. **16:** *A holy kiss,* a regular part of worship in the early church (1 Cor 16.20; 2 Cor 13.12; 1 Thess 5.26; 1 Pet 5.14).

16.17–20: A warning. *Those who cause dissensions,* otherwise unidentified, are clearly less central to the letter's purpose than those referred to in 1 Cor 5.1–13 or Gal 1.8–9; 6.17. *The teaching,* 6.17. **19:** 1.8. **20:** A concluding blessing (1 Cor 16.23; 1 Thess 5.28). **21:** *Timothy,* introduced in Acts 16.1–3. **22:** *Tertius* wrote down the letter as Paul dictated it; cf. 1 Cor 16.21n.; 1 Pet 5.12. **23:** *Gaius,* perhaps the same person mentioned in 1 Cor 1.14.

16.25–27: A concluding blessing, appearing in different ancient manuscripts after 14.23 or 15.33, or missing altogether. Many scholars consider these verses an addition by later scribes and editors. **25:** *My gospel,* 2.16. *The proclamation,* the Gk "kerygma" is another word for "gospel"; see 1 Cor 1.21–24. **25–26:** *Mystery,* 11.25–27. *The obedience of faith,* 1.5.

THE FIRST LETTER OF PAUL TO THE CORINTHIANS

NAME AND AUTHORSHIP

The letter is named for its recipients, the community of believers in Christ in the Greek city of Corinth (see map 14 in the color map section at the end of the volume). Scholars agree that Paul was its author.

HISTORICAL CONTEXT

First Corinthians affords an unparalleled glimpse into the life of an early Christian community in a Greco-Roman city. The richness of this portrait both reflects the ethical challenges faced by converts rooted in Greco-Roman polytheism, and signals intense experimentation with their new social identity discovered in Messiah Jesus.

Paul's Corinth was a Roman city, refounded by order of Julius Caesar in 44 BCE after its brutal destruction by Mummius in 146 BCE. Caesar populated the colony with numerous freedmen and legionary veterans, but the ethnic mix was more diverse by Paul's day, including Syrians and Egyptians, along with Greeks who had immigrated from surrounding cities. The first-century CE Jewish philosopher Philo speaks of a sizeable Jewish community in Corinth (cf. Acts 18.4,7). Corinth rapidly regained its ancient prosperity owing to its favorable location. By 27 BCE, Corinth was already the capital of the senatorial province of Achaia and the judicial seat of the Roman proconsul (see Acts 18.12). Sharp contrasts between rich and poor were apparent in this flourishing commercial center. But opportunities for social advancement also existed: even freedmen held civic office (see Rom 16.23b), something uncommon elsewhere. The Isthmian Games, hosted by Corinth every two years, drew large crowds. The theater, rehabilitated by the emperor Augustus in the late first century BCE, held more than fifteen thousand spectators. Cynic philosophers like Demetrius, a friend of the Roman thinker Seneca, frequented Corinth. The city was sacred to the goddess Aphrodite, protector of prostitutes, whose famous sanctuary stood on the Acrocorinth, the acropolis. The temple of Asclepius, the god of healing, had extensive dining facilities. Inscriptions and dedications attest to the importance of the worship of the Roman emperor. Paul's choice of this bustling cosmopolis as one of the principal centers of his missionary activity reveals the global reach of his missionary ambition.

The account of Paul's activity in Corinth in Acts 18.1–18 is incomplete and anecdotal, but can be supplemented by information from Paul's letters. Upon arrival in Corinth, Paul found lodging with Aquila and his wife Priscilla, both Jews and of the same trade as Paul. Paul preached in the synagogue every sabbath; were among those whom Paul tried to persuade. In response to opposition from some Jews, Paul withdrew from the synagogue and began preaching in the house of a "godfearer" named Titius Justus. Paul names Stephanas and his household as the first coverts of the Roman province of Achaia in southern Greece (1 Cor 16.15; 1.16). The author of Acts attributes sensational importance to the conversion of the synagogue president Crispus: "Many of the Corinthians who heard Paul became believers and were baptized" (Acts 18.8). As Paul represents it, most of his converts were lower class, lacking in education, wealth, and birth (1 Cor 1.26–28). But Paul also baptized a few elite persons, such as Gaius (1.14), who eventually became the "host . . . to the whole church" (Rom 16.23). After Paul left Corinth, confusion arose among the new converts regarding boundaries between the church and the larger society, prompting Paul to write the letter on association with "immoral" persons and "idolaters," to which reference is made in 1 Cor 5.9–10. While Paul was in Ephesus, the Corinthians sent him a letter, seeking his advice on several issues, including marriage, food sacrificed to idols, spiritual gifts, and other matters (7.1; 8.1; 12.1; 16.1,12). At some point after Paul's founding visit, another Christian teacher visited Corinth, an Alexandrian Jew named Apollos, "an eloquent man, well-versed in the scriptures" (Acts 18.24). Apollos made a strong impression upon the Corinthians, especially upon the elite who valued proficiency in philosophy and rhetoric. Factions formed within the church, with members declaring support for one teacher or another (1 Cor 1.10–12; 3.4).

LITERARY HISTORY

Most scholars view the writing known as 1 Corinthians as a single, unified composition. But its abrupt transitions, frequent changes of theme, and generally loose construction have raised questions about its integrity. Assigning portions of 1 Corinthians to separate letters would be justified only if the passages in question presupposed different situations. This appears possible in three instances: Paul's attitude toward the schisms (contrast 11.18–19 with 1.10–12), Paul's advice on food sacrificed to idols (contrast 10.1–11.1 with 8.1–13), and Paul's announcement of his travel plans (contrast 16.5–9 with 4.17–21). Hence, some scholars have divided 1 Corinthians into three letters, composed in the following order: Letter A, On Association with the Immoral and Idolaters (10.1–22; 6.12–20; 10.23–11.34); Letter B, In Response to the Corinthians' Questions (7–9; 12–16); Letter C, Counsel of Concord (1.1–6.11).

The strongest argument for the unity of the present text derives from rhetorical analysis, which identifies 1 Corinthians as a deliberative appeal for concord (1.1–4.21), with advice on divisive issues organized under subheadings (5.1–16.24). Yet a single letter may not be consistent with the several occasions and sources of information evident in the text: an anonymous report (11.18), the Corinthians' letter (7.1), a visit by Stephanas (16.17), and a report from "Chloe's people" (1.11).

INTERPRETATION

In 1 Corinthians Paul shows remarkable familiarity with the culture of his converts and his facility with its forms of discourse: for example, ch 7 shows Paul conversant with Cynic-Stoic views of marriage (like those of Musonius and Epictetus); 9.24–27 employs an athletic metaphor from the Isthmian Games; ch 13 praises *agape* ("love"), a Christian counterpart to the praise of *eros* ("sexual love") in Plato's *Symposium*; ch 15 offers a reasoned proof of the resurrection of the body, analogous to philosophical arguments for the immortality of the soul in Plato (*Phaedrus*) and Cicero (*Tusculan Disputations*); chs 1–4 utilize the rhetoric and arguments of Greco-Roman politics. In several passages, Paul addresses a group whose opinions on a variety of subjects—eating meat sacrificed to idols, the financial support of missionaries, speaking in tongues, the resurrection of the dead, going to court before unbelievers—diverge sharply from his own. The attitudes of this minority group ("the strong") correlate with those held by persons of high social status and education.

First Corinthians demonstrates Paul's capacity, even in this early period, to think through the social and ethical implications of the new being "in Christ": for example, his exhortation to share with the have-nots at the communal meal, so as to "discern the body" of Christ (11.17–34); and his insight into the paradoxical power of "the word of the cross" to call, redeem, and sanctify the low and despised of this world, "the nothings and nobodies"—a radical statement in the history of Western thought.

Laurence L. Welborn

1 Paul, called to be an apostle of Christ Jesus by the will of God, and our brother Sosthenes,

² To the church of God that is in Corinth, to those who are sanctified in Christ Jesus, called to be saints, together with all those who in every place call on the name of our Lord Jesus Christ, both their Lord[a] and ours:

³ Grace to you and peace from God our Father and the Lord Jesus Christ.

⁴ I give thanks to my[b] God always for you because of the grace of God that has been given you in Christ Jesus, ⁵ for in every way you have been enriched in him, in speech and knowledge of every kind— ⁶ just as the testimony of[c] Christ has been strengthened among you— ⁷ so that you are not lacking in any spiritual gift as you wait for the revealing of our Lord Jesus Christ. ⁸ He will also strengthen you to the end, so that you may be blameless on the day of our Lord Jesus Christ. ⁹ God is faithful; by him you were called into the fellowship of his Son, Jesus Christ our Lord.

¹⁰ Now I appeal to you, brothers and sisters,[d] by the name of our Lord Jesus Christ, that all of you be in agreement and that there be no divisions among you, but that you be united in the same mind and the same purpose. ¹¹ For it has been reported to me by Chloe's people that there are quarrels among you, my brothers and sisters.[e] ¹² What I mean is that each of you says, "I belong to Paul," or "I belong to Apollos," or "I belong to Cephas," or "I belong to Christ." ¹³ Has Christ been

a   Gk *theirs*
b   Other ancient authorities lack *my*
c   Or *to*
d   Gk *brothers*
e   Gk *my brothers*

1.1–3: Prescript and Greeting. The prescript of Paul's letters has the same form found in many papyrus letters of antiquity: the names of the sender and the addressees, with a short greeting. **1:** "Paulos" is the Greek form of a Latin surname or cognomen ("Paulus"), meaning "small, of little significance," perhaps a self-deprecatory nickname expressing the apostle's sense of humility. Paul's sense of being *called* as *an apostle* is vividly described in Gal 1.15–16. *Christ* is not part of the proper name of *Jesus*, but is the Gk translation of Heb "mashiah," "the anointed," that is, the Messiah; Paul is the emissary of Messiah Jesus. It is not certain whether *Sosthenes* named here as a Christian *brother* is the same person as the synagogue president of Acts 18.17. **2:** *Church of God* (Gk "ekklesia theou") may be a translation of Heb "qahal Yahweh" ("assembly of Yahweh") expressing a sense of divine election; but "ekklesia" was the designation of the city "assembly" of Corinth, so that *church of God* may have evoked a sense of belonging to an alternative community. **2b:** This phrase is likely an addition to the prescript, which seeks to make Paul's advice applicable to *all those who in every place call on the name of our Lord Jesus Christ*, an indication that the original letter has been edited. **3:** The greeting *grace and peace* derives from older Jewish formulas (see *Apoc. Bar.* 78.2), but embodies the essence of Paul's own experience of God in Christ.

1.4–9: Thanksgiving. The thanksgiving is a standard feature of the prescripts of Paul's letters, comparable to the assurance of prayer for the addressees of other ancient letters. **4:** Paul gives thanks for the *grace of God . . . given* to the Corinthians, not for their "labor of love" as in 1 Thess 1.3. **5:** Because *speech* and *knowledge* are attainments of which the Corinthians are proud (1.17; 8.1–2; 13.1–2), Paul's selective mention of these gifts has an ironic quality, enhanced by the hyperbolic phrases, *in every way . . . of every kind*. **8:** Paul's assurance that God *will . . . strengthen* the Corinthians contains a mild reproach of their instability. *The day of our Lord* is an apocalyptic term for the Second Coming of Christ, the day of judgment; see 3.13; 4.5.

1.10–17: Divisions in the church. Paul describes the situation in the church of Corinth in terms like those used by political orators to characterize conflicts within city-states: *divisions* and *quarrels* are synonyms for discord, and Paul's appeal to *be in agreement* and *be united in the same mind and the same purpose* echoes the language of speeches on concord. **11:** While *Chloe*, who is mentioned only here in the New Testament, may not have lived in Corinth, Paul's mention of her name without introduction indicates that she and her *people* (probably slaves) were known to the Corinthians. **12:** Paul caricatures the Corinthians' partisanship using slogans like those shouted by fans of star performers in the amphitheater. *Apollos*, from Alexandria in Egypt, was an eloquent early Christian preacher according to Acts 18.24–28; see also 1 Cor 3.4–6; 4.6; 16.12. *Cephas*, the Aramaic form of Peter's name. The climactic slogan, *I belong to Christ*, is added for ironic effect, and does not indicate the existence of a "Christ-party." **13:** Paul's rhetorical question, *Has Christ been divided?* uses a verb related to a

divided? Was Paul crucified for you? Or were you baptized in the name of Paul? [14] I thank God[a] that I baptized none of you except Crispus and Gaius, [15] so that no one can say that you were baptized in my name. [16] (I did baptize also the household of Stephanas; beyond that, I do not know whether I baptized anyone else.) [17] For Christ did not send me to baptize but to proclaim the gospel, and not with eloquent wisdom, so that the cross of Christ might not be emptied of its power.

[18] For the message about the cross is foolishness to those who are perishing, but to us who are being saved it is the power of God. [19] For it is written,

"I will destroy the wisdom of the wise,
   and the discernment of the discerning I
      will thwart."

[20] Where is the one who is wise? Where is the scribe? Where is the debater of this age? Has not God made foolish the wisdom of the world? [21] For since, in the wisdom of God, the world did not know God through wisdom, God decided, through the foolishness of our proclamation, to save those who believe. [22] For Jews demand signs and Greeks desire wisdom, [23] but we proclaim Christ crucified, a stumbling block to Jews and foolishness to Gentiles, [24] but to those who are the called, both Jews and Greeks, Christ the power of God and the wisdom of God. [25] For God's foolishness is wiser than human wisdom, and God's weakness is stronger than human strength.

[26] Consider your own call, brothers and sisters:[b] not many of you were wise by human standards,[c] not many were powerful, not many were of noble birth. [27] But God chose what is foolish in the world to shame the wise; God chose what is weak in the world to shame the strong; [28] God chose what is low and despised in the world, things that are not, to reduce to nothing things that are, [29] so that no one[d] might boast in the presence of

a   Other ancient authorities read *I am thankful*
b   Gk *brothers*
c   Gk *according to the flesh*
d   Gk *no flesh*

common Greek term for "party": "Has the body of Christ been split into parties?" **14:** Paul's thanksgiving that he *baptized none . . . except Crispus and Gaius* has a note of irony which suggests that Crispus and Gaius may have been involved in forming factions. *Crispus* is the former synagogue president (Acts 18.8), while *Gaius* is described as "the host to the whole church" (Rom 16.23); both are evidently of the highest social standing in the church. **16:** Paul employs the device of a feigned lapse of memory to separate *Stephanas*, his strongest supporter (see 16.15–18), from Crispus and Gaius. **17:** Paul formulates his commission as an apostle antithetically: *not to baptize but to proclaim*. The negative definition of the style and content of Paul's preaching (*not with eloquent wisdom*) suggests how the Corinthians have found Paul's proclamation deficient.

1.18–2.5: The folly of the message about the cross. Paul acknowledges that his preaching is *foolishness* to the educated elite, but asserts that God has confounded the *wisdom* of this world. **18:** Paul provocatively reduces the content of the gospel to a single, shameful event—*the cross*. Greek "moria" (*foolishness*) has a social stigma that does not attach to English "folly": better, "a vulgar joke." **19:** Isa 29.14 (LXX). This text is particularly apt, since it critiques those who take pride in wisdom and foretells the creation of a new order in which the deaf will hear and the blind will see. **20:** Paul's rhetorical questions mock the educated elite by means of culturally specific titles of dignity: the Jewish *scribe* is not merely a skilled copyist but an expert in the scriptures; the *debater* is a philosophical researcher highly esteemed in the Hellenic world. **21:** Paul shapes a playful contrast between two types of *wisdom*: on the one hand, a divine attribute; on the other, a human attainment (cf. Sir 1.9–10; Wis 7; 8). **22:** The *desire* for *wisdom* among the *Greeks* was proverbial: see Herodotus 4.77.1. **23:** The first-century BCE orator Cicero attests the constraint upon discourse about the cross among persons of higher social class: "The mere mention of the word 'cross' is shameful to a Roman citizen and a free man" (*Pro Rabirio* 5.16). **24–25:** In substantiation of the paradox of the *crucified Christ* as *the power* and *wisdom of God*, Paul employs phrases that sound positively blasphemous—*God's foolishness . . . God's weakness*. **26–31:** Paul expounds the social consequences of the divine reversal of wisdom and foolishness. **26–28:** The terms used by Paul to describe the makeup of the community are those employed by Greek writers to designate the major class divisions in civil strife: *wise, powerful*, and *of noble birth* are euphemisms for "the rich," while "the poor" are the *foolish, weak*, and *low* (born). Paul offers a radical explanation of why the majority of those who have been "called" by the gospel of the crucified are persons lacking in education, wealth, and birth: *God chose* (repeated three times for

God. [30] He is the source of your life in Christ Jesus, who became for us wisdom from God, and righteousness and sanctification and redemption, [31] in order that, as it is written, "Let the one who boasts, boast in[a] the Lord."

2 When I came to you, brothers and sisters,[b] I did not come proclaiming the mystery[c] of God to you in lofty words or wisdom. [2] For I decided to know nothing among you except Jesus Christ, and him crucified. [3] And I came to you in weakness and in fear and in much trembling. [4] My speech and my proclamation were not with plausible words of wisdom,[d] but with a demonstration of the Spirit and of power, [5] so that your faith might rest not on human wisdom but on the power of God.

[6] Yet among the mature we do speak wisdom, though it is not a wisdom of this age or of the rulers of this age, who are doomed to perish. [7] But we speak God's wisdom, secret and hidden, which God decreed before the ages for our glory. [8] None of the rulers of this age understood this; for if they had, they would not have crucified the Lord of glory. [9] But, as it is written,

"What no eye has seen, nor ear heard,
    nor the human heart conceived,
what God has prepared for those who love
    him"—

[10] these things God has revealed to us through the Spirit; for the Spirit searches everything, even the depths of God. [11] For what human being knows what is truly human except the human spirit that is within? So also no one comprehends what is truly God's except the Spirit of God. [12] Now we have received not the spirit of the world, but the Spirit that is from God, so that we may understand the gifts bestowed on us by God. [13] And we speak of these things in words not taught by human wisdom but taught by the Spirit, interpreting spiritual things to those who are spiritual.[e]

[14] Those who are unspiritual[f] do not receive the gifts of God's Spirit, for they are foolishness to them, and they are unable to understand them because they are spiritually discerned. [15] Those who are spiritual discern all things, and they are themselves subject to no one else's scrutiny.

[16] "For who has known the mind of the
        Lord
    so as to instruct him?"
But we have the mind of Christ.

a   Or of
b   Gk brothers
c   Other ancient authorities read testimony
d   Other ancient authorities read the persuasiveness of wisdom
e   Or interpreting spiritual things in spiritual language, or comparing spiritual things with spiritual
f   Or natural

emphasis). 31: Jer 9.23. 2.1–5: Paul's concession that he did not preach in lofty words or wisdom is a rejoinder to an anticipated objection against his assertion that the crucified Christ is the wisdom of God: "But little wisdom or eloquence was apparent when you came preaching among us!" Paul adopts the persona of the befuddled orator from comedy and mime in order to establish that, despite his stammering weakness, the message about Christ is the power of God. Paul's choice of terms belonging to the technical vocabulary of Hellenistic rhetoric (lofty words, plausible words, demonstration, power) makes a contrast between his proclamation and that of missionary rivals who have made use of the art of rhetoric. 2: Paul's use of the perfect participle, crucified, to describe more precisely the Christ whom he proclaims is a provocation to the elite: Paul insists that the present significance of Christ, even after his resurrection, consists in nothing other than that he is the crucified.

2.6–16: The wisdom Paul teaches. Paul's claim that he speaks wisdom among the mature is perplexing, in light of his previous assertion that he preaches the gospel without eloquent wisdom (1.17; 2.1,4). The seeming contradiction is resolved if 2.6–16 is regarded as Paul's self-parody as a teacher imparting secret wisdom to initiates. The brilliance of this strategy is that, by mocking himself and his proclamation, Paul undermines the idea that an apostle is a wise man as defined by the elite, while simultaneously asserting the existence of a paradoxical wisdom capable of transforming those who receive it, despite the ineptitude of its communicators. 6: Mature (Gk "teleios") is a technical term in the mystery religions, designating one who has been fully initiated. The rulers of this age may be spiritual, demonic powers, but more likely are political authorities. 9: The source of this citation is uncertain, but may come from the Apocalypse of Elijah (thus the second-century CE exegete Origen), cited here as scripture. 16: Isa 40.13.

3 And so, brothers and sisters,[a] I could not speak to you as spiritual people, but rather as people of the flesh, as infants in Christ. [2] I fed you with milk, not solid food, for you were not ready for solid food. Even now you are still not ready, [3] for you are still of the flesh. For as long as there is jealousy and quarreling among you, are you not of the flesh, and behaving according to human inclinations? [4] For when one says, "I belong to Paul," and another, "I belong to Apollos," are you not merely human?

[5] What then is Apollos? What is Paul? Servants through whom you came to believe, as the Lord assigned to each. [6] I planted, Apollos watered, but God gave the growth. [7] So neither the one who plants nor the one who waters is anything, but only God who gives the growth. [8] The one who plants and the one who waters have a common purpose, and each will receive wages according to the labor of each. [9] For we are God's servants, working together; you are God's field, God's building.

[10] According to the grace of God given to me, like a skilled master builder I laid a foundation, and someone else is building on it. Each builder must choose with care how to build on it. [11] For no one can lay any foundation other than the one that has been laid; that foundation is Jesus Christ. [12] Now if anyone builds on the foundation with gold, silver, precious stones, wood, hay, straw— [13] the work of each builder will become visible, for the Day will disclose it, because it will be revealed with fire, and the fire will test what sort of work each has done. [14] If what has been built on the foundation survives, the builder will receive a reward. [15] If the work is burned up, the builder will suffer loss; the builder will be saved, but only as through fire.

[16] Do you not know that you are God's temple and that God's Spirit dwells in you?[b] [17] If anyone destroys God's temple, God will destroy that person. For God's temple is holy, and you are that temple.

[18] Do not deceive yourselves. If you think that you are wise in this age, you should become fools so that you may become wise. [19] For the wisdom of this world is foolishness with God. For it is written,

"He catches the wise in their craftiness,"
[20] and again,

"The Lord knows the thoughts of the wise, that they are futile."

[21] So let no one boast about human leaders. For all things are yours, [22] whether Paul or Apollos or Cephas or the world or life or death or the present or the future—all belong to you, [23] and you belong to Christ, and Christ belongs to God.

4 Think of us in this way, as servants of Christ and stewards of God's mysteries. [2] Moreover, it is required of stewards that they be found trustworthy. [3] But with me it is a very small thing that I should be judged by you or by any human court. I do not even judge myself. [4] I am not aware of anything against myself, but I am not thereby acquit-

---

a   Gk *brothers*
b   In verses 16 and 17 the Greek word for *you* is plural

3.1–4.21: Apostles as servants of the Lord. 3.1–4: Paul chides the Corinthians in a derisive manner for their spiritual immaturity. **1:** Paul's description of the Corinthians as *infants* uses a metaphor from political rhetoric, comparing the factious with quarrelsome children. **4:** The reduction in the number of slogans from the four of 1.12 to two, *"I belong to Paul," "I to Apollos,"* suggests that Apollos is the focus of the Corinthians' partisanship.

3.5–4.5: In a series of well-constructed metaphors, Paul portrays himself and Apollos as farm workers (3.6–9), construction laborers (3.9–15), and household stewards (4.1–5), in order to emphasize collegiality against partisanship, and to diminish the importance attributed to them. **3.5:** Both Paul and Apollos have been *assigned* positions as *servants* by *the Lord*. **6:** The one who *planted* has priority over the one who has *watered*, and a greater claim upon the produce. **10:** Paul is a *skilled master builder* (Gk "sophos architekton," a technical term of construction work) who has laid the *foundation* of the community, while Apollos is, figuratively, one of the anonymous workers (*someone*) who has added something to the structure. **13:** *The Day*, the day of judgment; see 1.8n. **15:** The expression *as through fire* is a common Greek idiom describing a narrow escape from danger: as the fire ignites, the workers escape from the penalty to be imposed upon their shoddy construction by running through the walls of the burning building. **19:** Job 5.12–13. **20:** Ps 94.11. **22:** *Paul . . . Apollos . . . Cephas*, see 1.12n. **4.3:** Paul's indifference to the possibility that he may be *judged* by the Corinthians employs a Greek verb ("anakrinein") with a technical usage for the preliminary examination of political leaders to establish their

ted. It is the Lord who judges me. [5] Therefore do not pronounce judgment before the time, before the Lord comes, who will bring to light the things now hidden in darkness and will disclose the purposes of the heart. Then each one will receive commendation from God.

[6] I have applied all this to Apollos and myself for your benefit, brothers and sisters,[a] so that you may learn through us the meaning of the saying, "Nothing beyond what is written," so that none of you will be puffed up in favor of one against another. [7] For who sees anything different in you?[b] What do you have that you did not receive? And if you received it, why do you boast as if it were not a gift?

[8] Already you have all you want! Already you have become rich! Quite apart from us you have become kings! Indeed, I wish that you had become kings, so that we might be kings with you! [9] For I think that God has exhibited us apostles as last of all, as though sentenced to death, because we have become a spectacle to the world, to angels and to mortals. [10] We are fools for the sake of Christ, but you are wise in Christ. We are weak, but you are strong. You are held in honor, but we in disrepute. [11] To the present hour we are hungry and thirsty, we are poorly clothed and beaten and homeless, [12] and we grow weary from the work of our own hands. When reviled, we bless; when perse-

cuted, we endure; [13] when slandered, we speak kindly. We have become like the rubbish of the world, the dregs of all things, to this very day.

[14] I am not writing this to make you ashamed, but to admonish you as my beloved children. [15] For though you might have ten thousand guardians in Christ, you do not have many fathers. Indeed, in Christ Jesus I became your father through the gospel. [16] I appeal to you, then, be imitators of me. [17] For this reason I sent[c] you Timothy, who is my beloved and faithful child in the Lord, to remind you of my ways in Christ Jesus, as I teach them everywhere in every church. [18] But some of you, thinking that I am not coming to you, have become arrogant. [19] But I will come to you soon, if the Lord wills, and I will find out not the talk of these arrogant people but their power. [20] For the kingdom of God depends not on talk but on power. [21] What would you prefer? Am I to come to you with a stick, or with love in a spirit of gentleness?

5 It is actually reported that there is sexual immorality among you, and of a kind that is not found even among pagans; for a man is

a Gk *brothers*
b Or *Who makes you different from another?*
c Or *am sending*

qualifications, suggesting that the Corinthians plan to "examine" Paul's apostolic credentials. **5:** *Before the Lord comes,* see 1.8n.; 3.13.

4.6–13: Application. 6: Paul makes clear that he has been teaching with the aid of figures of speech *applied* to himself and Apollos (see 1.12n.). *"Nothing beyond what is written"* is a maxim of uncertain origin whose meaning must be pertinent to the following clause, *so that none of you will be puffed up.* **7–8:** With mounting sarcasm, Paul mocks the pretensions of leading figures in the Corinthian church (*king* was the client's term for a rich patron). Paul ironically reminds these patrons that everything they *have* (spiritually) they have *received* as a *gift*; they have nothing of which to *boast*. **9–13:** Paul expounds the consequences of the message about the cross for himself and his colleagues, who have conformed their lives to the fate of the crucified Christ: they are *fools* (Gk "moroi") in a *spectacle* (Gk "theatron") *exhibited* by God. Paul's vocabulary is explicitly theatrical: like the poor fools in the mime, Paul and his colleagues are *weak, hungry, poorly clothed, beaten* (literally, "given the knuckle-sandwich"), etc. **13:** *Rubbish* and *dregs* were the worst terms of abuse in Greek, originally applied to those unfortunate persons, mostly paupers and the deformed, who were put to death for the purification of the city, because life was assumed to be a burden for them.

4.14–21: Admonition. Paul portrays himself as a solicitous *father*, the Corinthians as unruly *children*, and other ministers of the gospel as *guardians* (Gk "paidagogoi"). That Paul is not altogether pleased with the performance of the guardians is suggested by his hyperbolic reference to their number, *ten thousand*, and by the need for parental intervention. If the Corinthians will not accept instruction from *faithful Timothy* (see Acts 18.5), Paul will come with his *stick* (Gk "rabdos"), standard equipment of the fool in the mime. Paul's warning to the Corinthians is imbued with an ironic consciousness of the possibility of his own discomfiture.

5.1–13: Sexual immorality in the community. 1: The expression *father's wife* is an idiom for "stepmother."

living with his father's wife. [2] And you are arrogant! Should you not rather have mourned, so that he who has done this would have been removed from among you?

[3] For though absent in body, I am present in spirit; and as if present I have already pronounced judgment [4] in the name of the Lord Jesus on the man who has done such a thing.[a] When you are assembled, and my spirit is present with the power of our Lord Jesus, [5] you are to hand this man over to Satan for the destruction of the flesh, so that his spirit may be saved in the day of the Lord.[b]

[6] Your boasting is not a good thing. Do you not know that a little yeast leavens the whole batch of dough? [7] Clean out the old yeast so that you may be a new batch, as you really are unleavened. For our paschal lamb, Christ, has been sacrificed. [8] Therefore, let us celebrate the festival, not with the old yeast, the yeast of malice and evil, but with the unleavened bread of sincerity and truth.

[9] I wrote to you in my letter not to associate with sexually immoral persons— [10] not at all meaning the immoral of this world, or the greedy and robbers, or idolaters, since you would then need to go out of the world. [11] But now I am writing to you not to associate with anyone who bears the name of brother or sister[c] who is sexually immoral or greedy, or is an idolater, reviler, drunkard, or robber. Do not even eat with such a one. [12] For what have I to do with judging those outside? Is it not those who are inside that you are to judge? [13] God will judge those outside. "Drive out the wicked person from among you."

6 When any of you has a grievance against another, do you dare to take it to court before the unrighteous, instead of taking it before the saints? [2] Do you not know that the saints will judge the world? And if the world is to be judged by you, are you incompetent to try trivial cases? [3] Do you not know that we are to judge angels—to say nothing of ordinary matters? [4] If you have ordinary cases, then, do you appoint as judges those who have no standing in the church? [5] I say this to your shame. Can it be that there is no one among you wise enough to decide between one believer[c] and another, [6] but a believer[c] goes to court against a believer[c]—and before unbelievers at that?

a   Or *on the man who has done such a thing in the name of the Lord Jesus*

b   Other ancient authorities add *Jesus*

c   Gk *brother*

Paul accurately reports that sexual relations with one's stepmother were prohibited by biblical law (Lev 18.7–8; 20.11; Deut 22.30) as well as by Roman law; according to the *Institutes of Gaius*, "neither can I marry her who has aforetime been my mother-in-law or stepmother." 2: That the church had taken no disciplinary action suggests that the sinner was a person of high social status. 3–5: While it is not clear precisely what was involved in the execution of this sentence, Paul's language (*hand this man over to Satan*) indicates a punishment that was drastic and permanent, such as excommunication. 5: *Flesh* for Paul does not refer to the human body but to an instinct toward sin, a way of life unredeemed by the spirit and oriented toward worldly advantages. *The day of the Lord,* see 1.8n. 6–8: Paul's metaphor compares immorality in the community with *old yeast* which must be cleansed from the house in preparation for the Jewish festival of Passover, when only *unleavened* bread was to be eaten (Ex 12.15–20). 7: Paul nowhere else describes *Christ* as *our paschal lamb*; but cf. Jn 1.29; 19.36; Rev 5.12. 9–13: **Clarifying a misunderstanding. 9:** Defenders of the unity of 1 Corinthians assume that the *letter* to which Paul refers has been lost. But would the Corinthians have treated one of Paul's letters with such disregard? Alternatively, the letter may be preserved in 1 Cor 10.1–22; 6.12–20; 10.23–11.34, passages which discuss association with the immoral and idolaters; see further Introduction, pp. 1999–2000. 13: *Drive out the wicked person,* following the instructions of Deut 13.5; 17.7; etc.

     6.1–11: **Lawsuits between believers.** Someone *dares* to do what should be unthinkable for a Christian: *to take another* Christian *to court before the unrighteous.* 1: The phrase *has a grievance against another* employs a technical expression of legal proceedings frequently attested in Greek sources. In general, only persons of more than moderate wealth had access to the courts. 2: For the idea that *the saints* (the believers) *will judge the world,* see Dan 7.22 (LXX); Wis 3.8; Rev 3.21; 20.4. 3: That the angels themselves are subject to judgment, see Jude 6; 2 Pet 2.4. 4: The lawsuits in question seem to have been *ordinary* civil *cases,* concerned with money or property.

7 In fact, to have lawsuits at all with one another is already a defeat for you. Why not rather be wronged? Why not rather be defrauded? 8 But you yourselves wrong and defraud—and believers[a] at that.

9 Do you not know that wrongdoers will not inherit the kingdom of God? Do not be deceived! Fornicators, idolaters, adulterers, male prostitutes, sodomites, 10 thieves, the greedy, drunkards, revilers, robbers—none of these will inherit the kingdom of God. 11 And this is what some of you used to be. But you were washed, you were sanctified, you were justified in the name of the Lord Jesus Christ and in the Spirit of our God.

12 "All things are lawful for me," but not all things are beneficial. "All things are lawful for me," but I will not be dominated by anything. 13 "Food is meant for the stomach and the stomach for food,"[b] and God will destroy both one and the other. The body is meant not for fornication but for the Lord, and the Lord for the body. 14 And God raised the Lord and will also raise us by his power. 15 Do you not know that your bodies are members of Christ? Should I therefore take the members of Christ and make them members of a prostitute? Never! 16 Do you not know that whoever is united to a prostitute becomes one body with her? For it is said, "The two shall be one flesh." 17 But anyone united to the Lord becomes one spirit with him. 18 Shun fornication! Every sin that a person commits is outside the body; but the fornicator sins against the body itself. 19 Or do you not know that your body is a temple[c] of the Holy Spirit within you, which you have from God, and that you are not your own? 20 For you were bought with a price; therefore glorify God in your body.

7 Now concerning the matters about which you wrote: "It is well for a man not to touch a woman." 2 But because of cases of sexual immorality, each man should have his own wife and each woman her own husband. 3 The

a Gk brothers
b The quotation may extend to the word other
c Or sanctuary

7: Paul's advice resembles that of Jesus in Mt 5.39–40; Lk 6.28–30: nonresistance. 9–11: Catalogues of vices and virtues are known from Jewish and Greek writers, especially the Stoic philosophers. 9: Male prostitutes (Gk "malakoi," lit., "soft men") were boys and men sodomized by other males, while sodomites (Gk "arsenokoitai," lit., "men who bed males"; a word first found here and based on LXX Lev 18.22; 20.13) were men who exercised the dominant role, pederasts.

6.12–20: Christians going to prostitutes. The abrupt beginning of 6.12, and differences of tone and content with 5.1–6.11, suggest that this paragraph originally belonged not here, but possibly between 10.22 and 10.23, with which 6.12–20 has much in common: in both passages, the temptation to immorality is strong and Christians are urged to "flee" (6.18; 10.8,14); in both passages, Paul quotes the Corinthian slogan, "All things are lawful for me" (6.12; 10.23). 12: Paul quotes a slogan of the Corinthians, a proud boast of freedom, asserting liberation from cultural taboos. Paul counters by insisting upon the mutually beneficial as the criterion of moral judgment. 13: Another slogan of the Corinthians, with a background in Cynic philosophy. Paul counters by affirming God's power over the body. 14: The resurrection of Jesus signals that the body is not meant for corruption but for more life. 15: Paul appeals to his characteristic idea of the church as the body of Christ (see 12.12–14,27) in order to exclude the possibility of contact with a dangerous polluting agent, the prostitute. 16: Gen. 2.24. 18: Cf. 10.14 (5.9). That the fornicator sins against himself, against his own person (reflected in his body), is an idea with Stoic parallels. 19: Like the community as a whole (cf. 3.16), each believer is a temple of the Holy Spirit. 20: Paul draws upon the custom of sacred manumission: the slave whose freedom was bought with a price with money previously deposited in the temple treasury was regarded as the property of the god.

7.1–40: Marriage and sexual relations. In response to the Corinthians' questions, Paul rethinks the most basic relationships, with the result that marriage and other statuses are relativized in importance by the eschatological "calling" from the Lord. 1: Now concerning, a formula introducing the first of several topics about which the Corinthians had asked Paul in their letter; see also 7.25; 8.1; 12.1; 16.1; 16.12. The words "It is well for a man not to touch a woman" are a quotation from the Corinthians' letter. Touch is an idiom for "have sex with." The quotation may be an expression of extreme asceticism, or may represent an ironic retort by those who claimed freedom from conventional morality (6.12n.) to Paul's warning against immorality in his previous letter.

husband should give to his wife her conjugal rights, and likewise the wife to her husband. ⁴ For the wife does not have authority over her own body, but the husband does; likewise the husband does not have authority over his own body, but the wife does. ⁵ Do not deprive one another except perhaps by agreement for a set time, to devote yourselves to prayer, and then come together again, so that Satan may not tempt you because of your lack of self-control. ⁶ This I say by way of concession, not of command. ⁷ I wish that all were as I myself am. But each has a particular gift from God, one having one kind and another a different kind.

⁸ To the unmarried and the widows I say that it is well for them to remain unmarried as I am. ⁹ But if they are not practicing self-control, they should marry. For it is better to marry than to be aflame with passion.

¹⁰ To the married I give this command—not I but the Lord—that the wife should not separate from her husband ¹¹ (but if she does separate, let her remain unmarried or else be reconciled to her husband), and that the husband should not divorce his wife.

¹² To the rest I say—I and not the Lord—that if any believerᵃ has a wife who is an unbeliever, and she consents to live with him, he should not divorce her. ¹³ And if any woman has a husband who is an unbeliever, and he consents to live with her, she should not divorce him. ¹⁴ For the unbelieving husband is made holy through his wife, and the unbelieving wife is made holy through her husband. Otherwise, your children would be unclean, but as it is, they are holy. ¹⁵ But if the unbelieving partner separates, let it be so; in such a case the brother or sister is not bound. It is to peace that God has called you.ᵇ ¹⁶ Wife, for all you know, you might save your husband. Husband, for all you know, you might save your wife.

¹⁷ However that may be, let each of you lead the life that the Lord has assigned, to which God called you. This is my rule in all the churches. ¹⁸ Was anyone at the time of his call already circumcised? Let him not seek to remove the marks of circumcision. Was anyone at the time of his call uncircumcised? Let him not seek circumcision. ¹⁹ Circumcision is nothing, and uncircumci-

ᵃ   Gk *brother*

ᵇ   Other ancient authorities read *us*

2: Against the temptation to immorality, Paul counsels monogamy and fidelity in marriage; cf. 1 Thess 4.3–5. **3:** *Conjugal rights,* lit., "debt," used here in a technical and euphemistic sense, to denote the obligation of spouses to each other. **4:** That the partnership of marriage includes the bodies of the husband and wife was also affirmed by the Stoic philosopher Musonius. **5:** Paul warns rather strongly (*deprive* is literally "defraud") against withholding conjugal relations, and allows for exceptions only within limits—*by* harmonious *agreement,* for a season, *to devote* oneself *to prayer* (cf. *T. Naph.* 8). **6:** To avoid the impression that he commands sexual relations within marriage, Paul clarifies the point of his previous statement: he has spoken *by way of concession,* to prevent temptation on account of *lack of self-control.* **7:** Paul's *wish* is that all were as he is—unmarried (v. 8) yet self-controlled, a state which he regards as a *gift from God;* yet Paul acknowledges that others have different gifts. **8–9:** Paul counsels celibacy *to the unmarried and widows,* unless they are "out of control." Greek writers describe *passion* as an internal burning; love spells in magical papyri send desire into the body of the beloved as "heat." **10–11:** The *command* of *the Lord* appears to refer to sayings about divorce like those attributed to Jesus in Mk 10.2–12; Mt 5.31–32; 19:3–9. Paul has formulated the command of Jesus in accordance with Roman law under which *the wife* could *divorce her husband*; according to biblical law, divorce was initiated only by the husband (Deut 24.1). To *separate* is a technical term for divorce in Greek sources. **12–16:** Paul offers advice to Christ-believers in mixed marriages. The advice is naturally offered on Paul's own authority, because such marriages were not envisioned by Jesus. If the non-Christian is sympathetically disposed to live with the believer, there should be no divorce. **14:** Paul's statement rests upon the notion that "holiness," like "uncleanness," is a quality transferable within relationships; cf. 1 Clem 46.2. **15:** For *peace* as the goal of Christian life, see 2 Cor 13.11; Rom 14.17. **16:** The term *save* is used here in the sense of conversion; cf. 1 Pet 3.1–2. **17–24:** Paul inserts a paragraph enunciating his general *rule in all the churches,* of which the preceding advice on marriage has been a special application: the *call* of God does not remove a Christian from his or her situation in society, but intensifies obedience to God in the midst of life. **18:** Paul envisions cases of a Jewish convert who might *seek to remove the marks of circumcision,* and of a Gentile convert who might *seek circumcision,* motivated by a desire

sion is nothing; but obeying the commandments of God is everything. [20] Let each of you remain in the condition in which you were called.

[21] Were you a slave when called? Do not be concerned about it. Even if you can gain your freedom, make use of your present condition now more than ever.[a] [22] For whoever was called in the Lord as a slave is a freed person belonging to the Lord, just as whoever was free when called is a slave of Christ. [23] You were bought with a price; do not become slaves of human masters. [24] In whatever condition you were called, brothers and sisters,[b] there remain with God.

[25] Now concerning virgins, I have no command of the Lord, but I give my opinion as one who by the Lord's mercy is trustworthy. [26] I think that, in view of the impending[c] crisis, it is well for you to remain as you are. [27] Are you bound to a wife? Do not seek to be free. Are you free from a wife? Do not seek a wife. [28] But if you marry, you do not sin, and if a virgin marries, she does not sin. Yet those who marry will experience distress in this life,[d] and I would spare you that. [29] I mean, brothers and sisters,[b] the appointed time has grown short; from now on, let even those who have wives be as though they had none, [30] and those who mourn as though they were not mourning, and those who rejoice as though they were not rejoicing, and those who buy as though they had no possessions, [31] and those who deal with the world as though they had no dealings with it. For the present form of this world is passing away.

a   Or *avail yourself of the opportunity*
b   Gk *brothers*
c   Or *present*
d   Gk *in the flesh*

for social acceptance in either group. **19:** Paul insists that *circumcision* and *uncircumcision* amount to *nothing*; what matters is keeping *the commandments of God*; cf. Gal 5.6; 6.15; Rom 2.25–26. **20:** Paul plays provocatively with the word "calling" to indicate that something has been added to every *condition*, by virtue of which the Christian can *remain* in his or her calling, yet with a higher vocation. **21:** A *slave* should *not be concerned* about his condition. But what if he is able to become free? Paul's advice has puzzled interpreters; the Greek literally reads "rather make use of" (the words "your present condition now more than ever" have been supplied by the NRSV translators), with the verb lacking an object in the Greek text, and either "slavery" or "freedom" must be supplied to complete the meaning. The context argues for the former, as indicated by the qualifying phrases *even if* and *now more than ever* (lit., "rather"): thus, *even if* a slave has the resources to purchase his freedom, he should rather *make use of* his *present condition*. But there may be a critique of slavery implicit in Paul's choice of the verb *make use of*: the Christian vocation is exercised by *use*, not by possession. **22:** The calling *in the Lord* results in a status reversal: the Christian *slave* has become a *freed person* of Christ, while the free man has become *a slave of Christ*. Paul's thought moves beyond the Stoic consolation of "inner freedom" and implies changes in social relationship and behavior; see Philem 16. **23:** As was the custom in sacred manumission, where the god was imagined to be the purchaser of the slave, so Christ has *bought* the Corinthians *with a price*, whether slave or free, so that they should no longer enslave themselves to *human masters*. **25–38:** Whether *virgins* should *marry* must have been a question raised in the Corinthians' letter to Paul, as indicated by the recurrence of the formula *now concerning* (see 7.1n.). **25:** Paul acknowledges that the advice that follows is his own *opinion*, since he has *no command of the Lord*; cf. 7.10,12. **26:** The *impending crisis* refers to the tribulations expected to occur in the last days before the Second Coming; see also vv. 29,31. **27:** What kind of "bond" is envisioned? Not, evidently, the bond of marriage, but a pledge to preserve the virginity of the young woman, to which the man addressed by Paul has committed himself. **28:** Paul reassures the man and his betrothed that the decision to *marry* is no *sin*, should they prove incapable of keeping their pledge to virginity. **29–31:** Paul shares his belief about the foreshortening of time as justification for urging an adjustment in social, emotional, and economic relations. The participle that Paul chooses (*grown short*) to describe what has happened to *time* in the Christ-event is from a verb used elsewhere in Greek literature of the furling of a ship's sails, of the folding of a bird's wings, of curtains gathered together. An apocalyptic parallel to Paul's account of life according to the principle of *as though . . . not* is found in 2 Esd 16.41b–44: "Let the one who buys like the one who will lose; . . . those who marry, like those who will have no children." But there are important differences: for Paul, the eschatological rupture occurs in the present, and is immanent to every action, whereas 2 Esdras distinguishes present from

³² I want you to be free from anxieties. The unmarried man is anxious about the affairs of the Lord, how to please the Lord; ³³ but the married man is anxious about the affairs of the world, how to please his wife, ³⁴ and his interests are divided. And the unmarried woman and the virgin are anxious about the affairs of the Lord, so that they may be holy in body and spirit; but the married woman is anxious about the affairs of the world, how to please her husband. ³⁵ I say this for your own benefit, not to put any restraint upon you, but to promote good order and unhindered devotion to the Lord.

³⁶ If anyone thinks that he is not behaving properly toward his fiancée,ᵃ if his passions are strong, and so it has to be, let him marry as he wishes; it is no sin. Let them marry. ³⁷ But if someone stands firm in his resolve, being under no necessity but having his own desire under control, and has determined in his own mind to keep her as his fiancée,ᵃ he will do well. ³⁸ So then, he who marries his fiancéeᵃ does well; and he who refrains from marriage will do better.

³⁹ A wife is bound as long as her husband lives. But if the husband dies,ᵇ she is free to marry anyone she wishes, only in the Lord. ⁴⁰ But in my judgment she is more blessed if she remains as she is. And I think that I too have the Spirit of God.

8 Now concerning food sacrificed to idols: we know that "all of us possess knowledge." Knowledge puffs up, but love builds up. ² Anyone who claims to know something does not yet have the necessary knowledge; ³ but anyone who loves God is known by him.

⁴ Hence, as to the eating of food offered to idols, we know that "no idol in the world really exists," and that "there is no God but one." ⁵ Indeed, even though there may be so-called gods in heaven or on earth—as in fact there are many gods and many lords— ⁶ yet for us there is one God, the Father, from whom are all things and for whom we exist, and one Lord, Jesus Christ, through whom are all things and through whom we exist.

ᵃ Gk *virgin*
ᵇ Gk *falls asleep*

future, and distributes the crisis across different actions. **32–35:** Paul wants his converts to be *free from anxieties*. Epictetus counseled the ideal Cynic to avoid the distractions of marriage; but the goal of Paul's advice is not philosophical self-mastery, but *unhindered devotion to the Lord*. **36–38:** Paul gives particular consideration to a situation which posed a special danger: when the desires of those who have pledged themselves to celibacy threaten to get out of control. In advising marriage in this case, Paul is not compromising his preference for the unmarried state. In Paul's hierarchy of virtue, marriage is good, but celibacy is better. **39–40:** The freedom of a Christian widow to remarry is affirmed, with one proviso: that she marry a fellow Christian. Yet Paul judges the widow to be *more blessed* who *remains* unmarried.

8.1–13: Eating food offered to idols. 1: The formula *now concerning* (see 7.1n.) indicates that this matter had been raised in the Corinthians' letter to Paul. The background was apparently this: Paul's advice in a previous letter (cf. 1 Cor 5.9) to shun the worship of idols (see 1 Cor 10.14–22) proved confusing and difficult for some to follow. What if one were invited to dine in the banquet hall of a sacred precinct? To decline such invitations would be socially disadvantageous (cf. 1 Cor 5.10). In reply, Paul quotes repeatedly from the Corinthians' letter (8.1,4,8), permitting a detailed reconstruction of the social location and religious beliefs of the disputants. *"All of us possess knowledge"* is a quotation from the Corinthians' letter. The content of their knowledge is quoted in 8.4: *"No idol . . . really exists."* As a consequence, eating idol meat is a matter of indifference: *"We are no worse off,"* etc. (8.8; but also see further, below). Perhaps the "strong" represented it as their duty to build up the conscience of the "weak," so that they would not cling to superstitious scruples (8.10). In seeking to identify the "strong" and the "weak," one should bear in mind that the poor seldom had meat as part of their diet, except when it was distributed at public religious festivals, whereas the rich could afford to buy meat in the market, and would have received invitations to dine in temples, owing to their social status. **1:** Paul counters the emphasis upon religious *knowledge* by exposing its tendency to self-inflation; *love* (Gk "agape") is the constructive force of Christian community, praised in ch 13. **3:** Cf. Rom 8.28–30; Gal 4.9; 1 Cor 13.12. **4:** The Corinthians' knowledge that *"no idol in the world really exists"* is grounded in the monotheistic faith to which they have been converted; cf. Deut 4.35; 6.4; Wis 7.17; 13.1; 15.2–3. **5:** Paul acknowledges not that *many gods* exist, but that

7 It is not everyone, however, who has this knowledge. Since some have become so accustomed to idols until now, they still think of the food they eat as food offered to an idol; and their conscience, being weak, is defiled. 8 "Food will not bring us close to God."[a] We are no worse off if we do not eat, and no better off if we do. 9 But take care that this liberty of yours does not somehow become a stumbling block to the weak. 10 For if others see you, who possess knowledge, eating in the temple of an idol, might they not, since their conscience is weak, be encouraged to the point of eating food sacrificed to idols? 11 So by your knowledge those weak believers for whom Christ died are destroyed.[b] 12 But when you thus sin against members of your family,[c] and wound their conscience when it is weak, you sin against Christ. 13 Therefore, if food is a cause of their falling,[d] I will never eat meat, so that I may not cause one of them[e] to fall.

9 Am I not free? Am I not an apostle? Have I not seen Jesus our Lord? Are you not my work in the Lord? 2 If I am not an apostle to others, at least I am to you; for you are the seal of my apostleship in the Lord.

3 This is my defense to those who would examine me. 4 Do we not have the right to our food and drink? 5 Do we not have the right to be accompanied by a believing wife,[f] as do the other apostles and the brothers of the Lord and Cephas? 6 Or is it only Barnabas and I who have no right to refrain from working for a living? 7 Who at any time pays the expenses for doing military service? Who plants a vineyard and does not eat any of its

a The quotation may extend to the end of the verse
b Gk *the weak brother . . . is destroyed*
c Gk *against the brothers*
d Gk *my brother's falling*
e Gk *cause my brother*
f Gk *a sister as wife*

they are worshiped as such by others. **6:** Paul quotes an early Christian confession; cf. Rom 11.36; Col 1.15–16. **7:** Paul confronts the "strong" with the reality that some do not share their enlightened attitude toward the gods. Those who have been *accustomed to idols until now* must be Gentiles rather than Jews. The Greek word translated *conscience* does not correspond to the modern conception of an internal guide to moral conduct in the future, but denotes a past misdeed which causes pain. The "strong" have asserted that their consumption of idol meat did not convict them of any wrongdoing, and have alleged that the *conscience* of other Christians is *weak* for harboring such scruples. Paul appropriates the term *conscience* from the "strong" and uses it to express his own true concern that someone for whom the *so-called gods* (v. 5) have existence might be *defiled* by eating *food offered to an idol*. **8:** The entire verse is another quotation from the Corinthians' letter, despite the NRSV's punctuation. **9:** The Greek word translated *liberty* has a meaning closer to "authority" or "right," as in 9.4–6,12,18. **10:** The situation envisioned here is illustrated by the temple of Asclepius at Corinth, which had three dining rooms on the east side of the courtyard. **11–12:** Paul formulates a radical conclusion regarding the relationship between *knowledge* and love: the proper object of religious concern is not an abstract truth about God, but *those weak believers for whom Christ died*. **13:** Paul formulates a general principle of Christian ethics: self-limiting regard for others.

9.1–27: Paul's defense of his means of subsistence, with implications for his legitimacy as an apostle. As if to illustrate the principle of renunciation articulated in 8.13, Paul launches into a spirited defense of his decision not to accept financial support from some at Corinth. The background of the controversy was as follows. While Paul was resident in Corinth, he provided for his own needs by working with his hands (Acts 18.1–3). When other apostles and evangelists subsequently arrived, they accepted patronage from wealthy persons. In retrospect, Paul's refusal of support appeared questionable. Did Paul know he was not entitled to support because he was not really an apostle? Moreover, labor of the sort by which Paul sustained himself was viewed as degrading by persons of high social status. These doubts and questions must have found expression in the Corinthians' letter to Paul. **1:** *Am I not free?* Paul responds to the insinuation that he is not "free" to evangelize because he is a "slave" of his labor. *An apostle . . . seen Jesus*; cf. 15.8; Gal 1.1,11–17. **3:** *Defense*, (Gk "apologia") a speech of defense before a court. On plans to *examine* Paul, see the allusion in 4.3–4. **5:** *The brothers of the Lord* are Jesus' brothers; cf. Mk 6.3; Gal 1.19. *Cephas*, the Aramaic form of Peter's name. **6:** *Barnabas* was Paul's first colleague in mission; see Gal.2.1–10; Acts 9.27; 11.25–26; 13–14. **7–14:** Why does Paul multiply examples of the exercise of a privilege

fruit? Or who tends a flock and does not get any of its milk?

[8] Do I say this on human authority? Does not the law also say the same? [9] For it is written in the law of Moses, "You shall not muzzle an ox while it is treading out the grain." Is it for oxen that God is concerned? [10] Or does he not speak entirely for our sake? It was indeed written for our sake, for whoever plows should plow in hope and whoever threshes should thresh in hope of a share in the crop. [11] If we have sown spiritual good among you, is it too much if we reap your material benefits? [12] If others share this rightful claim on you, do not we still more?

Nevertheless, we have not made use of this right, but we endure anything rather than put an obstacle in the way of the gospel of Christ. [13] Do you not know that those who are employed in the temple service get their food from the temple, and those who serve at the altar share in what is sacrificed on the altar? [14] In the same way, the Lord commanded that those who proclaim the gospel should get their living by the gospel.

[15] But I have made no use of any of these rights, nor am I writing this so that they may be applied in my case. Indeed, I would rather die than that—no one will deprive me of my ground for boasting! [16] If I proclaim the gospel, this gives me no ground for boasting, for an obligation is laid on me, and woe to me if I do not proclaim the gospel! [17] For if I do this of my own will, I have a reward; but if not of my own will, I am entrusted with a commission. [18] What then is my reward? Just this: that in my proclamation I may make the gospel free of charge, so as not to make full use of my rights in the gospel.

[19] For though I am free with respect to all, I have made myself a slave to all, so that I might win more of them. [20] To the Jews I became as a Jew, in order to win Jews. To those under the law I became as one under the law (though I myself am not under the law) so that I might win those under the law. [21] To those outside the law I became as one outside the law (though I am not free from God's law but am under Christ's law) so that I might win those outside the law. [22] To the weak I became weak, so that I might win the weak. I have become all things to all people, that I might by all means save some. [23] I do it all for the sake of the gospel, so that I may share in its blessings.

[24] Do you not know that in a race the runners all compete, but only one receives the prize? Run in such a way that you may win it. [25] Athletes exercise self-control in all things; they do it to receive a perishable wreath, but we an imperishable one. [26] So I do not run aimlessly, nor do I box as though beating the air; [27] but I punish my body and enslave it, so that after proclaiming to others I myself should not be disqualified.

(by the soldier, the planter, the herder, the priest) about which the Corinthians are in agreement, when it is not his exercise of the privilege which is in dispute, but his renunciation of it? For the key to Paul's argumentative strategy, see note on vv. 12b–14 below. **9:** Deut. 25.4. **12b–14:** Paul cleverly reinterprets *the Lord's command* as a *right* of which he has *not made use.* Paul's critics may have pointed out that, by working as a craftsman, Paul had violated the norms of Christian mission—*that those who proclaim the gospel should get their living by the gospel.* **14:** What *the Lord commanded* refers to a saying like that attributed to Jesus in Lk 10.7. **15:** Against those who find his occupation shameful, Paul asserts that it has provided him with *ground for boasting*; see also 2 Cor 11.7–10. **16:** Paul represents his preaching as an *obligation* (lit., "necessity"), not a choice; cf. Rom 1.14–15. **17–18:** By means of a series of well-chosen economic terms, Paul reverses the values of the Corinthian patrons: *reward* is literally "wages"; *commission* (Gk "oikonomia") is "the work of a household-manager"; *free of charge* is a characteristic of benefactors. Paul's point is that evangelists who accept financial support are mere hirelings, whereas he is the true benefactor of the community. **19–23:** Paul portrays himself as a populist leader who identifies with the interests of the common people. Paul justifies his self-lowering action *for the sake of the gospel*: by making himself *a slave to all,* he hopes to *save some.* Paul's upper-class critics may have regarded him as a demagogue, but the poor and weak would have found his self-presentation appealing. **24–27:** In an extended metaphor, Paul compares himself to an athlete in training for the games. His renunciation of financial support should be understood as a form of discipline, an exercise of *self-control.* **25:** The *perishable wreath* may allude specifically to the winner's crown of the Isthmian Games, which was made of withered celery.

10 I do not want you to be unaware, brothers and sisters,[a] that our ancestors were all under the cloud, and all passed through the sea, [2] and all were baptized into Moses in the cloud and in the sea, [3] and all ate the same spiritual food, [4] and all drank the same spiritual drink. For they drank from the spiritual rock that followed them, and the rock was Christ. [5] Nevertheless, God was not pleased with most of them, and they were struck down in the wilderness.

[6] Now these things occurred as examples for us, so that we might not desire evil as they did. [7] Do not become idolaters as some of them did; as it is written, "The people sat down to eat and drink, and they rose up to play." [8] We must not indulge in sexual immorality as some of them did, and twenty-three thousand fell in a single day. [9] We must not put Christ[b] to the test, as some of them did, and were destroyed by serpents. [10] And do not complain as some of them did, and were destroyed by the destroyer. [11] These things happened to them to serve as an example, and they were written down to instruct us, on whom the ends of the ages have come. [12] So if you think you are standing, watch out that you do not fall. [13] No testing has overtaken you that is not common to everyone. God is faithful, and he will not let you be tested beyond your strength, but with the testing he will also provide the way out so that you may be able to endure it.

[14] Therefore, my dear friends,[c] flee from the worship of idols. [15] I speak as to sensible people; judge for yourselves what I say. [16] The cup of blessing that we bless, is it not a sharing in the blood of Christ? The bread that we break, is it not a sharing in the body of Christ? [17] Because there is one bread, we who are many are one body, for we all partake of the one bread. [18] Consider the people of Israel;[d] are not those who eat the sacrifices

a Gk *brothers*
b Other ancient authorities read *the Lord*
c Gk *my beloved*
d Gk *Israel according to the flesh*

10.1–22: Warning against participation in the worship of idols. Paul's demand for a complete break with polytheistic sacrificial rituals is significantly more rigorous than his advice on food offered to idols in ch 8, suggesting that this passage belonged (with 6.12–20) to the letter on association with the immoral and idolaters mentioned in 5.9–10. Paul's admonition takes the form of a typological interpretation of Israel's Exodus and wilderness traditions, encouraging the Corinthians to see the danger to their community through the prism of Israel's calamitous idolatry. 1: The expression *our ancestors* reckons Gentile Christians as belonging to Israel. For Israel *under the cloud*, see Ps 105.39; Wis 10.17; 19.7; on passage *through the sea*, cf. Ex 14.21–22. 2: Paul typologically constructs Israel's Exodus experience as prefiguring Christian baptism. 3–4: *Spiritual food* refers to the "manna" of Ex 16.15; cf. Ps 78.24–25; *spiritual drink* is the water struck from the rock by Moses in Ex 17.6; Num 20.7–11; cf. Ps 78.15–16. The tradition that the *rock followed* Israel through the wilderness is found in *Tg. Ps.-J.* on Num 20.19. In a stunning typological substitution, Paul explains that *the rock was Christ.* Using a similar hermeneutical maneuver, the first-century CE Jewish interpreter Philo equates the "rock" with "wisdom" and "manna" with the divine "logos." 5: For the divine punishment of the wilderness generation, see Num 14.29–30; Jude 5; Heb 3.17. 6: Paul suggests that *evil desire* is the root of idolatry and immorality; for the background, see Num 11.4–6; Ps 106.14–15. 7: Paul quotes Ex 32.6, the only scripture cited explicitly in ch 10, because it epitomizes Paul's concern with idolatry and immorality among the Corinthians. 8: For the close connection of idolatry with sexual immorality, see *T. Reuben* 4. On the *twenty-three thousand* who died by the plague, cf. Num 25.1–9. 9: That Israel *put God to the test*, see Ps 78.18; for *destroyed by serpents*, see Num 21.6. 10: Num. 16.41,49. 11: Paul discerns a deeper "typological" purpose in the *things* that *happened* to Israel. Paul's capacity to grasp such correspondences depends upon his eschatological perspective. 12–13: Paul reassures the Corinthians that God *will provide the way out* of the temptation to participate in polytheistic rituals. 14: Paul formulates the point of the preceding typological interpretation as an urgent injunction; cf. the similarly formulated warning in 6.18. 15–22: To dissuade the Corinthians from participating in polytheistic rituals, Paul develops an argument that he hopes will appeal to the *sensible*. The argument rests upon the assumption that religious "fellowship" (Gk "koinonia") is mutually exclusive. 16: The elasticity of the Greek phrase translated *sharing in* allows both for the social concept "fellowship with" and for the sacramental idea of "participation in" *the blood . . . the body of Christ*. 17: More than an act of communal sharing, Christians become *one body* through partaking of the *one bread*; cf. 12.13. 20:

partners in the altar? [19] What do I imply then? That food sacrificed to idols is anything, or that an idol is anything? [20] No, I imply that what pagans sacrifice, they sacrifice to demons and not to God. I do not want you to be partners with demons. [21] You cannot drink the cup of the Lord and the cup of demons. You cannot partake of the table of the Lord and the table of demons. [22] Or are we provoking the Lord to jealousy? Are we stronger than he?

[23] "All things are lawful," but not all things are beneficial. "All things are lawful," but not all things build up. [24] Do not seek your own advantage, but that of the other. [25] Eat whatever is sold in the meat market without raising any question on the ground of conscience, [26] for "the earth and its fullness are the Lord's." [27] If an unbeliever invites you to a meal and you are disposed to go, eat whatever is set before you without raising any question on the ground of conscience. [28] But if someone says to you, "This has been offered in sacrifice," then do not eat it, out of consideration for the one who informed you, and for the sake of conscience— [29] I mean the other's conscience, not your own. For why should my liberty be subject to the judgment of someone else's conscience? [30] If I partake with thankfulness, why should I be denounced because of that for which I give thanks?

[31] So, whether you eat or drink, or whatever you do, do everything for the glory of God. [32] Give no offense to Jews or to Greeks or to the church of God, [33] just as I try to please everyone in everything I do, not seeking my own advantage, but that of many, so that they

11 may be saved. [1] Be imitators of me, as I am of Christ.

[2] I commend you because you remember me in everything and maintain the traditions just as I handed them on to you. [3] But I want you to understand that Christ is the head of every man, and the husband[a] is the head of his wife,[b] and God is the head of Christ. [4] Any man who prays or prophesies with something on his head disgraces his head, [5] but any woman who prays or prophesies with her head unveiled disgraces her head—it is one and the same thing as having her head shaved. [6] For if a woman will not veil herself,

a   The same Greek word means *man* or *husband*
b   Or *head of the woman*

Cf. Deut 32.17. **21:** Greek papyri furnish examples of invitations to dine upon the "couch" of deities such as lord Sarapis. **22:** Cf. Deut 32.19,21.

10.23–11.1: Limits upon religious exclusivity. Paul anticipates objections to his advice to shun idolatry and deals with two ambiguous cases; on the meaning of "conscience," see 8.7n. **23:** As in 6.12, Paul quotes a Corinthian slogan and counters with consideration of what is *beneficial* and edifying. **25:** Should all meat *sold in the market* be regarded as idol meat? The question was relevant, because meat markets were often located in the vicinity of temples. **27:** The *meal* is presumably in the private home of an unbeliever. **29b–30:** Because these questions stand in tension with what precedes and follows, some interpreters regard them as the objections of an imaginary interlocutor, while others suggest that they originated as a marginal gloss by one of the "strong" who read Paul's letter. **31–33:** Paul foregoes consideration of further cases and formulates a general rule of conduct.

11.2–16: Hairstyles in the assembly. The point at issue is difficult to determine. Paul seems to insist that charismatic women leaders wear the veil, in accordance with Jewish custom. But v. 15 allows that women have their *hair* as a *covering*. Hence, some interpreters construe *unveiled* (vv. 5,13) more generally as "uncovered," in reference to the loose, disheveled hair of women in the ecstatic worship of Dionysus. But there is little support for this in the text. More interesting than what Paul argues for is what he does not argue against—the Spirit-filled leadership of women. It is assumed that women will *pray* and *prophesy* in the worship assembly (v. 5). **2:** A problematic beginning: How will Paul *maintain the traditions* in the face of the new social identity given in Christ (cf. Gal 3.28)? **3–7:** Paul argues on the basis of a hierarchy of being: *God, Christ, man, woman.* **4:** Jewish men in the time of Paul did not wear a head-covering; see *Gen. Rab.* 17.8. **5–6:** On the potential disgrace of a *woman unveiled* in public, see the comment of Plutarch on Roman custom: "It is more usual for women to go forth in public with their heads covered and men with their heads uncovered" (*Quaestiones Romanae* 267a). For Paul's assumption that *it is disgraceful for a woman to have her hair cut* short, it may be relevant that Roman

then she should cut off her hair; but if it is disgraceful for a woman to have her hair cut off or to be shaved, she should wear a veil. [7] For a man ought not to have his head veiled, since he is the image and reflection[a] of God; but woman is the reflection[a] of man. [8] Indeed, man was not made from woman, but woman from man. [9] Neither was man created for the sake of woman, but woman for the sake of man. [10] For this reason a woman ought to have a symbol of[b] authority on her head,[c] because of the angels. [11] Nevertheless, in the Lord woman is not independent of man or man independent of woman. [12] For just as woman came from man, so man comes through woman; but all things come from God. [13] Judge for yourselves: is it proper for a woman to pray to God with her head unveiled? [14] Does not nature itself teach you that if a man wears long hair, it is degrading to him, [15] but if a woman has long hair, it is her glory? For her hair is given to her for a covering. [16] But if anyone is disposed to be contentious—we have no such custom, nor do the churches of God.

[17] Now in the following instructions I do not commend you, because when you come together it is not for the better but for the worse. [18] For, to begin with, when you come together as a church, I hear that there are divisions among you; and to some extent I believe it. [19] Indeed, there have to be factions among you, for only so will it become clear who among you are genuine. [20] When you come together, it is not really to eat the Lord's supper. [21] For when the time comes to eat, each of you goes ahead with your own supper, and one goes hungry and another becomes drunk. [22] What! Do you not have homes to eat and drink in? Or do you show contempt for the church of God and humiliate those who have nothing? What should I say to you? Should I commend you? In this matter I do not commend you!

[23] For I received from the Lord what I also handed on to you, that the Lord Jesus on the night when he was betrayed took a loaf of bread, [24] and when he had given thanks, he broke it and said, "This is my body that is for[d] you. Do this in remembrance of me." [25] In the same way he took the cup also, after supper,

[a] Or glory
[b] Gk lacks a symbol of
[c] Or have freedom of choice regarding her head
[d] Other ancient authorities read is broken for

portraiture generally depicts women with long hair braided and wound up around their heads. **7:** See Gen 1.27. **8–9:** An argument from the order of creation; see Gen 2.18–23. **10:** The angels are probably the "sons of God" in Gen 6.2 who had intercourse with mortal women and fathered a race of giants. Like other Jewish writers of the period (e.g., T. Reuben 5.6), Paul evidently fears that the angels will be aroused to lust by the sight of exposed women. **11–12:** Nevertheless indicates that Paul breaks off the preceding argument and moves on to emphasize what is important: in the Lord there is mutuality and reciprocity between woman and man. **13–16:** Paul's argument having collapsed, he hands the decision over to the Corinthians, invoking a Stoic argument from nature and finally appealing to custom.

11.17–34: Divisions at the Lord's Supper. A gulf between the "haves" and the "have-nots" emerged at the very place where the Corinthians should have been most capable of discerning the unity of the body of Christ—at the Lord's Supper. According to the conventions of Greco-Roman dinner parties, the host apportioned the fare according to the status of his guests, reserving the best food and wine for his social equals and intimate friends. **18:** The phrase come together as a church designates the weekly assembly of all the Christians of Corinth (cf. 14.23; 16.2), a larger gathering of the several subgroups, or "house churches," for the purpose of eating the Lord's Supper. The whole church evidently met in the home of a wealthy member, such as Gaius (Rom 16.23). **19:** Paul's assertion that there have to be factions may reflect an apocalyptic belief about the tribulation expected in the last days, but also may be meant ironically. **20–21:** The contrast between the Lord's supper and "the private supper" (NRSV: your own supper) makes clear how Paul sees the problem: the privatization of a meal intended for the community. The Greek verb translated goes ahead is ambiguous: it may suggest that some (the leisure class) began to eat before others (slaves, laborers) had arrived, but also that some selfishly ate their food while others looked on. In any case, the result is that one goes hungry and another becomes drunk. **22:** Paul's question Do you not have homes? is heavy with irony against the proprietary class. **23–26:** Paul reminds the Corinthians of the act of self-giving, which established the basis of their fellowship, on the basis of early

saying, "This cup is the new covenant in my blood. Do this, as often as you drink it, in remembrance of me." [26] For as often as you eat this bread and drink the cup, you proclaim the Lord's death until he comes.

[27] Whoever, therefore, eats the bread or drinks the cup of the Lord in an unworthy manner will be answerable for the body and blood of the Lord. [28] Examine yourselves, and only then eat of the bread and drink of the cup. [29] For all who eat and drink[a] without discerning the body,[b] eat and drink judgment against themselves. [30] For this reason many of you are weak and ill, and some have died.[c] [31] But if we judged ourselves, we would not be judged. [32] But when we are judged by the Lord, we are disciplined[d] so that we may not be condemned along with the world.

[33] So then, my brothers and sisters,[e] when you come together to eat, wait for one another. [34] If you are hungry, eat at home, so that when you come together, it will not be for your condemnation. About the other things I will give instructions when I come.

12 Now concerning spiritual gifts,[f] brothers and sisters,[e] I do not want you to be uninformed. [2] You know that when you were pagans, you were enticed and led astray to idols that could not speak. [3] Therefore I want you to understand that no one speaking by the Spirit of God ever says "Let Jesus be cursed!" and no one can say "Jesus is Lord" except by the Holy Spirit.

[4] Now there are varieties of gifts, but the same Spirit; [5] and there are varieties of services, but the same Lord; [6] and there are varieties of activities, but it is the same God who activates all of them in everyone. [7] To each is given the manifestation of the Spirit for the common good. [8] To one is given through the Spirit the utterance of wisdom, and to another the utterance of knowledge according to the same Spirit, [9] to another faith by the same Spirit, to another gifts of healing by the one Spirit, [10] to another the working of miracles, to another prophecy, to another the discernment of spirits, to another various kinds of tongues, to another the interpretation of tongues. [11] All these are activated by one and the same Spirit, who allots to each one individually just as the Spirit chooses.

a   Other ancient authorities add *in an unworthy manner,*
b   Other ancient authorities read *the Lord's body*
c   Gk *fallen asleep*
d   Or *When we are judged, we are being disciplined by the Lord*
e   Gk *brothers*
f   Or *spiritual persons*

tradition; cf. Mk 14.12–25. **25:** Paul's reference to *the cup, after supper* presupposes that a full meal was served between the bread and the wine. **26:** *Until he comes,* see 1.8n. **29:** What is meant by *discerning the body*—the eucharistic bread as Christ's body, or the gathered church as Christ's body, or perhaps both? **33–34:** Paul's counsel that the Corinthians *wait for one another* implies sharing, so as to alleviate the hunger and humiliation of those who have nothing (vv. 21–22).

12–14: On spiritual gifts. Paul counters an overemphasis upon glossolalia (speaking in tongues). Judging from the amount of space devoted to the subject, the gift of tongues must have been highly prized among the Corinthians. Not everyone in the church spoke in tongues (12.30); those who had the gift may have looked down upon those who did not. Paul does not deny the power of speaking in tongues, but interprets that power by ordering the gifts from the greatest (love) to the least (tongues), while affirming that all are necessary for the body of Christ. **12.1:** The formula *now concerning* (see 7.1n.) indicates that a question about *spiritual gifts* had been raised in the Corinthians' letter. **3:** Paul establishes criteria to determine whether a person is *speaking by the Spirit of God.* Did someone in the church at Corinth actually say *"Jesus be cursed!"* in an ecstatic trance? Did the Corinthians hesitate to expel this person because of an overvaluation of spiritual gifts? **4–11:** Paul affirms the diversity of *gifts* within unity. **7:** The guiding principle should be *the common good.* **8–11:** The nine named gifts are ranked: first *wisdom,* last *tongues.* **12–26:** Paul's metaphor of the church as a *body* is derived from Greco-Roman political discourse, where the figure functioned to urge concord. In the well-known fable of Menenius Agrippa, the Roman senator compared a strike by the common people to a revolt of the hands, mouth, and teeth against the belly, resulting in the death of the body. In ancient politics, the body analogy was essentially conservative, portraying the established order as "natural." Paul uses the metaphor subversively

[12] For just as the body is one and has many members, and all the members of the body, though many, are one body, so it is with Christ. [13] For in the one Spirit we were all baptized into one body—Jews or Greeks, slaves or free—and we were all made to drink of one Spirit.

[14] Indeed, the body does not consist of one member but of many. [15] If the foot would say, "Because I am not a hand, I do not belong to the body," that would not make it any less a part of the body. [16] And if the ear would say, "Because I am not an eye, I do not belong to the body," that would not make it any less a part of the body. [17] If the whole body were an eye, where would the hearing be? If the whole body were hearing, where would the sense of smell be? [18] But as it is, God arranged the members in the body, each one of them, as he chose. [19] If all were a single member, where would the body be? [20] As it is, there are many members, yet one body. [21] The eye cannot say to the hand, "I have no need of you," nor again the head to the feet, "I have no need of you." [22] On the contrary, the members of the body that seem to be weaker are indispensable, [23] and those members of the body that we think less honorable we clothe with greater honor, and our less respectable members are treated with greater respect; [24] whereas our more respectable members do not need this. But God has so arranged the body, giving the greater honor to the inferior member, [25] that there may be no dissension within the body, but the members may have the same care for one another. [26] If one member suffers, all suffer together with it; if one member is honored, all rejoice together with it.

[27] Now you are the body of Christ and individually members of it. [28] And God has appointed in the church first apostles, second prophets, third teachers; then deeds of power, then gifts of healing, forms of assistance, forms of leadership, various kinds of tongues. [29] Are all apostles? Are all prophets? Are all teachers? Do all work miracles? [30] Do all possess gifts of healing? Do all speak in tongues? Do all interpret? [31] But strive for the greater gifts. And I will show you a still more excellent way.

13 If I speak in the tongues of mortals and of angels, but do not have love, I am a noisy gong or a clanging cymbal. [2] And if I have prophetic powers, and understand all mysteries and all knowledge, and if I have all faith, so as to remove mountains, but do not have love, I am nothing. [3] If I give away all my possessions, and if I hand over my body so that I may boast,[a] but do not have love, I gain nothing.

[4] Love is patient; love is kind; love is not envious or boastful or arrogant [5] or rude.

---

a   Other ancient authorities read *body to be burned*

to question conventional assumptions about status and honor. **13:** Paul alludes to an early baptismal formula; cf. Gal 3.27–28. **14–21:** Ancient philosophers and orators referred to the *hands* and *feet*, the *eyes* and *ears* in elaborating the society-as-body metaphor, but Paul emphasizes mutuality rather than hierarchy. **22–26:** Paul reverses the values of ancient political rhetoric, which figured the parts of the body representing the ruling class, such as the head and the belly, as most honorable and indispensable. Paul claims, scandalously, that the weaker parts are actually more *indispensable* and *honorable*, that we acknowledge this fact when *we clothe* these private parts, and that *God has so arranged the body* in this paradoxical manner, *giving the greater honor to the inferior member*. **27:** Paul summarizes the argument and applies it to *the body of Christ* metaphor. **28–30:** Because God has established the diversity of gifts in the body, one should not succumb to the ambition to have others' gifts, or to the tendency to privilege one gift over others.

13.1–13: Praise of love. In the context of chs 12–14, Paul's encomium of love serves to devalue the gift of tongues by showing the Corinthians a "more excellent way." Yet, ch 13 is self-contained, and the transitions from 12.31 to 13.1 and from 13.13 to 14.1 are weak, so that some scholars conjecture that ch 13 was conceived and written earlier and independently (possibly as an essay for Paul's school in Ephesus; cf. Acts 19.9) and reused here because of its relevance. With Paul's speech in praise of love, compare Plato *Symp.* 197c–e. **1–3:** The gifts are *nothing* without *love*. **1:** *Tongues of mortals* refers to human speech; *tongues of angels* refers to glossolalia; cf. *T. Job* 48–52; 2 Cor 12.4. Paul's comparative terms, *noisy gong* and *clanging cymbal*, are derived from ancient religious rituals; such sounds lack the warmth of love. **3:** If the alternative reading *my body to be burned* (textual note *a*) is adopted, Paul is probably referring to the notorious Indian philosophers ("gymnosophists") who im-

It does not insist on its own way; it is not irritable or resentful; ⁶ it does not rejoice in wrongdoing, but rejoices in the truth. ⁷ It bears all things, believes all things, hopes all things, endures all things.

⁸ Love never ends. But as for prophecies, they will come to an end; as for tongues, they will cease; as for knowledge, it will come to an end. ⁹ For we know only in part, and we prophesy only in part; ¹⁰ but when the complete comes, the partial will come to an end. ¹¹ When I was a child, I spoke like a child, I thought like a child, I reasoned like a child; when I became an adult, I put an end to childish ways. ¹² For now we see in a mirror, dimly,ᵃ but then we will see face to face. Now I know only in part; then I will know fully, even as I have been fully known. ¹³ And now faith, hope, and love abide, these three; and the greatest of these is love.

14 Pursue love and strive for the spiritual gifts, and especially that you may prophesy. ² For those who speak in a tongue do not speak to other people but to God; for nobody understands them, since they are speaking mysteries in the Spirit. ³ On the other hand, those who prophesy speak to other people for their upbuilding and encouragement and consolation. ⁴ Those who speak in a tongue build up themselves, but those who prophesy build up the church. ⁵ Now I would like all of you to speak in tongues, but even more to prophesy. One who prophesies is greater than one who speaks in tongues, unless someone interprets, so that the church may be built up.

⁶ Now, brothers and sisters,ᵇ if I come to you speaking in tongues, how will I benefit you unless I speak to you in some revelation or knowledge or prophecy or teaching? ⁷ It is the same way with lifeless instruments that produce sound, such as the flute or the harp. If they do not give distinct notes, how will anyone know what is being played? ⁸ And if the bugle gives an indistinct sound, who will get ready for battle? ⁹ So with yourselves; if in a tongue you utter speech that is not intelligible, how will anyone know what is being said? For you will be speaking into the air. ¹⁰ There are doubtless many different kinds of sounds in the world, and nothing is without sound. ¹¹ If then I do not know the meaning of a sound, I will be a foreigner to the speaker and the speaker a foreigner to me. ¹² So with yourselves; since you are eager for spiritual gifts, strive to excel in them for building up the church.

¹³ Therefore, one who speaks in a tongue should pray for the power to interpret. ¹⁴ For if I pray in a tongue, my spirit prays but my mind is unproductive. ¹⁵ What should I do then? I will pray with the spirit, but I will pray with the mind also; I will sing praise with the spirit, but I will sing praise with the mind also. ¹⁶ Otherwise, if you say a blessing with the spirit, how can anyone in the position of an outsider say the "Amen" to your thanksgiving, since the outsider does not know what you are saying? ¹⁷ For you may give

ᵃ Gk *in a riddle*
ᵇ Gk *brothers*

molated themselves to demonstrate their contempt of death. **4–7:** The qualities of love: *patient*, cf. 1 Thess 5.14; Gal 5.22; *kind*, cf. Rom 2.4; *not envious*, cf. 3.3; not *arrogant*, cf. 4.18–19. **5:** Cf. 10.33. **8–13:** Paul emphasizes the imperishability of *love*, in contrast to the limitations of *prophecies*, *tongues*, and *knowledge*, which the Corinthians have overvalued. **8:** The Greek verb translated *ends* is used elsewhere in reference to the wind: love is like a wind that never "subsides." **12:** *In a mirror, dimly*: that is, one does not see the thing itself, but only its reflected image. **13:** For the triad *faith, hope, and love*, cf. 1 Thess 1.3; 5.8; Col 1.4–5.

14.1–40: Prophecy is more edifying than tongues-speaking. 1: *Prophesy*, not in the sense of "predict the future," but "edify" the church, as in v. 3. **2:** Paul shares with Plato, Philo, and others the belief in a higher form of Spirit-inspired speech directed to the divine, but incomprehensible to normal human intelligence. **5:** Paul's concession, *I would like all of you to speak in tongues*, reveals the high value that was set upon this gift, and how many Corinthians earnestly strove for it. By declaring that *one who prophesies is greater than one who speaks in tongues*, Paul reverses the hierarchy of speech-types assumed by the elite, elevating the comprehensible above the esoteric. The new criterion of value is whether the community is edified. **6–12:** Paul devalues the esoteric speech of tongues by comparison with the sounds produced *by lifeless instruments*. **13–19:** In praying, singing, and other acts of worship, Paul counsels cooperation between *spirit* and *mind*. **16:** The word translated *outsider*

thanks well enough, but the other person is not built up. [18] I thank God that I speak in tongues more than all of you; [19] nevertheless, in church I would rather speak five words with my mind, in order to instruct others also, than ten thousand words in a tongue.

[20] Brothers and sisters,[a] do not be children in your thinking; rather, be infants in evil, but in thinking be adults. [21] In the law it is written,

"By people of strange tongues
  and by the lips of foreigners
I will speak to this people;
    yet even then they will not listen to me,"

says the Lord. [22] Tongues, then, are a sign not for believers but for unbelievers, while prophecy is not for unbelievers but for believers. [23] If, therefore, the whole church comes together and all speak in tongues, and outsiders or unbelievers enter, will they not say that you are out of your mind? [24] But if all prophesy, an unbeliever or outsider who enters is reproved by all and called to account by all. [25] After the secrets of the unbeliever's heart are disclosed, that person will bow down before God and worship him, declaring, "God is really among you."

[26] What should be done then, my friends?[a] When you come together, each one has a hymn, a lesson, a revelation, a tongue, or an interpretation. Let all things be done for building up. [27] If anyone speaks in a tongue, let there be only two or at most three, and each in turn; and let one interpret. [28] But if there is no one to interpret, let them be silent in church and speak to themselves and to

God. [29] Let two or three prophets speak, and let the others weigh what is said. [30] If a revelation is made to someone else sitting nearby, let the first person be silent. [31] For you can all prophesy one by one, so that all may learn and all be encouraged. [32] And the spirits of prophets are subject to the prophets, [33] for God is a God not of disorder but of peace.

(As in all the churches of the saints, [34] women should be silent in the churches. For they are not permitted to speak, but should be subordinate, as the law also says. [35] If there is anything they desire to know, let them ask their husbands at home. For it is shameful for a woman to speak in church.[b] [36] Or did the word of God originate with you? Or are you the only ones it has reached?)

[37] Anyone who claims to be a prophet, or to have spiritual powers, must acknowledge that what I am writing to you is a command of the Lord. [38] Anyone who does not recognize this is not to be recognized. [39] So, my friends,[c] be eager to prophesy, and do not forbid speaking in tongues; [40] but all things should be done decently and in order.

15

Now I would remind you, brothers and sisters,[a] of the good news[d] that I proclaimed to you, which you in turn

a Gk brothers
b Other ancient authorities put verses 34-35 after verse 40
c Gk my brothers
d Or gospel

(Gk "idiotes") means someone untrained, i.e., not adept at understanding those speaking in tongues. **18–19:** As in the case of food (cf. 8.13), Paul adopts the ethical principle of self-limiting regard for others. **20–25:** The Corinthians have been naïve in failing to consider the effects of speaking in tongues upon nonadept believers as well as unbelievers. **21:** The point of the citation (not found in the law, as Paul says, but in Isa 28.11–12) is that the word of the Lord foretold not only the phenomenon of speaking in tongues but also its failure to convince. **22–23:** For unbelievers, tongues are a sign opposed and spoken against, leading outsiders to the conclusion that Christians are out of their minds. **26–33a:** Paul gives instructions for an orderly procedure involving tongues and prophecy in the worship assembly. **33b–36:** Many scholars regard this passage as a later non-Pauline addition, because it disrupts the flow of the argument from v. 33a to v. 37; it contradicts the assumption of 11.5 that women will pray and prophesy in the assembly; it resembles the viewpoint of the Deutero-Pauline letters (see 1 Tim 2.9–15); it exhibits non-Pauline sentiments, e.g., v. 34b, as the law also says; and vv. 34–35 appear after 14.40 in some manuscripts. **37–40:** Assertion of authority and summary of the argument of ch 14.

15.1–58: A reasoned proof of the resurrection of the dead. The issue that evokes this argument is identified in v. 12: some of the Corinthians have said, "There is no resurrection of the dead." Greeks and Romans who were not skeptical in the face of death tended to believe in the separation of the soul from the body, a belief sanctioned by the oracle at Delphi and popular philosophers. Enlightened persons found the idea of the resur-

received, in which also you stand, [2] through which also you are being saved, if you hold firmly to the message that I proclaimed to you—unless you have come to believe in vain.

[3] For I handed on to you as of first importance what I in turn had received: that Christ died for our sins in accordance with the scriptures, [4] and that he was buried, and that he was raised on the third day in accordance with the scriptures, [5] and that he appeared to Cephas, then to the twelve. [6] Then he appeared to more than five hundred brothers and sisters[a] at one time, most of whom are still alive, though some have died.[b] [7] Then he appeared to James, then to all the apostles. [8] Last of all, as to one untimely born, he appeared also to me. [9] For I am the least of the apostles, unfit to be called an apostle, because I persecuted the church of God. [10] But by the grace of God I am what I am, and his grace toward me has not been in vain. On the contrary, I worked harder than any of them—though it was not I, but the grace of God that is with me. [11] Whether then it was I or they, so we proclaim and so you have come to believe.

[12] Now if Christ is proclaimed as raised from the dead, how can some of you say there is no resurrection of the dead? [13] If there is no resurrection of the dead, then Christ has not been raised; [14] and if Christ has not been raised, then our proclamation has been in vain and your faith has been in vain. [15] We are even found to be misrepresenting God, because we testified of God that he raised Christ—whom he did not raise if it is true that the dead are not raised. [16] For if the dead are not raised, then Christ has not been raised. [17] If Christ has not been raised, your faith is futile and you are still in your sins. [18] Then those also who have died[b] in Christ have perished. [19] If for this life only we have hoped in Christ, we are of all people most to be pitied.

[20] But in fact Christ has been raised from the dead, the first fruits of those who have died.[b] [21] For since death came through a human being, the resurrection of the dead has also come through a human being; [22] for as all die in Adam, so all will be made alive in Christ. [23] But each in his own order: Christ the first fruits, then at his coming those who belong to Christ. [24] Then comes the end,[c] when he hands over the kingdom to God the Father, after he has destroyed every ruler and every authority and power. [25] For he must reign until he has put all his enemies under his feet. [26] The last enemy to be destroyed is death. [27] For "God[c] has put all things in subjection under his feet." But when it says,

a   Gk *brothers*
b   Gk *fallen asleep*
c   Or *Then come the rest*
d   Gk *he*

rection of the body laughable; cf. Acts 17.32. Paul constructs an argument for the resurrection of the body on the analogy of the philosophical proof of the immortality of the soul in Plato *Phaedr.* 245c–257d; Cicero *Tusculan Disputations* bk. 1; Plutarch *On the Soul*; etc. The major divisions of Paul's discourse are easily recognized and correspond to the sections of his philosophical models: 15.1–34, proof of the fact of the resurrection, established by reasoned arguments; and 15.35–58, discussion of the manner of the resurrection and the nature of the resurrection body, culminating in a "mythological hymn." **15.1–2**: Paul reminds the Corinthians that the resurrection faith belongs to the foundation of Christian tradition. **3–4**: Paul quotes an early creed; cf. Rom 4.24–25; 10.9–10; 1 Thess 5.10. The phrase, *he was buried*, is unique to this instance of the creed and may have been added by Paul for the context here. **5–7**: Within the argument of ch 15, the list of witnesses to Christ's resurrection, which belonged to the tradition that Paul had received, provides the evidential basis for what follows. **5**: *Cephas* is the Aramaic form of Peter's name. **8**: Paul adds his own witness to the tradition. The term translated *one untimely born* refers to an abortion or miscarriage. Paul may be taking up an insult hurled at him by his opponents. **9**: See 9.4–5; 22.4–5; Gal 1.13. **12–34**: **The reality of the resurrection of the dead. 13–19**: Paul employs a series of rhetorical syllogisms (*if . . . then*) to refute the denial of the resurrection by some at Corinth. **18–19**: Cf. 1 Thess 4.13. **20–28**: Paul argues positively for the resurrection based upon an order established by God. **20**: *The first fruits* guarantee the harvest to come. **21–23**: For the *Adam–Christ* typology, see also vv. 45–49; Rom 5.12–21. **23**: Cf. 1 Thess 4.16. **24–25**: On the apocalyptic scenario envisioned here, compare 2 Esd 7.29; Rev 20.4–6; *Pirke Eliezer* 11. **24**: Cf. Rom 5.17. **25**: See Ps 110.1. **26**: For the personification of death, see vv. 54–55; 2 Esd

"All things are put in subjection," it is plain that this does not include the one who put all things in subjection under him. [28] When all things are subjected to him, then the Son himself will also be subjected to the one who put all things in subjection under him, so that God may be all in all.

[29] Otherwise, what will those people do who receive baptism on behalf of the dead? If the dead are not raised at all, why are people baptized on their behalf?

[30] And why are we putting ourselves in danger every hour? [31] I die every day! That is as certain, brothers and sisters,[a] as my boasting of you—a boast that I make in Christ Jesus our Lord. [32] If with merely human hopes I fought with wild animals at Ephesus, what would I have gained by it? If the dead are not raised,

"Let us eat and drink,
    for tomorrow we die."

[33] Do not be deceived:

"Bad company ruins good morals."

[34] Come to a sober and right mind, and sin no more; for some people have no knowledge of God. I say this to your shame.

[35] But someone will ask, "How are the dead raised? With what kind of body do they come?" [36] Fool! What you sow does not come to life unless it dies. [37] And as for what you sow, you do not sow the body that is to be, but a bare seed, perhaps of wheat or of some other grain. [38] But God gives it a body as he has chosen, and to each kind of seed its own body. [39] Not all flesh is alike, but there is one flesh for human beings, another for animals, another for birds, and another for fish. [40] There are both heavenly bodies and earthly bodies, but the glory of the heavenly is one thing, and that of the earthly is another. [41] There is one glory of the sun, and another glory of the moon, and another glory of the stars; indeed, star differs from star in glory.

[42] So it is with the resurrection of the dead. What is sown is perishable, what is raised is imperishable. [43] It is sown in dishonor, it is raised in glory. It is sown in weakness, it is raised in power. [44] It is sown a physical body, it is raised a spiritual body. If there is a physical body, there is also a spiritual body. [45] Thus it is written, "The first man, Adam, became a living being"; the last Adam became a life-giving spirit. [46] But it is not the spiritual that is first, but the physical, and then the spiritual. [47] The first man was from the earth, a man of dust; the second man is[b] from heaven. [48] As was the man of dust, so are those who are of the dust; and as is the man of heaven, so are those who are of heaven. [49] Just as we have borne the image of the man of dust, we will[c] also bear the image of the man of heaven.

[50] What I am saying, brothers and sisters,[a] is this: flesh and blood cannot inherit the kingdom of God, nor does the perishable inherit the imperishable. [51] Listen, I will tell you a mystery! We will not all die,[d] but we

a   Gk brothers
b   Other ancient authorities add the Lord
c   Other ancient authorities read let us
d   Gk fall asleep

8.55. **27:** Ps 8.6. **29–34:** A personal attack on his opponents, appealing to practice, experience, and generally accepted wisdom. **29:** It is not clear what was involved in the Corinthian practice of *baptism on behalf of the dead*. Paul appeals to the practice to suggest to the Corinthians that they have an implicit faith in the resurrection. **32:** Does Paul refer to a real fight *with wild animals* in the arena *at Ephesus*, or to a figurative struggle with adversaries? The quotation is from Isa 22.13. **33:** Paul cites a proverb from a play by the Greek comic writer Menander (third century BCE). **35–50: The nature of the resurrection body.** Through analogies, Paul seeks to make comprehensible that there can be types of *bodies* other than bodies of *flesh*. **36–38:** The first analogy is drawn from a *seed*; the same analogy is used in Jn 12.24. **39:** The second analogy references the different kinds of *flesh* of lower beings. **40–41:** The third analogy points to the difference between *heavenly bodies* and *earthly bodies*, and references the various types of *glory* among celestial bodies. **42–44:** By means of four antitheses, Paul contrasts the resurrected *body* with the present, mortal body. **45:** Gen. 2.7. **45–49:** *The first man . . . the man of dust* is Adam; the *last Adam . . . the second man . . . the man of heaven* is Christ; cf. 15.21–23n. **49:** Christians will be transformed in the resurrection: they will exchange the *image of the man of dust*, which they currently bear as descendants of Adam, for the *image of the man of heaven*, which they will receive through participation in Christ. **50:** Paul clarifies that a resurrection of *flesh and blood* is impossible. **51–57:** Paul discloses a *mystery*, a

will all be changed, [52] in a moment, in the twinkling of an eye, at the last trumpet. For the trumpet will sound, and the dead will be raised imperishable, and we will be changed. [53] For this perishable body must put on imperishability, and this mortal body must put on immortality. [54] When this perishable body puts on imperishability, and this mortal body puts on immortality, then the saying that is written will be fulfilled:

"Death has been swallowed up in victory."
[55] "Where, O death, is your victory?
    Where, O death, is your sting?"
[56] The sting of death is sin, and the power of sin is the law. [57] But thanks be to God, who gives us the victory through our Lord Jesus Christ.

[58] Therefore, my beloved,[a] be steadfast, immovable, always excelling in the work of the Lord, because you know that in the Lord your labor is not in vain.

16 Now concerning the collection for the saints: you should follow the directions I gave to the churches of Galatia. [2] On the first day of every week, each of you is to put aside and save whatever extra you earn, so that collections need not be taken when I come. [3] And when I arrive, I will send any whom you approve with letters to take your gift to Jerusalem. [4] If it seems advisable that I should go also, they will accompany me.

[5] I will visit you after passing through Macedonia—for I intend to pass through Macedonia— [6] and perhaps I will stay with you or even spend the winter, so that you may send me on my way, wherever I go. [7] I do not want to see you now just in passing, for I hope to spend some time with you, if the Lord permits. [8] But I will stay in Ephesus until Pentecost, [9] for a wide door for effective work has opened to me, and there are many adversaries.

[10] If Timothy comes, see that he has nothing to fear among you, for he is doing the work of the Lord just as I am; [11] therefore let no one despise him. Send him on his way in peace, so that he may come to me; for I am expecting him with the brothers.

[12] Now concerning our brother Apollos, I strongly urged him to visit you with the other brothers, but he was not at all willing[b] to come now. He will come when he has the opportunity.

[13] Keep alert, stand firm in your faith, be courageous, be strong. [14] Let all that you do be done in love.

[15] Now, brothers and sisters,[c] you know that members of the household of Stephanas were the first converts in Achaia, and they

a   Gk *beloved brothers*
b   Or *it was not at all God's will for him*
c   Gk *brothers*

lyrical account of the destiny of those who survive until the resurrection, a Pauline counterpart to the mythological hymn which concludes the philosophical proofs of the immortality of the soul. **52:** Cf. 1 Thess 4.16. **54:** Isa 25.7. **55:** Hos 13.14. **56:** A later gloss reflecting thorough acquaintance with Paul's mature theology; cf. Rom 5.12; 7.7–8,13. **58:** Concluding exhortation.

16.1–24: Advice on administrative and personal matters. 1–4: Paul gives instructions for the implementation of a charitable *collection* for the poor *saints* (believers) in Jerusalem. See further Gal 2.10; 2 Cor 8–9; Rom 15.25–29. **1:** The formula *now concerning* (see 7.1n.) indicates that a question about the collection had been raised in the Corinthians' letter to Paul. **4:** *If it seems advisable,* better "if it is considerable"—that is, the size of the collection: Paul will only take the collection to Jerusalem in person if the sum is worth the effort. **5–8:** Paul's account of his travel plans in this passage contrasts sharply with that in 4.18–19; cf. Acts 19.1, 21–22. **10–11:** Paul is doubtful whether Timothy (see 4.17n.) will be treated with respect by the Corinthians; thus Paul provides the strongest assurance: *he is doing the work of the Lord.* **12:** The formula *now concerning* (see 7.1n.) indicates that the Corinthians had asked about Apollos (see 1.12n.) in their letter to Paul. The eagerness of some in Corinth for Apollos's speedy return is illuminated by Acts 18.27–28. **13–14:** This concluding exhortation signals the end of the letter, after which the paragraph on Stephanas (vv. 15–18) makes a surprising new beginning. **15–18:** Appeal for *recognition* of *Stephanas.* On the *household of Stephanas,* see 1.16n. **15:** The direct address, *brothers* (*and sisters*), communicates a sense of urgency. Why should Paul need to appeal for recognition of *the first converts in Achaia* (the principal Roman province of southern Greece)? Evidently Paul assumed that the congregation, or some of its members, had no strong inclination to grant it. The phrase *devoted themselves to the service of the*

have devoted themselves to the service of the saints; [16] I urge you to put yourselves at the service of such people, and of everyone who works and toils with them. [17] I rejoice at the coming of Stephanas and Fortunatus and Achaicus, because they have made up for your absence; [18] for they refreshed my spirit as well as yours. So give recognition to such persons.

[19] The churches of Asia send greetings. Aquila and Prisca, together with the church in their house, greet you warmly in the Lord. [20] All the brothers and sisters[a] send greetings. Greet one another with a holy kiss.

[21] I, Paul, write this greeting with my own hand. [22] Let anyone be accursed who has no love for the Lord. Our Lord, come![b] [23] The grace of the Lord Jesus be with you. [24] My love be with all of you in Christ Jesus.[c]

[a] Gk *brothers*
[b] Gk *Marana tha*. These Aramaic words can also be read *Maran atha*, meaning *Our Lord has come*
[c] Other ancient authorities add *Amen*

saints (i.e., the believers) employs some of the same vocabulary used by Paul in describing the charitable collection in 16.1; 2 Cor 8.4; 9.1. **17:** *Fortunatus* ("Lucky") and *Achaicus* ("the Achaian") are probably Stephanas's slaves or freedmen; their names indicate servile origins. **19:** On *Aquila* and *Prisca* in *Asia* (Minor), see Acts 18.2,18–21,26. **20:** The *holy kiss* was a form of early Christian greeting; cf. 1 Thess 5.26; Rom 16.16; 1 Pet 5.14. **21:** Up to this point Paul had been dictating the letter; now he adds a few words in his *own hand.* **22:** *Our Lord, come!* An early Christian prayer, in Aramaic, expressing hope in an imminent Second Coming of Christ; cf. Rev 22.20.

THE SECOND LETTER OF PAUL TO THE CORINTHIANS

NAME, AUTHORSHIP, HISTORICAL CONTEXT

See the Introduction to 1 Corinthians.

LITERARY HISTORY

Second Corinthians switches topics and tone rapidly. After a conciliatory passage and before finishing his travelogue (2.5–13), Paul shifts into a self-defense (2.14–5.21) based on an exegetical discussion of Moses' veil in Exodus 34 (3.1–18) and ending in an anxious appeal for reconciliation (6.1–13; 7.2–4 [6.14–7.1 appears to be parenthetical]). Thereupon the travelogue resumes, picking up where it left off at 2.13, and Paul again sounds a conciliatory tone by expressing his complete confidence in the Corinthians (7.5–16). Two chapters (8 and 9) follow on the collection for the poor of Jerusalem that may well be separate solicitation letters. A highly charged polemical section, dripping with sarcasm and irony (10.1–13.10), concludes the letter. These considerations have convinced many scholars that 2 Corinthians is a composite of different letters, even if their precise extent and relative chronology are uncertain (see notes on 2.13; 6.14–7.1; 8.1–9.15; 10.1–18).

Nevertheless, because some motifs occur throughout the letter, some scholars do not subscribe to a partition theory. The relationship between affliction and consolation, for example, first raised in 1.3–11, is the backbone of the arguments in 4.7–10; 4.16–5.10; and 12.7–10. The twin themes of boasting and confidence intimated in 1.12–14 feature prominently in 3.4–18; 8.1–7,24; 9.1–5; and all of chs 10–13. The paradox of power in weakness informs the whole letter: Weakness, not extravagant power, authenticates true ministry, so much so that Paul would allow himself to boast only of his afflictions and sufferings (4.7–5.10; 11.23b–33; 12.1–10). Even if 2 Corinthians is a composite, the different letters were composed within a brief period to deal with specific controversial issues.

CONTENTS AND INTERPRETATION

Paul has a running dispute with the Corinthians over money. He rejects the congregation's patronage by refusing remuneration (1 Cor 9; 2 Cor 11.7,9; 12.16), but he is willing to accept gifts from their rivals in Macedonia (2 Cor 11.8–9; Phil 4.15–18). When he asks the Corinthians to contribute to the collection for Jerusalem (see notes on 8.1–9.15), a project Paul accepted at the Jerusalem meeting (Gal 2.10) and subsequently took to Galatia and Corinth (1 Cor 16.1–4), he and his companion are accused of being "crafty" and "deceitful" (2 Cor 12.16–18).

The arrival of outside missionaries (10.13–15; 11.4) makes a bad situation worse. These opponents of Paul, derisively called "super-apostles" (11.5; 12.11), "false apostles" (11.13), even "Satan's ministers" (11.15), boast of their Jewish credentials (11.22), their spiritual prowess manifested in ecstasies and visions (12.1) and in performing miracles (12.12), weighty recommendation (3.1; 5.12), and elegant speech (11.6). They also appear willing to accept Corinthian patronage (2.17). All of these qualities are perceived to be lacking in Paul (10.1–2,10).

Sensing he is on the verge of losing control of the congregation, Paul visits Corinth a second time, with disastrous results. A member of the congregation grievously offends him (2.5–6), and he departs from Corinth deeply hurt. After this "painful visit" (2.1; 7.2), Paul writes a "letter of tears" (2.4; 7.8), a letter that is either lost or partially preserved in chs 10–13. Despite or perhaps because of its severity, the letter succeeds in bringing the majority of the congregation back to Paul (7.6–7). Relieved at the resolution of the conflict, Paul resumes the collection and sends ahead of his third visit a delegation headed by Titus (8.6,16–24) with a solicitation letter (chs 8–9, which may also be a composite of two separate letters). In Rom 15.26, Paul writes, from Corinth, that he is about to embark on a journey to Jerusalem to deliver the collection from "Macedonia and Achaia." So he appears to have brought the project, finally, to a successful conclusion.

READING GUIDE

The letter is best read straight through, but one can note at various points where shifts in tone or subject occur, and therefore where different letters may have been joined together.

Sze-kar Wan

1 Paul, an apostle of Christ Jesus by the will of God, and Timothy our brother,

To the church of God that is in Corinth, including all the saints throughout Achaia:

² Grace to you and peace from God our Father and the Lord Jesus Christ.

³ Blessed be the God and Father of our Lord Jesus Christ, the Father of mercies and the God of all consolation, ⁴ who consoles us in all our affliction, so that we may be able to console those who are in any affliction with the consolation with which we ourselves are consoled by God. ⁵ For just as the sufferings of Christ are abundant for us, so also our consolation is abundant through Christ. ⁶ If we are being afflicted, it is for your consolation and salvation; if we are being consoled, it is for your consolation, which you experience when you patiently endure the same sufferings that we are also suffering. ⁷ Our hope for you is unshaken; for we know that as you share in our sufferings, so also you share in our consolation.

⁸ We do not want you to be unaware, brothers and sisters,ᵃ of the affliction we experienced in Asia; for we were so utterly, unbearably crushed that we despaired of life itself. ⁹ Indeed, we felt that we had received the sentence of death so that we would rely not on ourselves but on God who raises the dead. ¹⁰ He who rescued us from so deadly a peril will continue to rescue us; on him we have set our hope that he will rescue us again, ¹¹ as you also join in helping us by your prayers, so that many will give thanks on ourᵇ behalf for the blessing granted us through the prayers of many.

¹² Indeed, this is our boast, the testimony of our conscience: we have behaved in the world with franknessᶜ and godly sincerity, not by earthly wisdom but by the grace of God—and all the more toward you. ¹³ For we

---

ᵃ Gk *brothers*

ᵇ Other ancient authorities read *your*

ᶜ Other ancient authorities read *holiness*

1.1–2.13: Opening.

1.1–2: Salutation. A standard part of Paul's letters; see 1 Cor 1.1; Phil 1.1; Philem 1. **1:** An *apostle* was a special emissary, but Paul reminds the Corinthians that he was appointed *by* (lit., "through") *the will of God.* Cf. Rom 1.1; 1 Cor 1.1; Gal 1.1. For Paul's self-understanding of his call to be an apostle, see Gal 1.10–17 but also Rom 1.1–6; 1 Cor 9; 15.7–11. *Timothy,* along with Silvanus, was with Paul at the founding of the Corinthian congregation (v. 19; Acts 18.5) and acted as Paul's representative when troubles broke out (1 Cor 4.17; 16.10–11; cf. also Acts 19.22). Elsewhere Paul calls Timothy "my beloved child" (1 Cor 4.17), but here he calls him *brother,* a sign of respect. Elsewhere in 2 Cor the plural "churches" is used; the singular here, *the church of God,* is a collective designation of all the congregations in Corinth. *Saints* refers not to an elite group of believers but to followers of Christ set apart by God. *Achaia,* the Roman senatorial province of which *Corinth* was the capital. **2:** *Grace to you and peace from God . . . ,* a standard greeting found in all of Paul's letters except 1 Thess 1.1, where a short form is used.

1.3–7: Paul blesses God for rescuing him and consoling his afflictions. Not the standard thanksgiving that reinforces Paul's relationship with the recipients (e.g., Phil 1.3–11; 1 Thess 1.2–10), but a blessing in the Jewish liturgical tradition that emphasizes the attributes of God. Paul chooses the latter, partly because his relationship with the Corinthians is strained, and partly because he wants to introduce the themes of affliction and *consolation* that are repeated at key points in the letter (see Introduction). **3–4:** Calling God *Father of mercies* is common in Jewish worship; see Rom 12.1; Phil 2.1. *So that we may be able to console . . . ,* whatever Paul experienced is for the sake of the Corinthians. **5–7:** Paul invites the Corinthians to be partners in suffering by noting believers' identification with *the sufferings of Christ,* which *are abundant for us;* see 4.10–11; Phil 3.10–11.

1.8–11: God delivers Paul. In recounting God's deliverance, Paul stresses the Corinthians' participation in his ministry. **8:** *Asia,* a Roman senatorial province in modern-day western Turkey that included Ephesus. **9:** There is no consensus on what this ordeal was; possibilities include imprisonment (Phil 1.19–24) and the event behind "I fought with wild animals at Ephesus" (1 Cor 15.32).

1.12–2.13: Paul stresses his bond with the Corinthians. Paul recounts his past dealings with the Corinthians in hopes of cementing his relationship with them.

1.12–14: Paul claims his conduct is a basis of solidarity. 12: *Boast* or confidence is a prominent theme in Paul's letters (e.g., 1 Thess 2.19) but especially in the Corinthian correspondence; "sure" (2 Cor 1.15); "confidence" (3.4; 8.22); "boldness" (3.12; 10.2); "frankly" (6.11); "boasting" (9.2–3; 1 Cor 9.15). It is used here as a synonym of *con-*

write you nothing other than what you can read and also understand; I hope you will understand until the end— [14] as you have already understood us in part—that on the day of the Lord Jesus we are your boast even as you are our boast.

[15] Since I was sure of this, I wanted to come to you first, so that you might have a double favor;[a] [16] I wanted to visit you on my way to Macedonia, and to come back to you from Macedonia and have you send me on to Judea. [17] Was I vacillating when I wanted to do this? Do I make my plans according to ordinary human standards,[b] ready to say "Yes, yes" and "No, no" at the same time? [18] As surely as God is faithful, our word to you has not been "Yes and No." [19] For the Son of God, Jesus Christ, whom we proclaimed among you, Silvanus and Timothy and I, was not "Yes and No"; but in him it is always "Yes." [20] For in him every one of God's promises is a "Yes." For this reason it is through him that we say the "Amen," to the glory of God. [21] But it is God who establishes us with you in Christ and has anointed us, [22] by putting

his seal on us and giving us his Spirit in our hearts as a first installment.

[23] But I call on God as witness against me: it was to spare you that I did not come again to Corinth. [24] I do not mean to imply that we lord it over your faith; rather, we are workers with you for your joy, because you stand firm in the faith. 2 [1] So I made up my mind not to make you another painful visit. [2] For if I cause you pain, who is there to make me glad but the one whom I have pained? [3] And I wrote as I did, so that when I came, I might not suffer pain from those who should have made me rejoice; for I am confident about all of you, that my joy would be the joy of all of you. [4] For I wrote you out of much distress and anguish of heart and with many tears, not to cause you pain, but to let you know the abundant love that I have for you.

[5] But if anyone has caused pain, he has caused it not to me, but to some extent—not

a   Other ancient authorities read *pleasure*
b   Gk *according to the flesh*

science, the human capacity for self-judgment. **13**: *Until the end* can mean "completely," in contrast to "in part" in the next verse. **14**: *On the day of the Lord Jesus*, the Second Coming; see 1 Cor 5.5; Phil 1.6,10; 2.16. Because on that day Paul's sincerity and conscience will be proven blameless (cf. 1 Cor 1.8), that is his basis for boasting.

1.15–2.13: Paul remembers the Corinthians as he travels to Macedonia. Paul often shares his travel plans to stress his relationship with a congregation in spite of his absence (e.g., 1 Thess 2.17–3.3). Here he also responds to misunderstandings caused by his canceled visit. **1.15**: *Double favor* (lit., "double grace") likely refers to the two visits Paul would have made to Corinth on his way to Macedonia and by way of return, which he recounts in the next verse. **16**: *Macedonia*, a Roman province in northern Greece, which included the cities of Philippi and Thessalonica. *Send me on*, Gk "propempein," a technical term for provisioning for a journey or mission (Rom 15.24; 1 Cor 16.6,11; cf. Acts 15.3; 20.38; 21.5; Titus 3.13; 3 Jn 6), including finance, escorts, letters of recommendation. *Judea*, not just southern Palestine but especially Jerusalem. The visit has to do with delivering the collection for the poor in Jerusalem; see 2 Cor 8.1–9.15n.; Rom 15.25–26. Paul's decision to accompany the collection is a slight change of plan from 1 Cor 16.3–4. **17**: *Vacillating*, lit., "trifling." Paul defends himself and his co-workers against the charge that they changed their minds frivolously and claims that his actions cannot be evaluated according to human standards. **18–19**: *"Yes and No,"* a sign of equivocating; see Mt 5.37; Jas 5.12. **19**: *Silvanus*, or Silas, a companion of Paul (see Acts 15.40–18.5; 1 Thess 1.1; 2 Thess 1.1) is mentioned here as cofounder of the Corinthian congregation with *Timothy*; see also 1.1n. **20**: *Amen*, a Hebrew word meaning "certainly" or "let it be so," used in response to someone's statement and in liturgical settings; see Deut 27.14–26; 1 Chr 16.36; Neh 5.13; 8.6; 1 Cor 14.16. **22**: The reception of the *Spirit* as *first installment* (the same Gk word is translated "guarantee" in 5.5) is proof that God's promises will be fulfilled (v. 20). **23**: *I did not come again* refers to the canceled double visit of vv. 15–16. **2.1**: Paul evidently made an unplanned *painful visit* to Corinth, his second, perhaps referred to in 13.2, during which some member of the congregation grievously offended him (see 2.5–11; 7.12). A third visit is anticipated in 12.14,21; 13.1. **3–4**: *I wrote as I did. . . . I wrote you . . . with many tears* (also v. 9), the "letter of tears," written shortly after the "painful visit"; see 7.8,12. The combination of *tears* and *joy* here recalls the twin themes of affliction and consolation in 1.3–11. This letter is either lost or portions of it are preserved in chs 10–13. See Introduction for sequence of events. **5–11**: The "letter of tears" was evidently well received. Paul pleads that

to exaggerate it—to all of you. [6] This punishment by the majority is enough for such a person; [7] so now instead you should forgive and console him, so that he may not be overwhelmed by excessive sorrow. [8] So I urge you to reaffirm your love for him. [9] I wrote for this reason: to test you and to know whether you are obedient in everything. [10] Anyone whom you forgive, I also forgive. What I have forgiven, if I have forgiven anything, has been for your sake in the presence of Christ. [11] And we do this so that we may not be outwitted by Satan; for we are not ignorant of his designs.

[12] When I came to Troas to proclaim the good news of Christ, a door was opened for me in the Lord; [13] but my mind could not rest because I did not find my brother Titus there. So I said farewell to them and went on to Macedonia.

[14] But thanks be to God, who in Christ always leads us in triumphal procession, and through us spreads in every place the fragrance that comes from knowing him. [15] For we are the aroma of Christ to God among those who are being saved and among those who are perishing; [16] to the one a fragrance from death to death, to the other a fragrance from life to life. Who is sufficient for these things? [17] For we are not peddlers of God's word like so many;[a] but in Christ we speak as persons of sincerity, as persons sent from God and standing in his presence.

3 Are we beginning to commend ourselves again? Surely we do not need, as some do, letters of recommendation to you or from you, do we? [2] You yourselves are our letter, written on our[b] hearts, to be known and read by all; [3] and you show that you are a letter of Christ, prepared by us, written not with ink but with the Spirit of the living God, not on tablets of stone but on tablets of human hearts.

[4] Such is the confidence that we have through Christ toward God. [5] Not that we are

---

a Other ancient authorities read *like the others*
b Other ancient authorities read *your*

---

the offender be forgiven now that the whole congregation has meted out appropriate punishment (v. 6). **6:** The identity of *such a person* has never been established; see also 7.12. **11:** *Satan,* Heb "accuser"; see also 11.14; 12.7. Elsewhere in 2 Cor this evil figure is called "the god of this world" (4.4), "Beliar" (6.15), and "serpent" (11.3). **12:** *Troas,* a Roman colony in northwest modern Turkey, a short trip by sea to Philippi; see Acts 16.8–11. **13:** *Titus,* a co-worker like Timothy and Silvanus, was likely the carrier of the "letter of tears" mentioned in 2.3–4; 7.8. With Paul's anxious wait for Titus, the narrative drops off and does not resume until 7.5; see Introduction.

2.14–7.4: Real character of Paul's ministry.

2.14–4.6: The ministry of glory. God is the author of Paul's ministry of glory.

2.14–17: God equips competent ministers. 14: The image of *triumphal procession* is of God the victor leading Paul as captive in a Roman procession. *Fragrance,* and "aroma" (v. 15), could allude to the execution of prisoners at end of the procession, thus combining Roman customs with sacrificial language from the Hebrew Bible (e.g., Lev 1.9). It could also allude to the presence of divine wisdom (Sir 24.15). **15–16:** *Saved . . . perishing* describes the different effects Paul's preaching of the gospel has on his hearers. *Sufficient,* or competent. The rhetorical question suggests that only God can equip competent ministers; see 3.5–6. **17:** Paul disdainfully calls his opponents *peddlers of God's word,* probably alluding to their acceptance and Paul's refusal of financial support from the Corinthians; see 11.8–9n. *Sincerity* anticipates the charges of falsehood and cunning (see 4.2).

3.1–4.6: Ministers of the new covenant of Spirit. 1: *Letters of recommendation,* conventional introductions for itinerant missionaries to the writer's friends and wider circles; see Acts 18.27. Romans 16 is one such letter of recommendation for Phoebe in her travel to Rome. Paul's lack of such letters is seen as a weakness; see also 5.12. **2–3:** Paul reminds the Corinthians that because he founded the congregation, it serves as his *letter of Christ* that documents his qualifications. Mention of *Spirit* recalls the Corinthians' conversion experience; see Gal 3.2–3. *Tablets of stone . . . tablets of human hearts* contrasts the Ten Commandments (Ex 20.1–17; 24.12; 31.18; 34.1) with the "new covenant" of Jer 31.31–33; see also Ezek 36.26–27, where "heart of stone" is explicitly contrasted with "heart of flesh" and the spirit of God will be poured into the people. **4:** *Confidence,* see v. 12 and 1.12–14n. **5–6:** *Competence,* see 2.15–16n. In these two verses the adjective, noun, and verb forms of Gk "hikanos" are used to indicate that it is God who equipped *us* for the task of serving the *new covenant;* see 3.2–3n. *Spirit,* the Holy Spirit, recalls v. 3 and anticipates vv. 17–18. In Paul's binary thinking, since *the Spirit gives life,* i.e., raises to

competent of ourselves to claim anything as coming from us; our competence is from God, ⁶who has made us competent to be ministers of a new covenant, not of letter but of spirit; for the letter kills, but the Spirit gives life.

⁷Now if the ministry of death, chiseled in letters on stone tablets,ᵃ came in glory so that the people of Israel could not gaze at Moses' face because of the glory of his face, a glory now set aside, ⁸how much more will the ministry of the Spirit come in glory? ⁹For if there was glory in the ministry of condemnation, much more does the ministry of justification abound in glory! ¹⁰Indeed, what once had glory has lost its glory because of the greater glory; ¹¹for if what was set aside came through glory, much more has the permanent come in glory!

¹²Since, then, we have such a hope, we act with great boldness, ¹³not like Moses, who put a veil over his face to keep the people of Israel from gazing at the end of the glory thatᵇ was being set aside. ¹⁴But their minds were hardened. Indeed, to this very day, when they hear the reading of the old covenant, that same veil is still there, since only in Christ is it set aside. ¹⁵Indeed, to this very day whenever Moses is read, a veil lies over their minds; ¹⁶but when one turns to the Lord, the veil is removed.

¹⁷Now the Lord is the Spirit, and where the Spirit of the Lord is, there is freedom. ¹⁸And all of us, with unveiled faces, seeing the glory of the Lord as though reflected in a mirror, are being transformed into the same image from one degree of glory to another; for this comes from the Lord, the Spirit.

4 Therefore, since it is by God's mercy that we are engaged in this ministry, we do not lose heart. ²We have renounced the shameful things that one hides; we refuse to practice cunning or to falsify God's word; but by the open statement of the truth we commend ourselves to the conscience of everyone in the sight of God. ³And even if our gospel is veiled, it is veiled to those who are perishing. ⁴In their case the god of this world has blinded the minds of the unbelievers, to keep them from seeing the light of the gospel of the glory of Christ, who is the image of God. ⁵For we do not proclaim ourselves; we proclaim Jesus Christ as Lord and ourselves as your slaves for Jesus' sake. ⁶For it is the God who said, "Let light shine out of darkness," who has shone in our hearts to give the light of the knowledge of the glory of God in the face of Jesus Christ.

ᵃ Gk on stones
ᵇ Gk of what

resurrected life from death (Rom 4.17; 8.11; 1 Cor 15.22,36,45; Gal 3.21; cf. also Jn 5.21; 6.63; 1 Pet 3.18), its opposite, *the letter*, i.e., the written code, must mean death. The letter/Spirit contrast in this context does not mean literal versus inner meaning. *New covenant, not of letter but of spirit*, refers to two competing interpretations of Jeremiah's "new covenant." **7–11:** The controlling imagery is Moses' changed countenance in Ex 34.29–35, which Paul interprets using a rabbinic method of argumentation, from the lesser to the greater. **7:** *Ministry of death*, the fading glory of the old covenant. **12:** *Boldness* connotes fearlessness of appearing before God in the end time; see v. 4 and 1.12–14n. **13:** Paul interprets the *veil* of Moses as covering up the transitory nature of the *glory that was being set aside*, lit., "abolished." **14–15:** The *veil* becomes a metaphor for lack of enlightenment. *Old covenant* refers not to the Hebrew Bible in general but to the Sinai covenant (Ex 24.7) or to the law (2 Chr 34.30), i.e., the written code as such. **15:** *Moses* here refers to the Torah, the law or teaching of Moses that forms the first part of the Jewish scriptures, the first five books of the Bible; see 2 Chr 25.4; Mk 12.26; Acts 15.21. **16:** Paul modifies Ex 34.34 by removing "Moses" and changing "removed" to "is removed," resulting in *the Lord* removing *the veil*, with contrast to the veiled "minds" in vv. 14–15. **17:** Paul hastens to add that "the Lord" of the biblical text refers to *the Spirit*, which guarantees freedom. **18:** *Glory of the Lord* parallels *the Lord, the Spirit* (also vv. 16–17). *Being transformed* refers to a fundamental change in those who remove their veils. *Image*, see Rom 8.29; 1 Cor 15.49; Col 3.10. *From one degree of glory to another* reflects belief in the Greco-Roman world that an encounter with the divine transforms the beholder into its image.

4.1–6: Climax of Paul's self-defense. Paul returns to the question of competence first raised in 2.16. **2–3:** Answers to charges; see 2.17. *Cunning*, see 11.3; 12.16 "crafty." *Conscience*, see 1.12n. **4:** *This world*, see 1 Cor 3.19; 5.10; 7.31 (twice), a synonym in Paul for "the present age" (Gal 1.4) and "the present time" (Rom 3.26; 8.18; 11.5). *God of this world*, see "rulers of this age" (1 Cor 2.6,8; Eph 2.2) and 2.11n. **6:** A paraphrase of Gen 1.3; Ps 112.4; Isa 9.2.

⁷But we have this treasure in clay jars, so that it may be made clear that this extraordinary power belongs to God and does not come from us. ⁸We are afflicted in every way, but not crushed; perplexed, but not driven to despair; ⁹persecuted, but not forsaken; struck down, but not destroyed; ¹⁰always carrying in the body the death of Jesus, so that the life of Jesus may also be made visible in our bodies. ¹¹For while we live, we are always being given up to death for Jesus' sake, so that the life of Jesus may be made visible in our mortal flesh. ¹²So death is at work in us, but life in you.

¹³But just as we have the same spirit of faith that is in accordance with scripture—"I believed, and so I spoke"—we also believe, and so we speak, ¹⁴because we know that the one who raised the Lord Jesus will raise us also with Jesus, and will bring us with you into his presence. ¹⁵Yes, everything is for your sake, so that grace, as it extends to more and more people, may increase thanksgiving, to the glory of God.

¹⁶So we do not lose heart. Even though our outer nature is wasting away, our inner nature is being renewed day by day. ¹⁷For this slight momentary affliction is preparing us for an eternal weight of glory beyond all measure, ¹⁸because we look not at what can be seen but at what cannot be seen; for what can be seen is temporary, but what cannot be seen is eternal.

5 For we know that if the earthly tent we live in is destroyed, we have a building from God, a house not made with hands, eternal in the heavens. ²For in this tent we groan, longing to be clothed with our heavenly dwelling— ³if indeed, when we have taken it off[a] we will not be found naked. ⁴For while we are still in this tent, we groan under our burden, because we wish not to be unclothed but to be further clothed, so that what is mortal may be swallowed up by life. ⁵He who has prepared us for this very thing is God, who has given us the Spirit as a guarantee.

⁶So we are always confident; even though we know that while we are at home in the body we are away from the Lord— ⁷for we walk by faith, not by sight. ⁸Yes, we do have confidence, and we would rather be away from the body and at home with the Lord. ⁹So whether we are at home or away, we make it our aim to please him. ¹⁰For all of us must appear before the judgment seat of Christ, so that each may receive recompense for what has been done in the body, whether good or evil.

¹¹Therefore, knowing the fear of the Lord, we try to persuade others; but we ourselves are well known to God, and I hope that we are also well known to your consciences. ¹²We are not commending ourselves to you again, but giving you an opportunity to boast about us, so that you may be able to answer those who boast in outward appearance and not in the heart. ¹³For if we are beside ourselves, it is for God; if we are

---

a   Other ancient authorities read *put it on*

4.7–5.10: Ministry of hardship. Affliction and consolation, first raised in 1.3–11, are elaborated: Weakness points to God's empowering presence. **4.7:** *Clay jars,* once broken, cannot be mended but must be thrown away. The contrast with *treasure* demonstrates God's power. **8–9:** Catalogue of hardships formulated as antithetical pairs to show the incomparable power of God's glory. See also 6.4–10; 11.23–27; 12.10; Rom 8.35,38–39; 1 Cor 4.11–13; Phil 4.12. The Stoics used catalogues of hardship to demonstrate their indifference to adversity, but for Paul adversity demonstrates the unworthiness of the vessels and the overcoming of adversity documents the power of God. **10–11:** *Carrying . . . the death of Jesus,* the death of Jesus is replicated in Paul's bodily sufferings, with the result that *the life of Jesus may also be made visible;* cf. Gal 2.20. **13:** Ps 116.10. **4.16–5.10:** Paul uses the dualistic language current in Hellenistic thought to express the tension between present afflictions and ongoing renewal. **4.16:** *Lose heart,* see v. 1. The *outer nature* that is *wasting away* is the part that undergoes sufferings and hardships (vv. 8–9) and carries the death of Jesus (vv. 10–11). The *inner nature* is the part that *is being renewed* daily; cf. Rom 12.2. **18:** *Temporary* and *eternal* represent not consecutive but overlapping eras. **5.1:** Paul continues the temporary/permanent contrast with one between *earthly tent,* a reference to the body (see Wis 9.15), and *building from God,* which is *eternal in the heavens.* **5:** *Guarantee,* see 1.22n. **6–8:** *While . . . in the body we are away from the Lord,* see Phil 1.21,23; the body is a barrier to being with Christ more perfectly. **10:** See Rom 14.10.

5.11–6.10: Ministry of reconciliation. 5.11–13: Paul recalls his relationship to the Corinthians. **11:** *Consciences,* see 1.12n.; 4.2. **12:** *Commending,* see 3.1n. *Boast,* see 1.12n. and 3.12n. *Those who boast in outward appearance*

in our right mind, it is for you. [14] For the love of Christ urges us on, because we are convinced that one has died for all; therefore all have died. [15] And he died for all, so that those who live might live no longer for themselves, but for him who died and was raised for them.

[16] From now on, therefore, we regard no one from a human point of view;[a] even though we once knew Christ from a human point of view,[a] we know him no longer in that way. [17] So if anyone is in Christ, there is a new creation: everything old has passed away; see, everything has become new! [18] All this is from God, who reconciled us to himself through Christ, and has given us the ministry of reconciliation; [19] that is, in Christ God was reconciling the world to himself,[b] not counting their trespasses against them, and entrusting the message of reconciliation to us. [20] So we are ambassadors for Christ, since God is making his appeal through us; we entreat you on behalf of Christ, be reconciled to God. [21] For our sake he made him to be sin who knew no sin, so that in him we might become the righteousness of God.

6 As we work together with him,[c] we urge you also not to accept the grace of God in vain. [2] For he says,

"At an acceptable time I have listened to you,

and on a day of salvation I have helped you."

See, now is the acceptable time; see, now is the day of salvation! [3] We are putting no obstacle in anyone's way, so that no fault may be found with our ministry, [4] but as servants of God we have commended ourselves in every way: through great endurance, in afflictions, hardships, calamities, [5] beatings, imprisonments, riots, labors, sleepless nights, hunger; [6] by purity, knowledge, patience, kindness, holiness of spirit, genuine love, [7] truthful speech, and the power of God; with the weapons of righteousness for the right hand and for the left; [8] in honor and dishonor, in ill repute and good repute. We are treated as impostors, and yet are true; [9] as unknown, and yet are well known; as dying, and see—we are alive; as punished, and yet not killed; [10] as sorrowful, yet always rejoicing; as poor, yet making many rich; as having nothing, and yet possessing everything.

[11] We have spoken frankly to you Corinthians; our heart is wide open to you. [12] There is no restriction in our affections, but only in

a   Gk *according to the flesh*
b   Or *God was in Christ reconciling the world to himself*
c   Gk *As we work together*

likely refers to Paul's opponents who could well be advocating circumcision; 11.5–6,12–15; 12.11. **13:** Paul's opponents may have derided Paul for an apparent lack of ecstatic experiences (12.1,12), to which Paul answers by distinguishing between being *beside ourselves*, lit., "we are ecstatic," and being *in our right mind*. The former has to do with God; the latter has to do with his ministry with the Corinthians; cf. 1 Cor 14.2–5,18–19,27–28. **14–15:** *Love of Christ*, Christ's love for us. *Those who live . . . was raised*, Christ's death enlivens all who by right should be dead, so that they owe their lives to him; Gal 2.19–20; Rom 7.4; 14.7–9. **17:** The reality of *anyone* being *in Christ* documents the onset of the *new creation*, the eschatological cosmic reversal of the primordial fall. The *old* way of looking from a human point of view *has passed away* and is no longer valid. For new creation, see Gal 6.15; but also Eph 2.15; 2 Pet 3.13; Rev 21.1; cf. Rom 8.19–21. For background, see Isa 43.18–19; 65.17; 66.22. **18–19:** As a result of Christ's undoing the damage caused by the primordial rebellion, *trespasses* are canceled (see Rom 4.8) and human beings are *reconciled* to God; Rom 5.10–11; Col 1.20. **21:** *Made him to be sin*, a difficult phrase that may refer to Christ's identification with humanity. The saints can be so embraced by God's reconciliation that *we might become the righteousness of God*; see Rom 1.17; 3.5,21–22,25–26; 10.3 (twice); Phil 3.9; also Mt 6.33; Jas 1.20; 2 Pet 1.1.

6.1–10: Summary of defense. 2: Isa 49.8. **4–5:** Catalogue of hardships; see 4.8–9n. **6–7:** Catalogue of virtues; see Gal 5.22–23; Phil 4.8. **8–10:** These seven contrasting pairs, *impostors, and yet are true . . . having nothing, and yet possessing everything*, are not paradoxes to show the imperturbability of an ideal sage (as in Stoic philosophy), but antitheses answering charges against Paul. This is a summary of his self-defense that began in 2.14. From a human point of view (5.16), Paul and his co-workers might be accused of being *impostors, unknown*, etc., but in the context of the new creation (5.17), they are really *true, known*, etc.

yours. ¹³ In return—I speak as to children—open wide your hearts also.

¹⁴ Do not be mismatched with unbelievers. For what partnership is there between righteousness and lawlessness? Or what fellowship is there between light and darkness? ¹⁵ What agreement does Christ have with Beliar? Or what does a believer share with an unbeliever? ¹⁶ What agreement has the temple of God with idols? For we[a] are the temple of the living God; as God said,

"I will live in them and walk among them,
    and I will be their God,
    and they shall be my people.
¹⁷ Therefore come out from them,
    and be separate from them, says the
        Lord,
and touch nothing unclean;
    then I will welcome you,
¹⁸ and I will be your father,
    and you shall be my sons and
        daughters,
says the Lord Almighty."

7 Since we have these promises, beloved, let us cleanse ourselves from every defilement of body and of spirit, making holiness perfect in the fear of God.

² Make room in your hearts[b] for us; we have wronged no one, we have corrupted no one, we have taken advantage of no one. ³ I do not say this to condemn you, for I said before that you are in our hearts, to die together and to live together. ⁴ I often boast about you; I have great pride in you; I am filled with consolation; I am overjoyed in all our affliction.

⁵ For even when we came into Macedonia, our bodies had no rest, but we were afflicted in every way—disputes without and fears within. ⁶ But God, who consoles the downcast, consoled us by the arrival of Titus, ⁷ and not only by his coming, but also by the consolation with which he was consoled about you, as he told us of your longing, your mourning, your zeal for me, so that I rejoiced still more. ⁸ For even if I made you sorry with my letter, I do not regret it (though I did regret it, for I see that I grieved you with that letter, though only briefly). ⁹ Now I rejoice, not because you were grieved, but because your grief led to repentance; for you felt a godly grief, so that you were not harmed in any way by us. ¹⁰ For godly grief produces a repentance that leads to salvation and brings no regret, but worldly grief produces death. ¹¹ For see what earnestness this godly grief has produced in you, what eagerness to clear yourselves, what indignation, what alarm, what longing, what zeal, what punishment! At every point you have proved yourselves guiltless in the matter. ¹² So although I wrote to you, it was not on account of the one who did the wrong, nor on account of the one who

---

a Other ancient authorities read *you*
b Gk lacks *in your hearts*

6.11–7.4: Final appeal to the Corinthians. 6.11–13: *Frankly,* see 1.12n. **6.14–7.1:** An abrupt interruption of Paul's appeal in the present context, since 7.2–4 more naturally follows 6.11–13. This passage contains many words used nowhere else by Paul; the stark dualism is also uncharacteristic of him. **14:** *Mismatched,* lit., "misyoked," used only here in the New Testament; see Lev 19.19. *Partnership* (used only here in the New Testament), *fellowship,* and "share" (v. 15) are synonyms meaning "association" in general. *Righteousness and lawlessness,* see Rom 6.19, where the second word is translated "iniquity." *Light and darkness* (see Rom 2.19; 13.12; 1 Cor 4.5; 1 Thess 5.4–5) also undergirds the imagery of 4.3–6, where the same contrast between "believers" and *unbelievers* (v. 15) is also found. **15:** *Beliar,* another name for Satan; see 2.11n. **16a:** *Temple of the living God,* see 1 Cor 3.16. **16b–18:** A chain of citations from Lev 26.12; Ezek 37.27; Isa 52.11; 2 Sam 7.14; Isa 43.6 to show separation from defilement. **7.1:** *Defilement,* used only here in the New Testament. *Body* and *spirit* are not set in opposition here; contrast Gal 5.16–26. *Fear of God,* see 5.11. **7.2–4:** Resumption of appeal in 6.11–13. **3:** *Die . . . live,* Paul reverses the traditional declaration of friendship, "live . . . die," to emphasize his bond with the Corinthians through identification with Christ's death and life. **4:** *Boast,* see 1.12–14n. and 3.12n. *Consolation . . . affliction,* see 1.3–7n. All three themes are introduced in 1.3–14.

7.5–16: Resumption of travelogue (2.12–13). "Afflicted" (v. 5), "consoles" (vv. 6,7,13), "boasting" (v. 14 twice), "confidence" (v. 16), introduced in 1.3–14, are recapitulated throughout this passage; see notes there, and also 7.4n. **6–8:** *Titus* (see 2.13n.) brought news that Paul's *letter* (see 2.3–4n.) had been received favorably; see 2.5–11.

was wronged, but in order that your zeal for us might be made known to you before God. [13] In this we find comfort.

In addition to our own consolation, we rejoiced still more at the joy of Titus, because his mind has been set at rest by all of you. [14] For if I have been somewhat boastful about you to him, I was not disgraced; but just as everything we said to you was true, so our boasting to Titus has proved true as well. [15] And his heart goes out all the more to you, as he remembers the obedience of all of you, and how you welcomed him with fear and trembling. [16] I rejoice, because I have complete confidence in you.

8 We want you to know, brothers and sisters,[a] about the grace of God that has been granted to the churches of Macedonia; [2] for during a severe ordeal of affliction, their abundant joy and their extreme poverty have overflowed in a wealth of generosity on their part. [3] For, as I can testify, they voluntarily gave according to their means, and even beyond their means, [4] begging us earnestly for the privilege[b] of sharing in this ministry to the saints— [5] and this, not merely as we expected; they gave themselves first to the Lord and, by the will of God, to us, [6] so that we might urge Titus that, as he had already made a beginning, so he should also complete this generous undertaking[c] among you. [7] Now as you excel in everything—in faith, in

speech, in knowledge, in utmost eagerness, and in our love for you[d]—so we want you to excel also in this generous undertaking.[c]

[8] I do not say this as a command, but I am testing the genuineness of your love against the earnestness of others. [9] For you know the generous act[e] of our Lord Jesus Christ, that though he was rich, yet for your sakes he became poor, so that by his poverty you might become rich. [10] And in this matter I am giving my advice: it is appropriate for you who began last year not only to do something but even to desire to do something— [11] now finish doing it, so that your eagerness may be matched by completing it according to your means. [12] For if the eagerness is there, the gift is acceptable according to what one has—not according to what one does not have. [13] I do not mean that there should be relief for others and pressure on you, but it is a question of a fair balance between [14] your present abundance and their need, so that their abundance may be for your need, in order that there may be a fair balance. [15] As it is written,

"The one who had much did not have too much,

a Gk brothers
b Gk grace
c Gk this grace
d Other ancient authorities read your love for us
e Gk the grace

12: *The one who did the wrong*, the offender mentioned in 2.6. *The one who was wronged*, Paul himself. 16: *Confidence* concludes the narrative of vv. 5–16 and anticipates the appeal for the collection in chs 8–9.

8.1–9.15: The collection for the Jerusalem church was meant not only to bring relief to its economic plight but also to show unity between it and the often well-to-do, urban, largely Gentile congregations in the Diaspora; see Gal 2.10; 1 Cor 16.1–4; Rom 15.25–27. Chapters 8 and 9 are probably two separate letters to two different regions in Achaia; see 9.2n.

8.1–24: Letter of appeal to the Corinthians for the collection. 1–7: The Macedonian churches as an example of generosity. 1: *Grace* (Gk "charis"), used ten times in chs 8–9 to describe the collection, translated in 8.4 as "privilege"; in 8.6,7,19 as "generous undertaking"; in 8.9 as "generous act"; in 8.16 as "thanks"; in 9.8 as "blessing"; in 9.15 as "thanks." Other words used in this connection: Gk "eulogia," "bountiful gift" and "voluntary gift" (9.5); "bountifully" (9.6 twice); "ministry" (Gk "leitourgia"), 9.12; "sharing" (Gk "koinonia"), 8.4; 9.13. This attests to the rich theological significance Paul attaches to the collection. *Macedonia*, see 1.16n. Paul principally has the Philippian and Thessalonian churches in mind, but see 9.2. 2: *Severe ordeal*, possibly the same event as in Phil 1.29–30. 4: *Sharing* (Gk "koinonia"), used here to describe the collection (as also in 9.13 and Rom 15.26), also refers to participation in the Eucharist (1 Cor 10.16) and in Christ's suffering (Phil 3.10); see 8.1n. *Saints*, here and in 9.1,12, refers to the Jerusalem believers. 6: *Titus*, see 2.13n.; 8.16–24. 8–15: There should be a *fair balance* between those who have more and those who have less. 9: A close parallel of *though he was rich, . . . he became poor* is 5.21, "He made him into sin who knew no sin . . ."; see also Phil 2.6–8. 15: "*The one . . . too little,*" Ex 16.18.

and the one who had little did not have too little."

[16] But thanks be to God who put in the heart of Titus the same eagerness for you that I myself have. [17] For he not only accepted our appeal, but since he is more eager than ever, he is going to you of his own accord. [18] With him we are sending the brother who is famous among all the churches for his proclaiming the good news;[a] [19] and not only that, but he has also been appointed by the churches to travel with us while we are administering this generous undertaking[b] for the glory of the Lord himself[c] and to show our goodwill. [20] We intend that no one should blame us about this generous gift that we are administering, [21] for we intend to do what is right not only in the Lord's sight but also in the sight of others. [22] And with them we are sending our brother whom we have often tested and found eager in many matters, but who is now more eager than ever because of his great confidence in you. [23] As for Titus, he is my partner and co-worker in your service; as for our brothers, they are messengers[d] of the churches, the glory of Christ. [24] Therefore openly before the churches, show them the proof of your love and of our reason for boasting about you.

9 Now it is not necessary for me to write you about the ministry to the saints, [2] for I know your eagerness, which is the subject of my boasting about you to the people of Macedonia, saying that Achaia has been ready since last year; and your zeal has stirred up most of them. [3] But I am sending the brothers in order that our boasting about you may not prove to have been empty in this case, so that you may be ready, as I said you would be; [4] otherwise, if some Macedonians come with me and find that you are not ready, we would be humiliated—to say nothing of you—in this undertaking.[e] [5] So I thought it necessary to urge the brothers to go on ahead to you, and arrange in advance for this bountiful gift that you have promised, so that it may be ready as a voluntary gift and not as an extortion.

[6] The point is this: the one who sows sparingly will also reap sparingly, and the one who sows bountifully will also reap bountifully. [7] Each of you must give as you have made up your mind, not reluctantly or under compulsion, for God loves a cheerful giver. [8] And God is able to provide you with every blessing in abundance, so that by always having enough of everything, you may share abundantly in every good work. [9] As it is written,

"He scatters abroad, he gives to the poor;
his righteousness[f] endures forever."

[10] He who supplies seed to the sower and bread for food will supply and multiply your seed for sowing and increase the harvest of your righteousness.[f] [11] You will be enriched in every way for your great generosity, which will produce thanksgiving to God through us; [12] for the rendering of this ministry not only supplies the needs

a   Or *the gospel*
b   Gk *this grace*
c   Other ancient authorities lack *himself*
d   Gk *apostles*
e   Other ancient authorities add *of boasting*
f   Or *benevolence*

16–24: The sending of Titus and two unnamed *brothers* (vv. 18,22–23) might indicate that the collection is modeled after the Temple tax, which required an entourage representing major contributors for delivery.

9.1–15: A second letter of appeal for the collection. 1: Ch 9 starts the appeal afresh. **2:** *Macedonia*, compared to 8.1, now has to listen to Paul's boasting that *Achaia has been ready since last year.* The boasting might stand in contrast to the unfinished state of the Corinthian collection (8.10–11), which lends support to ch 9 being a separate letter, but in vv. 3–4 Paul is not sure that his boast will be substantiated. **3:** *Brothers,* also v. 5, are probably those mentioned in 8.18,22–23. **5:** *Bountiful gift* and *voluntary gift* both translate Gk "eulogia"; see 8.1n. **7:** *God loves a cheerful giver,* Prov 22.8. **8:** Abundance carries with it the responsibility of sharing. *Enough,* see 1 Tim 6.6 ("contentment"); cf. Phil 4.11, where a cognate word is translated "content." The word connotes the Hellenistic philosophical ideal of self-sufficiency transcending all shortcomings and hardships. In contrast, Paul states that God is the basis for such sufficiency. See 12.9n. **9:** Ps 112.9. **10:** *Seed, food,* Isa 55.10. *Harvest of your righteousness,* Hos 10.12. **11–12:** One possible motive for Paul's working tirelessly on the collection is the apocalyptic vision of Gentiles pouring into Jerusalem (Isa 60.4–7; 66.12,18–21; Mic 4.1–2), rendering overflowing *thanksgiving to God.*

of the saints but also overflows with many thanksgivings to God. ¹³ Through the testing of this ministry you glorify God by your obedience to the confession of the gospel of Christ and by the generosity of your sharing with them and with all others, ¹⁴ while they long for you and pray for you because of the surpassing grace of God that he has given you. ¹⁵ Thanks be to God for his indescribable gift!

10 I myself, Paul, appeal to you by the meekness and gentleness of Christ—I who am humble when face to face with you, but bold toward you when I am away!—²I ask that when I am present I need not show boldness by daring to oppose those who think we are acting according to human standards.ᵃ ³ Indeed, we live as human beings,ᵇ but we do not wage war according to human standards;ᵃ ⁴ for the weapons of our warfare are not merely human,ᶜ but they have divine power to destroy strongholds. We destroy arguments ⁵ and every proud obstacle raised up against the knowledge of God, and we take every thought captive to obey Christ. ⁶ We are ready to punish every disobedience when your obedience is complete.

⁷ Look at what is before your eyes. If you are confident that you belong to Christ, remind yourself of this, that just as you belong to Christ, so also do we. ⁸ Now, even if I boast a little too much of our authority, which the Lord gave for building you up and not for tearing you down, I will not be ashamed of it. ⁹ I do not want to seem as though I am trying to frighten you with my letters. ¹⁰ For they say, "His letters are weighty and strong, but his bodily presence is weak, and his speech contemptible." ¹¹ Let such people understand that what we say by letter when absent, we will also do when present.

¹² We do not dare to classify or compare ourselves with some of those who commend themselves. But when they measure themselves by one another, and compare themselves with one another, they do not show good sense. ¹³ We, however, will not boast beyond limits, but will keep within the field that God has assigned to us, to reach out even as far as you. ¹⁴ For we were not

ᵃ Gk *according to the flesh*
ᵇ Gk *in the flesh*
ᶜ Gk *fleshly*

10.1–13.13: Defense of apostolic authority.

10.1–18: Paul attacks his opponents. The ironic and polemical tone of chs 10–13 contrasts sharply with that of the preceding chapters. Paul no longer refers to his opponents obliquely (see 2.17n.; 5.12n.), but pointedly. For these reasons, many scholars think that chs 10–13 are part of another letter (see Introduction). 1–6: His opponents criticize Paul for lack of power, but Paul insists on demonstrating power through weakness; see 4.7–12n.; 11.30 (summarizing 11.21b–29); 12.9–10 (summarizing 12.1–8); 1 Cor 1.17–25. 1: *Meekness and gentleness of Christ*, the self-emptying state of Christ as depicted in 8.9; Phil 2.6–8. *I who am . . . when I am away*, alludes to the charge against him; see also v. 10. *Humble*, lit., "base" or "humiliated," see 11.7n. 2: *Those who think . . .*, opponents whom Paul addresses throughout the letter only in the third person; see 10.10–11,12; 11.5,12–15,22–23,26; 12.11. Paul appeals to the Corinthians directly and makes them choose between him and his opponents. 3–5: *Not merely human, but . . . divine power,* Paul admits that he and those like him live as *human beings,* but his *weapons* have superhuman power. *We destroy arguments,* the opponents are characterized as debaters; see also 1 Cor 1.19–20. *Wage war, destroy,* and *take . . . captive,* warfare imagery applied to the religious debate. 6: Paul hopes that the Corinthians' *obedience* may be *complete.* Paul's threat of "punishment" here is in marked contrast to his commendation of the Corinthians in 7.15 for obedience at the receipt of that letter, lending support to chs 10–13 belonging to a different letter. 7–11: Paul answers specific charges. 7: *Just as you belong to Christ, so also do we,* answers the opponents' boasting that they "belong to Christ." 8: *Boast,* Paul normally boasts of the Corinthians; see 1.12n., 3.12n., but here he boasts of himself, but only by claiming authority as their founder. The proper content of boasting is a bone of contention in chs 10–13. *Building you up . . . tearing you down,* cf. Jer 1.10; Eccl 3.3. 9–11: *Letters* answers direct charges by the opponents (v. 10) that his personal appearances and speech, unlike his *weighty* letter, are unimpressive. "*His speech contemptible,*" see 11.6. 12–18: The proper way to boast is within one's territory. 12: *We do not dare to classify or compare,* standard rhetorical device of calling attention to one's praiseworthy acts in comparison with persons of superiority. Paul denounces the practice here but

overstepping our limits when we reached you; we were the first to come all the way to you with the good news[a] of Christ. [15] We do not boast beyond limits, that is, in the labors of others; but our hope is that, as your faith increases, our sphere of action among you may be greatly enlarged, [16] so that we may proclaim the good news[a] in lands beyond you, without boasting of work already done in someone else's sphere of action. [17] "Let the one who boasts, boast in the Lord." [18] For it is not those who commend themselves that are approved, but those whom the Lord commends.

11 I wish you would bear with me in a little foolishness. Do bear with me! [2] I feel a divine jealousy for you, for I promised you in marriage to one husband, to present you as a chaste virgin to Christ. [3] But I am afraid that as the serpent deceived Eve by its cunning, your thoughts will be led astray from a sincere and pure[b] devotion to Christ. [4] For if someone comes and proclaims another Jesus than the one we proclaimed, or if you receive a different spirit from the one you received, or a different gospel from the one you accepted, you submit to it readily enough. [5] I think that I am not in the least inferior to these super-apostles. [6] I may be untrained in speech, but not in knowledge; certainly in every way and in all things we have made this evident to you.

[7] Did I commit a sin by humbling myself so that you might be exalted, because I proclaimed God's good news[c] to you free of charge? [8] I robbed other churches by accepting support from them in order to serve you. [9] And when I was with you and was in need, I did not burden anyone, for my needs were supplied by the friends[d] who came from Macedonia. So I refrained and will continue to refrain from burdening you in any way. [10] As the truth of Christ is in me, this boast of mine will not be silenced in the regions of Achaia. [11] And why? Because I do not love you? God knows I do!

[12] And what I do I will also continue to do, in order to deny an opportunity to those who want an opportunity to be recognized as our

a   Or *the gospel*
b   Other ancient authorities lack *and pure*
c   Gk *the gospel of God*
d   Gk *brothers*

parodies it later in his fool's speech; see 11.21b–12.10. **13–16:** *Field* (v. 13), lit., "(measure of) rule (Gk 'kanon')" (also vv. 15,16), probably refers to the proper jurisdiction, i.e., the Gentiles, assigned to Paul and Barnabas at the Jerusalem meeting (Gal 2.9). Paul reminds his Corinthian hearers that he founded the congregation legitimately, *without boasting of work already done in someone else's sphere of action* (v. 16, "kanon"). It is a polemic against the opponents whom Paul accuses of overstepping their bounds, going back on the Jerusalem agreement. *In lands beyond you,* indication that Paul had hoped to use Corinth as a base for further missionary work. If Rom 15.23–24,28 is any indication, a trip to Spain is in view. **17:** Jer 9.23–24, also cited in 1 Cor 1.31.

11.1–12.10: A fool's speech. Paul parodies his opponents' penchant for comparison right after criticizing them for doing the same (10.12).

11.1–15: Appeal to the Corinthians as a fool. 1: *Foolishness* (Gk "aphrosyne") is the opposite of "moderation" or "sober-mindedness" (Gk "sophrosyne"); see "madman" (Gk "paraphronon"), 11.23; 1 Cor 1–3 uses different words for "foolishness" (Gk "moria," "moros"), whose opposite is "wisdom" (Gk "sophia"). **2:** *I promised you in marriage,* Paul presents himself as father of the bride, that is, he is the founder of the Corinthian congregation; see 1.19. **3:** *Serpent,* Satan; see 2.11; 11.14; 1 Cor 7.5. *Deceived Eve,* Gen 3.13. In connection with "marriage" and "virginity" (v. 2), Paul is probably thinking of the Jewish tradition that Satan sexually seduced Eve (see *2 Enoch* 31.6). **4–5:** *Another Jesus, different spirit, different gospel,* reminiscent of language in Gal 1.6–9; see 10.13–16n. **6:** *Untrained in speech,* see 10.10. **7:** *Humbling myself,* lit., "debasing myself"; see also 12.21; Phil 4.12. The adjective is used in 10.1. Christ is said to be "debased" in Phil 2.8. Since Greco-Roman philosophers viewed craftsmen as debased, Paul's use of the word might refer to his continual activity as a craftsman (see 1 Cor 4.12; 1 Thess 2.9) to support himself. **9:** *I did not burden anyone,* see 12.13; 1 Cor 9 for Paul's refusal to accept support from the Corinthians; see 1 Thess 2.9; Phil 4.16,18, for Macedonian support. In the Roman world, accepting support was to place the recipient (client) under the immediate obligation of the benefactor (patron). By not accepting Corinthian support, Paul is refusing the Corinthians the status and authority of patronage; by accepting Macedonian support, Paul is seen as slighting the Corinthian congregation; and by pursuing the collection at

equals in what they boast about. [13] For such boasters are false apostles, deceitful workers, disguising themselves as apostles of Christ. [14] And no wonder! Even Satan disguises himself as an angel of light. [15] So it is not strange if his ministers also disguise themselves as ministers of righteousness. Their end will match their deeds.

[16] I repeat, let no one think that I am a fool; but if you do, then accept me as a fool, so that I too may boast a little. [17] What I am saying in regard to this boastful confidence, I am saying not with the Lord's authority, but as a fool; [18] since many boast according to human standards,[a] I will also boast. [19] For you gladly put up with fools, being wise yourselves! [20] For you put up with it when someone makes slaves of you, or preys upon you, or takes advantage of you, or puts on airs, or gives you a slap in the face. [21] To my shame, I must say, we were too weak for that!

But whatever anyone dares to boast of—I am speaking as a fool—I also dare to boast of that. [22] Are they Hebrews? So am I. Are they Israelites? So am I. Are they descendants of Abraham? So am I. [23] Are they ministers of Christ? I am talking like a madman—I am a better one; with far greater labors, far more imprisonments, with countless floggings, and often near death. [24] Five times I have received from the Jews the forty lashes minus one. [25] Three times I was beaten with rods. Once I received a stoning. Three times I was shipwrecked; for a night and a day I was adrift at sea; [26] on frequent journeys, in danger from rivers, danger from bandits, danger from my own people, danger from Gentiles, danger in the city, danger in the wilderness, danger at sea, danger from false brothers and sisters;[b] [27] in toil and hardship, through many a sleepless night, hungry and thirsty, often without food, cold and naked. [28] And, besides other things, I am under daily pressure because of my anxiety for all the churches. [29] Who is weak, and I am not weak? Who is made to stumble, and I am not indignant?

[30] If I must boast, I will boast of the things that show my weakness. [31] The God and Father of the Lord Jesus (blessed be he forever!) knows that I do not lie. [32] In Damascus, the governor[c] under King Aretas guarded the city of Damascus in order to[d] seize me, [33] but I was let down in a basket through a window in the wall,[e] and escaped from his hands.

12 It is necessary to boast; nothing is to be gained by it, but I will go on to visions and revelations of the Lord. [2] I know a person in Christ who fourteen years ago was caught up to the third heaven—whether in the body or out of the body I do not know; God knows. [3] And I know that such a person—whether in the body or out of the body I do not know;

a   Gk *according to the flesh*
b   Gk *brothers*
c   Gk *ethnarch*
d   Other ancient authorities read *and wanted to*
e   Gk *through the wall*

the same time, Paul could be accused of being unscrupulous; see 12.14–18n. **12–15:** Characterization of Paul's opponents. *Satan*, see 2.11n.

11.16–12.10: Paul compares himself to his opponents. 16–33: Paul lists his hardships as validation of his apostolic authenticity. **16:** *Fool*, see 11.1n. **17–18:** *Boast according to human standards*, a different type of boasting from that of 1.12–14 and much closer to the boasting of 10.8. **22:** *Hebrews . . . Israelites . . . descendants of Abraham*, suggests that they boast of their Jewish pedigree. Paul is proud of his Jewish heritage, ready to declare it unflinchingly whenever the situation calls for it; see Rom 9.4; 11.1; Gal 1.13; Phil 3.5. **23a:** *Madman*, see 11.1n. **23b–27:** Catalogue of hardships used ironically to show the extreme afflictions and weakness of Paul; see notes on 1.3–7; 4.8–9; 10.1. Little is known about details of these hardships. **24:** *Forty lashes minus one*, see Deut 25.3. **32–33:** See Acts 9.23–25. *Damascus*, site of Paul's first contact with the Jesus movement. *Aretas* IV ruled the Nabateans from 9 BCE until his death ca. 41 CE. The Nabateans took control of Damascus in 37 CE, soon after which Paul escaped from the city *in a basket*.

12.1–10: Paul relates an out-of-body experience, since his opponents have claimed such experiences as validation of their spiritual prowess; see 5.13n. **1:** *Visions and revelations*, extrasensory events that endow the seer with power and status; see v. 7; 1 Cor 9.1; 15.5–8; Gal 1.12; 2.1–2. **2–3:** *I know a person* (also v. 5), an oblique reference to himself, following the apocalyptic convention of anonymous authorship; see vv. 7–9. *Third heaven*,

God knows— [4] was caught up into Paradise and heard things that are not to be told, that no mortal is permitted to repeat. [5] On behalf of such a one I will boast, but on my own behalf I will not boast, except of my weaknesses. [6] But if I wish to boast, I will not be a fool, for I will be speaking the truth. But I refrain from it, so that no one may think better of me than what is seen in me or heard from me, [7] even considering the exceptional character of the revelations. Therefore, to keep[a] me from being too elated, a thorn was given me in the flesh, a messenger of Satan to torment me, to keep me from being too elated.[b] [8] Three times I appealed to the Lord about this, that it would leave me, [9] but he said to me, "My grace is sufficient for you, for power[c] is made perfect in weakness." So, I will boast all the more gladly of my weaknesses, so that the power of Christ may dwell in me. [10] Therefore I am content with weaknesses, insults, hardships, persecutions, and calamities for the sake of Christ; for whenever I am weak, then I am strong.

[11] I have been a fool! You forced me to it. Indeed you should have been the ones commending me, for I am not at all inferior to these super-apostles, even though I am nothing. [12] The signs of a true apostle were performed among you with utmost patience, signs and wonders and mighty works. [13] How have you been worse off than the other churches, except that I myself did not burden you? Forgive me this wrong!

[14] Here I am, ready to come to you this third time. And I will not be a burden, because I do not want what is yours but you; for children ought not to lay up for their parents, but parents for their children. [15] I will most gladly spend and be spent for you. If I love you more, am I to be loved less? [16] Let it be assumed that I did not burden you. Nevertheless (you say) since I was crafty, I took you in by deceit. [17] Did I take advantage of you through any of those whom I sent to you? [18] I urged Titus to go, and sent the brother with him. Titus did not take advantage of you, did he? Did we not conduct ourselves with the same spirit? Did we not take the same steps?

[19] Have you been thinking all along that we have been defending ourselves before you? We are speaking in Christ before God. Everything we do, beloved, is for the sake of building you up. [20] For I fear that when I come, I may find you not as I wish, and that you may find me not as you wish; I fear that there may perhaps be quarreling, jealousy, anger, selfishness, slander, gossip, conceit, and disorder. [21] I fear that when I come again, my God may humble me before you, and that I may have to mourn over many who previously sinned and have not repented of the impurity, sexual immorality, and licentiousness that they have practiced.

[a] Other ancient authorities read *To keep*
[b] Other ancient authorities lack *to keep me from being too elated*
[c] Other ancient authorities read *my power*

i.e., *Paradise* (v. 4), where according to mystical Judaism one is granted a vision of the blessed. *In the body or out of the body*, an ecstatic experience. **4:** *Not to be told*, esoteric knowledge not to be divulged to the uninitiated. **7:** Nature of the *thorn* is unknown. **9:** *Sufficient* (Gk "arkein"), a different word from that of 2.6,16; 3.5–6 and a cognate of "enough" of 9.8 (see note there). Unlike the Hellenistic ideal of sufficiency that transcends hardships regardless of one's circumstance (see 9.8), Paul accepts these hardships as real, because in their *weakness* they ironically manifest the *power* of God; see 10.1n. **10:** *Whenever I am weak, then I am strong*, Paul informs his hearers he is equally endowed with extravagant power, but he subordinates it to *weaknesses, insults, hardships, persecutions, and calamities*.

12.11–13: Conclusion of the fool's speech. **11:** *Super-apostles*, see 10.2n. *Commending*, see 3.1n. **12:** Paul is not above telling the Corinthians that he too has performed miracles. **13:** See 11.9n.

12.14–13.10: Paul prepares for a third visit. **12.14–18:** Paul answers charges that he has been enriching himself through the collection (chs 8–9). **14:** *Third* visit (also v. 21; 13.1), see 2.1n. for the "painful visit," Paul's second to Corinth. *I will not be a burden*, see 11.9n. *Parents*, for Paul as father to his converts, see 11.2. **16:** *(You say) . . . I took you in by deceit*, some Corinthians evidently accused Paul of skimming the collection funds. **18:** *Titus* was sent to oversee the collection in 8.6,16,23; see also 2.13n. *The brother* is the "brother" sent by Paul to accompany Titus in 8.22–23 and not the "brother" elected by the congregations in 8.18. **19–21:** Paul warns the Corinthians to repent before his third visit. **19:** *Building you up*, see 10.8; 13.10. **20–21:** Catalogue of vices, see Rom 1.29–31;

13 This is the third time I am coming to you. "Any charge must be sustained by the evidence of two or three witnesses." [2] I warned those who sinned previously and all the others, and I warn them now while absent, as I did when present on my second visit, that if I come again, I will not be lenient— [3] since you desire proof that Christ is speaking in me. He is not weak in dealing with you, but is powerful in you. [4] For he was crucified in weakness, but lives by the power of God. For we are weak in him,[a] but in dealing with you we will live with him by the power of God.

[5] Examine yourselves to see whether you are living in the faith. Test yourselves. Do you not realize that Jesus Christ is in you?—unless, indeed, you fail to meet the test! [6] I hope you will find out that we have not failed. [7] But we pray to God that you may not do anything wrong—not that we may appear to have met the test, but that you may do what is right, though we may seem to have failed. [8] For we cannot do anything against the truth, but only for the truth. [9] For we rejoice when we are weak and you are strong. This is what we pray for, that you may become perfect. [10] So I write these things while I am away from you, so that when I come, I may not have to be severe in using the authority that the Lord has given me for building up and not for tearing down.

[11] Finally, brothers and sisters,[b] farewell.[c] Put things in order, listen to my appeal,[d] agree with one another, live in peace; and the God of love and peace will be with you. [12] Greet one another with a holy kiss. All the saints greet you.

[13] The grace of the Lord Jesus Christ, the love of God, and the communion of[e] the Holy Spirit be with all of you.

[a] Other ancient authorities read *with him*
[b] Gk *brothers*
[c] Or *rejoice*
[d] Or *encourage one another*
[e] Or *and the sharing in*

13.13; 1 Cor 5.10–11; 6.9–10; Gal 5.19–21. **21:** Ironic use of *humble,* here meaning "humiliate"; see 11.7n. **13.1–10:** Previously mentioned themes are resumed in a severe warning of harsh discipline. **1:** *Third* visit, see 12.14n. *"Any . . . witnesses,"* Deut 19.15. **3–4:** *Christ . . . is not weak . . . but is powerful,* the weak/powerful paradox summarized; see 10.1n.; 12.10n. **10:** Strong warning while *away,* so that Paul will not have to resort to *severe* discipline, precisely what the opponents accused Paul of doing (10.10–11). Paul reminds the Corinthians that this is so for the purpose of *building up,* not *tearing down;* see 10.8; 12.19.

13.11–13: Final benediction. **11:** *Finally,* a standard device to conclude a discussion. *Farewell* (or "rejoice") . . . *put . . . listen . . . agree . . . live . . . ,* a series of parting exhortations. **12:** *Holy kiss,* see Rom 16.16; 1 Cor 16.20; 1 Thess 5.26. **13:** A full triadic benediction found nowhere else in Paul's letters.

THE LETTER OF PAUL TO THE GALATIANS

NAME, DATE, AND AUTHORSHIP

The addressees of the Letter to the Galatians are an unspecified number of "the churches of Galatia" (1.2), a Roman province in central Asia Minor where, according to Acts, Paul had preached (Acts 13.14–14.23; cf. 16.6; 18.23). Although Galatians follows the form of a letter to specific churches, there are no references to individuals and little information about Paul's mission in the region. Rather, the letter is Paul's defense of his Gentile mission as a whole and the understanding of the law on which it is based.

The date of the letter's composition is not given. It was written some time between the late 40s and mid 50s CE. Paul would develop his views on the law further in the Letter to the Romans. Paul's authorship is generally accepted by modern scholars.

HISTORICAL CONTEXT

By the middle of the first century CE, although the early Christian movement was still connected to Judaism, an increasing number of its members were Gentiles. The tireless missionary activity of Paul, who saw himself as the apostle to the Gentiles (1.16), had fostered this development. Inevitably the question arose of what relationship Gentile Christians should have toward Judaism. One critical issue concerned the law of Moses. Should Gentile Christians convert to Judaism in the process of becoming Christians? Were they required to observe the Jewish law, at least in part? The Letter to the Galatians belongs to this controversy, and in it Paul states a position on the Jewish law, which was to have far-reaching consequences.

CONTENTS AND INTERPRETATION

Prior to writing Galatians, Paul had been involved in discussions of Gentile observance of the law with the leaders of the Jerusalem church (2.1–10). This meeting may be identical with the council at Jerusalem, reported in Acts 15.1–29. Paul's account of his visit to Jerusalem is very different from the one in Acts. In Galatians Paul insists that no demand was made for Gentiles to observe the law. Subsequently, a conflict in Antioch ensued over table fellowship of Jews and Gentiles (2.11–14). Paul names as his opponents in Antioch "certain people . . . from James," the brother of Jesus (1.19) and leader of the Jerusalem church, and "the circumcision faction," but it is unclear whether the two groups are the same. Nonetheless, they persuaded the rest of the Jews, including Peter and Barnabas, to break off table fellowship with Gentile believers. Paul repeats his accusation against Peter that Peter himself no longer observed Jewish law and customs, yet he could be pressured to impose them on Gentiles.

In the confrontation with Peter, Paul had held that the demands of the Jewish law were an unnecessary burden for Gentiles when even Jewish Christians did not always observe them (2.11–14). Now he argues that the observance of the Jewish law by Gentile Christians is incompatible with acceptance of the gospel (2.15–21). Paul does not address the question of whether Jewish Christians should still keep the law. In an allegorical argument based upon the story of Hagar and Sarah (4.21–31; see Gen 16; 21.1–21) Paul suggests that the Sinai covenant and the community based upon the observance of the law is at odds with the authentic Israel, the community united with the one true heir of Abraham, Jesus Christ (3.16). Earlier in the letter Paul spoke about the law as a provisional measure, a means to discipline those who would inherit Abraham's promise (3.24; cf. 4.1–6). These passages imply that Judaism is redundant, perhaps even an obstacle to God's plan for human salvation. Paul does not draw this conclusion, and in Romans 9–11 he explicitly rebuts it. Paul agrees that Peter and James are "entrusted with the gospel to the circumcised" (2.7–8), and observance of the law was preserved at this time in Jewish Christian communities.

The context of Paul's formulations was a bitter struggle with opponents in Galatia. The content and sharp polemics of the letter were worked out in reply to what Paul knew of his opponents' teaching and of their attacks upon him. Despite the efforts of scholars to identify and reconstruct the arguments of Paul's opponents, they remain a shadowy group. Most commentators describe them as Judaizers because they insisted on circumcision. Whether they belonged to the same opposition that Paul had faced in Antioch or during his visit to the Jerusalem leaders (the "false believers" in 2.4) cannot be decided from Paul's letter. We also have no evidence that they were missionaries sent by the Jerusalem church and representing James, notwithstanding Paul's earlier conflict in Antioch. Nevertheless, the effect of their controversy with Paul is unmistakable. The opposition forced him to develop a defense of his mission to the Gentiles, which would provide the rationale for a later Christianity independent of its Jewish roots. In recent decades a more careful reading of ancient Jewish literature, supplemented by the discovery of new texts, notably those of the sect of Qumran, has undermined earlier understandings of ancient Judaism as a legalistic religion. We can now see that Paul was participating in internal Jewish debates about the nature and role of the law.

Toward the end of the letter Paul turns to moral exhortation (5.13–6.10) so that his position on the law does not leave the Galatians without ethical guidance. Christian freedom from the law is based on living in the realm of the Spirit. The Spirit is a connecting thread between Paul's law-free gospel and his vision of Christian behavior, between faith and love (5.5–6,18,22–25.).

Sheila Briggs

1 Paul an apostle—sent neither by human commission nor from human authorities, but through Jesus Christ and God the Father, who raised him from the dead— [2] and all the members of God's family[a] who are with me,

To the churches of Galatia:

[3] Grace to you and peace from God our Father and the Lord Jesus Christ, [4] who gave himself for our sins to set us free from the present evil age, according to the will of our God and Father, [5] to whom be the glory forever and ever. Amen.

[6] I am astonished that you are so quickly deserting the one who called you in the grace of Christ and are turning to a different gospel— [7] not that there is another gospel, but there are some who are confusing you and want to pervert the gospel of Christ. [8] But even if we or an angel[b] from heaven should proclaim to you a gospel contrary to what we proclaimed to you, let that one be accursed! [9] As we have said before, so now I repeat, if anyone proclaims to you a gospel contrary to what you received, let that one be accursed!

a   Gk *all the brothers*
b   Or *a messenger*

1.1–5: The salutation, in which Paul stresses his apostolic authority. **1:** *Apostle,* both a witness (Acts 1.22) and a proclaimer (1 Cor 12.28) of the resurrection of Jesus. Paul's apostleship results directly from his experience of the risen Christ. **2:** *Churches of Galatia,* the plural indicates that Paul was addressing several Christian communities; the specific locations are uncertain. Galatia, around modern Ankara in Turkey, was a region named after and occupied by a people of Celtic origins. But Galatia also gave its name to the larger Roman province that extended to the south, to the cities of Iconium, Lystra, and Derbe, where Paul and Barnabas also founded churches (Acts 14.1–23). First-century Jews considered Galatia as coextensive with the ancient land of the descendants of Gomer (Gen 10.2) and also understood it as encompassing the broader area of the Roman province. **3:** *Grace . . . peace,* the combined Greek and Hebrew greeting that Paul typically used (e.g., Rom 1.7; 1 Cor 1.3; 2 Cor 1.2). **4:** *Gave himself for our sins,* in sacrificial death (Mk 10.45) as a sin offering (Lev 4–5). Paul repeats this central early Christian tradition (see also 2.20; 1 Tim 2.6). The *present evil age* implies that there is another age, the "age to come" in Jewish apocalyptic thought (see also 2 Thess 2.7–8). Christ's death, therefore, cancels believers' sin and delivers them for this messianic era.

1.6–2.14: A recapitulation of Paul's life and ministry.

1.6–9: Paul rebukes the Galatians. Unlike Paul's other letters (Rom 1.8–15; 1 Cor 1.4–9), he does not offer thanksgiving for those addressed. Instead he immediately upbraids them for *deserting the one who called you—* not Paul here, but God or God through Christ. The new teaching that the Galatians have accepted is *a different gospel* and not compatible with Paul's instruction. **8–9:** Paul's opponents may have held that their teaching had been revealed by *an angel from heaven,* a common claim in Judaism (reflected in 3.19) and also in folk religions of Asia Minor, spread throughout Galatia. In any case, Paul's revelation comes from a higher source than any angel, Jesus Christ (1.11). *Accursed,* an anathema using a double curse for emphasis.

1.10–12: Paul states the defense of his gospel. His position is not based on expediency: He does not reject

¹⁰ Am I now seeking human approval, or God's approval? Or am I trying to please people? If I were still pleasing people, I would not be a servant^a of Christ.

¹¹ For I want you to know, brothers and sisters,^b that the gospel that was proclaimed by me is not of human origin; ¹² for I did not receive it from a human source, nor was I taught it, but I received it through a revelation of Jesus Christ.

¹³ You have heard, no doubt, of my earlier life in Judaism. I was violently persecuting the church of God and was trying to destroy it. ¹⁴ I advanced in Judaism beyond many among my people of the same age, for I was far more zealous for the traditions of my ancestors. ¹⁵ But when God, who had set me apart before I was born and called me through his grace, was pleased ¹⁶ to reveal his Son to me,^c so that I might proclaim him among the Gentiles, I did not confer with any human being, ¹⁷ nor did I go up to Jerusalem to those who were already apostles before me, but I went away at once into Arabia, and afterwards I returned to Damascus.

¹⁸ Then after three years I did go up to Jerusalem to visit Cephas and stayed with him fifteen days; ¹⁹ but I did not see any other apostle except James the Lord's brother. ²⁰ In what I am writing to you, before God, I do not lie! ²¹ Then I went into the regions of Syria and Cilicia, ²² and I was still unknown by sight to the churches of Judea that are in Christ; ²³ they only heard it said, "The one who formerly was persecuting us is now proclaiming the faith he once tried to destroy." ²⁴ And they glorified God because of me.

2 Then after fourteen years I went up again to Jerusalem with Barnabas, taking Titus along with me. ² I went up in response to a revelation. Then I laid before them (though only in a private meeting with the acknowledged leaders) the gospel that I proclaim among the Gentiles, in order to make sure that I was not running, or had not run, in vain. ³ But even Titus, who was with me, was

^a Gk *slave*
^b Gk *brothers*
^c Gk *in me*

observance of the Jewish law by Gentiles as a means of winning more converts through lax requirements. **11–12:** Paul's gospel was directly revealed to him by Jesus Christ. Paul implies that the teaching of his opponents, unlike his *gospel,* is of *human origin.*

1.13–2.14: Paul recounts his background in Judaism, his calling as an apostle, and his mission to the Gentiles. The purpose of this autobiographical sketch is to state the facts, as Paul saw them, of how he became the apostle to the Gentiles.

1.13–24: Paul's conversion, early life in the church, and defense of his apostleship. 13–14: *Persecuting the church of God,* see Acts 8.3; 9.21; 22.4. Paul insists that he was an exemplary Jew (Acts 22.3; Phil 3.4–6) who was *zealous for the traditions of my ancestors,* i.e., for the Jewish law, including its oral traditions, which were upheld in Pharisaic Judaism (Phil 3.5–6). **15–16:** Paul's conversion occurs as a direct result of divine intervention without human mediation in order to fulfill God's plan of revealing Christ to the Gentiles. *Set . . . born,* like a prophet in the Hebrew Bible (Isa 49.1; Jer 1.5). *To me* (lit., "in me"), links the ideas that Christ is revealed to Paul and through Paul to the Gentiles. **17:** *Arabia,* the Nabatean kingdom in Transjordan, of which the capital was Petra. *Damascus* is recorded in Acts 9.8–25 as the place where Paul went immediately after his conversion; see also 2 Cor 11.32–33. **18:** It is unclear whether the *three years* are to be counted from Paul's call or from his return to Damascus. *Cephas* is the Aramaic equivalent of "Peter" (Gk "Petros"; both names mean "rock") and the form of the name favored by Paul. **19:** *James* the brother of Jesus (Mk 6.3; Mt 13.55; 1 Cor 15.7) who became a leading member of the Jerusalem church (Acts 1.14; 15.13; 21.18–19). **21:** *Syria* had Antioch as its capital, and the chief city of *Cilicia* on the southeast coast of Asia Minor was Paul's hometown of Tarsus. **22–23:** Cf. Acts 9.26–30, which gives a different account of all these events.

2.1–10: Paul meets with the Jerusalem leaders. It is difficult to determine the relationship of the visit of Paul and Barnabas to Jerusalem, reported here, with the account of their visit in Acts 15.1–29. If the same events are being described, then we have two radically different versions. **1:** It is unclear whether the *fourteen years* are to be counted from his call or his first Jerusalem visit (1.18). *Barnabas,* a Jewish Christian and Paul's co-missionary, who participated in the mission to Antioch and brought Paul there (see Acts 4.36; 9.27; 11.22–30; 13.1–15.41). *Titus,* a Greek, possibly converted by Paul himself, who also becomes Paul's co-missionary. **3–5:** Paul's opponents,

Black Sea

GALATIA

*Aegean
Sea*

CILICIA
• Tarsus

• Antioch

SYRIA

*Mediterranean
Sea*

• Damascus

JUDEA
• Jerusalem

ARABIA
(NABATEAN
KINGDOM)

| 0 | 100 | 200 Miles |
| 0 | 100 | 200 Kilometers |

30° 35° 40°

Places mentioned in Galatians 1–2.

not compelled to be circumcised, though he was a Greek. ⁴ But because of false believersᵃ secretly brought in, who slipped in to spy on the freedom we have in Christ Jesus, so that they might enslave us— ⁵ we did not submit to them even for a moment, so that the truth of the gospel might always remain with you. ⁶ And from those who were supposed to be acknowledged leaders (what they actually were makes no difference to me; God shows no partiality)—those leaders contributed nothing to me. ⁷ On the contrary, when they saw that I had been entrusted with the gospel for the uncircumcised, just as Peter had been entrusted with the gospel for the circumcised ⁸ (for he who worked through Peter making him an apostle to the circumcised also worked through me in sending me to the Gentiles),

ᵃ Gk *false brothers*

the *false believers,* both in this earlier conflict and in Galatia, claim that conversion to Judaism is a precondition for membership in the Christian community and therefore demand Titus's circumcision. 6–9: *Uncircumcised . . . circumcised,* Gentiles and Jews. Paul asserts that the Jerusalem leaders agreed with him in distinguishing between their mission to their fellow Jews and his to the Gentiles, thus conceding his apostolic authority over the latter. The division of labor may not have been so sharply defined (Acts 10). *John,* probably the apostle (Acts

⁹ and when James and Cephas and John, who were acknowledged pillars, recognized the grace that had been given to me, they gave to Barnabas and me the right hand of fellowship, agreeing that we should go to the Gentiles and they to the circumcised. ¹⁰ They asked only one thing, that we remember the poor, which was actually what I was[a] eager to do.

¹¹ But when Cephas came to Antioch, I opposed him to his face, because he stood self-condemned; ¹² for until certain people came from James, he used to eat with the Gentiles. But after they came, he drew back and kept himself separate for fear of the circumcision faction. ¹³ And the other Jews joined him in this hypocrisy, so that even Barnabas was led astray by their hypocrisy. ¹⁴ But when I saw that they were not acting consistently with the truth of the gospel, I said to Cephas before them all, "If you, though a Jew, live like a Gentile and not like a Jew, how can you compel the Gentiles to live like Jews?"[b]

¹⁵ We ourselves are Jews by birth and not Gentile sinners; ¹⁶ yet we know that a person is justified[c] not by the works of the law but through faith in Jesus Christ.[d] And we have come to believe in Christ Jesus, so that we might be justified by faith in Christ,[e] and not by doing the works of the law, because no one will be justified by the works of the law. ¹⁷ But if, in our effort to be justified in Christ, we ourselves have been found to be sinners, is Christ then a servant of sin? Certainly not! ¹⁸ But if I build up again the very things that I once tore down, then I demonstrate that I am a transgressor. ¹⁹ For through the law I died to the law, so that I might live to God. I have been crucified with

a   Or *had been*
b   Some interpreters hold that the quotation extends into the following paragraph
c   Or *reckoned as righteous;* and so elsewhere
d   Or *the faith of Jesus Christ*
e   Or *the faith of Christ*

3–4). **10:** Paul organized a collection among the churches he founded to be sent to Jerusalem (Acts 11.29–30; 24.17; Rom 15.25–29; 1 Cor 16.1–3, 2 Cor 8.1–9.15). *The poor* may be a religious expression which identified the Jerusalem Christians as the righteous, humble ones of God (Lk 1.48; Mt 5.3), a usage which we also find in the contemporary Jewish sect of Qumran (1QpHab 12.2–6). It could also be a reference to the physical neediness of the community after the famine of 46/48 CE (Josephus, *Ant.* 20.51).

2.11–14: Paul's confrontation with Peter at Antioch. Some interpreters of the Jewish law, e.g., rabbis in the more liberal school of Hillel, allowed the table fellowship of Jew and non-Jew at the time of Paul. It was possible for Jews to observe dietary and purity laws while eating with Gentiles. Biblical stories of Jews refusing to eat Gentile food take place in hostile or foreign environments where the observance of the dietary laws could not be guaranteed (Dan 1.8–16; Tob 1.10–13; Jdt 10.5). Sharing, or not sharing, a meal was a strong indication of acceptance or nonacceptance (Acts 10.14; 11.3,8). **12:** The *people . . . from James,* messengers from the Jerusalem apostle who insisted on a stricter interpretation of the law, forbidding such table fellowship. **14:** Paul attacks Peter's behavior because it might *compel the Gentiles to live like Jews.* Although the ban on table fellowship did not prohibit Gentiles from being members of the Christian community, it could have relegated those who did not choose full conversion to Judaism to second-class status.

2.15–5.12: Paul's gospel: faith in Christ frees us from law.

2.15–21: Jews and Gentiles are both justified through Christ. Paul states his basic principle: Trusting in Christ, including the sacrifice of his death, is what makes one righteous. **15:** *Gentile sinners,* Gentiles were sinners in Jewish eyes because they were idolaters, i.e., adherents of non-Jewish religions. **16:** *Works of the law,* the exact meaning of this phrase is much debated. In this context it certainly refers to practices such as dietary laws and sabbath observance that marked Jewish identity. But it might also include the ethical as well as the ritual requirements of the law, or it might characterize the particular standard of observance being advocated by Paul's opponents as a condition of belonging to the Christian community. *Faith in Jesus Christ* stresses the believer's trust in Christ. The alternative translation (textual notes *d* and *e*), *faith of Jesus Christ,* emphasizes the saving effect of Jesus' obedience, culminating in his death on the cross. **17:** Paul gives an ironic presentation of an objection to his view. If we who are seeking justification in Christ are, in the view of our opponents, sinners, i.e., living like Gentiles (see vv. 14–15), then does that mean that Christ works for sin? The implication is that for a Christian failure to observe the law is not sin. **18:** *Things,* i.e., observance of the law as the only path to righteousness. **19:** *Through the law I died to the law,* a summary statement of arguments that Paul will make in

Christ; [20] and it is no longer I who live, but it is Christ who lives in me. And the life I now live in the flesh I live by faith in the Son of God,[a] who loved me and gave himself for me. [21] I do not nullify the grace of God; for if justification[b] comes through the law, then Christ died for nothing.

3 You foolish Galatians! Who has bewitched you? It was before your eyes that Jesus Christ was publicly exhibited as crucified! [2] The only thing I want to learn from you is this: Did you receive the Spirit by doing the works of the law or by believing what you heard? [3] Are you so foolish? Having started with the Spirit, are you now ending with the flesh? [4] Did you experience so much for nothing?—if it really was for nothing. [5] Well then, does God[c] supply you with the Spirit and work miracles among you by your doing the works of the law, or by your believing what you heard?

[6] Just as Abraham "believed God, and it was reckoned to him as righteousness," [7] so, you see, those who believe are the descendants of Abraham. [8] And the scripture, foreseeing that God would justify the Gentiles by faith, declared the gospel beforehand to Abraham, saying, "All the Gentiles shall be blessed in you." [9] For this reason, those who believe are blessed with Abraham who believed.

[10] For all who rely on the works of the law are under a curse; for it is written, "Cursed is everyone who does not observe and obey all the things written in the book of the law." [11] Now it is evident that no one is justified before God by the law; for "The one who is righteous will live by faith."[d] [12] But the law does not rest on faith; on the contrary, "Whoever does the works of the law[e] will live by them." [13] Christ redeemed us from the curse of the law by becoming a curse for us—for it is written, "Cursed is everyone who hangs on a tree"— [14] in order that in Christ Jesus the blessing of Abraham might come to the Gentiles, so that we might receive the promise of the Spirit through faith.

[15] Brothers and sisters,[f] I give an example from daily life: once a person's will[g] has

a   Or *by the faith of the Son of God*
b   Or *righteousness*
c   Gk *he*
d   Or *The one who is righteous through faith will live*
e   Gk *does them*
f   Gk *Brothers*
g   Or *covenant* (as in verse 17)

chs 3–4. *Crucified with Christ*, see 5.24; 6.14; Rom 6.5–11; 2 Cor 4.7–12. **20:** *Christ who lives in me*, see Rom 8.9–11; 2 Cor 13.5; Col 1.27. *Gave himself for me*, see 1.4n.

3.1–5: Paul's challenge to the Galatians. Paul asks the Galatians whether they received the gift of the Spirit through fulfilling practices required by Jewish law, or through accepting the gospel preached by Paul (*believing what you heard*, vv. 2,5). **1:** *Jesus Christ was publicly exhibited as crucified*, a reference to the graphic description of the crucifixion in Paul's preaching. **3:** *Ending with the flesh*, an oblique reference to circumcision. The opposition of *Spirit* and *flesh* is an important theme in Paul (4.29; 5.16–25; 6.8; Rom 8.1–12; 3.1; 1 Cor 15.35–55; Phil 3.2–6). **5:** *Miracles* are associated with apostolic preaching and the presence of the Spirit (Rom 15.19; 1 Cor 12.10; 2 Cor 12.12).

3.6–14: Abraham the model for Christian faith. Paul contrasts the believer, whose exemplar is Abraham and who is justified by faith, with those who seek justification through performing the practices of the Jewish law. **6:** Gen 15.6; see also Rom 4.3. Paul again uses Abraham as a model of faith in Rom 4. **8:** Gen 12.3; 18.18; 22.18. **10:** Deut 27.36. In Paul's time the general Jewish view was that perfect fulfillment of the law was not a requirement of belonging to God's covenant people but observance of the law expressed faithfulness to God's covenant. **11:** Hab 2.4; Rom 1.17. **12:** Lev 18.5; see also Rom 10.5. **13:** Deut 21.23 concerns execution by hanging but the Jewish sect at Qumran had apparently already interpreted it to include crucifixion (11QTemple 64.12). Paul takes *tree* as a reference to Jesus' cross.

3.15–18: The inheritance of Abraham. Paul argues that Christ is the one heir of Abraham and that what was promised to Abraham cannot be inherited through the law. **15:** *Will*, the Gk means "covenant" as well as a person's document of bequest (see textual note g). **16:** *Offspring*, lit., "seed" (see textual notes a and b on this verse). Paul uses the same Greek word as the Septuagint (LXX) text of God's promises to Abraham in Genesis (Gen 12.7; 15.5; 17.8; 22.17). Paul contrasts the singular *seed* in the text with the common (and in his view mistaken) inter-

been ratified, no one adds to it or annuls it. [16] Now the promises were made to Abraham and to his offspring;[a] it does not say, "And to offsprings,"[b] as of many; but it says, "And to your offspring,"[a] that is, to one person, who is Christ. [17] My point is this: the law, which came four hundred thirty years later, does not annul a covenant previously ratified by God, so as to nullify the promise. [18] For if the inheritance comes from the law, it no longer comes from the promise; but God granted it to Abraham through the promise.

[19] Why then the law? It was added because of transgressions, until the offspring[a] would come to whom the promise had been made; and it was ordained through angels by a mediator. [20] Now a mediator involves more than one party; but God is one.

[21] Is the law then opposed to the promises of God? Certainly not! For if a law had been given that could make alive, then righteousness would indeed come through the law. [22] But the scripture has imprisoned all things under the power of sin, so that what was promised through faith in Jesus Christ[c] might be given to those who believe.

[23] Now before faith came, we were imprisoned and guarded under the law until faith would be revealed. [24] Therefore the law was our disciplinarian until Christ came, so that we might be justified by faith. [25] But now that faith has come, we are no longer subject to a disciplinarian, [26] for in Christ Jesus you are all children of God through faith. [27] As many of you as were baptized into Christ have clothed yourselves with Christ. [28] There is no longer Jew or Greek, there is no longer slave or free, there is no longer male and female; for all of you are one in Christ Jesus. [29] And if you belong to Christ, then you are Abraham's offspring,[a] heirs according to the promise.

4 My point is this: heirs, as long as they are minors, are no better than slaves, though they are the owners of all the property; [2] but they remain under guardians and trustees until the date set by the father. [3] So with us; while we were minors, we were enslaved to

a Gk *seed*
b Gk *seeds*
c Or *through the faith of Jesus Christ*

pretation of it as a plural, *seeds.* **17:** Paul follows the Septuagint, not the Hebrew, text of Ex 12.40 by including within the *four hundred thirty years* not only the Israelite sojourn in Egypt but also the earlier period in Canaan.

3.19–25: The purpose of the law of Moses. The law does not replace God's promise to Abraham but is a temporary means of discipline for God's people. **19:** *Added because of transgressions* allows several interpretations. It can mean to make aware of sin (Rom 3.20; 7.7). It can also carry the further sense of restraining transgressions (vv. 23–25). The phrase can also signify that the law provoked sin (Rom 5.20; 7.7–12). *Ordained through angels* reflects a later Jewish belief that the law was delivered on Sinai not directly from God but by angels; see Deut 33.2 (Septuagint); Acts 7.38,53; Heb 2.2, also *Jub.* 1.26–2.1. *A mediator,* Moses (see Lev 26.46; Num 36.13). **20:** An obscure verse that links monotheism with there being no need for a mediator of God's promise. **22:** *Faith in Jesus Christ* stresses the believer's faith as necessary for obtaining the promise, while the alternative, *faith of Jesus Christ* (see textual note c), emphasizes Jesus' faith as that which grants the promise; see 2.16n. **24–25:** *Disciplinarian,* the slave who accompanied a boy to school and who often harshly punished the boy for his behavior.

3.26–29: Baptism into Christ. Through baptism believers are incorporated into Christ, abolishing social distinctions, and are made with him the offspring of Abraham and heirs to the promise. **26–28:** Paul is likely here quoting from an early Christian baptismal formula. **26:** Christians are adopted children of God and therefore co-heirs with Christ (Rom 8.14–17). **27:** Baptism unites the believer with Christ (Rom 6.3–11). *Clothed . . . with Christ,* see Rom 13.14; Col 3.10. **28:** A similar erasure of social distinctions is proclaimed in 1 Cor 12.13; Col 3.11, where baptismal formulas also seem to be quoted, but without the phrase *male and female.* That phrase is taken from Gen 1.27. **29:** Christ alone is *Abraham's offspring* or seed (see 3.16n.) but now includes all those united in baptism with him.

4.1–7: Christ brings believers into their inheritance as adopted children of God. 1: After a father's death the guardian took over the father's virtually unlimited power over minor children in the ancient family. **3:** *Elemental spirits of the world* refers probably to cosmic powers that dominate human beings (see also 4.8; Col 2.8,20). The phrase (alternatively translated as *rudiments,* textual note a on this verse) can also denote the four elements (earth, air, fire, water), which in Paul's time were seen as controlling human destiny. The *rudiments* can addition-

the elemental spirits[a] of the world. [4] But when the fullness of time had come, God sent his Son, born of a woman, born under the law, [5] in order to redeem those who were under the law, so that we might receive adoption as children. [6] And because you are children, God has sent the Spirit of his Son into our[b] hearts, crying, "Abba![c] Father!" [7] So you are no longer a slave but a child, and if a child then also an heir, through God.[d]

[8] Formerly, when you did not know God, you were enslaved to beings that by nature are not gods. [9] Now, however, that you have come to know God, or rather to be known by God, how can you turn back again to the weak and beggarly elemental spirits?[e] How can you want to be enslaved to them again? [10] You are observing special days, and months, and seasons, and years. [11] I am afraid that my work for you may have been wasted.

[12] Friends,[f] I beg you, become as I am, for I also have become as you are. You have done me no wrong. [13] You know that it was because of a physical infirmity that I first announced the gospel to you; [14] though my condition put you to the test, you did not scorn or despise me, but welcomed me as an angel of God, as Christ Jesus. [15] What has become of the goodwill you felt? For I testify that, had it been possible, you would have torn out your eyes and given them to me. [16] Have I now become your enemy by telling you the truth? [17] They

make much of you, but for no good purpose; they want to exclude you, so that you may make much of them. [18] It is good to be made much of for a good purpose at all times, and not only when I am present with you. [19] My little children, for whom I am again in the pain of childbirth until Christ is formed in you, [20] I wish I were present with you now and could change my tone, for I am perplexed about you.

[21] Tell me, you who desire to be subject to the law, will you not listen to the law? [22] For it is written that Abraham had two sons, one by a slave woman and the other by a free woman. [23] One, the child of the slave, was born according to the flesh; the other, the child of the free woman, was born through the promise. [24] Now this is an allegory: these women are two covenants. One woman, in fact, is Hagar, from Mount Sinai, bearing children for slavery. [25] Now Hagar is Mount Sinai in Arabia[g] and corresponds to the present Jerusalem, for she is in slavery with her

a Or *the rudiments*
b Other ancient authorities read *your*
c Aramaic for *Father*
d Other ancient authorities read *an heir of God through Christ*
e Or *beggarly rudiments*
f Gk *Brothers*
g Other ancient authorities read *For Sinai is a mountain in Arabia*

ally be the basic principles of a philosophy or code (see Heb 5.12). 4: *Born of a woman, born under the law* stresses Jesus' human and Jewish birth, seen by Paul as the enslaved human condition, in contrast to the freedom Christ brings to those adopted as God's children. 6: *Abba*, see textual note *c* and Mk 14.36; Rom 8.15.

4.8–11: The Galatians slip back into bondage. Paul brands the Galatians' observance of the law as equivalent to a return to their pre-Christian enslavement. 9: *Elemental spirits*, see 4.3n. 10: The Galatians are observing the Jewish calendar.

4.12–20: Paul reminds the Galatians of their close relationship to him. 13: Paul may be alluding to one or both visits he made to Galatia as mentioned in Acts 16.6; 18.23. The *infirmity* is not known; efforts to identify it as eye trouble, based on v. 15, may be based on too literal a reading. The adverb *first* can also be translated as "formerly." 17: *They*, i.e., Paul's opponents, may have threatened to exclude from the Christian community Gentiles who did not follow their example of observing the law. 19: Paul uses as a metaphor of his apostolic activity a mother giving birth. Elsewhere Paul calls the members of the churches he founded his "children" (1 Cor 4.14; 2 Cor 6.13; 1 Thess 2.11).

4.21–5.1: The allegory of Hagar and Sarah. 4.21: *The law* in the Hebrew Bible comprises the first five books, the Pentateuch or Torah. 22–23: Gen 16.1–4,15; 21.1–7. 24: *Allegory*, literally, "these things are spoken allegorically." Paul takes the Genesis story and sees some of its elements as substitutes in the past for how the covenant is being fulfilled in his own day. *These women are two covenants*, i.e., Hagar represents those descendants of Abraham who observe the law and Sarah those who through Christ are the true heirs to God's promise to Abraham. 25: *Now Hagar is Mount Sinai in Arabia*, see textual note *g*. Paul is unique in identifying Hagar directly

children. ²⁶ But the other woman corresponds to the Jerusalem above; she is free, and she is our mother. ²⁷ For it is written,

"Rejoice, you childless one, you who bear
no children,
burst into song and shout, you who
endure no birth pangs;
for the children of the desolate woman are
more numerous
than the children of the one who is
married."

²⁸ Now you,ᵃ my friends,ᵇ are children of the promise, like Isaac. ²⁹ But just as at that time the child who was born according to the flesh persecuted the child who was born according to the Spirit, so it is now also. ³⁰ But what does the scripture say? "Drive out the slave and her child; for the child of the slave will not share the inheritance with the child of the free woman." ³¹ So then, friends,ᵇ we are children, not of the slave but of the free woman. ¹ For freedom Christ has set us free. Stand firm, therefore, and do not submit again to a yoke of slavery.

²Listen! I, Paul, am telling you that if you let yourselves be circumcised, Christ will be of no benefit to you. ³ Once again I testify to every man who lets himself be circumcised that he is obliged to obey the entire law. ⁴ You who want to be justified by the law have cut yourselves off from Christ; you have fallen away from grace. ⁵ For through the Spirit,

by faith, we eagerly wait for the hope of righteousness. ⁶ For in Christ Jesus neither circumcision nor uncircumcision counts for anything; the only thing that counts is faith workingᶜ through love.

⁷ You were running well; who prevented you from obeying the truth? ⁸ Such persuasion does not come from the one who calls you. ⁹ A little yeast leavens the whole batch of dough. ¹⁰ I am confident about you in the Lord that you will not think otherwise. But whoever it is that is confusing you will pay the penalty. ¹¹ But my friends,ᵇ why am I still being persecuted if I am still preaching circumcision? In that case the offense of the cross has been removed. ¹² I wish those who unsettle you would castrate themselves!

¹³ For you were called to freedom, brothers and sisters;ᵇ only do not use your freedom as an opportunity for self-indulgence,ᵈ but through love become slaves to one another. ¹⁴ For the whole law is summed up in a single commandment, "You shall love your neighbor as yourself." ¹⁵ If, however, you bite and devour one another, take care that you are not consumed by one another.

ᵃ Other ancient authorities read we
ᵇ Gk brothers
ᶜ Or made effective
ᵈ Gk the flesh

with Mount Sinai, where the law was given to Israel. **26:** *The Jerusalem above . . . our mother,* Paul draws on the prophets' vision of the pilgrimage of the nations to the restored Jerusalem (Isa 51.2–6; 60; 62.1–2; Zech 2.10–12). Ps 86.5 (Septuagint) (cf. Ps 87.5) has the phrase "mother Zion." **27:** Isa 54.1; see also Isa 51.2–3. **29–30:** Gen 21.9–10. Genesis does not mention Ishmael persecuting Isaac but the idea is found in some later Jewish interpretations of this text.

5.2–12: Paul's case against circumcision. Paul argues that a Gentile who accepts circumcision is seeking righteousness through the law, an act incompatible with faith in Christ. **3-4:** See 2.16; 3.10–12. **6:** *Neither circumcision nor uncircumcision,* 6.15; 1 Cor 7.19. The alternative *faith made effective through love* (textual note c) gives faith a passive sense. It is instigated through love, presumably God's love. **8:** *The one who calls you,* God through Christ; see 1.6–9n. **9:** Paul uses the same proverb in 1 Cor 5.6. He is concerned that his opponents will win over the whole Galatian community. **11:** Some of Paul's opponents may have alleged he was inconsistent in his position on Gentile circumcision, perhaps pointing out that he had Timothy circumcised (Acts 16.1–3). **12:** A negative and bitterly sarcastic allusion to circumcision; see Phil 3.2. Paul may also be insulting his opponents through a comparison between circumcision and a pagan religious practice of Galatia, in which the priests of the Anatolian mother goddess Cybele, the Galli, emasculated themselves.

5.13–6.10: The behavior of those called in freedom to live by the Spirit. Paul presents a Christian ethic in reply to those demanding observance of the law from the Galatians.

5.13–26: Christian liberty. 13: See vv. 1,6. *Slaves to one another,* mutual submission is an important theme for

16 Live by the Spirit, I say, and do not gratify the desires of the flesh. 17 For what the flesh desires is opposed to the Spirit, and what the Spirit desires is opposed to the flesh; for these are opposed to each other, to prevent you from doing what you want. 18 But if you are led by the Spirit, you are not subject to the law. 19 Now the works of the flesh are obvious: fornication, impurity, licentiousness, 20 idolatry, sorcery, enmities, strife, jealousy, anger, quarrels, dissensions, factions, 21 envy,[a] drunkenness, carousing, and things like these. I am warning you, as I warned you before: those who do such things will not inherit the kingdom of God.

22 By contrast, the fruit of the Spirit is love, joy, peace, patience, kindness, generosity, faithfulness, 23 gentleness, and self-control. There is no law against such things. 24 And those who belong to Christ Jesus have crucified the flesh with its passions and desires. 25 If we live by the Spirit, let us also be guided by the Spirit. 26 Let us not become conceited, competing against one another, envying one another.

6 My friends,[b] if anyone is detected in a transgression, you who have received the Spirit should restore such a one in a spirit of gentleness. Take care that you yourselves are not tempted. 2 Bear one another's burdens, and in this way you will fulfill[c] the law of Christ. 3 For if those who are nothing think they are something, they deceive themselves. 4 All must test their own work; then that work, rather than their neighbor's work, will become a cause for pride. 5 For all must carry their own loads.

6 Those who are taught the word must share in all good things with their teacher.

7 Do not be deceived; God is not mocked, for you reap whatever you sow. 8 If you sow to your own flesh, you will reap corruption from the flesh; but if you sow to the Spirit, you will reap eternal life from the Spirit. 9 So let us not grow weary in doing what is right, for we will reap at harvest time, if we do not give up. 10 So then, whenever we have an opportunity, let us work for the good of all, and especially for those of the family of faith.

11 See what large letters I make when I am writing in my own hand! 12 It is those who want to make a good showing in the flesh that try to compel you to be circumcised—only that they may not be persecuted for the cross of Christ. 13 Even the circumcised do not themselves obey the law, but they want you to be circumcised so that they may boast about your flesh. 14 May I never boast of anything except the cross of our Lord Jesus Christ, by which[d] the world has been crucified to me, and I to the world. 15 For[e] neither circumcision nor uncircumcision is anything; but a new creation is everything! 16 As for those who will

a   Other ancient authorities add *murder*
b   Gk *Brothers*
c   Other ancient authorities read *in this way fulfill*
d   Or *through whom*
e   Other ancient authorities add *in Christ Jesus*

Paul and his followers; see Eph 5.21; Phil 2.3. **14**: Lev 19.18; Mt 22.39; Rom 13.8–10. **16**: *Desires of the flesh*, the self-indulgence (lit., "flesh"; see textual note *d* on v. 13) warned against in v. 13; see Eph 2.3. **16–17**: The opposition of the Spirit to the flesh (3.3; Rom 8.1–17) leads to inner conflict (Rom 7.14–24). **18**: Rom 6.14. **19–23**: Catalogues of vices and virtues were a common form of ethical instruction in the Greco-Roman world (see Mk 7.21–22; Mt 15.19; Rom 1.29–31; 1 Cor 6.9–10; 2 Cor 6.6–7; 12.20–21; Phil 4.8; Col 3.5–14; 1 Tim 1.9–10; 6.11; 2 Tim 3.2–5; 1 Pet 2.1; 4.3; 2 Pet 1.5–7; Rev 21.8; 22.15). The idea of two opposing forces leading to either righteous or wicked behavior was prominent in the Qumran sect (1QS 3.13–4.26).

6.1–10: Paul offers the Galatians several maxims by which to judge their behavior. **2**: *The law of Christ* may be a phrase Paul borrowed from his opponents; see also 1 Cor 9.21; Rom 8.2. The Spirit enables the believer to live out the principle of love, thus fulfilling the law without observing its requirements. **6**: Christian teachers are entitled to financial support from their church (1 Cor 9.14). **8**: Rom 8.5–8. **9**: *Not grow weary*, Paul uses the same Greek verb in 2 Cor 4.1,16 (translated as "not lose heart"); see also Lk 18.1. **10**: *The family of faith*, lit., "members of the household of faith"; compare the phrase "household of God" in Eph 2.19; 1 Tim 3.15; 1 Pet 4.17.

6.11–18: Postscript. **11**: Paul had dictated this letter to a secretary, but writes the conclusion in his *own hand*; see 1 Cor 16; 2 Thess 3.17. **12–14**: *Boast about . . . flesh/boast . . . about the cross of our Lord Jesus Christ*, see also 1 Cor 1.29–31; Phil 3.2–4. *The flesh* may be a double reference to circumcision and his opponents' pride in the

follow this rule—peace be upon them, and mercy, and upon the Israel of God.

¹⁷ From now on, let no one make trouble for me; for I carry the marks of Jesus branded on my body.

¹⁸ May the grace of our Lord Jesus Christ be with your spirit, brothers and sisters.ᵃ Amen.

ᵃ Gk *brothers*

success of their mission. **15:** 3.28; 5.6. *New creation,* Rom 8.19–23; 2 Cor 5.17; also Rev 21.5. **16–18:** A two-part blessing. Verse 16 has the form of a traditional Jewish benediction and is conditional, bestowed on those who follow Paul's teaching. As such it is the counterpart to the curse in 1.8. The address *brothers and sisters* in v. 18 does not appear in the final blessing of Paul's other letters and expresses the hope that the former warm relationship between the apostle and the community will be restored. **16:** *This rule* has been summarized in v. 15 but is in fact the standards of Christian faith and behavior Paul has advocated throughout the letter. *Israel of God,* a phrase unique to this verse, equivalent to the "true Israel," i.e., those who follow Paul's *rule* and not the teachings of his opponents. **17:** *Marks of Jesus,* the scars from injuries inflicted on Paul during his mission (2 Cor 6.4–5; 11.23–25). Paul may also be suggesting that his scars identify him as belonging to Christ like the brand marks on a slave.

THE LETTER OF PAUL TO THE EPHESIANS

NAME

This letter is named for its recipients, the Christian community in the city of Ephesus, a major city on the Aegean coast of Asia Minor, where Paul spent a considerable amount of time (Acts 18–19). However, some early manuscripts of Ephesians, as well as some early Christian writers, lack the opening reference to Ephesus in 1.1 (see note *a*), and since the text does not seem to address problems specific to a single congregation, some scholars think that Ephesians was a circular letter sent to a number of churches, perhaps in Asia Minor. Others, noting the similarities to the letter to the Colossians, believe the original audience was the churches of Hierapolis and Laodicea (see Col 4.13,16).

AUTHORSHIP, LITERARY HISTORY, AND DATE

Significant contrasts between Ephesians and the letters certainly ascribed to Paul raise questions about the identity of its author. Many important terms in Ephesians are not used by Paul elsewhere (e.g., "heavenly places," "dividing wall," "fellow citizen"), and some of Paul's characteristic terms and emphases either are given new meaning (e.g., "mystery," "church") or are completely absent (e.g., "the Jews," "justify"). In addition, the verbose rhetorical style of Ephesians, especially the use of complex, long sentences (many of which have been divided in the NRSV), is not characteristic of Paul. Theological differences are also evident, especially Ephesians' emphasis on believers' present salvation (1.3–12; 2.4–10) and the use of household rules as ethical teaching (5.22–6.9). Because of these differences, many scholars hold that Ephesians was written in the late first century by a Jewish-Christian admirer of Paul who sought to apply Paul's thought to the situation of the church in his own day. A minority of scholars hold that Paul composed this letter at the end of his career while imprisoned, probably in Rome. This position attributes different theological emphases to developments in Paul's thinking and the situation addressed.

There are many verbal parallels between the letters to the Ephesians and the Colossians, as the following list shows:

EPHESIANS	COLOSSIANS
1.1–2	1.1–2
1.15–16	1.3–4,9
5.6	3.6
5.18–20	3.16–17
5.22	3.18
5.25	3.19
6.1	3.20
6.5–9	3.22–25; 4.1
6.18–20	4.2–4
6.21–22	4.7–8

These close connections, along with others given in the annotations, suggest a literary relationship between the two letters. If Paul was the author of both, they likely would have been written at the same time, probably in the late 50s; if Ephesians was written by a later follower of Paul, then it seems he drew upon the already established authority of the letter to the Colossians and modeled his work on it. Possible allusions to other Pauline letters such as Romans and 1 Corinthians are not as close as those to Colossians.

HISTORICAL CONTEXT

Establishing a historical context for Ephesians has proven extremely difficult. In contrast to many of Paul's letters and even to Colossians, Ephesians contains few hints of specific events or issues that might have triggered its composition. Since unity between Jews and Gentiles within the church is a major theme, some scholars believe that the text is meant to address the alienation of Jewish Christians from their Gentile counterparts, either in theory or arising from a conflict in the churches of Asia Minor. Other scholars suggest external events, such as Roman persecution, as the impetus for the letter's composition. A more fruitful approach may be to employ a rhetorical analysis, paying close attention to how the author presents himself and his readers, especially his desire for their maturity as believers. This approach reveals that the author sees his readers as deficient in a number of key areas, including knowledge of God's plan for salvation, the power of the Spirit, and the purpose of the church as the body of Christ.

STRUCTURE AND INTERPRETATION

Ephesians begins with a greeting (1.1–2) and an introductory thanksgiving prayer (1.15–23) and ends with an epilogue (6.21–24), but it lacks many features typical of the Pauline letter form (see p. 1973) and is better classified as a sermon. The text can be divided into two parts: theological teaching (chs 1–3), and ethical exhortation (chs 4–6). The first part focuses on the church as a new community in which Jews and Gentiles equally share in God's blessings. The second part is an appeal for the church to maintain that new unity and press on toward complete maturity by rejecting former lifestyles and displaying Christian values of truth, love, forgiveness, and sexual purity. However, rather than advocating a complete transformation of household relationships based on love, forgiveness, and mutual submission, the author's Christology is used to justify the structure and duties of the ideal ancient patriarchal family through an adaptation of the familiar household code.

In powerful poetic language drawn from early Christian hymns and the Jewish scriptures, Ephesians celebrates a vision of the universal church. According to God's eternal plan for humanity, Christ's death brought together Jews and Gentiles into a new, unified community: the Jewish law, which previously divided Jew from Gentile, was rendered irrelevant by the cross, and Christ thus reconciled both groups to each other and to God (2.14–16). Whether Ephesians is intended to encourage Gentiles to recognize their position as full partners in the church or whether Gentiles are being admonished to respect their Jewish fellow believers more highly is not clear. According to Ephesians, human existence is beset by the malevolent influence of demonic beings. Christ has been given power over them, and through God's grace human beings are freed from their immoral and deceitful influences. The new life of believers is one of knowledge and spiritual power, and thus there is the recurring contrast of the old life with the new (2.1–6,11–13,19; 4.22–24; 5.8). Another prominent theme is Paul's role as revealer of God's previously hidden plan for the salvation of humankind (3.1–12). The church must recognize Christ as its Lord and exemplar (4.12–16,20–24; 5.1–2), and also its own exalted status as a spirit-filled community that brings the power and presence of God to the world (1.22–23; 2.22; 3.10,19; 4.24). Conflict with demonic forces continues (6.10–20), but the church looks forward to the complete reestablishment of God's sovereignty over creation (1.10) and the perfection of the church as the body of Christ (4.12–16). Because Ephesians describes the church in such universal and glorious terms, it has been used by theologians (including Thomas Aquinas, Luther, and Calvin) throughout the centuries to establish their vision of the church and its mission.

GUIDE TO READING

The first chapter of Ephesians introduces nearly all the theological ideas and themes developed in the letter. The first section (1.3–14) gives a sweeping overview of God's plan for salvation, while the second (1.15–23) focuses upon how this plan should be realized in believers' lives. Readers may find it helpful to keep this passage in mind as they read the rest of Ephesians and to note how subsequent passages fill out the meaning of its poetic evocation.

Jennifer K. Berenson

1

Paul, an apostle of Christ Jesus by the will of God,

To the saints who are in Ephesus and are faithful[a] in Christ Jesus:

[2] Grace to you and peace from God our Father and the Lord Jesus Christ.

[3] Blessed be the God and Father of our Lord Jesus Christ, who has blessed us in Christ with every spiritual blessing in the heavenly places, [4] just as he chose us in Christ[b] before the foundation of the world to be holy and blameless before him in love. [5] He destined us for adoption as his children through Jesus Christ, according to the good pleasure of his will, [6] to the praise of his glorious grace that he freely bestowed on us in the Beloved. [7] In him we have redemption through his blood, the forgiveness of our trespasses, according to the riches of his grace [8] that he lavished on us. With all wisdom and insight [9] he has made known to us the mystery of his will, according to his good pleasure that he set forth in Christ, [10] as a plan for the fullness of time, to gather up all things in him, things in heaven and things on earth. [11] In Christ we have also obtained an inheritance,[c] having been destined according to the purpose of him who accomplishes all things according to his counsel and will, [12] so that we, who were the first to set our hope on Christ, might live for the praise of his glory. [13] In him you also, when you had heard the word of truth, the gospel of your salvation, and had believed in him, were marked with the seal of the promised Holy Spirit; [14] this[d] is the pledge of our inheritance toward redemption as God's own people, to the praise of his glory.

[15] I have heard of your faith in the Lord Jesus and your love[e] toward all the saints, and for this reason [16] I do not cease to give thanks for you as I remember you in my prayers. [17] I pray that the God of our Lord Jesus Christ, the Father of glory, may give you a spirit of wisdom and revelation as you come to know him, [18] so that, with the eyes of your heart enlightened, you may know what is the hope to which he has called you, what are the riches

a   Other ancient authorities lack *in Ephesus*, reading *saints who are also faithful*
b   Gk *in him*
c   Or *been made a heritage*
d   Other ancient authorities read *who*
e   Other ancient authorities lack *and your love*

1.1–2: **Salutation** (cf. Col 1.1–2). *Apostle*, see Rom 1.1n. *By the will of God*, see 3.2–13. *Saints . . . faithful*, emphasizing two foundational aspects of Christian existence: holiness (see Col 1.2n.) and steadfast loyalty to Jesus. *Ephesus*, an important city on the west coast of Asia Minor, where Paul had a successful ministry (see the Introduction and Acts 18.19–21; 19; 1 Cor 16.8–9). **2:** A common Pauline greeting drawing upon and transforming conventional Greek (*grace*) and Hebrew (*peace*) salutations.

1.3–14: **Blessing of God for his blessings to the church** (cf. Rom 8.15–34). **3:** *Blessed be*, this extended praise of God is based on a traditional Jewish form of worship that enumerates God's actions on behalf of Israel (1 Kings 8.15,56; Lk 1.68–75). *In Christ*, a theme throughout this section, indicating Christ's mediation of divine blessings. *In the heavenly places*, anticipates the letter's interest in heavenly realities accessible in the present (1.20–23; 2.6–7; 3.11–12). **4:** *Chose us*, the language of Israel's election as God's people (Deut 7.6–8) is used here for Christian believers. *Before the foundation . . . to be holy and blameless*, God's election of and care for believers extends from before creation through the coming judgment. **5:** *Adoption*, a privileged status allowing intimacy and full inheritance rights (see 1.11–14; Rom 8.15–17; Gal 4.5). **6:** *Beloved*, a title for Christ; cf. "beloved son," Mk 1.11; Col 1.13. **7:** *Redemption*, the first hint of opposition to God's plan (see Col 1.14n. and Eph 1.21; 2.2; 6.10–17). *His blood*, Christ's sacrificial death brings divine *forgiveness* for moral failures. **9:** *Mystery*, the previously hidden plan of God, which here encompasses all creation (Dan 2.17–30; Rom 8:18–23; cf. Eph 3.1–6; Col 1.26–27). **10:** God's plan culminates in the unification of the cosmos under and through Christ (1.20–22; cf. Col 1.15–20). **13:** *You*, Gentiles (2.11; 3.1) have also been included in God's blessings. According to Paul the promise of the *Spirit* came through Abraham (Gal 3.14,22); the Spirit is also associated with the prophet Joel (Joel 2.28–32; Acts 2.14–21) and Jesus' promise (Lk 24.49; Jn 14.26; Acts 1.4–5). *Seal*, a mark of ownership and protection; see also 4.30. **14:** *Pledge*, the same Gk word is translated "first installment" in 2 Cor 1.22.

1.15–23: **Thanksgiving prayer for wisdom and power** (cf. Col 1.3–14). **15:** *Faith . . . love*, two central Christian virtues (1 Cor 13.13; 1 Thess 5.8; Col 1.3–5). **17–18:** *Hope*, the third virtue, is here not just eschatological, but also the ability to understand (*wisdom, revelation, enlightened*) God's purposes and how to live rightly in response (cf. 4.18).

of his glorious inheritance among the saints, [19] and what is the immeasurable greatness of his power for us who believe, according to the working of his great power. [20] God[a] put this power to work in Christ when he raised him from the dead and seated him at his right hand in the heavenly places, [21] far above all rule and authority and power and dominion, and above every name that is named, not only in this age but also in the age to come. [22] And he has put all things under his feet and has made him the head over all things for the church, [23] which is his body, the fullness of him who fills all in all.

2 You were dead through the trespasses and sins [2] in which you once lived, following the course of this world, following the ruler of the power of the air, the spirit that is now at work among those who are disobedient. [3] All of us once lived among them in the passions of our flesh, following the desires of flesh and senses, and we were by nature children of wrath, like everyone else. [4] But God, who is rich in mercy, out of the great love with which he loved us [5] even when we were dead through our trespasses, made us alive together with Christ[b]—by grace you have been saved— [6] and raised us up with him and seated us with him in the heavenly places in Christ Jesus, [7] so that in the ages to come he might show the immeasurable riches of his grace in kindness toward us in Christ Jesus. [8] For by grace you have been saved through faith, and this is not your own doing; it is the gift of God— [9] not the result of works, so that no one may boast. [10] For we are what he has made us, created in Christ Jesus for good works, which God prepared beforehand to be our way of life.

[11] So then, remember that at one time you Gentiles by birth,[c] called "the uncircumcision" by those who are called "the circumcision"—a physical circumcision made in the flesh by human hands— [12] remember that you were at that time without Christ, being aliens from the commonwealth of Israel, and strangers to the covenants of promise, having no hope and without God in the world. [13] But now in Christ Jesus you who once were far off have been brought near by the blood of Christ. [14] For he is our peace; in his flesh he has made both groups

a   Gk *He*
b   Other ancient authorities read *in Christ*
c   Gk *in the flesh*

19   20: An emphatic assertion that God's *power* is available to believers to live out their calling (cf. 2.6; 3.7,16,20). *At his right hand*, a common early Christian description, dependent on Ps 110.1, of Christ's exaltation (Acts 2.34–35; Rom 8.34; Col 3.1; Heb 8.1). **21:** *Rule . . . dominion*, hostile spiritual powers subjected to Christ (Col 1.16; cf. 1 Cor 15.20–28). *Name*, see Phil 2.9. **22:** *Under his feet*, see Ps 8:6; 1 Cor 15.27; cf. Ps 110.1. **22–23:** *Head . . . body*, see Col 1.18n. Scholars disagree on the origin of the head-body metaphor developed here (see also Eph 4.12,15–16), which is found in various forms of cosmic speculation in Hellenistic, Jewish, and Gnostic thought. **23:** *Fullness*, the church expresses God's power and presence to the world or perhaps the church has been completed by Christ (3.19; Col 1.19n.; 2.9–10; see also Jer 23.24).

2.1–10: The old life contrasted with the new (cf. Col 1.21–23). **1–5:** Formerly both Gentile (*you*) and Jewish (*all of us*) Christians habitually sinned and lacked God's protection and blessings (*were dead/children of wrath*). **2:** *Course*, literally "age," a reference to the present as a limited period in which human life is pervaded and perverted by the devil (*the ruler . . . air*; 6.10–17; see also Rom 6.12–13). **3:** *Children of wrath*, those who will be punished at the future judgment (1 Thess 5.4–10). **5,8:** *By grace . . . saved*, deliverance to a new life is due solely to God's mercy and benevolence (1.7). **5–6:** *Made us alive . . . raised us . . . seated us*, believers have been exalted like Christ himself (1.20). **9:** *Works*, individual achievement (*your own doing*, v. 8), not "works of the law" as in Gal 2.16. **10:** *Good works*, the ethical *way of life* imperative in God's plan is emphasized here (1.4; 1 Tim 6.18; Titus 2.14; 3.8). *Prepared beforehand*, see 1.4.

2.11–22: The unity of Jews and Gentiles in the church. **11:** *The uncircumcision*, a derogatory term for Gentiles. *The circumcision*, Jews, but often used for those who required all believers to obey the law of Moses (Acts 10.45; Gal 2.12; Col 4.11; cf. Phil 3.3). **12–13:** *You were . . . But now*, another contrast of old and new (2.1–5), focused on the Gentiles' plight as *aliens* and *strangers* from Israel and God. **12:** *Covenants of promise*, God promised Abraham (Gen 15.18; 17.2–8), Israel/Jacob (Gen 28.13–15), and David (2 Sam 7; Ps 89) his presence and protection (see Ps 105). **13:** *Far off . . . brought near*, Christ's death reconciles Gentiles with God (v. 17; cf. Isa

into one and has broken down the dividing wall, that is, the hostility between us. ¹⁵ He has abolished the law with its commandments and ordinances, that he might create in himself one new humanity in place of the two, thus making peace, ¹⁶ and might reconcile both groups to God in one body[a] through the cross, thus putting to death that hostility through it.[b] ¹⁷ So he came and proclaimed peace to you who were far off and peace to those who were near; ¹⁸ for through him both of us have access in one Spirit to the Father. ¹⁹ So then you are no longer strangers and aliens, but you are citizens with the saints and also members of the household of God, ²⁰ built upon the foundation of the apostles and prophets, with Christ Jesus himself as the cornerstone.[c] ²¹ In him the whole structure is joined together and grows into a holy temple in the Lord; ²² in whom you also are built together spiritually[d] into a dwelling place for God.

3 This is the reason that I Paul am a prisoner for[e] Christ Jesus for the sake of you Gentiles— ² for surely you have already heard of the commission of God's grace that was given me for you, ³ and how the mystery was made known to me by revelation, as I wrote above in a few words, ⁴ a reading of which will enable you to perceive my understanding of the mystery of Christ. ⁵ In former generations this mystery[f] was not made known to humankind, as it has now been revealed to his holy apostles and prophets by the Spirit:

⁶ that is, the Gentiles have become fellow heirs, members of the same body, and sharers in the promise in Christ Jesus through the gospel.

⁷ Of this gospel I have become a servant according to the gift of God's grace that was given me by the working of his power. ⁸ Although I am the very least of all the saints, this grace was given to me to bring to the Gentiles the news of the boundless riches of Christ, ⁹ and to make everyone see[g] what is the plan of the mystery hidden for ages in[h] God who created all things; ¹⁰ so that through the church the wisdom of God in its rich variety might now be made known to the rulers and authorities in the heavenly places. ¹¹ This was in accordance with the eternal purpose that he has carried out in Christ Jesus our Lord, ¹² in whom we have access to God in boldness and confidence through faith in him.[i] ¹³ I pray therefore that you[j] may not lose heart over my sufferings for you; they are your glory.

a Or *reconcile both of us in one body for God*
b Or *in him*, or *in himself*
c Or *keystone*
d Gk *in the Spirit*
e Or *of*
f Gk *it*
g Other ancient authorities read *to bring to light*
h Or *by*
i Or *the faith of him*
j Or *I*

57.19). **14:** *Made both groups into one*, a second result of Christ's death is uniting Jews and Gentiles in a new community. *Dividing wall*, the Jewish law; perhaps also the balustrade in the Jerusalem Temple, beyond which Gentiles were forbidden to go. **15:** *Abolished the law*, in the author's view the primary function of the law is to distinguish Jews from Gentiles, thus promoting *hostility* (Acts 10.28); this harsh conclusion is later softened by direct quotation from the law (6.2–3) **16:** A summary of vv. 11–15. **17:** *Proclaimed peace*, see Isa 52.7. **19:** *Citizens*, a civic metaphor for their full inclusion among God's children (1.5,11–14). **20–22:** The author uses a mixture of architectural and agricultural metaphors to describe the dependence of God's people on each other and on the Lord Jesus (4.15–16). **20:** *Prophets*, early Christian prophets (3.5; 4.11; 1 Cor 14). *Cornerstone*, either the foundation (Isa 28.16), or the capstone (*T. Sol.* 22.7) that completes a building. **21–22:** *A holy temple*, the community embodies the presence of God; the Essenes held a similar view of themselves in direct contrast with the Jerusalem Temple (1QS 8.4–10).

3.1–13: Paul reveals God's plan (cf. Col 1.24–29). **1:** A prayer is interrupted by vv. 2–13 and resumed in v. 14. **2:** *Commission*, Paul's encounter with Christ (Gal 1.15–16). **3:** *Mystery*, see 1.9n.; here, the uniting of Jews and Gentiles into a single community (3.6,9–12; Col 1.27; 2.2). *Above*, literally, "previously," either in 1.9–10 or perhaps in an earlier letter. **8:** *Least*, 1 Cor 15.8–9. **10:** *Wisdom of God . . . heavenly places*, the church embodies and thus reveals God's plan (*wisdom*) and Christ's supremacy to hostile spiritual powers. **13:** *Sufferings . . . glory*, imprisonment on behalf of the Gentiles (3.1) has secured their new life and future glorification (2 Cor 1.6; 4.12; Col 1.24).

[14] For this reason I bow my knees before the Father,[a] [15] from whom every family[b] in heaven and on earth takes its name. [16] I pray that, according to the riches of his glory, he may grant that you may be strengthened in your inner being with power through his Spirit, [17] and that Christ may dwell in your hearts through faith, as you are being rooted and grounded in love. [18] I pray that you may have the power to comprehend, with all the saints, what is the breadth and length and height and depth, [19] and to know the love of Christ that surpasses knowledge, so that you may be filled with all the fullness of God.

[20] Now to him who by the power at work within us is able to accomplish abundantly far more than all we can ask or imagine, [21] to him be glory in the church and in Christ Jesus to all generations, forever and ever. Amen.

4 I therefore, the prisoner in the Lord, beg you to lead a life worthy of the calling to which you have been called, [2] with all humility and gentleness, with patience, bearing with one another in love, [3] making every effort to maintain the unity of the Spirit in the bond of peace. [4] There is one body and one Spirit, just as you were called to the one hope of your calling, [5] one Lord, one faith, one baptism, [6] one God and Father of all, who is above all and through all and in all.

[7] But each of us was given grace according to the measure of Christ's gift. [8] Therefore it is said,

"When he ascended on high he made
    captivity itself a captive;
he gave gifts to his people."

[9] (When it says, "He ascended," what does it mean but that he had also descended[c] into the lower parts of the earth? [10] He who descended is the same one who ascended far above all the heavens, so that he might fill all things.) [11] The gifts he gave were that some would be apostles, some prophets, some evangelists, some pastors and teachers, [12] to equip the saints for the work of ministry, for building up the body of Christ, [13] until all of us come to the unity of the faith and of the knowledge of the Son of God, to maturity, to the measure of the full stature of Christ. [14] We must no longer be children, tossed to and fro and blown about by every wind of doctrine, by people's trickery, by their craftiness in deceitful scheming. [15] But speaking the truth in love, we must grow up in every way into him who is the head, into Christ, [16] from whom the whole body, joined and knit together by every ligament with which it is equipped, as each part is working properly, promotes the body's growth in building itself up in love.

[17] Now this I affirm and insist on in the Lord: you must no longer live as the Gentiles live, in the futility of their minds. [18] They are darkened in their understanding, alienated from the life of God because of their ignorance and hardness of heart. [19] They have lost all sensitivity and have abandoned themselves to licentiousness, greedy to practice every kind of impurity. [20] That is not the way you learned Christ! [21] For surely you have heard about him

a Other ancient authorities add *of our Lord Jesus Christ*
b Gk *fatherhood*
c Other ancient authorities add *first*

3.14–21: Prayer for the church to live up to its destiny. 14–15: *Father . . . family*, a play on words in Greek ("pater," "patria," see note *b*); God is the Father (creator and ruler) of all nations and spiritual powers. **16–18:** The author returns to themes found in 1.15–20. **18–19:** *Breadth, length, height, depth*, the dimensions of God's wisdom or Christ's love; in either case emphasizing immensity. **19:** *Filled with all the fullness*, 1.23n. **20–21:** A doxology celebrating God's ability to accomplish his plan for the church through the Spirit's power.

4.1–6.20: Ethical exhortation. 4.1–16: Appeal for unity amid diversity. 1: This exhortation balances the divine *calling* with human responsibility. **2–3:** See a similar list of virtues in Gal 5.22–23. **3:** *Unity* and *peace*, made possible by Christ (2.11–22), must be consciously maintained. **4–6:** Seven bases of unity. **8–11:** Ps 68.18 is interpreted as revealing Christ's exaltation over the spiritual powers (1.20–22) and *gifts* of leadership for the church. **9:** *Lower parts of the earth*, either the earth itself or Hades. **12:** *To equip the saints*, literally, "for the completion of the saints." *For the work of ministry*, highlighting the purpose of Christian leadership. **14:** *Wind of doctrine*, Jas 1.6; Jude 12,13. **15:** A vision of the church as an organic, interrelated whole, whose goal is to reflect fully its head, Christ (2.20–22).

4.17–5.21: Appeal for a changed way of life (cf. Col 3.5–17). **4.17–18:** On the plight of the Gentiles, see 2.1–

and were taught in him, as truth is in Jesus. [22] You were taught to put away your former way of life, your old self, corrupt and deluded by its lusts, [23] and to be renewed in the spirit of your minds, [24] and to clothe yourselves with the new self, created according to the likeness of God in true righteousness and holiness.

[25] So then, putting away falsehood, let all of us speak the truth to our neighbors, for we are members of one another. [26] Be angry but do not sin; do not let the sun go down on your anger, [27] and do not make room for the devil. [28] Thieves must give up stealing; rather let them labor and work honestly with their own hands, so as to have something to share with the needy. [29] Let no evil talk come out of your mouths, but only what is useful for building up,[a] as there is need, so that your words may give grace to those who hear. [30] And do not grieve the Holy Spirit of God, with which you were marked with a seal for the day of redemption. [31] Put away from you all bitterness and wrath and anger and wrangling and slander, together with all malice, [32] and be kind to one another, tenderhearted, forgiving one another, as God in Christ has forgiven

5 you.[b] [1] Therefore be imitators of God, as beloved children, [2] and live in love, as Christ loved us[c] and gave himself up for us, a fragrant offering and sacrifice to God.

[3] But fornication and impurity of any kind, or greed, must not even be mentioned among you, as is proper among saints. [4] Entirely out of place is obscene, silly, and vulgar talk; but instead, let there be thanksgiving. [5] Be sure of this, that no fornicator or impure person, or one who is greedy (that is, an idolater), has any inheritance in the kingdom of Christ and of God.

[6] Let no one deceive you with empty words, for because of these things the wrath of God comes on those who are disobedient. [7] Therefore do not be associated with them. [8] For once you were darkness, but now in the Lord you are light. Live as children of light— [9] for the fruit of the light is found in all that is good and right and true. [10] Try to find out what is pleasing to the Lord. [11] Take no part in the unfruitful works of darkness, but instead expose them. [12] For it is shameful even to mention what such people do secretly; [13] but everything exposed by the light becomes visible, [14] for everything that becomes visible is light. Therefore it says,

"Sleeper, awake!
Rise from the dead,
and Christ will shine on you."

[15] Be careful then how you live, not as unwise people but as wise, [16] making the most of the time, because the days are evil. [17] So do not be foolish, but understand what the will of the Lord is. [18] Do not get drunk with wine, for that is debauchery; but be filled with the Spirit, [19] as you sing psalms and hymns and spiritual songs among yourselves, singing and making melody to the Lord in your hearts, [20] giving thanks to God the Father at all times and for everything in the name of our Lord Jesus Christ.

[21] Be subject to one another out of reverence for Christ.

[22] Wives, be subject to your husbands as you are to the Lord. [23] For the husband is the

---

a   Other ancient authorities read *building up faith*
b   Other ancient authorities read *us*
c   Other ancient authorities read *you*

3,11–12. 19: *Licentiousness . . . impurity*, excessive and inappropriate sexual behavior (5.3,5). **22–24:** The *old* lifestyle, like worn-out clothing, must be replaced by a *new* lifestyle guided by one's knowledge of Christ. **25:** *Speak the truth*, see 4.15; Zech 8.16. **26:** On *anger*, see also 1 Cor 13.5; Jas 1.19. **29:** *Building up*, see 2.20–22; 4.16. **30:** *Seal*, see 1.13n. **4:32–5.2:** *Kindness* and *love* are identified as central virtues stemming from imitation of God and Christ. **5.2:** *Fragrant offering*, see Ex 29.18; Ezek 20.41. **3–5:** Sexual sins are the primary focus in these verses (4.19). **4:** Proper speech is a recurring theme (4.15,29). **8:** *Darkness/light*, opposing images for the domains of hostile spiritual powers and unrepentant Gentiles, and of God and believers. **11–13:** See John 3.20. **14:** *Sleeper . . . you*, perhaps a fragment of a baptismal hymn. **21:** Some feminist scholars see this call to mutual subjection as a principle that moderates the subordination of wives prescribed by the conventional household code that follows; others fault the author for failing to challenge female subordination in any significant way.

5.22–6.9: Rules for household relationships (cf. Col 3.18–4.1). On the form of these rules, see Col 3.18–4.1n. **5.22–33:** Relations between *wives* and *husbands*. The subordination of *wives* to *husbands* is legitimized by an

head of the wife just as Christ is the head of the church, the body of which he is the Savior. [24] Just as the church is subject to Christ, so also wives ought to be, in everything, to their husbands.

[25] Husbands, love your wives, just as Christ loved the church and gave himself up for her, [26] in order to make her holy by cleansing her with the washing of water by the word, [27] so as to present the church to himself in splendor, without a spot or wrinkle or anything of the kind—yes, so that she may be holy and without blemish. [28] In the same way, husbands should love their wives as they do their own bodies. He who loves his wife loves himself. [29] For no one ever hates his own body, but he nourishes and tenderly cares for it, just as Christ does for the church, [30] because we are members of his body.[a] [31] "For this reason a man will leave his father and mother and be joined to his wife, and the two will become one flesh." [32] This is a great mystery, and I am applying it to Christ and the church. [33] Each of you, however, should love his wife as himself, and a wife should respect her husband.

6 Children, obey your parents in the Lord,[b] for this is right. [2] "Honor your father and mother" this is the first commandment with a promise: [3] "so that it may be well with you and you may live long on the earth."

[4] And, fathers, do not provoke your children to anger, but bring them up in the discipline and instruction of the Lord.

[5] Slaves, obey your earthly masters with fear and trembling, in singleness of heart, as you obey Christ; [6] not only while being watched, and in order to please them, but as slaves of Christ, doing the will of God from the heart. [7] Render service with enthusiasm, as to the Lord and not to men and women, [8] knowing that whatever good we do, we will receive the same again from the Lord, whether we are slaves or free.

[9] And, masters, do the same to them. Stop threatening them, for you know that both of you have the same Master in heaven, and with him there is no partiality.

[10] Finally, be strong in the Lord and in the strength of his power. [11] Put on the whole armor of God, so that you may be able to stand against the wiles of the devil. [12] For our[c] struggle is not against enemies of blood and flesh, but against the rulers, against the authorities, against the cosmic powers of this present darkness, against the spiritual forces of evil in the heavenly places. [13] Therefore take up the whole armor of God, so that you may be

a Other ancient authorities add *of his flesh and of his bones*

b Other ancient authorities lack *in the Lord*

c Other ancient authorities read *your*

extended analogy: The husband's role is aligned with Christ's authority over the church (*head*; see 1.22; 4.15 and Col 1.18n.), while wives are to imitate the church as the obedient recipient of Christ's blessings (*body*). **22:** *Be subject*, accept a position of subordination to the husband's authority. **25–29:** The marriage relationship is to be modeled on that between Christ and the church, in which the church's purity was achieved through Christ's death and continual care. *Husbands* are to imitate Christ's self-sacrifice, a standard elsewhere held up for all (5.2). Feminist criticism points out that granting divine authority to the male and expecting passivity of women may legitimate abusive relationships. **26:** Baptism is compared to the Jewish custom of a bride's prenuptial bath. **28–30:** Here the author draws upon the identity of the church as Christ's body to motivate the husband's deep care for his wife. **30–32:** *Mystery*, the unity of Christ and the church as revealed through interpretation of Gen 2.24. Note the scribal addition from Gen 2.23 (see note *a*). **33:** See Lev 19.18. **6.1–4:** Relations between *children* and *fathers*. Note that children are to obey their parents, but instructions are only given to fathers concerning their upbringing. Legally, all children were property of their father. **2–3:** Ex 20.12; Deut 5.16. **5–9:** Relations between *slaves* and *masters*. Like wives, *slaves* are not to imitate Christ but obey their masters' divinely sanctioned authority; see Col 3.22–4.1; Titus 2.9–10. **6:** *Not only while being watched*, a stereotypical accusation made against slaves. **8:** An eschatological reward is used to motivate Christian slaves; cf. Gal 3.28. **9:** *Masters* must recognize their own subjection to God, who despite sanctioning these social differences shows no *partiality*.

6.10–20: Appeal for strength in spiritual battle. 12: The Christian's enemies are not human (*blood and flesh*), but spiritual (1.21; 2.2). **13–17:** The *armor* of Israel's divine protector (Isa 11.4–5; 52.7; 59.17; Wis 5.17–20). **13:**

able to withstand on that evil day, and having done everything, to stand firm. [14] Stand therefore, and fasten the belt of truth around your waist, and put on the breastplate of righteousness. [15] As shoes for your feet put on whatever will make you ready to proclaim the gospel of peace. [16] With all of these,[a] take the shield of faith, with which you will be able to quench all the flaming arrows of the evil one. [17] Take the helmet of salvation, and the sword of the Spirit, which is the word of God.

[18] Pray in the Spirit at all times in every prayer and supplication. To that end keep alert and always persevere in supplication for all the saints. [19] Pray also for me, so that when I speak, a message may be given to me to make known with boldness the mystery of the gospel,[b] [20] for which I am an ambassador

in chains. Pray that I may declare it boldly, as I must speak.

[21] So that you also may know how I am and what I am doing, Tychicus will tell you everything. He is a dear brother and a faithful minister in the Lord. [22] I am sending him to you for this very purpose, to let you know how we are, and to encourage your hearts.

[23] Peace be to the whole community,[c] and love with faith, from God the Father and the Lord Jesus Christ. [24] Grace be with all who have an undying love for our Lord Jesus Christ.[d]

[a] Or *In all circumstances*
[b] Other ancient authorities lack *of the gospel*
[c] Gk *to the brothers*
[d] Other ancient authorities add *Amen*

That evil day, all Christian existence is situated within an ongoing spiritual conflict (5.16). **14**: *Truth*, 4.15,25. *Righteousness*, here appropriate Christian behavior. **15**: *Gospel of peace*, 2.14–18. **17**: *Salvation*, deliverance from evil powers. *The sword*, the only offensive weapon mentioned, is the proclamation of the gospel. **20**: *In chains*, see 3.1; 4.1.

6.21–24: Epilogue (Cf. Col 4.7–8.) **21**: *Tychicus*, Paul's associate; see Acts 20.4; Col 4.7; 2 Tim 4.12. **23**: *Whole community*, the Greek "brothers" (note c) includes both men and women. **24**: *Undying*, the final words of the letter are "in immortality," perhaps instead pointing toward God's unending grace in the age to come.

THE LETTER OF PAUL TO THE PHILIPPIANS

NAME AND AUTHORSHIP

The letter to the Philippians is one of the richest of Paul's letters and has never been seriously questioned as genuine. Philippi was a major city of Macedonia in northern Greece and a Roman colony on the Via Egnatia, the Roman road linking Byzantium in the East to the western coast of Macedonia, from which ships could easily reach Italy. The Christian community in Philippi was the westernmost Pauline church at the time of its founding (Acts 16.11–13). The mutual affection between Paul and the Philippians is evident in the letter and contrasts with the problems Paul faced in other churches.

DATE AND PLACE OF COMPOSITION

Except that Paul was in prison and awaiting trial at the time of writing (1.2–26), it is impossible to speak confidently of the time and place of the writing of this letter. Because of references to the imperial guard or praetorium (1.13) and to the emperor's household (4.22), and also because the situation reflected in the letter bears some resemblance to that described at the end of Acts, the traditional date of the letter has been during Paul's imprisonment at Rome (about 61–63 CE). The indications are by no means conclusive, however, and more recently some scholars have thought that the place of composition is perhaps Caesarea before Paul's arrival in Rome (Acts 24–26) or Ephesus at an earlier stage in Paul's career, especially because of the several goings and comings between Paul and Philippi implied in the letter (2.19,25–26; 4.10,18) that seem to be inconsistent with the great distance from Philippi to Rome. The terms referring to the emperor's household were also used for provincial government centers and the imperial civil service outside Rome. Elsewhere Paul notes an unhappy situation in Ephesus (1 Cor 15.32) and in the Roman province of Asia, of which Ephesus was a major center (2 Cor 1.8), and in Acts 20.16 he bypasses Ephesus on his way south down the coast. These indicators suggest an Ephesian imprisonment and the occasion of the letter.

The immediate occasion of Paul's writing was the return to Philippi of Epaphroditus (2.25–30), who was sent by the Philippian church with gifts for Paul (4.18), and who then became seriously ill while staying with him. Paul took this opportunity to thank them for their gifts and to set their mutual difficulties in a wider framework by describing his and their situation in light of the reality of Christ.

STRUCTURE AND INTERPRETATION

The letter follows the usual pattern of Paul's letters, but some abrupt changes of topic (especially between 3.1 and 2, and 4.3 and 4), in addition to the fact that an early Christian writer (Polycarp, *Philippians* 2.3) speaks of "letters" of Paul to the Philippians, have led some scholars to conclude that our present Philippians is composed of as many as three letters that Paul wrote to Philippi. Many scholars, however, find that Philippians is a coherent whole as it stands. After the greeting (1.1–2) and thanksgiving (1.3–11), Paul lays out the situation (1.12–26) and exhorts the community to unity (1.27–4.3) with many arguments, including proposing Christ (2.5–11), Timothy and Epaphroditus (2.19–30), and himself (3.4–14) as models of self-giving for the good of the whole. He thanks them for their recent gift (4.10–20) and concludes the letter (4.21–23).

Paul writes from prison uncertain of the outcome for himself (1.12–26). The themes of opposition and the possibility of death are therefore prominent. Yet in the midst of suffering and uncertainty, the theme of joy emerges quite clearly and remarkably (1.4,18,25; 2.2,17–18,28; 4.4,10). The Philippians too are experiencing opposition (1.29), but Paul's major concern is to bring them together and thus to overcome the threat of internal disharmony. In keeping with that purpose, he uses a hymnic passage that celebrates the self-emptying of Christ even to death, for which God bestowed on him the name of "Lord," the "name above all names" (2.6–11). The hymn was probably composed by a prior author, perhaps originally in Aramaic, and was known to both Paul and the Philippians. Here it serves as the prime example of why they should be willing also to empty themselves of their own opinions. The example of Paul himself follows and supports the argument (3.4–16). Paul offers both Christ and himself as examples of courage and self-surrender in the face of suffering and death. Thus he exhorts the Philippians to turn away from partisan interest to unity.

Carolyn Osiek

1 Paul and Timothy, servants[a] of Christ Jesus,

To all the saints in Christ Jesus who are in Philippi, with the bishops[b] and deacons:[c]

[2] Grace to you and peace from God our Father and the Lord Jesus Christ.

[3] I thank my God every time I remember you, [4] constantly praying with joy in every one of my prayers for all of you, [5] because of your sharing in the gospel from the first day until now. [6] I am confident of this, that the one who began a good work among you will bring it to completion by the day of Jesus Christ. [7] It is right for me to think this way about all of you, because you hold me in your heart,[d] for all of you share in God's grace[e] with me, both in my imprisonment and in the defense and confirmation of the gospel. [8] For God is my witness, how I long for all of you with the compassion of Christ Jesus. [9] And this is my prayer, that your love may overflow more and more with knowledge and full insight [10] to help you to determine what is best, so that in the day of Christ you may be pure and blameless, [11] having produced the harvest of righteousness that comes through Jesus Christ for the glory and praise of God.

[12] I want you to know, beloved,[f] that what has happened to me has actually helped to spread the gospel, [13] so that it has become known throughout the whole imperial guard[g] and to everyone else that my imprisonment

is for Christ; [14] and most of the brothers and sisters,[f] having been made confident in the Lord by my imprisonment, dare to speak the word[h] with greater boldness and without fear. [15] Some proclaim Christ from envy and rivalry, but others from goodwill. [16] These proclaim Christ out of love, knowing that I have been put here for the defense of the gospel; [17] the others proclaim Christ out of selfish ambition, not sincerely but intending to increase my suffering in my imprisonment. [18] What does it matter? Just this, that Christ is proclaimed in every way, whether out of false motives or true; and in that I rejoice.

Yes, and I will continue to rejoice, [19] for I know that through your prayers and the help of the Spirit of Jesus Christ this will turn out for my deliverance. [20] It is my eager expectation and hope that I will not be put to shame in any way, but that by my speaking with all boldness, Christ will be exalted now as always in my body, whether by life or by death. [21] For to me, living is Christ and dying is gain. [22] If I am to live in the flesh, that means fruit-

[a] Gk *slaves*
[b] Or *overseers*
[c] Or *overseers and helpers*
[d] Or *because I hold you in my heart*
[e] Gk *in grace*
[f] Gk *brothers*
[g] Gk *whole praetorium*
[h] Other ancient authorities read *word of God*

1.1–2: Salutation. 1: *Bishops and deacons,* the alternate translation *overseers and helpers* is preferable. These functions are not yet the church offices that they will later become.

1.3–11: Thanksgiving. A common feature of a Pauline letter. **5:** *Sharing,* "koinônia," an important Pauline concept (2.1; 3.10; 4.15) that was key to his understanding of Christian unity. *From the first day,* when Paul first preached at Philippi (Acts 16.12). **6:** *The day of Jesus Christ,* when he will return and the present age will end (2.16; see 1 Cor 1.8; cf. 2 Thess 2.3 and 2 Pet 3.10). **10:** Rom 2.18.

1.12–26: Paul's situation in chains. 13: Paul is confined in some Roman administrative center, where he has had the opportunity to preach the gospel. **15–18:** Not all Christian preachers agreed with Paul or liked him; this is clear in Galatians and 1 and 2 Corinthians (especially 2 Cor 10–13), and here Paul questions their motives. Accusations against opponents was a common rhetorical tactic. **19:** This will turn out for my deliverance, quoting Job 13.16. **21–24:** His life is not his own but is given over to Christ, so that he is indifferent to the outcome of life or death; nevertheless, his death would mean loss to his churches.

ful labor for me; and I do not know which I prefer. ²³ I am hard pressed between the two: my desire is to depart and be with Christ, for that is far better; ²⁴ but to remain in the flesh is more necessary for you. ²⁵ Since I am convinced of this, I know that I will remain and continue with all of you for your progress and joy in faith, ²⁶ so that I may share abundantly in your boasting in Christ Jesus when I come to you again.

²⁷ Only, live your life in a manner worthy of the gospel of Christ, so that, whether I come and see you or am absent and hear about you, I will know that you are standing firm in one spirit, striving side by side with one mind for the faith of the gospel, ²⁸ and are in no way intimidated by your opponents. For them this is evidence of their destruction, but of your salvation. And this is God's doing. ²⁹ For he has graciously granted you the privilege not only of believing in Christ, but of suffering for him as well— ³⁰ since you are having the same struggle that you saw I had and now hear that I still have.

2 If then there is any encouragement in Christ, any consolation from love, any sharing in the Spirit, any compassion and sympathy, ² make my joy complete: be of the same mind, having the same love, being in full accord and of one mind. ³ Do nothing from selfish ambition or conceit, but in humility regard others as better than yourselves. ⁴ Let each of you look not to your own interests, but to the interests of others. ⁵ Let the same mind be in you that was^a in Christ Jesus,

> ⁶ who, though he was in the form of God,
> did not regard equality with God
> as something to be exploited,
> ⁷ but emptied himself,
> taking the form of a slave,
> being born in human likeness.

And being found in human form,
> ⁸ he humbled himself
> and became obedient to the point of
> death—
> even death on a cross.

> ⁹ Therefore God also highly exalted him
> and gave him the name
> that is above every name,
> ¹⁰ so that at the name of Jesus
> every knee should bend,
> in heaven and on earth and under the
> earth,
> ¹¹ and every tongue should confess
> that Jesus Christ is Lord,
> to the glory of God the Father.

¹² Therefore, my beloved, just as you have always obeyed me, not only in my presence, but much more now in my absence, work out your own salvation with fear and trembling; ¹³ for it is God who is at work in you, enabling you both to will and to work for his good pleasure.

¹⁴ Do all things without murmuring and arguing, ¹⁵ so that you may be blameless and innocent, children of God without blemish in the midst of a crooked and perverse generation, in which you shine like stars in the world. ¹⁶ It is by your holding fast to the word of life that I can boast on the day of Christ that I did not run in vain or labor in vain. ¹⁷ But even if I am being poured out as a libation over the sacrifice and the offering of your faith, I am glad and rejoice with all of you— ¹⁸ and in the same way you also must be glad and rejoice with me.

¹⁹ I hope in the Lord Jesus to send Timothy to you soon, so that I may be cheered by news of you. ²⁰ I have no one like him who will be

a Or *that you have*

1.27–4.4: Appeal to unity, to be followed by examples. 2.1–18: First example: self-emptying of Christ. 6: *In the form of God, equality with God,* may refer to divine status, or simply preexistence as a heavenly being (Dan 7.14), or Adam's original immortality (Wis 2.23–24), which Christ renounced by becoming subject to death. **7:** *But emptied himself,* the extreme limit of self-denial. **8:** Mt 26.39; Jn 10.18; Rom 5.19; Heb 5.8; 12.2. **9:** *Exalted,* in raising him from the dead. *The name . . . above every name* is Lord. **10–11:** Cf. Isa 45.23. **12:** *With fear and trembling,* a frequent biblical expression (Ex 15.16; Deut 2.25; Ps 2.11; Isa 19.6; 4 Macc 4.10) that had become commonplace (1 Cor 2.3; 2 Cor 7.15; Eph 6.5). **15:** *Shine like stars,* Dan 12.3. **16:** *Day of Christ,* see 1.6n. **17:** Paul's possible death is compared to a temple sacrifice.

2.19–3.1a: Second example: Timothy and Epaphroditus. 2.19: *Timothy,* Acts 16.1–3; 1 Cor 16.10–11. **24:** *I trust*

genuinely concerned for your welfare. [21] All of them are seeking their own interests, not those of Jesus Christ. [22] But Timothy's[a] worth you know, how like a son with a father he has served with me in the work of the gospel. [23] I hope therefore to send him as soon as I see how things go with me; [24] and I trust in the Lord that I will also come soon.

[25] Still, I think it necessary to send to you Epaphroditus—my brother and co-worker and fellow soldier, your messenger[b] and minister to my need; [26] for he has been longing for[c] all of you, and has been distressed because you heard that he was ill. [27] He was indeed so ill that he nearly died. But God had mercy on him, and not only on him but on me also, so that I would not have one sorrow after another. [28] I am the more eager to send him, therefore, in order that you may rejoice at seeing him again, and that I may be less anxious. [29] Welcome him then in the Lord with all joy, and honor such people, [30] because he came close to death for the work of Christ,[d] risking his life to make up for those services that you could not give me.

3 Finally, my brothers and sisters,[e] rejoice[f] in the Lord.

To write the same things to you is not troublesome to me, and for you it is a safeguard. [2] Beware of the dogs, beware of the evil workers, beware of those who mutilate the flesh![g] [3] For it is we who are the circumcision, who worship in the Spirit of God[h] and boast in Christ Jesus and have no confidence in the flesh— [4] even though I, too, have reason for confidence in the flesh.

If anyone else has reason to be confident in the flesh, I have more: [5] circumcised on the eighth day, a member of the people of Israel, of the tribe of Benjamin, a Hebrew born of Hebrews; as to the law, a Pharisee; [6] as to zeal, a persecutor of the church; as to righteousness under the law, blameless.

[7] Yet whatever gains I had, these I have come to regard as loss because of Christ. [8] More than that, I regard everything as loss because of the surpassing value of knowing Christ Jesus my Lord. For his sake I have suffered the loss of all things, and I regard them as rubbish, in order that I may gain Christ [9] and be found in him, not having a righteousness of my own that comes from the law, but one that comes through faith in Christ,[i] the righteousness from God based on faith. [10] I want to know Christ[j] and the power of his resurrection and the sharing of his sufferings by becoming like him in his death, [11] if somehow I may attain the resurrection from the dead.

[12] Not that I have already obtained this or have already reached the goal;[k] but I press on to make it my own, because Christ Jesus has made me his own. [13] Beloved,[l] I do not con-

---

a Gk *his*
b Gk *apostle*
c Other ancient authorities read *longing to see*
d Other ancient authorities read *of the Lord*
e Gk *my brothers*
f Or *farewell*
g Gk *the mutilation*
h Other ancient authorities read *worship God in spirit*
i Or *through the faith of Christ*
j Gk *him*
k Or *have already been made perfect*
l Gk *Brothers*

. . . *that I will also come soon,* an argument against Rome as place of writing (see Rom 15.23–25). **25:** *Epaphroditus,* apostle and co-worker of Paul who brought the gift from Philippi (4.18), now being sent home.

3.1b–3: A digression about those who preach the necessity of circumcision, requiring Christians to observe the laws of Judaism. They were Paul's bitter opponents elsewhere, especially in Galatia, and are introduced here as a negative example (cf. Gal 5.1–12). **3:** *The flesh,* emphasis on physical rituals.

3.4–4.1: Third example: Paul himself. 3.5: *Hebrew,* a more preferred self-designation than "Jew," which was used more often by and for outsiders. *Pharisee,* member of the group most concerned with interpretation of the Jewish law. **6:** *A persecutor,* Acts 9.1–2; 1 Cor 15.9; Gal 1.13. *As to righteousness under the law, blameless,* Paul did not see himself as guilty or incomplete before his encounter with Christ. **8:** *Rubbish,* or excrement. **9:** *The righteousness from God based on faith,* a free gift bestowed by God through the grace of Christ (Rom 1.16–4.25). **10–11:** Actually to know Christ as risen and living is to have power to suffer like him, and to possess the hope of rising and living with him. **12–14:** *The goal* and *the prize,* allusion to popular sports, the Greek footraces, their

sider that I have made it my own;[a] but this one thing I do: forgetting what lies behind and straining forward to what lies ahead, [14] I press on toward the goal for the prize of the heavenly[b] call of God in Christ Jesus. [15] Let those of us then who are mature be of the same mind; and if you think differently about anything, this too God will reveal to you. [16] Only let us hold fast to what we have attained.

[17] Brothers and sisters,[c] join in imitating me, and observe those who live according to the example you have in us. [18] For many live as enemies of the cross of Christ; I have often told you of them, and now I tell you even with tears. [19] Their end is destruction; their god is the belly; and their glory is in their shame; their minds are set on earthly things. [20] But our citizenship[d] is in heaven, and it is from there that we are expecting a Savior, the Lord Jesus Christ. [21] He will transform the body of our humiliation[e] that it may be conformed to the body of his glory,[f] by the

4 power that also enables him to make all things subject to himself. [1] Therefore, my brothers and sisters,[g] whom I love and long for, my joy and crown, stand firm in the Lord in this way, my beloved.

[2] I urge Euodia and I urge Syntyche to be of the same mind in the Lord. [3] Yes, and I ask you also, my loyal companion,[h] help these women, for they have struggled beside me in the work of the gospel, together with Clement and the rest of my co-workers, whose names are in the book of life.

[4] Rejoice[i] in the Lord always; again I will say, Rejoice.[i] [5] Let your gentleness be known to everyone. The Lord is near. [6] Do not worry about anything, but in everything by prayer and supplication with thanksgiving let your requests be made known to God. [7] And the peace of God, which surpasses all understanding, will guard your hearts and your minds in Christ Jesus.

[8] Finally, beloved,[j] whatever is true, whatever is honorable, whatever is just, whatever is pure, whatever is pleasing, whatever is commendable, if there is any excellence and if there is anything worthy of praise, think about[k] these things. [9] Keep on doing the things that you have learned and received and heard and seen in me, and the God of peace will be with you.

[10] I rejoice[l] in the Lord greatly that now at last you have revived your concern for me; indeed, you were concerned for me, but had no opportunity to show it.[m] [11] Not that I am referring to being in need; for I have learned to be content with whatever I have. [12] I know what it is to have little, and I know what it is to have plenty. In any and all circumstances I have learned the secret of being well-fed and of going hungry, of hav-

a   Other ancient authorities read *my own yet*
b   Gk *upward*
c   Gk *Brothers*
d   Or *commonwealth*
e   Or *our humble bodies*
f   Or *his glorious body*
g   Gk *my brothers*
h   Or *loyal Syzygus*
i   Or *Farewell*
j   Gk *brothers*
k   Gk *take account of*
l   Gk *I rejoiced*
m   Gk lacks *to show it*

finishing post, and the award to the winner (see 2.16; 1 Cor 9.24–27). **18–19:** *Many live as enemies of the cross of Christ,* presumably professing Christians who cannot accept Paul's theology of the cross. **20:** *Our citizenship,* our ultimate political loyalty and real homeland, contrasting with the status of most of the Philippians as Roman citizens. **21:** Rom 8.23; 1 Cor 15.47–57; 2 Cor 5.1–5; Col 3.1–4. **4.1:** 1 Thess 2.19–20. A *crown* was often awarded to the winner of a race (see 3.12–14n.).

4.2–9: Heart of the problem. 2: *Euodia . . . Syntyche,* two women leaders in the Philippian church, most likely heads of house-churches and therefore among the overseers and helpers (1.1) whose disagreement has had a disastrous effect on the church; the factions into which they have broken are the major concern of the letter. **3:** *My loyal companion,* an unknown but influential figure who could serve as mediator between the two. Less likely, the Greek word for *companion* may be understood as a proper name, *Syzygus. Book of life,* a book kept by God containing names of those to be saved (Ps 69.28; Dan 12.1; Lk 10.20; Rev 3.5; etc.).

4.10–20: Acknowledgment of their gifts. 11: *Content,* Paul here expresses the Stoic ideal of indifference, but

ing plenty and of being in need. ¹³ I can do all things through him who strengthens me. ¹⁴ In any case, it was kind of you to share my distress.

¹⁵ You Philippians indeed know that in the early days of the gospel, when I left Macedonia, no church shared with me in the matter of giving and receiving, except you alone. ¹⁶ For even when I was in Thessalonica, you sent me help for my needs more than once. ¹⁷ Not that I seek the gift, but I seek the profit that accumulates to your account. ¹⁸ I have been paid in full and have more than enough; I am fully satisfied, now that I have received from Epaphroditus the gifts you sent, a

fragrant offering, a sacrifice acceptable and pleasing to God. ¹⁹ And my God will fully satisfy every need of yours according to his riches in glory in Christ Jesus. ²⁰ To our God and Father be glory forever and ever. Amen.

²¹ Greet every saint in Christ Jesus. The friends[a] who are with me greet you. ²² All the saints greet you, especially those of the emperor's household.

²³ The grace of the Lord Jesus Christ be with your spirit.[b]

[a] Gk *brothers*
[b] Other ancient authorities add *Amen*

with new motivation because of Christ. **15–16:** *Macedonia, Thessalonica,* according to Acts 17.1, Paul had gone to Thessalonica in Greece immediately after his stay in Philippi. **15,17,18:** *Giving and receiving, profit . . . account, paid in full,* a series of business terms used metaphorically here and in other contexts of friendship. **18:** *Fragrant offering,* Gen 8.21; Ex 29.18; Ezek 20.41.

4.21–23: Conclusion. 22: *The emperor's household,* members of the imperial civil service who are believers where Paul is confined. This need not be in Rome, but wherever there was a Roman administrative center.

THE LETTER OF PAUL TO THE COLOSSIANS

NAME

This letter is named for its recipients, the Christian community in the city of Colossae (1.2), a community that had been founded by a Colossian associate of Paul named Epaphras (1.7–8; 4.12–13). Colossae, once a thriving town on the Lycus River in the Roman province of Asia, fell into decay after an earthquake ca. 60 CE; the site has not yet been excavated.

AUTHORSHIP AND DATE

Despite its similarity to the undisputed letters of Paul in structure, language, and theology, the letter to the Colossians lacks some central Pauline terms, uses new theological vocabulary, and is composed in a more elevated, liturgical style. Two theological differences stand out: first, the vision of believers' present lives as almost completely transformed by Christ's death and resurrection (3.1–4), instead of Paul's usual tension between the partial experience of salvation in the present and the future resurrection that ushers in the full enjoyment of Christ's benefits (e.g., Rom 6.4); second, the use of household rules to define ethical norms (3.18–4.1), which is more characteristic of other post-Pauline literature, such as Ephesians, the Pastoral Letters, and 1 Peter, than of Paul's own ethical instructions on similar themes (e.g., 1 Cor 7). Such differences have led some scholars to conclude that Colossians was written in Paul's name by one of his disciples—either during Paul's lifetime or shortly after his death (ca. 65 CE)—in order to authorize the application of Paul's thought to a new situation. Other scholars, noting its close similarities to the letter to Philemon, think the letter was written by Paul himself while imprisoned (4.3,10,18) at Rome near the end of his life, and attribute theological contrasts to shifts in Paul's thinking and the particular situation addressed in the letter. Colossians also has significant similarities to Ephesians and was probably used as a model by the author of that letter (see p. 2053).

HISTORICAL CONTEXT

Although the letter begins with a highly complimentary description of the Colossians' lives, unnamed teachers pose a threat to their faith. The lack of an independent description of these teachings makes their precise identification difficult. It appears that these teachings advocated observance of Jewish rituals and pursuit of mystical experiences through asceticism (2.8–23) and that they are best understood as a form of Jewish apocalyptical mysticism, although some scholars have preferred to see a synthesis of Judaism with proto-Gnostic thought, local Phrygian religious practices, or Hellenistic philosophy. The attractiveness of Jewish elements in this spirituality reflects the ongoing close connections between Jewish and Christian communities; the polemical tone of this letter (for instance, "empty deceit, according to human tradition," 2.8), however, represents an emerging first-century Christian ambivalence toward Judaism among non-Jewish believers. This tension is exemplified in Colossians where a Jewish eschatological outlook and moral commitments are central to the author's Christian vision, and yet Jewish practices, including celebrating holy days and observing dietary laws, are rejected as incompatible with Christ.

STRUCTURE AND INTERPRETATION

Colossians follows the usual structure of a Pauline letter (see p. 1973), beginning with a greeting (1.1–2), an introductory thanksgiving (1.3–8) and prayer (1.9–14), and ending with greetings and instructions (4.7–18). The body of the letter includes both a theological argument (2.6–23) and ethical instructions (3.1–4.6). The basis of the theological argument is presented in 1.12–2.5. In the elevated words of an early Christian hymn, Christ is praised as the supreme power over the cosmos and the church (1.15–20). Although demonic forces enslaved humanity in the past, Christians have been freed from their influence, forgiven through Christ's death, and made full citizens of the kingdom of Christ, to whom they now owe complete allegiance (1.12–14,21–23). Christ's identity as the perfect revelation of God (1.19; 2.9–10) and as the single source of wisdom about how to live rightly (1.9–10; 2.2–3) is emphasized. The main theological argument focuses on the change in believers' existence achieved by Christ's death on the cross (2.9–15); the recurring contrasts of death and life (2.12–13,20; 3.1–5), old and new (3.9–10), and past and present (1.12–14,21–23) emphasize the fundamental psychological and moral reorientation required of the faithful. Because Jewish rituals and mystical experiences of angelic worship do not foster allegiance to Christ and belong to the old order as well as to pagan superstitions about astrological powers, the author argues they must be rejected as implicit denials of Christ's lordship. The members of a true Christian community, rejecting their previous immoral lifestyle (3.5–11) and reorienting their entire lives around Christ as Lord (3.1–4), are to live in harmony with each other as they worship and give thanks to God and Christ (3.12–17). However, the description of the ideal household (3.18–4.1), as presented by the author, is only a mildly Christianized version of the ancient patriarchal family rather than a reconsideration of family relationships based on the equality of all in the new community and the principles of mutual love and forgiveness (3.10–15). Colossians has provided fertile ground for theological speculation from the second century CE on; perhaps most significant is the role of 1.15–20 in the christological debates of the fourth century.

GUIDE TO READING

The argument of Colossians rests upon a series of contrasts (hidden/revealed; above/below; shadow/substance; human/divine; once/now; strip off/clothe), each of which hinges upon the author's understanding of Jesus' death. This key event is understood in apocalyptic terms, and the reader will benefit by keeping in mind that this letter is rooted in a world thought to be populated by a multitude of spiritual entities enmeshed in cosmic conflict and awaiting the final judgment of God.

Jennifer K. Berenson

1 Paul, an apostle of Christ Jesus by the will of God, and Timothy our brother, ² To the saints and faithful brothers and sisters[a] in Christ in Colossae:
Grace to you and peace from God our Father.

³ In our prayers for you we always thank God, the Father of our Lord Jesus Christ, ⁴ for we have heard of your faith in Christ Jesus and of the love that you have for all the saints, ⁵ because of the hope laid up for you in heaven. You have heard of this hope before in the word of the truth, the gospel ⁶ that has come to you. Just as it is bearing fruit and growing in the whole world, so it has been bearing fruit among yourselves from the day you heard it and truly comprehended the grace of God. ⁷ This you learned from Epaphras, our beloved fellow servant.[b] He is a faithful minister of Christ on your[c] behalf, ⁸ and he has made known to us your love in the Spirit.

⁹ For this reason, since the day we heard it, we have not ceased praying for you and asking that you may be filled with the knowledge of God's[d] will in all spiritual wisdom and understanding, ¹⁰ so that you may lead lives worthy of the Lord, fully pleasing to him, as you bear fruit in every good work and as you grow in the knowledge of God. ¹¹ May you

a Gk *brothers*
b Gk *slave*
c Other ancient authorities read *our*
d Gk *his*

1.1–2: **Salutation.** 1: *Apostle . . . by the will of God,* see 1.25; Rom 1.1n. *Timothy,* Paul's fellow missionary and emissary (Philem 1; 2 Cor 1.1; Phil 1.1; 2.19–24). *Brother* indicates a bond of affection and loyalty. 2: *Saints,* literally "holy ones," refers to all believers. *Brothers and sisters,* the Greek "brothers" (see note *a*) includes both men and women. *Grace . . . peace,* a common Pauline greeting drawing upon and transforming conventional Greek (*grace*) and Hebrew (*peace*) salutations.

1.3–8: **Thanksgiving for prior obedience.** 3–5: *Faith, hope,* and *love,* a summary of Christian virtues (1 Cor 13.13; 1 Thess 5.8). 4: *Faith,* here allegiance or loyalty. 5: *Gospel,* in general, proclamation of good news, as of a military victory; here referring to Christ's victory over death and cosmic powers (see 2.15). 6: *The whole world,* hyperbole for all the Christian communities in Roman cities. 7: *Epaphras,* founder of the church in Colossae (4.12–13; Philem 23).

1.9–14: **Prayer for future growth** in knowledge (v. 9), moral maturity (v. 10), and endurance (v. 11). 9: *Spiritual*

be made strong with all the strength that comes from his glorious power, and may you be prepared to endure everything with patience, while joyfully [12] giving thanks to the Father, who has enabled[a] you[b] to share in the inheritance of the saints in the light. [13] He has rescued us from the power of darkness and transferred us into the kingdom of his beloved Son, [14] in whom we have redemption, the forgiveness of sins.[c]

[15] He is the image of the invisible God, the firstborn of all creation; [16] for in[d] him all things in heaven and on earth were created, things visible and invisible, whether thrones or dominions or rulers or powers—all things have been created through him and for him. [17] He himself is before all things, and in[d] him all things hold together. [18] He is the head of the body, the church; he is the beginning, the firstborn from the dead, so that he might come to have first place in everything. [19] For in him all the fullness of God was pleased to dwell, [20] and through him God was pleased to reconcile to himself all things, whether on earth or in heaven, by making peace through the blood of his cross.

[21] And you who were once estranged and hostile in mind, doing evil deeds, [22] he has now reconciled[e] in his fleshly body[f] through death, so as to present you holy and blame-less and irreproachable before him— [23] provided that you continue securely established and steadfast in the faith, without shifting from the hope promised by the gospel that you heard, which has been proclaimed to every creature under heaven. I, Paul, became a servant of this gospel.

[24] I am now rejoicing in my sufferings for your sake, and in my flesh I am complet-ing what is lacking in Christ's afflictions for the sake of his body, that is, the church. [25] I became its servant according to God's com-mission that was given to me for you, to make the word of God fully known, [26] the mystery that has been hidden throughout the ages and generations but has now been revealed to his saints. [27] To them God chose to make known how great among the Gentiles are the riches of the glory of this mystery, which is Christ in you, the hope of glory. [28] It is he whom we proclaim, warning everyone and teaching everyone in all wisdom, so that we

a   Other ancient authorities read *called*
b   Other ancient authorities read *us*
c   Other ancient authorities add *through his blood*
d   Or *by*
e   Other ancient authorities read *you have now been reconciled*
f   Gk *in the body of his flesh*

wisdom and understanding, a major theme of the letter (1.25–28; 2.2–4,9–15). **12–14:** Perhaps a fragment of a bap-tismal hymn. **12–13:** *Light . . . darkness,* apocalyptic imagery for the opposing domains of God and malevolent spiritual beings (see 1.16n.; 1 Thess 5.5). **12:** *Inheritance,* a metaphor for God's blessings based on Israel's inheri-tance of the land as a gift of God. **14:** *Redemption,* release from slavery to demonic powers.

   1.15–20: The supremacy of Christ over the cosmos (vv. 15–17) and the church (vv. 18–20), expressed as a hymn in which Jesus' relationship to creation is based on the Jewish figure Wisdom/Sophia (Prov 8; Sir 24; Wis 6–9; see also Jn 1.1–18; Phil 2.6–11). **15:** *Image,* the perfect, visible manifestation of God. *Firstborn* expresses pri-ority and supremacy. **16:** *Thrones . . . powers,* hostile spiritual beings (1.13; 2.15; Eph 6.12). **18:** *Head,* ruling author-ity or originator; see Eph 1.22; 5.23. *The body, the church,* both terms stem from ancient political discourse for a community assembly and its unity and coherence; see Rom 12.4–5; 1 Cor 12.27. See also Eph 1.22–23n. *Firstborn from the dead,* the first of those to be resurrected from the dead (1 Cor 15.20,23; Acts 26.23; Rev 1.5). **19:** *Full-ness of God,* the power and presence of God in Christ (see also 1.29; 2.9–10). **20:** *Reconcile . . . making peace,* the enslavement of humanity to demonic powers is presupposed here (1.13–14; 2.15).

   1.21–23: Assurance and warning. 21: *Hostile in mind, doing evil deeds,* interrelated aspects of the former life (Rom 1.18–32). **22:** *Fleshly body,* an emphatic contrast with Christ's heavenly origins (2.11; cf. 1.15–17). *To present you . . . before him,* reconciliation is completed by Christ's approval at the eschatological judgment (v. 28). **23:** Concern for continued allegiance to Christ is the motivation for the letter (see 2.6–20).

   1.24–2.5: Paul's mission and pastoral commitment. 1.24: *Sufferings,* imprisonment (4.3,10,18) and hardships experienced while preaching the gospel (2 Cor 4.7–12; 11.23–28). *Completing . . . afflictions,* not a denigration of Christ's death but a reflection of the belief that God's people must suffer before the culmination of history (1 Cor 4.9; Rev 6.9–11). **26–27:** *Mystery,* the previously hidden plan of God; here, the gospel proclaimed to Gen-

may present everyone mature in Christ. [29] For this I toil and struggle with all the energy that he powerfully inspires within me.

2 For I want you to know how much I am struggling for you, and for those in Laodicea, and for all who have not seen me face to face. [2] I want their hearts to be encouraged and united in love, so that they may have all the riches of assured understanding and have the knowledge of God's mystery, that is, Christ himself,[a] [3] in whom are hidden all the treasures of wisdom and knowledge. [4] I am saying this so that no one may deceive you with plausible arguments. [5] For though I am absent in body, yet I am with you in spirit, and I rejoice to see your morale and the firmness of your faith in Christ.

[6] As you therefore have received Christ Jesus the Lord, continue to live your lives[b] in him, [7] rooted and built up in him and established in the faith, just as you were taught, abounding in thanksgiving.

[8] See to it that no one takes you captive through philosophy and empty deceit, according to human tradition, according to the elemental spirits of the universe,[c] and not according to Christ. [9] For in him the whole fullness of deity dwells bodily, [10] and you have come to fullness in him, who is the head of every ruler and authority. [11] In him also you were circumcised with a spiritual circumcision,[d] by putting off the body of the flesh in the circumcision

of Christ; [12] when you were buried with him in baptism, you were also raised with him through faith in the power of God, who raised him from the dead. [13] And when you were dead in trespasses and the uncircumcision of your flesh, God[e] made you[f] alive together with him, when he forgave us all our trespasses, [14] erasing the record that stood against us with its legal demands. He set this aside, nailing it to the cross. [15] He disarmed[g] the rulers and authorities and made a public example of them, triumphing over them in it.

[16] Therefore do not let anyone condemn you in matters of food and drink or of observing festivals, new moons, or sabbaths. [17] These are only a shadow of what is to come, but the substance belongs to Christ. [18] Do not let anyone disqualify you, insisting on self-abasement and worship of angels, dwelling[h] on visions,[i] puffed up without cause by a

---

a   Other ancient authorities read *of the mystery of God, both of the Father and of Christ*

b   Gk *to walk*

c   Or *the rudiments of the world*

d   Gk *a circumcision made without hands*

e   Gk *he*

f   Other ancient authorities read *made us*; others, *made*

g   Or *divested himself of*

h   Other ancient authorities read *not dwelling*

i   Meaning of Gk uncertain

---

tiles (2.2; 4.3; Rom 16.25–26; cf. Eph 1.10; 3.2–6). *Hope of glory*, the expectation of eschatological approval. **2.1:** *Laodicea*, see 4.13n. **2:** *Mystery* here refers to Christ as preached to Gentiles. **5:** *Morale, firmness*, terminology evoking military discipline.

2.6–23: Theological Argument. 2.6–15: Instruction on Christ and the cross. 6–7: Thematic statement of the letter (see Introduction; 1.21–23; 3.1–4). **6:** *Received*, a technical term for the reception of oral tradition; here, that Jesus is Lord (Rom 10.9). **8:** *Philosophy* includes ethical and religious teachings. *Human tradition*, in contrast to God's revelation through Paul. *Elemental spirits*, spiritual entities or perhaps the four primal elements; they are associated with the Jewish law in Gal 4.1–5,9–10. **9–10:** See 1.19n. **11:** *Circumcision* was a physical mark of membership in Israel. *By putting off . . . flesh*, a graphic description of Christ's death and the event of baptism (*spiritual circumcision*). **12:** *You were also raised*, Paul is usually reluctant to speak of a spiritual resurrection of believers in the present (see Introduction). **13:** *Uncircumcision of your flesh*, the Colossians were Gentiles. **14:** *Record . . . demands*, a document detailing transgressions, perhaps similar to that in Dan 7.10 and Rev 20.12. **15:** *Rulers and authorities*, see 1.16n. *Disarmed . . . public example*, as Rome's vanquished enemies were displayed in a victorious parade or "triumph."

2.16–23: Warnings against outmoded religious practices. 16: *Matters of food and drink*, observance of Jewish dietary laws. *Festivals, new moons, or sabbaths*, summary of the Jewish religious calendar (e.g., 2 Chr 8.13; Neh 10.33). *New moons* mark the beginning of each lunar month. **17:** *Shadow . . . substance*, Platonic language indicating the superiority of Christ (see Heb 8.5n.). **18:** Through rigorous asceticism (*self-abasement*) achieving a mystical ascent to heaven (*dwelling on visions*); *worship of angels* may refer to participating in angelic worship

human way of thinking,[a] [19] and not holding fast to the head, from whom the whole body, nourished and held together by its ligaments and sinews, grows with a growth that is from God.

[20] If with Christ you died to the elemental spirits of the universe,[b] why do you live as if you still belonged to the world? Why do you submit to regulations, [21] "Do not handle, Do not taste, Do not touch"? [22] All these regulations refer to things that perish with use; they are simply human commands and teachings. [23] These have indeed an appearance of wisdom in promoting self-imposed piety, humility, and severe treatment of the body, but they are of no value in checking self-indulgence.[c]

3 So if you have been raised with Christ, seek the things that are above, where Christ is, seated at the right hand of God. [2] Set your minds on things that are above, not on things that are on earth, [3] for you have died, and your life is hidden with Christ in God. [4] When Christ who is your[d] life is revealed, then you also will be revealed with him in glory.

[5] Put to death, therefore, whatever in you is earthly: fornication, impurity, passion, evil desire, and greed (which is idolatry). [6] On account of these the wrath of God is coming on those who are disobedient.[e] [7] These are the ways you also once followed, when you were living that life.[f] [8] But now you must get rid of all such things—anger, wrath, malice, slander, and abusive[g] language from your mouth. [9] Do not lie to one another, seeing that you have stripped off the old self with its practices [10] and have clothed yourselves with the new self, which is being renewed in knowledge according to the image of its creator. [11] In that renewal[h] there is no longer Greek and Jew, circumcised and uncircumcised, barbarian, Scythian, slave and free; but Christ is all and in all!

[12] As God's chosen ones, holy and beloved, clothe yourselves with compassion, kindness, humility, meekness, and patience. [13] Bear with one another and, if anyone has a complaint against another, forgive each other; just as the Lord[i] has forgiven you, so you also must forgive. [14] Above all, clothe yourselves with love, which binds everything together in perfect harmony. [15] And let the peace of Christ rule in your hearts, to which indeed you were called in the one body. And be thankful. [16] Let

a   Gk *by the mind of his flesh*
b   Or *the rudiments of the world*
c   Or *are of no value, serving only to indulge the flesh*
d   Other authorities read *our*
e   Other ancient authorities lack *on those who are disobedient* (Gk *the children of disobedience*)
f   Or *living among such people*
g   Or *filthy*
h   Gk *its creator,* [11]*where*
i   Other ancient authorities read *just as Christ*

of God or to revering angels. **19**: *Head, body,* see 1.18n. **20**: *Died to the elemental spirits,* no longer under their authority (vv. 8–15). *As if . . . world,* see 2.11; 3.1–3. **21**: Jewish purity regulations. **22**: See Mk 7.7,19. **23**: *They are of no value,* the criticism is either that such practices do not address the author's moral concerns (3.5,8) or that they inappropriately focus on the body.

3.1–4.6: Ethical implications. 3.1–4: Maintain a heavenly perspective. 1: *Raised,* 2.12. *Seated,* see Eph 1.19–20n. **1–2:** *Seek . . . above . . . set . . . above,* commands to orient one's life around the heavenly reality of Christ's exaltation and authority. **3:** *Died,* see 2.20n. *Hidden,* not disclosed to outsiders, but already revealed to believers (1.26; 2.3). **4:** *Is revealed,* to all at the eschatological judgment (1 Cor 2.6–16).

3.5–11: Reject sins of previous life. 5: *Put to death,* vehemently refuse to engage in. *Fornication . . . evil desire,* inappropriate sexual behavior. *Idolatry,* often linked with sexual sins in Jewish thought (Hos 4.12–19; Rom 1.23–27; 1 Cor 10.7–8). **6:** *Wrath,* God's eschatological judgment. **8:** *Anger . . . abusive language,* a list of vices commonly condemned in antiquity (cf. 1 Cor 6.9; Gal 5.19–21). **9–10:** *Old self . . . new self,* another contrast emphasizing the new act of creation (*image of its creator* recalls Gen 1.26–27) brought about by baptism (2.12). *Stripped off . . . clothed,* metaphor for adopting a new way of life (3.12–14; Eph 4.22–24). **11:** An eloquent rejection of privileges based on ethnicity and socioeconomic status; cf. the additional abrogation of a gender hierarchy in Gal 3.28. *Barbarian . . . Scythian,* shorthand in antiquity for uncultured peoples.

3.12–17: Adopt virtues of the new life. 12: *Compassion . . . patience,* virtues emphasizing a proper attitude toward oneself and genuine concern for others. **13:** *Forgive,* Eph 4.32; cf. Mt 6.14–15. **14–15:** For some modern

the word of Christ[a] dwell in you richly; teach and admonish one another in all wisdom; and with gratitude in your hearts sing psalms, hymns, and spiritual songs to God.[b] [17] And whatever you do, in word or deed, do everything in the name of the Lord Jesus, giving thanks to God the Father through him.

[18] Wives, be subject to your husbands, as is fitting in the Lord. [19] Husbands, love your wives and never treat them harshly.

[20] Children, obey your parents in everything, for this is your acceptable duty in the Lord. [21] Fathers, do not provoke your children, or they may lose heart. [22] Slaves, obey your earthly masters[c] in everything, not only while being watched and in order to please them, but wholeheartedly, fearing the Lord.[c] [23] Whatever your task, put yourselves into it, as done for the Lord and not for your masters,[d] [24] since you know that from the Lord you will receive the inheritance as your reward; you serve[e] the Lord Christ. [25] For the wrongdoer will be paid back for whatever wrong has been done, and there is no partiality. [1] Masters, treat your slaves justly and fairly, for you know that you also have a Master in heaven.

[2] Devote yourselves to prayer, keeping alert in it with thanksgiving. [3] At the same time pray for us as well that God will open to us a door for the word, that we may declare the mystery of Christ, for which I am in prison, [4] so that I may reveal it clearly, as I should.

[5] Conduct yourselves wisely toward outsiders, making the most of the time.[f] [6] Let your speech always be gracious, seasoned with salt, so that you may know how you ought to answer everyone.

[7] Tychicus will tell you all the news about me; he is a beloved brother, a faithful minister, and a fellow servant[g] in the Lord. [8] I have sent him to you for this very purpose, so that you may know how we are[h] and that he may encourage your hearts; [9] he is coming with Onesimus, the faithful and beloved brother, who is one of you. They will tell you about everything here.

[10] Aristarchus my fellow prisoner greets you, as does Mark the cousin of Barnabas, concerning whom you have received instructions—if he comes to you, welcome him. [11] And Jesus who is called Justus greets you. These are the only ones of the circumcision among my co-workers for the kingdom of God, and they have been a comfort to me. [12] Epaphras, who is one of you, a servant[g] of Christ Jesus, greets you. He is always wrestling in his prayers on your behalf, so that you may stand mature and

---

a Other ancient authorities read *of God*, or *of the Lord*

b Other ancient authorities read *to the Lord*

c In Greek the same word is used for *master* and *Lord*

d Gk *not for men*

e Or *you are slaves of*, or *be slaves of*

f Or *opportunity*

g Gk *slave*

h Other authorities read *that I may know how you are*

---

readers this call for unity will be at odds with the imposition of unity through authority (see 3.18–4.1). **16:** *Word of Christ*, teachings concerning Christ.

3.18–4.1: Rules for household relationships. This passage adopts a popular philosophical format of paired commands (wife/husband, etc.) for describing the ancient ideal of the patriarchal family and defends it as appropriate for a community dedicated to Christ as Lord (see the more extensive theological justification in Eph 5.22–6.9). The commands to the male figure somewhat moderate his traditional prerogatives (see 3.19,21; 4.1). **18–19:** Relations between *wives* and *husbands*. **18:** *Be subject*, accept a position of subordination to the husband's authority. The role of Nympha (4.15n) may indicate that these rules were not consistently enforced. **19:** *Never treat them harshly*, alternatively, "do not be embittered against them." **20–21:** Relations between *children* and *fathers*, see Eph 6.1–4 and notes. **3.22–4.1:** Relations between *slaves* and *masters*, see Eph 6.5–9 and notes.

4.2–6: Final admonitions. 3: *Door for the word*, an opportunity to preach. *Mystery*, see 1.26–27n. *Prison*, see 1.24n. **5:** *Making the most*, recognizing the eschatological urgency. **6:** *Salt*, graciousness or wit.

4.7–18: Final greetings and instructions. 7: *Tychicus*, Paul's associate (Acts 20.4; 2 Tim 4.12), commended like Epaphras (cf. 1.7). **9:** *Onesimus*, Philem 10–21. **10:** *Aristarchus*, Acts 20.4; 27.2; Philem 24. *Welcome him*, cf. Paul's conflict with Mark in Acts 13.13; 15.37–39. **11:** *The circumcision*, the Jews, here without negative connotations (cf.

fully assured in everything that God wills. [13] For I testify for him that he has worked hard for you and for those in Laodicea and in Hierapolis. [14] Luke, the beloved physician, and Demas greet you. [15] Give my greetings to the brothers and sisters[a] in Laodicea, and to Nympha and the church in her house. [16] And when this letter has been read among you, have it read also in the church of the Laodiceans; and see that you read also the letter from Laodicea. [17] And say to Archippus, "See that you complete the task that you have received in the Lord."

[18] I, Paul, write this greeting with my own hand. Remember my chains. Grace be with you.[b]

a Gk *brothers*
b Other ancient authorities add *Amen*

Gal 2.12). **12:** *Epaphras*, see 1.7n. **13:** *Laodicea, Hierapolis*, cities located 10 and 15 miles (16 and 24 km), respectively, northwest of Colossae. **14:** *Luke*, 2 Tim 4.11; Philem 24. Traditionally identified as the author of the Gospel of Luke and Acts (see respective Introductions). *Demas*, 2 Tim 4.10; Philem 24. **15:** *Brothers and sisters*, see Eph 6.23n. *Nympha*, probably the leader of the church that met in her home (see Philem 1–2). **16:** *The letter from Laodicea*, a letter of Paul that has not survived, although some scholars identify it with Ephesians. **17:** *Archippus*, Philem 2. **18:** A final word in the author's handwriting to authenticate the letter (cf. 1 Cor 16.21; Gal 6.11); the rest of the letter would have been dictated to a secretary (see Rom 16.22).

THE FIRST LETTER OF PAUL TO THE THESSALONIANS

NAME AND CANONICAL STATUS

This letter is named for its recipients, the Christian community in Thessalonica in Macedonia in northern Greece. The title is not an original part of the text itself, but was added when the letters of Paul were copied and collected together. The title in the earliest Greek manuscripts is the simple form "To the Thessalonians 1." From the second century on this letter has been accepted as part of the collection of letters of Paul within what became the New Testament canon.

AUTHORSHIP, DATE, AND HISTORICAL CONTEXT

Like 2 Thessalonians, 1 Thessalonians identifies its senders as Paul, Silvanus, and Timothy (1.1), though Paul is clearly the leading author (see 2.18; 3.1–5; 5.27). Its authenticity as a genuine letter of Paul is seldom questioned.

First Thessalonians is widely regarded as Paul's earliest letter, written from Corinth during his founding mission there; Athens, mentioned in 1 Thess 3:1, has sometimes been seen as the letter's place of origin, especially by early Christian interpreters. Acts 17–18 records Paul's visits to Thessalonica and then, via Athens, to Corinth. The date of the letter therefore corresponds with Paul's Corinthian mission, usually dated about 49–51 CE, but sometimes earlier, between 41–44 CE. Thessalonica was the capital of the Roman province of Macedonia, while Corinth lay farther south in the province of Achaia. Both cities were located on important land and sea routes; Paul's mission focused on such urban centers.

LITERARY HISTORY, STRUCTURE, AND CONTENTS

It has sometimes been argued that the letter as we now have it is composed of earlier letters, later woven into one. Some sections of the letter (especially 2.14–16) have been proposed as later additions to the text. Most scholars, however, agree that what we have is a single letter, not a composite.

The structure and contents of 1 Thessalonians may be outlined as follows:

1.1	Opening greeting
1.2–10	Opening thanksgiving and remembrance of the Thessalonians' response to the gospel
2.1–12	Recalling the conduct of Paul and his co-workers toward the Thessalonians, despite hardships
2.13–16	The Thessalonians' response to the gospel, and their hardships
2.17–3.13	Paul's desire to see the Thessalonians, and Timothy's good report about them
4.1–12	Ethical instructions on the Christian life
4.13–5.11	Teaching about the fate of those who have died and about the coming day of the Lord
5.12–24	Practical instruction about life in the church
5.25–28	Closing greeting

INTERPRETATION

A pastoral letter of encouragement and exhortation, 1 Thessalonians reflects a warm and affectionate relationship between Paul and the Christians at Thessalonica. Unlike some other letters of Paul, it is not concerned to combat what Paul sees as false teaching or immoral conduct. The first three chapters recall the enthusiastic response of the Thessalonians to the gospel, and the mutual affection between them and the apostolic missionaries. Both groups have faced hardships but have remained faithful. Paul longs to visit them again and is heartened by the good reports of their "faith and love" (3.6) that Timothy has brought. The last two chapters are more focused on instruction, but even here Paul is concerned to commend the Thessalonians' good conduct (4.1,9). The main issue addressed in these chapters is Thessalonian worries about those who have died. Paul seeks to reassure and comfort them, while also exhorting them to readiness for the coming day of salvation. This instruction about the coming of the Lord, and the salvation of believers both living and dead, has been influential in the development of doctrine concerning the nature of Christian hope and future expectation.

GUIDE TO READING

It is important to read this text as a letter, appreciating its origins in the relationship between the apostolic missionaries and the community they founded. Paul expresses a warm parental and pastoral concern for his converts. The theme of imitation is significant: the Thessalonians have suffered, yet have remained faithful and joyful, a pattern found in other churches (2.14), in Paul, and in the Lord himself (1.6). The teaching on the coming of the Lord and the fate of believers needs to be interpreted in the context of lively early Christian belief: the return of Christ was expected very soon. Consequently this first generation of converts had to face the question of why some of their number had died before the day of salvation had arrived. A significant issue for contemporary Christian readers is what kind of expectation is appropriate now, two thousand years later.

David G. Horrell

1 Paul, Silvanus, and Timothy,
To the church of the Thessalonians in God the Father and the Lord Jesus Christ:
Grace to you and peace.

[2] We always give thanks to God for all of you and mention you in our prayers, constantly [3] remembering before our God and Father your work of faith and labor of love and steadfastness of hope in our Lord Jesus Christ. [4] For we know, brothers and sisters[a] beloved by God, that he has chosen you, [5] because our message of the gospel came to you not in word only, but also in power and in the Holy Spirit and with full conviction; just as you know what kind of persons we proved to be among you for your

sake. [6] And you became imitators of us and of the Lord, for in spite of persecution you received the word with joy inspired by the Holy Spirit, [7] so that you became an example to all the believers in Macedonia and in Achaia. [8] For the word of the Lord has sounded forth from you not only in Macedonia and Achaia, but in every place your faith in God has become known, so that we have no need to speak about it. [9] For the people of those regions[b] report about us what kind of welcome we had among you, and how you turned to God from idols, to serve a living and true God, [10] and to

a Gk *brothers*
b Gk *For they*

1.1: Greeting. The opening follows the basic pattern of ancient Greek letters, listing the senders and recipients and expressing a greeting. *Silvanus* is the Latin form of Silas, one of Paul's companions (Acts 15.22,40; 17.1). *Timothy* was also a co-worker with Paul and an important emissary (3.2,6; cf. 1 Cor 16.10–11; Phil 2.19–24). *Church:* the Greek word "ekklesia" refers to an assembly, originally of citizens in the city-state. The phrase *grace and peace* reflects both Greek and Jewish forms of greeting.

1.2–10: Opening thanksgiving. Greek letters typically opened with a prayer or an expression of thanks for the health of the recipients. Paul and his coauthors express their thanks for the Thessalonians' response to the gospel. **3:** *Faith . . . love . . . hope,* cf. 5.8; 1 Cor 13.13. **4:** *Brothers and sisters,* the Greek word "adelphoi" refers to all members of the community; this is Paul's most common way of addressing recipients of his letters and suggests that they form a family of siblings. This and other descriptions—especially *chosen*—draw on biblical terms for the people of Israel (Deut 7.6–7; 14.2). **5:** The presentation of the gospel involved not only words but also deeds that demonstrated the Spirit's power (cf. Rom 15.19; 2 Cor 12.12). **6–8:** The Thessalonians have experienced *persecution* or suffering, though the precise cause or nature of this suffering is not made clear (cf. 2.14; 3.3–4,7); their faithful perseverance in this marks them as *imitators* of Paul and of the Lord. In turn they have become an *example,* or role model, for Christians elsewhere in *Macedonia* and *Achaia,* the two Roman provinces in Greece (see Introduction). **9–10:** A summary of what the Thessalonians' response to the gospel meant. *Turned . . . from idols* indicates that the converts were Gentiles. The expectation of salvation on the imminent day of judgment is also evident.

2.1–12: The conduct of Paul and his co-workers. 1–8: This description emphasizes the integrity and pastoral

wait for his Son from heaven, whom he raised from the dead—Jesus, who rescues us from the wrath that is coming.

2 You yourselves know, brothers and sisters,[a] that our coming to you was not in vain, [2] but though we had already suffered and been shamefully mistreated at Philippi, as you know, we had courage in our God to declare to you the gospel of God in spite of great opposition. [3] For our appeal does not spring from deceit or impure motives or trickery, [4] but just as we have been approved by God to be entrusted with the message of the gospel, even so we speak, not to please mortals, but to please God who tests our hearts. [5] As you know and as God is our witness, we never came with words of flattery or with a pretext for greed; [6] nor did we seek praise from mortals, whether from you or from others, [7] though we might have made demands as apostles of Christ. But we were gentle[b] among you, like a nurse tenderly caring for her own children. [8] So deeply do we care for you that we are determined to share with you not only the gospel of God but also our own selves, because you have become very dear to us.

[9] You remember our labor and toil, brothers and sisters;[a] we worked night and day, so that we might not burden any of you while we proclaimed to you the gospel of God. [10] You are witnesses, and God also, how pure, upright, and blameless our conduct was toward you believers. [11] As you know, we dealt with each one of you like a father with his children, [12] urging and encouraging you and pleading that you lead a life worthy of God, who calls you into his own kingdom and glory.

[13] We also constantly give thanks to God for this, that when you received the word of God that you heard from us, you accepted it not as a human word but as what it really is, God's word, which is also at work in you believers. [14] For you, brothers and sisters,[a] became imitators of the churches of God in Christ Jesus that are in Judea, for you suffered the same things from your own compatriots as they did from the Jews, [15] who killed both the Lord Jesus and the prophets,[c] and drove us out; they displease God and oppose everyone [16] by hindering us from speaking to the Gentiles so that they may be saved. Thus they have constantly been filling up the measure of their sins; but God's wrath has overtaken them at last.[d]

[17] As for us, brothers and sisters,[a] when, for a short time, we were made orphans by being separated from you—in person, not in heart—we longed with great eagerness to see you face to face. [18] For we wanted to come to you—certainly I, Paul, wanted to again and again—but Satan blocked our way. [19] For what is our hope or joy or crown of boasting before

---

a   Gk *brothers*
b   Other ancient authorities read *infants*
c   Other ancient authorities read *their own prophets*
d   Or *completely* or *forever*

---

concern of Paul and his fellow missionaries. **2:** Despite *opposition* (Gk "agon," meaning "contest"), they struggled on. On the mistreatment at *Philippi*, see Acts 16.19–40. **3–6:** Other traveling missionaries might do things from baser motives (cf. 2 Cor 2.17; 11.20; *Did.* 11–12). **7:** *Like a nurse,* a wet nurse or nursing mother, a striking image of the character of Paul's pastoral concern. **9:** As elsewhere, Paul insisted on working to support himself rather than depending on the congregation for support (1 Cor 9.1–18; 2 Thess 3.7–8). **11:** *Like a father,* another image of care for children (cf. v. 7; 1 Cor 4.15; 2 Cor 12.14). **12:** Paul's main aim as founding father of the community is to enable the Thessalonians to *lead a life worthy of God* (see 4.1–12).

2.13–16: The Thessalonians' response to the gospel, and their hardships. The opposition the Thessalonians have encountered from their non-Christian neighbors (primarily Gentiles) is paralleled with Jewish opposition to the Christian movement in Judea, and more generally to the *prophets* that God had sent (see Lk 11.47; 13.34; Acts 7.52). This opposition has brought *God's wrath* upon the perpetrators: Paul apparently has in mind a judgment of particular Jews at some specific time, perhaps their expulsion from Rome in 41 or 49 CE.

2.17–3.13: Paul's desire to see the Thessalonians and Timothy's good report about them. The strong and affectionate bond between Paul and the Thessalonians is again clearly displayed. **2.18:** *Satan,* the adversary, who deceives and tempts (1 Cor 7.5; 2 Cor 2.11; 11.14). **19:** A *crown* is the laurel wreath won by an athlete. The *coming*

our Lord Jesus at his coming? Is it not you? [20] Yes, you are our glory and joy!

3 Therefore when we could bear it no longer, we decided to be left alone in Athens; [2] and we sent Timothy, our brother and co-worker for God in proclaiming[a] the gospel of Christ, to strengthen and encourage you for the sake of your faith, [3] so that no one would be shaken by these persecutions. Indeed, you yourselves know that this is what we are destined for. [4] In fact, when we were with you, we told you beforehand that we were to suffer persecution; so it turned out, as you know. [5] For this reason, when I could bear it no longer, I sent to find out about your faith; I was afraid that somehow the tempter had tempted you and that our labor had been in vain.

[6] But Timothy has just now come to us from you, and has brought us the good news of your faith and love. He has told us also that you always remember us kindly and long to see us—just as we long to see you. [7] For this reason, brothers and sisters,[b] during all our distress and persecution we have been encouraged about you through your faith. [8] For we now live, if you continue to stand firm in the Lord. [9] How can we thank God enough for you in return for all the joy that we feel before our God because of you? [10] Night and day we pray most earnestly that we may see you face to face and restore whatever is lacking in your faith.

[11] Now may our God and Father himself and our Lord Jesus direct our way to you. [12] And may the Lord make you increase and abound in love for one another and for all, just as we abound in love for you. [13] And may he so strengthen your hearts in holiness that you may be blameless before our God and Father at the coming of our Lord Jesus with all his saints.

4 Finally, brothers and sisters,[b] we ask and urge you in the Lord Jesus that, as you learned from us how you ought to live and to please God (as, in fact, you are doing), you should do so more and more. [2] For you know what instructions we gave you through the Lord Jesus. [3] For this is the will of God, your sanctification: that you abstain from fornication; [4] that each one of you know how to control your own body[c] in holiness and honor, [5] not with lustful passion, like the Gentiles who do not know God; [6] that no one wrong or exploit a brother or sister[d] in this matter, because the Lord is an avenger in all these things, just as we have already told you beforehand and solemnly warned you. [7] For God did not call us to impurity but in holiness. [8] Therefore whoever rejects this rejects not human authority but God, who also gives his Holy Spirit to you.

[9] Now concerning love of the brothers and sisters,[b] you do not need to have anyone write to you, for you yourselves have been taught by God to love one another; [10] and indeed you do love all the brothers and sisters[b] throughout Macedonia. But we urge you, beloved,[b] to do so more and more, [11] to aspire to live quietly, to mind your own affairs, and to work with your hands, as we directed you, [12] so that you may behave

---

a   Gk lacks *proclaiming*
b   Gk *brothers*
c   Or *how to take a wife for himself*
d   Gk *brother*

(Gk "parousia") of the Lord is a key theme for the letter (see 1.10; 3.13; 4.15; 5.2,23). **3.1** On Paul in *Athens*, see Acts 17.15–18.1. **5**: *The tempter*, another reference to Satan (2.18). **11–13**: The prayer which concludes this first main section of the letter (1.1–3.13) anticipates the themes to be developed in the instruction to follow: love (4.9–12), holiness (4.3–5), and the parousia (4.15; 5.2,23). **13**: *Saints*, Christian believers.

    4.1–12: Ethical instructions. 1: *To live*, lit., "to walk" (cf. 2.12; 4.12), a Jewish metaphor for a way of life, a pattern of moral conduct. Idolatry and sexual immorality are a focus of Jewish concern (e.g., Wis 14.12), as is *sanctification* (v. 3), that is, "holiness" (v. 7; the same Gk word is used). **4**: *Body*, lit., "vessel," which could refer to the man's body, or specifically his sexual organ, or to his wife. **9–12**: *Love of the brothers and sisters* (Gk "philadelphia") is the primary responsibility toward those in the church (cf. Rom 12.10); behaving in a decent and inoffensive way will, it is hoped, lessen hostility from outsiders. **11**: Working *with your own hands* would imitate Paul's own practice (2.9).

properly toward outsiders and be dependent on no one.

[13] But we do not want you to be uninformed, brothers and sisters,[a] about those who have died,[b] so that you may not grieve as others do who have no hope. [14] For since we believe that Jesus died and rose again, even so, through Jesus, God will bring with him those who have died.[b] [15] For this we declare to you by the word of the Lord, that we who are alive, who are left until the coming of the Lord, will by no means precede those who have died.[b] [16] For the Lord himself, with a cry of command, with the archangel's call and with the sound of God's trumpet, will descend from heaven, and the dead in Christ will rise first. [17] Then we who are alive, who are left, will be caught up in the clouds together with them to meet the Lord in the air; and so we will be with the Lord forever. [18] Therefore encourage one another with these words.

5 Now concerning the times and the seasons, brothers and sisters,[a] you do not need to have anything written to you. [2] For you yourselves know very well that the day of the Lord will come like a thief in the night. [3] When they say, "There is peace and security," then sudden destruction will come upon them, as labor pains come upon a pregnant woman, and there will be no escape! [4] But you, beloved,[a] are not in darkness, for that day to surprise you like a thief; [5] for you are all children of light and children of the day; we are not of the night or of darkness. [6] So then let us not fall asleep as others do, but let us keep awake and be sober; [7] for those who sleep sleep at night, and those who are drunk get drunk at night. [8] But since we belong to the day, let us be sober, and put on the breastplate of faith and love, and for a helmet the hope of salvation. [9] For God has destined us not for wrath but for obtaining salvation through our Lord Jesus Christ, [10] who died for us, so that whether we are awake or asleep we may live with him. [11] Therefore encourage one another and build up each other, as indeed you are doing.

[12] But we appeal to you, brothers and sisters,[a] to respect those who labor among you, and have charge of you in the Lord and admonish you; [13] esteem them very highly in love because of their work. Be at peace among yourselves. [14] And we urge you, beloved,[a] to admonish the idlers, encourage the fainthearted, help the weak, be patient with all of them. [15] See that none of you repays evil for evil, but always seek to do good to one another and to all. [16] Rejoice always, [17] pray without ceasing, [18] give thanks in all circumstances; for this is the will of God in Christ Jesus for you. [19] Do not quench the Spirit. [20] Do not despise the words of

a Gk brothers
b Gk fallen asleep

4.13–5.11: Teaching about the fate of those who have died and about the coming day of the Lord. Paul seeks to comfort and encourage his readers. The dead are not lost but will rise first (cf. 1 Cor 15.12–22). The imagery here (clouds, angels, trumpets, the thief in the night) is similar to that found in Mt 23.30–43, and may reflect knowledge of this traditional material; see also Isa 27.13; Zeph 1.16. 4.15 By the word of the Lord may indicate that this teaching stems from Jesus. 17: We who are alive, Paul expects the end to come while he and some of his Thessalonian addressees are still living. Caught up . . . in the air: the basis for belief among some Christians in the Rapture, the physical ascension of those still living at the parousia; Paul's main point is reassurance that both living and dead will be with the Lord forever. 5.3: Peace and security may specifically target the achievements of the Roman empire (the "pax Romana"), with a warning of sudden destruction. 5: The contrasts of light and darkness are found also in the Dead Sea scrolls (1QS 1.9–10; 3.20–21). 6–8: For the imagery of staying armed and awake, see Rom 13.11–13; Eph 6.13–17.

5.12–24: Practical instruction about life in the church. 12–13: There are clearly some who exercise leadership in the church. 14: Idlers, refusal to work may be a problem in the community (cf. 4.11; 2 Thess 3.6–12), though the word here (Gk "ataktos") means disorderly or undisciplined. 15: This verse is similar to Rom 12.17 and 1 Pet 3.9, as

prophets,[a] [21] but test everything; hold fast to what is good; [22] abstain from every form of evil.

[23] May the God of peace himself sanctify you entirely; and may your spirit and soul and body be kept sound[b] and blameless at the coming of our Lord Jesus Christ. [24] The one who calls you is faithful, and he will do this.

[25] Beloved,[c] pray for us.

[26] Greet all the brothers and sisters[d] with a holy kiss. [27] I solemnly command you by the Lord that this letter be read to all of them.[e]

[28] The grace of our Lord Jesus Christ be with you.[f]

a Gk *despise prophecies*
b Or *complete*
c Gk *Brothers*
d Gk *brothers*
e Gk *to all the brothers*
f Other ancient authorities add *Amen*

well as to a saying from the gospel tradition (Mt 5.44; Lk 6.27–28). **19–20:** Prophecies are one of the indications of the Spirit's activity in the congregation (cf. 1 Cor 14.1–40).

5.25–28: Closing greeting. 26: The *holy kiss* became an established greeting in the Pauline churches (see Rom 16.16; 1 Cor 16.20; 2 Cor 13.12; also 1 Pet 5.14). *To all of them,* that is, to the whole community, which may have included several house churches. **28:** This closing became a standard ending in Paul's letters (e.g., Rom 16.20; 1 Cor 16.23); a fuller and now liturgical form occurs in 2 Cor 13.13.

THE SECOND LETTER OF PAUL TO THE THESSALONIANS

NAME AND CANONICAL STATUS

As with 1 Thessalonians, the name was given to the letter when Pauline letters were copied and collected together. The title in the earliest Greek manuscripts is the simple form: "To the Thessalonians 2."

From the second century on this letter has been uncontroversially accepted as part of the collection of letters of Paul within what became the New Testament canon.

AUTHORSHIP, DATE, AND HISTORICAL CONTEXT

Second Thessalonians has a close relationship to 1 Thessalonians; in terms of both structure and content it has much in common with the first letter. One such similarity is the identification of the authors as Paul, Silvanus, and Timothy (1.1). Again, a single authorial voice, that of Paul, is dominant (2.5; 3.17). However, since the nineteenth century the authenticity of this letter has been seriously challenged, and modern commentators are divided over whether this letter is genuinely from Paul himself or was composed by a later follower to correct misunderstandings of Paul's teaching. The main reasons some scholars doubt the letter's authenticity are: its close relationship to 1 Thessalonians (which it may be imitating); its more formal, impersonal style; the hints that inauthentic letters of Paul are in circulation, coupled with the attempt to stress this letter's genuineness (2.2; 3.17); and its distinctive eschatological outlook.

Dating the letter depends on decisions about its authorship. If it is by Paul, it was probably written shortly after 1 Thessalonians and addressed to the same group of churches in Thessalonica. If it is a letter written in Paul's name by someone else, then it probably dates from the late first (or perhaps early second) century CE and may not even have been intended specifically for Thessalonica. Rather, it was intended to clarify and correct a reading of 1 Thessalonians by Christians whom the author regarded as in error.

LITERARY HISTORY, STRUCTURE, AND CONTENTS

As with 1 Thessalonians, so this letter has sometimes been seen as a compilation of more than one original letter. However, it was most likely composed as a single letter in the form we have it now.

The structure and content of 2 Thessalonians may be outlined as follows:

1.1–2	Opening greeting
1.3–12	Opening thanksgiving and prayer
2.1–12	Warning and instruction about the coming of Christ
2.13–17	Further thanksgiving and prayer
3.1–5	A request for prayer
3.6–16	Warning and instruction about believers who are unruly and idle
3.17–18	Closing greeting

INTERPRETATION

Second Thessalonians has generally been interpreted as a follow-up letter to 1 Thessalonians. It repeats some of the material from 1 Thessalonians, though it casts it in a somewhat more formal way (compare, e.g., 1.3 and 1 Thess 1.2). Like 1 Thessalonians, 2 Thessalonians encourages Christians facing suffering and hardship (1.4–6; 2.13–15; 3.3–5,13). More evident in 2 Thessalonians, though, is a concern to address problems in the churches. There are two in particular, which may be linked, since one is primarily a doctrinal issue, the other a behavioral one. The doctrinal issue concerns those who say "that the day of the Lord is already here" (2.2); the behavioral issue concerns those who refuse to work and are (in the author's view, at least) causing trouble (3.6–12). It is possible that a belief that the final day had already come (cf. 2 Tim 2.18) led people to abandon their normal daily commitments. The author addresses the problem of this false eschatological belief by describing a series of events that must take place before the day of the Lord can happen (see notes on 2.3–12). This section of the letter draws on motifs from Jewish apocalyptic literature (e.g., *Jub.* 23.14–21; Dan 8.24–25) and has some parallels with other early Christian texts (e.g., Mk 13; Jude 14–19; Rev 20.1–15). But the specific scenario outlined in 2 Thessalonians is distinctive and—to modern readers, at least—enigmatic.

GUIDE TO READING

This letter needs to be read in conjunction with 1 Thessalonians, not only to appreciate the similarities between the two but also to see how 2 Thessalonians addresses problems that have seemingly arisen, or developed, following the receipt of that letter. Whether this is a response by Paul himself, or by another author some time later, remains open to debate. But the eschatological scenario outlined in 2 Thessalonians is clearly different from that set out in 1 Thessalonians. As with other apocalyptic and eschatological writings, such as the book of Revelation, a major question for modern readers is how to interpret the imagery here and the sequence of events which the writer sees as necessary preludes to the final day of salvation.

David G. Horrell

1 Paul, Silvanus, and Timothy,
To the church of the Thessalonians in God our Father and the Lord Jesus Christ:
[2] Grace to you and peace from God our[a] Father and the Lord Jesus Christ.
[3] We must always give thanks to God for you, brothers and sisters,[b] as is right, because your faith is growing abundantly, and the love of every one of you for one another is increasing. [4] Therefore we ourselves boast of you among the churches of God for your steadfastness and faith during all your persecutions and the afflictions that you are enduring.
[5] This is evidence of the righteous judgment of God, and is intended to make you worthy of the kingdom of God, for which you are also suffering. [6] For it is indeed just of God to repay with affliction those who afflict you, [7] and to give relief to the afflicted as well as to us, when the Lord Jesus is revealed from heaven with his mighty angels [8] in flaming fire, inflicting

vengeance on those who do not know God and on those who do not obey the gospel of our Lord Jesus. [9] These will suffer the punishment of eternal destruction, separated from the presence of the Lord and from the glory of his might, [10] when he comes to be glorified by his saints and to be marveled at on that day among all who have believed, because our testimony to you was believed. [11] To this end we always pray for you, asking that our God will make you worthy of his call and will fulfill by his power every good resolve and work of faith, [12] so that the name of our Lord Jesus may be glorified in you, and you in him, according to the grace of our God and the Lord Jesus Christ.

2 As to the coming of our Lord Jesus Christ and our being gathered together to him, we beg you, brothers and sisters,[b] [2] not to be

a Other ancient authorities read *the*
b Gk *brothers*

1.1–2: Greeting. The opening of the letter is identical to that of 1 Thessalonians, apart from the longer phrase at the end of the greeting; see 1 Thess 1.1n.

1.3–12: Opening thanksgiving and prayer. One long sentence in Greek, these verses begin with a thanksgiving for the believers' faith and then speak of their vindication and the punishment awaiting unbelievers before ending with a prayer. **3–4:** The thanksgiving echoes the content of 1 Thess 1.2–10, mentioning *persecutions and afflictions* and the *faith, love,* and *steadfastness* (cf. "steadfastness of hope" in 1 Thess 1.3), which the readers have shown. **5–10:** The focus here is on the *affliction* God will cause to those who currently *afflict you*, that is, the Christian readers of the letter. Imagery drawn from biblical descriptions of the coming day of judgment, referring to God, is here used to depict *the Lord Jesus* at his coming (cf. Zech 14.5; Isa 66.15–16). Compare the depictions of judgment and punishment in Jude 5–16 and 2 Pet 2.4–22, though there the focus is on false teachers; here the focus is those who do not believe. **10:** *Saints,* Christian believers.

2.1–12: Warning and instruction about the coming of Christ. The writer is concerned to refute the idea that *the day of the Lord* (cf. Isa 13.6; Joel 2.1; Am 5.18) has already come, and to set out a sequence of events that

quickly shaken in mind or alarmed, either by spirit or by word or by letter, as though from us, to the effect that the day of the Lord is already here. [3] Let no one deceive you in any way; for that day will not come unless the rebellion comes first and the lawless one[a] is revealed, the one destined for destruction.[b] [4] He opposes and exalts himself above every so-called god or object of worship, so that he takes his seat in the temple of God, declaring himself to be God. [5] Do you not remember that I told you these things when I was still with you? [6] And you know what is now restraining him, so that he may be revealed when his time comes. [7] For the mystery of lawlessness is already at work, but only until the one who now restrains it is removed. [8] And then the lawless one will be revealed, whom the Lord Jesus[c] will destroy[d] with the breath of his mouth, annihilating him by the manifestation of his coming. [9] The coming of the lawless one is apparent in the working of Satan, who uses all power, signs, lying wonders, [10] and every kind of wicked deception for those who are perishing, because they refused to love the truth and so be saved. [11] For this reason God sends them a powerful delusion, leading them to believe what is false, [12] so that all who have not believed the truth but took pleasure in unrighteousness will be condemned.

[13] But we must always give thanks to God for you, brothers and sisters[e] beloved by the Lord, because God chose you as the first fruits[f] for salvation through sanctification by the Spirit and through belief in the truth. [14] For this purpose he called you through our proclamation of the good news,[g] so that you may obtain the glory of our Lord Jesus Christ. [15] So then, brothers and sisters,[e] stand firm and hold fast to the traditions that you were taught by us, either by word of mouth or by our letter.

[16] Now may our Lord Jesus Christ himself and God our Father, who loved us and through grace gave us eternal comfort and good hope, [17] comfort your hearts and strengthen them in every good work and word.

3 Finally, brothers and sisters,[e] pray for us, so that the word of the Lord may spread rapidly and be glorified everywhere, just as it is among you, [2] and that we may be rescued from wicked and evil people; for not all have faith. [3] But the Lord is faithful; he will strengthen you and guard you from the evil one.[h] [4] And we have confidence in the Lord concerning you, that you are doing and will go on doing the things that we command. [5] May the Lord direct your hearts

---

a   Gk *the man of lawlessness*; other ancient authorities read *the man of sin*
b   Gk *the son of destruction*
c   Other ancient authorities lack *Jesus*
d   Other ancient authorities read *consume*
e   Gk *brothers*
f   Other ancient authorities read *from the beginning*
g   Or *through our gospel*
h   Or *from evil*

---

must happen first. This implies that the coming of Christ must be some time away (contrast 1 Thess 4.15). **2:** *As though from us* is ambiguous and difficult: it might refer to 1 Thessalonians, to correct a misreading of it, or it might imply that forgeries attributed to Paul are in circulation and that the readers should not be led astray by them. **3–4:** It is uncertain to whom *the lawless one* refers; possibilities include a false prophet or an emperor, such as had been encountered in earlier Jewish history (cf. Dan 8.24–25; 11.36; 1 Macc 1.1–64; Mk 13.14). Roman emperors were often given a form of divine status and were worshiped in imperial ritual. **6–7:** It is uncertain who or what is "the restrainer," although presumably someone or thing on the side of good, since its purpose is to restrain evil (cf. Rev 20.2–3). **8:** *Breath of his mouth*, see Ps 33.3; Job 4.9; Isa 11.4. **9–10:** *Satan*, who deceives: see 1 Thess 2.18n.

2.13–17: Further thanksgiving and prayer. 13: The opening of the thanksgiving closely follows 1.3, which in turn echoes 1 Thess 1.2–10. On God's election (*chose you*), see 1 Thess 1.4n., and on *sanctification* see 1 Thess 4.1n. **15:** *The traditions*, that is, those that Paul taught, which might hint that this letter is written at a later period, but see 1 Cor 11.2. *Our letter* probably refers to 1 Thess, and to the need for its correct interpretation (see 2.2n.). **16–17:** This prayer echoes the phrasing of 1 Thess 3.2 and 3.11–13.

3.1–5: A request for prayer. 1: The opening echoes 1 Thess 4.1 and 5.25. **2:** Cf. 2 Tim 4.17–18. **3:** *The evil one*,

to the love of God and to the steadfastness of Christ.

⁶ Now we command you, beloved,ᵃ in the name of our Lord Jesus Christ, to keep away from believers who areᵇ living in idleness and not according to the tradition that theyᶜ received from us. ⁷ For you yourselves know how you ought to imitate us; we were not idle when we were with you, ⁸ and we did not eat anyone's bread without paying for it; but with toil and labor we worked night and day, so that we might not burden any of you. ⁹ This was not because we do not have that right, but in order to give you an example to imitate. ¹⁰ For even when we were with you, we gave you this command: Anyone unwilling to work should not eat. ¹¹ For we hear that some of you are living in idleness, mere busybodies, not doing any work. ¹² Now such persons we command and exhort in the Lord Jesus Christ to do their work quietly and to earn their own living. ¹³ Brothers and sisters,ᵈ do not be weary in doing what is right.

¹⁴ Take note of those who do not obey what we say in this letter; have nothing to do with them, so that they may be ashamed. ¹⁵ Do not regard them as enemies, but warn them as believers.ᵉ

¹⁶ Now may the Lord of peace himself give you peace at all times in all ways. The Lord be with all of you.

¹⁷ I, Paul, write this greeting with my own hand. This is the mark in every letter of mine; it is the way I write. ¹⁸ The grace of our Lord Jesus Christ be with all of you.ᶠ

ᵃ Gk brothers
ᵇ Gk from every brother who is
ᶜ Other ancient authorities read you
ᵈ Gk Brothers
ᵉ Gk a brother
ᶠ Other ancient authorities add Amen

see Mt 6.13. **5**: *Of God . . . of Christ,* in both cases the construction is ambiguous: it could mean the believers' love for God and steadfastness in following Christ, or God's love and Christ's own steadfastness. Perhaps both meanings are intended here.

3.6–16: Warning and instruction about believers who are unruly and idle. Here the writer confronts the issue of those who refuse to work and urges the readers to shun those who refuse to follow his teaching. **6:** *In idleness* (here and in v. 11) translates the Greek adverb "ataktos," which essentially means being disorderly (see 1 Thess 5.14n.). Clearly here the main way this is evident is in some people's refusal to work (see vv. 7–12). This conduct may perhaps have been motivated by the belief that the day of the Lord had already come (see 2.1–12n.). *The tradition,* cf. 2.15, though here the word is singular, and refers specifically to the pattern of conduct of Paul and his associates. **7–10:** This pattern (cf. 1 Thess 2.9) is now held up as a model to imitate. On the apostles' *right* to support, see 1 Cor 9.4–15, and on the problem of some taking advantage of such support, see *Did.* 11–12. **12:** Cf. 1 Thess 4.11. **14–15:** A strong warning to heed this teaching; nonetheless, the purpose of shunning the disobedient is that they may be won back, not excluded forever (cf. Jude 22–23).

3.17–18: Closing greeting. 17: The opening phrase is identical to that in 1 Cor 16.21 and Col 4.18; see also Gal 6.11. Here, however, the second sentence reflects a perceived need to stress the authenticity of the letter (cf. note on 2.2). **18:** See 1 Thess 5.28n.

INTRODUCTION
TO THE PASTORAL EPISTLES

The term "Pastoral Epistles" has been applied, since the eighteenth century, to the three letters from Paul to his two co-workers and envoys, Timothy and Titus. The name reflects the central concern in these three epistles for the internal life, governance, and behavior of Christian communities and their members. Scholars have long debated whether these letters were written by the apostle Paul himself, or by a later disciple who sought to provide guidance for Pauline churches in new times and places. While most scholars today regard them as pseudepigraphical (that is, ascribed to the authority of a major figure but not actually written by him, a custom well attested in ancient literature), there is not complete unanimity on the question.

The conclusion that these three epistles were not written by Paul is based upon literary, historical, and theological criteria. First and Second Timothy and Titus share a common Greek vocabulary and style that diverges in many ways from the other Pauline epistles. Historically, the Pastoral Epistles presume an institutionalized leadership in local communities and internal dissent over faith and practice, which better fits a period late in the first or early in the second century CE when Paul was no longer alive. It is possible to see how some passages may have been written to explain or definitively interpret passages in the authentic letters already in circulation (such as 1 Tim 2.9–19; cf. 1 Cor 14.33–36). Theologically these letters minimize or lack characteristic Pauline themes (such as justification by faith, and the church as the body of Christ) in favor of a new emphasis on adherence to tradition and regulation as signs of the Christian piety they seek to inculcate in their readers. Although Timothy and Titus had been Paul's trusted co-workers for decades, the first letter to Timothy and the letter to Titus present the recipients as needing basic instructions for community leadership. Second Timothy is less concerned with regulating the life of the Christian communities than Titus and 1 Timothy. It has been described as a "testament," the last words of the apostle to a close associate. It looks forward to the difficulties facing Timothy and others after Paul's death with foreboding, and bears some similarity to the genuine Philippians in this regard.

Recent challenges to the pseudepigraphical nature of all three letters have come from scholars who argue that each should be judged separately, that the letters contain fragments of original Pauline material, or that the very concept of "authorship" of a Pauline letter requires nuance, given that Paul used secretaries and served as a member of a cooperative missionary team. Neither is there scholarly unanimity about which other letters are certainly authentic nor which parts of those are most tellingly "Pauline" for comparison with these epistles. Each reader should consider the evidence about the authorship of the Pastorals cumulatively, first as a question of historical fact—did Paul write them or not? Then, and separately, one should reflect on the interpretative and theological implications of such a decision, for the denial of Pauline authorship may or may not entail a loss of authoritative status for that document within a particular religious community.

Regardless of authorship, the Pastoral Epistles share a common rhetorical strategy: Each is addressed to a single individual among Paul's co-workers but also has in mind a wider circle of readers. In each the author presents himself as a Paul who speaks in the epistolary medium as an unambiguously authoritative figure of the past to church leaders and members of later generations who did not know him personally.

Margaret M. Mitchell

THE FIRST LETTER OF PAUL TO TIMOTHY

NAME, AUTHORSHIP, AND BACKGROUND

This letter is named for its recipient, Paul's "loyal child" Timothy (1.2); for further information on Timothy, see the Introduction to 2 Timothy, p. 2091. The letter presents Paul as a wise and sure teacher who hands on to his student his deposit of tradition, his "sound teaching" (1.10; 4.6), so that this fixed legacy will be passed down with fidelity to the next generation. (On the authorship and date of this letter, see p. 2084.) The text presents a vision of household ethics that brings together instructions on Christian "godliness" (or "piety"; 2.2) for the individual with a church order of regulations and qualifications for various roles (bishops, deacons, widows, elders) in the church, designated "the household of God" (3.15). This advice is set in a dual context formed, positively, by the warmly remembered relationship between Paul and Timothy, and, negatively, by the frequent allusions to purveyors of alternate teachings in or near Timothy's church in Ephesus.

STRUCTURE

After an epistolary prescript (1.1–2) the author launches (without the customary thanksgiving) into the body of the letter, which is roughly arranged with alternating sections of contrast between true and false teaching (1.3–2.15; 4.1–5.2; 6.2b–21a) and instructions for church order and governance, understood as the means for living in the church of God (3.1–16; 5.3–6.2a). The letter concludes with summary exhortations to Timothy to guard this tradition with which he has been entrusted (6.11–21). As with all Pauline letters a final benediction (6.21) seals the letter, perhaps in anticipation of liturgical use.

INTERPRETATION AND GUIDE TO READING

Although the author names two of his Christian opponents (1.20), exactly what they taught, and why, is only hazily sketched here in vituperative terms: They have "deviated" from the truth (1.6); they have "suffered shipwreck in the faith" (1.19). No definitive reconstruction is possible from these verbal assaults, but it seems that these opponents have some connection with Judaism and Torah observance, "myths and endless genealogies" (1.4), and ascetic practices, such as rejecting marriage and abstaining from certain foods (4.3). Recent research has suggested a link between the Christians whom this author opposes and those who held to traditions found in the later apocryphal *Acts of Paul and Thecla*, which validates women's ministries and claimed Paul as the champion of an ascetic and celibate lifestyle. In this view, 1 Timothy is a kind of "corrective composition" whose author is seeking to "fix" Paul's authentic legacy for an early second-century audience.

In the authorial rhetoric of this text, at times Timothy is directly addressed, but more often he recedes into the background, and the author speaks to a more universal audience. As ethical instruction (parenesis), 1 Timothy is cast in characteristic forms of Greco-Roman moral exhortation, such as Seneca's *Moral Epistles* and the pseudepigraphical Socratic and Neopythagorean letters. These include letters between friends or teachers and students about progress in the ethical life, lists of virtues and vices, and contrasts between illustrious examples and notorious counterexamples. Likewise, the content is in many ways similar to moralizing literature of the time, with emphasis on decorum and decency, on the hierarchical, orderly disposition of the patriarchal household, on reliable speech, and against accumulation of wealth. But the letter's theological universe, which is punctuated by shorthand terminology and quotations from established traditions, is distinctly Christian.

Margaret M. Mitchell

1

Paul, an apostle of Christ Jesus by the command of God our Savior and of Christ Jesus our hope, [2] To Timothy, my loyal child in the faith:

Grace, mercy, and peace from God the Father and Christ Jesus our Lord.

[3] I urge you, as I did when I was on my way to Macedonia, to remain in Ephesus so that you may instruct certain people not to teach any different doctrine, [4] and not to occupy themselves with myths and endless genealogies that promote speculations rather than the divine training[a] that is known by faith. [5] But the aim of such instruction is love that comes from a pure heart, a good conscience, and sincere faith. [6] Some people have deviated from these and turned to meaningless talk, [7] desiring to be teachers of the law, without understanding either what they are saying or the things about which they make assertions.

[8] Now we know that the law is good, if one uses it legitimately. [9] This means understanding that the law is laid down not for the innocent but for the lawless and disobedient, for the godless and sinful, for the unholy and profane, for those who kill their father or mother, for murderers, [10] fornicators, sodomites, slave traders, liars, perjurers, and whatever else is contrary to the sound teaching [11] that conforms to the glorious gospel of the blessed God, which he entrusted to me.

[12] I am grateful to Christ Jesus our Lord, who has strengthened me, because he judged me faithful and appointed me to his service, [13] even though I was formerly a blasphemer, a persecutor, and a man of violence. But I received mercy because I had acted ignorantly in unbelief, [14] and the grace of our Lord overflowed for me with the faith and love that are in Christ Jesus. [15] The saying is sure and worthy of full acceptance, that Christ Jesus came into the world to save sinners—of whom I am the foremost. [16] But for that very reason I received mercy, so that in me, as the foremost, Jesus Christ might display the utmost patience, making me an example to those who would come to believe in him for eternal life. [17] To the King of the ages, immortal, invisible, the only God, be honor and glory forever and ever.[b] Amen.

[18] I am giving you these instructions, Timothy, my child, in accordance with the prophecies made earlier about you, so that by following them you may fight the good fight, [19] having faith and a good conscience. By rejecting conscience, certain persons have suffered shipwreck in the faith; [20] among them are Hymenaeus and Alexander, whom

---

a Or *plan*
b Gk *to the ages of the ages*

1.1–2: Epistolary prescript: sender, addressees, and salutation, following the typical form of a Pauline letter (see Philem 1.1–3), with the addition of mercy in the greeting (cf. 2 Tim 1.2).

1.3–2.15: The contrast of true and false teaching (part one).

1.3–11: Opening warning against false teachers, in place of a thanksgiving formula (cf. Philem 4–9), signaling the urgency of the problem, as the author sees it. **3:** *Instruct,* the author's main purpose (1.5,18; 4.11; 5.7; 6.13,17). **4:** *Myths and endless genealogies,* uncertain, but probably speculations on biblical texts (cf. 4.7; Titus 1.14; 3.9). *Divine training,* or "plan," or "stewardship." **5:** *Love . . . conscience . . . faith,* for Paul's usual triad of faith, love, and hope (1 Thess 1.3; 5.8; 1 Cor 13.13). **6:** *Deviated,* see 6.21n. **7:** *The law,* presumably the Torah. **9–10:** Implicitly, a stereotypical depiction of the false teachers as ethically depraved; cf. other catalogues of vice in Rom 1.29–31; 1 Cor 5.11; 6.9–10; Gal 5.19–21.

1.12–20: Contrasting portraits of faithfulness and faithlessness. 12–17: A portrait of Paul, the blasphemer transformed into the faithful proclaimer (cf. the different portrayals in Paul's letters [1 Cor 15.8–10; Gal 1.13–24; Phil 3.5–11], and in Acts 9). **15:** *The saying is sure,* a favored formula in the Pastorals (see 3.1; 4.9; 2 Tim 2.11; Titus 3.8). **17:** Theology cast as doxology (cf. 6.15–16). **18:** *Prophecies,* see 4.14. **19:** *Conscience,* the seat of self-awareness of guilt or innocence (a key theme; see 1.5; 3.9; 4.2; 2 Tim 1.3; Titus 1.15). **20:** *Hymenaeus* (unknown apart from here and 2 Tim 2.17) and *Alexander* (likely to be identified with "Alexander the coppersmith" in 2 Tim 4.14; perhaps Acts 19.33), characterized as blasphemers (cf. 1.13). *Turned over to Satan,* for correction or possibly for punishment (cf. 1 Cor 5.5). Satan or the devil is mentioned frequently in the Pastorals; see 3.6,7; 5.15; 2 Tim 2.26.

2.1–8: Instruction on prayer. 1–3: Accommodation with worldly authorities urged for the sake of peace for the church (see Rom 13.1–7). The irenic tone circumvents the difficult question of the limits of Christian acqui-

I have turned over to Satan, so that they may learn not to blaspheme.

2 First of all, then, I urge that supplications, prayers, intercessions, and thanksgivings be made for everyone, [2] for kings and all who are in high positions, so that we may lead a quiet and peaceable life in all godliness and dignity. [3] This is right and is acceptable in the sight of God our Savior, [4] who desires everyone to be saved and to come to the knowledge of the truth. [5] For

there is one God;
there is also one mediator between God
      and humankind,
Christ Jesus, himself human,
    [6] who gave himself a ransom for all

—this was attested at the right time. [7] For this I was appointed a herald and an apostle (I am telling the truth,[a] I am not lying), a teacher of the Gentiles in faith and truth.

[8] I desire, then, that in every place the men should pray, lifting up holy hands without anger or argument; [9] also that the women should dress themselves modestly and decently in suitable clothing, not with their hair braided, or with gold, pearls, or expensive clothes, [10] but with good works, as is proper for women who profess reverence for God. [11] Let a woman[b] learn in silence with full submission. [12] I permit no woman[b] to teach or to have authority over a man;[c] she is to keep silent. [13] For Adam was formed first, then Eve; [14] and Adam was not deceived,

but the woman was deceived and became a transgressor. [15] Yet she will be saved through childbearing, provided they continue in faith and love and holiness, with modesty.

3 The saying is sure:[d] whoever aspires to the office of bishop[e] desires a noble task. [2] Now a bishop[f] must be above reproach, married only once,[g] temperate, sensible, respectable, hospitable, an apt teacher, [3] not a drunkard, not violent but gentle, not quarrelsome, and not a lover of money. [4] He must manage his own household well, keeping his children submissive and respectful in every way— [5] for if someone does not know how to manage his own household, how can he take care of God's church? [6] He must not be a recent convert, or he may be puffed up with conceit and fall into the condemnation of the devil. [7] Moreover, he must be well thought of by outsiders, so that he may not fall into disgrace and the snare of the devil.

[8] Deacons likewise must be serious, not double-tongued, not indulging in much wine, not greedy for money; [9] they must hold fast to the mystery of the faith with a clear con-

a   Other ancient authorities add *in Christ*
b   Or *wife*
c   Or *her husband*
d   Some interpreters place these words at the end of the previous paragraph. Other ancient authorities read *The saying is commonly accepted*
e   Or *overseer*
f   Or *an overseer*
g   Gk *the husband of one wife*

escence to an emperor who was honored as a god by daily worship and oaths of allegiance. *Godliness*, or "piety" ("eusebeia"), a predominant concern of the Pastoral epistles (3.16, translated "religion"; 4.7,8; 6.3,5,6; 2 Tim 3.5; Titus 1.1). The rationale given for such prayer is both strategic (2.2b) and theological (2.3–7).**4:** Strong emphasis on God as universal savior (cf. 4.10). *Knowledge of the truth*, as found in the gospel proclamation (see 2 Tim 2.25; 3.7; Titus 1.1). **5:** *One God . . . one mediator*, a reformulation of the Shema (see Deut 6.4–9n.; cf. 1 Cor 8.6; Eph 4.5–6). **7:** The title *herald*, although sometimes implied (e.g., 2 Cor 4.5; 5.20), is not found in the undisputed letters of Paul (unlike *apostle*); cf. 2 Tim 1.11.

    2.9–15: The proper demeanor of faithful women. The author objects to the current practice of women holding leadership and teaching positions because it threatens conventional domestic order (also 5.3–16). **9:** *Dress themselves modestly*, a standard concern of Stoic and other Hellenistic moralists. *And decently*, Gk "sophrosune" ("moderation"), one of the four cardinal virtues of Greek philosophical thought. **11–12:** Very similar to the contested passage 1 Cor 14.34–35 (see note there). **13–14:** A "strong" reading of Gen 2–3 assigning all the blame to the woman (contrast Rom 5.12–21). **15:** *She will be saved through childbearing*, a soteriology (theology of salvation) at odds with Paul's justification by faith (Gal 2.16; Rom 1.16–17). *Modesty*, Gk "sophrosune"; see 2.9n.

    3.1–16: Living in the church of God (part one). Qualifications for prospective bishops (3.1–7) and deacons (3.8–13), already established ecclesial offices (contrast 1 Cor 12.28; Phil 1.1n.). **1,2:** *Bishop*, (Gk "episkopos"), "overseer," one who looks after church affairs (see note e). **5:** *God's church* (cf. v. 15, "the household of God"), the church is en-

science. ¹⁰ And let them first be tested; then, if they prove themselves blameless, let them serve as deacons. ¹¹ Womenª likewise must be serious, not slanderers, but temperate, faithful in all things. ¹² Let deacons be married only once,ᵇ and let them manage their children and their households well; ¹³ for those who serve well as deacons gain a good standing for themselves and great boldness in the faith that is in Christ Jesus.

¹⁴ I hope to come to you soon, but I am writing these instructions to you so that, ¹⁵ if I am delayed, you may know how one ought to behave in the household of God, which is the church of the living God, the pillar and bulwark of the truth. ¹⁶ Without any doubt, the mystery of our religion is great:

He^c was revealed in flesh,
   vindicated^d in spirit,^e
     seen by angels,
proclaimed among Gentiles,
   believed in throughout the world,
     taken up in glory.

4 Now the Spirit expressly says that in later^f times some will renounce the faith by paying attention to deceitful spirits and teachings of demons, ² through the hypocrisy of liars whose consciences are seared with a hot iron. ³ They forbid marriage and demand abstinence from foods, which God created to be received with thanksgiving by those who believe and know the truth. ⁴ For everything created by God is good, and nothing is to be rejected, provided it is received with thanksgiving; ⁵ for it is sanctified by God's word and by prayer.

⁶ If you put these instructions before the brothers and sisters,^g you will be a good servant^h of Christ Jesus, nourished on the words

of the faith and of the sound teaching that you have followed. ⁷ Have nothing to do with profane myths and old wives' tales. Train yourself in godliness, ⁸ for, while physical training is of some value, godliness is valuable in every way, holding promise for both the present life and the life to come. ⁹ The saying is sure and worthy of full acceptance. ¹⁰ For to this end we toil and struggle,ⁱ because we have our hope set on the living God, who is the Savior of all people, especially of those who believe.

¹¹ These are the things you must insist on and teach. ¹² Let no one despise your youth, but set the believers an example in speech and conduct, in love, in faith, in purity. ¹³ Until I arrive, give attention to the public reading of scripture,ʲ to exhorting, to teaching. ¹⁴ Do not neglect the gift that is in you, which was given to you through prophecy with the laying on of hands by the council of elders.ᵏ ¹⁵ Put these things into practice, devote yourself to them, so that all may see your progress. ¹⁶ Pay close attention to yourself and to your teaching; continue in these things, for in doing this you will save both yourself and your hearers.

ª Or *Their wives,* or *Women deacons*
ᵇ Gk *be husbands of one wife*
ᶜ Gk *Who;* other ancient authorities read *God;* others, *Which*
ᵈ Or *justified*
ᵉ Or *by the Spirit*
ᶠ Or *the last*
ᵍ Gk *brothers*
ʰ Or *deacon*
ⁱ Other ancient authorities read *suffer reproach*
ʲ Gk *to the reading*
ᵏ Gk *by the presbytery*

visioned as an orderly patriarchal Greco-Roman household. **11:** *Women* deacons (but see note a for the ambiguity), such as Phoebe (Rom 16.1). If women deacons are intended, the short treatment may be due to the author's anxiety about female leadership (see 2.9–15; 5.3–16). **14–15:** *If I am delayed,* an epistolary commonplace, here suggesting verisimilitude (cf. Rom 15.24; 1 Cor 16.7; Philem 22; Phil 2.24). Whether he is dead or alive, the letter takes Paul's place.

4.1–5.2: The contrast of true and false teaching (part two). 1: The *later times* (see note f) were often associated with false teachings (Mk 13.21–23; 2 Thess 2.1–16; cf. 2 Tim 4.3–4). **3:** *They forbid marriage and demand abstinence from foods,* clearest statement of the opponents' ascetic practices. **6:** The sound teaching, the reliable tradition the Pastoral epistles pass on (1.10; 4.1,6,13,16; 5.17; 6.1,3; 2 Tim 1.13; 3.10,16; 4.3; Titus 1.9; 2.1,7,10). **7:** *Myths,* see 1.4n. **7–10:** The life of faith compared to training for an athletic contest (cf. 1 Cor 9.24–27; 2 Tim 2.5). **13:** A glimpse into the content of an early Christian worship service. **14:** *The laying on of hands,* a gesture marking the succession of ministerial authorization (see 5.22; 2 Tim 1.6; Acts 6.6). **15:** *Your progress,* "prokope," the Stoic concept of ethical advancement, which will be expressed negatively in 2 Tim 2.16; 3.9,13.

5 Do not speak harshly to an older man,[a] but speak to him as to a father, to younger men as brothers, [2] to older women as mothers, to younger women as sisters—with absolute purity.

[3] Honor widows who are really widows. [4] If a widow has children or grandchildren, they should first learn their religious duty to their own family and make some repayment to their parents; for this is pleasing in God's sight. [5] The real widow, left alone, has set her hope on God and continues in supplications and prayers night and day; [6] but the widow[b] who lives for pleasure is dead even while she lives. [7] Give these commands as well, so that they may be above reproach. [8] And whoever does not provide for relatives, and especially for family members, has denied the faith and is worse than an unbeliever.

[9] Let a widow be put on the list if she is not less than sixty years old and has been married only once;[c] [10] she must be well attested for her good works, as one who has brought up children, shown hospitality, washed the saints' feet, helped the afflicted, and devoted herself to doing good in every way. [11] But refuse to put younger widows on the list; for when their sensual desires alienate them from Christ, they want to marry, [12] and so they incur condemnation for having violated their first pledge. [13] Besides that, they learn to be idle, gadding about from house to house; and they are not merely idle, but also gossips and busybodies, saying what they should not say. [14] So I would have younger widows marry, bear children, and manage their households, so as to give the adversary no occasion to revile us. [15] For some have already turned away to follow Satan. [16] If any believing woman[d] has relatives who are really widows, let her assist them; let the church not be burdened, so that it can assist those who are real widows.

[17] Let the elders who rule well be considered worthy of double honor,[e] especially those who labor in preaching and teaching; [18] for the scripture says, "You shall not muzzle an ox while it is treading out the grain," and, "The laborer deserves to be paid." [19] Never accept any accusation against an elder except on the evidence of two or three witnesses. [20] As for those who persist in sin, rebuke them in the presence of all, so that the rest also may stand in fear. [21] In the presence of God and of Christ Jesus and of the elect angels, I warn you to keep these instructions without prejudice, doing nothing on the basis of partiality. [22] Do not ordain[f] anyone hastily, and do not participate in the sins of others; keep yourself pure.

[23] No longer drink only water, but take a little wine for the sake of your stomach and your frequent ailments.

[24] The sins of some people are conspicuous and precede them to judgment, while the sins of others follow them there. [25] So also good works are conspicuous; and even when they are not, they cannot remain hidden.

6 Let all who are under the yoke of slavery regard their masters as worthy of all honor, so that the name of God and the teaching may not be blasphemed. [2] Those who have believing masters must not be disrespectful to them on the ground that they are members of the church;[g] rather they must serve them

---

a Or *an elder*, or *a presbyter*
b Gk *she*
c Gk *the wife of one husband*
d Other ancient authorities read *believing man or woman*; others, *believing man*
e Or *compensation*
f Gk *Do not lay hands on*
g Gk *are brothers*

5.3–6.2a: Living in the church of God (part two). Three groups of persons are singled out for instructions: widows (vv. 3–16), elders (vv. 17–20), and slaves (6.1–2). **3–16:** *Real widows* (vv. 3,5,16), an attempt to legislate the practice of widowhood—women living on the support of the church while dedicating their time to a ministry of continual prayer—by insisting on the maintenance of the conventional patriarchal household. **9:** *Put on the list,* designated for communal support. **13:** Stereotypical caricature of idle women as busybodies. **14:** *The adversary,* see 1.20n.; 3.7. Also can be a reference to human opponents (cf. 1 Cor 16.9; Phil 1.28).

18b: A saying of Jesus, according to Lk 10.7. **19:** *Two or three witnesses,* Deut 19.15; 2 Cor 13.1. **23:** A little wine, in contrast to the asceticism of the opponents; see 4.3n. **6.1–2:** Reminiscent of the exhortations in Eph 6.5–9; Col 3.22–4.1, but lacking a reciprocal exhortation to the owners.

all the more, since those who benefit by their service are believers and beloved.[a]

Teach and urge these duties. [3] Whoever teaches otherwise and does not agree with the sound words of our Lord Jesus Christ and the teaching that is in accordance with godliness, [4] is conceited, understanding nothing, and has a morbid craving for controversy and for disputes about words. From these come envy, dissension, slander, base suspicions, [5] and wrangling among those who are depraved in mind and bereft of the truth, imagining that godliness is a means of gain.[b] [6] Of course, there is great gain in godliness combined with contentment; [7] for we brought nothing into the world, so that[c] we can take nothing out of it; [8] but if we have food and clothing, we will be content with these. [9] But those who want to be rich fall into temptation and are trapped by many senseless and harmful desires that plunge people into ruin and destruction. [10] For the love of money is a root of all kinds of evil, and in their eagerness to be rich some have wandered away from the faith and pierced themselves with many pains.

[11] But as for you, man of God, shun all this; pursue righteousness, godliness, faith, love, endurance, gentleness. [12] Fight the good fight of the faith; take hold of the eternal life, to which you were called and for which you made[d] the good confession in the presence of many witnesses. [13] In the presence of God, who gives life to all things, and of Christ Jesus, who in his testimony before Pontius Pilate made the good confession, I charge you [14] to keep the commandment without spot or blame until the manifestation of our Lord Jesus Christ, [15] which he will bring about at the right time—he who is the blessed and only Sovereign, the King of kings and Lord of lords. [16] It is he alone who has immortality and dwells in unapproachable light, whom no one has ever seen or can see; to him be honor and eternal dominion. Amen.

[17] As for those who in the present age are rich, command them not to be haughty, or to set their hopes on the uncertainty of riches, but rather on God who richly provides us with everything for our enjoyment. [18] They are to do good, to be rich in good works, generous, and ready to share, [19] thus storing up for themselves the treasure of a good foundation for the future, so that they may take hold of the life that really is life.

[20] Timothy, guard what has been entrusted to you. Avoid the profane chatter and contradictions of what is falsely called knowledge; [21] by professing it some have missed the mark as regards the faith.

Grace be with you.[e]

a   Or *since they are believers and beloved, who devote themselves to good deeds*
b   Other ancient authorities add *Withdraw yourself from such people*
c   Other ancient authorities read *world—it is certain that*
d   Gk *confessed*
e   The Greek word for *you* here is plural; in other ancient authorities it is singular. Other ancient authorities add *Amen*

6.2b–21: **The contrast of true and false teaching (part three).** 3–5: A portrait of the unsound teacher, with many resonances to 1.3–11. 6–10: The catchword *gain* leads to a favorite philosophical and biblical (Job 1.21; Eccl 5.15) commonplace about the false security of riches (taken up again in 6.17–19). 6: *Contentment* (also v. 8), "autarkeia," a Stoic term meaning "self-sufficiency." 11–12: *Fight the good fight,* compare 1.18 and 2 Tim 4.7. 13: *Pontius Pilate,* the only New Testament reference to the Roman governor of Judea (see Mt 27.2; Lk 3.1) outside the Gospels and Acts. *The good confession,* see Jn 18.33–38, but cf. Mt 27.11–13. 14: *Commandment,* a reference to the testimony in this letter, or perhaps the same as the "good confession" in v. 12, the vow Timothy made at his ordination. Manifestation (lit., "epiphany"), a reference to the Second Coming (a favored term in the Pastorals: 2 Tim 1.10; 4.1,8; Titus 2.13). 15–16: A hymn to the sovereignty of God as all-powerful, immortal, and invisible (Ex 33.20; Rom 1.23; Col 1.15; Jn 1.18). 19: *The treasure,* for the theme, see Mt 6.19–20; Lk 12.21; 2 Esd 7.77.

6.20–21: **Timothy the guardian of the true teaching.** 20: *What has been entrusted to you* (lit., "the deposit"), the teachings in this letter, seen as a vaccination against false teaching. *What is falsely called knowledge,* perhaps a reference to Gnostics, religious persons who claimed sole possession of divine insight based on a complex dualistic cosmology, mythology, and anthropology. 21: *Missed the mark,* a characterization of all opponents, which frames the letter (see also 1.6, "have deviated from," more literally, "being off the mark," and 2 Tim 2.18).

6.21b: **Concluding benediction.**

THE SECOND LETTER OF PAUL TO TIMOTHY

NAME, AUTHORSHIP, AND BACKGROUND

The second letter addressed to Paul's "beloved child" Timothy, despite its similarities in address and diction, has a more personal tone than the first. (On the authorship and date of this letter, see p. 2084.) Less concerned with church order and roles, here Paul is portrayed as near death. In testamentary fashion the apostle hands on to his spiritual heir, Timothy, the wisdom accumulated through a life of mission, ministry, and, above all, suffering for the gospel. The letter is set within a carefully scripted historical scenario marked by Paul's imminent death and Timothy's bereavement, at a time of distortions to the apostle's "sound teaching" (1.13; see 4.3).

Timothy is named as co-sender of six Pauline letters (2 Cor 1.1; Phil 1.1; Col 1.1; 1 Thess 1.1; 2 Thess 1.1; Philem 1). They present Timothy as one of his most loyal disciples (Phil 2.19–22), who acted as a trusted delegate to churches (1 Thess 3.2–6; 1 Cor 4.17, "beloved and faithful child"; 16.10). According to Acts 16, Timothy's mother was Jewish and his father Greek. That later account imagines that Paul had him circumcised in the face of anticipated Jewish hostility (an event not corroborated in Paul's epistles). This letter sketches Timothy's life in broad strokes, from his early immersion in the scriptures (2 Tim 3.15) and matrilineal Christian pedigree (1.5), to his authorization for ministry by the laying on of Paul's hands (1.6), and his present ecclesiastical challenges. Most prominent in the letter, however, is the detailed and moving portrait of Paul, imprisoned for the gospel in Rome (1.8,16–17; 2.9), and forsaken by even his close friends (1.15; 4.10,16), yet empowered by his Lord not only to endure suffering and death but to celebrate it as the fitting culmination to a life of ministry and service (4.6–8,17–18).

STRUCTURE AND INTERPRETATION

The theme of 2 Timothy is announced in 1.8: Timothy and all who follow him should not be ashamed of the gospel or its representative, Paul, but should stand in fidelity to them, even to the point of suffering. Second Timothy follows a regular epistolary structure with an opening prescript (1.1–2), thanksgiving (1.3–7), body (1.8–4.18), greetings and closing (4.19-22). Timothy is urged to contemplate the positive example of Paul (1.8–14) and the negative one afforded by those who deserted Paul in time of need (1.15–18). The essential principle of the argument is appeal to example (Paul as one who suffered for the gospel: 1.12; 2.9–10; 3.11; 4.6-7, 16-18), and call for imitation, by Timothy (2.3; 4.5), and by all readers through him (see especially 2.11-12). Further, the exhortation to Timothy to be strong and teach others correctly (2.1–13) is contrasted with false teachers who must be contended with (2.14–26), for, as expected at the end time, signs of their appearance are already here (3.1–9). But Timothy is to follow in Paul's footsteps (3.10–4.5). These exhortations culminate in the depiction of the dying apostle's reflections on his life and its imminent conclusion (4.6–8; cf. Phil 1.12–26). The letter ends on a hopeful note as the imprisoned Paul exults in divine deliverance (both past and future) and issues spirited directives for the ministry, including a future visit from Timothy (4.8–18).

Margaret M. Mitchell

1 Paul, an apostle of Christ Jesus by the will of God, for the sake of the promise of life that is in Christ Jesus,

[2] To Timothy, my beloved child:

Grace, mercy, and peace from God the Father and Christ Jesus our Lord.

[3] I am grateful to God—whom I worship with a clear conscience, as my ancestors did—when I remember you constantly in my prayers night and day. [4] Recalling your tears, I long to see you so that I may be filled with joy. [5] I am reminded of your sincere faith, a faith that lived first in your grandmother Lois and your mother Eunice and now, I am sure, lives in you. [6] For this reason I remind you to rekindle the gift of God that is within you through the laying on of my hands; [7] for God did not give us a spirit of cowardice, but rather a spirit of power and of love and of self-discipline.

[8] Do not be ashamed, then, of the testimony about our Lord or of me his prisoner, but join with me in suffering for the gospel, relying on the power of God, [9] who saved us and called us with a holy calling, not according to our works but according to his own purpose and grace. This grace was given to us in Christ Jesus before the ages began, [10] but it has now been revealed through the appearing of our Savior Christ Jesus, who abolished death and brought life and immortality to light through the gospel. [11] For this gospel I was appointed a herald and an apostle and a teacher,[a] [12] and for this reason I suffer as I do. But I am not ashamed, for I know the one in whom I have put my trust, and I am sure that he is able to guard until that day what I have entrusted to him.[b] [13] Hold to the standard of sound teaching that you have heard from me, in the faith and love that are in Christ Jesus. [14] Guard the good treasure entrusted to you, with the help of the Holy Spirit living in us.

[15] You are aware that all who are in Asia have turned away from me, including Phygelus and Hermogenes. [16] May the Lord grant mercy to the household of Onesiphorus, because he often refreshed me and was not ashamed of my chain; [17] when he arrived in Rome, he eagerly[c] searched for me and found me [18]—may the Lord grant that he will find mercy from the Lord on that day! And you know very well how much service he rendered in Ephesus.

2 You then, my child, be strong in the grace that is in Christ Jesus; [2] and what you have heard from me through many witnesses entrust to faithful people who will be able to teach others as well. [3] Share in suffering like a good soldier of Christ Jesus. [4] No one serving in the army gets entangled in everyday affairs; the soldier's aim is to please the enlisting officer. [5] And in the case of an athlete, no one is crowned without competing according to the rules. [6] It is the farmer who does the

---

a   Other ancient authorities add *of the Gentiles*

b   Or *what has been entrusted to me*

c   Or *promptly*

1.1–2: Epistolary prescript (see 1 Tim 1.1n.) *The promise of life*, see 1 Tim 4.8.

1.3–7: Thanksgiving for Timothy's faith. 3: *I remember you constantly in my prayers*, cf. 1 Thess 1.2–3; Philem 4; Rom 1.9; Phil 1.3–4. **5:** Faith *lives* in Timothy (as does the Holy Spirit in 1.14). **6:** *I remind you*, memory plays a key role in the exhortation (also 2.8,14). *Laying on of my hands*, cf. 1 Tim 4.14n.

1.8–14: Theme: co-suffering, rather than shame, for the gospel and its apostle. 8: *Ashamed*, see also 1.12,16; 2.15; cf. Rom 1.16. **9–10:** Gospel proclamation in shorthand form, with characteristic themes. **9:** *Before the ages began*, see Titus 1.2; cf. Jn 1.2–3. **10:** *Appearing*, see 1 Tim 6.14n. *Abolished death*, cf. 1 Cor 15.26,54–57. **11.** *Herald and an apostle*, see 1 Tim 2.7n. **12:** *The one in whom I have put my trust*, Timothy, and each subsequent reader who stands in his place. *What I have entrusted to him* (lit., "the deposit"), as in 1.14; 1 Tim 6.20; cf. 2.2, a major theme of the Pastorals. *That day*, the Second Coming of Christ, the eschaton, see v. 18; 4.8; 2 Thess 1.10. **13:** *Sound teaching*, see 1 Tim 4.6n.

1.15–18: Examples, worthy and unworthy. 15: Asia, a Roman province in Asia Minor. *Phygelus and Hermogenes*, named only here. *Turned away from me*, Paul's abandonment is depicted again in 4.10,16. **16:** *Onesiphorus*, see 4.19; *my chain*, i.e., imprisonment; see 2.9. **18:** *That day*, see v. 12n.

2.1–13: Timothy's charge to suffer for the gospel. 2: *Entrust*, Timothy is to hand on the deposit he receives from Paul to the next generation. **4–6:** *Soldier, athlete, farmer*, commonplaces from three professions about

work who ought to have the first share of the crops. [7] Think over what I say, for the Lord will give you understanding in all things.

[8] Remember Jesus Christ, raised from the dead, a descendant of David—that is my gospel, [9] for which I suffer hardship, even to the point of being chained like a criminal. But the word of God is not chained. [10] Therefore I endure everything for the sake of the elect, so that they may also obtain the salvation that is in Christ Jesus, with eternal glory. [11] The saying is sure:

If we have died with him, we will also live
     with him;
[12] if we endure, we will also reign with him;
if we deny him, he will also deny us;
[13] if we are faithless, he remains faithful—
for he cannot deny himself.

[14] Remind them of this, and warn them before God[a] that they are to avoid wrangling over words, which does no good but only ruins those who are listening. [15] Do your best to present yourself to God as one approved by him, a worker who has no need to be ashamed, rightly explaining the word of truth. [16] Avoid profane chatter, for it will lead people into more and more impiety, [17] and their talk will spread like gangrene. Among them are Hymenaeus and Philetus, [18] who have swerved from the truth by claiming that the resurrection has already taken place. They are upsetting the faith of some. [19] But God's firm foundation stands, bearing this inscription: "The Lord knows those who are his," and, "Let everyone who calls on the name of the Lord turn away from wickedness."

[20] In a large house there are utensils not only of gold and silver but also of wood and clay, some for special use, some for ordinary. [21] All who cleanse themselves of the things I have mentioned[b] will become special utensils, dedicated and useful to the owner of the house, ready for every good work. [22] Shun youthful passions and pursue righteousness, faith, love, and peace, along with those who call on the Lord from a pure heart. [23] Have nothing to do with stupid and senseless controversies; you know that they breed quarrels. [24] And the Lord's servant[c] must not be quarrelsome but kindly to everyone, an apt teacher, patient, [25] correcting opponents with gentleness. God may perhaps grant that they will repent and come to know the truth, [26] and that they may escape from the snare of the devil, having been held captive by him to do his will.[d]

3 You must understand this, that in the last days distressing times will come. [2] For people will be lovers of themselves, lovers of money, boasters, arrogant, abusive, disobedient to their parents, ungrateful, unholy, [3] inhuman, implacable, slanderers, profligates, brutes, haters of good, [4] treacherous, reckless, swollen with conceit, lovers of pleasure rather than lovers of God, [5] holding to the outward form of godliness but denying its power. Avoid them! [6] For among them are

[a]   Other ancient authorities read the Lord
[b]   Gk of these things
[c]   Gk slave
[d]   Or by him, to do his (that is, God's) will

the cost of securing divine favor. **8:** Another encapsulation of the gospel (cf. Rom 1.3). **11:** *The saying is sure,* see 1 Tim 1.15n. **11–13:** A series of parallel clauses, suggesting to some scholars a quotation from a hymn. *Died with him . . . live with him,* Rom 6.5–11; 2 Cor 5.14–15. *Reign with him,* in glory at the end-time (1 Cor 4.8). *Deny him,* Mt 10.33; Mk 8.38; 1 Jn 2.22–23.

   2.14–26: Strategies for proper combat with false teachers. 14: wrangling over words, Gk "logomachia," a special concern of the Pastoral epistles (see 1 Tim 6.4). **17:** *Hymenaeus,* 1 Tim 1.20. *Philetus,* otherwise unknown. *Gangrene,* the opposite of "healthy" teaching (see 1.13n.). **18:** *Swerved from the truth,* see 1 Tim 6.21n. *The resurrection has already taken place,* a glimpse at the eschatology of the opponents, though not the theology behind it. They apparently spiritualized the future apocalyptic hope of resurrection, believing it to be a present reality. **19:** *God's firm foundation* (cf. 1 Tim 6.19), as known in scripture. *This inscription,* a quotation from Num 16.5; the second sentence has resonances with Isa 26.13; Job 36.10; Sir 17.26. **20–21:** *Utensils . . . some for special use, some for ordinary* (lit., "some for honor, some for dishonor"), contrast Rom 9.19–23. **23:** *Stupid and senseless controversies,* see 1 Tim 6.4; Titus 3.9. **26:** *Held captive,* "captured and kept alive" (the same verb is used in Lk 5.10).

   3.1–9: End-time now: a close-up picture of the opposition. 1: *The last days,* seen as both future and already

those who make their way into households and captivate silly women, overwhelmed by their sins and swayed by all kinds of desires, [7] who are always being instructed and can never arrive at a knowledge of the truth. [8] As Jannes and Jambres opposed Moses, so these people, of corrupt mind and counterfeit faith, also oppose the truth. [9] But they will not make much progress, because, as in the case of those two men,[a] their folly will become plain to everyone.

[10] Now you have observed my teaching, my conduct, my aim in life, my faith, my patience, my love, my steadfastness, [11] my persecutions, and my suffering the things that happened to me in Antioch, Iconium, and Lystra. What persecutions I endured! Yet the Lord rescued me from all of them. [12] Indeed, all who want to live a godly life in Christ Jesus will be persecuted. [13] But wicked people and impostors will go from bad to worse, deceiving others and being deceived. [14] But as for you, continue in what you have learned and firmly believed, knowing from whom you learned it, [15] and how from childhood you have known the sacred writings that are able to instruct you for salvation through faith in Christ Jesus. [16] All scripture is inspired by God and is[b] useful for teaching, for reproof, for correction, and for training in righteousness, [17] so that everyone who belongs to God may be proficient, equipped for every good work.

4 In the presence of God and of Christ Jesus, who is to judge the living and the dead, and in view of his appearing and his kingdom, I solemnly urge you: [2] proclaim the message; be persistent whether the time is favorable or unfavorable; convince, rebuke, and encourage, with the utmost patience in teaching. [3] For the time is coming when people will not put up with sound doctrine, but having itching ears, they will accumulate for themselves teachers to suit their own desires, [4] and will turn away from listening to the truth and wander away to myths. [5] As for you, always be sober, endure suffering, do the work of an evangelist, carry out your ministry fully.

[6] As for me, I am already being poured out as a libation, and the time of my departure has come. [7] I have fought the good fight, I have finished the race, I have kept the faith. [8] From now on there is reserved for me the crown of righteousness, which the Lord, the righteous judge, will give me on that day, and not only to me but also to all who have longed for his appearing.

[9] Do your best to come to me soon, [10] for Demas, in love with this present world, has deserted me and gone to Thessalonica; Crescens has gone to Galatia,[c] Titus to Dalmatia. [11] Only Luke is with me. Get Mark and bring him with you, for he is useful in my ministry. [12] I have sent Tychicus to Ephesus. [13] When you come, bring the cloak that I left

a   Gk lacks *two men*
b   Or *Every scripture inspired by God is also*
c   Other ancient authorities read *Gaul*

present. **2–4:** Vice catalogue (see 1 Tim 1.9–10n.). **5:** *Godliness,* see 1 Tim 2.1–3n. **6:** *Captivate silly women,* common negative ancient caricature of women, employed as part of the invective against the opponents (cf. 1 Tim 2.11–12; 4.7). **7:** *Knowledge of the truth,* see 1 Tim 2.4n. **8:** *Jannes and Jambres,* the names of the Egyptian magicians who opposed Moses (Ex 7.11), according to postbiblical Jewish tradition.

3.10–4.5: Timothy's charge to steadfastness in his ministry. 11: *Antioch, Iconium, and Lystra,* Acts 13.14–14.23 recounts persecutions of Paul in these three cities in Asia Minor, in the same order (which may suggest knowledge of Acts by this author). **15–16:** *Sacred writings, scripture,* the Jewish scriptures (the Hebrew Bible in the ancient Greek version, the Septuagint, abbreviated LXX), which Christians will later call the Old Testament. **4.1:** *Appearing,* see 1 Tim 6.14n. *Kingdom,* also 4.18. **2:** A succinct list of the tasks of bishops. **3–4:** The false teachers as purveyors of myths (cf. 1 Tim 1.4; 4.7; Titus 1.14). **5:** *Evangelist,* Eph 4.11; Acts 21.8.

4.6–8: Paul's reflections on his impending death. 6–7: Sacrificial (Phil 2.17) and athletic (1 Cor 9.24–27; Phil 2.16; 1 Tim 6.12; Acts 20.24) metaphors applied to Paul's ministerial life. **8:** *Crown of righteousness,* the winner's prize, a symbol of positive judgment from the Lord at his Second Coming (1 Thess 2.19; 1 Cor 9.25; Phil 4.1).

4.8–18: An update from prison. 9: An abrupt shift from the previous indication of Paul's imminent death (also 4.21). **10–11:** Paul's abandonment at the end (also 1.15; 4.16). **10–12:** *Demas, Luke, Mark,* mentioned together also in Philem 24 and Col 4.10–14. *Crescens,* mentioned only here. On *Titus,* see Introduction to Titus. **12:**

with Carpus at Troas, also the books, and above all the parchments. [14] Alexander the coppersmith did me great harm; the Lord will pay him back for his deeds. [15] You also must beware of him, for he strongly opposed our message.

[16] At my first defense no one came to my support, but all deserted me. May it not be counted against them! [17] But the Lord stood by me and gave me strength, so that through me the message might be fully proclaimed and all the Gentiles might hear it. So I was rescued from the lion's mouth. [18] The Lord will rescue me from every evil attack and save me for his heavenly king-dom. To him be the glory forever and ever. Amen.

[19] Greet Prisca and Aquila, and the household of Onesiphorus. [20] Erastus remained in Corinth; Trophimus I left ill in Miletus. [21] Do your best to come before winter. Eubulus sends greetings to you, as do Pudens and Linus and Claudia and all the brothers and sisters.[a]

[22] The Lord be with your spirit. Grace be with you.[b]

[a] Gk *all the brothers*

[b] The Greek word for *you* here is plural. Other ancient authorities add *Amen*

Tychicus, see Col 4.7; cf. Eph 6.21–22; Acts 20.4; Titus 3.12. **13:** *Troas,* ancient Troy, the departure point from Asia to Europe (2 Cor 2.12–13; Acts 16.8–12). *Carpus* is mentioned only here. *The books, and above all the parchments,* a suggestive reference, but what is being referred to is unknown. **14:** *Alexander,* see 1 Tim 1.20n. **16:** *My first defense,* formal "apology" against judicial charges. **17:** *The Lord . . . gave me strength,* as he will Timothy (2.1; also 1 Tim 1.12). *Rescued from the lion's mouth,* Ps 21.22 (LXX); Dan 6.21; 1 Macc 2.60.

4.19–21: Epistolary Greetings. 19: *Prisca and Aquila,* prominent missionary team, who were close to Paul (Rom 16.3; 1 Cor 16.19; Acts 18.2,18). *Onesiphorus,* 1.16–17. **20:** *Erastus,* the city-treasurer of Corinth (Rom 16.23; cf. Acts 19.22). *Trophimus,* Acts 20.4; 21.29. **21:** All of these people who are with Paul (despite 4.11!) are found only here. *Come before winter,* while a sea voyage is possible.

4.22: Concluding benediction.

THE LETTER OF PAUL TO TITUS

NAME, AUTHORSHIP, AND BACKGROUND

This letter, which has many similarities to 1 Timothy, is named for its recipient, Paul's envoy and co-worker Titus. It is cast as a reminder and incitement to Titus to complete his mission on Crete (1.5). Acts and the other Pauline letters do not mention any apostolic mission on this, the largest of the Aegean islands and home to a large Jewish community. Those who argue that the letter is genuine contend that such a mission could have taken place after Paul's imprisonment at Rome recounted in Acts 28, while those who regard it as pseudepigraphical (see further Introduction to the Pastoral Epistles, p. 2084) think the author has chosen Crete as a locale representing quintessential disobedience (1.12), or because of a later tradition associating Titus with the island.

Although Titus is not mentioned in Acts, Paul's letters provide information about a co-worker named Titus. According to Gal 2.3 Titus was a Gentile who accompanied Paul to the conference with the Jerusalem apostles, where Titus served as a litmus test for the acceptability of uncircumcised Gentile converts. Titus played a crucial role in the pastoral ministry to Corinth, first as a key administrator of the collection for the church in Jerusalem (2 Cor 8.6,16–17,23; 12.18), and later as Paul's diplomatic envoy who successfully brokered a reconciliation between the apostle and the Corinthian church, which had harbored doubts about Paul's legitimacy and financial reliability (2 Cor 2.13; 7.6–7,13–16).

STRUCTURE AND INTERPRETATION

The letter to Titus is framed as a commissioning letter. After the usual epistolary prescript (1.1–4, which is expanded with a theological creed), the body of the letter focuses on Titus's dual commission to correct things on Crete and to appoint elders (1.5–16). The basis for his ministry follows in sections devoted to the submission expected of various groups in the church (2.1–10), the theological basis for pious living (2.11–15), and a final section bringing the two themes—submission and good works—together (3.1–11). The letter concludes with a discussion of travel plans (3.12–13), a final exhortation to good works (3.14), epistolary greetings (3.15a), and a benediction (3.15b).

Paul delegates two tasks to Titus, under the heading of "putting things in order" (1.5): exhorting the faithful in sound teaching (1.9,13; 2.1–2,8), and refuting the opposition (2.2,15; cf. 1.9). The mainstay of sound teaching, as the author defines it, is strict maintenance of a patriarchal church order and the proper submission it demands (2.5,9; 3.1; contrast the characterization of the opponents as "insubordinate" or "rebellious" in 1.6,10). This ethic of the "household code" as applied to the Christian house church reflects the wider cultural context of the Greco-Roman world and is characteristic of the Pastoral epistles. The second task, the refutation of opponents (fellow Christians of Jewish background who adhere to the requirements of the law of Moses, the Torah, such as dietary laws), is addressed by the author in a negative fashion, through sharp invective and ridicule (1.10–16; 2.8; 3.9–11) rather than theological debate, which the author appears to eye largely with suspicion (1.13–14; 3.9–11).

GUIDE TO READING

Though short, this letter is theologically packed, requiring readers to pause and reconstruct the underlying gospel narrative and theological concepts, which the author often invokes by terse shorthand. Passages such as 1.1–3; 2.11–14; and 3.4–7 allow for instructive comparison with other tight Pauline formulations (see Gal 4.1–11; Rom 3.21–26; 2 Tim 1.9–10), so the theology constructed here can be appreciated both for its distinctiveness and for its continuity with earlier traditions.

Margaret M. Mitchell

1 Paul, a servant[a] of God and an apostle of Jesus Christ, for the sake of the faith of God's elect and the knowledge of the truth that is in accordance with godliness, [2] in the hope of eternal life that God, who never lies, promised before the ages began— [3] in due time he revealed his word through the proclamation with which I have been entrusted by the command of God our Savior,

[4] To Titus, my loyal child in the faith we share:

Grace[b] and peace from God the Father and Christ Jesus our Savior.

[5] I left you behind in Crete for this reason, so that you should put in order what remained to be done, and should appoint elders in every town, as I directed you: [6] someone who is blameless, married only once,[c] whose children are believers, not accused of debauchery and not rebellious. [7] For a bishop,[d] as God's steward, must be blameless; he must not be arrogant or quick-tempered or addicted to wine or violent or greedy for gain; [8] but he must be hospitable, a lover of goodness, prudent, upright, devout, and self-controlled. [9] He must have a firm grasp of the word that is trustworthy in accordance with the teaching, so that he may be able both to preach with sound doctrine and to refute those who contradict it.

[10] There are also many rebellious people, idle talkers and deceivers, especially those of the circumcision; [11] they must be silenced, since they are upsetting whole families by teaching for sordid gain what it is not right to teach. [12] It was one of them, their very own prophet, who said,

"Cretans are always liars, vicious brutes,
lazy gluttons."

[13] That testimony is true. For this reason rebuke them sharply, so that they may become sound in the faith, [14] not paying attention to Jewish myths or to commandments of those who reject the truth. [15] To the pure all things are pure, but to the corrupt and unbelieving nothing is pure. Their very minds and consciences are corrupted. [16] They profess to know God, but they deny him by their actions. They are detestable, disobedient, unfit for any good work.

2 But as for you, teach what is consistent with sound doctrine. [2] Tell the older men to be temperate, serious, prudent, and sound in faith, in love, and in endurance.

[3] Likewise, tell the older women to be reverent in behavior, not to be slanderers or slaves to drink; they are to teach what is good, [4] so that they may encourage the young women to love their husbands, to love their children, [5] to be self-controlled, chaste, good managers of the household, kind, being submissive to their husbands, so that the word of God may not be discredited.

---

a   Gk *slave*
b   Other ancient authorities read *Grace, mercy,*
c   Gk *husband of one wife*
d   Or *an overseer*

1.1–4: Epistolary prescript, sender, addressee, and salutation with theological expansion reminiscent of Rom 1.2–6 (cf. 1 Cor 2.7; Col 1.26; 2 Tim 1.10). **2:** *God, who never lies,* cf. v. 12. *Before the ages began,* see 2 Tim 1.9; cf. Jn 1.2–3. **3:** *God our Savior* (also 2.10; 3.4; 1 Tim 1.1; 2.3; 4.10). **4:** *Christ Jesus our Savior* (also 2.13; 3.6; 2 Tim 1.10).

1.5–16: Titus's commission in Crete. **5–7:** *Elders . . . bishop,* here apparently regarded as synonymous or at least overlapping categories (cf. 1 Tim 3.1–7; 5.17–20). **6:** *Rebellious,* lit., "insubordinate" (also 1.10). **7:** *Steward,* manager of the household (cf. 1 Cor 4.1–2). **9:** *Sound doctrine,* the reliable tradition the Pastoral epistles pass on; see 1 Tim 4.6n. **10:** *Those of the circumcision,* Jewish Christians who teach adherence to Torah, the law of Moses (see Gal 2.12), including dietary laws (see v. 15). **11:** *Upsetting whole families,* lit., "households," the basic unit of civic and church life. **12:** Invective against opponents supported by a hexameter from the Cretan poet Epimenides (ca. 600 BCE). **13:** *Sound in the faith,* having a "healthy" faith (also 2.2; see 1 Tim 4.6n.). **14:** *Jewish myths,* probably speculations on biblical texts; see 3.9; 1 Tim 1.4; 4.7. **15:** Cf. Rom 14.14. **16:** *Good work,* see 2.7,14; 3.1,8,14 (also 3.8n.).

2.1–10: The proclamation of sound teaching in submission. A catalogue of virtues reflecting and inscribing the hierarchical order of the Greco-Roman household (v. 2, older men; vv. 3–5 women, older and younger; vv. 6–8 younger men; vv. 9–10, slaves). **2:** *Faith . . . love . . . endurance,* a variation on Paul's usual triad of faith, love, and hope (1 Cor 13.13; 1 Thess 1.3; 5.8; cf. 1 Tim 1.5). **5:** *Being submissive,* the author seeks to rein in the insubor-

⁶ Likewise, urge the younger men to be self-controlled. ⁷ Show yourself in all respects a model of good works, and in your teaching show integrity, gravity, ⁸ and sound speech that cannot be censured; then any opponent will be put to shame, having nothing evil to say of us.

⁹ Tell slaves to be submissive to their masters and to give satisfaction in every respect; they are not to talk back, ¹⁰ not to pilfer, but to show complete and perfect fidelity, so that in everything they may be an ornament to the doctrine of God our Savior.

¹¹ For the grace of God has appeared, bringing salvation to all,ᵃ ¹² training us to renounce impiety and worldly passions, and in the present age to live lives that are self-controlled, upright, and godly, ¹³ while we wait for the blessed hope and the manifestation of the glory of our great God and Savior,ᵇ Jesus Christ. ¹⁴ He it is who gave himself for us that he might redeem us from all iniquity and purify for himself a people of his own who are zealous for good deeds.

¹⁵ Declare these things; exhort and reprove with all authority.ᶜ Let no one look down on you.

3 Remind them to be subject to rulers and authorities, to be obedient, to be ready for every good work, ² to speak evil of no one, to avoid quarreling, to be gentle, and to show every courtesy to everyone. ³ For we ourselves were once foolish, disobedient, led astray, slaves to various passions and pleasures, passing our days in malice and envy, despicable, hating one another. ⁴ But when the goodness and loving kindness of God our Savior appeared, ⁵ he saved us, not because of any works of righteousness that we had done, but according to his mercy, through the waterᵈ of rebirth and renewal by the Holy Spirit. ⁶ This Spirit he poured out on us richly through Jesus Christ our Savior, ⁷ so that, having been justified by his grace, we might become heirs according to the hope of eternal life. ⁸ The saying is sure.

I desire that you insist on these things, so that those who have come to believe in God may be careful to devote themselves to good works; these things are excellent and profitable to everyone. ⁹ But avoid stupid controversies, genealogies, dissensions, and quarrels about the law, for they are unprofitable and worthless. ¹⁰ After a first and second admonition, have nothing more to do with anyone who causes divisions, ¹¹ since you know that such a person is perverted and sinful, being self-condemned.

¹² When I send Artemas to you, or Tychicus, do your best to come to me at Nicopolis, for I have decided to spend the winter there.

ᵃ Or *has appeared to all, bringing salvation*
ᵇ Or *of the great God and our Savior*
ᶜ Gk *commandment*
ᵈ Gk *washing*

dinate (1.6,10) by calling for obedience to each one's superiors (also 2.9; 3.1) and for adherence to the model of Titus (v. 7).

2.11–15: The theological basis for present pious living. 11: *The grace of God has appeared* (lit., "been manifested"), in the life, death, and resurrection of Christ (cf. 3.4). **13:** *The manifestation* (lit., "epiphany"), a reference to the Second Coming, as elsewhere in the Pastoral epistles (1 Tim 6.14; 2 Tim 1.10; 4.1,8). *Our great God and Savior, Jesus Christ,* if translated this way (see note *b*), is one of the rare places in the New Testament where Christ may be referred to as God (Jn 1.18; 20.28; Rom 9.5). **14:** *Who gave himself,* Gal 1.4; 2.20; Eph 5.2; 1 Tim 2.6. *Redeem us,* buy back from slavery (Rom 3.24; 1 Cor 1.30; 6.20; 7.23; Eph 1.7; Col 1.14; cf. Mk 10.45). *A people of his own,* appropriation of the biblical promise to Israel (Deut 7.6–8; Ex 9.5–16); cf. 1 Pet 2.9.

3.1–11: Submission and good works are the marks of the saved. 1: *Subject to rulers and authorities,* advice for Christians to accommodate to the larger social order (similar to Rom 13.1–7; 1 Tim 2.1–3). **4–7:** A tight credal formulation, perhaps from an early hymn. **5:** *The water of rebirth and renewal,* baptism, as both promise of resurrection (Rom 6.3–5) and power for present transformation (Rom 12.2). **8:** *The saying is sure,* a frequent formula in the Pastoral epistles (1 Tim 1.15; 3.1; 4.9; 2 Tim 2.11). *Good works,* as distinguished from "works of righteousness" in v. 5 (the works of the law); see 1.16n. **9–11:** Condemnatory attitude toward the opponents (cf. 1 Tim 6.3–5; 2 Tim 2.14–18), as contrasted with the gentler disposition of 1 Tim 2.4; 2 Tim 2.24–26. **9:** *Genealogies,* linked with "myths" (see 1.4n.) in 1 Tim 1.4.

3.12–13: Travel plans. 12: *Artemas,* otherwise unknown. *Tychicus,* one of Paul's companions (Acts 20.4; Eph

¹³ Make every effort to send Zenas the lawyer and Apollos on their way, and see that they lack nothing. ¹⁴ And let people learn to devote themselves to good works in order to meet urgent needs, so that they may not be unproductive.

¹⁵ All who are with me send greetings to you. Greet those who love us in the faith. Grace be with all of you.ᵃ

ᵃ Other ancient authorities add *Amen*

6.21–22; Col 4.7; 2 Tim 4.12). *Nicopolis*, probably in western Greece.. **13**: *Zenas the lawyer*, named only here. *Apollos*, an early Christian leader; see Acts 18.24; 1 Cor 1.12; 16.12. *See that they lack nothing*, providing hospitality for itinerant missionaries, as in Rom 16.2; 3 Jn 6.

3.14: Concluding exhortation to good works.
3.15a: Epistolary greetings.
3.15b: Concluding benediction.

THE LETTER OF PAUL TO PHILEMON

NAME AND AUTHORSHIP

This enigmatic letter is named for its first-named recipient, Philemon. It is a piece of the apostle Paul's business correspondence, a curious but intentional blend of personal and public appeal, addressed to three individuals (Philemon, Apphia, and Archippus) and to the church that meets in one of their houses (v. 2).

STRUCTURE AND CONTENTS

The structure of Philemon is straightforward. After the epistolary prescript (vv. 1–3) and thanksgiving (vv. 4–7), which praise Philemon for his past benefactions, in the epistolary body (vv. 8–22) Paul makes a fresh request for the present situation involving Philemon's slave Onesimus through various forms of subtle and not-so-subtle appeal, ending with the suggestion that he will soon visit Philemon (v. 22). He closes the letter with epistolary greetings from missionary co-workers that accent the public arena of Philemon's decision (vv. 23–24), and a final benediction (v. 25).

INTERPRETATION AND GUIDE TO READING

The letter shows Paul's epistolary style at its best and employs a subtle rhetoric to make a request of one of the recipients—probably Philemon. The exact nature of the request is the basis for the enigma that the letter to Philemon represents.

In order to interpret this letter, one must reconstruct the situation it presupposes, but to do so the reader must depend upon the letter itself. Paul writes this letter from prison (vv. 1,9–10; a location is not specified), where he has been joined by someone named Onesimus, whom Paul has converted to the gospel there (v. 10). This Onesimus, who is the slave of Philemon (v. 16), is the object of Paul's appeal (v. 10). While the circumstances that led to Onesimus's encounter with Paul are not described in the letter, two quite different possibilities suggest themselves: Either Onesimus ran away from his master, perhaps after causing him some financial loss (vv. 15,18), or Onesimus was sent by his owner to serve Paul in prison (v. 13), much as Epaphroditus was sent to Paul in prison by the Philippians (Phil 2.25–30). The advantage of the latter possibility is that it explains how Onesimus came to be in prison with Paul, whereas the former option must explain why a slave would run away to a prison. Perhaps Onesimus, according to legal precedent, sought out a friend of his master's to act as an intermediary in a dispute between himself and his owner. The precise occasion of the letter is the moment of Paul's sending Onesimus back to his master (v. 12). The letter will accompany Onesimus and register a plea on his behalf (v. 10).

What is Paul asking Philemon to do? Because Paul formulates his request in intentionally vague and rhetorical terms, a definitive judgment is hard to make. Readers should explore at least three possible interpretations: (1) Paul is asking Philemon to receive Onesimus back as a slave and forgive whatever transgressions he had committed (vv. 17–18); (2) Paul is asking Philemon to send Onesimus back to continue serving the apostle's physical needs while in prison (vv. 13–14); (3) Paul is strongly hinting that Philemon should not only receive Onesimus back but grant this new Christian brother his freedom (vv. 16,21). Each of these options has some grounding in the text, and which one the reader adopts depends upon which verses are thought to be the focal point of the argument and upon how one assesses Paul's tone at various points. One thing, however, is certain about this letter: Paul engages in full-strength arm-twisting of Philemon to do his "good deed" (v. 14). But the final decision of what to do is left up to Philemon himself—in the context of a host of on-lookers among his fellow Christians! One of the most remarkable things about this letter is that it was preserved and ultimately incorporated into the canonical collection of Paul's letters. This may be a hint that Philemon's ultimate decision answered Paul's request.

This letter has played a role in the history of Christian social ethics disproportionate to its size. The adequacy of Paul's attitude and actions toward the institution of slavery, both in his context and as a legacy for Christian social thought, continues to be debated.

Margaret M. Mitchell

[1] Paul, a prisoner of Christ Jesus, and Timothy our brother,[a]

To Philemon our dear friend and co-worker, [2] to Apphia our sister,[b] to Archippus our fellow soldier, and to the church in your house:

[3] Grace to you and peace from God our Father and the Lord Jesus Christ.

[4] When I remember you[c] in my prayers, I always thank my God [5] because I hear of your love for all the saints and your faith toward the Lord Jesus. [6] I pray that the sharing of your faith may become effective when you perceive all the good that we[d] may do for Christ. [7] I have indeed received much joy and encouragement from your love, because the hearts of the saints have been refreshed through you, my brother.

[8] For this reason, though I am bold enough in Christ to command you to do your duty, [9] yet I would rather appeal to you on the basis of love—and I, Paul, do this as an old man, and now also as a prisoner of Christ Jesus.[e] [10] I am appealing to you for my child, Onesimus, whose father I have become during my imprisonment. [11] Formerly he was useless to you, but now he is indeed useful[f] both to you and to me. [12] I am sending him, that is, my own heart, back to you. [13] I wanted to keep him with me, so that he might be of service to me in your place during my imprisonment for the gospel; [14] but I preferred to do nothing without your consent, in order that your good deed might be voluntary and not something forced. [15] Perhaps this is the reason he was separated from you for a while, so that you might have him back forever, [16] no longer as a slave but more than a slave, a beloved brother—especially to me but how much more to you, both in the flesh and in the Lord.

[17] So if you consider me your partner, welcome him as you would welcome me. [18] If he has wronged you in any way, or owes you anything, charge that to my account. [19] I, Paul, am writing this with my own hand: I will repay it. I say nothing about your owing me even your own self. [20] Yes, brother, let me have this benefit from you in the Lord! Re-

---

a   Gk *the brother*
b   Gk *the sister*
c   From verse 4 through verse 21, *you* is singular
d   Other ancient authorities read *you* (plural)
e   Or *as an ambassador of Christ Jesus, and now also his prisoner*
f   The name Onesimus means *useful* or (compare verse 20) *beneficial*

1–3: Epistolary prescript (senders, addressees, and salutation), with each sender and recipient carefully designated. **1:** *Timothy,* see Introduction to 2 Timothy. **2:** *Our sister,* fellow Christian. *Apphia,* named only here. *Archippus,* see Col 4.17. *And to the church in your house,* Paul puts Philemon's decision in a more public context.

4–7: Thanksgiving for Philemon's past good deeds. In vv. 4–22a Paul uses the singular address (*you*). Because he calls him "brother" in v. 20, it must refer either to Philemon or Archippus; tradition and current scholarship almost unanimously choose Philemon, on the grounds that he is the first named. **4:** *Remember you in my prayers,* cf 2 Tim 1.3. **7:** *Hearts,* "splanchna," lit., "inner organs," refers to the emotional center of a person (see vv. 12,20).

8–22: Paul's appeal for another good deed from Philemon. 10: *Whose father I have become,* lit., "whom I begot" to new life in the gospel (cf. 1 Cor 4.15). **11:** *Useful* ("eu-chrestos") is a double pun, referring both to Onesimus's name (see textual note *f*) and his identity in Christ ("eu-Christos" = "good in Christ"). **14:** *Voluntary,* Paul does not command (cf. v. 8), but prefers to persuade. **15:** *Was separated,* a perhaps deliberately vague reference to Onesimus's absence. **16:** *No longer as a slave,* finally the problem is stated: status dissonance (i.e., when a person occupies two or more social positions simultaneously). What happens when a slave of a Christian master becomes a Christian? Some scholars take Paul to mean the slave stops being a slave by becoming a brother, but others think Paul considers the new status of *brother* as relativizing, but not changing, the slave's station in the world. *In the flesh and in the Lord,* in the world and in the church. **17–19:** *Partner, charge . . . to my account, repay,* business terminology signaling Paul's financial obligations to Philemon. *Writing this with my own hand,* cf. 1 Cor 16.21; Gal 6.11. *Owing me even your own self,* Philemon's spiritual obligation to the one who converted him. **21:** *More than I say,* a mere commonplace or a diplomatically framed hint to release him from slavery? **22b:** *Your prayers,* in the plural. Paul here joins the co-recipients (v. 2) with him in registering his plea to Philemon.

fresh my heart in Christ. [21] Confident of your obedience, I am writing to you, knowing that you will do even more than I say.

[22] One thing more—prepare a guest room for me, for I am hoping through your prayers to be restored to you.

[23] Epaphras, my fellow prisoner in Christ Jesus, sends greetings to you,[a] [24] and so do Mark, Aristarchus, Demas, and Luke, my fellow workers.

[25] The grace of the Lord Jesus Christ be with your spirit.[b]

[a] Here *you* is singular
[b] Other ancient authorities add *Amen*

23–24: Greetings, the same five people are named in Col 4.10–14. *Epaphras,* Col 1.7; 4.12.
25: Concluding benediction.

THE LETTER TO THE HEBREWS

NAME AND AUTHORSHIP

During the collection of the New Testament books into a canon, the Letter to the Hebrews got its name from its implied addressees, the "Hebrews." Although the text itself does not name its addressees, its emphasis on Jewish scripture and ritual in making its argument may have suggested the title. By the end of the second century CE Hebrews began to be attributed to Paul. In the earliest collection of Paul's letters (P46) this one followed Paul's letter to the Romans. In the canon lists of the fourth century it was included with the Pauline letters. Consequently, the name "Paul" came to be used for the author of the work, appearing first in the Vulgate. The title "The Epistle of Paul to the Hebrews" reflects the authority attained by both the figure of Paul the apostle as author and the literary genre of the letter.

Despite the traditional attribution to Paul, early church writers questioned its authorship. Clement, Tertullian, and Origen acknowledged differences in style and theology between Hebrews and Paul's own letters. Clement argued that Luke had translated Paul's Hebrew original into Greek, while Origen suggested that a disciple of Paul wrote the letter based on Paul's notes. Modern interpreters have suggested other authors, including Apollos and Priscilla (see Acts 18.24–26). There is not sufficient evidence to identify any person named in the New Testament as the author; thus it is held to be anonymous.

DATE

Like the name of the author, the precise date of Hebrews cannot be determined. Because the argument depends on Jewish liturgical practice, some scholars argue that it must have been written before the destruction of the Temple in Jerusalem in 70 CE. The work alludes to the rites as described in scripture, however, and does not presume knowledge of current practice in the Temple. Composed after the first generation of Christian leaders, but not later than the mid-90s when Hebrews is quoted in 1 Clement, the work is to be dated somewhere between 60 and 90 CE.

CONTENT, GENRE, AND STRUCTURE

Hebrews addresses an audience of both Jewish and Gentile background that has suffered hardship and persecution (10.32). Some may have renounced their faith (2.3; 6.4–6, 12.25). The work is written to encourage and exhort them to ongoing confidence and faith. The author grounds the argument in scripture and argues that Jesus is superior to earlier Jewish traditions. Because of its highly structured exegetical and exhortatory style, and the author's claim to present a "word of exhortation" (13.32), the literary genre of Hebrews is best described as an early Christian sermon, rather than a letter. Typical features of letters, such as opening and closing greetings, make the work resemble a letter. Images, themes, and motifs anticipate and reinforce each other as the argument unfolds. The structure falls into four main sections. Chapters 1.1–4.13 explore the word of God spoken through the Son; chs 4.14–10.31 interpret Jesus as the eternal high priest against the background of the Israelite priesthood. The third part, 10.32–12.29, describes faith as insight into a heavenly world of reality. Chapter 13 gives practical advice and greetings.

GUIDE TO READING

Because so many of the standard historical introductory questions about Hebrews are uncertain, Hebrews is best read by leaving those questions open and exploring the work as a distinctive Christian writing. In a manner unique among New Testament books, the sermon develops the image of Christ as the great high priest who fulfills and completes the Jewish system of sacrifice. It interprets the significance of Jesus Christ and his death in categories of ritual and sacrifice familiar to both its author and its audience. Ancient readers could appreciate the sophisticated rhetorical style, follow the repetition and development of images and vocabulary, and understand the logic of the author's argument in the context of Platonic and allegorical interpretation and of other early Christian language. Reading with particular attention to repetition and patterns of imagery and to the allusions to scripture and liturgy will help the contemporary reader to appreciate the sermon's rhetorical effectiveness to strengthen flagging faith and encourage hope in God's promised salvation.

Cynthia Briggs Kittredge

1

Long ago God spoke to our ancestors in many and various ways by the prophets, [2] but in these last days he has spoken to us by a Son,[a] whom he appointed heir of all things, through whom he also created the worlds. [3] He is the reflection of God's glory and the exact imprint of God's very being, and he sustains[b] all things by his powerful word. When he had made purification for sins, he sat down at the right hand of the Majesty on high, [4] having become as much superior to angels as the name he has inherited is more excellent than theirs.

[5] For to which of the angels did God ever say,

"You are my Son;
    today I have begotten you"?

Or again,

"I will be his Father,
    and he will be my Son"?

[6] And again, when he brings the firstborn into the world, he says,

"Let all God's angels worship him."

[7] Of the angels he says,

"He makes his angels winds,
    and his servants flames of fire."

[8] But of the Son he says,

"Your throne, O God, is[c] forever and
    ever,
and the righteous scepter is the scepter
    of your[d] kingdom.
[9] You have loved righteousness and hated
    wickedness;

therefore God, your God, has anointed you
    with the oil of gladness beyond your
    companions."

[10] And,

"In the beginning, Lord, you founded the
    earth,
and the heavens are the work of your
    hands;
[11] they will perish, but you remain;
    they will all wear out like clothing;
[12] like a cloak you will roll them up,
    and like clothing[e] they will be changed.
But you are the same,
    and your years will never end."

[13] But to which of the angels has he ever said,

"Sit at my right hand
    until I make your enemies a footstool
        for your feet"?

[14] Are not all angels[f] spirits in the divine service, sent to serve for the sake of those who are to inherit salvation?

2

Therefore we must pay greater attention to what we have heard, so that we do not drift away from it. [2] For if the message declared through angels was valid, and every transgression or disobedience received a just

a Or *the Son*
b Or *bears along*
c Or *God is your throne*
d Other ancient authorities read *his*
e Other ancient authorities lack *like clothing*
f Gk *all of them*

1.1–4.13: Word of God spoken through the Son.

1.1–4: The prologue: God has spoken through a Son. The formal, rhythmic prologue contrasts God's mode of speaking in the past with God's mode of speaking *in these last days*. The contrast assumes that the one *Son* of the present is better than the many *prophets* of *long ago*. The relationship of the Son to God is elaborated in a hymn, similar to other Christological hymns in the New Testament (Phil 2.6–11; Col 1.15–20). **3:** The Son is described as participating in the creation and as one who *sustains all things. The reflection of God's glory and the exact imprint of God's very being,* language derived from Jewish wisdom speculation about the female figure of Wisdom, who was present at the time of creation (Prov 8.22–31; Wis 9.9), came to earth to dwell (Sir 24.8; Bar 3.37), and returned to her place in the heavens (*1 Enoch* 42.1–2). In Wis 7.26 wisdom is described as "a reflection . . . of God." See also Jn 1.1–3. When the Son had accomplished the priestly work of *purification* (9.14,26–28), he sat down at God's right hand (Ps 110.1). **4:** *The name* may be "Son" or possibly "Lord" (Phil 2.9–11).

1.5–2.18: The superiority of the Son to the angels. *Angels,* thought to be mediators of God's word in giving the law to Israel and imagined to be in attendance at the enthronement of the Son, are inferior to the Son because their role is to serve (v. 14). Seven quotations from Jewish scripture are cited as speaking about or to Jesus. **1.5:** Ps 2.7; 2 Sam 7.14. **6:** Deut 32.43. **7:** Ps 104.4. **8:** Ps 45.6–7. **10–12:** Ps 102.25–27. **13:** Ps 110.1. The author alludes to Ps 110.1 in 8.1; 10.12; 12.2. Ps 110.1 is interpreted messianically elsewhere in the New Testament (Acts 2.24; 1 Cor 15.25).

2.1–4: Exhortation not to fall away. The superiority of the Son to the angels makes it more necessary to obey

penalty, ³ how can we escape if we neglect so great a salvation? It was declared at first through the Lord, and it was attested to us by those who heard him, ⁴ while God added his testimony by signs and wonders and various miracles, and by gifts of the Holy Spirit, distributed according to his will.

⁵ Now God[a] did not subject the coming world, about which we are speaking, to angels. ⁶ But someone has testified somewhere,

"What are human beings that you are
       mindful of them,[b]
   or mortals, that you care for them?[c]
⁷ You have made them for a little while
       lower[d] than the angels;
   you have crowned them with glory and
       honor,[e]
⁸ subjecting all things under their feet."

Now in subjecting all things to them, God[a] left nothing outside their control. As it is, we do not yet see everything in subjection to them, ⁹ but we do see Jesus, who for a little while was made lower[f] than the angels, now crowned with glory and honor because of the suffering of death, so that by the grace of God[g] he might taste death for everyone.

¹⁰ It was fitting that God,[a] for whom and through whom all things exist, in bringing many children to glory, should make the pioneer of their salvation perfect through sufferings. ¹¹ For the one who sanctifies and those who are sanctified all have one Father.[h] For this reason Jesus[a] is not ashamed to call them brothers and sisters,[i] ¹² saying,

"I will proclaim your name to my brothers
       and sisters,[i]

   in the midst of the congregation I will
       praise you."
¹³ And again,
   "I will put my trust in him."
And again,
   "Here am I and the children whom God
       has given me."

¹⁴ Since, therefore, the children share flesh and blood, he himself likewise shared the same things, so that through death he might destroy the one who has the power of death, that is, the devil, ¹⁵ and free those who all their lives were held in slavery by the fear of death. ¹⁶ For it is clear that he did not come to help angels, but the descendants of Abraham. ¹⁷ Therefore he had to become like his brothers and sisters[i] in every respect, so that he might be a merciful and faithful high priest in the service of God, to make a sacrifice of atonement for the sins of the people. ¹⁸ Because he himself was tested by what he suffered, he is able to help those who are being tested.

a   Gk he
b   Gk What is man that you are mindful of him?
c   Gk or the son of man that you care for him? In the
    Hebrew of Psalm 8.4-6 both man and son of man
    refer to all humankind
d   Or them only a little lower
e   Other ancient authorities add and set them over the
    works of your hands
f   Or who was made a little lower
g   Other ancient authorities read apart from God
h   Gk are all of one
i   Gk brothers

the message of salvation he brought than the law of Moses, which came through the angels. 2: *The message declared through angels*, see Acts 7.53; Gal 3.19; Josephus, *Ant.* 15.5.3. 3: *Attested to us by those who heard,* the message has come to this community through an earlier generation. 4: *Signs and wonders,* see Acts 2.43; 15.12; cf. Deut 6.22. *Miracles,* see Acts 8.13; 19.11; cf. Ps 105.27. *Gifts of the Holy Spirit,* see 1 Cor 12.4–11.

2.5–18: Jesus' exaltation through abasement. 5: *The coming world,* the age to come. 6–9: Quoting Ps 8.4–6, the author interprets the verses as referring to Jesus, the human being. Unlike the original psalm which said that God created human beings "a little lower than the angels," the author understands that Jesus the human being is superior to angels but was made *for a little while lower* than them in his death (cf. Phil 2.6–11). 10–18: Jesus shares humanity with all human beings (*children,* lit., "sons"). In order to liberate his *brothers and sisters* from *slavery* to the power of death, Jesus had to share their human experience *in every respect.* 10: The expression, *make . . . perfect,* is characteristic of this letter (5.9; 7.19,28; 9.9; 10.1,14; 11.40; 12.23) and means "to make complete, to bring to maturity." Christ as *pioneer* goes before and points out the way to his followers (12.2); the same Gk word is translated "author" (Acts 3.15) and "leader" (Acts 5.31). 12: Ps 22.22. 13: Isa 8.17–18. 14: See Wis 2.24; Rom 6.23. 17: As *high priest* the Son is both *merciful* (cf. 5.2–3) and *faithful* (cf. 3.2,6), *to make a sacrifice of*

3 Therefore, brothers and sisters,[a] holy partners in a heavenly calling, consider that Jesus, the apostle and high priest of our confession, [2] was faithful to the one who appointed him, just as Moses also "was faithful in all[b] God's[c] house." [3] Yet Jesus[d] is worthy of more glory than Moses, just as the builder of a house has more honor than the house itself. [4] (For every house is built by someone, but the builder of all things is God.) [5] Now Moses was faithful in all God's[c] house as a servant, to testify to the things that would be spoken later. [6] Christ, however, was faithful over God's[c] house as a son, and we are his house if we hold firm[e] the confidence and the pride that belong to hope.

[7] Therefore, as the Holy Spirit says,
"Today, if you hear his voice,
[8] do not harden your hearts as in the
	rebellion,
	as on the day of testing in the
		wilderness,
[9] where your ancestors put me to the
		test,
	though they had seen my works [10] for
		forty years.
Therefore I was angry with that
		generation,
and I said, 'They always go astray in their
		hearts,
	and they have not known my ways.'
[11] As in my anger I swore,
	'They will not enter my rest.'"

[12] Take care, brothers and sisters,[a] that none of you may have an evil, unbelieving heart that turns away from the living God. [13] But exhort one another every day, as long as it is called "today," so that none of you may be hardened by the deceitfulness of sin. [14] For we have become partners of Christ, if only we hold our first confidence firm to the end. [15] As it is said,

	"Today, if you hear his voice,
	do not harden your hearts as in the
			rebellion."

[16] Now who were they who heard and yet were rebellious? Was it not all those who left Egypt under the leadership of Moses? [17] But with whom was he angry forty years? Was it not those who sinned, whose bodies fell in the wilderness? [18] And to whom did he swear that they would not enter his rest, if not to those who were disobedient? [19] So we see that they were unable to enter because of unbelief.

4 Therefore, while the promise of entering his rest is still open, let us take care that none of you should seem to have failed to reach it. [2] For indeed the good news came to us just as to them; but the message they heard did not benefit them, because they

---

a Gk *brothers*
b Other ancient authorities lack *all*
c Gk *his*
d Gk *this one*
e Other ancient authorities add *to the end*

---

atonement continually for *sins* that bring death and the fear of it to God's *people* (vv. 14–15). **18:** Jesus was *tested* by suffering (5.7–8); therefore he can help the community this sermon addresses, which is also being tested.

3.1–6: Comparison of Jesus and Moses. The author argues for Jesus' superiority to Moses, who, like the angels, is another intermediary of God's word or law. **1:** *Holy partners,* the readers or hearers are addressed in terms that remind them of their position and responsibility in sharing *in a heavenly calling,* as Jesus is in the heavens. As *apostle,* Jesus is the one sent by God to humankind; as *high priest,* he is their representative before God. **2:** The author first refers to what Jesus and Moses have in common: faithfulness to their respective tasks. *Was faithful in all God's house* alludes to the Septuagint (LXX) version of Num 12.7–8. **3–5:** As to position, Christ (a "son," v. 6) is superior to Moses (a *servant* in God's house; Num 12.7). **6:** *We are his house,* the community of faithful believers. *That belong to hope,* hope is a key theme in the sermon (see 6.11,18; 7.19; 10.23).

3.7–4.13: Entering God's rest. The author makes an extended commentary on Ps 95.7–11 and applies it to the lives of the audience. **3.8:** *Rebellion* and *testing* are translations of the Hebrew names Meribah and Massah in Ps 95.8 (Ex 17.1–7; Num 20.1–13; Deut 33.8). **11:** *My rest,* the possession of the promised land of Canaan. **13:** *The deceitfulness of sin,* disobedience (Num 14.1–4,34,41), leading to apostasy or renunciation of faith. **15:** Ps 95.7. **16–19:** A series of questions refers to Israel, *those who left Egypt under the leadership of Moses* and who did not *enter* the *rest.* The *unbelief* of the Israelites will be compared with the necessary faithfulness of the Christian community.

4.1–13: The faithfulness required of Christians. 1: God's promise, which must be fulfilled, remains for faith-

were not united by faith with those who listened.[a] [3] For we who have believed enter that rest, just as God[b] has said,

"As in my anger I swore,
'They shall not enter my rest,'"

though his works were finished at the foundation of the world. [4] For in one place it speaks about the seventh day as follows, "And God rested on the seventh day from all his works." [5] And again in this place it says, "They shall not enter my rest." [6] Since therefore it remains open for some to enter it, and those who formerly received the good news failed to enter because of disobedience, [7] again he sets a certain day—"today"—saying through David much later, in the words already quoted,

"Today, if you hear his voice,
do not harden your hearts."

[8] For if Joshua had given them rest, God[b] would not speak later about another day. [9] So then, a sabbath rest still remains for the people of God; [10] for those who enter God's rest also cease from their labors as God did from his. [11] Let us therefore make every effort to enter that rest, so that no one may fall through such disobedience as theirs.

[12] Indeed, the word of God is living and active, sharper than any two-edged sword, piercing until it divides soul from spirit, joints from marrow; it is able to judge the thoughts and intentions of the heart. [13] And before him

no creature is hidden, but all are naked and laid bare to the eyes of the one to whom we must render an account.

[14] Since, then, we have a great high priest who has passed through the heavens, Jesus, the Son of God, let us hold fast to our confession. [15] For we do not have a high priest who is unable to sympathize with our weaknesses, but we have one who in every respect has been tested[c] as we are, yet without sin. [16] Let us therefore approach the throne of grace with boldness, so that we may receive mercy and find grace to help in time of need.

5 Every high priest chosen from among mortals is put in charge of things pertaining to God on their behalf, to offer gifts and sacrifices for sins. [2] He is able to deal gently with the ignorant and wayward, since he himself is subject to weakness; [3] and because of this he must offer sacrifice for his own sins as well as for those of the people. [4] And one does not presume to take this honor, but takes it only when called by God, just as Aaron was.

[5] So also Christ did not glorify himself in becoming a high priest, but was appointed by the one who said to him,

a Other ancient authorities read it did not meet with faith in those who listened
b Gk he
c Or tempted

ful Christians to inherit. **2:** *Those who listened,* Num 13.30–14.10. **3:** Ps 95.11. **4:** Gen 2.2. The meaning of "rest" is enlarged to include God's sabbath rest. **5:** Ps 95.11. **7–8:** *Today,* see 3.13–15. The possession of Canaan under Joshua was not the promised *rest,* otherwise *David,* understood to be the author of the psalm, would not have spoken centuries later of a rest still remaining (Ps 95.7–8). **9–10:** *Sabbath rest,* points back to God's rest after the work of creation (Gen 2.2), and forward to rest as the ultimate destiny of followers in heaven. **11–13:** The author exhorts the community to enter into the rest and concludes the opening section, which has explored the theme of God's speaking, with a statement about *the word of God* which is living. **13:** The Gk word translated *account* is "logos," the same word translated as "word" in v. 12.

4.14–10.31: Jesus as the eternal high priest. 4.14–5.10: Christ as great high priest. The author understands Jesus' life, death, and present heavenly role through the category of "high priest" who perfects the ancient sacrificial system of Judaism. Having discussed Jesus' "faithfulness"(2.17; 3.1–6), the author turns to reflect on his "mercy." **4.14:** *Through the heavens,* Jesus has passed through the series of heavens above the earth (cf. 2 Cor 12.2) and entered into the highest where God dwells. His entry is the basis for the confidence and hope of Christians. **16:** *Approach the throne of grace,* the sermon's imagery shifts from holding fast (3.6,14; 4.14) to moving forward, an image that will be explored as the sermon proceeds. **5.1:** The author defines what a *high priest* is and shows how the definition fits Jesus. A priest is *chosen from among* human beings and represents them before God in sacrifices he offers. **2:** He can effectively represent them because he shares human *weakness.* **3:** See Lev 9.7. **4:** He is called by God to this office. *Aaron,* Ex 28.1. **5:** Citing Ps 2.7, the author demonstrates that Christ is *ap-*

"You are my Son,
today I have begotten you";
[6] as he says also in another place,
"You are a priest forever,
according to the order of Melchizedek."
[7] In the days of his flesh, Jesus[a] offered up prayers and supplications, with loud cries and tears, to the one who was able to save him from death, and he was heard because of his reverent submission. [8] Although he was a Son, he learned obedience through what he suffered; [9] and having been made perfect, he became the source of eternal salvation for all who obey him, [10] having been designated by God a high priest according to the order of Melchizedek.

[11] About this[b] we have much to say that is hard to explain, since you have become dull in understanding. [12] For though by this time you ought to be teachers, you need someone to teach you again the basic elements of the oracles of God. You need milk, not solid food; [13] for everyone who lives on milk, being still an infant, is unskilled in the word of righteousness. [14] But solid food is for the mature, for those whose faculties have been trained by practice to distinguish good from evil.

6 Therefore let us go on toward perfection,[c] leaving behind the basic teaching about Christ, and not laying again the foundation: repentance from dead works and faith toward God, [2] instruction about baptisms, laying on of hands, resurrection of the dead, and eternal judgment. [3] And we will do[d] this, if God permits. [4] For it is impossible to restore again to repentance those who have once been enlightened, and have tasted the heavenly gift, and have shared in the Holy Spirit, [5] and have tasted the goodness of the word of God and the powers of the age to come, [6] and then have fallen away, since on their own they are crucifying again the Son of God and are holding him up to contempt. [7] Ground that drinks up the rain falling on it repeatedly, and that produces a crop useful to those for whom it is cultivated, receives a blessing from God. [8] But if it produces thorns and thistles, it is worthless and on the verge of being cursed; its end is to be burned over.

[9] Even though we speak in this way, beloved, we are confident of better things in your case, things that belong to salvation. [10] For God is not unjust; he will not overlook your work and the love that you showed for his sake[e] in serving the saints, as you still do. [11] And we want each one of you to show the

a Gk *he*
b Or *him*
c Or *toward maturity*
d Other ancient authorities read *let us do*
e Gk *for his name*

pointed by God (cf. Lk 3.22). **6:** The author quotes Ps 110.4. *According to the order of Melchizedek* is interpreted to mean "like" Melchizedek. The sermon will return to this element in 7.1–22. **7–9:** The author refers to an example of Jesus' sharing human weakness and suffering in order to show how that makes him a source of salvation for human beings. **7:** Traditionally, this verse has been understood to refer to Gethsemane (Mk.14.32–42 and parallels). However, the description resembles the portrayal of the typical Jewish hero, such as Abraham or Moses, who prays loudly to God for deliverance (2 Macc 11.6; Philo, *Rer. div. her.* 19). **10:** *Melchizedek,* see 7.1–10n. Although simply called a "priest according to the order of Melchizedek" in the psalm citation, the author elaborates that Jesus is a "high priest according to the order of Melchizedek."

5.11–6.20: Exhortation to hope. The author's tone shifts from critical to complimentary in this hortatory passage. The community is encouraged to move forward, first *toward perfection* (6.1), then *to seize the hope set before us* (6.18). **5.12–14:** Common in Hellenistic rhetoric, the comparison between *milk* as rudimentary teaching and *solid food* as more advanced teaching is used to encourage the community to move beyond basic teachings (cf. 1 Cor 3.1–2). **6.1:** *Dead works,* "works that lead to death" or "sin." **2:** *Baptisms,* ritual washings used in both Jewish and Christian practice (see 9.10). *Laying on of hands* was a ritual of commissioning (see Acts 6.6; 8.17–19; 9.17; 13.3; 1 Tim 4.14; 2 Tim 1.6). Teaching about *resurrection of the dead* would have been accepted by both Jews and Christians. The author understands all these as "basic teaching," while the priesthood of Christ is the more advanced teaching explored by the sermon. **4–6:** Those who have *fallen away* cannot be restored to repentance; they therefore share in *crucifying . . . the Son of God.* These verses describe the dire consequence for one who loses hope and falls away. **7–8:** *Thorns and thistles* could refer to the curse of Gen 3.18; the blessings of the Promised Land require fidelity to God's covenant (Deut 11.11; 28.1–5). **9–12:** The author reassures the audience

same diligence so as to realize the full assurance of hope to the very end, [12] so that you may not become sluggish, but imitators of those who through faith and patience inherit the promises.

[13] When God made a promise to Abraham, because he had no one greater by whom to swear, he swore by himself, [14] saying, "I will surely bless you and multiply you." [15] And thus Abraham,[a] having patiently endured, obtained the promise. [16] Human beings, of course, swear by someone greater than themselves, and an oath given as confirmation puts an end to all dispute. [17] In the same way, when God desired to show even more clearly to the heirs of the promise the unchangeable character of his purpose, he guaranteed it by an oath, [18] so that through two unchangeable things, in which it is impossible that God would prove false, we who have taken refuge might be strongly encouraged to seize the hope set before us. [19] We have this hope, a sure and steadfast anchor of the soul, a hope that enters the inner shrine behind the curtain, [20] where Jesus, a forerunner on our behalf, has entered, having become a high priest forever according to the order of Melchizedek.

7 This "King Melchizedek of Salem, priest of the Most High God, met Abraham as he was returning from defeating the kings and blessed him"; [2] and to him Abraham apportioned "one-tenth of everything." His name,

in the first place, means "king of righteousness"; next he is also king of Salem, that is, "king of peace." [3] Without father, without mother, without genealogy, having neither beginning of days nor end of life, but resembling the Son of God, he remains a priest forever.

[4] See how great he is! Even[b] Abraham the patriarch gave him a tenth of the spoils. [5] And those descendants of Levi who receive the priestly office have a commandment in the law to collect tithes[c] from the people, that is, from their kindred,[d] though these also are descended from Abraham. [6] But this man, who does not belong to their ancestry, collected tithes[c] from Abraham and blessed him who had received the promises. [7] It is beyond dispute that the inferior is blessed by the superior. [8] In the one case, tithes are received by those who are mortal; in the other, by one of whom it is testified that he lives. [9] One might even say that Levi himself, who receives tithes, paid tithes through Abraham, [10] for he was still in the loins of his ancestor when Melchizedek met him.

[11] Now if perfection had been attainable through the levitical priesthood—for the people received the law under this priest-

a Gk *he*
b Other ancient authorities lack *Even*
c Or *a tenth*
d Gk *brothers*

that they are not among those who are lost. **10:** *Saints,* fellow Christians. **13–18:** As a basis for hope, the author refers to God's promise to Abraham that he would bless Abraham's descendants (Gen 22.16–18). The promise made to Abraham applies to all Christians. **18:** *Two unchangeable things,* God's promise and God's oath. **19–20:** The author summarizes the theme of *hope* and introduces the next topic: a *priest* like *Melchizedek* and the entry of the priest into the holy of holies. **19:** *The inner shrine,* the holy of holies (9.3) of the tabernacle, behind the *curtain* or veil (Ex 26.31–35), restricted to the high priest alone (Lev 16.2). **20:** As *forerunner,* however, Jesus goes ahead on behalf of human beings. *Melchizedek,* here the author picks up the argument of 5.10.

7.1–28: The priesthood of Melchizedek and the levitical priesthood compared. Having referred to Ps 110.4 (see 5.6,10; 6.20), the author proceeds to show how Christ is a priest *according to the order of* ("like") *Melchizedek.* The Dead Sea Scrolls give evidence of Jewish speculation on Melchizedek as an angelic, heavenly figure who rescues the righteous (11QMelch). **1–10:** From Gen 14.17–20 the author deduces that the mysterious priest-king Melchizedek was greater than either Abraham or his descendent, Levi. **3:** *Without father, without mother, without genealogy,* the Bible makes no mention of Melchizedek's ancestors, birth, and death. **5:** See Num 18.21–24; Deut 26.12. **8:** *Those who are mortal,* the levitical priests (Num 18). One who *lives,* Melchizedek, whose death is not recorded.

7.11–25: The levitical priesthood is inadequate because it is provisional and temporary (vv. 11–14). On the other hand, a priest resembling Melchizedek is eternal (Ps 110.4), and the office is neither inherited nor trans-

hood—what further need would there have been to speak of another priest arising according to the order of Melchizedek, rather than one according to the order of Aaron? [12] For when there is a change in the priesthood, there is necessarily a change in the law as well. [13] Now the one of whom these things are spoken belonged to another tribe, from which no one has ever served at the altar. [14] For it is evident that our Lord was descended from Judah, and in connection with that tribe Moses said nothing about priests.

[15] It is even more obvious when another priest arises, resembling Melchizedek, [16] one who has become a priest, not through a legal requirement concerning physical descent, but through the power of an indestructible life. [17] For it is attested of him,

"You are a priest forever,
according to the order of Melchizedek."
[18] There is, on the one hand, the abrogation of an earlier commandment because it was weak and ineffectual [19] (for the law made nothing perfect); there is, on the other hand, the introduction of a better hope, through which we approach God.

[20] This was confirmed with an oath; for others who became priests took their office without an oath, [21] but this one became a priest with an oath, because of the one who said to him,

"The Lord has sworn
and will not change his mind,
'You are a priest forever'"—
[22] accordingly Jesus has also become the guarantee of a better covenant.

[23] Furthermore, the former priests were many in number, because they were prevented by death from continuing in office; [24] but he holds his priesthood permanently, because he continues forever. [25] Consequently he is able for all time to save[a] those who approach God through him, since he always lives to make intercession for them.

[26] For it was fitting that we should have such a high priest, holy, blameless, undefiled, separated from sinners, and exalted above the heavens. [27] Unlike the other[b] high priests, he has no need to offer sacrifices day after day, first for his own sins, and then for those of the people; this he did once for all when he offered himself. [28] For the law appoints as high priests those who are subject to weakness, but the word of the oath, which came later than the law, appoints a Son who has been made perfect forever.

8 Now the main point in what we are saying is this: we have such a high priest, one who is seated at the right hand of the throne of the Majesty in the heavens, [2] a minister in the sanctuary and the true tent[c] that the Lord, and not any mortal, has set up. [3] For every high priest is appointed to offer gifts and sacrifices; hence it is necessary for this priest also to have something to offer. [4] Now if he were on earth, he would not be a priest at all, since there are priests who offer gifts according to the law. [5] They offer worship in

a Or *able to save completely*
b Gk lacks *other*
c Or *tabernacle*

mitted (vv. 15–19). Unlike the levitical priests, Jesus was appointed with a divine oath (v. 17; Ps 110.4); furthermore, being immortal, Jesus holds his priesthood permanently (vv. 20–25). **14:** *From Judah,* Jesus, as a descendant of David, belonged to the tribe of Judah (1 Chr 2.3–15; Sir 45.25). **17:** Ps 110.2. **20:** Oath, see 6.17. **21:** Ps 110.4. **25:** Christ's *intercession,* see 9.24.

7.26–28: Summary of the merits of the high priest, Jesus the Son of God. The theme of perfection and completeness concludes this section (see also vv. 11,19). The law has been incapable of bringing the priesthood to perfection because the Israelite priests were mortal (vv. 23–24). The author has established the eternal character of Christ's priesthood.

8.1–6: Old and new ministry. The author asserts that Christians have an eternal high priest who has been exalted into heaven (1.3). Christ exercises his priestly ministry only in heaven, since on earth he is not a Levite, and therefore not a priest. **4–5:** The author refers to the scripture that describes these rituals rather than to the Jewish practice of his day. **5:** Ex 25.40. Popular Platonic ideas of the time held that true realities existed in the heavenly world, while earthly ones were copies or shadows of the real. The author argues that Christ's ministry is superior because it takes place in that true heavenly world.

a sanctuary that is a sketch and shadow of the heavenly one; for Moses, when he was about to erect the tent,[a] was warned, "See that you make everything according to the pattern that was shown you on the mountain." [6] But Jesus[b] has now obtained a more excellent ministry, and to that degree he is the mediator of a better covenant, which has been enacted through better promises. [7] For if that first covenant had been faultless, there would have been no need to look for a second one.

[8] God[c] finds fault with them when he says:
"The days are surely coming, says the
        Lord,
    when I will establish a new covenant
        with the house of Israel
        and with the house of Judah;
[9] not like the covenant that I made with
        their ancestors,
    on the day when I took them by the
            hand to lead them out of the land
            of Egypt;
for they did not continue in my
        covenant,
    and so I had no concern for them, says
        the Lord.
[10] This is the covenant that I will make
        with the house of Israel
    after those days, says the Lord:
I will put my laws in their minds,
    and write them on their hearts,
and I will be their God,
    and they shall be my people.
[11] And they shall not teach one another
    or say to each other, 'Know the Lord,'
for they shall all know me,
    from the least of them to the greatest.
[12] For I will be merciful toward their
        iniquities,
    and I will remember their sins no
        more."

[13] In speaking of "a new covenant," he has made the first one obsolete. And what is obsolete and growing old will soon disappear.

9 Now even the first covenant had regulations for worship and an earthly sanctuary. [2] For a tent[a] was constructed, the first one, in which were the lampstand, the table, and the bread of the Presence;[d] this is called the Holy Place. [3] Behind the second curtain was a tent[a] called the Holy of Holies. [4] In it stood the golden altar of incense and the ark of the covenant overlaid on all sides with gold, in which there were a golden urn holding the manna, and Aaron's rod that budded, and the tablets of the covenant; [5] above it were the cherubim of glory overshadowing the mercy seat.[e] Of these things we cannot speak now in detail.

[6] Such preparations having been made, the priests go continually into the first tent[a] to carry out their ritual duties; [7] but only the high priest goes into the second, and he but once a year, and not without taking the blood that he offers for himself and for the sins committed unintentionally by the people. [8] By this the Holy Spirit indicates that the way into the sanctuary has not yet been disclosed as long as the first tent[a] is still standing. [9] This is a symbol[f] of the present time, during which gifts and sacrifices are offered that cannot perfect the conscience of the worshiper, [10] but deal only with food and drink and various baptisms, regulations for the body imposed until the time comes to set things right.

a   Or *tabernacle*
b   Gk *he*
c   Gk *He*
d   Gk *the presentation of the loaves*
e   Or *the place of atonement*
f   Gk *parable*

8.7–13: Old and new covenant. The announcement of a "new covenant" in Jer 31.31–34 causes a comparison with the old covenant, with Moses on Mount Sinai. Jer 31.31–34 is quoted and commented upon here and in 9.15–20 and 10.9–18. **13:** The old covenant will be replaced by the new.

9.1–10: The earthly sanctuary. The author describes the wilderness tabernacle of Ex 25–26 and its ritual. **2:** *The bread of the Presence,* Lev 24.5. **3:** Ex 26.31–33. **4:** *The golden altar of incense* stood in the Holy Place (Ex 30.6). *Ark of the covenant,* the chest containing the tablets of the law (Ex 25.10–22). *Urn . . . manna,* Ex 16.32–34. *Aaron's rod,* Num 17.1–10. **5:** *Mercy seat,* see Ex 25.17–22; 37.6–9. **7:** The ritual for the day of atonement (Yom Kippur), in which the high priest enters the holy of holies, is described; see Lev 16. **10:** *The time . . . to set things right,* the period of the new covenant, inaugurated by the death of Christ.

[11] But when Christ came as a high priest of the good things that have come,[a] then through the greater and perfect[b] tent[c] (not made with hands, that is, not of this creation), [12] he entered once for all into the Holy Place, not with the blood of goats and calves, but with his own blood, thus obtaining eternal redemption. [13] For if the blood of goats and bulls, with the sprinkling of the ashes of a heifer, sanctifies those who have been defiled so that their flesh is purified, [14] how much more will the blood of Christ, who through the eternal Spirit[d] offered himself without blemish to God, purify our[e] conscience from dead works to worship the living God!

[15] For this reason he is the mediator of a new covenant, so that those who are called may receive the promised eternal inheritance, because a death has occurred that redeems them from the transgressions under the first covenant.[f] [16] Where a will[f] is involved, the death of the one who made it must be established. [17] For a will[f] takes effect only at death, since it is not in force as long as the one who made it is alive. [18] Hence not even the first covenant was inaugurated without blood. [19] For when every commandment had been told to all the people by Moses in accordance with the law, he took the blood of calves and goats,[g] with water and scarlet wool and hyssop, and sprinkled both the scroll itself and all the people, [20] saying, "This is the blood of the covenant that God has ordained for you." [21] And in the same way he sprinkled with the blood both the tent[c] and all the vessels used in worship. [22] Indeed, under the law almost everything is purified with blood, and without the shedding of blood there is no forgiveness of sins.

[23] Thus it was necessary for the sketches of the heavenly things to be purified with these rites, but the heavenly things themselves need better sacrifices than these. [24] For Christ did not enter a sanctuary made by human hands, a mere copy of the true one, but he entered into heaven itself, now to appear in the presence of God on our behalf. [25] Nor was it to offer himself again and again, as the high priest enters the Holy Place year after year with blood that is not his own; [26] for then he would have had to suffer again and again since the foundation of the world. But as it is, he has appeared once for all at the end of the age to remove sin by the sacrifice of himself. [27] And just as it is appointed for mortals to die once, and after that the judgment, [28] so Christ, having been offered once to bear the sins of many, will appear a second time, not to deal with sin, but to save those who are eagerly waiting for him.

10 Since the law has only a shadow of the good things to come and not the true form of these realities, it[h] can never, by the same sacrifices that are continually

a   Other ancient authorities read *good things to come*
b   Gk *more perfect*
c   Or *tabernacle*
d   Other ancient authorities read *Holy Spirit*
e   Other ancient authorities read *your*
f   The Greek word used here means both *covenant* and *will*
g   Other ancient authorities lack *and goats*
h   Other ancient authorities read *they*

9.11–28: The sacrifice of Christ. The author applies the categories of priestly ministry, covenant, and sanctuary ritual to the saving death of Christ. Christ's death is interpreted as the one effective sacrifice that atones for the sins of humanity (vv. 14,26,28). **12–13:** The day of atonement ritual (Lev 16.1–19), the sacrifice of the red *heifer* (Num 19.1–10), and the sacrificial ratification of the Sinai covenant (Ex 24.3–8) all have to do with the shedding of blood and contribute to the imagery of this argument. **14:** *The eternal Spirit,* the spiritual aspects of Christ's sacrifice. **15–17:** Shifts between meanings of Gk "diatheke" from "covenant" to "will"; see note *f.* Cf. Gal 3.15–18. **18:** Ex 24.3–8. The blood with which Moses seals the covenant will be assotiated with Jesus' death. **19:** *Scarlet wool and hyssop,* cf. Lev 14.4; Num 19.6. **20:** Ex 24.8. **28:** *The sins of many,* Isa 53.12; Mk 10.45. *A second time,* a reference to the Second Coming of Christ is not wholly consistent with the understanding that Christ has entered into heaven and made salvation available in the present (v. 11).

10.1–18: Old and new sacrifice. The author summarizes the comparison between Christ's sacrifice and Israelite ritual. Evidence is found in scripture both for the limitations of the ritual and for the meaning of the word spoken in the Son. **1:** The *shadow* of the *law* is understood to be inferior to *the true form* that is in the future.

offered year after year, make perfect those who approach. [2] Otherwise, would they not have ceased being offered, since the worshipers, cleansed once for all, would no longer have any consciousness of sin? [3] But in these sacrifices there is a reminder of sin year after year. [4] For it is impossible for the blood of bulls and goats to take away sins. [5] Consequently, when Christ[a] came into the world, he said,

"Sacrifices and offerings you have not
    desired,
    but a body you have prepared for me;
[6] in burnt offerings and sin offerings
    you have taken no pleasure.
[7] Then I said, 'See, God, I have come to do
    your will, O God'
    (in the scroll of the book[b] it is written
    of me)."

[8] When he said above, "You have neither desired nor taken pleasure in sacrifices and offerings and burnt offerings and sin offerings" (these are offered according to the law), [9] then he added, "See, I have come to do your will." He abolishes the first in order to establish the second. [10] And it is by God's will[c] that we have been sanctified through the offering of the body of Jesus Christ once for all.

[11] And every priest stands day after day at his service, offering again and again the same sacrifices that can never take away sins. [12] But when Christ[d] had offered for all time a single sacrifice for sins, "he sat down at the right hand of God," [13] and since then has been waiting "until his enemies would be made a footstool for his feet." [14] For by a single offering he has perfected for all time those who are sanctified. [15] And the Holy Spirit also testifies to us, for after saying,

[16] "This is the covenant that I will make
    with them
    after those days, says the Lord:
I will put my laws in their hearts,
    and I will write them on their minds,"
[17] he also adds,
    "I will remember[e] their sins and their
    lawless deeds no more."
[18] Where there is forgiveness of these, there is no longer any offering for sin.

[19] Therefore, my friends,[f] since we have confidence to enter the sanctuary by the blood of Jesus, [20] by the new and living way that he opened for us through the curtain (that is, through his flesh), [21] and since we have a great priest over the house of God, [22] let us approach with a true heart in full assurance of faith, with our hearts sprinkled clean from an evil conscience and our bodies washed with pure water. [23] Let us hold fast to the confession of our hope without wavering, for he who has promised is faithful. [24] And let us consider how to provoke one another to love and good deeds, [25] not neglecting to meet together, as is the habit of some, but encouraging one another, and all the more as you see the Day approaching.

[26] For if we willfully persist in sin after having received the knowledge of the truth, there no longer remains a sacrifice for sins, [27] but a fearful prospect of judgment, and a fury of

a Gk *he*
b Meaning of Gk uncertain
c Gk *by that will*
d Gk *this one*
e Gk *on their minds and I will remember*
f Gk *Therefore, brothers*

4–9: The proof for the idea that it is *impossible* for animal sacrifices to *take away sins* is found in interpretation of Ps 40.6–8 (Septuagint) in which the speaker is understood to be Christ. **8:** 1 Sam 15.22; Ps 50.8–15; Isa 1.10–17; Jer 7.21–26; Hos 6.6. **10:** *Sanctified,* ceremonially cleansed and perfected through Christ's blood (10.29). **12–13:** Ps 110.1. **15–18:** The Holy Spirit is understood to be speaking a paraphrase of Jer 31.33–34. The new covenant assures full and final forgiveness of sins.

10.19–31: Exhortations and warnings. Compare the exhortation in 4.14–16. **20:** *That he opened for us through the curtain (that is, through his flesh),* perhaps the curtain symbolizes Jesus' physical existence, which separates the holy of holies from the outer sanctuary; or the physical existence of Jesus symbolizes the path of access to God. The *flesh* of Jesus is the means for approaching God. **22–25:** Three privileges and duties of Christians: *Let us approach* God in faith and worship (vv. 22,25); *let us hold fast* the public *confession of our hope* (v. 23); *let us consider* how we can help others in love (v. 24). **23:** *Confession of our hope,* the basic attitude of Christians. In Hebrews, faith undergirds hope (see 3.6; 6.11,18; 7.19). **25:** *The Day* of Christ's Second Coming, see 9.28n. **26:**

fire that will consume the adversaries. [28] Anyone who has violated the law of Moses dies without mercy "on the testimony of two or three witnesses." [29] How much worse punishment do you think will be deserved by those who have spurned the Son of God, profaned the blood of the covenant by which they were sanctified, and outraged the Spirit of grace? [30] For we know the one who said, "Vengeance is mine, I will repay." And again, "The Lord will judge his people." [31] It is a fearful thing to fall into the hands of the living God.

[32] But recall those earlier days when, after you had been enlightened, you endured a hard struggle with sufferings, [33] sometimes being publicly exposed to abuse and persecution, and sometimes being partners with those so treated. [34] For you had compassion for those who were in prison, and you cheerfully accepted the plundering of your possessions, knowing that you yourselves possessed something better and more lasting. [35] Do not, therefore, abandon that confidence of yours; it brings a great reward. [36] For you need endurance, so that when you have done the will of God, you may receive what was promised. [37] For yet

"in a very little while,
    the one who is coming will come and
        will not delay;
[38] but my righteous one will live by faith.
    My soul takes no pleasure in anyone
        who shrinks back."

[39] But we are not among those who shrink back and so are lost, but among those who have faith and so are saved.

11 Now faith is the assurance of things hoped for, the conviction of things not seen. [2] Indeed, by faith[a] our ancestors received approval. [3] By faith we understand that the worlds were prepared by the word of God, so that what is seen was made from things that are not visible.[b]

[4] By faith Abel offered to God a more acceptable[c] sacrifice than Cain's. Through this he received approval as righteous, God himself giving approval to his gifts; he died, but through his faith[d] he still speaks. [5] By faith Enoch was taken so that he did not experience death; and "he was not found, because God had taken him." For it was attested before he was taken away that "he had pleased God." [6] And without faith it is impossible to please God, for whoever would approach him must believe that he exists and that he rewards those who seek him. [7] By faith Noah, warned by God about events as yet unseen, respected the warning and built an ark to save his household; by this he condemned the world and became an heir to the righteousness that is in accordance with faith.

[8] By faith Abraham obeyed when he was called to set out for a place that he was to receive as an inheritance; and he set out, not knowing where he was going. [9] By faith he stayed for a time in the land he had been promised, as in a foreign land, living in tents, as did Isaac and Jacob, who were heirs with him of the same promise. [10] For he looked forward to the city that has foundations, whose architect and builder is God. [11] By faith he received power of procreation, even

a Gk *by this*
b Or *was not made out of visible things*
c Gk *greater*
d Gk *through it*

Solemn warning about deliberate sin (see 5.2; 6.4–6). **28:** Paul uses this citation to make a different point in Rom 12.19. Deut 17.2–6. **30:** Deut 32.35–36; Ps 135.14.

10.32–12.29: The power of faith.

10.32–39: Living by faith. This transitional passage shifts from a focus on hope and confidence (vv. 35–36) to faith (vv. 38–39). **37:** Isa 26.20 (Septuagint). **37–38:** Hab 2.3–4 (cf. Rom 1.17; Gal 3.11).

11.1–12.2: A cloud of witnesses to faith. A series of examples of models of faith from the Hebrew Bible, culminating in the example of Jesus in 12.1–2. **11.1:** The Gk word translated *assurance* has an objective quality and might be translated "reality." Likewise, *conviction* has the connotation of "evidence." The people of faith who follow all possess insight into the reality of the invisible divine world. **3:** Ps 33.6; Wis 9.1. **4:** Gen 4.3–10. **5:** Gen 5.21–24. **6:** A general axiom referring to the existence and moral government of God. **7:** *Noah,* Gen 6.13–22. *Righteousness,* Gen 15.6. **8–9:** Gen 12.1–8. **10:** *The city,* the heavenly Jerusalem. *Foundations,* contrasted with tents (v. 9). **11:** In some manuscripts, Sarah is the subject of the sentence: "By faith, Sarah received the power of procreation . . ." Sarah's faith in the unseen is parallel to Abraham's, and she is one of the heroic people of

though he was too old—and Sarah herself was barren—because he considered him faithful who had promised.[a] [12] Therefore from one person, and this one as good as dead, descendants were born, "as many as the stars of heaven and as the innumerable grains of sand by the seashore."

[13] All of these died in faith without having received the promises, but from a distance they saw and greeted them. They confessed that they were strangers and foreigners on the earth, [14] for people who speak in this way make it clear that they are seeking a homeland. [15] If they had been thinking of the land that they had left behind, they would have had opportunity to return. [16] But as it is, they desire a better country, that is, a heavenly one. Therefore God is not ashamed to be called their God; indeed, he has prepared a city for them.

[17] By faith Abraham, when put to the test, offered up Isaac. He who had received the promises was ready to offer up his only son, [18] of whom he had been told, "It is through Isaac that descendants shall be named for you." [19] He considered the fact that God is able even to raise someone from the dead—and figuratively speaking, he did receive him back. [20] By faith Isaac invoked blessings for the future on Jacob and Esau. [21] By faith Jacob, when dying, blessed each of the sons of Joseph, "bowing in worship over the top of his staff." [22] By faith Joseph, at the end of his life, made mention of the exodus of the Israelites and gave instructions about his burial.[b]

[23] By faith Moses was hidden by his parents for three months after his birth, because they saw that the child was beautiful; and they were not afraid of the king's edict.[c] [24] By faith Moses, when he was grown up, refused to be called a son of Pharaoh's daughter, [25] choosing rather to share ill-treatment with the people of God than to enjoy the fleeting pleasures of sin. [26] He considered abuse suffered

for the Christ[d] to be greater wealth than the treasures of Egypt, for he was looking ahead to the reward. [27] By faith he left Egypt, unafraid of the king's anger; for he persevered as though[e] he saw him who is invisible. [28] By faith he kept the Passover and the sprinkling of blood, so that the destroyer of the firstborn would not touch the firstborn of Israel.[f]

[29] By faith the people passed through the Red Sea as if it were dry land, but when the Egyptians attempted to do so they were drowned. [30] By faith the walls of Jericho fell after they had been encircled for seven days. [31] By faith Rahab the prostitute did not perish with those who were disobedient,[g] because she had received the spies in peace.

[32] And what more should I say? For time would fail me to tell of Gideon, Barak, Samson, Jephthah, of David and Samuel and the prophets— [33] who through faith conquered kingdoms, administered justice, obtained promises, shut the mouths of lions, [34] quenched raging fire, escaped the edge of the sword, won strength out of weakness, became mighty in war, put foreign armies to flight. [35] Women received their dead by resurrection. Others were tortured, refusing to accept release, in order to obtain a better resurrection. [36] Others suffered mocking and flogging, and even chains and imprisonment. [37] They were stoned to death,

a   Or By faith Sarah herself, though barren, received power to conceive, even when she was too old, because she considered him faithful who had promised.

b   Gk his bones

c   Other ancient authorities add By faith Moses, when he was grown up, killed the Egyptian, because he observed the humiliation of his people (Gk brothers)

d   Or the Messiah

e   Or because

f   Gk would not touch them

g   Or unbelieving

faith. Gen 17.19; 18.11–14; 21.2. 12: Gen 15.5–6; 22.17; 32.12; Rom 4.19. 16: A city, see v. 10n. 17: Gen 22.1–10. 18: Gen 21.12. 19: Abraham received Isaac back when he was told to offer a ram instead of his son (Gen 22.13). 20: Gen 27.27–29,39–40. 21: Gen 48; 47.31 (Septuagint). 22: Gen 50.24–25; Ex 13.19. 23: Ex 2.2; 1.22. 24–27: Ex 2.10–15. 26: Abuse suffered for the Christ (cf. 13.13); see also Ps 89.52 where "the anointed one" refers to the people of God. 27: Him who is invisible, Jn 1.18; Col 1.15; 1 Tim 1.17; 6.16. 28: Sprinkling of blood, on the lintels and doorposts; see Ex 12.21–30. 29: Ex 14.21–31. 30: Josh 6.12–21. 31: Rahab, Josh 2.1–21; 6.22–25. Rahab is referred to as a hero in Mt 1.5; Jas 2.25; 1 Clem 12. 32: Gideon, Judg 6–8; Barak, Judg 4–5; Samson, Judg 13–16; Jephthah, Judg 11–12; David, 1 Sam 16–30; 2 Sam 1–24; 1 Kings 1.1–2.11; Samuel, 1 Sam 1–12; 15.1–16.13. 33: Lions, Dan 6. 34: Fire, Dan 3. 35: Resurrection,

they were sawn in two,[a] they were killed by the sword; they went about in skins of sheep and goats, destitute, persecuted, tormented— [38] of whom the world was not worthy. They wandered in deserts and mountains, and in caves and holes in the ground.

[39] Yet all these, though they were commended for their faith, did not receive what was promised, [40] since God had provided something better so that they would not, apart from us, be made perfect.

12 Therefore, since we are surrounded by so great a cloud of witnesses, let us also lay aside every weight and the sin that clings so closely,[b] and let us run with perseverance the race that is set before us, [2] looking to Jesus the pioneer and perfecter of our faith, who for the sake of[c] the joy that was set before him endured the cross, disregarding its shame, and has taken his seat at the right hand of the throne of God.

[3] Consider him who endured such hostility against himself from sinners,[d] so that you may not grow weary or lose heart. [4] In your struggle against sin you have not yet resisted to the point of shedding your blood. [5] And you have forgotten the exhortation that addresses you as children—

"My child, do not regard lightly the
    discipline of the Lord,
  or lose heart when you are punished by
    him;
[6] for the Lord disciplines those whom he
    loves,
  and chastises every child whom he
    accepts."

[7] Endure trials for the sake of discipline. God is treating you as children; for what child is there whom a parent does not discipline? [8] If you do not have that discipline in which all children share, then you are illegitimate and not his children. [9] Moreover, we had human parents to discipline us, and we respected them. Should we not be even more willing to be subject to the Father of spirits and live? [10] For they disciplined us for a short time as seemed best to them, but he disciplines us for our good, in order that we may share his holiness. [11] Now, discipline always seems painful rather than pleasant at the time, but later it yields the peaceful fruit of righteousness to those who have been trained by it.

[12] Therefore lift your drooping hands and strengthen your weak knees, [13] and make straight paths for your feet, so that what is lame may not be put out of joint, but rather be healed.

[14] Pursue peace with everyone, and the holiness without which no one will see the Lord. [15] See to it that no one fails to obtain the grace of God; that no root of bitterness springs up and causes trouble, and through it many become defiled. [16] See to it that no one becomes like Esau, an immoral and godless person, who sold his birthright for a single meal. [17] You know that later, when he wanted to inherit the blessing, he was rejected, for he found no chance to repent,[e] even though he sought the blessing[f] with tears.

a   Other ancient authorities add *they were tempted*
b   Other ancient authorities read *sin that easily distracts*
c   Or *who instead of*
d   Other ancient authorities read *such hostility from sinners against themselves*
e   Or *no chance to change his father's mind*
f   Gk *it*

1 Kings 17.17–24; 2 Kings 4.25–37; *tortured*, 2 Macc 7.9,14. **37:** 2 Chr 24.20–22; Jer 26.23; 2 Macc 5.27; 6.12–7.42. **38:** *Caves*, 2 Macc 6.11; 10.6.

12.1–2: Jesus, the ultimate example of faith. Jesus is the supreme model of faith in God and an example for those who follow him. **1:** *Witnesses*, those mentioned in ch 11. **2:** *Pioneer and perfecter*, see 2.10n.

12.3–17: The discipline of God. The author develops the metaphors of the athletic contest or race (vv. 1,12–13), the father disciplining his children (vv. 5–11), and the "bitter root" (v. 15). **5–8:** Prov 3.11–12. In the family structure of the ancient world, the father's (*parent's*) obligation to punish sons (*children*) and so recognize their legitimacy is the background of the comparison between suffering and discipline from God. *Illegitimate* children were not disciplined. The author understands the scripture to be speaking to Christians as "sons" or "children" of the Father (cf. 5.8). *All . . . share*, namely, all children of God (v. 6). **9:** *Father of spirits*, God is traditionally understood to have power over the world of spirits (see Num 16.22; Rev 22.6). **12:** Isa 35.3. **14–17:** The necessity of *peace* and purity. **15:** *Root of bitterness*, Deut 29.18 (Septuagint). **16:** Gen 25.29–34. **17:** Gen 27.30–40.

12.18–29: Mount Sinai and Mount Zion contrasted. **18–19:** *Something that can be touched*, Mount Sinai (Ex

¹⁸ You have not come to something[a] that can be touched, a blazing fire, and darkness, and gloom, and a tempest, ¹⁹ and the sound of a trumpet, and a voice whose words made the hearers beg that not another word be spoken to them. ²⁰ (For they could not endure the order that was given, "If even an animal touches the mountain, it shall be stoned to death." ²¹ Indeed, so terrifying was the sight that Moses said, "I tremble with fear.") ²² But you have come to Mount Zion and to the city of the living God, the heavenly Jerusalem, and to innumerable angels in festal gathering, ²³ and to the assembly[b] of the firstborn who are enrolled in heaven, and to God the judge of all, and to the spirits of the righteous made perfect, ²⁴ and to Jesus, the mediator of a new covenant, and to the sprinkled blood that speaks a better word than the blood of Abel.

²⁵ See that you do not refuse the one who is speaking; for if they did not escape when they refused the one who warned them on earth, how much less will we escape if we reject the one who warns from heaven! ²⁶ At that time his voice shook the earth; but now he has promised, "Yet once more I will shake not only the earth but also the heaven." ²⁷ This phrase, "Yet once more," indicates the removal of what is shaken—that is, created things—so that what cannot be shaken may remain. ²⁸ Therefore, since we are receiving a kingdom that cannot be shaken, let us give thanks, by which we offer to God an acceptable worship with reverence and awe; ²⁹ for indeed our God is a consuming fire.

13 Let mutual love continue. ² Do not neglect to show hospitality to strangers, for by doing that some have entertained angels without knowing it. ³ Remember those who are in prison, as though you were in prison with them; those who are being tortured, as though you yourselves were being tortured.[c] ⁴ Let marriage be held in honor by all, and let the marriage bed be kept undefiled; for God will judge fornicators and adulterers. ⁵ Keep your lives free from the love of money, and be content with what you have; for he has said, "I will never leave you or forsake you." ⁶ So we can say with confidence,

"The Lord is my helper;
 I will not be afraid.
What can anyone do to me?"

⁷ Remember your leaders, those who spoke the word of God to you; consider the outcome of their way of life, and imitate their faith. ⁸ Jesus Christ is the same yesterday and today and forever. ⁹ Do not be carried away by all kinds of strange teachings; for it is well for the heart to be strengthened by grace, not by regulations about food,[d] which have not benefited those who observe them. ¹⁰ We have an altar from which those who officiate in the tent[e] have no right to eat. ¹¹ For the bodies of those animals whose blood is brought into the sanctuary by the high priest as a sacrifice for sin are burned outside the camp. ¹² Therefore Jesus also suffered outside the city gate in order to sanctify the people by his own blood. ¹³ Let us then go to him outside the camp and bear the abuse he endured. ¹⁴ For here we have no lasting city, but we are looking for the city that is to come. ¹⁵ Through him, then, let us continually offer a sacrifice of praise to God, that is, the fruit of

a Other ancient authorities read *a mountain*
b Or *angels, and to the festal gathering* ²³*and assembly*
c Gk *were in the body*
d Gk *not by foods*
e Or *tabernacle*

19.12–22; 20.18–21; Deut 4.11–12; 5.22–27). **20:** Ex 19.12–13. **21:** Deut 9.19. **24:** Abel's *blood* cried for vengeance (11.4; Gen 4.10); the *sprinkled blood* of Jesus, which established the new covenant (9.14; 13.20), *speaks . . . better* for forgiveness. **25:** Cf. 19.26–31. The theme of responding to the one who speaks recalls the beginning of the sermon. **26:** Hag 2.6. **29:** Deut 4.24; 9.3.
   13.1–25: Practical instructions to the community and greetings.
   13.1–17: The sermon concludes with specific ethical exhortation to show *mutual love.* **2:** *Entertained angels,* Gen 18.1–8; 19.1. **3:** Mt 25.35–46. **5:** Josh 1.5. **6:** Ps 118.6. **7:** *Your leaders,* former leaders who proclaimed God's word to the community in the past. **9:** Whether *regulations about food* refers to Jewish food laws or ritual dining practices is not clear. The author contrasts these to *grace,* which is effective. **11:** Lev 16.27. Cf. Col 2.16,20–23. **12:** As the sacrificed animals are burned outside the camp, so Jesus died outside the gate of Jerusalem (Jn 19.20). **14:**

lips that confess his name. [16] Do not neglect to do good and to share what you have, for such sacrifices are pleasing to God.

[17] Obey your leaders and submit to them, for they are keeping watch over your souls and will give an account. Let them do this with joy and not with sighing—for that would be harmful to you.

[18] Pray for us; we are sure that we have a clear conscience, desiring to act honorably in all things. [19] I urge you all the more to do this, so that I may be restored to you very soon.

[20] Now may the God of peace, who brought back from the dead our Lord Jesus, the great shepherd of the sheep, by the blood of the eternal covenant, [21] make you complete in everything good so that you may do his will, working among us[a] that which is pleasing in his sight, through Jesus Christ, to whom be the glory forever and ever. Amen.

[22] I appeal to you, brothers and sisters,[b] bear with my word of exhortation, for I have written to you briefly. [23] I want you to know that our brother Timothy has been set free; and if he comes in time, he will be with me when I see you. [24] Greet all your leaders and all the saints. Those from Italy send you greetings. [25] Grace be with all of you.[c]

a   Other ancient authorities read you
b   Gk brothers
c   Other ancient authorities add Amen

The city . . . to come, see 11.10. 15: A sacrifice of thanksgiving (Lev 7.12; Ps 50.14,23; Hos 14.2). 17: Leaders, those at the head of the community who protect people from harm.

13.18–25: Greetings, blessing, and postscript. 20–21: Blessing (see Isa 63.11). Brought back, lit., "led up." The verb refers to the exaltation of Jesus to the right hand of God. 22: Word of exhortation, a sermon, rather than a letter (see Acts 13.22); for I have written to you briefly, mention of the "briefness" of a letter is conventional in ancient letters. 23: Timothy is referred to in Paul's letters and Acts of the Apostles as a companion to Paul (1 Cor 4.17; Acts 16.1–3).

THE LETTER OF JAMES

NAME

The letter of James gets its name from the epistolary opening (1.1) that identifies the author by the Greek "Iakobos" (from the common Jewish name "Jacob") translated into English as "James."

CANONICAL STATUS

The early fourth-century CE church historian Eusebius noted that the letter found slow acceptance into the Christian canon despite the fact that it was "regularly used in very many churches" as one of the "'general' epistles" (*Hist. eccl.* 2.23; 3.25). The *Muratorian Canon* (late second century) does not mention James, but the letter was included in Bishop Athanasius's influential canon list ca. 367 CE. Its canonicity was then largely secure until the Protestant Reformation in the sixteenth century when Martin Luther moved it (along with Hebrews, Jude, and Revelation) to the end of the New Testament; in Luther's view it lacked essential elements of the gospel. But John Calvin and Philip Melanchthon, like the Council of Trent (1546), defended both the canonical status and theological value of the letter.

AUTHORSHIP

From among the several individuals named "James" who figure prominently in the early church, Christian tradition has held that the opening salutation refers to the brother of Jesus (Mt 13.55; Mk 6.3; Gal 1.19) and who was a leader in the Jerusalem church (Gal 2.9; Acts 15.13). Yet scholars have challenged this identification since antiquity. Those who defend the tradition argue that only such a well-known figure could refer to himself as James without an additional epithet, and that the absence of any biographical details differs significantly from other works considered pseudepigraphical (cf. 2 Tim 4.9–18). Modern critics of authenticity often cite doubts voiced in the early church: indications the letter dates to after James's martyrdom (ca. 62 CE), and a Greek literary style well beyond the likely capabilities of a Galilean villager. Recent commentators have suggested that material originating from James was reworked by a disciple after his martyrdom to create the letter as we know it. However, it remains possible that the author was an otherwise unknown James only later identified with Jesus' brother.

DATE AND HISTORICAL CONTEXT

The letter offers no decisive clues as to the time of its composition. If the specific language that a person is "not [justified] by faith alone" (2.24) is a direct response to Paul's assertion in Romans 3.28, it must be dated sometime later than ca. 57 CE. *First Clement* (ca. 95 CE), which shows some evidence of dependence on the text of James (compare *1 Clem.* 30.3; 31.2 with Jas 2.14–26; *1 Clem.* 29.1; 30.1–5 with Jas. 4.1–10), sets a latest possible date.

There are likewise no solid indications of the historical context that prompted the letter. The symbolic nature of addressing the recipients as the "twelve tribes" (see 1.1n.) raises the possibility that the language of "Dispersion" (1.1) is likewise symbolic (note the conclusion regarding the need to bring back anyone who "wanders from the truth," 5.19–20; but cf. 1 Pet 1.1). Certainly the choice of these particular images together with the esteem for the "law" (Gk "nomos," corresponding to Heb "torah"; 1.25; 2.8–12; 4.11), the reference to their "assembly" by Gk "synagoges" (lit., "synagogue"; 2.2), and the use of many examples from, as well as the style of, the Septuagint (LXX) convince most interpreters the letter was directed to ethnic Jews who believed Jesus was the Messiah/Christ (1.1; 2.1). Yet even these indicators are ambiguous. The Septuagint was scripture for both ethnically Gentile and Jewish Christian communities. Such writers as Ignatius, Hermas, Justin, Origen, and Eusebius used the terms "synagoges" and "ekklesia" ("church") both in parallel and interchangeably for exclusively Gentile communities well after the first century. Though each factor may be inconclusive taken by itself, their cumulative presence in a letter by an author named Jacob/James makes it very likely the letter is the product of Jewish Christianity.

STRUCTURE AND CONTENTS

Although the letter was once thought to be a loosely organized collection of teachings similar to the book of Proverbs, recent literary analyses using both ancient and modern approaches have converged on an understanding of the letter's structure. Following its epistolary salutation (1.1), there is a two-fold introduction (1.2–11; 1.12–21) that sets out in parallel fashion some major themes of the book (testing, wisdom, and consistency). The introduction is followed by several longer units that develop specific themes: consistency of word and action (1.22–2.13); faith and works (2.14–26); proper speech (3.1–18); relations with others and God (4.1–12); and coming judgment (4.13–5.9). The letter concludes (5.10–20) with brief exhortations regarding the recipients' responsibilities toward other members of the community.

INTERPRETATION AND GUIDE TO READING

Too often the Letter of James has not been heard on its own terms because it was read either contra Paul's theology of justification in particular or as representing Jewish Christianity contra the Gentile church more generally. While there are grounds for concluding that 2.14–26 may be a reaction against libertine readings of Paul's teaching that justification was "by faith apart from works" (see Rom 3.28; note not only the similar phrasing but also the use of Abraham as an example in Rom 4.1–25 and Jas 2.20–24), it is less clear that James and Paul are in fundamental disagreement with each other. Both see faith primarily as trust in God (Rom 4.5; Jas 1.5–6), and both agree that it should produce a response in one's manner of life (Rom 2.13; Phil 2.12–13; Jas 2.18). Yet however one understands the relationship between James and Paul, neither the issues of justification nor relations between Jews and Gentiles within the church dominate the content of this letter as a whole. Reading James on its own terms requires seeing how the understanding of consistently living out "the implanted word" (1.21) developed in the first two chapters leads to the specific ethical teachings at both personal (1.19–21,26; 3.13–18) and communal (2.2–4; 4.11–12) levels and a strong stand in favor of social justice (1.27; 2.5; 5.4) in the second half of the book.

Timothy B. Cargal

1 James, a servant[a] of God and of the Lord Jesus Christ,
To the twelve tribes in the Dispersion: Greetings.

[2] My brothers and sisters,[b] whenever you face trials of any kind, consider it nothing but joy, [3] because you know that the testing of your faith produces endurance; [4] and let endurance have its full effect, so that you may be mature and complete, lacking in nothing.

[5] If any of you is lacking in wisdom, ask God, who gives to all generously and ungrudgingly, and it will be given you. [6] But ask in faith, never doubting, for the one who doubts is like a wave of the sea, driven and tossed by the wind; [7, 8] for the doubter, being double-minded and unstable in every way, must not expect to receive anything from the Lord.

[9] Let the believer[c] who is lowly boast in being raised up, [10] and the rich in being brought low, because the rich will disappear like a flower in the field. [11] For the sun rises with its scorching heat and withers the field; its flower falls, and its beauty perishes. It is the same way with the rich; in the midst of a busy life, they will wither away.

a Gk *slave*
b Gk *brothers*
c Gk *brother*

1.1: Salutation. *Servant of God and . . . Christ,* a unique dual designation in the New Testament, where identifications of people as either "servant of God" (Titus 1.1; 1 Pet 2.16; Rev 7.3), "of Christ" (Rom 1.1; Eph 6.6; Jude 1), or "of the Lord" (2 Tim 2.24) are common. *Twelve tribes,* symbolic reference to the church as a new Israel (cf. Rev 7.4–8). *Dispersion,* scattered either geographically (cf. 1 Pet 1.1) or symbolically (5.19–20n.). **1.2–11: Trials and wisdom. 2:** *Trials,* or "temptations" as in 1.12 (Gk "peirasmos"). *Consider,* in Greek, either a command or statement of usual practice ("you considered"). **3:** *You know . . . testing . . . produces endurance,* common teaching of Jewish wisdom tradition (cf. Rom 5.3–4). **4–5:** *Lacking in nothing . . . lacking in wisdom,* suggests against their view that wisdom is a gift from God rather than learned through "trials" (cf. 1 Kings 3). **6:** *Ask in faith,* trusting God to give the "gift" (1.17) rather than "temptation" (1.13–14). **7–8:** *Double-minded,* not knowing what God will do. **9–11:** Reversal of fortunes between poor and rich (2.5; 5.1–3; cf. 1 Sam 2.7; Lk 6.20–26).

¹² Blessed is anyone who endures temptation. Such a one has stood the test and will receive the crown of life that the Lord[a] has promised to those who love him. ¹³ No one, when tempted, should say, "I am being tempted by God"; for God cannot be tempted by evil and he himself tempts no one. ¹⁴ But one is tempted by one's own desire, being lured and enticed by it; ¹⁵ then, when that desire has conceived, it gives birth to sin, and that sin, when it is fully grown, gives birth to death. ¹⁶ Do not be deceived, my beloved.[b]

¹⁷ Every generous act of giving, with every perfect gift, is from above, coming down from the Father of lights, with whom there is no variation or shadow due to change.[c] ¹⁸ In fulfillment of his own purpose he gave us birth by the word of truth, so that we would become a kind of first fruits of his creatures.

¹⁹ You must understand this, my beloved:[b] let everyone be quick to listen, slow to speak, slow to anger; ²⁰ for your anger does not produce God's righteousness. ²¹ Therefore rid yourselves of all sordidness and rank growth of wickedness, and welcome with meekness the implanted word that has the power to save your souls.

²² But be doers of the word, and not merely hearers who deceive themselves. ²³ For if any are hearers of the word and not doers, they are like those who look at themselves[d] in a mirror; ²⁴ for they look at themselves and, on going away, immediately forget what they were like. ²⁵ But those who look into the perfect law, the law of liberty, and persevere, being not hearers who forget but doers who act—they will be blessed in their doing.

²⁶ If any think they are religious, and do not bridle their tongues but deceive their hearts, their religion is worthless. ²⁷ Religion that is pure and undefiled before God, the Father, is this: to care for orphans and widows in their distress, and to keep oneself unstained by the world.

2 My brothers and sisters,[e] do you with your acts of favoritism really believe in our glorious Lord Jesus Christ?[f] ² For if a person with gold rings and in fine clothes comes into your assembly, and if a poor person in dirty clothes also comes in, ³ and if you take notice of the one wearing the fine clothes and say, "Have a seat here, please," while to the one who is poor you say, "Stand there," or, "Sit at my feet,"[g] ⁴ have you not made distinctions among yourselves, and become judges with evil thoughts? ⁵ Listen, my beloved brothers and sisters.[h] Has not God chosen the poor in the world to be rich in faith and to be heirs of the kingdom that he has promised to those who love him? ⁶ But you have dishonored the poor. Is it not the rich who oppress you? Is it not they who drag you into

a Gk *he*; other ancient authorities read *God*
b Gk *my beloved brothers*
c Other ancient authorities read *variation due to a shadow of turning*
d Gk *at the face of his birth*
e Gk *My brothers*
f Or *hold the faith of our glorious Lord Jesus Christ without acts of favoritism*
g Gk *Sit under my footstool*
h Gk *brothers*

1.12–21: Life through the word. 12: *Crown*, victor's laurel wreath rather than royal diadem (cf. Rev 2.10). **14–15:** *Desire . . . sin . . . death*, certain progression of acting consistent with one's corrupted will. **18:** God's opposite desire (*purpose*) to use *the word of truth* to give *birth* to a new will within us (cf. 1.21). **19:** Need for self-control; cf. Sir 5.10–14. **20:** Greek explicitly contrasts *anger* that originates in people ("orge andros") with *righteousness* that is from God ("dikaiosunen theou"). **21:** Consistency with God's *implanted word* both checks improper action and *saves* one's *soul*/life.

1.22–2.13: Consistency of word and action. Section framed by references to speech, actions, and God's law. **1.22–25:** Here *the word* that must be done is the "implanted word" (1.21) from God (Mt 7.24; Rom 2.13), not their own words. **24:** *Immediately forget* in the sense that behavior will not change unless there is a unity of word and deed. **25:** *Perfect . . . law of liberty*, God's revealed will makes one "mature and complete" (1.4) and free from the lure of improper desire (1.14). **26:** *Bridle their tongues*, now the focus shifts to consistency between their own speech and actions (2.16n.; 3.2). **27:** *Religion* should assist others and thereby one's self as well (cf. Mic 6.8). **2.1–4:** Discriminatory actions rooted in socio-economic *distinctions*. **5:** They claim to "believe" (see 2.1) *God chose the poor* (see 1.9–10), but their actions reveal they have chosen the rich. **6:** *Oppress you*, see 5.1–6. **7:** *The excellent name*, the "glorious Lord Jesus Christ" (2.1), *invoked* in their baptism. **8:** Lev 19.18 as hallmark of God's

court? [7] Is it not they who blaspheme the excellent name that was invoked over you?

[8] You do well if you really fulfill the royal law according to the scripture, "You shall love your neighbor as yourself." [9] But if you show partiality, you commit sin and are convicted by the law as transgressors. [10] For whoever keeps the whole law but fails in one point has become accountable for all of it. [11] For the one who said, "You shall not commit adultery," also said, "You shall not murder." Now if you do not commit adultery but if you murder, you have become a transgressor of the law. [12] So speak and so act as those who are to be judged by the law of liberty. [13] For judgment will be without mercy to anyone who has shown no mercy; mercy triumphs over judgment.

[14] What good is it, my brothers and sisters,[a] if you say you have faith but do not have works? Can faith save you? [15] If a brother or sister is naked and lacks daily food, [16] and one of you says to them, "Go in peace; keep warm and eat your fill," and yet you do not supply their bodily needs, what is the good of that? [17] So faith by itself, if it has no works, is dead.

[18] But someone will say, "You have faith and I have works." Show me your faith apart from your works, and I by my works will show you my faith. [19] You believe that God is one; you do well. Even the demons believe—and shudder. [20] Do you want to be shown, you senseless person, that faith apart from works is barren? [21] Was not our ancestor Abraham justified by works when he offered his son Isaac on the altar? [22] You see that faith was active along with his works, and faith was brought to completion by the works. [23] Thus the scripture was fulfilled that says, "Abraham believed God, and it was reckoned to him as righteousness," and he was called the friend of God. [24] You see that a person is justified by works and not by faith alone. [25] Likewise, was not Rahab the prostitute also justified by works when she welcomed the messengers and sent them out by another road? [26] For just as the body without the spirit is dead, so faith without works is also dead.

3 Not many of you should become teachers, my brothers and sisters,[a] for you know that we who teach will be judged with greater strictness. [2] For all of us make many mistakes. Anyone who makes no mistakes in speaking is perfect, able to keep the whole body in check with a bridle. [3] If we put bits into the mouths of horses to make them obey us, we guide their whole bodies. [4] Or look at ships: though they are so large that it takes strong winds to drive them, yet they are guided by a very small rudder wherever the will of the pilot directs. [5] So also the tongue is a small member, yet it boasts of great exploits.

How great a forest is set ablaze by a small fire! [6] And the tongue is a fire. The tongue is placed among our members as a world of iniquity; it stains the whole body, sets on fire the cycle of nature,[b] and is itself set on fire

a   Gk *brothers*
b   Or *wheel of birth*

reign revealed in Jesus (Mk 12.28–31; Jn 13.34; Gal 5.14). **10:** Unity of the law in the command to love (Rom 13.8–9; cf. Deut 27.26; 4 Macc 5.19–21). **11:** *You murder,* charge possibly based on actions in 5.6; cf. 4.2. **12:** Summary conclusion of section. **13:** Cf. Mt 6.14–15.

2.14–26: Faith and works. 14: *Works,* or "deeds," which may avoid overstating differences between James and Paul (see Introduction). *Can faith save,* i.e., faith only spoken about but not acted on cannot make one spiritually alive (see 2.17,26). **16:** *Keep warm* and *eat* in Greek are passive verbs ("be warm and well fed"), expressing what one wants and expects God to do. Stating God's desire for the needy, they fail to act on it (cf. 1.22). **18:** James rejects separating *faith* and *works*, insisting on a both/and relationship between them. **21–22:** Abraham's *works* in offering Isaac (see Gen 22.1–19) may bring his *faith . . . to completion* by showing absolute trust in God's promise that Isaac was the heir (cf. Heb 11.17–19). **23:** Quoting Gen 15.6. *Friend of God,* contrast 4.4. **25:** *Rahab* also acted on faith in God's promise (Josh 2.8–13; cf. Heb 11.31).

3.1–18: Proper use of speech is teaching God's wisdom. 1: *Judged with greater strictness,* both for consistency between words and actions, and for mercy toward others (2.12–13). **2:** *Perfect,* or "mature" as in 1.4 (Greek "teleios"). **3–4:** *Bits* and *rudder* exercise control far beyond what might be expected from their size because they express *the will of the pilot* or rider. **5:** *The tongue* likewise expresses the person's will and directs one's actions (Lk 6.45). **6:** *Tongue is . . . set on fire by hell,* destructive impact of will and actions opposed to God's will (cf.

by hell.[a] [7] For every species of beast and bird, of reptile and sea creature, can be tamed and has been tamed by the human species, [8] but no one can tame the tongue—a restless evil, full of deadly poison. [9] With it we bless the Lord and Father, and with it we curse those who are made in the likeness of God. [10] From the same mouth come blessing and cursing. My brothers and sisters,[b] this ought not to be so. [11] Does a spring pour forth from the same opening both fresh and brackish water? [12] Can a fig tree, my brothers and sisters,[c] yield olives, or a grapevine figs? No more can salt water yield fresh.

[13] Who is wise and understanding among you? Show by your good life that your works are done with gentleness born of wisdom. [14] But if you have bitter envy and selfish ambition in your hearts, do not be boastful and false to the truth. [15] Such wisdom does not come down from above, but is earthly, unspiritual, devilish. [16] For where there is envy and selfish ambition, there will also be disorder and wickedness of every kind. [17] But the wisdom from above is first pure, then peaceable, gentle, willing to yield, full of mercy and good fruits, without a trace of partiality or hypocrisy. [18] And a harvest of righteousness is sown in peace for[d] those who make peace.

4 Those conflicts and disputes among you, where do they come from? Do they not come from your cravings that are at war within you? [2] You want something and do not have it; so you commit murder. And you covet[e] something and cannot obtain it; so you engage in disputes and conflicts. You do not have, because you do not ask. [3] You ask and do not receive, because you ask wrongly, in order to spend what you get on your pleasures. [4] Adulterers! Do you not know that friendship with the world is enmity with God? Therefore whoever wishes to be a friend of the world becomes an enemy of God. [5] Or do you suppose that it is for nothing that the scripture says, "God[f] yearns jealously for the spirit that he has made to dwell in us"? [6] But he gives all the more grace; therefore it says,

"God opposes the proud,
    but gives grace to the humble."

[7] Submit yourselves therefore to God. Resist the devil, and he will flee from you. [8] Draw near to God, and he will draw near to you. Cleanse your hands, you sinners, and purify your hearts, you double-minded. [9] Lament and mourn and weep. Let your laughter be turned into mourning and your joy into dejection. [10] Humble yourselves before the Lord, and he will exalt you.

[11] Do not speak evil against one another, brothers and sisters.[g] Whoever speaks evil

a   Gk *Gehenna*
b   Gk *My brothers*
c   Gk *my brothers*
d   Or *by*
e   Or *you murder and you covet*
f   Gk *He*
g   Gk *brothers*

1.14–15,26–27). **8:** *No one can tame,* an implicit call to do the very thing said to be impossible. **9:** *Lord and Father,* both titles referring to God. *Likeness of God,* human beings who should act as God's agents (see Gen 1.26). **10:** *Blessing and cursing,* another indication of "double-mindedness" (1.7–8; 4.8). **11–12:** Cf. Mt 7.16–18. **13:** *Who is wise,* teachers should be those whose *good life* shows both *works* of the word (1.22) and the *gentleness* of mercy (2.13) arising from God's will *born of wisdom* (cf. 1.18). **15–16:** *Earthly, unspiritual, devilish,* what some might call *wisdom* is proven by its effects (*envy, selfish ambition, disorder,* and *wickedness*) not to be wisdom at all. **17–18:** Genuine *wisdom* is likewise proven by its origins (*from above,* see 1.5,17) and effects (cf. these virtues and preceding vices with Gal 5.19–24).

4.1–12: Relations with God and others. 1: *Your cravings,* improper desire brings destruction to the community as well as the self (cf. 1.14–15). **2:** *Murder,* probably hyperbole, although the charge is leveled three times in the letter (see 2.11; 5.6n.). **3:** *Ask and do not receive,* here the problem is the purpose of the request (*pleasures*) rather than "doubt" (see 1.6–8). **4:** *Adulterers,* Greek is feminine ("Adulteresses!"), recalling prophetic tradition of casting Israel as God's unfaithful wife (Jer 3.6–10; Ezek 16.8–52; Hos 1–3; cf. Mk 8.38). *Friend of the world . . . enemy of God,* contrast 2.23. **5:** *Scripture says,* quotation either from an unknown source or a general statement setting up citation in next verse. **6:** Quotation from Prov 3.34. **8:** *Purify your hearts,* the seat of will and intellect (Mt 13.15; Jn 13.2), and so a correction to *double-mindedness* that results from nearness with God (cf. 1.7–8). **9–10:**

against another or judges another, speaks evil against the law and judges the law; but if you judge the law, you are not a doer of the law but a judge. [12] There is one lawgiver and judge who is able to save and to destroy. So who, then, are you to judge your neighbor?

[13] Come now, you who say, "Today or tomorrow we will go to such and such a town and spend a year there, doing business and making money." [14] Yet you do not even know what tomorrow will bring. What is your life? For you are a mist that appears for a little while and then vanishes. [15] Instead you ought to say, "If the Lord wishes, we will live and do this or that." [16] As it is, you boast in your arrogance; all such boasting is evil. [17] Anyone, then, who knows the right thing to do and fails to do it, commits sin.

5 Come now, you rich people, weep and wail for the miseries that are coming to you. [2] Your riches have rotted, and your clothes are moth-eaten. [3] Your gold and silver have rusted, and their rust will be evidence against you, and it will eat your flesh like fire. You have laid up treasure[a] for the last days. [4] Listen! The wages of the laborers who mowed your fields, which you kept back by fraud, cry out, and the cries of the harvesters have reached the ears of the Lord of hosts. [5] You have lived on the earth in luxury and in pleasure; you have fattened your hearts in a day of slaughter. [6] You have condemned and murdered the righteous one, who does not resist you.

[7] Be patient, therefore, beloved,[b] until the coming of the Lord. The farmer waits for the precious crop from the earth, being patient with it until it receives the early and the late rains. [8] You also must be patient. Strengthen your hearts, for the coming of the Lord is near.[c] [9] Beloved,[d] do not grumble against one another, so that you may not be judged. See, the Judge is standing at the doors! [10] As an example of suffering and patience, beloved,[b] take the prophets who spoke in the name of the Lord. [11] Indeed we call blessed those who showed endurance. You have heard of the endurance of Job, and you have seen the purpose of the Lord, how the Lord is compassionate and merciful.

[12] Above all, my beloved,[b] do not swear, either by heaven or by earth or by any other oath, but let your "Yes" be yes and your "No" be no, so that you may not fall under condemnation.

[13] Are any among you suffering? They should pray. Are any cheerful? They should sing songs of praise. [14] Are any among you sick? They should call for the elders of the church and have them pray over them,

---

[a] Or *will eat your flesh, since you have stored up fire*
[b] Gk *brothers*
[c] Or *is at hand*
[d] Gk *Brothers*

Repentance in anticipation of the great reversal at the last day (see 1.9–10). **11:** *Not a doer of the law but a judge,* the law properly rules over the readers (2.8; cf. 1.25). **12:** God is *able to save* by changing one's will (1.18,21) or to *destroy* by being left to one's "desire . . . sin . . . [and] death" (1.14–15).

4.13–5.9: Coming judgment. 4.14: *You do not . . . know,* Christ's return "is near" (5.8–9), but the precise time is unknown (Mk 13.32). *Mist that . . . vanishes,* the impermanence of this age and its ways of life (1.11). **15:** *If the Lord wishes,* actions are properly determined by God's will and word (1.22). **17:** Theologically termed "sins of omission" arising from failing to do what one knows God desires (2.16n.). **5.2–4:** *Gold and silver have rusted,* while these metals do not rust or corrode, the imagery suggests deterioration (*rotted, moth-eaten;* cf. Mt 6.19–21) from lack of use by both the rich and those from whom they have been *kept back by fraud* (cf. 2.15–16). *Wages* were to be paid daily according to Jewish law (Deut 24.14–15). **6:** *Condemned and murdered the righteous one,* possibly a reference to Jesus' crucifixion but more likely to the general mistreatment of the poor by the rich as elsewhere in the letter (2.6b–7; 5.4; cf. Sir 34.26–27). **7:** *Precious crop,* possibly a sign of hope that repentance by the rich may yet lead to their inclusion in the spiritual harvest (5.19–20; cf. Mt 9.37–38).

5.10–20: Closing exhortations. The letter ends with brief exhortations to fulfill responsibilities to other members of the community. **10–11:** As in 1.2–5 and 1.12–18, God's *purpose* during times of *endurance* is not to put people through "trials" or "temptations" but to be *compassionate and merciful.* **12:** If one's actions are consistent with one's words there will be no need for an *oath* (cf. Mt 5.33–37). **13–16:** Both prayer and praise are here placed

anointing them with oil in the name of the Lord. [15] The prayer of faith will save the sick, and the Lord will raise them up; and anyone who has committed sins will be forgiven. [16] Therefore confess your sins to one another, and pray for one another, so that you may be healed. The prayer of the righteous is powerful and effective. [17] Elijah was a human being like us, and he prayed fervently that it might not rain, and for three years and six months it did not rain on the earth. [18] Then he prayed again, and the heaven gave rain and the earth yielded its harvest.

[19] My brothers and sisters,[a] if anyone among you wanders from the truth and is brought back by another, [20] you should know that whoever brings back a sinner from wandering will save the sinner's[b] soul from death and will cover a multitude of sins.

[a] Gk My brothers
[b] Gk his

in communal context. **15:** *Will save . . . will raise,* these verbs can refer both to temporal physical healing and to spiritual salvation and resurrection at the end of the age; given other uses of *save* in the letter (1.21; 2.14; 4.12; 5.20), James probably intends both senses in this context. **17–18:** Since Elijah (1 Kings 17.1; 18.41–45) was *like us,* he is a typical rather than extraordinary example (but see Jesus' remarks at Lk 4.25–27). **19–20:** *From wandering,* lit., "from the error of his way," recalling Rahab's actions in saving herself and the messengers (2.25). *Sinner's,* lit., "his," referring either to one who *wanders from the truth* or *whoever brings back* the wanderer. If Rahab provides the pattern, the ambiguity may be deliberate and express James's understanding of what the letter has accomplished.

THE FIRST LETTER OF PETER

NAME, AUTHORSHIP, AND DATE

The First Letter of Peter presents itself as a pastoral letter written by the apostle Peter from "Babylon," where he is accompanied by Silvanus (= Silas) and Mark (5.12–13), to churches in five provinces of Asia Minor (1.1). Since it is addressed to churches in a large area, it was placed among the Catholic (or general) Letters, and its canonical status was never disputed, in contrast to 2 Peter.

Some scholars still treat Simon Peter as the letter's author, with Silvanus as secretary (5.12); others consider Silvanus as the actual author, who wrote at Peter's instruction. However, the situation that the letter indirectly describes points to a time after Peter's death. Its language, style, content, and thought-world seem inappropriate to Peter, a Galilean fisherman and missionary to the Jews (Gal 2.9). The sophisticated Greek prose, the lack of references to the life and teaching of the earthly Jesus, the Christological emphasis on the cosmic Christ, and the address to Gentile Christians who had previously lived a sinful, idolatrous life (1.14,18,21; 2.1,9–11,25; 4.3) all point to a later disciple of Peter writing in the name of the revered apostle. Thus most scholars interpret the document as a letter from the last decade of the first century CE, written in Peter's name to support the claim that its teaching represented the apostolic faith.

HISTORICAL CONTEXT

The letter itself claims to be written by a presbyter (elder; 5.1) of the Roman church—the "Babylon" of 5.13 was a common cryptogram for Rome at the end of the first century (cf., e.g., Rev 17.5,9; 18.2,10,21). The references to Silvanus and Mark, both known companions of Paul (1 Thess 1.1; Philem 24), are part of a literary picture that combines elements of Pauline tradition with the figure of Peter. First Peter contains numerous points of contact with Paul's letters (compare, e.g. 2.1–5 and Rom 12.1; 2.7–10 and Rom 9–11; 2.13–14 and Rom 13.1–7). The Pauline letter form itself, including its distinctive structure and expressions, is adopted by 1 Peter (see 1.1–2n.; 4.10n.). The letter thus represents the combination of Pauline and Petrine traditions in the church of Rome at the end of the first century, set forth in a pastoral letter to churches struggling in difficult social situations.

STRUCTURE

The structure of First Peter represents an adaptation of the Pauline letter form: epistolary greeting (1.1–2); thanksgiving (1.3–12); the body of the letter (1.13–5.11) portraying the new identity of the people of God (1.13–2.10), Christian conduct in the given structures of society (2.11–3.12), and responsible suffering in the face of society (3.13–5.11); epistolary conclusion (5.12–14).

CONTENTS AND INTERPRETATION

First Peter is a real letter, a cohesive composition, and not, as some scholars have thought, a baptismal homily to which epistolary elements were added secondarily. The letter addresses a critical situation in the lives of the recipients, who once participated in the social and cultural life of their communities, but since their conversion to Christ are marginalized and abused. The society to which they once belonged now considers them an unwelcome, even dangerous sectarian movement (cf. Acts 28.22—"the sect everywhere spoken against"). While Christians are called to suffer "for the name" (4.15–16), the abuse is mostly verbal (2.22–23; 3.9–12,16). The positive attitude toward the state (2.13–17) suggests that there is as yet no overt government persecution, except perhaps for occasional arbitrary acts by subordinate officials. First Peter offers realistic encouragement and instruction to Christians attempting to live faithfully in such a situation.

The author does not present a programmatic theological essay, but the instructions he gives are based on theological reflection, expressed indirectly by the narrative world the letter projects: God created the world (4.19), God chose an elect people (2.9–10), God sent the Christ who was rejected by humans but exalted by God (2.4), God sent the Spirit and Christian evangelists who established a new people of God and converted the addressees (1.12), and God will send Christ in the near future to conduct the final judgment (1.7,13; 4.7). Christians live their lives in the time between Christ's resurrection and return. The Christological pattern of suffering and rejection is foundational for the ethic 1 Peter commends: just as Christ was misunderstood and suffered unjustly for the sake of others, so Christians are now called to follow "in his steps" (2.21). Just as all Christians are instructed to respect the government authorities (2.13–17), so the most vulnerable Christians, slaves of unbelieving masters and wives of unbelieving husbands, are instructed to fit uncomplainingly into the given structures of society as a testimony to the faith (2.18–3.6). Such behavior may convert the oppressor (3.1–2), but if not it is still following the example set by Christ and will be vindicated soon at the last judgment (4.5–7).

M. Eugene Boring

1 Peter, an apostle of Jesus Christ,
To the exiles of the Dispersion in Pontus, Galatia, Cappadocia, Asia, and Bithynia, [2] who have been chosen and destined by God the Father and sanctified by the Spirit to be obedient to Jesus Christ and to be sprinkled with his blood:

May grace and peace be yours in abundance.

[3] Blessed be the God and Father of our Lord Jesus Christ! By his great mercy he has given us a new birth into a living hope through the resurrection of Jesus Christ from the dead, [4] and into an inheritance that is imperishable, undefiled, and unfading, kept in heaven for you, [5] who are being protected by the power of God through faith for a salvation ready to be revealed in the last time. [6] In this you rejoice,[a] even if now for a little while you have had to suffer various trials, [7] so that the genuineness of your faith—being more precious than gold that, though perishable, is tested by fire—may be found to result in praise and glory and honor when Jesus Christ is revealed. [8] Although you have not seen[b] him, you love him; and even though you do not see him now, you believe in him and rejoice with an indescribable and glorious joy, [9] for you are receiving the outcome of your faith, the salvation of your souls.

[10] Concerning this salvation, the prophets who prophesied of the grace that was to be yours made careful search and inquiry, [11] inquiring about the person or time that the Spirit of Christ within them indicated when it testified in advance to the sufferings destined for Christ and the subsequent glory. [12] It was revealed to them that they were serving not themselves but you, in regard to the things that have now been announced to you through those who brought you good news by the Holy Spirit sent from heaven—things into which angels long to look!

[13] Therefore prepare your minds for action;[c] discipline yourselves; set all your hope on the grace that Jesus Christ will bring you when he is revealed. [14] Like obedient children, do not be conformed to the desires that you formerly had in ignorance. [15] Instead, as

[a] Or *Rejoice in this*
[b] Other ancient authorities read *known*
[c] Gk *gird up the loins of your mind*

1.1–2: Salutation. The author adapts the form used by Paul (see Rom 1.1–7n.). **1:** An *apostle* is an authorized representative. *Exiles of the Dispersion,* applying images of Israel to Christians (see Jas 1.1n.). *Pontus . . . Bithynia,* Roman provinces in Asia Minor. **2:** A proto-Trinitarian formula. *Obedience* and being *sprinkled with his blood* are covenant language (see Ex 24.3–8).

1.3–12: Thanksgiving. As in 2 Cor 1.3 and Eph 1.3, the customary thanksgiving (see Rom 1.8–15n.) becomes a doxological expression of praise that constitutes the theological basis for the imperatives to follow. **3:** *Hope* expresses the present confidence in the reality of future redemption founded on the *resurrection of Jesus Christ.* *New birth* is related to baptism (see 1.23; 2.2; 3.20–22; John 3.3–5). **5:** *Salvation ready to be revealed* at the end time. The present experience has a future consummation. The believer does not go "up" to heaven, but "forward" to the future reward to be revealed at the last time. **12:** The readers' Christian lives, though beset with difficulties (1.6; 2.19–24; 3.14–15; 4.12–19; 5.10) represent the climax of God's plan for the ages, which even the prophets and the angels could only long to share.

1.13–5.11: Body of the letter, a unified whole, although incorporating elements of earlier biblical and Christian tradition.

1.13–2.10: The new identity as the elect and holy people of God. The preceding indicative statements of God's mighty acts lead to imperatives for the Christian life. **1.13:** In the Greek text, the first imperative in the

he who called you is holy, be holy yourselves in all your conduct; [16] for it is written, "You shall be holy, for I am holy."

[17] If you invoke as Father the one who judges all people impartially according to their deeds, live in reverent fear during the time of your exile. [18] You know that you were ransomed from the futile ways inherited from your ancestors, not with perishable things like silver or gold, [19] but with the precious blood of Christ, like that of a lamb without defect or blemish. [20] He was destined before the foundation of the world, but was revealed at the end of the ages for your sake. [21] Through him you have come to trust in God, who raised him from the dead and gave him glory, so that your faith and hope are set on God.

[22] Now that you have purified your souls by your obedience to the truth[a] so that you have genuine mutual love, love one another deeply[b] from the heart.[c] [23] You have been born anew, not of perishable but of imperishable seed, through the living and enduring word of God.[d] [24] For

"All flesh is like grass
    and all its glory like the flower of grass.
The grass withers,
    and the flower falls,
[25] but the word of the Lord endures
    forever."

That word is the good news that was announced to you.

2 Rid yourselves, therefore, of all malice, and all guile, insincerity, envy, and all slander. [2] Like newborn infants, long for the pure, spiritual milk, so that by it you may grow into salvation— [3] if indeed you have tasted that the Lord is good.

[4] Come to him, a living stone, though rejected by mortals yet chosen and precious in God's sight, and [5] like living stones, let yourselves be built[e] into a spiritual house, to be a holy priesthood, to offer spiritual sacrifices acceptable to God through Jesus Christ. [6] For it stands in scripture:

"See, I am laying in Zion a stone,
    a cornerstone chosen and precious;
and whoever believes in him[f] will not be
    put to shame."

[7] To you then who believe, he is precious; but for those who do not believe,

"The stone that the builders rejected
    has become the very head of the corner,"

[8] and

"A stone that makes them stumble,
    and a rock that makes them fall."

They stumble because they disobey the word, as they were destined to do.

[9] But you are a chosen race, a royal priesthood, a holy nation, God's own people,[g] in order that you may proclaim the mighty acts of him who called you out of darkness into his marvelous light.

[10] Once you were not a people,
    but now you are God's people;
once you had not received mercy,
    but now you have received mercy.

[11] Beloved, I urge you as aliens and exiles to abstain from the desires of the flesh that

a Other ancient authorities add *through the Spirit*
b Or *constantly*
c Other ancient authorities read *a pure heart*
d Or *through the word of the living and enduring God*
e Or *you yourselves are being built*
f Or *it*
g Gk *a people for his possession*

letter is the command to *hope* for Christ's triumphal appearance. **15:** The second imperative to *be holy* means to live a life set apart for God's service, though in the midst of the world. **16:** Quoting Lev 11.44–45; 19.2; 20.7. **17:** The third imperative is to *live* in reverent fear of God rather than of the oppressive culture (cf. 2.17; 3.14). **19:** *Lamb without . . . blemish*, see Ex 12.5; Lev 23.12; Num 6.14; etc. **21:** Christian faith is theocentric, in God who has acted definitively in Christ. **22:** The fourth imperative is the command of *love*, unselfish caring for others (see Mt 22.34–40; Rom 13.8–10; 1 Cor 13). **24–25:** Isa 40.6–8. **2.1–10:** The fifth imperative is to *long for* the means of spiritual nourishment so that they may *grow* (2.2). After the new birth comes nurture that leads to maturity. **3:** Ps 34.8 **4:** Ps 118.22; Isa 28.16; Mt 21.42. **5–8:** The imagery shifts from birth and growth to the construction of a *spiritual house* (temple) and then to a *holy priesthood*. The images of the Christian life are communal rather than individualistic. **6:** Isa 28.16 **7:** Ps 118.22 **8:** Isa 8.14–15. **9–10:** Hos 2.23; Ex 19.6. *Chosen race . . . royal priesthood . . . holy nation . . . God's own people*, biblical language for Israel is applied to the readers, who were formerly Gentiles (1.18).

wage war against the soul. [12] Conduct your-selves honorably among the Gentiles, so that, though they malign you as evildoers, they may see your honorable deeds and glorify God when he comes to judge.[a]

[13] For the Lord's sake accept the author-ity of every human institution,[b] whether of the emperor as supreme, [14] or of gover-nors, as sent by him to punish those who do wrong and to praise those who do right. [15] For it is God's will that by doing right you should silence the ignorance of the foolish. [16] As servants[c] of God, live as free people, yet do not use your freedom as a pretext for evil. [17] Honor everyone. Love the family of believers.[d] Fear God. Honor the emperor.

[18] Slaves, accept the authority of your mas-ters with all deference, not only those who are kind and gentle but also those who are harsh. [19] For it is a credit to you if, being aware of God, you endure pain while suffering un-justly. [20] If you endure when you are beaten for doing wrong, what credit is that? But if you endure when you do right and suffer for it, you have God's approval. [21] For to this you have been called, because Christ also suffered for you, leaving you an example, so that you should follow in his steps.

[22] "He committed no sin,
   and no deceit was found in his mouth."
[23] When he was abused, he did not return abuse; when he suffered, he did not threaten; but he entrusted himself to the one who judges justly. [24] He himself bore our sins in his body on the cross,[e] so that, free from sins, we might live for righteousness; by his wounds[f] you have been healed. [25] For you were going astray like sheep, but now you have returned to the shepherd and guardian of your souls.

3 Wives, in the same way, accept the author-ity of your husbands, so that, even if some of them do not obey the word, they may be won over without a word by their wives' con-duct, [2] when they see the purity and reverence of your lives. [3] Do not adorn yourselves out-wardly by braiding your hair, and by wearing gold ornaments or fine clothing; [4] rather, let your adornment be the inner self with the last-ing beauty of a gentle and quiet spirit, which is very precious in God's sight. [5] It was in this way long ago that the holy women who hoped in God used to adorn themselves by accepting the authority of their husbands. [6] Thus Sarah obeyed Abraham and called him lord. You have become her daughters as long as you do what is good and never let fears alarm you.

[7] Husbands, in the same way, show consid-eration for your wives in your life together, paying honor to the woman as the weaker sex,[g] since they too are also heirs of the gra-cious gift of life—so that nothing may hinder your prayers.

[8] Finally, all of you, have unity of spirit, sympathy, love for one another, a tender heart, and a humble mind. [9] Do not repay evil for evil or abuse for abuse; but, on the contrary, repay with a blessing. It is for this that you were called—that you might inherit a blessing. [10] For

"Those who desire life
   and desire to see good days,

a   Gk *God on the day of visitation*
b   Or *every institution ordained for human beings*
c   Gk *slaves*
d   Gk *Love the brotherhood*
e   Or *carried up our sins in his body to the tree*
f   Gk *bruise*
g   Gk *vessel*

2.11–3.12: Christian existence and conduct in society. Cf. Col 3.18–4.1; Eph 5.22–6.9; Titus 2.1–10; 1 Tim 2–3; 5.1–3. The Roman empire, the institution of slavery, and the patriarchal family are accepted as the present order of things that is soon to pass away (see 1.17; 2.11; 4.7). **2.11–12:** Christian conduct within social structures is to be a testimony to others. **13–17:** Instructions to all on the proper attitude to God, the state, and each other. *Gover-nors,* of provinces of the Roman empire. **17:** Cf. Rom 13.7. **18–25:** Instructions to slaves, leading to more general comments addressed to a wider audience (cf. 3.8–12n.). Though resembling the typical household codes of Hellenistic moralists, the author's instruction is based on the example of Christ who suffered unjustly, in words that reflect the suffering servant of Isa 53.5–12. **22:** Isa 53.9. **3.1–7:** Instructions to wives and husbands. **1:** Un-believing husbands may be converted without preaching or argument by the Christian example of their wives; cf. 1 Cor 7.12–16. **6:** See Gen 18.12 (where NRSV translates the word for "lord" as "husband"). **8–12:** Concluding instructions to all. The more vulnerable members of the church, slaves and wives, are examples of the conduct

let them keep their tongues from evil
  and their lips from speaking deceit;
[11] let them turn away from evil and do good;
  let them seek peace and pursue it.
[12] For the eyes of the Lord are on the
  righteous,
  and his ears are open to their prayer.
But the face of the Lord is against those
  who do evil."

[13] Now who will harm you if you are eager to do what is good? [14] But even if you do suffer for doing what is right, you are blessed. Do not fear what they fear,[a] and do not be intimidated, [15] but in your hearts sanctify Christ as Lord. Always be ready to make your defense to anyone who demands from you an accounting for the hope that is in you; [16] yet do it with gentleness and reverence.[b] Keep your conscience clear, so that, when you are maligned, those who abuse you for your good conduct in Christ may be put to shame. [17] For it is better to suffer for doing good, if suffering should be God's will, than to suffer for doing evil. [18] For Christ also suffered[c] for sins once for all, the righteous for the unrighteous, in order to bring you[d] to God. He was put to death in the flesh, but made alive in the spirit, [19] in which also he went and made a proclamation to the spirits in prison, [20] who in former times did not obey, when God waited patiently in the days of Noah, during the building of the ark, in which a few, that is, eight persons, were saved through water. [21] And baptism, which this prefigured, now saves you—not as a removal of dirt from the body, but as an appeal to God for[e] a good conscience, through the resurrection

of Jesus Christ, [22] who has gone into heaven and is at the right hand of God, with angels, authorities, and powers made subject to him.

4 Since therefore Christ suffered in the flesh,[f] arm yourselves also with the same intention (for whoever has suffered in the flesh has finished with sin), [2] so as to live for the rest of your earthly life[g] no longer by human desires but by the will of God. [3] You have already spent enough time in doing what the Gentiles like to do, living in licentiousness, passions, drunkenness, revels, carousing, and lawless idolatry. [4] They are surprised that you no longer join them in the same excesses of dissipation, and so they blaspheme.[h] [5] But they will have to give an accounting to him who stands ready to judge the living and the dead. [6] For this is the reason the gospel was proclaimed even to the dead, so that, though they had been judged in the flesh as everyone is judged, they might live in the spirit as God does.

[7] The end of all things is near;[i] therefore be serious and discipline yourselves for the sake of your prayers. [8] Above all, maintain constant love for one another, for love covers a mul-

a Gk *their fear*
b Or *respect*
c Other ancient authorities read *died*
d Other ancient authorities read *us*
e Or *a pledge to God from*
f Other ancient authorities add *for us*; others, *for you*
g Gk *rest of the time in the flesh*
h Or *they malign you*
i Or *is at hand*

required of the whole church, which is in a vulnerable position in a hostile society. **10–12:** Ps 34.12–16.

  3.13–5.11: Responsible suffering in the face of hostility.

  3.13–17: Suffering for doing good (= doing right). Following the example of Christ's unjust suffering does not mean passivity but actively doing good. **15:** In word as well as action, Christians are to be able to give a *defense* (Gk "apologia") for the Christian faith, here summarized as "hope" (1.2,13,21).

  3.18–22: Christological grounding. 18: *Put to death in the flesh* means that Jesus really died in the human sphere; *made alive in the spirit* does not refer to a "part" of Christ that survived death, but that God raised Christ to a new life in the divine realm (cf. 1.3; 2.4; 3.21–22). **19–20:** The precise meaning of this fragment of an ancient Christological picture is unclear, but probably refers to Christ's preaching to the imprisoned evil spirits after his resurrection to announce his own victory (cf. Gen 6.1–4 as interpreted in *1 Enoch* 10.4–6). The picture is unrelated to 4.6 and the "descent to the world of the dead" of the Apostles' Creed. **20:** *Noah*, see Gen 6–8. *Eight persons*, Noah and his wife, and his three sons and their wives. **22:** See Eph 1.20; Heb 1:3.

  4.1–6: Application to the Christian life. 3: As in 2.9–10, the church is the continuing people of God, and outsiders are *Gentiles*. **6:** The *dead* are probably Christians who heard the gospel while they were alive.

  4.7–11: Eschatological exhortation. 9: Cf. Heb 13.2; 3 Jn 5–8. **10:** *Gift* is the distinctive Pauline word "cha-

titude of sins. [9] Be hospitable to one another without complaining. [10] Like good stewards of the manifold grace of God, serve one another with whatever gift each of you has received. [11] Whoever speaks must do so as one speaking the very words of God; whoever serves must do so with the strength that God supplies, so that God may be glorified in all things through Jesus Christ. To him belong the glory and the power forever and ever. Amen.

[12] Beloved, do not be surprised at the fiery ordeal that is taking place among you to test you, as though something strange were happening to you. [13] But rejoice insofar as you are sharing Christ's sufferings, so that you may also be glad and shout for joy when his glory is revealed. [14] If you are reviled for the name of Christ, you are blessed, because the spirit of glory,[a] which is the Spirit of God, is resting on you.[b] [15] But let none of you suffer as a murderer, a thief, a criminal, or even as a mischief maker. [16] Yet if any of you suffers as a Christian, do not consider it a disgrace, but glorify God because you bear this name. [17] For the time has come for judgment to begin with the household of God; if it begins with us, what will be the end for those who do not obey the gospel of God? [18] And

"If it is hard for the righteous to be saved,
what will become of the ungodly and
the sinners?"

[19] Therefore, let those suffering in accordance with God's will entrust themselves to a faithful Creator, while continuing to do good.

5 Now as an elder myself and a witness of the sufferings of Christ, as well as one who shares in the glory to be revealed, I exhort the elders among you [2] to tend the flock of God that is in your charge, exercising the oversight,[c] not under compulsion but willingly, as God would have you do it[d]—not for sordid gain but eagerly. [3] Do not lord it over those in your charge, but be examples to the flock. [4] And when the chief shepherd appears, you will win the crown of glory that never fades away. [5] In the same way, you who are younger must accept the authority of the elders.[e] And all of you must clothe yourselves with humility in your dealings with one another, for

"God opposes the proud,
but gives grace to the humble."

[6] Humble yourselves therefore under the mighty hand of God, so that he may exalt you in due time. [7] Cast all your anxiety on him, because he cares for you. [8] Discipline yourselves, keep alert.[f] Like a roaring lion your adversary the devil prowls around, looking for someone to devour. [9] Resist him, steadfast in your faith, for you know that your brothers and sisters[g] in all the world are undergoing the same kinds of suffering. [10] And after you have suffered for a little while, the God of all grace, who has called you to his eternal glory in Christ, will himself restore, support, strengthen, and establish you. [11] To him be the power forever and ever. Amen.

[12] Through Silvanus, whom I consider a faithful brother, I have written this short letter to encourage you and to testify that this is the true grace of God. Stand fast in it. [13] Your sister church[h] in Babylon, chosen together with you, sends you greetings; and so does my son Mark. [14] Greet one another with a kiss of love.

Peace to all of you who are in Christ.[i]

---

a   Other ancient authorities add *and of power*
b   Other ancient authorities add *On their part he is blasphemed, but on your part he is glorified*
c   Other ancient authorities lack *exercising the oversight*
d   Other ancient authorities lack *as God would have you do it*
e   Or *of those who are older*
f   Or *be vigilant*
g   Gk *your brotherhood*
h   Gk *She who is*
i   Other ancient authorities add *Amen*

---

risma," found outside the Pauline tradition only here in the New Testament.

4.12–19: Suffering in joy and hope. Suffering is to be a witness to the truth of the faith, not the result of one's own antisocial behavior. *Fiery ordeal* refers to persecutions (1.6–7). On the name *Christian*, cf. Acts 11.26; 26.28. **18:** Prov 11.31.

5.1–11: Concluding exhortation. 1: *Elders*, church officials (Acts 14.23; 20.17–38; Jas 5.14; 2 Jn 1; 3 Jn 1). **5:** Prov 3.34.

5.12–14: Conclusion of the Letter. *Silvanus* and *Mark* were companions of Paul (Acts 15.22; 2 Cor 1.19; Philem 24). *Babylon* was a cryptic name for Rome (Rev 17.1).

THE SECOND LETTER OF PETER

NAME, AUTHORSHIP, AND DATE

Like 1 Peter, 2 Peter is named for its supposed author, Simon Peter, the most prominent figure among the twelve apostles of Jesus. But there is little historical or literary evidence to connect the author of this letter either to Simon Peter or to the author of 1 Peter. The author wrote in the name of Peter, not to transmit a particular form of tradition associated with him, but to defend the common apostolic tradition of the church against a challenge to that tradition. Such pseudepigraphical attribution is frequent in the Bible and in other ancient literatures. The writer takes pains to appeal to the teaching of the apostles (3.2), explicitly including Paul's letters as apostolic (3.15–16). Second Peter was likely written from Rome at the end of the first century CE or the beginning of the second, and is probably the latest book of the New Testament.

CANONICAL STATUS

The place of this letter among the Catholic Epistles (those addressed to all Christians rather than to specific churches or individuals) was contested in the early church, and it was excluded from Syriac translations until the fourth century CE, when it became widely accepted. Its canonicity was again challenged during the Reformation.

LITERARY FORM AND BACKGROUND

Second Peter has the typical form of a letter (see p. 1973), except that it lacks the customary final greeting. It also has characteristics of a testament, the last words of advice and warning given by a patriarch to his children before his death; see especially 1.12–14, and compare Paul's final address to the elders of the church in Ephesus (Acts 20.17–35). Testaments are usually a third-person narrative, and conclude with an account of the patriarch's death; 2 Peter, however, is presented as a first-person, written delivery of the final words of Peter to all who share his faith (1.1). The writer uses a rhetorical style, characterized by grandiose language, and draws on a rich cultural heritage, including the Hebrew Bible, Jewish exegetical traditions, Hellenistic philosophical speculation, traditions about Jesus, a collection of Paul's letters, and the letter of Jude.

Second Peter has a direct literary relationship to the letter of Jude. Its author freely borrowed the language and content of the letter to Jude, as these parallels show:

2 Peter	Jude
2.1	4
2.4	6
2.6	7
2.10a	7–8
2.10b–11	8–9
2.12	10
2.13	12
2.15	11
2.17	12–13, 16
3.2	17
3.3	18

CONTENTS AND INTERPRETATION

Second Peter is characterized by an apocalyptic vision of this world as corrupt—because of lust (1.4)—and bound for destruction. It urges the reader to escape by means of the knowledge of Christ and of God and to pursue virtues based on the all-sufficient promises and gifts of God and achieved through knowledge and remembering (1.1–11). The goal is to participate in the divine nature (1.4) and to enter the eternal kingdom (1.11).

These exhortations are based on the authority of Peter's final testament (1.12–15); the heavenly voice (1.16–18); and scripture (1.19–21). Chapter 2 is a warning against false teachers whose condemnation is contrasted with the salvation of the righteous. The writer's opponents are characterized using language drawn from the letter of Jude and from polemical arguments against Epicurean philosophy. One cannot infer details about the identity of the "false teachers" (2.1) beyond noting that the writer found appropriate ammunition in these two sources.

Chapter 3 warns against denying the future coming of the Lord and twisting the meaning of Paul's letters. As in earlier Jewish traditions, the flood in the time of Noah is seen as an earlier, lesser destruction of the earth which anticipated the ultimate final destruction. As the flood was followed by a restoration of life on earth, so there will be "new heavens and a new earth, where righteousness is at home" (3.13). Those who await these events should abstain from the defilement of the world, avoid being led astray by the error of the lawless, and grow in grace and knowledge.

Patrick A. Tiller

1 Simeon[a] Peter, a servant[b] and apostle of Jesus Christ,

To those who have received a faith as precious as ours through the righteousness of our God and Savior Jesus Christ:[c]

[2] May grace and peace be yours in abundance in the knowledge of God and of Jesus our Lord.

[3] His divine power has given us everything needed for life and godliness, through the knowledge of him who called us by[d] his own glory and goodness. [4] Thus he has given us, through these things, his precious and very great promises, so that through them you may escape from the corruption that is in the world because of lust, and may become participants of the divine nature. [5] For this very reason, you must make every effort to support your faith with goodness, and goodness with knowledge, [6] and knowledge with self-control, and self-control with endurance, and endurance with godliness, [7] and godliness with mutual[e] affection, and mutual[e] affection with love. [8] For if these things are yours and are increasing among you,

they keep you from being ineffective and unfruitful in the knowledge of our Lord Jesus Christ. [9] For anyone who lacks these things is short-sighted and blind, and is forgetful of the cleansing of past sins. [10] Therefore, brothers and sisters,[f] be all the more eager to confirm your call and election, for if you do this, you will never stumble. [11] For in this way, entry into the eternal kingdom of our Lord and Savior Jesus Christ will be richly provided for you.

[12] Therefore I intend to keep on reminding you of these things, though you know them already and are established in the truth that has come to you. [13] I think it right, as long as I am in this body,[g] to refresh your memory,

a   Other ancient authorities read *Simon*
b   Gk *slave*
c   Or *of our God and the Savior Jesus Christ*
d   Other ancient authorities read *through*
e   Gk *brotherly*
f   Gk *brothers*
g   Gk *tent*

1.1–2: Salutation, see Rom 1.1–7n. 1: *Simeon* is Peter's Hebrew name, which more frequently occurs as Simon (e.g., Mt 4.18).

1.3–11: Opening exhortation. The major themes of the letter are introduced: *knowledge* of God and of Jesus, *effort* (variously translated as "be eager," "make every effort," or "strive"), stability (*confirm*), *godliness*, *corruption*, *lust*, and remembering. The readers should exchange this corrupt world (1.4; cf. 2.20) for *the eternal kingdom* (1.11) by means of the *knowledge* of God (1.3), the *promises* of God (1.4), and earnest moral striving (1.5–7). 4: *The divine nature* refers primarily to immortality, which is the opposite of *corruption*.

1.12–21: Three solemn appeals. The writer uses Peter's final words before his death, the Transfiguration of Jesus, and prophetic scripture to reinforce the reliability of the message. 12–15: The reference to Peter's death transforms the letter into a kind of testament in which a dying person gives ethical advice and warnings to his

¹⁴ since I know that my death[a] will come soon, as indeed our Lord Jesus Christ has made clear to me. ¹⁵ And I will make every effort so that after my departure you may be able at any time to recall these things.

¹⁶ For we did not follow cleverly devised myths when we made known to you the power and coming of our Lord Jesus Christ, but we had been eyewitnesses of his majesty. ¹⁷ For he received honor and glory from God the Father when that voice was conveyed to him by the Majestic Glory, saying, "This is my Son, my Beloved,[b] with whom I am well pleased." ¹⁸ We ourselves heard this voice come from heaven, while we were with him on the holy mountain.

¹⁹ So we have the prophetic message more fully confirmed. You will do well to be attentive to this as to a lamp shining in a dark place, until the day dawns and the morning star rises in your hearts. ²⁰ First of all you must understand this, that no prophecy of scripture is a matter of one's own interpretation, ²¹ because no prophecy ever came by human will, but men and women moved by the Holy Spirit spoke from God.[c]

2 But false prophets also arose among the people, just as there will be false teachers among you, who will secretly bring in destructive opinions. They will even deny the Master who bought them—bringing swift destruction on themselves. ² Even so, many will follow their licentious ways, and because of these teachers[d] the way of truth will be maligned. ³ And in their greed they will exploit you with deceptive words. Their condemnation, pronounced against them long ago, has not been idle, and their destruction is not asleep.

⁴ For if God did not spare the angels when they sinned, but cast them into hell[e] and committed them to chains[f] of deepest darkness to be kept until the judgment; ⁵ and if he did not spare the ancient world, even though he saved Noah, a herald of righteousness, with seven others, when he brought a flood on a world of the ungodly; ⁶ and if by turning the cities of Sodom and Gomorrah to ashes he condemned them to extinction[g] and made them an example of what is coming to the ungodly;[h] ⁷ and if he rescued Lot, a righteous man greatly distressed by the licentiousness of the lawless ⁸ (for that righteous man, living among them day after day, was tormented in his righteous soul by their lawless deeds that he saw and heard), ⁹ then the Lord knows how to rescue the godly from trial, and to keep the unrighteous under punishment until the day of judgment ¹⁰ —especially those

a Gk *the putting off of my tent*
b Other ancient authorities read *my beloved Son*
c Other ancient authorities read *but moved by the Holy Spirit saints of God spoke*
d Gk *because of them*
e Gk *Tartaros*
f Other ancient authorities read *pits*
g Other ancient authorities lack *to extinction*
h Other ancient authorities read *an example to those who were to be ungodly*

survivors or followers. **16–18:** Peter's presence at the Transfiguration of Jesus (Mt 17.1–8; Mk 9.2–8; Lk 9.28–36) makes him an *eyewitness* of the voice from heaven, which confirms the apostles' statements about Christ's *power and coming*. The wording of the heavenly voice differs slightly from that in the Gospels; the writer may be relying on oral tradition rather than a written gospel. **19:** *Morning star,* see Rev 2.28; 22.16 for similar language.

2.1–22: Warnings against false teachers. Beginning in 2.1 the author borrows language from the letter of Jude with extensive modifications (see p. 2132). The ethical condemnations are standard polemical attacks all adapted from Jude: greed, lack of moral restraint, deception (2.2–3), and disregard for authority (2.10). **1:** They *deny the Master* most likely by their immoral conduct (2.2,10,14,18). Jesus' death is understood as the purchase price for which he *bought* his followers as one buys a slave (either for freedom or for service). **4–10a:** Jude's examples of judgment (cf. Sir 16.6–17) are rearranged, abbreviated, and supplemented to remove Jude's concern with falling from grace, to follow the order of the biblical events, and to introduce a balanced emphasis on judgment and salvation. **4:** The *angels* who *sinned* are probably the "sons of God" of Gen 6.2 as popularized by the books of Enoch (see Jude 14–16n.). The allusive use of the noncanonical Enoch traditions contrasts with Jude's explicit quotation from them. *Tartaros* (*hell*) is the prison of the Titans of Greek myth. **5:** Gen 6.6–8; 8.18. **6:** Gen 19.24; cf. 3 Macc 2.5. **7:** Gen 19.16,29. **10b–11:** The *authority* that they despise may be either God's authority or angelic authorities. The *glorious ones* are probably angelic dignitaries. Jude's example of Michael's dispute with the devil (see Jude 9n.) is transformed into an example of angels, who refrain from bringing a *slanderous*

who indulge their flesh in depraved lust, and who despise authority.

Bold and willful, they are not afraid to slander the glorious ones,[a] [11] whereas angels, though greater in might and power, do not bring against them a slanderous judgment from the Lord.[b] [12] These people, however, are like irrational animals, mere creatures of instinct, born to be caught and killed. They slander what they do not understand, and when those creatures are destroyed,[c] they also will be destroyed, [13] suffering[d] the penalty for doing wrong. They count it a pleasure to revel in the daytime. They are blots and blemishes, reveling in their dissipation[e] while they feast with you. [14] They have eyes full of adultery, insatiable for sin. They entice unsteady souls. They have hearts trained in greed. Accursed children! [15] They have left the straight road and have gone astray, following the road of Balaam son of Bosor,[f] who loved the wages of doing wrong, [16] but was rebuked for his own transgression; a speechless donkey spoke with a human voice and restrained the prophet's madness.

[17] These are waterless springs and mists driven by a storm; for them the deepest darkness has been reserved. [18] For they speak bombastic nonsense, and with licentious desires of the flesh they entice people who have just[g] escaped from those who live in error. [19] They promise them freedom, but they themselves are slaves of corruption; for people are slaves to whatever masters them. [20] For if, after they have escaped the defilements of the world through the knowledge of our Lord and Savior Jesus Christ, they are again entangled in them and over-

powered, the last state has become worse for them than the first. [21] For it would have been better for them never to have known the way of righteousness than, after knowing it, to turn back from the holy commandment that was passed on to them. [22] It has happened to them according to the true proverb,

"The dog turns back to its own vomit," and,

"The sow is washed only to wallow in the mud."

3 This is now, beloved, the second letter I am writing to you; in them I am trying to arouse your sincere intention by reminding you [2] that you should remember the words spoken in the past by the holy prophets, and the commandment of the Lord and Savior spoken through your apostles. [3] First of all you must understand this, that in the last days scoffers will come, scoffing and indulging their own lusts [4] and saying, "Where is the promise of his coming? For ever since our ancestors died,[h] all things continue as they were from the beginning of creation!" [5] They deliberately ignore this fact, that by the word of God heavens existed long ago and an earth

a   Or *angels*; Gk *glories*
b   Other ancient authorities read *before the Lord*; others lack the phrase
c   Gk *in their destruction*
d   Other ancient authorities read *receiving*
e   Other ancient authorities read *love-feasts*
f   Other ancient authorities read *Beor*
g   Other ancient authorities read *actually*
h   Gk *our fathers fell asleep*

judgment from (or *before*) *the Lord*. 15–16: The account of Balaam's sin (see Num 22.7,21–35), as in Jude, is taken directly from postbiblical Jewish traditions, which uniformly make Balaam a greedy villain. 17–18: The seemingly excessive piling up of accusations functions as the necessary and proportionate response to the dangers inherent in their false teachings. 19: *Slaves of corruption,* compare Rom 6.6,16; 8.21; John 8.34. 21: Mt 12.45; Lk 11.26. 22: The first quotation is from Prov 26.11; the second is from an unknown source..

3.1–13: A defense of the expectation of the coming of Christ. The most troublesome of the false teachings is that the present world will continue eternally. These scoffers were predicted long ago by the prophets and by the Lord. Furthermore, from God's point of view, the delay is not long at all, and it is motivated by God's patience and desire for repentance. 3: *Indulging their own lusts,* if there is no judgment, then one may do as one pleases. 5–13: The flood (Gen 6–8) destroyed the first world and made way for the present one. In the same way, fire will destroy the present world, and a third world will replace it. The destruction of the earth by fire, a concept well known in Jewish tradition, is here described in the language of Stoic philosophical speculation. 4: *Our ancestors* are probably the biblical patriarchs since Adam. 5: *They deliberately ignore* in contrast to the repeated exhortation to *remember* (1.9,12–15; 3.1–2,8). On creation by God's *word,* and an original watery state, see Gen

was formed out of water and by means of water, [6] through which the world of that time was deluged with water and perished. [7] But by the same word the present heavens and earth have been reserved for fire, being kept until the day of judgment and destruction of the godless.

[8] But do not ignore this one fact, beloved, that with the Lord one day is like a thousand years, and a thousand years are like one day. [9] The Lord is not slow about his promise, as some think of slowness, but is patient with you,[a] not wanting any to perish, but all to come to repentance. [10] But the day of the Lord will come like a thief, and then the heavens will pass away with a loud noise, and the elements will be dissolved with fire, and the earth and everything that is done on it will be disclosed.[b]

[11] Since all these things are to be dissolved in this way, what sort of persons ought you to be in leading lives of holiness and godliness, [12] waiting for and hastening[c] the coming of the day of God, because of which the heavens will be set ablaze and dissolved, and the elements will melt with fire? [13] But, in accordance with his promise, we wait for new heavens and a new earth, where righteousness is at home.

[14] Therefore, beloved, while you are waiting for these things, strive to be found by him at peace, without spot or blemish; [15] and regard the patience of our Lord as salvation. So also our beloved brother Paul wrote to you according to the wisdom given him, [16] speaking of this as he does in all his letters. There are some things in them hard to understand, which the ignorant and unstable twist to their own destruction, as they do the other scriptures. [17] You therefore, beloved, since you are forewarned, beware that you are not carried away with the error of the lawless and lose your own stability. [18] But grow in the grace and knowledge of our Lord and Savior Jesus Christ. To him be the glory both now and to the day of eternity. Amen.[d]

a   Other ancient authorities read *on your account*
b   Other ancient authorities read *will be burned up*
c   Or *earnestly desiring*
d   Other ancient authorities lack *Amen*

1.2,6–10; Ps 33.6–7. 6: Gen 7.11. 8: Ps 90.4. 10: *Day of the Lord,* Am 5.18–20; Joel 2.2–32. *Like a thief* in the night, 1 Thess 5.2; Mt 24.43–44; Lk 12.39–40. The *elements* (see also v. 12) are probably the heavenly bodies (possibly including the earth as well). 13: Isa 65.17; 66.22; Rev 21.1.

3.14–17: Final exhortation. One ought to live blamelessly and take advantage of the opportunity to repent. 14–16: Paul also taught that the delay of judgment is an opportunity to strive for moral purity and to repent (Rom 2.4; 9.22). Any other understanding of Paul is a destructive misinterpretation. The use of the term "scriptures" does not necessarily imply a concept of canonicity. 18: Doxology. Cf. Rom 16.25; Eph 3.20–21; Phil 4.20; 1 Tim 1.17; 2 Tim 4.18; Heb 13.21; 1 Pet 5.11; Jude 24–25; Rev 5.13.

THE FIRST LETTER OF JOHN

NAME

Ancient manuscripts title this work "the first letter of John" even though its literary form is not that of an ancient letter (see pp. 1973-74). Its author provides no greeting or conclusion in which he identifies himself or its recipients. Yet repeated references to writing (1.4; 2.1,7–8,12–14,21,26) and the two letters attributed to the same author (2–3 John) provided early scribes with the title.

CANONICAL STATUS AND AUTHORSHIP

First John opens with echoes of the prologue to the Gospel of John (compare 1.1–4 and Jn 1.1–18) and focuses its ethical teaching on the love command, which Jesus gives his disciples at the Last Supper in the Gospel (Jn 13.31–35; 1 Jn 3.11–17,23; 4.7–21). It came into the Christian canon as an authoritative interpretation of the Gospel.

The anonymous voice of 1 John was identified with the author of the Fourth Gospel by the end of the second century CE (Eusebius, *Hist. eccl.* iii.39.17; *Muratorian Canon*, lines 26–31; Irenaeus, *Adv. Haer.* 3.16.5). Since the Gospel was attributed to the apostle John, the son of Zebedee, early Christians concluded that he had composed 1 John near the end of his long life (Jn 21.22–23). Modern scholars have a more complex view of the development of the Johannine community and its writings. The opening verses of 1 John employ a first person plural "we" as witnesses to the truth revealed in Jesus (1.1–4). That "we" probably refers to a circle of teachers faithful to the apostolic testimony of the Beloved Disciple and evangelist. A prominent member of that group composed this introduction.

DATE AND HISTORICAL CONTEXT

The earliest allusions to 1 John occur in the mid-second century CE (Polycarp, *To the Philippians* 6.3; 7.1; compare 1 Jn 4.2–3; also used by Papias according to Eusebius, *Hist. eccl.* iii. 36,1–2). Irenaeus (ca. 180 CE) cites 1 John explicitly. The date of 1 John depends upon its relationship to the Gospel of John. Its author employs language, images, and themes evocative of the Gospel but does not cite it as a text. Therefore it is possible to imagine that the Gospel as we know it had not yet taken its final form when 1 John was written. A date around 100 CE is plausible. Other scholars focus on the fact that 1 John appears less theologically developed than the Gospel in some respects. Attributes such as "light" and "life" are associated with God rather than the Son. Concern for forgiveness of sin and salvation in the final judgment has not been transformed by the Gospel's picture of the presence of eternal life in the believer. They conclude that 1 John should be dated earlier than the Gospel.

Although theological differences make 1 John appear to be earlier, the author's concerns suggest a historical context later than that of the Gospel. Jews and their hostility to faith in Jesus as Son of God, a major element in the Gospel (see Jn 9.13–41; 10.31–39), have disappeared from the discussion. So have references to the Hebrew Bible. Instead, the community has been shaken by schism (1 Jn 2.18–19). Those who have departed from the fellowship are said to be denying the reality of Jesus' coming in the flesh (1.1–4; 4.1–3) and the saving significance of the death ("blood") of Jesus (5.6). In addition, 1 John describes a communal discipline of prayer for members who sin (5.16–17). Therefore 1 John speaks to a historical setting later than the Gospel. A community that had been unified through a period of persecution by Jewish authorities has split over interpretation of Jesus and salvation. Its author seeks to reassure readers that they possess the truth revealed through Jesus.

LITERARY HISTORY

The rhetorical power of 1 John stems from its appeals to received tradition shared by the author and his readers. The phrase "what was from the beginning" (1.1) not only imitates the Gospel opening (Jn 1.1) but the teaching that follows (2.7,21,24; 3.11). Since 1 John does not speak to specific details of the readers' situation as letters usually do, or develop a sustained theological argument as Paul does in his letters, some scholars suggest that it was assembled from earlier written traditions. Often a core that concludes at 2.29 is thought to have been supplemented with the homiletic reflections on love and polemic against dissidents in the remaining chapters. First John 5.13 concludes the work in a fashion similar to the Gospel. Therefore 1 John 5.14–21 appear to be an epilogue added to the completed work.

STRUCTURE AND CONTENTS

First John lacks a clearly defined structure that carries its argument from the opening witness to the shared tradition (1.1–4) to the concluding statement of purpose (5.13) and appended remarks (5.14–21). Fellowship with the author and other Johannine witnesses requires belief in the teachings presented, which alternate between truths about the coming of Jesus and ethical exhortation focused on holiness and love within the community. Both aspects of the tradition are threatened by dissidents, who are characterized as "antichrists" emblematic of the evils predicted for the last days (4.1–6). The author often concludes one reflection and begins the next in the same sentence, so it is not entirely clear how to divide the units that comprise the work even when looking at verbal clues such as "I am writing" or "this is the message" or direct address to the readers such as "little children" or "beloved." The outline in the annotations is based on thematic shifts. Another proposal finds a repetition of the macrostructure of the Gospel in 1 John: prologue (1.1–4; Jn 1.1–18); God's light, truth, and life present in darkness (1.5–2.29; Jn 1.19–12.50); the Father's beloved children, the love command, and Spirit abiding with the community (3.1–5.12; Jn 13.1–17.26); blood and water at the cross (5.6–8; Jn 19.34–35); conclusion (5.13; Jn 20.31) and epilogue (5.14–21; Jn 21).

INTERPRETATION

First John speaks only indirectly about the views of dissidents as denying truths about Jesus as messiah (2.22–23), as coming in the flesh (4.2), and as bringing salvation through his death (5.6). The author treats their departure from the communion of Johannine believers as a violation of the love command equivalent to Cain murdering his brother (3.11–12). In addition, 1 John corrects false understandings of sin, holiness, and forgiveness (1.5–2.6). Christians are reminded that their obligation to love one another is grounded not only in God's command (2.7–17) but in God's nature as love (4.7–12). At least some readers need to be reassured about their salvation on the day of judgment (3.18–24). The community is encouraged to rely on the Spirit it has received from God (2.26–27). Interpreters face the problem of how to fit these varied concerns into a framework. Should they all be considered as responses to the false teaching of dissidents? Or is the author speaking to diverse concerns? In the latter perspective, the schism may be viewed as a crisis that had undermined confidence in other areas that had not been challenged by the false teachers.

Even if the false teachers had claimed the Spirit as basis for an interpretation of Jesus that in some way denied his humanity and his saving death, it remains difficult to decide how to situate such claims theologically. Irenaeus employed 1 John to refute the sharp divide between the Jesus of the Gospels and the Savior/Christ of various Gnostic teachers. Some scholars see the opponents of 1 John in the figure of Cerinthus (ca. 100 CE). He argued that the divine Christ descended upon the righteous man, Jesus, at his baptism and bestowed the Spirit, enabling Jesus to work miracles. Jesus also revealed a previously unknown Father, the true God superior to the creator of Genesis 1. Since the divine cannot suffer, Christ departed from Jesus prior to his death on the cross (see Irenaeus, *Adv. Haer.* 1.26.1). Such a theological position suits the hints that false teachers deny that Jesus is a messiah in the flesh as well as the comment that they accept a coming in water (= baptism) as salvific but not "water and blood" (= cross). But if 1 John had a Gnostic such as Cerinthus in view, one would expect some opposition to the depiction of God as "unknown Father" distinct from the creator. If the opponents cannot be identified with a known group or teaching, then the best one can say is that their views about Jesus and salvation were presented as teaching based on the Fourth Gospel.

Even without quoting the Gospel, the thick texture of Johannine allusions in 1 John provides its readers with an authentic understanding of the evangelist's message. But since the most important part of the Gospel for readers of 1 John is the Farewell Discourses (Jn 13–17), their emphasis on unity (15.1–10; 17.6–19) must have heightened the crisis of faith posed by a schism. Did the breakup among believers undermine the promise of eternal life through union with the Father and Son at the heart of their faith? First John replies by denying that those who left ever really belonged to the community. Their departure broke the mutual bond of love that lies at the heart of its union with God. The author also retrieved an apocalyptic tradition depicting the rise of false prophets, schism, and even false messiahs in a satanic attempt to delude the righteous in the last days (2.22;

4.1; cf. Mk 13.22). A number of the other concerns found in 1 John, such as authenticating one's faith so as to be confident in God's judgment, may reflect the consequences of the schism rather than the theological views that provoked it.

GUIDE TO READING

The interpretative setting of 1 John as a reflection on Johannine traditions for a church whose faith has been jarred by schism provides one approach to reading the text. Echoes of the Gospel are identified in the annotations. The pain and uncertainty of the audience come through in the sections of exhortation to mutual love and reassurance. However, the apocalyptic scenario that enables the author to demonize the dissident teachers, even branding them with a newly minted term "antichrists" (4.1–6) appears to encourage a hostility incompatible with the teaching on love.

Use of 1 John in the cycle of Christian liturgical readings during the Christmas season focuses on the positive notes: Jesus as messiah come in the flesh, and the love command grounded in the love God has shown in the Son. This emphasis reflects a tradition of reading that goes back to Augustine's comment, "in it John speaks at length and almost the whole time about love" (*In Epistolam Ioannis*, prologue). First John 3.1–3 is a popular selection at funerals, particularly when the Gospel reading is taken from John. It highlights another motif in the work, the confidence that believers should have in eternal life.

Pheme Perkins

1 We declare to you what was from the beginning, what we have heard, what we have seen with our eyes, what we have looked at and touched with our hands, concerning the word of life— [2] this life was revealed, and we have seen it and testify to it, and declare to you the eternal life that was with the Father and was revealed to us— [3] we declare to you what we have seen and heard so that you also may have fellowship with us; and truly our fellowship is with the Father and with his Son Jesus Christ. [4] We are writing these things so that our[a] joy may be complete.

[5] This is the message we have heard from him and proclaim to you, that God is light and in him there is no darkness at all. [6] If we say that we have fellowship with him while we are walking in darkness, we lie and do not do what is true; [7] but if we walk in the light as he himself is in the light, we have fellowship with one another, and the blood of Jesus his Son cleanses us from all sin. [8] If we say that we have no sin, we deceive ourselves, and the truth is not in us. [9] If we confess our sins, he who is faithful and just will forgive us our sins and cleanse us from all unrighteousness. [10] If we say that we have not sinned, we make him a liar, and his word is not in us.

2 My little children, I am writing these things to you so that you may not sin. But if anyone does sin, we have an advocate with

[a] Other ancient authorities read *your*

1.1–4: Introduction. 1–2: *From the beginning* echoes the opening of John's Gospel (Jn 1.1–18) in which Jesus is the Word made flesh, life, and light. Here *beginning* refers to the beginning of Christian faith. *We*, teachers in the community, charged with handing on the tradition. *Heard, seen, looked at, touched* insist on the human reality of the Son against false teachers (see Introduction). 3–4: Fellowship with the Father and Son and abiding joy are signs of genuine Christian community in the Johannine tradition (Jn 15.11; 17.13).

1.5–10: Holiness in the community. 5: Light is a common symbol for the holiness and perfection of God (Ps 4.6; Isa 60.1–2). God's light guides the righteous (Ps 27.1). 6–7: No one can claim fellowship with God who does not follow God's commands (Jn 3.19; 1 Jn 2.11). Christians do not claim to be perfect. Jesus' death has brought forgiveness of sins (cf. Rev 1.5; 5.9). 8–10: False teachers, who reject the saving death of Jesus (see Introduction), may have claimed that true believers were sinless. Such teaching makes God a liar (v. 10). The wicked have false views about God and sin (Ps 53).

2.1–6: Christ our advocate. 1–2: A similar image of the risen Christ interceding for believers describes Christ as high priest in Heb 4.15–5.4. Here Christ is the *advocate*, who defends the faithful in the divine court (for the

the Father, Jesus Christ the righteous; [2] and he is the atoning sacrifice for our sins, and not for ours only but also for the sins of the whole world.

[3] Now by this we may be sure that we know him, if we obey his commandments. [4] Whoever says, "I have come to know him," but does not obey his commandments, is a liar, and in such a person the truth does not exist; [5] but whoever obeys his word, truly in this person the love of God has reached perfection. By this we may be sure that we are in him: [6] whoever says, "I abide in him," ought to walk just as he walked.

[7] Beloved, I am writing you no new commandment, but an old commandment that you have had from the beginning; the old commandment is the word that you have heard. [8] Yet I am writing you a new commandment that is true in him and in you, because[a] the darkness is passing away and the true light is already shining. [9] Whoever says, "I am in the light," while hating a brother or sister,[b] is still in the darkness. [10] Whoever loves a brother or sister[c] lives in the light, and in such a person[d] there is no cause for stumbling. [11] But whoever hates another believer[e] is in the darkness, walks in the darkness, and does not know the way to go, because the darkness has brought on blindness.

[12] I am writing to you, little children,
  because your sins are forgiven on
    account of his name.
[13] I am writing to you, fathers,
  because you know him who is from the
    beginning.
I am writing to you, young people,
  because you have conquered the evil one.
[14] I write to you, children,
  because you know the Father.
I write to you, fathers,
  because you know him who is from the
    beginning.
I write to you, young people,
  because you are strong
  and the word of God abides in you,
    and you have overcome the evil one.

[15] Do not love the world or the things in the world. The love of the Father is not in those who love the world; [16] for all that is in the world—the desire of the flesh, the desire of the eyes, the pride in riches—comes not from the Father but from the world. [17] And the world and its desire[f] are passing away, but those who do the will of God live forever.

[18] Children, it is the last hour! As you have heard that antichrist is coming, so now many antichrists have come. From this we know that it is the last hour. [19] They went

a Or that
b Gk hating a brother
c Gk loves a brother
d Or in it
e Gk hates a brother
f Or the desire for it

Holy Spirit as *advocate* see Jn 14.15–16). **3–5:** Knowledge of God requires obedience to God's commandments (cf. Ezek 36.26–27). **6:** Jesus exemplifies the love which is God's commandment (Jn 13.1; 15.11–13).

2.7–11: The love commandment. 7: *I am writing you* repeats 2.1. Fidelity to Christ's *new commandment* to love one another (Jn 13.34) is freedom from sin. **8:** *The true light is already shining* echoes the portrayal of Jesus as light of the world in the Gospel (Jn 8.12; 9.5; 12.35–36).

2.12–17: Victory over evil. 12–14: A rhythmic series of phrases reminds all from the youngest (or newest) members to the most senior (*little children . . . fathers . . . young people*) that they share Christ's victory over the world and its ruling power, *the evil one* (see Jn 12.31; 16.11,33b). **15–17:** Jesus came to save the world (2.2; Jn 3.16), but the world also represents false values, love of wealth or honor, and passions that separate people from God and one another (3.17).

2.18–29: Victory over false teaching. 18–23: *Many antichrists have come* refers to the secessionists as agents of the evil one, trying to deceive God's people (v. 18; 4.1–3). The appearance of such false prophets signals the *last hour* in apocalyptic texts (Mt 24.4–5,24; CD 5.20; *T. Moses* 7.4; Rev 20.10). The term "antichrist" occurs in the New Testament only in 1–2 John. It may be a variant of the "false messiah" (Gk "pseudochristos") in the Synoptic apocalypse (Mk 13.22; Mt 24.24). The figure of an opponent of God who arises in the last days combines the image of the mythical chaos monster defeated by God (Isa 27.1; 51.9; Ps 74.13; Job 26.12), the figure of Satan as an angelic adversary (Zech 3.1; Dan 12.1; *Jub.* 1.20; 1QS 1.18; 3.20–21), a human ruler who embodies evil

2nd Generation

out from us, but they did not belong to us; for if they had belonged to us, they would have remained with us. But by going out they made it plain that none of them belongs to us. [20] But you have been anointed by the Holy One, and all of you have knowledge.[a] [21] I write to you, not because you do not know the truth, but because you know it, and you know that no lie comes from the truth. [22] Who is the liar but the one who denies that Jesus is the Christ?[b] This is the antichrist, the one who denies the Father and the Son. [23] No one who denies the Son has the Father; everyone who confesses the Son has the Father also. [24] Let what you heard from the beginning abide in you. If what you heard from the beginning abides in you, then you will abide in the Son and in the Father. [25] And this is what he has promised us,[c] eternal life.

[26] I write these things to you concerning those who would deceive you. [27] As for you, the anointing that you received from him abides in you, and so you do not need anyone to teach you. But as his anointing teaches you about all things, and is true and is not a lie, and just as it has taught you, abide in him.

[28] And now, little children, abide in him, so that when he is revealed we may have confidence and not be put to shame before him at his coming. [29] If you know that he is righteous, you may be sure that everyone who does right

3 has been born of him. [1] See what love the Father has given us, that we should be called children of God; and that is what we are. The reason the world does not know us is that it did not know him. [2] Beloved, we are God's children now; what we will be has not yet been revealed. What we do know is this: when he[d] is revealed, we will be like him, for we will see him as he is. [3] And all who have

this hope in him purify themselves, just as he is pure.

[4] Everyone who commits sin is guilty of lawlessness; sin is lawlessness. [5] You know that he was revealed to take away sins, and in him there is no sin. [6] No one who abides in him sins; no one who sins has either seen him or known him. [7] Little children, let no one deceive you. Everyone who does what is right is righteous, just as he is righteous. [8] Everyone who commits sin is a child of the devil; for the devil has been sinning from the beginning. The Son of God was revealed for this purpose, to destroy the works of the devil. [9] Those who have been born of God do not sin, because God's seed abides in them;[e] they cannot sin, because they have been born of God. [10] The children of God and the children of the devil are revealed in this way: all who do not do what is right are not from God, nor are those who do not love their brothers and sisters.[f]

[11] For this is the message you have heard from the beginning, that we should love one another. [12] We must not be like Cain who was from the evil one and murdered his brother. And why did he murder him? Because his own deeds were evil and his brother's righteous. [13] Do not be astonished, brothers and sisters,[g] that the world hates you. [14] We know that we have passed from death to life because we love one another. Whoever does not love abides in death. [15] All who hate

a Other ancient authorities read *you know all things*
b Or *the Messiah*
c Other ancient authorities read *you*
d Or *it*
e Or *because the children of God abide in him*
f Gk *his brother*
g Gk *brothers*

(Dan 8.25; Ezek 38.1; 39.6; 2 Macc 9.12; 2 Esd 5.6–13), and the false prophet (Deut 13.2–6; 18.30). **24–27:** The Holy Spirit ("the Holy One," v. 20) present within the community ("anointing that you received") enables believers to distinguish true faith from lies about Jesus (Jn 14.26; 16.13). **28–29:** *At his coming* refers to Christ coming in judgment. Those who remain true to the Johannine teaching have nothing to fear (cf. Jn 3.36).

3.1–10: God's children are holy. 1–3: As God's children, believers become like Christ (Jn 1.12–13; 13.15–16; 17.16–19). **4–6:** Jesus' coming has taken away the sin of those who remain faithful (1.5–2.2). **7–8:** Those who are deceived about sin (2.1) become children of the devil (cf. Jn 8.44). **9–10:** *God's seed*, the Holy Spirit (2.26–27), and mutual love (Jn 13.35) distinguish God's children.

3.11–18: Moral examples. 11: See 2.7. **12:** Cain shows that hating a brother leads to murder (Gen 4.8). **13–14:** Though righteous like Abel, believers should expect to be hated by outsiders (Jn 15.18–19). **15:** The phrase, *do*

2nd Generation

a brother or sister[a] are murderers, and you know that murderers do not have eternal life abiding in them. [16] We know love by this, that he laid down his life for us—and we ought to lay down our lives for one another. [17] How does God's love abide in anyone who has the world's goods and sees a brother or sister[b] in need and yet refuses help?

[18] Little children, let us love, not in word or speech, but in truth and action. [19] And by this we will know that we are from the truth and will reassure our hearts before him [20] whenever our hearts condemn us; for God is greater than our hearts, and he knows everything. [21] Beloved, if our hearts do not condemn us, we have boldness before God; [22] and we receive from him whatever we ask, because we obey his commandments and do what pleases him.

[23] And this is his commandment, that we should believe in the name of his Son Jesus Christ and love one another, just as he has commanded us. [24] All who obey his commandments abide in him, and he abides in them. And by this we know that he abides in us, by the Spirit that he has given us.

4 Beloved, do not believe every spirit, but test the spirits to see whether they are from God; for many false prophets have gone out into the world. [2] By this you know the Spirit of God: every spirit that confesses that Jesus Christ has come in the flesh is from God, [3] and every spirit that does not confess Jesus[c] is not from God. And this is the spirit of the antichrist, of which you have heard that it is coming; and now it is already

in the world. [4] Little children, you are from God, and have conquered them; for the one who is in you is greater than the one who is in the world. [5] They are from the world; therefore what they say is from the world, and the world listens to them. [6] We are from God. Whoever knows God listens to us, and whoever is not from God does not listen to us. From this we know the spirit of truth and the spirit of error.

[7] Beloved, let us love one another, because love is from God; everyone who loves is born of God and knows God. [8] Whoever does not love does not know God, for God is love. [9] God's love was revealed among us in this way: God sent his only Son into the world so that we might live through him. [10] In this is love, not that we loved God but that he loved us and sent his Son to be the atoning sacrifice for our sins. [11] Beloved, since God loved us so much, we also ought to love one another. [12] No one has ever seen God; if we love one another, God lives in us, and his love is perfected in us. [13] By this we know that we abide in him and he in us, because he has given us of his Spirit. [14] And we have seen and do testify that the Father has sent his Son as the Savior of the world. [15] God abides in those who confess that Jesus is the Son of God, and they abide in God. [16] So we have known and believe the love that God has for us.

[a] Gk *his brother*

[b] Gk *brother*

[c] Other ancient authorities read *does away with Jesus* (Gk *dissolves Jesus*)

---

not have eternal life abiding in them, invites readers to apply this lesson to the secessionists. Their break with the community is equivalent to murder (4.5; cf. Mt 5.21–22). **16–18:** Jesus' death is the supreme example of love (Jn 13.1; 15.9,13).

3.19–24: Love as confidence before God. 19–20: Love is the basis for God's judgment despite the doubts caused by the schism (2.28). **21–22:** Jesus promised that God would answer believers' prayer (Jn 16.23–24). **23–24:** Belief in the Son and love establish a permanent relationship between believers and God (Jn 16.26–27).

4.1–6: Testing spirits. 1–3: Since false teachers can appear genuine (cf. Mt 7.15–23), Christians must *test* such persons by their faith in Jesus (cf. 1 Cor 12.1–3). The dissidents changed the Johannine tradition by denying that Christ *has come in the flesh*. **4–6:** The Holy Spirit verifies 1 John as testimony to the true Johannine tradition (cf. Jn 16.13–14). **5:** *The world listens* could imply that the dissident teachers enjoy more success than the Johannine circle (cf. Jn 15.19).

4.7–21: God's love as the basis of salvation. 7–9: Believers are to imitate the love God has shown in sending the Son to give life (3.16–22; Jn 3.16). **10–12:** God's love has been shown in the death of Jesus (Jn 13.1). It is the basis of the love command (Jn 15.12–13). **12:** See Jn 1.18; 6.46. **13–16a:** See 3.23–24. **14:** See Jn 4.42. **16b–18:** *God is love* (4.8; cf. Rom 8.32,39; 1 Cor 13.11). When Christian life corresponds to the nature of God (1.5–7), there is no

God is love, and those who abide in love abide in God, and God abides in them. [17] Love has been perfected among us in this: that we may have boldness on the day of judgment, because as he is, so are we in this world. [18] There is no fear in love, but perfect love casts out fear; for fear has to do with punishment, and whoever fears has not reached perfection in love. [19] We love[a] because he first loved us. [20] Those who say, "I love God," and hate their brothers or sisters,[b] are liars; for those who do not love a brother or sister[c] whom they have seen, cannot love God whom they have not seen. [21] The commandment we have from him is this: those who love God must love their brothers and sisters[b] also.

[5] Everyone who believes that Jesus is the Christ[d] has been born of God, and everyone who loves the parent loves the child. [2] By this we know that we love the children of God, when we love God and obey his commandments. [3] For the love of God is this, that we obey his commandments. And his commandments are not burdensome, [4] for whatever is born of God conquers the world. And this is the victory that conquers the world, our faith. [5] Who is it that conquers the world but the one who believes that Jesus is the Son of God?

[6] This is the one who came by water and blood, Jesus Christ, not with the water only but with the water and the blood. And the Spirit is the one that testifies, for the Spirit is the truth. [7] There are three that testify:[e] [8] the Spirit and the water and the blood, and these three agree. [9] If we receive human testimony,

the testimony of God is greater; for this is the testimony of God that he has testified to his Son. [10] Those who believe in the Son of God have the testimony in their hearts. Those who do not believe in God[f] have made him a liar by not believing in the testimony that God has given concerning his Son. [11] And this is the testimony: God gave us eternal life, and this life is in his Son. [12] Whoever has the Son has life; whoever does not have the Son of God does not have life.

[13] I write these things to you who believe in the name of the Son of God, so that you may know that you have eternal life.

[14] And this is the boldness we have in him, that if we ask anything according to his will, he hears us. [15] And if we know that he hears us in whatever we ask, we know that we have obtained the requests made of him. [16] If you see your brother or sister[g] committing what is not a mortal sin, you will ask, and God[h] will give life to such a one—to those whose sin is not mortal. There is sin that is mortal; I do

---

a   Other ancient authorities add *him*; others add *God*
b   Gk *brothers*
c   Gk *brother*
d   Or *the Messiah*
e   A few other authorities read (with variations) [7]*There are three that testify in heaven, the Father, the Word, and the Holy Spirit, and these three are one.* [8]*And there are three that testify on earth:*
f   Other ancient authorities read *in the Son*
g   Gk *your brother*
h   Gk *he*

---

reason to fear God's judgment (2.1–6,28; 3.18–20). **19:** 4.7,11. **20:** Love shown to others demonstrates true knowledge and love for God (2.3–11; 3.23–24). **21:** *Those who love God must love their brothers and sisters* is a Johannine formulation of the command to love God and neighbor (Mt 22.34–40, quoting Deut 6.5 and Lev 19.18).

5.1–13: Concluding appeal to keep the true faith. 1–3: Belief in Jesus as the messiah (*the Christ*) (4.2–3; Jn 1.12–13; 20.31) and mutual love (4.20–21; Jn 13.35) are the hallmarks of the true Johannine community. **2:** *We know that we love the children of God, when we love God* reverses 4.12. It serves as polemic against the secessionists, since schism implies hating God's children (3.11–16). **4–5:** See 2.12–14; 4.4. **6–8:** *One who came by water and blood* refers to the death of Jesus as atonement for sin (1.7; 2.2; 4.10; Jn 1.29). The witnesses, *water, blood,* and *Spirit,* appear in John's account of Jesus' death (Jn 19.34–35; for water as Spirit, see Jn 7.38–39). **9–12:** The true faith is not based on human testimony alone (1.1–4; Jn 1.7–8) but on God's as well (cf. Jn 5.31–38; 16.6–11). **13:** *I write . . . that you have eternal life* echoes the ending of Jn 20.31.

5.14–21: Epilogue. Sin and forgiveness in the community. 14–15: God's children can be certain that God will hear their prayers (3.21–22; Jn 14.14–16; 15.16; 16.23–24; Mt 18.19–20). **16–17:** Communal prayer can elicit God's forgiveness and restore sinners (2.1–2; Mt 18.15–20; Jas 5.15b,19–20). *To those whose sin is not mortal* distinguishes a category of sin that cannot be forgiven. Elsewhere such sin is denying that God's Spirit is working through Jesus (Mk 3.28–30) or apostasy (Heb 6.4–6). Here the expression probably refers to those who have separated

not say that you should pray about that. [17] All wrongdoing is sin, but there is sin that is not mortal.

[18] We know that those who are born of God do not sin, but the one who was born of God protects them, and the evil one does not touch them. [19] We know that we are God's children, and that the whole world lies under the power of the evil one. [20] And we know that the Son of God has come and has given us understanding so that we may know him who is true;[a] and we are in him who is true, in his Son Jesus Christ. He is the true God and eternal life.

[21] Little children, keep yourselves from idols.[b]

---

[a] Other ancient authorities read *know the true God*

[b] Other ancient authorities add *Amen*

---

themselves from the Johannine community. They no longer dwell with God or have the Spirit (2.19–25). **18:** See 3.8–10. **19:** See 2.12–15; 5.4–5. **20:** *Him who is true* probably refers to the knowledge of the true God as some manuscripts suggest (see textual note *a* and cf. Jn 1.18; 14.7,9–10). Knowledge of the *true God* (Father and Son) confers *eternal life* (Jn 17.3). **21:** In a general sense, *keep yourselves from idols* probably refers to the false gods of non-Christian neighbors (Jn 10.14). Traveling missionaries were to reject non-Christian hospitality (3 Jn 7). In this context, the phrase may refer to association with the secessionists and their teaching (2 Jn 7–9).

THE SECOND LETTER OF JOHN

NAME

Titled "the second (letter) of John" in ancient codices, this short letter belonged to a collection led by 1 John.

CANONICAL STATUS AND AUTHORSHIP

By the fourth century CE (Eusebius, *Hist. eccl.* ii.23.25) three Johannine "letters" along with four others said to be written by apostles were included in the canon as "catholic" or universal. Some second-century Christians identified the "elder" (v. 1) with the apostle John, the son of Zebedee, considered the author of the Gospel and 1 John (cf. Peter as "fellow elder" in 1 Pet 5.1). However, Papias distinguished between John, the disciple, and another, the "elder." Most contemporary scholars identify the elder as the Johannine teacher who composed 1 John.

DATE AND HISTORICAL CONTEXT

Since 2 John refers to dissident teaching like that opposed in 1 John, it must have been written during the crisis provoked by the schism in the Johannine churches (ca. 100 CE). Because the elder warns the recipients against receiving dissident teachers, some scholars date 2 John earlier than the definitive break in 1 John. Others hold that the schism that had occurred in the city from which the elder writes (Ephesus) had not yet occurred in outlying regions.

STRUCTURE AND CONTENTS

Second John follows the conventions of a private letter: opening greeting identifies sender, addressees (vv. 1–3); letter body, beginning with an expression of joy at how recipients are faring, and concluding with future plans (vv. 4–12); final greeting from sender and associates to recipients (v. 13).

INTERPRETATION AND GUIDE TO READING

The letter opens with a summary of the mutual love that was the hallmark of Johannine Christians (Jn 13.34–35). It serves the ancient rhetorical standard of enlisting the goodwill of an audience at the beginning of a speech. The business of the letter follows, a warning against false teachers and the demand that no one associate with them in any way (vv. 7–11).

The elder's harsh treatment of false teachers strikes modern readers as contradicting the earlier teaching on mutual love. If 2 John was written when the full impact of the schism described in 1 John was being felt, this requirement could be viewed differently. To the elder it appeared necessary to quarantine other churches against this disease. Some scholars think that a copy of 1 John was sent along with this letter.

Pheme Perkins

¹The elder to the elect lady and her children, whom I love in the truth, and not only I but also all who know the truth, ²because of the truth that abides in us and will be with us forever:

³Grace, mercy, and peace will be with us from God the Father and from[a] Jesus Christ, the Father's Son, in truth and love.

⁴I was overjoyed to find some of your children walking in the truth, just as we have been commanded by the Father. ⁵But now, dear lady, I ask you, not as though I were writing you a new commandment, but one we have had from the beginning, let us love one another. ⁶And this is love, that we walk according to his commandments; this is the commandment just as you have heard it from the beginning—you must walk in it.

⁷Many deceivers have gone out into the world, those who do not confess that Jesus Christ has come in the flesh; any such person is the deceiver and the antichrist! ⁸Be on your guard, so that you do not lose what we[b] have worked for, but may receive a full reward. ⁹Everyone who does not abide in the teaching of Christ, but goes beyond it, does not have God; whoever abides in the teaching has both the Father and the Son. ¹⁰Do not receive into the house or welcome anyone who comes to you and does not bring this teaching; ¹¹for to welcome is to participate in the evil deeds of such a person.

¹²Although I have much to write to you, I would rather not use paper and ink; instead I hope to come to you and talk with you face to face, so that our joy may be complete.

¹³The children of your elect sister send you their greetings.[c]

a   Other ancient authorities add *the Lord*
b   Other ancient authorities read *you*
c   Other ancient authorities add *Amen*

1–3: Letter opening. *Elect lady* refers to a local church. *Love in the truth* sets out the Johannine vision of the church as a community whose members are united by Jesus' command to love one another (vv. 4–6; 1 Jn 2.22–23; 3.23) and reject false teaching about the Son (vv. 7–9).

4–11: Letter body. 4–6: The *new commandment* to love one another was central to Johannine Christianity (Jn 13.34–35; 1 Jn 2.7–10). **7–9:** False teachers do not *abide in the teaching of Christ* because they reject the humanity of Jesus (v. 7; see 1 Jn 4.2) and have destroyed Christian fellowship (1 Jn 2.19). False teaching is a sign that the *antichrist* is at work in the world (1 Jn 2.18–23; 4.1–3). **10–11:** The severity of this demand, *do not receive into the house* (i.e., church) anyone connected with the secessionists, follows from the view that their activities are Satan's final effort against God's people.

12–13: Letter closing. Ancient letters frequently end with a notice of the sender's future travel plans (cf. Rom 15.22,33).

THE THIRD LETTER OF JOHN

NAME

The title given in ancient manuscripts identifies this private letter with 1–2 John, which circulated more widely.

CANONICAL STATUS AND AUTHORSHIP

Though included in canon lists of the fourth century CE, 3 John was not widely used, perhaps because it is addressed to an individual, not a church. Identification of the "elder" (v. 1) with the author of 2 John is supported by the nearly identical concluding verses of the two letters. In antiquity 1–3 John were attributed to the apostle John, the son of Zebedee, as was the Gospel. Modern scholars distinguish the author of 1–3 John from the evangelist.

DATE AND HISTORICAL CONTEXT

The social setting of Johannine churches presumed in 2 and 3 John is similar, although there is no hint of the secessionist controversy in the latter. The "elder" lives in a church (possibly at Ephesus) with ties to other house churches in the surrounding region. Christian missionaries depended upon the hospitality of house churches when they traveled (cf. Rom 16.1–2). Diotrephes, apparently the head of such a church, had refused to receive emissaries associated with the elder. This letter seeks such support from another Christian in the same region, Gaius.

STRUCTURE AND CONTENTS

Third John follows the model of the ancient letter: an opening greeting from sender to recipient followed by the health wish (vv. 1–4); letter body (vv. 3–12); conclusion with travel plans and additional greetings (vv. 13–15). Rhetorically the body opens with praise for the recipient's well-known hospitality to traveling Christians (vv. 5–8) before addressing the business at hand (vv. 9–12).

INTERPRETATION AND GUIDE TO READING

In ancient diplomacy, refusing hospitality to an envoy was an insult to the sender. Third John does not indicate what led Diotrephes to prohibit members of his house church from having anything to do with persons sent by the elder (vv. 9–10). Some interpreters have seen a dispute between the elder, a teacher in the Johannine school, and an emerging monarchic episcopacy. Others propose that the elder is on the receiving end of the policy he had proposed to exclude false teachers in 2 John 10–11. From the letter itself, one can only infer that Gaius has no personal relationship with Diotrephes and that when Diotrephes rejected envoys from the elder, he was refusing to participate in their mission.

Whatever the basis for Diotrephes' lack of hospitality, 3 John provides a glimpse into the early Christian mission ca. 100 CE. Personal networks of hospitality maintained by traveling envoys linked small house church communities together. Travelers preferred the hospitality of believers to that of outsiders (v. 7).

Pheme Perkins

[1] The elder to the beloved Gaius, whom I love in truth.

[2] Beloved, I pray that all may go well with you and that you may be in good health, just as it is well with your soul. [3] I was overjoyed when some of the friends[a] arrived and testified to your faithfulness to the truth, namely how you walk in the truth. [4] I have no greater joy than this, to hear that my children are walking in the truth.

[5] Beloved, you do faithfully whatever you do for the friends,[a] even though they are strangers to you; [6] they have testified to your love before the church. You will do well to send them on in a manner worthy of God; [7] for they began their journey for the sake of Christ,[b] accepting no support from non-believers.[c] [8] Therefore we ought to support such people, so that we may become co-workers with the truth.

[9] I have written something to the church; but Diotrephes, who likes to put himself first, does not acknowledge our authority. [10] So if I come, I will call attention to what he is doing in spreading false charges against us. And not content with those charges, he refuses to welcome the friends,[a] and even prevents those who want to do so and expels them from the church.

[11] Beloved, do not imitate what is evil but imitate what is good. Whoever does good is from God; whoever does evil has not seen God. [12] Everyone has testified favorably about Demetrius, and so has the truth itself. We also testify for him,[d] and you know that our testimony is true.

[13] I have much to write to you, but I would rather not write with pen and ink; [14] instead I hope to see you soon, and we will talk together face to face.

[15] Peace to you. The friends send you their greetings. Greet the friends there, each by name.

[a] Gk *brothers*
[b] Gk *for the sake of the name*
[c] Gk *the Gentiles*
[d] Gk lacks *for him*

1–4: Letter opening and health wish. This secular opening (contrast 2 Jn 1–3) indicates that this is a private letter, not a communication read to an assembled church (contrast Philem 1–3). **4:** *My children* is the elder's designation for Christians in fellowship with his teaching (1 Jn 2.1).

5–12: Letter body. 5–8: Rhetorically the elder enlists the good will of Gaius, whom he does not know personally, by praising the reputation he has gained among traveling missionaries for hospitality. The axiom that such hospitality gains a share in the good work of evangelization was common in early Christianity (see Phil 4.10–20; Mt 10.40–42). **9–11:** The elder asks Gaius to supply his associates with the hospitality that Diotrephes has recently refused. **9:** *Does not acknowledge our authority* is diplomatic language for not receiving the envoy sent by an authority. It does not mean that the elder once had direct authority over Diotrephes or that house church. **12:** A note of recommendation for Demetrius, who may have carried the letter (cf. Rom 16.1–2).

13–15: Letter closing. See 2 Jn 12–13.

THE LETTER OF JUDE

NAME, AUTHORSHIP, AND DATE

This letter is named for its author Jude, identified in v. 1 as the brother of James, who was Jesus' brother and leader of the Jerusalem church (Gal 1.19). The author himself is not identified either as Jesus' brother (see Mt 13.55; Mk 6.3) or as Judas Thomas (Jesus' twin in the Syrian *Acts of Thomas*), as might be expected if the attribution to Jude were a later claim to Jude's authority. This may indicate that the letter was written by Jude. On the other hand, attribution of authorship to a major figure is well attested in the Bible and in other ancient literature. The date of composition is uncertain. It must be earlier than 2 Peter, which uses Jude (see p. 2132). The reference to "the predictions of the apostles" (v. 17) suggests a period when the apostles were a well-known group from the past. If so, a date late in the first century CE is likely, although some scholars have dated the letter as early as the 50s.

CANONICAL STATUS

The place of this letter among the Catholic Epistles (those addressed to all Christians rather than to specific churches or individuals) was contested in the early church, and it was excluded from Syriac translations until the fourth century CE, when it became widely accepted. Its canonicity was again challenged during the Reformation.

LITERARY FORM AND BACKGROUND

Jude has the typical form of a letter (see p. 1973), except that it lacks the customary final greeting. It uses a variety of biblical and nonbiblical sources; prominent among the latter is *1 Enoch*, a collection of apocalyptic writings attributed to Enoch (Gen 5.21–24) but written from the third century BCE to the first century CE. The author of the letter considered these writings to be authoritative, but it would be anachronistic to suppose that he considered them canonical.

Nothing can be known about the specific occasion for which the letter was written, or about the identity of the author's opponents since they are described in standard language taken from polemical rhetoric.

CONTENTS AND INTERPRETATION

The purpose of the letter is to encourage those to whom it is addressed "to contend for the faith" by maintaining moral purity against those who "pervert the grace of our God into licentiousness" (vv. 3–4). The rhetorical strategy is to warn people of God's judgment on the lustful, blasphemous, arrogant, greedy, rebellious opponents and to contrast it with the mercy of God for those who remain loyal to the faith as delivered by the apostles.

The letter is organized in concentric circles. It begins with a standard letter greeting and ends with an elaborate and beautiful prayer (vv. 24–25). Within these two formal elements are two exhortations: one to "contend for the faith" (v. 3), and one to keep oneself "in the love of God" (v. 21) and have "mercy" on others who are erring (vv. 22–23). Between these two exhortations, a series of biblical and nonbiblical stories and prophecies are presented as evidence of the error and eventual doom of the opponents. This material incorporates an interpretation of selected judgment scenes from Genesis and Exodus (vv. 5–8) with a note on Michael the archangel (vv. 9–10), an interpretation of selected errors from Genesis and Numbers (vv. 11–13), an application of the prophecy of *1 Enoch* 1.9 to the opponents (vv. 14–16), and an application of apostolic prophecy (vv. 17–19). In each case the transition from citation to interpretation is marked by the word "these" as subject of the sentence: "these dreamers" (v. 8); "these people" (v. 10); "these" (vv. 12,16).

Patrick A. Tiller

¹Jude,ᵃ a servantᵇ of Jesus Christ and brother of James,

To those who are called, who are belovedᶜ inᵈ God the Father and kept safe forᵈ Jesus Christ:

²May mercy, peace, and love be yours in abundance.

³Beloved, while eagerly preparing to write to you about the salvation we share, I find it necessary to write and appeal to you to contend for the faith that was once for all entrusted to the saints. ⁴For certain intruders have stolen in among you, people who long ago were designated for this condemnation as ungodly, who pervert the grace of our God into licentiousness and deny our only Master and Lord, Jesus Christ.ᵉ

⁵Now I desire to remind you, though you are fully informed, that the Lord, who once for all savedᶠ a people out of the land of Egypt, afterward destroyed those who did not believe. ⁶And the angels who did not keep their own position, but left their proper dwelling, he has kept in eternal chains in deepest darkness for the judgment of the great day. ⁷Likewise, Sodom and Gomorrah and the surrounding cities, which, in the same manner as they, indulged in sexual immorality and pursued unnatural lust,ᵍ serve as an example by undergoing a punishment of eternal fire. ⁸Yet in the same way these dreamers also defile the flesh, reject authority, and slander

the glorious ones.ʰ ⁹But when the archangel Michael contended with the devil and disputed about the body of Moses, he did not dare to bring a condemnation of slanderⁱ against him, but said, "The Lord rebuke you!" ¹⁰But these people slander whatever they do not understand, and they are destroyed by those things that, like irrational animals, they know by instinct. ¹¹Woe to them! For they go the way of Cain, and abandon themselves to Balaam's error for the sake of gain, and perish in Korah's rebellion. ¹²These are blemishesʲ on your love-feasts, while they feast with you without fear, feeding themselves.ᵏ They are waterless clouds carried along by the winds; autumn trees without fruit, twice dead, uprooted; ¹³wild waves of the sea, casting up the foam of their own shame; wandering stars,

ᵃ Gk *Judas*
ᵇ Gk *slave*
ᶜ Other ancient authorities read *sanctified*
ᵈ Or *by*
ᵉ Or *the only Master and our Lord Jesus Christ*
ᶠ Other ancient authorities read *though you were once for all fully informed, that Jesus* (or *Joshua*) *who saved*
ᵍ Gk *went after other flesh*
ʰ Or *angels*; Gk *glories*
ⁱ Or *condemnation for blasphemy*
ʲ Or *reefs*
ᵏ Or *without fear. They are shepherds who care only for themselves*

1–2: Salutation. See Rom 1.1–7n.

3–4: Occasion. The writer writes in response to what he considers to be a dangerous level of moral failure on the part of some leaders in the church. *Saints,* "holy ones," consecrated to God. The immoral behavior of the *intruders* is presumably the basis of the charge that they *deny* Jesus.

5–8: Three examples of judgment. God judged the Israelites who went out of Egypt with Moses (v. 5; see Num 14.20–23) but did not believe, angels (v. 6; see Gen 6.1–4; *1 Enoch* 6–16) who left *their own position,* and Sodom and Gomorrah (Gen 19) for their *sexual immorality.* **8:** *These dreamers* will suffer a similar fate for their similar misdeeds. The intruders apparently claim to experience revelatory dreams. The *authority* that they despise may be either God's authority or angelic authorities. The *glorious ones* are probably angelic dignitaries.

9–10: A further example of the impropriety of slander. According to nonbiblical Jewish tradition, when the archangel Michael was about to bury the body of Moses, Satan accused Moses of being a murderer, not worthy of an honorable burial. Michael sent Satan off with the words, "May the Lord rebuke you" (Zech 3.2).

11–13: Three examples of error. *Cain* the murderer: Gen 4.8; Heb 11.4; 1 Jn 3.12. *Balaam* who prophesied for gain: Num 22; Rev 2.14 (see 2 Pet 2.15n.). *Korah* who rebelled: Num 16. Similarly, the opponents lead their followers astray for gain and rebel against the (apostolic) leadership of the church. **12:** That they participate in their *love-feasts* (see 1 Cor 11.20–21n.) shows that they are members of the group. The author calls them *intruders* (v. 4) because their membership is illegitimate. Metaphors of *blemishes, shepherds* (see note *k* and Ezek 34.2,10), *clouds* (see Prov 25.14), *trees, waves,* and *stars* illustrate their uselessness, destructiveness, and selfishness. **13:** In the

for whom the deepest darkness has been reserved forever.

[14] It was also about these that Enoch, in the seventh generation from Adam, prophesied, saying, "See, the Lord is coming[a] with ten thousands of his holy ones, [15] to execute judgment on all, and to convict everyone of all the deeds of ungodliness that they have committed in such an ungodly way, and of all the harsh things that ungodly sinners have spoken against him." [16] These are grumblers and malcontents; they indulge their own lusts; they are bombastic in speech, flattering people to their own advantage.

[17] But you, beloved, must remember the predictions of the apostles of our Lord Jesus Christ; [18] for they said to you, "In the last time there will be scoffers, indulging their own ungodly lusts." [19] It is these worldly people, devoid of the Spirit, who are causing divisions. [20] But you, beloved, build yourselves up on your most holy faith; pray in the Holy Spirit; [21] keep yourselves in the love of God; look forward to the mercy of our Lord Jesus Christ that leads to[b] eternal life. [22] And have mercy on some who are wavering; [23] save others by snatching them out of the fire; and have mercy on still others with fear, hating even the tunic defiled by their bodies.[c]

[24] Now to him who is able to keep you from falling, and to make you stand without blemish in the presence of his glory with rejoicing, [25] to the only God our Savior, through Jesus Christ our Lord, be glory, majesty, power, and authority, before all time and now and forever. Amen.

a   Gk *came*
b   Gk *Christ to*
c   Gk *by the flesh*. The Greek text of verses 22-23 is uncertain at several points

books of Enoch, *wandering stars* (planets) were understood to be disobedient angels. For Jude the phrase serves as a metaphor for the activity of the opponents.

14–16: A prophecy of judgment. *1 Enoch* 1.9.

17–19: An apostolic prophecy. See 2 Thess 2.3; 1 Tim 4.1; 2 Tim 3.1; 4.3 for similar prophetic announcements.

20–23: Exhortations. 20–21: The promised encouragement "to contend for the faith" (v. 3) consists of traditional Christian ethical teaching. Jude incorporates a Trinitarian formula. **22–23:** The difficulties in interpreting these verses have given rise to several scribal simplifications that reduce the three clauses to two: to *have mercy on some* by rescuing them from *fire* (by getting them to repent; cf. Zech 3.24) and to *have mercy on others with fear* (of being corrupted oneself).

24–25: Doxology. Cf. Rom 16.25; Eph 3.20–21; Phil 4.20; 1 Tim 1.17; 2 Tim 4.18; Heb 13.21; 1 Pet 5.11; 2 Pet 3.18; Rev 5.13.

THE REVELATION TO JOHN

NAME

The Revelation to John is also known as the Apocalypse or the Apocalypse of John, from the Greek word meaning "disclosure" or "unveiling." While the book presents itself as a work of prophecy (1.3; 22.10), it has lent its name to a literary genre, the "apocalypse," that characterizes a range of Jewish and Christian writings that first appeared about 250 BCE.

CANONICAL STATUS

With its vivid visions of the consummation of God's divine plan of judgment and salvation, the book of Revelation brings the canon of the New Testament to a close. While the book of Revelation is not the only early Christian apocalypse, it is the only one that was included in the canon of the New Testament. The question of whether it should be considered canonical was a matter of some controversy in the early centuries of Christianity. Eusebius of Caesarea (ca. 263–339 CE), for example, writes that some reject Revelation but that others accept it as genuine (*Hist. eccl.* 3.25.4–5). The third-century writer Dionysius of Alexandria maintained that the book of Revelation could be considered orthodox only if it is read allegorically. Dionysius also recognized that the book of Revelation could not have been written by the same John to whom the Gospel according to John was attributed.

AUTHORSHIP

Unlike other Jewish and Christian apocalypses, which are pseudonymous, with their authors writing in the name of some revered figure from antiquity, the author of the book of Revelation identifies himself by name as John (1.1,4,9; 22.8). While some ancient authorities (e.g., Justin, *Dialogue with Trypho* 81.4) suggested that this is the apostle John, the son of Zebedee (see Mk 3.17), internal evidence from the book itself is inconclusive. The author's familiarity with the Jerusalem Temple and its rituals, the depth of his knowledge of the Hebrew Bible (of the 405 verses in Revelation, some 275 include allusions to passages in the Hebrew Bible, or to its Greek translation, the Septuagint), as well as his adoption of a literary genre that was familiar in Palestinian Judaism, combine to suggest that the John of Revelation may have been a Palestinian Jewish Christian who fled to the Diaspora as a consequence of the First Jewish Revolt against the Romans (66–73 CE). His self-identification to the "seven churches that are in Asia" (1.4) as "your brother who share with you in Jesus the persecution and the kingdom and the patient endurance" (1.9) suggests that he was well known to his audience, probably because he exercised a prophetic ministry among them (see 22.9). He mentions the twelve apostles as figures from the past (21.14), and does not refer to himself as one of them. The traditional identification of the John of the book of Revelation with the apostle of the same name is thus highly questionable, as is the connection of the John of the book of Revelation with the Gospel According to John or with the Letters of John.

DATE OF COMPOSITION AND HISTORICAL CONTEXT

There have been two main positions regarding the date of the book of Revelation. The first is that the book was composed between 64 and 70 CE, prior to the destruction of the Temple in 70 CE and prompted by the persecution of Christians toward the end of the reign of the Roman emperor Nero (54–68 CE). The second view is that while the book of Revelation draws on traditional material and on sources written prior to the fall of Jerusalem in 70 CE (e.g., chs. 11 and 12), it probably reached its final form toward the end of the reign of the Roman emperor Domitian (81–96 CE). The book is addressed to "the seven churches that are in Asia" (1.4), Christian communities in the Roman proconsular province of Asia, located in the western portion of present-day Turkey (see map on p. 2157). The book demonstrates its author's familiarity with the specific situation of each of the seven churches, beginning with Ephesus, the city that was the administrative capital of the province. The seven cities were complex and diverse in economic, social, political, and religious terms. Whether or not Christians faced organized and widespread persecutions sanctioned by Roman imperial authorities at the time the book was written, Christians in the province of Asia were living under the threat of serious oppression, facing the danger of being "slaughtered for the word of God and the testimony they had given" (6.9). One such victim is Antipas, identified by name in the message to the church at Pergamum (2.13). John himself establishes his solidarity with his audience, sharing with them "the persecution and the kingdom and the patient endurance" (1.9), finding himself on the island of Patmos "because of the word of God and the testimony of Jesus" (1.9). According to many commentators, including a number of early Christian writers (e.g., Eusebius, *Hist. eccl.* 3.18), John had been exiled to Patmos by Roman imperial authorities as a penalty for his testimony to Jesus. However, others suggest that John went to Patmos to spread the word of God.

A variety of voices and viewpoints competed for the attention of the late first-century Christians to whom the book of Revelation was originally addressed. John exhorts them to stand firm in their convictions, to resist "with patient endurance" (2.2,19; 3.10) and at any cost the overwhelming pressures to accommodation and compromise with the dominant culture. The destruction of Jerusalem by the Romans in 70 CE gave John ample cause to identify Rome as Babylon, recalling the Babylonian destruction of Jerusalem in 586 BCE. The breadth and depth of Rome's political and economic power found religious expression in the widespread worship of the emperor in the provinces of Asia, with temples built in honor of the emperor and of Rome personified as the goddess Roma. The book of Revelation takes sides in a battle over sovereignty, where the Roman emperor competes with God and Christ in a contest for the allegiance of the faithful. Warning that those who worship the emperor, symbolized by "the beast" (13.1–10), will suffer ultimate defeat, the book urges its audience to "hold fast to the faith of Jesus" (14.12) and thereby to share in the paradoxical victory of his death and resurrection.

LITERARY HISTORY

Interpreters of the book of Revelation through the centuries have puzzled over how to explain the many parallel passages and apparent repetitions throughout the book. The number seven, for example figures prominently throughout the book as a way of ordering the sequence of the book's visionary narratives: seven seals, seven bowls, seven trumpets. Some authors understand this as a matter of recapitulation, that is, the repeated description of the same events from several different vantage points. Thus, the series of seven trumpets (8.16–9.21; 11.14–19) and seven bowls (16:1–21), for example, furnish two parallel perspectives on God's cataclysmic judgment against the world and its inhabitants. Others have sought to unravel the complex literary structure of the Apocalypse by appealing to source theories, arguing that the book is a composite that reflects significant editorial work by its final author, who drew on earlier material, including some written sources.

STRUCTURE AND CONTENTS

The structure of the book of Revelation is widely debated among scholars, yet there is general agreement that it involves a series of parallel, interconnected, and yet ever progressing sections. It begins with a prologue (1.1–3), an epistolary salutation (1.4–8), and an inaugural vision (1.9–20), which are followed by messages to each of the seven churches (2.1–3.22). There follows (4.1–5.14) a vision of God enthroned and of Jesus depicted as a Lamb, who receives the seven-sealed scroll from the hand of God. A series of sevenfold visions commences at 6.1, beginning with the opening of each of the seven seals (6.1–8.5), followed by the sounding of each of seven trumpets (8.6–11.19). The sounding of the seventh trumpet is followed by the vision of the woman, the child, and the dragon (12.1–17), the vision of the two beasts (13.1–18), a threefold vision of the victory, and vindication of the faithful (14.1–20). These are followed by a final sevenfold series, the outpouring of the bowls of divine wrath (16.1–21). 17.1–18.24 presents the vision of the fall of Babylon, followed by the great doxology of 19.1–10 that also looks forward to the eschatological victory (19.11–21), the defeat of Satan (20.1–10), the last judgment (20:11–15), and the vision of the new Jerusalem (21.1–22.5). The book concludes with an epilogue (22.6–21).

INTERPRETATION

Over the centuries, the book of Revelation has been interpreted from a wide variety of approaches, ranging from literal readings of the book as predictive prophecy to readings that recognize in its utopian language the promise of hope in the midst of contemporary situations of suffering and oppression. There have been three main tendencies in the interpretation of Revelation: historical, prophetic-predictive, and symbolic. According to those who interpret the book historically, Revelation refers to events that took place during the first century CE. The prophetic-predictive tendency in the interpretation of the book reads Revelation for clues about the future, especially with regard to God's impending judgment on the world. Those who focus on symbolic interpretations of the book understand the Apocalypse neither as a window to the past nor as a visionary presentation of what is yet to come in the future, but as a work that speaks to readers of every time and place to offer them the vision of a universe symbolically transformed.

GUIDE TO READING

The book of Revelation is a work of extremes, ranging from soaring heights of hymnody inspired by Hebrew psalms and canticles to the gruesome language of plagues, warfare, and bloodshed. It uses the dualistic language characteristic of the apocalyptic genre to paint vivid portraits of the opposing sides in the eschatological conflict that will culminate in the definitive victory of God and the final defeat of all evil. With its symbolic numbers and colors, animals, and angelic and demonic beings, replete with echoes and images drawn from the literature of the ancient Near East, the Hebrew Bible, Greece, and Rome, the book of Revelation is so notoriously complex that the church father Jerome (345–420 CE) was led to remark that it contains as many mysteries as it contains words. Origen (185–254 CE) exclaimed, "Who can read the revelations granted to John without being amazed at the hidden depth of the ineffable mysteries, a depth apparent even to the person who does not understand what the text says?" (*On First Principles* 4.2.4). Many centuries later, the English author D. H. Lawrence (1885–1930) wrote, "When we read Revelation, we feel at once there are meanings behind meanings."

The symbolic visions of the book are by no means self-explanatory, and even John reports the need for the intervention of an angelic mediator to explain the meaning of mystery disclosed to him (17.7). This characteristic, common in other works of the same literary genre, serves to emphasize that there are transcendent levels of meaning that must be discerned. The significance of events on earth is to be sought above and beyond what is immediately apparent, and it is ultimately to God that believers must turn to receive the meaning and guidance that strengthen their resolve to persevere in the face of adversity.

Jean-Pierre Ruiz

1 The revelation of Jesus Christ, which God gave him to show his servants[a] what must soon take place; he made[b] it known by sending his angel to his servant[c] John, [2] who testified to the word of God and to the testimony of Jesus Christ, even to all that he saw.

[3] Blessed is the one who reads aloud the words of the prophecy, and blessed are those who hear and who keep what is written in it; for the time is near.

[4] John to the seven churches that are in Asia:

Grace to you and peace from him who is and who was and who is to come, and from the seven spirits who are before his throne, [5] and from Jesus Christ, the faithful witness, the firstborn of the dead, and the ruler of the kings of the earth.

a   Gk *slaves*
b   Gk *and he made*
c   Gk *slave*

1.1–3: The prologue. This revelation came from God through Jesus Christ and was communicated to John by an angel (referred to again in 22.16). **1:** *Revelation* (Gk "apokalypsis"; see Dan 2.28–30,45), a literary form in which a vision from God, often under the guidance of an angel or other heavenly messenger, communicates in symbolic language God's hidden plan for history. Apocalypses also include visions of the heavenly world. **3:** *Blessed is . . . ,* the first of seven beatitudes in the book of Revelation (cf. 14.13; 16.15; 19.9; 20.6; 22.7,14) is pronounced on the reader of this prophetic book and on those who hear it read and who heed its message. In antiquity, texts were commonly read aloud even among those who were literate. *The time is near* (repeated in 22.10) motivates obedience by announcing the imminence of the end-time.

1.4–8: Epistolary salutation to seven representative churches in the Roman province of Asia (in western Asia Minor). *Seven*, a number associated with heavenly realities, suggests the divine authority of the message delivered by John. **4:** *Grace . . . and peace* (see 2 Thess 1.2), combining the conventional Greek and Hebrew salutations, though John offers not his own greetings but those of God; *is . . . was . . . to come*, lit., "the being . . . the was . . . the coming." The seven spirits are either a symbolic reference to the manifold energies of the spirit of God (Isa 11.2), or a reference to the seven principal angels of God (Tob 12.15; 1 Enoch 20.1–8). Seven, the number of completion (of a ritual in Lev 4.6; of divine punishment in Lev 26.27–28) or wholeness, is the most important symbolic number in the book of Revelation. **5:** *Faithful witness*, Jesus testifies to the truth (Jn 18.37) and is the

To him who loves us and freed[a] us from our sins by his blood, [6] and made[b] us to be a kingdom, priests serving[c] his God and Father, to him be glory and dominion forever and ever. Amen.

[7] Look! He is coming with the clouds;
    every eye will see him,
even those who pierced him;
    and on his account all the tribes of the
        earth will wail.
So it is to be. Amen.

[8] "I am the Alpha and the Omega," says the Lord God, who is and who was and who is to come, the Almighty.

[9] I, John, your brother who share with you in Jesus the persecution and the kingdom and the patient endurance, was on the island called Patmos because of the word of God and the testimony of Jesus.[d] [10] I was in the spirit[e] on the Lord's day, and I heard behind me a loud voice like a trumpet [11] saying, "Write in a book what you see and send it to the seven churches, to Ephesus, to Smyrna, to Pergamum, to Thyatira, to Sardis, to Philadelphia, and to Laodicea."

[12] Then I turned to see whose voice it was that spoke to me, and on turning I saw seven golden lampstands, [13] and in the midst of the lampstands I saw one like the Son of Man, clothed with a long robe and with a golden sash across his chest. [14] His head and his hair were white as white wool, white as snow; his eyes were like a flame of fire, [15] his feet were like burnished bronze, refined as in a furnace, and his voice was like the sound of many waters. [16] In his right hand he held seven stars, and from his mouth came a sharp, two-edged sword, and his face was like the sun shining with full force.

[17] When I saw him, I fell at his feet as though dead. But he placed his right hand on me, saying, "Do not be afraid; I am the first and the last, [18] and the living one. I was dead, and see, I am alive forever and ever; and I have the keys of Death and of Hades. [19] Now write what you have seen, what is, and what is to take place after this. [20] As for the mystery of the seven stars that you saw in my right hand, and the seven golden lampstands:

a Other ancient authorities read *washed*
b Gk *and he made*
c Gk *priests to*
d Or *testimony to Jesus*
e Or *in the Spirit*

model for Christians who died as "witnesses" (2.13; 11.7; 17.6). *Firstborn . . . ruler of the kings*, Ps 119.27. He *loves* continually; he *freed* us once for all by his death (Rom 6.10). **6**: *Kingdom, priests*, the vocation promised to Israel (Ex 19.6; Isa 61.6) is extended to the followers of Jesus (1 Pet 2.9). *Glory and dominion*, Dan 7.14. **7**: Dan 7.13; Zech 12.10–12. *So it is to be. Amen*, a formal affirmation of this prophetic oracle announcing the coming of Christ. **8**: *Alpha and Omega*, the first and last letters of the Greek alphabet (like "A" and "Z" in English); hence, the beginning and end of all things (see v. 17; 22.13; Isa 44.6; 48.12).

1.9–20: Inaugural vision and commission on Patmos, a small island in the Aegean Sea where John found himself (see Introduction), ca. 55 mi (90 km) southwest of Ephesus (see map on p. 2157). **10**: *In the spirit*, in a state of prophetic ecstasy, a state of altered consciousness (also 4.2; Ezek 2.2). *The Lord's day*, the weekly day of Christian worship, Sunday. **11**: *The seven churches*, see 2.1–3.22. **12–16**: In the midst of the churches (see v. 20) stands the exalted Christ, whose royalty, eternity, wisdom, and immutability are suggested by means of symbols; the effect is that of terrifying majesty (compare v. 17 with Isa 6.5). *Seven golden lampstands*, reminiscent of those that stood in the wilderness tabernacle and in the Jerusalem Temple (cf. Zech 4.1–14). *Son of Man* (cf. 14.14; Mk 2.10), a title Jesus used of himself, had two meanings: (1) a typical human being in accordance with a common extended meaning of "son of" (see Mt 5.45); (2) a reference to the heavenly figure of Dan 7.13–14 who was to embody God's rule over the nations. **13–15**: *Golden sash*, Dan 10.5; *white . . . snow*, Dan 7.10; *eyes . . . fire*, Dan 10.6; *feet . . . bronze*, Dan 10.6; *sound of many waters*, a frequent accompaniment of divine appearance; see Ps 29.3; 93.4; Ezek 1.24; 43.2; cf. Dan 10.6. The figure is a combination of attributes of the heavenly messenger from Dan 10 and the Ancient One from Dan 7. *From his mouth came a sharp, two-edged sword* (cf. 19.15,21), the word of God (Isa 49.2; cf. Heb 4.12). **18**: *Hades*, used here with its synonym *Death*, is the abode of the dead; Jesus has the keys to release those confined within its gates (Mt 16.18; Jn 5.25–29). **20**: *Mystery*, hidden meanings that human beings cannot grasp without the assistance of divine revelation (Rev 1.20; 10.7; 17.5,7; Dan 2.29,45). Angel guardians are assigned to the seven churches, as also to nations (Dan 10.20–21; 12.1) and individuals (Dan 11.1).

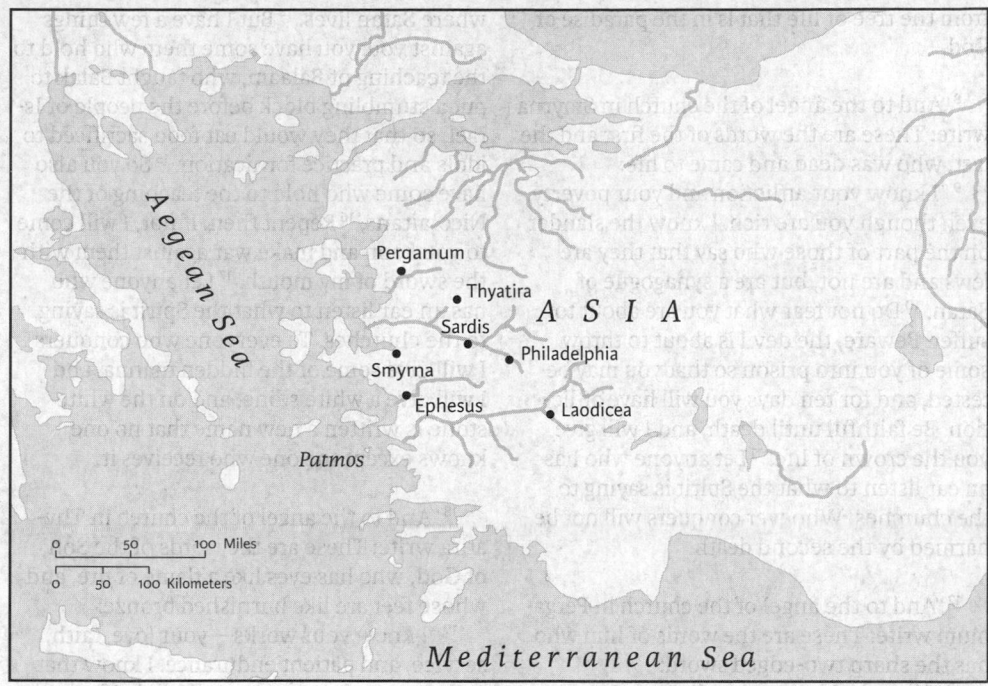

Chs 2–3: The seven churches.

the seven stars are the angels of the seven churches, and the seven lampstands are the seven churches.

2 "To the angel of the church in Ephesus write: These are the words of him who holds the seven stars in his right hand, who walks among the seven golden lampstands: ² "I know your works, your toil and your patient endurance. I know that you cannot tolerate evildoers; you have tested those who claim to be apostles but are not, and have found them to be false. ³ I also know that you are enduring patiently and bearing up for the sake of my name, and that you have not grown weary. ⁴ But I have this against you, that you have abandoned the love you had at first. ⁵ Remember then from what you have fallen; repent, and do the works you did at first. If not, I will come to you and remove your lampstand from its place, unless you repent. ⁶ Yet this is to your credit: you hate the works of the Nicolaitans, which I also hate. ⁷ Let anyone who has an ear listen to what the Spirit is saying to the churches. To everyone who conquers, I will give permission to eat

2.1–3.22: The messages to the seven churches, each containing an address, a descriptive phrase referring to the risen Christ, a commendation or condemnation of the church addressed, an admonition, and a concluding promise and exhortation to the faithful. For the location of the seven churches, see map above.

2.1–7: The first message is appropriately sent to *Ephesus*, the seaport city that was the administrative and commercial hub of the Roman province of Asia; Paul had labored here (Acts 19.8–10; 1 Cor 15.32; 16.8; cf. Eph 1.1). 1: Jesus *walks among* the churches (1.20). 2: *Evildoers*, compare the warning to the Ephesian elders in Acts 20.29–30; cf. 2 Cor 11.13. 6: *To hate evil* is the counterpart of the love of what God approves (Isa 61.8; Zech 8.17; 1QS 1.4). The *Nicolaitans* (probably not connected with the Nicolaus of Acts 6.5, contrary to Irenaeus, *Adv. Haer*. 1.26.3) are also mentioned in the message to the church in Pergamum (v. 15). It is not known what their *works* were, or what they may have taught, though it is possible that they permitted some accommodation to the local religious practices that the book of Revelation opposes. 7: *What the Spirit is saying*, speaking through Jesus to John, and through John to the churches (cf. Rev 2.11,17,29; 3.6,13,22). *Conquers*, a military term, suggesting

from the tree of life that is in the paradise of God.

[8] "And to the angel of the church in Smyrna write: These are the words of the first and the last, who was dead and came to life:

[9] "I know your affliction and your poverty, even though you are rich. I know the slander on the part of those who say that they are Jews and are not, but are a synagogue of Satan. [10] Do not fear what you are about to suffer. Beware, the devil is about to throw some of you into prison so that you may be tested, and for ten days you will have affliction. Be faithful until death, and I will give you the crown of life. [11] Let anyone who has an ear listen to what the Spirit is saying to the churches. Whoever conquers will not be harmed by the second death.

[12] "And to the angel of the church in Pergamum write: These are the words of him who has the sharp two-edged sword:

[13] "I know where you are living, where Satan's throne is. Yet you are holding fast to my name, and you did not deny your faith in me[a] even in the days of Antipas my witness, my faithful one, who was killed among you,

where Satan lives. [14] But I have a few things against you: you have some there who hold to the teaching of Balaam, who taught Balak to put a stumbling block before the people of Israel, so that they would eat food sacrificed to idols and practice fornication. [15] So you also have some who hold to the teaching of the Nicolaitans. [16] Repent then. If not, I will come to you soon and make war against them with the sword of my mouth. [17] Let anyone who has an ear listen to what the Spirit is saying to the churches. To everyone who conquers I will give some of the hidden manna, and I will give a white stone, and on the white stone is written a new name that no one knows except the one who receives it.

[18] "And to the angel of the church in Thyatira write: These are the words of the Son of God, who has eyes like a flame of fire, and whose feet are like burnished bronze:

[19] "I know your works—your love, faith, service, and patient endurance. I know that your last works are greater than the first. [20] But I have this against you: you tolerate that woman Jezebel, who calls herself a prophet

[a] Or deny my faith

continuous vigilance. Tree of life, Gen 2.9; 3.24; cf. Rev 22.2,14.

2.8–11: The second message, sent to Smyrna, commends the church for its perseverance amid affliction and poverty. Smyrna (modern Izmir) was a port city 30 mi (50 km) north of Ephesus. 8: Isa 44.6; 48.12. 9: *Rich*, in spiritual things. *Those who say that they are Jews and are not*, this accusation reflects struggles over identity, with some groups rejecting the claims to Jewish identity made by other groups. The word translated "Jew" (Gk "Ioudaios") could refer both to someone from Judea, and to an adherent of Judaism whether from birth or by conversion. *Synagogue of Satan* (cf. 3.9) likewise reflects significant tensions (cf. Jn 8.44; 1QH 2.22 refers to apostate Jews as "a congregation of Belial"). *Synagogue* can refer to a congregation or to a meeting place for a congregation. 10: *Ten days*, a limited period of trial (Dan 1.12). *Crown of life*, the reward of eternal life (Jas 1.12; 1 Pet 5.4). 11: *The second death*, the final condemnation of the unfaithful (20.14).

2.12–17: The third message is sent to *Pergamum*, a noted center of Roman emperor worship ca. 60 mi (80 km) north of Smyrna. 12: *Sharp two-edged sword*, 1.16n. 13: *Where Satan's throne is*, in contrast to the throne of God in ch 4, this may be a reference either to the temple of the Roman emperor or to the monumental altar of Zeus, both at Pergamum. *Antipas* is otherwise unknown; he is the only martyr named in the book. 14–15: *The teaching of Balaam*, here the author vilifies an opponent by comparing him to the diviner Balaam of Num 22.5–24.25. After Balaam's oracles, the Israelites engaged in both sexual relations with outsiders and the worship of foreign gods (see Num 25). To *eat food sacrificed to idols* meant either to participate in ritual banquets or to purchase and then consume meat that had been sacrificed in the temples of Pergamum (1 Cor 8; 10). *Practice fornication* here is meant metaphorically, with sexual misconduct symbolizing religious infidelity (Wis 14.12). 15: *Nicolaitans*, see v. 6n. 17: *Hidden manna*, eschatological nourishment from heaven (Ex 16.33–34; Ps 78.24). *White*, the color symbolizing victory and joy. *A new name*, Isa 62.2.

2.18–29: The fourth message is sent to Thyatira, a commercial center renowned for its many trade guilds, ca. 70 mi (110 km) north-northeast of Ephesus. Lydia, one of Paul's converts, was a dealer in purple cloth from

and is teaching and beguiling my servants[a] to practice fornication and to eat food sacrificed to idols. [21] I gave her time to repent, but she refuses to repent of her fornication. [22] Beware, I am throwing her on a bed, and those who commit adultery with her I am throwing into great distress, unless they repent of her doings; [23] and I will strike her children dead. And all the churches will know that I am the one who searches minds and hearts, and I will give to each of you as your works deserve. [24] But to the rest of you in Thyatira, who do not hold this teaching, who have not learned what some call 'the deep things of Satan,' to you I say, I do not lay on you any other burden; [25] only hold fast to what you have until I come. [26] To everyone who conquers and continues to do my works to the end,

I will give authority over the nations;
[27] to rule[b] them with an iron rod,
    as when clay pots are shattered—
[28] even as I also received authority from my Father. To the one who conquers I will also give the morning star. [29] Let anyone who has an ear listen to what the Spirit is saying to the churches.

3 "And to the angel of the church in Sardis write: These are the words of him who has the seven spirits of God and the seven stars:

"I know your works; you have a name of being alive, but you are dead. [2] Wake up, and strengthen what remains and is on the point of death, for I have not found your works perfect in the sight of my God. [3] Remember then what you received and heard; obey it, and repent. If you do not wake up, I will come like a thief, and you will not know at what hour I will come to you. [4] Yet you have still a few persons in Sardis who have not soiled their clothes; they will walk with me, dressed in white, for they are worthy. [5] If you conquer, you will be clothed like them in white robes, and I will not blot your name out of the book of life; I will confess your name before my Father and before his angels. [6] Let anyone who has an ear listen to what the Spirit is saying to the churches.

[7] "And to the angel of the church in Philadelphia write:

These are the words of the holy one, the true one,
    who has the key of David,
    who opens and no one will shut,
        who shuts and no one opens:
[8] "I know your works. Look, I have set before you an open door, which no one is able to shut. I know that you have but little power, and yet you have kept my word and have not denied my name. [9] I will make those of the synagogue of Satan who say that they

a Gk *slaves*
b Or *to shepherd*

Thyatira (Acts 16.14–15). **18:** Dan 10.6. **20:** *That woman Jezebel, who calls herself a prophet*, John's characterization of a female opponent at Thyatira, here identified contemptuously with the Phoenician wife of King Ahab, the queen who worshiped Baal and who opposed the prophet Elijah (1 Kings 16.31; 19.1–2). **22:** *I am throwing her on a bed*, punishment with serious sickness is threatened for the Thyatiran Jezebel. *Those who commit adultery with her* are those who are complicit in her worship of other gods. In the Hebrew Bible marital infidelity is a frequent metaphor for worship of gods other than the LORD (Deut 31.16; Judg 2.17; 1 Chr 5.25; Jer 3.6–11); see also vv. 14–15n. **23:** *Her children*, those who follow her teachings. **24:** *Deep things of Satan*, a sarcastic reference to her teachings (contrast 1 Cor 2.10). **26–27:** The conquerors will share in Jesus' rule (Ps 2.8–9). **28:** *The morning star* is Jesus himself (22.16; cf. Num 24.17).

3.1–6: The fifth message is sent to Sardis, a prosperous city ca. 55 mi (85 km) northeast of Ephesus that had been the capital of the kingdom of Lydia. **1:** *Seven spirits*, see 1.4n. *Seven stars*, 1.20. *You have a name*, its commitment in faith was only nominal. **3:** *Received and heard*, the gospel. Like a thief, just when unexpected (16.15; Mt 24.42–44; 1 Thess 5.2). **4–5:** *Soiled . . . white*, not impurity/purity, but surrender/conquest (see 2.17n.). *White robes* are a frequent image; see 3.18; 4.4; 6.11; 7.9; 19.14; cf. Zech 3.3–5. **5:** *Book of life*, the register of God containing the names of the redeemed (13.8; 17.8; 20.12,15; Ex 32.32; Ps 69.28; Dan 12.1; Mal 3.16; Lk 10.20).

3.7–13: The sixth message is sent to *Philadelphia*, a small town 80 mi (50 km) southeast of Sardis. **7:** *Key of David*, a symbol of authority (Isa 22.22). **8:** *An open door*, of opportunity (1 Cor 16.9; 2 Cor 2.12). **9:** *Synagogue of Satan*, see 2.9n. On tension between Christians and Jews in Philadelphia see Ignatius, *Philad.* 6.1. *Bow down*

are Jews and are not, but are lying—I will make them come and bow down before your feet, and they will learn that I have loved you. [10] Because you have kept my word of patient endurance, I will keep you from the hour of trial that is coming on the whole world to test the inhabitants of the earth. [11] I am coming soon; hold fast to what you have, so that no one may seize your crown. [12] If you conquer, I will make you a pillar in the temple of my God; you will never go out of it. I will write on you the name of my God, and the name of the city of my God, the new Jerusalem that comes down from my God out of heaven, and my own new name. [13] Let anyone who has an ear listen to what the Spirit is saying to the churches.

[14] "And to the angel of the church in Laodicea write: The words of the Amen, the faithful and true witness, the origin[a] of God's creation:

[15] "I know your works; you are neither cold nor hot. I wish that you were either cold or hot. [16] So, because you are lukewarm, and neither cold nor hot, I am about to spit you out of my mouth. [17] For you say, 'I am rich, I have prospered, and I need nothing.' You do not realize that you are wretched, pitiable, poor, blind, and naked. [18] Therefore I counsel you to buy from me gold refined by fire so that you may be rich; and white robes to clothe you and to keep the shame of your nakedness from being seen; and salve to anoint your eyes so that you may see. [19] I reprove and discipline those whom I love. Be earnest, therefore, and repent. [20] Listen! I am standing at the door, knocking; if you hear my voice and open the door, I will come in to you and eat with you, and you with me. [21] To the one who conquers I will give a place with me on my throne, just as I myself conquered and sat down with my Father on his throne. [22] Let anyone who has an ear listen to what the Spirit is saying to the churches."

4 After this I looked, and there in heaven a door stood open! And the first voice, which I had heard speaking to me like a trumpet, said, "Come up here, and I will show you what must take place after this." [2] At once I was in the spirit,[b] and there in heaven stood a throne, with one seated on the throne! [3] And the one seated there looks like jasper and carnelian, and around the throne is a rainbow that looks like an emerald. [4] Around the throne are twenty-four thrones, and seated on the thrones are twenty-four elders, dressed in white robes, with golden crowns on their heads. [5] Coming from the throne are flashes of lightning, and rumblings and peals

---

a   Or *beginning*
b   Or *in the Spirit*

---

before your feet, Isa 43.4; 60.14. **10:** Despite its weakness (v. 8), the Philadelphian church will be safeguarded during the eschatological tribulation. **11:** *I am coming soon*, 22.7,12,20. **12:** *A pillar*, steadfast and permanent (Gal 2.9). *New Jerusalem*, 21.2. *The name of my God*, marking the one inscribed as God's possession and as specially dedicated to God. *The name of the city of my God*, signifying citizenship in the new Jerusalem; see 21.2,10.

 3.14–22: The seventh message is sent to Laodicea, a wealthy city near Colossae (Col 2.1; 4.13–16), 95 mi (155 km) east of Ephesus. **14:** *The Amen* is Jesus Christ (2 Cor 1.20). *The faithful and true witness*, 1.5. The list of titles may derive from a Greek translation of Isa 65.16. The origin of God's creation, Jesus Christ is the principle and source of all creation (Jn 1.3; Col 1.15,18). **15–16:** Their lukewarm commitment is nauseating: *spit you out of my mouth*. **17:** Complacent and self-satisfied, they are spiritually poverty-stricken (Hos 12.8). **18:** *Buy from me gold refined by fire*, an idiom for removing sin from one's life (Job 23.10; Prov 27.21). A commercial transaction is used here as a metaphor for accepting salvation. *Eyes*, Laodicea was noted for its manufacture of a medication for ophthalmic disorders. **19:** God's chastening has beneficent motives (Prov 3.12; Heb 12.5–11). **20:** An invitation to participate in the messianic banquet in the coming age (cf. Mt 26.29). **21:** *A place with me*, a promise of reigning with Jesus in glory (22.5; Lk 22.30).

 4.1–5.14: Vision of God enthroned and of the Lamb. 4.1: *The first voice*, the voice of the exalted Jesus mentioned in 1.10. *Come up*, John is invited to ascend to heaven, to behold visions of God (Ezek 3.12; 8.3; 11.1). *What must take place*, Dan 2.29. **2:** *A throne*, Ezek 1.26–28; Dan 7.9. **3:** The glory of the divine presence is described in terms of precious gemstones; cf. Ex 24.10. *Twenty-four elders*, attendants around God's heavenly throne, probably symbolizing the twelve tribes of Israel and the twelve apostles. **5:** *Flashes of lightning*, expressive of the

of thunder, and in front of the throne burn seven flaming torches, which are the seven spirits of God; ⁶ and in front of the throne there is something like a sea of glass, like crystal.

Around the throne, and on each side of the throne, are four living creatures, full of eyes in front and behind: ⁷ the first living creature like a lion, the second living creature like an ox, the third living creature with a face like a human face, and the fourth living creature like a flying eagle. ⁸ And the four living creatures, each of them with six wings, are full of eyes all around and inside. Day and night without ceasing they sing,

"Holy, holy, holy,
the Lord God the Almighty,
    who was and is and is to come."

⁹ And whenever the living creatures give glory and honor and thanks to the one who is seated on the throne, who lives forever and ever, ¹⁰ the twenty-four elders fall before the one who is seated on the throne and worship the one who lives forever and ever; they cast their crowns before the throne, singing,

¹¹ "You are worthy, our Lord and God,
    to receive glory and honor and power,
for you created all things,
    and by your will they existed and were
        created."

5 Then I saw in the right hand of the one seated on the throne a scroll written on the inside and on the back, sealed[a] with seven seals; ² and I saw a mighty angel proclaiming with a loud voice, "Who is worthy to open the scroll and break its seals?" ³ And no one in heaven or on earth or under the earth was able to open the scroll or to look into it. ⁴ And I began to weep bitterly because no one was found worthy to open the scroll or to look into it. ⁵ Then one of the elders said to me, "Do not weep. See, the Lion of the tribe of Judah, the Root of David, has conquered, so that he can open the scroll and its seven seals."

⁶ Then I saw between the throne and the four living creatures and among the elders a Lamb standing as if it had been slaughtered, having seven horns and seven eyes, which are the seven spirits of God sent out into all the earth. ⁷ He went and took the scroll from the right hand of the one who was seated on the throne. ⁸ When he had taken the scroll, the four living creatures and the twenty-four elders fell before the Lamb, each holding a harp and golden bowls full of incense, which are the prayers of the saints. ⁹ They sing a new song:

"You are worthy to take the scroll
    and to open its seals,
for you were slaughtered and by your
        blood you ransomed for God
    saints from[b] every tribe and language
        and people and nation;
¹⁰ you have made them to be a kingdom
        and priests serving[c] our God,
    and they will reign on earth."

---

a Or *written on the inside, and sealed on the back*
b Gk *ransomed for God from*
c Gk *priests to*

---

majesty of God (Ex 19.16; Ezek 1.13; Rev 11.19). *Seven flaming torches,* Zech 4.2–3. *Seven spirits,* 1.4. **6:** *A sea of glass,* Ex 24.10; Ezek 1.22. *Four living creatures,* heavenly beings representing humankind and all animals (Ezek 1.5,10). *Full of eyes,* symbolizing unceasing watchfulness (Ezek 1.18). **8:** *Six wings . . . "Holy, holy, holy,"* Isa 6.2–3. **10:** *Cast their crowns,* an act of homage and submission, acknowledging that all power comes from God. **11:** *Our Lord and God,* titles that were also attributed to the Roman emperor (Suetonius, *Domitian* 13). **5.1:** *A scroll,* containing the divine plan of judgment and salvation (Ezek 2.9–10). *Sealed,* therefore both unalterable and unknown to others (Dan 12.4). **3–5:** No created being is worthy to carry out God's plan; only the messiah can do so. *Lion of . . . Judah,* Gen 49.9–10. *Root of David,* Isa 11.1,10. *Has conquered,* the paradoxical victory of the cross and resurrection (Jn 16.33). **6–9:** The *Lamb . . . slaughtered,* the crucified messiah, a reference to Jesus' death, by which God's purposes contained in the scroll are accomplished (Isa 53.7; Jn 1.29,36; 1 Pet 1.19). *Seven horns,* fullness of power (Deut 33.17; Ps 89.17; Dan 7.7–8.24; *1 Enoch* 80.6–12,37). *Seven eyes,* Zech 3.9; 4.10; 2 Chr 16.9. *Seven spirits,* 1.4. **8:** *Harp and golden bowls,* objects used in worship. *The prayers of the saints* on earth are joined with the worship rendered to the *Lamb* by the heavenly creatures. **9–10:** *A new song* is sung because Jesus by his death has inaugurated a new era (14.3). New hymns of praise mark and celebrate special occasions (Ps 33.3; 40.3; 96.1; 98.1; 144.9; 149.1; Isa 42.10). The Lamb is adored in terms similar to the adoration rendered to God (4.11). *A kingdom and priests,* see

¹¹ Then I looked, and I heard the voice of many angels surrounding the throne and the living creatures and the elders; they numbered myriads of myriads and thousands of thousands, ¹² singing with full voice,

"Worthy is the Lamb that was slaughtered
to receive power and wealth and wisdom
        and might
and honor and glory and blessing!"

¹³ Then I heard every creature in heaven and on earth and under the earth and in the sea, and all that is in them, singing,

"To the one seated on the throne and to
        the Lamb
be blessing and honor and glory and
        might
forever and ever!"

¹⁴ And the four living creatures said, "Amen!" And the elders fell down and worshiped.

6 Then I saw the Lamb open one of the seven seals, and I heard one of the four living creatures call out, as with a voice of thunder, "Come!"ᵃ ² I looked, and there was a white horse! Its rider had a bow; a crown was given to him, and he came out conquering and to conquer.

³ When he opened the second seal, I heard the second living creature call out, "Come!"ᵃ ⁴ And out cameᵇ another horse, bright red; its rider was permitted to take peace from the earth, so that people would slaughter one another; and he was given a great sword.

⁵ When he opened the third seal, I heard the third living creature call out, "Come!"ᵃ I looked, and there was a black horse! Its rider held a pair of scales in his hand, ⁶ and I heard what seemed to be a voice in the midst of the four living creatures saying, "A quart of wheat for a day's pay,ᶜ and three quarts of barley for a day's pay,ᶜ but do not damage the olive oil and the wine!"

⁷ When he opened the fourth seal, I heard the voice of the fourth living creature call out, "Come!"ᵃ ⁸ I looked and there was a pale green horse! Its rider's name was Death, and Hades followed with him; they were given authority over a fourth of the earth, to kill with sword, famine, and pestilence, and by the wild animals of the earth.

⁹ When he opened the fifth seal, I saw under the altar the souls of those who had been slaughtered for the word of God and for the testimony they had given; ¹⁰ they cried out with a loud voice, "Sovereign Lord, holy and true, how long will it be before you judge and avenge our blood on the inhabitants of the earth?" ¹¹ They were each given a white

---

ᵃ Or "Go!"
ᵇ Or went
ᶜ Gk a denarius

1.6n. **11–12:** The sevenfold praise of *myriads* (tens of thousands; Dan 7.10) in heaven honoring the sacrificial *Lamb*. **13:** Universal praise to God and to the *Lamb* as equal in majesty.

6.1–17: The opening of the first six seals of the scroll, and the enactment of what is written in it.

6.1–8: Four seals of destruction. 1: *Come!* Addressed successively to each of the four riders (Zech 6.1–8) who accomplish God's purposes. **2:** The *white horse* symbolizes a conquering power that none can resist; in 19.11–13 the reference is to Jesus. The *crown* given to the rider as he is sent forth suggests a guarantee of victory. **4:** The *red horse* symbolizes war and bloodshed. *Permitted to take peace from the earth,* effectively annulling the "pax Romana," the self-congratulatory designation of Roman imperial rule as "the Roman peace." **5:** The *black horse* symbolizes famine, which follows upon war. **6:** *A quart of wheat . . . three quarts of barley,* sold at exorbitantly inflated prices because of war and famine (cf. 2 Kings 6.24–25). The prohibition against harming the *olive oil* and the *wine* (neither olive trees nor grape vines are newly planted each year) suggests that the famine is limited. **8:** The *pale green horse* symbolizes pestilence and death. *Hades,* the Greek god of the underworld; cf. 1.18. A *fourth* part indicates wide but not total devastation. *Pestilence,* Ex 9.3; 2 Sam 24.13; Ezek 5.12. *Wild animals,* Ezek 6.17; 29.5; 33.27.

6.9–8.1: Three seals of judgment.

6.9–11: The fifth seal describes the appeal for divine justice and retribution by the martyrs (v. 10), and the heavenly response to their plea (v. 11). **9:** The *souls* of the martyrs are said to be *under the altar* because they had been martyred for the sake of Jesus (2.10; Mt 24.9; Phil 2.17; 2 Tim 4.6). **10:** *How long?* is a cry for divine vindication uttered by those who have suffered unbearable oppression (e.g., Ps 6.3; 13.2; 90.13; Zech 1.12–16). *Avenge*

robe and told to rest a little longer, until the number would be complete both of their fellow servants[a] and of their brothers and sisters,[b] who were soon to be killed as they themselves had been killed.

[12] When he opened the sixth seal, I looked, and there came a great earthquake; the sun became black as sackcloth, the full moon became like blood, [13] and the stars of the sky fell to the earth as the fig tree drops its winter fruit when shaken by a gale. [14] The sky vanished like a scroll rolling itself up, and every mountain and island was removed from its place. [15] Then the kings of the earth and the magnates and the generals and the rich and the powerful, and everyone, slave and free, hid in the caves and among the rocks of the mountains, [16] calling to the mountains and rocks, "Fall on us and hide us from the face of the one seated on the throne and from the wrath of the Lamb; [17] for the great day of their wrath has come, and who is able to stand?"

7 After this I saw four angels standing at the four corners of the earth, holding back the four winds of the earth so that no wind could blow on earth or sea or against any tree. [2] I saw another angel ascending from the rising of the sun, having the seal of the living God, and he called with a loud voice to the four angels who had been given power to damage earth and sea, [3] saying, "Do not damage the earth or the sea or the trees, until we have marked the servants[a] of our God with a seal on their foreheads."

[4] And I heard the number of those who were sealed, one hundred forty-four thousand, sealed out of every tribe of the people of Israel:

[5] From the tribe of Judah twelve thousand sealed,
   from the tribe of Reuben twelve thousand,
   from the tribe of Gad twelve thousand,
[6] from the tribe of Asher twelve thousand,
   from the tribe of Naphtali twelve thousand,
   from the tribe of Manasseh twelve thousand,
[7] from the tribe of Simeon twelve thousand,
   from the tribe of Levi twelve thousand,
   from the tribe of Issachar twelve thousand,
[8] from the tribe of Zebulun twelve thousand,
   from the tribe of Joseph twelve thousand,
   from the tribe of Benjamin twelve thousand sealed.

[9] After this I looked, and there was a great multitude that no one could count, from every nation, from all tribes and peoples and languages, standing before the throne and before the Lamb, robed in white, with palm branches in their hands. [10] They cried out in a loud voice, saying,

"Salvation belongs to our God who is seated on the throne, and to the Lamb!"

[11] And all the angels stood around the throne and around the elders and the four living creatures, and they fell on their faces before the throne and worshiped God, [12] singing,

[a] Gk slaves
[b] Gk brothers

our blood, God is the one who takes up the cause of those killed for the sake of justice (Ps 78.1–10 [LXX]). **11:** White robe, see 2.17n.; 3.4–5n.; 7.9n.

6.12–17: The opening of the sixth seal unleashes *a great earthquake,* and its catastrophic effects on the cosmos and on human society are described. **12:** *Black as sackcloth . . . ,* Joel 2.30–31. **13–14:** Isa 34.4; Mk 13.25. **15–17:** All classes of society seek to escape from the wrath of God (Isa 2.10,19). **16:** *Fall on us,* Hos 10.8; Lk 23.30. **17:** *The great day of their wrath,* the time of judgment (Joel 2.11).

7.1–17: An interlude between the sixth and seventh seals: two visions that provide the promise of divine protection for the faithful during the time of tribulation (vv. 1–8) and assurance of ultimate salvation (vv. 9–17). **1:** *The four winds* are destructive forces to be unleashed by God (Jer 49.36). They correspond to the four horsemen in 6.1–8 (see Zech 6.5). **3:** A *seal* (Ezek 9.4–6) marks those under God's protection. Seals were used to signify ownership or authorship. **4:** The symbolic number 144,000, which is the square of 12 multiplied by 1,000, has been interpreted variously as a reference to: the faithful remnant of Israel; the church; the martyrs; the remnant of Christians who survive the eschatological turmoil; all the redeemed (14.1,3). *Every tribe,* but the tribes of Dan and Ephraim are not mentioned. **9:** *A great multitude* (see Dan 7.14), in contrast with the 144,000 in v. 4 (5.9).

"Amen! Blessing and glory and wisdom
and thanksgiving and honor
and power and might
be to our God forever and ever! Amen."
[13] Then one of the elders addressed me,
saying, "Who are these, robed in white, and
where have they come from?" [14] I said to him,
"Sir, you are the one that knows." Then he
said to me, "These are they who have come
out of the great ordeal; they have washed
their robes and made them white in the blood
of the Lamb.
[15] For this reason they are before the
   throne of God,
   and worship him day and night within
      his temple,
   and the one who is seated on the throne
      will shelter them.
[16] They will hunger no more, and thirst no
      more;
   the sun will not strike them,
   nor any scorching heat;
[17] for the Lamb at the center of the throne
      will be their shepherd,
   and he will guide them to springs of the
      water of life,
and God will wipe away every tear from
      their eyes."

8 When the Lamb opened the seventh seal,
there was silence in heaven for about half
an hour. [2] And I saw the seven angels who
stand before God, and seven trumpets were
given to them.
[3] Another angel with a golden censer
came and stood at the altar; he was given a
great quantity of incense to offer with the
prayers of all the saints on the golden altar
that is before the throne. [4] And the smoke of
the incense, with the prayers of the saints,
rose before God from the hand of the angel.
[5] Then the angel took the censer and filled
it with fire from the altar and threw it on
the earth; and there were peals of thunder,
rumblings, flashes of lightning, and an
earthquake.
[6] Now the seven angels who had the seven
trumpets made ready to blow them.
[7] The first angel blew his trumpet, and
there came hail and fire, mixed with blood,
and they were hurled to the earth; and a third
of the earth was burned up, and a third of the
trees were burned up, and all green grass was
burned up.
[8] The second angel blew his trumpet, and
something like a great mountain, burning
with fire, was thrown into the sea. [9] A third
of the sea became blood, a third of the living
creatures in the sea died, and a third of the
ships were destroyed.
[10] The third angel blew his trumpet, and
a great star fell from heaven, blazing like a
torch, and it fell on a third of the rivers and
on the springs of water. [11] The name of the
star is Wormwood. A third of the waters
became wormwood, and many died from the
water, because it was made bitter.
[12] The fourth angel blew his trumpet, and
a third of the sun was struck, and a third of
the moon, and a third of the stars, so that a
third of their light was darkened; a third of

White robes and *palm branches* symbolize righteousness and victory (see 3.4–5n.; Dan 11.35). **12:** A sevenfold
ascription of praise to God. **14:** *The blood of the Lamb* cleanses from sin (Jn 1.29; 1 Jn 1.7); in the symbolism of the
book, *blood* (violent death) can make *robes . . . white* (lead to victory); cf. Isa 1.18. **15:** *Before the throne of God*, in
God's presence because of their faithfulness. Their ceaseless *worship* takes place in God's temple in heaven.
Shelter them, lit., "spread his tabernacle over them." **16:** Isa 49.10; Ps 121.6. **17:** A paradox: The *Lamb* is a *shepherd*
(Ps 23.1–2; Ezek 34.23–24; Jn 10.11). *Springs of . . . life*, 21.6; 22.1,17; Jn 4.10; 7.37. *Wipe away every tear*, 21.4; Isa 25.8.

8.1–5: The seventh seal is opened. The opening of the last of the seven seals (5.1; 6.1) leads to an awesome
and reverent *silence*, as response to divine judgment (Hab 3.3–6; Zech 2.13–3.2). A return to "primeval silence"
prior to the judgment appears in 2 Esd 7.30. **2:** The seven angels *stand before God* ready to do God's will (Tob
12.15). **3:** *Incense . . . prayers*, Ps 141.2. **5:** Ezek 10.2. The *earthquake* announces the divine judgment about to be
executed.

8.6–9.21: The first six trumpets unleash new convulsions of nature, patterned after the plagues inflicted on
Egypt in the book of Exodus (Ex 7.14–10.23).

8.6–13: Four trumpets of destruction. 7: *Hail and fire*, Ex 9.23–25; both destroyers of crops. *A third*, the devastation wrought by the trumpet plagues is not total. **9:** Ex 7.20. **11:** *Wormwood*, a bitter herb, poisons the waters
into which it falls (Jer 9.15; 23.15). It is associated with the constellation Scorpio. **12:** Ex 10.21–22; cf. Joel 3.15;

the day was kept from shining, and likewise the night.

¹³ Then I looked, and I heard an eagle crying with a loud voice as it flew in midheaven, "Woe, woe, woe to the inhabitants of the earth, at the blasts of the other trumpets that the three angels are about to blow!"

9 And the fifth angel blew his trumpet, and I saw a star that had fallen from heaven to earth, and he was given the key to the shaft of the bottomless pit; ² he opened the shaft of the bottomless pit, and from the shaft rose smoke like the smoke of a great furnace, and the sun and the air were darkened with the smoke from the shaft. ³ Then from the smoke came locusts on the earth, and they were given authority like the authority of scorpions of the earth. ⁴ They were told not to damage the grass of the earth or any green growth or any tree, but only those people who do not have the seal of God on their foreheads. ⁵ They were allowed to torture them for five months, but not to kill them, and their torture was like the torture of a scorpion when it stings someone. ⁶ And in those days people will seek death but will not find it; they will long to die, but death will flee from them.

⁷ In appearance the locusts were like horses equipped for battle. On their heads were what looked like crowns of gold; their faces were like human faces, ⁸ their hair like women's hair, and their teeth like lions'

teeth; ⁹ they had scales like iron breastplates, and the noise of their wings was like the noise of many chariots with horses rushing into battle. ¹⁰ They have tails like scorpions, with stingers, and in their tails is their power to harm people for five months. ¹¹ They have as king over them the angel of the bottomless pit; his name in Hebrew is Abaddon,ᵃ and in Greek he is called Apollyon.ᵇ

¹² The first woe has passed. There are still two woes to come.

¹³ Then the sixth angel blew his trumpet, and I heard a voice from the fourᶜ horns of the golden altar before God, ¹⁴ saying to the sixth angel who had the trumpet, "Release the four angels who are bound at the great river Euphrates." ¹⁵ So the four angels were released, who had been held ready for the hour, the day, the month, and the year, to kill a third of humankind. ¹⁶ The number of the troops of cavalry was two hundred million; I heard their number. ¹⁷ And this was how I saw the horses in my vision: the riders wore breastplates the color of fire and of sapphireᵈ and of sulfur; the heads of the horses were like lions' heads, and fire and smoke

ᵃ That is, *Destruction*
ᵇ That is, *Destroyer*
ᶜ Other ancient authorities lack *four*
ᵈ Gk *hyacinth*

Am 8.9. **13:** *An eagle* announces impending judgment. The threefold *woe* refers to the plagues unleashed at the sounding of the next three trumpets.

9.1–11.19: Three trumpets of woe.

9.1–12: The plague of monstrous locusts, which combine the terrors of evil spirits and of invading cavalry (perhaps a reference to the Parthians, an Iranian dynasty that ruled from Mesopotamia to India, at war with the Romans from the first century BCE to the second century CE). **1:** *A star . . . fallen from heaven,* a heavenly being, possibly an angel, identified by name in v. 11 (cf. Isa 14.12; Lk 10.18). The *bottomless pit* is the underworld, the abyss from which the beast arises (11.7; 17.8). **3:** *Locusts,* Ex 10.12–15; cf. Joel 1.4. **4:** God's servants are not to be harmed (7.3). **5:** *Five months,* while this might be a reference to the life cycle of locusts, which are hatched in spring and live until the end of summer, the more likely significance of this time period is symbolic, indicating the limited time span of this plague. **6:** *Will seek death,* in utter despair because of the torments (cf. Job 3.21). **7–10:** These are monstrous locusts, described in anthropomorphic terms (as in Joel 1 and 2), combining human features with the features of other creatures into a terrifying composite. *Teeth like lions',* Joel 1.6; *iron breastplates,* of a soldier or war horse (Job 39.19–20; *Tg. Nah.* 3.17, compares armor of Assyrian soldiers to locusts).

11: The name *Abaddon,* which means "Destruction," is a name for Sheol, the abode of the dead (see Job 26.6; Prov 15.11); here, as in Job 28,22, it is personified.

9.13–21: The plague of monstrous cavalry. 14: The *Euphrates* marked the eastern border of the Roman Empire, where invasion by its Parthian enemies threatened. **16–19:** These fire-breathing, lion-headed, serpent-tailed monsters are composite creatures, like the fire-breathing Chimera of Greek and Roman mythology. Also

and sulfur came out of their mouths. [18] By these three plagues a third of humankind was killed, by the fire and smoke and sulfur coming out of their mouths. [19] For the power of the horses is in their mouths and in their tails; their tails are like serpents, having heads; and with them they inflict harm.

[20] The rest of humankind, who were not killed by these plagues, did not repent of the works of their hands or give up worshiping demons and idols of gold and silver and bronze and stone and wood, which cannot see or hear or walk. [21] And they did not repent of their murders or their sorceries or their fornication or their thefts.

10 And I saw another mighty angel coming down from heaven, wrapped in a cloud, with a rainbow over his head; his face was like the sun, and his legs like pillars of fire. [2] He held a little scroll open in his hand. Setting his right foot on the sea and his left foot on the land, [3] he gave a great shout, like a lion roaring. And when he shouted, the seven thunders sounded. [4] And when the seven thunders had sounded, I was about to write, but I heard a voice from heaven saying, "Seal up what the seven thunders have said, and do not write it down." [5] Then the angel whom I saw standing on the sea and the land raised his right hand to heaven
> [6] and swore by him who lives forever and ever,

who created heaven and what is in it, the earth and what is in it, and the sea and what is in it: "There will be no more delay, [7] but in the days when the seventh angel is to blow his trumpet, the mystery of God will be fulfilled, as he announced to his servants[a] the prophets."

[8] Then the voice that I had heard from heaven spoke to me again, saying, "Go, take the scroll that is open in the hand of the angel who is standing on the sea and on the land." [9] So I went to the angel and told him to give me the little scroll; and he said to me, "Take it, and eat; it will be bitter to your stomach, but sweet as honey in your mouth." [10] So I took the little scroll from the hand of the angel and ate it; it was sweet as honey in my mouth, but when I had eaten it, my stomach was made bitter.

[11] Then they said to me, "You must prophesy again about many peoples and nations and languages and kings."

11 Then I was given a measuring rod like a staff, and I was told, "Come and measure the temple of God and the altar and those who worship there, [2] but do not measure the court outside the temple; leave that out, for it is given over to the nations, and they will trample over the holy city for forty-two months. [3] And I will grant my two witnesses authority to prophesy for one thousand two hundred sixty days, wearing sackcloth."

[a]   Gk *slaves*

---

see the description of conquering soldiers in Jer 46.2–23. **20–21:** The trumpet plagues fail to provoke the repentance that is their purpose. Compare the hardness of Pharaoh's heart despite the plagues (Ex 8.15,19). **20:** *Idols,* Dan 5.23. **21:** *Murders . . . thefts,* sins associated with the idolatrous worship of other gods, Wis 12.3–6.

10.1–11.13: An interlude between the sixth and seventh trumpets; two visions (10.1–11 and 11.1–13) present a renewal of John's prophetic commission (10.1–11) and describe what becomes of the two prophetic witnesses in the holy city (11.1–13).

10.1–11: The commission renewed. 1: *Another mighty angel,* in addition to the mighty angel in 5.2. **2:** The *little scroll* is distinct from the seven-sealed scroll in the right hand of God in 5.1. This scroll is in the angel's left hand, since in 10.5 he raises his right hand to heaven to swear an oath (Dan 12.7). *Sea* and *land* indicate the scope of the angel's authority. **4:** John is prohibited from disclosing what the *seven thunders have said,* but he "must prophesy again" (v. 11) after eating the little scroll. **6:** There will be *no more delay* in the accomplishment of God's will—the sounding of the seventh trumpet is imminent. **7:** *The mystery of God,* Rom 16.25–26; Eph 1.9; 3.3–9; Col 1.26–27. *His servants the prophets,* Am 3.7. **8–10:** Ezek 2.9–3.3. **10:** *Sweet,* because it contains God's words; *bitter* because it involves God's terrible judgments (Ezek 2.10). **11:** *You must,* an inescapable obligation, in accord with the divine will, *prophesy again;* the second part of the book (chs 12–22) contains these prophecies. *Peoples and nations and languages and kings* (Dan 3.4,7 [LXX]; 7.14; Rev 5.9; 7.9) suggests the broad range of John's prophetic activity.

11.1–13: The measuring of the temple and the two witnesses. 1: The symbolic act of the measurement of the sanctuary *and those who worship there* emphasizes the protection and preservation of the faithful who are within

4 These are the two olive trees and the two lampstands that stand before the Lord of the earth. 5 And if anyone wants to harm them, fire pours from their mouth and consumes their foes; anyone who wants to harm them must be killed in this manner. 6 They have authority to shut the sky, so that no rain may fall during the days of their prophesying, and they have authority over the waters to turn them into blood, and to strike the earth with every kind of plague, as often as they desire.

7 When they have finished their testimony, the beast that comes up from the bottomless pit will make war on them and conquer them and kill them, 8 and their dead bodies will lie in the street of the great city that is prophetically[a] called Sodom and Egypt, where also their Lord was crucified. 9 For three and a half days members of the peoples and tribes and languages and nations will gaze at their dead bodies and refuse to let them be placed in a tomb; 10 and the inhabitants of the earth will gloat over them and celebrate and exchange presents, because these two prophets had been a torment to the inhabitants of the earth.

11 But after the three and a half days, the breath[b] of life from God entered them, and they stood on their feet, and those who saw them were terrified. 12 Then they[c] heard a loud voice from heaven saying to them, "Come up here!" And they went up to heaven in a cloud while their enemies watched them. 13 At that moment there was a great earth-quake, and a tenth of the city fell; seven thousand people were killed in the earthquake, and the rest were terrified and gave glory to the God of heaven.

14 The second woe has passed. The third woe is coming very soon.

15 Then the seventh angel blew his trumpet, and there were loud voices in heaven, saying,

"The kingdom of the world has become
    the kingdom of our Lord
    and of his Messiah,[d]
and he will reign forever and ever."

16 Then the twenty-four elders who sit on their thrones before God fell on their faces and worshiped God, 17 singing,

"We give you thanks, Lord God Almighty,
    who are and who were,
for you have taken your great power
    and begun to reign.
18 The nations raged,
    but your wrath has come,
    and the time for judging the dead,
for rewarding your servants,[e] the prophets
    and saints and all who fear your name,
    both small and great,
and for destroying those who destroy the
    earth."

a   Or *allegorically*; Gk *spiritually*
b   Or *the spirit*
c   Other ancient authorities read *I*
d   Gk *Christ*
e   Gk *slaves*

(as in Zech 2.1–5; cf. Ezek 40.3–42.20). **2:** *The court outside,* the court of the Gentiles. *The holy city,* Jerusalem (Neh 11.1; Isa 52.1; Mt 4.5; 27.53). *Forty-two months* = 1,260 days (v. 3) = 3 1/2 years, a number that symbolizes the period of eschatological tribulation (Dan 7.25; 9.27; 12.7,11–12). As half of seven, the number of completeness, it also symbolizes radical incompleteness. **3:** Although the *two witnesses* are unnamed here, they may be prophetic figures who were expected to return in the end–time, possibly Enoch (Gen 5.24) and Elijah (2 Kings 2.1–11; Mal 4.5), or Moses (Deut 18.15,18) and Elijah. They are clothed in *sackcloth,* a sign that their prophetic message was a call to repentance. **4:** *Two olive trees,* supplying oil for the lamps in the temple (Zech 4.3–14). **6:** *Shut the sky,* cause a drought, as did Elijah (1 Kings 17.1). *Authority over the waters . . . ,* as did Moses and Aaron (Ex 7.17–21). **7:** *The beast,* 13.1; 17.8. *The bottomless pit,* see 9.1n. *Will make war on them,* Dan 7.21. **8:** *The great city* is identified here *prophetically,* i.e., allegorically or spiritually rather than literally by its proper name. While the majority of scholars identify this city as Jerusalem, others suggest that the city is Rome, as is Babylon in 17.1–6. The name *Sodom,* applied to Jerusalem in Isa 1.10; Jer 23.14; Ezek 16.46–56, alludes to that city's legendary wickedness (Gen 18.16–19.29). *Egypt* is associated with idolatry and is the land from which God delivered the enslaved people of Israel. *Where also their Lord was crucified,* Jerusalem. **10:** The *prophets had been a torment,* preaching an unpopular message of repentance. **11–12:** The witnesses are resuscitated (cf. Ezek 37.5,10) and taken to heaven (2 Kings 2.11). **12:** *Come up here,* 4.1. **13:** *Gave glory to the God of heaven,* a positive outcome of the *great earthquake.*
    11.14–19: The seventh trumpet announces (v. 15) the consummation of God's reign (10.7). **16:** *Elders,* 4.4n.

¹⁹ Then God's temple in heaven was opened, and the ark of his covenant was seen within his temple; and there were flashes of lightning, rumblings, peals of thunder, an earthquake, and heavy hail.

12 A great portent appeared in heaven: a woman clothed with the sun, with the moon under her feet, and on her head a crown of twelve stars. ² She was pregnant and was crying out in birth pangs, in the agony of giving birth. ³ Then another portent appeared in heaven: a great red dragon, with seven heads and ten horns, and seven diadems on his heads. ⁴ His tail swept down a third of the stars of heaven and threw them to the earth. Then the dragon stood before the woman who was about to bear a child, so that he might devour her child as soon as it was born. ⁵ And she gave birth to a son, a male child, who is to rule[a] all the nations with a

rod of iron. But her child was snatched away and taken to God and to his throne; ⁶ and the woman fled into the wilderness, where she has a place prepared by God, so that there she can be nourished for one thousand two hundred sixty days.

⁷ And war broke out in heaven; Michael and his angels fought against the dragon. The dragon and his angels fought back, ⁸ but they were defeated, and there was no longer any place for them in heaven. ⁹ The great dragon was thrown down, that ancient serpent, who is called the Devil and Satan, the deceiver of the whole world—he was thrown down to the earth, and his angels were thrown down with him.

¹⁰ Then I heard a loud voice in heaven, proclaiming,

---

[a] Or *to shepherd*

17–18: A song of triumph. **19:** Divine self-revelation concludes the vision of the seven trumpets and introduces the vision of ch 12. *The ark of [the] covenant* was constructed according to divine instruction at Mount Sinai (Ex 25.10–16) and eventually installed in the innermost room of the Temple by Solomon (1 Kings 8.1–12). It was presumably destroyed when the Babylonians captured Jerusalem in 586 BCE (but see 2 Macc 2.4–8).

12.1–17: The vision of the woman, the child, and the dragon is rich in symbolism drawn from mythological traditions found in ancient Babylonia, Egypt, Greece, and Rome, as well as in the Hebrew Bible. One well-known version of the story tells of the goddess Leto, pregnant with Apollo, who is menaced by the dragon Python, who pursues her because he knows that Apollo is destined to kill him (Hyginus, *Fabulae* 140). Here this material is reinterpreted in terms of Jewish traditions and expectations as the story of the birth of the messiah. **1:** *A great portent,* a sign or omen *in heaven* that points to a momentous event on earth; see v. 3; 15.1; cf. Lk 21.11; *Didache* 16.6. The *woman* is unnamed, and her precise identity is uncertain. Many scholars understand her as the symbolic representation of Israel, from whom the messiah is born (v. 5); the *twelve stars* thus refer to the twelve tribes. Patristic and medieval Christian interpreters most often took her to be Mary, or sometimes the church. Elements of her description are characteristic of several ancient goddesses. **3:** The *dragon,* identified in v. 9 as "the Devil" and "Satan," is Leviathan, the great sea monster of Canaanite tradition and of the Hebrew Bible (Job 40.25; Isa 27.1), one specification of the primeval watery chaos. *Seven heads and ten horns,* 13.1; 17.3; cf. Ps 74.13–14. These details are probably drawn from Dan 7.1–8, where they represent various empires and rulers; it is unclear what they symbolize here; cf. 17.9–10. **4:** *A third of the stars,* a proportion analogous to the destruction caused by the trumpet plagues (8.7–9.19; Dan 8.10). *Threw them to the earth,* Dan 8.20. **5:** *Rule . . . with a rod of iron,* an allusion to Ps 2.9, originally concerning the king of Israel, and interpreted as referring to a future anointed ruler or messiah (*Psalms of Solomon* 17.23–24). The messianic child is *snatched away and taken to God*: The resurrection and exaltation of Jesus denies the demonic dragon victory over its prey. **6:** *The wilderness* is a place where God provides refuge and sustenance amidst adversity (e.g., Gen 21.14–21; Deut 8.15–16; 29.5; 32.10; 1 Kings 17.1–2). *One thousand, two hundred sixty days,* the equivalent of "a time, and times, and half a time" (v. 14), "forty-two months" (11.2; 13.5), amounts to three and a half years. This symbolic number suggests a period of time limited by divine design. **7–12:** The *war* in *heaven* and its outcome offers, in symbolic language, the reason for the persecution and oppression of believers (v. 17). **7:** *Michael,* an archangel and the champion of Israel (Dan 10.13,21; 12.1; Jude 9) engages in combat against *the dragon and his angels* (Dan 10.20). **8:** *Defeated . . . in heaven,* see 9.1–2. Both passages may allude to Isa 14.12–20. **9:** Lk 10.18. *That ancient serpent,* see Gen 3.1–7; Isa 27.1. *Satan* means adversary, accuser (see Job 1.6–12; 2.1–7; Zech 3.1–2). *The deceiver,* 20.10. **10:** *The accuser,*

"Now have come the salvation and the
power
and the kingdom of our God
and the authority of his Messiah,[a]
for the accuser of our comrades[b] has been
thrown down,
who accuses them day and night before
our God.
[11] But they have conquered him by the
blood of the Lamb
and by the word of their testimony,
for they did not cling to life even in the
face of death.
[12] Rejoice then, you heavens
and those who dwell in them!
But woe to the earth and the sea,
for the devil has come down to you
with great wrath,
because he knows that his time is short!"
[13] So when the dragon saw that he had
been thrown down to the earth, he pursued[c]
the woman who had given birth to the male
child. [14] But the woman was given the two
wings of the great eagle, so that she could
fly from the serpent into the wilderness, to
her place where she is nourished for a time,
and times, and half a time. [15] Then from his
mouth the serpent poured water like a river
after the woman, to sweep her away with the
flood. [16] But the earth came to the help of the
woman; it opened its mouth and swallowed
the river that the dragon had poured from his
mouth. [17] Then the dragon was angry with the
woman, and went off to make war on the rest
of her children, those who keep the commandments of God and hold the testimony
of Jesus.

[18] Then the dragon[d] took his stand on
the sand of the seashore. [1] And I
saw a beast rising out of the sea,
having ten horns and seven heads; and
on its horns were ten diadems, and on its
heads were blasphemous names. [2] And the
beast that I saw was like a leopard, its feet
were like a bear's, and its mouth was like
a lion's mouth. And the dragon gave it his
power and his throne and great authority.
[3] One of its heads seemed to have received
a death-blow, but its mortal wound[e] had
been healed. In amazement the whole earth
followed the beast. [4] They worshiped the
dragon, for he had given his authority to the
beast, and they worshiped the beast, saying,
"Who is like the beast, and who can fight
against it?"
[5] The beast was given a mouth uttering
haughty and blasphemous words, and it was
allowed to exercise authority for forty-two
months. [6] It opened its mouth to utter blasphemies against God, blaspheming his name
and his dwelling, that is, those who dwell in
heaven. [7] Also it was allowed to make war on
the saints and to conquer them.[f] It was given
authority over every tribe and people and
language and nation, [8] and all the inhabitants
of the earth will worship it, everyone whose

13

[a] Gk *Christ*
[b] Gk *brothers*
[c] Or *persecuted*
[d] Gk *Then he*; other ancient authorities read *Then I
stood*
[e] Gk *the plague of its death*
[f] Other ancient authorities lack this sentence

as in Job 1.9–11. **11:** *They have conquered,* the paradoxical victory of the crucified Jesus (see 5.6–9n.) and of the
martyrs, who were faithful unto death. **12:** *Rejoice,* Ps 96.11; Isa 49.13. **14:** *Eagle,* Ex 19.4; Deut 32.11. *A time . . . half
a time,* see v. 6n. **15:** *Water . . . flood,* the chaos of the primeval sea monster (Isa 27.1; Ps 74.13; see 12.3n.). **16:** *Earth*
helps the woman, as in Ex 15.12 the earth swallows up the pursuing Egyptian armies. **17:** The frustrated *dragon*
redirects its anger toward *the rest of* the woman's *children,* namely, those who *keep the commandments . . . and
hold the testimony of Jesus* (14.12).

    12.18–13.18: The two beasts. 13.1–10: The *beast* from *the sea* combines the powers of the four beasts of Dan
7 and represents the Roman Empire, incited by the *dragon* (v. 2) to oppress *the saints* (v. 7). **1–2:** Based on Dan
7.1–7; see also 12.3n. *The sea,* primeval chaos. *Blasphemous names,* Roman emperors were deified, and worshiped
as gods. **3:** *Death-blow,* perhaps an allusion to the assassination of Julius Caesar in 44 BCE, or a reference to the
belief that the emperor Nero, who committed suicide in 68 CE, would be restored to life and rule (see 17.8n.).
The *mortal wound* (to the beast as a whole) did not destroy the empire. *Amazement,* as of one astonished by a
remarkable victory or portent (Jdt 11.16; 2 Esd 12.3). **5:** The sovereignty of God, even amid the oppression of the
faithful, is implied by the use of passive verbs here and in vv. 7,10,14,15 (cf. 6.4; see 17.17n.). *Forty-two months,* see

name has not been written from the foundation of the world in the book of life of the Lamb that was slaughtered.[a]

[9] Let anyone who has an ear listen:

[10] If you are to be taken captive,
　　into captivity you go;
if you kill with the sword,
　　with the sword you must be killed.
Here is a call for the endurance and faith of the saints.

[11] Then I saw another beast that rose out of the earth; it had two horns like a lamb and it spoke like a dragon. [12] It exercises all the authority of the first beast on its behalf, and it makes the earth and its inhabitants worship the first beast, whose mortal wound[b] had been healed. [13] It performs great signs, even making fire come down from heaven to earth in the sight of all; [14] and by the signs that it is allowed to perform on behalf of the beast, it deceives the inhabitants of earth, telling them to make an image for the beast that had been wounded by the sword[c] and yet lived; [15] and it was allowed to give breath[d] to the image of the beast so that the image of the beast could even speak and cause those who would not worship the image of the beast to be killed. [16] Also it causes all, both small and great, both rich and poor, both free and slave, to be marked on the right hand or the forehead, [17] so that no one can buy or sell who does not have the mark, that is, the name of the beast or the number of its name. [18] This calls for wisdom: let anyone with understanding calculate the number of the beast, for it is the number of a person. Its number is six hundred sixty-six.[e]

14 Then I looked, and there was the Lamb, standing on Mount Zion! And with him were one hundred forty-four thousand who had his name and his Father's name written on their foreheads. [2] And I heard a voice from heaven like the sound of many waters and like the sound of loud thunder; the voice I heard was like the sound of harpists playing on their harps, [3] and they sing a new song before the throne and before the four living creatures and before the elders. No one could learn that song except the one hundred forty-four thousand who have been redeemed from the earth. [4] It is these who have not defiled themselves with women, for they are virgins; these follow

a　Or *written in the book of life of the Lamb that was slaughtered from the foundation of the world*
b　Gk *whose plague of its death*
c　Or *that had received the plague of the sword*
d　Or *spirit*
e　Other ancient authorities read *six hundred sixteen*

11.2n. 8: *From the foundation of the world,* this phrase would most naturally qualify *slaughtered* (see textual note *a*). A *name* can be removed from *the book of life* (3.5n.); later, judgment seems to depend on one's conduct of life (20.12). The translation here is a harmonization with 17.8. **10:** Jer 15.2; 43.11; Mt 26.52. **11–18:** The *beast* from *the earth,* associated with the false prophet (16.13; 19.20), enforces emperor worship (v. 12) and produces *great signs* (v. 13) or portents to deceive the people (v. 14); cf. Mt 24.24; 2 Thess 2.9–10. **14:** The *image,* a statue of the deified emperor. **16–17:** *Marked* in imitation of the sealing of God's servants (7.2–4). The *mark* of the beast (also 14.9,11; 16.2; 19.20; 20.4) is different from the seal of God with which the faithful are identified (7.3; 9.4). Those who do not bear the mark of the beast suffer economic oppression. *Right hand . . . forehead,* phylacteries or "tephillin" were worn on the left arm and forehead (*Ep. Arist.* 159; Josephus, *Ant.* 4.213). Egyptian Jews were branded by Ptolemy IV (3 Macc 2.28–29). **18:** *This calls for wisdom,* Dan 12.10. *The number of a person* can be understood either as a number that stands for a specific person, or as a number that can be calculated by human beings, not a hidden number known only to God (cf. 21.17). In the ancient practice of gematria, the numerical equivalents of the letters of the Hebrew or Greek alphabets were added together, and the resulting sum was seen as giving a clue to the nature of the name. Thus *the number of the beast* (666) is the sum of the separate letters of its name. Of countless explanations, the most probable is "Neron Caesar" (in Hebrew letters), i.e., Emperor Nero, which, if spelled without the final "n", also accounts for the variant reading, 616 (see textual note *e*). The number six represents what falls short of the number of completeness, seven.

14.1–20: **A series of three visions** intended to reassure the faithful of ultimate victory and vindication. **1–5:** *The Lamb* and those redeemed from the earth; as in 7.4, the *one hundred forty-four thousand* is a symbolic expression. **1:** *Mount Zion,* Jerusalem, the center of God's eschatological reign (Heb 12.22). *Written on their foreheads,* 7.3n.; 22.4. **2:** *Many waters,* see 1.15n. **3:** *They,* the one hundred forty-four thousand. *New song,* 5.8–10.

the Lamb wherever he goes. They have been redeemed from humankind as first fruits for God and the Lamb, [5] and in their mouth no lie was found; they are blameless.

[6] Then I saw another angel flying in mid-heaven, with an eternal gospel to proclaim to those who live[a] on the earth—to every nation and tribe and language and people. [7] He said in a loud voice, "Fear God and give him glory, for the hour of his judgment has come; and worship him who made heaven and earth, the sea and the springs of water."

[8] Then another angel, a second, followed, saying, "Fallen, fallen is Babylon the great! She has made all nations drink of the wine of the wrath of her fornication."

[9] Then another angel, a third, followed them, crying with a loud voice, "Those who worship the beast and its image, and receive a mark on their foreheads or on their hands, [10] they will also drink the wine of God's wrath, poured unmixed into the cup of his anger, and they will be tormented with fire and sulfur in the presence of the holy angels and in the presence of the Lamb. [11] And the smoke of their torment goes up forever and ever. There is no rest day or night for those who worship the beast and its image and for anyone who receives the mark of its name."

[12] Here is a call for the endurance of the saints, those who keep the commandments of God and hold fast to the faith of[b] Jesus.

[13] And I heard a voice from heaven saying, "Write this: Blessed are the dead who from now on die in the Lord." "Yes," says the Spirit, "they will rest from their labors, for their deeds follow them."

[14] Then I looked, and there was a white cloud, and seated on the cloud was one like the Son of Man, with a golden crown on his head, and a sharp sickle in his hand! [15] Another angel came out of the temple, calling with a loud voice to the one who sat on the cloud, "Use your sickle and reap, for the hour to reap has come, because the harvest of the earth is fully ripe." [16] So the one who sat on the cloud swung his sickle over the earth, and the earth was reaped.

[17] Then another angel came out of the temple in heaven, and he too had a sharp sickle. [18] Then another angel came out from the altar, the angel who has authority over fire, and he called with a loud voice to him who had the sharp sickle, "Use your sharp sickle and gather the clusters of the vine of the earth, for its grapes are ripe." [19] So the angel swung his sickle over the earth and gathered the vintage of the earth, and he threw it into the great wine press of the wrath of God. [20] And the wine press was trodden outside the city, and blood flowed from the wine press, as

a   Gk *sit*
b   Or *to their faith in*

Throne, 4.2n. *Four living creatures*, 4.6n. 4: *They are virgins*, a characterization of the 144,000 that perhaps should be understood metaphorically in terms of the sexual abstinence required before contact with the divine (Ex 19.15; Deut 23.10–14) and of warriors before battle (1 Sam 21.5; 2 Sam 11.9–13). *These follow the Lamb*, who is their shepherd (7.17). *First fruits*, Ex 23.19. *No lie*, cf. Zeph 3.13. **6–13**: Three angels announce the coming judgment. **6**: *Flying in midheaven*, 8.13. *Eternal gospel*, the message or proclamation that follows in v. 7, an announcement that God's judgment is imminent. **7**: *Fear God*, 15.4; Deut 10.12–15. *Judgment*, 16.7; 18.10; 19.2. *Worship* acknowledges God's cosmic sovereignty as Creator. **8**: *Fallen, fallen is Babylon* (Isa 21.9) *the great* (Dan 4.30), an anticipation of 18.2. *Babylon* is a symbolic name for Rome (2 Esd 3.1–2). The association of the two is based on the destruction of Jerusalem by Babylon in 586 BCE and by Rome in 70 CE. *The wine of the wrath*, 18.3; Jer 51.7. **9–11**: The sentence pronounced against those who *worship the beast* will be worse than what is suffered by those who do not worship it or bear its *mark* (13.15–17). **10**: *Wine of God's wrath*, Jer 25.15–16; 51.7. *Unmixed*, not diluted and therefore more potent (see 3 Macc 5.2). Wine was often mixed with water before being drunk. *Fire and sulfur* (19.20; 20.10; 21.8) are instruments of divine punishment (Gen 19.24; Ps 11.6; Ezek 38.22). *Holy angels*, Mk 8.38. **11**: *Smoke*, 18.9,18; 19.3. **12**: An exhortation to perseverance addressed to those against whom the dragon goes to make war in 12.17. **13**: *Blessed*, see 1.3n. A promise assured by *the Spirit*. *Their deeds*, 2.2,19; 3.1–2.15. **14–20**: The eschatological harvest, the final judgment of God (Joel 3.13), involves the ingathering of the saints by *one like the Son of Man* (vv. 14–16) and the assembling of the wicked for destruction (vv. 17–20). **14**: *White cloud . . . Son of Man*, Dan 7.13; Mt 24.30; Mk 14.62. **15–16**: A grain harvest. **18–20**: A scene of the grape harvest and winemaking. **20**: Metaphorically, *wine* is frequently associated with *blood* (Gen 49.11; Deut 32.14; Sir 39.26; 1 Macc 6.34). Here

high as a horse's bridle, for a distance of about two hundred miles.[a]

15 Then I saw another portent in heaven, great and amazing: seven angels with seven plagues, which are the last, for with them the wrath of God is ended.

[2] And I saw what appeared to be a sea of glass mixed with fire, and those who had conquered the beast and its image and the number of its name, standing beside the sea of glass with harps of God in their hands. [3] And they sing the song of Moses, the servant[b] of God, and the song of the Lamb:

"Great and amazing are your deeds,
Lord God the Almighty!
Just and true are your ways,
King of the nations![c]
[4] Lord, who will not fear
and glorify your name?
For you alone are holy.
All nations will come
and worship before you,
for your judgments have been revealed."

[5] After this I looked, and the temple of the tent[d] of witness in heaven was opened, [6] and out of the temple came the seven angels with the seven plagues, robed in pure bright linen,[e] with golden sashes across their chests. [7] Then one of the four living creatures gave the seven angels seven golden bowls full of the wrath of God, who lives forever and ever; [8] and the temple was filled with smoke from the glory of God and from his power, and no one could enter the temple until the seven plagues of the seven angels were ended.

16 Then I heard a loud voice from the temple telling the seven angels, "Go and pour out on the earth the seven bowls of the wrath of God."

[2] So the first angel went and poured his bowl on the earth, and a foul and painful sore came on those who had the mark of the beast and who worshiped its image.

[3] The second angel poured his bowl into the sea, and it became like the blood of a corpse, and every living thing in the sea died.

[4] The third angel poured his bowl into the rivers and the springs of water, and they became blood. [5] And I heard the angel of the waters say,

"You are just, O Holy One, who are and were,
for you have judged these things;
[6] because they shed the blood of saints and prophets,
you have given them blood to drink.
It is what they deserve!"

[7] And I heard the altar respond,

"Yes, O Lord God, the Almighty,
your judgments are true and just!"

[8] The fourth angel poured his bowl on the sun, and it was allowed to scorch people with fire; [9] they were scorched by the fierce heat, but they cursed the name of God, who had authority over these plagues, and they did not repent and give him glory.

---

[a] Gk *one thousand six hundred stadia*
[b] Gk *slave*
[c] Other ancient authorities read *the ages*
[d] Or *tabernacle*
[e] Other ancient authorities read *stone*

---

the enormous quantity of blood suggests the vast extent of the divine judgment (cf. Isa 63.3–6). Mention of the *horse's bridle* here foreshadows the combat in 19.11–21.

15.1–16.21: The seven bowls of the wrath of God.

15.1–8: The preparation for judgment. 1: *Portent,* a third heavenly sign (see 12.1n.,3). *The wrath of God,* 14.10,19; 15.1,7; 16.1; 19.15. *Is ended,* accomplished or come to its fulfillment. **15.2–4:** Vision of the victorious martyrs in heaven (8.3–5). **2:** *Sea of glass,* see 4.6n. **3:** *Song of Moses,* Ex 15.1–18; Deut 32. **5:** *The temple of the tent of witness,* the heavenly counterpart of the tent of witness that accompanied Israel's journey through the desert (Num 9.15). *Was opened,* cf. 11.19. On opening the heavenly gates as a prelude to judgment, see 3 Macc 6.18–19. In Rome, the Temple of Janus was opened as a prelude to war (Virgil, *Aeneid* 1.294). **7:** *Golden bowls,* libation vessels used in religious rituals. **8:** *Smoke,* Ex 19.18; 40.34–35; Isa 6.1–4; cf. 1 Kings 8.10–11.

16.1–21: The pouring of the bowls (cf. chs 8–9, and the plagues inflicted on Egypt, Ex 7–12). **2:** *A foul and painful sore,* Ex 9.8–12. **3–4:** 8.8–9; Ex 7.14–24. **5–6:** A judgment doxology. **5:** *The angel* that has control *of the waters,* implying a worldview in which different angels preside over different elements of the cosmos (1 En. 60.10–22; Rev 7.1–2, winds; Rev 14.18, fire). **6:** Divine retribution (Isa 49.26). *Blood to drink,* cf. 17.6. **7:** *The al-*

[10] The fifth angel poured his bowl on the throne of the beast, and its kingdom was plunged into darkness; people gnawed their tongues in agony, [11] and cursed the God of heaven because of their pains and sores, and they did not repent of their deeds.

[12] The sixth angel poured his bowl on the great river Euphrates, and its water was dried up in order to prepare the way for the kings from the east. [13] And I saw three foul spirits like frogs coming from the mouth of the dragon, from the mouth of the beast, and from the mouth of the false prophet. [14] These are demonic spirits, performing signs, who go abroad to the kings of the whole world, to assemble them for battle on the great day of God the Almighty. [15] ("See, I am coming like a thief! Blessed is the one who stays awake and is clothed,[a] not going about naked and exposed to shame.") [16] And they assembled them at the place that in Hebrew is called Harmagedon.

[17] The seventh angel poured his bowl into the air, and a loud voice came out of the temple, from the throne, saying, "It is done!" [18] And there came flashes of lightning, rumblings, peals of thunder, and a violent earthquake, such as had not occurred since people were upon the earth, so violent was that earthquake. [19] The great city was split into three parts, and the cities of the nations fell. God remembered great Babylon and gave her the wine-cup of the fury of his wrath. [20] And every island fled away, and no mountains were to be found; [21] and huge hailstones, each weighing about a hundred pounds,[b] dropped from heaven on people, until they cursed God for the plague of the hail, so fearful was that plague.

17 Then one of the seven angels who had the seven bowls came and said to me, "Come, I will show you the judgment of the great whore who is seated on many waters, [2] with whom the kings of the earth have committed fornication, and with the wine of whose fornication the inhabitants of the earth have become drunk." [3] So he carried me away in the spirit[c] into a wilderness, and I saw a woman sitting on a scarlet beast that was full of blasphemous names, and it had seven heads and ten horns. [4] The woman was clothed in purple and scarlet, and adorned with gold and jewels and pearls, holding in her hand a golden cup full of abominations and the impurities of her fornication; [5] and on her forehead was written a name, a mystery: "Babylon the great, mother of whores and of earth's abominations." [6] And I saw that the woman was drunk with the blood of the

a Gk *and keeps his robes*
b Gk *weighing about a talent*
c Or *in the Spirit*

tar, 6.9–11. **10**: 8.12; Ex 10.21. *Throne of the beast,* 13.2. **12**: *Euphrates,* see 9.14n. *Kings from the east,* perhaps a reference to the Parthians, who would be led by the Roman emperor Nero, restored to life; see 13.3n.; *Sib. Or.* 4.120,139. **13–14**: *Foul spirits like frogs,* Ex 8.1–15. **14**: *Performing signs,* 13.13. **15**: *Like a thief,* see 3.3n. *Blessed,* see 1.3n. **16**: *They,* the frog-like spirits, emissaries of the demonic trio, that is, the dragon, the beast, and the false prophet. *Harmagedon,* spelled variously in the manuscripts with "gg" and/or "dd"; also "Armagedon." This is likely an allusion to Megiddo, the site of several decisive battles in Israel's history (Judg 5.19; 2 Kings 9.27; 2 Chr 35.22); in Hebrew "har Megiddo" means "the mountain of Megiddo." Here it is the symbolic assembly point of the forces hostile to God as they prepare for the eschatological battle. **19**: *The great city,* Rome. *Great Babylon,* 14.8. *Wine-cup,* 14.10. **21**: *Hail,* 8.7; Ex 9.13–35; Wis 5.22.

17.1–18.24: The fall of Babylon, which is Rome, the city on seven hills (17.9,18) and the leading persecutor of the saints (17.6).

17.1–18: The vision of the woman. 1: *The great whore,* a symbol that builds both on the fact that cities were grammatically gendered as feminine and on the Hebrew prophets' metaphorical references to cities and nations as brides, wives, or harlots (e.g., Tyre in Isa 23.17–18). **2:** Jer 51.7. *Fornication,* sexual misconduct applied metaphorically to the city's international commercial and political dealings, which are judged illicit and unjust. **3:** *In the spirit,* 1.10; 4.2; 21.10 (Ezek 2.2; 3.12,14,24). *Into a wilderness,* Isa 21.1–20. *Scarlet beast,* the Roman empire (see 13.1n.). *Blasphemous names,* divine titles given to Roman emperors (see 13.1). **4:** *Gold and jewels and pearls,* 18.16. **5:** *On her forehead,* 13.16; 14.1; 20.4; 22.4. *A mystery,* indicating that the name is symbolic and that it requires interpretation, which the angel offers in vv. 7–18. *Mother of whores,* Hos 2.2–5. **6:** *Drunk with . . . blood,*

saints and the blood of the witnesses to Jesus.

When I saw her, I was greatly amazed.
[7] But the angel said to me, "Why are you so amazed? I will tell you the mystery of the woman, and of the beast with seven heads and ten horns that carries her. [8] The beast that you saw was, and is not, and is about to ascend from the bottomless pit and go to destruction. And the inhabitants of the earth, whose names have not been written in the book of life from the foundation of the world, will be amazed when they see the beast, because it was and is not and is to come.

[9] "This calls for a mind that has wisdom: the seven heads are seven mountains on which the woman is seated; also, they are seven kings, [10] of whom five have fallen, one is living, and the other has not yet come; and when he comes, he must remain only a little while. [11] As for the beast that was and is not, it is an eighth but it belongs to the seven, and it goes to destruction. [12] And the ten horns that you saw are ten kings who have not yet received a kingdom, but they are to receive authority as kings for one hour, together with the beast. [13] These are united in yielding their power and authority to the beast; [14] they will make war on the Lamb, and the Lamb will conquer them, for he is Lord of lords and King of kings, and those with him are called and chosen and faithful."

[15] And he said to me, "The waters that you saw, where the whore is seated, are peoples and multitudes and nations and languages. [16] And the ten horns that you saw, they and the beast will hate the whore; they will make her desolate and naked; they will devour her flesh and burn her up with fire. [17] For God has put it into their hearts to carry out his pur-

pose by agreeing to give their kingdom to the beast, until the words of God will be fulfilled. [18] The woman you saw is the great city that rules over the kings of the earth."

18 After this I saw another angel coming down from heaven, having great authority; and the earth was made bright with his splendor. [2] He called out with a mighty voice,
"Fallen, fallen is Babylon the great!
It has become a dwelling place of demons,
a haunt of every foul spirit,
a haunt of every foul bird,
a haunt of every foul and hateful beast.[a]
[3] For all the nations have drunk[b]
of the wine of the wrath of her fornication,
and the kings of the earth have committed fornication with her,
and the merchants of the earth have grown rich from the power[c] of her luxury."
[4] Then I heard another voice from heaven saying,
"Come out of her, my people,
so that you do not take part in her sins,
and so that you do not share in her plagues;
[5] for her sins are heaped high as heaven,
and God has remembered her iniquities.
[6] Render to her as she herself has rendered,

a Other ancient authorities lack the words *a haunt of every foul beast* and attach the words *and hateful* to the previous line so as to read *a haunt of every foul and hateful bird*
b Other ancient authorities read *She has made all nations drink*
c Or *resources*

Ezek 39.19. Persecution took the form of exile (1.9), imprisonment (2.10), or death (2.10,13; 11.3). **8:** *The beast* now represents the Roman emperor Nero, who was expected to return to life and power (v. 11). *Was and is not and is to come,* a parody of the designation of God in 1.4,8. *Book of life,* see 3.5n. **9:** *This calls for a mind that has wisdom,* like the formula in 13.18, this expression introduces the interpretation of the symbolism of the preceding verses. The *seven mountains* are the seven hills of Rome. The *seven kings* are Roman emperors (cf. Dan 11.2; 2 Esd 12.22–26), which interpreters have identified with various emperors from Julius Caesar to Domitian. **12:** *Ten horns* represent subordinate or client rulers (Dan 7.7–8). **14:** The eschatological victory of Jesus Christ. *Lord of lords and king of kings,* 19.16. **16:** Ezek 23.26–29. **17:** The ten kings are unwitting instruments of God's will, fulfilling the divine plan (compare the passive verbs in 6.4; see 13.5n.). **18:** An explicit identification of the woman of v. 1 as *the great city,* i.e., Rome.

18.1–24: Dirge over the fallen city (Rome), with echoes from the taunt songs in Isa 23–24; 47; Jer 50–51; Ezek 26–27. **1–3:** Angelic announcement of judgment (14.8; Isa 21.9; Jer 50.39; 51.8). **1:** *The earth was made bright,* Ezek 43.2. **2:** *A dwelling place . . . a haunt,* Isa 13.21–22. **4–8:** Summons to God's people to leave the doomed city; cf.

and repay her double for her deeds;
mix a double draught for her in the cup
she mixed.
[7] As she glorified herself and lived
luxuriously,
so give her a like measure of torment
and grief.
Since in her heart she says,
'I rule as a queen;
I am no widow,
and I will never see grief,'
[8] therefore her plagues will come in a
single day—
pestilence and mourning and famine—
and she will be burned with fire;
for mighty is the Lord God who judges
her."

[9] And the kings of the earth, who committed fornication and lived in luxury with her, will weep and wail over her when they see the smoke of her burning; [10] they will stand far off, in fear of her torment, and say,

"Alas, alas, the great city,
Babylon, the mighty city!
For in one hour your judgment has
come."

[11] And the merchants of the earth weep and mourn for her, since no one buys their cargo anymore, [12] cargo of gold, silver, jewels and pearls, fine linen, purple, silk and scarlet, all kinds of scented wood, all articles of ivory, all articles of costly wood, bronze, iron, and marble, [13] cinnamon, spice, incense, myrrh, frankincense, wine, olive oil, choice flour and wheat, cattle and sheep, horses and chariots, slaves—and human lives.[a]

[14] "The fruit for which your soul longed
has gone from you,
and all your dainties and your splendor
are lost to you,
never to be found again!"

[15] The merchants of these wares, who gained wealth from her, will stand far off, in fear of her torment, weeping and mourning aloud,

[16] "Alas, alas, the great city,

clothed in fine linen,
in purple and scarlet,
adorned with gold,
with jewels, and with pearls!
[17] For in one hour all this wealth has been
laid waste!"

And all shipmasters and seafarers, sailors and all whose trade is on the sea, stood far off [18] and cried out as they saw the smoke of her burning,

"What city was like the great city?"

[19] And they threw dust on their heads, as they wept and mourned, crying out,

"Alas, alas, the great city,
where all who had ships at sea
grew rich by her wealth!
For in one hour she has been laid waste."

[20] Rejoice over her, O heaven, you saints and apostles and prophets! For God has given judgment for you against her.

[21] Then a mighty angel took up a stone like a great millstone and threw it into the sea, saying,

"With such violence Babylon the great city
will be thrown down,
and will be found no more;
[22] and the sound of harpists and minstrels
and of flutists and trumpeters
will be heard in you no more;
and an artisan of any trade
will be found in you no more;
and the sound of the millstone
will be heard in you no more;
[23] and the light of a lamp
will shine in you no more;
and the voice of bridegroom and bride
will be heard in you no more;
for your merchants were the magnates of
the earth,
and all nations were deceived by your
sorcery.
[24] And in you[b] was found the blood of
prophets and of saints,

---

a   Or *chariots, and human bodies and souls*
b   Gk *her*

Jer 51.45; Mt 24.16. **5:** *High as heaven,* Jer 51.9. **6:** Jer 50.29; cf. Isa 40.2. **9–20:** Lamentation of those who have been enriched through their dealings with the corrupt city: kings (vv. 9–10), merchants (vv. 11–16), and mariners (vv. 17–20; cf. Ezek 27.29–36). **13:** *Slaves—and human lives,* through the practice of slavery, the Roman imperial economy reduced human beings to mere commodities that could be bought and sold like any other merchandise **20:** *Rejoice over her,* Jer 51.48. **21–24:** Symbolic action representing the total destruction of the city (Jer 51.63–64). **22:** *Sound of harpists,* Jer 25.10; Ezek 26.13. **24:** *Blood of prophets,* Mt 23.34–35; Lk 11.49–51; 13.33–34.

and of all who have been slaughtered
on earth."

19 After this I heard what seemed to be
the loud voice of a great multitude in
heaven, saying,
"Hallelujah!
Salvation and glory and power to our God,
² for his judgments are true and just;
he has judged the great whore
who corrupted the earth with her
fornication,
and he has avenged on her the blood of his
servants."ᵃ
³ Once more they said,
"Hallelujah!
The smoke goes up from her forever and
ever."
⁴ And the twenty-four elders and the four
living creatures fell down and worshiped God
who is seated on the throne, saying,
"Amen. Hallelujah!"
⁵ And from the throne came a voice saying,
"Praise our God,
all you his servants,ᵃ
and all who fear him,
small and great."
⁶ Then I heard what seemed to be the voice
of a great multitude, like the sound of many
waters and like the sound of mighty thunder-
peals, crying out,
"Hallelujah!
For the Lord our God
the Almighty reigns.
⁷ Let us rejoice and exult
and give him the glory,
for the marriage of the Lamb has come,
and his bride has made herself ready;
⁸ to her it has been granted to be clothed
with fine linen, bright and pure"—
for the fine linen is the righteous deeds of the
saints.

⁹ And the angel saidᵇ to me, "Write this:
Blessed are those who are invited to the marriage supper of the Lamb." And he said to me,
"These are true words of God." ¹⁰ Then I fell
down at his feet to worship him, but he said
to me, "You must not do that! I am a fellow
servantᶜ with you and your comradesᵈ who
hold the testimony of Jesus.ᵉ Worship God!
For the testimony of Jesusᵉ is the spirit of
prophecy."

¹¹ Then I saw heaven opened, and there
was a white horse! Its rider is called Faithful
and True, and in righteousness he judges
and makes war. ¹² His eyes are like a flame
of fire, and on his head are many diadems;
and he has a name inscribed that no one
knows but himself. ¹³ He is clothed in a robe
dipped inᶠ blood, and his name is called The
Word of God. ¹⁴ And the armies of heaven,
wearing fine linen, white and pure, were
following him on white horses. ¹⁵ From his
mouth comes a sharp sword with which to
strike down the nations, and he will ruleᵍ
them with a rod of iron; he will tread the
wine press of the fury of the wrath of God
the Almighty. ¹⁶ On his robe and on his thigh
he has a name inscribed, "King of kings and
Lord of lords."

¹⁷ Then I saw an angel standing in the
sun, and with a loud voice he called to all
the birds that fly in midheaven, "Come,
gather for the great supper of God, ¹⁸ to eat

ᵃ Gk *slaves*
ᵇ Gk *he said*
ᶜ Gk *slave*
ᵈ Gk *brothers*
ᵉ Or *to Jesus*
ᶠ Other ancient authorities read *sprinkled with*
ᵍ Or *will shepherd*

19.1–10: **Doxology** giving praise to God for the destruction of Rome (vv. 1–5) and for the marriage of the
Lamb (vv. 6–9). 1: *Hallelujah,* Heb for "Praise the Lᴏʀᴅ," as in Pss 104.25; 106.1; 111.1; etc. 3: *Smoke . . . forever,* i.e.,
destruction never to be rebuilt. 4: See 4.4,6. 5: Ps 115.13. 7: *His bride,* the new Jerusalem (21.2,9). 8: *Fine linen,* in
contrast to the attire of Babylon (17.4). 9: *Blessed,* see 1.3n. 10: God alone is the appropriate object of worship
(cf. 22.8–9).

19.11–21: **The victory of Jesus Christ and the heavenly armies** over the beast and its cohorts. 11: *Heaven
opened,* Ezek 1.1. *In righteousness he judges,* Isa 11.4. 12: *Many diadems,* in contrast to the diadems of the dragon
(12.3). *A name . . . that no one knows,* because the name stands for a person, knowledge of a name confers power
over the person. That his name is known only to himself implies that Jesus' power is sovereign and unlimited (cf.
2.17). 13: As revealer of God he is called *The Word of God* (Jn 1.1,14). 14: *Armies,* the angelic host (see Lk 2.13 note *c*).

the flesh of kings, the flesh of captains, the flesh of the mighty, the flesh of horses and their riders—flesh of all, both free and slave, both small and great." [19] Then I saw the beast and the kings of the earth with their armies gathered to make war against the rider on the horse and against his army. [20] And the beast was captured, and with it the false prophet who had performed in its presence the signs by which he deceived those who had received the mark of the beast and those who worshiped its image. These two were thrown alive into the lake of fire that burns with sulfur. [21] And the rest were killed by the sword of the rider on the horse, the sword that came from his mouth; and all the birds were gorged with their flesh.

20 Then I saw an angel coming down from heaven, holding in his hand the key to the bottomless pit and a great chain. [2] He seized the dragon, that ancient serpent, who is the Devil and Satan, and bound him for a thousand years, [3] and threw him into the pit, and locked and sealed it over him, so that he would deceive the nations no more, until the thousand years were ended. After that he must be let out for a little while.

[4] Then I saw thrones, and those seated on them were given authority to judge. I also saw the souls of those who had been beheaded for their testimony to Jesus[a] and for the word of God. They had not worshiped the beast or its image and had not received its mark on their foreheads or their hands. They came to life and reigned with Christ a thousand years. [5] (The rest of the dead did not come to life until the thousand years were ended.) This is the first resurrection. [6] Blessed and holy are those who share in the first resurrection. Over these the second death has no power, but they will be priests of God and of Christ, and they will reign with him a thousand years.

[7] When the thousand years are ended, Satan will be released from his prison [8] and will come out to deceive the nations at the four corners of the earth, Gog and Magog, in order to gather them for battle; they are as numerous as the sands of the sea. [9] They marched up over the breadth of the earth and surrounded the camp of the saints and the beloved city. And fire came down from heaven[b] and consumed them. [10] And the

a Or *for the testimony of Jesus*
b Other ancient authorities read *from God, out of heaven,* or *out of heaven from God*

Fine linen, 19.8. **15:** 1.16; 2.12,16; 19.21; Ps 2.9. **16:** 17.14; Deut 10.17. **17–18:** *An angel* summons the birds of prey (Ezek 39.4,17–20). **17:** *The great supper of God,* in gruesome contrast to the "marriage feast of the Lamb" (v. 9). **19–21:** The final battle between Jesus and the beast (anticipated in 16.13–16). **20:** *The beast,* the first beast, introduced in 13.1–8. *The false prophet* is the second beast of 13.11–15. *The lake of fire,* see 14.10n.; 20.10,14–15; 21.8; Dan 7.11. *Sulfur* was well known in the ancient world as a noxious substance; it was used to render land infertile (Deut 29.23; Job 18.15), and burning sulfur symbolized God's judgment (Gen 19.24; Ps 11.6; Ezek 38.22). See 9.17; 14.10; 20.10; 21.8. **21:** *The sword of the rider . . . the sword that came from his mouth,* suggesting that the victory is won not by violence but by "The Word of God" (19.13).

20.1–10: The defeat of Satan.

20.1–6: The temporary imprisonment of Satan and the reign of Christ and the martyrs. **1:** *Chain,* 2 Pet 2.4; Jude 6. **2–3:** The period of a *thousand years* is symbolic both here and in vv. 4–7, suggesting a temporary time of righteousness and tranquility before the final eschatological consummation. Cf. Ps 90.4; as the eternal time of blessing in *Jub.* 4:29–30; 23.27–30; a time far greater than the ten days during which the saints endured trials (2.10). **2:** *The dragon . . . serpent . . . Devil . . . Satan,* 12.9n. **3:** Satan is locked into the pit to prevent him from carrying out his demonic work as "the deceiver of the whole world" (12.9). After the *thousand years,* though, *he must be let out for a little while,* but even this limited period is under God's control (Dan 7.25). **4:** *Thrones* of judgment (Dan 7.9,22,27; Mt 19.28; Lk 22.30). *Those . . . beheaded for their testimony,* martyrs (in 6.9–10 the souls of the martyrs, under the altar, cry for vengeance). *Its mark,* 13.16–17; 14.9. *Reigned with Christ a thousand years,* this passage, which gave rise to Christian millennialism, suggests an interim messianic kingdom. **6:** *Blessed,* see 1.3n. *Priests,* 1.6; 5.10; Ex 19.6. *Second death,* see 2.11n.; 20.14; 21.8.

20.7–10: The release of Satan and the final conflict. *Gog and Magog,* gathering with the nations for war against Israel in Ezek 38–39 (a prophecy mentioned in 16.14–16 and 19.17–21). **9:** *The beloved city,* Jerusalem (Sir

devil who had deceived them was thrown into the lake of fire and sulfur, where the beast and the false prophet were, and they will be tormented day and night forever and ever.

[11] Then I saw a great white throne and the one who sat on it; the earth and the heaven fled from his presence, and no place was found for them. [12] And I saw the dead, great and small, standing before the throne, and books were opened. Also another book was opened, the book of life. And the dead were judged according to their works, as recorded in the books. [13] And the sea gave up the dead that were in it, Death and Hades gave up the dead that were in them, and all were judged according to what they had done. [14] Then Death and Hades were thrown into the lake of fire. This is the second death, the lake of fire; [15] and anyone whose name was not found written in the book of life was thrown into the lake of fire.

21 Then I saw a new heaven and a new earth; for the first heaven and the first earth had passed away, and the sea was no more. [2] And I saw the holy city, the new Jerusalem, coming down out of heaven from God, prepared as a bride adorned for her husband. [3] And I heard a loud voice from the throne saying,

"See, the home[a] of God is among mortals. He will dwell[b] with them;

they will be his peoples,[c] and God himself will be with them;[d] [4] he will wipe every tear from their eyes. Death will be no more; mourning and crying and pain will be no more, for the first things have passed away."

[5] And the one who was seated on the throne said, "See, I am making all things new." Also he said, "Write this, for these words are trustworthy and true." [6] Then he said to me, "It is done! I am the Alpha and the Omega, the beginning and the end. To the thirsty I will give water as a gift from the spring of the water of life. [7] Those who conquer will inherit these things, and I will be their God and they will be my children. [8] But as for the cowardly, the faithless,[e] the polluted, the murderers, the fornicators, the sorcerers, the idolaters, and all liars, their place will be in the lake that burns with fire and sulfur, which is the second death."

[9] Then one of the seven angels who had the seven bowls full of the seven last plagues came and said to me, "Come, I will show you the bride, the wife of the Lamb." [10] And in

---

a   Gk *the tabernacle*
b   Gk *will tabernacle*
c   Other ancient authorities read *people*
d   Other ancient authorities add *and be their God*
e   Or *the unbelieving*

24.11) or the city representing the whole land (Ezek 38.11 [LXX]). *Fire,* Ezek 38.22; 39.6; 2 Kings 1.9–12. **10:** *Was thrown into the lake of fire,* the final overthrow of Satan (*Test. Jud.* 25.3).

20.11–15: The last judgment. 11: The *great white throne,* 4.2; 20.4. **12:** *Books* of deeds, ledgers that record what everyone has done (Dan 7.10). The *book of life* is distinguished from the books of deeds just opened (see 3.5n). *Judged according to their works,* Mt 16.27; Rom 2.6; 2 Cor 5.10. **13–14:** Personified *Death and Hades* (see 1.18n.; 6.8n.) are the last enemies to be defeated. **14:** *The second death,* see 2.11n.; Mt 25.41.

21.1–22.5: Vision of the new Jerusalem.

21.1–8: The renewal of creation: 1: *A new heaven and a new earth,* Isa 65.17; 66.22. All creation will be renewed, freed from imperfections, and transformed by God (Rom 8.19–21). *The sea,* the primeval force of turbulence and unrest (Gen 1.2; Ps 29.3,10). **2:** *New Jerusalem,* 21.9–10; Heb 11.10. *Coming down out of heaven,* 3.12; Gal 4.26; 2 Esd 13.35–36. *Prepared as a bride,* 19.7–9; Isa 61.10. The image of the eschatological Jerusalem as a *bride* contrasts with the image of Rome as the whore Babylon in chs 17–18. **3:** Ezek 37.27. **4:** 7.16; Isa 25.8; 35.10. **5:** The speaker here is God (1.8). **6:** *Alpha* and *Omega,* see 1.8n. *Water of life,* Isa 55.1; Jn 4.13; 7.37. **7:** *Those who conquer,* compare the concluding words of each of the seven letters in chs 2 and 3. **8:** *Polluted, . . . murderers . . . idolaters,* a list of vices, commonly associated with idolatry (Ps 106.36–38), which also threaten the churches (2.14,20–21). *The second death,* contrasted to the water of life in v. 6 (see 2.11n.).

21.9–27: The measuring of the city. Cf. Ezek 40–42. Both the city and its measurements (which are multiples of 12) are symbolic. **9:** *The seven bowls,* see ch 16. *The bride, the wife of the Lamb,* 19.7; 21.2. Israel is por-

the spirit[a] he carried me away to a great, high mountain and showed me the holy city Jerusalem coming down out of heaven from God. [11] It has the glory of God and a radiance like a very rare jewel, like jasper, clear as crystal. [12] It has a great, high wall with twelve gates, and at the gates twelve angels, and on the gates are inscribed the names of the twelve tribes of the Israelites; [13] on the east three gates, on the north three gates, on the south three gates, and on the west three gates. [14] And the wall of the city has twelve foundations, and on them are the twelve names of the twelve apostles of the Lamb.

[15] The angel[b] who talked to me had a measuring rod of gold to measure the city and its gates and walls. [16] The city lies foursquare, its length the same as its width; and he measured the city with his rod, fifteen hundred miles;[c] its length and width and height are equal. [17] He also measured its wall, one hundred forty-four cubits[d] by human measurement, which the angel was using. [18] The wall is built of jasper, while the city is pure gold, clear as glass. [19] The foundations of the wall of the city are adorned with every jewel; the first was jasper, the second sapphire, the third agate, the fourth emerald, [20] the fifth onyx, the sixth carnelian, the seventh chrysolite, the eighth beryl, the ninth topaz, the tenth chrysoprase, the eleventh jacinth, the twelfth amethyst. [21] And the twelve gates are twelve pearls, each of the gates is a single pearl, and the street of the city is pure gold, transparent as glass.

[22] I saw no temple in the city, for its temple is the Lord God the Almighty and the Lamb. [23] And the city has no need of sun or moon to shine on it, for the glory of God is its light, and its lamp is the Lamb. [24] The nations will walk by its light, and the kings of the earth will bring their glory into it. [25] Its gates will never be shut by day—and there will be no night there. [26] People will bring into it the glory and the honor of the nations. [27] But nothing unclean will enter it, nor anyone who practices abomination or falsehood, but only those who are written in the Lamb's book of life.

22 Then the angel[e] showed me the river of the water of life, bright as crystal, flowing from the throne of God and of the Lamb [2] through the middle of the street of the city. On either side of the river is the tree of life[f] with its twelve kinds of fruit, producing its fruit each month; and the leaves of the tree are for the healing of the nations. [3] Nothing accursed will be found there any more. But the throne of God and of the Lamb will be in it, and his servants[g] will worship him; [4] they will see his face, and his name

---

a   Or *in the Spirit*

b   Gk *He*

c   Gk *twelve thousand stadia*

d   That is, almost seventy-five yards

e   Gk *he*

f   Or *the Lamb.* [2] *In the middle of the street of the city, and on either side of the river, is the tree of life*

g   Gk *slaves*

---

trayed as the bride of God in Isa 54.5; Hos 2.19–20; the antithesis of Babylon in 17.1–3. **10:** *In the spirit,* see 1.10n. *High mountain,* Ezek 40.2. *Jerusalem . . . out of heaven,* v. 2n. **11:** *Jasper,* 4.3; *glory of God* (Ezek 43.2–5). **12:** Ezek 48.30–34. **14:** See Eph 2.20. *Twelve apostles* added to the twelve tribes of Israel creates the symbolic number twenty-four (4.3–4). **15–18:** *The city* that *lies foursquare,* i.e., with streets that intersect at right angles, unlike the irregular walls of Palestinian cities (Ezek 42.20). The cube is a perfect, symmetrical shape (for the ideal Temple as a square, see Ezek 40.5; 45.1–5). This description of a city with a river running through it resembles ancient accounts of Babylon (Herodotus, *Hist.* 1.178–79). The precious stones, with the names of the twelve tribes, adorned the high priest's breastplate (Ex 28.17–20). **19:** Isa 54.11–12. **21:** *The street of the city is pure gold,* even more impressive than stone-paved Roman roads **22–23:** Unlike the cities of the Roman province of Asia, where monumental temples to the deified emperor reminded the population of the pervasive power of the distant imperial capital, in the new Jerusalem *no temple . . . no . . . sun* are needed because the presence and glory of God pervade the entire community (Isa 24.23; 60.1,19; 2 Esd 7.39–42). *Its lamp is the Lamb,* Ps 132.17. **25:** City gates would be closed at night and at the approach of enemies; perpetually open gates symbolize complete safety and security; see Isa 60.11; Zech 14.7; 1QM 12.13–15. **27:** *Book of life,* see 3.5n.

   22.1–5: The river and the tree of life. 1: *The river,* cf. Gen 2.10; Ps 46.4; Ezek 47.1; Zech 14.8. **2:** *The tree,* a collective reference to many trees *on either side of the river* (Ezek 47.12; see 2.7n.). **3:** *The throne of God and of the Lamb*

will be on their foreheads. [5] And there will be no more night; they need no light of lamp or sun, for the Lord God will be their light, and they will reign forever and ever.

[6] And he said to me, "These words are trustworthy and true, for the Lord, the God of the spirits of the prophets, has sent his angel to show his servants[a] what must soon take place."

[7] "See, I am coming soon! Blessed is the one who keeps the words of the prophecy of this book."

[8] I, John, am the one who heard and saw these things. And when I heard and saw them, I fell down to worship at the feet of the angel who showed them to me; [9] but he said to me, "You must not do that! I am a fellow servant[b] with you and your comrades[c] the prophets, and with those who keep the words of this book. Worship God!"

[10] And he said to me, "Do not seal up the words of the prophecy of this book, for the time is near. [11] Let the evildoer still do evil, and the filthy still be filthy, and the righteous still do right, and the holy still be holy."

[12] "See, I am coming soon; my reward is with me, to repay according to everyone's work. [13] I am the Alpha and the Omega, the first and the last, the beginning and the end."

[14] Blessed are those who wash their robes,[d] so that they will have the right to the tree of life and may enter the city by the gates. [15] Outside are the dogs and sorcerers and fornicators and murderers and idolaters, and everyone who loves and practices falsehood.

[16] "It is I, Jesus, who sent my angel to you with this testimony for the churches. I am the root and the descendant of David, the bright morning star."

[17] The Spirit and the bride say, "Come." And let everyone who hears say, "Come." And let everyone who is thirsty come. Let anyone who wishes take the water of life as a gift.

[18] I warn everyone who hears the words of the prophecy of this book: if anyone adds to them, God will add to that person the plagues described in this book; [19] if anyone takes away from the words of the book of this prophecy, God will take away that person's share in the tree of life and in the holy city, which are described in this book.

[20] The one who testifies to these things says, "Surely I am coming soon." Amen. Come, Lord Jesus!

[21] The grace of the Lord Jesus be with all the saints. Amen.[e]

a Gk *slaves*
b Gk *slave*
c Gk *brothers*
d Other ancient authorities read *do his commandments*
e Other ancient authorities lack *all*; others lack *the saints*; others lack *Amen*

---

is one throne, 3.21. 4: To *see* God's *face*, full awareness of God's immediate presence (Job 33.26; Ps 10.11; 42.2), an eschatological blessing (Ps 84.7; Mt 5.8; 1 Jn 3.2). *On their foreheads*, see 7.3n.; 14.1; contrast 13.16; 17.5. 5: Those who *worship* God (v. 3) *will reign* with God in eternal triumph (Dan 7.18,27).

22.6–21: Epilogue, consisting of warnings and exhortations. 6: *He said*, an angel (v. 8), perhaps the one referred to in 1.1. *These words*, the contents of this book. *The God of the spirits of the prophets*, the one who inspired the spirits of the prophets (1 *QH* 20.11–13). 7: A parenthesis, reporting the words of Jesus (cf. 16.15). *Blessed*, see 1.3n. 8–9: 19.10. 10: *Do not seal*, cf. Isa 8.16; Dan 12.4. This book is to remain unsealed because the end is imminent. 12: *My reward is with me*, Isa 40.10; Jer 17.10. 13: Jesus applies God's title to himself (see 1.8n.). 14: *Blessed*, the seventh beatitude of the book; see 1.3n. *Wash*, 7.14. *The city*, the heavenly Jerusalem. 15: A list of those who are not permitted to enter the city, characterized generally as *everyone who loves and practices falsehood*. 16: *Root . . . of David*, Isa 11.1,10; Mt 1.1. *Morning star*, see 2.28n. 17: *The bride*, 21.2,9. *Come*, singular in Greek, is addressed to Jesus, as in v. 20. 18–19: A solemn warning against altering the teachings of *this book* (cf. Deut 4.2; 12.21). 20: *The one who testifies*, Jesus Christ; see 1.2. *Amen. Come, Lord Jesus*, a response, with liturgical echoes (1 Cor 16.22), to *surely I am coming soon*. 21: An epistolary postscript.

Essays

Tables

Bibliography

Glossary

Index

THE CANONS OF THE BIBLE

The contents of the Bible differ depending on the particular community using it. The major difference is between Christian Bibles, which include the New Testament, and the Jewish Bible, which does not. But there are also differences between the Hebrew Bible in Judaism and the Old Testament in Christianity, and there are differences among Christians about the contents of the Old Testament (see chart p. 2187). The discussion below will explain, within the limits of what scholars now know, how these differences came about.

DEFINITIONS

"Canon," a Greek word meaning "reed," came to refer to any straight stick that could be used for measuring. This basic meaning was extended to refer to any rule or standard by which things could be compared or judged. The Alexandrian grammarians, classical Greek writers who were not simply grammarians but also what we would call literary critics, used "canon" as their term for the list of standard or classic authors who were worthy of attention and imitation. This was not a closed category, and there were disputes about adding or removing works from the list. Furthermore, inclusion on the list merely recognized a work's quality; it did not confer any new status. Nevertheless, a canon of writings came to denote those texts that were of central importance to a given group. When used in reference to the Bible, canon has an even stronger significance: Not only is a given set of texts included, but all other texts—no matter how worthy otherwise—are excluded. This sense is expressed in a rabbinic comment on Eccl 12.12. The biblical text reads:

> Of anything beyond these [Heb *mehemah*], my child, beware. Of making many books there is no end.

The rabbinic comment states:

> Those who bring more than twenty-four books [the standard number in the Hebrew Bible; see below] into their house introduce confusion [Heb *mehumah*] into their house (Qoh. Rab. 12.12).

This suggests not only that the works in the canon are important, but that they, along with their authoritative interpretation, are sufficient in and of themselves.

THE HEBREW BIBLE

It is extremely difficult to trace how this conception of canon developed, and how it is connected to related notions, such as the eventual stabilization of the biblical text. Until the mid-twentieth century, many scholars thought that the canon of the Hebrew Bible was established at Jabneh (Jamnia), a city near the Mediterranean coast, west of Jerusalem, which was a center of Jewish learning after the destruction of the Second Temple (70 CE). According to this theory, a group of rabbis met there in about 90 CE and voted on whether certain books were canonical; at the end of this meeting, the official contents of the Hebrew Bible were supposedly established. It is now acknowledged that this overly neat reconstruction is incorrect and was based on a misunderstanding of rabbinic texts. Unfortunately, evidence is not available to offer a clear picture of how the canon of the Hebrew Bible was formed. Much of the material from early Jewish sources (for instance, the Dead Sea Scrolls, rabbinic texts, and the first-century CE historian Josephus) and Christian sources is ambiguous. Furthermore, many of the sources were written several centuries after the canon was definitively established, and are more interested in fostering a particular viewpoint than in presenting the facts objectively; they must, therefore, be used with great caution.

This much is clear: The canon of the Hebrew Bible did not develop at a single moment in time but rather in stages. There is general agreement that the Torah or Pentateuch was the first section of the Hebrew Bible to be canonized, that is, to be recognized as central by the community. Exactly when this happened is uncertain. Many scholars had associated this development with Ezra, and they saw the "law of your God" (Ezra 7.14), with which Ezra was entrusted in the fifth century BCE, as the Pentateuch. We now recognize, however, that this assertion goes beyond the evidence of the text. Though the Jewish community had recognized the Torah as central to its identity by the Persian period (sixth to fourth centuries), a conclusion suggested by citations of Torah material as authoritative in biblical books from this period (e.g., Chronicles, Ezra-Nehemiah), it is unclear exactly how this happened, or whether this development should be associated primarily with a single individual such as Ezra, or should be seen as part of a larger, more complicated process.

According to rabbinic tradition, the Torah is the first part of a tripartite (three-part) canon, followed by Nevi'im (prophets) and Ketuvim (writings), forming a work that much later was known by the acronym Tanak(h), *Torah, Nevi'im, Ketuvim*. Nevi'im is composed of Joshua, Judges, Samuel (seen as one book), Kings (seen as one book)—historical works known as "the former prophets"—and "the latter prophets," consisting of Isaiah, Jeremiah, Ezekiel, and the twelve minor prophets (Hosea through Malachi, seen as one book). The order of these eight books has been relatively stable. Ketuvim is comprised of the following eleven books, which, by contrast, appear in a wide variety of orders in various book lists and biblical manuscripts: Psalms, Proverbs, Job; the "five scrolls," whose order has been especially variable, Ruth, Song of Solomon, Ecclesiastes, Lamentations, and Esther; Daniel, Ezra-Nehemiah (seen as one book), and Chronicles (seen as one book). The number of canonical books according to traditional Jewish sources is thus twenty-four (five in the Torah, eight in Nevi'im, eleven in Ketuvim).

The origin of the tripartite canon has been a topic of recent dispute, with several scholars suggesting that a two-part canon, the Torah and other works, was the original form, and that only later was it divided into three parts. It is more likely, however, that the tripartite canon is primary, and evidence for it appears in such sources as Lk 24.44, which refers to "the law of Moses, the prophets, and the psalms," and in parallel expressions in the Dead Sea Scrolls. The tripartite canon likely reflects the gradual nature of the canonization process, with Nevi'im canonized before Ketuvim. This would explain why the Ketuvim contain the book of Daniel (dating from the second century BCE), and several late historical books, such as Ezra-Nehemiah and Chronicles, which would seem more appropriately to belong with similar works such as Joshua and Kings. The tripartite canon most likely suggests, therefore, that Torah was canonized in the Persian period, followed by the canonization of Nevi'im in the late Persian or early Greek period, while the Ketuvim were canonized last, around the time of the destruction of the Second Temple (70 CE).

The tripartite order is not the only order known in antiquity, nor is the number of twenty-four books the only number mentioned in ancient Jewish sources. Josephus, the Jewish historian of the first century CE, refers to twenty-two biblical books (*Ag. Ap.* 1.42). It is not clear if he simply had a smaller canon or if, instead, his canon had the texts in a different order, combined in different ways. Some traditions put Ruth after Judges and Lamentations after Jeremiah, treating these smaller books as appendixes to the ones they follow, rather than as independent works. Such an arrangement would yield twenty-two books, a number that conveniently corresponds to the number of letters in the Hebrew alphabet; some early Christian sources also cite this as the number of books in the Bible. The arrangement of Ruth and Lamenta-

tions mentioned above is that of the Septuagint (LXX), the Greek translation of the Bible begun in Alexandria, Egypt, in the second century BCE (see "The Greek Bible" below). According to this tradition, mentioned by some early church fathers and reflected in the arrangement of the earliest comprehensive Septuagint manuscripts (fourth century CE), the Hebrew Bible is divided into four parts: Torah, Histories, Poetical and Wisdom books, and Prophets (see the Introduction to the Poetical and Wisdom Books, p. 721). This order continues to be used by Christians in their organization of the Hebrew Bible (Old Testament) materials. Older scholarship spoke of this four-part, twenty-two-book arrangement as the Alexandrian canon, in contrast to the tripartite, twenty-four-book Palestinian canon, but scholars now recognize that such a clear dichotomy never existed and therefore avoid the use of those terms.

Scholars also now recognize that even when canonization took place, the contents of the Bible did not absolutely freeze. This is true, first of all, about books whose status as scripture continued to be debated. The Bible had begun to stabilize significantly by the fourth century CE, with the development of explicit lists in the Christian community of books considered canonical (see the chart CANONS OF THE HEBREW BIBLE). Other groups, too, had their ideas about the canon; it is unlikely, for instance, that the Qumran community, most of whose texts date from the century or so immediately before and immediately after the Common Era, viewed Esther as canonical, since no clear biblical manuscript of that book has survived among the thousands of fragments discovered. In contrast, many manuscripts of *Jubilees*, a set of comments on Genesis and Exodus, have survived, and given this work's affinities with the practices of the Dead Sea community, it was probably a canonical text for them. Within rabbinic literature, the Wisdom of Jesus ben Sirach (Sirach or Ecclesiasticus) is sometimes cited with the same formula used for biblical texts and was thus, in some sense, canonical for some rabbis. Therefore, although we may speak of the canon as forming in the first century CE, there was flexibility and variation around the fringes.

This flexibility may also be seen in the extensive divergence with respect to the wording of the biblical text as shown in manuscripts from Qumran, in translations of the Hebrew Bible in the Septuagint and elsewhere, and to a lesser extent in early rabbinic citations. These differences are not just small, such as a variant spelling here or there, but are often major and affect the meaning of the text. There are cases where the text is found in two or more different recensions—identifiably different versions, revisions, or critical texts, not merely two different

CANONS OF THE HEBREW BIBLE

JEWISH CANON	PROTESTANT CANON	ROMAN CATHOLIC/ORTHODOX CANON
Torah (LAW)	PENTATEUCH	PENTATEUCH
Genesis	Genesis	Genesis
Exodus	Exodus	Exodus
Leviticus	Leviticus	Leviticus
Numbers	Numbers	Numbers
Deuteronomy	Deuteronomy	Deuteronomy
Nevi'im (PROPHETS)	HISTORIES	HISTORIES
FORMER PROPHETS	Joshua	Joshua
Joshua	Judges	Judges
Judges	Ruth	Ruth
Samuel (1 & 2)	1 & 2 Samuel	1 & 2 Samuel
Kings (1 & 2)	1 & 2 Kings	1 & 2 Kings
	1 & 2 Chronicles	1 & 2 Chronicles
LATTER PROPHETS	Ezra	Ezra
Isaiah	Nehemiah	Nehemiah
Jeremiah	Esther	Tobit
Ezekiel		Judith
The Twelve		Esther
Hosea	POETICAL/WISDOM BOOKS	1 & 2 Maccabees
Joel	Job	
Amos	Psalms	
Obadiah	Proverbs	POETICAL/WISDOM BOOKS
Jonah	Ecclesiastes	Job
Micah	Song of Solomon	Psalms
Nahum		Proverbs
Habakkuk	PROPHETS	Ecclesiastes
Zephaniah	Isaiah	Song of Solomon
Haggai	Jeremiah	Wisdom of Solomon
Zechariah	Lamentations	Sirach
Malachi	Ezekiel	
	Daniel	PROPHETS
	Hosea	Isaiah
Ketubim (WRITINGS)	Joel	Jeremiah
Psalms	Amos	Lamentations
Proverbs	Obadiah	Baruch
Job	Jonah	Ezekiel
(Five Scrolls):	Micah	Daniel
Song of Solomon	Nahum	Hosea
Ruth	Habakkuk	Joel
Lamentations	Zephaniah	Amos
Ecclesiastes	Haggai	Obadiah
Esther	Zechariah	Jonah
Daniel	Malachi	Micah
Ezra-Nehemiah		Nahum
Chronicles (1 & 2)	THE APOCRYPHA	Habakkuk
	1 & 2 Esdras	Zephaniah
There is no Apocrypha	Tobit	Haggai
in the Hebrew Bible	Judith	Zechariah
	Esther (with additions)	Malachi
	Wisdom of Solomon	
	Ecclesiasticus (Sirach)	Orthodox Canons generally include
	Baruch	1 & 2 Esdras
	Letter of Jeremiah (Baruch ch 6)	Prayer of Manasseh
	Prayer of Azariah and Song of Three	Psalm 151
	Daniel and Susanna	3 Maccabees
	Daniel, Bel, & Snake	4 Maccabees (as an Appendix)
	Prayer of Manasseh	
	1 & 2 Maccabees	

copies of the same original with minor variants—which may simply vary the order of materials or may exhibit fundamentally different text-types (for example, short types versus expansive types, as with the text of Jeremiah; see the Introduction to Jeremiah, p. 1057). Early in the first millennium, however, these variations subsided as canonization and types of rabbinic exposition that paid a great deal of attention to the exact spelling of the individual word developed. This eventually brought about textual stability, though here too this was a gradual process, and the means by which it was accomplished are largely unknown.

The most basic question is why particular texts were canonized while others were not. Canonized texts within Jewish tradition were considered part of "the holy scriptures" or "that which is read" (to use rabbinic designations). Excluded texts in some cases had been translated in the Septuagint and were therefore canonized in the Christian community (see "The Greek Bible," below); others were lost, or survived as pseudepigrapha (writings falsely attributed to major biblical figures), or were preserved only in fragmentary form in the Dead Sea Scrolls. Some of these excluded texts date from after the Persian period (later than 333 BCE) and thus were seen as too recent to be eligible.

In various ways, canonical status for a book or group of books has to do with the community's views on their centrality, authority, sacredness, and inspiration. Over time these characteristics have become connected, inseparably so in some traditions; yet they are not identical, and though they overlap, they must still be viewed distinctly. The Song of Solomon, for instance, was originally an erotic love poem; by the early rabbinic period, it came to be interpreted allegorically as a love poem between God and Israel. It was also seen as the inspired composition of Solomon himself. Was it canonized before it was seen as a holy, allegorical text? In that case, its canonization might reflect a central role that it held in culture or ritual. Or was it canonized only after it was viewed as allegorical and as a composition of Solomon? In that case its significance, whether of authorship or of ideas, could have played a more important part. There is no way to judge between these two paths to canonization, and the resulting difficulty is characteristic of the problems in dealing with issues of canonization in general.

Despite such major uncertainties in our understanding of the process of canonization, however, several points seem fairly certain. First, it is likely that the final stages of canonization were a reaction to the destruction of the Second Temple in 70 CE. This crisis intensified a development, which had begun over half a millennium earlier with the destruction of the First Temple (586

BCE). Through this development Israel gradually became the people of the Book. Second, it is unlikely that canonization represents a purely top-down process, through which a small group of leaders (rabbis) determined the canon; instead, the designation of works as canonical was more like the official recognition of the works that a large segment of the community had already held to be central, holy, or authoritative. Finally, the act of canonization was remarkably inclusive, creating a body of works richly textured by a wide variety of genres, ideologies, and theologies. This is, fundamentally, a typical ancient Near Eastern process: Instead of creating a small, highly consistent text, as we perhaps would now do, those responsible for the process made efforts to include many of the viewpoints in ancient Israel, incorporating differing and even contradictory traditions into this single, and singular, book.

THE GREEK BIBLE

When Christian writings began to circulate, during the second half of the first century CE, the Bible that the early Christians used for reading and quotation was the Septuagint, the Greek translation and expansion of the Hebrew Bible that had been produced in Alexandria and other Diaspora communities for the use of Greek-speaking Jews. Probably as a result of the as yet unsettled matter of which works were canonical for the Jewish community, the Septuagint included further works: historical books (1 and 2 Maccabees, 1 Esdras); wisdom writings (The Wisdom of Solomon, The Wisdom of Jesus Ben Sirach); short works of fiction, or novellas (Tobit, Judith); an apocalypse (2 Esdras); historical legend (3 Maccabees); philosophical diatribe (4 Maccabees); an addendum to Jeremiah (Baruch and the Letter of Jeremiah); and expansions to Esther, Daniel (the Prayer of Azariah and the Song of the Three Jews, Susanna, Bel and the Dragon), and Psalms (Prayer of Manasseh and Psalm 151). (For further details see the Introduction to the Apocryphal/ Deuterocanonical Books, p. 1361, and the introductions to the individual books.)

Greek-speaking Jews in the Diaspora granted this Greek Bible an authority equivalent to that of the Hebrew texts. The legend that God had directly inspired its seventy translators was familiar to Alexandrian Jews (Philo, *Life of Moses*, 2.40). Manuscripts discovered at Qumran include Greek texts as well as a Hebrew text closer to the Septuagint than to the Masoretic text (4QSam[a]; 4Q121 Num 3.30-4.14; see "Hebrew Bible: Texts and Versions," p. 2194, for information about the Masoretic Text). Toward the end of the first century BCE, some books of the Septuagint were revised in Palestine to bring them closer to the known Hebrew text. Some

New Testament citations whose wordings are between the Greek and Hebrew texts that we have today may also reflect local revisions.

Evidently the various Jewish communities in the Greek-speaking Diaspora knew their Greek Bible in versions that differed from each other. Jewish revisions in the second century CE sought to bring the Greek text closer to the Hebrew and in some cases to replace terms that Christians had seized upon in disputes with Jews, such as "virgin" in Isa 7.14. The Theodotion version of the second century CE forms the text of most surviving manuscripts. Citations in Christian writers of the fourth century CE, as well as the Old Latin versions, suggest that there were Christian recensions of the Greek Bible during this period as well. The Septuagint, therefore, is really an anthology of translations and revisions.

Although some early Christians were aware that the Greek Bible they used was more extensive than the Hebrew Bible, its authority remained intact. Origen (185–254) recommended Judith, Tobit, and Wisdom to beginning Bible readers before the Gospels and Epistles. Athanasius (296–374) may also have shared this view: He includes Wisdom, as well as the Didache and the *Shepherd of Hermas* (two noncanonical early Christian writings) in his list of works to be used in the instruction of catechumens. Jerome (ca. 345–420) continued to cite the Greek Bible, though arguing for the superiority of the Hebrew text and canon. It was Jerome who first separated these additional works in the Greek Bible from those for which he had Hebrew originals, placing them at the end of the Old Testament.

The result of this history was that the Christian church ended up with a set of writings for its Old Testament that differed from those that for Jews formed the Hebrew Bible. Without definitive specification, Christians in the Western (Latin, later Roman) and Eastern (Greek, later Orthodox) churches used not only the works regarded as canonical by the Jewish community but also those additional works, or a selection of them, included in the Septuagint. Most Christians naturally were unaware of the differences among the biblical books; most were illiterate, and of the literate, very few could read Hebrew, the language of the original texts. The Christian churches therefore entered the second millennium with an expanded Old Testament, in an order different from the Hebrew Bible.

The Protestant Reformation coincided with a greatly increased interest in the study of ancient languages other than Latin. Among the leaders of the Reformation churches there was, along with a desire to make the Bible itself the standard of theological inquiry, a heightened effort to go behind the Latin text to the original

languages in which the Bible had been written, since the Bible alone, and not the Bible plus its traditional interpretation, was being given much more importance in Reformation thought. This effort reopened the issue of the status of those Old Testament books that were not accepted by the Jews and did not have original Hebrew texts. The result was a sharp demarcation between those texts in the Hebrew Bible and all the others, with the reformers granting clear privilege to the Hebrew texts— though retaining the order of the Septuagint for them. In Martin Luther's translation, the additional works were kept in their separate section, as Jerome had originally intended, between the Hebrew Bible (Old Testament) and the New Testament. Luther wanted these texts to be available for reading and meditation, but he did not regard them as scripture. Among the Calvinist reformers the position was even more definitive: None of these additional works were acceptable, and therefore they were excluded from the Bible entirely. The Anglican church, while retaining most of them (and using some in lectionary readings and services of prayer and worship), also held that though these additional books were valuable for reading and study, they could not be used to establish doctrine.

In response to this critique of their canonical status, the Roman Catholic Counter-Reformation position was to declare these works definitively a part of the Bible. The Catholic church to this day maintains the canonical status of Tobit, Judith, the longer version of Esther, 1 and 2 Maccabees, the Wisdom of Solomon, Sirach, Baruch (including the Letter of Jeremiah), and the Additions to Daniel. The Orthodox churches also maintained the canonical status of these works, and in addition regarded some or all of the following books as canonical: 1 Esdras, the Prayer of Manasseh, Psalm 151, 3 Maccabees, 2 Esdras, and (in an appendix) 4 Maccabees. The NRSV includes headings within the Apocryphal/Deuterocanonical Books calling attention to the varying canonical status of these works.

THE NEW TESTAMENT

As noted above, the early Christian community soon began to produce writings dealing with its own history, beliefs, and traditions. By the end of the first century CE and the beginning of the second, various gospels, narratives, letters, didactic discourses, and apocalyptic writings circulated among regional Christian communities. The practice of reading from these works, along with selections from the Greek version of the Jewish Scriptures, soon arose in Christian worship. Use in this public setting implicitly began the process of attributing to these Christian writings an authority analogous to that of the

Jewish Scriptures. When disputes broke out, as they inevitably would, about beliefs or traditions, the canonical or noncanonical status of the various Christian writings became important.

The authority of smaller collections, the four Gospels and a ten-letter compilation of Pauline letters, was accepted by the second century CE. Other writings, Acts, Hebrews, Revelation, and the catholic epistles (2 and 3 John; Jude; 2 Peter) were not as widely attested in the early period. Still other Christian writings also appear as authorities in the second and third centuries, since official lists only appear in the fourth century CE as a consequence of theological polemics (see Athanasius, *Festal Letter* 39; Eusebius, *Hist. eccl.* 3.3.5; 3.25.3–4). Christian canon lists remained fluid through the sixth century with such inclusions as the *Shepherd of Hermas* or the spurious *Epistle to the Laodiceans* among the Pauline letters. The Muratorian canon, whose date and provenance are disputed (second-century Rome to fourth-century East), includes Wisdom of Solomon in the New Testament. Other collections omit Hebrews. (See the chart for a comparison of three New Testament canon lists.)

Arguments over apostolic authorship emerge as a consequence of second-century CE challenges to general Christian practice. Valentinus and other Gnostics—who taught an esoteric form of Christianity—asserted that the Jewish God was ignorant of the highest divine realms, and that therefore both the Jewish scriptures and Christian writings, which accept them, would mislead naïve believers. They claimed to possess the esoteric teaching that Jesus had given to a few favored followers including Peter, Thomas, James the brother of Jesus, and Mary Magdalene. In the second and third centuries, Gnostics produced a number of revelations said to contain that secret apostolic teaching. Marcion established a church that excluded the Old Testament because its God was not the father of Jesus. He proposed a "New Testament" comprised of a version of the Gospel of Luke and ten Pauline epistles that opened with Galatians, evidence for the difference between the Law and the gospel. Marcion's texts of the gospel and epistles were edited to erase passages contrary to his theological perspective. Some scholars credit him with the idea of a canon as a fixed, closed group of texts. Against both Gnostics and Marcionites, Irenaeus argued that the Spirit poured out on the Church enabled her to write scripture (*Adv. Haer.* 3.21.3–4) and affirmed the unity of the Old Testament and New Testament (*Adv. Haer.* 4.28.1–2). Tertullian refers to reading the "books of God" in Christian worship with no differentiation between Jewish and Christian writings (*Apology* 39.3).

Besides these disputes, in which different contents of authoritative writings clearly reflected underlying theological differences, the physical character of Christian texts contributed to the emergence of canon. From the beginning Christians used the codex (pl. codices) format—a bound volume of pages, similar to a present-day book—rather than the more traditional scroll for their writings. While a codex permits easier access than a scroll, codices were the medium of early drafts, assembled notes, and the like. Finished literary works and sacred texts like the Torah were copied onto scrolls. Scholars disagree over whether early Christian use of codices resulted from the moderate socioeconomic status of most Christians, or whether the choice of this format made a conscious statement about their contents. Perhaps the first- and second-century Christians thought that their writings differed from the ancient authority of the Torah and the prophets. Use of the codex made possible the smaller collections that would be combined in the larger canon of twenty-seven writings at the end of the fourth century CE. Early collections of Paul's letters would have been seen as relatively informal writings directed to different local churches. Gospel collections were seen as representative of the oral teaching of the apostles, not formal literary works. The codex would have been an appropriate form for such writings. Use of readings from the Gospels along with prophets in Christian worship indicates that the Gospels had come to enjoy equal authority with the Torah and the prophets by the mid-second century (see Justin Martyr, *1 Apology* 67.3–5).

Scrolls were made of papyrus or leather pieces glued or sewn together, and lengthy ones became inconvenient to handle: The average length is about 20–26 feet (6 to 8 m), though longer scrolls are known. The codex can accommodate a much longer text, so that collections of books could be bound into one volume. Codices containing the Old Testament and later the entire Christian scripture were produced from the fourth century CE on. There was not a uniform collection of books or a uniform order of presentation in the earliest codices, however. Individual Christian congregations may not have possessed copies of all writings included in canon lists. It would have been difficult to distinguish these texts from other early Christian writings also found in codices. Some Christians turned over apocryphal writings to imperial officials during the Diocletian persecution (303 CE). Confusion over unofficial and authorized writings in Christian worship persisted into the mid-fourth century CE. Canon 59 of the Synod of Laodicea (360 CE) decreed, "Private psalms should not be read in church, neither uncanon-

CANONS OF THE NEW TESTAMENT		
THE MURATORIAN CANON (SECOND TO FOURTH CENTURY)	THE LIST OF EUSEBIUS (EARLY FOURTH CENTURY)	THE CANONS OF ATHANASIUS (367 CE)
[Matthew][1]	Matthew	Matthew
[Mark]	Mark	Mark
Luke	Luke	Luke
John	John	John
Acts	Acts	Acts
1 & 2 Corinthians	Romans	James
Ephesians	1 & 2 Corinthians	1 & 2 Peter
Philippians	Ephesians	1, 2, & 3 John
Colossians	Philippians	Jude
Galatians	Colossians	Romans
1 & 2 Thessalonians	Galatians	1 & 2 Corinthians
Romans	1 & 2 Thessalonians	Galatians
Philemon	Philemon	Ephesians
Titus	Titus	Philippians
1 & 2 Timothy	1 & 2 Timothy	Colossians
Jude	[Hebrews][3]	1 & 2 Thessalonians
1 & 2 John[2]	1 Peter	Hebrews[5]
Wisdom of Solomon	1 John	1 & 2 Timothy
Revelation to John	[Revelation to John][4]	Titus
		Philemon
	Disputed books:	Revelation to John
	James	
	Jude	
	2 Peter	
	2 & 3 John	

1. The MS begins in the middle of a line, but the inclusion of Matthew and Mark is virtually certain. 2. Some scholars argue for a conjectural reading that would support inclusion of all three letters of John. 3. Elsewhere, Eusebius regards Hebrews as by Paul. 4. Also listed as "disputed." 5. Athanasius regards this as by Paul.

ized books, but only the canonical ones of the new and old covenant."

Origen's advice to those reading scripture privately presumes that the educated, Christian elite had copies of deuterocanonical writings, Gospels, epistles, psalms, and the Torah. He proposes an order of reading designed to overcome the difficulties in approaching biblical literature. First, he suggests, Esther, Judith, Tobit, or Wisdom. Then, the Gospels, epistles, and Psalms. Finally, the reader can tackle books that are difficult or seemingly without reward, such as Leviticus or Numbers (*Homilies on Numbers* 27.1). The biblical codices of the fourth and fifth centuries CE include different selections of Jewish apocrypha. In Codex Sinaiticus one finds Tobit, Judith, Wisdom, Sirach, 1 and 4 Maccabees; in Codex Vaticanus, Baruch, Letter of Jeremiah, Wisdom, Sirach, Judith, Tobit; in Codex Alexandrinus, Psalms of Solomon, 3 and 4 Maccabees. Athanasius's *Festal Letter* 39 omits the deuterocanonical writings from the Old Testament but accepts them for private reading. Though Athanasius includes all twenty-seven New Testament writings, the issue was not settled everywhere. Gregory of Nazianzus (d. 389) omits Revelation from his

catalogue as do the lectionaries of the Eastern church. Didymus of Alexandria omits 2 and 3 John but cites the apostolic fathers as authoritative. Such evidence indicates that despite consensus on the four Gospels and Pauline epistles, regional variations over the rest persisted.

By the end of the fourth century, however, there was widespread agreement about which books had scriptural status. Among the large number of early Christian writings in a diversity of genres, including gospels, letters, acts, apocalypses, and didactic treatises, a smaller number had come to be widely accepted. The criteria that were implicitly, and sometimes explicitly, operative were apostolic authority—that a work was written by or attributed to one of the first generation of Christian leaders, especially Paul and the twelve apostles—and consistency with their teaching, especially as determined by ecclesiastical authorities in major centers like Rome, Alexandria, Ephesus, and Byzantium. As a result, some of the writings that had come to be considered noncanonical were lost and only rediscovered in the late nineteenth and twentieth centuries.

TEXTUAL CRITICISM

THE NEED FOR TEXTUAL CRITICISM

No original manuscript of any biblical book has survived. This situation, which may seem unusual to us, is actually quite normal for ancient writings, and even for those from only a few centuries ago. For instance, none of Shakespeare's plays is available in the original manuscript from Shakespeare's hand, and for most of them there are two or more early printed versions with many differences between them. For the biblical books, numerous copies or partial copies, varying greatly in age and quality, have been preserved in various parts of the world. Occasionally, as with the discovery of the Dead Sea Scrolls (the Qumran documents) in the mid-twentieth century, new copies turn up. Nevertheless, for the entire text of the Bible, scholars are faced with a situation in which they have multiple manuscripts that have been copied by hand so that each is a unique product, unlike a modern printed book, and therefore the copies differ among themselves in many places, some differences being trivial and some important. Given this situation, scholars have had to develop a methodology for deciding which wording should be followed in cases where the copies disagree. This methodology is called *textual criticism* because it is a way of assessing a text through critical comparison of its different copies.

Textual criticism is not used only on religious writings. Any important text where there is not a definitive, printed edition backed up with an author's manuscript or corrected by the author may need to undergo textual criticism. Typographical errors, omitted words, even graphic elements like incorrect indentions of poetic lines, can all mean that a text does not reflect the original author's intentions completely. The methods may have to be adapted to differing circumstances, but the principles have been developed over centuries and have been checked when manuscripts have been found that can confirm or refute reconstructions of a text. Most important, there is widespread agreement among textual scholars on the methods and procedures that should be used, even when the results remain in dispute.

DEFINITIONS

Establishing a critical edition of the biblical text involves the collection of all the differences between manuscript copies of any text, and the publication of all significant ones. The manuscripts are in the form of collections of biblical books, usually bound leaves, called *codices* (the plural of *codex*); *scrolls*, or long strips of papyrus or parchment rolled up, of individual books, such as those found at Qumran near the Dead Sea; *lectionaries*, or passages excerpted from texts in order to be read in worship services; and *citations*, or quotations in ancient writers, such as the Dead Sea Scrolls, the rabbis, and early church theologians. These sources, taken all together, are called *witnesses* or *authorities*, and the differences among them are called *variant readings* or simply *variants*. Also important are ancient translations, or *versions*, of the Bible, which provide indirect evidence for the original text. More details on these different forms of the texts are given under the specific discussion of the texts for the Hebrew Bible, the Apocryphal/Deuterocanonical Books, and the New Testament.

REASONS FOR VARIANTS

Variants can be of several kinds. The copyist may have misseen or misheard a word, producing a simple spelling error, or perhaps a different word. For example, in Eph 4.32 (cf. 5.2), the variants alternate between the pronouns "us" and "you." In Greek these two words are quite close (*hemin* and *humin*), differing by only one letter, and when pronounced aloud they are almost indistinguishable. In other places, the copyist's eye may inadvertently have skipped a phrase or sentence, thereby leaving out a sequence of words. In Sir 30.11–12, for example, some manuscripts omit two lines ending " . . . in his youth," possibly because the immediately preceding line also ends ". . . in his youth" and the copyist picked up after the second occurrence, omitting what came in between. Conversely, the copyist may inadvertently have gone over a phrase twice, producing a repetition. Although it may be difficult to determine when these errors took place in particular instances, there is nothing complex about them, and many variants are of this kind.

Sometimes, however, copyists seem to have tried to improve the text they were reproducing. They might have done this in several ways. They may have tried to "correct" a word or phrase that was unacceptable for one reason or another by substituting a more acceptable word or phrase. At 1 Tim 5.16, for example, the text reads "believing woman," and the translators' note says that some manuscripts have "believing man or woman," others "believing man." Here the translators have chosen the variant that is the most unusual, assuming that a copyist would more likely expand the phrase, or substitute "man" for "woman," rather than the reverse, in a cultural context that tended to treat women as less important than men. Copyists might also have been aware of a similar passage in another biblical book, and tried to make the passage they were copying conform to that. For example, Lk 11.2, the beginning of the Lord's Prayer, has variant readings that are probably an effort to make it conform to Mt 6.9. Copyists might also have tried to make the text support a particular theological view or belief. For instance, at Deut 32.8, some manuscripts read "according to the number of the sons of God" (NRSV "the gods," a paraphrase), while others read "according to the number of the sons of Israel" (NRSV "Israelites"). There is general agreement that the second variant was introduced by a scribe trying to avoid a polytheistic wording. Copying a manuscript was not necessarily just a mechanical process, but could involve deliberate changes for a number of reasons.

ANCIENT TRANSLATIONS

These methods of trying to determine the correct reading do not always provide enough evidence, or it may be that none of the existing manuscripts seems to have preserved the exact wording of the original author. Another source of information that scholars turn to is very early translations of the Bible. These early translations are often called *versions*, and they were in use among Jews or Christians whose primary languages were other than the ones used in the original writings. They include translations of the Hebrew Bible into Greek (for instance, the Septuagint), Aramaic (translations and paraphrases called Targums), Syriac (the Peshitta), and Latin (the Vulgate), and translations of part or all of the Christian scriptures into Syriac, Coptic, and Latin.

These versions are useful to translators because the early stage at which they were made provides insight into forms of the biblical text that may be closer to the original writings. They can therefore be consulted for help in determining what is more likely to be an original reading, or when the best manuscripts of the original language texts have gaps or obvious errors. In many translations, including the NRSV, these ancient versions are cited in the footnotes of the Hebrew Bible to explain where and why the translators have chosen an alternative reading or translated something other than the Hebrew text that has come down to us. For readers unfamiliar with the nomenclature of these ancient documents, however, such notes may not convey very much information. The versions are discussed in more detail in the section on "The Hebrew Bible: Texts and Versions."

THE PROCESS OF TEXTUAL CRITICISM

In order to establish the best possible text, scholars must first collect all of the significant variants and information about the manuscripts in which they occur. As a practical matter, a *critical text*—one with a version of the Greek or Hebrew on the page and an *apparatus*, usually footnotes giving variants and their source manuscripts—is published. Scholars must then determine whether they will accept the readings in the text or adopt instead one of the alternatives.

They may first rely on external evidence. This would include matters such as the age of the manuscript in which the variant occurs, since older manuscripts are generally closer to the original than later ones; or whether the variant occurs in manuscripts from one region only or in those from widely different regions. They will also use internal evidence: In general, shorter readings are preferable to longer ones, since scribes are more likely to add to a text than to delete materials (though, in the case of offensive or theologically challenging texts, deletion must be considered); difficult readings, including awkward phrases, coarse words, and poor grammar, are preferable to smoother ones, since scribes might try to "correct" such difficulties; and stylistic considerations can help judgments about how a particular author would have written.

The task would be difficult enough if scholars could be sure that the original wording in any place with a variant reading was preserved in at least one manuscript; but even that is not necessarily the case. There are instances where no existing manuscript is likely to preserve the original wording: where none of the variants seem to be right, or where the original text does not make sense as far as current scholarship can determine. In such cases scholars must assume that the original wording of the text has been lost or distorted in the course of the copying process. They then have several options open to them. One (called *conjectural emendation*) is to conjecture, based on the text as it now stands, what the original wording might have been. This can often be based on a scholar's general knowledge of the ancient languages, just as an English speaker can notice, and mentally correct, a typographical error in a modern book without having access to the author's manuscript. Another possibility is to consult the ancient versions. Finally, scholars may have to admit defeat and acknowledge that, given the current state of our knowledge, it is impossible to determine what the original wording might have been. For instance, at 1 Sam 13.1, the translation shows, by the use of ellipsis, that a word (the age of Saul when he began to reign) is missing. The translators' note points out that this number is not in the Hebrew text, and that the obvious second place to look for it, the ancient Greek translation known as the Septuagint, does not include any part of the verse. It is therefore impossible to recover the original wording unless some other ancient manuscript source is discovered.

The translators' notes in the NRSV call attention to all of these matters and many others as well. These notes, printed in italic type and keyed to the text by superscript letters, can be found at the bottom of the right-hand column of the translation on each page. The abbreviations used in these notes are given in the discussion below, and are listed on p. xxii.

THE HEBREW BIBLE: TEXTS AND VERSIONS
The Masoretic Text

The basic text for the Hebrew Bible today is called the *Masoretic Text* (MT), an edition of the Hebrew that was standardized in the fifth to tenth centuries CE by rabbinic scholars (called *masoretes*, from *massorah*, probably "what is handed down," that is, "tradition"). The Masoretic Text accomplished two things: It settled upon a *consonantal* text, that is, it established specific choices for the letters of the Hebrew words in the text; and it *pointed* those letters with a system of markings that indicated which vowels should be read with the Hebrew letters. This two-part decision was necessary because classical Hebrew writing was in effect a system of consonants, with only a few ways of indicating vowel sounds. Words with the same consonants but different vowels would look the same, as would the English words "untrained" and "interned" if they were both spelled "ntrnd." In the notes to the Hebrew Bible of the NRSV, "Heb" may refer to the consonantal (unpointed) Hebrew text, and MT to the same text with the vowel pointings included. The distinction is an important one, because the consonants are more likely to represent the original text than are the vowel sounds, which were added later, though based on older traditions. If the same consonants will make more sense with different vowels, the NRSV (and most other modern translations) will assume that those different vowels yield a word that is closer to the original text.

When ancient scholars had gotten the Masoretic Text into its final form, it became the standard text-form and alternative text-traditions were lost. It was therefore the case that all copies of the Hebrew Bible that were known were based upon this Masoretic Text, and although there were variants among the different copies, there was no way to check independently on the textual basis of most of the Hebrew Bible. With a few exceptions, this remained the case until the discovery of the Dead Sea Scrolls (the documents of the Qumran community) in 1947. Among the scrolls were manuscripts of most books of the Hebrew Bible that were more than a thousand years older than the oldest manuscripts available up to that point. These more ancient copies of the Hebrew text

have shed light on some passages in the traditional form of the biblical text. For example, at 1 Sam 10.27–11.1 in the traditional text there is no indication of the background to the conflict between King Nahash of Ammon and the men of Jabesh-gilead. But in a Qumran manuscript of 2 Samuel there is a continuation of 10.27 and an opening phrase for 11.1 that explains the context, and the NRSV includes them.

Ancient Versions of the Hebrew Bible

In cases where no form of the Hebrew text gives a reading that is satisfactory, scholars can turn to the ancient versions. The assistance these ancient versions give to textual critics and translators is partly due to the situation with regard to the text of the Hebrew Bible explained above. These early translations were made from Greek or Hebrew texts that, for the most part, are earlier than those copies of the Masoretic Text that have survived to the present. They therefore can give guidance to scholars about the state of the text, and even choices of wording, that are not represented in existing manuscripts. They can also confirm readings as being more likely. Of course, these ancient translations are themselves preserved only in copies, so that all of the considerations that apply to the original language texts of the Bible also apply to them: It is necessary to establish a critical text for them by comparing variant readings. They must therefore be used with caution, and they cannot be relied upon absolutely. This is, of course, a standard of comparison at one remove from the text itself: Scholars must look at the Greek, for instance, in the Septuagint, and conjecture or assume what the Hebrew would have been in order to result in a particular rendition into Greek. Nevertheless, it is a valuable source of clues.

For example, at 1 Sam 10.1, the text of the Septuagint is longer than that of the Hebrew Bible. In examining the difference, scholars have theorized that a copyist of the Hebrew text inadvertently omitted part of the verse because the same phrase occurs twice in it, and the copyist went directly from one to the other, omitting what was in between.

Names and Character of the Ancient Versions

The ancient versions of the Bible are referred to in a variety of ways by scholars. Following is a list, by language, of the chief versions.

Greek: The most prominent Greek version, and the oldest surviving translation of the Hebrew Bible, is the Septuagint, which was translated beginning in the third century BCE for use of Jews who were living in the Diaspora in Alexandria, Egypt, and other places around the Mediterranean after the conquests of Alexander the Great, and who therefore spoke Greek. The Septuagint, from a word meaning "seventy" because of a legend that seventy or seventy-two scholars worked on it, is abbreviated LXX (the Roman numerals for seventy) and, in the notes to the NRSV of the Hebrew text, is referred to as "Gk." Three later Greek versions—by Aquila, Symmachus, and Theodotion—were produced for the use of Jews after Christians had taken over the Septuagint and the increasing conflict between Jews and Christians about the interpretation of the Jewish scriptures had led Jews to stop using the Septuagint. These versions are also sometimes used by translators, but none of them has survived in its entirety.

Aramaic: Aramaic was the official language of the Persian Empire, and the Jewish people who lived under Persian domination spoke Aramaic, which eventually supplanted Hebrew as the ordinary language of Jews. Aramaic is a Semitic language, like Hebrew, and shares some vocabulary with it, but Aramaic speakers cannot easily understand Hebrew. It was therefore necessary to provide translations of the Hebrew Bible for Aramaic speakers. Read aloud in liturgical contexts, after the Hebrew had been read (see Neh 8.7 for an early example), these translations, called Targums, are often more paraphrases than literal translations. Most date to the early centuries of the Common Era. They nevertheless provide useful information about earlier forms of the Hebrew text. In the NRSV notes they are abbreviated "Tg."

Syriac: The Syriac language is a form of Aramaic and was spoken by Jews in northern Syria who translated their Bible into it. The *Peshitta* (which means "simple," that is, a plain translation without textual comments) was prepared for the use of Jews and later taken over by Syriac-speaking Christians, who added a Syriac version of the New Testament to it. In the NRSV notes it is abbreviated "Syr." There is also a Syriac translation of the Septuagint that was part of a *hexapla* or "sixfold" Bible; in the NRSV notes this is abbreviated "Syr H."

Latin: Two Latin translations are used by scholars. The first, the "Old Latin" version, was actually a Latin translation of the Septuagint and of the New Testament dating from before the fourth century CE. More useful is the Vulgate, the translation prepared in the fourth century by the great Christian biblical scholar Jerome. Jerome, in translating his Old Testament, worked directly from the Hebrew text of the time, and his version therefore can be helpful in determining original readings in that text. In the NRSV notes the Old Latin version is abbreviated "OL," and the Vulgate is abbreviated "Vg."

THE APOCRYPHAL/DEUTEROCANONICAL BOOKS: TEXTS AND VERSIONS

For most of the Apocryphal/Deuterocanonical Books, the translational basis is the Septuagint text. Various manuscripts of the Septuagint have survived, and the complete text is available in a critical edition prepared by Alfred Rahlfs and published in 1935. A newer critical text is in process of publication—the Gottingen Septuagint project—but it is not yet complete. The NRSV has used the newer text when it is available, for example in Esther and Sirach. The translators used Theodotion's version for the Additions to Daniel. For the Wisdom of Jesus ben Sira (Sirach or Ecclesiasticus), Hebrew manuscripts of large parts of the text have been discovered, and the NRSV has therefore used the Hebrew text instead of the Greek when it seems to offer a better alternative; in addition, there are Syriac and Latin versions of this book that also shed light on the text. For 2 Esdras, scholars agree that the best text is the Latin; they also consult versions in Syriac, Ethiopic, Arabic, Armenian, and Georgian.

THE NEW TESTAMENT: TEXTS AND VERSIONS
New Testament Manuscripts

Text critics must evaluate the evidence of thousands of manuscripts in order to establish the wording of the Greek New Testament. (See "The Process of Textual Criticism," p. 2193) This is a very large number of surviving copies for a collection of ancient documents; many classical texts survive in only a few copies. The overwhelming majority of these New Testament manuscripts (ca. 2,400) contain full or partial Gospel texts, followed by texts containing all or portions of the Pauline epistles (ca. 800). Revelation survives in only 287 copies. The manuscripts consist of papyrus fragments (some of only a few pages, some even shorter, preserving only a few verses); *uncials*, very early manuscripts written in letters unconnected to each other and similar to upper-case letters; and *minuscules*, later manuscripts written in a script that connects the letters and in which lower-case letters predominate. In addition to manuscript evidence, citations in Christian writers, lectionaries (excerpted passages for liturgical reading), and translations into other languages may shed light on the earliest wording of the text. With such a wealth of evidence, there is no phrase in the New Testament for which there is not some variant. Most involve issues of grammar, style, or copyists' corrections. Textual variants that affect the theological meaning of the text are fewer.

With such a wealth of information about the New Testament text, scholars have had to develop ways of classifying not only individual manuscripts but groups of copies so that they can more readily deal with all of the variants. If they can determine, for example, that a group of copies all descended from a common ancestor, they can assess the variants for that group together and compare them with other groups that descend from different early copies. Variants that occur in two or more of these "families" have a much higher probability of being original than variants that may have arisen within only one group, for instance.

Most of the known variants to the text of the New Testament originated in the first two centuries of its existence. As Christianity spread throughout the Mediterranean, different groups had their own copies of the various New Testament documents, in some cases excluding books that are now included, or including books that are now excluded. (See the essay on "The Canons of the Bible.") In addition, the Greek copies began to diverge, and they also began to translate the texts into other languages: Latin, Syriac, and Coptic. The Latin text, because of the dominance of the Latin language in the western Roman Empire, became the most prevalent, and the Greek text was used consistently only in the east, in the area around Constantinople (modern Istanbul). This Greek text, preserved and copied in the Orthodox churches of the east, became known as the *Byzantine* text, and for many centuries it was the only or main version of the Greek text available. Beginning in the seventeenth and eighteenth centuries, however, scholars began to discover other early texts. Early in the twentieth century, text-critics proposed families or text-types linked to the major regions of Christianity: Alexandria in Egypt, to the south; the east represented by Caesarea, on the eastern coast of the Mediterranean; and the west represented by Italy/Gaul and Africa. At first scholars assumed that the Byzantine text resulted from combinations of these types, but such a genealogy of the various text-types could not explain the mixture of readings found in the papyri and the oldest surviving codices. The so-called *Alexandrian* tradition, texts from the area of Egypt that included many of the most ancient papyrus copies (preserved in the very dry climate of that area), became in the nineteenth century a favored basis for establishing original readings. But the complexity of variants has increasingly made this approach, too, untenable.

Since the papyri evidence from the earliest centuries represents copies of particular books of the New Testament, it is likely that the scribes who set out to produce codices containing the entire Bible in the fourth century would have had a variety of different text-types for the individual books. No codex, therefore, is of uniform reliability. Codex Alexandrinus (early fifth century CE) is, as it turns out, a poor witness for the Gospels, but many critics consider it the best text of Revelation, even superior to a third-century papyrus copy. The age of a manuscript, therefore, does not necessarily determine the value of its readings, although it is one factor among many that scholars need to take into account. Writings such as Rev-

elation and the shorter catholic epistles (2 and 3 John; Jude; 2 Peter), which were not widely used as scripture until the fourth century, have a different textual tradition than the Gospels and the Pauline epistles.

Consequently, most text critics do not begin with a particular manuscript tradition and correct it to establish the text. Instead, the wealth and diversity of manuscript evidence have enabled critics to produce a Greek text based on *eclectic* principles: choosing the best readings from a variety of manuscript sources. This range of choice has also meant that New Testament scholars do not need to make conjectural emendations of the text, a practice common in the editing of other ancient texts, including the Hebrew Bible, where few early manuscripts are available. The best text for a particular passage requires detailed study of all preserved variants. Internal principles of textual criticism include consideration of readings that are more likely to be scribal corrections or errors, that fit the theological biases of an author or later editors, or that could have given rise to the other known variants.

The NRSV translation is based on a modern eclectic edition of the Greek text, *Nestle-Aland* 26th edition (or the equivalent *United Bible Societies Greek New Testament* 3rd edition, but incorporating information from the 4th edition as well). Textual variants in wording, both stylistic and theologically significant, are indicated in the translators' notes as "other ancient authorities." In order to understand the basis for these alternative translations, readers should consult the text-critical notes in the Greek text or a commentary on the Greek text.

Versions of the New Testament

The early Christian orientation toward the written word led to translation of the Bible into other languages for converts who did not speak Greek. Evidence from Old Latin, Syriac, and Coptic translations from the late second and third centuries CE figures in text-criticism. Ethiopic (mid-fourth century), Armenian (early fifth century), and Old Slavonic (late ninth century) translations form key moments in the cultural life of the people. Many of the apocryphal writings are preserved in Syriac, Coptic, and Armenian, thus providing a wider literature associated with the Bible.

Often manuscript evidence for the earliest translations is scanty or only derived from quotations. Tertullian's quotations appear to be his own translation into Latin, so the first evidence for the text appears in Cyprian (250 CE). Augustine and Jerome both complain about the large number of poor translations in circulation. Jerome was commissioned by Pope Damascus to produce a Latin Bible (ca. 383). His revised Gospels and translation of the

Hebrew Bible were combined with other translations for the remaining books of the Old and New Testaments to produce a Latin version known as the Vulgate. The Vulgate enjoyed wide circulation from the seventh century CE and was officially promulgated as the text of the Roman Catholic Church by Pope Sixtus V (1590). A neo-Vulgate with alterations in the text, style, and corrections to bring the translation closer to the Greek text was promulgated by John Paul II (1979).

The earliest evidence for the Syriac New Testament comes from a harmony of the Gospels, *The Diatessaron*, composed by Tatian in the second century CE. It is the source of citations in the commentary by Ephraem (310–373 CE). Texts from Antioch contributed to revisions of the Syriac New Testament, the Peshitta or common version (earliest manuscripts from the mid-fifth century CE), and a translation by Philoxenus (507/508 CE). The oldest versions of the New Testament translated into the Sahidic dialect of Coptic emerge in the third century CE. In the fourth century the whole Bible was translated into the Bohairic dialect, which became the official language of Coptic Christianity. A number of manuscripts found in the twentieth century remain to be assembled, catalogued, and incorporated into editions of the Coptic text.

TRANSLATION OF THE BIBLE INTO ENGLISH

PRINCIPLES OF TRANSLATION

Bible translation, though in principle the same as any other translation, is distinguished from it by two considerations: First, the reverence in which adherents of Judaism and Christianity hold the text, leading to concerns whenever a new translation is published that the text be treated with the respect it deserves; and second, the great popularity of the Bible, which has led to the proliferation of translations to meet every conceivable need and audience. In order to find one's way among the great variety of Bible translations available today, it is important to understand the principles underlying all efforts at translation.

In any translation from one language to another—the "source" language, or the original, and the "target" language, or the translation—two basic approaches define the limits at either end of a continuum of methods. The technical names for these "pure" translation approaches are *formal equivalence* and *dynamic equivalence*. Formal equivalence is usually explained as "word-for-word" translation, and dynamic equivalence as "sense-for-sense" or "meaning-for-meaning." In general, formal equivalence places more importance on the qualities of the source language, and dynamic equivalence is more concerned with the resulting readability in the target language.

Except where the source and the target languages are closely related, however, a purely word-for-word approach would be almost unreadable. Such is the case with translations of the Bible: ancient Greek, Hebrew, Aramaic, and Latin (the languages of the original texts) are very different from modern English. Here, for example, is Mt 6.9–10 in a word-for-word rendering of the original Greek:

Father of us who in the heavens, be holy the name of
    you;
come the kingdom of you;
become the will of you as in heaven and upon earth.

While it would be possible to puzzle out some meaning from this, it is clear that it is not English, and that an entire Bible translated along these lines would never be read. Most translations, therefore, move in the direction of dynamic equivalence, at least far enough to make sure that their representation of the original text makes sense in English. Some are more strict, for example always trying to use the same English word to translate a given Greek or Hebrew word (a characteristic known as "consistency"); some are freer, trying to achieve a more colloquial English style and using what seems to be the best English word for a Greek or Hebrew word in each separate context, regardless of how the same Greek or Hebrew word might be translated elsewhere. The result is a great range of translation choices for the Bible in English, from those suited to close study to those designed for readability, and readers can usually find a translation that will make sense to them and fit their needs.

In the case of ancient documents, and especially those of religious significance like the Bible, there are further complicating factors. Translations must find ways to deal with cultural differences between the worlds of the ancient writers and modern readers; they often try to accommodate traditional phrasing or translations, especially in key passages; and they must take into account the actual uses to which the translation will be put, including uses on formal and significant occasions.

Cultural differences come into consideration when a passage to be translated presents, not a puzzle about the dictionary definition of a word, but one about the way the word was used in its original cultural environment. An example occurs in the following passages: "the two kidneys with the fat that is on them" (Lev 3.4); "He slashes open my kidneys" (Job 16.13); and "In the night also my heart instructs me" (Ps 16.7). The word translated "heart" in the Psalm and "kidneys" in Leviticus and Job is the same Hebrew word, *kelayot* (or *kilyotay*, "my kidneys"). Literally it means the bodily organs, and in the passage from Leviticus that is clearly its meaning: The passage is discussing which parts of an animal will be burnt as a sacrifice. As a metaphor, however, it means the inner life of the human person, and that meaning is represented in the Psalm. The verse from Job falls somewhere in between. In its context, it is part of a catalogue of images of physical torture, intended to express spiritual or psychological suffering, many of which cannot be taken literally. There is a question whether it should be translated literally here. An ancient Israelite listening to these passages would have differentiated among this range of meanings, just as we would differentiate among "stomach trouble" and "I have no stomach for that job," or "heart surgery," "My heart stood still," and "Have a heart." In the case of the Hebrew word, the translation has to make that distinction for us, since the literal rendering "kidneys" in the passage from Psalms would make no sense, or the wrong sense, to a modern reader.

A related problem sometimes arises when translators have to consider whether to add a word to the text to make something clear to a modern reader that the ancient audience would have understood without explanation. For example, in 2 Pet 2.14, the literal translation "children of a curse" is rendered in the NRSV as "Accursed children!" This conveys the correct meaning in idiomatic English, but it does not convey to the modern reader what ancient hearers would assume, that the curse is from God. The New English Bible translation does this effectively by adding a word to make this implicit meaning explicit: "God's curse is on them."

An example of a translation trying to accommodate traditional understanding occurs in Jn 1.18, where the NRSV translates a Greek phrase as "God the only Son," and a footnote calls attention to two other possibilities. The Greek in actuality has three variants: *monogenes theos*, "only God"; *ho monogenes theos*, "the only God"; and *ho monogenes huios*, "the only Son." The translators first must decide how to render the Greek adjective *mono-*

genes. Older versions translate it as "only-begotten," but it really means something like "only one of its kind," i.e., "unique." Then they must determine which noun—"God" or "Son"—this adjective is supposed to modify. The manuscript evidence tends to support "God," since that variant appears in two papyri from the early third century CE, and also in manuscripts and citations from the fourth century. The variant "Son" only appears in the fifth century, in Codex Alexandrinus, and in later manuscripts. Since "only God" is present earlier, closer to the original time of writing, and since it is awkward, whereas "only Son" could be an effort to smooth out the text, it would seem that "only God" is the original reading. The NRSV effort to combine the two phrases is probably not correct.

Variety of use affects Bible translation particularly because many translations are intended for audiences that are far beyond the classroom or the scholar's study. In particular, Bible translations are intended to be read aloud in worship services, and bearing this in mind, many translators will try to use an English style that is more formal or elevated than that in the underlying text. Passages from the Bible are used in ceremonies marking significant life events, like marriage; on important national occasions, like the inauguration of a president; and to help express and channel great communal emotions, as in the funeral of a national leader. A translation that is too colloquial could seem jarring in such contexts.

Translations, thus, rather than being static, fixed creations that plug in one word in English for one word in the original language, are dynamic mediations between different and sometimes opposing tendencies. Insofar as they take the original language seriously as a controlling factor, they will tend to be word-for-word renderings; insofar as they take English seriously, they will tend more toward a meaning-for-meaning approach. They will try to represent not just the language, but the thought and cultural background, of the original writers and audiences; but they must also be sensitive to, and aware of, the great variety of needs among contemporary readers.

ENGLISH VERSIONS OF THE BIBLE

Prior to the sixteenth century, translations of the Bible into English were made from the Latin Vulgate instead of from Hebrew or Greek, and existed only in manuscript copies. The first English versions of the entire Bible were the two associated with John Wycliffe, translated from the Vulgate between 1380 and 1397. Part of the work on the first version was done by Wycliffe himself, and the rest, including all of the second, by scholars who were his immediate associates. Nicholas Hereford was largely responsible for the first version, which was completed before Wycliffe's death. John Purvey, Wycliffe's secretary, was responsible for the second version, which was completed by 1397. In the "General Prologue" to the second version Purvey states that it is best "to translate after the sentence and not only after the words, so that the sentence be as open, or opener, in English as Latin"—that is, so that the meaning be as clear, or clearer.

The sixteenth century brought the Bible in English to the common people as a printed book. The first English version directly translated from the Hebrew and Greek was the work of William Tyndale: The New Testament was published in 1526, the Pentateuch in 1530, and Jonah in 1531. In 1534 and 1535 he published revised versions of the New Testament, which were the basis of all later revisions and the main source of the authorized versions of the New Testament in English. Tyndale was finally betrayed into the hands of his enemies and in October 1536 was strangled and burned at the stake.

Miles Coverdale's translation appeared in 1535, the first complete Bible in English. It was not a direct translation from the original languages, but was based on two Latin versions and the translations by Tyndale into English, and by the European reformers Luther and Zwingli into German. In 1537 Matthew's Bible was published. "Thomas Matthew" was a pseudonym of John Rogers, a friend of Tyndale, who took Tyndale's manuscript translations of the books of the Old Testament from Joshua to 2 Chronicles, together with Tyndale's printed translations of the Pentateuch and the New Testament, and published them in this one volume, which he completed by adding Coverdale's version of the rest of the Old Testament and the Apocrypha. In 1539 Richard Taverner, a layman and a lawyer, published a revision of Matthew's Bible, one edition of which was issued in parts so that people who could not afford to purchase the whole Bible might buy one or more parts. Taverner was a good Greek scholar and made some changes in the translation of the New Testament that have been kept in later versions. Meanwhile at Paris, in early 1538, Miles Coverdale had begun a new revision of Matthew's Bible, which had been commissioned by Sir Thomas Cromwell, Secretary to King Henry VIII and Vicar General. The Great Bible, as this was called, was published at London in 1539. It was the first authorized English version, and a copy was ordered to be placed in every church. Until very recently, the Psalms in the *Book of Common Prayer* were from this translation. A revision of the Great Bible under the auspices of the Anglican bishops, the Bishops' Bible, was published in 1568 and revised in 1572. This revised edition was to become the basis of the King James Version.

Under the Roman Catholic Queen Mary the printing of the English Bible ceased, and its use in the churches was forbidden. Many English Protestants sought refuge on the Continent, and a group of these at Geneva undertook the revision of the English Bible. The Geneva version appeared in 1560. It was a convenient size instead of an unwieldy folio and was the first English version to use numbered verses, each set off as a separate paragraph. The Geneva Bible was never authorized, but it became the household Bible of the English-speaking nations for three-quarters of a century. It was the Bible of Shakespeare, John Bunyan, and the Puritans.

In 1582 an English translation of the New Testament was published at Rheims in France, made from the Latin by Roman Catholic scholars who had been forced to leave England led by Gregory Martin, who had been trained at Oxford University. A similar translation of the Old Testament was published at Douay in France in 1609.

On February 10, 1604, after a conference "for hearing and for the determining things pretended to be amiss in the church," King James I ordained: "That a translation be made of the whole Bible, as consonant as can be to the original Hebrew and Greek; and this to be set out and printed without any marginal notes, and only to be used in all churches of England in time of divine service." He appointed fifty-four translators, forty-eight of whom are named in the records that have come down. They worked in six companies, to each of which was assigned a section of the Bible. Two companies met at Oxford, two at Cambridge, and two at Westminster. Each company would consider the work of the other companies, and differences would be resolved by correspondence if possible, and if not, be referred to the general meeting at the end. This was a meeting at London of a committee of six, made up of two representatives from the companies at each of the three centers, which devoted nine months to final editing. Dr. Myles Smith, of Oxford University, wrote an informative preface, "The Translators to the Reader." This Bible, with a dedication to King James, was published in 1611.

An outstanding merit of the King James Version is the music of its cadences, the result of a sure instinct for what would sound well when read aloud. For example, here are the successive translations of Prov 3.17, in praise of wisdom, where Coverdale, the Great Bible, and the Bishops' Bible agree in reading: "Her wayes are pleasant wayes and all her paths are peaceable." The Geneva Bible has: "Her wayes are wayes of pleasure and all her pathes prosperitie." The King James Version gives to the verse a perfect melody: "Her wayes are wayes of pleasantnesse, and all her pathes are peace."

The English Bible owes more to William Tyndale than to anyone else because the basic structure of his translation has endured. It has been estimated that about 60 percent of the text of the English Bible achieved its final literary form before the King James Version appeared, and that in the King James Version at least one-third of the New Testament is worded exactly as in Tyndale's New Testament, while the sentences of the remaining two-thirds follow Tyndale's general pattern.

For two and a half centuries the King James Version maintained its place as the Authorized Version of the English-speaking peoples, without any serious consideration of its revision, but in 1870 the Convocation of the Province of Canterbury appointed a committee to undertake a revision. The Revised Version of the New Testament was published in 1881, the Old Testament in 1885, and the Apocrypha in 1895. The American Standard Version, containing the renderings preferred by the American scholars who had cooperated in the work of revision, was published in 1901. In 1928 the copyright of the American Standard Version was acquired by the International Council of Religious Education, and thus passed into the ownership of the churches of the United States and Canada that were associated in this Council through their boards of education and publication. The Council appointed a committee of Protestant scholars to have charge of the text of the American Standard Version and to undertake inquiry as to whether further revision was necessary. After more than two years of study and experimental work, this committee decided that there was need for a thorough revision of the version of 1901, which would stay as close to the King James tradition as it could in the light of present knowledge of the Hebrew and Greek texts and their meaning on the one hand, and present usage of English on the other. In 1937 the revision was authorized by the Council. The Revised Standard Version of the New Testament was published in 1946, the Old Testament in 1952, and the Apocrypha in 1957. The Revised Standard Version took full account of the new knowledge of the history, geography, religions, and cultures of Bible lands, and of rich new resources for understanding the vocabulary, grammar, and idioms of the ancient languages. It also returned to the basic structure and more natural cadence of the Tyndale-King James tradition.

The second half of the twentieth century saw the publication of many translations and revisions of the English Bible. In fact, between 1952 and 1990, when the New Revised Standard Version was published, no fewer than twenty-six different renderings of the complete English Bible were issued, with twenty-five additional translations and revisions of the New Testament. Among these the following Jewish, Protestant, and Catholic translations are of special note.

In 1955 the Jewish Publication Society, whose first translation of the Hebrew Scriptures had appeared in 1917, initiated a new translation. *The Torah, The Five Books of Moses*, was published in 1962, *The Prophets (Nevi'im)* in 1978,

and *The Writings (Kethuvim)* in 1982. These three volumes, with revisions, were brought together in 1985 under the title *Tanakh, A New Translation of the Holy Scriptures According to the Traditional Hebrew Text*. The *Tanakh* has useful footnotes of three kinds—textual, translational, and explanatory—and is notable for its perceptive handling of Hebrew vocabulary and syntax in contemporary English.

A newer rendering of the Hebrew Bible, still in process, is that of Everett Fox, which tries to preserve as much as possible of Hebrew idiom in its English style. Portions that have so far appeared are Genesis (In the Beginning), 1983; Exodus (Now These are the Names), 1986; Torah (The Five Books of Moses), 1995; 1–2 Samuel (Give Us a King! Samuel, Saul, and David), 1999.

In the year that the RSV New Testament was published (1946), British Protestant churches embarked on a totally new translation of the scriptures, The New English Bible; the New Testament appeared in 1961, and a revised New Testament, along with the Old Testament and Apocrypha, in 1970. At that time, C. H. Dodd, director of the enterprise and chairman of the New Testament translation panel, stated that this was "not another revision of an old version, but a genuinely new translation of the original, which should be frankly contemporary in vocabulary, idiom, style and rhythm-not to supersede the Authorized Version, but as a second version alongside it." The rendering is free and vigorous, tending at places to be periphrastic. Here and there the translators have rearranged the sequence of verses and sections of the text. A revision, under the chairmanship of W. D. McHardy, was published as the Revised English Bible in 1989.

The first English Bible made from the original Hebrew and Greek languages that received Roman Catholic approval was The Revised Standard Version Catholic Edition, of which the New Testament was published in 1965 and the complete Bible in 1966. In it the Deuterocanonical Books were placed among the Old Testament books in accord with the Catholic canon. It was prepared by the Catholic Biblical Association of Great Britain with the consent of the Revised Standard Version Bible Committee and the Division of Christian Education of the National Council of Churches of Christ in the U.S.A. There are no changes in the Old Testament text; the sixty-seven changes in the New Testament, made for liturgical and theological reasons, are carefully noted in an appendix. A significant further advance toward a Common Bible was achieved with the publication of the RSV without any changes whatever in the Oxford Annotated Bible with the Apocrypha (1966), to which Richard Cardinal Cushing of Boston granted the imprimatur.

The first English translation of the Bible made from the original languages by Catholic scholars was The Jerusalem Bible, published in 1966. With close comparison with the Hebrew and Greek, it is based on the French translation made under the direction of l'École Biblique of Jerusalem by a committee of scholars headed by Père Roland de Vaux, O.P., and popularly known as La Bible de Jérusalem. The English translation was made by a British Committee headed by Alexander Jones, L.S.S., of Christ's College, Liverpool. The translation is well done and has been warmly received. At the same time it must be acknowledged that occasionally French idiom intrudes. "Yahweh" is used instead of the substitute, the LORD. The volume is provided with useful introductions and notes, and "thee," "thou," and "thine" disappear from the text. A full revision was published in 1985 as The New Jerusalem Bible under the supervision of Henry Wansbrough of Ampleforth Abbey, York.

The New American Bible, a translation by members of the Catholic Biblical Association of America sponsored by the U.S. Bishops' Conference, was published in 1970. The completed work renders the text into modern American language. A revision, now in process, completed the New Testament in 1987.

For readers new to English, the American Bible Society issued "Good News for Modern Man," a translation of the New Testament by Robert G. Bratcher, in 1966. Also called Today's English Version, it uses simplified syntax and a limited vocabulary. The Old Testament, prepared by a committee, came out in 1976, and the Deuterocanonical/Apocryphal books in 1979. The popularity of the Good News Bible spurred the preparation of another modern-speech Bible. This is the New International Version, sponsored by the New York Bible Society (subsequently the New York International Bible Society). The New Testament was published in 1973 and the complete Bible in 1978. Less colloquial than Today's English Version, and more literal than the New English Bible, the version was prepared by twenty teams of translators from evangelical Protestant traditions in the United States, Canada, Australia, New Zealand, and Great Britain.

The ecumenicity of our times is in various degrees represented in these newer translations, but perhaps most of all in the New Revised Standard Version. The committee that produced the Revised Standard Version is a continuing committee, holding meetings at regular intervals and having charge of the RSV text, and it has become both international and ecumenical, with the appointment of Catholic and Protestant members from Great Britain, Canada, and the United States. Since 1946 an American Jewish scholar had been a member of the Old Testament section. More recently a Greek Orthodox scholar joined. In 1974 the Division of Christian Education of the National Council of Churches directed that the Committee undertake a revision of the RSV Bible with the Apocrypha, mandating that necessary changes be made (1) in paragraph structure and punctuation; (2) in the elimination of archaisms while retaining the flavor of the Tyndale-King James Bible tradition; (3) in attaining a greater degree of accuracy, clarity, and euphony; and (4) in eliminating masculine-oriented language relating to people, so far as this could be done without distorting passages that reflect the historical situation of ancient patriarchal culture. Within the constraints set by the original text and the mandates given by the Division, the committee followed the maxim, "As literal as possible, as free as necessary." As a consequence, the New Revised Standard Version (1990) remains essentially a literal translation. Paraphrastic renderings were adopted only sparingly, and then chiefly to compensate for the lack of a common-gender third-person singular pronoun. The NRSV contains all of the books that are regarded as authoritative by Protestant, Roman Catholic, and Eastern Orthodox churches.

THE INTERPRETATION OF THE BIBLE
THE HEBREW BIBLE'S INTERPRETATION OF ITSELF

Since the different books that make up the Bible were written and became authoritative at various times, later books refer in various ways to earlier ones. From the beginning of this process, whenever the Bible or any section that eventually became part of the Bible was read or recited, it was interpreted. This is a natural process; no text can be read purely in the abstract, since we all bring our lives and experiences to the text and often attempt to bring the text closer to our lives. It is thus not surprising that according to Neh 8.8, when sections of the biblical text were read to the postexilic community in the fifth century, "They read from the book, from the law of God, with interpretation. They gave the sense, so that the people understood the reading." Like any book, the Bible required interpretation. Since it was to them an authoritative book, the people needed to hear not only the text itself but also its correct interpretation because, like any literary work, the Bible is at some points ambiguous.

Since the covenant-making ceremony mentioned above occurred in the fall, it was likely that one reading from the Torah would have been Lev 23.33–43, which outlines the commemoration of the fall harvest festival of booths (Sukkot), beginning on the fifteenth day of the seventh month (counting from Nisan, in the spring, not Tishri, in the fall). According to v. 40, proper commemoration of the festival includes the following: "On the first day you shall take the fruit of majestic trees, branches of palm trees, boughs of leafy trees, and willows of the brook; and you shall rejoice before the LORD your God for seven days." This passage is ambiguous on at least two points: What should the worshipers do after they "take" these various greens? What is meant by "the fruit of majestic trees" and "boughs of leafy trees," which are interspersed with very specific tree names ("palm," "willow")?

The treatment of Lev 23.33–43 in the later passage in Neh. 8.14–15 shows how this postexilic community interpreted the text of Leviticus, resolving these ambiguities: "And they found it written in the law [Heb torah], which the LORD had commanded by Moses, that the people of Israel should live in booths during the festival of the seventh month, and that they should publish and proclaim in all their towns and in Jerusalem as follows, 'Go out to the hills and bring branches of olive, wild olive, myrtle, palm, and other leafy trees to make booths, as it is written.'" Thus, the term "take" from Lev 23.40 is interpreted in the context of the immediately following legislation (v. 42)—"You shall live in booths for seven days"—to mean "take" for the construction of "booths." Furthermore, the ambiguous trees are specified as olive trees and myrtles. The way in which this later text clarifies how the earlier text should be understood is not at all remarkable: The types of branches to be used are clarified and, naturally enough, the broader context of the fall festival laws of Lev 23 is used to explicate the purpose for which these branches are taken.

The process of inner-biblical interpretation, where we can see a later biblical text interpreting an earlier one, began early in the history of the development of the Bible. But it was certainly accelerated by the canonization of the Torah (see the essay "The Canons of the Bible" on p. 2185 and the Introduction to the Pentateuch, p. 3). It is especially obvious in Deuteronomy, which in both its legal and its narrative sections reuses and interprets earlier biblical traditions. One example from each genre will illustrate the pervasive interpretive nature of Deuteronomy.

The law of a Hebrew slave is found in Ex 21.2–11, the Covenant Collection, and in Deut 15.12–18 as part of the Deuteronomic Law Collection. A quick glance indicates that these two texts are closely related and interdependent. Moreover, biblical scholars agree that the Deuteronomic Law Collection (D) is later than the Covenant Code (C). It is thus significant that the words "without debt" from Ex 21.2 are missing in D's retelling of this law. Instead we find the following, which, based on its placement and context, is most likely D's interpretation of C's "without debt": "And when you send a male slave out from you a free person, you shall not send him out empty-handed. Provide liberally out of your flock, your threshing floor, and your wine press, thus giving to him some of the bounty with which the LORD your God has blessed you" (Deut 15.13–14). The Deuteronomist has naturally subsumed the text of C into his own intellectual-theological framework, which includes the idea that the underprivileged must be looked after carefully. For the Deuteronomist, "without debt" could not be interpreted literally and narrowly; instead it suggested that the slave must be released with resources to enable him to be self-sufficient so that he will not immediately find himself in debt again; thus the slave must be provided for. While this is not an obvious interpretation of Exodus and is certainly not what the author of Exodus intended by the phrase, it offers a good example of how a word may be reinterpreted by a later writer to fit a later ideology.

In fact, this particular reinterpretation is mild when compared with other, more radical reworkings of the earlier law in Deuteronomy. Take, for example, the insistence that the same law applies to both male and female slaves, in contrast to Ex 21.2–6,7–11. Note that the ear-piercing ceremony, which transpires if the slave opts to stay with the master, must take place at the owner's house (Deut 15.17), while Exodus suggests that it happens "before God," namely at the local shrine (Ex 21.6). According to Deuteronomy, the local shrines were illegitimate, and worship was permitted only at the Jerusalem Temple. This suggests that later writers, facing differing circumstances, did not always feel bound by the letter of earlier laws and could "interpret" them into new laws which the earlier legislators would hardly have recognized.

These same tendencies can be seen in Deuteronomy's reinterpretation of earlier narratives. Both Ex 18 and Deut 1.9–18 narrate the establishment of a judicial system in ancient Israel so that Moses would not be responsible for all legal cases. The theme and vocabulary of the two stories are so similar that it is clear that Deuteronomy has created its story by "interpreting" Exodus. Some of this interpretation is quite reasonable; for example, Deut 1.17, "Any case that is too hard for you," clarifies the somewhat ambiguous "every important [lit. "great"] case" of Ex 18.22. However, the change of Ex 18.21, "able men . . . who fear God, are trustworthy, and hate dishonest gain" to Deut 1.13, "individuals who are wise, discerning, and reputable," is not based on a straightforward interpretation of the earlier text. It is as if the author of this passage thought: Is it reasonable that righteousness in religious observance is the most important quality of judges? Surely not. Surely he meant "wise" when he said "men who fear God"! There are other cases of radical revision in this interpretive passage in Deut 1. The Deuteronomist, for example, "ignores" the fact that this judicial system was set up at the instigation of Moses' father-in-law, and transfers the initiative to Moses. Like any reader, the Deuteronomist interprets the story within his own mental framework, even if this means that a "new" story quite distinct from the original is created.

The previous illustrations show how ambiguities in texts are resolved, and how a text can be (consciously or unconsciously) removed from its original context and reinterpreted within the framework of the later reader's context. They reflect cases where the later biblical interpreters are simply acting as readers of texts, and these readings, though at points radical, have parallels to the way contemporary readers might engage secular works. As a composite canonical text, however, the Bible presents challenges of interpretation which are quite different from contemporary literary works. In particular, the Bible contains diverse legal traditions that are ultimately incorporated into a single work and thus somehow need to be read together or reconciled. Additionally, particular parts of the Bible, especially prophetic texts, present themselves as divine truths; when these seem not to have come true, they must be interpreted differently.

A simple case where laws are contradictory occurs in the legislation concerning the cooking of the Passover lamb. Exodus 12.8–9 notes, "They shall eat the lamb that same night; they shall eat it roasted over the fire with unleavened bread and bitter herbs. Do not eat any of it raw or boiled in water, but roasted over the fire, with its head, legs, and inner organs." Deuteronomy 16.7, however, insists, "You shall boil it [NRSV "cook it" reflects an incorrect attempt at harmonizing the various laws] and eat it at the place that the LORD your God will choose." These differences are not at all surprising within a source-critical model, which suggests that they reflect different practices of different groups of people at different times. But what are we to do when both texts enter the canonical Bible?

We are not the first to appreciate this problem; it was already felt, for example, in the postexilic book of Chronicles, for which the Torah (more or less in the form that we know it) was authoritative. The Chronicler depicts the Passover celebration under King Josiah (2 Chr 35.13): "They boiled the passover lamb with fire according to the ordinance" [a literal translation; NRSV is harmonistic and incorrect]. The Chronicler has thus reconciled the two traditions by choosing elements from both: The offering is "boiled," following Deut 16.7, but "with fire" reflects the "roasted over the fire" of Ex 12.8–9. Through the brilliant (but problematic) expression "boiled . . . with fire," the two variant authoritative traditions are retained, and in some sense reconciled.

The manner in which various problematic prophecies are already interpreted within the Bible, so that they become true, is quite remarkable. The clearest example of this is from one of the latest texts of the Hebrew Bible, Dan 9. The background of this text is the prophecy in Jer 25.11, which suggests that Babylon will be given dominion over the world for seventy years; Jer 29.10 builds upon that prophecy, suggesting that after these seventy years are completed, Israel will be restored. This presented a serious problem for the author of Dan 9, living during the reign of the (Seleucid) Greek king, Antiochus IV Epiphanes, who persecuted the Jews and forbade them to follow the most fundamental laws (see Introduction to Daniel, p. 1233). In this period, between 167 and 164 BCE, it seemed that Jeremiah's word, which claimed that a complete restoration would transpire, was false. But also by that time it is likely that Jeremiah was already considered a true prophet, whose book was canonical. How could this true prophet utter an oracle that was so patently and painfully false?

This explains why Daniel "intensively consulted [NRSV "perceived in" is incorrect] the books concerning the number of years that, according to the word of the LORD to the prophet Jeremiah, must be fulfilled for the devastation of Jerusalem, namely, seventy years" (9.2). Because Jeremiah's prophecy seemed not to be true, intensive consultation was needed, so that the real meaning, the proper interpretation of the seemingly unambiguous "seventy years" [Heb shib'im shanah] could be deciphered. The angel Gabriel (v. 21) finally offers Daniel the correct interpretation (v. 24): "Seventy weeks [Heb shabu'im shib'im] are decreed for your people and your holy city: to finish the transgression, to put an end to sin, and to atone for iniquity, to bring in everlasting righteousness, to seal both vision and prophet, and to anoint a most holy place." The consonants of Jeremiah's shib'im ("seventy"), are read twice, first as shabu'im, ("weeks"), then, as expected, as shib'im ("seventy"). (In the period when Daniel was written, Hebrew used consonants only, so the same word could be pronounced, and understood as, two different words with different vowels.) The result of this intensive consultation is that Jeremiah's "seventy" means "seventy weeks of years": seventy times seven or four hundred and ninety years. Thus, Daniel updated the prophecy and gave Jeremiah a four-hundred-twenty-year extension so that his prophecy could still be true.

The author has here engaged in what one scholar has called (in reference to similar rabbinic texts) "creative philology," reading and interpreting words in a highly creative fashion. Here, as in later rabbinic texts, this is not frivolous but is done out of necessity, in order to maintain the status of Jeremiah and his prophecies. Closely related to "creative philology" is "creative historiography," where an interpreter rearranges or adds to earlier texts, thereby creating a fundamentally new historical tradition. This may be seen very often in Chronicles, which frequently and ingeniously rearranges or adds to its sources, typically the books of Samuel and Kings. A classic example of this type of interpretation through "creative historiography" may be seen in 2 Chr 8.2, which claims that "Solomon rebuilt the cities that Huram [a variant spelling of Hiram] had given to him, and settled the people of Israel in them." This is an imaginative revision of 1 Kings 9.11–12, which tells of cities that Solomon gave to Hiram! The Chronicler read his source within his own interpretive framework and theology, which included the notion that the righteous Solomon could not possibly give away cities from the holy land of Israel; 2 Chr 8.2 is an interpretive attempt to deal with this theological problem.

These examples illustrate how later biblical passages interpret earlier passages. Many other examples from almost every biblical book could be offered, including more subtle cases where the interpretation is accomplished through textual juxtaposition, or the interpretive tradition is not found in a separate text (like Chronicles), but has entered as a type of gloss in the original text that it is interpreting. The examples cited above are meant to illustrate the range of inner-biblical interpretations; some are rather straightforward, clarifying ambiguities, while others are remarkably radical, transforming legal or narrative traditions in a quite extreme fashion. Finally, when seen in combination with the following essay on the premodern Jewish interpretation of the Bible (p. 2208), these illustrations highlight the continuity between inner-biblical interpretation and early rabbinic interpretation. This continuity should not be surprising; not only are the two historically contiguous, but both work within a canonical framework. As a result, both are beset by all the problems, as well as the opportunities, that the canonization of the Hebrew Bible presented.

THE INTERPRETATION OF THE BIBLE
THE NEW TESTAMENT INTERPRETS THE JEWISH SCRIPTURES

SCRIPTURE IN THE NEW TESTAMENT

The second-century CE satirist Lucian of Samosata, in Asia Minor, attacked the early Christian movement in the person of a charlatan prophet, Peregrinus. Peregrinus feigned conversion, rose to the position of local bishop, and gained considerable prestige among his naïve coreligionists when he was imprisoned for the faith, before assuming another career. How did Peregrinus achieve his exalted position? According to Lucian, "He interpreted and explained some of their books and even composed many and they revered him as a god, made use of him as a lawgiver" (*On the Death of Peregrinus* 11). By the mid-second century CE, then, Christians could be mocked for their preoccupation with interpreting sacred texts as well as for composing their own writings. At least in part, such interpretation was understood to involve the promulgation of laws. Whether "a lawgiver" pronounced legal rulings on community discipline or codified ethical norms is not clear. From the point of view of the educated elite, Christians who followed such unlearned bishops could be duped because they, as well as their leaders, lacked the advanced rhetorical training required for the interpretation of texts.

Similar objections are given voice within the New Testament. In the Gospel of John, local Pharisees scorn the blind man's confession that Jesus is from God, not a sinner, on the grounds that he has no standing to interpret the Torah (Jn 9.24–34). Matthew has the scribe trained for the kingdom of heaven able to bring from his store-house both new things and old ones (Mt 13.52). He defends Jesus' understanding of the Torah and the prophets as attending to the substantive matters—justice, mercy, and faithfulness—rather than making burdens of details about tithing as the Pharisees do (Mt 23.23–24). Paul insists that the true meaning of the law remains veiled, like Moses' face, from his fellow Israelites. They can only understand its meaning by turning to Christ (2 Cor 3.7–18).

Thus, most biblical interpretation in the New Testament serves a polemical or apologetic purpose: to defend Christian claims about Jesus. Neither the assertions themselves nor the presuppositions employed to derive them from scripture would be acceptable to those who did not share Christian beliefs. Nevertheless, the interpretative methods used, especially by Matthew and Paul, have much in common with those used by other Jews in the same period.

Though mid-second century Christians had begun to consider their own writings as sacred texts, that was not yet true when the New Testament was being written. Only the latest of the New Testament texts, 2 Peter, suggests that a collection of Paul's letters was regarded as authoritative (2 Pet 3.15–16). Thus, whenever a New Testament writer refers to or quotes scripture, he is interpreting texts so regarded by the Jewish community. The scriptures were not known to these writers in their original Hebrew, but in Greek translation, the Septuagint (see "Hebrew Bible: Texts and Versions," p. 2194 and "The Greek Bible," p. 2188). Since various text forms of the Septuagint were known in Judea itself, it was clearly used by Jews and not only by Gentile converts to Christianity. In many cases, the text that a New Testament author quotes or interprets differs from that found in a modern translation of the Hebrew Bible. We cannot tell if the author is quoting from memory, misquoting, or altering the text unless we have compared it with the Septuagint and not only with the Hebrew.

The writings that counted as scripture for the New Testament writers are those they held in common with Diaspora Jews: the Torah, prophets, Psalms, and assorted texts from the Writings. In frequency of quotation and allusion in the New Testament, Psalms and Isaiah predominate, followed by Deuteronomy and other passages from the Torah. Some are introduced with a formula such as "it is written" (Mt 2.5; Lk 20.17; Acts 15.15–18) or "it was said" (Mt 5.21). In other cases, the expression "that is" combined with application of the text to reading the community's experience as part of God's eschatological plan resembles the interpretation of prophetic passages in the interpretive commentaries ("pesharim") among the Dead Sea Scrolls from Qumran (Mt 3.3; 11.10;

Jn 6.31,50; Acts 2.16; 4.11; Rom 9.7–9; 10.6–8; Heb 7.5; 1 Pet 1.24–25; see 1 QpHab 12.6; CD 7.14–15; 4Q174 1.11–14). Use of an adversative expression to correct a prior tradition of interpretation, as in Matthew's "you have heard . . . but I say" (Mt 5.21–22,27–28,31–32,33–34,38–39 43–44) resembles a rabbinic formula (*Midr. Pss.* 119.26). Matthew does not continue in the rabbinic mode, however, which would require that Jesus establish his interpretation by appealing to other texts from scripture.

CHRISTOLOGICAL READING OF SCRIPTURE

The primary focus of New Testament biblical interpretation is the belief that Jesus is God's messiah, the agent of God's eschatological salvation. Some texts are repeatedly interpreted with a strong messianic meaning: Ps 2; 8; 110; Deut 18.15,18–19; and 2 Sam 7.14. Prophecies from Joel 2–3 (Acts 2.16–21), Zech 9–14 (Mark 11.1–2; Heb 10.19), Dan 7 (Mk 13.26), and Dan 12 (Jn 5.29) play a major role in understanding the risen and exalted Jesus as the one who has inaugurated the end-time. Daniel 7.13–14 lies behind the Christological confession of Jesus as the Son of Man who will come in judgment (see Mk 14.62). In many cases, the reference to Daniel is not explicitly marked. Readers who do not recognize the allusion—or are not aided by the notes found in a modern edition—may miss the use of allusions or partial quotations to support a claim about Jesus.

Even when the text being employed is evident, one cannot always determine whether the author is using the passage as an isolated prooftext or intends readers to incorporate elements from its larger biblical context into the interpretation. Among the Qumran texts, testimony collections gather biblical passages on a particular topic. Some combine references to a future prophet (4Q175: Deut 5.28–29; 18.18–19; 33.8–11; Num 24.15–17; 4Q174: 2 Sam 7.10–14; Ps 1.1; 2.1–2). If early Christians used similar collections of texts on a theme, the larger context of any quotation (which would not have been given in the collection) is irrelevant. When the same texts are quoted in the same combination by different authors, such a source may well be behind all of them. Christ as the stumbling stone based on Isa 8.14; 28.16; and Ps 118.22 appears in several places (Mt 21.42; Acts 4.11; Eph 2.20; 1 Pet 2.6). Matthew's set of fulfillment quotations, which assert that events in the life of Jesus were foretold by the prophets (1.23 [Isa 7.14; 8.8]; 2.6 [Mic 5.2], 18 [Jer 31.15], 23 [source uncertain; see Judg 13.5,7; Isa 11.1; 53.2]; 4.14 [Isa 9.1–2]; 8.17 [Isa 53.4]; 12.17–21 [Isa 42.1–4]; 21.4–5 [Zech 9.9]) may have been taken from a collection of prooftexts. They exhibit the particular significance of Isaiah in early Christian understanding of the suffering and death of Jesus.

Christians, using the Septuagint translation, were able to read Isaiah's original reference to a young woman who will soon bear a child as a reference to the miraculous birth of God's messiah from a virgin (Isa 7.14). When Matthew embedded this text into the story of Jesus' birth, he fixed its Christian interpretation in the imagination. Similar reinterpretations arose in dealing with the end of Jesus' life: The necessity of explaining how Jesus' death fit into God's plan drew Christian attention to passages describing God's suffering righteous one. Early interpretation matched details in the story of Jesus' passion to passages in Isaiah (for example, abuse of the prisoner from Isa 50.6 and 53.5; see Mt 27.67–68). Some scholars think that Jesus himself may have begun this process by applying texts concerning the suffering righteous one and the coming "son of man" (Dan 7.13–14) to his ministry.

Isaiah's prophecies about the salvation that is coming to Zion also play an important role in the Gospel narratives. The announcement of salvation to the suffering ones in Isa 61.1–3 has been embedded in an inaugural speech of Jesus (Lk 4.17–19). The same passage is reflected in Matthew's Beatitudes (Mt 5.3–12). Images of the day of salvation from Isaiah dominate the Christian liturgical celebrations of Advent, Christmas, Lent, and Easter. So firmly are these passages fixed within a Christological interpretive tradition that many Christians find it impossible to imagine that they could refer to anything other than the coming of salvation in Jesus.

As Christians came to articulate claims about Jesus' identity as the unique Son of God, they used biblical texts to support this view in a more polemical way. Jesus is shown to prove his own superiority to the human descendants of David with a clever twist on Ps 110.1 (Mk 12.35–37): David himself (the presumed author of the Psalm) uses the title "Lord" of the messiah. Hebrews 1.5-14 attaches a number of other Psalm texts to Ps 2.7 as evidence that Jesus is God's Son and as such exalted above the angels. John 10.31-39 has Jesus cite Ps 82.6 in self-defense when he is accused of blasphemy for claiming to be the unique representative of God. In all of these examples, interpreting the Bible is not pursued for its own sake. Rather, Christian beliefs about Jesus are prior to the biblical passages produced to support them. The result, however, is that many passages from the prophets and Psalms have become so embedded in the gospel narrative that for the Christian imagination they are the story of Jesus.

SCRIPTURE AND CHRISTIAN PRACTICE

Matthew 5.17–20 defends the teaching of Jesus against the charge of dissolving the Torah and the prophets. The Torah is identified with the exact words of the written Hebrew, and Matthew affirms its divine authority in every particular. The Christian understanding represents the fulfillment of the Torah and prophets by establishing a righteousness superior to that taught by scribes and Pharisees. What principle underlies the adversative readings that follow in Mt 5.21–28? A common explanation attributes to Jesus the authority of a messianic interpreter of the law. He can determine its intent with an authority greater than that of those Jewish interpreters who appeal to the oral tradition that was presumed to have been given by Moses. Disputed points are to be resolved once and for all based on the "prophet like Moses" of Deut 18.15–18 (see Jn 4.19,25). In what follows, Jesus and his followers are to do more, not less, than the Torah requires. The debate over divorce in Mt 19.3–13 employs a related argument. Though the Torah contains provisions for granting a divorce (Deut 21.1), Jesus claims that Moses introduced such stipulations as a concession. They do not reflect the will of God as revealed in Gen 1.27. The Genesis text also figures in a critique of social laxity about divorce in the Dead Sea Scrolls (see CD 4.19–21). Thus it was used to indicate God's intention concerning marriage prior to the time of the Qumran community (second century BCE through first century CE). The Qumran tradition, however, does not use it, as the New Testament does, to negate the legal standing of another text of the Torah. This passage from Matthew implies that the point of "messianic" interpretation is to restore the intention of the original lawgiver, namely God. Matthew 5.48 concludes on a similar note: Righteousness implies assimilation to God's own perfection.

New Testament authors do not interpret the details of legal traditions found in the Jewish scriptures. Rather a series of "summary principles" serves to demonstrate that the intention of the Torah has been realized in the Christian community. Matthew 7.12 uses the "golden rule" as such a summary, for instance. The most common Christian summary focuses on the injunction to love God and the neighbor, the love command (see Mk 12.28–34; Jn 13.34–35; Rom 13.8–10; Gal 5.14; Eph 5.1–2; 1 Thess 4.9–10; Heb 13.1; Jas 2.8). Matthew 23.23–24 employs the distinction between attention to observance of detailed precepts concerning tithing and the "weightier matters"—justice, mercy, and faithfulness. This passage has, apparently, been reformulated from Matthew's Jewish Christian perspective, since it presupposes the development of the law on tithing (Deut 14.22–29, later taken to include dill and cumin). The parallel in Lk 11.42 fits the more common New Testament pattern. Those condemned fail in justice and love of God, that is, the obligation to love God and neighbor. Though the text is not quoted exactly, Matthew's formula probably reflects Mic 6.8.

Christians presume that the stories concerning Israel provide instructional examples for their community. Tales of unfaithfulness or grumbling in the wilderness were particularly popular (see 1 Cor 10.1–13; Heb 3.7–4.13). Abraham serves as an example of the works (such as hospitality) appropriate to faith (Jas 2.21–26 includes Rahab as an example). The heading "faith" introduces a catalogue of biblical models in Heb 11.1–40, which serves as a summary of the biblical story from Abel through the prophets. Though "by faith" has been inserted into each example, the particular story that follows does not always represent faith, at least not in the same way. The Christological exegesis by which Hebrews argued that Jesus as exalted Son of God was foreseen by the Psalms and prophets and that the sacrificial death of Jesus ended the need for Jewish sacrificial rituals (Heb 7.1–10.18) shapes this catalogue as well. Each of the heroes in the catalogue merits a promised reward for fidelity to God, which has been deferred until the establishment of a heavenly people of God through Jesus (11.13–16).

SCRIPTURE IN CHRISTIAN POLEMIC

The Christian conviction that scripture spoke to and about their community even when it was made up largely of Gentiles (as in 1 Pet 1.10–23) resulted in polemical use of the biblical text against its literal meaning. The strategies employed in several of the more striking re-readings became fixed principles in early Christian exegesis: typology, allegory, and the distinction between the "spirit" and the "letter" of the text. Typology is a method of reading a text that sees characters, incidents, or themes within it as representing "types," or impressions, of a central form, the "antitype." When a coin or medallion was struck, the copies produced were called types, and the name therefore came to signify all of the related images based on one master design. Typological readings already occurred in the Hebrew Bible; the prophet known as Second Isaiah, for instance, interpreted the return from exile typologically as a second Exodus (Isa 48.20–21, alluding to Ex 17.1–7). In the New Testament, interpreting a biblical text typologically presumes that persons or events in the narrative provide a pattern of Christian experience; for instance, Israel's passage through the Red Sea and eating manna foreshadow Christian baptism and eucharist (1 Cor 10.1–4). In other cases, the relationship of the Christian person, idea, or event may be antithetical to the person, idea, or event found in scripture; for instance, Paul contrasts Adam and Christ (Rom 5.12–21), part of Paul's argument for faith rather than observance of the law as the principle of salvation.

Paul's use of the Abraham story to defend the thesis moves into terrain foreign to the obvious meaning of the story. Genesis 15.6 is taken to mean that Abraham's righteousness depends only on faith (Rom 4.1–25). Some scholars call this type of argument "midrash," a traditional Jewish form of interpretation, in which one text is supplemented by others to extract a further meaning. Psalm 32.1–2 plays this role in Rom 4.7–8. John 6.30–51 contains a lengthy dispute in which the incarnate Christ is said to be the meaning of Exodus. Biblical references in the Fourth Gospel are notoriously indefinite. John 6.31 reflects some combination of Ex 16.4,15; Ps 78.24; and Wis 16.28. Such typologies do not deny that scripture refers to persons and events that belong to Israel's past. Their significance in God's plan of salvation, however, requires that they be recognized as prefiguring the Christian reality.

Paul's treatment of the Abraham story in Gal 4.21–31 moves beyond simple typology to a method of interpretation that becomes more prevalent in later Christian writers: allegory. Allegory in its pure sense is an extended comparison between two different levels, usually a narrative level and a psychological or spiritual level, in which the writer, speaking directly about the narrative incidents and characters, intends and is understood to mean to speak about the symbolic level. This kind of reading had already been adapted from Greek interpretive practice by the Jewish writer Philo of Alexandria (ca. 15 BCE–50 CE). In Galatians, the son born of a slave woman is rather shockingly associated with the Sinai covenant and all those who seek to be bound by it. Descendants of Isaac are not physical descendants of Abraham but children of a promise. Paul concludes that since Gen 21.10 permits the slave woman and her son to be cast out, his audience should do the same to any Christians who insist upon belonging to Israel "according to the flesh." Even in what appears a blatant misreading of the Abraham story, Paul presumes that the text has a literal sense as well. Abraham, Isaac, Sarah, and Hagar are not merely symbolic figures representative of the two parties to the conflict in Galatia.

Later theories of allegorical meaning found support in Paul's distinction between "the letter that kills" and the life-giving "Spirit" in 2 Cor 3.6. The polemical context of this passage sets Paul and his preaching over against what appear to have been Jewish Christian missionaries. Again Paul's version of Ex 34.28–35 in the argument which follows inverts the Jewish traditions of the Targums. The standard Jewish explanations of this passage assume that the splendor on Moses' face either remained permanently or increased. For Paul's Jewish contemporaries the glory on Moses' face and the eternity of the Sinai covenant are closely associated (see Pseudo-Philo, *Biblical Antiquities* 11.5; 19.10–16; 32.7; 1Q34 2.5–8). Israel's sin makes it impossible for the people to look upon the glory reflected in the face of Moses. Paul instead assumes that the veiling of Moses' face was a means of hiding the evidence of a fading glory, that is, an impermanent covenant. He asserts that he is the servant of a new, eternal covenant established through the Spirit (Jer 31.18,33; Ezek 36.26), not the letters carved on the tablets of stone.

With the Latin rendering of Greek *gramma* ("letter") as *littera*, its identification with the carved tablets of Torah gave way to "letter" as meaning the entire writ-

ten text. Paul's antithesis of Spirit and letter was taken to be a hermeneutical principle rather than a polemical attack on the eternity of the law (also see Rom 2.27–29; 7.6). From this perspective, a literal reading of the text fails to convey its deepest truth. Only the spiritual interpretation that associates scripture with the revelation of God in Christ conveys life. Israel may then stand for any persons who are trapped by the literal sense of the text and who therefore fail to interpret all of the scriptures in light of Christ.

THE INTERPRETATION OF THE BIBLE
JEWISH INTERPRETATION IN THE PREMODERN ERA

There is a strong continuity of approaches between the inner-biblical interpretation of the Hebrew Bible (see above, p. 2201) and its interpretation in later Jewish tradition. The later interpreters faced the same issues as those from the end of the biblical period: the ambiguity of many words, the desire to bring the text closer to Jewish life, and the fact that they now had to deal with these texts as canonical, that is, both authoritative and closed to further additions. Not surprisingly, they adopted and adapted many of the same solutions, especially the use of creative philology and creative historiography, in order to give the static text greater elasticity. Some interpretive innovations appeared at particular periods, either as creative breakthroughs within the Jewish tradition or as a response to outside influences; among the latter were the use of the Old Testament in the Christian community for Christological purposes and the study of Muslim interpreters of the Koran. By and large, however, continuity rather than discontinuity characterized the premodern interpretation of the Bible. The connection between early postbiblical interpretation and the preceding late inner-biblical interpretation was also uniform.

There is, however, major discontinuity in the genres through which the interpretations are expressed. Postbiblical interpretation recognizes the Bible as a canonical text, and it thus introduces the genre of commentary, in which a biblical passage is quoted with an introductory phrase separating the canonical text from its gloss or interpretation. This separation of text from commentary highlights the significance of the biblical text. It is fundamentally different from inner-biblical interpretation, in which the interpretive addition is often inserted

into the text itself without differentiating text and commentary, or in which scripture is rewritten; for example, Deuteronomy rewrites sections of Exodus, or Chronicles rewrites Samuel-Kings (see above, pp. 2202–2203). Although the practice of interpreting the text by rewriting it continued for a short period after the canonization of the Hebrew Bible, it was largely replaced by commentaries of various sorts. For clear theological reasons, these commentaries were interested in differentiating between the canonical biblical text and its interpretation.

TRANSLATION AS INTERPRETATION

The earliest postbiblical interpretive traditions, however, are found in another new genre, Bible translation. In the postexilic period, after the return from the Babylonian exile where the common language was Aramaic, many Jews were no longer fluent in Hebrew, and the Bible was for the first time translated into Aramaic. Though these earliest translations are no longer extant, we do have later translations of sections of the Bible that predate the destruction of the Second Temple (70 CE) from the Dead Sea community of Qumran, as well as a set of Aramaic translations, called Targums, that crystallized at a later date in both Babylon and Israel. In addition, the Bible was translated into Greek in Alexandria, Egypt, beginning in the third century BCE. This translation, called the Septuagint (the translation of the seventy), is of great value and is supplemented by a variety of other Greek translations, some of which were found at Qumran. (See "Hebrew Bible: Texts and Versions," p. 2194.)

These translations illustrate the truism that all translations are interpretations. More particularly, they demonstrate the range of translation approaches, from literal interpretation to free paraphrase. (See the essay on "Translation of the Bible into English," p. 2194, for a discussion of translation approaches.) For example, the Septuagint and the Aramaic translation called Targum Onqelos are typically word-for-word, literal versions, as far as that is possible. Yet even these "literal" translations show nonliteral tendencies at points. For example, Onqelos was aware of the fact that the biblical verse, "You shall not boil a kid in its mother's milk" (Ex 23.19; 34.26; Deut 14.21), was generalized in early Jewish tradition and served as the basis for the prohibition of eating dairy products and meat together. For this reason, Onqelos translates the biblical text according to the rabbinic tradition, rendering it, "Do not eat meat with milk." The interpretive nature of the Septuagint is especially obvious in Psalms. Following an interpretive tendency that already existed in the Hebrew Bible, whereby several psalms were given historical superscriptions that contextualized them in the life of David (e.g., Ps 51, "To the leader. A Psalm of David, when the prophet Nathan came to him, after he had gone in to Bathsheba"), superscriptions were added to several additional psalms (e.g., Ps 27, introduced in the Septuagint with "A Psalm of David, before he was anointed"). Thus, a biblical model was followed, and new introductions, which provided new interpretive "Davidic" frameworks for these psalms, were composed.

In other cases, nonliteral translations were offered because the theology of the author and his community disagreed with what the text explicitly said; this is the philosophical equivalent of the translation by Onqelos of "You shall not boil a kid in its mother's milk" as "Do not eat meat with milk." For example, Num 12.8 says of Moses, "he beholds the form of the LORD," a notion that was very disturbing to the translator of the Septuagint, for whom the predominant image of Deuteronomy, that God has no form (see esp. Deut 4.12,15), was normative. The translator thus assimilated what the text explicitly says into his theology (and into the Priestly theology, which emphasizes the manifestation of God through his "glory"), and rendered this section of the verse as "and he saw the glory of the LORD." This was the same sort of change discussed above (p. 2202) when both Deuteronomy and Chronicles rewrote (rather than translated) earlier texts, changing them so that they conform to the later theology.

These cases of nonliteral, exegetical translations are rather tame when compared to some of the highly expansionistic translations seen in the Targums, especially those originating in Palestine. Most remarkable is the case where the Targums "translate" the *Akedah* or the binding of Isaac (Gen 22). In the biblical account, Isaac has a relatively minor role and is a character who is acted upon rather than one who acts. The Targums, however, interpret the story in such a way that Isaac now plays a major role. For example, Targum Pseudo-Jonathan glosses v. 10 as follows: "Abraham put forth his hand and took the knife to slaughter his son. Isaac spoke up and said to his father: 'Tie me well lest I struggle because of the anguish of my soul, with the result that a blemish will be found in your offering, and I will be thrust into the pit of destruction.' The eyes of Abraham were looking at the eyes of Isaac, and the eyes of Isaac were looking at the angels on high. Isaac saw them but Abraham did not see them. The angels on high exclaimed: 'Come, see two unique ones who are in the world; one is slaughtering, and one is being slaughtered; the one who slaughters does not hesitate, and the one who is being slaughtered stretches forth his neck'" (*Targum Pseudo-Jonathan: Genesis*, trans. Michael Maher. Collegeville, Minn: Liturgical, 1992, p. 79). (The translation in Targum Neofiti is similar.)

The Targum to Song of Solomon is even more remarkable in the way in which it assimilates the text to its general understanding that the book should be interpreted as a historical allegory. Thus, its "translation" of 1.2, "Let him kiss me with the kisses of his mouth! For your love is better than wine," reads as follows: "Solomon the prophet said: 'Blessed be the name of God who gave us the law via Moses the scribe, a law inscribed on two tablets of stone, and six orders of the Mishnah and the Talmud by oral tradition, and spoke to us face to face as a man kisses his companion, from the abundance of the love with which he loved us, more than the seventy nations'" (Marvin Pope, *Song of Songs* [*Anchor Bible*], New York: Doubleday, 1977, p. 299). A similar, very expansionistic translation of Genesis may also be seen in the much earlier Aramaic Genesis Apocryphon, found among the Dead Sea Scrolls.

PESHARIM

Though rabbinic interpretation is seen as the normative or mainstream type of premodern Jewish interpretation, that mode of interpretation is really not new, but shows much continuity with the postbiblical interpretation seen in the Dead Sea Scrolls and in Greek Jewish writing as well. The genre of Qumran literature called Pesher literature, in which a biblical text is first quoted, and then its interpretation is adduced, is structurally similar to rabbinic Midrash (see below) and medieval commentary. Pesher literature is distinct, however, from rabbinic literature (though not from the type of Jewish interpretation evidenced in much of the New Testament) in that it typically applies (mostly prophetic) texts to the author's current situation with the assumption that the biblical text, though written long ago, refers to the later author's time period. For example, Pesher Habakkuk quotes (in a slightly different form) the words of the seventh-century prophet Habakkuk (2.15), "Alas for you who make your neighbors drink, pouring out your wrath until they are drunk, in order to gaze on their nakedness," and then continues: "Its interpretation concerns the Wicked Priest who pursued the Teacher of Righteousness [the leader of the Qumran community] to consume him with the ferocity of his anger in the place of his banishment, in festival time, during the day of Atonement. He paraded in front of them, to consume them and make them fall on the day of fasting, the sabbath of their rest (trans. Florentino García Martínez and Elbert J. C. Tigchelaar, The Dead Sea Scrolls Study Edition, Leiden: Brill, 1977, vol. 1, pp. 19,21).

An example of (proto)rabbinic interpretation of legal material already found in this prerabbinic community is illustrated by the following interpretation from the Damascus Covenant, another key text of the Qumran community: "No one should do work on the sixth day, from the moment when the sun's disc is at a distance of its diameter from the gate [= the horizon], for this is what it says [Deut 5.12], 'Observe the sabbath day and keep it holy'" (CD X.15) (Dead Sea Scrolls Study Edition, ibid., pp. 567,569). This legal text is quoting the Decalogue from Deuteronomy, and is interpreting the first word, shamor, in a more literal sense as "guard"; it continues by suggesting that the way in which one guards the sabbath day is by ceasing from work a bit before the sabbath actually begins, the time when the sun is one diameter away from setting. This would, of course, help to prevent violation of the sabbath, which, according to the Bible, is a capital offense. Yet such stringent observance is never actually required by the biblical text; rather, it is "found" in the text through a slightly unusual reading, using (only mildly) creative philology on the Hebrew word shamor, "observe," which is understood as "guard."

CREATIVE HISTORIOGRAPHY

Prerabbinic texts are also useful in terms of tracing the notion of "creative historiography" from the late biblical through the early rabbinic periods. Jubilees, a pseudepigraphic book written in the second century BCE, at about the same time as Daniel, is filled with examples of creative historiography. For example, in retelling the creation story, Jubilees adds to the biblical text, noting among other additions that angels are fashioned on the first day of creation. Law is of paramount importance for this author, and he therefore retrojects many legal obligations from Exodus-Deuteronomy into his retelling of the book of Genesis, so that Genesis would not be "merely" a narrative work. (This

shows, incidentally, that the emphasis on "law" was not a rabbinic or Pharisaic innovation.) In addition, because the Torah was canonical for the author of Jubilees, the two different creation stories, which critical scholars see as separate (Gen 1.1–2.4a; 2.4b–3.24), are read canonically as a single story by one divine author. As a result, the second (Yahwistic) story is used to fill in the details of the more laconic first (Priestly) story. There is nothing remarkable about this development: Once the Bible is read canonically and the existence of sources forgotten, it becomes natural to interpret the stories in this fashion.

Josephus, the Jewish historian of the first century CE, also offers many examples of creative historiography in his Jewish Antiquities. He often remolds biblical characters so that they better fit the ideals of his Greco-Roman audience. He also restructures biblical texts, so that problems inherent in the text as it is currently ordered are resolved. For example, Gen 10 contains a genealogical description of the nations of the world that recounts their dispersion. Yet this is followed by the Tower of Babel story, which begins with the geographical unity of humanity. Josephus brilliantly solves this problem by reversing the order of these chapters, putting the genealogies after the story of the Tower of Babel. This is an early example of what would later become a fundamental principle of Jewish interpretation, that the narrative order of the biblical text does not necessarily represent the chronological order of the events it is depicting.

Jubilees and Josephus are also important because they offer explicit justifications for their radical rewriting of earlier traditions. Jubilees presents itself as revealed to Moses on Sinai with the help of a mediating angel. Josephus notes in the introduction to Antiquities: "The precise details of our scripture will, then, be set forth, each in its place, as my narrative proceeds, that being the procedure that I have promised to follow throughout this work, neither adding nor omitting anything" (Josephus, Jewish Antiquities, Books I–IV, trans. Henry St. John Thackeray [Loeb Classical Library], Cambridge, Mass: Harvard University Press, 1967, p. 9). If these two ideas may be combined, we have much of the basis for the rabbinic interpretation of the Bible, which understood itself as (1) the legitimate (oral) law revealed to Moses on Sinai, which was passed down from generation to generation; and (2) the authoritative law, which might differ in word from the phraseology of the biblical text, but is, in reality, "neither adding nor omitting anything."

RABBINIC INTERPRETATION

There is a final, crucial assumption of the classical rabbinic world, which is best represented by the Mishnah (codified ca. 200 CE), the Babylonian Talmud (ca. 500), and the slightly earlier Talmud of the Land of Israel, as well as the various *Midrashim* (commentary or homily collections) from these periods: The Bible is divine speech, and as such should not be limited to the normal rules of human speech. The interpretation of Jer 25.11 in Dan 9 (see p. 2203) indicates that this idea, which would encourage extensively creative philology, did not first develop with the rabbis. Indeed, it was greatly fostered already by the creation from various sources of a "unified" Torah. How else but through the assumption that God-talk is fundamentally different from human-talk can we explain, for example, why the two versions of the Decalogue (Ex 20, Deut 5) are different? God, and only God, can speak two things simultaneously! How else can we explain the fact that there "seems" to be a contradiction between various texts concerning slavery, about whether a Hebrew slave may remain a slave forever, or must be released at the jubilee (see below)? Obviously, this apparent contradiction must be reconciled by creative reinterpretation, based on the assumption that God does not use words in the same way we do.

The rabbis, in expressing this assumption, typically insisted that there is a superconcentration of meaning in the Bible as divine word. This meant for them that it cannot be interpreted as a "normal" text, which might have a stable meaning; rather, it has seventy (an indeterminate, but large, number of) faces or meanings. Interpretation for the rabbis is like striking a rock with a hammer: Many different types of pieces, each of which is a legitimate part of the whole, are broken off. Also, as divine speech superendowed with meaning, there are no extra words in the text; nor, for some, are there even extra letters—all is significant as the word of God.

Not all rabbis subscribed to these views to the same degree, and it might even be possible to isolate a group that saw the Bible as composed in more normal language. As a result, a tension developed between the desire to take the text at its face value and the desire to see it as overendowed with meaning. This tension continued throughout later Jewish interpretation. Yet all agreed that as a divine text, the Bible may not be interpreted just like any other text. This is true whether the rabbinic comments are found in a Midrash (plural: Midrashim), where they are organized around a particular text, or whether they are found in the Talmud and thus are organized (more or less) according to legal topics.

A particular interest of classical rabbinic interpretation was reconciling divergent legal traditions found in the Torah, and "expanding" the Torah through creative interpretation. This "expansion" allowed ambiguities to be clarified and the text to be contemporized despite its antiquated nature. For example, a Midrash to Ex 21.6,

which states that the Hebrew slave under some circumstances shall stay with his master "for life," is glossed "until the jubilee year." "Life" ordinarily means "forever," or at least until death; the Midrash, however, is "forced" into this reading, using creative philology, because Lev 25.40 says: "They shall serve with you until the year of the jubilee." The Torah, as the unified word of God, cannot contain different ideas of when a slave is released, so it is "obvious" that the "forever" of Ex 21.6 must "really mean" until the jubilee. Again, though this interpretation might seem forced to us, it is almost natural within the framework of a society that reads the Torah as a unified, divine work.

As noted earlier, the rabbis also often extend and clarify biblical laws. Thus, the biblical text states that "work" is prohibited on the sabbath day, and anyone who works has committed a capital offense (e.g., Ex 31.14–15). But what is work? The problem is the same as that discussed above in reference to the festival of booths, where Lev 23.40 says that you must "take" branches of various trees but does not explicitly say what is to be done with them (see p. 2202). In the case of the branches, the context was used to provide the answer, and thus Neh 8.15 suggested that the branches should be taken to build booths, most likely based on the fact that the booth legislation (Lev 23.42) immediately follows the branch legislation. Similarly, Ex 31.12–17, which concerns the general sabbath prohibition, is found immediately after the instruction to construct the tabernacle; the classical rabbis adduced from this juxtaposition that "work" is any type of labor involved with the construction of the tabernacle. This is a reasonable, though not fully compelling, interpretation, which takes the text in its final form very seriously. Not only is every letter significant, but even the juxtaposition of adjacent units yields meaning.

The vast literature of the classical rabbinic period is replete with examples of creative historiography, many of which are based on overly careful readings, what we might consider overreading the biblical text; but of course a divine text cannot be read too carefully. For example, the binding of Isaac opens with the phrase, "After these things God tested Abraham" (Gen 22.1). Modern, critical commentators might see the phrase "After these things" as a type of filler, or paragraph marker, but this was an unlikely choice within the rabbinic mindset. This created a problem, since Gen 22 is not obviously, causally related to the previous chapter. Thus, "these things" must be discovered through creative historiography. As is typical, there is no single rabbinic answer to what "these things" were. Various Midrashim, preserved both in Midrashic texts like Genesis Rabbah and in the Babylonian Talmud, create a dialogue between Isaac and Ishmael in which Ishmael boasts that he endured the pain of circumcision at the age of thirteen (Gen 17.25), while Isaac was circumcised at eight days; Isaac counters by saying that Ishmael just gave an organ to God, whereas he, Isaac, is willing to give all of his organs to God. It is, according to this view, "after these things," namely after Isaac expressed his willingness to be sacrificed, that God tested Abraham. Another view creates a dialogue between God and Satan, in which God says that Abraham would even be willing to sacrifice his son. This brings Genesis closer to the dialogue between God and the Satan (adversary) in Job 1–2; indeed, it is common for the rabbis to use one canonical story to fully explore the meaning of another. Finally, it is noteworthy that these two expansions are not merely silly, nor do they simply "fill in" the details lacking in the original story. They both help to explain the major problem of the text: How could a good God make such a request of Abraham?

Although the Midrashic inclination was deeply attuned to the text, its meaning as the Bible, and its connection to the life of community, it accomplished these goals with some violence to the context of the text. Thus, many rabbinic interpretations concentrate on the meaning of the individual word and the significance of the single letter (for example, the comments in the Midrash Genesis Rabbah, which explain why the Bible opened with a bet, the second letter of the Hebrew alphabet), so that the broader contextual story is often lost. The eleventh century saw a reaction against this type of interpretation in the development of the peshat school of interpretation.

MEDIEVAL COMMENTATORS

Peshat is a notoriously difficult term to define, and it seems to change meaning depending on the commentator involved. For Rabbi Solomon (Heb Shelomoh) son of Isaac, or Rashi, who lived in France from 1040 to 1105, peshat meant "contextual meaning." Rashi's commentary, covering almost the entire Hebrew Bible, is a type of medieval Reader's Digest of classical rabbinic interpretation. Very little in Rashi is original; his brilliance, and extreme popularity (Rashi on the Torah was the first Hebrew book printed, before the Torah itself!) lay in his ability to select and rework rabbinic traditions, largely ignoring the many rabbinic traditions that overly strained the context of the text and those which used the text as a type of peg on which to hang various ideas that are not at all connected to the context. More than that, the traditional Midrashim were so atomistic and filled with diverse opinions that it is almost always impossible to answer a simple question of how the Midrash understood the text. Rashi, through his judicious selection process, chose Midrashim that

were relatively close to the text and were mutually reinforcing. Thus, we have peshat where the broader text, as well as each letter or word, has a clear meaning. This accomplishment was so significant that the commentary of Rashi, especially on the Torah, is one of the most significant Jewish postbiblical texts; it profoundly influenced Jewish understanding of the Bible, especially in European communities, as well as that of medieval Christians, for whom Rashi epitomized Jewish exegesis.

The method of peshat was taken one step further by Rashi's son-in-law, Rabbi Samuel (Heb Shmuel) son of Meir, or Rashbam (1080–1174), who understood peshat in a more radical sense as the simple meaning of the text. Rashbam, though a leading scholar of Jewish law, felt free to offer interpretations of the text in his commentary on the Torah that disagreed with rabbinic law. For example, in contrast to his father-in-law Rashi who, following the rabbinic tradition, interprets the words "for life" concerning the Hebrew slave in Ex 21.6 as until the jubilee year, Rashbam glosses "according to the peshat, all the days of his life." It remains unclear how Rashbam would have reconciled this peshat with what he understood to be the requirements of rabbinic law. In any case, the type of very literal, non-Midrashic way of reading the text, which characterized Rashbam, found new followers.

Rashbam is also noteworthy for the way in which some of his comments are clearly the product of a reaction against the Christians, especially the persecution of Jews during the Crusades. Though anti-Christian polemic existed in Rashi as well, it was relatively mild; the Crusades, which marked a significant change in the status of the Jews in medieval Europe, would leave a deep impact on many commentators. Nevertheless, Jewish commentary should not be seen as predominantly reactive.

Much of the rest of medieval Jewish interpretation may be understood within the context provided above, as a continuum on which the classical atomistic Midrashim and the search for peshat existed as opposite poles. Several additional influences are noteworthy. Especially in countries where Arabic was spoken, a new serious study of the Hebrew language was begun, likely in an effort to counter the Muslim claim that the Arabic of the Koran is the most beautiful language. Arabic paradigms were applied to Hebrew by scholars in the Arab orbit (e.g., Sa'adya [882–942] in Babylon, Abraham ibn Ezra [1089–1164] in Spain and elsewhere), and commentaries that were more philological in nature, exploring the meaning of grammatical forms and lexical terms, developed. Spinoza offers a picture of ibn Ezra as a medieval radical, doubting the Mosaic authorship of several verses from the Torah. In reality, despite some atypical positions that include the suggestion that Isa 40–66, what scholars now call Second and Third Isaiah, are not by the same author as chs 1–39, ibn Ezra was quite traditional in his outlook, and deeply philological in his perspective. Rabbi David Kimchi (Radak), who lived in Provence from 1160 to 1235, systematized many of these interpretations, and his understanding of biblical grammar continues to have a major influence on the scientific study of Hebrew. More than any other medieval exegete, Radak also showed a deep interest in what would later be called textual criticism, namely deciding what the correct text of the Bible was, and many of his views in this area are remarkably modern.

The world of premodern interpretation is, of course, much richer than indicated here. There was a very significant strain of mystical interpretation of the text, exemplified in the Zohar (late thirteenth century), and in the commentary of Nachmanides, Rabbi Moses son of Nachman (active in the thirteenth century). Philosophical interpretations also developed; most notable are those found in *The Guide to the Perplexed* by Maimonides (1135–1204). With the Renaissance, Jewish scholars were influenced by the new science; this is especially seen in the extremely lengthy commentary by Don Isaac Abravanel (1437–1508), who also synthesizes and to an extent harmonizes the many commentators of all types and from various geographical locations who preceded him.

Postbiblical Jewish exegesis does not neatly divide into the schools through which medieval Christian interpretation is often defined. It is essentially different from much of the work of its Christian counterparts. Part of this is because they were studying different works: the Hebrew Bible studied alone, or in relation to rabbinic traditions, is fundamentally different from the Old Testament as part of the Bible, followed by the New Testament. The allegorical and especially the typological methods, which had a very significant role in Christian interpretation, played a much less weighty role in Jewish interpretation. Finally, direct access to the text in its original Hebrew typically distinguished Jewish biblical interpretation from that of the Christians. Despite these differences, which are very significant, most Jewish and Christian premodern interpretation shares a set of basic assumptions that make them fundamentally premodern. These include the idea that the Bible is an authoritative canonical work, which is revealed divine speech, and, as such, must be interpreted in a special way. Though set in history, it is in a sense timeless, speaking to every generation and to every individual. Although several medieval rabbis cast some small doubts on one aspect or another of these premises of interpretation, only in the seventeenth century would these shared assumptions begin to erode, and only then would we slowly move from premodern to modern biblical interpretation.

THE INTERPRETATION OF THE BIBLE
CHRISTIAN INTERPRETATION IN THE PREMODERN ERA

As the article on New Testament interpretation of the Jewish Scriptures (p. 2204) indicates, Christian interpretation of scripture begins in the New Testament. The New Testament writers developed two of the interpretive approaches that remained central to Christian biblical interpretation until the rise of modern historical criticism: (1) a christocentric focus, that is, a tendency to interpret Hebrew Bible texts, especially prophetic texts, as referring to Christ; and (2) typology, the recognition of a person or event in the Hebrew Bible as a type or figure of Christ or Christian salvation. A third approach, allegory, is also present in rudimentary form.

In order to understand the development of early Christian interpretation, it is important to consider the contexts within which and the purposes for which

Christians interpreted the scriptures. First, teaching and pastoral care of Christian communities was one important focus, and much early interpretation occurs in the context of sermons and pastoral letters (e.g., the letters of Ignatius [ca. 35–ca.107 CE] and the homilies of Melito [d. ca. 190]). Second, missionary activity and Christian apologetics (the defense of Christianity before pagan detractors) provided a quite different context. In this situation the biblical writings had to be interpreted to an audience, which often found these texts crude and out of keeping with the intellectual tastes of Greek-speaking culture. Thus there was a strong impetus to interpret the scriptures in a way that would enhance their intellectual respectability. For this purpose Christian apologists used the tradition of allegorical interpretation that had been developed within Greek philosophical circles as a means of interpreting Homer and the other early Greek poets. Even before the rise of Christianity, the Jewish philosopher Philo of Alexandria (ca. 20 BCE–42 CE) had undertaken a detailed allegorical interpretation of Jewish scriptures, and Philo's influence upon the Alexandrian school of Christian interpreters was profound.

A third context for interpretation emerged from Christianity's attempts to define itself in comparison to Judaism. Since both religions laid claim to the same body of scripture (the Hebrew Bible for Jews, the Old Testament for Christians), Christian interpretation addressed itself to the competing interpretations made by Judaism and Christianity. The harshly polemical *Epistle of Barnabas* (early second century) rejects the claims of Judaism to the covenant and so does not even begin to struggle with the interpretive problem that engages other Christian writers of the early centuries, the problem of the nature of the relationship between the old and new covenants, and the scriptures that witness to them. Much richer and more reflective is Justin Martyr's (ca. 100–165) *Dialogue with Trypho the Jew*. The work takes the form of a long conversation between Justin and Trypho, a learned rabbi, each of whom tries to persuade the other of the superiority of his claims and the interpretation of the scriptures upon which they are based. Justin attempts to establish a unity for the Old and New Testaments by arguing that the eternal Logos, fully revealed as Christ in the New Testament, was already the revealer of God's will to the prophets. Though the old covenant was valid, Justin claims that the Jewish scriptures themselves foresee its being superseded by a new covenant. Justin's approach, which anticipates the classic Christian understanding of the Old Testament, exhibits a historical perspective absent from Barnabas, but it is equally christocentric.

The fourth context of early Christian interpretation was provided by disputes among Christians. For early Christian communities, two questions above all others exercised exegetical and theological thought: namely, (a) how does Jesus relate to God, and subsequently, (b) how does Jesus' relationship to God affect his status as a human being? Since many biblical texts seem to present quite different answers to these questions, interpreters pored over any hint at a theological solution. The debate surrounding the former question, termed the "Trinitarian controversy," centered on analyzing and systematizing texts that mention God, Jesus, and the Holy Spirit at the same time, such as Jesus' baptism in Mark 1:10–11 and triadic formulations such as in 2 Corinthians 13:13 and Matthew 28:19. Justin Martyr argued that, according to biblical texts, Jesus was "another God and Lord," thus

sacrificing clear monotheism to preserve Jesus' divinity. By contrast, monarchianists such as Sabellius (ca. 220) and Adoptionists such as Theodotus of Byzantium (ca. 190) emphasized biblical texts that supposedly revealed Jesus' humanity in order to protect monotheism.

For the most part, early Christian theologians worked with a clear assumption of a unified and coherent witness of the entire canon of scripture as well as an expectation that exegesis results in necessarily logical and systematic doctrine. These hermeneutical guidelines, inherited from in part from Jewish sources, directed early Christian exegetes to resolve in some manner the various discrepancies found in the disparate texts within and between both Old and New Testaments. For example, early Christians recognized that a coherent doctrine of God and a definitively unambiguous statement of Jesus' relationship to God are not found in the Bible. Thus, the Bible's various ways of presenting God, Jesus and the Holy Spirit, were reconciled by formulations hammered out by the imperially backed councils of Nicea (325 CE) and Chalcedon (381 CE). From its very beginnings, Christian biblical interpretation thus became the driving force of theological reflection throughout the history of Christianity.

Although Christian theological disputes often focused upon biblical interpretation, other arguments focused on the nature of scripture itself. One challenge was posed by Marcion of Pontus (mid-second century), who rejected the Hebrew Bible entirely, claiming it was the revelation of an alien God and accepted only the Gospel of Luke and ten Pauline epistles as the authentic "Gospel and apostle." Even these texts, he insisted, were corrupted by interpolations. To argue his case, Marcion invoked the principles of text criticism developed for the study of Greek poets. He also argued for a literal rather than an allegorical interpretation of the Old Testament (especially Genesis) in his attempts to discredit it as a crude and offensive book. Even more than the debate with Judaism, Marcion's claims required the church to articulate clearly its understanding of the revelatory significance of the Old Testament and its relationship to the New. A further challenge was posed by various Gnostic Christians. Like Marcion they also tended to reject the Old Testament, but in contrast to him, they engaged in a highly developed form of allegorical interpretation, which appealed strongly to one type of Hellenistic intellectualism.

Some of the liveliest of early Christian writings are those composed to refute Marcion and the Gnostics. The most notable is Irenaeus's (ca. 130–ca. 200) *Against All Heresies* (*Adv. Haer.*). Irenaeus argued for the validity of the revelation of God in the Old Testament and its law but also claimed that in the New Testament God is revealed in a new way. He demonstrated the unity of the scriptures by means of typology, so that the Old Testament serves as a witness to the New. Irenaeus also attacked the interpretive methods of his Gnostic opponents, such as Valentinus (ca. 100–ca. 160), objecting that they ignored the context of passages, overlooking the clear and obvious in favor of the obscure, and reading into the text their fanciful theories. Significantly, Irenaeus not only argued on the basis of interpretive principles but also invoked what comes to be known as "the rule of faith." As a defense against an anarchy of interpretation, there is a standard of correct interpretation, which Irenaeus claimed is that which had been preserved in those churches that stand in the apostolic succession. Interpretation, which differs from that of the apostolic churches, cannot be deemed true.

The argument for the authoritative interpretation of the church was definitively established by Tertullian (ca. 160–ca. 225) in the early third century in *The Prescription against Heretics* (*De praescriptione haereticorum*). In making orthodoxy the norm for the interpretation of scripture, Tertullian, the lawyer with no taste for philosophy, may have thought that he was establishing a narrow and simple standard. But even as the threat from heretical interpretation receded, more philosophically oriented Christian interpreters, such as Origen (ca. 185–ca. 254) and Augustine (354–430), developed more profound and supple understandings of the nature of interpretation and the relation of scripture to orthodox theology.

Questions also arose concerning the definitive and authoritative version of the biblical texts. In the second century, some theologians apparently worried about the conflicting accounts of the four canonical gospels; one popular solution was the creation of Gospel harmonies. For example, Tatian's *Diatesseron* (ca. 150) was a second-century synthesis of the four canonical gospels so as to present one unified story. While Tatian's harmony was very popular in the East until the fifth century, other early Christian exegetes such as Irenaeus urged Christians to hold all four canonical gospels in tension. Retaining the separate works requires exegetical energy, since the conflicts must be explained in some way, but the tradition of four separate gospels continues to this day.

Another conflict developed concerning the textual source from which one should translate the Bible. Until the last decades of the fourth century, most early Christian interpreters assumed the priority of the Greek Septuagint and its derivative translations. When Jerome moved to Palestine about 390 CE, he decided to retranslate his Latin version of the Old Testament from the Hebrew text instead of the Greek; he reasoned that the Hebrew text was closer to the original version, and thus was more authoritative. In response, Augustine confronted him with a series of letters imploring him to retain the Greek text as his source, since switching texts could cause great theological confusion, disrupt the seeming prophetic continuity of Old and New Testaments, and perhaps cause a schism between Greeks and Latins within the Church. Jerome retained his view that his translation gained access to the "Hebrew Truth," and eventually his new version, known as the "Vulgate," rose to prominence in the Latin West. Though Jerome often relied upon the Greek version of traditionally Christological texts in his new, and ostensibly Hebrew-based, translation (cf. Isa 7 and Job 19:25–27), the Vulgate required that at least nominal deference be paid to the Hebrew text as the "true" text of the Hebrew Bible.

In addition to looking at early Christian biblical interpretation in the light of various contexts for interpretation, one should also take account of the two rival schools of interpretation that flourished in Alexandria and Antioch during the early Common Era. As noted above, the sophisticated intellectual environment of Alexandria was already home to a lively tradition of allegorical exegesis before the emergence of Christianity. Thus it was inevitable that Christians would adapt this method of interpretation to their scriptures. Among the most eminent of the Alexandrian school were Clement (ca. 150–ca. 215) and Origen. Allegorical interpretation reads a text as if the narrative incidents, characters, and other elements of its literal meaning are all intended to convey to the reader, by means of an extended comparison, another level of meaning entirely, usually a moral or spiritual one. Although many rather different types of interpretation may be called allegorical, all share a conviction that the authoritative text being interpreted has a deeper meaning than what appears on the surface, the literal reading. Thus *allegory* assumes that a text has multiple meanings, though interpreters may differ as to their worth. (Origen, for example, distinguished among literal, moral, and spiritual meanings.) Typically, allegorical interpretation shows little interest in meanings that are historically specific, preferring those that disclose timeless truths. Allegory is often invoked as an interpretive method when an ancient text that is undeniably authoritative has come to seem alien to the cultural sensitivities and intellectual values of a later age. Since the revered text must contain truth (which is often unconsciously equated with the highest and best values of the interpreter's own time), a method must be employed that will allow those truths to be found in the text. In this manner the Christian allegorists of the Alexandrian school interpreted those aspects of the scriptures that seemed morally offensive, obscure, or simply of little literal interest. Thus Origen could interpret the narrative of the Exodus as an allegory of the journey of the soul as it leaves the sensual world (Egypt) and journeys toward the promised land of blessedness (Canaan). Origen was the most sophisticated of the allegorists, and the one who first gave allegory its theoretical foundations. Moreover, he was the first Christian to compose what can properly be called a *commentary* on a biblical book, a mode of interpretation that flourished in the fourth and fifth centuries.

Despite the prestige that allegorical exegesis enjoyed in some circles, it was also the subject of strong criticism. In part it attracted suspicion because it was the method of interpretation favored by Gnostics. But allegory was also vulnerable to the charge that it was arbitrary and obscure. The strongest critique of the allegorical method favored by the Alexandrian school came from the rival tradition of biblical interpretation associated with the Syrian city of Antioch. Like Alexandria, Antioch was also heir to a long tradition of Hellenistic scholarship. But Antioch was influenced more by Aristotelian traditions and by Jewish rabbinic exegesis. Thus, even though the *Antiochene* interpreters sought a spiritual meaning in the text, understanding also required, in their view, a grasp of the historical context within which the texts were written, as well as an appreciation of the literal sense of the text. Diodore of Tarsus (d. ca. 390), for example, sought to arrange the Psalms in historical sequence, using information found internally and in the titles. He understood the Song of Songs as love poetry written by Solomon for the Queen of Sheba.

The most radical and most creative interpreter of the school of Antioch was Bishop Theodore of Mopsuestia (ca. 350–428). Theodore challenged the inspired character of several books of the canon, including Job, Song of Songs, Chronicles, and Ezra-Nehemiah, claiming that they reflected only human wisdom and learning. In reaction, the Second Council of Constantinople, in 553, ordered his exegetical works to be burned. In general, the Antiochene school aroused suspicion because several church leaders judged heretical, most notably Nestorius (d. ca. 451), were associated with it. Despite opposition to the more radical interpreters, however, many of the insights and understandings of the Antiochene approach were popularized by the influential sermon collections of the moderate John Chrysostom (ca. 347–407) and by the manuals of biblical interpretation written by Adrian (425) and Junilius Africanus (550).

The stance of the allegorists and that of the more literal-historical interpreters were not necessarily mutually exclusive. Many interpreters employed both methods. Jerome (ca. 345–420), the translator of the Vulgate, began as an allegorist in the style of Origen but increasingly came under the influence of the Antiochene approach.

Even so, he never entirely abandoned allegory in his writings. Similarly, Augustine was troubled by the Manichean use of a literal-historical approach to discredit the Jewish scriptures on the grounds that they contained immoralities. He was unable to embrace Christianity until he saw how the allegorical method could provide a spiritual interpretation for such troubling passages. Like Jerome, however, Augustine moved beyond allegory to a more nuanced position that recognized the place of allegory but required the interpreter to distinguish between passages that can be understood in a literal interpretation and those requiring a figurative one. Moreover, all interpretation must be guided by the rule of faith and the law of love: "If it seems to anyone that he has understood the divine scriptures, or any part of them, in such a way that by that understanding he does not build up that double love of God and neighbor, he has not yet understood" (*On Christian Teaching*, 1.35.39–36.40).

Examples of early Christian biblical interpretation are also evident well beyond the writings of professional theological exegetes. From the production of visual art, liturgy, and music to the realms of ethics, politics, and legal theory, biblical interpretation in some sense undergirded, was filtered through, and occurred within almost every cultural practice of the Christian movement from its inception until the early modern period. For example, early Christian production of visual art generally depicts biblical narratives, characters, and themes, and as such the artifacts reflect the basic typological and Christological patterns explored by biblical exegetes. While Christian images often reveal common interpretive motifs, at times fresh exegetical thought emerges from creative iconographic juxtapositions. It is clear that Christians employed images exegetically as early as the second century, when Clement of Alexandria (ca. 150–215) exhorted Christians to choose pagan iconographies carefully, presumably in order to attribute biblical themes to the generic motifs. In one classic example, the pagan iconography of the "Good Shepherd" provided an easily recognizable but also inconspicuous mode of presenting the Johannine theme of Christ as the Good Shepherd. Around the year 200 CE, Roman Christians developed the earliest known identifiably Christian art as they began to paint the walls of their newly acquired catacombs. Generally, they juxtaposed elements from a limited catalogue of pagan images, scenes from the Hebrew Bible, and imagery derived from the New Testament. A third-century mosaic in the necropolis underneath St. Peter's Basilica in Rome depicts a beardless Christ with a cross-nimbus imaged as Helios, the sun god, driving a chariot surrounded by grape vines. Surrounding this figure are an image of a shepherd with a sheep around his neck, an image of Jonah emerging from the belly of the fish, an image of fish and fishing lures, and another image of Christ telling Peter to "fish for people" (Matt 4:19). Together, these images offer a complex network of biblical exegesis, systematic theology, and pastoral care. The pagan theme of the sun-chariot's daily ascent from the realm of darkness at daybreak recalls Christ's resurrection and ascension, as does Jonah's deliverance from the fish's belly. The good shepherd, as noted above, invokes Christ's mission to find and care for the lost, while the vines of Dionysius are implicitly reinterpreted as the vine of Christ (John 15). In the funerary context of the catacomb, this program of images offers hope for the deceased in the final Resurrection by depicting biblical themes, characters, and narrative scenes. While extant images from the first few centuries of the Christian era are rare, Christian art quickly became widespread after the imperial sponsorship of Christianity by Constantine the Great in the fourth century.

Similarly, early Christian liturgy relied upon biblical exegesis for the production and justification of its practices while offering interpretations of the Bible within its rites. By the second century, there are well-established manuals for church leadership and liturgy, such as the Syrian Didache; its baptismal liturgy, for example, is a pastiche of biblical texts designed to interpret, legitimate, and actualize the baptismal act. Like the ubiquitous Christian act of writing hymns, liturgy has also proven a fruitful space for reenacting and recontextualizing biblical text, thus offering new meanings for various communities.

THE MIDDLE AGES

During the early Middle Ages scholars of the Bible mainly preserved and transmitted the understandings developed in earlier centuries. In the west most interpreters were no longer able to read Greek, the Irish scholar John Scotus Erigena (ca. 810–ca. 877) being a noteworthy exception. Moreover, there was no significant interchange with Jewish interpreters, such as had been possible at Antioch. The works of Jerome, Augustine, and other patristic writers, however, were widely studied. As in earlier centuries, both literal and allegorical exegesis was practiced. Most commonly, four senses of scripture were recognized: the literal or historical, the allegorical, the anagogical (a mystical sense signifying heaven, the afterlife, or communion with God), and the moral or tropological. Thus "Jerusalem" could signify, literally, the historical city; allegorically, the church; anagogically, the heavenly city; and morally, the human soul. Though no author is consistent and rigorous in their application of all senses to all texts, Pope Gregory I's Morals in Job (ca. 595) is the most thorough and famous example of the four senses in medieval exegesis. The influence of this four-level interpretive method extended beyond scriptural interpretation; most notably, Dante deliberately constructed his Divine Comedy in order to allow, as far as possible, all four levels of interpretation to be applied to it.

The primary institutional context for the study of the Bible in the early medieval period was the monastery. Among the early monastic scholars the most prominent was the Venerable Bede (ca. 673–725), who composed commentaries and biblical aids as well as his influential Ecclesiastical History. An important impetus to the study of the Bible came from the religious and educational reforms sponsored by the Carolingian monarchs. Charlemagne (ca. 742–814) and his grandson Charles the Bald (d. 877) attracted the best scholars of the day, including Alcuin (ca. 735–804) and John Scotus Erigena (ca. 810–ca. 877), to supervise education at the palace and cathedral schools. The growth of such schools created a demand for resources, and the scholars of the Carolingian renaissance produced an impressive number of biblical manuscripts, annotations and aids to study, commentaries, and historical work. These works were largely digests and compilations of glosses on the biblical text drawn from writings produced in late antiquity by the Latin fathers. The culmination of this type of scholarship was the production of the Glossa ordinaria, compiled by Anselm of Laon (d. 1117) in collaboration with other scholars.

The twelfth and thirteenth centuries saw the beginning of a more creative phase of medieval biblical scholarship, located first in the cathedral schools and subsequently in the universities. One important innovation was the division of the biblical books into chapters, first developed in England by Stephen Langton (d. 1228). (The numbering of the verses, or smaller units within the chapters, was developed in the fifteenth and sixteenth centuries by both Jewish and Christian scholars.) This system was used in another innovation, the production of concordances to the Bible, the most influential of which was that prepared by the Dominicans of St. Jacques in Paris, under the supervision of Hugo of St. Cher (ca. 1195–1263). Perhaps the most important of the cathedral schools was that of the Abbey of St. Victor, also in Paris, where a series of influential scholars taught during the twelfth century. The school, which was known for the rigor of study under the direction of its founder, Hugh of St. Victor (d. 1142), fostered both literal and allegorical (or mystical) exegesis. Later teachers tended to emphasize one or the other, Richard of St. Victor (d. 1173) developing allegorical interpretation, and Andrew of St. Victor (d. 1175) emphasizing the careful investigation of the literal and historical sense. Significantly, Andrew knew

Hebrew and was influenced by Jewish scholars and traditions of Jewish exegesis. During the following centuries an appreciation of the importance of such knowledge became more common among Christian exegetes of the Bible. Although the presence of significant Jewish communities in the major medieval cities made the study of Hebrew and Jewish exegesis somewhat more accessible, such knowledge did not flourish among Christian biblical scholars until the Renaissance. Greek was still relatively little known at this time, although Robert Grosseteste (ca. 1175–1253) translated several works, including the *Testaments of the Twelve Patriarchs*, from Greek into Latin.

Along with the development of important schools in the twelfth century, there was also a shift in the form in which biblical study was presented. In contrast to the earlier compendia of glosses, which were organized as a running comment on the text of the Bible itself, in the twelfth century a different form of commentary developed, one that was organized according to theological topics and issues. This change in literary form both signaled and facilitated a closer relationship between the study of scripture and the development of theological doctrine. The most significant of these works, the *Sentences* of Peter Lombard (ca. 1100–1160), eventually became the standard theological textbook during the Middle Ages.

The establishment of universities in the thirteenth century marks an important shift in the social location of biblical study. In this context biblical interpretation became more specialized and was drawn even more closely into dialogue with theology and philosophy. Although some scholars continued to engage in allegorical exegesis, both the prominence of Aristotelian thought in the universities and the emphasis on doctrinal theology pushed biblical interpretation more strongly in the direction of literal exegesis. Albertus Magnus (1193–1280) and especially Thomas Aquinas (ca. 1225–1274) were the most eminent of these Aristotelian-influenced scholastic theologians and biblical interpreters. The harvest of this form of literal biblical exegesis can best be appreciated in the *Postilla literalis* of Nicholas of Lyra (ca. 1270–1349), which covers the entire Bible. Lyra's knowledge not only of biblical Hebrew, but also of the commentaries of Rashi (1040–1105) and other Jewish scholars (see "Jewish Interpretation in the Premodern Era"), gives his work a linguistic and exegetical precision lacking in many other medieval commentaries.

THE RENAISSANCE AND REFORMATION

The emphasis on original languages and a respect for the role of reason in interpretation, which had already become influential in late medieval scholarship, became the hallmarks of the new humanistic learning of the Renaissance. These values, however, which had previously been invoked in the service of scholastic theology in the Middle Ages, led in some rather different directions in the fifteenth and sixteenth centuries. The scholar Erasmus (ca. 1466–1536) is something of a transitional figure. Though he used his incomparable humanistic knowledge to produce a new critical edition of the Greek New Testament and drew on classical Roman rhetorical traditions in his interpretation of Ecclesiastes, he also defended allegorical interpretation of scripture and had a high regard for scholastic theology, that of Thomas Aquinas in particular. For the most part, the Christian humanist scholars did not set out to challenge the authority of the church. Yet sometimes the claims of reason brought them into conflict with church authority and traditions. In 1440 Lorenzo Valla (1407–1457) published his *Declamation on the Donation of Constantine*, in which he used reason to argue that the so-called donation of Constantine, which had underwritten papal authority in Rome, was in fact a forgery. Similarly, he demonstrated that a letter supposedly written by Jesus to Abgar, king of Edessa, which had been considered genuine at least since the fourth century, was in fact spurious. His approach to such ancient documents, and to the New Testament itself in his other writings, anticipated the critical study of the Bible that was to develop in later centuries. The audience for such critical works on the text of the New Testament text was facilitated by the publication of several Greek grammars between 1495 and 1520.

Fueling the explosive growth in Renaissance scholarship was the new availability of texts and critical works made possible by the development of the printing press. Following the publication of Johannes Gutenberg's Latin Bible in 1454, a wide range of books became available, not only in Latin and vernacular languages but in Greek and Hebrew as well. During the early sixteenth century several polyglot Bibles were published, that is, Bibles in which Greek, Latin, Hebrew, and Aramaic texts of the Bible were printed side by side to facilitate critical comparison.

The characteristic Renaissance interest in ancient languages and texts led some scholars, such as Giovanni Pico della Mirandola (1463–1494), Johannes Reuchlin (1455–1522), and Guillaume Postel (ca. 1510–1581), to explore the esoteric traditions of Jewish kabbalistic mysticism. Postel even translated the *Bahir* and the *Zohar* into Latin. These Christian kabbalists drew together elements of Jewish mysticism, Neoplatonic philosophy, Christian theology, and the Renaissance interest in the occult into a spiritual synthesis, which, as one might expect, was condemned by church authorities. Reuchlin, however, can be called the father of Christian Renaissance study of Hebrew. He published an influential Hebrew grammar, based on the work of the medieval Jewish Rabbi David Kimchi (Radak) (see "Jewish Interpretation in the Premodern Era," p. 2208), and other aids that facilitated the increasing interest in the study of Hebrew by Christians. Reuchlin also played an important role in resisting some attempts by the church to suppress Jewish writings, including the Talmud.

With the Reformation, biblical interpretation increasingly took place within an intense debate about the role of scripture in relation to Christian faith. To a large extent, however, both the early Protestant reformers and the scholars who remained within the Catholic tradition incorporated the new linguistic and philological training in their interpretation of the Bible. Though Martin Luther (1483–1546) was not the first to argue that the Bible is the ultimate authority in matters of doctrine, the Protestant movement is distinctive in insisting that the Bible is the sole foundation for faith, doctrine, and church practices. In their refutation of the Protestants, Catholic scholars also appealed to biblical exegesis in support of the authority of the church and the papacy. Thus in the sixteenth century biblical interpretation reflects both the rich legacy of Renaissance humanism's linguistic and philological knowledge and a context of highly charged theological argument.

Although Protestant biblical interpreters in general rejected allegory in favor of the literal-historical sense, their interpretation of the Hebrew Bible was usually Christological and typological. Luther, for example, attended both to the literal-historical sense and to the literal-prophetic sense of scripture (i.e., the typological meaning foreshadowed in the text). Thus, since David was considered to be a prophet, the Psalms referred not only to David's life and circumstances but also to Christ who was to come. Luther's writings also reflect both continuity and discontinuity with the medieval tradition in his treatment of the tropological or moral meaning of scripture. Traditionally, this concern had been with the way in which the text addressed the nature and practice of the virtue of love. For Luther, the moral meaning is that aspect of the text that has to do with the nurture of faith, that is, trust in God's promises. Other Protestants, however, such as Zwingli and Bucer, follow Erasmus in understanding the moral meaning of scripture as providing paradigms for human behavior.

The issue of the relation of the two testaments also provoked a variety of responses among Protestant interpreters. Given Luther's theological distinction between law and gospel, his interpretation tends to posit a significant degree of tension between the testaments.

In contrast, many other Protestant theologians saw an essential continuity between the testaments. Henrich Bullinger (1504–1575), for example, treated covenant as a hermeneutical principle, which unifies the scriptures. Before the advent of Christ the sign of the covenant is circumcision; after the advent, baptism. But the covenant is one and the same, the New Testament only presenting it with greater clarity. The nature and extent of the canon of the Old Testament also became an issue of controversy between Protestants and the Roman Catholic Church. Like Jerome before them, the Protestant reformers argued that the church's Old Testament canon should be that of the Hebrew scriptures, that is, without the Apocrypha. At the Council of Trent (1546) the Roman Catholic church reaffirmed the inspired nature of some of these books, which were termed "deuterocanonical." The term does not denote a difference in status from the "protocanonical" books but signifies that their canonical status was clarified at a second stage. (See the essay "The Canons of the Bible," p. 2185, and the introductions to individual books among the Apocryphal/Deuterocanonical Books for more details on the canonical status of particular books and the development of the differing canons of the Old Testament among the various Christian communities.)

Concern for historical context and for an understanding of biblical rhetoric was also prominent in early Protestant interpretation. The biblical interpretation of John Calvin (1509–1564), who had legal training, was influenced by Renaissance humanism's approach to clarifying ancient law by means of an appeal to the original historical contexts and the intentions of the authors. As Calvin observes in the dedicatory preface to his commentary on Romans, "almost [the commentator's] only task [is] to unfold the mind of the writer whom he has undertaken to expound." Calvin's interpretation thus tends to be contextual rather than atomistic and attends not only to history but also to the cultural institutions and background of biblical texts and to the rhetorical forms in which biblical language expresses itself. Indeed, disagreement over a proper understanding of biblical rhetoric lies at the heart of one of the most important doctrinal disputes within early Protestantism. Luther contended that the word "is" in the biblical phrase "this *is* my body" (Mt 26.26) is to be interpreted literally, whereas Zwingli (1484–1531) argued that its natural sense must be understood rhetorically as nonliteral, "this *signifies* my body." Out of that interpretive dispute emerged two different theological understandings of the Eucharist.

Although Protestant theology's emphasis on scripture as the sole foundation of belief provided the impetus for intense interpretive activity, Roman Catholic scholars also produced a large amount of biblical scholarship, some provoked by controversies with Protestants and some not. Cardinal Cajetan (Thomas de Vio, 1469–1534) shared several views with Protestants, such as the preference for the Hebrew text over the Vulgate, the advocacy of a shorter canon (excluding the Apocrypha), and a literal form of interpretation. But much of his exegetical work was devoted to demonstrating biblical support for papal authority and traditional church doctrine.

The spread of literacy, the increased availability of translations of the Bible into European languages, and the Protestant emphasis on the sufficiency of scripture alone contributed to the spread of biblical interpretation not only among those trained in theological institutions and having linguistic skills but also among laity with modest training or only a bare literacy. Thus in the sixteenth century and beyond one begins to see an increase in popular interpretations, often of a millenarian slant. Although Luther and the other reformers had believed that the Bible was so clear that all reasonable readers would agree as to its meaning, as matters actually developed the democratization of interpretation led to a bewildering array of readings of scripture, nowhere more so than in England in the late sixteenth century. From the plowmaker Matthew Hamond to the clerk John Hilton, those who claimed that the New Testament was "a mere fable" were seen as a threat to decency and social order. Later, during the English revolution and the period of the Commonwealth (1640–1660), biblical interpretation became a primary mode of political argument among partisans of all factions.

THE SEVENTEENTH AND EIGHTEENTH CENTURIES

At the same time that Protestant orthodoxy was developing a complex and minute exegesis of the Bible in support of various church doctrines, rationalists of diverse theological allegiances were developing ideas, which many saw as challenging traditional understandings of the Bible. Both the new scientific discoveries and those resulting from the exploration of previously unknown lands raised questions about how this new knowledge was to be understood in relation to the Bible. The conflict between the astronomer Galileo Galilei (1564–1642) and the Catholic Church over the heliocentric view of the universe is only the most famous example. The perplexing problem of how to account for the existence of nations and peoples not mentioned by the Bible prompted the French reformer Isaac de la Peyrère (ca. 1596–1676) to suggest that Adam was not in fact the first human but was only the ancestor of the Israelites (*The Pre-Adamites . . . By which are prov'd that the first men were created before Adam*). At about the same time, along with oth-

ers the philosopher Thomas Hobbes in *Leviathan* (1651) questioned Moses' authorship of the entire Pentateuch and in general emphasized the human mediation between God's word and the scriptures as they are available to be read in the Bible. The French Catholic scholar Richard Simon (1638–1712), often called the father of modern biblical scholarship, wrote a *Critical History of the Old Testament* (1678), in which he discussed the various versions of the Bible with respect to their relationship and authority. Empirical in his approach, Simon also denied Moses' authorship of the Pentateuch and suggested that national archives preserved by prophets and scribes provided the sources from which the biblical books were composed long after the date of the events described in them. A similar rationalist criticism of the Bible was developed by the Jewish philosopher Baruch (Benedict) Spinoza (1632–1677).

Moral criticism of the Bible, which had in part given rise to the allegorical method of interpretation in antiquity, was also practiced. Pierre Bayle (1647–1706), a French Protestant, published a highly influential historical and critical dictionary that contained an article on David widely perceived as scandalous, since it drew attention to the themes of adultery, murder, treachery, and injustice in the story of the "man after God's own heart" (see 1 Sam 13.14). Both moral and rational criticism of the Bible, including a critique of the claims to miraculous events, is found to varying degrees in the Deists of the eighteenth century, some of the more radical of whom challenged even the resurrection of Christ. In France, Voltaire (1694–1778) popularized some of the more extreme notions concerning the Bible and its claims, and a similar radical stance was taken by the American Thomas Paine (1736–1809).

Although discussion and interpretation of the Bible was conducted by intellectuals of every stripe, as well as at a more popular level, the seventeenth and eighteenth centuries saw an enormous development of technical biblical scholarship, which was almost always related to theological and cultural debates. For instance, the controversy as to the date and origin of the vowel points in the traditional Hebrew text of the Bible was fueled largely by disputes concerning the inspiration of the Bible and the relative reliability of the Hebrew text versus the Septuagint and the Vulgate. The study of text criticism was significantly advanced by the publication of the London Polyglot (1655–1657), which included Hebrew, Greek, Vulgate, Syriac, Ethiopic, Arabic, and Persian versions, the Samaritan Pentateuch, and several Targums, along with a wealth of critical notes and aids. A large number of critical and historically oriented commentaries were published during the seventeenth century.

With the eighteenth century there developed what can be called modern criticism of the Bible. The theory of the composition of the Pentateuch from a number of still identifiable sources, an idea that has been central to modern criticism, was first advanced by French scholar Jean Astruc (1684–1766). Bishop and Oxford professor Robert Lowth (1710–1787) in England developed an analysis of the nature of Hebrew poetry, which is still widely accepted. But it was German scholarship that systematized and gave a distinctively modern character to historical-critical study of the Bible. Two landmarks of this emergent discipline were J. D. Michaelis's (1717–1791) introduction to the New Testament and J. G. Eichhorn's (1752–1827) introduction to the Old Testament.

THE INTERPRETATION OF THE BIBLE
FROM THE NINETEENTH TO THE MID-TWENTIETH CENTURIES

THE HISTORICAL-CRITICAL METHOD

The philosophical developments of the seventeenth and eighteenth centuries had prompted an approach to the Bible that is often characterized as critical. It was critical not in a negative sense, although that would often seem to be the case, but in the sense that it was free of presuppositions, especially those derived from either theology or tradition. To fully understand the Bible, scholars increasingly adopted an inductive approach, interpreting the Bible in an almost secular way, setting aside received views of its authority and authorship. This critical approach, an outgrowth of attitudes fostered during the Enlightenment, was very much in the spirit of the times and, like other legacies of the Enlightenment, was influenced by larger intellectual currents, such as Romanticism and the theory of evolution.

The overriding goal was historical: to determine what had actually taken place, and to recover the actual persons and events of the Bible as they had been preserved in the various stages of biblical tradition. The nature and development of these stages were to be understood through critical scholarship. This was the aim of "higher criticism," as distinguished from "lower," or textual criticism, and this higher criticism was essentially the historical-critical method.

With its many subdisciplines, the historical-critical method dominated biblical interpretation through the mid-twentieth century, and it continues to be influential. The scholars whose work is surveyed in the following pages were immensely learned, often experts in a variety of fields, including philology, textual criticism, comparative literature, and the study of ancient cultures contemporaneous with the biblical traditions. Moreover, also in keeping with the intellectual mood of the nineteenth and early twentieth centuries, they were optimistic, in retrospect even overconfident, operating on the assured conviction that with sufficient data and careful analysis of the data an objective, accurate, and complete understanding of the Bible was possible.

SOURCE CRITICISM

The critical study of the Bible had been begun in the seventeenth century by Hobbes, Spinoza, and Richard Simon, and it continued to gain momentum during the Enlightenment. In many respects the conclusions of scholars working on the Hebrew Bible were paralleled by those who worked on the New Testament, and the methods and preoccupations of both were similar to those of classical scholarship. In all three disciplines there was a growing concentration upon history. And scholars in all three disciplines recognized that historical reconstruction needed to begin with a careful analysis of sources.

This was true first of all of the analysis of the Pentateuch into several literary strands. Jean Astruc had proposed in 1753 that the different names used for God in different parts of the book of Genesis were due to different sources that antedated the final composition of the book. Astruc's insight was elaborated and refined mainly by German scholars, especially W. M. L. de Wette and K. H. Graf, who extended the analysis of sources to the rest of the Pentateuch (and in some cases to the book of Joshua, leading to the term "Hexateuch"; see below).

The results of more than a century of this source criticism were brilliantly synthesized in 1878 by the German Old Testament scholar Julius Wellhausen in his book (*Prolegomena to*) *The History of Israel*. Wellhausen's goal was to write a history of ancient Israel, especially its religion, and he followed an evolutionary model. The religion of Israel, Wellhausen argued, had developed in three stages: a primitive, spontaneous phase in the era before the monarchy; an ethical monotheism expressed especially by the preexilic prophets; and a sterile legalism characteristic of the Second Temple period. To support this reconstruction, he engaged in a careful analysis of the biblical traditions and, drawing especially on the earlier work of de Wette and Graf, gave the classic formulation to what is called the Documentary Hypothesis. According to the Documentary Hypothesis as elaborated by Wellhausen, the Pentateuch was an unreliable source for reconstructing the history of the time periods it narrated, but the traditions that comprised it, identified as J, E, D, and P, were datable and important evidence for the periods in which they were compiled. (See further "Introduction to the Pentateuch," pp. 3–6.) These "documents" are hypothetical, that is, they do not actually exist, but they are the best explanation of the evidence—the parallels, repetitions, and inconsistencies in the final form of the Pentateuch.

Wellhausen's historical reconstruction is clearly a product of its time, and it reflects the biases of the late nineteenth century. His view of early Israel as a fresh, undefiled religious spirit has a Romantic flavor, and his characterization of postexilic Judaism as a decline into dead legalism has an anti-Semitic cast. But his formulation of the Documentary Hypothesis became a classic statement, the theory that subsequent scholars up to the present have built upon, accepted, modified, or rejected. Despite initial and continuing conservative opposition, and, in the case of Roman Catholics especially, institutional interdict, it was widely adopted by liberal Protestant scholars and eventually by Roman Catholic and Jewish scholars as well, resulting in a large consensus that is still dominant.

Source criticism was not an end in itself but a method to be used in historical reconstruction. It recognized the inherent complexity of biblical traditions, and attempted to disentangle the prior stages of their development. Among the many significant results of source criticism was the recognition that the book of Isaiah is a composite work. The isolated insights of earlier scholars, including Rabbi Ibn Ezra in the twelfth century, and J. G. Eichhorn and others in the eighteenth, were expanded and elaborated in the commentary on Isaiah by Bernhard Duhm in 1892. The book of Isaiah, Duhm argued, was in effect an anthology spanning several centuries. First Isaiah (chs 1–39) was a product of the preexilic period and was itself a composite, including authentic oracles of the eighth-century BCE prophet Isaiah of Jerusalem, addi-

tions to those oracles and biographical materials added by his disciples, and historical narratives largely spliced in from 2 Kings. Chapters 40–55, Deutero-Isaiah or Second Isaiah, were a product of the mid-sixth century BCE, as the historical references in those chapters indicated. And the remainder of the book, chs 56–66, was to be dated a century or more later, despite similarities of language and themes to chs 40–55. In the Romantic spirit, Duhm was motivated to distinguish the genuine words of Isaiah himself, as well as those of the anonymous prophets responsible for the latter two divisions of the book, especially the author of the "Servant Songs" (Isa 42.1–4; 49.1–6; 50.4–9; 52.13–53.12).

Similar preoccupations and approaches characterized the study of the New Testament. Drawing on the work of earlier scholars, especially Simon (again!) and H. S. Reimarus, in 1835 David F. Strauss published his "life of Jesus critically examined," soon to be translated from German to English by George Eliot, in which he attempted to strip the Gospels of the miraculous and mythical in order to recover the real Jesus. This inaugurated a "quest" for the historical Jesus that continued in the work of Ernst Renan in the mid-nineteenth century and Albert Schweitzer at the beginning of the twentieth, and that remains unfulfilled, as the lack of consensus at the beginning of the twenty-first century demonstrates.

This quest was accompanied by a source-critical analysis of the Synoptic Gospels. While debate about which Gospel was written first was never fully resolved, the literary priority of Mark was argued by a succession of scholars in the nineteenth century. According to this view, held by a majority of New Testament scholars but by no means all, Mark was used as a source by both Matthew and Luke (or, more properly, the authors of the Gospels to whom those names are traditionally given). Many passages in Matthew and Luke other than those based on Mark also share a verbatim correspondence, and another source was hypothesized for them. Known as Q, from the German word Quelle ("source"), it consists almost entirely of sayings of Jesus and, though hypothetical, is the earliest source for the life of Jesus. This "Two-Source Hypothesis" was given classic formulation in English by B. H. Streeter in 1924. (See further "Introduction to the Gospels," p. 1743.)

Source criticism in the New Testament was also applied to the Gospel of John and the Acts of the Apostles. Careful analysis of the letters attributed to Paul led to the conclusion that some of them, especially the "Pastoral Epistles" (1 and 2 Timothy and Titus), and probably Ephesians and 2 Thessalonians as well, had not been written by Paul himself, and that others (such as 2 Corinthians) may be combinations of two or more originally distinct writings.

THE RECOVERY OF THE ANCIENT WORLD

The recovery of extensive written remains from the ancient Near East, and also to a lesser extent from the classical world, the latter especially in the form of papyri that document ordinary life, coincided with the development of the disciplines of anthropology, sociology, linguistics, and folklore. Both new data and new methods were applied to the biblical communities, resulting in works of extraordinary insight and, in retrospect, often of considerable naïveté. Biblical studies, however labeled, became a subject not just in denominational, seminary curriculums but a discipline recognized in larger university contexts as well, often as part of religious studies or *Religionswissenschaft*.

The process of recovery began with the decipherment of ancient Egyptian hieroglyphic writing in the early nineteenth century, which was made possible when a member of Napoleon's army discovered the Rosetta Stone in Egypt in 1799. This opened up the vast literature of Egypt, including valuable historical texts that provided synchronisms with biblical data relating especially to the first millennium BCE, and provided the basis for what would eventually be a comprehensive absolute chronology of the ancient Near East. Egyptian literature also provided parallels to such biblical genres as love poetry and wisdom literature.

In the mid-nineteenth century, British and French explorers began to unearth hundreds of thousands of cuneiform texts in Mesopotamia, and these too were rapidly deciphered, giving access to the literature and written remains of ancient Babylon, Assyria, and Persia. Like the Egyptian texts, they could often be correlated with biblical history, but their impact on biblical studies was more profound. In 1872 George Smith, working in the British Museum, discovered on one of the tablets that had been sent to London a flood narrative remarkably similar to the account in Genesis. While some took this as a simple historical confirmation of the Flood, it soon became clear that the biblical account was a literary descendant of earlier Mesopotamian accounts. Further discoveries provided many other parallels between Babylonian and Israelite literature, law, institutions, and beliefs, and in most cases Babylon again appeared to be the source. Sparked by a series of lectures by the German Assyriologist Friedrich Delitzsch in 1902–1904, a heated controversy developed, pitting "Babel" against the Bible. Ultimately many of the simplistic conclusions concerning the priority, and the superiority, of the traditions of "Babel" were rejected, and in retrospect they seem clearly anti-Semitic. But the controversy not only marks the emergence of Assyriology (the study of the cultures of ancient Mesopotamia) as an independent discipline but also established the importance of nonbiblical materials for the understanding of the Bible.

For the study of the New Testament, the most important discovery was that of the Oxyrhynchus Papyri, a large collection of documents dating to the early centuries of the Common Era. Among the thousands of mostly Greek texts excavated between 1897 and 1934 were fragments of very early manuscripts of parts of the New Testament, along with three collections of sayings of Jesus, some of which, though not found in the canonical Gospels, are apparently authentic. The latter were of considerable importance in the debate about the prehistory of the Gospels, that is, the reconstruction of the stages between Jesus himself and the earliest written traditions. The papyri also included hundreds of documents from ordinary life in Roman times, illuminating both the form of Greek used in the New Testament and the social world of its writers and audiences.

FORM CRITICISM

While source criticism became a dominant interpretive method, the influx of nonbiblical data prompted a more nuanced investigation of the prehistory of the written biblical traditions. The pioneer in this work was the German scholar Hermann Gunkel (1862–1932), perhaps the most influential biblical interpreter of the twentieth century. While accepting Wellhausen's analysis as valid, Gunkel incorporated evidence both from Babylonian literature and from comparative folklore to propose a shift in emphasis from history to the history of literature. Prior to the formation of the Pentateuchal "documents," there was discernible a long process of development and transmission of "forms," or genres, which had parallels in nonbiblical sources. They were also vehicles for preserving very ancient traditions. These forms have their own history and chronological and cross-cultural continuity.

Central to the study of these forms, known as "form criticism," was the identification of the *Sitz im Leben* ("setting in life"), the original and subsequent contexts in which the forms were developed and used. Gunkel first applied form criticism to the book of Genesis in his commentary published in 1901, in which he isolated such forms as saga, legend, taunt, curse, hymn, etiology, and proverb. His studies on the Psalms (1928–1933) were also groundbreaking, setting the terms of the discussion for the rest of the century by his classification of the various genres (hymn, individual and communal laments, individual and communal thanksgivings, royal psalms, wisdom psalms, etc.). Although there is a kind of idealism about the definition of the forms, parallels from outside the Bible confirmed their applicability and enhanced the understanding of the particulars of biblical traditions.

Gunkel had not hesitated to apply his insights to the New Testament, as in his important monograph on creation and chaos as central themes in prophetic and especially apocalyptic literature, including the book of Revelation. Two of his students, Martin Dibelius and Rudolf Bultmann, applied the principles of form criticism more systematically to the Gospels. They refined the definitions of forms such as parables and miracle stories, and Bultmann especially identified similar forms in other ancient sources. Although the question of the historical Jesus was still an issue, New Testament form criticism moved beyond what could be hypothesized about the original setting in the life of Jesus himself and focused more on the role that the forms played in various settings in earliest Christianity.

ARCHAEOLOGY

Serious exploration of the Levant began in the early nineteenth century, and notable advances were made in mapping the region and in identifying ancient sites. In the decades before World War I, extensive and, by the standards of the time, scientific excavations were undertaken by British, German, French, and American archaeologists. In Palestine attention was focused on the major cities of ancient Israel, as Jerusalem, Samaria, Megiddo, Shechem, Jericho, Taanach, and Gezer were all partially excavated. An overriding preoccupation of the excavators was historical, even apologetic: to verify, by independent data, the historicity of biblical traditions.

In the 1920s and 1930s many more projects were initiated, and excavation techniques were improved. Greater accuracy in dating excavated remains was made possible through the refinement of ceramic typology, especially as elaborated by the American scholar W. F. Albright in his excavations at Tell Beit Mirsim. But very little of the vast amount of material that was excavated and published could be related directly to the Bible, and debates often ensued about how to synthesize archaeological and biblical data.

When work resumed after World War II in the 1950s and 1960s, new projects were undertaken and many sites that had been earlier—and fortunately only partially—excavated were redug, especially by British, American, and Israeli archaeologists. In part because of the flood of material from periods long before and after biblical times or having little direct relevance to the Bible, archaeology began to develop as an independent discipline, as had already happened in the classical world. More attention was given to what archaeology actually produced, the material culture of the region in various periods, and in some circles there developed a theoretical tension between archaeology and biblical studies, as many earlier archaeologists were also biblical scholars. Now, more and more archaeologists were acquiring interest and expertise in periods and regions not directly relevant to biblical history. The result, by the late twentieth century, was that some archaeologists lacked sufficient expertise to connect what they excavated with the written sources, and many biblical scholars simply ignored the potential contributions of archaeology to the interpretation of the Bible. This was especially true in the case of the New Testament. Apart from continuing efforts since the late nineteenth century to identify sites associated with the life of Jesus, until the 1970s the study of the New Testament was largely restricted to texts, with little attention to the growing body of information about Palestine and the entire eastern Mediterranean world derived from archaeology.

ETHNOGRAPHY, SOCIOLOGY, AND ANTHROPOLOGY

As explorers and archaeologists began to make the ancient Near East known, they also observed those living there in the present. While many of the descriptions published were little more than naïve catalogues of perceived parallels between Arab customs and details of life in biblical times, there were serious works of scholarship, including W. Robertson Smith's Lectures on the Religion of the Semites (1889) and Gustaf Dalman's extensive survey of Palestinian social life and customs (Arbeit [work] und Sitte [customs] in Palästina, 1928–39). At the same time, the disciplines of sociology and anthropology were becoming more sophisticated. An early sociological interpretation of the Hebrew Bible was Max Weber's Ancient Judaism (1917–19), and there were sporadic applications of sociological method to early Christianity as well. Not until the later twentieth century, however, would it become important in biblical interpretation.

Anthropological research had a more immediate impact. Typical of early efforts was the encyclopedic work of James G. Frazer. In The Golden Bough: A Study in Comparative Religion (1890; revised and abridged by Theodor Gaster in 1959) and subsequent works such as Folk-lore in the Old Testament (1919), Frazer organized a staggering amount of data in support of his understanding of the evolution of society from primitive beginnings to civilization. His principal focus was on myth and rituals, especially the essential role of the king in the welfare of the larger society, and he included both the Hebrew Bible and the New Testament in his analysis.

While Frazer's work was subsequently criticized for its failure to pay sufficient attention to specific cultural contexts and for his cavalier treatment of the data to fit his theories, his influence was considerable. In particular, British and Scandinavian scholars developed and refined his approach, developing what has been characterized as a "myth and ritual" school. The work of Sigmund Mowinckel of Norway is representative. Using form criticism as a method (he had been Gunkel's student) and the function of the king as an organizing principle, and drawing heavily on Babylonian sources, his study of the Psalms (1921–24) focused on their use in what he suggested was an annual enthronement festival of Yahweh, like the Babylonian New Year festival. He also identified the individual speaker in many of the psalms as the king himself, and found evidence for prophets giving oracular messages to the king or to the community as part of the New Year ceremony. In *He That Cometh* (1951), Mowinckel examined the reuse of these royal ritual traditions in postexilic Judaism and in the New Testament.

REDACTION CRITICISM

The impression left by source criticism was that the final forms of the Pentateuch and other biblical books or collections for which multiple sources were hypothesized were pedestrian compilations with little literary merit. Beginning in the 1930s, again mainly in Germany, attention began to be paid to the larger units as creative works in their own right. In several influential essays, and in his commentaries on Genesis and Deuteronomy, Gerhard von Rad argued that the Hexateuch (the Pentateuch plus Joshua) was itself a literary form. Its *Sitz im Leben* was the feast of weeks (see Deut 16.9; 26.1–2), where the key events of the nation's "salvation history"—the Exodus, the conquest of the land, and the covenant—were recited and reenacted. The Hexateuch for von Rad is the final, literary product of a long development of such narrative creeds, earlier forms of which are found in such texts as Deut 26.5–9; Ps 136; Ex 15.

One reason that von Rad included the book of Joshua in his analysis was that the promise of the land, a central theme especially in J and P, was unfulfilled in the Pentateuch. Martin Noth took another approach. The original conclusion to the Pentateuch, he proposed, had been replaced by a "Deuteronomistic History." With the book of Deuteronomy as a kind of theological preface, the books of Joshua through 2 Kings comprised a carefully written history of Israel in the promised land. Since 2 Kings ended with the destruction of Jerusalem and the end of Israel's autonomy in the land, Noth argued that this history was

an exilic composition, which explained the catastrophe as the inevitable result of Israel's failure to live up to the obligations of its covenant with God as detailed in Deuteronomy. Subsequent scholars revised Noth's views, suggesting that while the final form of the Deuteronomistic History was, as he had suggested, a product of the mid-sixth century BCE, it had its own literary history and had existed in one or more editions during the monarchy before the exile. But his essential insight concerning the underlying unity of the books of Deuteronomy through 2 Kings remained the foundation for subsequent interpretation of the historical books.

Attention to larger units developed in the study of the New Testament as well, beginning in the 1950s. In important commentaries on Matthew and Mark, Günther Bornkamm and Willi Marxsen understood those Gospels as creative literary works, with distinctive theologies and themes. In his study of the theology of Luke, Hans Conzelmann showed how the Gospel of Luke and the book of Acts together formed a carefully composed narrative, with thematic unity provided by an understanding of the life of Jesus as the center of history and Jerusalem as the geographical center of the story. Similar approaches were undertaken for the Gospel of John and the letters of Paul, and for both the Hebrew Bible and the New Testament, redaction criticism's focus on larger units anticipates the methods of literary criticism and canonical criticism later in the twentieth century.

DISCOVERIES OF TEXTS BETWEEN THE WORLD WARS

The discovery and decipherment of cuneiform texts of ancient Assyria and Babylon during the second half of the nineteenth century had profoundly changed the understanding of the Hebrew Bible. On the historical level, the repeated references especially in Assyrian annals to kings of Israel and Judah and to events mentioned in the Bible enabled the construction of a detailed chronology. But for the most part, connections between the cuneiform texts and biblical traditions were indirect. This is not surprising, given the distance and often the time that separated those Mesopotamian cultures from ancient Israel. And apart from a scattering of inscriptions in Hebrew, Phoenician, Aramaic, and Moabite, there were no significant written remains from Israel itself or its most immediate neighbors. That changed in the 1920s and 1930s, as excavations uncovered more collections of ancient texts, and further decipherment shed light on such groups as the Sumerians, the Hittites, and the Hurrians. While there were seldom direct correlations with the Bible, the tablets from Nuzi in northern Iraq and Mari and Ugarit in northern Syria were especially important in expanding the knowledge of the larger world to which ancient Israel belonged.

In many respects the mythological texts from Ugarit are the most important because of their geographical proximity to ancient Israel and the direct light they shed on the Hebrew Bible. Written in a previously unknown Semitic language belonging to the same subfamily as Hebrew, they are composed in poetry that is often remarkably close in diction and in form to biblical poetry. The myths feature gods and goddesses such as El, Baal, and Asherah, all frequently mentioned in the Bible but hitherto incompletely known, largely because of the biblical writers' antagonism toward gods other than Yahweh. Moreover, similar motifs—for example, the childless patriarch, the theophany of the storm god, the council of the gods, the sacred mountain—and innumerable smaller details illustrate the shared commonalties between the culture of Israel and those of its neighbors. Despite undeniable chronological and geographical discontinuities, the literary, religious, and institutional traditions of the Levant, including ancient Israel, are best understood as part of a cultural continuum that, allowing for local particularities, is remarkably consistent and pervasive.

THE DEAD SEA SCROLLS

Another discovery that sent scholarship in new directions was that of a cache of manuscripts in caves near Qumran at the northwest corner of the Dead Sea. Over the course of several years, beginning in 1947, the remains of hundreds of manuscripts were discovered, first by local Bedouin and subsequently by archaeologists. Some of the manuscripts were largely intact, including an almost complete scroll of the Hebrew text of the book of Isaiah, and others were preserved only in fragments. Written mostly in Hebrew and Aramaic, with a few in Greek, they are generally agreed to have been a library deposited in the caves for safekeeping during the First Jewish Revolt (66–73 CE) by the inhabitants of the nearby settlement. Most scholars identify these inhabitants as Essenes, one of the major groups within Judaism in the Roman period, according to the first-century CE Jewish historian Josephus. Among many important aspects of the scrolls, three may be highlighted here. First are the manuscripts of the Hebrew Bible, more than a thousand years older than any previously known, giving new impetus to text criticism (see p. 2192). Second is their contribution to the understanding of both Hebrew and Aramaic in the Roman period. And third is the glimpse they provide—especially in what have been termed "sectarian documents," that is, various community regulations, hymns, eschato-

logical texts, and biblical commentaries (*pesharim*; see p. 2209)—of one group within Judaism around the turn of the era. What had earlier been oversimplified as a kind of monolithic Judaism is now, on the basis of these texts and other sources reexamined in their light, understood rather as a complex spectrum of various "Judaisms," one of which was earliest Christianity. And while there are no direct links between the Dead Sea Scrolls and the New Testament, they do reveal a rich and complicated background for the emergence of Christianity as well as for the development of rabbinic Judaism after 70 CE.

THE NAG HAMMADI TEXTS

In 1945 at Nag Hammadi, some 300 mi (500 km) south of Cairo, Egyptian peasants unearthed a large jar containing thirteen codices. Most of the texts contained within these volumes were Christian Gnostic texts, and although written in Coptic many had been translated from Greek. One of the most important was *The Gospel of Thomas*, a collection of the sayings of Jesus perhaps originally compiled before the end of the first century CE. Fragments of *The Gospel of Thomas* had earlier been found among the Oxyrhynchus Papyri (see above). Less than half of the sayings attributed to Jesus in this text are paralleled in the New Testament, and the *Gospel of Thomas* thus provides both an important independent source and an example of how earliest Christian tradition was collected and expanded by a particular writer within a specific community, a process more and more recognized in the study of the canonical Gospels.

CONCLUSION

With few exceptions, until after World War II historical-critical scholarship was engaged in by Protestant scholars. With the promulgation of the papal encyclical *Divino Afflante Spiritu* in 1943, Roman Catholic scholars began to become practitioners as well. Likewise, both in the United States and in Israel, with the development there of the Hebrew University and later other institutions of higher education, Jewish scholars also made significant contributions. Facilities at major denominational graduate centers increasingly recruited scholars without regard to their religious affiliations. By the mid-twentieth century it was possible to speak of a consensus of interpretation: a general agreement on methods and results that largely transcended national and confessional differences. That consensus was evidenced in important ecumenical endeavors, especially in the United States, including several ongoing translation and commentary projects. In the next several decades that consensus would begin to unravel.

CONTEMPORARY METHODS IN BIBLICAL STUDY

In its development during the eighteenth and nineteenth centuries, biblical criticism was often in conversation with other disciplines, including linguistics, anthropology, the history of religion, sociology, philosophical hermeneutics, and literary aesthetics, as well as with theology. Yet as biblical studies became a discipline in its own right, it developed a set of classical methods and questions that set the parameters for research. These methods were largely concerned with the history of the text and of the cultures that produced the texts. The consensus that these were the relevant questions and the methods by which they should be pursued lasted until well after the middle of the twentieth century. Since the 1970s, however, many biblical scholars have questioned the adequacy of an almost exclusive orientation to questions with a historical focus. Also, in keeping with a trend characteristic of most of the humanities and social sciences, there has been a strong movement toward interdisciplinary conversation. Although it is difficult to give a simple overview of the proliferating approaches to biblical studies since the 1970s, they can be roughly grouped under the categories of literary, social-scientific, and cultural hermeneutical approaches.

LITERARY APPROACHES

A popular appreciation of the narrative art of the Bible has always existed. Its stories were represented in the sculpture and stained-glass windows of medieval churches, and Western literature has been profoundly influenced by its characters, themes, and symbols. In both Judaism and Christianity the reading and retelling of the stories in devotional and liturgical contexts made them deeply familiar. Yet even though biblical Hebrew poetry had been the subject of academic study since the eighteenth century (most notably in Bishop Robert Lowth's *Lectures on the Sacred Poetry of the Hebrews*), little attention had been paid to the poetics of biblical narrative. One impetus to the interest in biblical narrative that developed in the 1970s can be traced to a development in American higher education: the creation of departments of religious studies in nondenominational colleges and public universities in the 1960s and 1970s. In such contexts the study of the Bible "as literature" was deemed especially appropriate to a secular curriculum. Such interest was not restricted to scholars in secular contexts, however. In 1968 James Muilenberg, who for much of his career had been a professor at Union Theological Seminary in

New York, delivered a presidential address to the Society of Biblical Literature titled "Form Criticism and Beyond." Here he called for a type of literary-theological approach to the poetry and prose of the Bible, which he referred to as "rhetorical criticism." Giving further impetus to literary study of the Bible was the work of several scholars of English and comparative literature, who extended their expertise in the analysis of literature to biblical texts. Most prominent were Northrop Frye (*The Great Code: The Bible and Literature*), Robert Alter (*The Art of Biblical Narrative* and *The Art of Biblical Poetry*), and Frank Kermode (*The Genesis of Secrecy*, a study of the Gospel of Mark). Alter and Kermode later collaborated to edit *The Literary Guide to the Bible*.

This literary approach differed from historical study in significant ways. Whereas historical study tended to be concerned with the prehistory of the text (oral traditions and written source materials) and with its development through successive redactions, literary study focused on the final form of the text. Whereas historical study was interested in the world referred to by the text, literary study directed its attention to the world constructed in the text. Nevertheless, there were historical dimensions to this early work in biblical literature. Both Alter and Meir Sternberg attempted to isolate distinctive features of ancient Israelite narrative art (e.g., modes of characterization, the use of type-scenes, techniques of repetition, forms of plot development), which were not necessarily the same as the techniques used in modern Western narrative. Similarly, New Testament literary study has included a strong interest in the comparative analysis of Greco-Roman literary genres and techniques and those used in the Gospels, Acts, and early noncanonical Christian literature.

Much of the early literary study of the Bible was influenced by the "New Criticism," an approach that had dominated Anglo-American literary scholarship from the 1930s through the 1950s. In New Criticism the literary text was considered an autonomous work of art, to be studied independently of its author's intentions and of the sociopolitical currents of the time in which it was produced. New Criticism was a reaction both to a methodology arising out of the history of literature, in which new literary movements are seen as developing from those of previous eras, and to biographical criticism, which reads literary texts as expressions of the life experiences of the writers. The focus in New Criticism is rather on the way in which the text itself is structured so as to produce the observed or expected effects and understandings. Thus, the plot, characters, setting, point of view, and other aspects of the story's rhetoric are analyzed. As the literary study of the Bible was gaining ground, however, rapid changes were taking place in the larger field of literary study, changes that were quickly reflected in biblical studies.

Structuralism was the first of these new movements to make an impact. The origins of structuralism are in the work of the early twentieth-century linguist Ferdinand de Saussure, who attempted to analyze the system of relationships within a language that make acts of speech possible. In particular, he stressed that meanings are produced not so much by simple definition as by a network of contrasts (e.g., a tree is a woody plant that is not a bush or a shrub). The anthropologist Claude Lévi-Strauss argued that symbolic structures within human societies, including their kinship systems and their mythologies, could be analyzed in the same way, as systems of differences structured according to binary oppositions (e.g., life/death; male/female; hunting/farming; outside/inside). In a parallel development A. J. Greimas attempted to use Saussure's insights to develop a "grammar" of narrative in much the same way as Saussure attempted to develop a grammar of sentences. Biblical scholars, anthropologists, and literary theorists were quick to apply these approaches to the Bible. The mythic narratives and genealogical accounts of Genesis, the symbolic geography of the Gospel narratives, and even the theological vocabulary of Paul offered opportunities for analyzing the patterns of binary opposition that structuralists argued were the key to the meaning of the texts.

Even as structuralism was being adapted for the study of biblical literature, its assumptions and claims were being challenged in the wider world of philosophical and literary studies. Structuralism claimed that the binary oppositions that structure human thought are essentially universal and unaffected by culture or history. Though the surface features of texts might vary with different societies and over time, the underlying structures did not. Such claims proved difficult to sustain. Just as structuralism dispensed with history, so it also had no place for the reader in the production of meaning. Structuralism understood itself as a kind of scientific method. Yet different readers regularly reached different understandings of the same text. Finally, although structuralism seemed to lend itself well to myths, folktales, and highly formulaic narratives, it seemed unable to deal with more complex narratives.

Against the focus on a supposedly objective and stable text in narrative criticism and against structuralism's focus on impersonal and universal codes, reader-response criticism argued for the essential role of the reader in the process of making meaning. Structuralism tended to display its results in terms of charts, an implicitly spatial understanding of the text. But reader-response theory insisted that reading is essentially a temporal affair. In reading, one only gradually gathers information that is progressively organized and reorganized by the reader to produce meaning. Moreover, the text often contains "gaps" that the reader, consciously or unconsciously, fills in (e.g., details concerning characters, aspects of motivation or causality, connections between events). As the reader becomes actively involved in the process of reading, what the reader engages is not simply the issues of plot and character but also matters of norms and values, which the reader may embrace or resist. Reader-response criticism thus accounts for the different understandings of and reactions to the "same" text by different readers by claiming a necessary place for the subjective element in reading. Subjectivity is limited, however, by what the reader's community considers to be a plausible or implausible inference. Thus it is not so much individual readers as "interpretive communities" who set the parameters according to which interpretation takes place.

Although important reader-response studies of Hebrew Bible texts have been produced, the method found its most enthusiastic reception in the study of the New Testament Gospels. Yet it has been one of the most controversial of methods, challenged by historical critics for neglect of the intentions of the author and the horizon of the original audience, and by postmodern critics for its failure to break decisively with such historical assumptions as the understanding of the text as a stable "object" opposed to the readerly "subject." One of the consequences of reader-response criticism's focus on the role of interpretive communities, however, has been a renewed appreciation for the forms of interpretation practiced by Jewish and Christian communities before the rise of modern biblical studies during the Enlightenment. Instead of seeing such traditional readings as naive or simply wrong, interpreters now ask about the assumptions and values that govern the reading practices of Christian typological and allegorical exegesis and of Rabbinic midrash. Midrash in particular has engaged contemporary literary scholars, because some of its interpretive practices bear an intriguing resemblance to forms of postmodern interpretation (for example, the acceptance of multiple, even contradictory, interpretations of the same text, and the interpretation of one text by another without regard to historical influence).

If reader-response criticism represented one reaction to the limitations of traditional narratology and to structuralism, a more pervasive criticism emerged under the rubric of poststructuralism, or deconstruction. This movement, associated with the French philosopher Jacques Derrida, is above all a critique of the metaphysical assumptions of Western philosophy, and only secondarily an analysis of the nature of texts and the interpretive process. Derrida noted the attempt of philosophy to posit a central term (God, reason, the human being) in relation to which all of reality can be organized. This organization characteristically takes place by means of binary oppositions (e.g., rational/irrational, oral/written, presence/absence), in which the first term is accepted as superior to the second. Deconstruction attempts to dismantle such structures in order to show their artificiality and the inevitable ways in which any such structure of thought implicitly "decenters" its central term and undermines itself through internal inconsistency and contradiction. When applied to texts, deconstruction begins with the perception that language is inevitably incomplete and surprisingly fluid. It then analyzes how even a text's ostensible argument is rendered problematic, if not outright self-contradictory, by extraneous details or slippages in meaning that at first appear peripheral and unimportant. For deconstruction the point of reading is not to restate the meaning intended by the author but to engage the text in creative thought, often by means of punning play with the text. Deconstruction's very style serves to undermine the binary opposition serious/frivolous, for its aim is in part to uncover the ways in which various forms of thought attempt to inscribe power and privilege.

The perspectives of deconstruction have been combined with other intellectual currents (most notably Freudianism and Marxism) to produce a variety of related approaches that are often referred to comprehensively by the term "postmodernism." Along with Derrida's deconstruction, Michel Foucault's study of the complex nature of power and truth and Fredric Jameson's neo-Marxist analysis of ideology have been deeply influential on postmodernism in biblical studies. For an overview of these trends as well as other forms of postmodernism, see *The Postmodern Bible* by The Bible and Culture Collective.

Since one of the features of postmodernism is its tendency to dissolve boundaries, it is scarcely surprising that its characteristic approaches have combined with a wide variety of other impulses within biblical studies, most notably feminist criticism, but also various forms of ideological criticism (see below under CULTURAL HERMENEUTICS). Similarly, postmodern analysis is not restricted to narrative but employed in relation to all sorts of texts. Indeed, the self-conscious study of the literary artistry of the Bible, such a controversial novelty in 1970, has been all but put aside in the rapidly shifting mix of methods and approaches that have been developed alongside the classical forms of biblical interpretation.

SOCIAL-SCIENTIFIC CRITICISM

Social-scientific criticism, another form of biblical criticism that has arisen in more recent years, applies insights and methods from the fields of sociology, anthropology, and ethnography to describe aspects of ancient social life manifested in the biblical texts and to reconstruct the social worlds behind the text. To some extent historical criticism has always had a social dimension, since the objects of its interest included nations, states, social groupings, and religious movements. Yet self-conscious social-scientific investigation, though not unknown in earlier stages of biblical studies, has come into its own since the 1960s.

As early as the Renaissance, students of the Bible sought to make cross-cultural comparisons between ancient Israel and the nations of the ancient Near East. With the development of critical biblical study in the nineteenth century, this interest in cross-cultural study focused particularly on the comparison between Israel and the pre-Islamic Bedouin Arabs, as well as with contemporary Bedouin society, especially in the work of Julius Wellhausen and William Robertson Smith. Similarly, Martin Noth compared Israel's premonarchical tribal confederacy with ancient Greek tribal leagues. In retrospect, these early attempts at social-scientific analysis were hampered by a lack of rigorous method, by erroneous assumptions about the economic and social organization of ancient Israel, and by an overly static model of ancient culture. More sophisticated was the work of the sociologist Max Weber, whose *Ancient Judaism* (compiled from lectures given in 1917–19) attempted to incorporate the dimensions of historical and institutional change in his account of the social organization of ancient Israel. Sociological investigation was not as prominent in New Testament studies, although the Chicago school of social analysis (leaders of which were Shailer Mathews and Shirley Jackson Case) did investigate the social location of early Christians and attempted to account for the success of Christianity among Gentiles but not among Jews.

These early attempts at social-scientific criticism were largely displaced by interest in other questions and methods, and for almost forty years little was published in this field. By the 1960s and 1970s, however, interest in it revived. Since the issues posed by Hebrew Bible and New Testament materials are significantly different, each literature will be discussed separately. In studies concentrating on the Hebrew Bible, several areas have proven fruitful for analysis. The first issue to be examined, and one still sharply debated, is that of the socioeconomic and political nature of the formation of the Israelite tribal confederacy. Social historians rejected the conquest model of Israel's entry into Canaan as it is described in the biblical narrative. Both George Mendenhall and Norman Gottwald argued that Israel's origins were to be sought instead in a peasant revolt against urban Canaanite overlords. The peasant movement was a revolt against the hierarchical socioeconomic structure and developed as a retribalization along egalitarian lines in the central highlands. What differentiated Mendenhall and Gottwald, however, was Gottwald's explicit use of Marxist social theory. Although both of their proposals have been sharply criticized for reliance more on presupposed models than on textual or material evidence, they served to open the question of Israel's origins for fresh investigation. Since the 1970s archaeology has also generated increasing information about social organization, population patterns, domestic architecture, agricultural practices, and trade patterns for the period preceding the monarchy. This information, together with a wider array of possible comparative models for the development of noncentralized peasant societies, has begun to generate new ways of understanding early Israel, though none has yet achieved consensus.

Similarly, attempts to understand the movement from a loose tribal confederation to the eventual formation of royal states has been aided by comparative social analysis. Social anthropologists have documented the development of chieftainships as an intermediate stage between these two forms of social organization. A chiefdom is a hierarchically organized society that lacks the strong central governmental apparatus characteristic of a true state. Though some aspects of the process are still debated, it is now widely thought that Saul's "kingship" and at least the early stages of David's rule should be thought of as chieftainships.

Prophecy is another area of Israel's religious and social life that has proven fruitful for social-scientific analysis. Apart from texts of prophetic oracles recovered from neighboring nations, archaeology does not contribute to this question. Rather, the biblical texts are analyzed in light of sociological models and comparative ethnographic evidence. Though the limited evidence makes many conclusions elusive, it has been possible to clarify the social location of the prophets and their relationship or nonrelationship to established religious institutions and to the monarchy. How a prophet secures legitimation, the role of ecstasy and other phenomena of abnormally heightened consciousness, and the relation of oral and written communication have all been examined in social-scientific perspective. The later development of

apocalypticism and the question of its social location—whether it was, for example, an outgrowth of prophecy, a scribal phenomenon, or a movement of the social margins or of the priestly elite—has been debated as the biblical texts are reread in light of apocalyptic and millenarian movements in the medieval and modern periods.

The biblical text also contains significant information about purity laws and kinship and family patterns, topics that lend themselves to comparative social analysis. In the 1960s the anthropologist Mary Douglas pioneered such studies with her analysis of the food laws in Leviticus, interpreting them as a symbolic system for organizing the world and correlating purity laws in general with the social concern for boundaries. More recently the genealogies and ancestral narratives in Genesis, the family laws in Deuteronomy, and the reports on the postexilic community in Ezra-Nehemiah have been investigated in an attempt to discern the basic structures of family organization, as well as changes over time in the patterns of family life. As modern interest in gender constructs and roles has grown, so has the investigation of such issues in ancient Israel. Although the resources are mainly the texts of the Hebrew Bible, attempts have been made to use the findings of archaeology to determine the patterns of life and activity characteristic of males and females in biblical times (see C. Meyers, *Discovering Eve: Ancient Israelite Women in Context*).

In the field of New Testament, insights from sociology were first used in the 1970s to analyze the nature of the early Christian movement. The anthropological study of millenarian movements and sociological typologies of sects were employed to clarify the dynamics of the Christian communities that emerged in the first two centuries of the era. One of the watersheds in the use of sociological and anthropological perspectives in New Testament studies was the publication of *The First Urban Christians* by Wayne Meeks, which was a comprehensive attempt to describe the social context and organization of the early Pauline communities. Also significant was the application to biblical texts of cultural anthropological studies of the roles of honor and shame in Mediterranean societies, and the functioning of patron-client forms of social relations. These studies not only illumined structural aspects of early Christian society and its context but also showed how aspects of discourse and categories of thought were organized in characteristic patterns that reflected these social values and assumptions. In such cases social-scientific and traditional theological investigation of the New Testament may converge, as the latter recognizes the need to understand the meaning and context of key terms by means of social-scientific analysis.

The rich comparative material available from the classical world has facilitated many types of sociological investigation. Slavery, as social phenomenon and as metaphor, has been an important topic, as has the role of prophets and prophecy, the practice of magic, and the class status of early converts to Christianity. As in the field of Hebrew Bible, the social study of family structures and gender roles has yielded important insights.

Although disputes concerning appropriate methodology for social analysis have not been absent in Hebrew Bible studies, they have been particularly prominent in New Testament studies. Even the terminology has been contested. Some scholars prefer to describe their work as social history, that is, as an extension of traditional historical criticism that is informed by categories and questions from sociology and cultural anthropology. Others have insisted that their work is social-scientific in the strong sense of the term, that is, as work guided by the correlation of models and data, as are more purely sociological and social-psychological studies. More significant than the disagreement over terminology, however, has been the issue of which sociological or anthropological methods and approaches are most suitable. Social conflict is a topic that has long been of interest to sociologists, though it has been studied from two quite different perspectives. Social functionalism examines the ways in which society, considered as an organism, attempts to contain and manage conflict, integrating disparate members and subgroups into the whole. This approach was used by Gerd Theissen to explore the primary stages of the early Christian movement and its subsequent evolution. By contrast, conflict models in sociological theory emphasize the ways in which different groups in a society pursue their own interests and the ways in which different ideologies struggle with one another. More recent work in the sociology of early Christianity has favored conflict models over social functionalism. The nature of the textual sources has also influenced the choice of methods. Since much early Christian literature is self-consciously theological or ideological, cultural anthropology and the sociology of knowledge have proven particularly fruitful. Both of these approaches pay attention to the way in which societies create "symbolic universes" by which to negotiate issues of identity, legitimacy, and the creation or resolution of conflict. This focus on the social functions of language has drawn together literary and social criticism toward something of a convergence on what might be termed ideological criticism, an issue also central to the third methodological movement to be discussed, cultural hermeneutics.

CULTURAL HERMENEUTICS

Classical biblical studies, as it emerged from its Enlightenment roots, understood itself as a form of critical analysis that was objective, disinterested, and even "scientific." Though biblical theology might make normative claims, even those claims were based on a preliminary act of interpretation that was grounded in objective scholarship. In recent years the claim of classic biblical scholarship to be a quasi-scientific enterprise has been questioned by those who insist that the enterprise of historical criticism of the Bible is unconsciously shaped and informed by cultural assumptions specific to the time and place in which that method was developed. Pure objectivity is an illusion. In the interpretation of texts and cultures there is no "view from nowhere." All interpreters, whether or not they are aware of it, frame their questions and perceive the data from some perspective, which helps to shape their understanding of the text or culture in question. Rather than seeing the influence of the interpreter's social and cultural location as a problem, some have claimed it as a positive value. Thus the term "cultural hermeneutics" serves as an umbrella term for a variety of approaches to biblical interpretation (e.g., liberationist, feminist, postcolonial) in which the social location of the interpreter is not only made explicit but serves as a normative principle in interpretation. The primary categories that have figured in such interpretation are those of class, ethnicity, and gender.

The earliest and most methodologically self-conscious of these approaches is that of Latin American liberation theology, which emerged in the 1960s and 1970s. This approach did not begin as an academic perspective but rather emerged out of the concrete experience of the poor and of those pastors and other religious professionals who lived and worked with them. They insisted that the starting point for reading and interpreting the Bible must not be a stance of "objectivity" but rather the experience of the crushing poverty and oppression of the lowest social classes. Interpreted from the perspective of material poverty, the Bible discloses itself as a text of liberation and serves to further a revolutionary process of emancipation.

Much of the work of liberation hermeneutics took place in the Bible studies of Christian base communities, in which groups of the poor were encouraged to read and interpret the Bible for themselves, with the assistance of a priest or teacher. Although this oral interpretation was seldom recorded, Ernesto Cardenal's *The Gospel in Solentiname* provides an example. The interpretation developed in the base communities was paralleled by the work of theologians and biblical scholars, who articulated the principles of liberation hermeneutics in a series of important studies (see, especially, L. Boff and C. Boff, *Introducing Liberation Theology*; and J. Severino Croatto, *Biblical Hermeneutics: Toward a Theory of Reading in the*

Production of Meaning). Liberation theology has tended to place special emphasis on such specific portions of the Bible as the story of the Exodus, the social criticism of the prophets, the figure of Mary (as singer of the Magnificat, with its imagery of social transformation; Lk 1), Jesus' preaching of the kingdom of God in the Gospels, the depiction of the liberating Christian community in Acts, and the struggle against evil in its imperialist and cosmic guise in the book of Revelation.

In the wake of Latin American liberation hermeneutics, religious communities and academics in the various countries of Africa and Asia have developed analogous forms of biblical interpretation that work from the particular experiences of those nations. A related movement, which is indebted to liberation hermeneutics but which also draws on other sources, is postcolonial hermeneutics (see R. S. Sugirtharajah, ed., *Voices from the Margin: Interpreting the Bible in the Third World*). As European countries colonized various parts of the globe from the sixteenth to the nineteenth centuries, the Bible was an important aspect of the sometimes forced assimilation of indigenous peoples to European cultural values. The desire of European churches to spread Christianity meant that the Bible, as interpreted by Europeans, accompanied the colonizers. Where conversion took place, the Bible displaced indigenous traditions, even as it buttressed European dominance. In recent years biblical scholars in the Third World (and increasingly in Europe and North America) have examined this complex history and heritage. They have attempted to analyze the roles that the Bible and its interpretation have played in these colonized countries. Not only have the colonizers' interpretations been examined and critiqued (e.g., the use of the Exodus/Conquest story in North America and South Africa to justify the displacement of the indigenous peoples), but increasingly, attempts have been made to recover the forms of interpretation developed by the newly Christianized indigenous peoples themselves. Elements of "hybrid interpretation," that is, the mixing of indigenous traditions with Christian biblical narratives, are not only identified but often encouraged as a continuing creative practice. Thus, part of the resistance to the effects of the colonization experience is to read the Bible along with rather than above other religious and cultural traditions.

Within North America several ethnic communities, including Hispanics, Asian Americans, and Native Americans, have also developed self-conscious traditions of biblical interpretation. The earliest and most developed of these is African American biblical hermeneutics. The Bible has played a particularly significant role in the African American community, and popular forms of African American biblical interpretation have been embedded in the songs and sermons of the community for centuries. In the 1960s and 1970s, as the Black Theology movement developed, African American biblical scholars began to turn their attention both to the recovery and analysis of this traditional interpretation and to the development of a critical, academic form of African American biblical interpretation (see C. H. Felder, ed., *Stony the Road We Trod: African-American Biblical Interpretation*). Afrocentric interpretation has drawn attention to the historical role played by African countries (especially Egypt and Ethiopia) and by Africans in the biblical text. But African American biblical hermeneutics has also attended to texts and issues that have been important to the lives of the African American community: for instance, the Exodus narratives, the place of slavery in Israelite and early Christian reflection, and the preaching of Jesus. African American biblical studies has also been marked by a deep reflection on the nature of interpretation itself, especially the ways in which an oppressed community appropriates for its own liberation a text that also serves as the authorizing document of the society within which its members have been oppressed.

Whereas the various perspectives discussed so far under the rubric of cultural hermeneutics are distinctively Christian, the same cannot be said for feminist biblical hermeneutics. Here, although Christian feminist biblical interpretation emerged slightly earlier, Jewish and Christian feminist interpretation has largely developed in tandem, and the critical conversation between Jewish and Christian feminists has been one of the distinctive features of this movement. In the 1950s and 1960s Protestant seminaries began to admit women in significantly larger numbers than before, followed soon after by an increase in the number of Catholic and Jewish women pursuing theological education. The emergence of the women's movement in the 1960s and its criticism of the role of the Bible in the oppression of women posed a challenge to those who identified themselves as both Christian or Jewish and feminist. One early position, which still continues to be important in the Christian evangelical community, is to affirm that the Bible, when correctly interpreted, affirms women's full humanity. Other feminists, more critical of the Bible itself, have attempted to expose and analyze the patriarchal elements in the biblical text itself in order to show how the patriarchal values can be separated from the essentially liberating values that form its primary message. More radical feminists, however, have attempted to show that the biblical traditions are thoroughly and irredeemably antifeminist.

Feminist interpretation of the Bible has embraced a variety of methodologies. The include the approaches of historical-critical and sociological biblical scholarship,

since it attempts to recover and reconstruct the historical reality of women's lives in ancient Israel and in the Greco-Roman world of early Christianity and early Judaism. Some Christian feminists, in an attempt to make a case for the liberating nature of early Christianity, did so in ways that played off the egalitarian message of Jesus against his Jewish background. Jewish feminists challenged the accuracy of the representation of Judaism, and as a result considerably more nuanced pictures of gender relations in both early Christianity and Judaism have been developed.

Not all feminist interpretation has been concerned with historical reconstruction, however. A significant strand of feminism has used literary methods, exploring the ways in which biblical texts construct and represent an image of women that may function in the service of particular ideologies. In many instances this literary approach has involved reading against the grain of the text. For instance, a character whom the text treats as a subsidiary character may become for feminist analysis the central character of the text (e.g., Jephthah's daughter in Judg 11 or the Levite's concubine in Judg 19). Of particular concern to feminists has been the issue of women and violence, for many of the biblical texts do represent violence against women, and a smaller but significant number represent women engaged in violence. While much of this literary work has also had a historical focus, in that it has been concerned with how the ancient texts have represented women, increasingly attention has been drawn to what is called cultural studies, i.e., how Western traditions in art and, more recently, film have themselves depicted the biblical representations of women.

Since feminism made women aware of their own particular perspective as women in the process of interpretation, it is not surprising that feminism has also become aware that particular women occupy very different positions in society, depending on their social and economic class and their ethnicity. Consequently, it has become more problematic to refer to a single "feminist" movement, for women of color and Third World women have insisted that gender, class, and ethnicity must all be considered in their complex interrelationships. African American women, for instance, have complicated the Anglo-European interpretation of the Abraham/Sarah narratives by focusing on the character of Hagar—the ethnic outsider, the slave, the surrogate mother—and her role in creating the narrative's moral complexity. Similarly, Latina, African, and Asian women have taken up the challenge of understanding the ways in which the practices of reading and interpreting the Bible serve to constrain or to emancipate women in their particular social and cultural contexts.

Finally, two different types of theological interpretation of the Bible can also be classified as forms of cultural hermeneutics, since they foreground the community context of the formation and interpretation of the Bible. The first of these is canonical criticism. Though the forms of canonical criticism developed by its two major proponents, Brevard Childs and James Sanders, differ, one can identify common elements. Specifically, canonical criticism is concerned with how scripture's final form was created within a believing community and how the meanings created by that final form continue to guide the reading practices of the community. The canonical shaping of the Jewish Bible, for instance—which places the Writings in the final position and concludes with the call of 2 Chronicles for the exiles to go up to Jerusalem to rebuild the Temple—tells a different story from that produced by the shaping of the Christian Old Testament, which places the prophets last and concludes with Malachi's reference to the return of the prophet Elijah to announce the coming Day of the Lord.

In one sense canonical criticism is an extension of historical criticism's interest in the development of traditions. But in contrast to historical criticism's tendency to investigate the earliest stages of development, canonical criticism explicitly privileges the latest stage, the canon in its final form. This concern with reading the text of scripture in its final form gives canonical criticism some similarity to the literary approaches of the "New Criticism." Thus, where historical criticism, reading the book of Isaiah, tries to distinguish which materials come from the eight-century prophet, the sixth-century prophet, and the fifth-century prophet, literary and canonical critics focus on how the final form of the book has created the context within which all of its materials are now to be read, as a movement from judgment to salvation. While canonical criticism's self-conscious attention to what it means to read scripture as a member of a religious tradition links it with cultural hermeneutics, it also differs from some of the other forms of cultural hermeneutics discussed earlier. Just as those forms of interpretation make repeated reference to the specific experience of the reader as a guide to interpretation, canonical hermeneutics finds the clues to a proper reading in the ways in which the text of scripture was shaped by the believing community at the time its canon was fixed.

Perhaps closer to other forms of cultural hermeneutics is the type of theological interpretation often called "postcritical." Like canonical criticism, it is a reaction against historical criticism's inability to articulate the meaning of scripture for a believing community. In contrast to canonical criticism, which focuses on the final stages of the composition of the biblical text and the meaning of the biblical books in that context, postcritical interpretation orients itself to the early interpretive practices of Rabbinic Judaism and patristic Christianity. Thus Rabbinic midrash and Christian allegorical and typological exegesis are reclaimed as valid ways of understanding the biblical texts as scripture. These traditional interpretive practices are also used as patterns for the development of new postcritical ways of reading and interpreting scripture, as one can see in Peter Ochs's *The Return to Scripture in Judaism and Christianity.*

In the Christian tradition postcritical interpretation is also deeply influenced by Hans Frei's *The Eclipse of Biblical Narrative* and George Lindbeck's *The Nature of Doctrine.* Both authors claim that before the rise of historical criticism the normative way of reading scripture in Christianity was as a grand narrative from Genesis to Revelation, with the Old Testament related to the New not only by plot but also by forms of typological interpretation that linked figures and events. Thus scripture does not simply tell a story but is rather a master narrative, that is, a narrative within which persons can live and by means of which they understand reality. The forms of postcritical interpretation that attempt to recover this way of reading scripture are not only self-consciously literary in orientation but also draw on ethnographic models. Lindbeck characterizes his approach as "cultural-linguistic." That is to say, one learns to enter the world of scripture as one learns to speak a language or to live in another culture. What makes this approach to scripture *post*critical and *post*modern is that the symbolic worlds of classical Judaism and Christianity are no longer the native worlds even for most believers. Modernity, with its different forms of critical understanding, has displaced them. The retrieval and reappropriation that is the goal of postcritical interpretation occur self-consciously in the shadow of modernity. Moreover, as Lindbeck's cultural-linguistic analogy suggests, postcritical interpretation is not simply about interpretation but also about participation in the practices of a living religious community shaped by the symbolic world of scripture.

If anything ties together the various strands of newly developing approaches to biblical interpretation, it is a concern for the relationship of language, meaning, and power. More historically oriented literary and social methods increasingly examine the ways in which issues of conflict and access to power can be traced in the texts of the Hebrew Bible and the New Testament. Cultural hermeneutics, though not uninterested in historical reconstruction, also focuses on the ways in which access to the power to interpret the text and construe its meaning serves to empower those who have traditionally been marginalized. And postmodernism has attempted to underscore the ironies of all such interpretive strategies, since in its view a stable and definitive meaning always eludes the interpreter. Yet its very skepticism about any final and objective understanding is what opens up space for a reappropriation of traditional forms of interpretation that attempt to challenge the interpretive power of modernity itself.

THE GEOGRAPHY OF THE BIBLE

The geographical territory encompassed by the Bible (if one includes all identifiable places that are mentioned in it) includes most countries that border the Mediterranean Sea as well as those to its east. The majority of the narratives of the Hebrew Bible and the Apocrypha, as well as the Gospels in the New Testament, are set in that subregion of the Middle East known as the Levant and now governed by Lebanon, Syria, Jordan, Israel, and the Palestinian Authority. Egypt to the southwest, Asia Minor (modern Turkey) to the north, and Mesopotamia (largely modern Iraq) and Persia (Iran) to the northeast are also part of the biblical landscape.

In Mesopotamia—the Greek term for the region between the Euphrates and Tigris Rivers (see color Maps 6 and 14 at the end of this volume)—as in Egypt, urban civilization developed by the fourth millennium BCE in the river valleys that provided the essential water for a region where rainfall was at best seasonal and at worst, especially in the case of Egypt, insufficient for agriculture. But the regular summer flooding of the Nile Valley enabled the early and continuous existence of a remarkably long-lasting culture in Egypt, which because of its proximity to the Middle East was an important player in that region's history and the locale for several episodes in biblical narrative, most notably the Exodus. In Mesopotamia the inhabitants had harnessed the two rivers to provide, by means of an elaborate irrigation system, sufficient water for agriculture as well as for consumption. The successive imperial powers that originated in Mesopotamia were able to use this productive region as a base for expansion, especially to the west, over which they exercised control throughout most of the first millennium BCE, until the Hellenistic period.

Although surrounded by vast deserts, there is a narrow stretch of land where agriculture can flourish, which extends from the Nile Valley around to the Persian Gulf. The western part of this "fertile crescent," the Levant, has the same environment as much of the rest of the region adjacent to the Mediterranean, which today as for the last several millennia is characterized by almost ideal growing conditions for grapes and olives and for raising sheep and goats; grains and legumes and other fruits can also be grown in much of the region. Its climate is moderate, without excessively high or low temperatures for the most part, and with abundant rainfall that occurs mainly during the winter months. Jerusalem, for example, receives on average about 22 in (550 mm) of rain annually, most of it falling between November and February, with January being the rainiest month. Higher elevations to the north receive still more rainfall, and the southern and easternmost regions considerably less.

Within the Levant itself, the primary focus of biblical narratives, there is a wide variety of environments, the result of the geological substructure of the region, which presents dramatic changes in a relatively small area. Moving from west to east, the Mediterranean coast is occupied by a coastal plain that is about 15 mi (25 km) wide in the south but narrows as one moves north. It is interrupted by Mount Carmel, which juts into it, and virtually disappears in northern Israel and Lebanon. The coast itself has several excellent harbors in the north, from which the Canaanites and their successors the Phoenicians conducted a flourishing maritime trade. Farther south the coast is relatively even, and there are few natural harbors. Phoenician influence eventually extended to such port cities as Acco, Dor, Joppa, and Ashkelon, and in the late first century Herod the Great constructed an impressive artificial harbor at Caesarea. Along the coastal plain was a major route used by traders and by armies of conquest between Egypt and Damascus. This route ran to the point where the coast narrows below Mount Carmel, from which passes led from the coastal plain to the Jezreel (Esdraelon) Valley; from there, several routes could be taken to the northeast.

Adjacent to the coastal plain in the south is an uplift of smaller, gentler hills called "the Shephelah" ("lowland"). As the natural western boundary of the kingdom of Judah in the Iron Age, and of other entities in the same region before and after, it was protected by such important cities as Lachish and Gezer. The Shephelah forms the foothills of the mountainous region immediately to its east. This is the "hill country" of the biblical writers, with higher elevations to the north. For example, Jerusalem, about 35 mi (55 km) east of the Mediterranean, is 2,500 ft (760 m) above sea level, and many mountains in northern Galilee have elevations of over 3,300 ft (1,000 m). The highest peak in the region is Mount Hermon, which at 9,200 ft (2,800 m) is snow-covered year-round. The hill country is the setting for many of the key locales in biblical narrative, including the relatively inaccessible sites of Jerusalem, the capital of the kingdom of Judah (later Judea), and Samaria, the capital of the Northern Kingdom of Israel and later of the province with the same name. This central mountainous ridge is bisected by the broad, fertile Jezreel Valley, the major route to the interior and hence the location of important ancient cities, including Jokneam, Megiddo, Taanach, Ibleam, and Jezreel. Mount Tabor rises from the floor of the Jezreel Valley in splendid isolation to an elevation of 1,929 ft (588 m) above sea level. The village of Nazareth, home of Jesus, is in the hills on the northern side of the valley.

To the north of the Jezreel Valley lies Galilee. Because of its abundant springs, Galilee was dotted by settlements from prehistoric times, but it plays little role in biblical narratives until the end of the first millennium BCE, when it is the setting both for some of the campaigns of the Maccabees and, in the early first century CE, of the ministry of Jesus in the Gospels.

Just east of this central mountainous region is the Rift Valley. This major depression in the earth's crust extends from southern Turkey into East Africa; in Israel and Jordan it is almost entirely below sea level. Included in it are the Huleh Basin in northern Galilee, 230 ft (70 m) above sea level, where the site of Hazor was a major fortified city from early in the second millennium BCE until its destruction by the Assyrians in 732 BCE. Some 12 mi (20 km) south of Lake Huleh is the Sea of Chinnereth, or the Sea of Galilee (also called the Sea of Tiberias), a large freshwater lake about 12 mi (20 km) long that fills the valley. It lies 210 m (700 ft) below sea level, and is fed by the Jordan River, which flows into it from the north. It is habitat to nearly two dozen species of fish, and the fishing industry has been an important part of the local economy since prehistoric times. Many of the events narrated in the Gospels are set in the many towns and cities near the lake; the region was a center of resistance against the Romans during the First Jewish Revolt of 66–73 CE.

The Jordan River continues its flow south from the Sea of Galilee 65 mi (105 km) to the Dead Sea. The valley itself is about 12 mi (20 km) wide and is entirely below sea level, with a semitropical climate that produces lush vegetation, even though because of its low elevation it receives relatively little rain. Important cities in the valley include Beth-shan (later Scythopolis) in the north and Jericho in the south. The valley was another important north-south route, especially during the Roman period, when Jews often avoided the district controlled by the Samaritans between Galilee and Judea.

The Dead Sea, lying 1,300 ft (400 m) below sea level, is the lowest point on the land mass of the earth. Because of evaporation due to high temperatures (a record 124°F [51°C] was measured here), the composition of the water is about 25 percent salt and other minerals, making organic life impossible and giving this lake its ancient name, "the salt sea" (Num 34.3,12; NRSV "Dead Sea"). The desolate region that surrounds it is the narrative setting for the legendary cities of Sodom and Gomorrah. On its western shore are Qumran, where the Dead Sea Scrolls were found, and Masada, a palace constructed by Herod that was the last Jewish outpost to be captured in the First Jewish Revolt.

East of the Rift Valley there is a rapid rise to the relatively level Transjordanian plateau to the east, with the elevation of modern Amman (ancient Rabbah, later Philadelphia) at ca. 2,700 ft (820 m) about average. This region also receives sufficient rainfall to sustain agriculture and, moreover, is watered by two tributaries of the Jordan, the Yarmuk and the Jabbok, and by the Arnon, which flows into the Dead Sea. The northern part of the plateau, biblical Bashan, was famous for its cattle and for its oak forests, and in the Hellenistic and Roman periods was the location of several of the cities of the Decapolis. Traversing the Transjordanian plateau from south to north is another major route, called in the Bible the "King's Highway" (Num 20.17), used throughout antiquity

as a conduit for the incense and spice trade from Arabia to Damascus. East of the plateau is a vast desert region, a continuation of the Arabian desert that extends northward to the Euphrates Valley, and thus limits the Fertile Crescent on both east and west. Apart from a few oases, especially Tadmor (later Palmyra) northeast of Damascus, this desert was mostly uninhabited in historic times.

South of the hill country of Judah lies the Negeb, a region of limited rainfall and hence marginal agriculture. The city of Beer-sheba is located in the extreme northern Negeb, just south of the Judean hill country. The Negeb merges into the Sinai peninsula, which is formed by the two northern arms of the Red Sea, separating the Sinai from the North African desert to its west and the Arabian desert to its east.

The small size of this region is out of proportion to its importance in ancient times and to the importance of the biblical texts which are set in it. West of the Jordan, the traditional limits of ancient Israel were Dan in the north and Beer-sheba in the south, separated by a distance of about 150 mi (240 km). Between these two cities, and between the Mediterranean and the Rift Valley, is a region with an area approximately the same as that of the state of Vermont. From another perspective, Jerusalem is about 35 mi (55 km) east of the Mediterranean and 16 mi (25 km) west of the Dead Sea. In the right conditions, both bodies of water are visible from Jerusalem's hills.

CULTURAL CONTEXTS
THE ANCIENT NEAR EAST AND ANCIENT ISRAEL TO THE MID-FIRST MILLENNIUM BCE

BEGINNINGS

By the time Israel appeared on the stage of the ancient Near East, civilization and the patterns of empires and of the larger shared culture of the Levant were already well established. Before the end of the fourth millennium BCE, full urbanization had developed in the great river valleys of Egypt and Mesopotamia. The development of sophisticated technology to exploit the flooding of the Nile and to channel the waters of the Euphrates and Tigris enabled the production of regular food supplies and led to regional hegemonies. In Egypt, centered in the Nile Valley and oriented according to the south-to-north

direction of the Nile's flow, this culminated in the unification of Upper (southern) and Lower (northern) Egypt at the beginning of the Early Dynastic Period toward the end of the fourth millennium. In southern Mesopotamia the kings of Sumer ruled that region from a succession of dominant city-states beginning at about the same time.

The stages that preceded urbanization are prehistoric in the sense that they antedate the development of writing. Archaeologists have been able to trace the slow, and often independent, progress from hunter-gatherer economies throughout the Near East to stable cultures that relied on domesticated crops and animals for their sustenance. Dependable supplies of food led to increases of population and eventually to competition for resources. These factors combined to necessitate specialization of tasks, centralized control, and record-keeping. For these purposes, writing was invented, again toward the end of the fourth millennium and, once introduced, was widely adopted (although using different systems) in Egypt and Mesopotamia. By 3000 BCE, then, written history may be said to have begun.

One result of more than two centuries of discovery, excavation, and decipherment of ancient texts is that a detailed chronology of the ancient Near East has been established. While there are occasional gaps in the sequence of rulers for Egypt and for the various Mesopotamian city-states, those sequences are relatively complete. For regions peripheral to the centers of power the historical record is more spotty, but still substantial. Allowing for minor scholarly disagreements, the chronology is secure and provides a framework for the history of the entire ancient Near East, including Israel. Although there remain some small groups of undeciphered texts, including a few in what is apparently the Philistine language, and although much of cuneiform literature is still underground, it is unlikely that new discoveries will require substantial revision of our current understanding of the essential chronology of the ancient Near East.

Nor is the knowledge of the historical record restricted to kings and princes. Hundreds of thousands of nonelite texts have been found. These are not great myths and royal inscriptions but mundane business and commercial records, which shed valuable light on the lives of ordinary men and women and have begun to make possible a reconstruction of the social world of the ancient Near East.

Ancient cultures were as intrigued as we are by beginnings, and they constructed elaborate myths to explain their own prehistory. The establishment of the natural and social orders is typically presented in these myths as the work of a deity, usually the principal god or goddess of the political entity in which they were written. Both Egyptian and Mesopotamian literatures have many such creation myths, features of which have parallels in biblical traditions. Like their more powerful neighbors to the southwest and northeast, the ancient Israelites had their own accounts of origins, some of which were ultimately collected and edited in the book of Genesis. The early chapters of Genesis deal with prehistory and are largely mythical. In these Israelite expressions of the origins of the world, of society, and of civilization, the principal agent is the god of Israel. And although intended as the prologue to a larger historical narrative, they are not his-

torical in any modern sense; that is, they do not accurately represent what the archaeological record shows to have taken place, whether in terms of chronology, or the origin of species, or a universal flood.

Egypt and Mesopotamia have their own complex histories during the third millennium, now relatively well known thanks to textual and archaeological data. In the Levant this is the period known as the Early Bronze Age, when northern Syria was largely in the orbit of Mesopotamia, and Egypt exercised direct control over southern Canaan. For complex reasons not fully understood, toward the end of the third millennium Egypt experienced some internal disruption, reflected in the decline of city-states in southern Canaan but not in Syria farther to the north. By 2000 BCE, however, centralized control had been reestablished, and the textual and artifactual evidence is abundant. Trade flourished, as is indicated by both the archaeological record and commercial and diplomatic correspondence among larger urban centers, and between them and Mesopotamia and Egypt. The Levant was spanned by a cultural continuum, with Syria and northern Canaan being more closely linked with Mesopotamia, and southern Canaan with Egypt. Canaan itself had a relatively homogeneous culture, and its inhabitants, especially in rural and village settings, went about their lives with relatively few changes despite the struggles of the urban centers with each other. From as far back as the end of the fourth millennium, and into the first, there appears to have been continuity of population, whose patterns of material culture develop rather than being replaced by successive waves of invaders, as earlier historical reconstructions suggested.

It is in this larger context that Israel placed its own beginnings, centered on the lives of four generations of ancestors, the families of Abraham and Sarah, of Isaac and Rebekah, and of Jacob and Leah, Rachel, Bilhah, and Zilpah, and their offspring.

THE HISTORICITY OF THE ANCESTRAL NARRATIVES IN GENESIS

In the biblical account of the origins of Israel, narratives concerning Israel's ancestors in Gen 12–50 follow the mythic material in chs 1–11. The chronology of the narratives themselves is set by the biblical writers in the early second millennium BCE, but there are no direct connections between the biblical traditions and nonbiblical sources. No person or event known from Egyptian, Mesopotamian, or other sources is even mentioned in the biblical narrative. At the relatively few points where the Bible does name rulers (as in Gen 14; 20.2; 26.8), none of them are found in any nonbiblical sources. Moreover, at many points in the narrative the Bible is tantalizingly vague. If the biblical writers had just named, for example, the pharaoh who took Sarah into his house (Gen 12.15), or the pharaoh in whose court Joseph rose to power (Gen 41), we would know when the biblical writers thought those events took place, and could correlate them with Egyptian chronology.

The biblical narratives themselves are the result of a lengthy and complicated process of formation, transmission, and editing (see "Introduction to the Pentateuch," p. 3). Although the reconstruction of that process is hypothetical, there is no doubt that the process itself has caused the inclusion of many anachronisms. These reflect the times when the transmission and editing took place rather than the times in which the narratives are presumably set.

As a result of these factors, not surprisingly, scholars are divided on the question of historicity, with proposed dates for the ancestors of Israel, if in fact they even existed, spanning the entire second millennium BCE. A cautious positive assessment would be at best a convergence of possibilities. Allowing for anachronisms, the data are not inconsistent with the Middle to Late Bronze Ages (ca. 2000–1200), with some clues pointing to earlier rather than later in that time span. These clues are admittedly indirect, and include the forms of personal names used and the identification of the god of the ancestors as El (see Ex 6.3), also known in texts from Ugarit in northwest Syria as the head of the Canaanite pantheon from Ugarit. The account of Joseph's elevation to a position of prominence in the Egyptian court is not incompatible with the rise to power of the Hyksos, the Fifteenth Dynasty rulers of Semitic origin who controlled much of Lower Egypt at the end of the Middle Bronze Age (ca. 1650–1550).

Yet most of the details of the lives of the ancestors of Israel, both as pastoral seminomads and as periodically migrating to Egypt, fit not only the mid-second millennium but other times as well. Biblical writings probably do preserve some authentic historical memories, but these have been so refracted by the processes of transmission and the idealization of the ancestors that it is impossible to designate any of the individuals mentioned in Genesis as historical or to establish anything resembling a precise chronology.

THE HISTORICITY OF THE EXODUS FROM EGYPT

As with the ancestral narratives in Genesis, there is no direct connection between biblical traditions and other ancient sources. Egyptian records contain no mention of the major individuals and events of the narrative in Ex 1–15: Moses, Aaron, the plagues, and the defeat of the Egyptian army at the sea are completely absent from the ex-

tensive documentation we have for ancient Egypt. Again, the biblical sources are frustratingly unspecific. Neither the pharaoh "who did not know Joseph" (Ex 1.8) nor the pharaoh of the Exodus itself (Ex 5–15) is named. The only precise detail in the narrative is the store cities named in Ex 1.11, but their precise location and the dates when they were founded and occupied are uncertain, and their inclusion could also be anachronistic. In addition, biblical chronology is both vague and inconsistent. Moreover, as with the ancestral narratives in Gen 12–50, the narrative has been shaped by centuries of transmission and redaction. Finally, although the importance of the Exodus is evident from the amount of space devoted to the generation of the Exodus (the books of Exodus through Deuteronomy), the narrative framework was supplemented by the attachment of large chunks of legal and ritual material from subsequent periods. Once again, then, it is hardly surprising that scholars have divergent views about the date and even the historicity of the Exodus and of its principal characters. And, again, we do best to speak of a convergence of probabilities based on indirect evidence.

The first fixed datum, one of great importance, is a victory stele of Pharaoh Merneptah (1213–1203). In it he claims to have defeated various enemies in Canaan, including the identifiable cities of Gezer, Yanoam, and Ashkelon, and in the same geographical region, a group identified as Israel. Whether the victory celebrated on the stele is as complete as claimed, it is clear that by the end of the thirteenth century BCE the Egyptians knew of the existence of a geopolitical entity called Israel in the land of Canaan. Thus, the Exodus, or some movement of Hebrews out of Egypt, and their entry into Canaan, where they formed at least part of the group that called itself Israel, must have occurred before that date.

The biblical narrative is composite, and when critically analyzed suggests that what the Bible presents as a single episode may in fact have been several, and that more than one group of "Hebrews" eventually moved from Egypt to Canaan, probably entering it at several different places. Most of the details of the account of the forced labor of the Hebrews and of the glimpses of the Egyptian court that we get in the narratives would fit almost any period in ancient Egyptian history.

A majority of modern scholars, but by no means all, date the central episode, associated with Moses, to the thirteenth century, during the reign of Rameses II (1279–1213). An earlier date, toward the beginning of the Late Bronze Age, would link the Exodus with the expulsion of the Hyksos Dynasties from Egypt in the mid-sixteenth century and better fits the chronology in the biblical text, which dates the Exodus to 480 years prior to the construction of the Solomonic Temple in the mid-tenth century (1 Kings 6.1). This correlation was first proposed by the first-century CE Jewish historian Josephus, and has many modern adherents. Among the arguments against it is the absence of any mention of Israel in the land of Canaan before the Merneptah inscription. This is especially true in the case of the Amarna Letters, which are diplomatic correspondence from the fourteenth century between the Egyptian court and the rulers of city-states in Canaan. Furthermore, the biblical accounts of the period after the entry into the land found in the books of Joshua and Judges (see further below) contain no hint of Egyptian presence in the land, although both archaeological and written sources indicate that it was significant throughout the Late Bronze Age. It thus seems more probable to most current scholars that the Exodus took place during the thirteenth century.

That some Exodus took place is a responsible inference, given the persistence of the Exodus tradition in the Bible and its presence in the earliest biblical poetry (notably Ex 15), and some smaller details, such as the Egyptian names of Moses, Aaron, and Phinehas. The event must have involved fewer people than the exaggerated biblical numbers (see Ex 12.37) indicate, and may have constituted little more than the escape of a relatively small group of Hebrews from forced labor in the eastern Nile delta, most likely in the thirteenth century BCE. Given the lack of historical data it is impossible to say more.

That group, whatever its size, interpreted its escape as the direct intervention of the deity Yahweh on its behalf, to be celebrated in hymns and magnified in importance as it was told and retold. When the group eventually entered Canaan, at a time when there was no centralized power to oppose it, it joined with others and eventually became the twelve-tribe confederation of Israel.

THE EARLY HISTORY OF ISRAEL IN THE LAND OF CANAAN

Perhaps no period in the history of Israel is more controversial than the first two centuries of the Iron Age. The beginning and end of this era are framed by two synchronisms: the mention of Israel in the Merneptah Stele in the late thirteenth century (see above), and the campaign of Pharaoh Shishak in the southern Levant in 925 (see below), an event documented both in Egyptian sources and in the Bible. During the intervening three centuries, according to the chronology accepted by the majority of scholars, Israel developed from a loose confederation of tribes into a relatively stable dynastic monarchy. But of the principal events and individuals that figure in biblical narratives, none occur in other sources. Once more, a historical reconstruction must be inferential.

One reconstruction of the beginning of this period that was dominant from the early to the mid-twentieth century is that of conquest. The book of Joshua describes how the large group of Israelites crossed the Jordan under the leadership of Joshua and, in a series of swift and relentless campaigns, defeated the kings of the major Canaanite cities and annihilated most of the indigenous population. This view seemed to be confirmed by the presence of destruction layers at key sites, all dated to the very end of the Late Bronze Age.

Reexcavation of many of those sites and more refined ceramic chronology, however, made it clear that some of the sites had not in fact been occupied at that time, and that the destructions were not all contemporaneous. Moreover, the opening chapters of the book of Judges presents a very different picture. While some Israelite tribes were apparently successful in defeating their Canaanite neighbors, many others coexisted alongside them. This is apparently confirmed even in the book of Joshua, where such Canaanite groups as the family of Rahab (Josh 6.25) and the Gibeonites (Josh 9) were incorporated into Israel. Thus the conquest model has largely been abandoned by scholars, but no other reconstruction has gained general acceptance.

One plausible scenario is to combine elements of various models to suggest that Israel as we know it emerged in the land of Canaan and was made up of diverse groups. One of these was the Exodus group, whose allegiance to the god who had brought them out of Egypt, Yahweh, would become the central religious tenet of the confederation. They were joined by others, some who were apparently their kin who had never gone down to Egypt, and some who may have been Canaanites disaffected from the centers of power. These disparate elements united in a confederation or league, whose primary principles of sole worship of Yahweh and mutual support were expressed in a social compact or covenant. The elements are called tribes, and they are associated with specific subregions in the land. While the number of twelve tribes is constant, both the names of the tribes and the territories with which they were associated shifted in response to historical vicissitudes. The religious symbol of the confederation was a movable shrine, the ark of the covenant, which seems to have been based at different tribal centers at different times. The confederation was decentralized, with no overarching authority, and the tribes were relatively independent. In time of crisis, however, tribes were expected to come to the assistance of a beleaguered member, as in the very ancient poem in Judg 5, or to punish one of their own for breach of the compact, as in the account of the Benjaminite war in Judg 19–21. In situations like these a volunteer militia was mustered.

This reconstruction takes into account a variety of biblical data that are embedded in a later historical work, the Deuteronomistic History (see "Introduction to the Historical Books," p. 313). It also incorporates recent archaeological evidence, including both significant elements of cultural continuity between the Late Bronze Age and the Iron Age, and the proliferation of small rural settlements in the hill country both west and east of the Jordan. Not all of these settlements would have been Israelite, nor would tribal territory necessarily entail complete control. Several important urban centers remained outside the confederation, and Israel did not achieve total control of the promised land until the end of the eleventh century at the earliest.

At the beginning of the Iron Age (ca. 1200 BCE), shortly after the likely date for the Exodus, another group had arrived in Canaan. These were the Philistines, one component of the "Sea Peoples" well documented in Egyptian sources and in the archaeological record. Of Aegean origin, they had repeatedly failed in their attempts to invade Egypt, and one or more of these Sea Peoples, including the Philistines, settled in Canaan. According to the biblical account, they formed a pentapolis in the five cities of Gaza, Ashkelon, Ashdod, Gath, and Ekron, and the four of these cities that have been securely identified (Gath is the exception) show a remarkably homogenous material culture at this time.

The broad outline of the biblical account, in Judg 13–16 (the Samson stories) and in 1 and 2 Samuel (the stories of Samuel, Saul, and David), and the archaeological record are in considerable agreement. The Philistines had a superior technology, especially in metallurgy (see 1 Sam 13.20) and military hardware, and a professional standing army. By the mid-eleventh century they had considerably expanded their territory to the north and east, and their presence is evident at important centers beyond it, including Beth-shan in the Jordan Valley, and at military outposts in the heart of Judah, the dominant southern tribe, and in the north as well. The Philistines and the Israelites were thus on a collision course, both vying for control of the same region, and Israel's survival was at stake.

THE UNITED MONARCHY (CA. 1020–928 BCE)

The emergence of Israel as a nation-state is part of a larger pattern of the development of regional geopolitical and ethnic entities throughout the region, such as those of the Edomites, Moabites, and Ammonites in Transjordan, the Arameans in Damascus and other centers in central and northern Syria, and the Phoenicians in Tyre. For this development there is both archaeological and scattered written evidence. In the case of Israel, the major source is the Bible itself, especially the narrative of the Deuteronomistic Historians in 1 and 2 Samuel and 1 Kings

1–11. Judging from these sources, at least in part because of the Philistine threat, toward the end of the eleventh century Israel profoundly changed its form of government from a loose confederation of tribes to a monarchy, according to the terminology of the biblical writers. The first ruler, Saul, seems to have been more a military chief than a full-fledged king. And despite initial successes, he was unable to check the Philistine advance and died in a battle with them deep in Israel's territory in the Jezreel Valley. He was succeeded by a former commander in his army, David, who moved swiftly to contain the Philistines within their original territory and to unite Israel around himself and a newly chosen capital, Jerusalem.

Biblical historians describe additional military successes, which enabled David, and his son and successor Solomon, to subject kingdoms adjacent to Israel to vassal status, including the Edomites, the Moabites, and the Ammonites in Transjordan and the Arameans in Damascus. Whether the extent of the territory controlled by David and Solomon is as large as biblical sources suggest is questionable. Clearly the biblical historians have magnified the period of the United Monarchy, the reigns of David and Solomon, viewing them in many respects as an ideal age, made possible by divine grant. Underlying the sometimes hyperbolic biblical accounts, however, is authentic historical memory of increasing centralized control and concomitant administrative complexity, a picture indirectly confirmed by the archaeological record. When textual and archaeological data are added to the synchronisms between the Israelite monarchy and those of its neighbors, beginning in the tenth century, there is little doubt that the outlines of the biblical narrative are essentially correct.

The most important of these synchronisms comes just after the death of Solomon. The Egyptian pharaoh Shishak (Sheshonq I) undertook a campaign in Western Asia in 925, a date based on established Egyptian chronology. Mentioned in 1 Kings 14.25–26 (cf. 2 Chr 12.2–9), this campaign is further documented in Egyptian sources and is confirmed by destruction layers at key cities in Israel. This synchronism is the basis for the chronology of the first three kings of Israel, Saul (ca. 1025–1005), David (1005–965), and Solomon (968–928, allowing for a coregency with David at the beginning of his reign).

To be sure, the biblical account of the reigns of these three kings, found in 1 and 2 Samuel and 1 Kings 1–11, is shaped by theological concerns and also displays a pervading interest in the characters of the narrative—the tragically inadequate Saul, the heroic David, the ambitious but flawed Solomon—and in the intrigues of the royal court. But it is also significantly different from narratives about earlier periods in Israel's history. Divine intervention is minimal, with most events taking place largely on the human plane. Moreover, a careful reading of the biblical text discloses archival and other details that can be correlated with the archaeological record and are consistent with the framework of events presupposed by the narrative. Thus, the skepticism of some modern historians, who argue that the biblical accounts of the United Monarchy are fictional retroversions from a later time, seems unwarranted.

David also seems to have initiated the transformation of the monarchy into a dynastic kingship, which, consistent with other Near Eastern models, was promulgated as the result of divine choice. With the establishment of the monarchy came social and religious innovation. The older structures of the decentralized premonarchic confederation were now coopted by royal institutions. The ark of the covenant was enshrined in the Temple in Jerusalem built by Solomon, providing in effect divine sanction for the monarchy. Priests became royal appointees, and there was a growing movement toward centralization of worship in the capital. Yet this centralized administration formed a kind of overlay, a veneer, on the social systems of the nation as a whole. Individuals still identified themselves as members of a family, clan, and tribe, and disputes between them were usually settled at the local level. Apart from the requirement of paying taxes and providing personnel for royal projects and for the army, life in the villages probably proceeded much as it had for centuries.

The establishment of the monarchy, however, had entailed the formation of an elite, wealthy class. Life in the capital of Jerusalem and, after the split of the kingdom into two, in the northern capital of Samaria as well, was characterized by conspicuous consumption. This is evident in the accounts of Solomon's court (1 Kings 4.22–28; 10.14–22), and in the description of the Temple and royal palace complex he constructed (1 Kings 6–7). That the extravagances documented in these accounts are not entirely an exaggeration is evident from archaeological data at Samaria and at royal cities such as Megiddo, Hazor, Gezer, and Dan. With the concentration of political power in the hands of a ruling aristocracy came abuse. One of the constants of the biblical traditions is opposition to the exploitation of the poorer classes. This opposition was frequently expressed in prophetic rebukes of the aristocracy, as in the legendary traditions concerning Elijah (2 Kings 20), and in the books of the prophets themselves. While their own relationship to the centers of power was not always antagonistic, prophets such as Amos, Isaiah, and Micah in the eighth century and Jeremiah in the late seventh to early sixth centuries were harsh in their denunciation of social injustice. In a

sense they were conservatives, even reactionaries, insisting that the older premonarchic tradition of covenant was still binding, a tradition that commanded not only exclusive worship of Yahweh but also fair treatment of every Israelite.

THE DIVIDED MONARCHIES (CA. 928 TO THE LATE SEVENTH CENTURY BCE)

The union of north and south had been fragile, even during the United Monarchy, and it disintegrated at Solomon's death. The reason implied in 1 Kings 12 is the northerners' anger at the cost of the extravagances of the capital, and this must have been part of the motivation. Solomon's son and successor Rehoboam was unable to gain the allegiance of the ten northern tribes, who seceded and formed a separate kingdom. This inaugurates the period of the Divided Monarchy, the two kingdoms of Israel in the north and Judah in the south. The dynasty that David had established remained in power in Judah for nearly four centuries, while Israel was ruled by a succession of royal families, many of whose rulers came to power in military coups. The parts were less than their sum had been, and the two kingdoms had mixed relations, sometimes friendly, sometimes hostile. Neither was able to control effectively the regions that bordered them, and the Davidic empire, such as it was, ceased to exist.

Changes on the larger international scene would increasingly affect these two kingdoms. Pressure from a revived Egypt is already evident in the above-mentioned campaign of Shishak to the north in 925. Meanwhile, in northern Mesopotamia, the kingdom of Assyria had consolidated its control over Babylon in the south and adjacent regions to the north and east, and by the ninth century was poised to expand into the Levant. At this point the fairly complete Assyrian annals enable the construction of a relatively exact chronology and provide numerous synchronisms with biblical texts. Beginning with Ahab, king of Israel in the mid-ninth century, many of the rulers of both Israel and Judah are mentioned in Assyrian sources, an indication of the growing Assyrian interest in the region and a coincidence of ominous significance.

The Assyrians were establishing an empire, a process that reached its zenith with the Assyrian king Esarhaddon's subjugation of Egypt in 671. They accomplished this by virtue of a technologically sophisticated army, which in relatively rapid advance overwhelmed the smaller kingdoms to their west, usually incorporating their territories into the empire as provinces and deporting the elite of their populations to other regions. By the late eighth century this subjugation was virtually complete. The Syrian kingdoms had been taken, including that of the Arameans in Damascus in 732. In 722 Samaria fell, its ruling class was exiled to Assyria, and the Northern Kingdom of Israel became an Assyrian province. Judah's territory was curtailed and, in part because of the remote location of Jerusalem, was allowed to exist in vassal status. Toward the end of the eighth century King Hezekiah attempted to reassert Judean independence, but this was ruthlessly quashed by the Assyrian king Sennacherib in a campaign (701) which is well documented in both biblical and Assyrian sources. Jerusalem avoided destruction only by payment of a heavy tribute, and the Davidic dynasty survived.

Beginning with Amos and Hosea in the mid-eighth century, the prophets, and the later authors of the Deuteronomistic History (Joshua–2 Kings) interpreted these events as a deserved punishment inflicted by God on his rebellious people. For them, the repeated experiences of attack, siege, and exile were ultimately caused not by the inexorable progress of the Assyrian armies but by divine agency, imposing the fulfillment of the curses attached to the covenant made by God with Israel on Mount Sinai.

THE END OF THE KINGDOM OF JUDAH (LATE SEVENTH TO EARLY SIXTH CENTURIES BCE)

By the late seventh century the Assyrian Empire was overextended and thus unable to prevent first independence and eventually overthrow by a resurgent Babylonia to its south. The Babylonians captured the Assyrian capital of Nineveh in 612, and in effect took over the Assyrian Empire. In the initial years, Egypt and Judah attempted to take advantage of the transfer of power by reasserting their independence. This was the time of the reign of the Judean king Josiah (640–609), whom biblical sources compare to David and whose accomplishments are magnified like those of his illustrious predecessor. While it seems likely that Judah was able to reestablish control over some of the territory to the north and west that had been under direct Assyrian rule, its autonomy, such as it was, was short-lived. After Josiah's death in battle at Megiddo in 609, in a failed attempt to prevent the Egyptians from moving north to reinforce the tottering Assyrians, Judah was again reduced to the status of a vassal, first to Egypt, and then, by the end of the seventh century, to Babylon. Caught between two greater powers, the Judean kings Jehoiakim and Zedekiah successively allied themselves with Egypt, which proved to be the weaker partner. Under Nebuchadrezzar (also called Nebuchadnezzar) II, the Babylonians laid siege to Jerusalem in 597 and 586, in the second instance destroying the city, burning down the Temple, and ending the Davidic dynasty.

Despite the extravagant propaganda of the royal establishment, neither the Davidic dynasty nor its capital city were impregnable. Jerusalem was destroyed, its dynastic Temple burned, and its population decimated by death and exile. Autonomous control of the promised land became only a memory. And despite partial restoration later in the sixth century, exile in Babylon forever transformed the religion of Judah-Judaism. From this point on, a significant proportion of Jews would be living outside the promised land, without king, Temple, or priesthood.

CULTURAL CONTEXTS
THE PERSIAN AND HELLENISTIC PERIODS

THE PERSIAN PERIOD (539–333 BCE)

The Babylonian exile and the period of Persian domination that followed was a time of great transformation for Judean institutions, religious practices, and culture, but it was equally a time in which the fundamental continuity with preexilic traditions was reaffirmed and secured. When Nebuchadrezzar put down the rebellion of Judah in 586 BCE, he exiled to Babylonia a portion of the population, including the ruling class and the skilled artisans. Some, however, remained in Judah, where a subsistence economy was soon reestablished.

Although the system of regular sacrifices at the Temple was disrupted, the ruined Temple remained a focus for religious observances. The book of Lamentations may preserve liturgical poems used on days commemorating the destruction of Jerusalem and its Temple. Little is known about the circumstances of those who went into exile, although it appears that the exiles were settled in many local communities in Babylonia, where they were able to oversee their own internal and cultural affairs under the leadership of Jewish elders and prophets (see Ezek; Isa 40–55).

The conquest of Babylon by the Persian king Cyrus the Great in 539 BCE brought significant changes. In keeping with his policy of respecting the various deities worshiped throughout the empire, a decree by Cyrus in 538 (see Ezra 1.1–4; 6.1–5) authorized the rebuilding of the Temple in Jerusalem and the return of the Temple vessels captured by Nebuchadrezzar. In addition, Cyrus allowed any of the exiles who wished to return to Judah to do so. Within the exilic community in Babylon the anonymous prophet known as "Second Isaiah" (Isa 40–55) strongly supported Cyrus and urged the exiles to return to Judah. Although the historical sources are few and not always easy to interpret, it appears that only a small minority of the exiles and their descendants returned to Judah, most choosing to remain in Babylonia. This latter group became the nucleus of a large and highly significant Jewish Diaspora community (Jews of "the dispersion," that is, living outside the promised land), which strongly influenced the development of Judaism and Jewish culture during the following centuries.

Despite the decree of Cyrus, the Temple in Jerusalem was not rebuilt until 520–515 BCE. The reasons for the delay were various. Persian control over the western territories may actually have been tentative until after the Persians conquered Egypt in 525. The economy of Yehud (the name by which the Persian province of Judah was known) was weak, and there appears to have been friction between the population that had remained in the land and the small but powerful group who returned from exile with the authorization and financial backing of the Persian king. Conflicts with the neighboring territories of Samaria and Geshur and Ammon in Transjordan also complicated the situation. Within the Bible the prophetic books of Haggai and Zechariah and portions of Ezra 1–6 refer to this period, but these sources have to be read and interpreted critically, for they are neither consistent with one another nor easy to understand on their own terms. At least during the early part of Persian rule the governors of Judah appear to have been prominent Jews from the Diaspora community, one of whom, Zerubbabel, was actually a member of the Davidic royal family. The province of Yehud itself was very small, consisting of Jerusalem and the territory surrounding it within a radius of about 15–20 mi (24–32 km).

Once the Temple was rebuilt, it became the nucleus of the restored community, and consequently a focus of conflict (Isa 56–66; Mal). The high priestly family, which had also returned from the Diaspora, became very powerful, and at least on occasion was in conflict with the governor appointed by the Persian king. Although the details are often not clear, there appears to have been continuing conflict during the fifth century between those Jews whose ancestors had been in exile and those whose ancestors had remained in the land. Those who returned from the Diaspora styled themselves the "children of the exile" and referred rather contemptuously to the rest as "people of the land," as though their very status as Jews was in question. In fact, the question of the limits of the community was one of the most contentious issues of the period, reflected both in the controversy over mixed marriages between Jewish men and ethnically foreign women (Ezra 10; Neh 13) and also in conflicts within the Jewish community over who had the right to claim the traditional identity as descendants of "Abraham" and "Israel" (see Isa 63.16 and more generally "Third Isaiah," Isa 56–66). Although the conflicts between various contending groups in early Persian period Yehud are largely cast in religious terms, there is no question that they were also in part socioeconomic (see Neh 5). All of these conflicts and efforts toward redefinition of the community, however, took place within the reality of Persian imperial control. Thus it is not by accident that the two most prominent figures involved in various reforms of mid-fifth century Yehud, Ezra and Nehemiah, were Diaspora Jews of high standing, carrying out tasks that had been specifically authorized by the Persian kings.

Because this was a period of self-conscious reconstruction, it was also a time of immense literary activity, as traditional materials were collected, revised, and edited, and new works composed. Although much of the Pentateuch may have existed in various forms during the time of the monarchy, it was probably reworked during the Persian period into something close to its final form. Indeed, some scholars have suggested that this revision may have been undertaken under the sponsorship of the Persian government, reflecting Persia's interest in achieving stability throughout its empire by means of religious and legal reforms in the provinces. Although a history of Israel and Judah known as the Deuteronomistic History (Deut through 2 Kings) had been composed during the latter years of the monarchy and updated during the exile, a new version of that history, 1–2 Chronicles, was prepared during the Persian period (ca. 350 BCE). It clearly reflects the concerns of the postexilic community, focusing almost exclusively on the history of Judah and giving particular emphasis to the institution of the Temple. The books of Ezra and Nehemiah interpret events from the decree of Cyrus in 538 until the late fifth century.

In addition to the prophetic books composed at this time (Isa 56–66, Hag, Zech, Mal, and perhaps Joel), there is evidence that the texts of older prophets were also edited and reinterpreted. Psalmody had been an important element of worship at the First Temple but appears to have taken on an even more significant role in the Second Temple. Although the expansion and revision of the book of Psalms may have continued until well into the Hellenistic or even Roman period, an important shaping of the psalter, perhaps including its division into five "books," was part of Persian period activity. Wisdom writing, too, flourished during this time. The book of Job, parts of the book of Proverbs, and perhaps Ecclesiastes were likely composed then.

THE HELLENISTIC PERIOD (333–363 BCE)

The westward expansion of the Persian Empire into the area of Asia Minor had brought it into conflict with Greece, since many of the cities of Asia Minor that came under Persian control had been founded and populated by Greeks. Twice the Persians had even invaded the Greek mainland but were defeated on both occasions. Eventually, Philip of Macedon developed a plan to free the Greek cities of Asia Minor from Persian domination. Although he died before he could undertake the campaign, it was taken up by his son Alexander the Great in 334 BCE. Alexander, however, did not stop with the accomplishment of that initial goal. In 333 he continued down the Phoenician coast, subduing any city that resisted, conquered Egypt, then turned to the Persian heartland, defeating Darius III, the last Persian emperor, in 331. Alexander continued his conquest into the eastern reaches of the Persian Empire before returning in 324 to Babylon, which he apparently intended to establish as the capital of the empire he now controlled. He died in 323 before he could successfully organize his enormous territory. After Alexander's death, his generals fought for control of portions of the empire. By 301 an agreement gave Egypt to Ptolemy and Mesopotamia and Syria-Palestine to Seleucus. Ptolemy, however, occupied Palestine and southern Syria. Through a series of five wars extending over more than a hundred years, the Ptolemaic kings managed to hold onto their Palestinian territory, finally losing it to the Seleucids in 198 BCE.

Jerusalem had surrendered to Alexander in 333 and was relatively undisturbed by the events of his conquest. Samaria, too, surrendered but rebelled in 332 and was severely punished, its inhabitants killed or sold into slavery, and the city refounded as a Macedonian military colony. Documents belonging to a group of Samaritans who fled and were later tracked down and killed by Alexander's troops have been excavated from the Wadi Daliyeh in the Jordan Valley. In contrast to the relatively settled conditions following Alexander's conquest, however, the dispute between the Ptolemies and the Seleucids over control of Palestine had serious consequences for Jerusalem and Judea. Not only did the wars sometimes affect Judean territory, but the nation's leaders had to make difficult choices concerning which power to support. The conflict between pro-Ptolemaic and pro-Seleucid factions within the Judean community was a significant factor in internal politics during the third century BCE.

Although the high priest was the primary representative of the Judeans, the Ptolemaic system of government and taxation had significant effects on the power structure of the country. The Ptolemies considered their territories primarily as a source of revenue. Rather than collecting funds directly, they employed "tax farmers," often local persons who bought the right to collect taxes for a specified area. Their profit was the difference between the amount they raised and the amount they had pledged to the government. Some of these positions were quite lucrative. Moreover, the Ptolemies also engaged prominent landowners to keep the peace as the heads of locally organized military villages. The Jewish historian Josephus preserves a long account of the Tobiad family, which served the Ptolemaic government in both capacities. From his lively narrative one has a sense not only of the power and wealth such positions could afford but also of the dangers and conflict they often entailed.

Culturally, the most significant effect of Ptolemaic rule was the establishment of a large Jewish Diaspora community in Egypt, centered in the new city of Alexandria, founded by Alexander the Great. Jews had often migrated to Egypt during times of economic or political trouble (see Jer 42–44). In the fifth century a Jewish military colony in the service of the Persian army was established at Elephantine (near modern Aswan). They had their own temple, though they remained in correspondence with Jerusalem concerning various religious matters, including the proper celebration of Passover and assistance in securing Persian permission for the rebuilding of the Elephantine temple after it was destroyed by local Egyptians. The various Aramaic documents found there (letters, contracts, marriage documents, records of legal disputes, etc.) provide an important glimpse into the daily life of this Jewish community in Egypt. Among the papyri was a copy of the book of Ahikar, a legendary story about an official in the Assyrian court at the time of Sennacherib and Esarhaddon (late eighth to early seventh century). Although the story was not Jewish in origin, it became popular among the Jews. The book of Tobit in the Apocrypha makes reference to Ahikar, even calling him Tobit's nephew (Tob 1.21–22).

The Hellenistic-era Egyptian Diaspora, however, was much larger and more influential than the previous small communities of Jews living in Egypt. Its origins are not clear, but during the initial Ptolemaic conquest of Palestine, Ptolemy I apparently captured Jerusalem and took many prisoners back to Egypt, where they settled. Later many other Jews migrated there, presumably for economic reasons. The community continued to grow, both in numbers and in prosperity, until in the Roman period the Jewish population numbered in the hundreds of thousands, including many wealthy and prominent families.

By the middle of the third century BCE the largely Greek-speaking Jewish community in Egypt had translated the books of the Torah (Genesis–Deuteronomy) into Greek, and over the next century or so, the other books of the Hebrew Bible were also translated. A legendary account of this project is contained in the Letter of Aristeas. According to that narrative, the impetus for the project came from the king himself, Ptolemy II Philadelphus (285–246 BCE), who wished to have a copy for the library of Alexandria. Seventy-two Jewish translators were brought to Egypt from Jerusalem for the task; hence the translation came to be known as the Septuagint, from the Greek word for "seventy." Scholars largely reject this account as unhistorical and maintain that the translation was undertaken for the religious needs of a Jewish community that no longer understood Hebrew. (See the essays "The Canons of the Bible" and "Hebrew Bible: Texts and Versions" for more information about the Septuagint.)

In addition to the translation of the scriptures, the Jewish Diaspora in Egypt produced a rich and varied literature in Greek. One should not assume, however, that every Jewish writing in Greek originated in Alexandria, for during the Hellenistic period Greek became the most important international language. Educated Jews in Palestine and in the eastern Diaspora were nearly as likely to speak Greek as their counterparts in Egypt. Nevertheless, Alexandria remained unparalleled in the richness of its intellectual culture.

Throughout the Hellenistic world the increasing contact between different ethnic groups led to a new self-consciousness within communities about their own historical traditions and how these traditions related to those of other peoples. Thus historiographical writing, from the scholarly to the popular, became an important type of literary activity. In the late third century BCE an Alexandrian Jew named Demetrius investigated the chronologies of the biblical tradition, attempting to explain apparent contradictions and logical inconsistencies. A more entertaining work is Eupolemus's *Concerning the Kings in Judea*. A friend of Judas Maccabeus (see below), Eupolemus retold the biblical narrative with many embellishments and legendary details in an attempt to glorify Israel's traditions and accomplishments. In Eupolemus's history Moses appears as a culture-bringer, the inventor of the alphabet, which the Phoenicians and the Greeks later borrowed. Eupolemus particularly emphasizes the power and influence of the Israelite kingdom

under David and Solomon, as well as the splendor of the Solomonic Temple. Not only was the Temple decorated with gifts from the kings of Tyre and Egypt, but Solomon reciprocated, sending a golden pillar to the temple of Zeus in Tyre.

The tendency to make connections between one's own traditions and those of other ethnic groups and to claim priority in the arts of civilization is reflected in the highly legendary history written in the second century BCE by an anonymous Samaritan. He identifies Enoch with Greek Atlas and claims that Abraham was the inventor of astrology, which he taught to the Egyptians when he sojourned there. A similar tendency is evident in the work of Artapanus. In his history Moses becomes the inventor of the technologies basic to civilization. Moreover, this Moses serves as a general in the Egyptian army, organizes Egyptian religion, and comes to be treated virtually as a god by the Egyptians, who identify him with Hermes (the Greek equivalent of the Egyptian god Thoth). The interest of Egyptian Jews in the biblical figure of Joseph is reflected in the romance, *Joseph and Asenath*, which tells the story of Joseph's marriage to the Egyptian noblewoman Asenath. She is depicted as a model convert to Judaism, and the story depicts some of the complications that attended Jewish-Gentile relations in Hellenistic Egypt.

Jewish poetic works composed in Greek also reflect a blending of cultural traditions. The Hellenistic genre of poetry praising cities and countries is represented in the work of Theodotus and Philo the Epic Poet, who wrote poems about Shechem and Jerusalem, respectively. Even more ambitious was the work of Ezekiel the Tragedian, whose play *The Exodus* retold the account of Ex 1–15 in a style influenced by the Greek dramatists Aeschylus and Euripides.

Greek philosophy, too, left its imprint on Hellenistic Jewish culture. Already in the second century BCE an Alexandrian Jew named Aristobulus produced a philosophical commentary on the Torah in which he claimed that the law of Moses anticipated many of the fundamental tenets of Greek philosophy and that the Greek philosophers Pythagoras, Socrates, and Plato derived their ideas from the Jewish law. Written toward the end of the Hellenistic period, the Wisdom of Solomon continues the biblical tradition of wisdom books like Proverbs but incorporates many elements of Greek rhetoric, philosophy, and literary style.

Less is known about the Jews of the eastern Diaspora who remained under Seleucid control than about the Jews of Egypt and Palestine, but it appears that peoples of various ethnic groups had access to economic and political advancement within the Seleucid Empire.

Several writings from this time—Tobit, Dan 1–6, and Esther—suggest something of the outlook of Jews in the eastern Diaspora. Written originally in Hebrew or Aramaic and later enlarged when they were translated into Greek, these books are works of fiction, edifying entertainments that tell the stories of Jews who achieved high status in foreign courts, were threatened by jealous rivals, and yet succeeded in securing personal power and the good will of the king. Though the stories are all set in the pre-Hellenistic period (Tobit in the Assyrian Empire, Daniel in the Babylonian exile, and Esther in the Persian court), they were probably written during the Seleucid period. While they acknowledge that faithful Jews may be vulnerable because of their religion, on the whole these are optimistic stories with a positive view of the Gentile kings.

The eastern Diaspora was also the conduit for important religious developments that arose from the contact between Judaism and the religions of Babylon and Persia. This influence is most clearly seen in the development of apocalyptic literature. Parts of the book of *1 Enoch* composed in the third century BCE reflect astronomical lore and traditions about antediluvian sages that derive from Babylonian sources. Although it is more difficult to trace the path of influence in its earliest stages, the dualistic religious beliefs of Persian Zoroastrianism almost certainly contributed to the development of Jewish apocalyptic thought and to some of the ideas of the sectarians at Qumran.

The eventual triumph of the Seleucid kingdom over the Ptolemies in the fifth Syrian war (198 BCE) obviously had a greater significance for the Jews of Judea than for those of Egypt. The Seleucid ruler Antiochus III treated the Judeans generously in appreciation for the support he received from the pro-Seleucid faction, granting an allowance for the Temple and various tax concessions, as well as confirming the Judeans' right to live "according to the laws of their country." Although relations began well, the way the Seleucid Empire governed its territories set the stage for a terrible conflict. Unlike the Ptolemaic system of centralized government administered with the cooperation of local leaders, the Seleucid regime was more decentralized. It derived some unity, however, from a network of Greek cities established throughout the empire. These were not necessarily ethnically Greek but were cities that had received a charter to organize as a *polis*, the Greek form of city government. Cultural prestige and economic advantages often led the leadership of Near Eastern cities to request such a charter.

The events leading up to the conflict between Judea and the Seleucid king Antiochus IV Epiphanes (175–164 BCE) are complex and not fully understood. In part they involved a struggle for succession to the high priesthood and the attempts of various contenders to secure the support of the king by paying him large sums of money. The first of the contenders, Jason, also paid to have Jerusalem established as a Greek *polis*, Antioch at Jerusalem. Neither of these acts in itself seems to have aroused much opposition in Jerusalem. The conflict was not a cultural conflict between Judaism and Hellenism, for Palestinian Jews had already incorporated significant elements of Hellenistic culture, which they considered quite compatible with their religious identity.

The crisis was sparked by the attempt by another contender, Menelaus, to buy the office of high priest. When he promised the king more than he could pay, he attempted to raise the money by taking golden vessels from the Temple. At this, a riot broke out in Jerusalem. Subsequent fighting between the forces of Jason and Menelaus convinced Antiochus that Judea was in revolt, and he retook the city and plundered the Temple, either in 169 or 168. Sometime later there were further disturbances, and Antiochus sent Syrian troops, which remained garrisoned in Jerusalem. Whether the status of Jerusalem at this point was a *polis* or a military colony is uncertain, but in either case in 167 the Temple was reorganized to accommodate the religious needs of the Syrian troops. The Temple was dedicated to Zeus Olympius, the Greek name for the Syrian god Baal Shamem, and an altar established for sacrifice to him. Though Menelaus continued to preside as high priest, most Jews considered these actions to have profaned the Temple. In addition, the traditional practice of Judaism was suppressed by Antiochus, perhaps with the cooperation of Menelaus. Since religious persecution was virtually unknown in antiquity, it is difficult to know how Antiochus understood this repression and what he hoped to accomplish by it. Its actual result was to ignite the resistance known as the Maccabean revolt.

The Hasmoneans, Mattathias and his sons Judas Maccabeus, Jonathan, Simon, John, and Eleazar, were the leaders of the revolt. Although Judas managed to retake control of the Temple in 164 (its rededication being the occasion for the institution of the festival of Hanukkah), it was not until 142 that the last of the Seleucid army was expelled and actual independence was secured by Simon. From then until the Roman conquest of Judea in 63 BCE the small kingdom was ruled by the Hasmonean family, which in addition to being kings also assumed the office of high priest.

Religious and cultural life in Judea during the Seleucid and Hasmonean periods was rich and varied, with a remarkable quantity of literature produced in Hebrew, Aramaic, and to some extent in Greek. Sirach (Ecclesiasticus), Jesus Ben Sira's book of wisdom teachings, was probably composed in Hebrew about 180 BCE. Though largely traditional, it embodies several innovations: Ben Sira's identification of wisdom with the law of Moses, his praise of the contemporary high priest Simon II, and his own explicit claim to authorship. Ben Sira disapproved of apocalyptic speculation, but the crisis under Antiochus IV produced an upsurge in apocalyptic writings, not only Dan 7–12, but also *1 Enoch* 83–90 and *The Testament of Moses*. After the establishment of the Hasmonean monarchy, a supporter of the dynasty composed an account of the war in Hebrew (1 Maccabees), modeling it after the earlier books of Kings and Chronicles. An Egyptian Jewish writer, Jason of Cyrene, also wrote a history of the war in Greek (2 Maccabees), which was strongly influenced by forms of Hellenistic history writing.

Our knowledge of the literature of this time has been greatly increased by the discovery of the Dead Sea Scrolls at Qumran. Although this library was the property of a sectarian religious group related to the Essenes, it contained many Hebrew and Aramaic texts that were not sectarian compositions. Several of these scrolls contain noncanonical psalms, blessings, and other liturgical material. There are also many examples of what is called "the rewritten Bible," fairly free retellings of parts of the biblical story, embellished with new narrative episodes, prayers, and other elements (e.g., *Jubilees*, *The Genesis Apocryphon*, *The Apocryphon of Joshua*). Some texts elaborate on the apocalyptic elements of the books of Ezekiel and Daniel or place apocalyptic pronouncements in the mouths of other biblical figures, such as Levi, Qahat, and Amram. Several texts, often having to do with matters of religious law, purport to be discourses of Moses. Perhaps the most remarkable document is the Temple Scroll, which apparently takes the form of an address by God to Moses. Al-

though it incorporates material from the books of Exodus through Deuteronomy, it also contains much new material, including detailed instructions for building the Temple.

These documents and others pertaining to the Qumran sect itself help to clarify issues of religious controversy that shaped the period of Hasmonean rule. The Temple and the Torah were central institutions for Judaism, which made them focal points for conflict. The Qumran scrolls show that conflict over the proper calendar (i.e., a solar or lunar calendar) for the conduct of Temple sacrifices was a major issue dividing the Qumran Essenes from their rivals, the Pharisees. Though the Hasmoneans were not always on good terms with the Pharisees, they adopted the lunar calendar favored by them. Many other writings from Qumran also elaborate their understanding of disputed issues such as purity, marriage, and sabbath observance, concerning which they were at odds with the Pharisees. Although the Qumran community did not compose apocalypses (i.e., reports of revelatory visions), they were strongly influenced by apocalyptic ideas and considered themselves to be living in the last times, just before God would intervene to restore proper order to the world. They supported their ideas in part by writing commentaries (*pesharim*) on biblical texts, which they read as referring to themselves and their opponents.

In general, the Hellenistic period presents a picture of Judaism that is much more diverse than is often imagined. Not only did Jews live in a vast range of lands from Egypt to Parthia, they also creatively adapted many elements from the varied Hellenistic cultures of these lands. Nevertheless, important symbols and institutions, including the Temple in Jerusalem, the scriptures, and common religious practices based in the Torah, provided a sense of unity and common identity.

CULTURAL CONTEXTS
THE ROMAN PERIOD

The Roman conquest of Judea in 63 BCE was part of a centuries-long expansion of the power of Rome. The destruction of Carthage in North Africa in 146 BCE concluded the Punic Wars and secured the western Mediterranean, and the destruction of Corinth in the same year demonstrated Rome's control of Greece. In the next century, a series of conflicts with the successors of Alexander the Great in Asia and Egypt brought Roman rule to the entire eastern Mediterranean. The events that led to the replacement of the Roman republic by autocratic rule

culminated with the installation of Julius Caesar's nephew Octavian (later Augustus) as the first emperor in 27 BCE, and included the conquest of Egypt. The Mediterranean was now, as it has aptly been called, "a Roman lake."

Within the Roman Empire, especially in the east, client states were allowed considerable autonomy as long as their rulers maintained order and paid tribute to Rome. In Judea, Herod the Great, king of Judea from 37 to 4 BCE, succeeded on both counts, and with Roman sanction his control eventually extended to all of the region west of the Jordan and over much of Transjordan. His successors were not so adept, and direct Roman rule of Judea itself began in 6 CE. Thus began an uneasy détente between a series of Roman governors and the leaders of the Jewish community, based in the Temple in Jerusalem. This broke down during the First Jewish Revolt (66–73 CE), prompting the Roman destruction of Jerusalem in 70 CE. A brief resurgence of Jewish nationalism in the Second Jewish Revolt (132–135 CE) was easily crushed, and Jerusalem became Aelia Capitolina, a fully Hellenized city from which Jews were banned.

This is the historical setting for the life of Jesus and the development of earliest Christianity, one of several "Judaisms" that coexisted in Palestine before 70. For most of them the Temple was the primary place of worship and the locus of authority in religious and intracommunity issues. The priesthood in the Temple was hereditary, but from the time of Herod on the high priest was appointed by a ruler or governor. The high priest was head of a council, called the Sanhedrin, which had jurisdiction in religious and, to a limited extent, in civic matters. Other groups that comprised Judaism, with boundaries not always sharply drawn, included the Sadducees, members of the priesthood whose social status was aristocratic and whose views were conservative. The Pharisees were a lay movement concerned with observance of the Torah and hence with its interpretation, often through local houses of assembly; these "synagogues," however, did not supplant the Temple as the place of sacrifice and pilgrimage. The Pharisees were forerunners of the Rabbinic Judaism that developed after the Temple's destruction in 70. Outside of these groups, but still part of the broad spectrum of Judaism, were the Essenes, who had seceded from the Temple-based priesthood during the early Hasmonean period (mid-first century BCE), and the Samaritans, whose rejection of the Jerusalem Temple as the proper place for sacrificial worship had crystallized by the same time.

WITHIN THE ROMAN EMPIRE

Readers encounter two different cultural spaces within the New Testament: the village economy of agriculture and fishing in the Galilee, and the mobile economy of merchants and tradesmen in the urban centers of the empire. The first, the village economy, forms the context of Jesus' ministry and of the itinerant disciples who formulated the collections of sayings, stories, and miracles that underlie the Gospels. The second, the merchant economy, constitutes the world of Paul's missions as well as that of countless unknown disciples like those responsible for bringing the gospel message to Rome around 41 CE. This larger, urban world is that of the epistles and the

book of Acts. It is also evident in the expansions and reformulations of Mark and "Q" that are found in Matthew and Luke. Both the village agriculturists and the traveling merchants view from below a third cultural space: that of the wealthy, educated elite who are responsible for most of the architectural, artistic, literary, legal, philosophical, and religious remains that represent the Roman world and its influence within Western history and culture.

The predominance of this third, elite world in its cultural influence creates a problem for historians. We must be cautious in using the productions of an elite minority to describe the religious or social world of ordinary people in ancient societies. Anthropologists, for instance, make a distinction between the high tradition of sacred texts, temple rites, and the learned commentary upon them that centers upon the great urban cultural milieu, and the humbler, smaller traditions of religious belief, story, and practice that villagers hand on to one another. The story of the young Jesus remaining in the Temple to debate the teachers (Lk 2.41–52) exemplifies this distinction. For the Galilean peasants, religious devotion is focused on, and expressed in, the act of pilgrimage to Jerusalem for Passover. For the religious elite, it rather consists of learned interpretation of the sacred texts.

The thousands of papyri that have been found in the dry climate of Egypt have yielded new insights into the lives of ordinary people in ancient times. Scholars also study texts for nonelite forms of storytelling, popular belief, and everyday life; these aspects of experience are reflected in novels, in expansions of the biblical text in the Targums (Aramaic paraphrases of the Hebrew Bible), in Jewish and Christian apocryphal writings, and within the New Testament itself, as well as in the remains of material culture recovered by archaeologists.

Roman rule constituted the overarching political reality for both the village agricultural society in the Gospels and the urban context of Acts and the epistles. Its most immediate impact within Palestine was the accession of the Idumean Herod as king. Rome, not the Jewish populace, established the terms of Herodian rule. Herod's massive building projects—including the city of Caesarea, his own mausoleum at Herodion, and the Temple complex in Jerusalem—followed Greek and Roman models. Further consequences of Herod's rule included the severing of ties between tenant farmers and landholders who were no longer local patrons (see Mk 12.1–9). The pressure on the tax system to meet Roman demands and to finance Herod's building projects must have been considerable; this, and the possibilities for corruption and extortion inherent in the system itself, resulted in the cultural disdain reflected in the phrase "tax collector and sinner" (Lk 15.1–2; Mt 18.17 uses the alternative, equally dismissive, "tax collector and Gentile"). The presence of Roman soldiers might mean that goods and services were extorted at random from the local populace (Mt 5.41), but retired centurions might also be valuable local patrons (Lk 7.1–10). Physicians who were attached to the army units could also serve the populace on the side (Mk 5.26).

Most of Galilee seems to have been a prosperous region of small landholders and grazing herds of sheep and goats. Families in the villages where Jesus preached were largely self-sufficient. Craftsmen, such as Jesus himself, may have worked in the cities that were being built in the region, like Tiberias and Sepphoris. Even the rebellion against Rome, which zealots in Judea ignited in 66 CE, had a short life in Galilee. Within a year its populace had given up and returned to everyday life. Further evidence for the general prosperity of the region emerges when one turns to the occupation of Jesus' core disciples, Peter, James, and John (Mk 1.16–20). The fishing industry around the Sea of Galilee was a flourishing one, as the archaeological remains of extensive harbor installations indicate. Fishing involved families or partners who owned the boats working with hired hands. Fish was salted, dried, smoked, or pickled, and packed in jars for export. Thus Jesus and his disciples were neither naïve isolated pastoralists nor poor peasants, but were engaged in economic enterprises crucial to Galilee's place in the larger world.

For Jerusalem, a city whose chief economic asset was its Temple, the crowds of pilgrims at major feasts and the massive new complex of buildings were both an economic boon and a source of civic pride. The major cities in the eastern Mediterranean, such as Antioch, Ephesus, Philippi, Corinth, and Thessalonica, also enjoyed increased prosperity as a consequence of Roman rule and the growing numbers of travelers on land and sea. Without the possibility of such routine travel, the Christian mission could not have taken place. It was also furthered by the existence of Jewish communities in those cities, which provided an initial network (e.g., see Acts 13.5; 14.1). Many of the peoples incorporated into the Roman Empire, Jew and non-Jew alike, would have shared positive sentiments toward its authority (see Rom 13.1–7; 1 Pet 2.13–17).

On the other hand, civic discord, rioting, and full-scale rebellion against Roman rule remained real possibilities. Alexandria in Egypt had a large Jewish population that included highly educated, cultured, and wealthy individuals like the philosopher and exegete Philo of Alexandria (d. ca. 50 CE). Yet non-Jewish residents rioted in 41 CE when the Jewish elite sought the same citizenship rights as the citizen descendants of the Greek founders. Despite the appeals of a delegation of prominent Jewish Alexandrians, the emperor Claudius refused to grant their request, and threatened severe punishment if further civil discord occurred. Claudius also expelled members of Rome's Jewish community for "rioting at the name of Chrestus," presumably local discord occasioned by Christian missionaries (see Acts 18.1–2). Nero, in 65, executed some members of the new sect of undesirables, the Christians—including, according to tradition, Peter and Paul—as scapegoats for a fire that destroyed blocks of wooden tenements in Rome. He became the focus of anti-Roman sentiment, the demonic persecutor of faithful Christians in later generations (see Rev 13.1–18).

Despite the counsel of moderate voices and the opposition of Herod Agrippa, the Roman-appointed ruler of Galilee and northern Transjordan, and zealous leaders led Palestinian Jews to revolt against Rome in 66; by August of 70, Titus led Roman troops in burning and destroying the Temple. Christians living in Jerusalem appear to have fled the city prior to its fall. Jews living in the Diaspora did not support the rebellion; this did not keep the Romans from penalizing all Jews after the defeat. The Romans forced Jews who once paid a tax to support the Temple (see Mt 17.24–27) to pay instead an increased tax to the temple of Jupiter Capitolinus in Rome.

THE TYPICAL ROMAN CITY

A brief tour of Caesarea Maritima, the residence of the Roman governor of Judea (Acts 8.40; 9.30; 10.1,24; 11.11; 12.19–23; 18.22; 21.8; 23.23; 25.1–13), reveals the outline of an ancient city from the perspective of the rich. It was originally a small military settlement dating from the mid-third century BCE; Augustus gave it to Herod, who built a magnificent city of some 8,000 acres and a harbor to rival that of Alexandria. Two breakwaters created a sheltered harbor of 40 acres. An area with a temple, on a raised mound, dedicated to Rome and Augustus, faced the harbor at the south end of the forum that runs along the harborside. To the south of the city, a theater faced the sea, although the structure that has been unearthed is a later, rebuilt one. Among the discoveries there is a stone with an inscription referring to Pontius Pilate as prefect. There was also a large amphitheater similar to the Colosseum and a large racecourse (hippodrome).

An aqueduct supplied the city with water from springs on Mount Carmel, and an elaborate sewer system under the city drained away waste. Walkways were decorated with mosaics, and promenades were lined with columns. Herod spared no expense on his showcase; builders used imported marbles from Italy and Egypt, and pink granite from Aswan. There were warehouses facing the harbor to store the goods that passed through the city from extensive maritime trade, which reached as far as south Asia.

The residents of Palestine did not have to journey to Alexandria, Corinth, or Rome to see the world's riches on display for a wealthy elite.

Capernaum on the northern shore of the Sea of Galilee was the base for Jesus' preaching activities around Galilee. It lay on the road that connected Caesarea and Ptolemais (Acco) on the coast with Damascus in Syria. Even if they never visited the new city of Caesarea, the traffic along the highway between the coast and Damascus would have alerted Jesus and his contemporaries to the cultural realities of Greco-Roman cities. Two other city foundations within Galilee itself, Sepphoris and Tiberias, contributed to the growth of urbanization. Herod Antipas, tetrarch of Galilee and Perea from 4 BCE to 39 CE, resided at Sepphoris, a mere 4 mi (4 mi7 km) from Nazareth, until he moved to the newly built Tiberias on the lake in 19–20 CE. The term "tekton" used for Joseph and his sons (Mk 6.3; Mt 13.55) is usually translated "carpenter," but there is no reason to assume that Jesus and his family were restricted to the carpenter's shop of a village. They are just as likely to have been employed in the building that occurred in Sepphoris and Tiberias. Jesus' view of the rich could have been shaped by such experiences, and his followers probably included some connected to the Herodian court (see Lk 8.3).

STATUS AND SOCIAL CLASS IN THE CITY

The artisans, manual laborers, and merchants who lived in a typical Roman city had little time for the pleasures of the city's main streets. Long days in cramped and often dark shops would have been more typical of Paul's life as a tentmaker, for instance (Acts 18.3; 2 Cor 6.5; 11.27). This trade involved creating the awnings, made of a rough, thick fabric like sailcloth, which provided cover from the sun in theaters and the forum, and in front of the booths from which goods were sold. When crowds thronged the city for a festival, such as the biennial Isthmian games outside Corinth in honor of Poseidon (see Dio Chrysostom, *Discourses* 8.9), there would be no shortage of work for tentmakers.

The members of the wealthy elite and the educated scribes, Pharisees, or philosophers who were attached to them despised such lowly occupations, as well as those who collected the taxes. The tensions between rich and poor that were evident in Corinth (1 Cor 11.17–34) show how difficult it could be to cross social divisions of class and status. Those in whose homes the community assembled would have thought it their right to provide a feast for the others who were from their own group; as for the rest—artisans who had to work from dawn to dusk, as well as slave members of the community—they should be glad for the meager rations provided for them.

Similarly, the letter of James (2.1–13) excoriates Christians for showing deference to a rich man, giving him a comfortable seat and asking the poor to squat on the floor in the assembly. Although Paul's letters lack the sharp attacks on wealth found in the teaching of Jesus or in the letter of James, Paul does attack the privileges of social superiority to one's fellows when they surface in the Christian community.

Although most Christians did not belong to the local civic elite (1 Cor 1.26–30), a few individuals associated with the Corinthian church could claim such status. Acts 18.8 refers to Crispus (1 Cor 1.14) as *archisynagogos*, "head of the synagogue," a title that he may have been accorded as a benefactor, perhaps by contributing funds for a synagogue building. Women can appear as patronesses and *archisynagogoi* as well. Paul recommends Phoebe, a deaconess from the Corinthian port city Cenchrea (Rom 16.1–2). Such recommendations were a common letter form in the ancient world, in which patronage relationships were essential to success. Gaius (1 Cor 1.14) was wealthy enough to host all the Christians in Corinth at once (Rom 16.23).

Paul also conveys greetings from a certain Erastus, who is *oikonomos* ("city treasurer") of Corinth (Rom 16.23), the only convert who is known to have held a civic office. A pavement in Corinth from the area between the north market and the theater bears an inscription stating that Erastus paved the area at his own expense in return for the office of *aedile* (one of the four magistrates who governed the city, and particularly the public officers in charge of the streets). Since the name is an unusual one (no other instances are known), scholars think it possible that it was the same person mentioned by Paul. The term that Paul uses is not the Greek equivalent for *aedile*, so it may represent a lesser position in the municipal government that was an intermediate step on the way to becoming a magistrate.

Since Corinth had been refounded as a Roman colony under Julius Caesar less than a century before, and therefore would have had no long-entrenched ruling class, the opportunities offered for civic advancement may have encouraged competition. In other cities, the ranks of citizens—those enrolled who could hold various public offices—were strictly limited to a particular group of aristocratic families. Other residents, no matter how wealthy or influential, were excluded. Jews who sought to be included on the citizen rolls of Alexandria were rebuffed. Since Roman citizens and the Greek citizens of Alexandria were exempt from poll taxes levied by the Roman state, this status carried some economic advantage. Most Jews, who were laborers and artisans, would not have been eligible for enrollment in any case.

Whether Jewish families succeeded in joining the citizen elite elsewhere in the Diaspora is less clear. Luke has Paul claim to be a citizen of Tarsus (Acts 21.39), but this may be mistaken or imprecise.

LITERACY AND EDUCATION

Scholars remain divided over how to assess the extent of literacy in the Greco-Roman period. Portraits showing girls holding the stylus and wax tablet of the student suggest that among the elite some level of education extended to women, but on the evidence of documentary papyri, far fewer women than men were able to sign their names, and women who were able to write often pointed out that fact explicitly. The cities and larger villages of Egypt had teachers who drilled children in the rudiments of reading and writing Greek as well as the study of classic texts. Further education would require sending each young person, accompanied by a family slave, off to Alexandria in search of a suitable tutor.

Even among those who could read, the difficulty of deciphering texts in which all the letters were run together (the standard way in which ancient texts are written) often made it preferable to listen to a slave who was trained to read such texts aloud. We can deduce which texts were most in demand by studying the literary papyri. Texts of Homer are by far the most frequently found, with considerable numbers of texts by Demosthenes, Euripides, and Hesiod as well. Technical manuals on such subjects as medicine and astrology also show up in papyri fragments. Among the papyri that have been discovered are some that were orders to and from a book dealer in Oxyrhynchus: Outgoing orders seek dialogues of Plato and works of Homer, Menander, Euripides, and Aristophanes. The dealer acknowledges receipt of treatises on such edifying subjects as "On Training," "On Marriage," "On Freedom from Pain," "On the Uses of Parents," "On the Uses of Domestic Slaves," and Book 3 of a work by Poseidonius, "On Persuasion" (see P. Oxy. 1153; 2192). Apparently this dealer's clientele read for self-improvement and practical purposes as much as for entertainment and philosophical enlightenment.

The requirements of reading Torah may have made basic schooling even more necessary for Jewish boys, for whom the Bible would replace Homer as the primary text. Assimilated Jews in cities like Tarsus and Alexandria, however, saw to it that their sons received instruction in the classics as well. Philo defends the practice of sending Jewish students on to the more advanced instruction in arithmetic, geometry, music, and philosophy at the equivalent of a secondary school, the gymnasium (Special Laws 2.229–30). Educational centers like Alexandria and Tarsus had numerous schools of rhetoric to further

a young man's ability to take his place in public affairs by training him to speak fluently and write persuasively. Although Paul insists that eloquence ("wisdom") is not needed to communicate the truth of the gospel (1 Cor 1.17) and disclaims any use of such methods (1 Cor 2.4; 2 Cor 11.6), both his opponents (2 Cor 10.10) and contemporary scholars notice a high degree of rhetorical art in his letters. Even his refusal to engage in the sort of rhetorical discourse that would please his audience exhibits familiarity with such arts (see the "fool's speech," 2 Cor 11.1–12.13).

It is more difficult to assess the kind of education received by boys growing up in the Galilean towns and villages. In an oral society, persons can be highly skilled and even have extensive cultural knowledge, such as Jesus' knowledge of scripture, without being able to read or write. Luke 4.16 presumes that Jesus was literate, though Luke may be speaking from the perspective of an urban class that assumes literate habits as a normal part of education. The Jewish historian Josephus writing in the 90s CE makes no such assumption. Weekly Torah study can be accomplished orally: "He [Moses] appointed the Law to be most excellent and a necessary form of instructions, ordaining that it be heard not once or twice or several times, but that every week men should quit their other occupations and assemble to listen to the Law and obtain a thorough and accurate knowledge of it" (Ag. Ap. 2.175).

The first-century CE synagogue building at Gamla in the Golan lacks the elaborate religious features of later synagogues like that at Capernaum. It consists of a central nave created by two rows of columns and four levels of stone benches set in steps along the walls. Without the ritual bath attached to the complex, there would be nothing to distinguish it from an ordinary assembly hall. There is no evidence of a Torah shrine built into the walls, of a fixed elevated podium from which Torah was read, or of a seat of honor near the center; presumably Torah reading and instruction took place in the central area. The architectural space of the synagogue could serve a variety of community functions, from teaching and worship to legal proceedings and social gathering.

Another form of education required by Jesus and his disciples involves skills specific to their individual trades. Measuring, counting, and recording skills necessary to building or running a fishing business could have been taught on an apprentice basis. Tax collectors had to keep records of persons and amounts. Officials in the local Jewish community also had to collect the annual half-shekel paid to the Temple by all Jewish males (Ex 30.11–16; Mt 17.24–27). Such practical skills must have been taught, but little evidence of the process survives. Though not considered "education" by the literate, rhetorically trained elite of the Greco-Roman cities or by the literate scribes learned in Jewish Torah, such skills would have distinguished Jesus and his disciples from others in their villages.

RELIGION, ASTROLOGY, AND MAGIC

When Herod the Great built Caesarea Maritima, he placed the temple to Rome and Augustus in a prominent place. The city was dedicated to the emperor; its civic life would include festive sacrifices in the ruler's honor. Herod's renovations to the Jerusalem Temple and his expansions of its surroundings were planned to enhance the prestige of the city. Other cities also had famous shrines and festivals that drew visitors from abroad. Acts 19.21–40 tells a story of a riot at Ephesus that occurred when those who sold silver models of its famous temple to the goddess Artemis (Diana) claimed that the effectiveness of Paul's preaching had cut into their business.

Christianity did not deliver the death blow to the established civic worship that Luke seems to suggest. Most of his readers lived in cities, and they could easily witness the ongoing enthusiasm for sacrifices and festivals. What individual residents actually believed about the gods was not an issue; their participation, not their internal assent, was the key, and that participation (or lack of it) was observed by the authorities. To join in sacrifices honoring the Roman emperor, for example, demonstrated that the city and its populace were loyal subjects of the empire. Jews refused to participate in these events, and this refusal often brought on them accusations of "hatred of humanity." At Alexandria some argued that Jews could never be admitted to the citizen rolls because they did not worship the city's gods. Nevertheless, through long-tolerated practice, Jews were not often persecuted for this failure to participate in civic rituals. When Christians who were not of Jewish origin began to withdraw from such public activities, however, it caused comment, suspicion, and even persecution. A story like that of Paul's deeds in Ephesus, leading some to abandon the worship of Artemis, would have highlighted the superiority of Christ to one of Asia Minor's most famous religious shrines and might increase Christian resolve to remain separate. Not all Christians would choose persecution, however. Some clearly followed the lead of educated pagans, who often did not believe in the real existence of the gods, or in their myths. They would join public religious activities as required by their social status or civic office, as a social bond rather than as a religious profession. When faced with Christians who obstinately refused to participate, magistrates had no qualms about sentencing them to exile or death.

Astrologers, diviners, and magicians could be visited in the marketplace. Though such activities were frowned upon by those higher in the social scale, the large number of horoscopes, amulets, and magic spells recovered shows that these methods of making decisions, predicting the future, and bringing good luck (or guarding against bad) continued to be popular. Astrologers to the upper classes justified their practices with a philosophical veneer based on Stoic physical doctrines explaining the relations between earthly and heavenly bodies by means of an all-pervading "rational spirit." Christian insistence that the glorified and exalted Christ is above all the demonic powers and planetary forces (see Col 2.8–23; Eph 1.15–2.2; 6.12) did little to curb popular enthusiasm for these beliefs and practices. Biblical texts show up in Christian magical amulets. Jesus' exorcisms led to accusations that his powers were a consequence of an alliance with the leader of the demonic world (Mk 3.22–30), and Acts describes conflicts between Christian missionaries and local magicians (8.4–25; 13.4–12).

PHILOSOPHY AS HEALING THE SOUL

Unlike the monotheistic faith of Jews and Christians, which placed a high premium on hearing, interpreting, and acting on divine revelation preserved in sacred texts, Greco-Roman religions did not produce texts, legal and ethical codes, or theological doctrines. Those who sought teaching about the divine and its relationship to the observable cosmos, or moral guidance and advice about how to live a good life, turned to philosophy. Formal study of the philosophical systems that emerged from the schools of classical and Hellenistic Athens—especially Platonism, Stoicism, and Epicureanism—could only be pursued by the elite, who had the leisure time to devote to them. Luke's tale of Paul's visit to Athens (Acts 17.16–31) shows its first-century reputation as a destination for intellectuals, not the powerful center of commerce and art that it had been.

More ordinary citizens learned what they knew of philosophy from anthologies of moralistic tales, treatises on how to cope with various problems in life, public discourses offered by itinerant philosophical preachers, and the like. The philosopher-teacher saw himself as a physician for the soul. Under his guidance, people might be converted from the mindless, destructive pursuit of the passions, from fears about a future they could not control, even from superstitious belief in the gods. Some treatises, like Plutarch's "Advice on Marriage" (*Mor.* 12.138–46) even recommend that the young husband share his knowledge with his wife. Such knowledge will protect her against the passion for luxuries, foolish behavior, and talk common among women. If she knows something of Plato, Xenophon, and astronomy, she will not be taken in by the common practices of magic or witchcraft. Such treatises also presume that in the properly ordered household the husband governs the life of his wife, his children, and his slaves in accordance with a reason that has been schooled by philosophical instruction. Similar kinds of assumptions appear in sections of the New Testament often referred to as "household codes" (Col 3.18–4.1; Eph 5.21–6.9; 1 Pet 2.18–3.7). They also inform the descriptions of requirements for leadership (1 Tim 3.1-11), including those that exclude women from teaching or supervising men (1 Tim 2.9–15; 1 Cor 14.34–36).

Scholars have become particularly interested in a movement of rough-spoken, anti-establishment street preachers called Cynics, from the Greek word for dog, originally a derogatory name that referred to their unrefined public behavior. Claiming as their inspiration Socrates, the impoverished stone mason who went about Athens challenging all its citizens, representatives of this movement could be found in the public marketplaces. They rejected the comforts that could be offered by wealthy patrons and lived on as little as possible. They were known for sharp sayings intended to wound an opponent, not persuasive speeches to soothe one into agreement. If the harsh medicine worked, the hearer might convert to a philosophical way of life. If not, he might become angry, even murderously so, as had Socrates's opponents. Some scholars think that this movement provides the best ancient analogy for the itinerant mission of Jesus and his disciples, as depicted in the Gospels. Others have proposed that Paul's description of himself as the solicitous nurse or the father to his fledgling converts (1 Thess 2.1–12) is analogous to the Cynics' relationship to their own followers. Although these cultural models may not have dictated the content of early Christian preaching, they provide a context for understanding what missionaries like Paul were doing in the cities that they visited, and how they would have appeared to their first hearers.

TIMELINE

DATE	PERIOD	EGYPT
Ca. 3300–2000 BCE	EARLY BRONZE AGE	
3300–3100	Early Bronze I	Earliest forms of writing
3100–2700	Early Bronze II	Political unification; Early Dynastic period
2700–2300	Early Bronze III	Old Kingdom; Dynasties 3–5
2300–2000	Early Bronze IV	First Intermediate Period
Ca. 2000–1550 BCE	MIDDLE BRONZE AGE	
2000–1650	Middle Bronze I–II	Middle Kingdom; Dynasties 11–12
1650–1550	Middle Bronze III	Second Intermediate/ Hyksos Period
Ca. 1550–1200 BCE	LATE BRONZE AGE	New Kingdom; Dynasties 18–19: Thutmose III (1479–1425), Akenhaten (1352–1336), Seti I (1294–1279), Rameses II (1279–1213), Merneptah (1213–1203); Sea Peoples (groups including Philistines) invasions begin
Ca. 1200–586 BCE	IRON AGE	
Ca. 1200–1025	Iron I	Rameses III (1184–1153)[1]
Ca. 1025–586	Iron II	
Ca. 1025–928	Iron IIA	
Ca. 928–722	Iron IIB	Shishak I invades Palestine (925)

1. For a more complete list of rulers, see "Chronological Table of Rulers," pp. 2258–61.

SYRIA-PALESTINE		MESOPOTAMIA, ASIA MINOR
		Earliest forms of writing; Full urbanization; Sumerian culture develops
In Egyptian sphere		High point of Sumerian culture
Flourishing city-states		Sargon of Akkad; Naram-Sin of Akkad; Gudea of Lagash
Decline/abandonment of city-states		Third Dynasty of Ur
Revival of urbanism; Invention of alphabet		Amorite kingdoms: Shamshi-Adad of Assyria (ca. 1813–1781); Hammurapi of Babylon (ca. 1792–1750); Rise of Hittites
In Egyptian sphere; Rise of Mitanni in north; Uqarit flourishes;		
Exodus of the Hebrews from Egypt;		Hittites challenge Egypt for control of Syria;
Collapse of city-states		Hittite empire collapses; Trojan War
Israel emerges in Canaan; Philistines settle on SW coast; Small city-states develop in Phoenicia, Syria, Transjordan		Resurgence of Assyria: Tiglath-pileser I (1114–1076)
United Monarchy in Israel: Saul (1025–1005); David (1005–965); Solomon (968–928)		
Divided Monarchy:		
JUDAH:	ISRAEL:	
Rehoboam (928–911)	Jeroboam I (928–907)	Rise of Neo-Assyrian Empire
	Omri (882–871); Capital at Samaria	Shalmaneser III (858–824);
	Ahab (873–852)	Battle of Qarqar (853)
Jehoshaphat (867–846)	Prophet Elijah (mid-ninth century)	
	Prophet Elisha (mid- to late ninth century)	
Athaliah (842–836)	Jehu (842–814)	
Jehoash (836–798)	Jehoash (800–788)	Adad-nirari III (811–783)
	Jeroboam II (788–747)	
	Prophet Amos (mid-eighth century)	
	Prophet Hosea (mid-eighth century)	Tiglath-pileser III (745–727); Assyrian conquest of the Levant
Ahaz (743/735–727/715)	Hoshea (732–722)	Shalmaneser V (727–722)
		Samaria captured (722)

DATE	PERIOD	EGYPT
Ca. 722–586	Iron IIC	
		Egypt conquered by Assyria (671)
		Psammetichus I (664–610)
		Neco II (610–595)
Ca. 586–539	NEO-BABYLONIAN	

		GREECE AND ROME
539–333	PERSIAN	
		Greeks repel Persian invasions
		Peloponnesian War (431–404)
333–63	HELLENISTIC	Alexander the Great (336–323); Defeats Persians at Issus (332); Occupies the Levant and Egypt
		Rome gains control over Greece (ca. 188–146);
		Sack of Carthage and Corinth (146)
63 BCE–330 CE	ROMAN	Julius Caesar named dictator (49); assassinated (44)
		Octavian (Augustus) defeats Antony at Actium (31); (Emperor 27 BCE–14 CE)
		Tiberius (14–37 CE)
		Gaius (Caligula) (37–41)
		Claudius (41–54)
		Nero (54–68)
		Vespasian (69–79)
		Titus (79–81)
		Domitian (81–96)
		Nerva (96–98)
		Trajan (98–117)
		Hadrian (117–138)

SYRIA-PALESTINE	MESOPOTAMIA
JUDAH:	Sargon II (722–705)
Prophet Isaiah (late eighth to early seventh centuries)	Sennacherib (705–681); Attack on Judah and
Prophet Micah (late eighth century)	seige of Jerusalem (701)
Hezekiah (727/715–698/687)	Esar-haddon (681–669)
Manasseh (698/687–642)	Ashurbanipal (669–627)
Josiah (639–609)	
Prophet Zephaniah (late seventh century)	
Prophet Jeremiah (late seventh to early sixth centuries)	Rise of Babylon
Jehoahaz (609)	Assyrian capital of Nineveh captured (612)
Jehoiakim (608–598)	
Jehoiachin (597)	Nebuchadrezzar II (604–562) of Babylon
Prophet Ezekiel (early sixth century)	
Zedekiah (597–586); Capture of Jerusalem (586)	
	Nabonidus (556–539)

EASTERN AND MEDITERRANEAN	
	Cyrus II (the Great) (559–530);
	Capture of Babylon
Some exiles return from Babylon (538)	Cambyses (530–522); Capture of Egypt (525)
Second Temple built (520–515)	Darius I (522–486)
Prophet Haggai (520); Prophet Zechariah (520–518)	Xerxes I (486–465)
Nehemiah governor of Judah (ca. 445–430)	Artaxerxes I (465–424)
Mission of Ezra the scribe (mid-fifth [or early fourth] century)	Artaxerxes II (405–359)

Seleucus I (312/311–281) controls Syria and Mesopotamia
Ptolemy I (323–282) controls Egypt, Palestine, Phoenicia
Antiochus III (223–187) gains control of southern Syria,
Phoenicia, and Judea from Ptolemy IV (202–198)
Ben Sira (Sirach) (early second century)
Antiochus IV Epiphanes (175–164)
Revolt of the Maccabees (167–164)

HASMONEAN RULE OF JUDEA (165–37):
John Hyrcanus (135–104); Alexander Janneus (103–76);
Salome Alexandra (76–67)

Pompey conquers the Levant (66–62); Enters Jerusalem (63)
Herod the Great king of Judea (37–4);
Rebuilds Second Temple
(Herod) Antipas (4 BCE–39 CE)
Life of Jesus of Nazareth (ca. 4 BCE–30 CE)
Pontius Pilate governor of Judea (26–36)
(Herod) Agrippa I (39–44)
Missionary activity of Paul (mid-first century)
(Herod) Agrippa II (53–93)
First Jewish Revolt in Judea against Rome (66–73); Jerusalem is
captured (70)
Jewish revolts in Egypt, Libya, Cyprus (115–118)
Second Jewish Revolt in Judea against Rome (132–135)

CHRONOLOGICAL TABLE OF RULERS

DATE	EGYPT	ASSYRIA	BABYLONIA
1300 BCE	DYNASTY 19 (1295–1186): Seti I (1294–1279) Rameses II (1279–1213) Merneptah (1213–1203)		
1200	DYNASTY 20 (1186–1069)		
		Tiglath-pileser I (1114–1076)	
	DYNASTY 21 (1069–945)		
1000	DYNASTIES 22–24 (945–715): Shoshenq I (**Shishak**) (945–924)		
		Shalmaneser III (858–824)	
		Shamshi-Adad V (824–811)	
	DYNASTY 25 (780–656):		
800		Adad-nirari III (811–783)	
		Shalmaneser IV (783–773)	
		Ashur-dan III (773–755) Ashur-nirari V (755–745)	
		Tiglath-pileser III (**Pul**) (745– 727) **Shalmaneser** V (727–722) **Sargon** II (722–705)	Marduk-apal-iddina II (**Merodach-baladan**) (721–710, 703)
700		**Sennacherib** (705–681)	
	Taharqa (**Tirhakah**) (690–664)	**Esar-haddon** (681–669) Ashurbanipal (669–627)	
	DYNASTY 26 (664–525):	Ashur-etil-ilani Sin-shum-lishir } (627–612) Sin-shar-ishkun	Nabo-polassar (625–605)
	Psammetichus I (664–610) **Neco** II (610–595) Psammetichus II (595–589) Apries (**Hophra**) (589–570) Amasis II (570–526) Psammetichus III (526–525)	Ashur-uballit II (612–609)	**Nebuchadrezzar** II (**Nebuchadnezzar**) (605–562) Amel-Marduk (**Evil- merodach**) (562–560) Neriglissar (560–556) Labashi-Marduk (556) **Nabonidus** (556–539) **Belshazzar** (coregent 553–543)
400			
325 BCE			

Note: Names in boldface occur in the Bible. Overlapping dates indicate coregencies. Date ranges are reigns, not life spans.
1. The data are inconsistent for the dates of the reigns of Ahaz, Hezekiah, and Manasseh.

PERSIA	ISRAEL

UNITED MONARCHY:
Saul (1025–1005); **David** (1005–965);
Solomon (Yedidiah) (968–928)

DIVIDED MONARCHY:

JUDAH:	ISRAEL:
Rehoboam (928–911)	**Jeroboam** I (928–907)
Abijam (Abijah) (911–908)	**Nadab** (907–906)
Asa (908–867)	**Baasha** (906–883)
Jehoshaphat (870–846)	**Elah** (883–882); **Zimri** (882)
	Omri (882–871)
	Ahab (873–852)
Jehoram (Joram) (851–843)	**Ahaziah** (852–851)
Ahaziah (Jehoahaz) (843–842)	**Jehoram** (Joram) (851–842)
Athaliah (842–836)	**Jehu** (842–814)
Jehoash (Joash) (836–798)	**Jehoahaz** (817–800)
Amaziah (798–769)	**Jehoash** (Joash) (800–784)
Azariah (Uzziah) (785–733)	**Jeroboam** II (788–747)
	Zechariah (747); **Shallum** (747)
	Menahem (747–737)
Jotham (759–743)	**Pekahiah** (737–735)
Ahaz (743/735–727/715)[1]	**Pekah** (735–732)
	Hoshea (732–722)
Hezekiah (727/715–698/687)[1]	

Manasseh (698/687–642)1
Amon (641–640)
Josiah (640–609)
Jehoahaz (Shallum) (609)
Jehoiakim (Eliakim) (608–598)
Jehoiachin (Jeconiah, etc.) (597)
Zedekiah (Mattaniah) (597–586)

Cyrus II (559–530)
Cambyses (530–522)
Darius I (522–486)
Xerxes I (**Ahasuerus**) (486–465)
Artaxerxes I (465–424)
Darius II (423–405)
Artaxerxes II (405–359)
Artaxerxes III (359–338)
Artaxerxes IV (338–336)
Darius III (336–330)

DATE	EGYPT		SYRIA
		HELLENISTIC PERIOD	Alexander (the Great) (336–323)
300 BCE	Ptolemy I Soter (305–282)		Seleucus I Nicator (305–281)
	Ptolemy II Philadelphus (285–246)		Antiochus I Soter (281–261)
			Antiochus II Theos (261–246)
	Ptolemy III Euergetes (246–221)		Seleucus II Callinicus (246–225)
	Ptolemy IV Philopator (221–204)		Seleucus III Soter Ceraunos (225–223)
	Ptolemy V Epiphanes (204–180);		Antiochus III (the Great) (223–187)
	Cleopatra I (180–176)		Seleucus IV Philopator (187–175)
			Antiochus IV Epiphanes (175–164)
	Ptolemy VI Philometor (180–145);		Antiochus V Eupator (164–162)
	Cleopatra II (175–116)		Demetrius I Soter (162–150)
	Ptolemy VII Neos Philopator (145)		Alexander Epiphanes (Balas) (150–145)
	Ptolemy VIII Euergetes II Physcon (170–116)		Demetrius II Nicator (145–141 and 129–125)
			Antiochus VI Epiphanes (145–142)
			Trypho (142–138)
			Antiochus VII Sidetes (138–129)
			Cleopatra Thea (126–121)
			Antiochus VIII Grypus (125–121 and 121–96)
	Cleopatra III (116–101)		Seleucus V (125)
	Ptolemy IX Soter II (116–107 and 88–80)		Antiochus IX Cyzicenus (115–95)
100 BCE	Ptolemy X Alexander I (107–88)		Seleucus VI (95)
			Antiochus X Eusebes (95–83)
			Antiochus XI Philadelphus (95)
	Cleopatra Berenice (101–88)		Demetrius III Eukairos (95–88)
			Philip I Epiphanes Philadelphus (95–84)
	Ptolemy XI Alexander II (80)		Antiochus XII Dionysus Epiphanes (87–84)
			Philip II (67–66)
	Ptolemy XII Auletes (80–59 and 55–51)		Antiochus XIII Asiaticus (69–68 and 65–64)
50 BCE	Cleopatra VII (51–30)		
	Ptolemy XIII (51–47)		
	Ptolemy XIV (47–44)		
			ROMAN EMPIRE
			ROMAN EMPERORS:
			Octavian (Augustus) (27 BCE–14 CE)
25 CE			Tiberius (14–37)
50 CE			Gaius Caligula (37–41)
			Claudius (41–54)
			Nero (54–68)
			Galba (68–69); Otho (69); Vitellius (69)
			Vespasian (69–79)
			Titus (79–81)
100 CE			Domitian (81–96)
			Nerva (96–98)
			Trajan (98–117)
			Hadrian (117–138)

PALESTINE

HASMONEAN RULERS

[Mattathias d. 166]

Judas Maccabeus, son of Mattathias (165–160)

Jonathan, son of Mattathias (160–142)

Simon, son of Mattathias (142–135)

John Hyrcanus I, son of Simon (135–104)

Judah Aristobulus I , son of John Hyrcanus (104–103)

Alexander Janneus, son of John Hyrcanus (103–76)

Salome Alexandra, wife of Alexander Jannaeus (76–67)

Aristobulus II, son of Alexander Jannaeus and
    Salome Alexandra (67–63)

Hyrcanus II, son of Alexander Jannaeus and
    Salome Alexandra (63–40)

Mattathias Antigonus, son of Aristobulus II (40–37)

HERODIAN DYNASTY

Herod the Great, king of the Jews (37–4)

Herod Archelaus, son of Herod the Great,
    ethnarch of Judea, Samaria, Idumea (4 BCE–6 CE)

Herod Antipas, son of Herod the Great,
    tetrarch of Galilee and Perea (4 BCE–39 CE)

Herod **Philip**, son of Herod the Great, tetrarch of
Batanea, Trachonitis, Auranitis (4 BCE–34 CE)

Herod Agrippa I, grandson of Herod the Great, king of Batanea, Trachonitis, Aurantis (37–44) and of Judea, Galilee,
and Perea (41–44)

Herod **Agrippa** II, son of Herod Agrippa I, king of
    Chalcis (50–53), king of Batanea, Trachonitis,
    Auranitis, Galilee, Perea (53–ca. 93)

ROMAN GOVERNORS OF JUDEA

Coponius (6–8 CE)

M. Ambivius (9–12)

Annius Rufus (12–15)

Valerius Gratus (15–26)

Pontius Pilate (26–36)

Marcellus (36–37)

Marullus (37–41)[2]

Cuspius Fadus (44–46)

Tiberius Julius Alexander (46–48)

Ventidius Cumanus (48–52)

M. Antonius **Felix** (52–60?)

Porcius Festus (60?–62)

Clodius Albinus (62–64)

Gessius Florus (64–66)

2. In 41 Judea was made part of the kingdom of Herod Agrippa I, grandson of Herod the Great (see Herodian Dynasty,
above). At his death in 44 it became a province again.

WEIGHTS AND MEASURES

The modern equivalents for biblical measures and weights are presented in the following tables.

HEBREW WEIGHTS

HEBREW	NRSV	EQUIVALENCE	U.S. AVOIRDUPOIS	METRIC UNITS
kikkar	talent	60 minas	75.558 pounds	34.3 kilograms
maneh	mina	50 shekels	20.148 ounces	571.2 grams
sheqel	shekel	2 bekas	176.29 grains	11.42 grams
pim (or payim)	pim	.667 shekel	117.52 grains	7.61 grams
beqa'	beka, half a shekel	10 gerahs	88.14 grains	5.71 grams
gerah	gerah		8.81 grains	.57 gram

The practice of weighing unmarked ingots of metal used in commercial transactions prior to the invention of money explains that the names of the units of weight were used later as indications of value, and as names for monetary standards. There is, however, no direct relation between the shekel-weight and the weight of a shekel piece.

WEIGHTS IN THE NEW TESTAMENT

GREEK	NRSV	EQUIVALENCE	U.S. AVOIRDUPOIS	METRIC UNITS
talenton	talent	(Hebrew) talent	75.558 pounds	34.3 kilograms
mna	pound	(Hebrew) mina	20.148 ounces	571.2 grams
litra	pound	(Latin) libra	0.719 pound	326.4 grams

HEBREW MEASURES OF LENGTH

HEBREW	NRSV	EQUIVALENCE	U.S. MEASURES	METRIC UNITS
'ammah	cubit	2 spans	17.49 inches	.443 meter
zeret	span	3 handbreadths	8.745 inches	.221 meter
topah, tepah	handbreadth	4 fingers	2.915 inches	.074 meter
'etsba'	finger		0.728 inch	.019 meter

The cubit described in Ezekiel 40.5; 43.13 is equal to seven (not six) handbreadths, namely 20.405 inches.

MEASURES OF LENGTH IN THE NEW TESTAMENT

GREEK	NRSV	U.S. MEASURES	METRIC UNITS
pechus	cubit	about 1.5 feet	.456 meter
orguia	fathom	about 72.44 inches	1.839 meters
stadion	stadia, or the equivalent in miles	about 606 feet	184.7 meters
milion	mile	about 4,854 feet	1.482 kilometers

HEBREW MEASURES OF CAPACITY: LIQUID MEASURES

HEBREW	NRSV	EQUIVALENCE	U.S. MEASURES	METRIC UNITS
kor	measure, cor	10 baths	60.738 gallons	230 liters
bat	bath	6 hins	6.073 gallons	23 liters
hin	hin	3 kabs	1.012 gallons	3.829 liters
qab	kab	4 logs	1.4349 quarts	1.276 liters
log	log		0.674 pint	.32 liter

HEBREW MEASURES OF CAPACITY: DRY MEASURES

HEBREW	NRSV	EQUIVALENCE	U.S. MEASURES	METRIC UNITS
ḥomer	homer	2 lethechs	6.524 bushels	229.7 liters
kor	measure, cor	2 lethechs	6.524 bushels	229.7 liters
letek	lethech, measure	5 ephahs	3.262 bushels	114.8 liters
ʾepah	ephah, measure	3 seahs	20.878 quarts	22.9 liters
seʾah	measure	3.33 omers	6.959 quarts	7.7 liters
ʿomer	omer	1.8 kabs	2.087 quarts	2.3 liters
ʾissaron	tenth part (of ephah)			
qab	kab		1.159 quarts	1.3 liters

MEASURES OF CAPACITY IN THE NEW TESTAMENT

GREEK	NRSV	EQUIVALENCE	U.S. MEASURES	METRIC UNITS
batos	measure	(Hebrew) bat	6.073 gallons	23 liters
koros	measure	(Hebrew) kor	60.738 gallons or 6.524 bushels	230 liters
saton	measure	(Hebrew) seʾah	6.959 dry quarts	7.71 liters
metretes	measure		10.3 gallons	39 liters
choinix	quart		0.98 dry quart	1.079 liters
modios	bushel	(Latin) modius	7.68 dry quarts	8.458 liters
xestes	pot	(Latin) sextarius	0.96 dry pint, or 1.12 fluid pints	.53 liter

CALENDAR

The year was composed of twelve lunar months (beginning on the day of the new moon), with an intercalary month added periodically (see perhaps 1 Kings 12.33). In some traditions, and perhaps originally, the year began in the fall, at the autumnal equinox (see Ex 23.16; 34.22). In others, following Babylonian practice, the new year was celebrated in the spring. The fall new year became standard in postbiblical Judaism.

Months in the Bible are usually identified by ordinal numbers, beginning with the spring new year. Some months (in boldface in the following list) are also designated with names derived either from a Canaanite calendar or, in postexilic texts, from a Babylonian one; the names of months not found in the Bible are known from other ancient sources.

	CANAANITE NAME	BABYLONIAN NAME	MODERN EQUIVALENT
First	**Abib**	**Nisan**	March–April
Second	**Ziv**	Iyyar	April–May
Third		**Sivan**	May–June
Fourth		Tammuz	June–July
Fifth		Ab	July–August
Sixth		**Elul**	August–September
Seventh	**Ethanim**	Tishri	September–October
Eighth	**Bul**	Marheshvan	October–November
Ninth		Chislev	November–December
Tenth		**Tebeth**	December–January
Eleventh		**Shebat**	January–February
Twelfth		**Adar**	February–March

PARALLEL TEXTS

Alongside the widespread evidence of alternative traditions in the Bible, in which two or more authors or traditions deal with the same general subjects (e.g., the two accounts of creation in Gen 1–3; the Gospel of John as compared with the first three Gospels), throughout the Bible there are also literary relationships between one book or part of a book and another. Sometimes the authors or editors of one book simply reproduced their sources verbatim; sometimes they were retouched. Often called "synoptic passages," because when viewed together their common elements can be seen, these texts are important in understanding the specific purposes and themes of a writer by analyzing what was included, added, omitted, revised, and rearranged. There follows a listing of the larger synoptic passages throughout the Bible. These texts have a demonstrable literary relationship with each other, either direct, where a source can be identified, or indirect, where a source that no longer survives but must be presumed is quoted at length and verbatim, or with only minor modifications in one or more places.

HEBREW BIBLE

	SYNOPTIC PASSAGES		SUBJECT MATTER
EXODUS	Ex 20.2–17	Deut 5.6–21	Ten Commandments
JOSHUA	Josh 21.1–39	1 Chr 6.54–81	Levitical cities
2 SAMUEL	2 Sam 22	Ps 18	Thanksgiving hymn
1 CHRONICLES	1 Chr 1.1–4	Gen 5	Descendants of Adam
	1 Chr 1.5–23	Gen 10.1–32	Descendants of Noah
	1 Chr 1.24–27	Gen 11.10–32	Descendants of Shem
	1 Chr 1.28–33	Gen 25.1–6,12–18	Descendants of Ishmael and Keturah
	1 Chr 1.34–54	Gen 36.1–43	Descendants of Esau
	1 Chr 3.1–9	2 Sam 3.2–5; 5.5,13–16	Sons of David
	1 Chr 6.54–81	Josh 21.1–39	Levitical cities
	1 Chr 10	1 Sam 31	Death of Saul
	1 Chr 11.1–9	2 Sam 5.1–10	David's early reign
	1 Chr 11.10–47	2 Sam 23.8–39	David's heroes
	1 Chr 13.5–14	2 Sam 6.1–11	David retrieves the ark
	1 Chr 14.1–17	2 Sam 5.11–25	David's reign in Jerusalem
	1 Chr 15.25–16.3	2 Sam 6.12–19	David brings the ark to Jerusalem
	1 Chr 16.8–36	Ps 105.1–15; 96.1–13;	Thanksgiving hymn
	1 Chr 17–21	2 Sam 7; 8; 10; 11.1; 12.26,30–31; 21.18–22; 24	David's reign in Jerusalem
2 CHRONICLES	2 Chr 1.3–13	1 Kings 3.4–15	Solomon's prayer for wisdom
	2 Chr 1.14–17	1 Kings 10.26–29	Solomon's wealth
	2 Chr 2.1–18	1 Kings 5.1–18	Preparations for building Temple
	2 Chr 3.1–4	1 Kings 6.1–3	Temple dimensions
	2 Chr 4.1–5.1	1 Kings 7.23–26,39–51	Temple metalwork
	2 Chr 5.2–7.10	1 Kings 8	Dedication of the Temple
	2 Chr 7.11–9.29	1 Kings 9–10	Solomon's reign
	2 Chr 9.29–31	1 Kings 11.41–42	Solomon's death
	2 Chr 10.1–11.4	1 Kings 12.1–24	Rehoboam's accession
	2 Chr 12.2–16	1 Kings 14.25–31	Shishak's invasion
	2 Chr 15.16–17.1	1 Kings 15.17–24	Asa's reign
	2 Chr 18.2–34; 20.31–21.1	1 Kings 22	Jehoshaphat's reign
2 CHRONICLES	2 Chr 21.2–10	2 Kings 8.16–22	Jehoram's reign
	2 Chr 22.2–6	2 Kings 8.25–29	Ahaziah's reign
	2 Chr 22.10–23.21	2 Kings 11	Athaliah's reign

	SYNOPTIC PASSAGES		SUBJECT MATTER
	2 Chr 24.1–14	2 Kings 12.1–14	Jehoash's reign
	2 Chr 25.1–4,17–28; 26.1–2	2 Kings 14.1–22	Amaziah's reign
	2 Chr 26.3–4,21–23	2 Kings 15.1–7	Uzziah's reign
	2 Chr 27.1–9	2 Kings 15.32–38	Jotham's reign
	2 Chr 28.1–4,26–27	2 Kings 16.1–4,19–20	Ahaz's reign
	2 Chr 29.1–2; 32.1, 9–12,15	2 Kings 18.1–3,13,17–22, 29–30	Hezekiah's reign
	2 Chr 33.1–9,18–20	2 Kings 21.1–9,17–18	Manasseh's reign
	2 Chr 33.21–25	2 Kings 21.19–26	Amon's reign
	2 Chr 34.1–2,8–31; 35.20	2 Kings 22.1–23.3,29	Josiah's reign
	2 Chr 36.1–4	2 Kings 23.30–34	Jehoahaz's reign
	2 Chr 36.5,6,8	2 Kings 23.36–37; 24.1,5	Jehoiakim's reign
	2 Chr 36.9	2 Kings 24.8	Jehoiakin's reign
	2 Chr 36.11–12	2 Kings 24.18–19	Zedekiah's reign
	2 Chr 36.22–23	Ezra 1.1–2	Decree of Cyrus
EZRA	Ezra 1.1–2	2 Chr 36.22–23	Decree of Cyrus
	Ezra 2.1–70	Neh 7.7–69	List of returning exiles
PSALMS	Ps 14	Ps 53	Lament
	Ps 18	2 Sam 22	Thanksgiving hymn
ISAIAH	Isa 2.2–4	Mic 4.1–3	Oracle of future age
	Isa 15–16	Jer 48.29–38	Oracle against Moab
	Isa 36–39	2 Kings 18.13–20.19	Events in Hezekiah's reign
JEREMIAH	Jer 39.1–10	2 Kings 25.1–12	The fall of Jerusalem
	Jer 48.29–38	Isa 16.6–10; 15.2–7; 16.11–12	Oracle against Moab
	Jer 49.9–10,14–16	Ob 5–6,1–4	Oracle against Edom
	Jer 52	2 Kings 24.18–25.30	The fall of Jerusalem
OBADIAH	Ob 1–6	Jer 49.14–16,9–10	Oracle against Edom
MICAH	Mic 4.1–3	Isa 2.2–4	Oracle of future age

APOCRYPHA

	SYNOPTIC PASSAGES		SUBJECT MATTER
1 ESDRAS	1 Esd 1.1–55	2 Chr 35.1–36.21	Last days of Judah
	1 Esd 2.1–15	Ezra 1.1–11	Cyrus's decree
	1 Esd 2.16–30	Ezra 4.7–24	Opposition to rebuilding Temple
	1 Esd 5.7–46	Ezra 2.1–70; Neh 7.7–69	List of returning exiles
	1 Esd 5.47–73	Ezra 3.1–4.5	Rebuilding Temple
	1 Esd 6.1–7.15	Ezra 4.24–6.22	Completion of Temple
	1 Esd 8.1–9.55	Ezra 7.1–10.44; Neh 7.73–8.12	Ezra's mission

NEW TESTAMENT

A majority of scholars think that the Gospel of Mark was independently used as a source by Matthew and Luke.

	SYNOPTIC PASSAGES		SUBJECT MATTER
Mk 1.2–8	Mt 3.1–6,11–12	Lk 3.1–6,16	John the Baptist
Mk 1.9–11	Mt 3.13–17	Lk 3.21–22	Baptism of Jesus
Mk 1.12–13	Mt 4.1–2,11	Lk 4.1–2,13	Temptation of Jesus
Mk 1.16–20	Mt 4.18–22	(Lk 5.1–11)	Call of disciples
Mk 1.21–38	(Mt 7.28–29; 8.14–17)	Lk 4.31–43	Teaching and healing by Jesus
Mk 1.40–45	Mt 8.1–4	Lk 5.12–16	Healing of a leper
Mk 2.1–22	Mt 9.1–17	Lk 5.17–39	Events in Jesus' ministry
Mk 2.23–3.30	Mt 12.1–37; 10.1–4	Lk 6.1–19; 11.14–23; 12.10; 6.43–45	Events in Jesus' ministry
Mk 3.31–4.25	Mt 12.46–50; 13.1–13, 18–23	Lk 8.4–21	Sayings of Jesus
Mk 4.30–34	Mt 13.31–32,34–35	Lk 13.18–19	Sayings of Jesus
Mk 4.35–41	Mt 8.23–27	Lk 8.22–35	Stilling the storm
Mk 5.1–43	Mt 8.28–34; 9.18–26	Lk 8.26–56	Healings by Jesus
Mk 6.1–6	Mt 13.51–52		Rejection in Nazareth
Mk 6.7–14	Mt 10.1,9–11; 14.1–2	Lk 9.1–9	Events in Jesus' ministry
Mk 6.17–29	Mt 14.3–12		Death of John the Baptist
Mk 6.30–44	Mt 14.13–21	Lk 9.10–17	Feeding of five thousand
Mk 6.45–8.10	Mt 14.22–15.39		Events in Jesus' ministry
Mk 8.11–21	Mt 16.1–12	(Lk 11.29; 12.1)	Sayings of Jesus
Mk 8.27–9.48	Mt 16.13–17.23; 18.1–9	Lk 9.18–50; 17.1–2	Events in Jesus' ministry
Mk 12.28–31	Mt 22.34–40	Lk 10.25–38	Sayings of Jesus
Mk 10.1–12	Mt 19.1–12		On marriage
Mk 10.13–52	Mt 19.13–30; 20.17–34	Lk 18.15–43; 22.24–27	Sayings of Jesus
Mk 11.1–12.37	Mt 21.1–27,33–46; 22.15-46	Lk 19.28–38,45–48; 20.1–44; (10.25–28)	Jesus in Jerusalem
Mk 12.41–44		Lk 21.1–4	The poor widow
Mk 13.1–32	Mt 24.1–36	Lk 21.5–33	Sayings of Jesus about the end
Mk 14.1–15.47	Mt 26.1–27.2; 27.11–61	Lk 22.1–34,39–71; 23.1–5,18–55	Passion of Jesus
Mk 16.1–8	Mt 28.1–10	Lk 24.1–11	The empty tomb

A majority of scholars think that Matthew and Luke used a source that has not survived (known as "Q").

	SYNOPTIC PASSAGES	SUBJECT MATTER
Mt 3.7–10,12	Lk 3.7–9,17	John the Baptist's preaching
Mt 4.3–10	Lk 3.3–12	Temptation of Jesus
Mt 5.3–12	Lk 6.20–23	Beatitudes
Mt 5.13–16	Lk 14.34–35; 11.33	Sayings of Jesus
Mt 5.21–26	Lk 12.57–59	Sayings of Jesus
Mt 5.38–48	Lk 6.27–36	Sayings of Jesus
Mt 6.9–15	Lk 11.2–4	Lord's Prayer
Mt 6.19–7.27	Lk 12.33–36; 16.13; 12.22–31; 6.37–38, 41–42; 11.9–13; 6.31; 13.23–24; 6.43–49	Sayings of Jesus
Mt 8.5–15	Lk 7.1–10	Healing of a centurion's servant
Mt 8.18–22	Lk 9.57–60	Sayings of Jesus
Mt 10.26–39	Lk 12.2–9,51–53; 14.26–27	Sayings of Jesus
Mt 11.2–19	Lk 7.18–35	On John the Baptist

	SYNOPTIC PASSAGES	SUBJECT MATTER
Mt 11.20–27	Lk 10.13–15,21–22	Sayings of Jesus
Mt 12.38–45	Lk 11.29–32; 11.24–26	Sayings of Jesus
Mt 13.16–17	Lk 10.23–24	Sayings of Jesus
Mt 13.33	Lk 13.20–21	Sayings of Jesus
Mt 18.10–14	Lk 15.3–7	Sayings of Jesus
Mt 22.1–4	Lk 14.16–22	Parable of the marriage feast
Mt 23.37–39	Lk 13.34–35	Lament over Jerusalem
Mt 24.37–51	Lk 17.26–35; 12.39–46	Sayings of Jesus about the end
Mt 25.14–30	Lk 19.12–27	Parable of the talents

TRANSLATIONS OF ANCIENT TEXTS

INTRODUCTORY

Evans, Craig A. *Ancient Texts for New Testament Studies: A Guide to the Background Literature.* Peabody, Mass. Hendrickson, 2005.

Sparks, Kenton L. *Ancient Texts for the Study of the Hebrew Bible: A Guide to the Background Literature.* Peabody, Mass. Hendrickson, 2005.

ANCIENT NEAR EASTERN

Chavalas, Mark W., ed. *The Ancient Near East: Historical Sources in Translation.* Oxford: Blackwell, 2006.

Hallo, William W., and K. Lawson Younger, eds. *The Context of Scripture.* Vol. 1, *Canonical Compositions from the Biblical World.* Vol. 2, *Monumental Inscriptions from the Biblical World.* Vol. 3, *Archival Documents from the Biblical World.* Leiden: E. J. Brill, 1997; 1999; 2003.

Lewis, Theodore I., ed. *Writings from the Ancient World.* A series produced by the Society of Biblical Literature (Atlanta, Ga.), with each volume devoted to a particular genre and language.

Pritchard, James B., ed. *Ancient Near Eastern Texts Relating to the Old Testament.* Princeton, N.J.: Princeton University Press, 3d ed., 1969.

EARLY JEWISH
General

Bartlett, John R. *Jews in the Hellenistic World: Josephus, Aristeas, the Sibylline Oracles, Eupolemus.* Cambridge, Eng.: Cambridge University Press, 1985.

Maccoby, Hyam. *Early Rabbinic Writings.* Cambridge, Eng.: Cambridge University Press, 1988.

Septuagint

Pietersma, Albert, and Benjamin G. Wright, eds. *A New English Translation of the Septuagint and the Other Greek Translations Traditionally included under That Title.* New York: Oxford University Press, 2007.

Dead Sea Scrolls

Abegg, Martin, Jr.; Peter Flint; and Eugene Ulrich, eds. *The Dead Sea Scrolls Bible: The Oldest Known Bible.* San Francisco: HarperSanFrancisco, 1999.

García Martínez, Florentino, ed. *The Dead Sea Scrolls Study Edition.* 2 vols. Grand Rapids, Mich.: Eerdmans, 2000.

Vermes, Geza. *The Complete Dead Sea Scrolls in English.* Rev. ed. New York: Penguin, 2004.

Apocrypha and Pseudepigrapha

Charles, R. H., ed. *The Apocrypha and Pseudepigrapha of the Old Testament.* 2 vols. Oxford: Clarendon, 1913.

Charlesworth, James H., ed. *The Old Testament Pseudepigrapha.* 2 vols. New York: Doubleday, 1983; 1985.

Josephus

Mason, Steve, ed. *Flavius Josephus: Translation and Commentary.* Leiden: E. J. Brill, 2000– .

Whiston, William, trans. *The Works of Josephus Complete and Unabridged.* 1736. New updated edition, Peabody, Mass.: Hendrickson, 1987.

Williamson, G. A., trans. *Josephus: The Jewish War.* New York: Penguin, 1984.

Loeb Classical Library

Philo of Alexandria

Williamson, Ronald. *Jews in the Hellenistic World: Philo.* Cambridge, Eng.: Cambridge University Press, 1989.

Yonge, C. D., trans. *The Works of Philo.* 1854. New updated edition, Peabody, Mass.: Hendrickson, 1993.

Loeb Classical Library

TRANSLATIONS OF ANCIENT TEXTS

Mishnah

Danby, Herbert. *The Mishnah*. Oxford: Clarendon, 1933.
Neusner, Jacob. *The Mishnah: A New Translation*. New Haven: Yale University Press, 1988.

Talmud

Epstein, I. *The Babylonian Talmud*. 30 vols. London: Soncino, 1935–48.
Steinsaltz, Adin. *The Talmud*. New York: Random House, 1989–99.

EARLY CHRISTIAN
General

Barrett, C. K. *The New Testament Background: Writings from Ancient Greece and the Roman Empire That Illuminate Christian Origins*. Rev. ed. San Francisco: HarperCollins, 1987.
Cartlidge, David R., and David L. Dungan, eds. *Documents for the Study of the Gospels*. Rev. ed. Minneapolis: Fortress, 1994.
Elliott, J. K. *The Apocryphal New Testament: A Collection of Apocryphal Christian Literature in an English Translation*. Rev ed. Oxford: Oxford University Press, 1999.
Richardson, Cyril D., ed. *Early Christian Fathers*. New York: Macmillan, 1970.
Staniforth, Maxwell, trans. *Early Christian Writings*. New York: Penguin, 1987.

Nag Hammadi

Barnstone, Willis, and Marvin Meyer, eds. *The Gnostic Bible*. Boston: Shambhala, 2003.
Layton, Bentley. *The Gnostic Scriptures: A New Translation*. Garden City, N.Y.: Doubleday, 1987.
Robinson, J. M., ed. *The Nag Hammadi Library in English*. 4th rev. ed. Leiden: E. J. Brill, 1996.

ANCIENT TRANSLATIONS OF THE BIBLE
Greek

Brenton, Lancelot C. L. *The Septuagint with Apocrypha: Greek and English*. 1851. Reprint, Peabody, Mass.: Hendrickson, 1986.

Aramaic

McNamara, Martin, et al. *The Aramaic Bible: The Targums*. Collegeville, Minn.: Liturgical, 1987– .

CLASSICAL SOURCES

Beard, Mary; John North; and Simon Price. *Religions of Rome*. Vol. 2: *A Sourcebook*. Cambridge, Eng.: Cambridge University Press, 1998.
Translations of the writings of most Greek and Roman authors are available in the Loeb Classical Library.

GLOSSARY

A

Aaron the first high priest, brother of Moses and Levite (Ex 4.14); he is inaugurated in Ex chs 28–29. Although it is unclear how, or whether, Aaron was supposed to be the progenitor of later priests, he is regarded as the prototype. See **Levite, Zadokite**

Abaddon (Heb "place of destruction"), the realm of the dead (Job 26.6; Prov 15.11; Ps 88.10–12; Rev 9.11)

Abba (Aram. "father"), the word Jesus (Mk 14.36) and the early church (Rom 8.15) used to address God

accession the act of taking one's place as a ruler

acropolis (Gk "height of the city") the fortified upper area of a Greek city; "the Acropolis" refers to this area in Athens

acrostic a literary device in which the first letter of each line of poetry occurs according to a predetermined pattern. In the poetry of the Hebrew Bible all acrostics are alphabetical: the individual lines of a poem (or occasionally small groups of lines) begin with the twenty-two letters of the Hebrew alphabet in order. (This would be equivalent to the first line of an English poem beginning with A, the second with B, etc.) The acrostic form, besides giving the esthetic pleasure of a pattern, may have been intended to make memorization easier. It may also have been intended as a way of expressing completeness: in Lamentations, for instance, the acrostic format of the individual chs might have been used to express the completeness of the outpouring of grief. The following poems in the Bible are acrostics: Pss. 9–10, 25, 34, 37, 111, 112, 119, 145; Prov. 31.10–31; Lam 1, 2, 3, 4 (ch 5 is not an acrostic, but preserves part of the form by having 22 lines, the number of letters in the Hebrew alphabet); Nah 1.2–8 (or 9) (incomplete). In the Hebrew text of Sirach, 51.13–30 is acrostic.

Adar the twelfth month (February-March) in the Jewish year. In order to bring the lunar calendar into alignment with the solar year, a leap year, in which there are two months of Adar, occurs seven times during each nineteen-year cycle of years (see Calendar)

Adonai (Heb "my Lord") a divine title and the word generally substituted for **YHWH** when the Bible is read aloud

Ahikar an ancient Near Eastern story of a prime minister to the king of Assyria, who is betrayed by an ungrateful nephew but ultimately vindicated. It is alluded to in Tob 1.21–22.

Akedah (Heb "binding") the story of the binding of Isaac (Gen 22)

Akkadian the language of Assyria and Babylonia. Akkadian is a Semitic language related to Hebrew, and is written in cuneiform, wedge-shaped writing.

alien see **resident alien**

allegory an extended comparison, which directly describes one reality while indirectly describing something entirely different. An allegory as a narrative uses action, setting, and characters to point symbolically to something else.

alleluia a Greek and Latin form of a Hebrew phrase that means "Praise the LORD." See **hallelujah**.

Amarna Letters diplomatic correspondence from the reigns of the Egyptian pharaohs Amenophis III and Akhenaten, written in **Akkadian** cuneiform, that provide information about **Canaan** in the fourteenth century BCE

Ammon, Ammonites, the territory and its inhabitants east of the Jordan River

Amorites according to the Bible, one of the native nations of Canaan. Amorites are attested in other ancient Near Eastern documents from the third millennium BCE and onward as residents of Syria who migrated to Mesopotamia and other areas. Their language was related to Hebrew.

amphictyony a social organization in ancient Greece in which groups were united around a central sanctuary and serviced this sanctuary on a rotating basis. Some scholars think that a similar system existed in Israel in premonarchic times.

anachronism an element in a story that is out of place because it did not exist at the time in which the story is set. Anachronisms can be valuable clues to when a narrative was written.

Anat a Canaanite goddess often depicted as a warrior

anathema (Gk "devoted [to evil]," "accursed") a solemn pronouncement by a recognized religious authority banning or condemning a person, thing, or idea as false or evil

aniconic (Gk "not representational") worship without the use of statues or images; also a symbolic or suggestive presentation of a divine being, rather than a literal or realistic rendition

anoint touch or rub with oil. Anointing was a sign that a person or thing was dedicated to God. See also **messiah**.

anthropomorphic (Gk "in human form") the description or representation of a divine being in the form of a human person

antichrist the apocalyptic figure presented as opposing God, battling the heavenly angels serving God, or fighting against God's anointed ruler

antithesis the contrast of ideas through closely contrasted words

antithetic parallelism two parallel lines related to one another by opposition or contrast

aphorism a short, memorable saying

apocalypse (Gr. *apokalypsis*, "removal of the veil, revelation") a literary genre in which an angel or other heavenly being communicates to a human being the divine plan for history, especially the end of time

apocalyptic having the character of an apocalypse

Apocrypha (Gk "hidden things") a group of about twenty mostly Jewish works, many of which were included in the **Septuagint**, but which are not included in the Jewish or Protestant canons of the Bible. Most of these works are canonical for Roman Catholics; a few more are canonical for Orthodox Christians. See **deuterocanon**.

apodictic law law stated absolutely, as in the Decalogue's "you shall not," rather than casuistically, "if a person . . . ." See **casuistic law**.

apologia (Gk "explanation") a defense of one's actions or beliefs, usually in a formal speech or written document

apostasy abandoning a set of beliefs, or the position of having abandoned them

apostle (Gk "one who is sent"), a delegate or representative. In the New Testament, an apostle was one who had known Jesus and could witness to the resurrection (Acts 1.21–2), or a preacher of the gospel who had been called by God (1 Cor 12.28; Rom 16.7).

apostrophe (Gk "turn from") a direct address to someone or something not present

apotropaic (Gk "turn away from") an action intended to ward off evil

Aramaic a Semitic language used widely in the Near East during the Persian period, though it developed earlier. It became the ordinary language of Jews, and was used by Jesus. An Aramaic translation of the Hebrew Bible is called a **Targum**.

Aramaism the use in another language of a word or grammatical form derived from Aramaic.

Arameans a Semitic people living in Syria from the second millennium BCE onward. Damascus was a principal city of the Arameans.

aretalogy (Gk "words about virtue") praise of virtues, either of a hero or of oneself

ark of the covenant the chest in the tabernacle or Temple that contained the text or tablets of the covenant, and that served as part of the throne of the LORD

Armageddon the traditional site of the final battle between good and evil (Rev 16.6), possibly derived from Megiddo, a strategically located site where many battles occurred

ascension going up, particularly to a divine realm but also literally climbing a hill (as to Jerusalem)

asceticism (Gk "training") deliberate self-denial or self-punishment for religious purpose

Asherah (pl. Asherim) Canaanite goddess, wife or consort of **El**; her sacred symbol, a pole or tree, was the object of prophetic condemnation.

Assyria a Mesopotamian world power in the second and first millennia BCE. Its capital cities included Ashur and Nineveh. The Assyrian empire conquered the Northern Kingdom of Israel in 722 BCE and exiled its people. The Assyrians were well-known for their massive building projects, and for their cruelty in war.

Astarte the Canaanite goddess of love and fertility

atbash a form of code in Hebrew in which the last letter of the alphabet is substituted for the first, the next-to-last for the second, and so on: *alep* becomes *taw*, *bet* becomes *shin*, *gimel* becomes *resh*, etc. (In English, *A* would become *Z*, *B* would become *Y*, etc.) In Jer 25.26; 51.41, Babylon (b-b-l) is written Sheshach (sh-sh-k).

atonement expiation for sin, or reparation for an injury committed against another

Atrahasis hero of the Mesopotamian epic named for him, who survives the god Enlil's efforts to destroy humankind by a flood. See also **Gilgamesh**.

B

Baal ("master," "lord," "husband") the chief god of Canaanite religion, a storm god

Babylonia a Mesopotamian world power. It often competed against Assyria, which it conquered in 612 BCE. Its major city was Babylon (Akkadian "gate of the gods"). Its main god became Marduk. Babylonia destroyed Jerusalem in 586, and was conquered by the Persian king **Cyrus** the Great in 539.

Babylonian exile the forced relocation of some of the population of Judah, especially the elite, after the conquest by Babylonia in the early sixth century BCE. The exile ended with the permitted return to the land under **Cyrus** in 538 BCE.

Babylonian Talmud see **Talmud**

ban (Heb *herem*) the dedication or sacrifice of war booty (including people) to the deity

baptism ritual purification by immersion in water, used by Christians as an initiation into the community

BCE Before the Common Era, equivalent to BC

Beelzebul (also Baalzebul, Baalzebub, Beelzebub) the ruler of the demons (Mt 12.24–27). It is based on the Hebrew *Baalzebul*, "Baal the exalted," a title of the Phoenician god at Ekron (2 Kings 1.2–18), changed probably as a derogatory name into Baalzebub, "lord of flies."

Behemoth a mythical beast in Job 40.15–24 who represents violent forces in the world

Bel (Akkadian "master," cognate to **Baal**) title of **Marduk**

belomancy a method of divination by choosing or tossing down arrows on which names of potential victims are inscribed

berît (Heb "treaty, contract, covenant") a term that may be used of a legal agreement between two individuals, groups, or nations, or between God and Israel (see **covenant**)

bicolon unit of Hebrew poetry composed of two *cola*, or lines (sometimes called a *dístich*)

Binding (of Isaac) see **Akedah**

Book of the Covenant see **Covenant Collection**

booths, festival of (Heb *Sukkot*) the autumn harvest festival, also called the festival of ingathering), so named because the harvesters lived in the fields in makeshift tents or booths, also called tabernacles

bulla a clay seal with the impression of a signet ring or other symbol of authority

C

Cairo Geniza the storeroom (see **geniza**) of a synagogue in Old Cairo in which were discovered many thousands of fragments of texts, including a portion of the book of Sirach (Ecclesiasticus) in Hebrew

Cambyses son of **Cyrus** and king of Persia 529–522 BCE. He conquered Egypt in 525

Canaan in Mesopotamian and Egyptian documents and in some biblical texts, a name for the region in the southern Levant part of which became biblical Israel, whose inhabitants are called Canaanites. Also a grandson of Noah.

canon (Gk "measuring rod") the rule by which something is determined to belong or not to a category. Christian tradition uses the word for the official list of the books that make up the Bible.

canonical criticism the interpretation of a biblical text based upon its final form, rather than viewing it as an assemblage of preexisting units

casuistic law (also called "case law") the form of law dealing with the treatment of specific cases. It is frequently in the form of "if/when . . . then" formulae. Most ancient Near Eastern law collections are formulated this way.

catchword, catchphrase a representative or repeated word or group of words that stands for an argument

or point of view; that word or phrase picked up and used in a subsequent or related text

Catholic Epistles (also "Epistles General") the New Testament letters, from James to 3 John, identified not by their recipients but by their authors and therefore presumed to be addressed to the universal ("catholic" means "entire") church

CE Common Era, equivalent to AD

centurion in the Roman army, an officer commanding a century, a maximum of a hundred soldiers; there were sixty centuries in a legion

ceramic typology dating different levels of an archaeological site by classifying the pieces of pottery found in them according to the approximate eras in which they were made

Chaldean(s) a collective name for the tribes that were dominant in Babylon from the late sixth century BCE; Chaldea is frequently associated with the area of southern Mesopotamia

chaos complete lack of order. In ancient Near Eastern mythology, chaos was sometimes personified as divine beings who had to be conquered by other gods in order to establish an orderly, habitable universe.

charismatic (Gr. "gifted, graced") characterized by the ability to influence or lead others; personally magnetic; talented

chattel possessions or persons owned by someone else and therefore at that person's complete disposal

Chemosh the chief god of Moab

cherubim (sing. "cherub") mythical, composite creatures with body parts from various animals; they often had wings and human heads. They were commonly guardians of temples and palaces in the ancient Near East.

chiasm, chiasmus (from Gr. *chi*, the letter that resembles an *X*) inverting the second pair of terms in a parallel structure, so that the corresponding terms, if laid out in a square, would form an *X*. The resultant pattern is *abba, abcba, abccba*, etc.

Christ (Gk "anointed"), the translation of Heb *mashiah*, "messiah." In the New Testament and in general usage, Christ always refers to Jesus of Nazareth.

christology the theological doctrines concerning the nature of Christ

chronicle an account of events in the order in which they occurred

Chronicler the name for the unknown author of the books of Chronicles; sometimes also applied to the author of Ezra and Nehemiah

church (see also house church) the community of believers in a particular area; the later use of "church" to mean a building where people worship does not occur in the New Testament

church fathers see **patristic writers**

circumcision the removal of the foreskin of the penis

Cisjordan Latin for "this side of Jordan," that is, the region west of the Jordan river

citadel a stronghold or fortress, whether standing alone or serving as the inner fortification of a city

clan a social unit, composed of several families considered to be descended from a common ancestor; several clans constituted a tribe

climax (Gk "ladder"), a series of clauses in which each succeeding clause repeats the important term from the previous clause, each clause in turn making a more important point

codex a manuscript of separate pages, bound along one edge. Modern books are a development of the codex.

colon (pl. *cola*) a single line of poetry (also known as a *stich*)

colophon (Gk "summit," by extension "finishing touch") a notice, usually found at the end of an ancient text, giving information about details such as authorship

concordance a word index to a given text, listing each occurrence of a given word along with its context

concubine a woman who is the sexual partner of a man, and is legally recognized as such, but who does not have the full status of a wife

corvée forced labor for the state

cosmology an account of the origins of the cosmos

cosmopolis (Gk "world city") a major metropolis, usually the main city of an empire, to which peoples from different countries or ethnic groups came or in which they resided

cosmos (Gk "order, regularity") the created world of order, stability, relative permanence; the opposite of chaos

Council of Trent the twenty-ninth ecumenical council of the Roman Catholic Church (1545–1563), held after the Protestant Reformation had begun. Among other decisions, it defined the books that are included in the Catholic canon of Scripture.

covenant (Heb *berit*) a contract or treaty. Some covenants have specific conditions or treaty stipulations, while others are covenants of grant; often used of the relationship between God and Israel

Covenant Code another term for **Covenant Collection**

Covenant Collection an ancient set of laws (Ex 20.19–23.33), which details the terms of the covenant between God and Israel

cult prostitute one available for sexual intercourse with worshipers at the temple of a god

cult rituals and religious practices at a place of worship. The cult of the Jerusalem Temple means the religious practices carried out there, with no judgment about their value.

Cynics (Gk "dogs, doglike ones") a nickname for a Greek philosophical movement of the fourth century BCE aimed at achieving happiness by lessening desires, and therefore needing less; it also taught contempt (or at least disregard) for social conventions and consequent lack of shame about meeting one's physical needs (hence the nickname, since dogs were popularly supposed to have no shame)

Cyrus Cylinder an Akkadian inscription describing the conquest of Babylon by **Cyrus**

Cyrus king of Persia (559–530 BCE). He defeated Media in 550 and conquered most of the ancient Near East, including **Babylonia**, allowing the Jewish exiles in Babylonia to return to Judah in 538

D

D according to the **Documentary Hypothesis**, the Deuteronomic source, which covers almost the entire book of Deuteronomy

Davidic dynasty the direct descendents of King David, who ruled in Jerusalem from the tenth to the early sixth centuries BCE

Davidic having to do with the monarchic dynasty founded by David that ruled over Israel and, after the division of the kingdom, the southern part (Judah) until the Babylonian conquest and exile of the sixth century BCE; also the movement to restore that monarchy or to reproduce the self-rule that it represented

Day of Atonement, Heb **Yom Kippur**, the tenth day of the seventh month in the fall, a day of fasting and repentance

Day of the Lord the time mentioned in many prophetic books when God will appear as a warrior, sometimes fighting against Israel, sometimes against Israel's enemies

Dead Sea Scrolls a group of manuscripts found beginning in 1947 in caves near the Dead Sea, at Wadi Qumran. The scrolls were probably the library of an Essene settlement that flourished at the site from the second century BCE until it was destroyed by the Romans in 68 CE. The library included Hebrew manuscripts of biblical books older than those previously known, and other scrolls regulating the life of the community that shed light on the variety of Jewish belief and practice in the Roman period.

Decalogue (Gk "ten words") a traditional name for the list of ten commandments in Ex 20.1–17, Deut 5.6–21

defective spelling the form of a word in the Hebrew text that is missing one or more optional vowel letters

defilement a state of ritual impurity caused by contact with a corpse or other impure object. Priestly literature in the Torah is especially concerned with defilement and removing defilement.

demon, demonic (Gk "spirit") a being of the spiritual realm, or a quality of that realm, particularly one opposed or hostile to human beings

deuterocanon, deuterocanonical (Gk "second canon"), those books or portions of books not included in the Jewish or Protestant canons but accepted as canonical by some Christian churches (Roman Catholic and Orthodox) because they were included in the **Septuagint**. The NRSV places notices within the Apocryphal/ Deuterocanonical Books explaining which ones are accepted by which groups.

Deutero-Isaiah see **Second Isaiah**

Deuteronomistic History the account in the books of Deuteronomy, Joshua, Judges, Samuel, and Kings that presents the history of Israel in the promised land, interpreting it a partial failure to keep the covenant faithfully, and the consequences of that failure. These books show significant theological and linguistic similarities, suggesting that they have a common editor or editors.

Deuteronomistic pertaining to the editor(s) of the history comprised in the books of Joshua, Judges, Samuel, and Kings, as prefaced by the book of Deuteronomy. The term is also applied to the style of these books, reflecting concern for such matters as obedience to the laws given in Deuteronomy, centralized worship in Jerusalem, and support for the **Davidic dynasty**.

Deutero-Pauline (Gk "secondary [letters] of Paul") the writings (Ephesians, Colossians, 1 and 2 Timothy, Titus, and sometimes Hebrews) traditionally attributed to Paul but which many modern scholars now classify as written by others, perhaps some of them disciples of Paul

devil a spiritual being opposed to God or to the angels of God

diaspora (Gk "dispersal") the scattering of Jews from the promised land Israel, and hence any Jews living outside Israel. Also dispersion.

diatribe an argument against a position, or one critical of a person or group. Diatribe often includes an imagined dialogue between opposing viewpoints.

Didache (Gk "teaching") an early Christian writing, dating from around 150 CE but including earlier materials. It consists of moral exhortation, a manual of church order, and guidance for community life. It is valuable for providing insight into the concerns of early Christian communities, and contains material similar to that in the **Pastoral Epistles**.

dietary laws see **kosher**

disciple a follower, an adherent of a particular teaching

dispersion see **diaspora**

divination the effort to learn about the present or the future, by consulting mediums, interpreting omens, and the like

divine warrior God in the role of leader of the heavenly armies, usually seen as fighting for Israel. See also **holy war**.

Documentary Hypothesis a theory about the formation of the first five books of the Bible, Genesis through Deuteronomy. The hypothesis holds that there are four traditions underlying these books, naming them after a chief characteristic of each: ""*J* or the "Yahwist" (""*J* from the German spelling "Jahveh") uses the divine name "YHWH" (the Lord) consistently and contains much of the oldest material; ""*E* or the "Elohist" uses the divine name "Elohim" (God) fairly consistently and contains traditions from the Northern Kingdom of Israel; ""*P* or the "Priestly" writer is concerned largely with legal codes and matters of religious practice; and ""*D* or the "Deuteronomist" represents the traditions gathered mostly in Deuteronomy.

doxology (Gk "word of glory") a prayer of praise to God, or one glorifying God

dualism the religious or philosophical view that reality consists of two basic elements, often seen as "good" and "evil"

dynasty a ruling family; when a leader dies, the next leader is always chosen from among the family members

E

E according to the **Documentary Hypothesis**, the Elohist source, which in Genesis refers to God as *elohim*. It is general though to have originated in the Northern Kingdom of Israel.

Edom, Edomites the territory and people to the southeast and south of Judah, first attested in late second-millennium BCE texts. Edom is identified in Genesis 36 with Esau, Jacob's brother. The enmity between these brothers and between Judah and Edom mirror each other. Edom was later called **Idumea**.

El a Canaanite deity popular in the second millennium BCE. In the texts from Ugarit, he is a significant deity, but is often depicted as old and is largely supplanted by **Baal**.

elect, election those whom God has chosen (Matt 24.22,24; Rom 8.33) or the process of God's having chosen a group (Rom 9.11); these terms do not imply the later (Calvinist) teaching of predestination

Elephantine Papyri Aramaic documents, mostly from the fifth century BCE, found on the island of Elephantine, near Syene (modern Aswan) in Egypt. The papyri show that among those who inhabited the colony on Elephantine were Jews who kept up religious observances, such as Passover, and had their own temple.

elohim the Hebrew word usually translated "God," though its plural form is sometimes also translated "gods." It is originally a common noun (a god), though it is often used as a proper noun for the God of Israel, even though it is a plural form.

Elohist the presumed author of the **E** source according to the **Documentary Hypothesis**

encomium a formal speech praising someone, as in a funeral oration

Enuma Elish a Babylonian text in which the god Marduk becomes king of the gods after creating the cosmos from the body of the goddess of the deep, Tiamat, whom Marduk defeated

ephod (1) the linen apron worn by priests in the Temple; (2) a device used to divine the will of God. The second kind of ephod was carried in priestly garments, which may explain why the same word can be used for both.

Ephraim son of Joseph, for whom the most important tribe of the **Northern Kingdom** is named

Epicureans a Greek philosophical school, founded by Epicurus (341–270 BCE), who taught that human beings naturally seek pleasure, and that the best way to achieve this pursuit was in moderation, since moderation permits the longest possible life of pleasure-seeking

Epiphanes a title, "[God] made manifest," adopted by Antiochus IV, the ruler of the part of the Greek empire that included Judea during the second century BCE. He was the king who forced pagan worship to occur in the Jerusalem Temple, thus provoking the revolt of the Maccabees.

epiphany (Gk "appearing") the manifestation or visual presence of a divine being

epiphany (Gk "manifestation, appearance") usually the appearance of a god or divine being in a form that can be seen by human beings

episcopacy, episcopate (Gk "overseer") a form of church governance in which one authority is responsible for the Christians in a particular geographical area

epistle a letter, sometimes intended for public reading and therefore written according to a particular literary form

Epistles General see **Catholic Epistles**

epistolary prescript a standard salutation or opening phrase at the beginning of a letter

epithet a word or phrase that characterizes a person or thing, and that can often be used by itself to refer to the person

eponymous (Gk "regarding the name") person for whom something is named; Judas Maccabeus is the eponymous main character of the books of 1 and 2 Maccabees

eschatological, eschatology (Gr. *eschata*, "last things") a concern with the end time, or the end of the world as we know it, whether that involves a new historical era radically discontinuous from this one, or an entirely new cosmos after the destruction of the current one

eschaton (Gk "final thing") the end of a period or era; the final stage of history

Essenes a communal society in Judaism from the second century BCE to the first century CE whose members lived apart in communities that were similar in some respects to later monastic groups. It is generally agreed that the **Dead Sea Scrolls** were collected and preserved by an Essene community.

ethics, ethical (Gk "custom") rules of behavior or moral standards expected in a particular place or among a particular group; behavior conforming to those rules or standards

etiology (Gr. *aition*, "cause") an explanation for a name, an event, a custom or ritual, or a natural phenomenon. An etiological story is one that posits a particular cause (not necessarily correctly) for something.

etymology (Gk "study of origins") the study of the derivation of words from their root meanings

Eucharist a ritual or service of thanksgiving, centering on the sharing of bread and wine, based on the final meal Jesus shared with his followers before his trial and crucifixion; also called Communion, the Lord's Supper, and the Mass.

eunuch a castrated male, sometimes a guard for a ruler's concubines and sometimes an official in a court or government

euphemism the substitution of an inoffensive word for one that is too explicit or impolite

evangelist (from Gk *euangelion*, "good news") the author of a gospel

exegesis (Gk "lead into") the explanation or interpretation of the meaning of a written text

exhortation urging a particular course of action or behavior by argument or advice

exile the forced removal of a people from its land, and the community in which they lived in the foreign land. The Israelites of the Northern Kingdom were exiled by the Assyrians in the late eighth century BCE, and the Judeans were exiled by the Babylonians in the early sixth century. Specifically, "the Exile" is the period from 586 to 538 BCE, when much of the population of Judah was deported from Judah to Babylon. See **Babylonian Exile**.

F

fable an illustrative story in which animals or plants have speaking parts.

Fertile Crescent the agriculturally fertile areas of the Near East and Mesopotamia, forming an arc through the modern countries of Israel, Palestine, Jordan, Lebanon, Syria, and Iraq

festival scrolls the five short books that are read on five holy days in the Jewish calendar: Song of Songs on Passover, Ruth on the festival of weeks, Lamentations on 9 Ab (the date of the Temple's destruction), Ecclesiastes on the festival of booths, and Esther on Purim

First Temple the Temple in Jerusalem built by King Solomon in the tenth century BCE and destroyed by the Babylonians in 586 BCE

form criticism the interpretation of a text with particular attention to its genre and structure and to the original setting (**Sitz im Leben**) out of which it arose

Former Prophets the name in the Hebrew Bible for the first part of the longer section called "the Prophets." The Former Prophets are the books of Joshua, Judges, Samuel, and Kings.

forty in biblical usage, a conventional number for a lengthy or completed time period: forty years of wandering in the wilderness (Num 14.33–34), forty years of kingship for David (1Kings 2.11), and Solomon (1 Kings 11.42), forty days of fasting for Moses (Ex 34.28) or Jesus (Mt 4.2 and parallels)

G

Galilee the northernmost geographical area of Israel

Gehenna originally the valley of (the son of) Hinnom, a place outside of Jerusalem where children were burnt as sacrificial offerings. Its associations with burning and evil developed into the image of a place of fiery punishment.

gematria (Heb *gimatriya*, likely from Gk *geometria*) a procedure for interpreting a word or phrase by its numerical value. Hebrew letters may represent numbers (*alef* = 1; *bet* = 2, etc.), and the letters of a word or phrase are added up and equated with other words having the same total.

genealogy a list or history of the ancestors of an individual or group

geniza a storeroom in a synagogue used for keeping old books and objects, especially those too sacred to be discarded. See also **Cairo Geniza**.

genre a form of literature with particular characteristics

gentile a non-Jew

Gilgamesh the Mesopotamian epic, whose hero, Gilgamesh, travels the world in search of immortality. Among the characters he encounters is Utnapishtim, whose tale of the flood has parallels with the biblical account of Noah.

glean to gather or collect, usually by hand, grain that is left behind by reapers

glossolalia the phenomenon of ecstatic speech, or "speaking in tongues" that characterized some early Christian worship (1 Cor 12.10,28,30); it occurs in some Pentecostal Christian worship in the present day. The report of the speeches on the Feast of Weeks (Pentecost) in Acts 2.4–11 maintains that the languages spoken were human languages that could be understood by those in attendance; the reports in the letters reflect not a known, spoken language but a transitory occurrence during worship when one or more worshipers would break into speech (perhaps regarded as the speech of heavenly beings) that neither they nor their hearers could understand.

Gnosticism (from Gk *gnosis*, "knowledge") a philosophy that regards spirit and matter as opposites. According to Gnostic teaching, human beings are spirits trapped or imprisoned in matter; the material world is an illusion or the work of an inferior, even demonic, divine being; and the purpose of life is to learn how to free oneself from material things (including the body) and attain eternal life in the spiritual realm. This is accomplished by learning specialized or secret knowledge about the nature of reality; it is from this emphasis on knowledge that gnosticism gets its name.

Greek Bible a general term for the variety of ancient translations of the Hebrew Bible into Greek in antiquity, including the **Septuagint** and the translations of Aquila, **Symmachus**, and **Theodotion**

H

H see **Holiness Collection**

Hades the Greek name for the underworld, to which the disembodied souls of the dead went; it was similar to **Sheol** (see)

hallelujah a Hebrew acclamation, "Praise Yah!" It is frequent in the Psalms.

Hammurabi (or **Hammurapi**) king of Babylon in the eighteenth century BCE, responsible for the formulation of a legal collection (the Code [or Laws] of Hammurabi) that is one of the earliest collections of case law

Hanukkah see **Hasmonean revolt**

haruspex a practicer of divination who examines inner organs of chickens for guidance

Hasmonean Revolt the uprising led by the family of Mattathias Heshmon against the **Seleucid** ruler Antiochus IV Epiphanes beginning in 166 BCE, particularly by Mattathias's son Judah (or Judas) Maccabeus ("the hammer"), which succeeded in liberating Jerusalem and the surrounding territory from Seleucid rule in 164. When the Temple, which had been desecrated by Antiochus, was retaken by the Jews it was rededicated, an event commemorated in the festival of Hanukkah ("dedication").

Hasmonean the dynasty descended from the Maccabee brothers. It ruled Judea from 135 to 36 BCE; the last Hasmonean was overthrown by Herod the Great

Hebrew Bible a term used to refer to what Christians call the (Protestant) Old Testament. Though the two terms refer to the same body of writings, the order of books in the Hebrew Bible (that is, the Jewish Bible) differs from that found in the Old Testament.

Hellenism the spread of Greek culture, politics, and language around the Mediterranean in the period after the conquests of Alexander the Great (d. 323 BCE)

Hellenistic Greek-speaking or influenced by Greek culture after the time of Alexander

Hellenize bring under the influence of Greek language and culture

hepatoscopy the practice of divination by examining animal livers for guidance

herem see **ban**

hermeneutics (Gk "interpretation") the theory and practice of interpretation

Herodian followers and members of the court of Herod the Great and his sons (late first century BCE to late first century CE)

Hexapla the compendium of six Bible versions (in columns: 1. Hebrew, 2. Hebrew transliterated into Greek, 3. Greek [Aquila], 4. Greek [**Symmachus**], 5. **Septuagint**, 6. Greek [**Theodotion**]) compiled by the early Christian scholar Origen (d. 254). The original was lost, but quotations from and translations of it have survived.

Hexateuch (Gr. "six scrolls") a scholarly grouping of the first six books in the Bible, Genesis through Joshua. See **Pentateuch**, **Tetrateuch**

high places shrines, usually on a hill or a raised platform, where worship, especially sacrifices, took place

higher criticism the effort to distinguish among the sources of biblical documents, and to trace them back to their origins; distinguished from "lower criticism" or textual criticism, which is concerned with establishing the most accurate text in its final

form. See **Documentary Hypothesis**; **synoptic problem.**

historical-critical method interpreting a text by trying to understand its original setting and audience, and what it would have meant when it was originally written or spoken. This method uses the tools of historical research to understand the conditions of the past, and critical tools to understand the traditions and developments that lie behind the surface of the text. It is also a general term that includes such methods as form criticism and redaction criticism.

Holiness Code, Collection, School, Source the ritual and ethical laws in Lev 17–26, named from the repeated exhortation to the Israelites to be holy, or the purported authors or collectors of the material in those chapters. "Collection" is preferred in the annotations herein. "Code" implies a definitive, legal corpus, whereas "Collection" acknowledges the coherence of the chapters without implying a particular purpose in bringing the materials together. "Source" posits a particular document that is reproduced in the chapters, a document produced by a "School" that aimed at inculcating holiness among the people. The authors of this group of laws (sometimes called the Holiness School) were affiliated with the Priestly school and also wrote small sections dispersed throughout the first four books of the Bible; the entire work is often abbreviated *H*.

holocaust a sacrifice entirely consumed by fire, a whole burnt offering

holy war battles conducted under divine guidance in which the LORD fought for Israel in the role of **divine warrior**

homily a sermon

Horeb possibly another name for **Sinai** (see), primarily though not exclusively in Deuteronomy (e.g., Deut 1.2; Ex 3.1)

hortatory characteristic of writing or speech that aims at changing the behavior of the hearers or inspiring them to a particular course of action

hosanna a Hebrew word, meaning "Save!" that was used as a cry of acclamation

house church a descriptive term (not used in the NT itself) for a worship gathering of early Christians in a home rather than a separate building such as a synagogue

household rules the codes of behavior and hierarchy that governed domestic relations in the Roman world, particularly a patriarchal authority system, the subordination of women, children, and slaves, and the rights and responsibilities of various parties in a familial relationship; see Eph 6.1–9; Titus 2.1–10

Hyksos rulers in Egypt of Semitic origin in the mid-second millennium BCE

hyperbole exaggeration for effect

hypostatization speaking of an abstract quality as if it were an object or a living being. See also **personification**.

hyssop a shrub related to mint. It was used as a medicine and, because of its leafy branches, for ritual sprinkling of water or blood.

I

idolatry the worship of anything other than what the worshiper defines as the true God

Idumea later name for **Edom,** a kingdom located south of Judah, between the Dead Sea and the Mediterranean

Ignatius, Letters of early Christian writings of instruction. The author, Ignatius, bishop of Antioch in the late first century CE, wrote them (seven are known to have survived) on his way to martyrdom in Rome. They are largely concerned with overcoming divisions in local churches, combating false teaching, and conducting one's life properly.

imprecation a curse or other prayer for harm to another; the opposite of blessing

impurity a ritual state which prevented an individual from participating in religious rituals (see **defilement**)

incarnation (Latin, "enfleshment") the belief that a divine being has become human in some form

inclusio the use of the same word or phrase at the end of a passage as appeared at the beginning, thus rounding off or completing it. Also called inclusion, frame, and envelope structure.

incubation the practice of sleeping in a particular place, or in contact with particular things (animal skins, the ground) in order to induce dreams that might provide divine guidance

inspiration the belief that the words uttered by a human being are really the words of a divine being. In the ancient world, prophets and oracles were thought to be inspired. In Christian tradition, the notion of inspiration was eventually applied to the whole Bible.

intercalation adding a day or month to a calendar to compensate for the inexact fit between the solar year and the daily or lunar cycle. In the Jewish calendar, an extra month (a repetition of **Adar**) is intercalated in seven years of the nineteen-year cycle.

interpolation an insertion of material into a previously existent text

irony (adj., ironic) a characteristic of literature in which the reader or listener knows more than the characters about the situation in the story. By extension, an ironic aspect of a story, situation, or fact is one that from the outside looks very different than it does from the inside. Irony thus becomes a rhetorical technique in which the author's literal meaning differs from the author's intended meaning.

Ishtar Mesopotamian goddess of fertility and war

Isis Egyptian goddess, wife of Osiris, the god of vegetation and hence of regeneration

Israel the name for both the union of twelve tribal groups, of which David and Solomon were kings, and for the northern section of this kingdom, which split off after the death of Solomon and began a separate political existence under Jeroboam (1 Kings 12). See **Northern Kingdom, Southern Kingdom.**

J

J (from Jahvist, German for Yahwist) according to the **Documentary Hypothesis,** the document or source that uses the divine name (see **YHWH**). J is usually understood to be the earliest source, and to have been written in Judah. It frequently depicts God in very anthropomorphic terms.

Jerome (ca. 345–420) Christian theologian and translator. He translated the Bible into Latin, in the case of the Old Testament directly from the Hebrew. His version became known as the Vulgate ("common") because it was commonly used in Western Christianity. With the Protestant Reformation, its authority was questioned, but was reaffirmed by the Roman Catholic Church at the **Council of Trent.**

Johannine characteristic of, or having to do with, the NT literature associated with the Gospel of John and 1, 2, 3 John; sometimes (though not in more recent scholarship) also applied to the book of Revelation

Joseph and Aseneth (also spelled Asenath) a Jewish novel written in Greek in the first century BCE or the first century CE about Joseph's life in Egypt; his marriage to Asenath, the daughter of an Egyptian priest (see Gen 41.45); her conversion to faith in Joseph's God; and their triumph over a plot to kill them.

Josephus a Jewish historian who lived from ca. 37 CE to ca. 100 CE. Four of his works, all written in Greek, have survived: *The Jewish War*, an account of the rebellion against Rome in 66–70 CE, with background information starting at ca. 200 BCE; *The Antiquities of the Jews*, a complete history from the creation up to the point where *The Jewish War* begins; *Against Apion*, a defense of Judaism; and an autobiography, the *Life*.

jubilee (Heb *yovel*, perhaps "ram" from the sounding of the ram's horn to mark the beginning of the observance) the year of release for slaves and return of ancestral lands to their original owners (or descendants of the owners), to occur every fifty years (after seven sabbaths of years). It is a cornerstone of Priestly ideology, but it is uncertain if it was ever practiced.

Jubilees, book of a retelling, attributed to Moses, of much of Genesis and Exodus and representing itself as a hidden revelation from the Angel of the Presence. It was most likely written in the second century BCE in Judea. The book gets its name from its concern with cycles of time. Jubilees was apparently considered authoritative by the Qumran community.

Judah, Yehud, Judea, Judean when the kingdom of Israel was divided, after the death of Solomon (1 Kings 12.1–20), the southern portion (Southern Kingdom) took the name of its major tribe, Judah (Heb *Yehudah*). That proper noun became "Yehud" during the Persian period (536–333 BCE), "Ioudaia" during Greek rule (333–67), and "Judaea" or Judea under the Romans. The geographical territory had also been diminished, until by the time of the Romans it consisted of the area around Jerusalem, south of Samaria, west of Perea and the Dead Sea, and north of Idumea (though administratively "Judea and Samaria" could also be referred to as "Judea" simply). The inhabitants of the territory were Judeans (just as the inhabitants of the northern area west of the Sea of Galilee were Galileans). The terms "Judaism" and "Jew" are derived from this name.

jussive a verb form in the third person expressing a command

justification translation of the underlying Gk term "making righteous," expressing the restoration of one's proper relationship to the moral realm or to God (see Rom 5.1–21)

K

kere see qere.

ketib ("what is written"; also *ketiv*) the biblical text in its written form, in contrast, in certain cases, to the way it is to be read aloud (**qere**)

Ketubim (also Kethubim, Ketuvim) The Writings, the third division of the Hebrew Bible

kosher (Heb "fit" or "proper") a general term used in postbiblical texts for dietary laws; usually applied to food, but also to other ritual objects and practices.

L

lament a poem of grief or mourning (see also **qinah**)

Last Supper the name for the meal that Jesus shared with his closest followers on the night before his crucifixion (Mt 26.20–29 and parallels)

Latter Prophets the canonical division of **Nevi'im** that includes the books of Isaiah, Jeremiah, Ezekiel, and the Twelve **Minor Prophets**

law the usual English translation of Hebrew *torah*, which more generally means "teaching, instruction." *Torah* is also the name for the first five books of the Hebrew Bible, Genesis through Deuteronomy.

laying on hands a gesture of healing, blessing, or setting something or someone apart for religious purposes

lectionary a list of readings of scripture passages for sabbaths and holy days (in Judaism) or Sundays and holy days (in Christianity). Christian lectionaries also sometimes include readings for weekdays. Lectionaries are partly designed to read certain portions of the Bible—for instance, the Torah, in Jewish lectionaries, or the first three Gospels, in many Christian lectionaries—completely through, in order, over a lectionary cycle of a year or several years. In addition, in Christian lectionaries important seasons (for instance, Christmas or Easter) have their own specific readings outside the continuous readings. In the synagogue, the Torah reading is followed by what is called a Haftarah reading (*haphtarah* is Hebrew for "conclusion, completion") from one of the prophets; in addition, the **festival scrolls** are read on five holy days.

legate an official representative

legend a popular story, sometimes exaggerated or romanticized, about a holy or important person or place.

Levant (Lat "rising") the east as the direction of the rising sun; more usually, the lands at the eastern end of the Mediterranean

Leviathan a monster of the sea in Canaanite mythology, who is defeated by Baal. It is sometimes identified with the crocodile (Job 41.1) and represents the forces of watery chaos which must be overcome at creation (Ps 74.1–17) and that will be finally defeated at the end of time (Isa 27.1). In the book of Revelation, the dragon, the enemy of God, is identified with the sea (17.1,3), and in the new creation there is no more sea (21.1).

levirate marriage (from Latin *levir*, "husband's brother") the provision that if a man died without an heir to carry on his name, his brother would marry the widow and the first son she bore would be regarded as the dead brother's heir

Levites the priests of Israel were deemed to be descendants of Levi, therefore members of the tribe of Levi, or Levites (sometimes levites). There is little evidence for this tribe, but the religious authorities in early Israel claimed descent from **Aaron** (see), the first high priest. Perhaps during the reform of Josiah, however, the levites were demoted to Temple assistants, probably when their local shrines were suppressed, and the Jerusalem priesthood, claiming descent from Zadok (see **Zadokites**) gained greater power and wealth.

lex talionis (Latin "law [of retribution] in kind") punishment fitting the crime; see **talion**

lingua franca a common tongue or shared language that enables people with different native languages to converse, carry on commercial relationships, etc. In the Persian period **Aramaic** replaced Akkadian as a lingua franca around the Near East; during the Hellenistic period Greek did the same for the lands surrounding the eastern Mediterranean.

litany (Gk "entreaty") a prayer form consisting of a series of petitions or supplications, often following each with a repeated congregational response

littoral a region along the shore of a large body of water

liturgical characteristic of an order for worship, either directions for action (rituals) or texts for speaking (rites)

liturgy the form or ritual for communal, public worship

Lord's Supper a term (used in the NT only at 1 Cor 11.20) for the commemoration or re-enactment of Jesus' last meal with his followers (see **Last Supper**)

lot(s) any method of choosing something by random chance, as by tossing a marked stone (similar to flipping a coin) or choosing an arrow or a stick from a group of similar objects. "Casting lots" was used to select candidates for a position (Acts 1.15–26), to determine who had transgressed a vow or law (1 Sam 14.41–42), or in other ways to determine the divine will, since it was assumed that an event that was random from the human perspective could be determined by divine direction.

lower criticism or **textual criticism**, as distinguished from **higher criticism**

LXX the roman numeral 70, the standard abbreviation for the **Septuagint**

M

Maat Egyptian goddess of reason and order; her name literally means "truth"

Major Prophets a convenient title for the three longest prophetic books, Isaiah, Jeremiah, and Ezekiel (in Christian Bibles, also Daniel); in contrast to **Minor Prophets** (see)

makarism (Gk "happy, blessed") a statement of blessing or an attribution of happiness to one who follows the exhortation of the speaker; the Beatitudes (Mt 5.3–11) are makarisms, perhaps following the form of

many Psalms such as Ps 1.1, "Happy are those who do not follow the advice of the wicked. . . ."

malediction curse; opposite of benediction, "blessing"

manumission release from servitude

Marduk chief god of Babylon; according to **Enuma Elish**, he formed the cosmos from the corpse of **Tiamat**, goddess of the deep

martyr (Gk "witness") a person who demonstrates loyalty by remaining faithful to his or her religion even when being threatened with death or being killed

martyrology (Gk "list of witnesses [to their faith]") an account of the martyrdoms of various individuals, or an official list of those accounted as martyrs, that is, who were killed because of their religious beliefs

Masorah (Heb "tradition") the system of markings (vowel signs, marginal notes, cantillation and accent marks, etc.) that were added to the consonantal Hebrew text by scribal scholars (**Masoretes**) in the early Middle Ages

Masorete a scholar of the scribal schools that in the early Middle Ages established the basic Hebrew text for the Bible, fixed its accepted pronunciation, and ensured its accurate copying and transmission by a system of markings (**Masorah**)

Masoretic Text the text of the Hebrew Bible, established by Jewish scholars (**Masoretes**). The text consists of the Hebrew consonants, vowel signs, accent markings, and other notes. Texts derived from this effort date from circa 900 to 1000 CE. The Masoretic Text is the only complete form of the Hebrew Bible that has survived, though individual manuscripts of books are among the **Dead Sea Scrolls**.

matrilineal tracing descent through female ancestors; see **patrilineal**

matzah unleavened bread, associated with **Passover**, but also used with certain sacrifices.

Megillot Heb "scrolls," in Jewish tradition the five festival scrolls, the books of Song of Solomon (read at Passover), Ruth (on Shavuot [Weeks/Pentecost]), Lamentations (on Tisha B'Ab, commemorating the destruction of Jerusalem in 586 BCE and 70 CE), Ecclesiastes (on Sukkot [Tabernacles]), and Esther (on Purim)

merism a figure of speech in which opposing terms, e.g., "good and bad," are combined to convey the idea of including both terms and everything in between

Merneptah Stele an Egyptian inscribed stone that includes the first mention of Israel outside the Bible. It celebrates victories of Pharaoh Merneptah (ca. 1200 BCE) in Canaan.

Merodach a Hebrew version of **Marduk**, chief god of Babylon

Mesha Stele (also called the Moabite Stone) a monument dating from about 830 BCE with engraved text celebrating the reign of King Mesha of **Moab** (2 Kings 3.4–5). Besides an account of the dealings of Mesha with the descendants of Omri, king of the Northern Kingdom of Israel, the text mentions the god of Moab, Chemosh, and the favor that Chemosh has shown to Mesha in contrast to his predecessors in allowing Mesha to reclaim territory from Israel. It also contains a reference to the **herem** or ban.

Mesopotamia (Gk "between the rivers") the area between the Tigris and Euphrates rivers

messiah (Heb *mashiah*, "anointed [one]") a title for a king or other servant or agent of God (priest, prophet, or even the non-Israelite Cyrus in Isa. 45.1). In the Hebrew Bible, *mashiah* never refers to the future ideal king. Later the term came to be used of the expected savior of the Jewish people, and was taken over by Christians to refer to Jesus, whom they believed to be the messiah (Gk *christos*, "anointed"). See also **Christ**.

messianic having to do with the **messiah** or with the era that the messiah was inaugurating

Messianic Secret conventional term for Jesus' commands, primarily in Mark (1.44; 3.12; 8.30 and elsewhere), not to proclaim his status or deeds publicly

metaphor a direct comparison between two things

metonymy a figure of speech in which a word is used in place of another word to which it is closely related: "The coastlands have seen and are afraid" (Isa 41.5) means "the inhabitants of the coasts, foreigners."

mezuzah (Heb "doorpost") a parchment on which are written the paragraphs of the **Shema**

midrash, midrashic (Heb *derash* "inquire") interpretation that finds meanings in a text that are other than, or go beyond, the "plain sense" (see **peshat**)

Milcom the principal god of the **Ammonites**; also called **Molech**

Minor Prophets the twelve shorter prophetic books from Hosea to Malachi, seen as a collection; also known as the Book of the Twelve

Mishnah (Heb "oral instruction," from *shanah* "repeat") the compilation of oral law and rabbinic commentary, edited ca. 200 CE, that is the basis of the **Talmud**

Moab, Moabites the territory and its inhabitants east of the Dead Sea

Moabite Stone see **Mesha Stele**

Molech a Canaanite god whose worship according to the biblical writers included child sacrifice

Mosaic having to do with Moses or with the teaching that Moses is purported to have proclaimed in the Torah (Pentateuch)

Mot the **Canaan**ite god of death

motif an image or character type that recurs throughout a literary work

mystery in the New Testament, a divine truth that is kept hidden or secret by God until the right moment for it to be revealed

mystery religion any one of various religious groups in the Greek and Roman empires which practiced secret rites of initiation. Mystery religions taught that the real meaning of life could not be learned without divine guidance and that such guidance was available in their secret teachings and practices. These secret rites were themselves known as "mysteries," and had the sense of a revelation from the divine realm that is similar to some of the New Testament uses of "mystery."

mysticism the effort to be in direct contact with a divine realm, as opposed to the view that the divine must always be mediated—by subordinate beings such as angels or by a human being, a sacred text, or some other bridge

N

narrative a connected, orderly account of an incident, or a longer account including many incidents. Narratives can be historical, fictional, legendary, mythical, or a combination of types.

Nebi'im see **Nevi'im**

necromancy (Gk "divination [by means of] the dead") the effort to determine the unknown or the future by consulting those who are dead, as in Saul's questioning of the dead Samuel through the medium of Endor (1 Sam 28.3–25). If **teraphim** (see) are images of ancestors, then divination by their means would be a form of necromancy.

Negeb, Negev the region south of the central hill country of Israel

Nevi'im (also Nebi'im) the Prophets, the second division of the Hebrew Bible, subdivided into the **Former Prophets** and the **Latter Prophets**

new moon the beginning of any month in the Jewish calendar

Northern Kingdom the political assembly of tribal groups that split off from the kingdom of Israel after Solomon's death. This newly formed kingdom was itself called Israel, and in some texts also **Ephraim**, after its largest tribe.

novel a fictional work in prose. Ancient novels were often **romances**.

O

obelisk a four-sided stone shaft, usually tapered and topped with a pyramid, characteristic of ancient Egypt

Old Latin the Latin translation of the Bible based on the Greek text, the Septuagint. The Old Latin version was replaced by the Vulgate, the Latin translation by Jerome.

oracle (usually translates Heb *masa'*, literally "burden") a statement uttered by a prophet or other sacred person, purporting to be the words of a deity

oracular having the qualities of an oracle or sacred speech

Oral Torah a synonym for the **Mishnah** and **Talmud**. According to traditional rabbinic belief, the Oral Law was given to Moses on Mount Sinai along with the written law, the Torah. It was committed to writing by the rabbis in the first millennium CE.

ordination a formal ceremony and process by which certain members of the community are set apart for religious service, for instance as priests

oxymoron (Gk "clever-foolish") combining two terms that appear contradictory.

P

P according to the **Documentary Hypothesis,** the Priestly source in the Pentateuch, comprised of both narratives and laws. It is concerned, among other things, with laws and regulations, ritual practices, the proper conduct of the Temple worship, holiness and purity, and genealogies.

Palestine a name first used by the fifth-century BCE historian Herodotus and adopted by the Romans in the designation *Provincia Syria Palaestina* ("Syro-Palestinian Province"), which replaced *Provincia Judaea* ("Judean Province") after 135 CE. The word is derived from the term translated "**Philistine**," and the Latin spelling of "Philistine," and the Roman designation was probably intended as a derogation of Jewish claims to the territory.

pantheon (Gk "all gods") the complete community of divine beings worshiped or honored in a particular culture

papyrus (pl. **papyri**) the paper made from reeds that grow along the Nile and other rivers in the Near East; the reeds were split, soaked, laid side-by-side in one layer with another layer, also side-by-side, at right angles, and then pounded together until the matted fibers had meshed into a flat, somewhat flexible sheet. Papyri were one of the writing surfaces (others being clay and animal skins) in use in antiquity. Early Gk manuscripts of the NT are on papyri, and many significant texts—such as P46, an important textual source of Paul's letters that also includes the Letter to the Hebrews—are in this form.

parable a statement or story that uses figurative or imaginative language to evoke a reality that lies beyond the literal level of the story of statement. A parable makes its point by analogy, or the comparison of a known fact, situation, or experience with one that is less familiar.

parallelism a characteristic feature of biblical Hebrew poetry in which the second line of a unit in some way echoes the meaning or grammatical structure of the first line. This can take the form of a repetition of the meaning, or of a statement of opposites, or of a further statement that serves to extend or modify the first line in some way.

parenesis moral exhortation

parousia (Gk "coming") the second coming of Christ; the expected return of the **messiah** at the end of the age or the end of the world

Paschal pertaining to the **Passover** (ultimately from Gk *pascha,* derived from Heb *pesah*)

Passover (Heb *pesah*) the festival that commemorates the Exodus of the Israelites from Egypt

Pastoral Epistles or **Pastoral Letters** a term used for three letters attributed to Paul, 1 and 2 Timothy and Titus

patriarchs the ancestors of Israel: Abraham, Isaac, and Jacob

patriarchy the social and cultural arrangements and conventions in which the father of a family, older males, or males generally, exercise authority over females, children, slaves, and those younger; characteristic of Israelite and Roman social practice

patrilineal tracing one's descent through male ancestors; see also **matrilineal**

patristic writers theologians of the early Christian centuries, including Clement, Irenaeus, Origen, and Jerome

patronym, patronymic (Gk "father's name") the designation of a person or group by the name of their father or ancestor

Pauline characteristic of the thought or writings of Paul; those letters generally accepted to be by Paul: Romans, 1 and 2 Corinthians, Galatians, Philippians, 1 and 2 Thessalonians, and Philemon

penitential psalms Psalms 6, 32, 38, 51, 102, 130, and 143, used in Christian services of repentance from the earliest times

Pentapolis the five cities of the **Philistines:** Ashdod, Ashkelon, Ekron, Gath, Gaza

Pentateuch (Gk "five scrolls") the first five books of the Bible, Genesis through Deuteronomy; the Torah

Pentecost see **weeks, festival of**

periphrasis, periphrastic the use of more words than necessary to express a thought

Persian period the era from 539 to 333 BCE, from Cyrus until Alexander

personification representing an idea, a value, or other abstract thought as a person.

Pesah see **passover**

peshat (Heb "simple") the "plain sense" or "contextual sense" of a text, often contrasted with *derash*, the homiletical meaning

pesher (pl. *pesharim*; "interpretation") a type of commentary on the Bible in the **Dead Sea Scrolls** in which the biblical text is understood to be fulfilled in the interpreter's time

Peshitta (Syriac, "simple") the name of the **Syriac** translation of the Bible (called "simple" because it was a plain translation from Hebrew, not a translation with textual apparatus like the **Syrohexapla**). The Peshitta contains books of the Bible translated by Jews for Jewish worshipers who spoke Syriac, but it was taken over and completed (including a New Testament) by Syriac-speaking Christians.

Pharisees a Jewish sect in the first century CE, according to Josephus and the New Testament. The Pharisees were concerned to extend Jewish practice into all areas of life, and followed the tradition of interpretation (**Oral Torah**) associated with the schools of Hillel and Shammai. They were opponents of the more conservative **Sadducees**, who did not accept their traditions of oral law.

Philistines a group of the **Sea Peoples,** who invaded and settled in on the southeastern coast of the Mediterranean in the late second millennium BCE, having been repulsed in an invasion of Egypt (ca. 1190 BCE). The five major Philistine cities (the **Pentapolis**) were Ashkelon, Ashdod, Ekron, Gath, and Gaza.

Philo a Hellenistic Jewish philosopher and interpreter of scripture, who lived in Alexandria, Egypt, from about 20 BCE to 50 CE. He wrote works in philosophy, scriptural interpretation, and history. In Philo's view, the best insights of Greek philosophy could be found in the Bible by means of allegorical interpretation. He influenced Jewish writers like the author of the Wisdom of Solomon and Christian theologians such as Clement, Origen, and Ambrose.

Phoenicia(n) (Gk "red-purple") the territory occupied by a Semitic group along the eastern Mediterranean coast, in an area roughly where modern Lebanon now is. The Phoenicians were seagoing and engaged in trade across a wide area; their main cities in biblical times, Tyre and Sidon, are prominent on the coast. They manufactured cloth dyed purple using a mollusk that grew along the shore (these "Tyrian purple" robes were worn by kings). The Phoenicians

were also responsible for the spread westward across the Mediterranean of a form of alphabetical writing, from which all later alphabets, including Hebrew and Greek, were derived.

phylacteries (Gk *phulakterion*, "amulet," from *phulax*, "guard") small black leather boxes containing biblical passages (Ex 13.1–10, 13.11–16; Deut 6.4–9, 11.13–21), worn during prayer on the head and on the left arm. Also called "tefillin."

Platonism a philosophy derived from the teaching of Plato, saying that there is a profound difference, even an opposition, between the realm of matter and the realm of spirit, and that the world of sense experience is essentially an illusion, deriving what reality it has from a correspondence with a true, ultimately real world of Forms

pogrom an officially encouraged, organized massacre of a minority group

polemic, polemical (Gk *polemos*, "war") an argument or debate in the form of an attack on one's opponent or on the opposing position. Polemical speech is characterized by verbal attacks, exaggerated language, and sometimes violent imagery

Polycarp, Letter of an early second-century CE Christian letter of instruction, written by Polycarp, bishop of Smyrna, and addressed to the church of Philippi

potsherd a broken piece of pottery. Examination of such pieces allows archaeologists to date the different levels of a site according to the type of pottery represented at a given level.

prescript (epistolary) see **epistolary prescript**

priest, high priest in the Hebrew Bible, the priest (Heb *kohen*) was the official set apart to preside at the worship in the Temple, particularly to offer sacrifices of various kinds. In the NT the term "priest" (primarily *hiereus*) is applied only to the Jewish priesthood of the Temple (*archiereus*, "high priest," "chief priest," e.g. Mt 2.4); a pagan priest (Acts 14.13); Melchizedek (e.g., Heb 7.1); Jesus Christ (Heb 10.21); or the whole of the Christian people ("priesthood," 1 Pet 2.5; "priests," Rev 1.6). The *Gk* term *presbyteros*, from which the English word "priest" is derived, means "elder" and is so translated in the NRSV (e.g., Jas 5.14; 2 John 1.1).

primogeniture the social tradition by which the eldest son inherits a father's title or the bulk of the father's property

proem a short introduction or preface to a literary text

Promised Land a conventional term for the Land of Israel, as it was promised to Abraham and to the descendants of Abraham ("this land that I have promised," Ex 32.13)

prophecy, prophesy the name for a prophetic utterance is "prophecy" (pronounced prah-feh-see, rhyming with "fee"); the activity of a prophet is to "prophesy" (pronounced prah-feh-sye, rhyming with "high")

prophet (Gk *prophetes*, "speak out" or "speak forth") the **Septuagint** translation of *nabi'* ("one who is called"), the standard Heb term for prophet. Synonyms include "seer," "man of God," and "visionary."

prophetic lawsuit (Heb *rib*) a literary form in the prophets and elsewhere in which the people are accused of breaking their covenant with God

Prophets, The, Heb **Nevi'im,** the second division of the **Hebrew Bible**

proselyte (Gk "come toward") one who has adopted a religion or belief system, often after leaving a previous religion; a convert

protreptic (Gk "turn toward, turn forward to") speech promoting a particular view; exhortation, persuasion

pseudepigrapha (Gk "writings with false attributions of authorship") a diverse group of Jewish or Christian religious writings attributed to notable biblical persons that are not included in the books of the Hebrew Bible, the New Testament, or the Apocrypha. These writings date from about 250 BCE to 200 CE, and some of them are quoted from or alluded to in the Bible.

pseudonymous written or published under a false name. Pseudonymous writing in antiquity is often attributed to someone much better known than the actual writer, in order to give the text the benefit of the presumed authority of the famous person.

Ptolemies the rulers of Egypt and its surrounding areas after the breakup of the Greek empire of Alexander the Great, following his death in 323

Purim the festival that commemorates the delivery of the Jews in Persia from destruction, as recounted in the book of Esther

Q

Q see **synoptic problem**

qeri ("what is read") in the **Masoretic text,** a word as it should be pronounced, in contrast to what is written (ketib) in the main text

qinah meter a metrical pattern consisting of a line with three stresses followed by a line with two stresses; it is primarily used in psalms of lament or complaint, and in the book of Lamentations.

Qumran community the settlement near Wadi Qumran at the Dead Sea, most likely composed of Essenes. The Qumran group was a sectarian Jewish community that kept its own practices in opposition to the established community in Jerusalem and Judea;

the library of this group was discovered beginning in 1947 and is known as the **Dead Sea Scrolls**.

R

rabbi (Aram. "teacher") a Jewish religious leader who studies the **Torah** and its associated commentaries, particularly the **Talmud,** and offers his own teaching based on that study

rapture the doctrine, based on an interpretation of 1 Thess 4.13–18, that when Jesus Christ returns in the **parousia** (see) those Christians who have not yet died will be "caught up" along with Christ and those who, having died, are raised from the dead. In its context, the passage is intended not as a literal description of events at the return of Christ, but as a reassurance that both those still living and those already dead would be reunited with Christ.

reader-response criticism analyzing a text by looking at the relationship between the text and its reader, including the clues within the text that guide the reader in drawing meaning from it

redaction criticism the study of how already existing textual units—narratives of incidents, laws, proverbs, or other isolatable pieces that can be disentangled by **source criticism**—were combined into larger texts by the activities of editors, called "redactors"

redactor an editor who works with already existing units to combine them into larger wholes

resident alien a foreigner with legal rights living in Israel or an Israelite residing in the territory of another tribe

revelation (Latin "remove the veil," translating Greek *apokalypsis*) belief or insight granted to a human being by a deity or heavenly being

rhetoric (Gk *rhetor*, "speaker, orator") the art or study of persuasive speech or writing

Rift Valley a major cleft or depression that extends from southeastern Turkey to East Africa, and at the point of the Dead Sea is the lowest place on the land mass of Earth

Ritual Decalogue a term for the commandments in Ex 34.10–28, in some cases paralleling those of the Decalogue (Ex 20.1–17) but mostly dealing with matters of worship or other religious observance, such as the offering of firstborn livestock or the observance of festivals

Roman Period the period of Roman ruke in Judea, beginning in 63 BCE

romance a popular storytelling technique in the ancient Mediterranean world that recounted the situation of young lovers and how they overcome obstacles to their marriage. In early Christianity the form was modified to tell the stories of early converts and martyrs and the obstacles to their faith.

Rule of the Community one of the Dead Sea scrolls (1QS) that sets out the arrangements under which the community functioned and those that they held up as an ideal: holding property in common; eating, blessing, and advising one another in unity; preparing for the end time; and training new members of the community in their responsibilities.

S

sackcloth rough cloth, often made from animal hair. A garment made of sackcloth is uncomfortable and is worn to indicate penitence or grief.

Sadducees a Jewish sect in the first century CE, according to Josephus and the New Testament. They held to a strict application of Torah and to maintaining Temple worship according to its mandate. They were opposed to the **Pharisees** in not accepting the traditions of oral law, and they were also opposed to the political activists who wished to rebel against Roman rule, fearing that any rebellion would bring an end to the limited autonomy under which they could maintain Temple worship.

saga popular narrative account of prehistory or events of the distant past. Sagas often involve stories of the ancestors of a group or the founders of a country.

saint(s) (Lat "holy one[s]") in the NT, the term for all Christians (2 Cor 1.1), or for what all Christians are "called" to be (Rom 1.7, 1 Cor 1.2)

Samaritan Pentateuch a Hebrew text of the first five books of the Bible used by the **Samaritans**. This text differs from the **Masoretic Text** at many points. Some of these disagreements reflect Samaritan beliefs, but others are supported by the **Dead Sea Scrolls** and reflect an alternate textual tradition.

Samaritans the descendants of the population of Samaria (the capital of the **Northern Kingdom** of Israel) after the Assyrian invasion of that kingdom and the deportation of its inhabitants in 722 BCE. The Samaritans regard themselves as descended from the Jewish remnant after the deportation, but the returning exiles from the Southern Kingdom of Judah (after the **Babylonian exile** in the early sixth century) did not regard them as Jews, seeing them rather as descendants of foreigners who had been settled there after the Jewish population had been removed. Therefore, beginning with Ezra and Nehemiah, the leadership forbade intermarriage between Samaritans and Jews. The Samaritans maintained worship (with a temple on Mount Gerizim) and the Pentateuch (but not the rest of the Bible), although their calendar is not the same as the Jewish calendar.

Sanhedrin (ultimately from Gk *synedria* from *syn-* and *hedra*, "with seat," i.e., "council") the religious court, whose membership was drawn from the Jewish ruling classes, that held ruling authority over the territory of Palestine under the Roman empire. The Sanhedrin was responsible for census-taking and taxation as well as for acting as a court that would decide cases on its own and also, after preliminary determination, send cases on to the Roman governors. "Sanhedrin" is also the title of a tractate of the **Mishnah** dealing with law courts in general.

Satan (Heb "adversary, accuser") the Satan (a title, not a name) in Job 1.6–12, 2.1–7 is a member of the divine council who serves as a prosecutor or tester of God's faithful (see also Zech 3.1). In the Gospels Satan serves as the chief tempter and head of the demonic realm (Mt 4.1–11; 12.26); in the book of Revelation Satan is identified with the serpent, the dragon, and the devil (12.9; 20.2).

school of prophets term for the followers of a prophet, who preserved the prophet's words and, it is presumed, applied them to new situations as they arose

scribe in general, one who could write, especially official documents, and take down dictation for letters, legal proceedings, etc. In the New Testament, a scribe was a lawyer, one who was expert in the requirements and meaning of Jewish law, especially the **Torah**.

scroll a long strip of parchment (treated leather) or papyrus (reeds split, moistened, and pressed together), on which a text was written in columns. The scroll was read by unrolling one side while rolling up the other, to expose successive columns of text. Besides the literal meaning, scrolls stand for the message or teaching of God that a prophet has internalized and will then deliver to the intended hearers. Jeremiah (15.16) eats the words of God, and following him Ezekiel (3.3) eats a scroll. The message of God in the book of Revelation (5.1ff.) is expressed in stages as the seals on a scroll are broken open.

Sea Peoples remnants of the Mycenean or Aegean civilizations, which collapsed toward the end of the second millennium BCE. Some of these people sailed eastward on the Mediterranean and attacked those living along the coast; they were repulsed from Egypt and settled in southwest Canaan. The biblical **Philistines** are among the Sea Peoples.

Second Coming the return of a glorified Christ to Earth in judgment and redemption. See **parousia**.

Second Isaiah, also **Deutero-Isaiah**, the general term for chs 40–55 of the book of Isaiah. These chs are primarily concerned with the events leading up to the decree of the Persian king Cyrus in 538 BCE permitting the exiles to return to Judah from Babylon and rebuild Jerusalem and the Temple. See also **Third Isaiah**.

Second Temple the Temple constructed beginning ca. 515 BCE by the returning exiles, and continued and expanded over the course of time, until its destruction by the Romans in 70 CE

sect a religious grouping that emphasizes strict adherence to particular teachings and excludes those who do not conform

seder (Heb "order") the ritual meal and recitation of Passover. Also, the major divisions of the **Mishnah** (pl. *sedarim*).

Seleucids the rulers of Syria and its surrounding areas after the breakup of the Greek empire of Alexander the Great, following his death, The Seleucid ruler Antiochus IV "Epiphanes" desecrated the Temple in 167 BCE, leading to the Maccabean revolt and the rededication of the Temple in 164 BCE, an event commemorated in the festival of Hanukkah.

Septuagint the ancient Greek translation of the Hebrew Scriptures. The Septuagint was translated over a lengthy period beginning probably in the third century BCE. Traditionally there were 72 translators, a number that was rounded off to 70 and, in Roman numerals, used as the abbreviation for this translation (LXX). The Septuagint was prepared for the use of Jews who lived in the **Diaspora** whose main language was Greek. It is important for several reasons: it translated a version of the Hebrew text that is older than the **Masoretic text**; it contains additional works, grouped in NRSV as the Apocryphal/Deuterocanonical Books, most of which were originally written in Greek; and it was the Old Testament of early Christians.

Shavuot see **festival of weeks**

Shema the first word, used as a title, of the exhortation "Hear, O Israel, the LORD is our God, the LORD alone" (Deut. 6.4), also the name of perhaps the most important and best-known prayer in Judaism, comprised of Deut. 6.4–9; 11.13–21; and Num. 15.37–41.

Sheol the underworld or abode of the dead

Shephelah the foothills leading to the central hill country of the land of Israel

shofar, also **shophar** the ram's horn for ceremonial use. In ancient Israel it was sounded to announce the anointing of a king or as a summons to war or to sound an alarm; today, in the synagogue, it is sounded on the High Holy Days.

signet ring a ring bearing a personal seal, used to make an indentation in clay as a sign of authenticity of authorship

simile a comparison, using "like" or "as" rather than, as in metaphor, linking two things directly

Sinai properly, the name of a peninsula bounded on the north by the Mediterranean Sea, on the east by the Gulf of Aqaba, and on the west by the Gulf of Suez. Traditionally the mountain of Sinai, purportedly the location where Moses received the Decalogue, is on this peninsula, but no mountain has been definitively identified as the biblical Sinai. See also **Horeb**.

Sitz im Leben (German, "setting in life") in **form criticism**, the original context in which a specific genre or form was used

sorites a philosophical argument in the form of linked propositions. The second part of each proposition forms the first part of the next, and the series therefore becomes an extended chain of reasoning

source criticism the effort to discover the sources or documents behind a text and to explore how the sources were combined into larger units. See **Documentary Hypothesis**.

Southern Kingdom see **Judah, Yehud**, etc.

step parallelism a form of poetic **parallelism** (see) in which successive lines do not repeat or reverse the structure of the preceding line, but build on it like a set of steps: "O send out your light and your truth; / let them lead me; / let them bring me to your holy hill/and to your dwelling. / Then I will go to the altar of God, / to God my exceeding joy; / and I will praise you with the harp, / O God, my God." (Ps 43.3–4)

Stoics Greek philosophers in the Hellenistic and Roman periods, who taught that emotions should be strictly controlled by reason

Sukkot see **booths, festival of**

Sumer a civilization that ruled southern Mesopotamia from the late fourth millennium to the early second millennium BCE. The Sumerians developed cuneiform writing, which involved using a wedge-shaped reed to press marks into wet clay; the clay was then baked.

superscription a heading or descriptive title before the actual beginning of a text; many of the Psalms have a superscription giving a purported setting for the Psalm (e.g. Ps 3) or instructions on how it is to be performed (Ps 4).

suzerain the lord or ruler to whom loyalty is due in a covenant relationship

Symmachus a second-century CE translator of the Bible into Greek, whose translation was included in Origen's **Hexapla** (a compendium of six Bible versions)

synagogue (Gk "coming together with") an assembly; a congregation. For Jews who were too distant from the Temple to worship at it, and for all Jews after the final destruction of the Temple by the Romans in 70 CE, the synagogue became the only form of worship. Services consisted of prayer, song, and study of the sacred text.

syncretism the incorporation into one religion of practices and teachings derived from another, or the effort to combine two different religious traditions into a third, composite religion

synecdoche (Gk "understand with") a figure of speech using a part of something to stand for the whole: in "Do not keep needy eyes waiting" (Sir 4.1) "needy eyes" stands for the whole needy person

synonymous parallelism a type of **parallelism** where the second line or **colon** of a **bicolon** echoes the meaning of the first in different terms.

Synoptic Gospels Matthew, Mark, and Luke. "Synoptic" means "view together," and is applied to these writings because they, unlike John, can be readily compared.

synoptic problem the observation that in many passages Matthew and Luke repeat with only minor changes what Mark says, yet in other passages they do not follow Mark, or include stories or sayings that Mark does not have, yet match each other very closely. According to the most widely held theory, Matthew and Luke relied on Mark and on another document (now lost) that contained mostly sayings of Jesus; this second document is referred to as "Q" (from the German word "Quelle," meaning "source"). In addition, Matthew and Luke each had their own sources.

Syriac an eastern form of **Aramaic** that was the language of some Jews and of some eastern Christian communities in the early centuries of the Common Era. It is the language of the **Peshitta**.

Syrohexapla (or Syriac hexapla) a Syriac translation of the Septuagint text that provides textual evidence about the nature of the Septuagint. Although the Hexapla was translated in the seventh century CE, it is based upon a **Septuagint** text dating from as early as the third century CE.

T

tabernacle the portable sanctuary used by the Israelites during their wanderings in the wilderness

tabernacles, feast of see **booths, festival of**

tablet a slab, typically of clay, with a smoothed surface that can be inscribed with a text

talion (Latin *talio*, "in kind" from *talis*, "like," "such like") a punishment that is of the same kind as the crime: exacting an equivalent penalty, such as an equal economic loss for theft, or death for murder, or "an eye

for an eye." Talion is well attested in Mesopotamian law, and in some biblical legal collections.

Talmud (Heb "teaching") the title of the two great collections of rabbinic teaching, the Jerusalem Talmud (also called the Palestinian Talmud or the Talmud of the Land of Israel) and the Babylonian Talmud. The Talmuds were compiled beginning after 200 CE. They consist of comments on, and extensions of, the Mishnah in order to apply Jewish teaching to everyday life, but they also include information on a wide range of topics. The two centers of rabbinic study (the land of Israel and Babylonia) were in contact with each other and the commentary therefore reflected a common effort; later, especially with the completion of the Talmud in Israel (ca. 400 CE), the Babylonian effort continued to refine and extend the applications, and it was the Talmud developed in Babylonia (completion after 500 CE) that was distributed worldwide, under the auspices of the academies that continued to work in Babylon until the beginning of the second millennium CE.

Tanakh an acronym formed from the beginning letters of the three divisions of the **Hebrew Bible**: Torah, Nevi'im, Ketubim

Targum translation of the Hebrew Bible into **Aramaic**. The Targums are important for textual criticism of the Hebrew text, since they provide evidence about it at a stage earlier than that of the **Masoretic text**.

tel (Heb), **tell** (Arabic) a mound formed by repeated construction, occupation, and destruction of buildings on a particular site

Temple the central place of worship for Israelite religion in Jerusalem, referring either to the **First Temple** or the **Second Temple**

teraphim a term (generally translated "household gods") for certain cultic objects in early Israel; their nature and function is unclear, and their size seems to be varied (in Gen 31.34 Rachel can conceal Laban's household gods by sitting on them; in 1 Sam 19.13, the "idol" is large enough to look like someone is in a bed). They may have been images of one's ancestors. One use to which they were put may have been divination (Ezek 21.21), but how this was done is not explained.

testament (Lat "*testamentum*," for Gk *diatheke*) a final disposition of one's personal property, but used in LXX to translate Heb *berith*, "covenant," and therefore applied to the "new covenant" or "new testament" as inaugurated by Jesus (recalling Jeremiah's promise of a "new covenant" in 31.31–34); testament therefore came to mean the collection of writings (the Hebrew Scriptures or the Christian Scriptures) that presented the covenant of God with the people of God

Tetragrammaton (Gk "four letters") the divine name, YHWH

Tetrateuch the first four books of the Bible, Genesis through Numbers, regarded by some scholars as an edited collection to which Deuteronomy was then attached. See **Pentateuch**

textual criticism the effort to establish, by scholarly assessment of manuscript copies and other sources, an accurate version of a text; also called "lower criticism"

theodicy the theological effort to justify the goodness of God in the face of suffering

Theodotion (ca. second century CE) a translator of the Hebrew Bible into Greek and reviser of the Septuagint

theophany (Gk "appearance of god") the temporary appearance or manifestation of a divine being in a form that can be apprehended by the human senses

Third Isaiah, also **Trito-Isaiah**, the scholarly term for chs 56–66 of the book of Isaiah, which are primarily concerned with the life of the returned exiles in the province of Yehud (the Persian name for Judah) after 538 BCE. Some scholars doubt the separate existence of Third Isaiah; others maintain that it is not the product of one author, but a collection of diverse oracles by different members of a "school of Isaiah" collected during the **Persian period**. See also **Second Isaiah**.

Thomas, Gospel of an early collection of sayings attributed to Jesus. It contains no miracle stories and no account of Jesus' deeds, his birth, his death, or the resurrection. Some of the sayings resemble those in the canonical Gospels, but others reflect **Gnosticism**.

thresh to beat gathered stalks of grain in order to separate the grain from the stems and husks. A threshing floor, a flat area used for threshing grain, was often built on a hilltop to catch the breeze necessary for **winnow**ing.

threshing floor see **thresh**

Tiamat goddess of the deep and mother of the Babylonian pantheon; she is sometimes portrayed as a dragon.

tithe the conventional religious due (traditionally 10 percent) of certain material goods, such as herbs (Deut 14.22; Mt 23.23); other produce, like fruit or livestock, required the donation of "first fruits" or the young that opened the womb (the firstborn kid or calf) to God (Ex 13.12)

Torah (Heb "teaching, instruction") the first division of the Hebrew Bible, consisting of Genesis through

Deuteronomy. The word (and hence the title) is sometimes translated "law," but this translation is misleading since the five books contain much more than law codes and regulations.

tradition criticism the investigation of the development of a text from its earliest stages (oral or original source documents) to the latest (canonical) stage

Transfiguration, the conventional title for narrative (Mk 9.2–8; Mt 17.1–8; Lk 9.28–36) in which Jesus, accompanied by Peter, James, and John, ascends a mountain and appears to the disciples in dazzling white, like a vindicated martyr, in the company of Moses and Elijah (founder and renewer of Israel)

Transjordan ("across Jordan") the region east of the Jordan River

transmission history an account, usually inferred, of how a text came down to the present from its originator. Steps in transmission history can include oral transmission, redaction, manuscript copying, and scribal emendation.

Trito-Isaiah see **Third Isaiah**

trope (Gk "turn [away]") use of a word or phrase in a sense differing from its usual or literal meaning, as in a figure of speech; "a stitch in time" is not about sewing, but about the advantages of timely or early action

Twelve, Book of the the **Minor Prophets**

Twelve, the conventional designation for Jesus' closest followers (Mk 3.14–16 and parallels; Mk 10.32)

typology (Gk *tupos*, the raised design on a seal for imprinting in wax, then by extension a pattern or model) understanding persons or events, especially in the New Testament, by referring them to earlier biblical precursors

U

Ugarit city on the Mediterranean coast (Ras-Shamra in present-day Syria), source of an important collection of Canaanite myths and other texts from the second half of the second millennium BCE in a language called Ugaritic, which was related to Hebrew

Ugaritic an ancient Semitic language closely related to Hebrew, which was used at the city of Ugarit on the coast of the Mediterranean in Syria in the second millennium BCE. Many Ugaritic texts have connections in style and content with the Bible.

unleavened bread (Heb *matzah*, pl. *matzot*) bread made without yeast; also the festival of unleavened bread associated with **passover**.

Urim and Thummim a method of **divination** used to discover God's response to "yes" or "no" questions

V

vassal the underlord in a covenant relationship, who is granted power and control over people in a particular area in return for loyalty to the **suzerain**

Vassal Treaty of Esarhaddon an Assyrian treaty document from the reign of the Assyrian king Esarhaddon (681–669 BCE), with parallels to parts of Deuteronomy

Vulgate see **Jerome**

W

wadi (Arabic) a stream bed or valley that is dry for part of the year; an arroyo or gulch

weeks, festival of (Heb *Shavuot*; "Pentecost," Gk for "fiftieth" [day]) the spring harvest, occurring according to Priestly texts fifty days (seven full weeks) after Passover

winnow to separate grain from its husks (called chaff) after it has been threshed. The threshed grain is placed in a wide, flat basket and tossed repeatedly into the air, allowing a breeze to blow away the lighter chaff while the grain drops back down into the basket.

wisdom literature Job, Proverbs, and Ecclesiastes in the Hebrew Bible, Sirach and Wisdom in the Apocrypha, and some Psalms. Wisdom literature is concerned with insight, instruction, meditation of the meaning of life, and moral exhortation. It does not generally concern itself with key events in Israel's history, such as the Exodus; central teachings, such as the covenant; or focal institutions, such as the Davidic monarchy, prophecy, or the Temple.

Writings the third division of the **Hebrew Bible**

Y

Yahweh see **YHWH**

Yahwistic characteristic of the religion of the worship of YHWH or of the teachings, Temple practices, etc., in the Pentateuch

Yehud designation of the province of Judah during Persian times; see **Judah**

YHWH (sometimes also YHVH) the name of God, which in Jewish tradition is conventionally unpronounced; moden scholars use the conventional pronunciation "Yahweh." The name is represented in the **Masoretic text** by the Hebrew letters *yod-he-vav-he* and the vowels for the title *Adonai*, "my Lord." In most English translations, following an ancient substitution, YHWH is represented by the word LORD written in capital and small capital letters. The original vocalization and meaning of the name YHWH is uncertain, though it is connected to the verb *h-y-h*, "be" or "become," most likely in a causative sense, "he who causes to be."

Yom Kippur see **Day of Atonement**

Z

Zadokites priests purportedly descended from Zadok, one of David's chief priests and the only chief priest under Solomon, who anointed Solomon king (1 Kings 1). Zadok was descended from Aaron (1 Chr 6). Ezekiel's vision of the restored Temple explicitly maintains that Zadokites will be the priests, differentiated from **Levites** (Ezek 48.11). The Qumran community wanted to restore the Zadokite priesthood; Zadok may also be the source of the name Sadducees, those who supported the religio-political elite centered on the Jerusalem Temple under the Roman occupation. See also **Aaron**.

Zealot a member of a Jewish revolutionary movement during the Roman occupation of Palestine in the first century CE

ziggurat a temple-tower in ancient Mesopotamia. Ziggurats are presumed to represent a mount, on the top of which the earthly and divine realms merged.

Zion the name of the fortified hill within Jerusalem and thus, by extension, an alternative name for Jerusalem itself, especially in biblical poetry

Zion theology a name for the view that God's ultimate plan for Israel is restoration of the monarchy under a Davidic king who rules from Jerusalem

INDEX TO THE STUDY MATERIALS

The index is to the introductions, annotations, and essays, not to the biblical text. It therefore refers not to biblical citations but to page numbers.

A

Aaron; *see also* priesthood
  appointment of, HB:91
  complaint of, HB:206–8
  genealogy of, HB:91
  and golden calf, HB:129–30
  priesthood of, HB:215
  Simon the High Priest and,
    AP:1518
  sprouting rod of, HB:215
Abraham
  as ancestor of Jesus, NT:1748
  and ancestral history in Genesis,
    HB:9; HB:26
  blessing of, HB:46; HB:66
  burial plot of, HB:42
  call of, HB:27
  circumcision and, AP:1517; HB:10;
    NT:1982
  covenant with, HB:31; HB:91
  death of, HB:45
  faith of, NT:1981–82
  and Lot, HB:29–30
  meaning of name, HB:34
  as model for Christian faith,
    NT:2046
  as model for returnees, HB:1006
  obedience of, HB:41
  promise to, HB:9; HB:27; HB:31;
    HB:32; HB:81; HB:91; NT:2055;
    NT:2109
  as prophet, HB:38
  testing of, HB:40–41
Absalom
  defeat of, HB:471–73
  return of, HB:464–66
  revolt of, HB:466–67
acrostics
  in Ecclesiasticus, AP:1527
  in Lamentations, HB:1147
  in Proverbs, HB:933–34
  in Psalms, HB:780; HB:800;
    HB:802; HB:867; HB:871; HB:890
Acts of the Apostles, NT:1919–71
  authorship of, NT:1919
  date of, NT:1919–20

and Gospel of Luke, NT:1919;
    NT:1921
  title of, NT:1919
  "we" passages in, NT:1919; NT:1950;
    NT:1951; NT:1958; NT:1959;
    NT:1960; NT:1967; NT:1970
'adam (human being), HB:13; HB:14;
    HB:17
Adam and Christ, NT:1983–84
Additions to Daniel, AP:1542
Additions to the Book of Esther,
    AP:1411–12; HB:707
adultery, AP:1549; HB:193; HB:260–61;
    HB:286–87; *see also* sexual
    offenses
  as capital offense, HB:286
  divorce and, NT:1810
  as metaphor for idolatry, NT:2159
  ordeal and, HB:193
  penalty for, HB:286
  perils of, HB:903–4
  stoning and, HB:65
  woman caught in, NT:1895–96
age, of human beings, HB:17; HB:18
agriculture, HB:22
  Hosea and, HB:1260–62
  seasons of, HB:21
Alcimus (high priest), AP:1574;
    AP:1579; AP:1628–30
Alexander the Great, AP:1364;
    AP:1555; HB:1249–50
aliens
  attitude toward, HB:170
  and Levites, HB:292
  resident, HB:244; HB:268; HB:277;
    HB:447
  and widows, HB:292
allegory
  in biblical interpretation, HB:950
  fable of eagles, HB:1182–83
  of Hagar and Sarah, NT:2048–49
  of the pot, HB:1193–94
  of the sisters, HB:1191–93
  of unfaithful wife, HB:1178–81
almsgiving, AP:1386–87; AP:1463–64;
    AP:1496

altar(s), HB:121; HB:190
  of burnt offerings, HB:1223;
    HB:1243
  of incense, HB:126; HB:137
  rebuilding of, HB:671–72
  sacrificial, HB:137
Amos
  meaning of name, HB:1284
  visions of, HB:1293–94
Amos, Book of, HB:1282–97
  and classical prophecy, HB:1284
  date of, HB:1284
anachronisms, AP:1564; HB:243;
    HB:416; HB:427
ancestors, HB:259
  of Israel, AP:1516
ancestral deities, HB:54
Ancient One, HB:1248
angel of God, divine presence and,
    HB:103; *see also* angel of the
    Lord; divine presence
angel of the Lord, HB:33; HB:39;
    HB:376, HB:564; HB:801; *see
    also* angel of God; divine
    presence
angels, HB:35; HB:36; HB:130
  in Matthean infancy narrative,
    NT:1748–49
  and stairway of Jacob, HB:50
  superiority of Son to, NT:2104–5
anger, divine, HB:1037–38; HB:1342;
    see also wrath
animals, unclean, HB:101
Anointed, the, HB:963; HB:1341; *see
    also* Messiah
  the Lord's, HB:1028
anointing
  of David, HB:423–24
  of Jesus, NT:1818; NT:1843–44;
    NT:1902–3
  of kings in ancient Israel, HB:489
antichrist, NT:2140–41
  and false teaching, NT:2146
Antiochus IV Epiphanes, AP:1364;
    AP:1457; AP:1543; AP:1544;
    AP:1556; AP:1557–62; AP:1563;